ZONDERVAN NIV

NAVE'S TOPICAL

BIBLE

About the Editors

John R. Kohlenberger III, general editor, is a specialist in the application of computers to Bible-related reference projects. He has taught at Multnomah School of Bible and Western Seminary in Portland and has produced *The NIV Interlinear Hebrew-English Old Testament*, *The Hebrew-English Concordance to the Old Testament*, *The Greek-English Concordance to the New Testament*, *The NRSV Concordance, Unabridged*, and, with Edward W. Goodrick, the *Zondervan NIV Exhaustive Concordance*.

David J. Jirak, associate editor, is a graduate of Multnomah School of the Bible. He is a business consultant on employee benefit plans.

PREMIER
REFERENCE
SERIES

ZONDERVAN NIV

NAVE'S TOPICAL

BIBLE

JOHN R. KOHLENBERGER III
GENERAL EDITOR

DAVID J. JIRAK
ASSOCIATE EDITOR

ZondervanPublishingHouse
Grand Rapids, Michigan

A Division of HarperCollins*Publishers*

Zondervan NIV Nave's Topical Bible
Copyright © 1994 by John R. Kohlenberger III

Requests for information should be addressed to:

ZondervanPublishingHouse
Grand Rapids, Michigan 49530

Library of Congress Cataloging-in-Publication Data

Zondervan NIV Nave's Topical Bible
    John R. Kohlenberger III, general editor; David J. Jirak, associate editor.
        p.   cm.
        ISBN: 0-310-57950-3
        1. Bible–Indexes.   I. Jirak, David J.   II. Nave, Orville J. (Orville
James), 1841–1917. Topical Bible.   III. Title.
    BS432.K65   1992
    220.5'208   92-11386
                                                CIP

This edition is printed on acid-free paper and meets the American National Standards
Institute Z39.48 standard.

Printed in the United States of America

00 01 02 03 04 / ❖ DC/ 14 13 12 11 10 9 8

CONTENTS

ACKNOWLEDGMENTS

Special thanks are due to Paul Hillman, former President of Zondervan Publishing House, who first gave me the commission to revise the classic *Nave's Topical Bible*. Thanks to Stan Gundry, Vice President and Publisher/Academic Books and Electronic Publishing and Bruce Ryskamp, Corporate Vice President/Book, Bible, and Electronic Group Executive, for their patience and support over the years.

Imprint Editor Ed van der Maas has been involved in all aspects of design and production and has been a special friend to me and my family. Verlyn D. Verbrugge provided many valuable suggestions in the final stages of editing and typesetting. Laura Weller once again did a great and humorous job of proofreading.

Special thanks to Doris Rikkers, Bible Editor of Zondervan Bible Publishers, for allowing us to use the excellent book outlines and several essays from the outstanding *NIV Study Bible*.

David J. Jirak, Associate Editor of this project, spent many years and endless hours of data input, evaluation, and editing. This book would not be the same without him. Kathy Jirak and Brian Wheeler also had a part in the data input.

James A. Swanson provided the definitions of proper names, checked KJV-specific headings against NIV vocabulary, and supplemented many articles.

Special thanks to my wife, Carolyn Kohlenberger, and to my son, Joshua, for valuable assistance in NIV text formatting.

Roger Green and Don Wills of Telios Systems in Portland, Oregon developed special programming to create a printout that assisted David J. Jirak in evaluating all of Nave's biblical citations against the NIV.

Dennis B. Thomas developed special programming to merge the NIV into our database and sort it all in alphabetical order.

Larry and Cyndi Stone and Aaron Jarrard of OmniTek Computers in Portland, Oregon provided technical assistance and allowed me generous use of their hardware.

Mike Petersen, Mary Beth Danneels, and the rest of the staff of Multnomah Graphics permitted me 24-hour access to their offices and equipment.

Through the talents of these individuals, *The NIV Nave's Topical Bible* is a far better book than the general editor alone could have made it. However, the editor does accept full responsiblity for any shortcomings or errors found in the book.

INTRODUCTION

What is a Topical Bible?

The NIV Nave's Topical Bible combines the most useful features of a Bible Handbook, a Bible Dictionary, and a Bible Concordance. Like a Bible Handbook, this Topical Bible introduces the reader to each book of the Bible and surveys its contents. Like a Bible Dictionary, this Topical Bible is an alphabetically organized presentation of biblical and extrabiblical information on Bible people, places, events, and objects. Like a Concordance, this Topical Bible indexes the Scriptures with thousands of biblical references and biblical text samplings.

The NIV Nave's Topical Bible is also much more than these other general reference works. A Bible Handbook offers only selected comments on the biblical text; this Topical Bible offers a thorough survey of most biblical topics, people, places, and events. A Bible Dictionary cites a handful of biblical texts to document its articles; this Topical Bible cites more than 100,000 verses. A Bible Concordance displays only a one-line context for the verses it indexes; this Topical Bible reproduces the full NIV text of nearly 33,000 verses.

A Concise History of *Nave's Topical Bible*

Orville James Nave (1841-1917) was an army chaplain who assembled the original *Nave's Topical Bible* while stationed at Fort McPherson in Georgia. With the assistance of his wife Anna Semans Nave, over a fourteen-year period Nave attempted to "classify everything found in the Scriptures." Nave covered thousands more topics than the earlier analyses of Matthew Talbot and Roswell D. Hitchcock. In fact, he believed it to be an "approximately exhaustive" digest of the King James Version.

Nave's Topical Bible was first published in 1896.

Nave saw it through seven editions over the next twenty years, including its reorganization into *Nave's Topical Study Bible* in 1907. It inspired several similar works. Notable among these were Thomas David Williams *A Textual Concordance of the Holy Scriptures* (1908) based on the Douay-Rheims translation and from a Catholic perspective. Harold E. Monser and twelve contributors created *The Cross-Reference Bible* to the American Standard Version (1910) and its spin-off, *Cross Reference Dictionary of Bible References* (1914), sometimes reprinted as *Topical Index and Digest of the Bible*. Walter A. Elwell revised *Hitchcock's New and Complete Analysis of the Holy Bible* of 1873, which was released as the *Topical Analysis of the Bible* using the New International Version (Baker, 1991).

Moody Press also issued a modestly revised and abridged edition in 1974, edited by S. Maxwell Coder. Their *Nave's Compact Topical Bible* (n.d.) presents 1,000 key topics in 255 pages. Tyndale House published *Nave's Topical Living Bible* in 1982.

Seventy-three years after the publication of the original, Zondervan commissioned an update and expansion of the best-selling *Nave's*. Edward Viening added new articles and supplemented many of the existing articles to create the *Zondervan Topical Bible* in 1969. Currently reprinted as *Nave's Topical Bible: Revised and Enlarged*, this was the most thorough revision of *Nave's* to appear until the present work.

In 1972 Zondervan released *The New Compact Topical Bible*, now *The Nave's Compact Topical Bible*, another revised and restructured edition of *Nave's*. Editor Gary Wharton added more than one hundred new articles and classified many of the descriptive texts Nave simply listed under the heading "Unclassified Scriptures." *The Nave's Compact* is not compact because it abridges Nave's content, but because it does not print out the text of the Scriptures it indexes. These two revisions are the basis of the current work.

A Concise History of
The NIV Nave's Topical Bible

The continuing popularity of *Nave's* and the growing acceptance of the New International Version suggested a marriage of the two standards. General editor John R. Kohlenberger III designed the project and assigned most of the early responsibilites to associate editor David J. Jirak. David and his wife Kathy created an electronic database from *The Nave's Compact Topical Bible*. David then compared these data to Zondervan enlarged edition of *Nave's* to note which verses had been printed out in full. Roger Green of Telios Systems created a computer program to generate a massive printout to assist David in evaluating every verse in *Nave's* against the NIV to be certain the translation appropriately represented each topic.

After this database had been settled, John evaluated each entry heading against the vocabulary of the NIV to create new headings, new cross-references, and new articles. John also created exhaustive lists indexing NIV vocabulary to the original Hebrew, Aramaic, and Greek, based on the materials he and Edward W. Goodrick developed for the *NIV Exhaustive Concordance*. James A. Swanson offered definitions for proper names, additional KJV to NIV referencing, and supplemented many articles. The restructured and redesigned materials were then proofed by Verlyn D. Verbrugge, Laura Weller, and David Jirak.

As a result, *The NIV Nave's Topical Bible* preserves the essence of the time-tested original, while adding more than 500 headings, 2,000 subtopics, 1,300 cross-references, and exhaustive referencing to the NIV and to the original biblical languages. The articles continue to represent Nave's conservative Christianity, while attempting to acknowledge a variety of interpretive perspectives on controversial subjects. New articles, such as Abuse, Ecology, and Homosexual, and revised articles, such as Abortion, Discipleship, Wine, and Women help make *The NIV Nave's Topical Bible* the new standard for the current generation.

How to Use *The NIV Nave's Topical Bible*

The NIV Nave's Topical Bible offers quick and easy access to more than 7,000 biblical topics. Simply look up any subject, person, place, or book of the Bible in alphabetical order. There you will find a concise summary of biblical insights, well documented with Scripture references and often with Scripture text.

Entry Headings

The following shows the three elements that can appear in an entry heading in addition to the entry word:

ABEDNEGO, ABED-NEGO [6284, 10524] (*servant of Nego* or *Nebo*).

Proper and place names are indexed according to NIV spelling. When KJV spelling differs, it follows after a comma. In brackets are the Goodrick-Kohlenberger (G/K) numbers of the *NIV Exhaustive Concordance*. These indicate every Hebrew, Aramaic, and Greek word translated by the entry word. If the list is preceded by an asterisk (*), it only represents the most frequent words; otherwise the list is exhaustive. (See below, pages ix-x.) The definition of the name follows in parentheses and italics. When sources disagree on the definitions, these differences are listed and documented:

ASA [654, *809*] (possibly *healer* BDB; *myrtle* KB).

The abbreviations are explained in the tables following the introduction on page xii.

·Sometimes an entry heading contains only a cross-reference to another article. This is often the case of KJV terms, such as:

ABEZ *See Ebez.*

WINEBIBBER *See Drunkard; Drunkenness; Wine.*

NIV+ References

Whenever an entry heading is a word used in the NIV, an exhaustive listing of related NIV words follows:

AARON [195, 2].
NIV+ AARON'S, AARONIC

This listing of NIV words and the index of G/K numbers gives you all the materials necessary to use the *NIV Exhaustive Concordance* to make an exhaustive study to supplement the selective resources of the *NIV Nave's*. (See below pages ix-x).

The Entry Proper

An entry can be as simple as:

JAGUR [3327]. A town of Judah (Jos 15:21).

or as complex as JESUS THE CHRIST, which fills 66 pages with 2,742 paragraphs of information including 84 primary subdivisions, 309 secondary subdivisions, 43 cross-references to 68 topics, and 2,296 verses printed in full.

Subdivisions

Short articles appear as single paragraphs. Longer articles are usually subdivided to one or two levels.

Proper names that refer to more than one person or place are subdivided by numbered paragraphs. For example, there are three listings for Abel; thirty-one for Zechariah. More than 3,000 proper name subdivisions are identified.

Primary subdivisions are set flush left in bold print. Secondary subdivisions are indented and followed by a dash:

JESUS THE CHRIST
. . .
Purpose of His Death:
To make reconciliation—

NIV Text

Of the more than 100,000 verses cited, nearly one-third are printed out in full. Biblical texts cited are enclosed in parentheses; texts printed in full are preceded by the reference in bold. Additional citations following a printed verse are enclosed in parentheses, but preceded by a plus mark:

Unjust weights and measures (Dt 25:13-16)—
Pr 20:10 Differing weights and differing measures—the LORD detests them both. (+Pr 20:23)

The paragraphing of the NIV is followed; however, poetic and other special indentations are not.

The ampersand symbol (&) and "w" (with) are used to indicate closely related texts that help in the understanding of the previously cited text, often a New Testament text that quotes from the Old or a parallel passage:

Jesus as Head of the church (Ps 118:22-23, w Mt 21:42-43, & Mk 12:10; Isa 28:16, w Eph 2:2-22, & 1Pe 2:6).

Although so many biblical selections are provided by the *NIV Nave's*, please do not limit your biblical study to these excerpts. The easiest way to misinterpret the Bible is to study its texts out of their contexts. The editors have taken great care to select only relevant texts, but we strongly encourage users not only to double-check our work, but to double-check your own insights by studying the larger context of each verse.

Cross-References

More than 3,700 cross-references to 6,100 entries are set in italics:

See Month, 1; Nisan.

See Jesus the Christ, Second Coming; Millennium.

Entry headings are separated by semicolons; subdivisions of entries follow commas.

How to Use *The NIV Nave's Topical Bible* with the *NIV Exhaustive Concordance*

The NIV Nave's Topical Bible and the *NIV Exhaustive Concordance* are made for each other. The *Concordance* provides an exhaustive index of every word in the NIV, listed in biblical order from Genesis to Revelation, and an exhaustive index of the relationship of the NIV to the original biblical languages. The *NIV Nave's* provides a biblical index that is organized by subjects, that is not limited to NIV vocabulary, and is arranged by thematic development rather than by biblical order. Together these works provide endless access to the riches of God's Word.

Exhaustive NIV Word Studies

The *Concordance* indexes every reference to every NIV word. The *NIV Nave's*, while not exhaustive in its treatment of NIV vocabulary, does list every person and place in the NIV and provides an exhaustive listing of NIV words for every NIV-specific entry heading.

When you want to study any NIV word in full, begin with the *Concordance*. Look up the word exactly as it is spelled in the NIV. The *Concordance* also gives you a complete listing of related NIV words you can work through as well. Then check the *NIV Nave's* for insights from its analysis.

Thorough Synonym Studies: Suggested by the NIV Nave's

While working through any entry in the *NIV Nave's*, you will notice that the verses cited regularly contain key words that are synonymns of the entry heading. This is one major advantage of the Topical Bible over the Concordance. For example, the entry on Truth contains the synonymns "faithful," "faithfulness," "just," "love," and "right." The *Concordance* indexes 224 verses on "truth" and another 142 on its related words. When you add the five synonymns identified in the *NIV Nave's*, you get another 1,546 references—and that does not even count their related words!

Thorough Synonym Studies: Suggested by the Original Languages

The NIV is an English translation of the original biblical languages: Hebrew, Aramaic, and Greek. The *NIV Exhaustive Concordance* identifies the relationship of the NIV to the original languages by means of a numbering system that is used in the *Concordance* and in the *NIV Nave's Topical Bible*. Hebrew words have a one- to four-digit number in normal type. Aramaic words have a five-digit number. Greek word numbers are in italics.

The biblical language indexes of the *Concordance* offer another source of words for synonym study. There are eighteen G/K numbers listed in the *NIV Nave's* entry on Love. (The asterisk indicates this is a selective list of only the most frequent words in the original languages.) If you looked up the first italicized number (*26*) in the Greek-English Index on page 1673 of the *Concordance*, you would find that every NIV word in the list is related to "love," except for "longed for." However, the first Hebrew word (170), indexed on page 1362 of the *Concordance*, lists the synonyms "adore," "allies," "ally," "attracted to," "desires," "friend," "friends," "like," "liked," and "value" in addition to related words to "love." Again, all these synonyms can be studied with the *Concordance* and many will appear in the *NIV Nave's*.

Thorough Study of the Original Languages

Both the *NIV Nave's* and the *Concordance* are based on the English of the NIV and are indexed to the original biblical languages. The discriminating student may wish at times to study a word or topic as indexed in the original languages and not only in the NIV.

The G/K numbers identify the relationship of the NIV to the original languages. The *Concordance* offers an index to the majority of occurrences of Hebrew, Aramaic, and Greek words by combining the information of its indexes and the main concordance.

Using the example of "Love" from the previous section, let's say you wanted to study through the words represented by the eighteen numbers listed in the *NIV Nave's*:

1. First you must locate the number in its proper index: Hebrew, Aramaic, or Greek.

2. Next make a list of all unique NIV words in the number's index. For example, Greek word *26* has eight lines in its index, but only five unique words. (The word "love" appears in the phrases "truly love" and "showed love.")

3. Look up each of these unique NIV spellings in the main concordance. At the end of each context line is a G/K number or an abbreviation. By locating all of the G/K numbers that match the number you are working with, you can make a thorough word study of any Hebrew, Aramaic, or Greek term—and study it in an English translation.

We have used the word "thorough" instead of "exhaustive" because the NIV does not always translate every word of the original languages in a way you can locate with the *NIV Exhaustive Concordance*. For example, the index to Hebrew word 170 notes that the word is "untranslated" two times. The index to Greek word *27* notes that the NIV uses the pronoun "it" to translate *agape* in one verse. Because "it" is not indexed with contexts in the *Concordance*, you cannot locate that one occurrence. Exhaustive NIV-based concordances to the Greek New Testament and the Hebrew-Aramaic Old Testament are scheduled for release in 1993 and 1995 respectively. With these concordances you will be able to locate those rare occurrences of untranslated or unindexed words for exhaustive study.

A 30-page Index of G/K to Strong's Numbers shows the relationship of this new numbering system to the old system developed by James A. Strong, which is still used in many reference books.

Selected Resources for Additional Studies

The NIV Nave's Topical Bible combines the best features of the most essential biblical reference books. But as useful as that combination is, it is not exhaustive. The following list suggests dozens of additional tools for further research. All works represent an evangelical approach to the Bible.

Study Bibles

The most essential companion to *The NIV Nave's Topical Bible* is a full-text Study Bible. *The NIV Study Bible* (Zondervan, 1985) is the finest academic evangelical Study Bible yet produced. For additional topical insights, the classic *Thompson Chain-Reference Bible* (Kirkbride, Revised NIV edition 1991) and the *NIV Topical Study Bible* (Zondervan, 1989) are most useful. The latter work, edited by Verlyn D. Verbrugge, is especially useful in identifying topics that are key to each book of the Bible and in noting prophecies and their fulfillments.

Bible Dictionaries and Encyclopedias

Bible dictionaries and encyclopedias provide biblical and historical information on people, places, customs, events, objects, and books of the Bible. On a basic level *The NIV Compact Bible Dictionary* (Zondervan, 1989) and *Young's Compact Dictionary of the Bible* (Tyndale, 1989) stand out. On an intermediate level, *The New International Dictionary of the Bible* (Zondervan, 1987) and *The New Unger's Bible Dictionary* (Moody, 1988) are standards. The five-volume *Zondervan Pictorial Encyclopedia of the Bible* (Zondervan, 1976) is accessible to all readers while the four-volume *International Standard Bible Encyclopedia* (Eerdmans, 1979-88) is written on a more technical level.

Bible Commentaries

Commentaries provide insights on the biblical text. They offer additional information on interpretation, history and culture, biblical languages, and even spiritual and devotional insights. Among the best one-volume commentaries on the whole

Bible is the *International Bible Commentary* (Zondervan, 1986). The twelve-volume *Expositor's Bible Commentary* (Zondervan, 1976-92) is among the best series for the general reader. The technical and as yet incomplete *Word Biblical Commentary* (Word, 1982-) is highly regarded for the serious researcher. Thousands of additional titles and series are recommended in Douglas Stuart's *A Guide to Selecting and Using Bible Commentaries* (Word, 1990), Tremper Longman's *Old Testament Commentary Survey* (Baker, 1991), and D. A. Carson's *New Testament Commentary Survey* (Baker, 1986).

Bible History and Archaeology

In addition to dictionaries and commentaries, several kinds of reference works offer additional information on Bible backgrounds. *Chronological and Background Charts of the Old Testament* (Zondervan, 1978) and *Chronological and Background Charts of the New Testament* (Zondervan, 1981) offer much historical information in chart form. *A Survey of Israel's History* (Zondervan, Revised 1986) and *New Testament History* (Doubleday, 1969) are standard textbooks. *The New International Dictionary of Biblical Archaeology* (Zondervan,

1983) is a specialized Bible dictionary of archaeological insights on biblical people, places, and events. *Handbook of Life in Bible Times* (IVP, 1986) is an excellent illustrated guide to customs and culture.

Theology and Ethics

The implications of biblical texts for theology and ethics are often covered in Bible dictionaries and commentaries. More thorough coverage is found in theological textbooks, such as Ericksen's *Christian Theology* (Baker, 1985). The *Evangelical Dictionary of Theology* (Baker, 1984) is one of the finest theological dictionaries, offering concise overviews and bibliographies on thousands of theological and ethical topics. The *Topical Analysis of the Bible* (Baker, 1991) offers 35,000 biblical citations to illustrate twenty-seven major theological topics, divided into over 6,000 subdivisions. *The Dictionary of the Ecumenical Movement* discusses many theological and ethical issues from a historical and modern ecumenical perspective. The *Dictionary of Charismatic and Pentecostal Movements* (Zondervan, 1988) offers a unique perspective on biography and theology.

ABBREVIATIONS AND SYMBOLS

Books of the Bible

1Ch	1 Chronicles
1Co	1 Corinthians
1Jn	1 John
1Ki	1 Kings
1Pe	1 Peter
1Sa	1 Samuel
1Th	1 Thessalonians
1Ti	1 Timothy
2Ch	2 Chronicles
2Co	2 Corinthians
2Jn	2 John
2Ki	2 Kings
2Pe	2 Peter
2Sa	2 Samuel
2Th	2 Thessalonians
2Ti	2 Timothy
3Jn	3 John
Ac	Acts
Am	Amos
Col	Colossians
Da	Daniel
Dt	Deuteronomy
Ecc	Ecclesiastes
Eph	Ephesians
Est	Esther
Ex	Exodus

Eze	Ezekiel
Ezr	Ezra
Gal	Galatians
Ge	Genesis
Hab	Habakkuk
Hag	Haggai
Heb	Hebrews
Hos	Hosea
Isa	Isaiah
Jas	James
Jdg	Judges
Jer	Jeremiah
Jn	John
Jnh	Jonah
Job	Job
Joel	Joel
Jos	Joshua
Jude	Jude
La	Lamentations
Lev	Leviticus
Lk	Luke
Mal	Malachi
Mic	Micah
Mk	Mark
Mt	Matthew
Na	Nahum
Ne	Nehemiah

Nu	Numbers
Ob	Obadiah
Phm	Philemon
Php	Philippians
Pr	Proverbs
Ps	Psalms
Rev	Revelation
Ro	Romans
Ru	Ruth
SS	Song of Songs
Tit	Titus
Zec	Zechariah
Zep	Zephaniah

Books of the Apocrypha

1Es	1 Esdras
1Mc	1 Maccabees
2Es	2 Esdras
2Mc	2 Maccabees
3Mc	3 Maccabees
4Mc	4 Maccabees
Bar	Baruch
Bel	Bel and the Dragon
Sir	Sirach
Tob	Tobit
Wis	Wisdom

Other

& ... "and"; read this biblical text with the preceding

Antiq. ... Josephus, *Antiquities of the Jews.*

BDB ... Brown, Driver and Briggs. *Hebrew and English Lexicon* (Oxford, 1907).

ISBE .... *International Standard Bible Encyclopedia* (Eerdmans, 1979-88).

KB ... Koehler and Baumgartner *Lexicon in Veteris Testamenti Libros* (Eerdmans, 1951-53).

JB ... Jerusalem Bible

KJV ... King James Version

NIV ... New International Version

NRSV ... New Revised Standard Version

w ... "with"; read this biblical text with the preceding

ZPBE ... *Zondervan Pictorial Bible Encyclopedia* (Zondervan, 1976).

The
NIV Nave's
Topical Bible

A

AARON [195, 2].
NIV+ AARON'S, AARONIC
Personal History:
Lineage of: a son of Amram of the Kohathites, and brother of Moses and Miriam (Ex 6:16-20; Nu 26:59-60; Jos 21:4,10; 1Ch 6:2-3). His marriage to Elisheba, daughter of Amminadab (Ex 6:23). The children of: Nadab, Abihu, Eleazar and Ithamar (Ex 6:23,25; 1Ch 6:3-4; 24:1-2). Descendants of (1Ch 6:3-15,50-53; 24).
Character of (Ps 106:16).
As a Leader Ordained by God:
Meets Moses in the wilderness and is made spokesman for Moses (Ex 4:14-16,27-31; 7:1-2,6-7). Commissioned as a deliverer of Israel (Ex 6:13,26-27; Jos 24:5; 1Sa 12:8; Ps 77:20; 105:26; Mic 6:4). Inspiration of (Ex 12:1; Lev 10:8; 11:1; 13:1; 15:1; Nu 2:1; 4:1,17; 18:1; 19:1; 20:12). Summoned to Sinai with Nadab, Abihu, and seventy elders (Ex 19:24; 24:1,9-10).
Events in the Life of:
Murmured against by the people (Ex 5:20-21; 16:2-12; Nu 14:2-5,10; 16:3-11,41; 20:2; Ps 106:16). Places pot of manna in the ark (Ex 16:34). With Hur supports the hands of Moses during battle (Ex 17:10-13). Judges Israel in the absence of Moses (Ex 24:13-14). Makes the golden calf (Ex 32; Dt 9:7-21; Ac 7:40-41).
His benedictions upon the people (Lev 9:22)—
Nu 6:23 "Tell Aaron and his sons, 'This is how you are to bless the Israelites. Say to them:
²⁴"'"The LORD bless you and keep you; ²⁵the LORD make his face shine upon you and be gracious to you; ²⁶the LORD turn his face toward you and give you peace."'
Forbidden to mourn the death of his sons Nadab and Abihu (Lev 10:6,19).
Gossips with Miriam about Moses because of jealousy (Nu 12:1). Intercedes for Miriam (Nu 12:11-12). Stops the plague started by Korah's rebellion, by priestly intercession (Nu 16:46-48).
Rod of, buds (Nu 17; Heb 9:4), preserved by storing in the ark of the covenant (Nu 17; Heb 9:4).
He and Moses dishonor God in the presence of the Israelites when the rock is struck (Nu 20:12,23-29). Moses and Aaron are not allowed to enter the land of Canaan because of this lack of faith at the waters of Meribah Kadesh in the Desert of Zin (Dt 32:51-52).
Dies at 123 years of age on Mt. Hor (Nu 33:38-39). Death and burial of (Nu 20:27-28; Dt 10:6; 32:50).
As a Priest:
Priesthood of (Ex 28:1; 29:9; Nu 17; 18:1; Ps 99:6; Heb 5:4). Consecration of, to the priesthood (Ex 28; 29; Lev 8). Enters the priestly office (Lev 9).
Descendants of, ordained priests forever (Ex 28:40-43; 29:9; Nu 3:3; 18:1; 1Ch 23:13; 2Ch 26:18). *See Priest, High Priest.*

AARONITES
Descendants of Aaron who were priests, numbering 3700 fighting men under Jehoiada who joined David at Hebron (1Ch 12:27). Their leader was Zadok (1Ch 27:17).

AB
The Babylonian name of the fifth month in sacred sequence, month eleven in civil sequence. In the Bible it is referred to only as "the fifth month" (Nu 33:38; Ezr 7:8; Jer 1:3). The dry season (July-August); ripening season for grapes, figs, and olives. *See Month, 5.*

ABADDON [3] (*destruction*).
A Hebrew word for the underworld, meaning the place of destruction (Job 31:12, ftn), and in the OT is a synonym of death (Hell) and Sheol. The abode of the dead (Job 26:6, ftn; Pr 15:11, ftn; 27:20, ftn).
The name of the angel of the bottomless pit (Rev 9:11, ftn), whose Greek name is Apollyon which means destroyer.

ABAGTHA [5].
One of seven eunuchs that served King Xerxes (Est 1:10).

ABANA [76].
A river of Damascus and one of the two mentioned by the leprous Naaman (2Ki 5:12).

ABARIM [6305] (*geographical regions beyond*).
NIV+ IYE ABARIM
Either a region east of the Jordan and SE of the Dead Sea, or a mountain range northwest of Moab (Nu 27:12; 33:47-48; Dt 32:49; Jer 22:20). *See Nebo, 2.*

ABBA [5] (*father*).
An Aramaic word meaning *father*, which is a customary title of God in prayer. It is found in the Babylonian Talmud where it is used, of a child to his father, and also as a type of address to rabbis. It is equivalent to *papa*. This term conveys a sense of warm intimacy and also respect for the father. The Jews found it too presumptuous and nearly blasphemous; they would therefore never address God in this manner.
Jesus called God "Father" and gave that same right to his disciples (Mt 6:5-15). Paul sees this as symbolic of the Christian's adoption as a child of God and of possession of the Spirit (Mk 14:36; Ro 8:15; Gal 4:6).

ABDA [6272] (*servant of Yahweh*).
1. Father of Adoniram (1Ki 4:6).
2. A Levite of the family of Jeduthun, the son of Shammua (Ne 11:17).

ABDEEL [6274] (*servant of God [El]*).
Father of Shelemiah, who was appointed by Jehoiakim, the king of Judah, "to arrest Baruch the scribe and Jeremiah the prophet" (Jer 36:26).

ABDI [6279] (*servant of Yahweh* or *my servant*).
1. A Levite in the reign of Hezekiah, the father of Kishi and grandfather of Ethan (1Ch 6:44; 2Ch 29:12).
2. A son of Elam (Ezr 10:26).

ABDIEL [6280] (*servant of God [El]*).
A Gadite chief, the father of Ahi (1Ch 5:15).

ABDON [6277, 6278] (*servant*).
1. A Levitical city given to the tribe of Asher (Jos 19:28, ftn; 21:30; 1Ch 6:74).
2. A son of Hillel, from Pirathon in Ephraim, the hill country of the Amalekites; a judge of Israel for eight years (Jdg 12:13-15).
3. A son of Shashak (1Ch 8:23,25,28).
4. Firstborn son of Jeiel of Gibeon (1Ch 8:30; 9:35-36).
5. The son of Micah, an official of King Josiah (2Ch 34:20). Also called Acbor, son of Micaiah (2Ki 22:12).

ABEDNEGO, ABED-NEGO [6284, 10524] (*servant of Nego* or *Nebo*).

His Hebrew name was Azariah. He was taken as a captive to Babylon with Daniel, Hananiah, and Mishael, where each was given a Babylonian name (Da 1:6-20; 2:17,49; 3:12-30). Azariah was given the Akkadian name Abednego, which was the Babylonian god of wisdom, connected with the planet Mercury.

Shadrach, Meshach, and Abednego were chosen to learn the language and the ways of the Chaldeans (Babylonians) so that they could enter the king's service (Da 1:3-5,17-20), c. 605 B.C. These three were eventually thrown into the king's furnace because they refused to bow down and worship Nebuchadnezzar's golden image (Da 3:1,4-6,8-30).

ABEL [64, 2040, 6] (proper name *morning mist;* place name *meadow* or *stream*).

1. The second son of Adam and Eve (Ge 4:1-2).
The history of (Ge 4:1-15,25).
NT references to the death of (Mt 23:35; Lk 11:51; Heb 11:4; 12:24; 1Jn 3:12).
2. A city in Naphtali (2Sa 20:14, ftn; 20:18).
3. An element of certain place names. *See seven place names following.*

ABEL, GREAT STONE OF KJV "the great *stone of* Abel" (1Sa 6:18) is "the large rock" in the NIV text and "Greater Abel" in the note.

ABEL BETH MAACAH, ABEL OF BETH MAACAH, ABEL BETHMAACHA [68] (*meadow of the house of Maacah [oppression]*). Sheba son of Bicri fled there from King David (2Sa 20:14-22). A town in Naphtali (2Sa 20:15). Ben-Hadad later seized it (1Ki 15:20). Tiglath-Pileser, king of Assyria captured it (2Ki 15:29).

ABEL-CHERAMIM See Abel Keramim.

ABEL KERAMIM [70] (*meadow of vineyards*). A place in Ammon, east of the Jordan, to which Jephthah pursued the Ammonites (Jdg 11:33).

ABEL MAIM, ABEL-MAIM [72] (*meadow of waters*). A city conquered by Ben-Hadad (2Ch 16:4). Also known as Abel Beth Maacah (2Ch 16:4, ftn).

ABEL MEHOLAH, ABEL-MEHOLAH [71] (*meadow of the round dance*).

NIV+MEHOLAH

A town probably in the Jordan Valley, named in conjunction with the retreat of the Midianites from Gideon (Jdg 7:22; 1Ki 4:12). Probably Elisha's birthplace (1Ki 19:16).

ABEL MIZRAIM, ABEL-MIZRAIM [73] (*meadow of Egypt*, or *mourning of Egypt*).

NIV+MIZRAIM

The place was the threshing floor of Atad where the Israelites and all Pharaoh's officials mourned for Jacob (Ge 50:11).

ABEL SHITTIM, ABEL-SHITTIM [69] (*meadow of the acacia trees*).

NIV+SHITTIM

A place where the Israelites made their final camp before crossing the Jordan into Canaan (Nu 33:49). *See Shittim.*

ABETTING See Complicity.

ABEZ See Ebez.

ABI See Abijah, 7.

ABIA, ABIAH See Abijah, 1 & 3.

ABI-ALBON [50] (*[my] father is Albon*). Also called Abiel (1Ch 11:32). *See Abiel.* One of David's mighty men (2Sa 23:31).

ABIASAPH [25] (*[my] father has gathered*). A Levite, and the last son of Korah (Ex 6:24). He is also identified as Ebiasaph (1Ch 6:23,37; 9:19). *See Ebiasaph.*

ABIATHAR [59, 8] (*[my] father gives abundance* or *the father is preeminent*).

1. High priest under David.

He is the son of Ahimelech and, like his father, a high priest at Nob; he alone escaped from the massacre of his family and all the priests at Nob by Saul to join with David at Keilah, bringing an ephod with him (1Sa 22:6-23). Consults the ephod for David (1Sa 23:9; 30:7). David did not depose Zadok whom Saul had appointed to the priesthood; instead, the two constituted a double high priesthood (2Sa 15:35; 20:25; 1Ki 4:4; 1Ch 15:11). Abiathar was loyal to David when Absalom rebelled; leaves Jerusalem with the ark of the covenant, but is directed by David to return with the ark (2Sa 15:24-29). Helps David by sending his son Jonathan from Jerusalem to David with secret information concerning the counsel of Ahithophel (2Sa 15:35-36; 17:15-22; 1Ki 2:26).

Later he supports Adonijah's attempt to succeed David to the royal throne at David's death (1Ki 1:7). Because of this he is forced out of office by Solomon and is banished to Anathoth (1Ki 2:26-27). With this, the priestly line was confined to Zadok, an Aaronite, and the rule of Eli's house ended in fulfillment of prophecy (1Sa 2:31-35).

The reference to "Ahimelech son of Abiathar" as priest with Zadok is confusing because in other places "Abiathar son of Ahimelech" is known as the high priest. This problem is sometimes solved by saying that the names were transposed by a copyist error; many find this to be an improbable solution since the reference to Ahimelech, the son of Abiathar, as priest is too clear to make a mistake (2Sa 8:17; 1Ch 18:16; 24:3,6,31). One of the best explanations is that as the aged Abiathar came near to the end of David's reign, and his life, the responsibilities of office became heavy enough for him to shift many of those duties over to his oldest son Ahimelech; Ahimelech therefore became the functioning high priest.

When Jesus refers to "Abiathar as high priest" at Nob (instead of his father Ahimelech), it is perhaps best understood as Jesus referring to the "passage concerning Abiathar as high priest," by analogy with the way he refers to the burning bush (Mk 12:26).

2. *See Ahimelech, 3.*

ABIB [26] (*heads or spikes of grain*).

Hebrew name of the first month in sacred sequence, month seven in civil sequence (Ex 12:2). The name was changed to Nisan after the Exile (Ne 2:1; Est 3:7). The season of later rains (March-April); beginning of the barley and flax harvest.

The Passover and the Feast of Unleavened Bread are instituted, and the Israelites depart from Egypt in (Ex 13:4; 23:15; 34:18; Dt 16:1). It was to become a memorial month to the deliverance of the Israelites from Egypt (Ex 12, w 13:3-4; Dt 16:1-8,16).

The order of events during the celebration month:
1. On the tenth day the Passover lamb was chosen.
2. On the fourteenth day the lamb was slain and eaten.
3. On the fifteenth day they began harvesting by gathering sheaves of the barley firstfruits.
4. On the sixteenth day they offered the sheaves.

The tabernacle, the Tent of Meeting, is set up in (Ex 40:2,17). The Israelites arrive at the Desert of Zin, staying at Kadesh (Nu 20:1). Canaan entered in (Jos 4:19). Jordan's overflow in (1Ch 12:15).

See Month, 1; Nisan.

ABIDA, ABIDAH [30] (*[my] father knows*). Fourth of five sons of Midian, and the grandson of Abraham and Keturah (Ge 25:4; 1Ch 1:33).

ABIDAN [29] (*[my] father is judge*). A son of Gideoni, and a prince of the tribe of Benjamin chosen to represent his tribe in the wilderness of Sinai (Nu 1:11; 2:22; 10:24). He was present at the dedication of the tabernacle (Nu 7:60,65).

ABIEL [24] (*[my] father is God [El]*).
1. The grandfather of Saul and Abner (1Sa 9:1; 14:51).
2. One of David's mighty men (1Ch 11:32), also called Abi-Albon (2Sa 23:31). Albon is a copyist's transference from the following verse; some mss of the LXX have Abiel here.

ABIEZER, ABIEZRITE(S) [48, 49] (*[my] father is help*).
1. Founder of a clan of Manasseh (Jos 17:2; Jdg 6:34; 8:2). He was the second son of Hammoleketh, sister of Gilead and granddaughter of Manasseh (1Ch 7:17-18). Also called Iezer, a shortened form, the progenitor of the Iezerites (Nu 26:30).
2. One of David's mighty men (2Sa 23:27; 1Ch 11:28; 27:12).

ABIGAIL [28] (*[my] father rejoices* or *father [cause] of joy*).
1. The wife of Nabal of Carmel, a Calebite, and, after Nabal's death, of David (1Sa 25:3,14-44; 27:3; 30:5; 2Sa 2:2), to whom she bore his second son, Kileab (2Sa 3:3), or Daniel (1Ch 3:1).
2. A sister of David, daughter of Nahash (Jesse), wife of Jether (Ithra, KJV) an Israelite (some Hebrew mss have Ishmaelite), and mother of Amasa, commander of David's army (2Sa 17:25; 1Ch 2:16-17).

ABIHAIL [35, 38] (*[my] father has strength/wealth* or *cause of strength/wealth*).
1. A Levite, the father of Zuriel, leader of the Merarite clans (Nu 3:35).
2. The wife of Abishur (1Ch 2:29).
3. A Gadite who lived in Gilead of Bashan and on the pasturelands of Sharon (1Ch 5:14).
4. The wife of Rehoboam, king of Judah. A daughter of Eliab, David's oldest brother (2Ch 11:18).
5. The father of Queen Esther (Est 2:15; 9:29).

ABIHU [33] (*he is [my] father*). Son of Aaron (Ex 6:23; Nu 3:2). Summoned by God to Sinai (Ex 24:1,9). Called to the priesthood (Ex 28:1). Died because he and Nadab offered unauthorized fire to the Lord (Lev 10:1-2; Nu 26:61). Died childless (Nu 3:4).

ABIHUD [34] (*[my] father has majesty*). A son of Bela, the oldest son of Benjamin (1Ch 8:3).

ABIJAH [23, 31, 32, 7] (*[my] father is Yahweh*).
NIV+ ABIJAH'S
1. The second son of Samuel; appointed, with his brother Joel, as judges but did not follow in Samuel's ways. They followed after dishonest gains, bribes, and perverted justice. Because of this the Israelites demanded a king to lead them (1Sa 8:1-5; 1Ch 6:28).
2. A son of Jeroboam I of Israel (1Ki 14:1-18). He died of illness when still a child, in fulfillment of a prediction by the prophet Ahijah.
3. The wife of Judah's grandson Hezron and mother of Ashhur the father of Tekoa (1Ch 2:24).
4. The seventh son of Beker, the son of Benjamin (1Ch 7:8).
5. The second king of Judah, the son and successor of Rehoboam, and the grandson of Solomon (1Ch 3:10). Name is spelled "Abijam" in 1 Kings 14 and 15 (See NIV ftn). He reigned three years (2Ch 12:16). Prosperity tempted him to follow the evil ways of his father (1Ki 15:3). He had fourteen wives by whom he had twenty-two sons and sixteen daughters (2Ch 13:21).

He made war on Jeroboam I, the king of Israel, in an effort to recover the ten tribes of Israel (2Ch 13). Before the battle, Abijah condemns the apostasy of the Northern kingdom and at the same time affirms a theocratic institution; he shows the folly of opposing Yahweh's kingdom and concludes by urging Israel not to fight against Yahweh. Jeroboam I, with a numerically stronger army, was routed by Yahweh; the two nations were not allied as they once were, but Jeroboam never made war with Abijah again (1Ki 15:1-8; 2Ch 11:22; 13). He was succeeded by Asa his son (1Ki 15:8; 2Ch 14:1).
6. A descendant of Aaron. The ancestral head of the eighth of the 24 groups into which David had divided the priests (1Ch 24:10).
7. The daughter of Zechariah, and mother of king Hezekiah (2Ch 29:1). Also called Abi (2Ki 18:2, ftn).
8. A priest of Nehemiah's time (Ne 10:7; 12:4,17).
9. A chief of the priests who returned from Babylon with Zerubbabel (Ne 12:4).

ABIJAM (*[my] father is the sea* or *father of the West*). *See Abijah, 5.*

ABILENE [9] (probably *meadow*). A territory surrounding the city of Abila NW of Damascus (Lk 3:1).

ABIMAEL [42] (*[my] father is God [El]*). The ninth of the thirteen sons or descendants of Joktan, who was descended from Shem (Ge 10:28; 1Ch 1:22).

ABIMELECH [43] (*[my] father is a king* or *[my] father is Molech*).
NIV+ ABIMELECH'S
1. A Philistine king of Gerar, S of Gaza in the foothills of the Judean mountains (Ge 20:1-18).
2. A second king of Gerar, probably the son of the one mentioned in 1, at whose court Isaac tried to pass off his wife Rebekah as his sister (Ge 26:1-11).
3. The son of Gideon by a concubine (Jdg 8:31; 9:1-57, w 6:32 & 7:1).
4. A Philistine king mentioned in the title of Psalm 34, who very likely is the same as Achish, king of Gath (1Sa 21:10-22:1), with whom David sought refuge when he fled from Saul.

5. A priest in the days of David. A son of Abiathar (2Sa 8:17; 1Ch 18:16). Also called Ahimelech in the LXX and in the Chronicles (1Ch 24:6).

6. *See Achish; Ahimelech.*

ABINADAB [44] (*[my] father is generous* or *[my] father is Nadab*).

NIV+ ABINADAB'S

1. A Levite, in whose house the ark of God rested twenty years (1Sa 7:1-2; 2Sa 6:3-4; 1Ch 13:7).

2. The second son of Jesse (1Sa 16:8; 17:13).

3. Son of Saul (1Sa 31:2), also called Ishvi (1Sa 14:49).

4. Father of one of Solomon's governors who supplied provisions for the king and the royal household. Also called Ben-Abinadab (1Ki 4:11).

ABINOAM [45] (*[my] father is graciousness*). The father of Barak (Jdg 4:6,12; 5:1,12).

ABIRAM [53] (*[my] father is exalted*).

1. One of the sons of Eliab, a Reubenite, who conspired with Dathan and with On against Moses and Aaron; the earth opened and swallowed them (Nu 16; 26:9-10; Dt 11:6; Ps 106:17).

2. The son of Hiel of Bethel; in rebuilding Jericho, Hiel's firstborn, Abiram, died, as well as his youngest son, Segub, in accordance with the word of the Lord spoken to Joshua (1Ki 16:34, w Jos 6:26).

ABISHAG [54] (*[my] father strays*). The Shunammite who looked after David in his old age (1Ki 1:3-4,15). After David died, Adonijah, his oldest son, wished to marry Abishag. He tried using Bathsheba as leverage to gain Abishag as his wife. Solomon saw this as an attempt to gain the throne by controlling and possessing the king's harem which was a royal right. Solomon had him killed (1Ki 2:13-25).

ABISHAI [57, 93] (*[my] father is Jesse* or *father exists*).

The son of Zeruiah, David's sister (1Sa 26:6; 1Ch 2:16). Became the chief of the Three, David's chief men, because he killed 300 men with his spear (2Sa 23:18-19).

Goes into Saul's camp with David; they find Saul asleep with his spear planted in the ground near his head; Abishai tells David that he will pin Saul to the ground with one thrust of the spear, which David does not allow (1Sa 26:6-8). Abishai and his brother Joab pursue Abner all day until they reach the hill of Ammah near Giah; later they murder Joab (2Sa 2:24; 3:30). Defeats the Ammonites (2Sa 10:10,14). Defeats 18,000 Edomites in the Valley of Salt (1Ch 18:12).

Seeks the life of Shimei son of Gera (2Sa 16:5-9; 19:18-23). Leads a division of David's army against Absalom (2Sa 18:2,5). Overthrows Sheba (2Sa 20:1-22). Saves David from being killed by Ishbi-Benob, one of the descendants of Rapha, a Philistine (2Sa 21:16-17). Obtains water from the well of Bethlehem for David (1Ch 11:15-20).

ABISHALOM [58] (*[my] father is peace*). (1Ki 15:2, 10). A longer form of Absalom. *See Absalom.*

ABISHUA [55] (*[my] father is salvation*).

1. The son of Phinehas the priest (1Ch 6:4-5,50; Ezr 7:5).

2. A Benjamite of the family of Bela (1Ch 8:4).

ABISHUR [56] (*[my] father is a wall*).

NIV+ ABISHUR'S

A man of Judah, the son of Shammai (1Ch 2:28-29).

ABITAL [40] (*[my] father is [the] night dew*). The fifth wife of David and mother of Shephatiah (2Sa 3:4; 1Ch 3:3).

ABITUB [39] (*[my] father is good*). A Benjamite, son of Shaharaim and Hushim (1Ch 8:8-11).

ABIUD [10] (*[my] father has majesty*). The son of Ze-rubbabel (Mt 1:13).

ABLUTION *See Washings.*

ABNER [46, 79] (*[my] father is Ner [lamp]*).

NIV+ ABNER'S

Son of Ner. Cousin of Saul (1Sa 14:50-51). Commander of the army of Saul (1Sa 14:50; 17:55; 26:5,14). Abner breaks with Ish-Bosheth and the house of Saul (2Sa 3:6-11) and transfers his loyalty to the house of David (2Sa 3:12-21). Murdered by Joab; David's sorrow for (2Sa 3:22-39). Dedicated spoils of war to the tabernacle (1Ch 26:27-28).

ABOMINATION [9199, 9359, *1007*].

NIV+ ABOMINABLE, ABOMINATIONS; See DETEST

This has to do with activities that are offensive in a moral, religious, or even a natural sense of repulsion.

God's Law Regarding:

Sexual relations, incest (Lev 18:6-18; Dt 27:20), lying with a woman in her monthly period (Lev 18:19; 20:18), adultery, your neighbor's wife (Lev 18:20), homosexuality (Lev 18:22; 20:13), bestiality (Lev 18:23; 20:15-16), idolatry (Dt 7:25-26; 27:15; 32:16-42), divination, sorcery, interpreting omens, witchcraft, casting spells, mediums or spiritists, those who consult the dead (Dt 18:9-15), offering children in sacrifice, by fire, to Molech (Dt 18:10, w Lev 18:21)

Wearing clothes of opposite sex—

Dt 22:5 A woman must not wear men's clothing, nor a man wear women's clothing, for the LORD your God detests anyone who does this.

The earnings of a female or a male prostitute to pay a vow (Dt 23:18), remarriage of defiled wife (Dt 24:1-4)

Unjust weights and measures (Dt 25:13-16; Pr 11:1)—

Pr 20:10 Differing weights and differing measures—the LORD detests them both. (+Pr 20:23)

See Law.

Actions and Attitudes:

A false witness who pours out lies (Dt 19:15-21; Pr 6:19; 21:28)

Perverseness—

Pr 3:32 for the LORD detests a perverse man but takes the upright into his confidence.

Pr 11:20 The LORD detests men of perverse heart but he delights in those whose ways are blameless.

False pride (Pr 6:17)—

Pr 16:5 The LORD detests all the proud of heart. Be sure of this: They will not go unpunished.

Murder (Pr 6:17)

Lying—

Pr 6:17 haughty eyes, a lying tongue, hands that shed innocent blood,

Pr 6:19 a false witness who pours out lies and a man who stirs up dissension among brothers.

Pr 12:22 The LORD detests lying lips, but he delights in men who are truthful.

One who devises wicked schemes (Pr 6:18)

Wicked imaginations, *i.e.,* the thoughts of the wicked—
Pr 6:18 a heart that devises wicked schemes, feet that are quick to rush into evil, (+Pr 15:26)
Pr 21:27 The sacrifice of the wicked is detestable—how much more so when brought with evil intent!

Wickedness—
Pr 8:7 My mouth speaks what is true, for my lips detest wickedness.

The sacrifice of the wicked (Pr 15:8; 21:27; Isa 1:13).
See Falsehood.

Idols, a General View:

(Dt 7:25-26; 27:15; 29:17-18; Eze 7:20-21). Solomon, in his old age, followed other gods and was punished (1Ki 11:1-12), Ashtoreth of the Sidonians, Molech of the Ammonites, Chemosh of the Moabites (1Ki 11:5-8; 11:33; 2Ki 23:13).

There are no gods apart from God—
Dt 6:4 Hear, O Israel: The LORD our God, the LORD is one. (+1Ch 17:20; Isa 43:10-13; 44:6-28)

Conditions for blessing: Return to God and turn from worthless gods (Jer 4:1-2), or receive disaster (Eze 5:5ff).

Idols, the worship of, and related practices: (Eze 16:1-63; Hos 9:10).
See Idol; Idolatry.

People, Types:

False witness (Pr 6:19; 17:15), trouble maker (Pr 6:19)

Mocker—
Pr 24:9 The schemes of folly are sin, and men detest a mocker.

Dishonest—
Pr 29:27 The righteous detest the dishonest; the wicked detest the upright.

Of Wicked:

Sacrifice—
Pr 15:8 The LORD detests the sacrifice of the wicked, but the prayer of the upright pleases him. (+Pr 21:27)

The way of—
Pr 15:9 The LORD detests the way of the wicked but he loves those who pursue righteousness.

The thoughts of—
Pr 15:26 The LORD detests the thoughts of the wicked, but those of the pure are pleasing to him.

Prayer—
Pr 28:9 If anyone turns a deaf ear to the law, even his prayers are detestable.
See Wicked.

ABOMINATION THAT CAUSES DESOLATION
[9037+9199, *1007+2247*]. An utterly abhorrent abomination (Da 9:27; 11:31; 12:11). Daniel's prophecies may refer to one or all of three events: to Antiochus' desecration of the temple in 167-169 B.C. (1Mc 1:21-61), to the destruction of Jerusalem in A.D. 70 (Mt 24:15; Mk 13:14), and to the setting up of the image of the beast (Rev 13:14-15). *See Antiochus, 4.*

ABORTION
Induced termination of pregnancy by killing the fetus. Clinical abortions are not addressed in the Bible. But the value of the unborn is clearly seen in texts that speak of their value and of judgments on those who kill them.

The value of the unborn (Job 31:15)—
Ps 139:13 For you created my inmost being; you knit me together in my mother's womb. [14]I praise you because I am fearfully and wonderfully made; your works are wonderful, I know that full well. [15]My frame was not hidden from you when I was made in the secret place. When I was woven together in the depths of the earth, [16]your eyes saw my unformed body. All the days ordained for me were written in your book before one of them came to be. (+Ecc 11:5; Isa 44:2,24; 49:1,5; Jer 1:4)
Lk 1:41 When Elizabeth heard Mary's greeting, the baby leaped in her womb, and Elizabeth was filled with the Holy Spirit. [42]In a loud voice she exclaimed: "Blessed are you among women, and blessed is the child you will bear! [43]But why am I so favored, that the mother of my Lord should come to me? [44]As soon as the sound of your greeting reached my ears, the baby in my womb leaped for joy. [45]Blessed is she who has believed that what the Lord has said to her will be accomplished!"

Punishment for injury to a pregnant mother and her unborn child—
Ex 21:22 "If men who are fighting hit a pregnant woman and she gives birth prematurely but there is no serious injury, the offender must be fined whatever the woman's husband demands and the court allows. [23]But if there is serious injury, you are to take life for life, [24]eye for eye, tooth for tooth, hand for hand, foot for foot, [25]burn for burn, wound for wound, bruise for bruise.

Punishment for the atrocity of ripping open pregnant women (2Ki 8:12; 15:16; Hos 13:16)—
Am 1:13 This is what the LORD says: "For three sins of Ammon, even for four, I will not turn back [my wrath]. Because he ripped open the pregnant women of Gilead in order to extend his borders, [14]I will set fire to the walls of Rabbah that will consume her fortresses amid war cries on the day of battle, amid violent winds on a stormy day. [15]Her king will go into exile, he and his officials together," says the LORD.
See Miscarry.

ABRAHAM, ABRAM
[90, 92, *11*] *(father of many or exalted father).*
NIV+ ABRAHAM'S, ABRAM, ABRAM'S

Events in the Life of:

Called Abram, son of Terah (Ge 11:26-27). Abram marries Sarai (Ge 11:29). Dwells in Ur of the Chaldeans, but moves. Terah, his father, took Abram and the rest of the family, intending to move to Canaan. On the way they stop and settle in Haran in NW Mesopotamia, where Terah dies (Ge 11:31; Ne 9:7; Ac 7:4). Eventually Abram, at seventy-five, sets out from Haran for the land of Canaan (Ge 12:1-6; Ac 7:4).

The divine call of—
Ge 12:1 The LORD had said to Abram, "Leave your country, your people and your father's household and go to the land I will show you.

[2]"I will make you into a great nation and I will bless you; I will make your name great, and you will be a blessing. [3]I will bless those who bless you, and whoever curses you I will curse; and all peoples on earth will be blessed through you." (+Jos 24:3; Ne 9:7-8; Isa 51:2)
Ac 7:2 To this he replied: "Brothers and fathers, listen to me! The God of glory appeared to our father Abraham while he was still in Mesopotamia, before he lived in Haran. [3]'Leave your country and your people,' God said, 'and go to the land I will show you.'

[4]"So he left the land of the Chaldeans and settled in Haran. After the death of his father, God sent him to this land where you are now living. (+Heb 11:8) *See Call.*

Canaan given to (Ge 12:1,6-7; 15:7-21; Eze 33:24). Dwells in the hills E of Bethel and W of Ai (Ge 12:8). Relocates to Egypt because of a famine in Canaan (Ge 12:10-20; 26:1). Upon leaving Egypt, they travel to the Negev and on to Bethel; since there is not enough land in one place to support their large herds of sheep, Abram gives Lot his choice of land; Lot chooses the plain of Jordan, leaving Abram to live at the great trees of Mamre the Amorite at Hebron (Ge 13; 14:13; 35:27). Dwells in Gerar and Beersheba (Ge 20; 21:22-34).

Defeats Kedorlaomer king of Elam (Ge 14:5-16; Heb 7:1). Is blessed by Melchizedek (Ge 14:18-20; Heb 7:1-10). *See Melchizedek.*

God's covenant with (Ge 15; 17:1-22; Mic 7:20; Lk 1:73; Ro 4:13; 15:8; Heb 6:13-15)—

Gal 3:6 Consider Abraham: "He believed God, and it was credited to him as righteousness." [7]Understand, then, that those who believe are children of Abraham. [8]The Scripture foresaw that God would justify the Gentiles by faith, and announced the gospel in advance to Abraham: "All nations will be blessed through you." [9]So those who have faith are blessed along with Abraham, the man of faith.

[10]All who rely on observing the law are under a curse, for it is written: "Cursed is everyone who does not continue to do everything written in the Book of the Law." [11]Clearly no one is justified before God by the law, because, "The righteous will live by faith." [12]The law is not based on faith; on the contrary, "The man who does these things will live by them." [13]Christ redeemed us from the curse of the law by becoming a curse for us, for it is written: "Cursed is everyone who is hung on a tree." [14]He redeemed us in order that the blessing given to Abraham might come to the Gentiles through Christ Jesus, so that by faith we might receive the promise of the Spirit.

[15]Brothers, let me take an example from everyday life. Just as no one can set aside or add to a human covenant that has been duly established, so it is in this case. [16]The promises were spoken to Abraham and to his seed. The Scripture does not say "and to seeds," meaning many people, but "and to your seed," meaning one person, who is Christ. [17]What I mean is this: The law, introduced 430 years later, does not set aside the covenant previously established by God and thus do away with the promise. [18]For if the inheritance depends on the law, then it no longer depends on a promise; but God in his grace gave it to Abraham through a promise. (+Gal 3:19-28)

Gal 3:29 If you belong to Christ, then you are Abraham's seed, and heirs according to the promise. (+Gal 4:22-31) *See Covenants, Major in the Old Testament.*

Ishmael born to (Ge 16:3,7-16). Renamed Abraham by the Lord (Ge 17:5; Ne 9:7). Circumcision of (Ge 17:10-14,23-27). *See Circumcision.* Angels appear to (Ge 18:1-16; 22:11-12,15; 24:7). His questions and intercession concerning the destruction of the righteous and wicked in Sodom (Ge 18:23-32). Witnesses the destruction of Sodom (Ge 19:27-29). Dwells in Gerar; deceives Abimelech concerning Sarah, his wife (Ge 20). Isaac born to Abraham when he is 100 years old according to the promise of Yahweh (Ge 21:1-5; Gal 4:22-30). Sends Hagar and Ishmael away (Ge 21:10-14; Gal 4:22-30).

Trial of his faith in the offering of Isaac (Ge 22:1-19; Heb 11:17-19; Jas 2:21). *See Faith, Instances of trial of.* Sarah, his wife, dies (Ge 23:1-2). He purchases a place for her burial and buries her in a cave (Ge 23:3-20). *See Burial; Burying Places.* Provides a wife for Isaac (Ge 24). Marries Keturah (Ge 25:1). Death (Ge 15:15; 25:8-10). In Paradise (Mt 8:11; Lk 13:28; 16:22-31).

Wealth of (Ge 13:2; 24:35). Children of (Ge 16:15; 21:2-3; 25:1-4; 1Ch 1:32-34). Inheritance of (Ge 25:5-6). *See Inheritance.* Age of at different periods (Ge 12:4; 16:16; 21:5; 25:7).

Character Qualities of:

Personal piety of and promises to (Ge 12:7-8; 13:4,18; 18:18-33; 20:7; 21:33; 22:3-13; 26:5; Ne 9:7-8; 2Ch 20:7; Isa 41:8; Ro 4:16-18; Jas 2:23). *See Worship.* Unselfishness of (Ge 13:9; 21:25-30). Independence of, in character (Ge 14:23; 23:6-16). Faith of (Ge 15:6; Ro 4:1-22; Gal 3:6-9; Heb 11:8-19; Jas 2:21-24). *See Faith, Instances of.* A prophet (Ge 20:7). Friend of God (2Ch 20:7; Isa 41:8; Jas 2:23).

How regarded by his descendants (Mt 3:9; Lk 13:16,28; 19:9; Jn 8:33-40,52-59).

ABRAHAM'S SIDE In the Lukan account of the rich man and Lazarus, Lazarus is being comforted at Abraham's side [KJV "bosom"] while the rich man is being tormented in the fires of hell (Lk 16:22-23). *See Lazarus.*

In the Talmudic language, to sit in Abraham's side is to enter Paradise (compare 4Mc 13:17). It is the place where the righteous go at the moment of death and where judgment is enacted as preliminary and perhaps probationary, to the Final Judgment at the end of the age.

See Hades; Hell; Immortality; Paradise; Righteous, Promises to; Sheol; Spirit; Wicked, Punishment of.

ABRAM *See Abraham, Abram.*

ABRECH, ABREK Transliteration of a term, perhaps of Egyptian origin, translated "make way" or "bow down" in the NIV (Ge 41:43; see NRSV ftn).

ABRONAH [6307]. A place where the Israelites camped (Nu 33:34-35).

ABSALOM [94] (*father is peace*).

NIV+ ABSALOM'S

1. The third son of David by Maacah, daughter of Talmai, king of Geshur (2Sa 3:3; 1Ch 3:2), also known as Abishalom (1Ki 15:2,10, w 1Ch 11:20-21).

Absalom hates Amnon, one of his stepbrothers and David's first son, because Amnon had raped his sister Tamar; after two years, Absalom avenges Tamar (2Sa 13:1-29). He flees to Geshur and stays there three years (2Sa 13:37-38). He is permitted by David to return to Jerusalem (2Sa 14:1-24). He is more handsome than anyone in all Israel (2Sa 14:25). Children of (2Sa 14:27; 1Ki 15:2,10; 2Ch 11:20). He is not allowed to see David for two years after his return from exile in Geshur (2Sa 14:28), at which time he forces Joab to get him an audience with the king (2Sa 14:31-33).

His Popularity:

(2Sa 15:2-6,13). Conspiracy (2Sa 15-17). Death and burial (2Sa 18:9-17). Pillar of (2Sa 18:18). David's mourning for (2Sa 18:33; 19:1-8).

2. Rehoboam's father-in-law (2Ch 11:20-21).

3. In the Apocrypha, an ambassador of Judas Maccabaeus, the father of Mattathias and Jonathan (1Mc 11:70; 13:11; 2Mc 11:17).

ABSTEMIOUSNESS *See Abstinence; Temperance.*

ABSTINENCE

From Intoxicating Beverages:

Abuse of alcohol condemned—

Pr 23:20 Do not join those who drink too much wine or gorge themselves on meat,

Pr 23:31 Do not gaze at wine when it is red, when it sparkles in the cup, when it goes down smoothly! ³²In the end it bites like a snake and poisons like a viper. ³³Your eyes will see strange sights and your mind imagine confusing things. ³⁴You will be like one sleeping on the high seas, lying on top of the rigging. ³⁵"They hit me," you will say, "but I'm not hurt! They beat me, but I don't feel it! When will I wake up so I can find another drink?" (+Lk 21:34)

Aaron and the Levitical priesthood, while on duty—

Lev 10:8 Then the LORD said to Aaron, ⁹"You and your sons are not to drink wine or other fermented drink whenever you go into the Tent of Meeting, or you will die. This is a lasting ordinance for the generations to come. ¹⁰You must distinguish between the holy and the common, -between the unclean and the clean, ¹¹and you must teach the Israelites all the decrees the LORD has given them through Moses." (+Eze 44:21)

Nazirites, while taking a special vow—

Nu 6:2 "Speak to the Israelites and say to them: 'If a man or woman wants to make a special vow, a vow of separation to the LORD as a Nazirite, ³he must abstain from wine and other fermented drink and must not drink vinegar made from wine or from other fermented drink. He must not drink grape juice or eat grapes or raisins. ⁴As long as he is a Nazirite, he must not eat anything that comes from the grapevine, not even the seeds or skins. (+Nu 6:20)

Manoah's wife, Samson's mother, during pregnancy—

Jdg 13:2 A certain man of Zorah, named Manoah, from the clan of the Danites, had a wife who was sterile and remained childless. ³The angel of the LORD appeared to her and said, "You are sterile and childless, but you are going to conceive and have a son. ⁴Now see to it that you drink no wine or other fermented drink and that you do not eat anything unclean, ⁵because you will conceive and give birth to a son. No razor may be used on his head, because the boy is to be a Nazirite, set apart to God from birth, and he will begin the deliverance of Israel from the hands of the Philistines."

Jdg 13:13 The angel of the LORD answered, "Your wife must do all that I have told her. ¹⁴She must not eat anything that comes from the grapevine, nor drink any wine or other fermented drink nor eat anything unclean. She must do everything I have commanded her."

Kings and princes—

Pr 31:4 "It is not for kings, O Lemuel—not for kings to drink wine, not for rulers to crave beer, ⁵lest they drink and forget what the law decrees, and deprive all the oppressed of their rights.

John the Baptist—

Lk 1:15 for he will be great in the sight of the Lord. He is never to take wine or other fermented drink, and he will be filled with the Holy Spirit even from birth.

Instances of:

Israelites in the wilderness (Dt 29:6). Samson (Jdg 16:17, w 13:3-5,13-14 & Nu 6:3-4).

Recabites, honoring an ancestral commitment—

Jer 35:1 This is the word that came to Jeremiah from the LORD during the reign of Jehoiakim son of Josiah king of Judah: ²"Go to the Recabite family and invite them to come to one of the side rooms of the house of the LORD and give them wine to drink."

³So I went to get Jaazaniah son of Jeremiah, the son of Habazziniah, and his brothers and all his sons—the whole family of the Recabites. ⁴I brought them into the house of the LORD, into the room of the sons of Hanan son of Igdaliah the man of God. It was next to the room of the officials, which was over that of Maaseiah son of Shallum the doorkeeper. ⁵Then I set bowls full of wine and some cups before the men of the Recabite family and said to them, "Drink some wine."

⁶But they replied, "We do not drink wine, because our forefather Jonadab son of Recab gave us this command: 'Neither you nor your descendants must ever drink wine. ⁷Also you must never build houses, sow seed or plant vineyards; you must never have any of these things, but must always live in tents. Then you will live a long time in the land where you are nomads.' ⁸We have obeyed everything our forefather Jonadab son of Recab commanded us. Neither we nor our wives nor our sons and daughters have ever drunk wine ⁹or built houses to live in or had vineyards, fields or crops. ¹⁰We have lived in tents and have fully obeyed everything our forefather Jonadab commanded us. ¹¹But when Nebuchadnezzar king of Babylon invaded this land, we said, 'Come, we must go to Jerusalem to escape the Babylonian and Aramean armies.' So we have remained in Jerusalem."

¹²Then the word of the LORD came to Jeremiah, saying: ¹³"This is what the LORD Almighty, the God of Israel, says: Go and tell the men of Judah and the people of Jerusalem, 'Will you not learn a lesson and obey my words?' declares the LORD. ¹⁴'Jonadab son of Recab ordered his sons not to drink wine and this command has been kept. To this day they do not drink wine, because they obey their forefather's command. But I have spoken to you again and again, yet you have not obeyed me.

Daniel (Da 1:8,12). John the Baptist (Mt 11:18; Lk 1:15; 7:33).

See Temperance.

Other Things Abstained From:

Food, in fasting (Lev 16:29; 23:27; 1Sa 7:6; Ne 9:1; Joel 2:12; Mt 6:16-18). *See Fasting.* Sexual contact within marriage, temporarily (Ex 19:15; 1Co 7:1-5).

In Israel—

The use of blood or fat (Ge 9:4; Lev 3:17). The tendon of the hip (Ge 32:32). Meat not properly bled and prepared (Ex 22:31; Dt 14:21). Whole groups of animals (Lev 11). Contact with unclean person (Lev 15) *See Unclean.*

Christians—

From evil and immorality (Ac 15:20,29; Eph 4:17-5:21; Col 3:1-11; 1Pe 2:11-12). For the sake of a weaker brother (Ro 14; 1Co 8). Wrongly used as a form of self-righteousness (Col 2:20-23; 1Ti 4:1-3). From an appearance of evil (1Th 5:22).

ABUNDANT, ABUNDANCE [*8041, 8044, 8425, 10678].

NIV+ ABOUND, ABOUNDING, ABOUNDS, ABUNDANCE, ABUNDANTLY

General:

(Ecc 5:9-20; Isa 15:7; Mt 13:12; 25:29; Mk 12:42-44; Lk 21:1-4; 2Co 8:12-15). Steadfast love (Ex 34:6-7; Ps 69:13; 103; Jnh 4:2). Peace (Lev 26:3,6; Ps 37:10-11; Jer 33:6-9).

Pardon (Nu 14:17-19)—

2Ch 30:18 Although most of the many people who came

from Ephraim, Manasseh, Issachar and Zebulun had not purified themselves, yet they ate the Passover, contrary to what was written. But Hezekiah prayed for them, saying, "May the LORD, who is good, pardon everyone [19]who sets his heart on seeking God—the LORD, the God of his fathers—even if he is not clean according to the rules of the sanctuary." [20]And the LORD heard Hezekiah and healed the people.

Isa 1:18 "Come now, let us reason together," says the LORD. "Though your sins are like scarlet, they shall be as white as snow; though they are red as crimson, they shall be like wool.

Isa 55:7 Let the wicked forsake his way and the evil man his thoughts. Let him turn to the LORD, and he will have mercy on him, and to our God, for he will freely pardon. (+Joel 3:20-21)

Mic 7:18 Who is a God like you, who pardons sin and forgives the transgression of the remnant of his inheritance? You do not stay angry forever but delight to show mercy. [19]You will again have compassion on us; you will tread our sins underfoot and hurl all our iniquities into the depths of the sea. [20]You will be true to Jacob, and show mercy to Abraham, as you pledged on oath to our fathers in days long ago.

Prosperity (Dt 28:47). Anguish (1Sa 1:16). Wealth (2Ch 17:3-6; 18:1; 20:25-27; 24:8-14; Ps 37:16; 52:6-7; Jer 48:36-38; 51:12-13). Honor (2Ch 17:5; 18:1; 1Co 12:23-24). Glory of Zion (Isa 66:11). Overflow of the heart (Mt 12:34; Lk 6:45). Life (Jn 5:39-40; 10:10; 20:30-31), is not in the abundance of possessions (Lk 12:15). Grace (Ro 5; 2Co 4:15), of giving (2Co 8:1-15), through the knowledge of our God and Savior Jesus Christ (2Pe 1:2). Affection, brotherly (2Co 7:15). Plunder (2Ch 20:25). Immeasurably more than we ask (Eph 3:20). Holy Spirit (Tit 3:5-6).

Participation in the divine nature and a rich welcome into the eternal kingdom—

2Pe 1:3 His divine power has given us everything we need for life and godliness through our knowledge of him who called us by his own glory and goodness. [4]Through these he has given us his very great and precious promises, so that through them you may participate in the divine nature and escape the corruption in the world caused by evil desires.

[5]For this very reason, make every effort to add to your faith goodness; and to goodness, knowledge; [6]and to knowledge, self-control; and to self-control, perseverance; and to perseverance, godliness; [7]and to godliness, brotherly kindness; and to brotherly kindness, love. [8]For if you possess these qualities in increasing measure, they will keep you from being ineffective and unproductive in your knowledge of our Lord Jesus Christ. [9]But if anyone does not have them, he is nearsighted and blind, and has forgotten that he has been cleansed from his past sins.

[10]Therefore, my brothers, be all the more eager to make your calling and election sure. For if you do these things, you will never fall, [11]and you will receive a rich welcome into the eternal kingdom of our Lord and Savior Jesus Christ.

From God:

Provisions, *i.e.* needs—

Lev 26:3 "'If you follow my decrees and are careful to obey my commands, [4]I will send you rain in its season, and the ground will yield its crops and the trees of the field their fruit. [5]Your threshing will continue until grape harvest and the grape harvest will continue until planting, and

you will eat all the food you want and live in safety in your land.

Dt 30:9 Then the LORD your God will make you most prosperous in all the work of your hands and in the fruit of your womb, the young of your livestock and the crops of your land. The LORD will again delight in you and make you prosperous, just as he delighted in your fathers, [10]if you obey the LORD your God and keep his commands and decrees that are written in this Book of the Law and turn to the LORD your God with all your heart and with all your soul.

Ps 132:13 For the LORD has chosen Zion, he has desired it for his dwelling: [14]"This is my resting place for ever and ever; here I will sit enthroned, for I have desired it— [15]I will bless her with abundant provisions; her poor will I satisfy with food.

Pr 3:9 Honor the LORD with your wealth, with the first-fruits of all your crops; [10]then your barns will be filled to overflowing, and your vats will brim over with new wine.

Isa 30:23 He will also send you rain for the seed you sow in the ground, and the food that comes from the land will be rich and plentiful. In that day your cattle will graze in broad meadows. (+Eze 36:29-30)

Am 9:13 "The days are coming," declares the LORD, "when the reaper will be overtaken by the plowman and the planter by the one treading grapes. New wine will drip from the mountains and flow from all the hills. (+Zec 8:12)

Php 4:19 And my God will meet all your needs according to his glorious riches in Christ Jesus.

Joys—

Ps 36:8 They feast on the abundance of your house; you give them drink from your river of delights.

Life—

Jn 10:10 The thief comes only to steal and kill and destroy; I have come that they may have life, and have it to the full.

Power—

Eph 3:20 Now to him who is able to do immeasurably more than all we ask or imagine, according to his power that is at work within us,

Grace—

2Co 9:8 And God is able to make all grace abound to you, so that in all things at all times, having all that you need, you will abound in every good work.

ABUSE

Substance Abuse:

1Co 6:12 "Everything is permissible for me"—but not everything is beneficial. "Everything is permissible for me"—but I will not be mastered by anything. [13]"Food for the stomach and the stomach for food"—but God will destroy them both. The body is not meant for sexual immorality, but for the Lord, and the Lord for the body.

Of alcohol—

Biblical condemnation of alcohol abuse may be generalized to apply to abuse of any mind- or behavior-altering substance. Condemned (Pr 20:1; 21:17; 23:20,30-35; Isa 5:22; Eph 5:18; 1Ti 3:8; Tit 2:3). Examples of (Ge 9:20-24; 19:30-36; Isa 28:7-8; 1Co 11:20-22). *See Abstinence; Temperance.*

Of food (Pr 23:1-3,20-21; 25:16; 30:22; Isa 56:10-11; Am 6:4-7; 1Co 6:12-13; 1Co 11:20-22; Php 3:18-19).

Sexual Abuse:

Rape punished by death (Dt 22:25-27). Examples of:

rape (Ge 34:1-7; Jdg 19:25-20:13; 2Sa 13:1-20; Zec 14:2), attempted homosexual rape (Ge 19:4-9; Jdg 19:22-24).

Abuse of Persons:

Physical injury was punished in like kind (Ex 21:22-25; Lev 24:19-20).

Servants and slaves—

Set free if physically abused (Ex 21:26-27)

Family—

Under the law, an unfavored wife still had to be cared for (Ex 21:10-11; Dt 21:15-17). A child could be put to death for abuse of parents (Ex 21:15,17; Dt 21:18-21). Corporal punishment, if done out of the motivation of love, is not abuse (Pr 3:11-12; 13:24; 29:15; Heb 12:7-11).

ABYSS [*12, 5853*] (*unfathomable depth*).

The abode of demons (Lk 8:31) and the place of the dead (Ro 10:7). The bottomless pit; a place of torment and of imprisoned demons (Rev 9:1-2,11; 11:7; 17:8; 20:1-3).

ACACIA WOOD [8847].

NIV+ ACACIAS

A tree (Isa 41:19). The ark of the covenant made of it wood (Ex 25:10), poles of the ark (Ex 25:13; 38:6), boards in the tabernacle (Ex 26:15-37), the altar of burnt offerings (Ex 38:1,6).

ACBOR, ACHBOR [6570] (*mouse* or *jerboa*).

1. The father of Baal-Hanan, a king of Edom (Ge 36:38-39; 1Ch 1:49).

2. The son of Micaiah, a messenger of King Josiah (2Ki 22:12-14). Also called Abdon the son of Micah (2Ch 34:20). *See Abdon, 5.*

3. The father of Elnathan (Jer 26:22; 36:12).

ACCAD *See Akkad.*

ACCEPTED BY GOD The worshiper's prayers (Ge 19:19-21), willing praise (Ps 119:108). Children of Israel (Ex 28:38; Eze 20:40-41; 43:27). Job's prayers (Job 42:9). The OT prophets continually affirmed that offerings were only acceptable when the person was acceptable; the offerer never became acceptable to God by giving him gifts (Hos 8:13; Mal 1:6-14).

NT Believers:

People from every nation who fear God and do what is right (Ac 10:34-35). The believer's goal is to please God (2Co 5:9). Through Christ (Eph 1:4-6).

ACCEPTED TIME The time favorable for seeking God. When forgiven (Ps 32:5-6). When in trouble (Ps 69:13). Today, *i.e.*, now (Ps 95:7-8; Isa 49:8; 2Co 6:2).

ACCESS TO GOD

Exemplified (Ex 24:2; 34:4-7). Typified (Lev 16:12-15, w Heb 10:19-22). In prayer (Dt 4:7; 2Ki 4:33; Mt 6:6; 1Pe 1:17). *See Prayer.* A privilege of believers (Dt 4:7; Ps 15; 23:6; 24:3-5). In his temple (Ps 15:1; 27:4-5; 43:3; 65:4). Blessedness of (Ps 16:11; 65:4; 73:28). Believers earnestly seek (Ps 27:4; 42:1-2; 43:3-4; 84:1-2). Is of God (Ps 65:4). Promises connected with (Ps 145:18-20; Isa 55:1-5; Mt 6:6; Jas 4:8). Urge others to seek (Isa 2:3; Jer 31:6). The wicked commanded to seek (Isa 55:6; Jas 4:8). Promised to repenting sinners (Hos 14:2; Joel 2:14). *See Repentance.* Is by Christ (Jn 10:7-10; 14:6-7; Ro 5:1-2; Eph 2:13; 3:12; Heb 7:18-19; 10:1-25; 1Pe 3:18). Obtained through faith (Ac 14:27; Ro 5:1-2; Eph 3:12; Heb 11:6). Is by the Holy Spirit (Eph 2:18). Believers have with confidence (Eph 3:12; Heb 4:16; 10:19-22). Follows upon

reconciliation to God (Col 1:21-22). To obtain mercy and grace (Heb 4:16).

ACCESSORY *See Complicity.*

ACCO, ACCHO [6573]. A town on the Mediterranean coast c. thirty miles south of Tyre, and ten from Mt. Carmel (Jdg 1:31, NIV). Also called Ptolemais by the ancient Greeks and Romans because Ptolemy, the Egyptian king, rebuilt the city in c. 100 B.C.; a town of Phoenicia (Ac 21:7, NIV, Ptolemais). *See Ptolemais.*

ACCOMPLICE *See Complicity.*

ACCOUNTABILITY *See Responsibility.*

ACCURSED [460, 2404, 7837, 7839, *2932*].

NIV+ CURSE

People that are cursed (Dt 21:23; Jos 6:18; 7:1,11,13,15; 1Ch 2:7; Isa 65:20; Ro 9:3; 1Co 12:3; Gal 1:8).

Things that are cursed (Jos 6:17-18; 7:12).

See Abomination; Anathema; Idolatry.

ACCUSATION, FALSE [*8189, 8357, 8476, 1592, 2989, 2991*].

NIV+ ACCUSE, ACCUSATIONS, ACCUSED, ACCUSER, ACCUSERS, ACCUSES, ACCUSING

Forbidden

Ex 23:1 "Do not spread false reports. Do not help a wicked man by being a malicious witness.

Ex 23:7 Have nothing to do with a false charge and do not put an innocent or honest person to death, for I will not acquit the guilty.

Lev 19:16 "'Do not go about spreading slander among your people. "'Do not do anything that endangers your neighbor's life. I am the LORD.

Lk 3:14 Then some soldiers asked him, "And what should we do?" He replied, "Don't extort money and don't accuse people falsely—be content with your pay." (+Tit 2:3)

Consolation for falsely accused—

Mt 5:11 "Blessed are you when people insult you, persecute you and falsely say all kinds of evil against you because of me. (+Jn 15:19-21)

1Pe 4:14 If you are insulted because of the name of Christ, you are blessed, for the Spirit of glory and of God rests on you.

Instances of False Accusation:

Joseph by Potiphar's wife (Ge 39:7-20); Joseph's brothers by Joseph (Ge 42:6-14); Moses by Korah (Nu 16:1-3,13); the prophet Ahimelech by Saul (1Sa 22:11-16); Abner by Joab (2Sa 3:24-27); Elijah by Ahab (1Ki 18:17-18); Naboth by Jezebel (1Ki 21:1-14); the Jews who returned under Ezra, accused by the men of Trans-Euphrates (Ezr 4:6-16; Ne 6:5-9); Job by Satan (Job 1:9-10; 2:4-5)

David—

Ps 41:5 My enemies say of me in malice, "When will he die and his name perish?" [6]Whenever one comes to see me, he speaks falsely, while his heart gathers slander; then he goes out and spreads it abroad.

[7]All my enemies whisper together against me; they imagine the worst for me, saying, [8]"A vile disease has beset him; he will never get up from the place where he lies." [9]Even my close friend, whom I trusted, he who shared my bread, has lifted up his heel against me.

By the princes of Ammon (2Sa 10:1-4; 1Ch 19:1-4), Jeremiah (Jer 26:8-15; 37:12-15; 43:1-4), Amos (Am 7:10-11), Mary (Mt 1:19), Jesus (Mt 9:34; 10:25; 12:2-14;

26:59-61; Mk 3:22; 14:53-65; Lk 23:2; Jn 18:30), Stephen (Ac 6:11-14), Paul (Ac 17:6-7; 21:27-29; 24:1-9,12-13; 25:1-2,7; Ro 3:8), Paul and Silas (Ac 16:19-21).

In last days, people will be slanderous—

2Ti 3:3 without love, unforgiving, slanderous, without self-control, brutal, not lovers of the good,

See *Conspiracy; Evidence; False Witness; Persecution; Speaking; Evil; Talebearer.*

ACELDAMA See *Akeldama.*

ACHAIA [*938*]. A region of Greece, on the S coast of the gulf of Corinth. Paul visits (Ac 18; 19:21; 1Co 16:15; 2Co 1:1). Generosity of the Christians in (Ro 15:26; 2Co 9:2; 11:10).

ACHAICUS [*939*] (*belonging to Achaia*). A Corinthian Christian who helped Paul, visited him at Ephesus and was commended for his good will toward Paul (1Co 16:17-19).

ACHAN [6575] (a word play from Achar: *troubler*). The son of Carmi and a Judahite of Zerah's clan who participated in the assault upon Jericho; he also violated the sacrificial ban by stealing gold, silver, and a beautiful robe from the spoil taken. After Israel failed to take Ai, inquiry was made by lot, and Achan was found to be guilty. Sin and punishment of (Jos 7; 22:20; 1Ch 2:7).

ACHAR [6580] (*trouble*). A variant spelling of Achan (1Ch 2:7).

ACHAZ See *Ahaz.*

ACHBOR See *Acbor.*

ACHIM See *Akim.*

ACHISH [429] (*the king gives*). King of the Philistines, also called Abimelech (Ps 34, title). David escapes to (1Sa 21:10-15; 27; 28:1-2; 29). Achish continues as king of Gath during the reign of Solomon (1Ki 2:39-40).

ACHMETHA See *Ecbatana.*

ACHOR [6574] (*trouble*). A valley near Jericho in which Achan was stoned (Jos 7:24-26; 15:7; Isa 65:10; Hos 2:15).

ACHSA, ACHSAH See *Acsah.*

ACHSHAPH See *Acshaph.*

ACHZIB See *Aczib.*

ACKNOWLEDGE [*1981, 3359, 5795, 10313, 3933*].

NIV+ ACKNOWLEDGED, ACKNOWLEDGES, ACKNOWLEDGMENT

General (Isa 61:9; 63:16; 1Co 14:37-38).

Acknowledging, in an imperative sense, that the Lord is God and that there is no other (Dt 4:39; Pr 3:5-6), in an imprecatory sense (Ps 79:6-7; Jer 10:23-25).

We acknowledge our sins (Ps 32:5; 51:1-6; Isa 59:12-13), our rebellion, idolatry, and wickedness (Jer 3:13; 14:20).

Recognition (1Co 16:17-18).

ACRE [5103+7538].

NIV+ TEN-ACRE

The amount of land a pair of oxen could plow in a day (1Sa 14:14; Isa 5:10).

ACROPOLIS (*crest of city, high ground of city*). The upper or higher city, citadel, or castle of a Greek city. Especially the high rocky promontory in Athens where the treasury of the city and its finest temples were located.

ACROSTIC A literary device by which the first letter of each line of poetry forms either a word or the successive letters of the alphabet. An outstanding example is Psalm 119, in which each successive set of eight verses begins with a different letter of the Hebrew alphabet. The effect is not apparent in the English translation, but the Hebrew letters are given between the lines in order to show the construction. NIV notes identify other acrostic poems (Ps. 9-10; 24; 34; 37; 111; 112; 145; Pr 31:10-31; La 1; 2; 3; 4).

ACROSTIC POETRY See *Poetry.*

ACSAH [6578] (*decorative anklet*). Caleb's daughter (1Ch 2:49). Caleb offered her as a reward, to be married, to the man who would capture the city of Debir, which was formerly called Kiriath Sepher. Caleb's nephew, Othniel, took the city and won the prize (Jos 15:16-19; Jdg 1:9-15).

ACSHAPH [439] (*fascination*). An important Canaanite city which Joshua captured with its king (Jos 11:1; 12:7,20). It is named as being on the border of the lot assigned to Asher (Jos 19:24-25).

ACTIONS AT LAW Duty of defendant (Mt 5:40; 1Co 6:7). See *Adjudication at Law; Arbitration.*

ACTIVITY, EVIL

Of sinners in general (Pr 1:10-16)—

Pr 4:14 Do not set foot on the path of the wicked or walk in the way of evil men. [15]Avoid it, do not travel on it; turn from it and go on your way. [16]For they cannot sleep till they do evil; they are robbed of slumber till they make someone fall. [17]They eat the bread of wickedness and drink the wine of violence.

Pr 6:18 a heart that devises wicked schemes, feet that are quick to rush into evil,

Isa 59:7 Their feet rush into sin; they are swift to shed innocent blood. Their thoughts are evil thoughts; ruin and destruction mark their ways.

Mic 2:1 Woe to those who plan iniquity, to those who plot evil on their beds! At morning's light they carry it out because it is in their power to do it. [2]They covet fields and seize them, and houses, and take them. They defraud a man of his home, a fellowman of his inheritance.

Mic 7:3 Both hands are skilled in doing evil; the ruler demands gifts, the judge accepts bribes, the powerful dictate what they desire—they all conspire together.

Ro 3:15 "Their feet are swift to shed blood; [16]ruin and misery mark their ways, [17]and the way of peace they do not know." [18]"There is no fear of God before their eyes."

Of Pharisees—

Mt 23:15 "Woe to you, teachers of the law and Pharisees, you hypocrites! You travel over land and sea to win a single convert, and when he becomes one, you make him twice as much a son of hell as you are.

Of Paul in persecuting the church (Ac 9:2)—

Ac 26:11 Many a time I went from one synagogue to another to have them punished, and I tried to force them to blaspheme. In my obsession against them, I even went to foreign cities to persecute them. (+Gal 1:13)

Php 3:6 as for zeal, persecuting the church; as for legalistic righteousness, faultless.

Of busybodies in the church, stirring up strife—

2Th 3:10 For even when we were with you, we gave you

this rule: "If a man will not work, he shall not eat." [11]We hear that some among you are idle. They are not busy; they are busybodies. [12]Such people we command and urge in the Lord Jesus Christ to settle down and earn the bread they eat.

1Ti 5:13 Besides, they get into the habit of being idle and going about from house to house. And not only do they become idlers, but also gossips and busybodies, saying things they ought not to.

1Pe 4:15 If you suffer, it should not be as a murderer or thief or any other kind of criminal, or even as a meddler.

Of Satan—

1Pe 5:8 Be self-controlled and alert. Your enemy the devil prowls around like a roaring lion looking for someone to devour.

ACTS OF THE APOSTLES

Author: Anonymous; traditionally Luke, the companion of Paul.

Date: Probably between A.D. 63 and 67.

Outline:

I. Peter and the Beginnings of the Church in Israel (chs. 1-12).
  A. "Throughout Judea, Galilee and Samaria" (1:1-9:31; see 9:31).
    1. Introduction (1:1-2).
    2. Christ's post-resurrection ministry (1:3-11).
    3. The period of waiting for the Holy Spirit (1:12-26).
    4. The filling with the Spirit (ch. 2).
    5. The healing of the lame man and the resultant arrest of Peter and John (3:1-4:31).
    6. The community of goods (4:32-5:11).
    7. The arrest of the twelve apostles (5:12-42).
    8. The choice of the Seven (6:1-7).
    9. Stephen's arrest and martyrdom (6:8-7:60).
    10. The scattering of the Jerusalem believers (8:1-4).
    11. Philip's ministry (8:5-40).
      a. In Samaria (8:5-25).
      b. To the Ethiopian eunuch (8:26-40).
    12. Saul's conversion (9:1-31).
  B. "As far as Phoenicia, Cyprus and Antioch" (9:32-12:25; see 11:19).
    1. Peter's ministry on the Mediterranean coast (9:32-11:18).
      a. To Aeneas and Dorcas (9:32-43).
      b. To Cornelius (10:1-11:18).
    2. The new Gentile church in Antioch (11:19-30).
    3. Herod's persecution of the church and his subsequent death (ch. 12).

II. Paul and the Expansion of the Church from Antioch to Rome (chs. 13-28).
  A. "Throughout the region of Phrygia and Galatia" (13:1-15:35; see 16:6).
    1. Paul's first missionary journey (chs. 13-14).
    2. The Jerusalem conference (15:1-35).
  B. "Over to Macedonia" (15:36-21; see 16:9).
    1. Paul's second missionary journey (15:36-18:22).
    2. Paul's third missionary journey (18:23-21:16).
  C. "To Rome" (21:17-28:31; see 28:14).
    1. Paul's imprisonment in Jerusalem (21:17-23:35).
      a. Arrest (21:17-22:29).
      b. Trial before the Sanhedrin (22:30-23:11).
      c. Transfer to Caesarea (23:12-35).
    2. Paul's imprisonment in Caesarea (chs. 24-26).
      a. Trial before Felix (ch. 24).
      b. Trial before Festus (25:1-12).

c. Hearing before Festus and Agrippa (25:13-26:32).
    3. Voyage to Rome (27:1-28:15).
    4. Two years under house arrest in Rome (28:16-31).
See Missionary Journeys of Paul.

ACZIB, ACHZIB [424] (*deceit*).

1. A city of Judah in the Shephelah (Jos 15:44; Mic 1:14) perhaps the same as modern Tell el-Beida, which is SW of Adullam. Taken by Sennacherib, c. 701 B.C. Also called Kezib (Ge 38:5) and Cozeba (1Ch 4:22).

2. A town in Asher on the coast N of Acco (Jos 19:29; Jdg 1:31).

ADADAH [6368]. A city in Judah (Jos 15:22).

ADAH [6336] (*adornment*).

1. The wife of Lamech and mother of Jabal (Ge 4:19-20,23).

2. The daughter of Elon the Hittite, and the first of three wives of Esau; she was the mother of Eliphaz (Ge 36:2,4, 10,12,16).

ADAIAH [6347, 6348] (*adornment of Yahweh*).

1. A native of Bozkath; the father of Jedidah, the mother of Josiah, the king of Judah (2Ki 22:1).

2. A Levite of the family of Gershom; the son of Ethni and father of Zerah, in the ancestry of Asaph (1Ch 6:41-43).

3. The son of Shimei and one of the chief Benjamites in pre-captivity Jerusalem (1Ch 8:1,21).

4. A priest and a Levite; the son of Jeroham (1Ch 9:10-12), also in the parallel list in Nehemiah, although the genealogies do not agree in all details (Ne 11:12).

5. The father of Maaseiah, an army officer who helped make Joash king in the overthrow of Athaliah (2Ch 23:1).

6. A man who married a foreign wife during the Exile and divorced her after the Captivity (Ezr 10:29).

7. Another man who did the same thing (Ezr 10:39).

8. A descendant of Judah whose posterity lived in Jerusalem after the captivity (Ne 11:5).

ADALIA [130] (possibly *honorable*). The fifth son of Haman (Est 9:8).

ADAM [134, 136, 77] (*[red] earth,* or *[ruddy] skin color*).

NIV+ ADAM'S

1. The first man. His creation (Ge 1:26-28; 2:7; 1Co 15:45; 1Ti 2:13). The history of, before he sinned (Ge 1:26-30; 2:16-25). His temptation and sin (Ge 3; Job 31:33, ftn; Isa 43:27; Hos 6:7; Ro 5:14-21; 1Ti 2:14). The subsequent history of (Ge 3:20-24; 4:1-2,25; 5:1-5). His death (Ge 5:5). Progenitor of the human race (Dt 32:8; Mal 2:10). A type of Christ (Ro 5:14). Brought sin and death into the world (1Co 15:22,45).

2. Christ: the last Adam (1Co 15:45).

3. A city in the Jordan Valley where the Israelites entered the promised land (Jos 3:16).

ADAMAH [142] (*[red] earth*). A city of Naphtali (Jos 19:36). The location is disputed, yet it may be the modern city of Tell ed-Damiyeh.

ADAMANT NIV "hardest stone" (Eze 3:9; Zec 7:12).

See Diamond; Flint, 2; Hardest Stone; Minerals of the Bible, 1; Stones.

ADAMI NEKEB [146] (*the ground of piercing*). A place on the border of Naphtali (Jos 19:33).

ADAR [160, 10009] (possibly *dark, clouded*).

Month twelve in sacred sequence, six in civil sequence (Ezr 6:15; Est 3:7; 8:12; 9:1,15-21). The rainy season (February-March); the season for harvesting citrus fruit. *See Month, 12.*

ADAR SHENI (*Second Adar*). This intercalary month (not in Bible) was added about every three years so the lunar calendar would correspond to the solar year. *See Month, 13.*

ADBEEL [118] (*[the] grief of God [El]*). The third son of Ishmael (Ge 25:13; 1Ch 1:29).

ADDAN *See Addon.*

ADDAR [161, 162] (*glorious*).
NIV+ HAZAR ADDAR, ATAROTH ADDAR
1. Also called Ard (Ge 46:21; Nu 26:40).
A son of Bela, and grandson of Benjamin (1Ch 8:3). Counted as a son of Benjamin and head of a family in the tribe.
2. A place on the S border of Judah (Jos 15:3).
See Hazar Addar, Hazar-Addar; Ataroth Addar, Ataroth-Adar.

ADDER [704].
NIV+ ADDERS
A poisonous snake (Job 20:16; Isa 30:6; 59:5). *See Cobra; Serpent.*

ADDI [79] (*my witness,* or *adorned*). An ancestor of Joseph, the husband of Mary (Lk 3:28).

ADDICTION
1Co 6:12 "Everything is permissible for me"—but not everything is beneficial. "Everything is permissible for me"—but I will not be mastered by anything. 13"Food for the stomach and the stomach for food"—but God will destroy them both. The body is not meant for sexual immorality, but for the Lord, and the Lord for the body.
2Pe 2:19 They promise them freedom, while they themselves are slaves of depravity— for a man is a slave to whatever has mastered him. (+Ro 6:16-21)
See Abuse.

ADDON [124, 150]. The inhabitants of Addon came up after the Babylonian captivity, but were unable to prove their lineage as descendants of Israel (Ezr 2:59; Ne 7:61).

ADER *See Eder.*

ADIEL [6346] (*adornment of God [El]*).
1. A descendant of Simeon who gained more pastoral land for himself in the region of Gedor in the time of Hezekiah (1Ch 4:36).
2. A priest, son of Jahzerah and the father of Maasai; Maasai returned after the Babylonian captivity and was very active in reconstructing the temple (1Ch 9:12).
3. Father of Azmaveth, who was supervisor of David's treasuries (1Ch 27:25).

ADIN [6350] (*voluptuous, luxurious*).
1. One whose family returned from exile with Zerubbabel (Ezr 2:15; Ne 7:20).
2. One whose posterity came back with Ezra (Ezr 8:6).
3. The name of a family sealing the covenant (Ne 10:16).

ADINA [6351] (*adorned*). The son of Shiza, a Reubenite; one of David's mighty men (1Ch 11:42).

ADINO (*his adorned one*). KJV "Adino the Eznite" is a variant reading in the NIV (2Sa 23:8, ftn). *See Josheb-Bas-shebeth.*

ADITHAIM [6353] (*double [row] of adornments*). A city in the Shephelah in the district of Zorah-Azekah (Jos 15:36).

ADJUDICATION AT LAW To be avoided

Pr 17:14 Starting a quarrel is like breaching a dam; so drop the matter before a dispute breaks out.

Pr 20:3 It is to a man's honor to avoid strife, but every fool is quick to quarrel.

Pr 25:8 do not bring hastily to court, for what will you do in the end if your neighbor puts you to shame? 9If you argue your case with a neighbor, do not betray another man's confidence, 10or he who hears it may shame you and you will never lose your bad reputation.

Mt 5:25 "Settle matters quickly with your adversary who is taking you to court. Do it while you are still with him on the way, or he may hand you over to the judge, and the judge may hand you over to the officer, and you may be thrown into prison. (+Mt 5:40; Lk 12:58)

See Actions at Law; Arbitration; Compromise; Court, of Law; Justice; Litigation.

ADJURATION KJV "adjure" is in the NIV to "pronounce" or "bind under oath," to "make someone swear an oath". It is an act or appeal in which a person in authority imposes some obligation upon another with the strength and solemnity of an oath (Jos 6:26; 1Sa 14:24; 1Ki 22:16; 2Ch 18:15). In the NT the high priest calls upon Jesus to acknowledge that he was the Messiah (Mk 5:7). The oath was binding and required a reply. *See Oath.*

It is also used to exorcise demons (Ac 19:13).

ADLAI [6354] (*be just*). The father of Shaphat, who was David's chief herdsman (1Ch 27:29).

ADMAH [144] (*[red] earth*). A city near Gomorrah and Zeboiim (Ge 10:19). The king was Shinab (Ge 14:2,8). Admah was destroyed along with Sodom and Gomorrah (Dt 29:23, w Ge 19:24-28; Hos 11:8).

ADMATHA [148] (*unrestrained*). The third named prince of Persia and Media (Est 1:14).

ADMINISTRATORS [*6913, 10518, *1354, 3873*].
NIV+ ADMINISTER, ADMINISTERED, ADMINISTERING, ADMINISTRATION, ADMINISTRATORS
Officers who ruled in Darius's kingdom; satraps report to (Da 6:2-7).

ADMONITION [5184, 6386, *3805*]. *See Wicked, Warned.*

ADNA [6363] (*delight*).
1. A son of Pahath-Moab who had married a foreign wife during the Exile (Ezr 10:30).
2. A chief priest, and the head of his father's house in the days of Joiakim (Ne 12:12-15).

ADNAH [6365, 6367] (*delight*).
1. One of the captains of the tribe of Manasseh who joined David at Ziklag (1Ch 12:20).
2. A man of Judah who held high military rank under Jehoshaphat (2Ch 17:14).

ADONI-BEZEK [152] (*lord of Bezek*).

NIV+ BEZEK

The king of Bezek, who had the thumbs and big toes of 70 kings cut off: when the Israelites routed the Canaanites and Perizzites and captured Adoni-Bezek, they had his thumbs and big toes cut off (Jdg 1:4-7).

See Bezek.

ADONIJAH [153, 154] (*[my] lord is Yahweh*).

NIV+ ADONIJAH'S

1. The fourth son of David by his wife Haggith (2Sa 3:4; 1Ki 1:5-6; 1Ch 3:2). Usurpation of, and downfall (1Ki 1). Executed by Solomon (1Ki 2:13,25).

2. A Levite whom Jehoshaphat sent to assist in teaching the law to the people of Judah (2Ch 17:8).

3. A leader who with Nehemiah sealed the covenant (Ne 10:16). *See Adonikam.*

ADONIKAM [156] (*[my] lord arises*). One of the Jews who returned with Ezra from Babylon with Zerubbabel (Ezr 2:13). Later three of his descendants came with Ezra (Ne 7:18). Probably the same as Adonijam, 3 (Ne 10:16).

ADONIRAM [157, 2067] (*[my] Lord is exalted*). A man in charge of forced labor during the reigns of David (2Sa 20:24, ftn) and later under Solomon (1Ki 4:6; 5:14), and then Solomon's son, Rehoboam (1Ki 12:18; 2Ch 10:18, ftn). He was stoned to death by the people of Israel as their first act of rebellion and revolt, which was lead by Jeroboam, son of Nebat, during the division of the monarchy.

ADONI-ZEDEK, ADONI-ZEDEC [155] (*[my] lord is righteousness*). The Amorite king of Jerusalem who with four other kings was defeated in battle and slain by Joshua at Gibeon (Jos 10:1-27).

ADOPTION [*1047, 4340, 5625].

NIV+ ADOPT, ADOPTED

Explained: (2Co 6:18).

Of Children:

Instances of: Of one born in Abram's house (Ge 15:3), of Joseph's sons (Ge 48:5,14,16,22), of Moses (Ex 2:5-10; Ac 7:20-21; Heb 11:24), of Esther (Est 2:7).

Spiritual Adoption:

Of Israel (Ex 4:22-23)—

Nu 6:27 "So they will put my name on the Israelites, and I will bless them." (+Dt 14:1-2; 26:18-19; 27:9; 28:9-10; 32:5-6)

2Ch 7:14 if my people, who are called by my name, will humble themselves and pray and seek my face and turn from their wicked ways, then will I hear from heaven and will forgive their sin and will heal their land. (+Isa 63:8)

Isa 63:16 But you are our Father, though Abraham does not know us or Israel acknowledge us; you, O LORD, are our Father, our Redeemer from of old is your name. (+Jer 3:19; 31:9,20; Hos 1:9-10; 11:1; Ro 9:4)

Of Solomon (2Sa 7:14; 1Ch 22:10; 28:6).

Of the righteous—

Pr 14:26 He who fears the LORD has a secure fortress, and for his children it will be a refuge. (+Isa 43:1-6; 63:8,16; Mt 5:9,44-45; 12:50; 13:43; Lk 6:35)

Jn 11:52 and not only for that nation but also for the scattered children of God, to bring them together and make them one.

Ro 9:8 In other words, it is not the natural children who are God's children, but it is the children of the promise who are regarded as Abraham's offspring. (+Ro 9:26)

2Co 6:17 "Therefore come out from them and be separate, says the Lord. Touch no unclean thing, and I will receive you."

[18] "I will be a Father to you, and you will be my sons and daughters, says the Lord Almighty." (+Eph 2:19; Php 2:15; Heb 12:6-7,9)

1Jn 3:1 How great is the love the Father has lavished on us, that we should be called children of God! And that is what we are! The reason the world does not know us is that it did not know him. [2] Dear friends, now we are children of God, and what we will be has not yet been made known. But we know that when he appears, we shall be like him, for we shall see him as he is. (+1Jn 3:10; 4:4)

Of the Gentiles promised—

Hos 2:23 I will plant her for myself in the land; I will show my love to the one I called 'Not my loved one.' I will say to those called 'Not my people,' 'You are my people'; and they will say, 'You are my God.'"

Ro 9:24 even us, whom he also called, not only from the Jews but also from the Gentiles? [25] As he says in Hosea:

"I will call them 'my people' who are not my people; and I will call her 'my loved one' who is not my loved one," [26] and,

"It will happen that in the very place where it was said to them, 'You are not my people,' they will be called 'sons of the living God.'" (+Eph 3:6)

Eph 3:6 This mystery is that through the gospel the Gentiles are heirs together with Israel, members together of one body, and sharers together in the promise in Christ Jesus. (+Eph 3:14-15; Heb 2:10-11,13)

Testified to by the Holy Spirit (Ro 8:14-17,19,21,29; Gal 4:5-7), through the gospel (Eph 3:6).

The Means of Adoption:

By God's grace—

Eze 16:3 and say, 'This is what the Sovereign LORD says to Jerusalem: Your ancestry and birth were in the land of the Canaanites; your father was an Amorite and your mother a Hittite. [4] On the day you were born your cord was not cut, nor were you washed with water to make you clean, nor were you rubbed with salt or wrapped in cloths. [5] No one looked on you with pity or had compassion enough to do any of these things for you. Rather, you were thrown out into the open field, for on the day you were born you were despised.

[6] "Then I passed by and saw you kicking about in your blood, and as you lay there in your blood I said to you, "Live!"

Ro 4:16 Therefore, the promise comes by faith, so that it may be by grace and may be guaranteed to all Abraham's offspring—not only to those who are of the law but also to those who are of the faith of Abraham. He is the father of us all. [17] As it is written: "I have made you a father of many nations." He is our father in the sight of God, in whom he believed—the God who gives life to the dead and calls things that are not as though they were.

Eph 1:5 he predestined us to be adopted as his sons through Jesus Christ, in accordance with his pleasure and will— [6] to the praise of his glorious grace, which he has freely given us in the One he loves.

Eph 1:11 In him we were also chosen, having been predestined according to the plan of him who works out everything in conformity with the purpose of his will,

By faith—

Jn 1:12 Yet to all who received him, to those who believed in his name, he gave the right to become children of God—

[13]children born not of natural descent, nor of human decision or a husband's will, but born of God.

Gal 3:7 Understand, then, that those who believe are children of Abraham.

Gal 3:26 You are all sons of God through faith in Christ Jesus,

Gal 3:29 If you belong to Christ, then you are Abraham's seed, and heirs according to the promise. (+Eph 1:5)

Through Christ (Jn 1:12-13)—

Jn 1:12 Yet to all who received him, to those who believed in his name, he gave the right to become children of God— [13]children born not of natural descent, nor of human decision or a husband's will, but born of God. (+Gal 3:26)

Gal 4:4 But when the time had fully come, God sent his Son, born of a woman, born under law, [5]to redeem those under law, that we might receive the full rights of sons.

Eph 1:5 he predestined us to be adopted as his sons through Jesus Christ, in accordance with his pleasure and will—

Heb 2:10 In bringing many sons to glory, it was fitting that God, for whom and through whom everything exists, should make the author of their salvation perfect through suffering. [11]Both the one who makes men holy and those who are made holy are of the same family. So Jesus is not ashamed to call them brothers.

Heb 2:13 And again, "I will put my trust in him." And again he says, "Here am I, and the children God has given me."

According to promise (Ro 9:8; Gal 3:29; Eph 3:6), through the gospel (Eph 3:6).

Role of the Holy Spirit:

Witnessed to by the Spirit—

Ro 8:16 The Spirit himself testifies with our spirit that we are God's children.

Led by the Spirit as evidence of—

Ro 8:14 because those who are led by the Spirit of God are sons of God.

They have received the Spirit of sonship—

Ro 8:15 For you did not receive a spirit that makes you a slave again to fear, but you received the Spirit of sonship. And by him we cry, *"Abba,* Father."

Gal 4:6 Because you are sons, God sent the Spirit of his Son into our hearts, the Spirit who calls out, *"Abba,* Father."

Results:

A new name (Nu 6:27)—

Isa 62:2 The nations will see your righteousness, and all kings your glory; you will be called by a new name that the mouth of the LORD will bestow.

Ac 15:17 that the remnant of men may seek the Lord, and all the Gentiles who bear my name, says the Lord, who does these things'

Disciplined by the Father—

Dt 8:5 Know then in your heart that as a man disciplines his son, so the LORD your God disciplines you. (+2Sa 7:14)

Pr 3:11 My son, do not despise the LORD's discipline and do not resent his rebuke, [12]because the LORD disciplines those he loves, as a father the son he delights in.

Heb 12:5 And you have forgotten that word of encouragement that addresses you as sons:

"My son, do not make light of the Lord's discipline, and do not lose heart when he rebukes you, [6]because the Lord disciplines those he loves, and he punishes everyone he accepts as a son."

[7]Endure hardship as discipline; God is treating you as sons. For what son is not disciplined by his father? [8]If you are not disciplined (and everyone undergoes discipline), then you are illegitimate children and not true sons. [9]Moreover, we have all had human fathers who disciplined us and we respected them for it. How much more should we submit to the Father of our spirits and live! [10]Our fathers disciplined us for a little while as they thought best; but God disciplines us for our good, that we may share in his holiness. [11]No discipline seems pleasant at the time, but painful. Later on, however, it produces a harvest of righteousness and peace for those who have been trained by it.

Safety (Pr 14:26), God is Father-Redeemer (Isa 63:16)

Recipient of God's long-suffering mercy—

Jer 31:1 "At that time," declares the LORD, "I will be the God of all the clans of Israel, and they will be my people."

Jer 31:19 After I strayed, I repented; after I came to understand, I beat my breast. I was ashamed and humiliated because I bore the disgrace of my youth.' [20]Is not Ephraim my dear son, the child in whom I delight? Though I often speak against him, I still remember him. Therefore my heart yearns for him; I have great compassion for him," declares the LORD.

A new inheritance—

Mt 13:43 Then the righteous will shine like the sun in the kingdom of their Father. He who has ears, let him hear.

Ro 8:17 Now if we are children, then we are heirs—heirs of God and co-heirs with Christ, if indeed we share in his sufferings in order that we may also share in his glory.

The new birth (Jn 1:12-13)

Will become brothers and sisters of Christ—

Jn 20:17 Jesus said, "Do not hold on to me, for I have not yet returned to the Father. Go instead to my brothers and tell them, 'I am returning to my Father and your Father, to my God and your God.'"

Heb 2:11 Both the one who makes men holy and those who are made holy are of the same family. So Jesus is not ashamed to call them brothers. [12]He says, "I will declare your name to my brothers; in the presence of the congregation I will sing your praises."

A new future: Gathered as one by Christ (Jn 11:52)

Final consummation—

Ro 8:19 The creation waits in eager expectation for the sons of God to be revealed.

Ro 8:23 Not only so, but we ourselves, who have the firstfruits of the Spirit, groan inwardly as we wait eagerly for our adoption as sons, the redemption of our bodies.

1Jn 3:2 Dear friends, now we are children of God, and what we will be has not yet been made known. But we know that when he appears, we shall be like him, for we shall see him as he is.

A New Lifestyle:

A love of peace—

Mt 5:9 Blessed are the peacemakers, for they will be called sons of God.

Desire for God's glory—

Mt 5:16 In the same way, let your light shine before men, that they may see your good deeds and praise your Father in heaven.

Likeness to God—

Mt 5:44 But I tell you: Love your enemies and pray for those who persecute you, [45]that you may be sons of your Father in heaven. He causes his sun to rise on the evil and the good, and sends rain on the righteous and the unrighteous.

Mt 5:48 Be perfect, therefore, as your heavenly Father is perfect.

An avoiding of pretense—

Mt 6:1 "Be careful not to do your 'acts of righteousness' before men, to be seen by them. If you do, you will have no reward from your Father in heaven.

²"So when you give to the needy, do not announce it with trumpets, as the hypocrites do in the synagogues and on the streets, to be honored by men. I tell you the truth, they have received their reward in full. ³But when you give to the needy, do not let your left hand know what your right hand is doing, ⁴so that your giving may be in secret. Then your Father, who sees what is done in secret, will reward you.

A forgiving spirit—

Mt 6:14 For if you forgive men when they sin against you, your heavenly Father will also forgive you.

Confidence in God—

Mt 6:25 "Therefore I tell you, do not worry about your life, what you will eat or drink; or about your body, what you will wear. Is not life more important than food, and the body more important than clothes? ²⁶Look at the birds of the air; they do not sow or reap or store away in barns, and yet your heavenly Father feeds them. Are you not much more valuable than they? ²⁷Who of you by worrying can add a single hour to his life?

²⁸"And why do you worry about clothes? See how the lilies of the field grow. They do not labor or spin. ²⁹Yet I tell you that not even Solomon in all his splendor was dressed like one of these. ³⁰If that is how God clothes the grass of the field, which is here today and tomorrow is thrown into the fire, will he not much more clothe you, O you of little faith? ³¹So do not worry, saying, 'What shall we eat?' or 'What shall we drink?' or 'What shall we wear?' ³²For the pagans run after all these things, and your heavenly Father knows that you need them. ³³But seek first his kingdom and his righteousness, and all these things will be given to you as well. ³⁴Therefore do not worry about tomorrow, for tomorrow will worry about itself. Each day has enough trouble of its own.

A spirit of prayer—

Mt 7:7 "Ask and it will be given to you; seek and you will find; knock and the door will be opened to you. ⁸For everyone who asks receives; he who seeks finds; and to him who knocks, the door will be opened.

⁹"Which of you, if his son asks for bread, will give him a stone? ¹⁰Or if he asks for a fish, will give him a snake? ¹¹If you, then, though you are evil, know how to give good gifts to your children, how much more will your Father in heaven give good gifts to those who ask him!

A merciful spirit—

Lk 6:35 But love your enemies, do good to them, and lend to them without expecting to get anything back. Then your reward will be great, and you will be sons of the Most High, because he is kind to the ungrateful and wicked. ³⁶Be merciful, just as your Father is merciful.

Holiness—

2Co 6:17 "Therefore come out from them and be separate, says the Lord. Touch no unclean thing, and I will receive you."

¹⁸"I will be a Father to you, and you will be my sons and daughters, says the Lord Almighty."

2Co 7:1 Since we have these promises, dear friends, let us purify ourselves from everything that contaminates body and spirit, perfecting holiness out of reverence for God. (+Php 2:15)

Following God—

Eph 5:1 Be imitators of God, therefore, as dearly loved children

ADORAIM
[126] (possibly *pair of knolls*). A fortified city in SW Judah, five miles SW of Hebron, fortified by Rehoboam, son of Solomon (2Ch 11:9).

ADORAM
(*[my] lord is exalted*). An alternate form of Adoniram. *See Adoniram.*

ADORNING
[*3636, 6335, 6995, *3175, 3180*].

NIV+ ADORN, ADORNED, ADORNMENT, ADORNS

Physical:

Bracelets (Ge 24:22; Nu 31:50; 2Sa 1:10). Earrings (Ge 35:4; Ex 32:2; 35:22; Nu 31:50; Jdg 8:24; Pr 25:12; Eze 16:12). Chains, used as ornaments (Ge 41:42; Pr 1:9; Eze 16:11; Da 5:29). Rings, for the fingers (Ge 41:42; Ex 35:22; Est 3:10; 8:8; Job 42:11; Isa 3:21; Hos 2:13; Lk 15:22). Ornaments, wearing of (Ex 33:4; Isa 3:18; Jer 2:32; 4:30; Eze 16:11; 23:40).

Jewels:

General references to (Ex 35:22; Nu 31:50). Discarded or refusal to wear (Ge 35:4; Ex 33:4; 1Pe 3:3). Brought as offerings to God (Ex 35:22; Nu 31:50; Mt 2:1-2,9-11).

Spiritual:

Clothed in righteousness, salvation, strength (Job 29:14; Ps 132:16; Isa 52:1; 61:10; Zec 3:4; Mt 22:11). General references to (Ps 45:13; Pr 1:9; 4:9; SS 1:10; Isa 61:10; 1Pe 3:3-4; Rev 21:2). White clothing, the heavenly garment (Mt 17:2; Rev 3:5; 3:18; 4:4; 7:9; 19:8).

ADRAMMELECH
[165, 166] (*nobility of Molech [king]*).

1. The name given to Adar, the god brought to Samaria from Assyria by the Sepharvites (2Ki 17:31).

2. One of the sons of Sennacherib, who along with his brother Sharezer, killed their father while he was worshiping in the temple of his god Nisroch (2Ki 19:37; Isa 37:38).

ADRAMYTTIUM
[*101*] (*the mansion of death*). A port city of Mysia, in the NW part of the Roman province of Asia (Ac 27:2).

ADRIATIC, ADRIA
[*102*]. The Adriatic Sea, a body of water between Italy on the W and Dalmatia, Macedonia, and Achaia on the E (Ac 27:27).

ADRIEL
[6377] (*[my] help is God [El]*). The son of Barzillai the Meholathite; Saul's son-in-law (1Sa 18:19; 2Sa 21:8-9).

ADULLAM, ADULLAMITE
[6355, 6356] (*retreat or refuge; possibly [they are] just*).

1. A cave near the Dead Sea. David takes refuge in (1Sa 22:1; 2Sa 23:13; 1Ch 11:15). *See also the titles of Pss 57 and 142.*

2. An ancient city of Canaan (Ge 38:1; Jos 12:15; 15:35), fortified by Rehoboam (2Ch 11:5-7), inhabited after the Exile (Ne 11:25-30), referred to by Micah (Mic 1:15).

3. The people of Adullam, used of Hirah, Judah's friend (Ge 38:1,12,20).

ADULLAMITE
See Adullam, Adullamite, 3.

ADULTERY [*2388, 2393, 2424, 5537, *3655, 3656, 3657, 3658, 3659, 4518, 4519, 4521].

NIV+ ADULTERER, ADULTERERS, ADULTERESS, ADULTERIES, ADULTEROUS

Defined:

Mt 5:28 But I tell you that anyone who looks at a woman lustfully has already committed adultery with her in his heart.

Mt 5:32 But I tell you that anyone who divorces his wife, except for marital unfaithfulness, causes her to become an adulteress, and anyone who marries the divorced woman commits adultery.

Mt 19:9 I tell you that anyone who divorces his wife, except for marital unfaithfulness, and marries another woman commits adultery." (+Mk 10:11-12; Lk 16:18)

Ro 7:1 Do you not know, brothers—for I am speaking to men who know the law—that the law has authority over a man only as long as he lives? [2]For example, by law a married woman is bound to her husband as long as he is alive, but if her husband dies, she is released from the law of marriage. [3]So then, if she marries another man while her husband is still alive, she is called an adulteress. But if her husband dies, she is released from that law and is not an adulteress, even though she marries another man.

Laws concerning (Nu 5:11-31)—

Dt 22:13 If a man takes a wife and, after lying with her, dislikes her [14]and slanders her and gives her a bad name, saying, "I married this woman, but when I approached her, I did not find proof of her virginity," [15]then the girl's father and mother shall bring proof that she was a virgin to the town elders at the gate. [16]The girl's father will say to the elders, "I gave my daughter in marriage to this man, but he dislikes her. [17]Now he has slandered her and said, 'I did not find your daughter to be a virgin.' But here is the proof of my daughter's virginity." Then her parents shall display the cloth before the elders of the town, [18]and the elders shall take the man and punish him. [19]They shall fine him a hundred shekels of silver and give them to the girl's father, because this man has given an Israelite virgin a bad name. She shall continue to be his wife; he must not divorce her as long as he lives.

[20]If, however, the charge is true and no proof of the girl's virginity can be found, [21]she shall be brought to the door of her father's house and there the men of her town shall stone her to death. She has done a disgraceful thing in Israel by being promiscuous while still in her father's house. You must purge the evil from among you.

[22]If a man is found sleeping with another man's wife, both the man who slept with her and the woman must die. You must purge the evil from Israel.

[23]If a man happens to meet in a town a virgin pledged to be married and he sleeps with her, [24]you shall take both of them to the gate of that town and stone them to death—the girl because she was in a town and did not scream for help, and the man because he violated another man's wife. You must purge the evil from among you.

[25]But if out in the country a man happens to meet a girl pledged to be married and rapes her, only the man who has done this shall die. [26]Do nothing to the girl; she has committed no sin deserving death. This case is like that of someone who attacks and murders his neighbor, [27]for the man found the girl out in the country, and though the betrothed girl screamed, there was no one to rescue her.

[28]If a man happens to meet a virgin who is not pledged to be married and rapes her and they are discovered, [29]he shall pay the girl's father fifty shekels of silver. He must marry the girl, for he has violated her. He can never divorce her as long as he lives.

Repulsive to the righteous—

Job 31:1 "I made a covenant with my eyes not to look lustfully at a girl. [2]For what is man's lot from God above, his heritage from the Almighty on high? [3]Is it not ruin for the wicked, disaster for those who do wrong? [4]Does he not see my ways and count my every step?

[5]"If I have walked in falsehood or my foot has hurried after deceit— [6]let God weigh me in honest scales and he will know that I am blameless— [7]if my steps have turned from the path, if my heart has been led by my eyes, or if my hands have been defiled, [8]then may others eat what I have sown, and may my crops be uprooted.

[9]"If my heart has been enticed by a woman, or if I have lurked at my neighbor's door, [10]then may my wife grind another man's grain, and may other men sleep with her. [11]For that would have been shameful, a sin to be judged. [12]It is a fire that burns to Destruction; it would have uprooted my harvest. (+Eze 18:5-6,9)

Fatal consequences of—

Pr 2:16 It will save you also from the adulteress, from the wayward wife with her seductive words, (+Pr 2:17)

Pr 2:18 For her house leads down to death and her paths to the spirits of the dead. [19]None who go to her return or attain the paths of life.

Pr 5:3 For the lips of an adulteress drip honey, and her speech is smoother than oil; [4]but in the end she is bitter as gall, sharp as a double-edged sword. (+Pr 5:5-23)

Pr 6:23 For these commands are a lamp, this teaching is a light, and the corrections of discipline are the way to life, [24]keeping you from the immoral woman, from the smooth tongue of the wayward wife. [25]Do not lust in your heart after her beauty or let her captivate you with her eyes, [26]for the prostitute reduces you to a loaf of bread, and the adulteress preys upon your very life. [27]Can a man scoop fire into his lap without his clothes being burned? [28]Can a man walk on hot coals without his feet being scorched? [29]So is he who sleeps with another man's wife; no one who touches her will go unpunished.

[30]Men do not despise a thief if he steals to satisfy his hunger when he is starving. [31]Yet if he is caught, he must pay sevenfold, though it costs him all the wealth of his house. [32]But a man who commits adultery lacks judgment; whoever does so destroys himself. [33]Blows and disgrace are his lot, and his shame will never be wiped away; [34]for jealousy arouses a husband's fury, and he will show no mercy when he takes revenge. [35]He will not accept any compensation; he will refuse the bribe, however great it is.

Pr 7:1 My son, keep my words and store up my commands within you. [2]Keep my commands and you will live; guard my teachings as the apple of your eye. [3]Bind them on your fingers; write them on the tablet of your heart. [4]Say to wisdom, "You are my sister," and call understanding your kinsman; [5]they will keep you from the adulteress, from the wayward wife with her seductive words.

[6]At the window of my house I looked out through the lattice. [7]I saw among the simple, I noticed among the young men, a youth who lacked judgment. [8]He was going down the street near her corner, walking along in the direction of her house [9]at twilight, as the day was fading, as the dark of night set in.

[10]Then out came a woman to meet him, dressed like a prostitute and with crafty intent. [11](She is loud and defiant, her feet never stay at home; [12]now in the street, now in the

squares, at every corner she lurks.) ¹³She took hold of him and kissed him and with a brazen face she said:

¹⁴"I have fellowship offerings at home; today I fulfilled my vows. ¹⁵So I came out to meet you; I looked for you and have found you! ¹⁶I have covered my bed with colored linens from Egypt. ¹⁷I have perfumed my bed with myrrh, aloes and cinnamon. ¹⁸Come, let's drink deep of love till morning; let's enjoy ourselves with love! ¹⁹My husband is not at home; he has gone on a long journey. ²⁰He took his purse filled with money and will not be home till full moon."

²¹With persuasive words she led him astray; she seduced him with her smooth talk. ²²All at once he followed her like an ox going to the slaughter, like a deer stepping into a noose ²³till an arrow pierces his liver, like a bird darting into a snare, little knowing it will cost him his life.

²⁴Now then, my sons, listen to me; pay attention to what I say. ²⁵Do not let your heart turn to her ways or stray into her paths. ²⁶Many are the victims she has brought down; her slain are a mighty throng. ²⁷Her house is a highway to the grave, leading down to the chambers of death.

Pr 9:13 The woman Folly is loud; she is undisciplined and without knowledge. ¹⁴She sits at the door of her house, on a seat at the highest point of the city, ¹⁵calling out to those who pass by, who go straight on their way. ¹⁶"Let all who are simple come in here!" she says to those who lack judgment. ¹⁷"Stolen water is sweet; food eaten in secret is delicious!" ¹⁸But little do they know that the dead are there, that her guests are in the depths of the grave.

Pr 22:14 The mouth of an adulteress is a deep pit; he who is under the LORD's wrath will fall into it.

Pr 23:26 My son, give me your heart and let your eyes keep to my ways, ²⁷for a prostitute is a deep pit and a wayward wife is a narrow well. ²⁸Like a bandit she lies in wait, and multiplies the unfaithful among men.

Moral and spiritual corruption by—

Jer 3:1 "If a man divorces his wife and she leaves him and marries another man, should he return to her again? Would not the land be completely defiled? But you have lived as a prostitute with many lovers—would you now return to me?" declares the LORD. ²"Look up to the barren heights and see. Is there any place where you have not been ravished? By the roadside you sat waiting for lovers, sat like a nomad in the desert. You have defiled the land with your prostitution and wickedness.

Jer 5:7 "Why should I forgive you? Your children have forsaken me and sworn by gods that are not gods. I supplied all their needs, yet they committed adultery and thronged to the houses of prostitutes. ⁸They are well-fed, lusty stallions, each neighing for another man's wife.

Hos 4:1 Hear the word of the LORD, you Israelites, because the LORD has a charge to bring against you who live in the land: "There is no faithfulness, no love, no acknowledgment of God in the land. ²There is only cursing, lying and murder, stealing and adultery; they break all bounds, and bloodshed follows bloodshed.

Hos 4:9 And it will be: Like people, like priests. I will punish both of them for their ways and repay them for their deeds.

¹⁰"They will eat but not have enough; they will engage in prostitution but not increase, because they have deserted the LORD to give themselves ¹¹to prostitution, to old wine and new, which take away the understanding ¹²of my people. They consult a wooden idol and are answered by a stick of wood. A spirit of prostitution leads them astray; they are unfaithful to their God. ¹³They sacrifice on the

mountaintops and burn offerings on the hills, under oak, poplar and terebinth, where the shade is pleasant. Therefore your daughters turn to prostitution and your daughters-in-law to adultery.

¹⁴"I will not punish your daughters when they turn to prostitution, nor your daughters-in-law when they commit adultery, because the men themselves consort with harlots and sacrifice with shrine prostitutes—a people without understanding will come to ruin!

¹⁵"Though you commit adultery, O Israel, let not Judah become guilty. "Do not go to Gilgal; do not go up to Beth Aven. And do not swear, 'As surely as the LORD lives!'

¹⁶The Israelites are stubborn, like a stubborn heifer. How then can the LORD pasture them like lambs in a meadow? ¹⁷Ephraim is joined to idols; leave him alone! ¹⁸Even when their drinks are gone, they continue their prostitution; their rulers dearly love shameful ways. ¹⁹A whirlwind will sweep them away, and their sacrifices will bring them shame.

Figurative:

(Jer 3:1-2; 9:2; 23:10; Eze 16:15-16; Hos 1; 2:1-2; 3:1; 7:1-4; Ro 7:1-6).

Forbidden:

Ex 20:14 "You shall not commit adultery.

Lev 18:20 "'Do not have sexual relations with your neighbor's wife and defile yourself with her.

Lev 19:29 "'Do not degrade your daughter by making her a prostitute, or the land will turn to prostitution and be filled with wickedness. (+Dt 5:18)

Dt 23:17 No Israelite man or woman is to become a shrine prostitute.

Pr 31:3 do not spend your strength on women, your vigor on those who ruin kings. (+Mt 5:27-28; 19:16-19)

Mk 10:17 As Jesus started on his way, a man ran up to him and fell on his knees before him. "Good teacher," he asked, "what must I do to inherit eternal life?"

¹⁸"Why do you call me good?" Jesus answered. "No one is good—except God alone. ¹⁹You know the commandments: 'Do not murder, do not commit adultery, do not steal, do not give false testimony, do not defraud, honor your father and mother.'" (+Lk 18:18-20)

Ac 15:20 Instead we should write to them, telling them to abstain from food polluted by idols, from sexual immorality, from the meat of strangled animals and from blood. (+Ac 15:29; Ro 13:9)

Ro 13:13 Let us behave decently, as in the daytime, not in orgies and drunkenness, not in sexual immorality and debauchery, not in dissension and jealousy.

1Co 5:9 I have written you in my letter not to associate with sexually immoral people— ¹⁰not at all meaning the people of this world who are immoral, or the greedy and swindlers, or idolaters. In that case you would have to leave this world. ¹¹But now I am writing you that you must not associate with anyone who calls himself a brother but is sexually immoral or greedy, an idolater or a slanderer, a drunkard or a swindler. With such a man do not even eat.

1Co 6:13 "Food for the stomach and the stomach for food"—but God will destroy them both. The body is not meant for sexual immorality, but for the Lord, and the Lord for the body. ¹⁴By his power God raised the Lord from the dead, and he will raise us also. ¹⁵Do you not know that your bodies are members of Christ himself? Shall I then take the members of Christ and unite them with a prostitute? Never! ¹⁶Do you not know that he who unites himself with a prostitute is one with her in body? For it is said, "The two will become one flesh." (+1Co 6:17)

1Co 6:18 Flee from sexual immorality. All other sins a man commits are outside his body, but he who sins sexually sins against his own body.

1Co 10:7 Do not be idolaters, as some of them were; as it is written: "The people sat down to eat and drink and got up to indulge in pagan revelry." [8]We should not commit sexual immorality, as some of them did—and in one day twenty-three thousand of them died. (+Eph 4:17-19)

Eph 5:3 But among you there must not be even a hint of sexual immorality, or of any kind of impurity, or of greed, because these are improper for God's holy people.

Col 3:5 Put to death, therefore, whatever belongs to your earthly nature: sexual immorality, impurity, lust, evil desires and greed, which is idolatry.

1Th 4:3 It is God's will that you should be sanctified: that you should avoid sexual immorality; [4]that each of you should learn to control his own body in a way that is holy and honorable, [5]not in passionate lust like the heathen, who do not know God; [6]and that in this matter no one should wrong his brother or take advantage of him. The Lord will punish men for all such sins, as we have already told you and warned you. [7]For God did not call us to be impure, but to live a holy life. (+1Ti 1:9-10; Jas 2:10-11)

Forgiveness of:

Jdg 19:1 In those days Israel had no king. Now a Levite who lived in a remote area in the hill country of Ephraim took a concubine from Bethlehem in Judah.

[2]But she was unfaithful to him. She left him and went back to her father's house in Bethlehem, Judah. After she had been there four months, [3]her husband went to her to persuade her to return. He had with him his servant and two donkeys. She took him into her father's house, and when her father saw him, he gladly welcomed him. [4]His father-in-law, the girl's father, prevailed upon him to stay; so he remained with him three days, eating and drinking, and sleeping there. (+Jn 4:16-26,39-42)

Jn 8:10 Jesus straightened up and asked her, "Woman, where are they? Has no one condemned you?"

[11]"No one, sir," she said. "Then neither do I condemn you," Jesus declared. "Go now and leave your life of sin."

Lack of Repentance in:

Pr 30:20 "This is the way of an adulteress: She eats and wipes her mouth and says, 'I've done nothing wrong.'

Isa 57:3 "But you—come here, you sons of a sorceress, you offspring of adulterers and prostitutes! [4]Whom are you mocking? At whom do you sneer and stick out your tongue? Are you not a brood of rebels, the offspring of liars?

Jer 7:9 "'Will you steal and murder, commit adultery and perjury, burn incense to Baal and follow other gods you have not known, [10]and then come and stand before me in this house, which bears my Name, and say, "We are safe"—safe to do all these detestable things? [11]Has this house, which bears my Name, become a den of robbers to you? But I have been watching! declares the Lord.

[12]"'Go now to the place in Shiloh where I first made a dwelling for my Name, and see what I did to it because of the wickedness of my people Israel. [13]While you were doing all these things, declares the Lord, I spoke to you again and again, but you did not listen; I called you, but you did not answer. [14]Therefore, what I did to Shiloh I will now do to the house that bears my Name, the temple you trust in, the place I gave to you and your fathers. [15]I will

thrust you from my presence, just as I did all your brothers, the people of Ephraim.'

Ro 1:28 Furthermore, since they did not think it worthwhile to retain the knowledge of God, he gave them over to a depraved mind, to do what ought not to be done. [29]They have become filled with every kind of wickedness, evil, greed and depravity. They are full of envy, murder, strife, deceit and malice. They are gossips, [30]slanderers, God-haters, insolent, arrogant and boastful; they invent ways of doing evil; they disobey their parents; [31]they are senseless, faithless, heartless, ruthless. [32]Although they know God's righteous decree that those who do such things deserve death, they not only continue to do these very things but also approve of those who practice them. (+2Co 12:21)

1Pe 4:3 For you have spent enough time in the past doing what pagans choose to do—living in debauchery, lust, drunkenness, orgies, carousing and detestable idolatry. [4]They think it strange that you do not plunge with them into the same flood of dissipation, and they heap abuse on you.

Rev 9:20 The rest of mankind that were not killed by these plagues still did not repent of the work of their hands; they did not stop worshiping demons, and idols of gold, silver, bronze, stone and wood—idols that cannot see or hear or walk. [21]Nor did they repent of their murders, their magic arts, their sexual immorality or their thefts.

Instances of:

The Sodomites (Ge 19:4-8; Jude 7). Lot and his two daughters (Ge 19:31-38). Shechem (Ge 34:1-2). Reuben (Ge 35:22). Judah (Ge 38:1-26). Potiphar's wife (Ge 39:6-12).

Israelites (Ex 32:6)—

Jer 23:10 The land is full of adulterers; because of the curse the land lies parched and the pastures in the desert are withered. The [prophets] follow an evil course and use their power unjustly.

[11]"Both prophet and priest are godless; even in my temple I find their wickedness," declares the Lord. (+Jer 29:23; Eze 22:9-11; 33:26; Hos 7:4)

Gilead, the father of Jephthah (Jdg 11:1). Samson (Jdg 16:1). The Levite's concubine (Jdg 19:1-2). The men of Gibeah (Jdg 19:22-25). The sons of Eli (1Sa 2:22). David (2Sa 11:1-5). Amnon, David's oldest son by Ahinoam (2Sa 13:1-20). Absalom, David's third son by Maacah (2Sa 16:22). Herod (Mt 14:3-4; Mk 6:17-18; Lk 3:19). The Samaritan woman (Jn 4:17-18). The woman brought to Jesus in the temple (Jn 8:3-11). The Corinthians (1Co 5:1-5).

Heathen—

Eph 4:17 So I tell you this, and insist on it in the Lord, that you must no longer live as the Gentiles do, in the futility of their thinking. (+Eph 4:18)

Eph 4:19 Having lost all sensitivity, they have given themselves over to sensuality so as to indulge in every kind of impurity, with a continual lust for more.

[20]You, however, did not come to know Christ that way. (+1Pe 4:3-4)

Those living in the last days—

2Ti 3:6 They are the kind who worm their way into homes and gain control over weak-willed women, who are loaded down with sins and are swayed by all kinds of evil desires,

Penalties for:

Death—

Ge 20:3 But God came to Abimelech in a dream one night

and said to him, "You are as good as dead because of the woman you have taken; she is a married woman."

Ge 20:7 Now return the man's wife, for he is a prophet, and he will pray for you and you will live. But if you do not return her, you may be sure that you and all yours will die."

Ge 26:11 So Abimelech gave orders to all the people: "Anyone who molests this man or his wife shall surely be put to death."

Ge 38:24 About three months later Judah was told, "Your daughter-in-law Tamar is guilty of prostitution, and as a result she is now pregnant." Judah said, "Bring her out and have her burned to death!"

Lev 20:10 "'If a man commits adultery with another man's wife—with the wife of his neighbor—both the adulterer and the adulteress must be put to death.

¹¹"'If a man sleeps with his father's wife, he has dishonored his father. Both the man and the woman must be put to death; their blood will be on their own heads.

¹²"'If a man sleeps with his daughter-in-law, both of them must be put to death. What they have done is a perversion; their blood will be on their own heads.

Lev 21:9 "'If a priest's daughter defiles herself by becoming a prostitute, she disgraces her father; she must be burned in the fire. (+Dt 22:13-27)

2Sa 12:7 Then Nathan said to David, "You are the man! This is what the LORD, the God of Israel, says: 'I anointed you king over Israel, and I delivered you from the hand of Saul. 8I gave your master's house to you, and your master's wives into your arms. I gave you the house of Israel and Judah. And if all this had been too little, I would have given you even more. 9Why did you despise the word of the LORD by doing what is evil in his eyes? You struck down Uriah the Hittite with the sword and took his wife to be your own. You killed him with the sword of the Ammonites. ¹⁰Now, therefore, the sword will never depart from your house, because you despised me and took the wife of Uriah the Hittite to be your own.'

¹¹"This is what the LORD says: 'Out of your own household I am going to bring calamity upon you. Before your very eyes I will take your wives and give them to one who is close to you, and he will lie with your wives in broad daylight. ¹²You did it in secret, but I will do this thing in broad daylight before all Israel.'"

¹³Then David said to Nathan, "I have sinned against the LORD." Nathan replied, "The LORD has taken away your sin. You are not going to die.

¹⁴But because by doing this you have made the enemies of the LORD show utter contempt, the son born to you will die."

Eze 23:45 But righteous men will sentence them to the punishment of women who commit adultery and shed blood, because they are adulterous and blood is on their hands.

⁴⁶"This is what the Sovereign LORD says: Bring a mob against them and give them over to terror and plunder. ⁴⁷The mob will stone them and cut them down with their swords; they will kill their sons and daughters and burn down their houses.

⁴⁸"So I will put an end to lewdness in the land, that all women may take warning and not imitate you.

Jn 8:4 and said to Jesus, "Teacher, this woman was caught in the act of adultery. 5In the Law Moses commanded us to stone such women. Now what do you say?"

Fines—

Ex 22:16 "If a man seduces a virgin who is not pledged to be married and sleeps with her, he must pay the bride-price, and she shall be his wife. ¹⁷If her father absolutely refuses to give her to him, he must still pay the bride-price for virgins. (+Dt 22:19,28-29)

Make a guilt offering—

Lev 19:20 "'If a man sleeps with a woman who is a slave girl promised to another man but who has not been ransomed or given her freedom, there must be due punishment. Yet they are not to be put to death, because she had not been freed. ²¹The man, however, must bring a ram to the entrance to the Tent of Meeting for a guilt offering to the LORD. ²²With the ram of the guilt offering the priest is to make atonement for him before the LORD for the sin he has committed, and his sin will be forgiven.

Curses—

The law of jealousy regarding an unfaithful wife (Nu 5:11-31).

Dt 27:20 "Cursed is the man who sleeps with his father's wife, for he dishonors his father's bed." Then all the people shall say, "Amen!"

²¹"Cursed is the man who has sexual relations with any animal." Then all the people shall say, "Amen!"

²²"Cursed is the man who sleeps with his sister, the daughter of his father or the daughter of his mother." Then all the people shall say, "Amen!"

²³"Cursed is the man who sleeps with his mother-in-law." Then all the people shall say, "Amen!"

Job 24:15 The eye of the adulterer watches for dusk; he thinks, 'No eye will see me,' and he keeps his face concealed. ¹⁶In the dark, men break into houses, but by day they shut themselves in; they want nothing to do with the light. ¹⁷For all of them, deep darkness is their morning; they make friends with the terrors of darkness.

¹⁸"Yet they are foam on the surface of the water; their portion of the land is cursed, so that no one goes to the vineyards.

Divine judgments—

2Sa 12:10 Now, therefore, the sword will never depart from your house, because you despised me and took the wife of Uriah the Hittite to be your own.'

¹¹"This is what the LORD says: 'Out of your own household I am going to bring calamity upon you. Before your very eyes I will take your wives and give them to one who is close to you, and he will lie with your wives in broad daylight. ¹²You did it in secret, but I will do this thing in broad daylight before all Israel.'"

Jer 29:22 Because of them, all the exiles from Judah who are in Babylon will use this curse: 'The LORD treat you like Zedekiah and Ahab, whom the king of Babylon burned in the fire.' ²³For they have done outrageous things in Israel; they have committed adultery with their neighbors' wives and in my name have spoken lies, which I did not tell them to do. I know it and am a witness to it," declares the LORD.

Eze 16:38 I will sentence you to the punishment of women who commit adultery and who shed blood; I will bring upon you the blood vengeance of my wrath and jealous anger. ³⁹Then I will hand you over to your lovers, and they will tear down your mounds and destroy your lofty shrines. They will strip you of your clothes and take your fine jewelry and leave you naked and bare. ⁴⁰They will bring a mob against you, who will stone you and hack you to pieces with their swords. ⁴¹They will burn down your houses and inflict punishment on you in the sight of many women. I will put a stop to your prostitution, and you will no longer pay your lovers.

Mal 3:5 "So I will come near to you for judgment. I will be quick to testify against sorcerers, adulterers and perjurers, against those who defraud laborers of their wages, who oppress the widows and the fatherless, and deprive aliens of justice, but do not fear me," says the LORD Almighty.

1Co 10:8 We should not commit sexual immorality, as some of them did—and in one day twenty-three thousand of them died.

Heb 13:4 Marriage should be honored by all, and the marriage bed kept pure, for God will judge the adulterer and all the sexually immoral.

2Pe 2:9 if this is so, then the Lord knows how to rescue godly men from trials and to hold the unrighteous for the day of judgment, while continuing their punishment. [10]This is especially true of those who follow the corrupt desire of the sinful nature and despise authority. Bold and arrogant, these men are not afraid to slander celestial beings;

2Pe 2:14 With eyes full of adultery, they never stop sinning; they seduce the unstable; they are experts in greed—an accursed brood!

Rev 2:20 Nevertheless, I have this against you: You tolerate that woman Jezebel, who calls herself a prophetess. By her teaching she misleads my servants into sexual immorality and the eating of food sacrificed to idols. [21]I have given her time to repent of her immorality, but she is unwilling. [22]So I will cast her on a bed of suffering, and I will make those who commit adultery with her suffer intensely, unless they repent of her ways.

Rev 18:9 "When the kings of the earth who committed adultery with her and shared her luxury see the smoke of her burning, they will weep and mourn over her. [10]Terrified at her torment, they will stand far off and cry: "'Woe! Woe, O great city, O Babylon, city of power! In one hour your doom has come!'

Excommunication (1Co 5:1-10)—

1Co 5:11 But now I am writing you that you must not associate with anyone who calls himself a brother but is sexually immoral or greedy, an idolater or a slanderer, a drunkard or a swindler. With such a man do not even eat. [12]What business is it of mine to judge those outside the church? Are you not to judge those inside? [13]God will judge those outside. "Expel the wicked man from among you."

Eph 5:11 Have nothing to do with the fruitless deeds of darkness, but rather expose them. [12]For it is shameful even to mention what the disobedient do in secret.

Exclusion from the kingdom of God—

1Co 6:9 Do you not know that the wicked will not inherit the kingdom of God? Do not be deceived: Neither the sexually immoral nor idolaters nor adulterers nor male prostitutes nor homosexual offenders [10]nor thieves nor the greedy nor drunkards nor slanderers nor swindlers will inherit the kingdom of God.

Gal 5:19 The acts of the sinful nature are obvious: sexual immorality, impurity and debauchery;

Gal 5:21 and envy; drunkenness, orgies, and the like. I warn you, as I did before, that those who live like this will not inherit the kingdom of God.

Eph 5:5 For of this you can be sure: No immoral, impure or greedy person—such a man is an idolater—has any inheritance in the kingdom of Christ and of God. [6]Let no one deceive you with empty words, for because of such things God's wrath comes on those who are disobedient.

Jude 7 In a similar way, Sodom and Gomorrah and the surrounding towns gave themselves up to sexual im-

morality and perversion. They serve as an example of those who suffer the punishment of eternal fire.

Rev 21:8 But the cowardly, the unbelieving, the vile, the murderers, the sexually immoral, those who practice magic arts, the idolaters and all liars—their place will be in the fiery lake of burning sulfur. This is the second death."

Rev 22:14 "Blessed are those who wash their robes, that they may have the right to the tree of life and may go through the gates into the city. [15]Outside are the dogs, those who practice magic arts, the sexually immoral, the murderers, the idolaters and everyone who loves and practices falsehood.

Source of:

The heart—

Mt 15:19 For out of the heart come evil thoughts, murder, adultery, sexual immorality, theft, false testimony, slander. (+Mk 7:21-23)

The sinful nature (Gal 5:19-21).

See Fornication; Idolatry; Lasciviousness; Prostitute; Rape; Sensuality; Homosexual; Prostitute.

ADUMMIM [147] (*red [streaks]*). A pass on the road between Jerusalem and Jericho (Jos 15:7; 18:17), on the north border of Judah and the south border of Benjamin. Held to be the scene of Jesus' parable of the Good Samaritan (Lk 10:30-35).

ADVENT *See Jesus the Christ, Second Coming; Millennium.*

ADVERSARY [*7640, 7756, 8477, 8533, *508*].
NIV+ ADVERSARIES, ADVERSITY

In general, an enemy; personal, national, or supernatural (Ex 23:22; 1Sa 2:10; Na 1:2; Mt 5:25). Specifically, Satan is the enemy of all mankind (1Pe 5:8).

ADVERSITY *See Afflictions.*

ADVICE *See Counsel.*

ADVOCATE [8446, *2858, 2859*] (*helper, Paraclete*).
NIV+ ADVOCATING

An advocate is one who pleads the case or the cause of another. The Holy Spirit or Counselor (Jn 14:16-17,26; 15:26; 16:7), Jesus Christ himself (1Jn 2:1).

AENEAS [*138*] (possibly *praise*). A paralytic, healed at Lydda by Peter (Ac 9:32-35).

AENON [*143*] (*spring*). A place probably N of Jerusalem to the W of the Jordan Valley because the Johannine account indicates that there was "plenty of water." Some scholars identify ancient Salim with present-day Salim, which is about three to four miles E of Nablus (Shechem). A place near Salim, W of the Jordan, where John the Baptist baptized (Jn 3:22-23).

AEON [*172*] (*a segment of time, eternity*). A Greek word indicating a period of time, usually translated ever or forever (Eph 3:21; Jn 6:51,58), age or ages (Eph 1:21; Col 1:26), world (Ro 12:2; 2Ti 4:10).

AFFECTIONS [3137, 5883, *5073*].
NIV+ AFFECTION

Set Upon God:

Of believers, supremely set on God—

Dt 6:5 Love the LORD your God with all your heart and with all your soul and with all your strength.

Ps 42:1 As the deer pants for streams of water, so my soul pants for you, O God.

Ps 73:23 Yet I am always with you; you hold me by my right hand. ²⁴You guide me with your counsel, and afterward you will take me into glory. ²⁵Whom have I in heaven but you? And earth has nothing I desire besides you. ²⁶My flesh and my heart may fail, but God is the strength of my heart and my portion forever.

Ps 119:9 How can a young man keep his way pure? By living according to your word. ¹⁰I seek you with all my heart; do not let me stray from your commands. ¹¹I have hidden your word in my heart that I might not sin against you. ¹²Praise be to you, O LORD; teach me your decrees. ¹³With my lips I recount all the laws that come from your mouth. ¹⁴I rejoice in following your statutes as one rejoices in great riches. ¹⁵I meditate on your precepts and consider your ways. ¹⁶I delight in your decrees; I will not neglect your word.

¹⁷Do good to your servant, and I will live; I will obey your word. ¹⁸Open my eyes that I may see wonderful things in your law. ¹⁹I am a stranger on earth; do not hide your commands from me. ²⁰My soul is consumed with longing for your laws at all times.

Mk 12:30 Love the Lord your God with all your heart and with all your soul and with all your mind and with all your strength.'

Of the wicked, not sincerely set on God (Isa 58:1-2; Eze 33:31-32; Lk 8:13), are unnatural and perverted (Ro 1:18-32; 2Ti 3:1-9; 2Pe 2:10-22). Desires of the flesh, crucified in believers (Ro 6:5-7; Gal 5:24), should be put to death by the Spirit (Ro 8:12-13; 13:14; 1Co 9:27; Col 3:5-6; 1Th 4:3-7). False teachers seek to captivate (Gal 1:9-10; 4:17; 2Ti 3:6; 2Pe 2:3,18; Rev 2:14,20).

Should Be Set Upon:

The house and worship of God (1Ch 29:3; Ps 26:8; 27:4; 84:1-2), the people of God (Ps 16:3; Ro 12:10; 2Co 7:13-16; 1Th 2:8), the commandments and statutes of God (Ps 19:8-10; 119), heavenly things (Col 3:1-2).

In General:

Should be zealously engaged for God (Ps 69:9; 119:139; Gal 4:18). Blessedness of making God the object of our affections (Ps 91:14). Should not grow cold (Ps 106:12-13; Mt 24:12; Gal 4:14-16; Rev 2:4). Christ claims the first place in (Mt 10:37; Lk 14:26). Stirred up by communion with Christ (Lk 24:32).

AFFLICTED [1868, 1895, 2688, 2703, 5595, 5597, 5782, 6700, 6705, 6714].

NIV+ AFFLICT, AFFLICTING, AFFLICTION, AFFLICTIONS

In General:

Sympathy with (Job 6:14; Mt 25:34-40). Help for (Job 22:29; Isa 58:6-7; Lk 10:30-37; 1Ti 5:9-10). Rewards of service to (Isa 53:10; Mt 25:34-45). Exhorted to pray (Jas 5:13). Prayer for healing (Jas 5:14-15).

Duty to:

Pity (Job 6:14), comfort (Job 16:5; 29:25; 2Co 1:3-5; 1Th 4:18), relieve (Job 31:19-20; Isa 58:9-12; Php 4:14; 1Ti 5:10), protect the poor (Ps 82:3; Pr 22:22; 31:5), pray (Ac 12:5; Php 1:19; Jas 5:14-16), sympathize (Ro 12:15; Gal 6:2), remember those in prison and those who are mistreated (Heb 13:3).

AFFLICTED BELIEVERS

God is a refuge and strength to (Ps 27:5-6; Isa 25:4; Jer 16:19; Na 1:7), delivers (Ps 34:4,19; Pr 12:13; Jer 39:17-

18), protects (Ps 34:20), is with (Ps 46:5,7; Isa 43:2-3), comforts (Isa 49:13; Jer 31:13; Mt 5:4; 2Co 1:3-5; 7:6).

Christ comforts (Isa 61:2, w Lk 4:18-19; Mt 11:28-30; Lk 7:13; Jn 14:1; 16:33), preserves (Isa 63:9; Lk 21:18), is with (Jn 14:18), supports (2Ti 4:17; Heb 2:18), delivers (Rev 3:10).

Should be resigned (1Sa 3:18; 2Ki 20:19; Job 1:21; Ps 39:9), acknowledge the justice of their discipline (Ne 9:33; Job 2:10; Isa 64:5-7; La 3:39; Mic 7:9), not despise discipline (Job 5:17-18; Pr 3:11-12; Heb 12:5-6), trust in the goodness of God (Job 13:15; Ps 71:20; 2Co 1:9), avoid sin (Job 34:31-32; Jn 5:14; 1Pe 2:12), praise God (Ps 13:5-6; 56:8-11; 57:6-7; 71:20-23), take encouragement from former mercy (Ps 27:9; 2Co 1:10), call upon God in the day of trouble (Ps 50:15; 55:16-17). *See Affliction, Prayer under.* Turn and devote themselves to God (Ps 116:7-9; Jer 50:3-5; Hos 6:1), be patient (Lk 21:19; Ro 12:12; 2Th 1:4-7; Jas 1:4; 1Pe 2:20), imitate Christ (Heb 12:1-3; 1Pe 2:21-23), imitate the prophets (Jas 5:10).

Examples of Afflicted Believers:

Joseph (Ge 39:20-23; Ps 105:17-19), Eli (1Sa 3:11-18), David (2Sa 12:15-23), Nehemiah (Ne 1:3-4), Job (Job 1:20-22), Paul (Ac 20:22-24; 21:13), the apostles (1Co 4:13; 2Co 6:4-10), Moses (Heb 11:24-29).

AFFLICTION [2716, 4316, 6411, 6700, 6715, 2568].
NIV+ See AFFLICTED

Consolation Under:

God is the Author and Giver of (Ps 23:4; Ro 15:5; 2Co 1:3-4; 7:6-7; Col 1:11; 2Th 2:16-17).

Christ is the Author and Giver of (Isa 61:1-3; Jn 14:18; 2Co 1:5).

The Holy Spirit is the Author and Giver of (Jn 14:16-17; 15:26; 16:7; Ac 9:31).

In the prospect of death (Job 19:25-27; Ps 23:4; Jn 14:1-3; 2Co 5:1; 1Th 4:12-13; Heb 4:9-10; Rev 7:14-17; 14:13). Through the Holy Scriptures (Ps 119:50,76; Ro 15:4). Pray for (Ps 119:81-83). By ministers of the gospel (Isa 40:1-2; 1Co 14:3; 2Co 1:4,6). Promised (Ps 119:76; Isa 51:3,12; 66:13; Eze 14:22-23; Hos 2:14; Zec 1:17). Believers should administer to each other (1Th 4:18; 5:11,14).

Under the infirmities of age (Ps 71:9,18).

Is sought in vain from the world (Ps 69:20; Ecc 4:1; La 1:2), abundant (Ps 71:21; Isa 66:10-11), a cause of praise (Isa 12:1; 49:13), everlasting (2Th 2:16-17), firm and secure (Heb 6:17-20).

To the persecuted (Dt 33:27), the poor (Ps 10:14; 34:6, 9-10), those deserted by friends or family (Ps 27:10; 41:9-12; Jn 14:18; 15:18-19), the sick (Ps 41:3), the troubled in mind (Ps 42; 94:19; Jn 14:1,27; 16:20-22)

Those who mourn for sin—

Ps 51:17 The sacrifices of God are a broken spirit; a broken and contrite heart, O God, you will not despise. (+Isa 1:18; 40:1-2; 61:1-3)

Mic 7:18 Who is a God like you, who pardons sin and forgives the transgression of the remnant of his inheritance? You do not stay angry forever but delight to show mercy. ¹⁹You will again have compassion on us; you will tread our sins underfoot and hurl all our iniquities into the depths of the sea. (+Lk 4:18-19)

The tempted (Ro 16:17-20)—

1Co 10:13 No temptation has seized you except what is common to man. And God is faithful; he will not let you be tempted beyond what you can bear. But when you are tempted, he will also provide a way out so that you can stand up under it. (+2Co 12:9; Jas 1:12; 4:7-10; 2Pe 2:9; Rev 2:10)

Prayer Under:

For the presence and support of God—

Ps 10:1 Why, O LORD, do you stand far off? Why do you hide yourself in times of trouble?

Ps 102:2 Do not hide your face from me when I am in distress. Turn your ear to me; when I call, answer me quickly.

Exhortation to—

Jas 5:13 Is any one of you in trouble? He should pray. Is anyone happy? Let him sing songs of praise.

That, God would consider our trouble (2Ki 19:16; Ne 9:32; Ps 9:13; La 5), we may be taught the uncertainty of life (Ps 39:4), the Holy Spirit may not be withdrawn (Ps 51:11), we may be turned to God (Ps 51:12-15; 80:7; 85:4-7; Jer 31:18).

For, protection and preservation from enemies (2Ki 19:19; 2Ch 20:12; Ps 17:8-9; 143:11-12)

Divine teaching and direction (Job 34:32)—

Ps 27:11 Teach me your way, O LORD; lead me in a straight path because of my oppressors.

Ps 143:10 Teach me to do your will, for you are my God; may your good Spirit lead me on level ground.

Divine comfort (Ps 4:6)—

Ps 119:76 May your unfailing love be my comfort, according to your promise to your servant. 77Let your compassion come to me that I may live, for your law is my delight.

Mercy (Ps 6:2; Hab 3:2)

Deliverance from troubles (Ps 25:17,22; 39:10)—

Isa 64:9 Do not be angry beyond measure, O LORD; do not remember our sins forever. Oh, look upon us, we pray, for we are all your people. 10Your sacred cities have become a desert; even Zion is a desert, Jerusalem a desolation. 11Our holy and glorious temple, where our fathers praised you, has been burned with fire, and all that we treasured lies in ruins. 12After all this, O LORD, will you hold yourself back? Will you keep silent and punish us beyond measure?

Jer 17:14 Heal me, O LORD, and I will be healed; save me and I will be saved, for you are the one I praise.

Pardon and deliverance from sin (Ps 39:8)—

Ps 51:1 Have mercy on me, O God, according to your unfailing love; according to your great compassion blot out my transgressions. 2Wash away all my iniquity and cleanse me from my sin.

3For I know my transgressions, and my sin is always before me. 4Against you, you only, have I sinned and done what is evil in your sight, so that you are proved right when you speak and justified when you judge. 5Surely I was sinful at birth, sinful from the time my mother conceived me. 6Surely you desire truth in the inner parts; you teach me wisdom in the inmost place.

7Cleanse me with hyssop, and I will be clean; wash me, and I will be whiter than snow. 8Let me hear joy and gladness; let the bones you have crushed rejoice. 9Hide your face from my sins and blot out all my iniquity.

10Create in me a pure heart, O God, and renew a steadfast spirit within me. 11Do not cast me from your presence or take your Holy Spirit from me. 12Restore to me the joy of your salvation and grant me a willing spirit, to sustain me.

13Then I will teach transgressors your ways, and sinners will turn back to you. 14Save me from bloodguilt, O God, the God who saves me, and my tongue will sing of your righteousness. 15O Lord, open my lips, and my mouth will

declare your praise. 16You do not delight in sacrifice, or I would bring it; you do not take pleasure in burnt offerings. 17The sacrifices of God are a broken spirit; a broken and contrite heart, O God, you will not despise. (+Ps 79:8-9)

Relief from troubles (Ps 39:12-13), restoration of joy (Ps 51:8,12; 69:29; 90:14-15), increase of faith (Mk 9:24).

AFFLICTIONS [4804, 5596, *2568*].

NIV+ See AFFLICTED

In General:

God, determines the continuance of (Ge 15:13-14; Nu 14:33; Isa 10:25; Jer 29:10), appoints (2Ki 6:33; Job 5:6,17; Ps 66:10-11; Am 3:6; Mic 6:9), dispenses as he will (Job 11:10; Isa 10:15-16; 45:7), regulates the measure of (Ps 80:5; Isa 9:1; Jer 46:28), does not willingly send (La 3:33).

Consequent upon the Fall (Ge 3:16-19). Frequently end in good (Ge 50:20; Ex 1:11-12; Dt 8:15-18; Jer 24:5-7; Eze 20:37). Sin visited with (2Sa 12:14; Ps 89:30-32; Isa 57:17; Ac 13:10-11).

Always less than we deserve—

Ezr 9:13 "What has happened to us is a result of our evil deeds and our great guilt, and yet, our God, you have punished us less than our sins have deserved and have given us a remnant like this.

Ps 103:10 he does not treat us as our sins deserve or repay us according to our iniquities.

Sin produces (Job 4:8; 20:11; Pr 1:31). Man is born to (Job 5:6-7; 14:1). Often severe (Job 16:7-16; Ps 42:7; 66:12; Rev 7:14).

Tempered with mercy (Ps 78:38-39; 106:43-46)—

Isa 30:18 Yet the LORD longs to be gracious to you; he rises to show you compassion. For the LORD is a God of justice. Blessed are all who wait for him!

19O people of Zion, who live in Jerusalem, you will weep no more. How gracious he will be when you cry for help! As soon as he hears, he will answer you. 20Although the Lord gives you the bread of adversity and the water of affliction, your teachers will be hidden no more; with your own eyes you will see them. 21Whether you turn to the right or to the left, your ears will hear a voice behind you, saying, "This is the way; walk in it." (+La 3:32)

Mic 7:7 But as for me, I watch in hope for the LORD, I wait for God my Savior; my God will hear me.

8Do not gloat over me, my enemy! Though I have fallen, I will rise. Though I sit in darkness, the LORD will be my light. 9Because I have sinned against him, I will bear the LORD's wrath, until he pleads my case and establishes my right. He will bring me out into the light; I will see his righteousness. (+Na 1:12)

Believers are to expect (Jn 16:33; Ac 14:22). Believers appointed to (1Th 3:3).

Of Believers:

Exhibit the love and faithfulness of God (Dt 8:5; Ps 119:75)—

Pr 3:11 My son, do not despise the LORD's discipline and do not resent his rebuke, 12because the LORD disciplines those he loves, as a father the son he delights in. (+1Co 11:32; Heb 12:6-11)

Rev 3:19 Those whom I love I rebuke and discipline. So be earnest, and repent. 20Here I am! I stand at the door and knock. If anyone hears my voice and opens the door, I will come in and eat with him, and he with me.

21To him who overcomes, I will give the right to sit with me on my throne, just as I overcame and sat down with my

Father on his throne. ²²He who has an ear, let him hear what the Spirit says to the churches."

Believers have joy under (Job 5:17-18; Jas 5:11).

Are but temporary (Ps 30:5; 103:9-10)—

Isa 54:7 "For a brief moment I abandoned you, but with deep compassion I will bring you back. ⁸In a surge of anger I hid my face from you for a moment, but with everlasting kindness I will have compassion on you," says the LORD your Redeemer. (+Jn 16:20; 1Pe 1:6; 5:10)

End in joy and blessedness (Ps 126:5-6; Isa 61:2-3; Mt 5:4; 1Pe 4:13-14). Often comes from the profession of the gospel (Mt 24:9; Jn 15:21; 2Ti 3:11-12). Are comparatively light (Ac 20:23-24; Ro 8:18; 2Co 4:17-18).

Benefits to Believers:

In, trying our faith and obedience (Ge 22:1-2, w Heb 11:17-18; Ex 15:23-25; Dt 8:2-3,16; 1Pe 1:7; Rev 2:10)

Humbling us (Dt 8:3,16; 2Ch 7:13-14)—

La 3:19 I remember my affliction and my wandering, the bitterness and the gall. ²⁰I well remember them, and my soul is downcast within me. ²¹Yet this I call to mind and therefore I have hope:

²²Because of the LORD's great love we are not consumed, for his compassions never fail. ²³They are new every morning; great is your faithfulness. ²⁴I say to myself, "The LORD is my portion; therefore I will wait for him." (+2Co 12:7)

Leading us to confession of sin (Nu 21:7; Ps 32:4-5; 51:3-6), turning us to God (Dt 4:30-31; Ne 1:8-9; Ps 78:34-38; Isa 10:20-21; Hos 2:6-7), leading us to seek God in prayer (Jdg 4:3; Jer 31:18; La 2:17-19; Hos 5:14-15; Jnh 2:1), testing and exhibiting our sincerity (Job 23:10; Ps 66:10; Pr 17:3), keeping us from again departing from God (Job 34:31-32; Isa 10:20; Eze 14:10-11), convincing us of sin (Job 36:8-10; Ps 119:67; Lk 15:16,18), exhibiting the power and faithfulness of God (Ps 34:19-20; 2Co 4:8-11), exercising our patience (Ps 40:1; Ro 5:3; Jas 1:3; 1Pe 2:20), teaching us the will of God (Ps 119:71; Isa 26:9), purifying us (Ecc 7:2-3; Isa 1:25-26; 48:10; Jer 9:6-7; Zec 13:9; Mal 3:2-3), promoting the glory of God (Jn 9:1-3; 11:3-4; 21:18-19), rendering us fruitful in good works (Jn 15:2; Heb 12:10-11)

Furthering the Gospel (Ac 8:3-4; 11:19-21)—

Php 1:12 Now I want you to know, brothers, that what has happened to me has really served to advance the gospel. ¹³As a result, it has become clear throughout the whole palace guard and to everyone else that I am in chains for Christ.

2Ti 2:8 Remember Jesus Christ, raised from the dead, descended from David. This is my gospel, ⁹for which I am suffering even to the point of being chained like a criminal. But God's word is not chained. ¹⁰Therefore I endure everything for the sake of the elect, that they too may obtain the salvation that is in Christ Jesus, with eternal glory. (+2Ti 4:16-18)

Examples of benefits to believers—

Joseph's brothers (Ge 42:21), Joseph (Ge 45:5-8), Israel (Dt 8:3-5), Josiah (2Ki 22:19), Hezekiah (2Ch 32:25-26), Manasseh (2Ch 33:12), Jonah (Jnh 2:7), Prodigal son (Lk 15:21).

Of the Wicked:

Are ineffective of themselves, for their conversion (Ex 9:30; Isa 9:13; Jer 2:30; Hag 2:17). God is glorified in (Ex 14:4; Eze 38:22-23). Their persecution of believers, a cause of (Dt 30:7; Ps 55:19; Zec 2:9; 2Th 1:6). Are multi-

plied (Dt 31:17; Job 20:12-18; Ps 32:10). Sometimes humble them (1Ki 21:27).

Frequently harden—

Ne 9:28 "But as soon as they were at rest, they again did what was evil in your sight. Then you abandoned them to the hand of their enemies so that they ruled over them. And when they cried out to you again, you heard from heaven, and in your compassion you delivered them time after time.

²⁹"You warned them to return to your law, but they became arrogant and disobeyed your commands. They sinned against your ordinances, by which a man will live if he obeys them. Stubbornly they turned their backs on you, became stiff-necked and refused to listen. ³⁰For many years you were patient with them. By your Spirit you admonished them through your prophets. Yet they paid no attention, so you handed them over to the neighboring peoples. ³¹But in your great mercy you did not put an end to them or abandon them, for you are a gracious and merciful God. (+Jer 5:3)

Are continual (Job 15:20; Ecc 2:23; Isa 32:10). Produce slavish fear (Job 15:24; Ps 73:19; Jer 49:3,5). Are often judicially sent (Job 21:17; Ps 107:17; Jer 30:15). God holds in derision (Ps 37:13; Pr 1:26-27).

Are for examples to others (Ps 64:7-9; Zep 3:6-7)—

1Co 10:5 Nevertheless, God was not pleased with most of them; their bodies were scattered over the desert.

⁶Now these things occurred as examples to keep us from setting our hearts on evil things as they did. ⁷Do not be idolaters, as some of them were; as it is written: "The people sat down to eat and drink and got up to indulge in pagan revelry." ⁸We should not commit sexual immorality, as some of them did—and in one day twenty-three thousand of them died. ⁹We should not test the Lord, as some of them did—and were killed by snakes. ¹⁰And do not grumble, as some of them did—and were killed by the destroying angel.

¹¹These things happened to them as examples and were written down as warnings for us, on whom the fulfillment of the ages has come. ¹²So, if you think you are standing firm, be careful that you don't fall! ¹³No temptation has seized you except what is common to man. And God is faithful; he will not let you be tempted beyond what you can bear. But when you are tempted, he will also provide a way out so that you can stand up under it. (+2Pe 2:6)

Are often sudden (Ps 73:19)—

Pr 6:15 Therefore disaster will overtake him in an instant; he will suddenly be destroyed—without remedy. (+Isa 30:12-13; Rev 18:10)

Failure to repent is a cause of (Pr 1:30-31)—

Eze 24:13 "'Now your impurity is lewdness. Because I tried to cleanse you but you would not be cleansed from your impurity, you will not be clean again until my wrath against you has subsided. (+Am 4:6-12; Zec 7:11-12; Rev 2:21-22)

Believers should not be alarmed at (Pr 3:25-26).

Examples of afflictions of the wicked—

Pharaoh and the Egyptians (Ex 9:14-15; 14:24-25), Ahaziah (2Ki 1:1-4), Gehazi (2Ki 5:27), Jehoram (2Ch 21:12-16), Uzziah (2Ch 26:19-21), Ahaz (2Ch 28:5-8,22).

AFTERWARD [*339, 928, 2256, 3869, 4200, 4946, 2779, *3552*, *3958*].

NIV+ AFTER, AFTERWARD

(Ps 73:24; Pr 20:17; Mt 25:11; Jn 13:36; 1Co 15:46; Gal 3:23; Heb 12:11,17).

AGABUS [*13*]. A prophet living in Jerusalem who prophesied a world-wide famine which was fulfilled during the reign of Claudius (Ac 11:27-30). He also met Paul in Caesarea and warned him that he would be arrested in Jerusalem (Ac 21:10-11).

AGAG [97] (possibly *violent*).
NIV+ AGAGITE

1. The king of Amalek, referred to by Balaam (Nu 24:2-3,7).

2. Another king of Amalek. Saul spared Agag when he should have killed him. When Samuel came into the camp, he rebuked Saul and ordered that Agag be brought to him. Samuel killed Agag as Saul should have according to God's command (1Sa 15:8-33).

AGAGITE [98] (possibly *violent*).
NIV+ AGAG

A description of Haman (Est 3:1,10; 8:3,5; 9:24). The LXX understood the term to mean "enemy." Josephus explains it as a synonym of Amalek, a descendant of Agag (Ant. xi,6,5). *See Agag, 2.*

AGAPE [*26, 27*] (*love; volitional and self-sacrificial love*).
NIV+ LOVE

A Greek word meaning "love" and "love-feasts." *See Love; Love Feast.*

AGAR *See Hagar.*

AGATE [8648]. A precious stone used in the high priest's breastpiece (Ex 28:19; 39:12). KJV "agates" is also translated "rubies" in the NIV (Isa 54:12; Eze 27:16).
See Minerals of the Bible, 1; Ruby; Stones.

AGE *See Aeon.*

AGE (OLD), AGED *See Old Age.*

AGEE [96] (possibly *fugitive*). A Hararite and the father of Shammah (2Sa 23:11).

AGENCY The duties entrusted to God's servants.

In Salvation of People:
Job 33:14 For God does speak—now one way, now another—though man may not perceive it. ¹⁵In a dream, in a vision of the night, when deep sleep falls on men as they slumber in their beds, ¹⁶he may speak in their ears and terrify them with warnings, ¹⁷to turn man from wrongdoing and keep him from pride, ¹⁸to preserve his soul from the pit, his life from perishing by the sword. ¹⁹Or a man may be chastened on a bed of pain with constant distress in his bones, ²⁰so that his very being finds food repulsive and his soul loathes the choicest meal. ²¹His flesh wastes away to nothing, and his bones, once hidden, now stick out. ²²His soul draws near to the pit, and his life to the messengers of death.

²³"Yet if there is an angel on his side as a mediator, one out of a thousand, to tell a man what is right for him, ²⁴to be gracious to him and say, 'Spare him from going down to the pit; I have found a ransom for him'— ²⁵then his flesh is renewed like a child's; it is restored as in the days of his youth. ²⁶He prays to God and finds favor with him, he sees God's face and shouts for joy; he is restored by God to his righteous state. ²⁷Then he comes to men and says, 'I sinned, and perverted what was right, but I did not get what I deserved. ²⁸He redeemed my soul from going down to the pit, and I will live to enjoy the light.'

²⁹"God does all these things to a man—twice, even three times— ³⁰to turn back his soul from the pit, that the light of life may shine on him.

Ps 8:2 From the lips of children and infants you have ordained praise because of your enemies, to silence the foe and the avenger.

Mt 4:19 "Come, follow me," Jesus said, "and I will make you fishers of men."

Mt 5:13 "You are the salt of the earth. But if the salt loses its saltiness, how can it be made salty again? It is no longer good for anything, except to be thrown out and trampled by men.

¹⁴"You are the light of the world. A city on a hill cannot be hidden. ¹⁵Neither do people light a lamp and put it under a bowl. Instead they put it on its stand, and it gives light to everyone in the house. ¹⁶In the same way, let your light shine before men, that they may see your good deeds and praise your Father in heaven. (+Lk 1:17; 5:10; 10:17; 1Co 1:26-29; 1Th 2:4; 1Ti 1:11; 6:20; Jas 5:20)

In Executing Judgments:
(Ge 3:15; 1Sa 15:18; 2Sa 7:14; 2Ki 9:6-9; 19:25-26; 2Ch 22:7; Ps 17:13-14; Isa 10:5-6; 13:5; 41:15; Jer 27:8; 51:20-23).

AGONY [987, 1631, 2655, 7815, 8358, *990, 3849, 4506, 6047*] (*anguish*). Occurs only in Luke's account of Jesus' agony in Gethsemane (Lk 22:44).

AGORA [*59*] (*marketplace*).
NIV+ MARKETPLACE, MARKETPLACES

In ancient cities the town meeting place was the market where the public met for the exchange of merchandise, information, and ideas (Mk 6:56; Ac 17:17).

AGRAPHA (*unwritten things*). Sayings ascribed to Jesus transmitted to us outside of the canonical Gospels. The number is not large, and most are obviously apocryphal or spurious. They are found in the NT outside of the Gospels (Ac 1:4ff; 11:16; 20:35; 1Co 7:10), ancient manuscripts of the NT, patristic literature, papyri, and apocryphal gospels.

AGRICULTURE The occupation of man before the Fall (Ge 2:15). Rendered laborious by the curse on the earth (Ge 3:17-19). Man condemned to labor in, after the Fall (Ge 3:23). Contributes to the support of all (Ecc 5:9). The providence of God to be acknowledged in the produce of (Jer 5:24; Hos 2:8).

Requires:
Hard work will be abundantly recompensed (Pr 12:11; 13:23; 28:19; Heb 6:7). Diligence (Pr 27:23-27; Ecc 11:6). Wisdom (Isa 28:26). Hard work (2Ti 2:6). Patience in waiting (Jas 5:7).

Persons Engaged in, Called:
Workers of the ground (Ge 4:2). Workers or hired men (Mt 9:37; 20:1).

In General:
Patriarchs engaged in (Ge 4:2; 9:20). The labor of, supposed to be lessened by Noah (Ge 5:29, w Ge 9:20). Soil of Canaan suited to (Ge 13:10; Dt 8:7-10). Climate of Canaan favorable to (Dt 11:10-12). The Israelites loved and followed (2Ch 26:10). Peace favorable to (Jer 31:24). War destructive to (Jer 5:16-17; 51:23).

Was Promoted Among the Israelites by:
The prohibition against usury (Ex 22:25). The right of redemption (Lev 25:23-28). The promises of God's

blessing on (Lev 26:4; Dt 7:13; 11:14-15). Allotments to each family (Nu 36:7-9).

Enactments to Protect:

Against, the trespass of cattle (Ex 22:5), injuring the produce of (Ex 22:6). Not to, be engaged in during the Sabbatical year (Ex 23:10-11), covet the fields of another (Dt 5:21), move landmarks (Dt 19:14; Pr 22:28), cut down crops of another (Dt 23:25). Produce of, exported (1Ki 5:11; Eze 27:17). Often performed by hired help (1Ch 27:26; 2Ch 26:10; Mt 20:8; Lk 17:7). Produce of, often reduced in yield because of sin (Isa 5:10; 7:23; Jer 12:13; Joel 1:10-12). Grief resulted from the failure of the fruits of (Joel 1:11; Am 5:16-17).

Activities in:

Binding sheaves of grain or weeds into bundles (Ge 37:7; Mt 13:30). Stacking (Ex 22:6). Gleaning (Lev 19:9; Ru 2:3). Pruning (Lev 25:3; Isa 5:6; Jn 15:2). Watering (Dt 11:10; 1Co 3:6-8). Threshing (Dt 25:4; Jdg 6:11). Winnowing (Ru 3:2; Job 39:12; Mt 3:12). Plowing (Job 1:14). Harrowing (Job 39:10; Isa 28:24). Mowing (Ps 72:6; Am 7:1; Jas 5:4). Planting (Pr 31:16; Isa 44:14; Jer 31:5). Sowing (Ecc 11:4; Isa 32:20; Mt 13:3). Clearing out the stones (Isa 5:2). Hedging (Isa 5:2,5; Hos 2:6). Digging (Lk 13:8; 16:3). Reaping (Isa 17:5). Fertilizing (Isa 25:10; Lk 14:34-35). Storing in barns (Mt 6:26; 13:30). Weeding (Mt 13:28). Grafting (Ro 11:17-19,24).

Animals Used in:

The donkey (Dt 22:10), ox (Dt 22:10; 25:4), horse (Isa 28:28).

Tools of:

The sickle (Dt 16:9; 23:25), cart (1Sa 6:7; Isa 28:27-28), mattock (1Sa 13:20), ax (1Sa 13:20), plow (1Sa 13:20), fork (1Sa 13:21), iron pick (2Sa 12:31), hoe (Isa 7:25), pruning knives (Isa 18:5; Joel 3:10), rod (Isa 28:27), winnowing fork (Jer 15:7; Mt 3:12; Lk 3:17), shovel (Isa 30:24), threshing sledge (Isa 41:15), sieve (Am 9:9).

Illustrative of the:

Cultivating the heart (Jer 4:3; Hos 10:12). Cultivating the church (1Co 3:9).

AGRIPPA I [68]. Known in history as King Herod Agrippa I or Herod Agrippa, and in the NT as Herod, 10 B.C. to A.D. 44 He was the grandson of Herod the Great and ruled over the whole of Judea from A.D. 41 to 44. He killed James to please the Jews and intended to do the same to Peter (Ac 12:1-5). He died suddenly in Caesarea (Ac 12:19-23; Jos. Antiq. XIX.viii.2), A.D. 44.

AGRIPPA II [68]. Known in history as King Herod Agrippa II, Marcus Julius Agrippa, and in the NT as Agrippa, A.D. 28 to after A.D. 93, probably c. A.D. 100. He was the son of Agrippa I, and ruled over only a small part of his father's territory. Paul appeared before the tribunal of Agrippa and Festus (Ac 25:23-26). He died in c. A.D. 100.

AGUE NIV "fever"; a disease "that will destroy your sight and drain away your life" (Lev 26:16). *See Fever.*

AGUR [101] (*gatherer, possibly wage earner*). The author or "collector" of the wise sayings of the Proverbs (Pr 30). He is named as the son of Jakeh (Pr 30:1).

AHA [177, 208, 2027, 2098, 8011].

NIV+ AH

A term of derision (Ps 35:21; 40:15; 70:3; Eze 25:3; 26:2; 36:2).

AHAB [281, 282] (*brother of father*).

NIV+ AHAB'S

1. King of Israel for twenty-two years, reigning in Samaria (1Ki 16:29). Idolatry of (1Ki 16:30-33; 18:18-20; 21:25-26). Marries Jezebel (1Ki 16:31). Reproved by Elijah; assembles the prophets of Baal (1Ki 18:15-46). Defeats Ben-Hadad (1Ki 20). Illegally confiscates Naboth's vineyard (1Ki 21). Closing history and death of (1Ki 22:1-41; 2Ch 18). Succeeded by his son, Ahaziah (1Ki 22:40). Prophecies against (1Ki 20:42; 21:19-24; 22:19-28; 2Ki 9:8,25-26). Other wickedness of (2Ki 3:2; 2Ch 21:6; 22:3-4; Mic 6:16). The seventy sons of, all his chief men, his close friends, and his priest were murdered (2Ki 10:1-11).

2. A false prophet (Jer 29:21-22).

AHARAH [341] (*brother of Rah*). Also called Ashbel, Ahiram, and Aher, the third son of Benjamin (Ge 46:21; Nu 26:38; 1Ch 7:12; 8:1).

AHARHEL [342] (*brother of Rachel*). A son of Harum, and the founder of a family enrolled in the tribe of Judah (1Ch 4:8).

AHASAI *See Ahzai.*

AHASBAI [335] (*I seek refuge in Yahweh*). A Maacathite and the father of Eliphelet, one of David's heroes (2Sa 23:34). Possibly the same as Ur (1Ch 11:35). *See Ur.*

AHASUERUS *Ahasuerus is a Hebrew transliteration of the name of the Persian king Xerxes. See Xerxes.*

AHAVA [178]. A Babylonian town on the Ahava Canal (Ezr 8:15,21,31).

AHAZ [298, 937] (*he has grasped*).

1. King of Judah, son and successor of Jotham (2Ki 15:38; 16:1; 2Ch 27:9; 28:1). Idolatrous abominations of (2Ki 16:3-4; 2Ch 28:2-4,22-25). Kingdom of, invaded by the kings of Syria and Samaria (2Ki 16:5-6; 2Ch 28:5-8). Robs the temple to purchase aid from the king of Assyria (2Ki 16:7-9,17-18; 2Ch 28:21). Visits Damascus, obtains a unique pattern of an altar, which he substitutes for the altar in the temple in Jerusalem and otherwise perverts the forms of worship (2Ki 16:10-16). Stairway of (2Ki 20:11; Isa 38:8). Prophets in the reign of (Isa 1:1; Hos 1:1; Mic 1:1). Prophecies concerning (Isa 7:13-25). Succeeded by Hezekiah (2Ki 16:20).

2. Son of Micah and great-grandson of Jonathan (1Ch 8:35; 9:41-42).

AHAZIAH [301, 302, 3370] (*Yahweh has upheld*).

NIV+ AHAZIAH'S

1. King of Judah. Also called Azariah (2Ch 22:6, ftn) and Jehoahaz (2Ch 21:17, ftn). History of (2Ki 8:25-29; 9:16-29). Gifts of, to the temple (2Ki 12:18). Brothers of, slain (2Ki 10:13-14). Succeeded by Athaliah (2Ch 22:10-12).

2. King of Israel. History of (1Ki 22:40,49,51-53; 2Ch 20:35-37; 2Ki 1). Succeeded by Jehoram (2Ki 3:1).

AHBAN [283] (*brother of intelligent one*). A man of Judah, of the house of Jerahmeel (1Ch 2:29).

AHER [338] (*another, a substitute*). A Benjamite (1Ch 7:12). *See Aharah.*

AHI [306] (*my brother*, possibly *Yahweh is [my] brother*).

1. Chief of the Gadites in Gilead (1Ch 5:15).

2. A man of Asher, son of Shomer (1Ch 7:34).

AHIAH [308] (*brother of Yahweh*).

1. A leader of Israel who agreed to the covenant of Nehemiah (Ne 10:26).

2. *See Ahijah.*

AHIAM [307] (*brother of mother*). One of David's heroes (2Sa 23:33). The son of Sacar (1Ch 11:35).

AHIAN [319] (*little brother*). Son of Shemida (1Ch 7:19).

AHIEZER [323] (*[my] brother is a help*).

1. Captain of the tribe of Dan (Nu 1:12; 2:25-26). Contributes to the tabernacle (Nu 7:66-71).

2. One of David's valiant men (1Ch 12:3).

AHIHUD [310, 312] (*[my] brother has majesty*).

1. A prince of Asher, assists in allotting the land of Canaan among the tribes (Nu 34:27).

2. A son of Bela (1Ch 8:7).

AHIJAH [308, 309] (*[my] brother is Yahweh*).

NIV+ AHIJAH'S

1. Son of Bela (1Ch 8:7).

2. Son of Jerahmeel (1Ch 2:25).

3. A priest in Shiloh, probably identified with Ahimelech (1Sa 22:11). Was priest in Saul's reign (1Sa 14:3,18). Killed (1Sa 22:11-19).

4. One of David's heroes (1Ch 11:36). Also called Eliam (2Sa 23:34).

5. A Levite who was treasurer in the tabernacle (1Ch 26:20).

6. Son of Shisha, secretary of Solomon (1Ki 4:3).

7. A prophet in Shiloh (1Ki 11:29-39; 12:15).

8. Father of Baasha (1Ki 15:27,33; 2Ki 9:9).

See Ahiah.

AHIKAM [324] (*[my] brother stands*). Son of Shaphan (2Ki 22:12-14; 25:22; 2Ch 34:20; Jer 26:24; 39:14; 40:5-16; 41:1-18; 43:6).

AHILUD [314] (*[my] brother is born*).

Father of: Baana (1Ki 4:12). Jehoshaphat (2Sa 8:16; 20:24; 1Ki 4:3; 1Ch 18:15).

AHIMAAZ [318] (*[my] brother is fury*).

1. Father-in-law of king Saul (1Sa 14:50).

2. Son of Zadok, the high priest. Loyal to David (2Sa 15:36; 17:17-20; 18:19-33; 1Ch 6:8-9,53).

3. One of Solomon's twelve district governors (1Ki 4:15). He married Basemath, the daughter of Solomon. Some suggest that he should be identified with the son of Zadok.

AHIMAN [317] (possibly *[my] brother is a gift*).

1. One of the three giant sons of Anak seen in Mt. Hebron by the spies (Nu 13:22). The three sons, Sheshai, Ahiman, and Talmai, were driven by Caleb from Hebron (Jos 15:14) and killed (Jdg 1:10).

2. A Levite gatekeeper (1Ch 9:17).

AHIMELECH [316] (*[my] brother is king*).

1. Saul's high priest who helped David by giving him the bread of the Presence and Goliath's sword. Upon hearing this, Saul ordered the death of Ahimelech and the other priests with him (1Sa 21-22). Abiathar, son of Ahimelech, escaped.

2. A Hittite who, with Abishai, was asked to accompany David to Saul's camp (1Sa 26:6).

3. Son of Abiathar, and grandson of Ahimelech (2Sa 8:17; 1Ch 18:16; 24:6). *See Abiathar.*

AHIMOTH [315] (*[my] brother is my support* possibly *my brother is Mot*). Son of Elkanah (1Ch 6:25), descendant of Kohath and a Levite.

AHINADAB [320] (*[my] brother is willing*). Son of Iddo (1Ki 4:14).

AHINOAM [321] (*[my] brother is pleasant*).

1. Wife of King Saul (1Sa 14:50).

2. One of David's wives, a Jezreelitess (1Sa 25:43), who lived with him at Gath (1Sa 27:3). She and Abigail were captured by the Amalekites at Ziklag (1Sa 30:5) but rescued by David (1Sa 30:18). Ahinoam bore Amnon, David's first son (2Sa 3:2).

AHIO [311] (*[my] brother is Yahweh*).

1. A Levite, who drove the cart bearing the ark (2Sa 6:3-4; 1Ch 13:7).

2. A Benjamite (1Ch 8:14).

3. Son of Jeiel (1Ch 8:31; 9:37).

AHIRA [327] (*[my] brother is my friend*, or *[my] brother is evil*). Prince captain of the tribe of Naphtali (Nu 1:15; 2:29; 7:78,83; 10:27).

AHIRAM, AHIRAMITE [325, 326] (*[my] brother is exalted*). Son of Benjamin (Nu 26:38). *See Aharah.*

AHISAMACH [322] (*[my] brother is a support*). A Danite, the father of Oholiab (Ex 31:6; 35:34; 38:23).

AHISHAHAR [328] (*[my] brother was born at early dawn*). A descendant of Benjamin through Jediael and Bilhan (1Ch 7:10).

AHISHAR [329] (*[my] brother is upright*, or *[my] brother has sung*). An official over Solomon's household (1Ki 4:6).

AHITHOPHEL [330] (possibly *[my] brother is in the desert* or *[my] brother is foolishness*).

NIV+ AHITHOPHEL'S

One of David's counselors (2Sa 15:12; 1Ch 27:33). Joins Absalom (2Sa 15:31,34; 16:15,20-23; 17:1-23). Probably referred to by David in Ps 55:12-14. Suicide of (2Sa 17:1-14,23).

AHITUB [313] (*[my] brother is goodness*).

1. High Priest, father of Ahiah (1Sa 14:3; 22:9,11-12, 20).

2. Father of Zadok (2Sa 8:17; 1Ch 18:16).

3. Ruler of the house of God (1Ch 9:11; Ne 11:11).

4. The Ahitub mentioned (1Ch 6:8,11-12) is probably identical with the last described above, or else he is confused with Azariah (2Ch 31:10).

AHLAB [331] (*fat, fruitful, healthy*). A town of Asher from which the Israelites were not able to drive the inhabitants (Jdg 1:31).

AHLAI [333] (*Alas! I wish that!*).

1. The father of Zabad, one of David's soldiers (1Ch 11:41).

2. A daughter of Sheshan who married her father's Egyptian slave Jarha. They had a son Attai (1Ch 2:31-35).

AHOAH [291] (*brotherly*). A son of Bela (1Ch 8:4) and his descendants (2Sa 23:9,28; 1Ch 11:12). *See Ahohite.* Also called Ahijah (1Ch 8:7) and Iri (1Ch 7:7).

AHOHITE [292]. A name given to the descendants of Ahoah, Dodo (2Sa 23:9), Zalmon (2Sa 23:28), Ilai (1Ch 11:29).

AHOLAH, AHOLA *See Oholah.*

AHOLIAB *See Oholiab.*

AHOLIBAH *See Oholah; Oholibah.*

AHOLIBAMAH *See Oholibamah.*

AHUMAI [293]. Son of Jahath (1Ch 4:2).

AHUZZAM, AHUZAM [303] (*possessor*). Son of Ashhur (1Ch 4:6).

AHUZZATH [304] (*possession*). A "friend" of Abimelech, who made a peace treaty with Isaac at Beersheba after they saw that the Lord had blessed him (Ge 26:23-33).

AHZAI [300] (*Yahweh has grasped*). A priest who lived in Jerusalem (Ne 11:13).

AI [6504] (*the ruin, the heap*).
1. A royal city of the Canaanites. Conquest and destruction of (Jos 7; 8). Population of (Jos 8:25). Rebuilt (Ezr 2:28).
Also called Aija (Ne 11:31) and Aiath (Isa 10:28).
2. A city of the Ammonites (Jer 49:3).

AIAH, AJAH [371] (*black kite [a type of hawk]*).
NIV+ AIAH'S
1. A Horite (Ge 36:24; 1Ch 1:40).
2. The father of Rizpah, Saul's concubine (2Sa 3:7; 21:8).

AIATH [6569] (possibly *ruin, heap*). Feminine form of the city Ai (Isa 10:28).

AIJA [6509] (*ruin, heap*). Another spelling of Ai (Ne 11:31). *See Ai, 1.*

AIJALON, AJALON [389] (*[the] place of the deer*).
1. A city of Dan (Jos 19:42). Assigned to the Levites (Jos 21:24; 1Sa 14:31; 1Ch 6:69). Amorites of, not exterminated (Jdg 1:35).
2. A city of Zebulun (Jdg 12:12).
3. A city of Judah (2Ch 28:18; 11:10).
4. A valley (Jos 10:12).

AIJELETH SHAHAR In the KJV title of Psalm 22; NIV "The Doe of the Morning." A musical term which probably indicated the tune to which the psalm was sung. *See Music, Symbols Used in.*

AIN [6526] (*an eye[ball]* or *spring [of water]*).
1. A city of Simeon (Jos 19:7; 15:32; 21:16; 1Ch 4:32). Also called Ashan (1Ch 6:59). Possibly identical with En Rimmon (Ne 11:29).
2. A landmark on the northern boundary of Israel (Nu 34:11).

AIN FESHKA (*spring of Feshka*). Oasis on the W side of the Dead Sea, S of Khirbet Qumran. Used for farming by the community that produced the Dead Sea Scrolls.

AJAH *See Aiah, Ajah.*

AJALON *See Aijalon, Ajalon.*

AKAN [6826]. A Horite (Ge 36:27; 1Ch 1:42). Also spelled Jaakan (1Ch 1:42, ftn).

AKELDAMA [*192*] (*field of blood*). The "Field of Blood" (Mt 27:8) purchased with money which Judas received for betraying Jesus (Ac 1:18-19).

AKHENATEN (*blessed spirit of [the god] Aten*). The name chosen by Amenhotep IV (1379-1362 B.C.), ruler in the Eighteenth Dynasty of Egypt, during the biblical era of the judges. He was a monotheist, demanding that all worship only the sun god under the name Aten. The Amarna Letters date from his era. *See Amarna, Tell El.*

AKIM [*943*] (*Yahweh is my brother*). A descendant of Zerubbabel (Mt 1:14). Ancestor of Christ.

AKKAD [422]. An ancient center of Hamitic imperial power conquered by Nimrod (Ge 10:10). The city is evidently Agade which Sargon I brought into prominence as the capital of his Semitic empire, c. 2360-2180.

AKKUB [6822] (*guard*).
1. Son of Elioenai (1Ch 3:24).
2. A Levite who founded a family of temple gatekeepers (1Ch 9:17).
3. The head of a family of the temple servants (Ezr 2:45).
4. A Levite who helped expound the Law (Ne 8:7).

AKRABBIM (*scorpions*). *See Scorpion Pass.*

ALABASTER [223]. A white stone. Vessels made of (Mt 26:7; Mk 14:3; Lk 7:37).

ALAMETH *See Alemeth.*

ALAMMELECH *See Allammelech.*

ALAMOTH [6628]. A musical term (1Ch 15:20). In title to Ps 46. *See Music, Symbols Used in.*

ALCOHOL *See Abstinence; Abuse, Substance Abuse; Beer; Drunkenness; Fermented Drink; Wine.*

ALEMETH [6630, 6631] (*concealment*).
1. A son of Beker and grandson of Benjamin (1Ch 7:8).
2. Son of Jehoaddah or Jadah (1Ch 8:36; 9:42).
3. A Levitical city (1Ch 6:60).
See Almon.

ALEXANDER [235] (*man's defender*).
1. Son of Simon who carried the cross of Jesus (Mk 15:21).
2. A relative of the high priest, present at the defense of Peter and John (Ac 4:6).
3. A Jew of Ephesus (Ac 19:33).
4. A metalworker (1Ti 1:20; 2Ti 4:14).

ALEXANDER THE GREAT (*man's defender*). Son of Philip, King of Macedon. Lived from 356-323 B.C. He conquered the civilized world from Greece eastward to India. He is the "shaggy goat" of Da 8:5-8,21. His hellenization of the world changed the trade language from Aramaic to Greek, the language of the NT. *See Testaments, Time Between.*

ALEXANDRA Wife of Aristobulus, King of the Jews (104-103 B.C.).

ALEXANDRIA [233].

NIV+ ALEXANDRIAN

A city of Egypt (Ac 6:9). Ships of (Ac 27:6; 28:11). Apollos born in (Ac 18:24).

ALGUM, ALGUMWOOD [454].

NIV+ ALMUGWOOD

Probably a variant of almugwood (1Ki 10:11-12, ftn; 2Ch 2:8; 9:10-11). *See Almug, Almugwood.*

ALIAH *See Alvah.*

ALIAN *See Alvan.*

ALIENS [1591, 1731, 2424, 4472, 5797, 5799, *3828, 4230*] (*sojourner, stranger, foreigner*).

NIV+ ALIEN, ALIEN'S, ALIENATE, ALIENATED

To be treated with justice (Ex 22:21; 23:9; Lev 19:33-34; Dt 1:16; 10:19 24:14,17; 27:19; Jer 7:6; 22:3; Eze 22:29; Mal 3:5). Religious privileges of (Ex 12:48-49; Nu 9:14; 15:14-15). Kindness to Edomites, commanded (Dt 23:7).

Israelites Authorized:

To purchase, as slaves (Lev 25:44-45). To take usury from (Dt 15:3; 23:20). Not permitted to make kings of (Dt 17:15).

Forbidden to eat the passover (Ex 12:45). Partially exempt from the law (Dt 14:21). Numerous in times of David and Solomon (2Sa 22:45-46; 2Ch 2:17; 15:9). Oppressed (Eze 22:29). Rights of (Nu 35:15; Jos 20:9; Eze 47:22-23). David's kindness to (2Sa 15:19-20). Hospitality to, required by Jesus (Mt 25:35,38,43).

See Glean; Heathen; Hospitality; Inhospitableness; Proselyte; Strangers.

ALL THINGS [*3972, 6017, 10353, *570, 3910, 4246*].

The whole created order. God created and rules over (1Ch 29:12; Ps 119:91; Ecc 11:5; Isa 44:24; Jer 10:16; 51:19; Jn 1:3; Ro 8:28; 1Co 8:6; Rev 4:11). Under Jesus' authority (Mt 11:27; 28:20; Lk 10:22; Jn 13:3; Eph 1:10, 22; Col 1:16,17,20; Heb 1:2,3). All things are possible with God (Mt 19:26; Mk 10:27).

ALLAMMELECH [526] (*oak of the king* or *oak of [the god] Molech*). A town of Asher (Jos 19:26).

ALLEGORY [2648].

Explained:

Allegory is a literary genre that attempts to explain spiritual truths in pictorial forms. Some parables, for example, are a type of allegory. Allegory is also a method of interpretation that searches for a mysterious, hidden meaning beyond the literal understanding of the text.

In the OT:

Of the trees seeking a king (Jdg 9:8-15). Israel is a vine brought from Egypt (Ps 80). Wisdom is pictured as a noble woman (Pr 1:2-33); folly as a harlot (Pr 9:13-18). Messiah's kingdom represented by the wolf and the lamb dwelling together (Isa 11:6-8).

In the NT:

Jesus used allegory, as in the interpretation of his parable of the sower (Mt 13:18-23; Mk 4:14-20; Lk 8:11-15). Paul used allegory in using Hagar and Sarah to represent the differences between the Old and New Covenants (Gal 4:21-31). Many events and characters in the book of Revelation are used allegorically; most are clear or explained in context. For example, the Lamb and the Lion of Judah are both Jesus (Rev 5:5-14); the dragon is Satan (Rev 12:9).

Allegory in Interpretation:

Allegory is used as a literary device in the Bible. But, with the exception of Gal 4:21-31, allegory is not used in the NT to interpret the OT. However, allegory became increasingly important during the Apostolic period and into the Ante-Nicene period. The Alexandrian Jews of this period wished to reconcile Christianity with Greek thought. Origen taught a threefold sense of Scripture, corresponding to the body, soul, and the spirit.

In the Middle Ages four senses were found: historical, allegorical, moral, and anagogical (mystical). Jerusalem is *literally* a city in Israel, *allegorically* the church, *morally* the believing soul, *anagogically* the heavenly Jerusalem. The conquests of Joshua have been understood to be an allegory of the soul's victory over sin and self. Many Jewish scholars understand the Song of Songs to be allegorical, depicting God's love for Israel. On the other hand, many Christian scholars understand this as Christ's love for his church.

See Fable; Parable; Symbols and Similitudes.

ALLELUIA *See Hallelujah.*

ALLIANCES [*170, 907, 2489, 6468].

NIV+ ALLEGIANCE, ALLIANCE, ALLIED, ALLIES, ALLY

Forbidden (Ex 23:32; 34:12; Dt 7:2-3; 13:6,8; Jos 23:6-7; Jdg 2:2; Ezr 9:12; Pr 1:10,15; 2Co 6:14-17; Eph 5:11). Lead to idolatry (Ex 34:15-16; Nu 25:1-8; Dt 7:4; Jdg 3:5-7; Rev 2:20). Have led to murder and human sacrifice (Ps 106:37-38). Provoke the anger of God (Dt 7:4; 31:16-17; 2Ch 19:2; Ezr 9:13-14; Ps 106:29,40; Isa 2:6). Provoke God to leave people to reap the fruits of them (Jos 23:12-13; Jdg 2:1-3). Are ensnaring (Ex 23:33; Nu 25:18; Dt 12:30; 13:6; Ps 106:36). Are enslaving (2Pe 2:18-19). Are defiling (Ezr 9:1-2). Are degrading (Isa 1:23). Are ruinous to spiritual interests (Pr 29:24; Heb 12:14-15; 2Pe 3:17). Are ruinous to moral character (1Co 15:33). Are a proof of folly (Pr 12:11). Children who enter into, bring shame upon their parents (Pr 28:7). Evil consequences of (Pr 28:19; Jer 51:7). The wicked are prone to (Ps 50:18; Jer 2:25). The wicked tempt believers to (Ne 6:2-4). Sin of, to be confessed, deeply repented of, and forsaken (Ezr 10).

Involve Believers:

In their guiltiness (2Jn 9-11; Rev 18:4). In their punishment (Nu 16:26; Jer 51:6; Rev 18:4). Unbecoming in those called believers (2Ch 19:2; 2Co 6:14,16; Php 2:15). Exhortations to shun all inducements to (Pr 1:10-15; 4:14-15; 2Pe 3:17). Exhortations to hate and avoid (Pr 14:7; Ro 16:17; 1Co 5:9-11; Eph 5:6-7; 1Ti 6:5; 2Ti 3:5). A call to come out from (Nu 16:26; Ezr 10:11; Jer 51:6,45; 2Co 6:17; 2Th 3:6; Rev 18:4). Means of preservation from (Pr 2:10-20; 19:27). Blessedness of avoiding (Ps 1:1). Blessedness of forsaking (Ezr 9:12; Pr 9:6; 2Co 6:17-18). Believers grieve to meet with, in their dealings with the world (Ps 57:4; 120:5-6; 2Pe 2:7-8). Believers grieve to witness in their brothers (Ge 26:35; Ezr 9:3; 10:6). Believers hate and avoid (Ps 26:4-5; 31:6; 101:7; Rev 2:2). Believers deprecate (Ge 49:6; Ps 6:8; 15:4; 101:4,7; 119:115; 139:19). Believers are separate from (Ex 33:16; Ezr 6:21). Believers should be careful when accidentally thrown into (Mt 10:16; Col 4:5; 1Pe 2:12). Pious parents prohibit, to their children (Ge 28:1). Persons in authority should denounce (Ezr 10:9-11; Ne 13:23-27). Punishment of (Nu 33:56; Dt 7:4; Jos 23:13; Jdg 2:3; 3:5-8; Ezr 9:7,14; Ps 106:41-42; Rev 2:16,22-23).

Exemplified:

Solomon (1Ki 11:1-8). Rehoboam (1Ki 12:8-9). Jehoshaphat (2Ch 18:3; 19:2; 20:35-38). Jehoram (2Ch 21:6). Ahaziah (2Ch 22:3-5). Israelites (Ezr 9:1-2). Israel (Eze 44:7). Judas Iscariot (Mt 26:14-16).

Examples of Avoiding:

Man of God (1Ki 13:7-10). Nehemiah (Ne 6:2-4; 10:29-31). David (Ps 101:4-7; 119:115). Jeremiah (Jer 15:17). Joseph of Arimathea (Lk 23:51). Church of Ephesus (Rev 2:6).

Examples of Forsaking:

Israelites (Nu 16:27; Ezr 6:21-22; 10:3-4,16-17). Sons of the priests (Ezr 10:18-19).

Examples of the Judgments of God Against:

Korah (Nu 16:32). Ahaziah (2Ch 22:7-8). Judas Iscariot (Ac 1:18).

ALLON [474] (*oak*).

1. Son of Jedaiah (1Ch 4:37).
2. KJV Allon, a city of Naphtali (Jos 19:33), is "the large tree" in the NIV.

ALLON BACUTH, ALLON-BACHUTH [475]

(*oak of weeping*). Place where Rebekah was buried (Ge 35:8).

ALLOY See *Refining*.

ALMIGHTY [7372, 8724, *4120, 4877*] (NIV rendering of *Shaddai* in the OT, *Pantokrator* in the NT).

NIV+ MIGHT

Used 56 Times for: Identification (Ge 17:1). Invocation (Ge 28:3). Description (Eze 10:5). Praise (Rev 4:8). *See God, Names of.*

ALMODAD [525] (*God [El] is loved*). First mentioned of Joktan's thirteen sons (Ge 10:26; 1Ch 1:20).

ALMON [6626]. Levitical city of Benjamin (Jos 21:18). Called Alemeth (1Ch 6:60).

ALMON DIBLATHAIM, ALMON-DIBLATHAIM [6627] (*way of the double fig cakes*).

NIV+ BETH DIBLATHAIM

A stopping place in the wilderness journeys of the Israelites in Moab (Nu 33:46-47). Probably the same as Beth Diblathaim (Jer 48:22), and Diblah (Eze 6:14). *See Beth Diblathaim.*

ALMOND [4280, 5481, 9196].

NIV+ ALMONDS

A tree (Ge 30:37). Fruit of (Ge 43:11). Aaron's rod of the (Nu 17:8). Bowls of lampstand in the tabernacle fashioned after the flowers of the (Ex 25:33-34; 37:19-20).

Figurative:

Of old age (Ecc 12:5), of God's watching (Jer 1:11-12).

ALMS KJV "alms" is rendered "give (to the poor)" and "acts of righteousness" in the NIV.

To be Given:

Without public show (Mt 6:1-4; Ro 12:8). Freely (2Co 9:6-7). Commanded (Dt 15:7-11; Mt 5:42; 19:21; Lk 12:33; 2Co 9:5-7; Gal 2:10; 1Ti 6:18; Heb 13:16). Asked by the unfortunate (Jn 9:8; Ac 3:2). Withholding, not of love (1Jn 3:17).

Instances of Giving:

Zacchaeus (Lk 19:8). Dorcas (Ac 9:36). Cornelius (Ac 10:2). The early Christians (Ac 2:44-45; 4:34-37; 6:1-3; 11:29-30; 24:17; Ro 15:25-28; 1Co 16:1-4; 2Co 8:1-4; 9:1; Heb 6:10).

See Beneficence; Charitableness; Gifts From God; Giving; Liberality; Neighbor; Poor; Works, Good.

ALMUG, ALMUGWOOD [523].

NIV+ ALGUM

Probably a variant of algum and algumwood (1Ki 10:11-12; 2Ch 2:8; 9:10-11, ftn). Trees of Ophir and Lebanon used in building the temple and musical instruments. *See Algum, Algumwood.*

ALOES [189, 193, *264*]. Used as perfume (Ps 45:8; Pr 7:17; SS 4:14). In embalming the dead (Jn 19:39). Descriptive of the camping places of the Israelites (Nu 24:6).

ALOTH [6599]. One of the districts in Israel during the reign of Solomon who shared the responsibility of contributing provisions for the king and the royal household for one month in the year (1Ki 4:16).

ALPHA AND OMEGA [*270+6042*]. A title of Christ, meaning "First and Last" and "Beginning and End" (Rev 1:8, cf. 17; 21:6; 22:13; cf. Isa 41:4; 44:6; 48:12).

ALPHAEUS [*271*].

1. Father of James (Mt 10:3; Mk 3:18).
2. Father of Levi (Mk 2:14).
3. Possibly Clopas, husband of the Mary at the cross (Jn 19:25; also Mk 15:40), as Clopas and Alphaeus are of Semitic derivation. Unlikely the Cleopas of the Emmaus road (Lk 24:18) since Clopas was a common Greek name.

ALTAR OF BURNT OFFERING, THE

Dimensions of (Ex 27:1; 38:1). Horns on the corners of (Ex 27:2; 38:2). Covered with bronze (Ex 27:2). All its vessels of bronze (Ex 27:3; 38:3). A network grating of bronze placed in (Ex 27:4-5; 38:4). Furnished with rings and poles (Ex 27:6-7; 38:5-7). Made after a divine pattern (Ex 27:8).

Called:

The brazen altar (Ex 39:39; 1Ki 8:64). The altar of God (Ps 43:4). The altar of the Lord (Mal 2:13). Placed in the court before the door of the tabernacle (Ex 40:6,29). Sanctified by God (Ex 29:44). Anointed and sanctified with holy oil (Ex 40:10; Lev 8:10-11). Cleansed and purified with blood (Ex 29:36-37). Was most holy (Ex 40:10). Sanctified whatever touched it (Ex 29:37). All sacrifices to be offered on (Ex 29:38-42; Isa 56:7). All gifts to be presented at (Mt 5:23-24). Nothing polluted or defective to be offered on (Lev 22:22; Mal 1:7-8). Offering at the dedication of (Nu 7).

The Fire Upon:

Came from before the Lord (Lev 9:24). Was continually burning (Lev 6:13). Consumed the sacrifices (Lev 1:8-9). Sacrifices bound to the horns of (Ps 118:27, ftn). The blood of sacrifices put on the horns and poured at the foot of (Ex 29:12; Lev 4:7,18,25; 8:15).

The Priests:

Alone to serve (Nu 18:3,7). Derived support from (1Co 9:13). Ahaz removed and profaned (2Ki 16:10-16). The Jews were condemned for swearing lightly by (Mt 23:18-19). A type of Christ (Heb 13:10).

ALTAR OF INCENSE Dimensions of (Ex 30:1-2; 37:25). Covered with gold (Ex 30:3; 37:26). Top of, surrounded with a crown of gold (Ex 30:3; 37:26). Had four rings of gold under the crown for the poles (Ex 30:4; 37:27). Poles of, covered with gold (Ex 30:5). Called the golden altar (Ex 39:38). Placed before the veil in the outer sanctuary (Ex 30:6; 40:5,26). Said to be before the Lord (Lev 4:7; 1Ki 9:25). Anointed with holy oil (Ex 30:25-27). The priest burned incense on, every morning and evening (Ex 30:7-8). No strange incense nor any sacrifice to be offered on (Ex 30:9). Atonement made for, by the high priest once every year (Ex 30:10; Lev 16:18-19). The blood of all sin offerings put on the horns of (Lev 4:7,18). Covered by the priests before removal from the sanctuary (Nu 4:11). A type of Christ (Rev 8:3; 9:3).

Punishment for: Offering strange fire on (Lev 10:1-2). Unauthorized offering on (2Ch 26:16-19).

ALTARS [789, 2219, 2802, 4246, 4640, 5232, 10401, *1117, 2593, 2603*].

NIV+ ALTAR

Designed for sacrifice (Ex 20:24). To be made of earth or uncut stone (Ex 20:24-25; Dt 27:5-6). Of brick, detestable to God (Isa 65:3). Natural rocks sometimes used as (Jdg 6:19-21; 13:19-20). Were not to have steps up to them (Ex 20:26). For idolatrous worship, often built on roofs of houses (2Ki 23:12; Jer 19:13; 32:29). Idolaters raised Asherah poles near (Jdg 6:30; 1Ki 16:32-33; 2Ki 21:3). The Israelites not to raise Asherah poles (Dt 16:21). For idolatrous worship, to be destroyed (Ex 34:13; Dt 7:5). Probable origin of inscriptions on (Dt 27:8).

Mentioned in Scripture:

Of Noah (Ge 8:20). Of Abraham (Ge 12:7-8; 13:18; 22:9). Of Isaac (Ge 26:25). Of Jacob (Ge 33:20; 35:1,3,7). Of Moses (Ex 17:15; 24:4). Of Balaam (Nu 23:1,14,29). Of Joshua (Jos 8:30-31). Of the temple of Solomon (2Ch 4:1,19). Of the second temple (Ezr 3:2-3). Of Reubenites, E of Jordan (Jos 22:10). Of Gideon (Jdg 6:26-27). Of the people of Israel (Jdg 21:4). Of Samuel (1Sa 7:17). Of David (2Sa 24:21,25). Of Jeroboam at Bethel (1Ki 12:33). Of Ahaz (2Ki 16:10-12). Of the Athenians (Ac 17:23). For burnt offering (Ex 27:1-8). For incense (Ex 30:1-6). Protection afforded by (1Ki 1:50-51). Afforded no protection to murderers (Ex 21:14; 1Ki 2:18-34).

AL-TASCHITH (*[do] not destroy*). In KJV titles of Pss 57-59; 75; NIV "Do Not Destroy". Probably the tune to which each of these psalms was sung. The phrase occurs in Isa 65:8, leading some to deduce it is the name of a vintage or wine-making song. *See Music, Symbols Used in.*

ALTRUISM (*concern and actions for the welfare of others*).

Jesus Commends:

By teaching—

Mt 20:26 Not so with you. Instead, whoever wants to become great among you must be your servant, [27]and whoever wants to be first must be your slave—

Mt 23:11 The greatest among you will be your servant.

Mk 9:35 Sitting down, Jesus called the Twelve and said, "If anyone wants to be first, he must be the very last, and the servant of all." (+Mk 10:43-45; Lk 22:26-27; Jn 13:4-11)

Jn 13:12 When he had finished washing their feet, he put on his clothes and returned to his place. "Do you understand what I have done for you?" he asked them. [13]"You

call me 'Teacher' and 'Lord,' and rightly so, for that is what I am. [14]Now that I, your Lord and Teacher, have washed your feet, you also should wash one another's feet. [15]I have set you an example that you should do as I have done for you. (+Jn 13:16-17; Ac 20:35)

By example (Jn 13:4-17). Came to serve (Mt 20:28; Php 2:7), went about doing good works (Ac 10:38)

Pleased not himself—

Ro 15:3 For even Christ did not please himself but, as it is written: "The insults of those who insult you have fallen on me."

Became poor for others (2Co 8:9).

Paul Commends:

By teaching, to help the weak—

Ac 20:33 I have not coveted anyone's silver or gold or clothing. [34]You yourselves know that these hands of mine have supplied my own needs and the needs of my companions. [35]In everything I did, I showed you that by this kind of hard work we must help the weak, remembering the words the Lord Jesus himself said: 'It is more blessed to give than to receive.'"

Ro 15:1 We who are strong ought to bear with the failings of the weak and not to please ourselves. [2]Each of us should please his neighbor for his good, to build him up.

To promote the welfare of others—

1Co 10:24 Nobody should seek his own good, but the good of others. (+1Co 10:31-32)

1Co 10:33 even as I try to please everybody in every way. For I am not seeking my own good but the good of many, so that they may be saved. (+Gal 6:1-2)

Gal 6:10 Therefore, as we have opportunity, let us do good to all people, especially to those who belong to the family of believers. (+Php 2:4-9)

By example, became servant of all—

1Co 9:18 What then is my reward? Just this: that in preaching the gospel I may offer it free of charge, and so not make use of my rights in preaching it. [19]Though I am free and belong to no man, I make myself a slave to everyone, to win as many as possible. [20]To the Jews I became like a Jew, to win the Jews. To those under the law I became like one under the law (though I myself am not under the law), so as to win those under the law. [21]To those not having the law I became like one not having the law (though I am not free from God's law but am under Christ's law), so as to win those not having the law. [22]To the weak I became weak, to win the weak. I have become all things to all men so that by all possible means I might save some.

2Co 4:5 For we do not preach ourselves, but Jesus Christ as Lord, and ourselves as your servants for Jesus' sake.

Made many rich (2Co 6:10).

Motives Inspiring to:

Love of neighbor (Lk 10:25-37). To save people (1Co 9:22). For Jesus' sake (2Co 4:5).

Example of Jesus—

2Co 8:9 For you know the grace of our Lord Jesus Christ, that though he was rich, yet for your sakes he became poor, so that you through his poverty might become rich.

Php 2:3 Do nothing out of selfish ambition or vain conceit, but in humility consider others better than yourselves. [4]Each of you should look not only to your own interests, but also to the interests of others.

[5]Your attitude should be the same as that of Christ Jesus: [6]Who, being in very nature God, did not consider equality with God something to be grasped, [7]but made himself

nothing, taking the very nature of a servant, being made in human likeness. ⁸And being found in appearance as a man, he humbled himself and became obedient to death—even death on a cross!

See Alms; Beneficence; Charitableness; Duty of People to People; Liberality; Love.

ALUSH [478]. Camping place of the Israelites (Nu 33:13).

ALVAH [6595]. Chief of Edom, descended from Esau (Ge 36:40; 1Ch 1:51).

ALVAN [6597] (possibly *ascending one,* or *tall*). Son of Shobal, a descendant of Seir (Ge 36:23). Also spelled Alian (1Ch 1:40, ftn).

AMAD [6675]. A town of Asher (Jos 19:26).

AMAL [6663] (*laborer, troubler*). Son of Helem (1Ch 7:35).

AMALEK [6667].
NIV+ AMALEKITE, AMALEKITES
Son of Eliphaz (Ge 36:12; 1Ch 1:36). Probably not the ancestor of the Amalekites mentioned in the time of Abraham (Ge 14:7).

AMALEKITE(S) [6667, 6668].
NIV+ AMALEK
Descent of (Ge 36:12,16).

Character of:
Wicked (1Sa 15:18). Oppressive (Jdg 10:12). Warlike and cruel (1Sa 15:33). Governed by kings (1Sa 15:20,32). A powerful and influential nation (Nu 24:7). Possessed cities (1Sa 15:5).

Country of:
In the south of Canaan (Nu 13:29; 1Sa 27:8). Extended from Havilah to Shur (1Sa 15:7). Was the scene of ancient warfare (Ge 14:7). Part of the Kenites dwelt among (1Sa 15:6). Were the first to oppose Israel (Ex 17:8). Beaten at Rephidim, through the intercession of Moses (Ex 17:9-13). Doomed to utter destruction foretold (Nu 24:20). Presumption of Israel punished by (Nu 14:45). United with Eglon against Israel (Jdg 3:13). Part of their possessions taken by Ephraim (Jdg 5:14, w Jdg 12:15). With Midian, oppressed Israel (Jdg 6:3-5).

Saul:
Overcame, and delivered Israel (1Sa 14:48). Commissioned to destroy (1Sa 15:1-3). Massacred (1Sa 15:4-8). Condemned for not utterly destroying (1Sa 15:9-26; 28:18). Agag, king of, slain by Samuel (1Sa 15:32-33). Invaded by David (1Sa 27:8-9). Pillaged and burned Ziklag (1Sa 30:1-2). Pursued and slain by David (1Sa 30:10-20). Spoil taken from, consecrated (2Sa 8:11-12). Confederated against Israel (Ps 83:5-7). Remnant of, completely destroyed during the reign of Hezekiah (1Ch 4:41-43).

AMAM [585]. A city of Judah (Jos 15:26). Probably within the district later assigned to Simeon (Jos 19:1-9).

AMANA [592] (*constant*). A mountain near Lebanon (SS 4:8), from which flows the Abana River (2Ki 5:12). *See Abana.*

AMANUENSIS A secretary employed to write from dictation or to copy manuscripts. Examples: Baruch (Jer 36:4; 45:1), Tertius (Ro 16:22), perhaps Silas (1Th 1:1;

2Th 1:1; 1Pe 5:12) and Timothy (2Co 1:1; Php 1:1; Col 1:1; 1Th 1:1; 2Th 1:1; Phm 1:1).

AMARANTHINE A type of straw flower that does not shrivel when picked. NIV "can never fade" (1Pe 1:4; 5:4).

AMARIAH [618, 619] (*Yahweh has said*).
NIV+ AMARIAH'S
1. Two Levites (1Ch 6:7,52; 23:19; 24:23).
2. Chief priest in the reign of Jehoshaphat (2Ch 19:11).
3. A high priest, father of Ahitub (1Ch 6:11; Ezr 7:3).
4. A Levite, who assisted in distributing temple gifts (2Ch 31:15-19).
5. Son of Hezekiah (Zep 1:1).
6. Father of Zechariah (Ne 11:4).
7. A priest, returned from exile (Ne 10:3; 12:2). Probably identical with one mentioned in Ne 12:13.
8. A returned exile. Divorces his idolatrous wife (Ezr 10:42).

AMARNA, TELL EL (*the hill Amarna*). The modern name for the ancient capital of Amenhotep IV (c. 1379-1362 B.C.), where in 1887 a large number of clay tablets containing the private correspondence between the ruling Egyptian pharaohs and the political leaders in Canaan were discovered. *See Akhenaten; Texts, Ancient Near Eastern Non-Biblical Texts Relating to the Old Testament..*

AMASA [6690] (*[my] people are from Jesse*).
1. Nephew of David (2Sa 17:25; 1Ch 2:17). Joins Absalom (2Sa 17:25). Returns to David and is made captain of the host (2Sa 19:13). Slain (2Sa 20:8-12; 1Ki 2:5,32).
2. Son of Hadlai (2Ch 28:12).

AMASAI [6691] (*[my] people are from Jesse*).
1. A Levite and ancestor of Samuel (1Ch 6:25,35).
2. Leader of a body of men unhappy with Saul, who joined David (1Ch 12:18).
3. A priest and trumpeter (1Ch 15:24).
4. A Levite of the Kohathites (2Ch 29:12).

AMASHAI, AMASHSAI [6692]. Priest in Nehemiah's time (Ne 11:13).

AMASIAH [6674] (*Yahweh carries a load*). A captain under Jehoshaphat (2Ch 17:16).

AMAZIAH [604, 605] (*Yahweh is powerful*).
NIV+ AMAZIAH'S
1. A Levite (1Ch 6:45).
2. King of Judah. History of (2Ki 14; 2Ch 25).
3. An idolatrous priest at Bethel (Am 7:10-17).
4. Father of Joshah (1Ch 4:34).

AMBASSADORS [7495, *4563*].
NIV+ AMBASSADOR
Sent by:
Moses to Edom (Nu 20:14), to the Amorites (Nu 21:21), by Gibeonites to the Israelites (Jos 9:4), Israelites to various nations (Jdg 11:12-28).
Hiram to: David (2Sa 5:11), Solomon (1Ki 5:1).
Ben-Hadad to Ahab (1Ki 20:2-6), Amaziah to Jehoash (2Ki 14:8), Ahaz to Tiglath-Pileser (2Ki 16:7), Hoshea to So, king of Egypt (2Ki 17:4), Sennacherib through the field commander, to Hezekiah (2Ki 19:9), Merodach-Baladan to Hezekiah (2Ki 20:12; 2Ch 32:31), Zedekiah to Egypt (Eze 17:15).
Other references to (Pr 13:17; Isa 18:2; 30:4; 33:7; 36:11; 39:1-2; Lk 14:32).

Figurative:

(Job 33:23; Ob 1; 2Co 5:20; Eph 6:20).

AMBER NIV "glowing metal" (Eze 1:4,27; 8:2). *See Glowing Metal; Minerals of the Bible, 1; Stones.*

AMBITION [2249, 5818].

Worthy:

1Ti 3:1 Here is a trustworthy saying: If anyone sets his heart on being an overseer, he desires a noble task.

Worldly:

Jas 4:1 What causes fights and quarrels among you? Don't they come from your desires that battle within you? ²You want something but don't get it. You kill and covet, but you cannot have what you want. You quarrel and fight. You do not have, because you do not ask God.

1Jn 2:16 For everything in the world—the cravings of sinful man, the lust of his eyes and the boasting of what he has and does—comes not from the Father but from the world.

Cursed—

Isa 5:8 Woe to you who add house to house and join field to field till no space is left and you live alone in the land. (+Heb 2:9)

False accusation against Moses (Nu 16:13).

Insatiable—

Hab 2:5 indeed, wine betrays him; he is arrogant and never at rest. Because he is as greedy as the grave and like death is never satisfied, he gathers to himself all the nations and takes captive all the peoples.

⁶"Will not all of them taunt him with ridicule and scorn, saying, "'Woe to him who piles up stolen goods and makes himself wealthy by extortion! How long must this go on?'

Hab 2:9 "Woe to him who builds his realm by unjust gain to set his nest on high, to escape the clutches of ruin!

Parable illustrating (2Ki 14:9)

Perishable—

Job 20:6 Though his pride reaches to the heavens and his head touches the clouds, ⁷he will perish forever, like his own dung; those who have seen him will say, 'Where is he?'

Ps 49:11 Their tombs will remain their houses forever, their dwellings for endless generations, though they had named lands after themselves.

¹²But man, despite his riches, does not endure; he is like the beasts that perish.

¹³This is the fate of those who trust in themselves, and of their followers, who approve their sayings. *Selah*

Rebuked by Jesus—

Mt 16:26 What good will it be for a man if he gains the whole world, yet forfeits his soul? Or what can a man give in exchange for his soul? (+Mt 18:1-3)

Mt 20:20 Then the mother of Zebedee's sons came to Jesus with her sons and, kneeling down, asked a favor of him.

²¹"What is it you want?" he asked. She said, "Grant that one of these two sons of mine may sit at your right and the other at your left in your kingdom."

²²"You don't know what you are asking," Jesus said to them. "Can you drink the cup I am going to drink?" "We can," they answered.

²³Jesus said to them, "You will indeed drink from my cup, but to sit at my right or left is not for me to grant. These places belong to those for whom they have been prepared by my Father."

²⁴When the ten heard about this, they were indignant with the two brothers. ²⁵Jesus called them together and said, "You know that the rulers of the Gentiles lord it over them, and their high officials exercise authority over them. ²⁶Not so with you. Instead, whoever wants to become great among you must be your servant, ²⁷and whoever wants to be first must be your slave— ²⁸just as the Son of Man did not come to be served, but to serve, and to give his life as a ransom for many."

Mt 23:5 "Everything they do is done for men to see: They make their phylacteries wide and the tassels on their garments long; ⁶they love the place of honor at banquets and the most important seats in the synagogues; ⁷they love to be greeted in the marketplaces and to have men call them 'Rabbi.'

Mt 23:12 For whoever exalts himself will be humbled, and whoever humbles himself will be exalted.

Mk 9:33 They came to Capernaum. When he was in the house, he asked them, "What were you arguing about on the road?" ³⁴But they kept quiet because on the way they had argued about who was the greatest.

³⁵Sitting down, Jesus called the Twelve and said, "If anyone wants to be first, he must be the very last, and the servant of all."

³⁶He took a little child and had him stand among them. Taking him in his arms, he said to them, ³⁷"Whoever welcomes one of these little children in my name welcomes me; and whoever welcomes me does not welcome me but the one who sent me." (+Mk 10:35-45)

Mk 12:38 As he taught, Jesus said, "Watch out for the teachers of the law. They like to walk around in flowing robes and be greeted in the marketplaces, ³⁹and have the most important seats in the synagogues and the places of honor at banquets. (+Lk 9:25,46-48; 11:43)

Lk 22:24 Also a dispute arose among them as to which of them was considered to be greatest. ²⁵Jesus said to them, "The kings of the Gentiles lord it over them; and those who exercise authority over them call themselves Benefactors. ²⁶But you are not to be like that. Instead, the greatest among you should be like the youngest, and the one who rules like the one who serves. ²⁷For who is greater, the one who is at the table or the one who serves? Is it not the one who is at the table? But I am among you as one who serves. ²⁸You are those who have stood by me in my trials. ²⁹And I confer on you a kingdom, just as my Father conferred one on me, ³⁰so that you may eat and drink at my table in my kingdom and sit on thrones, judging the twelve tribes of Israel.

Jn 5:44 How can you believe if you accept praise from one another, yet make no effort to obtain the praise that comes from the only God?

Temptation by Satan—

Mt 4:8 Again, the devil took him to a very high mountain and showed him all the kingdoms of the world and their splendor. ⁹"All this I will give you," he said, "if you will bow down and worship me."

¹⁰Jesus said to him, "Away from me, Satan! For it is written: 'Worship the Lord your God, and serve him only.'" (+Lk 4:5-8)

Instances of:

King of Babylon (Isa 14:12-15), Eve (Ge 3:5-6), Korah and his followers (Nu 16:3-35), Abimelech (Jdg 9:1-6), Absalom (2Sa 15:1-13; 18:18), Haman (Est 5:9-13)

Disciples of Jesus (Mt 18:1-3; 20:20-24; Mk 9:33-37)—

Mk 10:35 Then James and John, the sons of Zebedee,

came to him. "Teacher," they said, "we want you to do for us whatever we ask."

36"What do you want me to do for you?" he asked.

37They replied, "Let one of us sit at your right and the other at your left in your glory."

38"You don't know what you are asking," Jesus said. "Can you drink the cup I drink or be baptized with the baptism I am baptized with?"

39"We can," they answered.

Jesus said to them, "You will drink the cup I drink and be baptized with the baptism I am baptized with, 40but to sit at my right or left is not for me to grant. These places belong to those for whom they have been prepared."

41When the ten heard about this, they became indignant with James and John. 42Jesus called them together and said, "You know that those who are regarded as rulers of the Gentiles lord it over them, and their high officials exercise authority over them. 43Not so with you. Instead, whoever wants to become great among you must be your servant, 44and whoever wants to be first must be slave of all. 45For even the Son of Man did not come to be served, but to serve, and to give his life as a ransom for many." (+Lk 9:46-48; 22:24-30)

Diotrephes (3Jn 9-10).

Disappointed:

Ahithophel (2Sa 17:23), Adonijah (1Ki 1:5), Haman (Est 6:6-9).

AMBUSH [741, 2675, 4422, 5041, 6811, *1909, 1910*].
NIV+ AMBUSHES

Instances of:

At Ai (Jos 8:2-22), Shechem (Jdg 9:25,34), Gibeah (Jdg 20:29-41), near Zemaraim (2Ch 13:13).

By Jehoshaphat (2Ch 20:21-22).

See Armies.

Figurative: (Jer 51:12).

AMEN [589, 297] (*so be it*).

A word used to reinforce a statement (Nu 5:22; Dt 27:12-26; Ne 5:13; 2Co 1:20; Rev 5:14; 22:20).

Used in prayer (1Ki 1:36; 1Ch 16:36; Ne 8:6; Ps 41:13; 72:19; 89:52; 106:48; Jer 28:6; Mt 6:13; 1Co 14:16; Rev 5:14; 19:4).

A title of Christ (Rev 3:14).

AMETHYST [334, *287*]. A precious stone (Ex 28:19; 39:12; Rev 21:20). *See Minerals of the Bible, 1; Stones.*

AMI [577] (*trustworthy, reliable, faithful*). A servant of Solomon (Ezr 2:57). Also called Amon (Ne 7:59). *See Amon.*

AMINADAB *See Amminadab.*

AMITTAI [624] (*true*). Father of Jonah (2Ki 14:25; Jnh 1:1).

AMMAH [565] (*cubit*).
NIV+ METHEG AMMAH

A hill around Gibeon where Joab and Abishai halted in their pursuit of Abner and his forces after they defeated him in the battle of Gibeon (2Sa 2:24-32).

AMMI (*my people*). Name given to Israel symbolizing acceptance (Hos 2:1, KJV); opposite of Lo-Ammi, "not my people" (Hos 1:9).

AMMIEL [6653] (*God [El] is my kinsman*).

1. The son of Gemalli and spy sent out by Moses (Nu 13:12).

2. The father of Makir of Lo Debar (2Sa 9:4-5; 17:27).

3. The father of Bathsheba, one of David's wives (1Ch 3:5). Called also Eliam (2Sa 11:3).

4. The sixth son of Obed-Edom who, with his family, was associated with the temple gatekeepers (1Ch 26:5).

AMMIHUD [6654] (*[my] people have majesty*).

1. The father of Elishama, chief of Ephraim (Nu 1:10; 2:18; 7:48,53), and the son of Ladan (1Ch 7:26).

2. A man of Simeon and father of Shemuel (Nu 34:20).

3. A Naphtalite whose son, Pedahel, also assisted in the division of the land (Nu 34:28).

4. Father of Talmai and king of Geshur. Absalom fled to Talmai after he killed his brother Amnon (2Sa 13:37).

5. Son of Omri, father of Uthai (1Ch 9:4).

AMMIHUR *See Ammihud.*

AMMINADAB [6657, *300*] (*my people are generous*).

1. A Levite. Aaron's father-in-law (Ex 6:23).

2. A prince of Judah (Nu 1:7; 2:3; 7:12,17; 10:14; Ru 4:19-20; 1Ch 2:10; Mt 1:4; Lk 3:33).

3. A son of Kohath, son of Levi (1Ch 6:22). Perhaps the same as 1.

4. A Kohathite who assisted in the return of the ark from the house of Obed-Edom (1Ch 15:10-11).

AMMINADIB KJV "chariots of Amminadib" are "royal chariots of my people" in the NIV (SS 6:12, see also ftn). *See Amminadab.*

AMMISHADDAI [6659] (*Shaddai is [my] kinsman*). Father of Abiezer, captain of the tribe of Dan in Moses' time (Nu 1:12; 2:25; 7:66,71; 10:25).

AMMIZABAD [6655] (*[my] people have given a gift*). Son of Benaiah, third of David's captains (1Ch 27:6).

AMMON [6648, 6649] (*people*).
NIV+ AMMONITE, AMMONITES

Ammon or Ben-Ammi is the name of one of the sons of Lot born to him by his youngest daughter in Zoar (Ge 19:38). *See Ammonite(s).*

AMMONI *See Kephar Ammoni.*

AMMONITE(S) [1201+6648, 6648, 6649].
NIV+ AMMON

Descendants of Ben-Ammi, one of the sons of Lot (Ge 19:38). Character of (Jdg 10:6; 2Ki 23:13; 2Ch 20:22-23; Jer 27:3,9; Eze 25:1-7; Am 1:13; Zep 2:10). Territory of (Nu 21:24; Dt 2:19; Jos 12:2; 13:10,25; Jdg 11:13).

Israelites forbidden to disturb (Dt 2:19,37). Excluded from the congregation of Israel (Dt 23:3-6). Confederate with Moabites and Amalekites against Israel (Jdg 3:12-13). Defeated by the Israelites (Jdg 10:7-18; 11:32-33; 12:1-3; 1Sa 11; 2Sa 8:12; 10; 11:1; 12:26-31; 17:27; 1Ch 18:11; 20:1-3; 2Ch 20; 26:7-8; 27:5). Conspire against the Jews (Ne 4:7-8).

Solomon takes wives from (1Ki 11:1; Ne 13:26). Rehoboam takes wives from (2Ch 12:13). Jews intermarry with (Ezr 9:1,10-12; 10:10-44; Ne 13:23).

Kings of: Baalis (Jer 40:14; 41:10)

Idols of:

Molech (2Ki 23:13). *See Molech.* Prophecies concerning (Isa 11:14; Jer 9:25-26; 25:15-21; 27:1-11; 49:1-6; Eze

21:20,28-32; 25:1-11; Da 11:41; Am 1:13-15; Zep 2:8-11).

AMNESTY For political offenses: Shimei (2Sa 19:16-23). Amasa (2Sa 19:13, w 17:25).

AMNON [578, 596] (*trustworthy*).

NIV+ AMNON'S

1. Son of David (2Sa 3:2; 1Ch 3:1). Incest of, and death (2Sa 13).

2. Son of Shimon (1Ch 4:20).

AMOK [6651] (*capable* KB).

NIV+ AMOK'S

Priest who returned with Zerubbabel from exile (Ne 12:7,20).

AMON [571, 572, *321*] (*trustworthy*).

NIV+ AMON'S

1. Governor of the city of Samaria (1Ki 22:26; 2Ch 18:25).

2. King of Judah (2Ki 21:18-26; 2Ch 33:21-25; Zep 1:1; Mt 1:10).

3. Ancestor of one of the families of the temple servants (Ne 7:59). Called Ami (Ezr 2:57). *See Ami.*

4. A city thought by most scholars to be the same as the city of No (Hebrew) (Jer 46:25). It was the capital of Egypt. Thebes is the Greek name.

AMORITE(S) [616] (possibly *hill dwellers* BDB; *westerners* KB). Descendants of Canaan (Ge 10:15-6; 1Ch 1:13-14). Were giants (Am 2:9). Conquered by Kedorlaomer and rescued by Abraham (Ge 14).

Territory of (Ge 14:7; Nu 13:29; 21:13; Dt 1:4,7,19; 3:8-9; Jos 5:1; 10:5; 12:2-3; Jdg 1:35-36; 11:22), given to descendants of Abraham (Ge 15:21; 48:22; Dt 1:20; 2:26-36; 7:1; Jos 3:10; Jdg 11:23; Am 2:10), allotted to Reuben, Gad, and Manasseh (Nu 32:33-42; Jos 13:15-21), conquest of (Nu 21:21-30; Jos 10:11; Jdg 1:34-36).

Chiefs of (Jos 13:21). Wickedness of (Ge 15:16; 2Ki 21:11; Ezr 9:1). Idolatry of (Jdg 6:10; 1Ki 21:26). Judgments denounced against (Ex 23:23-24; 33:2; 34:10-11; Dt 20:17-18). Hornets sent among (Jos 24:12). Not exterminated (Jdg 1:34-36; 3:1-3,5-8; 1Sa 7:14; 2Sa 2:2; 1Ki 9:20-21; 2Ch 8:7). Intermarry with Jews (Ezr 9:1-2; 10:18-44). Kings of (Jos 10:3-26).

AMOS [6650, *322*] (*burden bearer*). A prophet (Am 1:1). Forbidden to prophesy in Israel (Am 7:10-17). Vision of (Am 8:2).

AMOS, BOOK OF

Author: Amos of Tekoa

Date: probably between 760-750 B.C.

Outline:

I. Superscription (1:1).

II. Introduction to Amos's Message (1:2).

III. Judgments on the Nations (1:3-2:16).
  A. Judgment on Aram (1:3-5).
  B. Judgment on Philistia (1:6-8).
  C. Judgment on Phoenicia (1:9-10).
  D. Judgment on Edom (1:11-12).
  E. Judgment on Ammon (1:13-15).
  F. Judgment on Moab (2:1-3).
  G. Judgment on Judah (2:4-5).
  H. Judgment on Israel (2:6-16).
    1. Ruthless oppression of the poor (2:6-7a).
    2. Unbridled profanation of religion (2:7b-8).

3. Contrasted position of the Israelites (2:9-12).
    4. The oppressive system will perish (2:13-16).
IV. Oracles against Israel (3:1-5:17).
  A. Judgment on the Chosen People (ch. 3).
    1. God's punishment announced (3:1-2).
    2. The announcement vindicated (3:3-8).
    3. The punishment vindicated (3:9-15).
  B. Judgment on an Unrepentant People (ch. 4).
    1. Judgment on the socialites (4:1-3).
    2. Perversion of religious life (4:4-5).
    3. Past calamities brought no repentance (4:6-11).
    4. No hope for a hardened people (4:12-13).
  C. Judgment on an Unjust People (5:1-17).
    1. The death dirge (5:1-3).
    2. Exhortation to life (5:4-6).
    3. Indictment of injustices (5:7-13).
    4. Exhortation to life (5:14-15).
    5. Prosperity will turn to grief (5:16-17).
V. Announcements of Exile (5:18-6:14).
  A. A Message of Woe against Israel's Perverted Religion (5:18-27).
  B. A Message of Woe against Israel's Complacent Pride (6:1-7).
  C. A Sworn Judgment on the Proud and Unjust Nation (6:8-14).
VI. Visions of Divine Retribution (7:1-9:10).
  A. Judgment Relented (7:1-6).
    1. A swarm of locusts (7:1-3).
    2. A consuming fire (7:4-6).
  B. Judgment Unrelented (7:7-9:10).
    1. The plumb line (7:7-17).
      a. The vision (7:7-9).
      b. Challenged and vindicated (7:10-17).
    2. The basket of ripe fruit (ch. 8).
      a. The vision (8:1-3).
      b. The exposition (8:4-14).
    3. The Lord by the altar (9:1-10).
      a. The vision (9:1-4).
      b. The exposition (9:5-10).
VII. Restored Israel's Blessed Future (9:11-15).
  A. Revival of the House of David (9:11-12).
  B. Restoration of Israel to an Edenic Promised Land (9:13-15).
  See Prophets, The Minor.

AMOZ [576] (*strong*). Father of Isaiah (2Ki 19:2,20; 20:1; Isa 1:1; 13:1).

AMPHIPOLIS [*315*] (*a city surrounded* or *a city conspicuous*). City of Macedonia not far from Philippi. Paul passed through it (Ac 17:1).

AMPLIATUS, AMPLIAS [*309*]. A Christian to whom Paul sent a greeting (Ro 16:8).

AMRAM, AMRAMITES [6688, 6689] (*exalted people*).

1. Father of Moses (Ex 6:18,20; Nu 26:58-59; 1Ch 6:3,18; 23:12-13). Head of one of the branches of Levites (Nu 3:19,27; 1Ch 26:23). Age of, at death (Ex 6:20).

2. Son of Bani (Ezr 10:34).

3. *See Hemdan.*

AMRAPHEL [620]. King of Shinar (Ge 14:1,9).

AMULET *See Charmers and Charming.*

AMUN *See Amon.*

AMUSEMENTS AND WORLDLY PLEASURES

Belong to the works of the flesh (Gal 5:19,21).

Are transitory (Job 21:12-13; Heb 11:25), vain (Ecc 2:11), choke the Word of God in the heart (Lk 8:14), formed a part of idolatrous worship (Ex 32:4,6,19, w 1Co 10:7; Jdg 16:23-25).

Lead to:

Rejection of God (Job 21:12-15), poverty (Pr 21:17), disregard of the judgments and works of God (Isa 5:12; Am 6:1-6), sorrow (Pr 14:13), greater evil (Job 1:5; Mt 14:6-8), attempting to find fulfillment in (Ecc 2:1-8).

Indulgence in:

A proof of folly (Ecc 7:4), a characteristic of the wicked (Isa 47:8; Eph 4:17,19; 2Ti 3:4; Tit 3:3; 1Pe 4:3), a proof of spiritual death (1Ti 5:6), an abuse of riches (Jas 5:1,5), wisdom of abstaining from (Ecc 7:2-3), shunned by the early believers (1Pe 4:3).

Abstinence From:

Seems strange to the wicked (1Pe 4:4), denounced by God (Isa 5:11-12), exclude from the kingdom of God (Gal 5:21), punishment of (Ecc 11:9; 2Pe 2:13), renunciation of, exemplified by Moses (Heb 11:25).

See Dancing; Games; Pleasure, Worldly; Worldliness.

AMZI [603] (possibly *Yahweh is my strength*).

1. A descendant of Merari and of Levi, and progenitor of Ethan, whom David set over the service of song (1Ch 6:44-46).

2. An ancestor of Adaiah, a priest in the second temple (Ne 11:12).

ANAB [6693] (*grape*). A city of the Anakites taken by Joshua (Jos 11:21). It fell to Judah (Jos 15:50). SE of Debir, SW of Hebron. It retains its ancient name.

ANAH [6704].

1. Daughter of Zibeon and mother of Oholibamah, Esau's wife (Ge 36:2,14,25).

2. Son of Seir, chief of Edom (Ge 36:20,29; 1Ch 1:38).

3. Son Zibeon (Ge 36:24; 1Ch 1:40-41). Also called Beeri (Ge 26:34).

ANAHARATH [637]. City on the border of Issachar (Jos 19:19). Modern en-Naura.

ANAIAH [6717] (*Yahweh responds*).

1. A prince or priest who assisted in the reading of the law to the people (Ne 8:4).

2. A Jew who, with Nehemiah, sealed the covenant (Ne 10:22). Nos. 1 and 2 may be the same person.

ANAK [6710, 6737] (*[long] necked, tall*).

NIV+ ANAKITES

Descendant of Arba (Jos 15:13), and the ancestor of the Anakites (Nu 13:22,28,33).

ANAKITES, ANAKIM [1201+6737, 6737] (*[long] necked, tall*).

NIV+ ANAK

Descent of (Nu 13:22; Jos 15:13).

Called: The descendants of Anak (Nu 13:33). Anakites (Dt 1:28; 9:2).

Divided into three tribes (Jos 15:14). Inhabited the mountains of Judah (Jos 11:21). Hebron, chief city of (Jos 14:15, w 21:11). Of gigantic strength and stature (Dt 2:10-11,21). Israel terrified by (Nu 14:1, w 13:33). Hebron a

possession of, given to Caleb for his faithfulness (Jos 14:6-14). Driven from Hebron by Caleb (Jos 15:13-14). Driven from Kiriath Sepher or Debir by Othniel (Jos 15:15-17; Jdg 1:12-13). Almost annihilated (Jos 11:21-22).

ANAMITES, ANAMIM [6723]. A tribe descended from Mizraim (Ge 10:13; 1Ch 1:11).

ANAMMELECH [6724] (*Anath is king*). An Assyrian idol (2Ki 17:31).

ANAN [6728] (*cloud*). A Jew, returned from Babylonian captivity (Ne 10:26).

ANANI [6730] (*Yahweh is a covering*). A descendant of David (1Ch 3:24).

ANANIAH [6731, 6732] (*Yahweh is a covering*).

1. Son of Maaseiah (Ne 3:23).

2. Town of Benjamin (Ne 11:32).

ANANIAS [393] (*Yahweh is gracious*).

1. High priest, before whom Paul was tried (Ac 23:2-5; 24:1; 25:2).

2. A covetous member of church at Jerusalem. Falsehood and death of (Ac 5:1-11).

3. A Christian in Damascus (Ac 9:10-18; 22:12-16).

ANARCHY

In Israel:

Isa 3:5 People will oppress each other—man against man, neighbor against neighbor. The young will rise up against the old, the base against the honorable.

[6]A man will seize one of his brothers at his father's home, and say, "You have a cloak, you be our leader; take charge of this heap of ruins!" [7]But in that day he will cry out, "I have no remedy. I have no food or clothing in my house; do not make me the leader of the people."

[8]Jerusalem staggers, Judah is falling; their words and deeds are against the LORD, defying his glorious presence.

In the Early Church:

Warned against—

Gal 5:13 You, my brothers, were called to be free. But do not use your freedom to indulge the sinful nature; rather, serve one another in love. [14]The entire law is summed up in a single command: "Love your neighbor as yourself."

Insubordinate members hostile to authority—

2Pe 2:10 This is especially true of those who follow the corrupt desire of the sinful nature and despise authority.

Bold and arrogant, these men are not afraid to slander celestial beings; [11]yet even angels, although they are stronger and more powerful, do not bring slanderous accusations against such beings in the presence of the Lord. [12]But these men blaspheme in matters they do not understand. They are like brute beasts, creatures of instinct, born only to be caught and destroyed, and like beasts they too will perish.

[13]They will be paid back with harm for the harm they have done. Their idea of pleasure is to carouse in broad daylight. They are blots and blemishes, reveling in their pleasures while they feast with you. [14]With eyes full of adultery, they never stop sinning; they seduce the unstable; they are experts in greed—an accursed brood! [15]They have left the straight way and wandered off to follow the way of Balaam son of Beor, who loved the wages of wickedness. [16]But he was rebuked for his wrongdoing by a donkey—a

beast without speech—who spoke with a man's voice and restrained the prophet's madness.

[17]These men are springs without water and mists driven by a storm. Blackest darkness is reserved for them. [18]For they mouth empty, boastful words and, by appealing to the lustful desires of sinful human nature, they entice people who are just escaping from those who live in error. [19]They promise them freedom, while they themselves are slaves of depravity—for a man is a slave to whatever has mastered him.

Jude 8 In the very same way, these dreamers pollute their own bodies, reject authority and slander celestial beings. [9]But even the archangel Michael, when he was disputing with the devil about the body of Moses, did not dare to bring a slanderous accusation against him, but said, "The Lord rebuke you!" [10]Yet these men speak abusively against whatever they do not understand; and what things they do understand by instinct, like unreasoning animals— these are the very things that destroy them.

[11]Woe to them! They have taken the way of Cain; they have rushed for profit into Balaam's error; they have been destroyed in Korah's rebellion.

[12]These men are blemishes at your love feasts, eating with you without the slightest qualm—shepherds who feed only themselves. They are clouds without rain, blown along by the wind; autumn trees, without fruit and uprooted—twice dead. [13]They are wild waves of the sea, foaming up their shame; wandering stars, for whom blackest darkness has been reserved forever.

ANATH [6742] (*a Semitic goddess*).

1. Father of the judge Shamgar (Jdg 3:31; 5:6).

2. A Canaanite goddess of war and of love, sometimes identified with Astarte, Asherah, and Ashtoreth. She was the sister and consort of Baal. The name is reflected in the city Beth Anath (Jos 19:38; Jdg 1:33) *See Asherah; Ashtoreth; Beth Anath.*

ANATHEMA [353] (*devoted to destruction*).

NIV+ CONDEMNED, CURSE, CURSED

A thing devoted to God becomes his and is therefore irrevocably withdrawn from common use (Lev 27:28-29; Ro 9:3; 1Co 12:3; 16:22; Gal 1:9).

ANATHEMA MARANATHA These words from

1Co 16:22 were formerly interpreted as a double curse. *Anathema* does mean cursed (1Co 12:3). *Marana tha* is Aramaic for "Come, O Lord!" (cf. Rev 22:20).

See Blasphemy; Cursing; God, Name of; Oath.

ANATHOTH, ANATHOTHITE [6743, 6744, 6745] (*plural of Anath*).

1. A Levitical city in Benjamin (Jos 21:18; 1Ch 6:60). Abiathar confined in (1Ki 2:26).

Birthplace: Of Jeremiah (Jer 1:1; 32:7-12), of Abiezer (2Sa 23:27), of Jehu (1Ch 12:3). Prophecies against (Jer 11:21-23). Inhabitants of, after Babylonian captivity (Ezr 2:23; Ne 7:27).

2. Son of Beker (1Ch 7:8).

3. A Jew, who returned from Babylon (Ne 10:19).

ANCHOR [46, 149, 4694, 5007].

NIV+ ANCHORED, ANCHORS

Literal (Ac 27:17,29,30,40). Figurative (Heb 6:19).

ANCIENT OF DAYS A title of Yahweh (Da 7:9, 13,22).

ANCIENT TEXTS RELATING TO THE OLD TESTAMENT See Texts, Ancient Near Eastern Non-Biblical Texts Relating to the Old Testament.

ANCIENTS [4565].

NIV+ ANCIENT

Those of the past (1Sa 24:13). *See Elders.*

ANDREW [436] (*manly*). An apostle. A fisherman (Mt 4:18). Of Bethsaida (Jn 1:44). A disciple of John (Jn 1:40). Finds Peter, his brother, and brings him to Jesus (Jn 1:40-42). Call of (Mt 4:18; Mk 1:16). His name appears in the list of the apostles (Mt 10:2; Mk 3:18; Lk 6:14). Asks the Master privately about the destruction of the temple (Mk 13:3-4). Tells Jesus of the Greeks who wanted to see him (Jn 12:20-22). Reports the number of loaves at the feeding of the five thousand (Jn 6:8). Meets with the disciples after the Lord's ascension (Ac 1:13).

ANDRONICUS [438] (*victor [over] man*). Kinsman of Paul (Ro 16:7).

ANEM [6722] (*springs*). A Levitical city (1Ch 6:73).

ANER [6738, 6739].

1. A Canaanite chief and brother of Mamre (Ge 14:13,24).

2. A Levitical city of Manasseh (1Ch 6:70).

ANGEL [OF THE LORD] [4855, 10417, 34] (*messenger*).

NIV+ ANGEL'S, ANGELS, ARCHANGEL

In addition to 54 occurrences of "the angel of the LORD" (Ex 3:2; Jdg 2:1), many uses of "angel" indicate a manifestation of God himself. These include: angel (Ac 7:30,35 w Ex 3:2), my angel (Ex 23:20-23; 32:34), angel of God (Ex 14:19; Jdg 13:6; 2Sa 14:17,20), angel of his Presence (Isa 63:9).

ANGEL OF THE CHURCHES Heavenly messengers and guardians or earthly messengers and pastors (Rev 1:20; 2:1,8,18; 3:1,7,14).

ANGELS [52, 466+1201, 466+1201+2021, 4855, 34, 2694].

NIV+ ANGEL, ANGEL'S, ARCHANGEL

Created by God and Christ (Ne 9:6; Col 1:16). Worship God and Christ (Ne 9:6; Php 2:9-11; Heb 1:6). Are ministering spirits (1Ki 19:5; Ps 68:17; 104:4; Lk 16:22; Ac 12:7-11; 27:23; Heb 1:7,14). Communicate the will of God and Christ (Da 8:16-17; 9:21-23; 10:11; 12:6-7; Mt 2:13,20; Lk 1:19,28; Ac 5:20; 8:26; 10:5; 27:23; Rev 1:1). Obey the will of God (Ps 103:20; Mt 6:10). Execute the purposes of God (Nu 22:22; Ps 103:21; Mt 13:39-42; 28:2; Jn 5:4; Rev 5:2). Execute the judgments of God (2Sa 24:16; 2Ki 19:35; Ps 35:5-6; Ac 12:23; Rev 16:1). Celebrate the praises of God (Job 38:7; Ps 148:2; Isa 6:3; Lk 2:13-14; Rev 5:11-12; 7:11-12). The law given by the mediation of (Ps 68:17; Ac 7:53; Heb 2:2).

Announced:

The conception of Christ (Mt 1:20-21; Lk 1:31). The birth of Christ (Lk 2:10-12). The resurrection of Christ (Mt 28:5-7; Lk 24:23). The ascension and second coming of Christ (Ac 1:11). The conception of John the Baptist (Lk 1:13,36). Minister to Christ (Mt 4:11; Lk 22:43; Jn 1:51). Are subject to Christ (Eph 1:21; Col 1:16; 2:10; 1Pe 3:22). Shall execute the purposes of Christ (Mt 13:41; 24:31). Shall attend Christ at his second coming (Mt

16:27; 25:31; Mk 8:38; 2Th 1:7). Know and delight in the gospel of Christ (Eph 3:9-10; 1Ti 3:16; 1Pe 1:12). Mediation of, in response to prayer (Mt 26:53; Ac 12:5,7). Rejoice over every repentant sinner (Lk 15:7,10). Have charge over the children of God (Ps 34:7; 91:11-12; Da 6:22; Mt 18:10). Are of different orders (Isa 6:2; 1Th 4:16; 1Pe 3:22; Jude 9; Rev 12:7). Not to be worshiped (Col 2:18; Rev 19:10; 22:9). Are examples of meekness (2Pe 2:11; Jude 9). Are wise (2Sa 14:20). Are mighty (Ps 103:20). Are holy (Mt 25:31). Are elect (1Ti 5:21). Are innumerable (Job 25:3; Heb 12:22).

Fallen: (Job 4:18; Mt 25:41; 2Pe 2:4; Jude 6; Rev 2:9).

ANGER [678, 2405, 2779, 3019, 4087, 4088, 4089, 5757, 6301, 6939, 7287, 7861, 7863, 7911, 7912, 8074, 8120, *2596, 3973, 3974*].

NIV+ ANGERED, ANGERS, ANGRY

Forbidden (Ecc 7:9; Mt 5:22; Ro 12:19). A work of the flesh (Gal 5:20). A characteristic of fools (Pr 12:16; 14:29; 27:3; Ecc 7:9).

Connected With:

Pride (Pr 21:24). Cruelty (Ge 49:7; Pr 27:3-4). Clamor and evil-speaking (Eph 4:31). Malice and blasphemy (Col 3:8). Strife and contention (Pr 21:19; 29:22; 30:33). Brings its own punishment (Job 5:2; Pr 19:19; 25:28). Grievous words stir up (Jdg 12:4; 2Sa 19:43; Pr 15:1). Should not betray us into sin (Ps 37:8; Eph 4:26). In prayer be free from (1Ti 2:8). May be averted by wisdom (Pr 29:8). Meekness pacifies (Pr 15:1; Ecc 10:4). Children should not be provoked to (Eph 6:4; Col 3:21). Be slow to (Pr 15:18; 16:32; 19:11; Tit 1:7; Jas 1:19). Avoid those given to (Ge 49:6; Pr 22:24).

Justifiable, Exemplified:

Our Lord (Mk 3:5). Jacob (Ge 31:36). Moses (Ex 11:8; 32:19; Lev 10:16; Nu 16:15). Nehemiah (Ne 5:6; 13:17,25).

Sinful, Exemplified:

Cain (Ge 4:5-6). Esau (Ge 27:45). Simeon and Levi (Ge 49:5-7). Moses (Nu 20:10-11). Balaam (Nu 22:27). Saul (1Sa 20:30). Ahab (1Ki 21:4). Naaman (2Ki 5:11). Asa (2Ch 16:10). Uzziah (2Ch 26:19). Haman (Est 3:5). Nebuchadnezzar (Da 3:13). Jonah (Jnh 4:4). Herod (Mt 2:16). Jews (Lk 4:28). High Priest (Ac 5:17; 7:54).

ANGER OF GOD

NIV+ ANGERED, ANGERS, ANGRY, WRATH

Turned away by Christ (Lk 2:11,14; Ro 5:9; 2Co 5:18-19; Eph 2:14,17; Col 1:20; 1Th 1:10). Is turned away from them that believe (Jn 3:14-18; Ro 3:25; 5:1). Is turned away upon confession of sin and repentance (Job 33:27-28; Ps 106:43-45; Jer 3:12-13; 18:7-8; 31:18-20; Joel 2:12-14; Lk 15:18-20). Is slow (Ps 103:8; Isa 48:9; Jnh 4:2; Na 1:3). Is righteous (Ps 58:10-11; La 1:18; Ro 2:6,8; 3:5-6; Rev 16:6-7). The justice of, not to be questioned (Ro 9:18,20,22). Manifested in terrors (Ex 14:24; Ps 76:6-8; Jer 10:10; La 2:20-22). Manifested in judgments and afflictions (Job 21:17; Ps 78:49-51; 90:7; Isa 9:19; Jer 7:20; Eze 7:19; Heb 3:17). Cannot be resisted (Job 9:13; 14:13; Ps 76:7; Na 1:6). Aggravated by continual provocation (Nu 32:14). Specially reserved for the day of wrath (Zep 1:14-18; Mt 25:41; Ro 2:5,8; 2Th 1:8; Rev 6:17; 11:18; 19:15).

Against:

The wicked (Ps 7:11; 21:8-9; Isa 3:8; 13:9; Na 1:2-3; Ro 1:18; 2:8; Eph 5:6; Col 3:6). Those who forsake him (Ezr

8:22; Isa 1:4). Unbelief (Ps 78:21-22; Jn 3:36; Heb 3:18-19). Impenitence (Ps 7:12; Pr 1:30-31; Isa 9:13-14; Ro 2:5). Apostasy (Heb 10:26-27). Idolatry (Dt 29:20,27-28; 32:19-20,22; Jos 23:16; 2Ki 22:17; Ps 78:58-59; Jer 44:3). Sin, in believers (Ps 89:30-32; 90:7-9; 99:8; 102:9-10; Isa 47:6). Extreme, against those who oppose the gospel (Ps 2:2-3,5; 1Th 2:16). Folly of provoking (Jer 7:19; 1Co 10:22). To be dreaded (Ps 2:12; 76:7; 90:11; Mt 10:28). To be deprecated (Ex 32:11; Ps 6:1; 38:1; 74:1-2; Isa 64:9). Removal of, should be prayed for (Ps 39:10; 79:5; 80:4; Da 9:16; Hab 3:2). Tempered with mercy to believers (Ps 30:5; Isa 26:20; 54:8; 57:15-16; Jer 30:11; Mic 7:11). To be borne with submission (2Sa 24:17; La 3:39,43; Mic 7:9). Should lead to repentance (Isa 42:24-25; Jer 4:8).

Exemplified Against:

The old world (Ge 7:21-23). Builders of Babel (Ge 11:8). Cities of the plain (Ge 19:24-25). Egyptians (Ex 7:20; 8:6,16,24; 9:3,9,23; 10:13,22; 12:29; 14:27). Israelites (Ex 32:35; Nu 11:1,33; 14:40-45; 21:6; 25:9; 2Sa 24:1,15). Enemies of Israel (1Sa 5:6; 7:10). Nadab (Lev 10:2). The Spies (Nu 14:37). Korah (Nu 16:31,35). Aaron and Miriam (Nu 12:9-10). Five Kings (Jos 10:25). Abimelech (Jdg 9:56). Men of Beth Shemesh (1Sa 6:19). Saul (1Sa 31:6). Uzzah (2Sa 6:7). Saul's family (2Sa 21:1). Sennacherib (2Ki 19:28,35,37).

ANIAM [642] (*I am kinsman*). A son of Shemida, a Manassehite (1Ch 7:19).

ANIM [6719] (*springs*). A city of Judah (Jos 15:50).

ANIMALS [*989, 2651, 3274, 7366, 8802, 10263, 4465, 5488*].

NIV+ ANIMAL, CREATURE, CREATURES

Creation of:

(Ge 1:24-25; 2:19; Jer 27:5). Food of (Ge 1:30). Named (Ge 2:20). Ordained as food for man (Ge 9:2-3; Lev 11:3, 9,21-22; Dt 14:4-6,9,11,20). God's care of (Ge 9:9-10; Dt 25:4; Job 38:41; Ps 36:6; 104:11,21; 145:15-16; 147:9; Jn 4:11; Mt 6:26; 10:29; Lk 12:6,24; 1Co 9:9). Under the curse (Ge 3:14; 6:7,17). Suffer under divine judgments sent upon man (Jer 7:20; 14:4; 21:6; Eze 14:13,17,19-21; Joel 1:18-20). Two of every kind preserved in the ark (Ge 6:19-20; 7:2,9,14-15; 8:19). Seven clean, of every sort, preserved in the ark (Ge 7:2-3). Suffered the plagues of Egypt (Ex 8:17; 9:9-10,19; 11:5). Perish at death (Ecc 3:21). Possessed of demons (Mt 8:31-32; Mk 5:13; Lk 8:33). Clean and unclean (Ge 7:2,8; 8:20; Lev 7:21; 11; 20:25; Dt 14:3-20; Ac 10:11-15; 1Ti 4:3-5).

God's Control of:

(Ps 91:13; Lk 10:19). Instruments of God's will (Ex 8; 10:4-15,19; Nu 21:6; 22:28; Jos 24:12; Joel 1:4). Belong to God (Ps 50:10-12). Sent in judgment (Lev 26:22; Nu 21:6-7; Dt 8:15; Eze 5:17; 14:15; Rev 6:8). Nature of (Job 41; Ps 32:9; Jas 3:7). Habits of (Job 12:7-8; 37:8; 39; 40:20-21; Ps 104:20-25; Isa 13:21-22; 34:14). Breeding of (Ge 30:35-43; 31:8-9). Instincts of (Dt 32:11; Job 35:11; 39; 40:15-24; Ps 104:11-30; Pr 6:5-8; 30:25-28; Isa 1:3; Jer 2:24; 8:7; La 4:3; Mt 24:28). Abodes of (Job 24:5; 37:8; 39:5-10,27-29; Ps 104:20,22,25; Isa 34:14-15; Jer 2:24; 50:39; Mk 1:13).

Cruelty to:

Of Balaam to his donkey (Nu 22:22-33). Hamstringing horses (2Sa 8:4; 1Ch 18:4).

Kindness to:

By the righteous (Pr 12:10). In not muzzling an ox while

threshing (Dt 25:4; 1Ti 5:18). In relieving the overburdened (Ex 23:5; Dt 22:4). In rescuing from pits (Mt 12:11; Lk 13:15; 14:5). In feeding (Ge 24:32; 43:24; Jdg 19:21).

Instances of:

Jacob in making shelters for his cattle (Ge 33:17). People of Gerar in providing tents for cattle (2Ch 14:15).

Laws Concerning:

Sabbath rest for (Ex 20:10; Dt 5:14).

Treatment of vicious (Ex 21:28-32,35-36). Penalty for injury of (Ex 21:33-34). Hybridizing of, forbidden (Lev 19:19). Working of (Dt 22:10). Mother birds and their young (Dt 22:6-7).

Names of:

Antelopes (Dt 14:5; Isa 51:20). Apes (1Ki 10:22). Baboons (1Ki 10:22; 2Ch 9:21). Donkeys, beasts of burden (Ge 22:3; Nu 22:28; Dt 22:10; Jdg 5:10; 10:4 1Sa 9:3; Mt 21:2). Bears (1Sa 17:34; 2Sa 17:8; 2Ki 2:24; Pr 17:12; 28:15; Isa 11:7). Behemoth (Job 40:15-24). Boars (Ps 80:13). Bull, as offerings (Ex 29:10-11,36; Lev 4:4; Nu 15:8; 1Ki 18:33; 2Ch 13:9; Ezr 6:17; Ps 66:15). Calves (Ge 18:7; 1Sa 28:24; Am 6:4; Lk 15:23). Camels (Ge 12:16; 30:43; Lev 11:4; Jdg 6:5; 1Sa 30:17; 1Ch 5:21; Job 1:3; Mt 19:24; 23:24). Cattle, livestock (Ge 1:25; 31:18; Ex 9:4; 20:10; Nu 32:1; Jos 14:4; Eze 39:18; Am 4:1). Coneys, rock badgers (Lev 11:5; Ps 104:18; Pr 30:26). Cows (Ge 32:15; Dt 7:13; 1Sa 6:7). Deer (Dt 14:5; 2Sa 2:18; 22:34; 1Ch 12:8; Ps 42:1; Pr 5:19; 6:5; Isa 35:6; Jer 14:5). Dogs (1Ki 14:11; 22:38; Ps 59:6; Pr 26:17; Ecc 9:4; Lk 16:21). Dragons (Rev 12:3-17). Elephants (Job 40:15, ftn). Foxes (Jdg 15:4; Ne 4:3; Ps 63:10; SS 2:15; Mt 8:20). Gecko (Lev 11:30). Goats, as offerings (Ge 15:9; Lev 4:24; 16:15; Jdg 13:19; 2Ch 29:23). Heifers, offered as sacrifices (Ge 15:9; Nu 19:2; Dt 21:3; Heb 9:13). Horses (Dt 17:16; 2Ki 23:11; Job 39:19; Ps 32:9; 33:17; Isa 31:1). Lambs, for offerings (Ex 29:38-39; Lev 3:7; 4:32; 5:6; Nu 6:12). Leopards (SS 4:8; Isa 11:6; Jer 5:6; 13:23; Hos 13:7; Hab 1:8). Lions, general references to (Jdg 14:5; 1Sa 17:34; 1Ki 13:24; Da 6:19), characteristics of (Dt 33:22; Jdg 14:18; 2Sa 17:10; Job 10:16; Ps 17:12; Pr 30:30; Isa 31:4; Na 2:12). Lizards (Lev 11:30). Mountain sheep (Dt 14:5). Mules (2Sa 13:29; 18:9; 1Ki 1:33; Ps 32:9; Zec 14:15). Oxen, laws concerning (Ex 21:28; 22:1; 23:4; Lev 17:3; Dt 5:14; 22:1; 25:4; Lk 13:15; 1Co 9:9; 1Ti 5:18). Pigs (Lev 11:7; Isa 65:4; 66:17; Mt 7:6; 8:30; Lk 15:15; 2Pe 2:22). Rabbit (Lev 11:6). Rams, used in sacrifices (Ge 15:9; 22:13; Ex 29:15; Lev 5:15; Nu 5:8). Rats (Lev 11:29; 1Sa 6:4; Isa 66:17). Rooster (Pr 30:31). Sheep (Ge 4:4; 30:32; Dt 18:4; 32:14; 2Ch 7:5; 15:11; Job 1:3; 42:12; Mt 12:11). Wild oxen (Nu 23:22; Dt 33:17; Job 39:9; Ps 29:6; Isa 34:7). Vipers, poisonous serpents (Job 20:16; Isa 30:6; 59:5). Weasel (Lev 11:29). Wolves, illustrative of the wicked (Mt 7:15; 10:16; Jn 10:12; Ac 20:29).

See Birds; Insects.

ANISE *See Dill.*

ANKLET An ornament worn by women on the ankles (Isa 3:16,20). *See Jewel, Jewelry.*

ANNA [*483*] (*grace*). A widow and prophetess who at the age of 84 recognized Jesus as the Messiah when He was brought into the Temple (Lk 2:36-38).

ANNAS [*483, 484*] (*grace*). Associate high priest with Caiaphas (Lk 3:2; Jn 18:13,19,24; Ac 4:6).

ANNIHILATION The belief that there is no existence after death or that there is no existence for the wicked after death.

Some texts seem to imply death as final (Job 14:12,18-22; Ps 6:5; 88:10; Isa 26:14). The resurrection is the hope of all believers (Ps 16:9-11; Isa 53:11; Da 12:1-3). In the teaching of Jesus (Mt 22:23-32; Lk 14:14; Jn 11:24-26), of the apostles (Ac 4:1-4,33; 23:6-8; 24:10-21; 1Co 15). *See Resurrection.*

The eternal punishment of the wicked is also clearly taught (Da 12:2; Mt 18:8-9; Jn 3:36; 2Th 1:9; Rev 14:11; 20:4-15). *See Wicked, Punishment of.*

ANNUAL FEASTS All but Purim and Dedication instituted by Moses.

Designated as:

Solemn feasts (Nu 15:3; 2Ch 8:13; La 2:6; Eze 46:9). Set feasts (Nu 29:39; Ezr 3:5). Appointed feasts (Isa 1:14). Holy convocations (Lev 23:4). First and last days were Sabbatic (Lev 23:39-40; Nu 28:18-25; 29:12,35; Ne 8:1-18). Kept with rejoicing (Lev 23:40; Dt 16:11-14; 2Ch 30:21-26; Ezr 6:22; Ne 8:9-12,17; Ps 122:4; Isa 30:29; Zec 8:19). Divine protection given during (Ex 34:24).

All males were required to attend (Ex 23:17; 34:23; Dt 16:16; Eze 36:38; Lk 2:41-42; Jn 4:45; 7). Aliens permitted to attend (Jn 12:20; Ac 2:1-11). Attended by women (1Sa 1:3,9; Lk 2:41).

Observed:

By Jesus (Mt 26:17-20; Lk 2:41-42; 22:15; Jn 2:13,23; 5:1; 7:10; 10:22). By Paul (Ac 20:6,16; 24:11,17).

New Moon:

(Nu 10:10; 28:11-15; 1Ch 23:31; 2Ch 31:3; Ezr 3:5). Buying and selling at time of, suspended (Am 8:5).

The Passover:

Institution of (Ex 12:3-49; 23:15-18; 34:18; Lev 23:4-8; Nu 9:2-5,13-14; 28:16-25; Dt 16:1-8,16; Ps 81:3,5). Design of (Ex 12:21-28).

Special Passover, for those who were unclean, or on journey to be held in second month (Nu 9:6-12; 2Ch 30:2-4). Lamb killed by Levites, for those who were ceremonially unclean (2Ch 30:17; 35:3-11; Ezr 6:20). Strangers authorized to celebrate (Ex 12:48-49; Nu 9:14).

Observed at place designated by God (Dt 16:5-7). With unleavened bread (Ex 12:8,15-20; 13:3,6; 23:15; Lev 23:6; Nu 9:11; 28:17; Dt 16:3-4; Mk 14:12; Lk 22:7; Ac 12:3; 1Co 5:8). Penalty for neglecting to observe (Nu 9:13).

Reinstituted by Ezekiel (Eze 45:21-24).

Observation of—

Renewed, by the Israelites on entering Canaan (Jos 5:10-11). By Hezekiah (2Ch 30:1). By Josiah (2Ki 23:22-23; 2Ch 35:1,18). After return from captivity (Ezr 6:19-20). Observed by Jesus (Mt 26:17-20; Lk 22:15; Jn 2:13, 23; 13). Jesus when twelve years old, in the temple at time of (Lk 2:41-50). Jesus crucified at time of (Mt 26:2; Mk 14:1-2; Jn 18:28). Lord's Supper ordained at (Mt 26:26-28; Mk 14:12-25; Lk 22:7-20). The lamb of, a type of Christ (1Co 5:7).

Prisoners released at, by the Romans (Mt 27:15; Mk 15:6; Lk 23:16-17; Jn 18:39). Peter imprisoned at time of (Ac 12:3).

Christ called—

Our Passover lamb (1Co 5:7; see also Jn 1:36; Rev 5:6-14).

Pentecost:

Called Feast of Weeks (Ex 34:22; Dt 16:10). Feast of

Harvest (Ex 23:16). Day of First Fruits (Nu 28:26). Day of Pentecost (Ac 2:1; 20:16; 1Co 16:8).

Institution of (Ex 23:16; 34:22; Lev 23:15-21; Nu 28:26-31; Dt 16:9-12,16).

Holy Spirit given to the apostles on the day of (Ac 2).

Purim:

Instituted by Esther and Mordecai to commemorate the deliverance of the Jews from the plot of Haman (Est 9:20-32).

Tabernacles:

Also called Feast of Ingathering. Instituted (Ex 23:16; 34:22; Lev 23:34-43; Nu 29:12-40; Dt 16:13-16). Design of (Lev 23:42-43). The law read in connection with, every seventh year (Dt 31:10-12; Ne 8:18).

Observance of—

After the captivity (Ezr 3:4; Ne 8:14-18). By Jesus (Jn 7:2,14). Observance of, omitted (Ne 8:17). Penalty for not observing (Zec 14:16-19).

Jeroboam institutes an idolatrous feast parallel to, in the eighth month (1Ki 12:32-33).

Trumpets:

When and how observed (Lev 23:24-25; Nu 29:1-6). Celebrated after the captivity with joy (Ne 8:2,9-12).

Dedication or Hanukkah:

Instituted in the Intertestamental era, commemorating the dedication of the temple by Judas Maccabeus (1Mc 4:59). Observed by Jesus (Jn 10:22-39).

See Feasts; also each feast by name.

ANOINTING [*5417, 5418, 5431, *230, 5987, 5984].

NIV+ ANOINT, ANOINTED

Of the body (Dt 28:40; Ru 3:3; Est 2:12; Ps 92:10; 104:15; 141:5; Pr 27:9,16; Ecc 9:8; SS 1:3; 4:10; Isa 57:9; Am 6:6; Mic 6:15). Of guests (2Ch 28:15; Lk 7:46). The sick (Isa 1:6; Mk 6:13; Lk 10:34; Jas 5:14; Rev 3:18). The dead (Mt 26:12; Mk 14:8; 16:1; Lk 23:56). Of Jesus, as a token of love (Lk 7:37-38,46; Jn 11:2; 12:3). Omitted in mourning (2Sa 12:20; 14:2; Isa 61:3; Da 10:3). God preserves those who receive (Ps 18:50; 20:6; 89:20-23). Believers receive (Isa 61:3; 1Jn 2:20).

In Consecration:

Of high priests (Ex 29:7,29; 40:13; Lev 6:20; 8:12; 16:32; Nu 35:25; Ps 133:2).

Of priests (Ex 28:41; 30:30; 40:15; Lev 4:3; 8:30; Nu 3:3).

Of kings (Jdg 9:8,15), Saul (1Sa 9:16; 10:1; 15:1), David (1Sa 16:3,12-13; 2Sa 2:4; 5:3; 12:7; 9:21; 1Ch 11:3). Solomon (1Ki 1:39; 1Ch 29:22), Jehu (1Ki 19:16; 2Ki 9:1-3,6,12). Hazael (1Ki 19:15), Joash (2Ki 11:12; 2Ch 23:11), Jehoahaz (2Ki 23:30), Cyrus (Isa 45:1).

Of prophets (1Ki 19:16).

Of the tabernacle (Ex 30:26; 40:9; Lev 8:10; Nu 7:1), altars of (Ex 30:26-28; 40:10; Lev 8:11; Nu 7:1), vessels of (Ex 30:27-28; 40:9-10; Lev 8:10-11; Nu 7:1).

Jacob's pillar at Bethel (Ge 28:18; 31:13; 35:14).

See Dedication.

Figurative:

Of Christ's kingly and priestly office (Ps 45:7; 89:20; Isa 61:1; Da 9:24; Lk 4:18; Ac 4:27; 10:38; Heb 1:9). Of spiritual gifts (2Co 1:21; 1Jn 2:20,27). Of God's choice and enabling of leaders (Ex 40:13-15; Lev 8:12; 1Sa 16:13; 1Ki 19:16).

Symbolic of Jesus' death (Mt 26:7-12; Jn 12:3-7).

ANOINTING OIL [5418]. Formula of, given by Moses (Ex 30:22-25,31-33). *See Oil; Ointment.*

ANOTH *See Beth Anoth.*

ANT [5805].

NIV+ ANTS

Illustrate work ethic (Pr 6:6-8; 30:25).

ANTEDILUVIANS *(those who lived before the flood).*
Worship God (Ge 4:3-4,26). Occupations of (Ge 4:2-3,20-22). Arts of (Ge 4:2-3,20-22; 6:14-22). Enoch prophesies to (Jude 14-15). Noah preaches to (2Pe 2:5). Wickedness of (Ge 6:5-7). Destruction of (Ge 7:1,21-23; Job 22:15-17; Mt 24:37-39; Lk 17:26-27; 2Pe 2:5). *See Flood.*

Longevity of. *See Longevity.*

Giants among. *See Giants.*

ANTELOPE [9293]. (Dt 14:5; Isa 51:20). *See Deer.*

ANTHOTHIJAH, ANTOTHIJAH [6746]. Son of Shashak, a Benjamite (1Ch 8:24-25).

ANTHROPOMORPHISMS Figures of speech that attribute human anatomy, acts, and affections to God.

Anatomy:

Arm (Ps 89:13), body or form (Nu 11:25), ear (Ps 34:15)

Eye (2Ch 16:9)—

Isa 1:15 When you spread out your hands in prayer, I will hide my eyes from you; even if you offer many prayers, I will not listen. Your hands are full of blood;

Mouth—

Ps 33:6 By the word of the LORD were the heavens made, their starry host by the breath of his mouth.

Voice—

Eze 1:24 When the creatures moved, I heard the sound of their wings, like the roar of rushing waters, like the voice of the Almighty, like the tumult of an army. When they stood still, they lowered their wings.

Eze 1:28 Like the appearance of a rainbow in the clouds on a rainy day, so was the radiance around him. This was the appearance of the likeness of the glory of the LORD. When I saw it, I fell facedown, and I heard the voice of one speaking.

Wings—

Ps 36:7 How priceless is your unfailing love! Both high and low among men find refuge in the shadow of your wings.

Ps 57:1 Have mercy on me, O God, have mercy on me, for in you my soul takes refuge. I will take refuge in the shadow of your wings until the disaster has passed.

See terms for human body parts, e.g., Arm, Eye, Hand.

Intellectual Facilities:

Knowing—

Ge 18:17 Then the LORD said, "Shall I hide from Abraham what I am about to do? [18]Abraham will surely become a great and powerful nation, and all nations on earth will be blessed through him. [19]For I have chosen him, so that he will direct his children and his household after him to keep the way of the LORD by doing what is right and just, so that the LORD will bring about for Abraham what he has promised him."

Reason (Isa 1:18).

Remembering—

Ge 9:16 Whenever the rainbow appears in the clouds, I

will see it and remember the everlasting covenant between God and all living creatures of every kind on the earth."

Ge 19:29 So when God destroyed the cities of the plain, he remembered Abraham, and he brought Lot out of the catastrophe that overthrew the cities where Lot had lived.

Ex 2:24 God heard their groaning and he remembered his covenant with Abraham, with Isaac and with Jacob. (+Isa 43:26; 63:11)

Understanding (Ps 147:5). Will (Ro 9:19).

Acts:

Breathing (Ps 33:6), fainting not (Isa 40:28), grasping, with hand (Ps 35:2)

Hearing—

Ps 94:9 Does he who implanted the ear not hear? Does he who formed the eye not see?

Laughing (Ps 2:4; 37:13; 59:8; Pr 1:26).

Resting—

Ge 2:2 By the seventh day God had finished the work he had been doing; so on the seventh day he rested from all his work. ³And God blessed the seventh day and made it holy, because on it he rested from all the work of creating that he had done.

Ge 2:19 Now the Lord God had formed out of the ground all the beasts of the field and all the birds of the air. He brought them to the man to see what he would name them; and whatever the man called each living creature, that was its name. (+Ex 20:11)

Ex 31:17 It will be a sign between me and the Israelites forever, for in six days the Lord made the heavens and the earth, and on the seventh day he abstained from work and rested.'" (+Dt 5:14; Heb 4:4,10)

Seeing—

Ge 18:21 that I will go down and see if what they have done is as bad as the outcry that has reached me. If not, I will know."

Ex 14:24 During the last watch of the night the Lord looked down from the pillar of fire and cloud at the Egyptian army and threw it into confusion. (+Ps 94:9)

Sleeping (Ps 44:23; 78:65)—

Ps 121:4 indeed, he who watches over Israel will neither slumber nor sleep.

Speaking—

Ge 18:33 When the Lord had finished speaking with Abraham, he left, and Abraham returned home. (+Nu 11:25; Ps 33:6)

Standing—

Ps 35:2 Take up shield and buckler; arise and come to my aid.

Walking (Ge 3:8; Lev 26:12; Dt 23:14; Job 22:14; Hab 3:15).

Affections and Emotions:

Amazement (Isa 59:16; 63:5; Mk 6:6)

Grief—

Ge 6:6 The Lord was grieved that he had made man on the earth, and his heart was filled with pain. (+Jdg 10:16; Ps 95:10; Heb 3:10,17)

Jealousy—

Ex 20:5 You shall not bow down to them or worship them; for I, the Lord your God, am a jealous God, punishing the children for the sin of the fathers to the third and fourth generation of those who hate me, (+Ex 34:13-14; Nu 25:11; Dt 29:20; 32:16,21; 1Ki 14:22; Ps 78:58; 79:5; Isa 30:1-2; 31:1,3; Eze 16:42; 23:25; 36:5-6; 38:19; Zep 1:18; 3:8; Zec 1:14; 8:2; 1Co 10:22)

Swearing an oath (Isa 62:8; Heb 6:16-17; 7:21,28). *See Anger of God; Oath.*

ANTICHRIST(S) [532] (*against Christ*). (Mt 24:5,23-24,26; Mk 13:6,21-22; Lk 21:8; 2Th 2:3-12; 1Jn 2:18,22; 4:3; 2Jn 7). To be destroyed (Rev 19:20; 20:10,15).

ANTI-LEBANON *See Lebanon.*

ANTIOCH [522, 523].

1. A city of Syria. Disciples first called Christians in (Ac 11:19-30). Church in (Ac 13:1; 14:26-27). Barnabas and Paul make second visit to (Ac 14:26-28). Dissension in church of (Ac 15:22, w 15:1-35). Paul and Peter's controversy at (Gal 2:11-15).

2. A city of Pisidia. Persecutes Paul (Ac 13:14-52; Ac 14:19-22; 18:22; 2Ti 3:11).

ANTIOCHUS (*opposer*). A favorite name of the Seleucid kings of Syria, referred to as the kings of the North in Da 11.

1. Antiochus II Theos (286-246 B.C.) married Berenice, daughter of Ptolemy II, the "king of the South" (Da 11:6).

2. Antiochus III, the Great (242-187 B.C.) gained control of Israel in 198 (Da 11:10-19).

3. Antiochus IV (Epiphanes), son of III (215-163 B.C.); his attempt to hellenize the Jews led to the Maccabean revolt (Da 8:9-12,23-25; 11:21-35; see also 1 and 2Mc). *See Abomination That Causes Desolation; Testaments, Time Between.*

ANTIPAS [525] (possibly *a contraction of Antipater*).

1. An early Christian martyr of Pergamum (Rev 2:13).

2. Herod Antipas, son of Herod the Great; ruled Galilee and Perea from 4 B.C. to A.D. 39. *See Herod.*

ANTIPATER *See Herod.*

ANTIPATRIS [526]. A city in Samaria (Ac 23:31).

ANTITYPE *See Types.*

ANTONIA, TOWER OF A fortress connected with the temple at Jerusalem, built by Herod the Great. It was garrisoned by Roman soldiers who watched the temple area (Ac 21:30ff).

ANTOTHIJAH *See Anthothijah, Antothijah.*

ANTOTHITE *See Anathoth, Anathothite.*

ANUB [6707] (*fruitful*). Son of Koz of the tribe of Judah (1Ch 4:8).

ANVIL [7193]. (Isa 41:7).

ANXIETY [1796, 4088, 8595, *267, 3533, 3849*].
NIV+ ANXIETIES, ANXIOUS, ANXIOUSLY

Forbidden (Mt 6:25-34; Lk 12:11-12,22-28; 1Co 7:32; Php 4:6; 1Pe 5:7).

Unavailing (Ps 39:6; Mt 6:27; Lk 12:25-26). Proceeds from unbelief (Mt 6:26,28-30; Lk 12:24,27-28). Martha rebuked for (Lk 10:40-41).

Remedy for (Ps 37:5; 55:22; Heb 13:5; 1Pe 5:6-7). *See Care, Worldly.*

APARTMENT [1074]. (Jer 36:22). *See Winter Apartment, Winter House.*

APES [7761]. In Solomon's zoological collections (1Ki 10:22; 2Ch 9:21).

APELLES [*593*]. A disciple in Rome (Ro 16:10).

APHARSACHITES, APHARSATHCHITES, APHARSITES
Aramaic terms transliterated as proper names in the KJV are translated "officials" in the NIV (Ezr 5:6; 6:6).

APHEK [707] (stronghold).
1. A city of the tribe of Asher (Jos 19:30). A city whose inhabitants were not driven out by Asher (Jdg 1:31).

2. A city of the tribe of Issachar. Philistines defeat Israelites at (1Sa 4:1-11). Saul slain at (1Sa 29:1, w 1Sa 31). Probably the same as the royal city of the Canaanites (Jos 12:18).

3. A city between Damascus and Israel. Ben-Hadad defeated at (1Ki 20:26-30).

APHEKAH [708] (the fortress). A city in the mountains of Judah (Jos 15:53).

APHIAH [688]. Ancestor of Saul (1Sa 9:1).

APHIK See Aphek.

APHRAH See Beth Ophrah; Ophrah.

APHSES See Happizzez.

APOCALYPSE (disclosure). Greek title of the book of Revelation. See Apocalyptic Literature; Revelation, Book of.

APOCALYPTIC LITERATURE
A type of prophetic literature that communicates the ultimate triumph of God over evil through dreams, visions, and symbols. Daniel and Revelation and parts of Ezekiel and Zechariah are canonical apocalypses. Many non-canonical apocalypses appeared between c. 200 B.C. and A.D. 200 in the style of Daniel, also claiming to have been written by a famous OT character. Major examples are 1 and 2 Enoch, Jubilees, Assumption of Moses, 2 Esdras, Apocalypse of Baruch, The Testaments of the Twelve Prophets, and the Psalms of Solomon.

APOCRYPHA (hidden, obscure). Books and chapters interspersed among the canonical books of the OT in the LXX and Vulgate, but not found in the Hebrew OT. The Jewish people, who produced them, and Protestants do not consider them canonical. The Roman Catholic Church received the following as deuterocanonical at the Council of Trent (1546): Tobit, Judith, Additions to Esther, Wisdom of Solomon, Ecclesiasticus, Baruch, Letter of Jeremiah, The Prayer of Azariah and the Song of the Three Young Men, Susanna, Bel and the Dragon, and 1 and 2 Maccabees. Other works are considered deuterocanonical by the Orthodox Church: 1 and 2 Esdras, The Prayer of Manasseh, Psalm 151, 3 and 4 Maccabees. See Testaments, Time Between.

APOLLONIA [662]. A city of Macedonia (Ac 17:1).

APOLLOS [663]. An eloquent Christian convert at Corinth (Ac 18:24-28; 19:1; 1Co 1:12; 3:4-7). Refuses to return to Rome (1Co 16:12). Paul writes Titus about (Tit 3:13). Born in Alexandria (Ac 18:24).

APOLLYON [661] (destroyer). Angel of the bottomless pit (Rev 9:11).

APOSTASY (abandoning God).
Described (Dt 13:13,32)—

Dt 32:15 Jeshurun grew fat and kicked; filled with food, he became heavy and sleek. He abandoned the God who made him and rejected the Rock his Savior. (+Isa 65:11-12; Mt 12:45)

Lk 11:24 "When an evil spirit comes out of a man, it goes through arid places seeking rest and does not find it. Then it says, 'I will return to the house I left.' [25]When it arrives, it finds the house swept clean and put in order. [26]Then it goes and takes seven other spirits more wicked than itself, and they go in and live there. And the final condition of that man is worse than the first."

Ac 7:39 "But our fathers refused to obey him. Instead, they rejected him and in their hearts turned back to Egypt. [40]They told Aaron, 'Make us gods who will go before us. As for this fellow Moses who led us out of Egypt—we don't know what has happened to him!' [41]That was the time they made an idol in the form of a calf. They brought sacrifices to it and held a celebration in honor of what their hands had made. [42]But God turned away and gave them over to the worship of the heavenly bodies. This agrees with what is written in the book of the prophets: "'Did you bring me sacrifices and offerings forty years in the desert, O house of Israel? [43]You have lifted up the shrine of Molech and the star of your god Rephan, the idols you made to worship. Therefore I will send you into exile' beyond Babylon. (+1Ti 4:1-3; 2Ti 3:6-9)

2Ti 4:3 For the time will come when men will not put up with sound doctrine. Instead, to suit their own desires, they will gather around them a great number of teachers to say what their itching ears want to hear. [4]They will turn their ears away from the truth and turn aside to myths. (+Heb 3:12)

2Pe 2:15 They have left the straight way and wandered off to follow the way of Balaam son of Beor, who loved the wages of wickedness. [16]But he was rebuked for his wrongdoing by a donkey—a beast without speech—who spoke with a man's voice and restrained the prophet's madness.

[17]These men are springs without water and mists driven by a storm. Blackest darkness is reserved for them. [18]For they mouth empty, boastful words and, by appealing to the lustful desires of sinful human nature, they entice people who are just escaping from those who live in error. [19]They promise them freedom, while they themselves are slaves of depravity—for a man is a slave to whatever has mastered him. [20]If they have escaped the corruption of the world by knowing our Lord and Savior Jesus Christ and are again entangled in it and overcome, they are worse off at the end than they were at the beginning. [21]It would have been better for them not to have known the way of righteousness, than to have known it and then to turn their backs on the sacred command that was passed on to them. [22]Of them the proverbs are true: "A dog returns to its vomit," and, "A sow that is washed goes back to her wallowing in the mud." (+Jude 8)

Foretold (Mt 24:12)—

2Th 2:3 Don't let anyone deceive you in any way, for that day will not come until the rebellion occurs and the man of lawlessness is revealed, the man doomed to destruction.

1Ti 4:1 The Spirit clearly says that in later times some will abandon the faith and follow deceiving spirits and things taught by demons. [2]Such teachings come through hypocritical liars, whose consciences have been seared as with a hot iron. (+1Ti 4:3)

2Ti 3:1 But mark this: There will be terrible times in the last days. [2]People will be lovers of themselves, lovers of money, boastful, proud, abusive, disobedient to their parents, ungrateful, unholy, [3]without love, unforgiving, slanderous, without self-control, brutal, not lovers of the good, **4**treacherous, rash, conceited, lovers of pleasure rather than lovers of God— **5**having a form of godliness but denying its power. Have nothing to do with them.

6They are the kind who worm their way into homes and gain control over weak-willed women, who are loaded down with sins and are swayed by all kinds of evil desires, **7**always learning but never able to acknowledge the truth. **8**Just as Jannes and Jambres opposed Moses, so also these men oppose the truth—men of depraved minds, who, as far as the faith is concerned, are rejected. **9**But they will not get very far because, as in the case of those men, their folly will be clear to everyone. (+2Ti 4:3-4)

2Pe 2:1 But there were also false prophets among the people, just as there will be false teachers among you. They will secretly introduce destructive heresies, even denying the sovereign Lord who bought them—bringing swift destruction on themselves.

Admonitions against (Mt 24:4-5; Mk 13:5-6; Heb 3:12)—

2Pe 3:17 Therefore, dear friends, since you already know this, be on your guard so that you may not be carried away by the error of lawless men and fall from your secure position. (+2Jn 8)

Jude 4 For certain men whose condemnation was written about long ago have secretly slipped in among you. They are godless men, who change the grace of our God into a license for immorality and deny Jesus Christ our only Sovereign and Lord.

5Though you already know all this, I want to remind you that the Lord delivered his people out of Egypt, but later destroyed those who did not believe. **6**And the angels who did not keep their positions of authority but abandoned their own home—these he has kept in darkness, bound with everlasting chains for judgment on the great Day.

No remedy for—

Heb 6:4 It is impossible for those who have once been enlightened, who have tasted the heavenly gift, who have shared in the Holy Spirit, **5**who have tasted the goodness of the word of God and the powers of the coming age, **6**if they fall away, to be brought back to repentance, because to their loss they are crucifying the Son of God all over again and subjecting him to public disgrace.

7Land that drinks in the rain often falling on it and that produces a crop useful to those for whom it is farmed receives the blessing of God. **8**But land that produces thorns and thistles is worthless and is in danger of being cursed. In the end it will be burned.

Heb 10:26 If we deliberately keep on sinning after we have received the knowledge of the truth, no sacrifice for sins is left, **27**but only a fearful expectation of judgment and of raging fire that will consume the enemies of God. **28**Anyone who rejected the law of Moses died without mercy on the testimony of two or three witnesses. **29**How much more severely do you think a man deserves to be punished who has trampled the Son of God under foot, who has treated as an unholy thing the blood of the covenant that sanctified him, and who has insulted the Spirit of grace?

Punishment—

1Ch 28:9 "And you, my son Solomon, acknowledge the God of your father, and serve him with wholehearted devotion and with a willing mind, for the LORD searches every heart and understands every motive behind the thoughts. If you seek him, he will be found by you; but if you forsake him, he will reject you forever.

Isa 1:28 But rebels and sinners will both be broken, and those who forsake the LORD will perish.

Isa 65:12 I will destine you for the sword, and you will all bend down for the slaughter; for I called but you did not answer, I spoke but you did not listen. You did evil in my sight and chose what displeases me."

13Therefore this is what the Sovereign LORD says: "My servants will eat, but you will go hungry; my servants will drink, but you will go thirsty; my servants will rejoice, but you will be put to shame. **14**My servants will sing out of the joy of their hearts, but you will cry out from anguish of heart and wail in brokenness of spirit. **15**You will leave your name to my chosen ones as a curse; the Sovereign LORD will put you to death, but to his servants he will give another name.

Jer 17:5 This is what the LORD says: "Cursed is the one who trusts in man, who depends on flesh for his strength and whose heart turns away from the LORD. **6**He will be like a bush in the wastelands; he will not see prosperity when it comes. He will dwell in the parched places of the desert, in a salt land where no one lives.

Eze 3:20 "Again, when a righteous man turns from his righteousness and does evil, and I put a stumbling block before him, he will die. Since you did not warn him, he will die for his sin. The righteous things he did will not be remembered, and I will hold you accountable for his blood.

Eze 18:24 "But if a righteous man turns from his righteousness and commits sin and does the same detestable things the wicked man does, will he live? None of the righteous things he has done will be remembered. Because of the unfaithfulness he is guilty of and because of the sins he has committed, he will die.

Eze 18:26 If a righteous man turns from his righteousness and commits sin, he will die for it; because of the sin he has committed he will die.

Eze 33:12 "Therefore, son of man, say to your countrymen, 'The righteousness of the righteous man will not save him when he disobeys, and the wickedness of the wicked man will not cause him to fall when he turns from it. The righteous man, if he sins, will not be allowed to live because of his former righteousness.' **13**If I tell the righteous man that he will surely live, but then he trusts in his righteousness and does evil, none of the righteous things he has done will be remembered; he will die for the evil he has done.

Eze 33:18 If a righteous man turns from his righteousness and does evil, he will die for it. (+Zep 1:4-6)

Jn 15:6 If anyone does not remain in me, he is like a branch that is thrown away and withers; such branches are picked up, thrown into the fire and burned.

2Th 2:11 For this reason God sends them a powerful delusion so that they will believe the lie **12**and so that all will be condemned who have not believed the truth but have delighted in wickedness. (+Heb 10:25-31,38-39)

2Pe 2:17 These men are springs without water and mists driven by a storm. Blackest darkness is reserved for them.

2Pe 2:20 If they have escaped the corruption of the world by knowing our Lord and Savior Jesus Christ and are again entangled in it and overcome, they are worse off at the end than they were at the beginning. **21**It would have been better for them not to have known the way of righteousness, than to have known it and then to turn their backs on the sacred command that was passed on to them. **22**Of them the proverbs are true: "A dog returns to its vomit," and, "A sow that is washed goes back to her wallowing in the mud." (+Jude 6)

Caused by:

Persecution—

Mt 13:20 The one who received the seed that fell on rocky places is the man who hears the word and at once receives it with joy. [21]But since he has no root, he lasts only a short time. When trouble or persecution comes because of the word, he quickly falls away.

Mt 24:9 "Then you will be handed over to be persecuted and put to death, and you will be hated by all nations because of me. [10]At that time many will turn away from the faith and will betray and hate each other, [11]and many false prophets will appear and deceive many people. [12]Because of the increase of wickedness, the love of most will grow cold, (+Mk 4:5-17; Lk 8:13)

Worldliness (2Ti 4:10).

Instances of:

Israelites (Ex 32; Nu 14; Ac 7:39-43), Saul (1Sa 15:26-29; 18:12; 28:15,18), Amaziah (2Ch 25:14,27), disciples (Jn 6:66), Judas (Mt 26:14-16; 27:3-5; Mk 14:10-11; Lk 22:3-6,47-48; Ac 1:16-18), Hymenaeus and Alexander (1Ti 1:19-20), Phygelus and Hermogenes (2Ti 1:15).

See Antichrist(s); Apostates; Backsliding, Instances of Israel's Backsliding; Backsliders; Reprobacy; Reprobates.

APOSTATES Described (Dt 13:13; Heb 3:12). Persecution tends to make (Mt 24:9-10; Lk 8:13). A worldly spirit tends to make (2Ti 4:10). Never belonged to Christ (1Jn 2:19). Believers do not become (Ps 44:18-19; Heb 6:9; 10:39). It is impossible to restore (Heb 6:4-6). Guilt and punishment of (Zep 1:4-6; Heb 10:25-31,39; 2Pe 2:17, 20-22). Cautions against becoming (Heb 3:12; 2Pe 3:17). Shall abound in the latter days (Mt 24:12; 2Th 2:3; 1Ti 4:1-3).

Exemplified:

Amaziah (2Ch 25:14,27). Professed disciples (Jn 6:66). Hymenaeus and Alexander (1Ti 1:19-20). *See Apostasy.*

APOSTLE [*692, 693*] (*to send off* or *out*).
NIV+ APOSTLES, APOSTLES', APOSTLESHIP, APOSTOLIC, SUPER-APOSTLES

An title of Jesus (Heb 3:1). *See Apostles.*

APOSTLES [*693, 6013*] (*to send off* or *out*).
NIV+ See APOSTLE

A title distinguishing the twelve disciples, whom Jesus selected to be intimately associated with himself (Lk 6:13).

Names of the twelve—

Mt 10:2 These are the names of the twelve apostles: first, Simon (who is called Peter) and his brother Andrew; James son of Zebedee, and his brother John; [3]Philip and Bartholomew; Thomas and Matthew the tax collector; James son of Alphaeus, and Thaddaeus; [4]Simon the Zealot and Judas Iscariot, who betrayed him.

For more information (Mk 3:16-19; Lk 6:13-16; Ac 1:13,26).

Selection of (Mt 4:18,22; 9:9-10; 10:2-4; Mk 3:13-19; Lk 6:13-16; Jn 1:43).

Commission of (Mt 10; 28:19-20; Mk 3:14-15; 6:7-11; 16:15; Lk 9:1-5; 22:28-30; Jn 20:23; 21:15-19; Ac 1; 2; 10:42). Uneducated (Mt 11:25; Ac 4:13). Miraculous power given to (Mt 10:1; Mk 3:15; 6:7; 16:17; Lk 9:1-2;

10:9,17; Ac 2:4,43; 5:12-16; 1Co 14:18; 2Co 12:12). Authority of (Mt 16:19; 18:18; 19:28).

Inspiration of (Mt 10:27; 16:17-19; Lk 24:45; Ac 1:2; 13:9). Duties of. *See above, Commission of.* For more information see Lk 24:48; Jn 15:27; Ac 1:8,21-22; 2:32; 3:15; 4:33; 5:32; 10:39-41; 13:31; 2Pe 1:16,18; 1Jn 1:1-3. *See Minister.*

Moral state of, before Pentecost (Mt 17:17; 18:3; 20:20-22; Lk 9:54-55). Slow to receive Jesus as Messiah (Mt 14:33). Forsake Jesus (Mk 14:50).

Fail to comprehend the nature and mission of Jesus, and the nature of the kingdom he came to establish (Mt 8:25-27; 15:23; 16:8-12,21-22; 19:25; Mk 4:13; 6:51-52; 8:17-18; 9:9-10,31-32; 10:13-14; Lk 9:44-45; 18:34; 24:19,21; Jn 4:32-33; 10:6; 11:12-13; 12:16; 13:6-8; 14:5-9,22; 16:6,17-18,32; 20:9; 21:12; Ac 1:6).

See Barnabas; Matthias; Minister; Paul.

False: (2Co 11:13; Rev 2:2). *See Teachers, False.*

APOTHECARY *See Perfume, Perfumer.*

APPAIM [691] (*[a pair of] nostrils*). Son of Nadab (1Ch 2:30-31).

APPAREL *See Dress.*

APPEAL [2011, 2704, 7924, *2126, 4151, 4155*].
NIV+ APPEALED, APPEALING, APPEALS

Paul makes, to Caesar (Ac 25:10-11,21-27; 26:32; 28:19). *See Change of Venue; Court, of Law.*

APPEAL TO GOD To witness (Ge 31:50; Dt 30:19; Jdg 11:10; 1Sa 12:5; Job 16:19; Ro 1:9; 2Co 1:23; Php 1:8; 1Th 2:5).

APPEARANCES [*2118, 2180, 5260, 8011, 1586, 1872, 2210, 2211, 3972, 4134, 5743, 5746*].
NIV+ APPEAR, APPEARANCE, APPEARED, APPEARING, APPEARS, REAPPEARS

Of God to people (Ge 12:7; 17:1; 18:1; 26:2; 35:9; Ex 3:16; 1Ki 3:5; 9:2; 2Ch 3:1).

APPEARING *See Eschatology.*

APPELLATIO The judicial process of appealing to a higher magistrate, as Paul did to Festus (Ac 25:1-12).

APPETITE [5883, *3120*].
NIV+ APPETITES

Kept in subjection (Pr 23:1-2; Da 1:8-16; 1Co 9:27). *See Temperance.*

APPHIA [722]. A Christian at Colosse (Phm 2).

APPIAN WAY An ancient Roman road on which Paul traveled (Ac 28:13-16).

APPIUS, FORUM OF, APPII FORUM [*716*]. A market town forty-three miles from Rome, where Paul met a delegation of Roman Christians (Ac 28:15).

APPLE [413, 949, 9515].
NIV+ APPLES

A fruit (Pr 25:11; SS 2:3,5; 7:8; 8:5; Joel 1:12).

APPLE OF THE EYE The eyeball; symbolizing that which is precious and protected (Dt 32:10; Ps 17:8; Pr 7:2; Zec 2:8).

APRON *See Dress.*

AQABAH, GULF OF The eastern arm of the Red

Sea, where Solomon's seaport was located (1Ki 9:26). *See Ezion Geber.*

AQUEDUCT [9498] (*water channel*). A channel made of stone to convey water to places where the water is to be used (2Ki 18:17; Isa 7:3; 36:1). Many fine Roman aqueducts survive.

AQUILA [*217*] (*eagle*). A Jewish Christian, a tentmaker by trade, who with his wife Priscilla labored with Paul at Corinth and was of help to Apollos and many others (Ac 18:2,18,26; Ro 16:3-4; 1Co 16:19; 2Ti 4:19).

AR [6840] (possibly *city*). A city of Moab (Nu 21:15; Dt 2:9,18,24,29). Destruction of (Nu 21:26-30; Isa 15:1).

ARA [736]. Son of Jether (1Ch 7:38).

ARAB [742, 6861, 6862] (*desert* or *steppe*).
NIV+ ARABIA, ARABIAN, ARABS
1. A city of Judah (Jos 15:52).
2. *See Arabia; Arabians.*

ARABAH [6858] (*desert*).
NIV+ BETH ARABAH
A name applying to the rift running from Mt. Hermon to the Gulf of Aqabah. It is a narrow valley of varying breadth and productivity. The Israelites made stops there in their wilderness wanderings, and Solomon got iron and copper from its mines (Dt 1:1,7; 11:30; Jos 3:16; 1Sa 23:24; Jer 39:4).

ARABIA [6851, *728*] (*desert* or *steppe*).
NIV+ ARAB, ARABIAN, ARABS
Paid tribute to Solomon (2Ch 9:14) and Jehoshaphat (2Ch 17:11). Exports of (Eze 27:21). Prophecies against (Isa 21:13; Jer 25:24). Paul visits (Gal 1:17).

ARABIANS, ARABS [6861, *732*] (*desert plateau dwellers*).
NIV+ ARAB, ARABIA, ARABIAN
Paid tribute to Solomon (2Ch 9:14) and Jehoshaphat (2Ch 17:11). Invade and defeat Judah (2Ch 21:16-17; 22:1). Defeated by Uzziah (2Ch 26:7). Oppose Nehemiah's rebuilding the walls of Jerusalem (Ne 2:19; 4:7). Commerce of (Eze 27:21). Gospel preached to (Ac 2:11; Gal 1:17). Prophecies concerning (Isa 21:13-17; 42:11; 60:7; Jer 25:24).

ARAD [6865, 6866] (*wild donkey*).
1. A city on the S of Canaan (Nu 21:1; 33:40). Subdued by Joshua (Jos 12:14; Jdg 1:16).
2. Son of Beriah (1Ch 8:15).

ARAH [783, 6869] (*he wanders*).
1. An Asherite (1Ch 7:39).
2. Father of a family that returned from exile (Ezr 2:5; Ne 7:10).
3. Jew whose granddaughter became the wife of Tobiah the Ammonite (Ne 6:18).
4. Town in NE Palestine belonging to Sidonians (Jos 13:4).

ARAM [806].
NIV+ ARAM MAACAH, ARAM NAHARAIM, ARAM ZOBAH, ARAMAIC, ARAMEAN, ARAMEANS, PADDAN ARAM
1. Son of Shem (Ge 10:22-23).
2. Son of Kemuel, Abraham's nephew (Ge 22:21).
3. An Asherite (1Ch 7:34).
4. Ancestor of Jesus (Mt 1:3-4; Lk 3:33). *See Ram, 1.*

5. Place in Gilead (1Ch 2:23).
6. Region corresponding to modern Syria (Nu 23:7; 2Sa 8:5; 1Ki 20:20; Am 1:5). The Aramean people spread from Phoenicia to the Fertile Crescent and were closely related to Israel, with whom their history was intertwined. *See Syria.*

ARAM MAACAH [807].
NIV+ ABEL BETH MAACAH, ARAM, MAACAH
Also called Maacah. A small kingdom in Northwest Mesopotamia (1Ch 19:6, ftn). The states of Aram Maacah, Aram Naharaim, and Zobah were N and NE of Israel and formed a solid block from the region of Lake Huleh through the Anti-Lebanons to beyond the Euphrates.
See Aram Naharaim; Aram Zobah; Zobah.

ARAM NAHARAIM [808].
NIV+ ARAM
A state in Northwest Mesopotamia (Ge 24:10; Dt 23:4; Jdg 3:8; 1Ch 19:6 and notes). *See Aram Maacah.*

ARAM ZOBAH [809].
NIV+ ARAM, ZOBAH
Only in the Title of Ps 60 (Ps 60, ftn). *See Aram Maacah; Zobah.*

ARAMAIC [811, *1365+1579, 1580*].
NIV+ ARAM
A Semitic language closely related to Hebrew, which developed various dialects and spread to all of SW Asia. Aramaic portions in the OT are Da 2:4-7:28; Ezr 4:8-6:18; 7:12-26; Jer 10:11. Aramaic words occur in the NT (Mk 5:41; 15:34; Mt 27:46; Ro 8:15; Gal 4:6; 1Co 16:22). Aramaic was the colloquial language of Israel from the time of the return from the Exile.

ARAN [814] (*wild goat*). Son of Dishan (Ge 36:28; 1Ch 1:42).

ARARAT [827]. Modern Armenia (2Ki 19:37; Isa 37:38, KJV) and to its mountain range (Ge 8:4), the resting place of Noah's ark. The region is now part of Turkey.

ARATUS A Cilician poet (315-240 B.C.). Paul quotes from his *Phaenomena* (Ac 17:28). *See Asceticism; Cleanthes; Stoicism; Stoics.*

ARAUNAH [779, 821] (*strong*). A Jebusite from whom David bought a site for an altar (2Sa 24:16-24). Also spelled Ornan (1Ch 21:15 ftn, 18-28).

ARBA (*four*).
NIV+ KIRIATH ARBA
Giant ancestor of Anak (Jos 14:15; 15:13; 21:11).

ARBATHITE [6863] (*person from Arabah*). A native of Beth Arabah (2Sa 23:31; 1Ch 11:32).

ARBEL *See Beth Arbel.*

ARBITE [750]. One of David's mighty men (2Sa 23:35).

ARBITRATION [3519, *3537*].
NIV+ ARBITER, ARBITRATE
The two prostitutes before Solomon (1Ki 3:16-28). Urged by Paul as a mode of action for Christians (1Co 6:1-8).
See Court, of Law.

ARCH *See Architecture.*

ARCHAEOLOGY (*study of ancient things*). Study of the material remains of the past by excavating ancient buried cities and examining their remains; deciphering inscriptions; and evaluating the language, literature, art, architecture, monuments, and other aspects of human life and achievement. Biblical archaeology is concerned with Israel and the countries with which the Hebrews and early Christians came into contact. Modern archaeology began with Napoleon's expedition to Egypt, on which many scholars accompanied him to study Egyptian monuments (1798), and with the work of Edward Robinson in Palestine (1838, 1852). Discoveries of great importance which throw much light upon the patriarchal period are the Mari Tablets, the Nuzi Tablets, the Tell-el Amarna Tablets, and the Ras Shamra Tablets. The discovery of the Dead Sea Scrolls and the excavation of Qumran are among the more recent archaeological finds of importance. Archaeology is of great help in better understanding the Bible, in dealing with critical questions regarding the Bible, and in gaining an appreciation of the ancient world.

ARCHANGEL [*791*] (*ruling angel*).

NIV+ See ANGEL

A high order of angels (1Th 4:16). Michael called a "prince" (Da 10:13,21; 12:1; Jude 9; Rev 12:7). *See Angels.*

ARCHELAUS [*793*] (*ruler of people*). The son of Herod the Great. He ruled over Judea, Samaria, and Idumea from 4 B.C. to A.D. 6 (Mt 2:22).

ARCHERS [1251+2932, 2005, 3452, 4619, 8008+, 8043].

NIV+ ARCHER

Hunters or warriors with bow and arrow, weapons universally used in ancient times (Ge 21:20; 1Sa 20:17-42; Isa 21:17). "Arrow" is often used figuratively (Job 6:4; Jer 9:8), as is also "bow" (Ps 7:12). *See Archery.*

ARCHERY

Practiced by:

Ishmael (Ge 21:20), Esau (Ge 27:3), Jonathan (1Sa 20:20,36-37), Sons of Ulam (1Ch 8:40), Philistines (1Sa 31:1-3; 1Ch 10:3), Persians (Isa 13:17-18), people of Kedar (Isa 21:17), Syrians (1Ki 22:31-34), Israelites (2Sa 1:18; 1Ch 5:18; 12:2; 2Ch 14:8; 26:14; Ne 4:13; Zec 9:13), Lydians (Jer 46:9).

In war (Ge 49:23; Jdg 5:11; 1Sa 31:3; Isa 22:3; Jer 4:29; Zec 10:4).

See Archers; Armies; Arrows; Bow; War.

ARCHEVITES *See Erech, 2.*

ARCHI, ARCHITES *See Arkite(s).*

ARCHIPPUS [*800*] (*master of the horse*). An office bearer in the church at Colosse (Col 4:17; Phm 2).

ARCHITECTURE The materials of architecture in antiquity were wood, clay, brick (formed of clay, whether sun-baked or kiln-fired), and stone. The determining factor in the choice of material used was local availability. The homes of the poor had no artistic distinction. The wealthy and the nobility, however, adorned their palatial homes ornately with gold and ivory. Architectural remains—temples, city gates, arches, ziggurats, pyramids—survive intact in great abundance, and archaeology has uncovered the foundations of countless buildings. Each country had its own distinctive style of architecture. No architecture has surpassed that of Greece, although the temple of Solomon and the one rebuilt by Herod were universally admired.

ARCHIVES [10103+10148; 10103+10515]. Storage place for royal documents (Ezr 4:15; 5:17; 6:1).

ARCTURUS A constellation: "the Bear" (Job 9:9; 38:32). *See Astronomy; Bear, Illustrative of.*

ARD, ARDITE [764, 766] (*hunchbacked*).
1. Son of Benjamin (Ge 46:21).
2. Son of Bela and his clan (Nu 26:40).

ARDON [765] (*hunchbacked*). Son of Caleb (1Ch 2:18).

ARELI, ARELITE [739, 740]. Son of Gad (Ge 46:16) and his clan (Nu 26:17).

AREOPAGITE A member of the Areopagus (Ac 17:34).

AREOPAGUS [*740, 741*] (*hill of the Greek god, Ares*).
1. The rocky hill of the Greek god of war Ares (Mars) on the Acropolis at Athens.
2. The name of a council which met on Mars Hill. In NT times it was primarily concerned with morals and education. Paul was brought before it (Ac 17:19-34).

ARETAS [*745*] (*virtuous*). A Nabataean king, father-in-law of Herod Antipas (2Co 11:32).

ARGOB [758, 759] (*mound*).
1. A region in Bashan taken by the Israelites under Moses (Dt 3:4) and given to the half-tribe of Manasseh (Dt 3:13).
2. Could also be a place or a person (2Ki 15:25). The Hebrew text is uncertain.

ARIDAI [767] (perhaps *delight of Hari*). Son of Haman killed by the Jews (Est 9:9).

ARIDATHA [792] (perhaps *given by Hari*). A son of Haman killed by the Jews (Est 9:8).

ARIEH [794] (*lion*). Either a person or a place. The text is uncertain (2Ki 15:25).

ARIEL [790, 791] (*lioness of God [El]*).
1. Leader under Ezra (Ezr 8:16-17).
2. Figurative name for Jerusalem (Isa 29:1-2,7).
3. In 2Sa 23:20 and 1Ch 11:22 "best men" (KJV "lion-like men") translates a word similar to Ariel.

ARIMATHEA [*751*]. Home of Joseph who buried Jesus in his own tomb (Mt 27:57; Mk 15:43; Lk 23:51; Jn 19:38). Its location is in doubt, but it is conjectured to be Ramathaim-Zophim, c. twenty miles NW of Jerusalem.

ARIOCH [796, 10070].
1. King of Ellasar (Ge 14:1,9).
2. Captain of Nebuchadnezzar's guard (Da 2:14-15, 24-25).

ARISAI [798]. Son of Haman (Est 9:9).

ARISTARCHUS [*752*] (*best ruler*). A Thessalonian traveling companion of Paul (Ac 19:29; 20:4; 27:2; Col 4:10; Phm 24).

ARISTOBULUS [*755*] (*best adviser*). A Roman Christian greeted by Paul (Ro 16:10).

ARK [778, 9310, *3066*] (*box*).

1. Directions for building of (Ge 6:14-16). Noah and family preserved in (Ge 6:18; 7:8; Mt 24:38; Heb 11:7; 1Pe 3:20). Animals saved in (Ge 6:19-20; 7:1-16).

2. Of bulrushes (Ex 2:3).

ARK OF THE COVENANT

Description of:

Dimensions of (Ex 25:10; 37:1). Entirely covered with gold (Ex 25:11; 37:2). Surrounded with a crown of gold (Ex 25:11). Furnished with rings and poles (Ex 25:12-15; 37:3-5). Tables of testimony alone placed in (Ex 25:16,21; 1Ki 8:9,21; 2Ch 5:10; Heb 9:4). Atonement cover laid upon (Ex 25:21; 26:34). Placed in the Most Holy Place (Ex 26:33; 40:21; Heb 9:3-4). The pot of manna and Aaron's rod laid up before (Heb 9:4, w Ex 16:33-34; Nu 17:10). A copy of the law laid in the side of (Dt 31:26). Anointed with sacred oil (Ex 30:26). Covered with the veil by the priests before removal (Nu 4:5-6).

A symbol of the presence and glory of God (Nu 14:43-44; Jos 7:6; 1Sa 14:18-19; Ps 132:8). Considered the glory of Israel (1Sa 4:21-22). Was holy (2Ch 35:3). Sanctified its resting-place (2Ch 8:11). The Israelites inquired of the Lord before (Jos 7:6-9; Jdg 20:27; 1Ch 13:3). Profanation of, punished (Nu 4:5,15; 1Sa 6:19; 1Ch 15:13). Protecting of, rewarded (1Ch 13:14).

Was Called the:

Ark of God (1Sa 3:3). Ark of God's might (2Ch 6:41; Ps 132:8). Ark of the covenant of the Lord (Nu 10:33). Ark of the testimony (Ex 30:6; Nu 7:89).

Was Carried:

By priests or Levites alone (Dt 10:8; Jos 3:14; 2Sa 15:24; 1Ch 15:2). Before the Israelites in their journeys (Nu 10:33; Jos 3:6). Sometimes to the camp in war (1Sa 4:4-5).

History and Miracles Connected With:

Jordan divided (Jos 4:7). Fall of the walls of Jericho (Jos 6:6-20). Captured by the Philistines (1Sa 4:11). Fall of Dagon (1Sa 5:1-4). Philistines plagued (1Sa 5:6-12). Manner of its restoration (1Sa 6:1-18). At Kiriath Jearim twenty years (1Sa 7:1-2). Removed from Kiriath Jearim to the house of Obed-Edom (2Sa 6:1-11). David made a tent for (2Sa 6:17; 1Ch 15:1). Brought into the city of David (2Sa 6:12-15; 1Ch 15:25-28). Brought by Solomon into the temple with great solemnity (1Ki 8:1-6; 2Ch 5:2-9). A type of Christ (Ps 40:8; Rev 11:19).

ARKITE(S) [805, 6909]. Descendants of Canaan (Ge 10:17; 1Ch 1:15). Member of a clan in Ephraim (Jos 16:2; 1Ch 27:33).

ARM [274, 2432, 2741, 3338, 4190, 7396, *1098*, *3959*].
NIV+ ARMLETS, ARMRESTS, ARMS

Figurative:

Of divine providence—

Ex 6:6 "Therefore, say to the Israelites: 'I am the LORD, and I will bring you out from under the yoke of the Egyptians. I will free you from being slaves to them, and I will redeem you with an outstretched arm and with mighty acts of judgment. (+Ex 15:16)

Dt 4:34 Has any god ever tried to take for himself one nation out of another nation, by testings, by miraculous signs and wonders, by war, by a mighty hand and an outstretched arm, or by great and awesome deeds, like all the things the LORD your God did for you in Egypt before your very eyes?

Dt 5:15 Remember that you were slaves in Egypt and that the LORD your God brought you out of there with a mighty hand and an outstretched arm. Therefore the LORD your God has commanded you to observe the Sabbath day. (+Dt 7:19; 9:29)

Dt 11:2 Remember today that your children were not the ones who saw and experienced the discipline of the LORD your God: his majesty, his mighty hand, his outstretched arm; (+Dt 26:8)

Dt 33:27 The eternal God is your refuge, and underneath are the everlasting arms. He will drive out your enemy before you, saying, 'Destroy him!'

1Ki 8:42 for men will hear of your great name and your mighty hand and your outstretched arm—when he comes and prays toward this temple,

2Ki 17:36 But the LORD, who brought you up out of Egypt with mighty power and outstretched arm, is the one you must worship. To him you shall bow down and to him offer sacrifices. (+2Ch 6:32)

Ps 77:15 With your mighty arm you redeemed your people, the descendants of Jacob and Joseph. *Selah*

Ps 89:10 You crushed Rahab like one of the slain; with your strong arm you scattered your enemies.

Ps 89:13 Your arm is endued with power; your hand is strong, your right hand exalted.

Ps 89:21 My hand will sustain him; surely my arm will strengthen him. (+Ps 98:1; 136:12)

SS 2:6 His left arm is under my head, and his right arm embraces me.

Isa 33:2 O LORD, be gracious to us; we long for you. Be our strength every morning, our salvation in time of distress.

Isa 40:10 See, the Sovereign LORD comes with power, and his arm rules for him. See, his reward is with him, and his recompense accompanies him. [11]He tends his flock like a shepherd: He gathers the lambs in his arms and carries them close to his heart; he gently leads those that have young.

Isa 51:5 My righteousness draws near speedily, my salvation is on the way, and my arm will bring justice to the nations. The islands will look to me and wait in hope for my arm.

Isa 51:9 Awake, awake! Clothe yourself with strength, O arm of the LORD; awake, as in days gone by, as in generations of old. Was it not you who cut Rahab to pieces, who pierced that monster through?

Isa 52:10 The LORD will lay bare his holy arm in the sight of all the nations, and all the ends of the earth will see the salvation of our God.

Isa 53:1 Who has believed our message and to whom has the arm of the LORD been revealed?

Isa 59:16 He saw that there was no one, he was appalled that there was no one to intervene; so his own arm worked salvation for him, and his own righteousness sustained him.

Isa 62:8 The LORD has sworn by his right hand and by his mighty arm: "Never again will I give your grain as food for your enemies, and never again will foreigners drink the new wine for which you have toiled;

Isa 63:5 I looked, but there was no one to help, I was appalled that no one gave support; so my own arm worked salvation for me, and my own wrath sustained me.

Isa 63:12 who sent his glorious arm of power to be at Moses' right hand, who divided the waters before them, to gain for himself everlasting renown,

Jer 21:5 I myself will fight against you with an

outstretched hand and a mighty arm in anger and fury and great wrath.

Jer 27:5 With my great power and outstretched arm I made the earth and its people and the animals that are on it, and I give it to anyone I please.

Jer 32:17 "Ah, Sovereign LORD, you have made the heavens and the earth by your great power and outstretched arm. Nothing is too hard for you. (+Eze 20:33)

Lk 1:51 He has performed mighty deeds with his arm; he has scattered those who are proud in their inmost thoughts. (+Ac 13:17)

See Anthropomorphisms.

ARMAGEDDON [762] (*Mount Megiddo*). Found only in Rev 16:16; the final battlefield between the forces of good and evil. Located on the S rim of Esdraelon, the scene of many decisive battles in the history of Israel (Jdg 5:19-20; 6:33; 1Sa 31; 2Ki 23:29-30). *See Megiddo.*

ARMENIA *See Ararat.*

ARMIES [2657, 4722, 5120, 7372, *4213, 5128, 5136*].
NIV+ See ARMY

Who of the Israelites were subject to service in (Nu 1:2-3; 26:2; 2Ch 25:5), Who were exempt from service in (Nu 1:47-50; 2:33; Dt 20:5-9; Jdg 7:3). Numbering of Israel's military forces (Nu 1:2-3; 26:2; 1Sa 11:8; 2Sa 18:1-2; 24:1,9; 1Ki 20:15; 2Ch 25:5). Levies for (Nu 31:4; Jdg 20:10). Compulsory service in (1Sa 14:52).

See Cowardice.

How Commanded:

Commander-in-chief (1Sa 14:50; 2Sa 2:8; 8:16; 17:25; 19:13; 20:23), Generals of corps and divisions (Nu 2:3-31; 1Ch 27:1-22; 2Ch 17:12-19), Captains of thousands (Nu 31:14,48; 1Sa 17:18; 1Ch 28:1; 2Ch 25:5), of hundreds (Nu 31:14,48; 2Ki 11:15; 1Ch 28:1; 2Ch 25:5), of fifties (2Ki 1:9; Isa 3:3).

See Cavalry; Chariot.

Mustering of:

Methods employed in mustering: Sounding a trumpet (Nu 10:9; Jdg 3:27; 6:34; 1Sa 13:3-4), Cutting oxen in pieces, and sending the pieces throughout Israel (1Sa 11:7). Refusal to obey the summons, instance of (Jdg 21:5-11, w Jdg 20).

Tactics:

Camp and march (Nu 2). March in ranks (Joel 2:7). Move in attack in three divisions (Jdg 7:16; 9:43; 1Sa 11:11; 13:17,18; 2Sa 18:2; Job 1:17). Flanks called wings (Isa 8:8). Orders delivered with trumpets (2Sa 2:28; 18:16; 20:1,22; Ne 4:18,20). *See Strategy.*

Stratagems:

Ambushes at: Ai (Jos 8:2-22), Shechem (Jdg 9:25,34), Gibeah (Jdg 20:29-43), Zemaraim (2Ch 13:4,13). By Jehoshaphat (2Ch 20:20-22).

Reconnaissances:

Of Jericho (Jos 2:1-24), Ai (Jos 7:2-3), Bethel (Jdg 1:23-24), Laish (Jdg 18:2-10). Night attacks (Ge 14:15; Jdg 7:16-22). Decoy (Jos 8:4-22; Jdg 20:29-43; Ne 6). Delay (2Sa 17:7-14).

Speed of action:

Abraham, in pursuit of Kedorlaomer (Ge 14:14-15). Joshua, against the Amorites (Jos 10:6,9), the confederated kings (Jos 11:7). David's attack upon the Philistines (2Sa 5:23-25). Forced marches (Isa 5:26-27). Sieges (Jer 39:1), of Jericho (Jos 6), Samaria (2Ki 6:24-33:7), Jerusalem (2Ki 25:1-3).

Machines used (2Ch 26:15; Jer 6:6; Eze 26:9). Fortifications (Jdg 9:31; 2Sa 5:9; 2Ki 25:1; 2Ch 11:11; 26:9; Ne 3:8; 4:2; Isa 22:10; 25:12; 29:3; 32:14; Jer 6:6; 32:24; 33:4; 51:53; Eze 4:2; 17:17; 21:22; 26:8; 33:27; Da 11:15, 19; Na 2:1; 3:14).

Standards (Nu 2:2-3,10,17-18,25,31,34; 10:14,18,22, 25). Uniforms of (Eze 23:6,12; Na 2:3). Standing armies (1Sa 13:2; 1Ch 27; 2Ch 1:14; 17:12-19; 26:11-15).

Religious Ceremonies Attending:

Seeking counsel from God before battle (Nu 27:21; Jdg 1:1; 1Sa 14:19,37-41; 23:2-12; 30:8; 2Sa 2:1; 5:19,23; 1Ki 22:7-28; 2Ki 3:11-19; 1Ch 14:10,14; Jer 37:7-10). Sacrifices (1Sa 13:11-12). Purifications (Nu 31:19-24). Prophets prophesy before (2Ch 20:14-17). Holiness required (Dt 23:9). Officers consecrate themselves to God (2Ch 17:16). Army choir and songs (2Ch 20:21-22). Ark taken to battle (Jos 6:6-7,13; 1Sa 4:4-11).

Divine Assistance to:

When Aaron and Hur held up Moses' hands (Ex 17:11-12). In siege of Jericho (Jos 6). Sun stands still (Jos 10:11-14). Gideon's victory (Jdg 7). Samaria's deliverances (1Ki 20; 2Ki 7). Jehoshaphat's victories (2Ki 3; 2Ch 20). Angel of the Lord puts to death the Assyrians (2Ki 19:35).

Determine royal succession (2Sa 2:8-10; 1Ki 16:16; 2Ki 11:4-12).

Composed of insurgents (1Sa 22:1-2). Mercenaries (2Sa 10:6; 1Ch 19:6-7; 2Ch 25:5-6). Confederated (Jos 10:1-5; 11:1-5; Jdg 1:3; 2Sa 10:6,15-16,19; 1Ki 15:20; 22:1-4; 2Ki 16:9; 18:19-21; 1Ch 19:6-7; 2Ch 16:2-9; 18:1,3; 20:1; 22:5; 28:16,20; Ps 83:1-12; Isa 7:1-9; 8:9-12; 54:15). Exhorted before battle (Dt 20:1-9). Battle shouts (Jdg 7:18; 1Sa 17:20,52).

Triumphs of, Celebrated:

With songs (Jdg 5; 1Sa 18:6-7) music (2Ch 20:28), dancing (1Sa 18:6-7).

Rewards for Meritorious Conduct:

The general offers his daughter in marriage (Jos 15:16-17). King offers his daughter (1Sa 17:25; 18:17-28). Promotion (2Sa 23:8-39; 1Ch 11:6,10-47), Share the spoils (Nu 31:25-47).

Insubordination in, punished, Achan (Jos 7). Check roll-call (1Sa 14:17; Nu 31:48-49).

Panics (Isa 30:17), Among the Midianites (Jdg 7:21), Philistines (1Sa 14:15-19), Syrians (2Ki 7:7-15). Soldiers destroy each other to escape captivity (1Sa 14:20; 31:4-6). Champions fight instead of (1Sa 17:8-53; 2Sa 2:14-17; 21:15-22). Confidence in vain (Ps 33:16; 44:6). Escort duty performed by (2Ki 1:9; Ac 23:23-24,31-33).

Roman Army:

Commanders of (Ac 22:24-29). Centurions (Mt 8:5,8; 27:54; Lk 7:2; 23:47; Ac 10:1,7,22; 21:32; 22:26; 23:17, 23; 24:23; 27:1,11,43; 28:16). Divided into regiments (Ac 10:1; 27:1).

For other than armies of the Israelites and Romans: *See Amalekite(s); Assyria; Babylon; Egyptians; Midianite(s); Persia; Syria.*

For commissaries of: *See Commissary.*

For weapons used: *See Armor.*

See Ambush; Cavalry; Fort; Garrison; Herald; Hostage; Navy; Reconnaissance; Siege; Soldiers; Spies; Standard; Strategy; Truce; War.

Figurative: (Dt 33:2; 2Ki 6:17; Ps 34:7; 68:17; Rev 9:16).

See Army.

ARMLET, BRACELET [731].

NIV+ ARM, ARMS

An ornament usually for the upper arm, worn by both men and women (Ex 35:22; Nu 31:50; 2Sa 1:10; Isa 3:20).

ARMONI [813] (*[one] born in the dwelling tower, the palace*). A son of Saul by his concubine Rizpah, slain by the Gibeonites to satisfy justice (2Sa 21:8-11).

ARMOR [2520, 3998, 5516, 6246, 7989+9234, 9234, *3960, 4110*].

NIV+ See ARMY

The equipment of a soldier (1Sa 13:22; Jer 46:3-4; Eph 6:14-17).

Defensive:

Helmet (1Sa 17:5,38; 2Ch 17:17; 26:14; Jer 46:4; Eze 23:24). Breastplate (Rev 9:9-17). Coat of armor (1Sa 17:5,38; 1Ki 22:34; 2Ch 18:33). Greaves, protection for the leg (1Sa 17:6). Shield (2Sa 1:21; 8:7; 1Ki 10:16,17; 14:27; 2Ch 9:16; 26:14; Ne 2:3).

Offensive:

Bows (Ge 21:16,20). Made of bronze (2Sa 22:35; Job 20; Ps 18:34). Of wood (Eze 39:9). David instructed the Israelites in the use of, by writing war song (2Sa 1:18). Arrows (1Sa 31:3; 2Sa 22:15; 1Ki 22:34; 2Ki 19:32; 2Ch 17:17; Ps 7:13; Isa 22:3; Jer 51:3).

War club (Job 41:29; Jer 51:20). Spear (Nu 25:7; 1Sa 18:10; 2Sa 18:14). Javelin, a heavy lance (Eze 39:9). Used by Goliath (1Sa 17:6). By Saul (1Sa 18:11; 19:9-10).

Sling, used for throwing stones (Pr 26:8). David slays Goliath with (1Sa 17:40-50). Skilled use of (Jdg 20:16). Used in war (Jdg 20:16; 2Ki 3:25; 2Ch 26:14).

Sword, used by Gibeon (Jdg 7:20). By Peter (Mt 26:51; Jn 18:10). David's army equipped with (1Ch 21:5).

Figurative:

(Ro 13:12; 2Co 6:7; 10:4; Eph 6:11-17; 1Th 5:8).

ARMOR-BEARER [3998+5951].

NIV+ See ARMY

An attendant who carried a soldier's equipment.

Of Abimelech (Jdg 9:54), Jonathan (1Sa 14:6-7,12,14,17), Saul (1Sa 16:21; 31:6), Goliath (1Sa 17:7), Joab (2Sa 18:15).

ARMORY [1074+3998, 5977].

NIV+ See ARMY

A place for the storage of armor (Ne 3:19; SS 4:4; Isa 22:8; 39:2). In different parts of the kingdom (1Ki 10:17; 2Ch 11:12).

See Jerusalem.

Figurative: (Jer 50:25).

ARMY [408, 408+4878, 554, 824, 1201, 2162+, 2432, 2657+, 2741, 4595, 4713, 4722, 6639+, 7372, 7736+, 10264, *5128*].

NIV+ ARM, ARMED, ARMIES, ARMOR, ARMOR-BEARER, ARMOR-BEARERS, ARMORY, ARMS

In Israel males (except Levites) were subject to military duty at the age of twenty (Nu 1:3,17). Army divisions were subdivided into thousands and hundreds, with respective officers (Nu 31:14). Until Israel got its first king it had no standing army, but whenever there was need, God raised up men of special ability to save the country from its enemies. Down to the time of Solomon, Israel's armies were composed mostly of footmen (1Sa 4:10); later horsemen and chariots were added (2Sa 8:4; 1Ki 10:26,28-29).

The Roman army was composed of legions divided into cohorts, maniples, and centuries (Ac 10:1; 21:31).

See Armies.

ARNAN [820]. Name of a family descended from David (1Ch 3:21).

ARNON [818].

NIV+ ARNON'S

A river emptying into the Dead Sea from the east. Boundary between Moabites and Amorites (Nu 21:13-14,26; 22:36; Dt 2:24,36; 3:8,16; Jos 12:1). Fords of (Isa 16:2). Miracles at (Nu 21:14).

ARODI, ARODITE, AROD [771, 772] (*hunchback-ed*). The sixth son of Gad (Ge 46:16) and his clan (Nu 26:17).

AROER, AROERITE [6876, 6901] (*juniper*).

1. A city of the Amorites in the valley of the Arnon River (Dt 4:48). Conquered by Israelites (Dt 2:36; 3:12; Jdg 11:26). Taken by Hazael (2Ki 10:33).

2. A city built, or, probably more correctly, rebuilt, by the Gadites (Nu 32:34; Jos 13:25). Jephthah kills the Ammonites at (Jdg 11:33).

3. A city in Judah (1Sa 30:28). Birthplace of two of David's heroes (1Ch 11:44).

AROMATIC RESIN [978]. Fragrant gum or resin listed with precious stones (Ge 2:12; Nu 11:7). See Minerals of the Bible, 1; Resin.

ARPAD, ARPHAD [822]. A fortified city of Syria, perhaps identical with Arvad (2Ki 18:34; 19:13). Idols of (Isa 36:19).

ARPHAXAD [823, *790*]. Son of Shem (Ge 10:22; 11:10-13; 1Ch 1:17-18,24; Lk 3:36).

ARREST [*9530, 2095+3836+5931, 3195, 4140, 4389, 5197*].

NIV+ ARRESTED, ARRESTING

Of Jesus (Mt 26:57; Mk 14:46; Lk 22:54; Jn 18:12), apostles (Ac 5:17-18; 6:12), Paul and Silas (Ac 16:19), Paul (Ac 21:30). Paul authorized to arrest Christians (Ac 9:2).

See Extradition; Prison; Prisoners.

ARROGANCE [*1454, 1452, 2147, 2294, 2295, 2326, 3400, 5881*].

NIV+ ARROGANT, ARROGANTLY

1Sa 2:3 "Do not keep talking so proudly or let your mouth speak such arrogance, for the LORD is a God who knows, and by him deeds are weighed. (+Pr 8:13)

Isa 13:11 I will punish the world for its evil, the wicked for their sins. I will put an end to the arrogance of the haughty and will humble the pride of the ruthless.

See Pride.

ARROWS [2932, 2943, 3721, 4751, 8008, *1018*].

NIV+ ARROW

Deadly and destructive weapons (Pr 26:18). Called shafts (Isa 49:2). Sharp (Ps 120:4; Isa 5:28). Bright and polished (Isa 49:2; Jer 51:11). Sometimes poisoned (Job 6:4). Carried in a quiver (Ge 27:3; Isa 49:2; Jer 5:16; La 3:13).

Discharged:

From a bow (Ps 11:2; Isa 7:24). From machines (2Ch 26:15). At a mark for amusement (1Sa 20:20-22). At the beasts of the earth (Ge 27:3). Against enemies (2Ki 19:32; Jer 50:14). With great force (Nu 24:8; 2Ki 9:24).

Swiftness of, alluded to (Zec 9:14). The ancients divined by (Eze 21:21).

Figurative:

Of Christ (Isa 49:2). Of the word of Christ (Ps 45:5). Of God's judgment (Dt 32:23-42; Ps 7:13; 21:12; 64:7; Eze 5:16). Of severe afflictions (Job 6:4; Ps 38:2). Of bitter words (Ps 64:3). Of slanderous tongues (Jer 9:8). Of false witnesses (Pr 25:18). Of devices of the wicked (Ps 11:2). Of young children (Ps 127:4). Of lightning (Ps 77:17-18; Hab 3:11). Broken, of destruction of power (Ps 76:3). Falling from the hand, of the paralyzing power (Eze 39:3).

ARSON (Ps 74:7-8). Law concerning (Ex 22:6).

Instances of: By Samson (Jdg 15:4-5), Absalom (2Sa 14:30), Zimri (1Ki 16:18).

ART Seen in the gifting of Bezalel and Oholiab to build the tabernacle and its furnishings (Ex 31:1-12; 35:30-39:43); of Huram(-abi) and his work on the temple of Solomon (1Ki 7:13-45; 2Ch 2:13-4:16).

Israel was not to apply artistic talents to create idols (Ex 20:4,23; 32:1-24; 34:17; Lev 26:1). *See Arts and Crafts; Bezalel; Huram; Tabernacle; Temple.*

ARTAXERXES [831, 10078] (*kingdom of righteousness*). There are three kings with the name of Artaxerxes.

1. Artaxerxes I (465-425 B.C.), son of Xerxes I; known as Macrocheir or Longimanus. He overcame revolts in Egypt, where, with Athenian support, unrest started in 460 and lasted until 454, and in other parts of the Persian Empire. During that time some of the eastern possessions were lost. By the peace treaty of Callias (449), signed at Susa, the relations between Athens and Persia were stabilized on a *status quo ante bellum* basis. Artaxerxes was buried at Naqsi Rustam next to the tombs of his father and grandfather.

Artaxerxes I authorized Ezra's mission to Jerusalem in 458 (Ezr 7:8,11-26). He temporarily halted the reconstruction of Jerusalem (4:7-23). Nehemiah's two missions were under his reign and with his permission, the first in 445 (Ne 2:1ff; 13:6).

2. Artaxerxes II (404-359 B.C.), son of Darius II and grandson of Artaxerxes I; known as Mnemon. He crushed the rebellion of his brother Cyrus (Battle of Cunaxa, 401), as related by Xenophon in his *Anabasis*. He lost Egypt probably in 402 or 401, repelled the meddling of Sparta in the affairs of Asia Minor (Peace of Antalcidas, 386), and suppressed other rebellious movements led by local satraps. Several of his inscriptions refer to his building activities. The palace he built at Susa is considered by some authorities to be identical with the palace described in Esther (Est 1:5-6).

3. Artaxerxes III (359-338 B.C.), son of Artaxerxes II; known as Ochus. By the use of skillful diplomacy and military force he succeeded in maintaining a superficially strong empire, until the time when he was murdered as the result of a conspiracy led by Bagoas (338).

ARTEMAS [782] (*[given by] Artemis*). A companion of Paul (Tit 3:12).

ARTEMIS [783]. The Greek goddess of hunting, corresponding to the Roman Diana. Her largest and most famous temple was at Ephesus; it was regarded as one of the wonders of the ancient world (Ac 19:23-41).

ARTIFICER *See Arts and Crafts; Occupations and Professions.*

ARTILLERY *See Armory.*

ARTISANS [4994]. *See Occupations.*

ARTS AND CRAFTS Armorer (1Sa 8:12). Baker (Ge 40:1; 1Sa 8:13). Brickmaker (Ge 11:3; Ex 5:7-8,18). Blacksmith (Ge 4:22; 1Sa 13:19). Carver (Ex 31:5; 1Ki 6:18). Carpenter (2Sa 5:11; Mk 6:3). Caulker (Eze 27:9, 27). Dyer (Ex 25:5). Embroiderer (Ex 35:35; 38:23). Embalmer (Ge 50:2-3,26). Engraver (Ex 28:11; Isa 49:16; 2Co 3:7). Gardener (Ge 4:2; 9:20; Jer 29:5; Jn 20:15). Goldsmith (Isa 40:19; Jer 10:9). Launderer (2Ki 18:17; Mk 9:3). Mariner (Eze 27:8-9). Mason (2Sa 5:11; 2Ch 24:12). Musician (1Sa 18:6; 1Ch 15:16). Perfumer (Ex 30:25,35; 1Sa 8:13). Potter (Isa 64:8; Jer 18:3; La 4:2; Zec 11:13). Refiner of metals (1Ch 28:18; Mal 3:2-3). Rope-maker (Jdg 16:11). Silversmith (Jdg 17:4; Ac 19:24). Stonecutter (Ex 20:25; 1Ch 22:15). Ship-builder (1Ki 9:26). Smelter of metals (Job 28:2). Spinner (Ex 35:25; Pr 31:19). Tailor (Ex 28:3). Tanner (Ac 9:43; 10:6). Tentmaker (Ge 4:20; Ac 18:3). Tool-maker (Ge 4:22; 2Ti 4:14). Weaver (Ex 35:35; Jn 19:23). Wine-maker (Ne 13:15; Isa 63:3).

ARUBBOTH, ARUBOTH [749]. A district laid under tribute to Solomon's governor (1Ki 4:10).

ARUMAH [777] (*lofty*). Place near Shechem where Abimelech lived (Jdg 9:41).

ARVAD, ARVADITES [770, 773]. Island off the coast of Phoenicia (Eze 27:8,11). Its people were descendants of Ham (Ge 10:18; 1Ch 1:16; Eze 27:8,11).

ARZA [825] (perhaps *gracious*). A steward of Elah (1Ki 16:9).

ASA [654, 809] (possibly *healer* BDB; *myrtle* KB).
NIV+ ASA'S

1. King of Judah (1Ki 15:8-24; 1Ch 3:10; 2Ch 14; 15; 16; Mt 1:7).

2. A Levite (1Ch 9:16).

ASAHEL [6915] (*God [El] has made*).
NIV+ ASAHEL'S

1. Nephew of David and one of his captains (2Sa 2:18-24,32; 3:27; 23:24; 1Ch 2:16; 11:26; 27:7).

2. A Levite commissioned by Jehoshaphat to teach the law to Judah (2Ch 17:8).

3. A Levite who had charge of tithes (2Ch 31:13).

4. Father of Jonathan (Ezr 10:15).

ASAIAH, ASAHIAH [6919] (*Yahweh has made*).

1. An officer of King Josiah (2Ki 22:12-20; 2Ch 34:20-28).

2. A Simeonite (1Ch 4:36).

3. Levite in the time of David (1Ch 6:30).

4. A Shilonite (1Ch 9:5).

5. Chief Levite in David's day who helped bring the ark to Jerusalem (1Ch 15:6,11).

ASAPH [666] (*gatherer*).
NIV+ ASAPH'S

1. Father of Joah (2Ki 18:18; Isa 36:3,22).

2. Son of Berekiah. One of the three leaders of music in David's organization of the tabernacle service (1Ch 15:16-19; 16:5-7; 25:1-9; 2Ch 5:12; 35:15; Ne 12:46). Appointed

to sound the cymbals in the temple choir (1Ch 15:17,19; 16:5,7). A composer of sacred lyrics (2Ch 29:13-30). *See titles of Pss 50; 73-83.* Descendants of, in the temple choir (1Ch 25:1-9; 2Ch 20:14; 29:13; Ezr 2:41; 3:10; Ne 7:44; 11:22).

3. A Levite whose descendants lived in Jerusalem after the exile (1Ch 9:15).

4. A Kohath Levite (1Ch 26:1).

5. Keeper of forests (Ne 2:8).

ASAREL, ASAREEL [832]. Son of Jehallelel (1Ch 4:16).

ASARELAH [833]. One of the temple choir (1Ch 25:2, 14), Probably identical with Azarel, Azareel.

ASCENSION OF CHRIST, THE

Prophecies respecting (Ps 24:7; 68:18, w Eph 4:7-8). Foretold by himself (Jn 6:62; 7:33; 14:28; 16:5; 20:17). Forty days after his resurrection (Ac 1:3). Described (Ac 1:9). From Mount of Olives (Lk 24:50; w Mk 11:1; Ac 1:12). While blessing his disciples (Lk 24:50). When he had atoned for sin (Heb 9:12; 10:12). Was triumphant (Ps 68:18). Was to supreme power and dignity (Lk 24:26; Eph 1:20-21; 1Pe 3:22). As the Forerunner of His people (Heb 6:20). To intercede (Ro 8:34; Heb 9:24). To send the Holy Spirit (Jn 16:7; Ac 2:33). To receive gifts for people (Ps 68:18, w Eph 4:8-11). To prepare a place for his people (Jn 14:2). His second coming shall be in like manner as (Ac 1:10-11).

Typified: (Lev 16:15, w Heb 6:20; Heb 9:7,9,12).

ASCENTS, SONGS OF Title given Psalms 120 to 134. These psalms were, with 135 and 136, part of the liturgical collection "The Great Hallel." They were probably sung during the pilgrimage or "ascent" to Jerusalem required by the annual feasts.

ASCETICISM A philosophy that leads to severe self-discipline in subordinating the body to the control of the moral attributes of the mind. Extreme application of, rebuked by Jesus (Mt 11:19; Lk 7:34), by Paul (Col 2:20-23; 1Ti 4:1-4,8). *See Stoicism; Stoics.*

Instances of the practice of:

John the Baptist (Mt 11:18; Lk 7:33). Those who practiced celibacy for the kingdom of heaven (Mt 19:12).

ASENATH [664] (*belonging to] the goddess Neith*). Wife of Joseph and mother of Manasseh and Ephraim (Ge 41:45,50; 46:20).

ASER *See Asher.*

ASH *See Pine.*

ASHAN [6941] (*smoke*).
    NIV+ BOR ASHAN
A Levitical city of Judah, later of Simeon (Jos 15:42; 19:7; 1Ch 4:32; 6:59). *See Ain, 1.*

ASHBEA *See Beth Ashbea.*

ASHBEL, ASHBELITE [839, 840] (possibly a form of *man of Baal* BDB; *having a long upper lip* KB). Son of Benjamin (Ge 46:21; 1Ch 8:1) and his clan (Nu 26:38).

ASHCHENAZ *See Ashkenaz.*

ASHDOD, ASHDODITES [846, 847, 848] (perhaps *fortress*). A city of the Philistines (Jos 13:3; 1Sa 6:17; Am 3:9). Anakites inhabit (Jos 11:22). Assigned to Judah (Jos

15:47). Dagon's temple in, in which was deposited the ark (1Sa 5).

Conquest of:

By Uzziah (2Ch 26:6), By Assyria supreme commander (Isa 20:1).

People of, conspire against the Jews (Ne 4:7-8). Jews intermarry with (Ne 13:23-24). Prophecies concerning (Jer 25:20; Am 1:8; 3; Zep 2:4; Zec 9:6). Called Azotus in NT times (Ac 8:40).

ASHDOTH-PISGAH (*slopes of Pisgah*). *See Pisgah.*

ASHER, ASHERITES [888, 888+1201, 896, *818*] (*Happy One!*).
    NIV+ ASHER'S
1. Son of Jacob, by Zilpah (Ge 30:13; 35:26; 49:20; Ex 1:4; 1Ch 2:2). Descendants of (Ge 46:17; Nu 26:44-47; Lk 2:36).

2. Tribe of.

Census of, by families (Nu 1:40-41; 26:44-47; 1Ch 7:40; 12:36). Station of, in camp (Nu 2:25,27). Prophecies concerning by Moses (Dt 33:24-25), by John (Rev 7:6). Allotment to, of land in Canaan (Jos 19:24-31; Eze 48:2). Criticized by Deborah (Jdg 5:17). Summoned by Gideon (Jdg 6:35; 7:23). Join Hezekiah (2Ch 30:11).

3. A city of Shechem (Jos 17:7; 1Ki 4:16).

ASHERAH [895].
    NIV+ ASHERAHS
1. Canaanite goddess, sometimes identified with Anath and Ashtoreth. *See Anath; Ashtoreth.*

2. Asherah poles: images of or trees planted to the goddess Asherah. Forbidden to be established (Ex 34:13; Dt 7:5; 16:21; Isa 1:29; 17:8; 27:9; Mic 5:14). Worshiped by Israelites (Jdg 3:7; 1Ki 14:15,23; 15:13; 2Ki 13:6; 17:10,16; 21:3-7; 2Ch 24:18; Jer 17:2). Destroyed by Gideon (Jdg 6:28), Hezekiah (2Ki 18:4), Josiah (2Ki 23:14; 2Ch 34:3-4), Asa (2Ch 14:3), Jehoshaphat (2Ch 17:6; 19:3).

See High Places; Idolatry.

ASHES [709, 2014, 2016, 6760, *5075, 5491*].
    NIV+ ASH
Uses of, in purification (Nu 19:9-10,17; Heb 9:13). A symbol of mourning (2Sa 13:19; Est 4:1,3). Sitting in (Job 2:8; Isa 58:5; Jer 6:26; Eze 27:30; Jnh 3:6; Lk 10:13). Repenting in (Job 42:6; Da 9:3; Jnh 3:6; Mt 11:21; Lk 10:13). Disguises of (1Ki 20:38,41).

ASHHUR Son of Hezron (1Ch 2:24; 4:5).

ASHHUR, ASHUR [858] (possibly *darkness, dawn* BDB; *a Babylonian goddess* KB). Son of Hezron (1Ch 2:24; 4:5).

ASHIMA [860]. An idol (2Ki 17:30).

ASHKELON [884, 885]. One of the five chief cities of the Philistines (Jos 13:3). Captured by the people of Judah (Jdg 1:18). Samson slays thirty men of (Jdg 14:19). Tumors of (1Sa 6:17). Prophecies concerning (Jer 25:20; 47:5,7; Am 1:8; Zep 2:4,7; Zec 9:5).

ASHKENAZ [867]. Son of Gomer (Ge 10:3; 1Ch 1:6). Descendants of (Jer 51:27).

ASHNAH [877]. A name of two towns in Judah (Jos 15:33,43).

ASHPENAZ [881] (*guest*). A prince in Nebuchadnezzar's court (Da 1:3).

ASHRIEL *See Asriel, Ashriel.*

ASHTAROTH [6958].

1. Plural form of Ashtoreth. *See Ashtoreth.*

2. The capital city of Bashan (Dt 1:4; Jos 9:10). Giants dwell at (Jos 12:4). Allotted to Manasseh (Jos 13:31; 1Ch 6:71). Possibly identical with Ashteroth Karnaim (Ge 14:5).

ASHTERATHITE [6960]. A native of Ashtaroth (1Ch 11:44).

ASHTEROTH KARNAIM [6959] (*Ashteroth of the pair of horns, [two peaks?]*). An ancient city of Palestine taken by Kedorlaomer (Ge 14:5).

ASHTORETH [6956].

NIV+ ASHTORETHS

An idol of the Philistines, Sidonians, and Phoenicians, sometimes identified with Anath and Asherah. *See Anath; Asherah.* Probably identical with queen of heaven (Jer 7:18). Worshiped by Israelites (Jdg 2:13; 10:6; 1Sa 7:3-4; 12:10; 1Ki 11:5,33; 2Ki 23:13). Temple of (1Sa 31:10). High places of, at Jerusalem, destroyed (2Ki 23:13).

ASHUR *See Ashhur.*

ASHURBANIPAL [10055] (*Ashur creates a son*). King of Assyria who colonized the cities of Samaria after the Israelites were taken captive to Assyria (Ezr 4:10). Reigned from 688-626 B.C. He was a great lover of learning—his library (over 22,000 tablets) survives.

ASHURI, ASHURITES [856]. A tribal region, possibly Asher (2Sa 2:9).

ASHURNASIRPAL II Ruthless king of Assyria, reigned early in ninth century B.C.

ASHVATH [6937] (possibly *wrought iron*). Son of Japhlet (1Ch 7:33).

ASIA [*823, 824*]. Inhabitants of, in Jerusalem, at Pentecost (Ac 2:9; 21:27; 24:19). Paul and Silas forbidden by the Holy Spirit to preach in (Ac 16:6). Gospel preached in, by Paul (Ac 19; 20:4). Paul leaves (Ac 20:16). Churches of (1Co 16:19; Rev 1:4,11). High officials of Asia were friends of Paul (Ac 19:31).

ASIARCHS High officials of Asia. *See Asia.*

ASIEL [6918] (*God [El] has made*). Grandfather of Jehu (1Ch 4:35).

ASKELON *See Ashkelon.*

ASNAH [663] (possibly *thornbush* BDB; *he who belongs to [the god] Nah* IDB). Descendants of, return to Jerusalem (Ezr 2:50).

ASNAPPER *See Ashurbanipal; Samaria.*

ASP *See Cobra; Serpent; Viper.*

ASPATHA [672] (possibly *given from a sacred horse*). Son of Haman (Est 9:7).

ASPHALTUM *See Caulkers; Pitch; Tar.*

ASRIEL, ASHRIEL [835] (either *God has filled with joy*, or *[the object of] joy is God*).

NIV+ ASRIELITE

1. Descendant of Manasseh (Nu 26:31; Jos 17:2).

2. Son of Manasseh, Asriel (1Ch 7:14).

ASS, DOMESTIC *See Donkey, Domestic.*

ASS, WILD *See Donkey, Wild.*

ASSAR *See Tel Assar.*

ASSASSINATION [4637, 5782].

NIV+ ASSASSINATE, ASSASSINATED, ASSASSINS

David's abhorrence of (2Sa 4:9-12). Laws prohibiting (Dt 27:24).

Instances of:

Of Eglon, by Ehud (Jdg 3:15-22), Abner, by Joab (2Sa 3:27), Ish-Bosheth, by the sons of Rimmon (2Sa 4:5-7), Amnon, by Absalom (2Sa 13:28-29), Amasa, by Joab (2Sa 20:9-10), Joash, by his servants (2Ki 12:19-20), Sennacherib, by his sons (2Ki 19:37; Isa 37:38).

ASSAULT AND BATTERY

NIV+ ASSAULTS

Laws Concerning:

Ex 21:15 "Anyone who attacks his father or his mother must be put to death.

Ex 21:18 "If men quarrel and one hits the other with a stone or with his fist and he does not die but is confined to bed, ¹⁹the one who struck the blow will not be held responsible if the other gets up and walks around outside with his staff; however, he must pay the injured man for the loss of his time and see that he is completely healed.

Ex 21:22 "If men who are fighting hit a pregnant woman and she gives birth prematurely but there is no serious injury, the offender must be fined whatever the woman's husband demands and the court allows. ²³But if there is serious injury, you are to take life for life, ²⁴eye for eye, tooth for tooth, hand for hand, foot for foot, ²⁵burn for burn, wound for wound, bruise for bruise.

²⁶"If a man hits a manservant or maidservant in the eye and destroys it, he must let the servant go free to compensate for the eye. ²⁷And if he knocks out the tooth of a manservant or maidservant, he must let the servant go free to compensate for the tooth.

Dt 17:8 If cases come before your courts that are too difficult for you to judge—whether bloodshed, lawsuits or assaults—take them to the place the LORD your God will choose. ⁹Go to the priests, who are Levites, and to the judge who is in office at that time. Inquire of them and they will give you the verdict. ¹⁰You must act according to the decisions they give you at the place the LORD will choose. Be careful to do everything they direct you to do. ¹¹Act according to the law they teach you and the decisions they give you. Do not turn aside from what they tell you, to the right or to the left. ¹²The man who shows contempt for the judge or for the priest who stands ministering there to the LORD your God must be put to death. You must purge the evil from Israel.

Mt 5:39 But I tell you, Do not resist an evil person. If someone strikes you on the right cheek, turn to him the other also. (+Lk 6:29)

Damages and compensation for (Ex 21:18-19,22).

See Bruise, Bruises; Flog, Flogging; Scourging; Stripes, 1-3; Stoning.

The Beating of Jesus:

Prophecies of (Isa 50:6; La 3:30). The attacks upon (Mt 26:67; 27:30; Mk 14:65; Lk 22:63; Jn 19:3).

ASSHUR [855].

NIV+ ASSHURITES

Son of Shem, and ancestor of the Assyrians (Ge 10:11,22; 1Ch 1:17; Eze 32:22). *See Assyria.*

ASSHURITES, ASSHURIM [857].

NIV+ ASSHUR

Descendants of Dedan (Ge 25:3).

ASSIR [661] (*prisoner*).

1. Son of Korah (Ex 6:24; 1Ch 6:22).
2. Son of Ebiasaph (1Ch 6:23,37).
3. Son of Jehoiachin (1Ch 3:17).

ASSOCIATION-SEPARATION

Evil associations—

Warnings concerning (Ex 23:2; 34:12; Ps 1:1; Pr 4:14; 24:1; 1Co 5:11; 2Co 6:14). Results of (Nu 33:55; 1Ki 11:2; 2Ch 19:2; Pr 28:7; Jn 18:18; 18:25; 1Co 15:33).

Contact with impurity (Lev 5:2; 15:11; Nu 19:13; Isa 52:11; 2Co 6:17; Col 2:21).

Separation from unclean (Lev 13:5,21,33,46; Nu 5:3). Israel from nations (Lev 20:26; Nu 23:9; Dt 7:2; Jos 23:7; Jdg 2:2; Ezr 9:12; 10:11; Isa 52:11; Jer 15:19). Believers from evil associations (Jn 15:19; Ac 2:40; Eph 5:11; 2Th 3:6). Final separation of evil from good (Mt 13:30,49; 25:32; Lk 16:26; 17:34).

Good associations—

Companionship (Ps 119:63; Pr 2:20; 13:20; 2Th 3:14). Personal contact with Jesus (Mt 9:20,25; 14:34-36; Mk 3:10; 9:27; Lk 6:19), Peter (Ac 3:7; 9:41).

ASSOS [840]. A seaport in Mysia (Ac 20:13-14).

ASSURANCE [586, 622, 6859, 4244, 4443].

NIV+ ASSURE, ASSURED, ASSUREDLY, ASSURES, REASSURE, REASSURED

Produced by faith (Eph 3:12; 2Ti 1:12; Heb 10:22). Made full by hope (Heb 6:11,19). Confirmed by love (1Jn 3:14,19; 4:18). Is the effect of righteousness (Isa 32:17). Is abundant in the understanding of the gospel (Col 2:2; 1Th 1:5).

Believers Privileged to Have:

Their election (Ps 4:3; 1Th 1:4). Their redemption (Job 19:25). Their adoption (Ro 8:16; 1Jn 3:2). Their salvation (Isa 12:2). Eternal life (1Jn 5:13). The unalienable love of God (Ro 8:38-39). Union with God and Christ (1Co 6:15; 2Co 13:5; Eph 5:30; 1Jn 2:5; 4:13). Peace with God by Christ (Ro 5:1). Preservation (Ps 3:6,8; 27:3-5; 46:3). Answers to prayer (1Jn 3:22; 5:14-15). Continuance in grace (Php 1:6). Comfort in affliction (Ps 73:26; Lk 4:18-19; 2Co 4:8-10,16-18). Support in death (Ps 23:4). A glorious resurrection (Job 19:26; Ps 17:15; Php 3:21; 1Jn 3:2). A kingdom (Heb 12:28; Rev 5:10). A crown (2Ti 4:7-8; Jas 1:12). Give diligence to attain to (2Pe 1:10-11). Strive to maintain (Heb 3:14,18). Confident hope in God restores (Ps 42:11).

Exemplified:

David (Ps 23:4; 73:24-26). Paul (2Ti 1:12; 4:18).

ASSYRIA [824+855, 855].

NIV+ ASSYRIA'S, ASSYRIAN, ASSYRIANS

Antiquity and origin of (Ge 10:8-11). Situated beyond the Euphrates (Isa 7:20). Watered by the Tigris River (Ge 2:14).

Called:

The land of Nimrod (Mic 5:6). Shinar (Ge 11:2; 14:1). Asshur (Nu 24:22,24). Nineveh, chief city of (Ge 10:11; 2Ki 19:36). Governed by kings (2Ki 15:19,29).

Celebrated for:

Fertility (2Ki 18:32; Isa 36:17). Extent of conquests (2Ki 18:33-35; 19:11-13; Isa 10:9-14). Extensive commerce (Eze 27:23-24). Idolatry, the religion of (2Ki 19:37).

As a Power, Was:

Most formidable (Isa 28:2). Intolerant and oppressive (Na 3:19). Cruel and destructive (Isa 10:7). Selfish and reserved (Hos 8:9). Unfaithful (2Ch 28:20-21). Proud and haughty (2Ki 19:22-24; Isa 10:8). An instrument of God's vengeance (Isa 7:18-19; 10:5-6). Chief men of, described (Eze 23:6,12,23). Armies of, described (Isa 5:26-29).

Invaded Israel (2Ki 15:19). Bought off by Menahem (2Ki 15:19-20).

Tiglath-Pileser, King of:

Ravaged Israel (2Ki 15:29). Asked to aid Ahaz against Syria (2Ki 16:7-8). Took money from Ahaz, but did not strengthen him (2Ch 28:20-21). Conquered Syria (2Ki 16:9).

Shalmaneser, King of:

Reduced Israel to tribute (2Ki 17:3). Was conspired against by Hoshea (2Ki 17:4). Imprisoned Hoshea (2Ki 17:4). Carried Israel captive (2Ki 17:5-6). Repopulated Samaria from Assyria (2Ki 17:24).

Sennacherib, King of:

Invaded Judah (2Ki 18:13). Bought off by Hezekiah (2Ki 18:14-16). Insulted and threatened Judah (2Ki 18:17-32; 19:10-13). Blasphemed the Lord (2Ki 18:33-35). Prayed against by Hezekiah (2Ki 19:14-19). Reproved for pride and blasphemy (2Ki 19:20-34; Isa 37:21-29). His army destroyed by God (2Ki 19:35). Assassinated by his sons (2Ki 19:37). Condemned for oppressing God's people (Isa 52:4). Manasseh taken captive to (2Ch 33:11). The repopulating of Samaria from, completed by Ashurbanipal (Ezr 4:10). Idolatry of, brought into Samaria (2Ki 17:29). Judah condemned for trusting (Jer 2:18,36). Israel condemned for trusting (Hos 5:13; 7:11; 8:9). The Jews condemned for following the idolatries of (Eze 16:28; 23:5,7). The greatness, extent, duration, and fall of, illustrated (Eze 31:3-17).

Predictions Respecting:

Conquest of the Kenites by (Nu 24:22). Conquest of Syria by (Isa 8:4). Conquest and captivity of Israel by (Isa 8:4; Hos 9:3; 10:6; 11:5). Invasion of Judah by (Isa 5:26; 7:17-20; 8:8; 10:5-6,12). Restoration of Israel from (Isa 27:12-13; Hos 11:11; Zec 10:10). Destruction of (Isa 10:12-19; 14:24-25; 30:31-33; 31:8-9; Zec 10:11). Participation in the blessings of the gospel (Isa 19:23-25; Mic 7:12).

ASTARTE See Anath; Ashtaroth, 1; Ashtoreth.

ASTONISHMENT [*7099, 9449, 1742, 2014, 2513].

NIV+ ASTONISHED, ASTONISHING, ASTOUND, ASTOUNDED, ASTOUNDING

Christ causes (Mt 13:54; 15:31; 22:22,33; Mk 2:12; 4:41; 7:37; 10:24; Lk 2:48; 4:22,26; 8:25).

ASTROLOGERS, ASTROLOGY [2042+9028, 4169, 10373].

NIV+ ASTROLOGER

Those who try to find out the influence of the stars upon human affairs or to foretell events by their positions and aspects (Isa 47:13; Jer 10:1-2; Da 1:20; 2:27; 4:7; 5:7,11; Isa 47:12-13).

See Astronomy; Sorcery.

ASTRONOMY

Phenomena Concerning the Universe:

God the creator of—

Job 9:6 He shakes the earth from its place and makes its pillars tremble. [7]He speaks to the sun and it does not shine; he seals off the light of the stars. [8]He alone stretches out the heavens and treads on the waves of the sea. [9]He is the Maker of the Bear and Orion, the Pleiades and the constellations of the south.

Job 26:7 He spreads out the northern [skies] over empty space; he suspends the earth over nothing.

Job 26:13 By his breath the skies became fair; his hand pierced the gliding serpent.

Job 37:18 can you join him in spreading out the skies, hard as a mirror of cast bronze?

Ps 8:3 When I consider your heavens, the work of your fingers, the moon and the stars, which you have set in place,

Ps 136:5 who by his understanding made the heavens, *His love endures forever.* [6]who spread out the earth upon the waters, *His love endures forever.* [7]who made the great lights—*His love endures forever.* [8]the sun to govern the day, *His love endures forever.* [9]the moon and stars to govern the night; *His love endures forever.*

Isa 40:22 He sits enthroned above the circle of the earth, and its people are like grasshoppers. He stretches out the heavens like a canopy, and spreads them out like a tent to live in.

Isa 40:26 Lift your eyes and look to the heavens: Who created all these? He who brings out the starry host one by one, and calls them each by name. Because of his great power and mighty strength, not one of them is missing.

God the ruler of—

Job 38:31 "Can you bind the beautiful Pleiades? Can you loose the cords of Orion? [32]Can you bring forth the constellations in their seasons or lead out the Bear with its cubs? [33]Do you know the laws of the heavens? Can you set up [God's] dominion over the earth?

Ps 68:33 to him who rides the ancient skies above, who thunders with mighty voice.

Eze 32:7 When I snuff you out, I will cover the heavens and darken their stars; I will cover the sun with a cloud, and the moon will not give its light. [8]All the shining lights in the heavens I will darken over you; I will bring darkness over your land, declares the Sovereign LORD.

Am 5:8 (he who made the Pleiades and Orion, who turns blackness into dawn and darkens day into night, who calls for the waters of the sea and pours them out over the face of the land—the LORD is his name—

Immeasurable—

Jer 31:37 This is what the LORD says: "Only if the heavens above can be measured and the foundations of the earth below be searched out will I reject all the descendants of Israel because of all they have done," declares the LORD.

Jer 33:22 I will make the descendants of David my servant and the Levites who minister before me as countless as the stars of the sky and as measureless as the sand on the seashore.'"

Laws of, permanent—

Ecc 1:5 The sun rises and the sun sets, and hurries back to where it rises.

Jer 31:35 This is what the LORD says, he who appoints the sun to shine by day, who decrees the moon and stars to shine by night, who stirs up the sea so that its waves roar—the LORD Almighty is his name: [36]"Only if these decrees vanish from my sight," declares the LORD, "will the descendants of Israel ever cease to be a nation before me."

Declares God's glory—

Ps 19:1 The heavens declare the glory of God; the skies proclaim the work of his hands. [2]Day after day they pour forth speech; night after night they display knowledge. [3]There is no speech or language where their voice is not heard. [4]Their voice goes out into all the earth, their words to the ends of the world.

In the heavens he has pitched a tent for the sun, [5]which is like a bridegroom coming forth from his pavilion, like a champion rejoicing to run his course. [6]It rises at one end of the heavens and makes its circuit to the other; nothing is hidden from its heat.

Destruction of—

Isa 34:4 All the stars of the heavens will be dissolved and the sky rolled up like a scroll; all the starry host will fall like withered leaves from the vine, like shriveled figs from the fig tree. (+Mt 24:35)

2Pe 3:10 But the day of the Lord will come like a thief. The heavens will disappear with a roar; the elements will be destroyed by fire, and the earth and everything in it will be laid bare.

Rev 6:12 I watched as he opened the sixth seal. There was a great earthquake. The sun turned black like sackcloth made of goat hair, the whole moon turned blood red, [13]and the stars in the sky fell to earth, as late figs drop from a fig tree when shaken by a strong wind. [14]The sky receded like a scroll, rolling up, and every mountain and island was removed from its place.

Rev 21:1 Then I saw a new heaven and a new earth, for the first heaven and the first earth had passed away, and there was no longer any sea.

Celestial Phenomena:

Fire from heaven, on the cities of the plain (Ge 19:24-25), On the two captains and their fifties (2Ki 1:10-14), On the flocks and servants of Job (Job 1:16).

Staying of the sun and moon—

Jos 10:12 On the day the LORD gave the Amorites over to Israel, Joshua said to the LORD in the presence of Israel:

"O sun, stand still over Gibeon, O moon, over the Valley of Aijalon." [13]So the sun stood still, and the moon stopped, till the nation avenged itself on its enemies,

as it is written in the Book of Jashar.

The sun stopped in the middle of the sky and delayed going down about a full day. [14]There has never been a day like it before or since, a day when the LORD listened to a man. Surely the LORD was fighting for Israel!

Hail on the Egyptians (Ex 9:22-34). Darkness on the Egyptians (Ex 10:21-23)

Darkness at crucifixion of Christ—

Mt 27:45 From the sixth hour until the ninth hour darkness came over all the land.

Lk 23:44 It was now about the sixth hour, and darkness came over the whole land until the ninth hour, [45]for the sun stopped shining. And the curtain of the temple was torn in two.

Pillar of cloud and fire (Ex 13:21-22; 14:19,24; 40:38; Nu 9:15-23; Ps 78:14). Thunder and lightning on Mt. Sinai (Ex 19:16,18; 20:18).

Signs in the Sun, Moon and Stars: (Joel 2:30-31):

Isa 13:10 The stars of heaven and their constellations will not show their light. The rising sun will be darkened and the moon will not give its light.

Foretold by Jesus as part of his second coming—

Mt 24:29 "Immediately after the distress of those days " 'the sun will be darkened, and the moon will not give its light; the stars will fall from the sky, and the heavenly bodies will be shaken.'

Mt 24:35 Heaven and earth will pass away, but my words will never pass away.

Mk 13:24 "But in those days, following that distress,

" 'the sun will be darkened, and the moon will not give its light; ²⁵the stars will fall from the sky, and the heavenly bodies will be shaken.'

Lk 21:25 "There will be signs in the sun, moon and stars. On the earth, nations will be in anguish and perplexity at the roaring and tossing of the sea.

Ac 2:19 I will show wonders in the heaven above and signs on the earth below, blood and fire and billows of smoke. ²⁰The sun will be turned to darkness and the moon to blood before the coming of the great and glorious day of the Lord.

In the final judgments—

Rev 8:10 The third angel sounded his trumpet, and a great star, blazing like a torch, fell from the sky on a third of the rivers and on the springs of water— ¹¹the name of the star is Wormwood. A third of the waters turned bitter, and many people died from the waters that had become bitter.

¹²The fourth angel sounded his trumpet, and a third of the sun was struck, a third of the moon, and a third of the stars, so that a third of them turned dark. A third of the day was without light, and also a third of the night.

Rev 9:1 The fifth angel sounded his trumpet, and I saw a star that had fallen from the sky to the earth. The star was given the key to the shaft of the Abyss. ²When he opened the Abyss, smoke rose from it like the smoke from a gigantic furnace. The sun and sky were darkened by the smoke from the Abyss.

Rev 10:1 Then I saw another mighty angel coming down from heaven. He was robed in a cloud, with a rainbow above his head; his face was like the sun, and his legs were like fiery pillars. ²He was holding a little scroll, which lay open in his hand. He planted his right foot on the sea and his left foot on the land,

Rev 12:3 Then another sign appeared in heaven: an enormous red dragon with seven heads and ten horns and seven crowns on his heads. ⁴His tail swept a third of the stars out of the sky and flung them to the earth. The dragon stood in front of the woman who was about to give birth, so that he might devour her child the moment it was born.

Rev 13:13 And he performed great and miraculous signs, even causing fire to come down from heaven to earth in full view of men.

Rev 16:8 The fourth angel poured out his bowl on the sun, and the sun was given power to scorch people with fire. ⁹They were seared by the intense heat and they cursed the name of God, who had control over these plagues, but they refused to repent and glorify him.

Rev 19:11 I saw heaven standing open and there before

me was a white horse, whose rider is called Faithful and True. With justice he judges and makes war. ¹²His eyes are like blazing fire, and on his head are many crowns. He has a name written on him that no one knows but he himself. ¹³He is dressed in a robe dipped in blood, and his name is the Word of God. ¹⁴The armies of heaven were following him, riding on white horses and dressed in fine linen, white and clean.

Constellations: (Isa 13:10)

Glory of—

1Co 15:41 The sun has one kind of splendor, the moon another and the stars another; and star differs from star in splendor.

Sun seemingly rotating (Ecc 1:5)

Wandering—

Jude 13 They are wild waves of the sea, foaming up their shame; wandering stars, for whom blackest darkness has been reserved forever.

The serpent (Job 26:13), Orion and Pleiades (Job 9:9; 38:31; Am 5:8).

See Constellations; Eclipse; Heaven; Meteorology; Moon; Stars; Sun.

ASUPPIM NIV "storehouses" at the S gate of the temple (1Ch 26:15,17; Ne 12:25).

ASWAN [6059]. Egyptian town on border of Egypt and Ethiopia (Isa 49:12; Eze 29:10; 30:6).

ASYNCRITUS [850] (*incomparable*). A disciple at Rome (Ro 16:14).

ATAD [354] (*thornbush*). The place where the sons of Jacob mourned for their father (Ge 50:10-11).

ATARAH [6499] (*circlet, wreath*). Wife of Jerahmeel (1Ch 2:26).

ATAROTH [6500] (*circlets, wreaths*).

NIV+ ATAROTH ADDAR

Also called Atroth.

1. A city E of Jordan (Nu 32:3,34).

2. A city, or possibly two different cities, of Ephraim (Jos 16:2,5,7; 18:13).

3. A city of Judah (1Ch 2:54). Called Atroth Beth Joab. *See Atroth Beth Joab; Joab, 4.*

4. A city of Gad (Nu 32:35).

ATAROTH ADDAR, ATAROTH-ADAR [6501] (*wreaths of majesty*).

NIV+ ADDAR, ATAROTH

See Ataroth, 2.

ATER [359] (possibly *crippled one, left-handed one,* or *the proper name Etir*).

1. A descendant of Hezekiah who returned from Babylon (Ezr 2:16; Ne 7:21; 10:17).

2. A gatekeeper (Ezr 2:42; Ne 7:45).

3. An Israelite who agreed to Nehemiah's covenant (Ne 10:17).

ATHACH [6973]. A city of Judah (1Sa 30:30).

ATHAIAH [6970] (possibly *[the] superiority of Yahweh*). Son of Uzziah (Ne 11:4).

ATHALIAH [6975, 6976] (possibly *Yahweh is exalted* BDB; *oldest of Yahweh* KB).

1. Wife of Jehoram, king of Judah (2Ki 8:18,26; 11:1-3,12-16,20; 2Ch 22:10-12; 23:12-15,21).

2. Son of Jehoram (1Ch 8:26).

3. Father of Jeshaiah (Ezr 8:7).

ATHARIM [926] (traditionally *way of the spies*). The Israelites, under Moses, were attacked by the king of Arad, and some were taken captive (Nu 21:1ff).

ATHEISM

Instances of—

Ps 10:4 In his pride the wicked does not seek him; in all his thoughts there is no room for God.

Ps 14:1 The fool says in his heart, "There is no God." They are corrupt, their deeds are vile; there is no one who does good. (+Ps 53:1)

Arguments against—

Job 12:7 "But ask the animals, and they will teach you, or the birds of the air, and they will tell you; [8]or speak to the earth, and it will teach you, or let the fish of the sea inform you. [9]Which of all these does not know that the hand of the LORD has done this? [10]In his hand is the life of every creature and the breath of all mankind. [11]Does not the ear test words as the tongue tastes food? [12]Is not wisdom found among the aged? Does not long life bring understanding? [13]"To God belong wisdom and power; counsel and understanding are his. [14]What he tears down cannot be rebuilt; the man he imprisons cannot be released. [15]If he holds back the waters, there is drought; if he lets them loose, they devastate the land. [16]To him belong strength and victory; both deceived and deceiver are his. [17]He leads counselors away stripped and makes fools of judges. [18]He takes off the shackles put on by kings and ties a loincloth around their waist. [19]He leads priests away stripped and overthrows men long established. [20]He silences the lips of trusted advisers and takes away the discernment of elders. [21]He pours contempt on nobles and disarms the mighty. [22]He reveals the deep things of darkness and brings deep shadows into the light. [23]He makes nations great, and destroys them; he enlarges nations, and disperses them. [24]He deprives the leaders of the earth of their reason; he sends them wandering through a trackless waste. [25]They grope in darkness with no light; he makes them stagger like drunkards.

Ro 1:19 since what may be known about God is plain to them, because God has made it plain to them. [20]For since the creation of the world God's invisible qualities—his eternal power and divine nature—have been clearly seen, being understood from what has been made, so that men are without excuse.

See God; Faith; Unbelief.

ATHENS, ATHENIANS [121, 122].

A leading city of Greece and its inhabitants (Ac 17:15-34; 1Th 3:1).

ATHLAI [6974] (possibly *Yahweh is exalted* BDB; *oldest of Yahweh* KB). A son of Bebai (Ezr 10:28).

ATHLETE, ATHLETICS *See Games.*

ATOMS OF MATTER NIV "dust of the world" (Pr 8:26).

ATONEMENT [4105, 4113, 4114, *2661, 2662, 2663*].

NIV+ ATONE, ATONED, ATONING

The divine act of grace in which God accepts an offering as a substitute for the punishment for sin. In the OT, the shed blood of sacrificial offerings effected atonement. The blood shed in the sacrifices was sacred. It epitomized the life of the sacrificial victim. Since life was sacred, blood (a symbol of life) had to be treated with respect (Ge 9:5-6). Eating blood was therefore strictly forbidden (Lev 7:26-27; Dt 12:16,23-25; 15:23; 1Sa 14:32-34). Lev 17:14 stresses the intimate relationship between blood and life by twice declaring that "the life of every creature is its blood." Life is the precious and mysterious gift of God, and people are not to seek to preserve it or increase their life-force by eating "life" that is "in the blood" (Lev 17:11)—as many pagan peoples throughout history have thought they could do (Ge 9:4).

Practically every sacrifice included the sprinkling or smearing of blood on the altar or within the tabernacle (Lev 1:5; 3:2; 4:6,25; 7:2; 17:6), thus teaching that atonement involves the substitution of life for life. The blood of the OT sacrifice pointed forward to the blood of the Lamb of God, who obtained for his people "eternal redemption" (Heb 9:12). "Without the shedding of blood there is no forgiveness" (Heb 9:22).

For tabernacle and furniture (Lev 16:15-20,33). In consecration of the Levites (Nu 8:21). For those defiled by the dead (Nu 6:11). Made for houses (Lev 14:53). Sin. *See below, Sin.*

By:

Meat offerings (Lev 5:11-13), jewels (Nu 31:50), money (Ex 30:12-16; Lev 5:15-16; 2Ki 12:16), incense (Nu 16:46-50). By animals. *See below, Made by Animal Sacrifices.* By Jesus. *See below, Made by Jesus.*

Day of:

Time of (Ex 30:10; Lev 23:27; 25:9; Nu 29:7). How observed (Ex 30:10; Lev 16:2-34; 23:27-32; Nu 29:7-11; Heb 5:3; 9:7).

Made by Animal Sacrifices:

In the blood shed—

Lev 17:11 For the life of a creature is in the blood, and I have given it to you to make atonement for yourselves on the altar; it is the blood that makes atonement for one's life.

In burnt offerings—

Lev 1:4 He is to lay his hand on the head of the burnt offering, and it will be accepted on his behalf to make atonement for him.

For unintentional sin (Lev 4:13-21; Nu 15:22-28; 28:27-31; 29), for purification after childbirth (Lev 12:6-8).

In guilt offerings—

For sin (Lev 5:6-10; 6:7), for cleansing from a skin disease (Lev 14:12-32).

In sin offerings—

Ex 29:36 Sacrifice a bull each day as a sin offering to make atonement. Purify the altar by making atonement for it, and anoint it to consecrate it. (+Lev 4:20)

For unintentional sins of a leader (Lev 4:22-35), of the descendants of Aaron (Lev 9:7; 10:17; 16:6-9).

The scapegoat (Lev 16:10-34). On festival days (Nu 28:22; 29).

Forgiveness of sins through (Lev 5:10)—

Lev 19:22 With the ram of the guilt offering the priest is to make atonement for him before the LORD for the sin he has committed, and his sin will be forgiven.

Made by Jesus:

Through his blood shed (Lk 22:20)—

1Co 1:23 but we preach Christ crucified: a stumbling block to Jews and foolishness to Gentiles,

Eph 2:13 But now in Christ Jesus you who once were far away have been brought near through the blood of Christ.

[14]For he himself is our peace, who has made the two one and has destroyed the barrier, the dividing wall of hostility, [15]by abolishing in his flesh the law with its commandments and regulations. His purpose was to create in himself one new man out of the two, thus making peace,

Heb 9:12 He did not enter by means of the blood of goats and calves; but he entered the Most Holy Place once for all by his own blood, having obtained eternal redemption. [13]The blood of goats and bulls and the ashes of a heifer sprinkled on those who are ceremonially unclean sanctify them so that they are outwardly clean. [14]How much more, then, will the blood of Christ, who through the eternal Spirit offered himself unblemished to God, cleanse our consciences from acts that lead to death, so that we may serve the living God!

[15]For this reason Christ is the mediator of a new covenant, that those who are called may receive the promised eternal inheritance—now that he has died as a ransom to set them free from the sins committed under the first covenant.

Heb 9:25 Nor did he enter heaven to offer himself again and again, the way the high priest enters the Most Holy Place every year with blood that is not his own. [26]Then Christ would have had to suffer many times since the creation of the world. But now he has appeared once for all at the end of the ages to do away with sin by the sacrifice of himself.

Heb 12:24 to Jesus the mediator of a new covenant, and to the sprinkled blood that speaks a better word than the blood of Abel.

Heb 13:12 And so Jesus also suffered outside the city gate to make the people holy through his own blood.

Heb 13:20 May the God of peace, who through the blood of the eternal covenant brought back from the dead our Lord Jesus, that great Shepherd of the sheep, [21]equip you with everything good for doing his will, and may he work in us what is pleasing to him, through Jesus Christ, to whom be glory for ever and ever. Amen.

1Jn 5:6 This is the one who came by water and blood—Jesus Christ. He did not come by water only, but by water and blood. And it is the Spirit who testifies, because the Spirit is the truth.

Rev 1:5 and from Jesus Christ, who is the faithful witness, the firstborn from the dead, and the ruler of the kings of the earth. To him who loves us and has freed us from our sins by his blood,

Rev 5:9 And they sang a new song: "You are worthy to take the scroll and to open its seals, because you were slain, and with your blood you purchased men for God from every tribe and language and people and nation.

Rev 7:14 I answered, "Sir, you know." And he said, "These are they who have come out of the great tribulation; they have washed their robes and made them white in the blood of the Lamb.

Rev 12:11 They overcame him by the blood of the Lamb and by the word of their testimony; they did not love their lives so much as to shrink from death.

Through his death—

Ro 3:24 and are justified freely by his grace through the redemption that came by Christ Jesus. [25]God presented him as a sacrifice of atonement, through faith in his blood. He did this to demonstrate his justice, because in his forbearance he had left the sins committed beforehand unpunished— [26]he did it to demonstrate his justice at the present time, so as to be just and the one who justifies

those who have faith in Jesus. (+Ro 5:11-15; 1Th 1:10; Heb 13:12)

1Jn 2:2 He is the atoning sacrifice for our sins, and not only for ours but also for the sins of the whole world.

1Jn 3:5 But you know that he appeared so that he might take away our sins. And in him is no sin.

1Jn 4:10 This is love: not that we loved God, but that he loved us and sent his Son as an atoning sacrifice for our sins. (+Rev 5:6,9; 13:8)

Typified—

In Passover lamb (Ex 12:5,11,14; 1Co 5:7). In sacrifices (Ex 24:8; Lev 16:30,34; 17:11; 19:22; Heb 9:11-28) Compare Ge 4:4, w Heb 11:4; Ge 22:2, w Heb 11:17,19; Ex 12:5,11,14, w 1Co 5:7; Ex 24:8, w Heb 9:10; Lev 16:30, 34, w Heb 9:7,12,28; Lev 17:11, w Heb 9:22.

Divinely inspired (Lk 2:30-31)—

Gal 4:4 But when the time had fully come, God sent his Son, born of a woman, born under law, [5]to redeem those under law, that we might receive the full rights of sons. (+Eph 1:3-12,17-22; 2:4-10)

Col 1:19 For God was pleased to have all his fullness dwell in him, [20]and through him to reconcile to himself all things, whether things on earth or things in heaven, by making peace through his blood, shed on the cross.

1Pe 1:20 He was chosen before the creation of the world, but was revealed in these last times for your sake. (+Rev 13:8)

A mystery (1Co 2:7; 1Pe 1:8-12).

Once for all (Heb 7:27; 9:24-28; 10:10,12,14)—

1Pe 3:18 For Christ died for sins once for all, the righteous for the unrighteous, to bring you to God. He was put to death in the body but made alive by the Spirit,

Made on our behalf—

Isa 53:4 Surely he took up our infirmities and carried our sorrows, yet we considered him stricken by God, smitten by him, and afflicted. [5]But he was pierced for our transgressions, he was crushed for our iniquities; the punishment that brought us peace was upon him, and by his wounds we are healed. [6]We all, like sheep, have gone astray, each of us has turned to his own way; and the LORD has laid on him the iniquity of us all.

[7]He was oppressed and afflicted, yet he did not open his mouth; he was led like a lamb to the slaughter, and as a sheep before her shearers is silent, so he did not open his mouth. [8]By oppression and judgment he was taken away. And who can speak of his descendants? For he was cut off from the land of the living; for the transgression of my people he was stricken. (+Isa 53:9)

Isa 53:10 Yet it was the LORD's will to crush him and cause him to suffer, and though the LORD makes his life a guilt offering, he will see his offspring and prolong his days, and the will of the LORD will prosper in his hand. [11]After the suffering of his soul, he will see the light [of life] and be satisfied; by his knowledge my righteous servant will justify many, and he will bear their iniquities. [12]Therefore I will give him a portion among the great, and he will divide the spoils with the strong, because he poured out his life unto death, and was numbered with the transgressors. For he bore the sin of many, and made intercession for the transgressors. (+Mt 20:28)

Jn 6:51 I am the living bread that came down from heaven. If anyone eats of this bread, he will live forever. This bread is my flesh, which I will give for the life of the world."

Jn 11:49 Then one of them, named Caiaphas, who was high priest that year, spoke up, "You know nothing at all!

⁵⁰You do not realize that it is better for you that one man die for the people than that the whole nation perish."

⁵¹He did not say this on his own, but as high priest that year he prophesied that Jesus would die for the Jewish nation, (+Gal 3:13)

Eph 5:2 and live a life of love, just as Christ loved us and gave himself up for us as a fragrant offering and sacrifice to God.

1Th 5:9 For God did not appoint us to suffer wrath but to receive salvation through our Lord Jesus Christ. **¹⁰**He died for us so that, whether we are awake or asleep, we may live together with him.

Heb 2:9 But we see Jesus, who was made a little lower than the angels, now crowned with glory and honor because he suffered death, so that by the grace of God he might taste death for everyone.

1Pe 2:24 He himself bore our sins in his body on the tree, so that we might die to sins and live for righteousness; by his wounds you have been healed.

For reconciliation—

Da 9:24 "Seventy 'sevens' are decreed for your people and your holy city to finish transgression, to put an end to sin, to atone for wickedness, to bring in everlasting righteousness, to seal up vision and prophecy and to anoint the most holy.

²⁵"Know and understand this: From the issuing of the decree to restore and rebuild Jerusalem until the Anointed One, the ruler, comes, there will be seven 'sevens,' and sixty-two 'sevens.' It will be rebuilt with streets and a trench, but in times of trouble. **²⁶**After the sixty-two 'sevens,' the Anointed One will be cut off and will have nothing. The people of the ruler who will come will destroy the city and the sanctuary. The end will come like a flood: War will continue until the end, and desolations have been decreed. **²⁷**He will confirm a covenant with many for one 'seven.' In the middle of the 'seven' he will put an end to sacrifice and offering. And on a wing [of the temple] he will set up an abomination that causes desolation, until the end that is decreed is poured out on him."

Ro 5:1 Therefore, since we have been justified through faith, we have peace with God through our Lord Jesus Christ, **²**through whom we have gained access by faith into this grace in which we now stand. And we rejoice in the hope of the glory of God. (+Ro 5:3-5)

Ro 5:6 You see, at just the right time, when we were still powerless, Christ died for the ungodly. **⁷**Very rarely will anyone die for a righteous man, though for a good man someone might possibly dare to die. **⁸**But God demonstrates his own love for us in this: While we were still sinners, Christ died for us.

⁹Since we have now been justified by his blood, how much more shall we be saved from God's wrath through him! **¹⁰**For if, when we were God's enemies, we were reconciled to him through the death of his Son, how much more, having been reconciled, shall we be saved through his life! **¹¹**Not only is this so, but we also rejoice in God through our Lord Jesus Christ, through whom we have now received reconciliation. (+Ro 5:12-21)

2Co 5:18 All this is from God, who reconciled us to himself through Christ and gave us the ministry of reconciliation: **¹⁹**that God was reconciling the world to himself in Christ, not counting men's sins against them. And he has committed to us the message of reconciliation. (+2Co 5:20-21)

Eph 2:16 and in this one body to reconcile both of them to God through the cross, by which he put to death their

hostility. **¹⁷**He came and preached peace to you who were far away and peace to those who were near.

Col 1:20 and through him to reconcile to himself all things, whether things on earth or things in heaven, by making peace through his blood, shed on the cross.

²¹Once you were alienated from God and were enemies in your minds because of your evil behavior. **²²**But now he has reconciled you by Christ's physical body through death to present you holy in his sight, without blemish and free from accusation—

Heb 2:17 For this reason he had to be made like his brothers in every way, in order that he might become a merciful and faithful high priest in service to God, and that he might make atonement for the sins of the people.

For remission of sins—

Zec 13:1 "On that day a fountain will be opened to the house of David and the inhabitants of Jerusalem, to cleanse them from sin and impurity.

Mt 26:28 This is my blood of the covenant, which is poured out for many for the forgiveness of sins. (+Lk 22:20)

Lk 24:46 He told them, "This is what is written: The Christ will suffer and rise from the dead on the third day, **⁴⁷**and repentance and forgiveness of sins will be preached in his name to all nations, beginning at Jerusalem.

Jn 1:29 The next day John saw Jesus coming toward him and said, "Look, the Lamb of God, who takes away the sin of the world!

Ro 4:25 He was delivered over to death for our sins and was raised to life for our justification.

1Co 15:3 For what I received I passed on to you as of first importance: that Christ died for our sins according to the Scriptures,

Gal 1:3 Grace and peace to you from God our Father and the Lord Jesus Christ, **⁴**who gave himself for our sins to rescue us from the present evil age, according to the will of our God and Father,

Eph 1:7 In him we have redemption through his blood, the forgiveness of sins, in accordance with the riches of God's grace

Col 1:14 in whom we have redemption, the forgiveness of sins.

Heb 1:3 The Son is the radiance of God's glory and the exact representation of his being, sustaining all things by his powerful word. After he had provided purification for sins, he sat down at the right hand of the Majesty in heaven.

Heb 10:1 The law is only a shadow of the good things that are coming—not the realities themselves. For this reason it can never, by the same sacrifices repeated endlessly year after year, make perfect those who draw near to worship. **²**If it could, would they not have stopped being offered? For the worshipers would have been cleansed once for all, and would no longer have felt guilty for their sins. **³**But those sacrifices are an annual reminder of sins, **⁴**because it is impossible for the blood of bulls and goats to take away sins.

⁵Therefore, when Christ came into the world, he said:

"Sacrifice and offering you did not desire, but a body you prepared for me; **⁶**with burnt offerings and sin offerings you were not pleased. **⁷**Then I said, 'Here I am—it is written about me in the scroll—I have come to do your will, O God.'"

⁸First he said, "Sacrifices and offerings, burnt offerings and sin offerings you did not desire, nor were you pleased with them" (although the law required them to be made).

⁹Then he said, "Here I am, I have come to do your will." He sets aside the first to establish the second. ¹⁰And by that will, we have been made holy through the sacrifice of the body of Jesus Christ once for all.

¹¹Day after day every priest stands and performs his religious duties; again and again he offers the same sacrifices, which can never take away sins. ¹²But when this priest had offered for all time one sacrifice for sins, he sat down at the right hand of God. (+Heb 10:13-17)

Heb 10:18 And where these have been forgiven, there is no longer any sacrifice for sin.

¹⁹Therefore, brothers, since we have confidence to enter the Most Holy Place by the blood of Jesus, ²⁰by a new and living way opened for us through the curtain, that is, his body,

1Jn 1:7 But if we walk in the light, as he is in the light, we have fellowship with one another, and the blood of Jesus, his Son, purifies us from all sin. (+1Jn 3:5)

For redemption (Mt 20:28)—

Ac 20:28 Keep watch over yourselves and all the flock of which the Holy Spirit has made you overseers. Be shepherds of the church of God, which he bought with his own blood. (+Gal 3:13)

1Ti 2:6 who gave himself as a ransom for all men—the testimony given in its proper time. (+Heb 9:12; Rev 5:9)

See Blood; Jesus the Christ, Death of, Mission of, Sufferings of; Redemption; Salvation.

ATONEMENT COVER [4114, *2663*]. KJV "mercy seat." Description of (Ex 25:17-22). Placed on the ark of the testimony (Ex 26:34; 30:6; 31:7; 40:20; Heb 9:5). Materials of, to be a freewill offering (Ex 35:4-12). Made by Bezalel (Ex 37:1,6-9).

Sprinkled with blood (Lev 16:14-15). There God met with his people (Ex 25:22; 30:6,36; Lev 16:2; Nu 7:89; 17:4; 1Sa 4:4; 2Sa 6:2; 2Ki 19:15; 1Ch 13:6; Ps 80:1; Ps 99:1; Isa 37:16; Heb 4:16).

In Solomon's temple (1Ch 28:11).

See Tabernacle.

ATONEMENT, DAY OF *See Day of Atonement.*

ATONING SACRIFICE [*2662*]. *See Propitiation.*

ATROPHY *See Disease; Shriveled Hand.*

ATROTH BETH JOAB [6502] (*circlets, folds of the house of Joab*). Descendants of Salma; the house of Joab, occurs in the genealogy of Judah (1Ch 2:54).

ATROTH SHOPHAN [6503] (*circlets, folds of Shophan*). Town built by Gadites E of Jordan (Nu 32:35).

ATTAI [6968] (*timely*, or perhaps *an abbreviation of Athaiah*).
1. A Gadite warrior (1Ch 12:11).
2. Son of Rehoboam (2Ch 11:20).
3. Grandson of Sheshan (1Ch 2:35-36).

ATTALIA [*877*]. A seaport of Pamphylia (Ac 14:25).

ATTORNEY *See Lawyer.*

ATTRIBUTES OF GOD *See God.*

AUGUSTUS [*880*] (*reverent, holy*). A title of Roman emperors (Lk 2:1). "Emperor" and "Imperial" [*4935*] in Ac 25:21,25; 27:1 are rendered Augustus in the KJV.

AUL *See Awl.*

AVA *See Avva, Ava.*

AVARICE

Love of money: a root of evil—

1Ti 6:10 For the love of money is a root of all kinds of evil. Some people, eager for money, have wandered from the faith and pierced themselves with many griefs.

Insatiable—

Ecc 4:7 Again I saw something meaningless under the sun: ⁸There was a man all alone; he had neither son nor brother. There was no end to his toil, yet his eyes were not content with his wealth. "For whom am I toiling," he asked, "and why am I depriving myself of enjoyment?" This too is meaningless—a miserable business!

Ecc 5:10 Whoever loves money never has money enough; whoever loves wealth is never satisfied with his income. This too is meaningless.

¹¹As goods increase, so do those who consume them. And what benefit are they to the owner except to feast his eyes on them?

Forbidden in overseer—

1Ti 3:2 Now the overseer must be above reproach, the husband of but one wife, temperate, self-controlled, respectable, hospitable, able to teach, ³not given to drunkenness, not violent but gentle, not quarrelsome, not a lover of money.

Tit 1:7 Since an overseer is entrusted with God's work, he must be blameless—not overbearing, not quick-tempered, not given to drunkenness, not violent, not pursuing dishonest gain.

Instances of: Descendants of Joseph (Jos 17:14-18).

See Covetousness; Greed; Rich, The; Riches.

AVEN [225] (*evil power, wickedness*).

NIV+ BETH AVEN
1. Valley of Aven (Am 1:5, ftn).
2. Bethel (Am 5:5, ftn)
3. Beth Aven (Hos 10:8, ftn).
4. A possible spelling for On or Heliopolis (Eze 30:17, ftn).

See Beth Aven, Beth-Aven.

AVENGER OF BLOOD [1457].

Premosaic:

Edict of God—

Ge 9:5 And for your lifeblood I will surely demand an accounting. I will demand an accounting from every animal. And from each man, too, I will demand an accounting for the life of his fellow man.

⁶"Whoever sheds the blood of man, by man shall his blood be shed; for in the image of God has God made man.

Cain fears (Ge 4:14-15), Lamech fears (Ge 4:24).

Mosaic Law Concerning:

Cities of refuge from (Nu 35:6-34; Dt 19:1-13; Jos 20:1-9; 21:13,21,27,32,38; 1Ch 6:57,67).

Set aside by David (2Sa 14:4-11).

Figurative: (Ps 8:2; 44:16; Ro 13:4; 1Th 4:6).

See Homicide.

AVITH [6400]. Capital city of the Edomites (Ge 36:35; 1Ch 1:46).

AVVA, AVA [6379]. Also called Ivvah. A district near Babylon (2Ki 17:24; 18:34; 19:13; Isa 37:13).

AVVIM, AVIM [6399].
1. A city of Benjamin (Jos 18:23).
2. A tribe in southern Palestine. *See Avvites, Avites.*

AVVITES, AVITES [6398].
1. A people driven out of Canaan by the Philistines (Dt 2:23; Jos 13:3).
2. Colonists of Samaria (2Ki 17:31).

AWAKENINGS, REFORMS
General references (1Ki 18:39; 2Ch 30:11; Ezr 10:1; Lk 3:7-10; Jn 4:39; Ac 2:40-41; 8:6; 9:35; 11:21; 13:48; 18:8; 19:18).

Instances: Asa (1Ki 15:12). Jehu (1Ki 10:27). Jehoiada (2Ki 11:18). Josiah (2Ki 23:4). Jehoshaphat (2Ch 19:3). Hezekiah (2Ch 31:1). Manasseh (2Ch 33:15). Ezra (Ezr 10:3). Nehemiah (Ne 13:19).

AWL [5345]. A sharp piercing tool (Ex 21:6; Dt 15:17).

AX, AXE [1366, 1749, 4172, 4477, 4490, 7935, *544*].
NIV+ AXES, AXHEAD
A tool for cutting wood (Dt 19:5; 20:19; 1Sa 13:20-21; 2Sa 12:31; Ps 74:5-6). A weapon of war (Jer 46:22). Elisha causes an axhead to float (2Ki 6:5-6).
Figurative of judgment (Jer 46:22; Mt 3:10).

AXLES, AXLETREE [3338, 6248]. Part of a wheeled vehicle, like the movable stands (1Ki 7:30-33).

AYYAH [6509]. A city n Ephraim (1Ch 7:28).

AZAL See Azel, Azal, 1.

AZALIAH [729] (*Yahweh is keeping in reserve*). Father of Shaphan (2Ki 22:3; 2Ch 34:8).

AZANIAH [271] (*Yahweh has listened*). Father of Jeshua (Ne 10:9).

AZAREL, AZARAEL, AZAREEL [6475] (*God [El] has helped*).
1. An Aaronite of the family of Korah (1Ch 12:6).
2. A musician in the temple (1Ch 25:18), also called Uzziel. See *Uzziel 4.*
3. A Danite prince (1Ch 27:22).
4. A son of Bani (Ezr 10:41).
5. A priest (Ne 11:13; 12:36).

AZARIAH [6481, 6482, 10538] (*Yahweh has helped*).
NIV+ AZARIAH'S
1. Man of Judah (1Ch 2:8).
2. King of Judah. See *Uzziah, 1.*
3. Son of Jehu (1Ch 2:38).
4. Son of Ahimaaz (1Ch 6:9).
5. Levite (1Ch 6:36).
6. Son of Zadok (1Ki 4:2).
7. High priest (1Ch 6:10).
8. Son of Nathan (1Ki 4:5).
9. Prophet (2Ch 15:1-8).
10. Son of King Jehoshaphat (2Ch 21:2).
11. Son of Jehoram (2Ch 22:6, ftn). See *Ahaziah.*
12. Son of Jehoram (2Ch 23:1).
13. Son of Johanan (2Ch 28:12).
14. Levite (2Ch 29:12).
15. High priest (2Ch 26:16-20).
16. Son of Hilkiah (1Ch 6:13-14).
17. Opponent of Jeremiah (Jer 43:2).
18. Jewish captive of Babylon (Da 1:7). See *Abednego.*
19. Son of Maaseiah (Ne 3:23).
20. Levite (Ne 8:7).
21. Priest (Ne 10:2).
22. Prince of Judah (Ne 12:32-33).

AZARIAHU [6482]. A son of Jehoshaphat (2Ch 21:2).

AZAZ [6452] (*strong*). Father of Bela (1Ch 5:8).

AZAZEL [6439]. NIV "scapegoat," one of the goats chosen for the service of the Day of Atonement (Lev 16:8,10,26). It has been interpreted both personally and impersonally as meaning: 1. remission of sin, 2. a place name, 3. an evil spirit, 4. the devil. See *Scapegoat.*

AZAZIAH [6453] (*Yahweh is strong*).
1. A harpist in the temple (1Ch 15:21).
2. Father of Hoshea (1Ch 27:20).
3. An overseer in the temple (2Ch 31:13).

AZBUK [6443]. The father of Nehemiah (Ne 3:16).

AZEKAH [6467] (possibly *hoe [the ground]*). A town of Judah (Jos 10:10-11; 15:35; 1Sa 17:1; 2Ch 11:9; Ne 11:30; Jer 34:7).

AZEL, AZAL [727, 728] (*noble*).
1. A place near Jerusalem (Zec 14:5).
2. A Benjamite (1Ch 8:37-38; 9:43-44).

AZEM See *Ezem.*

AZGAD [6444] (*strong is Gad*).
1. Ancestor of certain captives who returned from Babylon (Ezr 2:12; Ne 7:17).
2. A returned exile (Ezr 8:12).
3. A chief who signed Nehemiah's covenant (Ne 10:15).

AZIEL [6456] (*God is my strength*). A temple musician (1Ch 15:20).

AZIZA [6461] (*powerful*). Son of Zattu (Ezr 10:27).

AZMAVETH [6462, 6463] (*strong one of death* ISBE; *camel fodder, a plant of the plumose family* KB).
NIV+ BETH AZMAVETH
1. One of David's heroes (2Sa 23:31).
2. Benjamite (1Ch 12:3).
3. David's treasurer (1Ch 27:25).
4. Descendant of Jonathan (1Ch 8:36).
5. Place N of Anathoth (Ezr 2:24; Ne 12:29).

AZMON [6801] (*strongly [built body]*). A place on the S of Canaan (Nu 34:4,5; Jos 15:4).

AZNOTH TABOR, AZNOTH-TABOR [268] (possibly *peaks of Tabor*).
NIV+ TABOR
A town in Naphtali (Jos 19:34).

AZOR [110] (*help*). Ancestor of Jesus (Mt 1:13-14). Perhaps identical with Azrikam (1Ch 3:23).

AZOTUS [111]. The name of Ashdod in NT times (Ac 8:40). See *Ashdod.*

AZRIEL [6480] (*God [El] is [my] help*).
1. A chief of Manasseh (1Ch 5:24).
2. Father of Jerimoth (1Ch 27:19).
3. Father of Seraiah (Jer 36:26).

AZRIKAM [6483] (*[my] help arises*).
1. Son of Neariah (1Ch 3:23).
2. Son of Azel (1Ch 8:38; 9:44).
3. A Levite (1Ch 9:14; Ne 11:15).
4. Governor of the house of Ahaz (2Ch 28:7).

AZUBAH [6448] (*abandonment*).
  1. Mother of Jehoshaphat (1Ki 22:42; 2Ch 20:31).
  2. Wife of Caleb (1Ch 2:18-19).

AZUR *See Azzur.*

AZZAH *See Gaza, 1.*

AZZAN [6464] (*strong*). Father of Paltiel of the tribe of Issachar; chosen to help distribute the territory W of the Jordan among the various tribes who settled there (Nu 34:26).

AZZUR, AZUR [6473] (*help*).
  1. An Israelite, who sealed Nehemiah's covenant (Ne 10:17).
  2. A Gibeonite, the father of Hananiah, a false prophet of Gibeon in the days of King Zedekiah (Jer 28:1).
  4. Father of Jaazaniah, an Israelite prince (Eze 11:1).

B

BAAL [1251, 1252, 955] (*master, owner, lord*).
NIV+ BAAL-BERITH, BAAL GAD, BAAL HAMON, BAAL-HANAN, BAAL HAZOR, BAAL HERMON, BAAL MEON, BAAL PEOR, BAAL PERAZIM, BAAL SHALISHAH, BAAL TAMAR, BAAL ZEPHON, BAAL-ZEBUB, BAAL'S, BAALS, BAMOTH BAAL

1. A god worshiped by the Canaanites and the Phoenicians; a god of storms and fertility. Often in the plural (Jdg 2:11; 3:7).

Wickedly Worshiped—

By the Israelites in the time of the judges (Jdg 2:10-23; 1Sa 7:3-4), by the kingdom of Israel (2Ki 17:16; Jer 23:13; Hos 11:2; 13:1), under Ahab (1Ki 16:31-33; 18:18; 19:18), Jehoram (2Ki 3:2), by the Israelites (2Ki 21:3; 2Ch 22:2-4; 24:7; 28:2; 33:3). Jeremiah preaches against the worship of (Jer 2:8,23; 7:9).

Altars of, destroyed by Gideon (Jdg 6:25-32), by Jehoiada (2Ki 11:18), by Josiah (2Ki 23:4-5).

Prophets of, slain by Elijah (2Ki 18:4). All worshipers of, destroyed by Jehu (2Ki 10:18-25).

2. A Benjamite (1Ch 8:30; 9:36).

3. A Reubenite (1Ch 5:5).

4. A city in the tribe of Simeon (1Ch 4:33). Called Baalath Beer (Jos 19:8).

BAAL-BERITH [1253] (*lord [Baal] of a covenant*).
NIV+ BAAL

A god of the Shechemites (Jdg 9:4). Worshiped by Israelites (Jdg 8:33). Also called El-Berith (Jdg 9:46). *See El-Berith.*

BAAL GAD, BAAL-GAD [1254] (*lord [Baal] of good luck*).
NIV+ BAAL, GAD

A city of the Canaanites (Jos 11:17; 12:7; 13:5). Probably identical with Baal Hermon (Jdg 3:3; 1Ch 5:23).

BAAL-GUR *See Gur Baal.*

BAAL HAMON, BAAL-HAMON [1255] (*lord [Baal] of Hamon*, or *possessor of abundance*).
NIV+ BAAL

A place where Solomon had a vineyard (SS 8:11). Its location is unknown. Called Hammon (Jos 19:28).

BAAL-HANAN [1257] (*lord [Baal] is gracious*).
NIV+ BAAL

1. The son of Acbor and king of Edom (Ge 36:38; 1Ch 1:49).

2. An official under David (1Ch 27:28).

BAAL HAZOR, BAAL-HAZOR [1258] (*lord [Baal] of Hazor*).
NIV+ BAAL, HAZOR

Where Absalom had a sheep-range and where he brought about the death of Amnon in revenge for the rape of his sister (2Sa 13:23).

BAAL HERMON, BAAL-HERMON [1259] (*lord [Baal] of Hermon*).
NIV+ BAAL, HERMON, SENIR

1. A city near Mt. Hermon (1Ch 5:23). Identical with Baal Gad. *See Baal Gad.*

2. A mountain of Lebanon (Jdg 3:3).

BAAL MEON, BAAL-MEON [1260].
NIV+ BETH BAAL MEON, BETH MEON

A city of the Reubenites (Nu 32:38; 1Ch 5:8; Eze 25:9). Also called: Beth Meon (Jer 48:23), Beth Baal Meon (Jos 13:17), Beon (Nu 32:3).

BAAL PEOR, BAAL-PEOR [1261] (*lord [Baal] of Peor*).
NIV+ BAAL, PEOR

An idol of Moab (Nu 25:3,5; Dt 4:3; Ps 106:28; Hos 9:10).

BAAL PERAZIM, BAAL-PERAZIM [1262] (*lord [Baal] of making a breach, breaking through*).
NIV+ BAAL, PERAZIM

A place in the valley of Rephaim (2Sa 5:20; 1Ch 14:11). Called Mt. Perazim (Isa 28:21).

BAAL SHALISHAH, BAAL-SHALISHA [1264] (*lord [Baal] of Shalisha*).
NIV+ BAAL

A place near Gilgal (1Sa 9:4; 2Ki 4:42).

BAAL TAMAR, BAAL-TAMAR [1265] (*lord [Baal] of the palm tree*).
NIV+ BAAL, TAMAR

A place near Gibeah (Jdg 20:33).

BAAL-ZEBUB [1256] (*lord [Baal] of the flies*).
NIV+ BAAL, BEELZEBUB

Name under which Baal was worshiped by the Philistines of Ekron (2Ki 1:2-3,6). An intentional biblical corruption of the original name Baal-Zebul, "Baal the prince." *See Beelzebub.*

BAAL ZEPHON, BAAL-ZEPHON [1263] (*lord [Baal] of the North*).
NIV+ BAAL, ZEPHON

A place near which the Israelites encamped just before they crossed the Red Sea (Ex 14:2,9; Nu 33:7). The site is unknown.

BAALAH [1267] (feminine of Baal "lord" *lady*).
NIV+ KIRIATH JEARIM

1. A city in the S of Judah (Jos 15:29). Apparently identical with Balah (Jos 19:3) and Bilhah (1Ch 4:29).

2. A city in the N of Judah called also Kiriath Jearim. *See Kiriath Jearim.*

3. A mountain in Judah (Jos 15:11). Probably identical with Mt. Jearim.

BAALAH OF JUDAH, BAALE OF JUDAH (*lords [Baals] of Judah*). Town on N border of Judah; the same as Baalah and Kiriath Baal and Kiriath Jearim (2Sa 6:2; 1Ch 13:6).

BAALATH [1272] (feminine of Baal "lord" *lady*).
NIV+ BAALATH BEER

A city of Dan (Jos 19:44; 1Ki 9:18; 2Ch 8:6).

BAALATH BEER, BAALATH-BEER [1273]

(*lord [Baal] of the well*).

NIV+ BAALATH

A city in the tribe of Simeon (Jos 19:8). *See Baal, 4.*

BAALBEK (*city of Baal*).
City of Coele-Syria, c. forty miles NW of Damascus, famous for its ruins.

BAALI (*my lord* or *my husband*).
Name often given to Yahweh by Israel, no longer to be used when Baal worship is eradicated (Hos 2:16, ftn).

BAALIM
Plural form of Baal in KJV (Jdg 2:11; 1Sa 7:4; Hos 2:13,17; 11:2). *See Baal.*

BAALIS [1271]
(possibly *son of delight*, or *Baals*). King of the Ammonites (Jer 40:14).

BAANA [1275]
(*son of affliction*).
1. Son of Ahilud (1Ki 4:12).
2. Father of Zadok (Ne 3:4).
3. A son of Hushai (1Ki 4:16).

BAANAH [1276]
(*son of affliction*).
1. A captain of Ish-Bosheth's army (2Sa 4:2,5-6,9).
2. Father of Heled (also Heleb) (2Sa 23:29, ftn; 1Ch 11:30).
3. A chief Jew of the Exile (Ezr 2:2; Ne 7:7; 10:27).
4. *See Baana, 3.*

BAARA [1281]
(*passionate [burning] one*). Wife of Shaharaim (1Ch 8:8). Called Hodesh.

BAASEIAH [1283]
(*the Lord is bold*). An ancestor of Asaph, the musician (1Ch 6:40).

BAASHA [1284]
(*boldness*).

NIV+ BAASHA'S

King of Israel (1Ki 15:16-22,27-34; 16:1-7; 21:22; 2Ki 9:9; 2Ch 16:1-6; Jer 41:9).

BABBLER [5066].

NIV+ BABBLING

A sarcastic title applied to Paul (Ac 17:18).

BABBLING [1006].

NIV+ BABBLER

Condemned (Mt 6:7; 1Ti 6:20; 2Ti 2:16).

BABEL [951]
(*gate of god[s]*; Ge 11:9 *confused*).

NIV+ BABYLON, BABYLON'S, BABYLONIA, BABYLONIAN, BABYLONIANS, BABYLONIANS'

A city in the plain of Shinar. Tower built and tongues confused at (Ge 11:1-9). *See Babylon.*

BABIES [1201, 3528, 3529, 6403, 1100, 4086, 5503].

NIV+ BABY, BABY'S

In the mouths of, praise is ordained (Mt 21:16).

Symbolize—

Those without guile (Ps 8:2; Mt 11:25; Lk 10:21), the children of the kingdom of heaven (Mt 18:2-6; Mk 10:15; Lk 18:17), weak Christians (Ro 2:20; 1Co 3:1; Heb 5:13; 1Pe 2:2).

See Children; Parents.

BABOONS [9415].
Imported by Solomon (1Ki 10:22; 2Ch 9:21).

BABYLON, BABYLONIA [824+951, 824+4169, 951, 9114, 10093, 10094, 10373, 956] (*gate of god[s]*).

NIV+ BABEL, BABYLON'S, BABYLONIA, BABYLONIAN, BABYLONIANS, BABYLONIANS'

Described:

Origin of (Ge 10:8,10). Origin of the name (Ge 11:8-9). Land of the Chaldeans (Eze 12:13). Land of Shinar in (Da 1:2; Zec 5:11, ftn). Land of Merathaim (Jer 50:21). Desert of the sea (Isa 21:1,9). Sheshach, a cryptic term for Babylon (Jer 25:12,26, ftn). Lady of kingdoms (Isa 47:5). Situated beyond the Euphrates (Ge 11:31, w Jos 24:2-3). Formerly a part of Mesopotamia (Ac 7:2). Conquered by the Assyrians and a part of their empire (2Ki 17:24, w Isa 23:13). Watered by the rivers Euphrates and Tigris (Ps 137:1; Jer 51:13). Composed of many nations (Da 3:4,29). Governed by Kings (2Ki 20:12; Da 5:1). Languages spoken in (Da 1:4; 2:4). With Media and Persia divided by Darius into 120 provinces (Da 6:1). Administrators placed over (Da 2:48; 6:2). Babylon the chief province of (Da 3:1).

Babylon the Capital of:

Its antiquity (Ge 11:4,9). Enlarged by Nebuchadnezzar (Da 4:30). Surrounded with a great wall and fortified (Jer 51:53,58). Called the jewel of kingdoms and the glory of Babylonians' pride (Isa 13:19), the golden city (Isa 14:4, KJV), the city of merchants (Eze 17:4), Babylon the great (Da 4:30).

Remarkable for:

Antiquity (Jer 5:15). Naval power (Isa 43:14). Military power (Jer 5:16; 50:23). National greatness (Isa 13:19; Jer 51:41). Wealth (Jer 50:37; 51:13). Commerce (Eze 17:4). Manufacture of garments (Jos 7:21). Wisdom of officials (Isa 47:10; Jer 50:35).

Inhabitants of:

Idolatrous (Jer 50:38; Da 3:18). Addicted to magic (Isa 47:9,12-13; Da 2:1-2). Profane and sacrilegious (Da 5:1-3). Wicked (Isa 47:10).

As a Power Was:

Arrogant (Isa 14:13-14; Jer 50:29,31-32). Secure and self-confident (Isa 47:7-8). Grand and stately (Isa 47:1,5). Covetous (Jer 51:13). Oppressive (Isa 14:4). Cruel and destructive (Isa 14:17; 47:6; Jer 51:25; Hab 1:6-7). An instrument of God's vengeance on other nations (Jer 51:7; Isa 47:6). Armies of, described (Hab 1:7-9).

Represented by:

A great eagle (Eze 17:3). A head of gold (Da 2:32,37-38). A lion with eagle's wings (Da 7:4). Ambassadors of, sent to Hezekiah (2Ki 20:12). Figure of a woman (Rev 17).

Nebuchadnezzar, King of:

Made Jehoiakim vassal (2Ki 24:1). Besieged Jerusalem (2Ki 24:10-11). Took Jehoiachin captive to Babylon (2Ki 24:12,14-16; 2Ch 36:10). Sacked the temple (2Ki 24:13). Made Zedekiah king (2Ki 24:17). Besieged and took Jerusalem (2Ki 24:20; 25:1-4). Burned Jerusalem (2Ki 25:9-10). Took Zedekiah captive to Babylon (2Ki 25:7,11, 18-21; 2Ch 36:20). Sacked and burned the temple (2Ki 25:9,13-17; 2Ch 36:18-19). Revolt of the Israelites from, and their punishment illustrated (Eze 17). The Israelites exhorted to be subject to, and settle in (Jer 27:17; 29:1-7). Treatment of the Israelites in (2Ki 25:27-30; Da 1:3-7). Grief of the Israelites in (Ps 137:1-6). Destroyed by the Medes (Da 5:30-31). Restoration of the Israelites from (2Ch 36:23; Ezr 1; 2:1-67). The gospel preached in (1Pe 5:13). A type of Antichrist (Rev 16:19; 17:5).

Predictions Respecting:

Conquests by (Jer 21:3-10; 27:2-6; 49:28-33; Eze 21:19-32; 29:18-20). Captivity of the Israelites by (Jer 20:4-6; 22:20-26; 25:9-11; Mic 4:10). Restoration of the Israelites from (Isa 14:1-4; 44:28; 48:20; Jer 29:10; 50:4, 8,19). Destruction of (Isa 13; 14:4-22; 21:1-10; 47; Jer 25:12; 50; 51). Perpetual desolation of (Isa 13:19-22; 14:22-23; Jer 50:13,39; 51:37). Acknowledgment of Yahweh (Ps 87:4).

BACA [1133] (*balsam tree,* or *weeping*). An unknown valley of Israel (Ps 84:6). It refers figuratively to an experience of sorrow turned into joy.

BACHRITES *See Beker, Bekerite.*

BACKBITING

Evil of—

Ps 15:1 LORD, who may dwell in your sanctuary? Who may live on your holy hill?

²He whose walk is blameless and who does what is righteous, who speaks the truth from his heart ³and has no slander on his tongue, who does his neighbor no wrong and casts no slur on his fellowman,

Pr 25:23 As a north wind brings rain, so a sly tongue brings angry looks.

Ro 1:29 They have become filled with every kind of wickedness, evil, greed and depravity. They are full of envy, murder, strife, deceit and malice. They are gossips, ³⁰ slanderers, God-haters, insolent, arrogant and boastful; they invent ways of doing evil; they disobey their parents;

2Co 12:20 For I am afraid that when I come I may not find you as I want you to be, and you may not find me as you want me to be. I fear that there may be quarreling, jealousy, outbursts of anger, factions, slander, gossip, arrogance and disorder.

See Accusation, False; Slander; Speaking, Evil.

BACKSLIDERS

NIV+ BACKSLIDING, BACKSLIDINGS

Described as:

Blind—

2Pe 1:9 But if anyone does not have them, he is nearsighted and blind, and has forgotten that he has been cleansed from his past sins. (+Rev 3:17)

Godless—

2Jn 9 Anyone who runs ahead and does not continue in the teaching of Christ does not have God; whoever continues in the teaching has both the Father and the Son.

Idolaters—

1Co 10:7 Do not be idolaters, as some of them were; as it is written: "The people sat down to eat and drink and got up to indulge in pagan revelry."

Lukewarm (Rev 3:15-16)

Grumblers—

Ex 17:7 And he called the place Massah and Meribah because the Israelites quarreled and because they tested the LORD saying, "Is the LORD among us or not?"

1Co 10:10 And do not grumble, as some of them did—and were killed by the destroying angel.

Forsaking God—

Jer 17:13 O LORD, the hope of Israel, all who forsake you will be put to shame. Those who turn away from you will be written in the dust because they have forsaken the LORD, the spring of living water.

Tempting Christ—

1Co 10:9 We should not test the Lord, as some of them did—and were killed by snakes.

Forsaking God's covenant—

Ps 78:10 they did not keep God's covenant and refused to live by his law. ¹¹They forgot what he had done, the wonders he had shown them.

Pr 2:17 who has left the partner of her youth and ignored the covenant she made before God.

Turned aside to evil—

Ps 125:5 But those who turn to crooked ways the LORD will banish with the evildoers. Peace be upon Israel.

1Ti 5:15 Some have in fact already turned away to follow Satan.

Unfit for God's kingdom—

Lk 9:62 Jesus replied, "No one who puts his hand to the plow and looks back is fit for service in the kingdom of God."

God's Forbearance With:

Dt 32:5 They have acted corruptly toward him; to their shame they are no longer his children, but a warped and crooked generation. ⁶Is this the way you repay the LORD, O foolish and unwise people? Is he not your Father, your Creator, who made you and formed you?

Dt 32:26 I said I would scatter them and blot out their memory from mankind, ²⁷but I dreaded the taunt of the enemy, lest the adversary misunderstand and say, 'Our hand has triumphed; the LORD has not done all this.'"

Ezr 9:10 "But now, O our God, what can we say after this? For we have disregarded the commands (+Ezr 9:14)

Isa 42:3 A bruised reed he will not break, and a smoldering wick he will not snuff out. In faithfulness he will bring forth justice;

God's Concern for:

Dt 32:28 They are a nation without sense, there is no discernment in them. ²⁹If only they were wise and would understand this and discern what their end will be!

Ps 81:13 "If my people would but listen to me, if Israel would follow my ways, ¹⁴how quickly would I subdue their enemies and turn my hand against their foes!

Isa 1:4 Ah, sinful nation, a people loaded with guilt, a brood of evildoers, children given to corruption! They have forsaken the LORD; they have spurned the Holy One of Israel and turned their backs on him.

⁵Why should you be beaten anymore? Why do you persist in rebellion? Your whole head is injured, your whole heart afflicted. ⁶From the sole of your foot to the top of your head there is no soundness—only wounds and welts and open sores, not cleansed or bandaged or soothed with oil.

⁷Your country is desolate, your cities burned with fire; your fields are being stripped by foreigners right before you, laid waste as when overthrown by strangers. (+Isa 1:8-9)

Isa 1:21 See how the faithful city has become a harlot! She once was full of justice; righteousness used to dwell in her—but now murderers! ²²Your silver has become dross, your choice wine is diluted with water.

Isa 65:2 All day long I have held out my hands to an obstinate people, who walk in ways not good, pursuing their own imaginations— ³a people who continually provoke me to my very face, offering sacrifices in gardens and burning incense on altars of brick;

Jer 2:5 This is what the LORD says: "What fault did your fathers find in me, that they strayed so far from me? They followed worthless idols and became worthless themselves.

Jer 2:11 Has a nation ever changed its gods? (Yet they are not gods at all.) But my people have exchanged their Glory for worthless idols. [12]Be appalled at this, O heavens, and shudder with great horror," declares the LORD. [13]"My people have committed two sins: They have forsaken me, the spring of living water, and have dug their own cisterns, broken cisterns that cannot hold water.

Jer 2:17 Have you not brought this on yourselves by forsaking the LORD your God when he led you in the way?

Jer 2:31 "You of this generation, consider the word of the LORD: "Have I been a desert to Israel or a land of great darkness? Why do my people say, 'We are free to roam; we will come to you no more'? [32]Does a maiden forget her jewelry, a bride her wedding ornaments? Yet my people have forgotten me, days without number.

Jer 18:13 Therefore this is what the LORD says: "Inquire among the nations: Who has ever heard anything like this? A most horrible thing has been done by Virgin Israel. [14]Does the snow of Lebanon ever vanish from its rocky slopes? Do its cool waters from distant sources ever cease to flow? [15]Yet my people have forgotten me; they burn incense to worthless idols, which made them stumble in their ways and in the ancient paths. They made them walk in bypaths and on roads not built up.

Jer 50:6 "My people have been lost sheep; their shepherds have led them astray and caused them to roam on the mountains. They wandered over mountain and hill and forgot their own resting place. (+Hos 6:4-11; 11:1-4)

Hos 11:7 My people are determined to turn from me. Even if they call to the Most High, he will by no means exalt them.

[8]"How can I give you up, Ephraim? How can I hand you over, Israel? How can I treat you like Admah? How can I make you like Zeboiim? My heart is changed within me; all my compassion is aroused. (+Hos 11:9)

Mt 23:37 "O Jerusalem, Jerusalem, you who kill the prophets and stone those sent to you, how often I have longed to gather your children together, as a hen gathers her chicks under her wings, but you were not willing.

Warnings to:

Dt 4:25 After you have had children and grandchildren and have lived in the land a long time—if you then become corrupt and make any kind of idol, doing evil in the eyes of the LORD your God and provoking him to anger, [26]I call heaven and earth as witnesses against you this day that you will quickly perish from the land that you are crossing the Jordan to possess. You will not live there long but will certainly be destroyed. [27]The LORD will scatter you among the peoples, and only a few of you will survive among the nations to which the LORD will drive you. [28]There you will worship man-made gods of wood and stone, which cannot see or hear or eat or smell. (+Dt 28:58-59)

Dt 29:18 Make sure there is no man or woman, clan or tribe among you today whose heart turns away from the LORD our God to go and worship the gods of those nations; make sure there is no root among you that produces such bitter poison.

Dt 31:16 And the LORD said to Moses: "You are going to rest with your fathers, and these people will soon prostitute themselves to the foreign gods of the land they are entering. They will forsake me and break the covenant I made with them. [17]On that day I will become angry with them and forsake them; I will hide my face from them, and they will be destroyed. Many disasters and difficulties will

come upon them, and on that day they will ask, 'Have not these disasters come upon us because our God is not with us?' [18]And I will certainly hide my face on that day because of all their wickedness in turning to other gods. (+1Ki 9:6-9; 2Ch 7:19-22; Jer 7:13-34; 11:9-17; Mk 9:50)

Corrective Judgments Upon:

Dt 32:16 They made him jealous with their foreign gods and angered him with their detestable idols. [17]They sacrificed to demons, which are not God—gods they had not known, gods that recently appeared, gods your fathers did not fear. [18]You deserted the Rock, who fathered you; you forgot the God who gave you birth.

[19]The LORD saw this and rejected them because he was angered by his sons and daughters. [20]"I will hide my face from them," he said, "and see what their end will be; for they are a perverse generation, children who are unfaithful. [21]They made me jealous by what is no god and angered me with their worthless idols. I will make them envious by those who are not a people; I will make them angry by a nation that has no understanding. [22]For a fire has been kindled by my wrath, one that burns to the realm of death below. It will devour the earth and its harvests and set afire the foundations of the mountains.

[23]"I will heap calamities upon them and spend my arrows against them. [24]I will send wasting famine against them, consuming pestilence and deadly plague; I will send against them the fangs of wild beasts, the venom of vipers that glide in the dust. [25]In the street the sword will make them childless; in their homes terror will reign. Young men and young women will perish, infants and gray-haired men.

1Ki 8:33 "When your people Israel have been defeated by an enemy because they have sinned against you, and when they turn back to you and confess your name, praying and making supplication to you in this temple, (+2Ch 7:19-22)

Ne 9:26 "But they were disobedient and rebelled against you; they put your law behind their backs. They killed your prophets, who had admonished them in order to turn them back to you; they committed awful blasphemies. (+Ne 9:27-30)

Job 34:26 He punishes them for their wickedness where everyone can see them, [27]because they turned from following him and had no regard for any of his ways. (+Isa 50:1; Jer 8:1-4)

Jer 8:5 Why then have these people turned away? Why does Jerusalem always turn away? They cling to deceit; they refuse to return. (+Jer 8:6-13)

Jer 8:14 "Why are we sitting here? Gather together! Let us flee to the fortified cities and perish there! For the LORD our God has doomed us to perish and given us poisoned water to drink, because we have sinned against him. [15]We hoped for peace but no good has come, for a time of healing but there was only terror. (+Jer 16:22; Eze 22:18-22; Hos 8:14; 9:1-17)

Called to Repentance:

Isa 30:9 These are rebellious people, deceitful children, children unwilling to listen to the LORD's instruction.

Isa 30:15 This is what the Sovereign LORD, the Holy One of Israel, says: "In repentance and rest is your salvation, in quietness and trust is your strength, but you would have none of it.

Isa 31:6 Return to him you have so greatly revolted against, O Israelites.

Jer 3:4 Have you not just called to me: 'My Father, my friend from my youth, [5]will you always be angry? Will your wrath continue forever?' This is how you talk, but you do all the evil you can."

⁶During the reign of King Josiah, the LORD said to me, "Have you seen what faithless Israel has done? She has gone up on every high hill and under every spreading tree and has committed adultery there. ⁷I thought that after she had done all this she would return to me but she did not, and her unfaithful sister Judah saw it.

Jer 3:12 Go, proclaim this message toward the north: "'Return, faithless Israel,' declares the LORD, 'I will frown on you no longer, for I am merciful,' declares the LORD, 'I will not be angry forever. ¹³Only acknowledge your guilt—you have rebelled against the LORD your God, you have scattered your favors to foreign gods under every spreading tree, and have not obeyed me,'" declares the LORD.

¹⁴"Return, faithless people," declares the LORD, "for I am your husband. I will choose you—one from a town and two from a clan—and bring you to Zion.

Jer 3:21 A cry is heard on the barren heights, the weeping and pleading of the people of Israel, because they have perverted their ways and have forgotten the LORD their God.

²²"Return, faithless people; I will cure you of backsliding." "Yes, we will come to you, for you are the LORD our God.

Jer 4:14 O Jerusalem, wash the evil from your heart and be saved. How long will you harbor wicked thoughts?

Jer 6:16 This is what the LORD says: "Stand at the crossroads and look; ask for the ancient paths, ask where the good way is, and walk in it, and you will find rest for your souls. But you said, 'We will not walk in it.'

Hos 14:1 Return, O Israel, to the LORD your God. Your sins have been your downfall!

Mal 3:7 Ever since the time of your forefathers you have turned away from my decrees and have not kept them. Return to me, and I will return to you," says the LORD Almighty. "But you ask, 'How are we to return?'

Rev 2:4 Yet I hold this against you: You have forsaken your first love. ⁵Remember the height from which you have fallen! Repent and do the things you did at first. If you do not repent, I will come to you and remove your lampstand from its place.

Rev 2:20 Nevertheless, I have this against you: You tolerate that woman Jezebel, who calls herself a prophetess. By her teaching she misleads my servants into sexual immorality and the eating of food sacrificed to idols. ²¹I have given her time to repent of her immorality, but she is unwilling. ²²So I will cast her on a bed of suffering, and I will make those who commit adultery with her suffer intensely, unless they repent of her ways.

Rev 3:2 Wake up! Strengthen what remains and is about to die, for I have not found your deeds complete in the sight of my God. ³Remember, therefore, what you have received and heard; obey it, and repent. But if you do not wake up, I will come like a thief, and you will not know at what time I will come to you. (+Rev 3:18-19)

Promises to Penitent:

Hos 14:4 "I will heal their waywardness and love them freely, for my anger has turned away from them.

Of finding the Lord—

Dt 4:29 But if from there you seek the LORD your God, you will find him if you look for him with all your heart and with all your soul. ³⁰When you are in distress and all these things have happened to you, then in later days you will return to the LORD your God and obey him. (+Dt 4:31)

2Ch 15:2 He went out to meet Asa and said to him, "Listen to me, Asa and all Judah and Benjamin. The LORD is with you when you are with him. If you seek him, he will be found by you, but if you forsake him, he will forsake you. ³For a long time Israel was without the true God, without a priest to teach and without the law. ⁴But in their distress they turned to the LORD, the God of Israel, and sought him, and he was found by them.

Of spiritual enlightenment—

Isa 29:24 Those who are wayward in spirit will gain understanding; those who complain will accept instruction." (+Jer 3:14-19)

Hos 6:3 Let us acknowledge the LORD; let us press on to acknowledge him. As surely as the sun rises, he will appear; he will come to us like the winter rains, like the spring rains that water the earth."

Of restoration (Dt 30:1-10)—

Pr 24:16 for though a righteous man falls seven times, he rises again, but the wicked are brought down by calamity.

Isa 57:18 I have seen his ways, but I will heal him; I will guide him and restore comfort to him, ¹⁹creating praise on the lips of the mourners in Israel. Peace, peace, to those far and near," says the LORD. "And I will heal them." (+Hos 14:4)

Zec 10:6 "I will strengthen the house of Judah and save the house of Joseph. I will restore them because I have compassion on them. They will be as though I had not rejected them, for I am the LORD their God and I will answer them.

Of temporal prosperity—

Lev 26:40 "'But if they will confess their sins and the sins of their fathers—their treachery against me and their hostility toward me, ⁴¹which made me hostile toward them so that I sent them into the land of their enemies—then when their uncircumcised hearts are humbled and they pay for their sin, ⁴²I will remember my covenant with Jacob and my covenant with Isaac and my covenant with Abraham, and I will remember the land. (+Dt 30:1-5,7-10; Job 22:23-30)

Return of (Jer 31:18-19)—

Jer 50:4 "In those days, at that time," declares the LORD, "the people of Israel and the people of Judah together will go in tears to seek the LORD their God. ⁵They will ask the way to Zion and turn their faces toward it. They will come and bind themselves to the LORD in an everlasting covenant that will not be forgotten.

Hos 3:5 Afterward the Israelites will return and seek the LORD their God and David their king. They will come trembling to the LORD and to his blessings in the last days.

Jnh 2:4 I said, 'I have been banished from your sight; yet I will look again toward your holy temple.'

Punishment of:

By temporal loss (Dt 28:15-62)—

Dt 28:63 Just as it pleased the LORD to make you prosper and increase in number, so it will please him to ruin and destroy you. You will be uprooted from the land you are entering to possess. (+Dt 28:64-68)

Ezr 8:22 I was ashamed to ask the king for soldiers and horsemen to protect us from enemies on the road, because we had told the king, "The gracious hand of our God is on everyone who looks to him, but his great anger is against all who forsake him."

Jer 13:24 "I will scatter you like chaff driven by the desert wind. ²⁵This is your lot, the portion I have decreed for you," declares the LORD, "because you have forgotten me and trusted in false gods. (+Eze 15)

Am 2:4 This is what the LORD says: "For three sins of Judah, even for four, I will not turn back [my wrath]. Because they have rejected the law of the LORD and have not kept his decrees, because they have been led astray by false gods, the gods their ancestors followed, **5**I will send fire upon Judah that will consume the fortresses of Jerusalem."

6This is what the LORD says: "For three sins of Israel, even for four, I will not turn back [my wrath]. They sell the righteous for silver, and the needy for a pair of sandals.

By being overthrown by enemies (Nu 14:43; Dt 4:27-28; Jdg 2:12-15; 2Ki 18:11,; 12; 2Ch 29:6-8)—

Ps 78:40 How often they rebelled against him in the desert and grieved him in the wasteland! **41**Again and again they put God to the test; they vexed the Holy One of Israel. **42**They did not remember his power—the day he redeemed them from the oppressor, **43**the day he displayed his miraculous signs in Egypt, his wonders in the region of Zoan.

Ps 78:56 But they put God to the test and rebelled against the Most High; they did not keep his statutes. **57**Like their fathers they were disloyal and faithless, as unreliable as a faulty bow. **58**They angered him with their high places; they aroused his jealousy with their idols. **59**When God heard them, he was very angry; he rejected Israel completely. **60**He abandoned the tabernacle of Shiloh, the tent he had set up among men. **61**He sent [the ark of] his might into captivity, his splendor into the hands of the enemy. **62**He gave his people over to the sword; he was very angry with his inheritance. **63**Fire consumed their young men, and their maidens had no wedding songs; **64**their priests were put to the sword, and their widows could not weep.

By being forsaken of God—

2Ch 24:20 Then the Spirit of God came upon Zechariah son of Jehoiada the priest. He stood before the people and said, "This is what God says: 'Why do you disobey the LORD's commands? You will not prosper. Because you have forsaken the LORD, he has forsaken you.'"

Isa 2:6 You have abandoned your people, the house of Jacob. They are full of superstitions from the East; they practice divination like the Philistines and clasp hands with pagans.

Jer 6:30 They are called rejected silver, because the LORD has rejected them."

Jer 12:7 "I will forsake my house, abandon my inheritance; I will give the one I love into the hands of her enemies.

Jer 14:7 Although our sins testify against us, O LORD, do something for the sake of your name. For our backsliding is great; we have sinned against you. (+Jer 14:10)

Jer 15:1 Then the LORD said to me: "Even if Moses and Samuel were to stand before me, my heart would not go out to this people. Send them away from my presence! Let them go!

Hos 4:6 my people are destroyed from lack of knowledge. "Because you have rejected knowledge, I also reject you as my priests; because you have ignored the law of your God, I also will ignore your children. (+Hos 4:10)

By bearing the fruits of their sin—

Pr 14:14 The faithless will be fully repaid for their ways, and the good man rewarded for his.

Eze 11:21 But as for those whose hearts are devoted to their vile images and detestable idols, I will bring down on their own heads what they have done, declares the Sovereign LORD."

Eze 16:43 "'Because you did not remember the days of your youth but enraged me with all these things, I will

surely bring down on your head what you have done, declares the Sovereign LORD. Did you not add lewdness to all your other detestable practices?

Eze 23:35 "Therefore this is what the Sovereign LORD says: Since you have forgotten me and thrust me behind your back, you must bear the consequences of your lewdness and prostitution."

Instances of:

Saul (1Sa 15:11,26-28). Solomon (1Ki 11:4-40; Ne 13:26). Amon (2Ki 21:22-23). Rehoboam (2Ch 12:1-2). Joash (2Ch 24:24). Amaziah (2Ch 25:27). Jonah (Jnh 1:3). Disciples of Jesus (Jn 6:66). Peter (Mt 26:69-75). Corinthian Christians (1Co 5:1-8).

Galatians—

Gal 1:6 I am astonished that you are so quickly deserting the one who called you by the grace of Christ and are turning to a different gospel—

Gal 3:1 You foolish Galatians! Who has bewitched you? Before your very eyes Jesus Christ was clearly portrayed as crucified.

Gal 4:9 But now that you know God—or rather are known by God—how is it that you are turning back to those weak and miserable principles? Do you wish to be enslaved by them all over again? **10**You are observing special days and months and seasons and years! **11**I fear for you, that somehow I have wasted my efforts on you.

Gal 5:6 For in Christ Jesus neither circumcision nor uncircumcision has any value. The only thing that counts is faith expressing itself through love.

7You were running a good race. Who cut in on you and kept you from obeying the truth?

Hymenaeus and Alexander (1Ti 1:20). Phygelus and Hermogenes (2Ti 1:15).

Demas—

2Ti 4:10 for Demas, because he loved this world, has deserted me and has gone to Thessalonica. Crescens has gone to Galatia, and Titus to Dalmatia.

Churches of Asia (2Ti 1:15; Rev 2:4; 3:2-3)—

Rev 3:15 I know your deeds, that you are neither cold nor hot. I wish you were either one or the other! **16**So, because you are lukewarm—neither hot nor cold—I am about to spit you out of my mouth. **17**You say, 'I am rich; I have acquired wealth and do not need a thing.' But you do not realize that you are wretched, pitiful, poor, blind and naked. **18**I counsel you to buy from me gold refined in the fire, so you can become rich; and white clothes to wear, so you can cover your shameful nakedness; and salve to put on your eyes, so you can see.

See Apostasy; Backsliding; Church, The Body of Believers, Evil Conditions of; Reprobacy.

BACKSLIDING [294, 5412].

NIV+ BACKSLIDINGS

Is turning from God (1Ki 11:9). Is leaving the first love (Rev 2:4). Is departing from the simplicity of the gospel (2Co 11:3; Gal 3:1-3; 5:4,7). God is displeased at (Ps 78:57,59). Warnings against (Ps 85:8; 1Co 10:12). Guilt and consequences of (Nu 14:43; Ps 125:5; Isa 59:2,9-11; Jer 5:6; 8:5,13; 15:6; Lk 9:62). Brings its own punishment (Pr 14:14; Jer 2:19). A haughty spirit leads to (Pr 16:18). Leaning to (Pr 24:16; Hos 11:7). Liable to continue and increase (Jer 8:5; 14:7). Exhortations to return from (2Ch 30:6; Isa 31:6; Jer 3:12,14,22; Hos 6:1). Pray to be restored from (Ps 80:3; 85:4; La 5:21). Punishment of tempting others to the sin of (Pr 28:10; Mt 18:6). Not hopeless (Ps 37:24; Pr 24:16). Attempt to bring back those guilty of

(Gal 6:1; Jas 5:10,20). Sin of, to be confessed (Isa 59:12-14; Jer 3:13,14; 14:7-9). Pardon of, promised (2Ch 7:14; Jer 3:12; 31:20; 36:3). Healing of, promised (Jer 3:22; Hos 14:4). Afflictions sent to heal (Hos 5:15). Blessedness of those who keep from (Pr 28:15; Isa 26:3-4; Col 1:21-23). Despised by believers (Ps 101:3).

Instances of Israel's Backsliding:
At Meribah (Ex 17:1-7), when Aaron made the golden calf (Ex 32), after Joshua's death (Jdg 2), during Asa's reign (2Ch 15), Hezekiah's reign (2Ch 30:2-12).
See Apostasy; Backsliders.

BACUTH *See Allon Bacuth.*

BAD COMPANY *See Company, Evil.*

BADGER *See Sea Cow.*

BAG [3038, 3967, 3998, 7655, *1186+2400, 4385*].
NIV+ BAGS, BAGGAGE
Sack or pouch made for holding anything. Many kinds are mentioned in Scripture (Dt 25:13; 2Ki 5:23; Mt 10:10).

BAGPIPE (RSV); NIV "pipes." A musical instrument (Da 3:5,7,10,15). *See Music, Instruments of.*

BAHURIM, BAHARUMITE [1038, 1049] (*young men*). A village between Jericho and Jerusalem, on the eastern slope of the Mount of Olives; modern Ras et-Tmim (2Sa 3:16; 16:5; 17:18; 19:16; 1Ki 2:8).

BAIL *See Creditor; Debt; Debtor; Security, For Debt.*

BAJITH NIV "temple"; a place of idolatrous worship in Moab (Isa 15:2). *See Idolatry; Sanctuary, 4; Shrine.*

BAKBAKKAR [1320] (*investigator*). A Levite (1Ch 9:15).

BAKBUK [1317] (*gurgling [sound coming out of a bottle]*). The founder of a family of temple servants who returned from the Captivity with Zerubbabel (Ezr 2:51; Ne 7:53).

BAKBUKIAH [1319] (*Yahweh pours out*). A name occurring three times in Nehemiah (Ne 11:17; 12:9,25), a Levite in high office in Jerusalem right after the Exile.

BAKER [685].
NIV+ BAKE, BAKED, BAKERS, BAKES, BAKING
(1Sa 8:13; Jer 37:21; Hos 7:4,6). Pharaoh's chief baker (Ge 40).
See Bread.

BALAAM [1189, 962] (possibly *Baal [lord] of the people* BDB; possibly *the clan brings forth* IDB; *devourer, glutton* KB).
NIV+ BALAAM'S
Son of Beor. From Mesopotamia (Dt 23:4). A soothsayer (Jos 13:22). A prophet (Nu 24:2-9; 2Pe 2:15-16). Balak sends for, to curse Israel (Nu 22:5-7; Jos 24:9; Ne 13:2; Mic 6:5). Anger of, rebuked by his donkey (Nu 22:22-35; 2Pe 2:16). Counsel of, an occasion of Israel's corruption with the Midianites (Nu 31:16; Rev 2:14-15). Greed of (2Pe 2:15; Jude 11). Death of (Nu 31:8; Jos 13:22).

BALAC *See Balak.*

BALADAN [1156] Father of Merodach-Baladan (2Ki 20:12; Isa 39:1).

BALAH [1163] (*old, worn out*). A city of Simeon (Jos 19:3). Called Bilhah (1Ch 4:29).

BALAK [1192, *963*] (*devastator*).
NIV+ BALAK'S
King of Moab (Nu 22:4; Jos 24:9; Jdg 11:25; Mic 6:5). Tries to bribe Balaam to curse Israel (Nu 22:5-7,15-17).
See Balaam.

BALANCES [4404, 6369, 7144].
NIV+ BALANCE
Used for weighing (Job 31:6; Isa 40:12,15; Eze 5:1). Money weighed with (Isa 46:6; Jer 32:10). Must be just (Lev 19:36; Pr 16:11; Eze 45:10).

False Balance:
Used (Hos 12:7; Am 8:5; Mic 6:11), an abomination (Pr 11:1; 20:23).

Figurative:
(Job 6:2; 31:6; Ps 62:9; Isa 40:12; Da 5:27; Rev 6:5).

BALD LOCUST *See Insects.*

BALDNESS [1477, 6867, 7944, 7947+, 7949].
NIV+ BALD, BALDHEAD
(Lev 13:40,41). A judgment (Isa 3:24; Jer 47:5; 48:37; Eze 7:18). Artificial, a sign of mourning (Isa 22:12; Jer 16:6; Eze 27:31; 29:18; Am 8:10; Mic 1:16). Artificial, as an idolatrous practice, forbidden (Lev 21:5; Dt 14:1).
Instance of: Elisha (2Ki 2:23).

BALL [1885]. Playing at (Isa 22:18).

BALM [6057, 7661]. A medicinal balsam (Ge 37:25; 43:11; Jer 8:22; 46:11; 51:8; Eze 27:17).

BALSAM TREES *See Tree.*

BAMAH [1196] (*high location [for cultic worship]*). A high place (Eze 20:29).

BAMOTH [1199] (*high locations [for cultic worship]*).
NIV+ BAMOTH BAAL
A camping place of the Israelites (Nu 21:19-20).

BAMOTH BAAL [1200] (*high places for Baal [worship]*).
NIV+ BAAL, BAMOTH
A city assigned to Reuben as part of his inheritance (Jos 13:17).

BANI [1220] (*descendant*).
1. KJV a Gadite; NIV "son of" (2Sa 23:36).
2. Levite (1Ch 6:46).
3. Descendant of Judah (1Ch 9:4).
4. Levite (Ne 3:17).
5. Levite (Ne 9:4).
6. Levite (Ne 11:22).
7. Levite (Ne 10:13).
8. Man who signed covenant (Ne 10:14).
9. Ancestor of Jews who returned from the Captivity (Ezr 10:29).
10. KJV Bani; NIV "descendants of" (Ezr 10:38).

BANISHMENT [*1763, 5610, 5927, 5615*].
NIV+ BANISH, BANISHED
(Ezr 7:26). Of Adam and Eve, from Eden (Ge 3:22-24). Of Cain, to be "a restless wanderer" (Ge 4:14). Of Jews, from Rome (Ac 18:2). Of John, to Patmos (Rev 1:9).
See Exile.

BANK [1473, 1536, 3338, 8557, *3204*].

NIV+ BANKERS, BANKS, EMBANKMENT

A primitive kind of banking was known in ancient times. Israelites could not charge each other interest (Ex 22:25) but could charge Gentiles (Dt 23:20). The concept of a bank as a savings institution was unknown. *See Borrowing; Interest; Lending.*

BANNER [253, 1839, 1840, 5812].

NIV+ BANNERS

Banners, ensigns, or standards (not flags) were used in ancient times for military, national, and ecclesiastical purposes very much as they are today (Nu 2:2; Isa 5:26; 11:10; Jer 4:21).

BANQUET [3516+, 5492, 10389, 10447, *804, 1141, 1270, 1531*].

NIV+ BANQUETS

Social feasting was common among the Hebrews. There were feasts on birthdays (Ge 40:20), marriages (Ge 29:22), funerals (2Sa 3:35), grape-gatherings (Jdg 9:27), sheep-shearing (1Sa 25:2,36), sacrifices (Ex 34:15), and on other occasions. Often a second invitation was sent on the day of the feast (Lk 7:45), and their feet were washed (Lk 7:44). Banquets were often invigorated with music, singing, and dancing (Lk 15:23-25).

BAPTISM [966+, *967, 968*] (*dip,* or *immerse*).

NIV+ BAPTIZE, BAPTISMS, BAPTIST, BAPTIZED, BAPTIZING

As administered by John (Mt 3:5-12; Jn 3:23; Ac 13:24; 19:4). Sanctioned by Christ's submission to it (Mt 3:13-15; Lk 3:21). Adopted by Christ (Jn 3:22; 4:1-2). Appointed an ordinance of the Christian church (Mt 28:19-20; Mk 16:15-16). To be administered in the name of the Father, the Son, and the Holy Spirit (Mt 28:19). Water, the outward and visible sign in (Ac 8:36; 10:47). Regeneration, the inward and spiritual grace of (Jn 3:3,5-6; Ro 6:3-4,11). Remission of sins, signified by (Ac 2:38; 22:16). Unity of the church effected by (1Co 12:13; Gal 3:27-28). Confession of sin necessary to (Mt 3:6). Repentance necessary to (Ac 2:38). Faith necessary to (Ac 8:37; 18:8). There is but one (Eph 4:5).

Administered to:

Individuals (Ac 8:38; 9:18). Households (Ac 16:15; 1Co 1:16). Emblematic of the influences of the Holy Spirit (Mt 3:11; Tit 3:5). Typified (1Co 10:2; 1Pe 3:20-21).

BAR An Aramaic word meaning "son"; in the NT used as a prefix (Mt 16:17, KJV). *See Barabbas; Barnabas; Barsabbas; Bartholomew; Bar-Jesus; Bar-Jona.*

BARABBAS [972] (*son of a father,* possibly *son of a rabbi [teacher]*). A prisoner released by Pilate (Mt 27:16-26; Mk 15:7-15; Lk 23:18-25; Jn 18:40; Ac 3:14).

BARACHEL *See Barakel.*

BARACHIAH, BARAKIAH *See Berekiah, 5.*

BARAH *See Beth Barah, Beth-Barah.*

BARAK [1399, *973*] (*lightning*).

NIV+ BARAK'S

Israelite who defeated Sisera at the command of Deborah the judge (Jdg 4-5; 1Sa 12:11; Heb 11:32).

BARAKEL [1387]. (*God [El] blesses*). A Buzite, whose son Elihu was the last of Job's friends to reason with him (Job 32:2,6).

BARBARIAN [975]. A foreigner (Ac 28:2-4; Ro 1:14; 1Co 14:11; Col 3:11). *See Strangers.*

BARBER [1647].

NIV+ BARBER'S

A barber's razor (Eze 5:1)

BARHUMITE [1372]. Azmaveth the Barhumite, one of the Thirty (2Sa 23:31)

BARIAH [1377] (possibly *board, bar; fugitive* ISBE; *descendant* KB). Son of Shecaniah (1Ch 3:22).

BAR-JESUS [979] (*son of Joshua*). A false prophet (Ac 13:6).

BAR-JONA NIV "Simon son of Jonah," surname of Peter (Mt 16:17).

BARKOS [1401] (*son of [pagan god] Kos*). A Jew whose descendants returned from the Exile (Ezr 2:53; Ne 7:55).

BARLEY [8555, *3208, 3209*].

A product of: Egypt (Ex 9:31), Israel (Dt 8:8; 1Ch 11:13; Jer 41:8).

Fed to horses (1Ki 4:28). Used in offerings (Nu 5:15; Eze 45:15). Selling of (2Ch 2:10; Hos 3:2). Tribute in (2Ch 27:5). Priests estimated value of (Lev 27:16; 2Ki 7:1; Rev 6:6). Absalom burns Joab's field of (2Sa 14:30).

Loaves of (Jn 6:9,13).

BARN [662, 4476, *630*].

NIV+ BARNS

A storehouse for crops (Dt 28:8; Ps 144:13; Pr 3:10; Hag 2:19; Mt 3:12; 6:26; 13:30; Lk 12:18,24).

See Granary; Storehouse.

BARNABAS [982] (*son of comfort*). Also called Joseph (Ac 4:36). A prophet (Ac 13:1). An apostle (Ac 14:14). A Levite who gave his possessions to be owned in common with other disciples (Ac 4:36-37). Goes to Tarsus to find Paul, brings him to Antioch (Ac 11:25-26). Accompanies Paul to Jerusalem (Ac 11:30). Returns with Paul to Antioch (Ac 12:25).

Goes With Paul: To, Seleucia (Ac 13), Iconium (Ac 14:1-7).

Called Jupiter (Ac 14:12-18). Goes to Derbe (Ac 14:20). Is sent as delegate to Jerusalem (Ac 15; Gal 2:1-9). Estranged from Paul (Ac 15:36-39). Is reconciled to Paul (1Co 9:6). Piety of (Ac 11:22-24). Devotion of, to Jesus (Ac 15:25-26).

BARNEA *See Kadesh Barnea.*

BARREL An clay jar (1Ki 17:12,14,16; 18:33). *See Jar(s); Pottery.*

BARRENNESS [1678, 4497, 6808, 6829, 9039, 9155, 9332, *5096*].

NIV+ BARREN

Inability of women to bear children. A reproach (Ge 30:22-23; 1Sa 1:6,7; 2:1-11; Isa 4:1; Lk 1:25). Miraculously removed. *See Childlessness.*

Instances of:

Sarai (Ge 17:15-21), Rebekah (Ge 25:21), Manoah's wife (Jdg 13), Hannah (1Sa 1:6-20), Elizabeth (Lk 1:5-25).

Sent as a judgment (Ge 20:17-18).

BARSABBAS, BARSABAS *[984]* (*son of the Sabbath* or *son of Saba*).
1. Surname of Joseph (Ac 1:23).
2. Judas (Ac 15:22).

BARTER [4126, 5989]. (Job 6:27; 41:6; La 1:11). *See Commerce.*

BARTHOLOMEW *[978]* (*son of Talmai*). One of the apostles (Mt 10:3; Mk 3:18; Lk 6:14; Ac 1:13).

BARTIMAEUS *[985]* (*son of Timai*, or *son of uncleanness*). A blind man (Mt 20:29-34; Mk 10:46-52; Lk 18:35-43).

BARUCH [1358] (*be blessed*).
1. An amanuensis of Jeremiah (Jer 32:12-16; 36:4-32; 43:3-6; 45:1-2).
2. Son of Zabbai (Ne 3:20; 10:6).
3. A descendant of Perez (Ne 11:5).

BARUCH, BOOK OF Jewish pseudepigraphal book found in the Apocrypha; alleging to be a treatise by Jeremiah's scribe Baruch to Jewish exiles in Babylon.

BARZILLAI [1367] (*[made] of iron*).
1. A friend of David (2Sa 17:27-29; 19:31-39; 1Ki 2:7; Ezr 2:61; Ne 7:63).
2. Father of Adriel (2Sa 21:8).
3. A priest (Ezr 2:61; Ne 7:63).

BASE FELLOWS Hebrew derogatory term "sons of Belial"; NIV "evil" or "wicked men" (Dt 13:13; 1Sa 2:12; 10:27; 25:17; 30:22; 1Ki 21:10; 2Ch 13:7). *See Wicked.*

BASEMATH, BASHEMATH, BASMATH [1412] (*fragrant*).
1. Wife of Esau (Ge 26:34).
2. Ishmael's daughter (Ge 36:3-4,13,17). Also called Mahalath (Ge 28:9).
3. Solomon's daughter, called Basemath (1Ki 4:15).

BASHAN [824+1421, 1421] (*fertile stoneless plain*). A region E of the Jordan and N of Arnon (Ge 14:5); modern Golan Heights. Og, king of (Jos 13:12). Allotted to the two and one half tribes, which had their possession E of the Jordan (Nu 32:33; Dt 3:10-14; Jos 12:4-6; 13:29-31; 17:1). Invaded and taken by Hazael, king of Syria (2Ki 10:32-33). Retaken by Jehoash (2Ki 13:25). Fertility and productivity of (Isa 33:9; Jer 50:19; Na 1:4). Forests of famous (Isa 2:13; Eze 27:6; Zec 11:2). Distinguished for its fine cattle (Dt 32:14; Ps 22:12; Eze 39:18; Am 4:1; Mic 7:14).
See Argob; Ashtoreth; Edrei; Jair.

BASHAN-HAVOTH-JAIR *See Havvoth Jair.*

BASIC PRINCIPLES OF THIS WORLD [5122+3180]. Legalism and human traditions opposed to faith in Christ (Gal 4:3; Col 2:8,20). *See Commandments and Statutes, of Men; Legalism.*

BASIN [3963, 6195, *3781*].
NIV+ BASINS, WASHBASIN
Made of gold (1Ki 7:50; 1Ch 28:17; 2Ch 4:8,22; Ezr 1:10; 8:27), bronze (Ex 27:3; 38:3; 1Ki 7:45).
See Bronze Basin; Bronze Sea; Tabernacle.

BASKET [406, 1857, 3244, 3990, 3998, 6130, 8955, 9310, *4914*, *5083*].
NIV+ BASKETFULS, BASKETS
(Ge 40:16-17; Ex 29:3,23,32; Lev 8:2; Nu 6:15; Dt

26:2; 28:5, 17; 2Ki 10:7). Received the fragments after the miracles of the loaves (Mt 14:20; 15:37; 16:9-10). Paul let down from the wall in (Ac 9:25; 2Co 11:33).

BASON *See Basin.*

BASTARD *See Illegitimate.*

BAT [6491].
NIV+ BATS
Unclean for food (Lev 11:19; Dt 14:18; Isa 2:20).

BATH [1427, *3374*, 8175, 10126].
NIV+ BATH, BATHED, BATHING, BATHS
1. Bathing for physical cleanliness or refreshment is not often mentioned in the Bible, where most references to bathing are to partial washing. Bathing in the Bible stands primarily for ritual acts—purification of ceremonial defilement (Ex 30:19-21; Lev 16:4,24; Mk 7:3-4).
2. A Hebrew measure for liquids, containing about six gallons or twenty-two liters (1Ki 7:26,38; Ezr 7:22; Isa 5:10; Eze 45:10-11,14). *See Measure.*

BATH RABBIM, BATH-RABBIM [1442] (*daughter of a multitude*). A gate in the city of Heshbon (SS 7:4).

BATHSHEBA, BATH-SHEBA [1444] (*seventh daughter,* or *daughter of an oath*). Wife of Uriah and later wife of David. Also spelled Bathshua (1Ch 3:5, ftn). Adultery of (2Sa 11:2-5). Solomon's mother (1Ki 1:11-31; 2:13-21; 1Ch 3:5).

BATHSHUA, BATH-SHUA (possibly *daughter of opulence* BDB).
1. The daughter of Shua (Ge 38:2; 1Ch 2:3).
2. *See Bathsheba.*

BATTERING RAM [4119, 7692]. (2Sa 20:15; Eze 4:2; 21:22).

BATTERY *See Assault and Battery.*

BATTLE [*4309, 4878, 5120, 7372, 7930, 8131, 9558, 4483*].
NIV+ BATTLEMENTS, BATTLES
Shouting in (Jdg 7:20; 1Sa 17:20). Priests in (2Ch 13:12). Prayer before: by Asa (2Ch 14:11), Jehoshaphat (2Ch 20:3-12). *See Armies; War.*

BATTLE OF LIFE

Ancient Heroes:
Joshua (Jos 11:23). Gideon (Jdg 7:14). Jonathan (1Sa 14:6). David (1Sa 17:45). Elisha (2Ki 6:17). Jehoshaphat (2Ch 20:20).

The Spiritual Conflict:
An inward battle (Ro 7:23). Spiritual weapons (2Co 10:4). Invisible foes (Eph 6:12). Young soldiers enlisted (1Ti 1:18). A fight of faith (1Ti 6:12). Demands entire consecration (2Ti 2:4).

The Soul's Enemies:
(Ps 86:14; Jer 2:34; 18:20; Eze 13:18; 22:25; Lk 22:31; Eph 6:12; 1Pe 5:8).

Weapons and Armor:
(1Sa 17:45; 2Co 10:4; Eph 6:17; Heb 4:12; Rev 12:11).

Divine Protection:
Promised to believers (2Ch 16:9; Ps 34:7; 91:4; 125:2; Zec 2:5; Lk 21:18).

Examples of:

(Ge 35:5; Ex 14:20; 2Ki 6:17; Ezr 8:31; Da 6:22; Rev 7:3).

The Victory:

(Isa 53:12; Mt 12:20; Jn 16:33; 1Co 15:24; Rev 3:21; 6:2; 17:14).

BATTLE-AX *See Club.*

BATTLEMENTS [9087].
NIV+ BATTLE, BATTLE
Parapets on the tops of walls (Isa 54:11).

BAVAI *See Binnui, 1.*

BAY TREE NIV "tree" (Ps 37:35). *See Tree.*

BAZLUTH [1296]. One of the temple servants (Ezr 2:52; Ne 7:54).

BDELLIUM *See Aromatic Resin; Minerals of the Bible.*

BE ESHTARAH, BEESH-TERAH [1285].
A Levitical city (Jos 21:27). Called Ashtaroth (1Ch 6:71).

BEACON NIV "flagstaff" (Isa 30:17). *See Ensign; Standard.*

BEALIAH [1270] (*Yahweh is Lord*). A Benjamite soldier who joined David at Ziklag (1Ch 12:5).

BEALOTH [1268] (*feminine plural of Baal "lord" lady*). A town in Judah (Jos 15:24).

BEAM [781, 1464, 4096, 4164, 6770, 7521, 7771, 7936, 10058].
NIV+ BEAMS
Large long piece of timber for use in houses (1Ki 6:9-10; 7:3). Used for impaling (Ezr 6:11). Used in figurative sense by Jesus; NIV "plank" (Mt 7:3; Lk 6:41).

BEANS [7038]. Part of a simple diet (2Sa 17:28; Eze 4:9).

BEAR, THE [1800, 10155].
Described as:
Voracious (Da 7:5). Cunning (La 3:10). Cruel (Am 5:19). Often attacks men (2Ki 2:24; Am 5:19). Attacks the flock in the presence of the shepherd (1Sa 17:34). Particularly fierce when deprived of its young (2Sa 17:8; Pr 17:12). Growls when annoyed (Isa 59:11). Miraculously killed by David (1Sa 17:36-37).

Illustrative of:
God in his judgments (La 3:10; Hos 13:8). Peace in the Messianic era (Isa 11:7). Wicked rulers (Pr 28:15). The kingdom of the Medes (Da 7:5). The kingdom of Antichrist (Rev 13:2).
A constellation (Job 9:9; 38:32).

BEARD [2417, 5307].
NIV+ BEARDS
Worn Long by—
Aaron (Ps 133:2), Samson (Jdg 16:17), David (1Sa 21:13; Eze 5:1).
Cut by—
Shaven by Egyptians (Ge 41:14). Untrimmed in mourning (2Sa 19:24). Plucked (Ezr 9:3). Cut (Isa 7:20; 15:2; Jer 41:5; 48:37). Lepers required to shave (Lev 13:29-33; 14:9). Idolatrous practice of marring forbidden (Lev 19:27; 21:5). Beards of David's ambassadors half shaven by the king of the Amorites (2Sa 10:4).

BEAST [*989, 2651, 3274, 10263, *2563*].
NIV+ ANIMAL, BEASTS
1. A mammal, not man, distinguished from birds and fish (Ge 1:29-30).
2. A wild, as distinguished from a domesticated animal (Lev 26:22; Isa 13:21-22).
3. Any of the inferior animals, as distinguished from man (Ps 147:9; Ecc 3:19).
4. Apocalyptic symbol of brute force—sensual, lawless, and God-opposing (Da 7; Rev 13:11-18).

BEATEN WORK Of metals (Ex 25:18; 37:17,22; Nu 8:4).

BEATING [4547, 4804, 5782, *1296*, *2710*, *3139*, *4435*, *5597*].
NIV+ BEAT, BEATEN, BEATINGS, BEATS
As a punishment (Ex 5:14; Dt 25:3; Mk 13:9; Ac 5:40; 16:22,37; 18:17; 21:32; 22:19).
See Assault and Battery; Punishment; Scourging.

BEATITUDES [*897, 1385, *2328*, *3421*] (*divine favor*).
NIV+ BLESS, BLESSED, BLESSEDNESS, BLESSES, BLESSING, BLESSINGS
A word not found in the English Bible, but meaning either:
1. The joys of heaven.
2. A declaration of blessedness. Beatitudes occur frequently in the OT (Ps 32:1-2; 41:1). The Gospels contain isolated beatitudes by Christ (Mt 11:6; 13:16; Jn 20:29), but the word is most commonly used of those in Mt 5:3-11 and Lk 6:20-22, which set forth the qualities that should characterize his disciples. *See Graces; Sermon on the Mount.*

BEAUTY [*3202+, 3636, 3642, 3637+, 7382, *2819*, *6053*].
NIV+ BEAUTIFUL, BEAUTIFULLY
Vanity of (Ps 39:11; Pr 6:25; 31:30; Isa 3:24; Eze 16:14; 28:17). Consume away (Ps 39:11; 49:14).

Instances of:
Sarah (Ge 12:11). Rebekah (Ge 24:16). Rachel (Ge 29:17). Joseph (Ge 39:6). Moses (Ex 2:2; Heb 11:23). David (1Sa 16:12,18). Bathsheba (2Sa 11:2). Tamar (2Sa 13:1). Absalom (2Sa 14:25). Abishag (1Ki 1:4). Vashti (Est 1:11). Esther (Est 2:7).

Spiritual:
(1Ch 16:29; Ps 27:4; 29:2; 45:11; 90:17; 110:3; Eze 16:14; Zec 9:17).

BEAUTY AND BANDS NIV "Favor" and "Union"; staffs representing God's favor and the union of Israel and Judah; broken (Zec 11:7-14).

BEBAI [950] (*child*). The name of three Jews whose descendants came from exile (Ezr 2:11; 8:11; 10:28; Ne 7:16; 10:15).

BECHER *See Beker, Bekerite.*

BECORATH, BECHORATH [1138] (*firstborn*).
Son of Aphiah (1Sa 9:1).

BED [1655+, 3661, 3667, 4753, 5201, 5267, 5435, 6911+, 8886+, 10444, *2879, 3109, 3130*].

NIV+ BEDDING, BEDRIDDEN, BEDROOM, BEDROOMS, BEDS, SICKBED

Made of: iron (Dt 3:11), ivory (Am 6:4), gold and silver (Est 1:6). Used at meals (Am 6:4). Exempt from execution for debt (Pr 22:27). Perfumed (Pr 7:17).

Figurative (Ps 139:8).

BEDAD [971] (*solitary*). Father of Hadad (Ge 36:35).

BEDAN [979] (*son of judgment*).

1. In 1Sa 12:11 *See Barak.*
2. Son of Ulam (1Ch 7:17).

BEDEIAH [973] (*servant of Yahweh*). A son of Bani who had taken a foreign wife (Ezr 10:35).

BEE [1805].

NIV+ BEES

In Israel (Dt 1:44; Jdg 14:8; Ps 118:12; Isa 7:18). Figurative of the Assyrians summoned for judgment (Isa 7:18). *See Honey.*

BEELIADA [1269] (*the lord [Baal] knows*). Son of David (1Ch 14:7). Called Eliada (2Sa 5:16; 1Ch 3:8).

BEELZEBUB [*1015*] (*lord of the flies*).

NIV+ BAAL-ZEBUB

The prince of demons (Mt 10:25; 12:24,27; Mk 3:22; Lk 11:15,18-19). *See Baal-Zebub.*

BEELZEBUL *See Baal-Zebub.*

BEER [932, 8911] (as a place name *cistern, well*).

NIV+ BAALATH BEER, BEER LAHAI ROI, BEER ELIM

1. A stopping place of the Israelites (Nu 21:16-18).
2. A town in the tribe of Judah (Jdg 9:21).
3. A fermented, intoxicating beverage; its abuse condemned (1Sa 1:15; Pr 20:1; 31:4-6; Isa 28:7; 56:12; Mic 2:11). *See Abuse, Substance Abuse; Drunkenness; Fermented Drink; Wine.*

BEER ELIM, BEER-ELIM [935] (*cistern, well of Elim*).

NIV+ BEER, ELIM

A city of Moab (Isa 15:8).

BEER LAHAI ROI, BEER-LA-HAI-ROI [936] (*well that belongs to the Living One seeing me*).

NIV+ BEER

A well, probably near Kadesh, where the Lord appeared to Hagar (Ge 16:7,14) and where Isaac lived for some time (Ge 24:62; 25:11).

BEERA [938] (*cistern, well*). Son of Zophah (1Ch 7:37).

BEERAH [939] (*cistern, well*). A Reubenite (1Ch 5:6).

BEERI [941] (*[my] cistern, well*).

1. A Hittite (Ge 26:34).
See Anah.
2. Father of Hosea (Hos 1:1).

BEEROTH, BEEROTHITE [940, 943] (*cisterns, wells*).

1. NIV "wells" (Dt 10:6). *See Bene Jaakan.*
2. A city of the Hivites (Jos 9:17; 18:25; 2Sa 4:2; Ezr 2:25; Ne 7:29).
3. Inhabitants of Beeroth (2Sa 4:2,5,9; 23:37).

BEERSHEBA, BEER-SHEBA [937] (*the seventh well*).

1. The most southern city of Israel (Jdg 20:1). Named by Abraham, who dwelt there (Ge 21:31-33; 22:19). The dwelling place of Isaac (Ge 26:23). Jacob went out from, toward Haran (Ge 28:10). Sacrifices offered at, by Jacob when traveling to Egypt (Ge 46:1). In the inheritance of Judah (Jos 15:20,28; 2Sa 24:7). Afterward assigned to Simeon (Jos 19:2,9; 1Ch 4:28). Two sons of Samuel were judges at (1Sa 8:2). Became a seat of idolatrous worship (Am 5:5; 8:14).

2. Well of, belonged to Abraham and Isaac (Ge 21:25-26).

3. Wilderness of, Hagar miraculously sees a well in (Ge 21:14-19). An angel fed Elijah in (1Ki 19:5,7).

BEETLE NIV "cricket" (Lev 11:22). *See Insects.*

BEGGAR [8626, *4777*].

NIV+ BEG, BEGGARS, BEGGED, BEGGING

Set among princes (1Sa 2:8). Not the seed of the righteous (Ps 37:25). The children of the wicked (Ps 109:10; Pr 20:4; Lk 16:3).

Instances of:

Bartimaeus (Mk 10:46), Lazarus (Lk 16:20-22), the blind man (Jn 9:8), the lame man (Ac 3:2-5).
See Poor.

BEHEADING [*642, 4284*].

NIV+ BEHEADED

Execution by:

John the Baptist (Mt 14:10; Mk 6:27), James (Ac 12:2), martyrs (Rev 20:4).
See Punishment.

BEHEMOTH [990]. The word is a Hebrew plural and means "beast par excellence," referring to a large land animal, possibly the hippopotamus or the elephant (Job 40:15, ftn). Much of the language used to describe it in vv. 16-24 is highly poetic and hyperbolic (Job 40:15-24).

BEKA, BEKAH [1325].

NIV+ BEKAS

A half shekel (Ex 38:26). *See Measure.*

BEKER, BEKERITE [1146, 1151] (*young male camel*).

1. Son of Benjamin (Ge 46:21; 1Ch 7:6,8).
2. A family of Ephraim (Nu 26:35). Called Bered (1Ch 7:20).

BEL [1155] (Babylonian deity *Bel*). A Babylonian god (Isa 46:1; Jer 50:2; 51:44).

BELA, BELAITE, BELAH [1185, 1186, 1188] (*swallower, devourer*).

NIV+ ZOAR

1. A city called also Zoar (Ge 14:2,8).
2. King of Edom (Ge 36:32-33; 1Ch 1:43-44).
3. Son of Benjamin (Ge 46:21; Nu 26:38,40; 1Ch 7:6-7; 8:1,3).
4. Son of Azaz (1Ch 5:8).

BELIAL [*1016*] (*wicked, without use*). A word meaning "worthlessness," "wickedness," "lawlessness" translated as a proper noun in the KJV (Dt 13:13; Jdg 19:22; 1Sa 25:25). Personified (2Co 6:15). *See Base Fellows; Wicked.*

BELIEVER *See Righteous.*

BELIEVING *See Faith.*

BELLOWS [5135]. Used with the refiner's furnace (Jer 6:29).

BELLS [5197, 7194]. Attached to the hem of the priest's robe (Ex 28:33-34; 39:25-26). On horses (Zec 14:20).

BELLY [1061, 1623, 2824, 10435, *3120*]. Used figuratively for the seat of the affections (Job 15:2,35; 20:20; Ps 44:25; Pr 18:20; 20:27,30; Hab 3:16; Jn 7:38; Tit 1:12).

BELOVED DISCIPLE [*26, 5797*]. John spoken of as (Jn 13:23; 19:26; 20:2; 21:7,20).

BELSHAZZAR [1157, 10105, 10109] (*Bel protect the king*).
NIV+ BELSHAZZAR'S
King of Babylon (Da 5:1-30).

BELT [*258, 2512, 2513, 2514, 2520, *2438*].
NIV+ BELTS
Made of leather (2Ki 1:8; Mt 3:4), linen (Jer 13:1), gold (Da 10:5). Warrior's belt, used to bear arms (2Sa 18:11; 20:8), Jonathan gives his to David (1Sa 18:4).
Figurative: (Isa 11:5; Eph 6:14).
Symbolic: (Jer 13:1-11; Ac 21:11; Rev 15:6). *See Dress; Sash.*

BELTESHAZZAR [1171, 10108] (*protect his life*).
NIV+ DANIEL
His Hebrew name was Daniel. He was taken as a captive to Babylon with Hananiah, Mishael, and Azariah, where each one was given a Babylonian name (Da 1:6-20; 2:17,49; 3:12-30). Daniel was given the name Belteshazzar.
See Daniel.

BEMA *See Judgment Seat.*

BEN Hebrew word meaning "son" or "descendant"; possibly the name of a Levite (1Ch 15:18, ftn).

BEN-ABINADAB [1203] (*son of Abinadab*). *See Abinadab.*

BEN-AMMI [1214] (*son of my people*). Son of one of Lot's daughters; progenitor of Ammonites (Ge 19:38).

BEN-DEKER, BEN-DEKAR [1206] (*son of Deker [pierces]*). The father of one of Solomon's suppliers (1Ki 4:9).

BEN-GEBER [1205] (*son of strength*).
NIV+ GEBER
See Geber.

BEN-HADAD [1207] (*son of Hadad*).
NIV+ BEN-HADAD'S, HADAD
1. King of Syria (1Ki 15:18-20; 2Ch 16:2-4).
2. A king of Syria, who reigned in the time of Ahab, son of Ben-Hadad I (1Ki 20; 2Ki 5-7; 8:7-15).
3. Son of Hazael and king of Syria (2Ki 13:3,24-25; Am 1:4).

BEN-HAIL [1211] (*son of strength*). A prince of Judah (2Ch 17:7).

BEN-HANAN [1212] (*son of grace*).
NIV+ HANAN
A son of Shimon (1Ch 4:20).

BEN-HESED [1213] (*loyal love*). Father of one of Solomon's officers (1Ki 4:10).

BEN HINNOM [1208] (*valley of the son [or sons] of Hinnom*). A valley on the W and SW of Jerusalem which formed part of the border between Judah and Benjamin (Jos 15:8; 18:16; Ne 11:30-31). It later became the place of pagan sacrifice (2Ch 28:3; 33:6; Jer 32:35). Josiah defiled it by making it the city dump, where fires were kept constantly burning to consume the refuse (2Ki 23:10). Jewish apocalyptic writers called it the entrance to hell, and it became a figure of hell itself. Jesus used the term *gehenna* (NIV "hell") in this sense (Mt 5:22; 18:9; 23:15).
See Hades; Hell; Hinnom, Valley of; Topheth, Tophet.

BEN-HUR [1210] (*son of Hur*). *See Hur, 4.*

BEN-ONI [1204] (*son of my sorrow*). Name given Benjamin by Rachel (Ge 35:18).

BEN-ZOHETH [1209] (*son of Zoheth*). Son of Ishi (1Ch 4:20).

BENAIAH [1225, 1226] (*Yahweh has built*).
1. Son of Jehoiada, commander of the Kerethites and Pelethites (2Sa 8:18; 1Ki 1:38). A distinguished warrior (2Sa 23:20-23; 1Ch 11:22-25; 27:5-6). Loyal to Solomon (1Ki 1:8,10; 4:4).
2. An Ephraimite and distinguished warrior (2Sa 23:30; 1Ch 11:31; 27:14).
3. A Levitical musician (1Ch 15:18,20; 16:5).
4. A priest (1Ch 15:24; 16:6).
5. Son of Jeiel (2Ch 20:14).
6. A Levite in time of Hezekiah (2Ch 31:13).
7. A chief of the Simeonites (1Ch 4:36).
8. Son of Parosh (Ezr 10:25).
9. Son of Pahath-Moab (Ezr 10:30).
10. Son of Bani (Ezr 10:35).
11. Son of Nebo (Ezr 10:43).
12. Father of Pelatiah (Eze 11:1,13).

BENCHES [2756]. Of those selling doves in the temple (Mt 21:12; Mk 11:15).

BENE BERAK, BENE-BERAK [1222] (*sons of Barak [lightning]*). A city of Dan (Jos 19:45).

BENE JAAKAN, BENE-JAAKAN [1223] (possibly *son of Jaakan*).
NIV+ JAAKANITES
A tribe that gave its name to certain wells in the wilderness (Nu 33:31-32; Dt 10:6). *See Jaakan, Jaakanites.*

BENEDICTIONS Divinely appointed (Dt 10:8; 21:5; Nu 6:23-26).
By God:
Upon creatures he had made (Ge 1:22), mankind (Ge 1:28), Noah (Ge 9:1-2).
Instances of:
By Melchizedek upon Abraham (Ge 14:19-20; Heb 7:7).
By Bethuel's household upon Rebekah (Ge 24:60).
By Isaac upon Jacob (Ge 27:23-29,37; 28:1-4), Esau (Ge 27:39-40).
By Jacob upon Pharaoh (Ge 47:7-10), Joseph's sons (Ge 48), his own sons (Ge 49).
By Moses upon the tribes of Israel (Dt 33).
By Aaron (Lev 9:22-23), half the tribes who stood on Mt. Gerizim (Dt 11:29-30; 27:11-13; Jos 8:33).

By Joshua upon Caleb (Jos 14:13), the Reubenites and Gadites, and the half tribe of Manasseh (Jos 22:6-7).

By Naomi upon Ruth and Orpah (Ru 1:8-9).

By the elders and people upon Ruth (Ru 4:11-12).

By Eli upon Ruth (1Sa 1:17), upon Elkanah (1Sa 2:20).

By David upon the people (2Sa 6:18), upon Barzillai (2Sa 19:39).

By Araunah upon David (2Sa 24:23).

By Solomon upon the people (1Ki 8:14,55-58; 2Ch 6:3).

By Simeon upon Jesus (Lk 2:34).

By Jesus (Lk 24:50).

Levitical:

Nu 6:23 "Tell Aaron and his sons, 'This is how you are to bless the Israelites. Say to them:

²⁴" 'The LORD bless you and keep you; ²⁵the LORD make his face shine upon you and be gracious to you; ²⁶the LORD turn his face toward you and give you peace."'

Apostolic:

Ro 1:7 To all in Rome who are loved by God and called to be saints: Grace and peace to you from God our Father and from the Lord Jesus Christ.

Ro 15:5 May the God who gives endurance and encouragement give you a spirit of unity among yourselves as you follow Christ Jesus,

Ro 15:13 May the God of hope fill you with all joy and peace as you trust in him, so that you may overflow with hope by the power of the Holy Spirit.

Ro 15:33 The God of peace be with you all. Amen.

Ro 16:20 The God of peace will soon crush Satan under your feet. The grace of our Lord Jesus be with you. (+1Co 1:3; 16:23; 2Co 1:2)

2Co 13:14 May the grace of the Lord Jesus Christ, and the love of God, and the fellowship of the Holy Spirit be with you all. (+Gal 1:3)

Gal 6:16 Peace and mercy to all who follow this rule, even to the Israel of God.

Gal 6:18 The grace of our Lord Jesus Christ be with your spirit, brothers. Amen. (+Eph 1:2)

Eph 6:23 Peace to the brothers, and love with faith from God the Father and the Lord Jesus Christ. ²⁴Grace to all who love our Lord Jesus Christ with an undying love. (+Php 1:2; 4:23; Col 1:2; 1Th 1:1; 5:23; 2Th 1:2)

2Th 3:16 Now may the Lord of peace himself give you peace at all times and in every way. The Lord be with all of you.

2Th 3:18 The grace of our Lord Jesus Christ be with you all.

1Ti 1:2 To Timothy my true son in the faith: Grace, mercy and peace from God the Father and Christ Jesus our Lord.

1Ti 6:21 which some have professed and in so doing have wandered from the faith. Grace be with you. (+2Ti 1:2)

2Ti 4:22 The Lord be with your spirit. Grace be with you.

Tit 3:15 Everyone with me sends you greetings. Greet those who love us in the faith. Grace be with you all. (+Phm 3,25)

Heb 13:20 May the God of peace, who through the blood of the eternal covenant brought back from the dead our Lord Jesus, that great Shepherd of the sheep, ²¹equip you with everything good for doing his will, and may he work in us what is pleasing to him, through Jesus Christ, to whom be glory for ever and ever. Amen.

Heb 13:25 Grace be with you all.

1Pe 1:2 who have been chosen according to the foreknowledge of God the Father, through the sanctifying work of the Spirit, for obedience to Jesus Christ and sprinkling by his blood: Grace and peace be yours in abundance.

1Pe 5:10 And the God of all grace, who called you to his eternal glory in Christ, after you have suffered a little while, will himself restore you and make you strong, firm and steadfast. ¹¹To him be the power for ever and ever. Amen.

1Pe 5:14 Greet one another with a kiss of love. Peace to all of you who are in Christ.

2Pe 1:2 Grace and peace be yours in abundance through the knowledge of God and of Jesus our Lord.

³His divine power has given us everything we need for life and godliness through our knowledge of him who called us by his own glory and goodness. ⁴Through these he has given us his very great and precious promises, so that through them you may participate in the divine nature and escape the corruption in the world caused by evil desires.

2Jn 3 Grace, mercy and peace from God the Father and from Jesus Christ, the Father's Son, will be with us in truth and love.

Jude 2 Mercy, peace and love be yours in abundance. (+Rev 22:21)

BENEFACTOR [2309].

NIV+ BENEFACTORS

A title of honor bestowed by ancient states upon those famous for notable deeds of benevolence (Lk 22:25).

BENEFICENCE (*goodness, kindness*).

Commanded: (Lev 25:35-43)

Dt 15:7 If there is a poor man among your brothers in any of the towns of the land that the LORD your God is giving you, do not be hardhearted or tightfisted toward your poor brother. ⁸Rather be openhanded and freely lend him whatever he needs. ⁹Be careful not to harbor this wicked thought: "The seventh year, the year for canceling debts, is near," so that you do not show ill will toward your needy brother and give him nothing. He may then appeal to the LORD against you, and you will be found guilty of sin. ¹⁰Give generously to him and do so without a grudging heart; then because of this the LORD your God will bless you in all your work and in everything you put your hand to. ¹¹There will always be poor people in the land. Therefore I command you to be openhanded toward your brothers and toward the poor and needy in your land.

¹²If a fellow Hebrew, a man or a woman, sells himself to you and serves you six years, in the seventh year you must let him go free. ¹³And when you release him, do not send him away empty-handed. ¹⁴Supply him liberally from your flock, your threshing floor and your winepress. Give to him as the LORD your God has blessed you. ¹⁵Remember that you were slaves in Egypt and the LORD your God redeemed you. That is why I give you this command today.

Dt 15:18 Do not consider it a hardship to set your servant free, because his service to you these six years has been worth twice as much as that of a hired hand. And the LORD your God will bless you in everything you do.

Pr 3:27 Do not withhold good from those who deserve it, when it is in your power to act. ²⁸Do not say to your neighbor, "Come back later; I'll give it tomorrow"—when you now have it with you.

Pr 25:21 If your enemy is hungry, give him food to eat; if he is thirsty, give him water to drink. ²²In doing this, you will heap burning coals on his head, and the LORD will reward you.

Mt 5:42 Give to the one who asks you, and do not turn away from the one who wants to borrow from you.

Mt 19:21 Jesus answered, "If you want to be perfect, go, sell your possessions and give to the poor, and you will have treasure in heaven. Then come, follow me."

Mt 25:35 For I was hungry and you gave me something to eat, I was thirsty and you gave me something to drink, I was a stranger and you invited me in, 36I needed clothes and you clothed me, I was sick and you looked after me, I was in prison and you came to visit me.'

37"Then the righteous will answer him, 'Lord, when did we see you hungry and feed you, or thirsty and give you something to drink? 38When did we see you a stranger and invite you in, or needing clothes and clothe you? 39When did we see you sick or in prison and go to visit you?'

40"The King will reply, 'I tell you the truth, whatever you did for one of the least of these brothers of mine, you did for me.'

41"Then he will say to those on his left, 'Depart from me, you who are cursed, into the eternal fire prepared for the devil and his angels. 42For I was hungry and you gave me nothing to eat, I was thirsty and you gave me nothing to drink, 43I was a stranger and you did not invite me in, I needed clothes and you did not clothe me, I was sick and in prison and you did not look after me.'

44"They also will answer, 'Lord, when did we see you hungry or thirsty or a stranger or needing clothes or sick or in prison, and did not help you?'

45"He will reply, 'I tell you the truth, whatever you did not do for one of the least of these, you did not do for me.' (+Mk 10:21)

Lk 3:11 John answered, "The man with two tunics should share with him who has none, and the one who has food should do the same." (+Ro 15:27)

1Co 13:3 If I give all I possess to the poor and surrender my body to the flames, but have not love, I gain nothing.

1Co 16:1 Now about the collection for God's people: Do what I told the Galatian churches to do. 2On the first day of every week, each one of you should set aside a sum of money in keeping with his income, saving it up, so that when I come no collections will have to be made. 3Then, when I arrive, I will give letters of introduction to the men you approve and send them with your gift to Jerusalem. (+2Co 8:7-15)

2Co 8:24 Therefore show these men the proof of your love and the reason for our pride in you, so that the churches can see it.

2Co 9:1 There is no need for me to write to you about this service to the saints. 2For I know your eagerness to help, and I have been boasting about it to the Macedonians, telling them that since last year you in Achaia were ready to give; and your enthusiasm has stirred most of them to action. 3But I am sending the brothers in order that our boasting about you in this matter should not prove hollow, but that you may be ready, as I said you would be. 4For if any Macedonians come with me and find you unprepared, we—not to say anything about you—would be ashamed of having been so confident. 5So I thought it necessary to urge the brothers to visit you in advance and finish the arrangements for the generous gift you had promised. Then it will be ready as a generous gift, not as one grudgingly given.

6Remember this: Whoever sows sparingly will also reap sparingly, and whoever sows generously will also reap

generously. 7Each man should give what he has decided in his heart to give, not reluctantly or under compulsion, for God loves a cheerful giver. 8And God is able to make all grace abound to you, so that in all things at all times, having all that you need, you will abound in every good work. 9As it is written:

"He has scattered abroad his gifts to the poor; his righteousness endures forever."

10Now he who supplies seed to the sower and bread for food will also supply and increase your store of seed and will enlarge the harvest of your righteousness. 11You will be made rich in every way so that you can be generous on every occasion, and through us your generosity will result in thanksgiving to God.

12This service that you perform is not only supplying the needs of God's people but is also overflowing in many expressions of thanks to God. 13Because of the service by which you have proved yourselves, men will praise God for the obedience that accompanies your confession of the gospel of Christ, and for your generosity in sharing with them and with everyone else. 14And in their prayers for you their hearts will go out to you, because of the surpassing grace God has given you. 15Thanks be to God for his indescribable gift!

Gal 2:10 All they asked was that we should continue to remember the poor, the very thing I was eager to do.

1Ti 5:8 If anyone does not provide for his relatives, and especially for his immediate family, he has denied the faith and is worse than an unbeliever.

1Ti 5:16 If any woman who is a believer has widows in her family, she should help them and not let the church be burdened with them, so that the church can help those widows who are really in need.

Heb 13:16 And do not forget to do good and to share with others, for with such sacrifices God is pleased.

Jas 2:15 Suppose a brother or sister is without clothes and daily food. 16If one of you says to him, "Go, I wish you well; keep warm and well fed," but does nothing about his physical needs, what good is it?

1Jn 3:17 If anyone has material possessions and sees his brother in need but has no pity on him, how can the love of God be in him?

Results:

Blessed—

Ps 41:1 Blessed is he who has regard for the weak; the LORD delivers him in times of trouble.

Pr 22:9 A generous man will himself be blessed, for he shares his food with the poor.

Rewarded—

Ps 112:9 He has scattered abroad his gifts to the poor, his righteousness endures forever; his horn will be lifted high in honor.

Pr 11:25 A generous man will prosper; he who refreshes others will himself be refreshed.

Pr 28:27 He who gives to the poor will lack nothing, but he who closes his eyes to them receives many curses.

Isa 58:6 "Is not this the kind of fasting I have chosen: to loose the chains of injustice and untie the cords of the yoke, to set the oppressed free and break every yoke? 7Is it not to share your food with the hungry and to provide the poor wanderer with shelter—when you see the naked, to clothe him, and not to turn away from your own flesh and blood? (+Isa 58:8-9)

Isa 58:10 and if you spend yourselves in behalf of the hungry and satisfy the needs of the oppressed, then your light will rise in the darkness, and your night will become like the noonday. ¹¹The LORD will guide you always; he will satisfy your needs in a sun-scorched land and will strengthen your frame. You will be like a well-watered garden, like a spring whose waters never fail.

Eze 18:5 "Suppose there is a righteous man who does what is just and right. (+Eze 18:6)

Eze 18:7 He does not oppress anyone, but returns what he took in pledge for a loan. He does not commit robbery but gives his food to the hungry and provides clothing for the naked. ⁸He does not lend at usury or take excessive interest. He withholds his hand from doing wrong and judges fairly between man and man. ⁹He follows my decrees and faithfully keeps my laws. That man is righteous; he will surely live, declares the Sovereign LORD. (+Mt 19:21)

Mk 9:41 I tell you the truth, anyone who gives you a cup of water in my name because you belong to Christ will certainly not lose his reward. (+Mk 10:21)

Heb 6:10 God is not unjust; he will not forget your work and the love you have shown him as you have helped his people and continue to help them.

Examples: (Mt 25:35-45)—

Ac 11:29 The disciples, each according to his ability, decided to provide help for the brothers living in Judea. ³⁰This they did, sending their gift to the elders by Barnabas and Saul.

Ro 15:25 Now, however, I am on my way to Jerusalem in the service of the saints there. ²⁶For Macedonia and Achaia were pleased to make a contribution for the poor among the saints in Jerusalem. ²⁷They were pleased to do it, and indeed they owe it to them. For if the Gentiles have shared in the Jews' spiritual blessings, they owe it to the Jews to share with them their material blessings.

2Co 8:1 And now, brothers, we want you to know about the grace that God has given the Macedonian churches. ²Out of the most severe trial, their overflowing joy and their extreme poverty welled up in rich generosity. ³For I testify that they gave as much as they were able, and even beyond their ability. Entirely on their own, ⁴they urgently pleaded with us for the privilege of sharing in this service to the saints. ⁵And they did not do as we expected, but they gave themselves first to the Lord and then to us in keeping with God's will. ⁶So we urged Titus, since he had earlier made a beginning, to bring also to completion this act of grace on your part. ⁷But just as you excel in everything— in faith, in speech, in knowledge, in complete earnestness and in your love for us—see that you also excel in this grace of giving.

⁸I am not commanding you, but I want to test the sincerity of your love by comparing it with the earnestness of others. ⁹For you know the grace of our Lord Jesus Christ, that though he was rich, yet for your sakes he became poor, so that you through his poverty might become rich.

¹⁰And here is my advice about what is best for you in this matter: Last year you were the first not only to give but also to have the desire to do so. ¹¹Now finish the work, so that your eager willingness to do it may be matched by your completion of it, according to your means. ¹²For if the willingness is there, the gift is acceptable according to what one has, not according to what he does not have.

¹³Our desire is not that others might be relieved while you are hard pressed, but that there might be equality. ¹⁴At the present time your plenty will supply what they need, so that in turn their plenty will supply what you need. Then there will be equality, ¹⁵as it is written: "He who gathered much did not have too much, and he who gathered little did not have too little."

Php 4:10 I rejoice greatly in the Lord that at last you have renewed your concern for me. Indeed, you have been concerned, but you had no opportunity to show it. ¹¹I am not saying this because I am in need, for I have learned to be content whatever the circumstances. ¹²I know what it is to be in need, and I know what it is to have plenty. I have learned the secret of being content in any and every situation, whether well fed or hungry, whether living in plenty or in want. ¹³I can do everything through him who gives me strength.

¹⁴Yet it was good of you to share in my troubles. ¹⁵Moreover, as you Philippians know, in the early days of your acquaintance with the gospel, when I set out from Macedonia, not one church shared with me in the matter of giving and receiving, except you only; ¹⁶for even when I was in Thessalonica, you sent me aid again and again when I was in need. ¹⁷Not that I am looking for a gift, but I am looking for what may be credited to your account. ¹⁸I have received full payment and even more; I am amply supplied, now that I have received from Epaphroditus the gifts you sent. They are a fragrant offering, an acceptable sacrifice, pleasing to God.

1Ti 6:18 Command them to do good, to be rich in good deeds, and to be generous and willing to share.

See Alms; Liberality; Poor, Duty to; Rich, The; Riches.

Instances of:

The old man of Gibeah (Jdg 19:16-21). Boaz (Ru 2). The Jews returned from Exile (Ne 5:8-12; 8:10-11). Job (Job 29:11-17; 31:16-23). The Temanites (Isa 21:14). The good Samaritan (Lk 10:33-35). Zacchaeus (Lk 19:8). The first Christians (Ac 2:44-46; 4:32-37). Cornelius (Ac 10:2, 4). Onesiphorus (2Ti 1:16-18).

See Alms; Poor, Duties to.

BENEVOLENCE *See Alms; Beneficence; Charitableness; Liberality; Love.*

BENINU [1231] (*our son*). A Levite (Ne 10:13).

BENJAMIN, BENJAMITE(S) [278+2157, 408+, 1228+, 1229, 3549, *1021*] (*son of [the] right hand* BDB; *southerner* KB).

NIV+ BENJAMIN'S

1. Son of Jacob by Rachel (Ge 35:18,24; 46:19). Taken into Egypt (Ge 42-45). Prophecy concerning (Ge 49:27). Descendants of (Ge 46:21; Nu 26:38-41).

2. Tribe of. Census of, at Sinai (Nu 1:37), in the plain of Moab (Nu 26:41). Clans of (Nu 26:38-40; 1Ch 7:6-12; 8). Position of, in camp and march (Nu 2:18,22). Moses' benediction upon (Dt 33:12). Allotment in the land of Canaan (Jos 18:11-28). Reallotment (Eze 48:23). Did not exterminate the Jebusites (Jdg 1:21). Join Deborah in the war against Sisera (Jdg 5:14). Territory of, invaded by the Ammonites (Jdg 10:9). Did not avenge the crime of the Gibeonites against the Levite's concubine, the war that followed (Jdg 19-20). Saul, the first king of Israel, from (1Sa 9:1,17; 10:20-21). Its rank in the time of Samuel (1Sa 9:21). Jerusalem within the territory of (Jer 6:1). A company of, joins David at Ziklag (1Ch 12:1-2,16). Not enrolled by Joab when he took a census of the military forces of Israel (1Ch 21:6). Loyal to Ish-Bosheth, the son of Saul (2Sa 2:9,15,31; 1Ch 12:29). Subsequently joins David (2Sa 3:19; 19:16-19). Loyal to Rehoboam (1Ki 12:21; 2Ch 11:1). Military forces of, in the reign of Asa (2Ch 14:8), of Jehoshaphat (2Ch 17:17). Skill in archery and as slingers of stones (Jdg 3:15; 20:16; 1Ch 8:40; 12:2). Return to Israel from the Exile in Babylon (Ezr 1:5). Saints of, seen

in John's vision (Rev 7:8). Paul, of the tribe of (Ro 11:1; Php 3:5).

See Israel.

3. Grandson of Benjamin (1Ch 7:10).

4. A son of Harim (Ezr 10:32). Probably identical with the man mentioned in Ne 3:23.

5. A Jew who assisted in purifying the wall of Jerusalem (Ne 12:34).

6. A gate of Jerusalem (Jer 20:2; 37:13; 38:7; Zec 14:10).

BENO [1217] (*his son*). A descendant of Merari (1Ch 24:26-27).

BENOTH *See Succoth Benoth.*

BEON [1274]. A place E of Jordan, probably the same as Baal Meon (Nu 32:3,38).

See Baal Meon.

BEOR [1242, *1027*] (perhaps *a burning*).

1. Father of Bela (Ge 36:32; 1Ch 1:43).

2. Father of Balaam (Nu 22:5; 24:3,15; 31:8; Dt 23:4; Jos 13:22; 24:9; Mic 6:5; 2Pe 2:15).

BERA [1396] (*gift*). King of Sodom, defeated by Kedorlaomer in the days of Abraham (Ge 14:2,8).

BERACAH, BERACHAH, VALLEY OF [1389, 1390] (*blessing*).

1. An Israelite, who joined David at Ziklag (1Ch 12:3).

2. A valley in the S of Judah, where Jehoshaphat assembled the Israelites to offer praise to God for victory over the Ammonites and Moabites (2Ch 20:26). Between Bethlehem and Hebron.

BERACHIAH, BERECHIAH *See Berekiah.*

BERAIAH [1349] (*Yahweh creates*). Son of Shimei (1Ch 8:21).

BERAK *See Bene Berak.*

BEREA, BEREANS [*1023, 1024*]. A city in the S of Macedonia (Ac 17:10,13; 20:4). Its inhabitants are important as an example of comparing new teaching to the received Scriptures.

BEREAVEMENT [8892, 8897, 8898].

NIV+ BEREAVE, BEREAVED, BEREAVES

From God (Hos 9:12). Mourning in, forbidden to Aaron, on account of his son's wickedness (Lev 10:6). To Ezekiel, for his wife (Eze 24:16-18).

Instances of:

Abraham, of Sarah (Ge 23:2). Jacob, of Joseph (Ge 37:34-35). Joseph, of his father (Ge 50:1,4). The Egyptians, of their firstborn (Ex 12:29-33). Naomi, of her husband (Ru 1:3,5,20-21).

David, of his child by Bathsheba (2Sa 12:15-21)—

2Sa 12:22 He answered, "While the child was still alive, I fasted and wept. I thought, 'Who knows? The LORD may be gracious to me and let the child live.' ²³But now that he is dead, why should I fast? Can I bring him back again? I will go to him, but he will not return to me."

Of Absalom (2Sa 18:33; 19:4).

Resignation in:

Job—

Job 1:18 While he was still speaking, yet another messenger came and said, "Your sons and daughters were feasting and drinking wine at the oldest brother's house,

¹⁹when suddenly a mighty wind swept in from the desert and struck the four corners of the house. It collapsed on them and they are dead, and I am the only one who has escaped to tell you!"

²⁰At this, Job got up and tore his robe and shaved his head. Then he fell to the ground in worship ²¹and said: "Naked I came from my mother's womb, and naked I will depart. The LORD gave and the LORD has taken away; may the name of the LORD be praised."

David (2Sa 12:22,30)

Solomon—

Ecc 7:2 It is better to go to a house of mourning than to go to a house of feasting, for death is the destiny of every man; the living should take this to heart. ³Sorrow is better than laughter, because a sad face is good for the heart. ⁴The heart of the wise is in the house of mourning, but the heart of fools is in the house of pleasure.

Christians—

1Th 4:13 Brothers, we do not want you to be ignorant about those who fall asleep, or to grieve like the rest of men, who have no hope. ¹⁴We believe that Jesus died and rose again and so we believe that God will bring with Jesus those who have fallen asleep in him. ¹⁵According to the Lord's own word, we tell you that we who are still alive, who are left till the coming of the Lord, will certainly not precede those who have fallen asleep. ¹⁶For the Lord himself will come down from heaven, with a loud command, with the voice of the archangel and with the trumpet call of God, and the dead in Christ will rise first. ¹⁷After that, we who are still alive and are left will be caught up together with them in the clouds to meet the Lord in the air. And so we will be with the Lord forever. ¹⁸Therefore encourage each other with these words.

See Affliction, Consolation Under, Prayer Under; Resignation.

BERED [1354, 1355] (possibly *freezing rain*).

1. A town in the S of Israel (Ge 16:14).

2. A son of Shuthelah (1Ch 7:20). Probably the same as Beker (Nu 26:35).

BEREKIAH, BERACHIAH [1392, 1393, *974*] (*Yahweh blesses*).

1. Father of Asaph (1Ch 6:39; 15:17,23).

2. A warrior of Ephraim (2Ch 28:12).

3. A brother of Zerubbabel (1Ch 3:20).

4. Son of Asa (1Ch 9:16).

5. Son of Iddo, father of Zechariah (Zec 1:1,7; Mt 23:35).

6. Son of Meshullam (Ne 3:4,30; 6:18).

BERI [1373] (*wisdom*).

NIV+ BERITES

Son of Zophah (1Ch 7:36).

BERIAH, BERIITE [1380, 1381] (*prominent, excellent*).

1. Son of Asher (Ge 46:17; 1Ch 7:30) and his clan (Nu 26:44-45).

2. Son of Ephraim (1Ch 7:20-23).

3. A Benjamite (1Ch 8:13).

4. Son of Shimei (1Ch 23:10-11).

BERITES [1379] (*choice young men*).

NIV+ BERI

Followed Sheba in his rebellion against David (2Sa 20:14).

BERITH *See Baal-Berith.*

BERNICE [*1022*] (*victorious*). Daughter of Agrippa (Ac 25:13,23; 26:30).

BERODACH-BALADAN *See Merodach-Baladan.*

BEROTHAH [1363] (*well*). Part of the northern boundary of Canaan (Eze 47:16).

BEROTHAI, BEROTHITE [1408]. A city of Zobah (2Sa 8:8) and its inhabitants (1Ch 11:39).

BERYL [1403, 1404, *1039*] (*yellow jasper*).
   1. Set in the priestly breastplate (Ex 28:17; 39:10).
   2. A precious stone (Eze 28:13).
   3. John saw, in the foundation of the new Jerusalem (Rev 21:20).
   See Minerals of the Bible, 1; Stones.

BESAI [1234] (*in secret council of Yahweh* KB). One of the temple servants (Ezr 2:49; Ne 7:52).

BESODEIAH [1233] (*in secret council of Yahweh*). Father of Meshullam (Ne 3:6).

BESOM *See Broom.*

BESOR [1410]. A brook near Gaza (1Sa 30:9-10,21).

BESTIALITY (*Sexual relations between a human and an animal*).
Ex 22:19 "Anyone who has sexual relations with an animal must be put to death.
Lev 18:23 "'Do not have sexual relations with an animal and defile yourself with it. A woman must not present herself to an animal to have sexual relations with it; that is a perversion.
Lev 20:16 "'If a woman approaches an animal to have sexual relations with it, kill both the woman and the animal. They must be put to death; their blood will be on their own heads.

BETAH *See Tebah, 2.*

BETEN [1062] (*womb, bowels*). A city of Asher (Jos 19:25).

BETH The most common OT word for house, family or dynasty. Used in the more than fifty place names that follow.

BETH ANATH, BETH-ANATH [1117] (*house of Anath*).
   NIV+ ANATH
   A fortified city of Naphtali (Jos 19:38; Jdg 1:33).

BETH ANOTH, BETH-ANOTH [1116] (*house of Anath [plural]*). A city in Judah (Jos 15:59).

BETH ARABAH, BETH-ARABAH [1098] (*house of Arabah [desert plain]*).
   NIV+ ARABAH
   A city in the valley of the Dead Sea (Jos 15:6,61; 18:22). Called Arabah (Jos 18:18).

BETH-ARAM *See Beth Haram.*

BETH ARBEL, BETH-ARBEL [1079] (*house of Arbel*). A city devastated by Shalman (Hos 10:14).

BETH ASHBEA [1080] (*house of Ashbea*). A descendant of Shelah (1Ch 4:21).

BETH AVEN, BETH-AVEN [1077] (*house of idolatry*).
   NIV+ AVEN
   A place on the mountains of Benjamin (Jos 7:2; 18:12; 1Sa 13:5; 14:23; Hos 4:15; 5:8; 10:5).

BETH AZMAVETH, BETH-AZMAVETH [1115] (*strong of death* ISBE; *house of Azmaveth [camel fodder, a plant of the plumose family]* KB).
   NIV+ AZMAVETH
   A town of Benjamin (Ne 7:28). Called Azmaveth (Ne 12:29; Ezr 2:24).

BETH BAAL MEON, BETH-BAAL-MEON [1081] (*house of Baal Meon*).
   NIV+ BAAL MEON
   A place in the tribe of Reuben (Jos 13:17).
   Called Baal Meon (Nu 32:38; Eze 25:9), Beon (Nu 32:3), Beth Meon (Jer 48:23).
   Subdued by the Israelites (Nu 32:3-4). Assigned to the Reubenites (Jos 13:17).

BETH BARAH, BETH-BARAH [1083] (*house of Barah [the river ford]*). A city E of the Jordan (Jdg 7:24).

BETH BIRI, BETH-BIREI [1082] (*house of Biri* or *den of a lioness*). A town of Simeon S of Judah (1Ch 4:31).
   See Beth Lebaoth, Beth-Lebaoth.

BETH CAR, BETH-CAR [1105] (*site [house] of a lamb*). A place W of Mizpah (1Sa 7:11).

BETH DAGON, BETH-DAGON [1087] (*temple [house] of Dagon*).
   NIV+ DAGON
   1. A city of Judah (Jos 15:41).
   2. A city of Asher (Jos 19:27).

BETH DIBLATHAIM, BETH-DIBLATHAIM [1086] (*house of Diblathaim*).
   NIV+ ALMON DIBLATHAIM
   A city of Moab (Jer 48:22).
   See Almon Diblathaim.

BETH EDEN [1114] (*house of Eden; garden place*) Probably another name for Damascus (Am 1:5). *See Damascus.*

BETH EKED [1118]. Forty-two relatives of Ahaziah slaughtered there (2Ki 10:12-14).

BETH EMEK, BETH-EMEK [1097] (*house of Emek* or *site of the valley*). A city of Asher (Jos 19:27).

BETH EZEL, BETH-EZEL [1089] (*house of Ezel* or *site nearby*).
   NIV+ EZEL
   A town of Judah (Mic 1:11).

BETH GADER, BETH-GADER [1084] (*house of Gader* or *site of a stone hedge*). A place in Judah (1Ch 2:51). Probably identical with Geder (Jos 12:13); and with Gedor (Jos 15:58).

BETH GAMUL, BETH-GAMUL [1085] (*house of recompense*).
   NIV+ GAMUL
   A city of Moab (Jer 48:23).

BETH GILGAL [1090]. Perhaps an alternate name for Gilgal, 1 or 2 (Ne 12:29). *See Gilgal.*

BETH-HACCEREM *See Beth Hakkerem.*

BETH HAGGAN [1091] (*house of Haggan* or *site of the garden*). A garden house (2Ki 9:27). Probably identical with En Gannim (Jos 19:21).

BETH HAKKEREM [1094] (*house of Hakkerem* or *site of the vineyard*). A mountain in Judah (Ne 3:14; Jer 6:1).

BETH HARAM [1099]. A fortified city of Gad, E of the Jordan, between Succoth and Debir (Jos 13:27).

BETH HARAN, BETH-HARAN [1100] (*house of the mountaineer*).

NIV+ HARAN

A fortified city E of Jordan (Nu 32:36).

BETH HOGLAH, BETH-HOGLA [1102] (*house of Hoglah* or *site of the partridge*).

NIV+ HOGLAH

A place on the border of Judah (Jos 15:6; 18:19,21).

BETH HORON, BETH-HORON [1103] (*house of Horon* or *site of a ravine*).

NIV+ HORONITE

Two ancient cities of Canaan, near which Joshua defeated the Amorites (Jos 10:10-11; 16:3,5; 18:13-14; 1Sa 13:18; 1Ch 7:24). Solomon builds (1Ki 9:17; 2Ch 8:5). Taken from Judah by the ten tribes (2Ch 25:13).

BETH JESHIMOTH, BETH-JESHIMOTH
[1093] (*house of Jeshimoth* or *site of desolation*). A place in the plains of Moab, the S limit of Israel's encampment (Nu 33:49). It was assigned to the Reubenites (Jos 13:20), but was later in Moabite possession (Eze 25:9). Modern Tell el-Azeimeh, about twelve miles SE of Jericho (Jos 12:3).

BETH JOAB *See Atroth Beth Joab.*

BETH LEBAOTH, BETH-LEBAOTH [1106]
(*house of Lebaoth* or *den of the lioness*). A town of Simeon in the S part of Judah (Jos 19:6). Called Lebaoth (Jos 15:32), and the same as Beth Biri (1Ch 4:31).

BETH-LEHEM-JUDAH *See Bethlehem; Judah.*

BETH-MAACHAH (*house of Maacah*). *See Abel Beth Maacah.*

BETH MARCABOTH, BETH-MARCABOTH
[1096, 1112] (*site [house] of Marcaboth [chariots]*). A town of Simeon (Jos 19:5; 1Ch 4:31). Probably identical with Madmannah, which may have been its older name (Jos 15:31).

BETH MEON, BETH-MEON [1110] (*house of habitation*).

NIV+ BAAL MEON

A city of Moab (Jer 48:23); the same as Beth Baal Meon (Jos 13:17).

BETH MILLO [1109] (*house of Millo* or *site of earth fill*).

1. Beth Millo probably refers to the earthen fill used to erect a platform on which walls and other large structures were built (Jdg 9:6,20). It may be identical to the "stronghold" of v. 46 (Jdg 9:46).

2. A name given to part of the citadel of Jerusalem, NIV "supporting terraces" (2Sa 5:9, ftn; 1Ch 11:8, ftn). King

Solomon raises a levy to repair (1Ki 9:15,24, ftn; 11:27, ftn). King Joash murdered at (2Ki 12:20). Repaired by King Hezekiah (2Ch 32:5, ftn).

BETH NIMRAH, BETH-NIMRAH [1113] (*house of Nimrah [spotted leopard]* BDB; *house of a basin of clear, limpid water* KB).

NIV+ NIMRAH

A fortified city E of Jordan (Nu 32:36; Jos 13:27).

BETH OPHRAH [1108] (*house of Ophrah* or *house of dust*).

NIV+ OPHRAH

A city found in the Shephelah (Mic 1:10, ftn).

BETH-PALET *See Beth Pelet.*

BETH PAZZEZ [1122]. A city in Issachar (Jos 19:21).

BETH PELET [1120] (*house of Pelet [escape]*).

NIV+ PELET

A city in Judah (Jos 15:27; Ne 11:26).

BETH PEOR, BETH-PEOR [1121] (*house of Peor*).

NIV+ PEOR

A place in the tribe of Reuben (Dt 3:29; 4:46; 34:6). Near the burial place of Moses (Jos 13:20).

BETH RAPHA, BETH-RAPHA [1125] (*house of Rapha [healing]*).

NIV+ RAPHA

Son of Eshton (1Ch 4:12).

BETH REHOB, BETH-REHOB [1124] (*house of Rehob [main street, market]*).

NIV+ REHOB

A place in Dan (Jdg 18:28; 2Sa 10:6). Called Rehob.

BETH SHAN, BETH-SHAN [1126] (*site [house] of Shan [repose]*). A city of Manasseh (Jos 17:11; 1Ch 7:29). Not subdued (Jdg 1:27). Bodies of Saul and his sons exposed in (1Sa 31:10,12). District of, under tribute to Solomon's governor (1Ki 4:12).

BETH-SHEAN *See Beth Shan, Beth-Shan.*

BETH SHEMESH, BETH-SHEMESH [1127, 1128] (*temple [house] of Shemesh [pagan sun god]*).

1. A priestly city of Dan (Jos 21:16; 1Sa 6:15; 1Ch 6:59). On the northern border of Judah (Jos 15:10; 1Sa 6:9,12). In later times transferred to Judah (2Ki 14:11). Mentioned in Solomon's governed districts (1Ki 4:9). Amaziah taken prisoner at (2Ki 14:11-13; 2Ch 25:21-23). Retaken by the Philistines (2Ch 28:18). Called Ir Shemesh (Jos 19:41).

2. A city near Jerusalem (Jos 19:22).

3. A fortified city of Naphtali (Jos 19:38; Jdg 1:33).

4. Literally "Beth Shemesh in Egypt," with the qualifying phrase being used to distinguish it from "Beth Shemesh in Judah" (2Ki 14:11). Called On (in Hebrew) in Egypt; also known as Heliopolis, about five miles NE of Cairo, where there was a temple of Ra (Jer 43:13, ftn).

BETH SHITTAH, BETH-SHITTAH [1101] (*house of Shittah [acacias]*). A place near the Jordan (Jdg 7:22).

BETH TAPPUAH, BETH-TAPPUAH [1130]
(*house of Tappuah [apricot;apple tree]*).

NIV+ TAPPUAH

A town of Judah (Jos 15:53).

BETH TOGARMAH [1129]. A city in eastern Asia
Minor (Eze 27:14; 38:6). *See Togarmah.*

BETH ZUR, BETH-ZUR [1123] (*cliff house*).

NIV+ ZUR

A town in Judah (Jos 15:58; 1Ch 2:45; 2Ch 11:7; Ne 3:16).

BETHANY [*1029*] (*house of Ananiah* or *poor ones* or *unripe figs*). A village on the eastern slope of the Mount of Olives (Jn 11:18). Mary, Martha, and Lazarus dwell at (Lk 10:38-41). Lazarus dies and is raised to life at (Jn 11). Jesus attends a feast in (Mt 26:6-13; Jn 12:1-9). The colt on which Jesus made his triumphal entry into Jerusalem obtained at (Mk 11:1-11). Jesus stays at (Mt 21:17; Mk 11:11-12,19).

BETHEL, BETH-EL [1078, 1088] (*temple [house] of God [El]*).

NIV+ EL BETHEL, LUZ

1. A city N of Jerusalem. The ancient city next to, and finally embraced in, was called Luz (Jos 18:13; Jdg 1:23-26). Abraham establishes an altar at (Ge 12:8; 13:3-4). The place where Jacob saw the vision of the stairway (Ge 28:10-22; 31:13; Hos 12:4), and builds an altar at (Ge 35:1-15). Deborah dies at (Ge 35:8). Conquered by Joshua (Jos 8:17, w 12:16), by the house of Joseph (Jdg 1:22-26). Allotted to Benjamin (Jos 18:13,22). Court of justice held at, by Deborah (Jdg 4:5), by Samuel (1Sa 7:16).

Tabernacle at, and called House of God (Jdg 20:18,31; 21:2). Jeroboam institutes idolatrous worship at (1Ki 12:25-33; 2Ki 10:29). Idolatry at (Jer 48:13; Am 4:4). Shalmaneser sends a priest to (2Ki 17:27-28). Prophecies against the idolatrous altars at (1Ki 13:1-6,32; 2Ki 23:4,15-20; Am 3:14). The company of prophets at (2Ki 2:3). Children of, mock Elisha (2Ki 2:23-24). People of, return from Babylon (Ezr 2:28; Ne 7:32). Prophecies against (Am 5:5).

2. A city in the S of Judah (1Sa 30:27).

3. A mountain (1Sa 13:2).

BETHER (perhaps *house [shrine] of the mountain*). Mountains of (SS 2:17, ftn, text "rugged hills").

BETHESDA [*1031*] (*site [house] of mercy*). A spring-fed pool in Jerusalem (Jn 5:1-16) into which the sick went for healing.

BETHHANAN *See Elon Bethhanan.*

BETHLEHEM [1095, 1107, *1033*] (*house of bread; possibly temple [house] of Lakhmu [pagan deity]*).

NIV+ BETHLEHEMITE, EPHRATH

1. A city SW of Jerusalem (Jdg 17:7; 19:18). Called Ephrathah and Ephrath (Ge 48:7; Ps 132:6; Mic 5:2), and Bethlehem in Judah (Jdg 17:7-9; 19:1,18; Ru 1:1; 1Sa 17:12). Rachel dies and is buried at (Ge 35:16,19; 48:7). The city of Boaz (Ru 1:1,19; 2:4; 4). Taken and held by the Philistines (2Sa 23:14-16). Jeroboam converts it into a military stronghold (2Ch 11:6). The city of Joseph (Mt 2:5-6; Lk 2:4). Birthplace of Jesus (Mic 5:2; Mt 2; Lk 2:4,15). Herod slays the children of (Mt 2:16-18).

2. A town of Zebulun, six miles W of Nazareth (Jos 19:15). Israel judged at (Jdg 12:10).

BETHPHAGE [*1036*] (*house of unripe figs*). A village on the Mount of Olives (Mt 21:1; Mk 11:1; Lk 19:29).

BETHSAIDA [*1034*] (*site [house] of fishing*).

1. A city of Galilee. The city of Philip, Andrew, and Peter (Jn 1:44; 12:21). Jesus visits (Mk 6:45), cures a blind man in (Mk 8:22), prophesies against (Mt 11:21; Lk 10:13).

2. Secluded area E of the sea of Galilee; Jesus feeds five thousand people in (Mt 14:13; Mk 6:32; Lk 9:10).

BETHUEL [1432, 1433] (*man of God [El]*). Son of Nahor, father of Rebekah (Ge 22:22-23; 24:15,24; 25:20; 28:2,5).

BETHUL [1434]. A city of Simeon (Jos 19:4). Called Kesil (Jos 15:30) and Bethuel (1Ch 4:30).

BETONIM [1064] (*pistachio nuts*). A town of Gad (Jos 13:26).

BETRAYAL [953, 1655, 5085, 8228, 9213, *4140*+].

NIV+ BETRAY, BETRAYED, BETRAYER, BETRAYING, BETRAYS

Of Jesus (Mt 26:14-16,45-50; Mk 14:10-11; Lk 22:3-6; 22:47-48; Jn 13:21). Of others, foretold (Mt 20:18; 24:10). Of David, by Doeg (1Sa 22:9-10, w 1Sa 21:1-10). Of cities (Jdg 1:24-25).

See Confidence, Betrayed.

BETROTHAL [829].

NIV+ BETROTH, BETROTHED

Of Jacob (Ge 29:18-30). Exempts from military duty (Dt 20:7). A quasi marriage (Mt 1:18; Lk 1:27).

Figurative: (Isa 62:4; Hos 2:19-20; 2Co 11:2).

See Marriage.

BETTING By Samson (Jdg 14:12-19).

BEULAH [1241] (*married*). Poetic name for restored Israel (Isa 62:4).

BEZAI [1291].

1. Head of a Jewish family that returned from Babylon (Ezr 2:17; Ne 7:23).

2. A family that sealed the covenant with Nehemiah (Ne 10:18).

BEZALEL, BEZALEEL [1295] (*in the shadow of God [El]*).

1. A divinely inspired architect and master craftsman who built the tabernacle (Ex 31:2; 35:30-35; 36:1; 37:1; 38:1-7,22).

2. Son of Pahath-Moab (Ezr 10:30).

BEZEK [1028] (*scattering, sowing*).

NIV+ ADONI-BEZEK

1. Residence of Adoni-Bezek (Jdg 1:5). *See Adoni-Bezek.*

2. A rendezvous of Israel under Saul (1Sa 11:8).

BEZER [1310, 1311] (*[metallic] ore,* or *place of refuge*).

1. A city of refuge, E of the Jordan (Dt 4:43; Jos 20:8; 21:36; 1Ch 6:78).

2. Son of Zophah (1Ch 7:37).

BIBLE, THE General references to (2Sa 22:31; Ps 12:6; 119:9,50; 147:15; Mk 12:24; Lk 8:11; Eph 6:17). The Book of the ages (Ps 119:89; Mt 5:18; 24:35; 1Pe

1:25). Food for the soul (Dt 8:3; Job 23:12; Ps 119:103; Jer 15:16; 1Pe 2:2). Divinely inspired (Jer 36:2; Eze 1:3; Ac 1:16; 2Ti 3:16; 2Pe 1:21; Rev 14:13). Precepts written in the heart (Dt 6:6; 11:18; Ps 119:11; Lk 2:51; Ro 10:8; Col 3:16). Furnishes a light (Ps 19:8; 119:105,130; Pr 6:23; 2Pe 1:19). Loved by the believers (Ps 119:47,72,82,97, 140; Jer 15:16).

Mighty in its influence: a devouring flame (Jer 5:14), a crushing hammer (Jer 23:29), a life-giving force (Eze 37:7), a saving power (Ro 1:16), a penetrating sword (Eph 6:17; Heb 4:12).

Blessings to those who reverence it (Jos 1:8; Ps 19:11; Mt 7:24; Lk 11:28; Jn 5:24; 8:31; Rev 1:3). Purifies the life (Ps 119:9; Jn 15:3; 17:17; Eph 5:26; 1Pe 1:22). Written with a purpose (Jn 20:31; Ro 15:4; 1Co 10:11; 1Jn 5:13). The standard of faith (Pr 29:18; Isa 8:20; Jn 12:48; Gal 1:8; 1Th 2:13). Its words sacred (Dt 4:2; 12:32; Pr 30:6; Rev 22:19). The study of it commanded (Dt 17:19; Isa 34:16; Jn 5:39; Ac 17:11; Ro 15:4). Contains seed for the sower (Ps 126:6; Mk 4:14-15; 2Co 9:10). Absolutely trustworthy (1Ki 8:56; Ps 111:7; Eze 12:25; Mt 5:18; Lk 21:33). Profitable for instruction (Dt 4:10; 11:19; 2Ch 17:9; Ne 8:13; Isa 2:3). Ignorance of, dangerous (Mt 22:29; Jn 20:9; Ac 13:27; 2Co 3:15).

See Word of God.

BICRI, BICHRI (*first born*). Father of Sheba (2Sa 20:1).

BIDKAR [982] (*son of Deker [piercing]*). Jehu's captain (2Ki 9:25).

BIER [4753, 5435]. (2Sa 3:31; Lk 7:14).

BIGAMY *See Polygamy.*

BIGOTRY

Exhibited:

In self-righteousness—

Isa 65:5 who say, 'Keep away; don't come near me, for I am too sacred for you!' Such people are smoke in my nostrils, a fire that keeps burning all day.

Mk 2:16 When the teachers of the law who were Pharisees saw him eating with the "sinners" and tax collectors, they asked his disciples: "Why does he eat with tax collectors and 'sinners'?" (+Lk 15:2)

Lk 18:9 To some who were confident of their own righteousness and looked down on everybody else, Jesus told this parable: [10]"Two men went up to the temple to pray, one a Pharisee and the other a tax collector. [11]The Pharisee stood up and prayed about himself: 'God, I thank you that I am not like other men—robbers, evildoers, adulterers—or even like this tax collector. [12]I fast twice a week and give a tenth of all I get.'

[13]"But the tax collector stood at a distance. He would not even look up to heaven, but beat his breast and said, 'God, have mercy on me, a sinner.'

[14]"I tell you that this man, rather than the other, went home justified before God. For everyone who exalts himself will be humbled, and he who humbles himself will be exalted."

In intolerance—

Lk 9:49 "Master," said John, "we saw a man driving out demons in your name and we tried to stop him, because he is not one of us."

[50]"Do not stop him," Jesus said, "for whoever is not against you is for you."

Ac 18:12 While Gallio was proconsul of Achaia, the Jews made a united attack on Paul and brought him into court. [13]"This man," they charged, "is persuading the people to worship God in ways contrary to the law."

Rebuke of:

Ac 10:28 He said to them: "You are well aware that it is against our law for a Jew to associate with a Gentile or visit him. But God has shown me that I should not call any man impure or unclean.

Ac 10:45 The circumcised believers who had come with Peter were astonished that the gift of the Holy Spirit had been poured out even on the Gentiles.

Paul's argument against:

Ro 3:1 What advantage, then, is there in being a Jew, or what value is there in circumcision? [2]Much in every way! First of all, they have been entrusted with the very words of God.

[3]What if some did not have faith? Will their lack of faith nullify God's faithfulness? [4]Not at all! Let God be true, and every man a liar. As it is written:

"So that you may be proved right when you speak and prevail when you judge."

[5]But if our unrighteousness brings out God's righteousness more clearly, what shall we say? That God is unjust in bringing his wrath on us? (I am using a human argument.) [6]Certainly not! If that were so, how could God judge the world? [7]Someone might argue, "If my falsehood enhances God's truthfulness and so increases his glory, why am I still condemned as a sinner?" [8]Why not say—as we are being slanderously reported as saying and as some claim that we say—"Let us do evil that good may result"? Their condemnation is deserved.

[9]What shall we conclude then? Are we any better? Not at all! We have already made the charge that Jews and Gentiles alike are all under sin. [10]As it is written:

"There is no one righteous, not even one; [11]there is no one who understands, no one who seeks God. [12]All have turned away, they have together become worthless; there is no one who does good, not even one." [13]"Their throats are open graves; their tongues practice deceit." "The poison of vipers is on their lips." [14]"Their mouths are full of cursing and bitterness." [15]"Their feet are swift to shed blood; [16]ruin and misery mark their ways, [17]and the way of peace they do not know." [18]"There is no fear of God before their eyes."

[19]Now we know that whatever the law says, it says to those who are under the law, so that every mouth may be silenced and the whole world held accountable to God. [20]Therefore no one will be declared righteous in his sight by observing the law; rather, through the law we become conscious of sin.

[21]But now a righteousness from God, apart from law, has been made known, to which the Law and the Prophets testify. [22]This righteousness from God comes through faith in Jesus Christ to all who believe. There is no difference, [23]for all have sinned and fall short of the glory of God,

Ro 4:1 What then shall we say that Abraham, our forefather, discovered in this matter? [2]If, in fact, Abraham was justified by works, he had something to boast about—but not before God. [3]What does the Scripture say? "Abraham believed God, and it was credited to him as righteousness."

[4]Now when a man works, his wages are not credited to him as a gift, but as an obligation. [5]However, to the man who does not work but trusts God who justifies the wicked, his faith is credited as righteousness. [6]David says the

same thing when he speaks of the blessedness of the man to whom God credits righteousness apart from works:

[7]"Blessed are they whose transgressions are forgiven, whose sins are covered. [8]Blessed is the man whose sin the Lord will never count against him."

[9]Is this blessedness only for the circumcised, or also for the uncircumcised? We have been saying that Abraham's faith was credited to him as righteousness. [10]Under what circumstances was it credited? Was it after he was circumcised, or before? It was not after, but before! [11]And he received the sign of circumcision, a seal of the righteousness that he had by faith while he was still uncircumcised. So then, he is the father of all who believe but have not been circumcised, in order that righteousness might be credited to them. [12]And he is also the father of the circumcised who not only are circumcised but who also walk in the footsteps of the faith that our father Abraham had before he was circumcised.

[13]It was not through law that Abraham and his offspring received the promise that he would be heir of the world, but through the righteousness that comes by faith. [14]For if those who live by law are heirs, faith has no value and the promise is worthless, [15]because law brings wrath. And where there is no law there is no transgression.

[16]Therefore, the promise comes by faith, so that it may be by grace and may be guaranteed to all Abraham's off-spring—not only to those who are of the law but also to those who are of the faith of Abraham. He is the father of us all. (+Ro 4:17-22)

Ro 4:23 The words "it was credited to him" were written not for him alone, [24]but also for us, to whom God will credit righteousness—for us who believe in him who raised Jesus our Lord from the dead. [25]He was delivered over to death for our sins and was raised to life for our justification.

Instances of:

Joshua (Nu 11:27-29).

The Jews with, the Samaritans (Jn 4:9,27), Jesus (Lk 4:28; 7:39; 11:38-39; 15:22; 19:5-7; Jn 5:18), the blind man (Jn 9:29-34), Paul (Ac 21:28-29; 22:22).

John (Mk 9:38-40; Lk 9:49-50). James and John (Lk 9:51-56). The early Christians (Ac 10:45; 11:2-3; 15:1-10,24; Gal 2:3-5). Paul (Ac 9:1-2; 22:3-4; 26:9-11; Gal 1:13-14; Php 3:6).

See *Intolerance, Religious; Persecution; Respect of Persons; Uncharitableness.*

BIGTHA [960] (*gift of God*). Eunuch and servant of Xerxes (Est 1:10).

BIGTHANA, BIGTHAN [961, 962] (*gift of God*). A conspiring Persian officer (Est 2:21-23: 6:2).

BIGVAI [958] (*fortunate*).

1. Man who returned from the Captivity (Ezr 2:2; Ne 7:19).

2. Ancestor of family that returned from the Captivity (Ezr 2:14; Ne 7:19).

3. Probably the same as 2 above (Ezr 8:14).

BILDAD [1161] (*Bel has loved*). One of Job's friends (Job 2:11; 8:1; 18:1; 25:1).

BILEAM [1190] (*[a gift] brought to the people*). A town of Manasseh (1Ch 6:70). Called Ibleam (Jos 17:11) and Gath Rimmon (Jos 21:25).

BILGAH [1159] (*gleam, smile*).

NIV+ BILGAH'S

1. One of the chiefs of the priestly courses in the temple (1Ch 24:14).

2. A priest (Ne 12:5,18), perhaps identical with Bilgai (Ne 10:8).

BILGAI [1160] (*gleam, smile*). A priest (Ne 10:8).

BILHAH [1167, 1168] (perhaps *simplicity,* or *modesty,* or *to be without concern*).

1. Rachel's servant, bears children by Jacob (Ge 29:29; 30:3-4; 37:2). Mother of Dan and Naphtali (Ge 30:1-8; 35:25; 46:23,25). Reuben's incest with (Ge 35:22; 49:4).

2. A place in the land of Simeon (1Ch 4:29). Called Balah (Jos 19:3) and Baalah (Jos 15:29).

BILHAN [1169] (*foolish*).

1. A Horite chief (Ge 36:27; 1Ch 1:42).

2. A Benjamite (1Ch 7:10).

BILL OF DIVORCE See *Divorce.*

BILSHAN [1193] (*their Bel [lord]*). A Jew of the Cap-tivity (Ezr 2:2; Ne 7:7).

BIMHAL [1197] (*son of circumcision*). Son of Japhlet (1Ch 7:33).

BINDING AND LOOSING [*1313, 3395*].

NIV+ BIND, BINDINGS, BINDS, BOUND

The carrying of a key or keys was a symbol of the delegated power of opening and closing (Mt 16:19; Rev 1:18). See *Key.*

The apostles were given power to bind and to loose (Mt 16:19; 18:18). Peter loosed the feet of the lame man at the temple gate (Ac 3:1-10), and Paul bound the sight of Elymas (Ac 13:8-11). Peter was present when the Holy Spirit was poured out on the Jews (Ac 2), Samaritans (Ac 8:14-17), and Gentiles (Ac 10:34-48).

BINEA [1232]. A descendant of King Saul (1Ch 8:37; 9:43).

BINNUI [1218] (*a son*).

1. Man who helped rebuild walls of Jerusalem (Ne 3:18, ftn).

2. A Jew of the Captivity (Ne 7:15). Called Bani (Ezr 2:10).

3. A Levite of the Captivity (Ne 3:24; 12:8; 10:9).

4. Father of Noadiah (Ezr 8:33).

5. Descendant of Pahath-Moab who married a foreign wife (Ezr 10:30).

6. A Jew of the Captivity whose descendants married foreign wives (Ezr 10:38).

BIRDS [1251+4053, 3687, 4053+7606, 6416, 6514, 7256, 7606, 10533, 10616, *3997, 4374, 4764*].

NIV+ BIRD, BIRD'S

Creation of, on the fifth creative day (Ge 1:20-30). Man's rule over (Ge 1:26,28; 9:2-3; Ps 8:5-8; Jer 27:6; Da 2:38; Jas 3:7). Given for food (Ge 9:2-3; Dt 14:11-20). What species were unclean (Lev 11:13-20; Dt 14:12-19).

Used for sacrifice. See *Dove; Pigeon.* Divine care of (Job 38:41; Ps 147:9; Mt 10:29; Lk 12:6,24). Songs of, at the break of day (Ps 104:12; Ecc 12:4; SS 2:12). Domesti-cated (Job 41:5; Jas 3:7). Solomon's proverbs of (1Ki 4:33). Nests of (Ps 104:17; Mt 8:20; 13:32). Instincts of

(Pr 1:17). Habits of (Job 39:13-18,26-30). Migrate (Jer 8:7).

Mosaic law protected the mother from being taken with the young (Dt 22:6-7). Cages of (Jer 5:27; Rev 18:2). *See Snare.*

Figurative: (Isa 16:2; 46:11; Jer 12:9; Eze 39:4).

Symbolic: (Da 7:6).

See Cormorant; Dove; Eagle; Falcon; Gull; Hawk; Hen, 2; Heron; Hoopoe; Kite; Osprey; Ostrich; Owl; Partridge; Pigeon; Quail; Raven; Red Kite; Screech Owl; Sparrow; Stork; Swallow; Swift; Thrush; Vulture; White Owl.

BIRSHA [1407] (*disagreeable in taste*). A king of Gomorrah (Ge 14:2-10).

BIRTH [*1061, 1800, 2655, 3528, 3533, 3535, 5951, 6584+7924, 6913, 8167, *1002, 1164, 1181, 2844, 3120+3613, 4472, 5503, 5770*].

NIV+ BEAR, BEARING, BEARS, BIRTHDAY, BORE, BORN, CHILDBEARING, CHILDBIRTH, FIRSTBORN, NEWBORN, STILLBORN, UNBORN

Pangs in giving (Ps 48:6; Isa 13:8; 21:3; Jer 4:31; 6:24; 30:6; 31:8). Giving, ordained to be in sorrow (Ge 3:16).

Famous births: Cain (Ge 4:1), Abel (Ge 4:2), Noah (Ge 5:28-29), Isaac (Ge 21:1-5), Esau and Jacob (Ge 25:24-26), the children of Jacob (Ge 29:31-30:24; 35:16-18), Moses (Ex 2:1-4), John the Baptist (Lk 1:5-25,57), Jesus (Mt 1:18-25; Lk 1:26-38; 2:1-20).

See Abortion; Children.

BIRTHDAY [3427+3528, *1160*].

NIV+ See BIRTH

Celebrated by feasts (Ge 40:20; Mt 14:6). Cursed (Job 3; Jer 20:14,18).

BIRTHRIGHT [1148]

NIV+ See BIRTH

Described—

Belonged to the firstborn (Dt 21:15-16). Entitled the firstborn to a double portion of inheritance (Dt 21:15-17), a royal succession (2Ch 21:3). An honorable title (Ex 4:22; Ps 89:27; Jer 31:9; Ro 8:29; Col 1:15; Heb 1:6; 12:23; Rev 1:5).

Lost by firstborn—

Sold by Esau (Ge 25:29-34; 27:36, w 25:33; Heb 12:16; Ro 9:12-13). Forfeited by Reuben (1Ch 5:1-2). Set aside: that of Manasseh (Ge 48:15-20), Adonijah (1Ki 2:15), Hosah's son (1Ch 26:10).

See Firstborn.

BIRZAITH, BIRZAVITH [1365] (*well of olive oil*). A descendant of Asher (1Ch 7:31).

BISHLAM [1420] (*son of Shalom [peace]*). A Samaritan who obstructed the rebuilding of the temple at Jerusalem (Ezr 4:7-24).

BISHOP The same as elder or overseer (Ac 20:28; Php 1:1; 1Ti 3:1; Tit 1:7, ftns). *See Elders; Overseer.*

BIT [1323, 5496, 8270, *5903*].

NIV+ BITS

Part of a bridle (Ps 32:9; Jas 3:3).

BITHIAH [1437] (possibly *worshiper of Yahweh* BDB; *[female pagan god] queen* KB). Daughter of Pharaoh and wife of Mered of Judah (1Ch 4:18).

BITHRON [1443] (*gully*). A district bordering on the Jordan (2Sa 2:29).

BITHYNIA [*1049*]. A Roman province in Asia Minor (Ac 16:7; 1Pe 1:1).

BITTER HERBS Eaten symbolically with the Passover (Ex 12:8; Nu 9:11).

BITTER WATER At Marah (Ex 15:23). A ceremonial water used by the priest (Nu 5:18-27).

BITTERN *See Owl.*

BITTERNESS [4360, 4933, 5253, 5289, 5352, 5353, 8032, *4394*].

NIV+ BITTER, BITTERLY, EMBITTER, EMBITTERED

A poisonous and bitter plant (Hos 10:4; Am 6:12). *See Gall, 3.*

Of spirit (Dt 32:32; Jer 4:18; Ac 8:23; Ro 3:14; Eph 4:31; Heb 12:5; Jas 3:14).

BITUMEN *See Tar.*

BIZIOTHIAH, BIZJOTHJAH [1026] (*contempt of Yahweh*). A town in Judah (Jos 15:28). Baalath Beer (Jos 19:8), and Balah (Jos 19:3).

BIZTHA [1030] (perhaps *eunuch,* or *bound*). A eunuch and servant of the Persian king Xerxes (Est 1:10).

BLACK VULTURE An unclean bird, not to be eaten under the law (Lev 11:13; Dt 14:13). *See Vulture.*

BLACKNESS [370, 3124, 3125, 4025, 6465, 6906, 7516, 7722, 8837, 8839, *3506*].

NIV+ BLACK, BLACKENED, BLACKER, BLACKEST

Figurative:

(Job 30:30; Joel 2:6). Blackness of darkness (Jude 13). *See Colors, Figurative and Symbolic.*

BLACKSMITH [3093]. *See Smith.*

BLAIN *See Boil.*

BLASPHEMY [*1552, 5542, 5919, 7837, *1059, 1060, 1061*] (*speak reviling*).

NIV+ BLASPHEME, BLASPHEMED, BLASPHEMER, BLASPHEMES, BLASPHEMIES, BLASPHEMING, BLASPHEMOUS

Reproaching God—

2Ki 19:22 Who is it you have insulted and blasphemed? Against whom have you raised your voice and lifted your eyes in pride? Against the Holy One of Israel!

2Ch 32:19 They spoke about the God of Jerusalem as they did about the gods of the other peoples of the world—the work of men's hands.

Ps 73:9 Their mouths lay claim to heaven, and their tongues take possession of the earth.

Ps 73:11 They say, "How can God know? Does the Most High have knowledge?"

Ps 74:18 Remember how the enemy has mocked you, O LORD, how foolish people have reviled your name.

Ps 139:20 They speak of you with evil intent; your adversaries misuse your name.

Pr 30:9 Otherwise, I may have too much and disown you and say, 'Who is the LORD?' Or I may become poor and steal, and so dishonor the name of my God. (+Isa 5:19)

Isa 8:21 Distressed and hungry, they will roam through the land; when they are famished, they will become enraged and, looking upward, will curse their king and their

God. ²²Then they will look toward the earth and see only distress and darkness and fearful gloom, and they will be thrust into utter darkness. (+Isa 37:23)

Isa 45:9 "Woe to him who quarrels with his Maker, to him who is but a potsherd among the potsherds on the ground. Does the clay say to the potter, 'What are you making?' Does your work say, 'He has no hands'?

Isa 52:5 "And now what do I have here?" declares the LORD. "For my people have been taken away for nothing, and those who rule them mock," declares the LORD. "And all day long my name is constantly blasphemed.

Eze 35:12 Then you will know that I the LORD have heard all the contemptible things you have said against the mountains of Israel. You said, "They have been laid waste and have been given over to us to devour." ¹³You boasted against me and spoke against me without restraint, and I heard it.

Da 7:25 He will speak against the Most High and oppress his saints and try to change the set times and the laws. The saints will be handed over to him for a time, times and half a time.

Mt 10:25 It is enough for the student to be like his teacher, and the servant like his master. If the head of the house has been called Beelzebub, how much more the members of his household!

Defying God—

Isa 29:15 Woe to those who go to great depths to hide their plans from the LORD, who do their work in darkness and think, "Who sees us? Who will know?" ¹⁶You turn things upside down, as if the potter were thought to be like the clay! Shall what is formed say to him who formed it, "He did not make me"? Can the pot say of the potter, "He knows nothing"?

Isa 36:15 Do not let Hezekiah persuade you to trust in the LORD when he says, 'The LORD will surely deliver us; this city will not be given into the hand of the king of Assyria.' (+Isa 36:16-17)

Isa 36:18 "Do not let Hezekiah mislead you when he says, 'The LORD will deliver us.' Has the god of any nation ever delivered his land from the hand of the king of Assyria? (+Isa 36:19)

Isa 36:20 Who of all the gods of these countries has been able to save his land from me? How then can the LORD deliver Jerusalem from my hand?"

²¹But the people remained silent and said nothing in reply, because the king had commanded, "Do not answer him."

Isa 37:10 "Say to Hezekiah king of Judah: Do not let the god you depend on deceive you when he says, 'Jerusalem will not be handed over to the king of Assyria.'

Eze 8:12 He said to me, "Son of man, have you seen what the elders of the house of Israel are doing in the darkness, each at the shrine of his own idol? They say, 'The LORD does not see us; the LORD has forsaken the land.'"

Eze 9:9 He answered me, "The sin of the house of Israel and Judah is exceedingly great; the land is full of bloodshed and the city is full of injustice. They say, 'The LORD has forsaken the land; the LORD does not see.'

Mal 3:13 "You have said harsh things against me," says the LORD. "Yet you ask, 'What have we said against you?'

¹⁴"You have said, 'It is futile to serve God. What did we gain by carrying out his requirements and going about like mourners before the LORD Almighty?

Denying God's word—

Jer 17:15 They keep saying to me, "Where is the word of the LORD? Let it now be fulfilled!"

Speaking lies against God—

Hos 7:13 Woe to them, because they have strayed from me! Destruction to them, because they have rebelled against me! I long to redeem them but they speak lies against me.

Attributing ignorance to God—

Ps 10:11 He says to himself, "God has forgotten; he covers his face and never sees."

Ps 10:13 Why does the wicked man revile God? Why does he say to himself, "He won't call me to account"?

Isa 40:27 Why do you say, O Jacob, and complain, O Israel, "My way is hidden from the LORD; my cause is disregarded by my God"?

Exalting oneself above God—

Da 11:36 "The king will do as he pleases. He will exalt and magnify himself above every god and will say unheard-of things against the God of gods. He will be successful until the time of wrath is completed, for what has been determined must take place. ³⁷He will show no regard for the gods of his fathers or for the one desired by women, nor will he regard any god, but will exalt himself above them all. (+2Th 2:4)

Calling Jesus accursed—

1Co 12:3 Therefore I tell you that no one who is speaking by the Spirit of God says, "Jesus be cursed," and no one can say, "Jesus is Lord," except by the Holy Spirit.

Jas 2:7 Are they not the ones who are slandering the noble name of him to whom you belong?

Occasioned by sins of believers (2Sa 12:14)—

Ro 2:24 As it is written: "God's name is blasphemed among the Gentiles because of you."

Foretold by Peter—

2Pe 3:3 First of all, you must understand that in the last days scoffers will come, scoffing and following their own evil desires. ⁴They will say, "Where is this 'coming' he promised? Ever since our fathers died, everything goes on as it has since the beginning of creation."

Foretold by John (Rev 13:1,5-6)—

Rev 16:9 They were seared by the intense heat and they cursed the name of God, who had control over these plagues, but they refused to repent and glorify him. (+Rev 16:11)

Rev 16:21 From the sky huge hailstones of about a hundred pounds each fell upon men. And they cursed God on account of the plague of hail, because the plague was so terrible.

Rev 17:3 Then the angel carried me away in the Spirit into a desert. There I saw a woman sitting on a scarlet beast that was covered with blasphemous names and had seven heads and ten horns.

Forbidden—

Ex 20:7 "You shall not misuse the name of the LORD your God, for the LORD will not hold anyone guiltless who misuses his name. (+Ex 22:28)

Lev 19:12 "'Do not swear falsely by my name and so profane the name of your God. I am the LORD. (+Lev 22:32)

Jas 3:10 Out of the same mouth come praise and cursing. My brothers, this should not be.

Jas 5:12 Above all, my brothers, do not swear—not by heaven or by earth or by anything else. Let your "Yes" be yes, and your "No," no, or you will be condemned.

Against the Holy Spirit—

Mt 12:31 And so I tell you, every sin and blasphemy will be forgiven men, but the blasphemy against the Spirit will not be forgiven. [32]Anyone who speaks a word against the Son of Man will be forgiven, but anyone who speaks against the Holy Spirit will not be forgiven, either in this age or in the age to come. (+Mk 3:29-30; Lk 12:10)

Punishment for—

Lev 24:10 Now the son of an Israelite mother and an Egyptian father went out among the Israelites, and a fight broke out in the camp between him and an Israelite. [11]The son of the Israelite woman blasphemed the Name with a curse; so they brought him to Moses. (His mother's name was Shelomith, the daughter of Dibri the Danite.) [12]They put him in custody until the will of the LORD should be made clear to them.

[13]Then the LORD said to Moses: [14]"Take the blasphemer outside the camp. All those who heard him are to lay their hands on his head, and the entire assembly is to stone him. [15]Say to the Israelites: 'If anyone curses his God, he will be held responsible; [16]anyone who blasphemes the name of the LORD must be put to death. The entire assembly must stone him. Whether an alien or native-born, when he blasphemes the Name, he must be put to death.

Isa 65:7 both your sins and the sins of your fathers," says the LORD. "Because they burned sacrifices on the mountains and defied me on the hills, I will measure into their laps the full payment for their former deeds."

Heb 10:29 How much more severely do you think a man deserves to be punished who has trampled the Son of God under foot, who has treated as an unholy thing the blood of the covenant that sanctified him, and who has insulted the Spirit of grace?

Instances of:

Israel—

Eze 20:27 "Therefore, son of man, speak to the people of Israel and say to them, 'This is what the Sovereign LORD says: In this also your fathers blasphemed me by forsaking me: [28]When I brought them into the land I had sworn to give them and they saw any high hill or any leafy tree, there they offered their sacrifices, made offerings that provoked me to anger, presented their fragrant incense and poured out their drink offerings.

The depraved son of Shelomith, who, in a fight with an Israelite, cursed God (Lev 24:10-16). Of the Israelites, in grumbling against God (Nu 21:5-6). Infidels who used the adultery of David as an occasion to blaspheme (2Sa 12:14). Shimei, in his malice toward David (2Sa 16:5). One of Sennacherib's field commanders, in the siege of Jerusalem (2Ki 18:22; 19; Isa 36:15-20; 37:10-33). Job's wife, when she exhorted Job to curse God and die (Job 2:9). Peter, when accused of being a disciple of Jesus (Mt 26:74; Mk 14:71). The revilers of Jesus, when He was crucified (Mt 27:40-44,63). The early Christians, persecuted by Saul of Tarsus compelled to blaspheme the name of Jesus (Ac 26:11; 1Ti 1:13). Two disciples, Hymenaeus and Alexander, who were delivered to Satan that they might learn not to blaspheme (1Ti 1:20).

Man of sin (2Th 2:3)—

2Th 2:4 He will oppose and will exalt himself over everything that is called God or is worshiped, so that he sets himself up in God's temple, proclaiming himself to be God.

Backslidden Ephesians (Rev 2:9).

False Accusations of:

Against Naboth (1Ki 21:13).

Against Jesus (Mt 9:3; 26:65; Mk 2:7; 14:58; Lk 5:21; 22:70-71; Jn 5:18; 10:33)—

Jn 19:7 The Jews insisted, "We have a law, and according to that law he must die, because he claimed to be the Son of God."

Against Stephen (Ac 6:11,13).

Prophecy of—

Rev 13:1 And the dragon stood on the shore of the sea. And I saw a beast coming out of the sea. He had ten horns and seven heads, with ten crowns on his horns, and on each head a blasphemous name. (+Rev 13:5)

Rev 13:6 He opened his mouth to blaspheme God, and to slander his name and his dwelling place and those who live in heaven. (+Rev 16:9,11,21; 17:3)

BLAST [*5870, 5972, 7754, 7938, 8120].

NIV+ BLASTS

1. From God's nostrils, figurative of judgment (Ex 15:8; 2Sa 22:16; Job 4:9; Ps 18:15).

2. From a horn, a call to assemble (Ex 19:13,16; Lev 23:24) or to battle (Jos 6:5,16; Job 39:25).

BLASTUS [*1058*] (*sprout [of a vine, branch]*). One of Herod's officers (Ac 12:20).

BLEEDING, SUBJECT TO A woman who had been bleeding for twelve years could not be healed by physicians (Mt 9:20; Mk 5:25; Lk 8:43, ftn). The precise nature of the woman's problem is not known. Her existence was wretched because she was shunned by people generally, since anyone having contact with her was made ceremonially unclean (Lev 15:25-33). Jesus healed her (both physically, "be freed from your suffering," and spiritually, "go in peace"; Mk 5:34) as a result of her simple act of faith.

BLEMISH [4583, 8845, *320, 3700, 5069*].

NIV+ BLEMISHED, BLEMISHES

A physical deformity. Barred sons of Aaron from exercise of priestly offices (Lev 21:17-23). Animals with, forbidden to be used for sacrifice (Lev 22:19-25).

Figurative: (Eph 5:27; 1Pe 1:19).

BLESSING [*887, 897, 1385, 1388, *1922, 2328, 2330, 3421*].

NIV+ BLESS, BLESSED, BLESSEDNESS, BLESSES, BLESSINGS

For blessing before eating. *See Benedictions; Prayer, Thanksgiving, and Before Taking Food.*

BLESSINGS, SPIRITUAL

From God:

Dt 33:25 The bolts of your gates will be iron and bronze, and your strength will equal your days. (+Dt 33:27)

Ps 18:28 You, O LORD, keep my lamp burning; my God turns my darkness into light. (+Ps 18:29-31)

Ps 18:32 It is God who arms me with strength and makes my way perfect. (+Ps 18:33-34)

Ps 18:35 You give me your shield of victory, and your right hand sustains me; you stoop down to make me great. [36]You broaden the path beneath me, so that my ankles do not turn.

Ps 29:11 The LORD gives strength to his people; the LORD blesses his people with peace.

Ps 37:6 He will make your righteousness shine like the dawn, the justice of your cause like the noonday sun.

Ps 37:17 for the power of the wicked will be broken, but the LORD upholds the righteous.

Ps 37:24 though he stumble, he will not fall, for the LORD upholds him with his hand.

Ps 37:39 The salvation of the righteous comes from the LORD; he is their stronghold in time of trouble.

Ps 63:8 My soul clings to you; your right hand upholds me. (+Ps 66:8)

Ps 66:9 he has preserved our lives and kept our feet from slipping.

Ps 68:18 When you ascended on high, you led captives in your train; you received gifts from men, even from the rebellious—that you, O LORD God, might dwell there.

Ps 68:28 Summon your power, O God; show us your strength, O God, as you have done before.

Ps 68:35 You are awesome, O God, in your sanctuary; the God of Israel gives power and strength to his people. Praise be to God!

Ps 84:5 Blessed are those whose strength is in you, who have set their hearts on pilgrimage.

Ps 84:11 For the LORD God is a sun and shield; the LORD bestows favor and honor; no good thing does he withhold from those whose walk is blameless.

Isa 40:11 He tends his flock like a shepherd: He gathers the lambs in his arms and carries them close to his heart; he gently leads those that have young.

Isa 40:29 He gives strength to the weary and increases the power of the weak.

Isa 40:31 but those who hope in the LORD will renew their strength. They will soar on wings like eagles; they will run and not grow weary, they will walk and not be faint.

Isa 41:10 So do not fear, for I am with you; do not be dismayed, for I am your God. I will strengthen you and help you; I will uphold you with my righteous right hand.

Isa 41:13 For I am the LORD, your God, who takes hold of your right hand and says to you, Do not fear; I will help you. (+Isa 41:16; Ac 3:19)

1Co 2:9 However, as it is written: "No eye has seen, no ear has heard, no mind has conceived what God has prepared for those who love him"— (+Php 4:13)

Jas 1:17 Every good and perfect gift is from above, coming down from the Father of the heavenly lights, who does not change like shifting shadows.

Jude 24 To him who is able to keep you from falling and to present you before his glorious presence without fault and with great joy—

Guidance—

Ex 33:16 How will anyone know that you are pleased with me and with your people unless you go with us? What else will distinguish me and your people from all the other people on the face of the earth?"

Ps 23:2 He makes me lie down in green pastures, he leads me beside quiet waters, ³he restores my soul. He guides me in paths of righteousness for his name's sake.

Ps 119:102 I have not departed from your laws, for you yourself have taught me. (+Isa 40:11)

Isa 58:11 The LORD will guide you always; he will satisfy your needs in a sun-scorched land and will strengthen your frame. You will be like a well-watered garden, like a spring whose waters never fail.

Sanctification (Ex 31:13)—

Lev 21:8 Regard them as holy, because they offer up the food of your God. Consider them holy, because I the LORD am holy—I who make you holy.

Isa 1:25 I will turn my hand against you; I will thoroughly purge away your dross and remove all your impurities.

Isa 4:3 Those who are left in Zion, who remain in Jerusalem, will be called holy, all who are recorded among the living in Jerusalem. ⁴The Lord will wash away the filth of the women of Zion; he will cleanse the bloodstains from Jerusalem by a spirit of judgment and a spirit of fire.

Isa 6:6 Then one of the seraphs flew to me with a live coal in his hand, which he had taken with tongs from the altar. ⁷With it he touched my mouth and said, "See, this has touched your lips; your guilt is taken away and your sin atoned for."

1Jn 1:9 If we confess our sins, he is faithful and just and will forgive us our sins and purify us from all unrighteousness.

Jude 1 Jude, a servant of Jesus Christ and a brother of James, To those who have been called, who are loved by God the Father and kept by Jesus Christ:

The perfecting of salvation—

2Co 1:21 Now it is God who makes both us and you stand firm in Christ. He anointed us,

Php 1:6 being confident of this, that he who began a good work in you will carry it on to completion until the day of Christ Jesus.

Php 2:13 for it is God who works in you to will and to act according to his good purpose.

Php 4:19 And my God will meet all your needs according to his glorious riches in Christ Jesus.

Col 1:11 being strengthened with all power according to his glorious might so that you may have great endurance and patience, and joyfully ¹²giving thanks to the Father, who has qualified you to share in the inheritance of the saints in the kingdom of light.

1Th 5:24 The one who calls you is faithful and he will do it. (+Heb 13:20-21)

1Pe 1:5 who through faith are shielded by God's power until the coming of the salvation that is ready to be' revealed in the last time.

2Pe 1:2 Grace and peace be yours in abundance through the knowledge of God and of Jesus our Lord.

³His divine power has given us everything we need for life and godliness through our knowledge of him who called us by his own glory and goodness. ⁴Through these he has given us his very great and precious promises, so that through them you may participate in the divine nature and escape the corruption in the world caused by evil desires.

The deposit of the Spirit, guaranteeing what is to come—

2Co 1:22 set his seal of ownership on us, and put his Spirit in our hearts as a deposit, guaranteeing what is to come.

2Co 5:5 Now it is God who has made us for this very purpose and has given us the Spirit as a deposit, guaranteeing what is to come.

Peace—

Isa 26:12 LORD, you establish peace for us; all that we have accomplished you have done for us.

Isa 57:19 creating praise on the lips of the mourners in Israel. Peace, peace, to those far and near," says the LORD. "And I will heal them."

Mal 4:2 But for you who revere my name, the sun of righteousness will rise with healing in its wings. And you will go out and leap like calves released from the stall.

Php 4:7 And the peace of God, which transcends all understanding, will guard your hearts and your minds in Christ Jesus.

From Christ:

Jn 1:16 From the fullness of his grace we have all received one blessing after another. (+Ro 1:7; 16:20; 1Co 1:3;

16:23; 2Co 1:2; 13:14; Gal 1:3; 6:16,18; Eph 1:2; 6:23-24; Php 1:2; 4:23; 1Th 5:28; 2Th 1:2; 3:16,18; 1Ti 1:2; 2Ti 1:2; Phm 3,25; 2Pe 1:1; 2Jn 3)

Contingent Upon Obedience and Resulting in:

Divine favor—

Ex 19:5 Now if you obey me fully and keep my covenant, then out of all nations you will be my treasured possession. Although the whole earth is mine, (+Jer 7:23)

Mercy—

Ex 20:6 but showing love to a thousand [generations] of those who love me and keep my commandments.

Dt 5:10 but showing love to a thousand [generations] of those who love me and keep my commandments. (+Dt 5:16)

Dt 7:9 Know therefore that the LORD your God is God; he is the faithful God, keeping his covenant of love to a thousand generations of those who love him and keep his commands.

1Ki 8:23 and said: "O LORD, God of Israel, there is no God like you in heaven above or on earth below—you who keep your covenant of love with your servants who continue wholeheartedly in your way.

2Ch 30:9 If you return to the LORD, then your brothers and your children will be shown compassion by their captors and will come back to this land, for the LORD your God is gracious and compassionate. He will not turn his face from you if you return to him."

Holiness (Dt 28:9; 30:1-3)—

Dt 30:6 The LORD your God will circumcise your hearts and the hearts of your descendants, so that you may love him with all your heart and with all your soul, and live. (+Col 1:22-23)

Eternal salvation—

Mt 10:22 All men will hate you because of me, but he who stands firm to the end will be saved.

Mt 24:13 but he who stands firm to the end will be saved. (+Mk 13:13)

Heb 3:6 But Christ is faithful as a son over God's house. And we are his house, if we hold on to our courage and the hope of which we boast.

Heb 3:14 We have come to share in Christ if we hold firmly till the end the confidence we had at first.

Heb 10:36 You need to persevere so that when you have done the will of God, you will receive what he has promised.

Rev 2:10 Do not be afraid of what you are about to suffer. I tell you, the devil will put some of you in prison to test you, and you will suffer persecution for ten days. Be faithful, even to the point of death, and I will give you the crown of life.

See Contingencies; Faithfulness; Regeneration; Salvation.

BLESSINGS, TEMPORAL

From God: (Ps 136:25).

Rain (Dt 11:14; 28:12)—

Job 37:6 He says to the snow, 'Fall on the earth,' and to the rain shower, 'Be a mighty downpour.'

Job 38:25 Who cuts a channel for the torrents of rain, and a path for the thunderstorm, ²⁶to water a land where no man lives, a desert with no one in it, ²⁷to satisfy a desolate wasteland and make it sprout with grass?

Ps 68:9 You gave abundant showers, O God; you refreshed your weary inheritance.

Ps 135:7 He makes clouds rise from the ends of the earth;

he sends lightning with the rain and brings out the wind from his storehouses.

Ps 147:8 He covers the sky with clouds; he supplies the earth with rain and makes grass grow on the hills.

Jer 10:13 When he thunders, the waters in the heavens roar; he makes clouds rise from the ends of the earth. He sends lightning with the rain and brings out the wind from his storehouses.

Jer 14:22 Do any of the worthless idols of the nations bring rain? Do the skies themselves send down showers? No, it is you, O LORD our God. Therefore our hope is in you, for you are the one who does all this. (+Jer 51:16)

Joel 2:23 Be glad, O people of Zion, rejoice in the LORD your God, for he has given you the autumn rains in righteousness. He sends you abundant showers, both autumn and spring rains, as before.

Am 4:7 "I also withheld rain from you when the harvest was still three months away. I sent rain on one town, but withheld it from another. One field had rain; another had none and dried up.

Zec 10:1 Ask the LORD for rain in the springtime; it is the LORD who makes the storm clouds. He gives showers of rain to men, and plants of the field to everyone.

Zec 10:12 I will strengthen them in the LORD and in his name they will walk," declares the LORD.

Mt 5:45 that you may be sons of your Father in heaven. He causes his sun to rise on the evil and the good, and sends rain on the righteous and the unrighteous. (+Ac 14:17)

Seedtime and harvest—

Ge 8:22 "As long as the earth endures, seedtime and harvest, cold and heat, summer and winter, day and night will never cease."

Lev 25:20 You may ask, "What will we eat in the seventh year if we do not plant or harvest our crops?" ²¹I will send you such a blessing in the sixth year that the land will yield enough for three years. ²²While you plant during the eighth year, you will eat from the old crop and will continue to eat from it until the harvest of the ninth year comes in.

Lev 26:4 I will send you rain in its season, and the ground will yield its crops and the trees of the field their fruit. ⁵Your threshing will continue until grape harvest and the grape harvest will continue until planting, and you will eat all the food you want and live in safety in your land.

Ps 107:35 He turned the desert into pools of water and the parched ground into flowing springs; ³⁶there he brought the hungry to live, and they founded a city where they could settle. ³⁷They sowed fields and planted vineyards that yielded a fruitful harvest; ³⁸he blessed them, and their numbers greatly increased, and he did not let their herds diminish.

Isa 55:10 As the rain and the snow come down from heaven, and do not return to it without watering the earth and making it bud and flourish, so that it yields seed for the sower and bread for the eater,

Jer 5:24 They do not say to themselves, 'Let us fear the LORD our God, who gives autumn and spring rains in season, who assures us of the regular weeks of harvest.'

Eze 36:30 I will increase the fruit of the trees and the crops of the field, so that you will no longer suffer disgrace among the nations because of famine. (+Mal 3:11; Ac 14:17)

Food and clothing—

Ge 9:1 Then God blessed Noah and his sons, saying to them, "Be fruitful and increase in number and fill the earth. ²The fear and dread of you will fall upon all the beasts of the earth and all the birds of the air, upon every creature that moves along the ground, and upon all the fish of the sea; they are given into your hands. [3]Everything that lives and moves will be food for you. Just as I gave you the green plants, I now give you everything.

Ge 28:20 Then Jacob made a vow, saying, "If God will be with me and will watch over me on this journey I am taking and will give me food to eat and clothes to wear [21]so that I return safely to my father's house, then the LORD will be my God

Dt 8:3 He humbled you, causing you to hunger and then feeding you with manna, which neither you nor your fathers had known, to teach you that man does not live on bread alone but on every word that comes from the mouth of the LORD. [4]Your clothes did not wear out and your feet did not swell during these forty years.

Dt 10:18 He defends the cause of the fatherless and the widow, and loves the alien, giving him food and clothing.

Dt 29:5 During the forty years that I led you through the desert, your clothes did not wear out, nor did the sandals on your feet.

Ru 1:6 When she heard in Moab that the LORD had come to the aid of his people by providing food for them, Naomi and her daughters-in-law prepared to return home from there.

2Ch 31:10 and Azariah the chief priest, from the family of Zadok, answered, "Since the people began to bring their contributions to the temple of the LORD, we have had enough to eat and plenty to spare, because the LORD has blessed his people, and this great amount is left over."

Ps 65:9 You care for the land and water it; you enrich it abundantly. The streams of God are filled with water to provide the people with grain, for so you have ordained it.

Ps 68:1 May God arise, may his enemies be scattered; may his foes flee before him. [2]As smoke is blown away by the wind, may you blow them away; as wax melts before the fire, may the wicked perish before God. [3]But may the righteous be glad and rejoice before God; may they be happy and joyful.

[4]Sing to God, sing praise to his name, extol him who rides on the clouds—his name is the LORD—and rejoice before him. [5]A father to the fatherless, a defender of widows, is God in his holy dwelling. [6]God sets the lonely in families, he leads forth the prisoners with singing; but the rebellious live in a sun-scorched land.

[7]When you went out before your people, O God, when you marched through the wasteland, *Selah* [8]the earth shook, the heavens poured down rain, before God, the One of Sinai, before God, the God of Israel. [9]You gave abundant showers, O God; you refreshed your weary inheritance. [10]Your people settled in it, and from your bounty, O God, you provided for the poor.

Ps 81:16 But you would be fed with the finest of wheat; with honey from the rock I would satisfy you."

Ps 104:14 He makes grass grow for the cattle, and plants for man to cultivate—bringing forth food from the earth: [15]wine that gladdens the heart of man, oil to make his face shine, and bread that sustains his heart.

Ps 104:27 These all look to you to give them their food at the proper time. [28]When you give it to them, they gather it up; when you open your hand, they are satisfied with good things.

Ps 111:5 He provides food for those who fear him; he remembers his covenant forever.

Ps 132:15 I will bless her with abundant provisions; her poor will I satisfy with food.

Ps 145:15 The eyes of all look to you, and you give them their food at the proper time. [16]You open your hand and satisfy the desires of every living thing.

Ps 146:7 He upholds the cause of the oppressed and gives food to the hungry. The LORD sets prisoners free,

Ecc 2:24 A man can do nothing better than to eat and drink and find satisfaction in his work. This too, I see, is from the hand of God,

Ecc 3:13 That everyone may eat and drink, and find satisfaction in all his toil—this is the gift of God.

Isa 33:15 He who walks righteously and speaks what is right, who rejects gain from extortion and keeps his hand from accepting bribes, who stops his ears against plots of murder and shuts his eyes against contemplating evil— [16]this is the man who will dwell on the heights, whose refuge will be the mountain fortress. His bread will be supplied, and water will not fail him.

Joel 2:26 You will have plenty to eat, until you are full, and you will praise the name of the LORD your God, who has worked wonders for you; never again will my people be shamed.

Mt 6:26 Look at the birds of the air; they do not sow or reap or store away in barns, and yet your heavenly Father feeds them. Are you not much more valuable than they?

Mt 6:30 If that is how God clothes the grass of the field, which is here today and tomorrow is thrown into the fire, will he not much more clothe you, O you of little faith? [31]So do not worry, saying, 'What shall we eat?' or 'What shall we drink?' or 'What shall we wear?' [32]For the pagans run after all these things, and your heavenly Father knows that you need them. [33]But seek first his kingdom and his righteousness, and all these things will be given to you as well.

Lk 12:22 Then Jesus said to his disciples: "Therefore I tell you, do not worry about your life, what you will eat; or about your body, what you will wear. [23]Life is more than food, and the body more than clothes. [24]Consider the ravens: They do not sow or reap, they have no storeroom or barn; yet God feeds them. And how much more valuable you are than birds! [25]Who of you by worrying can add a single hour to his life? [26]Since you cannot do this very little thing, why do you worry about the rest?

[27]"Consider how the lilies grow. They do not labor or spin. Yet I tell you, not even Solomon in all his splendor was dressed like one of these. [28]If that is how God clothes the grass of the field, which is here today, and tomorrow is thrown into the fire, how much more will he clothe you, O you of little faith! [29]And do not set your heart on what you will eat or drink; do not worry about it. [30]For the pagan world runs after all such things, and your Father knows that you need them. [31]But seek his kingdom, and these things will be given to you as well.

Jn 6:31 Our forefathers ate the manna in the desert; as it is written: 'He gave them bread from heaven to eat.'"

Preservation of life—

Dt 4:1 Hear now, O Israel, the decrees and laws I am about to teach you. Follow them so that you may live and may go in and take possession of the land that the LORD, the God of your fathers, is giving you.

Dt 4:40 Keep his decrees and commands, which I am giving you today, so that it may go well with you and your children after you and that you may live long in the land the LORD your God gives you for all time. (+Dt 5:33)

Dt 7:15 The LORD will keep you free from every disease. He will not inflict on you the horrible diseases you knew in Egypt, but he will inflict them on all who hate you.

Ps 21:4 He asked you for life, and you gave it to him—length of days, for ever and ever. (+Ps 3:6; 91:16)

Ps 103:2 Praise the LORD, O my soul, and forget not all his benefits— ³who forgives all your sins and heals all your diseases, ⁴who redeems your life from the pit and crowns you with love and compassion, ⁵who satisfies your desires with good things so that your youth is renewed like the eagle's.

Da 6:20 When he came near the den, he called to Daniel in an anguished voice, "Daniel, servant of the living God, has your God, whom you serve continually, been able to rescue you from the lions?" (+Da 6:22)

Children—

Ps 113:9 He settles the barren woman in her home as a happy mother of children. Praise the LORD.

Ps 127:3 Sons are a heritage from the LORD, children a reward from him. ⁴Like arrows in the hands of a warrior are sons born in one's youth. ⁵Blessed is the man whose quiver is full of them. They will not be put to shame when they contend with their enemies in the gate.

Prosperity (Ge 24:56; 26:24)—

Ge 49:24 But his bow remained steady, his strong arms stayed limber, because of the hand of the Mighty One of Jacob, because of the Shepherd, the Rock of Israel, (+Ge 49:25; Nu 10:29)

Dt 8:7 For the LORD your God is bringing you into a good land—a land with streams and pools of water, with springs flowing in the valleys and hills; ⁸a land with wheat and barley, vines and fig trees, pomegranates, olive oil and honey; ⁹a land where bread will not be scarce and you will lack nothing; a land where the rocks are iron and you can dig copper out of the hills.

¹⁰When you have eaten and are satisfied, praise the LORD your God for the good land he has given you. (+Dt 8:18)

1Sa 2:7 The LORD sends poverty and wealth; he humbles and he exalts. ⁸He raises the poor from the dust and lifts the needy from the ash heap; he seats them with princes and has them inherit a throne of honor. "For the foundations of the earth are the LORD's; upon them he has set the world.

1Ch 29:12 Wealth and honor come from you; you are the ruler of all things. In your hands are strength and power to exalt and give strength to all.

1Ch 29:14 "But who am I, and who are my people, that we should be able to give as generously as this? Everything comes from you, and we have given you only what comes from your hand.

1Ch 29:16 O LORD our God, as for all this abundance that we have provided for building you a temple for your Holy Name, it comes from your hand, and all of it belongs to you.

2Ch 1:12 therefore wisdom and knowledge will be given you. And I will also give you wealth, riches and honor, such as no king who was before you ever had and none after you will have."

Ezr 8:22 I was ashamed to ask the king for soldiers and horsemen to protect us from enemies on the road, because we had told the king, "The gracious hand of our God is on everyone who looks to him, but his great anger is against all who forsake him."

Ps 147:13 for he strengthens the bars of your gates and blesses your people within you. ¹⁴He grants peace to your borders and satisfies you with the finest of wheat.

Ecc 5:19 Moreover, when God gives any man wealth and possessions, and enables him to enjoy them, to accept his lot and be happy in his work—this is a gift of God.

Isa 30:23 He will also send you rain for the seed you sow in the ground, and the food that comes from the land will be rich and plentiful. In that day your cattle will graze in broad meadows.

Hos 2:8 She has not acknowledged that I was the one who gave her the grain, the new wine and oil, who lavished on her the silver and gold—which they used for Baal.

National greatness—

Ge 22:17 I will surely bless you and make your descendants as numerous as the stars in the sky and as the sand on the seashore. Your descendants will take possession of the cities of their enemies, (+Ge 26:3)

Ge 26:4 I will make your descendants as numerous as the stars in the sky and will give them all these lands, and through your offspring all nations on earth will be blessed,

Dt 1:10 The LORD your God has increased your numbers so that today you are as many as the stars in the sky.

Dt 7:13 He will love you and bless you and increase your numbers. He will bless the fruit of your womb, the crops of your land—your grain, new wine and oil—the calves of your herds and the lambs of your flocks in the land that he swore to your forefathers to give you. ¹⁴You will be blessed more than any other people; none of your men or women will be childless, nor any of your livestock without young.

Dt 15:4 However, there should be no poor among you, for in the land the LORD your God is giving you to possess as your inheritance, he will richly bless you,

Dt 15:6 For the LORD your God will bless you as he has promised, and you will lend to many nations but will borrow from none. You will rule over many nations but none will rule over you. (+Dt 26:18-19)

Dt 32:13 He made him ride on the heights of the land and fed him with the fruit of the fields. He nourished him with honey from the rock, and with oil from the flinty crag, ¹⁴with curds and milk from herd and flock and with fattened lambs and goats, with choice rams of Bashan and the finest kernels of wheat. You drank the foaming blood of the grape.

Job 12:23 He makes nations great, and destroys them; he enlarges nations, and disperses them.

Ps 69:35 for God will save Zion and rebuild the cities of Judah. Then people will settle there and possess it; ³⁶the children of his servants will inherit it, and those who love his name will dwell there. (+Isa 51:2)

Jer 30:19 From them will come songs of thanksgiving and the sound of rejoicing. I will add to their numbers, and they will not be decreased; I will bring them honor, and they will not be disdained.

Eze 36:36 Then the nations around you that remain will know that I the LORD have rebuilt what was destroyed and have replanted what was desolate. I the LORD have spoken, and I will do it.' (+Eze 36:37)

Eze 36:38 as numerous as the flocks for offerings at Jerusalem during her appointed feasts. So will the ruined cities be filled with flocks of people. Then they will know that I am the LORD."

Da 5:18 "O king, the Most High God gave your father Nebuchadnezzar sovereignty and greatness and glory and splendor.

Social peace (Lev 26:6; 1Ch 22:9)

Victory over enemies—

Ex 23:22 If you listen carefully to what he says and do all that I say, I will be an enemy to your enemies and will oppose those who oppose you.

Lev 26:6 "'I will grant peace in the land, and you will lie down and no one will make you afraid. I will remove savage beasts from the land, and the sword will not pass through your country. [7]You will pursue your enemies, and they will fall by the sword before you. [8]Five of you will chase a hundred, and a hundred of you will chase ten thousand, and your enemies will fall by the sword before you.

[9]" 'I will look on you with favor and make you fruitful and increase your numbers, and I will keep my covenant with you. (+Dt 28:7)

Ps 44:3 It was not by their sword that they won the land, nor did their arm bring them victory; it was your right hand, your arm, and the light of your face, for you loved them.

Worldly honors—

2Sa 7:8 "Now then, tell my servant David, 'This is what the LORD Almighty says: I took you from the pasture and from following the flock to be ruler over my people Israel. [9]I have been with you wherever you have gone, and I have cut off all your enemies from before you. Now I will make your name great, like the names of the greatest men of the earth. (+1Ch 17:7-8)

Exemplified to:

Noah at the time of the Flood (Ge 7:1),,Abraham (Ge 24:1). Isaac (Ge 26:12-24,28). Jacob (Ge 35:9-15). Israelites in Egypt (Ex 11:3)

In the wilderness, supplying water—

Ex 17:1 The whole Israelite community set out from the Desert of Sin, traveling from place to place as the LORD commanded. They camped at Rephidim, but there was no water for the people to drink. [2]So they quarreled with Moses and said, "Give us water to drink." Moses replied, "Why do you quarrel with me? Why do you put the LORD to the test?"

[3]But the people were thirsty for water there, and they grumbled against Moses. They said, "Why did you bring us up out of Egypt to make us and our children and livestock die of thirst?"

[4]Then Moses cried out to the LORD, "What am I to do with these people? They are almost ready to stone me."

[5]The LORD answered Moses, "Walk on ahead of the people. Take with you some of the elders of Israel and take in your hand the staff with which you struck the Nile, and go. [6]I will stand there before you by the rock at Horeb. Strike the rock, and water will come out of it for the people to drink." So Moses did this in the sight of the elders of Israel. [7]And he called the place Massah and Meribah because the Israelites quarreled and because they tested the LORD saying, "Is the LORD among us or not?" (+Nu 20:10-11; Ps 78:15-20)

Ps 105:4 Look to the LORD and his strength; seek his face always.

Manna (Ex 16:14,31; Nu 11:7-9; Ne 9:15; Ps 78:23-24). Quail (Nu 11:31-33; Ps 78:23-30; 105:40). To David (2Sa 5:10; 1Ch 14:17). Obed-Edom (2Sa 6:11). Solomon (1Ki 3:13; 1Ch 29:25; 2Ch 1:1). Elijah, fed by ravens (1Ki 17:2-7). By an angel (1Ki 19:5-8). To the widow of Zarephath (1Ki 17:12-16). Hezekiah prospered (2Ki 18:6-7; 2Ch 32:29). Restored to health (2Ki 20:1-7). Asa (2Ch 14:6-7). Jehoshaphat (2Ch 17:3-5; 20:30). Uzziah (2Ch 26:5-15). Jotham (2Ch 27:6). Job (Job 1:10; 42:10,12). Daniel (Da 1:9).

Prayer for:

Rain (1Ki 8:36; 2Ch 6:27).

Plentiful harvests—

Ge 27:28 May God give you of heaven's dew and of

earth's richness—an abundance of grain and new wine. (+Dt 26:15)

Dt 33:13 About Joseph he said: "May the LORD bless his land with the precious dew from heaven above and with the deep waters that lie below; (+Dt 33:14-15)

Dt 33:16 with the best gifts of the earth and its fullness and the favor of him who dwelt in the burning bush. Let all these rest on the head of Joseph, on the brow of the prince among his brothers.

Daily bread (Mt 6:11; Lk 11:3).

Prosperity (Ge 28:3-4)—

1Ch 4:10 Jabez cried out to the God of Israel, "Oh, that you would bless me and enlarge my territory! Let your hand be with me, and keep me from harm so that I will be free from pain." And God granted his request. (+Ne 1:11)

3Jn 2 Dear friend, I pray that you may enjoy good health and that all may go well with you, even as your soul is getting along well.

Providential guidance (Ge 24:12-14,42-44)—

Ro 1:10 in my prayers at all times; and I pray that now at last by God's will the way may be opened for me to come to you.

1Th 3:11 Now may our God and Father himself and our Lord Jesus clear the way for us to come to you.

Instances of Prayer for:

Abraham (Ge 15:2-4). Abraham's servant (Ge 24:12). Laban (Ge 24:60). Isaac (Ge 25:21). Hannah (1Sa 1:11). Elijah (1Ki 17:20-21; 18:42,44; Jas 5:17-18). Ezra (Ezr 8:21-23). Nehemiah (Ne 1:11; 2:4; 6:9).

Contingent Upon Obedience and Resulting in:

Longevity (Ex 20:12; Dt 4:40; 5:16)—

1Ki 3:14 And if you walk in my ways and obey my statutes and commands as David your father did, I will give you a long life."

Pr 3:1 My son, do not forget my teaching, but keep my commands in your heart, [2]for they will prolong your life many years and bring you prosperity.

Deliverance from enemies (Ex 23:22)—

Lev 26:6 " 'I will grant peace in the land, and you will lie down and no one will make you afraid. I will remove savage beasts from the land, and the sword will not pass through your country. [7]You will pursue your enemies, and they will fall by the sword before you. [8]Five of you will chase a hundred, and a hundred of you will chase ten thousand, and your enemies will fall by the sword before you. (+Dt 28:7; 30:1-4)

Pr 16:7 When a man's ways are pleasing to the LORD, he makes even his enemies live at peace with him.

Jer 15:19 Therefore this is what the LORD says: "If you repent, I will restore you that you may serve me; if you utter worthy, not worthless, words, you will be my spokesman. Let this people turn to you, but you must not turn to them. [20]I will make you a wall to this people, a fortified wall of bronze; they will fight against you but will not overcome you, for I am with you to rescue and save you," declares the LORD. [21]"I will save you from the hands of the wicked and redeem you from the grasp of the cruel."

Prosperity—

Lev 26:3 " 'If you follow my decrees and are careful to obey my commands, [4]I will send you rain in its season, and the ground will yield its crops and the trees of the field their fruit. [5]Your threshing will continue until grape harvest and the grape harvest will continue until planting, and you will eat all the food you want and live in safety in your land.

Dt 7:12 If you pay attention to these laws and are careful to follow them, then the Lord your God will keep his covenant of love with you, as he swore to your forefathers. [13]He will love you and bless you and increase your numbers. He will bless the fruit of your womb, the crops of your land—your grain, new wine and oil—the calves of your herds and the lambs of your flocks in the land that he swore to your forefathers to give you. [14]You will be blessed more than any other people; none of your men or women will be childless, nor any of your livestock without young.

Dt 15:4 However, there should be no poor among you, for in the land the Lord your God is giving you to possess as your inheritance, he will richly bless you, [5]if only you fully obey the Lord your God and are careful to follow all these commands I am giving you today.

Dt 28:2 All these blessings will come upon you and accompany you if you obey the Lord your God:

[3]You will be blessed in the city and blessed in the country.

[4]The fruit of your womb will be blessed, and the crops of your land and the young of your livestock—the calves of your herds and the lambs of your flocks.

[5]Your basket and your kneading trough will be blessed.

[6]You will be blessed when you come in and blessed when you go out.

[7]The Lord will grant that the enemies who rise up against you will be defeated before you. They will come at you from one direction but flee from you in seven.

[8]The Lord will send a blessing on your barns and on everything you put your hand to. The Lord your God will bless you in the land he is giving you.

[9]The Lord will establish you as his holy people, as he promised you on oath, if you keep the commands of the Lord your God and walk in his ways. [10]Then all the peoples on earth will see that you are called by the name of the Lord, and they will fear you. [11]The Lord will grant you abundant prosperity—in the fruit of your womb, the young of your livestock and the crops of your ground—in the land he swore to your forefathers to give you.

[12]The Lord will open the heavens, the storehouse of his bounty, to send rain on your land in season and to bless all the work of your hands. You will lend to many nations but will borrow from none. (+Dt 29:9)

Dt 30:1 When all these blessings and curses I have set before you come upon you and you take them to heart wherever the Lord your God disperses you among the nations, [2]and when you and your children return to the Lord your God and obey him with all your heart and with all your soul according to everything I command you today, [3]then the Lord your God will restore your fortunes and have compassion on you and gather you again from all the nations where he scattered you. [4]Even if you have been banished to the most distant land under the heavens, from there the Lord your God will gather you and bring you back. [5]He will bring you to the land that belonged to your fathers, and you will take possession of it. He will make you more prosperous and numerous than your fathers. (+Dt 30:9-20)

Jos 1:8 Do not let this Book of the Law depart from your mouth; meditate on it day and night, so that you may be careful to do everything written in it. Then you will be prosperous and successful.

1Ki 2:3 and observe what the Lord your God requires: Walk in his ways, and keep his decrees and commands, his laws and requirements, as written in the Law of Moses, so

that you may prosper in all you do and wherever you go, [4]and that the Lord may keep his promise to me: 'If your descendants watch how they live, and if they walk faithfully before me with all their heart and soul, you will never fail to have a man on the throne of Israel.'

1Ki 9:3 The Lord said to him:

"I have heard the prayer and plea you have made before me; I have consecrated this temple, which you have built, by putting my Name there forever. My eyes and my heart will always be there.

[4]"As for you, if you walk before me in integrity of heart and uprightness, as David your father did, and do all I command and observe my decrees and laws, [5]I will establish your royal throne over Israel forever, as I promised David your father when I said, 'You shall never fail to have a man on the throne of Israel.'

[6]"But if you or your sons turn away from me and do not observe the commands and decrees I have given you and go off to serve other gods and worship them, [7]then I will cut off Israel from the land I have given them and will reject this temple I have consecrated for my Name. Israel will then become a byword and an object of ridicule among all peoples. [8]And though this temple is now imposing, all who pass by will be appalled and will scoff and say, 'Why has the Lord done such a thing to this land and to this temple?' [9]People will answer, 'Because they have forsaken the Lord their God, who brought their fathers out of Egypt, and have embraced other gods, worshiping and serving them—that is why the Lord brought all this disaster on them.'"

1Ch 22:13 Then you will have success if you are careful to observe the decrees and laws that the Lord gave Moses for Israel. Be strong and courageous. Do not be afraid or discouraged.

1Ch 28:7 I will establish his kingdom forever if he is unswerving in carrying out my commands and laws, as is being done at this time.'

[8]"So now I charge you in the sight of all Israel and of the assembly of the Lord, and in the hearing of our God: Be careful to follow all the commands of the Lord your God, that you may possess this good land and pass it on as an inheritance to your descendants forever. (+2Ch 7:17-22)

2Ch 26:5 He sought God during the days of Zechariah, who instructed him in the fear of God. As long as he sought the Lord, God gave him success.

2Ch 27:6 Jotham grew powerful because he walked steadfastly before the Lord his God.

2Ch 31:10 and Azariah the chief priest, from the family of Zadok, answered, "Since the people began to bring their contributions to the temple of the Lord, we have had enough to eat and plenty to spare, because the Lord has blessed his people, and this great amount is left over."

Job 36:11 If they obey and serve him, they will spend the rest of their days in prosperity and their years in contentment.

Isa 1:19 If you are willing and obedient, you will eat the best from the land;

Jer 7:3 This is what the Lord Almighty, the God of Israel, says: Reform your ways and your actions, and I will let you live in this place. [4]Do not trust in deceptive words and say, "This is the temple of the Lord, the temple of the Lord, the temple of the Lord!" [5]If you really change your ways and your actions and deal with each other justly, [6]if you do not oppress the alien, the fatherless or the widow and do not shed innocent blood in this place, and if you do not follow other gods to your own harm, [7]then I will let you live in this place, in the land I gave your forefathers for ever and ever.

Jer 11:1 This is the word that came to Jeremiah from the LORD: ²"Listen to the terms of this covenant and tell them to the people of Judah and to those who live in Jerusalem. ³Tell them that this is what the LORD, the God of Israel, says: 'Cursed is the man who does not obey the terms of this covenant— ⁴the terms I commanded your forefathers when I brought them out of Egypt, out of the iron-smelting furnace.' I said, 'Obey me and do everything I command you, and you will be my people, and I will be your God. ⁵Then I will fulfill the oath I swore to your forefathers, to give them a land flowing with milk and honey'—the land you possess today." I answered, "Amen, LORD."

Jer 12:16 And if they learn well the ways of my people and swear by my name, saying, 'As surely as the LORD lives'—even as they once taught my people to swear by Baal—then they will be established among my people.

Jer 17:24 But if you are careful to obey me, declares the LORD, and bring no load through the gates of this city on the Sabbath, but keep the Sabbath day holy by not doing any work on it, ²⁵then kings who sit on David's throne will come through the gates of this city with their officials. They and their officials will come riding in chariots and on horses, accompanied by the men of Judah and those living in Jerusalem, and this city will be inhabited forever. ²⁶People will come from the towns of Judah and the villages around Jerusalem, from the territory of Benjamin and the western foothills, from the hill country and the Negev, bringing burnt offerings and sacrifices, grain offerings, incense and thank offerings to the house of the LORD. ²⁷But if you do not obey me to keep the Sabbath day holy by not carrying any load as you come through the gates of Jerusalem on the Sabbath day, then I will kindle an unquenchable fire in the gates of Jerusalem that will consume her fortresses.' "

Jer 22:4 For if you are careful to carry out these commands, then kings who sit on David's throne will come through the gates of this palace, riding in chariots and on horses, accompanied by their officials and their people. ⁵But if you do not obey these commands, declares the LORD, I swear by myself that this palace will become a ruin.' "

Jer 22:15 "Does it make you a king to have more and more cedar? Did not your father have food and drink? He did what was right and just, so all went well with him. ¹⁶He defended the cause of the poor and needy, and so all went well. Is that not what it means to know me?" declares the LORD.

Mal 3:10 Bring the whole tithe into the storehouse, that there may be food in my house. Test me in this," says the LORD Almighty, "and see if I will not throw open the floodgates of heaven and pour out so much blessing that you will not have room enough for it. ¹¹I will prevent pests from devouring your crops, and the vines in your fields will not cast their fruit," says the LORD Almighty. ¹²"Then all the nations will call you blessed, for yours will be a delightful land," says the LORD Almighty.

Favors to children (Dt 4:1,40)—

Dt 5:29 Oh, that their hearts would be inclined to fear me and keep all my commands always, so that it might go well with them and their children forever! (+Dt 7:9; 12:25,28)

Preeminent honors—

Dt 28:1 If you fully obey the LORD your God and carefully follow all his commands I give you today, the LORD your God will set you high above all the nations on earth.

Dt 28:13 The LORD will make you the head, not the tail. If you pay attention to the commands of the LORD your God that I give you this day and carefully follow them, you will always be at the top, never at the bottom.

Zec 3:7 "This is what the LORD Almighty says: 'If you will walk in my ways and keep my requirements, then you will govern my house and have charge of my courts, and I will give you a place among these standing here.

Averted judgments—

Ex 15:26 He said, "If you listen carefully to the voice of the LORD your God and do what is right in his eyes, if you pay attention to his commands and keep all his decrees, I will not bring on you any of the diseases I brought on the Egyptians, for I am the LORD, who heals you." (+Dt 7:15)

See God, Goodness of, Providence of; Prosperity.

BLIGHT [5782, 8730].

NIV+ BLIGHTED

Destructive plant disease, sent as a judgment (Dt 28:22; 1Ki 8:37; Am 4:9; Hag 2:17).

BLIND [*6177, 6422, 6426, *5603, 5604*].

NIV+ BLINDED, BLINDFOLDS, BLINDNESS, BLINDS

Cruelty to, forbidden (Lev 19:14; Dt 27:18). Hated by David (2Sa 5:8). *See Blindness.*

BLINDNESS [6177, 6427].

NIV+ See BLIND

Disqualified for priestly office (Lev 21:18). Of animals, disqualified for a sacrifice (Lev 22:22; Dt 15:21; Mal 1:8).

Miraculously inflicted upon the Sodomites (Ge 19:11), Syrians (2Ki 6:18-23), Saul of Tarsus (Ac 9:8-9), Elymas (Ac 13:11).

Sent as a judgment (Dt 28:28).

Miraculous healing of (Mt 9:27-30; 11:5; 12:22; 21:14), Bartimaeus (Mt 20:30-34; Mk 10:46-52), a man of Bethsaida (Mk 8:22-25), a man born blind (Jn 9:1-7).

Instances of:

Isaac (Ge 27:1). Jacob (Ge 48:10). Eli (1Sa 4:14-15). Ahijah (1Ki 14:4).

Spiritual:

Instances of—

Dt 29:4 But to this day the LORD has not given you a mind that understands or eyes that see or ears that hear. (+Job 5:14)

Isa 29:10 The LORD has brought over you a deep sleep: He has sealed your eyes (the prophets); he has covered your heads (the seers).

¹¹For you this whole vision is nothing but words sealed in a scroll. And if you give the scroll to someone who can read, and say to him, "Read this, please," he will answer, "I can't; it is sealed." ¹²Or if you give the scroll to someone who cannot read, and say, "Read this, please," he will answer, "I don't know how to read." (+Isa 56:10; 59:10)

Jer 2:8 The priests did not ask, 'Where is the LORD?' Those who deal with the law did not know me; the leaders rebelled against me. The prophets prophesied by Baal, following worthless idols.

Jer 5:21 Hear this, you foolish and senseless people, who have eyes but do not see, who have ears but do not hear: (+Jer 9:3)

Eze 12:2 "Son of man, you are living among a rebellious people. They have eyes to see but do not see and ears to hear but do not hear, for they are a rebellious people. (+Ro 11:8)

Foretold (Isa 60:2)—

Ro 2:4 Or do you show contempt for the riches of his kindness, tolerance and patience, not realizing that God's kindness leads you toward repentance? (+Ro 11:10)

Manifested:

In ignorance of God—

Ex 5:2 Pharaoh said, "Who is the LORD, that I should obey him and let Israel go? I do not know the LORD and I will not let Israel go."

Isa 1:3 The ox knows his master, the donkey his owner's manger, but Israel does not know, my people do not understand."

Jer 4:22 "My people are fools; they do not know me. They are senseless children; they have no understanding. They are skilled in doing evil; they know not how to do good."

Hos 4:1 Hear the word of the LORD, you Israelites, because the LORD has a charge to bring against you who live in the land: "There is no faithfulness, no love, no acknowledgment of God in the land. (+Hos 4:6)

Jn 7:28 Then Jesus, still teaching in the temple courts, cried out, "Yes, you know me, and you know where I am from. I am not here on my own, but he who sent me is true. You do not know him,

Jn 15:21 They will treat you this way because of my name, for they do not know the One who sent me.

Jn 16:2 They will put you out of the synagogue; in fact, a time is coming when anyone who kills you will think he is offering a service to God. ³They will do such things because they have not known the Father or me.

Jn 17:25 "Righteous Father, though the world does not know you, I know you, and they know that you have sent me.

Ac 17:23 For as I walked around and looked carefully at your objects of worship, I even found an altar with this inscription: TO AN UNKNOWN GOD. Now what you worship as something unknown I am going to proclaim to you.

1Co 1:18 For the message of the cross is foolishness to those who are perishing, but to us who are being saved it is the power of God. (+1Co 1:19)

1Co 1:20 Where is the wise man? Where is the scholar? Where is the philosopher of this age? Has not God made foolish the wisdom of the world? ²¹For since in the wisdom of God the world through its wisdom did not know him, God was pleased through the foolishness of what was preached to save those who believe.

1Co 2:8 None of the rulers of this age understood it, for if they had, they would not have crucified the Lord of glory.

1Co 2:14 The man without the Spirit does not accept the things that come from the Spirit of God, for they are foolishness to him, and he cannot understand them, because they are spiritually discerned. ¹⁵The spiritual man makes judgments about all things, but he himself is not subject to any man's judgment:

1Co 15:34 Come back to your senses as you ought, and stop sinning; for there are some who are ignorant of God— I say this to your shame.

Gal 4:8 Formerly, when you did not know God, you were slaves to those who by nature are not gods. (+Eph 4:17)

Eph 4:18 They are darkened in their understanding and separated from the life of God because of the ignorance that is in them due to the hardening of their hearts. (+Eph 4:19)

1Th 4:4 that each of you should learn to control his own body in a way that is holy and honorable, ⁵not in passionate lust like the heathen, who do not know God;

1Jn 4:8 Whoever does not love does not know God, because God is love.

3Jn 11 Dear friend, do not imitate what is evil but what is good. Anyone who does what is good is from God. Anyone who does what is evil has not seen God.

In ignorance of Christ (Mt 16:3,9)—

Lk 23:34 Jesus said, "Father, forgive them, for they do not know what they are doing." And they divided up his clothes by casting lots.

Jn 1:5 The light shines in the darkness, but the darkness has not understood it.

Jn 1:10 He was in the world, and though the world was made through him, the world did not recognize him.

Jn 4:10 Jesus answered her, "If you knew the gift of God and who it is that asks you for a drink, you would have asked him and he would have given you living water." (+Jn 4:11,15)

Jn 4:22 You Samaritans worship what you do not know; we worship what we do know, for salvation is from the Jews.

Jn 8:15 You judge by human standards; I pass judgment on no one.

Jn 8:19 Then they asked him, "Where is your father?" "You do not know me or my Father," Jesus replied. "If you knew me, you would know my Father also."

Jn 8:27 They did not understand that he was telling them about his Father.

Jn 8:33 They answered him, "We are Abraham's descendants and have never been slaves of anyone. How can you say that we shall be set free?"

Jn 8:42 Jesus said to them, "If God were your Father, you would love me, for I came from God and now am here. I have not come on my own; but he sent me. ⁴³Why is my language not clear to you? Because you are unable to hear what I say.

Jn 8:52 At this the Jews exclaimed, "Now we know that you are demon-possessed! Abraham died and so did the prophets, yet you say that if anyone keeps your word, he will never taste death. (+Jn 8:53)

Jn 8:54 Jesus replied, "If I glorify myself, my glory means nothing. My Father, whom you claim as your God, is the one who glorifies me. ⁵⁵Though you do not know him, I know him. If I said I did not, I would be a liar like you, but I do know him and keep his word. (+Jn 8:56)

Jn 8:57 "You are not yet fifty years old," the Jews said to him, "and you have seen Abraham!"

Jn 9:29 We know that God spoke to Moses, but as for this fellow, we don't even know where he comes from." ³⁰The man answered, "Now that is remarkable! You don't know where he comes from, yet he opened my eyes. (+Jn 9:31-38)

Jn 9:39 Jesus said, "For judgment I have come into this world, so that the blind will see and those who see will become blind." (+Ac 3:14)

Ac 3:17 "Now, brothers, I know that you acted in ignorance, as did your leaders. (+Ro 11:7-8)

Ro 11:25 I do not want you to be ignorant of this mystery, brothers, so that you may not be conceited: Israel has experienced a hardening in part until the full number of the Gentiles has come in.

1Pe 1:14 As obedient children, do not conform to the evil desires you had when you lived in ignorance.

1Jn 3:1 How great is the love the Father has lavished on us, that we should be called children of God! And that is what we are! The reason the world does not know us is that it did not know him.

1Jn 3:6 No one who lives in him keeps on sinning. No one who continues to sin has either seen him or known him.

In ignorance of the Holy Spirit—

Jn 14:17 the Spirit of truth. The world cannot accept him, because it neither sees him nor knows him. But you know him, for he lives with you and will be in you.

Ac 19:2 and asked them, "Did you receive the Holy Spirit when you believed?" They answered, "No, we have not even heard that there is a Holy Spirit."

In ignorance of the Scriptures—

Mt 22:29 Jesus replied, "You are in error because you do not know the Scriptures or the power of God. (+Mk 12:24)

Ac 13:27 The people of Jerusalem and their rulers did not recognize Jesus, yet in condemning him they fulfilled the words of the prophets that are read every Sabbath.

2Co 3:14 But their minds were made dull, for to this day the same veil remains when the old covenant is read. It has not been removed, because only in Christ is it taken away. [15]Even to this day when Moses is read, a veil covers their hearts.

Heb 5:11 We have much to say about this, but it is hard to explain because you are slow to learn. [12]In fact, though by this time you ought to be teachers, you need someone to teach you the elementary truths of God's word all over again. You need milk, not solid food!

2Pe 3:16 He writes the same way in all his letters, speaking in them of these matters. His letters contain some things that are hard to understand, which ignorant and unstable people distort, as they do the other Scriptures, to their own destruction.

In ignorance of moral truth—

Dt 32:28 They are a nation without sense, there is no discernment in them.

Pr 4:19 But the way of the wicked is like deep darkness; they do not know what makes them stumble.

Pr 28:5 Evil men do not understand justice, but those who seek the LORD understand it fully.

Isa 5:13 Therefore my people will go into exile for lack of understanding; their men of rank will die of hunger and their masses will be parched with thirst.

Da 12:10 Many will be purified, made spotless and refined, but the wicked will continue to be wicked. None of the wicked will understand, but those who are wise will understand.

Mt 15:14 Leave them; they are blind guides. If a blind man leads a blind man, both will fall into a pit." (+Mt 15:16)

Mt 16:3 and in the morning, 'Today it will be stormy, for the sky is red and overcast.' You know how to interpret the appearance of the sky, but you cannot interpret the signs of the times. (+Mt 16:9)

Mt 23:19 You blind men! Which is greater: the gift, or the altar that makes the gift sacred?

Mt 23:24 You blind guides! You strain out a gnat but swallow a camel.

Mt 23:26 Blind Pharisee! First clean the inside of the cup and dish, and then the outside also will be clean.

Mk 7:18 "Are you so dull?" he asked. "Don't you see that nothing that enters a man from the outside can make him 'unclean'? (+Lk 6:39)

Lk 12:48 But the one who does not know and does things deserving punishment will be beaten with few blows. From everyone who has been given much, much will be demanded; and from the one who has been entrusted with much, much more will be asked.

Lk 12:57 "Why don't you judge for yourselves what is right?

2Ti 3:7 always learning but never able to acknowledge the truth.

Jude 10 Yet these men speak abusively against whatever they do not understand; and what things they do understand by instinct, like unreasoning animals—these are the very things that destroy them.

In ignorance of the way of salvation—

Lk 19:42 and said, "If you, even you, had only known on this day what would bring you peace—but now it is hidden from your eyes.

Jn 3:4 "How can a man be born when he is old?" Nicodemus asked. "Surely he cannot enter a second time into his mother's womb to be born!"

Jn 6:52 Then the Jews began to argue sharply among themselves, "How can this man give us his flesh to eat?"

Jn 6:60 On hearing it, many of his disciples said, "This is a hard teaching. Who can accept it?"

2Pe 1:9 But if anyone does not have them, he is near-sighted and blind, and has forgotten that he has been cleansed from his past sins.

1Jn 1:6 If we claim to have fellowship with him yet walk in the darkness, we lie and do not live by the truth.

1Jn 1:8 If we claim to be without sin, we deceive ourselves and the truth is not in us.

1Jn 2:4 The man who says, "I know him," but does not do what he commands is a liar, and the truth is not in him.

1Jn 2:9 Anyone who claims to be in the light but hates his brother is still in the darkness.

1Jn 2:11 But whoever hates his brother is in the darkness and walks around in the darkness; he does not know where he is going, because the darkness has blinded him.

Rev 3:17 You say, 'I am rich; I have acquired wealth and do not need a thing.' But you do not realize that you are wretched, pitiful, poor, blind and naked.

In ignorance of God's ways—

Ps 95:10 For forty years I was angry with that generation; I said, "They are a people whose hearts go astray, and they have not known my ways."

Jer 5:4 I thought, "These are only the poor; they are foolish, for they do not know the way of the LORD, the requirements of their God.

Jer 8:7 Even the stork in the sky knows her appointed seasons, and the dove, the swift and the thrush observe the time of their migration. But my people do not know the requirements of the LORD.

[8]"How can you say, "We are wise, for we have the law of the LORD," when actually the lying pen of the scribes has handled it falsely? [9]The wise will be put to shame; they will be dismayed and trapped. Since they have rejected the word of the LORD, what kind of wisdom do they have?

Mic 4:12 But they do not know the thoughts of the LORD; they do not understand his plan, he who gathers them like sheaves to the threshing floor.

In unbelief—

Ps 14:1 The fool says in his heart, "There is no God." They are corrupt, their deeds are vile; there is no one who does good.

Ps 14:4 Will evildoers never learn—those who devour my people as men eat bread and who do not call on the LORD? (+Isa 15:1; Mk 16:14; Jn 12:35)

Jn 12:38 This was to fulfill the word of Isaiah the prophet: "Lord, who has believed our message and to whom has the arm of the Lord been revealed?" (+Ac 28:25,27)

2Co 4:3 And even if our gospel is veiled, it is veiled to those who are perishing. **4**The god of this age has blinded the minds of unbelievers, so that they cannot see the light of the gospel of the glory of Christ, who is the image of God.

2Co 4:6 For God, who said, "Let light shine out of darkness," made his light shine in our hearts to give us the light of the knowledge of the glory of God in the face of Christ.

2Th 2:11 For this reason God sends them a powerful delusion so that they will believe the lie **12**and so that all will be condemned who have not believed the truth but have delighted in wickedness.

In insensibility (Dt 29:4)—

Jdg 16:20 Then she called, "Samson, the Philistines are upon you!" He awoke from his sleep and thought, "I'll go out as before and shake myself free." But he did not know that the LORD had left him. (+Pr 7:7-23)

Pr 17:16 Of what use is money in the hand of a fool, since he has no desire to get wisdom?

Isa 6:9 He said, "Go and tell this people:

" 'Be ever hearing, but never understanding; be ever seeing, but never perceiving.' **10**Make the heart of this people calloused; make their ears dull and close their eyes. Otherwise they might see with their eyes, hear with their ears, understand with their hearts, and turn and be healed."

Isa 42:18 "Hear, you deaf; look, you blind, and see! **19**Who is blind but my servant, and deaf like the messenger I send? Who is blind like the one committed to me, blind like the servant of the LORD? **20**You have seen many things, but have paid no attention; your ears are open, but you hear nothing."

Isa 44:18 They know nothing, they understand nothing; their eyes are plastered over so they cannot see, and their minds closed so they cannot understand. **19**No one stops to think, no one has the knowledge or understanding to say, "Half of it I used for fuel; I even baked bread over its coals, I roasted meat and I ate. Shall I make a detestable thing from what is left? Shall I bow down to a block of wood?" **20**He feeds on ashes, a deluded heart misleads him; he cannot save himself, or say, "Is not this thing in my right hand a lie?"

Isa 48:8 You have neither heard nor understood; from of old your ear has not been open. Well do I know how treacherous you are; you were called a rebel from birth.

Jer 16:10 "When you tell these people all this and they ask you, 'Why has the LORD decreed such a great disaster against us? What wrong have we done? What sin have we committed against the LORD our God?'

Hos 7:11 "Ephraim is like a dove, easily deceived and senseless—now calling to Egypt, now turning to Assyria.

Mt 6:23 But if your eyes are bad, your whole body will be full of darkness. If then the light within you is darkness, how great is that darkness!

Mt 13:13 This is why I speak to them in parables:

"Though seeing, they do not see; though hearing, they do not hear or understand.

14In them is fulfilled the prophecy of Isaiah:

" 'You will be ever hearing but never understanding; you will be ever seeing but never perceiving. **15**For this people's heart has become calloused; they hardly hear with their ears, and they have closed their eyes. Otherwise they might see with their eyes, hear with their ears, understand with their hearts and turn, and I would heal them.'

Mk 4:11 He told them, "The secret of the kingdom of God has been given to you. But to those on the outside everything is said in parables **12**so that,

" 'they may be ever seeing but never perceiving, and ever

hearing but never understanding; otherwise they might turn and be forgiven!' "

Mk 6:52 for they had not understood about the loaves; their hearts were hardened. (+Mk 8:18; Lk 8:10; Jn 12:40; Ac 28:25-27)

In presumption—

Ps 10:5 His ways are always prosperous; he is haughty and your laws are far from him; he sneers at all his enemies. **6**He says to himself, "Nothing will shake me; I'll always be happy and never have trouble."

Ps 94:7 They say, "The LORD does not see; the God of Jacob pays no heed."

8Take heed, you senseless ones among the people; you fools, when will you become wise? (+Isa 28:10-12)

Isa 28:13 So then, the word of the LORD to them will become: Do and do, do and do, rule on rule, rule on rule; a little here, a little there—so that they will go and fall backward, be injured and snared and captured. (+Isa 28:14)

Isa 28:15 You boast, "We have entered into a covenant with death, with the grave we have made an agreement. When an overwhelming scourge sweeps by, it cannot touch us, for we have made a lie our refuge and falsehood our hiding place."

Isa 40:21 Do you not know? Have you not heard? Has it not been told you from the beginning? Have you not understood since the earth was founded?

Isa 40:27 Why do you say, O Jacob, and complain, O Israel, "My way is hidden from the LORD; my cause is disregarded by my God"? **28**Do you not know? Have you not heard? The LORD is the everlasting God, the Creator of the ends of the earth. He will not grow tired or weary, and his understanding no one can fathom. (+Jer 8:8-9)

Am 9:10 All the sinners among my people will die by the sword, all those who say, 'Disaster will not overtake or meet us.'

In perversity—

Job 21:14 Yet they say to God, 'Leave us alone! We have no desire to know your ways. (+Job 21:15)

Pr 1:7 The fear of the LORD is the beginning of knowledge, but fools despise wisdom and discipline.

Pr 1:22 "How long will you simple ones love your simple ways? How long will mockers delight in mockery and fools hate knowledge?

Pr 1:29 Since they hated knowledge and did not choose to fear the LORD, **30**since they would not accept my advice and spurned my rebuke,

Pr 13:18 He who ignores discipline comes to poverty and shame, but whoever heeds correction is honored.

Pr 19:2 It is not good to have zeal without knowledge, nor to be hasty and miss the way.

3A man's own folly ruins his life, yet his heart rages against the LORD.

Isa 5:20 Woe to those who call evil good and good evil, who put darkness for light and light for darkness, who put bitter for sweet and sweet for bitter.

Isa 26:10 Though grace is shown to the wicked, they do not learn righteousness; even in a land of uprightness they go on doing evil and regard not the majesty of the LORD. **11**O LORD, your hand is lifted high, but they do not see it. Let them see your zeal for your people and be put to shame; let the fire reserved for your enemies consume them.

Jer 9:3 "They make ready their tongue like a bow, to shoot lies; it is not by truth that they triumph in the land. They go from one sin to another; they do not acknowledge me," declares the LORD.

Jer 9:6 You live in the midst of deception; in their deceit they refuse to acknowledge me," declares the LORD. (+Eze 12:2-3)

Hos 5:4 "Their deeds do not permit them to return to their God. A spirit of prostitution is in their heart; they do not acknowledge the LORD. (+Mt 21:32; Mk 3:5)

Lk 11:52 "Woe to you experts in the law, because you have taken away the key to knowledge. You yourselves have not entered, and you have hindered those who were entering." (+Jn 3:19)

Ro 1:19 since what may be known about God is plain to them, because God has made it plain to them. ²⁰For since the creation of the world God's invisible qualities—his eternal power and divine nature—have been clearly seen, being understood from what has been made, so that men are without excuse.

²¹For although they knew God, they neither glorified him as God nor gave thanks to him, but their thinking became futile and their foolish hearts were darkened. ²²Although they claimed to be wise, they became fools (+Ro 1:23)

Ro 1:28 Furthermore, since they did not think it worthwhile to retain the knowledge of God, he gave them over to a depraved mind, to do what ought not to be done. ²⁹They have become filled with every kind of wickedness, evil, greed and depravity. They are full of envy, murder, strife, deceit and malice. They are gossips, ³⁰slanderers, God-haters, insolent, arrogant and boastful; they invent ways of doing evil; they disobey their parents; ³¹they are senseless, faithless, heartless, ruthless.

In hypocrisy (Tit 1:15)—

Tit 1:16 They claim to know God, but by their actions they deny him. They are detestable, disobedient and unfit for doing anything good.

Consequences of:

Pr 10:21 The lips of the righteous nourish many, but fools die for lack of judgment.

Pr 14:12 There is a way that seems right to a man, but in the end it leads to death.

Isa 27:11 When its twigs are dry, they are broken off and women come and make fires with them. For this is a people without understanding; so their Maker has no compassion on them, and their Creator shows them no favor. (+Hos 4:6)

Hos 4:14 "I will not punish your daughters when they turn to prostitution, nor your daughters-in-law when they commit adultery, because the men themselves consort with harlots and sacrifice with shrine prostitutes—a people without understanding will come to ruin!

2Th 1:8 He will punish those who do not know God and do not obey the gospel of our Lord Jesus.

Remedy for:

Isa 9:2 The people walking in darkness have seen a great light; on those living in the land of the shadow of death a light has dawned. (+Isa 25:7; 35:5)

Isa 42:6 "I, the LORD, have called you in righteousness; I will take hold of your hand. I will keep you and will make you to be a covenant for the people and a light for the Gentiles, ⁷to open eyes that are blind, to free captives from prison and to release from the dungeon those who sit in darkness.

Lk 4:18 "The Spirit of the Lord is on me, because he has anointed me to preach good news to the poor. He has sent me to proclaim freedom for the prisoners and recovery of sight for the blind, to release the oppressed,

Jn 8:12 When Jesus spoke again to the people, he said, "I am the light of the world. Whoever follows me will never walk in darkness, but will have the light of life."

Ac 26:18 to open their eyes and turn them from darkness to light, and from the power of Satan to God, so that they may receive forgiveness of sins and a place among those who are sanctified by faith in me.' (+2Co 4:6)

Eph 5:8 For you were once darkness, but now you are light in the Lord. Live as children of light

Col 1:13 For he has rescued us from the dominion of darkness and brought us into the kingdom of the Son he loves,

1Pe 2:9 But you are a chosen people, a royal priesthood, a holy nation, a people belonging to God, that you may declare the praises of him who called you out of darkness into his wonderful light.

See Affliction, Prayer Under; God, Providence of, Mysterious and Misinterpreted.

BLOOD [408+1460, 1414+8638, 1414, 1947, 2446, 2743+3655+4946, 3655+3870+4946, 5906, 6795, *135+, 136*].

NIV+ AKELDAMA, BLEEDING, BLOOD-STAINED, BLOODSHED, BLOODSHOT, BLOODSTAINS, BLOODTHIRSTY, LIFEBLOOD

Is the life (Ge 9:4; Lev 17:11,14; 19:16; Dt 12:23; Mt 27:4,24). Forbidden to be used as food (Ge 9:4; Lev 3:17; 7:26-27; 17:10-14; 19:26; Dt 12:16,23; 15:23; Eze 33:25; Ac 15:20,29; 21:25). Plague of (Ex 7:17-25; Ps 78:44; 105:29).

Sacrificial:

Sprinkled on altar and people (Ex 24:6-8; Eze 43:18, 20). Sprinkled on door posts (Ex 12:7-23; Heb 11:28). Without shedding of, no remission (Heb 9:22).

Of Sin Offering:

Sprinkled seven times before the veil (Lev 4;5-6,17), on horns of the altar of sweet incense, and at the bottom of the altar of burnt offering (Ex 30:10; Lev 4:7,18,25,30; 5:9; 9:9,12). Of bull of sin offering, put on the horns of the altar (Ex 29:12; Lev 8:15), poured at the bottom of the altar (Ex 29:12; Lev 8:15). *See Offerings.*

Of Trespass Offering: Sprinkled on the altar (Lev 7:2). *See Offerings.*

Of Burnt Offering:

Sprinkled round about, and upon the altar (Ex 29:16; Lev 1:5,11,15; 8:19; Dt 12:27). *See Offerings.* Used for cleansing of leprosy (Lev 14:6-7,17,28,51-52). *See Offerings.*

Of Peace Offering:

Sprinkled about the altar (Lev 3:2,8,13; 9:19). Blood of the ram of consecration put on tip of right ear, thumb, and large toe of, and sprinkled upon, Aaron and his sons (Ex 29:20-21; Lev 8:23-24,30). *See Offerings.*

Blood of the Covenant: (Ex 24:5-8; Zec 9:11)

Mt 26:28 This is my blood of the covenant, which is poured out for many for the forgiveness of sins. (+Heb 9:18-19,22; 10:29; 13:20)

See Offerings.

Of Atonement:

Sprinkled on atonement cover (Lev 16:14-15,18-19,27; 17:11).

Figurative:

Of, victories (Ps 58:10), oppression and cruelty (Hab 2:12), destruction (Eze 35:6), guilt (Lev 20:9; 2Sa 1:16; Eze 18:13), judgments (Eze 16:38; Rev 16:6).

Of Jesus:

Shed on the Cross (Jn 19:18)—

Jn 19:34 Instead, one of the soldiers pierced Jesus' side with a spear, bringing a sudden flow of blood and water.

Atoning (Mt 26:28; Mk 14:24; Lk 22:20; Ro 3:24-25)—

Ro 5:9 Since we have now been justified by his blood, how much more shall we be saved from God's wrath through him!

Eph 2:13 But now in Christ Jesus you who once were far away have been brought near through the blood of Christ.

Eph 2:16 and in this one body to reconcile both of them to God through the cross, by which he put to death their hostility.

Heb 10:19 Therefore, brothers, since we have confidence to enter the Most Holy Place by the blood of Jesus, [20]by a new and living way opened for us through the curtain, that is, his body,

Heb 12:24 to Jesus the mediator of a new covenant, and to the sprinkled blood that speaks a better word than the blood of Abel.

Heb 13:20 May the God of peace, who through the blood of the eternal covenant brought back from the dead our Lord Jesus, that great Shepherd of the sheep,

1Jn 5:6 This is the one who came by water and blood— Jesus Christ. He did not come by water only, but by water and blood. And it is the Spirit who testifies, because the Spirit is the truth.

1Jn 5:8 the Spirit, the water and the blood; and the three are in agreement.

Redeeming—

Ac 20:28 Keep watch over yourselves and all the flock of which the Holy Spirit has made you overseers. Be shepherds of the church of God, which he bought with his own blood.

Eph 1:7 In him we have redemption through his blood, the forgiveness of sins, in accordance with the riches of God's grace

Col 1:14 in whom we have redemption, the forgiveness of sins.

Col 1:20 and through him to reconcile to himself all things, whether things on earth or things in heaven, by making peace through his blood, shed on the cross.

Heb 9:12 He did not enter by means of the blood of goats and calves; but he entered the Most Holy Place once for all by his own blood, having obtained eternal redemption. [13]The blood of goats and bulls and the ashes of a heifer sprinkled on those who are ceremonially unclean sanctify them so that they are outwardly clean. [14]How much more, then, will the blood of Christ, who through the eternal Spirit offered himself unblemished to God, cleanse our consciences from acts that lead to death, so that we may serve the living God!

1Pe 1:18 For you know that it was not with perishable things such as silver or gold that you were redeemed from the empty way of life handed down to you from your forefathers, [19]but with the precious blood of Christ, a lamb without blemish or defect.

Rev 1:5 and from Jesus Christ, who is the faithful witness, the firstborn from the dead, and the ruler of the kings of the earth. To him who loves us and has freed us from our sins by his blood,

Rev 5:9 And they sang a new song: "You are worthy to take the scroll and to open its seals, because you were slain, and with your blood you purchased men for God from every tribe and language and people and nation.

Rev 7:14 I answered, "Sir, you know." And he said, "These are they who have come out of the great tribulation; they have washed their robes and made them white in the blood of the Lamb.

Sanctifying—

Heb 10:29 How much more severely do you think a man deserves to be punished who has trampled the Son of God under foot, who has treated as an unholy thing the blood of the covenant that sanctified him, and who has insulted the Spirit of grace?

Heb 13:12 And so Jesus also suffered outside the city gate to make the people holy through his own blood.

Justification through—

Ro 3:24 and are justified freely by his grace through the redemption that came by Christ Jesus. [25]God presented him as a sacrifice of atonement, through faith in his blood. He did this to demonstrate his justice, because in his forbearance he had left the sins committed beforehand unpunished— (+Ro 5:9)

Victory through—

Rev 12:11 They overcame him by the blood of the Lamb and by the word of their testimony; they did not love their lives so much as to shrink from death.

Eternal life by—

Jn 6:53 Jesus said to them, "I tell you the truth, unless you eat the flesh of the Son of Man and drink his blood, you have no life in you. [54]Whoever eats my flesh and drinks my blood has eternal life, and I will raise him up at the last day. [55]For my flesh is real food and my blood is real drink. [56]Whoever eats my flesh and drinks my blood remains in me, and I in him.

Typified by the blood of sacrifices—

Heb 9:6 When everything had been arranged like this, the priests entered regularly into the outer room to carry on their ministry. [7]But only the high priest entered the inner room, and that only once a year, and never without blood, which he offered for himself and for the sins the people had committed in ignorance. [8]The Holy Spirit was showing by this that the way into the Most Holy Place had not yet been disclosed as long as the first tabernacle was still standing. [9]This is an illustration for the present time, indicating that the gifts and sacrifices being offered were not able to clear the conscience of the worshiper. [10]They are only a matter of food and drink and various ceremonial washings—external regulations applying until the time of the new order.

[11]When Christ came as high priest of the good things that are already here, he went through the greater and more perfect tabernacle that is not man-made, that is to say, not a part of this creation. [12]He did not enter by means of the blood of goats and calves; but he entered the Most Holy Place once for all by his own blood, having obtained eternal redemption. [13]The blood of goats and bulls and the ashes of a heifer sprinkled on those who are ceremonially unclean sanctify them so that they are outwardly clean. [14]How much more, then, will the blood of Christ, who through the eternal Spirit offered himself unblemished to God, cleanse our consciences from acts that lead to death, so that we may serve the living God!

[15]For this reason Christ is the mediator of a new covenant, that those who are called may receive the promised

eternal inheritance—now that he has died as a ransom to set them free from the sins committed under the first covenant.

[16]In the case of a will, it is necessary to prove the death of the one who made it, [17]because a will is in force only when somebody has died; it never takes effect while the one who made it is living. [18]This is why even the first covenant was not put into effect without blood. [19]When Moses had proclaimed every commandment of the law to all the people, he took the blood of calves, together with water, scarlet wool and branches of hyssop, and sprinkled the scroll and all the people. [20]He said, "This is the blood of the covenant, which God has commanded you to keep." [21]In the same way, he sprinkled with the blood both the tabernacle and everything used in its ceremonies. [22]In fact, the law requires that nearly everything be cleansed with blood, and without the shedding of blood there is no forgiveness.

[23]It was necessary, then, for the copies of the heavenly things to be purified with these sacrifices, but the heavenly things themselves with better sacrifices than these. [24]For Christ did not enter a man-made sanctuary that was only a copy of the true one; he entered heaven itself, now to appear for us in God's presence. [25]Nor did he enter heaven to offer himself again and again, the way the high priest enters the Most Holy Place every year with blood that is not his own. [26]Then Christ would have had to suffer many times since the creation of the world. But now he has appeared once for all at the end of the ages to do away with sin by the sacrifice of himself. [27]Just as man is destined to die once, and after that to face judgment, [28]so Christ was sacrificed once to take away the sins of many people; and he will appear a second time, not to bear sin, but to bring salvation to those who are waiting for him.

Symbolized by the wine of the Lord's Supper—
1Co 10:16 Is not the cup of thanksgiving for which we give thanks a participation in the blood of Christ? And is not the bread that we break a participation in the body of Christ?
1Co 11:25 In the same way, after supper he took the cup, saying, "This cup is the new covenant in my blood; do this, whenever you drink it, in remembrance of me."

See Atonement; Jesus the Christ, Mission of, Sufferings of.

BLOOD, AVENGER
One who took it upon himself to avenge the blood of a slain kinsman (Ge 9:6; Nu 35:6). *See Avenger of Blood.*

BLOOD, ISSUE OF
See Bleeding, Subject to; Disease.

BLOOD MONEY
[135+5507]. Paid to Judas for betraying Jesus (Mt 27:6). *See Conscience Money*

BLOODY SWEAT
See Disease; Sweat, Bloody.

BLUE
[9418, 5610]. *See Colors, Figurative and Symbolic.*

BLUSHING
[4007].
NIV+ BLUSH
With shame (Ezr 9:6; Jer 6:15; 8:12).

BOANERGES
[1065] (*sons of thunder*). Surname of the sons of Zebedee (Mk 3:17).

BOARS, WILD
[2614]. (Ps 80:13). *See Pig.*

BOASTING
[*606, 607, 966, 2146, 9514, 10647, 225, 2878, 3016, 3017, 3018, 3306*].
NIV+ BOAST, BOASTED, BOASTERS, BOASTFUL, BOASTFULLY, BOASTS

Folly of—
Ps 49:6 those who trust in their wealth and boast of their great riches? [7]No man can redeem the life of another or give to God a ransom for him— [8]the ransom for a life is costly, no payment is ever enough— [9]that he should live on forever and not see decay. (+Pr 27:1; Isa 10:15; Jas 4:16)

Deceitful (Pr 20:14; 25:14). Of the wicked (Ps 52:1; 94:4; Ro 1:30). Of the tongue (Jas 3:5).

Forbidden (Jer 9:23).

Spiritual—
Ps 52:1 Why do you boast of evil, you mighty man? Why do you boast all day long, you who are a disgrace in the eyes of God?
Ps 94:4 They pour out arrogant words; all the evildoers are full of boasting.
Ro 3:27 Where, then, is boasting? It is excluded. On what principle? On that of observing the law? No, but on that of faith.
Ro 11:17 If some of the branches have been broken off, and you, though a wild olive shoot, have been grafted in among the others and now share in the nourishing sap from the olive root, [18]do not boast over those branches. If you do, consider this: You do not support the root, but the root supports you. [19]You will say then, "Branches were broken off so that I could be grafted in." [20]Granted. But they were broken off because of unbelief, and you stand by faith. Do not be arrogant, but be afraid. [21]For if God did not spare the natural branches, he will not spare you either.
1Co 1:29 so that no one may boast before him.
1Co 4:6 Now, brothers, I have applied these things to myself and Apollos for your benefit, so that you may learn from us the meaning of the saying, "Do not go beyond what is written." Then you will not take pride in one man over against another. [7]For who makes you different from anyone else? What do you have that you did not receive? And if you did receive it, why do you boast as though you did not?
2Co 10:12 We do not dare to classify or compare ourselves with some who commend themselves. When they measure themselves by themselves and compare themselves with themselves, they are not wise. [13]We, however, will not boast beyond proper limits, but will confine our boasting to the field God has assigned to us, a field that reaches even to you. [14]We are not going too far in our boasting, as would be the case if we had not come to you, for we did get as far as you with the gospel of Christ. [15]Neither do we go beyond our limits by boasting of work done by others. Our hope is that, as your faith continues to grow, our area of activity among you will greatly expand, [16]so that we can preach the gospel in the regions beyond you. For we do not want to boast about work already done in another man's territory. [17]But, "Let him who boasts boast in the Lord." [18]For it is not the one who commends himself who is approved, but the one whom the Lord commends.
Eph 2:8 For it is by grace you have been saved, through faith—and this not from yourselves, it is the gift of God— [9]not by works, so that no one can boast. [10]For we are God's workmanship, created in Christ Jesus to do good works, which God prepared in advance for us to do.

Instances of:

Goliath (1Sa 17). Ben-Hadad (1Ki 20:10). Amaziah (2Ch 25:17-20). Sennacherib (2Ki 18:19,28-35; 19:8-13; Isa 10:8-15). The disciples (Lk 10:17,20).

See Ostentation.

BOAT [641, 3998, *4449, 4450*].
NIV+ BOATS, LIFEBOAT
See Ship.

BOAZ [1244, 1245, *1067, 1078*] (perhaps *in him is strength*).

1. An ancestor of Jesus (Mt 1:5; Lk 3:32). History of, Ruth (Ru 2-4).

2. One of Solomon's brazen pillars erected at the temple. It stood on the left (north) side of the porch (1Ki 7:21; 2Ch 3:17).

BOAZ AND JAKIN, JACHIN *See Boaz, 2; Jakin, Jachin, 2; Temple, Solomon's.*

BOCHERU *See Bokeru, Bocheru.*

BOCHIM *See Bokim, Bochim.*

BODY [*1061, 1414, 1581, 2728, 5055, 5516, 5577, 5883, 6795, 7007, 10151, *3517, 4773, 4922, 5393*].
NIV+ BODIES, BODILY, EMBODIMENT

Called: house (2Co 5:1), house of clay (Job 4:19), golden bowl (Ecc 12:6), earthen vessel (2Co 4:7), tabernacle (2Pe 1:13), temple of God (1Co 3:16-17; 6:19), member of Christ (1Co 6:15).

Perishable (Job 17:14; 1Co 15:53-54). To be consecrated to God (Ro 12:1). To be kept unto holiness (1Co 6:13-20).

Resurrection of, to a spiritual body (1Co 15:19-54; 2Co 5:14; Php 3:21).

See Resurrection.

BOHAN [992] (*thumb, big toe*). A Reubenite (Jos 15:6; 18:17).

BOIL [1240, 1418, 1419, 5870, 8409+8410, 8825].
NIV+ BOILED, BOILING, BOILS

A tumor. Plague of Egyptians (Ex 9:9-10; Dt 28:27,35), of the Philistines, (1Sa 5:6,9; 1Sa 6:5). Of Hezekiah, healed (2Ki 20:7; Isa 38:21). Of Job (Job 2:7-8). Levitical ceremonies prescribed for (Lev 13:18-23).

BOILING POT Parable of (Eze 24:3-5).

BOKERU, BOCHERU [1150] (*his first born*). Son of Azel (1Ch 8:38; 9:44).

BOKIM, BOCHIM [1141] (*weepings*). A place W of Jordan, near Gilgal (Jdg 2:1,5).

BOLDNESS OF THE RIGHTEOUS [*3283, *2509, 4244, 4245*].
NIV+ BOLD, BOLDLY, EMBOLDENED

Exemplified:

Pr 28:1 The wicked man flees though no one pursues, but the righteous are as bold as a lion. (+Ac 18:26; 19:8)

Heb 13:6 So we say with confidence, "The Lord is my helper; I will not be afraid. What can man do to me?"

In prayer—

Heb 4:16 Let us then approach the throne of grace with confidence, so that we may receive mercy and find grace to help us in our time of need.

Heb 10:19 Therefore, brothers, since we have confidence

to enter the Most Holy Place by the blood of Jesus, (+1Jn 3:21-22; 5:14-15)

Inspired by, fear of the Lord—

Pr 14:26 He who fears the LORD has a secure fortress, and for his children it will be a refuge.

Faith in Christ—

Eph 3:12 In him and through faith in him we may approach God with freedom and confidence.

Instances of, in Prayer:

Abraham (Ge 18:23-32). Moses (Ex 33:12-18).

In the day of judgment—

1Jn 2:28 And now, dear children, continue in him, so that when he appears we may be confident and unashamed before him at his coming.

1Jn 4:17 In this way, love is made complete among us so that we will have confidence on the day of judgment, because in this world we are like him.

Its effect on others (Ac 4:13).

See Courage.

BOLSTER *See Pillow.*

BOLT, FIERY (Hab 3:5).

BOND [673, 4593, 5037, *2653, 5278*].
NIV+ BONDAGE, BONDS

To keep the peace (Ac 17:9).

BONDAGE [6268, 6269, 6275, 6285, *1525*].
NIV+ BOND, BONDS

Of Israelites, in Egypt (Ex 1:14; 2:23; 6:6), in Persia (Ezr 9:9). *See Emancipation; Servant.*

BONDMAN *See Servant.*

BONES [1752, 4157, 6793, 6795, 10150, *4014*].
NIV+ BONE, BACKBONE

Vision of the dry (Eze 37:1-14). None of Christ's broken (Ps 34:20; Jn 19:36).

BONNET *See Dress; Turban.*

BOOK [4181, 6219, 10515, *1046, 1047, 3364*].
NIV+ BOOKS, SCROLL

Genealogies kept in (Ge 5:1). Law of Moses written in (Nu 5:23; Dt 17:18; 31:9,24,26; 2Ki 22:8). Topography of Israel, recorded in (Jos 18:9).

Non-biblical books cited in the Bible:

Book of Jashar (Jos 10:13; 2Sa 1:18), records of Samuel, Nathan, and Gad (1Sa 10:25; 1Ch 29:29), Iddo (2Ch 12:15; 13:22), Isaiah (2Ch 26:22; 32:32; Isa 8:1).

Annals of the Kings of Judah and Israel:

Of David (1Ch 27:24), Solomon (1Ki 11:41), Jehu (2Ch 20:34), other kings (2Ch 24:27; 16:11; 25:26; 27:7; 28:26; 35:27; 36:8), the kings of Israel (1Ki 14:19; 2Ch 20:34; 33:18).

Other records kept in (Ezr 4:15; 6:1-2; Est 6:1; 9:32; Jer 32:12; Ac 19:19). Prophecies written in, by Jeremiah (Jer 25:13; 30:2; 45:1; 51:60,63; Da 9:2). Other prophecies written in (2Ch 33:18-19). Lamentations written in (2Ch 35:25). Numerous (Ecc 12:12). Eating of (Jer 15:16; Eze 2:8-10; 3:1-3; Rev 10:2-10). Of magic (Ac 19:19). Paul's left at Troas (2Ti 4:13).

Made in a roll (Jer 36:4; Zec 5:1). Sealed (Isa 29:11; Da 12:4; Rev 5:1-5).

Kiriath Jearim was called Kiriath Sepher, which signifies a city of books (Jos 15:15-16; Jdg 1:11-12).

Figurative:

Of Life: Names of, righteous written in—

Ex 32:32 But now, please forgive their sin—but if not, then blot me out of the book you have written."

Da 12:1 "At that time Michael, the great prince who protects your people, will arise. There will be a time of distress such as has not happened from the beginning of nations until then. But at that time your people—everyone whose name is found written in the book—will be delivered.

Lk 10:20 However, do not rejoice that the spirits submit to you, but rejoice that your names are written in heaven."

Php 4:3 Yes, and I ask you, loyal yokefellow, help these women who have contended at my side in the cause of the gospel, along with Clement and the rest of my fellow workers, whose names are in the book of life. (+Heb 12:23)

Rev 3:5 He who overcomes will, like them, be dressed in white. I will never blot out his name from the book of life, but will acknowledge his name before my Father and his angels.

Rev 21:27 Nothing impure will ever enter it, nor will anyone who does what is shameful or deceitful, but only those whose names are written in the Lamb's book of life.

Of Life: Wicked blotted out of—

Ex 32:33 The LORD replied to Moses, "Whoever has sinned against me I will blot out of my book. (+Rev 22:18-4228540)

Of Life: Wicked not written in—

Rev 13:8 All inhabitants of the earth will worship the beast—all whose names have not been written in the book of life belonging to the Lamb that was slain from the creation of the world.

Rev 17:8 The beast, which you saw, once was, now is not, and will come up out of the Abyss and go to his destruction. The inhabitants of the earth whose names have not been written in the book of life from the creation of the world will be astonished when they see the beast, because he once was, now is not, and yet will come.

Rev 20:15 If anyone's name was not found written in the book of life, he was thrown into the lake of fire.

Of remembrance—

Ps 56:8 Record my lament; list my tears on your scroll—are they not in your record?

Ps 139:16 your eyes saw my unformed body. All the days ordained for me were written in your book before one of them came to be.

Mal 3:16 Then those who feared the LORD talked with each other, and the LORD listened and heard. A scroll of remembrance was written in his presence concerning those who feared the LORD and honored his name.

Rev 20:12 And I saw the dead, great and small, standing before the throne, and books were opened. Another book was opened, which is the book of life. The dead were judged according to what they had done as recorded in the books.

BOOTH [6109, *5468*].

NIV+ BOOTHS

Made of boughs (Jnh 4:5), for cattle (Ge 33:17), watchmen (Job 27:18; Isa 1:8; 24:20). Prescribed for the Israelites to dwell in during the Feast of Tabernacles to remember their wanderings in the wilderness (Lev 23:40-43; Ne 8:15-16).

BOOTY [1023, 8965]. Spoils of war. Property and per-sons were sometimes preserved and sometimes completely destroyed (Jos 6:18-21; Dt 20:14,16-18). Abraham gave a tenth (Ge 14:20), David ordered that booty be shared with baggage guards (1Sa 30:21-25).

BOOZ *See Boaz, 1.*

BOR ASHAN [1016] (*pit of smoke*).

NIV+ ASHAN

A town in Judah (1Sa 30:30). Perhaps identical with Ashan (Jos 15:42). *See Ain, 1; Ashan.*

BORING THE EAR *See Piercing the Ear.*

BORN AGAIN *See New Birth.*

BORROWING [4278, 928+5957, 6292, 8626, *1247*].

NIV+ BORROW, BORROWED, BORROWER, BORROWS

Dishonesty in—

Ps 37:21 The wicked borrow and do not repay, but the righteous give generously;

Obligations in—

Ex 22:14 "If a man borrows an animal from his neighbor and it is injured or dies while the owner is not present, he must make restitution. ¹⁵But if the owner is with the animal, the borrower will not have to pay. If the animal was hired, the money paid for the hire covers the loss.

Distress from—

Ne 5:1 Now the men and their wives raised a great outcry against their Jewish brothers. ²Some were saying, "We and our sons and daughters are numerous; in order for us to eat and stay alive, we must get grain."

³Others were saying, "We are mortgaging our fields, our vineyards and our homes to get grain during the famine."

⁴Still others were saying, "We have had to borrow money to pay the king's tax on our fields and vineyards. ⁵Although we are of the same flesh and blood as our countrymen and though our sons are as good as theirs, yet we have to subject our sons and daughters to slavery. Some of our daughters have already been enslaved, but we are powerless, because our fields and our vineyards belong to others."

Pr 22:7 The rich rule over the poor, and the borrower is servant to the lender.

Compassion toward debtors commanded—

Ne 5:6 When I heard their outcry and these charges, I was very angry. ⁷I pondered them in my mind and then accused the nobles and officials. I told them, "You are exacting usury from your own countrymen!" So I called together a large meeting to deal with them ⁸and said: "As far as possible, we have bought back our Jewish brothers who were sold to the Gentiles. Now you are selling your brothers, only for them to be sold back to us!" They kept quiet, because they could find nothing to say.

⁹So I continued, "What you are doing is not right. Shouldn't you walk in the fear of our God to avoid the reproach of our Gentile enemies? ¹⁰I and my brothers and my men are also lending the people money and grain. But let the exacting of usury stop! ¹¹Give back to them immediately their fields, vineyards, olive groves and houses, and also the usury you are charging them—the hundredth part of the money, grain, new wine and oil."

¹²"We will give it back," they said. "And we will not demand anything more from them. We will do as you say." Then I summoned the priests and made the nobles and officials take an oath to do what they had promised.

¹³I also shook out the folds of my robe and said, "In this way may God shake out of his house and possessions

every man who does not keep this promise. So may such a man be shaken out and emptied!" At this the whole assembly said, "Amen," and praised the LORD. And the people did as they had promised.

Christ's rule concerning—

Mt 5:42 Give to the one who asks you, and do not turn away from the one who wants to borrow from you.

See Lending; Interest.

Instances of:

Israelites from the Egyptians (Ex 3:22; 11:2; 12:35), iron axhead (2Ki 6:5); returned exiles from each other (Ne 5:1-13).

Borrowing trouble. *See Security, For Debt.*

BOSCATH *See Bozkath.*

BOSOM [1843, 2668].

NIV+ BOSOMS

In Scripture the word is generally used in an affectionate sense (Isa 40:11; Jn 1:18). Sometimes it is almost synonymous with "heart" (Ps 35:13; Ecc 7:9).

BOSOR *See Beor; Bozrah.*

BOSS *See Shield.*

BOTANICAL GARDENS Garden of Eden (Ge 2:8-3:24), of Uzza (2Ki 21:18,25), king's garden (2Ki 25:4; Ne 3:15 w Ecc 2:5), of Susa (Est 1:5-6;7:7-8).

BOTANY Laws of nature in the vegetable kingdom uniform in action (Mt 7:16-18,20; Lk 6:43-44; 1Co 15:36-38; Gal 6:7). Lily, beauty of (Mt 6:28-29). The size of the harvest is related to the amount of seed sown (2Co 9:6).

See Algum; Almond; Aloes; Apple; Balm; Barley; Bay Tree; Beans; Bramble; Broom Tree; Bush; Cane; Caraway; Cassia; Cedar; Cinnamon; Citron Wood; Coriander; Cucumbers; Cummin; Cypress Wood; Date; Ebony; Fig Tree; Fir Tree; Flax; Frankincense; Galbanum; Gall, 3; Garlic; Gourd; Grain; Grass; Gum Resin; Hemlock; Henna Blossoms; Husk; Hyssop; Leek; Lentil(s); Lily; Mandrake; Melon; Millet; Mint; Mulberry Tree; Mustard Seed; Myrrh; Myrtle; Nard; Nettles; Nut; Oak; Olive; Onion; Palm Tree; Perfume; Pine; Plants of the Bible; Pomegranate; Poplar; Reed; Rose; Rue; Salt Herbs; Shittim; Spelt; Sycamore-Fig; Terebinth; Thistle; Thorn; Tree; Vine; Weeds; Wheat; Willow; Wormwood.

BOTCH *See Boil.*

BOTTLE [1074, 4202+7337].

NIV+ BOTTLED-UP, BOTTLES, JAR, SKINS

Perfume bottles (Isa 3:20). *See Wine; Wineskin.*

BOTTOMLESS PIT *See Abyss.*

BOUNDARY STONES [1473, 1474]. Stones used, to mark the boundary of property (Jos 13:21), to remove them was forbidden (Dt 27:17).

BOW [995, 2005, 2556, 3857, 4104, 4156, 4798, 5989, 6032, 8000, 8008, 8820, 9413, *2828, 4406, 4749, 5534*].

NIV+ BOWED, BOWING, BOWMEN, BOWS, BOWSHOT

A Weapon:

(Ge 21:16,20). Made of, bronze (2Sa 22:35; Job 20:24; Ps 18:34), wood (Eze 39:9). Used in war (Isa 13:18; La 2:4; Eze 39:3) and in hunting (Ge 27:3). David's lament of the bow (2Sa 1:18-27). Used by the Elamites (Jer 49:35). *See Archery; Arrows.*

Figurative:

(Ge 49:24; Job 16:13; 29:20; Ps 78:57; La 3:12; Hos 1:5; Hab 3:9; Rev 6:2).

Rainbow:

A sign from God—

Ge 9:8 Then God said to Noah and to his sons with him: **9**"I now establish my covenant with you and with your descendants after you **10**and with every living creature that was with you—the birds, the livestock and all the wild animals, all those that came out of the ark with you—every living creature on earth. **11**I establish my covenant with you: Never again will all life be cut off by the waters of a flood; never again will there be a flood to destroy the earth."

12And God said, "This is the sign of the covenant I am making between me and you and every living creature with you, a covenant for all generations to come: **13**I have set my rainbow in the clouds, and it will be the sign of the covenant between me and the earth. **14**Whenever I bring clouds over the earth and the rainbow appears in the clouds, **15**I will remember my covenant between me and you and all living creatures of every kind. Never again will the waters become a flood to destroy all life. **16**Whenever the rainbow appears in the clouds, I will see it and remember the everlasting covenant between God and all living creatures of every kind on the earth."

A likeness of God's glory—

Eze 1:28 Like the appearance of a rainbow in the clouds on a rainy day, so was the radiance around him. This was the appearance of the likeness of the glory of the LORD. When I saw it, I fell facedown, and I heard the voice of one speaking.

Rev 4:3 And the one who sat there had the appearance of jasper and carnelian. A rainbow, resembling an emerald, encircled the throne.

Rev 10:1 Then I saw another mighty angel coming down from heaven. He was robed in a cloud, with a rainbow above his head; his face was like the sun, and his legs were like fiery pillars.

BOWELS [5055]. Diseased (2Ch 21:15-20). Judas's gushed out (Ac 1:18).

Figurative:

Of the sensibilities (Ge 43:30; 1Ki 3:26; Job 30:27; Ps 22:14; SS 5:4; Jer 4:19; 31:20; La 1:20; Php 1:8; 2:1; Col 3:12; 1Jn 3:17).

See Heart.

BOWING [2556, 4104, 8820].

NIV+ BOW, BOWED, BOWS

In worship (2Ch 7:3). *See Obeisance; Worship, Attitudes in.*

BOWL [*110, 1657, 4094, 4670, 4932, 4984, *3654, 5581, 5786*].

NIV+ BOWL-SHAPED, BOWLFUL, BOWLS

Made of gold:

For the tabernacle (Ex 25:29; 37:16). Temple (1Ki 7:50; 1Ch 28:17; 2Ch 4:8). Of silver (Nu 4:7; 7:13,9,25,31, 37,43,49,55,61,67,73,79,84). Stamped "HOLY TO THE LORD" (Zec 14:20-21).

See Basin.

Figurative: Of fragile life (Ecc 12:6).

Symbolic:

Of prayer (Rev 5:8). Seven bowls of judgment (Rev 15:7-16:17).

BOX Containing portions of Scripture (Mt 23:5, ftn). *See Jar(s).*

BOX TREE *See Cypress Wood.*

BOXING Figurative of personal discipline (1Co 9:26-27). *See Games.*

BOZEZ [1010] (*oozing place*). A rock near Gibeah (1Sa 14:4).

BOZKATH [1304] (*[swollen,] elevated spot*). A city of Judah (Jos 15:39; 2Ki 22:1).

BOZRAH [1313] (*enclosure [for sheep], fortress*).

1. A city of Edom (Ge 36:33). Prophecies concerning (Isa 34:6; 63:1; Jer 49:13,22; Am 1:12).

2. A town of Moab (Jer 48:24).

BRACELET [7543, 9217].

NIV+ BRACELETS

Present of (Ge 24:22). Worn by women (Ge 24:30; Isa 3:19); men, NIV "cord" (Ge 38:18,25). Dedicated to the tabernacle (Ex 35:22; Nu 31:50). Taken as spoils (Nu 31:50; 2Sa 1:10).

Figurative of God's care for Israel (Eze 16:11).

BRAMBLE [2560].

NIV+ BRAMBLES

(Isa 34:13; Lk 6:44). Allegory of (Jdg 9:14-15).

BRANCH [*1936, 2367, 4093, 4751, 5234, 5746, 5916, 6733, 6997, 7542, 7866, 7908, 8585, 10561, *3080, 3097*].

NIV+ BRANCHES

Figurative:

(Pr 11:28; Hos 14:6; Isa 60:21; Jn 15:2-5). Pruning of (Isa 18:5; Da 4:14; Jn 15:6; Ro 11:17,21). Fruitless, cut off (Jn 15:2,6). A title of Christ (Ps 80:15; Isa 4:2; 11:1; Jer 23:5; 33:15; Zec 3:8; 6:12). Symbolic name of Joshua (Zec 6:12).

See Graft.

BRASS *See Bronze.*

BRAVERY *See Boldness of the Righteous; Courage.*

BRAY [5640].

NIV+ BRAYED

The sound of a hungry donkey; a metaphor of humans crying out in need (Job 6:5; 30:7).

BRAZEN SEA *See Bronze Basin.*

BRAZEN SERPENT *See Bronze Snake.*

BRAZIER *See Coppersmith; Craftsman; Occupations and Professions.*

BREAD [*4312, 5121, 5174, 6314, *109, 788, 6040*].

Kinds of:

Bread of affliction (1Ki 22:27; Ps 127:2; Hos 9:4; Isa 30:20), leavened (Lev 7:13; 23:17; Hos 7:4; Am 4:5; Mt 13:33), unleavened (Ge 19:3; Ex 29:2; Jdg 6:19; 1Sa 28:24).

Made of wheat flour (Ex 29:2; 1Ki 4:22; 5:11; Ps 81:16), manna (Nu 11:8), meal (1Ki 17:12), barley (Jdg 7:13).

How Prepared:

Mixed with oil (Ex 29:2,23), honey (Ex 16:31), with yeast. *See Yeast; see above, Kinds of.* Kneaded (Ge 18:6; Ex 8:3; 12:34; 1Sa 28:24; 2Sa 13:8; Jer 7:18; Hos 7:4).

Made into loaves (1Sa 10:3; 17:17; 25:18; 1Ki 14:3; Mk 8:14), cakes (2Sa 6:19; 1Ki 14:3; 17:12), wafers (Ex 16:21; 29:23).

Baked in ovens (Ex 8:3; Lev 2:4; 7:9; 11:35; 26:26; Hos 7:4), in pans (Lev 2:5,7; 2Sa 13:6-9),on hearths (Ge 18:6), on coals (1Ki 19:6; Isa 44:19; Jn 21:9).

Made by men (Ge 40:2), women (Lev 26:26; 1Sa 8:13; Jer 7:18). Trade in (Jer 37:21; Mk 6:35-37).

Offered in sacrifice (Lev 21:6,8,17,21-22; 22:25; 1Sa 2:36; 2Ki 23:9). By idolaters (Jer 7:18; 44:19).

See Bread, Consecrated; Offerings.

Figurative:

(Isa 55:2; 1Co 10:17; 2Co 9:10). Christ: the bread of life (Jn 6:32-59).

Symbolic:

Of the body of Christ (Mt 26:26; Ac 20:7; 1Co 11:23-24).

BREAD, CONSECRATED

Called "consecrated bread" (1Sa 21:4,6; 1Ch 28:16; 2Ch 2:4; 29:18; Mt 12:4; Mk 2:26; Lk 6:4; Heb 9:2).

Required to be kept before the Lord continually (Ex 25:30; 2Ch 2:4). Placed on the table "in the Tent of Meeting" (Ex 40:22-23). *See Table of, below.* Ordinance concerning (Lev 24:5-9). Unlawfully eaten by David (1Sa 21:6; Mt 12:3-4; Mk 2:25-26; Lk 6:3-4). Prepared by the Levites (1Ch 9:32; 23:29). Provided by a yearly per capita tax (Ne 10:32-33).

Table of:

(Heb 9:2). Ordinances concerning (Ex 25:23-28; 37:10-15). Its situation in the tabernacle (Ex 26:35; 40:22). Furniture of (Ex 25:29-30; 37:16; Nu 4:7). Consecration of (Ex 30:26-27,29). How removed (Nu 4:7,15). For the temple (1Ki 7:48,50; 2Ch 4:19,22).

BREAST [1843, 2601, 3751, 4422, 6403, 8716, 8718, *3466, 5111*].

NIV+ BREASTPIECE, BREASTPLATES, BREASTS

Breast in the Bible can simply refer to the chest area of the body (Lk 18:13). It can also refer to the female mammary glands (Ge 49:25; La 4:3; Lk 23:29), both in nurturing (Ps 22:9; Joel 2:16; Isa 60:16) and erotic contexts (SS 4:5; 7:7; Eze 23:3,21). To beat one's breast with a fist was a sign of sorrow or repentence (Eze 21:12; Lk 18:13; 23:48).

BREASTPLATE [3136, 9234, *2606*].

NIV+ BREASTPIECE, BREASTPLATES

1. For high priest (Ex 25:7). Directions for the making of (Ex 28:15-30). Made by Bezalel (Ex 31:2-5; 39:8,21). Freewill offering of materials for (Ex 35:9,27). Worn by Aaron (Ex 29:5; Lev 8:8).

2. Armor for soldiers (Rev 9:9,17).

Figurative:

Isa 59:17 He put on righteousness as his breastplate, and the helmet of salvation on his head; he put on the garments of vengeance and wrapped himself in zeal as a cloak.

Eph 6:14 Stand firm then, with the belt of truth buckled around your waist, with the breastplate of righteousness in place,

1Th 5:8 But since we belong to the day, let us be

self-controlled, putting on faith and love as a breastplate, and the hope of salvation as a helmet.

BREATH [678, 2039, 3640, 5883, 5972, 8120, *4460*, *4466*].

NIV+ BREATHE, BREATHED, BREATHES, BREATHING, GOD-BREATHED

Of life (Ge 2:7; 7:22; Ac 17:25). Of God (2Sa 22:16; Job 4:9; 15:30; 33:4; 37:10; Ps 18:15; 33:6; Isa 30:33).

Figurative: (Eze 37:9).

BREECHES *See Dress; Undergarments.*

BRETHREN *See Brother; Brothers of Our Lord.*

BRIBERY [4111, 5510, 8815, 8816, 8936, 9556, *5975*].

NIV+ BRIBE, BRIBES, BRIBING

Ps 26:9 Do not take away my soul along with sinners, my life with bloodthirsty men, [10]in whose hands are wicked schemes, whose right hands are full of bribes.

Pr 15:27 A greedy man brings trouble to his family, but he who hates bribes will live.

Isa 33:15 He who walks righteously and speaks what is right, who rejects gain from extortion and keeps his hand from accepting bribes, who stops his ears against plots of murder and shuts his eyes against contemplating evil— [16]this is the man who will dwell on the heights, whose refuge will be the mountain fortress. His bread will be supplied, and water will not fail him.

Corrupts conscience—

Ex 23:8 "Do not accept a bribe, for a bribe blinds those who see and twists the words of the righteous.

Dt 16:18 Appoint judges and officials for each of your tribes in every town the LORD your God is giving you, and they shall judge the people fairly. [19]Do not pervert justice or show partiality. Do not accept a bribe, for a bribe blinds the eyes of the wise and twists the words of the righteous.

Ecc 7:7 Extortion turns a wise man into a fool, and a bribe corrupts the heart.

Perverts justice—

1Sa 8:1 When Samuel grew old, he appointed his sons as judges for Israel.

1Sa 8:3 But his sons did not walk in his ways. They turned aside after dishonest gain and accepted bribes and perverted justice. (+1Sa 12:3)

Pr 17:23 A wicked man accepts a bribe in secret to pervert the course of justice.

Pr 28:21 To show partiality is not good—yet a man will do wrong for a piece of bread.

Isa 1:23 Your rulers are rebels, companions of thieves; they all love bribes and chase after gifts. They do not defend the cause of the fatherless; the widow's case does not come before them.

Isa 5:22 Woe to those who are heroes at drinking wine and champions at mixing drinks, [23]who acquit the guilty for a bribe, but deny justice to the innocent. (+Eze 22:12)

Am 5:12 For I know how many are your offenses and how great your sins. You oppress the righteous and take bribes and you deprive the poor of justice in the courts.

Mic 7:3 Both hands are skilled in doing evil; the ruler demands gifts, the judge accepts bribes, the powerful dictate what they desire—they all conspire together.

Destroys national welfare—

Pr 29:4 By justice a king gives a country stability, but one who is greedy for bribes tears it down.

Profanes God—

Eze 13:19 You have profaned me among my people for a

few handfuls of barley and scraps of bread. By lying to my people, who listen to lies, you have killed those who should not have died and have spared those who should not live.

Condemnation of—

Job 15:34 For the company of the godless will be barren, and fire will consume the tents of those who love bribes.

Eze 22:12 In you men accept bribes to shed blood; you take usury and excessive interest and make unjust gain from your neighbors by extortion. And you have forgotten me, declares the Sovereign LORD.

[13]"'I will surely strike my hands together at the unjust gain you have made and at the blood you have shed in your midst.

Punishment for—

Dt 27:25 "Cursed is the man who accepts a bribe to kill an innocent person." Then all the people shall say, "Amen!"

Am 2:6 This is what the LORD says: "For three sins of Israel, even for four, I will not turn back [my wrath]. They sell the righteous for silver, and the needy for a pair of sandals.

Instances of:

Delilah (Jdg 16:4-5). Samuel's sons (See above). The false prophet, Shemaiah (Ne 6:10-13). Ben-Hadad (1Ki 15:18-19). Haman bribes Xerxes to destroy the Jews (Est 3:8-9). Chief priests bribe Judas (Mt 26:15; 27:3-9; Mk 14:11; Lk 22:5). Soldiers bribed to declare that the disciples stole the body of Jesus (Mt 28:12-15). Felix seeks a bribe from Paul (Ac 24:26).

BRICK [4236, 4246, 4861].

NIV+ BRICKMAKING, BRICKS, BRICKWORK

Used in building: Babel (Ge 11:3), cities in Egypt (Ex 1:11,14), houses (Isa 9:10), altars (Isa 65:3). Made by Israelites (Ex 5:7-19), slave labor (2Sa 12:31), Ninevites (Na 3:14).

BRICKKILN *See Brick.*

BRIDE [3987, 3994, 4558, 8712, *1222*, *3811*].

NIV+ BRIDAL

Presents to (Ge 24:53). Maids of (Ge 24:59,61; 29:24, 29). Ornaments of (Isa 49:18; 61:10; Jer 2:32; Rev 21:2).

Figurative:

(Ps 45:10-17; Eze 16:8-14; Rev 19:7-8; 21:2,9; 22:17).

BRIDECHAMBER *See Bridegroom; Wedding.*

BRIDEGROOM [1033, 3163, *3812*, *3813*].

NIV+ BRIDEGROOM'S, BRIDEGROOMS

Ornaments of (Isa 61:10). Exempt from military duty (Dt 24:5). Companions of (Jdg 14:11). Joy with (Mt 9:15; Mk 2:19-20; Lk 5:34-35).

Parable of (Mt 25:1-13; SS 4:7-16).

Figurative: (Eze 16:8-14).

BRIDGE "River crossings" (Jer 51:32) may have included bridges or ferries. The Israelites generally crossed streams at a ford (Ge 32:22; 2Sa 19:18).

BRIDLE [8270+, *5903*].

NIV+ BRIDLES

To control an animal (Ps 32:9; Pr 26:3; Rev 14:20).

Figurative: (2Ki 19:28; Ps 39:1; Jas 1:26).

See Bit.

BRIER [1402, 2537, 2560, 6141, 6235, 6252, 7853, 9031, *1003*].

NIV+ BRIERS

Figurative (Isa 5:6; 55:13; Eze 2:6; 28:24).

BRIGANDINE *See Armor.*

BRIMSTONE *See Sulfur.*

BRONZE [4607, 5702, 5703, 5733, 10473, *5905, 5909, 5910*].

NIV+ BRONZE-TIPPED, COPPER

An alloy of copper and tin. Smelted (Eze 22:20; Job 28:2). Found in Canaan (Dt 8:9; Jos 22:8), Syria (2Sa 8:8). Tyrians traded in (Eze 27:13). Abundance of, for the temple (1Ki 7:47; 1Ch 22:14).

Articles made of:

Altar, vessels, and other articles of the tabernacle and temple (Ex 38:28-31; 1Ki 7:14-47; Ezr 8:27), cymbals (1Ch 15:19), trumpets (1Co 13:1), armor (1Sa 17:5-6; 2Ch 12:10), bows *See Bow,* fetters (Jdg 16:21; 2Ki 25:7), gates (Ps 107:16; Isa 45:2), bars (1Ki 4:13), idols (Da 5:4; Rev 9:20), mirrors (Ex 38:8), household vessels (Mk 7:4).

Workers in: Tubal-Cain (Ge 4:22), Hiram (1Ki 7:13-14), Alexander (2Ti 4:14).

See Bronze Basin; Bronze Sea; Copper; Molding.

Figurative:

(Lev 26:19; Dt 33:25; Isa 48:4; Jer 1:18; Eze 1:7; Da 2:32,39; 7:19; 10:6; Zec 6:1; Rev 1:15).

BRONZE BASIN [3963]. Directions for making (Ex 30:18-20). Situation of, in the tabernacle, tent of the congregation, and the altar (Ex 40:7). Sanctified (Ex 30:28; 40:11; Lev 8:11). Used for washing (Ex 40:30-32).

Figurative (Rev 4:6; 15:2, w Ex 38:8).

See Bronze Sea; Tabernacle.

BRONZE SEA [3542]. Made by Solomon for the temple (1Ki 7:23-26,30,38-39; 2Ch 4:2-14). Altered by Ahaz (2Ki 16:17). Broken and carried to Babylon by the Chaldeans (2Ki 25:13,16; Jer 52:17,20).

Figurative (Rev 4:6; 15:2, w 1Ki 7:23).

See Bronze Basin; Temple.

BRONZE SNAKE Made by Moses for the healing of the Israelites (Nu 21:8-9). Worshiped by Israelites (2Ki 18:4). A symbol of Christ's crucifixion (Jn 3:14-15).

BROOK [4782+4784, 5707]. *See River; River of Egypt.*

BROOM

A metaphor of Babylon swept away in judgment (Isa 14:23).

BROOM TREE [8413]. A desert shrub (1Ki 19:4-5; Job 30:4; Ps 120:4).

BROTH [5348]. (Jdg 6:19-20; 2Ki 4:38; Isa 65:4). Symbolic (Eze 24:5).

BROTHEL *See Groves; High Places; Idolatry; Prostitute.*

BROTHER [278+, 288, 408, 3303, 3304, 10017, *81, 82, 5789, 5790, 6012*].

NIV+ BROTHER-IN-LAW, BROTHER'S, BROTHERHOOD, BROTHERLY, BROTHERS

Signifies a relative (Ge 14:16; 29:12), a neighbor (Dt 23:7; Jdg 21:6; Ne 5:7), any Israelite (Jer 34:9; Ob 10), an inclusive term for all mankind (Ge 9:5; Mt 18:35; 1Jn 3:15), a companion (2Sa 1:26; 1Ki 13:30; 20:33).

Love of (Pr 17:17; 18:24; SS 8:1). Unfaithful (Pr 27:10). Reuben's love for Joseph (Ge 37:21-22). Joseph's, for his brothers (Ge 43:30-34; 45:1-5; 50:19-25).

A fraternal title, especially among Christians. Instituted by Christ (Mt 12:50; 25:40; Heb 2:11-12). Used by disciples (Ac 9:17; 21:20; Ro 16:23; 1Co 7:12; 2Co 2:13), Peter (1Pe 1:22). Used among the Israelites (Lev 19:17; Dt 22:1-4).

Brother's widow, law concerning Levirate marriage of (Dt 25:5-10; Mt 22:24; Mk 12:19; Lk 20:28).

See Fraternity.

BROTHERLY KINDNESS *See Brother; Charitableness; Fellowship; Fraternity; Friendship; Love.*

BROTHERS OF OUR LORD

James, Joseph, Simon, and Judas are called the Lord's brothers (Mt 13:55). He also had sisters (Mt 13:56). John records that his brothers did not believe in him (Jn 7:1-10). There are differences of opinion as to whether the "brothers" were full brothers, cousins, or children of Joseph by a former marriage.

BRUISE, BRUISES [2467, 5080, 6700, 7205, 7206, 8368, 8691, *5341*].

NIV+ BRUISED

1. The so-called law of retaliation was meant to limit the punishment to fit the crime (Ex 21:25). By invoking the law of love, Jesus corrected the popular misunderstanding of the law of retaliation (Mt 5:38-42).

2. Castrated animals were not acceptable sacrifices (Lev 22:24).

3. Wounds inflicted, by shackles (Ps 105:18), because of drunkenness (physical and psychological effects) (Pr 29-35), by God upon Israel, because of the sins of the people, will be healed by the Lord (Isa 30:26). *See Bruised Reed, 1.*

BRUISED REED

1. Descriptive of someone who is weak; the "servant of the Lord" will mend broken lives (Isa 42:3; Mt 12:20).

2. NIV "splintered reed"; descriptive of depending on weak political alliances rather than relying on the Lord (2Ki 18:21; cf Isa 30:1-5; 31:1-3).

See Bruise, Bruises.

BUBASTIS [7083] (*house of the cat goddess Basht*). One time capital of Lower Egypt; about forty miles NE of Cairo; modern Tel Basta. Prophesied against by Ezekiel (Eze 30:17, ftn). KJV Phi-Beseth.

BUCKET [1932].

NIV+ BUCKETS

For water (Ex 7:19; Nu 24:7; Isa 40:15).

BUCKLER [7558]. *See Shield.*

BUILDER [802, *1321, 2941*].

NIV+ BUILD, BUILDERS, BUILDING, BUILDINGS, BUILDS, BUILT, REBUILD, REBUILDING, REBUILT, WELL-BUILT

Of the tabernacle. *See Bezalel; Master Craftsman.* Of the temple (2Ki 12:11; 22:6; Ezr 3:10). Of the wall of Jerusalem (Ne 4:18). Of the church (1Co 3:10). God (Heb 3:4; 11:10). Who rejected the capstone (Ps 118:22; Mt 21:42; Ac 4:11; 1Pe 2:7). *See Carpentry; Foundation.*

BUILDING [1074, 1215, 1224, 1230, 4445, 4856, 5016, 6590, 10111, 10112, *2224, 3868, 3871, 3869*].

NIV+ See BUILDER

The church as God's building (1Co 3:9; Eph 2:21). The eternal body compared to the earthly tent (2Co 5:1).

BUKKI [1321] (*proved of Yahweh* BDB; *mouth [gurgle sounds] of Yahweh* ISBE).

1. Son of Abishua (1Ch 6:5,51; Ezr 7:4).

2. A prince of Dan (Nu 34:22).

BUKKIAH [1322] (*proved of Yahweh*). A Levite (1Ch 25:4,13).

BUL [1004].

Month eight in sacred sequence, month two in civil sequence. Also called Marcheshvan (not in Bible). The temple completed in (1Ki 6:38). Jeroboam institutes an idolatrous feast in, to correspond with the Feast of Tabernacles (1Ki 12:32-33). Time for planting wheat and barley (October-November).

See Month, 8.

BULL [52, 1330+, 7228, 8802, 10756, *5436*].

NIV+ BULL'S, BULLS

Uses of: For sacrifice (Ex 29:3,10-14,36; Lev 4:8,16; Nu 7:87-88; 28:11-31; 29; Heb 9:13; 10:4), plowing (1Sa 14:14; 1Ki 19:19; Pr 14:4; Isa 32:20; Jer 31:18), treading out grain (Dt 25:4), with wagons (Nu 7:3-8; 2Sa 6:3-6).

Laws concerning: trespass by (Ex 21:28-36), theft of (Ex 22:1-10), rest for (Ex 23:12), not to be muzzled when treading grain (Dt 25:4; 1Co 9:9; 1Ti 5:18), not to be yoked with a donkey (Dt 22:10).

Twelve bronze, under the cast metal Sea in Solomon's temple (1Ki 7:25; 2Ch 4:4; Jer 52:20).

See Cattle; Offerings.

Symbolic: (Eze 1:10; Rev 4:7).

BULRUSH *See Papyrus; Reed.*

BULWARK (Dt 20:20; 2Ch 26:15; Ecc 9:14). Figurative (Ps 48:13; Isa 26:1).

BUNAH [1007]. Son of Jerahmeel (1Ch 2:25).

BUNNI [1221].

1. A Levite, a teacher with Ezra (Ne 9:4).

2. Ancestor of Shemaiah (Ne 11:15).

3. A family of Jews (Ne 10:15).

BURDEN [*3877, 5362, 6024, 6268, 6673, 6701+6721, 976, 983, 2096, 2915, 5845*].

NIV+ BURDENED, BURDENS, BURDENSOME

Figurative:

Of oppressions (Isa 58:6; Mt 23:4; Lk 11:46; Gal 6:2). Of the prophetic message (Isa 13:1; 15:1; 17:1; 19:1).

BURGLARY *See Theft.*

BURIAL [*3243, 7690, 7699, 7700, *1946, 1947, 2507, 5313*].

NIV+ BURIED, BURIES, BURY, BURYING

Rites of (Jer 34:5). Soon after death (Dt 21:23; Jos 8:29; Jn 19:38-42; Ac 5:9-10). With spices (2Ch 16:14; Mk 16:1; Lk 23:56). Bier used at (2Sa 3:31; Lk 7:14).

Attended by relatives and friends: Of Jacob (Ge 50:5-9), Abner (2Sa 3:31), child of Jeroboam (1Ki 14:13), the son of the widow of Nain (Lk 7:12-13), Stephen (Ac 8:2).

Lack of, a disgrace (2Ki 9:10; Pr 30:17; Jer 16:4; 22:19;

Eze 39:15). Directions given about, before death, by Jacob (Ge 49:29-30), Joseph (Ge 50:25). Burial of Gog (multitude) requiring 7 months (Eze 39:12-13).

BURNING [*202, 430, 836+, 1277, 1624, 1730, 2779, 3013, 3019, 3081, 3675, 3678, 3918, 4003, 4805, 6590, 6592, 7787, 8596, 8599, 9462, *2794, 2876, 3906, 4786, 4792, 4796*].

NIV+ BURN, BURNED, BURNED-OUT, BURNS, BURNT

As a punishment (Ge 19:28; Jos 6:24; 8:20; 11:13; Jdg 18:27; 1Sa 30:1; 1Ki 9:16; 2Ch 36:19; Job 1:16). *See Punishment.*

BURNING BUSH The LORD appears to Moses (Ex 3:2-5; Ac 7:30).

BURNT OFFERING *See Offerings, Burnt.*

BURYING PLACES Bought by Abraham (Ge 23; 25:9).

Prepared by Jacob (Ge 50:5), Asa (2Ch 16:14), Joseph (Mt 27:60).

On hills (2Ki 23:16; Jos 24:33). In valleys (Jer 7:32).

Family (Ge 47:30; 49:29; Ac 7:16). Of kings (1Ki 2:10; 2Ch 32:33), a place of honor (2Ch 24:16,25; 21:20). For poor and strangers (Jer 26:23; Mt 27:7).

Tombs: In houses (1Sa 25:1; 1Ki 2:34), gardens (2Ki 21:18,26; Jn 19:41), caves (Ge 23:9), under trees. Deborah's (Ge 35:8), King Saul's (1Sa 31:13).

Closed with stones (Mt 27:60,66; Jn 11:38; 20:1). Sealed (Mt 27:66).

Marked with pillars: Rachel's (Ge 35:20). Inscriptions (2Ki 23:17).

Painted and decorated (Mt 23:27,29). Demon-possessed lived in (Mt 8:28). Any who touched were unclean (Nu 19:16,18; Isa 65:4). Refused to the dead (Rev 11:9). Robbed (Jer 8:1).

See Cremation; Dead; Death, Physical; Elegy; Grave; Mourning.

Figurative: (Isa 22:16; Ro 6:4; Col 2:12).

BUSH [6174, 6899, 8489, *1003+*].

NIV+ BUSHES

Desert shrubs (Ge 21:15; Jer 17:6). *See Burning Bush.*

BUSHELS [*1669+3174*]. (Lk 16:7). *See Measure.*

BUSINESS LIFE

Virtues found in—

Diligence (Pr 10:4; 13:4; 22:29; 2Pe 3:14). Fidelity (Ge 39:6; 2Ch 34:11-12; Ne 13:13; Da 6:4; 1Co 4:2; Heb 3:5). Honesty (Lev 19:35-36; Dt 25:15; Pr 11:1; Ro 12:17; 13:8). Industry (Ge 2:15; Pr 6:6; 10:5; 12:11; 13:11; 20:13; Ro 12:11). Giving of just weights (Lev 19:36; Dt 25:13; Pr 11:1; 16:11; 20:10; Eze 45:10; Mic 6:11). Integrity (Ps 41:12; Pr 11:3; 19:1; 20:7).

Vices found in—

Breach of trust (Lev 6:2; SS 1:6; Eze 16:17; Lk 16:12). Dishonesty (Dt 25:13; Pr 11:1; 20:14; 21:6; Hos 12:7). Extortion (Isa 10:2; Eze 22:12; Am 5:11; Mt 18:28; 23:25; Lk 3:13). Fraud (Lev 19:13; Mk 10:19; 1Co 6:8). Unjust gain (Pr 16:8; 21:6; 22:16; Jer 17:11; 22:13; Eze 22:13; Jas 5:4). Slothfulness (Pr 18:9; 24:30-31; Ecc 10:18; 2Th 3:11; Heb 6:12).

BUSYBODY [*4318, 4319*].

NIV+ BUSYBODIES

Meddlers denounced (Pr 26:17)—

1Ti 5:13 Besides, they get into the habit of being idle and going about from house to house. And not only do they become idlers, but also gossips and busybodies, saying things they ought not to.

2Th 3:11 We hear that some among you are idle. They are not busy; they are busybodies. [12]Such people we command and urge in the Lord Jesus Christ to settle down and earn the bread they eat.

    Command against—

Lev 19:16 "'Do not go about spreading slander among your people. "'Do not do anything that endangers your neighbor's life. I am the LORD.

1Pe 4:15 If you suffer, it should not be as a murderer or thief or any other kind of criminal, or even as a meddler.

    See Backbiting; Talebearer; Speaking, Evil.

BUTLER Pharaoh's, imprisoned and released (Ge 40; 1Ki 10:5; 2Ch 9:4; Ne 1:11; 2:1).

BUTTER [2772, 4717]. (Ge 18:8; Dt 32:14; Jdg 5:25; 2Sa 17:29; Job 20:17; Isa 7:15,22). Made by churning (Pr 30:33).

BUZ [998] (*contempt*).
    NIV+ BUZITE
    1. Son of Nahor (Ge 22:21).
    2. Father of Jahdo (1Ch 5:14).

BUZI [1001] (*contempt*). The father of Ezekiel (Eze 1:3).

BYBLOS *See Gebal.*

BYWAYS Literally "winding paths," traveled to avoid danger (Jdg 5:6).

C

CAB [7685]. A dry measure containing about two quarts (2Ki 6:25). *See Measure.*

CABBON [3887]. A place in Judah (Jos 15:40).

CABINET Heads of departments in government. David's (2Sa 8:15-18; 15:12; 20:23-26; 1Ch 27:32-34), Solomon's (1Ki 4:1-7), Hezekiah's (Isa 36:3), Artaxerxes' (Ezr 7:14). *See Counselor.*

CABUL [3886] (*good for nothing*).
1. A city in the N of Israel (Jos 19:27).
2. Name given by Hiram to certain cities in Galilee (1Ki 9:13).

CAESAR [*2790*].
NIV+ CAESAR'S
1. Augustus (Lk 2:1).
2. Tiberius (Lk 3:1; 20:22).
3. Claudius (Ac 11:28).
4. Nero (Php 4:22).

CAESAREA [*2791*]. A seaport in Israel.
Home of Philip (Ac 8:40; 21:8), Cornelius, the centurion (Ac 10:1,24), Herod (Ac 12:19-23), Felix (Ac 23:23-24).
Paul taken to, by the disciples to save him from his enemies (Ac 9:30), by Roman soldiers to be tried by Felix (Ac 23:23-35).

CAESAREA PHILIPPI [*2791*+*5805*]. A city in the N of Israel, visited by Jesus (Mt 16:13; Mk 8:27).

CAGE [3990, 6050].
NIV+ CAGES
For birds (Jer 5:27; Rev 18:2).

CAIAPHAS [*2780*]. High priest (Lk 3:2), son-in-law of Annas (Jn 18:13). Prophesies concerning Jesus (Jn 11:49-51; 18:14). Jesus tried before (Mt 26:2-3,57,63-65; Jn 18:24,28). Peter and other disciples accused before (Ac 4:1-22).

CAIN [7803, *2782*] (*metal worker* BDB KB; *brought forth, acquired* Ge. 4:1).
1. Son of Adam (Ge 4:1). Jealousy and crime of (Ge 4:3-15; Heb 11:4; 1Jn 3:12; Jude 11). Settles in the land of Nod (Ge 4:16). Children and descendants of (Ge 4:17-18).
2. *See Kain, 1.*

CAINAN [*2783*] (*worker in iron, metal worker*).
1. Also called Kenan. Son of Enos (Ge 5:9-15; 1Ch 1:2; Lk 3:37).
2. Son of Arphaxad (Lk 3:36).

CAKES [862, 882, 1811, 2705+, 3924, 5926, 6314, 7540, 7811].
NIV+ CAKE
Of unleavened bread (Ex 12:39), mixed with oil for offerings (Ex 29:2), offered to the Queen of Heaven (Jer 7:18); of raisins and figs (1Sa 25:18); of dates (2Sa 6:19); of barley (Eze 4:12).

CALAH [3996] (*strength, vigor*). An ancient city of Assyria (Ge 10:11-12).

CALAMUS [7866]. A sweet cane (SS 4:14; Eze 27:19). An ingredient of the holy ointment (Isa 43:24). Imported (Jer 6:20; Eze 27:19).

CALCOL [4004]. Son of Mahol (1Ki 4:31). Son of Zerah (1Ch 2:6).

CALDRON [1857, 6105, 7831].
NIV+ CALDRONS
In the tabernacle (1Sa 2:14), the temple (2Ch 35:13; Jer 52:18-19). Figurative of judgment (Eze 11:3-11).

CALEB [3979, 3992] (*dog* BDB; *snappish, warding off* KB).
NIV+ CALEB'S, CALEBITE
1. Son of Jephunneh. Also spelled Kelubai (1Ch 2:9, ftn). One of the two survivors of the Israelites permitted to enter the land of promise (Nu 14:30,38; 26:63-65; 32:11-13; Dt 1:34-36; Jos 14:6-15). Sent to Canaan as a spy (Nu 13:6). Brings favorable report (Nu 13:26-30; 14:6-9). Assists in dividing Canaan (Nu 34:19). Life of, miraculously saved (Nu 14:10-12). Leader of the Israelites after Joshua's death (Jdg 1:11-12). Age of (Jos 14:7-10). Inheritance of (Jos 14:6-15; 15:13-16). Descendants of (1Ch 4:15).
2. Third son of Hezron (1Ch 2:9). Ancestor of Bezalel the craftsman who built the tabernacle (1Ch 2:18-20).
3. Brother of Jerahmeel (1Ch 2:42,50), possibly the same as 1.

CALEB EPHRATHAH, CALEB-EPHRATAH
[3980].
NIV+ EPHRATHAH
A place near Bethlehem (1Ch 2:24).

CALENDAR In Bible time was reckoned solely on astronomical observations. Days, months, and years were determined by the sun and moon.
1. Days of the week were not named by the Israelites, but were designated by ordinal numbers. Jewish day began in the evening with the appearance of the first stars. Days were subdivided into hours and watches. Israelites divided nights into three watches (Ex 14:24; Jdg 7:19; La 2:19), the Romans four (Mt 14:25).
2. Egyptians had a week of ten days. The seven-day week is of Semitic origin (the Creation account), and ran consecutively irrespective of lunar or solar cycles. This was done for man's physical and spiritual welfare. The biblical records are silent regarding the observance of the Sabbath day from creation to the time of Moses. Sabbath observance was either revived or given special emphasis by Moses (Ex 16:23; 20:8).
3. The Hebrew month began with the new moon. Before the Exile months were designated by numbers. After the Exile names adopted from the Babylonians were used.
4. The Jewish calendar had two concurrent years, the sacred year, beginning in the spring with the month Nisan, and the civic year, beginning with Tishri (see chart below). The sacred year was instituted by Moses and consisted of lunar months of twenty-nine or thirty days each, with an intercalary month called Adar Sheni added about every three years. Every seventh year was a sabbatical year for the Israelites—a year of solemn rest for landlords, slaves, beasts of burden, and land, and freedom for Hebrew slaves. Every fiftieth year was a Jubilee year, observed by

family reunions, canceled mortgages, and return of lands to original owners (Lev 25:8-17).

Synchronized Jewish Sacred Calendar			
Sacred	Name	Modern Equivalent	Civic
1	Nisan	March-April	7
2	Iyyar	April-May	8
3	Sivan	May-June	9
4	Tammuz	June-July	10
5	Ab	July-August	11
6	Elul	August-September	12
7	Tishri	September-October	1
8	Bul	October-November	2
9	Kislev	November-December	3
10	Tebeth	December-January	4
11	Shebat	January-February	5
12	Adar	February-March	6

See Month; Time; also see each month under its respective topic heading.

CALF [1201+1330, 5309, 6319, 8802, *3674, 3675*].

NIV+ CALF-IDOL, CALF-IDOLS, CALVE, CALVED, CALVES

Offered in sacrifice (Mic 6:6). Golden idol, made by Aaron (Ex 32; Dt 9:16; Ne 9:18; Ps 106:19; Ac 7:41).

Images of, set up in Bethel and Dan by Jeroboam (1Ki 12:28-33; 2Ki 10:29). Worshiped by Jehu (2Ki 10:29). Prophecies against the golden calves at Bethel (1Ki 13:1-5,32; Jer 48:13; Hos 8:5-6; 10:5-6,15; 13:2; Am 3:14; 4:4; 8:14). Altars of, destroyed (2Ki 23:4,15-20).

CALKERS *See Caulkers.*

CALL [*606, 887, 2011, 2410, 6386, 7590, 7695, 7837, 7924, 8775, 9005, 10637, 10721, *1639, 3306, 3104, 3189, 1066, 5157, 2126, 2126, 3105, 5888, 4673, 3306, 2813*].

NIV+ CALLED, CALLING, CALLS, SO-CALLED

Personal:

By Christ (Isa 55:5; Ro 1:6), his Spirit (Rev 22:17), his works (Ps 19:2-3; Ro 1:20), his ministers (Jer 35:15; 2Co 5:20), his gospel (2Th 2:14).

Is from darkness to light (1Pe 2:9). Addressed to all (Isa 45:22; Mt 20:16). Most reject (Pr 1:24; Mt 20:16). Effective to believers (Ps 110:3; Ac 13:48; 1Co 1:24). Not to many wise by human standards (1Co 1:26). To repentance (Isa 55:1).

To believers is of grace (Gal 1:6; 2Ti 1:9), according to the purpose of God (Ro 8:28; 9:11,23-24), without repentance (Ro 11:29), high (Php 3:14), holy (2Ti 1:9), heavenly (Heb 3:1), to fellowship with Christ (1Co 1:9), to holiness (1Th 4:7), to a prize (Php 3:14), to liberty (Gal 5:13), to peace (1Co 7:15; Col 3:15), to glory and virtue (2Pe 1:3), to the eternal glory of Christ (2Th 2:14; 1Pe 5:10), to eternal life (1Ti 6:12).

Partakers of justified (Ro 8:30), walk worthy of (Eph 4:1; 2Th 1:11), blessedness of receiving (Rev 19:9), is to be made sure (2Pe 1:10), praise God for (1Pe 2:9), illustrated (Pr 8:3-4; Mt 23:3-9).

Rejected (Jer 6:16; Mt 22:3-7).

Rejection of leads to judicial blindness (Isa 6:9, w Ac 28:24-27; Ro 11:8-10), delusion (Isa 66:4; 2Th 2:10-11), withdrawal of the means of grace (Jer 26:4-6; Ac 13:46; 18:6; Rev 2:5), temporal judgments (Isa 28:12; Jer 6:16,19; 35:17; Zec 7:12-14), rejection by God (Pr 1:24-

32; Jer 6:19,30), condemnation (Jn 12:48; Heb 2:1-3; 12:25), destruction (Pr 29:1; Mt 22:3-7).

To Special Religious Duty:

Abraham—

Ge 12:1 The LORD had said to Abram, "Leave your country, your people and your father's household and go to the land I will show you.

²"I will make you into a great nation and I will bless you; I will make your name great, and you will be a blessing. ³I will bless those who bless you, and whoever curses you I will curse; and all peoples on earth will be blessed through you."

Isa 51:2 look to Abraham, your father, and to Sarah, who gave you birth. When I called him he was but one, and I blessed him and made him many.

Heb 11:8 By faith Abraham, when called to go to a place he would later receive as his inheritance, obeyed and went, even though he did not know where he was going.

Moses—

Ex 3:2 There the angel of the LORD appeared to him in flames of fire from within a bush. Moses saw that though the bush was on fire it did not burn up.

Ex 3:4 When the LORD saw that he had gone over to look, God called to him from within the bush, "Moses! Moses!" And Moses said, "Here I am."

Ex 3:10 So now, go. I am sending you to Pharaoh to bring my people the Israelites out of Egypt."

Ex 4:1 Moses answered, "What if they do not believe me or listen to me and say, 'The LORD did not appear to you'?"

²Then the LORD said to him, "What is that in your hand?" "A staff," he replied.

³The LORD said, "Throw it on the ground." Moses threw it on the ground and it became a snake, and he ran from it.

⁴Then the LORD said to him, "Reach out your hand and take it by the tail." So Moses reached out and took hold of the snake and it turned back into a staff in his hand. ⁵"This," said the LORD, "is so that they may believe that the LORD, the God of their fathers—the God of Abraham, the God of Isaac and the God of Jacob—has appeared to you."

⁶Then the LORD said, "Put your hand inside your cloak." So Moses put his hand into his cloak, and when he took it out, it was leprous, like snow.

⁷"Now put it back into your cloak," he said. So Moses put his hand back into his cloak, and when he took it out, it was restored, like the rest of his flesh.

⁸Then the LORD said, "If they do not believe you or pay attention to the first miraculous sign, they may believe the second. ⁹But if they do not believe these two signs or listen to you, take some water from the Nile and pour it on the dry ground. The water you take from the river will become blood on the ground."

¹⁰Moses said to the LORD, "O Lord, I have never been eloquent, neither in the past nor since you have spoken to your servant. I am slow of speech and tongue."

¹¹The LORD said to him, "Who gave man his mouth? Who makes him deaf or mute? Who gives him sight or makes him blind? Is it not I, the LORD? ¹²Now go; I will help you speak and will teach you what to say."

¹³But Moses said, "O Lord, please send someone else to do it."

¹⁴Then the LORD's anger burned against Moses and he said, "What about your brother, Aaron the Levite? I know he can speak well. He is already on his way to meet you, and his heart will be glad when he sees you. ¹⁵You shall speak to him and put words in his mouth; I will help both

of you speak and will teach you what to do. ¹⁶He will speak to the people for you, and it will be as if he were your mouth and as if you were God to him.

Ps 105:26 He sent Moses his servant, and Aaron, whom he had chosen.

Ac 7:34 I have indeed seen the oppression of my people in Egypt. I have heard their groaning and have come down to set them free. Now come, I will send you back to Egypt.'

³⁵"This is the same Moses whom they had rejected with the words, 'Who made you ruler and judge?' He was sent to be their ruler and deliverer by God himself, through the angel who appeared to him in the bush.

Aaron and his sons (Ex 4:14-16)—

Ex 28:1 "Have Aaron your brother brought to you from among the Israelites, along with his sons Nadab and Abihu, Eleazar and Ithamar, so they may serve me as priests. (+Ps 105:26)

Heb 5:4 No one takes this honor upon himself; he must be called by God, just as Aaron was.

Joshua—

Nu 27:18 So the LORD said to Moses, "Take Joshua son of Nun, a man in whom is the spirit, and lay your hand on him. ¹⁹Have him stand before Eleazar the priest and the entire assembly and commission him in their presence.

Nu 27:22 Moses did as the LORD commanded him. He took Joshua and had him stand before Eleazar the priest and the whole assembly. ²³Then he laid his hands on him and commissioned him, as the LORD instructed through Moses.

Dt 31:14 The LORD said to Moses, "Now the day of your death is near. Call Joshua and present yourselves at the Tent of Meeting, where I will commission him." So Moses and Joshua came and presented themselves at the Tent of Meeting.

Dt 31:23 The LORD gave this command to Joshua son of Nun: "Be strong and courageous, for you will bring the Israelites into the land I promised them on oath, and I myself will be with you."

Jos 1:1 After the death of Moses the servant of the LORD, the LORD said to Joshua son of Nun, Moses' aide: ²"Moses my servant is dead. Now then, you and all these people, get ready to cross the Jordan River into the land I am about to give to them—to the Israelites. ³I will give you every place where you set your foot, as I promised Moses. ⁴Your territory will extend from the desert to Lebanon, and from the great river, the Euphrates—all the Hittite country—to the Great Sea on the west. ⁵No one will be able to stand up against you all the days of your life. As I was with Moses, so I will be with you; I will never leave you nor forsake you.

⁶"Be strong and courageous, because you will lead these people to inherit the land I swore to their forefathers to give them. ⁷Be strong and very courageous. Be careful to obey all the law my servant Moses gave you; do not turn from it to the right or to the left, that you may be successful wherever you go. ⁸Do not let this Book of the Law depart from your mouth; meditate on it day and night, so that you may be careful to do everything written in it. Then you will be prosperous and successful. ⁹Have I not commanded you? Be strong and courageous. Do not be terrified; do not be discouraged, for the LORD your God will be with you wherever you go."

Gideon—

Jdg 6:11 The angel of the LORD came and sat down under the oak in Ophrah that belonged to Joash the Abiezrite, where his son Gideon was threshing wheat in a winepress

to keep it from the Midianites. ¹²When the angel of the LORD appeared to Gideon, he said, "The LORD is with you, mighty warrior."

¹³"But sir," Gideon replied, "if the LORD is with us, why has all this happened to us? Where are all his wonders that our fathers told us about when they said, 'Did not the LORD bring us up out of Egypt?' But now the LORD has abandoned us and put us into the hand of Midian."

¹⁴The LORD turned to him and said, "Go in the strength you have and save Israel out of Midian's hand. Am I not sending you?"

¹⁵"But Lord," Gideon asked, "how can I save Israel? My clan is the weakest in Manasseh, and I am the least in my family."

¹⁶The LORD answered, "I will be with you, and you will strike down all the Midianites together."

Samuel—

1Sa 3:4 Then the LORD called Samuel. Samuel answered, "Here I am."

⁵And he ran to Eli and said, "Here I am; you called me." But Eli said, "I did not call; go back and lie down." So he went and lay down.

⁶Again the LORD called, "Samuel!" And Samuel got up and went to Eli and said, "Here I am; you called me." "My son," Eli said, "I did not call; go back and lie down."

⁷Now Samuel did not yet know the LORD: The word of the LORD had not yet been revealed to him.

⁸The LORD called Samuel a third time, and Samuel got up and went to Eli and said, "Here I am; you called me." Then Eli realized that the LORD was calling the boy.

⁹So Eli told Samuel, "Go and lie down, and if he calls you, say, 'Speak, LORD, for your servant is listening.'" So Samuel went and lay down in his place.

¹⁰The LORD came and stood there, calling as at the other times, "Samuel! Samuel!" Then Samuel said, "Speak, for your servant is listening."

Solomon—

1Ch 28:6 He said to me: 'Solomon your son is the one who will build my house and my courts, for I have chosen him to be my son, and I will be his father.

1Ch 28:10 Consider now, for the LORD has chosen you to build a temple as a sanctuary. Be strong and do the work."

Jehu—

2Ki 9:6 Jehu got up and went into the house. Then the prophet poured the oil on Jehu's head and declared, "This is what the LORD, the God of Israel, says: 'I anoint you king over the LORD's people Israel. ⁷You are to destroy the house of Ahab your master, and I will avenge the blood of my servants the prophets and the blood of all the LORD's servants shed by Jezebel.

2Ch 22:7 Through Ahaziah's visit to Joram, God brought about Ahaziah's downfall. When Ahaziah arrived, he went out with Joram to meet Jehu son of Nimshi, whom the LORD had anointed to destroy the house of Ahab.

Cyrus—

Isa 45:1 "This is what the LORD says to his anointed, to Cyrus, whose right hand I take hold of to subdue nations before him and to strip kings of their armor, to open doors before him so that gates will not be shut: ²I will go before you and will level the mountains; I will break down gates of bronze and cut through bars of iron. ³I will give you the treasures of darkness, riches stored in secret places, so that you may know that I am the LORD, the God of Israel, who summons you by name. ⁴For the sake of Jacob my servant, of Israel my chosen, I summon you by name and bestow on you a title of honor, though you do not acknowledge me.

Amos—

Am 7:14 Amos answered Amaziah, "I was neither a prophet nor a prophet's son, but I was a shepherd, and I also took care of sycamore-fig trees. ¹⁵But the LORD took me from tending the flock and said to me, 'Go, prophesy to my people Israel.'

Apostles—

Mt 4:18 As Jesus was walking beside the Sea of Galilee, he saw two brothers, Simon called Peter and his brother Andrew. They were casting a net into the lake, for they were fishermen. ¹⁹"Come, follow me," Jesus said, "and I will make you fishers of men." ²⁰At once they left their nets and followed him.

²¹Going on from there, he saw two other brothers, James son of Zebedee and his brother John. They were in a boat with their father Zebedee, preparing their nets. Jesus called them, ²²and immediately they left the boat and their father and followed him. (+Mt 9:9)

Mk 1:16 As Jesus walked beside the Sea of Galilee, he saw Simon and his brother Andrew casting a net into the lake, for they were fishermen. ¹⁷"Come, follow me," Jesus said, "and I will make you fishers of men."

Mk 2:14 As he walked along, he saw Levi son of Alphaeus sitting at the tax collector's booth. "Follow me," Jesus told him, and Levi got up and followed him. (+Mk 3:13-19; Lk 5:27; 6:13-16)

Jn 15:16 You did not choose me, but I chose you and appointed you to go and bear fruit—fruit that will last. Then the Father will give you whatever you ask in my name.

The rich young ruler—

Mk 10:21 Jesus looked at him and loved him. "One thing you lack," he said. "Go, sell everything you have and give to the poor, and you will have treasure in heaven. Then come, follow me."

²²At this the man's face fell. He went away sad, because he had great wealth.

Paul—

Ac 9:4 He fell to the ground and heard a voice say to him, "Saul, Saul, why do you persecute me?"

⁵"Who are you, Lord?" Saul asked. "I am Jesus, whom you are persecuting," he replied.

⁶"Now get up and go into the city, and you will be told what you must do."

Ac 9:15 But the Lord said to Ananias, "Go! This man is my chosen instrument to carry my name before the Gentiles and their kings and before the people of Israel. ¹⁶I will show him how much he must suffer for my name."

Ac 13:2 While they were worshiping the Lord and fasting, the Holy Spirit said, "Set apart for me Barnabas and Saul for the work to which I have called them." ³So after they had fasted and prayed, they placed their hands on them and sent them off.

Ro 1:1 Paul, a servant of Christ Jesus, called to be an apostle and set apart for the gospel of God— (+1Co 1:1; 2Co 1:1; Gal 1:1,15-16; Eph 1:1; Col 1:1; 1Ti 1:1; 2Ti 1:1)

To All Believers:

Ro 8:30 And those he predestined, he also called; those he called, he also justified; those he justified, he also glorified.

1Co 1:2 To the church of God in Corinth, to those sanctified in Christ Jesus and called to be holy, together with all those everywhere who call on the name of our Lord Jesus Christ—their Lord and ours:

1Co 1:9 God, who has called you into fellowship with his Son Jesus Christ our Lord, is faithful.

1Co 1:24 but to those whom God has called, both Jews and Greeks, Christ the power of God and the wisdom of God.

1Th 2:11 For you know that we dealt with each of you as a father deals with his own children, ¹²encouraging, comforting and urging you to live lives worthy of God, who calls you into his kingdom and glory.

2Th 2:13 But we ought always to thank God for you, brothers loved by the Lord, because from the beginning God chose you to be saved through the sanctifying work of the Spirit and through belief in the truth. ¹⁴He called you to this through our gospel, that you might share in the glory of our Lord Jesus Christ.

2Ti 1:9 who has saved us and called us to a holy life—not because of anything we have done but because of his own purpose and grace. This grace was given us in Christ Jesus before the beginning of time,

Heb 3:1 Therefore, holy brothers, who share in the heavenly calling, fix your thoughts on Jesus, the apostle and high priest whom we confess. ²He was faithful to the one who appointed him, just as Moses was faithful in all God's house.

Heb 3:7 So, as the Holy Spirit says:

"Today, if you hear his voice, ⁸do not harden your hearts as you did in the rebellion, during the time of testing in the desert,

1Pe 5:10 And the God of all grace, who called you to his eternal glory in Christ, after you have suffered a little while, will himself restore you and make you strong, firm and steadfast.

2Pe 1:3 His divine power has given us everything we need for life and godliness through our knowledge of him who called us by his own glory and goodness.

2Pe 1:10 Therefore, my brothers, be all the more eager to make your calling and election sure. For if you do these things, you will never fall,

Jude 1 Jude, a servant of Jesus Christ and a brother of James, To those who have been called, who are loved by God the Father and kept by Jesus Christ:

Rev 17:14 They will make war against the Lamb, but the Lamb will overcome them because he is Lord of lords and King of kings—and with him will be his called, chosen and faithful followers."

See Minister, Call of; Backsliders; Seekers.

CALLING, THE CHRISTIAN (1Co 1:26; Eph 1:18; 4:1; Php 3:14; 1Th 2:12; 2Th 2:14; 2Ti 1:9; Heb 3:1; 1Pe 5:10; 2Pe 1:10). *See Call.*

CALNEH [4011] (*all of them*). Also called Canneh and Calno, a city of Assyria (Ge 10:10; Isa 10:9; Eze 27:23; Am 6:2).

CALNO [4012] (*all of them*). City which tried to resist the Assyrians (Isa 10:9).

CALVARY *See Golgotha.*

CAMEL [1145, 1695, 4140, *2823*].
NIV+ CAMEL'S, CAMEL-LOADS, CAMELS, CAMELS', SHE-CAMEL

Herds of (Ge 12:16; 24:35; 30:43; 1Sa 30:17; 1Ch 27:30; Job 1:3,17; Isa 60:6). Docility of (Ge 24:11).

Uses of: For riding (Ge 24:10,61,64; 31:17), posts (Est

8:10,14; Jer 2:23), drawing chariots (Isa 21:7), for carrying burdens (Ge 24:10; 37:25; 1Ki 10:2; 2Ki 8:9; 1Ch 12:40; Isa 30:6), for cavalry (1Sa 30:17), for milk (Ge 32:15). Forbidden as food (Lev 11:4). Hair of, made into cloth (Mt 3:4; Mk 1:6). Ornaments of (Jdg 8:21,26). Stables for (Eze 25:5).

CAMEL'S HAIR [2823]. John the Baptist wore a garment made of camel's hair (Mt 3:4; Mk 1:6). Such garments are still used in the Near East.

CAMON See Kamon.

CAMP [2837, 4328, 4722, 4869, 5046, 5825+, 7155, 8905, 9381, 4213].

NIV+ CAMPED, CAMPFIRES, CAMPING, CAMPS, ENCAMP, ENCAMPED, ENCAMPS

Of the Israelites around the tabernacle (Nu 2; 3). *See Itinerary.*

CAMPHIRE See Henna Blossoms.

CANA [2830] (*reed*). Marriage at (Jn 2:1-11). Nobleman's son healed at (Jn 4:46-47). Nathanael's home at (Jn 21:2).

CANAAN [4046, 4050, 5913] (*land of purple* hence *merchant, trader*).

NIV+ CANAANITE, CANAANITES

1. Son of Ham (Ge 9:18,22,25-27). Descendants of (Ge 10:6,15; 1Ch 1:8,13).

2. Land of (Ge 11:31; 17:8; 23:2). Called Israel (Ex 15:14), the land of Israel (1Sa 13:19), of the Hebrews (Ge 40:15), of the Jews (Ac 10:39), of promise (Heb 11:9), the Beautiful Land (Da 8:9), the holy land (Zec 2:12), the Lord's land (Hos 9:3), Immanuel's land (Isa 8:8), Beulah (Isa 62:4).

Promised to Abraham and his seed (Ge 12:1-7; 13:14-17; 15:18-21; 17:8; Dt 12:9-10; Ps 105:11) and the promise renewed to Isaac (Ge 26:3). Extent of: According to the promise (Ge 15:18; Ex 23:31; Dt 11:24; Jos 1:4; 15:1), after the Conquest by Joshua (Jos 12:1-8), in Solomon's time (1Ki 4:21,24; 2Ch 7:8; 9:26). Prophecy concerning, after the restoration of Israel (Eze 47:13-20).

Fertility of (Dt 8:7-9; 11:10-13). Fruitfulness of (Nu 13:27; 14:7-8; Jer 2:7; 32:22). Products of: Fruits (Dt 8:8; Jer 40:10,12), minerals (Dt 8:9). Exports of (Eze 27:17).

Famines in (Ge 12:10; 26:1; 47:13; Ru 1:1; 2Sa 21:1; 1Ki 17). *See Famine.*

Spies sent into, by Moses (Nu 13:17-29). Conquest of, by the Israelites (Nu 21:21-35; Dt 3:3-6; Jos 6-12; Ps 44:1-3). Divided by lot among the twelve tribes and families (Nu 26:55-56; 33:54; 34:13), by Joshua, Eleazar, and a prince from each tribe (Nu 34:16-29; 35:1-8; Jos 14-19). Divided into twelve provinces by Solomon (1Ki 4:7-19). Into two kingdoms, Judah and Israel (1Ki 11:29-36; 12:16-21). Roman provinces of (Lk 3:1; Jn 4:3-4). *See Canaanite(s).*

CANAANITE, SIMON THE See Simon, 2; Zealot, Simon the.

CANAANITE(S) [4046, 4050, 5914] (*land of purple* hence *merchant, trader*).

NIV+ CANAAN

Eleven nations descended from Canaan (Ge 10:15-19; Dt 7:1; 1Ch 1:13-16). Territory of (Ge 10:19; 12:6; 15:18; Ex 23:31; Nu 13:29; 34:1-12; Jos 1:4; 5:1), given to the

Israelites (Ge 12:6-7; 15:18; 17:8; Ex 23:23; Dt 7:1-3; 32:49; Ps 135:11-12).

Wickedness of (Ge 13:13; Lev 18:25,27-28; 20:23). To be expelled from the land (Ex 33:2; 34:11). To be destroyed (Ex 23:23-24; Dt 19:1; 31:3-5). Not expelled (Jos 17:12-18; Jdg 1:1-33; 3:1-3). Defeat the Israelites (Nu 14:45; Jdg 4:1-3). Defeated by the Israelites (Nu 21:1-3; Jos 11:1-16; Jdg 4:4-24), by the Egyptians (1Ki 9:16). Chariots of (Jos 17:18).

Isaac forbidden by Abraham to take a wife from (Ge 28:1). Judah marries a woman of (Ge 38:2; 1Ch 2:3). The Jews intermarry with after the Exile (Ezr 9:2).

Prophecy concerning (Ge 9:25-27).

CANANAEAN See Zealot, Simon the.

CANDACE [2833] (roughly *queen*). Queen of Ethiopia (Ac 8:27).

CANDIDATE Instance of Absalom, campaigning for popular favor (2Sa 15:1-6).

CANDLE See Lamp.

CANDLESTICK See Lampstand.

CANE [5475, 7866]. Probably the sweet calamus (Isa 43:24; Jer 6:20).

CANKER See Gangrene.

CANKERWORM See Locust.

CANNEH [4034]. An alternate form of Calneh. A city of Assyria (Eze 27:23). *See Calneh.*

CANNIBALISM (Lev 26:29; Dt 28:53-57; 2Ki 6:28-29; Jer 19:9; La 2:20; 4:10; Eze 5:10).

CANONICITY By the canon is meant the list of the books of the Bible recognized by the Christian church as genuine and inspired. The Protestant canon includes thirty-nine books in the OT and twenty-seven in the New. The Roman Catholic canon has fourteen more books and additions to the OT; the Orthodox as many as eighteen. *See Apocrypha.* The Jewish canon is the same as the Protestant OT. The OT canon was formed before the time of Christ, as is evident from Josephus (*Against Apion* 1:8), who wrote c. A.D. 90. We know very little of the history of the acceptance of the OT books as canonical. There is much more documentary evidence regarding the formation of the NT canon. The Muratorian Canon (c. A.D. 170), which survives only as a fragment, lists most of the NT books. Some of the books were questioned for a time for various reasons, usually uncertainty of authorship, but by the end of the fourth century our present canon was almost universally accepted, and this was done not by arbitrary decree of bishops, but by the general consensus of the church.

CANTICLES See Song of Solomon.

CAPERNAUM [3019] (*village of Nahum*). A city on the shore of the Sea of Galilee. Jesus chose, as the place of his abode (Mt 4:13; Lk 4:31). Miracles of Jesus performed at (Mt 9:1-26; 17:24-27; Mk 1:21-45; 2; 3:1-6; Lk 7:1-10; Jn 4:46-53; 6:17-25,59).

Jesus' prophecy against (Mt 11:23; Lk 10:15).

CAPHTOR [4116].

NIV+ CAPHTORITES

Place from which the Philistines originally came (Am 9:7), probably from the island of Crete (Jer 47:4; Am 9:7).

CAPHTORITES, CAPHTORIM [4118].

NIV+ CAPHTOR

People of Caphtor (Ge 10:14; Dt 2:23; 1Ch 1:12).

CAPITAL [4196, 4638+5477, 7633].

NIV+ CAPITALS

The uppermost member of a column or pilaster crowning the shaft and taking the weight of the entablature (Ex 36:38; 1Ki 7:16-42; 2Ki 25:17; 2Ch 4:12-13; Jer 52:22).

CAPITAL AND LABOR Strife between (Mt 21:33-41; Mk 12:1-9; Lk 20:9-10).

See Employee; Employer; Master; Rich, The; Servant.

CAPITAL PUNISHMENT *See Punishment.*

CAPPADOCIA [2838]. Easternmost Roman province of Asia Minor (Ac 2:9; 1Pe 1:1).

CAPSTONE [7157+8031, 74+8036, *1224+3051*]. The keystone of an arch or the last stone put in place to complete a building. Figurative of Jesus: first rejected; finally taking his rightful place of supremacy (Ps 118:22; Zec 4:7; Mt 21:42; Mk 12:10; Lk 20:17; Ac 4:11; 1Pe 2:7). *See Cornerstone.*

CAPTAIN [1251, 2021+2480+8042, 2980, 6233, 8569+, 8957, *3237, 5130*].

NIV+ CAPTAINS

Commander-in-chief of an army (Dt 20:9; Jdg 4:2; 1Sa 14:50; 1Ki 2:35; 16:16; 1Ch 27:34). Of the tribes (Nu 2). Of thousands (Nu 31:48; 1Sa 17:18; 1Ch 28:1). Of hundreds (2Ki 11:15). *See Centurion.* Of fifties (2Ki 1:9; Isa 3:3). Of the guard (Ge 37:36; 2Ki 25:8). Of the ward (Jer 37:13).

Signifying any commander (1Sa 9:16; 22:2; 2Ki 20:5), leader (1Ch 11:21; 12:34; 2Ch 17:14-19; Jn 18:12).

David's captains or chief heroes (2Sa 23; 1Ch 11; 12). King appoints (1Sa 18:13; 2Sa 17:25; 18:1).

Angel of the Lord called (Jos 5:14; 2Ch 13:12).

See Armies.

CAPTIVE [*659, 660, 673, 1655, 4334, 4374, 8647, 8660, 8664, 9530, *168, 5197*].

NIV+ CAPTIVATE, CAPTIVATED, CAPTIVES, CAPTIVITY, CAPTORS, CAPTURE, CAPTURED, CAPTURES, CAPTURING, RECAPTURE, RECAPTURED

Prisoner of war (Ge 14:12; 1Sa 30:1-2).

Cruelty to: Putting to death (Nu 31:9-20; Dt 20:13; 21:10; Jos 8:29; 10:15-40; 11:11; Jdg 7:25; 8:21; 21:11; 1Sa 15:32-33; 2Sa 8:2; 2Ki 8:12; Jer 39:6), 20,000 by Amaziah (2Ch 25:11-12), ripping open pregnant women (2Ki 8:12; 15:16; Am 1:13), enslaved or tortured with picks and axes (2Sa 12:31; 1Ch 20:3), blinded (Jdg 16:21; Jer 39:7), maimed (Jdg 1:6-7), ravished (La 5:11-13; Zec 14:2), enslaved (Dt 20:14; 2Ki 5:2; Ps 44:12; Joel 3:6), robbed (Eze 23:25-26), confined in pits (Isa 51:14). Other indignities to (Isa 20:4).

Kindness to (2Ki 25:27-30; Ps 106:46). Advanced to positions in state (Ge 41:39-45; Est 2:8; Da 1).

CAPTIVITY [1655, 3448, 8654, 8660, 8664, *168*].

NIV+ See CAPTIVE

Of the, Israelites foretold (Lev 26:33; Dt 28:36), ten tribes (2Ki 17:6,23-24; 18:9-12).

Of Judah in Babylon, prophecy of (Isa 39:6; Jer 13:19; 20:4; 25:2-11; 32:28), fulfilled (2Ki 24:11-16; 25; 2Ch 36; Jer 52:28-30). Jews return from (Ezr 2; 3; 8).

Israelites in, promises to (Ne 1:9).

As a judgment (Ezr 5:12; 9:7; Isa 5:13; Jer 29:17-19; La 1:3-5; Eze 39:23-24).

Figurative:

(Isa 61:1; Ro 7:23; 1Co 9:27; 2Co 10:5; 2Ti 2:26; 3:6). "Take captive your captives" (Jdg 5:12), "led captives in your train" (Ps 68:18; Eph 4:8).

CAR *See Beth Car.*

CARAVAN [785, 2657].

NIV+ CARAVANS

Company of travelers united together for a common purpose or for mutual protection and generally equipped for a long journey, especially in desert country or through foreign and presumably hostile territory (Ge 32-33; 1Sa 30:1-20).

CARAWAY [7902]. (Isa 28:25-27).

CARBUNCLE NIV "sparkling jewels," (Isa 54:12), "beryl," and "chrysolite." *See Beryl; Chrysolite, 1; Minerals of the Bible, 1; Stones.*

CARCAS [4139] (perhaps *vulture*). A eunuch and servant of the Persian king Xerxes (Est 1:10).

CARCASS, CARCASE [1581, 5147, 5577, 7007, *4773*] (*carcass*).

NIV+ CARCASSES

The dead body of a human or animal. Israelites were ceremonially unclean if they touched a carcass (Lev 11:8-40; Nu 6:6-7; 9:10; Dt 14:8).

CARCHEMISH, CHARCHEMISH [4138]. A Babylonian city on the Euphrates, against which the king of Egypt made war (2Ch 35:20; Isa 10:9; Jer 46:2).

CARE, WORLDLY [*2011, 3338, 3359, 5466, 7212, 8286, 9068, *2150, 2499, 3508, 5555*].

NIV+ CARED, CAREFREE, CAREFUL, CAREFULLY, CARELESS, CARELESSLY, CARES, CARING

Ecc 4:8 There was a man all alone; he had neither son nor brother. There was no end to his toil, yet his eyes were not content with his wealth. "For whom am I toiling," he asked, "and why am I depriving myself of enjoyment?" This too is meaningless—a miserable business!

Mt 6:25 "Therefore I tell you, do not worry about your life, what you will eat or drink; or about your body, what you will wear. Is not life more important than food, and the body more important than clothes? [26]Look at the birds of the air; they do not sow or reap or store away in barns, and yet your heavenly Father feeds them. Are you not much more valuable than they? [27]Who of you by worrying can add a single hour to his life?

[28]"And why do you worry about clothes? See how the lilies of the field grow. They do not labor or spin. [29]Yet I tell you that not even Solomon in all his splendor was dressed like one of these. [30]If that is how God clothes the grass of the field, which is here today and tomorrow is thrown into the fire, will he not much more clothe you, O you of little faith? [31]So do not worry, saying, 'What shall we eat?' or 'What shall we drink?' or 'What shall we wear?' [32]For the pagans run after all these things, and your heavenly Father knows that you need them. [33]But seek first his kingdom and his righteousness, and all these things will be given to you as well. [34]Therefore do not worry about tomorrow, for tomorrow will worry about itself. Each day has enough trouble of its own.

Mt 13:22 The one who received the seed that fell among the thorns is the man who hears the word, but the worries of this life and the deceitfulness of wealth choke it, making it unfruitful. (+Mk 4:19; Lk 8:14; 12:27)

Lk 14:18 "But they all alike began to make excuses. The first said, 'I have just bought a field, and I must go and see it. Please excuse me.'

¹⁹"Another said, 'I have just bought five yoke of oxen, and I'm on my way to try them out. Please excuse me.'

Lk 21:34 "Be careful, or your hearts will be weighed down with dissipation, drunkenness and the anxieties of life, and that day will close on you unexpectedly like a trap.

1Co 7:32 I would like you to be free from concern. An unmarried man is concerned about the Lord's affairs— how he can please the Lord. ³³But a married man is concerned about the affairs of this world—how he can please his wife—

Php 4:6 Do not be anxious about anything, but in everything, by prayer and petition, with thanksgiving, present your requests to God.

2Ti 2:4 No one serving as a soldier gets involved in civilian affairs—he wants to please his commanding officer.

In vain—

Ps 39:6 Man is a mere phantom as he goes to and fro: He bustles about, but only in vain; he heaps up wealth, not knowing who will get it.

Ps 127:2 In vain you rise early and stay up late, toiling for food to eat—for he grants sleep to those he loves. (+Mt 6:27; Lk 12:25-26)

Proceeds from unbelief (Mt 6:26,28-30; Lk 12:24,27-28), Martha rebuked for (Lk 10:40-41).

Remedy for:

Ps 37:5 Commit your way to the LORD; trust in him and he will do this:

Ps 55:22 Cast your cares on the LORD and he will sustain you; he will never let the righteous fall.

Pr 16:3 Commit to the LORD whatever you do, and your plans will succeed.

Jer 17:7 "But blessed is the man who trusts in the LORD, whose confidence is in him. ⁸He will be like a tree planted by the water that sends out its roots by the stream. It does not fear when heat comes; its leaves are always green. It has no worries in a year of drought and never fails to bear fruit." (+Mt 6:26-34; Lk 12:22-32)

Php 4:6 Do not be anxious about anything, but in everything, by prayer and petition, with thanksgiving, present your requests to God. ⁷And the peace of God, which transcends all understanding, will guard your hearts and your minds in Christ Jesus.

Heb 13:5 Keep your lives free from the love of money and be content with what you have, because God has said, "Never will I leave you; never will I forsake you."

1Pe 5:6 Humble yourselves, therefore, under God's mighty hand, that he may lift you up in due time. ⁷Cast all your anxiety on him because he cares for you.

Instances of:

Martha (Lk 10:40-41). Certain ones who desired to follow Jesus (Mt 8:19-22; Lk 9:57-62).

See Anxiety; Carnal Mindedness; Rich, The; Riches; Worldliness.

CAREAH *See Kareah.*

CARITES [4133]. Mercenary soldiers from Caria in SW Asia Minor (2Ki 11:4, 19).

CARMEL [4150, 4151, 4153] (*orchard planted with vine and fruit trees*).

NIV+ CARMELITE

1. A fertile and lovely mountain in Israel (SS 7:5; Isa 33:9; 35:2; Jer 46:18; 50:19; Am 1:2). Forests of (2Ki 19:23). Caves of (Am 9:3). An idolatrous high place upon; Elijah builds an altar upon, and confronts the worshipers of Baal, putting to death 450 of its prophets (1Ki 18:17-46). Elisha's abode in (2Ki 2:25; 4:25).

2. A city of Judah (Jos 15:55). Saul erects a memorial at (1Sa 15:12). Nabal's possessions at (1Sa 25:2). King Uzziah, who delighted in agriculture, had vineyards at (2Ch 26:10).

CARMELITE [4153].

NIV+ CARMEL

Hezro, one of David's mighty men, a native of Judean Carmel (1Sa 27:3; 1Ch 11:37).

CARMI, CARMITE [4145, 4146] (possibly *[fruitful] vine, vineyard owner* IDB).

1. Son of Reuben (Ge 46:9; Ex 6:14).
2. Son of Hezron (1Ch 4:1).
3. Father of Achan (Jos 7:1,18; 1Ch 2:7) and his clan (Nu 26:6).

CARNAL MINDEDNESS

NIV+ MATERIAL, SINFUL, UNSPIRITUAL, WORLDLY

Is in conflict with, the inward man (Ro 7:14-22), the Holy Spirit (Gal 5:17).

Is at enmity with God—

Ro 8:6 The mind of sinful man is death, but the mind controlled by the Spirit is life and peace; ⁷the sinful mind is hostile to God. It does not submit to God's law, nor can it do so. ⁸Those controlled by the sinful nature cannot please God.

Jas 4:4 You adulterous people, don't you know that friendship with the world is hatred toward God? Anyone who chooses to be a friend of the world becomes an enemy of God.

In the children of wrath (Eph 2:3). To be crucified (Ro 8:13; Gal 5:24). Excludes from kingdom of God (Gal 5:19-21).

Reaps corruption—

Gal 6:8 The one who sows to please his sinful nature, from that nature will reap destruction; the one who sows to please the Spirit, from the Spirit will reap eternal life.

See Care, Worldly; Flesh; Riches; Sin, Fruits of; Worldliness.

CARNELIAN [4917]. Seen in John's vision of the glory of God (Rev 4:3) and the foundation of the New Jerusalem (Rev 21:20).

See Minerals of the Bible, 1; Stones.

CARPENTRY [3093, 6770, 5454].

NIV+ CARPENTER, CARPENTER'S, CARPENTERS

Building the ark (Ge 6:14-16). Tabernacle and furniture of (Ex 31:2-9). *See Tabernacle.* David's palace (2Sa 5:11). Temple (2Ki 12:11; 22:6). *See Temple.* Making idols (Isa 41:7; 44:13). Carpenters (Jer 24:1; Zec 1:20), Joseph (Mt 13:55), Jesus (Mk 6:3).

See Carving; Master Craftsman.

CARPET *See Tapestry.*

CARPUS *[2842]* (*fruit(ful)*). A Christian at Troas (2Ti 4:13).

CARRIAGE [712, 4753, *4832*].

NIV+ CARRIAGES

A richly adorned royal means of transportation, a palanquin (SS 3:7,9-10). In the description of fallen Babylon (Rev 18:13).

CARSHENA *[4161]* (possibly *black*). A Persian prince (Est 1:14).

CART, CARTS [5047, 6322].

NIV+ CARTWHEEL

Vehicle with wheels used for carrying goods as well as persons (Ge 45:19,21; 46:5; 1Sa 6:7-14; 2Sa 6:3; Isa 28:27-28).

CARVING [2977, 2634, 5237, 5381, 6913, 7178, 7180, 7181, 7334, 7338, 7844].

NIV+ CARVED, CARVES

Woodwork of the temple was decorated with carvings of flowers, cherubim, and palm trees (1Ki 6:18,29,32,35; Ps 74:6). Beds decorated with (Pr 7:16). Idols manufactured by (Dt 7:5; Isa 44:9-17; 45:20; Hab 2:18-19).

Persons skilled in: Bezalel (Ex 31:1-5), Huram (1Ki 7:13-51; 2Ch 2:13-14).

CASIPHIA *[4085]*. A place in the Persian Empire (Ezr 8:17).

CASLUHITES, CASLUHIM *[4078]*. A people whose progenitor was a son of Mizraim (Ge 10:14; 1Ch 1:12).

CASSIA *[7703, 7904]*. An aromatic plant, probably cinnamon (Ps 45:8; Eze 27:19). An ingredient of the sacred oil (Ex 30:24).

CASTING See *Molding.*

CASTING LOTS [*3214, 3721, 5877, 5989, 8959, 965, *1443*].

NIV+ CAST, CASTS

To get a decision from God (Lev 16:8; Jos 18:6-10; 1Sa 14:42; 1Ch 24:31; 26:13-14; Jnh 1:7; Ac 1:26). To set a date (Est 3:7). To settle disputes (Pr 18:18). In divination (Eze 21:21). In gambling (Job 6:27; Ps 22:18; Mt 27:35). The decision is from the LORD (Pr 16:33). See *Lot, The.*

CASTLE See *Fort; Tower.* For the concept "My house is my castle" see Dt 24:10-11.

CASTOR AND POLLUX [*1483*]. Twin sons of Zeus, Greek gods thought to have power over wind and wave (Ac 28:11).

CATACOMBS Subterranean burial places used by the early church. Most are in Rome, where they extend for 600 miles.

CATERPILLAR(S) See *Grasshopper; Locust.*

CATHOLIC EPISTLES See *General Letters.*

CATHOLICITY Liberality of religious sentiment, inclusiveness.

Taught:

In Christ's reproof of John—
Mk 9:38 "Teacher," said John, "we saw a man driving out

demons in your name and we told him to stop, because he was not one of us."

[39]"Do not stop him," Jesus said. "No one who does a miracle in my name can in the next moment say anything bad about me, [40]for whoever is not against us is for us. [41]I tell you the truth, anyone who gives you a cup of water in my name because you belong to Christ will certainly not lose his reward. (+Lk 9:49-50)

In Peter's vision of the sheet and visit to Cornelius (Ac 10:1-43)—

Ac 10:44 While Peter was still speaking these words, the Holy Spirit came on all who heard the message. [45]The circumcised believers who had come with Peter were astonished that the gift of the Holy Spirit had been poured out even on the Gentiles. [46]For they heard them speaking in tongues and praising God. Then Peter said, [47]"Can anyone keep these people from being baptized with water? They have received the Holy Spirit just as we have." [48]So he ordered that they be baptized in the name of Jesus Christ. Then they asked Peter to stay with them for a few days.

In Paul's commission—
Ro 1:1 Paul, a servant of Christ Jesus, called to be an apostle and set apart for the gospel of God— [2]the gospel he promised beforehand through his prophets in the Holy Scriptures [3]regarding his Son, who as to his human nature was a descendant of David, [4]and who through the Spirit of holiness was declared with power to be the Son of God by his resurrection from the dead: Jesus Christ our Lord. [5]Through him and for his name's sake, we received grace and apostleship to call people from among all the Gentiles to the obedience that comes from faith. [6]And you also are among those who are called to belong to Jesus Christ.

[7]To all in Rome who are loved by God and called to be saints: Grace and peace to you from God our Father and from the Lord Jesus Christ.

Ro 1:14 I am obligated both to Greeks and non-Greeks, both to the wise and the foolish. [15]That is why I am so eager to preach the gospel also to you who are at Rome.

[16]I am not ashamed of the gospel, because it is the power of God for the salvation of everyone who believes: first for the Jew, then for the Gentile.

In Paul's rebuke of Jewish exclusiveness—
Ro 3:20 Therefore no one will be declared righteous in his sight by observing the law; rather, through the law we become conscious of sin.

[21]But now a righteousness from God, apart from law, has been made known, to which the Law and the Prophets testify. [22]This righteousness from God comes through faith in Jesus Christ to all who believe. There is no difference, [23]for all have sinned and fall short of the glory of God, [24]and are justified freely by his grace through the redemption that came by Christ Jesus. [25]God presented him as a sacrifice of atonement, through faith in his blood. He did this to demonstrate his justice, because in his forbearance he had left the sins committed beforehand unpunished— [26]he did it to demonstrate his justice at the present time, so as to be just and the one who justifies those who have faith in Jesus.

[27]Where, then, is boasting? It is excluded. On what principle? On that of observing the law? No, but on that of faith. [28]For we maintain that a man is justified by faith apart from observing the law. [29]Is God the God of Jews only? Is he not the God of Gentiles too? Yes, of Gentiles too, [30]since there is only one God, who will justify the circumcised by faith and the uncircumcised through that

same faith. [31]Do we, then, nullify the law by this faith? Not at all! Rather, we uphold the law.

Ro 4:1 What then shall we say that Abraham, our forefather, discovered in this matter? [2]If, in fact, Abraham was justified by works, he had something to boast about—but not before God. [3]What does the Scripture say? "Abraham believed God, and it was credited to him as righteousness."

[4]Now when a man works, his wages are not credited to him as a gift, but as an obligation. [5]However, to the man who does not work but trusts God who justifies the wicked, his faith is credited as righteousness. [6]David says the same thing when he speaks of the blessedness of the man to whom God credits righteousness apart from works:

[7]"Blessed are they whose transgressions are forgiven, whose sins are covered. [8]Blessed is the man whose sin the Lord will never count against him."

[9]Is this blessedness only for the circumcised, or also for the uncircumcised? We have been saying that Abraham's faith was credited to him as righteousness. [10]Under what circumstances was it credited? Was it after he was circumcised, or before? It was not after, but before! [11]And he received the sign of circumcision, a seal of the righteousness that he had by faith while he was still uncircumcised. So then, he is the father of all who believe but have not been circumcised, in order that righteousness might be credited to them. [12]And he is also the father of the circumcised who not only are circumcised but who also walk in the footsteps of the faith that our father Abraham had before he was circumcised.

[13]It was not through law that Abraham and his offspring received the promise that he would be heir of the world, but through the righteousness that comes by faith. [14]For if those who live by law are heirs, faith has no value and the promise is worthless, [15]because law brings wrath. And where there is no law there is no transgression.

[16]Therefore, the promise comes by faith, so that it may be by grace and may be guaranteed to all Abraham's offspring—not only to those who are of the law but also to those who are of the faith of Abraham. He is the father of us all. (+Ro 4:17-25)

In the judgment of apostolic church—

Ac 15:1 Some men came down from Judea to Antioch and were teaching the brothers: "Unless you are circumcised, according to the custom taught by Moses, you cannot be saved." [2]This brought Paul and Barnabas into sharp dispute and debate with them. So Paul and Barnabas were appointed, along with some other believers, to go up to Jerusalem to see the apostles and elders about this question. [3]The church sent them on their way, and as they traveled through Phoenicia and Samaria, they told how the Gentiles had been converted. This news made all the brothers very glad. [4]When they came to Jerusalem, they were welcomed by the church and the apostles and elders, to whom they reported everything God had done through them.

[5]Then some of the believers who belonged to the party of the Pharisees stood up and said, "The Gentiles must be circumcised and required to obey the law of Moses."

[6]The apostles and elders met to consider this question. [7]After much discussion, Peter got up and addressed them: "Brothers, you know that some time ago God made a choice among you that the Gentiles might hear from my lips the message of the gospel and believe. [8]God, who knows the heart, showed that he accepted them by giving the Holy Spirit to them, just as he did to us. [9]He made no

distinction between us and them, for he purified their hearts by faith. [10]Now then, why do you try to test God by putting on the necks of the disciples a yoke that neither we nor our fathers have been able to bear? [11]No! We believe it is through the grace of our Lord Jesus that we are saved, just as they are."

[12]The whole assembly became silent as they listened to Barnabas and Paul telling about the miraculous signs and wonders God had done among the Gentiles through them. [13]When they finished, James spoke up: "Brothers, listen to me. [14]Simon has described to us how God at first showed his concern by taking from the Gentiles a people for himself. [15]The words of the prophets are in agreement with this, as it is written:

[16]" 'After this I will return and rebuild David's fallen tent. Its ruins I will rebuild, and I will restore it, [17]that the remnant of men may seek the Lord, and all the Gentiles who bear my name, says the Lord, who does these things' [18]that have been known for ages.

[19]"It is my judgment, therefore, that we should not make it difficult for the Gentiles who are turning to God. [20]Instead we should write to them, telling them to abstain from food polluted by idols, from sexual immorality, from the meat of strangled animals and from blood. [21]For Moses has been preached in every city from the earliest times and is read in the synagogues on every Sabbath."

[22]Then the apostles and elders, with the whole church, decided to choose some of their own men and send them to Antioch with Paul and Barnabas. They chose Judas (called Barsabbas) and Silas, two men who were leaders among the brothers. [23]With them they sent the following letter:

The apostles and elders, your brothers,

To the Gentile believers in Antioch, Syria and Cilicia: Greetings.

[24]We have heard that some went out from us without our authorization and disturbed you, troubling your minds by what they said. [25]So we all agreed to choose some men and send them to you with our dear friends Barnabas and Paul— [26]men who have risked their lives for the name of our Lord Jesus Christ. [27]Therefore we are sending Judas and Silas to confirm by word of mouth what we are writing. [28]It seemed good to the Holy Spirit and to us not to burden you with anything beyond the following requirements: [29]You are to abstain from food sacrificed to idols, from blood, from the meat of strangled animals and from sexual immorality. You will do well to avoid these things. Farewell.

[30]The men were sent off and went down to Antioch, where they gathered the church together and delivered the letter. [31]The people read it and were glad for its encouraging message.

In the unity of believers—

Ro 5:1 Therefore, since we have been justified through faith, we have peace with God through our Lord Jesus Christ, [2]through whom we have gained access by faith into this grace in which we now stand. And we rejoice in the hope of the glory of God.

Gal 3:27 for all of you who were baptized into Christ have clothed yourselves with Christ. [28]There is neither Jew nor Greek, slave nor free, male nor female, for you are all one in Christ Jesus.

Eph 2:14 For he himself is our peace, who has made the two one and has destroyed the barrier, the dividing wall of hostility, [15]by abolishing in his flesh the law with its commandments and regulations. His purpose was to create in himself one new man out of the two, thus making peace,

¹⁶and in this one body to reconcile both of them to God through the cross, by which he put to death their hostility. ¹⁷He came and preached peace to you who were far away and peace to those who were near.

Col 3:11 Here there is no Greek or Jew, circumcised or uncircumcised, barbarian, Scythian, slave or free, but Christ is all, and is in all.

¹²Therefore, as God's chosen people, holy and dearly loved, clothe yourselves with compassion, kindness, humility, gentleness and patience. ¹³Bear with each other and forgive whatever grievances you may have against one another. Forgive as the Lord forgave you. ¹⁴And over all these virtues put on love, which binds them all together in perfect unity.

¹⁵Let the peace of Christ rule in your hearts, since as members of one body you were called to peace. And be thankful.

In the gifts of Holy Spirit to Gentiles as well as to Jews (Ac 10:44-48)—

Ac 11:17 So if God gave them the same gift as he gave us, who believed in the Lord Jesus Christ, who was I to think that I could oppose God?"

¹⁸When they heard this, they had no further objections and praised God, saying, "So then, God has granted even the Gentiles repentance unto life."

See Heathen; Strangers.

Instances of:

Solomon, in his prayer (1Ki 8:41-43). Paul, in recognizing devout heathen (Ac 13:16,26,42-43). Peter (Ac 10:34-35). Rulers of the synagogue at Salamis, permitting the apostles to preach (Ac 13:5).

CATTLE [989+, 1248, 1330, 5238, 8802, 10756, *1091, 3229, 4990*]. Of the bovine species. Used for sacrifice (1Ki 8:63). *See Heifer; Offerings.* Sheltered (Ge 33:17). Pharaoh's dream of (Ge 41:2-7,26-30). Stall-fed (Pr 15:17).

Gilead adapted to the raising of (Nu 32:1-4), and Bashan (Ps 22:12; Eze 39:18; Am 4:1).

See Animals; Bull; Cow; Heifer; Offerings.

CAUDA [*3007*]. An island near Crete (Ac 27:16).

CAULKERS [2616].
NIV+ CAULK

Those who drive some suitable substance into the seams of a ship's planking to render them watertight (Eze 27:9). *See Pitch; Tar.*

CAUL(S)

1. NIV "covering" of the liver. Burnt with sacrifice (Ex 29:13,22; Lev 3:4,10,15; 4:9; 7:4; 8:16,25; 9:10,19).

2. NIV "headbands" (Isa 3:18). *See Headbands.*

CAUSE
NIV+ CAUSED, CAUSES, CAUSING

See Actions at Law.

CAUTION [9365, *4133*].
NIV+ CAUTIONED, CAUTIOUS

See Expediency; Prudence.

CAVALRY [7305, *2689*]. Mounted on, horses (Ex 14:23; 1Sa 13:5; 2Sa 8:4; 1Ki 4:26; 2Ch 8:6; 9:25; 12:3; Isa 30:16; 31:1; Jer 4:29; Zec 10:5; Rev 9:16-18), camels (1Sa 30:17).

See Armies.

CAVE [5117, 5942, 6186, 7074, *5068*].
NIV+ CAVERNS, CAVES

Used as a dwelling: By Lot (Ge 19:30), Elijah (1Ki 19:9), Israelites (Eze 33:27), believers (Heb 11:38). Place of refuge (Jos 10:16-27; Jdg 6:2; 1Sa 13:6; 1Ki 18:4,13; 19:9,13). Burial place (Ge 23:9-20; 25:9; 49:29-32; 50:13; Jn 11:38).

Of Adullam (1Sa 22:1; 2Sa 23:13; 1Ch 11:15). En Gedi (1Sa 24:3-8).

CEDAR [780, 781, 4248].
NIV+ CEDARS

Valuable for building purposes (Isa 9:10). David's ample provision of, in Jerusalem, for the temple (2Ch 1:15; 22:4). Furnished by Hiram, king of Tyre, for Solomon's temple (1Ki 5:6-10; 9:11; 2Ch 2:16).

Used in rebuilding, the temple (Ezr 3:7), David's palace (2Sa 5:11; 1Ch 17:1), Solomon's palace (1Ki 7:2), masts of ships (Eze 27:5). Used in purifications (Lev 14:4,6,49-52; Nu 19:6).

Figurative:

(Ps 72:16; 92:12; Isa 2:13; 14:8; Jer 22:7; Eze 31:3; Zec 11:2).

CEDRON *See Kidron.*

CEILING [6212, 7771, 7815]. A reference is to the walls of the temple (1Ki 6:15).

CELESTIAL PHENOMENA Fire from heaven, on the cities of the plain (Ge 19:24-25), on the two captains and their fifties (2Ki 1:10-14), on the flocks and servants of Job (Job 1:16). Hail, on the Egyptians (Ex 9:22-34).

Darkness, on the Egyptians (Ex 10:22-23), at the crucifixion of Jesus (Mt 27:45; Lk 23:44-45). Pillar of cloud and fire (Ex 13:21-22; 14:19,24; 40:38; Nu 9:15-23; Ps 78:14). Thunder and lightning on Mt. Sinai (Ex 19:16,18; 20:18). Sun stood still (Jos 10:12-13).

Prophecy of darkening of sun, moon, and stars (Joel 2:30,32; Mt 24:29; Lk 21:25; Ac 2:19-20).

See Astronomy.

CELIBACY (*Abstaining from marriage and sexual activity*).

Lamented by Jephthah's daughter (Jdg 11:38-39).

Not obligatory—

1Co 7:1 Now for the matters you wrote about: It is good for a man not to marry. ²But since there is so much immorality, each man should have his own wife, and each woman her own husband. (+1Co 7:3-6)

1Co 7:7 I wish that all men were as I am. But each man has his own gift from God; one has this gift, another has that.

⁸Now to the unmarried and the widows I say: It is good for them to stay unmarried, as I am. ⁹But if they cannot control themselves, they should marry, for it is better to marry than to burn with passion.

1Co 7:25 Now about virgins: I have no command from the Lord, but I give a judgment as one who by the Lord's mercy is trustworthy. ²⁶Because of the present crisis, I think that it is good for you to remain as you are.

1Co 9:5 Don't we have the right to take a believing wife along with us, as do the other apostles and the Lord's brothers and Cephas?

1Ti 4:1 The Spirit clearly says that in later times some will abandon the faith and follow deceiving spirits and things taught by demons. ²Such teachings come through hypocritical liars, whose consciences have been seared as with a hot iron. ³They forbid people to marry and order them to abstain from certain foods, which God created to be received with thanksgiving by those who believe and who know the truth.

Practiced for kingdom of heaven's sake—

Mt 19:10 The disciples said to him, "If this is the situation between a husband and wife, it is better not to marry."

¹¹Jesus replied, "Not everyone can accept this word, but only those to whom it has been given. ¹²For some are eunuchs because they were born that way; others were made that way by men; and others have renounced marriage because of the kingdom of heaven. The one who can accept this should accept it."

1Co 7:32 I would like you to be free from concern. An unmarried man is concerned about the Lord's affairs— how he can please the Lord. ³³But a married man is concerned about the affairs of this world—how he can please his wife— ³⁴and his interests are divided. An unmarried woman or virgin is concerned about the Lord's affairs: Her aim is to be devoted to the Lord in both body and spirit. But a married woman is concerned about the affairs of this world—how she can please her husband. ³⁵I am saying this for your own good, not to restrict you, but that you may live in a right way in undivided devotion to the Lord.

³⁶If anyone thinks he is acting improperly toward the virgin he is engaged to, and if she is getting along in years and he feels he ought to marry, he should do as he wants. He is not sinning. They should get married. ³⁷But the man who has settled the matter in his own mind, who is under no compulsion but has control over his own will, and who has made up his mind not to marry the virgin—this man also does the right thing. ³⁸So then, he who marries the virgin does right, but he who does not marry her does even better.

³⁹A woman is bound to her husband as long as he lives. But if her husband dies, she is free to marry anyone she wishes, but he must belong to the Lord. ⁴⁰In my judgment, she is happier if she stays as she is—and I think that I too have the Spirit of God.

The 144,000 (Rev 14:1-4).

CELLAR *See Storehouse.*

CENCHREA [*3020*]. A seaport near Corinth (Ac 18:18; Ro 16:1).

CENSER [4746, 5233, *3338*].
NIV+ CENSERS

Used for offering incense (Lev 16:12; Nu 16:6-7,16-18,46; Rev 8:3). For the temple, made of gold (1Ki 7:50; 2Ch 4:22; Heb 9:4). Those which Korah used were converted into plates (Nu 16:37-39). Used in idolatrous rites (Eze 8:11).

Symbolic: (Rev 8:3,5).

CENSORIOUSNESS *See Charitableness; Speaking, Evil; Uncharitableness.*

CENSUS [408+6296, 4948, 5031, 5951+8031, 6218+, 7212, *615, 616*]. Numbering of Israel by Moses (Ex 38:26; Nu 1; 3:14-43; 26), David (2Sa 24:1-9; 1Ch 21:1-8; 27:24).

A poll tax to be levied at each (Ex 30:12-16; 38:26).

Of the Roman Empire, by Caesar (Lk 2:1-3).

CENTURION [*1672, 3035*] (*ruler over 100*).
NIV+ CENTURION'S, CENTURIONS

A commander of 100 soldiers in the Roman army (Mk

15:44-45; Ac 21:32; 22:25-26; 23:17,23; 24:23). Of Capernaum, comes to Jesus in behalf of his servant (Mt 8:5-13; Lk 7:1-10). In charge of the soldiers who crucified Jesus, testifies, "Truly this was the Son of God" (Mt 27:54; Mk 15:39; Lk 23:47).

See Cornelius; Julius.

CEPHAS [*3064*] (*rock*). *See Peter, Simon.*

CEREMONIAL WASHING [3200, *49, 968, 2752, 4778*]. The Mosaic Law, relative to cleansing, stresses that sin defiles. To keep this great truth constantly before the Israelites, specific ordinances concerning washings were given to Moses. The purpose was to teach, by this object lesson, that sin pollutes the soul, and that only those who were cleansed from their sins could be pure in the sight of the Lord (Heb 9:10; 10:22).

Of Garments (Ex 19:10,14). Of priests (Ex 29:4; 30:18-21; 40:12,31-32; Lev 8:6; 16:4,24,26,28; Nu 19:7-10,19; 2Ch 4:6). Of burnt offerings (Lev 1:9,13; 9:14; 2Ch 4:6). Of the hands (Mt 15:2; Mk 7:2-5; Lk 11:38). Of the feet (1Ti 5:10).

For defilement (Lev 11:24-40). Of lepers (Lev 13:6; 14:9). Of those having bodily discharge (Lev 15:5-13). Of those having eaten or touched that which died (Lev 11:25, 40; 17:15-16).

Traditional forms of, not observed by Jesus (Lk 11:38-39).

See Defilement; Purification; Washings.

CERTIFICATE OF DIVORCE [6219, *687, 1046*]. Given by the husband to his wife upon divorce (Dt 24:1-4; Mt 5:31; 19:7; Mk 10:4). Figurative of God's judgment on Israel (Isa 50:1; Jer 3:8). *See Divorce.*

CESAR *See Caesar.*

CESAREA *See Caesarea.*

CESAREA PHILIPPI *See Caesarea Philippi.*

CHAFF [3143, 5161, 7990, 10534, *949*].
Figurative:

(Job 21:18; Ps 1:4; 35:5; Isa 17:13; Da 2:35; Hos 13:3; Mt 3:12; Lk 3:17).

CHAINS [*272, 2414, 4591, 4593, 6310, 9249, 10212, 268, 1301, 1313*].
NIV+ CHAIN, CHAINED

Used as ornaments. Worn by princes (Ge 41:42; Da 5:7,29), on ankles (Nu 31:50; Isa 3:19), on the breastplate of high priest (Ex 28:14; 39:15). As ornaments on camels (Jdg 8:26). A partition of, in the temple (1Ki 6:21; 7:17).

Used to confine prisoners (Ps 68:6; 149:8; Jer 40:4; Ac 12:6-7; 21:33; 28:20; 2Ti 1:16). *See Fetters.*

Figurative:

(Ps 73:6; Pr 1:9; La 3:7; Eze 7:23-27; Jude 6; 2Pe 2:4; Rev 20:1).

CHALCEDONY [*5907*]. A precious stone (Rev 21:19). *See Minerals of the Bible, 1; Stones.*

CHALCOL *See Calcol.*

CHALDEA [4169].
NIV+ CHALDEAN, CHALDEANS

The southern portion of Babylonia. Often used interchangeably with Babylon as the name of the empire founded in the valley of the Euphrates. Abraham a native of (Ge 11:28,31; 15:7). Founded by the Assyrians (Isa 23:13). Character of its people (Hab 1:6).

See Babylon; Chaldeans.

CHALDEAN ASTROLOGERS *See Wise Men.*

CHALDEANS [4169, 5900, 10373].

NIV+ CHALDEA, CHALDEAN

1. Virtually synonymous with the Babylonians (2Ki 25:4; 2Ch 36:17; Isa 13:19, ftns). *See Babylon; Chaldea.*

2. Learned and wise men of the east, NIV "astrologers" (Da 2:2,4,5,10; 3:8; 4:7; 5:7).

CHALDEES *See Chaldeans; Ur.*

CHALK [1732]. (Isa 27:9).

CHAMBERING *See Adultery; Fornication.*

CHAMBERLAIN *See Eunuch.*

CHAMBERS OF IMAGERY NIV "shrine of his own idol". Rooms in the temple where seventy elders of Israel worshiped idols (Eze 8:12).

CHAMELEON [9491]. Forbidden as food (Lev 11:30).

CHAMOIS NIV "mountain sheep"; permitted as food (Dt 14:5). *See Animals.*

CHAMPAIGN Dt 11:30, KJV. *See Arabah.*

CHAMPIONSHIP [408+1227+2021, 408+2657, 1475].

NIV+ CHAMPION, CHAMPIONS

Instances of battles decided by: Goliath and David (1Sa 17:8-53). Young men of David's and Abner's armies (2Sa 2:14-17). Representatives of the Philistines' and David's armies (2Sa 21:15-22).

CHANAAN *See Canaan.*

CHANCELLOR A state officer (Ezr 4:8-9,17). *See Cabinet; Officer.*

CHANGE OF VENUE Granted Paul (Ac 23:17-35). Declined by Paul (Ac 25:9,11).

CHANGERS OF MONEY *See Money Changers.*

CHAPITER *See Capital.*

CHAPMAN NIV "merchants" (2Ch 9:14). *See Merchant; Trade and Travel.*

CHARACTER [2657, 467, 1509, 2302, 2456].

NIV+ CHARACTERS

Of Believers:

Attentive to Christ's voice (Jn 10:3-4), blameless and harmless (Php 2:15), bold (Pr 28:1), contrite (Isa 57:15; 66:2), devout (Ac 8:2; 22:13), faithful (Rev 17:14), fearing God (Mal 3:16; Ac 10:2), following Christ (Jn 10:4,27), godly (Ps 4:3; 2Pe 2:9), without falsehood (Jn 1:47), holy (Dt 7:6; 14:2; Col 3:12), humble (Ps 34:2; 1Pe 5:5), hungering for righteousness (Mt 5:6), just (Ge 6:9; Hab 2:4; Lk 2:25), led by the Spirit (Ro 8:14), generous (Isa 32:8; 2Co 9:13), loathing themselves (Eze 20:43), loving (Col 1:4; 1Th 4:9), lowly (Pr 16:19), meek (Isa 29:19; Mt 5:5), merciful (Ps 37:26; Mt 5:7), new creatures (2Co 5:17; Eph 2:10), obedient (Ro 16:19; 1Pe 1:14), poor in spirit (Mt 5:3), prudent (Pr 16:21), pure in heart (Mt 5:8; 1Jn 3:3), righteous (Isa 60:21; Lk 1:6), sincere (2Co 1:12; 2:17), steadfast (Ac 2:42; Col 2:5), taught of God (Isa

54:13; 1Jn 2:27), true (2Co 6:8), undefiled (Ps 119:1), upright (1Ki 3:6; Ps 15:2), watchful (Lk 12:37), zealous of good works (Tit 2:14). *See Righteous, Described.*

Of the Wicked:

Abominable (Rev 21:8), alienated from God (Eph 4:18; Col 1:21), blasphemous (Lk 22:65; Rev 16:9), blinded (2Co 4:4; Eph 4:18), boastful (Ps 10:3; 49:6), conspiring against believers (Ne 4:8; 6:2; Ps 38:12), corrupt (Mt 7:17; Eph 4:22), covetous (Mic 2:2; Ro 1:29), deceitful (Ps 5:6; Ro 3:13), delighting in the iniquity of others (Pr 2:14; Ro 1:32), despising believers (Ne 2:19; 4:2; 2Ti 3:3-4), destructive (Isa 59:7), disobedient (Ne 9:26; Tit 3:3; 1Pe 2:7), enticing to evil (Pr 1:10-14; 2Ti 3:6), envious (Ne 2:10; Tit 3:3), evildoers (Jer 13:23; Mic 7:3), fearful (Pr 28:1; Rev 21:8), fierce (Pr 16:29; 2Ti 3:3), foolish (Dt 32:6; Ps 5:5), forgetting God (Job 8:13), fraudulent (Pr 21:8; Isa 57:17), glorying in their shame (Php 3:19), hard-hearted (Eze 3:7), hating the light (Job 24:13; Jn 3:20), heady and conceited (2Ti 3:4), hostile to God (Ro 8:7; Col 1:21), hypocritical (Isa 29:13; 2Ti 3:5), ignorant of God (Hos 4:1; 2Th 1:8), impudent (Eze 2:4), infidel (Ps 10:4; 14:1), loathsome (Pr 13:5), lovers of pleasure, not of God (2Ti 3:4), lying (Ps 58:3; 62:4; Isa 59:4), mischievous (Pr 24:8; Mic 7:3), murderous (Ps 10:8; 94:6; Ro 1:29), persecuting (Ps 69:26; 109:16), perverse (Dt 32:5), prayerless (Job 21:15; Ps 53:4), proud (Ps 59:12; Ob 3; 2Ti 3:2), rebellious (Isa 1:2; 30:9), rejoicing in the affliction of believers (Ps 35:15), reprobate (2Co 13:5; 2Ti 3:8; Tit 1:16), selfish (2Ti 3:2), sensual (Php 3:19; Jude 19), sold under sin (1Ki 21:20; 2Ki 17:17), stiff-hearted (Eze 2:4), stiff-necked (Ex 33:5; Ac 7:51), uncircumcised in heart (Jer 9:26), unclean (Isa 64:6; Eph 4:19), unjust (Pr 11:7; Isa 26:18), ungodly (Pr 16:27), unholy (2Ti 3:2), unmerciful (Ro 1:31), unprofitable (Mt 25:30; Ro 3:12), unruly (Tit 1:10), unthankful (Lk 6:35; 2Ti 3:2), unwise (Dt 32:6), without self-control (2Ti 3:3). *See Wicked, Described as.*

Good:

Pr 22:1 A good name is more desirable than great riches; to be esteemed is better than silver or gold. (+Ecc 7:1)

Defamation of, punished—

Dt 22:13 If a man takes a wife and, after lying with her, dislikes her [14]and slanders her and gives her a bad name, saying, "I married this woman, but when I approached her, I did not find proof of her virginity," [15]then the girl's father and mother shall bring proof that she was a virgin to the town elders at the gate. [16]The girl's father will say to the elders, "I gave my daughter in marriage to this man, but he dislikes her. [17]Now he has slandered her and said, 'I did not find your daughter to be a virgin.' But here is the proof of my daughter's virginity." Then her parents shall display the cloth before the elders of the town, [18]and the elders shall take the man and punish him. [19]They shall fine him a hundred shekels of silver and give them to the girl's father, because this man has given an Israelite virgin a bad name. She shall continue to be his wife; he must not divorce her as long as he lives.

Revealed in countenance—

Isa 3:9 The look on their faces testifies against them; they parade their sin like Sodom; they do not hide it. Woe to them! They have brought disaster upon themselves.

Steadfastness of:

Ps 57:7 My heart is steadfast, O God, my heart is steadfast; I will sing and make music. (+Ps 108:1; 112:7)

Mk 4:20 Others, like seed sown on good soil, hear the

word, accept it, and produce a crop—thirty, sixty or even a hundred times what was sown."

2Th 3:3 But the Lord is faithful, and he will strengthen and protect you from the evil one.

Exhortations to steadfastness—

1Co 7:20 Each one should remain in the situation which he was in when God called him. (+1Co 15:58; 16:13; Eph 4:14-15; Php 1:27; 4:1; Col 1:23; 1Th 3:8)

2Th 2:15 So then, brothers, stand firm and hold to the teachings we passed on to you, whether by word of mouth or by letter. (+Heb 3:6,14)

Heb 10:23 Let us hold unswervingly to the hope we profess, for he who promised is faithful.

Heb 13:9 Do not be carried away by all kinds of strange teachings. It is good for our hearts to be strengthened by grace, not by ceremonial foods, which are of no value to those who eat them. (+1Pe 5:9; 2Pe 3:17; Rev 3:11)

Reward of steadfastness—

Mt 10:22 All men will hate you because of me, but he who stands firm to the end will be saved.

Jas 1:25 But the man who looks intently into the perfect law that gives freedom, and continues to do this, not forgetting what he has heard, but doing it—he will be blessed in what he does.

Continuing of (Rev 22:11).

Instances of Firmness:

Joseph—

Ge 39:12 She caught him by his cloak and said, "Come to bed with me!" But he left his cloak in her hand and ran out of the house.

Moses (Heb 11:24-26). Joshua (Jos 24:15). Daniel (Da 1:8; 6:10). Three Hebrews (Da 3:16-18). Pilate (Jn 19:22). Peter and John (Ac 4:19-20). Paul (Ac 20:22-24; 21:13-14). *See Decision; Stability.*

Instability of:

Pr 27:8 Like a bird that strays from its nest is a man who strays from his home.

Jer 2:36 Why do you go about so much, changing your ways? You will be disappointed by Egypt as you were by Assyria.

Hos 6:4 "What can I do with you, Ephraim? What can I do with you, Judah? Your love is like the morning mist, like the early dew that disappears.

Hos 7:8 "Ephraim mixes with the nations; Ephraim is a flat cake not turned over.

Hos 10:2 Their heart is deceitful, and now they must bear their guilt. The Lord will demolish their altars and destroy their sacred stones.

Mt 13:19 When anyone hears the message about the kingdom and does not understand it, the evil one comes and snatches away what was sown in his heart. This is the seed sown along the path. ²⁰The one who received the seed that fell on rocky places is the man who hears the word and at once receives it with joy. ²¹But since he has no root, he lasts only a short time. When trouble or persecution comes because of the word, he quickly falls away. ²²The one who received the seed that fell among the thorns is the man who hears the word, but the worries of this life and the deceitfulness of wealth choke it, making it unfruitful. (+Mk 4:15-19; Lk 8:5-15; 2Pe 2:14; Rev 2:4)

Warnings against—

Pr 24:21 Fear the Lord and the king, my son, and do not join with the rebellious, ²²for those two will send sudden destruction upon them, and who knows what calamities they can bring?

Lk 9:59 He said to another man, "Follow me." But the man replied, "Lord, first let me go and bury my father."

⁶⁰Jesus said to him, "Let the dead bury their own dead, but you go and proclaim the kingdom of God."

⁶¹Still another said, "I will follow you, Lord; but first let me go back and say good-by to my family."

⁶²Jesus replied, "No one who puts his hand to the plow and looks back is fit for service in the kingdom of God."

Eph 4:14 Then we will no longer be infants, tossed back and forth by the waves, and blown here and there by every wind of teaching and by the cunning and craftiness of men in their deceitful scheming. (+Heb 6:4-6; 13:9)

Jas 1:6 But when he asks, he must believe and not doubt, because he who doubts is like a wave of the sea, blown and tossed by the wind. ⁷That man should not think he will receive anything from the Lord; ⁸he is a double-minded man, unstable in all he does.

Jas 4:8 Come near to God and he will come near to you. Wash your hands, you sinners, and purify your hearts, you double-minded.

2Pe 2:14 With eyes full of adultery, they never stop sinning; they seduce the unstable; they are experts in greed—an accursed brood!

Instances of Instability:

Reuben—

Ge 49:3 "Reuben, you are my firstborn, my might, the first sign of my strength, excelling in honor, excelling in power. ⁴Turbulent as the waters, you will no longer excel, for you went up onto your father's bed, onto my couch and defiled it.

Pharaoh—

Ex 8:15 But when Pharaoh saw that there was relief, he hardened his heart and would not listen to Moses and Aaron, just as the Lord had said.

Ex 8:32 But this time also Pharaoh hardened his heart and would not let the people go.

Ex 9:34 When Pharaoh saw that the rain and hail and thunder had stopped, he sinned again: He and his officials hardened their hearts.

Ex 14:5 When the king of Egypt was told that the people had fled, Pharaoh and his officials changed their minds about them and said, "What have we done? We have let the Israelites go and have lost their services!"

Israelites—

Ex 32:8 They have been quick to turn away from what I commanded them and have made themselves an idol cast in the shape of a calf. They have bowed down to it and sacrificed to it and have said, 'These are your gods, O Israel, who brought you up out of Egypt.'

Jdg 2:17 Yet they would not listen to their judges but prostituted themselves to other gods and worshiped them. Unlike their fathers, they quickly turned from the way in which their fathers had walked, the way of obedience to the Lord's commands. (+Jdg 2:18)

Jdg 2:19 But when the judge died, the people returned to ways even more corrupt than those of their fathers, following other gods and serving and worshiping them. They refused to give up their evil practices and stubborn ways.

2Ch 11:17 They strengthened the kingdom of Judah and supported Rehoboam son of Solomon three years, walking in the ways of David and Solomon during this time.

Saul—

1Sa 18:19 So when the time came for Merab, Saul's daughter, to be given to David, she was given in marriage to Adriel of Meholah.

Solomon—

1Ki 11:4 As Solomon grew old, his wives turned his heart after other gods, and his heart was not fully devoted to the LORD his God, as the heart of David his father had been. [5]He followed Ashtoreth the goddess of the Sidonians, and Molech the detestable god of the Ammonites. [6]So Solomon did evil in the eyes of the LORD; he did not follow the LORD completely, as David his father had done. [7]On a hill east of Jerusalem, Solomon built a high place for Chemosh the detestable god of Moab, and for Molech the detestable god of the Ammonites. [8]He did the same for all his foreign wives, who burned incense and offered sacrifices to their gods.

Rehoboam—

2Ch 12:1 After Rehoboam's position as king was established and he had become strong, he and all Israel with him abandoned the law of the LORD.

Pilate (Jn 18:37-40; 19:1-6). Demas (2Ti 4:10).

CHARASHIM *See Craftsman; Ge Harashim.*

CHARGE

NIV+ CHARGED, CHARGES, CHARGING

Delivered to ministers. *See Ministers.*

CHARGER *See Plate, Platter.*

CHARIOT [1649, 5323, 5324, 8206, 8207, 8208, 8213, 8224, 8957, 761].

NIV+ CHARIOTEERS, CHARIOTS

For war (Ex 14:7,9,25; Jos 11:4; 1Sa 13:5; 1Ki 20:1,25; 2Ki 6:14; 2Ch 12:2-3; Ps 20:7; Jer 46:9; 47:3; 51:21; Joel 2:5; Na 2:3-4; 3:2). Wheels of Pharaoh's, providentially taken off (Ex 14:25).

Commanded by captains (Ex 14:7; 1Ki 9:22; 22:31-33; 2Ki 8:21). Made of iron (Jos 17:18; Jdg 1:19). Introduced among Israelites by David (2Sa 8:4). Imported from Egypt by Solomon (1Ki 10:26-29). Cities for (1Ki 9:19; 2Ch 1:14; 8:6; 9:25). Royal (Ge 41:43; 46:29; 2Ki 5:9; 2Ch 35:24; Jer 17:25; Ac 8:29). Drawn by camels (Isa 21:7; Mic 1:13).

Kings ride in (2Ch 35:24; Jer 17:25; 22:4). Cherubim in Solomon's temple mounted on (1Ch 28:18).

Figurative:

Chariots of God (Ps 68:17; 104:3; 2Ki 6:17; Isa 66:15; Hab 3:8; Rev 9:9).

Symbolic: (Zec 6:1-8; 2Ki 2:11-12).

CHARISM, CHARISMA, CHARISMATA

[5922].

NIV+ GIFT, GIFTS

An inspired gift, bestowed on the apostles and early Christians without any claim of merit on the individual's part, for the good of the church (Mt 10:1,8; Mk 16:17-18; Lk 10:1,9,17,19; Ac 2:4; 10:44-46; 19:6; 1Co 12).

See Gifts From God; Miracles; Spiritual Gifts; -Tongues, Gift of.

CHARITABLENESS

Encouraged—

Pr 10:12 Hatred stirs up dissension, but love covers over all wrongs.

Pr 17:9 He who covers over an offense promotes love, but whoever repeats the matter separates close friends.

Commanded—

Mt 5:23 "Therefore, if you are offering your gift at the altar and there remember that your brother has something

against you, [24]leave your gift there in front of the altar. First go and be reconciled to your brother; then come and offer your gift.

Mt 7:1 "Do not judge, or you too will be judged. [2]For in the same way you judge others, you will be judged, and with the measure you use, it will be measured to you.

[3]"Why do you look at the speck of sawdust in your brother's eye and pay no attention to the plank in your own eye? [4]How can you say to your brother, 'Let me take the speck out of your eye,' when all the time there is a plank in your own eye? [5]You hypocrite, first take the plank out of your own eye, and then you will see clearly to remove the speck from your brother's eye.

Mt 18:21 Then Peter came to Jesus and asked, "Lord, how many times shall I forgive my brother when he sins against me? Up to seven times?"

[22]Jesus answered, "I tell you, not seven times, but seventy-seven times.

Lk 6:36 Be merciful, just as your Father is merciful.

[37]"Do not judge, and you will not be judged. Do not condemn, and you will not be condemned. Forgive, and you will be forgiven. (+Lk 6:38-42)

Lk 17:3 So watch yourselves. "If your brother sins, rebuke him, and if he repents, forgive him.

[4]If he sins against you seven times in a day, and seven times comes back to you and says, 'I repent,' forgive him."

Jn 7:24 Stop judging by mere appearances, and make a right judgment."

Ro 14:1 Accept him whose faith is weak, without passing judgment on disputable matters. [2]One man's faith allows him to eat everything, but another man, whose faith is weak, eats only vegetables. [3]The man who eats everything must not look down on him who does not, and the man who does not eat everything must not condemn the man who does, for God has accepted him. [4]Who are you to judge someone else's servant? To his own master he stands or falls. And he will stand, for the Lord is able to make him stand.

[5]One man considers one day more sacred than another; another man considers every day alike. Each one should be fully convinced in his own mind. [6]He who regards one day as special, does so to the Lord. He who eats meat, eats to the Lord, for he gives thanks to God; and he who abstains, does so to the Lord and gives thanks to God. [7]For none of us lives to himself alone and none of us dies to himself alone. [8]If we live, we live to the Lord; and if we die, we die to the Lord. So, whether we live or die, we belong to the Lord.

[9]For this very reason, Christ died and returned to life so that he might be the Lord of both the dead and the living. [10]You, then, why do you judge your brother? Or why do you look down on your brother? For we will all stand before God's judgment seat. [11]It is written:

"'As surely as I live,' says the Lord, 'every knee will bow before me; every tongue will confess to God.'"

[12]So then, each of us will give an account of himself to God.

[13]Therefore let us stop passing judgment on one another. Instead, make up your mind not to put any stumbling block or obstacle in your brother's way. [14]As one who is in the Lord Jesus, I am fully convinced that no food is unclean in itself. But if anyone regards something as unclean, then for him it is unclean. [15]If your brother is distressed because of what you eat, you are no longer acting in love. Do not by your eating destroy your brother for whom Christ died. [16]Do not allow what you consider good to be spoken of as

evil. [17]For the kingdom of God is not a matter of eating and drinking, but of righteousness, peace and joy in the Holy Spirit, [18]because anyone who serves Christ in this way is pleasing to God and approved by men.

[19]Let us therefore make every effort to do what leads to peace and to mutual edification. [20]Do not destroy the work of God for the sake of food. All food is clean, but it is wrong for a man to eat anything that causes someone else to stumble. [21]It is better not to eat meat or drink wine or to do anything else that will cause your brother to fall.

[22]So whatever you believe about these things keep between yourself and God. Blessed is the man who does not condemn himself by what he approves. [23]But the man who has doubts is condemned if he eats, because his eating is not from faith; and everything that does not come from faith is sin. (+Ro 15:1-2)

1Co 10:28 But if anyone says to you, "This has been offered in sacrifice," then do not eat it, both for the sake of the man who told you and for conscience' sake— [29]the other man's conscience, I mean, not yours. For why should my freedom be judged by another's conscience? [30]If I take part in the meal with thankfulness, why am I denounced because of something I thank God for?

[31]So whether you eat or drink or whatever you do, do it all for the glory of God. [32]Do not cause anyone to stumble, whether Jews, Greeks or the church of God— [33]even as I try to please everybody in every way. For I am not seeking my own good but the good of many, so that they may be saved.

1Co 16:14 Do everything in love. (+2Co 2:7)

Gal 6:1 Brothers, if someone is caught in a sin, you who are spiritual should restore him gently. But watch yourself, or you also may be tempted.

Eph 4:32 Be kind and compassionate to one another, forgiving each other, just as in Christ God forgave you.

Col 3:13 Bear with each other and forgive whatever grievances you may have against one another. Forgive as the Lord forgave you. [14]And over all these virtues put on love, which binds them all together in perfect unity.

1Ti 1:5 The goal of this command is love, which comes from a pure heart and a good conscience and a sincere faith.

1Ti 4:12 Don't let anyone look down on you because you are young, but set an example for the believers in speech, in life, in love, in faith and in purity.

2Ti 2:22 Flee the evil desires of youth, and pursue righteousness, faith, love and peace, along with those who call on the Lord out of a pure heart.

Jas 2:13 because judgment without mercy will be shown to anyone who has not been merciful. Mercy triumphs over judgment!

Jas 4:11 Brothers, do not slander one another. Anyone who speaks against his brother or judges him speaks against the law and judges it. When you judge the law, you are not keeping it, but sitting in judgment on it. [12]There is only one Lawgiver and Judge, the one who is able to save and destroy. But you—who are you to judge your neighbor?

1Pe 3:9 Do not repay evil with evil or insult with insult, but with blessing, because to this you were called so that you may inherit a blessing.

Described—

1Co 13:1 If I speak in the tongues of men and of angels, but have not love, I am only a resounding gong or a clanging cymbal. [2]If I have the gift of prophecy and can fathom all mysteries and all knowledge, and if I have a faith that can move mountains, but have not love, I am nothing. [3]If I give all I possess to the poor and surrender my body to the flames, but have not love, I gain nothing. [4]Love is patient, love is kind. It does not envy, it does not boast, it is not proud. [5]It is not rude, it is not self-seeking, it is not easily angered, it keeps no record of wrongs. [6]Love does not delight in evil but rejoices with the truth. [7]It always protects, always trusts, always hopes, always perseveres.

[8]Love never fails. But where there are prophecies, they will cease; where there are tongues, they will be stilled; where there is knowledge, it will pass away. [9]For we know in part and we prophesy in part, [10]but when perfection comes, the imperfect disappears. [11]When I was a child, I talked like a child, I thought like a child, I reasoned like a child. When I became a man, I put childish ways behind me. [12]Now we see but a poor reflection as in a mirror; then we shall see face to face. Now I know in part; then I shall know fully, even as I am fully known.

[13]And now these three remain: faith, hope and love. But the greatest of these is love.

Covers sins (Pr 10:12; 17:9; 19:11)—

1Pe 4:8 Above all, love each other deeply, because love covers over a multitude of sins.

Pleases God—

Mt 6:14 For if you forgive men when they sin against you, your heavenly Father will also forgive you. [15]But if you do not forgive men their sins, your Father will not forgive your sins.

Mt 18:23 "Therefore, the kingdom of heaven is like a king who wanted to settle accounts with his servants. [24]As he began the settlement, a man who owed him ten thousand talents was brought to him. [25]Since he was not able to pay, the master ordered that he and his wife and his children and all that he had be sold to repay the debt.

[26]"The servant fell on his knees before him. 'Be patient with me,' he begged, 'and I will pay back everything.' [27]The servant's master took pity on him, canceled the debt and let him go.

[28]"But when that servant went out, he found one of his fellow servants who owed him a hundred denarii. He grabbed him and began to choke him. 'Pay back what you owe me!' he demanded.

[29]"His fellow servant fell to his knees and begged him, 'Be patient with me, and I will pay you back.'

[30]"But he refused. Instead, he went off and had the man thrown into prison until he could pay the debt. [31]When the other servants saw what had happened, they were greatly distressed and went and told their master everything that had happened.

[32]"Then the master called the servant in. 'You wicked servant,' he said, 'I canceled all that debt of yours because you begged me to. [33]Shouldn't you have had mercy on your fellow servant just as I had on you?' [34]In anger his master turned him over to the jailers to be tortured, until he should pay back all he owed.

[35]"This is how my heavenly Father will treat each of you unless you forgive your brother from your heart."

See Love; Uncharitableness.

CHARITY *See Alms; Beneficence; Liberality; Love.*

CHARMERS AND CHARMING [1251+4383, 2834, 2858, 4086, 4317, 4318, 4318, 5833].

NIV+ CHARM, CHARMED, CHARMER, CHARMS

Prohibited (Dt 18:11). Of serpents (Ps 58:4-5; Jer 8:17).

Magic charms and amulets (Pr 17:8; Isa 3:20; Eze 13:18, 20). *See Sorcery.*

CHARRAN *See Haran, 4.*

CHASTISEMENT, FROM GOD [3519, 3579].

NIV+ CHASTENED

A blessing—

Job 5:17 "Blessed is the man whom God corrects; so do not despise the discipline of the Almighty.

Ps 94:12 Blessed is the man you discipline, O LORD, the man you teach from your law; [13]you grant him relief from days of trouble, till a pit is dug for the wicked.

Heb 12:11 No discipline seems pleasant at the time, but painful. Later on, however, it produces a harvest of righteousness and peace for those who have been trained by it.

Corrective—

Dt 11:2 Remember today that your children were not the ones who saw and experienced the discipline of the LORD your God: his majesty, his mighty hand, his outstretched arm; [3]the signs he performed and the things he did in the heart of Egypt, both to Pharaoh king of Egypt and to his whole country; [4]what he did to the Egyptian army, to its horses and chariots, how he overwhelmed them with the waters of the Red Sea as they were pursuing you, and how the LORD brought lasting ruin on them. [5]It was not your children who saw what he did for you in the desert until you arrived at this place, [6]and what he did to Dathan and Abiram, sons of Eliab the Reubenite, when the earth opened its mouth right in the middle of all Israel and swallowed them up with their households, their tents and every living thing that belonged to them. [7]But it was your own eyes that saw all these great things the LORD has done.

[8]Observe therefore all the commands I am giving you today, so that you may have the strength to go in and take over the land that you are crossing the Jordan to possess, [9]and so that you may live long in the land that the LORD swore to your forefathers to give to them and their descendants, a land flowing with milk and honey.

2Sa 7:14 I will be his father, and he will be my son. When he does wrong, I will punish him with the rod of men, with floggings inflicted by men. [15]But my love will never be taken away from him, as I took it away from Saul, whom I removed from before you.

2Ch 6:24 "When your people Israel have been defeated by an enemy because they have sinned against you and when they turn back and confess your name, praying and making supplication before you in this temple, [25]then hear from heaven and forgive the sin of your people Israel and bring them back to the land you gave to them and their fathers.

[26]"When the heavens are shut up and there is no rain because your people have sinned against you, and when they pray toward this place and confess your name and turn from their sin because you have afflicted them, [27]then hear from heaven and forgive the sin of your servants, your people Israel. Teach them the right way to live, and send rain on the land you gave your people for an inheritance.

[28]"When famine or plague comes to the land, or blight or mildew, locusts or grasshoppers, or when enemies besiege them in any of their cities, whatever disaster or disease may come, [29]and when a prayer or plea is made by any of your people Israel—each one aware of his afflictions and pains, and spreading out his hands toward this temple— [30]then hear from heaven, your dwelling place. Forgive, and deal with each man according to all he does, since you know his heart (for you alone know the hearts of

men), [31]so that they will fear you and walk in your ways all the time they live in the land you gave our fathers.

2Ch 7:13 "When I shut up the heavens so that there is no rain, or command locusts to devour the land or send a plague among my people, [14]if my people, who are called by my name, will humble themselves and pray and seek my face and turn from their wicked ways, then will I hear from heaven and will forgive their sin and will heal their land.

Job 33:19 Or a man may be chastened on a bed of pain with constant distress in his bones, (+Job 34:31)

Ps 73:14 All day long I have been plagued; I have been punished every morning.

Ps 118:18 The LORD has chastened me severely, but he has not given me over to death.

Ps 119:67 Before I was afflicted I went astray, but now I obey your word.

Ps 119:75 I know, O LORD, that your laws are righteous, and in faithfulness you have afflicted me.

Isa 57:16 I will not accuse forever, nor will I always be angry, for then the spirit of man would grow faint before me—the breath of man that I have created. [17]I was enraged by his sinful greed; I punished him, and hid my face in anger, yet he kept on in his willful ways. [18]I have seen his ways, but I will heal him; I will guide him and restore comfort to him, (+Jer 24:5-6)

Jer 46:28 Do not fear, O Jacob my servant, for I am with you," declares the LORD. "Though I completely destroy all the nations among which I scatter you, I will not completely destroy you. I will discipline you but only with justice; I will not let you go entirely unpunished." (+1Co 11:32)

Inflicted for sins—

Lev 26:28 then in my anger I will be hostile toward you, and I myself will punish you for your sins seven times over.

Ps 89:32 I will punish their sin with the rod, their iniquity with flogging; (+Ps 107:10-12,17; Isa 40:2)

Jer 30:14 All your allies have forgotten you; they care nothing for you. I have struck you as an enemy would and punished you as would the cruel, because your guilt is so great and your sins so many.

La 1:5 Her foes have become her masters; her enemies are at ease. The LORD has brought her grief because of her many sins. Her children have gone into exile, captive before the foe.

Hos 7:12 When they go, I will throw my net over them; I will pull them down like birds of the air. When I hear them flocking together, I will catch them.

Hos 10:10 When I please, I will punish them; nations will be gathered against them to put them in bonds for their double sin. (+Am 4:6)

Administered in love (Dt 8:5)—

Pr 3:11 My son, do not despise the LORD's discipline and do not resent his rebuke, [12]because the LORD disciplines those he loves, as a father the son he delights in.

Heb 12:5 And you have forgotten that word of encouragement that addresses you as sons: "My son, do not make light of the Lord's discipline, and do not lose heart when he rebukes you, [6]because the Lord disciplines those he loves, and he punishes everyone he accepts as a son."

[7]Endure hardship as discipline; God is treating you as sons. For what son is not disciplined by his father? [8]If you are not disciplined (and everyone undergoes discipline), then you are illegitimate children and not true sons. [9]Moreover, we have all had human fathers who disciplined us and we respected them for it. How much more should

we submit to the Father of our spirits and live! ¹⁰Our fathers disciplined us for a little while as they thought best; but God disciplines us for our good, that we may share in his holiness.

Rev 3:19 Those whom I love I rebuke and discipline. So be earnest, and repent.

Repentance under—

Ps 106:43 Many times he delivered them, but they were bent on rebellion and they wasted away in their sin.

⁴⁴But he took note of their distress when he heard their cry; (+Ps 107:10-13)

Ps 107:17 Some became fools through their rebellious ways and suffered affliction because of their iniquities. ¹⁸They loathed all food and drew near the gates of death. ¹⁹Then they cried to the LORD in their trouble, and he saved them from their distress.

Isa 26:16 LORD, they came to you in their distress; when you disciplined them, they could barely whisper a prayer.

Jer 31:18 "I have surely heard Ephraim's moaning: 'You disciplined me like an unruly calf, and I have been disciplined. Restore me, and I will return, because you are the LORD my God. ¹⁹After I strayed, I repented; after I came to understand, I beat my breast. I was ashamed and humiliated because I bore the disgrace of my youth.'

Failure to repent under—

Isa 42:25 So he poured out on them his burning anger, the violence of war. It enveloped them in flames, yet they did not understand; it consumed them, but they did not take it to heart.

Jer 2:30 "In vain I punished your people; they did not respond to correction. Your sword has devoured your prophets like a ravening lion.

Hag 2:17 I struck all the work of your hands with blight, mildew and hail, yet you did not turn to me,' declares the LORD.

Prayer to be spared from—

Ps 6:1 O LORD, do not rebuke me in your anger or discipline me in your wrath. (+Ps 38:1)

Ps 107:23 Others went out on the sea in ships; they were merchants on the mighty waters. ²⁴They saw the works of the LORD, his wonderful deeds in the deep. ²⁵For he spoke and stirred up a tempest that lifted high the waves. ²⁶They mounted up to the heavens and went down to the depths; in their peril their courage melted away. ²⁷They reeled and staggered like drunken men; they were at their wits' end. ²⁸Then they cried out to the LORD in their trouble, and he brought them out of their distress. ²⁹He stilled the storm to a whisper; the waves of the sea were hushed. ³⁰They were glad when it grew calm, and he guided them to their desired haven. ³¹Let them give thanks to the LORD for his unfailing love and his wonderful deeds for men.

Vicariously borne by Jesus (Isa 53:4-5).

See Afflictions; Judgments; Punishment; Wicked, Punishment of.

CHASTITY

Commanded:

Ex 20:14 "You shall not commit adultery.

Pr 2:10 For wisdom will enter your heart, and knowledge will be pleasant to your soul. ¹¹Discretion will protect you, and understanding will guard you.

Pr 2:16 It will save you also from the adulteress, from the wayward wife with her seductive words, ¹⁷who has left the partner of her youth and ignored the covenant she made before God. ¹⁸For her house leads down to death and her

paths to the spirits of the dead. ¹⁹None who go to her return or attain the paths of life.

²⁰Thus you will walk in the ways of good men and keep to the paths of the righteous. ²¹For the upright will live in the land, and the blameless will remain in it; ²²but the wicked will be cut off from the land, and the unfaithful will be torn from it. (+Pr 5:3-14)

Pr 5:15 Drink water from your own cistern, running water from your own well. ¹⁶Should your springs overflow in the streets, your streams of water in the public squares? ¹⁷Let them be yours alone, never to be shared with strangers. ¹⁸May your fountain be blessed, and may you rejoice in the wife of your youth. ¹⁹A loving doe, a graceful deer—may her breasts satisfy you always, may you ever be captivated by her love. ²⁰Why be captivated, my son, by an adulteress? Why embrace the bosom of another man's wife?

²¹For a man's ways are in full view of the LORD, and he examines all his paths.

Pr 6:24 keeping you from the immoral woman, from the smooth tongue of the wayward wife. ²⁵Do not lust in your heart after her beauty or let her captivate you with her eyes,

Pr 7:1 My son, keep my words and store up my commands within you. ²Keep my commands and you will live; guard my teachings as the apple of your eye. ³Bind them on your fingers; write them on the tablet of your heart. ⁴Say to wisdom, "You are my sister," and call understanding your kinsman; ⁵they will keep you from the adulteress, from the wayward wife with her seductive words.

Pr 31:3 do not spend your strength on women, your vigor on those who ruin kings. (+Mt 5:27)

Mt 5:28 But I tell you that anyone who looks at a woman lustfully has already committed adultery with her in his heart. (+Mt 5:29-32)

Ac 15:20 Instead we should write to them, telling them to abstain from food polluted by idols, from sexual immorality, from the meat of strangled animals and from blood.

Ro 13:13 Let us behave decently, as in the daytime, not in orgies and drunkenness, not in sexual immorality and debauchery, not in dissension and jealousy.

1Co 6:13 "Food for the stomach and the stomach for food"—but God will destroy them both. The body is not meant for sexual immorality, but for the Lord, and the Lord for the body. ¹⁴By his power God raised the Lord from the dead, and he will raise us also. ¹⁵Do you not know that your bodies are members of Christ himself? Shall I then take the members of Christ and unite them with a prostitute? Never! ¹⁶Do you not know that he who unites himself with a prostitute is one with her in body? For it is said, "The two will become one flesh." ¹⁷But he who unites himself with the Lord is one with him in spirit.

¹⁸Flee from sexual immorality. All other sins a man commits are outside his body, but he who sins sexually sins against his own body. ¹⁹Do you not know that your body is a temple of the Holy Spirit, who is in you, whom you have received from God? You are not your own;

1Co 7:1 Now for the matters you wrote about: It is good for a man not to marry. ²But since there is so much immorality, each man should have his own wife, and each woman her own husband.

1Co 7:7 I wish that all men were as I am. But each man has his own gift from God; one has this gift, another has that.

⁸Now to the unmarried and the widows I say: It is good for them to stay unmarried, as I am. ⁹But if they cannot

control themselves, they should marry, for it is better to marry than to burn with passion.

1Co 7:25 Now about virgins: I have no command from the Lord, but I give a judgment as one who by the Lord's mercy is trustworthy. ²⁶Because of the present crisis, I think that it is good for you to remain as you are.

1Co 7:36 If anyone thinks he is acting improperly toward the virgin he is engaged to, and if she is getting along in years and he feels he ought to marry, he should do as he wants. He is not sinning. They should get married. ³⁷But the man who has settled the matter in his own mind, who is under no compulsion but has control over his own will, and who has made up his mind not to marry the virgin— this man also does the right thing.

Eph 5:3 But among you there must not be even a hint of sexual immorality, or of any kind of impurity, or of greed, because these are improper for God's holy people.

Col 3:5 Put to death, therefore, whatever belongs to your earthly nature: sexual immorality, impurity, lust, evil desires and greed, which is idolatry.

1Th 4:3 It is God's will that you should be sanctified: that you should avoid sexual immorality;

1Th 4:7 For God did not call us to be impure, but to live a holy life.

Instances of:

Joseph (Ge 39:7-20). Boaz (Ru 3:6-13).

Job—

Job 31:1 "I made a covenant with my eyes not to look lustfully at a girl. (+Job 31:9-12)

Paul (1Co 7).

The 144,000—

Rev 14:1 Then I looked, and there before me was the Lamb, standing on Mount Zion, and with him 144,000 who had his name and his Father's name written on their foreheads. ²And I heard a sound from heaven like the roar of rushing waters and like a loud peal of thunder. The sound I heard was like that of harpists playing their harps. ³And they sang a new song before the throne and before the four living creatures and the elders. No one could learn the song except the 144,000 who had been redeemed from the earth. ⁴These are those who did not defile themselves with women, for they kept themselves pure. They follow the Lamb wherever he goes. They were purchased from among men and offered as firstfruits to God and the Lamb. ⁵No lie was found in their mouths; they are blameless.

See Celibacy; Self-Control.

CHEATING [5792, 6430, 6943, 9438, *691, 5193*].
NIV+ CHEAT, CHEATED, CHEATS
See Dishonesty.

CHEBAR *See Kebar.*

CHEDORLAOMER *See Kedorlaomer.*

CHEERFULNESS [3202, 3512, 4401, 8524, *1877+ 2660, 2510, 2659*]. *See Contentment.*

CHEESE [1482, 2692+3043, 9147].
NIV+ CHEESES
(1Sa 17:18; 2Sa 17:29; Job 10:10).

CHELAL *See Kelal.*

CHELLUH *See Keluhi.*

CHELUB *See Kelub.*

CHELUBAI *See Caleb, 1.*

CHEMARIM NIV "pagan [priests]" (Zep 1:4). *See Groves; High Places; Idol; Idolatry; Priest, Corrupt.*

CHEMOSH [4019]. An idol of the Moabites and Ammonites (1Ki 11:7,33; 2Ki 23:13; Jer 48:7,13,46), and Amorites (Jdg 11:24).

CHENAANAH *See Kenaanah.*

CHENANI *See Kenani.*

CHENANIAH *See Kenaniah.*

CHEPHAR-HAAMMONAI *See Kephar Ammoni.*

CHEPHIRAH *See Kephirah.*

CHERAN *See Keran.*

CHERETHIMS, CHERETHITES *See Kerethite(s).*

CHERITH *See Kerith.*

CHERUB *See Kerub.*

CHERUBIM [4131, *5938*].
NIV+ CHERUB
Eastward of the garden of Eden (Ge 3:24).
In the tabernacle (Ex 25:18-20; 37:7-9). Ark rested beneath the wings of (1Ki 8:6-7; 2Ch 5:7-8; Heb 9:5). Figures of, embroidered on walls of tabernacle (Ex 26:1; 36:8), and on the veil (Ex 26:31; 36:35).
In the temple (1Ki 6:23-29; 2Ch 3:10-13). Figures of, on the veil (2Ch 3:14), walls (1Ki 6:29-35; 2Ch 3:7), movable stands (1Ki 7:29,36).
In Ezekiel's vision of the temple (Eze 41:18-20,25).

Figurative: (Eze 28:14,16).

Symbolic: (Eze 1; 10).

CHESALON *See Kesalon.*

CHESED *See Kesed.*

CHESIL *See Kesil.*

CHEST [761, 778, 4213, 10249, *3466, 5111*].
NIV+ CHESTS
1. The ark of the covenant (Ex 25:10-14; Dt 10:1-2).
2. For money (2Ki 12:9-10; 2Ch 24:8-11).
3. The torso (Job 41:24; Da 2:32; Rev 1:13).

CHESTNUT TREE *See Plane Tree.*

CHESULLOTH *See Kesulloth.*

CHEZIB *See Kezib.*

CHICKEN *See Hen, 2.*

CHIDING *See Rebuke.*

CHIDON *See Kidon.*

CHILDBEARING [2228, 3528, *5349, 5450, 6048*].
NIV+ See BIRTH
An expression found only in Paul's letter to Timothy (1Ti 2:15), a verse of uncertain meaning.

CHILDLESSNESS [3528+4202, 6829, 6884, 8891, 8897, *866*].
NIV+ BARREN, CHILDLESS
A reproach (Ge 16:2; 29:32; 30:1-3,13; 1Sa 1:6; Isa 4:1; Lk 1:25).

See Barrenness.

CHILDREN [*1201, 2446, 3251, 3528, 3528, 3529, 5830, 5853, 6407, 6408, 6884, 8890, 8897, *3758, 4086, 5065, 5448, 5451, 5451, 5626*].

NIV+ CHILD, CHILD'S, CHILDHOOD, CHILDISH, CHILDLESS, CHILDREN'S, GRANDCHILDREN, INFANCY, INFANT, INFANT'S, INFANTS

A Blessing:

Ge 5:29 He named him Noah and said, "He will comfort us in the labor and painful toil of our hands caused by the ground the LORD has cursed."

Ge 30:1 When Rachel saw that she was not bearing Jacob any children, she became jealous of her sister. So she said to Jacob, "Give me children, or I'll die!"

Ps 127:3 Sons are a heritage from the LORD, children a reward from him. [4]Like arrows in the hands of a warrior are sons born in one's youth. [5]Blessed is the man whose quiver is full of them. They will not be put to shame when they contend with their enemies in the gate.

Pr 17:6 Children's children are a crown to the aged, and parents are the pride of their children.

The gift of God—

Ge 4:1 Adam lay with his wife Eve, and she became pregnant and gave birth to Cain. She said, "With the help of the LORD I have brought forth a man."

Ge 4:25 Adam lay with his wife again, and she gave birth to a son and named him Seth, saying, "God has granted me another child in place of Abel, since Cain killed him."

Ge 17:16 I will bless her and will surely give you a son by her. I will bless her so that she will be the mother of nations; kings of peoples will come from her."

Ge 17:20 And as for Ishmael, I have heard you: I will surely bless him; I will make him fruitful and will greatly increase his numbers. He will be the father of twelve rulers, and I will make him into a great nation. (+Ge 22:17)

Ge 28:3 May God Almighty bless you and make you fruitful and increase your numbers until you become a community of peoples.

Ge 29:32 Leah became pregnant and gave birth to a son. She named him Reuben, for she said, "It is because the LORD has seen my misery. Surely my husband will love me now."

[33]She conceived again, and when she gave birth to a son she said, "Because the LORD heard that I am not loved, he gave me this one too." So she named him Simeon.

[34]Again she conceived, and when she gave birth to a son she said, "Now at last my husband will become attached to me, because I have borne him three sons." So he was named Levi.

[35]She conceived again, and when she gave birth to a son she said, "This time I will praise the LORD." So she named him Judah. Then she stopped having children.

Ge 30:2 Jacob became angry with her and said, "Am I in the place of God, who has kept you from having children?"

Ge 30:6 Then Rachel said, "God has vindicated me; he has listened to my plea and given me a son." Because of this she named him Dan.

Ge 30:17 God listened to Leah, and she became pregnant and bore Jacob a fifth son. [18]Then Leah said, "God has rewarded me for giving my maidservant to my husband." So she named him Issachar.

[19]Leah conceived again and bore Jacob a sixth son. [20]Then Leah said, "God has presented me with a precious gift. This time my husband will treat me with honor, because I have borne him six sons." So she named him Zebulun.

Ge 30:22 Then God remembered Rachel; he listened to her and opened her womb. [23]She became pregnant and gave birth to a son and said, "God has taken away my disgrace." [24]She named him Joseph, and said, "May the LORD add to me another son."

Ge 30:5 and she became pregnant and bore him a son. (+Ge 48:9,16)

Ru 4:13 So Boaz took Ruth and she became his wife. Then he went to her, and the LORD enabled her to conceive, and she gave birth to a son.

Job 1:21 and said: "Naked I came from my mother's womb, and naked I will depart. The LORD gave and the LORD has taken away; may the name of the LORD be praised."

Ps 107:38 he blessed them, and their numbers greatly increased, and he did not let their herds diminish.

Ps 107:41 But he lifted the needy out of their affliction and increased their families like flocks.

Ps 113:9 He settles the barren woman in her home as a happy mother of children. Praise the LORD.

Ps 127:3 Sons are a heritage from the LORD, children a reward from him.

Promised to the righteous (Dt 7:12,14; Job 5:25; Ps 128:2-4,6).

Given in answer to prayer to, Abraham (Ge 15:2-5; 21:1-2), Isaac (Ge 25:21), Leah (Ge 30:17-22), Rachel (Ge 30:22-24), Hannah (1Sa 1:9-20), Zechariah (Lk 1:13).

In Infancy:

Circumcision of. *See Circumcision.* Dedicated to God, Samson (Jdg 13:5,7), Samuel (1Sa 1:24-28), Jesus (Lk 2:22). Nurses for (Ex 2:7-9; Ru 4:16; 2Sa 4:4; 2Ki 11:2; Ac 7:20). Treatment of (Eze 16:4-6; Lk 2:7,12). Weaning of (Ge 21:8; 1Sa 1:22; 1Ki 11:20; Ps 131:2; Isa 28:9).

In Early Childhood:

Amusements of (Job 21:11; Zec 8:5; Mt 11:16-17; Lk 7:31-32). Early piety of, Samuel (1Sa 2:18; 3), Jeremiah (Jer 1:5-7), John the Baptist (Lk 1:15,80), Jesus (Lk 2:40, 46-47,52). Taught to walk (Hos 11:3). Tutored (2Ki 10:1; Ac 22:3; Gal 3:24; 4:1-2). *See Tutor.*

God's Care Of:

Ex 22:22 "Do not take advantage of a widow or an orphan. [23]If you do and they cry out to me, I will certainly hear their cry. [24]My anger will be aroused, and I will kill you with the sword; your wives will become widows and your children fatherless.

Dt 10:18 He defends the cause of the fatherless and the widow, and loves the alien, giving him food and clothing.

Dt 14:29 so that the Levites (who have no allotment or inheritance of their own) and the aliens, the fatherless and the widows who live in your towns may come and eat and be satisfied, and so that the LORD your God may bless you in all the work of your hands.

Job 29:12 because I rescued the poor who cried for help, and the fatherless who had none to assist him.

Ps 10:14 But you, O God, do see trouble and grief; you consider it to take it in hand. The victim commits himself to you; you are the helper of the fatherless.

Ps 10:17 You hear, O LORD, the desire of the afflicted; you encourage them, and you listen to their cry, [18]defending the fatherless and the oppressed, in order that man, who is of the earth, may terrify no more.

Ps 27:10 Though my father and mother forsake me, the LORD will receive me.

Ps 68:5 A father to the fatherless, a defender of widows, is God in his holy dwelling.

Ps 146:9 The LORD watches over the alien and sustains the fatherless and the widow, but he frustrates the ways of the wicked.

Jer 49:11 Leave your orphans; I will protect their lives. Your widows too can trust in me."

Hos 14:3 Assyria cannot save us; we will not mount war-horses. We will never again say 'Our gods' to what our own hands have made, for in you the fatherless find compassion."

Mal 3:5 "So I will come near to you for judgment. I will be quick to testify against sorcerers, adulterers and perjurers, against those who defraud laborers of their wages, who oppress the widows and the fatherless, and deprive aliens of justice, but do not fear me," says the LORD Almighty.

Blessed by Jesus (Mt 19:13-15; Mk 10:13-16; Lk 18:15-17). Intercessional sacrifices in behalf of (Job 1:5).

Commandments to:

To honor and obey parents—

Ex 20:12 "Honor your father and your mother, so that you may live long in the land the LORD your God is giving you.

Lev 19:3 "'Each of you must respect his mother and father, and you must observe my Sabbaths. I am the LORD your God.

Lev 19:32 "'Rise in the presence of the aged, show respect for the elderly and revere your God. I am the LORD. (+Dt 5:16)

Pr 1:8 Listen, my son, to your father's instruction and do not forsake your mother's teaching. 9They will be a garland to grace your head and a chain to adorn your neck. (+Pr 6:20-23)

Pr 23:22 Listen to your father, who gave you life, and do not despise your mother when she is old. (+Mt 15:4; Mk 10:19; Lk 18:20)

Eph 6:1 Children, obey your parents in the Lord, for this is right. (+Eph 6:2-3)

Col 3:20 Children, obey your parents in everything, for this pleases the Lord. (+1Ti 3:4)

Commandments to seek wisdom—

Pr 4:1 Listen, my sons, to a father's instruction; pay attention and gain understanding. 2I give you sound learning, so do not forsake my teaching. 3When I was a boy in my father's house, still tender, and an only child of my mother, 4he taught me and said, "Lay hold of my words with all your heart; keep my commands and you will live. (+Pr 4:5-9)

Pr 4:10 Listen, my son, accept what I say, and the years of your life will be many. 11I guide you in the way of wisdom and lead you along straight paths.

Pr 4:20 My son, pay attention to what I say; listen closely to my words. 21Do not let them out of your sight, keep them within your heart; 22for they are life to those who find them and health to a man's whole body.

Pr 5:1 My son, pay attention to my wisdom, listen well to my words of insight, 2that you may maintain discretion and your lips may preserve knowledge.

Pr 8:21 bestowing wealth on those who love me and making their treasuries full.

22"The LORD brought me forth as the first of his works, before his deeds of old; 23I was appointed from eternity, from the beginning, before the world began. 24When there were no oceans, I was given birth, when there were no springs abounding with water; 25before the mountains were settled in place, before the hills, I was given birth,

26before he made the earth or its fields or any of the dust of the world. 27I was there when he set the heavens in place, when he marked out the horizon on the face of the deep, 28when he established the clouds above and fixed securely the fountains of the deep, 29when he gave the sea its boundary so the waters would not overstep his command, and when he marked out the foundations of the earth. 30Then I was the craftsman at his side. I was filled with delight day after day, rejoicing always in his presence, 31rejoicing in his whole world and delighting in mankind.

32"Now then, my sons, listen to me; blessed are those who keep my ways. 33Listen to my instruction and be wise; do not ignore it. (+Pr 27:11)

Commandments to praise the Lord—

Ps 148:12 young men and maidens, old men and children. 13Let them praise the name of the LORD, for his name alone is exalted; his splendor is above the earth and the heavens.

Commandments to remember their Creator—

Pr 23:26 My son, give me your heart and let your eyes keep to my ways,

Ecc 12:1 Remember your Creator in the days of your youth, before the days of trouble come and the years approach when you will say, "I find no pleasure in them"—

Commandments to obey—

Ps 119:9 How can a young man keep his way pure? By living according to your word.

Pr 3:1 My son, do not forget my teaching, but keep my commands in your heart, 2for they will prolong your life many years and bring you prosperity.

3Let love and faithfulness never leave you; bind them around your neck, write them on the tablet of your heart.

Pr 6:20 My son, keep your father's commands and do not forsake your mother's teaching. 21Bind them upon your heart forever; fasten them around your neck. 22When you walk, they will guide you; when you sleep, they will watch over you; when you awake, they will speak to you. 23For these commands are a lamp, this teaching is a light, and the corrections of discipline are the way to life, 24keeping you from the immoral woman, from the smooth tongue of the wayward wife. 25Do not lust in your heart after her beauty or let her captivate you with her eyes,

Commandments to be pure—

Ecc 11:9 Be happy, young man, while you are young, and let your heart give you joy in the days of your youth. Follow the ways of your heart and whatever your eyes see, but know that for all these things God will bring you to judgment. 10So then, banish anxiety from your heart and cast off the troubles of your body, for youth and vigor are meaningless.

La 3:27 It is good for a man to bear the yoke while he is young.

1Ti 4:12 Don't let anyone look down on you because you are young, but set an example for the believers in speech, in life, in love, in faith and in purity.

2Ti 2:22 Flee the evil desires of youth, and pursue righteousness, faith, love and peace, along with those who call on the Lord out of a pure heart.

Tit 2:6 Similarly, encourage the young men to be self-controlled. *See Young Men.*

Miracles on behalf of: Raised from the dead, by Elijah (1Ki 17:17-23), Elisha (2Ki 4:17-36), Jesus (Mt 9:18,24-26; Mk 5:35-42; Lk 7:13-15; 8:49-56). Healing of (Mt 15:28; 17:18; Mk 7:29-30; 9:23-27; Lk 8:42-56; 9:38-42; Jn 4:46-54).

Prayer in behalf of:

For healing—

2Sa 12:16 David pleaded with God for the child. He fasted and went into his house and spent the nights lying on the ground.

For divine favor—

Ge 17:18 And Abraham said to God, "If only Ishmael might live under your blessing!"

For spiritual wisdom—

1Ch 22:12 May the LORD give you discretion and understanding when he puts you in command over Israel, so that you may keep the law of the LORD your God.

1Ch 29:19 And give my son Solomon the wholehearted devotion to keep your commands, requirements and decrees and to do everything to build the palatial structure for which I have provided."

For sins—

Job 1:5 When a period of feasting had run its course, Job would send and have them purified. Early in the morning he would sacrifice a burnt offering for each of them, thinking, "Perhaps my children have sinned and cursed God in their hearts." This was Job's regular custom.

Promises and assurances to:

Promise of divine instruction—

Isa 54:13 All your sons will be taught by the LORD, and great will be your children's peace.

Promise of long life to the obedient (Ex 20:12; Dt 5:16)—

Pr 3:1 My son, do not forget my teaching, but keep my commands in your heart, ²for they will prolong your life many years and bring you prosperity.

³Let love and faithfulness never leave you; bind them around your neck, write them on the tablet of your heart. ⁴Then you will win favor and a good name in the sight of God and man.

⁵Trust in the LORD with all your heart and lean not on your own understanding; ⁶in all your ways acknowledge him, and he will make your paths straight.

⁷Do not be wise in your own eyes; fear the LORD and shun evil. ⁸This will bring health to your body and nourishment to your bones.

⁹Honor the LORD with your wealth, with the firstfruits of all your crops; ¹⁰then your barns will be filled to overflowing, and your vats will brim over with new wine. (+Eph 6:2-3)

Promise of love and peace—

Pr 8:17 I love those who love me, and those who seek me find me.

Pr 8:32 "Now then, my sons, listen to me; blessed are those who keep my ways. (+Isa 40:11; 54:13)

Promise of acceptance by Jesus—

Mt 18:4 Therefore, whoever humbles himself like this child is the greatest in the kingdom of heaven.

⁵"And whoever welcomes a little child like this in my name welcomes me.

Mt 18:10 "See that you do not look down on one of these little ones. For I tell you that their angels in heaven always see the face of my Father in heaven.

Mt 19:14 Jesus said, "Let the little children come to me, and do not hinder them, for the kingdom of heaven belongs to such as these."

¹⁵When he had placed his hands on them, he went on from there. (+Mk 9:37)

Mk 10:16 And he took the children in his arms, put his hands on them and blessed them. (+Lk 9:48; 18:15-16)

Promise of joy to parents of wise children—

Pr 23:15 My son, if your heart is wise, then my heart will be glad; ¹⁶my inmost being will rejoice when your lips speak what is right.

Pr 23:24 The father of a righteous man has great joy; he who has a wise son delights in him. ²⁵May your father and mother be glad; may she who gave you birth rejoice!

Pr 29:3 A man who loves wisdom brings joy to his father, but a companion of prostitutes squanders his wealth.

Promise of forgiven sins—

1Jn 2:12 I write to you, dear children, because your sins have been forgiven on account of his name. ¹³I write to you, fathers, because you have known him who is from the beginning. I write to you, young men, because you have overcome the evil one. I write to you, dear children, because you have known the Father.

Of the righteous, blessed by God:

In escaping judgments—

Ge 6:18 But I will establish my covenant with you, and you will enter the ark—you and your sons and your wife and your sons' wives with you.

Ge 7:1 The LORD then said to Noah, "Go into the ark, you and your whole family, because I have found you righteous in this generation.

Ge 19:12 The two men said to Lot, "Do you have anyone else here—sons-in-law, sons or daughters, or anyone else in the city who belongs to you? Get them out of here,

Ge 19:15 With the coming of dawn, the angels urged Lot, saying, "Hurry! Take your wife and your two daughters who are here, or you will be swept away when the city is punished." ¹⁶When he hesitated, the men grasped his hand and the hands of his wife and of his two daughters and led them safely out of the city, for the LORD was merciful to them. (+Lev 26:44-45)

1Ki 11:13 Yet I will not tear the whole kingdom from him, but will give him one tribe for the sake of David my servant and for the sake of Jerusalem, which I have chosen."

2Ki 8:19 Nevertheless, for the sake of his servant David, the LORD was not willing to destroy Judah. He had promised to maintain a lamp for David and his descendants forever.

Pr 11:21 Be sure of this: The wicked will not go unpunished, but those who are righteous will go free.

Pr 12:7 Wicked men are overthrown and are no more, but the house of the righteous stands firm.

Blessed by God: In temporal prosperity—

Ge 12:7 The LORD appeared to Abram and said, "To your offspring I will give this land." So he built an altar there to the LORD, who had appeared to him.

Ge 13:15 All the land that you see I will give to you and your offspring forever.

Ge 17:7 I will establish my covenant as an everlasting covenant between me and you and your descendants after you for the generations to come, to be your God and the God of your descendants after you. ⁸The whole land of Canaan, where you are now an alien, I will give as an everlasting possession to you and your descendants after you; and I will be their God."

Ge 21:13 I will make the son of the maidservant into a nation also, because he is your offspring."

Ge 26:3 Stay in this land for a while, and I will be with you and will bless you. For to you and your descendants I will give all these lands and will confirm the oath I swore to your father Abraham. ⁴I will make your descendants as numerous as the stars in the sky and will give them all these lands, and through your offspring all nations on earth will be blessed,

Ge 26:24 That night the LORD appeared to him and said, "I am the God of your father Abraham. Do not be afraid, for I am with you; I will bless you and will increase the number of your descendants for the sake of my servant Abraham."

Dt 4:37 Because he loved your forefathers and chose their descendants after them, he brought you out of Egypt by his Presence and his great strength,

Dt 10:15 Yet the LORD set his affection on your forefathers and loved them, and he chose you, their descendants, above all the nations, as it is today.

Dt 12:28 Be careful to obey all these regulations I am giving you, so that it may always go well with you and your children after you, because you will be doing what is good and right in the eyes of the LORD your God.

1Ki 15:4 Nevertheless, for David's sake the LORD his God gave him a lamp in Jerusalem by raising up a son to succeed him and by making Jerusalem strong.

Ps 37:26 They are always generous and lend freely; their children will be blessed.

Ps 102:28 The children of your servants will live in your presence; their descendants will be established before you."

Ps 112:2 His children will be mighty in the land; the generation of the upright will be blessed. ³Wealth and riches are in his house, and his righteousness endures forever.

Pr 13:22 A good man leaves an inheritance for his children's children, but a sinner's wealth is stored up for the righteous.

Blessed by God: In divine mercy—

Ps 103:17 But from everlasting to everlasting the LORD's love is with those who fear him, and his righteousness with their children's children— ¹⁸with those who keep his covenant and remember to obey his precepts.

Pr 3:33 The LORD's curse is on the house of the wicked, but he blesses the home of the righteous.

Pr 20:7 The righteous man leads a blameless life; blessed are his children after him.

Isa 44:3 For I will pour water on the thirsty land, and streams on the dry ground; I will pour out my Spirit on your offspring, and my blessing on your descendants. ⁴They will spring up like grass in a meadow, like poplar trees by flowing streams. ⁵One will say, 'I belong to the LORD'; another will call himself by the name of Jacob; still another will write on his hand, 'The LORD's,' and will take the name Israel.

Isa 65:23 They will not toil in vain or bear children doomed to misfortune; for they will be a people blessed by the LORD, they and their descendants with them.

Jer 32:39 I will give them singleness of heart and action, so that they will always fear me for their own good and the good of their children after them.

Ac 2:39 The promise is for you and your children and for all who are far off—for all whom the Lord our God will call."

1Co 7:14 For the unbelieving husband has been sanctified through his wife, and the unbelieving wife has been sanctified through her believing husband. Otherwise your children would be unclean, but as it is, they are holy.

Parental Relationships:

Love of, for parents: Ruth (Ru 1:16-18), Jesus (Jn 19:26-27).

Counsel of parents to—

1Ki 2:1 When the time drew near for David to die, he gave a charge to Solomon his son.

²"I am about to go the way of all the earth," he said. "So be strong, show yourself a man, ³and observe what the LORD your God requires: Walk in his ways, and keep his decrees and commands, his laws and requirements, as written in the Law of Moses, so that you may prosper in all you do and wherever you go, ⁴and that the LORD may keep his promise to me: 'If your descendants watch how they live, and if they walk faithfully before me with all their heart and soul, you will never fail to have a man on the throne of Israel.'

1Ch 22:6 Then he called for his son Solomon and charged him to build a house for the LORD, the God of Israel. ⁷David said to Solomon: "My son, I had it in my heart to build a house for the Name of the LORD my God. ⁸But this word of the LORD came to me: 'You have shed much blood and have fought many wars. You are not to build a house for my Name, because you have shed much blood on the earth in my sight. ⁹But you will have a son who will be a man of peace and rest, and I will give him rest from all his enemies on every side. His name will be Solomon, and I will grant Israel peace and quiet during his reign. ¹⁰He is the one who will build a house for my Name. He will be my son, and I will be his father. And I will establish the throne of his kingdom over Israel forever.'

¹¹"Now, my son, the LORD be with you, and may you have success and build the house of the LORD your God, as he said you would. ¹²May the LORD give you discretion and understanding when he puts you in command over Israel, so that you may keep the law of the LORD your God. ¹³Then you will have success if you are careful to observe the decrees and laws that the LORD gave Moses for Israel. Be strong and courageous. Do not be afraid or discouraged. (+1Ch 28:9-10,20)

Of ministers (1Ti 3:4; Tit 1:6).

Instruction of: The law—

Dt 6:6 These commandments that I give you today are to be upon your hearts. ⁷Impress them on your children. Talk about them when you sit at home and when you walk along the road, when you lie down and when you get up. ⁸Tie them as symbols on your hands and bind them on your foreheads. ⁹Write them on the doorframes of your houses and on your gates.

Dt 11:19 Teach them to your children, talking about them when you sit at home and when you walk along the road, when you lie down and when you get up. ²⁰Write them on the doorframes of your houses and on your gates,

Dt 31:12 Assemble the people—men, women and children, and the aliens living in your towns—so they can listen and learn to fear the LORD your God and follow carefully all the words of this law. ¹³Their children, who do not know this law, must hear it and learn to fear the LORD your God as long as you live in the land you are crossing the Jordan to possess."

Jos 8:35 There was not a word of all that Moses had commanded that Joshua did not read to the whole assembly of Israel, including the women and children, and the aliens who lived among them.

Ps 78:1 O my people, hear my teaching; listen to the words of my mouth. ²I will open my mouth in parables, I will utter hidden things, things from of old— ³what we have heard and known, what our fathers have told us. ⁴We will not hide them from their children; we will tell the next generation the praiseworthy deeds of the LORD, his power, and the wonders he has done. **5**He decreed statutes for Jacob and established the law in Israel, which he commanded our forefathers to teach their children, **6**so the next generation would know them, even the children yet to be born, and they in turn would tell their children. **7**Then they would put their trust in God and would not forget his deeds but would keep his commands. **8**They would not be like their forefathers—a stubborn and rebellious generation, whose hearts were not loyal to God, whose spirits were not faithful to him.

Instruction of: The fear of the Lord—

Ps 34:11 Come, my children, listen to me; I will teach you the fear of the LORD.

Instruction of: The providence of God (Ex 10:2; 12:26-27)—

Ex 13:8 On that day tell your son, 'I do this because of what the LORD did for me when I came out of Egypt.' **9**This observance will be for you like a sign on your hand and a reminder on your forehead that the law of the LORD is to be on your lips. For the LORD brought you out of Egypt with his mighty hand. **10**You must keep this ordinance at the appointed time year after year.

Ex 13:14 "In days to come, when your son asks you, 'What does this mean?' say to him, 'With a mighty hand the LORD brought us out of Egypt, out of the land of slavery. **15**When Pharaoh stubbornly refused to let us go, the LORD killed every firstborn in Egypt, both man and animal. This is why I sacrifice to the LORD the first male offspring of every womb and redeem each of my firstborn sons.' **16**And it will be like a sign on your hand and a symbol on your forehead that the LORD brought us out of Egypt with his mighty hand."

Dt 4:9 Only be careful, and watch yourselves closely so that you do not forget the things your eyes have seen or let them slip from your heart as long as you live. Teach them to your children and to their children after them. **10**Remember the day you stood before the LORD your God at Horeb, when he said to me, "Assemble the people before me to hear my words so that they may learn to revere me as long as they live in the land and may teach them to their children."

Joel 1:3 Tell it to your children, and let your children tell it to their children, and their children to the next generation.

Instruction of: Righteousness—

Pr 1:1 The proverbs of Solomon son of David, king of Israel: (+Pr 1:4)

Pr 22:6 Train a child in the way he should go, and when he is old he will not turn from it.

Isa 28:9 "Who is it he is trying to teach? To whom is he explaining his message? To children weaned from their milk, to those just taken from the breast? **10**For it is: Do and do, do and do, rule on rule, rule on rule; a little here, a little there." (+Isa 38:19)

Instruction of: The Scriptures—

Ac 22:3 "I am a Jew, born in Tarsus of Cilicia, but brought up in this city. Under Gamaliel I was thoroughly trained in the law of our fathers and was just as zealous for God as any of you are today. (+Eph 6:4; 2Ti 3:15)

See Instruction; Tutor; Young Men.

Correction and punishment: By discipline—

Pr 19:18 Discipline your son, for in that there is hope; do not be a willing party to his death. (+Pr 23:13; 29:15)

Eph 6:4 Fathers, do not exasperate your children; instead,

bring them up in the training and instruction of the Lord. (+Col 3:2)

Correction and punishment: By the rod—

Pr 13:24 He who spares the rod hates his son, but he who loves him is careful to discipline him.

Pr 22:15 Folly is bound up in the heart of a child, but the rod of discipline will drive it far from him.

Pr 23:13 Do not withhold discipline from a child; if you punish him with the rod, he will not die. **14**Punish him with the rod and save his soul from death.

Pr 29:15 The rod of correction imparts wisdom, but a child left to himself disgraces his mother.

Correction and punishment: By death—

Ex 21:15 "Anyone who attacks his father or his mother must be put to death.

Ex 21:17 "Anyone who curses his father or mother must be put to death.

Lev 20:9 " 'If anyone curses his father or mother, he must be put to death. He has cursed his father or his mother, and his blood will be on his own head. (+Dt 21:21; 27:16; Pr 20:20; 22:15)

Pr 30:17 "The eye that mocks a father, that scorns obedience to a mother, will be pecked out by the ravens of the valley, will be eaten by the vultures.

Mt 15:4 For God said, 'Honor your father and mother' and 'Anyone who curses his father or mother must be put to death.' (+Mk 7:10)

Differences and partiality: Differences made between male and female (Lev 12). Partiality of parents, Rebekah for Jacob (Ge 27:6-17), Jacob for Joseph (Ge 37:3-4). Partiality among, forbidden (Dt 21:15-17).

Death and Mistreatment:

Death, as a judgment upon parents: Firstborn of Egypt (Ex 12:29; Nu 8:17; Ps 78:5), sons of Eli (1Sa 3:13-14), sons of Saul (1Sa 28:18-19), David's child by Uriah's wife (2Sa 12:14-19). Eaten. *See Cannibalism.*

Edict to murder: Of Pharaoh (Ex 1:22), Jehu (2Ki 10:1-8), Herod (Mt 2:16-18). Caused to pass through fire (2Ki 16:3; 17:7; Jer 32:35; Eze 16:21). Sacrificed (2Ki 17:31; Eze 16:20-21). Sold for debt (2Ki 4:1; Ne 5:5; Job 24:9; Mt 18:25). Sold in marriage, law concerning (Ex 21:7-11). Instance of Leah and Rachel (Ge 29:15-30).

Religious Involvement:

Attend divine worship (Ex 34:23; Jos 8:35)—

2Ch 20:13 All the men of Judah, with their wives and children and little ones, stood there before the LORD.

2Ch 31:16 In addition, they distributed to the males three years old or more whose names were in the genealogical records—all who would enter the temple of the LORD to perform the daily duties of their various tasks, according to their responsibilities and their divisions.

Ezr 8:21 There, by the Ahava Canal, I proclaimed a fast, so that we might humble ourselves before our God and ask him for a safe journey for us and our children, with all our possessions.

Ne 8:2 So on the first day of the seventh month Ezra the priest brought the Law before the assembly, which was made up of men and women and all who were able to understand. **3**He read it aloud from daybreak till noon as he faced the square before the Water Gate in the presence of the men, women and others who could understand. And all the people listened attentively to the Book of the Law.

Ne 12:43 And on that day they offered great sacrifices, rejoicing because God had given them great joy. The women and children also rejoiced. The sound of rejoicing in Jerusalem could be heard far away.

Mt 21:15 But when the chief priests and the teachers of the law saw the wonderful things he did and the children shouting in the temple area, "Hosanna to the Son of David," they were indignant.

Lk 2:46 After three days they found him in the temple courts, sitting among the teachers, listening to them and asking them questions.

Entitled to enjoy religious privileges (Dt 12:12-13). Illegitimate excluded from privilege of congregation (Dt 23:2; Heb 12:8).

Covenant involvement: Bound by covenants of parents (Ge 17:9-14). Share benefits of parents' covenant privileges (Ge 6:18; 12:7; 13:15; 17:7-8; 19:12; 21:23; 26:3-5,24; Lev 26:44-45; Isa 65:23; 1Co 7:14). Involved in guilt of parents (Ex 20:5; 34:7; Lev 20:5; 26:39-42; Nu 14:18,33; 1Ki 16:12; 21:29; Job 21:19; Ps 37:28; Isa 14:20-21; 65:6-7; Jer 32:18; Da 6:24). Not punished for parent's sake (2Ki 14:6; Jer 31:29-30; Eze 18:1-30).

Character of: Known by conduct (Pr 20:11). Future state (Mt 18:10; 19:14). Status of minors (Gal 4:1-2).

Alienated: Ishmael, to gratify Sarah (Ge 21:9-15). Adopted. *See Adoption; Parents.*

Good:

Have Lord's presence (1Sa 3:19). Blessed of God (Pr 3:1-4; Eph 6:2-3). Honor the aged (Job 32:6-7).

Honor father—

Mal 1:6 "A son honors his father, and a servant his master. If I am a father, where is the honor due me? If I am a master, where is the respect due me?" says the LORD Almighty. "It is you, O priests, who show contempt for my name. "But you ask, 'How have we shown contempt for your name?'

A joy to parents (Pr 10:1; 15:20; 23:24; 29:3)—

Pr 29:17 Discipline your son, and he will give you peace; he will bring delight to your soul.

Keep the law (Pr 28:7). Know the scriptures (2Ti 3:15). Love parents (Ge 46:29). Obey parents (Ge 28:7; 47:30; Pr 13:1), which pleases God (Col 3:20). Attend to parental teaching (Pr 13:1). Partake of God's promises (Ac 2:39).

Extol the Savior—

Mt 21:15 But when the chief priests and the teachers of the law saw the wonderful things he did and the children shouting in the temple area, "Hosanna to the Son of David," they were indignant.

¹⁶"Do you hear what these children are saying?" they asked him.

"Yes," replied Jesus, "have you never read,

" 'From the lips of children and infants you have ordained praise'?" (+Ps 8:2)

Take care of parents (Ge 45:9-11; 47:12; Mt 15:5). Wise—

Ecc 4:13 Better a poor but wise youth than an old but foolish king who no longer knows how to take warning.

Illustrative of conversion (Mt 18:3), of a teachable spirit (Mt 18:4).

Symbolic of regeneration—

Mt 18:2 He called a little child and had him stand among them. ³And he said: "I tell you the truth, unless you change and become like little children, you will never enter the kingdom of heaven. ⁴Therefore, whoever humbles himself like this child is the greatest in the kingdom of heaven.

⁵"And whoever welcomes a little child like this in my name welcomes me. ⁶But if anyone causes one of these

little ones who believe in me to sin, it would be better for him to have a large millstone hung around his neck and to be drowned in the depths of the sea. (+Mt 18:10; 19:14-15)

Mk 9:36 He took a little child and had him stand among them. Taking him in his arms, he said to them, ³⁷"Whoever welcomes one of these little children in my name welcomes me; and whoever welcomes me does not welcome me but the one who sent me." (+Mk 10:13-14)

Mk 10:15 I tell you the truth, anyone who will not receive the kingdom of God like a little child will never enter it." (+Mk 10:16)

Lk 9:46 An argument started among the disciples as to which of them would be the greatest. ⁴⁷Jesus, knowing their thoughts, took a little child and had him stand beside him. ⁴⁸Then he said to them, "Whoever welcomes this little child in my name welcomes me; and whoever welcomes me welcomes the one who sent me. For he who is least among you all—he is the greatest." (+Lk 18:15,17)

Instances of. Shem and Japheth (Ge 9:23). Isaac (Ge 22:6-12). Esau (Ge 28:6-9). Jacob (Ge 28:7). Judah (Ge 44:18-34). Joseph (Ge 45:9-13; 46:29; 47:11-12,29-30; 48:12; 50:1-13). Moses (Ex 15:2; 18:7). Jephthah's daughter (Jdg 11:36-39). Ruth (Ru 1:15-17). Samuel (1Sa 2:26; 3:10).

David (1Sa 22:3-4; Ps 71:5,17). Solomon (1Ki 2:19-20; 3:3-13). Abijah (1Ki 14:13). Obadiah (1Ki 18:12). Jehoshaphat (1Ki 22:43; 2Ch 17:3). The captive maid (2Ki 5:2-4). Jewish children (2Ch 20:13; Ne 8:3; 12:43). Josiah (2Ch 34:1-3). Job (Job 29:4). Elihu (Job 32:4-7). Jeremiah (Jer 1:5-7). The Recabites (Jer 35:18-19). Daniel and the three Hebrews (Da 1:8-20). Children in the temple (Mt 21:15). John (Lk 1:80). Jesus (Lk 2:51-52). Timothy (2Ti 1:5; 3:15).

Wicked:

Disrespectful, to parents—

Dt 27:16 "Cursed is the man who dishonors his father or his mother." Then all the people shall say, "Amen!"

Pr 15:20 A wise son brings joy to his father, but a foolish man despises his mother.

Pr 30:11 "There are those who curse their fathers and do not bless their mothers;

Eze 22:7 In you they have treated father and mother with contempt; in you they have oppressed the alien and mistreated the fatherless and the widow.

Mic 7:6 For a son dishonors his father, a daughter rises up against her mother, a daughter-in-law against her mother-in-law—a man's enemies are the members of his own household.

Job 19:18 Even the little boys scorn me; when I appear, they ridicule me. (+2Ki 2:23)

Disobedient to parents—

Dt 21:18 If a man has a stubborn and rebellious son who does not obey his father and mother and will not listen to them when they discipline him, ¹⁹his father and mother shall take hold of him and bring him to the elders at the gate of his town. ²⁰They shall say to the elders, "This son of ours is stubborn and rebellious. He will not obey us. He is a profligate and a drunkard." ²¹Then all the men of his town shall stone him to death. You must purge the evil from among you. All Israel will hear of it and be afraid.

Pr 13:1 A wise son heeds his father's instruction, but a mocker does not listen to rebuke.

Pr 15:5 A fool spurns his father's discipline, but whoever heeds correction shows prudence. (+Pr 30:13)

Ro 1:30 slanderers, God-haters, insolent, arrogant and

boastful; they invent ways of doing evil; they disobey their parents;

2Ti 3:2 People will be lovers of themselves, lovers of money, boastful, proud, abusive, disobedient to their parents, ungrateful, unholy,

Defraud parents—

Pr 28:7 He who keeps the law is a discerning son, but a companion of gluttons disgraces his father.

Pr 28:24 He who robs his father or mother and says, "It's not wrong"—he is partner to him who destroys.

Mk 7:9 And he said to them: "You have a fine way of setting aside the commands of God in order to observe your own traditions! ¹⁰For Moses said, 'Honor your father and your mother,' and, 'Anyone who curses his father or mother must be put to death.' ¹¹But you say that if a man says to his father or mother: 'Whatever help you might otherwise have received from me is Corban' (that is, a gift devoted to God), ¹²then you no longer let him do anything for his father or mother. ¹³Thus you nullify the word of God by your tradition that you have handed down. And you do many things like that."

Disgrace parents—

Pr 10:1 The proverbs of Solomon: A wise son brings joy to his father, but a foolish son grief to his mother.

Pr 17:2 A wise servant will rule over a disgraceful son, and will share the inheritance as one of the brothers.

Pr 17:21 To have a fool for a son brings grief; there is no joy for the father of a fool.

Pr 17:25 A foolish son brings grief to his father and bitterness to the one who bore him. (+Pr 19:13)

Pr 19:26 He who robs his father and drives out his mother is a son who brings shame and disgrace.

Pr 23:22 Listen to your father, who gave you life, and do not despise your mother when she is old.

Betray parents—

Mk 13:12 "Brother will betray brother to death, and a father his child. Children will rebel against their parents and have them put to death.

Instances of. Canaan (Ge 4:25). Lot's daughters (Ge 19:14,30-38). Ishmael (Ge 21:9). Eli's sons (1Sa 2:12,22-25). Samuel's sons (1Sa 8:3). Absalom (2Sa 15). Adonijah (1Ki 1:5). Abijah (1Ki 15:3). Ahaziah (1Ki 22:52). Children at Bethel (2Ki 2:23-24). Samaritan's descendants (2Ki 17:41). Adrammelech and Sharezer (2Ki 19:37; 2Ch 32:31). Amon (2Ki 21:21).

See Babies; Young Men.

CHILDREN OF GOD *See Righteous.*

CHILEAB *See Kileab.*

CHILION *See Kilion.*

CHILMAD *See Kilmad.*

CHIMHAM *See Kimham.*

CHIMNEY NIV "window" (Hos 13:3). *See Window.*

CHINESE KJV "Sinim" is believed by some to be a reference to the Chinese; NIV has "Aswan" (Isa 49:12). *See Aswan.*

CHINNERETH, CHINNEROTH *See Kinnereth.*

CHIOS *See Kios.*

CHISLEU *See Kislev.*

CHISLON *See Kislon.*

CHISLOTH-TABOR *See Kisloth Tabor.*

CHITTIM *See Kittim.*

CHIUN NIV "pedestal"; perhaps the proper name "Kaiwan" (Am 5:26, ftn). *See Rephan.*

CHLOE [*5951*] (*tender shoot*).
NIV+ CHLOE'S
A Christian of Corinth (1Co 1:11).

CHOICE [*1040, 1047, 1374, 1405, 2773, 3202, 3359, 3519, 4269, 4334, 4374, 4436, 4458, 8011, 8040, 8603, 145, 1089, 1721, 1723, 1724, 2527*].
NIV+ CHOICEST, CHOOSE, CHOOSES, CHOOSING, CHOSE, CHOSEN

Between life and death—

Dt 30:19 This day I call heaven and earth as witnesses against you that I have set before you life and death, blessings and curses. Now choose life, so that you and your children may live ²⁰and that you may love the LORD your God, listen to his voice, and hold fast to him. For the LORD is your life, and he will give you many years in the land he swore to give to your fathers, Abraham, Isaac and Jacob.

God and false gods—

Jos 24:15 But if serving the LORD seems undesirable to you, then choose for yourselves this day whom you will serve, whether the gods your forefathers served beyond the River, or the gods of the Amorites, in whose land you are living. But as for me and my household, we will serve the LORD."

¹⁶Then the people answered, "Far be it from us to forsake the LORD to serve other gods! ¹⁷It was the LORD our God himself who brought us and our fathers up out of Egypt, from that land of slavery, and performed those great signs before our eyes. He protected us on our entire journey and among all the nations through which we traveled. ¹⁸And the LORD drove out before us all the nations, including the Amorites, who lived in the land. We too will serve the LORD, because he is our God."

Judgments by David (2Sa 24:12-14; 1Ch 21:11-13)

Between God and Baal—

1Ki 18:21 Elijah went before the people and said, "How long will you waver between two opinions? If the LORD is God, follow him; but if Baal is God, follow him." But the people said nothing. (+1Ki 18:39-40)

Of Moses (Heb 11:24-25).

See Contingencies; Blessings, Spiritual Contingent Upon Obedience.

CHOIR [8876, 9343].
NIV+ CHOIRS

Leaders of (1Ch 25:2-6; Ne 12:42). Presided over by chief musician (Ps 4; Hab 3:19). Instructed by teachers (1Ch 15:22,27; 25:7-8).

In the tabernacle (1Ch 6:31-47). Composed of singers and instrumentalists (1Ch 15:16-21; 25:1-7; 2Ch 5:12-13; 23:13; Isa 38:20). Mixed choirs (2Ch 35:15,25; Ezr 2:64-65).

Sang every morning and evening (1Ch 9:33; 23:5,30), during offering of sacrifices (1Ch 16:41-42; 2Ch 29:27-28), at restoration of the temple (Ezr 2:41; 3:10-11), at the dedication of the wall of Jerusalem (Ne 12:27-30).

Appointed from the army to sing praises to God as a military strategy (2Ch 20:21).

See Music.

CHOOSING *See Choice.*

CHOR-ASHAN *See Bor Ashan.*

CHORAZIN *See Korazin.*

CHORUSES *See Music.*

CHOSEN [*1405, 3519, 3359, 4334, *1721, 1723, 1724*].

NIV+ See CHOICE

Also referred to as elect (Mt 24:22,24,31). Few (Mt 20:16).

Called—

1Pe 2:9 But you are a chosen people, a royal priesthood, a holy nation, a people belonging to God, that you may declare the praises of him who called you out of darkness into his wonderful light.

Rev 17:14 They will make war against the Lamb, but the Lamb will overcome them because he is Lord of lords and King of kings—and with him will be his called, chosen and faithful followers."

See Elect; Election; Foreknowledge of God; Predestination.

CHOZEBA *See Cozeba.*

CHRIST [5986] *(the Anointed One). See Jesus the Christ.*

CHRISTIAN [5985] *(follower of Christ).*

NIV+ BELIEVER, BELIEVERS, CHRIST, CHRIST'S, CHRISTIAN, CHRISTIANS, CHRISTS

Believers called (Ac 11:26; 26:28; 1Pe 4:16).

See Righteous.

CHRISTIANITY The word does not occur in the Bible. It was first used by Ignatius, in the first half of the second century. It designates all that which Jesus Christ brings to people of faith, life, and salvation.

CHRISTMAS The anniversary of the birth of Christ and its observance. Celebrated by most Protestants and by Roman Catholics on December 25, by Eastern Orthodox churches on January 6, and by the Armenian church on January 19. The first mention of its observance on December 25 is in the time of Constantine, c. A.D. 325. The date of the birth of Christ is not known. The word *Christmas* is formed of *Christ* plus *Mass*, meaning a religious service in commemoration of the birth of Christ. It is not clear whether the early Christians thought of or observed Christmas, but once introduced, the observance spread throughout Christendom. Some Christian groups disapprove of the festival.

CHRONICLES, 1 and 2

Author: Anonymous; according to ancient Jewish tradition, Ezra.

Date: Latter half of the fifth century B.C.

Outline:

I. Genealogies: Creation to Restoration (1Ch 1-9).
   A. The Patriarchs (ch. 1).
   B. The 12 Sons of Jacob/Israel (2:1-2).
   C. The Family of Judah (2:3-4:23).
   D. The Sons of Simeon (4:24-43).
   E. Reuben, Gad and the Half-Tribe of Manasseh (ch. 5).
   F. Levi and Families (ch. 6).
   G. Issachar, Benjamin, Naphtali, Manasseh, Ephraim and Asher (chs. 7-9).

II. The Reign of David (1Ch 10-29).
   A. Death of Saul (ch. 10).
   B. Capture of Jerusalem; David's Power Base (chs. 11-12).
   C. Return of the Ark; Establishment of David's Kingdom (chs. 13-16).
   D. Dynastic Promise (ch. 17).
   E. David's Conquest (chs. 18-20).
   F. The Census (ch. 21).
   G. Preparations for the Temple (ch. 22).
   H. Organization of the Temple Service (chs. 23-26).
   I. Administrative Structures of the Kingdom (ch. 27).
   J. David's Final Preparations for Succession and the Temple (28:1-29:20).

III. The Reign of Solomon (2Ch 1-9).
   A. The Gift of Wisdom (ch. 1).
   B. Building the Temple (2:1-5:1).
   C. Dedication of the Temple (5:2-7:22).
   D. Solomon's Other Activities (ch. 8).
   E. Solomon's Wisdom, Splendor and Death (ch. 9).

IV. The Schism, and the History of the Kings of Judah (2Ch 10-36).
   A. Rehoboam (chs. 10-12).
   B. Abijah (13:1-14:1).
   C. Asa (14:2-16:14).
   D. Jehoshaphat (17:1-21:3).
   E. Jehoram and Ahaziah (21:4-22:9).
   F. Joash (22:10-24:27).
   G. Amaziah (ch. 25).
   H. Uzziah (ch. 26).
   I. Jotham (ch. 27).
   J. Ahaz (ch. 28).
   K. Hezekiah (chs. 29-32).
   L. Manasseh (33:1-20).
   M. Amon (33:21-25).
   N. Josiah (34:1-36:1).
   O. Josiah's Successors (36:2-14).
   P. Exile and Restoration (36:15-23).

CHRONOLOGY, NEW TESTAMENT

In ancient times historians were not accustomed to recording history under exact dates, but were satisfied when some specific event was related to the reign of a noted ruler or a famous contemporary. Our method of dating events in reference to the birth of Christ was started by Dionysius Exiguus, a monk who lived in the sixth century, but who wrongly calculated Jesus' birth year. The birth of Christ must be dated in or before 5 B.C., as it is known that Herod the Great died in 4 B.C., and according to the Gospels Jesus was born some time before the death of the king. Luke gives the age of Jesus at his baptism as "about thirty years" (Lk 3:23). This would bring the baptism at c. A.D. 26 or 27. Since Herod began the reconstruction of the temple in 20 B.C., the "forty-six years" mentioned by the Jews during the first Passover of Jesus' public ministry (Jn 2:13-22), brings us to A.D. 27 for this first Passover. The ministry of John the Baptist began about the middle of A.D. 26. The time of the Crucifixion is determined by the length of the ministry of Jesus. Mark's gospel seems to require at least two years. John's gospel explicitly mentions three Passovers (Jn 2:23; 6:4; 11:55). If the feast (Jn 5:1) is also a Passover, as seems probable, then the length of the ministry of Jesus was a full three years and a little over. This places the Crucifixion at the Passover of A.D. 30.

As for the Apostolic Age the chronological data are

very limited and uncertain. The death of Herod Agrippa I in A.D. 44 is one of the fixed dates of the NT. This was the year of Peter's arrest and miraculous escape from prison. The proconsulship of Gallio was between 51 and 53, and this would bring the beginning of Paul's ministry at Corinth to c. A.D. 50. The accession of Festus as governor, under whom Paul was sent to Rome, probably took place c. 59/60.

New Testament Chronology	
Birth of Jesus	7-5 B.C.
Baptism of Jesus	A.D. 26
Crucifixion of Jesus	30
Conversion of Saul	34/35
Death of Herod Agrippa I	44
James written	before 50 (?)
First Missionary Journey	46-48
Galatians written	48/49
Jerusalem Conference	49/50
Second Missionary Journey	50-52
Paul at Corinth	50-52
1 and 2 Thessalonians written	51
Arrival of Gallio as Proconsul	52
Third Missionary Journey	53-57
Paul at Ephesus	54-57
1 and 2 Corinthians written	55
Romans written	57
Paul's Arrest in Jerusalem	57
Imprisonment at Caesarea	57-59
On Island of Malta	59
Arrival at Rome	59
Roman Imprisonment	59-61/62
Colossians, Philemon, Ephesians written	60
Philippians written	61
Paul's Release and Further Work	62-67
1 Timothy and Titus written	63-65
Synoptic Gospels and Acts written	before 67
1 and 2 Peter written	67/68
Peter's Death at Rome	67/68
Paul's Second Roman Imprisonment	67/68
2 Timothy written	67/68
Paul's Death at Rome	67/68
Jude written	c. 65-80
Writings of John	c. 90-100
Death of John	c. 100

CHRONOLOGY, OLD TESTAMENT

For the period from the Creation to the Flood the only Biblical data are the ages of the patriarchs in the genealogical tables of Genesis 5, 7, and 11. Extrabiblical sources for this period are almost completely lacking. For the period from the Flood to Abraham we are again dependent upon the genealogical data in the Bible. The numbers vary in the Masoretic text, the LXX, and the Samaritan Pentateuch. The construction of an absolute chronology from Adam to Abraham is not now possible on the basis of the available data.

The following chart is based on the early date of the Exodus. The later date (c. 1230 B.C.) only affects the dating of the patriarchs and judges.

Old Testament Chronology (From Abraham)	
Abram born	2166 B.C.
Abraham dies	1991
Jacob and family in Egypt	1876
Moses born	1526
The Exodus	1446
Moses dies; Israelites enter Canaan	1406
The Judges	1375-1050
Saul as king	10501010
David as king	1010-970
Solomon as king	970-930
Northern kingdom of Israel	930-722
Southern kingdom of Judah	930-586
Exile	586-538
First return under Zerubbabel	538
Temple rebuilt	536-516
Second return under Ezra	458
Wall of Jerusalem rebuilt	445
Third return under Nehemiah	432
Close of OT history and prophecy	c. 400

For the chronology of the kings, *See Kings.* For the approximate dates of OT books, see each by name.

CHRYSOLITE, CHRYSOLYTE [9577, 5994].

1. One of the precious stones set in the priestly breastplate (Ex 28:17; 39:10).

2. A precious stone used in poetic, prophetic, and apocalyptic literature (SS 5:14; Eze 1:16; 10:9; 28:13; Da 10:6; Rev 21:20).

See Minerals of the Bible, 1; Stones.

CHRYSOPRASE, CHRYSOPRASUS [5995]. A
precious stone (Rev 21:20).

See Minerals of the Bible, 1; Stones.

CHUB *See Libya.*

CHUN *See Cun.*

CHURCH, PLACE OF WORSHIP [1711, 4436].
NIV+ CHURCHES

Note: Nowhere in scripture does the word "church" identify a place of worship, but rather a group (or body) of believers, and that only in the NT.

The place where God was worshiped was called:

Courts (Ps 65:4; 84:2,10; 92:13; 96:8; 100:4; 116:19; Isa 1:12; 62:9; Zec 3:7). Holy Oracle (Ps 28:2). Holy place (Ex 28:29; 38:24; Lev 6:16; 10:17; 14:13; 16:2-24; Jos 5:15; 1Ki 8:8; 1Ch 23:32; 2Ch 29:5; 30:27; 35:5; Ezr 9:8; Ps 24:3; 46:4; 68:17; Ecc 8:10; Isa 57:15; Eze 41:4; 42:13; 45:4; Mt 24:15; Ac 6:13; 21:28; Heb 9:12,25). Holy temple (Ps 5:7; 11:4; 65:4; 79:1; 138:2; Jnh 2:4,7; Mic 1:2; Hab 2:20; Eph 2:21; 3:17).

House of God (Ge 28:17,22; Jos 9:23; Jdg 18:31; 20:18,26; 21:2; 1Ch 9:11; 24:5; 2Ch 5:14; 22:12; 24:13; 33:7; 36:19; Ezr 5:8,15; 7:20,23; Ne 6:10; 11:11; 13:11; Ps 42:4; 52:8; 55:14; 84:10; Ecc 5:1; Isa 2:3; Hos 9:8; Joel 1:16; Mic 4:2; Zec 7:2; Mt 12:4; 1Ti 3:15; Heb 10:21; 1Pe

4:17). House of the Lord (Ex 23:19; 34:26; Dt 23:18; Jos 6:24; Jdg 19:18; 1Sa 1:7,24; 2Sa 12:20; 1Ki 3:1; 6:37; 7:40; 8:10,63; 10:5; 2Ki 11:3-4,15,18-19; 12:4,9-10,13, 16; 16:18; 20:8; 23:2,7,11; 25:9; 1Ch 6:31; 22:1,11,14; 23:4; 26:12; 2Ch 8:16; 26:21; 29:5,15; 33:15; 34:15; 36:14; Ezr 7:27; Ps 23:6; 27:4; 92:13; 116:19; 118:26; 122:1,9; 134:1; Isa 2:2; 37:14; Jer 17:26; 20:1-2; 26:2,7; 28:1,5; 29:26; 35:2; 36:5-6; 38:14; 41:5; 51:51; La 2:7; Eze 44:4; Hag 1:2; Zec 8:9). House of Prayer (Isa 56:7; Mt 21:13; Mk 11:17; Lk 19:46). My Father's House (Jn 2:16; 14:2).

Sanctuary (Ex 25:8; Lev 19:30; 21:12; Nu 3:28; 4:12; 7:9; 8:19; 10:21; 18:1,5; 19:20; 1Ch 9:29; 22:19; 24:5; 28:10; 2Ch 20:8; 26:18; 29:21; 30:8,19; Ne 10:39; Ps 20:2; 28:2; 63:2; 68:24; 73:17; 74:3,7; 77:13; 78:69; 150:1; Isa 16:12; 63:18; La 2:7,20; 4:1; Eze 5:11; 42:20; 44:5,27; 45:3; 48:8,21; Da 8:11,13-14; 9:17,26; 11:31; Heb 8:2; 9:1-2). Tabernacle (Ex 26:1; Lev 26:11; Jos 22:19; Ps 15:1; 61:4; 76:2; Heb 8:2,5; 9:2,11; Rev 13:6; 21:3). Temple (1Sa 1:9; 3:3; 2Ki 11:10,13; Ezr 4:1; Ps 5:7; 11:4; 27:4; 29:9; 48:9; 68:29; Isa 6:1; Mal 3:1; Mt 4:5; 23:16; Lk 18:10; 24:53).

Zion—

Ps 9:11 Sing praises to the LORD, enthroned in Zion; proclaim among the nations what he has done. (+Ps 48:11)

Ps 74:2 Remember the people you purchased of old, the tribe of your inheritance, whom you redeemed—Mount Zion, where you dwelt.

Ps 132:13 For the LORD has chosen Zion, he has desired it for his dwelling:

Ps 137:1 By the rivers of Babylon we sat and wept when we remembered Zion.

Isa 35:10 and the ransomed of the LORD will return. They will enter Zion with singing; everlasting joy will crown their heads. Gladness and joy will overtake them, and sorrow and sighing will flee away.

Jer 31:6 There will be a day when watchmen cry out on the hills of Ephraim, 'Come, let us go up to Zion, to the LORD our God.'" (+Jer 50:5)

Joel 2:1 Blow the trumpet in Zion; sound the alarm on my holy hill. Let all who live in the land tremble, for the day of the LORD is coming. It is close at hand—

Joel 2:15 Blow the trumpet in Zion, declare a holy fast, call a sacred assembly.

Buildings: *See Synagogue; Tabernacle; Temple.*

Nature:

Instituted by divine authority (Ex 25:8-9; Dt 12:11-14).

Holy—

Ex 30:26 Then use it to anoint the Tent of Meeting, the ark of the Testimony, ²⁷the table and all its articles, the lampstand and its accessories, the altar of incense, ²⁸the altar of burnt offering and all its utensils, and the basin with its stand. ²⁹You shall consecrate them so they will be most holy, and whatever touches them will be holy.

Ex 40:9 "Take the anointing oil and anoint the tabernacle and everything in it; consecrate it and all its furnishings, and it will be holy.

Lev 8:10 Then Moses took the anointing oil and anointed the tabernacle and everything in it, and so consecrated them. ¹¹He sprinkled some of the oil on the altar seven times, anointing the altar and all its utensils and the basin with its stand, to consecrate them.

Lev 16:33 and make atonement for the Most Holy Place, for the Tent of Meeting and the altar, and for the priests and all the people of the community.

Lev 19:30 "'Observe my Sabbaths and have reverence for my sanctuary. I am the LORD.

Lev 21:12 nor leave the sanctuary of his God or desecrate it, because he has been dedicated by the anointing oil of his God. I am the LORD. (+Lev 26:2)

Nu 7:1 When Moses finished setting up the tabernacle, he anointed it and consecrated it and all its furnishings. He also anointed and consecrated the altar and all its utensils. (+Nu 8:19)

1Ki 9:3 The LORD said to him: "I have heard the prayer and plea you have made before me; I have consecrated this temple, which you have built, by putting my Name there forever. My eyes and my heart will always be there.

1Ch 29:3 Besides, in my devotion to the temple of my God I now give my personal treasures of gold and silver for the temple of my God, over and above everything I have provided for this holy temple:

2Ch 3:8 He built the Most Holy Place, its length corresponding to the width of the temple—twenty cubits long and twenty cubits wide. He overlaid the inside with six hundred talents of fine gold.

Isa 64:11 Our holy and glorious temple, where our fathers praised you, has been burned with fire, and all that we treasured lies in ruins.

Eze 23:39 On the very day they sacrificed their children to their idols, they entered my sanctuary and desecrated it. That is what they did in my house. (+Eze 43:12)

Should be shown reverence (Lev 19:30; 26:2).

Figurative—

1Co 3:17 If anyone destroys God's temple, God will destroy him; for God's temple is sacred, and you are that temple.

CHURCH, THE BODY OF BELIEVERS [1711, 4436] (assembly).

"church" in this entry encompasses organized bodies of believers in both testaments. In the OT, the church was a group of "gathered together" Hebrew believers, a congregation. In the NT, the church (technically) was a group of "called out" Christian believers.

Called:

In the OT, the congregation, congregation of Israel, or community of Israel (Ex 12:3,6,19,47; 16:1,2,9-10,22; Lev 4:13,15; 10:17; 24:14)

Zion (2Ki 19:21,31; Ps 9:11; 48:2,11-12; 74:2; 132:13; 137:1; Isa 35:10)—

Isa 40:9 You who bring good tidings to Zion, go up on a high mountain. You who bring good tidings to Jerusalem, lift up your voice with a shout, lift it up, do not be afraid; say to the towns of Judah, "Here is your God!" (+Isa 49:14; 51:16)

Isa 52:1 Awake, awake, O Zion, clothe yourself with strength. Put on your garments of splendor, O Jerusalem, the holy city. The uncircumcised and defiled will not enter you again.

Isa 52:2 Shake off your dust; rise up, sit enthroned, O Jerusalem. Free yourself from the chains on your neck, O captive Daughter of Zion.

Isa 52:7 How beautiful on the mountains are the feet of those who bring good news, who proclaim peace, who bring good tidings, who proclaim salvation, who say to Zion, "Your God reigns!" ⁸Listen! Your watchmen lift up their voices; together they shout for joy. When the LORD returns to Zion, they will see it with their own eyes. (+Isa 60:14)

Isa 62:1 For Zion's sake I will not keep silent, for

Jerusalem's sake I will not remain quiet, till her righteousness shines out like the dawn, her salvation like a blazing torch.

Isa 62:11 The LORD has made proclamation to the ends of the earth: "Say to the Daughter of Zion, 'See, your Savior comes! See, his reward is with him, and his recompense accompanies him.'" (+Jer 31:6; 50:5; La 1:4; Joel 2:1,15)

Also (Ro 9:33; 11:26; 1Pe 2:16). Daughter of Zion (Isa 62:11; Zec 9:9). Also (Mt 21:5; Jn 12:15).

In the NT, church—

Mt 16:18 And I tell you that you are Peter, and on this rock I will build my church, and the gates of Hades will not overcome it. (+Mt 18:17; Ac 2:47)

Ac 7:38 He was in the assembly in the desert, with the angel who spoke to him on Mount Sinai, and with our fathers; and he received living words to pass on to us.

Ac 20:28 Keep watch over yourselves and all the flock of which the Holy Spirit has made you overseers. Be shepherds of the church of God, which he bought with his own blood. (+1Co 11:18; 14:19,23,28,33-34)

1Co 15:9 For I am the least of the apostles and do not even deserve to be called an apostle, because I persecuted the church of God. (+Gal 1:13; Eph 1:22)

1Ti 3:15 if I am delayed, you will know how people ought to conduct themselves in God's household, which is the church of the living God, the pillar and foundation of the truth.

Described as:

Assembly of believers (Ps 89:7)

The upright—

Ps 111:1 Praise the LORD. I will extol the LORD with all my heart in the council of the upright and in the assembly.

Body of Christ (1Co 12:27)—

Eph 1:22 And God placed all things under his feet and appointed him to be head over everything for the church, ²³which is his body, the fullness of him who fills everything in every way. (+Eph 4:12)

Col 1:24 Now I rejoice in what was suffered for you, and I fill up in my flesh what is still lacking in regard to Christ's afflictions, for the sake of his body, which is the church.

Branch of God's planting—

Isa 60:21 Then will all your people be righteous and they will possess the land forever. They are the shoot I have planted, the work of my hands, for the display of my splendor.

Bride (Gal 6:16). Bride of Christ (Rev 21:9). Christ's body (Ro 12:5; 1Co 12:12,27; Eph 1:22-23; 4:12; Col 1:24). Church of God (Ac 20:28). Church of the living God (1Ti 3:15). Church of the firstborn (Heb 12:23). Congregation of Believers (Ps 149:1). Congregation of the Lord's Poor (Ps 74:19). Dove (SS 2:14; 5:2).

Family in heaven and earth—

Eph 3:15 from whom his whole family in heaven and on earth derives its name.

Flock of God (Eze 34:15; 1Pe 5:2). Fold of Christ (Jn 10:16). General Assembly of the Firstborn (Heb 12:23). The God of Jacob (Isa 2:3).

Golden lampstand—

Rev 1:20 The mystery of the seven stars that you saw in my right hand and of the seven golden lampstands is this: The seven stars are the angels of the seven churches, and the seven lampstands are the seven churches.

God's building—

1Co 3:9 For we are God's fellow workers; you are God's field, God's building.

God's field (1Co 3:9). God's heritage (Joel 3:2; 1Pe 5:3). Habitation of God (Eph 2:22). Heavenly Jerusalem (Gal 4:26; Heb 12:22). Holy City (Rev 21:2).

Holy Mountain—

Zec 8:3 This is what the LORD says: "I will return to Zion and dwell in Jerusalem. Then Jerusalem will be called the City of Truth, and the mountain of the LORD Almighty will be called the Holy Mountain."

Holy hill—

Ps 2:6 "I have installed my King on Zion, my holy hill." (+Ps 15:1)

House—

Heb 3:6 But Christ is faithful as a son over God's house. And we are his house, if we hold on to our courage and the hope of which we boast.

House of God (1Ti 3:15; Heb 10:21). House of Christ (Heb 3:6). Household of God (Eph 2:19). Inheritance (Ps 28:9; Isa 19:25). Israel of God (Gal 6:16).

Joy of the whole earth—

Ps 48:1 Great is the LORD, and most worthy of praise, in the city of our God, his holy mountain. ²It is beautiful in its loftiness, the joy of the whole earth. Like the utmost heights of Zaphon is Mount Zion, the city of the Great King.

Ps 48:11 Mount Zion rejoices, the villages of Judah are glad because of your judgments.

¹²Walk about Zion, go around her, count her towers, ¹³consider well her ramparts, view her citadels, that you may tell of them to the next generation.

Kingdom of God (Mt 6:33; 12:28; 19:24; 21:31). Kingdom of heaven (Mt 3:2; 4:17; 5:3,10,19-20; 10:7). His kingdom (Ps 103:19; 145:12; Mt 16:28; Lk 1:33). My kingdom (Jn 18:36). Your kingdom (Ps 45:6; 145:11,13; Mt 6:10; Lk 23:42). Lamb's bride (Eph 5:22-32; Rev 22:17). Lamb's wife (Rev 19:7-9; 21:9).

The Lord's portion—

Dt 32:9 For the LORD's portion is his people, Jacob his allotted inheritance.

Lot of God's inheritance (Dt 32:9). Mount Zion (Heb 12:22). Mountain of the Lord's house (Isa 2:2).

New Jerusalem—

Rev 21:2 I saw the Holy City, the new Jerusalem, coming down out of heaven from God, prepared as a bride beautifully dressed for her husband.

Pillar and ground of the truth (1Ti 3:15).

Place of God's throne—

Eze 43:7 He said: "Son of man, this is the place of my throne and the place for the soles of my feet. This is where I will live among the Israelites forever. The house of Israel will never again defile my holy name—neither they nor their kings—by their prostitution and the lifeless idols of their kings at their high places.

Pleasant portion (Jer 12:10).

River of gladness—

Ps 46:4 There is a river whose streams make glad the city of God, the holy place where the Most High dwells. ⁵God is within her, she will not fall; God will help her at break of day.

Sanctuary of God—

Ps 114:2 Judah became God's sanctuary, Israel his dominion.

Sought out, a city not forsaken (Isa 62:12).

Spiritual house—

1Pe 2:5 you also, like living stones, are being built into a spiritual house to be a holy priesthood, offering spiritual sacrifices acceptable to God through Jesus Christ.

Spouse of Christ (SS 4:12; 5:1); Strength and Glory of God (Ps 78:61). Temple of God (1Co 3:16-17). Temple of the Living God (2Co 6:16). Vineyard (Jer 12:10; Mt 21:41).

Discipline in the Mosaic institution:

Ge 17:14 Any uncircumcised male, who has not been circumcised in the flesh, will be cut off from his people; he has broken my covenant."

Ex 12:15 For seven days you are to eat bread made without yeast. On the first day remove the yeast from your houses, for whoever eats anything with yeast in it from the first day through the seventh must be cut off from Israel.

Ex 30:33 Whoever makes perfume like it and whoever puts it on anyone other than a priest must be cut off from his people.'"

Ex 30:37 Do not make any incense with this formula for yourselves; consider it holy to the LORD. [38]Whoever makes any like it to enjoy its fragrance must be cut off from his people."

Lev 7:27 If anyone eats blood, that person must be cut off from his people.'"

Lev 17:8 "Say to them: 'Any Israelite or any alien living among them who offers a burnt offering or sacrifice [9]and does not bring it to the entrance to the Tent of Meeting to sacrifice it to the LORD—that man must be cut off from his people.

Lev 19:5 "'When you sacrifice a fellowship offering to the LORD, sacrifice it in such a way that it will be accepted on your behalf. [6]It shall be eaten on the day you sacrifice it or on the next day; anything left over until the third day must be burned up. [7]If any of it is eaten on the third day, it is impure and will not be accepted. [8]Whoever eats it will be held responsible because he has desecrated what is holy to the LORD; that person must be cut off from his people.

Lev 20:18 "'If a man lies with a woman during her monthly period and has sexual relations with her, he has exposed the source of her flow, and she has also uncovered it. Both of them must be cut off from their people.

Lev 22:3 "Say to them: 'For the generations to come, if any of your descendants is ceremonially unclean and yet comes near the sacred offerings that the Israelites consecrate to the LORD, that person must be cut off from my presence. I am the LORD.

Nu 9:13 But if a man who is ceremonially clean and not on a journey fails to celebrate the Passover, that person must be cut off from his people because he did not present the LORD's offering at the appointed time. That man will bear the consequences of his sin.

Nu 15:31 Because he has despised the LORD's word and broken his commands, that person must surely be cut off; his guilt remains on him.'"

Nu 19:13 Whoever touches the dead body of anyone and fails to purify himself defiles the LORD's tabernacle. That person must be cut off from Israel. Because the water of cleansing has not been sprinkled on him, he is unclean; his uncleanness remains on him.

Nu 19:20 But if a person who is unclean does not purify himself, he must be cut off from the community, because he has defiled the sanctuary of the LORD. The water of cleansing has not been sprinkled on him, and he is unclean.

Dt 13:12 If you hear it said about one of the towns the LORD your God is giving you to live in [13]that wicked men have arisen among you and have led the people of their town astray, saying, "Let us go and worship other gods" (gods you have not known), [14]then you must inquire, probe and investigate it thoroughly. And if it is true and it has been proved that this detestable thing has been done among you, [15]you must certainly put to the sword all who live in that town. Destroy it completely, both its people and its livestock. [16]Gather all the plunder of the town into the middle of the public square and completely burn the town and all its plunder as a whole burnt offering to the LORD your God. It is to remain a ruin forever, never to be rebuilt. [17]None of those condemned things shall be found in your hands, so that the LORD will turn from his fierce anger; he will show you mercy, have compassion on you, and increase your numbers, as he promised on oath to your forefathers, [18]because you obey the LORD your God, keeping all his commands that I am giving you today and doing what is right in his eyes. (+Dt 17:2-7)

Dt 17:8 If cases come before your courts that are too difficult for you to judge—whether bloodshed, lawsuits or assaults—take them to the place the LORD your God will choose. [9]Go to the priests, who are Levites, and to the judge who is in office at that time. Inquire of them and they will give you the verdict. [10]You must act according to the decisions they give you at the place the LORD will choose. Be careful to do everything they direct you to do. [11]Act according to the law they teach you and the decisions they give you. Do not turn aside from what they tell you, to the right or to the left. [12]The man who shows contempt for the judge or for the priest who stands ministering there to the LORD your God must be put to death. You must purge the evil from Israel. [13]All the people will hear and be afraid, and will not be contemptuous again.

Dt 19:16 If a malicious witness takes the stand to accuse a man of a crime, [17]the two men involved in the dispute must stand in the presence of the LORD before the priests and the judges who are in office at the time. [18]The judges must make a thorough investigation, and if the witness proves to be a liar, giving false testimony against his brother, [19]then do to him as he intended to do to his brother. You must purge the evil from among you. [20]The rest of the people will hear of this and be afraid, and never again will such an evil thing be done among you. [21]Show no pity: life for life, eye for eye, tooth for tooth, hand for hand, foot for foot.

Dt 21:1 If a man is found slain, lying in a field in the land the LORD your God is giving you to possess, and it is not known who killed him, [2]your elders and judges shall go out and measure the distance from the body to the neighboring towns. [3]Then the elders of the town nearest the body shall take a heifer that has never been worked and has never worn a yoke [4]and lead her down to a valley that has not been plowed or planted and where there is a flowing stream. There in the valley they are to break the heifer's neck. [5]The priests, the sons of Levi, shall step forward, for the LORD your God has chosen them to minister and to pronounce blessings in the name of the LORD and to decide all cases of dispute and assault. [6]Then all the elders of the town nearest the body shall wash their hands over the heifer whose neck was broken in the valley, [7]and they shall declare: "Our hands did not shed this blood, nor did our eyes see it done. [8]Accept this atonement for your people Israel, whom you have redeemed, O LORD, and do not hold your people guilty of the blood of an innocent man." And the bloodshed will be atoned for. [9]So you will purge from yourselves the guilt of shedding innocent blood, since you have done what is right in the eyes of the LORD.

Dt 21:18 If a man has a stubborn and rebellious son who does not obey his father and mother and will not listen to them when they discipline him, [19]his father and mother shall take hold of him and bring him to the elders at the gate of his town. [20]They shall say to the elders, "This son of ours is stubborn and rebellious. He will not obey us. He is a profligate and a drunkard." [21]Then all the men of his town shall stone him to death. You must purge the evil from among you. All Israel will hear of it and be afraid.

Dt 22:13 If a man takes a wife and, after lying with her, dislikes her [14]and slanders her and gives her a bad name, saying, "I married this woman, but when I approached her, I did not find proof of her virginity," [15]then the girl's father and mother shall bring proof that she was a virgin to the town elders at the gate. [16]The girl's father will say to the elders, "I gave my daughter in marriage to this man, but he dislikes her. [17]Now he has slandered her and said, 'I did not find your daughter to be a virgin.' But here is the proof of my daughter's virginity." Then her parents shall display the cloth before the elders of the town, [18]and the elders shall take the man and punish him. [19]They shall fine him a hundred shekels of silver and give them to the girl's father, because this man has given an Israelite virgin a bad name. She shall continue to be his wife; he must not divorce her as long as he lives.

[20]If, however, the charge is true and no proof of the girl's virginity can be found, [21]she shall be brought to the door of her father's house and there the men of her town shall stone her to death. She has done a disgraceful thing in Israel by being promiscuous while still in her father's house. You must purge the evil from among you.

[22]If a man is found sleeping with another man's wife, both the man who slept with her and the woman must die. You must purge the evil from Israel.

[23]If a man happens to meet in a town a virgin pledged to be married and he sleeps with her, [24]you shall take both of them to the gate of that town and stone them to death—the girl because she was in a town and did not scream for help, and the man because he violated another man's wife. You must purge the evil from among you.

[25]But if out in the country a man happens to meet a girl pledged to be married and rapes her, only the man who has done this shall die. [26]Do nothing to the girl; she has committed no sin deserving death. This case is like that of someone who attacks and murders his neighbor, [27]for the man found the girl out in the country, and though the betrothed girl screamed, there was no one to rescue her.

[28]If a man happens to meet a virgin who is not pledged to be married and rapes her and they are discovered, [29]he shall pay the girl's father fifty shekels of silver. He must marry the girl, for he has violated her. He can never divorce her as long as he lives.

Ezr 10:7 A proclamation was then issued throughout Judah and Jerusalem for all the exiles to assemble in Jerusalem. [8]Anyone who failed to appear within three days would forfeit all his property, in accordance with the decision of the officials and elders, and would himself be expelled from the assembly of the exiles.

Evil Conditions of:

Backslidden—

Rev 2:1 "To the angel of the church in Ephesus write: These are the words of him who holds the seven stars in his right hand and walks among the seven golden lampstands:

[2]I know your deeds, your hard work and your per-

severance. I know that you cannot tolerate wicked men, that you have tested those who claim to be apostles but are not, and have found them false. [3]You have persevered and have endured hardships for my name, and have not grown weary.

[4]Yet I hold this against you: You have forsaken your first love. [5]Remember the height from which you have fallen! Repent and do the things you did at first. If you do not repent, I will come to you and remove your lampstand from its place.

Rev 2:12 "To the angel of the church in Pergamum write: These are the words of him who has the sharp, double-edged sword.

[13]I know where you live—where Satan has his throne. Yet you remain true to my name. You did not renounce your faith in me, even in the days of Antipas, my faithful witness, who was put to death in your city—where Satan lives.

[14]Nevertheless, I have a few things against you: You have people there who hold to the teaching of Balaam, who taught Balak to entice the Israelites to sin by eating food sacrificed to idols and by committing sexual immorality. [15]Likewise you also have those who hold to the teaching of the Nicolaitans. [16]Repent therefore! Otherwise, I will soon come to you and will fight against them with the sword of my mouth. (+Rev 2:17)

Rev 2:18 "To the angel of the church in Thyatira write: These are the words of the Son of God, whose eyes are like blazing fire and whose feet are like burnished bronze.

[19]I know your deeds, your love and faith, your service and perseverance, and that you are now doing more than you did at first.

[20]Nevertheless, I have this against you: You tolerate that woman Jezebel, who calls herself a prophetess. By her teaching she misleads my servants into sexual immorality and the eating of food sacrificed to idols. [21]I have given her time to repent of her immorality, but she is unwilling. [22]So I will cast her on a bed of suffering, and I will make those who commit adultery with her suffer intensely, unless they repent of her ways. [23]I will strike her children dead. Then all the churches will know that I am he who searches hearts and minds, and I will repay each of you according to your deeds. [24]Now I say to the rest of you in Thyatira, to you who do not hold to her teaching and have not learned Satan's so-called deep secrets (I will not impose any other burden on you): [25]Only hold on to what you have until I come. (+Rev 3:1-4,14-20) *See Backsliders; Backsliding.*

Barren (Mt 21:19-20; Mk 11:13-14)—

Lk 13:6 Then he told this parable: "A man had a fig tree, planted in his vineyard, and he went to look for fruit on it, but did not find any. [7]So he said to the man who took care of the vineyard, 'For three years now I've been coming to look for fruit on this fig tree and haven't found any. Cut it down! Why should it use up the soil?'

[8]"'Sir,' the man replied, 'leave it alone for one more year, and I'll dig around it and fertilize it. [9]If it bears fruit next year, fine! If not, then cut it down.'"

Corrupt—

Isa 5:1 I will sing for the one I love a song about his vineyard: My loved one had a vineyard on a fertile hillside. (+Isa 5:2-7)

Mt 21:33 "Listen to another parable: There was a landowner who planted a vineyard. He put a wall around it, dug a winepress in it and built a watchtower. Then he rented the vineyard to some farmers and went away on a journey. ³⁴When the harvest time approached, he sent his servants to the tenants to collect his fruit.

³⁵"The tenants seized his servants; they beat one, killed another, and stoned a third. ³⁶Then he sent other servants to them, more than the first time, and the tenants treated them the same way. ³⁷Last of all, he sent his son to them. 'They will respect my son,' he said.

³⁸"But when the tenants saw the son, they said to each other, 'This is the heir. Come, let's kill him and take his inheritance.' ³⁹So they took him and threw him out of the vineyard and killed him.

⁴⁰"Therefore, when the owner of the vineyard comes, what will he do to those tenants?"

⁴¹"He will bring those wretches to a wretched end," they replied, "and he will rent the vineyard to other tenants, who will give him his share of the crop at harvest time." (+Mt 21:42-44)

Mt 21:45 When the chief priests and the Pharisees heard Jesus' parables, they knew he was talking about them. (+Mt 21:46; Mk 12:1-12; Lk 20:9-19)

Corruption in—

Hos 4:9 And it will be: Like people, like priests. I will punish both of them for their ways and repay them for their deeds.

Mic 3:1 Then I said, "Listen, you leaders of Jacob, you rulers of the house of Israel. Should you not know justice, ²you who hate good and love evil; who tear the skin from my people and the flesh from their bones; ³who eat my people's flesh, strip off their skin and break their bones in pieces; who chop them up like meat for the pan, like flesh for the pot?"

⁴Then they will cry out to the LORD, but he will not answer them. At that time he will hide his face from them because of the evil they have done.

Mic 3:9 Hear this, you leaders of the house of Jacob, you rulers of the house of Israel, who despise justice and distort all that is right;

Mic 3:11 Her leaders judge for a bribe, her priests teach for a price, and her prophets tell fortunes for money. Yet they lean upon the LORD and say, "Is not the LORD among us? No disaster will come upon us." (+Mt 21:33-41)

Mt 23:2 "The teachers of the law and the Pharisees sit in Moses' seat. ³So you must obey them and do everything they tell you. But do not do what they do, for they do not practice what they preach. ⁴They tie up heavy loads and put them on men's shoulders, but they themselves are not willing to lift a finger to move them.

⁵"Everything they do is done for men to see: They make their phylacteries wide and the tassels on their garments long; ⁶they love the place of honor at banquets and the most important seats in the synagogues; ⁷they love to be greeted in the marketplaces and to have men call them 'Rabbi.'

Mt 23:13 "Woe to you, teachers of the law and Pharisees, you hypocrites! You shut the kingdom of heaven in men's faces. You yourselves do not enter, nor will you let those enter who are trying to.

Mt 23:15 "Woe to you, teachers of the law and Pharisees, you hypocrites! You travel over land and sea to win a single convert, and when he becomes one, you make him twice as much a son of hell as you are.

¹⁶"Woe to you, blind guides! You say, 'If anyone swears by the temple, it means nothing; but if anyone swears by the gold of the temple, he is bound by his oath.' ¹⁷You blind fools! Which is greater: the gold, or the temple that makes the gold sacred? ¹⁸You also say, 'If anyone swears

by the altar, it means nothing; but if anyone swears by the gift on it, he is bound by his oath.' ¹⁹You blind men! Which is greater: the gift, or the altar that makes the gift sacred? ²⁰Therefore, he who swears by the altar swears by it and by everything on it. ²¹And he who swears by the temple swears by it and by the one who dwells in it. ²²And he who swears by heaven swears by God's throne and by the one who sits on it.

²³"Woe to you, teachers of the law and Pharisees, you hypocrites! You give a tenth of your spices—mint, dill and cummin. But you have neglected the more important matters of the law—justice, mercy and faithfulness. You should have practiced the latter, without neglecting the former. ²⁴You blind guides! You strain out a gnat but swallow a camel.

²⁵"Woe to you, teachers of the law and Pharisees, you hypocrites! You clean the outside of the cup and dish, but inside they are full of greed and self-indulgence. ²⁶Blind Pharisee! First clean the inside of the cup and dish, and then the outside also will be clean.

²⁷"Woe to you, teachers of the law and Pharisees, you hypocrites! You are like whitewashed tombs, which look beautiful on the outside but on the inside are full of dead men's bones and everything unclean. ²⁸In the same way, on the outside you appear to people as righteous but on the inside you are full of hypocrisy and wickedness.

²⁹"Woe to you, teachers of the law and Pharisees, you hypocrites! You build tombs for the prophets and decorate the graves of the righteous. ³⁰And you say, 'If we had lived in the days of our forefathers, we would not have taken part with them in shedding the blood of the prophets.' ³¹So you testify against yourselves that you are the descendants of those who murdered the prophets. ³²Fill up, then, the measure of the sin of your forefathers!

³³"You snakes! You brood of vipers! How will you escape being condemned to hell?

Mt 26:14 Then one of the Twelve—the one called Judas Iscariot—went to the chief priests ¹⁵and asked, "What are you willing to give me if I hand him over to you?" So they counted out for him thirty silver coins. ¹⁶From then on Judas watched for an opportunity to hand him over.

Mt 26:59 The chief priests and the whole Sanhedrin were looking for false evidence against Jesus so that they could put him to death. ⁶⁰But they did not find any, though many false witnesses came forward.

Finally two came forward ⁶¹and declared, "This fellow said, 'I am able to destroy the temple of God and rebuild it in three days.'"

⁶²Then the high priest stood up and said to Jesus, "Are you not going to answer? What is this testimony that these men are bringing against you?" ⁶³But Jesus remained silent. The high priest said to him, "I charge you under oath by the living God: Tell us if you are the Christ, the Son of God."

⁶⁴"Yes, it is as you say," Jesus replied. "But I say to all of you: In the future you will see the Son of Man sitting at the right hand of the Mighty One and coming on the clouds of heaven."

⁶⁵Then the high priest tore his clothes and said, "He has spoken blasphemy! Why do we need any more witnesses? Look, now you have heard the blasphemy! ⁶⁶What do you think?" "He is worthy of death," they answered.

⁶⁷Then they spit in his face and struck him with their fists. Others slapped him ⁶⁸and said, "Prophesy to us, Christ. Who hit you?" (+Mk 12:1-12; 14:10-11; Lk 22:3-6)

Dissensions in (1Co 1:11-13; 3:3-4; 11:18-19; 2Co 12:20-21). Divisions in, to be shunned (Ro 16:17; 1Co 1:10; 3:3). Persecution of (Ac 8:1-3; 1Co 15:9; 1Th 2:14-15). *See Persecution.*

God's Care for:

Clothed in righteousness (Rev 19:8). Defended by God (Ps 89:18; Isa 4:5; 49:25; Mt 16:18). Edified by the Word (Ro 12:6; 1Co 14:4,13; Eph 4:15-16; Col 3:16). Is glorious (Ps 45:13; Eph 5:27). Growth of continuous (Ac 2:47; 5:14; 11:24).

Harmonious fellowship—

Ps 133:1 How good and pleasant it is when brothers live together in unity! ²It is like precious oil poured on the head, running down on the beard, running down on Aaron's beard, down upon the collar of his robes. ³It is as if the dew of Hermon were falling on Mount Zion. For there the LORD bestows his blessing, even life forevermore. (+Jn 13:34; Ac 4:32; Php 1:4; 2:1; 1Jn 3:4)

Indwelt by God—

Ps 132:14 "This is my resting place for ever and ever; here I will sit enthroned, for I have desired it—

Loved. *See below, Loved.* Not to be Despised (1Co 11:22).

Privileges of (Ps 36:8)—

Ps 87:5 Indeed, of Zion it will be said, "This one and that one were born in her, and the Most High himself will establish her."

Provides leaders (Jer 3:15)—

Eph 4:11 It was he who gave some to be apostles, some to be prophets, some to be evangelists, and some to be pastors and teachers, ¹²to prepare God's people for works of service, so that the body of Christ may be built up

Punishment for defiling (1Co 3:17). Safe under God's care (Ps 46:1-2,5).

Triumphant (Gal 4:26; Heb 12:22-23)—

Rev 3:12 Him who overcomes I will make a pillar in the temple of my God. Never again will he leave it. I will write on him the name of my God and the name of the city of my God, the new Jerusalem, which is coming down out of heaven from my God; and I will also write on him my new name.

Rev 21:3 And I heard a loud voice from the throne saying, "Now the dwelling of God is with men, and he will live with them. They will be his people, and God himself will be with them and be their God.

Rev 21:10 And he carried me away in the Spirit to a mountain great and high, and showed me the Holy City, Jerusalem, coming down out of heaven from God.

Government:

Of the Mosaic institution (Dt 17:8-13).

Loved:

By God—

Isa 27:2 In that day—"Sing about a fruitful vineyard: ³I, the LORD, watch over it; I water it continually. I guard it day and night so that no one may harm it.

Isa 43:1 But now, this is what the LORD says—he who created you, O Jacob, he who formed you, O Israel: "Fear not, for I have redeemed you; I have summoned you by name; you are mine. ²When you pass through the waters, I will be with you; and when you pass through the rivers, they will not sweep over you. When you walk through the fire, you will not be burned; the flames will not set you ablaze. ³For I am the LORD, your God, the Holy One of Israel, your Savior; I give Egypt for your ransom, Cush and Seba in your stead. ⁴Since you are precious and

honored in my sight, and because I love you, I will give men in exchange for you, and people in exchange for your life. ⁵Do not be afraid, for I am with you; I will bring your children from the east and gather you from the west. ⁶I will say to the north, 'Give them up!' and to the south, 'Do not hold them back.' Bring my sons from afar and my daughters from the ends of the earth— ⁷everyone who is called by my name, whom I created for my glory, whom I formed and made."

Isa 49:14 But Zion said, "The LORD has forsaken me, the Lord has forgotten me."

¹⁵"Can a mother forget the baby at her breast and have no compassion on the child she has borne? Though she may forget, I will not forget you! ¹⁶See, I have engraved you on the palms of my hands; your walls are ever before me. ¹⁷Your sons hasten back, and those who laid you waste depart from you.

Jer 3:14 "Return, faithless people," declares the LORD, "for I am your husband. I will choose you—one from a town and two from a clan—and bring you to Zion. ¹⁵Then I will give you shepherds after my own heart, who will lead you with knowledge and understanding.

Jer 13:11 For as a belt is bound around a man's waist, so I bound the whole house of Israel and the whole house of Judah to me,' declares the LORD, 'to be my people for my renown and praise and honor. But they have not listened.'

By Christ (Jn 10:8,11,14; Eph 5:25-32; Rev 3:9).

By believers—

Ps 84:1 How lovely is your dwelling place, O LORD Almighty! ²My soul yearns, even faints, for the courts of the LORD; my heart and my flesh cry out for the living God. (+Ps 87:7)

Ps 102:14 For her stones are dear to your servants; her very dust moves them to pity.

Ps 137:5 If I forget you, O Jerusalem, may my right hand forget [its skill]. (+1Co 12:25; 1Th 4:9)

Manifested, by prayer for—

Ps 122:6 Pray for the peace of Jerusalem: "May those who love you be secure. (+Isa 62:6)

Manifested, by distress at misfortunes of—

Ps 137:1 By the rivers of Babylon we sat and wept when we remembered Zion. ²There on the poplars we hung our harps, ³for there our captors asked us for songs, our tormentors demanded songs of joy; they said, "Sing us one of the songs of Zion!" ⁴How can we sing the songs of the LORD while in a foreign land? ⁵If I forget you, O Jerusalem, may my right hand forget [its skill]. ⁶May my tongue cling to the roof of my mouth if I do not remember you, if I do not consider Jerusalem my highest joy.

Isa 22:4 Therefore I said, "Turn away from me; let me weep bitterly. Do not try to console me over the destruction of my people." (+Jer 9:1)

Jer 14:17 "Speak this word to them: "'Let my eyes overflow with tears night and day without ceasing; for my virgin daughter—my people—has suffered a grievous wound, a crushing blow.

Jer 51:50 You who have escaped the sword, leave and do not linger! Remember the LORD in a distant land, and think on Jerusalem."

⁵¹"We are disgraced, for we have been insulted and shame covers our faces, because foreigners have entered the holy places of the LORD's house."

La 2:11 My eyes fail from weeping, I am in torment within, my heart is poured out on the ground because my people are destroyed, because children and infants faint in the streets of the city.

La 3:48 Streams of tears flow from my eyes because my people are destroyed.

[49]My eyes will flow unceasingly, without relief, [50]until the LORD looks down from heaven and sees. [51]What I see brings grief to my soul because of all the women of my city.

Manifested, by joy at prosperity of—

Isa 66:10 "Rejoice with Jerusalem and be glad for her, all you who love her; rejoice greatly with her, all you who mourn over her.

Isa 66:13 As a mother comforts her child, so will I comfort you; and you will be comforted over Jerusalem."

[14]When you see this, your heart will rejoice and you will flourish like grass; the hand of the LORD will be made known to his servants, but his fury will be shown to his foes.

Manifested, by zeal for—

Isa 58:12 Your people will rebuild the ancient ruins and will raise up the age-old foundations; you will be called Repairer of Broken Walls, Restorer of Streets with Dwellings.

Isa 62:1 For Zion's sake I will not keep silent, for Jerusalem's sake I will not remain quiet, till her righteousness shines out like the dawn, her salvation like a blazing torch.

Isa 62:6 I have posted watchmen on your walls, O Jerusalem; they will never be silent day or night. You who call on the LORD, give yourselves no rest, [7]and give him no rest till he establishes Jerusalem and makes her the praise of the earth.

New Testament Church:

List of NT Churches—

Antioch (Ac 13:1). Asia (1Co 16:19; Rev 1:4). Babylon (1Pe 5:13). Cenchrea (Ro 16:1). Caesarea (Ac 18:22). Cilicia (Ac 15:41). Corinth (1Co 1:2). Ephesus (Eph 1:22; Rev 2:1). Galatia (Gal 1:2). Galilee (Ac 9:31). Jerusalem (Ac 15:4). Joppa (Ac 9:42). Judea (Ac 9:31). Laodicea (Rev 3:14). Pergamum (Rev 2:12). Philadelphia (Rev 3:7). Samaria (Ac 9:31). Sardis (Rev 3:1). Smyrna (Rev 2:8). Syria (Ac 15:41). Thessalonica (1Th 1:1). Thyatira (Rev 2:18).

Beneficence of. *See Beneficence; Giving; Liberality.*

Christ, the head of (Ps 118:22-23)—

Isa 28:16 So this is what the Sovereign LORD says: "See, I lay a stone in Zion, a tested stone, a precious cornerstone for a sure foundation; the one who trusts will never be dismayed.

Isa 33:22 For the LORD is our judge, the LORD is our lawgiver, the LORD is our king; it is he who will save us.

Isa 55:4 See, I have made him a witness to the peoples, a leader and commander of the peoples.

Mt 12:6 I tell you that one greater than the temple is here.

Mt 12:8 For the Son of Man is Lord of the Sabbath." (+Mt 21:42,43)

Mt 23:8 "But you are not to be called 'Rabbi,' for you have only one Master and you are all brothers.

Mt 23:10 Nor are you to be called 'teacher,' for you have one Teacher, the Christ. (+Mk 2:28; 12:10; Lk 6:5; 20:17-18)

Jn 13:13 "You call me 'Teacher' and 'Lord,' and rightly so, for that is what I am.

Jn 15:1 "I am the true vine, and my Father is the gardener. [2]He cuts off every branch in me that bears no fruit, while every branch that does bear fruit he prunes so that it will be even more fruitful. [3]You are already clean because of the word I have spoken to you. [4]Remain in me, and I will

remain in you. No branch can bear fruit by itself; it must remain in the vine. Neither can you bear fruit unless you remain in me.

[5]"I am the vine; you are the branches. If a man remains in me and I in him, he will bear much fruit; apart from me you can do nothing. [6]If anyone does not remain in me, he is like a branch that is thrown away and withers; such branches are picked up, thrown into the fire and burned. [7]If you remain in me and my words remain in you, ask whatever you wish, and it will be given you. [8]This is to my Father's glory, that you bear much fruit, showing yourselves to be my disciples.

Ac 2:36 "Therefore let all Israel be assured of this: God has made this Jesus, whom you crucified, both Lord and Christ."

Ro 8:29 For those God foreknew he also predestined to be conformed to the likeness of his Son, that he might be the firstborn among many brothers.

Ro 9:5 Theirs are the patriarchs, and from them is traced the human ancestry of Christ, who is God over all, forever praised! Amen.

1Co 3:11 For no one can lay any foundation other than the one already laid, which is Jesus Christ.

1Co 11:3 Now I want you to realize that the head of every man is Christ, and the head of the woman is man, and the head of Christ is God.

1Co 12:5 There are different kinds of service, but the same Lord.

Eph 1:10 to be put into effect when the times will have reached their fulfillment—to bring all things in heaven and on earth together under one head, even Christ.

Eph 1:22 And God placed all things under his feet and appointed him to be head over everything for the church, [23]which is his body, the fullness of him who fills everything in every way.

Eph 2:20 built on the foundation of the apostles and prophets, with Christ Jesus himself as the chief cornerstone. [21]In him the whole building is joined together and rises to become a holy temple in the Lord. [22]And in him you too are being built together to become a dwelling in which God lives by his Spirit.

Eph 4:15 Instead, speaking the truth in love, we will in all things grow up into him who is the Head, that is, Christ.

Eph 5:23 For the husband is the head of the wife as Christ is the head of the church, his body, of which he is the Savior. [24]Now as the church submits to Christ, so also wives should submit to their husbands in everything.

[25]Husbands, love your wives, just as Christ loved the church and gave himself up for her [26]to make her holy, cleansing her by the washing with water through the word, [27]and to present her to himself as a radiant church, without stain or wrinkle or any other blemish, but holy and blameless. (+Eph 5:28)

Eph 5:29 After all, no one ever hated his own body, but he feeds and cares for it, just as Christ does the church— (+Eph 5:30-32)

Col 1:13 For he has rescued us from the dominion of darkness and brought us into the kingdom of the Son he loves,

Col 1:18 And he is the head of the body, the church; he is the beginning and the firstborn from among the dead, so that in everything he might have the supremacy.

Col 2:10 and you have been given fullness in Christ, who is the head over every power and authority.

Col 2:19 He has lost connection with the Head, from

whom the whole body, supported and held together by its ligaments and sinews, grows as God causes it to grow.

Col 3:11 Here there is no Greek or Jew, circumcised or uncircumcised, barbarian, Scythian, slave or free, but Christ is all, and is in all.

Heb 3:3 Jesus has been found worthy of greater honor than Moses, just as the builder of a house has greater honor than the house itself.

Heb 3:6 But Christ is faithful as a son over God's house. And we are his house, if we hold on to our courage and the hope of which we boast. (+1Pe 2:7)

Rev 1:13 and among the lampstands was someone "like a son of man," dressed in a robe reaching down to his feet and with a golden sash around his chest.

Rev 2:1 "To the angel of the church in Ephesus write: These are the words of him who holds the seven stars in his right hand and walks among the seven golden lampstands: (+Rev 2,5)

Rev 2:6 But you have this in your favor: You hate the practices of the Nicolaitans, which I also hate. (+Rev 2:7-8)

Rev 2:9 I know your afflictions and your poverty—yet you are rich! I know the slander of those who say they are Jews and are not, but are a synagogue of Satan. (+Rev 2:10-11)

Rev 2:12 "To the angel of the church in Pergamum write: These are the words of him who has the sharp, double-edged sword.

¹³I know where you live—where Satan has his throne. Yet you remain true to my name. You did not renounce your faith in me, even in the days of Antipas, my faithful witness, who was put to death in your city—where Satan lives. (+Rev 2:14-17)

Rev 2:18 "To the angel of the church in Thyatira write: These are the words of the Son of God, whose eyes are like blazing fire and whose feet are like burnished bronze.

¹⁹I know your deeds, your love and faith, your service and perseverance, and that you are now doing more than you did at first. (+Rev 2:20-28)

Rev 3:1 "To the angel of the church in Sardis write: These are the words of him who holds the seven spirits of God and the seven stars. I know your deeds; you have a reputation of being alive, but you are dead.

Rev 3:7 "To the angel of the church in Philadelphia write: These are the words of him who is holy and true, who holds the key of David. What he opens no one can shut, and what he shuts no one can open.

Rev 5:6 Then I saw a Lamb, looking as if it had been slain, standing in the center of the throne, encircled by the four living creatures and the elders. He had seven horns and seven eyes, which are the seven spirits of God sent out into all the earth.

Rev 21:22 I did not see a temple in the city, because the Lord God Almighty and the Lamb are its temple. ²³The city does not need the sun or the moon to shine on it, for the glory of God gives it light, and the Lamb is its lamp.

Rev 22:16 "I, Jesus, have sent my angel to give you this testimony for the churches. I am the Root and the Off-spring of David, and the bright Morning Star." *See Jesus, Kingdom of.* Community in (Ac 4:32).

Decrees of—

Ac 15:28 It seemed good to the Holy Spirit and to us not to burden you with anything beyond the following require-ments: ²⁹You are to abstain from food sacrificed to idols, from blood, from the meat of strangled animals and from

sexual immorality. You will do well to avoid these things. Farewell.

Ac 16:4 As they traveled from town to town, they delivered the decisions reached by the apostles and elders in Jerusalem for the people to obey.

Design of—

Ro 3:2 Much in every way! First of all, they have been entrusted with the very words of God.

Ro 9:4 the people of Israel. Theirs is the adoption as sons; theirs the divine glory, the covenants, the receiving of the law, the temple worship and the promises. (+Eph 2:20-22)

1Ti 3:15 if I am delayed, you will know how people ought to conduct themselves in God's household, which is the church of the living God, the pillar and foundation of the truth.

Discipline. *See below, Discipline.*

Diversity of callings in—

1Co 12:5 There are different kinds of service, but the same Lord.

1Co 12:28 And in the church God has appointed first of all apostles, second prophets, third teachers, then workers of miracles, also those having gifts of healing, those able to help others, those with gifts of administration, and those speaking in different kinds of tongues. (+Eph 4:11-12)

Divinely established or instituted—

Mt 16:15 "But what about you?" he asked. "Who do you say I am?"

¹⁶Simon Peter answered, "You are the Christ, the Son of the living God."

¹⁷Jesus replied, "Blessed are you, Simon son of Jonah, for this was not revealed to you by man, but by my Father in heaven. ¹⁸And I tell you that you are Peter, and on this rock I will build my church, and the gates of Hades will not overcome it.

Eph 2:20 built on the foundation of the apostles and prophets, with Christ Jesus himself as the chief corner-stone. ²¹In him the whole building is joined together and rises to become a holy temple in the Lord. ²²And in him you too are being built together to become a dwelling in which God lives by his Spirit.

1Th 1:1 Paul, Silas and Timothy, To the church of the Thessalonians in God the Father and the Lord Jesus Christ: Grace and peace to you.

2Th 1:1 Paul, Silas and Timothy, To the church of the Thessalonians in God our Father and the Lord Jesus Christ:

1Ti 3:15 if I am delayed, you will know how people ought to conduct themselves in God's household, which is the church of the living God, the pillar and foundation of the truth.

Founded on the lordship of Christ (Mt 16:18). Duty. *See Responsibilities below.* Edification, by teachers (Eph 4:11-12). By public worship (Col 3:16; Heb 10:25). Govern-ment. *See below, Government.* Growth of, rapid (Ac 2:41, 47; 4:4; 5:14; 6:7; 9:35; 11:21,24; 14:1; 19:17-20).

Growth of, cut back (Isa 2:2)—

Eze 17:22 "'This is what the Sovereign LORD says: I myself will take a shoot from the very top of a cedar and plant it; I will break off a tender sprig from its topmost shoots and plant it on a high and lofty mountain. ²³On the mountain heights of Israel I will plant it; it will produce branches and bear fruit and become a splendid cedar. Birds of every kind will nest in it; they will find shelter in the shade of its branches. ²⁴All the trees of the field will know that I the LORD bring down the tall tree and make the low tree grow tall. I dry up the green tree and make the dry tree flourish.

"'I the LORD have spoken, and I will do it.'" (+Da 4:35)

Holiness of (2Co 11:2; Eph 5:27; 2Pe 3:14; Rev 19:8). Loved. *See above, Loved.*

Membership in—

Mt 12:50 For whoever does the will of my Father in heaven is my brother and sister and mother." (+Mt 19:14; Mk 10:14)

Lk 18:16 But Jesus called the children to him and said, "Let the little children come to me, and do not hinder them, for the kingdom of God belongs to such as these.

Jn 15:5 "I am the vine; you are the branches. If a man remains in me and I in him, he will bear much fruit; apart from me you can do nothing. ⁶If anyone does not remain in me, he is like a branch that is thrown away and withers; such branches are picked up, thrown into the fire and burned.

Ac 2:41 Those who accepted his message were baptized, and about three thousand were added to their number that day.

Ac 2:47 praising God and enjoying the favor of all the people. And the Lord added to their number daily those who were being saved.

Ac 4:4 But many who heard the message believed, and the number of men grew to about five thousand.

Ac 5:14 Nevertheless, more and more men and women believed in the Lord and were added to their number.

Ac 9:35 All those who lived in Lydda and Sharon saw him and turned to the Lord.

Ac 9:42 This became known all over Joppa, and many people believed in the Lord.

Ac 11:21 The Lord's hand was with them, and a great number of people believed and turned to the Lord.

Ro 12:4 Just as each of us has one body with many members, and these members do not all have the same function, ⁵so in Christ we who are many form one body, and each member belongs to all the others.

1Co 3:11 For no one can lay any foundation other than the one already laid, which is Jesus Christ. ¹²If any man builds on this foundation using gold, silver, costly stones, wood, hay or straw, ¹³his work will be shown for what it is, because the Day will bring it to light. It will be revealed with fire, and the fire will test the quality of each man's work. ¹⁴If what he has built survives, he will receive his reward. ¹⁵If it is burned up, he will suffer loss; he himself will be saved, but only as one escaping through the flames.

1Co 12:12 The body is a unit, though it is made up of many parts; and though all its parts are many, they form one body. So it is with Christ. ¹³For we were all baptized by one Spirit into one body—whether Jews or Greeks, slave or free—and we were all given the one Spirit to drink.

¹⁴Now the body is not made up of one part but of many. ¹⁵If the foot should say, "Because I am not a hand, I do not belong to the body," it would not for that reason cease to be part of the body. ¹⁶And if the ear should say, "Because I am not an eye, I do not belong to the body," it would not for that reason cease to be part of the body. ¹⁷If the whole body were an eye, where would the sense of hearing be? If the whole body were an ear, where would the sense of smell be? ¹⁸But in fact God has arranged the parts in the body, every one of them, just as he wanted them to be. ¹⁹If they were all one part, where would the body be? ²⁰As it is, there are many parts, but one body.

²¹The eye cannot say to the hand, "I don't need you!"

And the head cannot say to the feet, "I don't need you!" ²²On the contrary, those parts of the body that seem to be weaker are indispensable, ²³and the parts that we think are less honorable we treat with special honor. And the parts that are unpresentable are treated with special modesty, ²⁴while our presentable parts need no special treatment. But God has combined the members of the body and has given greater honor to the parts that lacked it, ²⁵so that there should be no division in the body, but that its parts should have equal concern for each other. ²⁶If one part suffers, every part suffers with it; if one part is honored, every part rejoices with it.

²⁷Now you are the body of Christ, and each one of you is a part of it. ²⁸And in the church God has appointed first of all apostles, second prophets, third teachers, then workers of miracles, also those having gifts of healing, those able to help others, those with gifts of administration, and those speaking in different kinds of tongues.

Eph 4:25 Therefore each of you must put off falsehood and speak truthfully to his neighbor, for we are all members of one body.

Eph 5:30 for we are members of his body.

Php 4:3 Yes, and I ask you, loyal yokefellow, help these women who have contended at my side in the cause of the gospel, along with Clement and the rest of my fellow workers, whose names are in the book of life.

Rev 21:27 Nothing impure will ever enter it, nor will anyone who does what is shameful or deceitful, but only those whose names are written in the Lamb's book of life.

Militancy of (SS 6:10; Php 2:25; 2Ti 2:3; 4:7; Phm 2). Mission of. *See below, Mission.* Pastoral care of (Ac 20:28). Responsibilities. *See below, Responsibilities.*

Unity of (Ps 133:1)—

Jn 10:16 I have other sheep that are not of this sheep pen. I must bring them also. They too will listen to my voice, and there shall be one flock and one shepherd.

Jn 17:11 I will remain in the world no longer, but they are still in the world, and I am coming to you. Holy Father, protect them by the power of your name—the name you gave me—so that they may be one as we are one.

Jn 17:21 that all of them may be one, Father, just as you are in me and I am in you. May they also be in us so that the world may believe that you have sent me. ²²I have given them the glory that you gave me, that they may be one as we are one: ²³I in them and you in me. May they be brought to complete unity to let the world know that you sent me and have loved them even as you have loved me.

Ro 12:4 Just as each of us has one body with many members, and these members do not all have the same function, ⁵so in Christ we who are many form one body, and each member belongs to all the others.

1Co 10:17 Because there is one loaf, we, who are many, are one body, for we all partake of the one loaf.

1Co 12:5 There are different kinds of service, but the same Lord.

1Co 12:12 The body is a unit, though it is made up of many parts; and though all its parts are many, they form one body. So it is with Christ. ¹³For we were all baptized by one Spirit into one body—whether Jews or Greeks, slave or free—and we were all given the one Spirit to drink. (+1Co 12:14-24)

1Co 12:25 so that there should be no division in the body, but that its parts should have equal concern for each other. ²⁶If one part suffers, every part suffers with it; if one part is honored, every part rejoices with it. (+1Co 12:27)

Gal 3:26 You are all sons of God through faith in Christ

Jesus, ²⁷for all of you who were baptized into Christ have clothed yourselves with Christ. ²⁸There is neither Jew nor Greek, slave nor free, male nor female, for you are all one in Christ Jesus.

Eph 1:10 to be put into effect when the times will have reached their fulfillment—to bring all things in heaven and on earth together under one head, even Christ.

Eph 2:14 For he himself is our peace, who has made the two one and has destroyed the barrier, the dividing wall of hostility, ¹⁵by abolishing in his flesh the law with its commandments and regulations. His purpose was to create in himself one new man out of the two, thus making peace, ¹⁶and in this one body to reconcile both of them to God through the cross, by which he put to death their hostility. ¹⁷He came and preached peace to you who were far away and peace to those who were near. ¹⁸For through him we both have access to the Father by one Spirit.

¹⁹Consequently, you are no longer foreigners and aliens, but fellow citizens with God's people and members of God's household, (+Eph 2:20)

Eph 2:21 In him the whole building is joined together and rises to become a holy temple in the Lord.

Eph 3:6 This mystery is that through the gospel the Gentiles are heirs together with Israel, members together of one body, and sharers together in the promise in Christ Jesus.

Eph 3:15 from whom his whole family in heaven and on earth derives its name.

Eph 4:4 There is one body and one Spirit—just as you were called to one hope when you were called— ⁵one Lord, one faith, one baptism; ⁶one God and Father of all, who is over all and through all and in all.

Eph 4:12 to prepare God's people for works of service, so that the body of Christ may be built up ¹³until we all reach unity in the faith and in the knowledge of the Son of God and become mature, attaining to the whole measure of the fullness of Christ. (+Eph 4:14-15)

Eph 4:16 From him the whole body, joined and held together by every supporting ligament, grows and builds itself up in love, as each part does its work.

Eph 4:25 Therefore each of you must put off falsehood and speak truthfully to his neighbor, for we are all members of one body.

Col 3:11 Here there is no Greek or Jew, circumcised or uncircumcised, barbarian, Scythian, slave or free, but Christ is all, and is in all.

Col 3:15 Let the peace of Christ rule in your hearts, since as members of one body you were called to peace. And be thankful.

Union of, with Christ (Jn 15:1-7; Ro 11:17; 2Co 11:2; Eph 5:30,32; Rev 19:7; 21:9). Worship, to be attended (Heb 10:25).

To be conducted with order (Ecc 5:1,3; 1Co 11:4-5,33)—

1Co 14:26 What then shall we say, brothers? When you come together, everyone has a hymn, or a word of instruction, a revelation, a tongue or an interpretation. All of these must be done for the strengthening of the church.

1Co 14:33 For God is not a God of disorder but of peace. As in all the congregations of the believers,

1Co 14:40 But everything should be done in a fitting and orderly way. (+1Ti 3:15)

Discipline:

Designed to save the sinner—

Mt 18:15 "If your brother sins against you, go and show

him his fault, just between the two of you. If he listens to you, you have won your brother over.

1Co 5:1 It is actually reported that there is sexual immorality among you, and of a kind that does not occur even among pagans: A man has his father's wife. ²And you are proud! Shouldn't you rather have been filled with grief and have put out of your fellowship the man who did this? (+1Co 5:3)

1Co 5:4 When you are assembled in the name of our Lord Jesus and I am with you in spirit, and the power of our Lord Jesus is present, ⁵hand this man over to Satan, so that the sinful nature may be destroyed and his spirit saved on the day of the Lord.

⁶Your boasting is not good. Don't you know that a little yeast works through the whole batch of dough? ⁷Get rid of the old yeast that you may be a new batch without yeast— as you really are. For Christ, our Passover lamb, has been sacrificed. (+1Co 5:8-10)

1Co 5:11 But now I am writing you that you must not associate with anyone who calls himself a brother but is sexually immoral or greedy, an idolater or a slanderer, a drunkard or a swindler. With such a man do not even eat.

¹²What business is it of mine to judge those outside the church? Are you not to judge those inside? ¹³God will judge those outside. "Expel the wicked man from among you."

2Th 3:14 If anyone does not obey our instruction in this letter, take special note of him. Do not associate with him, in order that he may feel ashamed.

Designed to warn others—

1Ti 5:20 Those who sin are to be rebuked publicly, so that the others may take warning.

Designed to preserve sound doctrine—

Ro 16:17 I urge you, brothers, to watch out for those who cause divisions and put obstacles in your way that are contrary to the teaching you have learned. Keep away from them.

Gal 5:10 I am confident in the Lord that you will take no other view. The one who is throwing you into confusion will pay the penalty, whoever he may be.

1Ti 1:19 holding on to faith and a good conscience. Some have rejected these and so have shipwrecked their faith. ²⁰Among them are Hymenaeus and Alexander, whom I have handed over to Satan to be taught not to blaspheme.

Tit 1:13 This testimony is true. Therefore, rebuke them sharply, so that they will be sound in the faith

Exercised with kindness—

2Co 2:6 The punishment inflicted on him by the majority is sufficient for him. ⁷Now instead, you ought to forgive and comfort him, so that he will not be overwhelmed by excessive sorrow. ⁸I urge you, therefore, to reaffirm your love for him. (+2Co 2:9,10-11)

Gal 6:1 Brothers, if someone is caught in a sin, you who are spiritual should restore him gently. But watch yourself, or you also may be tempted.

Jude 22 Be merciful to those who doubt; ²³snatch others from the fire and save them; to others show mercy, mixed with fear—hating even the clothing stained by corrupted flesh.

Exercised with forbearance—

Ro 15:1 We who are strong ought to bear with the failings of the weak and not to please ourselves. (+Ro 15:2-3)

Reasons for discipline: Heresy (1Ti 6:3-5)—

Tit 3:10 Warn a divisive person once, and then warn him a second time. After that, have nothing to do with him.

¹¹You may be sure that such a man is warped and sinful; he is self-condemned.

2Jn 10 If anyone comes to you and does not bring this teaching, do not take him into your house or welcome him. ¹¹Anyone who welcomes him shares in his wicked work.

Reasons for discipline: Immorality—

Mt 18:17 If he refuses to listen to them, tell it to the church; and if he refuses to listen even to the church, treat him as you would a pagan or a tax collector.

¹⁸"I tell you the truth, whatever you bind on earth will be bound in heaven, and whatever you loose on earth will be loosed in heaven. (+1Co 5:1-7,11-13)

2Th 3:6 In the name of the Lord Jesus Christ, we command you, brothers, to keep away from every brother who is idle and does not live according to the teaching you received from us.

For schism (Ro 16:17).

Discipline by reproof—

2Co 7:8 Even if I caused you sorrow by my letter, I do not regret it. Though I did regret it—I see that my letter hurt you, but only for a little while— (+2Co 10:1-11)

2Co 13:2 I already gave you a warning when I was with you the second time. I now repeat it while absent: On my return I will not spare those who sinned earlier or any of the others,

2Co 13:10 This is why I write these things when I am absent, that when I come I may not have to be harsh in my use of authority—the authority the Lord gave me for building you up, not for tearing you down.

1Th 5:14 And we urge you, brothers, warn those who are idle, encourage the timid, help the weak, be patient with everyone.

2Th 3:15 Yet do not regard him as an enemy, but warn him as a brother.

1Ti 5:1 Do not rebuke an older man harshly, but exhort him as if he were your father. Treat younger men as brothers, ²older women as mothers, and younger women as sisters, with absolute purity.

2Ti 4:2 Preach the Word; be prepared in season and out of season; correct, rebuke and encourage—with great patience and careful instruction.

Tit 2:15 These, then, are the things you should teach. Encourage and rebuke with all authority. Do not let anyone despise you.

Witnesses required in —

Mt 18:16 But if he will not listen, take one or two others along, so that 'every matter may be established by the testimony of two or three witnesses.'

2Co 13:1 This will be my third visit to you. "Every matter must be established by the testimony of two or three witnesses."

1Ti 5:19 Do not entertain an accusation against an elder unless it is brought by two or three witnesses.

Government of the Christian Church:

Authority of apostles—

Mt 16:19 I will give you the keys of the kingdom of heaven; whatever you bind on earth will be bound in heaven, and whatever you loose on earth will be loosed in heaven."

Jn 20:23 If you forgive anyone his sins, they are forgiven; if you do not forgive them, they are not forgiven."

Ac 1:15 In those days Peter stood up among the believers (a group numbering about a hundred and twenty)

Ac 1:23 So they proposed two men: Joseph called Barsabbas (also known as Justus) and Matthias. ²⁴Then they prayed, "Lord, you know everyone's heart. Show us which of these two you have chosen ²⁵to take over this apostolic ministry, which Judas left to go where he belongs." ²⁶Then they cast lots, and the lot fell to Matthias; so he was added to the eleven apostles. (+Ac 5:1-11)

1Co 7:17 Nevertheless, each one should retain the place in life that the Lord assigned to him and to which God has called him. This is the rule I lay down in all the churches.

1Co 11:2 I praise you for remembering me in everything and for holding to the teachings, just as I passed them on to you.

1Co 11:33 So then, my brothers, when you come together to eat, wait for each other. ³⁴If anyone is hungry, he should eat at home, so that when you meet together it may not result in judgment. And when I come I will give further directions. (+Gal 2:9)

Authority of apostolic council—

Ac 15:1 Some men came down from Judea to Antioch and were teaching the brothers: "Unless you are circumcised, according to the custom taught by Moses, you cannot be saved." ²This brought Paul and Barnabas into sharp dispute and debate with them. So Paul and Barnabas were appointed, along with some other believers, to go up to Jerusalem to see the apostles and elders about this question. ³The church sent them on their way, and as they traveled through Phoenicia and Samaria, they told how the Gentiles had been converted. This news made all the brothers very glad. ⁴When they came to Jerusalem, they were welcomed by the church and the apostles and elders, to whom they reported everything God had done through them.

⁵Then some of the believers who belonged to the party of the Pharisees stood up and said, "The Gentiles must be circumcised and required to obey the law of Moses."

⁶The apostles and elders met to consider this question. ⁷After much discussion, Peter got up and addressed them: "Brothers, you know that some time ago God made a choice among you that the Gentiles might hear from my lips the message of the gospel and believe. ⁸God, who knows the heart, showed that he accepted them by giving the Holy Spirit to them, just as he did to us. ⁹He made no distinction between us and them, for he purified their hearts by faith. ¹⁰Now then, why do you try to test God by putting on the necks of the disciples a yoke that neither we nor our fathers have been able to bear? ¹¹No! We believe it is through the grace of our Lord Jesus that we are saved, just as they are."

¹²The whole assembly became silent as they listened to Barnabas and Paul telling about the miraculous signs and wonders God had done among the Gentiles through them. ¹³When they finished, James spoke up: "Brothers, listen to me. ¹⁴Simon has described to us how God at first showed his concern by taking from the Gentiles a people for himself. ¹⁵The words of the prophets are in agreement with this, as it is written:

¹⁶"'After this I will return and rebuild David's fallen tent. Its ruins I will rebuild, and I will restore it, ¹⁷that the remnant of men may seek the Lord, and all the Gentiles who bear my name, says the Lord, who does these things' ¹⁸that have been known for ages.

¹⁹"It is my judgment, therefore, that we should not make it difficult for the Gentiles who are turning to God. ²⁰Instead we should write to them, telling them to abstain from food polluted by idols, from sexual immorality, from the meat of strangled animals and from blood. ²¹For Moses has

been preached in every city from the earliest times and is read in the synagogues on every Sabbath."

²²Then the apostles and elders, with the whole church, decided to choose some of their own men and send them to Antioch with Paul and Barnabas. They chose Judas (called Barsabbas) and Silas, two men who were leaders among the brothers. ²³With them they sent the following letter:

The apostles and elders, your brothers,

To the Gentile believers in Antioch, Syria and Cilicia: Greetings.

²⁴We have heard that some went out from us without our authorization and disturbed you, troubling your minds by what they said. ²⁵So we all agreed to choose some men and send them to you with our dear friends Barnabas and Paul— ²⁶men who have risked their lives for the name of our Lord Jesus Christ. ²⁷Therefore we are sending Judas and Silas to confirm by word of mouth what we are writing. ²⁸It seemed good to the Holy Spirit and to us not to burden you with anything beyond the following requirements: ²⁹You are to abstain from food sacrificed to idols, from blood, from the meat of strangled animals and from sexual immorality. You will do well to avoid these things. Farewell.

³⁰The men were sent off and went down to Antioch, where they gathered the church together and delivered the letter. ³¹The people read it and were glad for its encouraging message.

Ac 16:4 As they traveled from town to town, they delivered the decisions reached by the apostles and elders in Jerusalem for the people to obey. ⁵So the churches were strengthened in the faith and grew daily in numbers.

Authority of congregation—

1Co 16:3 Then, when I arrive, I will give letters of introduction to the men you approve and send them with your gift to Jerusalem.

1Co 16:16 to submit to such as these and to everyone who joins in the work, and labors at it.

Jude 22 Be merciful to those who doubt; ²³snatch others from the fire and save them; to others show mercy, mixed with fear—hating even the clothing stained by corrupted flesh.

Leadership by apostles. *See above, Leadership by.*

Leadership by deacons—

Ac 6:2 So the Twelve gathered all the disciples together and said, "It would not be right for us to neglect the ministry of the word of God in order to wait on tables. ³Brothers, choose seven men from among you who are known to be full of the Spirit and wisdom. We will turn this responsibility over to them (+Ac 6:4)

Ac 6:5 This proposal pleased the whole group. They chose Stephen, a man full of faith and of the Holy Spirit; also Philip, Procorus, Nicanor, Timon, Parmenas, and Nicolas from Antioch, a convert to Judaism. ⁶They presented these men to the apostles, who prayed and laid their hands on them.

1Ti 3:8 Deacons, likewise, are to be men worthy of respect, sincere, not indulging in much wine, and not pursuing dishonest gain. ⁹They must keep hold of the deep truths of the faith with a clear conscience. ¹⁰They must first be tested; and then if there is nothing against them, let them serve as deacons.

¹¹In the same way, their wives are to be women worthy of respect, not malicious talkers but temperate and trustworthy in everything. ¹²A deacon must be the husband of but one wife and must manage his children and his household well. ¹³Those who have served well gain an

excellent standing and great assurance in their faith in Christ Jesus.

Leadership by elders—

Ac 14:23 Paul and Barnabas appointed elders for them in each church and, with prayer and fasting, committed them to the Lord, in whom they had put their trust.

Ac 20:17 From Miletus, Paul sent to Ephesus for the elders of the church.

Ac 20:28 Keep watch over yourselves and all the flock of which the Holy Spirit has made you overseers. Be shepherds of the church of God, which he bought with his own blood.

1Ti 5:1 Do not rebuke an older man harshly, but exhort him as if he were your father. Treat younger men as brothers,

1Ti 5:17 The elders who direct the affairs of the church well are worthy of double honor, especially those whose work is preaching and teaching.

1Ti 5:22 Do not be hasty in the laying on of hands, and do not share in the sins of others. Keep yourself pure.

Tit 1:5 The reason I left you in Crete was that you might straighten out what was left unfinished and appoint elders in every town, as I directed you.

Jas 5:14 Is any one of you sick? He should call the elders of the church to pray over him and anoint him with oil in the name of the Lord. ¹⁵And the prayer offered in faith will make the sick person well; the Lord will raise him up. If he has sinned, he will be forgiven.

1Pe 5:1 To the elders among you, I appeal as a fellow elder, a witness of Christ's sufferings and one who also will share in the glory to be revealed: ²Be shepherds of God's flock that is under your care, serving as overseers— not because you must, but because you are willing, as God wants you to be; not greedy for money, but eager to serve; ³not lording it over those entrusted to you, but being examples to the flock.

Leadership by overseers—

1Ti 3:1 Here is a trustworthy saying: If anyone sets his heart on being an overseer, he desires a noble task. ²Now the overseer must be above reproach, the husband of but one wife, temperate, self-controlled, respectable, hospitable, able to teach, (+1Ti 3:3-4)

1Ti 3:5 (If anyone does not know how to manage his own family, how can he take care of God's church?)

Leadership by prophets and teachers—

Ac 13:1 In the church at Antioch there were prophets and teachers: Barnabas, Simeon called Niger, Lucius of Cyrene, Manaen (who had been brought up with Herod the tetrarch) and Saul.

Ac 13:3 So after they had fasted and prayed, they placed their hands on them and sent them off.

Ac 13:5 When they arrived at Salamis, they proclaimed the word of God in the Jewish synagogues. John was with them as their helper.

1Ti 4:14 Do not neglect your gift, which was given you through a prophetic message when the body of elders laid their hands on you. (+2Ti 1:6)

Obedience to rulers—

Heb 13:17 Obey your leaders and submit to their authority. They keep watch over you as men who must give an account. Obey them so that their work will be a joy, not a burden, for that would be of no advantage to you.
Heb 13:24 Greet all your leaders and all God's people. Those from Italy send you their greetings.

Qualifications for Elders/Overseers and Deacons:		
Self-controlled	Elder	1Ti 3:2; Tit 1:8
Hospitable	Elder	1Ti 3:2; Tit 1:8
Able to teach	Elder	1Ti 3:2; 5:17; Tit 1:9
Not violent but gentle	Elder	1Ti 3:3; Tit 1:7
Not quarrelsome	Elder	1Ti 3:3
Not a lover of money	Elder	1Ti 3:3
Not a recent convert	Elder	1Ti 3:6
Good reputation with outsiders	Elder	1Ti 3:7
Not overbearing	Elder	Tit 1:7
Not quick-tempered	Elder	Tit 1:7
Loves what is good	Elder	Tit 1:8
Upright, holy	Elder	Tit 1:8
Disciplined	Elder	Tit 1:8
Above reproach (blameless)	Elder	1Ti 3:2; Tit 1:6
	Deacon	1Ti 3:9
Husband of one wife	Elder	1Ti 3:2; Tit 1:6
	Deacon	1Ti 3:12
Temperate	Elder	1Ti 3:2; Tit 1:7
	Deacon	1Ti 3:8
Respectable	Elder	1Ti 3:2
	Deacon	1Ti 3:8
Not given to drunkenness	Elder	1Ti 3:2; Tit 1:7
	Deacon	1Ti 3:8
Manages his own family well	Elder	1Ti 3:4
	Deacon	1Ti 3:12
Sees that his children obey him	Elder	1Ti 3:4-5; Tit 1:6
	Deacon	1Ti 3:12
Does not pursue dishonest gain	Elder	Tit 1:7
	Deacon	1Ti 3:8
Keeps hold of the deep truths	Elder	Tit 1:9
	Deacon	1Ti 3:9
Sincere	Deacon	1Ti 3:8
Tested	Deacon	1Ti 3:10

Mission of: To be entrusted with the oracles of God (Ro 3:2; 9:4).

Mission of: To bring peace—

Ps 22:27 All the ends of the earth will remember and turn to the LORD, and all the families of the nations will bow down before him, **28**for dominion belongs to the LORD and he rules over the nations.

29All the rich of the earth will feast and worship; all who go down to the dust will kneel before him—those who cannot keep themselves alive. **30**Posterity will serve him; future generations will be told about the Lord. **31**They will proclaim his righteousness to a people yet unborn—for he has done it.

Isa 2:2 In the last days the mountain of the LORD's temple will be established as chief among the mountains; it will be raised above the hills, and all nations will stream to it.

3Many peoples will come and say, "Come, let us go up to the mountain of the LORD, to the house of the God of Jacob. He will teach us his ways, so that we may walk in his paths." The law will go out from Zion, the word of the LORD from Jerusalem. **4**He will judge between the nations and will settle disputes for many peoples. They will beat their swords into plowshares and their spears into pruning

hooks. Nation will not take up sword against nation, nor will they train for war anymore. (+Isa 2:5)

Isa 11:6 The wolf will live with the lamb, the leopard will lie down with the goat, the calf and the lion and the yearling together; and a little child will lead them. **7**The cow will feed with the bear, their young will lie down together, and the lion will eat straw like the ox. **8**The infant will play near the hole of the cobra, and the young child put his hand into the viper's nest. **9**They will neither harm nor destroy on all my holy mountain, for the earth will be full of the knowledge of the LORD as the waters cover the sea. (+Isa 52:1,2,7-8)

Isa 61:1 The Spirit of the Sovereign LORD is on me, because the LORD has anointed me to preach good news to the poor. He has sent me to bind up the brokenhearted, to proclaim freedom for the captives and release from darkness for the prisoners, **2**to proclaim the year of the LORD's favor and the day of vengeance of our God, to comfort all who mourn, **3**and provide for those who grieve in Zion—to bestow on them a crown of beauty instead of ashes, the oil of gladness instead of mourning, and a garment of praise instead of a spirit of despair. They will be called oaks of righteousness, a planting of the LORD for the display of his splendor. (+Isa 65:25)

Mission of: To bring spiritual enlightenment (Isa 2:3)—

Isa 29:18 In that day the deaf will hear the words of the scroll, and out of gloom and darkness the eyes of the blind will see. **19**Once more the humble will rejoice in the LORD; the needy will rejoice in the Holy One of Israel. (+Joel 2:26-32; Hab 2:14; Ac 2:16-21)

Mission of: To bring moral transformation—

Isa 4:2 In that day the Branch of the LORD will be beautiful and glorious, and the fruit of the land will be the pride and glory of the survivors in Israel. **3**Those who are left in Zion, who remain in Jerusalem, will be called holy, all who are recorded among the living in Jerusalem. **4**The Lord will wash away the filth of the women of Zion; he will cleanse the bloodstains from Jerusalem by a spirit of judgment and a spirit of fire. **5**Then the LORD will create over all of Mount Zion and over those who assemble there a cloud of smoke by day and a glow of flaming fire by night; over all the glory will be a canopy. **6**It will be a shelter and shade from the heat of the day, and a refuge and hiding place from the storm and rain.

Isa 32:3 Then the eyes of those who see will no longer be closed, and the ears of those who hear will listen. **4**The mind of the rash will know and understand, and the stammering tongue will be fluent and clear. (+Isa 32:15-17)

Isa 35:1 The desert and the parched land will be glad; the wilderness will rejoice and blossom. Like the crocus, (+Isa 35:2,5-7; 44:3-4)

Isa 44:5 One will say, 'I belong to the LORD'; another will call himself by the name of Jacob; still another will write on his hand, 'The LORD's,' and will take the name Israel. (+Isa 55:10-13; Zep 3:9)

To be the salt and light of the world (Mt 5:13).

Responsibilities and Duties of Believers to Leaders:

To encourage—

1Co 16:10 If Timothy comes, see to it that he has nothing to fear while he is with you, for he is carrying on the work of the Lord, just as I am. **11**No one, then, should refuse to accept him. Send him on his way in peace so that he may return to me. I am expecting him along with the brothers.

To esteem—

Php 2:29 Welcome him in the Lord with great joy, and honor men like him,

1Th 5:12 Now we ask you, brothers, to respect those who work hard among you, who are over you in the Lord and who admonish you. ¹³Hold them in the highest regard in love because of their work. Live in peace with each other.

1Ti 5:17 The elders who direct the affairs of the church well are worthy of double honor, especially those whose work is preaching and teaching.

To imitate the example of (1Co 11:1; Php 3:17; 2Th 3:7)—

Heb 13:7 Remember your leaders, who spoke the word of God to you. Consider the outcome of their way of life and imitate their faith. (+1Pe 5:3)

To obey—

Heb 13:17 Obey your leaders and submit to their authority. They keep watch over you as men who must give an account. Obey them so that their work will be a joy, not a burden, for that would be of no advantage to you.

To receive (Php 2:29).

To reimburse (1Co 9:7-23; 2Co 12:13; Gal 6:6)—

Php 4:10 I rejoice greatly in the Lord that at last you have renewed your concern for me. Indeed, you have been concerned, but you had no opportunity to show it. ¹¹I am not saying this because I am in need, for I have learned to be content whatever the circumstances. ¹²I know what it is to be in need, and I know what it is to have plenty. I have learned the secret of being content in any and every situation, whether well fed or hungry, whether living in plenty or in want. (+Php 4:13)

Php 4:14 Yet it was good of you to share in my troubles. ¹⁵Moreover, as you Philippians know, in the early days of your acquaintance with the gospel, when I set out from Macedonia, not one church shared with me in the matter of giving and receiving, except you only; ¹⁶for even when I was in Thessalonica, you sent me aid again and again when I was in need. ¹⁷Not that I am looking for a gift, but I am looking for what may be credited to your account. ¹⁸I have received full payment and even more; I am amply supplied, now that I have received from Epaphroditus the gifts you sent. They are a fragrant offering, an acceptable sacrifice, pleasing to God. (+2Th 3:7-9; 1Ti 5:17-18)

To seek instruction from (Mal 2:7). Of leaders, to shepherd believers (Ac 20:28).

Prophecies Concerning:

Its universality—

Ge 12:3 I will bless those who bless you, and whoever curses you I will curse; and all peoples on earth will be blessed through you." (+Isa 2:2)

Isa 40:5 And the glory of the LORD will be revealed, and all mankind together will see it. For the mouth of the LORD has spoken."

Isa 42:3 A bruised reed he will not break, and a smoldering wick he will not snuff out. In faithfulness he will bring forth justice; ⁴he will not falter or be discouraged till he establishes justice on earth. In his law the islands will put their hope."

Isa 45:23 By myself I have sworn, my mouth has uttered in all integrity a word that will not be revoked: Before me every knee will bow; by me every tongue will swear. (+Isa 52:10,15; 54:1-5)

Isa 56:7 these I will bring to my holy mountain and give them joy in my house of prayer. Their burnt offerings and sacrifices will be accepted on my altar; for my house will

be called a house of prayer for all nations." ⁸The Sovereign LORD declares—he who gathers the exiles of Israel: "I will gather still others to them besides those already gathered."

Isa 59:19 From the west, men will fear the name of the LORD, and from the rising of the sun, they will revere his glory. For he will come like a pent-up flood that the breath of the LORD drives along.

Isa 60:1 "Arise, shine, for your light has come, and the glory of the LORD rises upon you. (+Isa 60:3-6)

Isa 60:7 All Kedar's flocks will be gathered to you, the rams of Nebaioth will serve you; they will be accepted as offerings on my altar, and I will adorn my glorious temple.

⁸"Who are these that fly along like clouds, like doves to their nests? ⁹Surely the islands look to me; in the lead are the ships of Tarshish, bringing your sons from afar, with their silver and gold, to the honor of the LORD your God, the Holy One of Israel, for he has endowed you with splendor. (+Isa 66:12,19,23)

Jer 3:17 At that time they will call Jerusalem The Throne of the LORD, and all nations will gather in Jerusalem to honor the name of the LORD. No longer will they follow the stubbornness of their evil hearts.

Jer 4:2 and if in a truthful, just and righteous way you swear, 'As surely as the LORD Lives,' then the nations will be blessed by him and in him they will glory."

Jer 16:19 O LORD, my strength and my fortress, my refuge in time of distress, to you the nations will come from the ends of the earth and say, "Our fathers possessed nothing but false gods, worthless idols that did them no good.

Jer 31:7 This is what the LORD says:

"Sing with joy for Jacob; shout for the foremost of the nations. Make your praises heard, and say, 'O LORD, save your people, the remnant of Israel.' ⁸See, I will bring them from the land of the north and gather them from the ends of the earth. Among them will be the blind and the lame, expectant mothers and women in labor; a great throng will return. ⁹They will come with weeping; they will pray as I bring them back. I will lead them beside streams of water on a level path where they will not stumble, because I am Israel's father, and Ephraim is my firstborn son.

Jer 31:34 No longer will a man teach his neighbor, or a man his brother, saying, 'Know the LORD,' because they will all know me, from the least of them to the greatest," declares the LORD. "For I will forgive their wickedness and will remember their sins no more."

Jer 33:22 I will make the descendants of David my servant and the Levites who minister before me as countless as the stars of the sky and as measureless as the sand on the seashore.' "

Da 2:35 Then the iron, the clay, the bronze, the silver and the gold were broken to pieces at the same time and became like chaff on a threshing floor in the summer. The wind swept them away without leaving a trace. But the rock that struck the statue became a huge mountain and filled the whole earth.

Da 2:44 "In the time of those kings, the God of heaven will set up a kingdom that will never be destroyed, nor will it be left to another people. It will crush all those kingdoms and bring them to an end, but it will itself endure forever.

Da 7:13 "In my vision at night I looked, and there before me was one like a son of man, coming with the clouds of heaven. He approached the Ancient of Days and was led into his presence. ¹⁴He was given authority, glory and sovereign power; all peoples, nations and men of every language worshiped him. His dominion is an everlasting dominion that will not pass away, and his kingdom is one that will never be destroyed.

Da 7:18 But the saints of the Most High will receive the kingdom and will possess it forever—yes, for ever and ever.'

Da 7:22 until the Ancient of Days came and pronounced judgment in favor of the saints of the Most High, and the time came when they possessed the kingdom.

Da 7:27 Then the sovereignty, power and greatness of the kingdoms under the whole heaven will be handed over to the saints, the people of the Most High. His kingdom will be an everlasting kingdom, and all rulers will worship and obey him.' (+Am 9:11-12)

Zep 2:11 The LORD will be awesome to them when he destroys all the gods of the land. The nations on every shore will worship him, every one in its own land. (+Zec 9:1,10; 14:6-9,16)

Mal 1:11 My name will be great among the nations, from the rising to the setting of the sun. In every place incense and pure offerings will be brought to my name, because my name will be great among the nations," says the LORD Almighty. (+Mt 8:11; Jn 10:16; Rev 11:15; 15:4)

Its prosperity—

Ps 72:7 In his days the righteous will flourish; prosperity will abound till the moon is no more.

8He will rule from sea to sea and from the River to the ends of the earth. **9**The desert tribes will bow before him and his enemies will lick the dust. **10**The kings of Tarshish and of distant shores will bring tribute to him; the kings of Sheba and Seba will present him gifts. **11**All kings will bow down to him and all nations will serve him.

Ps 72:16 Let grain abound throughout the land; on the tops of the hills may it sway. Let its fruit flourish like Lebanon; let it thrive like the grass of the field.

Ps 72:19 Praise be to his glorious name forever; may the whole earth be filled with his glory. Amen and Amen.

Ps 86:9 All the nations you have made will come and worship before you, O Lord; they will bring glory to your name.

Ps 102:15 The nations will fear the name of the LORD, all the kings of the earth will revere your glory. **16**For the LORD will rebuild Zion and appear in his glory.

Ps 102:18 Let this be written for a future generation, that a people not yet created may praise the LORD:

Ps 132:15 I will bless her with abundant provisions; her poor will I satisfy with food. **16**I will clothe her priests with salvation, and her saints will ever sing for joy.

17"Here I will make a horn grow for David and set up a lamp for my anointed one. **18**I will clothe his enemies with shame, but the crown on his head will be resplendent." (+Isa 4:2-6)

Isa 25:6 On this mountain the LORD Almighty will prepare a feast of rich food for all peoples, a banquet of aged wine—the best of meats and the finest of wines. **7**On this mountain he will destroy the shroud that enfolds all peoples, the sheet that covers all nations; **8**he will swallow up death forever. The Sovereign LORD will wipe away the tears from all faces; he will remove the disgrace of his people from all the earth. The LORD has spoken.

Isa 33:20 Look upon Zion, the city of our festivals; your eyes will see Jerusalem, a peaceful abode, a tent that will not be moved; its stakes will never be pulled up, nor any of its ropes broken. **21**There the LORD will be our Mighty One. It will be like a place of broad rivers and streams. No galley with oars will ride them, no mighty ship will sail them.

Isa 49:6 he says: "It is too small a thing for you to be my servant to restore the tribes of Jacob and bring back those of Israel I have kept. I will also make you a light for the Gentiles, that you may bring my salvation to the ends of the earth."

7This is what the LORD says—the Redeemer and Holy One of Israel—to him who was despised and abhorred by the nation, to the servant of rulers: "Kings will see you and rise up, princes will see and bow down, because of the LORD, who is faithful, the Holy One of Israel, who has chosen you."

8This is what the LORD says: "In the time of my favor I will answer you, and in the day of salvation I will help you; I will keep you and will make you to be a covenant for the people, to restore the land and to reassign its desolate inheritances, **9**to say to the captives, 'Come out,' and to those in darkness, 'Be free!' "They will feed beside the roads and find pasture on every barren hill.

10They will neither hunger nor thirst, nor will the desert heat or the sun beat upon them. He who has compassion on them will guide them and lead them beside springs of water. **11**I will turn all my mountains into roads, and my highways will be raised up. **12**See, they will come from afar—some from the north, some from the west, some from the region of Aswan." (+Isa 49:13-17)

Isa 49:18 Lift up your eyes and look around; all your sons gather and come to you. As surely as I live," declares the LORD, "you will wear them all as ornaments; you will put them on, like a bride.

Isa 51:3 The LORD will surely comfort Zion and will look with compassion on all her ruins; he will make her deserts like Eden, her wastelands like the garden of the LORD. Joy and gladness will be found in her, thanksgiving and the sound of singing. (+Isa 51:4)

Isa 51:5 My righteousness draws near speedily, my salvation is on the way, and my arm will bring justice to the nations. The islands will look to me and wait in hope for my arm. **6**Lift up your eyes to the heavens, look at the earth beneath; the heavens will vanish like smoke, the earth will wear out like a garment and its inhabitants die like flies. But my salvation will last forever, my righteousness will never fail. (+Isa 51:7)

Isa 51:8 For the moth will eat them up like a garment; the worm will devour them like wool. But my righteousness will last forever, my salvation through all generations."

Isa 52:1 Awake, awake, O Zion, clothe yourself with strength. Put on your garments of splendor, O Jerusalem, the holy city. The uncircumcised and defiled will not enter you again.

Isa 52:2 Shake off your dust; rise up, sit enthroned, O Jerusalem. Free yourself from the chains on your neck, O captive Daughter of Zion.

Isa 52:7 How beautiful on the mountains are the feet of those who bring good news, who proclaim peace, who bring good tidings, who proclaim salvation, who say to Zion, "Your God reigns!" **8**Listen! Your watchmen lift up their voices; together they shout for joy. When the LORD returns to Zion, they will see it with their own eyes.

Isa 52:10 The LORD will lay bare his holy arm in the sight of all the nations, and all the ends of the earth will see the salvation of our God.

Isa 52:15 so will he sprinkle many nations, and kings will shut their mouths because of him. For what they were not told, they will see, and what they have not heard, they will understand.

Isa 54:1 "Sing, O barren woman, you who never bore a

child; burst into song, shout for joy, you who were never in labor; because more are the children of the desolate woman than of her who has a husband," says the LORD. ²"Enlarge the place of your tent, stretch your tent curtains wide, do not hold back; lengthen your cords, strengthen your stakes. ³For you will spread out to the right and to the left; your descendants will dispossess nations and settle in their desolate cities.

⁴"Do not be afraid; you will not suffer shame. Do not fear disgrace; you will not be humiliated. You will forget the shame of your youth and remember no more the reproach of your widowhood. ⁵For your Maker is your husband—the LORD Almighty is his name—the Holy One of Israel is your Redeemer; he is called the God of all the earth.

Isa 54:11 "O afflicted city, lashed by storms and not comforted, I will build you with stones of turquoise, your foundations with sapphires. ¹²I will make your battlements of rubies, your gates of sparkling jewels, and all your walls of precious stones. ¹³All your sons will be taught by the LORD, and great will be your children's peace. ¹⁴In righteousness you will be established: Tyranny will be far from you; you will have nothing to fear. Terror will be far removed; it will not come near you.

Isa 55:5 Surely you will summon nations you know not, and nations that do not know you will hasten to you, because of the LORD your God, the Holy One of Israel, for he has endowed you with splendor."

Isa 55:10 As the rain and the snow come down from heaven, and do not return to it without watering the earth and making it bud and flourish, so that it yields seed for the sower and bread for the eater, ¹¹so is my word that goes out from my mouth: It will not return to me empty, but will accomplish what I desire and achieve the purpose for which I sent it. ¹²You will go out in joy and be led forth in peace; the mountains and hills will burst into song before you, and all the trees of the field will clap their hands. ¹³Instead of the thornbush will grow the pine tree, and instead of briers the myrtle will grow. This will be for the LORD's renown, for an everlasting sign, which will not be destroyed."

Isa 60:1 "Arise, shine, for your light has come, and the glory of the LORD rises upon you. ²See, darkness covers the earth and thick darkness is over the peoples, but the LORD rises upon you and his glory appears over you. ³Nations will come to your light, and kings to the brightness of your dawn.

⁴"Lift up your eyes and look about you: All assemble and come to you; your sons come from afar, and your daughters are carried on the arm. ⁵Then you will look and be radiant, your heart will throb and swell with joy; the wealth on the seas will be brought to you, to you the riches of the nations will come. ⁶Herds of camels will cover your land, young camels of Midian and Ephah. And all from Sheba will come, bearing gold and incense and proclaiming the praise of the LORD. (+Isa 60:7-9)

Isa 60:19 The sun will no more be your light by day, nor will the brightness of the moon shine on you, for the LORD will be your everlasting light, and your God will be your glory. ²⁰Your sun will never set again, and your moon will wane no more; the LORD will be your everlasting light, and your days of sorrow will end.

Isa 61:1 The Spirit of the Sovereign LORD is on me, because the LORD has anointed me to preach good news to the poor. He has sent me to bind up the brokenhearted, to proclaim freedom for the captives and release from dark-

ness for the prisoners, ²to proclaim the year of the LORD's favor and the day of vengeance of our God, to comfort all who mourn, ³and provide for those who grieve in Zion—to bestow on them a crown of beauty instead of ashes, the oil of gladness instead of mourning, and a garment of praise instead of a spirit of despair. They will be called oaks of righteousness, a planting of the LORD for the display of his splendor. (+Isa 61:4-5)

Isa 61:6 And you will be called priests of the LORD, you will be named ministers of our God. You will feed on the wealth of nations, and in their riches you will boast. (+Isa 61:7-8)

Isa 61:9 Their descendants will be known among the nations and their offspring among the peoples. All who see them will acknowledge that they are a people the LORD has blessed." (+Isa 61:10)

Isa 61:11 For as the soil makes the sprout come up and a garden causes seeds to grow, so the Sovereign LORD will make righteousness and praise spring up before all nations.

Isa 62:2 The nations will see your righteousness, and all kings your glory; you will be called by a new name that the mouth of the LORD will bestow. ³You will be a crown of splendor in the LORD's hand, a royal diadem in the hand of your God.

Isa 62:12 They will be called the Holy People, the Redeemed of the LORD; and you will be called Sought After, the City No Longer Deserted. (+Isa 65:18-19,23-25; 66:12,19,23; Jer 31:34; Eze 17:22-24)

Eze 34:26 I will bless them and the places surrounding my hill. I will send down showers in season; there will be showers of blessing.

Eze 34:29 I will provide for them a land renowned for its crops, and they will no longer be victims of famine in the land or bear the scorn of the nations. ³⁰Then they will know that I, the LORD their God, am with them and that they, the house of Israel, are my people, declares the Sovereign LORD. ³¹You my sheep, the sheep of my pasture, are people, and I am your God, declares the Sovereign LORD.'"

Eze 47:3 As the man went eastward with a measuring line in his hand, he measured off a thousand cubits and then led me through water that was ankle-deep. ⁴He measured off another thousand cubits and led me through water that was knee-deep. He measured off another thousand and led me through water that was up to the waist. ⁵He measured off another thousand, but now it was a river that I could not cross, because the water had risen and was deep enough to swim in—a river that no one could cross. (+Eze 47:6)

Eze 47:7 When I arrived there, I saw a great number of trees on each side of the river. ⁸He said to me, "This water flows toward the eastern region and goes down into the Arabah, where it enters the Sea. When it empties into the Sea, the water there becomes fresh. ⁹Swarms of living creatures will live wherever the river flows. There will be large numbers of fish, because this water flows there and makes the salt water fresh; so where the river flows everything will live. (+Eze 47:10-11)

Eze 47:12 Fruit trees of all kinds will grow on both banks of the river. Their leaves will not wither, nor will their fruit fail. Every month they will bear, because the water from the sanctuary flows to them. Their fruit will serve for food and their leaves for healing."

Joel 2:26 You will have plenty to eat, until you are full, and you will praise the name of the LORD your God, who has worked wonders for you; never again will my people be shamed. ²⁷Then you will know that I am in Israel, that I am the Lord your God, and that there is no other; never again will my people be shamed.

[28]"And afterward, I will pour out my Spirit on all people. Your sons and daughters will prophesy, your old men will dream dreams, your young men will see visions. [29]Even on my servants, both men and women, I will pour out my Spirit in those days. [30]I will show wonders in the heavens and on the earth, blood and fire and billows of smoke. [31]The sun will be turned to darkness and the moon to blood before the coming of the great and dreadful day of the Lord. [32]And everyone who calls on the name of the Lord will be saved; for on Mount Zion and in Jerusalem there will be deliverance, as the Lord has said, among the survivors whom the Lord calls.

Am 9:11 "In that day I will restore David's fallen tent. I will repair its broken places, restore its ruins, and build it as it used to be, [12]so that they may possess the remnant of Edom and all the nations that bear my name," declares the Lord, who will do these things.

Mic 4:3 He will judge between many peoples and will settle disputes for strong nations far and wide. They will beat their swords into plowshares and their spears into pruning hooks. Nation will not take up sword against nation, nor will they train for war anymore. [4]Every man will sit under his own vine and under his own fig tree, and no one will make them afraid, for the Lord Almighty has spoken.

Mic 5:2 "But you, Bethlehem Ephrathah, though you are small among the clans of Judah, out of you will come for me one who will be ruler over Israel, whose origins are from of old, from ancient times."

Mic 5:4 He will stand and shepherd his flock in the strength of the Lord, in the majesty of the name of the Lord his God. And they will live securely, for then his greatness will reach to the ends of the earth.

Mic 5:7 The remnant of Jacob will be in the midst of many peoples like dew from the Lord, like showers on the grass, which do not wait for man or linger for mankind.

Hab 2:14 For the earth will be filled with the knowledge of the glory of the Lord, as the waters cover the sea.

Zep 3:9 "Then will I purify the lips of the peoples, that all of them may call on the name of the Lord and serve him shoulder to shoulder.

Hag 2:7 I will shake all nations, and the desired of all nations will come, and I will fill this house with glory,' says the Lord Almighty. [8]'The silver is mine and the gold is mine,' declares the Lord Almighty. [9]'The glory of this present house will be greater than the glory of the former house,' says the Lord Almighty. 'And in this place I will grant peace,' declares the Lord Almighty."

Zec 2:10 "Shout and be glad, O Daughter of Zion. For I am coming, and I will live among you," declares the Lord. [11]"Many nations will be joined with the Lord in that day and will become my people. I will live among you and you will know that the Lord Almighty has sent me to you.

Zec 6:15 Those who are far away will come and help to build the temple of the Lord, and you will know that the Lord Almighty has sent me to you. This will happen if you diligently obey the Lord your God."

Zec 8:20 This is what the Lord Almighty says: "Many peoples and the inhabitants of many cities will yet come, [21]and the inhabitants of one city will go to another and say, 'Let us go at once to entreat the Lord and seek the Lord Almighty. I myself am going.' [22]And many peoples and powerful nations will come to Jerusalem to seek the Lord Almighty and to entreat him."

[23]This is what the Lord Almighty says: "In those days ten men from all languages and nations will take firm hold of one Jew by the hem of his robe and say, 'Let us go with you, because we have heard that God is with you.'"

Its lasting—

Isa 9:7 Of the increase of his government and peace there will be no end. He will reign on David's throne and over his kingdom, establishing and upholding it with justice and righteousness from that time on and forever. The zeal of the Lord Almighty will accomplish this.

Isa 33:20 Look upon Zion, the city of our festivals; your eyes will see Jerusalem, a peaceful abode, a tent that will not be moved; its stakes will never be pulled up, nor any of its ropes broken. (+Da 7:14,27; Mt 16:18)

Eph 1:10 to be put into effect when the times will have reached their fulfillment—to bring all things in heaven and on earth together under one head, even Christ.

Heb 12:23 to the church of the firstborn, whose names are written in heaven. You have come to God, the judge of all men, to the spirits of righteous men made perfect, [24]to Jesus the mediator of a new covenant, and to the sprinkled blood that speaks a better word than the blood of Abel.

Heb 12:27 The words "once more" indicate the removing of what can be shaken—that is, created things—so that what cannot be shaken may remain.

[28]Therefore, since we are receiving a kingdom that cannot be shaken, let us be thankful, and so worship God acceptably with reverence and awe,

Rev 5:10 You have made them to be a kingdom and priests to serve our God, and they will reign on the earth."

Rev 5:13 Then I heard every creature in heaven and on earth and under the earth and on the sea, and all that is in them, singing:

"To him who sits on the throne and to the Lamb be praise and honor and glory and power, for ever and ever!"

[14]The four living creatures said, "Amen," and the elders fell down and worshiped.

Rev 11:15 The seventh angel sounded his trumpet, and there were loud voices in heaven, which said: "The kingdom of the world has become the kingdom of our Lord and of his Christ, and he will reign for ever and ever."

Rev 12:10 Then I heard a loud voice in heaven say: "Now have come the salvation and the power and the kingdom of our God, and the authority of his Christ. For the accuser of our brothers, who accuses them before our God day and night, has been hurled down.

Rev 15:4 Who will not fear you, O Lord, and bring glory to your name? For you alone are holy. All nations will come and worship before you, for your righteous acts have been revealed."

Rev 20:4 I saw thrones on which were seated those who had been given authority to judge. And I saw the souls of those who had been beheaded because of their testimony for Jesus and because of the word of God. They had not worshiped the beast or his image and had not received his mark on their foreheads or their hands. They came to life and reigned with Christ a thousand years. [5](The rest of the dead did not come to life until the thousand years were ended.) This is the first resurrection. [6]Blessed and holy are those who have part in the first resurrection. The second death has no power over them, but they will be priests of God and of Christ and will reign with him for a thousand years. (+Rev 21:9)

Rev 21:10 And he carried me away in the Spirit to a mountain great and high, and showed me the Holy City, Jerusalem, coming down out of heaven from God. [11]It shone with the glory of God, and its brilliance was like that of a very precious jewel, like a jasper, clear as crystal. (+Rev 21:12-22)

Rev 21:23 The city does not need the sun or the moon to shine on it, for the glory of God gives it light, and the Lamb is its lamp. (+Rev 21:24-27)

Rev 22:1 Then the angel showed me the river of the water of life, as clear as crystal, flowing from the throne of God and of the Lamb ²down the middle of the great street of the city. On each side of the river stood the tree of life, bearing twelve crops of fruit, yielding its fruit every month. And the leaves of the tree are for the healing of the nations. ³No longer will there be any curse. The throne of God and of the Lamb will be in the city, and his servants will serve him. ⁴They will see his face, and his name will be on their foreheads. ⁵There will be no more night. They will not need the light of a lamp or the light of the sun, for the Lord God will give them light. And they will reign for ever and ever. *See Jesus the Christ, Kingdom of.*

State: Relationship of Church and State:

Ecclesiastical power superior to civil: Appoints kings (1Sa 10:1). Directs administration (1Sa 15:1-4). Reproves rulers (1Sa 15:14-35), withdraws support and anoints a successor (1Sa 16:1-13; 2Ki 9:1-26; 11:4-12). Attempted usurpation of ecclesiastical functions by civil authorities reproved (1Sa 13:8-14; 2Ch 26:16-21).

State superior to church: Evident, in David's appointments (1Ch 23-25; 2Ch 35:4). In Solomon's power (1Ki 2:26-27; 5-8). In Hezekiah reorganizing temple service (2Ch 31:2-19). In Jeroboam subverting the Jewish religion (1Ki 12:26-33). In Manasseh subverting and restoring the true religion (2Ch 33:2-9,15-17). In Joash supervising the repairs of the temple (2Ki 12:14-18). In Ahaz transforming the altars (2Ki 16:10-16). In Josiah exercising the function of a priest (2Ch 34:29-33).

State favorable to the church: Cyrus, in proclamation to restore the temple (2Ch 36:22-23; Ezr 1:1-11). Darius, in edict to further restoration of the temple (Ezr 6:1-14). Artaxerxes, in exempting religious institution from taxes (Ezr 7:24).

See Ecclesiasticism; Jesus the Christ, Kingdom of; Ministers; Usurpation, in Ecclesiastical Affairs.

CHURNING [1931, 2816, 4790, 8409, 8088, 10137].
NIV+ CHURN, CHURNED, CHURNS
(Pr 30:33). *See Butter.*

CHUSHAN-RISHATHAIM *See Cushan-Rishathaim.*

CHUZA *See Cuza.*

CILICIA [3070]. Maritime province of Asia Minor. Jews dwell in (Ac 6:9). Churches of (Ac 15:23,41; Gal 1:21).
Sea of (Ac 27:5).

CINNAMON [7872, 3077]. A spice (Pr 7:17; SS 4:14; Rev 18:13). An ingredient of the sacred oil (Ex 30:23).

CINNERETH, CINNEROTH *See Kinnereth; Galilee, Sea of.*

CIRCUMCISION [*4576, 213, 4362, 4364].
NIV+ CIRCUMCISE, CIRCUMCISED, CIRCUMCISING, MUTILATORS
Institution of (Ge 17:10-14; Lev 12:3; Jn 7:22; Ac 7:8; Ro 4:11). A seal of righteousness (Ro 2:25-29; 4:11). Performed on all males on the eighth day (Ge 17:12-13; Lev 12:3; Php 3:5). Rite of, observed on the Sabbath (Jn

7:23). A prerequisite of the privileges of the Passover (Ex 12:48). Child named at the time of (Ge 21:3-4; Lk 1:59; 2:21). Neglected (Jos 5:7). Covenant promises of (Ge 17:4,14; Ac 7:8; Ro 3:1; 4:11; 9:7-13; Gal 5:3). Necessity of, falsely taught by Judaizing Christians (Ac 15:1). Paul's argument against the continuance of (Ro 2:25,28; Gal 6:13). Characterized by Paul as a yoke (Ac 15:10). Abrogated (Ac 15:5-29; Ro 3:30; 4:9-11; 1Co 7:18-19; Gal 2:3-4; 5:2-11; 6:12; Eph 2:11,15; Col 2:11; 3:11).

Instances of:

Abraham (Ge 17:23-27; 21:3-4). Shechemites (Ge 34:24). Moses (Ex 4:25). Israelites at Gilgal (Jos 5:2-9). John the Baptist (Lk 1:59). Jesus (Lk 2:21). Paul (Php 3:5). Timothy (Ac 16:3).

Figurative:

(Ex 6:12, ftn; Dt 10:16; 30:6; Jer 4:4; 6:10, ftn; 9:26; Ro 2:28-29; 15:8, ftn; Php 3:3; Col 2:11; 3:11).

A designation of the Jews (Ac 10:45; 11:2; Ro 15:8, ftn; Eph 2:11; Col 4:11; Tit 1:10), of Christians (Php 3:3).

CIS *See Kish.*

CISTERN [1014, 1463, 1465].
NIV+ CISTERNS
An artificial reservoir dug in the earth or rock for the collection and storage of water from rain or spring (Pr 5:15; Ecc 12:6; Isa 36:16; Jer 2:13). Cisterns were a necessity in Israel with its long, dry summers. Empty cisterns were sometimes used as prisons (Ge 37:22; Jer 38:6; Zec 9:11).

Figurative:

(2Ki 18:31; Pr 5:15; Ecc 12:6). *See Wells.*

CITIES [4448, 6551, 7953, 9133, *4484*].
NIV+ CITY, CITY'S
Ancient (Ge 4:17; 10:10-12). Fortified (Nu 32:36; Dt 9:1; Jos 10:20; 14:12; 2Ch 8:5; 11:10-12; 17:2,19; 21:3; Isa 23:11). Gates of. *See Gates.*

Designated as:

Royal (Jos 10:2; 1Sa 27:5; 2Sa 12:26; 1Ch 11:7), treasure (Ge 41:48; Ex 1:11; 1Ki 9:19; 2Ch 8:4; 16:4; 17:12), chariot (2Ch 1:14; 8:6; 9:25), merchant (Isa 23:11; Eze 17:4; 27:3).

Town clerk of (Ac 19:35). Government of, by rulers (Ne 3:9,12,17-18; 7:2). *See Government.*

Suburbs of (Nu 35:3-5; Jos 14:4).

Watchmen of. *See Watchman.*

Figurative:

(Heb 11:10,16; 12:22; 13:14).

CITIES OF REFUGE Six cities set apart by Moses and Joshua as places of asylum for those who had accidentally committed manslaughter: Bezer (Benjamin), Ramoth Gilead (Gad), Golan (Manasseh), Hebron (Judah), Shechem (Ephraim), Kedesh (Naphtali). There they remained until a fair trial could be held. If proved innocent of willful murder, they had to remain in the city of refuge until the death of the high priest (Nu 35; Dt 4:43; 9:1-13; Jos 20).

CITIES OF THE PLAIN Cities near the Dead Sea, including Sodom, Gomorrah, Admah, Zeboiim, and Zoar. Lot lived in Sodom (Ge 13:10-12). They were destroyed because of their wickedness (Ge 19). Josephus (Wars, 4.8.4) identified the area of the five cities at the "Lake Asphaltitus" (the Dead Sea) and said traces of the five cities were still visible. No archaeological evidence, however, backs up that siting and so the sites remain unidentified.

CITIZENS [275, 1251, 3782, *4486, 4487, 4871+, 4889, 5232*].

NIV+ CITIZEN, CITIZENSHIP

Duties of:

Honors rulers—

Ex 22:28 "Do not blaspheme God or curse the ruler of your people.

Nu 27:20 Give him some of your authority so the whole Israelite community will obey him.

Job 34:18 Is he not the One who says to kings, 'You are worthless,' and to nobles, 'You are wicked,'

Pr 16:14 A king's wrath is a messenger of death, but a wise man will appease it.

¹⁵When a king's face brightens, it means life; his favor is like a rain cloud in spring.

Pr 24:21 Fear the LORD and the king, my son, and do not join with the rebellious,

Pr 25:6 Do not exalt yourself in the king's presence, and do not claim a place among great men; ⁷ᵃit is better for him to say to you, "Come up here," than for him to humiliate you before a nobleman.

Pr 25:15 Through patience a ruler can be persuaded, and a gentle tongue can break a bone.

Ecc 10:4 If a ruler's anger rises against you, do not leave your post; calmness can lay great errors to rest.

Ecc 10:20 Do not revile the king even in your thoughts, or curse the rich in your bedroom, because a bird of the air may carry your words, and a bird on the wing may report what you say. (+Ac 23:5)

1Pe 2:17 Show proper respect to everyone: Love the brotherhood of believers, fear God, honor the king.

Pray for rulers (Ezr 6:10; 1Ti 2:1-2). Promote peace (Jer 29:7). Obey the law (Ezr 7:26; 10:8; Ecc 4)

Pay taxes—

Mt 17:24 After Jesus and his disciples arrived in Capernaum, the collectors of the two-drachma tax came to Peter and asked, "Doesn't your teacher pay the temple tax?"

²⁵"Yes, he does," he replied.

When Peter came into the house, Jesus was the first to speak. "What do you think, Simon?" he asked. "From whom do the kings of the earth collect duty and taxes—from their own sons or from others?"

²⁶"From others," Peter answered.

"Then the sons are exempt," Jesus said to him. ²⁷"But so that we may not offend them, go to the lake and throw out your line. Take the first fish you catch; open its mouth and you will find a four-drachma coin. Take it and give it to them for my tax and yours."

Mt 22:17 Tell us then, what is your opinion? Is it right to pay taxes to Caesar or not?"

¹⁸But Jesus, knowing their evil intent, said, "You hypocrites, why are you trying to trap me? ¹⁹Show me the coin used for paying the tax." They brought him a denarius, ²⁰and he asked them, "Whose portrait is this? And whose inscription?"

²¹"Caesar's," they replied.

Then he said to them, "Give to Caesar what is Caesar's, and to God what is God's." (+Mk 12:14-17; Lk 20:22-25; Ro 13:5-7)

Rights of:

Public vindication when falsely accused—

Ac 16:37 But Paul said to the officers: "They beat us publicly without a trial, even though we are Roman citizens, and threw us into prison. And now do they want to get rid of us quietly? No! Let them come themselves and escort us out."

Protection from mob violence—

Ac 19:36 Therefore, since these facts are undeniable, you ought to be quiet and not do anything rash. (+Ac 19:37-41)

Fair trial—

Ac 22:25 As they stretched him out to flog him, Paul said to the centurion standing there, "Is it legal for you to flog a Roman citizen who hasn't even been found guilty?"

²⁶When the centurion heard this, he went to the commander and reported it. "What are you going to do?" he asked. "This man is a Roman citizen."

²⁷The commander went to Paul and asked, "Tell me, are you a Roman citizen?"

"Yes, I am," he answered.

²⁸Then the commander said, "I had to pay a big price for my citizenship."

"But I was born a citizen," Paul replied.

²⁹Those who were about to question him withdrew immediately. The commander himself was alarmed when he realized that he had put Paul, a Roman citizen, in chains. (+Ac 24:18-19; 25:5,10-11)

Ac 25:16 "I told them that it is not the Roman custom to hand over any man before he has faced his accusers and has had an opportunity to defend himself against their charges.

Loyal, Instances of:

Israelites (Jos 1:16-18; 2Sa 3:36-37; 15:23,30; 18:3; 21:17; 1Ch 12:38). David (1Sa 24:6-11; 26:6-16; 2Sa 1:14). Hushai (2Sa 17:15-16). David's soldiers (2Sa 18:12-13; 23:15-16). Joab (2Sa 19:5-6). Barzillai (2Sa 19:32). Jehoiada (2Ki 11:4-12). Isaiah (Isa 22:4). Jeremiah (La 1-5). Mordecai (Est 2:21-23).

Wicked and Treacherous: (Pr 17:11)

Pr 19:10 It is not fitting for a fool to live in luxury—how much worse for a slave to rule over princes!

Pr 19:12 A king's rage is like the roar of a lion, but his favor is like dew on the grass. (+Pr 20:2)

2Ti 3:1 But mark this: There will be terrible times in the last days. ²People will be lovers of themselves, lovers of money, boastful, proud, abusive, disobedient to their parents, ungrateful, unholy, ³without love, unforgiving, slanderous, without self-control, brutal, not lovers of the good, ⁴treacherous, rash, conceited, lovers of pleasure rather than lovers of God— (+2Pe 2:10)

Jude 8 In the very same way, these dreamers pollute their own bodies, reject authority and slander celestial beings.

Instances of:

Miriam and Aaron (Nu 12:1-11). Korah, Dathan, and Abiram (Nu 16:1-35; 26:9). Shechemites (Jdg 9:1-6,22-25,46-49). Ephraimites (Jdg 12:1-4). Israelites (1Sa 10:27; 1Ki 12:16-19). Absalom (2Sa 15:10-13). Ahithophel (2Sa 15:12; 17:1-4). Sheba (2Sa 20:1-2). Adonijah (1Ki 1:5-7). Jeroboam (1Ki 11:14-26; 12:20; 2Ch 13:5-9). Baasha (1Ki 15:27). Zimri (1Ki 16:9-10). Jozabad the son of Shimeath and Jehozabad son of Shomer (2Ki 12:19-21; 14:5). Shallum (2Ki 15:10). Menahem (2Ki 15:14). Pekah (2Ki 15:25). Hoshea (2Ki 15:30). Sons of Sennacherib (2Ki 19:37; 2Ch 32:21). Ishmael (Jer 40:14-16; 41). Bigthana and Teresh (Est 2:21). Jews (Eze 17:12-20). Barabbas (Mk 15:7). Theudas and 400 (Ac 5:36-37). An Egyptian (Ac 21:38).

Figurative:

Citizenship in heaven (Eph 2:12,19; Php 3:20; 1Pe 2:11).

CITRON WOOD [2591]. An aromatic wood; KJV "thyine" (Rev 18:12).

CITY CLERK [1208]. An official in Greco-Roman cities of the first century, as at Ephesus (Ac 19:35-41).

CITY OF DAVID

1. Jebusite stronghold of Zion captured by David and made by him his royal residence (2Sa 5:6-9).

2. Bethlehem, the home of David (Lk 2:4).

CITY OF DESTRUCTION A city of Egypt; exact location unknown (Isa 19:18, ftn). Some mss of the Massoretic Text, Dead Sea Scrolls, and the Vulgate have "City of the Sun" (Heliopolis). *See Heliopolis.*

CIVIL DAMAGES *See Damages and Compensations.*

CIVIL ENGINEERING (Jos 18:9; Job 28:9-11).

CIVIL SERVICE

School for—

Da 1:3 Then the king ordered Ashpenaz, chief of his court officials, to bring in some of the Israelites from the royal family and the nobility— **4**young men without any physical defect, handsome, showing aptitude for every kind of learning, well informed, quick to understand, and qualified to serve in the king's palace. He was to teach them the language and literature of the Babylonians. **5**The king assigned them a daily amount of food and wine from the king's table. They were to be trained for three years, and after that they were to enter the king's service. (+Da 1:6-16)

Da 1:17 To these four young men God gave knowledge and understanding of all kinds of literature and learning. And Daniel could understand visions and dreams of all kinds.

18At the end of the time set by the king to bring them in, the chief official presented them to Nebuchadnezzar. **19**The king talked with them, and he found none equal to Daniel, Hananiah, Mishael and Azariah; so they entered the king's service. **20**In every matter of wisdom and understanding about which the king questioned them, he found them ten times better than all the magicians and enchanters in his whole kingdom.

21And Daniel remained there until the first year of King Cyrus.

Appointment in, on account of merit—

Ge 39:1 Now Joseph had been taken down to Egypt. Potiphar, an Egyptian who was one of Pharaoh's officials, the captain of the guard, bought him from the Ishmaelites who had taken him there.

2The LORD was with Joseph and he prospered, and he lived in the house of his Egyptian master. **3**When his master saw that the LORD was with him and that the LORD gave him success in everything he did, **4**Joseph found favor in his eyes and became his attendant. Potiphar put him in charge of his household, and he entrusted to his care everything he owned. **5**From the time he put him in charge of his household and of all that he owned, the LORD blessed the household of the Egyptian because of Joseph. The blessing of the LORD was on everything Potiphar had, both in the house and in the field. **6**So he left in Joseph's care everything he had; with Joseph in charge, he did not

concern himself with anything except the food he ate. Now Joseph was well-built and handsome,

Ge 39:17 Then she told him this story: "That Hebrew slave you brought us came to me to make sport of me. **18**But as soon as I screamed for help, he left his cloak beside me and ran out of the house."

19When his master heard the story his wife told him, saying, "This is how your slave treated me," he burned with anger. **20**Joseph's master took him and put him in prison, the place where the king's prisoners were confined.

But while Joseph was there in the prison, **21**the LORD was with him; he showed him kindness and granted him favor in the eyes of the prison warden. (+Ge 41:38-44; 1Ki 11:28; Est 6:1-11; Da 1:7,17-21; 6:1-3)

Mt 25:14 "Again, it will be like a man going on a journey, who called his servants and entrusted his property to them. **15**To one he gave five talents of money, to another two talents, and to another one talent, each according to his ability. Then he went on his journey.

Mt 25:23 "His master replied, 'Well done, good and faithful servant! You have been faithful with a few things; I will put you in charge of many things. Come and share your master's happiness!'

24"Then the man who had received the one talent came. 'Master,' he said, 'I knew that you are a hard man, harvesting where you have not sown and gathering where you have not scattered seed. **25**So I was afraid and went out and hid your talent in the ground. See, here is what belongs to you.'

26"His master replied, 'You wicked, lazy servant! So you knew that I harvest where I have not sown and gather where I have not scattered seed? **27**Well then, you should have put my money on deposit with the bankers, so that when I returned I would have received it back with interest.

28"'Take the talent from him and give it to the one who has the ten talents. **29**For everyone who has will be given more, and he will have an abundance. Whoever does not have, even what he has will be taken from him. **30**And throw that worthless servant outside, into the darkness, where there will be weeping and gnashing of teeth.' (+Lk 19:12-27)

Corruption in—

Ne 5:15 But the earlier governors—those preceding me—placed a heavy burden on the people and took forty shekels of silver from them in addition to food and wine. Their assistants also lorded it over the people. But out of reverence for God I did not act like that.

Da 6:4 At this, the administrators and the satraps tried to find grounds for charges against Daniel in his conduct of government affairs, but they were unable to do so. They could find no corruption in him, because he was trustworthy and neither corrupt nor negligent. **5**Finally these men said, "We will never find any basis for charges against this man Daniel unless it has something to do with the law of his God."

6So the administrators and the satraps went as a group to the king and said: "O King Darius, live forever! **7**The royal administrators, prefects, satraps, advisers and governors have all agreed that the king should issue an edict and enforce the decree that anyone who prays to any god or man during the next thirty days, except to you, O king, shall be thrown into the lions' den. **8**Now, O king, issue the decree and put it in writing so that it cannot be altered—in accordance with the laws of the Medes and Persians, which cannot be repealed." ⁹So King Darius put the decree in writing.

¹⁰Now when Daniel learned that the decree had been published, he went home to his upstairs room where the windows opened toward Jerusalem. Three times a day he got down on his knees and prayed, giving thanks to his God, just as he had done before. ¹¹Then these men went as a group and found Daniel praying and asking God for help. ¹²So they went to the king and spoke to him about his royal decree: "Did you not publish a decree that during the next thirty days anyone who prays to any god or man except to you, O king, would be thrown into the lions' den?" The king answered, "The decree stands—in accordance with the laws of the Medes and Persians, which cannot be repealed."

¹³Then they said to the king, "Daniel, who is one of the exiles from Judah, pays no attention to you, O king, or to the decree you put in writing. He still prays three times a day." ¹⁴When the king heard this, he was greatly distressed; he was determined to rescue Daniel and made every effort until sundown to save him.

¹⁵Then the men went as a group to the king and said to him, "Remember, O king, that according to the law of the Medes and Persians no decree or edict that the king issues can be changed."

¹⁶So the king gave the order, and they brought Daniel and threw him into the lions' den. The king said to Daniel, "May your God, whom you serve continually, rescue you!"

¹⁷A stone was brought and placed over the mouth of the den, and the king sealed it with his own signet ring and with the rings of his nobles, so that Daniel's situation might not be changed.

Mk 15:15 Wanting to satisfy the crowd, Pilate released Barabbas to them. He had Jesus flogged, and handed him over to be crucified.

Ac 24:26 At the same time he was hoping that Paul would offer him a bribe, so he sent for him frequently and talked with him.

Reform in—

Ne 4:14 After I looked things over, I stood up and said to the nobles, the officials and the rest of the people, "Don't be afraid of them. Remember the Lord, who is great and awesome, and fight for your brothers, your sons and your daughters, your wives and your homes."

¹⁵When our enemies heard that we were aware of their plot and that God had frustrated it, we all returned to the wall, each to his own work.

Influence in (1Ki 1:5-10)—

1Ki 1:11 Then Nathan asked Bathsheba, Solomon's mother, "Have you not heard that Adonijah, the son of Haggith, has become king without our lord David's knowing it? ¹²Now then, let me advise you how you can save your own life and the life of your son Solomon. ¹³Go in to King David and say to him, 'My lord the king, did you not swear to me your servant: "Surely Solomon your son shall be king after me, and he will sit on my throne"? Why then has Adonijah become king?' ¹⁴While you are still there talking to the king, I will come in and confirm what you have said."

¹⁵So Bathsheba went to see the aged king in his room, where Abishag the Shunammite was attending him. ¹⁶Bathsheba bowed low and knelt before the king.

"What is it you want?" the king asked.

¹⁷She said to him, "My lord, you yourself swore to me your servant by the LORD your God: 'Solomon your son

shall be king after me, and he will sit on my throne.' ¹⁸But now Adonijah has become king, and you, my lord the king, do not know about it. (+1Ki 1:19)

1Ki 1:20 My lord the king, the eyes of all Israel are on you, to learn from you who will sit on the throne of my lord the king after him. ²¹Otherwise, as soon as my lord the king is laid to rest with his fathers, I and my son Solomon will be treated as criminals." (+1Ki 1:22-28)

1Ki 1:29 The king then took an oath: "As surely as the LORD lives, who has delivered me out of every trouble, ³⁰I will surely carry out today what I swore to you by the LORD, the God of Israel: Solomon your son shall be king after me, and he will sit on my throne in my place."

³¹Then Bathsheba bowed low with her face to the ground and, kneeling before the king, said, "May my lord King David live forever!" (+1Ki 1:32-40)

2Ki 4:13 Elisha said to him, "Tell her, 'You have gone to all this trouble for us. Now what can be done for you? Can we speak on your behalf to the king or the commander of the army?'" She replied, "I have a home among my own people."

Mt 20:20 Then the mother of Zebedee's sons came to Jesus with her sons and, kneeling down, asked a favor of him.

²¹"What is it you want?" he asked.

She said, "Grant that one of these two sons of mine may sit at your right and the other at your left in your kingdom."

²²"You don't know what you are asking," Jesus said to them. "Can you drink the cup I am going to drink?"

"We can," they answered.

²³Jesus said to them, "You will indeed drink from my cup, but to sit at my right or left is not for me to grant. These places belong to those for whom they have been prepared by my Father." (+Mk 10:35)

CLAIRVOYANCE See Sorcery.

CLAP [4673, 5782, 6215, 8492, 8562, 9546].

NIV+ CLAPPED, CLAPS

Clapping hands in joy (2Ki 11:12), in praise (Ps 47:1), in astonishment (Job 21:5), in scorn (Job 27:23; 34:37). Figurative of praise (Ps 98:8; Isa 55:12).

CLASP [7971, 8562, 3195].

NIV+ CLASPED, CLASPS

1. Used to fasten the curtains on the tabernacle (Ex 26:6,11,33; 35:11,13,18,33).

2. To shake hands in agreement and pledge for some obligation (Isa 2:6 w Pr 6:1).

3. Worshipers clasped Jesus' feet (Mt 28:9).

CLAUDA See Cauda.

CLAUDIA [3086] (possibly lame). A female disciple (2Ti 4:21).

CLAUDIUS [3087]. The fourth Roman emperor (c. A.D. 41-54). The famine foretold by Agabus took place in his reign (Ac 11:28). He banished all Jews from Rome (Ac 18:2).

CLAUDIUS LYSIAS [3087, 3385]. A Roman military officer (Ac 21:31-40; 22:23-30). Had Paul transferred from Jerusalem to Caesarea and wrote a letter to Governor Felix in order to protect him from an assassination plot (Ac 23:10-35; 24:7, ftn; 24:22).

CLAY [141, 824, 2817, 3084, 3226, 4246, 4879, 6760, 10279, *4017*, *5878*]. Man formed from (Job 33:6). Seals made of (Job 38:14). Used by a potter (Isa 29:16; 41:25; 45:9). Blind man's eyes anointed with (Jn 9:6).

Figurative:
(Job 4:19; Ps 40:2; Isa 45:9; 64:8; Jer 18:6; Ro 9:21).

Symbolic: (Da 2:33-41).

CLAY TABLETS Were made of clay which, while still wet, had wedge-shaped letters imprinted on them with a stylus, and then were kiln-fired or sun-dried. They were made of various shapes, and were often placed in a clay envelope. Vast quantities have been excavated in the Near East. The earliest examples date to 3000 B.C.

CLEAN AND UNCLEAN ANIMALS *See Animals; Birds; Fish; Insects.*

CLEANLINESS [430, 2342, 2899, 3196, 3197, 3198, 3200, 5470, 5929, 5931, *49, 2751, 2754, 2755, 4924*].
NIV+ CLEAN, CLEANNESS, CLEANSE, CLEANSED, CLEANSES, CLEANSING

Taught by frequent washings. *See Purification; Washing.*

Regulation relating to, in camp (Dt 23:12-14).

Figurative:
(Ps 51:7,10; 73:1; Pr 20:9; Isa 1:16; Eze 36:25; 1Jn 1:7,9; Rev 1:5).
See Sanitation and Hygiene

CLEANSING *See Washing.*

CLEANTHES The son of Phanius of Assos and head of the Stoic school in Athens from 263-232 B.C. His poem, *Hymn to Zeus*, is quoted by Paul before the Areopagus Court (Ac 17:28). He made Stoicism more religious in its orientation by teaching that the universe was a living being, that God was its soul, and that the sun was its heart. He taught detachment from moral concerns. Doing good for gain was like feeding cattle for meat. He also maintained that evil thoughts were worse than evil deeds, just as a tumor which does not break open is more dangerous than one which does.

See Aratus; Asceticism; Stoicism; Stoics.

CLEMENCY
Of David toward disloyal subjects: Shimei (2Sa 16:5-13; 19:16-23), Amasa (2Sa 19:13, w 2Sa 17:25).

Divine. *See God, Longsuffering of, and Mercy of; Kindness.*

CLEMENT [*3098*] (*mild*). A disciple at Philippi (Php 4:3).

CLEOPAS [*3093*] (*renowned father*). A disciple to whom Jesus appeared after his resurrection (Lk 24:18).

CLEOPHAS *See Clopas.*

CLERGYMAN *See Deacon; Elders; Minister; Pastor; Overseer.*

CLERK [*1208*]. Town (Ac 19:35).

CLOAK [168, 955, 2668, 4064, 4762, 5077, 5516+, 8100, 8515, 8529, *2668*, *5742*].
NIV+ CLOAKS

Outer garment, not to be taken in pledge for a loan (Ex 22:26-27). Elijah's (1Ki 18:46; 19:13); used in calling Elisha (1Ki 19:19); parting the Jordan (2Ki 2:8; 2Ki 2:14);

passes to Elisha (2Ki 2:13). Jesus' touched by the woman; her bleeding healed (Mt 9:20-21). Paul's left at Troas (2Ti 4:13).

Figurative of a curse (Ps 109:19).

CLOPAS [*3116*]. Husband of Mary (Jn 19:25). *See Mary, 2.*

CLOSET *See Room.*

CLOTH [955, 1865, 3156, 4802, 8391, 8529, 9271, 9418, *4527, 4820, 4984, 5051, 5058*].
NIV+ CLOTHS
(Mt 9:16; 27:59; Mk 14:51).

CLOTHING [*955, 4229, 4252, 4860, 8515, 8529, 10382, 10383, *1218, 1903, 1907, 2264, 2668, 2669, 4314*].
NIV+ CLOTHE, CLOTHED, CLOTHES
Of the Israelites, which did not grow old (Dt 8:4; 29:5; Ne 9:21).
See Dress.

CLOUD [2613, 5366, 5368, 5955, 6265, 6380, 6727, 6729, 6882, 6906, 6940, 7798, 8836, 10560, *3749, 3751*].
NIV+ CLOUDBURST, CLOUDLESS, CLOUDS, THUNDERCLOUD

Pillar of, With Fire:
Symbolic of the Lord's presence—

Ex 13:21 By day the Lord went ahead of them in a pillar of cloud to guide them on their way and by night in a pillar of fire to give them light, so that they could travel by day or night. [22]Neither the pillar of cloud by day nor the pillar of fire by night left its place in front of the people.

Ex 16:10 While Aaron was speaking to the whole Israelite community, they looked toward the desert, and there was the glory of the Lord appearing in the cloud.

Ex 19:9 The Lord said to Moses, "I am going to come to you in a dense cloud, so that the people will hear me speaking with you and will always put their trust in you." Then Moses told the Lord what the people had said.

Ex 19:16 On the morning of the third day there was thunder and lightning, with a thick cloud over the mountain, and a very loud trumpet blast. Everyone in the camp trembled.

Ex 24:16 and the glory of the Lord settled on Mount Sinai. For six days the cloud covered the mountain, and on the seventh day the Lord called to Moses from within the cloud. [17]To the Israelites the glory of the Lord looked like a consuming fire on top of the mountain. [18]Then Moses entered the cloud as he went on up the mountain. And he stayed on the mountain forty days and forty nights.

Ex 33:9 As Moses went into the tent, the pillar of cloud would come down and stay at the entrance, while the Lord spoke with Moses. [10]Whenever the people saw the pillar of cloud standing at the entrance to the tent, they all stood and worshiped, each at the entrance to his tent.

Ex 34:5 Then the Lord came down in the cloud and stood there with him and proclaimed his name, the Lord.

Lev 16:2 The Lord said to Moses: "Tell your brother Aaron not to come whenever he chooses into the Most Holy Place behind the curtain in front of the atonement cover on the ark, or else he will die, because I appear in the cloud over the atonement cover.

Nu 11:25 Then the Lord came down in the cloud and spoke with him, and he took of the Spirit that was on him and put the Spirit on the seventy elders. When the Spirit rested on them, they prophesied, but they did not do so again.

Nu 12:5 Then the LORD came down in a pillar of cloud; he stood at the entrance to the Tent and summoned Aaron and Miriam. When both of them stepped forward,

Nu 12:10 When the cloud lifted from above the Tent, there stood Miriam—leprous, like snow. Aaron turned toward her and saw that she had leprosy;

Nu 14:10 But the whole assembly talked about stoning them. Then the glory of the LORD appeared at the Tent of Meeting to all the Israelites.

Nu 16:19 When Korah had gathered all his followers in opposition to them at the entrance to the Tent of Meeting, the glory of the LORD appeared to the entire assembly.

Nu 16:42 But when the assembly gathered in opposition to Moses and Aaron and turned toward the Tent of Meeting, suddenly the cloud covered it and the glory of the LORD appeared.

Dt 31:15 Then the LORD appeared at the Tent in a pillar of cloud, and the cloud stood over the entrance to the Tent.

1Ki 8:10 When the priests withdrew from the Holy Place, the cloud filled the temple of the LORD. **11**And the priests could not perform their service because of the cloud, for the glory of the LORD filled his temple.

2Ch 7:1 When Solomon finished praying, fire came down from heaven and consumed the burnt offering and the sacrifices, and the glory of the LORD filled the temple. **2**The priests could not enter the temple of the LORD because the glory of the LORD filled it. **3**When all the Israelites saw the fire coming down and the glory of the LORD above the temple, they knelt on the pavement with their faces to the ground, and they worshiped and gave thanks to the LORD, saying, "He is good; his love endures forever."

Isa 6:1 In the year that King Uzziah died, I saw the Lord seated on a throne, high and exalted, and the train of his robe filled the temple.

Isa 6:4 At the sound of their voices the doorposts and thresholds shook and the temple was filled with smoke.

Mt 17:5 While he was still speaking, a bright cloud enveloped them, and a voice from the cloud said, "This is my Son, whom I love; with him I am well pleased. Listen to him!" (+Lk 9:34-35; 1Co 10:1)

A guide to Israel—

Ex 14:19 Then the angel of God, who had been traveling in front of Israel's army, withdrew and went behind them. The pillar of cloud also moved from in front and stood behind them,

Ex 14:24 During the last watch of the night the LORD looked down from the pillar of fire and cloud at the Egyptian army and threw it into confusion.

Ex 40:36 In all the travels of the Israelites, whenever the cloud lifted from above the tabernacle, they would set out; **37**but if the cloud did not lift, they did not set out—until the day it lifted. **38**So the cloud of the LORD was over the tabernacle by day, and fire was in the cloud by night, in the sight of all the house of Israel during all their travels.

Nu 9:15 On the day the tabernacle, the Tent of the Testimony, was set up, the cloud covered it. From evening till morning the cloud above the tabernacle looked like fire. **16**That is how it continued to be; the cloud covered it, and at night it looked like fire. **17**Whenever the cloud lifted from above the Tent, the Israelites set out; wherever the cloud settled, the Israelites encamped. **18**At the LORD's command the Israelites set out, and at his command they encamped. As long as the cloud stayed over the tabernacle, they remained in camp. **19**When the cloud remained over

the tabernacle a long time, the Israelites obeyed the LORD's order and did not set out. **20**Sometimes the cloud was over the tabernacle only a few days; at the LORD's command they would encamp, and then at his command they would set out. **21**Sometimes the cloud stayed only from evening till morning, and when it lifted in the morning, they set out. Whether by day or by night, whenever the cloud lifted, they set out. **22**Whether the cloud stayed over the tabernacle for two days or a month or a year, the Israelites would remain in camp and not set out; but when it lifted, they would set out. **23**At the LORD's command they encamped, and at the LORD's command they set out. They obeyed the LORD's order, in accordance with his command through Moses.

Nu 10:11 On the twentieth day of the second month of the second year, the cloud lifted from above the tabernacle of the Testimony. **12**Then the Israelites set out from the Desert of Sinai and traveled from place to place until the cloud came to rest in the Desert of Paran.

Nu 10:33 So they set out from the mountain of the LORD and traveled for three days. The ark of the covenant of the LORD went before them during those three days to find them a place to rest. **34**The cloud of the LORD was over them by day when they set out from the camp.

35Whenever the ark set out, Moses said,

"Rise up, O LORD! May your enemies be scattered; may your foes flee before you."

36Whenever it came to rest, he said,

"Return, O LORD, to the countless thousands of Israel."

Dt 1:33 who went ahead of you on your journey, in fire by night and in a cloud by day, to search out places for you to camp and to show you the way you should go.

Ne 9:12 By day you led them with a pillar of cloud, and by night with a pillar of fire to give them light on the way they were to take.

Ne 9:19 "Because of your great compassion you did not abandon them in the desert. By day the pillar of cloud did not cease to guide them on their path, nor the pillar of fire by night to shine on the way they were to take.

Ps 78:14 He guided them with the cloud by day and with light from the fire all night.

Ps 105:39 He spread out a cloud as a covering, and a fire to give light at night.

Isa 4:5 Then the LORD will create over all of Mount Zion and over those who assemble there a cloud of smoke by day and a glow of flaming fire by night; over all the glory will be a canopy.

In Isaiah's prophecy (Isa 4:5).

In Ezekiel's vision (Eze 10:3-4)—

Eze 10:18 Then the glory of the LORD departed from over the threshold of the temple and stopped above the cherubim. **19**While I watched, the cherubim spread their wings and rose from the ground, and as they went, the wheels went with them. They stopped at the entrance to the east gate of the LORD's house, and the glory of the God of Israel was above them.

Eze 11:22 Then the cherubim, with the wheels beside them, spread their wings, and the glory of the God of Israel was above them. **23**The glory of the LORD went up from within the city and stopped above the mountain east of it.

Figurative: (Jer 4:13; Hos 6:4; 13:3).

Symbolic: (Rev 14:14).

See Celestial Phenomena.

CLOUT *See Dress.*

CLUB [4751, 5138, 5151, 8657, 9371, *3833*].
NIV+ CLUBS

War club or club used by shepherds (2Sa 23:21; Job 41:29; Pr 25:18; Jer 51:20; Eze 39:9).

CNIDUS [*3118*] (*age*). A city in Asia Minor (Ac 27:7).

CO-HEIRS [*5169*].
NIV+ See INHERITANCE

As God's children Christians share in Christ's glory (Ro 8:17). *See Inheritance.*

COAL [836, 1624, 1625, 7073, 8363, *471, 472*].
NIV+ COALS

The Bible never refers to true mineral coal, which has not been found in Israel proper. The references are always either to charcoal or to live embers of any kind. Hebrews usually used charcoal for warmth or cooking (Isa 47:14; Jn 18:18; 21:9).

Figurative: (Pr 25:22).

Symbolic: (Isa 6:6-7; 2Sa 14:7).

COAL OIL *See Oil.*

COAT OF ARMOR (1Sa 17:5,38; 1Ki 22:34; 2Ch 18:33). *See Armor.*

COBRA [7352]
NIV+ COBRAS

A poisonous snake (Dt 32:33; Pr 23:32). Venom of, illustrates the speech of the wicked (Ps 58:4). Child playing with illustrates Messianic age (Isa 11:8-9).
See Serpent; Viper.

COCK *See Birds; Rooster.*

COCK CROWING *See Rooster.*

COCKATRICE *See Viper.*

COCKLE *See Weeds.*

COELE-SYRIA (*hollow Syria*). A name for that part of Syria that lay between the Lebanon and Anti-Lebanon Mountains.

COERCION
Religious:

Penalty for—
Ex 22:20 "Whoever sacrifices to any god other than the LORD must be destroyed.

Oath against—
2Ch 15:12 They entered into a covenant to seek the LORD, the God of their fathers, with all their heart and soul. **13**All who would not seek the LORD, the God of Israel, were to be put to death, whether small or great, man or woman. **14**They took an oath to the LORD with loud acclamation, with shouting and with trumpets and horns. **15**All Judah rejoiced about the oath because they had sworn it wholeheartedly. They sought God eagerly, and he was found by them. So the LORD gave them rest on every side.

Instances of:
Da 3:2 He then summoned the satraps, prefects, governors, advisers, treasurers, judges, magistrates and all the other provincial officials to come to the dedication of the image he had set up. **3**So the satraps, prefects, governors, advisers, treasurers, judges, magistrates and all the other provincial officials assembled for the dedication of the

image that King Nebuchadnezzar had set up, and they stood before it.
4Then the herald loudly proclaimed, "This is what you are commanded to do, O peoples, nations and men of every language: **5**As soon as you hear the sound of the horn, flute, zither, lyre, harp, pipes and all kinds of music, you must fall down and worship the image of gold that King Nebuchadnezzar has set up. **6**Whoever does not fall down and worship will immediately be thrown into a blazing furnace."
Da 3:29 Therefore I decree that the people of any nation or language who say anything against the God of Shadrach, Meshach and Abednego be cut into pieces and their houses be turned into piles of rubble, for no other god can save in this way." (+Da 6:26-27)
See Bigotry; Intolerance.

COFFER *See Chest, 2; Treasury.*

COFFIN [778, *5049*]. Joseph placed in for burial (Ge 50:26). *See Burial.*

COIN [*736, 1324, 1534, 3047, 3321, 3790, 5088*]. See *Money.*

COL-HOZEH [3997] (*every seer*). Father of Baruch (Ne 11:5).

COLLAR [7023, 9389]. *See Dress.*

COLLECTION [7689, *3356*].
NIV+ COLLECT, COLLECTED, COLLECTING, COLLECTIONS, COLLECTOR, COLLECTOR'S, COLLECTORS, COLLECTS

Of money for the poor.
See Alms; Beneficence; Giving; Liberality.

COLLEGE NIV "Second District" of the city of Jerusalem (2Ki 22:14; 2Ch 34:22). *See School.*

COLLOP NIV "bulges" of fat (Job 15:27).

COLLUSION
In Sin:
Lev 20:4 If the people of the community close their eyes when that man gives one of his children to Molech and they fail to put him to death, **5**I will set my face against that man and his family and will cut off from their people both him and all who follow him in prostituting themselves to Molech.
See Complicity; Connivance.

COLONIZATION Of conquered countries and people (2Ki 17:6,24; Ezr 4:9-10).

COLORS, FIGURATIVE AND SYMBOLIC
[2635, 7389, 8391].
NIV+ COLORED, COLORFUL, COLORS, DARK-COLORED, MULTICOLORED

Black:
Of affliction—
Job 3:5 May darkness and deep shadow claim it once more; may a cloud settle over it; may blackness overwhelm its light.
Ps 107:10 Some sat in darkness and the deepest gloom, prisoners suffering in iron chains, **11**for they had rebelled against the words of God and despised the counsel of the Most High.
Ps 143:3 The enemy pursues me, he crushes me to the

ground; he makes me dwell in darkness like those long dead.

Isa 9:19 By the wrath of the LORD Almighty the land will be scorched and the people will be fuel for the fire; no one will spare his brother.

Isa 24:11 In the streets they cry out for wine; all joy turns to gloom, all gaiety is banished from the earth.

Of calamity—

Isa 5:30 In that day they will roar over it like the roaring of the sea. And if one looks at the land, he will see darkness and distress; even the light will be darkened by the clouds.

Isa 8:22 Then they will look toward the earth and see only distress and darkness and fearful gloom, and they will be thrust into utter darkness.

Isa 50:3 I clothe the sky with darkness and make sackcloth its covering."

Joel 2:6 At the sight of them, nations are in anguish; every face turns pale.

Joel 2:10 Before them the earth shakes, the sky trembles, the sun and moon are darkened, and the stars no longer shine.

Joel 3:14 Multitudes, multitudes in the valley of decision! For the day of the LORD is near in the valley of decision. [15]The sun and moon will be darkened, and the stars no longer shine.

Na 2:10 She is pillaged, plundered, stripped! Hearts melt, knees give way, bodies tremble, every face grows pale.

Of the day of wrath—

Zep 1:14 "The great day of the LORD is near—near and coming quickly. Listen! The cry on the day of the LORD will be bitter, the shouting of the warrior there. [15]That day will be a day of wrath, a day of distress and anguish, a day of trouble and ruin, a day of darkness and gloom, a day of clouds and blackness,

Of death—

Job 10:20 Are not my few days almost over? Turn away from me so I can have a moment's joy [21]before I go to the place of no return, to the land of gloom and deep shadow, [22]to the land of deepest night, of deep shadow and disorder, where even the light is like darkness."

Am 5:8 (he who made the Pleiades and Orion, who turns blackness into dawn and darkens day into night, who calls for the waters of the sea and pours them out over the face of the land—the LORD is his name—

Of the abode of the lost—

Mt 8:12 But the subjects of the kingdom will be thrown outside, into the darkness, where there will be weeping and gnashing of teeth."

Mt 22:13 "Then the king told the attendants, 'Tie him hand and foot, and throw him outside, into the darkness, where there will be weeping and gnashing of teeth.'

Mt 25:30 And throw that worthless servant outside, into the darkness, where there will be weeping and gnashing of teeth.'

2Pe 2:4 For if God did not spare angels when they sinned, but sent them to hell, putting them into gloomy dungeons to be held for judgment;

Jude 13 They are wild waves of the sea, foaming up their shame; wandering stars, for whom blackest darkness has been reserved forever.

Rev 16:10 The fifth angel poured out his bowl on the throne of the beast, and his kingdom was plunged into darkness. Men gnawed their tongues in agony

Blue:

Of deity—

Ex 25:3 These are the offerings you are to receive from them: gold, silver and bronze; [4]blue, purple and scarlet yarn and fine linen; goat hair;

Ex 26:1 "Make the tabernacle with ten curtains of finely twisted linen and blue, purple and scarlet yarn, with cherubim worked into them by a skilled craftsman.

Ex 28:28 The rings of the breastpiece are to be tied to the rings of the ephod with blue cord, connecting it to the waistband, so that the breastpiece will not swing out from the ephod. (+Ex 28:37)

Ex 38:18 The curtain for the entrance to the courtyard was of blue, purple and scarlet yarn and finely twisted linen—the work of an embroiderer. It was twenty cubits long and, like the curtains of the courtyard, five cubits high,

Ex 39:1 From the blue, purple and scarlet yarn they made woven garments for ministering in the sanctuary. They also made sacred garments for Aaron, as the LORD commanded Moses.

[2]They made the ephod of gold, and of blue, purple and scarlet yarn, and of finely twisted linen. [3]They hammered out thin sheets of gold and cut strands to be worked into the blue, purple and scarlet yarn and fine linen—the work of a skilled craftsman. [4]They made shoulder pieces for the ephod, which were attached to two of its corners, so it could be fastened. [5]Its skillfully woven waistband was like it—of one piece with the ephod and made with gold, and with blue, purple and scarlet yarn, and with finely twisted linen, as the LORD commanded Moses.

Ex 39:21 They tied the rings of the breastpiece to the rings of the ephod with blue cord, connecting it to the waistband so that the breastpiece would not swing out from the ephod—as the LORD commanded Moses.

Ex 39:24 They made pomegranates of blue, purple and scarlet yarn and finely twisted linen around the hem of the robe.

Ex 39:29 The sash was of finely twisted linen and blue, purple and scarlet yarn—the work of an embroiderer—as the LORD commanded Moses.

Ex 39:31 Then they fastened a blue cord to it to attach it to the turban, as the LORD commanded Moses.

Nu 4:5 When the camp is to move, Aaron and his sons are to go in and take down the shielding curtain and cover the ark of the Testimony with it. [6]Then they are to cover this with hides of sea cows, spread a cloth of solid blue over that and put the poles in place.

[7]"Over the table of the Presence they are to spread a blue cloth and put on it the plates, dishes and bowls, and the jars for drink offerings; the bread that is continually there is to remain on it. [8]Over these they are to spread a scarlet cloth, cover that with hides of sea cows and put its poles in place.

[9]"They are to take a blue cloth and cover the lampstand that is for light, together with its lamps, its wick trimmers and trays, and all its jars for the oil used to supply it. [10]Then they are to wrap it and all its accessories in a covering of hides of sea cows and put it on a carrying frame.

[11]"Over the gold altar they are to spread a blue cloth and cover that with hides of sea cows and put its poles in place.

[12]"They are to take all the articles used for ministering in the sanctuary, wrap them in a blue cloth, cover that with hides of sea cows and put them on a carrying frame.

Nu 15:38 "Speak to the Israelites and say to them: 'Throughout the generations to come you are to make tassels on the corners of your garments, with a blue cord on each tassel. **³⁹**You will have these tassels to look at and so you will remember all the commands of the LORD, that you may obey them and not prostitute yourselves by going after the lusts of your own hearts and eyes. **⁴⁰**Then you will remember to obey all my commands and will be consecrated to your God.

2Ch 2:7 "Send me, therefore, a man skilled to work in gold and silver, bronze and iron, and in purple, crimson and blue yarn, and experienced in the art of engraving, to work in Judah and Jerusalem with my skilled craftsmen, whom my father David provided. (+2Ch 2:14; 3:14)

Of royalty (Est 8:15; Eze 23:6).

Predominant color in drapery and furnishings of the tabernacle, and in clothing of the priests—

Ex 24:10 and saw the God of Israel. Under his feet was something like a pavement made of sapphire, clear as the sky itself.

Jer 10:9 Hammered silver is brought from Tarshish and gold from Uphaz. What the craftsman and goldsmith have made is then dressed in blue and purple—all made by skilled workers.

Eze 1:26 Above the expanse over their heads was what looked like a throne of sapphire, and high above on the throne was a figure like that of a man.

Eze 10:1 I looked, and I saw the likeness of a throne of sapphire above the expanse that was over the heads of the cherubim.

Crimson, Red, Purple, and Scarlet:

Of iniquity (Isa 1:18; Rev 17:3-4; 18:12,16). Of prosperity (2Sa 1:24; Pr 31:21; La 4:5). Of conquest (Isa 63:2; Na 2:3; Rev 12:3). Of royalty (Jdg 8:26; Da 5:7,16, 29; Mt 27:28).

Types and shadows of the Atonement (Ex 25:3-4)—

Ex 25:5 ram skins dyed red and hides of sea cows; acacia wood;

Ex 26:1 "Make the tabernacle with ten curtains of finely twisted linen and blue, purple and scarlet yarn, with cherubim worked into them by a skilled craftsman.

Ex 26:14 Make for the tent a covering of ram skins dyed red, and over that a covering of hides of sea cows.

Ex 26:31 "Make a curtain of blue, purple and scarlet yarn and finely twisted linen, with cherubim worked into it by a skilled craftsman.

Ex 26:36 "For the entrance to the tent make a curtain of blue, purple and scarlet yarn and finely twisted linen—the work of an embroiderer.

Ex 27:16 "For the entrance to the courtyard, provide a curtain twenty cubits long, of blue, purple and scarlet yarn and finely twisted linen—the work of an embroiderer—with four posts and four bases.

Ex 28:4 These are the garments they are to make: a breastpiece, an ephod, a robe, a woven tunic, a turban and a sash. They are to make these sacred garments for your brother Aaron and his sons, so they may serve me as priests. **⁵**Have them use gold, and blue, purple and scarlet yarn, and fine linen.

⁶"Make the ephod of gold, and of blue, purple and scarlet yarn, and of finely twisted linen—the work of a skilled craftsman.

Ex 28:8 Its skillfully woven waistband is to be like it—of one piece with the ephod and made with gold, and with blue, purple and scarlet yarn, and with finely twisted linen.

Ex 28:15 "Fashion a breastpiece for making decisions—the work of a skilled craftsman. Make it like the ephod: of

gold, and of blue, purple and scarlet yarn, and of finely twisted linen.

Ex 28:31 "Make the robe of the ephod entirely of blue cloth,

Ex 28:33 Make pomegranates of blue, purple and scarlet yarn around the hem of the robe, with gold bells between them. (+Ex 28:37)

Ex 35:5 From what you have, take an offering for the LORD. Everyone who is willing is to bring to the LORD an offering of gold, silver and bronze; **⁶**blue, purple and scarlet yarn and fine linen; goat hair; **⁷**ram skins dyed red and hides of sea cows; acacia wood; (+Ex 35:23-25,35; 36:8, 19,35,37; 38:23)

Ex 39:1 From the blue, purple and scarlet yarn they made woven garments for ministering in the sanctuary. They also made sacred garments for Aaron, as the LORD commanded Moses.

²They made the ephod of gold, and of blue, purple and scarlet yarn, and of finely twisted linen. **³**They hammered out thin sheets of gold and cut strands to be worked into the blue, purple and scarlet yarn and fine linen—the work of a skilled craftsman. **⁴**They made shoulder pieces for the ephod, which were attached to two of its corners, so it could be fastened. **⁵**Its skillfully woven waistband was like it—of one piece with the ephod and made with gold, and with blue, purple and scarlet yarn, and with finely twisted linen, as the LORD commanded Moses. (+Ex 39:6-20)

Ex 39:21 They tied the rings of the breastpiece to the rings of the ephod with blue cord, connecting it to the waistband so that the breastpiece would not swing out from the ephod—as the LORD commanded Moses. (+Ex 39:22-23)

Ex 39:24 They made pomegranates of blue, purple and scarlet yarn and finely twisted linen around the hem of the robe. (+Ex 39:25-28)

Ex 39:29 The sash was of finely twisted linen and blue, purple and scarlet yarn—the work of an embroiderer—as the LORD commanded Moses. (+Ex 39:30)

Ex 39:31 Then they fastened a blue cord to it to attach it to the turban, as the LORD commanded Moses. (+Ex 39:32-43)

Lev 14:4 the priest shall order that two live clean birds and some cedar wood, scarlet yarn and hyssop be brought for the one to be cleansed. (+Lev 14:6,49-52)

Nu 4:7 "Over the table of the Presence they are to spread a blue cloth and put on it the plates, dishes and bowls, and the jars for drink offerings; the bread that is continually there is to remain on it. **⁸**Over these they are to spread a scarlet cloth, cover that with hides of sea cows and put its poles in place.

Nu 4:13 "They are to remove the ashes from the bronze altar and spread a purple cloth over it.

Nu 19:2 "This is a requirement of the law that the LORD has commanded: Tell the Israelites to bring you a red heifer without defect or blemish and that has never been under a yoke.

Nu 19:5 While he watches, the heifer is to be burned—its hide, flesh, blood and offal. **⁶**The priest is to take some cedar wood, hyssop and scarlet wool and throw them onto the burning heifer.

Isa 63:1 Who is this coming from Edom, from Bozrah, with his garments stained crimson? Who is this, robed in splendor, striding forward in the greatness of his strength? "It is I, speaking in righteousness, mighty to save."

²Why are your garments red, like those of one treading the winepress?

³"I have trodden the winepress alone; from the nations

no one was with me. I trampled them in my anger and trod them down in my wrath; their blood spattered my garments, and I stained all my clothing.

Heb 9:19 When Moses had proclaimed every commandment of the law to all the people, he took the blood of calves, together with water, scarlet wool and branches of hyssop, and sprinkled the scroll and all the people. **20**He said, "This is the blood of the covenant, which God has commanded you to keep." **21**In the same way, he sprinkled with the blood both the tabernacle and everything used in its ceremonies. **22**In fact, the law requires that nearly everything be cleansed with blood, and without the shedding of blood there is no forgiveness.

23It was necessary, then, for the copies of the heavenly things to be purified with these sacrifices, but the heavenly things themselves with better sacrifices than these.

White:

Of Holiness—

Lev 16:4 He is to put on the sacred linen tunic, with linen undergarments next to his body; he is to tie the linen sash around him and put on the linen turban. These are sacred garments; so he must bathe himself with water before he puts them on.

Lev 16:32 The priest who is anointed and ordained to succeed his father as high priest is to make atonement. He is to put on the sacred linen garments

Ps 51:7 Cleanse me with hyssop, and I will be clean; wash me, and I will be whiter than snow.

Ecc 9:8 Always be clothed in white, and always anoint your head with oil.

Isa 1:18 "Come now, let us reason together," says the LORD. "Though your sins are like scarlet, they shall be as white as snow; though they are red as crimson, they shall be like wool.

Da 7:9 "As I looked, "thrones were set in place, and the Ancient of Days took his seat. His clothing was as white as snow; the hair of his head was white like wool. His throne was flaming with fire, and its wheels were all ablaze.

Da 11:35 Some of the wise will stumble, so that they may be refined, purified and made spotless until the time of the end, for it will still come at the appointed time.

Da 12:10 Many will be purified, made spotless and refined, but the wicked will continue to be wicked. None of the wicked will understand, but those who are wise will understand.

Mt 17:1 After six days Jesus took with him Peter, James and John the brother of James, and led them up a high mountain by themselves. **2**There he was transfigured before them. His face shone like the sun, and his clothes became as white as the light.

Mt 28:2 There was a violent earthquake, for an angel of the Lord came down from heaven and, going to the tomb, rolled back the stone and sat on it. **3**His appearance was like lightning, and his clothes were white as snow. (+Mk 9:3)

Rev 1:13 and among the lampstands was someone "like a son of man," dressed in a robe reaching down to his feet and with a golden sash around his chest. **14**His head and hair were white like wool, as white as snow, and his eyes were like blazing fire.

Rev 2:17 He who has an ear, let him hear what the Spirit says to the churches. To him who overcomes, I will give some of the hidden manna. I will also give him a white stone with a new name written on it, known only to him who receives it.

Rev 3:4 Yet you have a few people in Sardis who have not soiled their clothes. They will walk with me, dressed in white, for they are worthy. **5**He who overcomes will, like them, be dressed in white. I will never blot out his name from the book of life, but will acknowledge his name before my Father and his angels.

Rev 3:18 I counsel you to buy from me gold refined in the fire, so you can become rich; and white clothes to wear, so you can cover your shameful nakedness; and salve to put on your eyes, so you can see.

Rev 4:4 Surrounding the throne were twenty-four other thrones, and seated on them were twenty-four elders. They were dressed in white and had crowns of gold on their heads.

Rev 6:2 I looked, and there before me was a white horse! Its rider held a bow, and he was given a crown, and he rode out as a conqueror bent on conquest.

Rev 6:11 Then each of them was given a white robe, and they were told to wait a little longer, until the number of their fellow servants and brothers who were to be killed as they had been was completed.

Rev 7:9 After this I looked and there before me was a great multitude that no one could count, from every nation, tribe, people and language, standing before the throne and in front of the Lamb. They were wearing white robes and were holding palm branches in their hands.

Rev 7:13 Then one of the elders asked me, "These in white robes—who are they, and where did they come from?"

14I answered, "Sir, you know."

And he said, "These are they who have come out of the great tribulation; they have washed their robes and made them white in the blood of the Lamb.

Rev 15:6 Out of the temple came the seven angels with the seven plagues. They were dressed in clean, shining linen and wore golden sashes around their chests.

Rev 19:8 Fine linen, bright and clean, was given her to wear." (Fine linen stands for the righteous acts of the saints.)

Rev 19:11 I saw heaven standing open and there before me was a white horse, whose rider is called Faithful and True. With justice he judges and makes war.

Rev 19:14 The armies of heaven were following him, riding on white horses and dressed in fine linen, white and clean.

Rev 20:11 Then I saw a great white throne and him who was seated on it. Earth and sky fled from his presence, and there was no place for them.

Choir singers arrayed in white (2Ch 5:12).

COLOSSE, COLOSSAE [*3145*] (*punishment*). A city of Phrygia (Col 1:2,7-8).

COLOSSIANS, BOOK OF

Author: The Apostle Paul

Date: c. A.D. 60

Outline:

I. Introduction (1:1-14).
  A. Greetings (1:1-2).
  B. Thanksgiving (1:3-8).
  C. Prayer (1:9-14).
II. The Supremacy of Christ (1:15-23).
III. Paul's Labor for the Church (1:24-2:7).
  A. A Ministry for the Sake of the Church (1:24-29).
  B. A Concern for the Spiritual Welfare of His Readers (2:1-7).
IV. Freedom from Human Regulations through Life with Christ (2:8-23).

A. Warning to Guard against the False Teachers (2:8-15).

B. Pleas to Reject the False Teachers (2:16-19).

C. An Analysis of the Heresy (2:20-23).

V. Rules for Holy Living (3:1-4:6).

A. The Old Self and the New Self (3:1-17).

B. Rules for Christian Households (3:18-4:1).

C. Further Instructions (4:2-6).

VI. Final Greetings (4:7-18).

COLT [912+1201, 6555, *4798*]. Ridden by Jesus (Mt 21:2,5,7; Mk 11:2; Jn 12:15).

COMFORT [5653, 5714, 5717, 5719, 5739, 5764, *4151, 4155, 4170, 4171, 4172, 4219*].

NIV+ COMFORTED, COMFORTER, COMFORTERS, COMFORTING, COMFORTS

See Affliction, Consolation Under; Righteous, Promises to.

COMFORTER *See God, Grace of; Holy Spirit.*

COMMANDMENT [1821, 5184, *1953*].

NIV+ COMMAND, COMMANDED, COMMANDING, COMMANDMENT, COMMANDMENTS, COMMANDS

Used in the English Bible to translate a number of Hebrew and Greek words meaning law, ordinance, statute, word, judgment, precept, saying, charge, etc.

COMMANDMENTS AND STATUTES, OF GOD

Admonishing Against:

Backsliding (Dt 8:11-17; 28:18; Eze 33:12-13,18; Lk 9:62; 1Co 10:12; Heb 3:12-13)—

Heb 12:15 See to it that no one misses the grace of God and that no bitter root grows up to cause trouble and defile many. (+2Pe 2:20-21)

Conspiracy (Ex 23:1-2). Hypocrisy (Mt 6:1-5,16; Lk 20:46-47; 1Pe 2:1).

Lusts (Pr 31:3; Ro 13:13-14)—

Gal 5:16 So I say, live by the Spirit, and you will not gratify the desires of the sinful nature. (+1Pe 2:11)

Oppression of foreigners (Ex 22:21; 23:9; Dt 24:14; Zec 7:10). Popular corruption (Ex 23:2). Reviling rulers (Ex 22:28; Ac 23:5).

Concerning:

Children, commanding obedience to parents—

Pr 6:20 My son, keep your father's commands and do not forsake your mother's teaching. (+Eph 6:1-3; Col 3:20) *See below, Commanding Reverence for Parents.*

Debtors' protection (Dt 24:10,12-13). Father's concern for children (Eph 6:4; Col 3:21). A husband's love for his wife (Eph 5:23; Col 3:19), honor for his wife (1Pe 3:7). Permanence of marriage (Ge 2:24; Mt 19:6; Mk 10:9; 1Co 7:1-16). Judges' justice in court (Dt 1:16). Lost property (Ex 23:4; Dt 22:1-3). Man's supremacy over animals (Ge 9:2). Masters', equity (Col 4:1), humane treatment of servants (Eph 6:9).

Ministers (Ac 20:31)—

1Ti 1:4 nor to devote themselves to myths and endless genealogies. These promote controversies rather than God's work—which is by faith.

1Ti 3:2 Now the overseer must be above reproach, the husband of but one wife, temperate, self-controlled, respectable, hospitable, able to teach, ³not given to drunkenness, not violent but gentle, not quarrelsome, not a lover of money. ⁴He must manage his own family well and see that his children obey him with proper respect. ⁵(If anyone does not know how to manage his own family, how can he take care of God's church?) ⁶He must not be a recent convert, or he may become conceited and fall under the same judgment as the devil. ⁷He must also have a good reputation with outsiders, so that he will not fall into disgrace and into the devil's trap.

⁸Deacons, likewise, are to be men worthy of respect, sincere, not indulging in much wine, and not pursuing dishonest gain. ⁹They must keep hold of the deep truths of the faith with a clear conscience. ¹⁰They must first be tested; and then if there is nothing against them, let them serve as deacons.

¹¹In the same way, their wives are to be women worthy of respect, not malicious talkers but temperate and trustworthy in everything.

¹²A deacon must be the husband of but one wife and must manage his children and his household well. ¹³Those who have served well gain an excellent standing and great assurance in their faith in Christ Jesus.

1Ti 4:12 Don't let anyone look down on you because you are young, but set an example for the believers in speech, in life, in love, in faith and in purity. ¹³Until I come, devote yourself to the public reading of Scripture, to preaching and to teaching. ¹⁴Do not neglect your gift, which was given you through a prophetic message when the body of elders laid their hands on you.

¹⁵Be diligent in these matters; give yourself wholly to them, so that everyone may see your progress. ¹⁶Watch your life and doctrine closely. Persevere in them, because if you do, you will save both yourself and your hearers.

1Ti 5:20 Those who sin are to be rebuked publicly, so that the others may take warning.

²¹I charge you, in the sight of God and Christ Jesus and the elect angels, to keep these instructions without partiality, and to do nothing out of favoritism. (+1Ti 5:22; 2Ti 2:1-3,14-16)

2Ti 2:22 Flee the evil desires of youth, and pursue righteousness, faith, love and peace, along with those who call on the Lord out of a pure heart. ²³Don't have anything to do with foolish and stupid arguments, because you know they produce quarrels. ²⁴And the Lord's servant must not quarrel; instead, he must be kind to everyone, able to teach, not resentful.

Tit 1:5 The reason I left you in Crete was that you might straighten out what was left unfinished and appoint elders in every town, as I directed you. ⁶An elder must be blameless, the husband of but one wife, a man whose children believe and are not open to the charge of being wild and disobedient. ⁷Since an overseer is entrusted with God's work, he must be blameless—not overbearing, not quick-tempered, not given to drunkenness, not violent, not pursuing dishonest gain. ⁸Rather he must be hospitable, one who loves what is good, who is self-controlled, upright, holy and disciplined. ⁹He must hold firmly to the trustworthy message as it has been taught, so that he can encourage others by sound doctrine and refute those who oppose it. (+Tit 2:1)

Tit 2:2 Teach the older men to be temperate, worthy of respect, self-controlled, and sound in faith, in love and in endurance.

³Likewise, teach the older women to be reverent in the way they live, not to be slanderers or addicted to much wine, but to teach what is good. ⁴Then they can train the younger women to love their husbands and children, ⁵to be self-controlled and pure, to be busy at home, to be kind,

and to be subject to their husbands, so that no one will malign the word of God. (+Tit 2:6-8)

Tit 2:9 Teach slaves to be subject to their masters in everything, to try to please them, not to talk back to them, [10]and not to steal from them, but to show that they can be fully trusted, so that in every way they will make the teaching about God our Savior attractive. (+Tit 2:15)

1Pe 5:2 Be shepherds of God's flock that is under your care, serving as overseers—not because you must, but because you are willing, as God wants you to be; not greedy for money, but eager to serve; [3]not lording it over those entrusted to you, but being examples to the flock.

Faithfulness (Col 4:17)—

1Ti 6:11 But you, man of God, flee from all this, and pursue righteousness, godliness, faith, love, endurance and gentleness. [12]Fight the good fight of the faith. Take hold of the eternal life to which you were called when you made your good confession in the presence of many witnesses.

1Ti 6:14 to keep this command without spot or blame until the appearing of our Lord Jesus Christ, (+2Ti 1:8)

2Ti 1:13 What you heard from me, keep as the pattern of sound teaching, with faith and love in Christ Jesus.

Fortitude (2Ti 2:3). Foolish questions (2Ti 2:23). Sanctification (1Th 4:3). Strife (2Ti 2:24). Places of public worship (Dt 12:11). Restitution (Ex 21:30-36; 22:1-15; Lev 6:4-5; 24:18; Nu 5:7). Servants' obedience (Eph 6:5-8; Col 3:22-25; Tit 2:9-10; 1Pe 2:18-19). Vicious animals (Ex 21:28-32,35-36). Wives' obedience (Eph 5:22; Col 3:18; 1Pe 3:1-4). Women (Eph 5:22,24; Tit 2:3-5; 1Pe 3:1-3). Young men's parental obedience (Pr 6:20; 23:22).

The Decalogue:

Ex 20:3 "You shall have no other gods before me. [4]"You shall not make for yourself an idol in the form of anything in heaven above or on the earth beneath or in the waters below. [5]You shall not bow down to them or worship them; for I, the LORD your God, am a jealous God, punishing the children for the sin of the fathers to the third and fourth generation of those who hate me, [6]but showing love to a thousand [generations] of those who love me and keep my commandments. [7]"You shall not misuse the name of the LORD your God, for the LORD will not hold anyone guiltless who misuses his name. [8]"Remember the Sabbath day by keeping it holy. [9]Six days you shall labor and do all your work, [10]but the seventh day is a Sabbath to the LORD your God. On it you shall not do any work, neither you, nor your son or daughter, nor your manservant or maidservant, nor your animals, nor the alien within your gates. [11]For in six days the LORD made the heavens and the earth, the sea, and all that is in them, but he rested on the seventh day. Therefore the LORD blessed the Sabbath day and made it holy. [12]"Honor your father and your mother, so that you may live long in the land the LORD your God is giving you. [13]"You shall not murder. [14]"You shall not commit adultery. [15]"You shall not steal. [16]"You shall not give false testimony against your neighbor. [17]"You shall not covet your neighbor's house. You shall not covet your neighbor's wife, or his manservant or maidservant, his ox or donkey, or anything that belongs to your neighbor." (+Dt 5:6-21) *See Decalogue; Tablets of the Law.*

Commanding:

Hate, of the abominations of the wicked (Dt 7:25-26)

Hatred of evil—

Ro 12:9 Love must be sincere. Hate what is evil; cling to what is good. [10]Be devoted to one another in brotherly love. Honor one another above yourselves. [11]Never be lacking in zeal, but keep your spiritual fervor, serving the Lord. [12]Be joyful in hope, patient in affliction, faithful in prayer. [13]Share with God's people who are in need. Practice hospitality.

[14]Bless those who persecute you; bless and do not curse. [15]Rejoice with those who rejoice; mourn with those who mourn. [16]Live in harmony with one another. Do not be proud, but be willing to associate with people of low position. Do not be conceited.

[17]Do not repay anyone evil for evil. Be careful to do what is right in the eyes of everybody. [18]If it is possible, as far as it depends on you, live at peace with everyone. [19]Do not take revenge, my friends, but leave room for God's wrath, for it is written: "It is mine to avenge; I will repay," says the Lord. [20]On the contrary:

"If your enemy is hungry, feed him; if he is thirsty, give him something to drink. In doing this, you will heap burning coals on his head."

[21]Do not be overcome by evil, but overcome evil with good.

Abiding in Christ (Jn 15:4,9)—

1Jn 2:28 And now, dear children, continue in him, so that when he appears we may be confident and unashamed before him at his coming.

Abstinence from evil—

1Th 5:22 Avoid every kind of evil.

Accord with Christ, and concord with one another—

Php 2:2 then make my joy complete by being like-minded, having the same love, being one in spirit and purpose. [3]Do nothing out of selfish ambition or vain conceit, but in humility consider others better than yourselves. [4]Each of you should look not only to your own interests, but also to the interests of others.

[5]Your attitude should be the same as that of Christ Jesus:

Admonition and encouragement—

1Th 5:14 And we urge you, brothers, warn those who are idle, encourage the timid, help the weak, be patient with everyone.

Altruistic service (Mt 20:26; Mk 9:35; 10:42-45; Lk 22:26; Jn 13:14)—

Ro 15:1 We who are strong ought to bear with the failings of the weak and not to please ourselves. [2]Each of us should please his neighbor for his good, to build him up.

1Co 10:24 Nobody should seek his own good, but the good of others. (+Gal 6:10; Php 2:3-4)

Assistance to the distressed (Ps 82:4; Pr 24:11).—

Building a sanctuary (Ex 25:8).

Casting anxiety upon the Lord (1Pe 5:7).

Charitableness (Mt 18:10; Lk 6:37-38; Ro 14:1-3,13)—

Ro 14:19 Let us therefore make every effort to do what leads to peace and to mutual edification.

Chastity (Pr 5:15-19; Mt 5:27-28). Cheerfulness (Ecc 9:7-9). Choice of wise men for rulers (Ex 18:21; Dt 1:13).

Christian graces (2Co 13:11)—

Col 3:12 Therefore, as God's chosen people, holy and dearly loved, clothe yourselves with compassion, kindness, humility, gentleness and patience. [13]Bear with each other and forgive whatever grievances you may have against one another. Forgive as the Lord forgave you. [14]And over all these virtues put on love, which binds them all together in perfect unity.

[15]Let the peace of Christ rule in your hearts, since as members of one body you were called to peace. And be thankful. [16]Let the word of Christ dwell in you richly as

you teach and admonish one another with all wisdom, and as you sing psalms, hymns and spiritual songs with gratitude in your hearts to God. [17]And whatever you do, whether in word or deed, do it all in the name of the Lord Jesus, giving thanks to God the Father through him. (+2Ti 2:22)

Christian tolerance toward the weak (Ro 15:1).

Confession of sin (Nu 8:12)—

Jas 5:16 Therefore confess your sins to each other and pray for each other so that you may be healed. The prayer of a righteous man is powerful and effective.

Contentment (Lk 3:14)—

Heb 13:5 Keep your lives free from the love of money and be content with what you have, because God has said, "Never will I leave you; never will I forsake you."

Courage (Dt 31:6-7; Jos 1:6-7,9; 1Ki 2:2-3; 1Ch 28:20; Ne 4:14; Jer 1:8; Eze 2:6). Cross bearing (Mt 16:24; Mk 8:34).

Destruction of idols (Ex 23:24; 34:13; Nu 33:52; Dt 7:25; 12:13). Diligence (Ecc 9:10; 11:6), in business (Pr 27:23). Discipleship (Mt 19:21; Mk 10:21; Lk 18:22).

Discipline of, disorderly church members—

2Th 3:6 In the name of the Lord Jesus Christ, we command you, brothers, to keep away from every brother who is idle and does not live according to the teaching you received from us.

Children (Mt 19:14; Mk 10:14; Lk 18:16-17).

Discreet conduct (Ro 12:17)—

Eph 4:1 As a prisoner for the Lord, then, I urge you to live a life worthy of the calling you have received. [2]Be completely humble and gentle; be patient, bearing with one another in love. [3]Make every effort to keep the unity of the Spirit through the bond of peace.

Eph 5:15 Be very careful, then, how you live—not as unwise but as wise, (+Eph 5:16)

Php 1:27 Whatever happens, conduct yourselves in a manner worthy of the gospel of Christ. Then, whether I come and see you or only hear about you in my absence, I will know that you stand firm in one spirit, contending as one man for the faith of the gospel

Php 4:5 Let your gentleness be evident to all. The Lord is near. (+1Pe 2:11-12)

Doing all to the glory of God—

1Co 10:31 So whether you eat or drink or whatever you do, do it all for the glory of God. (+Col 3:17)

Col 3:23 Whatever you do, work at it with all your heart, as working for the Lord, not for men,

Equity of servants (Col 4:1). Establishing and providing for the ordination of a holy ministry (Ex 28:1-3; 40:12-15; Lev 8:1-13).

Esteem for pastors—

1Th 5:12 Now we ask you, brothers, to respect those who work hard among you, who are over you in the Lord and who admonish you. (+1Th 5:13; 1Ti 5:17)

Heb 13:7 Remember your leaders, who spoke the word of God to you. Consider the outcome of their way of life and imitate their faith.

Evangelism (Mt 28:19).—

Faith (Ex 14:13; 2Ch 20:20; Ps 37:3,5; 62:8; 115:9,11; Pr 3:5; Isa 26:4; 50:10; Jer 49:11; Mk 1:15; 5:36; 11:22; Jn 6:29; 12:36; 14:1,11; 20:27), in Christ (1Jn 3:23). Faithfulness to ministers (Col 4:17; 1Ti 6:11-12,14; 2Ti 1:8,13), to friends (Pr 27:10).

Family support—

1Ti 5:8 If anyone does not provide for his relatives, and especially for his immediate family, he has denied the faith and is worse than an unbeliever.

Fear of God (Lev 19:14,32; 25:17; Dt 6:13; 10:12,20; 13:4; Jos 24:14; 1Sa 12:24; 2Ki 17:39; Pr 3:7; 23:17; 24:21; Ecc 12:13; Isa 8:13; 1Pe 2:17). Fidelity in marriage (Ge 2:24; Mt 19:6; Mk 10:8; 1Co 7:10-11), to God (1Sa 12:20; Mt 22:21), to God and government (Mt 22:21; Mk 12:17; Lk 20:25), to vows (Nu 30:2; Dt 23:21-23; Ps 50:14; Ecc 5:4). Forbearance (Eph 4:2; Col 3:13). Forgiveness (Mt 18:22; Mk 11:25; Lk 17:3-4; Ro 12:14; Eph 4:32; Col 3:13). Fortitude under persecution (Mt 10:26-28; Mk 13:9,11-13; 2Ti 2:3; Rev 2:10). Fraternal reproof (Mt 18:15-17; Lk 17:3-4). Fruits of righteousness (Lk 3:11,14).

Gentleness (Tit 3:2).

Godliness—

Eph 5:1 Be imitators of God, therefore, as dearly loved children

Golden Rule, in conduct (Mt 7:12; Lk 6:31).

Good works—

1Pe 3:21 and this water symbolizes baptism that now saves you also—not the removal of dirt from the body but the pledge of a good conscience toward God. It saves you by the resurrection of Jesus Christ,

Growth in grace—

Heb 6:1 Therefore let us leave the elementary teachings about Christ and go on to maturity, not laying again the foundation of repentance from acts that lead to death, and of faith in God,

2Pe 1:5 For this very reason, make every effort to add to your faith goodness; and to goodness, knowledge; [6]and to knowledge, self-control; and to self-control, perseverance; and to perseverance, godliness; [7]and to godliness, brotherly kindness; and to brotherly kindness, love. (+2Pe 1:8)

2Pe 3:18 But grow in the grace and knowledge of our Lord and Savior Jesus Christ. To him be glory both now and forever! Amen.

Jude 20 But you, dear friends, build yourselves up in your most holy faith and pray in the Holy Spirit. [21]Keep yourselves in God's love as you wait for the mercy of our Lord Jesus Christ to bring you to eternal life.

Heed to instruction (Pr 4:10; 19:20; 22:17), to parental instruction (Pr 1:8; 23:22), to the truth (Mt 11:15; Mk 4:9; Rev 2:7). Helpfulness (1Co 10:24; Gal 6:1-2; Php 2:4; 1Th 5:11).

Holiness (Ex 22:31; 30:29; Lev 11:44; 20:7,25-26; 21:7; Nu 15:40; Dt 18:13; Jos 7:13; Isa 1:16-17; Jer 6:16; Am 5:14-15; 1Co 5:7; 2Co 7:1; Eph 4:22-32)—

Col 3:5 Put to death, therefore, whatever belongs to your earthly nature: sexual immorality, impurity, lust, evil desires and greed, which is idolatry.

Col 3:8 But now you must rid yourselves of all such things as these: anger, rage, malice, slander, and filthy language from your lips. [9]Do not lie to each other, since you have taken off your old self with its practices

1Th 4:3 It is God's will that you should be sanctified: that you should avoid sexual immorality; [4]that each of you should learn to control his own body in a way that is holy and honorable, [5]not in passionate lust like the heathen, who do not know God; [6]and that in this matter no one should wrong his brother or take advantage of him. The Lord will punish men for all such sins, as we have already told you and warned you. (+1Th 4:7; 2Ti 2:19,22)

Heb 12:14 Make every effort to live in peace with all men and to be holy; without holiness no one will see the Lord.

Jas 1:21 Therefore, get rid of all moral filth and the evil that is so prevalent and humbly accept the word planted in you, which can save you. (+Jas 4:8; 1Pe 1:13-16; 2:11-12)

1Pe 3:15 But in your hearts set apart Christ as Lord. Always be prepared to give an answer to everyone who asks you to give the reason for the hope that you have. But do this with gentleness and respect,

3Jn 11 Dear friend, do not imitate what is evil but what is good. Anyone who does what is good is from God. Anyone who does what is evil has not seen God.

Holiness in ministers (Lev 21:6; Nu 8:14-15).

Honesty (Lev 19:35-36; Dt 25:13-16)—

1Th 4:12 so that your daily life may win the respect of outsiders and so that you will not be dependent on anybody.

In service (1Co 4:2; Eph 6:5-7; Col 3:22-23; Tit 2:9-10), in office (Lk 3:13). Honor, to civil rulers (1Pe 2:17), to wife (1Pe 3:7).

Hospitality (Ro 12:13)—

Heb 13:2 Do not forget to entertain strangers, for by so doing some people have entertained angels without knowing it. (+1Pe 4:9)

Humane treatment of servants (Eph 6:9). Humility (Ro 12:16; Php 2:3; Jas 4:10; 1Pe 3:8; 5:6-7).

Imitation of Christ—

Ro 13:14 Rather, clothe yourselves with the Lord Jesus Christ, and do not think about how to gratify the desires of the sinful nature.

Col 2:6 So then, just as you received Christ Jesus as Lord, continue to live in him, (+Col 2:7)

Industry (Pr 6:6; Eph 4:28; 1Th 4:11; 2Th 3:12).

Influence for righteousness (Mt 5:16)—

Php 2:15 so that you may become blameless and pure, children of God without fault in a crooked and depraved generation, in which you shine like stars in the universe

Joyfulness (Ro 12:12; Php 3:1)—

Php 4:4 Rejoice in the Lord always. I will say it again: Rejoice!

1Th 5:16 Be joyful always;

Justice (Lev 19:15; Isa 56:1; Zec 7:9-10; Jn 7:24), in courts (Dt 1:17; 25:1-2), to foreigners (Lev 19:33-34; 24:22).

Keeping the Sabbath holy (Ex 16:29; 20:8; 31:12-16; 35:2-3; Lev 19:3,30; 26:2; Dt 5:12).

Kindness (Pr 3:27-28; Eph 4:32; Col 3:12)—

1Th 5:15 Make sure that nobody pays back wrong for wrong, but always try to be kind to each other and to everyone else.

Kindness to animals (Dt 25:4). To enemies (Ex 23:4-5; Pr 25:21; Ro 12:20).

Labor (Ex 20:9; 35:2; Dt 5:13). Laying up treasure in heaven (Mt 6:20).

Liberality (Pr 3:9; Ecc 11:1; Mt 5:42; Lk 6:30; 12:33; 2Co 8:7)—

Heb 13:16 And do not forget to do good and to share with others, for with such sacrifices God is pleased.

Liberality in God's service (Mal 3:10), in support of religion (Dt 15:19; 16:17), toward the house of God (Ex 22:29; 30:12-16; 34:26; 35:4-9), to the poor (Lev 19:9-10; 23:22; Dt 15:7-15; 24:19-21; Ro 12:13; Heb 13:16; 1Jn 3:17).

Love, for enemies (Mt 5:44; Lk 6:27-29; Ro 12:14-15), for foreigners (Lev 19:34; Dt 10:19).

Love for God—

Dt 6:5 Love the LORD your God with all your heart and with all your soul and with all your strength. (+Dt 10:12;

11:1,8,13; 30:16; Jos 22:5; 23:11; Mt 22:37; Mk 12:30; Lk 10:27)

Love for other people (Lev 19:18,33-34; Mt 19:19; 22:39; Mk 12:31; Lk 10:27; Jn 13:34; 15:12,17; Ro 12:9-10)—

Ro 13:8 Let no debt remain outstanding, except the continuing debt to love one another, for he who loves his fellowman has fulfilled the law. [9]The commandments, "Do not commit adultery," "Do not murder," "Do not steal," "Do not covet," and whatever other commandment there may be, are summed up in this one rule: "Love your neighbor as yourself." [10]Love does no harm to its neighbor. Therefore love is the fulfillment of the law. (+1Co 16:14; Gal 5:14)

Eph 5:2 and live a life of love, just as Christ loved us and gave himself up for us as a fragrant offering and sacrifice to God. (+Col 3:14)

1Th 3:12 May the Lord make your love increase and overflow for each other and for everyone else, just as ours does for you.

1Th 4:9 Now about brotherly love we do not need to write to you, for you yourselves have been taught by God to love each other. (+Heb 13:1; Jas 2:8; 1Pe 2:17; 3:8; 4:8)

1Jn 3:11 This is the message you heard from the beginning: We should love one another.

1Jn 3:18 Dear children, let us not love with words or tongue but with actions and in truth.

1Jn 3:23 And this is his command: to believe in the name of his Son, Jesus Christ, and to love one another as he commanded us.

1Jn 4:7 Dear friends, let us love one another, for love comes from God. Everyone who loves has been born of God and knows God.

1Jn 4:21 And he has given us this command: Whoever loves God must also love his brother.

2Jn 5 And now, dear lady, I am not writing you a new command but one we have had from the beginning. I ask that we love one another.

Love for wife (Eph 5:23; Col 3:19). Loving truth and peace (Zec 8:19).

Maturity—

1Co 16:13 Be on your guard; stand firm in the faith; be men of courage; be strong. [14]Do everything in love.

Mature thinking—

1Co 14:20 Brothers, stop thinking like children. In regard to evil be infants, but in your thinking be adults. (+Tit 2:2)

Meekness (Mt 5:39-40; Lk 6:29; Eph 4:2; Col 3:12)—

Tit 3:2 to slander no one, to be peaceable and considerate, and to show true humility toward all men.

Mercy—

Pr 3:3 Let love and faithfulness never leave you; bind them around your neck, write them on the tablet of your heart.

Zec 7:9 "This is what the LORD Almighty says: 'Administer true justice; show mercy and compassion to one another. [10]Do not oppress the widow or the fatherless, the alien or the poor. In your hearts do not think evil of each other.' (+Lk 6:36)

Mercy to debtors (Dt 24:6).

Oaths in God's name (Dt 6:13; 10:20).

Obedience—

Pr 7:1 My son, keep my words and store up my commands within you. [2]Keep my commands and you will live; guard my teachings as the apple of your eye. [3]Bind them on your fingers; write them on the tablet of your heart. [4]Say to wisdom, "You are my sister," and call understanding your kinsman; (+Lev 18:4-5,26,30; 19:19,37; 20:8,22; 22:31; 25:18; Nu 15:40; Dt 4:1,6,23,30; 5:32-33; 6:17-18; 7:11; 8:1,6; 10:12-13; 11:1,8,13,32; 12:28,32; 13:4; 27:1,10; 29:9; 30:2,8,16; 1Sa 15:1; 1Ki 2:2-3; 2Ki 17:37-38; 1Ch 28:20; Pr 3:6; 4:20-21; 5:7; 7:5-14; Ecc 12:13; Jn 13:15)

Obedience of children (Pr 6:20; Eph 6:1-3; Col 3:20), of servants (Eph 6:5-8; Col 3:22-25; Tit 2:9-10; 1Pe 2:18-19), of soldiers (Dt 20:3; Lk 3:14), of wives (Eph 5:22; Col 3:18; 1Pe 3:1-4), of young men (Pr 6:20; 23:22), to Christ as Lord (1Pe 3:15)

To civil government (Ecc 8:2; Mk 12:17; Lk 20:25; Ro 13:1,7)—

Tit 3:1 Remind the people to be subject to rulers and authorities, to be obedient, to be ready to do whatever is good, (+1Pe 2:13)

Obedience to God's law (Dt 11:8,13,32; 30:16; Jos 22:5; 2Ki 17:37-38; 1Ch 28:8), to parents (Pr 6:20; Eph 6:1-3; Col 3:20). Orderly conduct of divine worship (1Co 14:26-33).

Patience (Jas 1:4)—

Jas 5:7 Be patient, then, brothers, until the Lord's coming. See how the farmer waits for the land to yield its valuable crop and how patient he is for the autumn and spring rains. [8]You too, be patient and stand firm, because the Lord's coming is near. [9]Don't grumble against each other, brothers, or you will be judged. The Judge is standing at the door!

Patience under afflictions (Pr 3:11)

Under tribulations (Ro 12:12; Jas 1:2-4)—

1Pe 4:1 Therefore, since Christ suffered in his body, arm yourselves also with the same attitude, because he who has suffered in his body is done with sin.

Peaceableness (Ro 12:18; Col 3:15)—

1Th 4:11 Make it your ambition to lead a quiet life, to mind your own business and to work with your hands, just as we told you, (+Heb 12:14)

Perfection (Ge 17:1; Mt 5:48). Praise (Ps 146-150). *See Praise.*

Prayer (Jer 33:3; Mt 7:7-11; Lk 11:9-13; Php 4:6; Col 4:2)—

1Th 5:17 pray continually; [18]give thanks in all circumstances, for this is God's will for you in Christ Jesus. (+1Ti 2:8)

For more laborers in the Lord's vineyard (Mt 9:38)

For rulers—

1Ti 2:1 I urge, then, first of all, that requests, prayers, intercession and thanksgiving be made for everyone— [2]for kings and all those in authority, that we may live peaceful and quiet lives in all godliness and holiness.

Prayerfulness (Lk 22:40; Ro 12:12; 1Th 5:17). Preparation for the Sabbath (Ex 16:23).

Preparedness (Mt 24:44; 25:13,1-12)—

1Th 5:8 But since we belong to the day, let us be self-controlled, putting on faith and love as a breastplate, and the hope of salvation as a helmet.

Propagation of children (Ge 9:1,7). Propriety in worship (1Co 14:26-33,40). Prudence (Col 4:5), in guests (Pr 23:1-2), in speech (Ecc 5:2,6; 7:21; 10:20). Public, instruction in the word of God (Dt 31:10-13). worship (Ex 34:23; Dt 12:5-7,11-14,17-18,26-27; 16:16). Pure conversation (Eph 4:29; 1Pe 3:10). Purity (2Co 7:1; Eph 5:1-4; 1Ti 5:22; Heb 13:4), in the family of a minister (Lev 21:9), of thought (Php 4:8).

Quietness (1Th 4:11).

Rebuke of sin (Lev 19:17; Eph 5:11). Reconciliation between Christian brothers (Mt 5:23-25).

Regard for consciences of others—

1Co 10:28 But if anyone says to you, "This has been offered in sacrifice," then do not eat it, both for the sake of the man who told you and for conscience' sake—

Regulated enjoyments (Ecc 11:9-10).

Religious instruction of children—

Dt 4:9 Only be careful, and watch yourselves closely so that you do not forget the things your eyes have seen or let them slip from your heart as long as you live. Teach them to your children and to their children after them. (+Dt 6:7-9)

Dt 11:19 Teach them to your children, talking about them when you sit at home and when you walk along the road, when you lie down and when you get up. [20]Write them on the doorframes of your houses and on your gates,

Dt 32:46 he said to them, "Take to heart all the words I have solemnly declared to you this day, so that you may command your children to obey carefully all the words of this law. (+Eph 6:4)

Remembrance, of God in youth (Ecc 12:1), of God's mercies (Dt 5:15; 8:2)

Of the law—

Dt 6:6 These commandments that I give you today are to be upon your hearts. [7]Impress them on your children. Talk about them when you sit at home and when you walk along the road, when you lie down and when you get up. [8]Tie them as symbols on your hands and bind them on your foreheads. [9]Write them on the doorframes of your houses and on your gates.

Dt 11:18 Fix these words of mine in your hearts and minds; tie them as symbols on your hands and bind them on your foreheads. (+Dt 32:46; 1Ch 16:15)

Renunciation of sources of temptation (Mt 5:29-30; 18:8-9; Mk 9:43-48).

Repentance (Pr 1:23; Eze 33:11; Mal 3:7; Mt 3:2; 7:13-14; Mk 1:15; Ac 2:38; 17:30)—

Rev 3:19 Those whom I love I rebuke and discipline. So be earnest, and repent.

Reproof of the erring (1Ti 5:20).

Resistance of evil—

Jas 4:7 Submit yourselves, then, to God. Resist the devil, and he will flee from you.

Respect for religious instruction—

1Th 5:20 do not treat prophecies with contempt.

Rest on the Sabbath (Ex 20:10; 23:12; 32:21; 35:2-3; Lev 23:3,24; Dt 5:14).

Restraint of temper (Ecc 7:9; Eph 4:26,31)—

Jas 1:19 My dear brothers, take note of this: Everyone should be quick to listen, slow to speak and slow to become angry,

Returning good for evil (Mt 5:4; 1Co 6:7; 1Pe 3:9). Reverence, for God's house (Lev 19:30; 26:2; Ecc 5:1), for holy places (Ex 3:5; Jos 5:15; Ac 7:33)

Reverence for parents (Ex 20:12; Lev 19:3; 20:9; Dt 5:16; Pr 23:22)—

Mt 15:4 For God said, 'Honor your father and mother' and 'Anyone who curses his father or mother must be put to death.' (+Mt 19:19; Lk 18:20; Eph 6:1-2)

For the aged (Lev 19:32). Right conduct (Dt 6:18; Pr 4:26-27; Php 1:27; Jas 1:19). Righteousness (Ex 23:7; Eze 45:9; Hos 12:6; Lk 13:24; Ro 13:7-8). Rulers to study God's law (Dt 17:18-20).

Secrecy in giving alms (Mt 6:3). Seeking, the Lord (1Ch

16:11; Isa 55:6; Am 5:4,6), the kingdom of God (Mt 16:24; Mk 8:34; 10:21; Lk 9:23; 18:22; Ro 15:2). Self-discipline (Mt 5:29-30; Mk 9:45-48). Self-examination (2Co 13:5). Service for God (Ex 23:25; Dt 6:13; 10:12,20). Simplicity in worship (Mt 6:7). Six days of labor, and one day of rest (Ex 20:9-11; 35:2). Sobermindedness (Tit 2:6). Sobriety (1Th 5:8; 1Pe 1:13; 4:7; 5:8-9). Social peace (1Th 5:13).

Spiritual diligence (Ro 12:11; 13:12; Heb 4:11)—

2Pe 1:10 Therefore, my brothers, be all the more eager to make your calling and election sure. For if you do these things, you will never fall,

2Pe 3:14 So then, dear friends, since you are looking forward to this, make every effort to be found spotless, blameless and at peace with him.

Spirituality (Gal 5:16).

Steadfastness (Dt 13:8,10; Ro 12:21; 1Co 15:58; 16:13)—

Gal 5:1 It is for freedom that Christ has set us free. Stand firm, then, and do not let yourselves be burdened again by a yoke of slavery. (+Eph 6:11,13-14,18; Php 1:27; 4:1)

1Th 5:21 Test everything. Hold on to the good.

2Th 2:15 So then, brothers, stand firm and hold to the teachings we passed on to you, whether by word of mouth or by letter. (+2Ti 1:13; 1Pe 1:13; Jude ; Rev 3:11)

Steadfastness in prayer (Ro 12:12; Eph 6:18; 1Th 5:17). Submission to God (2Ch 30:8; Pr 3:11; Jas 4:7), to fraternal counsel (Eph 5:21).

Suffering, one for another—

1Jn 3:16 This is how we know what love is: Jesus Christ laid down his life for us. And we ought to lay down our lives for our brothers. 17If anyone has material possessions and sees his brother in need but has no pity on him, how can the love of God be in him?

Sympathy (Ro 12:15)—

Heb 13:3 Remember those in prison as if you were their fellow prisoners, and those who are mistreated as if you yourselves were suffering. (+1Pe 3:8)

Support of ministers (Dt 12:19; Gal 6:6)—

1Ti 5:17 The elders who direct the affairs of the church well are worthy of double honor, especially those whose work is preaching and teaching. 18For the Scripture says, "Do not muzzle the ox while it is treading out the grain," and "The worker deserves his wages."

Thankfulness (Dt 8:10; Col 2:6-7; 3:15).

Thanksgiving (Eph 5:4)—

Eph 5:20 always giving thanks to God the Father for everything, in the name of our Lord Jesus Christ.

Php 4:6 Do not be anxious about anything, but in everything, by prayer and petition, with thanksgiving, present your requests to God. (+Col 3:17; 1Th 5:17-18; 1Ti 2:1)

Heb 13:15 Through Jesus, therefore, let us continually offer to God a sacrifice of praise—the fruit of lips that confess his name.

Tithing (Dt 12:6; 14:22).

Truthfulness (Pr 3:3)—

Zec 8:16 These are the things you are to do: Speak the truth to each other, and render true and sound judgment in your courts; 17do not plot evil against your neighbor, and do not love to swear falsely. I hate all this," declares the LORD. (+Zec 8:19; Eph 4:25)

Various Christian duties—

Ro 12:6 We have different gifts, according to the grace given us. If a man's gift is prophesying, let him use it in proportion to his faith. 7If it is serving, let him serve; if it is

teaching, let him teach; 8if it is encouraging, let him encourage; if it is contributing to the needs of others, let him give generously; if it is leadership, let him govern diligently; if it is showing mercy, let him do it cheerfully.

Eph 6:10 Finally, be strong in the Lord and in his mighty power. 11Put on the full armor of God so that you can take your stand against the devil's schemes. (+Eph 6:12)

Eph 6:13 Therefore put on the full armor of God, so that when the day of evil comes, you may be able to stand your ground, and after you have done everything, to stand. 14Stand firm then, with the belt of truth buckled around your waist, with the breastplate of righteousness in place, 15and with your feet fitted with the readiness that comes from the gospel of peace. 16In addition to all this, take up the shield of faith, with which you can extinguish all the flaming arrows of the evil one. 17Take the helmet of salvation and the sword of the Spirit, which is the word of God. 18And pray in the Spirit on all occasions with all kinds of prayers and requests. With this in mind, be alert and always keep on praying for all the saints. (+Eph 6:19-20)

Jas 4:8 Come near to God and he will come near to you. Wash your hands, you sinners, and purify your hearts, you double-minded. 9Grieve, mourn and wail. Change your laughter to mourning and your joy to gloom. 10Humble yourselves before the Lord, and he will lift you up.

11Brothers, do not slander one another. Anyone who speaks against his brother or judges him speaks against the law and judges it. When you judge the law, you are not keeping it, but sitting in judgment on it. (+Jas 5:7-9)

Jas 5:12 Above all, my brothers, do not swear—not by heaven or by earth or by anything else. Let your "Yes" be yes, and your "No," no, or you will be condemned. (+Jas 5:14)

1Pe 1:13 Therefore, prepare your minds for action; be self-controlled; set your hope fully on the grace to be given you when Jesus Christ is revealed. 14As obedient children, do not conform to the evil desires you had when you lived in ignorance. 15But just as he who called you is holy, so be holy in all you do; 16for it is written: "Be holy, because I am holy."

17Since you call on a Father who judges each man's work impartially, live your lives as strangers here in reverent fear.

1Pe 2:11 Dear friends, I urge you, as aliens and strangers in the world, to abstain from sinful desires, which war against your soul. 12Live such good lives among the pagans that, though they accuse you of doing wrong, they may see your good deeds and glorify God on the day he visits us.

13Submit yourselves for the Lord's sake to every authority instituted among men: whether to the king, as the supreme authority, 14or to governors, who are sent by him to punish those who do wrong and to commend those who do right. 15For it is God's will that by doing good you should silence the ignorant talk of foolish men. 16Live as free men, but do not use your freedom as a cover-up for evil; live as servants of God. 17Show proper respect to everyone: Love the brotherhood of believers, fear God, honor the king.

18Slaves, submit yourselves to your masters with all respect, not only to those who are good and considerate, but also to those who are harsh. 19For it is commendable if a man bears up under the pain of unjust suffering because he is conscious of God. 20But how is it to your credit if you receive a beating for doing wrong and endure it? But if you suffer for doing good and you endure it, this is commendable before God. [21]To this you were called, because Christ suffered for you, leaving you an example, that you should follow in his steps.

[22]"He committed no sin, and no deceit was found in his mouth."

[23]When they hurled their insults at him, he did not retaliate; when he suffered, he made no threats. Instead, he entrusted himself to him who judges justly. [24]He himself bore our sins in his body on the tree, so that we might die to sins and live for righteousness; by his wounds you have been healed. [25]For you were like sheep going astray, but now you have returned to the Shepherd and Overseer of your souls.

1Pe 3:8 Finally, all of you, live in harmony with one another; be sympathetic, love as brothers, be compassionate and humble. [9]Do not repay evil with evil or insult with insult, but with blessing, because to this you were called so that you may inherit a blessing. (+1Pe 3:15)

1Pe 4:7 The end of all things is near. Therefore be clear minded and self-controlled so that you can pray. [8]Above all, love each other deeply, because love covers over a multitude of sins. [9]Offer hospitality to one another without grumbling. [10]Each one should use whatever gift he has received to serve others, faithfully administering God's grace in its various forms. [11]If anyone speaks, he should do it as one speaking the very words of God. If anyone serves, he should do it with the strength God provides, so that in all things God may be praised through Jesus Christ. To him be the glory and the power for ever and ever. Amen.

[12]Dear friends, do not be surprised at the painful trial you are suffering, as though something strange were happening to you. [13]But rejoice that you participate in the sufferings of Christ, so that you may be overjoyed when his glory is revealed. [14]If you are insulted because of the name of Christ, you are blessed, for the Spirit of glory and of God rests on you. [15]If you suffer, it should not be as a murderer or thief or any other kind of criminal, or even as a meddler.

1Pe 5:5 Young men, in the same way be submissive to those who are older. All of you, clothe yourselves with humility toward one another, because, "God opposes the proud but gives grace to the humble."

[6]Humble yourselves, therefore, under God's mighty hand, that he may lift you up in due time. [7]Cast all your anxiety on him because he cares for you.

[8]Be self-controlled and alert. Your enemy the devil prowls around like a roaring lion looking for someone to devour. (+2Pe 1:5-7)

Watchfulness (Pr 4:23; Mt 24:42,44; 25:13; Mk 13:35-37; Lk 12:35-40; 21:36; 1Co 16:13-14; Eph 5:15; Php 3:2; Col 4:2)—

1Th 5:6 So then, let us not be like others, who are asleep, but let us be alert and self-controlled. (+1Pe 5:8)

1Pe 5:9 Resist him, standing firm in the faith, because you know that your brothers throughout the world are undergoing the same kind of sufferings. (+Rev 3:2)

Watchfulness against backsliding (Dt 4:9; 8:11; 11:16,28; 2Pe 3:17), against covetousness (Dt 15:9; Lk 12:15), against false Christs (Mt 24:23-26; Mk 13:21-23; Lk 17:23). Wholehearted service (Jos 22:5; 24:14; 1Sa 12:24; 1Ch 28:9; Ecc 9:10). Wisdom (Pr 3:21; 4:5,13; 5:1; 8:5-6,32-33; 23:12,23), in speech (Pr 23:9; 26:4-5; Col 4:6). Wise self-restraint (Ecc 7:16-18,21). Witnessing for Christ (Mk 5:19; 1Pe 3:15).

Worship (Ge 35:1; Ex 20:24; Rev 19:10; 22:9)—

Eph 5:19 Speak to one another with psalms, hymns and spiritual songs. Sing and make music in your heart to the Lord, (+Col 3:16)

Zeal for righteousness (Jn 6:27; 1Co 15:58)

Zeal for the faith—

Jude 3 Dear friends, although I was very eager to write to you about the salvation we share, I felt I had to write and urge you to contend for the faith that was once for all entrusted to the saints.

In one's calling (Ro 12:6-8).

Fixing Penalty for:

Adultery (Lev 20:10; 21:9; 1Co 6:9-10; Gal 5:19,21). Arson (Ex 22:6).

Bestiality (Ex 22:19; Lev 20:13,15-16). Blasphemy (Lev 24:16).

Carnality (Lev 19:20). Contempt of authority (Dt 17:12). Criminal neglect to safeguard life (Ex 21:28-36). Cursing parents (Ex 21:17; Lev 20:9).

Destruction of neighbor's property (Lev 24:18). Disobedience (Nu 15:30-31).

False Witness (Dt 19:18-19). Fornication (Ac 15:20; 1Co 6:18; 10:8).

Idolatry (Lev 20:2-5; Dt 17:2-5), enticement to idolatry (Dt 13:5,9-10,15). Impenitence (Lev 23:29). Incest (Lev 20:11-12,14,17,19-21).

Laziness (2Th 3:10). Loss of borrowed property (Ex 22:14-15), of property held in trust (Ex 22:7,13).

Kidnapping (Ex 21:16; Dt 24:7). Murder (Ex 21:12; Lev 24:17; Nu 35:31; Dt 19:11-13).

Personal injury (Ex 21:18-27; Lev 24:19-20).

Sabbath breaking (Ex 31:14; 35:2). Seduction (Ex 22:16).

Theft (Ex 22:1-4). Trespass (Ex 22:5).

Untimely cohabitation (Lev 20:18).

Witchcraft (Ex 22:18; Lev 20:27).

Forbidding:

Adultery (Ex 20:14; Lev 18:20; Dt 5:18; Mt 5:27; 19:18; Lk 18:20)—

Ro 13:9 The commandments, "Do not commit adultery," "Do not murder," "Do not steal," "Do not covet," and whatever other commandment there may be, are summed up in this one rule: "Love your neighbor as yourself."

1Co 10:8 We should not commit sexual immorality, as some of them did—and in one day twenty-three thousand of them died.

Anxiety (Mt 6:25-34; 10:19-23; Lk 12:11,22-32; Jn 14:27; Php 4:6). Association with evil company (Pr 1:10-19), with harlots (Pr 2:16; 5:3-21; 6:20,24-26; 7:1-27; 23:26-28).

Bestiality (Lev 18:23; 20:13,15-16). Boasting (Dt 9:4). Bribe taking (Ex 23:8; Dt 16:19; 27:25).

Causeless strife (Pr 3:30). Change in God's law (Dt 4:2; 12:32). Class distinction (Ex 23:3; Lev 19:15; Nu 15:29; Dt 16:19), legislation (Lev 24:22). Company with drunkards (Pr 23:20). Conformity to the world (Lev 20:23).

Contention (Ro 13:13)—

Php 2:14 Do everything without complaining or arguing, (+2Ti 2:14; Tit 3:2)

Corrupt conversation (Eph 4:29; 5:4; Col 3:8). Covetousness (Ex 20:17; Dt 5:21; 7:25-26; Lk 12:15; Ro 13:9; Eph 5:3; Col 3:5; 1Ti 6:10-11; Heb 13:5).

Dishonesty in business (Lev 19:13,35; 25:14; Dt 25:13-15; Mk 10:19). Divorce (1Co 7:10-11, w Mt 5:32; 19:9; Mk 10:11-12; Lk 16:18).

Drunkenness (Ro 13:13)—

Eph 5:18 Do not get drunk on wine, which leads to debauchery. Instead, be filled with the Spirit.

Envy (Pr 3:31; 23:17; 24:1,19; Ro 13:13; 1Pe 2:1). Evil speech (Ps 34:13; Pr 4:24; 30:10; Tit 3:2; 1Pe 3:10). Evil, to a neighbor (Ex 20:16; Lev 19:13,16; Pr 3:29).

False, dealing (Lev 6:1-5; 19:11), swearing (Lev 19:12), witness (Ex 20:16; 23:1; Lev 19:16; Dt 5:20; Pr 24:28; Mt 19:18; Lk 18:20). Falsehood (Lev 19:11; Eph 4:25; Col 3:9). Fellowship with the wicked (Pr 1:10-15; 4:14-15; Ro 16:17; 1Co 5:9-11; 2Co 6:14,17; Eph 5:11; 2Th 3:6; 2Ti 3:5). Foolish, unlearned questions (2Ti 2:23). Fraud (Lev 19:11,13,35; 1Th 4:6).

Giving cause for stumbling (1Co 8:9)—

1Co 10:32 Do not cause anyone to stumble, whether Jews, Greeks or the church of God—

Grudges (Lev 19:18). Haste for riches (Pr 23:4), in litigation (Pr 25:8-9). Hatred (Lev 19:17; Eph 4:31; Col 3:8). Heed to false teachers (Dt 13:1-18).

Idolatry (Ex 20:3-5,23; Lev 18:21; 20:2-5; 26:1; Dt 4:16-19,23; 5:7-9; 6:14; 13:2-3; 16:21-22; Jos 24:14; 2Ki 17:35; Eze 20:18)—

1Co 10:7 Do not be idolaters, as some of them were; as it is written: "The people sat down to eat and drink and got up to indulge in pagan revelry."

1Jn 5:21 Dear children, keep yourselves from idols.

Impure marriages (Lev 21:7). Incest (Lev 18:6; 20:11-12,13,17,19-21; Dt 22:30). Indulgence in wine (Pr 23:31; Eph 5:18; Tit 2:3). Injustice (Ex 23:2-3; Lev 19:15; 25:17; Dt 16:19), to foreigners (Ex 12:49; 22:21; Lev 19:33-34; Dt 1:16; 24:14,17), to the poor (Ex 23:6). Intolerance (Mk 9:39; Lk 9:49-50).

Improper respect of persons—

Jas 2:1 My brothers, as believers in our glorious Lord Jesus Christ, don't show favoritism. [2]Suppose a man comes into your meeting wearing a gold ring and fine clothes, and a poor man in shabby clothes also comes in. [3]If you show special attention to the man wearing fine clothes and say, "Here's a good seat for you," but say to the poor man, "You stand there" or "Sit on the floor by my feet," [4]have you not discriminated among yourselves and become judges with evil thoughts? (+Jas 2:5-7)

Jas 2:8 If you really keep the royal law found in Scripture, "Love your neighbor as yourself," you are doing right. [9]But if you show favoritism, you sin and are convicted by the law as lawbreakers.

Labor on the Sabbath (Ex 20:10; 23:12; 34:21; 35:2-3; Lev 23:3; Dt 5:14).

Lewdness (Pr 31:3; Ro 13:13; Eph 4:17-25)—

Eph 4:26 "In your anger do not sin": Do not let the sun go down while you are still angry, [27]and do not give the devil a foothold. [28]He who has been stealing must steal no longer, but must work, doing something useful with his own hands, that he may have something to share with those in need.

[29]Do not let any unwholesome talk come out of your mouths, but only what is helpful for building others up according to their needs, that it may benefit those who listen. [30]And do not grieve the Holy Spirit of God, with whom you were sealed for the day of redemption. [31]Get rid of all bitterness, rage and anger, brawling and slander, along with every form of malice. [32]Be kind and compassionate to one another, forgiving each other, just as in Christ God forgave you. (+Eph 5:3; 1Th 4:2-6; 2Ti 2:22)

Lawlessness (Dt 12:8). Laziness (2Th 3:10). Love of the world (1Jn 2:15).

Malice (Lev 19:17-18; Eph 4:31; Col 3:8; 1Pe 2:1). Malicious mischief (Lev 19:14). Meddling (1Pe 4:15). Murder (Ex 20:13; Dt 5:17; Mt 5:21; 19:18; Ro 13:9; Jas 2:11; 1Pe 4:15). Murmuring (1Co 10:10; Php 2:14; Jas 5:9).

Offerings with blemish implying insincere or imperfect service of God (Lev 1:3,10; 3:1,6; 4:3,23,28,32; 5:15,18; 6:6; 9:2-3; 22:18-22; Dt 15:21; 17:1). Oppression (Lev 19:13; Pr 22:22), of the poor (Dt 24:14), of the widows and orphans (Ex 22:22-24; Jer 22:3; Zec 7:10). Ostentation in giving, in fasting, and in prayer (Mt 6:1,5-6,17-18).

Perjury (Lev 19:12). Perversion of justice (Dt 16:19-20; 24:17). Prejudice (Ex 23:3). Profane swearing (Mt 5:34-36; Jas 5:12). Profaning God's name (Ex 20:7; Lev 18:21; 19:12; 21:6; 22:32; Dt 5:11). Prostitution of a daughter (Lev 19:29). Putting a neighbor's life in peril by false witness (Lev 19:16).

Removal of landmarks (Dt 19:14; Pr 22:28; 23:10). Resistance (Mt 5:39). Retaliation (Lev 19:18; Pr 24:29; Mt 5:38-42; Ro 12:17; 1Th 5:15; 1Pe 3:9). Robbery (Lev 19:13; Pr 22:22).

Sabbath breaking (Ex 31:14; Jer 17:21-22). Self-confidence (Pr 3:5,7).

Self-pride—

Ro 12:3 For by the grace given me I say to every one of you: Do not think of yourself more highly than you ought, but rather think of yourself with sober judgment, in accordance with the measure of faith God has given you.

Self-praise (Pr 27:2). Selfishness (1Co 10:24; Php 2:4). Strife (2Ti 2:24). Homosexuality (Lev 18:22; 20:13).

Taking of interest (Ex 22:25; Lev 25:35,37). Talebearing (Lev 19:16). Theft (Ex 20:15; Lev 19:11; Dt 5:19; Mt 19:18; Lk 18:20; Ro 13:9; Eph 4:28; 1Pe 4:15).

Uncharitable judgments (Mt 7:1-5; Lk 6:37,42)—

Ro 14:1 Accept him whose faith is weak, without passing judgment on disputable matters. [2]One man's faith allows him to eat everything, but another man, whose faith is weak, eats only vegetables. [3]The man who eats everything must not look down on him who does not, and the man who does not eat everything must not condemn the man who does, for God has accepted him.

Ro 14:13 Therefore let us stop passing judgment on one another. Instead, make up your mind not to put any stumbling block or obstacle in your brother's way.

Uncharitableness (Pr 24:17; Mt 18:10). Unholy ambition (Php 2:3). Unrighteous anger (Mt 5:22). Unrighteous judgments (Lev 19:15). Use of strong drink by priests (Lev 10:9).

Vain repetitions in prayer (Mt 6:7-8).

Various vices—

Ro 13:12 The night is nearly over; the day is almost here. So let us put aside the deeds of darkness and put on the armor of light. [13]Let us behave decently, as in the daytime, not in orgies and drunkenness, not in sexual immorality and debauchery, not in dissension and jealousy. (+Gal 5:19-21; Eph 4:28-31)

Eph 5:3 But among you there must not be even a hint of sexual immorality, or of any kind of impurity, or of greed, because these are improper for God's holy people. [4]Nor should there be obscenity, foolish talk or coarse joking, which are out of place, but rather thanksgiving. [5]For of this you can be sure: No immoral, impure or greedy person—such a man is an idolater—has any inheritance in the kingdom of Christ and of God. [6]Let no one deceive you with empty words, for because of such things God's wrath comes on those who are disobedient.

Eph 5:11 Have nothing to do with the fruitless deeds of darkness, but rather expose them. (+Eph 5:18; Col 3:5,8-9; 1Th 4:3-6; 5:15,22; 1Ti 3:3,8; 6:17)

2Ti 3:2 People will be lovers of themselves, lovers of money, boastful, proud, abusive, disobedient to their parents, ungrateful, unholy, [3]without love, unforgiving, slanderous, without self-control, brutal, not lovers of the good, [4]treacherous, rash, conceited, lovers of pleasure rather than lovers of God— [5]having a form of godliness but denying its power. Have nothing to do with them. (+Tit 2:3,10; Heb 13:5; Jas 1:21)

Jas 2:11 For he who said, "Do not commit adultery," also said, "Do not murder." If you do not commit adultery but do commit murder, you have become a lawbreaker. (+Jas 4:11; 5:9,12; 1Pe 2:11; 3:9)

1Pe 4:3 For you have spent enough time in the past doing what pagans choose to do—living in debauchery, lust, drunkenness, orgies, carousing and detestable idolatry.

Witchcraft (Lev 19:26,31; 20:6). Withholding a servant's wages (Lev 19:13).

Worldliness (Mt 6:19)—

Ro 12:2 Do not conform any longer to the pattern of this world, but be transformed by the renewing of your mind. Then you will be able to test and approve what God's will is—his good, pleasing and perfect will.

1Jn 2:15 Do not love the world or anything in the world. If anyone loves the world, the love of the Father is not in him.

Worldliness of ministers (2Ti 2:4-5).

Implied:

Commanding an exact conscience (Mt 6:22-24). Against self-righteousness (Mt 7:3).

Precepts of Jesus:

Stated or implied—

Mt 5:16 In the same way, let your light shine before men, that they may see your good deeds and praise your Father in heaven.

Mt 5:22 But I tell you that anyone who is angry with his brother will be subject to judgment. Again, anyone who says to his brother, 'Raca,' is answerable to the Sanhedrin. But anyone who says, 'You fool!' will be in danger of the fire of hell.

[23]"Therefore, if you are offering your gift at the altar and there remember that your brother has something against you, [24]leave your gift there in front of the altar. First go and be reconciled to your brother; then come and offer your gift.

Mt 5:27 "You have heard that it was said, 'Do not commit adultery.' [28]But I tell you that anyone who looks at a woman lustfully has already committed adultery with her in his heart. [29]If your right eye causes you to sin, gouge it out and throw it away. It is better for you to lose one part of your body than for your whole body to be thrown into hell. [30]And if your right hand causes you to sin, cut it off and throw it away. It is better for you to lose one part of your body than for your whole body to go into hell.

[31]"It has been said, 'Anyone who divorces his wife must give her a certificate of divorce.' [32]But I tell you that anyone who divorces his wife, except for marital unfaithfulness, causes her to become an adulteress, and anyone who marries the divorced woman commits adultery.

[33]"Again, you have heard that it was said to the people long ago, 'Do not break your oath, but keep the oaths you

have made to the Lord.' [34]But I tell you, Do not swear at all: either by heaven, for it is God's throne; [35]or by the earth, for it is his footstool; or by Jerusalem, for it is the city of the Great King. [36]And do not swear by your head, for you cannot make even one hair white or black. [37]Simply let your 'Yes' be 'Yes,' and your 'No,' 'No'; anything beyond this comes from the evil one.

[38]"You have heard that it was said, 'Eye for eye, and tooth for tooth.' [39]But I tell you, Do not resist an evil person. If someone strikes you on the right cheek, turn to him the other also. [40]And if someone wants to sue you and take your tunic, let him have your cloak as well. [41]If someone forces you to go one mile, go with him two miles. [42]Give to the one who asks you, and do not turn away from the one who wants to borrow from you.

[43]"You have heard that it was said, 'Love your neighbor and hate your enemy.' [44]But I tell you: Love your enemies and pray for those who persecute you, [45]that you may be sons of your Father in heaven. He causes his sun to rise on the evil and the good, and sends rain on the righteous and the unrighteous. [46]If you love those who love you, what reward will you get? Are not even the tax collectors doing that? [47]And if you greet only your brothers, what are you doing more than others? Do not even pagans do that? [48]Be perfect, therefore, as your heavenly Father is perfect.

Mt 6:1 "Be careful not to do your 'acts of righteousness' before men, to be seen by them. If you do, you will have no reward from your Father in heaven.

[2]"So when you give to the needy, do not announce it with trumpets, as the hypocrites do in the synagogues and on the streets, to be honored by men. I tell you the truth, they have received their reward in full. [3]But when you give to the needy, do not let your left hand know what your right hand is doing, [4]so that your giving may be in secret. Then your Father, who sees what is done in secret, will reward you.

Mt 6:6 But when you pray, go into your room, close the door and pray to your Father, who is unseen. Then your Father, who sees what is done in secret, will reward you. [7]And when you pray, do not keep on babbling like pagans, for they think they will be heard because of their many words. [8]Do not be like them, for your Father knows what you need before you ask him.

Mt 6:16 "When you fast, do not look somber as the hypocrites do, for they disfigure their faces to show men they are fasting. I tell you the truth, they have received their reward in full. [17]But when you fast, put oil on your head and wash your face, [18]so that it will not be obvious to men that you are fasting, but only to your Father, who is unseen; and your Father, who sees what is done in secret, will reward you.

[19]"Do not store up for yourselves treasures on earth, where moth and rust destroy, and where thieves break in and steal. [20]But store up for yourselves treasures in heaven, where moth and rust do not destroy, and where thieves do not break in and steal. [21]For where your treasure is, there your heart will be also.

[22]"The eye is the lamp of the body. If your eyes are good, your whole body will be full of light. [23]But if your eyes are bad, your whole body will be full of darkness. If then the light within you is darkness, how great is that darkness!

[24]"No one can serve two masters. Either he will hate the one and love the other, or he will be devoted to the one and despise the other. You cannot serve both God and Money.

[25]"Therefore I tell you, do not worry about your life,

what you will eat or drink; or about your body, what you will wear. Is not life more important than food, and the body more important than clothes?

Mt 6:31 So do not worry, saying, 'What shall we eat?' or 'What shall we drink?' or 'What shall we wear?' ³²For the pagans run after all these things, and your heavenly Father knows that you need them. ³³But seek first his kingdom and his righteousness, and all these things will be given to you as well. ³⁴Therefore do not worry about tomorrow, for tomorrow will worry about itself. Each day has enough trouble of its own. (+Mt 7:1-5)

Mt 7:6 "Do not give dogs what is sacred; do not throw your pearls to pigs. If you do, they may trample them under their feet, and then turn and tear you to pieces.

⁷"Ask and it will be given to you; seek and you will find; knock and the door will be opened to you. ⁸For everyone who asks receives; he who seeks finds; and to him who knocks, the door will be opened.

⁹"Which of you, if his son asks for bread, will give him a stone? ¹⁰Or if he asks for a fish, will give him a snake? ¹¹If you, then, though you are evil, know how to give good gifts to your children, how much more will your Father in heaven give good gifts to those who ask him! ¹²So in everything, do to others what you would have them do to you, for this sums up the Law and the Prophets.

¹³"Enter through the narrow gate. For wide is the gate and broad is the road that leads to destruction, and many enter through it. ¹⁴But small is the gate and narrow the road that leads to life, and only a few find it. (+Mt 7:15-20)

Mt 7:21 "Not everyone who says to me, 'Lord, Lord,' will enter the kingdom of heaven, but only he who does the will of my Father who is in heaven. ²²Many will say to me on that day, 'Lord, Lord, did we not prophesy in your name, and in your name drive out demons and perform many miracles?' ²³Then I will tell them plainly, 'I never knew you. Away from me, you evildoers!'

²⁴"Therefore everyone who hears these words of mine and puts them into practice is like a wise man who built his house on the rock. ²⁵The rain came down, the streams rose, and the winds blew and beat against that house; yet it did not fall, because it had its foundation on the rock. ²⁶But everyone who hears these words of mine and does not put them into practice is like a foolish man who built his house on sand. ²⁷The rain came down, the streams rose, and the winds blew and beat against that house, and it fell with a great crash."

²⁸When Jesus had finished saying these things, the crowds were amazed at his teaching, ²⁹because he taught as one who had authority, and not as their teachers of the law. (+Mt 10:5-42)

Mt 16:24 Then Jesus said to his disciples, "If anyone would come after me, he must deny himself and take up his cross and follow me.

Mt 18:8 If your hand or your foot causes you to sin cut it off and throw it away. It is better for you to enter life maimed or crippled than to have two hands or two feet and be thrown into eternal fire. ⁹And if your eye causes you to sin, gouge it out and throw it away. It is better for you to enter life with one eye than to have two eyes and be thrown into the fire of hell.

¹⁰"See that you do not look down on one of these little ones. For I tell you that their angels in heaven always see the face of my Father in heaven.

Mt 18:15 "If your brother sins against you, go and show him his fault, just between the two of you. If he listens to you, you have won your brother over. ¹⁶But if he will not

listen, take one or two others along, so that 'every matter may be established by the testimony of two or three witnesses.' ¹⁷If he refuses to listen to them, tell it to the church; and if he refuses to listen even to the church, treat him as you would a pagan or a tax collector.

Mt 18:21 Then Peter came to Jesus and asked, "Lord, how many times shall I forgive my brother when he sins against me? Up to seven times?"

²²Jesus answered, "I tell you, not seven times, but seventy-seven times.

Mt 19:16 Now a man came up to Jesus and asked, "Teacher, what good thing must I do to get eternal life?"

¹⁷"Why do you ask me about what is good?" Jesus replied. "There is only One who is good. If you want to enter life, obey the commandments."

¹⁸"Which ones?" the man inquired.

Jesus replied, " 'Do not murder, do not commit adultery, do not steal, do not give false testimony, ¹⁹honor your father and mother,' and 'love your neighbor as yourself.' "

Mt 20:25 Jesus called them together and said, "You know that the rulers of the Gentiles lord it over them, and their high officials exercise authority over them. ²⁶Not so with you. Instead, whoever wants to become great among you must be your servant, ²⁷and whoever wants to be first must be your slave— ²⁸just as the Son of Man did not come to be served, but to serve, and to give his life as a ransom for many." (+Mt 22:21)

Mt 22:34 Hearing that Jesus had silenced the Sadducees, the Pharisees got together. ³⁵One of them, an expert in the law, tested him with this question: ³⁶"Teacher, which is the greatest commandment in the Law?"

³⁷Jesus replied: " 'Love the Lord your God with all your heart and with all your soul and with all your mind.' ³⁸This is the first and greatest commandment. ³⁹And the second is like it: 'Love your neighbor as yourself.' ⁴⁰All the Law and the Prophets hang on these two commandments."

Mt 24:42 "Therefore keep watch, because you do not know on what day your Lord will come. ⁴³But understand this: If the owner of the house had known at what time of night the thief was coming, he would have kept watch and would not have let his house be broken into. ⁴⁴So you also must be ready, because the Son of Man will come at an hour when you do not expect him.

⁴⁵"Who then is the faithful and wise servant, whom the master has put in charge of the servants in his household to give them their food at the proper time? ⁴⁶It will be good for that servant whose master finds him doing so when he returns. ⁴⁷I tell you the truth, he will put him in charge of all his possessions. ⁴⁸But suppose that servant is wicked and says to himself, 'My master is staying away a long time,' ⁴⁹and he then begins to beat his fellow servants and to eat and drink with drunkards. ⁵⁰The master of that servant will come on a day when he does not expect him and at an hour he is not aware of. ⁵¹He will cut him to pieces and assign him a place with the hypocrites, where there will be weeping and gnashing of teeth.

Mt 25:34 "Then the King will say to those on his right, 'Come, you who are blessed by my Father; take your inheritance, the kingdom prepared for you since the creation of the world. ³⁵For I was hungry and you gave me something to eat, I was thirsty and you gave me something to drink, I was a stranger and you invited me in, ³⁶I needed clothes and you clothed me, I was sick and you looked after me, I was in prison and you came to visit me.'

³⁷"Then the righteous will answer him, 'Lord, when did we see you hungry and feed you, or thirsty and give you

something to drink? ³⁸When did we see you a stranger and invite you in, or needing clothes and clothe you? ³⁹When did we see you sick or in prison and go to visit you?'

⁴⁰"The King will reply, 'I tell you the truth, whatever you did for one of the least of these brothers of mine, you did for me.'

⁴¹"Then he will say to those on his left, 'Depart from me, you who are cursed, into the eternal fire prepared for the devil and his angels. ⁴²For I was hungry and you gave me nothing to eat, I was thirsty and you gave me nothing to drink, ⁴³I was a stranger and you did not invite me in, I needed clothes and you did not clothe me, I was sick and in prison and you did not look after me.'

⁴⁴"They also will answer, 'Lord, when did we see you hungry or thirsty or a stranger or needing clothes or sick or in prison, and did not help you?'

⁴⁵"He will reply, 'I tell you the truth, whatever you did not do for one of the least of these, you did not do for me.'

⁴⁶"Then they will go away to eternal punishment, but the righteous to eternal life."

Mk 6:7 Calling the Twelve to him, he sent them out two by two and gave them authority over evil spirits.

⁸These were his instructions: "Take nothing for the journey except a staff—no bread, no bag, no money in your belts. ⁹Wear sandals but not an extra tunic. ¹⁰Whenever you enter a house, stay there until you leave that town. ¹¹And if any place will not welcome you or listen to you, shake the dust off your feet when you leave, as a testimony against them." (+Mk 8:34)

Mk 9:35 Sitting down, Jesus called the Twelve and said, "If anyone wants to be first, he must be the very last, and the servant of all." (+Mk 9:36-37)

Mk 9:38 "Teacher," said John, "we saw a man driving out demons in your name and we told him to stop, because he was not one of us."

³⁹"Do not stop him," Jesus said. "No one who does a miracle in my name can in the next moment say anything bad about me, (+Mk 9:40-41)

Mk 9:42 "And if anyone causes one of these little ones who believe in me to sin, it would be better for him to be thrown into the sea with a large millstone tied around his neck. ⁴³If your hand causes you to sin, cut it off. It is better for you to enter life maimed than with two hands to go into hell, where the fire never goes out.

Mk 9:45 And if your foot causes you to sin, cut it off. It is better for you to enter life crippled than to have two feet and be thrown into hell.

Mk 9:47 And if your eye causes you to sin, pluck it out. It is better for you to enter the kingdom of God with one eye than to have two eyes and be thrown into hell, ⁴⁸where "'their worm does not die, and the fire is not quenched.' ⁴⁹Everyone will be salted with fire.

⁵⁰"Salt is good, but if it loses its saltiness, how can you make it salty again? Have salt in yourselves, and be at peace with each other."

Mk 10:9 Therefore what God has joined together, let man not separate." (+Mk 10:10)

Mk 10:11 He answered, "Anyone who divorces his wife and marries another woman commits adultery against her. ¹²And if she divorces her husband and marries another man, she commits adultery." (+Mk 10:17,22)

Mk 11:22 "Have faith in God," Jesus answered.

Mk 12:17 Then Jesus said to them, "Give to Caesar what is Caesar's and to God what is God's." And they were amazed at him.

Mk 13:33 Be on guard! Be alert! You do not know when

that time will come. ³⁴It's like a man going away: He leaves his house and puts his servants in charge, each with his assigned task, and tells the one at the door to keep watch.

³⁵"Therefore keep watch because you do not know when the owner of the house will come back—whether in the evening, or at midnight, or when the rooster crows, or at dawn. ³⁶If he comes suddenly, do not let him find you sleeping. ³⁷What I say to you, I say to everyone: 'Watch!'" (+Lk 6:27-36)

Lk 6:37 "Do not judge, and you will not be judged. Do not condemn, and you will not be condemned. Forgive, and you will be forgiven. ³⁸Give, and it will be given to you. A good measure, pressed down, shaken together and running over, will be poured into your lap. For with the measure you use, it will be measured to you."

³⁹He also told them this parable: "Can a blind man lead a blind man? Will they not both fall into a pit? ⁴⁰A student is not above his teacher, but everyone who is fully trained will be like his teacher.

⁴¹"Why do you look at the speck of sawdust in your brother's eye and pay no attention to the plank in your own eye? ⁴²How can you say to your brother, 'Brother, let me take the speck out of your eye,' when you yourself fail to see the plank in your own eye? You hypocrite, first take the plank out of your eye, and then you will see clearly to remove the speck from your brother's eye. (+Lk 10:28-37; 12:12-14)

Lk 12:15 Then he said to them, "Watch out! Be on your guard against all kinds of greed; a man's life does not consist in the abundance of his possessions." (+Lk 12:16-31; 13:24)

Jn 7:24 Stop judging by mere appearances, and make a right judgment."

Jn 13:34 "A new command I give you: Love one another. As I have loved you, so you must love one another. ³⁵By this all men will know that you are my disciples, if you love one another."

Jn 14:11 Believe me when I say that I am in the Father and the Father is in me; or at least believe on the evidence of the miracles themselves.

Jn 14:15 "If you love me, you will obey what I command.

Jn 14:23 Jesus replied, "If anyone loves me, he will obey my teaching. My Father will love him, and we will come to him and make our home with him. ²⁴He who does not love me will not obey my teaching. These words you hear are not my own; they belong to the Father who sent me.

Jn 15:2 He cuts off every branch in me that bears no fruit, while every branch that does bear fruit he prunes so that it will be even more fruitful. (+Jn 15:3)

Jn 15:4 Remain in me, and I will remain in you. No branch can bear fruit by itself; it must remain in the vine. Neither can you bear fruit unless you remain in me.

⁵"I am the vine; you are the branches. If a man remains in me and I in him, he will bear much fruit; apart from me you can do nothing. (+Jn 15:6)

Jn 15:7 If you remain in me and my words remain in you, ask whatever you wish, and it will be given you. ⁸This is to my Father's glory, that you bear much fruit, showing yourselves to be my disciples.

⁹"As the Father has loved me, so have I loved you. Now remain in my love. ¹⁰If you obey my commands, you will remain in my love, just as I have obeyed my Father's commands and remain in his love. ¹¹I have told you this so that my joy may be in you and that your joy may be

complete. [12]My command is this: Love each other as I have loved you.

Jn 15:17 This is my command: Love each other.

Jn 15:20 Remember the words I spoke to you: 'No servant is greater than his master.' If they persecuted me, they will persecute you also. If they obeyed my teaching, they will obey yours also. [21]They will treat you this way because of my name, for they do not know the One who sent me. [22]If I had not come and spoken to them, they would not be guilty of sin. Now, however, they have no excuse for their sin.

Prescribing:

Law of evidence (Dt 17:6; 19:15). Number of stripes in punishment (Dt 25:3). Priestly benedictions (Nu 6:23-26). Stimulants for the perishing (Pr 31:6).

Warning:

The rich—

1Ti 6:17 Command those who are rich in this present world not to be arrogant nor to put their hope in wealth, which is so uncertain, but to put their hope in God, who richly provides us with everything for our enjoyment. [18]Command them to do good, to be rich in good deeds, and to be generous and willing to share. [19]In this way they will lay up treasure for themselves as a firm foundation for the coming age, so that they may take hold of the life that is truly life.

Warning against:

Covetousness (Lk 12:15). False teachers (Mt 7:15; Eph 5:6-7; Col 2:8). Love of money (Heb 13:5).

Quenching the Spirit—

1Th 5:19 Do not put out the Spirit's fire;

Sensuality (Pr 6:24-25). Sinful indulgence (Lk 21:34). Sinning against the Holy Spirit (Eph 4:30; 1Th 5:19). Temptations (Pr 1:10-15; 19:27).

See Adultery; Children; Citizens; Homicide; Instruction; Ministers; Obedience, Commanded; Servant; Theft; Wife; Women.

COMMANDMENTS AND STATUTES, OF MEN

Traditions (Isa 29:13; Ro 14:1-6,10-19)—

Ro 14:20 Do not destroy the work of God for the sake of food. All food is clean, but it is wrong for a man to eat anything that causes someone else to stumble. [21]It is better not to eat meat or drink wine or to do anything else that will cause your brother to fall. (+Gal 1:14; Col 2:8)

1Ti 4:1 The Spirit clearly says that in later times some will abandon the faith and follow deceiving spirits and things taught by demons. [2]Such teachings come through hypocritical liars, whose consciences have been seared as with a hot iron. [3]They forbid people to marry and order them to abstain from certain foods, which God created to be received with thanksgiving by those who believe and who know the truth.

Rejected by Jesus (Mt 15:2-20; Mk 7:2-23).

COMMERCE
Laws concerning (Lev 19:36-37; 25:14,17). Carried on by means of caravans (Ge 37:25,27; Isa 60:6), ships (1Ki 9:27-28; 10:11; 22:48; Ps 107:23-30; Pr 31:14; Rev 18:19). Conducted in fairs (Eze 27:12,19; Mt 11:16). Of the Arabs (Isa 60:6; Jer 6:20; Eze 27:21-24), Egyptians (Ge 42:2-34), Ethiopians (Isa 45:14), Ishmaelites (Ge 37:27-28), Israelites (1Ki 9:26-28; Ne 3:31-32; Eze 27:17), Ninevites (Na 3:16), Syrians (Eze 27:16, 18), Tyrians (2Sa 5:11; 1Ki 5:6; Isa 23:8; Eze 27; 28:5), Sidonians (Isa 23:2; Eze 27:8), Babylonians (Rev 18:3,11-

13), Israelites (Eze 27:17). From Tarshish (Jer 10:9; Eze 27:25).

Evil practices connected with (Pr 29:14; Eze 22:13; Hos 12:7).

Articles of:

Apes and baboons (1Ki 10:22), balm (Ge 37:25), blue cloth (Eze 27:24), bronze (Eze 27:13; Rev 18:12), cinnamon (Rev 18:13), cattle (Eze 27:21), chest of rich apparel (Eze 27:24), citron wood (Rev 18:12), clothes for chariots (Eze 27:20), embroidery (Eze 27:16,24), frankincense (Jer 6:20; Rev 18:13), gold (1Ki 9:28; 10:22; 2Ch 8:18; Isa 60:6; Rev 18:12), honey (Eze 27:17), horses (1Ki 10:29; Eze 27:14; Rev 18:13), ivory (1Ki 10:22; 2Ch 9:21; Eze 27:15; Rev 18:12), iron (Eze 27:12,19), land (Ge 23:13-16; Ru 4:3), lead (Eze 27:12), linen (Rev 18:12), oil (1Ki 5:11; Eze 27:17), pearls (Rev 18:12), perfumes (SS 3:6), precious stones (Eze 27:16,22; 28:13,16; Rev 18:12), purple (Eze 27:16; Rev 18:12), sheep (Rev 18:13), slaves (Ge 37:28,36; Dt 24:7), silk (Rev 18:12), silver (1Ki 10:22; 2Ch 9:21; Rev 18:12), sweet cane (Jer 6:20), timber (1Ki 5:6,8), tin (Eze 27:12), wheat (1Ki 5:11; Eze 27:17; Rev 18:13), white wool (Eze 27:18), wine (2Ch 2:15; Eze 27:18; Rev 18:13), human bodies and souls (Rev 18:13).

Transportation of passengers (Jnh 1:3; Ac 21:2; 27:2, 6,37).

See Merchant; Tarshish, 2,3; Trade and Travel; Traffic.

COMMISSARY
For armies, cattle driven with (2Ki 3:9). *See Armies.* For royal households (2Ki 4:7-19,27-28).

COMMITMENT

Through the word of truth—

Jn 17:17 Sanctify them by the truth; your word is truth.

To the Lord—

Pr 16:3 Commit to the LORD whatever you do, and your plans will succeed.

1Co 1:2 To the church of God in Corinth, to those sanctified in Christ Jesus and called to be holy, together with all those everywhere who call on the name of our Lord Jesus Christ—their Lord and ours:

2Co 7:1 Since we have these promises, dear friends, let us purify ourselves from everything that contaminates body and spirit, perfecting holiness out of reverence for God.

1Pe 1:15 But just as he who called you is holy, so be holy in all you do; [16]for it is written: "Be holy, because I am holy."

COMMONWEALTH *See Citizens.*

COMMUNION

With God—

Ps 16:7 I will praise the LORD, who counsels me; even at night my heart instructs me. (+Jn 14:23)

2Co 6:16 What agreement is there between the temple of God and idols? For we are the temple of the living God. As God has said: "I will live with them and walk among them, and I will be their God, and they will be my people." (+1Jn 1:3)

With Christ—

Jn 14:23 Jesus replied, "If anyone loves me, he will obey my teaching. My Father will love him, and we will come to him and make our home with him.

1Jn 1:3 We proclaim to you what we have seen and heard, so that you also may have fellowship with us. And our fellowship is with the Father and with his Son, Jesus Christ.

Rev 3:20 Here I am! I stand at the door and knock. If anyone hears my voice and opens the door, I will come in and eat with him, and he with me.

With the Spirit—

Jn 14:16 And I will ask the Father, and he will give you another Counselor to be with you forever— [17]the Spirit of truth. The world cannot accept him, because it neither sees him nor knows him. But you know him, for he lives with you and will be in you. [18]I will not leave you as orphans; I will come to you.

2Co 13:14 May the grace of the Lord Jesus Christ, and the love of God, and the fellowship of the Holy Spirit be with you all.

Gal 4:6 Because you are sons, God sent the Spirit of his Son into our hearts, the Spirit who calls out, *"Abba, Father."*

Php 2:1 If you have any encouragement from being united with Christ, if any comfort from his love, if any fellowship with the Spirit, if any tenderness and compassion, [2]then make my joy complete by being like-minded, having the same love, being one in spirit and purpose. *See Fellowship.*

Instances of:

Enoch (Ge 5:22,24). Noah (Ge 6:9,13-22; 8:15-17). Abraham (Ge 12:1-3,7; 17:1-2; 18:1-33; 22:1-2,11-12,16-18). Hagar (Ge 16:8-12). Isaac (Ge 26:2,24), in dreams (Ge 28:13,15; 31:3; 35:1,7; 46:2-4). Moses (Ex 3; 4:1-17; 33:9,11; 34:28-35; Nu 12:8). Joshua (Jos 6:11-24; 7:10-15). Gideon (Jdg 6:11-24). Solomon (1Ki 3:5-14; 2Ch 1:7-12).

Of Believers:

Unity—

Ps 119:63 I am a friend to all who fear you, to all who follow your precepts.

Ps 133:1 How good and pleasant it is when brothers live together in unity! [2]It is like precious oil poured on the head, running down on the beard, running down on Aaron's beard, down upon the collar of his robes. [3]It is as if the dew of Hermon were falling on Mount Zion. For there the LORD bestows his blessing, even life forevermore.

Am 3:3 Do two walk together unless they have agreed to do so?

Jn 17:20 "My prayer is not for them alone. I pray also for those who will believe in me through their message, [21]that all of them may be one, Father, just as you are in me and I am in you. May they also be in us so that the world may believe that you have sent me.

1Co 10:16 Is not the cup of thanksgiving for which we give thanks a participation in the blood of Christ? And is not the bread that we break a participation in the body of Christ? (+1Co 10:17)

1Co 12:12 The body is a unit, though it is made up of many parts; and though all its parts are many, they form one body. So it is with Christ. [13]For we were all baptized by one Spirit into one body—whether Jews or Greeks, slave or free—and we were all given the one Spirit to drink.

Commanded—

Ro 12:15 Rejoice with those who rejoice; mourn with those who mourn.

2Co 6:14 Do not be yoked together with unbelievers. For what do righteousness and wickedness have in common? Or what fellowship can light have with darkness? [15]What harmony is there between Christ and Belial? What does a

believer have in common with an unbeliever? [16]What agreement is there between the temple of God and idols? For we are the temple of the living God. As God has said: "I will live with them and walk among them, and I will be their God, and they will be my people."

[17]"Therefore come out from them and be separate, says the Lord. Touch no unclean thing, and I will receive you."

[18]"I will be a Father to you, and you will be my sons and daughters, says the Lord Almighty."

Eph 4:1 As a prisoner for the Lord, then, I urge you to live a life worthy of the calling you have received. [2]Be completely humble and gentle; be patient, bearing with one another in love. [3]Make every effort to keep the unity of the Spirit through the bond of peace.

Eph 5:11 Have nothing to do with the fruitless deeds of darkness, but rather expose them.

Col 3:16 Let the word of Christ dwell in you richly as you teach and admonish one another with all wisdom, and as you sing psalms, hymns and spiritual songs with gratitude in your hearts to God.

1Th 4:18 Therefore encourage each other with these words.

1Th 5:11 Therefore encourage one another and build each other up, just as in fact you are doing.

1Th 5:14 And we urge you, brothers, warn those who are idle, encourage the timid, help the weak, be patient with everyone.

Heb 3:13 But encourage one another daily, as long as it is called Today, so that none of you may be hardened by sin's deceitfulness.

Heb 10:24 And let us consider how we may spur one another on toward love and good deeds. [25]Let us not give up meeting together, as some are in the habit of doing, but let us encourage one another—and all the more as you see the Day approaching.

Jas 5:16 Therefore confess your sins to each other and pray for each other so that you may be healed. The prayer of a righteous man is powerful and effective.

Exemplified—

1Sa 23:16 And Saul's son Jonathan went to David at Horesh and helped him find strength in God.

Ps 55:14 with whom I once enjoyed sweet fellowship as we walked with the throng at the house of God.

Mal 3:16 Then those who feared the LORD talked with each other, and the LORD listened and heard. A scroll of remembrance was written in his presence concerning those who feared the LORD and honored his name.

Lk 22:32 But I have prayed for you, Simon, that your faith may not fail. And when you have turned back, strengthen your brothers." (+Lk 24:17)

Lk 24:32 They asked each other, "Were not our hearts burning within us while he talked with us on the road and opened the Scriptures to us?"

Ac 2:42 They devoted themselves to the apostles' teaching and to the fellowship, to the breaking of bread and to prayer. (+1Jn 1:3,7) *See Eucharist; Fellowship.*

COMMUNITY [824, 6337, 7736, *2681+4436*].

NIV+ COMMUNITIES, COMMUNITY'S

Christian—

Ac 2:44 All the believers were together and had everything in common. [45]Selling their possessions and goods, they gave to anyone as he had need.

Ac 4:32 All the believers were one in heart and mind. No one claimed that any of his possessions was his own, but they shared everything they had.

Ac 4:34 There were no needy persons among them. For from time to time those who owned lands or houses sold them, brought the money from the sales ³⁵and put it at the apostles' feet, and it was distributed to anyone as he had need.

³⁶Joseph, a Levite from Cyprus, whom the apostles called Barnabas (which means Son of Encouragement), ³⁷sold a field he owned and brought the money and put it at the apostles' feet.

Ac 5:1 Now a man named Ananias, together with his wife Sapphira, also sold a piece of property. ²With his wife's full knowledge he kept back part of the money for himself, but brought the rest and put it at the apostles' feet.

³Then Peter said, "Ananias, how is it that Satan has so filled your heart that you have lied to the Holy Spirit and have kept for yourself some of the money you received for the land? ⁴Didn't it belong to you before it was sold? And after it was sold, wasn't the money at your disposal? What made you think of doing such a thing? You have not lied to men but to God."

⁵When Ananias heard this, he fell down and died. And great fear seized all who heard what had happened. ⁶Then the young men came forward, wrapped up his body, and carried him out and buried him. ⁷About three hours later his wife came in, not knowing what had happened. ⁸Peter asked her, "Tell me, is this the price you and Ananias got for the land?"

"Yes," she said, "that is the price."

⁹Peter said to her, "How could you agree to test the Spirit of the Lord? Look! The feet of the men who buried your husband are at the door, and they will carry you out also."

¹⁰At that moment she fell down at his feet and died. Then the young men came in and, finding her dead, carried her out and buried her beside her husband.

COMPANY [782+2495+4200, 907+2118, 1201, 1887, 2657, 4722, 6051, 6337, 6640, 7233, 7372, 7736, 8031, *253+608+714, 1855, 3918, 4436, 5061, 5322*].

NIV+ COMPANIES

Evil:

Perils of (Ge 19:14)—

Ge 19:15 With the coming of dawn, the angels urged Lot, saying, "Hurry! Take your wife and your two daughters who are here, or you will be swept away when the city is punished." (+Nu 16:21-25)

Nu 16:26 He warned the assembly, "Move back from the tents of these wicked men! Do not touch anything belonging to them, or you will be swept away because of all their sins."

Nu 33:55 "'But if you do not drive out the inhabitants of the land, those you allow to remain will become barbs in your eyes and thorns in your sides. They will give you trouble in the land where you will live. (+Jdg 2:1-3)

2Ch 19:2 Jehu the seer, the son of Hanani, went out to meet him and said to the king, "Should you help the wicked and love those who hate the LORD? Because of this, the wrath of the LORD is upon you.

Ezr 9:14 Shall we again break your commands and intermarry with the peoples who commit such detestable practices? Would you not be angry enough with us to destroy us, leaving us no remnant or survivor?

Ps 50:18 When you see a thief, you join with him; you throw in your lot with adulterers.

Ps 106:35 but they mingled with the nations and adopted their customs. (+Ps 106:36; Pr 13:20)

Hos 7:5 On the day of the festival of our king the princes become inflamed with wine, and he joins hands with the mockers.

Hos 7:8 "Ephraim mixes with the nations; Ephraim is a flat cake not turned over. ⁹Foreigners sap his strength, but he does not realize it. His hair is sprinkled with gray, but he does not notice.

Mic 6:16 You have observed the statutes of Omri and all the practices of Ahab's house, and you have followed their traditions. Therefore I will give you over to ruin and your people to derision; you will bear the scorn of the nations."

Evil company, seductive—

Pr 12:11 He who works his land will have abundant food, but he who chases fantasies lacks judgment.

Pr 12:26 A righteous man is cautious in friendship, but the way of the wicked leads them astray.

Pr 16:29 A violent man entices his neighbor and leads him down a path that is not good.

Ecc 9:18 Wisdom is better than weapons of war, but one sinner destroys much good.

Mt 24:12 Because of the increase of wickedness, the love of most will grow cold,

1Co 15:33 Do not be misled: "Bad company corrupts good character."

2Pe 2:7 and if he rescued Lot, a righteous man, who was distressed by the filthy lives of lawless men ⁸(for that righteous man, living among them day after day, was tormented in his righteous soul by the lawless deeds he saw and heard)—

2Pe 2:18 For they mouth empty, boastful words and, by appealing to the lustful desires of sinful human nature, they entice people who are just escaping from those who live in error.

Evil company, shunned by the righteous—

Ps 6:8 Away from me, all you who do evil, for the LORD has heard my weeping.

Ps 26:4 I do not sit with deceitful men, nor do I consort with hypocrites; ⁵I abhor the assembly of evildoers and refuse to sit with the wicked.

Ps 26:9 Do not take away my soul along with sinners, my life with bloodthirsty men,

Ps 28:3 Do not drag me away with the wicked, with those who do evil, who speak cordially with their neighbors but harbor malice in their hearts.

Ps 31:6 I hate those who cling to worthless idols; I trust in the LORD.

Ps 84:10 Better is one day in your courts than a thousand elsewhere; I would rather be a doorkeeper in the house of my God than dwell in the tents of the wicked.

Ps 101:4 Men of perverse heart shall be far from me; I will have nothing to do with evil.

Ps 101:7 No one who practices deceit will dwell in my house; no one who speaks falsely will stand in my presence.

Ps 119:115 Away from me, you evildoers, that I may keep the commands of my God!

Ps 120:5 Woe to me that I dwell in Meshech, that I live among the tents of Kedar! ⁶Too long have I lived among those who hate peace. ⁷I am a man of peace; but when I speak, they are for war.

Ps 139:19 If only you would slay the wicked, O God! Away from me, you bloodthirsty men! (+Ps 139:20)

Ps 139:21 Do I not hate those who hate you, O LORD, and abhor those who rise up against you? ²²I have nothing but hatred for them; I count them my enemies.

Ps 141:4 Let not my heart be drawn to what is evil, to take part in wicked deeds with men who are evildoers; let me not eat of their delicacies.

Pr 14:7 Stay away from a foolish man, for you will not find knowledge on his lips.

Pr 17:12 Better to meet a bear robbed of her cubs than a fool in his folly.

Jer 9:2 Oh, that I had in the desert a lodging place for travelers, so that I might leave my people and go away from them; for they are all adulterers, a crowd of unfaithful people.

Jer 15:17 I never sat in the company of revelers, never made merry with them; I sat alone because your hand was on me and you had filled me with indignation.

Hos 4:17 Ephraim is joined to idols; leave him alone!

Rev 2:2 I know your deeds, your hard work and your perseverance. I know that you cannot tolerate wicked men, that you have tested those who claim to be apostles but are not, and have found them false.

Warnings against evil company—

Ge 49:6 Let me not enter their council, let me not join their assembly, for they have killed men in their anger and hamstrung oxen as they pleased.

2Sa 23:6 But evil men are all to be cast aside like thorns, which are not gathered with the hand. **7**Whoever touches thorns uses a tool of iron or the shaft of a spear; they are burned up where they lie."

Pr 2:11 Discretion will protect you, and understanding will guard you. **12**Wisdom will save you from the ways of wicked men, from men whose words are perverse,

Pr 2:16 It will save you also from the adulteress, from the wayward wife with her seductive words,

Pr 2:19 None who go to her return or attain the paths of life.

Pr 4:14 Do not set foot on the path of the wicked or walk in the way of evil men. **15**Avoid it, do not travel on it; turn from it and go on your way.

Pr 5:8 Keep to a path far from her, do not go near the door of her house,

Pr 9:6 Leave your simple ways and you will live; walk in the way of understanding.

Pr 20:19 A gossip betrays a confidence; so avoid a man who talks too much.

Pr 22:5 In the paths of the wicked lie thorns and snares, but he who guards his soul stays far from them.

Pr 22:10 Drive out the mocker, and out goes strife; quarrels and insults are ended.

Pr 22:24 Do not make friends with a hot-tempered man, do not associate with one easily angered, **25**or you may learn his ways and get yourself ensnared. (+Pr 23:6)

Pr 23:20 Do not join those who drink too much wine or gorge themselves on meat,

Pr 24:1 Do not envy wicked men, do not desire their company;

Pr 28:7 He who keeps the law is a discerning son, but a companion of gluttons disgraces his father.

Pr 28:19 He who works his land will have abundant food, but the one who chases fantasies will have his fill of poverty.

Pr 29:24 The accomplice of a thief is his own enemy; he is put under oath and dare not testify.

1Ti 6:5 and constant friction between men of corrupt mind, who have been robbed of the truth and who think that godliness is a means to financial gain.

Evil company forbidden—

Ex 23:2 "Do not follow the crowd in doing wrong. When you give testimony in a lawsuit, do not pervert justice by siding with the crowd,

Ex 23:32 Do not make a covenant with them or with their gods. **33**Do not let them live in your land, or they will cause you to sin against me, because the worship of their gods will certainly be a snare to you." (+Ex 34:12-15)

Lev 18:3 You must not do as they do in Egypt, where you used to live, and you must not do as they do in the land of Canaan, where I am bringing you. Do not follow their practices. (+Lev 20:23; Dt 7:2-4)

Dt 12:30 and after they have been destroyed before you, be careful not to be ensnared by inquiring about their gods, saying, "How do these nations serve their gods? We will do the same." (+Jos 23:6-13)

Pr 1:10 My son, if sinners entice you, do not give in to them. **11**If they say, "Come along with us; let's lie in wait for someone's blood, let's waylay some harmless soul; (+Pr 1:13)

Pr 1:14 throw in your lot with us, and we will share a common purse"— **15**my son, do not go along with them, do not set foot on their paths;

Isa 8:11 The LORD spoke to me with his strong hand upon me, warning me not to follow the way of this people. He said: **12**"Do not call conspiracy everything that these people call conspiracy; do not fear what they fear, and do not dread it.

Jer 51:6 "Flee from Babylon! Run for your lives! Do not be destroyed because of her sins. It is time for the LORD's vengeance; he will pay her what she deserves.

Jer 51:45 "Come out of her, my people! Run for your lives! Run from the fierce anger of the LORD.

Ro 16:17 I urge you, brothers, to watch out for those who cause divisions and put obstacles in your way that are contrary to the teaching you have learned. Keep away from them. **18**For such people are not serving our Lord Christ, but their own appetites. By smooth talk and flattery they deceive the minds of naive people.

1Co 5:6 Your boasting is not good. Don't you know that a little yeast works through the whole batch of dough?

1Co 5:9 I have written you in my letter not to associate with sexually immoral people— **10**not at all meaning the people of this world who are immoral, or the greedy and swindlers, or idolaters. In that case you would have to leave this world. **11**But now I am writing you that you must not associate with anyone who calls himself a brother but is sexually immoral or greedy, an idolater or a slanderer, a drunkard or a swindler. With such a man do not even eat. (+2Co 6:14-15,16)

2Co 6:17 "Therefore come out from them and be separate, says the Lord. Touch no unclean thing, and I will receive you." (+Gal 5:9)

Eph 5:6 Let no one deceive you with empty words, for because of such things God's wrath comes on those who are disobedient. **7**Therefore do not be partners with them.

Eph 5:11 Have nothing to do with the fruitless deeds of darkness, but rather expose them.

2Th 3:6 In the name of the Lord Jesus Christ, we command you, brothers, to keep away from every brother who is idle and does not live according to the teaching you received from us.

1Ti 5:22 Do not be hasty in the laying on of hands, and do not share in the sins of others. Keep yourself pure.

2Ti 3:4 treacherous, rash, conceited, lovers of pleasure rather than lovers of God— **5**having a form of godliness but denying its power. Have nothing to do with them.

2Jn 10 If anyone comes to you and does not bring this

teaching, do not take him into your house or welcome him. [11]Anyone who welcomes him shares in his wicked work.

Rev 18:4 Then I heard another voice from heaven say: "Come out of her, my people, so that you will not share in her sins, so that you will not receive any of her plagues;

See Example; Influence, Evil.

Good:

Ps 1:1 Blessed is the man who does not walk in the counsel of the wicked or stand in the way of sinners or sit in the seat of mockers. (+Ps 15:1-3)

Ps 15:4 who despises a vile man but honors those who fear the LORD, who keeps his oath even when it hurts, (+Ps 15:5)

Pr 13:20 He who walks with the wise grows wise, but a companion of fools suffers harm. *See Communion, Of Believers; Example; Fellowship; Influence, Good.*

COMPASSES [4684]. Carpenter's (Isa 44:13).

COMPASSION [2571+6524, 2843, 2798, 5714, 5716, 5719, 6524+8317, 8163, 8171, 2359, 3880, 3882, 4499, 5072].

NIV+ COMPASSIONATE, COMPASSIONS

Of God: *See God, Mercy of.*

Of Christ: *See Jesus the Christ, Compassion of.*

COMPEL [706, 928, 7439, 10264, 337, 340+2130, 1313, 5309].

NIV+ COMPELLED, COMPELS, COMPULSION

As used by Jesus (Lk 14:23). Does not mean physical force, but zeal and moral urgency.

COMPLACENCY [1055, 7884, 8633, 8932].

NIV+ COMPLACENT

Indifference to God is judged—

Pr 1:32 For the waywardness of the simple will kill them, and the complacency of fools will destroy them; [33]but whoever listens to me will live in safety and be at ease, without fear of harm." (+Isa 32:9,11; Am 6:1; Zep 1:12).

Lk 11:23 "He who is not with me is against me, and he who does not gather with me, scatters.

See Lukewarmness.

COMPLAINT [606, 645, 1819, 8087, 8189, 8190, 8488, 8490, 9350, 9442]. *See Murmuring.*

COMPLICITY

Warnings against—

Ps 50:18 When you see a thief, you join with him; you throw in your lot with adulterers.

Pr 29:24 The accomplice of a thief is his own enemy; he is put under oath and dare not testify.

Ro 1:32 Although they know God's righteous decree that those who do such things deserve death, they not only continue to do these very things but also approve of those who practice them.

2Jn 10 If anyone comes to you and does not bring this teaching, do not take him into your house or welcome him. [11]Anyone who welcomes him shares in his wicked work.

Instances of—

Sarah, in deceiving, Pharaoh (Ge 12:11-19), Abimelech (Ge 20:2-5,11-14), Rebekah, in deceiving Isaac (Ge 27:5-17). The elders and nobles of Jezreel, in stoning Naboth (1Ki 21:7-14). Jews who opposed building the temple (Ne 6:10-19). Daughter of Herodias, in death of John the Baptist (Mt 14:8; Mk 6:25). Pilate, in the death of Christ (Mt

27:17-26; Mk 15:9-15; Lk 23:13-25; Jn 19:13-16). Paul, in death of Stephen (Ac 7:58).

See Collusion; Connivance; Conspiracy.

COMPROMISE

Before Litigation:

Commanded, by Solomon—

Pr 25:8 do not bring hastily to court, for what will you do in the end if your neighbor puts you to shame? [9]If you argue your case with a neighbor, do not betray another man's confidence, [10]or he who hears it may shame you and you will never lose your bad reputation.

By Christ (Mt 5:25-26)—

Lk 12:58 As you are going with your adversary to the magistrate, try hard to be reconciled to him on the way, or he may drag you off to the judge, and the judge turn you over to the officer, and the officer throw you into prison. [59]I tell you, you will not get out until you have paid the last penny."

See Adjudication at Law; Arbitration; Court, Of Law; Justice.

CONANIAH [4042] (*Yahweh sustains*).

1. A Levite (2Ch 31:12-13).
2. Another Levite (2Ch 35:9).

CONCEALMENT, EXPOSURE [*4059, 7621, 636, 649, 2821, 5158, 5745, 5746].

NIV+ CONCEAL, CONCEALED, CONCEALS, EXPOSE, EXPOSED, EXPOSES, EXPOSING

Concealment of Sin:

(Ge 3:8; Jos 7:21; Pr 28:13; Isa 29:15; 30:1).

Secret Sins:

Warning against (2Ki 17:9; Job 24:16; Ps 19:12; 90:8; Eze 8:12; Eph 5:12). Called works of darkness (Job 24:14; Pr 7:8-9; Jn 3:20; Ro 13:12; Eph 5:11; 1Th 5:7).

Exposure of Sin:

Inevitable (Nu 32:23; Job 20:27; Pr 26:26; Ecc 12:14; Lk 12:2; 1Co 4:5). Rendered doubly certain (Job 10:14; 14:16; Jer 16:17; Eze 11:5; Hos 7:2; Am 5:12).

CONCEIT [1452, 1470, 2295, 3029, 3030, 5605, 5643, 5861].

NIV+ CONCEITED, CONCEITS

Of the foolish—

Pr 12:15 The way of a fool seems right to him, but a wise man listens to advice.

Pr 26:5 Answer a fool according to his folly, or he will be wise in his own eyes.

Pr 26:12 Do you see a man wise in his own eyes? There is more hope for a fool than for him.

Pr 26:16 The sluggard is wiser in his own eyes than seven men who answer discreetly.

Pr 28:26 He who trusts in himself is a fool, but he who walks in wisdom is kept safe.

Ro 1:22 Although they claimed to be wise, they became fools

Of the rich—

Pr 28:11 A rich man may be wise in his own eyes, but a poor man who has discernment sees through him.

Of the self-righteous (Ps 36:2)—

Lk 18:11 The Pharisee stood up and prayed about himself: 'God, I thank you that I am not like other men—robbers, evildoers, adulterers—or even like this tax collector. [12]I fast twice a week and give a tenth of all I get.'

Warnings against—

Pr 3:5 Trust in the LORD with all your heart and lean not on your own understanding;

Pr 3:7 Do not be wise in your own eyes; fear the LORD and shun evil.

Pr 23:4 Do not wear yourself out to get rich; have the wisdom to show restraint.

Isa 5:21 Woe to those who are wise in their own eyes and clever in their own sight.

Jer 9:23 This is what the LORD says: "Let not the wise man boast of his wisdom or the strong man boast of his strength or the rich man boast of his riches,

Ro 11:25 I do not want you to be ignorant of this mystery, brothers, so that you may not be conceited: Israel has experienced a hardening in part until the full number of the Gentiles has come in.

Ro 12:16 Live in harmony with one another. Do not be proud, but be willing to associate with people of low position. Do not be conceited. (+1Co 3:18; Gal 6:3)

See Hypocrisy; Pride; Self-Exaltation.

CONCEPTION [1061, 2225, 2231, 2473, 3501, *326, 1164, 1877+3120+3836+5197, 5197*].

NIV+ CONCEIVE, CONCEIVED, CONCEIVES

Miraculous:

By Sarah (Ge 21:1-2), Rebekah (Ge 25:21), Rachel (Ge 30:22), Manoah's wife (Jdg 13:3-24), Hannah (1Sa 1:19-20), Elizabeth (Lk 1:24-25,36-37,58), Mary (Mt 1:18,20; Lk 1:31-35).

CONCISION *See Circumcision; Mutilators.*

CONCUBINAGE [7108, 10390].

NIV+ CONCUBINE, CONCUBINES

Laws Concerning:

(Ex 21:7-11; Lev 19:20-22; Dt 21:10-14). Concubines might be dismissed (Ge 21:9-14). Called wives (Ge 37:2; Jdg 19:3-5). Children of, not heirs (Ge 15:4; 21:10).

Practiced by Abraham (Ge 16:3; 25:6; 1Ch 1:32). Nahor (Ge 22:23-24), Jacob (Ge 30:4), Eliphaz (Ge 36:12), Gideon (Jdg 8:31), a Levite (Jdg 19:1), Caleb (1Ch 2:46-48), Manasseh (1Ch 7:14), Saul (2Sa 3:7), David (2Sa 5:13; 15:16), Solomon (1Ki 11:3), Rehoboam (2Ch 11:21), Abijah (2Ch 13:21), Belshazzar (Da 5:2).

See Marriage; Polygamy.

CONCUPISCENCE Intense longing for what God would not have us to have (Ro 7:8; Col 3:5; 1Th 4:5).

CONDEMNATION, SELF *See Self-Condemnation.*

CONDESCENSION, OF GOD

In reasoning with his creatures:

Sets forth his reasons for sending the flood (Ge 6:11-13). Enters into covenant with Abraham (Ge 15:1-21; 18:1-22). Indulges Abraham's intercession for Sodom (Ge 18:23-33). Warns Abimelech in a dream (Ge 20:3-7). Reasons with Moses (Ex 4:2-17). Sends flesh to the Israelites in consequence of their murmuring (Ex 16:12). Indulges Moses' prayer to see his glory (Ex 33:18-23). Indulges Gideon's tests (Jdg 6:36-40). Reasons with Job (Job 38; 39; 40; 41). Invites sinners, "Come now, let us reason together" (Isa 1:18-20). Expostulates with backsliding Israel (Isa 41:21-24; 43:1-19; 65:1-16; Jer 3:1-15; 4:1-31; 7:1-34; Eze 18:25-32; 33:10-20; Hos 2; Mic 6:1-9; Mal 3:7-15).

In his care, for mankind—

Ps 8:4 what is man that you are mindful of him, the son of

man that you care for him? **⁵**You made him a little lower than the heavenly beings and crowned him with glory and honor. **⁶**You made him ruler over the works of your hands; you put everything under his feet:

Ps 144:3 O LORD, what is man that you care for him, the son of man that you think of him?

For the world—

Ps 113:5 Who is like the LORD our God, the One who sits enthroned on high, **⁶**who stoops down to look on the heavens and the earth?

In redemption—

Isa 45:11 "This is what the LORD says—the Holy One of Israel, and its Maker: Concerning things to come, do you question me about my children, or give me orders about the work of my hands?

Jn 3:16 "For God so loved the world that he gave his one and only Son, that whoever believes in him shall not perish but have eternal life.

Ro 5:8 But God demonstrates his own love for us in this: While we were still sinners, Christ died for us.

Heb 2:11 Both the one who makes men holy and those who are made holy are of the same family. So Jesus is not ashamed to call them brothers.

Heb 6:17 Because God wanted to make the unchanging nature of his purpose very clear to the heirs of what was promised, he confirmed it with an oath. **¹⁸**God did this so that, by two unchangeable things in which it is impossible for God to lie, we who have fled to take hold of the hope offered to us may be greatly encouraged.

1Jn 4:10 This is love: not that we loved God, but that he loved us and sent his Son as an atoning sacrifice for our sins.

1Jn 4:19 We love because he first loved us.

Of Christ:

(Lk 22:27; Jn 13:5; 14; 2Co 8:9; Php 2:7-8; Heb 2:11).

CONDOLENCE

Instances of:

David, to Hanun (2Sa 10:2). King of Babylon, to Hezekiah (2Ki 20:12-13). The three friends of, to Job (Job 2:11). Jesus, to Mary and Martha (Jn 11:23-35).

See Affliction, Consolation Under; Sympathy.

CONDUCT, CHRISTIAN [784, 1821, 2006, 2143, 6913, 7189, *418, 4488*].

NIV+ CONDUCT, CONDUCTED, CONDUCTS

Believing God (Mk 11:22; Jn 14:11-12). Fearing God (Ecc 12:13; 1Pe 2:17). Loving God (Dt 6:5; Mt 22:37). Following God (Eph 5:1; 1Pe 1:15-16). Obeying God (Lk 1:6; 1Jn 5:3). Rejoicing in God (Ps 33:1; Hab 3:18). Believing in Christ (Jn 6:29; 1Jn 3:23). Loving Christ (Jn 21:15; 1Pe 1:7-8). Following the example of Christ (Jn 13:15; 1Pe 2:21-24). Obeying Christ (Jn 14:21; 15:14).

Living:

To Christ (Ro 14:8; 2Co 5:15). To righteousness (Mic 6:8; Ro 6:18; 1Pe 2:24). Soberly, righteously, and godly (Tit 2:12).

Walking:

Honestly (1Th 4:12). Worthy of God (1Th 2:12). Worthy of the Lord (Col 1:10). In the Spirit (Gal 5:25). After the Spirit (Ro 8:1). In newness of life (Ro 6:4). Worthy of our vocation (Eph 4:1). As children of light (Eph 5:8). Rejoicing in Christ (Php 3:1; 4:4). Loving one another (Jn 15:12; Ro 12:10; 1Co 13; Eph 5:2; Heb 13:1). Striving for the faith (Php 1:27; Jude 3). Putting away all sin (1Co 5:7; Heb 12:1). Abstaining from all appearance of evil (1Th

5:22). Perfecting holiness (Mt 5:48; 2Co 7:1; 2Ti 3:17). Hating defilement (Jude 23). Following after that which is good (Php 4:8; 1Th 5:15; 1Ti 6:11). Overcoming the world (1Jn 5:4-5). Adorning the gospel (Mt 5:16; Tit 2:10). Showing a good example (1Ti 4:12; Tit 2:7; 1Pe 2:12). Abounding in the work of the Lord (1Co 15:58; 2Co 8:7; 1Th 4:1). Shunning the wicked (Ps 1:1; 2Th 3:6). Controlling the body (1Co 9:27; Col 3:5). Subduing the temper (Eph 4:26; Jas 1:19). Submitting to injuries (Mt 5:39-41; 1Co 6:7). Forgiving injuries (Mt 6:14; Ro 12:20). Living peaceably with all (Ro 12:18; Heb 12:14). Visiting the afflicted (Mt 25:36; Jas 1:27). Doing as we would be done by (Mt 7:12; Lk 6:31). Sympathizing with others (Gal 6:2; 1Th 5:14). Honoring others (Ps 15:4; Ro 12:10). Fulfilling domestic duties (Eph 6:1-8; 1Pe 3:1-7). Submitting to authorities (Ro 13:1-7). Being liberal to others (Ac 20:35; Ro 12:13). Being contented (Php 4:11; Heb 13:4). Blessedness of maintaining (Ps 1:1-3; 19:9-11; 50:23; Mt 5:3-12; Jn 7:17; 15:10).

CONDUIT *See Aqueduct.*

CONEY [9176].

NIV+ CONEYS

Rock badger; unclean for food (Lev 11:5, ftn; Dt 14:7; Ps 104:18; Pr 30:26).

CONFECTION [7154].

NIV+ CONFECTIONS

A blend of incense or perfume (Ex 30:35; 1Sa 8:12). Difficult term transliterated "Pannag" in KJV (Eze 27:17). *See Perfume.*

CONFECTIONARY A perfumer (1Sa 8:13). *See Perfume.*

CONFEDERACIES Of kings (Ge 14:1-2; Jos 10:1-5; 11:1-5; 1Ki 20:1). *See Alliances.*

CONFESSION [606, 3344, 5583, 9343, *2018, 3933, 3934, 3951*].

NIV+ CONFESS, CONFESSED, CONFESSES, CONFESSING

To acknowledge one's faith in anything, as in the existence and authority of God, or the sins of which one has been guilty (Mt 10:32; Lev 5:5; Ps 32:5), to concede or allow (Jn 1:20; Ac 24:14; Heb 11:13), to praise God by thankfully acknowledging him (Ro 14:11; Heb 13:15).

Of Christ:

In baptism—

Ac 19:4 Paul said, "John's baptism was a baptism of repentance. He told the people to believe in the one coming after him, that is, in Jesus." **5**On hearing this, they were baptized into the name of the Lord Jesus. (+Gal 3:27)

To salvation—

Mt 10:32 "Whoever acknowledges me before men, I will also acknowledge him before my Father in heaven. (+Lk 12:8)

Ro 10:9 That if you confess with your mouth, "Jesus is Lord," and believe in your heart that God raised him from the dead, you will be saved. **10**For it is with your heart that you believe and are justified, and it is with your mouth that you confess and are saved. **11**As the Scripture says, "Anyone who trusts in him will never be put to shame."

Inspired by the Holy Spirit—

1Co 12:3 Therefore I tell you that no one who is speaking by the Spirit of God says, "Jesus be cursed," and no one can say, "Jesus is Lord," except by the Holy Spirit.

1Jn 4:2 This is how you can recognize the Spirit of God: Every spirit that acknowledges that Jesus Christ has come in the flesh is from God, **3**but every spirit that does not acknowledge Jesus is not from God. This is the spirit of the antichrist, which you have heard is coming and even now is already in the world.

Fellowship with the Father through (1Jn 2:23)—

1Jn 4:15 If anyone acknowledges that Jesus is the Son of God, God lives in him and he in God.

Timid believers deterred from—

Jn 12:42 Yet at the same time many even among the leaders believed in him. But because of the Pharisees they would not confess their faith for fear they would be put out of the synagogue; **43**for they loved praise from men more than praise from God.

Those refusing to make, rejected—

Mt 10:33 But whoever disowns me before men, I will disown him before my Father in heaven. (+Mk 8:38; Lk 12:9; 2Ti 2:12)

Hypocritical—

Mt 7:21 "Not everyone who says to me, 'Lord, Lord,' will enter the kingdom of heaven, but only he who does the will of my Father who is in heaven. **22**Many will say to me on that day, 'Lord, Lord, did we not prophesy in your name, and in your name drive out demons and perform many miracles?' **23**Then I will tell them plainly, 'I never knew you. Away from me, you evildoers!' (+Lk 13:26)

1Jn 1:6 If we claim to have fellowship with him yet walk in the darkness, we lie and do not live by the truth.

1Jn 2:4 The man who says, "I know him," but does not do what he commands is a liar, and the truth is not in him.

Commanded (2Ti 1:8).

Exemplified (Mt 3:11; 14:23; 16:16)—

Jn 1:15 John testifies concerning him. He cries out, saying, "This was he of whom I said, 'He who comes after me has surpassed me because he was before me.'" **16**From the fullness of his grace we have all received one blessing after another. **17**For the law was given through Moses; grace and truth came through Jesus Christ. **18**No one has ever seen God, but God the One and Only, who is at the Father's side, has made him known. (+Jn 6:29)

Jn 9:22 His parents said this because they were afraid of the Jews, for already the Jews had decided that anyone who acknowledged that Jesus was the Christ would be put out of the synagogue. **23**That was why his parents said, "He is of age; ask him."

24A second time they summoned the man who had been blind. "Give glory to God," they said. "We know this man is a sinner."

25He replied, "Whether he is a sinner or not, I don't know. One thing I do know. I was blind but now I see!"

26Then they asked him, "What did he do to you? How did he open your eyes?"

27He answered, "I have told you already and you did not listen. Why do you want to hear it again? Do you want to become his disciples, too?"

28Then they hurled insults at him and said, "You are this fellow's disciple! We are disciples of Moses! **29**We know that God spoke to Moses, but as for this fellow, we don't even know where he comes from."

30The man answered, "Now that is remarkable! You don't know where he comes from, yet he opened my eyes. **31**We know that God does not listen to sinners. He listens to the godly man who does his will. ³²Nobody has ever heard of opening the eyes of a man born blind. ³³If this man were not from God, he could do nothing."

³⁴To this they replied, "You were steeped in sin at birth; how dare you lecture us!" And they threw him out.

³⁵Jesus heard that they had thrown him out, and when he found him, he said, "Do you believe in the Son of Man?"

³⁶"Who is he, sir?" the man asked. "Tell me so that I may believe in him."

³⁷Jesus said, "You have now seen him; in fact, he is the one speaking with you."

³⁸Then the man said, "Lord, I believe," and he worshiped him. (+Jn 11:27; Ac 8:35-37; 9:20)

Ac 18:5 When Silas and Timothy came from Macedonia, Paul devoted himself exclusively to preaching, testifying to the Jews that Jesus was the Christ. (+Ro 1:16)

Of Sin: *See Sin, Confession of.*

CONFIDENCE [1053, 1055, 1059, 4073, 4074, 4440, 6051, 6164, *2509, 4244, 4275, 4301, 5712*].
NIV+ CONFIDENT, CONFIDENTLY, CONFIDES, CONFIDING, SELF-CONFIDENCE, SELF-CONFIDENT

In People:
Warned against (Jer 9:4; 12:6; Mic 7:5).

Betrayed:
Joshua, by the Gibeonites (Jos 9:3-15). Eglon, by Ehud (Jdg 3:15-23). Sisera, by Jael (Jdg 4:17-22). Samson, by Delilah (Jdg 16:17-20). Ahimelech, by David (1Sa 21:1-9). Abner, by Joab (2Sa 3:27). Amasa, by Joab (2Sa 20:9-10). Worshipers of Baal, by Jehu (2Ki 10:18-28). *See Betrayal.*

False: *See False Confidence.*

In God:
(Ps 118:8; Pr 3:26; 14:26; Ac 28:31; Eph 3:12; Heb 3:16; 10:35; 1Jn 2:28; 3:21; 5:14). *See Faith.*

CONFISCATION [10562, *771*].
Of property:
By David, that of Mephibosheth (2Sa 16:4). By Ahab, of Naboth's vineyard (1Ki 21:7-16). By Xerxes, of Haman's house (Est 8:1). As a penalty (Ezr 10:8).

CONFLAGRATIONS *See Burning.*

CONFORMITY [3869+6913, *2848, 5372*].
NIV+ CONFORM, CONFORMED, CONFORMS

Conformity to the World, Condemned:
Ro 12:1 Therefore, I urge you, brothers, in view of God's mercy, to offer your bodies as living sacrifices, holy and pleasing to God— this is your spiritual act of worship. ²Do not conform any longer to the pattern of this world, but be transformed by the renewing of your mind. Then you will be able to test and approve what God's will is—his good, pleasing and perfect will. (+Eze 5:7; 11:12)

1Pe 1:14 As obedient children, do not conform to the evil desires you had when you lived in ignorance. ¹⁵But just as he who called you is holy, so be holy in all you do; ¹⁶for it is written: "Be holy, because I am holy."

Conformity to Christ, Commanded:
Ro 8:29 For those God foreknew he also predestined to be conformed to the likeness of his Son, that he might be the firstborn among many brothers.

Eph 5:1 Be imitators of God, therefore, as dearly loved children ²and live a life of love, just as Christ loved us and gave himself up for us as a fragrant offering and sacrifice

to God. (+1Co 4:16; 1Th 1:6; 2:14; Heb 6:12; 13:7; 3Jn 11).

CONFUSION [1003, 1176, 1182, 2162, 2169, 2917, 4428, 4539, 9332, 9337, 9451, *5177, 5429*].
NIV+ CONFUSE, CONFUSED, CONFUSING

Of languages (Ge 11:1-9). Of Israel's enemies in battle (Ex 14:24; 23:27; Jos 10:10). Of Israel in judgment (Dt 28:20,28; Jer 51:34). Of believers by false teachers (Gal 1:7; 5:10).

CONGESTION NIV "swelling" (Lev 13:28) or "inflamation" (Dt 28:22). *See Disease.*

CONGREGATION, OF ISRAEL [5220,   7736, *1711, 5252*].
NIV+ CONGREGATIONS

Collective term for God's chosen in the OT, or an assembly of the people summoned for a definite purpose (1Ki 8:65), either the whole assembly, or a part (Nu 16:3; Ex 12:6; 35:1; Lev 4:13).

Often considered in a non-technical sense, as a gathering of believers or chosen, the church of the OT. For that purpose. *See Church, The Body of Believers.*

CONIAH (*Yahweh sustains*). A name given to Jehoiachin, king of Judah, who was carried captive by Nebuchadnezzar (Jer 22:24, ftn; 22:28; 37:1, ftn), c. 597 B.C. *See Jehoiachin.*

CONNIVANCE
Judged (Lev 20:4)—
1Sa 3:11 And the LORD said to Samuel: "See, I am about to do something in Israel that will make the ears of everyone who hears of it tingle. ¹²At that time I will carry out against Eli everything I spoke against his family—from beginning to end. ¹³For I told him that I would judge his family forever because of the sin he knew about; his sons made themselves contemptible, and he failed to restrain them.
Result—
Pr 10:10 He who winks maliciously causes grief, and a chattering fool comes to ruin.

CONONIAH *See Conaniah.*

CONQUESTS [*3769, 3771, 5782, 8647, *3771*].
NIV+ CONQUER, CONQUERED, CONQUEROR, CONQUERORS, CONQUERS

Of the heathen by Israel (Jos 6:20; 8:24; 10:28-29; 11:8,23; 12:7; Jdg 1:8; 3:30; 4:16; 8:28; 9:45; 11:33).

CONSCIENCE [4213, 4222, *4029+5323, 5287*].
NIV+ CONSCIENCE¹, CONSCIENCE-STRICKEN, CONSCIENCES, CONSCIENTIOUS

Guide (Ps 51:3)—
Pr 20:12 Ears that hear and eyes that see—the LORD has made them both.
Mt 6:22 "The eye is the lamp of the body. If your eyes are good, your whole body will be full of light. ²³But if your eyes are bad, your whole body will be full of darkness. If then the light within you is darkness, how great is that darkness!
Lk 11:33 "No one lights a lamp and puts it in a place where it will be hidden, or under a bowl. Instead he puts it on its stand, so that those who come in may see the light. ³⁴Your eye is the lamp of your body. When your eyes are good, your whole body also is full of light. But when they are bad, your body also is full of darkness. ³⁵See to it, then,

that the light within you is not darkness. ³⁶Therefore, if your whole body is full of light, and no part of it dark, it will be completely lighted, as when the light of a lamp shines on you."

Ro 2:14 (Indeed, when Gentiles, who do not have the law, do by nature things required by the law, they are a law for themselves, even though they do not have the law, ¹⁵since they show that the requirements of the law are written on their hearts, their consciences also bearing witness, and their thoughts now accusing, now even defending them.) (+Ro 7:18,22)

2Co 5:11 Since, then, we know what it is to fear the Lord, we try to persuade men. What we are is plain to God, and I hope it is also plain to your conscience.

Approves (Job 27:6; Pr 21:2)—

Ac 23:1 Paul looked straight at the Sanhedrin and said, "My brothers, I have fulfilled my duty to God in all good conscience to this day."

Ac 24:16 So I strive always to keep my conscience clear before God and man.

Ro 9:1 I speak the truth in Christ—I am not lying, my conscience confirms it in the Holy Spirit— (+1Co 4:4)

2Co 1:12 Now this is our boast: Our conscience testifies that we have conducted ourselves in the world, and especially in our relations with you, in the holiness and sincerity that are from God. We have done so not according to worldly wisdom but according to God's grace.

1Ti 1:5 The goal of this command is love, which comes from a pure heart and a good conscience and a sincere faith. (+1Ti 1:19)

1Ti 3:9 They must keep hold of the deep truths of the faith with a clear conscience. (+2Ti 1:3)

Heb 13:18 Pray for us. We are sure that we have a clear conscience and desire to live honorably in every way.

1Pe 2:19 For it is commendable if a man bears up under the pain of unjust suffering because he is conscious of God.

1Pe 3:16 keeping a clear conscience, so that those who speak maliciously against your good behavior in Christ may be ashamed of their slander.

1Pe 3:21 and this water symbolizes baptism that now saves you also—not the removal of dirt from the body but the pledge of a good conscience toward God. It saves you by the resurrection of Jesus Christ,

1Jn 3:20 whenever our hearts condemn us. For God is greater than our hearts, and he knows everything. ²¹Dear friends, if our hearts do not condemn us, we have confidence before God

Struggle with—

Job 15:21 Terrifying sounds fill his ears; when all seems well, marauders attack him.

Job 15:24 Distress and anguish fill him with terror; they overwhelm him, like a king poised to attack, (+Ps 51:3; Mt 6:22-23; Lk 11:33-36)

Ro 7:15 I do not understand what I do. For what I want to do I do not do, but what I hate I do. ¹⁶And if I do what I do not want to do, I agree that the law is good. ¹⁷As it is, it is no longer I myself who do it, but it is sin living in me. ¹⁸I know that nothing good lives in me, that is, in my sinful nature. For I have the desire to do what is good, but I cannot carry it out. ¹⁹For what I do is not the good I want to do; no, the evil I do not want to do—this I keep on doing. ²⁰Now if I do what I do not want to do, it is no longer I who do it, but it is sin living in me that does it. ²¹So I find this law at work: When I want to do good, evil is right there with me. ²²For in my inner being I delight

in God's law; ²³but I see another law at work in the members of my body, waging war against the law of my mind and making me a prisoner of the law of sin at work within my members.

Purged—

Heb 9:14 How much more, then, will the blood of Christ, who through the eternal Spirit offered himself unblemished to God, cleanse our consciences from acts that lead to death, so that we may serve the living God!

Heb 10:22 let us draw near to God with a sincere heart in full assurance of faith, having our hearts sprinkled to cleanse us from a guilty conscience and having our bodies washed with pure water. *See Honesty; Integrity.*

Of another, to be respected—

Ro 14:2 One man's faith allows him to eat everything, but another man, whose faith is weak, eats only vegetables. ³The man who eats everything must not look down on him who does not, and the man who does not eat everything must not condemn the man who does, for God has accepted him. ⁴Who are you to judge someone else's servant? To his own master he stands or falls. And he will stand, for the Lord is able to make him stand.

⁵One man considers one day more sacred than another; another man considers every day alike. Each one should be fully convinced in his own mind. ⁶He who regards one day as special, does so to the Lord. He who eats meat, eats to the Lord, for he gives thanks to God; and he who abstains, does so to the Lord and gives thanks to God. ⁷For none of us lives to himself alone and none of us dies to himself alone. ⁸If we live, we live to the Lord; and if we die, we die to the Lord. So, whether we live or die, we belong to the Lord.

⁹For this very reason, Christ died and returned to life so that he might be the Lord of both the dead and the living. ¹⁰You, then, why do you judge your brother? Or why do you look down on your brother? For we will all stand before God's judgment seat. ¹¹It is written:

"'As surely as I live,' says the Lord, 'every knee will bow before me; every tongue will confess to God.'"

¹²So then, each of us will give an account of himself to God.

¹³Therefore let us stop passing judgment on one another. Instead, make up your mind not to put any stumbling block or obstacle in your brother's way. ¹⁴As one who is in the Lord Jesus, I am fully convinced that no food is unclean in itself. But if anyone regards something as unclean, then for him it is unclean. ¹⁵If your brother is distressed because of what you eat, you are no longer acting in love. Do not by your eating destroy your brother for whom Christ died. ¹⁶Do not allow what you consider good to be spoken of as evil. ¹⁷For the kingdom of God is not a matter of eating and drinking, but of righteousness, peace and joy in the Holy Spirit, ¹⁸because anyone who serves Christ in this way is pleasing to God and approved by men. ¹⁹Let us therefore make every effort to do what leads to peace and to mutual edification. ²⁰Do not destroy the work of God for the sake of food. All food is clean, but it is wrong for a man to eat anything that causes someone else to stumble.

1Co 8:7 But not everyone knows this. Some people are still so accustomed to idols that when they eat such food they think of it as having been sacrificed to an idol, and since their conscience is weak, it is defiled. (+1Co 8:8)

1Co 8:9 Be careful, however, that the exercise of your freedom does not become a stumbling block to the weak. ¹⁰For if anyone with a weak conscience sees you who have this knowledge eating in an idol's temple, won't he be emboldened to eat what has been sacrificed to idols? [11]So this weak brother, for whom Christ died, is destroyed by your knowledge. [12]When you sin against your brothers in this way and wound their weak conscience, you sin against Christ. [13]Therefore, if what I eat causes my brother to fall into sin, I will never eat meat again, so that I will not cause him to fall.

1Co 10:27 If some unbeliever invites you to a meal and you want to go, eat whatever is put before you without raising questions of conscience. [28]But if anyone says to you, "This has been offered in sacrifice," then do not eat it, both for the sake of the man who told you and for conscience' sake— [29]the other man's conscience, I mean, not yours. For why should my freedom be judged by another's conscience? [30]If I take part in the meal with thankfulness, why am I denounced because of something I thank God for?

[31]So whether you eat or drink or whatever you do, do it all for the glory of God. [32]Do not cause anyone to stumble, whether Jews, Greeks or the church of God—

2Co 4:2 Rather, we have renounced secret and shameful ways; we do not use deception, nor do we distort the word of God. On the contrary, by setting forth the truth plainly we commend ourselves to every man's conscience in the sight of God.

Instances of Faithful:

Pharaoh, when he took Sarah into his harem (Ge 12:18-19). Abimelech, when he took Sarah for a concubine (Ge 26:9-11). Jacob, in his care of Laban's property (Ge 31:39), in his greeting of Esau (Ge 33:1-12). Joseph, with Potiphar's wife (Ge 39:7-12). Nehemiah, with taxes (Ne 5:15). Daniel, with the king's meat (Da 1:8). Peter, in his preaching (Ac 4:19-20; 5:29).

Unfaithful Conscience:

Corrupt (Mt 6:23; Lk 11:34; Jn 16:2-3).

Dead—

Pr 16:25 There is a way that seems right to a man, but in the end it leads to death.

Pr 30:20 "This is the way of an adulteress: She eats and wipes her mouth and says, 'I've done nothing wrong.'

Jer 6:15 Are they ashamed of their loathsome conduct? No, they have no shame at all; they do not even know how to blush. So they will fall among the fallen; they will be brought down when I punish them," says the LORD.

Am 6:1 Woe to you who are complacent in Zion, and to you who feel secure on Mount Samaria, you notable men of the foremost nation, to whom the people of Israel come! [2]Go to Calneh and look at it; go from there to great Hamath, and then go down to Gath in Philistia. Are they better off than your two kingdoms? Is their land larger than yours? [3]You put off the evil day and bring near a reign of terror. [4]You lie on beds inlaid with ivory and lounge on your couches. You dine on choice lambs and fattened calves. [5]You strum away on your harps like David and improvise on musical instruments. [6]You drink wine by the bowlful and use the finest lotions, but you do not grieve over the ruin of Joseph.

Ro 1:21 For although they knew God, they neither glorified him as God nor gave thanks to him, but their thinking became futile and their foolish hearts were darkened. [22]Although they claimed to be wise, they became fools [23]and exchanged the glory of the immortal God for images made to look like mortal man and birds and animals and reptiles.

[24]Therefore God gave them over in the sinful desires of their hearts to sexual impurity for the degrading of their bodies with one another. [25]They exchanged the truth of God for a lie, and worshiped and served created things rather than the Creator—who is forever praised. Amen.

Eph 4:17 So I tell you this, and insist on it in the Lord, that you must no longer live as the Gentiles do, in the futility of their thinking. [18]They are darkened in their understanding and separated from the life of God because of the ignorance that is in them due to the hardening of their hearts. [19]Having lost all sensitivity, they have given themselves over to sensuality so as to indulge in every kind of impurity, with a continual lust for more.

[20]You, however, did not come to know Christ that way. [21]Surely you heard of him and were taught in him in accordance with the truth that is in Jesus. [22]You were taught, with regard to your former way of life, to put off your old self, which is being corrupted by its deceitful desires; [23]to be made new in the attitude of your minds; [24]and to put on the new self, created to be like God in true righteousness and holiness.

[25]Therefore each of you must put off falsehood and speak truthfully to his neighbor, for we are all members of one body. [26]"In your anger do not sin": Do not let the sun go down while you are still angry, [27]and do not give the devil a foothold. [28]He who has been stealing must steal no longer, but must work, doing something useful with his own hands, that he may have something to share with those in need.

[29]Do not let any unwholesome talk come out of your mouths, but only what is helpful for building others up according to their needs, that it may benefit those who listen.

Defiled—

Tit 1:15 To the pure, all things are pure, but to those who are corrupted and do not believe, nothing is pure. In fact, both their minds and consciences are corrupted.

Seared—

1Ti 4:2 Such teachings come through hypocritical liars, whose consciences have been seared as with a hot iron.

Guilty (Job 15:21,24)—

Ps 51:1 Have mercy on me, O God, according to your unfailing love; according to your great compassion blot out my transgressions. [2]Wash away all my iniquity and cleanse me from my sin.

[3]For I know my transgressions, and my sin is always before me. [4]Against you, you only, have I sinned and done what is evil in your sight, so that you are proved right when you speak and justified when you judge. (+Ps 51:5-6)

Ps 51:7 Cleanse me with hyssop, and I will be clean; wash me, and I will be whiter than snow. [8]Let me hear joy and gladness; let the bones you have crushed rejoice. [9]Hide your face from my sins and blot out all my iniquity.

[10]Create in me a pure heart, O God, and renew a steadfast spirit within me. [11]Do not cast me from your presence or take your Holy Spirit from me. [12]Restore to me the joy of your salvation and grant me a willing spirit, to sustain me.

[13]Then I will teach transgressors your ways, and sinners will turn back to you. [14]Save me from bloodguilt, O God, the God who saves me, and my tongue will sing of your righteousness.

Ps 73:21 When my heart was grieved and my spirit embittered,

Pr 28:1 The wicked man flees though no one pursues, but the righteous are as bold as a lion.

Isa 59:9 So justice is far from us, and righteousness does not reach us. We look for light, but all is darkness; for brightness, but we walk in deep shadows. [10]Like the blind we grope along the wall, feeling our way like men without eyes. At midday we stumble as if it were twilight; among the strong, we are like the dead. [11]We all growl like bears; we moan mournfully like doves. We look for justice, but find none; for deliverance, but it is far away.

[12]For our offenses are many in your sight, and our sins testify against us. Our offenses are ever with us, and we acknowledge our iniquities: [13]rebellion and treachery against the LORD, turning our backs on our God, fomenting oppression and revolt, uttering lies our hearts have conceived. [14]So justice is driven back, and righteousness stands at a distance; truth has stumbled in the streets, honesty cannot enter. (+Mt 14:1-2)

Mt 27:3 When Judas, who had betrayed him, saw that Jesus was condemned, he was seized with remorse and returned the thirty silver coins to the chief priests and the elders. [4]"I have sinned," he said, "for I have betrayed innocent blood." "What is that to us?" they replied. "That's your responsibility."

[5]So Judas threw the money into the temple and left. Then he went away and hanged himself.

Mk 6:14 King Herod heard about this, for Jesus' name had become well known. Some were saying, "John the Baptist has been raised from the dead, and that is why miraculous powers are at work in him."

Mk 6:16 But when Herod heard this, he said, "John, the man I beheaded, has been raised from the dead!"

Jn 8:9 At this, those who heard began to go away one at a time, the older ones first, until only Jesus was left, with the woman still standing there.

Ac 2:37 When the people heard this, they were cut to the heart and said to Peter and the other apostles, "Brothers, what shall we do?"

1Ti 4:2 Such teachings come through hypocritical liars, whose consciences have been seared as with a hot iron.

Tit 1:15 To the pure, all things are pure, but to those who are corrupted and do not believe, nothing is pure. In fact, both their minds and consciences are corrupted.

Heb 9:14 How much more, then, will the blood of Christ, who through the eternal Spirit offered himself unblemished to God, cleanse our consciences from acts that lead to death, so that we may serve the living God!

Heb 10:26 If we deliberately keep on sinning after we have received the knowledge of the truth, no sacrifice for sins is left, [27]but only a fearful expectation of judgment and of raging fire that will consume the enemies of God. *See Blindness, Spiritual.*

Instances of Guilty—

Adam and Eve, after they sinned (Ge 3:7-8). Jacob, after defrauding Esau (Ge 33:1-12). Joseph's brothers (Ge 42:21; 44:16). Pharaoh, after the plagues (Ex 9:27). Micah, after stealing (Jdg 17:2). David, for his indignity to Saul (1Sa 24:5), for his adultery and for his murder of Uriah (Ps 32; 38; 40:11-12; 51), for numbering Israel (2Sa 24:10; 1Ch 21:1-8). The old prophet of Bethel (1Ki 13:18,29-32). The lepers of Samaria (2Ki 7:8-10). Jonah (Jnh 1:12). Herod, for beheading John the Baptist (Mt 14:2; Lk 9:7). Peter, after denying the Lord (Mt 26:75; Mk 14:72; Lk 22:62). Judas (Mt 27:3-5). The accusers of the women taken in adultery (Jn 8:9).

CONSCIENCE MONEY *See Money.*

CONSCIENTIOUSNESS *See Integrity.*

CONSCRIPTION [6218, 6590, 7371].

NIV+ CONSCRIPTED, CONSCRIPTING

Of soldiers (1Sa 14:52). Of forced labor (1Ki 5:13-18; 19:15-23; 2Ki 25:19).

CONSECRATED THINGS [3338+4848, 2883, 5121, 5692, 7705, 7727, 7731, 39, 41+2813, 4606].

NIV+ CONSECRATION

Laws regarding (Lev 27; Nu 18:8-32).
See Firstborn; Firstfruits.

CONSECRATION [7727].

NIV+ CONSECRATE, CONSECRATED, CONSECRATING, RECONSECRATED

Of Aaron. *See Aaron.* Of Priests. *See Priest.* Of the altar. *See Altar.* Of the temple. *See Temple, Solomon's; Offerings.*

Commanded (Ex 32:29).

Personal—

Ps 51:17 The sacrifices of God are a broken spirit; a broken and contrite heart, O God, you will not despise.

Mt 13:44 "The kingdom of heaven is like treasure hidden in a field. When a man found it, he hid it again, and then in his joy went and sold all he had and bought that field.

[45]"Again, the kingdom of heaven is like a merchant looking for fine pearls. [46]When he found one of great value, he went away and sold everything he had and bought it.

Ro 6:13 Do not offer the parts of your body to sin, as instruments of wickedness, but rather offer yourselves to God, as those who have been brought from death to life; and offer the parts of your body to him as instruments of righteousness.

Ro 6:16 Don't you know that when you offer yourselves to someone to obey him as slaves, you are slaves to the one whom you obey—whether you are slaves to sin, which leads to death, or to obedience, which leads to righteousness?

Ro 6:19 I put this in human terms because you are weak in your natural selves. Just as you used to offer the parts of your body in slavery to impurity and to ever-increasing wickedness, so now offer them in slavery to righteousness leading to holiness.

Ro 12:1 Therefore, I urge you, brothers, in view of God's mercy, to offer your bodies as living sacrifices, holy and pleasing to God—this is your spiritual act of worship.

2Co 8:5 And they did not do as we expected, but they gave themselves first to the Lord and then to us in keeping with God's will.

Conditional—

Ge 28:20 Then Jacob made a vow, saying, "If God will be with me and will watch over me on this journey I am taking and will give me food to eat and clothes to wear [21]so that I return safely to my father's house, then the LORD will be my God [22]and this stone that I have set up as a pillar will be God's house, and of all that you give me I will give you a tenth."

2Sa 15:7 At the end of four years, Absalom said to the king, "Let me go to Hebron and fulfill a vow I made to the LORD. [8]While your servant was living at Geshur in Aram, I made this vow: 'If the LORD takes me back to Jerusalem, I will worship the LORD in Hebron.'"

Instances of:

Cain and Abel (Ge 4:4-7). Abraham, of Isaac (Ge 22:9-12). Jephthah, of his daughter (Jdg 11:30-40). Hannah, of

Samuel (1Sa 1:11,24-28). David consecrates the water (2Sa 23:16; 1Ch 11:18). Zicri, of himself (2Ch 17:16).

See Dedication; Offerings.

CONSERVATION *See Ecology.*

CONSISTENCY

Encouraged—

Ne 5:9 So I continued, "What you are doing is not right. Shouldn't you walk in the fear of our God to avoid the reproach of our Gentile enemies?

Mt 6:24 "No one can serve two masters. Either he will hate the one and love the other, or he will be devoted to the one and despise the other. You cannot serve both God and Money. (+Lk 16:13)

Ro 14:22 So whatever you believe about these things keep between yourself and God. Blessed is the man who does not condemn himself by what he approves.

1Co 10:21 You cannot drink the cup of the Lord and the cup of demons too; you cannot have a part in both the Lord's table and the table of demons.

See Deceit; Expediency; Hypocrisy; Inconsistency; Obduracy; Prudence.

CONSOLATION [5714, 5717, 9487, 9488, *4155*].
NIV+ CONSOLE, CONSOLATIONS, CONSOLED, CONSOLING

See Affliction, Consolation Under; Holy Spirit.

CONSPIRACY [6051, 8003, 8004, *5371*].
NIV+ CONSPIRE, CONSPIRATORS, CONSPIRED

Law against—

Ex 23:1 "Do not spread false reports. Do not help a wicked man by being a malicious witness.

²"Do not follow the crowd in doing wrong. When you give testimony in a lawsuit, do not pervert justice by siding with the crowd,

Instances of:

Joseph's brothers, against Joseph (Ge 37:18-20). Miriam and Aaron, against Moses (Nu 12; 14:4; 16:1-35). Abimelech, against Gideon's sons (Jdg 9:1-6). Gaal, against Abimelech (Jdg 9:23-41). Delilah, against Samson (Jdg 16:4-21). Abner, against Ish-Bosheth (2Sa 3:7-21). Of Absalom (2Sa 15:10-13). Of Jeroboam (1Ki 14:2). Of Baasha (1Ki 15:27). Of Zimri (1Ki 16:9). Of Jezebel, against Naboth (1Ki 21:8-13). Of Jehu (2Ki 9:14-26). Of Jehoiada (2Ki 11:4-16). Of servants, against Joash (2Ki 12:20).

People in Jerusalem, against Amaziah (2Ki 14:19). Shallum, against Zechariah (2Ki 15:10). Pekahiah (2Ki 15:23-25). Pekah (2Ki 15:30). Amon (2Ki 21:23). Sennacherib (2Ki 19:37). Amaziah (2Ch 25:27). Xerxes (Est 2:21-23). Jeremiah (Jer 18:18). Daniel (Da 6:4-17). Shadrach, Meshach, and Abednego (Da 3:8-18).

Against Jesus (Jer 11:9,19; Mt 12:14; 21:38-41; 26:3-4; 27:1-2; Mk 3:6). Paul (Ac 18:12; 23:12-15).

Falsely accused of:

Jonathan (1Sa 22:8).

CONSTANCY [419, 1942+3265, 3429, 4296+9442, 4946+5584, 9458, *1384*].
NIV+ CONSTANT, CONSTANTLY

In obedience (Ps 119:31,33). In friendship (Pr 27:10). Under suffering (Mt 5:12; Heb 12:5; 1Pe 4:12-16). In prayer (Lk 18:1; Ro 12:12; Eph 6:18; Col 4:2; 1Th 5:17). In beneficence (Gal 6:9). In profession (Heb 10:23).

Instances of:

Ruth (Ru 1:14). Jonathan (1Sa 18:1; 20:16), Priscilla and Aquila (Ro 16:3-4).

See Character; Stability.

CONSTELLATIONS [2540, 4068, 4655, 4666]. (2Ki 23:5; Job 9:9; 38:32; Isa 13:10). The serpent (Job 26:13). Orion (Job 9:9; Am 5:8).

See Astronomy.

CONSTITUTION

Agreement Between the Ruler and the People:

King commanded to study and obey the Mosaic Law—

Dt 17:18 When he takes the throne of his kingdom, he is to write for himself on a scroll a copy of this law, taken from that of the priests, who are Levites. ¹⁹It is to be with him, and he is to read it all the days of his life so that he may learn to revere the LORD his God and follow carefully all the words of this law and these decrees ²⁰and not consider himself better than his brothers and turn from the law to the right or to the left. Then he and his descendants will reign a long time over his kingdom in Israel.

Made by David—

2Sa 5:3 When all the elders of Israel had come to King David at Hebron, the king made a compact with them at Hebron before the LORD, and they anointed David king over Israel. (+1Ch 11:3)

Made for Joash—

2Ch 23:2 They went throughout Judah and gathered the Levites and the heads of Israelite families from all the towns. When they came to Jerusalem, ³the whole assembly made a covenant with the king at the temple of God.

Jehoiada said to them, "The king's son shall reign, as the LORD promised concerning the descendants of David. (+2Ch 23:11)

Made by Zedekiah, proclaiming liberty—

Jer 34:8 The word came to Jeremiah from the LORD after King Zedekiah had made a covenant with all the people in Jerusalem to proclaim freedom for the slaves. ⁹Everyone was to free his Hebrew slaves, both male and female; no one was to hold a fellow Jew in bondage. ¹⁰So all the officials and people who entered into this covenant agreed that they would free their male and female slaves and no longer hold them in bondage. They agreed, and set them free. ¹¹But afterward they changed their minds and took back the slaves they had freed and enslaved them again.

King of Medes and Persians bound by—

Da 6:12 So they went to the king and spoke to him about his royal decree: "Did you not publish a decree that during the next thirty days anyone who prays to any god or man except to you, O king, would be thrown into the lions' den?"

The king answered, "The decree stands—in accordance with the laws of the Medes and Persians, which cannot be repealed."

¹³Then they said to the king, "Daniel, who is one of the exiles from Judah, pays no attention to you, O king, or to the decree you put in writing. He still prays three times a day." ¹⁴When the king heard this, he was greatly distressed; he was determined to rescue Daniel and made every effort until sundown to save him.

¹⁵Then the men went as a group to the king and said to him, "Remember, O king, that according to the law of the Medes and Persians no decree or edict that the king issues can be changed."

See Covenant.

CONSUMPTION NIV "wasting diseases" (Lev 26:16; Dt 28:22). *See Disease.*

CONTEMPT [997, 1022, 1994, 2295, 2725, 3070, 3075, 5540, 5542, 5571, 7837, *2024, 2969*].

NIV+ CONTEMPTIBLE, CONTEMPTUOUS, CONTEMPTUOUSLY

Sin of (Job 31:13-14; Pr 14:21). Folly of (Pr 11:12). A characteristic of the wicked (Pr 18:3; Isa 5:24; 2Ti 3:3).

Forbidden Toward:

Parents (Pr 23:22). Christ's little ones (Mt 18:10). Weak brothers (Ro 14:3). Young ministers (1Co 16:11). Believing masters (1Ti 6:2). The poor (Jas 2:1-3). Self-righteousness prompts to (Isa 65:5; Lk 18:9,11). Pride and prosperity prompt to (Ps 123:4). Ministers should give no occasion for (1Ti 4:12). Of ministers, is a despising of God (Lk 10:16; 1Th 4:8).

Toward the Church:

Often turned into respect (Isa 60:14). Often punished (Eze 28:26). Causes believers to cry to God (Ne 4:4; Ps 123:3).

The Wicked Exhibit Toward:

Christ (Ps 22:6; Isa 53:3; Mt 27:29). Believers (Ps 119:141). Authorities (2Pe 2:10; Jude 8). Parents (Pr 15:5,20). The afflicted (Job 19:18). The poor (Ps 14:6; Ecc 9:16). Believers sometimes guilty of (Jas 2:6).

Exemplified:

Hagar (Ge 16:4). Children of Belial (1Sa 10:27). Nabal (1Sa 25:10-11). Michal (2Sa 6:16). Sanballat (Ne 2:19; 4:2-3). False teachers (2Co 10:10).

CONTENTION [4506, *5809*]. *See Strife.*

CONTENTMENT [5833, 8934, 10710, *894*].

NIV+ CHEER, CHEERFUL, CHEERFULLY, CHEERING, CHEERS, CONTENT, CONTENTED, CONTENTMENT
Desirable—

Pr 14:14 The faithless will be fully repaid for their ways, and the good man rewarded for his.

Pr 15:13 A happy heart makes the face cheerful, but heartache crushes the spirit.

Pr 15:15 All the days of the oppressed are wretched, but the cheerful heart has a continual feast.

Pr 15:30 A cheerful look brings joy to the heart, and good news gives health to the bones.

Pr 16:8 Better a little with righteousness than much gain with injustice.

Pr 17:1 Better a dry crust with peace and quiet than a house full of feasting, with strife.

Pr 17:22 A cheerful heart is good medicine, but a crushed spirit dries up the bones.

Pr 30:8 Keep falsehood and lies far from me; give me neither poverty nor riches, but give me only my daily bread.

Ecc 2:24 A man can do nothing better than to eat and drink and find satisfaction in his work. This too, I see, is from the hand of God,

Ecc 4:6 Better one handful with tranquillity than two handfuls with toil and chasing after the wind.

Ecc 5:12 The sleep of a laborer is sweet, whether he eats little or much, but the abundance of a rich man permits him no sleep.

Ecc 6:9 Better what the eye sees than the roving of the appetite. This too is meaningless, a chasing after the wind.
Commanded—

Ps 37:7 Be still before the LORD and wait patiently for

him; do not fret when men succeed in their ways, when they carry out their wicked schemes.

Ecc 9:7 Go, eat your food with gladness, and drink your wine with a joyful heart, for it is now that God favors what you do. [8]Always be clothed in white, and always anoint your head with oil. [9]Enjoy life with your wife, whom you love, all the days of this meaningless life that God has given you under the sun—all your meaningless days. For this is your lot in life and in your toilsome labor under the sun.

Lk 3:14 Then some soldiers asked him, "And what should we do?" He replied, "Don't extort money and don't accuse people falsely—be content with your pay."

1Co 7:17 Nevertheless, each one should retain the place in life that the Lord assigned to him and to which God has called him. This is the rule I lay down in all the churches.

1Co 7:20 Each one should remain in the situation which he was in when God called him. [21]Were you a slave when you were called? Don't let it trouble you—although if you can gain your freedom, do so. (+1Co 7:22-23)

1Co 7:24 Brothers, each man, as responsible to God, should remain in the situation God called him to.

Gal 5:26 Let us not become conceited, provoking and envying each other.

1Ti 6:6 But godliness with contentment is great gain. [7]For we brought nothing into the world, and we can take nothing out of it. [8]But if we have food and clothing, we will be content with that.

Heb 13:5 Keep your lives free from the love of money and be content with what you have, because God has said, "Never will I leave you; never will I forsake you."

Instances of:

Esau (Ge 33:9). Barzillai (2Sa 19:33-37). The Shunammite (2Ki 4:13).

David—

Ps 16:6 The boundary lines have fallen for me in pleasant places; surely I have a delightful inheritance.

Paul—

Php 4:11 I am not saying this because I am in need, for I have learned to be content whatever the circumstances. [12]I know what it is to be in need, and I know what it is to have plenty. I have learned the secret of being content in any and every situation, whether well fed or hungry, whether living in plenty or in want.

See Affliction, Consolation Under; Resignation.

CONTINENCE *See Chastity; Self-Control.*

CONTINENTS (Ge 1:9-10; Job 26:7,10; 28:8-11; 38:4-18; Ps 95:5; 104:5-9; 136:6; Pr 8:29; 30:4).

See Geology.

CONTINGENCIES

In Divine Government of Mankind:

Conditional Rewards—

Ge 4:7 If you do what is right, will you not be accepted? But if you do not do what is right, sin is crouching at your door; it desires to have you, but you must master it."

Ge 18:19 For I have chosen him, so that he will direct his children and his household after him to keep the way of the LORD by doing what is right and just, so that the LORD will bring about for Abraham what he has promised him."

Ex 19:5 Now if you obey me fully and keep my covenant, then out of all nations you will be my treasured possession. Although the whole earth is mine,

Lev 26:3 "'If you follow my decrees and are careful to obey my commands, [4]I will send you rain in its season, and the ground will yield its crops and the trees of the field their fruit.

Dt 7:12 If you pay attention to these laws and are careful to follow them, then the LORD your God will keep his covenant of love with you, as he swore to your forefathers.

Dt 11:26 See, I am setting before you today a blessing and a curse— ²⁷the blessing if you obey the commands of the LORD your God that I am giving you today;

Dt 30:15 See, I set before you today life and prosperity, death and destruction. ¹⁶For I command you today to love the LORD your God, to walk in his ways, and to keep his commands, decrees and laws; then you will live and increase, and the LORD your God will bless you in the land you are entering to possess.

Dt 30:19 This day I call heaven and earth as witnesses against you that I have set before you life and death, blessings and curses. Now choose life, so that you and your children may live

1Ki 3:14 And if you walk in my ways and obey my statutes and commands as David your father did, I will give you a long life."

1Ch 28:7 I will establish his kingdom forever if he is unswerving in carrying out my commands and laws, as is being done at this time.' (+2Ch 26:5)

Job 36:11 If they obey and serve him, they will spend the rest of their days in prosperity and their years in contentment.

Jer 11:4 the terms I commanded your forefathers when I brought them out of Egypt, out of the iron-smelting furnace.' I said, 'Obey me and do everything I command you, and you will be my people, and I will be your God.

Jer 18:9 And if at another time I announce that a nation or kingdom is to be built up and planted,' ¹⁰and if it does evil in my sight and does not obey me, then I will reconsider the good I had intended to do for it.

Jer 22:4 For if you are careful to carry out these commands, then kings who sit on David's throne will come through the gates of this palace, riding in chariots and on horses, accompanied by their officials and their people. ⁵But if you do not obey these commands, declares the LORD, I swear by myself that this palace will become a ruin.'"

Mt 19:17 "Why do you ask me about what is good?" Jesus replied. "There is only One who is good. If you want to enter life, obey the commandments."

Mt 23:37 "O Jerusalem, Jerusalem, you who kill the prophets and stone those sent to you, how often I have longed to gather your children together, as a hen gathers her chicks under her wings, but you were not willing.

Jn 14:23 Jesus replied, "If anyone loves me, he will obey my teaching. My Father will love him, and we will come to him and make our home with him.

Jn 15:7 If you remain in me and my words remain in you, ask whatever you wish, and it will be given you.

Col 1:22 But now he has reconciled you by Christ's physical body through death to present you holy in his sight, without blemish and free from accusation— ²³if you continue in your faith, established and firm, not moved from the hope held out in the gospel. This is the gospel that you heard and that has been proclaimed to every creature under heaven, and of which I, Paul, have become a servant.

Heb 3:14 We have come to share in Christ if we hold firmly till the end the confidence we had at first.

Rev 22:17 The Spirit and the bride say, "Come!" And let him who hears say, "Come!" Whoever is thirsty, let him come; and whoever wishes, let him take the free gift of the water of life.

Conditional Punishment—

Ge 2:16 And the LORD God commanded the man, "You are free to eat from any tree in the garden; ¹⁷but you must not eat from the tree of the knowledge of good and evil, for when you eat of it you will surely die."

Ge 3:3 but God did say, 'You must not eat fruit from the tree that is in the middle of the garden, and you must not touch it, or you will die.'"

Lev 26:14 "'But if you will not listen to me and carry out all these commands, ¹⁵and if you reject my decrees and abhor my laws and fail to carry out all my commands and so violate my covenant, ¹⁶then I will do this to you: I will bring upon you sudden terror, wasting diseases and fever that will destroy your sight and drain away your life. You will plant seed in vain, because your enemies will eat it.

Dt 11:28 the curse if you disobey the commands of the LORD your God and turn from the way that I command you today by following other gods, which you have not known. (+Dt 30:15,19; 1Ki 3:14)

1Ki 20:42 He said to the king, "This is what the LORD says: 'You have set free a man I had determined should die. Therefore it is your life for his life, your people for his people.'"

Job 36:12 But if they do not listen, they will perish by the sword and die without knowledge.

Jer 12:17 But if any nation does not listen, I will completely uproot and destroy it," declares the LORD.

Jer 18:8 and if that nation I warned repents of its evil, then I will relent and not inflict on it the disaster I had planned.

Eze 33:14 And if I say to the wicked man, 'You will surely die,' but he then turns away from his sin and does what is just and right— ¹⁵if he gives back what he took in pledge for a loan, returns what he has stolen, follows the decrees that give life, and does no evil, he will surely live; he will not die. ¹⁶None of the sins he has committed will be remembered against him. He has done what is just and right; he will surely live.

Jnh 3:10 When God saw what they did and how they turned from their evil ways, he had compassion and did not bring upon them the destruction he had threatened.

Mt 6:15 But if you do not forgive men their sins, your Father will not forgive your sins.

Jn 9:41 Jesus said, "If you were blind, you would not be guilty of sin; but now that you claim you can see, your guilt remains.

Jn 15:6 If anyone does not remain in me, he is like a branch that is thrown away and withers; such branches are picked up, thrown into the fire and burned.

2Th 2:8 And then the lawless one will be revealed, whom the Lord Jesus will overthrow with the breath of his mouth and destroy by the splendor of his coming. ⁹The coming of the lawless one will be in accordance with the work of Satan displayed in all kinds of counterfeit miracles, signs and wonders, ¹⁰and in every sort of evil that deceives those who are perishing. They perish because they refused to love the truth and so be saved. (+2Th 2:11)

Rev 2:22 So I will cast her on a bed of suffering, and I will make those who commit adultery with her suffer intensely, unless they repent of her ways.

Rev 3:3 Remember, therefore, what you have received and heard; obey it, and repent. But if you do not wake up, I will come like a thief, and you will not know at what time I will come to you.

Instances of choice:

Joshua—

Jos 24:15 But if serving the LORD seems undesirable to you, then choose for yourselves this day whom you will serve, whether the gods your forefathers served beyond the River, or the gods of the Amorites, in whose land you are living. But as for me and my household, we will serve the LORD."

David—

2Sa 24:12 "Go and tell David, 'This is what the LORD says: I am giving you three options. Choose one of them for me to carry out against you.'"

[13]So Gad went to David and said to him, "Shall there come upon you three years of famine in your land? Or three months of fleeing from your enemies while they pursue you? Or three days of plague in your land? Now then, think it over and decide how I should answer the one who sent me."

[14]David said to Gad, "I am in deep distress. Let us fall into the hands of the LORD, for his mercy is great; but do not let me fall into the hands of men."

Jesus—

Mt 26:39 Going a little farther, he fell with his face to the ground and prayed, "My Father, if it is possible, may this cup be taken from me. Yet not as I will, but as you will."

See Blessings, Spiritual, Contingent Upon Obedience; Predestination; Will.

CONTRACTS

NIV+ See COVENANT

Binding force of (Jos 9:19; Pr 6:1-5)—

Mt 20:1 "For the kingdom of heaven is like a landowner who went out early in the morning to hire men to work in his vineyard. [2]He agreed to pay them a denarius for the day and sent them into his vineyard.

[3]"About the third hour he went out and saw others standing in the marketplace doing nothing. [4]He told them, 'You also go and work in my vineyard, and I will pay you whatever is right.' [5]So they went.

"He went out again about the sixth hour and the ninth hour and did the same thing. [6]About the eleventh hour he went out and found still others standing around. He asked them, 'Why have you been standing here all day long doing nothing?'

[7]"'Because no one has hired us,' they answered.

"He said to them, 'You also go and work in my vineyard.'

[8]"When evening came, the owner of the vineyard said to his foreman, 'Call the workers and pay them their wages, beginning with the last ones hired and going on to the first.'

[9]"The workers who were hired about the eleventh hour came and each received a denarius. [10]So when those came who were hired first, they expected to receive more. But each one of them also received a denarius. [11]When they received it, they began to grumble against the landowner. [12]'These men who were hired last worked only one hour,' they said, 'and you have made them equal to us who have borne the burden of the work and the heat of the day.'

[13]"But he answered one of them, 'Friend, I am not being unfair to you. Didn't you agree to work for a denarius? [14]Take your pay and go. I want to give the man who was hired last the same as I gave you. [15]Don't I have the right to do what I want with my own money? Or are you envious because I am generous?'

[16]"So the last will be first, and the first will be last."

Gal 3:15 Brothers, let me take an example from everyday life. Just as no one can set aside or add to a human covenant that has been duly established, so it is in this case.

Penalty for breach of—

Lev 6:1 The LORD said to Moses: [2]"If anyone sins and is unfaithful to the LORD by deceiving his neighbor about something entrusted to him or left in his care or stolen, or if he cheats him, (+Lev 6:3)

Lev 6:4 when he thus sins and becomes guilty, he must return what he has stolen or taken by extortion, or what was entrusted to him, or the lost property he found, [5]or whatever it was he swore falsely about. He must make restitution in full, add a fifth of the value to it and give it all to the owner on the day he presents his guilt offering. [6]And as a penalty he must bring to the priest, that is, to the LORD, his guilt offering, a ram from the flock, one without defect and of the proper value. [7]In this way the priest will make atonement for him before the LORD, and he will be forgiven for any of these things he did that made him guilty."

Dissolved:

By mutual consent (Ex 4:18), by blotting out (Col 2:14).

Ratified:

By giving presents (Ge 21:25-30; 1Sa 18:4), by consummating in the presence of the public at the gates of the city (Ge 23:17-18; Ru 4:1-11), by erecting a heap of stones (Ge 31:44-54), by oaths (Ge 26:3,28,31; Jos 9:15,20; 1Ch 16:16; Heb 6:16-17), by joining hands (Pr 6:1; 17:18; 22:26), with salt (Nu 18:19), by taking off the sandal (Ru 4:6-8), by written instrument (Jer 32:10-15)

By piercing the servant's ear—

Ex 21:2 "If you buy a Hebrew servant, he is to serve you for six years. But in the seventh year, he shall go free, without paying anything. [3]If he comes alone, he is to go free alone; but if he has a wife when he comes, she is to go with him. [4]If his master gives him a wife and she bears him sons or daughters, the woman and her children shall belong to her master, and only the man shall go free.

[5]"But if the servant declares, 'I love my master and my wife and children and do not want to go free,' [6]then his master must take him before the judges. He shall take him to the door or the doorpost and pierce his ear with an awl. Then he will be his servant for life.

Instances of:

Between Abraham and Abimelech, concerning wells of water (Ge 21:25-32), violated (Ge 26:15). Between Laban and Jacob, for Laban's daughter (Ge 29:15-20,27-30), violated (Ge 29:23-27), regarding sharing flocks and herds (Ge 30:28-34), violated (Ge 30:27-43; 31:7).

Between Joshua and Gibeonites—

Jos 9:3 However, when the people of Gibeon heard what Joshua had done to Jericho and Ai, [4]they resorted to a ruse: They went as a delegation whose donkeys were loaded with worn-out sacks and old wineskins, cracked and mended. [5]The men put worn and patched sandals on their feet and wore old clothes. All the bread of their food supply was dry and moldy. [6]Then they went to Joshua in the camp at Gilgal and said to him and the men of Israel, "We have come from a distant country; make a treaty with us."

[7]The men of Israel said to the Hivites, "But perhaps you live near us. How then can we make a treaty with you?"

[8]"We are your servants," they said to Joshua. But Joshua asked, "Who are you and where do you come from?"

⁹They answered: "Your servants have come from a very distant country because of the fame of the LORD your God. For we have heard reports of him: all that he did in Egypt, **Jos 9:15** Then Joshua made a treaty of peace with them to let them live, and the leaders of the assembly ratified it by oath.

¹⁶Three days after they made the treaty with the Gibeonites, the Israelites heard that they were neighbors, living near them. (+Jos 9:17)

Jos 9:18 But the Israelites did not attack them, because the leaders of the assembly had sworn an oath to them by the LORD, the God of Israel. The whole assembly grumbled against the leaders, ¹⁹but all the leaders answered, "We have given them our oath by the LORD, the God of Israel, and we cannot touch them now.

Between Solomon and Hiram (1Ki 5:8-12; 9:11).
See Covenant; Land; Vows.

CONTRITION [1917, 1918, 1920, 5783].

NIV+ CONTRITE

See Repentance; Sin, Confession of.

CONVENTION For counsel (Pr 15:22). *See Counsel.*

CONVERSATION [1821, *3364*].

Profane, forbidden—

Mt 5:37 Simply let your 'Yes' be 'Yes,' and your 'No,' 'No'; anything beyond this comes from the evil one.

Jas 5:12 Above all, my brothers, do not swear—not by heaven or by earth or by anything else. Let your "Yes" be yes, and your "No," no, or you will be condemned.

Corrupt, forbidden—

Eph 4:29 Do not let any unwholesome talk come out of your mouths, but only what is helpful for building others up according to their needs, that it may benefit those who listen.

Col 3:8 But now you must rid yourselves of all such things as these: anger, rage, malice, slander, and filthy language from your lips.

Edifying, commanded (Eph 4:29)—

Col 4:6 Let your conversation be always full of grace, seasoned with salt, so that you may know how to answer everyone.

People judged by—

Mt 12:36 But I tell you that men will have to give account on the day of judgment for every careless word they have spoken. ³⁷For by your words you will be acquitted, and by your words you will be condemned."

See Speaking. For KJV "conversation" *See Conduct, Christian.*

CONVERSION

A turning, which may be literal or figurative, ethical or religious, either from God, or, more frequently, to God. It implies a turning from and a turning to something, and is therefore associated with repentance (Ac 3:19; 26:20), and faith (Ac 11:21). On its negative side it is turning from sin, and on its positive side it is faith in Christ (Ac 20:21). Although it is an act of man, it is done by the power of God (Ac 3:26). In the process of salvation, it is the first step in the transition from sin to God. *See Converts.*

CONVERTS [*569*, *2189+3836*, *3745*, *4670*].

NIV+ CONVERT, CONVERTED

Parable illustrating four levels of receiving the Word: "Along the path" (Mt 13:4,19). "Rocky places" (Mt 13:5,20-21). "Choked" (Mt 13:7,22). "Good soil" (Mt 13:8,23; Lk 8:4-15).

See Backsliders; Conversion; Proselyte; Revivals.

Instances of:

Ruth (Ru 1:16). Nebuchadnezzar (Da 4). The mariners with Jonah (Jnh 1:5-6,14,16). Ninevites (Jnh 3). Gerasenes (Lk 8:35-39). The Samaritans (Jn 4:28-42). The thief on the cross (Lk 23:39-43). At Pentecost, three thousand (Ac 2:41). Post-Pentecostal (Ac 4:4). The eunuch (Ac 8:35-38). Saul of Tarsus (Ac 9:3-18). Sergius Paulus (Ac 13:7,12; 26:12-23). Cornelius (Ac 10). Jews and Greeks at Antioch (Ac 13:43). Lydia (Ac 16:14-15). Jailer (Ac 16:27-34). Greeks (Ac 17:4,12).

Zealous:

Instances of: Nebuchadnezzar (Da 3:29; 4:1-37). Andrew (Jn 1:40-41). Philip (Jn 1:43-45). The woman of Samaria (Jn 4:28-29). The man possessed of demons (Lk 8:39). The blind men (Mt 9:31; Jn 9:8-38). The mute man (Mk 7:36).

CONVEYANCE

Of Land: *See Land.*

CONVICTION, OF SIN [872, 3519, 7756, *1794, 4443*].

NIV+ CONVICT, CONVICTED, CONVICTIONS

To convince or prove guilty. The first stage of repentance.

Produced, by dreams—

Job 33:14 For God does speak—now one way, now another—though man may not perceive it. ¹⁵In a dream, in a vision of the night, when deep sleep falls on men as they slumber in their beds, ¹⁶he may speak in their ears and terrify them with warnings, ¹⁷to turn man from wrongdoing and keep him from pride,

By visions (Ac 9:3-5)—

Ac 9:6 "Now get up and go into the city, and you will be told what you must do." (+Ac 9:7-9)

By adversity (Job 33:18-30)—

La 1:20 "See, O LORD, how distressed I am! I am in torment within, and in my heart I am disturbed, for I have been most rebellious. Outside, the sword bereaves; inside, there is only death. (+Lk 15:17-21)

By the gospel—

Ac 2:37 When the people heard this, they were cut to the heart and said to Peter and the other apostles, "Brothers, what shall we do?"

1Co 14:24 But if an unbeliever or someone who does not understand comes in while everybody is prophesying, he will be convinced by all that he is a sinner and will be judged by all, ²⁵and the secrets of his heart will be laid bare. So he will fall down and worship God, exclaiming, "God is really among you!"

By conscience (Jn 8:9)—

Ro 2:15 since they show that the requirements of the law are written on their hearts, their consciences also bearing witness, and their thoughts now accusing, now even defending them.)

By the Holy Spirit—

Jn 16:7 But I tell you the truth: It is for your good that I am going away. Unless I go away, the Counselor will not come to you; but if I go, I will send him to you. ⁸When he comes, he will convict the world of guilt in regard to sin and righteousness and judgment: ⁹in regard to sin, because men do not believe in me; ¹⁰in regard to righteousness, because I am going to the Father, where you can see me no longer; **11**and in regard to judgment, because the prince of this world now stands condemned.

By God—

Dt 28:65 Among those nations you will find no repose, no resting place for the sole of your foot. There the LORD will give you an anxious mind, eyes weary with longing, and a despairing heart. **66**You will live in constant suspense, filled with dread both night and day, never sure of your life. **67**In the morning you will say, "If only it were evening!" and in the evening, "If only it were morning!"—because of the terror that will fill your hearts and the sights that your eyes will see. (+Ps 38:1-22; 51:1-4,7-17)

Instances of:

Adam and Eve, after their disobedience (Ge 3:8-10).

Cain, after he killed Abel—

Ge 4:13 Cain said to the LORD, "My punishment is more than I can bear.

Joseph's brothers, because of their cruelty to him (Ge 42:21-22; 44:16; 45:3; 50:15-21). Pharaoh, after the plague of hail (Ex 9:27-28), of locusts (Ex 10:16-17), after the death of the firstborn (Ex 12:31).

The Israelites, after worshiping the golden calf and being rebuked (Ex 33:4), after the death of ten spies and their sentence (Nu 14:39-40), after murmuring against God and being bitten by the serpents (Nu 21:7)

After being judged for disobedience (Dt 28:65-67)—

Eze 33:10 "Son of man, say to the house of Israel, 'This is what you are saying: "Our offenses and sins weigh us down, and we are wasting away because of them. How then can we live?"'

In the last days—

Eze 7:16 All who survive and escape will be in the mountains, moaning like doves of the valleys, each because of his sins. **17**Every hand will go limp, and every knee will become as weak as water. **18**They will put on sackcloth and be clothed with terror. Their faces will be covered with shame and their heads will be shaved.

Eze 7:25 When terror comes, they will seek peace, but there will be none. **26**Calamity upon calamity will come, and rumor upon rumor. They will try to get a vision from the prophet; the teaching of the law by the priest will be lost, as will the counsel of the elders.

Saul, after sparing Agag and the best of the spoils (1Sa 15:24). David, after the pestilence sent because he numbered the people (1Ch 21:8,30)

After his sin with Bathsheba (2Sa 9:12-13)—

Ps 51:1 Have mercy on me, O God, according to your unfailing love; according to your great compassion blot out my transgressions. **2**Wash away all my iniquity and cleanse me from my sin.

3For I know my transgressions, and my sin is always before me. **4**Against you, you only, have I sinned and done what is evil in your sight, so that you are proved right when you speak and justified when you judge. (+Ps 51:5-6)

Ps 51:7 Cleanse me with hyssop, and I will be clean; wash me, and I will be whiter than snow. **8**Let me hear joy and gladness; let the bones you have crushed rejoice. **9**Hide your face from my sins and blot out all my iniquity.

10Create in me a pure heart, O God, and renew a steadfast spirit within me. **11**Do not cast me from your presence or take your Holy Spirit from me. **12**Restore to me the joy of your salvation and grant me a willing spirit, to sustain me.

13Then I will teach transgressors your ways, and sinners will turn back to you. **14**Save me from bloodguilt, O God, the God who saves me, and my tongue will sing of your righteousness. **15**O Lord, open my lips, and my mouth will declare your praise. **16**You do not delight in sacrifice, or I would bring it; you do not take pleasure in burnt offerings. **17**The sacrifices of God are a broken spirit; a broken and contrite heart, O God, you will not despise.

In penitential Psalms—

Ps 31:10 My life is consumed by anguish and my years by groaning; my strength fails because of my affliction, and my bones grow weak.

Ps 38:1 O LORD, do not rebuke me in your anger or discipline me in your wrath. **2**For your arrows have pierced me, and your hand has come down upon me. **3**Because of your wrath there is no health in my body; my bones have no soundness because of my sin. **4**My guilt has overwhelmed me like a burden too heavy to bear.

5My wounds fester and are loathsome because of my sinful folly. **6**I am bowed down and brought very low; all day long I go about mourning. **7**My back is filled with searing pain; there is no health in my body. **8**I am feeble and utterly crushed; I groan in anguish of heart.

9All my longings lie open before you, O Lord; my sighing is not hidden from you. **10**My heart pounds, my strength fails me; even the light has gone from my eyes. **11**My friends and companions avoid me because of my wounds; my neighbors stay far away. **12**Those who seek my life set their traps, those who would harm me talk of my ruin; all day long they plot deception.

13I am like a deaf man, who cannot hear, like a mute, who cannot open his mouth; **14**I have become like a man who does not hear, whose mouth can offer no reply. **15**I wait for you, O LORD; you will answer, O Lord my God. **16**For I said, "Do not let them gloat or exalt themselves over me when my foot slips."

17For I am about to fall, and my pain is ever with me. **18**I confess my iniquity; I am troubled by my sin. **19**Many are those who are my vigorous enemies; those who hate me without reason are numerous. **20**Those who repay my good with evil slander me when I pursue what is good.

21O LORD, do not forsake me; be not far from me, O my God. **22**Come quickly to help me, O Lord my Savior. *See Psalms.*

Widow of Zarephath, when her son died (1Ki 17:18).

Job, in his distress—

Job 40:4 "I am unworthy—how can I reply to you? I put my hand over my mouth. **5**I spoke once, but I have no answer—twice, but I will say no more."

Isaiah, after his vision of God's throne—

Isa 6:5 "Woe to me!" I cried. "I am ruined! For I am a man of unclean lips, and I live among a people of unclean lips, and my eyes have seen the King, the LORD Almighty."

Belshazzar, after the handwriting on the wall (Da 5:6). Darius, when Daniel was in the lions' den (Da 6:18). Mariners, after casting Jonah into the sea (Jnh 1:16). Ninevites, at the preaching of Jonah (Jnh 3; Mt 12:41; Lk 11:32). Jonah, in the fish's belly (Jnh 2).

Herod, when he heard of the fame of Jesus (Mt 14:2; Mk 6:14; Lk 9:7). Jews, who condemned the woman taken in adultery (Jn 8:9). Judas, after his betrayal of Jesus (Mt 27:3-5).

Peter, after the large catch of fish—

Lk 5:8 When Simon Peter saw this, he fell at Jesus' knees and said, "Go away from me, Lord; I am a sinful man!"

Paul, on the way to Damascus (Ac 9:4-18). Felix, under the preaching of Paul (Ac 24:25).

Philippian jailer, after the earthquake—

Ac 16:29 The jailer called for lights, rushed in and fell trembling before Paul and Silas. **30**He then brought them out and asked, "Sirs, what must I do to be saved?"

See Penitent; Remorse; Repentance; Sin, Confession of; Wicked.

CONVOCATION [5246+7924].
NIV+ CONVOCATIONS

NIV "assembly"; a religious festival during which no work could be done (Ex 12:16; Lev 23:2-37; Isa 1:13).

COOKING [1418, 2326, 3184, 3185, 3968, 6105, 6913, 9462].
NIV+ COOK, COOKED, COOKS

A kid might not be cooked in the mother's milk (Dt 14:21). Spice used in (Eze 24:10). Ephraim, a cake unturned (Hos 7:8). In the temple (Eze 46:19-24).

See Bread; Oven.

COOS *See Cos.*

COPING NIV "eaves"; a parapet on the temple roof (1Ki 7:9).

COPPER [5703, 5733, 3321, 5910]. A mineral resource of Israel (Dt 8:9; Job 28:2). Refining, figurative of judgment (Eze 22:20; 24:11). Used as money (Mt 10:9; Mk 12:42). Alloyed with tin to make bronze. *See Bronze; Money.*

COPPERSMITH NIV Alexander the "metalworker" (2Ti 4:14).

COPULATION Forbidden between persons near of kin (Lev 18:6-16). During menses (Lev 15:19; 18:19), with animals (Ex 22:19).

See Adultery; Bestiality; Homosexual; Lasciviousness.

COR [4123, 10367].
NIV+ CORS

A measure of dry capacity, equal to the homer, containing ten ephahs or baths (1Ki 4:22; 5:11; 2Ch 2:10; 27:5; Ezr 7:22; Eze 45:14). *See Measure.*

CORAL [8029]. Ranked by Hebrews with precious stones (Job 28:18; Eze 27:16).

See Minerals of the Bible, 1; Stones.

CORBAN [3167] (*gift*). An offering dedicated to God (Lev 1:2-3; 2:1; 3:1; Nu 7:12-17; Mk 7:11).

CORD [99, 109, 2475, 2562, 3857, 4798, 5436, 6310, 7348, 9219, 9535, 5389].
NIV+ CORDS

Ancient Uses of:
In casting lots (Mic 2:5), fastening tents (Ex 35:18; 39:40; Isa 54:2), leading or binding animals (Ps 118:27, ftn; Hos 11:4), hitching to a cast or plow (Job 39:10), binding prisoners (Jdg 15:13), measuring ground (2Sa 8:2; Jos 17:14; Ps 78:55; Am 7:17; Zec 2:1), worn on the head as a sign of submission (1Ki 20:31).

Figurative:
Of spiritual blessings (Ps 16:6). Of sin (Pr 5:22). Of life (Ecc 12:6). Of friendship (Ecc 4:12; Hos 11:4).

Symbolic Uses of:
Tassels of thread on the corners of garments served as a

reminder to obey God's commands (Nu 15:38; cf Dt 6:4-9). Signifying an inheritance (Jos 17:14). Token in mourning (1Ki 20:31-33; Job 36:8). Ribbon used in poetic imagery (SS 4:3).

CORIANDER [1512]. A spice (Ex 16:31; Nu 11:7).

CORINTH [3172] (*decoration*).
NIV+ CORINTHIANS

A city of Achaia.

Visited:
By Paul (Ac 18; 2Co 12:14; 13:1, w 1Co 16:5-7 & 2Co 1:16). Apollos (Ac 19:1), Titus (2Co 8:16-17; 12:18). Erastus, a Christian of (Ro 16:23; 2Ti 4:20).

Church of:
Schism in (1Co 1:12; 3:4). Immoralities in (1Co 5; 11). Writes to Paul (1Co 7:1). Alienation of, from Paul (2Co 10). Abuse of ordinances in (1Co 11:22; 14). Heresies in (1Co 15:12; 2Co 11). Lawsuits in (1Co 6). Liberality of (2Co 9). Paul's letters to (1Co 1:2; 16:21-24; 2Co 1:1,13).

CORINTHIANS, 1 and 2
1 Corinthians:

Author: The Apostle Paul

Date: c. Spring A.D. 55

Outline:

I. Introduction (1:1-9).

II. Divisions in the Church (1:10-4:21).
  A. The Fact of the Divisions (1:10-17).
  B. The Causes of the Divisions (1:18-4:13).
    1. A wrong conception of the Christian message (1:18-3:4).
    2. A wrong conception of Christian ministry and ministers (3:5-4:5).
    3. A wrong conception of the Christian (4:6-13).
  C. The Exhortation to End the Divisions (4:14-21).

III. Moral and Ethical Disorders in the Life of the Church (chs. 5-6).
  A. Laxity in Church Discipline (ch. 5).
  B. Lawsuits before Non-Christian Judges (6:1-11).
  C. Sexual Immorality (6:12-20).

IV. Instruction on Marriage (ch. 7).
  A. The Prologue: General Principles (7:1-7).
  B. The Problems of the Married (7:8-24).
  C. The Problems of the Unmarried (7:25-40).

V. Instruction on the Questionable Practices (8:1-11:1).
  A. The Principles Involved (ch. 8).
  B. The Principles Illustrated (ch. 9).
  C. A Warning from the History of Israel (10:1-22).
  D. The Principles Applied (10:23-11:1).

VI. Instruction on Public Worship (11:2-14:40).
  A. Propriety in Worship (11:2-16).
  B. The Lord's Supper (11:17-34).
  C. Spiritual Gifts (chs. 12-14).
    1. The test of the gifts (12:1-3).
    2. The unity of the gifts (12:4-11).
    3. The diversity of the gifts (12:12-31a).
    4. The necessity of exercising the gifts in love (12:31b-13:13).
    5. The superiority of prophecy over tongues (14:1-25).
    6. Rules governing public worship (14:26-40).

VII. Instruction on the Resurrection (ch. 15).
  A. The Certainty of the Resurrection (15:1-34).
  B. The Consideration of Certain Objections (15:35-37).
  C. The Concluding Appeal (15:58).

VIII. Conclusion: Practical and Personal Matters (ch. 16).

2 Corinthians:

Author: The Apostle Paul

Date: c. Fall A.D. 55

Outline:

I. Primarily Apologetic: Paul's Explanation of His Conduct and Apostolic Ministry (chs. 1-7).

  A. Salutation (1:1-2).

  B. Thanksgiving for Divine Comfort in Affliction (1:3-11).

  C. The Integrity of Paul's Motives and Conduct (1:12-2:4).

  D. Forgiving the Offender at Corinth (2:5-11).

  E. God's Direction in the Ministry (2:12-17).

  F. The Corinthian Believers—a Letter from Christ (3:1-11).

  G. Seeing the Glory of God with Unveiled Faces (3:12-4:6).

  H. Treasure in Clay Jars (4:7-16a).

  I. The Prospect of Death and What It Means for the Christian (14:16b-5:10).

  J. The Ministry of Reconciliation (5:11-6:10).

  K. A Spiritual Father's Appeal to His Children (6:11-7:4).

  L. The Meeting with Titus (7:5-16).

II. Hortatory: The Collection for the Christians at Jerusalem (chs. 8-9).

  A. Generosity Encouraged (8:1-15).

  B. Titus and His Companions Sent to Corinth (8:16-9:5).

  C. Results of Generous Giving (9:6-15).

III. Polemical: Paul's Vindication of His Apostolic Authority (chs. 10-13).

  A. Paul's Defense of His Apostolic Authority and the Area of His Mission (ch. 10).

  B. Paul Forced into Foolish Boasting (chs. 11-12).

  C. Final Warnings (13:1-10).

  D. Conclusion (13:11-14).

CORMORANT [8960]. A bird forbidden as food (Lev 11:17; Dt 14:17). *See Birds.*

CORN *See Grain.*

CORNELIUS [*3173*] (*of a horn*). Roman centurion stationed at Caesarea, and the first Gentile convert (Ac 10:1).

CORNERSTONE [74+7157, 7157, *214, 214+1639*].
NIV+ CORNER, CORNERSTONES, STONE

Determined the design and structure of a building; the most important stone in the foundation (Isa 28:16). Figurative of Creation (Job 38:6). Of Christ (Isa 28:16; Zec 10:4; Eph 2:20; 1Pe 2:6).
See Capstone; Stones.

CORNET *See Music, Instruments of; Horn; Sistrums.*

CORPORAL PUNISHMENT *See Punishment.*

CORPULENCY Instances of: Eglon (Jdg 3:17), Eli (1Sa 4:18).

CORRECTION [3519, 3574, 3579, 4592, 9350, *1794, 2061*].
NIV+ CORRECT, CORRECTED, CORRECTING, CORRECTIONS, CORRECTLY, CORRECTS

See Afflictions, Of Believers; Chastisement, From God; Children, Correction of; Parents; Punishment; Reproof; Rod of Correction; Scourging.

CORRUPTION [480, 1175, 2095, 2866, 3237, 4299, 5422, 5614, 6074, 6838, 8845, 10705, *1425, 3620, 3621, 3622, 4922, 5021, 5780, 5785*].
NIV+ CORRUPT, CORRUPTED, CORRUPTLY, CORRUPTS

Physical Decomposition:

(Lev 22:25). After death (Ge 3:19; Job 17:14; 21:26; 34:15; Ps 16:10; 49:9; 104:29; Ecc 3:20; 12:7; Jnh 2:6; Ac 2:27,31; 13:34-37; 1Co 15:42,50).

Figurative:

Of sin (Isa 38:17; Ro 8:21; Gal 6:8; 2Pe 1:4; 2:12,19). Mount of (2Ki 23:13).

Judicial: *See Court, Of Law; Government; Judge.*

Ecclesiastical: *See Church, The Body of Believers, Corrupt; Ministers.*

Political: *See Bribery; Civil Service; Government; Politics.*

COS [*3271*] (*summit*). Island off the SW coast of Asia Minor (Ac 21:1).

COSAM [*3272*] (*diviner*). An ancestor of Christ (Lk 3:28).

COSMETICS [9043, 9475].
NIV+ COSMETIC

Any of the various preparations used for beautifying the hair and skin (2Ki 9:30; Jer 4:30; Eze 23:40).

COTTON *See Linen.*

COUCH [3661, 4753, 5435, 6911].
NIV+ COUCHES

A piece of furniture for reclining, but sometimes only a rolled-up mat (Am 6:4; Mt 9:6).

COULTER *See Plowshare.*

COUNCIL [4595, 4632, 6051, *1085, 4564, 5206, 5284*].
NIV+ COUNCILS

1. Group of people gathered for deliberation (Ge 49:6; 2Ki 9:5).

2. The Jewish Sanhedrin (Mt 26:59; Ac 5:34) and lesser courts (Mt 10:17; Mk 13:9).

COUNSEL [1821, 3446, 3619, 4600, 6051, 6783, *1089, 5205*].
NIV+ ADVICE, ADVISABLE, ADVISE, ADVISED, ADVISER, ADVISERS, COUNSELED, COUNSELOR, COUNSELORS, COUNSELS

Wisdom in (Ex 18:14-23)—

Pr 1:5 let the wise listen and add to their learning, and let the discerning get guidance—

Pr 11:14 For lack of guidance a nation falls, but many advisers make victory sure.

Pr 15:22 Plans fail for lack of counsel, but with many advisers they succeed.

Pr 19:20 Listen to advice and accept instruction, and in the end you will be wise.

Pr 20:18 Make plans by seeking advice; if you wage war, obtain guidance.

Pr 24:6 for waging war you need guidance, and for victory many advisers.

The wise profit by (Pr 1:5)—

Pr 9:9 Instruct a wise man and he will be wiser still; teach a righteous man and he will add to his learning.

Pr 12:15 The way of a fool seems right to him, but a wise man listens to advice.

Pr 27:9 Perfume and incense bring joy to the heart, and the pleasantness of one's friend springs from his earnest counsel.

Rejected, by Rehoboam (1Ki 12:8-16), by rich young ruler (Mt 19:22).

Consequences of rejecting divine—

Pr 1:24 But since you rejected me when I called and no one gave heed when I stretched out my hand, 25since you ignored all my advice and would not accept my rebuke, 26I in turn will laugh at your disaster; I will mock when calamity overtakes you— 27when calamity overtakes you like a storm, when disaster sweeps over you like a whirlwind, when distress and trouble overwhelm you.

28"Then they will call to me but I will not answer; they will look for me but will not find me. 29Since they hated knowledge and did not choose to fear the LORD, 30since they would not accept my advice and spurned my rebuke, 31they will eat the fruit of their ways and be filled with the fruit of their schemes. 32For the waywardness of the simple will kill them, and the complacency of fools will destroy them;

See Prudence.

COUNSELOR [408+6783, 3446, *4156, 5207*].

NIV+ See COUNSEL

A wise man, versed in law and diplomacy (1Ch 27:32-33). Ahithophel was, to David (2Sa 16:23; 1Ch 27:33), to Absalom (2Sa 16:23). A title of Christ (Isa 9:6). A title of the Holy Spirit (Jn 14:16,26; 15:26; 16:7).

COUNTENANCE [7156].

NIV+ See FACE

Angry (Pr 25:23). Cheerful (Job 29:24; Ps 4:6; 21:6; 44:3; Pr 15:13; 27:17). Fierce (Dt 28:50; Da 8:23). Guilty (Ge 4:5; Isa 3:9). Health indicated in (Ps 42:11; 43:5). Pride in (2Ki 5:1; Ps 10:4). Reading of (Ge 31:2,5). Sad (1Sa 1:18; Ne 2:2-3; Ecc 7:3; Eze 27:35; Da 1:15; 5:6). Transfigured (Ex 34:29-35; Lk 9:29; 2Co 3:7,13).

See Face.

COUNTRY [*141, 278, 824, 1473, 2215, 8276, 8441, 69, 1178, 3978, 4258, 4369, 6001*].

NIV+ COUNTRIES, COUNTRYSIDE, COUNTRYMAN, COUNTRYMAN

Loved by Israelites in Exile (Ne 1; 2; 5)—

Ps 137:1 By the rivers of Babylon we sat and wept when we remembered Zion. 2There on the poplars we hung our harps, 3for there our captors asked us for songs, our tormentors demanded songs of joy; they said, "Sing us one of the songs of Zion!"

4How can we sing the songs of the LORD while in a foreign land? 5If I forget you, O Jerusalem, may my right hand forget [its skill]. 6May my tongue cling to the roof of my mouth if I do not remember you, if I do not consider Jerusalem my highest joy.

See Church, The Body of Believers; Congregation, Of Israel; Patriotism.

COURAGE [599, 1201+2657, 2616, 3338+8332, 4213, 4222, 5162, 5883, 8120, *437, 2313, 2510, 4244*].

NIV+ COURAGEOUS, COURAGEOUSLY

Of the righteous—

Pr 28:1 The wicked man flees though no one pursues, but the righteous are as bold as a lion.

2Ti 1:7 For God did not give us a spirit of timidity, but a spirit of power, of love and of self-discipline.

Exhortations to (Ps 31:24; Isa 51:7,12-16)—

Eze 2:6 And you, son of man, do not be afraid of them or their words. Do not be afraid, though briers and thorns are all around you and you live among scorpions. Do not be afraid of what they say or terrified by them, though they are a rebellious house.

Eze 3:9 I will make your forehead like the hardest stone, harder than flint. Do not be afraid of them or terrified by them, though they are a rebellious house." (+Mt 10:28; Lk 12:4)

1Co 16:13 Be on your guard; stand firm in the faith; be men of courage; be strong.

Php 1:27 Whatever happens, conduct yourselves in a manner worthy of the gospel of Christ. Then, whether I come and see you or only hear about you in my absence, I will know that you stand firm in one spirit, contending as one man for the faith of the gospel 28without being frightened in any way by those who oppose you. This is a sign to them that they will be destroyed, but that you will be saved—and that by God.

Commanded:

Upon Joshua (Dt 31:7-8,22-23; Jos 1:1-9), the Israelites (Lev 26:6-8; Jos 23:6; 1Ch 19:13; 2Ch 32:7-8; Isa 41:10; 51:7,12-16), Solomon (1Ch 22:13; 28:20), Asa (2Ch 15:1-7), the disciples (Mt 10:26,28; Lk 12:4), Paul (Ac 18:9-10), other Christians (1Co 16:13; Php 1:27-28). By Jehoshaphat, upon judicial and executive officers (2Ch 19:11).

Instances of the Courage of Conviction:

Abraham, in leaving his fatherland (Ge 12:1-9), in offering Isaac (Ge 22:1-14). Gideon, in destroying the altar of Baal (Jdg 6:25-31). Ezra, in undertaking the perilous journey from Babylon to Israel without a guard (Ezr 8:22-23).

The Jews, in returning answer to Tattenai (Ezr 5:11). The three Hebrews who refused to bow down to the image of Nebuchadnezzar (Da 3:16-18). Daniel, in persisting in prayer, regardless of the edict against praying (Da 6:10). Peter and John, in refusing to obey men rather than God (Ac 4:19; 5:29).

Instances of Personal Bravery:

Joshua and Caleb, in advising that Israel go at once and possess the land (Nu 13:30; 14:6-12). Othniel, in killing Kiriath Sepher (Jos 15:16-17). Gideon, in attacking the confederate armies of the Midianites and Amalekites with 300 men (Jdg 7:7-23). Deborah, in leading Israel's armies (Jdg 4). Jael, in killing Sisera (Jdg 4:18-22). Agag, in the indifference with which he faced death (1Sa 15:32-33). David, in killing Goliath (1Sa 17:32-50), in entering the tent of Saul and carrying away Saul's spear (1Sa 26:7-12). David's captains (2Sa 23). Joab, in reproving King David (2Sa 19:5-7). Nehemiah, in refusing to take refuge in the temple (Ne 6:10-13). Esther, in going to the king to save her people (Est 4:8,16; 5-7).

Joseph of Arimathea, in caring for the body of Jesus (Mk 15:43). Thomas, in being willing to die with Jesus (Jn 11:16). Peter and other disciples (Ac 3:12-26; 4:9-13,19-20,31). The apostles, under persecution (Ac 5:21,29-32). Paul, in going to Jerusalem, despite his impressions that bonds and imprisonments awaited him (Ac 20:22-24; 24:14,25).

See Boldness of the Righteous; Ministers; Reproof, Faithfulness in; Cowardice.

COURSE OF PRIESTS AND LEVITES David
divided the priests and Levites into 24 groups, called courses (Lk 1:8), each with its own head (1Ch 24:1ff). Each
course officiated a week at a time.

COURT, OF BUILDINGS [*1074, 2958, 5477,
6247, 6478, 7232, 9133, 10170, *1037, 2639*].

NIV+ COURTS, COURTYARD, COURTYARDS

Of the Tabernacle:
(Ex 27:9,12,16-19; 35:17-18; 38:9,15-20,31; 39:40;
40:8,33; Lev 6:16,26; Nu 3:26,37; 4:26).

Of the Temple:
(1Ch 28:12; 2Ch 4:9; 6:13; 23:5; 33:5). The inner court
(1Ki 6:36; 7:12). The middle court (1Ki 8:64; 2Ch 7:7).

COURT, OF LAW [*1074, 2958, 5477, 6247, 6478,
7232, 9133, 10170, *1037, 2639*].

NIV+ COURTS, COURTYARD, COURTYARDS

Ecclesiastical:
1Ch 26:29 From the Izharites: Kenaniah and his sons were
assigned duties away from the temple, as officials and
judges over Israel. [30]From the Hebronites: Hashabiah and
his relatives—seventeen hundred able men—were responsible in Israel west of the Jordan for all the work of the
LORD and for the king's service. [31]As for the Hebronites,
Jeriah was their chief according to the genealogical
records of their families. In the fortieth year of David's
reign a search was made in the records, and capable men
among the Hebronites were found at Jazer in Gilead.
[32]Jeriah had twenty-seven hundred relatives, who were
able men and heads of families, and King David put them
in charge of the Reubenites, the Gadites and the half-tribe
of Manasseh for every matter pertaining to God and for the
affairs of the king.

2Ch 19:8 In Jerusalem also, Jehoshaphat appointed some
of the Levites, priests and heads of Israelite families to
administer the law of the LORD and to settle disputes. And
they lived in Jerusalem. [9]He gave them these orders: "You
must serve faithfully and wholeheartedly in the fear of the
LORD. [10]In every case that comes before you from your
fellow countrymen who live in the cities—whether bloodshed or other concerns of the law, commands, decrees or
ordinances—you are to warn them not to sin against the
LORD; otherwise his wrath will come on you and your
brothers. Do this, and you will not sin.
[11]"Amariah the chief priest will be over you in any
matter concerning the LORD, and Zebadiah son of Ishmael,
the leader of the tribe of Judah, will be over you in any
matter concerning the king, and the Levites will serve as
officials before you. Act with courage, and may the LORD
be with those who do well."

Mt 18:15 "If your brother sins against you, go and show
him his fault, just between the two of you. If he listens to
you, you have won your brother over. [16]But if he will not
listen, take one or two others along, so that 'every matter
may be established by the testimony of two or three witnesses.' [17]If he refuses to listen to them, tell it to the
church; and if he refuses to listen even to the church, treat
him as you would a pagan or a tax collector.

[18]"I tell you the truth, whatever you bind on earth will be
bound in heaven, and whatever you loose on earth will be
loosed in heaven.

Jn 20:23 If you forgive anyone his sins, they are forgiven;
if you do not forgive them, they are not forgiven."
See Church, The Body of Believers, Discipline.

Civil:
Held, outside the camp (Lev 24:14), at the tabernacle
(Nu 27:2), at the gates of the city (Dt 21:19; 22:15; 25:7;
Jos 20:4; Ru 4:1; Zec 8:16), under a palm tree (Jdg 4:5).

Circuit—
1Sa 7:15 Samuel continued as judge over Israel all the
days of his life. [16]From year to year he went on a circuit
from Bethel to Gilgal to Mizpah, judging Israel in all those
places. [17]But he always went back to Ramah, where his
home was, and there he also judged Israel. And he built an
altar there to the LORD.

Composition of, and mode of procedure—
Ex 18:25 He chose capable men from all Israel and made
them leaders of the people, officials over thousands,
hundreds, fifties and tens. [26]They served as judges for the
people at all times. The difficult cases they brought to
Moses, but the simple ones they decided themselves.

Dt 1:15 So I took the leading men of your tribes, wise and
respected men, and appointed them to have authority over
you—as commanders of thousands, of hundreds, of fifties
and of tens and as tribal officials. [16]And I charged your
judges at that time: Hear the disputes between your
brothers and judge fairly, whether the case is between
brother Israelites or between one of them and an alien.
[17]Do not show partiality in judging; hear both small and
great alike. Do not be afraid of any man, for judgment
belongs to God. Bring me any case too hard for you, and I
will hear it.

Dt 17:9 Go to the priests, who are Levites, and to the judge
who is in office at that time. Inquire of them and they will
give you the verdict.

Ru 4:2 Boaz took ten of the elders of the town and said,
"Sit here," and they did so. [3]Then he said to the kinsman-
redeemer, "Naomi, who has come back from Moab, is
selling the piece of land that belonged to our brother
Elimelech. [4]I thought I should bring the matter to your
attention and suggest that you buy it in the presence of
these seated here and in the presence of the elders of my
people. If you will redeem it, do so. But if you will not, tell
me, so I will know. For no one has the right to do it except
you, and I am next in line."

"I will redeem it," he said.

[5]Then Boaz said, "On the day you buy the land from
Naomi and from Ruth the Moabitess, you acquire the dead
man's widow, in order to maintain the name of the dead
with his property."

1Ch 26:29 From the Izharites: Kenaniah and his sons were
assigned duties away from the temple, as officials and
judges over Israel.

2Ch 19:8 In Jerusalem also, Jehoshaphat appointed some
of the Levites, priests and heads of Israelite families to
administer the law of the LORD and to settle disputes. And
they lived in Jerusalem. [9]He gave them these orders: "You
must serve faithfully and wholeheartedly in the fear of the
LORD. [10]In every case that comes before you from your
fellow countrymen who live in the cities—whether bloodshed or other concerns of the law, commands, decrees or
ordinances—you are to warn them not to sin against the
LORD; otherwise his wrath will come on you and your
brothers. Do this, and you will not sin.
[11]"Amariah the chief priest will be over you in any
matter concerning the LORD, and Zebadiah son of Ishmael,
the leader of the tribe of Judah, will be over you in any
matter concerning the king, and the Levites will serve as
officials before you. Act with courage, and may the LORD
be with those who do well." (+Mt 26:54-71)

Mk 14:53 They took Jesus to the high priest, and all the chief priests, elders and teachers of the law came together. **Mk 14:55** The chief priests and the whole Sanhedrin were looking for evidence against Jesus so that they could put him to death, but they did not find any. [56]Many testified falsely against him, but their statements did not agree.

[57]Then some stood up and gave this false testimony against him: [58]"We heard him say, 'I will destroy this man-made temple and in three days will build another, not made by man.'" [59]Yet even then their testimony did not agree.

[60]Then the high priest stood up before them and asked Jesus, "Are you not going to answer? What is this testimony that these men are bringing against you?" [61]But Jesus remained silent and gave no answer. Again the high priest asked him, "Are you the Christ, the Son of the Blessed One?"

[62]"I am," said Jesus. "And you will see the Son of Man sitting at the right hand of the Mighty One and coming on the clouds of heaven."

[63]The high priest tore his clothes. "Why do we need any more witnesses?" he asked. [64]"You have heard the blasphemy. What do you think?"

They all condemned him as worthy of death. [65]Then some began to spit at him; they blindfolded him, struck him with their fists, and said, "Prophesy!" And the guards took him and beat him.

Mk 15:1 Very early in the morning, the chief priests, with the elders, the teachers of the law and the whole Sanhedrin, reached a decision. They bound Jesus, led him away and handed him over to Pilate. (+Lk 22:50-71; Jn 18:13-28)

Ac 5:17 Then the high priest and all his associates, who were members of the party of the Sadducees, were filled with jealousy. [18]They arrested the apostles and put them in the public jail. [19]But during the night an angel of the Lord opened the doors of the jail and brought them out. [20]"Go, stand in the temple courts," he said, "and tell the people the full message of this new life."

[21]At daybreak they entered the temple courts, as they had been told, and began to teach the people.

When the high priest and his associates arrived, they called together the Sanhedrin—the full assembly of the elders of Israel—and sent to the jail for the apostles. **Ac 5:25** Then someone came and said, "Look! The men you put in jail are standing in the temple courts teaching the people." [26]At that, the captain went with his officers and brought the apostles. They did not use force, because they feared that the people would stone them.

[27]Having brought the apostles, they made them appear before the Sanhedrin to be questioned by the high priest. [28]"We gave you strict orders not to teach in this name," he said. "Yet you have filled Jerusalem with your teaching and are determined to make us guilty of this man's blood." **Ac 5:34** But a Pharisee named Gamaliel, a teacher of the law, who was honored by all the people, stood up in the Sanhedrin and ordered that the men be put outside for a little while.

Ac 5:38 Therefore, in the present case I advise you: Leave these men alone! Let them go! For if their purpose or activity is of human origin, it will fail. [39]But if it is from God, you will not be able to stop these men; you will only find yourselves fighting against God."

[40]His speech persuaded them. They called the apostles in and had them flogged. Then they ordered them not to speak in the name of Jesus, and let them go.

[41]The apostles left the Sanhedrin, rejoicing because they had been counted worthy of suffering disgrace for the Name.

Accused spoke in his own defense—

Jer 26:11 Then the priests and the prophets said to the officials and all the people, "This man should be sentenced to death because he has prophesied against this city. You have heard it with your own ears!"

[12]Then Jeremiah said to all the officials and all the people: "The LORD sent me to prophesy against this house and this city all the things you have heard. [13]Now reform your ways and your actions and obey the LORD your God. Then the LORD will relent and not bring the disaster he has pronounced against you. [14]As for me, I am in your hands; do with me whatever you think is good and right. [15]Be assured, however, that if you put me to death, you will bring the guilt of innocent blood on yourselves and on this city and on those who live in it, for in truth the LORD has sent me to you to speak all these words in your hearing."

[16]Then the officials and all the people said to the priests and the prophets, "This man should not be sentenced to death! He has spoken to us in the name of the LORD our God."

Mk 15:3 The chief priests accused him of many things. [4]So again Pilate asked him, "Aren't you going to answer? See how many things they are accusing you of."

[5]But Jesus still made no reply, and Pilate was amazed.

Ac 4:8 Then Peter, filled with the Holy Spirit, said to them: "Rulers and elders of the people! [9]If we are being called to account today for an act of kindness shown to a cripple and are asked how he was healed, [10]then know this, you and all the people of Israel: It is by the name of Jesus Christ of Nazareth, whom you crucified but whom God raised from the dead, that this man stands before you healed. [11]He is "'the stone you builders rejected, which has become the capstone.' [12]Salvation is found in no one else, for there is no other name under heaven given to men by which we must be saved."

Ac 4:18 Then they called them in again and commanded them not to speak or teach at all in the name of Jesus. [19]But Peter and John replied, "Judge for yourselves whether it is right in God's sight to obey you rather than God. [20]For we cannot help speaking about what we have seen and heard." **Ac 5:29** Peter and the other apostles replied: "We must obey God rather than men! [30]The God of our fathers raised Jesus from the dead—whom you had killed by hanging him on a tree. [31]God exalted him to his own right hand as Prince and Savior that he might give repentance and forgiveness of sins to Israel. [32]We are witnesses of these things, and so is the Holy Spirit, whom God has given to those who obey him."

Stephen before the Sanhedrin (Ac 7:1-60). Paul before the Sanhedrin (Ac 23:1-7), before Agrippa (Ac 26:1-32). *See Appeal; Punishment; Witness.*

Superior and Inferior—

Ex 18:21 But select capable men from all the people—men who fear God, trustworthy men who hate dishonest gain—and appoint them as officials over thousands, hundreds, fifties and tens. [22]Have them serve as judges for the people at all times, but have them bring every difficult case to you; the simple cases they can decide themselves. That will make your load lighter, because they will share it with you. [23]If you do this and God so commands, you will be able to stand the strain, and all these people will go home satisfied."

[24]Moses listened to his father-in-law and did everything

he said. [25]He chose capable men from all Israel and made them leaders of the people, officials over thousands, hundreds, fifties and tens. [26]They served as judges for the people at all times. The difficult cases they brought to Moses, but the simple ones they decided themselves. (+Ex 24:14)

Dt 1:15 So I took the leading men of your tribes, wise and respected men, and appointed them to have authority over you—as commanders of thousands, of hundreds, of fifties and of tens and as tribal officials. [16]And I charged your judges at that time: Hear the disputes between your brothers and judge fairly, whether the case is between brother Israelites or between one of them and an alien. [17]Do not show partiality in judging; hear both small and great alike. Do not be afraid of any man, for judgment belongs to God. Bring me any case too hard for you, and I will hear it.

Dt 17:8 If cases come before your courts that are too difficult for you to judge—whether bloodshed, lawsuits or assaults—take them to the place the LORD your God will choose. [9]Go to the priests, who are Levites, and to the judge who is in office at that time. Inquire of them and they will give you the verdict. [10]You must act according to the decisions they give you at the place the LORD will choose. Be careful to do everything they direct you to do. [11]Act according to the law they teach you and the decisions they give you. Do not turn aside from what they tell you, to the right or to the left. [12]The man who shows contempt for the judge or for the priest who stands ministering there to the LORD your God must be put to death. You must purge the evil from Israel. [13]All the people will hear and be afraid, and will not be contemptuous again. (+2Ch 19:5-10)

Justice required of—

Ex 23:2 "Do not follow the crowd in doing wrong. When you give testimony in a lawsuit, do not pervert justice by siding with the crowd, [3]and do not show favoritism to a poor man in his lawsuit.

Ex 23:6 "Do not deny justice to your poor people in their lawsuits. [7]Have nothing to do with a false charge and do not put an innocent or honest person to death, for I will not acquit the guilty.

[8]"Do not accept a bribe, for a bribe blinds those who see and twists the words of the righteous.

Dt 1:15 So I took the leading men of your tribes, wise and respected men, and appointed them to have authority over you—as commanders of thousands, of hundreds, of fifties and of tens and as tribal officials. [16]And I charged your judges at that time: Hear the disputes between your brothers and judge fairly, whether the case is between brother Israelites or between one of them and an alien. [17]Do not show partiality in judging; hear both small and great alike. Do not be afraid of any man, for judgment belongs to God. Bring me any case too hard for you, and I will hear it.

Dt 25:1 When men have a dispute, they are to take it to court and the judges will decide the case, acquitting the innocent and condemning the guilty. (+Dt 27:19)

2Ch 19:5 He appointed judges in the land, in each of the fortified cities of Judah. [6]He told them, "Consider carefully what you do, because you are not judging for man but for the LORD, who is with you whenever you give a verdict. [7]Now let the fear of the LORD be upon you. Judge carefully, for with the LORD our God there is no injustice or partiality or bribery."

[8]In Jerusalem also, Jehoshaphat appointed some of the Levites, priests and heads of Israelite families to administer the law of the LORD and to settle disputes. And they lived in Jerusalem. [9]He gave them these orders: "You must serve faithfully and wholeheartedly in the fear of the LORD. [10]In every case that comes before you from your fellow countrymen who live in the cities—whether bloodshed or other concerns of the law, commands, decrees or ordinances—you are to warn them not to sin against the LORD; otherwise his wrath will come on you and your brothers. Do this, and you will not sin. (+Ac 25:16)

Sentence of, final and obligatory—

Dt 17:8 If cases come before your courts that are too difficult for you to judge—whether bloodshed, lawsuits or assaults—take them to the place the LORD your God will choose. [9]Go to the priests, who are Levites, and to the judge who is in office at that time. Inquire of them and they will give you the verdict. [10]You must act according to the decisions they give you at the place the LORD will choose. Be careful to do everything they direct you to do. [11]Act according to the law they teach you and the decisions they give you. Do not turn aside from what they tell you, to the right or to the left. [12]The man who shows contempt for the judge or for the priest who stands ministering there to the LORD your God must be put to death. You must purge the evil from Israel.

Contempt of (Dt 17:8-12)—

Dt 17:13 All the people will hear and be afraid, and will not be contemptuous again.

Mic 5:1 Marshal your troops, O city of troops, for a siege is laid against us. They will strike Israel's ruler on the cheek with a rod.

Ac 23:1 Paul looked straight at the Sanhedrin and said, "My brothers, I have fulfilled my duty to God in all good conscience to this day." [2]At this the high priest Ananias ordered those standing near Paul to strike him on the mouth. [3]Then Paul said to him, "God will strike you, you whitewashed wall! You sit there to judge me according to the law, yet you yourself violate the law by commanding that I be struck!"

[4]Those who were standing near Paul said, "You dare to insult God's high priest?"

[5]Paul replied, "Brothers, I did not realize that he was the high priest; for it is written: 'Do not speak evil about the ruler of your people.'" *See Judge; Justice.*

Corrupt—

Pr 17:15 Acquitting the guilty and condemning the innocent—the LORD detests them both.

Pr 29:26 Many seek an audience with a ruler, but it is from the LORD that man gets justice.

Isa 1:23 Your rulers are rebels, companions of thieves; they all love bribes and chase after gifts. They do not defend the cause of the fatherless; the widow's case does not come before them.

Isa 5:23 who acquit the guilty for a bribe, but deny justice to the innocent.

Isa 10:1 Woe to those who make unjust laws, to those who issue oppressive decrees, [2]to deprive the poor of their rights and withhold justice from the oppressed of my people, making widows their prey and robbing the fatherless. (+Mic 3:11)

Mic 7:3 Both hands are skilled in doing evil; the ruler demands gifts, the judge accepts bribes, the powerful dictate what they desire—they all conspire together.

Zep 3:3 Her officials are roaring lions, her rulers are evening wolves, who leave nothing for the morning.

Mt 26:59 The chief priests and the whole Sanhedrin were

looking for false evidence against Jesus so that they could put him to death. ⁶⁰But they did not find any, though many false witnesses came forward.

Finally two came forward ⁶¹and declared, "This fellow said, 'I am able to destroy the temple of God and rebuild it in three days.'"

⁶²Then the high priest stood up and said to Jesus, "Are you not going to answer? What is this testimony that these men are bringing against you?"

Mt 27:18 For he knew it was out of envy that they had handed Jesus over to him.

¹⁹While Pilate was sitting on the judge's seat, his wife sent him this message: "Don't have anything to do with that innocent man, for I have suffered a great deal today in a dream because of him."

²⁰But the chief priests and the elders persuaded the crowd to ask for Barabbas and to have Jesus executed.

²¹"Which of the two do you want me to release to you?" asked the governor.

"Barabbas," they answered.

²²"What shall I do, then, with Jesus who is called Christ?" Pilate asked.

They all answered, "Crucify him!"

²³"Why? What crime has he committed?" asked Pilate. But they shouted all the louder, "Crucify him!"

²⁴When Pilate saw that he was getting nowhere, but that instead an uproar was starting, he took water and washed his hands in front of the crowd. "I am innocent of this man's blood," he said. "It is your responsibility!"

²⁵All the people answered, "Let his blood be on us and on our children!"

²⁶Then he released Barabbas to them. But he had Jesus flogged, and handed him over to be crucified.

Mk 14:53 They took Jesus to the high priest, and all the chief priests, elders and teachers of the law came together. (+Mk 14:54)

Mk 14:55 The chief priests and the whole Sanhedrin were looking for evidence against Jesus so that they could put him to death, but they did not find any. ⁵⁶Many testified falsely against him, but their statements did not agree.

⁵⁷Then some stood up and gave this false testimony against him: ⁵⁸"We heard him say, 'I will destroy this man-made temple and in three days will build another, not made by man.'" ⁵⁹Yet even then their testimony did not agree.

⁶⁰Then the high priest stood up before them and asked Jesus, "Are you not going to answer? What is this testimony that these men are bringing against you?" ⁶¹But Jesus remained silent and gave no answer. Again the high priest asked him, "Are you the Christ, the Son of the Blessed One?"

⁶²"I am," said Jesus. "And you will see the Son of Man sitting at the right hand of the Mighty One and coming on the clouds of heaven."

⁶³The high priest tore his clothes. "Why do we need any more witnesses?" he asked. ⁶⁴"You have heard the blasphemy. What do you think?"

They all condemned him as worthy of death. ⁶⁵Then some began to spit at him; they blindfolded him, struck him with their fists, and said, "Prophesy!" And the guards took him and beat him. (+Mk 15:10)

Ac 4:15 So they ordered them to withdraw from the Sanhedrin and then conferred together. ¹⁶"What are we going to do with these men?" they asked. "Everybody living in Jerusalem knows they have done an outstanding miracle, and we cannot deny it. ¹⁷But to stop this thing from spread-

ing any further among the people, we must warn these men to speak no longer to anyone in this name."

¹⁸Then they called them in again and commanded them not to speak or teach at all in the name of Jesus.

Ac 6:11 Then they secretly persuaded some men to say, "We have heard Stephen speak words of blasphemy against Moses and against God."

¹²So they stirred up the people and the elders and the teachers of the law. They seized Stephen and brought him before the Sanhedrin. ¹³They produced false witnesses, who testified, "This fellow never stops speaking against this holy place and against the law. ¹⁴For we have heard him say that this Jesus of Nazareth will destroy this place and change the customs Moses handed down to us."

Ac 24:26 At the same time he was hoping that Paul would offer him a bribe, so he sent for him frequently and talked with him.

²⁷When two years had passed, Felix was succeeded by Porcius Festus, but because Felix wanted to grant a favor to the Jews, he left Paul in prison. *See Bribery.*

See Judge; Justice; Priest.

COURTESY *See Manners.*

COURTSHIP

Ancient customs of: Suitor visited the woman (Jdg 14:7), women proposed marriage (Ru 3:9-13). *See Marriage.*

COVENANT [1382, 4162, 6343, *1347*] (*agreement, contract*).

NIV+ COVENANTED, COVENANTS

Of God With People:

See Covenants, Major in the Old Testament. Salt is an emblem of (Lev 2:13; Nu 18:19; 2Ch 13:5). Confirmed with an oath (Ge 22:16; 26:3; 50:24; Ex 34:27-28; Nu 32:11; Ps 89:35; 105:9; Lk 1:73; Heb 6:13,17-18). Binding (Lev 26; Jer 11:2-3; Gal 3:15). Everlasting (Ge 8:20-22; 9:1-17; Ps 105:8,10; Isa 54:10; 61:8). God faithful to (Lev 26:44-45; Dt 4:31; 7:8-9; Jdg 2:1; 1Ki 8:23; Ps 105:8-11; 106:45; 111:5; Mic 7:20).

Instances of, with individuals and groups—

With Adam (Ge 2:16-17), Noah (Ge 6:18; 8:16; 9:8-17), Abraham (Ge 12:1-3; 15; 17:1-22; Ex 6:4-8; Ps 105:8-11; Ro 9:7-13; Gal 3). *See Circumcision.* Isaac (Ge 17:19), Jacob (Ge 28:13-15). Israel, to deliver them from Egypt (Ex 6:4-8), to destroy Amalek (Ex 17:14-16). Phinehas (Nu 25:12-13). Levites (Ne 13:29; Mal 2:4-5).

Instances of, with Israel at Sinai—

At Horeb (Ex 34:27; Dt 5:2-3), in Moab (Dt 29:1-15). Blood of (Ex 24:8). *See Blood, Blood of the Covenant.* Book of (Ex 24:7). The Sabbath (Ex 31:16). The Ten Commandments (Ex 34:28; Dt 5:2-3; 9:9).

Major Social Concerns in the Sinaitic Covenant:

1. Personhood. Everyone's person is to be secure (Ex 20:13; 21:16-21,26-31; Lev 19:14; Dt 5:17; 24:7; 27:18).

2. False Accusation. Everyone is to be secure against slander and false accusation (Ex 20:16; 23:1-3; Lev 19:16; Dt 5:20; 19:15-21).

3. Woman. No woman is to be taken advantage of within her subordinate status in society (Ex 21:7-11,20,26-32; 22:16-17; Dt 21:10-14; 22:13-30; 24:1-5).

4. Punishment. Punishment for wrongdoing shall not be excessive so that the culprit is dehumanized (Dt 25:1-5).

5. Dignity. Every Israelite's dignity and right to be God's freedman and servant are to be honored and safeguarded (Ex 21:2,5-6; Lev 25; Dt 15:12-18).

6. Inheritance. Every Israelite's inheritance in the promised land is to be secure (Lev 25; Nu 27:5-7; 36:1-9; Dt 25:5-10).

7. Property. Everyone's property is to be secure (Ex 20:15; 21:33-36; 22:1-15; 23:4-5; Lev 19:35-36; Dt 5:19; 22:1-4; 25:13-15).

8. Fruit of Labor. Everyone is to receive the fruit of his labors (Lev 19:13; Dt 24:14; 25:4).

9. Fruit of the Ground. Everyone is to share the fruit of the ground (Ex 23:10-11; Lev 19:9-10; 23:22; 25:3-55; Dt 14:28-29; 24:19-21).

10. Rest on Sabbath. Everyone, down to the humblest servant and the resident alien, is to share in the weekly rest of God's Sabbath (Ex 20:8-11; 23:12; Dt 5:12-15).

11. Marriage. The marriage relationship is to be kept inviolate (Ex 20:14; Dt 5:18; see also Lev 18:6-23; 20:10-21; Dt 22:13-30).

12. Exploitation. No one, however disabled, impoverished or powerless, is to be oppressed or exploited (Ex 22:21-27; Lev 19:14,33-34; 25:35-36; Dt 23:19; 24:6,12-15,17; 27:18).

13. Fair Trial. Everyone is to be afforded a fair trial (Ex 23:6,8; Lev 19:15; Dt 1:17; 10:17-18; 16:18-20; 17:8-13; 19:15-21).

14. Social Order. Every person's God-given place in the social order is to be honored (Ex 20:12; 21:15,17; 22:28; Lev 19:3,32; 20:9; Dt 5:16; 17:8-13; 21:15-21; 27:16).

15. Law. No one shall be above the law, not even the king (Dt 17:18-20).

16. Animals. Concern for the welfare of other creatures is to be extended to the animal world (Ex 23:5,11; Lev 25:7; Dt 22:4,6-7; 25:4).

Repudiated by God on account of Israelite's idolatry (Jer 44:26-27; Heb 8:9). Broken by the Israelites (Jer 22:9; Eze 16:59; Heb 8:9). Punishment for breaking (Lev 26:25-46).David (2Sa 7:12-16; 1Ch 17:11-14; 2Ch 6:16), David and his house (2Sa 23:5; Ps 89:20-37; Jer 33:21), God's people (Isa 55:3; 59:21).

Of People With God:

Jacob (Ge 28:20-22). Joshua (Jos 24:25). Absalom (2Sa 15:7-8). Jehoiada and Joash (2Ki 11:17). Josiah (2Ki 23:3). Asa (2Ch 15:12-15). Nehemiah (Ne 9:38; 10). Israelites (Ex 24:3,7; 19:8; Dt 5:27; 26:17; Jer 50:5). *See Vows.*

Of People With People:

Sacred (Jos 9:18-21; Gal 3:15). Binding (Jos 9:18-20; Jer 34:8-21; Eze 17:14-18; Gal 3:15), on those represented as well (Dt 29:14-15). Breach of, punished (2Sa 21:1-6; Jer 34:8-22; Eze 17:13-19). National. *See Alliances.*

Ratified:

By giving the hand (Ezr 10:18; La 5:6; Eze 17:18), loosing the sandal (Ru 4:7-11), writing and sealing (Ne 9:38; Jer 32:10-12), giving presents (Ge 21:27-30; 1Sa 18:3-4), making a feast (Ge 26:30), erecting a monument (Ge 31:45-46,49-53), offering a sacrifice (Ge 15:9-17; Jer 34:18-19), salting (Lev 2:13; Nu 18:19; 2Ch 13:5), taking an oath (Ge 21:23-24; 25:33; 26:28-31; 31:53; Jos 2:12-14; 14:9). *See Oath.*

See Contracts; Vows.

Instances of:

Abraham and Abimelech (Ge 21:22-32). Abimelech and Isaac (Ge 26:26-31). Jacob and Laban (Ge 31:44-54). Jonathan and David (1Sa 18:3-4; 20:16,42; 2Sa 21:7). Jews with each other, to serve God (2Ch 15:12-15; Ne 10:28-32). King Zedekiah and his subjects (Jer 34:8).

Ahab with Ben-Hadad (1Ki 20:34). Subjects with sovereign (2Ch 23:1-3,16).

New Covenant:

Prophecy concerning—

Jer 31:31 "The time is coming," declares the LORD, "when I will make a new covenant with the house of Israel and with the house of Judah. ³²It will not be like the covenant I made with their forefathers when I took them by the hand to lead them out of Egypt, because they broke my covenant, though I was a husband to them," declares the LORD.

³³"This is the covenant I will make with the house of Israel after that time," declares the LORD. "I will put my law in their minds and write it on their hearts. I will be their God, and they will be my people. ³⁴No longer will a man teach his neighbor, or a man his brother, saying, 'Know the LORD,' because they will all know me, from the least of them to the greatest," declares the LORD.

"For I will forgive their wickedness and will remember their sins no more." (+Isa 59:21; 61:8-9; Eze 16:59-63; 34:25-31; 37:24-28)

Heb 8:4 If he were on earth, he would not be a priest, for there are already men who offer the gifts prescribed by the law. ⁵They serve at a sanctuary that is a copy and shadow of what is in heaven. This is why Moses was warned when he was about to build the tabernacle: "See to it that you make everything according to the pattern shown you on the mountain." ⁶But the ministry Jesus has received is as superior to theirs as the covenant of which he is mediator is superior to the old one, and it is founded on better promises.

⁷For if there had been nothing wrong with that first covenant, no place would have been sought for another. ⁸But God found fault with the people and said:

"The time is coming, declares the Lord, when I will make a new covenant with the house of Israel and with the house of Judah. ⁹It will not be like the covenant I made with their forefathers when I took them by the hand to lead them out of Egypt, because they did not remain faithful to my covenant, and I turned away from them, declares the Lord. ¹⁰This is the covenant I will make with the house of Israel after that time, declares the Lord. I will put my laws in their minds and write them on their hearts. I will be their God, and they will be my people. ¹¹No longer will a man teach his neighbor, or a man his brother, saying, 'Know the Lord,' because they will all know me, from the least of them to the greatest. ¹²For I will forgive their wickedness and will remember their sins no more."

¹³By calling this covenant "new," he has made the first one obsolete; and what is obsolete and aging will soon disappear.

Characterized by the Spirit rather than the letter (2Co 3:6-17). Purchased or ratified by the blood of Jesus (Mt 26:28; Mk 14:24; Lk 22:20; 1Co 11:25).

Jesus the mediator—

Heb 12:18 You have not come to a mountain that can be touched and that is burning with fire; to darkness, gloom and storm; ¹⁹to a trumpet blast or to such a voice speaking words that those who heard it begged that no further word be spoken to them, ²⁰because they could not bear what was commanded: "If even an animal touches the mountain, it must be stoned." ²¹The sight was so terrifying that Moses said, "I am trembling with fear."

²²But you have come to Mount Zion, to the heavenly Jerusalem, the city of the living God. You have come to thousands upon thousands of angels in joyful assembly, ²³to the church of the firstborn, whose names are written in

heaven. You have come to God, the judge of all men, to the spirits of righteous men made perfect, 24to Jesus the mediator of a new covenant, and to the sprinkled blood that speaks a better word than the blood of Abel.

See Covenants, Major in the Old Testament.

Everlasting—

Heb 13:20 May the God of peace, who through the blood of the eternal covenant brought back from the dead our Lord Jesus, that great Shepherd of the sheep,

COVENANTS, MAJOR IN THE OLD TESTAMENT

Major Types:

Royal Grant (*unconditional*)—

A king's grant (of land or some other benefit) to a loyal servant for faithful or exceptional service. The grant was normally perpetual and unconditional, but the servant's heirs benefited from it only as they continued their father's loyalty and service (1Sa 8:14; 22:7; 27:6; Est 8:1).

Parity (*conditional*)—

A covenant between equals, binding them to mutual friendship or at least to mutual respect for each other's spheres and interests. Participants called each other "brothers" (Ge 21:27; 26:31; 31:44-54; 1Ki 5:12; 15:19; 20:32-34; Am 1:9).

Suzerain-vassal (*unconditional*):

A covenant regulating the relationship between a great king and one of his subject kings. The great king claimed absolute right of sovereignty, demanded total loyalty and service (the vassal must "love" his suzerain) and pledged protection of the subject's realm and dynasty, conditional on the vassal's faithfulness and loyalty to him. The vassal pledged absolute loyalty to his suzerain—whatever service his suzerain demanded—and exclusive reliance on the suzerain's protection. Participants called each other "lord" and "servant" or "father" and "son" (Jos 9:6,8; Eze 17:13-18; Hos 12:1).

Major Instances:

1. Noahic—Ge 9:8-17.

Type: Royal Grant.

Participant: Made with "righteous" (Ge 6:9) Noah (and his descendants and every living thing on earth—all life that is subject to man's jurisdiction).

Description: An unconditional divine promise never to destroy all earthly life with some natural catastrophe; the covenant "sign" being the rainbow in the storm cloud.

2. Abrahamic A—Ge 15:9-21.

Type: Royal (land) Grant.

Participant: Made with "righteous" (his faith was "credited to him as righteousness," v. 6) Abram (and his descendants, v. 16).

Description: An unconditional divine promise to fulfill the grant of the land; a self-maledictory oath symbolically enacted it (v. 17).

3. Abrahamic B—Ge 17.

Type: Suzerain-vassal.

Participant: Made with Abraham as patriarchal head of his household.

Description: A conditional divine pledge to be Abraham's God and the God of his descendants (cf. "As for me," v. 4; "As for you," v. 9); the condition: total consecration to the Lord as symbolized by circumcision.

4. Sinaitic—Ex 19-24.

Type: Suzerain-vassal.

Participant: Made with Israel as the descendants of Abraham, Isaac and Jacob and as the people the Lord has redeemed from bondage to an earthly power.

Description: A conditional divine pledge to be Israel's God (as her Protector and the Guarantor of her blessed destiny); the condition: Israel's total consecration to the Lord as his people (his kingdom) who live by his rule and serve his purposes in history.

5. Phinehas—Nu 25:10-13.

Type: Royal Grant.

Participant: Made with the zealous priest Phinehas.

Description: An unconditionally divine promise to maintain the family of Phinehas in a "lasting priesthood" (implicitly a pledge to Israel to provide her forever with a faithful priesthood).

6. Davidic—2Sa 7:5-16.

Type: Royal Grant.

Participant: Made with faithful King David after his devotion to God as Israel's king and the Lord's anointed vassal had come to special expression (v. 2).

Description: An unconditional divine promise to establish and maintain the Davidic dynasty on the throne of Israel (implicitly a pledge to Israel) to provide her forever with a godly king like David and through that dynasty to do for her what he had done through David—bring her into rest in the promised land (1Ki 4:20-21; 5:3-4).

7. New—Jer 31:31-34.

Type: Royal Grant.

Participant: Promised to rebellious Israel as she is about to be expelled from the promised land in actualization of the most severe covenant curse (Lev 26:27-39; Dt 28:36-37,45-68).

Description: An unconditional divine promise to unfaithful Israel to forgive her sins and establish his relationship with her on a new basis by writing his law "on their hearts"—a covenant of pure grace.

See Covenant.

COVERING THE HEAD A symbol of sorrow and/or shame (2Sa 15:30; Est 6:12; Jer 14:3-4).

A symbol of authority (1Co 11:10). In Corinth men are commanded to pray and prophesy only with uncovered heads; women with heads covered with a veil or long hair (1Co 11:3-16).

COVETOUSNESS [2773, *2121, 2123, 2420*].

NIV+ COVET, COVETED, COVETING, COVETOUS

The Tenth Commandment against—

Ex 20:17 "You shall not covet your neighbor's house. You shall not covet your neighbor's wife, or his manservant or maidservant, his ox or donkey, or anything that belongs to your neighbor."

Dt 5:21 "You shall not covet your neighbor's wife. You shall not set your desire on your neighbor's house or land, his manservant or maidservant, his ox or donkey, or anything that belongs to your neighbor."

Ro 13:9 The commandments, "Do not commit adultery," "Do not murder," "Do not steal," "Do not covet," and whatever other commandment there may be, are summed up in this one rule: "Love your neighbor as yourself."

See Avarice; Bribery; Greed; Rich, The; Riches.

COW [1330, 7239, 8802, 9391].

NIV+ COWS, COWS'

Used for pulling carts (1Sa 6:7-12; Hos 10:11). Milk of, used for food. *See Milk; Cattle.*

Figurative: (Am 4:1).

COWARDICE [3950, 7579, 8820, *1264*].
NIV+ COWER, COWARDLY, COWERED, COWERING

Described—

Jos 7:5 who killed about thirty-six of them. They chased the Israelites from the city gate as far as the stone quarries and struck them down on the slopes. At this the hearts of the people melted and became like water.

Disqualified for military service—

Dt 20:8 Then the officers shall add, "Is any man afraid or fainthearted? Let him go home so that his brothers will not become disheartened too."

Jdg 7:3 announce now to the people, 'Anyone who trembles with fear may turn back and leave Mount Gilead.'" So twenty-two thousand men left, while ten thousand remained.

God inflicted on enemies—

Jos 23:10 One of you routs a thousand, because the LORD your God fights for you, just as he promised.

Inflicted as judgment—

Lev 26:36 "'As for those of you who are left, I will make their hearts so fearful in the lands of their enemies that the sound of a windblown leaf will put them to flight. They will run as though fleeing from the sword, and they will fall, even though no one is pursuing them. [37]They will stumble over one another as though fleeing from the sword, even though no one is pursuing them. So you will not be able to stand before your enemies.

Dt 32:30 How could one man chase a thousand, or two put ten thousand to flight, unless their Rock had sold them, unless the LORD had given them up?

Rebuke for—

Isa 51:12 "I, even I, am he who comforts you. Who are you that you fear mortal men, the sons of men, who are but grass, [13]that you forget the LORD your Maker, who stretched out the heavens and laid the foundations of the earth, that you live in constant terror every day because of the wrath of the oppressor, who is bent on destruction? For where is the wrath of the oppressor?

Cause of adversity—

Pr 29:25 Fear of man will prove to be a snare, but whoever trusts in the LORD is kept safe.

Caused by adversity—

Job 15:24 Distress and anguish fill him with terror; they overwhelm him, like a king poised to attack,

Job 18:11 Terrors startle him on every side and dog his every step.

Caused by wickedness—

Pr 28:1 The wicked man flees though no one pursues, but the righteous are as bold as a lion.

Instances of:

Adam, in attempting to shift responsibility for his sin upon Eve (Ge 3:12). Abraham, in calling his wife his sister (Ge 26:7-9). Jacob, in flying from Laban (Ge 31:31). Aaron, in yielding to the Israelites when they demanded an idol (Ex 32:22-24). The ten spies (Nu 13:28,31-33). Israelites, in fearing to attempt the conquest of Canaan (Nu 14:1-5; Dt 1:26-28), in the battle with the people of Ai (Jos 7:5), to meet Goliath (1Sa 17:24), to fight with the Philistines (1Sa 13:6-7). Twenty thousand of Gideon's army (Jdg 7:3). Ephraimites (Ps 78:9). Ephraimites and Manassites (Jos 17:14-18). Amorite kings (Jos 10:16). Canaanites (Jos 2:11; 5:1). Samuel, fearing to obey God's command to anoint a king in Saul's place (1Sa 16:2). David, in fleeing from Absalom (2Sa 15:13-17). Nicodemus, in coming to Jesus by night (Jn 3:1-2). Joseph

of Arimathea, secretly a disciple (Jn 19:38). Parents of the blind man, who was restored to sight (Jn 9:22). Early converts among the rulers (Jn 12:42-43). Disciples, in the storm at sea (Mt 8:26; Mk 4:38; Lk 8:25), when they saw Jesus walking on the water (Mt 14:25; Mk 6:50; Jn 6:19), when Jesus was apprehended (Mt 26:56). Peter, in denying the Lord (Mt 26:69-74; Mk 14:66-72; Lk 22:54-60; Jn 18:16-17,25,27). Pilate, in condemning Jesus, through fear of the people (Jn 19:12-16). Guards of the tomb of Jesus (Mt 28:4). The Philippian jailer (Ac 16:27). Peter and other Christians, at Antioch (Gal 2:11-14).

False teachers—

Gal 6:12 Those who want to make a good impression outwardly are trying to compel you to be circumcised. The only reason they do this is to avoid being persecuted for the cross of Christ.

Companions of Paul—

2Ti 4:16 At my first defense, no one came to my support, but everyone deserted me. May it not be held against them.

COZ *See Koz.*

COZBI [3944] (*deceitful* ISBE; *the luxuriant* KB). Daughter of Zur (Nu 25:15,18).

COZEBA [3943] (*liar*). A city of Judah (1Ch 4:22).
See Kezib; Aczib.

CRACKNEL *See Cakes.*

CRAFTINESS [4659, 5915, 6874, 6891, *4111*, *4112*].
NIV+ CRAFT, CRAFTY

Instances of:

Satan, in the temptation of Eve (Ge 3:1-5). Jacob, in the purchase of Esau's birthright (Ge 25:31-33), obtaining Isaac's blessing (Ge 27:6-29), in management of Laban's flocks and herds (Ge 30:31-43). Gibeonites, in deceiving Joshua and the Israelites into a treaty (Jos 9:3-15). Sanballat, in trying to deceive Nehemiah into a conference (Ne 6). Jews, in seeking to entangle the Master (Mt 22:15-17,24-28; Mk 12:13-14,18-23; Lk 20:19-26), in seeking to slay Jesus (Mt 26:4; Mk 14:1).

CRAFTSMAN [570, 588, 1215, 2682, 3086, 3093, 3110, *5493*]. Valley of (1Ch 4:14, ftn; Ne 11:35).
See Art; Ge Harashim; Master Craftsman.

CRANE *See Swift.*

CREATION [*1343, 7865, *2856*, *3231*, *3232*, *3233*].
NIV+ CREATE, CREATED, CREATES, CREATING, CREATOR

The Bible clearly teaches that the universe, "all things," came into existence through the will of the eternal God (Ge 1; 2; Jn 1:1-3; Heb 11:3; Rev 4:11). The Bible gives no information as to how long ago the original creation of matter occurred, or when the first day of creation began, or the sixth day ended. The two Creation accounts supplement each other (Ge 1; 2). Genesis 1 describes the creation of the universe as a whole, while Genesis 2 gives a more detailed account of the creation of man and says nothing about the creation of matter, light, heavenly bodies, plants, and animals, except to refer to the creation of animals as having taken place at an earlier time.

CREATOR [1343, 3670, 7865, *3231*, *3234*].
NIV+ See CREATION

Creator of the universe, God as (Ge 1:1; Ne 9:6; Job 26:7; Ps 102:25; Ac 14:15; Heb 11:3). The Word (Jesus) as

(Jn 1:1-3). Holy Spirit as (Ge 1:2; Job 26:13; 33:4; Ps 104:30). Creator of mankind, God as (Ge 1;26; 2:7; 5:2; Dt 4:32; Job 33:4; Ps 8:5; 100:3; Isa 51:13; Mal 2:10; Ac 17:28).

CREATURE [*1414, 2651, 5883, 7470, 8254, 9238, 2442].

NIV+ CREATURES

That which has been created (Ro 1:25; 8:39; Heb 4:13).

CREATURE LIVING Symbolic figure presented in (Eze 1:5ff; Rev 4:6-9; 5:6,8,11; 6:1,3,5-7). The living creatures in Revelation are somewhat modified from those in Ezekiel's vision.

CREDIT See Borrowing; Creditor; Debt; Lending; Security, For Debt.

CREDITOR [5957].

NIV+ ACCREDITED, CREDIT, CREDITED, CREDITORS, CREDITS

Mosaic laws concerning:

Release of debtor-servants—

Ex 21:2 "If you buy a Hebrew servant, he is to serve you for six years. But in the seventh year, he shall go free, without paying anything. ³If he comes alone, he is to go free alone; but if he has a wife when he comes, she is to go with him. ⁴If his master gives him a wife and she bears him sons or daughters, the woman and her children shall belong to her master, and only the man shall go free.

⁵"But if the servant declares, 'I love my master and my wife and children and do not want to go free,' ⁶then his master must take him before the judges. He shall take him to the door or the doorpost and pierce his ear with an awl. Then he will be his servant for life.

Must return cloak left as a pledge—

Ex 22:25 "If you lend money to one of my people among you who is needy, do not be like a moneylender; charge him no interest.

²⁶If you take your neighbor's cloak as a pledge, return it to him by sunset, ²⁷because his cloak is the only covering he has for his body. What else will he sleep in? When he cries out to me, I will hear, for I am compassionate.

Dt 24:10 When you make a loan of any kind to your neighbor, do not go into his house to get what he is offering as a pledge. ¹¹Stay outside and let the man to whom you are making the loan bring the pledge out to you. ¹²If the man is poor, do not go to sleep with his pledge in your possession. ¹³Return his cloak to him by sunset so that he may sleep in it. Then he will thank you, and it will be regarded as a righteous act in the sight of the LORD your God.

Must not take, widows' cloak for pledge—

Dt 24:17 Do not deprive the alien or the fatherless of justice, or take the cloak of the widow as a pledge.

Nor millstones—

Dt 24:6 Do not take a pair of millstones—not even the upper one—as security for a debt, because that would be taking a man's livelihood as security.

Must not extort interest of the poor—

Lev 25:35 "'If one of your countrymen becomes poor and is unable to support himself among you, help him as you would an alien or a temporary resident, so he can continue to live among you. ³⁶Do not take interest of any kind from him, but fear your God, so that your countryman may continue to live among you. ³⁷You must not lend him money at interest or sell him food at a profit.

Dt 15:2 This is how it is to be done: Every creditor shall cancel the loan he has made to his fellow Israelite. He shall not require payment from his fellow Israelite or brother, because the LORD's time for canceling debts has been proclaimed. ³You may require payment from a foreigner, but you must cancel any debt your brother owes you.

Dt 23:19 Do not charge your brother interest, whether on money or food or anything else that may earn interest. ²⁰You may charge a foreigner interest, but not a brother Israelite, so that the LORD your God may bless you in everything you put your hand to in the land you are entering to possess.

Must not oppress neighbor—

Lev 25:14 "'If you sell land to one of your countrymen or buy any from him, do not take advantage of each other. ¹⁵You are to buy from your countryman on the basis of the number of years since the Jubilee. And he is to sell to you on the basis of the number of years left for harvesting crops. ¹⁶When the years are many, you are to increase the price, and when the years are few, you are to decrease the price, because what he is really selling you is the number of crops. ¹⁷Do not take advantage of each other, but fear your God. I am the LORD your God.

Christ's injunctions to:

Mt 5:42 Give to the one who asks you, and do not turn away from the one who wants to borrow from you.

Lk 6:34 And if you lend to those from whom you expect repayment, what credit is that to you? Even 'sinners' lend to 'sinners,' expecting to be repaid in full.

Oppression by:

Seizing debtor's personal property—

Job 22:6 You demanded security from your brothers for no reason; you stripped men of their clothing, leaving them naked.

Job 24:3 They drive away the orphan's donkey and take the widow's ox in pledge.

Job 24:10 Lacking clothes, they go about naked; they carry the sheaves, but still go hungry.

Pr 22:26 Do not be a man who strikes hands in pledge or puts up security for debts; ²⁷if you lack the means to pay, your very bed will be snatched from under you.

Seizing debtor's houses—

Job 20:18 What he toiled for he must give back uneaten; he will not enjoy the profit from his trading. ¹⁹For he has oppressed the poor and left them destitute; he has seized houses he did not build.

²⁰"Surely he will have no respite from his craving; he cannot save himself by his treasure.

Imprisoning debtor—

Mt 5:25 "Settle matters quickly with your adversary who is taking you to court. Do it while you are still with him on the way, or he may hand you over to the judge, and the judge may hand you over to the officer, and you may be thrown into prison. ²⁶I tell you the truth, you will not get out until you have paid the last penny.

Mt 18:28 "But when that servant went out, he found one of his fellow servants who owed him a hundred denarii. He grabbed him and began to choke him. 'Pay back what you owe me!' he demanded.

²⁹"His fellow servant fell to his knees and begged him, 'Be patient with me, and I will pay you back.'

³⁰"But he refused. Instead, he went off and had the man thrown into prison until he could pay the debt. ³¹When the other servants saw what had happened, they were greatly

distressed and went and told their master everything that had happened.

[32]"Then the master called the servant in. 'You wicked servant,' he said, 'I canceled all that debt of yours because you begged me to. [33]Shouldn't you have had mercy on your fellow servant just as I had on you?' [34]In anger his master turned him over to the jailers to be tortured, until he should pay back all he owed.

[35]"This is how my heavenly Father will treat each of you unless you forgive your brother from your heart." (+Lk 12:58-59)

Enslaving debtor's children—

2Ki 4:1 The wife of a man from the company of the prophets cried out to Elisha, "Your servant my husband is dead, and you know that he revered the LORD. But now his creditor is coming to take my two boys as his slaves."

Ne 5:1 Now the men and their wives raised a great outcry against their Jewish brothers. [2]Some were saying, "We and our sons and daughters are numerous; in order for us to eat and stay alive, we must get grain."

[3]Others were saying, "We are mortgaging our fields, our vineyards and our homes to get grain during the famine."

[4]Still others were saying, "We have had to borrow money to pay the king's tax on our fields and vineyards. [5]Although we are of the same flesh and blood as our countrymen and though our sons are as good as theirs, yet we have to subject our sons and daughters to slavery. Some of our daughters have already been enslaved, but we are powerless, because our fields and our vineyards belong to others."

[6]When I heard their outcry and these charges, I was very angry. [7]I pondered them in my mind and then accused the nobles and officials. I told them, "You are exacting usury from your own countrymen!" So I called together a large meeting to deal with them [8]and said: "As far as possible, we have bought back our Jewish brothers who were sold to the Gentiles. Now you are selling your brothers, only for them to be sold back to us!" They kept quiet, because they could find nothing to say.

[9]So I continued, "What you are doing is not right. Shouldn't you walk in the fear of our God to avoid the reproach of our Gentile enemies? [10]I and my brothers and my men are also lending the people money and grain. But let the exacting of usury stop! [11]Give back to them immediately their fields, vineyards, olive groves and houses, and also the usury you are charging them—the hundredth part of the money, grain, new wine and oil."

[12]"We will give it back," they said. "And we will not demand anything more from them. We will do as you say." Then I summoned the priests and made the nobles and officials take an oath to do what they had promised.

[13]I also shook out the folds of my robe and said, "In this way may God shake out of his house and possessions every man who does not keep this promise. So may such a man be shaken out and emptied!" At this the whole assembly said, "Amen," and praised the LORD. And the people did as they had promised.

Job 24:9 The fatherless child is snatched from the breast; the infant of the poor is seized for a debt.

Merciful:

Ps 112:5 Good will come to him who is generous and lends freely, who conducts his affairs with justice.

Mt 18:23 "Therefore, the kingdom of heaven is like a king who wanted to settle accounts with his servants. [24]As he began the settlement, a man who owed him ten thousand talents was brought to him. [25]Since he was not able to pay,

the master ordered that he and his wife and his children and all that he had be sold to repay the debt.

[26]"The servant fell on his knees before him. 'Be patient with me,' he begged, 'and I will pay back everything.' [27]The servant's master took pity on him, canceled the debt and let him go.

Lk 7:41 "Two men owed money to a certain moneylender. One owed him five hundred denarii, and the other fifty. [42]Neither of them had the money to pay him back, so he canceled the debts of both. Now which of them will love him more?"

[43]Simon replied, "I suppose the one who had the bigger debt canceled."

"You have judged correctly," Jesus said.

See Debt; Debtor; Jubilee; Security, For Debt.

CREDULITY Willingness to trust too easily (Ge 3:6; Jos 9:14; Pr 14:15).

CREED A succinct statement of faith epitomizing the basic tenets of religious faith (Dt 4:4-6; 26:5-9). Various NT passages give the biblical foundation for the Christian creeds: the Apostles' Creed, the Nicene Creed, and the Athanasian Creed (Mt 16:16; 1Ti 3:16).

CREEK NIV "bay" (Ac 27:39). Identified as St. Paul's Bay, c. eight miles NW of the town of Zaletta on the island of Malta.

CREEPING THINGS NIV "creatures that move along the ground." A general term for animals (Ge 1:26; Lev 11:20-23,29-31,42; Ps 104:20,25; Ro 1:23). Unclean (Lev 5:2; 11:20,29-44; Dt 14:19). Clean (Lev 11:21-22). Used in idolatrous worship (Eze 8:10).

CREMATION (Jos 7:25; 1Sa 31:12; 2Ki 23:20; Am 2:1; 6:10).
See Burial.

CRESCENS [3206] (*increasing*). A disciple with Paul at Rome (2Ti 4:10).

CRETE, CRETAN [3205, 3207].
NIV+ CRETANS

An island in the Mediterranean, 165 miles long, 6 to 35 miles wide, forming a natural bridge between Europe and Asia Minor. It was the legendary birthplace of Zeus. Paul and Titus founded a church there (Tit 1:5-14). The Cretans in the OT are called Kerethites (1Sa 30:14; Eze 25:16). Cretans were in Jerusalem on the Day of Pentecost (Ac 2:11). According to Paul they were not of a high moral character (Tit 1:12).

CRIB *See Manger.*

CRICKET [3005]. Permitted as food (Lev 11:22). *See Insects.*

CRIME [2365, 2627, 2805, 6240, 6406, 6411, 7322, 8288, 8402, 93, 162, 2805, 4815].
NIV+ CRIMES, CRIMINAL, CRIMINALS
Some lists—

Eze 22:8 You have despised my holy things and desecrated my Sabbaths. [9]In you are slanderous men bent on shedding blood; in you are those who eat at the mountain shrines and commit lewd acts. [10]In you are those who dishonor their fathers' bed; in you are those who violate women during their period, when they are ceremonially unclean. [11]In you one man commits a detestable offense with his neighbor's wife, another shamefully defiles his daughter-in-law, and another violates his sister, his own father's daughter. [12]In you men accept bribes to shed blood; you take usury and excessive interest and make unjust gain from your neighbors by extortion. And you have forgotten me, declares the Sovereign LORD.

Eze 22:27 Her officials within her are like wolves tearing their prey; they shed blood and kill people to make unjust gain. [28]Her prophets whitewash these deeds for them by false visions and lying divinations. They say, 'This is what the Sovereign LORD says'—when the LORD has not spoken. [29]The people of the land practice extortion and commit robbery; they oppress the poor and needy and mistreat the alien, denying them justice.

[30]"I looked for a man among them who would build up the wall and stand before me in the gap on behalf of the land so I would not have to destroy it, but I found none.

Hos 4:1 Hear the word of the LORD, you Israelites, because the LORD has a charge to bring against you who live in the land: "There is no faithfulness, no love, no acknowledgment of God in the land. [2]There is only cursing, lying and murder, stealing and adultery; they break all bounds, and bloodshed follows bloodshed.

Mt 15:19 For out of the heart come evil thoughts, murder, adultery, sexual immorality, theft, false testimony, slander. (+Mk 7:21-22)

Ro 1:24 Therefore God gave them over in the sinful desires of their hearts to sexual impurity for the degrading of their bodies with one another.

Ro 1:29 They have become filled with every kind of wickedness, evil, greed and depravity. They are full of envy, murder, strife, deceit and malice. They are gossips, [30]slanderers, God-haters, insolent, arrogant and boastful; they invent ways of doing evil; they disobey their parents; [31]they are senseless, faithless, heartless, ruthless. [32]Although they know God's righteous decree that those who do such things deserve death, they not only continue to do these very things but also approve of those who practice them.

Ro 3:14 "Their mouths are full of cursing and bitterness." [15]"Their feet are swift to shed blood; [16]ruin and misery mark their ways, [17]and the way of peace they do not know." [18]"There is no fear of God before their eyes."

Ro 13:9 The commandments, "Do not commit adultery," "Do not murder," "Do not steal," "Do not covet," and whatever other commandment there may be, are summed up in this one rule: "Love your neighbor as yourself."

1Co 5:11 But now I am writing you that you must not associate with anyone who calls himself a brother but is sexually immoral or greedy, an idolater or a slanderer, a drunkard or a swindler. With such a man do not even eat.

Gal 5:19 The acts of the sinful nature are obvious: sexual immorality, impurity and debauchery; [20]idolatry and witchcraft; hatred, discord, jealousy, fits of rage, selfish ambition, dissensions, factions [21]and envy; drunkenness, orgies, and the like. I warn you, as I did before, that those who live like this will not inherit the kingdom of God.

See various crimes or sins, such as Adultery, Arson, Homicide. See also, Punishment.

CRIMINALS [2629, *2804, 2805+4472, 2806*].

NIV+ CRIME, CRIMES, CRIMINAL

Released at feasts (Mt 27:15,21; Mk 15:6; Lk 23:17). Confined in prisons (Ge 39:20-23; Ezr 7:26; Ac 4:3; 12:4-5; 16:19-40), in dungeons (Ge 40:15; 41:14; Ex 12:29; Isa 24:22; Jer 37:16; 38:10; La 3:53,55). Crucified with Jesus (Mt 27:38-44; Lk 23:32-39).

Cruelty to. *See Scourging; Stoning; Mocking.*

Punishment of. *See various crimes, such as Adultery, Arson, Homicide. See also, Punishments.*

CRIMINATION *See Self-Incrimination.*

CRIMSON [2808, 4147, 9355]. Brilliant red dye obtained from an insect (2Ch 2:7,14; Jer 4:30; Isa 1:18).

CRISPING PIN NIV "purses" (Isa 3:22). *See Purse.*

CRISPUS [*3214*] *(curled).* Former ruler of the Jewish synagogue at Corinth, converted by Paul (Ac 18:8; 1Co 1:14).

CRITICISM [4394, 7639, 8189, *1359, 3699*].

NIV+ CRITICAL, CRITICALLY, CRITICIZED

Unjust. *See Uncharitableness.*

CROCODILE *See Leviathan.*

CROCUS [2483]. A flower (Isa 35:1). *See Plants of the Bible.*

CROP [*3292, 5263, 6913, 9311, *2843, 2844*].

NIV+ CROP, CROPS

1. Pouch-like enlargement in the gullet of many birds in which food is partially prepared for digestion (Lev 1:16).

2. Produce of the land (Ge 26:12; Ex 23:10). Cursed (Ge 4:12). In the New Jerusalem (Rev 22:2).

CROSS [2005, 6015, 6296, *599, 1385, 4699, 5089*].

NIV+ CROSSES

Jesus crucified on (Mt 27:32; Mk 15:21; Lk 23:26; Ac 2:23,36; 4:10; 1Co 1:23; 2:2,8; Eph 2:16; Php 2:8; Col 1:20; 2:14; Heb 12:2). Borne by Simon (Mt 27:32; Mk 15:21; Lk 23:26), by Jesus (Jn 19:17). Death on, a disgrace (Gal 3:13).

Figurative:

Of duty—

Mt 10:38 and anyone who does not take his cross and follow me is not worthy of me.

Mt 16:24 Then Jesus said to his disciples, "If anyone would come after me, he must deny himself and take up his cross and follow me. (+Mk 8:34)

Mk 10:21 Jesus looked at him and loved him. "One thing you lack," he said. "Go, sell everything you have and give to the poor, and you will have treasure in heaven. Then come, follow me." (+Lk 9:23; 14:27)

Of Christ's vicarious death—

1Co 1:17 For Christ did not send me to baptize, but to preach the gospel—not with words of human wisdom, lest the cross of Christ be emptied of its power.

[18]For the message of the cross is foolishness to those who are perishing, but to us who are being saved it is the power of God.

Gal 5:11 Brothers, if I am still preaching circumcision, why am I still being persecuted? In that case the offense of the cross has been abolished.

Gal 6:14 May I never boast except in the cross of our Lord Jesus Christ, through which the world has been crucified to me, and I to the world.

Php 3:18 For, as I have often told you before and now say again even with tears, many live as enemies of the cross of Christ.

See Crucifixion; Self-Denial.

CROSS-EXAMINED [373]. Skill in cross-examining (Pr 20:5). Instance of (Ac 12:19) *See Witness.*

CROW [231, 5888].
NIV+ CROWED, CROWS
See Birds; Rooster.

CROWN [4194, 4195, 4200, 4887, 5694, 6497, 6498, 6584, 6996, 7619, 7721, 5109, 5110].
NIV+ CROWNED, CROWNS

Prescribed for priests (Ex 29:6; 39:30; Lev 8:9). Worn by kings (2Sa 1:10; 12:30; 2Ki 11:12; Est 6:8; SS 3:11; Rev 6:2), by queens (Est 1:11; 2:17; 8:15). Made of gold (Ps 21:3; Zec 6:11). An ornament (Eze 16:12; 23:42). Set with gems (2Sa 12:30; 1Ch 20:2; Zec 9:16; Isa 62:3). Given victor in games (1Co 9:25; 2Ti 2:5). Of thorns (Mt 27:29; Mk 15:17; Jn 19:5).

Figurative:

Of gracious visitation—
Isa 28:5 In that day the LORD Almighty will be a glorious crown, a beautiful wreath for the remnant of his people.

Of heavenly reward—
1Co 9:25 Everyone who competes in the games goes into strict training. They do it to get a crown that will not last; but we do it to get a crown that will last forever.
2Ti 4:8 Now there is in store for me the crown of right-eousness, which the Lord, the righteous Judge, will award to me on that day—and not only to me, but also to all who have longed for his appearing.
Jas 1:12 Blessed is the man who perseveres under trial, because when he has stood the test, he will receive the crown of life that God has promised to those who love him.
1Pe 5:4 And when the Chief Shepherd appears, you will receive the crown of glory that will never fade away.
Rev 2:10 Do not be afraid of what you are about to suffer. I tell you, the devil will put some of you in prison to test you, and you will suffer persecution for ten days. Be faithful, even to the point of death, and I will give you the crown of life.
Rev 3:11 I am coming soon. Hold on to what you have, so that no one will take your crown.
Symbolic: (Rev 4:4,10; 6:2; 9:7; 12:1,3; 13:1; 14:14; 19:12).

CRUCIBLE [5214]. The crucible in which ore is melted to be purified and separated from dross (Pr 17:3; 27:21).

CRUCIFIXION [416, 5090, 5365].
NIV+ CRUCIFY, CRUCIFIED, CRUCIFYING

The reproach of (Gal 3:13; 5:11). Of Jesus. *See Jesus the Christ, History of.* Of two criminals (Mt 27:38). Of disciples, foretold (Mt 23:34).

Figurative:

Of old nature—
Ro 6:6 For we know that our old self was crucified with him so that the body of sin might be done away with, that we should no longer be slaves to sin—
Gal 5:24 Those who belong to Christ Jesus have crucified the sinful nature with its passions and desires.

Of self-life—
Gal 2:20 I have been crucified with Christ and I no longer live, but Christ lives in me. The life I live in the body, I live by faith in the Son of God, who loved me and gave himself for me.

Gal 6:14 May I never boast except in the cross of our Lord Jesus Christ, through which the world has been crucified to me, and I to the world.
See Cross, Figurative.

CRUELTY [426, 427, 2807, 6883, 7996, 7997, 8273, 8288, 8368].
NIV+ CRUEL, CRUELLY

Instances of:

Of Sarah to Hagar (Ge 16:6; 21:9-14). Egyptians to the Israelites (Ex 5:6-18). Peninnah to Hannah (1Sa 1:4-7; 2:3). Of Jews to Jesus (Mt 26:67; 27:28-31), soldiers to Jesus (Lk 22:64; Jn 19:3). In war (Isa 13:16,18).
See Animals, Cruelty to; Kindness; Love; Malice; Prisoners, Of War.

CRUSE *See Jar(s).*

CRYING *See Mourning; Praise; Prayer; Weeping.*

CRYSTAL [2343, 3222, 3223]. A precious stone (Job 28:17 Rev 4:6; 21:11; 22:1).
See Minerals of the Bible, 1; Stones.

CUB [*1594, 1596, 8891].
NIV+ CUBS

The young of a dog or a beast of prey; a cub (Ge 49:9; Dt 33:22; Jer 51:38; Na 2:11-12).

CUBIT [564, 4388].
NIV+ CUBITS

A measure of distance, c. eighteen inches (Ge 6:16; Dt 3:11; Eze 40:5; 43:13; Rev 21:17). No one by worrying can add to his height (Mt 6:27; Lk 12:25 notes).

CUCKOO *See Gull.*

CUCUMBERS [7991]. Vegetables enjoyed by Israel in Egypt (Nu 11:5).

CUD [1742]. Chewing of, was one of the facts by which clean and unclean animals were distinguished (Lev 11:3-8; Dt 14:3-8).

CUMMIN [4021, 3248]. A plant bearing a small aromatic seed (Isa 28:25,27; Mt 23:23).

CUN [3923] (*chosen*). A Syrian city (1Ch 18:8).
See Tebah, 2; Berothai.

CUNEIFORM A system of writing by symbolic wedge-shaped characters upon clay tablets used primarily in Mesopotamia in ancient times. More than half a million such clay tablets have been found.

CUP [1483, 3926, 6195, 4539].
NIV+ CUPS

(Ge 40:11; 2Sa 12:3; 1Ki 7:26; Mt 23:25). Made of silver (Ge 44:2), gold (1Ch 28:17; Jer 52:19). Used in the institution of the Lord's Supper (Mt 26:27; Mk 14:23; Lk 22:20; 1Co 10:21). Of the table of demons (1Co 10:21).

Figurative:

Of sorrow (Ps 11:6; 73:10; 75:8; Isa 51:17,22; Jer 25:15-28; Eze 23:31-34; Mt 20:22-23; 26:39; Mk 14:36; Lk 22:42; Jn 18:11; Rev 14:10). Of consolation (Jer 16:7). Of joy (Ps 23:5). Of salvation (Ps 116:13).

CUPBEARER [5482].
NIV+ CUPBEARERS

A palace official who served wine at a king's table (Ge 40:11; 1Ki 10:5; 2Ch 9:4; Ne 1:11).

CUPIDITY *See Avarice; Covetousness; Lust.*

CURES [665, 8324, *557, 2543, 2751, 5392, 5618*]. Miraculous. *See Miracles; Disease; Physician.*

CURIOSITY Insatiable (Pr 27:20). Advised against (Ecc 7:21).

Instances of:

Of Eve (Ge 3:6). Of Abraham, to know whether God would destroy the righteous in Sodom (Ge 18:23-32). Of Jacob, to know the name of the angel (Ge 32:29). Of the Israelites, to see God (Ex 19:21,24), to witness the offering in the Most Holy Place (Nu 4:19-20). Of Manoah, to know the name of an angel (Jdg 13:17-18). Of the people of Beth Shemesh, to see inside the ark (1Sa 6:19). Of the Babylonians, to see Hezekiah's treasures (2Ki 20:13). Of Daniel, to know a vision (Da 12:8-9). Of Peter, to know what was being done with Jesus (Mt 26:58), to know what John would be appointed to do (Jn 21:21-22). A disciple, to know if there be few that be saved (Lk 13:23). Of Herod, to see Jesus (Lk 9:9; 23:8). Of the Jews, to see Lazarus, after he was raised from the dead (Jn 12:9), and to see Jesus (Jn 12:20-21). Of the disciples, to know whether Jesus would restore the kingdom of the Jews (Ac 1:6-7). Of the Athenians, to hear some new thing (Ac 17:19-21). Of angels, to look into the mysteries of salvation (1Pe 1:12).

CURSE [*457, 460, 826, 1385, 4423, 7686, 7837, 7839, 353, 1059, 2129, 2800, 2932, 2933*].

NIV+ ACCURSED, CURSED, CURSES, CURSING

Denounced against, the serpent (Ge 3:14-15). Adam and Eve (Ge 3:15-19), the ground (Ge 3:17-18), Cain (Ge 4:11-16), Canaan, Ham's son (Ge 9:24-27), the disobedient (Dt 28:15-68; Jer 11:3-17), Meroz (Jdg 5:23), Gehazi (2Ki 5:27). Barak commands Balaam to curse Israel (Nu 22:6; 23:11). Paternal (Ge 27:12-13; 49:5-7).

Of the Mosaic law—

Dt 27:15 "Cursed is the man who carves an image or casts an idol—a thing detestable to the LORD, the work of the craftsman's hands—and sets it up in secret."

Then all the people shall say, "Amen!"

¹⁶"Cursed is the man who dishonors his father or his mother."

Then all the people shall say, "Amen!"

¹⁷"Cursed is the man who moves his neighbor's boundary stone."

Then all the people shall say, "Amen!"

¹⁸"Cursed is the man who leads the blind astray on the road."

Then all the people shall say, "Amen!"

¹⁹"Cursed is the man who withholds justice from the alien, the fatherless or the widow."

Then all the people shall say, "Amen!"

²⁰"Cursed is the man who sleeps with his father's wife, for he dishonors his father's bed."

Then all the people shall say, "Amen!"

²¹"Cursed is the man who has sexual relations with any animal."

Then all the people shall say, "Amen!"

²²"Cursed is the man who sleeps with his sister, the daughter of his father or the daughter of his mother."

Then all the people shall say, "Amen!"

²³"Cursed is the man who sleeps with his mother-in-law."

Then all the people shall say, "Amen!"

²⁴"Cursed is the man who kills his neighbor secretly."

Then all the people shall say, "Amen!"

²⁵"Cursed is the man who accepts a bribe to kill an innocent person."

Then all the people shall say, "Amen!"

²⁶"Cursed is the man who does not uphold the words of this law by carrying them out."

Then all the people shall say, "Amen!"

Jos 8:30 Then Joshua built on Mount Ebal an altar to the LORD, the God of Israel, ³¹as Moses the servant of the LORD had commanded the Israelites. He built it according to what is written in the Book of the Law of Moses—an altar of uncut stones, on which no iron tool had been used. On it they offered to the LORD burnt offerings and sacrificed fellowship offerings. ³²There, in the presence of the Israelites, Joshua copied on stones the law of Moses, which he had written. ³³All Israel, aliens and citizens alike, with their elders, officials and judges, were standing on both sides of the ark of the covenant of the LORD, facing those who carried it—the priests, who were Levites. Half of the people stood in front of Mount Gerizim and half of them in front of Mount Ebal, as Moses the servant of the LORD had formerly commanded when he gave instructions to bless the people of Israel. ³⁴Afterward, Joshua read all the words of the law—the blessings and the curses—just as it is written in the Book of the Law.

Assumed for others (Mt 27:25). Paul wishes he could assume for Israel (Ro 9:3). *See Blessings.*

Christ assumed the curse of the Mosaic law for us (Gal 3:13). *See Jesus the Christ, Vicarious Death of.*

CURSING [457, 460, 7837, 7839, *725, 2932*].

NIV+ See CURSE

Of parents (Ex 21:17; Mt 15:4; Mk 7:10). Shimei curses David (2Sa 16:5-8). The precepts of Jesus concerning (Mt 5:44; Lk 6:28). Apostolic (Ro 12:14).

See Anathema Maranatha; Blasphemy; God, Name of; Oath.

CURTAINS [3749, 5009, 7267, *2925*].

NIV+ CURTAIN

Of the tabernacle:

Ten curtains formed the inner lining of the tabernacle, of embroidered linen (Ex 26:1-6). Eleven curtains of goat hair formed the tent over it (Ex 26:7-13). A single linen curtain covered the entrance (Ex 26:36-37). The courtyard was fenced by curtains (Ex 27:9-18). Made by Bezalel and Oholiab (Ex 36:8-38).

A single linen curtain divided the Most Holy Place from the Holy Place (Ex 26:31-33; 35:12; 39:34; 40:21), also in the temple (2Ch 3:14); called the second curtain (Heb 9:3); used to cover the ark (Nu 4:5). A type of the humanity or body of Christ (Heb 10:20). Figurative of the believer's access to God (Heb 6:19).

Of the temple:

Divided the Most Holy Place from the Holy Place (2Ch 3:14). Torn at the time of the crucifixion of Christ (Mt 27:51; Mk 15:38; Lk 23:45).

See Tabernacle; Tapestry.

CUSH [3932, 3933].

NIV+ CUSHITE, CUSHITES

1. Son of Ham (Ge 10:6-8; 1Ch 1:8-10).

2. A Benjamite, the title of the Psalm (Ps 7).

3. Land of (Ge 2:13; Ps 68:31; Isa 18:1). *See Cushite; Ethiopia.*

CUSHAN [3936]. Poetic form of Cush (Hab 3:7). *See Ethiopia.*

CUSHAN-RISHATHAIM [3937] (*man of Cush, doubly guilty*). King of Aram Naharaim; that is the king of NW Mesopotamia (Jdg 3:8-10).

CUSHI [3935].

1. *See Cushite, 2.*
2. Father of Shelemiah (Jer 36:14).
3. Father of Zephaniah (Zep 1:1).

CUSHITE [3932, 3934].

NIV+ CUSH, CUSHITES

1. Moses' wife (Nu 12:1).
2. A messenger who brought news to David (2Sa 18:21-32).
3. Tirhakah, king of Egypt. *See Tirhakah.*
4. Zerah, perhaps Pharaoh Oskoron I. *See Zerah, 7.*
5. Ebed-Melech, who pulled Jeremiah from the cistern (Jer 38:7-13). *See Ebed-Melech.*
6. A people, probably Ethiopians (2Ch 12:3; 14:12-13). *See Ethiopia.*

CUSTOM [*2978, 5477, 6913, *1621, 1665*].

NIV+ ACCUSTOMED, CUSTOMARY, CUSTOMS

When not referring to a tax, usually means "manner," "way," or "statute" (Ge 31:35; Jdg 11:39; Jer 32:11). In the NT it means "manner," "usage" (Lk 1:9; Ac 6:14), and "religious practices."

CUSTOM, RECEIPT OF *See Tax.*

CUTHAH, CUTH [3939, 3940]. A district of Asia, from which colonists were transported to Samaria (2Ki 17:24-30; Ezr 4:10).

CUTTINGS [1548, 3093, 4156, 4162, 5877, 7103, 7287, 7894, *149, 644, 904, 4311*].

NIV+ CUT, CUTS, CUTTER, CUTTING

A heathen practice, including tattooings, gashes, castrations, usually done in mourning for the dead and to propitiate deities. Forbidden to the Israelites (Lev 19:28; 21:5; Dt 14:1; Jer 16:6).

CUZA [*5966*] (*little judge*). Herod's steward (Lk 8:3).

CYLINDER SEALS *See Seal.*

CYMBAL [5199, 7529, *3247*].

NIV+ CYMBALS

A musical instrument. Of bronze (1Ch 15:19,28; 1Co 13:1). Used in the tabernacle service (2Sa 6:5; 1Ch 13:8; 15:16,19,28), in the temple service (2Ch 5:12-13; 1Ch 16:5,42; 25:1,6; Ps 150:5).

Used on special occasions:

The Day of Atonement (2Ch 29:25), laying of the foundation of the second temple (Ezr 3:10-11), dedication of the wall (Ne 12:27,36).

CYPRESS WOOD [1729, 9309, 9560]. (Isa 44:14; SS 1:14; 4:13). Probably the wood from which Noah's ark was made; KJV "gopher wood" (Ge 6:14). Used in making idols (Isa 44:12-17).

CYPRUS [4183, *3250, 3251*] (*copper*). An island (Ac 21:3; 27:4). Barnabas born in (Ac 4:36). Persecuted Jews preached the gospel at (Ac 11:19-20). Visited by Barnabas and Saul (Ac 13:4-12). Barnabas and Mark visit (Ac 15:39). Mnason, a disciple of (Ac 21:16).

CYRENE, CYRENIAN [*3254, 3255*] (*wall*). A city in N Africa, W of Egypt, c. ten miles from the coast. Originally a Greek city, it passed into the hands of the Romans. Simon, who helped Jesus carry his cross, came from there (Lk 23:26). People from Cyrene were in Jerusalem on the Day of Pentecost (Ac 2:10). Jews from the synagogue of the Cyrenians disputed with Stephen (Ac 6:9).

CYRENIUS *See Quirinius.*

CYRUS [3931, 10350]. King of Persia. Issues a decree for the emancipation of the Jews and rebuilding the temple (2Ch 36:22-23; Ezr 1; 3:7; 4:3; 5:13-14; 6:3). Prophecies concerning (Isa 13:17-22; 21:2; 41:2; 44:28; 45:1-4,13; 46:11; 48:14-15).

D

DABAREH *See Daberath.*

DABBESHETH, DABBASHETH [1833] (*hump*). A place on the boundary line of Zebulun (Jos 19:11).

DABERATH [1829] (*pasture*). A town of Issachar (Jos 19:12; 21:28). Assigned to the Levites (1Ch 6:72).

DAGGER [2995]. A short sword (Jdg 3:16-22).

DAGON [1837] (*[god of] grain* IDB; *fish* ISBE). NIV+ BETH DAGON, DAGON'S

A pagan deity with the body of a fish, head and hands of a man. Probably the god of agriculture. Worshiped in Mesopotamia and Canaan, with temples in Ashdod (1Sa 5:1-7), Gaza (Jdg 16:21-30), and in Israel (1Ch 10:10). Samson destroyed the temple in Gaza (Jdg 16:30).

DAILY SACRIFICE, THE Ordained in Mt. Sinai (Nu 28:6). A lamb as a burnt offering, morning and evening (Ex 29:38-39; Nu 28:3-4). Doubled on the Sabbath (Nu 28:9-10).

Required to be with a meat and drink offering (Ex 29:40-41; Nu 28:5-8). Slowly and entirely consumed (Lev 6:9-12). Perpetually observed (Ex 29:42; Nu 28:3,6). Pleasing (Nu 28:8; Ps 141:2). Secured God's presence and favor (Ex 29:43-44). Times of offering, were seasons of prayer (Ezr 9:5; Da 9:20-21, w Ac 3:1). Restored after the Captivity (Ezr 3:3). The abolition of, foretold (Da 9:26-27; 11:31).

Illustrative of:

Christ (Jn 1:29,36; 1Pe 1:19). Acceptable prayer (Ps 141:2).

See Sacrifices.

DALAIAH *See Delaiah.*

DALE, THE KING'S *See Valley, Vale.*

DALMANUTHA [*1236*]. South of the Plain of Gennesaret a cave has been found bearing the name "Talmanutha," perhaps the spot where Jesus landed. Matthew says Jesus went to the vicinity of Magadan (Mt 15:39). Dalmanutha and Magadan (of Magdala), located on the western shore of the Sea of Galilee, may be names for the same place or for two places located close to each other (Mk 8:10). *See Magadan.*

DALMATIA [*1237*] (*deceitful*). Province on the NE shore of the Adriatic Sea also called Illyricum (Ro 15:19; 2Ti 4:10).

DALPHON [1943] (*crafty* ISBE; *sleepless* KB). The son of Haman (Est 9:7).

DAMAGES AND COMPENSATIONS

Listed (Nu 5:5-8).

For assault—

Ex 21:18 "If men quarrel and one hits the other with a stone or with his fist and he does not die but is confined to bed, ¹⁹the one who struck the blow will not be held responsible if the other gets up and walks around outside with his staff; however, he must pay the injured man for the loss of his time and see that he is completely healed.

Ex 21:22 "If men who are fighting hit a pregnant woman and she gives birth prematurely but there is no serious injury, the offender must be fined whatever the woman's husband demands and the court allows.

For personal injury—

Ex 21:28 "If a bull gores a man or a woman to death, the bull must be stoned to death, and its meat must not be eaten. But the owner of the bull will not be held responsible. ²⁹If, however, the bull has had the habit of goring and the owner has been warned but has not kept it penned up and it kills a man or woman, the bull must be stoned and the owner also must be put to death. ³⁰However, if payment is demanded of him, he may redeem his life by paying whatever is demanded. ³¹This law also applies if the bull gores a son or daughter. ³²If the bull gores a male or female slave, the owner must pay thirty shekels of silver to the master of the slave, and the bull must be stoned.

³³"If a man uncovers a pit or digs one and fails to cover it and an ox or a donkey falls into it, ³⁴the owner of the pit must pay for the loss; he must pay its owner, and the dead animal will be his.

For deception—

Lev 6:1 The LORD said to Moses: ²"If anyone sins and is unfaithful to the LORD by deceiving his neighbor about something entrusted to him or left in his care or stolen, or if he cheats him, ³or if he finds lost property and lies about it, or if he swears falsely, or if he commits any such sin that people may do— ⁴when he thus sins and becomes guilty, he must return what he has stolen or taken by extortion, or what was entrusted to him, or the lost property he found, ⁵or whatever it was he swore falsely about. He must make restitution in full, add a fifth of the value to it and give it all to the owner on the day he presents his guilt offering.

For slander—

Dt 22:13 If a man takes a wife and, after lying with her, dislikes her ¹⁴and slanders her and gives her a bad name, saying, "I married this woman, but when I approached her, I did not find proof of her virginity," ¹⁵then the girl's father and mother shall bring proof that she was a virgin to the town elders at the gate. ¹⁶The girl's father will say to the elders, "I gave my daughter in marriage to this man, but he dislikes her. ¹⁷Now he has slandered her and said, 'I did not find your daughter to be a virgin.' But here is the proof of my daughter's virginity." Then her parents shall display the cloth before the elders of the town, ¹⁸and the elders shall take the man and punish him. ¹⁹They shall fine him a hundred shekels of silver and give them to the girl's father, because this man has given an Israelite virgin a bad name. She shall continue to be his wife; he must not divorce her as long as he lives.

For seduction—

Dt 22:28 If a man happens to meet a virgin who is not pledged to be married and rapes her and they are discovered, ²⁹he shall pay the girl's father fifty shekels of silver. He must marry the girl, for he has violated her. He can never divorce her as long as he lives.

See Fine.

DAMARIS [*1240*]. A female convert of Athens (Ac 17:34).

DAMASCUS, DAMASCENES [1877, 1966, 2008, *1241, 1242*].

An ancient city (Ge 14:15; 15:2). The capital of Syria

(1Ki 20:34; Isa 7:8; Jer 49:23-29; Eze 47:16-17). Laid under tribute to David (2Sa 8:5-6). Besieged by Rezon (1Ki 11:23-24). Recovered by Jeroboam (2Ki 14:28). Taken by the king of Assyria (2Ki 16:9). Walled (Jer 49:27; 2Co 11:33). Garrisoned (2Co 11:32). Luxury in (Am 3:12). Paul's experiences in (Ac 9; 22:5-16; 26:12-20; 2Co 11:32; Gal 1:17).

Prophecies concerning (Isa 8:4; 17:1-2; Jer 49:23-29; Am 1:3,5; Zec 9:1).

Wilderness of (1Ki 19:15).

See Syria.

DAMMIM *See Ephes Dammim, Pas Dammim.*

DAMNATION When referring to the future it means primarily eternal separation from God with accompanying punishments (Mt 5:29; 10:28; 23:33; 24:51). The severity of the punishment is determined by the degree of sin (Lk 12:36-48), and is eternal (Isa 66:24; Mk 3:29; 2Th 1:9; Jude 6-7). *See Punishment; Wicked, Punishment of.*

DAN, DANITE(S) [1201+1968, 1968, 1969, 1974] *(judge).*

NIV+ DAN JAAN, MAHANEH DAN

1. The fifth son of Jacob and Bilhah (Ge 30:6; 35:25). Descendants of (Ge 46:23; Nu 26:42-43). *See below, Tribe of.* Blessed of Jacob (Ge 49:16-17).

2. Tribe of: Census of (Nu 1:39; 26:42-43). Inheritance of, according to the allotment of Joshua (Jos 19:40-47), of Ezekiel (Eze 48:1). Position of, in journey and camp, during the exodus out of Egypt (Nu 2:25,31; 10:25). Blessed by Moses (Dt 33:22). Fail to conquer the Amorites (Jdg 1:34-35). Conquests by (Jos 19:47; Jdg 18:27-29). Deborah rebukes, for cowardice (Jdg 5:17). Idolatry of (Jdg 18). Commerce of (Jdg 5:17; Eze 27:19).

See Israel, Israelites.

3. A city of the tribe of Dan. Called Laish (Jdg 18:7,13, 27,29) and Leshem (Jos 19:47) and later known as Dan. *See Laish; Leshem.* Captured by the people of Dan (Jos 19:47). Idolatry established at (Jdg 18; 1Ki 12:28-29; Am 8:14). Captured by Ben-Hadad (1Ki 15:20; 2Ch 16:4).

DAN JAAN, DAN-JAAN [1970].

NIV+ DAN

A place, probably in Dan, covered by David's census (2Sa 24:6).

DANCING [2565, 4159, 4688, 4703, 7174, 8376, 8471, 4004, 5962].

NIV+ DANCE, DANCED, DANCES

Of children—

Job 21:11 They send forth their children as a flock; their little ones dance about.

Of women—

Ex 15:20 Then Miriam the prophetess, Aaron's sister, took a tambourine in her hand, and all the women followed her, with tambourines and dancing.

Jdg 11:34 When Jephthah returned to his home in Mizpah, who should come out to meet him but his daughter, dancing to the sound of tambourines! She was an only child. Except for her he had neither son nor daughter.

Jdg 21:19 But look, there is the annual festival of the LORD in Shiloh, to the north of Bethel, and east of the road that goes from Bethel to Shechem, and to the south of Lebonah."

[20]So they instructed the Benjamites, saying, "Go and hide in the vineyards [21]and watch. When the girls of Shiloh come out to join in the dancing, then rush from the vineyards and each of you seize a wife from the girls of Shiloh and go to the land of Benjamin.

1Sa 18:6 When the men were returning home after David had killed the Philistine, the women came out from all the towns of Israel to meet King Saul with singing and dancing, with joyful songs and with tambourines and lutes.

1Sa 21:11 But the servants of Achish said to him, "Isn't this David, the king of the land? Isn't he the one they sing about in their dances: "'Saul has slain his thousands, and David his tens of thousands'?"

Of David—

2Sa 6:14 David, wearing a linen ephod, danced before the LORD with all his might, [15]while he and the entire house of Israel brought up the ark of the LORD with shouts and the sound of trumpets.

[16]As the ark of the LORD was entering the City of David, Michal daughter of Saul watched from a window. And when she saw King David leaping and dancing before the LORD, she despised him in her heart. (+1Ch 15:29)

In the marketplace (Mt 11:16)—

Mt 11:17 "'We played the flute for you, and you did not dance; we sang a dirge, and you did not mourn.'

At feasts (Jdg 21:19-21; Mt 14:6; Mk 6:22)—

Lk 15:23 Bring the fattened calf and kill it. Let's have a feast and celebrate. [24]For this son of mine was dead and is alive again; he was lost and is found.' So they began to celebrate.

[25]"Meanwhile, the older son was in the field. When he came near the house, he heard music and dancing.

As a religious ceremony—

Ps 149:3 Let them praise his name with dancing and make music to him with tambourine and harp.

Ps 150:4 praise him with tambourine and dancing, praise him with the strings and flute,

Idolatrous—

Ex 32:19 When Moses approached the camp and saw the calf and the dancing, his anger burned and he threw the tablets out of his hands, breaking them to pieces at the foot of the mountain. (+Ex 32:25)

Figurative:

Of joy—

Ps 30:11 You turned my wailing into dancing; you removed my sackcloth and clothed me with joy,

Ecc 3:4 a time to weep and a time to laugh, a time to mourn and a time to dance,

Jer 31:4 I will build you up again and you will be rebuilt, O Virgin Israel. Again you will take up your tambourines and go out to dance with the joyful.

Jer 31:13 Then maidens will dance and be glad, young men and old as well. I will turn their mourning into gladness; I will give them comfort and joy instead of sorrow.

La 5:15 Joy is gone from our hearts; our dancing has turned to mourning.

DANIEL [1975, 10181, *1248*] *(God [El] is my judge).*

NIV+ DANIEL'S

1. An Israelite captive, also called Belteshazzar. *See Belteshazzar.* Educated at king's court (Da 1). Interprets visions (Da 2; 4; 5). Promotion and executive authority of (Da 2:48-49; 5:11,29; 6:2). Conspiracy against, cast into the lions' den (Da 6).

Prophecies of (Da 4:8-9; 7-12; Mt 24:15).

Special diet of (Da 1:8-16). Wisdom of (Da 1:17; Eze 28:3). Devoutness of (Da 2:18; 6; 9; 10; 12; Eze 14:14).

Courage and fidelity of (Da 4:27; 5:17-23; 6:10-23). Worshiped by Nebuchadnezzar (Da 2:6).

2. David's son. Also called Kileab (2Sa 3:3; 1Ch 3:1).

3. A descendant of Ithamar, and a companion of Ezra (Ezr 8:2; Ne 10:6).

DANIEL, BOOK OF

Author: Daniel

Date: c. 530 B.C.

Outline:

I. Prologue: The Setting (ch. 1; in Hebrew).
  A. Historical Introduction (1:1-2).
  B. Daniel and His Friends Are Taken Captive (1:3-7).
  C. The Young Men Are Faithful (1:8-16).
  D. The Young Men Are Elevated to High Positions (1:17-21).
II. The Destinies of the Nations of the World (chs. 2-7, in Aramaic, beginning at 2:4b).
  A. Nebuchadnezzar's Dream of a Large Statue (ch. 2).
  B. Nebuchadnezzar's Making of a Gold Image and His Decree That It Be Worshiped (ch. 3).
  C. Nebuchadnezzar's Dream of an Enormous Tree (ch. 4).
  D. Belshazzar's and Babylon's Downfall (ch. 5).
  E. Daniel's Deliverance (ch. 6).
  F. Daniel's Dream of Four Beasts (ch. 7).
III. The Destiny of the Nation of Israel (chs. 8-12; in Hebrew).
  A. Daniel's Vision of a Ram and a Goat (ch. 8).
  B. Daniel's Prayer and His Vision of the 70 "Sevens" (ch. 9).
  C. Daniel's Vision of Israel's Future (chs. 10-12).
   1. Revelation of things to come (10:1-3).
   2. Revelation from the angelic messenger (10:4-11:1).
   3. Prophecies concerning Persia and Greece (11:2-4).
   4. Prophecies concerning Egypt and Syria (11:5-35).
   5. Prophecies concerning the antichrist (11:36-45).
   6. Distress and deliverance (12:1).
   7. Two Resurrections (12:2-3).
   8. Instruction to Daniel (12:4).
   9. Conclusion (12:5-13).

DANNAH [1972] (*stronghold*). A city in the mountains of Judah (Jos 15:49).

DARA *See Darda.*

DARDA [1997]. Also called Dara. A famous wise man (1Ki 4:31; 1Ch 2:6).

DARIC [163].

NIV+ DARICS

Persian gold coin used in Israel after the return from the Captivity; said to have been named from the first Darius (1Ch 29:7; Ezr 8:27). Although the NIV has "drachmas" for the following references, some believe that the coin intended was the daric (Ezr 2:69; Ne 7:70-72). *See Drachma.*

DARIUS [2003, 10184] (Old Persian *he who upholds the good*). A common name for Medo-Persian rulers.

1. Darius the Mede (Gubaru), the son of Xerxes (Da 5:31; 9:1), made governor of Babylon by Cyrus, but he seems to have ruled for only a brief time (Da 10:1; 11:1), prominent in the book of Daniel (Da 6:1,6,9,25,28; 11:1).

2. Darius I called the Great (spelled variously Hystaspos, Hystaspis, or Hystaspes), fourth and greatest of the Persian rulers (522-486 B.C.); reorganized the government

into satraps and extended boundaries of the empire; a great builder; he was defeated by the Greeks at Marathon in 490 B.C.; renewed the edict of Cyrus and helped to rebuild the temple (Ezr 4:5,24; 5:5-7; 6:1-12; Hag 1:1; 2:1,10,18; Zec 1:1,7; 7:1). Died in 486 B.C. and was succeeded by Xerxes, the grandson of Cyrus the Great.

3. Darius, the Persian (spelled variously Codomanus or Codomannus), the last king of Persia (336-330 B.C.); defeated by Alexander the Great (330 B.C.) (Ne 12:22). Some scholars identify him with Darius II (Nothus), who ruled Persia and Babylon (423-404 B.C.).

DARKNESS [694, 696, 3124, 3125, 3127, 3128, 4419, 4420, 4743, 6547, 6602, 6906, 7223, 7516, 7725, 9507, 10286, *1190, 2432, 5027, 5028, 5030, 5031*].

NIV+ DARK, DARK-COLORED, DARKEN, DARKENED, DARKENING, DARKENS, DARKER, DARKEST, PITCH-DARK

Over the face of the earth (Ge 1:2; Job 38:9; Jer 4:23). Called "night" (Ge 1:5). God created (Isa 45:7). The NIV uses "[deep] darkness" to translate a word formerly translated "shadow of death," usually in a context of deep emotional despair or grief (Job 3:5; 10:21,22; 12:22; 16:16; 24:17,17; 28:3; 34:22; 38:17; Ps 23:4; 44:19; 107:10,14; Isa 9:2; Jer 2:6; 13:16; Am 5:8)

Miraculous:

In Egypt (Ex 10:21-22; Ps 105:28), at Sinai (Ex 20:21; Heb 12:18), at the Crucifixion (Mt 27:45; Mk 15:33).

Figurative:

Of judgments (Pr 20:20; Isa 8:22; 13:10; Jer 4:28; 13:16; La 3:2; Eze 32:7-8; Joel 2:2,10; Am 4:13; 5:18,20; 8:9; Mic 7:8; Mt 24:29; Mk 13:24; Lk 23:45; Rev 8:12; 9:2). Of powers of evil (Lk 22:53; Eph 6:12; Col 1:13; 1Th 5:5; Rev 16:10).

Of the abode of the lost (Mt 8:12; 22:13; 25:30).

Of spiritual blindness—

Isa 9:2 The people walking in darkness have seen a great light; on those living in the land of the shadow of death a light has dawned.

Isa 42:16 I will lead the blind by ways they have not known, along unfamiliar paths I will guide them; I will turn the darkness into light before them and make the rough places smooth. These are the things I will do; I will not forsake them.

Isa 50:10 Who among you fears the LORD and obeys the word of his servant? Let him who walks in the dark, who has no light, trust in the name of the LORD and rely on his God. (+Mt 4:16)

Mt 6:22 "The eye is the lamp of the body. If your eyes are good, your whole body will be full of light. ²³But if your eyes are bad, your whole body will be full of darkness. If then the light within you is darkness, how great is that darkness! (+Lk 1:79)

Lk 11:34 Your eye is the lamp of your body. When your eyes are good, your whole body also is full of light. But when they are bad, your body also is full of darkness.

Jn 1:5 The light shines in the darkness, but the darkness has not understood it.

Jn 3:19 This is the verdict: Light has come into the world, but men loved darkness instead of light because their deeds were evil. ²⁰Everyone who does evil hates the light, and will not come into the light for fear that his deeds will be exposed. ²¹But whoever lives by the truth comes into the light, so that it may be seen plainly that what he has done has been done through God."

Jn 8:12 When Jesus spoke again to the people, he said, "I am the light of the world. Whoever follows me will never walk in darkness, but will have the light of life."

Jn 11:9 Jesus answered, "Are there not twelve hours of daylight? A man who walks by day will not stumble, for he sees by this world's light. ¹⁰It is when he walks by night that he stumbles, for he has no light."

Ac 26:18 to open their eyes and turn them from darkness to light, and from the power of Satan to God, so that they may receive forgiveness of sins and a place among those who are sanctified by faith in me.'

Ro 1:21 For although they knew God, they neither glorified him as God nor gave thanks to him, but their thinking became futile and their foolish hearts were darkened.

Ro 13:12 The night is nearly over; the day is almost here. So let us put aside the deeds of darkness and put on the armor of light. ¹³Let us behave decently, as in the daytime, not in orgies and drunkenness, not in sexual immorality and debauchery, not in dissension and jealousy.

1Co 4:5 Therefore judge nothing before the appointed time; wait till the Lord comes. He will bring to light what is hidden in darkness and will expose the motives of men's hearts. At that time each will receive his praise from God.

2Co 4:6 For God, who said, "Let light shine out of darkness," made his light shine in our hearts to give us the light of the knowledge of the glory of God in the face of Christ.

2Co 6:14 Do not be yoked together with unbelievers. For what do righteousness and wickedness have in common? Or what fellowship can light have with darkness?

Eph 5:8 For you were once darkness, but now you are light in the Lord. Live as children of light

Eph 5:11 Have nothing to do with the fruitless deeds of darkness, but rather expose them.

1Th 5:4 But you, brothers, are not in darkness so that this day should surprise you like a thief. ⁵You are all sons of the light and sons of the day. We do not belong to the night or to the darkness.

1Pe 2:9 But you are a chosen people, a royal priesthood, a holy nation, a people belonging to God, that you may declare the praises of him who called you out of darkness into his wonderful light.

1Jn 1:5 This is the message we have heard from him and declare to you: God is light; in him there is no darkness at all. ⁶If we claim to have fellowship with him yet walk in the darkness, we lie and do not live by the truth. ⁷But if we walk in the light, as he is in the light, we have fellowship with one another, and the blood of Jesus, his Son, purifies us from all sin.

1Jn 2:8 Yet I am writing you a new command; its truth is seen in him and you, because the darkness is passing and the true light is already shining.

⁹Anyone who claims to be in the light but hates his brother is still in the darkness. ¹⁰Whoever loves his brother lives in the light, and there is nothing in him to make him stumble. ¹¹But whoever hates his brother is in the darkness and walks around in the darkness; he does not know where he is going, because the darkness has blinded him. *See Blindness, Spiritual.*

Symbolic:

Of divine inscrutability—

2Sa 22:10 He parted the heavens and came down; dark clouds were under his feet. ¹¹He mounted the cherubim and flew; he soared on the wings of the wind. ¹²He made darkness his canopy around him—the dark rain clouds of the sky.

Ps 18:11 He made darkness his covering, his canopy around him—the dark rain clouds of the sky.

Ps 97:2 Clouds and thick darkness surround him; righteousness and justice are the foundation of his throne.

On Mt. Sinai (Ex 19:16; 20:21; Dt 4:11; 5:22)—

Heb 12:18 You have not come to a mountain that can be touched and that is burning with fire; to darkness, gloom and storm;

In the Sanctuary (1Ki 8:12)—

2Ch 6:1 Then Solomon said, "The LORD has said that he would dwell in a dark cloud;

See Tabernacle.

DARKON [2010] (perhaps *rough,* or *stern*). A descendant of Solomon's servant, Jaala, who returned with Zerubbabel from Exile (Ezr 2:56; Ne 7:58).

DART [5025]. A weapon (Job 41:26). *See Armor; Arrows.*

DATE [882, 3427, *2789*].
NIV+ DATES
A fruit (2Ch 31:5).

DATHAN [2018] (*strong*). A conspirator against Moses (Nu 16:1-35; 26:9; Dt 11:6; Ps 106:17).

DAUGHTER [1426, 1435, 3528, 5922, *2588, 2589, 5451*].
NIV+ DAUGHTER'S, DAUGHTER-IN-LAW, DAUGHTERS, DAUGHTERS-IN-LAW, GRANDDAUGHTER, GRANDDAUGHTERS
Daughter can refer to both persons and things, often without regard to relationship or gender.
1. Daughter (Ge 11:29) or other female descendant (Ge 24:48).
2. Women in general (Ge 28:6; Nu 25:1).
3. Worshipers of the true God (Ps 45:10; Isa 62:11; Mt 21:5; Jn 12:15).
4. City (Isa 37:22).
5. Citizens (Zec 2:10).

DAUGHTER-IN-LAW [3987, *3811*].
NIV+ See DAUGHTER
Filial: Instance of, Ruth (Ru 1:11-18; 4:15).
Unfilial: Prophecy of (Mic 7:6; Mt 10:35).

DAVID [1858, *1253*] (*beloved one*).
NIV+ DAVID'S
1. King of Israel. Genealogy of (Ru 4:18-22; 1Sa 16:11; 17:12; 1Ch 2:3-15; Mt 1:1-6; Lk 3:31-38). A shepherd (1Sa 16:11). Kills a lion and a bear (1Sa 17:34-36). Anointed king, while a youth, by the prophet Samuel, and inspired (1Sa 16:1,13; Ps 89:19-37). Chosen of God (Ps 78:70).

Described to Saul (1Sa 16:18). Detailed as armor-bearer and musician at Saul's court (1Sa 16:21-23). Slays Goliath (1Sa 17). Love of Jonathan for (1Sa 18:1-4). Popularity and discretion of (1Sa 18). Saul's jealousy of (1Sa 18:8-30). Is defrauded of Merab and given Michal for his wife (1Sa 18:17-27). Jonathan intercedes for (1Sa 19:1-7). Probably writes Ps 11 at this period of his life.

Conducts a campaign against, and defeats, the Philistines (1Sa 19:8). Saul attempts to slay him; he escapes to Ramah and dwells at Naioth, where Saul pursues him (1Sa 19:9-24). About this time he writes Ps 59. He returns, and Jonathan makes a covenant with him (1Sa 20). He escapes by way of Nob, where he obtains some consecrated bread and Goliath's sword from Abimelech (1Sa 21:1-6; Mt 12:3-4), to Gath (1Sa 21:10-15). At this time he probably writes Pss 34, 35, 52, 56, and 120. He recruits an army of insurgents, goes to Moab, returning to Hereth (1Sa 22). Probably writes Pss 17, 58, 64, 109, and 142. He saves Keilah (1Sa 23:1-13). He makes a second covenant with Jonathan (1Sa 23:16-18). He goes to the wilderness of Ziph, and is betrayed to Saul (1Sa 23:13-26). He writes Ps 54 about the betrayal and probably Pss 22, 31, and 140. Saul is diverted from pursuit of (1Sa 23:27-28). At this time he probably writes Ps 12. Goes to En Gedi (1Sa 23:29). Writes Ps 57. Covenants with Saul (1Sa 26). Marries Nabal's widow, Abigail, and Ahinoam (1Sa 25). Dwells in the wilderness of Ziph, has the opportunity to kill Saul but takes his spear only, Saul is contrite (1Sa 26). Flees to Achish and dwells in Ziklag (1Sa 27). List of men who join him (1Ch 12:1-22). Conducts an expedition against Amalekites, misinforms Achish (1Sa 27:8-12). At this time probably writes Ps 141. Is refused permission to accompany the Philistines to battle against the Israelites (1Sa 28:1-2; 29). Rescues the people of Ziklag, who had been captured by the Amalekites (1Sa 30). Probably writes Ps 13. Death and burial of Saul and his sons (1Sa 31; 2Sa 21:1-14). Slays the murderer of Saul (2Sa 1:1-16). Lamentation over Saul (2Sa 1:17-27).

After dwelling one year and four months at Ziklag (1Sa 27:7), goes to Hebron, and is anointed king by Judah (2Sa 2:1-4,11; 5:5; 1Ki 2:11; 1Ch 3:4; 11:1-3). List of those who join him at Hebron (1Ch 12:23-40). Ish-Bosheth, the son of Saul, crowned (2Sa 2-4). David wages war against, and defeats, Ish-Bosheth (2Sa 2:13-32; 3:4). Demands the restoration of Michal, his wife (2Sa 3:14-16). Abner revolts from Ish-Bosheth, and joins David, but is slain by Joab (2Sa 3). David punishes Ish-Bosheth's murderers (2Sa 4).

Anointed king over all Israel, after reigning over Judah at Hebron seven years and six months, and reigns thirty-three years (2Sa 2:11; 5:5; 1Ch 3:4; 11:1-3; 12:23-40; 29:27). Makes a conquest of Jerusalem (2Sa 5:6; 1Ch 11:4-8; Isa 29:1). Builds a palace (2Sa 5:11; 2Ch 2:3). Friendship of, with Hiram, king of Tyre (2Sa 5:11; 1Ki 5:1). Prospered of God (2Sa 5:10,12; 1Ch 11:9). Fame of (1Ch 14:17). Philistines make war against, and are defeated by him (2Sa 5:17,25).

Assembles 30,000 men to escort the ark to Jerusalem with music and thanksgiving (2Sa 6:1-5). Uzzah is stricken when he attempts to steady the ark (2Sa 6:6-11). David is terrified and leaves the ark at the house of Obed-Edom (2Sa 6:9-11). After three months brings the ark to Jerusalem with dancing and great joy (2Sa 6:12-16; 1Ch 13). Organized the tabernacle service (1Ch 9:22; 15:16-24; 16:4-6,37-43). Offers sacrifice, distributes gifts, and blesses the people (2Sa 6:17-19). Michal rebukes him for his religious enthusiasm (2Sa 6:20-23). Desires to build a temple, is forbidden, but receives promise that his seed should reign forever (2Sa 7:12-16; 23:5; 1Ch 17:11-14; 2Ch 6:16; Ps 89:3-4; 132:11-12; Ac 15:16; Ro 15:12). See *Covenants, Major in the Old Testament*. Interpretation and fulfillment of this prophecy (Ac 13:22-23). At this time, probably writes Pss 15, 16, 24, 101, and 138. Conquers the Philistines, Moabites, and Syria (2Sa 8).

Treats Mephibosheth, the lame son of Jonathan, with great kindness (2Sa 9:6; 19:24-30). Sends commissioners with a message of sympathy to Hanun, son of the king of Ammon; the message is misinterpreted and commissioners treated with indignity; David retaliates by invading

his kingdom and defeating the combined armies of the Ammonites and Syrians (2Sa 10; 1Ch 19). Probably writes Pss 18, 20, and 21.

Commits adultery with Bathsheba (2Sa 11:2-5). Wickedly causes the death of Uriah (2Sa 11:6-25). Takes Bathsheba to be his wife (2Sa 11:26-27). Is rebuked by the prophet Nathan (2Sa 12:1-14). Repents of his crime and confesses his guilt (Pss 6; 32; 38; 39; 40; 51). Is disciplined on account of his crime (Ps 38; 41; 69). His infant son by Bathsheba dies (2Sa 12:15-23). Solomon is born (2Sa 12:24-25).

Ammonites defeated and tortured (2Sa 12:26-31). Amnon's crime, his murder by Absalom, and Absalom's flight (2Sa 13). Absalom's return (2Sa 14:1-24). Absalom's usurpation (2Sa 14-15). David's flight from Jerusalem (2Sa 15:13-37). He probably writes, at this time Pss 5, 7, 26, 61, 69, 70, 86, and 143. Shimei curses him (2Sa 16). Crosses the Jordan (2Sa 17:21-29). Absalom's defeat and death (2Sa 18). Laments the death of Absalom (2Sa 18:33; 19:1-4). Reprimanded by Joab (2Sa 19:5-7). David reprimands the priests for not showing loyalty amid the murmurings of the people against him (2Sa 19:9-15). Shimei sues for clemency (2Sa 19:16-23). Mephibosheth sues for the king's favor (2Sa 19:24-30). Barzillai rewarded (2Sa 19:31-40). Judah accused by the ten tribes of stealing him away (2Sa 19:41-43). Returns to Jerusalem (2Sa 20:1-3). At this time, probably composes Pss 27, 66, 122, and 144.

Sheba's conspiracy against David, and his death (2Sa 20). Makes Amasa general (2Sa 19:13). Amasa is slain (2Sa 20:4-10). Consigns seven sons of Saul to the Gibeonites to be slain to atone for Saul's persecution of the Gibeonites (2Sa 21:1-14). Buries the bones of Saul and his sons (2Sa 21:12-14).

Defeats the Philistines (2Sa 21:15-22; 1Ch 20:4-8). Takes the military strength of Israel without divine authority, and is reproved (2Sa 24; 1Ch 21; 27:24). Probably composes Pss 20, 131. Marries Abishag (1Ki 1:1-4). Probably composes Pss 19 and 111.

Reorganizes the tabernacle service (1Ch 22-26; 2Ch 7:6; 8:14; 23:18; 29:27-30; 35:15; Ezr 3:10; 8:20).

Adonijah usurps the scepter. Solomon is appointed to the throne (1Ki 1; 1Ch 23:1). Delivers his charge to Solomon (1Ki 2:1-11; 1Ch 22:6-19; 28; 29). Probably composes Pss 23 and 145.

Last words of (2Sa 23:1-7). Death probably (1Ki 2:10; 1Ch 29:28; Ac 2:29-30). Tomb of (Ac 2:29). Age of, at death (2Sa 5:4-5; 1Ch 29:28). Length of reign, forty years (1Ki 2:11; 1Ch 29:27-28).

Wives of (2Sa 3:2-5; 11:3,27; 1Ch 3:5). Children born at Hebron (2Sa 3:2-5; 1Ch 3:4), at Jerusalem (2Sa 5:14-16; 1Ch 3:5-8; 14:4-7). Descendants of (1Ch 3).

Civil and military officers of (2Sa 8:16-18). See *Cabinet*.

List of his heroes and of their exploits (2Sa 23; 1Ch 11; 12:23-40).

Devoutness of (1Sa 13:14; 2Sa 6:5,14-18; 7:18-29; 8:11; 24:25; 1Ki 3:14; 1Ch 17:16-27; 29:10; 2Ch 7:17; Zec 12:8; Ps 6; 7; 11; 13; 17; 22; 26; 27:7-14; 28; 31; 35; 37; 38; 39; 40:11-17; 42; 43; 51; 54; 55; 56; 57; 59; 60; 61; 62; 64:1-6; 66; 69; 70; 71; 86; 101; 108; 120:1-2; 140; 141; 142; 143; 144; Ac 13:22).

Justice in the administration of (2Sa 8:15; 1Ch 18:14). Discretion of (1Sa 18:14,30). Meekness of (1Sa 24:7; 26:11; 2Sa 16:11; 19:22-23). Merciful (2Sa 19:23).

David as a musician (1Sa 16:21-23; 1Ch 15:16; 23:5;

2Ch 7:6; 29:26; Ne 12:36; Am 6:5), poet (2Sa 22). *See Psalms.* David as a prophet (2Sa 23:2-7; 1Ch 28:19; Mt 22:41-46; Ac 2:25-38; 4:25).

Type of Christ (Ps 2; 16; 18:43; 69:7-9,20-21,26,29; 89:19-37). Jesus called son of (Mt 9:27; 12:23; 15:22; 20:30-31; 21:9; 22:42; Mk 10:47-48; Lk 18:37,39).

Prophecies concerning him and his kingdom (Nu 24:17, 19; 2Sa 7:11-16; 1Ch 17:9-14; 22; 2Ch 6:5-17; 13:5; 21:7; Ps 89:19-37; Isa 9:7; 16:5; 22:20-25; Jer 23:5; 33:15-26; Lk 1:32-33).

Chronicles of, written by Samuel, Nathan, and Gad (1Ch 29:29-30).

2. A prophetic name for Christ (Jer 30:9; Eze 34:23-24; 37:24-25; Hos 3:5).

DAVID, CITY OF

1. Portion of Jerusalem occupied by David in c. 1003 B.C.; 2500 feet above sea-level. Originally a Canaanite city (Eze 16:3), it dates back to the third millennium. Solomon enlarged the City of David for the temple and other buildings, and later kings enlarged the city still more (2Ch 32:4-5,30; 2Ki 20:20; Isa 22:9-11).

2. Bethlehem (Lk 2:11).

DAY [*2256, 3427, 3429, 4740, 8702, 8840, 10317, *892, 2069, 2465, 4187, 4879, 4958*].

NIV+ DAILY, DAY'S, DAYBREAK, DAYLIGHT, DAYS, DAYTIME, EVERYDAY, MIDDAY, SEVEN-DAY, THREE-DAY

A creative period (Ge 1:5,8,13,19,23,31; 2:2). Divided into twelve hours (Jn 11:9). Prophetic (Da 8:14,26; 12:11-12; Rev 9:15; 11:3; 12:6). Six working days ordained (Ex 20:9; Eze 46:1). Sixth day of the week called preparation day (Mk 15:42; Jn 19:14,31,42). First day of the week called the Lord's Day (Rev 1:10). With the Lord as a thousand years (2Pe 3:8).

Day's journey, eighteen or twenty miles (Ex 3:18; 1Ki 19:4; Jnh 3:4). Sabbath day's journey, about two thousand paces (Ac 1:12). The seventh of the week ordained as a day of rest. *See Sabbath.*

DAY OF ATONEMENT An annual Hebrew feast when the high priest offered sacrifices for the sins of the nation (Lev 23:27; 25:9). It was the only fast period required by Mosaic law (Lev 16:29; 23:31). The day marked the only entry of the high priest into the Most Holy Place (Lev 16). It was observed on the tenth day of the seventh month; a day of great solemnity and strictest conformity to the law.

DAY OF CHRIST The period connected with reward and blessing at the coming of Christ for believers (1Co 1:8; 5:5; 2Co 1:14; Php 1:6,10; 2:16). The correct translation is "The day of the Lord," signifying a time of judgment. *See below, Day of the Lord.*

DAY OF THE LORD The period commencing with the second advent of Christ and terminating with the making of a new heaven and a new earth (Isa 65:17-19; 66:22; 2Th 2:2; 2Pe 2:13; Rev 21:1). Preceded and introduced by apocalyptic judgments (Rev 4:1-19:6).

DAY'S JOURNEY Eighteen or twenty miles (Ex 3:18; 1Ki 19:4; Jnh 3:4). Sabbath day's journey, about two thousand paces (Ac 1:12).

DAYSMAN NIV "someone to arbitrate" (Job 9:33). *See Mediation.*

DAYSPRING NIV "dawn" (Job 38:12) and "rising sun" (Lk 1:78).

DAYSTAR *See Morning Star.*

DEACON [*1354, 1356*] (*serve*).
NIV+ DEACONS

An officer charged with the temporal affairs of the church. The seven men chosen to help the apostles are often considered deacons (Ac 6:1-6). Qualifications of (1Ti 3:8-13). The Greek word translated deacon signifies servant, and is so translated (Mt 23:11; Jn 12:26). Also translated minister (Mk 10:43; 1Co 3:5; 1Th 3:2).

DEACONESS [*1354, 1356*] (*serve*).
NIV+ DEACON, DEACONS

Phoebe is called a "servant of the church," which could be translated a "deaconess" (Ro 16:1, ftn).

1Ti 3:1-13 lists character qualities of deacons. V. 11 refers either to deacons' wives or to special qualities required of deaconesses (see ftn). *See Women, In Leadership.*

DEAD [*6, 1588, *1775, 2222, 2728, 4637, 4638, 5577, 5782, 5877, 5883, 7007, 7516, 8327, 8619, 10625, *633, 650, 1586, 2505, 2506, 2569, 3121, 3156, 3738, 5271, 5462*].

NIV+ DEADENED, DEADLY, DEATH, DEATH'S, DEATHLY, DEATHS, DIE, DIED, DIES, DYING

Raised to life, instances of:

Son of the widow of Zarephath (1Ki 17:17-23), Shunammite's son (2Ki 4:32-37), young man laid in Elisha's tomb (2Ki 13:21), widow's son (Lk 7:12-15), Jairus' daughter (Lk 8:49-55), Lazarus (Jn 11:43-44), Dorcas (Ac 9:37-40), Eutychus (Ac 20:9-12, w Heb 11:35).

Prepared for burial by washing (Ac 9:37), anointing (Mt 26:12), wrapping in linen (Mt 27:59). Burned. *See Cremation.* Burnings of incense made for (2Ch 16:14; 21:19; Jer 34:5).

See Burial; Cremation; Embalming.

Pictured as:

As rest—

Job 3:13 For now I would be lying down in peace; I would be asleep and at rest ¹⁴with kings and counselors of the earth, who built for themselves places now lying in ruins, ¹⁵with rulers who had gold, who filled their houses with silver. ¹⁶Or why was I not hidden in the ground like a stillborn child, like an infant who never saw the light of day? ¹⁷There the wicked cease from turmoil, and there the weary are at rest. ¹⁸Captives also enjoy their ease; they no longer hear the slave driver's shout. ¹⁹The small and the great are there, and the slave is freed from his master.

As sleep—

Job 14:11 As water disappears from the sea or a riverbed becomes parched and dry, ¹²so man lies down and does not rise; till the heavens are no more, men will not awake or be roused from their sleep. ¹³"If only you would hide me in the grave and conceal me till your anger has passed! If only you would set me a time and then remember me! ¹⁴If a man dies, will he live again? All the days of my hard service I will wait for my renewal to come. ¹⁵You will call and I will answer; you will long for the creature your hands have made.

Job 14:21 If his sons are honored, he does not know it; if they are brought low, he does not see it. (+Da 12:12)

As hopelessness—

Job 17:13 If the only home I hope for is the grave, if I spread out my bed in darkness, **14**if I say to corruption, 'You are my father,' and to the worm, 'My mother' or 'My sister,' **15**where then is my hope? Who can see any hope for me?

Ecc 9:5 For the living know that they will die, but the dead know nothing; they have no further reward, and even the memory of them is forgotten. **6**Their love, their hate and their jealousy have long since vanished; never again will they have a part in anything that happens under the sun. (+Eze 32:27,30)

As separation from God—

Ps 6:5 No one remembers you when he is dead. Who praises you from the grave?

Ps 30:9 "What gain is there in my destruction, in my going down into the pit? Will the dust praise you? Will it proclaim your faithfulness?

Ps 88:10 Do you show your wonders to the dead? Do those who are dead rise up and praise you? *Selah* **11**Is your love declared in the grave, your faithfulness in Destruction? **12**Are your wonders known in the place of darkness, or your righteous deeds in the land of oblivion?

Ps 115:17 It is not the dead who praise the Lord, those who go down to silence;

Life After: (Job 14:12-15)

Ps 49:15 But God will redeem my life from the grave; he will surely take me to himself. *Selah*

Da 12:2 Multitudes who sleep in the dust of the earth will awake: some to everlasting life, others to shame and everlasting contempt.

Lk 20:35 But those who are considered worthy of taking part in that age and in the resurrection from the dead will neither marry nor be given in marriage, **36**and they can no longer die; for they are like the angels. They are God's children, since they are children of the resurrection.

Jn 11:25 Jesus said to her, "I am the resurrection and the life. He who believes in me will live, even though he dies;

Understanding after—

Eze 32:31 "Pharaoh—he and all his army—will see them and he will be consoled for all his hordes that were killed by the sword, declares the Sovereign Lord.

Lk 16:19 "There was a rich man who was dressed in purple and fine linen and lived in luxury every day. **20**At his gate was laid a beggar named Lazarus, covered with sores **21**and longing to eat what fell from the rich man's table. Even the dogs came and licked his sores.

22"The time came when the beggar died and the angels carried him to Abraham's side. The rich man also died and was buried. **23**In hell, where he was in torment, he looked up and saw Abraham far away, with Lazarus by his side. **24**So he called to him, 'Father Abraham, have pity on me and send Lazarus to dip the tip of his finger in water and cool my tongue, because I am in agony in this fire.'

25"But Abraham replied, 'Son, remember that in your lifetime you received your good things, while Lazarus received bad things, but now he is comforted here and you are in agony. **26**And besides all this, between us and you a great chasm has been fixed, so that those who want to go from here to you cannot, nor can anyone cross over from there to us.'

27"He answered, 'Then I beg you, father, send Lazarus to my father's house, **28**for I have five brothers. Let him warn them, so that they will not also come to this place of torment.'

29"Abraham replied, 'They have Moses and the Prophets; let them listen to them.'

30" 'No, father Abraham,' he said, 'but if someone from the dead goes to them, they will repent.'

31"He said to him, 'If they do not listen to Moses and the Prophets, they will not be convinced even if someone rises from the dead.' "

Abode of:

The pit (Job 17:13-15), Abraham's side (Lk 16:22), hell (Lk 16:23). *See Hades; Hell; Grave; Sheol.*

Paradise—

Lk 23:43 Jesus answered him, "I tell you the truth, today you will be with me in paradise."

See Burial; Death, Physical; Mourning; Resurrection; Righteous, Promises to; Wicked, Punishment of.

DEAD SEA
Lies southeast of Jerusalem. Called the Salt Sea (Ge 14:3; Nu 34:12), Sea of the Plain (Dt 3:17; 4:49; Jos 3:16), eastern sea (Joel 2:20; Zec 14:8).

Prophecy concerning (Eze 47:7-10,18).

DEAD SEA SCROLLS
Discovered in 1947 by a Bedouin in caves a mile or so W of the NW corner of the Dead Sea, at Qumran. So far mss have been found in 11 caves, and they are mostly dated as coming from the last two centuries B.C. and the first century A.D. At least 382 mss are represented by the fragments of Cave Four alone, c. 100 of which are biblical mss. These include fragments of every book of the Hebrew Bible except Esther. Some of the books are represented in many copies. Not all the mss are in fragments; some are complete or nearly complete. In addition to biblical books, fragments of apocryphal and apocalyptic books, commentaries, psalms, and sectarian literature have been found. Near the caves are the remains of a monastery of huge size, possibly the headquarters of a monastic sect of Jews called the Essenes. The discoveries at Qumran are important for biblical studies in general. They are of great importance for a study of the OT text, both Hebrew and the LXX. They are also of importance in relation to the NT, as they furnish the background to the preaching of John the Baptist and Jesus. There is no evidence that either John the Baptist or Jesus was a member of the group. *See Testaments, Time Between.*

DEAFNESS
[263+4202, 3087, 3094, 4946+9048, 3273].

NIV+ DEAF

Law concerning (Lev 19:14). Inflicted by God (Ex 4:11). Miraculous cure of (Mt 11:5; Mk 7:32; 9:25).

Figurative:

Of moral insensitivity (Isa 6:10; 29:18; 35:5; Eze 12:2; Mt 13:15; Jn 12:40; Ac 28:26-27).

See Blindness, Spiritual; Conscience, Dead; Impenitence; Obduracy.

DEATH, PHYSICAL [*See DEAD].

NIV+ See DEAD

Universal to mankind—

Ecc 3:2 a time to be born and a time to die, a time to plant and a time to uproot,

Ecc 3:19 Man's fate is like that of the animals; the same fate awaits them both: As one dies, so dies the other. All have the same breath; man has no advantage over the animal. Everything is meaningless. **20**All go to the same place; all come from dust, and to dust all return. **21**Who knows if the spirit of man rises upward and if the spirit of the animal goes down into the earth?"

Ro 5:12 Therefore, just as sin entered the world through one man, and death through sin, and in this way death came to all men, because all sinned—

Ro 5:14 Nevertheless, death reigned from the time of Adam to the time of Moses, even over those who did not sin by breaking a command, as did Adam, who was a pattern of the one to come.

1Pe 1:24 For, "All men are like grass, and all their glory is like the flowers of the field; the grass withers and the flowers fall,

Time of, unknown—

Ge 27:2 Isaac said, "I am now an old man and don't know the day of my death.

Ps 39:4 "Show me, O LORD, my life's end and the number of my days; let me know how fleeting is my life. (+Ps 39:13)

Nearness to—

Jos 23:14 "Now I am about to go the way of all the earth. You know with all your heart and soul that not one of all the good promises the LORD your God gave you has failed. Every promise has been fulfilled; not one has failed.

1Sa 20:3 But David took an oath and said, "Your father knows very well that I have found favor in your eyes, and he has said to himself, 'Jonathan must not know this or he will be grieved.' Yet as surely as the LORD lives and as you live, there is only a step between me and death."

Separates spirit and body—

Ecc 12:5 when men are afraid of heights and of dangers in the streets; when the almond tree blossoms and the grasshopper drags himself along and desire no longer is stirred. Then man goes to his eternal home and mourners go about the streets.

Ecc 12:7 and the dust returns to the ground it came from, and the spirit returns to God who gave it.

Does not end conscious existence—

Lk 20:34 Jesus replied, "The people of this age marry and are given in marriage. [35]But those who are considered worthy of taking part in that age and in the resurrection from the dead will neither marry nor be given in marriage, [36]and they can no longer die; for they are like the angels. They are God's children, since they are children of the resurrection. [37]But in the account of the bush, even Moses showed that the dead rise, for he calls the Lord 'the God of Abraham, and the God of Isaac, and the God of Jacob.' [38]He is not the God of the dead, but of the living, for to him all are alive."

Lk 23:39 One of the criminals who hung there hurled insults at him: "Aren't you the Christ? Save yourself and us!"

[40]But the other criminal rebuked him. "Don't you fear God," he said, "since you are under the same sentence? [41]We are punished justly, for we are getting what our deeds deserve. But this man has done nothing wrong."

[42]Then he said, "Jesus, remember me when you come into your kingdom."

[43]Jesus answered him, "I tell you the truth, today you will be with me in paradise."

Rev 20:12 And I saw the dead, great and small, standing before the throne, and books were opened. Another book was opened, which is the book of life. The dead were judged according to what they had done as recorded in the books. [13]The sea gave up the dead that were in it, and death and Hades gave up the dead that were in them, and each person was judged according to what he had done.

Exemplified in the appearance of Moses and Elijah at the transfiguration of Jesus (Mt 17:2-3; Mk 9:4-5; Lk 9:30-33).

Not to be feared by the righteous—

Mt 10:28 Do not be afraid of those who kill the body but cannot kill the soul. Rather, be afraid of the One who can destroy both soul and body in hell.

Brings rest to the righteous—

Job 3:13 For now I would be lying down in peace; I would be asleep and at rest

Job 3:17 There the wicked cease from turmoil, and there the weary are at rest. [18]Captives also enjoy their ease; they no longer hear the slave driver's shout. [19]The small and the great are there, and the slave is freed from his master.

Dispossesses of earthly goods (Job 1:21; Ps 49:17; Lk 12:16-20)—

1Ti 6:7 For we brought nothing into the world, and we can take nothing out of it.

A judgment—

Ge 2:17 but you must not eat from the tree of the knowledge of good and evil, for when you eat of it you will surely die."

Ge 3:19 By the sweat of your brow you will eat your food until you return to the ground, since from it you were taken; for dust you are and to dust you will return." (+Ge 6:7,11-13; 19:12-13,24-25; Jos 5:4-6; 1Ch 10:13-14)

God's power over—

Dt 32:39 "See now that I myself am He! There is no god besides me. I put to death and I bring to life, I have wounded and I will heal, and no one can deliver out of my hand.

1Sa 2:6 "The LORD brings death and makes alive; he brings down to the grave and raises up.

Ps 68:20 Our God is a God who saves; from the Sovereign LORD comes escape from death.

2Ti 1:10 but it has now been revealed through the appearing of our Savior, Christ Jesus, who has destroyed death and has brought life and immortality to light through the gospel.

Christ's power over—

Heb 2:14 Since the children have flesh and blood, he too shared in their humanity so that by his death he might destroy him who holds the power of death—that is, the devil— [15]and free those who all their lives were held in slavery by their fear of death.

Rev 1:18 I am the Living One; I was dead, and behold I am alive for ever and ever! And I hold the keys of death and Hades.

To be destroyed—

Isa 25:8 he will swallow up death forever. The Sovereign LORD will wipe away the tears from all faces; he will remove the disgrace of his people from all the earth. The LORD has spoken.

Hos 13:14 "I will ransom them from the power of the grave; I will redeem them from death. Where, O death, are your plagues? Where, O grave, is your destruction? "I will have no compassion,

1Co 15:21 For since death came through a man, the resurrection of the dead comes also through a man. [22]For as in Adam all die, so in Christ all will be made alive.

1Co 15:26 The last enemy to be destroyed is death.

1Co 15:55 "Where, O death, is your victory? Where, O death, is your sting?"

[56]The sting of death is sin, and the power of sin is the law. [57]But thanks be to God! He gives us the victory through our Lord Jesus Christ.

Rev 20:14 Then death and Hades were thrown into the lake of fire. The lake of fire is the second death.

Rev 21:4 He will wipe every tear from their eyes. There will be no more death or mourning or crying or pain, for the old order of things has passed away."

Preparation for—

2Ki 20:1 In those days Hezekiah became ill and was at the point of death. The prophet Isaiah son of Amoz went to him and said, "This is what the LORD says: Put your house in order, because you are going to die; you will not recover."

Lk 12:35 "Be dressed ready for service and keep your lamps burning, ³⁶like men waiting for their master to return from a wedding banquet, so that when he comes and knocks they can immediately open the door for him. ³⁷It will be good for those servants whose master finds them watching when he comes. I tell you the truth, he will dress himself to serve, will have them recline at the table and will come and wait on them.

By Moses (Nu 27:12-23), by David (1Ki 2:1-10), by Ahithophel (2Sa 17:23). Apostrophe to (Hos 13:14; 1Co 15:55).

Called Sleep:

Dt 31:16 And the LORD said to Moses: "You are going to rest with your fathers, and these people will soon prostitute themselves to the foreign gods of the land they are entering. They will forsake me and break the covenant I made with them. (+1Ki 14:31; 15:8,24; 16:6,28)

Job 7:21 Why do you not pardon my offenses and forgive my sins? For I will soon lie down in the dust; you will search for me, but I will be no more."

Job 14:12 so man lies down and does not rise; till the heavens are no more, men will not awake or be roused from their sleep. (+Ps 76:5-6)

Jer 51:39 But while they are aroused, I will set out a feast for them and make them drunk, so that they shout with laughter—then sleep forever and not awake," declares the LORD.

Da 12:2 Multitudes who sleep in the dust of the earth will awake: some to everlasting life, others to shame and everlasting contempt.

Jn 11:11 After he had said this, he went on to tell them, "Our friend Lazarus has fallen asleep; but I am going there to wake him up."

Ac 7:60 Then he fell on his knees and cried out, "Lord, do not hold this sin against them." When he had said this, he fell asleep.

Ac 13:36 "For when David had served God's purpose in his own generation, he fell asleep; he was buried with his fathers and his body decayed.

1Co 15:6 After that, he appeared to more than five hundred of the brothers at the same time, most of whom are still living, though some have fallen asleep.

1Co 15:18 Then those also who have fallen asleep in Christ are lost.

1Co 15:51 Listen, I tell you a mystery: We will not all sleep, but we will all be changed— (+1Th 4:13)

1Th 4:14 We believe that Jesus died and rose again and so we believe that God will bring with Jesus those who have fallen asleep in him. ¹⁵According to the Lord's own word, we tell you that we who are still alive, who are left till the coming of the Lord, will certainly not precede those who have fallen asleep.

Described as:

"Breathing one's last" or "giving up one's spirit" (Ge 25:8; 35:29; La 1:19; Ac 5:10).

King of terrors—

Job 18:14 He is torn from the security of his tent and marched off to the king of terrors.

A change (Job 14:14). Going to your fathers (Ge 15:15; 25:8; 35:29). Putting off this tabernacle (2Pe 1:14). Requiring the soul (Lk 12:20). Going the way from which there is no return (Job 16:22). Being gathered to our people (Ge 49:33). In silence (Ps 94:17; 115:17). Returning to dust (Ge 3:19). Being cut down (Job 14:2). Fleeing as a shadow (Job 14:2). Departing (Php 1:23).

Desired: (Jer 8:3; Rev 9:6). By Moses (Nu 11:15). By Elijah (1Ki 19:4).

By Job (Job 3; 6:8-11)—

Job 7:1 "Does not man have hard service on earth? Are not his days like those of a hired man? ²Like a slave longing for the evening shadows, or a hired man waiting eagerly for his wages, ³so I have been allotted months of futility, and nights of misery have been assigned to me. (+Job 7:15-16; 10:1)

By Jonah (Jnh 4:8).

By Simeon—

Lk 2:29 "Sovereign Lord, as you have promised, you now dismiss your servant in peace.

By Paul (2Co 5:2,8)—

Php 1:20 I eagerly expect and hope that I will in no way be ashamed, but will have sufficient courage so that now as always Christ will be exalted in my body, whether by life or by death. ²¹For to me, to live is Christ and to die is gain. (+Php 1:22)

Php 1:23 I am torn between the two: I desire to depart and be with Christ, which is better by far;

Exemption from:

Enoch (Ge 5:24; Heb 11:5). Elijah (2Ki 2). Promised to saints, when Christ returns for believers (1Co 15:51; 1Th 4:15,17). No death in heaven (Lk 20:36; Rev 21:4).

Inevitable:

2Sa 14:14 Like water spilled on the ground, which cannot be recovered, so we must die. But God does not take away life; instead, he devises ways so that a banished person may not remain estranged from him. (+Job 7:1)

Job 7:8 The eye that now sees me will see me no longer; you will look for me, but I will be no more. ⁹As a cloud vanishes and is gone, so he who goes down to the grave does not return. ¹⁰He will never come to his house again; his place will know him no more. (+Job 7:21)

Job 10:21 before I go to the place of no return, to the land of gloom and deep shadow, ²²to the land of deepest night, of deep shadow and disorder, where even the light is like darkness."

Job 14:2 He springs up like a flower and withers away; like a fleeting shadow, he does not endure.

Job 14:5 Man's days are determined; you have decreed the number of his months and have set limits he cannot exceed.

Job 14:7 "At least there is hope for a tree: If it is cut down, it will sprout again, and its new shoots will not fail. ⁸Its roots may grow old in the ground and its stump die in the soil, ⁹yet at the scent of water it will bud and put forth shoots like a plant. ¹⁰But man dies and is laid low; he breathes his last and is no more. ¹¹As water disappears from the sea or a riverbed becomes parched and dry, ¹²so man lies down and does not rise; till the heavens are no more, men will not awake or be roused from their sleep.

Job 14:14 If a man dies, will he live again? All the days of my hard service I will wait for my renewal to come.

Job 14:19 as water wears away stones and torrents wash away the soil, so you destroy man's hope. ²⁰You overpower him once for all, and he is gone; you change his countenance and send him away. ²¹If his sons are honored, he does not know it; if they are brought low, he does not see it.

Job 16:22 "Only a few years will pass before I go on the journey of no return.

Job 21:23 One man dies in full vigor, completely secure and at ease,

Job 21:25 Another man dies in bitterness of soul, never having enjoyed anything good. ²⁶Side by side they lie in the dust, and worms cover them both.

Job 21:32 He is carried to the grave, and watch is kept over his tomb. ³³The soil in the valley is sweet to him; all men follow after him, and a countless throng goes before him.

Job 30:23 I know you will bring me down to death, to the place appointed for all the living.

Job 34:15 all mankind would perish together and man would return to the dust. (+Job 34:19)

Ps 49:7 No man can redeem the life of another or give to God a ransom for him— (+Ps 49:8)

Ps 49:9 that he should live on forever and not see decay. ¹⁰For all can see that wise men die; the foolish and the senseless alike perish and leave their wealth to others.

Ps 82:7 But you will die like mere men; you will fall like every other ruler."

Ps 89:48 What man can live and not see death, or save himself from the power of the grave? *Selah*

Ps 144:4 Man is like a breath; his days are like a fleeting shadow.

Ecc 2:14 The wise man has eyes in his head, while the fool walks in the darkness; but I came to realize that the same fate overtakes them both.

¹⁵Then I thought in my heart,

"The fate of the fool will overtake me also. What then do I gain by being wise?" I said in my heart, "This too is meaningless." ¹⁶For the wise man, like the fool, will not be long remembered; in days to come both will be forgotten. Like the fool, the wise man too must die!

¹⁷So I hated life, because the work that is done under the sun was grievous to me. All of it is meaningless, a chasing after the wind. ¹⁸I hated all the things I had toiled for under the sun, because I must leave them to the one who comes after me.

Ecc 5:15 Naked a man comes from his mother's womb, and as he comes, so he departs. He takes nothing from his labor that he can carry in his hand.

Ecc 8:8 No man has power over the wind to contain it; so no one has power over the day of his death. As no one is discharged in time of war, so wickedness will not release those who practice it.

Ecc 9:5 For the living know that they will die, but the dead know nothing; they have no further reward, and even the memory of them is forgotten.

Ecc 9:10 Whatever your hand finds to do, do it with all your might, for in the grave, where you are going, there is neither working nor planning nor knowledge nor wisdom.

Isa 51:12 "I, even I, am he who comforts you. Who are you that you fear mortal men, the sons of men, who are but grass,

Jer 9:21 Death has climbed in through our windows and has entered our fortresses; it has cut off the children from the streets and the young men from the public squares.

Zec 1:5 Where are your forefathers now? And the prophets, do they live forever?

Jn 9:4 As long as it is day, we must do the work of him who sent me. Night is coming, when no one can work.

Heb 9:27 Just as man is destined to die once, and after that to face judgment,

Heb 13:14 For here we do not have an enduring city, but we are looking for the city that is to come.

Jas 1:10 But the one who is rich should take pride in his low position, because he will pass away like a wild flower. ¹¹For the sun rises with scorching heat and withers the plant; its blossom falls and its beauty is destroyed. In the same way, the rich man will fade away even while he goes about his business.

Of the Righteous:

A transition—

Lk 16:22 "The time came when the beggar died and the angels carried him to Abraham's side. The rich man also died and was buried.

Lk 23:43 Jesus answered him, "I tell you the truth, today you will be with me in paradise."

Balaam extols—

Nu 23:10 Who can count the dust of Jacob or number the fourth part of Israel? Let me die the death of the righteous, and may my end be like theirs!"

Peaceful—

Ps 37:37 Consider the blameless, observe the upright; there is a future for the man of peace.

Precious in the sight of the Lord—

Ps 116:15 Precious in the sight of the LORD is the death of his saints.

A merciful providence in—

Isa 57:1 The righteous perish, and no one ponders it in his heart; devout men are taken away, and no one understands that the righteous are taken away to be spared from evil. ²Those who walk uprightly enter into peace; they find rest as they lie in death.

Anticipated with confidence—

Pr 14:32 When calamity comes, the wicked are brought down, but even in death the righteous have a refuge. (+Lk 2:29)

Ac 7:59 While they were stoning him, Stephen prayed, "Lord Jesus, receive my spirit."

Ro 14:7 For none of us lives to himself alone and none of us dies to himself alone. ⁸If we live, we live to the Lord; and if we die, we die to the Lord. So, whether we live or die, we belong to the Lord.

1Co 3:21 So then, no more boasting about men! All things are yours, ²²whether Paul or Apollos or Cephas or the world or life or death or the present or the future—all are yours, ²³and you are of Christ, and Christ is of God.

2Co 5:1 Now we know that if the earthly tent we live in is destroyed, we have a building from God, an eternal house in heaven, not built by human hands.

2Co 5:4 For while we are in this tent, we groan and are burdened, because we do not wish to be unclothed but to be clothed with our heavenly dwelling, so that what is mortal may be swallowed up by life.

2Co 5:8 We are confident, I say, and would prefer to be away from the body and at home with the Lord.

1Th 5:9 For God did not appoint us to suffer wrath but to receive salvation through our Lord Jesus Christ. ¹⁰He died for us so that, whether we are awake or asleep, we may live together with him.

2Ti 4:6 For I am already being poured out like a drink offering, and the time has come for my departure. ⁷I have fought the good fight, I have finished the race, I have kept the faith. ⁸Now there is in store for me the crown of righteousness, which the Lord, the righteous Judge, will award to me on that day—and not only to me, but also to all who have longed for his appearing.

Heb 11:13 All these people were still living by faith when they died. They did not receive the things promised; they only saw them and welcomed them from a distance. And they admitted that they were aliens and strangers on earth.

Hope in—

Da 12:13 "As for you, go your way till the end. You will rest, and then at the end of the days you will rise to receive your allotted inheritance."

1Co 15:51 Listen, I tell you a mystery: We will not all sleep, but we will all be changed— ⁵²in a flash, in the twinkling of an eye, at the last trumpet. For the trumpet will sound, the dead will be raised imperishable, and we will be changed. ⁵³For the perishable must clothe itself with the imperishable, and the mortal with immortality. ⁵⁴When the perishable has been clothed with the imperishable, and the mortal with immortality, then the saying that is written will come true: "Death has been swallowed up in victory." (+1Co 15:55-57)

2Co 1:9 Indeed, in our hearts we felt the sentence of death. But this happened that we might not rely on ourselves but on God, who raises the dead. ¹⁰He has delivered us from such a deadly peril, and he will deliver us. On him we have set our hope that he will continue to deliver us,

1Th 4:13 Brothers, we do not want you to be ignorant about those who fall asleep, or to grieve like the rest of men, who have no hope. ¹⁴We believe that Jesus died and rose again and so we believe that God will bring with Jesus those who have fallen asleep in him.

2Pe 1:11 and you will receive a rich welcome into the eternal kingdom of our Lord and Savior Jesus Christ.

2Pe 1:14 because I know that I will soon put it aside, as our Lord Jesus Christ has made clear to me.

Rev 14:13 Then I heard a voice from heaven say, "Write: Blessed are the dead who die in the Lord from now on." "Yes," says the Spirit, "they will rest from their labor, for their deeds will follow them."

Of the Wicked: (Job 18:14)

Job 18:18 He is driven from light into darkness and is banished from the world.

Job 20:4 "Surely you know how it has been from of old, ever since man was placed on the earth, ⁵that the mirth of the wicked is brief, the joy of the godless lasts but a moment.

Job 20:8 Like a dream he flies away, no more to be found, banished like a vision of the night.

Job 20:11 The youthful vigor that fills his bones will lie with him in the dust.

Job 21:13 They spend their years in prosperity and go down to the grave in peace.

Job 21:17 "Yet how often is the lamp of the wicked snuffed out? How often does calamity come upon them, the fate God allots in his anger? ¹⁸How often are they like straw before the wind, like chaff swept away by a gale?

Job 21:23 One man dies in full vigor, completely secure and at ease, ²⁴his body well nourished, his bones rich with marrow. ²⁵Another man dies in bitterness of soul, never

having enjoyed anything good. ²⁶Side by side they lie in the dust, and worms cover them both.

Job 24:20 The womb forgets them, the worm feasts on them; evil men are no longer remembered but are broken like a tree.

Job 24:24 For a little while they are exalted, and then they are gone; they are brought low and gathered up like all others; they are cut off like heads of grain.

Job 27:8 For what hope has the godless when he is cut off, when God takes away his life?

Job 27:19 He lies down wealthy, but will do so no more; when he opens his eyes, all is gone. ²⁰Terrors overtake him like a flood; a tempest snatches him away in the night. ²¹The east wind carries him off, and he is gone; it sweeps him out of his place. ²²It hurls itself against him without mercy as he flees headlong from its power. ²³It claps its hands in derision and hisses him out of his place.

Ps 37:1 Do not fret because of evil men or be envious of those who do wrong; ²for like the grass they will soon wither, like green plants they will soon die away.

Ps 37:9 For evil men will be cut off, but those who hope in the Lᴏʀᴅ will inherit the land. ¹⁰A little while, and the wicked will be no more; though you look for them, they will not be found.

Ps 37:35 I have seen a wicked and ruthless man flourishing like a green tree in its native soil, ³⁶but he soon passed away and was no more; though I looked for him, he could not be found.

Ps 49:7 No man can redeem the life of another or give to God a ransom for him—

Ps 49:9 that he should live on forever and not see decay. ¹⁰For all can see that wise men die; the foolish and the senseless alike perish and leave their wealth to others.

Ps 49:14 Like sheep they are destined for the grave, and death will feed on them. The upright will rule over them in the morning; their forms will decay in the grave, far from their princely mansions.

Ps 49:17 for he will take nothing with him when he dies, his splendor will not descend with him.

Ps 49:19 he will join the generation of his fathers, who will never see the light [of life]. ²⁰A man who has riches without understanding is like the beasts that perish.

Pr 5:22 The evil deeds of a wicked man ensnare him; the cords of his sin hold him fast. ²³He will die for lack of discipline, led astray by his own great folly.

Pr 11:7 When a wicked man dies, his hope perishes; all he expected from his power comes to nothing.

Pr 11:10 When the righteous prosper, the city rejoices; when the wicked perish, there are shouts of joy.

Pr 21:16 A man who strays from the path of understanding comes to rest in the company of the dead.

Ecc 8:10 Then too, I saw the wicked buried—those who used to come and go from the holy place and receive praise in the city where they did this. This too is meaningless.

Isa 14:11 All your pomp has been brought down to the grave, along with the noise of your harps; maggots are spread out beneath you and worms cover you.

Isa 14:15 But you are brought down to the grave, to the depths of the pit.

Sudden (Nu 16:32)—

Pr 10:25 When the storm has swept by, the wicked are gone, but the righteous stand firm forever.

Pr 10:27 The fear of the Lᴏʀᴅ adds length to life, but the years of the wicked are cut short.

Isa 17:14 In the evening, sudden terror! Before the

morning, they are gone! This is the portion of those who loot us, the lot of those who plunder us.

Ac 5:3 Then Peter said, "Ananias, how is it that Satan has so filled your heart that you have lied to the Holy Spirit and have kept for yourself some of the money you received for the land? ⁴Didn't it belong to you before it was sold? And after it was sold, wasn't the money at your disposal? What made you think of doing such a thing? You have not lied to men but to God." ⁵When Ananias heard this, he fell down and died. And great fear seized all who heard what had happened. ⁶Then the young men came forward, wrapped up his body, and carried him out and buried him.

⁷About three hours later his wife came in, not knowing what had happened. ⁸Peter asked her, "Tell me, is this the price you and Ananias got for the land?"

"Yes," she said, "that is the price."

⁹Peter said to her, "How could you agree to test the Spirit of the Lord? Look! The feet of the men who buried your husband are at the door, and they will carry you out also."

¹⁰At that moment she fell down at his feet and died. Then the young men came in and, finding her dead, carried her out and buried her beside her husband.

A judgment—

Nu 16:29 If these men die a natural death and experience only what usually happens to men, then the LORD has not sent me. (+Nu 16:30)

1Sa 25:38 About ten days later, the LORD struck Nabal and he died.

Job 36:12 But if they do not listen, they will perish by the sword and die without knowledge.

Job 36:14 They die in their youth, among male prostitutes of the shrines.

Job 36:18 Be careful that no one entices you by riches; do not let a large bribe turn you aside.

Job 36:20 Do not long for the night, to drag people away from their homes.

Ps 55:23 But you, O God, will bring down the wicked into the pit of corruption; bloodthirsty and deceitful men will not live out half their days. But as for me, I trust in you.

Ps 58:9 Before your pots can feel [the heat of] the thorns— whether they be green or dry—the wicked will be swept away.

Ps 78:50 He prepared a path for his anger; he did not spare them from death but gave them over to the plague.

Ps 92:7 that though the wicked spring up like grass and all evildoers flourish, they will be forever destroyed.

Pr 2:22 but the wicked will be cut off from the land, and the unfaithful will be torn from it. (+Pr 14:32)

Isa 26:14 They are now dead, they live no more; those departed spirits do not rise. You punished them and brought them to ruin; you wiped out all memory of them.

Jer 16:3 For this is what the LORD says about the sons and daughters born in this land and about the women who are their mothers and the men who are their fathers: ⁴"They will die of deadly diseases. They will not be mourned or buried but will be like refuse lying on the ground. They will perish by sword and famine, and their dead bodies will become food for the birds of the air and the beasts of the earth."

Eze 28:8 They will bring you down to the pit, and you will die a violent death in the heart of the seas.

Eze 28:10 You will die the death of the uncircumcised at the hands of foreigners. I have spoken, declares the Sovereign LORD.' "

Am 9:10 All the sinners among my people will die by the sword, all those who say, 'Disaster will not overtake or meet us.'

Lk 12:20 "But God said to him, 'You fool! This very night your life will be demanded from you. Then who will get what you have prepared for yourself?'

Scenes of:

Jacob blessing his sons (Ge 49:1-33; Heb 11:21).

Moses—

Dt 34:1 Then Moses climbed Mt. Nebo from the plains of Moab to the top of Pisgah, across from Jericho. There the LORD showed him the whole land—from Gilead to Dan, ²all of Naphtali, the territory of Ephraim and Manasseh, all the land of Judah as far as the western sea, ³the Negev and the whole region from the Valley of Jericho, the City of Palms, as far as Zoar. ⁴Then the LORD said to him, "This is the land I promised on oath to Abraham, Isaac and Jacob when I said, 'I will give it to your descendants.' I have let you see it with your eyes, but you will not cross over into it."

⁵And Moses the servant of the LORD died there in Moab, as the LORD had said. ⁶He buried him in Moab, in the valley opposite Beth Peor, but to this day no one knows where his grave is. (+Dt 34:7)

Samson (Jdg 16:25-30). Eli (1Sa 4:12-18). The wife of Phinehas (1Sa 4:19-21).

Zechariah—

2Ch 24:22 King Joash did not remember the kindness Zechariah's father Jehoiada had shown him but killed his son, who said as he lay dying, "May the LORD see this and call you to account."

Jesus—

Mt 27:34 There they offered Jesus wine to drink, mixed with gall; but after tasting it, he refused to drink it. ³⁵When they had crucified him, they divided up his clothes by casting lots. ³⁶And sitting down, they kept watch over him there. ³⁷Above his head they placed the written charge against him: THIS IS JESUS, THE KING OF THE JEWS. ³⁸Two robbers were crucified with him, one on his right and one on his left. ³⁹Those who passed by hurled insults at him, shaking their heads ⁴⁰and saying, "You who are going to destroy the temple and build it in three days, save yourself! Come down from the cross, if you are the Son of God!"

⁴¹In the same way the chief priests, the teachers of the law and the elders mocked him. ⁴²"He saved others," they said, "but he can't save himself! He's the King of Israel! Let him come down now from the cross, and we will believe in him. ⁴³He trusts in God. Let God rescue him now if he wants him, for he said, 'I am the Son of God.'" ⁴⁴In the same way the robbers who were crucified with him also heaped insults on him.

⁴⁵From the sixth hour until the ninth hour darkness came over all the land. ⁴⁶About the ninth hour Jesus cried out in a loud voice, *"Eloi, Eloi, lama sabachthani?"*—which means, "My God, my God, why have you forsaken me?"

⁴⁷When some of those standing there heard this, they said, "He's calling Elijah."

⁴⁸Immediately one of them ran and got a sponge. He filled it with wine vinegar, put it on a stick, and offered it to Jesus to drink. ⁴⁹The rest said, "Now leave him alone. Let's see if Elijah comes to save him."

⁵⁰And when Jesus had cried out again in a loud voice, he gave up his spirit.

⁵¹At that moment the curtain of the temple was torn in

two from top to bottom. The earth shook and the rocks split. ⁵²The tombs broke open and the bodies of many holy people who had died were raised to life. ⁵³They came out of the tombs, and after Jesus' resurrection they went into the holy city and appeared to many people. (+Mk 15:23-38; Lk 23:27-49; Jn 19:16-30)

Stephen—

Ac 7:59 While they were stoning him, Stephen prayed, "Lord Jesus, receive my spirit." ⁶⁰Then he fell on his knees and cried out, "Lord, do not hold this sin against them." When he had said this, he fell asleep.

Death Penalty:

Shall not be remitted (Nu 35:31). In the Mosaic law the death penalty was inflicted for murder (Ge 9:5-6; Nu 35:16-21,30-33; Dt 17:6), adultery (Lev 20:10; Dt 22:24), incest (Lev 20:11-12,14), bestiality (Ex 22:19; Lev 20:15-16), sodomy (Lev 18:22; 20:13), rape of a betrothed virgin (Dt 22:25), perjury (Zec 5:4), kidnapping (Ex 21:16; Dt 24:7), upon a priest's daughter, who committed immorality (Lev 21:9), witchcraft (Ex 22:18), offering human sacrifice (Lev 20:2-5), striking or cursing father or mother (Ex 21:15,17; Lev 20:9), disobedience to parents (Dt 21:18-21), theft (Zec 5:3-4), blasphemy (Lev 24:23), Sabbath desecration (Ex 35:2; Nu 15:32-36), prophesying falsely or propagating false doctrines (Dt 13:10), sacrificing to false gods (Ex 22:20), refusing to abide by the decision of the court (Dt 17:12), treason (1Ki 2:25; Est 2:23), sedition (Ac 5:36-37).

Not inflicted on the testimony of less than two witnesses (Nu 35:30; Dt 17:6; 19:15).

Modes of Execution of the Death Penalty:

Burning (Ge 38:24; Lev 20:14; 21:9; Jer 29:22; Eze 23:25; Da 3:19-23). Stoning (Lev 20:2,27; Nu 14:10; 15:33-36; Dt 13:10; 17:5; 22:21,24; Jos 7:25; 1Ki 21:10; Eze 16:40). Hanging (Ge 40:22; Dt 21:22-23; Jos 8:29; Est 7:10). Beheading (Mt 14:10; Mk 6:16,27-28). Crucifixion (Mt 27:35,38; Mk 15:24,27; Lk 23:33). The sword (Ex 32:27-28; 1Ki 2:25,34,46; Ac 12:2).

Executed, by the witnesses (Dt 13:9; 17:7; Ac 7:58), by the congregation (Nu 15:35-36; Dt 13:9).

Figurative:

Ro 6:2 By no means! We died to sin; how can we live in it any longer? ³Or don't you know that all of us who were baptized into Christ Jesus were baptized into his death? ⁴We were therefore buried with him through baptism into death in order that, just as Christ was raised from the dead through the glory of the Father, we too may live a new life.

⁵If we have been united with him like this in his death, we will certainly also be united with him in his resurrection. ⁶For we know that our old self was crucified with him so that the body of sin might be done away with, that we should no longer be slaves to sin— ⁷because anyone who has died has been freed from sin.

⁸Now if we died with Christ, we believe that we will also live with him. ⁹For we know that since Christ was raised from the dead, he cannot die again; death no longer has mastery over him. ¹⁰The death he died, he died to sin once for all; but the life he lives, he lives to God.

¹¹In the same way, count yourselves dead to sin but alive to God in Christ Jesus.

Ro 7:1 Do you not know, brothers—for I am speaking to men who know the law—that the law has authority over a man only as long as he lives? ²For example, by law a married woman is bound to her husband as long as he is alive, but if her husband dies, she is released from the law

of marriage. ³So then, if she marries another man while her husband is still alive, she is called an adulteress. But if her husband dies, she is released from that law and is not an adulteress, even though she marries another man.

⁴So, my brothers, you also died to the law through the body of Christ, that you might belong to another, to him who was raised from the dead, in order that we might bear fruit to God. ⁵For when we were controlled by the sinful nature, the sinful passions aroused by the law were at work in our bodies, so that we bore fruit for death. ⁶But now, by dying to what once bound us, we have been released from the law so that we serve in the new way of the Spirit, and not in the old way of the written code.

⁷What shall we say, then? Is the law sin? Certainly not! Indeed I would not have known what sin was except through the law. For I would not have known what coveting really was if the law had not said, "Do not covet." ⁸But sin, seizing the opportunity afforded by the commandment, produced in me every kind of covetous desire. For apart from law, sin is dead. ⁹Once I was alive apart from law; but when the commandment came, sin sprang to life and I died. ¹⁰I found that the very commandment that was intended to bring life actually brought death. ¹¹For sin, seizing the opportunity afforded by the commandment, deceived me, and through the commandment put me to death.

Ro 8:10 But if Christ is in you, your body is dead because of sin, yet your spirit is alive because of righteousness. ¹¹And if the Spirit of him who raised Jesus from the dead is living in you, he who raised Christ from the dead will also give life to your mortal bodies through his Spirit, who lives in you.

Col 2:20 Since you died with Christ to the basic principles of this world, why, as though you still belonged to it, do you submit to its rules: (+2Ti 2:11)

Symbolized: By the pale horse (Rev 6:8).

See Dead; Regeneration; Second Death; Spiritual Death.

DEBAR *See Lo Debar.*

DEBIR [1809, 1810] (*back room [of a shrine temple for oracle pronouncement]*).

NIV+ KIRIATH SANNAH

1. King of Eglon (Jos 10:3-27).

2. A town in the mountains of Judah. Also called Kiriath Sepher which signifies a city of books (Jos 15:15-16). Anakites expelled from, by Joshua (Jos 11:21). Taken by Othniel (Jos 15:15-17,49; Jdg 1:12-13). Allotted to the Aaronites (Jos 21:15).

3. A place near the Valley of Achor (Jos 15:7).

DEBORAH [1806] (*hornet, wasp, wild honey bee*).

1. A nurse to Rebekah (Ge 24:59). Buried beneath an oak under Bethel (Ge 35:8).

2. The prophetess, a judge of Israel (Jdg 4:4-5; 5:7). Inspires Barak to defeat Sisera (Jdg 4:6-16). Triumphant song of (Jdg 5).

DEBT [2471, 4200+5957, 5391, 5963, 9024, 9023, 625, 1245, 4051, 4052, 4053].

NIV+ DEBTOR

Teaching against—

Ro 13:8 Let no debt remain outstanding, except the continuing debt to love one another, for he who loves his fellowman has fulfilled the law.

Security for:

Warnings against becoming a guarantor for others—
Pr 11:15 He who puts up security for another will surely suffer, but whoever refuses to strike hands in pledge is safe.
Pr 22:26 Do not be a man who strikes hands in pledge or puts up security for debts;

Clothing taken as, must be returned by sundown—
Ex 22:25 "If you lend money to one of my people among you who is needy, do not be like a moneylender; charge him no interest. ²⁶If you take your neighbor's cloak as a pledge, return it to him by sunset, ²⁷because his cloak is the only covering he has for his body. What else will he sleep in? When he cries out to me, I will hear, for I am compassionate.
Dt 24:10 When you make a loan of any kind to your neighbor, do not go into his house to get what he is offering as a pledge. ¹¹Stay outside and let the man to whom you are making the loan bring the pledge out to you. ¹²If the man is poor, do not go to sleep with his pledge in your possession. ¹³Return his cloak to him by sunset so that he may sleep in it. Then he will thank you, and it will be regarded as a righteous act in the sight of the LORD your God.
Job 22:6 You demanded security from your brothers for no reason; you stripped men of their clothing, leaving them naked.
Am 2:8 They lie down beside every altar on garments taken in pledge. In the house of their god they drink wine taken as fines.

Houses and property—
Ne 5:3 Others were saying, "We are mortgaging our fields, our vineyards and our homes to get grain during the famine."
⁴Still others were saying, "We have had to borrow money to pay the king's tax on our fields and vineyards."

Children—
Job 24:9 The fatherless child is snatched from the breast; the infant of the poor is seized for a debt.

Millstones forbidden—
Dt 24:6 Do not take a pair of millstones—not even the upper one—as security for a debt, because that would be taking a man's livelihood as security.
See Debtor; Creditor; Security, For Debt.

DEBTOR [5967, 4050, 5971].
NIV+ DEBT, DEBTORS, DEBTS

Laws concerning—
Ex 21:2 "If you buy a Hebrew servant, he is to serve you for six years. But in the seventh year, he shall go free, without paying anything. ³If he comes alone, he is to go free alone; but if he has a wife when he comes, she is to go with him. ⁴If his master gives him a wife and she bears him sons or daughters, the woman and her children shall belong to her master, and only the man shall go free.
⁵"But if the servant declares, 'I love my master and my wife and children and do not want to go free,' ⁶then his master must take him before the judges. He shall take him to the door or the doorpost and pierce his ear with an awl. Then he will be his servant for life.
Ex 22:10 "If a man gives a donkey, an ox, a sheep or any other animal to his neighbor for safekeeping and it dies or is injured or is taken away while no one is looking, ¹¹the issue between them will be settled by the taking of an oath before the LORD that the neighbor did not lay hands on the other person's property. The owner is to accept this, and

no restitution is required. ¹²But if the animal was stolen from the neighbor, he must make restitution to the owner. ¹³If it was torn to pieces by a wild animal, he shall bring in the remains as evidence and he will not be required to pay for the torn animal.
¹⁴"If a man borrows an animal from his neighbor and it is injured or dies while the owner is not present, he must make restitution. ¹⁵But if the owner is with the animal, the borrower will not have to pay. If the animal was hired, the money paid for the hire covers the loss.
Lev 25:14 "'If you sell land to one of your countrymen or buy any from him, do not take advantage of each other. ¹⁵You are to buy from your countryman on the basis of the number of years since the Jubilee. And he is to sell to you on the basis of the number of years left for harvesting crops. ¹⁶When the years are many, you are to increase the price, and when the years are few, you are to decrease the price, because what he is really selling you is the number of crops. ¹⁷Do not take advantage of each other, but fear your God. I am the LORD your God.
Lev 25:25 "'If one of your countrymen becomes poor and sells some of his property, his nearest relative is to come and redeem what his countryman has sold. ²⁶If, however, a man has no one to redeem it for him but he himself prospers and acquires sufficient means to redeem it, ²⁷he is to determine the value for the years since he sold it and refund the balance to the man to whom he sold it; he can then go back to his own property. ²⁸But if he does not acquire the means to repay him, what he sold will remain in the possession of the buyer until the Year of Jubilee. It will be returned in the Jubilee, and he can then go back to his property.
²⁹"'If a man sells a house in a walled city, he retains the right of redemption a full year after its sale. During that time he may redeem it. ³⁰If it is not redeemed before a full year has passed, the house in the walled city shall belong permanently to the buyer and his descendants. It is not to be returned in the Jubilee. ³¹But houses in villages without walls around them are to be considered as open country. They can be redeemed, and they are to be returned in the Jubilee.
³²"'The Levites always have the right to redeem their houses in the Levitical towns, which they possess. ³³So the property of the Levites is redeemable—that is, a house sold in any town they hold—and is to be returned in the Jubilee, because the houses in the towns of the Levites are their property among the Israelites. ³⁴But the pastureland belonging to their towns must not be sold; it is their permanent possession.
³⁵"'If one of your countrymen becomes poor and is unable to support himself among you, help him as you would an alien or a temporary resident, so he can continue to live among you. ³⁶Do not take interest of any kind from him, but fear your God, so that your countryman may continue to live among you. ³⁷You must not lend him money at interest or sell him food at a profit. ³⁸I am the LORD your God, who brought you out of Egypt to give you the land of Canaan and to be your God.
³⁹"'If one of your countrymen becomes poor among you and sells himself to you, do not make him work as a slave. ⁴⁰He is to be treated as a hired worker or a temporary resident among you; he is to work for you until the Year of Jubilee. ⁴¹Then he and his children are to be released, and he will go back to his own clan and to the property of his forefathers.
Lev 25:47 "'If an alien or a temporary resident among you

becomes rich and one of your countrymen becomes poor and sells himself to the alien living among you or to a member of the alien's clan, ⁴⁸he retains the right of redemption after he has sold himself. One of his relatives may redeem him: ⁴⁹An uncle or a cousin or any blood relative in his clan may redeem him. Or if he prospers, he may redeem himself. ⁵⁰He and his buyer are to count the time from the year he sold himself up to the Year of Jubilee. The price for his release is to be based on the rate paid to a hired man for that number of years. ⁵¹If many years remain, he must pay for his redemption a larger share of the price paid for him. ⁵²If only a few years remain until the Year of Jubilee, he is to compute that and pay for his redemption accordingly. ⁵³He is to be treated as a man hired from year to year; you must see to it that his owner does not rule over him ruthlessly.

⁵⁴" 'Even if he is not redeemed in any of these ways, he and his children are to be released in the Year of Jubilee, ⁵⁵for the Israelites belong to me as servants. They are my servants, whom I brought out of Egypt. I am the LORD your God. (+Dt 24:10-13)

Ne 10:31 "When the neighboring peoples bring merchandise or grain to sell on the Sabbath, we will not buy from them on the Sabbath or on any holy day. Every seventh year we will forgo working the land and will cancel all debts.

Mt 5:25 "Settle matters quickly with your adversary who is taking you to court. Do it while you are still with him on the way, or he may hand you over to the judge, and the judge may hand you over to the officer, and you may be thrown into prison. ²⁶I tell you the truth, you will not get out until you have paid the last penny.

Mt 5:40 And if someone wants to sue you and take your tunic, let him have your cloak as well.

Mt 18:25 Since he was not able to pay, the master ordered that he and his wife and his children and all that he had be sold to repay the debt.

Sold for debt—

2Ki 4:1 The wife of a man from the company of the prophets cried out to Elisha, "Your servant my husband is dead, and you know that he revered the LORD. But now his creditor is coming to take my two boys as his slaves."

²Elisha replied to her, "How can I help you? Tell me, what do you have in your house?"

"Your servant has nothing there at all," she said, "except a little oil."

³Elisha said, "Go around and ask all your neighbors for empty jars. Don't ask for just a few. ⁴Then go inside and shut the door behind you and your sons. Pour oil into all the jars, and as each is filled, put it to one side."

⁵She left him and afterward shut the door behind her and her sons. They brought the jars to her and she kept pouring. ⁶When all the jars were full, she said to her son, "Bring me another one."

But he replied, "There is not a jar left." Then the oil stopped flowing.

⁷She went and told the man of God, and he said, "Go, sell the oil and pay your debts. You and your sons can live on what is left."

Ne 5:3 Others were saying, "We are mortgaging our fields, our vineyards and our homes to get grain during the famine."

⁴Still others were saying, "We have had to borrow money to pay the king's tax on our fields and vineyards. ⁵Although we are of the same flesh and blood as our countrymen and though our sons are as good as theirs, yet we have to subject our sons and daughters to slavery. Some of our daughters have already been enslaved, but we are powerless, because our fields and our vineyards belong to others." (+Mt 18:25)

Imprisoned for debt (Mt 18:30).

Oppressed (2Ki 4:1-7; Ne 5:3-5)—

Job 20:18 What he toiled for he must give back uneaten; he will not enjoy the profit from his trading. ¹⁹For he has oppressed the poor and left them destitute; he has seized houses he did not build.

Mt 18:28 "But when that servant went out, he found one of his fellow servants who owed him a hundred denarii. He grabbed him and began to choke him. 'Pay back what you owe me!' he demanded.

²⁹"His fellow servant fell to his knees and begged him, 'Be patient with me, and I will pay you back.'

³⁰"But he refused. Instead, he went off and had the man thrown into prison until he could pay the debt.

Mercy toward, commanded—

Mt 18:23 "Therefore, the kingdom of heaven is like a king who wanted to settle accounts with his servants. ²⁴As he began the settlement, a man who owed him ten thousand talents was brought to him. ²⁵Since he was not able to pay, the master ordered that he and his wife and his children and all that he had be sold to repay the debt.

²⁶"The servant fell on his knees before him. 'Be patient with me,' he begged, 'and I will pay back everything.' ²⁷The servant's master took pity on him, canceled the debt and let him go.

Wicked—

Lk 20:9 He went on to tell the people this parable: "A man planted a vineyard, rented it to some farmers and went away for a long time. ¹⁰At harvest time he sent a servant to the tenants so they would give him some of the fruit of the vineyard. But the tenants beat him and sent him away empty-handed. ¹¹He sent another servant, but that one also they beat and treated shamefully and sent away empty-handed. ¹²He sent still a third, and they wounded him and threw him out.

¹³"Then the owner of the vineyard said, 'What shall I do? I will send my son, whom I love; perhaps they will respect him.'

¹⁴"But when the tenants saw him, they talked the matter over. 'This is the heir,' they said. 'Let's kill him, and the inheritance will be ours.' ¹⁵So they threw him out of the vineyard and killed him.

"What then will the owner of the vineyard do to them? ¹⁶He will come and kill those tenants and give the vineyard to others."

When the people heard this, they said, "May this never be!"

See Creditor; Debt; Security, For Debt.

DECALOGUE *(ten words).* Written by God (Ex 24:12; 31:18; 32:16; Dt 5:22; 9:10; Hos 8:12). Divine authority of (Ex 20:1; 34:27-28; Dt 5:4-22). Called the Words of the Covenant (Ex 34:28; Dt 4:13). Tables of Testimony (Ex 31:18; 34:29; 40:20).

Listed—

Ex 20:1 And God spoke all these words:

²"I am the LORD your God, who brought you out of Egypt, out of the land of slavery.

³"You shall have no other gods before me.

⁴"You shall not make for yourself an idol in the form of anything in heaven above or on the earth beneath or in the waters below. ⁵You shall not bow down to them or

worship them; for I, the LORD your God, am a jealous God, punishing the children for the sin of the fathers to the third and fourth generation of those who hate me, [6]but showing love to a thousand [generations] of those who love me and keep my commandments.

[7]"You shall not misuse the name of the LORD your God, for the LORD will not hold anyone guiltless who misuses his name.

[8]"Remember the Sabbath day by keeping it holy. [9]Six days you shall labor and do all your work, [10]but the seventh day is a Sabbath to the LORD your God. On it you shall not do any work, neither you, nor your son or daughter, nor your manservant or maidservant, nor your animals, nor the alien within your gates. [11]For in six days the LORD made the heavens and the earth, the sea, and all that is in them, but he rested on the seventh day. Therefore the LORD blessed the Sabbath day and made it holy.

[12]"Honor your father and your mother, so that you may live long in the land the LORD your God is giving you.

[13]"You shall not murder.

[14]"You shall not commit adultery.

[15]"You shall not steal.

[16]"You shall not give false testimony against your neighbor.

[17]"You shall not covet your neighbor's house. You shall not covet your neighbor's wife, or his manservant or maidservant, his ox or donkey, or anything that belongs to your neighbor."

Dt 5:6 "I am the LORD your God, who brought you out of Egypt, out of the land of slavery."

[7]You shall have no other gods before me.

[8]"You shall not make for yourself an idol in the form of anything in heaven above or on the earth beneath or in the waters below. [9]You shall not bow down to them or worship them; for I, the LORD your God, am a jealous God, punishing the children for the sin of the fathers to the third and fourth generation of those who hate me, [10]but showing love to a thousand [generations] of those who love me and keep my commandments.

[11]"You shall not misuse the name of the LORD your God, for the LORD will not hold anyone guiltless who misuses his name.

[12]"Observe the Sabbath day by keeping it holy, as the LORD your God has commanded you. [13]Six days you shall labor and do all your work, [14]but the seventh day is a Sabbath to the LORD your God. On it you shall not do any work, neither you, nor your son or daughter, nor your manservant or maidservant, nor your ox, your donkey or any of your animals, nor the alien within your gates, so that your manservant and maidservant may rest, as you do. [15]Remember that you were slaves in Egypt and that the LORD your God brought you out of there with a mighty hand and an outstretched arm. Therefore the LORD your God has commanded you to observe the Sabbath day.

[16]"Honor your father and your mother, as the LORD your God has commanded you, so that you may live long and that it may go well with you in the land the LORD your God is giving you.

[17]"You shall not murder.

[18]"You shall not commit adultery.

[19]"You shall not steal.

[20]"You shall not give false testimony against your neighbor.

[21]"You shall not covet your neighbor's wife. You shall not set your desire on your neighbor's house or land, his manservant or maidservant, his ox or donkey, or anything that belongs to your neighbor."

Confirmed, by Jesus—

Mt 19:18 "Which ones?" the man inquired.

Jesus replied, " 'Do not murder, do not commit adultery, do not steal, do not give false testimony, [19]honor your father and mother,' and 'love your neighbor as yourself.' "

Mt 22:34 Hearing that Jesus had silenced the Sadducees, the Pharisees got together. [35]One of them, an expert in the law, tested him with this question: [36]"Teacher, which is the greatest commandment in the Law?"

[37]Jesus replied: " 'Love the Lord your God with all your heart and with all your soul and with all your mind.' [38]This is the first and greatest commandment. [39]And the second is like it: 'Love your neighbor as yourself.' [40]All the Law and the Prophets hang on these two commandments."

Lk 10:25 On one occasion an expert in the law stood up to test Jesus. "Teacher," he asked, "what must I do to inherit eternal life?"

[26]"What is written in the Law?" he replied. "How do you read it?"

[27]He answered: " 'Love the Lord your God with all your heart and with all your soul and with all your strength and with all your mind'; and, 'Love your neighbor as yourself.' "

[28]"You have answered correctly," Jesus replied. "Do this and you will live."

By Paul—

Ro 13:8 Let no debt remain outstanding, except the continuing debt to love one another, for he who loves his fellowman has fulfilled the law. [9]The commandments, "Do not commit adultery," "Do not murder," "Do not steal," "Do not covet," and whatever other commandment there may be, are summed up in this one rule: "Love your neighbor as yourself." [10]Love does no harm to its neighbor. Therefore love is the fulfillment of the law.

See Commandments and Statutes, of God.

DECAPOLIS [*1279*] (*[league of] ten cities*). Ten cities situated in one district on the east of the Sea of Galilee (Mt 4:25; Mk 5:20; 7:31).

DECEIT [*423, 1704, 2744, 3950, 5327, 5958, 6810, 7331, 8228, 8245, 8736, 9214, 9438, 9567, *572, 573, 1515, 1987, 4165, 4414, 4415, 4418, 5854, 5855, 6022*].

NIV+ DECEITFUL, DECEITFULLY, DECEITFULNESS, DECEIVE, DECEIVED, DECEIVER, DECEIVERS, DECEIVES, DECEIVING, DECEPTION, DECEPTIVE, DECEPTIVELY

Is falsehood (Ps 119:118). The tongue is an instrument of (Ro 3:13). Comes from the heart (Mk 7:22). Characteristic of the heart (Jer 17:9). God abhors (Ps 5:6). Forbidden (Pr 24:28; 1Pe 3:10). Christ was perfectly free from (Isa 53:9, w 1Pe 2:22).

Saints free from (Ps 24:4; Zep 3:13; Rev 14:5), purpose against (Job 27:4), avoid (Job 31:5), shun those addicted to (Ps 101:7), pray for deliverance from those who use (Ps 43:1; 120:2), delivered from those who use (Ps 72:14), should beware of those who teach (Eph 5:6; Col 2:8), should lay aside, in seeking truth (1Pe 2:1). Ministers should lay aside (2Co 4:2; 1Th 2:3).

The wicked are full of (Ro 1:29), devise (Ps 35:20; 38:12; Pr 12:5), utter (Ps 10:7; 36:3), work (Pr 11:18), increase in (2Ti 3:13), use, to themselves (Jer 37:9; Ob 7), delight in (Pr 20:17).

False teachers are workers of (2Co 11:13), preach (Jer 14:14; 23:26), impose on others by (Ro 16:18; Eph 4:14), sport themselves with (2Pe 2:13). Hypocrites practice (Hos 11:12). False witnesses use (Pr 12:17). A characteristic of Antichrist (2Jn 7). Characteristic of apostasy (2Th 2:10).

Evil of:

Hinders knowledge of God (Jer 9:6). Keeps from turning to God (Jer 8:5). Leads to pride and oppression (Jer 5:27-28), to lying (Pr 14:25). Often accompanied by fraud and injustice (Ps 10:7; 43:1). Hatred often concealed by (Pr 26:24-26). The folly of fools is (Pr 14:8). The kisses of an enemy are (Pr 27:6). Blessedness of being free from (Ps 24:4-5; 32:2). Punishment of (Ps 55:23; Jer 9:7-9).

See Confidence, False; Deception; Falsehood; Flattery; Hypocrisy.

DECEPTION [See DECEIT].

NIV+ See DECEIT

Instances of:

By Satan (Ge 3:4). Abraham, in saying that Sarah was his sister (Ge 12:13; 20:2). Isaac, in saying that his wife was his sister (Ge 26:7). Jacob and Rebekah, in imposing Jacob on his father, and Jacob's impersonating Esau (Ge 27:6-23). Jacob's sons, in entrapping the Shechemites (Ge 34:13-31), in representing to their father that Joseph had been destroyed by wild beasts (Ge 37:29-35). Joseph, in his ruse with his brothers (Ge 42-44). The Gibeonites, in misrepresenting their habitat (Jos 9:3-15). Ehud deceives Eglon, and slays him (Jdg 3:15-30). Delilah deceives Samson (Jdg 16:4-20). David feigns insanity (1Sa 21:10-15). Amnon deceives Tamar by feigning sickness (2Sa 13:6-14). Hushai deceives Absalom (2Sa 16:15-19). Sanballat tries to deceive Nehemiah (Ne 6). By Absalom, when he avenged his sister (2Sa 13:24-28), when he began his conspiracy (2Sa 15:7). The old prophet (1Ki 13:18). Gehazi (2Ki 5:20). Job's friends (Job 6:15). Doeg (Ps 52:2). Herod (Mt 2:8). Pharisees (Mt 22:16). Chief priests (Mk 14:1). Lawyer (Lk 10:25). Ananias and Sapphira (Ac 5:1).

See Deceit; Hypocrisy; Falsehood; False Witness.

Self: *See False Confidence; Flattery.*

DECISION [*3025, 3519, 5477, 9149, 10418, *3212*].

NIV+ DECIDE, DECIDED, DECISIONS

Teaching Concerning:

Choosing life—

Dt 30:19 This day I call heaven and earth as witnesses against you that I have set before you life and death, blessings and curses. Now choose life, so that you and your children may live

Committing to the Lord—

Jos 24:15 But if serving the LORD seems undesirable to you, then choose for yourselves this day whom you will serve, whether the gods your forefathers served beyond the River, or the gods of the Amorites, in whose land you are living. But as for me and my household, we will serve the LORD."

1Sa 12:20 "Do not be afraid," Samuel replied. "You have done all this evil; yet do not turn away from the LORD, but serve the LORD with all your heart.

1Ki 18:21 Elijah went before the people and said, "How long will you waver between two opinions? If the LORD is God, follow him; but if Baal is God, follow him." But the people said nothing.

Isa 50:7 Because the Sovereign LORD helps me, I will not

be disgraced. Therefore have I set my face like flint, and I know I will not be put to shame.

Mt 6:24 "No one can serve two masters. Either he will hate the one and love the other, or he will be devoted to the one and despise the other. You cannot serve both God and Money. (+Mt 8:21-22)

Lk 9:59 He said to another man, "Follow me."

But the man replied, "Lord, first let me go and bury my father."

[60]Jesus said to him, "Let the dead bury their own dead, but you go and proclaim the kingdom of God."

[61]Still another said, "I will follow you, Lord; but first let me go back and say good-by to my family."

[62]Jesus replied, "No one who puts his hand to the plow and looks back is fit for service in the kingdom of God." (+Lk 16:13)

1Co 15:58 Therefore, my dear brothers, stand firm. Let nothing move you. Always give yourselves fully to the work of the Lord, because you know that your labor in the Lord is not in vain.

Walking righteously—

Jos 1:7 Be strong and very courageous. Be careful to obey all the law my servant Moses gave you; do not turn from it to the right or to the left, that you may be successful wherever you go.

2Ch 19:11 "Amariah the chief priest will be over you in any matter concerning the LORD, and Zebadiah son of Ishmael, the leader of the tribe of Judah, will be over you in any matter concerning the king, and the Levites will serve as officials before you. Act with courage, and may the LORD be with those who do well." (+Pr 4:25-27; Mt 4:17)

2Th 3:13 And as for you, brothers, never tire of doing what is right.

1Ti 6:11 But you, man of God, flee from all this, and pursue righteousness, godliness, faith, love, endurance and gentleness. [12]Fight the good fight of the faith. Take hold of the eternal life to which you were called when you made your good confession in the presence of many witnesses. [13]In the sight of God, who gives life to everything, and of Christ Jesus, who while testifying before Pontius Pilate made the good confession, I charge you [14]to keep this command without spot or blame until the appearing of our Lord Jesus Christ,

Heb 12:1 Therefore, since we are surrounded by such a great cloud of witnesses, let us throw off everything that hinders and the sin that so easily entangles, and let us run with perseverance the race marked out for us.

1Pe 1:13 Therefore, prepare your minds for action; be self-controlled; set your hope fully on the grace to be given you when Jesus Christ is revealed.

2Pe 1:10 Therefore, my brothers, be all the more eager to make your calling and election sure. For if you do these things, you will never fall,

Remaining in Christ—

Jn 15:4 Remain in me, and I will remain in you. No branch can bear fruit by itself; it must remain in the vine. Neither can you bear fruit unless you remain in me.

[5]"I am the vine; you are the branches. If a man remains in me and I in him, he will bear much fruit; apart from me you can do nothing.

Jn 15:7 If you remain in me and my words remain in you, ask whatever you wish, and it will be given you.

Jn 15:9 "As the Father has loved me, so have I loved you. Now remain in my love.

1Jn 2:24 See that what you have heard from the beginning remains in you. If it does, you also will remain in the Son and in the Father.

1Jn 2:28 And now, dear children, continue in him, so that when he appears we may be confident and unashamed before him at his coming.

Endurance in:

In obedience—

Jn 8:31 To the Jews who had believed him, Jesus said, "If you hold to my teaching, you are really my disciples. (+1Co 15:58)

Col 2:6 So then, just as you received Christ Jesus as Lord, continue to live in him, [7]rooted and built up in him, strengthened in the faith as you were taught, and overflowing with thankfulness.

2Th 2:15 So then, brothers, stand firm and hold to the teachings we passed on to you, whether by word of mouth or by letter.

2Th 2:17 encourage your hearts and strengthen you in every good deed and word.

2Pe 3:17 Therefore, dear friends, since you already know this, be on your guard so that you may not be carried away by the error of lawless men and fall from your secure position. [18]But grow in the grace and knowledge of our Lord and Savior Jesus Christ. To him be glory both now and forever! Amen.

2Jn 8 Watch out that you do not lose what you have worked for, but that you may be rewarded fully.

In grace—

Ac 13:43 When the congregation was dismissed, many of the Jews and devout converts to Judaism followed Paul and Barnabas, who talked with them and urged them to continue in the grace of God.

2Ti 2:1 You then, my son, be strong in the grace that is in Christ Jesus.

2Ti 2:3 Endure hardship with us like a good soldier of Christ Jesus.

In faith—

Ac 14:22 strengthening the disciples and encouraging them to remain true to the faith. "We must go through many hardships to enter the kingdom of God," they said.

1Co 16:13 Be on your guard; stand firm in the faith; be men of courage; be strong.

Php 1:27 Whatever happens, conduct yourselves in a manner worthy of the gospel of Christ. Then, whether I come and see you or only hear about you in my absence, I will know that you stand firm in one spirit, contending as one man for the faith of the gospel

Col 1:23 if you continue in your faith, established and firm, not moved from the hope held out in the gospel. This is the gospel that you heard and that has been proclaimed to every creature under heaven, and of which I, Paul, have become a servant.

Heb 3:6 But Christ is faithful as a son over God's house. And we are his house, if we hold on to our courage and the hope of which we boast.

[7]So, as the Holy Spirit says: "Today, if you hear his voice, [8]do not harden your hearts as you did in the rebellion, during the time of testing in the desert,

Heb 3:14 We have come to share in Christ if we hold firmly till the end the confidence we had at first.

Heb 4:14 Therefore, since we have a great high priest who has gone through the heavens, Jesus the Son of God, let us hold firmly to the faith we profess.

Heb 10:23 Let us hold unswervingly to the hope we profess, for he who promised is faithful.

Heb 10:35 So do not throw away your confidence; it will be richly rewarded.

1Pe 5:8 Be self-controlled and alert. Your enemy the devil prowls around like a roaring lion looking for someone to devour. [9]Resist him, standing firm in the faith, because you know that your brothers throughout the world are undergoing the same kind of sufferings.

Jude 20 But you, dear friends, build yourselves up in your most holy faith and pray in the Holy Spirit. [21]Keep yourselves in God's love as you wait for the mercy of our Lord Jesus Christ to bring you to eternal life.

In Christian liberty—

Gal 5:1 It is for freedom that Christ has set us free. Stand firm, then, and do not let yourselves be burdened again by a yoke of slavery. (+Gal 5:2-9)

Gal 5:10 I am confident in the Lord that you will take no other view. The one who is throwing you into confusion will pay the penalty, whoever he may be. (+Gal 5:11-26)

In the Lord—

Php 4:1 Therefore, my brothers, you whom I love and long for, my joy and crown, that is how you should stand firm in the Lord, dear friends!

In holiness—

1Th 3:8 For now we really live, since you are standing firm in the Lord.

1Th 3:13 May he strengthen your hearts so that you will be blameless and holy in the presence of our God and Father when our Lord Jesus comes with all his holy ones.

In sound doctrine—

Eph 4:14 Then we will no longer be infants, tossed back and forth by the waves, and blown here and there by every wind of teaching and by the cunning and craftiness of men in their deceitful scheming.

2Ti 1:13 What you heard from me, keep as the pattern of sound teaching, with faith and love in Christ Jesus. [14]Guard the good deposit that was entrusted to you—guard it with the help of the Holy Spirit who lives in us.

Tit 1:7 Since an overseer is entrusted with God's work, he must be blameless—not overbearing, not quick-tempered, not given to drunkenness, not violent, not pursuing dishonest gain.

Tit 1:9 He must hold firmly to the trustworthy message as it has been taught, so that he can encourage others by sound doctrine and refute those who oppose it.

Heb 2:1 We must pay more careful attention, therefore, to what we have heard, so that we do not drift away.

Heb 13:9 Do not be carried away by all kinds of strange teachings. It is good for our hearts to be strengthened by grace, not by ceremonial foods, which are of no value to those who eat them.

Heb 13:13 Let us, then, go to him outside the camp, bearing the disgrace he bore.

Instances of:

Abel—

Heb 11:4 By faith Abel offered God a better sacrifice than Cain did. By faith he was commended as a righteous man, when God spoke well of his offerings. And by faith he still speaks, even though he is dead.

Enoch—

Heb 11:5 By faith Enoch was taken from this life, so that he did not experience death; he could not be found, because God had taken him away. For before he was taken, he was commended as one who pleased God. [6]And without faith it is impossible to please God, because anyone who comes to him must believe that he exists and that he rewards those who earnestly seek him.

Noah—

Heb 11:7 By faith Noah, when warned about things not yet seen, in holy fear built an ark to save his family. By his faith he condemned the world and became heir of the righteousness that comes by faith.

Abraham—

Heb 11:8 By faith Abraham, when called to go to a place he would later receive as his inheritance, obeyed and went, even though he did not know where he was going.

Heb 11:17 By faith Abraham, when God tested him, offered Isaac as a sacrifice. He who had received the promises was about to sacrifice his one and only son, [18]even though God had said to him, "It is through Isaac that your offspring will be reckoned." [19]Abraham reasoned that God could raise the dead, and figuratively speaking, he did receive Isaac back from death.

Jacob—

Ge 28:20 Then Jacob made a vow, saying, "If God will be with me and will watch over me on this journey I am taking and will give me food to eat and clothes to wear [21]so that I return safely to my father's house, then the LORD will be my God (+Ge 28:22)

Joseph—

Ge 39:9 No one is greater in this house than I am. My master has withheld nothing from me except you, because you are his wife. How then could I do such a wicked thing and sin against God?"

Moses—

Nu 12:7 But this is not true of my servant Moses; he is faithful in all my house. (+Heb 3:5)

Heb 11:24 By faith Moses, when he had grown up, refused to be known as the son of Pharaoh's daughter. [25]He chose to be mistreated along with the people of God rather than to enjoy the pleasures of sin for a short time. [26]He regarded disgrace for the sake of Christ as of greater value than the treasures of Egypt, because he was looking ahead to his reward. (+Heb 11:27)

Israelites—

Ex 19:7 So Moses went back and summoned the elders of the people and set before them all the words the LORD had commanded him to speak. [8]The people all responded together, "We will do everything the LORD has said." So Moses brought their answer back to the LORD.

Ex 24:3 When Moses went and told the people all the LORD's words and laws, they responded with one voice, "Everything the LORD has said we will do."

Ex 24:7 Then he took the Book of the Covenant and read it to the people. They responded, "We will do everything the LORD has said; we will obey."

Dt 4:4 but all of you who held fast to the LORD your God are still alive today.

Dt 5:27 Go near and listen to all that the LORD our God says. Then tell us whatever the LORD our God tells you. We will listen and obey.

Dt 26:17 You have declared this day that the LORD is your God and that you will walk in his ways, that you will keep his decrees, commands and laws, and that you will obey him.

Jos 22:34 And the Reubenites and the Gadites gave the altar this name: A Witness Between Us that the LORD is God.

Jos 24:21 But the people said to Joshua, "No! We will serve the LORD."

[22]Then Joshua said, "You are witnesses against yourselves that you have chosen to serve the LORD."

"Yes, we are witnesses," they replied.

[23]"Now then," said Joshua, "throw away the foreign gods that are among you and yield your hearts to the LORD, the God of Israel."

[24]And the people said to Joshua, "We will serve the LORD our God and obey him."

[25]On that day Joshua made a covenant for the people, and there at Shechem he drew up for them decrees and laws.

1Ki 19:18 Yet I reserve seven thousand in Israel—all whose knees have not bowed down to Baal and all whose mouths have not kissed him." (+2Ki 11:17)

2Ch 11:16 Those from every tribe of Israel who set their hearts on seeking the LORD, the God of Israel, followed the Levites to Jerusalem to offer sacrifices to the LORD, the God of their fathers.

2Ch 13:10 "As for us, the LORD is our God, and we have not forsaken him. The priests who serve the LORD are sons of Aaron, and the Levites assist them. [11]Every morning and evening they present burnt offerings and fragrant incense to the LORD. They set out the bread on the ceremonially clean table and light the lamps on the gold lampstand every evening. We are observing the requirements of the LORD our God. But you have forsaken him.

2Ch 15:12 They entered into a covenant to seek the LORD, the God of their fathers, with all their heart and soul.

2Ch 15:15 All Judah rejoiced about the oath because they had sworn it wholeheartedly. They sought God eagerly, and he was found by them. So the LORD gave them rest on every side. (+2Ch 23:16; 29:10; Ezr 10:3-44; Ne 9:38)

Ne 10:28 "The rest of the people—priests, Levites, gatekeepers, singers, temple servants and all who separated themselves from the neighboring peoples for the sake of the Law of God, together with their wives and all their sons and daughters who are able to understand— [29]all these now join their brothers the nobles, and bind themselves with a curse and an oath to follow the Law of God given through Moses the servant of God and to obey carefully all the commands, regulations and decrees of the LORD our Lord. (+Ne 10:30-31; Jer 34:15)

Jer 42:5 Then they said to Jeremiah, "May the LORD be a true and faithful witness against us if we do not act in accordance with everything the LORD your God sends you to tell us. [6]Whether it is favorable or unfavorable, we will obey the LORD our God, to whom we are sending you, so that it will go well with us, for we will obey the LORD our God."

Jer 50:5 They will ask the way to Zion and turn their faces toward it. They will come and bind themselves to the LORD in an everlasting covenant that will not be forgotten.

Hos 11:12 Ephraim has surrounded me with lies, the house of Israel with deceit. And Judah is unruly against God, even against the faithful Holy One.

Levites (Ex 32:26).

Caleb—

Nu 14:6 Joshua son of Nun and Caleb son of Jephunneh, who were among those who had explored the land, tore their clothes [7]and said to the entire Israelite assembly, "The land we passed through and explored is exceedingly good. [8]If the LORD is pleased with us, he will lead us into that land, a land flowing with milk and honey, and will give it to us. [9]Only do not rebel against the LORD. And do not be afraid of the people of the land, because we will swallow them up. Their protection is gone, but the LORD is with us. Do not be afraid of them."

[10]But the whole assembly talked about stoning them. Then the glory of the LORD appeared at the Tent of Meeting to all the Israelites.

Nu 14:24 But because my servant Caleb has a different spirit and follows me wholeheartedly, I will bring him into the land he went to, and his descendants will inherit it. (+Dt 1:36; Jos 14:14)

Balaam—

Nu 22:15 Then Balak sent other princes, more numerous and more distinguished than the first. [16]They came to Balaam and said:

"This is what Balak son of Zippor says: Do not let anything keep you from coming to me, [17]because I will reward you handsomely and do whatever you say. Come and put a curse on these people for me."

[18]But Balaam answered them, "Even if Balak gave me his palace filled with silver and gold, I could not do anything great or small to go beyond the command of the LORD my God. (+Nu 24:13)

Phinehas—

Nu 25:7 When Phinehas son of Eleazar, the son of Aaron, the priest, saw this, he left the assembly, took a spear in his hand [8]and followed the Israelite into the tent. He drove the spear through both of them—through the Israelite and into the woman's body. Then the plague against the Israelites was stopped; [9]but those who died in the plague numbered 24,000.

[10]The LORD said to Moses, [11]"Phinehas son of Eleazar, the son of Aaron, the priest, has turned my anger away from the Israelites; for he was as zealous as I am for my honor among them, so that in my zeal I did not put an end to them. [12]Therefore tell him I am making my covenant of peace with him. [13]He and his descendants will have a covenant of a lasting priesthood, because he was zealous for the honor of his God and made atonement for the Israelites."

Joshua—

Jos 24:15 But if serving the LORD seems undesirable to you, then choose for yourselves this day whom you will serve, whether the gods your forefathers served beyond the River, or the gods of the Amorites, in whose land you are living. But as for me and my household, we will serve the LORD."

Gideon—

Jdg 6:25 That same night the LORD said to him, "Take the second bull from your father's herd, the one seven years old. Tear down your father's altar to Baal and cut down the Asherah pole beside it. [26]Then build a proper kind of altar to the LORD your God on the top of this height. Using the wood of the Asherah pole that you cut down, offer the second bull as a burnt offering."

[27]So Gideon took ten of his servants and did as the LORD told him. But because he was afraid of his family and the men of the town, he did it at night rather than in the daytime. (+Jdg 6:28)

Ruth—

Ru 1:16 But Ruth replied, "Don't urge me to leave you or to turn back from you. Where you go I will go, and where you stay I will stay. Your people will be my people and your God my God.

Saul—

1Sa 11:4 When the messengers came to Gibeah of Saul and reported these terms to the people, they all wept aloud.

[5]Just then Saul was returning from the fields, behind his oxen, and he asked, "What is wrong with the people? Why are they weeping?" Then they repeated to him what the men of Jabesh had said.

[6]When Saul heard their words, the Spirit of God came upon him in power, and he burned with anger. [7]He took a pair of oxen, cut them into pieces, and sent the pieces by messengers throughout Israel, proclaiming, "This is what will be done to the oxen of anyone who does not follow Saul and Samuel." Then the terror of the LORD fell on the people, and they turned out as one man.

David—

1Sa 17:32 David said to Saul, "Let no one lose heart on account of this Philistine; your servant will go and fight him."

[33]Saul replied, "You are not able to go out against this Philistine and fight him; you are only a boy, and he has been a fighting man from his youth."

[34]But David said to Saul, "Your servant has been keeping his father's sheep. When a lion or a bear came and carried off a sheep from the flock, [35]I went after it, struck it and rescued the sheep from its mouth. When it turned on me, I seized it by its hair, struck it and killed it. [36]Your servant has killed both the lion and the bear; this uncircumcised Philistine will be like one of them, because he has defied the armies of the living God. [37]The LORD who delivered me from the paw of the lion and the paw of the bear will deliver me from the hand of this Philistine."

Saul said to David, "Go, and the LORD be with you." (+2Sa 22:22-24)

Psalmist (Ps 17:3)—

Ps 26:6 I wash my hands in innocence, and go about your altar, O LORD,

Ps 26:11 But I lead a blameless life; redeem me and be merciful to me. (+Ps 27:3-8)

Ps 40:9 I proclaim righteousness in the great assembly; I do not seal my lips, as you know, O LORD. [10]I do not hide your righteousness in my heart; I speak of your faithfulness and salvation. I do not conceal your love and your truth from the great assembly.

Ps 56:12 I am under vows to you, O God; I will present my thank offerings to you. (+Ps 57:7-8)

Ps 71:17 Since my youth, O God, you have taught me, and to this day I declare your marvelous deeds.

Ps 86:11 Teach me your way, O LORD, and I will walk in your truth; give me an undivided heart, that I may fear your name.

Ps 101:2 I will be careful to lead a blameless life—when will you come to me? I will walk in my house with blameless heart. [3]I will set before my eyes no vile thing. The deeds of faithless men I hate; they will not cling to me.

Ps 108:1 My heart is steadfast, O God; I will sing and make music with all my soul.

Ps 116:9 that I may walk before the LORD in the land of the living.

Ps 116:13 I will lift up the cup of salvation and call on the name of the LORD. [14]I will fulfill my vows to the LORD in the presence of all his people.

Ps 116:16 O LORD, truly I am your servant; I am your servant, the son of your maidservant; you have freed me from my chains.

Ps 119:8 I will obey your decrees; do not utterly forsake me.

Ps 119:30 I have chosen the way of truth; I have set my heart on your laws. [31]I hold fast to your statutes, O LORD; do not let me be put to shame.

Ps 119:38 Fulfill your promise to your servant, so that you may be feared.

Ps 119:33 Teach me, O LORD, to follow your decrees; then I will keep them to the end. **34**Give me understanding, and I will keep your law and obey it with all my heart. **35**Direct me in the path of your commands, for there I find delight. **36**Turn my heart toward your statutes and not toward selfish gain.

Ps 119:57 You are my portion, O LORD; I have promised to obey your words.

Ps 119:94 Save me, for I am yours; I have sought out your precepts.

Ps 119:106 I have taken an oath and confirmed it, that I will follow your righteous laws.

Ps 119:115 Away from me, you evildoers, that I may keep the commands of my God!

Ps 119:125 I am your servant; give me discernment that I may understand your statutes.

Ps 119:145 I call with all my heart; answer me, O LORD, and I will obey your decrees. **146**I call out to you; save me and I will keep your statutes.

A prophet of Judah—

1Ki 13:8 But the man of God answered the king, "Even if you were to give me half your possessions, I would not go with you, nor would I eat bread or drink water here. **9**For I was commanded by the word of the LORD: 'You must not eat bread or drink water or return by the way you came.'" **10**So he took another road and did not return by the way he had come to Bethel.

Elijah—

1Ki 18:22 Then Elijah said to them, "I am the only one of the LORD's prophets left, but Baal has four hundred and fifty prophets.

Jehoshaphat—

1Ki 22:7 But Jehoshaphat asked, "Is there not a prophet of the LORD here whom we can inquire of?"

8The king of Israel answered Jehoshaphat, "There is still one man through whom we can inquire of the LORD, but I hate him because he never prophesies anything good about me, but always bad. He is Micaiah son of Imlah."

"The king should not say that," Jehoshaphat replied. (+2Ch 18:6-7)

Micaiah (1Ki 22:13-14; 2Ch 18:6-7).

Naaman (2Ki 5:13-14)—

2Ki 5:15 Then Naaman and all his attendants went back to the man of God. He stood before him and said, "Now I know that there is no God in all the world except in Israel. Please accept now a gift from your servant." (+2Ki 5:16)

2Ki 5:17 "If you will not," said Naaman, "please let me, your servant, be given as much earth as a pair of mules can carry, for your servant will never again make burnt offerings and sacrifices to any other god but the LORD.

Hezekiah—

2Ki 18:6 He held fast to the LORD and did not cease to follow him; he kept the commands the LORD had given Moses. (+2Ch 15:17)

Josiah—

2Ki 22:2 He did what was right in the eyes of the LORD and walked in all the ways of his father David, not turning aside to the right or to the left.

2Ki 23:3 The king stood by the pillar and renewed the covenant in the presence of the LORD—to follow the LORD and keep his commands, regulations and decrees with all his heart and all his soul, thus confirming the words of the

covenant written in this book. Then all the people pledged themselves to the covenant.

2Ki 23:25 Neither before nor after Josiah was there a king like him who turned to the LORD as he did— with all his heart and with all his soul and with all his strength, in accordance with all the Law of Moses. (+2Ch 34:31)

Nehemiah—

Ne 6:11 But I said, "Should a man like me run away? Or should one like me go into the temple to save his life? I will not go!" (+Ne 2; 4:6)

Esther—

Est 4:16 "Go, gather together all the Jews who are in Susa, and fast for me. Do not eat or drink for three days, night or day. I and my maids will fast as you do. When this is done, I will go to the king, even though it is against the law. And if I perish, I perish."

Job (Job 2:9-10). Daniel (Da 1:8). The three Hebrews (Da 3:11-12,16-18).

Matthew—

Mt 9:9 As Jesus went on from there, he saw a man named Matthew sitting at the tax collector's booth. "Follow me," he told him, and Matthew got up and followed him.

Joseph—

Mk 15:43 Joseph of Arimathea, a prominent member of the Council, who was himself waiting for the kingdom of God, went boldly to Pilate and asked for Jesus' body.

Nathanael—

Jn 1:49 Then Nathanael declared, "Rabbi, you are the Son of God; you are the King of Israel."

Martha—

Jn 11:27 "Yes, Lord," she told him, "I believe that you are the Christ, the Son of God, who was to come into the world."

Disciples—

Lk 18:28 Peter said to him, "We have left all we had to follow you!"

Jn 6:68 Simon Peter answered him, "Lord, to whom shall we go? You have the words of eternal life. **69**We believe and know that you are the Holy One of God."

Ac 2:42 They devoted themselves to the apostles' teaching and to the fellowship, to the breaking of bread and to prayer.

Paul—

Ac 9:29 He talked and debated with the Grecian Jews, but they tried to kill him.

Ro 1:16 I am not ashamed of the gospel, because it is the power of God for the salvation of everyone who believes: first for the Jew, then for the Gentile.

Ro 8:38 For I am convinced that neither death nor life, neither angels nor demons, neither the present nor the future, nor any powers, **39**neither height nor depth, nor anything else in all creation, will be able to separate us from the love of God that is in Christ Jesus our Lord.

Php 1:20 I eagerly expect and hope that I will in no way be ashamed, but will have sufficient courage so that now as always Christ will be exalted in my body, whether by life or by death. **21**For to me, to live is Christ and to die is gain.

2Ti 4:7 I have fought the good fight, I have finished the race, I have kept the faith. **8**Now there is in store for me the crown of righteousness, which the Lord, the righteous Judge, will award to me on that day—and not only to me, but also to all who have longed for his appearing.

Church, of Ephesus—

Rev 2:2 I know your deeds, your hard work and your

perseverance. I know that you cannot tolerate wicked men, that you have tested those who claim to be apostles but are not, and have found them false. ³You have persevered and have endured hardships for my name, and have not grown weary.

Of Sardis—

Rev 3:4 Yet you have a few people in Sardis who have not soiled their clothes. They will walk with me, dressed in white, for they are worthy.

Rev 3:8 I know your deeds. See, I have placed before you an open door that no one can shut. I know that you have little strength, yet you have kept my word and have not denied my name.

Rev 3:10 Since you have kept my command to endure patiently, I will also keep you from the hour of trial that is going to come upon the whole world to test those who live on the earth.

Saints—

Rev 14:4 These are those who did not defile themselves with women, for they kept themselves pure. They follow the Lamb wherever he goes. They were purchased from among men and offered as firstfruits to God and the Lamb.

See Character.

DECISION, VALLEY OF [3025]. *See Jehoshaphat, Valley of.*

DECREE [*1819, 1821, 2976, 2978, 3076, 4180, 7422, 7756, 10057, 10186, 10302, *1504*].

NIV+ DECREED, DECREES

An official ruling or law (Da 2:9; Est 1:20; Jnh 3:7; Ac 16:4; Rev 13:8).

DEDAN [1847].

NIV+ DEDANITES

1. A son of Raamah (Ge 10:7; 1Ch 1:9).
2. A son of Jokshan (Ge 25:3; 1Ch 1:32).
3. A country, probably bordering on Edom (Jer 49:8; Eze 25:13; 27:15,20; 38:13).

DEDANITES, DEDANIM [1848].

NIV+ DEDAN

Descendants of Dedan (Isa 21:13).

DEDICATION [2853, 5694, 10273, *1589, 2952*].

NIV+ DEDICATE, DEDICATED, DEDICATES

Law concerning dedicated things (Lev 27; Nu 18:14; 1Ch 26:26-27). Must be without blemish (Lev 22:18-23; Mal 1:14). Not redeemable (Lev 27:28-29). Offering must be voluntary (Lev 1:3; 22:19). *See Offerings; Vows.*

Of the tabernacle (Nu 7). Solomon's temple (1Ki 8; 2Ch 7:5). Second temple (Ezr 6:16-17). Of the wall of Jerusalem (Ne 12:27-43). Of houses (Dt 20:5). Of Samuel by his mother (1Sa 1:11,22).

Of Self. *See Consecration.*

For instances of liberality in dedicated things. *See Liberality.*

DEDICATION, FEAST OF Annual Jewish feast celebrating the restoration of the temple following its desecration by Antiochus Epiphanes. Jesus delivered a discourse at this feast (Jn 10:22ff).

See Feasts; Hanukkah; Kislev; Maccabees; Month, 9.

DEED [1524, 1525, 1691, 1821, 3208, 3707, 4616, 4856, 5042, 5095, 5126, 5148, 6219, 6411, 6613, 6614,

6913, 7189, 7190, 7407, 8288, 8400, 9335, *2240, 3197, 4552, 4556*].

NIV+ DEEDED, DEEDS

To the land (Jer 32:12,14,44). *See Land.* For works. *See Works, Good.*

DEEP [*696, 1524, 4394, 5099, 5185, 6676, 6678, 6906, 7516, 8041, 8101, 8145, 9166, 9333, 9554, *958, 960*].

NIV+ ANKLE-DEEP, DEEPER, DEEPEST, DEEPLY, DEEPS, DEPTH, DEPTHS

The ocean (Ne 9:11), chaos (Ge 1:2), the deepest part of the sea (Ge 49:25), abyss (Lk 8:31; Rev 9:1; 11:7).

DEER [385, 387, 3502, 3607]. Also called doe, roe deer. Designated among the clean animals, to be eaten (Dt 12:15; 14:5). Provided for Solomon's household (1Ki 4:23). Swiftness of (2Sa 2:18; 1Ch 12:8; Pr 6:5; SS 8:14; Isa 35:6). Surefootedness of (2Sa 22:34). Gentleness of (Pr 5:19).

DEFENSE [*1462, 1713, 1906, 3519, 5911, 8189, 9149, *664, 665*].

NIV+ DEFEND, DEFENDED, DEFENDER, DEFENDERS, DEFENDING, DEFENDS, DEFENSES

An argument made before a court. Of Jeremiah (Jer 26:12-16), Peter (Ac 4:8-13; 5:23-29), Stephen (Ac 7), Paul (Ac 22; 23:1-6; 24:10-21; 26:1-23).

Military defenses. *See Fort; Armies.*

DEFILEMENT [*1458, 2725, 2729, 2866, 3237, 3238, 9210, *3662*].

NIV+ DEFILE, DEFILED, DEFILES, DEFILING

Laws relating to (Lev 7:18-21; 11:43; 22:2-7). Caused by, leprosy (Lev 13:3,44-46; 14; 22:4-7), copulation (Lev 15:17), discharges (Lev 15:1-17), childbirth (Lev 12:2-8; Lk 2:22), menses (Lev 15:19-33; 2Sa 11:4), touching the dead (Nu 19:11-22; 31:19-20), touching carcass of any unclean animal (Lev 11:39-40; 17:15-16; 22:8), touching carcass of any unclean thing (Lev 5:2-13; 11:8,24-28,31-38; 14:46-57; 15:5-11; Dt 23:10-11), slaying in battle (Nu 31:19-20). Contact with sinners falsely supposed to cause (Jn 18:28).

Of priests (Lev 16:26,28; Nu 19:7-10; Eze 44:25-26).

Egyptian perspective (Ge 43:32).

See Purification; Unclean, Uncleanness; Washings.

DEFORMITY [5426, 8594].

NIV+ DEFORMED

See Blemish.

DEGRADATION [2725, 7829, 9493, *869*].

NIV+ DEGRADE, DEGRADED, DEGRADING

Of God's people (Ex 32:25; Eze 16:6; 20:31; 2Pe 2:22).

DEGREES NIV "steps" on the stairway of Ahaz (2Ki 20:9-11).

DEGREES, SONGS OF Title given Psalms 120 to 134 in the KJV. *See Ascents, Songs of.*

DEHAVITES At the end of Ezra 4:9 the KJV lists three peoples: "the Susanchites, the Dehavites, *and* the Elamites," while the NIV reads "the Elamites of Susa." The KJV transliterated "the Dehavites" from a difficult Aramaic term, rightly rendered "of" in the NIV.

DEITY OF JESUS *See Jesus the Christ, Deity of.*

DEKAR *See Ben-Deker, Ben-Deker.*

DELAIAH [1933, 1934] (*Yahweh draws up [like water in a bucket]*).

1. Descendant of David (1Ch 3:1-24).

2. Head of the twenty-third course of priests (1Ch 24:18).

3. Prince who tried to save Jeremiah's roll from destruction (Jer 36:12,25).

4. An ancestor of the tribe that returned under Zerubbabel (Ezr 2:60; Ne 7:62).

5. The father of Shemaiah (Ne 6:10).

DELIGHTING IN GOD [*9503, 2773, 2911, 2913, 2914, 4718, 5375, 6695, 8193, 8354, 8356, 8464, 8523, 8524, 9130, 9141, *2305*, *5897*].

NIV+ DELIGHT, DELIGHTED, DELIGHTFUL, DELIGHTING, DELIGHTS

Commanded (Ps 37:4). Reconciliation leads to (Job 22:21,26). Observing the Sabbath leads to (Isa 58:13-14).

Saints' Experience in:

Communion with God (SS 2:3). The law of God (Ps 1:2; 119:24,35). The goodness of God (Ne 9:25). The comforts of God (Ps 94:19).

Hypocrites:

Pretend to (Isa 58:2). In heart despise (Job 27:10; Jer 6:10). Promises to (Ps 37:4). Blessedness of (Ps 112:1).

DELILAH [1935] (*tease*). A Philistine woman who lured Samson to his ruin (Jdg 16:4-20).

DELIVERANCE [2208, 3802, 3828, 5911, 7119, 7129, 9591, *5401*]. See *Affliction; God, Providence of; Prayer, Answer to.*

DELIVERER [3802, 4635, 7117, *3392*, *4861*].

NIV+ DELIVER, DELIVERANCE, DELIVERED, DELIVERERS, DELIVERING, DELIVERS, DELIVERY

A title of Jesus (Ro 11:26). See *Titles and Names.*

DELUGE See *Flood.*

DELUSION, SELF See *Self-Delusion.*

DEMAGOGISM

Instances of:

Absalom (2Sa 15:2-6). Pilate (Mt 27:17-26; Mk 15:15; Lk 23:13-24; Jn 18:38-40; 19:6-13). Felix (Ac 24:27). Herod (Ac 12:3).

DEMAS [*1318*] (*[common] folks*). Fellow laborer with Paul (Col 4:14; Phm 24), who later deserted him (2Ti 4:10).

DEMETRIUS [*1320*] (*of Demeter*).

1. A disciple praised by John (3Jn 12).

2. A silversmith at Ephesus who made trouble for Paul (Ac 19:23-27).

DEMONS [8717, *794*, *1227*, *1228*, *1230*].

NIV+ DEMON, DEMON-POSSESSED, DEMON-POSSESSION

Worship of (Lev 17:7; Dt 32:17; 2Ch 11:15; Ps 106:37; Mt 4:9; Lk 4:7; 1Co 10:20-21; 1Ti 4:1; Rev 13:4). Worship of, forbidden (Lev 17:7; Zec 13:2; Rev 9:20).

Possession by, instances of:

Saul (1Sa 16:14-23; 18:10-11; 19:9-10). Two men of the Gadarenes (Mt 8:28-34; Mk 5:2-20). The mute man (Mt 9:32-33). The blind and mute man (Mt 12:22; Lk 11:14). The daughter of the Syrian Phoenician (Mt 15:22-29; Mk 7:25-30). The child with seizures (Mt 17:14-18;

Mk 9:17-27; Lk 9:37-42). The man in the synagogue (Mk 1:23-26; Lk 4:33-35). Mary Magdalene (Mk 16:9; Lk 8:2-3). The herd of pigs (Mt 8:30-32).

Cast out by Jesus (Mt 4:24; 8:16; Mk 3:22; Lk 4:41).

Power over, given the disciples (Mt 10:1; Mk 6:7; 16:17). Cast out by the disciples (Mk 9:38; Lk 10:17), by Peter (Ac 5:16), by Paul (Ac 16:16-18; 19:12), by Philip (Ac 8:7). The disciples could not expel (Mk 9:18,28-29). Sceva's sons exorcise (Ac 19:13-16). The parable of the man repossessed (Mt 12:43-45).

Jesus falsely accused of being possessed of (Mk 3:22-30; Jn 7:20; 8:48; 10:20).

Testify to the deity of Jesus (Mt 8:29; Mk 1:23-24; 3:11; 5:7; Lk 8:28; Ac 19:15).

Adversaries of men (Mt 12:45). Sent to cause trouble between Abimelech and the Shechemites (Jdg 9:23). Messages given false prophets by (1Ki 22:21-23).

Believe and tremble (Jas 2:19). To be judged at the general judgment (Mt 8:29, w 2Pe 2:4; Jude 6).

Punishment of (Mt 8:29; 25:41; Lk 8:28; 2Pe 2:4; Jude 6; Rev 12:7-9).

See *Devil; Satan.*

DENARIUS [*1324*].

NIV+ DENARII

See *Money.*

DENS [4995, 5104, 10129, *5068*].

NIV+ DEN

Used as places of refuge (Jdg 6:2; Heb 11:38; Rev 6:15).

DENYING JESUS [4202, 5742, 6073, 6700, 237+2848+6017, 565, 766]. See *Jesus the Christ, Rejected.*

DEPRAVITY [8845, 99, *1406*, *2967*, *2798*, *5785*].

NIV+ DEPRAVED

In the Nature of Humanity:

Ge 6:5 The LORD saw how great man's wickedness on the earth had become, and that every inclination of the thoughts of his heart was only evil all the time. 6The LORD was grieved that he had made man on the earth, and his heart was filled with pain. 7So the LORD said, "I will wipe mankind, whom I have created, from the face of the earth—men and animals, and creatures that move along the ground, and birds of the air—for I am grieved that I have made them." 8But Noah found favor in the eyes of the LORD.

Ge 8:21 The LORD smelled the pleasing aroma and said in his heart: "Never again will I curse the ground because of man, even though every inclination of his heart is evil from childhood. And never again will I destroy all living creatures, as I have done.

Job 4:17 'Can a mortal be more righteous than God? Can a man be more pure than his Maker? 18If God places no trust in his servants, if he charges his angels with error, 19how much more those who live in houses of clay, whose foundations are in the dust, who are crushed more readily than a moth!

Job 9:2 "Indeed, I know that this is true. But how can a mortal be righteous before God? 3Though one wished to dispute with him, he could not answer him one time out of a thousand.

Job 9:20 Even if I were innocent, my mouth would condemn me; if I were blameless, it would pronounce me guilty.

Job 9:29 Since I am already found guilty, why should I

struggle in vain? ³⁰Even if I washed myself with soap and my hands with washing soda, ³¹you would plunge me into a slime pit so that even my clothes would detest me.

Job 11:12 But a witless man can no more become wise than a wild donkey's colt can be born a man.

Job 14:4 Who can bring what is pure from the impure? No one!

Job 15:14 "What is man, that he could be pure, or one born of woman, that he could be righteous? ¹⁵If God places no trust in his holy ones, if even the heavens are not pure in his eyes, ¹⁶how much less man, who is vile and corrupt, who drinks up evil like water!

Job 25:4 How then can a man be righteous before God? How can one born of woman be pure? ⁵If even the moon is not bright and the stars are not pure in his eyes, ⁶how much less man, who is but a maggot—a son of man, who is only a worm!"

Ps 5:9 Not a word from their mouth can be trusted; their heart is filled with destruction. Their throat is an open grave; with their tongue they speak deceit.

Ps 51:5 Surely I was sinful at birth, sinful from the time my mother conceived me.

Ps 58:1 Do you rulers indeed speak justly? Do you judge uprightly among men? ²No, in your heart you devise injustice, and your hands mete out violence on the earth. ³Even from birth the wicked go astray; from the womb they are wayward and speak lies. ⁴Their venom is like the venom of a snake, like that of a cobra that has stopped its ears, ⁵that will not heed the tune of the charmer, however skillful the enchanter may be.

Ps 94:11 The LORD knows the thoughts of man; he knows that they are futile.

Ps 130:3 If you, O LORD, kept a record of sins, O Lord, who could stand?

Pr 10:20 The tongue of the righteous is choice silver, but the heart of the wicked is of little value.

Pr 20:6 Many a man claims to have unfailing love, but a faithful man who can find?

Pr 20:9 Who can say, "I have kept my heart pure; I am clean and without sin"?

Pr 21:8 The way of the guilty is devious, but the conduct of the innocent is upright.

Isa 1:5 Why should you be beaten anymore? Why do you persist in rebellion? Your whole head is injured, your whole heart afflicted. ⁶From the sole of your foot to the top of your head there is no soundness—only wounds and welts and open sores, not cleansed or bandaged or soothed with oil.

Isa 51:1 "Listen to me, you who pursue righteousness and who seek the LORD: Look to the rock from which you were cut and to the quarry from which you were hewn;

Jer 13:23 Can the Ethiopian change his skin or the leopard its spots? Neither can you do good who are accustomed to doing evil.

Jer 16:12 But you have behaved more wickedly than your fathers. See how each of you is following the stubbornness of his evil heart instead of obeying me.

Jer 17:9 The heart is deceitful above all things and beyond cure. Who can understand it?

Hos 6:7 Like Adam, they have broken the covenant—they were unfaithful to me there.

Mic 7:2 The godly have been swept from the land; not one upright man remains. All men lie in wait to shed blood; each hunts his brother with a net. ³Both hands are skilled in doing evil; the ruler demands gifts, the judge accepts bribes, the powerful dictate what they desire—they all

conspire together. ⁴The best of them is like a brier, the most upright worse than a thorn hedge. The day of your watchmen has come, the day God visits you. Now is the time of their confusion.

Mt 7:17 Likewise every good tree bears good fruit, but a bad tree bears bad fruit.

Mt 12:34 You brood of vipers, how can you who are evil say anything good? For out of the overflow of the heart the mouth speaks. ³⁵The good man brings good things out of the good stored up in him, and the evil man brings evil things out of the evil stored up in him.

Mt 15:19 For out of the heart come evil thoughts, murder, adultery, sexual immorality, theft, false testimony, slander. (+Mk 7:21-23)

Jn 3:19 This is the verdict: Light has come into the world, but men loved darkness instead of light because their deeds were evil.

Jn 8:23 But he continued, "You are from below; I am from above. You are of this world; I am not of this world.

Jn 14:17 the Spirit of truth. The world cannot accept him, because it neither sees him nor knows him. But you know him, for he lives with you and will be in you. (+Ro 1:21-32)

Ro 2:1 You, therefore, have no excuse, you who pass judgment on someone else, for at whatever point you judge the other, you are condemning yourself, because you who pass judgment do the same things.

Ro 6:6 For we know that our old self was crucified with him so that the body of sin might be done away with, that we should no longer be slaves to sin—

Ro 6:19 I put this in human terms because you are weak in your natural selves. Just as you used to offer the parts of your body in slavery to impurity and to ever-increasing wickedness, so now offer them in slavery to righteousness leading to holiness. ²⁰When you were slaves to sin, you were free from the control of righteousness.

Ro 7:5 For when we were controlled by the sinful nature, the sinful passions aroused by the law were at work in our bodies, so that we bore fruit for death. (+Ro 7:11-15,18-25)

Ro 8:5 Those who live according to the sinful nature have their minds set on what that nature desires; but those who live in accordance with the Spirit have their minds set on what the Spirit desires. ⁶The mind of sinful man is death, but the mind controlled by the Spirit is life and peace; ⁷the sinful mind is hostile to God. It does not submit to God's law, nor can it do so. ⁸Those controlled by the sinful nature cannot please God.

Ro 8:13 For if you live according to the sinful nature, you will die; but if by the Spirit you put to death the misdeeds of the body, you will live,

1Co 2:14 The man without the Spirit does not accept the things that come from the Spirit of God, for they are foolishness to him, and he cannot understand them, because they are spiritually discerned.

1Co 3:3 You are still worldly. For since there is jealousy and quarreling among you, are you not worldly? Are you not acting like mere men?

1Co 5:9 I have written you in my letter not to associate with sexually immoral people— ¹⁰not at all meaning the people of this world who are immoral, or the greedy and swindlers, or idolaters. In that case you would have to leave this world.

2Co 5:14 For Christ's love compels us, because we are convinced that one died for all, and therefore all died.

Gal 5:17 For the sinful nature desires what is contrary to the Spirit, and the Spirit what is contrary to the sinful nature. They are in conflict with each other, so that you do not do what you want.

Gal 5:19 The acts of the sinful nature are obvious: sexual immorality, impurity and debauchery; [20]idolatry and witchcraft; hatred, discord, jealousy, fits of rage, selfish ambition, dissensions, factions [21]and envy; drunkenness, orgies, and the like. I warn you, as I did before, that those who live like this will not inherit the kingdom of God.

Eph 2:1 As for you, you were dead in your transgressions and sins, [2]in which you used to live when you followed the ways of this world and of the ruler of the kingdom of the air, the spirit who is now at work in those who are disobedient. [3]All of us also lived among them at one time, gratifying the cravings of our sinful nature and following its desires and thoughts. Like the rest, we were by nature objects of wrath.

Eph 2:12 remember that at that time you were separate from Christ, excluded from citizenship in Israel and foreigners to the covenants of the promise, without hope and without God in the world.

Eph 4:17 So I tell you this, and insist on it in the Lord, that you must no longer live as the Gentiles do, in the futility of their thinking. [18]They are darkened in their understanding and separated from the life of God because of the ignorance that is in them due to the hardening of their hearts. [19]Having lost all sensitivity, they have given themselves over to sensuality so as to indulge in every kind of impurity, with a continual lust for more. (+Eph 4:22)

Jas 4:5 Or do you think Scripture says without reason that the spirit he caused to live in us envies intensely?

1Pe 1:18 For you know that it was not with perishable things such as silver or gold that you were redeemed from the empty way of life handed down to you from your forefathers,

1Pe 2:25 For you were like sheep going astray, but now you have returned to the Shepherd and Overseer of your souls.

1Jn 1:8 If we claim to be without sin, we deceive ourselves and the truth is not in us.

1Jn 1:10 If we claim we have not sinned, we make him out to be a liar and his word has no place in our lives.

1Jn 2:16 For everything in the world—the cravings of sinful man, the lust of his eyes and the boasting of what he has and does—comes not from the Father but from the world.

Universal:

Ge 6:11 Now the earth was corrupt in God's sight and was full of violence. [12]God saw how corrupt the earth had become, for all the people on earth had corrupted their ways. [13]So God said to Noah, "I am going to put an end to all people, for the earth is filled with violence because of them. I am surely going to destroy both them and the earth. (+2Ch 6:36)

Ps 14:1 The fool says in his heart, "There is no God." They are corrupt, their deeds are vile; there is no one who does good.

[2]The LORD looks down from heaven on the sons of men to see if there are any who understand, any who seek God. [3]All have turned aside, they have together become corrupt; there is no one who does good, not even one. (+Ps 53:1-3)

Ps 143:2 Do not bring your servant into judgment, for no one living is righteous before you.

Ecc 7:20 There is not a righteous man on earth who does what is right and never sins.

Isa 53:6 We all, like sheep, have gone astray, each of us

has turned to his own way; and the LORD has laid on him the iniquity of us all.

Isa 64:6 All of us have become like one who is unclean, and all our righteous acts are like filthy rags; we all shrivel up like a leaf, and like the wind our sins sweep us away. (+Mic 7:2-4)

Ro 3:9 What shall we conclude then? Are we any better? Not at all! We have already made the charge that Jews and Gentiles alike are all under sin. [10]As it is written:

"There is no one righteous, not even one; [11]there is no one who understands, no one who seeks God. [12]All have turned away, they have together become worthless; there is no one who does good, not even one."

[13]"Their throats are open graves; their tongues practice deceit."

"The poison of vipers is on their lips."

[14]"Their mouths are full of cursing and bitterness."

[15]"Their feet are swift to shed blood; [16]ruin and misery mark their ways, [17]and the way of peace they do not know."

[18]"There is no fear of God before their eyes."

[19]Now we know that whatever the law says, it says to those who are under the law, so that every mouth may be silenced and the whole world held accountable to God.

Ro 3:23 for all have sinned and fall short of the glory of God,

Ro 5:6 You see, at just the right time, when we were still powerless, Christ died for the ungodly.

Ro 5:12 Therefore, just as sin entered the world through one man, and death through sin, and in this way death came to all men, because all sinned— [13]for before the law was given, sin was in the world. But sin is not taken into account when there is no law. [14]Nevertheless, death reigned from the time of Adam to the time of Moses, even over those who did not sin by breaking a command, as did Adam, who was a pattern of the one to come.

Ro 11:32 For God has bound all men over to disobedience so that he may have mercy on them all.

Gal 3:10 All who rely on observing the law are under a curse, for it is written: "Cursed is everyone who does not continue to do everything written in the Book of the Law." [11]Clearly no one is justified before God by the law, because, "The righteous will live by faith."

Gal 3:22 But the Scripture declares that the whole world is a prisoner of sin, so that what was promised, being given through faith in Jesus Christ, might be given to those who believe.

Jas 3:2 We all stumble in many ways. If anyone is never at fault in what he says, he is a perfect man, able to keep his whole body in check.

1Jn 5:19 We know that we are children of God, and that the whole world is under the control of the evil one.

See Fall of Mankind, The; Sin.

DEPRESSION *See Despondency.*

DEPUTY [5893, 7224]. An officer who administers the functions of a superior in his absence (1Ki 22:47; 2Ki 15:5; Ac 13:7-8; 18:12; 19:38).

DERBE [*1291, 1292*]. A city of Lycaonia. Paul fled to (Ac 14:6,20). Visited by Paul and Silas (Ac 16:1). Gaius born in (Ac 20:4).

DERISION [996, 4353, 7840, 7841, 8562, 9240].
NIV+ DERIDE, DERIDES

The wicked held in, by God (Ps 2:4; Pr 1:26).

Instances of:

Sarah, when the angels gave her the promise of a child (Ge 18:12). The evil children of Bethel deride Elisha (2Ki 2:23). The people of Israel scoff at Hezekiah (2Ch 30:1-10).

See Irony; Sarcasm; Scoffing.

DESERTS [2999, 4497, 5877, 6440, 6858, 7233, 7470, 7480, 7481, 7684, 7708, 9220, *2244, 2245*].

NIV+ DESERT

Vast barren plains (Ex 5:3; Jn 6:13). Uninhabited places (Mt 14:15; Mk 6:31).

Described as:

Uninhabited and lonesome (Jer 2:6). Uncultivated (Nu 20:5; Jer 2:2). Desolate (Eze 6:14). Dry and without water (Ex 17:1; Dt 8:15). Trackless (Isa 43:19). Great and terrible (Dt 1:19). Waste and howling (Dt 32:10). Infested with wild beasts (Isa 13:21; Mk 1:13). Infested with serpents (Dt 8:15). Infested with robbers (Jer 3:2; La 4:19). Danger of traveling in (Ex 14:3; 2Co 11:26). Guides required in (Nu 10:31; Dt 32:10).

Phenomena of, Alluded to:

Mirage or deceptive appearance of water (Jer 15:18). Scorching wind (Jer 4:11). Tornadoes or whirlwinds (Isa 21:1). Clouds of sand and dust (Dt 28:24; Jer 4:12-13).

Mentioned in Scripture:

Arabian or great desert (Ex 23:31). Beth Aven (Jos 18:12). Beersheba (Ge 21:14; 1Ki 19:3-4). Damascus (1Ki 19:15). Edom (2Ki 3:8). En Gedi (1Sa 24:1). Gibeon (2Sa 2:24). Judea (Mt 3:1). Jeruel (2Ch 20:16). Kedemoth (Dt 2:26). Kadesh (Ps 29:8). Maon (1Sa 23:24-25). Paran (Ge 21:21; Nu 10:12). Shur (Ge 16:7; Ex 15:22). Sin (Ex 16:1). Sinai (Ex 19:1-2; Nu 33:16). Ziph (1Sa 23:14-15). Zin (Nu 20:1; 27:14). Of the Red Sea (Ex 13:18). Near Gaza (Ac 8:26). Wastelands often found in (Jer 17:6). Parts of, afforded pasture (Ge 36:24; Ex 3:1). Inhabited by wandering tribes (Ge 21:20-21; Ps 72:9; Jer 25:24). The persecuted fled to (1Sa 23:14; Heb 11:38). The disaffected fled to (1Sa 22:2; Ac 21:38).

Illustrative of:

Barrenness (Ps 106:9; 107:33,35). Those deprived of all blessings (Hos 2:3). The world (SS 3:6; 8:5). The Gentiles (Isa 35:1,6; 41:19). What offers no support (Jer 2:31). Desolation by armies (Jer 12:10-13; 50:12).

DESIGN [3110, 4742, 5126, 5504, 7451, *1927*].

NIV+ DESIGNED, DESIGNER, DESIGNERS, DESIGNS

In nature, evidence of (Job 12:7-11; Pr 16:4).

DESIRED OF ALL NATIONS Some see as a title of Jesus (Hag 2:7). Others deny a messianic application and hold that it means the precious gifts of all nations (Hag 2:8 w Isa 60:5).

DESIRE, SPIRITUAL [*203, 2094, 2773, 2775, 2911, 2913, 2914, 5883, 8356, 9294, 9592, *2121, 2123, 2420, 2527*].

NIV+ DESIRABLE, DESIRED, DESIRES

For divine piety—

Ps 17:11 They have tracked me down, they now surround me, with eyes alert, to throw me to the ground.

Ps 51:1 Have mercy on me, O God, according to your unfailing love; according to your great compassion blot out my transgressions. ²Wash away all my iniquity and cleanse me from my sin.

³For I know my transgressions, and my sin is always before me. ⁴Against you, you only, have I sinned and done what is evil in your sight, so that you are proved right when you speak and justified when you judge.

Ps 51:7 Cleanse me with hyssop, and I will be clean; wash me, and I will be whiter than snow. ⁸Let me hear joy and gladness; let the bones you have crushed rejoice. ⁹Hide your face from my sins and blot out all my iniquity.

¹⁰Create in me a pure heart, O God, and renew a steadfast spirit within me. ¹¹Do not cast me from your presence or take your Holy Spirit from me. ¹²Restore to me the joy of your salvation and grant me a willing spirit, to sustain me.

¹³Then I will teach transgressors your ways, and sinners will turn back to you. (+Ps 119:82)

Hab 3:2 LORD, I have heard of your fame; I stand in awe of your deeds, O LORD. Renew them in our day, in our time make them known; in wrath remember mercy.

For divine fellowship—

Ps 62:1 My soul finds rest in God alone; my salvation comes from him.

Ps 63:1 O God, you are my God, earnestly I seek you; my soul thirsts for you, my body longs for you, in a dry and weary land where there is no water.

Ps 63:8 My soul clings to you; your right hand upholds me.

For divine help—

Ps 25:5 guide me in your truth and teach me, for you are God my Savior, and my hope is in you all day long.

Ps 25:15 My eyes are ever on the LORD, for only he will release my feet from the snare.

Ps 68:28 Summon your power, O God; show us your strength, O God, as you have done before.

Ps 119:77 Let your compassion come to me that I may live, for your law is my delight.

Ps 119:116 Sustain me according to your promise, and I will live; do not let my hopes be dashed. ¹¹⁷Uphold me, and I will be delivered; I will always have regard for your decrees.

Exhortations concerning—

Ps 70:4 But may all who seek you rejoice and be glad in you; may those who love your salvation always say, "Let God be exalted!"

Ps 105:4 Look to the LORD and his strength; seek his face always.

Isa 55:1 "Come, all you who are thirsty, come to the waters; and you who have no money, come, buy and eat! Come, buy wine and milk without money and without cost. ²Why spend money on what is not bread, and your labor on what does not satisfy? Listen, listen to me, and eat what is good, and your soul will delight in the richest of fare. (+Isa 55:3)

Isa 55:6 Seek the LORD while he may be found; call on him while he is near.

Hos 10:12 Sow for yourselves righteousness, reap the fruit of unfailing love, and break up your unplowed ground; for it is time to seek the LORD, until he comes and showers righteousness on you.

For God—

Ps 24:6 Such is the generation of those who seek him, who seek your face, O God of Jacob. *Selah*

Ps 27:8 My heart says of you, "Seek his face!" Your face, LORD, I will seek.

Ps 33:20 We wait in hope for the LORD; he is our help and our shield.

Ps 40:1 I waited patiently for the LORD; he turned to me and heard my cry.

Ps 42:1 As the deer pants for streams of water, so my soul pants for you, O God. ²My soul thirsts for God, for the living God. When can I go and meet with God? ³My tears have been my food day and night, while men say to me all day long, "Where is your God?" ⁴These things I remember as I pour out my soul: how I used to go with the multitude, leading the procession to the house of God, with shouts of joy and thanksgiving among the festive throng.

⁵Why are you downcast, O my soul? Why so disturbed within me? Put your hope in God, for I will yet praise him, my Savior and ⁶my God. My soul is downcast within me; therefore I will remember you from the land of the Jordan, the heights of Hermon—from Mount Mizar.

⁷Deep calls to deep in the roar of your waterfalls; all your waves and breakers have swept over me.

⁸By day the LORD directs his love, at night his song is with me—a prayer to the God of my life.

⁹I say to God my Rock, "Why have you forgotten me? Why must I go about mourning, oppressed by the enemy?" ¹⁰My bones suffer mortal agony as my foes taunt me, saying to me all day long, "Where is your God?"

¹¹Why are you downcast, O my soul? Why so disturbed within me? Put your hope in God, for I will yet praise him, my Savior and my God.

Ps 69:3 I am worn out calling for help; my throat is parched. My eyes fail, looking for my God. (+Ps 73:26)

Ps 119:10 I seek you with all my heart; do not let me stray from your commands. (+Ps 119:12,19)

Ps 119:20 My soul is consumed with longing for your laws at all times. (+Ps 119:25)

Ps 119:40 How I long for your precepts! Preserve my life in your righteousness. (+Ps 119:81,88,123,131-132,135-136)

Ps 119:149 Hear my voice in accordance with your love; preserve my life, O LORD, according to your laws.

Ps 119:156 Your compassion is great, O LORD; preserve my life according to your laws. (+Ps 119:174)

Ps 123:1 I lift up my eyes to you, to you whose throne is in heaven. ²As the eyes of slaves look to the hand of their master, as the eyes of a maid look to the hand of her mistress, so our eyes look to the LORD our God, till he shows us his mercy.

Ps 130:5 I wait for the LORD, my soul waits, and in his word I put my hope. ⁶My soul waits for the Lord more than watchmen wait for the morning, more than watchmen wait for the morning.

Ps 143:6 I spread out my hands to you; my soul thirsts for you like a parched land. *Selah*

⁷Answer me quickly, O LORD; my spirit fails. Do not hide your face from me or I will be like those who go down to the pit. ⁸Let the morning bring me word of your unfailing love, for I have put my trust in you. Show me the way I should go, for to you I lift up my soul. ⁹Rescue me from my enemies, O LORD, for I hide myself in you. ¹⁰Teach me to do your will, for you are my God; may your good Spirit lead me on level ground.

¹¹For your name's sake, O LORD, preserve my life; in your righteousness, bring me out of trouble. ¹²In your unfailing love, silence my enemies; destroy all my foes, for I am your servant.

Isa 8:17 I will wait for the LORD, who is hiding his face from the house of Jacob. I will put my trust in him.

Isa 8:19 When men tell you to consult mediums and spiritists, who whisper and mutter, should not a people inquire of their God? Why consult the dead on behalf of the living?

Isa 26:8 Yes, LORD, walking in the way of your laws, we wait for you; your name and renown are the desire of our hearts. ⁹My soul yearns for you in the night; in the morning my spirit longs for you. When your judgments come upon the earth, the people of the world learn righteousness. (+Mt 13:17)

Lk 10:42 but only one thing is needed. Mary has chosen what is better, and it will not be taken away from her."

Php 3:12 Not that I have already obtained all this, or have already been made perfect, but I press on to take hold of that for which Christ Jesus took hold of me. ¹³Brothers, I do not consider myself yet to have taken hold of it. But one thing I do: Forgetting what is behind and straining toward what is ahead, ¹⁴I press on toward the goal to win the prize for which God has called me heavenward in Christ Jesus. (+1Pe 1:10)

For his holy courts—

Ps 84:2 My soul yearns, even faints, for the courts of the LORD; my heart and my flesh cry out for the living God.

Reward of (Dt 4:29)—

Ps 34:10 The lions may grow weak and hungry, but those who seek the LORD lack no good thing.

Ps 37:4 Delight yourself in the LORD and he will give you the desires of your heart.

Ps 37:9 For evil men will be cut off, but those who hope in the LORD will inherit the land. (+Ps 37:34; 107:9)

Ps 119:2 Blessed are they who keep his statutes and seek him with all their heart.

Pr 2:3 and if you call out for insight and cry aloud for understanding, ⁴and if you look for it as for silver and search for it as for hidden treasure, ⁵then you will understand the fear of the LORD and find the knowledge of God.

Isa 40:31 but those who hope in the LORD will renew their strength. They will soar on wings like eagles; they will run and not grow weary, they will walk and not be faint.

Jer 29:13 You will seek me and find me when you seek me with all your heart.

Mt 5:6 Blessed are those who hunger and thirst for righteousness, for they will be filled. (+Lk 1:53; 6:21; Jn 6:35)

Heb 11:6 And without faith it is impossible to please God, because anyone who comes to him must believe that he exists and that he rewards those who earnestly seek him.

See Hunger, Figurative; Thirst.

Evil: *See Imagination; Lust.*

DESOLATION, ABOMINATION OF
See Abomination That Causes Desolation.

DESPAIR [631, 1017, 3286, 3707, 3910, 5000, 7041, 9039, 9041, *1989*]. *See Despondency.*

DESPISERS [*996, 1022, 1718, 2361, 4415, 5540, 9493, *2969*].

NIV+ DESPISE, DESPISED, DESPISES

General references to (Pr 1:30; 9:8; Mt 7:6; Ac 13:41; Ro 2:4; 2Ti 3:3; Heb 10:28; 2Pe 2:10).

DESPONDENCY
Isa 35:3 Strengthen the feeble hands, steady the knees that give way; ⁴say to those with fearful hearts, "Be strong, do not fear; your God will come, he will come with vengeance; with divine retribution he will come to save you."

Heb 12:12 Therefore, strengthen your feeble arms and weak knees. ¹³"Make level paths for your feet," so that the lame may not be disabled, but rather healed.

Caused by corrective judgments—

Nu 17:12 The Israelites said to Moses, "We will die! We

are lost, we are all lost! [13]Anyone who even comes near the tabernacle of the LORD will die. Are we all going to die?"

Dt 28:65 Among those nations you will find no repose, no resting place for the sole of your foot. There the LORD will give you an anxious mind, eyes weary with longing, and a despairing heart. [66]You will live in constant suspense, filled with dread both night and day, never sure of your life. [67]In the morning you will say, "If only it were evening!" and in the evening, "If only it were morning!"—because of the terror that will fill your hearts and the sights that your eyes will see.

Isa 2:19 Men will flee to caves in the rocks and to holes in the ground from dread of the LORD and the splendor of his majesty, when he rises to shake the earth.

Hos 10:8 The high places of wickedness will be destroyed—it is the sin of Israel. Thorns and thistles will grow up and cover their altars. Then they will say to the mountains, "Cover us!" and to the hills, "Fall on us!"

Mt 24:30 "At that time the sign of the Son of Man will appear in the sky, and all the nations of the earth will mourn. They will see the Son of Man coming on the clouds of the sky, with power and great glory.

Lk 23:29 For the time will come when you will say, 'Blessed are the barren women, the wombs that never bore and the breasts that never nursed!' [30]Then

"'they will say to the mountains, "Fall on us!" and to the hills, "Cover us!"'"

Rev 6:14 The sky receded like a scroll, rolling up, and every mountain and island was removed from its place.

[15]Then the kings of the earth, the princes, the generals, the rich, the mighty, and every slave and every free man hid in caves and among the rocks of the mountains. [16]They called to the mountains and the rocks, "Fall on us and hide us from the face of him who sits on the throne and from the wrath of the Lamb! [17]For the great day of their wrath has come, and who can stand?"

Rev 9:5 They were not given power to kill them, but only to torture them for five months. And the agony they suffered was like that of the sting of a scorpion when it strikes a man. [6]During those days men will seek death, but will not find it; they will long to die, but death will elude them.

Caused by deferred hope—

Pr 13:12 Hope deferred makes the heart sick, but a longing fulfilled is a tree of life.

Caused by adversity (Job 4:5; 9:16-35; 17:7-16).

Lament in—

Job 3:1 After this, Job opened his mouth and cursed the day of his birth. [2]He said: [3]"May the day of my birth perish, and the night it was said, 'A boy is born!' [4]That day—may it turn to darkness; may God above not care about it; may no light shine upon it. [5]May darkness and deep shadow claim it once more; may a cloud settle over it; may blackness overwhelm its light. [6]That night—may thick darkness seize it; may it not be included among the days of the year nor be entered in any of the months. [7]May that night be barren; may no shout of joy be heard in it. [8]May those who curse days curse that day, those who are ready to rouse Leviathan. [9]May its morning stars become dark; may it wait for daylight in vain and not see the first rays of dawn, [10]for it did not shut the doors of the womb on me to hide trouble from my eyes.

[11]"Why did I not perish at birth, and die as I came from the womb? [12]Why were there knees to receive me and breasts that I might be nursed? [13]For now I would be lying down in peace; I would be asleep and at rest [14]with kings and counselors of the earth, who built for themselves

places now lying in ruins, [15]with rulers who had gold, who filled their houses with silver. [16]Or why was I not hidden in the ground like a stillborn child, like an infant who never saw the light of day? [17]There the wicked cease from turmoil, and there the weary are at rest. [18]Captives also enjoy their ease; they no longer hear the slave driver's shout. [19]The small and the great are there, and the slave is freed from his master.

[20]"Why is light given to those in misery, and life to the bitter of soul, [21]to those who long for death that does not come, who search for it more than for hidden treasure, [22]who are filled with gladness and rejoice when they reach the grave? [23]Why is life given to a man whose way is hidden, whom God has hedged in? [24]For sighing comes to me instead of food; my groans pour out like water. [25]What I feared has come upon me; what I dreaded has happened to me. [26]I have no peace, no quietness; I have no rest, but only turmoil."

Job 17:13 If the only home I hope for is the grave, if I spread out my bed in darkness, [14]if I say to corruption, 'You are my father,' and to the worm, 'My mother' or 'My sister,' [15]where then is my hope? Who can see any hope for me? [16]Will it go down to the gates of death? Will we descend together into the dust?" (+Ps 6:6; 22:1-2; 55:4-7)

Ps 77:7 "Will the Lord reject forever? Will he never show his favor again? [8]Has his unfailing love vanished forever? Has his promise failed for all time? [9]Has God forgotten to be merciful? Has he in anger withheld his compassion?" *Selah* (+Ps 88:3-17; Ecc 2:20)

Jer 8:20 "The harvest is past, the summer has ended, and we are not saved."

La 3:1 I am the man who has seen affliction by the rod of his wrath.

[2]He has driven me away and made me walk in darkness rather than light; [3]indeed, he has turned his hand against me again and again, all day long.

[4]He has made my skin and my flesh grow old and has broken my bones. [5]He has besieged me and surrounded me with bitterness and hardship. [6]He has made me dwell in darkness like those long dead.

[7]He has walled me in so I cannot escape; he has weighed me down with chains. [8]Even when I call out or cry for help, he shuts out my prayer. [9]He has barred my way with blocks of stone; he has made my paths crooked.

[10]Like a bear lying in wait, like a lion in hiding, [11]he dragged me from the path and mangled me and left me without help. [12]He drew his bow and made me the target for his arrows.

[13]He pierced my heart with arrows from his quiver. [14]I became the laughingstock of all my people; they mock me in song all day long. [15]He has filled me with bitter herbs and sated me with gall.

[16]He has broken my teeth with gravel; he has trampled me in the dust. [17]I have been deprived of peace; I have forgotten what prosperity is. [18]So I say, "My splendor is gone and all that I had hoped from the LORD."

[19]I remember my affliction and my wandering, the bitterness and the gall. [20]I well remember them, and my soul is downcast within me. (+La 5:15-21)

La 5:22 unless you have utterly rejected us and are angry with us beyond measure.

Mic 7:1 What misery is mine! I am like one who gathers summer fruit at the gleaning of the vineyard; there is no cluster of grapes to eat, none of the early figs that I crave. [2]The godly have been swept from the land; not one upright man remains. All men lie in wait to shed blood; each hunts his brother with a net. ³Both hands are skilled in doing evil; the ruler demands gifts, the judge accepts bribes, the powerful dictate what they desire—they all conspire together. ⁴The best of them is like a brier, the most upright worse than a thorn hedge. The day of your watchmen has come, the day God visits you. Now is the time of their confusion. ⁵Do not trust a neighbor; put no confidence in a friend. Even with her who lies in your embrace be careful of your words. ⁶For a son dishonors his father, a daughter rises up against her mother, a daughter-in-law against her mother-in-law—a man's enemies are the members of his own household.

⁷But as for me, I watch in hope for the LORD, I wait for God my Savior; my God will hear me.

Instances of:

Cain, when God pronounced judgment upon him (Ge 4:13-14). Hagar, when cast out of the household of Abraham (Ge 21:15-16). Moses, when sent on his mission to the Israelites (Ex 4:1,10,13; 6:12), at the Red Sea (Ex 14:15), when the people lusted for flesh (Nu 11:15). The Israelites, on account of the cruel oppressions of the Egyptians (Ex 6:9). Joshua, over the defeat at Ai (Jos 7:7-9). Elijah, when he fled from Jezebel to the wilderness and sat under the broom tree and wished to die (1Ki 19:4). Jonah, after he had preached to the Ninevites (Jnh 4:3,8). The mariners with Paul (Ac 27:20).

See Affliction, Consolation Under; Righteous, Promises to.

DESPOTISM *See Government, Monarchical.*

DESTINY [344, 784, 4200, 4948, 4972, 5247, 6067, 9286, *641, 3023, 4633, 5465, 5502*].

1. Final determined end. Of all people (Ecc 7:2; 9:2-3; Heb 9:27). Of the wicked (Ps 73:17; Jer 15:2; 43:11). Of believers (1Co 2:7).

2. The pagan god of fate (Isa 65:11).

DETECTIVES *See Spies.*

DEUEL [1979] (*known of God [El]*). Also called Reuel (Nu 2:14, ftn). Captain of the tribe of Dan (Nu 1:14; 2:14; 7:42; 10:20).

DEUTERONOMY (*second [giving] of the law*).

Author: Moses, though the preamble (1:1-5) and report of Moses' death (ch. 34) were written by someone else.

Date: c. 1406 B.C.

Outline:

I. The Preamble (1:1-5).

II. The Historical Prologue (1:6-4:43).

III. The Stipulations of the Covenant (4:44-26:19).
  A. The Great Commandment: The Demand for Absolute Allegiance (4:44-11:32).
  B. Supplementary Requirements (chs. 12-26).
   1. Ceremonial consecration (12:1-16:17).
   2. Governmental leaders and a righteous nation (16:18-21:21).
   3. Sanctity of God's kingdom (21:22-25:19).
   4. Confession of God as Redeemer-King (ch. 26).

IV. Ratification; Curses and Blessings (chs. 27-30).

V. Covenant Leadership Succession (chs. 31-34).
  A. Change of Leadership (31:1-29).
  B. Song of Moses (31:30-32:47).
  C. Moses' Testamental Blessing on the Tribes (32:48-33:29).
  D. Death of Moses and Succession of Joshua (ch. 34).

The book is sometimes divided into three addresses:

I. First Address (1:1-4:43).

II. Second Address (4:44-28:68).

III. Third Address (chs. 29-33).

IV. Moses' Death (ch. 34).

DEVIL [*1229, 1333*] (*slanderer* or *liar*).

NIV+ DEVIL'S

One of the principal titles of Satan, the archenemy of God and of mankind. It is not known how he originated, unless Isaiah and Ezekiel give us a clue (Isa 14:12-20; Eze 28:12-19), but it is certain that he was not created evil. He rebelled against God when in a state of holiness and apparently led other angels into rebellion with him (Jude 6; 2Pe 2:4). He is a being of superhuman power and wisdom but is not omnipotent or omniscient. He tries to frustrate God's plans and purposes for human beings. His principal method of attack is by temptation. His power is limited, and he can go only as far as God permits. On the Judgment Day he will be cast into hell to remain there forever.

See Satan.

DEVOTED THING [1467, 2143, 2616, 2883, 3049, 3051, 3922, 5989, 8969, *41, 504, 1565, 1639+4674, 5082, 5309, 5435, 5816, 6067*].

NIV+ See DEVOTION

That which is set apart to the Lord and therefore no longer belongs to the former owner (Lev 27:29, and ftn; Jos 7:1-15). *See Corban.*

DEVOTION [2876, 6313, 8354, 8491, 8969+, *605, 2339*].

NIV+ DEVOTE, DEVOTED, DEVOTES, DEVOTING

To God: *See Religion.*

For conspicuous instances of, study Enoch, Noah, Abraham, Moses, David's later history, Solomon's earlier life, Josiah, Asa, Isaiah, Elijah, Jeremiah, Daniel, Shadrach, Meshach, and Abednego.

To Jesus: *See Peter, Simon; John; Paul; Mary, 3.*

For elaborated topics covering the subject, *See Love, Of People for God; Consecration; Zeal.*

DEW [3228, 10299]. A merciful providence (Dt 33:13). Forms imperceptibly (2Sa 17:12), in the night (Job 29:19). From the clouds (Pr 3:20). Called the dew of heaven (Da 4:15). Absence of (1Ki 17:1). Miraculous profusion and absence of (Jdg 6:36-40).

See Meteorology.

Figurative:

(Ps 110:3; Isa 26:19; Hos 6:4; 13:3; 14:5).

DIADEM [5694, 7565]. A golden plate worn on the turban of the high priest (Ex 29:6; 39:30; Lev 8:9). A royal crown (Isa 62:3). *See Crown.*

DIAL NIV "stairway" (2Ki 20:11; Isa 38:8). *See Stairs.*

DIAMOND *See Emerald; Flint; Minerals of the Bible, 1; Stones.*

DIANA Goddess of the Ephesians (Ac 19:24,27-28,35). *See Artemis.*

DIASPORA (*scattered [like] seed*). The name applied to the Jews living outside of Israel and maintaining their religious faith among the Gentiles (Jas 1:1; 1Pe 1:1). By the time of Christ the diaspora must have been several times the population of Israel. *See Dispersion; Testaments, Time Between.*

DIBLAH, DIBLATH [1812]. Probably an early copyist's error for Riblah, a town c. fifty miles S of Hamath (Eze 6:14).

DIBLAIM [1813] (*lump of [two dried fig] cakes*). Father of Hosea's wife (Hos 1:3).

DIBLATHAIM *See Almon Diblathaim; Beth Diblathaim.*

DIBON, DIBON GAD [1897, 1898].

1. Also called Dibon Gad and Dimon. A city on the northern banks of the Arnon (Nu 21:30). Israelites encamp at (Nu 33:45). Allotted to Gad and Reuben (Nu 32:3,34; Jos 13:9,17). Taken by Moab (Isa 15:2; Jer 48:18,22).

2. A city in the tribe of Judah (Ne 11:25), probably identical with Dimonah (Jos 15:22).

DIBRI [1828] (possibly *speak*). The father of Shelomith (Lev 24:11).

DIDRACHMA (*two drachma*). The annual temple tax was two drachmas (Mt 17:24). *See Drachma; Money.*

DIDYMUS [*1441*] (*twin*). The surname of Thomas (Jn 11:16; 20:24; 21:2).

DIKLAH [1989] (*[place of] date palms*). The son of Joktan, and the name of a district inhabited by his descendants (Ge 10:27; 1Ch 1:21).

DILEAN [1939] (*cucumber* ISBE; *protrude* KB). A city of Judah (Jos 15:38).

DILIGENCE [3026, 6913, 10012, 10056, *5082, 1639*].

NIV+ DILIGENT, DILIGENTLY

Jesus as an example of (Mk 1:35; Lk 2:49).

Required by God in seeking him (1Ch 22:19; Heb 11:6), obeying him (Dt 6:17; 11:13), listening to him (Isa 55:2), striving after perfection (Php 3:13-14), developing Christian qualities (2Pe 1:5), keeping the soul (Dt 4:9), keeping the heart (Pr 4:23), labors of love (Heb 6:10-12), following every good work (1Ti 3:10), guarding against defilement (Heb 12:15), seeking to be found spotless (2Pe 3:14), making our calling sure (2Pe 1:10), self-examination (Ps 77:6), lawful business (Pr 27:23; Ecc 9:10), teaching religion (2Ti 4:2; Jude 3), instructing children (Dt 6:7; 11:19), discharging official duties (Dt 19:18), saints should abound in (2Co 8:7).

Required in the service of God (Jn 9:4; Gal 6:9). Is not in vain (1Co 15:58). Preserves from evil (Ex 15:26). Leads to assured hope (Heb 6:11). God rewards (Dt 11:14; Heb 11:6).

In temporal matters leads to favor (Pr 11:27), prosperity (Pr 10:4; 13:4), honor (Pr 12:24; 22:29).

Figurative: (Pr 6:6-8).

Exemplified:

Ruth (Ru 2:17). Hezekiah (2Ch 31:21). Nehemiah and his helpers (Ne 4:6). Psalmist (Ps 119:60). Apostles (Ac 5:42). Apollos (Ac 18:25). Titus (2Co 8:22). Paul (1Th 2:9). Onesiphorus (2Ti 1:17).

See Industry; Zeal; Idleness; Slothfulness.

DILL [*464*]. A plant whose aromatic seeds are used in cooking (Mt 23:23).

DIMNAH [1962] (*manure*). A Levite town in Zebulun (Jos 21:35). May be the same as Rimmono (1Ch 6:77).

DIMON [1904].

NIV+ DIMON'S

A town in Moab, generally called "Dibon," but it is called Dimon two times (Isa 15:9, ftn), c. four miles N of Aroer.

DIMONAH [1905]. A town in the S of Judah (Jos 15:22), probably the same as the "Dibon" of Nehemiah (Ne 11:25).

DINAH [1909] (*female judge*).

NIV+ DINAH'S

The daughter of Jacob and Leah (Ge 30:21). Rape of (Ge 34).

DINAITES NIV "judges" (Ezr 4:9).

DINHABAH [1973]. A city of Edom (Ge 36:32; 1Ch 1:43).

DINNER [5492, 367, 756, 1270, 2266, 2879, 5263].

NIV+ DINE, DINED

Eaten at noon (Ge 43:16).

See Feasts.

DIONYSIUS, THE AREOPAGITE [*1477*] (*belonging to Dionysus*). A member of the Areopagus, Athenian supreme court; converted by Paul (Ac 17:34).

DIOSCURI *See Castor and Pollux.*

DIOTREPHES [*1485*] (*nurtured by Zeus*). A domineering Christian leader condemned by John (3Jn 9-10).

DIPLOMACY

Ecclesiastical:

Paul, in winning souls to Christ—

1Co 9:20 To the Jews I became like a Jew, to win the Jews. To those under the law I became like one under the law (though I myself am not under the law), so as to win those under the law. [21]To those not having the law I became like one not having the law (though I am not free from God's law but am under Christ's law), so as to win those not having the law. [22]To the weak I became weak, to win the weak. I have become all things to all men so that by all possible means I might save some. [23]I do all this for the sake of the gospel, that I may share in its blessings.

In circumcising Timothy (Ac 16:3), in performing certain temple services to placate the Jews (Ac 21:20-25, w Gal 6:12).

Corrupt practices in:

The officers of Nebuchadnezzar's court to secure the destruction of Daniel (Da 6:4-15).

Instances of:

Abimelech (Ge 21:22-23; 26:26-31). The Gibeonites, in securing a league with the Israelites through deception (Jos 9:3-16). Of Jephthah, with the king of Moab, unsuccessful (Jdg 11:12-28). Of Abigail (1Sa 25:23-31). Of Hiram, to secure the goodwill of David (2Sa 5:11). Of Tou, to promote the friendship of David (2Sa 8:10). David, in sending Hushai to Absalom's court (2Sa 15:32-37; 16:15-19; 17:1-14). The wise woman of Abel (2Sa 20:16-22). Absalom winning the people (2Sa 15:2-6). Solomon, in his alliance with Hiram (1Ki 5:1-12; 9:10-14,26-27; 10:11), by intermarriage with other nations (1Ki 1:1-5). Ambassadors from Ben-Hadad to Ahab (1Ki 20:31-34). Jehoash purchases peace from Hazael (2Ki 12:18). Ahaz purchases aid from the king of Assyria (2Ki 16:7-9). The king of Assyria's field commander, in trying to entice Jerusalem to surrender by bombastic harangue (2Ki 18:17-37; 19:1-13; Isa 36:11-22). Sanballat, in an attempt to prevent the rebuilding of Jerusalem by Nehemiah (Ne 6).

The people of Tyre and Sidon, in securing the favor of Herod (Ac 12:20-22). Paul, in turning the Pharisees and Sadducees against each other at his trial (Ac 23:6-10).

See Prudence; Tact.

DISASTERS *See Burning.*

DISBELIEF *See Unbelief.*

DISCERNING OF SPIRITS The ability to discern between those who spoke by the Spirit of God and those who were moved by false spirits (1Co 12:10).

DISCHARGE, BODILY [2307, 2308]. Caused ceremonial uncleanness. Of a male (Lev 15:2-15,32). Of a female (Lev 15:25-33). Of a priest (Lev 22:3). *See Disease.*

DISCIPLE [1201, 4341, *899, 3411, 3412, 3413, 5209*] (*student*).

NIV+ DISCIPLES, DISCIPLES'

A name given to the followers of any teacher. Of John the Baptist (Mt 9:14). Of the Pharisees (Lk 5:33). Of Jesus (Mt 10:1; 20:17; Ac 9:26; 14:20; 21:4). The seventy sent forth (Lk 10:1). First called Christians at Antioch (Ac 11:26).

See Apostles; Righteous.

DISCIPLESHIP Following Jesus.

Evangelism: Making Disciples

Mt 28:18 Then Jesus came to them and said, "All authority in heaven and on earth has been given to me. [19]Therefore go and make disciples of all nations, baptizing them in the name of the Father and of the Son and of the Holy Spirit, [20]and teaching them to obey everything I have commanded you. And surely I am with you always, to the very end of the age."

Ac 6:7 So the word of God spread. The number of disciples in Jerusalem increased rapidly, and a large number of priests became obedient to the faith.

Personal Growth: Being a Disciple

Characterized by putting Jesus first in all things—

Mk 8:34 Then he called the crowd to him along with his disciples and said: "If anyone would come after me, he must deny himself and take up his cross and follow me. [35]For whoever wants to save his life will lose it, but whoever loses his life for me and for the gospel will save it. [36]What good is it for a man to gain the whole world, yet forfeit his soul? [37]Or what can a man give in exchange for his soul? [38]If anyone is ashamed of me and my words in this adulterous and sinful generation, the Son of Man will be ashamed of him when he comes in his Father's glory with the holy angels." (+Mt 10:32-39; Lk 14:26-27,33; Jn 21:15-19).

By following Jesus' teaching—

Jn 8:31 To the Jews who had believed him, Jesus said, "If you hold to my teaching, you are really my disciples. [32]Then you will know the truth, and the truth will set you free."

By fruitfulness—

Jn 15:5 "I am the vine; you are the branches. If a man remains in me and I in him, he will bear much fruit; apart from me you can do nothing. [6]If anyone does not remain in me, he is like a branch that is thrown away and withers;

such branches are picked up, thrown into the fire and burned. [7]If you remain in me and my words remain in you, ask whatever you wish, and it will be given you. [8]This is to my Father's glory, that you bear much fruit, showing yourselves to be my disciples.

By love for other disciples—

Jn 13:34 "A new command I give you: Love one another. As I have loved you, so you must love one another. [35] By this all men will know that you are my disciples, if you love one another."

See Commandments and Statutes, of God; Identification.

DISCIPLINE [3519, 3579, 4592, *4082, 4084*].

NIV+ DISCIPLINED, DISCIPLINES

Of armies, for disobedience of orders (Jos 7:10-26; Jdg 21:5-12). *See Armies.*

Church Discipline: *See Church, The Body of Believers, Discipline.*

See Chastisement, From God; Graces; Self-Control; Self-Discipline.

DISCONTENTMENT *See Contentment; Murmuring.*

DISCOURAGEMENT [3169, 4206, 4213+5648, 7919+8120, 8368, *126, 1591*].

NIV+ DISCOURAGE, DISCOURAGED, DISCOURAGING

See Despondency.

DISEASE [1821, 2688, 2716, 4700, 4701, 5710, 7665, 7669, 8137, 8831, *3798*].

NIV+ DISEASED, DISEASES

Sent from God (Lev 14:34). As judgments (Ps 107:17; Isa 3:17).

Instances of:

Upon the Egyptians. *See Plague.* Upon Nabal (1Sa 25:38), David's child (2Sa 12:15), Gehazi (2Ki 5:27), Jeroboam (2Ch 13:20), Jehoram (2Ch 21:12-19), Uzziah (2Ch 26:17-20).

Threatened as judgments (Lev 26:16; Dt 7:15; 28:22,27-28,35; 29:22).

Healing of, from God (Ex 15:26; 23:25; Dt 7:15; 2Ch 16:12; Ps 103:3; 107:20).

In answer to prayer:

Of Hezekiah (2Ki 20:1-11; Isa 38:1-8), David (Ps 21:4; 116:3-8).

Miraculous healing *See Miracles.*

Physicians employed for (2Ch 16:12; Jer 8:22; Mt 9:12; Mk 5:26; Lk 4:23). Remedies used (Pr 17:22; 20:30; Isa 38:21; Jer 30:13; 46:11), medicinal compress (2Ki 20:7), ointments (Isa 1:6; Jer 8:22), wine and oil (Lk 10:34).

Of the sexual organs (Lev 15; 22:4; Nu 5:2; Dt 23:10). *See Bleeding, Subject to; Circumcision; Menstruation.* Treatment of fractures (Eze 30:21).

See Affliction.

Figurative: (Ps 38:7; Isa 1:6; Jer 30:12).

Various kinds of: *See Bleeding, Subject to; Blindness; Boil; Congestion; Consumption; Deafness; Demons; Discharge, Bodily; Dropsy; Dysentery; Fever; Gout; Hemorrhage; Hemorrhoids; Indigestion; Inflammation; Insanity; Itch; Lameness; Leprosy; Paralysis; Pestilence; Seizures; Sore; Stammering; Sunstroke; Tumor; Worm.*

Of the bowels. *See Bowels.*

DISFELLOWSHIP

From God and People:

Of the uncircumcised (Ge 17:14). Of violators of the law, of unleavened bread (Ex 12:15), of sacrifices (Lev 17:9; 19:5-7), of purification (Nu 19:20). Of those defiled, by eating prohibited food (Lev 7:25,27; 17:10; 19:8), by touching the dead (Nu 19:13), by committing abominations (Lev 18:29; 20:3-6).

Commanded:

For blasphemy (Nu 15:31). For schism (Ro 16:17). For heresy (1Ti 6:3-5; Tit 3:10-11; 2Jn 10-11). For immorality (Mt 18:17-18; 1Co 5:1-7,11,13; 2Th 3:6).

See Excommunication.

DISGUISES [2924, 5795, 6634, 9101].

NIV+ DISGUISE, DISGUISED

Examples of (Ge 38:14; 1Sa 28:8; 1Ki 14:2; 20:38; 22:30; 2Ch 35:22).

DISH [113, 3998, 4090, 4094, 7505, *4243, 4402*].

NIV+ DISHES

Usually made either of baked clay or of metal. Orientals ate from a central platter or dish (Mt 26:23). Dishes used in the tabernacle and temple were made of gold (Ex 37:16; Nu 7:14ff; 2Ch 4:22, 24:14) or bronze (1Ki 7:38-40; 2Ki 25:14).

DISHAN [1914, 1915] (*ibex [?]*). The son of Seir (Ge 36:21,30; 1Ch 1:38).

DISHON [1914] (*ibex [?]*).

1. The son of Seir (Ge 36:21,30; 1Ch 1:38).
2. The grandson of Seir (Ge 36:25; 1Ch 1:41).

DISHONESTY [1299, 2039, 5327, 6404, 8400, *94, 96, 153, 156*].

NIV+ DISHONEST, DISHONESTLY

In not paying debts (Ps 37:12)—

Ps 37:21 The wicked borrow and do not repay, but the righteous give generously;

Jas 5:4 Look! The wages you failed to pay the workmen who mowed your fields are crying out against you. The cries of the harvesters have reached the ears of the Lord Almighty.

In collusion with thieves—

Ps 50:18 When you see a thief, you join with him; you throw in your lot with adulterers.

In wicked devices for gain—

Job 24:2 Men move boundary stones; they pasture flocks they have stolen. ³They drive away the orphan's donkey and take the widow's ox in pledge. ⁴They thrust the needy from the path and force all the poor of the land into hiding. ⁵Like wild donkeys in the desert, the poor go about their labor of foraging food; the wasteland provides food for their children. ⁶They gather fodder in the fields and glean in the vineyards of the wicked. ⁷Lacking clothes, they spend the night naked; they have nothing to cover themselves in the cold. ⁸They are drenched by mountain rains and hug the rocks for lack of shelter. ⁹The fatherless child is snatched from the breast; the infant of the poor is seized for a debt. ¹⁰Lacking clothes, they go about naked; they carry the sheaves, but still go hungry. ¹¹They crush olives among the terraces; they tread the winepresses, yet suffer thirst. (+Pr 1:10-14)

Pr 20:14 "It's no good, it's no good!" says the buyer; then off he goes and boasts about his purchase.

Isa 32:7 The scoundrel's methods are wicked, he makes up evil schemes to destroy the poor with lies, even when the plea of the needy is just.

Jer 22:13 "Woe to him who builds his palace by unrighteousness, his upper rooms by injustice, making his countrymen work for nothing, not paying them for their labor.

Eze 22:29 The people of the land practice extortion and commit robbery; they oppress the poor and needy and mistreat the alien, denying them justice.

Hos 12:7 The merchant uses dishonest scales; he loves to defraud.

Am 3:10 "They do not know how to do right," declares the LORD, "who hoard plunder and loot in their fortresses."

Am 8:5 saying, "When will the New Moon be over that we may sell grain, and the Sabbath be ended that we may market wheat?"—skimping the measure, boosting the price and cheating with dishonest scales,

Mic 6:10 Am I still to forget, O wicked house, your ill-gotten treasures and the short ephah, which is accursed? ¹¹Shall I acquit a man with dishonest scales, with a bag of false weights?

Denounced—

Jer 7:8 But look, you are trusting in deceptive words that are worthless.

⁹"'Will you steal and murder, commit adultery and perjury, burn incense to Baal and follow other gods you have not known, ¹⁰and then come and stand before me in this house, which bears my Name, and say, "We are safe"— safe to do all these detestable things?

Jer 9:4 "Beware of your friends; do not trust your brothers. For every brother is a deceiver, and every friend a slanderer. ⁵Friend deceives friend, and no one speaks the truth. They have taught their tongues to lie; they weary themselves with sinning. ⁶You live in the midst of deception; in their deceit they refuse to acknowledge me," declares the LORD. (+Jer 9:8)

Hos 4:1 Hear the word of the LORD, you Israelites, because the LORD has a charge to bring against you who live in the land: "There is no faithfulness, no love, no acknowledgment of God in the land. ²There is only cursing, lying and murder, stealing and adultery; they break all bounds, and bloodshed follows bloodshed.

Na 3:1 Woe to the city of blood, full of lies, full of plunder, never without victims!

Forbidden—

Lev 19:13 "'Do not defraud your neighbor or rob him. "'Do not hold back the wages of a hired man overnight.

Lev 19:35 "'Do not use dishonest standards when measuring length, weight or quantity. ³⁶Use honest scales and honest weights, an honest ephah and an honest hin. I am the LORD your God, who brought you out of Egypt.

Dt 25:13 Do not have two differing weights in your bag— one heavy, one light. ¹⁴Do not have two differing measures in your house—one large, one small. ¹⁵You must have accurate and honest weights and measures, so that you may live long in the land the LORD your God is giving you. ¹⁶For the LORD your God detests anyone who does these things, anyone who deals dishonestly.

Ps 62:10 Do not trust in extortion or take pride in stolen goods; though your riches increase, do not set your heart on them.

Pr 3:27 Do not withhold good from those who deserve it, when it is in your power to act. ²⁸Do not say to your neighbor, "Come back later; I'll give it tomorrow"—when you now have it with you.

Pr 11:1 The LORD abhors dishonest scales, but accurate weights are his delight.

Pr 20:10 Differing weights and differing measures—the LORD detests them both.

Pr 20:23 The LORD detests differing weights, and dishonest scales do not please him.

1Th 4:6 and that in this matter no one should wrong his brother or take advantage of him. The Lord will punish men for all such sins, as we have already told you and warned you.

Penalties for—

Lev 6:2 "If anyone sins and is unfaithful to the LORD by deceiving his neighbor about something entrusted to him or left in his care or stolen, or if he cheats him, ³or if he finds lost property and lies about it, or if he swears falsely, or if he commits any such sin that people may do— ⁴when he thus sins and becomes guilty, he must return what he has stolen or taken by extortion, or what was entrusted to him, or the lost property he found, ⁵or whatever it was he swore falsely about. He must make restitution in full, add a fifth of the value to it and give it all to the owner on the day he presents his guilt offering. ⁶And as a penalty he must bring to the priest, that is, to the LORD, his guilt offering, a ram from the flock, one without defect and of the proper value. ⁷In this way the priest will make atonement for him before the LORD, and he will be forgiven for any of these things he did that made him guilty."

Pr 20:17 Food gained by fraud tastes sweet to a man, but he ends up with a mouth full of gravel.

Zep 1:9 On that day I will punish all who avoid stepping on the threshold, who fill the temple of their gods with violence and deceit.

Zec 5:3 And he said to me, "This is the curse that is going out over the whole land; for according to what it says on one side, every thief will be banished, and according to what it says on the other, everyone who swears falsely will be banished. ⁴The LORD Almighty declares, 'I will send it out, and it will enter the house of the thief and the house of him who swears falsely by my name. It will remain in his house and destroy it, both its timbers and its stones.'"

Parable concerning—

Lk 16:1 Jesus told his disciples: "There was a rich man whose manager was accused of wasting his possessions. ²So he called him in and asked him, 'What is this I hear about you? Give an account of your management, because you cannot be manager any longer.' ³"The manager said to himself, 'What shall I do now? My master is taking away my job. I'm not strong enough to dig, and I'm ashamed to beg— ⁴I know what I'll do so that, when I lose my job here, people will welcome me into their houses.' ⁵"So he called in each one of his master's debtors. He asked the first, 'How much do you owe my master?' ⁶"'Eight hundred gallons of olive oil,' he replied. "The manager told him, 'Take your bill, sit down quickly, and make it four hundred.' ⁷"Then he asked the second, 'And how much do you owe?' "'A thousand bushels of wheat,' he replied. "He told him, 'Take your bill and make it eight hundred.' ⁸"The master commended the dishonest manager because he had acted shrewdly. For the people of this world are more shrewd in dealing with their own kind than are the people of the light.

Instances of:

Abimelech's servants usurp a well of water (Ge 21:25; 26:15-22). Jacob obtains his brother's birthright by unjust advantage (Ge 25:29-33), steals his father's blessing (Ge 27:6-29), Laban's flocks by skillful manipulation (Ge

30:31-43). Rebekah's guile in Jacob's behalf (Ge 27:6-17). Laban's treatment of Jacob (Ge 29:21-30; 31:36-42). Rachel steals the household gods (Ge 31:19). Simeon and Levi deceive the Shechemites (Ge 34:15-31). Achan hides the wedge of gold and the Babylonian garment (Jos 7:11-26). Micah steals eleven hundred pieces of silver (Jdg 17:2). Micah's priest steals his images (Jdg 18:14-21). Joab's guile in securing Absalom's return (2Sa 14:2-20). Ahab usurps Naboth's vineyard (1Ki 21:2-16). Judas's hypocritical sympathy for the poor (Jn 12:6).

See Diplomacy; Hypocrisy; Injustice; Treason.

DISOBEDIENCE TO GOD [*4202+9048, 5286, 6296, 577, 578, 579, 4157].

NIV+ DISOBEY, DISOBEDIENT, DISOBEYED, DISOBEYING, DISOBEYS

Originated in Adam (Ro 5:19). Characteristic of all (Ro 1:32; Eph 2:2; 5:6; Col 3:6; Tit 1:16; 3:3; Heb 2:2; 1Pe 2:8). Temptation to (Ge 3:1-5).

Denunciations against—

Nu 14:11 The LORD said to Moses, "How long will these people treat me with contempt? How long will they refuse to believe in me, in spite of all the miraculous signs I have performed among them? ¹²I will strike them down with a plague and destroy them, but I will make you into a nation greater and stronger than they."

Nu 14:22 not one of the men who saw my glory and the miraculous signs I performed in Egypt and in the desert but who disobeyed me and tested me ten times— ²³not one of them will ever see the land I promised on oath to their forefathers. No one who has treated me with contempt will ever see it.

Nu 32:8 This is what your fathers did when I sent them from Kadesh Barnea to look over the land. ⁹After they went up to the Valley of Eshcol and viewed the land, they discouraged the Israelites from entering the land the LORD had given them. ¹⁰The LORD's anger was aroused that day and he swore this oath: ¹¹'Because they have not followed me wholeheartedly, not one of the men twenty years old or more who came up out of Egypt will see the land I promised on oath to Abraham, Isaac and Jacob— ¹²not one except Caleb son of Jephunneh the Kenizzite and Joshua son of Nun, for they followed the LORD wholeheartedly.' ¹³The LORD's anger burned against Israel and he made them wander in the desert forty years, until the whole generation of those who had done evil in his sight was gone.

Dt 18:19 If anyone does not listen to my words that the prophet speaks in my name, I myself will call him to account.

Punishment of:

Of the Israelites by covenant curses (Lev 26:14-46; Dt 28:15-68). *See Wicked.* Of the Egyptians by plagues. *See Plague; Sin, Punishment of.*

Instances of:

Of Adam and Eve, eating the forbidden fruit (Ge 3:6-11). Of Lot, in refusing to go to the mountain, as commanded by the angels (Ge 19:19-20). Of Lot's wife, in looking back upon Sodom (Ge 19:26). Of Moses, in making excuses when commissioned to deliver Israel (Ex 4:13-14), when he struck the rock (Nu 20:11,23-24). Of Aaron, at the striking of the rock by Moses (Nu 20:23-24). Of Pharaoh, in refusing to let the Israelites go (Ex 5:2; 7:13,22-23; 8:15,19,32; 9:12,34; 10:20,27; 11:10; 14:8). Of the Israelites, in gathering excessive quantities of manna (Ex 16:19-20), in refusing to enter the promised land (Dt 1:26, w Nu 14:1-10; Jos 5:6; Ps 106:24-25). Of Nadab and Abihu, in offering unauthorized fire (Lev 10:1-2). Of Balaam, in accompanying the messengers from Balak (Nu 22:22). Of Achan, in hiding the wedge of gold and the Babylonian garment (Jos 7:15-26). Of Saul, in offering a sacrifice (1Sa 13:13), in sparing Agag and the spoils of the Amalekites (1Sa 15; 28:18). Of David, in his adultery, and in the killing of Uriah (2Sa 12:9). Of Solomon, in building places for idolatrous worship (1Ki 11:7-10). Of the prophet of Judah, in not keeping the commandment to deliver his message to Jeroboam without delay (1Ki 13). Of a man of Israel, who refused to smite the prophet (1Ki 20:35-36). Of Ahab, in suffering the king of Assyria to escape out of his hands (1Ki 20:42). Of priests, in not performing their functions after the due order (1Ch 15:13). Of the people of Judah (Jer 43:7), in going to dwell in Egypt contrary to divine command (Jer 44:12-14). Of Jonah, in refusing to deliver the message to the Ninevites (Jnh 1). Of the blind men Jesus healed, and commanded not to tell of their healing (Mt 9:30-31). Of the leper whom Jesus healed, and commanded not to tell of the fact (Mk 1:45). Of Paul, in going to Jerusalem contrary to repeated admonitions (Ac 21:4,10-14).

Of the Righteous. See *Commandments and Statutes, of God.*

Children. See *Children, Commandments to.*

DISPENSATION (*law or arrangement of a house*). It means "stewardship," "office," "commission" (1Co 9:17; Eph 3:2; Col 1:25), words which involve the idea of administration. In Ephesians the word refers to God's plan of salvation (Eph 1:10). The NT used the word in a twofold sense: with respect to one in authority, it means an arrangement or plan; with respect to one under authority, it means a stewardship or administration.

DISPENSATIONS An era of time during which mankind's obedience to God is tested according to the revelation of God available to him. From two dispensations (or covenants) to seven (innocence, conscience, human government, promise, law, grace, the kingdom) are held by various schools of interpretation.

DISPERSION Of the descendants of Noah (Ge 10). After building the tower of Babel (Ge 11:1-9; Dt 32:8). Of the Jews, foretold (Jer 16:15; 24:9; Jn 7:35). *See Diaspora.*

DISPLAY [2555, 3359, 3723, 5989, 6995, 7098, 7298, 8011, *617*, *1892*].
NIV+ DISPLAYED, DISPLAYS

General References to:
(Est 1:4; 5:11; Isa 39:2; Lk 20:46; Ac 25:23).

In Religious Service:
(2Ki 10:16; Mt 6:2,5,16; 23:5).

DISPUTE [1821, 3519, 4506, 5477, 6699, 8189, 8190, 9149, *1359*, *2427*, *3215*, *4547*, *5087*, *5202*, *5808*].
NIV+ DISPUTABLE, DISPUTED, DISPUTES, DISPUTING

About property. *See Property.*

DISSEMBLING *See Deception; Hypocrisy.*

DISSENSION [4506, *1496*, *2251*].
NIV+ DISSENSIONS

In churches (1Co 1:10-13; 3:3-4; 11:18-19).

DISSIPATION [*861*, *3190*]. Dangers of (Job 1:5). *See Drunkenness.*

DISTAFF [3969]. Used in spinning thread (Pr 31:19).

DITCH [1463]. *See Pit.*

DIVES (*rich*). In the Vulgate, the name given to the rich man in the parable of the rich man and Lazarus (Lk 16:19-31).

DIVIDING WALL [*3546*]. The barrier between the Court of the Gentiles and the Court of the Jews in the temple in Jerusalem. For a Gentile to go beyond it meant death (Josephus, *Antiq.* 15.11.5). Figurative of Christ bringing Jews and Gentiles together as one in the church (Eph 2:14).

DIVINATION [5241, 5727, 6726, 7876, 7877, 10140].
NIV+ DIVINATIONS, DIVINE, DIVINER, DIVINERS

The practice of foreseeing or foretelling future events or discovering hidden knowledge; forbidden to Jews (Lev 19:26; Dt 18:10; Isa 19:3; Ac 16:16). Various means were used: reading omens, dreams, the use of the lot, astrology, necromancy, and others.

DIVINITY OF CHRIST See *Jesus the Christ, Deity of.*

DIVISIONS [477, 1074, 1522, 2745, 4713, 7372, 8031, 10585, *1375*, *1496*, *5388*].
NIV+ DIVIDE, DIVIDED, DIVIDES, DIVIDING, DIVISION, DIVISIVE

Forbidden in the church (1Co 1:10). Condemned in the church (1Co 1:11-13; 11:18). Improper in the church (1Co 12:24-25).

Are Contrary to the:

Unity of Christ (1Co 1:13; 12:13). Desire of Christ (Jn 17:21-23). Purpose of Christ (Jn 10:16). Spirit of the primitive church (1Co 11:16). Are a proof of a sinful spirit (1Co 3:3). Avoid those who cause (Ro 16:17). Evil of, illustrated (Mt 12:25).

DIVORCE [1763, 4135, 8938, *668*, *687*, *918*, *3386*].
NIV+ DIVORCED, DIVORCES

Mosaic laws concerning—

Ex 21:7 "If a man sells his daughter as a servant, she is not to go free as menservants do. [8]If she does not please the master who has selected her for himself, he must let her be redeemed. He has no right to sell her to foreigners, because he has broken faith with her. [9]If he selects her for his son, he must grant her the rights of a daughter. [10]If he marries another woman, he must not deprive the first one of her food, clothing and marital rights. [11]If he does not provide her with these three things, she is to go free, without any payment of money.

Dt 21:10 When you go to war against your enemies and the LORD your God delivers them into your hands and you take captives, [11]if you notice among the captives a beautiful woman and are attracted to her, you may take her as your wife. [12]Bring her into your home and have her shave her head, trim her nails [13]and put aside the clothes she was wearing when captured. After she has lived in your house and mourned her father and mother for a full month, then you may go to her and be her husband and she shall be your wife. [14]If you are not pleased with her, let her go wherever she wishes. You must not sell her or treat her as a slave, since you have dishonored her.

Dt 24:1 If a man marries a woman who becomes displeasing to him because he finds something indecent about her, and he writes her a certificate of divorce, gives it to her and sends her from his house, ²and if after she leaves his house she becomes the wife of another man, ³and her second husband dislikes her and writes her a certificate of divorce, gives it to her and sends her from his house, or if he dies, ⁴then her first husband, who divorced her, is not allowed to marry her again after she has been defiled. That would be detestable in the eyes of the LORD. Do not bring sin upon the land the LORD your God is giving you as an inheritance.

Authorized for marital unfaithfulness—

Mt 5:31 "It has been said, 'Anyone who divorces his wife must give her a certificate of divorce.' ³²But I tell you that anyone who divorces his wife, except for marital unfaithfulness, causes her to become an adulteress, and anyone who marries the divorced woman commits adultery.

Mt 19:3 Some Pharisees came to him to test him. They asked, "Is it lawful for a man to divorce his wife for any and every reason?"

⁴"Haven't you read," he replied, "that at the beginning the Creator 'made them male and female,' ⁵and said, 'For this reason a man will leave his father and mother and be united to his wife, and the two will become one flesh'? ⁶So they are no longer two, but one. Therefore what God has joined together, let man not separate."

⁷"Why then," they asked, "did Moses command that a man give his wife a certificate of divorce and send her away?"

⁸Jesus replied, "Moses permitted you to divorce your wives because your hearts were hard. But it was not this way from the beginning. ⁹I tell you that anyone who divorces his wife, except for marital unfaithfulness, and marries another woman commits adultery."

¹⁰The disciples said to him, "If this is the situation between a husband and wife, it is better not to marry."

¹¹Jesus replied, "Not everyone can accept this word, but only those to whom it has been given.

Unjust reproved—

Mal 2:14 You ask, "Why?" It is because the LORD is acting as the witness between you and the wife of your youth, because you have broken faith with her, though she is your partner, the wife of your marriage covenant.

¹⁵Has not [the LORD] made them one? In flesh and spirit they are his. And why one? Because he was seeking godly offspring. So guard yourself in your spirit, and do not break faith with the wife of your youth.

¹⁶"I hate divorce," says the LORD God of Israel, "and I hate a man's covering himself with violence as well as with his garment," says the LORD Almighty.

So guard yourself in your spirit, and do not break faith.

From Gentile wives, required by Ezra (Ezr 10:1-16). Disobedience, a cause for, among the Persians (Est 1:10-22).

Final, after remarriage of either party—

Jer 3:1 "If a man divorces his wife and she leaves him and marries another man, should he return to her again? Would not the land be completely defiled? But you have lived as a prostitute with many lovers—would you now return to me?" declares the LORD.

Christ's injunctions concerning (Mk 10:2-12)—

Lk 16:18 "Anyone who divorces his wife and marries another woman commits adultery, and the man who marries a divorced woman commits adultery.

Paul's injunctions concerning—

1Co 7:10 To the married I give this command (not I, but the Lord): A wife must not separate from her husband.

¹¹But if she does, she must remain unmarried or else be reconciled to her husband. And a husband must not divorce his wife.

¹²To the rest I say this (I, not the Lord): If any brother has a wife who is not a believer and she is willing to live with him, he must not divorce her. ¹³And if a woman has a husband who is not a believer and he is willing to live with her, she must not divorce him. ¹⁴For the unbelieving husband has been sanctified through his wife, and the unbelieving wife has been sanctified through her believing husband. Otherwise your children would be unclean, but as it is, they are holy.

¹⁵But if the unbeliever leaves, let him do so. A believing man or woman is not bound in such circumstances; God has called us to live in peace. ¹⁶How do you know, wife, whether you will save your husband? Or, how do you know, husband, whether you will save your wife?

¹⁷Nevertheless, each one should retain the place in life that the Lord assigned to him and to which God has called him. This is the rule I lay down in all the churches.

Figurative of God's Judgment of Israel:

(Isa 50:1; 54:4-8; Jer 3:8).

See Certificate of Divorce; Marriage.

DIZAHAB [1903] (*that which has gold*). A place in the region of Sinai where Moses gave a farewell address (Dt 1:1).

DOCTOR [2620].

NIV+ DOCTORS

A physician (Mt 9:12; Mk 2:17; 5:26; Lk 5:31. Luke (Col 4:14).

See Physician; Disease.

DOCTRINES [1436, 2281].

NIV+ DOCTRINE

Origin in God:

Jn 7:16 Jesus answered, "My teaching is not my own. It comes from him who sent me. ¹⁷If anyone chooses to do God's will, he will find out whether my teaching comes from God or whether I speak on my own.

Set forth by church councils (Ac 15:6-29).

False:

Jesus accuses scribes and Pharisees of false teaching—

Mt 5:19 Anyone who breaks one of the least of these commandments and teaches others to do the same will be called least in the kingdom of heaven, but whoever practices and teaches these commands will be called great in the kingdom of heaven. (+Mt 5:20)

Mt 15:9 They worship me in vain; their teachings are but rules taught by men.' "

False teachers, to be avoided—

Ro 16:17 I urge you, brothers, to watch out for those who cause divisions and put obstacles in your way that are contrary to the teaching you have learned. Keep away from them. ¹⁸For such people are not serving our Lord Christ, but their own appetites. By smooth talk and flattery they deceive the minds of naive people. (+1Co 3:11,21; 1Ti 1:3-7; 6:3-5,20-21)

Accursed (Gal 1:6-8; Jude 4,11), rejected (Tit 1:10-11,14; 3:10-11; 2Jn 9-11). Admonitions against (Ro 16:17-18; Eph 4:14; Col 2:4,8,18-23; 1Ti 1:3-7; 4:7; 6:20-21; 2Ti 2:16; Tit 3:10-11; Heb 13:9).

False doctrine called: heresies (1Co 11:18-19; 2Pe 2:1-2), corruption (2Co 2:17; 11:3-4; Gal 1:6-8; 2Ti 2:14-18; 3:6-9; 2Pe 2:14-19).

Origin of false doctrine: people (Mt 15:9; Ro 16:17-18; 1Co 3:11,21; 2Co 2:17; Eph 4:14; Col 2:4,8,18-23; 2Ti 3:6-9,13; Tit 1:10-11,14; 2Pe 2:1-3), Satan (2Co 11:3-4; 1Ti 4:1-3), Antichrist (1Jn 4:3; 2Jn 7,9-11).

See Minister, False and Corrupt; Schism; Teachers, False.

DODAI [1862] (*beloved*). An officer in David's army (1Ch 27:4).

DODANIM *See Rodanim.*

DODAVAHU, DODAVAH [1845] (*beloved of Yahweh*). Eliezer's father (2Ch 20:37).

DODO [1861] (*beloved*).
1. The grandfather of Tola (Jdg 10:1).
2. The son of Ahohite (2Sa 23:9).
3. The father of one of David's mighty men (2Sa 23:24).

DOEG [1795] (*anxious*). An Edomite, present when Ahimelech helped David (1Sa 21:7; 22:9,22; Ps 52, T). Killed eighty-five priests (1Sa 22:18-19).

DOER OF THE WORD Example of belief (Mt 7:21; 12:50; Lk 11:28; Ro 2:13-15; 2Co 8:11; Jas 1:22-27; 4:11).
See Hearers.

DOG [3978, 7046, *3249, 3264*].
NIV+ DOG'S, DOGS
Price of, not to be brought into the sanctuary (Dt 23:18). Shepherd dogs (Job 30:1).

Habits of:
Licking blood (1Ki 21:19; 22:38), licking sores (Lk 16:21), returns to his vomit (Pr 26:11; 2Pe 2:22), lapping of (Jdg 7:5). Mute and sleeping (Isa 56:10-11).
Title of contempt (1Sa 17:43; 24:14; 2Sa 3:8; 9:8; 16:9; 2Ki 8:13; Isa 56:10-11; Mt 15:26).

Figurative:
(Php 3:2; Rev 22:15).

DOGMATISM *See Commandments and Statutes, of Men.*

DOMICILE Rights of (Dt 24:10-11).

DOMINION, OF MANKIND [4867, 4939, 5428, 5440, 10424, 10717, *794, 2026, 3262*].
NIV+ DOMAIN
See Mankind, Design of.

DONATIONS *See Liberality.*

DONKEY, DOMESTIC [912, 2789, 6554, 6555, 7230, 7241, *3229, 3942, 3952, 5689*].
NIV+ DONKEY'S, DONKEYS, DONKEYS'
Unclean for food (Lev 11:2-3,26; Ex 13:13).

Described as:
Knowing its master (Isa 1:3). Strong (Ge 49:14). Fond of ease (Ge 49:14-15). Formed a part of patriarchal wealth (Ge 12:16; 30:43; Job 1:3; 42:12).

Was Used:
In agriculture (Isa 30:6,24). For bearing burdens (Ge 42:26; 1Sa 25:18). For riding (Ge 22:3; Nu 22:21-23). In harness (Isa 21:7). In war (2Ki 7:7,10). Governed by a bridle (Pr 26:3). Urged on with a staff (Nu 22:23,27). Women often rode on (Jos 15:18; 1Sa 25:20). Persons of rank rode on (Jdg 10:3-4; 2Sa 16:2). Judges of Israel rode on white (Jdg 5:10). Young, most valued for labor (Isa

30:6,24). Trustworthy persons appointed to take care of (Ge 36:24; 1Sa 9:3; 1Ch 27:30). Often taken unlawfully by corrupt rulers (Nu 16:15; 1Sa 8:16; 12:3). Sometimes counted an ignoble creature (Jer 22:19).

Laws Respecting:
Not to be coveted (Ex 20:17). Fall under a burden, to be assisted (Ex 23:5). Astray, to be brought back to its owner (Ex 23:4; Dt 22:1). Astray, to be taken care of till its owner appeared (Dt 22:2-3). Not to be yoked with an ox (Dt 22:10). To enjoy the Sabbath rest (Dt 5:14). Firstborn of, if not redeemed, to have its neck broken (Ex 13:13; 34:20). Christ entered Jerusalem on (Zec 9:9; Jn 12:14).

Miracles Connected With:
Mouth of Balaam's opened to speak (Nu 22:28; 2Pe 2:16). A thousand men slain by Samson with a jawbone of (Jdg 15:15-17). Not torn by a lion (1Ki 13:28). Eaten during famine in Samaria (2Ki 6:25).

DONKEY, WILD
NIV+ DONKEY'S, DONKEYS, DONKEYS'
Inhabits wild and solitary places (Job 39:6; Isa 32:14; Da 5:21). Ranges the mountains for food (Job 39:8). Brays when hungry (Job 6:5). Suffers in time of scarcity (Jer 14:6).

Described as:
Fond of liberty (Job 39:5). Intractable (Job 11:12). Unsocial (Hos 8:9). Despises his pursuers (Job 39:5-7). Supported by God (Ps 104:10-11).

Illustrative of:
Intractableness of natural man (Job 11:12). The wicked in their pursuit of sin (Job 24:5). Israel in their love of idols (Jer 2:23-24). The Assyrian power (Hos 8:9). The Ishmaelites (Ge 16:12).

DOOR [1923, 1946, 6197, 7339, *2598, 2601, 4784, 5327*].
NIV+ DOORFRAME, DOORFRAMES, DOORKEEPER, DOORKEEPERS, DOORPOST, DOORPOSTS, DOORS, DOORWAY, DOORWAYS
Posts of, sprinkled with the blood of the Passover lamb (Ex 12:22), the law to be written on (Dt 11:20). Hinges for (Pr 26:14), made of gold (1Ki 7:5). Doors of the temple made of two leaves, cherubim and flowers carved upon, covered with gold (1Ki 6:31-35).

Figurative:
Door of hope (Hos 2:15), of opportunity (1Co 16:9; Rev 3:8), closed (Mt 25:10; Lk 13:25; Rev 3:7).

DOORKEEPER [6197+9068, 6214, 8788].
NIV+ DOOR, DOORKEEPERS
Keeper of doors and gates in public buildings, temples, walled cities, etc., often called "gatekeepers" (2Ki 7:10; 1Ch 23:5; Ps 84:10; Ezr 7:24; Mk 13:34).
See Gatekeepers.

DOPHKAH [1986] (*drive [sheep]*). The first stopping place of the Israelites after they left the wilderness of Sin. It is usually identified with the Egyptian mining center at Serabit el-Khadim in Sinai (Nu 33:12).

DOR [1799, 1888].
NIV+ HAMMOTH DOR, NAPHOTH DOR
A town and district of Israel (Jos 11:2). Conquered by Joshua (Jos 12:23; 1Ki 4:11). Allotted to Manasseh, although situated in the territory of Asher (Jos 17:11; Jdg 1:27).

DORCAS [*1520*] (*gazelle*). A Christian woman living at Joppa whom Peter raised from the dead (Ac 9:36-43).

DOTHAN [*2019*] (*two wells*). A place c. thirteen miles N of Shechem near where Joseph was sold (Ge 37:17) and where Elisha saw a vision of angels (2Ki 6:13-23).

DOUBLE-MINDED [6189, *1500*]. One who is a doubter, hesitant (Ps 119:113; Jas 1:8; 4:8).

DOUBTING [*242, 517, 603+1181, 1359, 1369, 1491*].
NIV+ DOUBT, DOUBTED, DOUBTLESS, DOUBTS

In prayer (Mt 21:21; Jas 1:6-8). Admonishings against (Pr 24:10; Mt 8:26; 14:31; 17:17; Mk 4:40; 9:19; Lk 8:25; 9:40).

Instances of:

Job (Job 3; 4:3-6; 9:16-23; 30:20-21). Abraham (Ge 12:12-13; 15:8). Sarah (Ge 18:12-14). Lot (Ge 19:30). Moses (Ex 3:11; 4:1,10,13; 5:22-23; 6:12; Nu 11:21-22). Israelites (Ex 14:10-12,15; 1Sa 17:11,24; Isa 40:27-28; 49:14-15). Gideon (Jdg 6:13,15). Samuel (1Sa 16:1-2). Psalmists (Ps 22:2; 31:22; 42:5-6; 49:5; 73:13-17; 77:3,7-9). Obadiah (1Ki 18:7-14). Elijah (1Ki 19:13-18). Jeremiah (Jer 1:6; 8:18; 32:24-25; 45:3; La 3:8,17-18; 5:20).

Christ's disciples (Mt 8:23-27; 14:29-31; 17:14-21; 28:17; Mk 4:38,40; 9:14-29; 16:10-11; Lk 8:25; 9:40-41; Jn 14:8-11; 20:24-27). John the Baptist (Mt 11:2-3). Ananias (Ac 9:13-14). Peter (Mt 14:30-31). Thomas (Jn 20:25). Early believers (1Pe 1:6).

See Cowardice; Murmuring.

DOUGH [1302, *2435, 5878*]. First of, offered to God (Nu 15:19-21; Ne 10:37). Kneaded (Jer 7:18; Hos 7:4). Part of, for priest (Eze 44:30). *See Bread; Oven.*

DOVE [3433, 9367, *4361, 5583*].
NIV+ DOVES

Sent out from the ark by Noah (Ge 8:8-11). Mourning of (Isa 38:14; 59:11; Na 2:7). Domesticated (Isa 60:8). Nests of (Jer 48:28). Harmlessness of, typical of Christ's gentleness (Mt 10:16). Sacrificial uses of (Ge 15:9). Prescribed for purification, of women (Lev 12:6,8; Lk 2:24), of Nazirites (Nu 6:10), of lepers (Lev 14:22). Burnt offering of (Lev 1:14-17). Trespass offering of, for the poor (Lev 5:7-10; 12:8). Sin offering, for those who touched any dead body (Nu 6:10). Market for, in the temple (Mt 21:12; Jn 2:14).

Symbolic:

Of the Holy Spirit (Mt 3:16; Lk 3:22; Jn 1:32). *See Pigeon.*

DOVE'S DUNG NIV "seed pods" (2Ki 6:25 and ftn). *See Plants of the Bible.*

DOWRY Sum paid to parents for a daughter taken as wife (Ex 22:16-17), by Shechem for Dinah (Ge 34:12), by Boaz for Ruth (Ru 4:3-9), by David to Saul for Michal (1Sa 18:25).

DOXOLOGY *See Praise.*

DRACHMA [2007, *736*].
NIV+ DRACHMAS

A Greek silver coin worth about a day's wages (Lk 15:8; Ac 19:19). The temple tax was two drachmas (Mt 17:24). In Ezr 2:69 and Ne 7:70-72 the term may refer to the Persian daric. *See Daric; Money.*

DRAGON [*1532*]. Any terrible creature, as a venomous serpent (Dt 32:33; Ps 91:13), a sea monster (Ps 74:13; 148:7; Isa 27:1; Eze 29:3; 32:2). Figurative of forces opposed to God: Egypt (Isa 51:9), Satan (Rev 12; 13; 16:13; 20:2). *See Serpent.*

DRAM *See Daric.*

DRAMA *See Pantomime.*

DRAUGHT HOUSE *See Latrine.*

DRAWER OF WATER One who brought water from a well or a spring to a house (Dt 29:11; Jos 9:23-27).

DRAWING [*2980*]. Of pictures on tile (Eze 4:1).

DREAM [2111, 2612, 2706, 2731, 10267, *1965, 1966, 3941*].
NIV+ DREAMED, DREAMER, DREAMERS, DREAMING, DREAMS

Transitory (Job 20:8). Vanity of (Ecc 5:3,7).

Revelations by (Nu 12:6; Job 33:15-17; Jer 23:28; Joel 2:28; Ac 2:17). The dreams of the cupbearer and baker (Ge 40:8-23), of Pharaoh (Ge 41:1-36).

Interpreted by Joseph (Ge 40:12-13,18-19; 41:25-32), by Daniel (Da 2:16-23,28-30; 4). Delusive (Isa 29:7-8).

False prophets pretended to receive revelations through (Dt 13:1-5; Jer 23:25-32; 27:9; 29:8; Zec 10:2). *See Vision.*

Instances of:

Of Abimelech, concerning Sarah (Ge 20:3). Of Jacob, concerning the stairway (Ge 28:12), the speckled goats (Ge 31:10-13), concerning his going down into Egypt (Ge 46:2). Of Laban, concerning Jacob (Ge 31:24). Of Joseph, concerning the sheaves (Ge 37:5-10). Of the Midianite, concerning the cake of barley (Jdg 7:13). Of Solomon, concerning his choice of wisdom (1Ki 3:3-15). Of Eliphaz, of a spirit speaking to him (Job 4:12-21). Of Daniel, concerning the four beasts (Da 7). Of Joseph, concerning Mary's innocence (Mt 1:20-21), concerning the flight into Egypt (Mt 2:13), concerning the return into Israel (Mt 2:18-22). Of Pilate's wife, concerning Jesus (Mt 27:19). Cornelius's vision, concerning Peter (Ac 10:3-6). Peter's vision of the unclean beasts (Ac 10:10-16). Paul's vision of the man in Macedonia, crying, "Come over to Macedonia and help us" (Ac 16:9), relating to his going to Rome (Ac 23:11), concerning the shipwreck and the safety of all on board (Ac 27:23-24).

DRESS [*1607, 4229, 4252, 4732, 8324, *314, 1907, 2439, 2667, 4314*].
NIV+ DRESSED, DRESSING, WELL-DRESSED

Of fig leaves (Ge 3:7). Of skins (Ge 3:21). Of other materials. *See Hair; Goats' Hair; Leather; Linen; Sackcloth; Silk; Wool.* Mixed materials in, forbidden (Dt 22:11). Men forbidden to wear women's, and women forbidden to wear men's (Dt 22:5). Rules with respect to women's (1Ti 2:9-10; 1Pe 3:3). Not to be held over night as a pledge for debt (Ex 22:26). Ceremonial purification of (Lev 11:32; 13:47-59; Nu 31:20). Tearing of. *See Mourning.*

Of the head:

Turbans prescribed by Moses, for the priests (Ex 28:40; 29:9; 39:28), by Ezekiel (Eze 44:18). Turbans and headdresses worn by men (Da 3:21) and by women (Isa 3:20; Eze 24:17,23). Shawls (Isa 3:23). Veils (Eze 13:18,21).

Various articles of:

Mantle, robe, or cloak (Ezr 9:3; 1Ki 19:13; 1Ch 15:27; Job 1:20), richly ornamented (2Sa 13:18), purple (Jn

19:2,5). Robe (Ex 28:4; 1Sa 18:4). Capes (Isa 3:22). Embroidered coat (Ex 28:4,40; 1Sa 2:19; Da 3:21). Sleeveless shirt, called coat (Mt 5:40; Lk 6:29; Jn 19:23; Ac 9:39). Cloak (2Ti 4:13; Jn 19:2,5). Trousers (Da 3:21). Skirts (Eze 5:3). Sashes (Isa 3:20). *See Veil.*

Changes of clothing, the folly of excessive (Job 27:16). Uniform vestments kept in store for worshipers of Baal (2Ki 10:22-23; Zep 1:8), for wedding feast (Mt 22:11). Presents made of changes of clothing (Ge 45:22; 1Sa 18:4; 2Ki 5:5; Est 6:8; Da 5:7). Garments of priests. *See Priest.* Dress in mourning. *See Mourning.*

Symbolic:

Filthy, of unrighteousness and judgment (Isa 64:6; Zec 3:3-4). Clean, of acceptance (Zec 3:4-7).

See Colors, Figurative and Symbolic.

DRINK [*5172, 5492, 5821, 6010, 6011, 8115, 8893, 8910, 8911, 8912, 8913, 9197, 9198, 9272, 9275, 9276, 10302, 10483, 10748, *3494, 3499, 3500, 3501, 3884, 3886, 4232, 4403, 4503, 4530, 4540, 4975, 5064, 5228, 5621*].

NIV+ DRANK, DRINKERS, DRINKING, DRINKS, DRUNK, DRUNKARD, DRUNKARD'S, DRUNKARDS, DRUNKEN, DRUNKENNESS

Beverages of the Israelites were water (Ge 24:11-18), wine (Ge 14:18; Jn 2:3), and milk (Jdg 4:19).

DRINK OFFERING *See Offerings, Drink; Libation.*

DRIVING [*5627].

NIV+ DRIVE, DRIVEN, DRIVER, DRIVER'S, DRIVERS, DRIVES, DROVE

Rapid, by Jehu (2Ki 9:20).

DROMEDARY *See Camel.*

DROPSY [*5622*]. (Lk 14:2).

DROSS [6092]. Refuse separated from molten ore or metal. Figurative of divine judgment (Ps 119:119; Pr 25:4; 26:23; Isa 1:22; Eze 22:18-19).

DROUGHT [1314, 1316, 2996, 3312, 7480]. (Ge 31:40; 1Ki 17; 18; Jer 14:1-6). Sent by God as a judgment (Dt 28:23-24; 1Ki 8:35; 2Ch 6:26; 7:13; Hos 13:15).

See Famine; Meteorology; Rain.

Figurative: (Ps 32:4; Isa 44:3).

DRUG ABUSE Not mentioned in the Bible, but the principles derived from alcohol abuse would apply to drugs. *See Abuse, Substance Abuse; Drunkenness.*

DRUNKARD [6010, 8893, *3500, 3501, 3884*].

NIV+ See DRINK

Described: (Pr 23:29-35).

End result:

Poverty (Pr 23:21; Isa 28:1,3), cut off (Joel 1:5), destroyed (Na 1:10), trodden under feet (Isa 28:1,3), shame (Hab 2:16), death (Dt 21:20-21). Insatiable appetite of (Hab 2:5-6). Excluded from the kingdom (1Co 6:9-10).

The psalmist mocked by (Ps 69:12). Fellowship with, forbidden (1Co 5:11). Punishment of (Dt 21:20-21).

See Drunkenness; Wine; Temperance; Abstinence.

DRUNKENNESS [8893, 8913, 9275, *3494, 3886, 4232*].

NIV+ See DRINK

Repugnancy of (Isa 28:7-8; 56:12; Hos 7:5,14; Joel 1:5;

3:3; Am 2:8,12; Mt 24:49; Lk 12:45). Mockery of (Ps 69:12; Pr 20:1).

Consequences of (Pr 21:17; 23:21,29-35; Isa 19:14; 24:9-11; 28:7; Hos 4:11). Death penalty for (Dt 21:20-21; 29:19-20; Jer 25:27). Excludes from the kingdom of God (1Co 6:9-10; Gal 5:19-21).

Forbidden (1Sa 1:14; Pr 23:20,31-32; 31:4-7; Lk 21:34; Ro 13:13; 1Co 11:21-30; Eph 5:18; 1Th 5:7-8; 1Pe 4:3). Woes denounced against (Isa 5:11-12,22; 28:1,3,7-8; Am 6:1,6; Na 1:10; Hab 2:15-16).

Figurative:

(Isa 28:8; 51:17,21-23; 63:6; Jer 25:15-16,27-28; 51:7-9; La 3:15; Eze 23:31-34; Hab 2:15-16).

See Abstinence; Drunkard; Sobriety; Wine.

Instances of:

Noah (Ge 9:21). Lot (Ge 19:33). Nabal (1Sa 25:36). Uriah (2Sa 11:13). Amnon (2Sa 13:28). Elah (1Ki 16:9). Ben-Hadad and his thirty-two confederate kings (1Ki 20:16). Xerxes (Est 1:10-11). Belshazzar (Da 5:1-6). Believers (1Co 11:21).

Falsely Accused of:

Hannah (1Sa 1:12-16). Jesus (Mt 11:19). The apostles (Ac 2:13-15).

DRUSILLA [*1537*]. Daughter of Herod Agrippa I; married first to Azizus, king of Emesa; later to Felix, procurator of Judea (Ac 24:24-25).

DRY PLACES [62, 2427, 2893, 2990, 2992, 2996, 3000, 3019, 3143, 3312, 3313, 3317, 3318, 4908, 5172, 5980, 6877, 7480, 7534, 7535, 7546, *3831*]. (Nu 20:2; 2Ki 3:9; Ps 68:6; Isa 1:30; Jer 14:3; 17:6).

DUKE NIV "chief." Of Edom (Ge 36:15-43; Ex 15:15; 1Ch 1:51-54). Of the Midianites (Jos 13:21).

DULCIMER NIV "pipes" (Da 3:5,10,15). *See Music, Instruments of.*

DUMAH [1873, 1874] (*silence, name of underworld*).

1. Son of Ishmael (Ge 25:14; 1Ch 1:30; Isa 21:11-12).

2. A city of Canaan assigned to Judah (Jos 15:52).

DUMB *See Mute.*

DUNG [883, 1645, 1672]. Laws were made regarding excrement of human beings and animals used in sacrifice (Dt 23:12-14; Ex 29:14; Lev 8:17). Dry dung was often used as fuel (Eze 4:12-15), also fertilizer (Isa 25:10; Lk 13:8).

DUNG GATE A gate in the Jerusalem wall that led out to the Valley of Hinnom where rubbish was dumped (Ne 3:14).

DUNGEON [1014, 1074+3975, 8846, *4987*].

NIV+ DUNGEONS

In prisons (Jer 38:6; La 3:53). *See Prison.*

DURA [10164]. A plain of Babylon where Nebuchadnezzar set up his image (Da 3:1).

DUST [85, 141, 709, 824, 1919, 6760, 8836, *3155, 5954, 5967*]. Man made from (Ge 2:7; 3:19,23; Ecc 3:20). Casting of, in anger (2Sa 16:13). Shaking from feet (Mt 10:14; Ac 13:51). Put on the head in mourning (Jos 7:6; 1Sa 4:12; 2Sa 1:2; 15:30; Job 2:12; 42:6).

DUTY [995, 1460, 1821, 3302, 3655, 5096, 5466, 6584, 6641, 9068, 9250, 10208, *2601*, *2646*, *4051*, *4488*, *5465*].

NIV+ DUTIES

1. Tribute levied on foreign commerce by Solomon (1Ki 10:15).

2. Escape from, sought by Moses (Ex 3:11; 4:1,10,13; 6:12,30), by Jonah (Jnh 1:1-15), by Ananias (Ac 9:13-14).

Of People to God:

To love (Dt 6:5; 11:1; 30:15-20; Jos 23:11; Ps 31:23; Mt 22:37; Lk 12:27). To obey (Dt 10:12-13; 30:15-20; Jos 22:5; Pr 23:26; Mt 12:50; 22:21; 23:23; Lk 17:10; Jn 14:15,21; 15:14; Ac 4:19-20; 5:29).

Of People to People:

To love (Lev 19:18; Mt 19:19; 22:39; Mk 12:31; Jn 13:34; Ro 13:8-10; Gal 5:14; Jas 2:8). To help (Isa 58:6-7; Mt 25:34-46; Lk 10:23-36). To forgive (Mt 18:21-35; Lk 17:3-4; Eph 4:32; Col 3:13). To practice "the golden rule" toward (Mt 7:12). To respect a brother's conscience (Ro 14:1-23; 1Co 8:1-13). To restore a sinning brother (Gal 6:1-2).

See Commandments and Statutes, of God; Children; Husband; Minister, Duties of; Parents; Wife.

DWARFED [1987]. Could not officiate at the altar (Lev 21:20).

DYEING [131].

NIV+ DYED

Of fabric (Ex 25:5; 26:14; Isa 63:1; Eze 23:15).

DYING *See Death, Physical.*

DYSENTERY [*1548*]. (Ac 28:8).

DYSPEPSIA *See Indigestion.*

E

EAGLE [5979, 10495, *108*].
NIV+ EAGLE'S, EAGLES, EAGLES'

General:

As food: Forbidden as food, classified as detestable (Lev 11:13; Dt 14:12). *See Birds.*

Species of: Osprey (Lev 11:18; Dt 14:17). Vulture (Job 15:23; Pr 30:17; Mic 1:16; Mt 24:28; Lk 17:37).

Flight of: The swift flight of, as an analogy of the swiftness of destruction to come (Dt 28:49; Jer 4:13; 48:40; 49:22; La 4:19). Its soaring capability (Job 39:27; Isa 40:31; Jer 49:22; Ob 4). Their graceful flight as a simile for various themes (Pr 23:5; Isa 40:31; Ob 4).

Care of young: Nest of (Dt 32:11; Job 39:27-30; Jer 49:16). Bears young on her wings (Dt 32:11). Life is renewed like an eagle's (Ps 103:5; Isa 40:31).

Figurative:

Of God's care (Ex 19:4; Dt 32:11). Of warriors (2Sa 1:23; Jer 4:13; 48:40; Hos 8:1). Of the swiftness of life (Job 9:26). Of renewed life (Isa 40:31).

Symbolic:

Of the glory of God (Eze 1:10; 10:14). An allegory, the "seed of the land" (Zedekiah) is planted by a "great eagle" (Nebuchadnezzar) and grows up to be a "spreading vine"; this spreading vine is then transplanted by another eagle (Hophra) (Eze 17:1-8). A lion with wings of an eagle representing the majesty and strength of Babylon (Da 7:4). Of redeemed man (Rev 4:7). Of the church (Rev 12:14).

EAR [263, 265+, 3087, *198*, 4044, 6064, 6065]. ·
NIV+ EARS

Attentiveness:

To what God says, to what is right, to his voice, to his commands, and to keep all his decrees (Ex 15:26; 23:22; Dt 11:13; 15:5; 28:1; Jer 11:6; Mt 13:23; Lk 8:15; Ac 17:11). To a truth worthy of attention (Mt 11:15; 13:9,43; Mk 4:23; Lk 14:35). To Jesus' words (Lk 19:48). A stringent demand for attention to the utterances of prophets who were inspired by the Spirit (Rev 2:7,11,29; 3:6,13,22; 13:9).

Blocked:

God will listen to the righteous, not to sinners (Ge 18:23-32; 1Sa 8; Ps 34:15-16; 145:18-19; Pr 15:29; Isa 59:1-2; Jn 9:31; 15:7; Jas 5:16-18; 1Jn 5:14-15). *See God, Access to; Righteous, Promises to; Wicked, Prayers of.*

The result of ignoring, the law (Nu 15:30-31; Dt 1:43-46; Pr 28:9; Isa 1:10-15; 24:4-13)

Ignoring the Lord (1Sa 2:27-33; 8; Isa 65:12-15; 66:4; Zec 7:11-14; Lk 9:26; 2Ti 2:11-13)—

Heb 6:4 It is impossible for those who have once been enlightened, who have tasted the heavenly gift, who have shared in the Holy Spirit, **5**who have tasted the goodness of the word of God and the powers of the coming age, **6**if they fall away, to be brought back to repentance, because to their loss they are crucifying the Son of God all over again and subjecting him to public disgrace. (+2Pe 2:1) *See God, Rejected; Jesus the Christ, Rejected.*

The result of ignoring the plight of the poor (Dt 15:7-11; Pr 21:13; 22:16)—

Pr 22:22 Do not exploit the poor because they are poor and do not crush the needy in court, **23**for the LORD will take up their case and will plunder those who plunder them. (+Pr 28:8)

Isa 10:1 Woe to those who make unjust laws, to those who issue oppressive decrees, **2**to deprive the poor of their rights and withhold justice from the oppressed of my people, making widows their prey and robbing the fatherless. **3**What will you do on the day of reckoning, when disaster comes from afar? To whom will you run for help? Where will you leave your riches? **4**Nothing will remain but to cringe among the captives or fall among the slain. Yet for all this, his anger is not turned away, his hand is still upraised. (+Eze 16:49-50; Zec 7:9-14; Jas 2:1-13)

See Poor, Warning Against Neglect; Poor, Oppression of.

The inability of idols to hear (1Ki 18:22-39; Ps 115:4-8; 135:15-18; Isa 46:7; Jer 10:2-5; 1Co 8:4-6; 12:2). *See Idol; Idolatry, Folly of.*

Hearing blocked by life's troubles (Mt 13:18-23, esp. 22). *See Sower.*

Ceremonies:

Pierced as a sign of servitude (Ex 21:5-6; Dt 15:16-17). Blood put upon, in consecration of priests (Ex 29:20; Lev 8:23), in cleansing lepers (Lev 14:14,25). *See Leprosy.* Anointed with oil in purifications (Lev 14:17,28).

Deaf:

Hearing closed to prevent obedience and subsequent salvation (Jos 11:20; Isa 6:10; 63:17; Jn 12:37-41; Ro 9:10-18; 11:25). *See Deafness.* The Lord, in refusing to listen to a petition (Dt 1:45), is petitioned to hear and to not refuse to answer (1Ki 8:28-53, esp. vv. 28-30,32,34,36,39, 43,45,49,52; 2Ki 19:16; Ne 1:6).

Fearful:

The nations, because of reports of what God had accomplished (Ex 15:13-16; Dt 2:24-25; Jos 2:8-9; 1Sa 4:6-9; Est 8:15-17; Ps 48:4-7), from the knowledge of God's majesty (Ps 99:1-3; 114:7-8; Eze 38:20). *See Fear of God.*

Of hearing God speak (Ex 20:19; Dt 5:25)—

Heb 12:18 You have not come to a mountain that can be touched and that is burning with fire; to darkness, gloom and storm; **19**to a trumpet blast or to such a voice speaking words that those who heard it begged that no further word be spoken to them, **20**because they could not bear what was commanded: "If even an animal touches the mountain, it must be stoned." **21**The sight was so terrifying that Moses said, "I am trembling with fear."

See Voice, of God; Anthropomorphisms, Acts. Israel, from reports of punishment (Dt 13:11; 17:12-13; 19:18-21; 1Ti 5:20). *See Punishment.*

Figurative:

Anthropomorphic uses of:—

Ps 17:6 I call on you, O God, for you will answer me; give ear to me and hear my prayer.

Ps 39:12 "Hear my prayer, O LORD, listen to my cry for help; be not deaf to my weeping. For I dwell with you as an alien, a stranger, as all my fathers were.

Ps 77:1 I cried out to God for help; I cried out to God to hear me.

Ps 80:1 Hear us, O Shepherd of Israel, you who lead Joseph like a flock; you who sit enthroned between the cherubim, shine forth

Ps 84:8 Hear my prayer, O LORD God Almighty; listen to me, O God of Jacob. *Selah*

Misguided:

The value of listening to instruction (Pr 1:8-9)—

Pr 2:1 My son, if you accept my words and store up my commands within you, ²turning your ear to wisdom and applying your heart to understanding, ³and if you call out for insight and cry aloud for understanding, ⁴and if you look for it as for silver and search for it as for hidden treasure, ⁵then you will understand the fear of the LORD and find the knowledge of God. ⁶For the LORD gives wisdom, and from his mouth come knowledge and understanding. ⁷He holds victory in store for the upright, he is a shield to those whose walk is blameless, ⁸for he guards the course of the just and protects the way of his faithful ones.

⁹Then you will understand what is right and just and fair—every good path. ¹⁰For wisdom will enter your heart, and knowledge will be pleasant to your soul. ¹¹Discretion will protect you, and understanding will guard you.

¹²Wisdom will save you from the ways of wicked men, from men whose words are perverse, ¹³who leave the straight paths to walk in dark ways, ¹⁴who delight in doing wrong and rejoice in the perverseness of evil, ¹⁵whose paths are crooked and who are devious in their ways.

¹⁶It will save you also from the adulteress, from the wayward wife with her seductive words, ¹⁷who has left the partner of her youth and ignored the covenant she made before God. ¹⁸For her house leads down to death and her paths to the spirits of the dead. ¹⁹None who go to her return or attain the paths of life.

²⁰Thus you will walk in the ways of good men and keep to the paths of the righteous. ²¹For the upright will live in the land, and the blameless will remain in it; ²²but the wicked will be cut off from the land, and the unfaithful will be torn from it. (+Pr 3:1-2; 4; 5:1-6; 6:20-29; 7:1-5; 19:27; 22:17-19) *See Counsel; Instruction; Knowledge; Wisdom.*

Listening to the advice of fools (Pr 13:20; Ecc 7:5-6). *See Speaking, Speech, Foolish.*

Misunderstood:

Taking the words of others too seriously (Ecc 7:21-22). Those listening to Jesus' words from the cross (Mt 27:46-47; Mk 15:34-35). Those who heard the voice of God (Jn 12:29).

Quick to hear:

Listening carefully to what others say (Jas 1:19).

Rational:

Words are tested by hearing (Job 12:11; 34:3). Powerful presentation (Job 29:21-25; 32:11-12). God will teach men (Isa 54:13; Jer 31:33-34; Jn 6:45; 1Co 2:13; 1Th 4:9; 1Jn 2:26-27).

Refusal to listen:

A rebellious people (Eze 12:2; Zec 7:11-14). The Jews (Jn 8:43; 10:20; Ac 13:44-50). The Sanhedrin (Ac 7:57). Men will reject the truth and accept a lie (2Ti 4:2-4).

Unconcerned:

People are not concerned with the pleading of God by his Spirit or by his prophets (Ne 9:29-30; Zec 7:11-12). *See Holy Spirit, Sin Against; Holy Spirit, Withdrawn From Unrepentant Sinners.* Idols, are absolutely indifferent to the prayers of people (Ps 115:6).

Israel, with ears which are open yet unable to hear—

Isa 6:9 He said, "Go and tell this people: "'Be ever hearing, but never understanding; be ever seeing, but never

perceiving.' ¹⁰Make the heart of this people calloused; make their ears dull and close their eyes. Otherwise they might see with their eyes, hear with their ears, understand with their hearts, and turn and be healed." (+Isa 42:18-20; 43:8)

Those not concerned to take Jesus' words seriously—

Mt 7:26 But everyone who hears these words of mine and does not put them into practice is like a foolish man who built his house on sand. ²⁷The rain came down, the streams rose, and the winds blew and beat against that house, and it fell with a great crash."

The reason Jesus speaks in parables (Mt 13:13). Those who hear the word but do not do what it says (Jas 1:22-25).

Worthless:

The parable of the sower (Mt 13:20-22; Mk 4:16-19; Lk 8:13-14). John the Baptist and Herod (Mk 6:20). Paul, in Athens at the Areopagus (Ac 17:19,32), before Felix (Ac 24:24-26), before Agrippa and Festus (Ac 26:1-29).

EAR OF GRAIN *See Grain.*

EARLY RAIN *See Rain.*

EARLY RISING

General references to:

To rise early (Ge 19:27; 26:31; Ex 8:20; 34:4; Jos 3:1; Jdg 6:38; 1Sa 5:4; 15:12; 17:20; 2Ch 20:20). Daybreak (Jos 6:15; 1Sa 9:26; Ps 46:5; 57:8; Da 6:19; Mk 16:2; Lk 24:22). Prior to daybreak (Ru 3:14; Pr 31:15). Morning (Ps 90:14; 101:8). *See Morning.*

To do evil: (Ex 32:6; Nu 14:40; Job 24:14; Isa 5:11).

EARNEST A pledge or token (Ps 86:17). The Spirit, as a guarantee of the future redemption of our bodies (Ro 8:23), of our inheritance (Ro 8:23; Eph 1:13-14), of the promise to come (2Co 1:22).

See Inheritance; Token, 1.

EARNESTNESS [5883, 8626, 8838, *1699, 1755+ 1877, 1757, 2118, 2418, 4498, 4666+4667, 5081, 5082, 5655*].

NIV+ EARNEST, EARNESTLY

An intense desire which results in repentance, produced by godly sorrow (2Co 7:11). Sincerity in your love (2Co 8:7-8). *See Sincerity; Zeal.*

EARRING [5690, 5755, 6316, 9366].

NIV+ EARRINGS

As an offering:

Offering of, for the golden calf (Ex 32:2-3). As a wave offering for the tabernacle (Ex 35:22). As an offering to the Lord to make atonement (Nu 31:50).

Types of:

Gold (Ex 32:2-3; Jdg 8:24; Pr 25:12). Gold studded with silver (SS 1:11).

Worn:

By the Israelites (Ex 32:2-3; Jdg 8:24). By Ishmaelites, as a cultural habit (Jdg 8:24). For idolatrous purposes (Ge 35:4; Isa 3:19).

EARTH [141, 824, 6760, 8073, 9315, 10075, 10077, 10309, *1178, 2103, 2973, 3180, 4922, 5954*].

NIV+ EARTH'S, EARTHEN, EARTHLY

Creation of:

By God—

Ge 1:1 In the beginning God created the heavens and the earth. (+Ex 20:11; 31:17)

2Ki 19:15 And Hezekiah prayed to the LORD: O LORD, God of Israel, enthroned between the cherubim, you alone are God over all the kingdoms of the earth. You have made heaven and earth.

2Ch 2:12 And Hiram added: "Praise be to the LORD, the God of Israel, who made heaven and earth! He has given King David a wise son, endowed with intelligence and discernment, who will build a temple for the LORD and a palace for himself.

Ne 9:6 You alone are the LORD. You made the heavens, even the highest heavens, and all their starry host, the earth and all that is on it, the seas and all that is in them. You give life to everything, and the multitudes of heaven worship you. (+Job 38:4)

Ps 90:2 Before the mountains were born or you brought forth the earth and the world, from everlasting to everlasting you are God.

Ps 102:25 In the beginning you laid the foundations of the earth, and the heavens are the work of your hands. (+Ps 104:5)

Ps 115:15 May you be blessed by the LORD, the Maker of heaven and earth. (+Ps 124:8)

Ps 146:5 Blessed is he whose help is the God of Jacob, whose hope is in the LORD his God, ⁶the Maker of heaven and earth, the sea, and everything in them—the LORD, who remains faithful forever.

Pr 8:22 "The LORD brought me forth as the first of his works, before his deeds of old; ²³I was appointed from eternity, from the beginning, before the world began. ²⁴When there were no oceans, I was given birth, when there were no springs abounding with water; ²⁵before the mountains were settled in place, before the hills, I was given birth, ²⁶before he made the earth or its fields or any of the dust of the world.

Isa 37:16 "O LORD Almighty, God of Israel, enthroned between the cherubim, you alone are God over all the kingdoms of the earth. You have made heaven and earth.

Isa 45:18 For this is what the LORD says—he who created the heavens, he is God; he who fashioned and made the earth, he founded it; he did not create it to be empty, but formed it to be inhabited—he says: "I am the LORD, and there is no other. (+Isa 66:1-2)

Jer 10:12 But God made the earth by his power; he founded the world by his wisdom and stretched out the heavens by his understanding.

Jer 27:5 With my great power and outstretched arm I made the earth and its people and the animals that are on it, and I give it to anyone I please.

Jer 32:17 "Ah, Sovereign LORD, you have made the heavens and the earth by your great power and outstretched arm. Nothing is too hard for you.

Jer 51:15 "He made the earth by his power; he founded the world by his wisdom and stretched out the heavens by his understanding.

Ac 14:15 "Men, why are you doing this? We too are only men, human like you. We are bringing you good news, telling you to turn from these worthless things to the living God, who made heaven and earth and sea and everything in them.

Heb 11:3 By faith we understand that the universe was formed at God's command, so that what is seen was not made out of what was visible.

2Pe 3:5 But they deliberately forget that long ago by God's word the heavens existed and the earth was formed out of water and by water.

Rev 10:6 And he swore by him who lives for ever and

ever, who created the heavens and all that is in them, the earth and all that is in it, and the sea and all that is in it, and said, "There will be no more delay!

Rev 14:7 He said in a loud voice, "Fear God and give him glory, because the hour of his judgment has come. Worship him who made the heavens, the earth, the sea and the springs of water."

By Christ—

Jn 1:3 Through him all things were made; without him nothing was made that has been made.

Jn 1:10 He was in the world, and though the world was made through him, the world did not recognize him.

Heb 1:10 He also says, "In the beginning, O Lord, you laid the foundations of the earth, and the heavens are the work of your hands.

Primitive condition of (Ge 1:2,6-7; Job 26:7; 38:4-7; Ps 104:5-9; Pr 3:19-20; Isa 40:22; Jer 4:23-26). *See Creation; God, Creator.* Created to be inhabited (Isa 45:18). By design (Isa 45:18).

Belongs to:

The Lord (Ex 9:29; 19:5; Dt 10:14; 1Sa 2:8; Ps 24:1; 50:12; Isa 66:1; 1Co 10:26). God controls (Job 9:6; Rev 7:1). God's footstool (Isa 66:1; La 2:1; Mt 5:35; Ac 7:49).

Cursed:

Cursed by God (Ge 3:17-19; 5:29; Ro 8:19-22).

Early divisions of:

(Ge 10-11; Dt 32:8; Ps 74:17).

Future of:

Perpetuity of (Ge 49:26; Dt 33:15; Ps 78:69; 104:5; Ecc 1:4; Hab 3:6). Will be judged (1Sa 2:10; Ps 96:13; 98:9).

Destruction of, foretold—

Ps 102:25 In the beginning you laid the foundations of the earth, and the heavens are the work of your hands. ²⁶They will perish, but you remain; they will all wear out like a garment. Like clothing you will change them and they will be discarded. ²⁷But you remain the same, and your years will never end.

Isa 24:19 The earth is broken up, the earth is split asunder, the earth is thoroughly shaken. ²⁰The earth reels like a drunkard, it sways like a hut in the wind; so heavy upon it is the guilt of its rebellion that it falls—never to rise again.

Isa 51:6 Lift up your eyes to the heavens, look at the earth beneath; the heavens will vanish like smoke, the earth will wear out like a garment and its inhabitants die like flies. But my salvation will last forever, my righteousness will never fail.

Mt 5:17 "Do not think that I have come to abolish the Law or the Prophets; I have not come to abolish them but to fulfill them. ¹⁸I tell you the truth, until heaven and earth disappear, not the smallest letter, not the least stroke of a pen, will by any means disappear from the Law until everything is accomplished.

Mt 24:3 As Jesus was sitting on the Mount of Olives, the disciples came to him privately. "Tell us," they said, "when will this happen, and what will be the sign of your coming and of the end of the age?"

Mt 24:6 You will hear of wars and rumors of wars, but see to it that you are not alarmed. Such things must happen, but the end is still to come.

Mt 24:14 And this gospel of the kingdom will be preached in the whole world as a testimony to all nations, and then the end will come.

Mt 24:29 "Immediately after the distress of those days "'the sun will be darkened, and the moon will not give its light; the stars will fall from the sky, and the heavenly bodies will be shaken.'

³⁰"At that time the sign of the Son of Man will appear in the sky, and all the nations of the earth will mourn. They will see the Son of Man coming on the clouds of the sky, with power and great glory. ³¹And he will send his angels with a loud trumpet call, and they will gather his elect from the four winds, from one end of the heavens to the other.

Mt 24:35 Heaven and earth will pass away, but my words will never pass away.

³⁶"No one knows about that day or hour, not even the angels in heaven, nor the Son, but only the Father. ³⁷As it was in the days of Noah, so it will be at the coming of the Son of Man. ³⁸For in the days before the flood, people were eating and drinking, marrying and giving in marriage, up to the day Noah entered the ark; ³⁹and they knew nothing about what would happen until the flood came and took them all away. That is how it will be at the coming of the Son of Man. ⁴⁰Two men will be in the field; one will be taken and the other left. ⁴¹Two women will be grinding with a hand mill; one will be taken and the other left.

⁴²"Therefore keep watch, because you do not know on what day your Lord will come. (+Mk 13:24-37; Lk 21:26-36)

2Pe 3:10 But the day of the Lord will come like a thief. The heavens will disappear with a roar; the elements will be destroyed by fire, and the earth and everything in it will be laid bare.

¹¹Since everything will be destroyed in this way, what kind of people ought you to be? You ought to live holy and godly lives ¹²as you look forward to the day of God and speed its coming. That day will bring about the destruction of the heavens by fire, and the elements will melt in the heat. ¹³But in keeping with his promise we are looking forward to a new heaven and a new earth, the home of righteousness.

Rev 20:11 Then I saw a great white throne and him who was seated on it. Earth and sky fled from his presence, and there was no place for them.

Rev 21:1 Then I saw a new heaven and a new earth, for the first heaven and the first earth had passed away, and there was no longer any sea.

A new earth (Isa 65:17; 66:22; 2Pe 3:13; Rev 21:1).

Residence of mankind: (Ps 115:16).

EARTHENWARE [3084]. *See Pottery.*

EARTHQUAKES [8323, *4939*] (*shaking, trembling*).
NIV+ EARTHQUAKE, QUAKE, QUAKED, QUAKING

(Job 9:6; Ps 18:7; 46:2-3; 104:32; Jer 4:24). *See Mountain.* As judgments (Ps 18:15; 60:2; Isa 13:13; 24:18-20; 29:6; Na 1:5; Rev 6:12-14; 11:13; 16:18,20). *See Judgment.* Prophecies of (Eze 38:19-20; Zec 14:4; Mt 24:7; Mk 13:8; Lk 21:11; Rev 11:19).

Instances of:
At Sinai (Ex 19:18; Ps 68:8; 77:18; 114:4-7; Heb 12:26). When Korah, Dathan, and Abiram were swallowed up (Nu 16:31-34). When Jonathan and his armorbearer attacked the garrison at Gibeah (1Sa 14:15). When the Lord revealed himself to Elijah in the still small voice (1Ki 19:11). In Canaan, in the days of Uzziah, king of Judah (Am 1:1; Zec 14:5). At the crucifixion of Jesus (Mt 27:51). At the resurrection of Jesus (Mt 28:2). When Paul and Silas were in prison at Philippi (Ac 16:26).

EAST [*4667, 6298, 7156, 7708, 7710, 7711, 7713, 7719, *424*].
NIV+ EASTERN, EASTWARD

An Important Direction for God:
Glory of God from (Eze 43:2). Angel from (Rev 7:2).

An Important Direction for People:
The Garden of Eden (Ge 2:8; 3:24). *See Garden.* An east wind (Ge 41:6,23,27; Ex 10:13; 14:21; Job 15:2; 27:21; 38:24; Ps 48:7; 78:26; Isa 27:8; Jer 18:17; Eze 17:10; 19:12; 27:26; Hos 12:1; 13:15; Hab 1:9). *See Wind.* A significant direction for the Hebrews (Ex 38:13; Nu 3:38; 10:5; Eze 10:19; 11:23; 43:2,4). God has removed our transgressions (Ps 103:12). Faces toward in worship (Eze 8:16).

People of:
Eastern people (Ge 29:1; Jdg 6:3,33). Eastern people had a special reputation for wisdom (1Ki 4:30; Mt 2:1-12). "People of the east" denotes Arab groups who accompanied the Midianites and the Amalekites in attacking Israel (Job 1:3; Jer 49:28; Eze 25:4,10). Kings of (Rev 16:12).

EAST WIND Hot, dry wind coming from the S and SE of Israel (Jer 4:11; Hos 13:15), destructive (Ge 41:6; Ps 48:7; Eze 17:10; 27:26), used as a means of salvation for Israel by God (Ex 14:21), used as a means of judgment by God (Isa 27:8; Jer 18:17; Jnh 4:8).

EASTER The day on which the church celebrates the resurrection of Jesus Christ. KJV "Easter" should be "Passover" as in NIV (Ac 12:4). *See Feasts; Passover.*

EASTERN SEA *See Dead Sea.*

EATING [*430, 433, 1356, 4312, 4310, 8286, 8425, 10030, 10301, *753, 1109, 1111, 1174, 2266, 2879, 2983, 4689, 5263, 5303, 5592, 5963*].
NIV+ ATE, EAT, EATEN, EATER, EATS

The host acting as waiter (Ge 18:8). Favored guests served an extra portion (Ge 43:34). *See Hospitality.* Sitting at table (Ex 32:6). *See Table.* Table used in (Jdg 1:7). Reclining on couches (Am 6:4,7; Mt 26:7,20; Mk 14:3,18; Jn 12:2; 13:23). *See Couch.* Washing before (Mt 15:2).
See Feasts; Food; Gluttony.

EBAL [6506, 6507].
1. A Horite (Ge 36:23; 1Ch 1:40).

2. A mountain of Ephraim located N and directly opposite Mt. Gerizim. These two mountains form the two sides of an important E-W pass. Upon entering the land of Canaan, after the time of Moses, the Hebrews were to confirm their covenant with Yahweh. This required that half of the tribes were to be on Mt. Gerizim to proclaim the blessings, the other half of the tribes were to stand on Mt. Ebal to proclaim the curses of the covenant with the ark of the covenant between them (Dt 11:29; 27:12-13; Jos 8:33). Altar built on (Dt 27:4-6; Jos 8:30). They were to sacrifice a fellowship offering there, eating and rejoicing in the presence of the Lord (Dt 27:7). Traditionally these were called peace offerings (Dt 27:7, ftn). All the words of this covenant were to be written very clearly on the stones of the altar that they set up (Dt 27:8). *See Gerizim.*

3. Son of Joktan (1Ch 1:22). *See Obal.*

EBED [6270] (*servant*).
1. Father of Gaal, who led the rebellion against Abimelech at Shechem (Jdg 9:26-45).

2. The son of Jonathan, one of those who returned to Israel with Ezra (Ezr 8:6).

3. The title *Ebed* was adopted, apparently by David, from an Akkadian practice, which was also used in Edom and Ammon. It was a designation of the class of court officials as distinguished from the older institution of tribal elders. In Ebed-Melech it becomes a proper name.

EBED-MELECH [6283] (*servant of Melek [king]*). An Ethiopian eunuch in Zedekiah's court who interceded on Jeremiah's behalf before King Zedekiah to have Jeremiah pulled out of a mud filled cistern (Jer 38:1-13). The prophecy concerning Ebed-Melech promised that he would survive the destruction of the kingdom as a reward for his efforts (Jer 39:16-18).

EBENEZER [75] (*stone of help*). A town of Ephraim near Aphek where the Israelites fought two battles with the Philistines and were defeated, losing the ark in the second battle (1Sa 4:1-11; 5:1). Later, after defeating the Philistines, the Israelites erected a memorial stone, naming it Ebenezer (1Sa 7:12).

EBER [6299, 1576] (*[regions] beyond [the river]*, or source of the word *Hebrew*).

1. The probable founder of the Hebrew race (Ge 10:21-25; 11:14-17; 1Ch 1:18-19,25; Lk 3:35). Prophecy concerning (Nu 24:24). Perhaps Eber in this passage should be understood not as a proper name but as the word for "region beyond" (here, beyond the Euphrates), which is the same as the name Eber in Hebrew.

2. A Gadite (1Ch 5:13).

3. A Benjamite (1Ch 8:12).

4. Another family of the tribe of Benjamin (1Ch 8:22).

5. A postexilic priest (Ne 12:20).

6. Father of Peleg and Joktan (Lk 3:35).

EBEZ [82]. A town given by lot to Issachar (Jos 19:20).

EBIASAPH [47] (*[my] father has gathered*). A son of Korah (1Ch 6:23,37; 9:19; 26:1). *See Korah, 4.* Abiasaph is an alternate form (Ex 6:24). *See Abiasaph.* Called also Asaph (1Ch 26:1). *See Asaph.*

EBONY [2041]. A highly prized core wood of a tree imported from S India, Ceylon, and perhaps Ethiopia. It was valued by the Egyptians, Phoenicians, Babylonians, Greeks, and Romans for its use, along with ivory, in fine furniture, vessels, and turned objects. It was also used in the Near East for idols. *See Image; Idol; Idolatry; Temple, Idolatrous.* Merchandise in (Eze 27:15).

EBRONAH *See Abronah.*

ECBATANA [10020] (perhaps *place of gathering*). A city located at the foot of the Alvand Mountain which is now Hamadan. The capital of Media, where during the reign of Darius I, a copy of Cyrus's decree was found which authorized the rebuilding of the temple in Jerusalem (Ezr 6:2,3-12). *See Cyrus; Darius; Medes; Persia; Temple, The Second.*

ECCLESIASTES

Author and Date:

Several passages strongly suggest that King Solomon is the author (1:1,12,16; 2:4-9; 7:26-29; 12:9; cf. 1Ki 2:9; 3:12; 4:29-34; 5:12; 10:1-8). On the other hand, the writer's title ("Teacher," Hebrew *Qoheleth*), his unique style of Hebrew and his attitude toward rulers (suggesting that of a subject rather than a monarch—see, e.g., 4:1-2;

5:8-9; 8:2-4; 10:20) may point to another person and a later period.

Outline:

I. Author (1:1).

II. Theme: The meaninglessness of man's efforts on earth apart from God (1:2).

III. Introduction: The profitlessness of working to accumulate things to achieve happiness (1:3-11).

IV. Discourse, Part 1: In spite of life's apparent enigmas and meaninglessness, it is to be enjoyed as a gift from God (1:12-11:6).

V. Discourse, Part 2: Since old age and death will soon come, man should enjoy life in his youth, remembering that God will judge (11:7-12:7).

VI. Theme Repeated (12:8).

VII. Conclusion: Reverently trust in and obey God (12:9-14).

ECCLESIASTICISM Jewish, rebuked by Jesus (Mt 9:10-13; 23:2-35), to be overthrown (Mt 21:19-20,28-44). Arrogance of (Mt 12:2-8; 23:4). Traditional rules of the Jewish (Mt 15:1-20; Mk 7:2-23). *See Church, The Body of Believers; Commandments and Statutes, of Men; Minister, False and Corrupt; Usurpation, in Ecclesiastical Affairs.*

ECLIPSE Of the sun and moon (Isa 13:10; 60:19; Eze 32:7-8; Joel 2:10,31; 3:15; Am 8:9; Mic 3:6; Mt 24:29; Mk 13:24; Ac 2:20; Rev 6:12; 8:12). *See Sun; Moon.*

ECOLOGY

Mankind created to care for the earth (Ge 1:28; 2:15; Ps 8:6-8; 115:16). The land was to enjoy rest every seven years (Lev 25:1-7); the land enjoyed its rest during Israel's exile (2Ch 36:20-21). Animals were to rest on the Sabbath (Ex 20:10). Fruit trees were not to be cut down in war time (Dt 20:19-20). A bird and its young were not to be caught together (Dt 22:6-7). Babylon judged for violence to the forests of Lebanon and its animals (Hab 2:17 w Isa 14:8).

ECONOMICS Political (Ge 41:33-57). Household (Pr 24:27; 31:10-31; Ecc 11:4-6; Jn 6:12-13). *See Family; Frugality; Industry.*

ECONOMY *See Economics; Government.*

ECUMENICISM (*the inhabited earth*). A movement among Christian religious groups—Protestant, Eastern Orthodox, Roman Catholic—to bring about a closer unity in work and organization. The word is not found in the NIV, but backing for the movement may be found in John 17 where Jesus prays for the unity of his church.

ED KJV transliterates the name of the altar erected by the tribes Reuben, Gad, and Manasseh at the fords of the Jordan (Jos 22:34); NIV "Witness."

EDAR *See Eder.*

EDEN [6359, 6360, 6361] (*paradise, delight*, possibly *flat land*).

1. The Garden of Eden (Ge 2:8-17; 3:23-24; 4:16; Isa 51:3; Eze 28:13; 31:9,16,18; 36:35; Joel 2:3).

2. Gods of (2Ki 19:12; Isa 37:12; Am 1:5).

3. A Gershonite (2Ch 29:12).

4. A Levite (2Ch 31:15).

5. A marketplace of costly merchandise (Eze 27:23-24).

EDER [6374, 6375, 6376] (*flock*).

1. A tower near Ephrath where Jacob encamped on the way back to Canaan (Ge 35:21).

2. A city of Judah (Jos 15:21).

3. A son of Beriah, grandson of Shaharaim, a Benjamite (1Ch 8:15).

4. A grandson of Merari (1Ch 23:23; 24:30).

EDICT [1821, 2017, 7330, 10601, 10628, *1409*]. A public proclamation, written and sealed with the king's signet and publicly read (Ezr 6:11-12; Est 2:8; 8:8-13; 9:1,13). Penalties were severe for violating a Persian edict (Ezr 6:11). Moses' parents are listed as an example of those who were not afraid to transgress the royal edict (Heb 11:23).

EDIFICATION, EDIFY, EDIFYING [*3868*, *3869*]
(Latin *to build up*).

NIV+ EDIFIED, EDIFIES

The root of this Greek word is found in various words and compound words in the NT, i.e., build (Mt 23:29; 26:61), building (Jn 2:20), builder (1Co 3:10; Heb 3:3-4), builds up (1Co 8:1), strengthen (1Co 8:10), edified (1Co 14:5,17), edification (Ro 14:19).

Paul uses the word group frequently but never in the literal sense of "building" a building. He uses it often in the metaphorical sense of "building" or "building up" the church, and of "building up" fellow believers. Paul refers to the church as a building (1Co 3:9; Eph 2:21), and of building the church upon the foundation that he and the apostles and the prophets laid (1Co 3:10,12,14; Eph 2:20).

Paul uses the words more frequently in the sense of "strengthening, unifying, making for peace." Christians are to build up each other in this sense (1Th 5:11). It is primarily love that "builds up" (1Co 8:1).

EDOM [121+824, 121] (*red*).

NIV+ EDOM'S, EDOMITE, EDOMITES, ESAU

1. A name of Esau, possibly on account of his being covered with red hair (Ge 25:25,30; 36:1,8,19).

2. A name of the land occupied by the descendants of Esau. It extended from the Gulf of Aqabah to the Red Sea, and was also called Idumea (Ge 32:3; 36:16-17,21; Jer 40:11).

Prophecies concerning (Jer 25:21-23; 27:1-11; Da 11:41). Noted for its wise men (Ob 8). Sins of (Ob 10-14). Wilderness of (2Ki 3:8).

See Edomite(s).

Figurative:

Of the foes of Zion (Isa 63:1).

EDOMITE(S) [121+1201, 121, 122] (*red*).

NIV+ EDOM

Called also Edom. Land of (Ge 32:3; Dt 2:4-5,12). Descendants of Esau (Ge 36). Rulers of (Ge 36:9-43; Ex 15:15; 1Ch 1:51-54). Kings of (Ge 36:31-39; Nu 20:14; 1Ch 1:43-50; Eze 32:29; Am 2:1).

Prophecies concerning (Ge 25:23; 27:29,37-40; Nu 24:18; Isa 11:14; 21:11-12; 34; 63:1-6; Jer 9:25-26; 27:1-11; 49:7-22; La 4:21-22; Eze 25:12-14; 32:29-30; 36:5; Joel 3:19; Am 1:11-12; 9:12; Ob 1-21; Mal 1:2-5). Protected by divine command from desolation by the Israelites (Dt 2:4-6), from being held in abhorrence by the Israelites (Dt 23:7). Children of the third generation might be received into the congregation of Israel (Dt 23:8). Refuse the Israelites passage through their country (Nu 20:18-21). Saul makes war against (1Sa 14:47). Garrisons of (2Sa 8:14). David conquers (1Ki 11:14-16; 1Ch 18:11-13), writes battle songs concerning his conquest of (Ps 60:8-9; 108:9-10). Ruled by a deputy king (1Ki 22:47).

Become confederates of Jehoshaphat (2Ki 3:9,26). Revolt in the days of Jehoram (2Ki 8:20-22; 2Ch 21:8-10). Amaziah, king of Judah, invades the territory of Edom, defeating ten thousand Edomites (2Ki 14:7,10; 2Ch 25:11-12; 28:17). The Lord delivers the army of, into the hands of Jehoshaphat (2Ch 20:20,23). A Jewish prophet in Babylon denounces (Ps 137:7; Eze 25:12-14; 35). Join Babylon in the war against the Israelites (Eze 35:5; Am 1:9-11; Ob 11-16).

EDREI [167] (*strong*).

1. A chief city of Og, king of Bashan (Dt 1:4; Jos 12:4). Assigned to Manasseh (Jos 13:12,31). Located c. ten miles NE of Ramoth-Gilead.

2. A city of Naphtali, the location is unknown (Jos 19:37).

EDUCATION See *Instruction; Teachers; School.*

EGG [1070, 1842, 2733, 4880, *6051*] (*whiteness*).

NIV+ EGGS

(Job 6:6; Lk 11:12). Appears also in the plural (Dt 22:6; Job 39:14; Isa 10:14).

EGLAH [6321] (*heifer*). The wife of David (2Sa 3:5; 1Ch 3:3).

EGLAIM [104].

NIV+ EN EGLAIM

A city on the border of Moab (Isa 15:8).

EGLATH SHELISHIYAH [6326] (possibly *the third Eglath*). A town near Zoar mentioned in prophetic oracles of judgment on Moab (Isa 15:5; Jer 48:34).

EGLON [6323, 6324] (*circle* ISBE; *young bull* KB).

1. A city of Canaan located between Gaza and Lachish (Jos 10:3,5,23), captured by Joshua (Jos 10:36-37; 12:12), assigned to Judah (Jos 15:39).

2. The king of Moab who captured Jericho (the City of Palms) from the Israelites as a judgment against them, controlling it for eighteen years (Jdg 3:12-14). Eglon was assassinated by Ehud, a judge, because the Israelites cried out to the Lord (Jdg 3:15-23).

EGOTISM See *Conceit.*

EGYPT [5191, 5213+, 7356+, *131+*, *2016*].

NIV+ EGYPT'S, EGYPTIAN, EGYPTIAN'S, EGYPTIANS

The Country of:

Fertility of (Ge 13:10). Imports of (Ge 37:25,36). Productions of (Nu 11:5; Ps 78:47; Pr 7:16; Isa 19:5-10). Irrigation employed in (Dt 11:10). Called, Rahab which is the poetic name for Egypt (Ps 87:4; 89:10), the land of Ham (Ps 105:23; 106:21-22). Exports of (Pr 7:16; Eze 27:7), of horses (1Ki 10:28-29). Limits of (Ge 29:10).

Abraham dwells in (Ge 12:10-20; 13:1). The king acquires title to land of (Ge 47:18-26). Joseph's captivity in and subsequent rule over. *See Joseph, 1.* Israelites in bondage in. *See Israel, Israelites.* Plagues in. *See Plague.* Civil war in (Isa 19:2). Overflowed by the Nile (Am 8:8; 9:5). Joseph takes Jesus to (Mt 2:13-20).

Prophecies against (Ge 15:13-14; Isa 19; 20:2-6; 45:14; Jer 9:25-26; 43:8-13; 44:30; 46; Eze 29-32; Hos 8:13; Joel 3:19; Zec 10:11).

See Egyptians.

Famine in (Ge 41; Ac 7:11). *See Famine.* Magi of (Ge 41:8; Ex 7:11; 1Ki 4:30; Ac 7:22). *See Magi.* Priests of (Ge 41:45; 47:22). Army of destroyed in the Red Sea (Ex

14:5-31; Isa 43:17). *See Army.* Armies of (Ex 14:7; Isa 31:1). Idols of (Eze 20:7-8).

River, or Brook of:

Perhaps identical with Shihor. *See River of Egypt; Sihor, Shihor.* A small stream flowing into the Mediterranean Sea, the western boundary of the land promised to the Israelites (Ge 15:18; Nu 34:5; Jos 13:3; 15:4,47; 1Ki 8:65; 2Ki 24:7; Isa 27:12; Eze 47:19; 48:28).

Symbolic: (Rev 11:8).

EGYPTIANS [5212, 5213, *130*].

NIV+ See EGYPT

Descendants of the Mizraim (Ge 10:6,13-14, ftn). Hospitality of, to Abraham (Ge 12:10-20). Slaves bought by (Ge 37:36). The art of embalming the dead practiced by (Ge 50:2-3,26). Oppressed the Israelites (Ex 1-2). Refuse to release the Israelites (Ex 5-10). Judged by plagues (Ex 7-12; Ps 78:43-51), firstborn of destroyed (Ex 12:29; Ps 78:51; 105:36; 136:10). Sent the Israelites away (Ex 12:31-42). Army pursued the Israelites, and was destroyed (Ex 14:5-31; Ps 106:7; Heb 11:29). Wisdom of (1Ki 4:30).

Refused to eat with the Hebrews (Ge 43:32). Abhorred shepherds (Ge 46:34). Eligible to membership in Israelite congregation in the third generation (Dt 23:7-8). Alliances with, without first consulting God, forbidden to the Israelites (Isa 30:1-5; 31:1-3; 36:6; Eze 17:15). Intermarry with the Israelites (1Ki 3:1).

Invasions of Israel: Under Shishak (1Ki 14:25-26; 2Ch 12:2-9), Pharaoh Neco (2Ki 23:29-35; 2Ch 35:20-24; 36:2-4). Aid the Israelites against the Chaldeans (Jer 37:5-11). An enthusiastic Egyptian instigated a rebellion against the Roman government (Ac 21:38).

Conversion of, foretold (Isa 19:18). Prophecies of dispersion and restoration of (Eze 29:12-16; 30:23-26). *See Egypt.*

EHI [305] (*my brother [is exalted]*). A son of Benjamin (Ge 46:21).

EHUD [179, 287] (*united*).

1. A Benjamite judge, the assassin of Eglon (Jdg 3:15-30; 1Ch 8:6). *See Eglon, 2.*

2. Son of Bilhan (1Ch 7:10).

EKED *See Beth Eked.*

EKER [6831] (possibly *offspring*). The son of Ram, part of the postexilic clan of Jerahmeel (1Ch 2:27).

EKRON, EKRONITES [6833, 6834] (perhaps *barren place* or *fertile place*). One of the five chief cities of the Philistines (Jos 13:3). Conquered and allotted to Judah (Jos 15:11,45; Jdg 1:18). Allotted to Dan (Jos 19:43). The ark of God taken to (1Sa 5:10). Temple of Baal-Zebub, the god of Ekron, at (2Ki 1:2).

Prophecies against (Jer 25:20; Am 1:8; Zep 2:4; Zec 9:5).

EL (*God; Mighty One*). A generic word for God in the Semitic languages. The chief Canaanite god was El. The God of Israel is usually referred to in the plural form, *Elohim*, or in compound names, as in the following articles.

EL-BERITH [451] (*a god of a covenant*). An alternate name for the god worshiped at Shechem, in whose temple some of the people of Shechem took refuge when Abimelech destroyed the city (Jdg 9:46). *See Baal-Berith.*

EL BETHEL [450] (*God [El] of Bethel*).

NIV+ BETHEL

A name given by Jacob to Luz because God there revealed Himself to him (Ge 35:7).

EL ELOHE ISRAEL [449] (*God, the God of Israel*). Name of an altar erected by Jacob near Shechem (Ge 33:20).

EL PARAN [386] (*tree of Paran*).

NIV+ PARAN

A place in the wilderness of Paran (Ge 14:6).

EL SHADDAI (*God of mountains* or *God who is self-sufficient* KB or in older etymology *God of breasts*).

NIV+ GOD ALMIGHTY

Translated "God Almighty" in the NIV following the NT rendering of *Shaddai* by *pantokrator*. The name by which God appeared to Abraham, Isaac, and Jacob (Ex 6:3).

See God, Names of; Shaddai.

ELA [452]. The father of Shimei, one of Solomon's district governors (1Ki 4:18).

ELAH [462, 463] (*a species of a mighty tree*).

NIV+ ELAH'S

1. A chief of Edom (Ge 36:41).

2. The valley (valley of the terebinth), in which David killed Goliath (1Sa 17:2,19; 21:9).

3. The king of Israel, son of Baasha; killed by Zimri (1Ki 16:8-10).

4. The father of Hoshea, the last king of Israel (2Ki 15:30; 17:1; 18:1,9).

5. The son of Caleb (1Ch 4:15).

6. The Benjamite, son of Uzzi (1Ch 9:8).

7. *See Ela.*

ELAM [6520, 6521] (*highland*).

NIV+ ELAM'S, ELAMITES (*highland*).

1. The son of Shem (Ge 10:22; 1Ch 1:17).

2. The son of Shashak (1Ch 8:24).

3. The son of Meshelemiah (1Ch 26:3).

4. The ancestor of a family which returned from the Exile (Ezr 2:7; Ne 7:12).

5. Another ancestor of a returned family (Ezr 2:31; Ne 7:34).

6. The father of two sons returned from the Exile (Ezr 8:7).

7. The ancestor of a man who married a foreign woman (Ezr 10:2,26).

8. A chief who sealed a covenant with Nehemiah (Ne 10:14).

9. A priest who took part in the dedication of the wall (Ne 12:42).

10. A country situated on the E side of the Tigris opposite Babylonia; was one of the earliest civilizations; figures prominently in Babylonian and Assyrian history. Some of its people were brought to Samaria by the Assyrians (Ezr 4:9-10). Elamites at Jerusalem on the Day of Pentecost (Ac 2:9).

ELAMITES [10551, *1780*] (*highland*).

NIV+ ELAM

Descendants of Shem (Ge 10:22). They were present at Pentecost (Ac 2:9).

ELASAH [543] (*God has fashioned*).

1. The son of Pashhur the priest, and one of those with foreign wives (Ezr 10:22).

2. The son of Shaphan and one of Zedekiah's emissaries to Nebuchadnezzar who took a letter to the exiles in Babylon for Jeremiah (Jer 29:3).

ELATH [393, 397] (*grove of large trees*). A city on the coast of Edom situated at the head of the Gulf of Arabah (Dt 2:8; 1Ki 9:26; 2Ch 8:17).

The conquest of, by the Edomites (2Ki 16:6), by Uzziah (2Ch 26:1-2).

ELDAAH [456] (*God [El] is [my] desire*). A descendant of Abraham (Ge 25:4; 1Ch 1:33).

ELDAD [455] (*beloved of God [El]; possibly Dadi [pagan god] is god*). One of Moses' 70 elders (Nu 11:24-29).

ELDERS [2418, 10675, *1172, 4564, 4565, 5236*].

NIV+ ELDER, ELDERLY

In the Mosaic system: *See Elders, Council of; Government, Mosaic.*

In the NT church:

Received gifts on behalf of church—
Ac 11:29 The disciples, each according to his ability, decided to provide help for the brothers living in Judea. ³⁰This they did, sending their gift to the elders by Barnabas and Saul.

Ordained—
Ac 14:23 Paul and Barnabas appointed elders for them in each church and, with prayer and fasting, committed them to the Lord, in whom they had put their trust.
Tit 1:5 The reason I left you in Crete was that you might straighten out what was left unfinished and appoint elders in every town, as I directed you. ⁶An elder must be blameless, the husband of but one wife, a man whose children believe and are not open to the charge of being wild and disobedient. ⁷Since an overseer is entrusted with God's work, he must be blameless—not overbearing, not quick-tempered, not given to drunkenness, not violent, not pursuing dishonest gain. ⁸Rather he must be hospitable, one who loves what is good, who is self-controlled, upright, holy and disciplined. ⁹He must hold firmly to the trustworthy message as it has been taught, so that he can encourage others by sound doctrine and refute those who oppose it.

Overseers of the church (Ac 15:1-29)—
Ac 16:4 As they traveled from town to town, they delivered the decisions reached by the apostles and elders in Jerusalem for the people to obey. ⁵So the churches were strengthened in the faith and grew daily in numbers.
Ac 20:17 From Miletus, Paul sent to Ephesus for the elders of the church.
Ac 20:28 Keep watch over yourselves and all the flock of which the Holy Spirit has made you overseers. Be shepherds of the church of God, which he bought with his own blood. ²⁹I know that after I leave, savage wolves will come in among you and will not spare the flock. ³⁰Even from your own number men will arise and distort the truth in order to draw away disciples after them. ³¹So be on your guard! Remember that for three years I never stopped warning each of you night and day with tears.
³²"Now I commit you to God and to the word of his grace, which can build you up and give you an inheritance among all those who are sanctified.

Ac 21:18 The next day Paul and the rest of us went to see James, and all the elders were present.
1Ti 5:17 The elders who direct the affairs of the church well are worthy of double honor, especially those whose work is preaching and teaching. ¹⁸For the Scripture says, "Do not muzzle the ox while it is treading out the grain," and "The worker deserves his wages." ¹⁹Do not entertain an accusation against an elder unless it is brought by two or three witnesses.
1Pe 5:1 To the elders among you, I appeal as a fellow elder, a witness of Christ's sufferings and one who also will share in the glory to be revealed: ²Be shepherds of God's flock that is under your care, serving as overseers—not because you must, but because you are willing, as God wants you to be; not greedy for money, but eager to serve; ³not lording it over those entrusted to you, but being examples to the flock. ⁴And when the Chief Shepherd appears, you will receive the crown of glory that will never fade away.
⁵Young men, in the same way be submissive to those who are older. All of you, clothe yourselves with humility toward one another, because, "God opposes the proud but gives grace to the humble."

Performed ecclesiastical duties—
1Ti 4:14 Do not neglect your gift, which was given you through a prophetic message when the body of elders laid their hands on you.
Jas 5:14 Is any one of you sick? He should call the elders of the church to pray over him and anoint him with oil in the name of the Lord. ¹⁵And the prayer offered in faith will make the sick person well; the Lord will raise him up. If he has sinned, he will be forgiven.

Apocalyptic Vision of the Twenty-four Elders:
(Rev 4:4,10; 5:5-6,8,11,14; 7:11,13; 11:16; 14:3; 19:4).
See Bishop; Church, Government of the Christian Church; Deacon; Overseer.

ELDERS, COUNCIL OF

Chosen elders of the nation, vested with representative, judicial, and executive authority (Ex 4:29; 5:15,19; 6:14-25; 12:21; Nu 11:16-30). Called the council (Nu 16:2; Mk 15:43); council of the elders (Ps 107:32; Lk 22:66); elders of Israel (Ex 3:16,18), of Judah (1Sa 30:26), of the people (Ex 19:7), of the community (Lev 4:15), of the Jews (Ezr 5:5); Sanhedrin (Mt 5:22; 26:59; Ac 4:15; 5:21-41).

Closely associated with Moses and subsequent leaders (Ex 3:16-18; 4:29; 12:21; 17:5-6; 18:12; 19:7; 24:1,14; Nu 16:25; Dt 5:23; 27:1; 29:10; 31:9,28; Jos 7:6; 8:10,33; 23:2; 24:1; Jdg 11:5-11; Ac 5:17-18,21). Made confession of sin in behalf of the nation (Lev 4:15; 9:1).

Miscellaneous facts relating to—
Demands a king (1Sa 8:4-10,19-22). Saul pleads to be honored before (1Sa 15:30). Chooses David as king (2Sa 3:17-21; 5:3; 1Ch 11:3). Closely associated with David (2Sa 12:17; 1Ch 15:25; 21:16). Joins Absalom in his usurpation (2Sa 17:4). David rebukes (2Sa 19:11). Assists Solomon at the dedication of the temple (1Ki 8:1-3; 2Ch 5:2-4). Counsels King Rehoboam (1Ki 12:6-8,13). Counsels King Ahab (1Ki 20:7-8). Josiah assembles, to hear the law of the Lord (2Ki 23:1; 2Ch 34:29,31).

Legislates with Ezra in reforming certain marriages with the Gentiles (Ezr 10:8-14). Legislates in later times (Mt 15:2,7-9; Mk 7:1-13). Sits as a court (Jer 26:10-24). Constitutes, with priests and scribes, a court for the trial of both civil and ecclesiastical causes (Mt 21:23; 26:3-5,57-68; 27:1-2; Mk 8:31; 14:53-65; 15:1; Lk 22:52-71; Ac

4:1-21; 6:12-15). Seeks counsel from prophets (Eze 8:1; 14:1; 20:1,3). Corrupt (1Ki 21:8-14; Eze 8:11-12; Mt 26:14-15; 27:3-4).

A similar council existed among the Egyptians (Ge 50:7), the Midianites and Moabites (Nu 22:4,7-8), the Gibeonites (Jos 9:11).

ELEAD [537] (*God [El] has testified*). A descendant of Ephraim (1Ch 7:21).

ELEADAH [538] (*God [El] has adorned*). The son of Ephraim (1Ch 7:20).

ELEALEH [541, 542] (*God [El] is high*). A city in Transjordan, rebuilt by the tribe of Reuben (Nu 32:3,37). Repossessed by the Moabites (Isa 15:4; 16:9; Jer 48:34).

ELEASAH [543] (*God [El] has fashioned*).

1. A person or family of the clan of Jerahmeel of the tribe of Judah (1Ch 2:39-40).

2. A member of the tribe of Benjamin, descended from Saul (1Ch 8:37; 9:43).

ELEAZAR [540, *1789*] (*God [El] is a help*).

NIV+ ELEAZAR'S

1. The son of Aaron (Ex 6:23; 28:1). He married a daughter of Putiel, who bore him Phinehas (Ex 6:25). After the death of Nadab and Abihu he is made the chief of the tribe of Levi (Nu 3:32). The duties of (Nu 4:16).

He succeeds Aaron as the high priest (Nu 20:26,28; Dt 10:6). Assists Moses in the census (Nu 26:63). With Joshua, divides Israel (Nu 34:17). Death and burial of (Jos 24:33). Descendants of (1Ch 24:1-19).

2. An inhabitant of Kiriath Jearim who attended the ark (1Sa 7:1-2).

3. The son of Dodai the Ahohite, and one of David's three mighty men (2Sa 23:9-10,13; 1Ch 11:12).

4. A Merarite Levite (1Ch 23:21-22; 24:28).

5. The son of Phinehas (Ezr 8:33; Ne 12:42).

6. A returned Israelite exile (Ezr 10:25).

7. The great-grandfather of Joseph, the husband of Mary (Mt 1:15).

ELECT [*1723, 1724*] (*chosen*).

NIV+ ELECTION

Those chosen by God for some special purpose (Ps 106:23; Isa 43:10; 45:4). Among the elect mentioned in Scripture are Moses, the Israelites, Christ, the angels, Christ's disciples.

ELECTION [*1724*].

NIV+ ELECT

Of Israel (Dt 7:6; Isa 45:4). Of rulers (Ne 11:1). Of Christ as Messiah (Isa 42:1; 1Pe 2:6).

By grace (Mt 22:14)—

Jn 15:16 You did not choose me, but I chose you and appointed you to go and bear fruit—fruit that will last. Then the Father will give you whatever you ask in my name.

Jn 17:6 "I have revealed you to those whom you gave me out of the world. They were yours; you gave them to me and they have obeyed your word. (+Ro 11:5)

Eph 1:4 For he chose us in him before the creation of the world to be holy and blameless in his sight. In love

Eph 2:10 For we are God's workmanship, created in Christ Jesus to do good works, which God prepared in advance for us to do.

2Th 2:13 But we ought always to thank God for you,

brothers loved by the Lord, because from the beginning God chose you to be saved through the sanctifying work of the Spirit and through belief in the truth. (+1Pe 2:9)

Of ministers (Lk 6:13; Ac 9:15). Of good angels (1Ti 5:21). Of churches (1Pe 5:13).

See Chosen; Elect; Predestination.

ELECTIONEERING By Absalom (2Sa 15:1-6). Adonijah (1Ki 1:7). *See Candidate.*

ELEGY A song of sorrow.

By David, on Saul and Jonathan—

2Sa 1:17 David took up this lament concerning Saul and his son Jonathan,

2Sa 1:19 "Your glory, O Israel, lies slain on your heights. How the mighty have fallen!

²⁰"Tell it not in Gath, proclaim it not in the streets of Ashkelon, lest the daughters of the Philistines be glad, lest the daughters of the uncircumcised rejoice.

²¹"O mountains of Gilboa, may you have neither dew nor rain, nor fields that yield offerings [of grain]. For there the shield of the mighty was defiled, the shield of Saul—no longer rubbed with oil. ²²From the blood of the slain, from the flesh of the mighty, the bow of Jonathan did not turn back, the sword of Saul did not return unsatisfied.

²³"Saul and Jonathan—in life they were loved and gracious, and in death they were not parted. They were swifter than eagles, they were stronger than lions.

²⁴"O daughters of Israel, weep for Saul, who clothed you in scarlet and finery, who adorned your garments with ornaments of gold.

²⁵"How the mighty have fallen in battle! Jonathan lies slain on your heights. ²⁶I grieve for you, Jonathan my brother; you were very dear to me. Your love for me was wonderful, more wonderful than that of women.

²⁷"How the mighty have fallen! The weapons of war have perished!"

On Abner—

2Sa 3:33 The king sang this lament for Abner:

"Should Abner have died as the lawless die? ³⁴Your hands were not bound, your feet were not fettered. You fell as one falls before wicked men."

And all the people wept over him again.

See Lamentations, Book of; Poetry.

ELEMENTS [*5122*] (*rows, series, alphabet, first principles of a science, physical elements, heavenly bodies, planets, personal cosmic powers*).

NIV+ ELEMENTARY

Heathen deities and practices (Gal 4:3,9), rudiments (Col 2:8,20), first principles (Heb 5:12). *See Basic Principles of this World.*

ELEPH *See Haeleph.*

ELEPHANT The Hebrew *behemoth* may be the elephant or hippopotamus (Job 40:15, ftn). *See Ivory.*

ELEVEN, THE [*1894*]. The eleven apostles who remained after the defection of Judas (Mk 16:14; Lk 24:9,33; Ac 2:14).

ELHANAN [*481*] (*God [El] is gracious*).

1. The son of Dodo, one of David's heroes (2Sa 23:24; 1Ch 11:26).

2. A distinguished warrior in the time of David who killed Lahmi the brother of Goliath the Gittite (1Ch 20:5), or the Bethlehemite who killed Goliath (2Sa 21:19). The two accounts may be harmonized if an early copyist of

Samuel misread "Lahmi the brother of" as "the Bethlehemite."

ELI [6603] (*Yahweh is exalted* IDB; *[God [El]] is exalted* KB).

NIV+ ELI'S

Misjudges and rebukes Hannah (1Sa 1:13-14). His benediction upon Hannah (1Sa 1:17-18; 2:20). Officiates when Samuel is presented at the tabernacle (1Sa 1:24-28). High priest (1Sa 1:25; 2:11; 1Ki 2:27). Judge of Israel (1Sa 4:18, ftn). Indulgent of his corrupt sons (1Sa 2:22-25,29; 3:11-14). His concern for the ark (1Sa 4:11-18). Death of (1Sa 4:18).

Prophecies of judgments upon his house (1Sa 2:27-36; 3:11-14, w 1Ki 2:27).

ELI, ELI, LAMA SABACHTHANI See *Eloi, Eloi, Lama Sabachthani.*

ELIAB [482] (*God [El] is [my] father*).

1. Son of Helon (Nu 1:9; 2:7; 7:24,29; 10:16).

2. A Reubenite, progenitor of Dathan and Abiram (Nu 16:1,12; 26:8-9; Dt 11:6).

3. The son of Jesse, and eldest brother of David (1Sa 16:6; 17:13,28; 1Ch 2:13). Elihu, an officer over the tribe of Judah (1Ch 27:18).

4. An ancestor of Samuel (1Ch 6:27). Called also Elihu in the parallel genealogies (1Sa 1:1), and Eliel (1Ch 6:34).

5. A hero of the tribe of Gad (1Ch 12:9).

6. A Levite, a gatekeeper and musician (1Ch 15:18,20; 16:5).

ELIADA [486] (*God [El] knows*).

1. The son of David (2Sa 5:16; 1Ch 3:8).

2. Father of Rezon (1Ki 11:23).

3. Benjamite general (2Ch 17:17).

ELIAHBA [494] (*God [El] hides*). The Shaalbonite, one of David's heroes (2Sa 23:32; 1Ch 11:33).

ELIAKIM [509, *1806*] (*God [El] establishes*).

NIV+ ELIAKIM'S

1. The master of Hezekiah's household; sent by the king to negotiate with invading Assyrians (2Ki 18:17-37; Isa 36:1-22), and then to seek help of Isaiah the prophet (2Ki 19:2; Isa 37:2).

2. The original name of King Jehoiakim (2Ki 23:34; 2Ch 36:4). See *Jehoiakim.*

3. Priest (Ne 12:41).

4. The ancestor of Jesus (Mt 1:13).

5. Another and earlier ancestor of Jesus (Lk 3:30).

ELIAM [500] (*God [El] is [my] kinsman*).

1. The father of Bathsheba (2Sa 11:3). Called Ammiel (1Ch 3:5).

2. One of David's mighty men known as the "Thirty" (2Sa 23:34). Called Ahijah (1Ch 11:36).

ELIAS See *Elijah.*

ELIASAPH [498] (*God [El] has added*).

1. The son of Deuel, a leader of the tribe of Gad (Nu 1:14; 2:14; 7:42,47; 10:20).

2. The son of Lael, a leader of the families of the Gershonites (Nu 3:24).

ELIASHIB [513] (*God [El] restores*).

NIV+ ELIASHIB'S

1. A descendant of Zerubbabel and remotely related to David (1Ch 3:24).

2. A priest in the time of David (1Ch 24:12).

3. An ancestor of a man who helped Ezra (Ezr 10:6; Ne 12:10,22-23).

4. A Levite who put away his foreign wife (Ezr 10:24).

5. A man who married a foreign woman (Ezr 10:27).

6. Another man who married a foreign woman (Ezr 10:36).

7. A high priest in the time of Nehemiah (Ne 3:1,20-21; 13:4,7,28).

ELIATHAH [484, 517] (*God [El] comes*). A temple musician, the son of Heman (1Ch 25:4,27).

ELIDAD [485] (*God [El] is [my] beloved*). A Benjamite, the son of Kislon (Nu 34:21). Eleazar the priest and Joshua were appointed to assign the land west of the Jordan to the tribes who were to settle there. God also appointed one man from each of the tribes to help Eleazar and Joshua, Elidad being the leader from the tribe of Benjamin.

ELIEHOENAI [492] (*my eyes [look] to Yahweh*).

1. A Korahite gatekeeper of the tabernacle (1Ch 26:3).

2. One of the family heads who returned with Ezra; the son of Zerahiah (Ezr 8:4). See *Elioenai.*

ELIEL [483] (*God [El] is [my] God*).

1. The chief of Manasseh (1Ch 5:24).

2. The ancestor of Samuel (1Ch 6:34). Called Eliab (1Ch 6:27).

3. The son of Shimei (1Ch 8:20).

4. The son of Shashak (1Ch 8:22).

5. A Mahavite and a captain in David's army (1Ch 11:46).

6. One of David's heroes (1Ch 11:47).

7. A Gadite; perhaps the same as 5 or 6 (1Ch 12:11).

8. A chief Levite (1Ch 15:11).

9. A chief of Judah; perhaps the same as 5 (1Ch 15:9).

10. A Levite overseer (2Ch 31:13).

ELIENAI [501] (*my eyes [look] to Yahweh*). A Benjamite citizen of Jerusalem (1Ch 8:20).

ELIEZER [499, *1808*] (*God [El] is [my] help*).

1. Steward of Abraham, who in place of a son, would have become Abraham's heir (Ge 15:2). Perhaps the same as the servant mentioned in (Ge 24).

2. The son of Moses and Zipporah (Ex 18:4; 1Ch 23:15,17; 26:25).

3. The grandson of Benjamin (1Ch 7:8).

4. A priest (1Ch 15:24).

5. A Reubenite chief (1Ch 27:16).

6. A prophet who rebuked Jehoshaphat (2Ch 20:37).

7. A chieftain sent to induce the Israelites to return to Jerusalem (Ezr 8:16).

8. A priest who put away his foreign wife (Ezr 10:18).

9. A Levite who put away his foreign wife (Ezr 10:23).

10. A son of Harim who put away his foreign wife (Ezr 10:31).

11. An ancestor of Jesus (Lk 3:29).

ELIHOREPH [495]. A son of Shisha (1Ki 4:3).

ELIHU [490, 491] (*Yahweh is [my] God*).

1. A son of Tohu, an Ephraimite, an ancestor of Samuel

(1Sa 1:1). Probably identical with Eliab (1Ch 6:27), and Eliel (1Ch 6:34).

2. A Manassite warrior, who joined David at Ziklag (1Ch 12:20).

3. A Korahite gatekeeper of the tabernacle (1Ch 26:7).

4. A chief of the tribe of Judah and one of David's brothers (1Ch 27:18). Possibly Eliab, the oldest brother of David (1Sa 16:6).

5. A son of Barakel the Buzite who speaks to Job when his three friends have failed to silence him (Job 32-37).

ELIJAH [488, 489, 2460] (*Yahweh is [my] God*).

NIV+ ELIJAH'S

1. The Tishbite, a Gileadite and prophet. Announces to Ahab the coming of a disastrous drought (1Ki 17:2-7). The severity of Ahab, which is noted in secular literature as well, i.e., Jos. *Antiq.* VIII.xiii.2, prompts Elijah to escape into the wilderness, where he is miraculously fed by ravens (1Ki 17:1-6). By divine direction, he goes to Zarephath of Sidon where he is sustained in the household of a widow (1Ki 17:8-16). The widow's son becomes fatally ill; Elijah prays over him with the result that his life is restored (1Ki 17:16-24). Paul has a similar experience with a young man named Eutychus (Ac 20:7-12). He returns and sends a message to Ahab through Obadiah, a devout believer in the Lord, who was in charge of Ahab's palace (1Ki 18:1-16). Meets Ahab and directs him to assemble the prophets of Baal (1Ki 18:17-20). Derisively challenges the priests of Baal to offer sacrifices (1Ki 18:25-29). Slays the prophets of Baal (1Ki 18:40). Escapes to the wilderness from the fierceness of Jezebel (1Ki 19:1-18). Fasts forty days (1Ki 19:8). Despondency and murmuring of (1Ki 19:10,14). Consolation given to (1Ki 19:11-18). Flees to the wilderness of Damascus; directed to anoint Hazael as king over Aram, Jehu son of Nimshi king over Israel, and Elisha to be a prophet in his own place (1Ki 19:9-21). Personal aspect of (2Ki 1:8).

Piety of (1Ki 19:10,14; Lk 1:17; Ro 11:2; Jas 5:17). His translation to heaven in a whirlwind (2Ki 2:11). Antitype of John the Baptist (Mt 11:14; 17:10-13; Mk 9:11-13; Lk 1:17; Jn 1:21-25). Appears to Jesus at his transfiguration (Mt 17:1-4; Mk 9:2-5; Lk 9:28-33).

Miracles of:

Increases the oil of the widow of Zarephath (1Ki 17:14-16). Raises from the dead the son of the woman of Zarephath (1Ki 17:17-24). Causes fire to consume the sacrifice (1Ki 18:24,36-38). Causes rain after a drought of three and a half years (1Ki 18:41-45; Jas 5:17-18). Calls fire down upon the soldiers of Ahaziah (2Ki 1:10-14; Lk 9:54, ftn).

Prophecies of:

Foretells, a drought (1Ki 17:1), the destruction of Ahab and his house (1Ki 21:17-29; 2Ki 9:25-37), the death of Ahaziah (2Ki 1:2-17), the plague sent as a judgment upon the people in the time of Jehoram, king of Israel (2Ch 21:12-15).

2. A Benjamite chief, the son of Jeroham (1Ch 8:27).

3. A postexilic Jew who divorced his foreign wife; a descendant of Harim (Ezr 10:21).

4. A postexilic Jew who divorced his foreign wife; a descendant of Elam (Ezr 10:26).

ELIKA [508]. A Harodite, one of David's mighty men known as the "Thirty" (2Sa 23:25).

ELIM [396] (*big trees*).

NIV+ BEER ELIM

The fourth stopping place of the Israelites after they crossed the Red Sea; they found twelve springs and seventy palm trees (Ex 15:27; 16:1; Nu 33:9-10).

ELIMELECH [497] (*God [El] is [my] king*). An Ephrathite from Bethlehem of Judah who, with his wife, Naomi and his two sons, immigrated from Judah to Moab in the days of the judges to escape a famine in the land (Ru 1:2,3; 2:1,3; 4:3,9).

ELIOENAI [493] (*my eyes [look] to Yahweh*).

1. The son of Neariah (1Ch 3:23-24).

2. A Simeonite leader (1Ch 4:36).

3. A Benjamite (1Ch 7:8).

4. A man who divorced his foreign wife (Ezr 10:22).

5. A man who divorced his foreign wife (Ezr 10:27).

6. A priest, perhaps the same as 4 (Ne 12:41).

ELIPHAL [503] (*[my] God [El] sit in judgment*). Perhaps the same as Eliphelet (2Sa 23:34). One of David's mighty men known as the "Thirty" (1Ch 11:35).

ELIPHAZ [502] (*God [El] is fine gold* or *God crushes*).

1. The oldest son of Esau by his Hittite wife Adah (Ge 36:4,10-12,15-16; 1Ch 1:35-36).

2. One of Job's three friends; wise, rich, and a ruler of men. He was probably the leader of this trio (Job 42:7), and also the oldest. He took for granted that Job must have committed some major sin as the only explanation for his tremendous suffering. He tries to make it as easy as possible for Job to repent because of the powerful impact of the dream he had had concerning man's sinful condition in the presence of God (Job 4:12-21). In his second address, Eliphaz's point of view is that Job's problems stem from his strong sense of personal righteousness; that Job believes that he has all the wisdom that he needs, therefore, he has no need of input from God or wise men (Job 15). In his third address, Eliphaz condemns Job of many sins, calling him back to right relationship and the resultant blessing of God (Job 22).

ELIPHELEHU [504] (*God [El], distinguish him!*). A Levite musician (1Ch 15:18,21).

ELIPHELET [505] (*God [El] is [my] deliverance*).

1. A son of David, probably identical with #2 (2Sa 5:16; 1Ch 3:8; 14:7).

2. One of David's mighty men known as the "Thirty" (2Sa 23:34).

3. A son of David (1Ch 3:6; 14:7). Called Elpelet (1Ch 14:5).

4. A descendant of Saul (1Ch 8:39).

5. A companion of Ezra (Ezr 8:13).

6. A priest from among the Israelites who had married a foreign woman and had pledged to divorce his wife (Ezr 10:33).

ELISABETH See Elizabeth.

ELISHA, ELISEUS [515, 1811] (*God [El] is [my] salvation*).

NIV+ ELISHA'S

The successor to Elijah the prophet . Elijah is instructed to anoint (1Ki 19:16). Called by Elijah (1Ki 19:19). Ministers to Elijah (1Ki 19:21). Witnesses Elijah's translation, receives a double portion of his spirit (2Ki 2:1-15; 3:11). Mocked by the children of Bethel (2Ki 2:23-24). Causes the king to restore the property of the hospitable Shunammite (2Ki 8:1-6). Instructs that Jehu be anointed the king of Israel (2Ki 9:1-3). Life of, sought by Jehoram (2Ki 6:31-33). The death of (2Ki 13:14-20). Bones of, restore a dead man to life (2Ki 13:21).

Miracles of:

Divides the Jordan (2Ki 2:14). Purifies the waters of Jericho by casting salt into the fountain (2Ki 2:19-22). Increases the oil of the woman whose sons were to be sold for debt (2Ki 4:1-7). Raises from the dead the son of the Shunammite (2Ki 4:18-37). Neutralizes the poison of the stew (2Ki 4:38-41). Increases the bread to feed one hundred men (2Ki 4:42-44). Heals Naaman the leper (2Ki 5:1-19; Lk 4:27). Sends leprosy as a judgment upon Gehazi (2Ki 5:26-27). Recovers the axhead that had fallen into a stream by causing it to float (2Ki 6:6). Reveals the counsel of the king of Syria (2Ki 6:12). Opens the eyes of his servant to see the hosts of the Lord (2Ki 6:17). Brings blindness upon the army of Syria (2Ki 6:18).

Prophecies of:

Foretells a son to the Shunammite woman (2Ki 4:16); plenty to the starving in Samaria (2Ki 7:1); death of the unbelieving prince (2Ki 7:2); seven years' famine in the land of Canaan (2Ki 8:1-3); death of Ben-Hadad, king of Syria (2Ki 8:7-10); elevation of Hazael to the throne (2Ki 8:11-15); the victory of Jehoash over Syria (2Ki 13:14-19). Elisha is referred to once in the NT (Lk 4:27).

ELISHAH [511] (*God [El] saves*). The son of Javan, whose name was given to an ancient land and its people, not identified (Ge 10:4; 1Ch 1:7; Eze 27:7).

ELISHAMA [514] (*God [El] has heard*).

1. A leader of the tribe of Ephraim during the census in the wilderness. The grandfather of Joshua (Nu 1:10; 2:18; 7:48,53; 10:22; 1Ch 7:26).

2. A son of David (2Sa 5:16; 1Ch 3:8; 14:7).

3. KJV Elishama, another son of David, is NIV Elishua (1Ch 3:6, ftn). *See Elishua.*

4. The grandfather of the Ishmael who killed Gedaliah the governor of Israel appointed by Nebuchadnezzar (2Ki 25:25; Jer 41:1).

5. Of the tribe of Judah, descended from Sheshan (1Ch 2:41).

6. A priest sent by Jehoshaphat to teach the law in Judah (2Ch 17:8).

7. A secretary to Jehoiakim (Jer 36:12,20-21).

ELISHAPHAT [516] (*God [El] is [my] judge*). One of five Judean commanders who helped Jehoiada the priest in the overthrow of Athaliah to make Joash king (2Ch 23:1).

ELISHEBA [510] (*God [El] is an oath* BDB; *God [El] is [my] fill* KB). The daughter of Amminadab and wife of Aaron (Ex 6:23).

ELISHUA [512] (*God [El] is [my] salvation*). A son of David (2Sa 5:15; 1Ch 14:5). Elishama (1Ch 3:6, ftn) is probably a scribal error in Hebrew mss.

ELIUD [1809] (*God [El] is [my] grandeur*). An ancestor of Jesus; in the fifth generation before Jesus, he was the son of Akim and the father of Eleazar (Mt 1:14-15).

ELIZABETH (God [El] is [my] oath).[1810]. The wife of Zechariah and mother of John the Baptist (Lk 1:5-60).

ELIZAPHAN [507] (*God [El] is [my] hiding*).

1. A Levite (Ex 6:22; Lev 10:4). The son of Uzziel, the

leader of the families of the Kohathite clans who had the responsibility to take care of the ark, the table, the lampstand, and the vessels of the sanctuary (Nu 3:30; 1Ch 15:8; 2Ch 29:13).

2. A leader of Zebulun (Nu 34:25).

ELIZUR [506] (*God [El] is [my] rock*). A leader of Reuben, the son of Shedeur; one of the leaders who helped Moses take the census in the wilderness (Nu 1:5; 2:10; 7:30,35; 10:18).

ELKANAH [555] (*God [El] has possessed*).

1. The grandson of Korah (Ex 6:24; 1Ch 6:23).

2. The father of Samuel (1Sa 1:1,4,8,19,21,23; 2:11,20; 1Ch 6:27,34).

3. A Levite (1Ch 6:25,36).

4. Possibly identical with 3 (1Ch 6:26,35).

5. A Levite (1Ch 9:16).

6. A Levite who joined David at Ziklag (1Ch 12:6).

7. A doorkeeper for the ark, perhaps identical with 6 (1Ch 15:23).

8. A prince of Ahaz (2Ch 28:7).

ELKOSH [556].
NIV+ ELKOSHITE
The birthplace of Nahum the prophet (Na 1:1).

ELLASAR [536]. A city-state in Babylonia in the time of Abraham (Ge 14:1,9).

ELM *See Terebinth.*

ELMADAM [1825]. An ancestor of Jesus (Lk 3:28).

ELNAAM [534] (*God [El] is pleasantness*). The father of two of David's mighty men known as the "Thirty" (1Ch 11:46).

ELNATHAN [535] (*God [El] has given*).

1. The grandfather of Jehoiachin (2Ki 24:8).

2. Levites who helped Ezra (Ezr 8:16).

3. The son of Acbor and a high official of King Jehoiakim (Jer 26:22; 36:12,25).

ELOHE *See El Elohe Israel.*

ELOHIM (*a god, the God; Mighty One*). The most frequent Hebrew word for God, gods, angels, or magistrates. The plural *Elohim* when used for God in the OT is singular in meaning, and is often called "plural of majesty." *See God, Names of, Elohim.*

Used of heathen gods:

The Philistine god Dagon (Jdg 16:23-24), the Sidonian goddess Ashtoreth (1Ki 11:5,33), the Moabite god Chemosh (1Ki 11:33), the Ammonite god Chemosh (1Ki 11:33), and Baal-Zebub of Ekron (2Ki 1:2,3,6) are also referred to in the plural.

Used of other groups:

Judges (Ex 21:6; 22:8-9), heavenly beings (Ps 8:5), those high among people (Ps 36:7).

ELOI, ELOI, LAMA SABACHTHANI
[1830+3316+4876] (*My God, my God, why have you forsaken me?*). One of the seven cries of Jesus from the cross (Mt 27:46; Mk 15:34 w Ps 22:1).

ELON, ELONITE [390, 391, 472, 533] (*a species of a mighty tree*).

1. The father-in-law of Esau (Ge 26:34; 36:2).

2. A son of Zebulun (Ge 46:14) and his clan (Nu 26:26).

3. A town of Dan (Jos 19:43).

4. A Hebrew judge (Jdg 12:11-12).

ELON BETHHANAN [392] (*tree of Bethhanan*). A town of Dan (1Ki 4:9). Perhaps identical with Elon (Jos 19:43).

ELOTH *See Elath.*

ELPAAL [551] (*God [El] creates*). A Benjamite (1Ch 8:11-12,18).

ELPELET [550] (*God [El] is deliverance*). A son of David (1Ch 14:5). Called Eliphelet (1Ch 3:6).

ELTEKEH [558, 559] (*meeting place*). A city of Dan (Jos 19:44; 21:23).

ELTEKON [560] (*God [El] has arranged*). A city of Judah (Jos 15:59).

ELTOLAD [557] (*generation* IDB; *kindred of God [El]* ISBE; *God [El] + place where children could be obtained* KB). A city of Judah (Jos 15:30; 19:4). Called Tolad (1Ch 4:29).

ELUL [469].

The sixth month in sacred sequence, month twelve in civil sequence. The returned Jews finish the wall of Jerusalem in (Ne 6:15). Zerubbabel builds the temple in (Hag 1:14-15).

A transitional season from dry to rainy (August-September). The season for processing grapes, figs, and olives. *See Month, 6.*

ELUZAI [539] (*God [El] is my strength*). A Benjamite warrior who joined David while he was in exile from Saul at the Philistine city of Ziklag (1Ch 12:5). He was able to use a bow or sling with either hand.

ELYMAS [1829] (possibly *wise one* hence *magician*). A Jewish magician and false prophet associated with Proconsul Sergius Paulus at Paphos on Cyprus. He was punished with blindness when he opposed Paul and Barnabas and tried to turn the proconsul from the faith (Ac 13:8-11).

ELZABAD [479] (*God [El] has given*).

1. A Gadite warrior who joined David at Ziklag (1Ch 12:12).

2. A Korahite gatekeeper (1Ch 26:7).

ELZAPHAN *See Elizaphan.*

EMANCIPATION Of all Hebrew servants (Ex 21:2; Lev 25:8-17,39-41; Dt 15:12).

Proclamation of:

By Cyrus (2Ch 36:23; Ezr 1:1-4), by Zedekiah (Jer 34:8-11). *See Exodus; Jubilee.*

EMBALMING [2846, 2847].

NIV+ EMBALM, EMBALMED

Of Jacob (Ge 50:2-3), of Joseph (Ge 50:26), of Asa (2Ch 16:14), of Jesus (Mk 15:46; 16:1; Jn 19:39-40).

EMBEZZLEMENT (Lk 16:1-7). *See Dishonesty.*

EMBLEMS OF THE HOLY SPIRIT *See Holy Spirit, Emblems of.*

EMBROIDERY [8387, 8391].

NIV+ EMBROIDERED, EMBROIDERER, EMBROIDERERS

In blue, purple, and scarlet, on the curtains of the tabernacle (Ex 26:1,36; 27:16), on the ephod and coat of the high priest, mingled with gold (Ex 28:4-5,39). Bezalel and Oholiab divinely inspired for in the work of the tabernacle (Ex 35:30-35; 38:22-23). On the garments of Sisera (Jdg 5:30). On the garments of women (Ps 45:14; Eze 16:10,13,18). On the garments of princes (Eze 26:16).

See Tapestry.

EMEK *See Beth Emek; Emek Keziz.*

EMEK KEZIZ [6681] (*valley of Keziz*). A valley and city of Benjamin (Jos 18:21).

EMERALD [3402, 5039, 5040]. One of the jewels in the priestly breastplate (Ex 28:18; 39:11; Jer 17:1).

Figurative:

Ezekiel uses imagery of the Creation and the Fall to picture the career of the king of Tyre; unlike Adam, who was naked, the king is pictured as a fully clothed priest, ordained to guard God's holy place; the nine stones listed are among the twelve worn by the priest (Eze 28:13).

Since God dwells in "unapproachable light" and is one "whom no one has seen or can see" (1Ti 6:16), he is described in terms of the reflected brilliance of precious stones—an emerald rainbow around the throne (Rev 4:3).

Symbolic:

In the foundation of the holy city (Rev 21:19).

See Minerals of the Bible, 1; Stones.

EMERGENCY *See Decision.*

EMERODS *See Hemorrhoids.*

EMITES, EMIM [400] (*frightening beings*). Early inhabitants of the area around Kiriathaim which is E of the Dead Sea. They were defeated in the time of Abraham by the four invading kings (Ge 14:5). A race of giants who were "strong and numerous, and as tall as the Anakites" (Dt 2:10-11). *See Rephaites.*

EMMANUEL *See Immanuel.*

EMMAUS [1843] (*hot springs*). A village seven miles from Jerusalem (Lk 24:7-35).

EMPLOYEE

Character of Unrighteous:

Job 7:1 "Does not man have hard service on earth? Are not his days like those of a hired man? [2]Like a slave longing for the evening shadows, or a hired man waiting eagerly for his wages, [3]so I have been allotted months of futility, and nights of misery have been assigned to me.

Job 14:1 "Man born of woman is of few days and full of trouble. (+Job 14:6)

Mt 20:1 "For the kingdom of heaven is like a landowner who went out early in the morning to hire men to work in his vineyard. [2]He agreed to pay them a denarius for the day and sent them into his vineyard.

[3]"About the third hour he went out and saw others standing in the marketplace doing nothing. [4]He told them, 'You also go and work in my vineyard, and I will pay you whatever is right.' [5]So they went.

"He went out again about the sixth hour and the ninth hour and did the same thing. [6]About the eleventh hour he went out and found still others standing around. He asked them, 'Why have you been standing here all day long doing nothing?'

[7]"'Because no one has hired us,' they answered.

"He said to them, 'You also go and work in my vineyard.'

[8]"When evening came, the owner of the vineyard said to his foreman, 'Call the workers and pay them their wages, beginning with the last ones hired and going on to the first.'

[9]"The workers who were hired about the eleventh hour came and each received a denarius. [10]So when those came who were hired first, they expected to receive more. But each one of them also received a denarius. [11]When they received it, they began to grumble against the landowner. [12]'These men who were hired last worked only one hour,' they said, 'and you have made them equal to us who have borne the burden of the work and the heat of the day.'

[13]"But he answered one of them, 'Friend, I am not being unfair to you. Didn't you agree to work for a denarius? [14]Take your pay and go. I want to give the man who was hired last the same as I gave you. [15]Don't I have the right to do what I want with my own money? Or are you envious because I am generous?'

[16]"So the last will be first, and the first will be last."

Mt 21:33 "Listen to another parable: There was a landowner who planted a vineyard. He put a wall around it, dug a winepress in it and built a watchtower. Then he rented the vineyard to some farmers and went away on a journey. [34]When the harvest time approached, he sent his servants to the tenants to collect his fruit.

[35]"The tenants seized his servants; they beat one, killed another, and stoned a third. [36]Then he sent other servants to them, more than the first time, and the tenants treated them the same way. [37]Last of all, he sent his son to them. 'They will respect my son,' he said.

[38]"But when the tenants saw the son, they said to each other, 'This is the heir. Come, let's kill him and take his inheritance.' [39]So they took him and threw him out of the vineyard and killed him.

[40]"Therefore, when the owner of the vineyard comes, what will he do to those tenants?"

[41]"He will bring those wretches to a wretched end," they replied, "and he will rent the vineyard to other tenants, who will give him his share of the crop at harvest time."

Jn 10:12 The hired hand is not the shepherd who owns the sheep. So when he sees the wolf coming, he abandons the sheep and runs away. Then the wolf attacks the flock and scatters it. [13]The man runs away because he is a hired hand and cares nothing for the sheep.

Rights of an Employee:

Prompt payment—

Lev 19:13 "'Do not defraud your neighbor or rob him. "'Do not hold back the wages of a hired man overnight.

Participation of produce—

Lev 25:6 Whatever the land yields during the sabbath year will be food for you—for yourself, your manservant and maidservant, and the hired worker and temporary resident who live among you,

Just compensation—

Mt 10:10 take no bag for the journey, or extra tunic, or sandals or a staff; for the worker is worth his keep.

Lk 10:7 Stay in that house, eating and drinking whatever they give you, for the worker deserves his wages. Do not move around from house to house. (+Ro 4:4; Col 4:1)

1Ti 5:18 For the Scripture says, "Do not muzzle the ox while it is treading out the grain," and "The worker deserves his wages."

Oppression of—

Dt 24:14 Do not take advantage of a hired man who is poor and needy, whether he is a brother Israelite or an alien living in one of your towns. [15]Pay him his wages each day before sunset, because he is poor and is counting on it. Otherwise he may cry to the LORD against you, and you will be guilty of sin.

Pr 22:16 He who oppresses the poor to increase his wealth and he who gives gifts to the rich—both come to poverty.

Mal 3:5 "So I will come near to you for judgment. I will be quick to testify against sorcerers, adulterers and perjurers, against those who defraud laborers of their wages, who oppress the widows and the fatherless, and deprive aliens of justice, but do not fear me," says the LORD Almighty.

Lk 15:15 So he went and hired himself out to a citizen of that country, who sent him to his fields to feed pigs. [16]He longed to fill his stomach with the pods that the pigs were eating, but no one gave him anything. (+Lk 15:17)

Jas 5:4 Look! The wages you failed to pay the workmen who mowed your fields are crying out against you. The cries of the harvesters have reached the ears of the Lord Almighty.

Kindness to exemplified—

Ru 2:4 Just then Boaz arrived from Bethlehem and greeted the harvesters, "The LORD be with you!" "The LORD bless you!" they called back.

Lk 15:17 "When he came to his senses, he said, 'How many of my father's hired men have food to spare, and here I am starving to death!

Lk 15:19 I am no longer worthy to be called your son; make me like one of your hired men.'

See Employer; Master; Servant; Slave.

EMPLOYER

Required:

To grant a Sabbath rest (Ex 20:10)—

Dt 5:14 but the seventh day is a Sabbath to the LORD your God. On it you shall not do any work, neither you, nor your son or daughter, nor your manservant or maidservant, nor your ox, your donkey or any of your animals, nor the alien within your gates, so that your manservant and maidservant may rest, as you do.

To make prompt payment (Lev 19:13)—

Dt 24:15 Pay him his wages each day before sunset, because he is poor and is counting on it. Otherwise he may cry to the LORD against you, and you will be guilty of sin.

Jas 5:4 Look! The wages you failed to pay the workmen who mowed your fields are crying out against you. The cries of the harvesters have reached the ears of the Lord Almighty. [5]You have lived on earth in luxury and self-indulgence. You have fattened yourselves in the day of slaughter.

To be kind—

Lev 25:39 "'If one of your countrymen becomes poor among you and sells himself to you, do not make him work as a slave. [40]He is to be treated as a hired worker or a temporary resident among you; he is to work for you until the Year of Jubilee. [41]Then he and his children are to be released, and he will go back to his own clan and to the property of his forefathers. [42]Because the Israelites are my servants, whom I brought out of Egypt, they must not be sold as slaves. [43]Do not rule over them ruthlessly, but fear your God.

Job 31:13 "If I have denied justice to my menservants and maidservants when they had a grievance against me,

[14]what will I do when God confronts me? What will I answer when called to account? [15]Did not he who made me in the womb make them? Did not the same one form us both within our mothers?

Eph 6:9 And masters, treat your slaves in the same way. Do not threaten them, since you know that he who is both their Master and yours is in heaven, and there is no favoritism with him.

Phm 15 Perhaps the reason he was separated from you for a little while was that you might have him back for good— [16]no longer as a slave, but better than a slave, as a dear brother. He is very dear to me but even dearer to you, both as a man and as a brother in the Lord.

Not to oppress—

Dt 24:14 Do not take advantage of a hired man who is poor and needy, whether he is a brother Israelite or an alien living in one of your towns. [15]Pay him his wages each day before sunset, because he is poor and is counting on it. Otherwise he may cry to the LORD against you, and you will be guilty of sin.

Pr 22:16 He who oppresses the poor to increase his wealth and he who gives gifts to the rich—both come to poverty.

Mal 3:5 "So I will come near to you for judgment. I will be quick to testify against sorcerers, adulterers and perjurers, against those who defraud laborers of their wages, who oppress the widows and the fatherless, and deprive aliens of justice, but do not fear me," says the LORD Almighty.

To accord just compensation—

Jer 22:13 "Woe to him who builds his palace by unrighteousness, his upper rooms by injustice, making his countrymen work for nothing, not paying them for their labor.

Mt 10:10 take no bag for the journey, or extra tunic, or sandals or a staff; for the worker is worth his keep.

Mt 20:1 "For the kingdom of heaven is like a landowner who went out early in the morning to hire men to work in his vineyard. [2]He agreed to pay them a denarius for the day and sent them into his vineyard.

[3]"About the third hour he went out and saw others standing in the marketplace doing nothing. [4]He told them, 'You also go and work in my vineyard, and I will pay you whatever is right.' [5]So they went.

"He went out again about the sixth hour and the ninth hour and did the same thing. [6]About the eleventh hour he went out and found still others standing around. He asked them, 'Why have you been standing here all day long doing nothing?'

[7]" 'Because no one has hired us,' they answered.

"He said to them, 'You also go and work in my vineyard.'

[8]"When evening came, the owner of the vineyard said to his foreman, 'Call the workers and pay them their wages, beginning with the last ones hired and going on to the first.'

[9]"The workers who were hired about the eleventh hour came and each received a denarius. [10]So when those came who were hired first, they expected to receive more. But each one of them also received a denarius. [11]When they received it, they began to grumble against the landowner. [12]'These men who were hired last worked only one hour,' they said, 'and you have made them equal to us who have borne the burden of the work and the heat of the day.'

[13]"But he answered one of them, 'Friend, I am not being unfair to you. Didn't you agree to work for a denarius? [14]Take your pay and go. I want to give the man who was hired last the same as I gave you. [15]Don't I have the right to do what I want with my own money? Or are you envious because I am generous?'

Lk 10:7 Stay in that house, eating and drinking whatever they give you, for the worker deserves his wages. Do not move around from house to house.

Ro 4:4 Now when a man works, his wages are not credited to him as a gift, but as an obligation.

Col 4:1 Masters, provide your slaves with what is right and fair, because you know that you also have a Master in heaven.

1Ti 5:18 For the Scripture says, "Do not muzzle the ox while it is treading out the grain," and "The worker deserves his wages."

See Employee; Labor; Master; Servant.

EMULATION

To create a desire for salvation—

Ro 11:11 Again I ask: Did they stumble so as to fall beyond recovery? Not at all! Rather, because of their transgression, salvation has come to the Gentiles to make Israel envious.

Ro 11:14 in the hope that I may somehow arouse my own people to envy and save some of them.

To generosity in giving to aid others—

2Co 8:1 And now, brothers, we want you to know about the grace that God has given the Macedonian churches. [2]Out of the most severe trial, their overflowing joy and their extreme poverty welled up in rich generosity. [3]For I testify that they gave as much as they were able, and even beyond their ability. Entirely on their own, [4]they urgently pleaded with us for the privilege of sharing in this service to the saints. [5]And they did not do as we expected, but they gave themselves first to the Lord and then to us in keeping with God's will. [6]So we urged Titus, since he had earlier made a beginning, to bring also to completion this act of grace on your part. [7]But just as you excel in everything—in faith, in speech, in knowledge, in complete earnestness and in your love for us—see that you also excel in this grace of giving.

[8]I am not commanding you, but I want to test the sincerity of your love by comparing it with the earnestness of others.

2Co 9:1 There is no need for me to write to you about this service to the saints. [2]For I know your eagerness to help, and I have been boasting about it to the Macedonians, telling them that since last year you in Achaia were ready to give; and your enthusiasm has stirred most of them to action. [3]But I am sending the brothers in order that our boasting about you in this matter should not prove hollow, but that you may be ready, as I said you would be. [4]For if any Macedonians come with me and find you unprepared, we—not to say anything about you—would be ashamed of having been so confident. [5]So I thought it necessary to urge the brothers to visit you in advance and finish the arrangements for the generous gift you had promised. Then it will be ready as a generous gift, not as one grudgingly given.

To love and good works—

Heb 10:24 And let us consider how we may spur one another on toward love and good deeds.

Illustrated—

In Esau's marriages (Ge 28:6-9). In Jacob's household (Ge 30:1-24).

EN EGLAIM [6536] (*spring of two calves*).
NIV+ EGLAIM

Possibly modern Ain Feshka at the NW corner of the Dead Sea (Eze 47:10).

EN GANNIM [6528] (*spring of gardens*).
1. A city of Judah (Jos 15:34).
2. A city of Issachar (Jos 19:21; 21:29).

EN GEDI [6527] (*spring of young goat*).
NIV+ HAZAZON TAMAR

Called Hazazon Tamar. Built by the Amorites (Ge 14:7; 2Ch 20:2). A city allotted to Judah (Jos 15:62). Famous for its vineyards (SS 1:14).

Wilderness of, near the Dead Sea. David uses as a stronghold (1Sa 23:29; 24). Cave of (1Sa 24:3).

EN HADDAH [6532] (*spring of gladness*). A city of Issachar probably located c. six miles E of Mount Tabor (Jos 19:21).

EN HAKKORE [6530] (*spring of the partridge* or *spring of the caller*). A spring at Lehi from which Samson drank after slaughtering the Philistines (Jdg 15:19).

EN HAZOR [6533] (*spring of Hazor*).
NIV+ HAZOR

En Hazor was a fortified city assigned to Naphtali (Jos 19:37).

EN MISHPAT [6535] (*spring of judgment*).
NIV+ KADESH

The ancient name of Kadesh (Ge 14:7). *See Kadesh.*

EN RIMMON [6538] (*spring of Rimmon*).
NIV+ RIMMON

A city of Judah in the Negev, later assigned to Simeon (Jos 19:7; 1Ch 4:32). Probably identical with Ain and Rimmon (Jos 15:32; 1Ch 4:32). Those returning from the Exile resettled at En Rimmon (Ne 11:29).

EN ROGEL [6537] (*spring of the fuller,* or *wanderer,* or *spy*). A spring near Jerusalem (Jos 15:7; 18:16; 2Sa 17:17), possibly the Jackal Well (Ne 2:13). A rebellious feast at (1Ki 1:9).

EN SHEMESH [6539] (*spring of Shemesh,* [sun or pagan god]). A place on the N boundary of Judah and the S boundary of Benjamin (Jos 15:7; 18:17). The last spring on the road between Jerusalem and the Jordan Valley was found there. En Shemesh has been called the "Spring of the Apostles" since the fifteenth century.

EN TAPPUAH [6540] (*spring of apple*).
NIV+ TAPPUAH

A spring of uncertain location at the S border of Manasseh (Jos 17:7); usually identified with modern Sheikh Abu Zarad c. eight miles S of Shechem. The town was a Canaanite stronghold that held out against the Israelites for a period of time during the conquest of the land by the Israelites.

ENAIM [6542] (*two springs*). It is most likely located in the high hill country SE of Jerusalem between Adullam and Timnah; KJV "open place" (Ge 38:14,21).

ENAM [6543]. A town in the western foothills of Judah (Jos 15:34).

ENAN [6544] (*spring*).
NIV+ HAZAR ENAN

The father of Ahira who was a military leader of the tribe of Naphtali and one who assisted in the Sinai census (Nu 1:15; 2:29; 7:78,83; 10:27).

ENCAMPMENT [2837, 3655+4722, 8905].
NIV+ See CAMP

Places where the Israelites encamped on the way from Egypt to Canaan (Nu 33). Also headquarters of armies (1Sa 13:16; 2Ch 32:1). *See Camp.*

ENCHANTMENT [879, 2489+2490, 4318, 10081].
NIV+ ENCHANTER, ENCHANTERS

The use of any form of magic, including divination; forbidden to God's people (Dt 18:10; Ac 8:9,11; 13:8,10; 19:19). *See Divination; Magic; Sorcery.*

END OF THE WORLD Consummation of the age (Mt 13:39,49; 24:3; 28:20; Heb 9:26). *See Eschatology.*

ENDOR [6529] (*spring of Dor*). A city of Issachar allotted to Manasseh (Jos 17:11). Deborah triumphs at, over Sisera (Jdg 4; Ps 83:10). The medium of, consulted by Saul (1Sa 28:7-25).

ENDURANCE [*586, 2118, 3920, 5951, 6641, 7756, 8425, *3531, 5702, 5705*].
NIV+ ENDURE, ENDURED, ENDURES, ENDURING
See Perseverance.

ENEAS *See Aeneas.*

ENEMY [*367, 7640, 7675, 7756, 8533, *2398*].
NIV+ ENEMIES, ENEMY'S, ENMITY, FOE, FOES
Kindness to, commanded (Ex 23:4)—

Ex 23:5 If you see the donkey of someone who hates you fallen down under its load, do not leave it there; be sure you help him with it.

Pr 25:21 If your enemy is hungry, give him food to eat; if he is thirsty, give him water to drink. 22In doing this, you will heap burning coals on his head, and the LORD will reward you.

Mt 5:43 "You have heard that it was said, 'Love your neighbor and hate your enemy.' 44But I tell you: Love your enemies and pray for those who persecute you, 45that you may be sons of your Father in heaven. He causes his sun to rise on the evil and the good, and sends rain on the righteous and the unrighteous. 46If you love those who love you, what reward will you get? Are not even the tax collectors doing that? 47And if you greet only your brothers, what are you doing more than others? Do not even pagans do that? 48Be perfect, therefore, as your heavenly Father is perfect.

Lk 6:27 "But I tell you who hear me: Love your enemies, do good to those who hate you, 28bless those who curse you, pray for those who mistreat you. 29If someone strikes you on one cheek, turn to him the other also. If someone takes your cloak, do not stop him from taking your tunic. 30Give to everyone who asks you, and if anyone takes what belongs to you, do not demand it back. 31Do to others as you would have them do to you.

32"If you love those who love you, what credit is that to you? Even 'sinners' love those who love them. 33And if you do good to those who are good to you, what credit is that to you? Even 'sinners' do that. 34And if you lend to those from whom you expect repayment, what credit is that to you? Even 'sinners' lend to 'sinners,' expecting to be repaid in full. ³⁵But love your enemies, do good to them, and lend to them without expecting to get anything back. Then your reward will be great, and you will be sons of the Most High, because he is kind to the ungrateful and wicked. ³⁶Be merciful, just as your Father is merciful.

Ro 12:14 Bless those who persecute you; bless and do not curse.

Ro 12:20 On the contrary: "If your enemy is hungry, feed him; if he is thirsty, give him something to drink. In doing this, you will heap burning coals on his head."

Destruction of, requested by David—

Ps 35:1 Contend, O LORD, with those who contend with me; fight against those who fight against me. ²Take up shield and buckler; arise and come to my aid. ³Brandish spear and javelin against those who pursue me. Say to my soul, "I am your salvation."

⁴May those who seek my life be disgraced and put to shame; may those who plot my ruin be turned back in dismay. ⁵May they be like chaff before the wind, with the angel of the LORD driving them away; ⁶may their path be dark and slippery, with the angel of the LORD pursuing them. ⁷Since they hid their net for me without cause and without cause dug a pit for me,

See Prayer, Imprecatory.

Rejoicing at the destruction of, forbidden—

Pr 24:17 Do not gloat when your enemy falls; when he stumbles, do not let your heart rejoice, ¹⁸or the LORD will see and disapprove and turn his wrath away from him.

Rejoicing at the destruction of, not practiced by Job—

Job 31:29 "If I have rejoiced at my enemy's misfortune or gloated over the trouble that came to him— ³⁰I have not allowed my mouth to sin by invoking a curse against his life—

Forgiveness of:

Commanded (Mt 6:12-15; 18:21-35; Mk 11:25; Lk 17:3-4; Eph 4:31-32; Col 3:13; 1Pe 3:9).

Instances of:

Esau, of Jacob (Ge 33:4,11). Joseph, of his brothers (Ge 45:5-15; 50:19-21). Moses, of Miriam and Aaron (Nu 12:1-13). David, of Saul (1Sa 24:10-12; 26:9,23; 2Sa 1:14-17), of Shimei (2Sa 16:9-13; 19:23; 1Ki 2:8-9), of Absalom and his co-conspirators (2Sa 18:5,12,32-33; 19:6, 12-13). The prophet of Judah by Jeroboam (1Ki 13:3-6). Jesus, of his persecutors (Lk 23:34). Stephen, of his murderers (Ac 7:60).

The wickedness of David's (Ps 56:2,5-6; 57:4,6; 62:4; 69:4; 71:10; 102:8; 109:2-5; 129:1-3).

Figurative:

Of the devil (Mt 13:25,28,39).

ENGAGEMENT *See Betrothal.*

ENGINE NIV "machines" of war (2Ch 26:15) or "battering rams" (Eze 26:9). *See Armies; Fort.*

ENGRAFTING *See Graft.*

ENGRAVING [2933, 2980, 3100, 4180, 5237, 7334, 7338, *1963*].

NIV+ ENGRAVE, ENGRAVED, ENGRAVES

On the stones set in the priest's breastplate (Ex 28:9-11,21,36; 39:8-14). In making idols (Ex 32:4), in the priest's ephod (Ex 39:6), in the priest's crown (Ex 39:30).

ENOCH [2840, *1970*] (*initiated* ISBE; *follower* KB).

1. Cain's eldest son (Ge 4:17).

2. A city built by Cain (Ge 4:17).

3. The father of Methuselah (Ge 5:21-22). Walked with God and then was translated to heaven by God (Ge 5:24; Heb 11:5).

ENOCH, BOOKS OF Apocalyptic literature written by various authors and circulated under the name of Enoch; written c. 163 B.C. to A.D. 50. Possibly quoted in Jude 14-15.

ENON *See Aenon.*

ENOSH, ENOS [633, *1968*] (*[mortal] man*). The son of Seth (Ge 4:26; 5:6-11; 1Ch 1:1; Lk 3:38).

ENQUIRING OF GOD *See Affliction, Prayer Under; Prayer.*

ENSIGN A standard or banner (Ps 74:4; Isa 5:26; 11:10,12; 18:3; 30:17; 31:9; Zec 9:16). *See Banner; Standard.*

ENTERTAINMENTS [8471, 10166, *1926*, *3826*, *4138*, *5810*].

NIV+ ENTERTAIN, ENTERTAINED, ENTERTAINMENT

Often great (Ge 21:8; Da 5:1; Lk 5:29). Preparations made for (Ge 18:6-7; Mt 22:4; Lk 15:23).

Given on Occasions of:

Weaning children (Ge 21:8). Ratifying covenants (Ge 26:30; 31:54). Offering voluntary sacrifice (Ge 31:54; Dt 12:6-7; 1Sa 1:4-5). After wine was trodden (Jdg 9:27). Harvest home (Ru 3:2-7; Isa 9:3). Festivals (1Sa 20:5,24-26). Sheepshearing (1Sa 25:2,36; 2Sa 13:23). Return of friends (2Sa 12:4; Lk 15:23). Coronation of kings (1Ki 1:9,18-19; 1Ch 12:39-40; Hos 7:5). Taking leave of friends (1Ki 19:21). National deliverance (Est 8:17; 9:17-19). Marriage (Mt 22:2). Birth days (Mk 6:21).

Kinds of, Mentioned in Scripture:

Dinner (Ge 43:16; Mt 22:4; Lk 14:12). Banquet (Est 5:4-6). Served often by hired servants (Mt 22:3; Jn 2:5). Served often by members of the family (Lk 10:40; Jn 12:2). Supper (Lk 14:12; Jn 12:2). Under the direction of a master of the feast (Jn 2:8-9).

Invitations to:

Should be sent to the poor (Dt 14:29, w Lk 14:13). Often by the master in person (2Sa 13:24; Est 5:4; Zep 1:7; Lk 7:36). Often only to relatives and friends (1Ki 1:9; Lk 14:12). Often addressed to many (Lk 14:16). Repeated through servants when all things were ready (Lk 14:17).

Often Given in:

The house (Lk 5:29). Near landmarks (1Ki 1:9). The court of the house (Est 1:5-6; Lk 7:36-37). The upper room or guest chamber (Mk 14:14-15). The house (Lk 5:29).

Guests at:

Had their feet washed when they came a distance (Ge 18:4; 43:24; Lk 7:38,44). Arranged according to rank (Ge 43:33; 1Sa 9:22; Lk 14:10). Often had separate dishes (Ge 43:34; 1Sa 1:4). A choice portion reserved for principal guests (Ge 43:34; 1Sa 1:5; 9:23-24). Began with thanksgiving (1Sa 9:13; Mk 8:6). Often scenes of great intemperance (1Sa 25:36; Da 5:3-4; Hos 7:5). Portions often sent to the absent (Ne 8:10; Est 9:19). None asked to eat more than he liked (Est 1:8). Men and women did not usually meet at (Est 1:8-9; Mk 6:21, w Mt 14:11). Given by the guests in return (Job 1:4; Lk 14:12). Usually anointed (Ps 23:5; Lk 7:46). Music and dancing often introduced at (Am 6:5; Mk 6:22; Lk 15:25). Eager to take chief seats at, condemned (Mt 23:6; Lk 14:7-8). Often ate from the same dish (Mt 26:23). Concluded with a hymn (Mk 14:26). None admitted after the master had risen and shut the door (Lk 13:24-25). Offense given by refusing to go to (Lk 14:18,24). Anxiety to have many guests at, alluded to (Lk 14:22-23). *See Feasts.*

ENTHUSIASM [2419, 5080].

Instances of:

Gideon (Jdg 6-7), Jehu (2Ki 9:1-14; 10:1-28). *See Zeal.*

ENUMERATION *See Census.*

ENVY [7861, 7863, 8353, 2419, 2420, 4057+4505, 4143, 5784].

NIV+ ENVIED, ENVIES, ENVIOUS, ENVYING

Characteristic of:

Depravity—
Ro 1:29 They have become filled with every kind of wickedness, evil, greed and depravity. They are full of envy, murder, strife, deceit and malice. They are gossips,
Tit 3:3 At one time we too were foolish, disobedient, deceived and enslaved by all kinds of passions and pleasures. We lived in malice and envy, being hated and hating one another.

Worldliness—
Ro 13:13 Let us behave decently, as in the daytime, not in orgies and drunkenness, not in sexual immorality and debauchery, not in dissension and jealousy.
1Co 3:3 You are still worldly. For since there is jealousy and quarreling among you, are you not worldly? Are you not acting like mere men?
2Co 12:20 For I am afraid that when I come I may not find you as I want you to be, and you may not find me as you want me to be. I fear that there may be quarreling, jealousy, outbursts of anger, factions, slander, gossip, arrogance and disorder.
Gal 5:19 The acts of the sinful nature are obvious: sexual immorality, impurity and debauchery; 20idolatry and witchcraft; hatred, discord, jealousy, fits of rage, selfish ambition, dissensions, factions 21and envy; drunkenness, orgies, and the like. I warn you, as I did before, that those who live like this will not inherit the kingdom of God.
1Ti 6:4 he is conceited and understands nothing. He has an unhealthy interest in controversies and quarrels about words that result in envy, strife, malicious talk, evil suspicions
Jas 3:14 But if you harbor bitter envy and selfish ambition in your hearts, do not boast about it or deny the truth.
Jas 3:16 For where you have envy and selfish ambition, there you find disorder and every evil practice.
Jas 4:5 Or do you think Scripture says without reason that the spirit he caused to live in us envies intensely?

Not characteristic of love—
1Co 13:4 Love is patient, love is kind. It does not envy, it does not boast, it is not proud.

Described as:

Destructive—
Job 5:2 Resentment kills a fool, and envy slays the simple.

The cause of rotting bones—
Pr 14:30 A heart at peace gives life to the body, but envy rots the bones.

All consuming—
Pr 27:4 Anger is cruel and fury overwhelming, but who can stand before jealousy?
SS 8:6 Place me like a seal over your heart, like a seal on your arm; for love is as strong as death, its jealousy unyielding as the grave. It burns like blazing fire, like a mighty flame.

Drives people to achievement:

Ecc 4:4 And I saw that all labor and all achievement spring from man's envy of his neighbor. This too is meaningless, a chasing after the wind.

As unyielding as the grave (SS 8:6), where envy and selfish ambition are found, disorder and every evil practice will be found (Jas 3:16).

Forbidden:

Ps 37:1 Do not fret because of evil men or be envious of those who do wrong;
Ps 37:7 Be still before the LORD and wait patiently for him; do not fret when men succeed in their ways, when they carry out their wicked schemes.
Ps 49:16 Do not be overawed when a man grows rich, when the splendor of his house increases; 17for he will take nothing with him when he dies, his splendor will not descend with him. 18Though while he lived he counted himself blessed—and men praise you when you prosper— 19he will join the generation of his fathers, who will never see the light [of life].
20A man who has riches without understanding is like the beasts that perish.
Pr 3:31 Do not envy a violent man or choose any of his ways, 32for the LORD detests a perverse man but takes the upright into his confidence.
Pr 23:17 Do not let your heart envy sinners, but always be zealous for the fear of the LORD. 18There is surely a future hope for you, and your hope will not be cut off.
Pr 24:1 Do not envy wicked men, do not desire their company; 2for their hearts plot violence, and their lips talk about making trouble. (+Pr 24:19-20; Ro 13:13)
Gal 5:25 Since we live by the Spirit, let us keep in step with the Spirit. 26Let us not become conceited, provoking and envying each other.
Jas 5:8 You too, be patient and stand firm, because the Lord's coming is near. 9Don't grumble against each other, brothers, or you will be judged. The Judge is standing at the door!
1Pe 2:1 Therefore, rid yourselves of all malice and all deceit, hypocrisy, envy, and slander of every kind. 2Like newborn babies, crave pure spiritual milk, so that by it you may grow up in your salvation,

Punishment for:

Eze 35:11 therefore as surely as I live, declares the Sovereign LORD, I will treat you in accordance with the anger and jealousy you showed in your hatred of them and I will make myself known among them when I judge you.

Instances of:

Cain, of Abel (Ge 4:4-8). Sarah, of Hagar (Ge 16:5-6; 21:9-10). Philistines, of Isaac because of the large number of flocks and herds he owned (Ge 26:14). Rachel, of Leah (Ge 30:1). Leah, of Rachel (Ge 30:15). Laban's sons, of Jacob (Ge 31:1). Joseph's brothers, of Joseph (Ge 37:4-11,18-20; Ac 7:9). Joshua, of Eldad and Medad (Nu 11:28-30). Miriam and Aaron, of Moses (Nu 12:1-10). Korah, Dathan, and Abiram, of Moses (Nu 16:3; Ps 106:16-18). Saul, of David (1Sa 18:8-9,29; 1Sa 20:31). Haman, of Mordecai (Est 5:13).

Asaph, at prosperity of wicked—
Ps 73:2 But as for me, my feet had almost slipped; I had nearly lost my foothold. 3For I envied the arrogant when I saw the prosperity of the wicked.

The wicked, at the prosperity of the righteous—

Ps 112:10 The wicked man will see and be vexed, he will gnash his teeth and waste away; the longings of the wicked will come to nothing.

Isa 26:11 O LORD, your hand is lifted high, but they do not see it. Let them see your zeal for your people and be put to shame; let the fire reserved for your enemies consume them.

The princes of Babylon, of Daniel (Da 6:3-4). Priests, of Jesus (Mt 27:18; Mk 15:10; Jn 11:47-48). Jews, of Paul and Barnabas (Ac 13:45; 17:5).

See Jealousy.

EPAENETUS *See Epenetus.*

EPAPHRAS [2071] *(handsome).* A co-worker with Paul (Col 1:7; 4:12; Phm 23).

EPAPHRODITUS [2073] *(handsome).* A messenger of Paul (Php 2:25; 4:18). Sick at Rome (Php 2:26-27,30).

EPENETUS [2045] *(praised).* A convert to Christ in the province of Asia (Ro 16:5).

EPHAH [406, 6548, 6549] *(darkness).*
1. A son of Midian (Ge 25:4; 1Ch 1:33; Isa 60:6).
2. Caleb's concubine (1Ch 2:46).
3. A son of Jahdai (1Ch 2:47).
4. A measure of about 3/5 bushel. *See Measure, Dry Capacity.*

EPHAI [6550] *(my bird).* A Netophathite (Jer 40:8). Sons warned Gedaliah (Jer 40:8-16; 41:3).

EPHER [6761] *([small] gazelle).*
1. A son of Midian (Ge 25:4; 1Ch 1:33).
2. A son of Ezra (1Ch 4:17).
3. A chief of Manasseh (1Ch 5:24).

EPHES DAMMIM [702] *(border of Dammim [blood]).* A place between Socoh and Azekah in Judah, where David killed Goliath (1Sa 17:1). Called Pas Dammim (1Ch 11:13).

EPHESIANS, EPISTLE TO THE

Author: The Apostle Paul

Date: c. A.D. 60

Outline:

I. Greetings (1:1-2).

II. The Divine Purpose: The Glory and Headship of Christ (1:3-14).

III. Prayer That Christians May Realize God's Purpose and Power (1:15-23).

IV. Steps Toward the Fulfillment of God's Purpose (chs. 2-3).
  A. Salvation of Individuals by Grace (2:1-10).
  B. Reconciliation of Jew and Gentile through the Cross (2:11-18).
  C. Uniting of Jew and Gentile in One Household (2:19-22).
  D. Revelation of God's Wisdom through the Church (3:1-13).
  E. Prayer for Deeper Experience of God's Fullness (3:14-21).

V. Practical Ways to Fulfill God's Purpose in the Church (4:1-6:20).
  A. Unity (4:1-6).
  B. Maturity (4:7-16).
  C. Renewal of Personal Life (4:17-5:20).

D. Deference in Personal Relationships (5:21-6:9).
  1. Principle (5:21).
  2. Husbands and wives (5:22-33).
  3. Children and parents (6:1-4).
  4. Slaves and masters (6:5-9).
  E. Strength in the Spiritual Conflict (6:10-20).

VI. Conclusion, Final Greetings and Benediction (6:21-24).

EPHESUS [1650, 2386, 2387].
NIV+ EPHESIAN, EPHESIANS

Paul visits and preaches in (Ac 18:19-21; 19; 20:16-38). Apollos visits and preaches in (Ac 18:18-28). Sceva's sons attempt to expel a demon in (Ac 19:13-16). Timothy directed by Paul to remain at (1Ti 1:3). Onesiphorus lives at (2Ti 1:18). Paul sends Tychicus to (2Ti 4:12). Church at (Rev 1:11). Apocalyptic message to (Rev 2:1-7).

See Ephesians, Epistle to the.

EPHLAL [697] *(judgment, arbitration).* A descendant of Judah through Perez and the family of Jerahmeel (1Ch 2:37).

EPHOD [680, 681].
1. A sacred vestment worn by the high priest. Described (Ex 25:7; 28:6-14,31-35). Breastplate attached to (Ex 28:22-30). Making of (Ex 39:2-26). Worn by Aaron (Ex 39:5).

An ephod made by his mother was worn by Samuel as a young boy ministering before the Lord (1Sa 2:18), by the common priests (1Sa 22:18), by David (2Sa 6:14). Used as an oracle (1Sa 23:9,12; 30:7-8).

As an idol—

Gideon made an ephod out of gold, placing it in his hometown of Ophrah, the ephod subsequently becoming an idol to Israel (Jdg 8:27). Micah from the hill country of Ephraim made one of gold (Jdg 17:5; 18:14). Prophecy concerning the absence of an ephod from Israel (Hos 3:4).

2. A man of Manasseh (Nu 34:23).

EPHPHATHA [2395] *(to open).* An Aramaic passive imperative transliterated into the Greek (Mk 7:34).

EPHRAIM [713+, 2394] *(doubly fruitful).*
NIV+ EPHRAIM'S, EPHRAIMITE, EPHRAIMITES

1. The second son of Joseph (Ge 41:52). Adopted by Jacob (Ge 48:5). Blessed before Manasseh; prophecies concerning (Ge 48:14-20). Descendants of (Nu 26:35-37; 1Ch 7:20-27). Mourns for his sons (1Ch 7:21-22).

2. A tribe of Israel. Prophecy concerning (Ge 49:25-26; Isa 7; 9:18-21; 11:13; 28:1-6; Jer 31; Hos 5:13-14; Zec 9:10-13; 10:7-12). Numbered at Sinai and in the plains of Moab (Nu 1:33; 26:37). Place in camp and march (Nu 2:18,24; 10:22). Blessed by Moses (Dt 33:13-17).

Territory allotted to, after the conquest of Canaan (Jos 16:5-9; 17:9-10,15-18; 1Ch 7:28-29). Fail to expel the Canaanites (Jos 16:10). Take Bethel in battle (Jdg 1:22-25). Join Gideon against the Midianites (Jdg 7:24-25). Rebuke Gideon for not summoning them to join the war against the Midianites (Jdg 8:1). Their jealousy of Jephthah (Jdg 12:1). Defeated by him (Jdg 12:4-6). Receive Ish-Bosheth as king (2Sa 2:8-9). Revolt from the house of David (1Ki 12:25; 2Ch 10:16). Jeroboam set up a golden calf in Bethel (1Ki 12:29). Some of the tribe join Judah under Asa (2Ch 15:9). Chastise Ahaz and Judah (2Ch 28:7). Join Hezekiah in reinstituting the Passover (2Ch 30:18). Join in the destruction of idols in Jerusalem (2Ch 31:1). Submit to the scepter of Josiah (2Ch 34:1-6).

Envied other tribes (Isa 11:13). Exalted by other tribes (Hos 13:1). Reallotment of territory to, by Ezekiel (Eze 48:5). Worshiped Baal (Hos 13:1). Sin of, remembered by God (Hos 13:12).

Name of, applied to the ten tribes (2Ch 17:2; 25:6-7; Isa 7:8-9; 11:12-13; 17:3; Jer 31:18,20; Hos 4:17; 5:3,5; 6:4, 10; 8:11; 12:14). Tribe of, called Joseph (Rev 7:8).

3. Mount of. A range of low mountains (Jos 17:15-18). Joshua has his inheritance in (Jdg 2:9). Residence of Micah (Jdg 17:8). A place of hiding for the Israelites (1Sa 14:22). Sheba resides in (2Sa 20:21). Prophecy concerning its conversion (Jer 31:6). Noted for rich pastures (Jer 50:19).

4. A wood E of the Jordan. Absalom killed in (2Sa 18:6-17).

5. A gate of Jerusalem (2Ki 14:13; 2Ch 25:23; Ne 8:16; 12:39).

6. A city in the territory of Ephraim to which Jesus escapes to evade the persecution of Caiaphas (Jn 11:54).

EPHRAIMITE [713+, 718] (doubly fruitful).
NIV+ EPHRAIM, EPHRAIMITES

A member of the tribe of Ephraim (Jos 16:5-7)—

Jos 16:8 From Tappuah the border went west to the Kanah Ravine and ended at the sea. This was the inheritance of the tribe of the Ephraimites, clan by clan. ⁹It also included all the towns and their villages that were set aside for the Ephraimites within the inheritance of the Manassites. (+Jos 16:10; Jdg 12)

EPHRATH, EPHRATHAH [714, 715, 716, 717, 718] (fruitful land).
NIV+ BETHLEHEM, CALEB EPHRATHAH, EPHRATHITE, EPHRATHITES

1. A place near Bethel where Rachel died and was buried (Ge 35:16,19; 48:7).

2. A name of Bethlehem (Ru 4:11; Mic 5:2).

3. The second wife of Caleb, mother of Hur (1Ch 2:19,50; 4:4).

4. An area associated with Kiriath Jearim (Ps 132:6, ftn).

EPHRON [6766, 6767] (gazelle).
NIV+ EPHRON'S

1. The son of Zohar; the Hittite from whom Abraham purchased the field containing the cave of Machpelah, to the E of Mamre (Ge 23:8-17; 25:9; 49:29-30; 50:13).

2. Mount Ephron, a district whose cities were on the border of Judah (Jos 15:9).

3. A city near Bethel from which Abijah took Jeroboam I (2Ch 13:19).

4. A strongly fortified city between Karnaim and Beth Shan (Scythopolis) in the Maccabean period. It tried to prevent the passage of Judas and the Israelites with him, but Judas took the city, plundered it, and killed all its male inhabitants (1Mc 5:46-52; 2Mc 12:27-29).

EPIC Heroic poetry. Miriam's song (Ex 15:1-19,21). Deborah's song (Jdg 5). See Poetry.

EPICUREANS [2134].
NIV+ EPICUREAN

A style of life familiar to Solomon long before Epicurus (341-270 B.C.) defined the doctrine through his school of philosophy in Athens (Ecc 2:1-10). Paul confronts a group of Epicurean and Stoic philosophers at a meeting of the Court of the Areopagus (Mars Hill) which is NW of the

Acropolis and connected to it (Ac 17:16-34). See Aratus; Cleanthes; Stoicism; Stoics. It is suspected that by the Christian era the responsibility of the Court of the Areopagus was to censor the religious life of the community, and because of Paul's teaching concerning Jesus and the Resurrection they were exercising that right of censor.

See Sensuality.

EPILEPSY See Seizures.

EPISTLE (letter). Formal letters containing Christian doctrine and exhortation, referring particularly to the twenty-one epistles of the NT, divided into Pauline and General epistles. Not all the letters of the apostles have survived (1Co 5:9; Col 4:16).

EPISTLES, GENERAL See General Letters.

EPISTLES, PASTORAL See Pastoral Epistles.

EQUALITY See Mankind, Equality of All People.

EQUITY [4797]. See Justice.

ER [6841, 2474] (watcher, watchful).

1. The eldest son of Judah (Ge 38:3,6-7; 46:12; Nu 26:19; 1Ch 2:3).

2. A son of Judah's son Shelah (1Ch 4:21).

3. An ancestor of Jesus (Lk 3:28).

ERAN, ERANITE [6896, 6897] (watcher, watchful). A grandson of Ephraim and his clan (Nu 26:36).

ERASTUS [2235] (beloved).

1. A convert of Paul sent with Timothy from Ephesus into Macedonia on an errand (Ac 19:22).

2. The "city treasurer" or the "city director of public works" of Corinth; a Christian (Ro 16:23).

3. A companion of Paul who remained in Corinth (2Ti 4:20). Possibly the same as 1 above.

ERECH [804, 10074].

1. A Babylonian city founded by Nimrod (Ge 10:10), located forty miles NW of Ur toward Babylon.

2. The men of Erech along with the men of Tripolis, Persia, and Babylon were settled in the cities of Samaria and elsewhere in Trans-Euphrates by Ashurbanipal (Ezr 4:9-10).

ERI, ERITE [6878, 6879] (watcher). The fifth son of Gad, the grandson of Jacob (Ge 46:16) and his clan (Nu 26:16).

ERRORS [2628, 5413, 8704, 8705, 8706, 8709, 9334, 9360, 9494, 4414, 4415].
NIV+ ERROR, ERRED

In teachers and doctrines. See Teachers, False.

ESAIAS See Isaiah.

ESARHADDON [675] (Ashur has given a brother [for a lost son]). The son and successor of Sennacherib after Sennacherib was murdered by his sons Adrammelech and Sharezer in 681 B.C.; ruled Assyria 681-669 B.C. (2Ki 19:37; 2Ch 32:21; Isa 37:38); restored the city of Babylon; conquered Egypt; brought deportees into Samaria (Ezr 4:2); took Manasseh captive (2Ch 33:11).

ESAU [6916, 2481] (hairy).
NIV+ EDOM, ESAU'S

The eldest of twin sons born to Isaac and Rebekah. Birth of (Ge 25:19-26; 1Ch 1:34). A hunter (Ge 25:27-28).

Beloved by Isaac (Ge 25:27-28). Sold his birthright for a single meal of stew (Ge 25:29-34; 27:36; Heb 12:16). He was alternately called Edom because he had red coloring; Edom means red (Ge 25:25,30). Married two Hittite women (Ge 26:34). Polygamy of (Ge 26:34; 28:9; 36:2-3). His marriages a grief to Isaac and Rebekah (Ge 26:35). Was defrauded of his father's blessing by Jacob (Ge 27; Heb 11:20). Met Jacob on the return of the latter from Haran (Ge 33:1). With Jacob, buried his father (Ge 35:29). Descendants of (Ge 36; 1Ch 1:35-57). Called Edom (Ge 25:30; 36:1,8). His name used to denote his descendants and their country (Dt 2:5; Jer 49:8,10; Ob 6). Ancestor of Edomites (Jer 49:8). Enmity of descendants of, toward descendants of Jacob (Ob 10-14). Prophecies concerning (Ob 18).

ESCAPE [*3655, 4200+8965, 4880, 4946+, 5674, 5911, 7127, 7129, *709, *1767, *5771*].

NIV+ ESCAPED, ESCAPES, ESCAPING

None, from judgment of God:

Adam and Eve—

Ge 3:7 Then the eyes of both of them were opened, and they realized they were naked; so they sewed fig leaves together and made coverings for themselves.

⁸Then the man and his wife heard the sound of the LORD God as he was walking in the garden in the cool of the day, and they hid from the LORD God among the trees of the garden. ⁹But the LORD God called to the man, "Where are you?"

¹⁰He answered, "I heard you in the garden, and I was afraid because I was naked; so I hid."

¹¹And he said, "Who told you that you were naked? Have you eaten from the tree that I commanded you not to eat from?"

Cain—

Ge 4:9 Then the LORD said to Cain, "Where is your brother Abel?"

"I don't know," he replied. "Am I my brother's keeper?"

¹⁰The LORD said, "What have you done? Listen! Your brother's blood cries out to me from the ground. ¹¹Now you are under a curse and driven from the ground, which opened its mouth to receive your brother's blood from your hand. ¹²When you work the ground, it will no longer yield its crops for you. You will be a restless wanderer on the earth."

Mankind—

Job 34:21 "His eyes are on the ways of men; he sees their every step. ²²There is no dark place, no deep shadow, where evildoers can hide. ²³God has no need to examine men further, that they should come before him for judgment. ²⁴Without inquiry he shatters the mighty and sets up others in their place. ²⁵Because he takes note of their deeds, he overthrows them in the night and they are crushed. ²⁶He punishes them for their wickedness where everyone can see them, ²⁷because they turned from following him and had no regard for any of his ways. ²⁸They caused the cry of the poor to come before him, so that he heard the cry of the needy. ²⁹But if he remains silent, who can condemn him? If he hides his face, who can see him? Yet he is over man and nation alike, ³⁰to keep a godless man from ruling, from laying snares for the people.

Isa 10:1 Woe to those who make unjust laws, to those who issue oppressive decrees, ²to deprive the poor of their rights and withhold justice from the oppressed of my people, making widows their prey and robbing the fatherless. ³What will you do on the day of reckoning, when

disaster comes from afar? To whom will you run for help? Where will you leave your riches?

Mt 23:33 "You snakes! You brood of vipers! How will you escape being condemned to hell?

Ro 2:3 So when you, a mere man, pass judgment on them and yet do the same things, do you think you will escape God's judgment?

1Th 5:2 for you know very well that the day of the Lord will come like a thief in the night. ³While people are saying, "Peace and safety," destruction will come on them suddenly, as labor pains on a pregnant woman, and they will not escape.

Heb 2:2 For if the message spoken by angels was binding, and every violation and disobedience received its just punishment, ³how shall we escape if we ignore such a great salvation? This salvation, which was first announced by the Lord, was confirmed to us by those who heard him.

Heb 12:25 See to it that you do not refuse him who speaks. If they did not escape when they refused him who warned them on earth, how much less will we, if we turn away from him who warns us from heaven? ²⁶At that time his voice shook the earth, but now he has promised, "Once more I will shake not only the earth but also the heavens."

Rev 6:15 Then the kings of the earth, the princes, the generals, the rich, the mighty, and every slave and every free man hid in caves and among the rocks of the mountains. ¹⁶They called to the mountains and the rocks, "Fall on us and hide us from the face of him who sits on the throne and from the wrath of the Lamb! ¹⁷For the great day of their wrath has come, and who can stand?"

See Sin, Fruits of, Punishment of; Judgment; Judgments.

ESCHATOLOGY (*study of last events*). Division of systematic theology dealing with the doctrine of last things such as death, resurrection, second coming of Christ, end of the age, divine judgment, and the future state. The OT teaches a future resurrection and judgment day (Job 19:25-27; Isa 25:6-9; 26:19-21; Da 12:2-3). The NT interprets, enlarges, and completes the OT eschatology. It stresses the Resurrection (Ro 8:11; 1Co 15), the second coming of Christ (Mt 16:27; Lk 17:30; 1Co 1:7; 4:5; 1Th 2:19; 3:13; 4:13-18; 2Th 1:7-10; 2:1-6; 1Pe 1:7; 1Jn 2:28), the final judgment when the unsaved are cast into hell (Rev 20), and the righteous enter heaven (Mt 25:31-46). Christians differ on how the Millennium is to be interpreted, dividing themselves into amillennialists, postmillennialists, and premillennialists (Rev 20:1-6). *See Millennium.*

ESCHEAT *See Confiscation.*

ESDRAELON (*the valley of God's sowing* or *God will sow*). Mentioned as "Esdraelon" only in the Apocrypha. The Valley of Jezreel which lies between Galilee on the N and Samaria on the S (Jos 17:16; Jdg 6:33). Assigned to Issachar (Jos 15:56). Known as the "fertile valley."

ESDRAS, BOOKS OF *See Apocrypha.*

ESEK [6922] (*dispute*). A well dug by Isaac's servants in the valley near Gerar. A dispute arose between Isaac's herdsmen and the herdsmen of Gerar over rights to the water, so he named it Esek which means *dispute*. Isaac's men moved to another place and found the same problem, so he named it Sitnah which means *opposition*. Finally they dug a third well that no one quarreled over, so he named Rehoboth, which means *room* (Ge 26:19-22).

ESHAN [878] (*support*). A city in Judah (Jos 15:52).

ESH-BAAL, ESHBAAL [843] (man of Baal).

NIV+ BAAL

Ish-Bosheth, the youngest son of Saul; he was made king over Israel by Abner to repudiate David's claim to the throne; he ruled two years and then was murdered by David's men (2Sa 2:8-10; 4:5-12). He was originally called Esh-baal (1Ch 8:33; 9:39).

ESHBAN [841] (man of understanding). A son of Dishon, a Horite chief from the region of Mt. Seir (Ge 36:26; 1Ch 1:41).

ESHCOL [865, 866] ([grape] cluster).

1. An Amorite, and ally of Abraham (Ge 14:13,24).

2. A valley or brook near Hebron (Nu 13:23-24; 32:9; Dt 1:24).

ESHEK [6944] (oppressor). A descendant of Jonathan (1Ch 8:38-40).

ESHTAOL, ESHTAOLITES, ESHTAULITES

[900, 901] ([place of oracles] inquiry). A town of Judah (Jos 15:33). Allotted to Dan (Jos 19:41; Jdg 18:2,8,11). Samson moved by the Spirit of the Lord near (Jdg 13:25). Samson buried near (Jdg 16:31).

ESHTEMOA, ESHTEMOH [903, 904] ([place where oracle is] heard).

1. A town of Canaan assigned to Judah (Jos 15:50). Allotted to the Aaronites (Jos 21:14; 1Ch 6:57). David shared the spoil with (1Sa 30:28).

2. A descendant of Ezra (1Ch 4:17,19).

ESHTON [902] (possibly hen-pecked [husband] or effeminate). A son of Mehir, the son of Kelub (1Ch 4:11-12).

ESLI [2268] (Yahweh sets apart). An ancestor of Jesus (Lk 3:25).

ESROM See Hezron.

ESSENES An important Jewish community which was flourishing in Israel during the lifetime of Jesus. They were not mentioned in the Bible, but described in Josephus and Philo, and are presumed to be the inhabitants of Qumran, where Dead Sea Scrolls were discovered. Most lived communal, celibate lives. They observed the law strictly; they practiced ceremonial baptisms; they were apocalyptic; they opposed the temple priesthood. See Testaments, Time Between.

ESTATE [1074, 5709, 9165, 4045, 6005]. See Land.

ESTHER [676] (Persian star, possibly [Babylonian goddess] Ishtar).

NIV+ ESTHER'S, HADASSAH

Called also Hadassah (Est 2:7). The cousin of Mordecai (Est 2:7,15). Chosen to be queen (Est 2:17). Tells the king of the plot against his life (Est 2:22). Fasts on account of the decree to destroy the Israelites; accuses Haman to the king; intercedes for her people (Est 4-9).

ESTHER, BOOK OF

Author: Anonymous

Date: Shortly after the events narrated, c. 460 B.C.

Outline:

I. The Feasts of Xerxes (1:1-2:18).
A. Vashti Deposed (ch. 1).
B. Esther Made Queen (2:1-18).
II. The Feasts of Esther (2:19-7:10).

A. Mordecai Uncovers a Plot (2:19-23).
B. Haman's Plot (ch. 3).
C. Mordecai Persuades Esther to Help (ch. 4).
D. Esther's Request to the King: First Banquet (5:1-8).
E. A Sleepless Night (5:9-6:14).
F. Haman Hanged: The Second Banquet (ch. 7).
III. The Feasts of Purim (chs. 8-10).
A. The King's Edict in Behalf of the Jews (ch. 8).
B. The Institution of Purim (ch. 9).
C. The Promotion of Mordecai (ch. 10).

ETAM [6515] (possibly place of birds of prey).

1. A rock where Samson was bound and delivered to the Philistines (Jdg 15:8,11-13).

2. A name in the list of Judah's descendants, but probably referring to 4 (1Ch 4:3).

3. A village of Simeon (1Ch 4:32).

4. A city in Judah (2Ch 11:6).

ETERNAL LIFE [5905, 6329, 6409, 7710, 10550, 132, 172, 173].

NIV+ ETERNALLY, ETERNITY

Participation in the life of Jesus Christ, the eternal Son of God (Jn 1:4; 10:10; 17:3; Ro 6:23), which reaches its fruition in the life to come (Mt 25:46; Jn 6:54; Ro 2:7; Tit 3:7). It is endless in its duration and divine in quality. See Immortality; Life, Everlasting.

ETERNAL PUNISHMENT See Punishment, Eternal.

ETERNITY [5905, 6329, 6409, 7710, 10550, 132, 172, 173, 353].

NIV+ ETERNAL, ETERNALLY

God inhabits (Isa 57:15; Mic 5:2), rules (Jer 10:10).

God, adoration for (Ps 30:12; 41:13), steadfastness of (Ps 72:17; 90:2; Mt 6:13), righteousness of (Ps 119:142; 2Co 9:9). See God, Eternity of.

Priestly order of Melchizedek (Ps 110:4). See Christ, Eternity of.

Angels (Jude 6). See Life, Everlasting; Punishment, Eternal.

ETH KAZIN [6962]. A landmark in the boundary line of Zebulun (Jos 19:13).

ETHAM [918] (possibly fort). The second camping place of Israel (Ex 13:20; Nu 33:6-8).

ETHAN [420] (long lived, ever-flowing [streams]).

1. An exceptionally wise man in Solomon's time; an Ezrahite (1Ki 4:31; Ps 89:T).

2. A son of Zerah (1Ch 2:6,8).

3. A descendant of Gershon (1Ch 6:42-43).

4. A Levite singer (1Ch 6:44; 15:17,19).

ETHANIM [923] (ever-flowing [streams]).

Seventh month in sacred sequence, First in civil sequence. The Feast of Trumpets in (Lev 23:23-25). The Day of Atonement, on the tenth day of (Lev 23:26-32). The Feast of Tabernacles, beginning on the fifteenth day of (Lev 23:33-43). The Jubilee proclaimed on the tenth day of the fiftieth year (Lev 25:9). The temple dedicated in and the ark restored (1Ki 8:2). The altar restored in, after the Captivity (Ezr 3:1,6). Called Tishri in current Jewish calendar.

Beginning of the early rains (September-October), the time of plowing. See Month, 7.

ETHBAAL [909] (*with [him is] Baal*). The king of Sidon; the father of Jezebel (1Ki 16:31).

ETHER [6987] (perhaps *perfume*). A city of Canaan. Assigned to Judah (Jos 15:42). Subsequently allotted to Simeon (Jos 19:7). Called Token in the parallel passage (1Ch 4:32).

ETHIOPIA [3934, *134*].

NIV+ ETHIOPIAN, ETHIOPIANS

A region in Africa, inhabited by the descendants of Ham, S of Egypt. Was called the land of Cush (Ge 10:6; 1Ch 1:9; Isa 11:11). Rivers of (Ge 10:6; Isa 18:1). Moses marries a Cushite woman (Nu 12:1). Tirhakah, the king of Ethiopia, attempted to stop Sennacherib's invasion of Israel in the time of Hezekiah (2Ki 19:9). Zerah was defeated by Asa in the Valley of Zephathah near Mareshah (2Ch 14:9-15; 16:8). Was ruled by Xerxes as a part of the Babylonian Empire (Est 1:1). Prophecies concerning the submission of (Ps 68:31; 87:4; Isa 45:14; Da 11:43). Desolation of (Isa 20:2-6; 43:3; Eze 30:4-9; Hab 3:7; Zep 2:12). Merchandise of (Isa 45:14). Ebed-Melech, an official in the royal palace, probably a eunuch and keeper of the royal harem, a native of; treats Jeremiah with kindness by interceding on his behalf before Zedekiah (Jer 38:7-13; 39:15-18). Warriors of (2Ch 12:3; 16:8; Jer 46:9; Eze 38:5). Bordered Egypt on the S (Eze 29:10). Candace, queen of (Ac 8:27). A eunuch from, becomes a disciple under the preaching of Philip (Ac 8:27-39).

ETHIOPIAN EUNUCH Treasurer of Candace, queen of the Ethiopians (Ac 8:26-39), became a Christian through Philip.

ETHNAN [925] (*gift* or *hire*). One of the sons of Helah, of the tribe of Judah (1Ch 4:7); some identify him with Ithnan, a town in S Judah in the Negev (Jos 15:23).

ETHNI [922] (*gift* or *hire*). An ancestor of Asaph, a musician (1Ch 6:41).

ETIQUETTE *See Manners.*

EUBULUS [2300] (*good counsel*). A Roman Christian who was a friend of Paul's during his second Roman imprisonment; he sent greetings with Paul's letter to Timothy (2Ti 4:21). His name is common in papyri and inscriptions.

EUCHARIST (*thanksgiving*). One name for the Lord's Supper, meaning "giving of thanks." *See Lord's Supper.*

Instituted—

Mt 26:17 On the first day of the Feast of Unleavened Bread, the disciples came to Jesus and asked, "Where do you want us to make preparations for you to eat the Passover?"

[18]He replied, "Go into the city to a certain man and tell him, 'The Teacher says: My appointed time is near. I am going to celebrate the Passover with my disciples at your house.'" [19]So the disciples did as Jesus had directed them and prepared the Passover.

[20]When evening came, Jesus was reclining at the table with the Twelve. [21]And while they were eating, he said, "I tell you the truth, one of you will betray me."

[22]They were very sad and began to say to him one after the other, "Surely not I, Lord?"

[23]Jesus replied, "The one who has dipped his hand into the bowl with me will betray me. [24]The Son of Man will go just as it is written about him. But woe to that man who betrays the Son of Man! It would be better for him if he had not been born."

[25]Then Judas, the one who would betray him, said, "Surely not I, Rabbi?"

Jesus answered, "Yes, it is you."

[26]While they were eating, Jesus took bread, gave thanks and broke it, and gave it to his disciples, saying, "Take and eat; this is my body."

[27]Then he took the cup, gave thanks and offered it to them, saying, "Drink from it, all of you. [28]This is my blood of the covenant, which is poured out for many for the forgiveness of sins. [29]I tell you, I will not drink of this fruit of the vine from now on until that day when I drink it anew with you in my Father's kingdom." (+Mk 14:22-25; Lk 22:19-20; Jn 13:1-4)

Celebrated by the early Church—

Ac 2:42 They devoted themselves to the apostles' teaching and to the fellowship, to the breaking of bread and to prayer.

Ac 2:46 Every day they continued to meet together in the temple courts. They broke bread in their homes and ate together with glad and sincere hearts,

Ac 20:7 On the first day of the week we came together to break bread. Paul spoke to the people and, because he intended to leave the next day, kept on talking until midnight.

1Co 11:26 For whenever you eat this bread and drink this cup, you proclaim the Lord's death until he comes.

Bread and cup of, symbols of the body and blood of Christ (Mt 26:26-28)—

1Co 10:16 Is not the cup of thanksgiving for which we give thanks a participation in the blood of Christ? And is not the bread that we break a participation in the body of Christ? [17]Because there is one loaf, we, who are many, are one body, for we all partake of the one loaf.

1Co 10:21 You cannot drink the cup of the Lord and the cup of demons too; you cannot have a part in both the Lord's table and the table of demons. [22]Are we trying to arouse the Lord's jealousy? Are we stronger than he?

1Co 11:23 For I received from the Lord what I also passed on to you: The Lord Jesus, on the night he was betrayed, took bread, [24]and when he had given thanks, he broke it and said, "This is my body, which is for you; do this in remembrance of me." [25]In the same way, after supper he took the cup, saying, "This cup is the new covenant in my blood; do this, whenever you drink it, in remembrance of me."

Profanation of, forbidden—

1Co 11:20 When you come together, it is not the Lord's Supper you eat, [21]for as you eat, each of you goes ahead without waiting for anybody else. One remains hungry, another gets drunk. [22]Don't you have homes to eat and drink in? Or do you despise the church of God and humiliate those who have nothing? What shall I say to you? Shall I praise you for this? Certainly not!

1Co 11:33 So then, my brothers, when you come together to eat, wait for each other. [34]If anyone is hungry, he should eat at home, so that when you meet together it may not result in judgment. And when I come I will give further directions.

Self-examination before taking, commanded—

1Co 11:27 Therefore, whoever eats the bread or drinks the cup of the Lord in an unworthy manner will be guilty of sinning against the body and blood of the Lord. [28]A man ought to examine himself before he eats of the bread and drinks of the cup. [29]For anyone who eats and drinks without recognizing the body of the Lord eats and drinks judgment on himself. ³⁰That is why many among you are weak and sick, and a number of you have fallen asleep. ³¹But if we judged ourselves, we would not come under judgment. ³²When we are judged by the Lord, we are being disciplined so that we will not be condemned with the world.

EUNICE [2332] (*good victory*). The daughter of Lois, Timothy's mother, and the wife of a Gentile (Ac 16:1; 2Ti 1:5).

EUNUCH [6247, 2336] (*one emasculated*).

NIV+ EUNUCHS

Castrated males, used as custodians of royal harems and court officials (2Ki 20:18; Est 1:10-15; 2:21; Jer 41:16; Da 1:3; Ac 8:27). Not practiced by Israelites; eunuchs not allowed to enter the assembly of the Lord (Dt 23:1). *See Ethiopian Eunuch.*

Figurative of those who stay unmarried for the sake of the kingdom (Mt 19:10-12).

EUODIA [2337] (*good fragrance*). A Christian woman at Philippi (Php 4:2).

EUPHRATES [7310, 2371] (*to break forth*).

NIV+ TRANS-EUPHRATES

A river in the Garden of Eden (Ge 2:14). The eastern limit of the kingdom of Israel (Ge 15:18; Ex 23:31; Dt 1:7; 11:24; Jos 1:4; 2Sa 8:3; 1Ki 4:21; 1Ch 5:9; 18:3). Pharaoh Neco, king of Egypt, made conquest to (2Ki 24:7; Jer 46:2-10). On the banks of, Jeremiah symbolically buries his belt (Jer 13:1-7; see v.4, ftn). Jeremiah instructs staff officer Seraiah son of Neriah to cast the roll containing prophecies against Babylon into the Euphrates (Jer 51:59-64).

Symbolic:

The inundations of, of the extension of the empire of Assyria (Isa 8:6-8). In the symbolisms of the Apocalypse (Rev 9:14; 16:12).

EUROCLYDON, EURAQUILO *See Northeaster.*

EUTYCHUS [2366] (*fortunate*). A youth who fell asleep and fell out of the window to his death while Paul preached; was restored to life by Paul (Ac 20:9-10).

EVANGELISM *See Minister, Duties of; Zeal.*

EVANGELIST [2296] (*[a bringer of] good news*).

NIV+ EVANGELISTS

1. One who preached the good news of Jesus Christ from place to place (Ac 8:12,26-39; 14:7; 1Co 1:17; 3:6). Philip is a typical example (Ac 21:8). Timothy was encouraged by Paul to do the work of an evangelist (2Ti 4:5).

2. In biblical studies: the author of a Gospel.

EVAPORATION (Ps 135:7; Jer 10:13; 51:16; Am 5:8; 9:6).

EVE [2558, 2293] (*life*). Creation of (Ge 1:26-28; 2:21-24; 1Ti 2:13). Named by Adam (Ge 2:23; 3:20). Deceived by Satan (Ge 3; 2Co 11:3; 1Ti 2:14). Clothed with fig leaves (Ge 3:7), with skins (Ge 3:21). Messiah promised to (Ge 3:15). Curse denounced against (Ge 3:16). Children of (Ge 4:1-2,25; 5:3-4).

EVENING SACRIFICE One of two daily offerings prescribed in the Mosaic ritual (Ex 29:38-42; Nu 28:3-8).

EVENING, THE [*5742, 6845, 6847, 2270, 4067, 4070*].

NIV+ EVENINGS

The day originally began with (Ge 1:5). Divided into two, commencing at 3 o'clock, and sunset (Ex 12:6; Nu 9:3).

Called the cool of the day (Ge 3:8). People cease from labor in (Ru 2:17; Ps 104:23). Wild beasts come forth in (Ps 59:6,14). Where morning dawns and evening fades God calls forth songs of joy (Ps 65:8). The enemies of Jerusalem were so zealous to attack and defeat her that the soldiers encouraged each other to do battle at times of the day when attacks were rarely made, i.e., noon and evening (Jer 6:4-5).

A Time For:

Custom of sitting at the gates in (Ge 19:1). Meditation (Ge 24:63). Passover lamb killed in (Ex 12:6,18). The golden lampstand lighted in (Ex 27:21, w Ex 30:8). Part of the daily sacrifice offered in (Ex 29:41; Ps 141:2; Da 9:21). All defiled persons unclean until (Lev 11:24-28; 15:5-7; 17:15; Nu 19:19). Humiliation often continued until (Jos 7:6; Jdg 20:23,26; 21:2; Ezr 9:4-5). Exercise (2Sa 11:2). Prayer (Ps 55:17; Mt 14:15,23). Taking food (Mk 14:17-18; Lk 24:29-30). The sky red in, a token of fair weather (Mt 16:2).

EVERLASTING ARMS (Dt 33:27).

EVERLASTING FIRE *See Fire, Figurative.*

EVERLASTING LIFE *See Life, Everlasting.*

EVERLASTING PUNISHMENT *See Punishment, Eternal.*

EVI [209] (*desire*). One of five Midianite kings killed by the Israelites under Moses (Nu 31:8; Jos 13:21).

EVICTION Of tenants (Mt 21:41; Mk 12:9).

EVIDENCE [6332, 9149, *1182, 1328, 1891, 3456, 6019*].

NIV+ EVIDENT, EVIDENTLY

False, forbidden—

Ex 20:16 "You shall not give false testimony against your neighbor.

Ex 23:1 "Do not spread false reports. Do not help a wicked man by being a malicious witness.

Ex 23:7 Have nothing to do with a false charge and do not put an innocent or honest person to death, for I will not acquit the guilty.

Pr 24:28 Do not testify against your neighbor without cause, or use your lips to deceive.

Mt 19:18 "Which ones?" the man inquired. Jesus replied, "'Do not murder, do not commit adultery, do not steal, do not give false testimony,

Concealment of, punished—

Lev 5:1 "'If a person sins because he does not speak up when he hears a public charge to testify regarding something he has seen or learned about, he will be held responsible.

The entire community involved in—

Lev 24:14 "Take the blasphemer outside the camp. All those who heard him are to lay their hands on his head, and the entire assembly is to stone him.

Two or more witnesses required in to sustain an allegation—

Nu 35:30 "'Anyone who kills a person is to be put to death as a murderer only on the testimony of witnesses. But no one is to be put to death on the testimony of only one witness.

Dt 17:6 On the testimony of two or three witnesses a man shall be put to death, but no one shall be put to death on the testimony of only one witness. ⁷The hands of the witnesses must be the first in putting him to death, and then the hands of all the people. You must purge the evil from among you.

Dt 19:15 One witness is not enough to convict a man accused of any crime or offense he may have committed. A matter must be established by the testimony of two or three witnesses.

Mt 18:16 But if he will not listen, take one or two others along, so that 'every matter may be established by the testimony of two or three witnesses.'

Heb 10:28 Anyone who rejected the law of Moses died without mercy on the testimony of two or three witnesses.

Punishment for falsehood in—

Dt 19:16 If a malicious witness takes the stand to accuse a man of a crime, ¹⁷the two men involved in the dispute must stand in the presence of the LORD before the priests and the judges who are in office at the time. ¹⁸The judges must make a thorough investigation, and if the witness proves to be a liar, giving false testimony against his brother, ¹⁹then do to him as he intended to do to his brother. You must purge the evil from among you. ²⁰The rest of the people will hear of this and be afraid, and never again will such an evil thing be done among you. ²¹Show no pity: life for life, eye for eye, tooth for tooth, hand for hand, foot for foot.

Self-incriminating, demanded—

Jos 7:19 Then Joshua said to Achan, "My son, give glory to the LORD, the God of Israel, and give him the praise. Tell me what you have done; do not hide it from me."

²⁰Achan replied, "It is true! I have sinned against the LORD, the God of Israel. This is what I have done: ²¹When I saw in the plunder a beautiful robe from Babylonia, two hundred shekels of silver and a wedge of gold weighing fifty shekels, I coveted them and took them. They are hidden in the ground inside my tent, with the silver underneath."

See Witness; False Witness; Accusation, False; Self-Incrimination.

EVIL [*2365, 4659, 6401, 6404, 6406, 8273, 8278, 8288, 8317, 8399, 8400, 8401, *94, 176, 2123, 2798, 2803, 2805, 4504, 4505, 5765*].

NIV+ EVILDOER, EVILDOERS, EVILS

Tree of the knowledge of good and evil (Ge 2:9,17). Knowledge of (Ge 3:5,22). In the heart (Ge 6:5; 8:21; Lk 6:45).

To be forsaken (Ps 34:14; 37:27; Pr 3:7; 1Pe 3:11). To be abhorred (Ps 97:10; Am 5:15; Ro 12:9). You are not to repay evil for evil done to you (Ro 12:17; 1Th 5:15; 1Pe 3:9).

Appearance of to be avoided (Ro 14:1-23; 1Co 8:7-13; 10:28-33; 1Th 4:11-12; 5:22), exemplified by Paul, refusing to eat that which was offered to idols (1Co 8:13), in supporting himself (1Co 9:7-23).

See Company, Evil; Imagination, Of Mankind, Evil; Nonresistance.

EVIL-MERODACH [213] (*worshiper of Marduk[s]* changed in textual transmission to read *fool of [blessing]*). Son and successor of Nebuchadnezzar. Released Jehoiachin from prison (2Ki 25:27-30; Jer 52:31-34).

EVIL FOR EVIL *See Retaliation.*

EVIL FOR GOOD

Ps 7:4 if I have done evil to him who is at peace with me or without cause have robbed my foe— ⁵then let my enemy pursue and overtake me; let him trample my life to the ground and make me sleep in the dust. *Selah*

Ps 35:12 They repay me evil for good and leave my soul forlorn.

Ps 109:5 They repay me evil for good, and hatred for my friendship.

Pr 17:13 If a man pays back evil for good, evil will never leave his house.

Instances of:

Joseph accuses his brothers of rendering (Ge 44:4). Israelites, to Moses (Ex 5:21; 14:11; 15:24; 16:2-3; 17:3-4). Saul returns, to David (1Sa 19:1,4-5,10). Nabal returns, to David (1Sa 25:21), David, to Uriah (2Sa 11), to Joab (1Ki 2:4-6).

See Enemy; Good for Evil.

EVIL PUT AWAY (Dt 13:5; 17:7; 19:19; 21:21; 22:21; 24:7; Job 22:23; 1Co 5:13).

EVIL SPEAKING *See Speaking, Evil.*

EVIL SPIRITS *See Demons.*

EVILDOERS [224+7188, 1201+6594, 6913+8402, 8288, 8317, 8401, *94+2239, 96, 490+2237+3836*].

NIV+ EVIL

Warnings to (Ps 34:16; 37:9; 94:16; 119:115; Isa 9:17; 14:20; 31:2). Examples of (Jdg 2:11; 3:7; 4:1; 6:1; 10:6; 13:1; 1Ki 14:22; 15:26; 16:7; 2Ki 8:27; 13:2; 14:24; 15:9,28; 17:2; 21:2; 23:32; 24:9; Ne 9:28; Isa 65:12; 2Ti 4:14).

EWE [3898, 7366, 8161].

NIV+ EWES

Female sheep.

EXALTATION [*1467, 1540, 5294, 5951, 6590, 8123, 8435, *5738*].

NIV+ EXALT, EXALTED, EXALTS

Of Christ: *See Jesus the Christ, Exaltation of.*

Of Self: *See Self-Exaltation.*

EXAMPLE [*5596, 5682*].

NIV+ EXAMPLES

Bad:

Admonitions against (Lev 18:2-3; 20:23; Dt 18:9; 2Ch 30:7; Isa 8:11; Hos 4:9,15; Zec 1:4; Mt 23:1-3; 1Co 8:9-13; 10:6; Eph 4:17; 3Jn 11). Corrupting (Pr 22:24-25; Jer 16:12; 17:1-2; Eze 20:18; Hos 4:9; 5:5).

Good:

Commanded (1Ti 4:12; Tit 2:7-8; 1Pe 5:3). Inspiring (Ne 5:8-19; 1Th 1:6-8; 1Pe 2:11-25). To be imitated (Heb 13:7; Jas 5:10-11). Illustrated (Ps 101:2; 1Pe 3:5-6).

God, our:

In holiness (Lev 11:44; 19:2). In perfection (Mt 5:48). In mercy (Lk 6:36). In not discriminating (Eph 6:9).

Christ, our:

In service (Mt 20:28; Mk 10:43-45; Lk 22:27; Jn 13:13-17,34; Php 2:5-8). In meekness (2Co 10:1; 1Pe 2:20-25). In self-renunciation (Ro 15:2-7; 2Co 8:7; Eph 5:1-2; 1Jn 3:16). In enduring persecution (1Pe 3:17-18; 4:1). In forgiving (Col 3:13). In obedience (1Jn 2:6). In steadfastness

(Heb 12:2-3). In perseverance (Rev 3:21). *See Jesus the Christ, Our Example.*

Paul, our:

Commanded (1Co 4:16; 11:1; Php 3:17; 4:9; 1Ti 1:16; 2Ti 1:13). In self-control (1Co 7:7-8). In self-maintenance (1Th 3:7-10). In beneficence (Ac 20:35).

See Influence.

EXCHANGERS *See Money Changers.*

EXCOMMUNICATION Disciplinary exclusion from church fellowship. Jews had temporary and permanent excommunication (Jn 9:22; 12:42; 16:2). Early church practiced it (1Co 5:5; 1Ti 1:20). *See Disfellowship.*

EXCUSES [8200, *406, 2400+4148, 4733*].

NIV+ EXCUSE

For disobedience (Ge 3:12-13; Ex 32:22-24; Dt 30:11-14). For rejecting salvation (Lk 14:18-20; Jn 15:22; Ac 24:25; Ro 1:20-21; 3:19). Inexcusable (Ro 2:1).

Examples:

For release from duty: By Moses, when commissioned to deliver Israel (Ex 3:11; 4:1,10-14), by Gideon (Jdg 6:12-17), by Jesus' disciples (Mt 8:21; Lk 9:59-62).

When called to be a prophet: Elisha (1Ki 19:19-21), Isaiah (Isa 6:5-8), Jeremiah (Jer 1:5-10).

For physical healing: Naaman, the leper (2Ki 5:10-14).

EXECUTION *See Death, Death Penalty.*

EXECUTIONER [*5063*] (*punishment*).

NIV+ EXECUTE, EXECUTED, EXECUTING, EXECUTION

(Ge 37:36; Pr 16:14; Jer 39:9; Da 2:14; Mt 14:10). *See Punishment.*

EXHORTATIONS, SPECIAL [*4151, 4155*].

NIV+ EXHORT, EXHORTATION, EXHORTED

To avoid various forms (Pr 4:15; Ro 16:17; 1Ti 6:20; 2Ti 2:16,23; Tit 3:9). To choose between good and evil (Ex 32:26; Dt 30:19; Jos 24:15; 1Ki 18:21).

EXILE [1583, 1655, 1661, 2143, 5615, 8654, 8660, 8938, 10120+10145, *3578, 3579*].

NIV+ EXILED, EXILES

Usually refers to the period of time during which the Southern Kingdom (Judah) was forcibly detained in Babylon. Began in the reign of Jehoiakim (609-598 B.C.), culminating in the fall of Jerusalem (c. 586 B.C.). It ended with the decree of Cyrus permitting Jews to return to Israel c. 536 B.C. *See Diaspora; Outcasts.*

EXODUS [*2016*] (*a going out*). Departure of Israel from Egypt under Moses. *See Exodus, Book of.*

EXODUS, BOOK OF

Author: Moses

Date: c. 1445-1406 B.C.

Outline:

I. Divine Redemption (chs. 1-18).
   A. Fulfilled Multiplication (ch. 1).
      1. The promised increase (1:1-7).
      2. The first pogrom (1:8-14).
      3. The second pogrom (1:15-21).
      4. The third pogrom (1:22).
   B. Preparations for Deliverance (2:1-4:26).
      1. Preparing a leader (2:1-10).
      2. Extending the time of preparation (2:11-22).
      3. Preparing the people (2:23-25).

   4. Calling a deliverer (3:1-10).
      5. Answering inadequate objections (3:11-4:17).
      6. Preparing a leader's family (4:18-26).
   C. First Steps in Leadership (4:27-7:5).
      1. Reinforced by brothers (4:27-31).
      2. Rebuffed by the enemy (5:1-14).
      3. Rebuffed by the enslaved (5:15-21).
      4. Revisited by old objections (5:22-23).
      5. Reinforced by the name of God (6:1-8).
      6. Reminded of one's lowly origins (6:9-7:5).
   D. Judgment and Salvation through the Plagues (7:6-11:10).
      1. Presenting the signs of divine authority (7:6-13).
      2. First plague: water turned to blood (7:14-24).
      3. Second plague: frogs (7:25-8:15).
      4. Third plague: gnats (8:16-19).
      5. Fourth plague: flies (8:20-32).
      6. Fifth plague: against livestock (9:1-7).
      7. Sixth plague: boils (9:8-12).
      8. Seventh plague: hail (9:13-35).
      9. Eighth plague: locusts (10:1-20).
      10. Ninth plague: darkness (10:21-29).
      11. Tenth plague announced: death of the firstborn (ch. 11).
   E. The Passover (12:1-28).
      1. Preparations for the Passover (12:1-13).
      2. Preparations for Unleavened Bread (12:14-20).
      3. Celebration of the Passover (12:21-28).
   F. The Exodus from Egypt (12:29-51).
      1. Death at midnight (12:29-32).
      2. Expulsion from Egypt (12:33-42).
      3. Regulations for the Passover (12:43-51).
   G. The Consecration of the Firstborn (13:1-16).
   H. Crossing the "Red Sea" (13:17-15:21).
      1. Into the wilderness (13:17-22).
      2. At the "Red Sea" (14:1-14).
      3. Across the "Red Sea" (14:15-31).
      4. Song at the sea (15:1-21).
   I. Journey to Sinai (15:22-18:27).
      1. The waters of Marah (15:22-27).
      2. The manna and the quail (ch. 16).
      3. The waters of Meribah (17:1-7).
      4. The war with Amalek (17:8-16).
      5. The wisdom of Jethro (ch. 18).
II. Covenant at Sinai (chs. 19-24).
   A. The Covenant Proposed (ch. 19).
   B. The Decalogue (20:1-17).
   C. The Reaction of the People to God's Fiery Presence (20:18-21).
   D. The Book of the Covenant (20:22-23:33).
      1. Prologue (20:22-26).
      2. Laws on slaves (21:1-11).
      3. Laws on homicide (21:12-17).
      4. Laws on bodily injuries (21:18-32).
      5. Laws on property damage (21:33-22:15).
      6. Laws on society (22:16-31).
      7. Laws on justice and neighborliness (23:1-9).
      8. Laws on sacred seasons (23:10-19).
      9. Epilogue (23:20-33).
   E. Ratification of the Covenant (ch. 24).
III. Divine Worship (chs. 25-40).
   A. Instructions Concerning the Tabernacle (chs. 25-31).
      1. Collection of the materials (25:1-9).
      2. Ark and atonement cover (25:10-22).
      3. Table of the bread of the Presence (25:23-30).
      4. Gold lampstand (25:31-40).

5. Curtains and frames (ch. 26).
6. Altar of burnt offering (27:1-8).
7. Courtyard (27:9-19).
8. Priesthood (27:20-28:5).
9. Garments of the priests (28:6-43).
10. Ordination of the priests (ch. 29).
11. Altar of incense (30:1-10).
12. Census tax (30:11-16).
13. Bronze basin (30:17-21).
14. Anointing oil and incense (30:22-38).
15. Appointment of craftsmen (31:1-11).
16. Sabbath rest (31:12-18).
B.False Worship (chs. 32-34).
1. The golden calf (32:1-29).
2. Moses' mediation (32:30-35).
3. Threatened separation and Moses' prayer (ch. 33).
4. Renewal of the covenant (ch. 34).
C. The Building of the Tabernacle (chs. 35-40).
1. Summons to build (35:1-19).
2. Voluntary gifts (35:20-29).
3. Bezalel and his craftsmen (35:30-36:7).
4. Progress of the work (36:8-39:31).
5. Moses' blessing (39:32-43).
6. Erection of the tabernacle (40:34-38).
7. Dedication of the tabernacle (40:34-38).

EXORCISM (*to bind with an oath, to conjure*). The casting out of demons by means of magical formulas and ceremonies (Mt 12:27; Mk 9:38; Ac 19:13). *See Demons.*

EXPANSE [8385].
NIV+ EXPAND, EXPANSES
The heavens above the earth (Ge 1:6-8,14-17,20).

EXPECTATION [7595, 9536, *638, 1693*].
NIV+ EXPECT, EXPECTANT, EXPECTANTLY, EXPECTED, EXPECTING
Of the righteous (Ps 62:5; Pr 24:14; Php 1:20). Of the wicked (Pr 10:28; 11:7,23; Zec 9:5; Ac 12:11).

EXPEDIENCY To avoid offending others weaker (Ro 14:1-2,14-22; 1Co 6:12; 8:8-13; 9:22-23; 10:23-29,32-33). To save people (1Co 9:19-23). Rule governing (1Co 10:30-31).
Exemplified by Paul, in circumcising Timothy (Ac 16:3), in purifying himself at the temple (Ac 21:23-27). *See Evil; Prudence.*

EXPERIENCE [3359, 7212, *3972*].
NIV+ EXPERIENCED
Solomon's (Ecc 1:2). Religious, relating of. *See Testimony, Religious.*

EXPERIMENT In worldly pleasure, Solomon's (Ecc 1; 2).

EXPIATION The act or means of making amends or reparation for sin. *See Atonement.*

EXPORTS [3655].
NIV+ EXPORTED
From Egypt: horses and chariots, and linen yarn (1Ki 10:28-29; 2Ch 1:16-17), grain (Ge 42; 43).
From Gilead: spices (Ge 37:25).
From Ophir: gold (1Ki 10:11; 22:48; 1Ch 29:4).
From Tarshish: gold (1Ki 10:22), ivory, apes, and baboons (1Ki 10:22), silver, iron, tin, lead, bronze, slaves (Eze 27:12-13).
From Arabia: sheep and goats (Eze 27:21).

Israel: honey (Eze 27:17).
See Imports; Commerce.

EXPOSTULATION *See Reproof.*

EXTERMINATION [6, 3049, 9012].
NIV+ EXTERMINATE, EXTERMINATING
See War.

EXTORTION [5131, 5298, 6294, 6943+6945, 6945, *1398*].
NIV+ EXTORT
Prayed upon the wicked by David (Ps 109:11). Warning against (Pr 22:16). Purged out of the land (Isa 16:4). Judged by God (Eze 22:12). Cruel (Mic 2:3).
Scribes and Pharisees accused of by Christ (Mt 23:25). Pharisee judges himself not guilty of (Lk 18:11).
Forbidden (Lk 3:13-14). Cause for disfellowship (1Co 5:10-11). Excludes from the kingdom of God (1Co 6:10).
Instances of:
Jacob, in demanding Esau's birthright for a bowl of stew (Ge 25:31). Pharaoh in exacting of the Egyptians lands and persons for grain (Ge 47:13-26). The Jews after the Captivity (Ne 5:1-13).
See Interest; Usury.

EXTRADITION
Instances of: Elijah from hiding to Ahab by Obadiah (1Ki 18:7,10). Uriah from Egypt to Jehoiakim by Elnathan and company (Jer 26:21-23). Early believers from Damascus chief priests, in Jerusalem by Paul (Ac 9:2,14; 22:5).

EXTRAVAGANCE Not to be pursued (Pr 21:17,20; Lk 16:19). *See Gluttony.*

EYE [5260, 6523, 6524, 9193, 10540, *3669, 4056, 4057, 5557, 5584, 5585*].
NIV+ EYEBROWS, EYED, EYELIDS, EYES, EYESIGHT
Anthropomorphisms, figurative of God's omniscience (Ps 11:4; Pr 15:3), justice (Am 9:8), holiness (Hab 1:13), care (Ps 33:18-19; 34:15; 121:3-5; Isa 1:15; 1Pe 3:12), glory (Isa 3:8). *See Anthropomorphisms.*
Figurative:
Of the moral state (Mt 7:3-5; 13:15-16; Mk 7:22). Of moral perception (Mt 6:22-23; Mk 8:18; Lk 10:23; Ac 26:18).
Of insatiable desire (Pr 27:20; Ecc 1:18; 2Pe 2:14; Hos 2:16). Of evil pleasure (Mt 5:29; 18:9; Mk 9:27).

EYE FOR EYE *See Retaliation.*

EYES, OPENED (Ge 21:19; Nu 22:31; 2Ki 6:17; Lk 24:31).

EYES, PAINTING OF *See Cosmetics.*

EYESALVE A preparation for the eyes. Also used figuratively for restoration of spiritual vision.

EZBAI [256]. Father of Naarai (1Ch 11:37). Possibly identical with Paarai (2Sa 23:35).

EZBON [719].
1. A son of Gad (Ge 46:16). Called Ozni (Nu 26:16).
2. A son of Bela (1Ch 7:7).

EZEKIAS *See Hezekiah.*

EZEKIEL [3489] (*God [El] strengthens*). A priest. The time of his prophecy (Eze 1:1-3). Persecution of (Eze 3:25).

Visions of: Of God's glory (Eze 1; 8; 10; 11:22), of Israelites' abominations (Eze 8:5-6), of their punishment (Eze 9:10), of the valley of dry bones (Eze 37:1-14), of a man with a measuring line (Eze 40-48), of the river (Eze 47:1-5).

Teaches by pantomime: Feigns muteness (Eze 3:26; 24:27; 33:22), symbolizes the siege of Jerusalem by drawings on a tile (Eze 4), shaves himself (Eze 5:1-4), removes his belongings to illustrate the approaching Israelite captivity (Eze 12:3-7), sighs (Eze 21:6-7), employs a boiling pot to symbolize the destruction of Jerusalem (Eze 24:1-14), omits mourning at the death of his wife (Eze 24:16-27), prophesies by parable of an eagle (Eze 17:2-10). Other parables (Eze 15; 16; 19; 23).

Prophecies of concerning various nations (Eze 25-29). His popularity (Eze 33:31-32).

EZEKIEL, BOOK OF

Author: Ezekiel

Date: See chart below

Outline:

I. Oracles of Judgment against Israel (chs. 1-24).
A. Ezekiel's Inaugural Vision (chs. 1-3).
1. The divine overwhelming (ch. 1).
2. The equipping and commissioning (2:1-3:15).
3. The watchman 3:16-21).
4. Further stipulations (3:22-27).
B. Symbolic Acts Portraying the Siege of Jerusalem (chs. 4-5).
1. The city of Jerusalem on a clay tablet (4:1-3).
2. Prophetic immobility (4:4-8).
3. Diet for the siege and exile (4:9-17).
4. The divine razor and its consequences (ch. 5).
C. Oracles Explaining Divine Judgment (chs. 6-7).
1. Doom for the mountains of Israel (ch. 6).
2. The end (ch. 7).

D. Vision of the Corrupted Temple (chs. 8-11).
1. Four abominations (ch. 8).
2. Destruction of the city (ch. 9).
3. God's glory leaves Jerusalem (ch. 10).
4. Conclusion of the vision (ch. 11).
E. Symbolic Acts Portraying Jerusalem's Exile (ch. 12).
1. An exile's baggage (12:1-16).
2. Anxious eating (12:17-20).
3. The nearness of judgment (12:21-28).
F. Oracles Explaining Divine Judgment (chs. 13-24).
1. False prophets and magic charms (ch. 13).
2. The penalty for idolatry (14:1-11).
3. Noah, Daniel and Job (14:12-23).
4. Jerusalem as a burnt vine branch (ch. 15).
5. Jerusalem as a wayward founding (16:1-43).
6. Jerusalem compared to other cities (16:44-63).
7. Jerusalem's kings allegorized (17:1-21).
8. The new tree (17:22-24).
9. The lesson of three generations (ch. 18).
10. The twofold lament (ch. 19).
11. Israel as a hardened repeater (ch. 20).
12. The sword of the Lord (ch. 21).
13. Jerusalem the city of blood (ch. 22).
14. Oholah and Oholibah (ch. 23).
15. The final fire: Jerusalem's end (24:1-14).
16. The death of Ezekiel's wife and the destruction of the temple (24:15-27).
II. Oracles of Judgment against the Nations (chs. 25-32).
A. Against Ammon (25:1-7).
B. Against Moab (25:8-11).
C. Against Edom (25:12-14).
D. Against Philistia (25:15-17).
E. Against Tyre (26:1-28:19).
1. The end of the city (ch. 26).
2. A lament for Tyre (ch. 27).
3. Against the king of Tyre (28:1-19).

DATES IN EZEKIEL					
REFERENCE	YEAR	MONTH	DAY	MODERN RECKONING	EVENT
1. 1:1	3	4	5	July 31, 593 B.C.	Inaugural vision
1:2	5	-	5		
3:16	"At the end of seven days"				
2. 8:1	6	6	5	Sept. 17, 592	Transport to Jerusalem
3. 20:1-2	7	5	10	Aug. 14, 591	Negative view of Israel's history
4. 24:1	9	10	10	Jan. 15, 588	Beginning of siege (cf. 2 Ki 25:1)
5. 26:1	11	-	1	Apr. 23, 587 to Apr. 13, 586	Oracle against Tyre
6. 29:1	10	10	12	Jan. 7, 587	Oracle against Egypt
7. 29:17	27	1	1	Apr. 26, 571	Egypt in exchange for Tyre
8. 30:20	11	1	7	Apr. 29, 587	Oracle against Pharaoh
9. 31:1	11	3	1	June 21, 587	Oracle against Pharaoh
10. 32:1	12	12	1	Mar. 3, 585	Lament over Pharaoh
11. 32:17	12	-	15	Apr. 13, 586 to Apr. 1, 585	Egypt dead
12. 33:21	12	10	5	Jan. 8, 585	Arrival of first fugitive
13. 40:1	25	1	10	Apr. 28, 573	Vision of the future
40:1	"fourteenth year after the fall of the city"				

F. Against Sidon (28:20-24).

G. A Note of Promise for Israel (28:25-26).

H. Against Egypt (chs. 29-32).

  1. As a doomed monster (29:1-16).

  2. As a payment to Nebuchadnezzar (29:17-21).

  3. The approaching day (30:1-19).

  4. Pharaoh's arms are broken (30:20-26).

  5. As a felled cedar (ch. 31).

  6. A lament over Pharaoh (32:1-16).

  7. As consigned to the pit among the uncircumcised (32:17-32).

III. Oracles of Consolation for Israel (chs. 33-48).

A. The Watchman (33:1-20).

B. Jerusalem's Fall Reported and Explained (33:21-33).

C. The Lord as the Good Shepherd (ch. 34).

D. Oracles against Edom (ch. 35).

E. Consolations for the Mountains of Israel (36:1-15).

F. Summary of Ezekiel's Theology (36:16-38).

G. Vision of National Restoration (ch. 37).

  1. National resurrection (37:1-14).

  2. National reunification (37:15-28).

H. The Final Battle (chs. 38-39).

I. Vision of Renewed Worship (chs. 40-48).

  1. Wall around the temple (40:1-47).

  2. Temple exterior (40:48-41:26).

  3. Temple interior (ch. 42).

  4. The return of God's glory (ch. 43).

  5. The priesthood (ch. 44).

  6. Land allotment (ch. 45).

  7. The duties of the prince (ch. 46).

  8. Life-giving water (47:1-12).

  9. Land allotment (47:13-48:35).

EZEL *See Beth Ezel.*

EZEM [6796] (*bone [strength]*). A city in the S of Judah (Jos 15:29; 19:3; 1Ch 4:29).

EZER [733, 6470, 6472] (*help*).

1. The sixth son of Seir; a clan chief of the native Horite inhabitants of Edom (Ge 36:21,27,30; 1Ch 1:38,42).

2. A Judahite, father of Hushah (1Ch 4:4).

3. An Ephraimite slain by the men of Gath (1Ch 7:21).

4. A Gadite warrior who went over to David (1Ch 12:9).

5. A Levite, son of Jeshua, who repaired a section of the wall of Jerusalem under Nehemiah's direction (Ne 3:19).

6. A priest who participated in the dedication of the wall (Ne 12:42).

EZION GEBER, EZION-GEBER [6787] (*giant, the giant backbone*).

NIV+ GEBER

The last encampment of Israel before coming to the wilderness of Zin (Nu 33:35-36; Dt 2:8). Solomon, built a navy at (1Ki 9:26), visited (2Ch 8:17). Jehoshaphat's ships built at (2Ch 20:36), wrecked at (1Ki 22:48).

EZRA [6474, 10537] (*help*).

NIV+ EZRA'S

A famous scribe and priest (Ezr 7:1-6,10-12,21; Ne 12:36). Appoints a fast (Ezr 8:21). Commissioned by Artaxerxes to rebuild the temple in Jerusalem which he directs (Ezr 7:8). Persecuted by Tattenai the governor (Ezr 6:3-17). Darius renews the decree of Cyrus for rebuilding the temple which he directs to completion (Ezr 6:1-15). His charge to the priests (Ezr 8:29). Exhorts people to put away heathen wives (Ezr 10:1-17). Reads the law (Ne 8).

Reforms corruption (Ezr 10; Ne 13). Participates in the dedication of the wall of Jerusalem (Ne 12:27-43).

EZRA, BOOK OF

Author: According to Jewish tradition Ezra wrote Ezra and Nehemiah and also 1 and 2 Chronicles.

Date: c. 440 B.C.

Outline:

I. First Return from Exile and Rebuilding of the Temple (chs. 1-6).

A. First Return of the Exiles (ch. 1).

  1. The edict of Cyrus (1:1-4).

  2. The return under Sheshbazzar (1:5-11).

B. List of Returning Exiles (ch. 2).

C. Revival of Temple Worship (ch. 3).

  1. The rebuilding of the altar (3:1-3).

  2. The Feast of Tabernacles (3:4-6).

  3. The beginning of temple reconstruction (3:7-13).

D. Opposition to Rebuilding (4:1-23).

  1. Opposition during the reign of Cyrus (4:1-5).

  2. Opposition during the reign of Xerxes (4:6).

  3. Opposition during the reign of Artaxerxes (4:7-23).

E. Completion of the Temple (4:24-6:22).

  1. Resumption of work under Darius (4:24).

  2. A new beginning inspired by Haggai and Zechariah (5:1-2).

  3. Intervention of the governor, Tattenai (5:3-5).

  4. Report to Darius (5:6-17).

  5. Search for the decree of Cyrus (6:1-5).

  6. Darius's order for the rebuilding of the temple (6:6-12).

  7. Completion of the temple (6:13-15).

  8. Dedication of the temple (6:16-18).

  9. Celebration of Passover (6:19-22).

II. Ezra's Return and Reforms (chs. 7-10).

A. Ezra's Return to Jerusalem (chs. 7-8).

  1. Introduction (7:1-10).

  2. The authorization by Artaxerxes (7:11-26).

  3. Ezra's doxology (7:27-28).

  4. List of those returning with Ezra (8:1-14).

  5. The search for Levites (8:15-20).

  6. Prayer and fasting (8:21-23).

  7. The assignment of the sacred articles (8:24-30).

  8. The journey and arrival in Jerusalem (8:31-36).

B. Ezra's Reforms (chs. 9-10).

  1. The offense of mixed marriages (9:1-5).

  2. Ezra's confession and prayer (9:6-15).

  3. The people's response (10:1-4).

  4. The calling of a public assembly (10:5-15).

  5. Investigation of the offenders (10:16-17).

  6. The list of offenders (10:18-43).

  7. The dissolution of mixed marriages (10:44).

EZRAH [6477]. A Judahite (1Ch 4:17).

EZRAHITES [276].

NIV+ ZERAH

The family or clan of Ethan and Heman, legendary wise men and poets (1Ki 4:31; Ps 88:T; 89:T). The word is probably a gentilic form of "Zerah," since 1Ch 2:6 designates Ethan and Heman as sons of Zerah.

EZRI [6479] (*my help*). Son of Kelub; the steward in charge of the agriculture of the crown lands in the time of David (1Ch 27:26).

F

FABLE (talk, tale, legend, myth).

A type of literary genre in which animals and inanimate objects are used as persons or actors, speaking and using human behavior as if they actually were human beings. The fable is akin to the *allegory* and the *parable*. The fable is distinguished from the others in that there is a moral to the story; while the primary point of the allegory and the parable is to teach spiritual virtues.

There are two fables in the OT. In the first, the people of Shechem are warned by Jotham, the sole survivor of Abimelech's coup, that Abimelech is treacherous and will provide certain tyranny (Jdg 9:7-15). In the second, Jehoash, king of Israel, snubs Amaziah, king of Judah, with an insult, warning that he is courting disaster (2Ki 14:9).

In the NT, the debate among the parts of the body may be considered a fable (1Co 12:14-26). For KJV "fable" (1Ti 1:4; 4:7; 2Ti 4:4; Tit 1:14; 2Pe 1:16) *See Myths.*

See Allegory; Parable.

FACE [*678, 5260, 5790, 6524, 7155, 7156, 8011, 8559, 10228, *4725, *5125*].

NIV+ FACED, FACEDOWN, FACES, FACING, STERN-FACED

General References to:

Refers to the face of, the waters (Ge 1:2), the earth (Ge 1:29), a man (Ge 3:19; Jas 1:23), flocks (Ge 30:40), God (Nu 6:25), the moon (Job 26:9), the seraphs (Isa 6:2), and the sky (Mt 16:3), Christ (2Co 4:6), the living creatures around the throne (Rev 4:7). The man himself may be meant (Dt 7:10), as in the Oriental circumlocution for "I." Character revealed in (Isa 3:9). Disfiguring of, in fasting (Mt 6:16).

Reflects Feelings:

(Ge 4:5; Pr 15:13). Moses in the presence of God (Ex 3:6). Favors are granted when the face is lifted up (Nu 6:25). Ruth bowed with her face to the ground in humility (Ru 2:10). Mourning (2Sa 19:4). To turn away or to hide the face is rejection (Pr 13:1). To seek the face is a desire for an audience (Ps 105:4). To harden the face is to promise no appeal (Pr 21:29). To spit on the face is a serious insult (Mt 26:67). Determination was evident when Jesus set his face to go to Jerusalem (Lk 9:51).

Covered:

By a harlot (Ge 38:15). Moses, when talking to the people after he was in the presence of God (Ex 34:29-35; 2Co 3:13-18). David (2Sa 19:4). In the doom of Haman (Est 7:8).

Of God:

Applied to God, it denotes his presence. Jacob struggles with God until daybreak and lives; he names the place where he fought, Peniel, which means "face of God," because "I saw God face to face, and yet my life was spared" (Ge 32:30). God himself or his glory which could not be seen by Moses (or by any man) or he would die (Ex 33:20). God hides his face from sin to show his displeasure (Pr 27:9) and to show that he has forgiven sin (Ps 51:9). John says that the Son of God alone has ever seen God face to

face (Jn 1:18). The literal translation for the "bread of the Presence" would be the "bread of the face" (Ex 25:30).

Transfigured:

Moses (Ex 34:29-35), Jesus (Mt 17:2; Lk 9:29).
See Countenance.

FAIR [622, 3206, 3208, 3637, 4797, 9185, *2304, 2699*].

NIV+ FAIRLY, FAIRNESS

Meaning of:

Has the meaning of, just (Jdg 16:9; Pr 1:3; 2:9; 2Co 6:13; Col 4:1), clear skies (Job 26:13; Mt 16:2), persuasive (Pr 7:21), clean (Zec 3:5), beautiful (Hos 10:11; Ac 7:20). It is not used to describe complexion.

FAIR HAVENS [*2816*]. A small bay near Lasea on the S coast of Crete, about five miles E of Cape Matala. Paul stayed here for a short time on his way to Rome (Ac 27:8-12).

FAITH [574, 575, 586, 953, 5085+5086, 5085, 9459, *601, 602, 1650+4411+4411, 1666+4411, 3898, 3899, 4409, 4411, 4412*].

NIV+ BELIEF, BELIEVE, FAITHFUL, FAITHFULLY, FAITHFULNESS, FAITHLESS

General Explanation of:

Faith has both an active and a passive sense in the Bible. The former meaning relates to one's loyalty to a person or fidelity to a promise; the latter confidence in the word or assurance of another. Faith is not merely *what* a person believes, i.e., accurate doctrine or creed, but also and more importantly, that the object of his faith is valid. A man's life is governed by his thoughts; he will ultimately become that which he dwells most upon in his mind. This is the reason for Paul's instruction to the Romans, "Do not conform any longer to the pattern of this world, but be transformed by the renewing of your mind" (Ro 12:2). He wrote similar instruction to the Philippians, "Finally, brothers, whatever is true, whatever is noble, whatever is right, whatever is pure, whatever is lovely, whatever is admirable—if anything is excellent or praiseworthy— think about such things" (Php 4:8).

The Value of:

People are kept secure by (2Ch 20:20; Ro 11:20; 2Co 1:24; 1Jn 5:4), are established by (Isa 7:9), are saved by (Jn 3:15; Ac 16:31; Ro 9:30-32; Gal 2:16; Eph 2:8-9; Php 3:9), healed by (Ac 14:9; Jas 5:15), are sanctified by (Ac 26:18), receive the Holy Spirit by (Gal 3:5,14), live by (2Co 5:7). Causes men to be a blessing to others (Jn 7:38). Disbelieving God is a great sin (Jn 16:9; Ro 14:23). Faith is necessary to please God (Heb 11:6).

The Gift of God:

The apostles ask Jesus to increase (Lk 17:5). God gives a certain measure of (Ro 12:3; 1Co 2:4-5). Given by the Spirit (1Co 12:8-9).

The Purpose of:

To gain understanding and to grow in the truth (Ps 119:97-105,129-131; Jn 8:31-32; 2Ti 2:15; 1Jn 2:5,14). To grow in the grace of God (Ac 2:42-47; Ro 4:4-5; 5:2; 1Co 15:10; Eph 4:15; Heb 4:16). To help us to rejoice through our faith (Ro 5:2-5,11; 15:13; Php 1:18-19; 2:17-18). To strengthen the man of faith (Ro 6:12-14; 11:20; 1Co 9:27; Php 4:6-7; 2Th 3:3; 2Ti 4:7-8; 1Pe 1:3-5). To be transformed into the image of Christ (Ro 8:29; 1Co 15:49; 2Co 3:18; 4:3-6). To become strong people of faith (Eph 4:1-3,11-13,15-16).

The Effect of:

Faith not works (Gal 5:5-6). Produces good works (1Th 1:3; 2Th 1:11), internal changes (1Th 2:13), perseverance (Jas 1:3).

The Righteousness of:

The true righteousness of God comes from (Ro 1:17; 3:21-30; 4:3,11; 9:31-33; 10:4-11; Gal 2:16; Php 3:9; Heb 11:7).

The Biblical Position Concerning:

Credited as righteousness (Ge 15:6; Ro 4:3; Gal 3:6; Jas 2:23).

Inspired by God's goodness—

Ps 36:7 How priceless is your unfailing love! Both high and low among men find refuge in the shadow of your wings. (+Ps 36:9)

Inspired by the Holy Spirit—

1Co 12:8 To one there is given through the Spirit the message of wisdom, to another the message of knowledge by means of the same Spirit, [9]to another faith by the same Spirit, to another gifts of healing by that one Spirit,

Explained—

Ps 118:8 It is better to take refuge in the LORD than to trust in man. [9]It is better to take refuge in the LORD than to trust in princes. (+Lk 17:6)

Lk 18:8 I tell you, he will see that they get justice, and quickly. However, when the Son of Man comes, will he find faith on the earth?" (+1Ti 4:12)

Heb 11:1 Now faith is being sure of what we hope for and certain of what we do not see. [2]This is what the ancients were commended for.

[3]By faith we understand that the universe was formed at God's command, so that what is seen was not made out of what was visible.

Heb 11:6 And without faith it is impossible to please God, because anyone who comes to him must believe that he exists and that he rewards those who earnestly seek him.

Worry, doubt, and the lack of faith (Mt 6:25-34; 14:31; Lk 9:40; 17:5).

Prayer for increase of faith (Mk 9:24)—

Lk 17:5 The apostles said to the Lord, "Increase our faith!"

The gift of God (Ro 12:3).—

The righteous live by (Hab 2:4; Ro 1:17; Gal 3:11; Heb 10:38).

Miracles accomplished by (Mt 17:18-20)—

Mt 21:21 Jesus replied, "I tell you the truth, if you have faith and do not doubt, not only can you do what was done to the fig tree, but also you can say to this mountain, 'Go, throw yourself into the sea,' and it will be done. [22]If you believe, you will receive whatever you ask for in prayer." (+Mk 9:23; 11:23-24)

Secures salvation—

Col 2:12 having been buried with him in baptism and raised with him through your faith in the power of God, who raised him from the dead.

2Th 2:13 But we ought always to thank God for you, brothers loved by the Lord, because from the beginning God chose you to be saved through the sanctifying work of the Spirit and through belief in the truth.

Heb 4:1 Therefore, since the promise of entering his rest still stands, let us be careful that none of you be found to have fallen short of it. [2]For we also have had the gospel preached to us, just as they did; but the message they heard was of no value to them, because those who heard did not combine it with faith. [3]Now we who have believed enter that rest, just as God has said,

"So I declared on oath in my anger, 'They shall never enter my rest.'"

And yet his work has been finished since the creation of the world. [4]For somewhere he has spoken about the seventh day in these words: "And on the seventh day God rested from all his work." [5]And again in the passage above he says, "They shall never enter my rest."

[6]It still remains that some will enter that rest, and those who formerly had the gospel preached to them did not go in, because of their disobedience. [7]Therefore God again set a certain day, calling it Today, when a long time later he spoke through David, as was said before:

"Today, if you hear his voice, do not harden your hearts."

[8]For if Joshua had given them rest, God would not have spoken later about another day. [9]There remains, then, a Sabbath-rest for the people of God; [10]for anyone who enters God's rest also rests from his own work, just as God did from his. [11]Let us, therefore, make every effort to enter that rest, so that no one will fall by following their example of disobedience.

Heb 6:1 Therefore let us leave the elementary teachings about Christ and go on to maturity, not laying again the foundation of repentance from acts that lead to death, and of faith in God,

Heb 6:12 We do not want you to become lazy, but to imitate those who through faith and patience inherit what has been promised.

Heb 6:18 God did this so that, by two unchangeable things in which it is impossible for God to lie, we who have fled to take hold of the hope offered to us may be greatly encouraged.

The Old Testament use:

In the OT, the word "faith" in the sense of belief occurs only five times (2Ch 20:20,20; Isa 7:9; 26:2; Hab 2:4). Faith is also communicated by words such as "believe," "fear," "hope," "love," and "trust." Faith is seen in the examples of the servants of God who committed their lives to him in unwavering trust and obedience. OT faith is never mere assent to a set of doctrines or outward acceptance of the Law, but absolute confidence in the faithfulness of God and a loving obedience to his will.

The New Testament Use:

In the NT "faith" and "believe" occur almost 500 times. The NT makes the claim that the promised Messiah had come and that Jesus of Nazareth was this promised Messiah. To believe on him meant to become a Christian, and was pivotal in the experience of the individual. Jesus offered himself as the object of faith and made plain that faith in him was necessary for eternal life.

The first Christians called themselves believers (Ac 2:44) and endeavored to persuade others to believe in Jesus (Ac 6:7; 28:24). In the epistles of Paul, faith is contrasted with works as a means of salvation (Ro 3:20-22). Faith is trust in the person of Jesus, the truth of his teaching, and the redemptive work which he accomplished at Calvary.

Faith may also refer to the body of truth which constitutes the whole of the Christian message (Jude 3).

Examples in the NT: In God (Lk 1:38-55; Ac 27:25; Ro 4:24; Heb 6:1; 1Pe 1:21; 4:19; 1Jn 3:21).

Strengthened by Miracles:

Of Abraham (Ge 15:8-18), of Gideon (Jdg 6:17,36-40), of Hezekiah (2Ki 20:8-11), of Zechariah (Lk 1:18-20,64).

In Affliction:

Exemplified by Job (Job 13:15-16; 14:15; 16:19; 19:25-27).

In Adversity:

Exemplified, by Hagar (Ge 16:15), by Moses (Nu 14:8-9), by Asa (2Ch 14:11), by Jehoshaphat (2Ch 20:12), by Hezekiah (2Ch 32:7-8), by Nehemiah (Ne 1:10; 2:20)

Exemplified by the psalmist (Ps 3:3,5-6; 4:3,8; 6:8-9)— **Ps 7:1** O LORD my God, I take refuge in you; save and deliver me from all who pursue me, (+Ps 7:10; 9:3-4; 11:1; 13:5; 17:6; 20:5-7; 31:1,3-6,14-15; 32:7; 33:20-22; 35:10; 38:9,15; 42:5-6,8; 43:5; 44:5,8; 46:1-3,5,7; 54:4; 55:16-17,23; 56:3-4,8-9; 57:1-3; 59:9,17; 60:9-10,12; 61:2,4,6-7; 62:1,5-7; 63:6-7; 69:19,35-36; 70:5; 71:1,3,5-7,14,16,20-21; 73:23-24,26,28; 86:2,7; 89:18,26; 91:1-2,9-10; 92:10, 15; 94:14-15,17-18,22; 102:13; 108:10-13; 118:6-7,10,14, 17; 119:42,57,74,81,114,166; 121:2; 138:7-8; 140:6-7,12; 142:3,5; 143:8-9)

By Jeremiah (La 3:24), by Daniel (Da 3:16-17), by Jonah (Jnh 2:2), by Micah (Mic 7:7-9,20)

Exemplified by Paul (Ac 27:25; 2Co 1:10; 4:8-9,13,16-18; Php 1:19-21)—

1Ti 4:10 (and for this we labor and strive), that we have put our hope in the living God, who is the Savior of all men, and especially of those who believe. (+2Ti 1:12-13)
2Ti 4:7 I have fought the good fight, I have finished the race, I have kept the faith. [8]Now there is in store for me the crown of righteousness, which the Lord, the righteous Judge, will award to me on that day—and not only to me, but also to all who have longed for his appearing. (+2Ti 4:18)

By the author of the letter to the Hebrews (Heb 10:34).

Commanded:

Ps 4:5 Offer right sacrifices and trust in the LORD.
Ps 115:9 O house of Israel, trust in the LORD—he is their help and shield.
Ps 115:11 You who fear him, trust in the LORD—he is their help and shield. (+Ecc 11:1)
Isa 26:4 Trust in the LORD forever, for the LORD, the LORD, is the Rock eternal.
Mt 6:25 "Therefore I tell you, do not worry about your life, what you will eat or drink; or about your body, what you will wear. Is not life more important than food, and the body more important than clothes? [26]Look at the birds of the air; they do not sow or reap or store away in barns, and yet your heavenly Father feeds them. Are you not much more valuable than they? [27]Who of you by worrying can add a single hour to his life?
[28]"And why do you worry about clothes? See how the lilies of the field grow. They do not labor or spin. [29]Yet I tell you that not even Solomon in all his splendor was dressed like one of these. [30]If that is how God clothes the grass of the field, which is here today and tomorrow is thrown into the fire, will he not much more clothe you, O you of little faith? [31]So do not worry, saying, 'What shall we eat?' or 'What shall we drink?' or 'What shall we wear?' [32]For the pagans run after all these things, and your heavenly Father knows that you need them. [33]But seek first his kingdom and his righteousness, and all these things will be given to you as well. [34]Therefore do not worry about tomorrow, for tomorrow will worry about itself. Each day has enough trouble of its own.

Mk 1:15 "The time has come," he said. "The kingdom of God is near. Repent and believe the good news!"
Mk 11:22 "Have faith in God," Jesus answered.
Lk 12:32 "Do not be afraid, little flock, for your Father has been pleased to give you the kingdom.
1Ti 6:11 But you, man of God, flee from all this, and pursue righteousness, godliness, faith, love, endurance and gentleness. [12]Fight the good fight of the faith. Take hold of the eternal life to which you were called when you made your good confession in the presence of many witnesses.
1Ti 6:17 Command those who are rich in this present world not to be arrogant nor to put their hope in wealth, which is so uncertain, but to put their hope in God, who richly provides us with everything for our enjoyment.
Jas 1:6 But when he asks, he must believe and not doubt, because he who doubts is like a wave of the sea, blown and tossed by the wind.

In time of public danger—

Ex 14:13 Moses answered the people, "Do not be afraid. Stand firm and you will see the deliverance the LORD will bring you today. The Egyptians you see today you will never see again. (+Nu 21:34; Dt 1:21,29-30; 3:2,22; 7:17-21)
Dt 20:1 When you go to war against your enemies and see horses and chariots and an army greater than yours, do not be afraid of them, because the LORD your God, who brought you up out of Egypt, will be with you. (+Dt 31:8, 23; Jos 10:25; Jdg 6:14-16; 2Ki 19:6-7; 2Ch 20:15,17)
2Ch 20:20 Early in the morning they left for the Desert of Tekoa. As they set out, Jehoshaphat stood and said, "Listen to me, Judah and people of Jerusalem! Have faith in the LORD your God and you will be upheld; have faith in his prophets and you will be successful."
2Ch 32:7 "Be strong and courageous. Do not be afraid or discouraged because of the king of Assyria and the vast army with him, for there is a greater power with us than with him. [8]With him is only the arm of flesh, but with us is the LORD our God to help us and to fight our battles." And the people gained confidence from what Hezekiah the king of Judah said.
Ne 4:14 After I looked things over, I stood up and said to the nobles, the officials and the rest of the people, "Don't be afraid of them. Remember the Lord, who is great and awesome, and fight for your brothers, your sons and your daughters, your wives and your homes."
Isa 37:6 Isaiah said to them, "Tell your master, 'This is what the LORD says: Do not be afraid of what you have heard—those words with which the underlings of the king of Assyria have blasphemed me.
Jer 42:11 Do not be afraid of the king of Babylon, whom you now fear. Do not be afraid of him, declares the LORD, for I am with you and will save you and deliver you from his hands.

In time of adversity—

Ps 37:3 Trust in the LORD and do good; dwell in the land and enjoy safe pasture.
Ps 37:5 Commit your way to the LORD; trust in him and he will do this:
Ps 37:7 Be still before the LORD and wait patiently for him; do not fret when men succeed in their ways, when they carry out their wicked schemes.
Ps 55:22 Cast your cares on the LORD and he will sustain you; he will never let the righteous fall.
Ps 62:8 Trust in him at all times, O people; pour out your hearts to him, for God is our refuge. *Selah*
Isa 43:1 But now, this is what the LORD says—he who

created you, O Jacob, he who formed you, O Israel: "Fear not, for I have redeemed you; I have summoned you by name; you are mine. ²When you pass through the waters, I will be with you; and when you pass through the rivers, they will not sweep over you. When you walk through the fire, you will not be burned; the flames will not set you ablaze.

Isa 43:5 Do not be afraid, for I am with you; I will bring your children from the east and gather you from the west.

Isa 43:10 "You are my witnesses," declares the LORD, "and my servant whom I have chosen, so that you may know and believe me and understand that I am he. Before me no god was formed, nor will there be one after me.

Isa 44:2 This is what the LORD says—he who made you, who formed you in the womb, and who will help you: Do not be afraid, O Jacob, my servant, Jeshurun, whom I have chosen.

Isa 44:8 Do not tremble, do not be afraid. Did I not proclaim this and foretell it long ago? You are my witnesses. Is there any God besides me? No, there is no other Rock; I know not one."

Commanded upon public leaders—

Jos 1:9 Have I not commanded you? Be strong and courageous. Do not be terrified; do not be discouraged, for the LORD your God will be with you wherever you go." (+Jos 1:5-8)

2Ch 15:7 But as for you, be strong and do not give up, for your work will be rewarded."

Commanded upon the young—

Pr 3:5 Trust in the LORD with all your heart and lean not on your own understanding; ⁶in all your ways acknowledge him, and he will make your paths straight.

Pr 3:24 when you lie down, you will not be afraid; when you lie down, your sleep will be sweet. ²⁵Have no fear of sudden disaster or of the ruin that overtakes the wicked, ²⁶for the LORD will be your confidence and will keep your foot from being snared.

Commanded upon the discouraged—

Isa 35:3 Strengthen the feeble hands, steady the knees that give way; ⁴say to those with fearful hearts, "Be strong, do not fear; your God will come, he will come with vengeance; with divine retribution he will come to save you."

Isa 41:10 So do not fear, for I am with you; do not be dismayed, for I am your God. I will strengthen you and help you; I will uphold you with my righteous right hand.

Isa 41:13 For I am the LORD, your God, who takes hold of your right hand and says to you, Do not fear; I will help you. ¹⁴Do not be afraid, O worm Jacob, O little Israel, for I myself will help you," declares the LORD, your Redeemer, the Holy One of Israel.

Isa 50:10 Who among you fears the LORD and obeys the word of his servant? Let him who walks in the dark, who has no light, trust in the name of the LORD and rely on his God.

Commanded upon widows—

Jer 49:11 Leave your orphans; I will protect their lives. Your widows too can trust in me."

Exemplified:

By Asa—

2Ch 14:11 Then Asa called to the LORD his God and said, "LORD, there is no one like you to help the powerless against the mighty. Help us, O LORD our God, for we rely on you, and in your name we have come against this vast army. O LORD, you are our God; do not let man prevail against you."

By Jehoshaphat—

2Ch 20:12 O our God, will you not judge them? For we have no power to face this vast army that is attacking us. We do not know what to do, but our eyes are upon you."

By Hezekiah—

2Ch 32:8 With him is only the arm of flesh, but with us is the LORD our God to help us and to fight our battles." And the people gained confidence from what Hezekiah the king of Judah said.

By Job (Job 1:21-22; 2:10)—

Job 5:8 "But if it were I, I would appeal to God; I would lay my cause before him. ⁹He performs wonders that cannot be fathomed, miracles that cannot be counted.

Job 19:25 I know that my Redeemer lives, and that in the end he will stand upon the earth. ²⁶And after my skin has been destroyed, yet in my flesh I will see God; ²⁷I myself will see him with my own eyes—I, and not another. How my heart yearns within me!

By the psalmists, setting forth supreme confidence in God—

Ps 4:3 Know that the LORD has set apart the godly for himself; the LORD will hear when I call to him.

Ps 4:8 I will lie down and sleep in peace, for you alone, O LORD, make me dwell in safety.

Ps 11:1 In the LORD I take refuge. How then can you say to me: "Flee like a bird to your mountain.

Ps 13:5 But I trust in your unfailing love; my heart rejoices in your salvation. (+Ps 13:6)

Ps 16:1 Keep me safe, O God, for in you I take refuge. ²I said to the LORD, "You are my Lord; apart from you I have no good thing."

Ps 16:5 LORD, you have assigned me my portion and my cup; you have made my lot secure.

Ps 16:8 I have set the LORD always before me. Because he is at my right hand, I will not be shaken. (+Ps 16:9-10)

Ps 16:11 You have made known to me the path of life; you will fill me with joy in your presence, with eternal pleasures at your right hand.

Ps 18:1 I love you, O LORD, my strength.

²The LORD is my rock, my fortress and my deliverer; my God is my rock, in whom I take refuge. He is my shield and the horn of my salvation, my stronghold. ³I call to the LORD, who is worthy of praise, and I am saved from my enemies. (+Ps 18:30-50)

Ps 20:5 We will shout for joy when you are victorious and will lift up our banners in the name of our God. May the LORD grant all your requests.

⁶Now I know that the LORD saves his anointed; he answers him from his holy heaven with the saving power of his right hand. ⁷Some trust in chariots and some in horses, but we trust in the name of the LORD our God. (+Ps 20:8)

Ps 23:1 The LORD is my shepherd, I shall not be in want. (+Ps 23:2-6)

Ps 25:1 To you, O LORD, I lift up my soul; ²in you I trust, O my God. Do not let me be put to shame, nor let my enemies triumph over me. (+Ps 25:3-4)

Ps 25:5 guide me in your truth and teach me, for you are God my Savior, and my hope is in you all day long. (+Ps 25:6-14)

Ps 25:15 My eyes are ever on the LORD, for only he will release my feet from the snare.

Ps 27:1 The LORD is my light and my salvation—whom shall I fear? The LORD is the stronghold of my life—of whom shall I be afraid? (+Ps 27:2-4)

Ps 27:5 For in the day of trouble he will keep me safe in his dwelling; he will hide me in the shelter of his tabernacle and set me high upon a rock. ⁶Then my head will be exalted above the enemies who surround me; at his tabernacle will I sacrifice with shouts of joy; I will sing and make music to the LORD. (+Ps 27:7-9)

Ps 27:10 Though my father and mother forsake me, the LORD will receive me. (+Ps 27:11-13)

Ps 27:14 Wait for the LORD; be strong and take heart and wait for the LORD. (+Ps 31:1-2)

Ps 31:3 Since you are my rock and my fortress, for the sake of your name lead and guide me. ⁴Free me from the trap that is set for me, for you are my refuge. ⁵Into your hands I commit my spirit; redeem me, O LORD, the God of truth. (+Ps 31:22-23,24)

Ps 40:1 I waited patiently for the LORD; he turned to me and heard my cry. ²He lifted me out of the slimy pit, out of the mud and mire; he set my feet on a rock and gave me a firm place to stand. ³He put a new song in my mouth, a hymn of praise to our God. Many will see and fear and put their trust in the LORD.

⁴Blessed is the man who makes the LORD his trust, who does not look to the proud, to those who turn aside to false gods. (+Ps 40:5-11)

Ps 46:1 God is our refuge and strength, an ever-present help in trouble. ²Therefore we will not fear, though the earth give way and the mountains fall into the heart of the sea, ³though its waters roar and foam and the mountains quake with their surging. *Selah* (+Ps 46:4)

Ps 46:5 God is within her, she will not fall; God will help her at break of day. (+Ps 46:6)

Ps 46:7 The LORD Almighty is with us; the God of Jacob is our fortress. *Selah* (+Ps 46:8-11; 56:10-13)

Ps 57:1 Have mercy on me, O God, have mercy on me, for in you my soul takes refuge. I will take refuge in the shadow of your wings until the disaster has passed.

²I cry out to God Most High, to God, who fulfills [his purpose] for me. ³He sends from heaven and saves me, rebuking those who hotly pursue me; *Selah* God sends his love and his faithfulness. (+Ps 57:4-11; 60:6-8)

Ps 60:9 Who will bring me to the fortified city? Who will lead me to Edom? ¹⁰Is it not you, O God, you who have rejected us and no longer go out with our armies? (+Ps 60:11)

Ps 60:12 With God we will gain the victory, and he will trample down our enemies. (+Ps 61:1)

Ps 61:2 From the ends of the earth I call to you, I call as my heart grows faint; lead me to the rock that is higher than I. (+Ps 61:3)

Ps 61:4 I long to dwell in your tent forever and take refuge in the shelter of your wings. *Selah* (+Ps 61:5)

Ps 61:6 Increase the days of the king's life, his years for many generations. ⁷May he be enthroned in God's presence forever; appoint your love and faithfulness to protect him. (+Ps 61:8)

Ps 62:5 Find rest, O my soul, in God alone; my hope comes from him. ⁶He alone is my rock and my salvation; he is my fortress, I will not be shaken. ⁷My salvation and my honor depend on God; he is my mighty rock, my refuge. (+Ps 62:8-12; 63:1-5)

Ps 63:6 On my bed I remember you; I think of you through the watches of the night. ⁷Because you are my help, I sing in the shadow of your wings. (+Ps 63:8)

By the following Psalms in their entirety—

Ps 91:1 He who dwells in the shelter of the Most High will rest in the shadow of the Almighty. ²I will say of the LORD,

"He is my refuge and my fortress, my God, in whom I trust." (+Ps 91:3-8)

Ps 91:9 If you make the Most High your dwelling—even the LORD, who is my refuge— ¹⁰then no harm will befall you, no disaster will come near your tent. (+Ps 91:11-16; 95; 105:108; 115:1-8)

Ps 115:9 O house of Israel, trust in the LORD—he is their help and shield. (+Ps 115:10)

Ps 115:11 You who fear him, trust in the LORD—he is their help and shield. (+Ps 115:12-14,15-18; 116:1-6)

Ps 116:7 Be at rest once more, O my soul, for the LORD has been good to you. (+Ps 116:8-19; 118:1-5)

Ps 118:6 The LORD is with me; I will not be afraid. What can man do to me? ⁷The LORD is with me; he is my helper. I will look in triumph on my enemies. (+Ps 118:8-9)

Ps 118:10 All the nations surrounded me, but in the name of the LORD I cut them off. (+Ps 118:11-13)

Ps 118:14 The LORD is my strength and my song; he has become my salvation. (+Ps 118:15-16)

Ps 118:17 I will not die but live, and will proclaim what the LORD has done. (+Ps 118:18-29; 121:1)

Ps 121:2 My help comes from the LORD, the Maker of heaven and earth. (+Ps 121:3-8; 123:126; 130:1-4)

Ps 130:5 I wait for the LORD, my soul waits, and in his word I put my hope. ⁶My soul waits for the Lord more than watchmen wait for the morning, more than watchmen wait for the morning. (+Ps 130:7-8; 135:136; 138:1-6)

Ps 138:7 Though I walk in the midst of trouble, you preserve my life; you stretch out your hand against the anger of my foes, with your right hand you save me. ⁸The LORD will fulfill [his purpose] for me; your love, O LORD, endures forever—do not abandon the works of your hands. (+Ps 139; 140:1-5)

Ps 140:6 O LORD, I say to you, "You are my God." Hear, O LORD, my cry for mercy. ⁷O Sovereign LORD, my strong deliverer, who shields my head in the day of battle— (+Ps 140:8-11)

Ps 140:12 I know that the LORD secures justice for the poor and upholds the cause of the needy. (+Ps 140:13; 145:146; 147:1-10)

Ps 147:11 the LORD delights in those who fear him, who put their hope in his unfailing love. (+Ps 147:12-20; 148:150)

By Isaiah—

Isa 8:10 Devise your strategy, but it will be thwarted; propose your plan, but it will not stand, for God is with us.

Isa 8:17 I will wait for the LORD, who is hiding his face from the house of Jacob. I will put my trust in him.

Isa 12:2 Surely God is my salvation; I will trust and not be afraid. The LORD, the LORD, is my strength and my song; he has become my salvation." (+Isa 17:13-14)

Isa 25:9 In that day they will say, "Surely this is our God; we trusted in him, and he saved us. This is the LORD, we trusted in him; let us rejoice and be glad in his salvation."

Isa 26:1 In that day this song will be sung in the land of Judah: We have a strong city; God makes salvation its walls and ramparts.

Isa 26:8 Yes, LORD, walking in the way of your laws, we wait for you; your name and renown are the desire of our hearts. (+Isa 33:1)

Isa 33:22 For the LORD is our judge, the LORD is our lawgiver, the LORD is our king; it is he who will save us.

Isa 50:7 Because the Sovereign LORD helps me, I will not be disgraced. Therefore have I set my face like flint, and I know I will not be put to shame. ⁸He who vindicates me is near. Who then will bring charges against me? Let us face each other! Who is my accuser? Let him confront me! ⁹It is the Sovereign LORD who helps me. Who is he that will condemn me? They will all wear out like a garment; the moths will eat them up.

Isa 63:16 But you are our Father, though Abraham does not know us or Israel acknowledge us; you, O LORD, are our Father, our Redeemer from of old is your name.

Isa 64:8 Yet, O LORD, you are our Father. We are the clay, you are the potter; we are all the work of your hand.

By Jeremiah—

Jer 14:9 Why are you like a man taken by surprise, like a warrior powerless to save? You are among us, O LORD, and we bear your name; do not forsake us!

Jer 14:22 Do any of the worthless idols of the nations bring rain? Do the skies themselves send down showers? No, it is you, O LORD our God. Therefore our hope is in you, for you are the one who does all this.

Jer 16:19 O LORD, my strength and my fortress, my refuge in time of distress, to you the nations will come from the ends of the earth and say, "Our fathers possessed nothing but false gods, worthless idols that did them no good.

Jer 17:17 Do not be a terror to me; you are my refuge in the day of disaster.

Jer 20:11 But the LORD is with me like a mighty warrior; so my persecutors will stumble and not prevail. They will fail and be thoroughly disgraced; their dishonor will never be forgotten.

Instances of:

Noah, in building the ark (Ge 6:14-22; Heb 11:7).

Abraham, in forsaking the land of his birth at the command of God (Ge 12:1-4; Heb 11:8), in believing the promise of many descendants (Ge 12:7; 15:4-6; Ro 4:18-21; Heb 11:11-12), in the offering up of Isaac (Ge 22:1-10; Heb 11:17-19).

Jacob, in blessing Joseph's sons (Ge 48:8-21; Heb 11:21).

Joseph, concerning God's providence in his being sold into Egypt, and the final deliverance of Israel (Ge 50:20, 24; Heb 11:22).

Jochebed, in caring for Moses (Ex 2:2-3; Heb 11:23).

Pharaoh's servants, who obeyed the Lord (Ex 9:20).

Abel (Heb 11:4).

Moses, in espousing the cause of his people (Heb 11:24-28), at the death of Korah (Nu 16:28-29).

Israelites (Ps 22:4-5), when Aaron declared the mission of himself and Moses (Ex 4:31), for forty years wanderings (Dt 8:2), in the battle with the Canaanites (1Ch 5:20), and other conquests (2Ch 13:8-18), by the waters of Meribah (Ps 81:7).

Caleb, in advising to take the land of promise (Nu 13:30; 14:6-9), when he asked for Hebron (Jos 14:12).

Rahab, in hospitality to the spies (Jos 2:9,11; Heb 11:31). The spies sent to look over Jericho (Jos 2:24). Conquest of Jericho (Jos 6; Heb 11:30).

Manoah's wife (Jdg 13:23).

Hannah (1Sa 1).

Jonathan, in killing the Philistines (1Sa 14:6).

David, in killing Goliath, the hero of the Philistines (1Sa 17:37,45-47), in choosing to fall into the hands of the Almighty in his punishment for numbering Israel (2Sa 24:14), in believing God's promise that his kingdom would be a perpetual kingdom (Ac 2:30).

The widow of Zarephath, in feeding Elijah (1Ki 17:13-15).

Elijah, in his controversy with the priests of Baal (1Ki 18:32-38).

Hezekiah (2Ki 18:5,19).

Amaziah, in dismissing the Ephraimites in obedience to the command of God, and going alone to battle against the Edomites (2Ch 25:7-10).

Ezra, in making the journey from Babylon to Jerusalem without a military escort (Ezr 8:22).

Mordecai, in the deliverance of the Jews (Est 4:14).

Job (Job 1:21-22; 2:10). Eliphaz, in the overruling providence of God, that afflictions are for the good of the righteous (Job 5:6-27).

The three Hebrews who refused to worship Nebuchadnezzar's idol (Da 3:13-27). Daniel, in the lions' den (Da 6). Nebuchadnezzar (Da 6:16).

The Ninevites, in obeying Jonah (Jnh 3:5).

Habakkuk (Hab 3:17-19).

Joseph, in obeying the vision about Mary and to flee into Egypt (Mt 1:18-24; 2:13-14).

Mary, in believing the angel of the Lord, and in submitting to the Lord's will (Lk 1:38).

Simeon, when he saw Jesus in the temple (Lk 2:25-35).

Paul (Ro 8:18,28,38-39; 1Co 9:24-27; 2Co 5:7; Gal 5:5).

The great men of faith (Heb 11:32-34).

The Trial of:

To prove depth of faith (Dt 8:2; 1Ch 29:17; Ps 26:2). To test spirituality (Mt 13:9-22; Lk 8:13-14). By tribulations (Mt 24:21-25; 2Th 1:3-5). By deferred hope (Heb 6:13-15). By trials (Jas 1:3,12). Is precious (1Pe 1:7).

Instances of the trial of:

Noah (Ge 6:14-22; Heb 11:7).

Abraham, when commanded to leave his native land (Ge 12:1-4; Heb 11:8), when commanded to offer Isaac (Ge 22:1-19; Heb 11:17-19).

Moses, when sent to Pharaoh (Ex 3:11-12; 4:10-17; Heb 11:25-29), at the Red Sea, by the murmurings of the people (Ex 14:15; Heb 11:29).

Joshua and the Israelites, in the method of taking Jericho (Jos 6; Heb 11:30).

Gideon, when commanded to deliver Israel (Jdg 6:36-40; Heb 11:32).

Ezra, in leaving Babylon without a military escort (Ezr 8:22).

Job, by affliction and adversity (Job 1; 2).

The three Hebrews, when commanded to worship Nebuchadnezzar's image (Da 3:8-30; Heb 11:32-34).

Daniel, when forbidden by decree to pray to Yahweh (Da 6:4-23; Heb 11:32-33).

The two blind men who appealed to Jesus for sight (Mt 9:28).

The Syrian Phoenician woman (Mt 15:21-28; Mk 7:24-30).

The disciples, by the question of Jesus, in the storm at sea (Mt 8:23-27; Mk 4:36-41; Lk 8:22-26), as to who he was (Mt 16:15-20; Lk 9:20-21), by their inability to cast out the evil spirit from the boy (Mt 17:14-21; Mk 9:14-29; Lk 9:37-42)

Of Philip, when questioned by Jesus as to how the multitude would be fed (Jn 6:5-6). Of Peter, when asked whether he loved Jesus (Jn 21:15-17).

See Tribulation.

Rewards of:

Protection—

2Sa 22:31 "As for God, his way is perfect; the word of the LORD is flawless. He is a shield for all who take refuge in him.

Ps 5:11 But let all who take refuge in you be glad; let them ever sing for joy. Spread your protection over them, that those who love your name may rejoice in you.

Ps 9:9 The LORD is a refuge for the oppressed, a stronghold in times of trouble. [10]Those who know your name will trust in you, for you, LORD, have never forsaken those who seek you.

Ps 18:30 As for God, his way is perfect; the word of the LORD is flawless. He is a shield for all who take refuge in him.

Ps 33:18 But the eyes of the LORD are on those who fear him, on those whose hope is in his unfailing love, [19]to deliver them from death and keep them alive in famine. (+Ps 33:20)

Pr 29:25 Fear of man will prove to be a snare, but whoever trusts in the LORD is kept safe.

Pr 30:5 "Every word of God is flawless; he is a shield to those who take refuge in him.

Jer 39:18 I will save you; you will not fall by the sword but will escape with your life, because you trust in me, declares the LORD.'"

Na 1:7 The LORD is good, a refuge in times of trouble. He cares for those who trust in him,

Heb 13:5 Keep your lives free from the love of money and be content with what you have, because God has said, "Never will I leave you; never will I forsake you." [6]So we say with confidence, "The Lord is my helper; I will not be afraid. What can man do to me?"

Spiritual peace (Ps 2:12)—

Ps 32:10 Many are the woes of the wicked, but the LORD's unfailing love surrounds the man who trusts in him. (+Ps 40:4)

Ps 84:5 Blessed are those whose strength is in you, who have set their hearts on pilgrimage.

Ps 84:12 O LORD Almighty, blessed is the man who trusts in you.

Isa 26:3 You will keep in perfect peace him whose mind is steadfast, because he trusts in you.

Ro 15:13 May the God of hope fill you with all joy and peace as you trust in him, so that you may overflow with hope by the power of the Holy Spirit.

Prosperity—

Pr 28:25 A greedy man stirs up dissension, but he who trusts in the LORD will prosper.

Isa 57:13 When you cry out for help, let your collection [of idols] save you! The wind will carry all of them off, a mere breath will blow them away. But the man who makes me his refuge will inherit the land and possess my holy mountain."

Jer 17:7 "But blessed is the man who trusts in the LORD, whose confidence is in him. [8]He will be like a tree planted by the water that sends out its roots by the stream. It does not fear when heat comes; its leaves are always green. It has no worries in a year of drought and never fails to bear fruit."

Eternal life (2Ti 1:1,8).

See Faith in Christ.

FAITH, TEACHINGS OF JESUS Beliefs held in common by apostles and early believers (Ac 6:7; 16:5; 1Co 16:13; Gal 1:23; 3:23,25; 6:10; Php 1:27; 1Ti 3:9; 4:1;

5:8; 6:10,21; 2Ti 3:8; 4:7; Tit 1:1,4,13; 3:15; Jude 3; Rev 2:13).

FAITH IN CHRIST
General References Concerning:
Commanded—

Mt 17:7 But Jesus came and touched them. "Get up," he said. "Don't be afraid." (+Jn 6:20)

Jn 20:27 Then he said to Thomas, "Put your finger here; see my hands. Reach out your hand and put it into my side. Stop doubting and believe."

Jn 20:29 Then Jesus told him, "Because you have seen me, you have believed; blessed are those who have not seen and yet have believed."

1Jn 3:23 And this is his command: to believe in the name of his Son, Jesus Christ, and to love one another as he commanded us.

All things possible by (Mt 21:22)—

Mk 9:23 "'If you can'?" said Jesus. "Everything is possible for him who believes."

Lk 17:6 He replied, "If you have faith as small as a mustard seed, you can say to this mulberry tree, 'Be uprooted and planted in the sea,' and it will obey you.

Prayer for increase of (Mk 9:24).

Leads to salvation

Jn 1:12 Yet to all who received him, to those who believed in his name, he gave the right to become children of God—

Jn 3:14 Just as Moses lifted up the snake in the desert, so the Son of Man must be lifted up, [15]that everyone who believes in him may have eternal life.

[16]"For God so loved the world that he gave his one and only Son, that whoever believes in him shall not perish but have eternal life. (+Jn 3:17-18)

Jn 3:36 Whoever believes in the Son has eternal life, but whoever rejects the Son will not see life, for God's wrath remains on him."

Jn 5:24 "I tell you the truth, whoever hears my word and believes him who sent me has eternal life and will not be condemned; he has crossed over from death to life. (+Jn 6:40,47)

Jn 7:38 Whoever believes in me, as the Scripture has said, streams of living water will flow from within him."

Jn 12:36 Put your trust in the light while you have it, so that you may become sons of light." When he had finished speaking, Jesus left and hid himself from them.

Jn 12:46 I have come into the world as a light, so that no one who believes in me should stay in darkness.

Jn 20:31 But these are written that you may believe that Jesus is the Christ, the Son of God, and that by believing you may have life in his name.

Ac 10:43 All the prophets testify about him that everyone who believes in him receives forgiveness of sins through his name."

Ac 13:48 When the Gentiles heard this, they were glad and honored the word of the Lord; and all who were appointed for eternal life believed.

Ac 15:9 He made no distinction between us and them, for he purified their hearts by faith.

Ac 15:11 No! We believe it is through the grace of our Lord Jesus that we are saved, just as they are."

Ac 16:31 They replied, "Believe in the Lord Jesus, and you will be saved—you and your household."

Ac 20:21 I have declared to both Jews and Greeks that they must turn to God in repentance and have faith in our Lord Jesus.

Ac 26:18 to open their eyes and turn them from darkness

to light, and from the power of Satan to God, so that they may receive forgiveness of sins and a place among those who are sanctified by faith in me.'

Ro 1:16 I am not ashamed of the gospel, because it is the power of God for the salvation of everyone who believes: first for the Jew, then for the Gentile. [17]For in the gospel a righteousness from God is revealed, a righteousness that is by faith from first to last, just as it is written: "The righteous will live by faith."

Ro 3:22 This righteousness from God comes through faith in Jesus Christ to all who believe. There is no difference, [23]for all have sinned and fall short of the glory of God, [24]and are justified freely by his grace through the redemption that came by Christ Jesus. [25]God presented him as a sacrifice of atonement, through faith in his blood. He did this to demonstrate his justice, because in his forbearance he had left the sins committed beforehand unpunished— [26]he did it to demonstrate his justice at the present time, so as to be just and the one who justifies those who have faith in Jesus.

[27]Where, then, is boasting? It is excluded. On what principle? On that of observing the law? No, but on that of faith. [28]For we maintain that a man is justified by faith apart from observing the law.

Ro 4:1 What then shall we say that Abraham, our forefather, discovered in this matter? [2]If, in fact, Abraham was justified by works, he had something to boast about—but not before God. [3]What does the Scripture say? "Abraham believed God, and it was credited to him as righteousness."

[4]Now when a man works, his wages are not credited to him as a gift, but as an obligation. [5]However, to the man who does not work but trusts God who justifies the wicked, his faith is credited as righteousness. [6]David says the same thing when he speaks of the blessedness of the man to whom God credits righteousness apart from works:

[7]"Blessed are they whose transgressions are forgiven, whose sins are covered. [8]Blessed is the man whose sin the Lord will never count against him."

[9]Is this blessedness only for the circumcised, or also for the uncircumcised? We have been saying that Abraham's faith was credited to him as righteousness. [10]Under what circumstances was it credited? Was it after he was circumcised, or before? It was not after, but before! [11]And he received the sign of circumcision, a seal of the righteousness that he had by faith while he was still uncircumcised. So then, he is the father of all who believe but have not been circumcised, in order that righteousness might be credited to them. [12]And he is also the father of the circumcised who not only are circumcised but who also walk in the footsteps of the faith that our father Abraham had before he was circumcised.

[13]It was not through law that Abraham and his offspring received the promise that he would be heir of the world, but through the righteousness that comes by faith. [14]For if those who live by law are heirs, faith has no value and the promise is worthless, [15]because law brings wrath. And where there is no law there is no transgression.

[16]Therefore, the promise comes by faith, so that it may be by grace and may be guaranteed to all Abraham's offspring—not only to those who are of the law but also to those who are of the faith of Abraham. He is the father of us all. [17]As it is written: "I have made you a father of many nations." He is our father in the sight of God, in whom he believed—the God who gives life to the dead and calls things that are not as though they were.

[18]Against all hope, Abraham in hope believed and so became the father of many nations, just as it had been said to him, "So shall your offspring be." [19]Without weakening in his faith, he faced the fact that his body was as good as dead—since he was about a hundred years old—and that Sarah's womb was also dead. [20]Yet he did not waver through unbelief regarding the promise of God, but was strengthened in his faith and gave glory to God, [21]being fully persuaded that God had power to do what he had promised. [22]This is why "it was credited to him as righteousness." [23]The words "it was credited to him" were written not for him alone, [24]but also for us, to whom God will credit righteousness—for us who believe in him who raised Jesus our Lord from the dead. [25]He was delivered over to death for our sins and was raised to life for our justification.

Ro 5:1 Therefore, since we have been justified through faith, we have peace with God through our Lord Jesus Christ, (+Ro 5:2)

Ro 9:31 but Israel, who pursued a law of righteousness, has not attained it. [32]Why not? Because they pursued it not by faith but as if it were by works. They stumbled over the "stumbling stone." [33]As it is written: "See, I lay in Zion a stone that causes men to stumble and a rock that makes them fall, and the one who trusts in him will never be put to shame."

Ro 10:4 Christ is the end of the law so that there may be righteousness for everyone who believes. (+Ro 10:5)

Ro 10:6 But the righteousness that is by faith says: "Do not say in your heart, 'Who will ascend into heaven?'" (that is, to bring Christ down) [7]"or 'Who will descend into the deep?'" (that is, to bring Christ up from the dead). [8]But what does it say? "The word is near you; it is in your mouth and in your heart," that is, the word of faith we are proclaiming: [9]That if you confess with your mouth, "Jesus is Lord," and believe in your heart that God raised him from the dead, you will be saved. [10]For it is with your heart that you believe and are justified, and it is with your mouth that you confess and are saved.

Ro 11:20 Granted. But they were broken off because of unbelief, and you stand by faith. Do not be arrogant, but be afraid. (+1Co 1:21)

1Co 2:5 so that your faith might not rest on men's wisdom, but on God's power.

Gal 2:16 know that a man is not justified by observing the law, but by faith in Jesus Christ. So we, too, have put our faith in Christ Jesus that we may be justified by faith in Christ and not by observing the law, because by observing the law no one will be justified.

Gal 3:1 You foolish Galatians! Who has bewitched you? Before your very eyes Jesus Christ was clearly portrayed as crucified. [2]I would like to learn just one thing from you: Did you receive the Spirit by observing the law, or by believing what you heard? [3]Are you so foolish? After beginning with the Spirit, are you now trying to attain your goal by human effort? [4]Have you suffered so much for nothing—if it really was for nothing? [5]Does God give you his Spirit and work miracles among you because you observe the law, or because you believe what you heard?

[6]Consider Abraham: "He believed God, and it was credited to him as righteousness." [7]Understand, then, that those who believe are children of Abraham. [8]The Scripture foresaw that God would justify the Gentiles by faith, and announced the gospel in advance to Abraham: "All nations will be blessed through you." [9]So those who have faith are blessed along with Abraham, the man of faith.

[10]All who rely on observing the law are under a curse, for it is written: "Cursed is everyone who does not continue to do everything written in the Book of the Law." [11]Clearly no one is justified before God by the law, because, "The righteous will live by faith." [12]The law is not based on faith; on the contrary, "The man who does these things will live by them." [13]Christ redeemed us from the curse of the law by becoming a curse for us, for it is written: "Cursed is everyone who is hung on a tree." [14]He redeemed us in order that the blessing given to Abraham might come to the Gentiles through Christ Jesus, so that by faith we might receive the promise of the Spirit. (+Gal 3:15-29)

Gal 5:5 But by faith we eagerly await through the Spirit the righteousness for which we hope. [6]For in Christ Jesus neither circumcision nor uncircumcision has any value. The only thing that counts is faith expressing itself through love.

Eph 1:12 in order that we, who were the first to hope in Christ, might be for the praise of his glory. [13]And you also were included in Christ when you heard the word of truth, the gospel of your salvation. Having believed, you were marked in him with a seal, the promised Holy Spirit, [14]who is a deposit guaranteeing our inheritance until the redemption of those who are God's possession—to the praise of his glory.

Eph 2:8 For it is by grace you have been saved, through faith—and this not from yourselves, it is the gift of God—

Eph 3:12 In him and through faith in him we may approach God with freedom and confidence.

Eph 3:17 so that Christ may dwell in your hearts through faith. And I pray that you, being rooted and established in love,

1Ti 1:16 But for that very reason I was shown mercy so that in me, the worst of sinners, Christ Jesus might display his unlimited patience as an example for those who would believe on him and receive eternal life.

2Ti 1:13 What you heard from me, keep as the pattern of sound teaching, with faith and love in Christ Jesus.

2Ti 3:15 and how from infancy you have known the holy Scriptures, which are able to make you wise for salvation through faith in Christ Jesus. (+1Pe 1:9)

1Pe 2:6 For in Scripture it says: "See, I lay a stone in Zion, a chosen and precious cornerstone, and the one who trusts in him will never be put to shame."

[7]Now to you who believe, this stone is precious. But to those who do not believe, "The stone the builders rejected has become the capstone,"

2Pe 1:1 Simon Peter, a servant and apostle of Jesus Christ, To those who through the righteousness of our God and Savior Jesus Christ have received a faith as precious as ours:

Rev 3:20 Here I am! I stand at the door and knock. If anyone hears my voice and opens the door, I will come in and eat with him, and he with me.

Will result in good works—

Jn 14:12 I tell you the truth, anyone who has faith in me will do what I have been doing. He will do even greater things than these, because I am going to the Father.

Jas 2:14 What good is it, my brothers, if a man claims to have faith but has no deeds? Can such faith save him? [15]Suppose a brother or sister is without clothes and daily food. [16]If one of you says to him, "Go, I wish you well; keep warm and well fed," but does nothing about his physical needs, what good is it? [17]In the same way, faith by itself, if it is not accompanied by action, is dead.

[18]But someone will say, "You have faith; I have deeds." Show me your faith without deeds, and I will show you my faith by what I do.

[19]You believe that there is one God. Good! Even the demons believe that—and shudder.

[20]You foolish man, do you want evidence that faith without deeds is useless? [21]Was not our ancestor Abraham considered righteous for what he did when he offered his son Isaac on the altar? [22]You see that his faith and his actions were working together, and his faith was made complete by what he did. [23]And the scripture was fulfilled that says, "Abraham believed God, and it was credited to him as righteousness," and he was called God's friend. [24]You see that a person is justified by what he does and not by faith alone.

[25]In the same way, was not even Rahab the prostitute considered righteous for what she did when she gave lodging to the spies and sent them off in a different direction? [26]As the body without the spirit is dead, so faith without deeds is dead. (+Jas 2:1-13)

Christ, the focus of faith (Ps 2:12)—

Heb 12:2 Let us fix our eyes on Jesus, the author and perfecter of our faith, who for the joy set before him endured the cross, scorning its shame, and sat down at the right hand of the throne of God.

The Christian triumphs by (Ro 8:35,37)—

2Co 1:24 Not that we lord it over your faith, but we work with you for your joy, because it is by faith you stand firm.

Eph 4:13 until we all reach unity in the faith and in the knowledge of the Son of God and become mature, attaining to the whole measure of the fullness of Christ.

Eph 6:16 In addition to all this, take up the shield of faith, with which you can extinguish all the flaming arrows of the evil one.

Php 3:9 and be found in him, not having a righteousness of my own that comes from the law, but that which is through faith in Christ—the righteousness that comes from God and is by faith.

Col 1:23 if you continue in your faith, established and firm, not moved from the hope held out in the gospel. This is the gospel that you heard and that has been proclaimed to every creature under heaven, and of which I, Paul, have become a servant.

Col 2:7 rooted and built up in him, strengthened in the faith as you were taught, and overflowing with thankfulness.

Heb 10:22 let us draw near to God with a sincere heart in full assurance of faith, having our hearts sprinkled to cleanse us from a guilty conscience and having our bodies washed with pure water.

Heb 10:38 But my righteous one will live by faith. And if he shrinks back, I will not be pleased with him."

[39]But we are not of those who shrink back and are destroyed, but of those who believe and are saved.

Heb 13:7 Remember your leaders, who spoke the word of God to you. Consider the outcome of their way of life and imitate their faith.

1Pe 1:5 who through faith are shielded by God's power until the coming of the salvation that is ready to be revealed in the last time.

1Pe 1:7 These have come so that your faith—of greater worth than gold, which perishes even though refined by fire—may be proved genuine and may result in praise, glory and honor when Jesus Christ is revealed. [8]Though you have not seen him, you love him; and even though you do not see him now, you believe in him and are filled with an inexpressible and glorious joy, **⁹**for you are receiving the goal of your faith, the salvation of your souls.

1Jn 5:4 for everyone born of God overcomes the world. This is the victory that has overcome the world, even our faith. **⁵**Who is it that overcomes the world? Only he who believes that Jesus is the Son of God.

1Jn 5:10 Anyone who believes in the Son of God has this testimony in his heart. Anyone who does not believe God has made him out to be a liar, because he has not believed the testimony God has given about his Son.

1Jn 5:14 This is the confidence we have in approaching God: that if we ask anything according to his will, he hears us.

Exemplified by:

The wise men of the East as they worship the infant King Jesus (Mt 2:1-2,11).

The disciples in response to the call of Jesus (Mt 4:18-22; Mk 1:16-20; Lk 5:4)—

Lk 5:5 Simon answered, "Master, we've worked hard all night and haven't caught anything. But because you say so, I will let down the nets." (+Lk 5:6-11; Jn 1:35-49)

Jn 6:68 Simon Peter answered him, "Lord, to whom shall we go? You have the words of eternal life. **⁶⁹**We believe and know that you are the Holy One of God." (+Jn 16:27)

Jn 16:30 Now we can see that you know all things and that you do not even need to have anyone ask you questions. This makes us believe that you came from God." (+Jn 16:33)

Peter (Mt 4:18-22)—

Mt 16:16 Simon Peter answered, "You are the Christ, the Son of the living God." (+Mk 1:16-20; Lk 5:4-5; Jn 6:68-69)

Andrew (Mt 4:18-22; Mk 1:16-20; Jn 1:41). James and John (Mt 4:21-22; Mk 1:19-20). Philip (Jn 1:43-46). Nathanael (Jn 1:46-49).

In response to Jesus during his early ministry. The disciples, through the miracle at Cana of Galilee (Jn 2:11). Jews at Jerusalem (Jn 2:23; 8:30; 11:45; 12:11). The Samaritans, who believed through the preaching of Jesus (Jn 4:39-42), of Philip (Ac 8:9-12).

Those who were healed by Jesus: the leper—

Mt 8:2 A man with leprosy came and knelt before him and said, "Lord, if you are willing, you can make me clean." (+Mk 1:40; Lk 5:12-13)

The centurion, for the healing of his servant (Mt 8:5-10,13)—

Lk 7:3 The centurion heard of Jesus and sent some elders of the Jews to him, asking him to come and heal his servant. **⁴**When they came to Jesus, they pleaded earnestly with him, "This man deserves to have you do this, **⁵**because he loves our nation and has built us our synagogue." **⁶**So Jesus went with them. He was not far from the house when the centurion sent friends to say to him: "Lord, don't trouble yourself, for I do not deserve to have you come under my roof.

⁷That is why I did not even consider myself worthy to come to you. But say the word, and my servant will be healed. **⁸**For I myself am a man under authority, with soldiers under me. I tell this one, 'Go,' and he goes; and that one, 'Come,' and he comes. I say to my servant, 'Do this,' and he does it."

⁹When Jesus heard this, he was amazed at him, and turning to the crowd following him, he said, "I tell you, I have not found such great faith even in Israel."

Those who brought the paralytic to Jesus (Mt 9:1-2; Mk 2:1-5; Lk 5:18-20).

Jairus, for the healing of his daughter—

Mt 9:18 While he was saying this, a ruler came and knelt before him and said, "My daughter has just died. But come and put your hand on her, and she will live." (+Mt 9:23-25; Mk 5:22-43; Lk 8:41-56)

The woman subject to bleeding—

Mt 9:20 Just then a woman who had been subject to bleeding for twelve years came up behind him and touched the edge of his cloak. **²¹**She said to herself, "If I only touch his cloak, I will be healed." **²²**Jesus turned and saw her. "Take heart, daughter," he said, "your faith has healed you." And the woman was healed from that moment. (+Mk 5:25-34; Lk 8:43-47)

Lk 8:48 Then he said to her, "Daughter, your faith has healed you. Go in peace."

Two blind men (Mt 9:27)—

Mt 9:28 When he had gone indoors, the blind men came to him, and he asked them, "Do you believe that I am able to do this?" "Yes, Lord," they replied. (+Mt 9:29-30)

The disciples in the storm—

Mt 14:33 Then those who were in the boat worshiped him, saying, "Truly you are the Son of God."

The sick of Gennesaret (Mt 14:36; Mk 3:10; 6:54-56).

The Syrian Phoenician woman (Mt 15:22-26)—

Mt 15:27 "Yes, Lord," she said, "but even the dogs eat the crumbs that fall from their masters' table." (+Mt 15:28; Mk 7:25-30)

The people of Decapolis (Mt 15:30).

The father of the demon-possessed child (Mt 17:14-15)—

Mk 9:24 Immediately the boy's father exclaimed, "I do believe; help me overcome my unbelief!" (+Lk 9:38,42)

Blind Bartimaeus, and a fellow blind man (Mt 20:30-34; Mk 10:46-52; Lk 18:35-43). Those who brought the deaf and mute man to Jesus (Mk 7:32). The woman who was a sinner (Lk 7:38,44-48,50). Mary, the sister of Martha (Lk 10:38-42; Jn 11:32). The Samaritan leper (Lk 17:11-19). The nobleman, for the healing of his son (Jn 4:46-47,50).

The people who saw the feeding of the five thousand—

Jn 6:14 After the people saw the miraculous sign that Jesus did, they began to say, "Surely this is the Prophet who is to come into the world."

The blind man whom Jesus healed on the Sabbath (Jn 9:13-38).

The people in Bethany beyond the Jordan—

Jn 10:41 and many people came to him. They said, "Though John never performed a miraculous sign, all that John said about this man was true." **⁴²**And in that place many believed in Jesus.

Zacchaeus (Lk 19:1-6). The thief, on the cross (Lk 23:42). John, the disciple, after the resurrection (Jn 20:8).

Thomas, after the resurrection—

Jn 20:28 Thomas said to him, "My Lord and my God!"

Those in the early church. By three thousand, at Pentecost (Ac 2:41). By five thousand (Ac 4:4). By multitudes (Ac 5:14). By Stephen (Ac 6:8; 7:55-56). By the Ethiopian eunuch (Ac 8:36,38). By the cripple at Lystra (Ac 14:8-10).

Paul—

Ro 7:24 What a wretched man I am! Who will rescue me from this body of death? **²⁵**Thanks be to God—through Jesus Christ our Lord! So then, I myself in my mind am a slave to God's law, but in the sinful nature a slave to the law of sin.

2Co 12:9 But he said to me, "My grace is sufficient for you, for my power is made perfect in weakness." Therefore I will boast all the more gladly about my weaknesses, so that Christ's power may rest on me. **¹⁰**That is why, for Christ's sake, I delight in weaknesses, in insults, in hardships, in persecutions, in difficulties. For when I am weak, then I am strong.

Gal 2:20 I have been crucified with Christ and I no longer live, but Christ lives in me. The life I live in the body, I live by faith in the Son of God, who loved me and gave himself for me.

Php 4:13 I can do everything through him who gives me strength.

2Ti 1:12 That is why I am suffering as I am. Yet I am not ashamed, because I know whom I have believed, and am convinced that he is able to guard what I have entrusted to him for that day.

2Ti 4:18 The Lord will rescue me from every evil attack and will bring me safely to his heavenly kingdom. To him be glory for ever and ever. Amen.

Expressed as a response to the preaching of the gospel. Of Lydda and Sharon (Ac 9:35), of Joppa (Ac 9:42), of Antioch (Ac 11:21-24). Barnabas (Ac 11:24). Eunice, Lois, and Timothy (Ac 16:1; 2Ti 1:5). Lydia (Ac 16:14). Philippian jailer (Ac 16:31-34). Crispus (Ac 18:8). The Corinthians (Ac 18:8; 1Co 15:11). Jews at Rome (Ac 28:24). Ephesians (Eph 1:13,15). Colossians (Col 1:2,4). Thessalonians (1Th 1:6; 3:6-8; 2Th 1:3-4). Philemon (Phm 5). Church at Thyatira (Rev 2:19).

FAITHFUL SAYINGS These are trustworthy statements; words that you may depend upon as truthful and everlasting (1Ti 1:15; 3:1; 4:9; 2Ti 2:11; Tit 3:8).

FAITHFULNESS [*573, 574, 575, 586, 622, 2874, 2876, 2883, 9068, *4411, 4412*].

NIV+ See FAITH

Described:

Scarce—

Ps 12:1 Help, Lord, for the godly are no more; the faithful have vanished from among men.

Pr 20:6 Many a man claims to have unfailing love, but a faithful man who can find?

Tested—

Lk 16:10 "Whoever can be trusted with very little can also be trusted with much, and whoever is dishonest with very little will also be dishonest with much. ¹¹So if you have not been trustworthy in handling worldly wealth, who will trust you with true riches? ¹²And if you have not been trustworthy with someone else's property, who will give you property of your own?

A fruit of the Spirit (Gal 5:22).

Rewards of—

Ps 31:23 Love the Lord, all his saints! The Lord preserves the faithful, but the proud he pays back in full.

Pr 28:20 A faithful man will be richly blessed, but one eager to get rich will not go unpunished.

Mt 10:22 All men will hate you because of me, but he who stands firm to the end will be saved. (+Mt 13:12; 25:29; Mk 13:13; Heb 10:34)

Rev 2:10 Do not be afraid of what you are about to suffer. I tell you, the devil will put some of you in prison to test you, and you will suffer persecution for ten days. Be faithful, even to the point of death, and I will give you the crown of life.

Required:

Mt 24:45 "Who then is the faithful and wise servant, whom the master has put in charge of the servants in his household to give them their food at the proper time? ⁴⁶It will be good for that servant whose master finds him doing so when he returns. ⁴⁷I tell you the truth, he will put him in charge of all his possessions. (+Mt 24:48-51; Lk 12:36-48)

Mt 25:14 "Again, it will be like a man going on a journey, who called his servants and entrusted his property to them. ¹⁵To one he gave five talents of money, to another two talents, and to another one talent, each according to his ability. Then he went on his journey. ¹⁶The man who had received the five talents went at once and put his money to work and gained five more. ¹⁷So also, the one with the two talents gained two more. ¹⁸But the man who had received the one talent went off, dug a hole in the ground and hid his master's money.

¹⁹"After a long time the master of those servants returned and settled accounts with them. ²⁰The man who had received the five talents brought the other five. 'Master,' he said, 'you entrusted me with five talents. See, I have gained five more.'

²¹"His master replied, 'Well done, good and faithful servant! You have been faithful with a few things; I will put you in charge of many things. Come and share your master's happiness!'

²²"The man with the two talents also came. 'Master,' he said, 'you entrusted me with two talents; see, I have gained two more.'

²³"His master replied, 'Well done, good and faithful servant! You have been faithful with a few things; I will put you in charge of many things. Come and share your master's happiness!' (+Mt 25:24-30; Lk 19:12-27)

Of stewards—

1Co 4:2 Now it is required that those who have been given a trust must prove faithful.

Of servants (Eph 6:5-9)—

Col 3:22 Slaves, obey your earthly masters in everything; and do it, not only when their eye is on you and to win their favor, but with sincerity of heart and reverence for the Lord.

Instances of:

Abraham's servant (Ge 24:33). Moses (Nu 12:7; Heb 3:3,5). Ruth (Ru 1:15-18). Ittai the Gittite (2Sa 15:19-22). David (2Sa 22:22-25). Elijah (1Ki 19:10,14). Workmen in temple repairs (2Ki 12:15; 2Ch 34:12). Josiah (2Ki 22:2). Abijah (2Ch 13:10-12). Jehoshaphat (2Ch 20:1-30). Hanani and Hananiah (Ne 7:2). Abraham (Ne 9:7-8; Gal 3:9). Nehemiah's treasurer (Ne 13:13). Job (Job 1:21-22; 2:9-10). The three Hebrew captives (Da 3:16-18). Daniel (Da 6:10). Jesus (Jn 4:34; Heb 3:2). Abraham (Gal 3:9). Paul (1Ti 1:12; 2Ti 4:7).

See Reward, A Motive, To Faithfulness.

See also, Jesus the Christ, Faithfulness of; God, Faithfulness of; Minister, Faithful.

FALCON [370, 1901].

NIV+ FALCON'S, FALCONS

A bird of prey (Job 28:7; Isa 34:15), unclean for food (Dt 14:13). *See Birds.*

FALL OF MANKIND, THE The fall of mankind as related in Genesis 3 is the historical choice by which Adam and Eve sinned voluntarily, and consequently involved all the human race in evil. Since the Fall, there is no person who continually does what is right and never sins (1Ki 8:46; Ps 130:3; 143:2; Pr 20:9; Ecc 7:20; Ro 3:8-10; 5:12; 1Co 15:22; 1Jn 1:8). By the Fall mankind was alienated from God. Mankind was created in God's own image, with a rational and moral nature like God's, with no inner impulse to sin, and with a will free to choose the will of God. Yielding to the outward temptation turned mankind from God and created an environment in which sin became a potent factor. Redemption from the Fall is accomplished through the second Adam, Jesus Christ (Ro 5:12-21; 1Co 15:21-22,45-49).

Consequences of:

Knowledge of, nakedness—

Ge 3:7 Then the eyes of both of them were opened, and they realized they were naked; so they sewed fig leaves together and made coverings for themselves.

Guilt—

Ge 3:8 Then the man and his wife heard the sound of the LORD God as he was walking in the garden in the cool of the day, and they hid from the LORD God among the trees of the garden. **9**But the LORD God called to the man, "Where are you?"

10He answered, "I heard you in the garden, and I was afraid because I was naked; so I hid."

Cursing of, the serpent—

Ge 3:14 So the LORD God said to the serpent, "Because you have done this,

"Cursed are you above all the livestock and all the wild animals! You will crawl on your belly and you will eat dust all the days of your life. **15**And I will put enmity between you and the woman, and between your offspring and hers; he will crush your head, and you will strike his heel."

Cursing of the ground (Ge 3:17-18).

Multiplying of sorrows—

Ge 3:16 To the woman he said, "I will greatly increase your pains in childbearing; with pain you will give birth to children. Your desire will be for your husband, and he will rule over you."

17To Adam he said, "Because you listened to your wife and ate from the tree about which I commanded you, 'You must not eat of it,' "Cursed is the ground because of you; through painful toil you will eat of it all the days of your life. **18**It will produce thorns and thistles for you, and you will eat the plants of the field. **19**By the sweat of your brow you will eat your food until you return to the ground, since from it you were taken; for dust you are and to dust you will return."

Death, physical (Ge 3:19; Ro 5:12,14)—

1Co 15:21 For since death came through a man, the resurrection of the dead comes also through a man. **22**For as in Adam all die, so in Christ all will be made alive.

Spiritual—

Ro 5:12 Therefore, just as sin entered the world through one man, and death through sin, and in this way death came to all men, because all sinned—

Ro 5:14 Nevertheless, death reigned from the time of Adam to the time of Moses, even over those who did not sin by breaking a command, as did Adam, who was a pattern of the one to come.

Ro 5:18 Consequently, just as the result of one trespass was condemnation for all men, so also the result of one act of righteousness was justification that brings life for all men. (+Ro 5:19,21)

Means of:

By transgression of commandments (Ge 2:16-17)—

Ge 3:1 Now the serpent was more crafty than any of the wild animals the LORD God had made. He said to the woman, "Did God really say, 'You must not eat from any tree in the garden'?"

2The woman said to the serpent, "We may eat fruit from the trees in the garden, **3**but God did say, 'You must not eat fruit from the tree that is in the middle of the garden, and you must not touch it, or you will die.'"

Ge 3:6 When the woman saw that the fruit of the tree was good for food and pleasing to the eye, and also desirable for gaining wisdom, she took some and ate it. She also gave some to her husband, who was with her, and he ate it.

Ge 3:11 And he said, "Who told you that you were naked? Have you eaten from the tree that I commanded you not to eat from?"

12The man said, "The woman you put here with me—she gave me some fruit from the tree, and I ate it."

Job 31:33 if I have concealed my sin as men do, by hiding my guilt in my heart

Isa 43:27 Your first father sinned; your spokesmen rebelled against me.

Hos 6:7 Like Adam, they have broken the covenant—they were unfaithful to me there.

Through deception of Satan—

Ge 3:4 "You will not surely die," the serpent said to the woman. **5**"For God knows that when you eat of it your eyes will be opened, and you will be like God, knowing good and evil."

Ge 3:13 Then the LORD God said to the woman, "What is this you have done?" The woman said, "The serpent deceived me, and I ate."

2Co 11:3 But I am afraid that just as Eve was deceived by the serpent's cunning, your minds may somehow be led astray from your sincere and pure devotion to Christ.

1Ti 2:14 And Adam was not the one deceived; it was the woman who was deceived and became a sinner.

Through evil desire (Ge 3:6)—

Ecc 7:29 This only have I found: God made mankind upright, but men have gone in search of many schemes."

See Depravity.

FALLOW DEER *See Animals; Deer.*

FALLOW GROUND Land that is left idle for a growing season, after plowing and harrowing, so that weeds and insects are killed while the soil regains its fertility. *See Agriculture.*

Practical Application:

Israel is instructed to follow this practice every seventh year (Ex 23:11), but through much of its history, they failed to allow their land a sabbath rest (Lev 26:34-35).

Spiritual Application:

Israel is encouraged to seek God and to become spiritually active (Jer 4:3; Hos 10:12).

FALSE ACCUSATION *See Accusation, False.*

FALSE APOSTLES [6013]. Paul speaks of false apostles in 2 Corinthians only. These people "masquerade as apostles of Christ" (2Co 11:13). Paul denounces them as servants of Satan (2Co 11:14), "masquerading as servants of righteousness," which is not surprising, since their master "masquerades as an angel of light" (2Co 11:14-15). Yet they claim to be servants of Christ (2Co 11:23). Apparently they boasted of their Jewish heritage, using this to help justify their self-proclaimed position as "apostle of Christ" (2Co 11:22).

FALSE CHRISTS [6023].

These are people who make a false claim to be the Messiah. Jesus warned his disciples that imitators and pretenders would follow him who would try to deceive his followers (Mt 24:5-11,23-25; Mk 13:6,21,23; Lk 21:8). False Christs are to be distinguished from the Antichrist. The false Christ is an impostor while the latter is one who opposes Christ. His opposition is mainly through the doctrines about Jesus' person and work which are contrary to the truth.

FALSE CONFIDENCE

Described:

In self (Dt 29:19; 1Ki 20:11; Pr 3:5,7; 26:5,12; 28:26; Isa 5:21; Ro 12:16; 2Co 1:9). In outward resources (Ps 20:7; 33:17; 44:6; 49:6; Pr 11:28; Isa 22:9-11; 31:1-3; Jer 48:7; Zec 4:6; Mk 10:24, ftn). In man (Ps 33:16; 62:9; 118:8; 146:3-4; Isa 2:22; Jer 17:5; Hos 5:13; 7:11).

Instances of:

At the tower of Babel (Ge 11:4). Sennacherib, in the siege of Jerusalem (2Ki 19:23). Asa, in relying on Syria rather than on God (2Ch 16:7-9). Hezekiah, in the defenses of Jerusalem (Isa 22:11). Peter, in asserting his devotion to Jesus (Mt 26:35; Lk 22:33-34; Jn 13:37-38).

See Confidence.

FALSE PROPHET [967, 6021].

Any person pretending to possess a message from God, but not possessing a divine commission (Jer 29:9). Test for (Dt 13:1-5; 18:20-22).

The False Prophet of the Apocalypse:

The false prophet is mentioned in the book of Revelation (Rev 19:20) and is usually identified with the two-horned beast of Revelation (Rev 13:11-18).

FALSE TEACHERS See Teachers, False.

FALSE WITNESS [8736, 9214, 6018, 6019, 6020].

Described:

Punishment for—

Dt 19:16 If a malicious witness takes the stand to accuse a man of a crime, [17]the two men involved in the dispute must stand in the presence of the LORD before the priests and the judges who are in office at the time. [18]The judges must make a thorough investigation, and if the witness proves to be a liar, giving false testimony against his brother, [19]then do to him as he intended to do to his brother. You must purge the evil from among you. [20]The rest of the people will hear of this and be afraid, and never again will such an evil thing be done among you. (+Pr 19:5,9; 21:28)

Zec 5:3 And he said to me, "This is the curse that is going out over the whole land; for according to what it says on one side, every thief will be banished, and according to what it says on the other, everyone who swears falsely will be banished. [4]The LORD Almighty declares, 'I will send it out, and it will enter the house of the thief and the house of him who swears falsely by my name. It will remain in his house and destroy it, both its timbers and its stones.'"

Innocent suffer from—

Ps 27:12 Do not turn me over to the desire of my foes, for false witnesses rise up against me, breathing out violence.

Ps 35:11 Ruthless witnesses come forward; they question me on things I know nothing about.

Proverbs concerning (Pr 6:16-19)—

Pr 12:17 A truthful witness gives honest testimony, but a false witness tells lies.

Pr 14:5 A truthful witness does not deceive, but a false witness pours out lies.

Pr 14:8 The wisdom of the prudent is to give thought to their ways, but the folly of fools is deception.

Pr 14:25 A truthful witness saves lives, but a false witness is deceitful. (+Pr 19:5)

Pr 19:9 A false witness will not go unpunished, and he who pours out lies will perish.

Pr 21:28 A false witness will perish, and whoever listens to him will be destroyed forever.

Pr 24:28 Do not testify against your neighbor without cause, or use your lips to deceive.

Pr 25:18 Like a club or a sword or a sharp arrow is the man who gives false testimony against his neighbor.

God hates—

Pr 6:16 There are six things the LORD hates, seven that are detestable to him: [17]haughty eyes, a lying tongue, hands that shed innocent blood, [18]a heart that devises wicked schemes, feet that are quick to rush into evil, [19]a false witness who pours out lies and a man who stirs up dissension among brothers.

Results from a corrupt heart—

Mt 15:19 For out of the heart come evil thoughts, murder, adultery, sexual immorality, theft, false testimony, slander.

See Evidence; Falsehood; Perjury; Witness.

Forbidden:

Ex 20:16 "You shall not give false testimony against your neighbor.

Ex 23:1 "Do not spread false reports. Do not help a wicked man by being a malicious witness. (+Ex 23:2-3; Lev 6:1-2)

Lev 6:3 or if he finds lost property and lies about it, or if he swears falsely, or if he commits any such sin that people may do— (+Lev 6:4-5)

Lev 19:11 "'Do not steal.

"'Do not lie.

"'Do not deceive one another.

[12]"'Do not swear falsely by my name and so profane the name of your God. I am the LORD.

Lev 19:16 "'Do not go about spreading slander among your people. "'Do not do anything that endangers your neighbor's life. I am the LORD. (+Dt 5:20; Pr 24:28; Mt 19:18)

Lk 3:14 Then some soldiers asked him, "And what should we do?" He replied, "Don't extort money and don't accuse people falsely—be content with your pay." (+Lk 18:20)

1Ti 1:9 We also know that law is made not for the righteous but for lawbreakers and rebels, the ungodly and sinful, the unholy and irreligious; for those who kill their fathers or mothers, for murderers, [10]for adulterers and perverts, for slave traders and liars and perjurers—and for whatever else is contrary to the sound doctrine

Instances of:

Witnesses against, Naboth (1Ki 21:13), Jesus (Mt 26:59-61; Mk 14:54-59), Stephen (Ac 6:11,13), Paul (Ac 16:20-21; 17:5-7; 24:5; 25:7-8).

FALSEHOOD [5086, 8736, 9214, 4415, 6022, 6025].

NIV+ FALSE, FALSELY

Described:

Atonement for—

Lev 6:2 "If anyone sins and is unfaithful to the LORD by deceiving his neighbor about something entrusted to him or left in his care or stolen, or if he cheats him, ³or if he finds lost property and lies about it, or if he swears falsely, or if he commits any such sin that people may do— ⁴when he thus sins and becomes guilty, he must return what he has stolen or taken by extortion, or what was entrusted to him, or the lost property he found, ⁵or whatever it was he swore falsely about. He must make restitution in full, add a fifth of the value to it and give it all to the owner on the day he presents his guilt offering. ⁶And as a penalty he must bring to the priest, that is, to the LORD, his guilt offering, a ram from the flock, one without defect and of the proper value. ⁷In this way the priest will make atonement for him before the LORD, and he will be forgiven for any of these things he did that made him guilty."

Punishment for—

Ps 12:2 Everyone lies to his neighbor; their flattering lips speak with deception.

³May the LORD cut off all flattering lips and every boastful tongue ⁴that says, "We will triumph with our tongues; we own our lips—who is our master?"

Ps 52:4 You love every harmful word, O you deceitful tongue!

⁵Surely God will bring you down to everlasting ruin: He will snatch you up and tear you from your tent; he will uproot you from the land of the living. *Selah*

Ps 55:23 But you, O God, will bring down the wicked into the pit of corruption; bloodthirsty and deceitful men will not live out half their days. But as for me, I trust in you.

Ps 63:11 But the king will rejoice in God; all who swear by God's name will praise him, while the mouths of liars will be silenced.

Pr 10:10 He who winks maliciously causes grief, and a chattering fool comes to ruin.

Pr 10:31 The mouth of the righteous brings forth wisdom, but a perverse tongue will be cut out.

Pr 12:19 Truthful lips endure forever, but a lying tongue lasts only a moment. (+Pr 14:5,25)

Pr 19:5 A false witness will not go unpunished, and he who pours out lies will not go free. (+Pr 19:9)

Rev 21:8 But the cowardly, the unbelieving, the vile, the murderers, the sexually immoral, those who practice magic arts, the idolaters and all liars—their place will be in the fiery lake of burning sulfur. This is the second death."

Rev 21:27 Nothing impure will ever enter it, nor will anyone who does what is shameful or deceitful, but only those whose names are written in the Lamb's book of life.

Rev 22:15 Outside are the dogs, those who practice magic arts, the sexually immoral, the murderers, the idolaters and everyone who loves and practices falsehood.

Falsehood will be found out—

Pr 10:9 The man of integrity walks securely, but he who takes crooked paths will be found out. (+Pr 28:18)

See Accusation, False; Conspiracy; Deceit; Deception; False Witness; Flattery; Hypocrisy; Perjury; Teachers, False.

All guilty of—

Job 13:4 You, however, smear me with lies; you are worthless physicians, all of you!

Ps 116:11 And in my dismay I said, "All men are liars." (+Jer 9:3-5; Hos 7:13; Mic 6:12; Ro 3:4)

Refrained from by the righteous—

Job 27:4 my lips will not speak wickedness, and my tongue will utter no deceit.

Job 31:5 "If I have walked in falsehood or my foot has hurried after deceit— ⁶let God weigh me in honest scales and he will know that I am blameless—

Job 31:33 if I have concealed my sin as men do, by hiding my guilt in my heart

Job 36:4 Be assured that my words are not false; one perfect in knowledge is with you.

Pr 14:5 A truthful witness does not deceive, but a false witness pours out lies.

Pr 14:25 A truthful witness saves lives, but a false witness is deceitful.

Isa 63:8 He said, "Surely they are my people, sons who will not be false to me"; and so he became their Savior.

Practiced by the wicked—

Ps 10:7 His mouth is full of curses and lies and threats; trouble and evil are under his tongue.

Ps 28:3 Do not drag me away with the wicked, with those who do evil, who speak cordially with their neighbors but harbor malice in their hearts.

Ps 36:3 The words of his mouth are wicked and deceitful; he has ceased to be wise and to do good.

Ps 50:19 You use your mouth for evil and harness your tongue to deceit. ²⁰You speak continually against your brother and slander your own mother's son.

Ps 52:2 Your tongue plots destruction; it is like a sharpened razor, you who practice deceit. ³You love evil rather than good, falsehood rather than speaking the truth. *Selah* ⁴You love every harmful word, O you deceitful tongue!

Ps 58:3 Even from birth the wicked go astray; from the womb they are wayward and speak lies.

Ps 62:4 They fully intend to topple him from his lofty place; they take delight in lies. With their mouths they bless, but in their hearts they curse. *Selah*

Ps 109:2 for wicked and deceitful men have opened their mouths against me; they have spoken against me with lying tongues.

Pr 2:12 Wisdom will save you from the ways of wicked men, from men whose words are perverse, ¹³who leave the straight paths to walk in dark ways, ¹⁴who delight in doing wrong and rejoice in the perverseness of evil, ¹⁵whose paths are crooked and who are devious in their ways.

Pr 12:17 A truthful witness gives honest testimony, but a false witness tells lies.

Pr 12:20 There is deceit in the hearts of those who plot evil, but joy for those who promote peace.

Pr 21:6 A fortune made by a lying tongue is a fleeting vapor and a deadly snare.

Isa 28:15 You boast, "We have entered into a covenant with death, with the grave we have made an agreement. When an overwhelming scourge sweeps by, it cannot touch us, for we have made a lie our refuge and falsehood our hiding place."

Isa 57:11 "Whom have you so dreaded and feared that you have been false to me, and have neither remembered me nor pondered this in your hearts? Is it not because I have long been silent that you do not fear me?

Isa 59:3 For your hands are stained with blood, your fingers with guilt. Your lips have spoken lies, and your tongue mutters wicked things. ⁴No one calls for justice; no one pleads his case with integrity. They rely on empty arguments and speak lies; they conceive trouble and give birth to evil.

Isa 59:12 For our offenses are many in your sight, and our sins testify against us. Our offenses are ever with us, and we acknowledge our iniquities: ¹³rebellion and treachery against the LORD, turning our backs on our God, fomenting oppression and revolt, uttering lies our hearts have conceived.

Jer 7:8 But look, you are trusting in deceptive words that are worthless.

Jer 7:28 Therefore say to them, 'This is the nation that has not obeyed the LORD its God or responded to correction. Truth has perished; it has vanished from their lips.

Jer 9:3 "They make ready their tongue like a bow, to shoot lies; it is not by truth that they triumph in the land. They go from one sin to another; they do not acknowledge me," declares the LORD.

Jer 9:5 Friend deceives friend, and no one speaks the truth. They have taught their tongues to lie; they weary themselves with sinning. ⁶You live in the midst of deception; in their deceit they refuse to acknowledge me," declares the LORD.

Jer 9:8 Their tongue is a deadly arrow; it speaks with deceit. With his mouth each speaks cordially to his neighbor, but in his heart he sets a trap for him.

Jer 12:6 Your brothers, your own family—even they have betrayed you; they have raised a loud cry against you. Do not trust them, though they speak well of you.

Hos 4:1 Hear the word of the LORD, you Israelites, because the LORD has a charge to bring against you who live in the land: "There is no faithfulness, no love, no acknowledgment of God in the land. ²There is only cursing, lying and murder, stealing and adultery; they break all bounds, and bloodshed follows bloodshed.

Ob 7 All your allies will force you to the border; your friends will deceive and overpower you; those who eat your bread will set a trap for you, but you will not detect it.

Mic 6:12 Her rich men are violent; her people are liars and their tongues speak deceitfully.

Na 3:1 Woe to the city of blood, full of lies, full of plunder, never without victims!

Jn 8:44 You belong to your father, the devil, and you want to carry out your father's desire. He was a murderer from the beginning, not holding to the truth, for there is no truth in him. When he lies, he speaks his native language, for he is a liar and the father of lies. ⁴⁵Yet because I tell the truth, you do not believe me!

1Ti 4:2 Such teachings come through hypocritical liars, whose consciences have been seared as with a hot iron.

1Pe 3:16 keeping a clear conscience, so that those who speak maliciously against your good behavior in Christ may be ashamed of their slander.

Wicked easily misled by—

Pr 14:8 The wisdom of the prudent is to give thought to their ways, but the folly of fools is deception.

Pr 17:4 A wicked man listens to evil lips; a liar pays attention to a malicious tongue.

An abomination to the Lord—

Ps 5:6 You destroy those who tell lies; bloodthirsty and deceitful men the LORD abhors.

Ps 5:9 Not a word from their mouth can be trusted; their heart is filled with destruction. Their throat is an open grave; with their tongue they speak deceit.

Pr 6:12 A scoundrel and villain, who goes about with a corrupt mouth, ¹³who winks with his eye, signals with his feet and motions with his fingers,

Pr 6:16 There are six things the LORD hates, seven that are detestable to him: ¹⁷haughty eyes, a lying tongue, hands that shed innocent blood, ¹⁸a heart that devises wicked schemes, feet that are quick to rush into evil, ¹⁹a false witness who pours out lies and a man who stirs up dissension among brothers.

Pr 12:22 The LORD detests lying lips, but he delights in men who are truthful.

Abhorred by the righteous—

Ps 31:18 Let their lying lips be silenced, for with pride and contempt they speak arrogantly against the righteous.

Ps 59:12 For the sins of their mouths, for the words of their lips, let them be caught in their pride. For the curses and lies they utter,

Ps 101:5 Whoever slanders his neighbor in secret, him will I put to silence; whoever has haughty eyes and a proud heart, him will I not endure.

Ps 101:7 No one who practices deceit will dwell in my house; no one who speaks falsely will stand in my presence.

Ps 119:29 Keep me from deceitful ways; be gracious to me through your law.

Ps 119:69 Though the arrogant have smeared me with lies, I keep your precepts with all my heart.

Ps 119:163 I hate and abhor falsehood but I love your law.

Ps 120:2 Save me, O LORD, from lying lips and from deceitful tongues.

³What will he do to you, and what more besides, O deceitful tongue? ⁴He will punish you with a warrior's sharp arrows, with burning coals of the broom tree.

Ps 144:8 whose mouths are full of lies, whose right hands are deceitful.

Ps 144:11 Deliver me and rescue me from the hands of foreigners whose mouths are full of lies, whose right hands are deceitful.

Pr 10:18 He who conceals his hatred has lying lips, and whoever spreads slander is a fool.

Pr 13:5 The righteous hate what is false, but the wicked bring shame and disgrace.

Pr 20:17 Food gained by fraud tastes sweet to a man, but he ends up with a mouth full of gravel.

Forbidden:

Ex 20:16 "You shall not give false testimony against your neighbor.

Ex 23:1 "Do not spread false reports. Do not help a wicked man by being a malicious witness.

Lev 19:11 "'Do not steal.

"'Do not lie.

"'Do not deceive one another.

¹²"'Do not swear falsely by my name and so profane the name of your God. I am the LORD.

Lev 19:16 "'Do not go about spreading slander among your people. "'Do not do anything that endangers your neighbor's life. I am the LORD. (+Ps 34:13; 1Pe 3:10)

Pr 17:7 Arrogant lips are unsuited to a fool—how much worse lying lips to a ruler!

Ecc 5:6 Do not let your mouth lead you into sin. And do not protest to the [temple] messenger, "My vow was a mistake." Why should God be angry at what you say and destroy the work of your hands?

Zep 3:13 The remnant of Israel will do no wrong; they will speak no lies, nor will deceit be found in their mouths. They will eat and lie down and no one will make them afraid."

Eph 4:25 Therefore each of you must put off falsehood and speak truthfully to his neighbor, for we are all members of one body.

Eph 4:29 Do not let any unwholesome talk come out of your mouths, but only what is helpful for building others up according to their needs, that it may benefit those who listen.

Col 3:9 Do not lie to each other, since you have taken off your old self with its practices

1Ti 1:9 We also know that law is made not for the righteous but for lawbreakers and rebels, the ungodly and sinful, the unholy and irreligious; for those who kill their fathers or mothers, for murderers, [10]for adulterers and perverts, for slave traders and liars and perjurers—and for whatever else is contrary to the sound doctrine

Instances of:

Satan, in deceiving Eve (Ge 3:4-5), in impugning Job's motives for being righteous (Job 1:9-10; 2:4-5), in his tempting of Jesus (Mt 4:8-9; Lk 4:6-7). Adam and Eve, in attempting to avoid responsibility (Ge 3:12-13).

Cain, in denying knowledge of his brother (Ge 4:9).

Abraham, in denying that Sarah was his wife (Ge 12:11-19; 20:2).

Sarah, to the angels, denying her laugh of unbelief (Ge 18:15), in denying to the king of Gerar, that she was Abraham's wife (Ge 20:5,16).

Isaac, denying that Rebekah was his wife (Ge 26:7-10).

Rebekah and Isaac, in the conspiracy against Esau (Ge 27:6-24,46).

Jacob's sons, in the scheme to destroy the Shechemites by first having them circumcised (Ge 34).

Joseph's brothers in deceiving their father into a belief that Joseph was killed by wild beasts (Ge 37:29-35). Potiphar's wife, in falsely accusing Joseph (Ge 39:14-17). Joseph, in the deception he carried on with his brothers (Ge 42-44).

Pharaoh, in dealing deceitfully with the Israelites (Ex 7-12).

Aaron, in attempting to shift responsibility for the making of the golden calf (Ex 32:1-24).

Rahab, in denying that the spies were in her house (Jos 2:4-6).

The Gibeonites' ambassadors, in the deception they perpetrated upon Joshua and the elders of Israel in leading them to believe that they came from a distant region, when in fact they dwelt in the immediate vicinity (Jos 9).

Ehud, in pretending to bear secret messages to Eglon, king of Moab, while his object was to assassinate him (Jdg 3:16-22).

Sisera, who instructed Jael to mislead his pursuers (Jdg 4:20).

Saul, in professing to Samuel to have obeyed the commandment to destroy all spoils of the Amalekites, when in fact he had not obeyed (1Sa 15:1-20), in accusing Ahimelech of conspiring with David against himself (1Sa 22:11-16), in deceiving the medium of Endor as to his identity (1Sa 28:7-12).

Michal, in the false statement that David was sick, in order to save him from Saul's violence (1Sa 19:12-17).

David, who lied to Ahimelech, professing to have a mission from the king, in order that he might obtain provisions and armor (1Sa 21), in feigning madness (1Sa 21:13-15), and other deceits with the Philistines (1Sa 27:8-12), the falsehood he put in the mouth of Hushai, of friendship to Absalom (2Sa 15:34-37).

The Amalekite who claimed to have slain Saul (2Sa 1:10-12).

Hushai, in false professions to Absalom (2Sa 16:16-19), in his deceitful counsel to Absalom (2Sa 17:7-14).

The wife of the Baharumite who saved the lives of Hushai's messengers, sent to inform David of the movements of Absalom's army (2Sa 17:15-22).

The old prophet of Bethel who misguided the prophet of Judah (1Ki 13:11-22),

Jeroboam's wife, pretending to be another woman (1Ki 14:1-6).

Jezebel, Ahab, and the conspirators against Naboth (1Ki 21:7-13).

Gehazi, when he ran after Naaman and misrepresented that Elisha wanted a talent of silver and two changes of clothing (2Ki 5:20-24).

Hazael, servant of the king of Syria, lied to the king in misrepresenting the prophet Elisha's message in regard to the king's recovery (2Ki 8:7-15).

Jehu lied to the worshipers of Baal in order to gain advantage over them and destroy them (2Ki 10:18-28).

Zedekiah, in violating his oath of allegiance to Nebuchadnezzar (2Ch 36:13; Eze 16:59; 17:13-20).

Samaritans, in their efforts to hinder the rebuilding of the temple at Jerusalem (Ezr 4).

Sanballat, in trying to obstruct the rebuilding of Jerusalem (Ne 6).

Haman, in his conspiracy against the Jews (Est 3:8).

In the answers of Job's friends (Job 21:34).

Jeremiah's adversaries in accusing him of joining the Chaldeans (Jer 37:13-15).

Princes of Israel, when they went to Jeremiah for a vision from the Lord (Jer 42:20).

Herod, to the wise men, in professing to desire to worship Jesus (Mt 2:8).

Jews, in falsely accusing Jesus of blasphemy, when he forgave sin (Mt 9:2-8; Mk 2:5-12; Lk 5:21-26), in falsely accusing Jesus of being a glutton and a drunkard (Mt 11:19), in refusing to bear truthful testimony concerning John the Baptist (Mt 21:24-27), when he announced that he was the Son of God (Mt 26:65; Mk 14:64; Jn 10:33-38).

The disobedient son who promised to work in the vineyard but did not (Mt 21:30).

Peter, in denying Jesus (Mt 26:69-75; Mk 14:66-72; Jn 18:16-18,25-27).

The Roman soldiers, who said the disciples stole the body of Jesus (Mt 28:13,15).

Ananias and Sapphira falsely state that they had sold their land for a given sum (Ac 5:1-10).

Stephen's accusers, who falsely accused him of blaspheming Moses and God (Ac 6:11-14).

Paul's opponents, falsely accusing him of treason to Caesar (Ac 16:20-21; 17:5-7; 24:5; 25:7-8).

The Cretans, who *are* always liars, evil brutes, lazy gluttons (Tit 1:12).

Murder Under False Pretenses:

Of Adonijah (1Ki 2:23-24), of Shimei (1Ki 2:42-43).

Results of:

Destructive—

Pr 11:9 With his mouth the godless destroys his neighbor, but through knowledge the righteous escape.

Pr 26:18 Like a madman shooting firebrands or deadly arrows [19]is a man who deceives his neighbor and says, "I was only joking!"

Pr 26:24 A malicious man disguises himself with his lips, but in his heart he harbors deceit. [25]Though his speech is charming, do not believe him, for seven abominations fill his heart. [26]His malice may be concealed by deception, but his wickedness will be exposed in the assembly.

Pr 26:28 A lying tongue hates those it hurts, and a flattering mouth works ruin.

Isa 32:7 The scoundrel's methods are wicked, he makes

up evil schemes to destroy the poor with lies, even when the plea of the needy is just.

See Accusation, False; Conspiracy; False Witness; Hypocrisy; Perjury; Teachers, False.

FAME OF JESUS (Mt 4:24-25; 9:26,31; 14:1; Mk 1:28,45; Lk 4:14,37; 5:15; 7:17).

FAMILIAR SPIRITS *See Spiritists.*

FAMILY [*3, 3+1074, 278, 1074, 1215, 2446, 3509, 4580, 5476, 5476, 9352, *1169, 3836+, 3858, 3875*].

NIV+ FAMILIES

The concept of the family in the Bible differs from the modern institution. The Hebrew family was larger than families today, including the father of the household, his parents, if living, his wife or wives and children, his daughters and sons-in-law, slaves, guests, and foreigners under his protection. Marriage was arranged by the father of the groom, and the family of the bride, for whom a dowry or purchase money was paid to her father (Ge 24). Polygamy and concubinage were practiced, though not favored by God. A husband could divorce his wife, but she could not divorce him.

The father of a family had the power of life and death over his children. To dishonor a parent was punishable by death (Ex 21:15,17).

The NT concept followed that of the OT. Parents and children, husbands and wives, masters and slaves were commanded to live together in harmony and love (Eph 5:22-6:9; Col 3:18-4:1).

Good, Exemplified:

Abraham (Ge 18:19). Jacob (Ge 35:2). Joshua (Jos 24:15). David (2Sa 6:20). Job (Job 1:5). Lazarus of Bethany (Jn 11:1-5). Cornelius (Ac 10:2,33). Lydia (Ac 16:15). The Philippian jailer (Ac 16:31-34). Crispus (Ac 18:8). Lois (2Ti 1:5).

Unhappiness in:

Caused, by indiscreetness—

Pr 11:22 Like a gold ring in a pig's snout is a beautiful woman who shows no discretion.

Pr 12:4 A wife of noble character is her husband's crown, but a disgraceful wife is like decay in his bones.

Pr 14:1 The wise woman builds her house, but with her own hands the foolish one tears hers down.

Pr 30:21 "Under three things the earth trembles, under four it cannot bear up:

Pr 30:23 an unloved woman who is married, and a maidservant who displaces her mistress.

By hatred—

Pr 15:17 Better a meal of vegetables where there is love than a fattened calf with hatred.

By contention—

Pr 18:19 An offended brother is more unyielding than a fortified city, and disputes are like the barred gates of a citadel.

Pr 19:13 A foolish son is his father's ruin, and a quarrelsome wife is like a constant dripping.

Pr 21:9 Better to live on a corner of the roof than share a house with a quarrelsome wife.

Pr 21:19 Better to live in a desert than with a quarrelsome and ill-tempered wife. (+Pr 25:24)

Pr 27:15 A quarrelsome wife is like a constant dripping on a rainy day; [16]restraining her is like restraining the wind or grasping oil with the hand.

Instances of Unhappiness in:

Of Abraham, on account of Hagar (Ge 16:5; 21:10-11). Of Isaac, on account of disagreement between Jacob and Esau (Ge 27:4-46). Of Jacob, polygamous jealousy between Leah and Rachel (Ge 29:30-34; 30:1-25). Moses and Zipporah (Ex 4:25-26). Elkanah, on account of feuds (1Sa 1:4-7). David and Michal (2Sa 6:16,20-23). Xerxes, on account of Vashti's refusing to appear before his drunken officials (Est 1:10-22).

Instituted:

Ge 2:23 The man said, "This is now bone of my bones and flesh of my flesh; she shall be called 'woman,' for she was taken out of man."

[24]For this reason a man will leave his father and mother and be united to his wife, and they will become one flesh.

Government of—

Ge 3:16 To the woman he said, "I will greatly increase your pains in childbearing; with pain you will give birth to children. Your desire will be for your husband, and he will rule over you."

Ge 18:19 For I have chosen him, so that he will direct his children and his household after him to keep the way of the LORD by doing what is right and just, so that the LORD will bring about for Abraham what he has promised him."

Est 1:20 Then when the king's edict is proclaimed throughout all his vast realm, all the women will respect their husbands, from the least to the greatest." (+Est 1:22)

1Co 7:10 To the married I give this command (not I, but the Lord): A wife must not separate from her husband.

1Co 11:3 Now I want you to realize that the head of every man is Christ, and the head of the woman is man, and the head of Christ is God.

1Co 11:7 A man ought not to cover his head, since he is the image and glory of God; but the woman is the glory of man. [8]For man did not come from woman, but woman from man; [9]neither was man created for woman, but woman for man.

Eph 5:22 Wives, submit to your husbands as to the Lord. [23]For the husband is the head of the wife as Christ is the head of the church, his body, of which he is the Savior. [24]Now as the church submits to Christ, so also wives should submit to their husbands in everything.

Col 3:18 Wives, submit to your husbands, as is fitting in the Lord.

1Ti 3:2 Now the overseer must be above reproach, the husband of but one wife, temperate, self-controlled, respectable, hospitable, able to teach,

1Ti 3:4 He must manage his own family well and see that his children obey him with proper respect. [5](If anyone does not know how to manage his own family, how can he take care of God's church?) (+1Ti 3:12)

1Pe 3:1 Wives, in the same way be submissive to your husbands so that, if any of them do not believe the word, they may be won over without words by the behavior of their wives,

1Pe 3:6 like Sarah, who obeyed Abraham and called him her master. You are her daughters if you do what is right and do not give way to fear.

Husband should provide for (Ge 30:30; 1Ti 5:8). Duty to (Isa 58:7).

Idolatrous (Jer 7:18).

Persian customs in (Est 1:10-22). *See Harem.*

See Children; Husband; Orphan; Widow; Wife.

Of Saints:

Live in unity (Ge 45:24; Ps 133:1). Live in mutual

forbearance (Ge 50:17-21; Mt 18:21-22). Should be taught God's Word (Dt 4:9-10). Rejoice together before God (Dt 14:26). Warned against departing from God (Dt 29:18). Deceivers and liars should be removed from (Ps 101:7). Blessed (Ps 128:3,6). Should be managed wisely (Pr 31:27; 1Ti 3:4-5,12). Punishment of irreligious (Jer 10:25). Worship God together (1Co 16:19).

Religion in:

Observed by: Abraham—

Ge 12:7 The LORD appeared to Abram and said, "To your offspring I will give this land." So he built an altar there to the LORD, who had appeared to him.

⁸From there he went on toward the hills east of Bethel and pitched his tent, with Bethel on the west and Ai on the east. There he built an altar to the LORD and called on the name of the LORD.

Ge 13:3 From the Negev he went from place to place until he came to Bethel, to the place between Bethel and Ai where his tent had been earlier ⁴and where he had first built an altar. There Abram called on the name of the LORD.

Ge 18:19 For I have chosen him, so that he will direct his children and his household after him to keep the way of the LORD by doing what is right and just, so that the LORD will bring about for Abraham what he has promised him."

By Joshua (Jos 24:15), Job (Job 1:5)

By David—

Ps 101:2 I will be careful to lead a blameless life—when will you come to me? I will walk in my house with blameless heart.

Manifested in observance of religious rites—

Ge 17:12 For the generations to come every male among you who is eight days old must be circumcised, including those born in your household or bought with money from a foreigner—those who are not your offspring. ¹³Whether born in your household or bought with your money, they must be circumcised. My covenant in your flesh is to be an everlasting covenant. ¹⁴Any uncircumcised male, who has not been circumcised in the flesh, will be cut off from his people; he has broken my covenant." (+Ge 35:2-4,7; Lk 2:21; Ac 10:2)

Ac 10:47 "Can anyone keep these people from being baptized with water? They have received the Holy Spirit just as we have." ⁴⁸So he ordered that they be baptized in the name of Jesus Christ. Then they asked Peter to stay with them for a few days. (+Ac 16:15)

Ac 16:25 About midnight Paul and Silas were praying and singing hymns to God, and the other prisoners were listening to them. ²⁶Suddenly there was such a violent earthquake that the foundations of the prison were shaken. At once all the prison doors flew open, and everybody's chains came loose. ²⁷The jailer woke up, and when he saw the prison doors open, he drew his sword and was about to kill himself because he thought the prisoners had escaped. ²⁸But Paul shouted, "Don't harm yourself! We are all here!"

²⁹The jailer called for lights, rushed in and fell trembling before Paul and Silas. ³⁰He then brought them out and asked, "Sirs, what must I do to be saved?"

³¹They replied, "Believe in the Lord Jesus, and you will be saved—you and your household." ³²Then they spoke the word of the Lord to him and to all the others in his house. ³³At that hour of the night the jailer took them and washed their wounds; then immediately he and all his family were baptized. ³⁴The jailer brought them into his house and set a meal before them; he was filled with joy because he had come to believe in God—he and his whole family.

1Co 1:16 (Yes, I also baptized the household of Stephanas; beyond that, I don't remember if I baptized anyone else.)

Manifested in religious instruction of children—

Dt 4:9 Only be careful, and watch yourselves closely so that you do not forget the things your eyes have seen or let them slip from your heart as long as you live. Teach them to your children and to their children after them. ¹⁰Remember the day you stood before the LORD your God at Horeb, when he said to me, "Assemble the people before me to hear my words so that they may learn to revere me as long as they live in the land and may teach them to their children."

Dt 11:19 Teach them to your children, talking about them when you sit at home and when you walk along the road, when you lie down and when you get up. ²⁰Write them on the doorframes of your houses and on your gates,

Manifested in household consecration—

Dt 12:5 But you are to seek the place the LORD your God will choose from among all your tribes to put his Name there for his dwelling. To that place you must go; ⁶there bring your burnt offerings and sacrifices, your tithes and special gifts, what you have vowed to give and your freewill offerings, and the firstborn of your herds and flocks. ⁷There, in the presence of the LORD your God, you and your families shall eat and shall rejoice in everything you have put your hand to, because the LORD your God has blessed you.

⁸You are not to do as we do here today, everyone as he sees fit, ⁹since you have not yet reached the resting place and the inheritance the LORD your God is giving you. ¹⁰But you will cross the Jordan and settle in the land the LORD your God is giving you as an inheritance, and he will give you rest from all your enemies around you so that you will live in safety. ¹¹Then to the place the LORD your God will choose as a dwelling for his Name—there you are to bring everything I command you: your burnt offerings and sacrifices, your tithes and special gifts, and all the choice possessions you have vowed to the LORD. ¹²And there rejoice before the LORD your God, you, your sons and daughters, your menservants and maidservants, and the Levites from your towns, who have no allotment or inheritance of their own.

Jos 24:15 But if serving the LORD seems undesirable to you, then choose for yourselves this day whom you will serve, whether the gods your forefathers served beyond the River, or the gods of the Amorites, in whose land you are living. But as for me and my household, we will serve the LORD."

Ac 10:1 At Caesarea there was a man named Cornelius, a centurion in what was known as the Italian Regiment. ²He and all his family were devout and God-fearing; he gave generously to those in need and prayed to God regularly.

Ac 18:8 Crispus, the synagogue ruler, and his entire household believed in the Lord; and many of the Corinthians who heard him believed and were baptized.

Purpose: To keep the way of the Lord (Ge 18:19), to keep children from sinning (Job 1:5), to be an example to the household (Ps 101:2).

FAMINE [4103, 8279, 8280, 8282, *3350*].

NIV+ FAMINES

Described:

Pharaoh forewarned of, in dreams (Ge 41). Sent as a

judgment (Lev 26:19-29; Dt 28:23-24,38-42; 1Ki 17:1; 2Ki 8:1; 1Ch 21:12; Ps 105:16; 107:33-34; Isa 3:1-8; 14:30; Jer 14:15-22; 19:9; 29:17,19; La 5:4-5,10; Eze 4:16-17; 5:16-17; 14:13-14; Joel 1:15-16; Am 4:6-9; 5:16-17; Hag 1:10-11; Mt 24:7; Lk 21:11; Rev 6:5-8). Description of (Dt 28:53-57; Isa 5:13; 9:18-21; 17:11; Jer 5:17; 14:1-6; 48:33; La 1:11,19; 2:11-22; 4:4-10; Joel 1:17-20). Righteous delivered from (Job 5:20; Ps 33:19; 37:19).

Cannibalism in (Dt 28:53; 2Ki 6:28).

Figurative:

God will withdraw from those who will not listen to the words of his prophets in the same way that food and water is scarce during famine (Am 8:11).

Instances of:

In Canaan (Ge 12:10; 26:1; 2Sa 21:1; 1Ki 17; 18:1; 2Ki 6:25-29; 7:4). In Egypt (Ge 41:53-57). In Jerusalem, from siege (2Ki 25:3; Jer 52:6). Universal (Ac 11:28).

FAN *See Winnow; Winnowing.*

FANATICISM Absolute and aggressive devotion to religion. The prophets of Baal (1Ki 18:28). The Jews against Christ (Jn 19:15). The Jews in stoning Stephen (Ac 7:57). Saul in persecuting the church (Ac 9:1). The Jews in their rage against Paul (Ac 21:36; 22:23).

FAREWELLS Allusions to (Ru 1:14; Lk 9:61; Ac 18:21; 20:38; 21:6; 2Co 13:11).

FARMER [*438, 3086, 5749, *1177, 5062*].

NIV+ FARM, FARMED, FARMERS, FARMING

An agriculturalist (Isa 28:24; Jer 14:4; Mt 21:33-46; Mk 12:1-9; Jn 15:1; 1Co 3:9).

Parables of, describing the spread of the Gospel (Mt 13:3-23); describing the unfaithful Jews, given over to corruption and hypocrisy (Mt 21:33-46; Mk 12:1-12; Lk 20:9-19).

Figurative:

Of God as the master gardener (Jn 15:1). Of the spread of the Gospel (Mt 13:3-23); of Paul and Apollos 1Co 3:5-9). *See Agriculture; Farming.*

FARMING [438, 3086, 4494, 6268, 6275, *1175, 1177, 5062*].

NIV+ FARM, FARMED, FARMER, FARMERS

Was the chief occupation of the people of Israel after the conquest of Canaan. Each family received a piece of ground marked by boundaries that could not be removed (Dt 19:14). Plowing took place in the autumn when the ground was softened by the rain. Grain was sown during the month of February; harvest began in the spring and usually lasted from Passover to Pentecost. The grain was cut with a sickle, and gleanings were for the poor (Ru 2:2). The grain was threshed out on the threshing floor, a saucer-shaped area of beaten clay 25 or more feet in diameter, on which animals dragged a sledge over the sheaves to beat out the grain. The grain was winnowed by tossing it into the air to let the chaff blow away and was then sifted to remove impurities (Ps 1:4). Wheat and barley were the most important crops, but other grains and vegetables were cultivated as well. *See Agriculture; Fallow Ground.*

FARTHING NIV "penny." *See Money.*

FASTING [7426, 7427, *3763, 3764*].

NIV+ FAST, FASTED, FASTS

Accompanied by self-denial (Dt 9:18; Ne 9:1), confes-

sion of sin (1Sa 7:6; Ne 9:1-2), reading of the Scriptures (Jer 36:6), prayer (Da 9:3; Mt 17:21).

Commanded (Joel 1:14; 2:12-13). Precepts concerning (Mt 6:16-18).

Habitual, of the Israelites (Zec 8:19), by John's disciples (Mt 9:14), by Pharisees (Mt 9:14; Mk 2:18; Lk 18:12), by Anna (Lk 2:37), by Cornelius (Ac 10:30), by Paul (2Co 6:5; 11:27).

In times of bereavement, of the people of Jabesh Gilead, for Saul and his sons (1Sa 31:13; 1Ch 10:12), of David, at the time of Saul's death (2Sa 1:12), of Abner's death (2Sa 3:35), of his child's sickness (2Sa 12:16,21-23).

Observed on occasions of, public calamities (2Sa 1:12; Ac 27:33), private afflictions (2Sa 12:16), approaching danger (Est 4:16; Ac 27:9,33-34), afflictions (Ps 35:13; Da 6:18), religious observances (Zec 8:19), ordination of ministers (Ac 13:3; 14:23).

Of the disobedient, unacceptable (Isa 58:3-7; Jer 14:12; Zec 7:5; Mt 6:16).

Prolonged, forty days and nights, by Moses (Ex 24:18; 34:28; Dt 9:9,18), forty days and nights, by Elijah (1Ki 19:8), three weeks, by Daniel (Da 10:2-3), forty days and nights, by Jesus (Mt 4:2; Mk 1:12-13; Lk 4:1-2).

See Humiliation and Self-Affliction; Humility.

Instances of:

Of the Israelites, in the conflict between the other tribes with the tribe of Benjamin, on account of the wrong suffered by a Levite's concubine (Jdg 20:26), when they went to Mizpah for the ark (1Sa 7:6).

Of David, at the death of Saul (2Sa 1:12), during the sickness of the child born to him by Bathsheba (2Sa 12:16-22), while interceding in prayer for his friends (Ps 35:13), in his zeal for Zion (Ps 69:10), in prayer for himself and his adversaries (Ps 109:4,24).

Of Ahab, when Elijah prophesied the destruction of himself and his house (1Ki 21:27, w 21:20-29).

Of Jehoshaphat, at the time of the invasion of the confederated armies of the Canaanites and Syrians (2Ch 20:3).

Of the Jews, in Babylon, with prayer for divine deliverance and guidance (Ezr 8:21,23), when Jeremiah prophesied against Judea and Jerusalem (Jer 36:9).

Of Ezra, on account of the idolatrous marriages of the Jews (Ezr 10:6).

Of Nehemiah, on account of the desolation of Jerusalem and the temple (Ne 1:4).

Of Darius, when he put Daniel in the lions' den (Da 6:18).

Of Daniel, on account of the captivity of the people, with prayer for their deliverance (Da 9:3), at the time of his vision (Da 10:1-3).

Of the Ninevites, when Jonah preached to them (Jnh 3:5-10).

By Paul, at the time of his conversion (Ac 9:9).

Of the disciples, at the time of the consecration of Barnabas and Saul (Ac 13:2-3).

Of the consecration of the elders (Ac 14:23).

FAT [487, 1374, 2693, 4671, 4833, 5458, 7022, 9042, 9043].

NIV+ FATTENED, FATTENING

Described:

The layer of fat around the kidneys and other viscera of sacrificial animals which was forbidden for food, but which was burned as an offering to Yahweh (Lev 4:31). Offered in sacrifice (Ex 23:18; 29:13,22; Lev 1:8; 3:3-5, 9-11,14-17; 4:8-10; 7:3-5; 8:16,25-26; 10:15; 17:6; 1Sa

2:15-16; Isa 43:24). Belonged to the Lord (Lev 3:16). Forbidden as food (Lev 3:16-17; 7:23). Idolatrous sacrifices of (Dt 32:38).

Instances of fat people: Eglon king of Moab (Jdg 3:17, 22). Eli the priest (1Sa 4:18). *See Corpulency.*

FATHER [3, 408, 587, 3528, 8037, 10003, *574, 1164, 4252, 4257, 4260, 4262*].

NIV+ FATHER-IN-LAW, FATHER'S, FATHERED, FATHERLESS, FATHERS, FATHERS', FOREFATHER, FOREFATHER'S, FOREFATHERS, GRANDFATHER, GRANDFATHER'S

Described:

Has various meanings in the Bible:

1. The originator of a way of life (Ge 4:20).
2. A male ancestor, immediate or remote, the father of nations or peoples (Ge 17:4; Ro 9:5).
3. An immediate male progenitor (Ge 42:13).
4. An adviser (Jdg 17:10), or a source (Job 38:28).
5. A spiritual ancestor (Jn 8:44; Ro 4:11).

God is the Creator of the human race (Mal 2:10) and is called the Father of the universe (Jas 1:17).

FATHERHOOD, OF GOD *See God, Fatherhood of.*

FATHER-IN-LAW [2767, 3162, *4290*].

NIV+ See FATHER

Unjust, Laban to Jacob (Ge 29:21-23; 31:7,39-42). Hospitable to son-in-law, a man of Bethlehem in Judah (Jdg 19:3-9).

FATHERLESS [3+401, 3846]. *See Orphan.*

FATHERS' GOD (Ex 3:13; Dt 1:11; 4:1; Jos 18:3; 2Ch 28:9; 29:5). *See God.*

FATHOM *See Sounding.*

FATTENED CALF [80, 2693, 5272, 5309, *4988, 4990, 5555*]. A clean animal fattened for offering to God (1Sa 28:24; 2Sa 6:13; Lk 15:23).

FAULT FINDING [*3523*].

NIV+ FAULTFINDERS

(Jude 16). *See Murmuring; Rebuke; Uncharitableness.*

FAVOR [*1388, 2704+7156, 2834, 2858, 2876, 3202, 5840, 7155, 8354, 8356, 9120, 9373, *473, 1283, 5921*]. *See God, Grace of.*

FAVORITISM [2075+, *1639+4720, 2848+4680, 4719, 4721+*].

NIV+ FAVOR, FAVORITE

Instances of: Rebekah, for her son Jacob (Ge 27:6-17). Jacob, for Rachel (Ge 29:30,34). Israel (Jacob), for Joseph (Ge 37:3-4). Joseph, for Benjamin (Ge 43:34). Forbidden in parents (Dt 21:15-17). Elkanah, for Hannah (1Sa 1:4-5). *See Partiality.*

FEAR [*399, 1593, 1796, 3006, 3010, 3328, 3707, 3710, 3711, 4570, 4616, 5022, 6907, 7064, 7065, *925, 5828, 5832*]. *See Cowardice; Fear of God.*

FEAR OF GOD

NIV+ AFRAID, FEARED, FEARFUL, FEARFULLY, FEARING, FEARLESSLY, FEARS, FEARSOME, FRIGHT, FRIGHTEN, FRIGHTENED, FRIGHTENING, GOD-FEARING

Described:

As, wisdom (Job 28:28; Pr 15:33), pure (Ps 19:9), the beginning of wisdom (Ps 111:10; Pr 9:10; 15:33), the beginning of knowledge (Pr 1:7), hating evil (Pr 8:13), adding length to life (Pr 10:27), a fountain of life (Pr 14:27), leading to life (Pr 19:23).

Commanded (Lev 19:14,32; 25:36,43; Dt 6:13; 10:20; 13:4; Jos 24:14; 1Sa 12:24; 2Ki 17:36; 1Ch 16:30; 2Ch 19:7,9; Ne 5:9; Ps 2:11; 22:23; 34:9; 96:4; Pr 3:7; 23:17; 24:21; Ecc 5:7; 12:13)—

Isa 8:13 The LORD Almighty is the one you are to regard as holy, he is the one you are to fear, he is the one you are to dread, (+Isa 29:23; Ro 11:20-21; Col 3:22; 1Pe 2:17; Rev 14:7)

Cultivated by God—

Ex 3:5 "Do not come any closer," God said. "Take off your sandals, for the place where you are standing is holy ground."

Ex 19:12 Put limits for the people around the mountain and tell them, 'Be careful that you do not go up the mountain or touch the foot of it. Whoever touches the mountain shall surely be put to death. [13]He shall surely be stoned or shot with arrows; not a hand is to be laid on him. Whether man or animal, he shall not be permitted to live.' Only when the ram's horn sounds a long blast may they go up to the mountain."

Heb 12:18 You have not come to a mountain that can be touched and that is burning with fire; to darkness, gloom and storm; [19]to a trumpet blast or to such a voice speaking words that those who heard it begged that no further word be spoken to them, [20]because they could not bear what was commanded: "If even an animal touches the mountain, it must be stoned." [21]The sight was so terrifying that Moses said, "I am trembling with fear."

[22]But you have come to Mount Zion, to the heavenly Jerusalem, the city of the living God. You have come to thousands upon thousands of angels in joyful assembly, [23]to the church of the firstborn, whose names are written in heaven. You have come to God, the judge of all men, to the spirits of righteous men made perfect, [24]to Jesus the mediator of a new covenant, and to the sprinkled blood that speaks a better word than the blood of Abel.

Deters from sin—

Ex 20:18 When the people saw the thunder and lightning and heard the trumpet and saw the mountain in smoke, they trembled with fear. They stayed at a distance [19]and said to Moses, "Speak to us yourself and we will listen. But do not have God speak to us or we will die."

[20]Moses said to the people, "Do not be afraid. God has come to test you, so that the fear of God will be with you to keep you from sinning."

Pr 16:6 Through love and faithfulness sin is atoned for; through the fear of the LORD a man avoids evil.

Jer 32:39 I will give them singleness of heart and action, so that they will always fear me for their own good and the good of their children after them. [40]I will make an everlasting covenant with them: I will never stop doing good to them, and I will inspire them to fear me, so that they will never turn away from me.

Averts temporal calamity (Dt 28:47-49)—

Dt 28:58 If you do not carefully follow all the words of this law, which are written in this book, and do not revere this glorious and awesome name—the LORD your God— [59]the LORD will send fearful plagues on you and your descendants, harsh and prolonged disasters, and severe and lingering illnesses. (+Dt 28:60-68; 2Ki 17:36-39)

Secures divine blessing (Dt 5:29)—

Ps 25:12 Who, then, is the man that fears the LORD? He will instruct him in the way chosen for him. **13**He will spend his days in prosperity, and his descendants will inherit the land. **14**The LORD confides in those who fear him; he makes his covenant known to them. (+Ps 31:19-20; 33:18-19)

Ps 34:7 The angel of the LORD encamps around those who fear him, and he delivers them.

Ps 34:9 Fear the LORD, you his saints, for those who fear him lack nothing.

Ps 85:8 I will listen to what God the LORD will say; he promises peace to his people, his saints—but let them not return to folly. **9**Surely his salvation is near those who fear him, that his glory may dwell in our land.

Ps 103:11 For as high as the heavens are above the earth, so great is his love for those who fear him;

Ps 103:13 As a father has compassion on his children, so the LORD has compassion on those who fear him;

Ps 103:17 But from everlasting to everlasting the LORD's love is with those who fear him, and his righteousness with their children's children— (+Ps 111:5; 112:1; 115:11,13)

Ps 128:1 Blessed are all who fear the LORD, who walk in his ways. **2**You will eat the fruit of your labor; blessings and prosperity will be yours. **3**Your wife will be like a fruitful vine within your house; your sons will be like olive shoots around your table. **4**Thus is the man blessed who fears the LORD. (+Ps 145:18-19)

Pr 22:4 Humility and the fear of the LORD bring wealth and honor and life. (+Ecc 7:18)

Ecc 8:12 Although a wicked man commits a hundred crimes and still lives a long time, I know that it will go better with God-fearing men, who are reverent before God. **13**Yet because the wicked do not fear God, it will not go well with them, and their days will not lengthen like a shadow. (+Mal 4:2; Lk 1:50; Ac 10:34-35)

Universality of, foretold (Ps 76:11-12; 102:15).

A bond of fellowship among righteous—

Mal 3:16 Then those who feared the LORD talked with each other, and the LORD listened and heard. A scroll of remembrance was written in his presence concerning those who feared the LORD and honored his name.

17"They will be mine," says the LORD Almighty, "in the day when I make up my treasured possession. I will spare them, just as in compassion a man spares his son who serves him. **18**And you will again see the distinction between the righteous and the wicked, between those who serve God and those who do not.

Instances of Guilty Fear:

Adam and Eve (Ge 3:8-13).

The wicked—

Job 15:20 All his days the wicked man suffers torment, the ruthless through all the years stored up for him. **21**Terrifying sounds fill his ears; when all seems well, marauders attack him. **22**He despairs of escaping the darkness; he is marked for the sword. **23**He wanders about—food for vultures; he knows the day of darkness is at hand. **24**Distress and anguish fill him with terror; they overwhelm him, like a king poised to attack, **25**because he shakes his fist at God and vaunts himself against the Almighty,

Job 18:11 Terrors startle him on every side and dog his every step.

Pr 10:24 What the wicked dreads will overtake him; what the righteous desire will be granted.

Those without moral direction—

Pr 1:24 But since you rejected me when I called and no one gave heed when I stretched out my hand, **25**since you ignored all my advice and would not accept my rebuke, **26**I in turn will laugh at your disaster; I will mock when calamity overtakes you— **27**when calamity overtakes you like a storm, when disaster sweeps over you like a whirlwind, when distress and trouble overwhelm you.

Those without God in general (Isa 2:19-21; 33:14).

King Belshazzar—

Da 5:6 His face turned pale and he was so frightened that his knees knocked together and his legs gave way.

The nations (Mic 7:17). Judas (Mt 27:3-5). The guards at Jesus' tomb (Mt 28:4). Christians no longer fear (Ro 8:15; 2Ti 1:7).

Demons—

Jas 2:19 You believe that there is one God. Good! Even the demons believe that—and shudder.

The nations in the day of wrath (Rev 6:16).

Instances of Those Who Feared:

Abraham, tested in the offering of his son Isaac (Ge 22:12).

Jacob, in the vision of the stairway, and the covenant of God (Ge 28:16-17; 42:18).

The midwives of Egypt, in refusing to take the lives of the Hebrew children (Ex 1:17,21).

The Egyptians, at the time of the plague of thunder and hail and fire (Ex 9:20).

Phinehas, in turning away the anger of God at the time of the plague (Nu 25:11, w 25:6-15).

The nine and one-half tribes of Israel west of the Jordan (Jos 22:15-20).

Obadiah, in his devotion to God, sheltered one hundred prophets against Jezebel because he feared God more than he feared the wrath of Jezebel (1Ki 18:3-4).

Jehoshaphat, in proclaiming a fast when the land was about to be invaded by the armies of the Ammonites and Moabites (2Ch 20:3).

Nehemiah, in his reform of the public administration which had heavily taxed the people and lorded their rule over the people (Ne 5:15).

Hanani, which qualified him to be ruler over Jerusalem (Ne 7:2).

Job, according to the testimony of Satan (Job 1:8).

David (Ps 119:38).

Hezekiah, in his treatment of the prophet Micah, who prophesied evil against Jerusalem (Jer 26:19).

The Israelites, in obeying the voice of the Lord (Hag 1:12).

The women at the tomb (Mt 28:8).

Cornelius, who feared God with all his house (Ac 10:2).

Noah, in preparing the ark (Heb 11:7).

Motivates God's:

Power (Jos 4:24; Ps 99:1; Jer 5:22; Mt 10:28; Lk 12:5), providence (1Sa 12:2-4), power and justice (Job 37:19-24), wrath (Ps 90:11), forgiveness (Ps 130:4), majesty (Jer 10:7).

See Conviction, of Sin; Faith.

Motivates People:

To respect others—

Lev 19:14 " 'Do not curse the deaf or put a stumbling block in front of the blind, but fear your God. I am the LORD.

Lev 19:30 " 'Observe my Sabbaths and have reverence for my sanctuary. I am the LORD.

Lev 25:17 Do not take advantage of each other, but fear your God. I am the LORD your God.

Lev 25:36 Do not take interest of any kind from him, but fear your God, so that your countryman may continue to live among you.

Lev 25:43 Do not rule over them ruthlessly, but fear your God.

To obedience—

Nu 32:15 If you turn away from following him, he will again leave all this people in the desert, and you will be the cause of their destruction."

Dt 6:13 Fear the LORD your God, serve him only and take your oaths in his name. ¹⁴Do not follow other gods, the gods of the peoples around you; ¹⁵for the LORD your God, who is among you, is a jealous God and his anger will burn against you, and he will destroy you from the face of the land.

Dt 7:1 When the LORD your God brings you into the land you are entering to possess and drives out before you many nations—the Hittites, Girgashites, Amorites, Canaanites, Perizzites, Hivites and Jebusites, seven nations larger and stronger than you— ²and when the LORD your God has delivered them over to you and you have defeated them, then you must destroy them totally. Make no treaty with them, and show them no mercy. ³Do not intermarry with them. Do not give your daughters to their sons or take their daughters for your sons, ⁴for they will turn your sons away from following me to serve other gods, and the LORD's anger will burn against you and will quickly destroy you.

Dt 8:5 Know then in your heart that as a man disciplines his son, so the LORD your God disciplines you.

⁶Observe the commands of the LORD your God, walking in his ways and revering him.

Dt 10:12 And now, O Israel, what does the LORD your God ask of you but to fear the LORD your God, to walk in all his ways, to love him, to serve the LORD your God with all your heart and with all your soul, ¹³and to observe the LORD's commands and decrees that I am giving you today for your own good?

Dt 10:20 Fear the LORD your God and serve him. Hold fast to him and take your oaths in his name.

Dt 13:4 It is the LORD your God you must follow, and him you must revere. Keep his commands and obey him; serve him and hold fast to him.

Dt 13:6 If your very own brother, or your son or daughter, or the wife you love, or your closest friend secretly entices you, saying, "Let us go and worship other gods" (gods that neither you nor your fathers have known, ⁷gods of the peoples around you, whether near or far, from one end of the land to the other), ⁸do not yield to him or listen to him. Show him no pity. Do not spare him or shield him. ⁹You must certainly put him to death. Your hand must be the first in putting him to death, and then the hands of all the people. ¹⁰Stone him to death, because he tried to turn you away from the LORD your God, who brought you out of Egypt, out of the land of slavery. ¹¹Then all Israel will hear and be afraid, and no one among you will do such an evil thing again.

Dt 17:11 Act according to the law they teach you and the decisions they give you. Do not turn aside from what they tell you, to the right or to the left. ¹²The man who shows contempt for the judge or for the priest who stands ministering there to the LORD your God must be put to death. You must purge the evil from Israel. ¹³All the people will hear and be afraid, and will not be contemptuous again.

Dt 21:18 If a man has a stubborn and rebellious son who does not obey his father and mother and will not listen to them when they discipline him, ¹⁹his father and mother shall take hold of him and bring him to the elders at the gate of his town. ²⁰They shall say to the elders, "This son of ours is stubborn and rebellious. He will not obey us. He is a profligate and a drunkard." ²¹Then all the men of his town shall stone him to death. You must purge the evil from among you. All Israel will hear of it and be afraid.

Dt 28:14 Do not turn aside from any of the commands I give you today, to the right or to the left, following other gods and serving them.

¹⁵However, if you do not obey the LORD your God and do not carefully follow all his commands and decrees I am giving you today, all these curses will come upon you and overtake you: (+Dt 28:16-68)

Dt 31:11 when all Israel comes to appear before the LORD your God at the place he will choose, you shall read this law before them in their hearing. ¹²Assemble the people—men, women and children, and the aliens living in your towns—so they can listen and learn to fear the LORD your God and follow carefully all the words of this law. ¹³Their children, who do not know this law, must hear it and learn to fear the LORD your God as long as you live in the land you are crossing the Jordan to possess."

1Sa 12:24 But be sure to fear the LORD and serve him faithfully with all your heart; consider what great things he has done for you. ²⁵Yet if you persist in doing evil, both you and your king will be swept away."

Job 13:21 Withdraw your hand far from me, and stop frightening me with your terrors.

Job 31:1 "I made a covenant with my eyes not to look lustfully at a girl. ²For what is man's lot from God above, his heritage from the Almighty on high? ³Is it not ruin for the wicked, disaster for those who do wrong? ⁴Does he not see my ways and count my every step?

Job 31:13 "If I have denied justice to my menservants and maidservants when they had a grievance against me, ¹⁴what will I do when God confronts me? What will I answer when called to account? ¹⁵Did not he who made me in the womb make them? Did not the same one form us both within our mothers?

¹⁶"If I have denied the desires of the poor or let the eyes of the widow grow weary, ¹⁷if I have kept my bread to myself, not sharing it with the fatherless— ¹⁸but from my youth I reared him as would a father, and from my birth I guided the widow— ¹⁹if I have seen anyone perishing for lack of clothing, or a needy man without a garment, ²⁰and his heart did not bless me for warming him with the fleece from my sheep, ²¹if I have raised my hand against the fatherless, knowing that I had influence in court, ²²then let my arm fall from the shoulder, let it be broken off at the joint. ²³For I dreaded destruction from God, and for fear of his splendor I could not do such things.

Isa 1:20 but if you resist and rebel, you will be devoured by the sword." For the mouth of the LORD has spoken.

Jer 4:4 Circumcise yourselves to the LORD, circumcise your hearts, you men of Judah and people of Jerusalem, or my wrath will break out and burn like fire because of the evil you have done—burn with no one to quench it.

Jer 22:5 But if you do not obey these commands, declares the LORD, I swear by myself that this palace will become a ruin.'"

Mt 10:28 Do not be afraid of those who kill the body but cannot kill the soul. Rather, be afraid of the One who can destroy both soul and body in hell. (+Lk 12:4-5)

2Co 5:10 For we must all appear before the judgment seat of Christ, that each one may receive what is due him for the things done while in the body, whether good or bad.

¹¹Since, then, we know what it is to fear the Lord, we try to persuade men. What we are is plain to God, and I hope it is also plain to your conscience.

2Ti 4:1 In the presence of God and of Christ Jesus, who will judge the living and the dead, and in view of his appearing and his kingdom, I give you this charge: ²Preach the Word; be prepared in season and out of season; correct, rebuke and encourage—with great patience and careful instruction.

2Pe 3:10 But the day of the Lord will come like a thief. The heavens will disappear with a roar; the elements will be destroyed by fire, and the earth and everything in it will be laid bare.

¹¹Since everything will be destroyed in this way, what kind of people ought you to be? You ought to live holy and godly lives ¹²as you look forward to the day of God and speed its coming. That day will bring about the destruction of the heavens by fire, and the elements will melt in the heat.

Rev 14:9 A third angel followed them and said in a loud voice: "If anyone worships the beast and his image and receives his mark on the forehead or on the hand, ¹⁰he, too, will drink of the wine of God's fury, which has been poured full strength into the cup of his wrath. He will be tormented with burning sulfur in the presence of the holy angels and of the Lamb.

To truthfulness—

Dt 15:9 Be careful not to harbor this wicked thought: "The seventh year, the year for canceling debts, is near," so that you do not show ill will toward your needy brother and give him nothing. He may then appeal to the LORD against you, and you will be found guilty of sin.

Dt 19:16 If a malicious witness takes the stand to accuse a man of a crime, ¹⁷the two men involved in the dispute must stand in the presence of the LORD before the priests and the judges who are in office at the time. ¹⁸The judges must make a thorough investigation, and if the witness proves to be a liar, giving false testimony against his brother, ¹⁹then do to him as he intended to do to his brother. You must purge the evil from among you. ²⁰The rest of the people will hear of this and be afraid, and never again will such an evil thing be done among you.

To filial obedience (Dt 21:21).

Reverence:

Expressed in the Old Testament—

Ge 35:5 Then they set out, and the terror of God fell upon the towns all around them so that no one pursued them.

Ex 18:21 But select capable men from all the people— men who fear God, trustworthy men who hate dishonest gain—and appoint them as officials over thousands, hundreds, fifties and tens.

Ex 20:18 When the people saw the thunder and lightning and heard the trumpet and saw the mountain in smoke, they trembled with fear. They stayed at a distance ¹⁹and said to Moses, "Speak to us yourself and we will listen. But do not have God speak to us or we will die."

²⁰Moses said to the people, "Do not be afraid. God has come to test you, so that the fear of God will be with you to keep you from sinning." (+Ex 20:21-26)

Lev 22:32 Do not profane my holy name. I must be acknowledged as holy by the Israelites. I am the LORD, who makes you holy

Dt 4:10 Remember the day you stood before the LORD your God at Horeb, when he said to me, "Assemble the people before me to hear my words so that they may learn to revere me as long as they live in the land and may teach them to their children."

Dt 5:29 Oh, that their hearts would be inclined to fear me and keep all my commands always, so that it might go well with them and their children forever!

Dt 6:2 so that you, your children and their children after them may fear the LORD your God as long as you live by keeping all his decrees and commands that I give you, and so that you may enjoy long life.

Dt 10:12 And now, O Israel, what does the LORD your God ask of you but to fear the LORD your God, to walk in all his ways, to love him, to serve the LORD your God with all your heart and with all your soul, ¹³and to observe the LORD's commands and decrees that I am giving you today for your own good?

Dt 10:20 Fear the LORD your God and serve him. Hold fast to him and take your oaths in his name. ²¹He is your praise; he is your God, who performed for you those great and awesome wonders you saw with your own eyes. (+Dt 14:23; 17:13)

Dt 28:58 If you do not carefully follow all the words of this law, which are written in this book, and do not revere this glorious and awesome name—the LORD your God—

Jos 24:14 "Now fear the LORD and serve him with all faithfulness. Throw away the gods your forefathers worshiped beyond the River and in Egypt, and serve the LORD. ¹⁵But if serving the LORD seems undesirable to you, then choose for yourselves this day whom you will serve, whether the gods your forefathers served beyond the River, or the gods of the Amorites, in whose land you are living. But as for me and my household, we will serve the LORD."

1Sa 12:14 If you fear the LORD and serve and obey him and do not rebel against his commands, and if both you and the king who reigns over you follow the LORD your God—good! ¹⁵But if you do not obey the LORD, and if you rebel against his commands, his hand will be against you, as it was against your fathers.

1Sa 12:23 As for me, far be it from me that I should sin against the LORD by failing to pray for you. And I will teach you the way that is good and right. ²⁴But be sure to fear the LORD and serve him faithfully with all your heart; consider what great things he has done for you. ²⁵Yet if you persist in doing evil, both you and your king will be swept away."

2Sa 23:3 The God of Israel spoke, the Rock of Israel said to me: 'When one rules over men in righteousness, when he rules in the fear of God, ⁴he is like the light of morning at sunrise on a cloudless morning, like the brightness after rain that brings the grass from the earth.'

1Ki 8:40 so that they will fear you all the time they live in the land you gave our fathers.

2Ki 17:36 But the LORD, who brought you up out of Egypt with mighty power and outstretched arm, is the one you must worship. To him you shall bow down and to him offer sacrifices. ³⁷You must always be careful to keep the decrees and ordinances, the laws and commands he wrote for you. Do not worship other gods. ³⁸Do not forget the covenant I have made with you, and do not worship other gods. ³⁹Rather, worship the LORD your God; it is he who will deliver you from the hand of all your enemies."

1Ch 16:30 Tremble before him, all the earth! The world is firmly established; it cannot be moved.

2Ch 19:7 Now let the fear of the LORD be upon you. Judge carefully, for with the LORD our God there is no injustice or partiality or bribery."

2Ch 19:9 He gave them these orders: "You must serve faithfully and wholeheartedly in the fear of the LORD. **¹⁰**In every case that comes before you from your fellow countrymen who live in the cities—whether bloodshed or other concerns of the law, commands, decrees or ordinances—you are to warn them not to sin against the LORD; otherwise his wrath will come on you and your brothers. Do this, and you will not sin.

Ezr 10:3 Now let us make a covenant before our God to send away all these women and their children, in accordance with the counsel of my lord and of those who fear the commands of our God. Let it be done according to the Law.

Job 28:28 And he said to man, 'The fear of the Lord—that is wisdom, and to shun evil is understanding.'"

Job 37:24 Therefore, men revere him, for does he not have regard for all the wise in heart?"

Ps 2:11 Serve the LORD with fear and rejoice with trembling.

Ps 15:4 who despises a vile man but honors those who fear the LORD, who keeps his oath even when it hurts,

Ps 19:9 The fear of the LORD is pure, enduring forever. The ordinances of the LORD are sure and altogether righteous.

Ps 22:23 You who fear the LORD, praise him! All you descendants of Jacob, honor him! Revere him, all you descendants of Israel!

Ps 22:25 From you comes the theme of my praise in the great assembly; before those who fear you will I fulfill my vows.

Ps 31:19 How great is your goodness, which you have stored up for those who fear you, which you bestow in the sight of men on those who take refuge in you.

Ps 33:8 Let all the earth fear the LORD; let all the people of the world revere him. (+Ps 33:18; 34:11)

Ps 37:7 Be still before the LORD and wait patiently for him; do not fret when men succeed in their ways, when they carry out their wicked schemes.

Ps 37:9 For evil men will be cut off, but those who hope in the LORD will inherit the land.

Ps 37:11 But the meek will inherit the land and enjoy great peace.

Ps 46:10 "Be still, and know that I am God; I will be exalted among the nations, I will be exalted in the earth."

Ps 52:6 The righteous will see and fear; they will laugh at him, saying,

Ps 60:4 But for those who fear you, you have raised a banner to be unfurled against the bow. *Selah*

Ps 64:9 All mankind will fear; they will proclaim the works of God and ponder what he has done.

Ps 67:7 God will bless us, and all the ends of the earth will fear him.

Ps 72:5 He will endure as long as the sun, as long as the moon, through all generations.

Ps 76:7 You alone are to be feared. Who can stand before you when you are angry?

Ps 76:11 Make vows to the LORD your God and fulfill them; let all the neighboring lands bring gifts to the One to be feared.

Ps 85:9 Surely his salvation is near those who fear him, that his glory may dwell in our land.

Ps 86:11 Teach me your way, O LORD, and I will walk in your truth; give me an undivided heart, that I may fear your name.

Ps 89:7 In the council of the holy ones God is greatly feared; he is more awesome than all who surround him.

Ps 90:11 Who knows the power of your anger? For your wrath is as great as the fear that is due you.

Ps 96:4 For great is the LORD and most worthy of praise; he is to be feared above all gods. (+Ps 96:9)

Ps 99:1 The LORD reigns, let the nations tremble; he sits enthroned between the cherubim, let the earth shake.

Ps 102:15 The nations will fear the name of the LORD, all the kings of the earth will revere your glory.

Ps 103:11 For as high as the heavens are above the earth, so great is his love for those who fear him;

Ps 103:13 As a father has compassion on his children, so the LORD has compassion on those who fear him;

Ps 103:17 But from everlasting to everlasting the LORD's love is with those who fear him, and his righteousness with their children's children—

Ps 111:5 He provides food for those who fear him; he remembers his covenant forever.

Ps 111:10 The fear of the LORD is the beginning of wisdom; all who follow his precepts have good understanding. To him belongs eternal praise.

Ps 112:1 Praise the LORD. Blessed is the man who fears the LORD, who finds great delight in his commands.

Ps 115:11 You who fear him, trust in the LORD—he is their help and shield.

Ps 115:13 he will bless those who fear the LORD—small and great alike.

Ps 118:4 Let those who fear the LORD say: "His love endures forever."

Ps 119:63 I am a friend to all who fear you, to all who follow your precepts.

Ps 119:74 May those who fear you rejoice when they see me, for I have put my hope in your word.

Ps 119:79 May those who fear you turn to me, those who understand your statutes.

Ps 128:1 Blessed are all who fear the LORD, who walk in his ways.

Ps 128:4 Thus is the man blessed who fears the LORD.

Ps 130:4 But with you there is forgiveness; therefore you are feared.

Ps 135:20 O house of Levi, praise the LORD; you who fear him, praise the LORD.

Ps 145:19 He fulfills the desires of those who fear him; he hears their cry and saves them.

Ps 147:11 the LORD delights in those who fear him, who put their hope in his unfailing love.

Pr 1:7 The fear of the LORD is the beginning of knowledge, but fools despise wisdom and discipline.

Pr 2:5 then you will understand the fear of the LORD and find the knowledge of God.

Pr 3:7 Do not be wise in your own eyes; fear the LORD and shun evil.

Pr 8:13 To fear the LORD is to hate evil; I hate pride and arrogance, evil behavior and perverse speech. (+Pr 9:10)

Pr 10:27 The fear of the LORD adds length to life, but the years of the wicked are cut short.

Pr 14:2 He whose walk is upright fears the LORD, but whose ways are devious despises him.

Pr 14:16 A wise man fears the LORD and shuns evil, but a fool is hotheaded and reckless.

Pr 14:26 He who fears the LORD has a secure fortress, and for his children it will be a refuge. **²⁷**The fear of the LORD is a fountain of life, turning a man from the snares of death.

Pr 15:16 Better a little with the fear of the LORD than great wealth with turmoil.

Pr 15:33 The fear of the LORD teaches a man wisdom, and humility comes before honor.

Pr 16:6 Through love and faithfulness sin is atoned for; through the fear of the LORD a man avoids evil.

Pr 19:23 The fear of the LORD leads to life: Then one rests content, untouched by trouble.

Pr 22:4 Humility and the fear of the LORD bring wealth and honor and life.

Pr 23:17 Do not let your heart envy sinners, but always be zealous for the fear of the LORD.

Pr 24:21 Fear the LORD and the king, my son, and do not join with the rebellious,

Pr 28:14 Blessed is the man who always fears the LORD, but he who hardens his heart falls into trouble.

Pr 31:30 Charm is deceptive, and beauty is fleeting; but a woman who fears the LORD is to be praised. (+Ecc 3:14)

Ecc 7:18 It is good to grasp the one and not let go of the other. The man who fears God will avoid all [extremes].

Ecc 8:12 Although a wicked man commits a hundred crimes and still lives a long time, I know that it will go better with God-fearing men, who are reverent before God. ¹³Yet because the wicked do not fear God, it will not go well with them, and their days will not lengthen like a shadow.

Ecc 12:13 Now all has been heard; here is the conclusion of the matter: Fear God and keep his commandments, for this is the whole [duty] of man.

Isa 2:10 Go into the rocks, hide in the ground from dread of the LORD and the splendor of his majesty!

Isa 2:19 Men will flee to caves in the rocks and to holes in the ground from dread of the LORD and the splendor of his majesty, when he rises to shake the earth. ²⁰In that day men will throw away to the rodents and bats their idols of silver and idols of gold, which they made to worship. ²¹They will flee to caverns in the rocks and to the overhanging crags from dread of the LORD and the splendor of his majesty, when he rises to shake the earth.

Isa 25:3 Therefore strong peoples will honor you; cities of ruthless nations will revere you.

Isa 33:6 He will be the sure foundation for your times, a rich store of salvation and wisdom and knowledge; the fear of the LORD is the key to this treasure.

Isa 33:13 You who are far away, hear what I have done; you who are near, acknowledge my power!

Isa 50:10 Who among you fears the LORD and obeys the word of his servant? Let him who walks in the dark, who has no light, trust in the name of the LORD and rely on his God. ¹¹But now, all you who light fires and provide yourselves with flaming torches, go, walk in the light of your fires and of the torches you have set ablaze. This is what you shall receive from my hand: You will lie down in torment.

Isa 59:19 From the west, men will fear the name of the LORD, and from the rising of the sun, they will revere his glory. For he will come like a pent-up flood that the breath of the LORD drives along. (+Isa 60:5; Jer 5:22; 10:7; 32:39,40)

Jer 33:9 Then this city will bring me renown, joy, praise and honor before all nations on earth that hear of all the good things I do for it; and they will be in awe and will tremble at the abundant prosperity and peace I provide for it.'

Hos 3:5 Afterward the Israelites will return and seek the LORD their God and David their king. They will come trembling to the LORD and to his blessings in the last days.

Mic 7:16 Nations will see and be ashamed, deprived of all their power. They will lay their hands on their mouths and their ears will become deaf. ¹⁷They will lick dust like a snake, like creatures that crawl on the ground. They will come trembling out of their dens; they will turn in fear to the LORD our God and will be afraid of you. ¹⁸Who is a God like you, who pardons sin and forgives the transgression of the remnant of his inheritance? You do not stay angry forever but delight to show mercy. ¹⁹You will again have compassion on us; you will tread our sins underfoot and hurl all our iniquities into the depths of the sea. ²⁰You will be true to Jacob, and show mercy to Abraham, as you pledged on oath to our fathers in days long ago.

Zep 3:7 I said to the city, 'Surely you will fear me and accept correction!' Then her dwelling would not be cut off, nor all my punishments come upon her. But they were still eager to act corruptly in all they did.

Zec 2:13 Be still before the LORD, all mankind, because he has roused himself from his holy dwelling."

Mal 3:16 Then those who feared the LORD talked with each other, and the LORD listened and heard. A scroll of remembrance was written in his presence concerning those who feared the LORD and honored his name.

Mal 4:2 But for you who revere my name, the sun of righteousness will rise with healing in its wings. And you will go out and leap like calves released from the stall.

Expressed in the New Testament—

Mt 10:28 Do not be afraid of those who kill the body but cannot kill the soul. Rather, be afraid of the One who can destroy both soul and body in hell.

Lk 1:50 His mercy extends to those who fear him, from generation to generation.

Lk 12:5 But I will show you whom you should fear: Fear him who, after the killing of the body, has power to throw you into hell. Yes, I tell you, fear him.

Lk 23:40 But the other criminal rebuked him. "Don't you fear God," he said, "since you are under the same sentence?

Ac 10:34 Then Peter began to speak: "I now realize how true it is that God does not show favoritism ³⁵but accepts men from every nation who fear him and do what is right.

Ac 13:26 "Brothers, children of Abraham, and you God-fearing Gentiles, it is to us that this message of salvation has been sent.

Ro 11:20 Granted. But they were broken off because of unbelief, and you stand by faith. Do not be arrogant, but be afraid. (+2Co 5:11)

2Co 7:1 Since we have these promises, dear friends, let us purify ourselves from everything that contaminates body and spirit, perfecting holiness out of reverence for God.

Eph 5:21 Submit to one another out of reverence for Christ.

Eph 6:5 Slaves, obey your earthly masters with respect and fear, and with sincerity of heart, just as you would obey Christ.

Php 2:12 Therefore, my dear friends, as you have always obeyed—not only in my presence, but now much more in my absence—continue to work out your salvation with fear and trembling, ¹³for it is God who works in you to will and to act according to his good purpose.

Col 3:22 Slaves, obey your earthly masters in everything; and do it, not only when their eye is on you and to win their favor, but with sincerity of heart and reverence for the Lord.

Heb 5:7 During the days of Jesus' life on earth, he offered up prayers and petitions with loud cries and tears to the one who could save him from death, and he was heard because of his reverent submission.

Heb 12:28 Therefore, since we are receiving a kingdom that cannot be shaken, let us be thankful, and so worship God acceptably with reverence and awe, ²⁹for our "God is a consuming fire."

Jas 2:19 You believe that there is one God. Good! Even the demons believe that—and shudder.

1Pe 1:17 Since you call on a Father who judges each man's work impartially, live your lives as strangers here in reverent fear.

1Pe 3:1 Wives, in the same way be submissive to your husbands so that, if any of them do not believe the word, they may be won over without words by the behavior of their wives, ²when they see the purity and reverence of your lives.

1Jn 4:16 And so we know and rely on the love God has for us. God is love. Whoever lives in love lives in God, and God in him.

¹⁷In this way, love is made complete among us so that we will have confidence on the day of judgment, because in this world we are like him. ¹⁸There is no fear in love. But perfect love drives out fear, because fear has to do with punishment. The one who fears is not made perfect in love.

Rev 11:18 The nations were angry; and your wrath has come. The time has come for judging the dead, and for rewarding your servants the prophets and your saints and those who reverence your name, both small and great—and for destroying those who destroy the earth."

Rev 14:7 He said in a loud voice, "Fear God and give him glory, because the hour of his judgment has come. Worship him who made the heavens, the earth, the sea and the springs of water."

Rev 19:5 Then a voice came from the throne, saying: "Praise our God, all you his servants, you who fear him, both small and great!"

See Punishment, Design of, to Secure Obedience; Reward, A Motive, To Faithfulness.

FEASTS [*430, 2504, 4595, 5492, *109, 369, 2038*].
NIV+ FEAST, FEASTED, FEASTING

Described:

The host serves his guests (Ge 18:8). Men alone present at (Ge 40:20; 43:32,34; 1Sa 9:22; Est 1:8; Mk 6:21; Lk 14:24), women alone (Est 1:9). Guests arranged according to age (Ge 43:33), rank (1Sa 9:22; Lk 14:8-10). Men and women attend (Ex 32:6, w 2-3; Da 5:1-4). Marriage feasts provided by the bridegroom (Jdg 14:10,17). Given by kings (1Sa 20:5; 25:36; 2Sa 9:10; 1Ki 2:7; Est 1:3-8; Da 5:1-4). Drunkenness at (1Sa 25:36; Est 1:10; Da 5:1-4). Wine served at (Est 5:6; 7:7; Isa 5:12). Music at (Isa 5:12; Am 6:4-5; Lk 15:25). Reclined on couches (Am 6:4,7; Jn 13:23,25). Dancing at (Mt 14:6; Lk 15:25). Served in one dish (Mt 26:23). Were presided over by a master of the banquet (Jn 2:8-9). *See Entertainments.*

Covenants ratified by (Ge 26:28-31).

Annual Festivals:

Instituted by Moses: Divine protection given during (Ex 34:24). Designated as, sacred assemblies (Lev 23:4). First and last days were sabbatic (Lev 23:39-40; Nu 28:18-25; 29:12,35; Ne 8:1-18). Kept with rejoicing (Lev 23:40; Dt 16:11-14; 2Ch 30:21-26; Ezr 6:22; Ne 8:9-12,17; Ps 42:4; Isa 30:29; Zec 8:19). Solemn feasts (Nu 15:3; 2Ch 8:13; La 2:6; Eze 46:9), Appointed feasts (Nu 29:39; Ezr 3:5; Isa 1:14).

The three principal festivals were Passover, Pentecost,

and Tabernacles. All males were required to attend (Ex 23:17; 34:23; Dt 16:16; Ps 42:4; 122:4; Eze 36:38; Lk 2:41; Jn 4:45; 7). Attended by women (1Sa 1:3,9; Lk 2:41). Aliens permitted to attend (Jn 12:20; Ac 2:1-11).

Celebrations for:

Birthdays (Ge 40:20; Mk 6:21), coronations (1Ki 1:25; 1Ch 12:38-40), national deliverances (Est 8:17; 9:17-19).

Figurative: (Mt 22:1-14; Lk 14:16-24; Rev 19:9,17).

Observed:

By Jesus (Mt 26:17-20; Lk 2:41-42; 22:15; Jn 2:13,23; 5:1; 7:10; 10:22-23), by Paul (Ac 20:6,16; 24:11,17).

See for full treatment of annual feasts: Dedication; Hanukkah; Kislev; Passover; Pentecost; Purim; Tabernacles, Feast of; Trumpets, Feast of.

FEET [*564+, 892, 5274, 7193, 7895, 8079, 8081, 10039+, 10655, *4267, 4270, 4546*].
NIV+ See FOOT

Sitting at (Lk 8:35; 10:39; Jas 2:3). Washing of, as an example, by Jesus (Jn 13:4-14). *See Washings.*

FELIX [*5772] (*fortunate, lucky*). Governor of Judea. Paul tried before (Ac 23:24-35; 24). Trembles under Paul's preaching (Ac 24:25). Leaves Paul in bonds (Ac 24:26-27; 25:14).

FELLOES *See Rim.*

FELLOW [*278, 408, 8276, *476, 5257, 5281, 5301, 5369*].
NIV+ FELLOW'S, FELLOWMAN, FELLOWS, FELLOWSHIP

A term of reproach (Ge 19:9; 1Sa 21:15; Mt 12:24; 26:61).

FELLOWSHIP [6051, 8968, *3126, 3545*].
NIV+ See FELLOW, SHARE

Defined—

Ecc 4:9 Two are better than one, because they have a good return for their work:

Ecc 4:12 Though one may be overpowered, two can defend themselves. A cord of three strands is not quickly broken.

Am 3:3 Do two walk together unless they have agreed to do so?

Of the righteous:

In brotherhood (Lev 18:19; 1Sa 23:16-18)—

Mt 23:8 "But you are not to be called 'Rabbi,' for you have only one Master and you are all brothers.

Jn 13:34 "A new command I give you: Love one another. As I have loved you, so you must love one another. ³⁵By this all men will know that you are my disciples, if you love one another." (+Jn 15:17)

Ro 14:1 Accept him whose faith is weak, without passing judgment on disputable matters. ²One man's faith allows him to eat everything, but another man, whose faith is weak, eats only vegetables. ³The man who eats everything must not look down on him who does not, and the man who does not eat everything must not condemn the man who does, for God has accepted him. ⁴Who are you to judge someone else's servant? To his own master he stands or falls. And he will stand, for the Lord is able to make him stand.

Ro 14:10 You, then, why do you judge your brother? Or why do you look down on your brother? For we will all stand before God's judgment seat.

Ro 14:13 Therefore let us stop passing judgment on one

another. Instead, make up your mind not to put any stumbling block or obstacle in your brother's way. [14]As one who is in the Lord Jesus, I am fully convinced that no food is unclean in itself. But if anyone regards something as unclean, then for him it is unclean. [15]If your brother is distressed because of what you eat, you are no longer acting in love. Do not by your eating destroy your brother for whom Christ died. [16]Do not allow what you consider good to be spoken of as evil. (+Ro 14:17)

Ro 14:18 because anyone who serves Christ in this way is pleasing to God and approved by men.

[19]Let us therefore make every effort to do what leads to peace and to mutual edification. [20]Do not destroy the work of God for the sake of food. All food is clean, but it is wrong for a man to eat anything that causes someone else to stumble. [21]It is better not to eat meat or drink wine or to do anything else that will cause your brother to fall. (+1Co 1:10)

1Co 12:13 For we were all baptized by one Spirit into one body—whether Jews or Greeks, slave or free—and we were all given the one Spirit to drink.

1Co 16:19 The churches in the province of Asia send you greetings. Aquila and Priscilla greet you warmly in the Lord, and so does the church that meets at their house. [20]All the brothers here send you greetings. Greet one another with a holy kiss. (+Gal 6:10)

Eph 2:14 For he himself is our peace, who has made the two one and has destroyed the barrier, the dividing wall of hostility, [15]by abolishing in his flesh the law with its commandments and regulations. His purpose was to create in himself one new man out of the two, thus making peace, [16]and in this one body to reconcile both of them to God through the cross, by which he put to death their hostility. [17]He came and preached peace to you who were far away and peace to those who were near. [18]For through him we both have access to the Father by one Spirit.

[19]Consequently, you are no longer foreigners and aliens, but fellow citizens with God's people and members of God's household, [20]built on the foundation of the apostles and prophets, with Christ Jesus himself as the chief cornerstone. [21]In him the whole building is joined together and rises to become a holy temple in the Lord.

Eph 5:30 for we are members of his body.

1Th 4:9 Now about brotherly love we do not need to write to you, for you yourselves have been taught by God to love each other. [10]And in fact, you do love all the brothers throughout Macedonia. Yet we urge you, brothers, to do so more and more.

Heb 13:1 Keep on loving each other as brothers.

1Pe 1:22 Now that you have purified yourselves by obeying the truth so that you have sincere love for your brothers, love one another deeply, from the heart. [23]For you have been born again, not of perishable seed, but of imperishable, through the living and enduring word of God.

In worship—

Ps 55:13 But it is you, a man like myself, my companion, my close friend, [14]with whom I once enjoyed sweet fellowship as we walked with the throng at the house of God.

1Co 10:16 Is not the cup of thanksgiving for which we give thanks a participation in the blood of Christ? And is not the bread that we break a participation in the body of Christ? [17]Because there is one loaf, we, who are many, are one body, for we all partake of the one loaf.

Eph 5:19 Speak to one another with psalms, hymns and spiritual songs. Sing and make music in your heart to the Lord, (+Col 3:16)

In unity of purpose—

Ps 119:63 I am a friend to all who fear you, to all who follow your precepts. (+Ps 133:1-3)

Am 3:3 Do two walk together unless they have agreed to do so?

Mal 3:16 Then those who feared the LORD talked with each other, and the LORD listened and heard. A scroll of remembrance was written in his presence concerning those who feared the LORD and honored his name.

Jn 17:11 I will remain in the world no longer, but they are still in the world, and I am coming to you. Holy Father, protect them by the power of your name—the name you gave me—so that they may be one as we are one.

Jn 17:21 that all of them may be one, Father, just as you are in me and I am in you. May they also be in us so that the world may believe that you have sent me. [22]I have given them the glory that you gave me, that they may be one as we are one: [23]I in them and you in me. May they be brought to complete unity to let the world know that you sent me and have loved them even as you have loved me.

Ac 1:14 They all joined together constantly in prayer, along with the women and Mary the mother of Jesus, and with his brothers.

Ac 2:1 When the day of Pentecost came, they were all together in one place.

Ac 2:42 They devoted themselves to the apostles' teaching and to the fellowship, to the breaking of bread and to prayer.

Ac 2:44 All the believers were together and had everything in common. [45]Selling their possessions and goods, they gave to anyone as he had need. [46]Every day they continued to meet together in the temple courts. They broke bread in their homes and ate together with glad and sincere hearts, [47]praising God and enjoying the favor of all the people. And the Lord added to their number daily those who were being saved. (+Ro 15:6-7)

1Co 1:10 I appeal to you, brothers, in the name of our Lord Jesus Christ, that all of you agree with one another so that there may be no divisions among you and that you may be perfectly united in mind and thought.

Php 1:3 I thank my God every time I remember you. [4]In all my prayers for all of you, I always pray with joy [5]because of your partnership in the gospel from the first day until now, [6]being confident of this, that he who began a good work in you will carry it on to completion until the day of Christ Jesus.

Php 1:27 Whatever happens, conduct yourselves in a manner worthy of the gospel of Christ. Then, whether I come and see you or only hear about you in my absence, I will know that you stand firm in one spirit, contending as one man for the faith of the gospel [28]without being frightened in any way by those who oppose you. This is a sign to them that they will be destroyed, but that you will be saved—and that by God. [29]For it has been granted to you on behalf of Christ not only to believe on him, but also to suffer for him, [30]since you are going through the same struggle you saw I had, and now hear that I still have.

Php 2:1 If you have any encouragement from being united with Christ, if any comfort from his love, if any fellowship with the Spirit, if any tenderness and compassion, [2]then make my joy complete by being like-minded, having the same love, being one in spirit and purpose. [3]Do nothing out of selfish ambition or vain conceit, but in humility consider others better than yourselves. [4]Each of you should look not only to your own interests, but also to the interests of others.

Col 2:2 My purpose is that they may be encouraged in heart and united in love, so that they may have the full riches of complete understanding, in order that they may know the mystery of God, namely, Christ,

1Pe 3:8 Finally, all of you, live in harmony with one another; be sympathetic, love as brothers, be compassionate and humble. **9**Do not repay evil with evil or insult with insult, but with blessing, because to this you were called so that you may inherit a blessing.

In ministry—

Mt 20:25 Jesus called them together and said, "You know that the rulers of the Gentiles lord it over them, and their high officials exercise authority over them. **26**Not so with you. Instead, whoever wants to become great among you must be your servant, **27**and whoever wants to be first must be your slave— **28**just as the Son of Man did not come to be served, but to serve, and to give his life as a ransom for many."

Mk 10:42 Jesus called them together and said, "You know that those who are regarded as rulers of the Gentiles lord it over them, and their high officials exercise authority over them. **43**Not so with you. Instead, whoever wants to become great among you must be your servant, **44**and whoever wants to be first must be slave of all. **45**For even the Son of Man did not come to be served, but to serve, and to give his life as a ransom for many."

Lk 22:32 But I have prayed for you, Simon, that your faith may not fail. And when you have turned back, strengthen your brothers."

Ac 20:34 You yourselves know that these hands of mine have supplied my own needs and the needs of my companions. **35**In everything I did, I showed you that by this kind of hard work we must help the weak, remembering the words the Lord Jesus himself said: 'It is more blessed to give than to receive.'"

Ro 1:12 that is, that you and I may be mutually encouraged by each other's faith.

Ro 15:1 We who are strong ought to bear with the failings of the weak and not to please ourselves. **2**Each of us should please his neighbor for his good, to build him up. **3**For even Christ did not please himself but, as it is written: "The insults of those who insult you have fallen on me." **4**For everything that was written in the past was written to teach us, so that through endurance and the encouragement of the Scriptures we might have hope.

5May the God who gives endurance and encouragement give you a spirit of unity among yourselves as you follow Christ Jesus, **6**so that with one heart and mouth you may glorify the God and Father of our Lord Jesus Christ.

7Accept one another, then, just as Christ accepted you, in order to bring praise to God.

Gal 6:2 Carry each other's burdens, and in this way you will fulfill the law of Christ.

Gal 6:10 Therefore, as we have opportunity, let us do good to all people, especially to those who belong to the family of believers.

1Th 4:18 Therefore encourage each other with these words.

1Th 5:11 Therefore encourage one another and build each other up, just as in fact you are doing.

1Th 5:14 And we urge you, brothers, warn those who are idle, encourage the timid, help the weak, be patient with everyone.

Heb 3:13 But encourage one another daily, as long as it is

called Today, so that none of you may be hardened by sin's deceitfulness.

Heb 10:24 And let us consider how we may spur one another on toward love and good deeds. **25**Let us not give up meeting together, as some are in the habit of doing, but let us encourage one another—and all the more as you see the Day approaching.

1Pe 2:17 Show proper respect to everyone: Love the brotherhood of believers, fear God, honor the king.

1Jn 3:14 We know that we have passed from death to life, because we love our brothers. Anyone who does not love remains in death.

1Jn 4:7 Dear friends, let us love one another, for love comes from God. Everyone who loves has been born of God and knows God. **8**Whoever does not love does not know God, because God is love.

1Jn 4:11 Dear friends, since God so loved us, we also ought to love one another. **12**No one has ever seen God; but if we love one another, God lives in us and his love is made complete in us.

13We know that we live in him and he in us, because he has given us of his Spirit.

Exemplified—

Gal 2:9 James, Peter and John, those reputed to be pillars, gave me and Barnabas the right hand of fellowship when they recognized the grace given to me. They agreed that we should go to the Gentiles, and they to the Jews.

With Christ:

Attained, by receiving Christ—

Mk 9:37 "Whoever welcomes one of these little children in my name welcomes me; and whoever welcomes me does not welcome me but the one who sent me."

Rev 3:20 Here I am! I stand at the door and knock. If anyone hears my voice and opens the door, I will come in and eat with him, and he with me.

By doing God's will—

Mt 12:48 He replied to him, "Who is my mother, and who are my brothers?" **49**Pointing to his disciples, he said, "Here are my mother and my brothers. **50**For whoever does the will of my Father in heaven is my brother and sister and mother." (+Lk 8:21)

Through a gathering of believers (Mt 18:20; 28:20), commemorating Christ's death (1Co 10:16-17), by walking in the light (1Jn 1:3,5-7)

By abiding in Christ—

1Jn 2:6 Whoever claims to live in him must walk as Jesus did.

1Jn 2:24 See that what you have heard from the beginning remains in you. If it does, you also will remain in the Son and in the Father.

1Jn 2:28 And now, dear children, continue in him, so that when he appears we may be confident and unashamed before him at his coming.

1Jn 3:6 No one who lives in him keeps on sinning. No one who continues to sin has either seen him or known him.

1Jn 3:24 Those who obey his commands live in him, and he in them. And this is how we know that he lives in us: We know it by the Spirit he gave us.

By keeping God's commandments (1Jn 3:6,24)

By continuing in his teaching—

2Jn 9 Anyone who runs ahead and does not continue in the teaching of Christ does not have God; whoever continues in the teaching has both the Father and the Son.

General—

Mt 18:20 For where two or three come together in my name, there am I with them."

Lk 24:32 They asked each other, "Were not our hearts burning within us while he talked with us on the road and opened the Scriptures to us?"

1Co 1:9 God, who has called you into fellowship with his Son Jesus Christ our Lord, is faithful.

1Co 10:16 Is not the cup of thanksgiving for which we give thanks a participation in the blood of Christ? And is not the bread that we break a participation in the body of Christ? [17]Because there is one loaf, we, who are many, are one body, for we all partake of the one loaf. (+1Jn 1:3,5-7; Rev 3:20)

Signified in Christ dwelling with people—

Jn 6:56 Whoever eats my flesh and drinks my blood remains in me, and I in him.

Jn 14:23 Jesus replied, "If anyone loves me, he will obey my teaching. My Father will love him, and we will come to him and make our home with him. (+Eph 3:17)

Col 1:27 To them God has chosen to make known among the Gentiles the glorious riches of this mystery, which is Christ in you, the hope of glory. (+1Jn 3:24)

1Jn 4:13 We know that we live in him and he in us, because he has given us of his Spirit.

Signified in our union with Christ (Jn 15:1-3)—

Jn 15:4 Remain in me, and I will remain in you. No branch can bear fruit by itself; it must remain in the vine. Neither can you bear fruit unless you remain in me.

[5]"I am the vine; you are the branches. If a man remains in me and I in him, he will bear much fruit; apart from me you can do nothing. (+Jn 15:6)

Jn 15:7 If you remain in me and my words remain in you, ask whatever you wish, and it will be given you. (+Jn 15:8)

Jn 17:21 that all of them may be one, Father, just as you are in me and I am in you. May they also be in us so that the world may believe that you have sent me. [22]I have given them the glory that you gave me, that they may be one as we are one: [23]I in them and you in me. May they be brought to complete unity to let the world know that you sent me and have loved them even as you have loved me.

Jn 17:26 I have made you known to them, and will continue to make you known in order that the love you have for me may be in them and that I myself may be in them."

Ro 7:4 So, my brothers, you also died to the law through the body of Christ, that you might belong to another, to him who was raised from the dead, in order that we might bear fruit to God.

Ro 8:1 Therefore, there is now no condemnation for those who are in Christ Jesus,

Ro 8:10 But if Christ is in you, your body is dead because of sin, yet your spirit is alive because of righteousness.

Ro 8:17 Now if we are children, then we are heirs—heirs of God and co-heirs with Christ, if indeed we share in his sufferings in order that we may also share in his glory.

Ro 11:17 If some of the branches have been broken off, and you, though a wild olive shoot, have been grafted in among the others and now share in the nourishing sap from the olive root,

Ro 12:5 so in Christ we who are many form one body, and each member belongs to all the others.

1Co 6:13 "Food for the stomach and the stomach for food"—but God will destroy them both. The body is not meant for sexual immorality, but for the Lord, and the Lord for the body. [14]By his power God raised the Lord from the dead, and he will raise us also. [15]Do you not know

that your bodies are members of Christ himself? Shall I then take the members of Christ and unite them with a prostitute? Never!

1Co 6:17 But he who unites himself with the Lord is one with him in spirit.

1Co 12:12 The body is a unit, though it is made up of many parts; and though all its parts are many, they form one body. So it is with Christ.

1Co 12:27 Now you are the body of Christ, and each one of you is a part of it.

2Co 11:2 I am jealous for you with a godly jealousy. I promised you to one husband, to Christ, so that I might present you as a pure virgin to him.

2Co 13:5 Examine yourselves to see whether you are in the faith; test yourselves. Do you not realize that Christ Jesus is in you—unless, of course, you fail the test?

Eph 5:30 for we are members of his body.

Col 3:3 For you died, and your life is now hidden with Christ in God.

1Th 5:9 For God did not appoint us to suffer wrath but to receive salvation through our Lord Jesus Christ. [10]He died for us so that, whether we are awake or asleep, we may live together with him.

Heb 2:11 Both the one who makes men holy and those who are made holy are of the same family. So Jesus is not ashamed to call them brothers.

1Jn 5:12 He who has the Son has life; he who does not have the Son of God does not have life.

1Jn 5:20 We know also that the Son of God has come and has given us understanding, so that we may know him who is true. And we are in him who is true—even in his Son Jesus Christ. He is the true God and eternal life.

Through the Spirit (Jn 14:16; 1Jn 3:6,24; 4:13). *See Communion, With the Spirit.*

With God:

Signified in people walking with God—

Ge 5:22 And after he became the father of Methuselah, Enoch walked with God 300 years and had other sons and daughters.

Ge 5:24 Enoch walked with God; then he was no more, because God took him away.

Ge 6:9 This is the account of Noah. Noah was a righteous man, blameless among the people of his time, and he walked with God.

Signified in God dwelling with people—

Ex 29:45 Then I will dwell among the Israelites and be their God. (+Ps 101:6)

Isa 57:15 For this is what the high and lofty One says—he who lives forever, whose name is holy: "I live in a high and holy place, but also with him who is contrite and lowly in spirit, to revive the spirit of the lowly and to revive the heart of the contrite.

Zec 2:10 "Shout and be glad, O Daughter of Zion. For I am coming, and I will live among you," declares the LORD.

Jn 14:23 Jesus replied, "If anyone loves me, he will obey my teaching. My Father will love him, and we will come to him and make our home with him.

2Co 6:16 What agreement is there between the temple of God and idols? For we are the temple of the living God. As God has said: "I will live with them and walk among them, and I will be their God, and they will be my people."

1Jn 3:24 Those who obey his commands live in him, and he in them. And this is how we know that he lives in us: We know it by the Spirit he gave us. (+1Jn 4:13)

Rev 21:3 And I heard a loud voice from the throne saying, "Now the dwelling of God is with men, and he will live with them. They will be his people, and God himself will be with them and be their God. **⁴**He will wipe every tear from their eyes. There will be no more death or mourning or crying or pain, for the old order of things has passed away."

General (Ex 33:11)—

Ex 33:14 The LORD replied, "My Presence will go with you, and I will give you rest."

¹⁵Then Moses said to him, "If your Presence does not go with us, do not send us up from here. **¹⁶**How will anyone know that you are pleased with me and with your people unless you go with us? What else will distinguish me and your people from all the other people on the face of the earth?"

¹⁷And the LORD said to Moses, "I will do the very thing you have asked, because I am pleased with you and I know you by name."

Lev 26:12 I will walk among you and be your God, and you will be my people. (+Am 3:3)

2Co 13:11 Finally, brothers, good-by. Aim for perfection, listen to my appeal, be of one mind, live in peace. And the God of love and peace will be with you.

1Jn 1:3 We proclaim to you what we have seen and heard, so that you also may have fellowship with us. And our fellowship is with the Father and with his Son, Jesus Christ.

1Jn 1:5 This is the message we have heard from him and declare to you: God is light; in him there is no darkness at all. **⁶**If we claim to have fellowship with him yet walk in the darkness, we lie and do not live by the truth. **⁷**But if we walk in the light, as he is in the light, we have fellowship with one another, and the blood of Jesus, his Son, purifies us from all sin.

Possible only through Christ—

Mk 9:37 "Whoever welcomes one of these little children in my name welcomes me; and whoever welcomes me does not welcome me but the one who sent me."

Jn 17:21 that all of them may be one, Father, just as you are in me and I am in you. May they also be in us so that the world may believe that you have sent me.

Jn 17:23 I in them and you in me. May they be brought to complete unity to let the world know that you sent me and have loved them even as you have loved me. *See Communion, With God.*

With the Holy Spirit:

General (Jn 14:16-17)—

Ro 8:9 You, however, are controlled not by the sinful nature but by the Spirit, if the Spirit of God lives in you. And if anyone does not have the Spirit of Christ, he does not belong to Christ.

1Co 3:16 Don't you know that you yourselves are God's temple and that God's Spirit lives in you?

2Co 13:14 May the grace of the Lord Jesus Christ, and the love of God, and the fellowship of the Holy Spirit be with you. (+Gal 4:6; Php 2:1) *See Communion, With the Spirit.*

With the Wicked:

Abhorred by the righteous—

Ge 49:6 Let me not enter their council, let me not join their assembly, for they have killed men in their anger and hamstrung oxen as they pleased.

Ex 33:15 Then Moses said to him, "If your Presence does not go with us, do not send us up from here. **¹⁶**How will anyone know that you are pleased with me and with your people unless you go with us? What else will distinguish

me and your people from all the other people on the face of the earth?"

Ezr 6:21 So the Israelites who had returned from the exile ate it, together with all who had separated themselves from the unclean practices of their Gentile neighbors in order to seek the LORD, the God of Israel. **²²**For seven days they celebrated with joy the Feast of Unleavened Bread, because the LORD had filled them with joy by changing the attitude of the king of Assyria, so that he assisted them in the work on the house of God, the God of Israel.

Ezr 9:14 Shall we again break your commands and intermarry with the peoples who commit such detestable practices? Would you not be angry enough with us to destroy us, leaving us no remnant or survivor?

Ps 6:8 Away from me, all you who do evil, for the LORD has heard my weeping.

Ps 26:4 I do not sit with deceitful men, nor do I consort with hypocrites; **⁵**I abhor the assembly of evildoers and refuse to sit with the wicked.

Implicating—

Ps 50:18 When you see a thief, you join with him; you throw in your lot with adulterers.

Revelry (Ps 50:18; Pr 12:11)—

Pr 29:24 The accomplice of a thief is his own enemy; he is put under oath and dare not testify.

1Co 15:33 Do not be misled: "Bad company corrupts good character."

2Pe 2:18 For they mouth empty, boastful words and, by appealing to the lustful desires of sinful human nature, they entice people who are just escaping from those who live in error. **¹⁹**They promise them freedom, while they themselves are slaves of depravity—for a man is a slave to whatever has mastered him.

Impoverishing—

Pr 28:19 He who works his land will have abundant food, but the one who chases fantasies will have his fill of poverty.

Forbidden with those who provide the wrong type of influence—

Ex 23:32 Do not make a covenant with them or with their gods. **³³**Do not let them live in your land, or they will cause you to sin against me, because the worship of their gods will certainly be a snare to you."

Ex 34:12 Be careful not to make a treaty with those who live in the land where you are going, or they will be a snare among you. (+Ex 34:13-16)

Nu 16:26 He warned the assembly, "Move back from the tents of these wicked men! Do not touch anything belonging to them, or you will be swept away because of all their sins."

Dt 7:2 and when the LORD your God has delivered them over to you and you have defeated them, then you must destroy them totally. Make no treaty with them, and show them no mercy. **³**Do not intermarry with them. Do not give your daughters to their sons or take their daughters for your sons, (+Dt 12:30)

Dt 13:6 If your very own brother, or your son or daughter, or the wife you love, or your closest friend secretly entices you, saying, "Let us go and worship other gods" (gods that neither you nor your fathers have known, **⁷**gods of the peoples around you, whether near or far, from one end of the land to the other), **⁸**do not yield to him or listen to him. Show him no pity. Do not spare him or shield him. **⁹**You must certainly put him to death. Your hand must be the first in putting him to death, and then the hands of all the people. **¹⁰**Stone him to death, because he tried to turn you away from the LORD your God, who brought you out of Egypt, out of the land of slavery. ¹¹Then all Israel will hear and be afraid, and no one among you will do such an evil thing again.

Jos 23:6 "Be very strong; be careful to obey all that is written in the Book of the Law of Moses, without turning aside to the right or to the left. ⁷Do not associate with these nations that remain among you; do not invoke the names of their gods or swear by them. You must not serve them or bow down to them. ⁸But you are to hold fast to the LORD your God, as you have until now.

Jos 23:13 then you may be sure that the LORD your God will no longer drive out these nations before you. Instead, they will become snares and traps for you, whips on your backs and thorns in your eyes, until you perish from this good land, which the LORD your God has given you.

Ezr 9:12 Therefore, do not give your daughters in marriage to their sons or take their daughters for your sons. Do not seek a treaty of friendship with them at any time, that you may be strong and eat the good things of the land and leave it to your children as an everlasting inheritance.'

Ezr 10:11 Now make confession to the LORD, the God of your fathers, and do his will. Separate yourselves from the peoples around you and from your foreign wives."

Ps 1:1 Blessed is the man who does not walk in the counsel of the wicked or stand in the way of sinners or sit in the seat of mockers.

Pr 1:10 My son, if sinners entice you, do not give in to them. ¹¹If they say, "Come along with us; let's lie in wait for someone's blood, let's waylay some harmless soul; ¹²let's swallow them alive, like the grave, and whole, like those who go down to the pit; ¹³we will get all sorts of valuable things and fill our houses with plunder; ¹⁴throw in your lot with us, and we will share a common purse"— ¹⁵my son, do not go along with them, do not set foot on their paths; ¹⁶for their feet rush into sin, they are swift to shed blood.

Pr 4:14 Do not set foot on the path of the wicked or walk in the way of evil men. ¹⁵Avoid it, do not travel on it; turn from it and go on your way. ¹⁶For they cannot sleep till they do evil; they are robbed of slumber till they make someone fall. ¹⁷They eat the bread of wickedness and drink the wine of violence.

Pr 14:7 Stay away from a foolish man, for you will not find knowledge on his lips.

Mt 18:17 If he refuses to listen to them, tell it to the church; and if he refuses to listen even to the church, treat him as you would a pagan or a tax collector.

Ro 16:17 I urge you, brothers, to watch out for those who cause divisions and put obstacles in your way that are contrary to the teaching you have learned. Keep away from them.

1Co 5:9 I have written you in my letter not to associate with sexually immoral people— ¹⁰not at all meaning the people of this world who are immoral, or the greedy and swindlers, or idolaters. In that case you would have to leave this world. ¹¹But now I am writing you that you must not associate with anyone who calls himself a brother but is sexually immoral or greedy, an idolater or a slanderer, a drunkard or a swindler. With such a man do not even eat.

¹²What business is it of mine to judge those outside the church? Are you not to judge those inside? ¹³God will judge those outside. "Expel the wicked man from among you."

2Co 6:14 Do not be yoked together with unbelievers. For what do righteousness and wickedness have in common? Or what fellowship can light have with darkness? ¹⁵What harmony is there between Christ and Belial? What does a believer have in common with an unbeliever? ¹⁶What agreement is there between the temple of God and idols? For we are the temple of the living God. As God has said: "I will live with them and walk among them, and I will be their God, and they will be my people."

¹⁷"Therefore come out from them and be separate, says the Lord. Touch no unclean thing, and I will receive you."

Eph 5:11 Have nothing to do with the fruitless deeds of darkness, but rather expose them.

2Th 3:6 In the name of the Lord Jesus Christ, we command you, brothers, to keep away from every brother who is idle and does not live according to the teaching you received from us.

2Th 3:14 If anyone does not obey our instruction in this letter, take special note of him. Do not associate with him, in order that he may feel ashamed. ¹⁵Yet do not regard him as an enemy, but warn him as a brother.

1Ti 6:3 If anyone teaches false doctrines and does not agree to the sound instruction of our Lord Jesus Christ and to godly teaching, ⁴he is conceited and understands nothing. He has an unhealthy interest in controversies and quarrels about words that result in envy, strife, malicious talk, evil suspicions ⁵and constant friction between men of corrupt mind, who have been robbed of the truth and who think that godliness is a means to financial gain.

2Ti 3:2 People will be lovers of themselves, lovers of money, boastful, proud, abusive, disobedient to their parents, ungrateful, unholy, ³without love, unforgiving, slanderous, without self-control, brutal, not lovers of the good, ⁴treacherous, rash, conceited, lovers of pleasure rather than lovers of God— ⁵having a form of godliness but denying its power. Have nothing to do with them.

⁶They are the kind who worm their way into homes and gain control over weak-willed women, who are loaded down with sins and are swayed by all kinds of evil desires, ⁷always learning but never able to acknowledge the truth. ⁸Just as Jannes and Jambres opposed Moses, so also these men oppose the truth—men of depraved minds, who, as far as the faith is concerned, are rejected. ⁹But they will not get very far because, as in the case of those men, their folly will be clear to everyone.

2Pe 3:17 Therefore, dear friends, since you already know this, be on your guard so that you may not be carried away by the error of lawless men and fall from your secure position. ¹⁸But grow in the grace and knowledge of our Lord and Savior Jesus Christ. To him be glory both now and forever! Amen.

2Jn 9 Anyone who runs ahead and does not continue in the teaching of Christ does not have God; whoever continues in the teaching has both the Father and the Son. ¹⁰If anyone comes to you and does not bring this teaching, do not take him into your house or welcome him. ¹¹Anyone who welcomes him shares in his wicked work.

Rev 18:1 After this I saw another angel coming down from heaven. He had great authority, and the earth was illuminated by his splendor. ²With a mighty voice he shouted: "Fallen! Fallen is Babylon the Great! She has become a home for demons and a haunt for every evil spirit, a haunt for every unclean and detestable bird. ³For all the nations have drunk the maddening wine of her adulteries. The kings of the earth committed adultery with her, and the merchants of the earth grew rich from her excessive luxuries."

⁴Then I heard another voice from heaven say: "Come

out of her, my people, so that you will not share in her sins, so that you will not receive any of her plagues;

Punishment for fellowship with the wicked—

Nu 25:1 While Israel was staying in Shittim, the men began to indulge in sexual immorality with Moabite women, ²who invited them to the sacrifices to their gods. The people ate and bowed down before these gods. ³So Israel joined in worshiping the Baal of Peor. And the LORD's anger burned against them.

⁴The LORD said to Moses, "Take all the leaders of these people, kill them and expose them in broad daylight before the LORD, so that the LORD's fierce anger may turn away from Israel."

⁵So Moses said to Israel's judges, "Each of you must put to death those of your men who have joined in worshiping the Baal of Peor."

⁶Then an Israelite man brought to his family a Midianite woman right before the eyes of Moses and the whole assembly of Israel while they were weeping at the entrance to the Tent of Meeting. ⁷When Phinehas son of Eleazar, the son of Aaron, the priest, saw this, he left the assembly, took a spear in his hand ⁸and followed the Israelite into the tent. He drove the spear through both of them—through the Israelite and into the woman's body. Then the plague against the Israelites was stopped; (+Nu 33:55-56; Dt 31:16-17)

Jos 23:12 "But if you turn away and ally yourselves with the survivors of these nations that remain among you and if you intermarry with them and associate with them, ¹³then you may be sure that the LORD your God will no longer drive out these nations before you. Instead, they will become snares and traps for you, whips on your backs and thorns in your eyes, until you perish from this good land, which the LORD your God has given you. (+Jdg 3:5-8; Ezr 9:7,14; Ps 106:34-35,41-43; Rev 2:16,22-23)

Instances of Evil Fellowship With the Wicked:

By Solomon (1Ki 11:1-8), Rehoboam (1Ki 12:8-9), Jehoshaphat (2Ch 18:3; 19:2; 20:35-37), Jehoram (2Ch 21:6), Ahaziah (2Ch 22:3-5), Israelites (Ezr 9:1-2), Israel (Eze 44:7), Judas Iscariot (Mt 26:14-16).

Instances of Those Who Avoided Fellowship With the Wicked:

The man of God (1Ki 13:7-10). Nehemiah (Ne 6:2-4; 10:29-31). David (Ps 101:4-7; 119:115). Jeremiah (Jer 15:17). Joseph of Arimathea (Lk 23:51). Church of Ephesus (Rev 2:6).

See Company, Evil; Influence, Evil.

FELLOWSHIP OFFERINGS [8968]. Traditionally "peace" offerings (Ex 20:24; 24:5; Lev 3:6; 7:11; 19:5). Offered by the leaders (Nu 7:17), by Joshua (Jos 8:31), by David (2Sa 6:17; 24:25). *See Offerings.*

FENCE [1555]. Walls made of stone enclosing a field, town, etc. (Nu 22:24; Ps 62:3; Pr 24:30-31; Isa 5:2; Mic 7:11). Hedge (Job 1:10; Isa 5:5; Mic 7:4; Hos 2:6).

Figurative: (Eze 22:30).

FENCED CITY *See Walled Cities.*

FERMENTED DRINK [8911, 4975]. Intoxicating beverages, usually other than grape wine (Dt 14:26). Used in drink offerings (Nu 28:7).

Forbidden to priests on duty (Lev 10:9), to Nazirites while under a vow (Nu 6:3; cf. Jdg 13:4,7,14; Lk 1:15). *See Abstinence; Beer; Drunkenness; Wine.*

FERRET *See Gecko.*

FERTILE CRESCENT A modern description of the territory from the Persian Gulf to Egypt, which is watered by the Euphrates, Tigris, Orontes, Jordan, and Nile rivers. *See Canaan; Mesopotamia; Palestine.*

FESTIVALS [2136, 2504, 2510, 2544, 4595, *2037, 2038*].

NIV+ FESTIVAL, FESTAL, FESTIVE

See Feasts.

FESTUS, PORCIUS [5776] *(festal, joyful)*. Was the Roman governor who succeeded Felix in the province of Judea (Ac 24:27). He presided at the hearing of the apostle Paul when he made his defense before Herod Agrippa II (Ac 24:27; 26:32). When Paul appealed to Caesar, Festus sent him to Rome. The date of Festus's accession is uncertain, probably A.D. 59/60. He died in office in A.D. 62.

FETTERS [673, 2414, 6310].

NIV+ FETTERED

A translation of words which have the general meaning "anything that restricts or restrains" as well as those which bear the specific definition "shackle for the foot." Fetters were made from wood, bronze, or iron. The prisoner would have manacles on his wrists which were suspended from his neck by a rope. His feet would have been shackled and connected by a short piece of rope or chain so that the hobbled prisoner could take only short steps (2Sa 3:34; Job 36:13; Ps 2:3; 105:18; 149:8). Used for securing prisoners (2Ch 33:11; 36:6; Mk 5:4). *See Chains; Shackles.*

FEVER [2363, 2996, 7707, *4789, 4790*].

NIV+ FEVERISH

(Lev 26:16; Dt 28:22; Job 30:30; Mt 8:14; Ac 28:8).

FEW SAVED The number saved spoken of as few (Mt 7:14; 22:14; Lk 13:24; 1Pe 3:20; Rev 3:4).

FICKLENESS *See Instability.*

FIELD [*141, 824, 2575, 2754, 3320, 4149, 8072, 8441, 8442, 8727, 10119, *69, 2546, 6001, 6005*].

NIV+ BATTLEFIELD, FIELDS, FIELDSTONES, GRAINFIELD, GRAINFIELDS

The biblical field was generally not enclosed, but was marked off from its neighbors by boundary markers (Dt 19:14; 27:17; Job 24:2; Pr 22:28; 23:10; Hos 5:10). A cultivated area where crops are grown (Ru 2:2; Ps 107:37), a place where herds could graze (Ge 34:5; Ex 9:21; Nu 22:24).

FIG [1136, 1811, 7811, 9204, 9300, *5190, 5192*].

NIV+ FIGS, SYCAMORE-FIG, SYCAMORE-FIGS

Aprons made of fig leaves, by Adam and Eve (Ge 3:7). Common to Palestine (Nu 13:23; Dt 8:8), to Egypt (Ps 105:33). Two hundred cakes of, sent by Abigail to David (1Sa 25:18,19-35). Dried and preserved (1Sa 30:12). Employed as a remedy (2Ki 20:7; Isa 38:21). Trade in (Ne 13:15).

FIG TREE

NIV+ See FIG

In an allegory (Jdg 9:11). Jeremiah's parable of (Jer 24:1-10). Jesus' cursing of (Mt 21:18-22; Mk 11:12-14,20-26). Barren, parable of (Lk 13:6-9; 21:29-31).

Figurative:

Of signs of the end times (Mt 24:32; Rev 6:13).

FIGHT OF FAITH (1Ti 6:12; 2Ti 4:7; Heb 10:32; 11:32-34).

FIGURE See *"Figurative" under principal topics throughout the work. See also, Allegory; Pantomime; Parable; Symbols and Similitudes; Types.*

FILIGREE [5401, 8687]. Ornate gold settings for the jewels of the ephod and breastpiece (Ex 28:13,20; 39:6,13,16).

FINANCES Methods of raising money. *See Money; Temple; Tribute.*

FINE [*6740, 6741].

NIV+ FINE-LOOKING, FINE-SOUNDING, FINED, FINELY, FINERY, FINES, FINEST; See PENALTY

For personal injury (Ex 21:22,30).

For theft—

Ex 22:4 "If the stolen animal is found alive in his possession—whether ox or donkey or sheep—he must pay back double.

Ex 22:7 "If a man gives his neighbor silver or goods for safekeeping and they are stolen from the neighbor's house, the thief, if he is caught, must pay back double. **8**But if the thief is not found, the owner of the house must appear before the judges to determine whether he has laid his hands on the other man's property. **9**In all cases of illegal possession of an ox, a donkey, a sheep, a garment, or any other lost property about which somebody says, 'This is mine,' both parties are to bring their cases before the judges. The one whom the judges declare guilty must pay back double to his neighbor.

Pr 6:30 Men do not despise a thief if he steals to satisfy his hunger when he is starving. **31**Yet if he is caught, he must pay sevenfold, though it costs him all the wealth of his house.

When sinning unknowingly—

Lev 5:15 "When a person commits a violation and sins unintentionally in regard to any of the LORD's holy things, he is to bring to the LORD as a penalty a ram from the flock, one without defect and of the proper value in silver, according to the sanctuary shekel. It is a guilt offering. **16**He must make restitution for what he has failed to do in regard to the holy things, add a fifth of the value to that and give it all to the priest, who will make atonement for him with the ram as a guilt offering, and he will be forgiven. (+Lev 22:14)

For deception—

Lev 6:2 "If anyone sins and is unfaithful to the LORD by deceiving his neighbor about something entrusted to him or left in his care or stolen, or if he cheats him, **3**or if he finds lost property and lies about it, or if he swears falsely, or if he commits any such sin that people may do— **4**when he thus sins and becomes guilty, he must return what he has stolen or taken by extortion, or what was entrusted to him, or the lost property he found, **5**or whatever it was he swore falsely about. He must make restitution in full, add a fifth of the value to it and give it all to the owner on the day he presents his guilt offering. **6**And as a penalty he must bring to the priest, that is, to the LORD, his guilt offering, a ram from the flock, one without defect and of the proper value.

Restitution for any wrongdoing (Nu 5:5-8).

See Damages and Compensations.

FINGER [720, 3338, 4090, 7782, 10064, *1235, 5931*].

NIV+ FINGERS

Six on one hand (2Sa 21:20).

FINGER OF GOD Anthropomorphism, indicating God's interaction with his creation. Creation (Ps 8:3). Miracles (Ex 8:19). Writing the tablets of the law (Ex 31:18; Dt 9:10). Exorcism (Lk 11:20). *See Anthropomorphisms.*

FINGERS, FINGERBREADTH A unit of measurement. The two bronze pillars of Solomon's temple were four fingers thick and hollow in the center (Jer 52:21). *See Measure.*

FINING POT *See Crucible.*

FIR TREE [1361, 9329].

NIV+ FIRS

Wood of, used for building (SS 1:17).

FIRE [*239, 241, 836, 852, 1277, 8596, 8599, 10471, *471, 3106, 4786, 4787, 5824*].

NIV+ AFIRE, CAMPFIRES, FIERY, FIREBRANDS, FIRELIGHT, FIREPANS, FIREPOT, FIRES, FIREWOOD

Children sacrificed in (2Ki 16:3; 17:17). Used as a signal in war (Jer 6:1). Men were burned in a furnace (Jer 29:22; Heb 11:34). The threat of being thrown into a furnace is used by Nebuchadnezzar for all those who would not fall down and worship the image that he set up of (Da 3:6,11,15,21).

Figurative:

Of judgments (Dt 4:24; 32:22; Isa 33:14; Jer 23:29; Am 1:4,7,10,12,14; 2:2; Mal 3:2; Lk 12:49; Rev 20:9), spiritual power (Ps 104:4; Jer 20:9; Mt 3:11; Lk 3:16), cleansing (Isa 6:6-7), of the destruction of the wicked (Mt 13:42,50; 25:41; Mk 9:48; Rev 9:2; 21:8).

Everlasting fire (Isa 33:14; Mt 18:8; 25:41; Mk 9:48).

Miracles Connected With:

Miraculously descends upon and consumes Abraham's sacrifice (Ge 15:17), Elijah's (1Ki 18:38), David's (1Ch 21:26), Solomon's, at dedication of the temple (2Ch 7:1-3).

Pillar of fire (Ex 13:21-22; 14:19,24; 40:38; Nu 9:15-23).

Display of, at Elijah's translation (2Ki 2:11).

Consumes, the conspirators with Korah, Dathan, and Abiram (Nu 16:35), the captains and their fifties (2Ki 1:9-15).

Torture by (Jer 29:22; Eze 23:25,47; Da 3).

See Celestial Phenomena; Cloud, Pillar of.

Symbolic:

Of God's presence, with Abram in the covenant (Ge 15:17), in the burning bush (Ex 3:2), on Sinai (Ex 19:18).

Tongues of, on the apostles (Ac 2:3).

See Arson.

FIREBRAND [2415, 4365].

NIV+ FIRE, FIREBRANDS

Burning wood used for light (Jdg 7:16), torches used as weapons (Pr 26:18), a remnant of a burnt stick (Am 4:11). *See Torches.*

FIREPAN [279, 836+3963, 4746, 9486] (*to rake together*).

NIV+ FIRE, FIREPANS, FIREPOT

A vessel for carrying live coals (Ex 27:3; 38:3).

FIRKIN *See Gallon.*

FIRMAMENT *See Expanse.*

FIRST BEGOTTEN *See Firstborn.*

FIRST DAY OF THE WEEK *See Sunday.*

FIRSTBORN [1144, 1147, 1148, 7081+, 7082, *1380+3616, 4758*].

NIV+ See BEAR, BIRTHRIGHT, FIRST

The first male born, whether man or animal, was reserved by God for himself (Ex 13:2,12-16; 22:29-30; 34:19-20; Lev 27:26; Nu 3:13; 8:17-18; Dt 15:19-23; Ne 10:36).

Redemption of (Ex 13:13; 34:20; Lev 27:26-27; Nu 3:40-51; 18:15-17). Levites taken instead of firstborn of the families of Israel (Nu 3:12,40-45; 8:16-18).

Birthright of:
Had precedence over other sons of the family (Ge 4:1,5-7; Dt 21:15-17), a double portion of inheritance (Dt 21:15-17), royal succession (2Ch 21:3). Sold by Esau (Ge 25:29-34; 27:36; Ro 9:12-13; Heb 12:16). Set aside, that of Manasseh (Ge 48:15-20; 1Ch 5:1), Adonijah (1Ki 2:13-15), Hosah's son (1Ch 26:10). Forfeited by Reuben (Ge 49:3-4; 1Ch 5:1-2). Honorable distinction of (Ex 4:22; Ps 89:27; Jer 31:9; Ro 8:29; Col 1:15; Heb 1:6; 12:23; Rev 1:5).
See Birthright.

As applied to Jesus:
A term applied to the Lord Jesus Christ (Ro 8:29; Col 1:15,18; Heb 1:6; Rev 1:5).

FIRSTFRUITS [1137, 7262+8040, 8040, *569*].

Offerings of:
First ripe of fruits, grain, oil, wine, and first of the fleece, required as an offering (Ex 22:29; Lev 2:12-16; Nu 18:12; Dt 18:4; 2Ch 31:5; Ne 10:35,37,39; Pr 3:9; Jer 2:3; Ro 11:16).

Offerings of, presented at the tabernacle (Ex 22:29; 23:19; 34:26; Dt 26:3-10), belonged to the priests (Lev 23:20; Nu 18:12-13; Dt 18:3-5), must be free from blemish (Lev 22:21; Nu 18:12). Freewill offerings of, given to the prophets (2Ki 4:42).

Offerings described:
Drink (Ge 35:14; Ex 29:40-41; 30:9; 37:16; Lev 23:13,18,37; Nu 4:7; Nu 6:15,17; 15:5,7,10,24; 28:7-31; 29:6,11,16,18-39; Dt 32:38; 2Ki 16:13-15; 1Ch 29:21; 2Ch 29:35; Ezr 7:17; Isa 57:6; Jer 7:18; 19:13; 32:29; 44:17-25; 52:19; Eze 20:28; 45:17; Joel 1:9,13; 2:14; Php 2:17; 2Ti 4:6).

Freewill (Ex 35:29; 36:3; Lev 7:16; 22:18,21,23; 23:37-38; Nu 15:3; 29:39; Dt 12:6,17; 16:10; 2Ch 31:14; Ezr 1:4,6; 2:68; 3:5; 7:16; 8:28; Ps 54:6; Eze 46:12; Am 4:5).

Burnt (Lev 1; 6:8-13).

Grain (Lev 2; 6:14-23).

Fellowship (Lev 3; 7:11-21).

Sin (Lev 4-5:13; 6:24-30).

Guilt (Lev 5:14-6:7; 7:1-10).

Wave offering (Ex 29:22-26; 35:22; Lev 7:30; 23:10-14,17).

To be offered as a thank offering upon entrance into the Land of Promise (Dt 26:3-10; 2Ch 29:31; 33:16; Ps 50:14,23; 56:12; 107:22; 116:17; Jer 17:26; 33:11; Am 4:5).

Figurative: (Ro 8:23; 11:16; 1Co 15:20,23; Jas 1:18).
See Offerings.

FIRSTLING *See Firstborn.*

FISH [1794, 1834, 1836, *244, 2715, 2716, 3063, 4066, 4709*].

NIV+ FISHERMEN, FISHERS, FISHHOOK, FISHHOOKS, FISHING

Creation of (Ge 1:20-22).

As Food:
Appointed for food (Ge 9:2-3). Clean and unclean (Lev 11:9-12; Dt 14:9-10). Broiled (Jn 21:9-13; Lk 24:42).

Caught:
Taken with, spears (Job 41:7), nets (Ecc 9:12; Hab 1:14-17; Lk 5:2-6; Jn 21:6-8), hooks (Isa 19:8; Am 4:2; Hab 1:15; Mt 17:27).

Figurative:
(Eze 47:9-10).

Miracles Connected With:
Jonah swallowed by (Jnh 1:17; 2; Mt 12:40). The loaves and fishes (Mt 14:19; 15:36-38; Lk 9:13-17). Coin obtained from mouth of (Mt 17:27). Overflowing nets (Lk 5:6-7; Jn 21:6,8,11). Furnished for the disciples by Jesus after his resurrection (Lk 24:42; Jn 21:9-13).

Sold in the Marketplace:
Men from Tyre living in Jerusalem (Ne 13:16).

FISH GATE An ancient gate on the E side of Jerusalem near Gihon where Tyrians held a fish market (2Ch 33:14; Ne 3:3; 12:39; 13:16; Zep 1:10).

FISH POOL *See Pool.*

FISH SPEAR *See Spear.*

FISHERMEN [1854, 1900, *243*].

NIV+ See FISH

Certain apostles (Mt 4:18-21; Mk 1:16-20; Jn 21:2-3).

Figurative:
(Jer 16:16; Mt 4:19).

FISHHOOK [1855+6106, 2676]. *See Hooks.*

FITCH *See Caraway.*

FLAG *See Ensign; Reed.*

FLAGON *See Wine.*

FLATTERY [2728, 2744, 2747, 4033, 7331, *2330, 2513+4725, 3135*].

NIV+ FLATTER, FLATTERING, FLATTERS

Condemned and rebuked—

Job 32:21 I will show partiality to no one, nor will I flatter any man; ²²for if I were skilled in flattery, my Maker would soon take me away.

Ps 12:2 Everyone lies to his neighbor; their flattering lips speak with deception.

³May the LORD cut off all flattering lips and every boastful tongue ⁴that says, "We will triumph with our tongues; we own our lips—who is our master?"

Pr 28:23 He who rebukes a man will in the end gain more favor than he who has a flattering tongue.

Lk 6:26 Woe to you when all men speak well of you, for that is how their fathers treated the false prophets.

Deceives, self—

Ps 36:2 For in his own eyes he flatters himself too much to detect or hate his sin.

The simple (Ro 16:18).

Practiced by enemy (Ps 12:2)—

Pr 26:28 A lying tongue hates those it hurts, and a flattering mouth works ruin.

Pr 29:5 Whoever flatters his neighbor is spreading a net for his feet.

Jude 16 These men are grumblers and faultfinders; they follow their own evil desires; they boast about themselves and flatter others for their own advantage.

Against God—

Ps 78:36 But then they would flatter him with their mouths, lying to him with their tongues;

By seducing women—

Pr 5:3 For the lips of an adulteress drip honey, and her speech is smoother than oil; (+Pr 6:24)

Pr 7:5 they will keep you from the adulteress, from the wayward wife with her seductive words.

Pr 7:21 With persuasive words she led him astray; she seduced him with her smooth talk.

Not practiced by Paul—

1Th 2:4 On the contrary, we speak as men approved by God to be entrusted with the gospel. We are not trying to please men but God, who tests our hearts. ⁵You know we never used flattery, nor did we put on a mask to cover up greed—God is our witness. ⁶We were not looking for praise from men, not from you or anyone else. As apostles of Christ we could have been a burden to you,

Instances of:

By Jacob (Ge 33:10), Gideon (Jdg 8:1-3), Mephibosheth (2Sa 9:8), woman of Tekoa (2Sa 14:17-20), Absalom (2Sa 15:2-6), Israel and Judah (2Sa 19:41-43), Adonijah (1Ki 1:42), Ahab (1Ki 20:4), false prophets (1Ki 22:1-13), Darius's officials (Da 6:1-9), Herodians (Lk 20:21), Tyrians (Ac 12:22). Tertullus flatters Felix (Ac 24:2-4). Paul flatters Felix (Ac 24:10). Agrippa (Ac 26:2-3).

FLAX [7324, 7325]. In Egypt (Ex 9:31). In Palestine (Jos 2:6). Linen made from (Pr 31:13; Isa 19:9).

See Linen.

FLEA [7282] (*mosquito*). (1Sa 24:14; 26:20).

FLEECE [1600, 1603]. *See Prayer; Token, 1; Wool.*

FLESH [1414,   2693,   2743+3655+4946, 3655+3870+4946, 4695, 5055, 6425, 6889, 6913+7089, 8638, 10125, *4922*].

NIV+ CREATURES, EARTHLY, HUMAN, MAN, MANKIND, MEAT, MORTAL, NATURE, NATURAL, PEOPLE, PHYSICAL, SENSUAL, SINFUL, WORLD, WORLDLY

1. The physical part of the body of people or animals (Ge 17:13-14; 1Co 15:39).

2. Human nature, deprived of the Holy Spirit, and dominated by sin (Ro 7:5, ftn); usually "sinful [nature]" in the NIV.

See Body; Carnal Mindedness.

FLESHHOOK *See Meat Forks.*

FLIES [2279, 4031, 6414, 6856].

NIV+ FLY

Plague of (Ex 8:21-31; Ps 78:45; 105:31). Common sense analogy (Ecc 10:1). Figurative (Isa 7:18).

FLINT [2734, 7641, 7644, 9032].

NIV+ FLINTY

1. Knives of flint used for circumcision (Ex 4:25; Jos 5:2-3).

2. Judah's heart had been inscribed with the point of a flint (Jer 17:1). The Israelites make their hearts harder than flint (Zec 7:12).

Figurative: (Isa 5:28; 50:7; Jer 17:1; Eze 3:9; Zec 7:12).

See Hardest Stone; Minerals of the Bible, 1; Stones.

FLOCK [3105, 4166, 5238, 5338, 6337, 6373, 7366, 8286, 8445, *2576, 4479, 4480*].

NIV+ FLOCKING, FLOCKS

A collection of sheep under the care of a shepherd, sometimes including goats as well (Ge 27:9; 30:32). Used figuratively of Christ's disciples (Lk 12:32; 1Pe 5:2-3).

FLOG, FLOGGING [5596, 5782, *2666, 3463, 3464, 3465*].

NIV+ FLOGGED, FLOGGINGS

The practice or system of punishment by repeated lashes or blows, usually with a rod or whip; or an instance of such punishment.

1. Beating is recognized as a legitimate form of punishment (Dt 25:1-3). According to Proverbs, hasty and poor judgments, like careless talk, often lead to strife; the settling of strife involves punishment for those who have been wrong, and it should be recognized that flogging (beating) is "for the back of fools" (Pr 19:29, w 18:6; 20:3).

It is permissible to discipline a child, and parents are encouraged to apply the rod of punishment to drive out folly (Pr 22:15) so that the child will not follow a path of destruction (Pr 19:18; 23:13-14).

The rod "imparts wisdom" (Pr 29:15) and promotes a healthy and happy family (Pr 29:17). Discipline is rooted in love not anger (Pr 3:11-12). *See Abuse.*

2. Elsewhere in the OT it is recognized that even the innocent may sometimes be scourged and crushed by evil individuals (Isa 52:13-53:12, esp 53:5). The suffering of the innocent, often at the hands of evildoers, is a common theme in the Psalms (13; 22; 28; 31:9-24; 35; 38; 41; 69; 71; 86; 102; 109).

3. Jesus warned certain of his disciples that they would be beaten in the synagogues if they continued to preach the gospel (Mk 13:9). According to Ac 5:40, the apostles were beaten by representatives of the Sanhedrin and ordered not to speak in the name of Jesus, but only after Gamaliel had pleaded with his fellow members not to put the defendants to death (Ac 5:33-39). Paul, who himself had beaten and imprisoned many Christians (Ac 22:19-20), was flogged with rods three times (2Co 11:25). In Ac 16:11-24, both Paul and Silas were involved.

Flogging of Jesus:

Prophesied (Isa 50:6). Described (Mt 20:19; 26:67-68; 27:26,30; Mk 10:34; 15:15,19; Lk 22:63-64; 23:16; Jn 18:22; 19:1).

See Assault and Battery; Bruise, Bruises; Lashes; Scourging; Stoning; Stripes.

FLOOD [4059, 4429, 4784, 5643, 8466, 8851, 8852, 9180, *431, 2886, 4439*].

NIV+ FLOODED, FLOODGATES, FLOODING, FLOODS, FLOODWATERS

Foretold (Ge 6:13,17). History of (Ge 6-8). The promise that it should not recur (Ge 8:20-22; Isa 54:9). References to (Job 22:16; Mt 24:38-39; Lk 17:26-27; Heb 11:7; 1Pe 3:20; 2Pe 2:5).

See Meteorology.

FLOUR [6159, 7854, *236*, *4947*]. Fine-crushed and sifted grain, generally wheat, rye, or barley (Jdg 6:19).

FLOWER [5481, 5890, 7258, 5900, 7488, 7491, *470*].
NIV+ FLORAL, FLOWERLIKE, FLOWERS
See Plants of the Bible.

FLUTE [2720, 5704, 6385, 10446, *884*, *886*, *888*].
NIV+ FLUTES

A wind instrument (Da 3:5,7,10,15). *See Music, Instruments of.*

FOAL [1201, *5626*]. *See Animals.*

FODDER [1173, 5028] (*mix, mingle*). Food for animals consisting of a mixture of grains (Ge 24:25,32; 43:24; Jdg 19:19; Job 6:5; 24:6; Isa 30:24).

FOLLY [222, 4070, 4074, 5576, 6121, 8508, *486*, *932*].
See Fool.

FOOD [*431, 430, 433, 1376, 3272, 4312, 4407, 4761, 4950, 7329, 7474, 7476, 10410, *788*, *1109*, *1111*, *1628*, *2266*, *5575*].
NIV+ FOODS

Articles of:

Bread (Ge 18:5-6; 1Sa 17:17), milk (Ge 49:12; Pr 27:27), vinegar (Nu 6:3; Ru 2:14), oil (Dt 12:17; Pr 21:17,20; Eze 16:13,18-19), butter (Ps 55:21; Pr 30:33), roasted grain (Ru 2:14; 1Sa 17:17; 25:18), cheese (1Sa 17:18; Job 10:10), dried fruit (1Sa 25:18; 30:12), meat (Pr 9:2), wine (Jn 2:3-10), fruit (2Sa 16:2), herbs (Ex 12:8; Nu 9:11; 2Ki 4:39; Job 30:4; La 3:15; Lk 11:42), honey (SS 5:1; Isa 7:15), fish (Mt 7:10; Lk 24:42).

From God (Ge 1:29-30; 9:3; Job 36:31; Ps 23:5; 104:14-15; 111:5; 136:25; 145:15; 147:9; Pr 30:8; Isa 3:1; Mt 6:11; Ac 14:17; Ro 14:14,21; 1Ti 4:3-5).

Men and women did not partake together (Ge 18:8-9; Est 1:3,9). Prepared by females (Ge 27:9; 1Sa 8:13; Pr 31:15). A hymn sung after (Mt 26:30). Thanks given before (Mk 8:6; Ac 27:35).

Things prohibited as (Ex 22:31; Lev 11:4-8,10-20,41-42; 17:13-15). Peter's vision concerning (Ac 10:10-16). Paul's teaching concerning the eating of food offered to idols (Ro 14:2-23; 1Co 8:4-13; 10:18-32). Flesh unwarrantedly forbidden as (1Ti 4:3-4).
See Bread; Eating; Oven.

FOOL [211, 2147, 4067, 5571, 5572, 6118, 6119, 6618, 9438, *932*, *933*, *3704*].
NIV+ FOLLY, FOOL'S, FOOLISH, FOOLISHLY, FOOLISHNESS, FOOLS

In Scripture connotes conceit and pride, or deficiency in judgment rather than mental inferiority.

Described as:

Arrogant—
Ps 5:5 The arrogant cannot stand in your presence; you hate all who do wrong.

Iniquitous (Ps 107:17)—
Tit 3:3 At one time we too were foolish, disobedient, deceived and enslaved by all kinds of passions and pleasures. We lived in malice and envy, being hated and hating one another.

Atheistic—
Ps 14:1 The fool says in his heart, "There is no God." They are corrupt, their deeds are vile; there is no one who does good. (+Ps 53:1)

A reproach—
Ps 74:18 Remember how the enemy has mocked you, O LORD, how foolish people have reviled your name.
Ps 74:22 Rise up, O God, and defend your cause; remember how fools mock you all day long.

Despising wisdom—
Pr 1:7 The fear of the LORD is the beginning of knowledge, but fools despise wisdom and discipline.
Pr 1:22 "How long will you simple ones love your simple ways? How long will mockers delight in mockery and fools hate knowledge?
Pr 18:2 A fool finds no pleasure in understanding but delights in airing his own opinions.

Deceitful (Pr 1:14,18).

Contentious (Pr 1:18)—
Pr 18:6 A fool's lips bring him strife, and his mouth invites a beating. [7]A fool's mouth is his undoing, and his lips are a snare to his soul.
Pr 29:9 If a wise man goes to court with a fool, the fool rages and scoffs, and there is no peace.

Clamorous—
Pr 9:13 The woman Folly is loud; she is undisciplined and without knowledge.

An embarrassment to his father—
Pr 10:1 The proverbs of Solomon: A wise son brings joy to his father, but a foolish son grief to his mother.
Pr 15:20 A wise son brings joy to his father, but a foolish man despises his mother.
Pr 17:25 A foolish son brings grief to his father and bitterness to the one who bore him.
Pr 19:13 A foolish son is his father's ruin, and a quarrelsome wife is like a constant dripping.

Excessively talkative—
Pr 10:8 The wise in heart accept commands, but a chattering fool comes to ruin. (+Pr 10:10)
Pr 29:11 A fool gives full vent to his anger, but a wise man keeps himself under control.
Ecc 10:12 Words from a wise man's mouth are gracious, but a fool is consumed by his own lips. [13]At the beginning his words are folly; at the end they are wicked madness—[14]and the fool multiplies words. No one knows what is coming—who can tell him what will happen after him?

A mocker—
Pr 14:9 Fools mock at making amends for sin, but goodwill is found among the upright.

A dreamer—
Pr 17:24 A discerning man keeps wisdom in view, but a fool's eyes wander to the ends of the earth.

Quarrelsome—
Pr 20:3 It is to a man's honor to avoid strife, but every fool is quick to quarrel.

Wasteful—
Pr 21:20 In the house of the wise are stores of choice food and oil, but a foolish man devours all he has.

Idle—
Ecc 4:5 The fool folds his hands and ruins himself.

Causes sorrow (Pr 10:1; 17:25; 19:13).

Willful (Pr 1:7; 27:22).

Lacking in understanding (Pr 9:13)—
Pr 10:13 Wisdom is found on the lips of the discerning, but a rod is for the back of him who lacks judgment.
Pr 15:21 Folly delights a man who lacks judgment, but a man of understanding keeps a straight course. (+Pr 26:1)
Pr 26:3 A whip for the horse, a halter for the donkey, and a rod for the backs of fools!

[4]Do not answer a fool according to his folly, or you will be like him yourself.

[5]Answer a fool according to his folly, or he will be wise in his own eyes.

[6]Like cutting off one's feet or drinking violence is the sending of a message by the hand of a fool.

[7]Like a lame man's legs that hang limp is a proverb in the mouth of a fool.

[8]Like tying a stone in a sling is the giving of honor to a fool.

[9]Like a thornbush in a drunkard's hand is a proverb in the mouth of a fool.

[10]Like an archer who wounds at random is he who hires a fool or any passer-by.

[11]As a dog returns to its vomit, so a fool repeats his folly.

[12]Do you see a man wise in his own eyes? There is more hope for a fool than for him. (+Ecc 7:4-6)

Deficient in conscience—
Pr 10:23 A fool finds pleasure in evil conduct, but a man of understanding delights in wisdom.

Practice deception (Pr 14:8).

Gullible—
Pr 14:15 A simple man believes anything, but a prudent man gives thought to his steps.

Unknowledgeable—
Pr 15:7 The lips of the wise spread knowledge; not so the hearts of fools.

Angry—
Ecc 7:9 Do not be quickly provoked in your spirit, for anger resides in the lap of fools.

Unperceptive—
Mt 7:26 But everyone who hears these words of mine and does not put them into practice is like a foolish man who built his house on sand. [27]The rain came down, the streams rose, and the winds blew and beat against that house, and it fell with a great crash."

General:
To be forsaken—
Pr 9:6 Leave your simple ways and you will live; walk in the way of understanding.

To be avoided—
Pr 14:8 The wisdom of the prudent is to give thought to their ways, but the folly of fools is deception.

Some suffer affliction because of—
Ps 107:17 Some became fools through their rebellious ways and suffered affliction because of their iniquities.

Parables of:
The foolish virgins (Mt 25:1-13), the rich fool (Lk 12:16-20).

FOOT [*564+, 892, 5274, 7193, 7895, 8079, 8081, 10039+, 10655, *4267, 4270, 4546*].

NIV+ BAREFOOT, AFOOT, FLEET-FOOTED, FOOTHOLD, FOOTINGS, FOOTPRINTS, FOUR-FOOTED, UNDERFOOT

Washing the feet, of the disciples by Jesus (Jn 13:4-16), by disciples (1Ti 5:10). *See Purification; Washing.*

Figurative: (Mt 18:8).

For footwear. *See Sandal.*

FOOTMAN *See Runner.*

FOOTSTOOL [2071, 3900, *5711*].

NIV+ STOOL

A literal support for the feet (2Ch 9:18), a figure of subjection (Ps 110:1; Isa 66:1; Mt 5:35).

FORD [5044, 5045, 6296, 6302] (*pass over, through*).

NIV+ FORDED, FORDS

A shallow place in a stream where people and animals could cross on foot (Ge 32:22; Isa 16:2).

FOREHEAD [1068+6524, 1477, 1478, 5195, 6991, *3587*].

NIV+ FOREHEADS

The part of the face above the eyes.

Often revealing the character of the person—
Shamelessness (Jer 3:3), courage (Eze 3:9), or godliness (Rev 7:3).

FOREIGNER [1201+5797, 1201+2021+5797, 2424, 4927, 5799, 6850, *254, 975, 2283, 3828, 4230*].

NIV+ FOREIGN, FOREIGNERS, FOREIGNERS'

Among the Jewish people, anyone outside the nation was regarded as inferior (Ge 31:15) and possessed restricted rights.

He could not eat the Passover (Ex 12:43), intermarry on equal terms (Ex 34:12-16), become king (Dt 17:15), enter the sanctuary (Eze 44:9; Ac 21:28-29). They could be included in the nation by accepting the law and its requirements.

In the NT the word is applied to those who are not members of God's kingdom (Eph 2:19).

FOREKNOWLEDGE OF GOD [*4589, 4590*].

NIV+ FOREKNEW, FOREKNOWLEDGE

See God, Foreknowledge of, Wisdom of.

FOREMAN [5893+, 5904, 8853, *2208*].

NIV+ FOREMEN

See Master Craftsman.

FOREORDINATION *See Predestination.*

FORERUNNER Figurative of Christ (Heb 4:14; 6:20).

FORESKIN [6889].

NIV+ FORESKINS

The fold of skin cut off in the process of circumcision (Ge 17:11,14; Ex 4:25; 1Sa 18:25,27; 2Sa 3:14). *See Circumcision.*

FORESTS [3091, 3623, 7236, *5627*].

NIV+ FOREST, FORESTED

Abounded with wild honey (1Sa 14:25-26). Populated by wild beasts (Ps 50:10; 104:20; Isa 56:9; Jer 5:6; Mic 5:8). Undergrowth often in (Isa 9:18). Tracts of land covered with trees (Isa 44:14). Often afforded pasture (Mic 7:14).

Destroyed by Fire:
Of destruction of the wicked (Isa 9:18; 10:17-18; Jer 21:14).

Illustrative:
Prophecies concerning the coming invasion of Jerusalem by Sennacherib, its failure to withstand the invasion, and the unbelief of the Jews. The moral change in the Jewish nation shall be as great as if the wooded Lebanon were to become a fruitful field and vice versa (Isa 29:17). These prophecies are illustrative of those accustomed to a life of self-indulgence, who because of the devastations of the enemy would now go without (Isa 32:15,19).

Mentioned in Scripture:
Were places of refuge (1Sa 22:5; 23:16). Hereth (1Sa

22:5). Ephraim (2Sa 18:6,8). Supplied timber for building (1Ki 5:6-8). Lebanon (1Ki 7:2; 10:17). Carmel (Isa 33:9; 35:1-2; Na 1:4). Often destroyed by enemies (2Ki 19:23; Isa 37:24; Jer 46:23). Jotham built towers in (2Ch 27:4). Owned by King Artaxerxes and kept by Asaph (Ne 2:8). The power of God extends over (Ps 29:9). The oaks of Bashan (Isa 2:13; Eze 27:6; Zec 11:2). Arabia (Isa 21:13). Called on to rejoice at God's mercy (Isa 44:23). A prophecy against the people of the south, with trees representing the people of the densely populated area of Judea (Eze 20:46-47).

FORGERY *See Seal.*

FORGETTING GOD [*4213+4946+8894, 5960, 8894, 8895, *2140*, *1720*, *2144*, *3284+3330*, *3291*, *3648+4033*].

NIV+ FORGET, FORGETS, FORGOT, FORGOTTEN

A characteristic of the wicked (Pr 2:17; Isa 65:11). Backsliders guilty of (Jer 2:32; 3:21).

Is forgetting his covenant (Dt 4:23; 2Ki 17:38), past deliverances (Jdg 8:34; Ps 78:42-43), what he has done (Ps 78:7,11; 106:13), benefits (Ps 103:2), kindnesses (Ps 106:7), law (Ps 119:153,176; Hos 4:6), Jerusalem (Ps 137:5), power to deliver (Isa 51:13-15), word of encouragement (Heb 12:5), Word of God (Jas 1:22-25).

Cautions against (Dt 6:12; 8:11). Prosperity leads to (Dt 8:11-20; Hos 13:6). Trials should not lead to (Ps 44:17-22). Exhortation to those guilty of (Ps 50:22). Resolve against (Ps 119:16,93). Encouraged by false teachers (Jer 23:27).

Punishment of (Job 8:12-13; Ps 9:17; Isa 17:10-11; Eze 23:35; Hos 8:11-14), threatened (Ps 50:22).

See Apostasy; Backsliders; Forsaking God.

FORGIVENESS [*4105, 5951, 6142, 6145, 6296, *912, 668, 918, 3195, 5919*].

NIV+ FORGIVE, FORGAVE, FORGIVEN, FORGIVES, FORGIVING

Of enemies:

By showing kindness to enemy's animal—

Ex 23:4 "If you come across your enemy's ox or donkey wandering off, be sure to take it back to him. ⁵If you see the donkey of someone who hates you fallen down under its load, do not leave it there; be sure you help him with it.

By giving—

Pr 25:21 If your enemy is hungry, give him food to eat; if he is thirsty, give him water to drink. ²²In doing this, you will heap burning coals on his head, and the LORD will reward you.

Mt 5:39 But I tell you, Do not resist an evil person. If someone strikes you on the right cheek, turn to him the other also. ⁴⁰And if someone wants to sue you and take your tunic, let him have your cloak as well. ⁴¹If someone forces you to go one mile, go with him two miles. (+Ro 12:20)

Commanded—

Pr 24:17 Do not gloat when your enemy falls; when he stumbles, do not let your heart rejoice,

Mt 5:38 "You have heard that it was said, 'Eye for eye, and tooth for tooth.' ³⁹But I tell you, Do not resist an evil person. If someone strikes you on the right cheek, turn to him the other also. ⁴⁰And if someone wants to sue you and take your tunic, let him have your cloak as well. ⁴¹If someone forces you to go one mile, go with him two miles.

⁴²Give to the one who asks you, and do not turn away from the one who wants to borrow from you.

⁴³"You have heard that it was said, 'Love your neighbor and hate your enemy.' ⁴⁴But I tell you: Love your enemies and pray for those who persecute you, ⁴⁵that you may be sons of your Father in heaven. He causes his sun to rise on the evil and the good, and sends rain on the righteous and the unrighteous. ⁴⁶If you love those who love you, what reward will you get? Are not even the tax collectors doing that? (+Mt 5:47-48; 18:21-35; Mk 11:25; Lk 6:27-34)

Lk 6:35 But love your enemies, do good to them, and lend to them without expecting to get anything back. Then your reward will be great, and you will be sons of the Most High, because he is kind to the ungrateful and wicked. ³⁶Be merciful, just as your Father is merciful.

³⁷"Do not judge, and you will not be judged. Do not condemn, and you will not be condemned. Forgive, and you will be forgiven.

Each other:

Lk 17:3 So watch yourselves. "If your brother sins, rebuke him, and if he repents, forgive him.

⁴If he sins against you seven times in a day, and seven times comes back to you and says, 'I repent,' forgive him."

Eph 4:32 Be kind and compassionate to one another, forgiving each other, just as in Christ God forgave you.

Col 3:13 Bear with each other and forgive whatever grievances you may have against one another. Forgive as the Lord forgave you.

Phm 10 I appeal to you for my son Onesimus, who became my son while I was in chains. (+Phm 18)

A condition of divine forgiveness—

Mt 6:12 Forgive us our debts, as we also have forgiven our debtors. (+Mt 6:13)

Mt 6:14 For if you forgive men when they sin against you, your heavenly Father will also forgive you. ¹⁵But if you do not forgive men their sins, your Father will not forgive your sins.

Mt 18:21 Then Peter came to Jesus and asked, "Lord, how many times shall I forgive my brother when he sins against me? Up to seven times?"

²²Jesus answered, "I tell you, not seven times, but seventy-seven times.

²³"Therefore, the kingdom of heaven is like a king who wanted to settle accounts with his servants. ²⁴As he began the settlement, a man who owed him ten thousand talents was brought to him. ²⁵Since he was not able to pay, the master ordered that he and his wife and his children and all that he had be sold to repay the debt.

²⁶"The servant fell on his knees before him. 'Be patient with me,' he begged, 'and I will pay back everything.' ²⁷The servant's master took pity on him, canceled the debt and let him go.

²⁸"But when that servant went out, he found one of his fellow servants who owed him a hundred denarii. He grabbed him and began to choke him. 'Pay back what you owe me!' he demanded.

²⁹"His fellow servant fell to his knees and begged him, 'Be patient with me, and I will pay you back.'

³⁰"But he refused. Instead, he went off and had the man thrown into prison until he could pay the debt. ³¹When the other servants saw what had happened, they were greatly distressed and went and told their master everything that had happened.

³²"Then the master called the servant in. 'You wicked servant,' he said, 'I canceled all that debt of yours because you begged me to. ³³Shouldn't you have had mercy on

your fellow servant just as I had on you?' ³⁴In anger his master turned him over to the jailers to be tortured, until he should pay back all he owed.

³⁵"This is how my heavenly Father will treat each of you unless you forgive your brother from your heart."

Mk 11:25 And when you stand praying, if you hold anything against anyone, forgive him, so that your Father in heaven may forgive you your sins." (+Lk 11:4)

See Enemy.

Spirit of, disallows rejoicing (Pr 24:17-18)

Disallows retaliation—

Pr 24:29 Do not say, "I'll do to him as he has done to me; I'll pay that man back for what he did."

Ro 12:17 Do not repay anyone evil for evil. Be careful to do what is right in the eyes of everybody.

Ro 12:19 Do not take revenge, my friends, but leave room for God's wrath, for it is written: "It is mine to avenge; I will repay," says the Lord.

Blesses—

Ro 12:14 Bless those who persecute you; bless and do not curse.

1Co 4:12 We work hard with our own hands. When we are cursed, we bless; when we are persecuted, we endure it; ¹³when we are slandered, we answer kindly. Up to this moment we have become the scum of the earth, the refuse of the world.

1Pe 3:9 Do not repay evil with evil or insult with insult, but with blessing, because to this you were called so that you may inherit a blessing.

FORM [1215, 1952, 3670, 3922, 4162, 6886, 9307, 9322, 9454, *1626, 1639, 3671, 3673, 3674, 3929, 5386, 5395, 5596*].

In religious service—

1Ch 15:13 It was because you, the Levites, did not bring it up the first time that the LORD our God broke out in anger against us. We did not inquire of him about how to do it in the prescribed way." ¹⁴So the priests and Levites consecrated themselves in order to bring up the ark of the LORD, the God of Israel.

2Ch 29:34 The priests, however, were too few to skin all the burnt offerings; so their kinsmen the Levites helped them until the task was finished and until other priests had been consecrated, for the Levites had been more conscientious in consecrating themselves than the priests had been.

Irregularity in—

2Ch 30:2 The king and his officials and the whole assembly in Jerusalem decided to celebrate the Passover in the second month. ³They had not been able to celebrate it at the regular time because not enough priests had consecrated themselves and the people had not assembled in Jerusalem. ⁴The plan seemed right both to the king and to the whole assembly. ⁵They decided to send a proclamation throughout Israel, from Beersheba to Dan, calling the people to come to Jerusalem and celebrate the Passover to the LORD, the God of Israel. It had not been celebrated in large numbers according to what was written. (+2Ch 30:17,20)

Mt 12:3 He answered, "Haven't you read what David did when he and his companions were hungry? ⁴He entered the house of God, and he and his companions ate the consecrated bread—which was not lawful for them to do, but only for the priests.

See Church, The Body of Believers, State.

FORMALISM

Rejected by God for presenting sacrifices rather than:

Obedience—

1Sa 15:22 But Samuel replied: "Does the LORD delight in burnt offerings and sacrifices as much as in obeying the voice of the LORD? To obey is better than sacrifice, and to heed is better than the fat of rams. ²³For rebellion is like the sin of divination, and arrogance like the evil of idolatry. Because you have rejected the word of the LORD, he has rejected you as king."

Ecc 5:1 Guard your steps when you go to the house of God. Go near to listen rather than to offer the sacrifice of fools, who do not know that they do wrong. (+1Co 7:19; 1Jn 2:3-11)

Thanksgiving—

Ps 50:8 I do not rebuke you for your sacrifices or your burnt offerings, which are ever before me. ⁹I have no need of a bull from your stall or of goats from your pens, ¹⁰for every animal of the forest is mine, and the cattle on a thousand hills. ¹¹I know every bird in the mountains, and the creatures of the field are mine. ¹²If I were hungry I would not tell you, for the world is mine, and all that is in it. ¹³Do I eat the flesh of bulls or drink the blood of goats? ¹⁴Sacrifice thank offerings to God, fulfill your vows to the Most High, ¹⁵and call upon me in the day of trouble; I will deliver you, and you will honor me."

Ps 69:30 I will praise God's name in song and glorify him with thanksgiving. ³¹This will please the LORD more than an ox, more than a bull with its horns and hoofs.

Repentance—

Ps 51:16 You do not delight in sacrifice, or I would bring it; you do not take pleasure in burnt offerings. ¹⁷The sacrifices of God are a broken spirit; a broken and contrite heart, O God, you will not despise.

Mercy—

Hos 6:6 For I desire mercy, not sacrifice, and acknowledgment of God rather than burnt offerings.

Mic 6:6 With what shall I come before the LORD and bow down before the exalted God? Shall I come before him with burnt offerings, with calves a year old? ⁷Will the LORD be pleased with thousands of rams, with ten thousand rivers of oil? Shall I offer my firstborn for my transgression, the fruit of my body for the sin of my soul? ⁸He has showed you, O man, what is good. And what does the LORD require of you? To act justly and to love mercy and to walk humbly with your God.

Mt 9:13 But go and learn what this means: 'I desire mercy, not sacrifice.' For I have not come to call the righteous, but sinners."

Mt 12:7 If you had known what these words mean, 'I desire mercy, not sacrifice,' you would not have condemned the innocent.

Live a life characterized by:

Justice, mercy, and humility—

Mic 6:6 With what shall I come before the LORD and bow down before the exalted God? Shall I come before him with burnt offerings, with calves a year old? ⁷Will the LORD be pleased with thousands of rams, with ten thousand rivers of oil? Shall I offer my firstborn for my transgression, the fruit of my body for the sin of my soul? ⁸He has showed you, O man, what is good. And what does the LORD require of you? To act justly and to love mercy and to walk humbly with your God.

A pure heart—

Mt 15:8 " 'These people honor me with their lips, but their hearts are far from me. ⁹They worship me in vain; their teachings are but rules taught by men.'" (+Ro 2:17-29)

Despised by God:

Isa 1:11 "The multitude of your sacrifices—what are they to me?" says the LORD. "I have more than enough of burnt offerings, of rams and the fat of fattened animals; I have no pleasure in the blood of bulls and lambs and goats. ¹²When you come to appear before me, who has asked this of you, this trampling of my courts? ¹³Stop bringing meaningless offerings! Your incense is detestable to me. New Moons, Sabbaths and convocations—I cannot bear your evil assemblies. ¹⁴Your New Moon festivals and your appointed feasts my soul hates. They have become a burden to me; I am weary of bearing them. ¹⁵When you spread out your hands in prayer, I will hide my eyes from you; even if you offer many prayers, I will not listen. Your hands are full of blood;

Isa 29:13 The Lord says: "These people come near to me with their mouth and honor me with their lips, but their hearts are far from me. Their worship of me is made up only of rules taught by men. ¹⁴Therefore once more I will astound these people with wonder upon wonder; the wisdom of the wise will perish, the intelligence of the intelligent will vanish." ¹⁵Woe to those who go to great depths to hide their plans from the LORD, who do their work in darkness and think, "Who sees us? Who will know?" ¹⁶You turn things upside down, as if the potter were thought to be like the clay! Shall what is formed say to him who formed it, "He did not make me"? Can the pot say of the potter, "He knows nothing"? (+Ps 50:8-15)

Jer 6:20 What do I care about incense from Sheba or sweet calamus from a distant land? Your burnt offerings are not acceptable; your sacrifices do not please me."

Jer 14:12 Although they fast, I will not listen to their cry; though they offer burnt offerings and grain offerings, I will not accept them. Instead, I will destroy them with the sword, famine and plague."

Am 5:21 "I hate, I despise your religious feasts; I cannot stand your assemblies. ²²Even though you bring me burnt offerings and grain offerings, I will not accept them. Though you bring choice fellowship offerings, I will have no regard for them. ²³Away with the noise of your songs! I will not listen to the music of your harps.

Mal 1:6 "A son honors his father, and a servant his master. If I am a father, where is the honor due me? If I am a master, where is the respect due me?" says the LORD Almighty. "It is you, O priests, who show contempt for my name. "But you ask, 'How have we shown contempt for your name?' (+Mal 1:7)

Mal 1:8 When you bring blind animals for sacrifice, is that not wrong? When you sacrifice crippled or diseased animals, is that not wrong? Try offering them to your governor! Would he be pleased with you? Would he accept you?" says the LORD Almighty. (+Mal 1:9)

Mal 1:10 "Oh, that one of you would shut the temple doors, so that you would not light useless fires on my altar! I am not pleased with you," says the LORD Almighty, "and I will accept no offering from your hands. (+Mal 1:11-12)

Mal 1:13 And you say, 'What a burden!' and you sniff at it contemptuously," says the LORD Almighty. "When you bring injured, crippled or diseased animals and offer them as sacrifices, should I accept them from your hands?" says the LORD.

¹⁴"Cursed is the cheat who has an acceptable male in his flock and vows to give it, but then sacrifices a blemished animal to the Lord. For I am a great king," says the LORD

Almighty, "and my name is to be feared among the nations.

Lk 13:24 "Make every effort to enter through the narrow door, because many, I tell you, will try to enter and will not be able to. ²⁵Once the owner of the house gets up and closes the door, you will stand outside knocking and pleading, 'Sir, open the door for us.'

"But he will answer, 'I don't know you or where you come from.'

²⁶"Then you will say, 'We ate and drank with you, and you taught in our streets.'

²⁷"But he will reply, 'I don't know you or where you come from. Away from me, all you evildoers!'

2Ti 3:1 But mark this: There will be terrible times in the last days. ²People will be lovers of themselves, lovers of money, boastful, proud, abusive, disobedient to their parents, ungrateful, unholy, ³without love, unforgiving, slanderous, without self-control, brutal, not lovers of the good, ⁴treacherous, rash, conceited, lovers of pleasure rather than lovers of God— ⁵having a form of godliness but denying its power. Have nothing to do with them.

Empty: (Mt 15:8-9)

Ro 2:17 Now you, if you call yourself a Jew; if you rely on the law and brag about your relationship to God; ¹⁸if you know his will and approve of what is superior because you are instructed by the law; ¹⁹if you are convinced that you are a guide for the blind, a light for those who are in the dark, ²⁰an instructor of the foolish, a teacher of infants, because you have in the law the embodiment of knowledge and truth— ²¹you, then, who teach others, do you not teach yourself? You who preach against stealing, do you steal? ²²You who say that people should not commit adultery, do you commit adultery? You who abhor idols, do you rob temples? ²³You who brag about the law, do you dishonor God by breaking the law? ²⁴As it is written: "God's name is blasphemed among the Gentiles because of you."

²⁵Circumcision has value if you observe the law, but if you break the law, you have become as though you had not been circumcised. ²⁶If those who are not circumcised keep the law's requirements, will they not be regarded as though they were circumcised? ²⁷The one who is not circumcised physically and yet obeys the law will condemn you who, even though you have the written code and circumcision, are a lawbreaker.

²⁸A man is not a Jew if he is only one outwardly, nor is circumcision merely outward and physical. ²⁹No, a man is a Jew if he is one inwardly; and circumcision is circumcision of the heart, by the Spirit, not by the written code. Such a man's praise is not from men, but from God.

1Co 7:19 Circumcision is nothing and uncircumcision is nothing. Keeping God's commands is what counts.

Php 3:4 though I myself have reasons for such confidence.

If anyone else thinks he has reasons to put confidence in the flesh, I have more: ⁵circumcised on the eighth day, of the people of Israel, of the tribe of Benjamin, a Hebrew of Hebrews; in regard to the law, a Pharisee; ⁶as for zeal, persecuting the church; as for legalistic righteousness, faultless.

⁷But whatever was to my profit I now consider loss for the sake of Christ.

FORNICATION

Instructions concerning illicit sexual intercourse (Ac 15:20,29; 21:25; 1Co 5:1; 6:13,18; 7:2). More specifically and primarily unlawful intercourse of an unwed person

(Mt 15:19; Mk 7:21; 1Co 6:9,18; Gal 5:19). It was commonly associated with heathen worship (Jer 2:20; 3:6) and was used as a figure of disloyalty to God (Eze 16:3-22).

See Adultery; Prostitute.

FORSAKING GOD [*5759, 6440, *1593*].

NIV+ FORSAKE, FORSAKEN, FORSAKES, FORSOOK

The wicked guilty of (Dt 28:20). Idolaters guilty of (1Sa 8:8; 1Ki 11:33). Backsliders guilty of (Jer 15:6).

Exemplified:

Israelites (1Sa 12:10). Saul (1Sa 15:11). Ahab (1Ki 18:18). Amon (2Ki 21:22). Kingdom of Judah (2Ch 12:1, 5; 21:10; Isa 1:4; Jer 15:6). Kingdom of Israel (2Ch 13:11, w 2Ki 17:7-18). Many disciples (Jn 6:66). Phygelus and Hermogenes (2Ti 1:15). Balaam son of Beor (2Pe 2:15).

Is Forsaking:

His covenant (Dt 29:25; 1Ki 19:10; Jer 22:9; Da 11:30). Prosperity tempts to (Dt 31:20; 32:15). Provokes God to forsake people (Jdg 10:13; 2Ch 15:2; 24:20,24). Resolve against (Jos 24:16; Ne 10:29-39). Warnings against (Jos 24:20; 1Ch 28:9). His house (2Ch 29:6). His commandments (Ezr 9:10). Sin of, to be confessed (Ezr 9:10). Unreasonableness and ingratitude of (Jer 2:5-6). Leads men to follow their own devices (Jer 2:13). Wickedness of (Jer 2:13; 5:7). Trusting in man is (Jer 17:5). Curse pronounced upon (Jer 17:5). Brings confusion (Jer 17:13). Brings down his wrath (Ezr 3:12). Followed by remorse (Eze 6:9). The right way (2Pe 2:15).

See Forgetting God; Apostasy.

FORT [810, 1072, 1315, 4448, 5057, 5058, 5171, 5181, 5183, 5193, 5369, 6437].

NIV+ FORTIFICATIONS, FORTIFIED, FORTIFIES, FORTRESS, FORTRESSES, FORTS

A military defense.

Field fortifications (Dt 20:19-20; 2Ki 25:1; Eze 4:2; 17:17; 26:8). Caves used for (Jdg 6:2; 1Sa 23:29; Isa 33:16). Erected in, vineyards and herding grounds (Isa 5:2; Mt 21:33; Mk 12:1), the desert (2Ch 26:10). Defenses of cities (2Ch 26:15; Isa 25:12). *See Garrison; Tower; Walls.*

Figurative:

Of God's care (2Sa 22:2-3,47; Ps 18:2; 31:3; 71:3; 91:2; 144:2; Pr 18:10; Na 1:7).

FORTIFICATION [1215, 1290, 2616, 2658, 4448, 5190, 5193, 6434, 6437] (*a military defense*).

NIV+ See FORT

Caves used for (Jdg 6:2; 1Sa 23:26). Field made during military operations (Dt 20:19-20; 2Ki 25:1; Jer 6:6; 32:24; 33:4; Eze 4:2; 17:17; 26:8; Da 11:15). Defenses of cities (2Sa 5:9; 2Ch 11:10-11; 26:9,15; Ne 3:8; 4:2; Isa 22:10; 25:12; 29:3; Jer 51:53; Na 3:14). Erected in, vineyards and herding grounds (Isa 5:2; Mt 21:33; Mk 12:1), the desert (2Ch 26:10).

Figurative:

Of God's care (2Sa 22:2-3,47; Ps 18:2; 31:3; 71:3; 91:2; 144:2; Pr 18:10; Na 1:7).

FORTITUDE *See Courage.*

FORTUNATUS [*5847*] (*fortunate*). A Corinthian Christian, a friend of Paul (1Co 16:17).

FORTUNE [238, 1513, 3888, 7876, 8654, 8669].

NIV+ FORTUNATE, FORTUNE-TELLING, FORTUNES

1. Changes of. See illustrated in lives of Joseph, from slave to prime minister. *See Joseph, 1.* Pharaoh's butler

and baker (Ge 40). David, from shepherd boy to king, noting the changes (1Sa 15:3,7-16:13; 2Sa 2:1-7). *See David; also Jeroboam; Haman; Mordecai; Esther; Job; Daniel.*

2. A pagan god (Isa 65:11).

FORTUNE-TELLING [*3446*]. *See Sorcery.*

FORTY [752, *5477, 5478*].

NIV+ FORTIETH, 40

Highly significant number.

Days:

Of rain, at the time of the flood (Ge 7:17), of flood, before sending forth the raven (Ge 8:6). For embalming (Ge 50:3). Jesus in the desert (Mt 4:2; Mk 1:15; Lk 4:2), compare to Israel's forty years in the desert. Spies in the land of promise (Nu 13:25). Goliath challenged Israel (1Sa 17:16). Symbolic (Eze 4:6). Of probation, given to the Ninevites (Jn 3:4). Christ's stay after the Resurrection (Ac 1:3).

Days of fasting:

By Moses (Ex 24:18; 34:28; Dt 9:9,25), Elijah (1Ki 19:8), Jesus (Mt 4:2).

Years:

Isaac's and Esau's age at time of marriages (Ge 25:20; 26:34). Wandering of the Israelites in the desert (Ex 16:35; Nu 14:34). Caleb's age when he spied out the land (Jos 14:7). Peace in Israel (Jdg 3:11; 5:31; 8:28). Eli as judge (1Sa 4:17), Saul as king (Ac 31:21), David as king (2Sa 5:4), Solomon (1Ki 11:42), Joash (2Ki 12:1). Egypt, to be desolated (Eze 29:11), to be restored after (Eze 29:13).

Lashes:

Administered as punishment for criminals (Dt 25:3; 2Co 11:24).

FORUM OF APPIUS [*5842*]. The Forum of Appius was a place forty-three miles SE of Rome, where Paul was met by friends (Ac 28:15).

FOUNDATION [99, 575, 3569, 3572, 3573, 4586, 4587, 4588, 4589, 4806, 4807, 4996, 10079, *1613, 2528, 2529, 2530*].

NIV+ FOUNDATIONS, FOUNDED

The lowest part of a building, and on which it rests (Lk 14:29; Ac 16:26).

Described as:

Of stone (1Ki 5:17). Joined together by cornerstones (Ezr 4:12, w 1Pe 2:6, & Eph 2:20). Strongly laid (Ezr 6:3). Security afforded by (Mt 7:25; Lk 6:48). Deep laid (Lk 6:48).

Figuratively Applied to:

Kingdoms (Ex 9:18). The mountains (Dt 32:22). The heavens (2Sa 22:8). The earth (Job 38:4; Ps 104:5). The world (Mt 13:35). The ocean (Ps 104:8).

Illustrative of:

Hope of saints (Ps 87:1). The righteous (Pr 10:25). Christ (Isa 28:16; 1Co 3:11). Doctrines of the apostles (Eph 2:20). Decrees and purposes of God (2Ti 2:19). First principles of the gospel (Heb 6:1-2). Security of saints' inheritance (Heb 11:10).

Laid for:

Cities (Jos 6:26; 1Ki 16:34). Temples (1Ki 6:37; Ezr 3:10). Walls (Ezr 4:12; Rev 21:14). Houses (Lk 6:48). Towers (Lk 14:28-29).

FOUNDING *See Molding.*

FOUNTAIN [1644, 5078, 5227, 6524].

NIV+ FOUNTAINS

Figurative:

Of divine grace (Ps 36:9; Jer 2:13), of the salvation of the gospel (Joel 3:18; Zec 13:1; Rev 7:17). The polluted, of the debasement of character (Pr 25:26).

FOUNTAIN GATE A gate in the walls of Jerusalem (Ne 2:14; 3:15; 12:37).

FOUNTAIN OF LIFE (Ps 36:9; Pr 13:14; 14:27; Jer 2:13; 17:13; Zec 13:1; Rev 7:17).

FOWL *See Birds.*

FOWLER [3687, 3704].

NIV+ FOWL, FOWLER'S

A bird-catcher (Ps 91:3; 124:7).

The fowler's snares used figuratively:—

1. Of the calamities and plots which await (Job 22:10; Ps 91:3; 124:7; Pr 22:5; Isa 24:17; Jer 48:43; Hos 9:8).

2. As the source or agent of calamity (Jos 23:13; Ps 69:22; Isa 8:14; Hos 5:1).

FOX [8785, *273*].

NIV+ FOXES

Samson uses, to burn the field of the Philistines (Jdg 15:4-5). Depreciations of (SS 2:15). Dens of (Mt 8:20; Lk 9:58).

Figurative:

Of heretics (SS 2:15). Of unfaithful prophets (Eze 13:1-7). Of craftiness (Lk 13:32).

See Jackal.

FRACTURES [8691].

NIV+ FRACTURE

Treatment of (Eze 30:21).

Figurative:

David calling for God to break the arm of the wicked man (Ps 10:15). David claiming that the power of the wicked will be broken (Ps 37:17). The strength of Moab is broken (Jer 48:25).

FRAGRANCE [1411, 5351, 5767, 6160, 6986, 8193, 8194, *4011*].

NIV+ FRAGRANT

Fragrant offerings (Lev 4:7; Nu 4:16). Metaphorical of acceptable service to God (2Co 2:14,16; Eph 5:2; Php 4:18).

FRANKINCENSE [4247, *3337*].

NIV+ INCENSE

A fragrant gum resin consisting of small, white chunks and beads which are easily ground into a powder; this powder emits a sweet odor when burned. An ingredient of the sacred oil (Ex 30:34). Commerce in (Rev 18:11-13).

FRATERNITY

Commanded by:

Moses to the Israelites—

Dt 15:7 If there is a poor man among your brothers in any of the towns of the land that the LORD your God is giving you, do not be hardhearted or tightfisted toward your poor brother. ⁸Rather be openhanded and freely lend him whatever he needs. ⁹Be careful not to harbor this wicked thought: "The seventh year, the year for canceling debts, is near," so that you do not show ill will toward your needy brother and give him nothing. He may then appeal to the LORD against you, and you will be found guilty of sin. ¹⁰Give generously to him and do so without a grudging heart; then because of this the LORD your God will bless you in all your work and in everything you put your hand to. ¹¹There will always be poor people in the land. Therefore I command you to be openhanded toward your brothers and toward the poor and needy in your land.

¹²If a fellow Hebrew, a man or a woman, sells himself to you and serves you six years, in the seventh year you must let him go free. ¹³And when you release him, do not send him away empty-handed. ¹⁴Supply him liberally from your flock, your threshing floor and your winepress. Give to him as the LORD your God has blessed you. ¹⁵Remember that you were slaves in Egypt and the LORD your God redeemed you. That is why I give you this command today. (+Jos 1:14-15)

David—

Ps 22:22 I will declare your name to my brothers; in the congregation I will praise you.

Ps 133:1 How good and pleasant it is when brothers live together in unity! ²It is like precious oil poured on the head, running down on the beard, running down on Aaron's beard, down upon the collar of his robes. ³It is as if the dew of Hermon were falling on Mount Zion. For there the LORD bestows his blessing, even life forevermore.

Malachi—

Mal 2:10 Have we not all one Father? Did not one God create us? Why do we profane the covenant of our fathers by breaking faith with one another?

Jesus (Ps 22:22)—

Mt 5:22 But I tell you that anyone who is angry with his brother will be subject to judgment. Again, anyone who says to his brother, 'Raca,' is answerable to the Sanhedrin. But anyone who says, 'You fool!' will be in danger of the fire of hell.

²³"Therefore, if you are offering your gift at the altar and there remember that your brother has something against you, ²⁴leave your gift there in front of the altar. First go and be reconciled to your brother; then come and offer your gift.

²⁵"Settle matters quickly with your adversary who is taking you to court. Do it while you are still with him on the way, or he may hand you over to the judge, and the judge may hand you over to the officer, and you may be thrown into prison. ²⁶I tell you the truth, you will not get out until you have paid the last penny.

Mt 18:15 "If your brother sins against you, go and show him his fault, just between the two of you. If he listens to you, you have won your brother over. ¹⁶But if he will not listen, take one or two others along, so that 'every matter may be established by the testimony of two or three witnesses.' ¹⁷If he refuses to listen to them, tell it to the church; and if he refuses to listen even to the church, treat him as you would a pagan or a tax collector.

¹⁸"I tell you the truth, whatever you bind on earth will be bound in heaven, and whatever you loose on earth will be loosed in heaven.

Mt 18:21 Then Peter came to Jesus and asked, "Lord, how many times shall I forgive my brother when he sins against me? Up to seven times?"

²²Jesus answered, "I tell you, not seven times, but seventy-seven times.

Mt 18:35 "This is how my heavenly Father will treat each of you unless you forgive your brother from your heart."

Mt 23:8 "But you are not to be called 'Rabbi,' for you have only one Master and you are all brothers.

Mt 25:40 "The King will reply, 'I tell you the truth, whatever you did for one of the least of these brothers of mine, you did for me.'

Jn 13:34 "A new command I give you: Love one another. As I have loved you, so you must love one another. ³⁵By this all men will know that you are my disciples, if you love one another." (+Jn 15:12-14; 21:17)

Paul—

Ro 12:10 Be devoted to one another in brotherly love. Honor one another above yourselves.

1Co 6:1 If any of you has a dispute with another, dare he take it before the ungodly for judgment instead of before the saints? ²Do you not know that the saints will judge the world? And if you are to judge the world, are you not competent to judge trivial cases? ³Do you not know that we will judge angels? How much more the things of this life! ⁴Therefore, if you have disputes about such matters, appoint as judges even men of little account in the church! ⁵I say this to shame you. Is it possible that there is nobody among you wise enough to judge a dispute between believers? ⁶But instead, one brother goes to law against another—and this in front of unbelievers!

⁷The very fact that you have lawsuits among you means you have been completely defeated already. Why not rather be wronged? Why not rather be cheated? ⁸Instead, you yourselves cheat and do wrong, and you do this to your brothers. (+Gal 6:1-5; 1Th 4:9; 2Th 3:14-15)

In Hebrews—

Heb 13:1 Keep on loving each other as brothers.

Peter (1Pe 1:12)—

1Pe 2:17 Show proper respect to everyone: Love the brotherhood of believers, fear God, honor the king.

1Pe 3:8 Finally, all of you, live in harmony with one another; be sympathetic, love as brothers, be compassionate and humble.

2Pe 1:5 For this very reason, make every effort to add to your faith goodness; and to goodness, knowledge;

2Pe 1:7 and to godliness, brotherly kindness; and to brotherly kindness, love.

John—

1Jn 2:9 Anyone who claims to be in the light but hates his brother is still in the darkness. ¹⁰Whoever loves his brother lives in the light, and there is nothing in him to make him stumble. ¹¹But whoever hates his brother is in the darkness and walks around in the darkness; he does not know where he is going, because the darkness has blinded him.

Exemplified:

By Abraham and Lot—

Ge 13:8 So Abram said to Lot, "Let's not have any quarreling between you and me, or between your herdsmen and mine, for we are brothers.

By Jonathan and David (1Sa 18:1; 19:2-7; 20:17,41-42; 23:16-18). By early Christians (Ac 2:42-47). By Paul (Ro 9:2-3; 10:1-4; 1Co 9:20-23). By James, Peter, and John (Gal 2:9). By Epaphroditus (Php 2:25-26). By the Thessalonian church (2Th 1:3).

See Brother; Church, The Body of Believers; Fellowship; Friendship; Love.

Nazirites, vows of (Nu 6:1-21; La 4:7; Am 2:11-12; Ac 21:24-31). *See Nazirite(s), Nazarite(s).*

Unity (Ps 133:1-3)

Broken:

Zec 11:14 Then I broke my second staff called Union, breaking the brotherhood between Judah and Israel.

Incompatible with, pride of title (Mt 23:8)

Indifference to another's conscience—

1Co 8:1 Now about food sacrificed to idols: We know that we all possess knowledge. Knowledge puffs up, but love builds up. ²The man who thinks he knows something does not yet know as he ought to know. ³But the man who loves God is known by God.

⁴So then, about eating food sacrificed to idols: We know that an idol is nothing at all in the world and that there is no God but one. ⁵For even if there are so-called gods, whether in heaven or on earth (as indeed there are many "gods" and many "lords"), ⁶yet for us there is but one God, the Father, from whom all things came and for whom we live; and there is but one Lord, Jesus Christ, through whom all things came and through whom we live.

⁷But not everyone knows this. Some people are still so accustomed to idols that when they eat such food they think of it as having been sacrificed to an idol, and since their conscience is weak, it is defiled. ⁸But food does not bring us near to God; we are no worse if we do not eat, and no better if we do.

⁹Be careful, however, that the exercise of your freedom does not become a stumbling block to the weak. ¹⁰For if anyone with a weak conscience sees you who have this knowledge eating in an idol's temple, won't he be emboldened to eat what has been sacrificed to idols? ¹¹So this weak brother, for whom Christ died, is destroyed by your knowledge. ¹²When you sin against your brothers in this way and wound their weak conscience, you sin against Christ. ¹³Therefore, if what I eat causes my brother to fall into sin, I will never eat meat again, so that I will not cause him to fall. (+1Co 10:28-29)

Selfishness—

1Jn 3:17 If anyone has material possessions and sees his brother in need but has no pity on him, how can the love of God be in him?

See Brother.

FRATRICIDE One who kills or murders his own brother or sister.

Instances of: Cain (Ge 4:8). Abimelech (Jdg 9:5). Absalom (2Sa 13:28-29). Solomon (1Ki 2:23-25). Jehoram (2Ch 21:4). *See Homicide; Murder.*

FRAUD [9214]. *See Dishonesty.*

FREEDMAN [592].

NIV+ See FREEDOM

A slave who has been granted his freedom (1Co 7:22), or a free man as contrasted with a slave (Gal 4:22-23), among Christians (Col 3:11).

FREEDMEN [3339].

NIV+ See FREEDOM

One of a number of synagogues at Jerusalem, conducted for Jews who spoke Greek rather than Aramaic, the latter being the native language of Palestinian Jews (Ac 6:9).

See Emancipation.

FREEDOM [2002, 2928, 8146, 457, 912, 1181+1801, 1800, 2026, 4244].

NIV+ FREE, FREED, FREEDMAN, FREEDMEN, FREEING, FREELY

From servitude. *See Emancipation; Jubilee.*

FREEWILL [5605, 5607, 10461]. *See Blessings, Spiritual, Contingent Upon Obedience.*

FREEWILL OFFERINGS [5605, 5607, 10461]. In the category of gifts, freewill offerings were voluntary offerings prompted solely by the impulse of the donor (Lev 22:21,23; 23:38; Nu 29:39; Dt 12:6,17; 2Ch 31:14; Ezr 3:5; 7:16; 8:28; Ps 119:108; 2Co 8:1-15).

See Beneficence; Gift, Giving; Liberality; Offerings.

FRET [3013]. The verb means to be irritated, angry, or nervous (Ps 37:1,7-8; Pr 24:19).

FRIENDS [*170, 173, 278, 476, 2492, 3359, 5335, 8276, 8291, 8934, 10245, *28, *2279, *5813*].

NIV+ FRIEND, FRIENDLY, FRIENDSHIP

False: (Ps 41:9; 88:18; Zec 13:6).

Instances of: Pharaoh's chief cupbearer to Joseph (Ge 40:23). Delilah to Samson (Jdg 16:4-21). The wife of a Levite living in the hill country of Ephraim (Jdg 19:1-2). David, to Uriah (2Sa 11), to Joab (1Ki 2:5-6). Ahithophel to David (2Sa 15:12). Job's friends (Job 6:14-30; 19:13-22).

David's friends to David (Ps 31:11-12; 35:11-16; 41:9)—

Ps 55:12 If an enemy were insulting me, I could endure it; if a foe were raising himself against me, I could hide from him. **13**But it is you, a man like myself, my companion, my close friend, **14**with whom I once enjoyed sweet fellowship as we walked with the throng at the house of God. (+Ps 55:20-21; 88:8)

Judas (Mt 26:48-49; Mk 14:43-50; Lk 22:47-48; Ac 1:16-17). Jesus' disciples (Mt 26:56,58). Paul's friends (2Ti 4:16).

See Hypocrisy.

General:

Affectionate (Dt 13:6)—

1Sa 18:1 After David had finished talking with Saul, Jonathan became one in spirit with David, and he loved him as himself.

1Sa 20:17 And Jonathan had David reaffirm his oath out of love for him, because he loved him as he loved himself.

Jn 15:9 "As the Father has loved me, so have I loved you. Now remain in my love. **10**If you obey my commands, you will remain in my love, just as I have obeyed my Father's commands and remain in his love. **11**I have told you this so that my joy may be in you and that your joy may be complete. **12**My command is this: Love each other as I have loved you. **13**Greater love has no one than this, that he lay down his life for his friends. **14**You are my friends if you do what I command. **15**I no longer call you servants, because a servant does not know his master's business. Instead, I have called you friends, for everything that I learned from my Father I have made known to you. **16**You did not choose me, but I chose you and appointed you to go and bear fruit—fruit that will last. Then the Father will give you whatever you ask in my name. **17**This is my command: Love each other.

Sympathetic (Job 2:11; 6:14; Ps 35:14). Mercenary (Pr 14:20; 19:4,6). Forsaken (Pr 17:9; 27:14). Faithful (Pr 17:17; 18:24; 27:6). Of mutual help (Pr 27:9,19). Cause rejoicing (Pr 27:9). Not to forsake (Pr 27:10). *See Friendship.*

Jesus calls his disciples (Lk 12:4; Jn 15:14-15).

FRIENDSHIP [173, 2256+3208+8934, 6051, 8276, 5802].

NIV+ FRIEND, FRIENDS, FRIENDLY

General:

Promoted by, sympathy—

Job 6:14 "A despairing man should have the devotion of his friends, even though he forsakes the fear of the Almighty. **15**But my brothers are as undependable as intermittent streams, as the streams that overflow

Fidelity—

Pr 11:13 A gossip betrays a confidence, but a trustworthy man keeps a secret.

Not wearing out one's welcome—

Pr 25:17 Seldom set foot in your neighbor's house—too much of you, and he will hate you.

Mutual understanding—

Am 3:3 Do two walk together unless they have agreed to do so?

See Friends.

Trials growing out of—

Dt 13:6 If your very own brother, or your son or daughter, or the wife you love, or your closest friend secretly entices you, saying, "Let us go and worship other gods" (gods that neither you nor your fathers have known, **7**gods of the peoples around you, whether near or far, from one end of the land to the other), **8**do not yield to him or listen to him. Show him no pity. Do not spare him or shield him. **9**You must certainly put him to death. Your hand must be the first in putting him to death, and then the hands of all the people.

Pr 22:24 Do not make friends with a hot-tempered man, do not associate with one easily angered, **25**or you may learn his ways and get yourself ensnared.

Faithfulness in—

Ps 35:13 Yet when they were ill, I put on sackcloth and humbled myself with fasting. When my prayers returned to me unanswered, **14**I went about mourning as though for my friend or brother. I bowed my head in grief as though weeping for my mother.

Pr 17:9 He who covers over an offense promotes love, but whoever repeats the matter separates close friends.

Pr 17:17 A friend loves at all times, and a brother is born for adversity.

Pr 27:6 Wounds from a friend can be trusted, but an enemy multiplies kisses.

Pr 27:9 Perfume and incense bring joy to the heart, and the pleasantness of one's friend springs from his earnest counsel.

10Do not forsake your friend and the friend of your father, and do not go to your brother's house when disaster strikes you—better a neighbor nearby than a brother far away.

Pr 27:14 If a man loudly blesses his neighbor early in the morning, it will be taken as a curse.

Pr 27:17 As iron sharpens iron, so one man sharpens another.

Pr 27:19 As water reflects a face, so a man's heart reflects the man.

Value of—

Ecc 4:9 Two are better than one, because they have a good return for their work: **10**If one falls down, his friend can help him up. But pity the man who falls and has no one to help him up! **11**Also, if two lie down together, they will keep warm. But how can one keep warm alone? **12**Though one may be overpowered, two can defend themselves. A cord of three strands is not quickly broken.

Instances of:

Abraham and Lot (Ge 14:14-16). Ruth and Naomi (Ru 1:16-17). David and Jonathan (1Sa 18:1-4; 20; 23:16-18; 2Sa 1:17-27; 9:1-13). David and Abiathar (1Sa 22:23). David and Mephibosheth (2Sa 9). David and Nahash (2Sa 10:2). David and Ittai (2Sa 15:19-22). David and Hushai (2Sa 15:32-37; 16; 17:1-22). David and Hiram (1Ki 5:1). Joram and Ahaziah (2Ki 8:28-29; 9:16). Jehu and Jehonadab (2Ki 10:15-27). Job and his three friends (Job 2:11-13). Daniel and his three companions (Da 2:49).

The Marys, and Joseph of Arimathea, for Jesus (Mt 27:55-61; 28:1-8; Lk 24:10; Jn 20:11-18). Mary, Martha, and Lazarus, and Jesus (Lk 10:38-42; Jn 11:1-46). Luke and Theophilus (Ac 1:1). Paul and his nephew (Ac 23:16). Paul, Priscilla, and Aquila (Ro 16:3-4). Paul, Timothy, and Epaphroditus (Php 2:19-20,22,25).

FRINGES *See Tassel(s).*

FROGS [7630, *1005*]. Plague of (Ex 8:2-14; Ps 78:45; 105:30).

Symbolic: (Rev 16:13).

FRONTLETS A leather band worn on the forehead (Ex 13:6-16; Dt 6:1-8; 11:18).

See Phylactery.

FROST [4095, 7885, 7943]. Appeared in winter on the high elevations in Bible lands (Job 37:10; 38:29).

FROWARDNESS *See Disobedience to God.*

FRUGALITY

General:

Diligent—

Pr 12:27 The lazy man does not roast his game, but the diligent man prizes his possessions.

Good—

Pr 13:22 A good man leaves an inheritance for his children's children, but a sinner's wealth is stored up for the righteous.

Wise—

Pr 21:17 He who loves pleasure will become poor; whoever loves wine and oil will never be rich.

Pr 21:20 In the house of the wise are stores of choice food and oil, but a foolish man devours all he has.

Prudent—

Pr 22:3 A prudent man sees danger and takes refuge, but the simple keep going and suffer for it.

Industrious—

Eph 4:28 He who has been stealing must steal no longer, but must work, doing something useful with his own hands, that he may have something to share with those in need.

The mark of a virtuous woman—

Pr 31:27 She watches over the affairs of her household and does not eat the bread of idleness.

Admonition regarding—

Pr 23:20 Do not join those who drink too much wine or gorge themselves on meat, [21]for drunkards and gluttons become poor, and drowsiness clothes them in rags.

Pretense to cover greed—

Mk 14:4 Some of those present were saying indignantly to one another, "Why this waste of perfume? [5]It could have been sold for more than a year's wages and the money given to the poor." And they rebuked her harshly.

Commanded by Jesus (Jn 6:12).

Instances of:

The provisions made by the Egyptians against famine (Ge 41:48-54), the gathering of manna (Ex 16:17-18,22-24)

The gathering of bread and fish after the feeding of the multitudes—

Mt 14:20 They all ate and were satisfied, and the disciples picked up twelve basketfuls of broken pieces that were left over.

Mt 15:37 They all ate and were satisfied. Afterward the disciples picked up seven basketfuls of broken pieces that were left over.

See Extravagance; Industry.

FRUIT TREES

NIV+ See FRUITS

Planting and first harvest (Lev 19:23-25). Care for (Dt 20:19-20). In Ezekiel's vision, evergreen and with healing properties (Eze 47:12). *See Tree.*

FRUITS [*3330, 7238, 7262, 7811, 9482, 10004, *1163, 2843, 2844*].

NIV+ FRUIT, FIRSTFRUITS, FRUITAGE, FRUITFUL, FRUITFULNESS, FRUITION, FRUITLESS

Natural:

Created—

Ge 1:11 Then God said, "Let the land produce vegetation: seed-bearing plants and trees on the land that bear fruit with seed in it, according to their various kinds." And it was so. [12]The land produced vegetation: plants bearing seed according to their kinds and trees bearing fruit with seed in it according to their kinds. And God saw that it was good.

Ge 1:27 So God created man in his own image, in the image of God he created him; male and female he created them.

[28]God blessed them and said to them, "Be fruitful and increase in number; fill the earth and subdue it. Rule over the fish of the sea and the birds of the air and over every living creature that moves on the ground."

[29]Then God said, "I give you every seed-bearing plant on the face of the whole earth and every tree that has fruit with seed in it. They will be yours for food.

See the list of various fruit-producing trees at Tree.

Spiritual: *See Righteousness, Fruits of; Sin, Fruits of; Holy Spirit, Fruit of.*

FRYING PAN *See Pan(s).*

FUEL [433, 836+928+1896, 836+1198+8596, 836+1277, 1277, 4409]. Wood, charcoal, dried grass, and even the dung of animals and humans was used for fuel (Eze 4:12,15; Mt 6:30; Jn 18:18).

FUGITIVES [1371, 5610, 5615, 5674, 7127, 7128, 7129].

NIV+ FUGITIVE

From Servitude:

Not to be returned (Dt 23:15-16).

From Justice:

Moses (Ex 2:15), Absalom (2Sa 13:34-38).

From the Avenger of Blood:

See Avenger of Blood; Cities of Refuge.

From the Wrath of the King:

David (1Sa 21:10), Jeroboam (1Ki 11:40), Joseph, to Egypt (Mt 2:13-15).

Instances of:

From slavery, Shimei's servants (1Ki 2:39), Onesimus (Phm 10).

See Exodus.

FULLER NIV "launderer"; one who cleans or dyes cloth or garments. The word is also used at times for one who thickens and shrinks newly shorn wool and newly woven cloth after cleansing it of natural oils. He may also have traded in textiles (Mal 3:2; Mk 9:3). *See Soap.*

FULLER'S FIELD *See Washerman's Field.*

FULLNESS OF TIME The time appointed when God's purposes for men and history for a particular event have been fulfilled (Mk 1:15; Gal 4:4; Eph 1:10; 1Ti 2:6; Tit 1:3; Heb 9:26).

FUNERAL [5301, 5386]. The ceremonies used in disposing of a dead human body. In Palestine the body was buried within a few hours after death in a tomb or cave. The body was washed, anointed with spices, and wrapped in cloths (Jn 12:7; 19:39-40). Refusal of proper burial was utter disgrace (Jer 22:19).

FURLONG *See Stadia.*

FURNACE [3901, 3929, 6612, 9486, 10086, *2825*]. Furnaces of the biblical period were made of brick or stone and were designed for different purposes, from small domestic types to large commercial smelters as those at Ezion Geber.

Figurative:

Of affliction (Dt 4:20; 1Ki 8:51; Ps 12:6; Isa 48:10; Jer 11:4). Of the Lord who refines the heart (Pr 17:3). Of lust (Hos 7:4). Of hell (Mal 4:1; Mt 13:42,50; Rev 9:2).

Uses of:

For refining gold (Pr 17:3), silver (Eze 22:22; Mal 3:3). For melting lead and tin (Eze 22:20). For capital punishment, Shadrach, Meshach, and Abednego cast into by Nebuchadnezzar (Da 3:6-26).

FURNITURE The principle reference to furniture in the Bible concerns the articles in the tabernacle and temple. Common people had little furniture; kings had beds (Dt 3:11) and tables (Jdg 1:7).

FUTURE [294, 339, 340, 344, 344+3427, 995, 2118+ 4537+8611, 3427+4737, 3427+8041, 4737, 4946+8158, 6961, 10021+10180, *608+785*, *3516*, *4460+4780*].

See Immortality; Eschatology.

FUTURE PUNISHMENT *See Punishment, Eternal.*

G

GAAL [1720] (*loathing*). Son of Ebed, who led the men of Shechem in a revolt against Abimelech, the son of Gideon (Jdg 9:26-41).

GAASH [1724] (*rumble, quake*). A foothill of Mt. Ephraim. Joshua's inheritance embraced (Jos 24:30). Joshua buried on the north side of (Jos 24:30; Jdg 2:9). Brooks of (2Sa 23:30).

GABA *See Geba.*

GABBAI [1480] (*collector*). A chief of Benjamin (Ne 11:8).

GABBATHA [*1119*] (possibly *height, ridge*). The place called "the Stone Pavement" (Jn 19:13), where Jesus was tried before Pilate.

GABRIEL [1508, *1120*] (*[strong] man of God [El]*). A messenger of God. Appeared to Daniel (Da 8:16; 9:21), to Zechariah (Lk 1:11-19), to Mary (Lk 1:26-29).

GAD, GADITES [1201+1532, 1201+1514, 1514, 1532, *1122*] (*fortune*).
1. Jacob's seventh son (Ge 30:11; 35:26; Ex 1:4). Children of (Ge 46:16; Nu 26:15-18; 1Ch 5:11). Prophecy concerning (Ge 49:19).
2. A tribe of Israel. Blessed by Moses (Dt 33:20). Enumeration of, at Sinai (Nu 1:14,24-25), in the plains of Moab (Nu 26:15-18), in the reign of Jotham (1Ch 5:11-17). Place of, in camp and march (Nu 2:10,14,16). Wealth of, in cattle, and spoils (Nu 32:1; Jos 22:8). Petition for their portion of land E of the Jordan (Nu 32:1-5; Dt 3:12,16-17; 29:8). Boundaries of territory (Jos 13:24-28; 1Ch 5:11). Aid in the conquest of the region W of the Jordan (Nu 32:16-32; Jos 4:12-13; 22:1-8). Erect a monument to signify the unity of the tribes E of the Jordan with the tribes W of the river (Jos 22:10-14).
Disaffected toward Saul as king and joined the faction under David in the wilderness of Hebron (1Ch 12:8-15,37-38). Join the Reubenites in the war against the Hagrites (1Ch 5:10,18-22). Smitten by the king of Syria (2Ki 10:32-33). Carried into captivity to Assyria (1Ch 5:26). Land of, occupied by the Ammonites, after the tribe is carried into captivity (Jer 49:1). Reallotment of territory to, by Ezekiel (Eze 48:27,29).
3. A prophet of David (2Sa 24:11). Requests David leave Adullam (1Sa 22:5). Bears the divine message to David offering choice between three evils, for his presumption in numbering Israel (2Sa 24:11-14; 1Ch 21:9-13). Requests David build an altar on threshing floor of Araunah (2Sa 24:18-19; 1Ch 21:18-19). Assists David in organizing temple service (2Ch 29:25). Writings of (1Ch 29:29).

GADARENES [*1123*]. The region around the city of Gadara is six miles SE of the S end of the Sea of Galilee (Mt 8:28). Mark and Luke identify the region by the capital city Gerasa, located about thirty-five miles southeast of the Sea (Mk 5:1; Lk 8:26 and ftns). *See Gerasenes.*

GADDAH *See Hazar Gaddah.*

GADDI [1534] (*my fortune*). A chief of Manasseh. One of the twelve spies who explored Canaan (Nu 13:11).

GADDIEL [1535] (*God [El] is my fortune* BDB; *[pagan god] Gad is [my] god* KB). A chief of Zebulun. One of the twelve spies (Nu 13:10).

GADER *See Beth Gader.*

GADI [1533] (*my fortune*). Father of Menahem, a king of Israel (2Ki 15:14-20).

GAHAM [1626] (*burning brightly*). A son of Nahor by his concubine Reumah (Ge 22:24).

GAHAR, GAHER [1627] (*[born in the] year of little rain*). One of the temple servants (Ezr 2:47; Ne 7:49).

GAIUS [*1127*].
1. A Macedonian and companion of Paul. Seized at Ephesus (Ac 19:29).
2. A man of Derbe. Accompanied Paul from Macedonia (Ac 20:4).
3. A Corinthian, whom Paul baptized (Ro 16:23; 1Co 1:14).
4. Man to whom 3 John was addressed (3Jn 1).

GALAL [1674] (possibly *tortoise* IDB; *roll away* KB).
1. A Levite (1Ch 9:15).
2. Son of Jeduthun (1Ch 9:16; Ne 11:17).

GALATIA [*1130, 1131*].
NIV+ GALATIAN, GALATIANS
A province of Asia Minor. Its churches visited by Paul (Ac 16:6; 18:23). Collection taken in, for Christians at Jerusalem (1Co 16:1). Peter's address to (1Pe 1:1). Churches in (Gal 1:1-2). *See Galatians, Epistle to the.*

GALATIANS, EPISTLE TO THE

Author: The apostle Paul
Date:
If the letter was addressed to churches located in north-central Asia Minor (Pessinus, Ancyra and Tavium), Galatians was written between A.D. 53 and 57.
If the letter was addressed to churches in the southern area of the Roman province of Galatia (Antioch, Iconium, Lystra and Derbe), Galatians was written A.D. 48 or 49.
Outline:
I. Introduction (1:1-9).
  A. Salutation (1:1-5).
  B. Denunciation (1:6-9).
II. Personal: Authentication of the Apostle of Liberty and Faith (1:10-2:10).
  A. Paul's Gospel Was Received by Special Revelation (1:10-12).
  B. Paul's Gospel Was Independent of the Jerusalem Apostles and the Judean Churches (1:13-2:21).
  1. Evidenced by his early activities as a Christian (1:13-17).
  2. Evidenced by his first post-Christian visit to Jerusalem (1:18-24).
  3. Evidenced by his visit to Jerusalem fourteen years later (2:1-10).
  4. Evidenced by his rebuke of Peter at Antioch (2:11-21).
III. Doctrinal: Justification of the Doctrine of Liberty and Faith (chs. 3-4).
  A. The Galatians' Experience of the Gospel (3:1-5).
  B. The Experience of Abraham (3:6-9).

C. The Curse of the Law (3:10-14).
D. The Priority of the Promise (3:15-18).
E. The Purpose of the Law (3:19-25).
F. Sons, Not Slaves (3:26-4:11).
G. Appeal to Enter into Freedom from Law (4:12-20).
H. The Allegory of Hagar and Sarah (4:21-31).
IV. Practical: Practice of the Life of Liberty and Faith (5:1-6:10).
  A. Exhortation to Freedom (5:1-12).
  B. Life by the Spirit, Not by the Flesh (5:13-26).
  C. Call for Mutual Help (6:1-10).
V. Conclusion (6:11-18).

GALBANUM [2697]. A fragrant gum used in the sacred oil (Ex 30:34).

GALEED [1681] (*heap of [stones that are a] witness*). The name given by Jacob to the heap of stones which he and Laban raised as a memorial of their compact (Ge 31:47-48).

GALILEAN [*1134*].
NIV+ GALILEE, GALILEANS
A native of Galilee (Mt 26:69; Jn 4:45; Ac 1:11; 5:37).

GALILEE [824+1665, 1665, *1133, 1134*] (*ring, circle,* hence *region*).
NIV+ GALILEAN, GALILEANS, TIBERIAS
The northern district of Israel. A city of refuge in (Jos 20:7; 21:32; 1Ch 6:76). Cities in, given to Hiram (1Ki 9:11-12). Taken by king of Assyria (2Ki 15:29). Prophecy concerning (Isa 9:1; Mt 4:15). Called Galilee of the nations (Isa 9:1). Herod, tetrarch of (Mk 6:21; Lk 3:1; 23:6-7). Jesus resides in (Mt 17:22; 19:1; Jn 7:1,9). Teaching and miracles of Jesus in (Mt 4:23,25; 15:29-31; Mk 1:14,28,39; 3:7; Lk 4:14,44; 5:17; 23:5; Jn 1:43; 4:3,43-45; Ac 10:37). People of, receive Jesus (Jn 4:45,53). Disciples were chiefly from (Ac 1:11; 2:7). Women from, ministered to Jesus (Mt 27:55-56; Mk 15:41; Lk 23:49,55). Jesus appeared to his disciples in, after his resurrection (Mt 26:32; 28:7,10,16-17; Mk 14:28; 16:7; Jn 21).
Routes from, to Judea (Jdg 21:19; Jn 4:3-5). Dialect of (Mk 14:70). Called Gennesaret (Mt 14:34; Mk 6:53). Churches in (Ac 9:31).

GALILEE, SEA OF Also called the Lake of Gennesaret (Lk 5:1), the Sea of Kinnereth (Nu 34:11, ftn; Dt 3:17), and the Sea of Tiberias, because Herod's capital was on its shores (Jn 6:1; 21:1). The lake is thirteen miles long and eight miles wide, filled with fresh and clear water, and full of fish. Because it was located in a pocket in the hills, it was subject to sudden violent storms. *See Gennesaret, 2; Kinnereth, 3; Tiberias.*

GALL [4360, 5354, 8032, *5958*].
1. The secretion of the human gall bladder (Job 16:13).
2. The poison of serpents (Job 20:14).
3. A bitter and poisonous herb (Jer 9:15; Hos 10:4; Am 6:12), perhaps used to deaden pain (Mt 27:34).
Figurative of the bitter end of immorality (Pr 5:4).

GALLERY [916].
NIV+ GALLERIES
A balcony of the temple in Ezekiel's vision (Eze 41:16; 42:3,5-6).

GALLEY [639]. *See Ship.*

GALLIM [1668] (*heaps*). A town of Benjamin (Isa 10:30; 1Sa 25:44).

GALLIO [*1136*]. Proconsul of Achaia. Dismisses complaint of Jews against Paul (Ac 18:12-17).

GALLON A unit of liquid measure. Six gallons is equal to the biblical measure known as a bath. Four quarts (one gallon), which is one sixth of a bath, is known as a hin. John records that the water jars used to hold water for ceremonial washing would hold twenty to thirty gallons of water; Jesus used this water to replenish the wine supply at the marriage celebration at Cana in Galilee (Jn 2:6).

GALLOWS [6770]. Used for execution of criminals (Est 2:23; 5:14; 6:4; 7:9-10; 9:13,25). Reproach of being hanged upon (Gal 3:13).
See Punishment.

GAMALIEL [1697, *1137*] (*recompense of God [El]*).
1. Chief of tribe of Manasseh (Nu 1:10; 2:20; 10:23).
2. An eminent Pharisee and teacher of the law, the teacher of Paul (Ac 22:3). He was broadminded and tolerant toward early Christians (Ac 5:34-39).

GAMBLING *See Betting; Lot, The.*

GAMES [76]. Footraces (1Co 9:24,26; Gal 2:2; Php 2:16; Heb 12:1). Gladiatorial (1Co 4:9; 9:26; 15:32; 2Ti 4:7).
Figurative:
Of the Christian life (1Co 9:24,26; Gal 5:7; Php 2:16; 3:14; Heb 12:1). Of a successful ministry (Gal 2:2; Php 2:16). Fighting wild beasts, of spiritual conflict (1Co 4:9; 9:26; 15:32; 2Ti 4:7).

GAMMAD, GAMMADIM [1689]. (probably *valiant men*). Men of in the watchtowers of Tyre (Eze 27:11).

GAMUL [1690] (*weaned*).
NIV+ BETH GAMUL
The head of the twenty-second course of priests (1Ch 24:17).

GANGRENE [*1121*]. Perhaps in a running or festering sore (Ex 9:9-10; Lev 21:20, 22:22; Dt 28:27; Job 7:5). False teaching spreads like gangrene (2Ti 2:17).

GANNIM *See En Gannim.*

GARDEN [1703, 1708, 5750, *3057, 3303*].
NIV+ GARDENER, GARDENS
A cultivated piece of ground planted with flowers, vegetables, shrubs, or trees, fenced with a mud or stone wall (Pr 24:31) or with thorny hedges (Isa 5:5). Gardens were sometimes used for burial places (Ge 23:17; 2Ki 21:18,26; Jn 19:41). The future state of the saved is figuratively represented by a garden (Rev 22:1-5).

GARDENER [*1177, 3058*]. *See Occupations and Professions.*

GAREB [1735, 1736] (*scabby*).
1. One of David's warriors (2Sa 23:38; 1Ch 11:40).
2. A hill near Jerusalem (Jer 31:39).

GARLAND [4292]. A crown or wreath for the head; figurative of the rewards of wisdom (Pr 1:9; 4:9). *See Crown.*

GARLIC [8770]. (Nu 11:5).

GARMENT [*168, 955, 4053, 4189, 4230, 4503, 6041, 7389, 8515, 8529, *2668*, *4984*].

NIV+ GARMENTS, UNDERGARMENT, UNDERGARMENTS

Of righteousness (Isa 61:10; Mt 22:11; 2Co 5:3; Rev 3:18; 7:14; 16:15; 19:8). *See Dress; Robe.*

GARMITE [1753] (*bone, bony*). A title applied to Keilah (1Ch 4:19).

GARNER *See Barn; Granary; Storehouse.*

GARRISON [5163, 5907].

NIV+ GARRISONS

A fortress manned by soldiers, used chiefly for the occupation of a conquered country (1Sa 10:5; 13:3; 14:1,6; 2Sa 8:6,14). *See Fort.*

GASHMU *See Geshem.*

GATAM [1725]. Grandson of Esau (Ge 36:11,16; 1Ch 1:36).

GATE, INSPECTION Name of one of the gates of Jerusalem (Ne 3:31).

GATEKEEPERS [8788, 10777].

NIV+ See GATES

Guards at the city gates, the doors of the king's palace, and doors of the temple (1Ch 9:17-32; 2Ch 34:13; 35:15). Lodged round about the temple in order to be present for opening the doors (1Ch 9:27). One-third were gatekeepers of the temple (2Ch 23:4), one-third were gatekeepers of the king's house (2Ch 23:5), one-third were gatekeepers of the gate of the foundation (2Ch 23:5). They served, also, as gatekeepers of the gates of the walls (Ne 12:25). They served in twenty-four courses (1Ch 26:13-19). Their posts were determined by lot (1Ch 24:31; 26:13-19).

GATES [964, 1378, 1946, 4981, 7339, 9133, *2598*, *4783*, *4784*].

NIV+ GATE, GATEKEEPERS, GATEPOST, GATEPOSTS, GATEWAY, GATEWAYS

Of cities (Dt 3:5; Jos 6:26; 1Sa 23:7; 2Sa 18:24; 2Ch 8:5). Made of iron (Ac 12:10), wood (Ne 1:3), bronze (Ps 107:16; Isa 45:2). Double doors (Isa 45:1; Eze 41:24).

The open square of, a place for idlers (Ge 19:1; 1Sa 4:18; Ps 69:12; Pr 1:21; Jer 17:19-20). Religious services held at (Ac 14:13). The law read at (Ne 8). Place for the transaction of public business, announcement of legal transactions (Ge 23:10,16), conferences on public affairs (Ge 34:20), holding courts of justice (Dt 16:18; 21:19; 22:15; Jos 20:4; Ru 4:1; 2Sa 15:2; Pr 22:22; Zec 8:16). Place for public concourse (Ge 23:10; Pr 1:21; 8:3; Jer 14:2; 22:2). Thrones of kings at (1Ki 22:10; 2Ch 18:9; Jer 38:7; 39:3). Punishment of criminals outside of (Dt 17:5; Jer 20:2; Ac 7:58; Heb 13:12). Closed at night (Jos 2:5,7), on the Sabbath (Ne 13:19). Guards at (2Ki 7:17; Ne 13:19, 22). Jails made in the towers of (Jer 20:2). Bodies of criminals exposed to view at (Jos 8:2-9; 2Ki 10:8).

Figurative:

Of the people of a city (Isa 3:26). Of the gospel (Isa 60:11). Of the powers of hell (Mt 16:18). Of death (Job 38:17; Ps 9:13; Isa 38:10). Of the grave (Isa 38:10). Of righteousness (Ps 118:19). Of salvation (Ge 28:17; Ps 24:7; 118:19-20; Isa 26:2). Narrow gate, of the way to life (Mt 7:13-14).

Symbolic: (Rev 21:12-13,21,25).

See Jerusalem, Gates of.

GATH [1781, 1785] (*winepress*).

NIV+ GATH HEPHER, GATH RIMMON, MORESHETH GATH

One of the five chief cities of the Philistines (Jos 13:3; 1Sa 6:17; Am 6:2; Mic 1:10). Anakites, a race of giants, inhabitants of (Jos 11:22). Goliath dwelt in (1Sa 17:4; 1Ch 20:5-8). Obed-Edom belonged to (2Sa 6:10). The ark taken to (1Sa 5:8). Inhabitants of, called Gittites (Jos 13:3). David takes refuge at (1Sa 21:10-15; 27:2-7). Band of Gittites, attached to David (2Sa 15:18-22). Taken by David (1Ch 18:1). Shimei's servants escape to (1Ki 2:39-41). Fortified by Rehoboam (2Ch 11:8). Taken by Hazael (2Ki 12:17). Recovered by Jehoash (2Ki 13:25). Besieged by Uzziah (2Ch 26:6). Called Metheg Ammah (2Sa 8:1).

GATH HEPHER, GATH-HEPHER [1783]
(*winepress water pit*).

NIV+ GATH, HEPHER

A town on the border of Zebulun (Jos 19:12-13) and birthplace of Jonah the prophet (2Ki 14:25).

GATH RIMMON, GATH-RIMMON [1784]
(*winepress of pomegranate*).

NIV+ GATH, RIMMON

1. A city of Dan on the Philistine plain (Jos 19:45).
2. A town of Manasseh, W of Jordan, assigned to Levites (Jos 21:25).

GAULANITIS A province NE of the Sea of Galilee, ruled by Herod Antipas. It encompassed the region of OT Golan. *See Golan.*

GAZA [6445, 6484, *1124*] (*strong*).

1. A city of the Philistines (Jos 13:3; Jer 25:20). One of the border cities of the Canaanites (Ge 10:19). A city of the Avvim and Anakim (Dt 2:23; Jos 11:22). Allotted to Judah (Jos 15:47; Jdg 1:18). A temple of Dagon, situated at (Jdg 16:23). Samson dies at (Jdg 16:21-31). On the western boundary of the kingdom of Israel in the time of Solomon (1Ki 4:24). Smitten by Pharaoh (Jer 47:1). Prophecies relating to (Am 1:6-7; Zep 2:4; Zec 9:5). Desert of (Ac 8:26-39).
2. A city of Ephraim (Jdg 6:4; 1Ch 7:28).

GAZATHITES, GAZITES NIV "[people of] Gaza" (Jos 13:3; Jdg 16:2). *See Gaza, 1.*

GAZELLE [7373, 7374, 7383, 7386].

NIV+ GAZELLES

See Animals.

GAZER *See Gezer.*

GAZEZ [1606] (possibly *sheep shearer* IDB; possibly *one born at the time of shearing* KB). The name of the son and of the grandson of Ephah (1Ch 2:46).

GAZZAM [1613] (*some kind of bird or insect*). One of the temple servants (Ezr 2:48; Ne 7:51).

GE HARASHIM [1629]. It may be the broad valley between Lod and Ono (1Ch 4:14, ftn; Ne 11:35).

GEBA [1494] (*hill*). A town in the territory of Benjamin (Jos 18:24; Ezr 2:26; Ne 7:30), assigned to the Levites (Jos 21:17). Jonathan defeated the Philistines at Geba (1Sa 13:3). Asa fortified the city (1Ki 15:22), and in Hezekiah's time it was the northern most city of Judah (2Ki 23:8). Men from Geba returned after the Exile (Ezr 2:26).

GEBAL [1488, 1489, 1490] (possibly *border* BDB; *hill* KB).

NIV+ GEBALITES

1. A seaport of Phoenicia N of Sidon, also known as Byblos. Modern Jebeil, twenty-five miles N of Beirut. The land of the Gebalites is mentioned (Jos 13:5-6). The town was renowned for its expert stonemasons (1Ki 5:17-18) and for shipbuilding (Eze 27:9).

2. A land between the Dead Sea and Petra (Ps 83:6-8).

GEBALITES [1490].

NIV+ GEBAL

The inhabitants of Gebal or Byblos (Jos 13:5). *See Gebal.*

GEBER [1506] (*[strong young] man*).

NIV+ BEN-GEBER, EZION GEBER

1. One of Solomon's suppliers in Ramoth Gilead (1Ki 4:13). Called Ben-Geber.

2. The son of Uri (1Ki 4:19).

GEBIM [1481] (*ditches*). A place near Anathoth (Isa 10:31).

GECKO [652]. (Lev 11:30). *See Animals, Names of.*

GEDALIAH [1545, 1546] (*great is Yahweh*).

NIV+ GEDALIAH'S

1. Governor appointed by Nebuchadnezzar after carrying the Israelites into captivity (2Ki 25:22-24). Jeremiah committed to the care of (Jer 39:14; 40:5-6). Warned of the conspiracy of Ishmael by Johanan and the captains of his army (Jer 40:13-16). Slain by Ishmael (2Ki 25:25-26; Jer 41:1-10).

2. A musician (1Ch 25:3,9).

3. A priest, who divorced his Gentile wife after the Exile (Ezr 10:18).

4. Ancestor of Zephaniah (Zep 1:1).

5. A prince who caused imprisonment of Jeremiah (Jer 38:1).

GEDEON *See Gideon.*

GEDER [1554] (*wall [of stones]*).

NIV+ GEDERITE

An ancient city of Canaan (Jos 12:13). Possibly identical with Gedor, 2 or 3.

GEDERAH [1557] (*stone pen, sheep corral*).

NIV+ GEDERATHITE

Located between the valleys of Sorek and Aijalon in the hills of Judah (Jos 15:36). Often identified as modern Jedirah, though others identify it with Khirbet Judraya.

GEDEROTH [1558] (*stone pens, sheep corrals*). A city in the plain of Judah (Jos 15:41; 2Ch 28:18).

GEDEROTHAIM [1562] (*two stone pens, two sheep corrals*). A city in the plain of Judah (Jos 15:36).

GEDI *See En Gedi.*

GEDOR [1529, 1530] (*wall* BDB; *pock-marked* KB).

1. A city in mountains of Judah (Jos 15:58).

2. The town of Jeroham (1Ch 12:7). Possibly identical with Geder. *See Geder.*

3. Valley of, taken by Simeonites (1Ch 4:39). *See Geder.*

4. An ancestor of Saul (1Ch 8:31; 9:37).

5. Either a place or a person, authorities disagree (1Ch 4:4,18).

GEHAZI [1634] (possibly *valley of vision*). The servant of Elisha (2Ki 4:8-37; 5:1-27; 8:4-6). He was punished for greed by becoming a leper.

GEHENNA (*valley of Hinnom*). *See Ben Hinnom; Hell.*

GELILOTH [1667] (*region*). A place mentioned (Jos 18:17), as marking the boundary of Benjamin. Gilgal is substituted (Jos 15:7).

GEMALLI [1696] (*my reward* KB). Father of Ammiel, and one of the twelve spies (Nu 13:12).

GEMARIAH [1701, 1702] (*Yahweh has accomplished*).

1. Son of Shaphan the scribe and friend of Jeremiah (Jer 36:10-25).

2. A son of Hilkiah, sent as ambassador to Nebuchadnezzar (Jer 29:3).

GENEALOGY [3509, 3510, 9352, *37, 1157, 1161*] (*account of one's descent*).

NIV+ GENEALOGICAL, GENEALOGIES

(Nu 1:18; 2Ch 12:15; Ezr 2:59; Ne 7:5; Heb 7:3). Of no spiritual significance (Mt 3:9; 1Ti 1:4; Tit 3:9).

From Adam to Noah (Ge 4:16-22; 5; 1Ch 1:1-4; Lk 3:36-38), to Abraham (Ge 11:10-32; 1Ch 1:4-27; Lk 3:34-38), to Jesus (Mt 1:1-16; Lk 3:23-38). Of the descendants of Noah (Ge 10), of Nahor (Ge 22:20-24), of Abraham, by his wife Keturah (Ge 25:1-4; 1Ch 1:32-33), of Ishmael (Ge 25:12-16; 1Ch 1:28-31), of Esau (Ge 36; 1Ch 1:35-54), of Jacob (Ge 35:23-26; Ex 1:5; 6:14-27; Nu 26; 1Ch 2-9), of Perez to David (Ru 4:18-22). Of the Jews who returned from the Captivity (Ezr 7:1-5; 8:1-15; Ne 7; 11:12). Of Joseph (Mt 1; Lk 3:23-38).

GENEALOGY OF JESUS CHRIST

Two genealogies are given in the NT:

(Mt 1:1-17; Lk 3:23-28). Matthew traces the descent of Jesus from Abraham and David, and divides it into three sets of fourteen generations. He omits three generations after Joram, namely Ahaziah, Joash, and Amaziah (1Ch 3:11-12). Contrary to Hebrew practice, he names five women: Tamar, Rahab, Ruth, Bathsheba, and Mary. The sense of "became the father of" in Hebrew genealogies is not exact; it indicated immediate or remote descent, an adoptive relation, or legal heirship. Luke's genealogy moves from Jesus to Adam, agreeing with the accounts in 1 Chronicles between Abraham and Adam (1Ch 1:1-7,24-28). From David to Abraham he agrees with Matthew; from Jesus to David he differs from Matthew. Perhaps Matthew gives the line of legal heirship, while Luke gives the line of physical descent.

GENERAL LETTERS

The seven letters following Hebrews—James; 1 and 2 Peter; 1, 2, and 3 John and Jude—have often been designated as the General Letters. This term goes back to the early church historian Eusebius (c. A.D. 265-340), who in his *Ecclesiastical History* (2.23-25) first referred to these seven letters as Catholic Letters, using the word "catholic" to mean "universal."

The letters so designated may be said to be, for the most part, addressed to general audiences rather than to specific persons or localized groups. 2 and 3 John, the two letters that seem most obviously addressed to individuals, have long been viewed as appendages of 1 John, which is clearly general in its address. However, when compared with Paul's letters, all these letters except 3 John are clearly general in nature. By contrast, Paul addresses his letters to such recipients as the saints at Philippi, or the churches of Galatia, or Timothy or Titus.

As Eusebius noted long ago, one interesting fact connected with the General Letters is that most of them were at one time among the disputed books of the NT. James, 2 Peter, 2 John, 3 John, and Jude were all questioned extensively before being admitted to the canon of Scripture.

GENERALS [5941]. Roman military leaders (Rev 6:15; 19:18). *See Captain.*

GENERATION [1887, 8055, 8067, 9000, 10183, 1155].

NIV+ GENERATIONS

A period of time (Ex 3:15; Da 4:3; Lk 1:50), or all the people living in a given period (Jdg 2:10; Mt 11:16), or a class of people having a certain quality (Dt 32:5,20; Mt 8:38), or a company gathered together (Ps 49:19).

GENERATION, EVIL (Dt 32:5; Pr 30:12; Mt 3:7; 12:39,45; Lk 9:41; Ac 2:40).

GENEROSITY [*2858, 605, 2330, 2331].

NIV+ GENEROUS, GENEROUSLY

See Beneficence; Giving; Liberality.

GENESIS [1414] (*beginning*).

Author: Historically, Jews and Christians alike have held that Moses was the author/compiler of the first five books of the OT.

Date: c. 1446 to 1406

Outlines:

Literary Outline:
I. Introduction (1:1-2:3).
II. Body (2:4-50:26).
  A. "The account of the heavens and the earth" (2:4-4:26).
  B. "The written account of Adam's line" (5:1-6:8).
  C. "The account of Noah" (6:9-9:29).
  D. "The account of Shem, Ham and Japheth" (10:1-11:9).
  E. "The account of Shem" (1:10-26).
  F. "The account of Terah" (11:217-25:11).
  G. "The account of Abraham's son Ishmael" (25:12-18).
  H. "The account of Abraham's son Isaac" (25:19-35:29).
  I. "The account of Esau" (36:1-37:1).
  J. "The account of Jacob" (37:2-50:26).

Thematic Outline:
I. Primeval History (1:1-11:26).
  A. Creation (1:1-2:3).
    1. Introduction (1:1-2).
    2. Body (1:3-31).
    3. Conclusion (2:1-3).
  B. Adam and Eve in Eden (2:4-25).
  C. The Fall and Its Consequences (3:1-24).
  D. The Rapid "Progress" of Sin (4:1-16).
  E. Two Genealogies (4:17-5:32).
    1. The genealogy of pride (4:17-24).
    2. The genealogy of death (4:25-5:32).
  F. The Extent of Sin before the Flood (6:1-8).
  G. The Great Flood (6:9-9:29).
    1. Preparing for the Flood (6:9-7:10).
    2. Judgment and redemption (7:11-8:19).

    a. The rising of the waters (7:11-24).
    b. The receding of the waters (8:1-19).
    3. The flood's aftermath (8:20-9:29).
    a. A new promise (8:20-22).
    b. New ordinances (9:1-7).
    c. A new relationship (9:8-17).
    d. A new temptation (9:18-23).
    e. A final word (9:24-29).
  H. The Spread of the Nations (10:1-11:26).
    1. The diffusion of nations (10:1-32).
    2. The confusion of tongues (11:1-9).
    3. The first Semitic genealogy (11:10-26).
II. Patriarchal History (11:27-50:26).
  A. The Life of Abraham (11:27-25:11).
    1. Abraham's background (11:27-32).
    2. Abraham's land (12:1-14:24).
    3. Abraham's people (15:1-24:67).
    4. Abraham's last days (25:1-11).
  B. The Descendants of Ishmael (25:2-18).
  C. The Life of Jacob (25:19-35:29).
    1. Jacob at home (25:19-27:46).
    2. Jacob abroad (28:1-30:43).
    3. Jacob at home again (31:1-35:29).
  D. The Descendants of Esau (36:1-37:1).
  E. The Life of Joseph (37:2-50:26).
    1. Joseph's career (37:2-41:57).
    2. Jacob's migration (42:1-47:31).
    3. Jacob's last days (48:1-50:14).
    4. Joseph's last days (50:15-26).

GENIUS Mechanical, a divine inspiration (Ex 28:3; 31:2-11; 35:30-35; 36:1). *See Inspiration.*

GENNESARET [1166].

1. "The land of Gennesaret" is a plain on the NW shore of the Sea of Galilee (Mt 14:34; Mk 6:53).
2. "The Lake of Gennesaret" is the same as the Sea of Galilee (Lk 5:1). *See Galilee, Sea of.*

GENTILES [1580, 260, 1619, 1620, 1818] (*nation, people*).

NIV+ GENTILE

Usually meaning non-Israelite people. *See Heathen.*

General:

Ways of, condemned—

Jer 10:2 This is what the LORD says: "Do not learn the ways of the nations or be terrified by signs in the sky, though the nations are terrified by them. [3]For the customs of the peoples are worthless; they cut a tree out of the forest, and a craftsman shapes it with his chisel.

Eph 4:17 So I tell you this, and insist on it in the Lord, that you must no longer live as the Gentiles do, in the futility of their thinking. [18]They are darkened in their understanding and separated from the life of God because of the ignorance that is in them due to the hardening of their hearts. [19]Having lost all sensitivity, they have given themselves over to sensuality so as to indulge in every kind of impurity, with a continual lust for more.

God's forbearance toward—

Ac 14:16 In the past, he let all nations go their own way.

Impartiality toward—

Ro 2:9 There will be trouble and distress for every human being who does evil: first for the Jew, then for the Gentile; [10]but glory, honor and peace for everyone who does good: first for the Jew, then for the Gentile. [11]For God does not show favoritism.

Ignorant worship practices of—

Mt 6:7 And when you pray, do not keep on babbling like pagans, for they think they will be heard because of their many words. **8**Do not be like them, for your Father knows what you need before you ask him.

Mt 6:31 So do not worry, saying, 'What shall we eat?' or 'What shall we drink?' or 'What shall we wear?' **32**For the pagans run after all these things, and your heavenly Father knows that you need them.

Ac 17:4 Some of the Jews were persuaded and joined Paul and Silas, as did a large number of God-fearing Greeks and not a few prominent women.

Ac 17:16 While Paul was waiting for them in Athens, he was greatly distressed to see that the city was full of idols.

Ac 17:22 Paul then stood up in the meeting of the Areopagus and said: "Men of Athens! I see that in every way you are very religious. **23**For as I walked around and looked carefully at your objects of worship, I even found an altar with this inscription: TO AN UNKNOWN GOD. Now what you worship as something unknown I am going to proclaim to you.

24"The God who made the world and everything in it is the Lord of heaven and earth and does not live in temples built by hands. **25**And he is not served by human hands, as if he needed anything, because he himself gives all men life and breath and everything else. **26**From one man he made every nation of men, that they should inhabit the whole earth; and he determined the times set for them and the exact places where they should live. **27**God did this so that men would seek him and perhaps reach out for him and find him, though he is not far from each one of us.

1Co 10:20 No, but the sacrifices of pagans are offered to demons, not to God, and I do not want you to be participants with demons.

1Co 12:2 You know that when you were pagans, somehow or other you were influenced and led astray to mute idols.

Wicked practices of—

Ro 1:18 The wrath of God is being revealed from heaven against all the godlessness and wickedness of men who suppress the truth by their wickedness, **19**since what may be known about God is plain to them, because God has made it plain to them. **20**For since the creation of the world God's invisible qualities—his eternal power and divine nature—have been clearly seen, being understood from what has been made, so that men are without excuse.

21For although they knew God, they neither glorified him as God nor gave thanks to him, but their thinking became futile and their foolish hearts were darkened. **22**Although they claimed to be wise, they became fools **23**and exchanged the glory of the immortal God for images made to look like mortal man and birds and animals and reptiles.

24Therefore God gave them over in the sinful desires of their hearts to sexual impurity for the degrading of their bodies with one another. **25**They exchanged the truth of God for a lie, and worshiped and served created things rather than the Creator—who is forever praised. Amen.

26Because of this, God gave them over to shameful lusts. Even their women exchanged natural relations for unnatural ones. **27**In the same way the men also abandoned natural relations with women and were inflamed with lust for one another. Men committed indecent acts with other men, and received in themselves the due penalty for their perversion.

28Furthermore, since they did not think it worthwhile to retain the knowledge of God, he gave them over to a depraved mind, to do what ought not to be done. **29**They have become filled with every kind of wickedness, evil, greed and depravity. They are full of envy, murder, strife, deceit and malice. They are gossips, **30**slanderers, God-haters, insolent, arrogant and boastful; they invent ways of doing evil; they disobey their parents; **31**they are senseless, faithless, heartless, ruthless. **32**Although they know God's righteous decree that those who do such things deserve death, they not only continue to do these very things but also approve of those who practice them.

Gal 2:15 "We who are Jews by birth and not 'Gentile sinners'

Eph 5:12 For it is shameful even to mention what the disobedient do in secret.

1Th 4:5 not in passionate lust like the heathen, who do not know God;

1Pe 4:3 For you have spent enough time in the past doing what pagans choose to do—living in debauchery, lust, drunkenness, orgies, carousing and detestable idolatry. **4**They think it strange that you do not plunge with them into the same flood of dissipation, and they heap abuse on you.

Moral responsibility of—

Ro 2:14 (Indeed, when Gentiles, who do not have the law, do by nature things required by the law, they are a law for themselves, even though they do not have the law, **15**since they show that the requirements of the law are written on their hearts, their consciences also bearing witness, and their thoughts now accusing, now even defending them.)

See Idolatry; Missions.

Prophecies of the Conversion of:

Ge 12:3 I will bless those who bless you, and whoever curses you I will curse; and all peoples on earth will be blessed through you."

Ge 22:18 and through your offspring all nations on earth will be blessed, because you have obeyed me."

Ge 49:10 The scepter will not depart from Judah, nor the ruler's staff from between his feet, until he comes to whom it belongs and the obedience of the nations is his.

Dt 32:21 They made me jealous by what is no god and angered me with their worthless idols. I will make them envious by those who are not a people; I will make them angry by a nation that has no understanding.

Ps 2:8 Ask of me, and I will make the nations your inheritance, the ends of the earth your possession.

Ps 22:27 All the ends of the earth will remember and turn to the LORD, and all the families of the nations will bow down before him, **28**for dominion belongs to the LORD and he rules over the nations. **29**All the rich of the earth will feast and worship; all who go down to the dust will kneel before him—those who cannot keep themselves alive. **30**Posterity will serve him; future generations will be told about the Lord. **31**They will proclaim his righteousness to a people yet unborn—for he has done it.

Ps 46:4 There is a river whose streams make glad the city of God, the holy place where the Most High dwells.

Ps 46:10 "Be still, and know that I am God; I will be exalted among the nations, I will be exalted in the earth."

Ps 65:2 O you who hear prayer, to you all men will come.

Ps 65:5 You answer us with awesome deeds of righteousness, O God our Savior, the hope of all the ends of the earth and of the farthest seas,

Ps 66:4 All the earth bows down to you; they sing praise to you, they sing praise to your name." *Selah*

Ps 68:31 Envoys will come from Egypt; Cush will submit herself to God.

[32]Sing to God, O kingdoms of the earth, sing praise to the Lord, *Selah*

Ps 72:8 He will rule from sea to sea and from the River to the ends of the earth. [9]The desert tribes will bow before him and his enemies will lick the dust. [10]The kings of Tarshish and of distant shores will bring tribute to him; the kings of Sheba and Seba will present him gifts. [11]All kings will bow down to him and all nations will serve him.

Ps 72:16 Let grain abound throughout the land; on the tops of the hills may it sway. Let its fruit flourish like Lebanon; let it thrive like the grass of the field.

Ps 72:19 Praise be to his glorious name forever; may the whole earth be filled with his glory. Amen and Amen.

Ps 86:9 All the nations you have made will come and worship before you, O Lord; they will bring glory to your name.

Ps 102:15 The nations will fear the name of the Lord, all the kings of the earth will revere your glory.

Ps 102:18 Let this be written for a future generation, that a people not yet created may praise the Lord: [19]"The Lord looked down from his sanctuary on high, from heaven he viewed the earth, [20]to hear the groans of the prisoners and release those condemned to death." [21]So the name of the Lord will be declared in Zion and his praise in Jerusalem [22]when the peoples and the kingdoms assemble to worship the Lord.

Ps 145:10 All you have made will praise you, O Lord; your saints will extol you. [11]They will tell of the glory of your kingdom and speak of your might,

Isa 2:2 In the last days the mountain of the Lord's temple will be established as chief among the mountains; it will be raised above the hills, and all nations will stream to it.

[3]Many peoples will come and say, "Come, let us go up to the mountain of the Lord, to the house of the God of Jacob. He will teach us his ways, so that we may walk in his paths." The law will go out from Zion, the word of the Lord from Jerusalem. [4]He will judge between the nations and will settle disputes for many peoples. They will beat their swords into plowshares and their spears into pruning hooks. Nation will not take up sword against nation, nor will they train for war anymore.

Isa 9:2 The people walking in darkness have seen a great light; on those living in the land of the shadow of death a light has dawned.

Isa 9:6 For to us a child is born, to us a son is given, and the government will be on his shoulders. And he will be called Wonderful Counselor, Mighty God, Everlasting Father, Prince of Peace. [7]Of the increase of his government and peace there will be no end. He will reign on David's throne and over his kingdom, establishing and upholding it with justice and righteousness from that time on and forever. The zeal of the Lord Almighty will accomplish this.

Isa 11:6 The wolf will live with the lamb, the leopard will lie down with the goat, the calf and the lion and the yearling together; and a little child will lead them. [7]The cow will feed with the bear, their young will lie down together, and the lion will eat straw like the ox. [8]The infant will play near the hole of the cobra, and the young child put his hand into the viper's nest. [9]They will neither harm nor destroy on all my holy mountain, for the earth will be full of the knowledge of the Lord as the waters cover the sea.

[10]In that day the Root of Jesse will stand as a banner for the peoples; the nations will rally to him, and his place of rest will be glorious.

Isa 18:7 At that time gifts will be brought to the Lord Almighty from a people tall and smooth-skinned, from a people feared far and wide, an aggressive nation of strange speech, whose land is divided by rivers—the gifts will be brought to Mount Zion, the place of the Name of the Lord Almighty.

Isa 24:16 From the ends of the earth we hear singing: "Glory to the Righteous One." But I said, "I waste away, I waste away! Woe to me! The treacherous betray! With treachery the treacherous betray!"

Isa 35:1 The desert and the parched land will be glad; the wilderness will rejoice and blossom. Like the crocus, [2]it will burst into bloom; it will rejoice greatly and shout for joy. The glory of Lebanon will be given to it, the splendor of Carmel and Sharon; they will see the glory of the Lord, the splendor of our God.

Isa 35:5 Then will the eyes of the blind be opened and the ears of the deaf unstopped. [6]Then will the lame leap like a deer, and the mute tongue shout for joy. Water will gush forth in the wilderness and streams in the desert. [7]The burning sand will become a pool, the thirsty ground bubbling springs. In the haunts where jackals once lay, grass and reeds and papyrus will grow.

Isa 40:5 And the glory of the Lord will be revealed, and all mankind together will see it. For the mouth of the Lord has spoken."

Isa 42:1 "Here is my servant, whom I uphold, my chosen one in whom I delight; I will put my Spirit on him and he will bring justice to the nations. (+Isa 42:2-3)

Isa 42:4 he will not falter or be discouraged till he establishes justice on earth. In his law the islands will put their hope." (+Isa 42:5-12; 45:6)

Isa 45:8 "You heavens above, rain down righteousness; let the clouds shower it down. Let the earth open wide, let salvation spring up, let righteousness grow with it; I, the Lord, have created it.

Isa 45:22 "Turn to me and be saved, all you ends of the earth; for I am God, and there is no other. [23]By myself I have sworn, my mouth has uttered in all integrity a word that will not be revoked: Before me every knee will bow; by me every tongue will swear. [24]They will say of me, 'In the Lord alone are righteousness and strength.'" All who have raged against him will come to him and be put to shame.

Isa 49:1 Listen to me, you islands; hear this, you distant nations: Before I was born the Lord called me; from my birth he has made mention of my name.

Isa 49:5 And now the Lord says—he who formed me in the womb to be his servant to bring Jacob back to him and gather Israel to himself, for I am honored in the eyes of the Lord and my God has been my strength— [6]he says: "It is too small a thing for you to be my servant to restore the tribes of Jacob and bring back those of Israel I have kept. I will also make you a light for the Gentiles, that you may bring my salvation to the ends of the earth."

Isa 49:18 Lift up your eyes and look around; all your sons gather and come to you. As surely as I live," declares the Lord, "you will wear them all as ornaments; you will put them on, like a bride.

[19]"Though you were ruined and made desolate and your land laid waste, now you will be too small for your people, and those who devoured you will be far away. [20]The children born during your bereavement will yet say in your hearing, 'This place is too small for us; give us more space to live in.' [21]Then you will say in your heart, 'Who bore me these? I was bereaved and barren; I was exiled and

rejected. Who brought these up? I was left all alone, but these—where have they come from?'"

²²This is what the Sovereign LORD says: "See, I will beckon to the Gentiles, I will lift up my banner to the peoples; they will bring your sons in their arms and carry your daughters on their shoulders. ²³Kings will be your foster fathers, and their queens your nursing mothers. They will bow down before you with their faces to the ground; they will lick the dust at your feet. Then you will know that I am the LORD; those who hope in me will not be disappointed."

Isa 54:1 "Sing, O barren woman, you who never bore a child; burst into song, shout for joy, you who were never in labor; because more are the children of the desolate woman than of her who has a husband," says the LORD. ²"Enlarge the place of your tent, stretch your tent curtains wide, do not hold back; lengthen your cords, strengthen your stakes. ³For you will spread out to the right and to the left; your descendants will dispossess nations and settle in their desolate cities.

Isa 55:5 Surely you will summon nations you know not, and nations that do not know you will hasten to you, because of the LORD your God, the Holy One of Israel, for he has endowed you with splendor."

Isa 56:3 Let no foreigner who has bound himself to the LORD say, "The LORD will surely exclude me from his people." And let not any eunuch complain, "I am only a dry tree."

Isa 56:6 And foreigners who bind themselves to the LORD to serve him, to love the name of the LORD, and to worship him, all who keep the Sabbath without desecrating it and who hold fast to my covenant— ⁷these I will bring to my holy mountain and give them joy in my house of prayer. Their burnt offerings and sacrifices will be accepted on my altar; for my house will be called a house of prayer for all nations." ⁸The Sovereign LORD declares—he who gathers the exiles of Israel: "I will gather still others to them besides those already gathered."

Isa 60:1 "Arise, shine, for your light has come, and the glory of the LORD rises upon you. (+Isa 60:2)

Isa 60:3 Nations will come to your light, and kings to the brightness of your dawn.

⁴"Lift up your eyes and look about you: All assemble and come to you; your sons come from afar, and your daughters are carried on the arm. ⁵Then you will look and be radiant, your heart will throb and swell with joy; the wealth on the seas will be brought to you, to you the riches of the nations will come. (+Isa 60:6-7)

Isa 60:8 "Who are these that fly along like clouds, like doves to their nests? ⁹Surely the islands look to me; in the lead are the ships of Tarshish, bringing your sons from afar, with their silver and gold, to the honor of the LORD your God, the Holy One of Israel, for he has endowed you with splendor.

¹⁰"Foreigners will rebuild your walls, and their kings will serve you. Though in anger I struck you, in favor I will show you compassion. ¹¹Your gates will always stand open, they will never be shut, day or night, so that men may bring you the wealth of the nations—their kings led in triumphal procession. ¹²For the nation or kingdom that will not serve you will perish; it will be utterly ruined.

¹³"The glory of Lebanon will come to you, the pine, the fir and the cypress together, to adorn the place of my sanctuary; and I will glorify the place of my feet. ¹⁴The sons of your oppressors will come bowing before you; all

who despise you will bow down at your feet and will call you the City of the LORD, Zion of the Holy One of Israel.

Isa 65:1 "I revealed myself to those who did not ask for me; I was found by those who did not seek me. To a nation that did not call on my name, I said, 'Here am I, here am I.'

Isa 66:12 For this is what the LORD says: "I will extend peace to her like a river, and the wealth of nations like a flooding stream; you will nurse and be carried on her arm and dandled on her knees.

Isa 66:19 "I will set a sign among them, and I will send some of those who survive to the nations—to Tarshish, to the Libyans and Lydians (famous as archers), to Tubal and Greece, and to the distant islands that have not heard of my fame or seen my glory. They will proclaim my glory among the nations.

Isa 66:23 From one New Moon to another and from one Sabbath to another, all mankind will come and bow down before me," says the LORD.

Jer 3:17 At that time they will call Jerusalem The Throne of the LORD, and all nations will gather in Jerusalem to honor the name of the LORD. No longer will they follow the stubbornness of their evil hearts.

Jer 4:2 and if in a truthful, just and righteous way you swear, 'As surely as the LORD lives,' then the nations will be blessed by him and in him they will glory."

Jer 16:19 O LORD, my strength and my fortress, my refuge in time of distress, to you the nations will come from the ends of the earth and say, "Our fathers possessed nothing but false gods, worthless idols that did them no good. ²⁰Do men make their own gods? Yes, but they are not gods!"

²¹"Therefore I will teach them—this time I will teach them my power and might. Then they will know that my name is the LORD.

Da 2:35 Then the iron, the clay, the bronze, the silver and the gold were broken to pieces at the same time and became like chaff on a threshing floor in the summer. The wind swept them away without leaving a trace. But the rock that struck the statue became a huge mountain and filled the whole earth.

Da 2:44 "In the time of those kings, the God of heaven will set up a kingdom that will never be destroyed, nor will it be left to another people. It will crush all those kingdoms and bring them to an end, but it will itself endure forever. (+Da 2:45)

Da 7:13 "In my vision at night I looked, and there before me was one like a son of man, coming with the clouds of heaven. He approached the Ancient of Days and was led into his presence. ¹⁴He was given authority, glory and sovereign power; all peoples, nations and men of every language worshiped him. His dominion is an everlasting dominion that will not pass away, and his kingdom is one that will never be destroyed.

Hos 2:23 I will plant her for myself in the land; I will show my love to the one I called 'Not my loved one.' I will say to those called 'Not my people,' 'You are my people'; and they will say, 'You are my God.'"

Joel 2:28 "And afterward, I will pour out my Spirit on all people. Your sons and daughters will prophesy, your old men will dream dreams, your young men will see visions. ²⁹Even on my servants, both men and women, I will pour out my Spirit in those days. ³⁰I will show wonders in the heavens and on the earth, blood and fire and billows of smoke. ³¹The sun will be turned to darkness and the moon to blood before the coming of the great and dreadful day of the LORD. ³²And everyone who calls on the name of the

LORD will be saved; for on Mount Zion and in Jerusalem there will be deliverance, as the LORD has said, among the survivors whom the LORD calls.

Am 9:11 "In that day I will restore David's fallen tent. I will repair its broken places, restore its ruins, and build it as it used to be, ¹²so that they may possess the remnant of Edom and all the nations that bear my name," declares the LORD, who will do these things.

Mic 4:3 He will judge between many peoples and will settle disputes for strong nations far and wide. They will beat their swords into plowshares and their spears into pruning hooks. Nation will not take up sword against nation, nor will they train for war anymore. ⁴Every man will sit under his own vine and under his own fig tree, and no one will make them afraid, for the LORD Almighty has spoken.

Hag 2:7 I will shake all nations, and the desired of all nations will come, and I will fill this house with glory,' says the LORD Almighty.

Zec 2:10 "Shout and be glad, O Daughter of Zion. For I am coming, and I will live among you," declares the LORD. ¹¹"Many nations will be joined with the LORD in that day and will become my people. I will live among you and you will know that the LORD Almighty has sent me to you.

Zec 6:15 Those who are far away will come and help to build the temple of the LORD, and you will know that the LORD Almighty has sent me to you. This will happen if you diligently obey the LORD your God."

Zec 8:20 This is what the LORD Almighty says: "Many peoples and the inhabitants of many cities will yet come, ²¹and the inhabitants of one city will go to another and say, 'Let us go at once to entreat the LORD and seek the LORD Almighty. I myself am going.' ²²And many peoples and powerful nations will come to Jerusalem to seek the LORD Almighty and to entreat him."

²³This is what the LORD Almighty says: "In those days ten men from all languages and nations will take firm hold of one Jew by the hem of his robe and say, 'Let us go with you, because we have heard that God is with you.'"

Zec 9:1 The word of the LORD is against the land of Hadrach and will rest upon Damascus—for the eyes of men and all the tribes of Israel are on the LORD—

Zec 9:10 I will take away the chariots from Ephraim and the war-horses from Jerusalem, and the battle bow will be broken. He will proclaim peace to the nations. His rule will extend from sea to sea and from the River to the ends of the earth.

Zec 14:8 On that day living water will flow out from Jerusalem, half to the eastern sea and half to the western sea, in summer and in winter.

⁹The LORD will be king over the whole earth. On that day there will be one LORD, and his name the only name.

Zec 14:16 Then the survivors from all the nations that have attacked Jerusalem will go up year after year to worship the King, the LORD Almighty, and to celebrate the Feast of Tabernacles.

Mal 1:11 My name will be great among the nations, from the rising to the setting of the sun. In every place incense and pure offerings will be brought to my name, because my name will be great among the nations," says the LORD Almighty.

Mt 3:9 And do not think you can say to yourselves, 'We have Abraham as our father.' I tell you that out of these stones God can raise up children for Abraham.

Mt 8:11 I say to you that many will come from the east

and the west, and will take their places at the feast with Abraham, Isaac and Jacob in the kingdom of heaven.

Mt 12:17 This was to fulfill what was spoken through the prophet Isaiah:

¹⁸"Here is my servant whom I have chosen, the one I love, in whom I delight; I will put my Spirit on him, and he will proclaim justice to the nations. ¹⁹He will not quarrel or cry out; no one will hear his voice in the streets. ²⁰A bruised reed he will not break, and a smoldering wick he will not snuff out, till he leads justice to victory. ²¹In his name the nations will put their hope."

Mt 19:30 But many who are first will be last, and many who are last will be first. (+Mk 10:31)

Lk 13:29 People will come from east and west and north and south, and will take their places at the feast in the kingdom of God. ³⁰Indeed there are those who are last who will be first, and first who will be last."

Lk 21:24 They will fall by the sword and will be taken as prisoners to all the nations. Jerusalem will be trampled on by the Gentiles until the times of the Gentiles are fulfilled.

Jn 10:16 I have other sheep that are not of this sheep pen. I must bring them also. They too will listen to my voice, and there shall be one flock and one shepherd.

Ac 9:15 But the Lord said to Ananias, "Go! This man is my chosen instrument to carry my name before the Gentiles and their kings and before the people of Israel.

See Church, The Body of Believers, Prophecies Concerning.

Conversion of:

Ac 10:45 The circumcised believers who had come with Peter were astonished that the gift of the Holy Spirit had been poured out even on the Gentiles.

Ac 11:1 The apostles and the brothers throughout Judea heard that the Gentiles also had received the word of God. ²So when Peter went up to Jerusalem, the circumcised believers criticized him ³and said, "You went into the house of uncircumcised men and ate with them."

⁴Peter began and explained everything to them precisely as it had happened: ⁵"I was in the city of Joppa praying, and in a trance I saw a vision. I saw something like a large sheet being let down from heaven by its four corners, and it came down to where I was. ⁶I looked into it and saw four-footed animals of the earth, wild beasts, reptiles, and birds of the air. ⁷Then I heard a voice telling me, 'Get up, Peter. Kill and eat.'

⁸"I replied, 'Surely not, Lord! Nothing impure or unclean has ever entered my mouth.'

Ac 13:2 While they were worshiping the Lord and fasting, the Holy Spirit said, "Set apart for me Barnabas and Saul for the work to which I have called them."

Ac 13:46 Then Paul and Barnabas answered them boldly: "We had to speak the word of God to you first. Since you reject it and do not consider yourselves worthy of eternal life, we now turn to the Gentiles. ⁴⁷For this is what the Lord has commanded us:

"'I have made you a light for the Gentiles, that you may bring salvation to the ends of the earth.'"

⁴⁸When the Gentiles heard this, they were glad and honored the word of the Lord; and all who were appointed for eternal life believed.

Ac 14:27 On arriving there, they gathered the church together and reported all that God had done through them and how he had opened the door of faith to the Gentiles.

Ac 15:7 After much discussion, Peter got up and addressed them: "Brothers, you know that some time ago God made a choice among you that the Gentiles might hear from my lips the message of the gospel and believe. [8]God, who knows the heart, showed that he accepted them by giving the Holy Spirit to them, just as he did to us. [9]He made no distinction between us and them, for he purified their hearts by faith. (+Ac 15:10-11)

Ac 15:12 The whole assembly became silent as they listened to Barnabas and Paul telling about the miraculous signs and wonders God had done among the Gentiles through them. [13]When they finished, James spoke up: "Brothers, listen to me. [14]Simon has described to us how God at first showed his concern by taking from the Gentiles a people for himself. [15]The words of the prophets are in agreement with this, as it is written:

[16]"'After this I will return and rebuild David's fallen tent. Its ruins I will rebuild, and I will restore it, [17]that the remnant of men may seek the Lord, and all the Gentiles who bear my name, says the Lord, who does these things' [18]that have been known for ages.

[19]"It is my judgment, therefore, that we should not make it difficult for the Gentiles who are turning to God. [20]Instead we should write to them, telling them to abstain from food polluted by idols, from sexual immorality, from the meat of strangled animals and from blood. [21]For Moses has been preached in every city from the earliest times and is read in the synagogues on every Sabbath."

[22]Then the apostles and elders, with the whole church, decided to choose some of their own men and send them to Antioch with Paul and Barnabas. They chose Judas (called Barsabbas) and Silas, two men who were leaders among the brothers. [23]With them they sent the following letter:

The apostles and elders, your brothers,

To the Gentile believers in Antioch, Syria and Cilicia: Greetings.

[24]We have heard that some went out from us without our authorization and disturbed you, troubling your minds by what they said. [25]So we all agreed to choose some men and send them to you with our dear friends Barnabas and Paul— [26]men who have risked their lives for the name of our Lord Jesus Christ. [27]Therefore we are sending Judas and Silas to confirm by word of mouth what we are writing. [28]It seemed good to the Holy Spirit and to us not to burden you with anything beyond the following requirements: [29]You are to abstain from food sacrificed to idols, from blood, from the meat of strangled animals and from sexual immorality. You will do well to avoid these things. Farewell.

[30]The men were sent off and went down to Antioch, where they gathered the church together and delivered the letter. [31]The people read it and were glad for its encouraging message.

Ac 18:4 Every Sabbath he reasoned in the synagogue, trying to persuade Jews and Greeks.

[5]When Silas and Timothy came from Macedonia, Paul devoted himself exclusively to preaching, testifying to the Jews that Jesus was the Christ. [6]But when the Jews opposed Paul and became abusive, he shook out his clothes in protest and said to them, "Your blood be on your own heads! I am clear of my responsibility. From now on I will go to the Gentiles."

Ac 26:16 'Now get up and stand on your feet. I have appeared to you to appoint you as a servant and as a witness of what you have seen of me and what I will show you. [17]I will rescue you from your own people and from the Gentiles. I am sending you to them [18]to open their eyes and turn them from darkness to light, and from the power of Satan to God, so that they may receive forgiveness of

sins and a place among those who are sanctified by faith in me.'

Ac 28:28 "Therefore I want you to know that God's salvation has been sent to the Gentiles, and they will listen!"

Ro 1:5 Through him and for his name's sake, we received grace and apostleship to call people from among all the Gentiles to the obedience that comes from faith. [6]And you also are among those who are called to belong to Jesus Christ.

[7]To all in Rome who are loved by God and called to be saints: Grace and peace to you from God our Father and from the Lord Jesus Christ.

Ro 9:22 What if God, choosing to show his wrath and make his power known, bore with great patience the objects of his wrath—prepared for destruction? [23]What if he did this to make the riches of his glory known to the objects of his mercy, whom he prepared in advance for glory— [24]even us, whom he also called, not only from the Jews but also from the Gentiles? [25]As he says in Hosea:

"I will call them 'my people' who are not my people; and I will call her 'my loved one' who is not my loved one,"

[26]and, "It will happen that in the very place where it was said to them, 'You are not my people,' they will be called 'sons of the living God.'"

[27]Isaiah cries out concerning Israel:

"Though the number of the Israelites be like the sand by the sea, only the remnant will be saved. [28]For the Lord will carry out his sentence on earth with speed and finality."

[29]It is just as Isaiah said previously:

"Unless the Lord Almighty had left us descendants, we would have become like Sodom, we would have been like Gomorrah."

[30]What then shall we say? That the Gentiles, who did not pursue righteousness, have obtained it, a righteousness that is by faith;

Ro 10:19 Again I ask: Did Israel not understand? First, Moses says, "I will make you envious by those who are not a nation; I will make you angry by a nation that has no understanding."

[20]And Isaiah boldly says, "I was found by those who did not seek me; I revealed myself to those who did not ask for me."

Ro 11:11 Again I ask: Did they stumble so as to fall beyond recovery? Not at all! Rather, because of their transgression, salvation has come to the Gentiles to make Israel envious. [12]But if their transgression means riches for the world, and their loss means riches for the Gentiles, how much greater riches will their fullness bring!

[13]I am talking to you Gentiles. Inasmuch as I am the apostle to the Gentiles, I make much of my ministry

Ro 11:17 If some of the branches have been broken off, and you, though a wild olive shoot, have been grafted in among the others and now share in the nourishing sap from the olive root, [18]do not boast over those branches. If you do, consider this: You do not support the root, but the root supports you. [19]You will say then, "Branches were broken off so that I could be grafted in." [20]Granted. But they were broken off because of unbelief, and you stand by faith. Do not be arrogant, but be afraid. [21]For if God did not spare the natural branches, he will not spare you either.

Ro 15:9 so that the Gentiles may glorify God for his mercy, as it is written:

"Therefore I will praise you among the Gentiles; I will sing hymns to your name."

[10]Again, it says, "Rejoice, O Gentiles, with his people."

¹¹And again, "Praise the Lord, all you Gentiles, and sing praises to him, all you peoples."

¹²And again, Isaiah says, "The Root of Jesse will spring up, one who will arise to rule over the nations; the Gentiles will hope in him."

Gal 1:15 But when God, who set me apart from birth and called me by his grace, was pleased ¹⁶to reveal his Son in me so that I might preach him among the Gentiles, I did not consult any man,

Gal 2:2 I went in response to a revelation and set before them the gospel that I preach among the Gentiles. But I did this privately to those who seemed to be leaders, for fear that I was running or had run my race in vain.

Gal 3:14 He redeemed us in order that the blessing given to Abraham might come to the Gentiles through Christ Jesus, so that by faith we might receive the promise of the Spirit.

Eph 3:1 For this reason I, Paul, the prisoner of Christ Jesus for the sake of you Gentiles—

²Surely you have heard about the administration of God's grace that was given to me for you, ³that is, the mystery made known to me by revelation, as I have already written briefly. ⁴In reading this, then, you will be able to understand my insight into the mystery of Christ, ⁵which was not made known to men in other generations as it has now been revealed by the Spirit to God's holy apostles and prophets. ⁶This mystery is that through the gospel the Gentiles are heirs together with Israel, members together of one body, and sharers together in the promise in Christ Jesus.

⁷I became a servant of this gospel by the gift of God's grace given me through the working of his power. ⁸Although I am less than the least of all God's people, this grace was given me: to preach to the Gentiles the unsearchable riches of Christ,

Col 3:11 Here there is no Greek or Jew, circumcised or uncircumcised, barbarian, Scythian, slave or free, but Christ is all, and is in all.

1Th 2:16 in their effort to keep us from speaking to the Gentiles so that they may be saved. In this way they always heap up their sins to the limit. The wrath of God has come upon them at last.

1Ti 3:16 Beyond all question, the mystery of godliness is great: He appeared in a body, was vindicated by the Spirit, was seen by angels, was preached among the nations, was believed on in the world, was taken up in glory.

2Ti 1:11 And of this gospel I was appointed a herald and an apostle and a teacher.

Rev 11:15 The seventh angel sounded his trumpet, and there were loud voices in heaven, which said: "The kingdom of the world has become the kingdom of our Lord and of his Christ, and he will reign for ever and ever."

Rev 15:4 Who will not fear you, O Lord, and bring glory to your name? For you alone are holy. All nations will come and worship before you, for your righteous acts have been revealed."

See Jesus the Christ, Kingdom of.

GENTILES, COURT OF THE
The part of Herod's temple which the Gentiles could enter (not mentioned in the Bible). In the temple of Revelation (Rev 11:2).

GENTILES, INCLUSION OF
See Catholicity.

GENTLENESS
[351, 476, 1987, 6714, 8204, 8205, 2117, 2473, 4558, 4559, 5710].

NIV+ GENTLE, GENTLY

Of Christ: (Isa 40:11; Mt 11:29; 2Co 10:1). *See Jesus the Christ, Compassion of, Humility of, Meekness of.*

Of God: (2Sa 22:36; Ps 18:35; Isa 40:11). *See God, Compassion of, Longsuffering of.*

Of Paul: (1Th 2:7).

Exhortations to:

A fruit of the Spirit—

Gal 5:22 But the fruit of the Spirit is love, joy, peace, patience, kindness, goodness, faithfulness,

Jas 3:17 But the wisdom that comes from heaven is first of all pure; then peace-loving, considerate, submissive, full of mercy and good fruit, impartial and sincere.

Required in the Lord's servants—

2Ti 2:24 And the Lord's servant must not quarrel; instead, he must be kind to everyone, able to teach, not resentful. ²⁵Those who oppose him he must gently instruct, in the hope that God will grant them repentance leading them to a knowledge of the truth, ²⁶and that they will come to their senses and escape from the trap of the devil, who has taken them captive to do his will.

Required in all Christians—

Tit 3:1 Remind the people to be subject to rulers and authorities, to be obedient, to be ready to do whatever is good, ²to slander no one, to be peaceable and considerate, and to show true humility toward all men.

See Humility; Kindness; Meekness; Patience.

GENUBATH
[1707] (*thief*). A son of Hadad the Edomite (1Ki 11:20).

GEOLOGY

Origin, in God—

Ge 1:9 And God said, "Let the water under the sky be gathered to one place, and let dry ground appear." And it was so. ¹⁰God called the dry ground "land," and the gathered waters he called "seas." And God saw that it was good.

1Sa 2:8 He raises the poor from the dust and lifts the needy from the ash heap; he seats them with princes and has them inherit a throne of honor. "For the foundations of the earth are the LORD's; upon them he has set the world.

2Sa 22:16 The valleys of the sea were exposed and the foundations of the earth laid bare at the rebuke of the LORD, at the blast of breath from his nostrils.

Job 12:8 or speak to the earth, and it will teach you, or let the fish of the sea inform you. ⁹Which of all these does not know that the hand of the LORD has done this?

Ps 18:15 The valleys of the sea were exposed and the foundations of the earth laid bare at your rebuke, O LORD, at the blast of breath from your nostrils.

Ps 24:1 The earth is the LORD's, and everything in it, the world, and all who live in it; ²for he founded it upon the seas and established it upon the waters. (+Ps 104:5)

Ps 136:6 who spread out the earth upon the waters, *His love endures forever.*

Pr 30:4 Who has gone up to heaven and come down? Who has gathered up the wind in the hollow of his hands? Who has wrapped up the waters in his cloak? Who has established all the ends of the earth? What is his name, and the name of his son? Tell me if you know!

2Pe 3:5 But they deliberately forget that long ago by God's word the heavens existed and the earth was formed out of water and by water. **6**By these waters also the world of that time was deluged and destroyed. **7**By the same word the present heavens and earth are reserved for fire, being kept for the day of judgment and destruction of ungodly men.

Control, by God—

Job 28:9 Man's hand assaults the flinty rock and lays bare the roots of the mountains. **10**He tunnels through the rock; his eyes see all its treasures. **11**He searches the sources of the rivers and brings hidden things to light.

Ps 104:5 He set the earth on its foundations; it can never be moved. **6**You covered it with the deep as with a garment; the waters stood above the mountains. **7**But at your rebuke the waters fled, at the sound of your thunder they took to flight; **8**they flowed over the mountains, they went down into the valleys, to the place you assigned for them. **9**You set a boundary they cannot cross; never again will they cover the earth.

10He makes springs pour water into the ravines; it flows between the mountains. **11**They give water to all the beasts of the field; the wild donkeys quench their thirst. **12**The birds of the air nest by the waters; they sing among the branches. **13**He waters the mountains from his upper chambers; the earth is satisfied by the fruit of his work. (+Pr 30:4)

Hab 3:9 You uncovered your bow, you called for many arrows. *Selah* You split the earth with rivers;

Infinity of—

Jer 31:37 This is what the LORD says: "Only if the heavens above can be measured and the foundations of the earth below be searched out will I reject all the descendants of Israel because of all they have done," declares the LORD.

Destruction of (2Pe 3:5-7).

See Astronomy; Creation; Earth; Hot Springs; Meteorology.

GERA [1733] (perhaps *sojourner*). A name common to the tribe of Benjamin.

1. A son of Benjamin (Ge 46:21).
2. A grandson of Benjamin (1Ch 8:3,5).
3. The father of Ehud (Jdg 3:15).
4. A son of Ehud (1Ch 8:7).
5. Father of Shimei (2Sa 16:5).

GERAH [1743].

NIV+ GERAHS

A weight equal about 1/20 of a shekel or 1/2 gram (Ex 30:13; Lev 27:25; Nu 3:47). *See Measure.*

GERAR [1761] (*circle, region*).

1. A city of the Philistines (Ge 10:19). Abimelech, king of (Ge 20:1; 26:6). Visited by Abraham (Ge 20:1), by Isaac (Ge 26:1; 2Ch 14:13-14).
2. A valley (Ge 26:17-22).

GERASENES [*1170*]. The region around Gerasa, one of the cities of the Decapolis near the SE end of the Sea of Galilee, in which the demoniacs lived whom Jesus healed (Mt 8:28, ftn; Mk 5:1; Lk 8:26,37). *See Gadarenes.*

GERGESENES A variant reading probably harmonizing Gadarenes and Gerasenes, the region in which Jesus exorcized demons (Mt 8:28; Mk 5:1; Lk 8:26, ftns). *See Gadarenes; Gerasenes.*

GERIZIM [1748]. Mount of blessing (Dt 11:29; 27:12; Jos 8:33). Jotham addresses the Shechemites from, against

the conspiracy of Abimelech (Jdg 9:7). Samaritans worship at (Jn 4:20).

GERSHOM [1768] (*traveler there*).

1. Son of Moses (Ex 2:22; 18:3; 1Ch 23:15-16; 26:24).
2. *See Gershon.*
3. A descendant of Phinehas (Ezr 8:2).
4. A Levite (Jdg 18:30).

GERSHON [1767, 1768].

NIV+ GERSHONITE, GERSHONITES

Also called Gershom. Son of Levi (Ge 46:11; Ex 6:16-17; Nu 3:17-26; 4:22-28,38; 7:7; 26:57; Jos 21:6; 1Ch 6:1,16-17,20,43,62,71; 15:7; 23:6).

GERSHONITES [1201+1767, 1201+1768, 1201+ 1769, 1769].

NIV+ GERSHON, GERSHONITE

Descendants of Gershon (Nu 3:25; 4:24,38; 7:7).

GERUTH KIMHAM [1745] (*lodging place of Kimham*). An unidentified place near Bethlehem, at which Ishmael and his fellow assassins stopped during their flight to Egypt (Jer 41:17).

GESHAN [1642]. A descendant of Caleb (1Ch 2:47).

GESHEM [1774, 1776] (*rain shower*). An Arab who opposed the work of Nehemiah (Hebrew *Gashmu*, a variant of *Geshem*) (Ne 2:19; 6:1-2,6, ftn).

GESHUR, GESHURITES [1770, 1771] (*bridge*).

1. District E of the sources of the Jordan. The inhabitants of, not subdued by the Israelites (Dt 3:14; Jos 12:5; 1Ch 2:23). David marries a princess of (2Sa 3:3; 1Ch 3:2). Absalom takes refuge in, after the murder of Amnon (2Sa 13:37-38; 15:8).

2. A people living S of the Philistines near Sinai. Their land was not taken at the time of the Conquest (Jos 13:2-13). Inhabitants of one of the villages of, exterminated, and the spoils taken by David (1Sa 27:8).

GETHER [1788]. The third son of Aram (Ge 10:23; 1Ch 1:17).

GETHSEMANE [*1149*] (*olive oil press*). A garden near Jerusalem. Jesus betrayed in (Mt 26:36-50; Mk 14:32-46; Lk 22:39-49; Jn 18:1-2).

GEUEL [1451] (*splendor of God [El]*). A representative from the tribe of Gad sent to spy out Canaan (Nu 13:15).

GEZER [1618] (possibly *pieces*). A Canaanite royal city perhaps also called Gob (2Sa 21:18 w 1Ch 20:4).

The king of, defeated by Joshua (Jos 10:33; 12:12). Canaanites not all expelled from, but made to pay tribute (Jos 16:10; Jdg 1:29). Allotted to Ephraim (Jos 16:10; 1Ch 7:28). Assigned to Levites (Jos 21:21). Battle with Philistines at (1Ch 20:4; 2Sa 21:18). Struck by David (2Sa 5:25; 1Ch 14:16). Fortified by Solomon after Pharaoh, king of Egypt, drives out Canaanites, making Gezer a dowry for Pharaoh's daughter (1Ki 9:15-17). Pharaoh Shishak, invaded the land in Rehoboam's fifth year as king. He launched an attack from Gezer, and was able to threaten and plunder Jerusalem from there (1Ki 14:25-28; 2Ch 12:1-12). Gezer was twelfth on a list of 156 cities captured by Shishak in his twentieth year. This record is found on a huge relief in the Egyptian stele at Karnak. Shishak's raids went as far N as the Sea of Galilee.

GHOR, THE The Arabic name for the Jordan Valley, biblical Arabah. *See Arabah.*

GHOST [200+3869, *4460, 5753*].
NIV+ GHOSTLIKE

An apparition (Isa 29:4); Jesus mistaken for (Mt 14:26; Mk 6:49; Lk 24:37:39). KJV "give up the ghost," means to breathe one's last, to die (Ge 25:8; 35:29; 49:33; Job 11:20; Mt 27:50; Jn 19:30). KJV "Holy Ghost" is NIV "Holy Spirit." *See Holy Spirit; Spirit.*

GIAH [1632] (*bubbling spring*). A place on the way to the wilderness of Gibeon (2Sa 2:24).

GIANTS People of exceptional height and strength, such as Og, king of Bashan (Jos 12:4; 13:12), and Goliath, whom David killed (1Sa 17). The Nephilim and descendants of Anak were giants to the Israelites (Ge 6:4; Nu 13:33) as were the Rephaites (Dt 2:11,20; 3:11). *See Anakites; Nephilim; Rephaites.*

GIBBAR, GIBEON [1507] (*[young vigorous] man, hero*). A man whose children returned from captivity with Zerubbabel (Ezr 2:20).

GIBBETHON [1510] (*mound, hill*). A city of Dan (Jos 19:44). Allotted to the Levites (Jos 21:23). Besieged by Israel, while in possession of Philistines (1Ki 15:27; 16:15,17).

GIBEA [1495] (*mound, hill*). A Judah ite (1Ch 2:49).

GIBEAH [1497] (*mound, hill*).
NIV+ GIBEATHITE

1. Of Judah (Jos 15:57).
2. Of Saul. Also called Gibeah of Benjamin. The people's wickedness (Jdg 19:12-30; Hos 9:9; 10:9). Destroyed by the Israelites (Jdg 20). The city of Saul (1Sa 10:26; 15:34; 22:6). The ark of the covenant conveyed to, by the Philistines (1Sa 7:1; 2Sa 6:3). Deserted (Isa 10:29).
3. Another town in Benjamin, also called Gibeah (Jos 18:28).
4. Gibeah in the field (Jdg 20:31). Probably identical with Geba. *See Geba.*

GIBEATH HAARALOTH [1502] (*hill of foreskins*). Place where the Israelites were circumcised after the wilderness wanderings (Jos 5:3.).

GIBEATHITE [1503] (*of Gibeah*).
NIV+ GIBEAH

Shemaah, two of whose sons were among David's warriors (1Ch 12:3).

GIBEON [1498, 1500] (*mound, hill*).
NIV+ GIBEONITE, GIBEONITES

1. A city of the Hivites (Jos 9:3,17; 2Sa 21:2). The people of deceive Joshua into a treaty (Jos 9). Made servants by the Israelites when their deception was discovered (Jos 9:27). The sun stands still over, during Joshua's battle with the five confederated kings (Jos 10:12-14). Allotted to Benjamin (Jos 18:25). Assigned to the Aaronites (Jos 21:17). The tabernacle located at (1Ki 3:4; 1Ch 16:39; 21:29; 2Ch 1:2-3,13). Smitten by David (1Ch 14:16). Seven sons of Saul slain at, to avenge the inhabitants of (2Sa 21:1-9). Solomon worships at, and offers sacrifices (1Ki 3:4), God appears to him in dreams (1Ki 3:5; 9:2). Abner slays Asahel at (2Sa 2:18-32; 3:30). Ishmael, the son of Nethaniah, defeated at, by Johanan (Jer 41:11-16).

2. Pool of (2Sa 2:13; Jer 41:12).

GIBEONITE(S) [408+1500, 1498] (*people from Gibeon*).
NIV+ GIBEON

Descended from the Hivites and Amorites (Jos 9:3,7, w 2Sa 21:2). A mighty and warlike people (Jos 10:2). Cities of (Jos 9:17).

Israel:

Deceived by (Jos 9:4-13). Made a league with (Jos 9:15). Spared on account of their oath (Jos 9:18-19). Appointed woodcutters (Jos 9:20-27). Attacked by the kings of Canaan (Jos 10:1-5). Delivered by Israel (Jos 10:6-10). Saul sought to destroy (2Sa 21:2). Israel plagued for Saul's cruelty to (2Sa 21:1). Effected the destruction of the remnant of Saul's house (2Sa 21:4-9). The office of the temple servants probably originated in (1Ch 9:2, ftn). Part of, returned from the captivity (Ne 7:25).

GIBLITES *See Gebalites.*

GIDDALTI [1547] (*I pronounce [God as] Great* ISBE; *I reared up* KB). A son of Heman (1Ch 25:4,29).

GIDDEL [1543] (*big*).
1. One of the temple servants (Ezr 2:47; Ne 7:49).
2. One of Solomon's servants (Ezr 2:56; Ne 7:58).

GIDEON [1549, *1146*] (*one who cuts, hacks*).
NIV+ GIDEON'S, JERUB-BAAL, JERUB-BAAL'S

Call of, by an angel (Jdg 6:11,14). His excuses (Jdg 6:15). Promises of the Lord to (Jdg 6:16). Angel attests the call to, by miracle (Jdg 6:21-24). He destroys the altar of Baal and builds one to the Lord (Jdg 6:25-27). Tests God's word with a fleece (Jdg 6:36-40). Leads an army against and defeats the Midianites (Jdg 6:33-35; 7; 8:4-12). Ephraimites rebuke, for not inviting them to join in the campaign against the Midianites (Jdg 8:1-3). Avenges himself upon the people of Succoth (Jdg 8:14-17). Israel desires to make him king; he refuses (Jdg 8:22-23). Makes an ephod which becomes a snare to the Israelites (Jdg 8:24-27). Had seventy sons (Jdg 8:30). Death of (Jdg 8:32). Faith of (Heb 11:32).

GIDEONI [1551] (*one who cuts, hacks*). Father of Abidan (Nu 1:11; 2:22; 7:60,65; 10:24).

GIDOM [1550] (*a cutting off, stop pursuit*). Limit of pursuit after battle of Gibeah (Jdg 20:45).

GIER EAGLE *See Birds; Osprey.*

GIFT, GIVING [*1388, 4458, 4966, 5368, 5508, 5510, 5522, 5989, 7731, 7933, 8816, 8856, 8933, 9556, 10448, *1517, 1561, 1564, 1565, 1797, 2330, 5921, 5922*].
NIV+ GIFTED, GIFTS, GIVE

A gift can be a blessing (1Sa 25:27), given to gain a favor (Ge 34:12), as an act of submission (Ps 68:29), an offering (Ex 28:38), a bribe (Pr 18:16). In the NT, anything given (Lk 21:1; Jas 1:17), a present (Mt 7:11), special spiritual endowment (Ro 1:11; 1Ti 4:14). *See Gifts From God.*

GIFTS FROM GOD

Himself:

In Christ, the Savior (Isa 42:6; 55:4; Jn 3:16; 4:10; 6:32-33), in the Holy Spirit, the Comforter. *See Holy Spirit.*

Temporal:

Food and clothing (Mt 6:25,33). Rain and fruitful seasons (Ge 8:22; 27:28; Lev 26:4-5; Isa 30:23). Wisdom (2Ch 1:12). Peace (Lev 26:6; 1Ch 22:9).

Gladness—

Ps 4:7 You have filled my heart with greater joy than when their grain and new wine abound.

Strength and power (Ps 29:11)—

Ps 68:18 When you ascended on high, you led captives in your train; you received gifts from men, even from the rebellious—that you, O LORD God, might dwell there.

Wisdom and knowledge—

Ecc 2:26 To the man who pleases him, God gives wisdom, knowledge and happiness, but to the sinner he gives the task of gathering and storing up wealth to hand it over to the one who pleases God. This too is meaningless, a chasing after the wind.

Da 2:21 He changes times and seasons; he sets up kings and deposes them. He gives wisdom to the wise and knowledge to the discerning. [22]He reveals deep and hidden things; he knows what lies in darkness, and light dwells with him. [23]I thank and praise you, O God of my fathers: You have given me wisdom and power, you have made known to me what we asked of you, you have made known to us the dream of the king."

1Co 1:5 For in him you have been enriched in every way—in all your speaking and in all your knowledge— [6]because our testimony about Christ was confirmed in you. [7]Therefore you do not lack any spiritual gift as you eagerly wait for our Lord Jesus Christ to be revealed.

Talents, figurative of gifts and abilities (Mt 25:14-30).

All good things—

Ps 21:2 You have granted him the desire of his heart and have not withheld the request of his lips. *Selah*

Ps 34:10 The lions may grow weak and hungry, but those who seek the LORD lack no good thing.

Ps 84:11 For the LORD God is a sun and shield; the LORD bestows favor and honor; no good thing does he withhold from those whose walk is blameless.

Isa 42:5 This is what God the LORD says—he who created the heavens and stretched them out, who spread out the earth and all that comes out of it, who gives breath to its people, and life to those who walk on it:

Eze 11:19 I will give them an undivided heart and put a new spirit in them; I will remove from them their heart of stone and give them a heart of flesh.

Jn 16:23 In that day you will no longer ask me anything. I tell you the truth, my Father will give you whatever you ask in my name. [24]Until now you have not asked for anything in my name. Ask and you will receive, and your joy will be complete.

Ro 8:32 He who did not spare his own Son, but gave him up for us all—how will he not also, along with him, graciously give us all things?

1Ti 6:17 Command those who are rich in this present world not to be arrogant nor to put their hope in wealth, which is so uncertain, but to put their hope in God, who richly provides us with everything for our enjoyment.

Jas 1:17 Every good and perfect gift is from above, coming down from the Father of the heavenly lights, who does not change like shifting shadows.

2Pe 1:3 His divine power has given us everything we need for life and godliness through our knowledge of him who called us by his own glory and goodness.

To be used and enjoyed (Ecc 3:13; 5:19-20; 1Ti 4:4-5). Should cause us to remember God (Dt 8:18). All creatures partake of (Ps 136:25; 145:15-16). Prayer for (Zec 10:1; Mt 6:11). *See Presents.*

Spiritual:

Of the Spirit—

Ro 11:29 for God's gifts and his call are irrevocable.

Ro 12:6 We have different gifts, according to the grace given us. If a man's gift is prophesying, let him use it in proportion to his faith. [7]If it is serving, let him serve; if it is teaching, let him teach; [8]if it is encouraging, let him encourage; if it is contributing to the needs of others, let him give generously; if it is leadership, let him govern diligently; if it is showing mercy, let him do it cheerfully.

1Co 7:7 I wish that all men were as I am. But each man has his own gift from God; one has this gift, another has that.

1Co 12:4 There are different kinds of gifts, but the same Spirit. [5]There are different kinds of service, but the same Lord. [6]There are different kinds of working, but the same God works all of them in all men.

[7]Now to each one the manifestation of the Spirit is given for the common good. [8]To one there is given through the Spirit the message of wisdom, to another the message of knowledge by means of the same Spirit, [9]to another faith by the same Spirit, to another gifts of healing by that one Spirit, [10]to another miraculous powers, to another prophecy, to another distinguishing between spirits, to another speaking in different kinds of tongues, and to still another the interpretation of tongues. [11]All these are the work of one and the same Spirit, and he gives them to each one, just as he determines.

1Co 13:2 If I have the gift of prophecy and can fathom all mysteries and all knowledge, and if I have a faith that can move mountains, but have not love, I am nothing.

Eph 4:7 But to each one of us grace has been given as Christ apportioned it.

1Pe 4:10 Each one should use whatever gift he has received to serve others, faithfully administering God's grace in its various forms.

Life, eternal (Isa 42:5; Eze 11:19; Jn 3:16-17,36)—

Jn 6:27 Do not work for food that spoils, but for food that endures to eternal life, which the Son of Man will give you. On him God the Father has placed his seal of approval."

Ro 5:16 Again, the gift of God is not like the result of the one man's sin: The judgment followed one sin and brought condemnation, but the gift followed many trespasses and brought justification. [17]For if, by the trespass of the one man, death reigned through that one man, how much more will those who receive God's abundant provision of grace and of the gift of righteousness reign in life through the one man, Jesus Christ.

[18]Consequently, just as the result of one trespass was condemnation for all men, so also the result of one act of righteousness was justification that brings life for all men.

Ro 6:23 For the wages of sin is death, but the gift of God is eternal life in Christ Jesus our Lord.

Grace (Jas 4:6). Wisdom (Pr 2:6; Jas 1:5). Repentance (Ac 11:28). Faith (Eph 2:8; Php 1:29).

Rest—

Mt 11:28 "Come to me, all you who are weary and burdened, and I will give you rest.

Glory—

Jn 17:22 I have given them the glory that you gave me, that they may be one as we are one:

See Blessings, Spiritual, From God; Charism, Charisma, Charismata; Tongues, Gift of.

GIHON [1633] (*to gush forth*).

1. A river in Egypt (Ge 2:13).

2. Pools near Jerusalem (1Ki 1:33,38,45). Hezekiah brings the waters of the upper pool by an aqueduct into the city of Jerusalem (2Ch 32:4,30; 33:14; Ne 2:13-15; 3:13-16; Isa 7:3; 22:9-11; 36:2).

GILALAI [1675]. A priest and musician (Ne 12:36).

GILBOA [1648] (*bubbling*). A hill S of Jezreel, where Saul was defeated by the Philistines and died (1Sa 28:4; 31:1-8; 1Ch 10:1-8).

GILEAD [824+1680, 1201+1682, 1201+1680, 1680, 1682] (perhaps *monument of stones*).

NIV+ GILEAD'S, GILEADITE, GILEADITES, JABESH GILEAD, RAMOTH GILEAD

1. A region E of the Jordan allotted to the tribes of Reuben and Gad and the half tribe of Manasseh (Nu 32:1-30; Dt 3:13; 34:1; 2Ki 10:33). Reubenites expel the Hagrites from (1Ch 5:9-10,18-22). Ammonites make war against; defeated by Jephthah (Jdg 11; Am 1:13). The prophet Elijah a native of (1Ki 17:1). David retreats to, at the time of Absalom's rebellion (2Sa 17:16,22,24). Pursued into, by Absalom (2Sa 17:26). Absalom defeated and slain in the forests of (2Sa 18:9).

Hazael, king of Syria, attacks the land of (2Ki 10:32-33; Am 1:3). Invaded by Tiglath-Pileser, king of Syria (2Ki 15:29). A grazing country (Nu 32:1; 1Ch 5:9). Exported spices, balm, and myrrh (Ge 37:25; Jer 8:22; 46:11).

Figurative of prosperity (Jer 22:6; 50:19).

2. A mountain (Jdg 7:3; SS 4:1; 6:5).

3. A city (Hos 6:8; 12:11).

4. Grandson of Manasseh (Nu 26:29-30; 27:1; 36:1; Jos 17:1,3; 1Ch 2:21,23; 7:14,17).

5. Father of Jephthah (Jdg 11:1-2).

6. A chief of Gad (1Ch 5:14).

GILGAL [1652] (*circle of stones*).

NIV+ BETH GILGAL

1. Place of the first encampment of the Israelites W of the Jordan (Jos 4:19; 9:6; 10:6,43; 14:6). Monument erected in, to commemorate the passage of the Jordan by the Israelites (Jos 4:19-24). Circumcision renewed at (Jos 5:2-9). Passover kept at (Jos 5:10-11). Manna ceased at, after the Passover (Jos 5:12). Quarries at (Jdg 3:19). Eglon, king of Moab, resides and is slain at (Jdg 3:14-26). A judgment seat, where Israel, in that district, came to be judged by Samuel (1Sa 7:16). Saul proclaimed king over all Israel at (1Sa 11:15; 13:4-15; 15:6-23). Agag, king of the Amalekites, slain at, by Samuel (1Sa 15:33). Tribe of Judah assembles at, to proceed to the E side of the Jordan to conduct King David back after the defeat of Absalom (2Sa 19:14-15,40-43). A school of the prophets at (2Ki 4:38-40).

Prophecies concerning (Hos 4:15; 9:15; 12:11; Am 4:4; 5:5).

2. A royal city in Canaan. Conquered by Joshua (Jos 12:23).

GILOH [1656]. A town near Hebron in the western foothills of Judah (Jos 15:51; 2Sa 15:12).

GILONITE [1639]. Ahithophel, one of David's counselors from the town of Giloh (2Sa 15:12; 23:34).

GIMZO [1693] (*place of sycamore trees*). A town off the Jerusalem Highway, three miles SW of Lydda (2Ch 28:18).

GIN *See Snare; Trap.*

GINATH [1640] (*protector*). The father of Tibni (1Ki 16:21).

GINNETHO *See Ginnethon.*

GINNETHON [1715].

NIV+ GINNETHON'S

A priest who returned to Jerusalem with Zerubbabel (Ne 10:6; 12:4).

GIRDLE *See Belt; Sash.*

GIRGASHITES [1739]. A Canaanite people (Ge 10:15). Land of given to Abraham and his descendants (Ge 15:21; Dt 7:1; Jos 3:10; Ne 9:8). Driven out before the Israelites (Jos 24:11).

GIRZITES, GERZITES [1747] (*people from Gezer*). A tribe named with the Geshurites and the Amalekites (1Sa 27:8).

GISHPA [1778] (*listener*). An overseer of the temple servants (Ne 11:21).

GITTAH-HEPHER A prolonged form of Gath Hepher.

See Gath Hepher.

GITTAIM [1786] (*two winepresses*). A town of Benjamin to which the Beerothites fled (Ne 11:31,33; 2Sa 4:3). The site is unknown.

GITTITE(S) [1785] (*of Gath*). Natives of Gath (Jos 13:1-3; 2Sa 6:8-11; 15:18; 21:19).

GITTITH [1787]. A word found in the titles of Psalms 8, 81, 84. It may denote a musical instrument imported from Gath or may be the title of a tune.

GIVING [*5447, 5989, 7061, *1443, *1521, *1522, *1797].

NIV+ GIVE, GAVE, GIVEN, GIVER, GIVES, LIFE-GIVING

Rules for:

Without ostentation—

Mt 6:1 "Be careful not to do your 'acts of righteousness' before men, to be seen by them. If you do, you will have no reward from your Father in heaven.

²"So when you give to the needy, do not announce it with trumpets, as the hypocrites do in the synagogues and on the streets, to be honored by men. I tell you the truth, they have received their reward in full. ³But when you give to the needy, do not let your left hand know what your right hand is doing, ⁴so that your giving may be in secret. Then your Father, who sees what is done in secret, will reward you.

Regularly—

1Co 16:2 On the first day of every week, each one of you should set aside a sum of money in keeping with his income, saving it up, so that when I come no collections will have to be made.

Liberally—

2Co 9:6 Remember this: Whoever sows sparingly will also reap sparingly, and whoever sows generously will also reap generously. ⁷Each man should give what he has decided in his heart to give, not reluctantly or under compulsion, for God loves a cheerful giver. (+2Co 9:8-15)

Cheerfully—

2Co 8:11 Now finish the work, so that your eager willingness to do it may be matched by your completion of it, according to your means. ¹²For if the willingness is there, the gift is acceptable according to what one has, not according to what he does not have. (+2Co 9:7)

See Alms; Beneficence; Liberality.

GIZONITE [1604]. The title of the sons of Hashem, among David's bodyguards (1Ch 11:34).

GLADIATOR One who contends with wild beasts (1Co 15:32). *See Games.*

GLADNESS [448+1637+8524, 1637, 8523, 8525, 8607]. *See Joy.*

GLASS [*5612, 5613*]. Was manufactured as early as 2500 B.C. by the Egyptians, and later by the Phoenicians, who promoted its commercial use, especially in jewelry. In the KJV, the glass mentioned by Paul (2Co 3:18) and by James (Jas 1:23-24) was a mirror of polished bronze. *See Mirror.* The references in Revelation to the sea of glass (Rev 4:6; 15:2) and the new Jerusalem (Rev 21:18,21) emphasize the purity and clarity of crystal.

GLEAN, GLEANING [4377, 4378, 4380, 6618, 6622].

NIV+ GLEANED, GLEANING, GLEANINGS, GLEANS

Laws concerning

The Hebrew custom of allowing the poor to follow the reapers, and to gather the grain or grapes that remained after the harvest (Lev 19:9-10; 23:22; Dt 24:19-20). *See Orphan; Strangers; Widow.*

Figurative: (Jdg 8:2; Isa 17:6; Jer 49:9; Mic 7:1).

Instances of: Ruth in the field of Boaz (Ru 2:2-3).

GLEDE *See Red Kite.*

GLORIFIED SAINTS [*1519*]. Great cloud of witnesses (Heb 12:1), righteous people made perfect (Heb 12:23; Rev 6:11), 144,000 (Rev 14:1-5).

Under the altar (Rev 6:9), before the throne (Rev 14:3). Sing song of redemption (Rev 14:3), of worship (Rev 15:2-4).

GLORIFYING GOD [1540, 3877, 8655, 10198, *1443+1518, 1519, 3486*]. Commanded (1Ch 16:28; Ps 22:23; Isa 42:12). Due to him (1Ch 16:29) for his holiness (Ps 99:9; Rev 15:4), mercy and truth (Ps 115:1; Ro 15:9), faithfulness and truth (Isa 25:1), wondrous works (Mt 15:31; Ac 4:21), judgments (Isa 25:3; Eze 28:22; Rev 14:7), deliverances (Ps 50:15), grace to others (Ac 11:18; 2Co 9:13; Gal 1:24).

Accomplished by:

Relying on his promises (Ro 4:20), praising him (Ps 50:23), doing all to glorify him (1Co 10:31), dying for him (Jn 21:19), suffering for Christ (1Pe 4:14,16), glorifying Christ (Ac 19:17; 2Th 1:12), bringing forth fruits of righteousness (Jn 15:8; Php 1:11), patience in affliction (Isa 24:1-3,15), faithfulness (1Pe 4:11). Required in body and spirit (1Co 6:20). Shall be universal (Ps 86:9; Rev 5:13).

Believers:

Should resolve on (Ps 69:30; 118:28), unite in (Ps 34:3; Ro 15:6), persevere in (Ps 86:12). All the blessings of God are designed to lead to (Isa 60:21; 61:3). The holy example of the believers may lead others to (Mt 5:16; 1Pe 2:12).

All, by nature, fail in (Ro 3:23). The wicked averse to (Da 5:23; Ro 1:21). Punishment for not (Da 5:23,30; Mal 2:2; Ac 12:23; Ro 1:21). Heavenly hosts engaged in (Rev 4:11).

Exemplified:

By David (Ps 57:5), the multitude (Mt 9:8; 15:31), the virgin Mary (Lk 1:46), the angels (Lk 2:14), the shepherds (Lk 2:20), by Jesus (Jn 17:4), the paralyzed man (Lk 5:25), the woman with infirmity (Lk 13:13), the leper whom Jesus healed (Lk 17:15), the blind man (Lk 18:43), the centurion (Lk 23:47), the church at Jerusalem (Ac 11:18), the Gentiles at Antioch (Ac 13:48), Abraham (Ro 4:20), Paul (Ro 11:36).

See Praise.

GLORY [*1540, 2086, 2146, 3877, 3883, 7382, 8655, 9514, 10331, 1518, 1519, 1901*].

NIV+ GLORIES, GLORIFIED, GLORIFIES, GLORIFY, GLORIFYING, GLORIOUS, GLORIOUSLY

Concerning God, the exhibition of his divine attributes and perfections (Ps 19:1) or the radiance of his presence (Lk 2:9). Concerning people, the manifestation of their commendable qualities, such as wisdom, righteousness, self-control, ability, etc. Glory is destiny of believers (Php 3:21; Ro 8:21; 1Co 15:43).

Spiritual:

Is given by God (Ps 84:11), is the work of the Holy Spirit (2Co 3:18).

Eternal:

Secured by the death of Christ (Heb 2:10), accompanies salvation by Christ (2Ti 2:10), inherited by believers (1Sa 2:8; Ps 73:24; Pr 3:35; Col 3:4; 1Pe 5:10), believers called to (2Th 2:14; 1Pe 5:10), enhanced by afflictions (2Co 4:17), present afflictions not worthy to be compared with (Ro 8:18), of the church shall be rich and abundant (Isa 60:11-13), the bodies of believers shall be raised in (1Co 15:43; Php 3:21), believers shall be glory of their ministers (1Th 2:19-20), afflictions of ministers are glory to believers (Eph 3:13).

Temporal:

Is given by God (Da 2:37), passes away (1Pe 1:24). The devil tries to seduce by (Mt 4:8). Of hypocrites turned to shame (Hos 4:7). Seek not, from man (Mt 6:2; 1Th 2:6). Of the wicked is in their shame (Php 3:19). Ends in destruction (Isa 5:14).

Of God:

Exhibited in Christ (Jn 1:14; 2Co 4:6; Heb 1:3). Ascribed to God (Gal 1:5).

Exhibited in his name (Dt 28:58; Ne 9:5), his majesty (Job 37:22; Ps 93:1; 104:1; 145:5,12; Isa 2:10), his power (Ex 15:1,6; Ro 6:4), his works (Ps 19:1; 111:3), his holiness (Ex 15:11).

Described as great (Ps 138:5), eternal (Ps 104:31), rich (Eph 3:16), highly exalted (Ps 8:1; 113:4).

Exhibited to Moses (Ex 34:5-7, w 33:18-23). Stephen (Ac 7:55), his church (Dt 5:24; Ps 102:16).

Enlightens the church (Isa 60:1-2; Rev 21:11,23). Believers desire to behold (Ps 63:2; 90:16). God is jealous of (Isa 42:8). The earth is full of (Isa 6:3). The knowledge of, shall fill the earth (Hab 2:14).

GLOWING METAL [3133, *4792*].

1. *Glowing metal* used to describe the color of divine glory (Eze 1:4,27; 8:2).

2. *Bronze glowing in a furnace* used in John's description of the King of Glory (Rev 1:15).

See Amber; Minerals of the Bible, 1; Stones.

GLUTTONY [1251+5883, 2361, *1143*, *5741*].

NIV+ GLUTTON, GLUTTED, GLUTTONS

Impoverishes (Pr 23:21).

Deadens moral sensibilities—

Am 6:4 You lie on beds inlaid with ivory and lounge on your couches. You dine on choice lambs and fattened calves. [5]You strum away on your harps like David and improvise on musical instruments. [6]You drink wine by the bowlful and use the finest lotions, but you do not grieve over the ruin of Joseph. [7]Therefore you will be among the first to go into exile; your feasting and lounging will end.

Lk 12:19 And I'll say to myself, "You have plenty of good things laid up for many years. Take life easy; eat, drink and be merry." '

[20]"But God said to him, 'You fool! This very night your life will be demanded from you. Then who will get what you have prepared for yourself?'

Lk 12:45 But suppose the servant says to himself, 'My master is taking a long time in coming,' and he then begins to beat the menservants and maidservants and to eat and drink and get drunk. [46]The master of that servant will come on a day when he does not expect him and at an hour he is not aware of. He will cut him to pieces and assign him a place with the unbelievers.

Php 3:19 Their destiny is destruction, their god is their stomach, and their glory is in their shame. Their mind is on earthly things.

Loathsome—

Pr 30:21 "Under three things the earth trembles, under four it cannot bear up: [22]a servant who becomes king, a fool who is full of food,

Punished, by death (Dt 21:20-21), plagues (Nu 11:32-33).

Associated with drunkenness—

Dt 21:20 They shall say to the elders, "This son of ours is stubborn and rebellious. He will not obey us. He is a profligate and a drunkard." [21]Then all the men of his town shall stone him to death. You must purge the evil from among you. All Israel will hear of it and be afraid.

Pr 23:21 for drunkards and gluttons become poor, and drowsiness clothes them in rags.

Ecc 10:17 Blessed are you, O land whose king is of noble birth and whose princes eat at a proper time—for strength and not for drunkenness. (+Lk 12:45-46; Ro 13:13)

1Pe 4:3 For you have spent enough time in the past doing what pagans choose to do—living in debauchery, lust, drunkenness, orgies, carousing and detestable idolatry.

Proverb relating to—

Isa 22:13 But see, there is joy and revelry, slaughtering of cattle and killing of sheep, eating of meat and drinking of wine! "Let us eat and drink," you say, "for tomorrow we die!"

1Co 15:32 If I fought wild beasts in Ephesus for merely human reasons, what have I gained? If the dead are not raised, "Let us eat and drink, for tomorrow we die."

Jesus falsely accused of (Mt 11:19; Lk 7:34).

Warnings against (Pr 30:21-22)—

Lk 21:34 "Be careful, or your hearts will be weighed down with dissipation, drunkenness and the anxieties of life, and that day will close on you unexpectedly like a trap.

Ro 13:13 Let us behave decently, as in the daytime, not in orgies and drunkenness, not in sexual immorality and debauchery, not in dissension and jealousy. [14]Rather, clothe yourselves with the Lord Jesus Christ, and do not

think about how to gratify the desires of the sinful nature. (+1Pe 4:2-3)

Instances of:

Israelites—

Ex 16:20 However, some of them paid no attention to Moses; they kept part of it until morning, but it was full of maggots and began to smell. So Moses was angry with them.

[21]Each morning everyone gathered as much as he needed, and when the sun grew hot, it melted away. (+Nu 11:4)

Nu 11:32 All that day and night and all the next day the people went out and gathered quail. No one gathered less than ten homers. Then they spread them out all around the camp. [33]But while the meat was still between their teeth and before it could be consumed, the anger of the LORD burned against the people, and he struck them with a severe plague. (+Nu 11:34-35; Ps 78:18)

Sons of Eli (1Sa 2:12-17). Belshazzar (Da 5:1).

See Pleasure, Worldly.

GNASH [3080, *1106*, *1107*, *5563*].

NIV+ GNASHED, GNASHES, GNASHING

To grind the teeth together as an expression of rage (Job 16:9), hatred (Ps 37:12), frustration (Ps 112:10). In the NT it expresses anguish and failure rather than anger (Mt 8:12; 13:42,50; 25:30).

GNASHING OF TEETH [*1106*+*3848*]. Of the enemy, in maliciousness (Job 16:9; Ps 35:16; 37:12; 112:10; La 2:16). Of the lost, from anguish of spirit (Mt 8:12; 13:42; 22:13; 24:51; 25:30; Lk 13:28).

GNAT [4031, 4038, *3270*].

NIV+ GNATS

Plague of (Ex 8:16-19; Ps 105:31). *See Insects.*

GNOSTICISM A second-century heresy that was a mixture of Judaism, Christianity, and Greek mystery religions. Its forerunners are seen in the errors refuted in the books of Colossians, 1 and 2 Timothy, 2 Peter, and 1 John. Some of its major tenets were:

1. The human body is matter, and therefore is evil. It is to be contrasted with God, who is wholly spirit and therefore good.

2. Salvation is the escape from the body, achieved not by faith in Christ but by special knowledge (the Greek word for "knowledge" is *gnosis*, from which comes Gnosticism).

3. Christ's true humanity was denied in two ways: (1) Some said that Christ only seemed to have a body, a view called Docetism, and (2) others said that the divine Christ joined the man Jesus at baptism and left him before he died, a view called Cerinthianism, after its most prominent spokesman, Cerinthus. This view is the background of much of 1 John (see 1Jn 1:1; 2:22; 4:2-3).

4. Since the body was considered evil, it was to be treated harshly. This ascetic form of Gnosticism is the background of part Colossians (Col 2:21-23).

5. Paradoxically, this dualism also led to immorality. Since matter (and not the breaking of God's law) was considered evil, breaking his law was of no moral consequence.

GOAD [1995, 1996, *3034*].

NIV+ GOADS

An instrument for prodding animals (1Sa 13:21; Ac

26:14). Six hundred men slain with by Shamgar, a judge of Israel (Jdg 3:31). *See Oxgoad.*

Figurative: Of mental incentive (Ecc 12:11).

GOAH [1717]. A place near Jerusalem (Jer 31:39).

GOAT [735, 1531, 1537, 3604, 6436+, ~~7618~~, 8538, 8539, 10535+10615, *2252, 2253, 5543*].

NIV+ GOAT'S, GOATS, GOATS', GOATSKINS, HE-GOAT, SCAPEGOAT

Designated as one of the clean animals to be eaten (Lev 11:1-8; Dt 14:4). Used for food (Ge 27:9; 1Sa 16:20), for the passover feast (Ex 12:5; 2Ch 35:7), as a sacrifice by Abraham (Ge 15:9), by Gideon (Jdg 6:19), Manoah (Jdg 13:19). Milk of, used for food (Pr 27:27). Hair of, used for clothing (Nu 31:20), pillows (1Sa 19:13), curtains of the tabernacle (Ex 26:7; 35:23; 36:14). Used for tents. *See Curtains; Tabernacle.* Mosaic law required that a kid should not be killed for food before it was eight days old (Lev 22:27), nor should it be boiled in its mother's milk (Ex 23:19). Numerous (Dt 32:14; SS 4:1; 6:5; 1Sa 25:2; 2Ch 17:11). Wild, in Israel (1Sa 24:2; Ps 104:18).

GOATS' HAIR [6436+, *128+1293*]. (Ex 25:4; 26:7; 35:6; 36:14; Nu 31:20).

GOB [1570] (*cistern*). The site of two of David's battles with the Philistines (2Sa 21:18-19).

GOBLET [110, 3926+7694, 3998, 10398]. *See Cup.*

GOD [446, 466, 468, 1425, 2006, 3051, 5822, 9199, 9359, 10033, *117, 356, 620, 1467, 1565, 2516, 2531, 2534, 2536, 2537, 4666, 5806*].

NIV+ GOD'S, GOD-BREATHED, GOD-FEARING, GOD-HATERS, GODDESS, GODLESS, GODLESSNESS, GODLINESS, GODLY, GODS

Access to:

Israel—

Dt 4:7 What other nation is so great as to have their gods near them the way the LORD our God is near us whenever we pray to him?

The pure of heart—

Ps 24:3 Who may ascend the hill of the LORD? Who may stand in his holy place? ⁴He who has clean hands and a pure heart, who does not lift up his soul to an idol or swear by what is false.

The thirsty—

Isa 55:3 Give ear and come to me; hear me, that your soul may live. I will make an everlasting covenant with you, my faithful love promised to David.

Gentiles—

Ac 14:27 On arriving there, they gathered the church together and reported all that God had done through them and how he had opened the door of faith to the Gentiles.

Enemies of God (Col 1:21-22)

Believers—

Heb 4:16 Let us then approach the throne of grace with confidence, so that we may receive mercy and find grace to help us in our time of need.

1Pe 1:17 Since you call on a Father who judges each man's work impartially, live your lives as strangers here in reverent fear.

The cleansed—

Jas 4:8 Come near to God and he will come near to you. Wash your hands, you sinners, and purify your hearts, you double-minded.

Through hope—

Ps 27:4 One thing I ask of the LORD, this is what I seek: that I may dwell in the house of the LORD all the days of my life, to gaze upon the beauty of the LORD and to seek him in his temple.

Ps 43:2 You are God my stronghold. Why have you rejected me? Why must I go about mourning, oppressed by the enemy?

Through fear—

Ps 145:18 The LORD is near to all who call on him, to all who call on him in truth. ¹⁹He fulfills the desires of those who fear him; he hears their cry and saves them. (+1Pe 1:17)

Through prayer—

Mt 6:6 But when you pray, go into your room, close the door and pray to your Father, who is unseen. Then your Father, who sees what is done in secret, will reward you. (+Heb 4:10)

Through faith—

Heb 11:6 And without faith it is impossible to please God, because anyone who comes to him must believe that he exists and that he rewards those who earnestly seek him.

Through love—

1Jn 4:16 And so we know and rely on the love God has for us. God is love. Whoever lives in love lives in God, and God in him.

Through Christ—

Jn 10:7 Therefore Jesus said again, "I tell you the truth, I am the gate for the sheep.

Jn 10:9 I am the gate; whoever enters through me will be saved. He will come in and go out, and find pasture.

Jn 14:6 Jesus answered, "I am the way and the truth and the life. No one comes to the Father except through me."

Ro 5:2 through whom we have gained access by faith into this grace in which we now stand. And we rejoice in the hope of the glory of God.

Eph 2:13 But now in Christ Jesus you who once were far away have been brought near through the blood of Christ.

Eph 2:18 For through him we both have access to the Father by one Spirit.

Eph 3:12 In him and through faith in him we may approach God with freedom and confidence.

Col 1:21 Once you were alienated from God and were enemies in your minds because of your evil behavior. ²²But now he has reconciled you by Christ's physical body through death to present you holy in his sight, without blemish and free from accusation—

Heb 7:19 (for the law made nothing perfect), and a better hope is introduced, by which we draw near to God.

Heb 7:25 Therefore he is able to save completely those who come to God through him, because he always lives to intercede for them.

Heb 10:19 Therefore, brothers, since we have confidence to enter the Most Holy Place by the blood of Jesus,

Heb 10:22 let us draw near to God with a sincere heart in full assurance of faith, having our hearts sprinkled to cleanse us from a guilty conscience and having our bodies washed with pure water. (+1Pe 1:17)

Satisfying—

Ps 65:4 Blessed are those you choose and bring near to live in your courts! We are filled with the good things of your house, of your holy temple.

Anger of: *See Anger of God.*

Appearance of:

To Adam (Ge 3:8-21). To Abraham (Ge 17:1; 18:2-33).

To Jacob, at Peniel (Ge 32:30), at Bethel (Ge 35:7,9). To Moses, in the burning bush (Ex 3:2; Dt 33:16; Mk 12:26; Lk 20:37; Ac 7:30), at Sinai (Ex 19:16-24; 24:10; 33:18-23). To Moses and Joshua (Dt 31:14-15). To princes of Israel, at Sinai (Ex 24:9-11). To Gideon (Jdg 6:11-24). To Solomon (1Ki 3:5; 9:2; 11:9; 2Ch 1:7-12; 7:12-22). To Isaiah (Isa 6:1-5). To Ezekiel (Eze 1:26-28).

Compassion of: *See below, Longsuffering of; Mercy of.*

Condescension of: (Ps 113:5-6).

Manifested: In reasoning, with Noah (Ge 6:11-13), with Moses (Ex 4:2-17), with sinners (Isa 1:18-20). In entering into a covenant with Abraham (Ge 15:1-21; 18:1-22). In indulging Abraham's intercession for Sodom (Ge 18:2-33). In indulging Moses' prayer to behold his glory (Ex 33:18-23). In indulging Gideon's tests (Jdg 6:36-40). In his care of man (Ps 8:4-6; 144:3). In redemption (Jn 3:16; Ro 5:8; Heb 6:17-18).

Creator: (Ps 148:3-4)

Ps 148:5 Let them praise the name of the LORD, for he commanded and they were created.

Pr 16:4 The LORD works out everything for his own ends—even the wicked for a day of disaster. (+Isa 45:7)

Isa 66:2 Has not my hand made all these things, and so they came into being?" declares the LORD. "This is the one I esteem: he who is humble and contrite in spirit, and trembles at my word. (+Jer 51:19)

Am 4:13 He who forms the mountains, creates the wind, and reveals his thoughts to man, he who turns dawn to darkness, and treads the high places of the earth—the LORD God Almighty is his name. .

Mk 13:19 because those will be days of distress unequaled from the beginning, when God created the world, until now—and never to be equaled again.

Ac 7:50 Has not my hand made all these things?'

Ro 1:20 For since the creation of the world God's invisible qualities—his eternal power and divine nature—have been clearly seen, being understood from what has been made, so that men are without excuse. (+1Co 11:12)

Heb 2:10 In bringing many sons to glory, it was fitting that God, for whom and through whom everything exists, should make the author of their salvation perfect through suffering.

Heb 3:4 For every house is built by someone, but God is the builder of everything. (+Rev 4:11)

Creator of the earth—

Ge 1:1 In the beginning God created the heavens and the earth. ²Now the earth was formless and empty, darkness was over the surface of the deep, and the Spirit of God was hovering over the waters. (+Ge 1:9-10; 2:1-4)

Ex 20:11 For in six days the LORD made the heavens and the earth, the sea, and all that is in them, but he rested on the seventh day. Therefore the LORD blessed the Sabbath day and made it holy.

1Sa 2:8 He raises the poor from the dust and lifts the needy from the ash heap; he seats them with princes and has them inherit a throne of honor. "For the foundations of the earth are the LORD's; upon them he has set the world.

2Ki 19:15 And Hezekiah prayed to the LORD: "O LORD, God of Israel, enthroned between the cherubim, you alone are God over all the kingdoms of the earth. You have made heaven and earth. (+Ne 9:6)

Job 38:4 "Where were you when I laid the earth's foundation? Tell me, if you understand.

Job 38:7 while the morning stars sang together and all the angels shouted for joy?

⁸"Who shut up the sea behind doors when it burst forth from the womb, ⁹when I made the clouds its garment and wrapped it in thick darkness, ¹⁰when I fixed limits for it and set its doors and bars in place,

Ps 24:1 The earth is the LORD's, and everything in it, the world, and all who live in it; ²for he founded it upon the seas and established it upon the waters.

Ps 89:11 The heavens are yours, and yours also the earth; you founded the world and all that is in it.

Ps 90:2 Before the mountains were born or you brought forth the earth and the world, from everlasting to everlasting you are God.

Ps 95:5 The sea is his, for he made it, and his hands formed the dry land. (+Ps 102:25; 104:2-3,5-6,24,30)

Ps 119:90 Your faithfulness continues through all generations; you established the earth, and it endures. (+Ps 121:2; 124:8)

Ps 136:5 who by his understanding made the heavens, *His love endures forever.* ⁶who spread out the earth upon the waters, *His love endures forever.* ⁷who made the great lights—*His love endures forever.* ⁸the sun to govern the day, *His love endures forever.* (+Ps 136:9)

Ps 146:5 Blessed is he whose help is the God of Jacob, whose hope is in the LORD his God, ⁶the Maker of heaven and earth, the sea, and everything in them—the LORD, who remains faithful forever.

Pr 3:19 By wisdom the LORD laid the earth's foundations, by understanding he set the heavens in place;

Pr 8:26 before he made the earth or its fields or any of the dust of the world. ²⁷I was there when he set the heavens in place, when he marked out the horizon on the face of the deep, ²⁸when he established the clouds above and fixed securely the fountains of the deep, ²⁹when he gave the sea its boundary so the waters would not overstep his command, and when he marked out the foundations of the earth.

Isa 37:16 "O LORD Almighty, God of Israel, enthroned between the cherubim, you alone are God over all the kingdoms of the earth. You have made heaven and earth.

Isa 40:28 Do you not know? Have you not heard? The LORD is the everlasting God, the Creator of the ends of the earth. He will not grow tired or weary, and his understanding no one can fathom.

Isa 42:5 This is what God the LORD says—he who created the heavens and stretched them out, who spread out the earth and all that comes out of it, who gives breath to its people, and life to those who walk on it:

Isa 44:24 "This is what the LORD says—your Redeemer, who formed you in the womb: I am the LORD, who has made all things, who alone stretched out the heavens, who spread out the earth by myself,

Isa 45:12 It is I who made the earth and created mankind upon it. My own hands stretched out the heavens; I marshaled their starry hosts.

Isa 45:18 For this is what the LORD says—he who created the heavens, he is God; he who fashioned and made the earth, he founded it; he did not create it to be empty, but formed it to be inhabited—he says: "I am the LORD, and there is no other.

Isa 48:13 My own hand laid the foundations of the earth, and my right hand spread out the heavens; when I summon them, they all stand up together.

Isa 51:13 that you forget the LORD your Maker, who stretched out the heavens and laid the foundations of the earth, that you live in constant terror every day because of the wrath of the oppressor, who is bent on destruction? For where is the wrath of the oppressor?

Isa 51:16 I have put my words in your mouth and covered you with the shadow of my hand—I who set the heavens in place, who laid the foundations of the earth, and who say to Zion, 'You are my people.'"

Jer 10:12 But God made the earth by his power; he founded the world by his wisdom and stretched out the heavens by his understanding.

Jer 27:5 With my great power and outstretched arm I made the earth and its people and the animals that are on it, and I give it to anyone I please. (+Jer 32:17)

Jer 51:15 "He made the earth by his power; he founded the world by his wisdom and stretched out the heavens by his understanding.

Jnh 1:9 He answered, "I am a Hebrew and I worship the LORD, the God of heaven, who made the sea and the land."

Ac 4:24 When they heard this, they raised their voices together in prayer to God. "Sovereign Lord," they said, "you made the heaven and the earth and the sea, and everything in them. (+Ac 14:15; 17:24-25; Rev 10:6; 14:7)

Creator of the heavens (Ge 1:1)—

Ge 1:6 And God said, "Let there be an expanse between the waters to separate water from water." ⁷So God made the expanse and separated the water under the expanse from the water above it. And it was so. ⁸God called the expanse "sky." And there was evening, and there was morning—the second day.

Ge 2:1 Thus the heavens and the earth were completed in all their vast array. ²By the seventh day God had finished the work he had been doing; so on the seventh day he rested from all his work. ³And God blessed the seventh day and made it holy, because on it he rested from all the work of creating that he had done.

⁴This is the account of the heavens and the earth when they were created.

When the LORD God made the earth and the heavens— (+Ex 20:11; 2Ki 19:15)

1Ch 16:26 For all the gods of the nations are idols, but the LORD made the heavens.

Ne 9:6 You alone are the LORD. You made the heavens, even the highest heavens, and all their starry host, the earth and all that is on it, the seas and all that is in them. You give life to everything, and the multitudes of heaven worship you.

Job 9:8 He alone stretches out the heavens and treads on the waves of the sea. ⁹He is the Maker of the Bear and Orion, the Pleiades and the constellations of the south.

Job 37:16 Do you know how the clouds hang poised, those wonders of him who is perfect in knowledge?

Job 37:18 can you join him in spreading out the skies, hard as a mirror of cast bronze?

Ps 8:3 When I consider your heavens, the work of your fingers, the moon and the stars, which you have set in place,

Ps 19:1 The heavens declare the glory of God; the skies proclaim the work of his hands.

Ps 19:4 Their voice goes out into all the earth, their words to the ends of the world. In the heavens he has pitched a tent for the sun, (+Ps 96:5)

Ps 102:25 In the beginning you laid the foundations of the earth, and the heavens are the work of your hands.

Ps 104:2 He wraps himself in light as with a garment; he stretches out the heavens like a tent ³and lays the beams of his upper chambers on their waters. He makes the clouds his chariot and rides on the wings of the wind.

Ps 104:5 He set the earth on its foundations; it can never be moved. ⁶You covered it with the deep as with a garment; the waters stood above the mountains.

Ps 104:24 How many are your works, O LORD! In wisdom you made them all; the earth is full of your creatures.

Ps 104:30 When you send your Spirit, they are created, and you renew the face of the earth. (+Ps 121:2)

Ps 124:8 Our help is in the name of the LORD, the Maker of heaven and earth. (+Ps 136:5; 146:5-6; Pr 3:19; 8:26-28; Isa 37:16; 42:5; 44:24; 45:18)

Jer 32:17 "Ah, Sovereign LORD, you have made the heavens and the earth by your great power and outstretched arm. Nothing is too hard for you.

Am 5:8 (he who made the Pleiades and Orion, who turns blackness into dawn and darkens day into night, who calls for the waters of the sea and pours them out over the face of the land—the LORD is his name— (+Ac 4:24)

Ac 14:15 "Men, why are you doing this? We too are only men, human like you. We are bringing you good news, telling you to turn from these worthless things to the living God, who made heaven and earth and sea and everything in them. (+Rev 10:6; 14:7)

Creator of the sun, moon, and stars—

Ge 1:14 And God said, "Let there be lights in the expanse of the sky to separate the day from the night, and let them serve as signs to mark seasons and days and years, ¹⁵and let them be lights in the expanse of the sky to give light on the earth." And it was so. ¹⁶God made two great lights—the greater light to govern the day and the lesser light to govern the night. He also made the stars. ¹⁷God set them in the expanse of the sky to give light on the earth, ¹⁸to govern the day and the night, and to separate light from darkness. And God saw that it was good. ¹⁹And there was evening, and there was morning—the fourth day. (+Ps 136:7-9)

Creator of the seas—

Ge 1:9 And God said, "Let the water under the sky be gathered to one place, and let dry ground appear." And it was so. ¹⁰God called the dry ground "land," and the gathered waters he called "seas." And God saw that it was good. (+Ex 20:11; Ne 9:6; Ps 95:5; 146:5-6; Pr 8:26-29; Jnh 1:9; Ac 4:24; 14:15)

Rev 10:6 And he swore by him who lives for ever and ever, who created the heavens and all that is in them, the earth and all that is in it, and the sea and all that is in it, and said, "There will be no more delay!

Rev 14:7 He said in a loud voice, "Fear God and give him glory, because the hour of his judgment has come. Worship him who made the heavens, the earth, the sea and the springs of water."

Creator of vegetation—

Ge 1:11 Then God said, "Let the land produce vegetation: seed-bearing plants and trees on the land that bear fruit with seed in it, according to their various kinds." And it was so. ¹²The land produced vegetation: plants bearing seed according to their kinds and trees bearing fruit with seed in it according to their kinds. And God saw that it was good.

Creator of animals—

Ge 1:20 And God said, "Let the water teem with living creatures, and let birds fly above the earth across the expanse of the sky." ²¹So God created the great creatures of the sea and every living and moving thing with which the water teems, according to their kinds, and every winged bird according to its kind. And God saw that it was good. ²²God blessed them and said, "Be fruitful and increase in number and fill the water in the seas, and let the birds increase on the earth." [23]And there was evening, and there was morning—the fifth day. [24]And God said, "Let the land produce living creatures according to their kinds: livestock, creatures that move along the ground, and wild animals, each according to its kind." And it was so. [25]God made the wild animals according to their kinds, the livestock according to their kinds, and all the creatures that move along the ground according to their kinds. And God saw that it was good.

Job 12:7 "But ask the animals, and they will teach you, or the birds of the air, and they will tell you; [8]or speak to the earth, and it will teach you, or let the fish of the sea inform you. [9]Which of all these does not know that the hand of the LORD has done this? (+Jer 27:5)

Creator of Mankind:

Ge 1:26 Then God said, "Let us make man in our image, in our likeness, and let them rule over the fish of the sea and the birds of the air, over the livestock, over all the earth, and over all the creatures that move along the ground."

[27]So God created man in his own image, in the image of God he created him; male and female he created them.

[28]God blessed them and said to them, "Be fruitful and increase in number; fill the earth and subdue it. Rule over the fish of the sea and the birds of the air and over every living creature that moves on the ground."

Ge 2:7 the LORD God formed the man from the dust of the ground and breathed into his nostrils the breath of life, and the man became a living being.

Ge 5:1 This is the written account of Adam's line. When God created man, he made him in the likeness of God.

[2]He created them male and female and blessed them. And when they were created, he called them "man."

Ge 9:6 "Whoever sheds the blood of man, by man shall his blood be shed; for in the image of God has God made man.

Ex 4:11 The LORD said to him, "Who gave man his mouth? Who makes him deaf or mute? Who gives him sight or makes him blind? Is it not I, the LORD?

Dt 4:32 Ask now about the former days, long before your time, from the day God created man on the earth; ask from one end of the heavens to the other. Has anything so great as this ever happened, or has anything like it ever been heard of?

Dt 32:6 Is this the way you repay the LORD, O foolish and unwise people? Is he not your Father, your Creator, who made you and formed you?

Dt 32:15 Jeshurun grew fat and kicked; filled with food, he became heavy and sleek. He abandoned the God who made him and rejected the Rock his Savior.

Dt 32:18 You deserted the Rock, who fathered you; you forgot the God who gave you birth.

Job 10:3 Does it please you to oppress me, to spurn the work of your hands, while you smile on the schemes of the wicked?

Job 10:8 "Your hands shaped me and made me. Will you now turn and destroy me?

Job 10:9 Remember that you molded me like clay. Will you now turn me to dust again?

Job 10:11 clothe me with skin and flesh and knit me together with bones and sinews? [12]You gave me life and showed me kindness, and in your providence watched over my spirit.

Job 31:15 Did not he who made me in the womb make them? Did not the same one form us both within our mothers?

Job 33:4 The Spirit of God has made me; the breath of the Almighty gives me life.

Job 34:19 who shows no partiality to princes and does not favor the rich over the poor, for they are all the work of his hands?

Ps 94:9 Does he who implanted the ear not hear? Does he who formed the eye not see?

Ps 95:6 Come, let us bow down in worship, let us kneel before the LORD our Maker;

Ps 100:3 Know that the LORD is God. It is he who made us, and we are his; we are his people, the sheep of his pasture. (+Ps 119:73)

Ps 149:2 Let Israel rejoice in their Maker; let the people of Zion be glad in their King.

Pr 20:12 Ears that hear and eyes that see—the LORD has made them both.

Pr 22:2 Rich and poor have this in common: The LORD is the Maker of them all.

Ecc 7:29 This only have I found: God made mankind upright, but men have gone in search of many schemes."

Ecc 12:1 Remember your Creator in the days of your youth, before the days of trouble come and the years approach when you will say, "I find no pleasure in them"—

Isa 17:7 In that day men will look to their Maker and turn their eyes to the Holy One of Israel.

Isa 42:5 This is what God the LORD says—he who created the heavens and stretched them out, who spread out the earth and all that comes out of it, who gives breath to its people, and life to those who walk on it:

Isa 43:1 But now, this is what the LORD says—he who created you, O Jacob, he who formed you, O Israel: "Fear not, for I have redeemed you; I have summoned you by name; you are mine.

Isa 43:7 everyone who is called by my name, whom I created for my glory, whom I formed and made."

Isa 43:15 I am the LORD, your Holy One, Israel's Creator, your King."

Isa 44:2 This is what the LORD says—he who made you, who formed you in the womb, and who will help you: Do not be afraid, O Jacob, my servant, Jeshurun, whom I have chosen. (+Isa 44:24)

Isa 45:12 It is I who made the earth and created mankind upon it. My own hands stretched out the heavens; I marshaled their starry hosts.

Isa 51:13 that you forget the LORD your Maker, who stretched out the heavens and laid the foundations of the earth, that you live in constant terror every day because of the wrath of the oppressor, who is bent on destruction? For where is the wrath of the oppressor?

Isa 64:8 Yet, O LORD, you are our Father. We are the clay, you are the potter; we are all the work of your hand.

Jer 27:5 With my great power and outstretched arm I made the earth and its people and the animals that are on it, and I give it to anyone I please.

Zec 12:1 This is the word of the LORD concerning Israel. The LORD, who stretches out the heavens, who lays the foundation of the earth, and who forms the spirit of man within him, declares:

Mal 2:10 Have we not all one Father? Did not one God create us? Why do we profane the covenant of our fathers by breaking faith with one another?

Mk 10:6 "But at the beginning of creation God 'made them male and female.'

Ac 17:24 "The God who made the world and everything in it is the Lord of heaven and earth and does not live in temples built by hands. ²⁵And he is not served by human hands, as if he needed anything, because he himself gives all men life and breath and everything else. ²⁶From one man he made every nation of men, that they should inhabit the whole earth; and he determined the times set for them and the exact places where they should live. (+Ac 17:27)

Ac 17:28 'For in him we live and move and have our being.' As some of your own poets have said, 'We are his offspring.' (+Ac 17:29)

1Co 12:18 But in fact God has arranged the parts in the body, every one of them, just as he wanted them to be.

1Co 12:24 while our presentable parts need no special treatment. But God has combined the members of the body and has given greater honor to the parts that lacked it, ²⁵so that there should be no division in the body, but that its parts should have equal concern for each other.

Heb 12:9 Moreover, we have all had human fathers who disciplined us and we respected them for it. How much more should we submit to the Father of our spirits and live!

1Pe 4:19 So then, those who suffer according to God's will should commit themselves to their faithful Creator and continue to do good.

Creator of mankind through Christ—
Ro 11:36 For from him and through him and to him are all things. To him be the glory forever! Amen.

1Co 8:6 yet for us there is but one God, the Father, from whom all things came and for whom we live; and there is but one Lord, Jesus Christ, through whom all things came and through whom we live.

Eph 3:9 and to make plain to everyone the administration of this mystery, which for ages past was kept hidden in God, who created all things.

Heb 1:1 In the past God spoke to our forefathers through the prophets at many times and in various ways, ²but in these last days he has spoken to us by his Son, whom he appointed heir of all things, and through whom he made the universe. *See Jesus the Christ, Creator.*

Creator of mankind by his word—
Ps 33:6 By the word of the LORD were the heavens made, their starry host by the breath of his mouth. ⁷He gathers the waters of the sea into jars; he puts the deep into storehouses.

Ps 33:9 For he spoke, and it came to be; he commanded, and it stood firm.

2Co 4:6 For God, who said, "Let light shine out of darkness," made his light shine in our hearts to give us the light of the knowledge of the glory of God in the face of Christ.

Heb 11:3 By faith we understand that the universe was formed at God's command, so that what is seen was not made out of what was visible. (+2Pe 3:5)

Creator of mankind by his will—
Rev 4:11 "You are worthy, our Lord and God, to receive glory and honor and power, for you created all things, and by your will they were created and have their being."

Dissertations on:
His works and providence (Job 5:8-20). The administration of his government (Job 9:2-35; 10:1-22). His sovereignty (Job 12:7-20; 26:1-14). His providence and grace (Job 33:4-30; Ps 107). His righteousness (Job 34:10-30; 35:1-16; Na 1:2-9). His majesty and justice (Job 36:30-33). His majesty and works (Ps 104:10-15).

Dwells With the Righteous:
(Ex 25:8; 29:45; Lev 26:11-12; 1Ki 6:13; Eze 37:26-27; 2Co 6:16; Rev 21:3).

Eternity of:
Ge 21:33 Abraham planted a tamarisk tree in Beersheba, and there he called upon the name of the LORD, the Eternal God.

Ex 3:15 God also said to Moses, "Say to the Israelites, 'The LORD, the God of your fathers—the God of Abraham, the God of Isaac and the God of Jacob—has sent me to you.' This is my name forever, the name by which I am to be remembered from generation to generation. (+Ex 15:18)

Dt 32:40 I lift my hand to heaven and declare: As surely as I live forever,

Dt 33:27 The eternal God is your refuge, and underneath are the everlasting arms. He will drive out your enemy before you, saying, 'Destroy him!'

1Ch 16:36 Praise be to the LORD, the God of Israel, from everlasting to everlasting. Then all the people said "Amen" and "Praise the LORD."

1Ch 29:10 David praised the LORD in the presence of the whole assembly, saying, "Praise be to you, O LORD, God of our father Israel, from everlasting to everlasting.

Ne 9:5 And the Levites—Jeshua, Kadmiel, Bani, Hashabneiah, Sherebiah, Hodiah, Shebaniah and Pethahiah—said: "Stand up and praise the LORD your God, who is from everlasting to everlasting." "Blessed be your glorious name, and may it be exalted above all blessing and praise.

Job 36:26 How great is God—beyond our understanding! The number of his years is past finding out.

Ps 9:7 The LORD reigns forever; he has established his throne for judgment.

Ps 41:13 Praise be to the LORD, the God of Israel, from everlasting to everlasting. Amen and Amen.

Ps 90:1 Lord, you have been our dwelling place throughout all generations. ²Before the mountains were born or you brought forth the earth and the world, from everlasting to everlasting you are God.

Ps 90:4 For a thousand years in your sight are like a day that has just gone by, or like a watch in the night.

Ps 92:8 But you, O LORD, are exalted forever.

Ps 93:2 Your throne was established long ago; you are from all eternity.

Ps 102:12 But you, O LORD, sit enthroned forever; your renown endures through all generations.

Ps 102:24 So I said: "Do not take me away, O my God, in the midst of my days; your years go on through all generations. ²⁵In the beginning you laid the foundations of the earth, and the heavens are the work of your hands. ²⁶They will perish, but you remain; they will all wear out like a garment. Like clothing you will change them and they will be discarded. ²⁷But you remain the same, and your years will never end.

Ps 145:13 Your kingdom is an everlasting kingdom, and your dominion endures through all generations. The LORD is faithful to all his promises and loving toward all he has made.

Ps 146:10 The LORD reigns forever, your God, O Zion, for all generations. Praise the LORD.

Isa 40:28 Do you not know? Have you not heard? The LORD is the everlasting God, the Creator of the ends of the earth. He will not grow tired or weary, and his understanding no one can fathom.

Isa 44:6 "This is what the LORD says—Israel's King and Redeemer, the LORD Almighty: I am the first and I am the last; apart from me there is no God.

Isa 57:15 For this is what the high and lofty One says—he who lives forever, whose name is holy: "I live in a high and holy place, but also with him who is contrite and lowly in spirit, to revive the spirit of the lowly and to revive the heart of the contrite.

Isa 63:16 But you are our Father, though Abraham does not know us or Israel acknowledge us; you, O LORD, are our Father, our Redeemer from of old is your name.

Jer 10:10 But the LORD is the true God; he is the living God, the eternal King. When he is angry, the earth trembles; the nations cannot endure his wrath.

La 5:19 You, O LORD, reign forever; your throne endures from generation to generation. (+Da 4:3)

Da 4:34 At the end of that time, I, Nebuchadnezzar, raised my eyes toward heaven, and my sanity was restored. Then I praised the Most High; I honored and glorified him who lives forever. His dominion is an eternal dominion; his kingdom endures from generation to generation.

Hab 1:12 O LORD, are you not from everlasting? My God, my Holy One, we will not die. O LORD, you have appointed them to execute judgment; O Rock, you have ordained them to punish.

Ro 1:20 For since the creation of the world God's invisible qualities—his eternal power and divine nature—have been clearly seen, being understood from what has been made, so that men are without excuse. (+Ro 16:26)

Eph 3:21 to him be glory in the church and in Christ Jesus throughout all generations, for ever and ever! Amen.

1Ti 1:17 Now to the King eternal, immortal, invisible, the only God, be honor and glory for ever and ever. Amen.

1Ti 6:15 which God will bring about in his own time—God, the blessed and only Ruler, the King of kings and Lord of lords, [16]who alone is immortal and who lives in unapproachable light, whom no one has seen or can see. To him be honor and might forever. Amen.

2Pe 3:8 But do not forget this one thing, dear friends: With the Lord a day is like a thousand years, and a thousand years are like a day.

Rev 4:8 Each of the four living creatures had six wings and was covered with eyes all around, even under his wings. Day and night they never stop saying: "Holy, holy, holy is the Lord God Almighty, who was, and is, and is to come." [9]Whenever the living creatures give glory, honor and thanks to him who sits on the throne and who lives for ever and ever, (+Rev 4:10; 11:17)

Faithfulness of:

Ge 9:16 Whenever the rainbow appears in the clouds, I will see it and remember the everlasting covenant between God and all living creatures of every kind on the earth."

Ge 28:15 I am with you and will watch over you wherever you go, and I will bring you back to this land. I will not leave you until I have done what I have promised you."

Lev 26:44 Yet in spite of this, when they are in the land of their enemies, I will not reject them or abhor them so as to destroy them completely, breaking my covenant with them. I am the LORD their God. [45]But for their sake I will remember the covenant with their ancestors whom I brought out of Egypt in the sight of the nations to be their God. I am the LORD.'"

Dt 4:31 For the LORD your God is a merciful God; he will not abandon or destroy you or forget the covenant with your forefathers, which he confirmed to them by oath. (+Jdg 2:1)

1Sa 12:22 For the sake of his great name the LORD will not reject his people, because the LORD was pleased to make you his own.

Isa 42:16 I will lead the blind by ways they have not known, along unfamiliar paths I will guide them; I will turn the darkness into light before them and make the rough places smooth. These are the things I will do; I will not forsake them.

Isa 44:21 "Remember these things, O Jacob, for you are my servant, O Israel. I have made you, you are my servant; O Israel, I will not forget you.

Isa 49:7 This is what the LORD says—the Redeemer and Holy One of Israel—to him who was despised and abhorred by the nation, to the servant of rulers: "Kings will see you and rise up, princes will see and bow down, because of the LORD, who is faithful, the Holy One of Israel, who has chosen you." (+Isa 49:14-15)

Isa 49:16 See, I have engraved you on the palms of my hands; your walls are ever before me.

Jer 29:10 This is what the LORD says: "When seventy years are completed for Babylon, I will come to you and fulfill my gracious promise to bring you back to this place.

Jer 31:36 "Only if these decrees vanish from my sight," declares the LORD, "will the descendants of Israel ever cease to be a nation before me."

[37]This is what the LORD says: "Only if the heavens above can be measured and the foundations of the earth below be searched out will I reject all the descendants of Israel because of all they have done," declares the LORD.

Jer 32:40 I will make an everlasting covenant with them: I will never stop doing good to them, and I will inspire them to fear me, so that they will never turn away from me.

Jer 33:14 "'The days are coming,' declares the LORD, 'when I will fulfill the gracious promise I made to the house of Israel and to the house of Judah.

Jer 33:20 "This is what the LORD says: 'If you can break my covenant with the day and my covenant with the night, so that day and night no longer come at their appointed time, [21]then my covenant with David my servant—and my covenant with the Levites who are priests ministering before me—can be broken and David will no longer have a descendant to reign on his throne. (+Jer 33:25-26)

Eze 16:60 Yet I will remember the covenant I made with you in the days of your youth, and I will establish an everlasting covenant with you.

Hos 2:19 I will betroth you to me forever; I will betroth you in righteousness and justice, in love and compassion. [20]I will betroth you in faithfulness, and you will acknowledge the LORD.

Ro 3:3 What if some did not have faith? Will their lack of faith nullify God's faithfulness? [4]Not at all! Let God be true, and every man a liar. As it is written: "So that you may be proved right when you speak and prevail when you judge." (+Heb 6:10,13-19)

Confidence in (Nu 23:19)—

Dt 32:4 He is the Rock, his works are perfect, and all his ways are just. A faithful God who does no wrong, upright and just is he.

2Sa 7:28 O Sovereign LORD, you are God! Your words are trustworthy, and you have promised these good things to your servant.

1Ch 28:20 David also said to Solomon his son, "Be strong and courageous, and do the work. Do not be afraid or discouraged, for the LORD God, my God, is with you. He will not fail you or forsake you until all the work for the service of the temple of the LORD is finished. (+Ne 1:5)

Ps 36:5 Your love, O LORD, reaches to the heavens, your faithfulness to the skies.

Ps 40:10 I do not hide your righteousness in my heart; I speak of your faithfulness and salvation. I do not conceal your love and your truth from the great assembly.

Ps 89:1 I will sing of the Lord's great love forever; with my mouth I will make your faithfulness known through all generations. [2]I will declare that your love stands firm forever, that you established your faithfulness in heaven itself.

Ps 89:5 The heavens praise your wonders, O Lord, your faithfulness too, in the assembly of the holy ones.

Ps 89:8 O Lord God Almighty, who is like you? You are mighty, O Lord, and your faithfulness surrounds you.

Ps 89:14 Righteousness and justice are the foundation of your throne; love and faithfulness go before you.

Ps 89:24 My faithful love will be with him, and through my name his horn will be exalted.

Ps 89:28 I will maintain my love to him forever, and my covenant with him will never fail.

Ps 89:33 but I will not take my love from him, nor will I ever betray my faithfulness. (+Ps 89:34)

Ps 92:1 It is good to praise the Lord and make music to your name, O Most High, [2]to proclaim your love in the morning and your faithfulness at night,

Ps 92:15 proclaiming, "The Lord is upright; he is my Rock, and there is no wickedness in him."

Ps 94:14 For the Lord will not reject his people; he will never forsake his inheritance.

Ps 105:8 He remembers his covenant forever, the word he commanded, for a thousand generations,

Ps 105:42 For he remembered his holy promise given to his servant Abraham.

Ps 111:5 He provides food for those who fear him; he remembers his covenant forever.

Ps 111:7 The works of his hands are faithful and just; all his precepts are trustworthy. [8]They are steadfast for ever and ever, done in faithfulness and uprightness. [9]He provided redemption for his people; he ordained his covenant forever—holy and awesome is his name.

Ps 119:90 Your faithfulness continues through all generations; you established the earth, and it endures. (+Ps 119:91)

Ps 132:11 The Lord swore an oath to David, a sure oath that he will not revoke: "One of your own descendants I will place on your throne—

Isa 25:1 O Lord, you are my God; I will exalt you and praise your name, for in perfect faithfulness you have done marvelous things, things planned long ago.

La 3:23 They are new every morning; great is your faithfulness.

Da 9:4 I prayed to the Lord my God and confessed: "O Lord, the great and awesome God, who keeps his covenant of love with all who love him and obey his commands,

Mic 7:20 You will be true to Jacob, and show mercy to Abraham, as you pledged on oath to our fathers in days long ago.

1Co 1:9 God, who has called you into fellowship with his Son Jesus Christ our Lord, is faithful.

1Co 10:13 No temptation has seized you except what is common to man. And God is faithful; he will not let you be tempted beyond what you can bear. But when you are tempted, he will also provide a way out so that you can stand up under it. (+2Co 1:18-19)

2Co 1:20 For no matter how many promises God has made, they are "Yes" in Christ. And so through him the "Amen" is spoken by us to the glory of God.

1Th 5:24 The one who calls you is faithful and he will do it. (+2Th 3:3)

2Ti 2:13 if we are faithless, he will remain faithful, for he cannot disown himself.

2Ti 2:19 Nevertheless, God's solid foundation stands firm, sealed with this inscription: "The Lord knows those who are his," and, "Everyone who confesses the name of the Lord must turn away from wickedness."

Tit 1:2 a faith and knowledge resting on the hope of eternal life, which God, who does not lie, promised before the beginning of time,

Heb 10:23 Let us hold unswervingly to the hope we profess, for he who promised is faithful. (+Heb 11:11)

1Pe 4:19 So then, those who suffer according to God's will should commit themselves to their faithful Creator and continue to do good.

2Pe 3:9 The Lord is not slow in keeping his promise, as some understand slowness. He is patient with you, not wanting anyone to perish, but everyone to come to repentance.

1Jn 1:9 If we confess our sins, he is faithful and just and will forgive us our sins and purify us from all unrighteousness.

Faithfulness exemplified (Ge 21:1; 24:27; Ex 2:24)—

Ex 6:4 I also established my covenant with them to give them the land of Canaan, where they lived as aliens. [5]Moreover, I have heard the groaning of the Israelites, whom the Egyptians are enslaving, and I have remembered my covenant.

Dt 7:8 But it was because the Lord loved you and kept the oath he swore to your forefathers that he brought you out with a mighty hand and redeemed you from the land of slavery, from the power of Pharaoh king of Egypt. [9]Know therefore that the Lord your God is God; he is the faithful God, keeping his covenant of love to a thousand generations of those who love him and keep his commands.

Dt 9:5 It is not because of your righteousness or your integrity that you are going in to take possession of their land; but on account of the wickedness of these nations, the Lord your God will drive them out before you, to accomplish what he swore to your fathers, to Abraham, Isaac and Jacob. (+Jos 21:45)

Jos 23:14 "Now I am about to go the way of all the earth. You know with all your heart and soul that not one of all the good promises the Lord your God gave you has failed. Every promise has been fulfilled; not one has failed. (+1Ki 8:15,20)

1Ki 8:23 and said: "O Lord, God of Israel, there is no God like you in heaven above or on earth below—you who keep your covenant of love with your servants who continue wholeheartedly in your way. [24]You have kept your promise to your servant David my father; with your mouth you have promised and with your hand you have fulfilled it—as it is today.

1Ki 8:56 "Praise be to the Lord, who has given rest to his people Israel just as he promised. Not one word has failed of all the good promises he gave through his servant Moses.

2Ki 8:19 Nevertheless, for the sake of his servant David, the Lord was not willing to destroy Judah. He had promised to maintain a lamp for David and his descendants forever.

2Ki 13:23 But the Lord was gracious to them and had compassion and showed concern for them because of his covenant with Abraham, Isaac and Jacob. To this day he has been unwilling to destroy them or banish them from his presence. (+2Ch 6:4-15; 21:7; Ne 1:5; 9:7-8)

Ps 98:3 He has remembered his love and his faithfulness to the house of Israel; all the ends of the earth have seen the salvation of our God.

Hag 2:5 'This is what I covenanted with you when you came out of Egypt. And my Spirit remains among you. Do not fear.'

Lk 1:54 He has helped his servant Israel, remembering to be merciful ⁵⁵to Abraham and his descendants forever, even as he said to our fathers."

Lk 1:68 "Praise be to the Lord, the God of Israel, because he has come and has redeemed his people. ⁶⁹He has raised up a horn of salvation for us in the house of his servant David ⁷⁰(as he said through his holy prophets of long ago),

Lk 1:72 to show mercy to our fathers and to remember his holy covenant, ⁷³the oath he swore to our father Abraham:

Ac 13:32 "We tell you the good news: What God promised our fathers ³³he has fulfilled for us, their children, by raising up Jesus. As it is written in the second Psalm: "'You are my Son; today I have become your Father.'

Heb 6:10 God is not unjust; he will not forget your work and the love you have shown him as you have helped his people and continue to help them.

Heb 6:13 When God made his promise to Abraham, since there was no one greater for him to swear by, he swore by himself, ¹⁴saying, "I will surely bless you and give you many descendants." ¹⁵And so after waiting patiently, Abraham received what was promised.

¹⁶Men swear by someone greater than themselves, and the oath confirms what is said and puts an end to all argument. ¹⁷Because God wanted to make the unchanging nature of his purpose very clear to the heirs of what was promised, he confirmed it with an oath. ¹⁸God did this so that, by two unchangeable things in which it is impossible for God to lie, we who have fled to take hold of the hope offered to us may be greatly encouraged. ¹⁹We have this hope as an anchor for the soul, firm and secure. It enters the inner sanctuary behind the curtain,

Fatherhood of:

Taught in the Old Testament—

Ex 4:22 Then say to Pharaoh, 'This is what the LORD says: Israel is my firstborn son,

Dt 14:1 You are the children of the LORD your God. Do not cut yourselves or shave the front of your heads for the dead,

Dt 32:5 They have acted corruptly toward him; to their shame they are no longer his children, but a warped and crooked generation. ⁶Is this the way you repay the LORD, O foolish and unwise people? Is he not your Father, your Creator, who made you and formed you?

2Sa 7:14 I will be his father, and he will be my son. When he does wrong, I will punish him with the rod of men, with floggings inflicted by men.

1Ch 28:6 He said to me: 'Solomon your son is the one who will build my house and my courts, for I have chosen him to be my son, and I will be his father.

1Ch 29:10 David praised the LORD in the presence of the whole assembly, saying, "Praise be to you, O LORD, God of our father Israel, from everlasting to everlasting.

Ps 68:5 A father to the fatherless, a defender of widows, is God in his holy dwelling.

Ps 89:26 He will call out to me, 'You are my Father, my God, the Rock my Savior.'

Isa 1:2 Hear, O heavens! Listen, O earth! For the LORD has spoken: "I reared children and brought them up, but they have rebelled against me.

Isa 9:6 For to us a child is born, to us a son is given, and the government will be on his shoulders. And he will be

called Wonderful Counselor, Mighty God, Everlasting Father, Prince of Peace.

Isa 63:16 But you are our Father, though Abraham does not know us or Israel acknowledge us; you, O LORD, are our Father, our Redeemer from of old is your name.

Isa 64:8 Yet, O LORD, you are our Father. We are the clay, you are the potter; we are all the work of your hand.

Jer 3:19 "I myself said, "'How gladly would I treat you like sons and give you a desirable land, the most beautiful inheritance of any nation.' I thought you would call me 'Father' and not turn away from following me.

Hos 1:10 "Yet the Israelites will be like the sand on the seashore, which cannot be measured or counted. In the place where it was said to them, 'You are not my people,' they will be called 'sons of the living God.'

Hos 11:1 "When Israel was a child, I loved him, and out of Egypt I called my son.

Fatherhood of, taught by Jesus—

Mt 5:45 that you may be sons of your Father in heaven. He causes his sun to rise on the evil and the good, and sends rain on the righteous and the unrighteous.

Mt 6:4 so that your giving may be in secret. Then your Father, who sees what is done in secret, will reward you.

Mt 6:8 Do not be like them, for your Father knows what you need before you ask him.

⁹"This, then, is how you should pray: "'Our Father in heaven, hallowed be your name,

Mt 7:11 If you, then, though you are evil, know how to give good gifts to your children, how much more will your Father in heaven give good gifts to those who ask him!

Mt 10:20 for it will not be you speaking, but the Spirit of your Father speaking through you.

Mt 10:29 Are not two sparrows sold for a penny? Yet not one of them will fall to the ground apart from the will of your Father.

Mt 10:32 "Whoever acknowledges me before men, I will also acknowledge him before my Father in heaven. ³³But whoever disowns me before men, I will disown him before my Father in heaven.

Mt 11:25 At that time Jesus said, "I praise you, Father, Lord of heaven and earth, because you have hidden these things from the wise and learned, and revealed them to little children. ²⁶Yes, Father, for this was your good pleasure.

²⁷"All things have been committed to me by my Father. No one knows the Son except the Father, and no one knows the Father except the Son and those to whom the Son chooses to reveal him.

Mt 12:50 For whoever does the will of my Father in heaven is my brother and sister and mother."

Mt 13:43 Then the righteous will shine like the sun in the kingdom of their Father. He who has ears, let him hear.

Mt 15:13 He replied, "Every plant that my heavenly Father has not planted will be pulled up by the roots.

Mt 16:17 Jesus replied, "Blessed are you, Simon son of Jonah, for this was not revealed to you by man, but by my Father in heaven.

Mt 16:27 For the Son of Man is going to come in his Father's glory with his angels, and then he will reward each person according to what he has done.

Mt 18:10 "See that you do not look down on one of these little ones. For I tell you that their angels in heaven always see the face of my Father in heaven.

Mt 18:14 In the same way your Father in heaven is not willing that any of these little ones should be lost.

Mt 18:19 "Again, I tell you that if two of you on earth

agree about anything you ask for, it will be done for you by my Father in heaven.

Mt 20:23 Jesus said to them, "You will indeed drink from my cup, but to sit at my right or left is not for me to grant. These places belong to those for whom they have been prepared by my Father."

Mt 26:29 I tell you, I will not drink of this fruit of the vine from now on until that day when I drink it anew with you in my Father's kingdom."

Mt 26:39 Going a little farther, he fell with his face to the ground and prayed, "My Father, if it is possible, may this cup be taken from me. Yet not as I will, but as you will."

Mk 8:38 If anyone is ashamed of me and my words in this adulterous and sinful generation, the Son of Man will be ashamed of him when he comes in his Father's glory with the holy angels."

Mk 11:25 And when you stand praying, if you hold anything against anyone, forgive him, so that your Father in heaven may forgive you your sins."

Mk 13:32 "No one knows about that day or hour, not even the angels in heaven, nor the Son, but only the Father.

Lk 2:49 "Why were you searching for me?" he asked. "Didn't you know I had to be in my Father's house?"

Lk 10:21 At that time Jesus, full of joy through the Holy Spirit, said, "I praise you, Father, Lord of heaven and earth, because you have hidden these things from the wise and learned, and revealed them to little children. Yes, Father, for this was your good pleasure.

[22]"All things have been committed to me by my Father. No one knows who the Son is except the Father, and no one knows who the Father is except the Son and those to whom the Son chooses to reveal him." (+Lk 11:2)

Lk 11:13 If you then, though you are evil, know how to give good gifts to your children, how much more will your Father in heaven give the Holy Spirit to those who ask him!"

Lk 22:29 And I confer on you a kingdom, just as my Father conferred one on me,

Lk 23:46 Jesus called out with a loud voice, "Father, into your hands I commit my spirit." When he had said this, he breathed his last.

Lk 24:49 I am going to send you what my Father has promised; but stay in the city until you have been clothed with power from on high."

Jn 1:14 The Word became flesh and made his dwelling among us. We have seen his glory, the glory of the One and Only, who came from the Father, full of grace and truth.

Jn 1:18 No one has ever seen God, but God the One and Only, who is at the Father's side, has made him known.

Jn 2:16 To those who sold doves he said, "Get these out of here! How dare you turn my Father's house into a market!"

Jn 4:21 Jesus declared, "Believe me, woman, a time is coming when you will worship the Father neither on this mountain nor in Jerusalem.

Jn 4:23 Yet a time is coming and has now come when the true worshipers will worship the Father in spirit and truth, for they are the kind of worshipers the Father seeks.

Jn 5:17 Jesus said to them, "My Father is always at his work to this very day, and I, too, am working." [18]For this reason the Jews tried all the harder to kill him; not only was he breaking the Sabbath, but he was even calling God his own Father, making himself equal with God.

[19]Jesus gave them this answer: "I tell you the truth, the Son can do nothing by himself; he can do only what he

sees his Father doing, because whatever the Father does the Son also does. [20]For the Father loves the Son and shows him all he does. Yes, to your amazement he will show him even greater things than these. [21]For just as the Father raises the dead and gives them life, even so the Son gives life to whom he is pleased to give it. [22]Moreover, the Father judges no one, but has entrusted all judgment to the Son, [23]that all may honor the Son just as they honor the Father. He who does not honor the Son does not honor the Father, who sent him.

Jn 5:36 "I have testimony weightier than that of John. For the very work that the Father has given me to finish, and which I am doing, testifies that the Father has sent me. [37]And the Father who sent me has himself testified concerning me. You have never heard his voice nor seen his form,

Jn 5:43 I have come in my Father's name, and you do not accept me; but if someone else comes in his own name, you will accept him.

Jn 6:27 Do not work for food that spoils, but for food that endures to eternal life, which the Son of Man will give you. On him God the Father has placed his seal of approval."

Jn 6:32 Jesus said to them, "I tell you the truth, it is not Moses who has given you the bread from heaven, but it is my Father who gives you the true bread from heaven.

Jn 6:44 "No one can come to me unless the Father who sent me draws him, and I will raise him up at the last day. [45]It is written in the Prophets: 'They will all be taught by God.' Everyone who listens to the Father and learns from him comes to me. [46]No one has seen the Father except the one who is from God; only he has seen the Father.

Jn 8:19 Then they asked him, "Where is your father?" "You do not know me or my Father," Jesus replied. "If you knew me, you would know my Father also."

Jn 8:27 They did not understand that he was telling them about his Father.

Jn 8:38 I am telling you what I have seen in the Father's presence, and you do what you have heard from your father."

Jn 8:41 You are doing the things your own father does."

"We are not illegitimate children," they protested."The only Father we have is God himself."

[42]Jesus said to them, "If God were your Father, you would love me, for I came from God and now am here. I have not come on my own; but he sent me.

Jn 8:49 "I am not possessed by a demon," said Jesus, "but I honor my Father and you dishonor me.

Jn 10:15 just as the Father knows me and I know the Father—and I lay down my life for the sheep.

Jn 10:29 My Father, who has given them to me, is greater than all; no one can snatch them out of my Father's hand. [30]I and the Father are one."

Jn 10:32 but Jesus said to them, "I have shown you many great miracles from the Father. For which of these do you stone me?"

[33]"We are not stoning you for any of these," replied the Jews, "but for blasphemy, because you, a mere man, claim to be God."

Jn 10:36 what about the one whom the Father set apart as his very own and sent into the world? Why then do you accuse me of blasphemy because I said, 'I am God's Son'? [37]Do not believe me unless I do what my Father does. [38]But if I do it, even though you do not believe me, believe the miracles, that you may know and understand that the Father is in me, and I in the Father."

Jn 12:26 Whoever serves me must follow me; and where I am, my servant also will be. My Father will honor the one who serves me.

²⁷"Now my heart is troubled, and what shall I say? 'Father, save me from this hour'? No, it was for this very reason I came to this hour. ²⁸Father, glorify your name!"

Then a voice came from heaven, "I have glorified it, and will glorify it again."

Jn 12:50 I know that his command leads to eternal life. So whatever I say is just what the Father has told me to say." (+Jn 13:1)

Jn 13:3 Jesus knew that the Father had put all things under his power, and that he had come from God and was returning to God;

Jn 14:2 In my Father's house are many rooms; if it were not so, I would have told you. I am going there to prepare a place for you.

Jn 14:6 Jesus answered, "I am the way and the truth and the life. No one comes to the Father except through me. ⁷If you really knew me, you would know my Father as well. From now on, you do know him and have seen him."

⁸Philip said, "Lord, show us the Father and that will be enough for us."

⁹Jesus answered: "Don't you know me, Philip, even after I have been among you such a long time? Anyone who has seen me has seen the Father. How can you say, 'Show us the Father'? ¹⁰Don't you believe that I am in the Father, and that the Father is in me? The words I say to you are not just my own. Rather, it is the Father, living in me, who is doing his work. ¹¹Believe me when I say that I am in the Father and the Father is in me; or at least believe on the evidence of the miracles themselves. ¹²I tell you the truth, anyone who has faith in me will do what I have been doing. He will do even greater things than these, because I am going to the Father. ¹³And I will do whatever you ask in my name, so that the Son may bring glory to the Father.

Jn 14:20 On that day you will realize that I am in my Father, and you are in me, and I am in you. ²¹Whoever has my commands and obeys them, he is the one who loves me. He who loves me will be loved by my Father, and I too will love him and show myself to him."

Jn 14:23 Jesus replied, "If anyone loves me, he will obey my teaching. My Father will love him, and we will come to him and make our home with him. ²⁴He who does not love me will not obey my teaching. These words you hear are not my own; they belong to the Father who sent me. (+Jn 14:26)

Jn 14:31 but the world must learn that I love the Father and that I do exactly what my Father has commanded me. "Come now; let us leave.

Jn 15:8 This is to my Father's glory, that you bear much fruit, showing yourselves to be my disciples.

⁹"As the Father has loved me, so have I loved you. Now remain in my love. ¹⁰If you obey my commands, you will remain in my love, just as I have obeyed my Father's commands and remain in his love.

Jn 15:16 You did not choose me, but I chose you and appointed you to go and bear fruit—fruit that will last. Then the Father will give you whatever you ask in my name.

Jn 15:23 He who hates me hates my Father as well. ²⁴If I had not done among them what no one else did, they would not be guilty of sin. But now they have seen these miracles, and yet they have hated both me and my Father.

Jn 15:26 "When the Counselor comes, whom I will send to you from the Father, the Spirit of truth who goes out from the Father, he will testify about me.

Jn 16:3 They will do such things because they have not known the Father or me.

Jn 16:10 in regard to righteousness, because I am going to the Father, where you can see me no longer;

Jn 16:15 All that belongs to the Father is mine. That is why I said the Spirit will take from what is mine and make it known to you.

Jn 16:23 In that day you will no longer ask me anything. I tell you the truth, my Father will give you whatever you ask in my name.

Jn 16:25 "Though I have been speaking figuratively, a time is coming when I will no longer use this kind of language but will tell you plainly about my Father. ²⁶In that day you will ask in my name. I am not saying that I will ask the Father on your behalf. ²⁷No, the Father himself loves you because you have loved me and have believed that I came from God. ²⁸I came from the Father and entered the world; now I am leaving the world and going back to the Father."

Jn 17:1 After Jesus said this, he looked toward heaven and prayed: "Father, the time has come. Glorify your Son, that your Son may glorify you.

Jn 17:5 And now, Father, glorify me in your presence with the glory I had with you before the world began.

Jn 17:11 I will remain in the world no longer, but they are still in the world, and I am coming to you. Holy Father, protect them by the power of your name—the name you gave me—so that they may be one as we are one.

Jn 17:21 that all of them may be one, Father, just as you are in me and I am in you. May they also be in us so that the world may believe that you have sent me.

Jn 17:24 "Father, I want those you have given me to be with me where I am, and to see my glory, the glory you have given me because you loved me before the creation of the world.

Jn 20:17 Jesus said, "Do not hold on to me, for I have not yet returned to the Father. Go instead to my brothers and tell them, 'I am returning to my Father and your Father, to my God and your God.'"

Jn 20:21 Again Jesus said, "Peace be with you! As the Father has sent me, I am sending you."

Fatherhood of, taught by the apostles—

Ac 1:4 On one occasion, while he was eating with them, he gave them this command: "Do not leave Jerusalem, but wait for the gift my Father promised, which you have heard me speak about.

Ac 2:33 Exalted to the right hand of God, he has received from the Father the promised Holy Spirit and has poured out what you now see and hear.

Ro 1:3 regarding his Son, who as to his human nature was a descendant of David, ⁴and who through the Spirit of holiness was declared with power to be the Son of God by his resurrection from the dead: Jesus Christ our Lord.

Ro 1:7 To all in Rome who are loved by God and called to be saints: Grace and peace to you from God our Father and from the Lord Jesus Christ. (+Ro 8:14)

Ro 8:15 For you did not receive a spirit that makes you a slave again to fear, but you received the Spirit of sonship. And by him we cry, "Abba, Father." (+Ro 8:16; 1Co 1:3)

1Co 8:6 yet for us there is but one God, the Father, from whom all things came and for whom we live; and there is but one Lord, Jesus Christ, through whom all things came and through whom we live.

1Co 15:24 Then the end will come, when he hands over

the kingdom to God the Father after he has destroyed all dominion, authority and power.

2Co 1:3 Praise be to the God and Father of our Lord Jesus Christ, the Father of compassion and the God of all comfort,

2Co 6:18 "I will be a Father to you, and you will be my sons and daughters, says the Lord Almighty."

Gal 1:1 Paul, an apostle—sent not from men nor by man, but by Jesus Christ and God the Father, who raised him from the dead— (+Gal 1:3)

Gal 1:4 who gave himself for our sins to rescue us from the present evil age, according to the will of our God and Father,

Gal 4:4 But when the time had fully come, God sent his Son, born of a woman, born under law, ⁵to redeem those under law, that we might receive the full rights of sons. ⁶Because you are sons, God sent the Spirit of his Son into our hearts, the Spirit who calls out, *"Abba,* Father." ⁷So you are no longer a slave, but a son; and since you are a son, God has made you also an heir. (+Eph 1:2)

Eph 1:3 Praise be to the God and Father of our Lord Jesus Christ, who has blessed us in the heavenly realms with every spiritual blessing in Christ.

Eph 1:17 I keep asking that the God of our Lord Jesus Christ, the glorious Father, may give you the Spirit of wisdom and revelation, so that you may know him better.

Eph 2:18 For through him we both have access to the Father by one Spirit.

Eph 3:14 For this reason I kneel before the Father,

Eph 4:6 one God and Father of all, who is over all and through all and in all.

Eph 5:20 always giving thanks to God the Father for everything, in the name of our Lord Jesus Christ. (+Eph 6:23; Php 1:2; Col 1:2)

Col 1:3 We always thank God, the Father of our Lord Jesus Christ, when we pray for you,

Col 1:12 giving thanks to the Father, who has qualified you to share in the inheritance of the saints in the kingdom of light.

Col 3:17 And whatever you do, whether in word or deed, do it all in the name of the Lord Jesus, giving thanks to God the Father through him.

1Th 1:1 Paul, Silas and Timothy,

To the church of the Thessalonians in God the Father and the Lord Jesus Christ:

Grace and peace to you.

1Th 1:3 We continually remember before our God and Father your work produced by faith, your labor prompted by love, and your endurance inspired by hope in our Lord Jesus Christ.

1Th 3:11 Now may our God and Father himself and our Lord Jesus clear the way for us to come to you.

1Th 3:13 May he strengthen your hearts so that you will be blameless and holy in the presence of our God and Father when our Lord Jesus comes with all his holy ones.

2Th 1:1 Paul, Silas and Timothy, To the church of the Thessalonians in God our Father and the Lord Jesus Christ: ²Grace and peace to you from God the Father and the Lord Jesus Christ.

2Th 2:16 May our Lord Jesus Christ himself and God our Father, who loved us and by his grace gave us eternal encouragement and good hope, (+1Ti 1:2; 2Ti 1:2; Tit 1:4)

Heb 1:5 For to which of the angels did God ever say, "You are my Son; today I have become your Father"?

Or again, "I will be his Father, and he will be my Son"?

⁶And again, when God brings his firstborn into the world, he says, "Let all God's angels worship him."

Heb 12:9 Moreover, we have all had human fathers who disciplined us and we respected them for it. How much more should we submit to the Father of our spirits and live!

Jas 1:17 Every good and perfect gift is from above, coming down from the Father of the heavenly lights, who does not change like shifting shadows.

Jas 1:27 Religion that God our Father accepts as pure and faultless is this: to look after orphans and widows in their distress and to keep oneself from being polluted by the world.

Jas 3:9 With the tongue we praise our Lord and Father, and with it we curse men, who have been made in God's likeness.

1Pe 1:2 who have been chosen according to the foreknowledge of God the Father, through the sanctifying work of the Spirit, for obedience to Jesus Christ and sprinkling by his blood:

Grace and peace be yours in abundance.

³Praise be to the God and Father of our Lord Jesus Christ! In his great mercy he has given us new birth into a living hope through the resurrection of Jesus Christ from the dead,

1Pe 1:17 Since you call on a Father who judges each man's work impartially, live your lives as strangers here in reverent fear.

1Jn 1:2 The life appeared; we have seen it and testify to it, and we proclaim to you the eternal life, which was with the Father and has appeared to us.

1Jn 2:1 My dear children, I write this to you so that you will not sin. But if anybody does sin, we have one who speaks to the Father in our defense—Jesus Christ, the Righteous One.

1Jn 2:13 I write to you, fathers, because you have known him who is from the beginning. I write to you, young men, because you have overcome the evil one. I write to you, dear children, because you have known the Father.

1Jn 2:15 Do not love the world or anything in the world. If anyone loves the world, the love of the Father is not in him.

1Jn 2:22 Who is the liar? It is the man who denies that Jesus is the Christ. Such a man is the antichrist—he denies the Father and the Son. ²³No one who denies the Son has the Father; whoever acknowledges the Son has the Father also.

²⁴See that what you have heard from the beginning remains in you. If it does, you also will remain in the Son and in the Father.

1Jn 3:1 How great is the love the Father has lavished on us, that we should be called children of God! And that is what we are! The reason the world does not know us is that it did not know him.

1Jn 4:14 And we have seen and testify that the Father has sent his Son to be the Savior of the world.

2Jn 3 Grace, mercy and peace from God the Father and from Jesus Christ, the Father's Son, will be with us in truth and love.

⁴It has given me great joy to find some of your children walking in the truth, just as the Father commanded us.

2Jn 9 Anyone who runs ahead and does not continue in the teaching of Christ does not have God; whoever continues in the teaching has both the Father and the Son.

Jude 1 Jude, a servant of Jesus Christ and a brother of

James, To those who have been called, who are loved by God the Father and kept by Jesus Christ:

Rev 1:5 and from Jesus Christ, who is the faithful witness, the firstborn from the dead, and the ruler of the kings of the earth.

To him who loves us and has freed us from our sins by his blood, ⁶and has made us to be a kingdom and priests to serve his God and Father—to him be glory and power for ever and ever! Amen.

Rev 3:5 He who overcomes will, like them, be dressed in white. I will never blot out his name from the book of life, but will acknowledge his name before my Father and his angels.

Rev 14:1 Then I looked, and there before me was the Lamb, standing on Mount Zion, and with him 144,000 who had his name and his Father's name written on their foreheads. *See Adoption, Spiritual Adoption.*

Favor of: *See below, Grace of.*

Foreknowledge of:

Ac 15:18 that have been known for ages.

Of contingencies—

1Sa 23:10 David said, "O LORD, God of Israel, your servant has heard definitely that Saul plans to come to Keilah and destroy the town on account of me. ¹¹Will the citizens of Keilah surrender me to him? Will Saul come down, as your servant has heard? O LORD, God of Israel, tell your servant."

And the LORD said, "He will."

¹²Again David asked, "Will the citizens of Keilah surrender me and my men to Saul?"

And the LORD said, "They will."

Of future events—

Isa 42:9 See, the former things have taken place, and new things I declare; before they spring into being I announce them to you."

Isa 44:7 Who then is like me? Let him proclaim it. Let him declare and lay out before me what has happened since I established my ancient people, and what is yet to come— yes, let him foretell what will come.

Isa 45:11 "This is what the LORD says—the Holy One of Israel, and its Maker: Concerning things to come, do you question me about my children, or give me orders about the work of my hands?

Isa 46:9 Remember the former things, those of long ago; I am God, and there is no other; I am God, and there is none like me. ¹⁰I make known the end from the beginning, from ancient times, what is still to come. I say: My purpose will stand, and I will do all that I please.

Isa 48:5 Therefore I told you these things long ago; before they happened I announced them to you so that you could not say, 'My idols did them; my wooden image and metal god ordained them.' ⁶You have heard these things; look at them all. Will you not admit them? "From now on I will tell you of new things, of hidden things unknown to you.

Jer 1:5 "Before I formed you in the womb I knew you, before you were born I set you apart; I appointed you as a prophet to the nations."

Da 2:28 but there is a God in heaven who reveals mysteries. He has shown King Nebuchadnezzar what will happen in days to come. Your dream and the visions that passed through your mind as you lay on your bed are these:

²⁹"As you were lying there, O king, your mind turned to things to come, and the revealer of mysteries showed you what is going to happen. (+Ac 2:23)

Of human needs—

Mt 6:8 Do not be like them, for your Father knows what you need before you ask him.

Of the day of judgment—

Mt 24:36 "No one knows about that day or hour, not even the angels in heaven, nor the Son, but only the Father. (+Mk 13:32)

Of the redeemed—

Ro 8:29 For those God foreknew he also predestined to be conformed to the likeness of his Son, that he might be the firstborn among many brothers.

Ro 11:2 God did not reject his people, whom he foreknew. Don't you know what the Scripture says in the passage about Elijah—how he appealed to God against Israel:

1Pe 1:2 who have been chosen according to the foreknowledge of God the Father, through the sanctifying work of the Spirit, for obedience to Jesus Christ and sprinkling by his blood: Grace and peace be yours in abundance.

Glory of:

Ps 24:8 Who is this King of glory? The LORD strong and mighty, the LORD mighty in battle. ⁹Lift up your heads, O you gates; lift them up, you ancient doors, that the King of glory may come in. (+Ps 24:10)

Ps 57:5 Be exalted, O God, above the heavens; let your glory be over all the earth. (+Ps 57:11)

Ps 72:18 Praise be to the LORD God, the God of Israel, who alone does marvelous deeds. ¹⁹Praise be to his glorious name forever; may the whole earth be filled with his glory. Amen and Amen.

Isa 40:5 And the glory of the LORD will be revealed, and all mankind together will see it. For the mouth of the LORD has spoken."

Php 1:11 filled with the fruit of righteousness that comes through Jesus Christ—to the glory and praise of God.

Described—

Eze 1:26 Above the expanse over their heads was what looked like a throne of sapphire, and high above on the throne was a figure like that of a man. ²⁷I saw that from what appeared to be his waist up he looked like glowing metal, as if full of fire, and that from there down he looked like fire; and brilliant light surrounded him. ²⁸Like the appearance of a rainbow in the clouds on a rainy day, so was the radiance around him. This was the appearance of the likeness of the glory of the LORD. When I saw it, I fell facedown, and I heard the voice of one speaking.

Hab 3:3 God came from Teman, the Holy One from Mount Paran. *Selah* His glory covered the heavens and his praise filled the earth. ⁴His splendor was like the sunrise; rays flashed from his hand, where his power was hidden. ⁵Plague went before him; pestilence followed his steps. (+Hab 3:6)

Transcendent (Ps 113:4).

Shall endure forever—

Ps 104:31 May the glory of the LORD endure forever; may the LORD rejoice in his works—

Ascribed by angels—

Lk 2:14 "Glory to God in the highest, and on earth peace to men on whom his favor rests."

To be ascribed by people—

Ps 29:2 Ascribe to the LORD the glory due his name; worship the LORD in the splendor of his holiness. (+Ro 11:36)

Manifested in the burning bush—

Ex 3:2 There the angel of the LORD appeared to him in

flames of fire from within a bush. Moses saw that though the bush was on fire it did not burn up.

Manifested in Mount Sinai—

Ex 19:18 Mount Sinai was covered with smoke, because the LORD descended on it in fire. The smoke billowed up from it like smoke from a furnace, the whole mountain trembled violently, (+Ex 20:18-19)

Ex 24:10 and saw the God of Israel. Under his feet was something like a pavement made of sapphire, clear as the sky itself.

Ex 24:17 To the Israelites the glory of the LORD looked like a consuming fire on top of the mountain. (+Ex 33:18-19)

Ex 33:20 But," he said, "you cannot see my face, for no one may see me and live." (+Ex 33:21)

Ex 33:22 When my glory passes by, I will put you in a cleft in the rock and cover you with my hand until I have passed by. (+Ex 33:23)

Ex 34:5 Then the LORD came down in the cloud and stood there with him and proclaimed his name, the LORD. (+Ex 34:29-35; Dt 4:11-12,33,36; 5:5,24-25)

Heb 12:18 You have not come to a mountain that can be touched and that is burning with fire; to darkness, gloom and storm; [19]to a trumpet blast or to such a voice speaking words that those who heard it begged that no further word be spoken to them, [20]because they could not bear what was commanded: "If even an animal touches the mountain, it must be stoned." [21]The sight was so terrifying that Moses said, "I am trembling with fear."

Manifested in the tabernacle—

Ex 40:34 Then the cloud covered the Tent of Meeting, and the glory of the LORD filled the tabernacle. [35]Moses could not enter the Tent of Meeting because the cloud had settled upon it, and the glory of the LORD filled the tabernacle.

Manifested in the heavens (2Sa 22:10-15)—

Ps 18:9 He parted the heavens and came down; dark clouds were under his feet. [10]He mounted the cherubim and flew; he soared on the wings of the wind. [11]He made darkness his covering, his canopy around him—the dark rain clouds of the sky. (+Ps 18:12-14)

Ps 19:1 The heavens declare the glory of God; the skies proclaim the work of his hands.

Manifested in his sovereignty—

Ps 97:2 Clouds and thick darkness surround him; righteousness and justice are the foundation of his throne. (+Ps 97:3-5)

Ps 97:6 The heavens proclaim his righteousness, and all the peoples see his glory.

Ps 145:5 They will speak of the glorious splendor of your majesty, and I will meditate on your wonderful works.

Ps 145:11 They will tell of the glory of your kingdom and speak of your might, [12]so that all men may know of your mighty acts and the glorious splendor of your kingdom.

Isa 6:1 In the year that King Uzziah died, I saw the Lord seated on a throne, high and exalted, and the train of his robe filled the temple. (+Isa 6:2)

Isa 6:3 And they were calling to one another: "Holy, holy, holy is the LORD Almighty; the whole earth is full of his glory." (+Isa 6:4,5)

Isa 24:23 The moon will be abashed, the sun ashamed; for the LORD Almighty will reign on Mount Zion and in Jerusalem, and before its elders, gloriously. (+Jude 24)

Jude 25 to the only God our Savior be glory, majesty, power and authority, through Jesus Christ our Lord, before all ages, now and forevermore! Amen.

Manifested in the church—

Isa 35:2 it will burst into bloom; it will rejoice greatly and shout for joy. The glory of Lebanon will be given to it, the splendor of Carmel and Sharon; they will see the glory of the LORD, the splendor of our God.

Isa 60:1 "Arise, shine, for your light has come, and the glory of the LORD rises upon you. [2]See, darkness covers the earth and thick darkness is over the peoples, but the LORD rises upon you and his glory appears over you.

Isa 60:19 The sun will no more be your light by day, nor will the brightness of the moon shine on you, for the LORD will be your everlasting light, and your God will be your glory. [20]Your sun will never set again, and your moon will wane no more; the LORD will be your everlasting light, and your days of sorrow will end. [21]Then will all your people be righteous and they will possess the land forever. They are the shoot I have planted, the work of my hands, for the display of my splendor.

Isa 61:3 and provide for those who grieve in Zion—to bestow on them a crown of beauty instead of ashes, the oil of gladness instead of mourning, and a garment of praise instead of a spirit of despair. They will be called oaks of righteousness, a planting of the LORD for the display of his splendor.

Eph 3:21 to him be glory in the church and in Christ Jesus throughout all generations, for ever and ever! Amen.

Manifested in Christ—

Jn 13:31 When he was gone, Jesus said, "Now is the Son of Man glorified and God is glorified in him. [32]If God is glorified in him, God will glorify the Son in himself, and will glorify him at once.

Jn 14:13 And I will do whatever you ask in my name, so that the Son may bring glory to the Father.

Jn 17:1 After Jesus said this, he looked toward heaven and prayed: "Father, the time has come. Glorify your Son, that your Son may glorify you.

Manifested to Ezekiel—

Eze 3:12 Then the Spirit lifted me up, and I heard behind me a loud rumbling sound—May the glory of the LORD be praised in his dwelling place!—

Eze 3:23 So I got up and went out to the plain. And the glory of the LORD was standing there, like the glory I had seen by the Kebar River, and I fell facedown.

Eze 8:4 And there before me was the glory of the God of Israel, as in the vision I had seen in the plain.

Manifested to Stephen—

Ac 7:55 But Stephen, full of the Holy Spirit, looked up to heaven and saw the glory of God, and Jesus standing at the right hand of God.

Goodness of:

Ex 33:19 And the LORD said, "I will cause all my goodness to pass in front of you, and I will proclaim my name, the LORD, in your presence. I will have mercy on whom I will have mercy, and I will have compassion on whom I will have compassion.

Dt 30:9 Then the LORD your God will make you most prosperous in all the work of your hands and in the fruit of your womb, the young of your livestock and the crops of your land. The LORD will again delight in you and make you prosperous, just as he delighted in your fathers,

Ps 25:8 Good and upright is the LORD; therefore he instructs sinners in his ways. (+Ps 25:9-10; 31:19)

Ps 33:5 The LORD loves righteousness and justice; the earth is full of his unfailing love.

Ps 36:7 How priceless is your unfailing love! Both high

and low among men find refuge in the shadow of your wings.

Ps 86:5 You are forgiving and good, O Lord, abounding in love to all who call to you.

Ps 100:5 For the LORD is good and his love endures forever; his faithfulness continues through all generations.

Ps 106:1 Praise the LORD. Give thanks to the LORD, for he is good; his love endures forever.

Ps 119:68 You are good, and what you do is good; teach me your decrees.

Na 1:7 The LORD is good, a refuge in times of trouble. He cares for those who trust in him, (+Mt 5:45; Ac 14:17)

Jas 1:17 Every good and perfect gift is from above, coming down from the Father of the heavenly lights, who does not change like shifting shadows.

Enduring—

Ps 52:1 Why do you boast of evil, you mighty man? Why do you boast all day long, you who are a disgrace in the eyes of God?

Leads to repentance—

Ro 2:4 Or do you show contempt for the riches of his kindness, tolerance and patience, not realizing that God's kindness leads you toward repentance?

Gratefully acknowledged (1Ch 16:34)—

2Ch 5:13 The trumpeters and singers joined in unison, as with one voice, to give praise and thanks to the LORD. Accompanied by trumpets, cymbals and other instruments, they raised their voices in praise to the LORD and sang: "He is good; his love endures forever." Then the temple of the LORD was filled with a cloud, (+2Ch 7:3)

Ps 68:19 Praise be to the Lord, to God our Savior, who daily bears our burdens. *Selah*

Ps 107:8 Let them give thanks to the LORD for his unfailing love and his wonderful deeds for men, 9for he satisfies the thirsty and fills the hungry with good things.

Ps 107:43 Whoever is wise, let him heed these things and consider the great love of the LORD.

Ps 118:29 Give thanks to the LORD, for he is good; his love endures forever. (+Ps 135:3; 136:1)

Ps 145:7 They will celebrate your abundant goodness and joyfully sing of your righteousness.

Ps 145:9 The LORD is good to all; he has compassion on all he has made.

Isa 63:7 I will tell of the kindnesses of the LORD, the deeds for which he is to be praised, according to all the LORD has done for us—yes, the many good things he has done for the house of Israel, according to his compassion and many kindnesses.

Manifested: In gracious providence—

Mt 7:11 If you, then, though you are evil, know how to give good gifts to your children, how much more will your Father in heaven give good gifts to those who ask him!

To the righteous (Ps 31:19)—

La 3:25 The LORD is good to those whose hope is in him, to the one who seeks him;

Ro 11:22 Consider therefore the kindness and sternness of God: sternness to those who fell, but kindness to you, provided that you continue in his kindness. Otherwise, you also will be cut off.

To the wicked—

Lk 6:35 But love your enemies, do good to them, and lend to them without expecting to get anything back. Then your reward will be great, and you will be sons of the Most High, because he is kind to the ungrateful and wicked.

Grace of:

Unmerited favor (Dt 7:7-8; 2Ch 30:9)—

Eph 1:6 to the praise of his glorious grace, which he has freely given us in the One he loves. (+Tit 2:11)

Heb 4:16 Let us then approach the throne of grace with confidence, so that we may receive mercy and find grace to help us in our time of need.

Divine help—

Ps 84:11 For the LORD God is a sun and shield; the LORD bestows favor and honor; no good thing does he withhold from those whose walk is blameless. (+1Co 10:13; 2Co 1:12; 12:9; 1Pe 1:5)

No warrant for sinful indulgence (Ro 6:1,15). Intercessory prayer for (Jn 17:11-12,15; 1Th 1:1; 5:28; 2Pe 1:2). Exhortation against rejecting (2Co 6:1-2). Exemplified with respect to Jacob and Esau (Ro 9:10-16).

Manifested: In drawing men to Christ (Jn 6:44-45), in redemption (Eph 1:5-9,11-12), in justification (Ge 15:6; Ro 3:22-24; 4:4-5,16; 5:2,6-8,15-21; Tit 3:7)

In passing over transgression—

Nu 23:20 I have received a command to bless; he has blessed, and I cannot change it.

21"No misfortune is seen in Jacob, no misery observed in Israel. The LORD their God is with them; the shout of the King is among them. (+Ne 9:17; Ro 3:25)

In salvation (Ro 11:5-6; Eph 2:8-9; 2Ti 1:9), in calling to service (Gal 1:15-16), in spiritual growth (Eph 3:16)

In spiritual gifts (1Co 1:4-8; Eph 4:7,11).—

Manifested: In character and conduct (2Co 1:12; Php 2:13), in the character and conduct of the righteous (1Co 15:10; 2Co 1:12; Php 2:13), in sustaining the righteous (1Ch 17:8; 2Co 12:9; 1Pe 1:5; Jude 24), in sustaining in temptation (1Co 10:13; Rev 3:10).

Manifestation of: To Enoch (Ge 5:24).

To Noah—

Ge 6:8 But Noah found favor in the eyes of the LORD. (+Ge 6:17-18)

To Abraham (Ge 12:2; 21:22). To Ishmael (Ge 21:20). To Isaac (Ge 26:24).

To Jacob (Ge 46:3)—

Ge 46:4 I will go down to Egypt with you, and I will surely bring you back again. And Joseph's own hand will close your eyes." (+Ge 48:16)

To Joseph (Ge 39:2-3,23).

To Moses—

Ex 3:12 And God said, "I will be with you. And this will be the sign to you that it is I who have sent you: When you have brought the people out of Egypt, you will worship God on this mountain." (+Ex 33:12-16)

Ex 33:17 And the LORD said to Moses, "I will do the very thing you have asked, because I am pleased with you and I know you by name."

To Israel—

Dt 4:7 What other nation is so great as to have their gods near them the way the LORD our God is near us whenever we pray to him?

To Naphtali—

Dt 33:23 About Naphtali he said: "Naphtali is abounding with the favor of the LORD and is full of his blessing; he will inherit southward to the lake."

To Joshua—

Jos 1:5 No one will be able to stand up against you all the days of your life. As I was with Moses, so I will be with you; I will never leave you nor forsake you.

Jos 1:9 Have I not commanded you? Be strong and

courageous. Do not be terrified; do not be discouraged, for the LORD your God will be with you wherever you go."

To Job—

Job 10:12 You gave me life and showed me kindness, and in your providence watched over my spirit.

To David (1Sa 25:26,34; 2Sa 7:8-16).

To Jeremiah—

Jer 15:20 I will make you a wall to this people, a fortified wall of bronze; they will fight against you but will not overcome you, for I am with you to rescue and save you," declares the LORD.

To the righteous—

Ps 5:12 For surely, O LORD, you bless the righteous; you surround them with your favor as with a shield.

Ac 4:33 With great power the apostles continued to testify to the resurrection of the Lord Jesus, and much grace was upon them all.

Guidance of:

Ge 12:1 The LORD had said to Abram, "Leave your country, your people and your father's household and go to the land I will show you. (+Ge 24:27)

Ps 23:2 He makes me lie down in green pastures, he leads me beside quiet waters, ³he restores my soul. He guides me in paths of righteousness for his name's sake.

Ps 48:14 For this God is our God for ever and ever; he will be our guide even to the end.

Ps 73:24 You guide me with your counsel, and afterward you will take me into glory. (+Pr 3:6)

Jer 3:4 Have you not just called to me: 'My Father, my friend from my youth, (+Jer 32:19)

Lk 1:79 to shine on those living in darkness and in the shadow of death, to guide our feet into the path of peace."

Jn 10:3 The watchman opens the gate for him, and the sheep listen to his voice. He calls his own sheep by name and leads them out. ⁴When he has brought out all his own, he goes on ahead of them, and his sheep follow him because they know his voice.

By pillars of cloud and fire—

Ex 13:21 By day the LORD went ahead of them in a pillar of cloud to guide them on their way and by night in a pillar of fire to give them light, so that they could travel by day or night.

Ne 9:19 "Because of your great compassion you did not abandon them in the desert. By day the pillar of cloud did not cease to guide them on their path, nor the pillar of fire by night to shine on the way they were to take.

By his presence—

Ex 15:13 "In your unfailing love you will lead the people you have redeemed. In your strength you will guide them to your holy dwelling.

Ex 33:13 If you are pleased with me, teach me your ways so I may know you and continue to find favor with you. Remember that this nation is your people."

¹⁴The LORD replied, "My Presence will go with you, and I will give you rest."

¹⁵Then Moses said to him, "If your Presence does not go with us, do not send us up from here.

Dt 32:10 In a desert land he found him, in a barren and howling waste. He shielded him and cared for him; he guarded him as the apple of his eye,

Dt 32:12 The LORD alone led him; no foreign god was with him.

Ps 78:52 But he brought his people out like a flock; he led them like sheep through the desert.

Ps 80:1 Hear us, O Shepherd of Israel, you who lead Joseph like a flock; you who sit enthroned between the cherubim, shine forth

Ps 107:7 He led them by a straight way to a city where they could settle.

By the ark of the covenant—

Nu 10:33 So they set out from the mountain of the LORD and traveled for three days. The ark of the covenant of the LORD went before them during those three days to find them a place to rest.

By his counsel—

2Sa 22:29 You are my lamp, O LORD; the LORD turns my darkness into light.

Ps 5:8 Lead me, O LORD, in your righteousness because of my enemies—make straight your way before me.

Ps 25:9 He guides the humble in what is right and teaches them his way.

Isa 48:17 This is what the LORD says—your Redeemer, the Holy One of Israel: "I am the LORD your God, who teaches you what is best for you, who directs you in the way you should go.

By his Spirit—

Jn 16:13 But when he, the Spirit of truth, comes, he will guide you into all truth. He will not speak on his own; he will speak only what he hears, and he will tell you what is yet to come.

Prayed for—

Ps 25:5 guide me in your truth and teach me, for you are God my Savior, and my hope is in you all day long.

Ps 27:11 Teach me your way, O LORD; lead me in a straight path because of my oppressors.

Ps 31:3 Since you are my rock and my fortress, for the sake of your name lead and guide me.

Ps 61:2 From the ends of the earth I call to you, I call as my heart grows faint; lead me to the rock that is higher than I.

Promised—

Ps 32:8 I will instruct you and teach you in the way you should go; I will counsel you and watch over you.

Isa 40:11 He tends his flock like a shepherd: He gathers the lambs in his arms and carries them close to his heart; he gently leads those that have young.

Isa 42:16 I will lead the blind by ways they have not known, along unfamiliar paths I will guide them; I will turn the darkness into light before them and make the rough places smooth. These are the things I will do; I will not forsake them.

Isa 58:11 The LORD will guide you always; he will satisfy your needs in a sun-scorched land and will strengthen your frame. You will be like a well-watered garden, like a spring whose waters never fail.

Holiness of:

Jos 24:19 Joshua said to the people, "You are not able to serve the LORD. He is a holy God; he is a jealous God. He will not forgive your rebellion and your sins.

1Sa 6:20 and the men of Beth Shemesh asked, "Who can stand in the presence of the LORD, this holy God? To whom will the ark go up from here?"

1Ch 16:10 Glory in his holy name; let the hearts of those who seek the LORD rejoice.

Job 6:10 Then I would still have this consolation—my joy in unrelenting pain—that I had not denied the words of the Holy One.

Job 15:15 If God places no trust in his holy ones, if even the heavens are not pure in his eyes,

Job 25:5 If even the moon is not bright and the stars are not pure in his eyes,

Ps 11:7 For the LORD is righteous, he loves justice; upright men will see his face.

Ps 22:3 Yet you are enthroned as the Holy One; you are the praise of Israel.

Ps 36:6 Your righteousness is like the mighty mountains, your justice like the great deep. O LORD, you preserve both man and beast.

Ps 47:8 God reigns over the nations; God is seated on his holy throne.

Ps 60:6 God has spoken from his sanctuary: "In triumph I will parcel out Shechem and measure off the Valley of Succoth.

Ps 89:35 Once for all, I have sworn by my holiness—and I will not lie to David— (+Ps 98:1; 105:3)

Ps 111:9 He provided redemption for his people; he ordained his covenant forever—holy and awesome is his name.

Ps 119:142 Your righteousness is everlasting and your law is true.

Ps 145:17 The LORD is righteous in all his ways and loving toward all he has made.

Pr 9:10 "The fear of the LORD is the beginning of wisdom, and knowledge of the Holy One is understanding.

Isa 5:16 But the LORD Almighty will be exalted by his justice, and the holy God will show himself holy by his righteousness.

Isa 6:3 And they were calling to one another: "Holy, holy, holy is the LORD Almighty; the whole earth is full of his glory."

Isa 29:19 Once more the humble will rejoice in the LORD; the needy will rejoice in the Holy One of Israel.

Isa 29:23 When they see among them their children, the work of my hands, they will keep my name holy; they will acknowledge the holiness of the Holy One of Jacob, and will stand in awe of the God of Israel. (+Isa 41:14)

Isa 43:14 This is what the LORD says—your Redeemer, the Holy One of Israel: "For your sake I will send to Babylon and bring down as fugitives all the Babylonians, in the ships in which they took pride. ¹⁵I am the LORD, your Holy One, Israel's Creator, your King." (+Isa 45:19)

Isa 47:4 Our Redeemer—the LORD Almighty is his name—is the Holy One of Israel.

Isa 49:7 This is what the LORD says—the Redeemer and Holy One of Israel—to him who was despised and abhorred by the nation, to the servant of rulers: "Kings will see you and rise up, princes will see and bow down, because of the LORD, who is faithful, the Holy One of Israel, who has chosen you."

Isa 52:10 The LORD will lay bare his holy arm in the sight of all the nations, and all the ends of the earth will see the salvation of our God.

Isa 57:15 For this is what the high and lofty One says—he who lives forever, whose name is holy: "I live in a high and holy place, but also with him who is contrite and lowly in spirit, to revive the spirit of the lowly and to revive the heart of the contrite. (+Eze 36:21-22)

Eze 39:7 "'I will make known my holy name among my people Israel. I will no longer let my holy name be profaned, and the nations will know that I the LORD am the Holy One in Israel. (+Eze 39:25)

Da 4:8 Finally, Daniel came into my presence and I told him the dream. (He is called Belteshazzar, after the name of my god, and the spirit of the holy gods is in him.)

Hos 11:9 I will not carry out my fierce anger, nor will I turn and devastate Ephraim. For I am God, and not man— the Holy One among you. I will not come in wrath.

Hab 1:12 O LORD, are you not from everlasting? My God, my Holy One, we will not die. O LORD, you have appointed them to execute judgment; O Rock, you have ordained them to punish. ¹³Your eyes are too pure to look on evil; you cannot tolerate wrong. Why then do you tolerate the treacherous? Why are you silent while the wicked swallow up those more righteous than themselves?

Lk 1:49 for the Mighty One has done great things for me—holy is his name.

Jn 17:11 I will remain in the world no longer, but they are still in the world, and I am coming to you. Holy Father, protect them by the power of your name—the name you gave me—so that they may be one as we are one.

Ro 1:23 and exchanged the glory of the immortal God for images made to look like mortal man and birds and animals and reptiles.

1Jn 2:20 But you have an anointing from the Holy One, and all of you know the truth.

Rev 4:8 Each of the four living creatures had six wings and was covered with eyes all around, even under his wings. Day and night they never stop saying: "Holy, holy, holy is the Lord God Almighty, who was, and is, and is to come."

Rev 6:10 They called out in a loud voice, "How long, Sovereign Lord, holy and true, until you judge the inhabitants of the earth and avenge our blood?"

Rev 15:4 Who will not fear you, O Lord, and bring glory to your name? For you alone are holy. All nations will come and worship before you, for your righteous acts have been revealed."

Incomparable—

Ex 15:11 "Who among the gods is like you, O LORD? Who is like you—majestic in holiness, awesome in glory, working wonders?

1Sa 2:2 "There is no one holy like the LORD; there is no one besides you; there is no Rock like our God.

Job 4:17 'Can a mortal be more righteous than God? Can a man be more pure than his Maker? (+Job 4:18-19)

Without iniquity—

Dt 32:4 He is the Rock, his works are perfect, and all his ways are just. A faithful God who does no wrong, upright and just is he. (+2Ch 19:7)

Job 34:10 "So listen to me, you men of understanding. Far be it from God to do evil, from the Almighty to do wrong.

Job 36:23 Who has prescribed his ways for him, or said to him, 'You have done wrong'?

Ps 92:15 proclaiming, "The LORD is upright; he is my Rock, and there is no wickedness in him."

Jer 2:5 This is what the LORD says: "What fault did your fathers find in me, that they strayed so far from me? They followed worthless idols and became worthless themselves.

La 3:38 Is it not from the mouth of the Most High that both calamities and good things come?

Mt 19:17 "Why do you ask me about what is good?" Jesus replied. "There is only One who is good. If you want to enter life, obey the commandments." (+Mk 10:18; Lk 18:19)

Jas 1:13 When tempted, no one should say, "God is tempting me." For God cannot be tempted by evil, nor does he tempt anyone;

A reason for personal holiness (Lev 11:44)—

Lev 19:2 "Speak to the entire assembly of Israel and say to them: 'Be holy because I, the LORD your God, am holy. (+Lev 20:26; 21:8; 2Ch 19:7)

Mt 5:48 Be perfect, therefore, as your heavenly Father is perfect.

1Pe 1:15 But just as he who called you is holy, so be holy in all you do; ¹⁶for it is written: "Be holy, because I am holy."

A reason for thanksgiving—

Ps 30:4 Sing to the LORD, you saints of his; praise his holy name.

Ps 99:3 Let them praise your great and awesome name—he is holy.

Ps 99:5 Exalt the LORD our God and worship at his footstool; he is holy. (+Ps 99:9)

Isa 12:6 Shout aloud and sing for joy, people of Zion, for great is the Holy One of Israel among you."

A reason for reverent approach to God—

Ex 3:5 "Do not come any closer," God said. "Take off your sandals, for the place where you are standing is holy ground." (+Jos 5:15)

Light, figurative of. *See below, Light.*

See Sin, Separates from God; below, God, Perfections of, Righteousness of.

Human Forms and Appearances of:

See Anthropomorphisms.

Immanence of: (Ge 26:24; 28:15; Ex 3:12; Dt 4:7; Jos 3:7; Ac 17:27-28).

Immutable:

Nu 23:19 God is not a man, that he should lie, nor a son of man, that he should change his mind. Does he speak and then not act? Does he promise and not fulfill? ²⁰I have received a command to bless; he has blessed, and I cannot change it.

1Sa 15:29 He who is the Glory of Israel does not lie or change his mind; for he is not a man, that he should change his mind." (+Ps 102:27)

Isa 40:28 Do you not know? Have you not heard? The LORD is the everlasting God, the Creator of the ends of the earth. He will not grow tired or weary, and his understanding no one can fathom.

Jas 1:17 Every good and perfect gift is from above, coming down from the Father of the heavenly lights, who does not change like shifting shadows.

In purpose—

Job 23:13 "But he stands alone, and who can oppose him? He does whatever he pleases.

Ps 33:11 But the plans of the LORD stand firm forever, the purposes of his heart through all generations.

Pr 19:21 Many are the plans in a man's heart, but it is the LORD's purpose that prevails.

Ecc 3:14 I know that everything God does will endure forever; nothing can be added to it and nothing taken from it. God does it so that men will revere him.

Ecc 7:13 Consider what God has done: Who can straighten what he has made crooked?

Isa 31:2 Yet he too is wise and can bring disaster; he does not take back his words. He will rise up against the house of the wicked, against those who help evildoers.

Heb 6:17 Because God wanted to make the unchanging nature of his purpose very clear to the heirs of what was promised, he confirmed it with an oath. ¹⁸God did this so that, by two unchangeable things in which it is impossible for God to lie, we who have fled to take hold of the hope offered to us may be greatly encouraged.

In faithfulness—

Ps 119:89 Your word, O LORD, is eternal; it stands firm in the heavens. ⁹⁰Your faithfulness continues through all generations; you established the earth, and it endures. ⁹¹Your laws endure to this day, for all things serve you.

In mercy—

Isa 59:1 Surely the arm of the LORD is not too short to save, nor his ear too dull to hear.

Hos 13:14 "I will ransom them from the power of the grave; I will redeem them from death. Where, O death, are your plagues? Where, O grave, is your destruction? "I will have no compassion,

Mal 3:6 "I the LORD do not change. So you, O descendants of Jacob, are not destroyed. (+Ro 11:29)

Impartial:

Dt 10:17 For the LORD your God is God of gods and Lord of lords, the great God, mighty and awesome, who shows no partiality and accepts no bribes.

Despises none—

Job 36:5 "God is mighty, but does not despise men; he is mighty, and firm in his purpose.

Does not show favoritism (2Ch 19:7; Job 34:19)—

Job 37:24 Therefore, men revere him, for does he not have regard for all the wise in heart?"

Ac 10:34 Then Peter began to speak: "I now realize how true it is that God does not show favoritism ³⁵but accepts men from every nation who fear him and do what is right.

Ro 2:6 God "will give to each person according to what he has done."

Ro 2:11 For God does not show favoritism.

Eph 6:8 because you know that the Lord will reward everyone for whatever good he does, whether he is slave or free. (+Eph 6:9)

Col 3:25 Anyone who does wrong will be repaid for his wrong, and there is no favoritism.

1Pe 1:17 Since you call on a Father who judges each man's work impartially, live your lives as strangers here in reverent fear.

Incomparable:

Ex 16:11 Who among the gods is like you, O LORD? Who is like you—majestic in holiness, awesome in glory, working wonders? (+Dt 33:26; 2Sa 7:22; 1Ki 8:23; Ps 35:10; 71:19; 89:6-8; 113:5; Mic 7:18)

Incomprehensible:

Job 15:8 Do you listen in on God's council? Do you limit wisdom to yourself?

Job 37:1 "At this my heart pounds and leaps from its place. ²Listen! Listen to the roar of his voice, to the rumbling that comes from his mouth. ³He unleashes his lightning beneath the whole heaven and sends it to the ends of the earth. ⁴After that comes the sound of his roar; he thunders with his majestic voice. When his voice resounds, he holds nothing back. ⁵God's voice thunders in marvelous ways; he does great things beyond our understanding. ⁶He says to the snow, 'Fall on the earth,' and to the rain shower, 'Be a mighty downpour.' ⁷So that all men he has made may know his work, he stops every man from his labor. ⁸The animals take cover; they remain in their dens. ⁹The tempest comes out from its chamber, the cold from the driving winds. ¹⁰The breath of God produces ice, and the broad waters become frozen. ¹¹He loads the clouds with moisture; he scatters his lightning through them. ¹²At his direction they swirl around over the face of the whole earth to do whatever he commands them. ¹³He brings the clouds to punish men, or to water his earth and show his love.

[14]"Listen to this, Job; stop and consider God's wonders. [15]Do you know how God controls the clouds and makes his lightning flash? [16]Do you know how the clouds hang poised, those wonders of him who is perfect in knowledge? [17]You who swelter in your clothes when the land lies hushed under the south wind, [18]can you join him in spreading out the skies, hard as a mirror of cast bronze?

[19]"Tell us what we should say to him; we cannot draw up our case because of our darkness. [20]Should he be told that I want to speak? Would any man ask to be swallowed up? [21]Now no one can look at the sun, bright as it is in the skies after the wind has swept them clean. [22]Out of the north he comes in golden splendor; God comes in awesome majesty. [23]The Almighty is beyond our reach and exalted in power; in his justice and great righteousness, he does not oppress. [24]Therefore, men revere him, for does he not have regard for all the wise in heart?"

Isa 40:12 Who has measured the waters in the hollow of his hand, or with the breadth of his hand marked off the heavens? Who has held the dust of the earth in a basket, or weighed the mountains on the scales and the hills in a balance? [13]Who has understood the mind of the LORD, or instructed him as his counselor? [14]Whom did the LORD consult to enlighten him, and who taught him the right way? Who was it that taught him knowledge or showed him the path of understanding?

[15]Surely the nations are like a drop in a bucket; they are regarded as dust on the scales; he weighs the islands as though they were fine dust. [16]Lebanon is not sufficient for altar fires, nor its animals enough for burnt offerings. [17]Before him all the nations are as nothing; they are regarded by him as worthless and less than nothing.

[18]To whom, then, will you compare God? What image will you compare him to? [19]As for an idol, a craftsman casts it, and a goldsmith overlays it with gold and fashions silver chains for it. [20]A man too poor to present such an offering selects wood that will not rot. He looks for a skilled craftsman to set up an idol that will not topple.

[21]Do you not know? Have you not heard? Has it not been told you from the beginning? Have you not understood since the earth was founded? [22]He sits enthroned above the circle of the earth, and its people are like grasshoppers. He stretches out the heavens like a canopy, and spreads them out like a tent to live in. [23]He brings princes to naught and reduces the rulers of this world to nothing. [24]No sooner are they planted, no sooner are they sown, no sooner do they take root in the ground, than he blows on them and they wither, and a whirlwind sweeps them away like chaff.

[25]"To whom will you compare me? Or who is my equal?" says the Holy One. [26]Lift your eyes and look to the heavens: Who created all these? He who brings out the starry host one by one, and calls them each by name. Because of his great power and mighty strength, not one of them is missing.

[27]Why do you say, O Jacob, and complain, O Israel, "My way is hidden from the LORD; my cause is disregarded by my God"? [28]Do you not know? Have you not heard? The LORD is the everlasting God, the Creator of the ends of the earth. He will not grow tired or weary, and his understanding no one can fathom. [29]He gives strength to the weary and increases the power of the weak. [30]Even youths grow tired and weary, and young men stumble and fall; [31]but those who hope in the LORD will renew their strength. They will soar on wings like eagles; they will run and not grow weary, they will walk and not be faint.

Isa 55:8 "For my thoughts are not your thoughts, neither are your ways my ways," declares the LORD. [9]"As the heavens are higher than the earth, so are my ways higher than your ways and my thoughts than your thoughts. (+Mt 11:27)

1Co 2:16 "For who has known the mind of the Lord that he may instruct him?" But we have the mind of Christ.

Infinite:

1Ki 8:27 "But will God really dwell on earth? The heavens, even the highest heaven, cannot contain you. How much less this temple I have built! (+2Ch 2:6; 6:1,18)

Ps 147:5 Great is our Lord and mighty in power; his understanding has no limit.

Jer 23:24 Can anyone hide in secret places so that I cannot see him?" declares the LORD. "Do not I fill heaven and earth?" declares the LORD.

Invisible:

Ex 20:21 The people remained at a distance, while Moses approached the thick darkness where God was.

Ex 33:20 But," he said, "you cannot see my face, for no one may see me and live."

Dt 4:11 You came near and stood at the foot of the mountain while it blazed with fire to the very heavens, with black clouds and deep darkness. (+Dt 4:12)

Dt 4:15 You saw no form of any kind the day the LORD spoke to you at Horeb out of the fire. Therefore watch yourselves very carefully,

Dt 5:22 These are the commandments the LORD proclaimed in a loud voice to your whole assembly there on the mountain from out of the fire, the cloud and the deep darkness; and he added nothing more. Then he wrote them on two stone tablets and gave them to me.

1Ki 8:12 Then Solomon said, "The LORD has said that he would dwell in a dark cloud; (+2Ch 6:1)

Job 9:11 When he passes me, I cannot see him; when he goes by, I cannot perceive him.

Job 23:8 "But if I go to the east, he is not there; if I go to the west, I do not find him. [9]When he is at work in the north, I do not see him; when he turns to the south, I catch no glimpse of him.

Ps 18:11 He made darkness his covering, his canopy around him—the dark rain clouds of the sky.

Ps 97:2 Clouds and thick darkness surround him; righteousness and justice are the foundation of his throne.

Jn 1:18 No one has ever seen God, but God the One and Only, who is at the Father's side, has made him known.

Jn 5:37 And the Father who sent me has himself testified concerning me. You have never heard his voice nor seen his form,

Jn 6:46 No one has seen the Father except the one who is from God; only he has seen the Father.

Ro 1:20 For since the creation of the world God's invisible qualities—his eternal power and divine nature—have been clearly seen, being understood from what has been made, so that men are without excuse.

Col 1:13 For he has rescued us from the dominion of darkness and brought us into the kingdom of the Son he loves, [14]in whom we have redemption, the forgiveness of sins.

[15]He is the image of the invisible God, the firstborn over all creation.

1Ti 1:17 Now to the King eternal, immortal, invisible, the only God, be honor and glory for ever and ever. Amen.

1Ti 6:16 who alone is immortal and who lives in unapproachable light, whom no one has seen or can see. To him be honor and might forever. Amen.

Heb 11:27 By faith he left Egypt, not fearing the king's anger; he persevered because he saw him who is invisible.

1Jn 4:12 No one has ever seen God; but if we love one another, God lives in us and his love is made complete in us.

Jealous: (Ex 20:5,7)

Ex 34:14 Do not worship any other god, for the LORD, whose name is Jealous, is a jealous God.

Dt 4:24 For the LORD your God is a consuming fire, a jealous God. (+Dt 5:9,11; 6:15)

Dt 29:20 The LORD will never be willing to forgive him; his wrath and zeal will burn against that man. All the curses written in this book will fall upon him, and the LORD will blot out his name from under heaven.

Dt 32:16 They made him jealous with their foreign gods and angered him with their detestable idols.

Dt 32:21 They made me jealous by what is no god and angered me with their worthless idols. I will make them envious by those who are not a people; I will make them angry by a nation that has no understanding.

Jos 24:19 Joshua said to the people, "You are not able to serve the LORD. He is a holy God; he is a jealous God. He will not forgive your rebellion and your sins.

2Ch 16:7 At that time Hanani the seer came to Asa king of Judah and said to him: "Because you relied on the king of Aram and not on the LORD your God, the army of the king of Aram has escaped from your hand. ⁸Were not the Cushites and Libyans a mighty army with great numbers of chariots and horsemen? Yet when you relied on the LORD, he delivered them into your hand. ⁹For the eyes of the LORD range throughout the earth to strengthen those whose hearts are fully committed to him. You have done a foolish thing, and from now on you will be at war."

Isa 30:1 "Woe to the obstinate children," declares the LORD, "to those who carry out plans that are not mine, forming an alliance, but not by my Spirit, heaping sin upon sin; ²who go down to Egypt without consulting me; who look for help to Pharaoh's protection, to Egypt's shade for refuge.

Eze 23:25 I will direct my jealous anger against you, and they will deal with you in fury. They will cut off your noses and your ears, and those of you who are left will fall by the sword. They will take away your sons and daughters, and those of you who are left will be consumed by fire.

Eze 36:5 this is what the Sovereign LORD says: In my burning zeal I have spoken against the rest of the nations, and against all Edom, for with glee and with malice in their hearts they made my land their own possession so that they might plunder its pastureland.'

Eze 39:25 "Therefore this is what the Sovereign LORD says: I will now bring Jacob back from captivity and will have compassion on all the people of Israel, and I will be zealous for my holy name.

Joel 2:18 Then the LORD will be jealous for his land and take pity on his people.

Na 1:2 The LORD is a jealous and avenging God; the LORD takes vengeance and is filled with wrath. The LORD takes vengeance on his foes and maintains his wrath against his enemies.

Zec 1:14 Then the angel who was speaking to me said, "Proclaim this word: This is what the LORD Almighty says: 'I am very jealous for Jerusalem and Zion,

1Co 10:22 Are we trying to arouse the Lord's jealousy? Are we stronger than he?

Judge:

Ge 16:5 Then Sarai said to Abram, "You are responsible for the wrong I am suffering. I put my servant in your arms, and now that she knows she is pregnant, she despises me. May the LORD judge between you and me."

Jdg 11:27 I have not wronged you, but you are doing me wrong by waging war against me. Let the LORD, the Judge, decide the dispute this day between the Israelites and the Ammonites."

1Sa 2:3 "Do not keep talking so proudly or let your mouth speak such arrogance, for the LORD is a God who knows, and by him deeds are weighed.

1Sa 2:10 those who oppose the LORD will be shattered. He will thunder against them from heaven; the LORD will judge the ends of the earth. "He will give strength to his king and exalt the horn of his anointed."

1Sa 24:12 May the LORD judge between you and me. And may the LORD avenge the wrongs you have done to me, but my hand will not touch you.

1Sa 24:15 May the LORD be our judge and decide between us. May he consider my cause and uphold it; may he vindicate me by delivering me from your hand."

1Ch 16:33 Then the trees of the forest will sing, they will sing for joy before the LORD, for he comes to judge the earth.

Job 21:22 "Can anyone teach knowledge to God, since he judges even the highest?

Ps 11:4 The LORD is in his holy temple; the LORD is on his heavenly throne. He observes the sons of men; his eyes examine them. ⁵The LORD examines the righteous, but the wicked and those who love violence his soul hates.

Ps 26:1 Vindicate me, O LORD, for I have led a blameless life; I have trusted in the LORD without wavering. ²Test me, O LORD, and try me, examine my heart and my mind;

Ps 35:24 Vindicate me in your righteousness, O LORD my God; do not let them gloat over me.

Ps 43:1 Vindicate me, O God, and plead my cause against an ungodly nation; rescue me from deceitful and wicked men.

Ps 50:4 He summons the heavens above, and the earth, that he may judge his people:

Ps 50:6 And the heavens proclaim his righteousness, for God himself is judge. *Selah*

Ps 58:11 Then men will say, "Surely the righteous still are rewarded; surely there is a God who judges the earth." (+Ps 75:7)

Ps 76:8 From heaven you pronounced judgment, and the land feared and was quiet— ⁹when you, O God, rose up to judge, to save all the afflicted of the land. *Selah* (+Ps 82:8)

Ps 94:1 O LORD, the God who avenges, O God who avenges, shine forth. ²Rise up, O Judge of the earth; pay back to the proud what they deserve.

Ps 135:14 For the LORD will vindicate his people and have compassion on his servants.

Pr 16:2 All a man's ways seem innocent to him, but motives are weighed by the LORD.

Pr 29:26 Many seek an audience with a ruler, but it is from the LORD that man gets justice.

Ecc 3:17 I thought in my heart, "God will bring to judgment both the righteous and the wicked, for there will be a time for every activity, a time for every deed."

Ecc 11:9 Be happy, young man, while you are young, and let your heart give you joy in the days of your youth. Follow the ways of your heart and whatever your eyes see, but know that for all these things God will bring you to judgment.

Ecc 12:14 For God will bring every deed into judgment, including every hidden thing, whether it is good or evil.

Isa 3:13 The LORD takes his place in court; he rises to judge the people. **14**The LORD enters into judgment against the elders and leaders of his people: "It is you who have ruined my vineyard; the plunder from the poor is in your houses.

Isa 28:17 I will make justice the measuring line and righteousness the plumb line; hail will sweep away your refuge, the lie, and water will overflow your hiding place.

Isa 28:21 The LORD will rise up as he did at Mount Perazim, he will rouse himself as in the Valley of Gibeon—to do his work, his strange work, and perform his task, his alien task.

Isa 30:18 Yet the LORD longs to be gracious to you; he rises to show you compassion. For the LORD is a God of justice. Blessed are all who wait for him!

Isa 30:27 See, the Name of the LORD comes from afar, with burning anger and dense clouds of smoke; his lips are full of wrath, and his tongue is a consuming fire.

Isa 33:22 For the LORD is our judge, the LORD is our lawgiver, the LORD is our king; it is he who will save us.

Jer 32:19 great are your purposes and mighty are your deeds. Your eyes are open to all the ways of men; you reward everyone according to his conduct and as his deeds deserve.

Da 7:9 "As I looked, "thrones were set in place, and the Ancient of Days took his seat. His clothing was as white as snow; the hair of his head was white like wool. His throne was flaming with fire, and its wheels were all ablaze. **10**A river of fire was flowing, coming out from before him. Thousands upon thousands attended him; ten thousand times ten thousand stood before him. The court was seated, and the books were opened. (+Na 1:3)

Mal 3:5 "So I will come near to you for judgment. I will be quick to testify against sorcerers, adulterers and perjurers, against those who defraud laborers of their wages, who oppress the widows and the fatherless, and deprive aliens of justice, but do not fear me," says the LORD Almighty.

Ac 17:31 For he has set a day when he will judge the world with justice by the man he has appointed. He has given proof of this to all men by raising him from the dead." (+1Co 5:13)

Heb 10:30 For we know him who said, "It is mine to avenge; I will repay," and again, "The Lord will judge his people." **31**It is a dreadful thing to fall into the hands of the living God.

Heb 12:22 But you have come to Mount Zion, to the heavenly Jerusalem, the city of the living God. You have come to thousands upon thousands of angels in joyful assembly, **23**to the church of the firstborn, whose names are written in heaven. You have come to God, the judge of all men, to the spirits of righteous men made perfect,

Rev 6:16 They called to the mountains and the rocks, "Fall on us and hide us from the face of him who sits on the throne and from the wrath of the Lamb! **17**For the great day of their wrath has come, and who can stand?"

Rev 11:18 The nations were angry; and your wrath has come. The time has come for judging the dead, and for rewarding your servants the prophets and your saints and those who reverence your name, both small and great— and for destroying those who destroy the earth."

Rev 16:5 Then I heard the angel in charge of the waters

say: "You are just in these judgments, you who are and who were, the Holy One, because you have so judged;

Rev 18:8 Therefore in one day her plagues will overtake her: death, mourning and famine. She will be consumed by fire, for mighty is the Lord God who judges her.

Just Judge—

Ge 18:21 that I will go down and see if what they have done is as bad as the outcry that has reached me. If not, I will know."

Ge 18:25 Far be it from you to do such a thing—to kill the righteous with the wicked, treating the righteous and the wicked alike. Far be it from you! Will not the Judge of all the earth do right?"

Nu 16:22 But Moses and Aaron fell facedown and cried out, "O God, God of the spirits of all mankind, will you be angry with the entire assembly when only one man sins?"

Dt 32:4 He is the Rock, his works are perfect, and all his ways are just. A faithful God who does no wrong, upright and just is he. (+Ne 9:33)

Job 4:17 'Can a mortal be more righteous than God? Can a man be more pure than his Maker?

Job 8:3 Does God pervert justice? Does the Almighty pervert what is right?

Job 34:10 "So listen to me, you men of understanding. Far be it from God to do evil, from the Almighty to do wrong. **11**He repays a man for what he has done; he brings upon him what his conduct deserves. **12**It is unthinkable that God would do wrong, that the Almighty would pervert justice.

Ps 7:9 O righteous God, who searches minds and hearts, bring to an end the violence of the wicked and make the righteous secure.

Ps 7:11 God is a righteous judge, a God who expresses his wrath every day.

Ps 9:4 For you have upheld my right and my cause; you have sat on your throne, judging righteously.

Ps 9:7 The LORD reigns forever; he has established his throne for judgment. **8**He will judge the world in righteousness; he will govern the peoples with justice.

Ps 67:4 May the nations be glad and sing for joy, for you rule the peoples justly and guide the nations of the earth. *Selah* (+Ps 96:10)

Ps 96:13 they will sing before the LORD, for he comes, he comes to judge the earth. He will judge the world in righteousness and the peoples in his truth. (+Ps 98:9)

Isa 26:7 The path of the righteous is level; O upright One, you make the way of the righteous smooth.

Isa 45:21 Declare what is to be, present it—let them take counsel together. Who foretold this long ago, who declared it from the distant past? Was it not I, the LORD? And there is no God apart from me, a righteous God and a Savior; there is none but me. (+Jer 32:19)

Ro 2:2 Now we know that God's judgment against those who do such things is based on truth.

Ro 2:5 But because of your stubbornness and your unrepentant heart, you are storing up wrath against yourself for the day of God's wrath, when his righteous judgment will be revealed. **6**God "will give to each person according to what he has done." **7**To those who by persistence in doing good seek glory, honor and immortality, he will give eternal life. **8**But for those who are self-seeking and who reject the truth and follow evil, there will be wrath and anger. **9**There will be trouble and distress for every human being who does evil: first for the Jew, then for the Gentile; **10**but glory, honor and peace for everyone who does good: first for the Jew, then for the Gentile. **11**For God does not show favoritism.

¹²All who sin apart from the law will also perish apart from the law, and all who sin under the law will be judged by the law. ¹³For it is not those who hear the law who are righteous in God's sight, but it is those who obey the law who will be declared righteous. ¹⁴(Indeed, when Gentiles, who do not have the law, do by nature things required by the law, they are a law for themselves, even though they do not have the law, ¹⁵since they show that the requirements of the law are written on their hearts, their consciences also bearing witness, and their thoughts now accusing, now even defending them.) ¹⁶This will take place on the day when God will judge men's secrets through Jesus Christ, as my gospel declares.

Ro 3:4 Not at all! Let God be true, and every man a liar. As it is written: "So that you may be proved right when you speak and prevail when you judge." ⁵But if our unrighteousness brings out God's righteousness more clearly, what shall we say? That God is unjust in bringing his wrath on us? (I am using a human argument.) ⁶Certainly not! If that were so, how could God judge the world?

Ro 3:26 he did it to demonstrate his justice at the present time, so as to be just and the one who justifies those who have faith in Jesus.

Ro 11:22 Consider therefore the kindness and sternness of God: sternness to those who fell, but kindness to you, provided that you continue in his kindness. Otherwise, you also will be cut off. (+Ro 11:23)

Eph 6:8 because you know that the Lord will reward everyone for whatever good he does, whether he is slave or free.

⁹And masters, treat your slaves in the same way. Do not threaten them, since you know that he who is both their Master and yours is in heaven, and there is no favoritism with him.

1Pe 1:17 Since you call on a Father who judges each man's work impartially, live your lives as strangers here in reverent fear.

Rev 19:2 for true and just are his judgments. He has condemned the great prostitute who corrupted the earth by her adulteries. He has avenged on her the blood of his servants."

Incorruptible Judge—

Dt 10:17 For the LORD your God is God of gods and Lord of lords, the great God, mighty and awesome, who shows no partiality and accepts no bribes.

2Ch 19:7 Now let the fear of the LORD be upon you. Judge carefully, for with the LORD our God there is no injustice or partiality or bribery." (+Job 8:3)

Job 34:19 who shows no partiality to princes and does not favor the rich over the poor, for they are all the work of his hands?

Justice of: (Dt 32:4)

2Sa 22:25 The LORD has rewarded me according to my righteousness, according to my cleanness in his sight.

1Ki 8:32 then hear from heaven and act. Judge between your servants, condemning the guilty and bringing down on his own head what he has done. Declare the innocent not guilty, and so establish his innocence.

Job 31:13 "If I have denied justice to my menservants and maidservants when they had a grievance against me, ¹⁴what will I do when God confronts me? What will I answer when called to account? ¹⁵Did not he who made me in the womb make them? Did not the same one form us both within our mothers?

Ps 51:4 Against you, you only, have I sinned and done what is evil in your sight, so that you are proved right when you speak and justified when you judge.

Ps 62:12 and that you, O Lord, are loving. Surely you will reward each person according to what he has done.

Ps 89:14 Righteousness and justice are the foundation of your throne; love and faithfulness go before you.

Ps 97:2 Clouds and thick darkness surround him; righteousness and justice are the foundation of his throne.

Ps 145:17 The LORD is righteous in all his ways and loving toward all he has made.

Pr 21:2 All a man's ways seem right to him, but the LORD weighs the heart.

³To do what is right and just is more acceptable to the LORD than sacrifice.

Pr 24:12 If you say, "But we knew nothing about this," does not he who weighs the heart perceive it? Does not he who guards your life know it? Will he not repay each person according to what he has done?

Isa 61:8 "For I, the LORD, love justice; I hate robbery and iniquity. In my faithfulness I will reward them and make an everlasting covenant with them.

Jer 9:24 but let him who boasts boast about this: that he understands and knows me, that I am the LORD, who exercises kindness, justice and righteousness on earth, for in these I delight," declares the LORD.

Jer 11:20 But, O LORD Almighty, you who judge righteously and test the heart and mind, let me see your vengeance upon them, for to you I have committed my cause. (+Jer 20:12; 32:19)

Jer 50:7 Whoever found them devoured them; their enemies said, 'We are not guilty, for they sinned against the LORD, their true pasture, the LORD, the hope of their fathers.'

Eze 14:23 You will be consoled when you see their conduct and their actions, for you will know that I have done nothing in it without cause, declares the Sovereign LORD."

Eze 18:25 "Yet you say, 'The way of the Lord is not just.' Hear, O house of Israel: Is my way unjust? Is it not your ways that are unjust? (+Eze 18:29)

Eze 18:30 "Therefore, O house of Israel, I will judge you, each one according to his ways, declares the Sovereign LORD. Repent! Turn away from all your offenses; then sin will not be your downfall.

Eze 33:7 "Son of man, I have made you a watchman for the house of Israel; so hear the word I speak and give them warning from me. ⁸When I say to the wicked, 'O wicked man, you will surely die,' and you do not speak out to dissuade him from his ways, that wicked man will die for his sin, and I will hold you accountable for his blood. ⁹But if you do warn the wicked man to turn from his ways and he does not do so, he will die for his sin, but you will have saved yourself.

¹⁰"Son of man, say to the house of Israel, 'This is what you are saying: "Our offenses and sins weigh us down, and we are wasting away because of them. How then can we live?"' ¹¹Say to them, 'As surely as I live, declares the Sovereign LORD, I take no pleasure in the death of the wicked, but rather that they turn from their ways and live. Turn! Turn from your evil ways! Why will you die, O house of Israel?'

¹²"Therefore, son of man, say to your countrymen, 'The righteousness of the righteous man will not save him when he disobeys, and the wickedness of the wicked man will not cause him to fall when he turns from it. The righteous man, if he sins, will not be allowed to live because of his former righteousness.' ¹³If I tell the righteous man that he

will surely live, but then he trusts in his righteousness and does evil, none of the righteous things he has done will be remembered; he will die for the evil he has done. ¹⁴And if I say to the wicked man, 'You will surely die,' but he then turns away from his sin and does what is just and right— ¹⁵if he gives back what he took in pledge for a loan, returns what he has stolen, follows the decrees that give life, and does no evil, he will surely live; he will not die. ¹⁶None of the sins he has committed will be remembered against him. He has done what is just and right; he will surely live.

¹⁷"Yet your countrymen say, 'The way of the Lord is not just.' But it is their way that is not just. ¹⁸If a righteous man turns from his righteousness and does evil, he will die for it. ¹⁹And if a wicked man turns away from his wickedness and does what is just and right, he will live by doing so.

Da 9:7 "Lord, you are righteous, but this day we are covered with shame—the men of Judah and people of Jerusalem and all Israel, both near and far, in all the countries where you have scattered us because of our unfaithfulness to you.

Da 9:14 The Lord did not hesitate to bring the disaster upon us, for the Lord our God is righteous in everything he does; yet we have not obeyed him.

Na 1:3 The Lord is slow to anger and great in power; the Lord will not leave the guilty unpunished. His way is in the whirlwind and the storm, and clouds are the dust of his feet.

Na 1:6 Who can withstand his indignation? Who can endure his fierce anger? His wrath is poured out like fire; the rocks are shattered before him.

Zep 3:5 The Lord within her is righteous; he does no wrong. Morning by morning he dispenses his justice, and every new day he does not fail, yet the unrighteous know no shame. (+Ac 17:31; Ro 2:2,5-16)

Heb 6:10 God is not unjust; he will not forget your work and the love you have shown him as you have helped his people and continue to help them. (+1Pe 1:17)

2Pe 2:9 if this is so, then the Lord knows how to rescue godly men from trials and to hold the unrighteous for the day of judgment, while continuing their punishment.

1Jn 1:9 If we confess our sins, he is faithful and just and will forgive us our sins and purify us from all unrighteousness.

Jude 6 And the angels who did not keep their positions of authority but abandoned their own home—these he has kept in darkness, bound with everlasting chains for judgment on the great Day. (+Rev 11:18)

Rev 15:3 and sang the song of Moses the servant of God and the song of the Lamb: "Great and marvelous are your deeds, Lord God Almighty. Just and true are your ways, King of the ages.

Knowledge of: (Ge 6:5)

1Sa 2:3 "Do not keep talking so proudly or let your mouth speak such arrogance, for the Lord is a God who knows, and by him deeds are weighed.

Job 12:13 "To God belong wisdom and power; counsel and understanding are his.

Job 12:22 He reveals the deep things of darkness and brings deep shadows into the light.

Job 21:22 "Can anyone teach knowledge to God, since he judges even the highest?

Job 22:13 Yet you say, 'What does God know? Does he judge through such darkness? ¹⁴Thick clouds veil him, so he does not see us as he goes about in the vaulted heavens.'

Job 26:6 Death is naked before God; Destruction lies uncovered. (+Job 28:23)

Job 28:24 for he views the ends of the earth and sees everything under the heavens.

Job 36:4 Be assured that my words are not false; one perfect in knowledge is with you.

⁵"God is mighty, but does not despise men; he is mighty, and firm in his purpose.

Job 37:16 Do you know how the clouds hang poised, those wonders of him who is perfect in knowledge?

Ps 147:4 He determines the number of the stars and calls them each by name. ⁵Great is our Lord and mighty in power; his understanding has no limit.

Pr 3:19 By wisdom the Lord laid the earth's foundations, by understanding he set the heavens in place; ²⁰by his knowledge the deeps were divided, and the clouds let drop the dew.

Isa 40:13 Who has understood the mind of the Lord, or instructed him as his counselor? ¹⁴Whom did the Lord consult to enlighten him, and who taught him the right way? Who was it that taught him knowledge or showed him the path of understanding? (+Isa 40:26)

Isa 40:27 Why do you say, O Jacob, and complain, O Israel, "My way is hidden from the Lord; my cause is disregarded by my God"? ²⁸Do you not know? Have you not heard? The Lord is the everlasting God, the Creator of the ends of the earth. He will not grow tired or weary, and his understanding no one can fathom. (+Isa 46:9)

Isa 46:10 I make known the end from the beginning, from ancient times, what is still to come. I say: My purpose will stand, and I will do all that I please.

Mt 24:36 "No one knows about that day or hour, not even the angels in heaven, nor the Son, but only the Father. (+Mk 13:32)

Ro 11:33 Oh, the depth of the riches of the wisdom and knowledge of God! How unsearchable his judgments, and his paths beyond tracing out! ³⁴"Who has known the mind of the Lord? Or who has been his counselor?"

1Co 1:25 For the foolishness of God is wiser than man's wisdom, and the weakness of God is stronger than man's strength.

1Jn 1:5 This is the message we have heard from him and declare to you: God is light; in him there is no darkness at all.

Knows the human state and condition (Ge 16:13)—

Ex 3:7 The Lord said, "I have indeed seen the misery of my people in Egypt. I have heard them crying out because of their slave drivers, and I am concerned about their suffering.

Dt 2:7 The Lord your God has blessed you in all the work of your hands. He has watched over your journey through this vast desert. These forty years the Lord your God has been with you, and you have not lacked anything.

2Ki 19:27 "'But I know where you stay and when you come and go and how you rage against me.

2Ch 16:9 For the eyes of the Lord range throughout the earth to strengthen those whose hearts are fully committed to him. You have done a foolish thing, and from now on you will be at war."

Job 23:10 But he knows the way that I take; when he has tested me, I will come forth as gold.

Job 31:4 Does he not see my ways and count my every step?

Job 34:21 "His eyes are on the ways of men; he sees their every step.

Job 34:25 Because he takes note of their deeds, he overthrows them in the night and they are crushed.

Ps 1:6 For the LORD watches over the way of the righteous, but the way of the wicked will perish.

Ps 11:4 The LORD is in his holy temple; the LORD is on his heavenly throne. He observes the sons of men; his eyes examine them.

Ps 33:13 From heaven the LORD looks down and sees all mankind; [14]from his dwelling place he watches all who live on earth— [15]he who forms the hearts of all, who considers everything they do.

Ps 37:18 The days of the blameless are known to the LORD, and their inheritance will endure forever.

Ps 38:9 All my longings lie open before you, O Lord; my sighing is not hidden from you.

Ps 66:7 He rules forever by his power, his eyes watch the nations—let not the rebellious rise up against him. *Selah*

Ps 69:19 You know how I am scorned, disgraced and shamed; all my enemies are before you.

Ps 103:14 for he knows how we are formed, he remembers that we are dust.

Ps 119:168 I obey your precepts and your statutes, for all my ways are known to you.

Ps 139:1 O LORD, you have searched me and you know me. [2]You know when I sit and when I rise; you perceive my thoughts from afar. [3]You discern my going out and my lying down; you are familiar with all my ways. [4]Before a word is on my tongue you know it completely, O LORD.

Ps 139:6 Such knowledge is too wonderful for me, too lofty for me to attain.

Ps 139:12 even the darkness will not be dark to you; the night will shine like the day, for darkness is as light to you.

Ps 139:14 I praise you because I am fearfully and wonderfully made; your works are wonderful, I know that full well. [15]My frame was not hidden from you when I was made in the secret place. When I was woven together in the depths of the earth, [16]your eyes saw my unformed body. All the days ordained for me were written in your book before one of them came to be.

Ps 142:3 When my spirit grows faint within me, it is you who know my way. In the path where I walk men have hidden a snare for me.

Pr 5:21 For a man's ways are in full view of the LORD, and he examines all his paths.

Pr 15:3 The eyes of the LORD are everywhere, keeping watch on the wicked and the good.

Pr 15:11 Death and Destruction lie open before the LORD—how much more the hearts of men!

Isa 29:15 Woe to those who go to great depths to hide their plans from the LORD, who do their work in darkness and think, "Who sees us? Who will know?" [16]You turn things upside down, as if the potter were thought to be like the clay! Shall what is formed say to him who formed it, "He did not make me"? Can the pot say of the potter, "He knows nothing"?

Isa 37:28 "But I know where you stay and when you come and go and how you rage against me.

Isa 66:18 "And I, because of their actions and their imaginations, am about to come and gather all nations and tongues, and they will come and see my glory.

Jer 23:24 Can anyone hide in secret places so that I cannot see him?" declares the LORD. "Do not I fill heaven and earth?" declares the LORD.

Jer 32:19 great are your purposes and mighty are your deeds. Your eyes are open to all the ways of men; you reward everyone according to his conduct and as his deeds deserve.

Am 9:2 Though they dig down to the depths of the grave,

from there my hand will take them. Though they climb up to the heavens, from there I will bring them down. [3]Though they hide themselves on the top of Carmel, there I will hunt them down and seize them. Though they hide from me at the bottom of the sea, there I will command the serpent to bite them. [4]Though they are driven into exile by their enemies, there I will command the sword to slay them. I will fix my eyes upon them for evil and not for good."

Mt 10:29 Are not two sparrows sold for a penny? Yet not one of them will fall to the ground apart from the will of your Father. [30]And even the very hairs of your head are all numbered.

1Co 8:3 But the man who loves God is known by God.

Knows the human heart (Ge 20:6)—

Dt 31:21 And when many disasters and difficulties come upon them, this song will testify against them, because it will not be forgotten by their descendants. I know what they are disposed to do, even before I bring them into the land I promised them on oath."

1Sa 16:7 But the LORD said to Samuel, "Do not consider his appearance or his height, for I have rejected him. The LORD does not look at the things man looks at. Man looks at the outward appearance, but the LORD looks at the heart."

2Sa 7:20 "What more can David say to you? For you know your servant, O Sovereign LORD.

1Ki 8:39 then hear from heaven, your dwelling place. Forgive and act; deal with each man according to all he does, since you know his heart (for you alone know the hearts of all men),

1Ch 28:9 "And you, my son Solomon, acknowledge the God of your father, and serve him with wholehearted devotion and with a willing mind, for the LORD searches every heart and understands every motive behind the thoughts. If you seek him, he will be found by you; but if you forsake him, he will reject you forever. (+1Ch 29:17; 2Ch 6:30)

Job 11:11 Surely he recognizes deceitful men; and when he sees evil, does he not take note?

Ps 7:9 O righteous God, who searches minds and hearts, bring to an end the violence of the wicked and make the righteous secure.

Ps 44:21 would not God have discovered it, since he knows the secrets of the heart?

Ps 94:9 Does he who implanted the ear not hear? Does he who formed the eye not see? [10]Does he who disciplines nations not punish? Does he who teaches man lack knowledge? [11]The LORD knows the thoughts of man; he knows that they are futile. (+Pr 15:11)

Pr 16:2 All a man's ways seem innocent to him, but motives are weighed by the LORD.

Pr 17:3 The crucible for silver and the furnace for gold, but the LORD tests the heart. (+Pr 21:2)

Pr 24:12 If you say, "But we knew nothing about this," does not he who weighs the heart perceive it? Does not he who guards your life know it? Will he not repay each person according to what he has done?

Jer 11:20 But, O LORD Almighty, you who judge righteously and test the heart and mind, let me see your vengeance upon them, for to you I have committed my cause. (+Jer 16:17)

Jer 17:10 "I the LORD search the heart and examine the mind, to reward a man according to his conduct, according to what his deeds deserve." (+Jer 20:12)

Eze 11:5 Then the Spirit of the LORD came upon me, and

he told me to say: "This is what the LORD says: That is what you are saying, O house of Israel, but I know what is going through your mind.

Am 4:13 He who forms the mountains, creates the wind, and reveals his thoughts to man, he who turns dawn to darkness, and treads the high places of the earth—the LORD God Almighty is his name.

Mt 6:4 so that your giving may be in secret. Then your Father, who sees what is done in secret, will reward you.

Mt 6:8 Do not be like them, for your Father knows what you need before you ask him.

Mt 6:18 so that it will not be obvious to men that you are fasting, but only to your Father, who is unseen; and your Father, who sees what is done in secret, will reward you.

Mt 6:32 For the pagans run after all these things, and your heavenly Father knows that you need them.

Lk 16:15 He said to them, "You are the ones who justify yourselves in the eyes of men, but God knows your hearts. What is highly valued among men is detestable in God's sight.

Ac 1:24 Then they prayed, "Lord, you know everyone's heart. Show us which of these two you have chosen

Ac 15:8 God, who knows the heart, showed that he accepted them by giving the Holy Spirit to them, just as he did to us.

1Co 3:20 and again, "The Lord knows that the thoughts of the wise are futile."

1Th 2:4 On the contrary, we speak as men approved by God to be entrusted with the gospel. We are not trying to please men but God, who tests our hearts.

Heb 4:13 Nothing in all creation is hidden from God's sight Everything is uncovered and laid bare before the eyes of him to whom we must give account.

1Jn 3:20 whenever our hearts condemn us. For God is greater than our hearts, and he knows everything. *See above, Foreknowledge of; below, Wisdom of.*

Light: (Da 2:22; Jas 1:17).

1Jn 1:5 This is the message we have heard from him and declare to you: God is light; in him there is no darkness at all.

Longsuffering:

Ge 6:3 Then the LORD said, "My Spirit will not contend with man forever, for he is mortal; his days will be a hundred and twenty years."

Ge 15:16 In the fourth generation your descendants will come back here, for the sin of the Amorites has not yet reached its full measure."

Ex 34:6 And he passed in front of Moses, proclaiming, "The LORD, the LORD, the compassionate and gracious God, slow to anger, abounding in love and faithfulness,

Nu 14:18 'The LORD is slow to anger, abounding in love and forgiving sin and rebellion. Yet he does not leave the guilty unpunished; he punishes the children for the sin of the fathers to the third and fourth generation.'

Ps 86:15 But you, O Lord, are a compassionate and gracious God, slow to anger, abounding in love and faithfulness.

Ps 103:8 The LORD is compassionate and gracious, slow to anger, abounding in love. ⁹He will not always accuse, nor will he harbor his anger forever; ¹⁰he does not treat us as our sins deserve or repay us according to our iniquities.

Isa 5:1 I will sing for the one I love a song about his vineyard: My loved one had a vineyard on a fertile hillside. ²He dug it up and cleared it of stones and planted it with the choicest vines. He built a watchtower in it and cut

out a winepress as well. Then he looked for a crop of good grapes, but it yielded only bad fruit.

³"Now you dwellers in Jerusalem and men of Judah, judge between me and my vineyard. ⁴What more could have been done for my vineyard than I have done for it? When I looked for good grapes, why did it yield only bad?

Isa 30:18 Yet the LORD longs to be gracious to you; he rises to show you compassion. For the LORD is a God of justice. Blessed are all who wait for him!

Isa 48:9 For my own name's sake I delay my wrath; for the sake of my praise I hold it back from you, so as not to cut you off.

Isa 48:11 For my own sake, for my own sake, I do this. How can I let myself be defamed? I will not yield my glory to another. (+Isa 57:16)

Jer 7:13 While you were doing all these things, declares the LORD, I spoke to you again and again, but you did not listen; I called you, but you did not answer.

Jer 7:23 but I gave them this command: Obey me, and I will be your God and you will be my people. Walk in all the ways I command you, that it may go well with you. ²⁴But they did not listen or pay attention; instead, they followed the stubborn inclinations of their evil hearts. They went backward and not forward. ²⁵From the time your forefathers left Egypt until now, day after day, again and again I sent you my servants the prophets. (+Jer 9:24)

Eze 20:17 Yet I looked on them with pity and did not destroy them or put an end to them in the desert.

Joel 2:13 Rend your heart and not your garments. Return to the LORD your God, for he is gracious and compassionate, slow to anger and abounding in love, and he relents from sending calamity.

Hab 1:2 How long, O LORD, must I call for help, but you do not listen? Or cry out to you, "Violence!" but you do not save? ³Why do you make me look at injustice? Why do you tolerate wrong? Destruction and violence are before me; there is strife, and conflict abounds. ⁴Therefore the law is paralyzed, and justice never prevails. The wicked hem in the righteous, so that justice is perverted.

Mt 21:33 "Listen to another parable: There was a landowner who planted a vineyard. He put a wall around it, dug a winepress in it and built a watchtower. Then he rented the vineyard to some farmers and went away on a journey. ³⁴When the harvest time approached, he sent his servants to the tenants to collect his fruit.

³⁵"The tenants seized his servants; they beat one, killed another, and stoned a third. ³⁶Then he sent other servants to them, more than the first time, and the tenants treated them the same way. ³⁷Last of all, he sent his son to them. 'They will respect my son,' he said.

³⁸"But when the tenants saw the son, they said to each other, 'This is the heir. Come, let's kill him and take his inheritance.' ³⁹So they took him and threw him out of the vineyard and killed him.

⁴⁰"Therefore, when the owner of the vineyard comes, what will he do to those tenants?"

⁴¹"He will bring those wretches to a wretched end," they replied, "and he will rent the vineyard to other tenants, who will give him his share of the crop at harvest time." (+Mk 12:1-9; Lk 20:9-16)

Ac 14:16 In the past, he let all nations go their own way.

Ro 3:25 God presented him as a sacrifice of atonement, through faith in his blood. He did this to demonstrate his justice, because in his forbearance he had left the sins committed beforehand unpunished—

Ro 15:5 May the God who gives endurance and

encouragement give you a spirit of unity among your-selves as you follow Christ Jesus,

1Pe 3:20 who disobeyed long ago when God waited patiently in the days of Noah while the ark was being built. In it only a few people, eight in all, were saved through water,

Abused by people—

Ne 9:28 "But as soon as they were at rest, they again did what was evil in your sight. Then you abandoned them to the hand of their enemies so that they ruled over them. And when they cried out to you again, you heard from heaven, and in your compassion you delivered them time after time.

²⁹"You warned them to return to your law, but they became arrogant and disobeyed your commands. They sinned against your ordinances, by which a man will live if he obeys them. Stubbornly they turned their backs on you, became stiff-necked and refused to listen. ³⁰For many years you were patient with them. By your Spirit you admonished them through your prophets. Yet they paid no attention, so you handed them over to the neighboring peoples. ³¹But in your great mercy you did not put an end to them or abandon them, for you are a gracious and merciful God.

Pr 1:24 But since you rejected me when I called and no one gave heed when I stretched out my hand, ²⁵since you ignored all my advice and would not accept my rebuke, ²⁶I in turn will laugh at your disaster; I will mock when calamity overtakes you— ²⁷when calamity overtakes you like a storm, when disaster sweeps over you like a whirlwind, when distress and trouble overwhelm you.

Pr 29:1 A man who remains stiff-necked after many rebukes will suddenly be destroyed—without remedy.

Ecc 8:11 When the sentence for a crime is not quickly carried out, the hearts of the people are filled with schemes to do wrong. (+Isa 5:1-4; Jer 7:13,23-25)

Mt 24:48 But suppose that servant is wicked and says to himself, 'My master is staying away a long time,' ⁴⁹and he then begins to beat his fellow servants and to eat and drink with drunkards. ⁵⁰The master of that servant will come on a day when he does not expect him and at an hour he is not aware of. ⁵¹He will cut him to pieces and assign him a place with the hypocrites, where there will be weeping and gnashing of teeth. *See below, Mercy of.*

Manifested in deferring judgments (Mic 7:18)—

Lk 13:6 Then he told this parable: "A man had a fig tree, planted in his vineyard, and he went to look for fruit on it, but did not find any. ⁷So he said to the man who took care of the vineyard, 'For three years now I've been coming to look for fruit on this fig tree and haven't found any. Cut it down! Why should it use up the soil?'

⁸"'Sir,' the man replied, 'leave it alone for one more year, and I'll dig around it and fertilize it. ⁹If it bears fruit next year, fine! If not, then cut it down.'"

Ac 17:30 In the past God overlooked such ignorance, but now he commands all people everywhere to repent.

Ro 9:22 What if God, choosing to show his wrath and make his power known, bore with great patience the objects of his wrath—prepared for destruction? ²³What if he did this to make the riches of his glory known to the objects of his mercy, whom he prepared in advance for glory—

2Pe 3:9 The Lord is not slow in keeping his promise, as some understand slowness. He is patient with you, not wanting anyone to perish, but everyone to come to repentance.

2Pe 3:15 Bear in mind that our Lord's patience means salvation, just as our dear brother Paul also wrote you with the wisdom that God gave him.

Manifested in giving time for repentance (Jer 11:7)—

Mt 23:37 "O Jerusalem, Jerusalem, you who kill the prophets and stone those sent to you, how often I have longed to gather your children together, as a hen gathers her chicks under her wings, but you were not willing. (+Lk 13:34)

Ro 2:4 Or do you show contempt for the riches of his kindness, tolerance and patience, not realizing that God's kindness leads you toward repentance?

Love of:

Dt 4:37 Because he loved your forefathers and chose their descendants after them, he brought you out of Egypt by his Presence and his great strength,

Dt 7:7 The LORD did not set his affection on you and choose you because you were more numerous than other peoples, for you were the fewest of all peoples. ⁸But it was because the LORD loved you and kept the oath he swore to your forefathers that he brought you out with a mighty hand and redeemed you from the land of slavery, from the power of Pharaoh king of Egypt.

Dt 7:13 He will love you and bless you and increase your numbers. He will bless the fruit of your womb, the crops of your land—your grain, new wine and oil—the calves of your herds and the lambs of your flocks in the land that he swore to your forefathers to give you.

Dt 10:15 Yet the LORD set his affection on your forefathers and loved them, and he chose you, their descendants, above all the nations, as it is today.

Dt 10:18 He defends the cause of the fatherless and the widow, and loves the alien, giving him food and clothing.

Dt 23:5 However, the LORD your God would not listen to Balaam but turned the curse into a blessing for you, because the LORD your God loves you.

Dt 33:3 Surely it is you who love the people; all the holy ones are in your hand. At your feet they all bow down, and from you receive instruction,

Dt 33:12 About Benjamin he said: "Let the beloved of the LORD rest secure in him, for he shields him all day long, and the one the LORD loves rests between his shoulders."

2Sa 12:24 Then David comforted his wife Bathsheba, and he went to her and lay with her. She gave birth to a son, and they named him Solomon. The LORD loved him;

Job 7:17 "What is man that you make so much of him, that you give him so much attention,

Ps 42:8 By day the LORD directs his love, at night his song is with me—a prayer to the God of my life.

Ps 47:4 He chose our inheritance for us, the pride of Jacob, whom he loved. *Selah* (+Ps 69:16)

Hos 11:1 "When Israel was a child, I loved him, and out of Egypt I called my son.

Mal 1:2 "I have loved you," says the LORD. "But you ask, 'How have you loved us?' "Was not Esau Jacob's brother?" the LORD says. "Yet I have loved Jacob,

2Co 13:11 Finally, brothers, good-by. Aim for perfection, listen to my appeal, be of one mind, live in peace. And the God of love and peace will be with you. (+2Co 13:14)

1Jn 3:1 How great is the love the Father has lavished on us, that we should be called children of God! And that is what we are! The reason the world does not know us is that it did not know him.

1Jn 4:12 No one has ever seen God; but if we love one another, God lives in us and his love is made complete in us.

1Jn 4:16 And so we know and rely on the love God has for us. God is love. Whoever lives in love lives in God, and God in him.

1Jn 4:19 We love because he first loved us.

Jude 21 Keep yourselves in God's love as you wait for the mercy of our Lord Jesus Christ to bring you to eternal life.

Everlasting (2Ch 20:21)—

Jer 31:3 The LORD appeared to us in the past, saying: "I have loved you with an everlasting love; I have drawn you with loving-kindness.

Better than life—

Ps 63:3 Because your love is better than life, my lips will glorify you.

For the wicked (Mt 18:12-14; Lk 15:4-7,11-27)—

Ro 5:8 But God demonstrates his own love for us in this: While we were still sinners, Christ died for us.

Eph 2:4 But because of his great love for us, God, who is rich in mercy, ⁵made us alive with Christ even when we were dead in transgressions—it is by grace you have been saved.

For the righteous—

Ps 103:13 As a father has compassion on his children, so the LORD has compassion on those who fear him;

Ps 146:8 the LORD gives sight to the blind, the LORD lifts up those who are bowed down, the LORD loves the righteous.

Pr 15:9 The LORD detests the way of the wicked but he loves those who pursue righteousness.

Jn 14:21 Whoever has my commands and obeys them, he is the one who loves me. He who loves me will be loved by my Father, and I too will love him and show myself to him."

Jn 14:23 Jesus replied, "If anyone loves me, he will obey my teaching. My Father will love him, and we will come to him and make our home with him.

Jn 16:27 No, the Father himself loves you because you have loved me and have believed that I came from God.

Jn 17:10 All I have is yours, and all you have is mine. And glory has come to me through them.

Jn 17:23 I in them and you in me. May they be brought to complete unity to let the world know that you sent me and have loved them even as you have loved me.

Jn 17:26 I have made you known to them, and will continue to make you known in order that the love you have for me may be in them and that I myself may be in them."

Ro 1:7 To all in Rome who are loved by God and called to be saints: Grace and peace to you from God our Father and from the Lord Jesus Christ.

Ro 9:13 Just as it is written: "Jacob I loved, but Esau I hated."

Ro 11:28 As far as the gospel is concerned, they are enemies on your account; but as far as election is concerned, they are loved on account of the patriarchs,

2Th 2:16 May our Lord Jesus Christ himself and God our Father, who loved us and by his grace gave us eternal encouragement and good hope,

For the cheerful giver—

2Co 9:7 Each man should give what he has decided in his heart to give, not reluctantly or under compulsion, for God loves a cheerful giver.

Exemplified—

Ex 19:4 'You yourselves have seen what I did to Egypt, and how I carried you on eagles' wings and brought you to myself. ⁵Now if you obey me fully and keep my covenant, then out of all nations you will be my treasured possession.

Although the whole earth is mine, ⁶you will be for me a kingdom of priests and a holy nation.' These are the words you are to speak to the Israelites." (+Lev 20:24)

Lev 20:26 You are to be holy to me because I, the LORD, am holy, and I have set you apart from the nations to be my own.

Dt 32:9 For the LORD's portion is his people, Jacob his allotted inheritance.

¹⁰In a desert land he found him, in a barren and howling waste. He shielded him and cared for him; he guarded him as the apple of his eye, ¹¹like an eagle that stirs up its nest and hovers over its young, that spreads its wings to catch and carries them on its pinions. ¹²The LORD alone led him; no foreign god was with him.

2Sa 7:23 And who is like your people Israel—the one nation on earth that God went out to redeem as a people for himself, and to make a name for himself, and to perform great and awesome wonders by driving out nations and their gods from before your people, whom you redeemed from Egypt? ²⁴You have established your people Israel as your very own forever, and you, O LORD, have become their God.

Ps 48:9 Within your temple, O God, we meditate on your unfailing love.

Ps 48:14 For this God is our God for ever and ever; he will be our guide even to the end.

Isa 43:1 But now, this is what the LORD says—he who created you, O Jacob, he who formed you, O Israel: "Fear not, for I have redeemed you; I have summoned you by name; you are mine. ²When you pass through the waters, I will be with you; and when you pass through the rivers, they will not sweep over you. When you walk through the fire, you will not be burned; the flames will not set you ablaze. ³For I am the LORD, your God, the Holy One of Israel, your Savior; I give Egypt for your ransom, Cush and Seba in your stead. ⁴Since you are precious and honored in my sight, and because I love you, I will give men in exchange for you, and people in exchange for your life.

Isa 49:13 Shout for joy, O heavens; rejoice, O earth; burst into song, O mountains! For the LORD comforts his people and will have compassion on his afflicted ones.

¹⁴But Zion said, "The LORD has forsaken me, the Lord has forgotten me."

¹⁵"Can a mother forget the baby at her breast and have no compassion on the child she has borne? Though she may forget, I will not forget you! ¹⁶See, I have engraved you on the palms of my hands; your walls are ever before me.

Isa 54:5 For your Maker is your husband—the LORD Almighty is his name—the Holy One of Israel is your Redeemer; he is called the God of all the earth. ⁶The LORD will call you back as if you were a wife deserted and distressed in spirit—a wife who married young, only to be rejected," says your God.

Isa 54:10 Though the mountains be shaken and the hills be removed, yet my unfailing love for you will not be shaken nor my covenant of peace be removed," says the LORD, who has compassion on you.

Isa 62:4 No longer will they call you Deserted, or name your land Desolate. But you will be called Hephzibah, and your land Beulah; for the LORD will take delight in you, and your land will be married. ⁵As a young man marries a maiden, so will your sons marry you; as a bridegroom rejoices over his bride, so will your God rejoice over you.

Isa 63:7 I will tell of the kindnesses of the LORD, the deeds for which he is to be praised, according to all the LORD has done for us—yes, the many good things he has done for the house of Israel, according to his compassion and many kindnesses. (+Isa 63:8)

Isa 63:9 In all their distress he too was distressed, and the angel of his presence saved them. In his love and mercy he redeemed them; he lifted them up and carried them all the days of old.

Isa 66:13 As a mother comforts her child, so will I comfort you; and you will be comforted over Jerusalem."

Jer 3:14 "Return, faithless people," declares the LORD, "for I am your husband. I will choose you—one from a town and two from a clan—and bring you to Zion. ¹⁵Then I will give you shepherds after my own heart, who will lead you with knowledge and understanding.

Eze 16:8 "'Later I passed by, and when I looked at you and saw that you were old enough for love, I spread the corner of my garment over you and covered your naked- ness. I gave you my solemn oath and entered into a cove- nant with you, declares the Sovereign LORD, and you became mine.

Hos 2:19 I will betroth you to me forever; I will betroth you in righteousness and justice, in love and compassion. ²⁰I will betroth you in faithfulness, and you will acknow- ledge the LORD.

Hos 2:23 I will plant her for myself in the land; I will show my love to the one I called 'Not my loved one.' I will say to those called 'Not my people,' 'You are my people'; and they will say, 'You are my God.'"

Zec 2:8 For this is what the LORD Almighty says: "After he has honored me and has sent me against the nations that have plundered you—for whoever touches you touches the apple of his eye—

Exemplified in forgiveness of sins—

Isa 38:17 Surely it was for my benefit that I suffered such anguish. In your love you kept me from the pit of destruc- tion; you have put all my sins behind your back.

Tit 3:4 But when the kindness and love of God our Savior appeared, ⁵he saved us, not because of righteous things we had done, but because of his mercy. He saved us through the washing of rebirth and renewal by the Holy Spirit,

Exemplified in the gift of his Son—

Jn 3:16 "For God so loved the world that he gave his one and only Son, that whoever believes in him shall not perish but have eternal life.

1Jn 4:8 Whoever does not love does not know God, because God is love. ⁹This is how God showed his love among us: He sent his one and only Son into the world that we might live through him. ¹⁰This is love: not that we loved God, but that he loved us and sent his Son as an atoning sacrifice for our sins.

Exemplified in chastisements—

Heb 12:6 because the Lord disciplines those he loves, and he punishes everyone he accepts as a son."

Mercy of:

Ex 20:2 "I am the LORD your God, who brought you out of Egypt, out of the land of slavery.

Ex 20:6 but showing love to a thousand [generations] of those who love me and keep my commandments. (+Dt 5:10)

Ex 33:19 And the LORD said, "I will cause all my good- ness to pass in front of you, and I will proclaim my name, the LORD, in your presence. I will have mercy on whom I will have mercy, and I will have compassion on whom I will have compassion.

Dt 4:31 For the LORD your God is a merciful God; he will not abandon or destroy you or forget the covenant with your forefathers, which he confirmed to them by oath.

Dt 7:9 Know therefore that the LORD your God is God; he is the faithful God, keeping his covenant of love to a thousand generations of those who love him and keep his commands.

1Ki 8:23 and said: "O LORD, God of Israel, there is no God like you in heaven above or on earth below—you who keep your covenant of love with your servants who con- tinue wholeheartedly in your way.

2Ch 30:9 If you return to the LORD, then your brothers and your children will be shown compassion by their captors and will come back to this land, for the LORD your God is gracious and compassionate. He will not turn his face from you if you return to him." (+Ezr 9:9)

Ps 18:50 He gives his king great victories; he shows unfailing kindness to his anointed, to David and his de- scendants forever.

Ps 25:6 Remember, O LORD, your great mercy and love, for they are from of old.

Ps 25:8 Good and upright is the LORD; therefore he in- structs sinners in his ways.

Ps 31:7 I will be glad and rejoice in your love, for you saw my affliction and knew the anguish of my soul. (+Ps 32:10)

Ps 36:5 Your love, O LORD, reaches to the heavens, your faithfulness to the skies.

Ps 57:10 For great is your love, reaching to the heavens; your faithfulness reaches to the skies.

Ps 62:12 and that you, O Lord, are loving. Surely you will reward each person according to what he has done.

Ps 69:16 Answer me, O LORD, out of the goodness of your love; in your great mercy turn to me. (+Ps 98:3)

Ps 108:4 For great is your love, higher than the heavens; your faithfulness reaches to the skies.

Ps 111:4 He has caused his wonders to be remembered; the LORD is gracious and compassionate.

Ps 116:5 The LORD is gracious and righteous; our God is full of compassion.

Ps 117:2 For great is his love toward us, and the faithful- ness of the LORD endures forever. Praise the LORD.

Ps 119:64 The earth is filled with your love, O LORD; teach me your decrees.

Ps 119:156 Your compassion is great, O LORD; preserve my life according to your laws.

Ps 138:2 I will bow down toward your holy temple and will praise your name for your love and your faithfulness, for you have exalted above all things your name and your word.

Ps 146:7 He upholds the cause of the oppressed and gives food to the hungry. The LORD sets prisoners free, ⁸the LORD gives sight to the blind, the LORD lifts up those who are bowed down, the LORD loves the righteous.

Isa 60:10 "Foreigners will rebuild your walls, and their kings will serve you. Though in anger I struck you, in favor I will show you compassion.

Jer 9:24 but let him who boasts boast about this: that he understands and knows me, that I am the LORD, who exercises kindness, justice and righteousness on earth, for in these I delight," declares the LORD. (+Jer 31:20)

Jer 32:18 You show love to thousands but bring the punishment for the fathers' sins into the laps of their children after them. O great and powerful God, whose name is the LORD Almighty,

Da 9:4 I prayed to the LORD my God and confessed: "O

Lord, the great and awesome God, who keeps his covenant of love with all who love him and obey his commands,

Hos 2:23 I will plant her for myself in the land; I will show my love to the one I called 'Not my loved one.' I will say to those called 'Not my people,' 'You are my people'; and they will say, 'You are my God.'"

Zec 10:6 "I will strengthen the house of Judah and save the house of Joseph. I will restore them because I have compassion on them. They will be as though I had not rejected them, for I am the LORD their God and I will answer them.

Lk 6:36 Be merciful, just as your Father is merciful.

Ac 17:30 In the past God overlooked such ignorance, but now he commands all people everywhere to repent. (+Ro 9:15)

Ro 11:32 For God has bound all men over to disobedience so that he may have mercy on them all.

Ro 15:9 so that the Gentiles may glorify God for his mercy, as it is written: "Therefore I will praise you among the Gentiles; I will sing hymns to your name."

2Co 1:3 Praise be to the God and Father of our Lord Jesus Christ, the Father of compassion and the God of all comfort,

Heb 4:16 Let us then approach the throne of grace with confidence, so that we may receive mercy and find grace to help us in our time of need.

1Pe 1:3 Praise be to the God and Father of our Lord Jesus Christ! In his great mercy he has given us new birth into a living hope through the resurrection of Jesus Christ from the dead,

2Pe 3:9 The Lord is not slow in keeping his promise, as some understand slowness. He is patient with you, not wanting anyone to perish, but everyone to come to repentance.

Everlasting—

1Ch 16:34 Give thanks to the LORD, for he is good; his love endures forever. (+1Ch 16:41)

2Ch 5:13 The trumpeters and singers joined in unison, as with one voice, to give praise and thanks to the LORD. Accompanied by trumpets, cymbals and other instruments, they raised their voices in praise to the LORD and sang: "He is good; his love endures forever." Then the temple of the LORD was filled with a cloud,

2Ch 7:3 When all the Israelites saw the fire coming down and the glory of the LORD above the temple, they knelt on the pavement with their faces to the ground, and they worshiped and gave thanks to the LORD, saying, "He is good; his love endures forever."

2Ch 7:6 The priests took their positions, as did the Levites with the LORD's musical instruments, which King David had made for praising the LORD and which were used when he gave thanks, saying, "His love endures forever." Opposite the Levites, the priests blew their trumpets, and all the Israelites were standing.

2Ch 7:14 if my people, who are called by my name, will humble themselves and pray and seek my face and turn from their wicked ways, then will I hear from heaven and will forgive their sin and will heal their land. (+Ezr 3:11; Ps 89:1)

Ps 89:2 I will declare that your love stands firm forever, that you established your faithfulness in heaven itself.

Ps 89:28 I will maintain my love to him forever, and my covenant with him will never fail.

Ps 100:5 For the LORD is good and his love endures forever; his faithfulness continues through all generations.

Ps 103:17 But from everlasting to everlasting the LORD's love is with those who fear him, and his righteousness with their children's children—

Ps 106:1 Praise the LORD. Give thanks to the LORD, for he is good; his love endures forever. (+Ps 107:1; 118:1-4,29; 136:1-26)

Manifested in withholding punishment—

Ge 8:21 The LORD smelled the pleasing aroma and said in his heart: "Never again will I curse the ground because of man, even though every inclination of his heart is evil from childhood. And never again will I destroy all living creatures, as I have done.

Ge 18:26 The LORD said, "If I find fifty righteous people in the city of Sodom, I will spare the whole place for their sake." (+Ge 18:30-32)

Ex 32:14 Then the LORD relented and did not bring on his people the disaster he had threatened.

Nu 16:48 He stood between the living and the dead, and the plague stopped.

2Sa 24:14 David said to Gad, "I am in deep distress. Let us fall into the hands of the LORD, for his mercy is great; but do not let me fall into the hands of men."

2Sa 24:16 When the angel stretched out his hand to destroy Jerusalem, the LORD was grieved because of the calamity and said to the angel who was afflicting the people, "Enough! Withdraw your hand." The angel of the LORD was then at the threshing floor of Araunah the Jebusite.

2Ki 13:23 But the LORD was gracious to them and had compassion and showed concern for them because of his covenant with Abraham, Isaac and Jacob. To this day he has been unwilling to destroy them or banish them from his presence.

Ezr 9:13 "What has happened to us is a result of our evil deeds and our great guilt, and yet, our God, you have punished us less than our sins have deserved and have given us a remnant like this. (+Job 11:6)

Isa 12:1 In that day you will say: "I will praise you, O LORD. Although you were angry with me, your anger has turned away and you have comforted me.

Isa 54:9 "To me this is like the days of Noah, when I swore that the waters of Noah would never again cover the earth. So now I have sworn not to be angry with you, never to rebuke you again.

Eze 16:6 " 'Then I passed by and saw you kicking about in your blood, and as you lay there in your blood I said to you, "Live!"

Eze 16:42 Then my wrath against you will subside and my jealous anger will turn away from you; I will be calm and no longer angry.

Eze 16:63 Then, when I make atonement for you for all you have done, you will remember and be ashamed and never again open your mouth because of your humiliation, declares the Sovereign LORD.' "

Eze 20:17 Yet I looked on them with pity and did not destroy them or put an end to them in the desert.

Hos 11:8 "How can I give you up, Ephraim? How can I hand you over, Israel? How can I treat you like Admah? How can I make you like Zeboiim? My heart is changed within me; all my compassion is aroused. ⁹I will not carry out my fierce anger, nor will I turn and devastate Ephraim. For I am God, and not man—the Holy One among you. I will not come in wrath.

Joel 2:13 Rend your heart and not your garments. Return to the LORD your God, for he is gracious and compassionate, slow to anger and abounding in love, and he relents from sending calamity.

Joel 2:18 Then the LORD will be jealous for his land and take pity on his people.

Jnh 4:2 He prayed to the LORD, "O LORD, is this not what I said when I was still at home? That is why I was so quick to flee to Tarshish. I knew that you are a gracious and compassionate God, slow to anger and abounding in love, a God who relents from sending calamity.

Jnh 4:10 But the LORD said, "You have been concerned about this vine, though you did not tend it or make it grow. It sprang up overnight and died overnight. ¹¹But Nineveh has more than a hundred and twenty thousand people who cannot tell their right hand from their left, and many cattle as well. Should I not be concerned about that great city?"

Mal 3:6 "I the LORD do not change. So you, O descendants of Jacob, are not destroyed.

Manifested in rescuing from destruction—

Ge 19:16 When he hesitated, the men grasped his hand and the hands of his wife and of his two daughters and led them safely out of the city, for the LORD was merciful to them.

Nu 21:8 The LORD said to Moses, "Make a snake and put it up on a pole; anyone who is bitten can look at it and live."

Jdg 2:18 Whenever the LORD raised up a judge for them, he was with the judge and saved them out of the hands of their enemies as long as the judge lived; for the LORD had compassion on them as they groaned under those who oppressed and afflicted them.

2Ki 14:26 The LORD had seen how bitterly everyone in Israel, whether slave or free, was suffering; there was no one to help them. ²⁷And since the LORD had not said he would blot out the name of Israel from under heaven, he saved them by the hand of Jeroboam son of Jehoash.

Ne 1:10 "They are your servants and your people, whom you redeemed by your great strength and your mighty hand.

Ne 9:17 They refused to listen and failed to remember the miracles you performed among them. They became stiff-necked and in their rebellion appointed a leader in order to return to their slavery. But you are a forgiving God, gracious and compassionate, slow to anger and abounding in love. Therefore you did not desert them, (+Ne 9:18-20)

Ne 9:27 So you handed them over to their enemies, who oppressed them. But when they were oppressed they cried out to you. From heaven you heard them, and in your great compassion you gave them deliverers, who rescued them from the hand of their enemies.

²⁸"But as soon as they were at rest, they again did what was evil in your sight. Then you abandoned them to the hand of their enemies so that they ruled over them. And when they cried out to you again, you heard from heaven, and in your compassion you delivered them time after time.

²⁹"You warned them to return to your law, but they became arrogant and disobeyed your commands. They sinned against your ordinances, by which a man will live if he obeys them. Stubbornly they turned their backs on you, became stiff-necked and refused to listen. ³⁰For many years you were patient with them. By your Spirit you admonished them through your prophets. Yet they paid no attention, so you handed them over to the neighboring peoples. ³¹But in your great mercy you did not put an end to them or abandon them, for you are a gracious and merciful God.

Manifested in leading his people—

Ex 15:13 "In your unfailing love you will lead the people you have redeemed. In your strength you will guide them to your holy dwelling.

Manifested in comforting the afflicted—

2Co 12:9 But he said to me, "My grace is sufficient for you, for my power is made perfect in weakness." Therefore I will boast all the more gladly about my weaknesses, so that Christ's power may rest on me.

Manifested in hearing prayer—

Ex 22:27 because his cloak is the only covering he has for his body. What else will he sleep in? When he cries out to me, I will hear, for I am compassionate. (+Heb 4:16)

Manifested in desire to save sinners—

Dt 5:29 Oh, that their hearts would be inclined to fear me and keep all my commands always, so that it might go well with them and their children forever!

Dt 32:29 If only they were wise and would understand this and discern what their end will be!

Jdg 10:16 Then they got rid of the foreign gods among them and served the LORD. And he could bear Israel's misery no longer.

2Ch 36:15 The LORD, the God of their fathers, sent word to them through his messengers again and again, because he had pity on his people and on his dwelling place.

Isa 65:2 All day long I have held out my hands to an obstinate people, who walk in ways not good, pursuing their own imaginations—

Isa 65:8 This is what the LORD says: "As when juice is still found in a cluster of grapes and men say, 'Don't destroy it, there is yet some good in it,' so will I do in behalf of my servants; I will not destroy them all.

Jer 2:9 "Therefore I bring charges against you again," declares the LORD. "And I will bring charges against your children's children. (+Jer 7:25)

Eze 18:23 Do I take any pleasure in the death of the wicked? declares the Sovereign LORD. Rather, am I not pleased when they turn from their ways and live?

Eze 18:31 Rid yourselves of all the offenses you have committed, and get a new heart and a new spirit. Why will you die, O house of Israel? ³²For I take no pleasure in the death of anyone, declares the Sovereign LORD. Repent and live!

Eze 33:11 Say to them, 'As surely as I live, declares the Sovereign LORD, I take no pleasure in the death of the wicked, but rather that they turn from their ways and live. Turn! Turn from your evil ways! Why will you die, O house of Israel?'

Mt 18:12 "What do you think? If a man owns a hundred sheep, and one of them wanders away, will he not leave the ninety-nine on the hills and go to look for the one that wandered off? ¹³And if he finds it, I tell you the truth, he is happier about that one sheep than about the ninety-nine that did not wander off. ¹⁴In the same way your Father in heaven is not willing that any of these little ones should be lost. (+Lk 15:4-7; 1Ti 2:4,6)

Manifested in forbearance toward sinners (2Ch 24:18-19)—

Ps 145:8 The LORD is gracious and compassionate, slow to anger and rich in love. ⁹The LORD is good to all; he has compassion on all he has made.

La 3:22 Because of the LORD's great love we are not consumed, for his compassions never fail. ²³They are new every morning; great is your faithfulness.

La 3:31 For men are not cast off by the Lord forever. ³²Though he brings grief, he will show compassion, so great is his unfailing love. ³³For he does not willingly bring affliction or grief to the children of men.

Da 4:22 you, O king, are that tree! You have become great and strong; your greatness has grown until it reaches the sky, and your dominion extends to distant parts of the earth.

²³"You, O king, saw a messenger, a holy one, coming down from heaven and saying, 'Cut down the tree and destroy it, but leave the stump, bound with iron and bronze, in the grass of the field, while its roots remain in the ground. Let him be drenched with the dew of heaven; let him live like the wild animals, until seven times pass by for him.'

²⁴"This is the interpretation, O king, and this is the decree the Most High has issued against my lord the king: ²⁵You will be driven away from people and will live with the wild animals; you will eat grass like cattle and be drenched with the dew of heaven. Seven times will pass by for you until you acknowledge that the Most High is sovereign over the kingdoms of men and gives them to anyone he wishes. ²⁶The command to leave the stump of the tree with its roots means that your kingdom will be restored to you when you acknowledge that Heaven rules. ²⁷Therefore, O king, be pleased to accept my advice: Renounce your sins by doing what is right, and your wickedness by being kind to the oppressed. It may be that then your prosperity will continue."

Na 1:3 The LORD is slow to anger and great in power; the LORD will not leave the guilty unpunished. His way is in the whirlwind and the storm, and clouds are the dust of his feet.

Manifested in granting forgiveness—

Ex 34:6 And he passed in front of Moses, proclaiming, "The LORD, the LORD, the compassionate and gracious God, slow to anger, abounding in love and faithfulness, ⁷maintaining love to thousands, and forgiving wickedness, rebellion and sin. Yet he does not leave the guilty unpunished; he punishes the children and their children for the sin of the fathers to the third and fourth generation."

Nu 14:18 'The LORD is slow to anger, abounding in love and forgiving sin and rebellion. Yet he does not leave the guilty unpunished; he punishes the children for the sin of the fathers to the third and fourth generation.' ¹⁹In accordance with your great love, forgive the sin of these people, just as you have pardoned them from the time they left Egypt until now."

²⁰The LORD replied, "I have forgiven them, as you asked.

2Sa 12:13 Then David said to Nathan, "I have sinned against the LORD." Nathan replied, "The LORD has taken away your sin. You are not going to die. (+2Ch 7:14; Job 33:14-30)

Ps 32:1 Blessed is he whose transgressions are forgiven, whose sins are covered. ²Blessed is the man whose sin the LORD does not count against him and in whose spirit is no deceit.

Ps 32:5 Then I acknowledged my sin to you and did not cover up my iniquity. I said, "I will confess my transgressions to the LORD"—and you forgave the guilt of my sin. *Selah*

Ps 65:3 When we were overwhelmed by sins, you forgave our transgressions.

Ps 78:38 Yet he was merciful; he forgave their iniquities and did not destroy them. Time after time he restrained his anger and did not stir up his full wrath. ³⁹He remembered that they were but flesh, a passing breeze that does not return.

Ps 85:2 You forgave the iniquity of your people and

covered all their sins. *Selah* ³You set aside all your wrath and turned from your fierce anger.

Ps 86:5 You are forgiving and good, O Lord, abounding in love to all who call to you.

Ps 86:13 For great is your love toward me; you have delivered me from the depths of the grave.

Ps 86:15 But you, O Lord, are a compassionate and gracious God, slow to anger, abounding in love and faithfulness.

Ps 99:8 O LORD our God, you answered them; you were to Israel a forgiving God, though you punished their misdeeds.

Ps 103:3 who forgives all your sins and heals all your diseases,

Ps 103:8 The LORD is compassionate and gracious, slow to anger, abounding in love. ⁹He will not always accuse, nor will he harbor his anger forever; ¹⁰he does not treat us as our sins deserve or repay us according to our iniquities. ¹¹For as high as the heavens are above the earth, so great is his love for those who fear him; ¹²as far as the east is from the west, so far has he removed our transgressions from us. ¹³As a father has compassion on his children, so the LORD has compassion on those who fear him; ¹⁴for he knows how we are formed, he remembers that we are dust.

Ps 130:3 If you, O LORD, kept a record of sins, O Lord, who could stand? ⁴But with you there is forgiveness; therefore you are feared.

Ps 130:7 O Israel, put your hope in the LORD, for with the LORD is unfailing love and with him is full redemption. ⁸He himself will redeem Israel from all their sins.

Pr 16:6 Through love and faithfulness sin is atoned for; through the fear of the LORD a man avoids evil.

Pr 28:13 He who conceals his sins does not prosper, but whoever confesses and renounces them finds mercy.

Isa 55:7 Let the wicked forsake his way and the evil man his thoughts. Let him turn to the LORD, and he will have mercy on him, and to our God, for he will freely pardon. ⁸"For my thoughts are not your thoughts, neither are your ways my ways," declares the LORD. ⁹"As the heavens are higher than the earth, so are my ways higher than your ways and my thoughts than your thoughts.

Jer 3:12 Go, proclaim this message toward the north: "'Return, faithless Israel,' declares the LORD, 'I will frown on you no longer, for I am merciful,' declares the LORD, 'I will not be angry forever.

Jer 3:22 "Return, faithless people; I will cure you of backsliding." "Yes, we will come to you, for you are the LORD our God.

Jer 31:20 Is not Ephraim my dear son, the child in whom I delight? Though I often speak against him, I still remember him. Therefore my heart yearns for him; I have great compassion for him," declares the LORD.

Jer 31:34 No longer will a man teach his neighbor, or a man his brother, saying, 'Know the LORD,' because they will all know me, from the least of them to the greatest," declares the LORD. "For I will forgive their wickedness and will remember their sins no more."

Jer 33:8 I will cleanse them from all the sin they have committed against me and will forgive all their sins of rebellion against me.

Jer 33:11 the sounds of joy and gladness, the voices of bride and bridegroom, and the voices of those who bring thank offerings to the house of the LORD, saying, "Give thanks to the LORD Almighty, for the LORD is good; his love endures forever." For I will restore the fortunes of the land as they were before,' says the LORD.

Jer 36:3 Perhaps when the people of Judah hear about every disaster I plan to inflict on them, each of them will turn from his wicked way; then I will forgive their wickedness and their sin."

Jer 50:20 In those days, at that time," declares the LORD, "search will be made for Israel's guilt, but there will be none, and for the sins of Judah, but none will be found, for I will forgive the remnant I spare.

Eze 36:25 I will sprinkle clean water on you, and you will be clean; I will cleanse you from all your impurities and from all your idols.

Da 9:9 The Lord our God is merciful and forgiving, even though we have rebelled against him;

Hos 14:4 "I will heal their waywardness and love them freely, for my anger has turned away from them.

Mic 7:18 Who is a God like you, who pardons sin and forgives the transgression of the remnant of his inheritance? You do not stay angry forever but delight to show mercy. (+Mic 7:19)

Mt 6:14 For if you forgive men when they sin against you, your heavenly Father will also forgive you.

Mt 18:23 "Therefore, the kingdom of heaven is like a king who wanted to settle accounts with his servants. 24As he began the settlement, a man who owed him ten thousand talents was brought to him. 25Since he was not able to pay, the master ordered that he and his wife and his children and all that he had be sold to repay the debt.

26"The servant fell on his knees before him. 'Be patient with me,' he begged, 'and I will pay back everything.' 27The servant's master took pity on him, canceled the debt and let him go.

Lk 1:50 His mercy extends to those who fear him, from generation to generation.

Lk 1:77 to give his people the knowledge of salvation through the forgiveness of their sins, 78because of the tender mercy of our God, by which the rising sun will come to us from heaven

Ac 3:19 Repent, then, and turn to God, so that your sins may be wiped out, that times of refreshing may come from the Lord,

Ac 26:18 to open their eyes and turn them from darkness to light, and from the power of Satan to God, so that they may receive forgiveness of sins and a place among those who are sanctified by faith in me.'

Ro 10:12 For there is no difference between Jew and Gentile—the same Lord is Lord of all and richly blesses all who call on him, 13for, "Everyone who calls on the name of the Lord will be saved." (+2Co 5:19)

Eph 1:6 to the praise of his glorious grace, which he has freely given us in the One he loves. 7In him we have redemption through his blood, the forgiveness of sins, in accordance with the riches of God's grace 8that he lavished on us with all wisdom and understanding.

Eph 2:4 But because of his great love for us, God, who is rich in mercy, 5made us alive with Christ even when we were dead in transgressions—it is by grace you have been saved. 6And God raised us up with Christ and seated us with him in the heavenly realms in Christ Jesus, 7in order that in the coming ages he might show the incomparable riches of his grace, expressed in his kindness to us in Christ Jesus.

1Ti 1:13 Even though I was once a blasphemer and a persecutor and a violent man, I was shown mercy because I acted in ignorance and unbelief.

Tit 3:5 he saved us, not because of righteous things we had

done, but because of his mercy. He saved us through the washing of rebirth and renewal by the Holy Spirit,

Heb 8:12 For I will forgive their wickedness and will remember their sins no more."

1Jn 1:9 If we confess our sins, he is faithful and just and will forgive us our sins and purify us from all unrighteousness.

Symbolized: In the atonement cover—

Ex 25:17 "Make an atonement cover of pure gold—two and a half cubits long and a cubit and a half wide. 18And make two cherubim out of hammered gold at the ends of the cover. 19Make one cherub on one end and the second cherub on the other; make the cherubim of one piece with the cover, at the two ends. 20The cherubim are to have their wings spread upward, overshadowing the cover with them. The cherubim are to face each other, looking toward the cover. 21Place the cover on top of the ark and put in the ark the Testimony, which I will give you. 22There, above the cover between the two cherubim that are over the ark of the Testimony, I will meet with you and give you all my commands for the Israelites. (+Ex 37:6-9)

Lev 16:1 The LORD spoke to Moses after the death of the two sons of Aaron who died when they approached the LORD. 2The LORD said to Moses: "Tell your brother Aaron not to come whenever he chooses into the Most Holy Place behind the curtain in front of the atonement cover on the ark, or else he will die, because I appear in the cloud over the atonement cover.

3"This is how Aaron is to enter the sanctuary area: with a young bull for a sin offering and a ram for a burnt offering. 4He is to put on the sacred linen tunic, with linen undergarments next to his body; he is to tie the linen sash around him and put on the linen turban. These are sacred garments; so he must bathe himself with water before he puts them on. 5From the Israelite community he is to take two male goats for a sin offering and a ram for a burnt offering.

6"Aaron is to offer the bull for his own sin offering to make atonement for himself and his household. 7Then he is to take the two goats and present them before the LORD at the entrance to the Tent of Meeting. 8He is to cast lots for the two goats—one lot for the LORD and the other for the scapegoat. 9Aaron shall bring the goat whose lot falls to the LORD and sacrifice it for a sin offering. 10But the goat chosen by lot as the scapegoat shall be presented alive before the LORD to be used for making atonement by sending it into the desert as a scapegoat.

11"Aaron shall bring the bull for his own sin offering to make atonement for himself and his household, and he is to slaughter the bull for his own sin offering. 12He is to take a censer full of burning coals from the altar before the LORD and two handfuls of finely ground fragrant incense and take them behind the curtain. 13He is to put the incense on the fire before the LORD, and the smoke of the incense will conceal the atonement cover above the Testimony, so that he will not die. 14He is to take some of the bull's blood and with his finger sprinkle it on the front of the atonement cover; then he shall sprinkle some of it with his finger seven times before the atonement cover. (+Nu 7:89; Heb 9:5)

Name of:

To be revered (Ex 20:7; Dt 5:11; 28:58; Ps 111:9; Mic 4:5; 1Ti 6:1). To be praised (Ps 34:3; 72:17). Not to be profaned (Ex 20:7; Lev 18:21; 19:12; 20:3; 21:6; 22:2,32; Dt 5:11; Ps 139:20; Isa 52:5; Ro 2:24; Rev 16:9). Profaned (Ps 139:20).

Names of:

In the ancient world a name was not merely a label but the meaning of the name was virtually equivalent to whoever or whatever bore it (1Sa 25:25). Giving a name to anyone or anything was tantamount to owning or controlling it (Ge 1:5,8,10; 2:19-20; 2Sa 12:28). Changing a name could signify a promotion to a higher status (Ge 17:5; 32:28) or a demotion (2Ki 23:34-35; 24:17), and blotting out or cutting off the name of a person or thing meant that that person or thing was destroyed (2Ki 14:27; Isa 14:22; Zep 1:4; cf. Ps 83:4).

The name and being of God are often used in parallelism with each other (Ps 18:49; 68:4; 74:18; 86:12; 92:1; Isa 25:1; Mal 3:16), which stresses their essential identity. Believing in Jesus' name (Jn 3:18) is therefore the same as believing in Jesus himself. Prayer in his name would be prayer in concert with his character, mind, and purpose.

The name Jesus is the Greek form for the Hebrew Joshua or "*salvation of Yahweh.*" As Yahweh's Savior his name accurately describes his work and purpose (Mt 1:21).

El and its compounds—

El [446] is the generic Semitic name for "God" or "deity." *El* is one of the oldest designations for deity in the ancient world. The word is found in several Semitic languages such as, Akkadian, Phoenician, and South Arabic. Even though the derivation of the word is uncertain, the root meaning is "power and authority" (Ge 1:1; Ps 19:1).

El Berith [451] means "god of the covenant" (Jdg 9:46) and is an alternate form of the name *Baal-Berith* (Jdg 8:33; 9:4). These are names of pagan gods and not the God of Israel. The remains of the Canaanite temple to Baal-Berith at Shechem, has been recovered.

El Bethel [450] means "God of Bethel," but is a place name, not a name of God. God directs Jacob to return to Bethel and build an altar there (Ge 35:1,6-7).

El Elohe Israel [449] means "God [El], the God of Israel" or "mighty is the God of Israel." Though a statement about God, it is actually the name of an altar, also associated with the travels of Jacob (Ge 33:18-20).

El Elyon; See below Elyon.

El Olam [446+6409] means "God the Everlasting One" or "God of Eternity." While living among the Philistines, Abraham calls upon the name of Yahweh, the Eternal God (Ge 21:33). Isaiah quotes God as saying, "The LORD is the everlasting God, the Creator of the ends of the earth" (Isa 40:28). The Psalmist expresses that, "from everlasting to everlasting you are God" (Ps 90:1-2; cf 93:2; Isa 26:4).

El Roi [446+8011 or 8024] means "God who sees me." As Hagar wandered in the desert, the angel of the LORD appeared to her (Ge 16:7-12). After his appearance she gave Yahweh this name saying, "You are the One who sees me." The well at that place was named "Beer Lahai Roi," which means "well of the Living One who sees me" (Ge 16:14).

El Shaddai [446+8724] appears seven times (Ge 17:1; 28:3; 35:11; 43:14; 48:3; Ex 6:3; Eze 10:5). It probably means "God the Mountain," similar to "God the Rock" (Dt 32:4). Older etymology defined it as "God the Provider," understanding *Shaddai* to be derived from the word for "breast." *See below Shaddai.*

Eloah—

Eloah [468] is thought to be a singular form of "Elohim." It is used primarily in Job (42 times) as a way to refer to God, but without referring to him as the "God of Israel." In other references it is usually synonymous in

meaning with *Elohim* (Ps 50:22-23), or *Yahweh* (Ps 139:19,21), or *Adonay* (Ps 114:7). It also appears in the exilic and postexilic periods (2Ch 32:15; Ne 9:17; Da 11:37-39).

Elohim (and its compounds) and *Theos*—

Elohim [466], the plural form of *El, Eloah* is used as a plural to refer to the many gods of the nations. But *Elohim* is used in a singular sense in the great majority of instances, and is thus referred to as "plural of majesty." In the singular sense *Elohim* is sometimes applied to the god of another people as in Chemosh, the god of the Amorites (Jdg 11:24), or Ashtoreth (Ishtar), the goddess of Sidon (1Ki 11:5), or Baal-Zebub, the god of Ekron (2Ki 1:2), but is used overwhelmingly (over 2300 times) in the OT to refer to Israel's God, meaning "the true God."

Theos [2536] is the NT counterpart of *Elohim* (Mt 22:32 w Ex 3:6). It usually refers to the true God, but can refer to pagan deities (Ac 17:18,23; 1Co 8:5).

Yahweh, Yah, and compounds—

Yahweh [3378] is the personal covenant name of Israel's God, the most common name for God in the OT (6829 times). *Yah* [3363] is its shortened form. The NIV consistently renders Yahweh as LORD. The name sounds like and may be derived from the Hebrew for the word "I AM" (Ex 3:14-15). The basic meaning of his name is "He who is" or "He who is truly present." or "I will be to you all that I am." For Israel, Yahweh is not merely one god among many; he is the Creator and Ruler of heaven and earth, who is worthy of and demands the exclusive homage of his people. It is important to understand that this is God's intensely personal name. The respect with which it was treated bears witness to the national feeling of Israel and also their fear of the God who is among them. This was recognized by the scribes who even avoided pronunciation of the name. They would use circumlocutions and alternate names where possible. *See below on Adonay.* In the NT, John records that Jesus made seven self-descriptions (Jn 6:35; 8:12 w 9:5; 10:7,9; 10:11,14; 11:25; 14:6; 15:1,5), each one being introduced by "I am." The Greek text makes this statement solemnly emphatic and echoes God's self-revelation to Moses (Ex 3:14). In a similar fashion, Jesus expressed the eternity of his being and his oneness with the Father by saying, "I tell you the truth," Jesus answered, "before Abraham was born, I am!" (Jn 8:58). The people listening knew exactly what he meant by what he said: I AM GOD. The penalty for such blasphemy was stoning (Lev 24:16), which they fully intended to carry out (Jn 8:59).

Yahweh Nissi [3378+5812] means "Yahweh is my banner or standard." This was the name given to the altar which Moses erected to commemorate the defeat of the Amalekites at Rephidim (Ex 17:8-15).

Yahweh Rapha [3378+8324]. At Marah, on the way to Sinai, the LORD promised Israel that if they fully obeyed him, he would not bring on them the diseases he brought on Egypt. His name of assurance means "[I am] Yahweh who heals you" (Ex 15:26).

Yahweh Shalom [3378+8934] means "Yahweh is peace." The angel of the LORD appeared to Gideon to commission him to liberate Israel from the Midianites (Jdg 6:1-22). The LORD greeted him with peace, so Gideon built an altar and named it "The LORD is Peace" (Jdg 6:23-24).

Yahweh Shammah [3378+9004] means "The LORD is There." Not a name of God, this is the name given to the restored Jerusalem (Eze 48:35). The glory of God will return and Messiah will rule from New Jerusalem forever

(Eze 43; cf. Rev 21). God's name is inseparably linked with Jerusalem.

Yahweh Tsabbaoth [3378+7372] means "LORD of Hosts" and is consistently translated "LORD Almighty" in the NIV (e.g., 1Sa 1:3,11). "Hosts" can refer to, human armies (Ex 7:4; Ps 44:9), celestial bodies (Ge 2:1; Dt 4:19; Isa 40:26), or heavenly creatures such as angels (Jos 5:14; 1Ki 22:19; Ps 148:2). This title is probably best understood as a general reference to the sovereignty of God over all powers in the universe. In the NT *Tsabbaoth* is twice transliterated by the Greek "Sabaoth" [4877] (Ro 9:29; Jas 5:4), but is usually *Pantokrator* [4120] (2Co 6:18; Rev 1:8; 4:8).

Yahweh Tsidkenu [3378+7406] means "Yahweh our Righteousness." This is the designation of the future king who will rise up from the line of David to rule over Israel (Jer 23:5-6). Righteousness is the divine attribute of the Messiah who imputes his righteousness to his followers and therefore is able to reconcile them to God (2Co 5:21). In a second reference, Jeremiah directs attention to Jerusalem, the capital of the King, which because of her intimate relationship to Messiah, will be given the same name and nature of the righteous monarch (Jer 33:15-16).

Yahweh Yireh [3378+8011] means "Yahweh will provide," "Yahweh will see [to it]." *Yireh* comes from the same Hebrew root as *Moriah,* the name of the region to which God sent Abraham to sacrifice Isaac (Ge 22:2; 2Ch 3:1). Both words are place names that confess Yahweh as the provider of a substitutionary sacrifice (Ge 22:14, cf. v. 8).

Adon, Adonay, and *Kurios*

Adon [123] or *Adonay* [151] is a title for God that emphasizes his sovereignty, that is "Lord." *Adon* is basically a title of honor. Out of respect one might address a superior with this title in the same way that we would say "sir" or "your honor." It would be used by a subject addressing a king (1Sa 24:8), a wife to her husband (Ge 18:12), a daughter or son to their father (Ge 31:35), a slave to his master (Ge 24:12; Ex 21:5), a subordinate to his leader (Nu 11:28). It therefore refers to one's position of authority and prestige (Ge 23:6; 45:8). The special spelling *Adonay* belongs preeminently to Yahweh, because he alone is the "Lord of the earth" (Jos 3:11,13; Ps 97:5; Mic 4:13; Zec 4:14; 6:5). In the years after the Exile (after 538 B.C.), with reverence for the name of God increasing, the name *Yahweh* began to be pronounce as *Adonay* in the reading of the Scriptures. The LXX translators, out of fear of profaning the name of God, were led to translate *Yahweh* as *kurios* or "Lord." The Massoretic pronunciation of the Hebrew text continued this tradition by using the vowels of *Adonay* with the consonants of *Yahweh* as a signal that the proper name of God should be pronounced as *Adonay.* The misreading of this convention led to the misunderstanding of the name of God as *Jehovah.*

Kurios [3261] is the NT counterpart of both *Adonay* (Mt 22:44 w Ps 110:1) and *Yahweh* (Mt 4:10 w Dt 6:13). It is used as a term of respect (Mt 13:27) and submission (Jn 13:16; 15:20) as well as the title "Lord" (Mt 1:20,22).

Shaddai—

Shaddai [8724] is used forty-eight times as a name of God, thirty-two times in Job (Job 5:17; 6:4,14; etc.), seven times in the compound name *El Shaddai. See above El..* It probably means "[God] the Mountain," similar to "God the Rock" (Dt 32:4). Older etymology defined it as "[God] the Provider," understanding *Shaddai* to be derived from

the word for "breast." The NIV consistently translates *Shaddai* as "Almighty" (Ge 17:1; Ps 91:1).

Elyon and *Upsistos—*

Elyon [6610] means "the Most High" or "the exalted One" (Ge 14:17-20; Ps 18:13; Isa 14:13-14). The NT Greek uses the form *hupsistos* [5736], meaning "highest," or "most exalted." Jesus was known as, and called, the Son of the Most High God (Mk 5:7; Lk 1:32-33; 6:28). The Holy Spirit is the power of the Most High (Lk 1:35). John the Baptist would be known as a prophet of the Most High God (Lk 1:76). Jesus taught his disciples to "love your enemies, do good to them, and lend to them without expecting to get anything back," because in so doing, their reward will be great and they will prove that they are "sons of the Most High, because he is kind to the ungrateful and wicked" (Lk 6:35). The Most High God is far too great and magnificent to be limited to houses made by men (Ac 7:48-50). The early apostles were known as servants of the Most High God (Ac 16:17). Melchizedek was king of Salem and priest of the Most High God (Heb 7:1 w Ge 14:17-20).

Other descriptive titles—

The Ancient of Days (Da 7:9,13,22). Deliverer (2Sa 22:2; Ps 18:2). Father (Ps 89:26; Mt 16:17; Mk 14:36; Lk 22:29; Jn 5:17; 8:54; 10:29; 14:23; Ro 8:15; Gal 4:6), Everlasting Father (Isa 9:6). The First and the Last (Isa 44:6; 48:12; Rev 1:17; 2:8; 22:13). God of gods (Dt 10:17; Ps 136:2; Da 2:47; 11:36), the God of heaven and earth (Ge 24:3,7). The Holy One (Isa 41:14; 43:14-15; 48:17), a God whose name is Holy (Isa 57:15). A Jealous God (Ex 34:14). Judge (Ge 18:25; Dt 32:36; Jdg 11:26). King of kings (1Ti 6:15; Rev 17:14; 19:16). The Living God (Jer 10:10; Da 6:26; Hos 1:10; Mt 16:16). Lord of lords (Dt 10:17; Ps 136:3; 1Ti 6:15; Rev 17:14; 19:16). Lord of kings (Da 2:47). The Mighty One (Isa 49:26; 60:16), Mighty God (Isa 9:6; 10:21; Lk 22:69). Prince (Ac 5:31), Prince of Peace (Isa 9:6). Redeemer (Job 19:25; Ps 19:14; 78:35; Isa 41:14; 43:14; 44:6; Jer 50:34). Righteous One (1Sa 45:21; Ps 4:1; 7:9). Rock appears five times in the Song of Moses (Dt 32:4,15,18,30,31), and several times in the Psalms (Ps 18:2,31,46; 19:14; 28:1; 78:35; 89:26), Isaiah (Isa 17:10; 26:4; 30:29; 44:8), and Habakkuk (Hab 1:12); in the NT Paul says that the Rock of Israel was Christ (1Co 10:4). The blessed and only Ruler (1Ti 6:15). Savior (Dt 32:15; 1Ch 16:35; Ps 89:26; Isa 43:3; Jn 4:42; Lk 1:47; Ac 5:31; 1Ti 1:1; 2:3; 4:10; Tit 1:3). Shield (Ps 3:3; 18:30). Strength (Ps 22:19). A Warrior (Ex 15:3). Wonderful Counselor (Isa 9:6).

Omnipotent:

Ge 17:1 When Abram was ninety-nine years old, the LORD appeared to him and said, "I am God Almighty; walk before me and be blameless.

Ge 18:14 Is anything too hard for the LORD? I will return to you at the appointed time next year and Sarah will have a son."

Job 42:2 "I know that you can do all things; no plan of yours can be thwarted.

Ac 26:8 Why should any of you consider it incredible that God raises the dead?

Rev 19:6 Then I heard what sounded like a great multitude, like the roar of rushing waters and like loud peals of thunder, shouting: "Hallelujah! For our Lord God Almighty reigns.

Rev 21:22 I did not see a temple in the city, because the Lord God Almighty and the Lamb are its temple. *See below, Power of.*

Omnipresent:

Ge 28:16 When Jacob awoke from his sleep, he thought, "Surely the LORD is in this place, and I was not aware of it."

1Ki 8:27 "But will God really dwell on earth? The heavens, even the highest heaven, cannot contain you. How much less this temple I have built! (+2Ch 2:6; Ac 7:48-49)

Ps 139:3 You discern my going out and my lying down; you are familiar with all my ways.

Ps 139:5 You hem me in—behind and before; you have laid your hand upon me.

Ps 139:7 Where can I go from your Spirit? Where can I flee from your presence? ⁸If I go up to the heavens, you are there; if I make my bed in the depths, you are there. ⁹If I rise on the wings of the dawn, if I settle on the far side of the sea, ¹⁰even there your hand will guide me, your right hand will hold me fast.

Jer 23:23 "Am I only a God nearby," declares the LORD, "and not a God far away? ²⁴Can anyone hide in secret places so that I cannot see him?" declares the LORD. "Do not I fill heaven and earth?" declares the LORD.

Ac 17:24 "The God who made the world and everything in it is the Lord of heaven and earth and does not live in temples built by hands.

Ac 17:27 God did this so that men would seek him and perhaps reach out for him and find him, though he is not far from each one of us. ²⁸'For in him we live and move and have our being.' As some of your own poets have said, 'We are his offspring.' *See below, Presence of.*

Omniscient: *See above, Knowledge of; below, Wisdom of.*

Perfection of:

Dt 32:4 He is the Rock, his works are perfect, and all his ways are just. A faithful God who does no wrong, upright and just is he.

2Sa 22:31 "As for God, his way is perfect; the word of the LORD is flawless. He is a shield for all who take refuge in him. (+Ps 18:30)

Mt 5:48 Be perfect, therefore, as your heavenly Father is perfect.

Ro 12:2 Do not conform any longer to the pattern of this world, but be transformed by the renewing of your mind. Then you will be able to test and approve what God's will is—his good, pleasing and perfect will.

Jas 1:17 Every good and perfect gift is from above, coming down from the Father of the heavenly lights, who does not change like shifting shadows. (+1Jn 1:5; Rev 15:3) *See above, Holiness of; below, Righteousness of.*

Personality of: *See below, Unity of.*

Power of: (Ex 9:16)

Ex 15:6 "Your right hand, O LORD, was majestic in power. Your right hand, O LORD, shattered the enemy. ⁷In the greatness of your majesty you threw down those who opposed you. You unleashed your burning anger; it consumed them like stubble.

Ex 15:11 "Who among the gods is like you, O LORD? Who is like you—majestic in holiness, awesome in glory, working wonders? ¹²You stretched out your right hand and the earth swallowed them.

Nu 11:23 The LORD answered Moses, "Is the LORD's arm too short? You will now see whether or not what I say will come true for you."

Dt 7:21 Do not be terrified by them, for the LORD your God, who is among you, is a great and awesome God. (+Dt 11:2; Job 37:1-22)

Job 37:23 The Almighty is beyond our reach and exalted in power; in his justice and great righteousness, he does not oppress.

Ps 21:13 Be exalted, O LORD, in your strength; we will sing and praise your might.

Ps 29:3 The voice of the LORD is over the waters; the God of glory thunders, the LORD thunders over the mighty waters. ⁴The voice of the LORD is powerful; the voice of the LORD is majestic. ⁵The voice of the LORD breaks the cedars; the LORD breaks in pieces the cedars of Lebanon. ⁶He makes Lebanon skip like a calf, Sirion like a young wild ox. ⁷The voice of the LORD strikes with flashes of lightning. ⁸The voice of the LORD shakes the desert; the LORD shakes the Desert of Kadesh. ⁹The voice of the LORD twists the oaks and strips the forests bare. And in his temple all cry, "Glory!"

Ps 62:11 One thing God has spoken, two things have I heard: that you, O God, are strong, (+Ps 68:34-35)

Ps 74:13 It was you who split open the sea by your power; you broke the heads of the monster in the waters.

Ps 74:15 It was you who opened up springs and streams; you dried up the ever flowing rivers.

Ps 77:14 You are the God who performs miracles; you display your power among the peoples.

Ps 77:16 The waters saw you, O God, the waters saw you and writhed; the very depths were convulsed.

Ps 77:18 Your thunder was heard in the whirlwind, your lightning lit up the world; the earth trembled and quaked. (+Ps 78:12-25)

Ps 78:26 He let loose the east wind from the heavens and led forth the south wind by his power. (+Ps 78:27-51)

Ps 79:11 May the groans of the prisoners come before you; by the strength of your arm preserve those condemned to die.

Ps 89:8 O LORD God Almighty, who is like you? You are mighty, O LORD, and your faithfulness surrounds you.

Ps 89:13 Your arm is endued with power; your hand is strong, your right hand exalted.

Ps 93:1 The LORD reigns, he is robed in majesty; the LORD is robed in majesty and is armed with strength. The world is firmly established; it cannot be moved.

Ps 93:4 Mightier than the thunder of the great waters, mightier than the breakers of the sea—the LORD on high is mighty. (+Ps 105:26-41)

Ps 106:8 Yet he saved them for his name's sake, to make his mighty power known.

Ps 111:6 He has shown his people the power of his works, giving them the lands of other nations.

Ps 135:6 The LORD does whatever pleases him, in the heavens and on the earth, in the seas and all their depths. (+Ps 135:8-12)

Ps 147:5 Great is our Lord and mighty in power; his understanding has no limit.

Ps 147:16 He spreads the snow like wool and scatters the frost like ashes. ¹⁷He hurls down his hail like pebbles. Who can withstand his icy blast? ¹⁸He sends his word and melts them; he stirs up his breezes, and the waters flow.

Isa 26:4 Trust in the LORD forever, for the LORD, the LORD, is the Rock eternal.

Isa 40:12 Who has measured the waters in the hollow of his hand, or with the breadth of his hand marked off the heavens? Who has held the dust of the earth in a basket, or weighed the mountains on the scales and the hills in a balance?

Isa 40:22 He sits enthroned above the circle of the earth, and its people are like grasshoppers. He stretches out the heavens like a canopy, and spreads them out like a tent to live in.

Isa 40:24 No sooner are they planted, no sooner are they sown, no sooner do they take root in the ground, than he blows on them and they wither, and a whirlwind sweeps them away like chaff.

Isa 40:26 Lift your eyes and look to the heavens: Who created all these? He who brings out the starry host one by one, and calls them each by name. Because of his great power and mighty strength, not one of them is missing.

Isa 40:28 Do you not know? Have you not heard? The LORD is the everlasting God, the Creator of the ends of the earth. He will not grow tired or weary, and his understanding no one can fathom.

Isa 51:10 Was it not you who dried up the sea, the waters of the great deep, who made a road in the depths of the sea so that the redeemed might cross over? (+Isa 51:15)

Isa 63:12 who sent his glorious arm of power to be at Moses' right hand, who divided the waters before them, to gain for himself everlasting renown,

Jer 5:22 Should you not fear me?" declares the LORD. "Should you not tremble in my presence? I made the sand a boundary for the sea, an everlasting barrier it cannot cross. The waves may roll, but they cannot prevail; they may roar, but they cannot cross it.

Jer 27:5 With my great power and outstretched arm I made the earth and its people and the animals that are on it, and I give it to anyone I please.

Jer 32:17 "Ah, Sovereign LORD, you have made the heavens and the earth by your great power and outstretched arm. Nothing is too hard for you.

Jer 32:27 "I am the LORD, the God of all mankind. Is anything too hard for me?

Da 2:20 and said: "Praise be to the name of God for ever and ever; wisdom and power are his. (+Mt 19:26; Mk 10:27)

Mk 14:36 *"Abba*, Father," he said, "everything is possible for you. Take this cup from me. Yet not what I will, but what you will." (+Lk 18:27)

Lk 1:49 for the Mighty One has done great things for me—holy is his name.

Lk 1:51 He has performed mighty deeds with his arm; he has scattered those who are proud in their inmost thoughts. (+Lk 22:29; 1Co 6:14)

Rev 19:1 After this I heard what sounded like the roar of a great multitude in heaven shouting: "Hallelujah! Salvation and glory and power belong to our God,

Supreme—

Dt 32:39 "See now that I myself am He! There is no god besides me. I put to death and I bring to life, I have wounded and I will heal, and no one can deliver out of my hand.

Jos 4:24 He did this so that all the peoples of the earth might know that the hand of the LORD is powerful and so that you might always fear the LORD your God."

1Sa 2:6 "The LORD brings death and makes alive; he brings down to the grave and raises up. 7The LORD sends poverty and wealth; he humbles and he exalts.

1Sa 14:6 Jonathan said to his young armor-bearer, "Come, let's go over to the outpost of those uncircumcised fellows. Perhaps the LORD will act in our behalf. Nothing can hinder the LORD from saving, whether by many or by few."

1Ch 29:11 Yours, O LORD, is the greatness and the power and the glory and the majesty and the splendor, for everything in heaven and earth is yours. Yours, O LORD, is the

kingdom; you are exalted as head over all. 12Wealth and honor come from you; you are the ruler of all things. In your hands are strength and power to exalt and give strength to all.

2Ch 14:11 Then Asa called to the LORD his God and said, "LORD, there is no one like you to help the powerless against the mighty. Help us, O LORD our God, for we rely on you, and in your name we have come against this vast army. O LORD, you are our God; do not let man prevail against you."

2Ch 25:8 Even if you go and fight courageously in battle, God will overthrow you before the enemy, for God has the power to help or to overthrow."

9Amaziah asked the man of God, "But what about the hundred talents I paid for these Israelite troops?"

The man of God replied, "The LORD can give you much more than that." (+Job 5:9)

Job 23:13 "But he stands alone, and who can oppose him? He does whatever he pleases. 14He carries out his decree against me, and many such plans he still has in store. (+Job 26:7-10)

Job 26:11 The pillars of the heavens quake, aghast at his rebuke. (+Job 26:12-13)

Job 26:14 And these are but the outer fringe of his works; how faint the whisper we hear of him! Who then can understand the thunder of his power?"

Job 36:5 "God is mighty, but does not despise men; he is mighty, and firm in his purpose.

Job 36:22 "God is exalted in his power. Who is a teacher like him? (+Job 36:27-33)

Job 38:8 "Who shut up the sea behind doors when it burst forth from the womb,

Job 38:11 when I said, 'This far you may come and no farther; here is where your proud waves halt'?

Job 40:9 Do you have an arm like God's, and can your voice thunder like his?

Job 42:2 "I know that you can do all things; no plan of yours can be thwarted.

Ps 104:7 But at your rebuke the waters fled, at the sound of your thunder they took to flight;

Ps 104:9 You set a boundary they cannot cross; never again will they cover the earth.

Ps 104:29 When you hide your face, they are terrified; when you take away their breath, they die and return to the dust. 30When you send your Spirit, they are created, and you renew the face of the earth.

Ps 104:32 he who looks at the earth, and it trembles, who touches the mountains, and they smoke.

Da 4:35 All the peoples of the earth are regarded as nothing. He does as he pleases with the powers of heaven and the peoples of the earth. No one can hold back his hand or say to him: "What have you done?"

Irresistible power (Dt 32:39; Job 10:7)—

1Sa 2:10 those who oppose the LORD will be shattered. He will thunder against them from heaven; the LORD will judge the ends of the earth. "He will give strength to his king and exalt the horn of his anointed."

2Ch 20:6 and said: "O LORD, God of our fathers, are you not the God who is in heaven? You rule over all the kingdoms of the nations. Power and might are in your hand, and no one can withstand you.

Job 9:4 His wisdom is profound, his power is vast. Who has resisted him and come out unscathed? 5He moves mountains without their knowing it and overturns them in his anger. 6He shakes the earth from its place and makes its pillars tremble. **⁷**He speaks to the sun and it does not shine; he seals off the light of the stars.

Job 9:10 He performs wonders that cannot be fathomed, miracles that cannot be counted.

Job 9:12 If he snatches away, who can stop him? Who can say to him, 'What are you doing?' **¹³**God does not restrain his anger; even the cohorts of Rahab cowered at his feet.

Job 9:19 If it is a matter of strength, he is mighty! And if it is a matter of justice, who will summon him?

Job 11:10 "If he comes along and confines you in prison and convenes a court, who can oppose him?

Job 12:14 What he tears down cannot be rebuilt; the man he imprisons cannot be released. (+Job 12:15)

Job 12:16 To him belong strength and victory; both deceived and deceiver are his.

Job 14:20 You overpower him once for all, and he is gone; you change his countenance and send him away.

Job 41:10 No one is fierce enough to rouse him. Who then is able to stand against me? **¹¹**Who has a claim against me that I must pay? Everything under heaven belongs to me.

Ps 66:3 Say to God, "How awesome are your deeds! So great is your power that your enemies cringe before you.

Ps 66:7 He rules forever by his power, his eyes watch the nations—let not the rebellious rise up against him. *Selah*

Ps 76:7 You alone are to be feared. Who can stand before you when you are angry?

Isa 14:24 The LORD Almighty has sworn, "Surely, as I have planned, so it will be, and as I have purposed, so it will stand.

Isa 14:27 For the LORD Almighty has purposed, and who can thwart him? His hand is stretched out, and who can turn it back?

Isa 31:3 But the Egyptians are men and not God; their horses are flesh and not spirit. When the LORD stretches out his hand, he who helps will stumble, he who is helped will fall; both will perish together.

Isa 43:13 Yes, and from ancient days I am he. No one can deliver out of my hand. When I act, who can reverse it?"

Isa 43:16 This is what the LORD says—he who made a way through the sea, a path through the mighty waters, **¹⁷**who drew out the chariots and horses, the army and reinforcements together, and they lay there, never to rise again, extinguished, snuffed out like a wick:

Isa 46:10 I make known the end from the beginning, from ancient times, what is still to come. I say: My purpose will stand, and I will do all that I please. **¹¹**From the east I summon a bird of prey; from a far-off land, a man to fulfill my purpose. What I have said, that will I bring about; what I have planned, that will I do.

Isa 50:2 When I came, why was there no one? When I called, why was there no one to answer? Was my arm too short to ransom you? Do I lack the strength to rescue you? By a mere rebuke I dry up the sea, I turn rivers into a desert; their fish rot for lack of water and die of thirst. **³**I clothe the sky with darkness and make sackcloth its covering."

Na 1:3 The LORD is slow to anger and great in power; the LORD will not leave the guilty unpunished. His way is in the whirlwind and the storm, and clouds are the dust of his feet. **⁴**He rebukes the sea and dries it up; he makes all the rivers run dry. Bashan and Carmel wither and the blossoms of Lebanon fade. **⁵**The mountains quake before him and the hills melt away. The earth trembles at his presence, the world and all who live in it. **⁶**Who can withstand his indignation? Who can endure his fierce anger? His wrath is poured out like fire; the rocks are shattered before him.

Incomparable—

Dt 3:24 "O Sovereign LORD, you have begun to show to your servant your greatness and your strong hand. For what god is there in heaven or on earth who can do the deeds and mighty works you do? (+Job 40:9; Ps 89:8)

Omnipotent (Ge 18:14; Jer 32:27)—

Mt 19:26 Jesus looked at them and said, "With man this is impossible, but with God all things are possible."

Everlasting—

Ro 1:20 For since the creation of the world God's invisible qualities—his eternal power and divine nature—have been clearly seen, being understood from what has been made, so that men are without excuse.

Creation by (Jer 10:12).

The resurrection of Christ by God's power (1Co 6:14)—

2Co 13:4 For to be sure, he was crucified in weakness, yet he lives by God's power. Likewise, we are weak in him, yet by God's power we will live with him to serve you.

The resurrection of believers by God's power—

1Co 6:14 By his power God raised the Lord from the dead, and he will raise us also.

Power manifested in behalf of believers—

Dt 33:26 "There is no one like the God of Jeshurun, who rides on the heavens to help you and on the clouds in his majesty. **²⁷**The eternal God is your refuge, and underneath are the everlasting arms. He will drive out your enemy before you, saying, 'Destroy him!'

2Ch 16:9 For the eyes of the LORD range throughout the earth to strengthen those whose hearts are fully committed to him. You have done a foolish thing, and from now on you will be at war."

Ezr 8:22 I was ashamed to ask the king for soldiers and horsemen to protect us from enemies on the road, because we had told the king, "The gracious hand of our God is on everyone who looks to him, but his great anger is against all who forsake him."

Ne 1:10 "They are your servants and your people, whom you redeemed by your great strength and your mighty hand.

Jer 20:11 But the LORD is with me like a mighty warrior; so my persecutors will stumble and not prevail. They will fail and be thoroughly disgraced; their dishonor will never be forgotten.

Da 3:17 If we are thrown into the blazing furnace, the God we serve is able to save us from it, and he will rescue us from your hand, O king.

Power manifested in his works (Dt 3:24)—

Ps 33:9 For he spoke, and it came to be; he commanded, and it stood firm.

Ps 107:25 For he spoke and stirred up a tempest that lifted high the waves.

Ps 107:29 He stilled the storm to a whisper; the waves of the sea were hushed.

Ps 114:7 Tremble, O earth, at the presence of the Lord, at the presence of the God of Jacob, **⁸**who turned the rock into a pool, the hard rock into springs of water.

Pr 30:4 Who has gone up to heaven and come down? Who has gathered up the wind in the hollow of his hands? Who has wrapped up the waters in his cloak? Who has established all the ends of the earth? What is his name, and the name of his son? Tell me if you know!

Isa 48:13 My own hand laid the foundations of the earth, and my right hand spread out the heavens; when I summon them, they all stand up together.

Jer 10:12 But God made the earth by his power; he founded the world by his wisdom and stretched out the heavens by his understanding. ¹³When he thunders, the waters in the heavens roar; he makes clouds rise from the ends of the earth. He sends lightning with the rain and brings out the wind from his storehouses. (+Jer 51:15; Ro 1:20) *See above, Omnipotent.*

Presence of:

Ge 16:13 She gave this name to the LORD who spoke to her: "You are the God who sees me," for she said, "I have now seen the One who sees me."

Ge 28:16 When Jacob awoke from his sleep, he thought, "Surely the LORD is in this place, and I was not aware of it."

Ex 20:24 "'Make an altar of earth for me and sacrifice on it your burnt offerings and fellowship offerings, your sheep and goats and your cattle. Wherever I cause my name to be honored, I will come to you and bless you. (+Ex 29:42-43; 30:6; 33:14)

Dt 4:34 Has any god ever tried to take for himself one nation out of another nation, by testings, by miraculous signs and wonders, by war, by a mighty hand and an outstretched arm, or by great and awesome deeds, like all the things the LORD your God did for you in Egypt before your very eyes?

³⁵You were shown these things so that you might know that the LORD is God; besides him there is no other. ³⁶From heaven he made you hear his voice to discipline you. On earth he showed you his great fire, and you heard his words from out of the fire.

Dt 4:39 Acknowledge and take to heart this day that the LORD is God in heaven above and on the earth below. There is no other.

1Ki 8:27 "But will God really dwell on earth? The heavens, even the highest heaven, cannot contain you. How much less this temple I have built!

Ps 139:3 You discern my going out and my lying down; you are familiar with all my ways.

Ps 139:5 You hem me in—behind and before; you have laid your hand upon me.

Ps 139:7 Where can I go from your Spirit? Where can I flee from your presence? ⁸If I go up to the heavens, you are there; if I make my bed in the depths, you are there. ⁹If I rise on the wings of the dawn, if I settle on the far side of the sea, ¹⁰even there your hand will guide me, your right hand will hold me fast.

Isa 57:15 For this is what the high and lofty One says—he who lives forever, whose name is holy: "I live in a high and holy place, but also with him who is contrite and lowly in spirit, to revive the spirit of the lowly and to revive the heart of the contrite.

Isa 66:1 This is what the LORD says: "Heaven is my throne, and the earth is my footstool. Where is the house you will build for me? Where will my resting place be?

Jer 23:23 "Am I only a God nearby," declares the LORD, "and not a God far away? ²⁴Can anyone hide in secret places so that I cannot see him?" declares the LORD. "Do not I fill heaven and earth?" declares the LORD.

Jer 32:18 You show love to thousands but bring the punishment for the fathers' sins into the laps of their children after them. O great and powerful God, whose name is the LORD Almighty, ¹⁹great are your purposes and mighty are your deeds. Your eyes are open to all the ways of men; you reward everyone according to his conduct and as his deeds deserve.

Jnh 1:3 But Jonah ran away from the LORD and headed for Tarshish. He went down to Joppa, where he found a ship bound for that port. After paying the fare, he went aboard and sailed for Tarshish to flee from the LORD.

⁴Then the LORD sent a great wind on the sea, and such a violent storm arose that the ship threatened to break up.

Ac 17:24 "The God who made the world and everything in it is the Lord of heaven and earth and does not live in temples built by hands.

Ac 17:27 God did this so that men would seek him and perhaps reach out for him and find him, though he is not far from each one of us. ²⁸'For in him we live and move and have our being.' As some of your own poets have said, 'We are his offspring.'

1Co 12:6 There are different kinds of working, but the same God works all of them in all men.

Manifested on the atonement cover. *See Shekinah.*

Preserver:

Ne 9:6 You alone are the LORD. You made the heavens, even the highest heavens, and all their starry host, the earth and all that is on it, the seas and all that is in them. You give life to everything, and the multitudes of heaven worship you.

Job 33:18 to preserve his soul from the pit, his life from perishing by the sword.

Ps 3:3 But you are a shield around me, O LORD; you bestow glory on me and lift up my head.

Ps 12:7 O LORD, you will keep us safe and protect us from such people forever.

Ps 17:7 Show the wonder of your great love, you who save by your right hand those who take refuge in you from their foes.

Ps 68:6 God sets the lonely in families, he leads forth the prisoners with singing; but the rebellious live in a sun-scorched land.

Ps 73:23 Yet I am always with you; you hold me by my right hand.

Isa 27:3 I, the LORD, watch over it; I water it continually. I guard it day and night so that no one may harm it. (+Isa 49:8)

Jer 2:6 They did not ask, 'Where is the LORD, who brought us up out of Egypt and led us through the barren wilderness, through a land of deserts and rifts, a land of drought and darkness, a land where no one travels and no one lives?' (+Da 5:23)

Mt 10:29 Are not two sparrows sold for a penny? Yet not one of them will fall to the ground apart from the will of your Father. ³⁰And even the very hairs of your head are all numbered. ³¹So don't be afraid; you are worth more than many sparrows. (+Lk 12:6-7)

Lk 21:18 But not a hair of your head will perish. (+Jn 17:11,15)

1Pe 3:12 For the eyes of the Lord are on the righteous and his ears are attentive to their prayer, but the face of the Lord is against those who do evil."

¹³Who is going to harm you if you are eager to do good?

2Pe 2:9 if this is so, then the Lord knows how to rescue godly men from trials and to hold the unrighteous for the day of judgment, while continuing their punishment.

Of the righteous (Ge 15:1)—

Ge 28:15 I am with you and will watch over you wherever you go, and I will bring you back to this land. I will not leave you until I have done what I have promised you."

Ge 49:24 But his bow remained steady, his strong arms stayed limber, because of the hand of the Mighty One of Jacob, because of the Shepherd, the Rock of Israel, ²⁵because of your father's God, who helps you, because of the

Almighty, who blesses you with blessings of the heavens above, blessings of the deep that lies below, blessings of the breast and womb. (+Ex 8:22-23)

Ex 9:26 The only place it did not hail was the land of Goshen, where the Israelites were.

Ex 11:7 But among the Israelites not a dog will bark at any man or animal.' Then you will know that the LORD makes a distinction between Egypt and Israel.

Ex 12:13 The blood will be a sign for you on the houses where you are; and when I see the blood, I will pass over you. No destructive plague will touch you when I strike Egypt.

Ex 12:17 "Celebrate the Feast of Unleavened Bread, because it was on this very day that I brought your divisions out of Egypt. Celebrate this day as a lasting ordinance for the generations to come.

Ex 12:23 When the LORD goes through the land to strike down the Egyptians, he will see the blood on the top and sides of the doorframe and will pass over that doorway, and he will not permit the destroyer to enter your houses and strike you down.

Ex 15:2 The LORD is my strength and my song; he has become my salvation. He is my God, and I will praise him, my father's God, and I will exalt him.

Ex 15:13 "In your unfailing love you will lead the people you have redeemed. In your strength you will guide them to your holy dwelling.

Ex 15:16 terror and dread will fall upon them. By the power of your arm they will be as still as a stone—until your people pass by, O LORD, until the people you bought pass by. ¹⁷You will bring them in and plant them on the mountain of your inheritance—the place, O LORD, you made for your dwelling, the sanctuary, O Lord, your hands established. (+Ex 19:4)

Ex 23:20 "See, I am sending an angel ahead of you to guard you along the way and to bring you to the place I have prepared. (+Ex 23:21-31)

Dt 1:30 The LORD your God, who is going before you, will fight for you, as he did for you in Egypt, before your very eyes, ³¹and in the desert. There you saw how the LORD your God carried you, as a father carries his son, all the way you went until you reached this place."

Dt 32:10 In a desert land he found him, in a barren and howling waste. He shielded him and cared for him; he guarded him as the apple of his eye,

Dt 33:12 About Benjamin he said: "Let the beloved of the LORD rest secure in him, for he shields him all day long, and the one the LORD loves rests between his shoulders."

Dt 33:25 The bolts of your gates will be iron and bronze, and your strength will equal your days.

²⁶"There is no one like the God of Jeshurun, who rides on the heavens to help you and on the clouds in his majesty. ²⁷The eternal God is your refuge, and underneath are the everlasting arms. He will drive out your enemy before you, saying, 'Destroy him!' ²⁸So Israel will live in safety alone; Jacob's spring is secure in a land of grain and new wine, where the heavens drop dew.

Jos 23:10 One of you routs a thousand, because the LORD your God fights for you, just as he promised.

1Sa 2:9 He will guard the feet of his saints, but the wicked will be silenced in darkness. "It is not by strength that one prevails; (+2Sa 22:1-27)

2Sa 22:28 You save the humble, but your eyes are on the haughty to bring them low. (+2Sa 22:29-51)

2Ch 16:9 For the eyes of the LORD range throughout the earth to strengthen those whose hearts are fully committed

to him. You have done a foolish thing, and from now on you will be at war."

Job 1:10 "Have you not put a hedge around him and his household and everything he has? You have blessed the work of his hands, so that his flocks and herds are spread throughout the land.

Job 5:11 The lowly he sets on high, and those who mourn are lifted to safety.

Job 5:18 For he wounds, but he also binds up; he injures, but his hands also heal. ¹⁹From six calamities he will rescue you; in seven no harm will befall you. ²⁰In famine he will ransom you from death, and in battle from the stroke of the sword. ²¹You will be protected from the lash of the tongue, and need not fear when destruction comes. (+Job 5:22-24)

Job 10:12 You gave me life and showed me kindness, and in your providence watched over my spirit.

Ps 9:9 The LORD is a refuge for the oppressed, a stronghold in times of trouble. (+Ps 18:14; 23:1-6)

Ps 31:20 In the shelter of your presence you hide them from the intrigues of men; in your dwelling you keep them safe from accusing tongues.

Ps 31:23 Love the LORD, all his saints! The LORD preserves the faithful, but the proud he pays back in full.

Ps 32:6 Therefore let everyone who is godly pray to you while you may be found; surely when the mighty waters rise, they will not reach him.

Ps 32:8 I will instruct you and teach you in the way you should go; I will counsel you and watch over you. (+Ps 34:7)

Ps 34:15 The eyes of the LORD are on the righteous and his ears are attentive to their cry;

Ps 34:17 The righteous cry out, and the LORD hears them; he delivers them from all their troubles.

Ps 34:19 A righteous man may have many troubles, but the LORD delivers him from them all;

Ps 34:20 he protects all his bones, not one of them will be broken. (+Ps 34:21-22)

Ps 37:17 for the power of the wicked will be broken, but the LORD upholds the righteous.

Ps 37:23 If the LORD delights in a man's way, he makes his steps firm; ²⁴though he stumble, he will not fall, for the LORD upholds him with his hand.

Ps 37:28 For the LORD loves the just and will not forsake his faithful ones. They will be protected forever, but the offspring of the wicked will be cut off;

Ps 37:32 The wicked lie in wait for the righteous, seeking their very lives; ³³but the LORD will not leave them in their power or let them be condemned when brought to trial.

Ps 41:1 Blessed is he who has regard for the weak; the LORD delivers him in times of trouble. ²The LORD will protect him and preserve his life; he will bless him in the land and not surrender him to the desire of his foes. ³The LORD will sustain him on his sickbed and restore him from his bed of illness.

Ps 46:1 God is our refuge and strength, an ever-present help in trouble.

Ps 46:7 The LORD Almighty is with us; the God of Jacob is our fortress. *Selah*

Ps 50:15 and call upon me in the day of trouble; I will deliver you, and you will honor me."

Ps 84:11 For the LORD God is a sun and shield; the LORD bestows favor and honor; no good thing does he withhold from those whose walk is blameless.

Ps 91:1 He who dwells in the shelter of the Most High will rest in the shadow of the Almighty.

Ps 91:3 Surely he will save you from the fowler's snare and from the deadly pestilence. [4]He will cover you with his feathers, and under his wings you will find refuge; his faithfulness will be your shield and rampart.

Ps 91:7 A thousand may fall at your side, ten thousand at your right hand, but it will not come near you.

Ps 91:9 If you make the Most High your dwelling—even the LORD, who is my refuge— [10]then no harm will befall you, no disaster will come near your tent.

Ps 91:14 "Because he loves me," says the LORD, "I will rescue him; I will protect him, for he acknowledges my name. [15]He will call upon me, and I will answer him; I will be with him in trouble, I will deliver him and honor him.

Ps 102:19 "The LORD looked down from his sanctuary on high, from heaven he viewed the earth, [20]to hear the groans of the prisoners and release those condemned to death."

Ps 103:2 Praise the LORD, O my soul, and forget not all his benefits— [3]who forgives all your sins and heals all your diseases, [4]who redeems your life from the pit and crowns you with love and compassion, [5]who satisfies your desires with good things so that your youth is renewed like the eagle's.

Ps 107:9 for he satisfies the thirsty and fills the hungry with good things.

[10]Some sat in darkness and the deepest gloom, prisoners suffering in iron chains, (+Ps 107:13)

Ps 116:6 The LORD protects the simplehearted; when I was in great need, he saved me.

Ps 118:13 I was pushed back and about to fall, but the LORD helped me.

Ps 121:3 He will not let your foot slip—he who watches over you will not slumber; [4]indeed, he who watches over Israel will neither slumber nor sleep.

Ps 121:7 The LORD will keep you from all harm—he will watch over your life; [8]the LORD will watch over your coming and going both now and forevermore.

Ps 125:1 Those who trust in the LORD are like Mount Zion, which cannot be shaken but endures forever. [2]As the mountains surround Jerusalem, so the LORD surrounds his people both now and forevermore.

[3]The scepter of the wicked will not remain over the land allotted to the righteous, for then the righteous might use their hands to do evil.

Ps 145:14 The LORD upholds all those who fall and lifts up all who are bowed down.

Ps 145:19 He fulfills the desires of those who fear him; he hears their cry and saves them. [20]The LORD watches over all who love him, but all the wicked he will destroy.

Ps 146:7 He upholds the cause of the oppressed and gives food to the hungry. The LORD sets prisoners free, [8]the LORD gives sight to the blind, the LORD lifts up those who are bowed down, the LORD loves the righteous.

Pr 2:7 He holds victory in store for the upright, he is a shield to those whose walk is blameless, [8]for he guards the course of the just and protects the way of his faithful ones.

Pr 10:3 The LORD does not let the righteous go hungry but he thwarts the craving of the wicked.

Pr 10:30 The righteous will never be uprooted, but the wicked will not remain in the land. (+Isa 25:4)

Isa 30:21 Whether you turn to the right or to the left, your ears will hear a voice behind you, saying, "This is the way; walk in it."

Isa 30:26 The moon will shine like the sun, and the sunlight will be seven times brighter, like the light of seven full days, when the LORD binds up the bruises of his people and heals the wounds he inflicted.

Isa 33:16 this is the man who will dwell on the heights, whose refuge will be the mountain fortress. His bread will be supplied, and water will not fail him.

Isa 40:11 He tends his flock like a shepherd: He gathers the lambs in his arms and carries them close to his heart; he gently leads those that have young.

Isa 40:29 He gives strength to the weary and increases the power of the weak.

Isa 40:31 but those who hope in the LORD will renew their strength. They will soar on wings like eagles; they will run and not grow weary, they will walk and not be faint.

Isa 42:16 I will lead the blind by ways they have not known, along unfamiliar paths I will guide them; I will turn the darkness into light before them and make the rough places smooth. These are the things I will do; I will not forsake them.

Isa 43:2 When you pass through the waters, I will be with you; and when you pass through the rivers, they will not sweep over you. When you walk through the fire, you will not be burned; the flames will not set you ablaze. (+Isa 46:3)

Isa 46:4 Even to your old age and gray hairs I am he, I am he who will sustain you. I have made you and I will carry you; I will sustain you and I will rescue you.

Isa 52:12 But you will not leave in haste or go in flight; for the LORD will go before you, the God of Israel will be your rear guard.

Isa 58:11 The LORD will guide you always; he will satisfy your needs in a sun-scorched land and will strengthen your frame. You will be like a well-watered garden, like a spring whose waters never fail.

Isa 63:9 In all their distress he too was distressed, and the angel of his presence saved them. In his love and mercy he redeemed them; he lifted them up and carried them all the days of old.

Jer 31:9 They will come with weeping; they will pray as I bring them back. I will lead them beside streams of water on a level path where they will not stumble, because I am Israel's father, and Ephraim is my firstborn son.

[10]"Hear the word of the LORD, O nations; proclaim it in distant coastlands: 'He who scattered Israel will gather them and will watch over his flock like a shepherd.'

Jer 31:28 Just as I watched over them to uproot and tear down, and to overthrow, destroy and bring disaster, so I will watch over them to build and to plant," declares the LORD.

Eze 11:16 "Therefore say: 'This is what the Sovereign LORD says: Although I sent them far away among the nations and scattered them among the countries, yet for a little while I have been a sanctuary for them in the countries where they have gone.'

Eze 34:11 "'For this is what the Sovereign LORD says: I myself will search for my sheep and look after them. [12]As a shepherd looks after his scattered flock when he is with them, so will I look after my sheep. I will rescue them from all the places where they were scattered on a day of clouds and darkness. (+Eze 34:13-14)

Eze 34:15 I myself will tend my sheep and have them lie down, declares the Sovereign LORD. [16]I will search for the lost and bring back the strays. I will bind up the injured and strengthen the weak, but the sleek and the strong I will destroy. I will shepherd the flock with justice.

Eze 34:22 I will save my flock, and they will no longer be plundered. I will judge between one sheep and another.

Eze 34:31 You my sheep, the sheep of my pasture, are

people, and I am your God, declares the Sovereign LORD.'"

Da 3:27 and the satraps, prefects, governors and royal advisers crowded around them. They saw that the fire had not harmed their bodies, nor was a hair of their heads singed; their robes were not scorched, and there was no smell of fire on them.

²⁸Then Nebuchadnezzar said, "Praise be to the God of Shadrach, Meshach and Abednego, who has sent his angel and rescued his servants! They trusted in him and defied the king's command and were willing to give up their lives rather than serve or worship any god except their own God.

Joel 2:18 Then the LORD will be jealous for his land and take pity on his people.

Zec 2:5 And I myself will be a wall of fire around it,' declares the LORD, 'and I will be its glory within.'

Zec 2:8 For this is what the LORD Almighty says: "After he has honored me and has sent me against the nations that have plundered you—for whoever touches you touches the apple of his eye—

Mt 4:6 "If you are the Son of God," he said, "throw yourself down. For it is written: "'He will command his angels concerning you, and they will lift you up in their hands, so that you will not strike your foot against a stone.'"

1Co 10:13 No temptation has seized you except what is common to man. And God is faithful; he will not let you be tempted beyond what you can bear. But when you are tempted, he will also provide a way out so that you can stand up under it. (+2Ti 34:13-18)

2Th 3:3 But the Lord is faithful, and he will strengthen and protect you from the evil one.

Jas 4:15 Instead, you ought to say, "If it is the Lord's will, we will live and do this or that."

His preserving care exemplified: To Noah and his family, at the time of the flood (Ge 6:8,13-21; 7; 8:1,15-16). To Abraham and Sarah, in Egypt (Ge 12:17), in Gerar (Ge 20:3). To Lot, when Sodom was destroyed (Ge 19). To Hagar, when Abraham cast her out (Ge 21:17,19). To Jacob, when he fled from home (Ge 35:3), when he fled from Laban, his father-in-law (Ge 31:24,29), when he met Esau (Ge 33:3-10), as he journeyed in the land of Canaan (Ge 35:3). To Joseph, in Egypt (Ge 39:2,21). To Moses, in his infancy (Ex 2:1-10).

To the Israelites: In bringing about their deliverance from bondage (Ex 1:9-12; 2:23-25; 3:7-9).

In exempting the land of Goshen from the plague of flies—

Ex 8:22 "'But on that day I will deal differently with the land of Goshen, where my people live; no swarms of flies will be there, so that you will know that I, the LORD, am in this land.

In preserving their cattle from the plague (Ex 9:4-7). In exempting the land of Goshen from the plague of darkness (Ex 10:21-23). In saving the firstborn, when the plague of death destroyed the firstborn of Egypt (Ex 12:13,23).

In deliverance from Egypt (Ex 13:3,17-20)—

Ex 13:21 By day the LORD went ahead of them in a pillar of cloud to guide them on their way and by night in a pillar of fire to give them light, so that they could travel by day or night. ²²Neither the pillar of cloud by day nor the pillar of fire by night left its place in front of the people. (+Ex 14)

Ex 19:4 'You yourselves have seen what I did to Egypt,

and how I carried you on eagles' wings and brought you to myself. (+Lev 26:13)

In the wilderness (Ex 40:36-38; Nu 9:17-23)—

Nu 10:33 So they set out from the mountain of the LORD and traveled for three days. The ark of the covenant of the LORD went before them during those three days to find them a place to rest. (+Nu 22:12; 23:8; Dt 1:31; 23:5; 26:7-9)

In victories under Joshua, over the Canaanites (Jos 6-11; 24:11-13), under Othniel (Jdg 3:9-11), under Ehud (Jdg 3:15-30), under Shamgar (Jdg 3:31), under Deborah (Jdg 4:5), under Gideon (Jdg 7; 8:1-23), under Jephthah (Jdg 11:29-40), under David (1Sa 17:45-49), under Ahab (1Ki 20). In delivering the kingdom of Israel from Syria (2Sa 8). In delivering Israel by Jeroboam II (2Ki 14:26-27), by Abijah (2Ch 13:4-18). In delivering from the oppressions of the king of Syria (2Ki 13:2-5).

To the kingdom of Judah: In delivering from Egypt (2Ch 12:2-12), from the Ethiopian host (2Ch 14:11-14). In giving peace with other nations (2Ch 17). In delivering them from the army of the Assyrians (2Ki 19).

To David (1Sa 17:32,45-47; 2Sa 7; 1Ch 11:13-14). To Hezekiah (2Ki 19). To Job (Job 1:9-12; 2:6). To Jeremiah and Baruch (Jer 36:26). To Daniel and the three Hebrew captives (Da 2:18-23; 3:27-28; 6). To Jonah (Jnh 1:17). To the wise men of the east (Mt 2:12). To Jesus and his parents (Mt 2:13,19-22). To Peter (Ac 12:3-17). To Paul and Silas (Ac 16:26-39). To Paul (Ac 27:24; 28:5-6, w Mk 16:18). *See below, Providence of; See Poor, God's Care.*

Providence of: (Ge 24:7,40-50,56; 26:24)

Lev 26:4 I will send you rain in its season, and the ground will yield its crops and the trees of the field their fruit. ⁵Your threshing will continue until grape harvest and the grape harvest will continue until planting, and you will eat all the food you want and live in safety in your land.

⁶"'I will grant peace in the land, and you will lie down and no one will make you afraid. I will remove savage beasts from the land, and the sword will not pass through your country.

Lev 26:10 You will still be eating last year's harvest when you will have to move it out to make room for the new.

Dt 8:18 But remember the LORD your God, for it is he who gives you the ability to produce wealth, and so confirms his covenant, which he swore to your forefathers, as it is today.

Dt 11:12 It is a land the LORD your God cares for; the eyes of the LORD your God are continually on it from the beginning of the year to its end. (+Dt 11:13-15)

Dt 15:4 However, there should be no poor among you, for in the land the LORD your God is giving you to possess as your inheritance, he will richly bless you, ⁵if only you fully obey the LORD your God and are careful to follow all these commands I am giving you today. ⁶For the LORD your God will bless you as he has promised, and you will lend to many nations but will borrow from none. You will rule over many nations but none will rule over you.

Dt 32:11 like an eagle that stirs up its nest and hovers over its young, that spreads its wings to catch them and carries them on its pinions. ¹²The LORD alone led him; no foreign god was with him.

¹³He made him ride on the heights of the land and fed him with the fruit of the fields. He nourished him with honey from the rock, and with oil from the flinty crag, ¹⁴with curds and milk from herd and flock and with fattened lambs and goats, with choice rams of Bashan and the

finest kernels of wheat. You drank the foaming blood of the grape.

1Sa 2:6 "The LORD brings death and makes alive; he brings down to the grave and raises up. ⁷The LORD sends poverty and wealth; he humbles and he exalts. ⁸He raises the poor from the dust and lifts the needy from the ash heap; he seats them with princes and has them inherit a throne of honor. "For the foundations of the earth are the LORD's; upon them he has set the world.

⁹He will guard the feet of his saints, but the wicked will be silenced in darkness. "It is not by strength that one prevails; (+1Ki 11:14-40)

1Ch 29:14 "But who am I, and who are my people, that we should be able to give as generously as this? Everything comes from you, and we have given you only what comes from your hand.

1Ch 29:16 O LORD our God, as for all this abundance that we have provided for building you a temple for your Holy Name, it comes from your hand, and all of it belongs to you.

Ps 23:1 The LORD is my shepherd, I shall not be in want. ²He makes me lie down in green pastures, he leads me beside quiet waters, ³he restores my soul. He guides me in paths of righteousness for his name's sake. ⁴Even though I walk through the valley of the shadow of death, I will fear no evil, for you are with me; your rod and your staff, they comfort me.

⁵You prepare a table before me in the presence of my enemies. You anoint my head with oil; my cup overflows. ⁶Surely goodness and love will follow me all the days of my life, and I will dwell in the house of the LORD forever.

Ps 34:7 The angel of the LORD encamps around those who fear him, and he delivers them.

Ps 34:9 Fear the LORD, you his saints, for those who fear him lack nothing. ¹⁰The lions may grow weak and hungry, but those who seek the LORD lack no good thing.

Ps 71:6 From birth I have relied on you; you brought me forth from my mother's womb. I will ever praise you. ⁷I have become like a portent to many, but you are my strong refuge.

Ps 71:15 My mouth will tell of your righteousness, of your salvation all day long, though I know not its measure. (+Ps 107:1-43)

Ps 127:1 Unless the LORD builds the house, its builders labor in vain. Unless the LORD watches over the city, the watchmen stand guard in vain. ²In vain you rise early and stay up late, toiling for food to eat—for he grants sleep to those he loves. (+Ps 127:3-5; 136:5-24)

Ps 136:25 and who gives food to every creature. *His love endures forever.*

Ps 144:12 Then our sons in their youth will be like well-nurtured plants, and our daughters will be like pillars carved to adorn a palace. ¹³Our barns will be filled with every kind of provision. Our sheep will increase by thousands, by tens of thousands in our fields; ¹⁴our oxen will draw heavy loads. There will be no breaching of walls, no going into captivity, no cry of distress in our streets.

¹⁵Blessed are the people of whom this is true; blessed are the people whose God is the LORD.

Ps 147:8 He covers the sky with clouds; he supplies the earth with rain and makes grass grow on the hills. ⁹He provides food for the cattle and for the young ravens when they call.

Ps 147:13 for he strengthens the bars of your gates and

blesses your people within you. ¹⁴He grants peace to your borders and satisfies you with the finest of wheat.

Pr 16:33 The lot is cast into the lap, but its every decision is from the LORD.

Ecc 2:24 A man can do nothing better than to eat and drink and find satisfaction in his work. This too, I see, is from the hand of God, (+Ecc 3:13)

Ecc 5:19 Moreover, when God gives any man wealth and possessions, and enables him to enjoy them, to accept his lot and be happy in his work—this is a gift of God.

Isa 46:4 Even to your old age and gray hairs I am he, I am he who will sustain you. I have made you and I will carry you; I will sustain you and I will rescue you.

Isa 51:2 look to Abraham, your father, and to Sarah, who gave you birth. When I called him he was but one, and I blessed him and made him many.

Isa 55:10 As the rain and the snow come down from heaven, and do not return to it without watering the earth and making it bud and flourish, so that it yields seed for the sower and bread for the eater, (+Eze 36:28-29)

Eze 36:30 I will increase the fruit of the trees and the crops of the field, so that you will no longer suffer disgrace among the nations because of famine. (+Eze 36:31-35)

Eze 36:36 Then the nations around you that remain will know that I the LORD have rebuilt what was destroyed and have replanted what was desolate. I the LORD have spoken, and I will do it.' (+Eze 36:37)

Eze 36:38 as numerous as the flocks for offerings at Jerusalem during her appointed feasts. So will the ruined cities be filled with flocks of people. Then they will know that I am the LORD." (+Joel 2:18-20)

Joel 2:21 Be not afraid, O land; be glad and rejoice. Surely the LORD has done great things. (+Joel 2:22)

Joel 2:23 Be glad, O people of Zion, rejoice in the LORD your God, for he has given you the autumn rains in righteousness. He sends you abundant showers, both autumn and spring rains, as before. (+Joel 2:24-25)

Joel 2:26 You will have plenty to eat, until you are full, and you will praise the name of the LORD your God, who has worked wonders for you; never again will my people be shamed.

Mt 5:45 that you may be sons of your Father in heaven. He causes his sun to rise on the evil and the good, and sends rain on the righteous and the unrighteous.

Ro 8:28 And we know that in all things God works for the good of those who love him, who have been called according to his purpose.

Jas 4:15 Instead, you ought to say, "If it is the Lord's will, we will live and do this or that."

In providing for temporal necessities—

Ge 1:29 Then God said, "I give you every seed-bearing plant on the face of the whole earth and every tree that has fruit with seed in it. They will be yours for food. ³⁰And to all the beasts of the earth and all the birds of the air and all the creatures that move on the ground—everything that has the breath of life in it—I give every green plant for food." And it was so.

Ge 2:16 And the LORD God commanded the man, "You are free to eat from any tree in the garden;

Ge 8:22 "As long as the earth endures, seedtime and harvest, cold and heat, summer and winter, day and night will never cease."

Ge 9:1 Then God blessed Noah and his sons, saying to them, "Be fruitful and increase in number and fill the earth. (+Ge 9:2)

Ge 9:3 Everything that lives and moves will be food for

you. Just as I gave you the green plants, I now give you everything.

Ge 28:20 Then Jacob made a vow, saying, "If God will be with me and will watch over me on this journey I am taking and will give me food to eat and clothes to wear ²¹so that I return safely to my father's house, then the LORD will be my God (+Ge 48:15-16)

Ge 49:24 But his bow remained steady, his strong arms stayed limber, because of the hand of the Mighty One of Jacob, because of the Shepherd, the Rock of Israel, ²⁵because of your father's God, who helps you, because of the Almighty, who blesses you with blessings of the heavens above, blessings of the deep that lies below, blessings of the breast and womb. (+Ex 16:15)

Lev 25:20 You may ask, "What will we eat in the seventh year if we do not plant or harvest our crops?" ²¹I will send you such a blessing in the sixth year that the land will yield enough for three years. ²²While you plant during the eighth year, you will eat from the old crop and will continue to eat from it until the harvest of the ninth year comes in.

Dt 2:7 The LORD your God has blessed you in all the work of your hands. He has watched over your journey through this vast desert. These forty years the LORD your God has been with you, and you have not lacked anything.

Dt 7:13 He will love you and bless you and increase your numbers. He will bless the fruit of your womb, the crops of your land—your grain, new wine and oil—the calves of your herds and the lambs of your flocks in the land that he swore to your forefathers to give you. ¹⁴You will be blessed more than any other people; none of your men or women will be childless, nor any,of your livestock without young. ¹⁵The LORD will keep you free from every disease. He will not inflict on you the horrible diseases you knew in Egypt, but he will inflict them on all who hate you. (+Dt 8:4)

Dt 10:18 He defends the cause of the fatherless and the widow, and loves the alien, giving him food and clothing. (+Dt 28:2-13)

Dt 29:5 During the forty years that I led you through the desert, your clothes did not wear out, nor did the sandals on your feet.

Ru 1:6 When she heard in Moab that the LORD had come to the aid of his people by providing food for them, Naomi and her daughters-in-law prepared to return home from there. (+Ne 9:24)

Ne 9:25 They captured fortified cities and fertile land; they took possession of houses filled with all kinds of good things, wells already dug, vineyards, olive groves and fruit trees in abundance. They ate to the full and were well-nourished; they reveled in your great goodness.

Job 5:8 "But if it were I, I would appeal to God; I would lay my cause before him. ⁹He performs wonders that cannot be fathomed, miracles that cannot be counted. ¹⁰He bestows rain on the earth; he sends water upon the countryside. ¹¹The lowly he sets on high, and those who mourn are lifted to safety.

Job 22:18 Yet it was he who filled their houses with good things, so I stand aloof from the counsel of the wicked.

Job 22:25 then the Almighty will be your gold, the choicest silver for you.

Ps 36:6 Your righteousness is like the mighty mountains, your justice like the great deep. O LORD, you preserve both man and beast. ⁷How priceless is your unfailing love! Both high and low among men find refuge in the shadow of your wings.

Ps 37:3 Trust in the LORD and do good; dwell in the land and enjoy safe pasture.

Ps 37:19 In times of disaster they will not wither; in days of famine they will enjoy plenty.

Ps 37:22 those the LORD blesses will inherit the land, but those he curses will be cut off.

Ps 37:25 I was young and now I am old, yet I have never seen the righteous forsaken or their children begging bread.

Ps 37:34 Wait for the LORD and keep his way. He will exalt you to inherit the land; when the wicked are cut off, you will see it.

Ps 65:9 You care for the land and water it; you enrich it abundantly. The streams of God are filled with water to provide the people with grain, for so you have ordained it. ¹⁰You drench its furrows and level its ridges; you soften it with showers and bless its crops. ¹¹You crown the year with your bounty, and your carts overflow with abundance. ¹²The grasslands of the desert overflow; the hills are clothed with gladness. ¹³The meadows are covered with flocks and the valleys are mantled with grain; they shout for joy and sing.

Ps 67:6 Then the land will yield its harvest, and God, our God, will bless us.

Ps 85:12 The LORD will indeed give what is good, and our land will yield its harvest.

Ps 104:10 He makes springs pour water into the ravines; it flows between the mountains. ¹¹They give water to all the beasts of the field; the wild donkeys quench their thirst. ¹²The birds of the air nest by the waters; they sing among the branches. ¹³He waters the mountains from his upper chambers; the earth is satisfied by the fruit of his work. ¹⁴He makes grass grow for the cattle, and plants for man to cultivate—bringing forth food from the earth: ¹⁵wine that gladdens the heart of man, oil to make his face shine, and bread that sustains his heart.

Ps 111:5 He provides food for those who fear him; he remembers his covenant forever. (+Ps 136:25)

Ps 145:15 The eyes of all look to you, and you give them their food at the proper time. ¹⁶You open your hand and satisfy the desires of every living thing.

Isa 43:20 The wild animals honor me, the jackals and the owls, because I provide water in the desert and streams in the wasteland, to give drink to my people, my chosen,

Isa 48:21 They did not thirst when he led them through the deserts; he made water flow for them from the rock; he split the rock and water gushed out.

Jer 5:24 They do not say to themselves, 'Let us fear the LORD our God, who gives autumn and spring rains in season, who assures us of the regular weeks of harvest.'

Jer 27:6 Now I will hand all your countries over to my servant Nebuchadnezzar king of Babylon; I will make even the wild animals subject to him.

Hos 2:8 She has not acknowledged that I was the one who gave her the grain, the new wine and oil, who lavished on her the silver and gold—which they used for Baal.

Jnh 4:6 Then the LORD God provided a vine and made it grow up over Jonah to give shade for his head to ease his discomfort, and Jonah was very happy about the vine.

Zec 10:1 Ask the LORD for rain in the springtime; it is the LORD who makes the storm clouds. He gives showers of rain to men, and plants of the field to everyone.

Mt 6:26 Look at the birds of the air; they do not sow or reap or store away in barns, and yet your heavenly Father feeds them. Are you not much more valuable than they?

Mt 6:30 If that is how God clothes the grass of the field, which is here today and tomorrow is thrown into the fire, will he not much more clothe you, O you of little faith? ³¹So do not worry, saying, 'What shall we eat?' or 'What shall we drink?' or 'What shall we wear?' ³²For the pagans run after all these things, and your heavenly Father knows that you need them. ³³But seek first his kingdom and his righteousness, and all these things will be given to you as well.

Mt 10:29 Are not two sparrows sold for a penny? Yet not one of them will fall to the ground apart from the will of your Father. ³⁰And even the very hairs of your head are all numbered. ³¹So don't be afraid; you are worth more than many sparrows. (+Lk 12:6-7,24-28)

Lk 22:35 Then Jesus asked them, "When I sent you without purse, bag or sandals, did you lack anything?" "Nothing," they answered.

Jn 6:31 Our forefathers ate the manna in the desert; as it is written: 'He gave them bread from heaven to eat.'"

Ac 14:17 Yet he has not left himself without testimony: He has shown kindness by giving you rain from heaven and crops in their seasons; he provides you with plenty of food and fills your hearts with joy."

2Co 9:10 Now he who supplies seed to the sower and bread for food will also supply and increase your store of seed and will enlarge the harvest of your righteousness.

In sending prosperity (Ps 75:7; 127:1-2)—

Isa 48:14 "Come together, all of you, and listen: Which of [the idols] has foretold these things? The LORD's chosen ally will carry out his purpose against Babylon; his arm will be against the Babylonians. ¹⁵I, even I, have spoken; yes, I have called him. I will bring him, and he will succeed in his mission.

Isa 54:16 "See, it is I who created the blacksmith who fans the coals into flame and forges a weapon fit for its work. And it is I who have created the destroyer to work havoc; ¹⁷no weapon forged against you will prevail, and you will refute every tongue that accuses you. This is the heritage of the servants of the LORD, and this is their vindication from me," declares the LORD.

Eze 29:19 Therefore this is what the Sovereign LORD says: I am going to give Egypt to Nebuchadnezzar king of Babylon, and he will carry off its wealth. He will loot and plunder the land as pay for his army. ²⁰I have given him Egypt as a reward for his efforts because he and his army did it for me, declares the Sovereign LORD.

In sending adversity (1Sa 2:6-9)—

2Sa 17:14 Absalom and all the men of Israel said, "The advice of Hushai the Arkite is better than that of Ahithophel." For the LORD had determined to frustrate the good advice of Ahithophel in order to bring disaster on Absalom.

Ps 75:7 But it is God who judges: He brings one down, he exalts another.

Ecc 3:10 I have seen the burden God has laid on men.

In saving from adversity (Ge 7:1; Ex 9:26; 15:26; 23:25-26)—

Ps 103:3 who forgives all your sins and heals all your diseases, ⁴who redeems your life from the pit and crowns you with love and compassion, ⁵who satisfies your desires with good things so that your youth is renewed like the eagle's.

Ps 116:1 I love the LORD, for he heard my voice; he heard my cry for mercy. ²Because he turned his ear to me, I will call on him as long as I live.

³The cords of death entangled me, the anguish of the grave came upon me; I was overcome by trouble and sorrow. ⁴Then I called on the name of the LORD: "O LORD, save me!"

⁵The LORD is gracious and righteous; our God is full of compassion. ⁶The LORD protects the simplehearted; when I was in great need, he saved me.

⁷Be at rest once more, O my soul, for the LORD has been good to you.

⁸For you, O LORD, have delivered my soul from death, my eyes from tears, my feet from stumbling, ⁹that I may walk before the LORD in the land of the living. ¹⁰I believed; therefore I said, "I am greatly afflicted." ¹¹And in my dismay I said, "All men are liars."

¹²How can I repay the LORD for all his goodness to me? ¹³I will lift up the cup of salvation and call on the name of the LORD. ¹⁴I will fulfill my vows to the LORD in the presence of all his people.

¹⁵Precious in the sight of the LORD is the death of his saints.

Ps 118:5 In my anguish I cried to the LORD, and he answered by setting me free. ⁶The LORD is with me; I will not be afraid. What can man do to me?

Ps 118:13 I was pushed back and about to fall, but the LORD helped me. ¹⁴The LORD is my strength and my song; he has become my salvation.

Ps 146:7 He upholds the cause of the oppressed and gives food to the hungry. The LORD sets prisoners free, ⁸the LORD gives sight to the blind, the LORD lifts up those who are bowed down, the LORD loves the righteous. ⁹The LORD watches over the alien and sustains the fatherless and the widow, but he frustrates the ways of the wicked.

Da 6:20 When he came near the den, he called to Daniel in an anguished voice, "Daniel, servant of the living God, has your God, whom you serve continually, been able to rescue you from the lions?"

²¹Daniel answered, "O king, live forever! ²²My God sent his angel, and he shut the mouths of the lions. They have not hurt me, because I was found innocent in his sight. Nor have I ever done any wrong before you, O king."

In delivering from enemies (Ge 14:20; Ex 3:17; 6:7; 14:29-30)—

Ex 23:22 If you listen carefully to what he says and do all that I say, I will be an enemy to your enemies and will oppose those who oppose you.

Ex 34:24 I will drive out nations before you and enlarge your territory, and no one will covet your land when you go up three times each year to appear before the LORD your God. (+Dt 20:4; 23:14; 30:4,20; 31:3,8; 2Ki 20:6; 2Ch 20:3-16)

2Ch 20:17 You will not have to fight this battle. Take up your positions; stand firm and see the deliverance the LORD will give you, O Judah and Jerusalem. Do not be afraid; do not be discouraged. Go out to face them tomorrow, and the LORD will be with you.'" (+2Ch 20:18-30; 32:8)

Ezr 8:22 I was ashamed to ask the king for soldiers and horsemen to protect us from enemies on the road, because we had told the king, "The gracious hand of our God is on everyone who looks to him, but his great anger is against all who forsake him." (+Ezr 8:23; Ps 18:17,27)

Ps 44:1 We have heard with our ears, O God; our fathers have told us what you did in their days, in days long ago. ²With your hand you drove out the nations and planted our fathers; you crushed the peoples and made our fathers flourish. ³It was not by their sword that they won the land, nor did their arm bring them victory; it was your right hand, your arm, and the light of your face, for you loved them. (+Ps 61:3)

Ps 78:52 But he brought his people out like a flock; he led them like sheep through the desert. ⁵³He guided them safely, so they were unafraid; but the sea engulfed their enemies. ⁵⁴Thus he brought them to the border of his holy land, to the hill country his right hand had taken. ⁵⁵He drove out nations before them and allotted their lands to them as an inheritance; he settled the tribes of Israel in their homes. (+Ps 97:10)

Ps 105:14 He allowed no one to oppress them; for their sake he rebuked kings: ¹⁵"Do not touch my anointed ones; do my prophets no harm."

¹⁶He called down famine on the land and destroyed all their supplies of food; ¹⁷and he sent a man before them— Joseph, sold as a slave. ¹⁸They bruised his feet with shackles, his neck was put in irons, ¹⁹till what he foretold came to pass, till the word of the LORD proved him true. ²⁰The king sent and released him, the ruler of peoples set him free. ²¹He made him master of his household, ruler over all he possessed, ²²to instruct his princes as he pleased and teach his elders wisdom.

²³Then Israel entered Egypt; Jacob lived as an alien in the land of Ham. ²⁴The LORD made his people very fruitful; he made them too numerous for their foes, ²⁵whose hearts he turned to hate his people, to conspire against his servants. ²⁶He sent Moses his servant, and Aaron, whom he had chosen. ²⁷They performed his miraculous signs among them, his wonders in the land of Ham. ²⁸He sent darkness and made the land dark—for had they not rebelled against his words? ²⁹He turned their waters into blood, causing their fish to die. ³⁰Their land teemed with frogs, which went up into the bedrooms of their rulers. ³¹He spoke, and there came swarms of flies, and gnats throughout their country. ³²He turned their rain into hail, with lightning throughout their land; ³³he struck down their vines and fig trees and shattered the trees of their country. ³⁴He spoke, and the locusts came, grasshoppers without number; ³⁵they ate up every green thing in their land, ate up the produce of their soil. ³⁶Then he struck down all the firstborn in their land, the firstfruits of all their manhood.

³⁷He brought out Israel, laden with silver and gold, and from among their tribes no one faltered. ³⁸Egypt was glad when they left, because dread of Israel had fallen on them. ³⁹He spread out a cloud as a covering, and a fire to give light at night. ⁴⁰They asked, and he brought them quail and satisfied them with the bread of heaven. ⁴¹He opened the rock, and water gushed out; like a river it flowed in the desert.

⁴²For he remembered his holy promise given to his servant Abraham. ⁴³He brought out his people with rejoicing, his chosen ones with shouts of joy; ⁴⁴he gave them the lands of the nations, and they fell heir to what others had toiled for— ⁴⁵that they might keep his precepts and observe his laws. Praise the LORD. (+Ac 7:34-36; 12:1-12)

Pr 16:7 When a man's ways are pleasing to the LORD, he makes even his enemies live at peace with him.

In thwarting evil purpose (Ge 37:5-20; 45:5-7; Ps 105:17; Ac 7:9-10)—

Ex 14:4 And I will harden Pharaoh's heart, and he will pursue them. But I will gain glory for myself through Pharaoh and all his army, and the Egyptians will know that I am the LORD." So the Israelites did this.

Nu 23:7 Then Balaam uttered his oracle: "Balak brought me from Aram, the king of Moab from the eastern mountains. 'Come,' he said, 'curse Jacob for me; come,

denounce Israel.' ⁸How can I curse those whom God has not cursed? How can I denounce those whom the LORD has not denounced?

Nu 23:23 There is no sorcery against Jacob, no divination against Israel. It will now be said of Jacob and of Israel, 'See what God has done!' (+Nu 22:12-18; 24:10-13)

Ezr 5:5 But the eye of their God was watching over the elders of the Jews, and they were not stopped until a report could go to Darius and his written reply be received.

Ne 6:16 When all our enemies heard about this, all the surrounding nations were afraid and lost their self-confidence, because they realized that this work had been done with the help of our God.

Est 7:10 So they hanged Haman on the gallows he had prepared for Mordecai. Then the king's fury subsided. (+Est 6:1-12; 9:25)

Job 5:12 He thwarts the plans of the crafty, so that their hands achieve no success. ¹³He catches the wise in their craftiness, and the schemes of the wily are swept away. (+Isa 8:9-10)

Ps 33:10 The LORD foils the plans of the nations; he thwarts the purposes of the peoples.

Ac 5:38 Therefore, in the present case I advise you: Leave these men alone! Let them go! For if their purpose or activity is of human origin, it will fail. ³⁹But if it is from God, you will not be able to stop these men; you will only find yourselves fighting against God."

In turning the curse into blessing—

Dt 23:4 For they did not come to meet you with bread and water on your way when you came out of Egypt, and they hired Balaam son of Beor from Pethor in Aram Naharaim to pronounce a curse on you. (+Dt 23:6)

Php 1:12 Now I want you to know, brothers, that what has happened to me has really served to advance the gospel.

Php 1:19 for I know that through your prayers and the help given by the Spirit of Jesus Christ, what has happened to me will turn out for my deliverance.

In exalting the lowly—

2Sa 7:8 "Now then, tell my servant David, 'This is what the LORD Almighty says: I took you from the pasture and from following the flock to be ruler over my people Israel. ⁹I have been with you wherever you have gone, and I have cut off all your enemies from before you. Now I will make your name great, like the names of the greatest men of the earth. (+1Ch 17:7-8)

Ps 68:6 God sets the lonely in families, he leads forth the prisoners with singing; but the rebellious live in a sunscorched land.

Ps 113:7 He raises the poor from the dust and lifts the needy from the ash heap; ⁸he seats them with princes, with the princes of their people.

In leading people to repentance—

Am 4:7 "I also withheld rain from you when the harvest was still three months away. I sent rain on one town, but withheld it from another. One field had rain; another had none and dried up. ⁸People staggered from town to town for water but did not get enough to drink, yet you have not returned to me," declares the LORD. ⁹"Many times I struck your gardens and vineyards, I struck them with blight and mildew. Locusts devoured your fig and olive trees, yet you have not returned to me," declares the LORD. ¹⁰"I sent plagues among you as I did to Egypt. I killed your young men with the sword, along with your captured horses. I filled your nostrils with the stench of your camps, yet you have not returned to me," declares the LORD. ¹¹"I overthrew some of you as I overthrew Sodom and Gomorrah.

You were like a burning stick snatched from the fire, yet you have not returned to me," declares the LORD.

Am 4:12 "Therefore this is what I will do to you, Israel, and because I will do this to you, prepare to meet your God, O Israel."

In punishing evildoers—

Dt 2:30 But Sihon king of Heshbon refused to let us pass through. For the LORD your God had made his spirit stubborn and his heart obstinate in order to give him into your hands, as he has now done. (+Jos 10:10-11,19)

Jdg 9:23 God sent an evil spirit between Abimelech and the citizens of Shechem, who acted treacherously against Abimelech. ²⁴God did this in order that the crime against Jerub-Baal's seventy sons, the shedding of their blood, might be avenged on their brother Abimelech and on the citizens of Shechem, who had helped him murder his brothers.

1Ch 5:26 So the God of Israel stirred up the spirit of Pul king of Assyria (that is, Tiglath-Pileser king of Assyria), who took the Reubenites, the Gadites and the half-tribe of Manasseh into exile. He took them to Halah, Habor, Hara and the river of Gozan, where they are to this day.

Isa 41:2 "Who has stirred up one from the east, calling him in righteousness to his service? He hands nations over to him and subdues kings before him. He turns them to dust with his sword, to windblown chaff with his bow.

Isa 41:4 Who has done this and carried it through, calling forth the generations from the beginning? I, the LORD— with the first of them and with the last—I am he."

In punishing rulers—

Da 5:18 "O king, the Most High God gave your father Nebuchadnezzar sovereignty and greatness and glory and splendor. (+Da 5:22)

In punishing nations (Dt 9:4-5)—

Job 12:23 He makes nations great, and destroys them; he enlarges nations, and disperses them. (+Eze 29:19-20)

In ordaining instruments of discipline—

Isa 13:3 I have commanded my holy ones; I have summoned my warriors to carry out my wrath—those who rejoice in my triumph.

⁴Listen, a noise on the mountains, like that of a great multitude! Listen, an uproar among the kingdoms, like nations massing together! The LORD Almighty is mustering an army for war. ⁵They come from faraway lands, from the ends of the heavens—the LORD and the weapons of his wrath—to destroy the whole country.

In using the heathen to execute his purpose—

Ezr 6:22 For seven days they celebrated with joy the Feast of Unleavened Bread, because the LORD had filled them with joy by changing the attitude of the king of Assyria, so that he assisted them in the work on the house of God, the God of Israel.

Isa 44:28 who says of Cyrus, 'He is my shepherd and will accomplish all that I please; he will say of Jerusalem, "Let it be rebuilt," and of the temple, "Let its foundations be laid." ' (+Isa 45:1-4)

Isa 45:5 I am the LORD, and there is no other; apart from me there is no God. I will strengthen you, though you have not acknowledged me, ⁶so that from the rising of the sun to the place of its setting men may know there is none besides me. I am the LORD, and there is no other.

Isa 45:13 I will raise up Cyrus in my righteousness: I will make all his ways straight. He will rebuild my city and set my exiles free, but not for a price or reward, says the LORD Almighty."

In fulfilling prophecy—

1Ki 12:15 So the king did not listen to the people, for this turn of events was from the LORD, to fulfill the word the LORD had spoken to Jeroboam son of Nebat through Ahijah the Shilonite. (+2Ch 10:15)

2Ch 36:22 In the first year of Cyrus king of Persia, in order to fulfill the word of the LORD spoken by Jeremiah, the LORD moved the heart of Cyrus king of Persia to make a proclamation throughout his realm and to put it in writing:

²³"This is what Cyrus king of Persia says:

" 'The LORD, the God of heaven, has given me all the kingdoms of the earth and he has appointed me to build a temple for him at Jerusalem in Judah. Anyone of his people among you—may the LORD his God be with him, and let him go up.' " (+Ezr 1:1)

Ac 3:17 "Now, brothers, I know that you acted in ignorance, as did your leaders. ¹⁸But this is how God fulfilled what he had foretold through all the prophets, saying that his Christ would suffer.

In nature (Job 12:7-20)—

Job 37:6 He says to the snow, 'Fall on the earth,' and to the rain shower, 'Be a mighty downpour.' ⁷So that all men he has made may know his work, he stops every man from his labor. ⁸The animals take cover; they remain in their dens. ⁹The tempest comes out from its chamber, the cold from the driving winds. ¹⁰The breath of God produces ice, and the broad waters become frozen. ¹¹He loads the clouds with moisture; he scatters his lightning through them. ¹²At his direction they swirl around over the face of the whole earth to do whatever he commands them. ¹³He brings the clouds to punish men, or to water his earth and show his love.

¹⁴"Listen to this, Job; stop and consider God's wonders. ¹⁵Do you know how God controls the clouds and makes his lightning flash? ¹⁶Do you know how the clouds hang poised, those wonders of him who is perfect in knowledge? ¹⁷You who swelter in your clothes when the land lies hushed under the south wind, ¹⁸can you join him in spreading out the skies, hard as a mirror of cast bronze?

¹⁹"Tell us what we should say to him; we cannot draw up our case because of our darkness. ²⁰Should he be told that I want to speak? Would any man ask to be swallowed up? ²¹Now no one can look at the sun, bright as it is in the skies after the wind has swept them clean. ²²Out of the north he comes in golden splendor; God comes in awesome majesty. ²³The Almighty is beyond our reach and exalted in power; in his justice and great righteousness, he does not oppress. ²⁴Therefore, men revere him, for does he not have regard for all the wise in heart?"

Job 38:25 Who cuts a channel for the torrents of rain, and a path for the thunderstorm, ²⁶to water a land where no man lives, a desert with no one in it, ²⁷to satisfy a desolate wasteland and make it sprout with grass?

Job 38:41 Who provides food for the raven when its young cry out to God and wander about for lack of food?

Job 39:5 "Who let the wild donkey go free? Who untied his ropes? ⁶I gave him the wasteland as his home, the salt flats as his habitat.

Ps 104:16 The trees of the LORD are well watered, the cedars of Lebanon that he planted. ¹⁷There the birds make their nests; the stork has its home in the pine trees. ¹⁸The high mountains belong to the wild goats; the crags are a refuge for the coneys.

¹⁹The moon marks off the seasons, and the sun knows when to go down.

Ps 104:24 How many are your works, O LORD! In wisdom you made them all; the earth is full of your creatures. ²⁵There is the sea, vast and spacious, teeming with creatures beyond number—living things both large and small. ²⁶There the ships go to and fro, and the leviathan, which you formed to frolic there.

²⁷These all look to you to give them their food at the proper time. ²⁸When you give it to them, they gather it up; when you open your hand, they are satisfied with good things. ²⁹When you hide your face, they are terrified; when you take away their breath, they die and return to the dust. ³⁰When you send your Spirit, they are created, and you renew the face of the earth.

Ps 135:7 He makes clouds rise from the ends of the earth; he sends lightning with the rain and brings out the wind from his storehouses.

Jer 10:13 When he thunders, the waters in the heavens roar; he makes clouds rise from the ends of the earth. He sends lightning with the rain and brings out the wind from his storehouses. (+Jer 51:16; 14:22; 31:35)

Instances of: Saving Noah (Ge 7:1; 2Pe 2:5). The call of Abraham (Ge 12:1). Protecting Abraham, Sarah, and Abimelech (Ge 20:3-6). Deliverance of Lot (Ge 19). Care of Isaac (Ge 26:2-3), of Jacob (Ge 31:7).

Instances of providence: The mission of Joseph—

Ge 50:20 You intended to harm me, but God intended it for good to accomplish what is now being done, the saving of many lives. (+Ge 37:5-10; 39:2-3,21,23; 45:7-8; Ps 105:17-22)

Warning Pharaoh of famine (Ge 41). Delivering the Israelites (Ex 3:8; 11:3; 13:18; Ac 7:34-36). The pillar of cloud (Ex 13:21; 14:19-20). Dividing the Red Sea (Ex 14:21). Delaying and destroying Pharaoh (Ex 14:25-30). Purifying the waters of Marah (Ex 15:25). Supplying manna and quail (Ex 16:13-15; Nu 11:31-32). Supplying water at Meribah (Nu 20:7-11; Ne 9:10-25). Protection of homes while at feasts (Ex 34:24). In the conquest of Canaan (Ps 44:2-3). Saving David's army (2Sa 5:23-25). The revolt of the ten tribes (1Ki 12:15,24; 2Ch 10:15). Fighting the battles of Israel (2Ch 13:12,18; 14:9-14; 16:7-9; 20:15,17; 22; 23; 32:21-22). Restoring Manasseh after his conversion (2Ch 33:12-13). Feeding Elijah and the widow (1Ki 17; 19:1-8). In prospering Hezekiah (2Ki 18:6-7; 2Ch 32:29), and Asa (2Ch 14:6-7), and Jehoshaphat (2Ch 17:3,5; 20:30), and Uzziah (2Ch 26:5-15), and Jotham (2Ch 27:6), and Job (Job 1:10; 42:10,12), and Daniel (Da 1:9). In turning the heart of the king of Assyria to favor the Jews (Ezr 6:22). In rescuing Jeremiah (La 3:52-58; Jer 38:6-13). Restoration of the Jews (2Ch 36:22-23; Ezr 1:1). Rescuing the Jews from Haman's plot (Esther). Rebuilding the walls of Jerusalem (Ne 6:16). Warning Joseph in dreams (Mt 1:20; 2:13,19-20), and the wise men of the east (Mt 2:12-13). Deliverance of Paul (2Co 1:10). Restoring Epaphroditus (Php 2:27). Banishment of John to Patmos (Rev 1:9).

Providence, Mysterious and misinterpreted: The silence of God—

Job 33:13 Why do you complain to him that he answers none of man's words?

The adversity of the righteous—

Ecc 7:15 In this meaningless life of mine I have seen both of these: a righteous man perishing in his righteousness, and a wicked man living long in his wickedness.

Ecc 8:14 There is something else meaningless that occurs on earth: righteous men who get what the wicked deserve,

and wicked men who get what the righteous deserve. This too, I say, is meaningless.

The prosperity of the wicked—

Job 12:6 The tents of marauders are undisturbed, and those who provoke God are secure—those who carry their god in their hands.

Job 21:7 Why do the wicked live on, growing old and increasing in power?

Job 24:1 "Why does the Almighty not set times for judgment? Why must those who know him look in vain for such days?

Ps 73:2 But as for me, my feet had almost slipped; I had nearly lost my foothold. ³For I envied the arrogant when I saw the prosperity of the wicked. (+Ps 73:4-5,12)

Ps 73:13 Surely in vain have I kept my heart pure; in vain have I washed my hands in innocence. ¹⁴All day long I have been plagued; I have been punished every morning.

¹⁵If I had said, "I will speak thus," I would have betrayed your children. ¹⁶When I tried to understand all this, it was oppressive to me ¹⁷till I entered the sanctuary of God; then I understood their final destiny. (+Ecc 7:15; 8:14)

Jer 12:1 You are always righteous, O LORD, when I bring a case before you. Yet I would speak with you about your justice: Why does the way of the wicked prosper? Why do all the faithless live at ease? ²You have planted them, and they have taken root; they grow and bear fruit. You are always on their lips but far from their hearts.

Mal 3:14 "You have said, 'It is futile to serve God. What did we gain by carrying out his requirements and going about like mourners before the LORD Almighty? ¹⁵But now we call the arrogant blessed. Certainly the evildoers prosper, and even those who challenge God escape.'"

Likeness in the lot of the righteous and the wicked—

Ecc 9:2 All share a common destiny—the righteous and the wicked, the good and the bad, the clean and the unclean, those who offer sacrifices and those who do not. As it is with the good man, so with the sinner; as it is with those who take oaths, so with those who are afraid to take them.

Ecc 9:11 I have seen something else under the sun: The race is not to the swift or the battle to the strong, nor does food come to the wise or wealth to the brilliant or favor to the learned; but time and chance happen to them all.

Permitting the violence of the wicked toward the righteous (Job 24:1-12)—

Hab 1:2 How long, O LORD, must I call for help, but you do not listen? Or cry out to you, "Violence!" but you do not save? ³Why do you make me look at injustice? Why do you tolerate wrong? Destruction and violence are before me; there is strife, and conflict abounds.

Hab 1:11 Then they sweep past like the wind and go on—guilty men, whose own strength is their god."

Hab 1:13 Your eyes are too pure to look on evil; you cannot tolerate wrong. Why then do you tolerate the treacherous? Why are you silent while the wicked swallow up those more righteous than themselves? ¹⁴You have made men like fish in the sea, like sea creatures that have no ruler.

Rejected:

By Israel (1Sa 8:7-8; Isa 65:12; 66:4). By Saul (1Sa 15:26). *See Jesus the Christ, Rejected.*

Repentance Attributed to:

(Ge 6:6-7; Ex 32:14; Jdg 2:18; 1Sa 15:35; 2Sa 24:16;

1Ch 21:15; Ps 106:45; Jer 26:19; Am 7:3; Jnh 3:10). *See Anthropomorphisms; Relent.*

Righteousness of: (Ge 18:25)

Jdg 5:11 the voice of the singers at the watering places. They recite the righteous acts of the LORD, the righteous acts of his warriors in Israel. "Then the people of the LORD went down to the city gates.

Ps 7:9 O righteous God, who searches minds and hearts, bring to an end the violence of the wicked and make the righteous secure.

Ps 72:1 Endow the king with your justice, O God, the royal son with your righteousness.

Ps 88:12 Are your wonders known in the place of darkness, or your righteous deeds in the land of oblivion?

Ps 89:16 They rejoice in your name all day long; they exult in your righteousness.

Ps 119:40 How I long for your precepts! Preserve my life in your righteousness.

Ps 143:1 O LORD, hear my prayer, listen to my cry for mercy; in your faithfulness and righteousness come to my relief.

Isa 41:10 So do not fear, for I am with you; do not be dismayed, for I am your God. I will strengthen you and help you; I will uphold you with my righteous right hand.

Isa 56:1 This is what the LORD says: "Maintain justice and do what is right, for my salvation is close at hand and my righteousness will soon be revealed.

Jer 4:2 and if in a truthful, just and righteous way you swear, 'As surely as the LORD lives,' then the nations will be blessed by him and in him they will glory."

Jer 9:24 but let him who boasts boast about this: that he understands and knows me, that I am the LORD, who exercises kindness, justice and righteousness on earth, for in these I delight," declares the LORD.

Mic 7:9 Because I have sinned against him, I will bear the LORD's wrath, until he pleads my case and establishes my right. He will bring me out into the light; I will see his righteousness.

Ac 17:31 For he has set a day when he will judge the world with justice by the man he has appointed. He has given proof of this to all men by raising him from the dead."

Ascribed by people (Ex 9:27)—

Ezr 9:15 O LORD, God of Israel, you are righteous! We are left this day as a remnant. Here we are before you in our guilt, though because of it not one of us can stand in your presence."

Job 36:3 I get my knowledge from afar; I will ascribe justice to my Maker.

Ps 5:8 Lead me, O LORD, in your righteousness because of my enemies—make straight your way before me. (+Ps 48:10)

Ps 71:15 My mouth will tell of your righteousness, of your salvation all day long, though I know not its measure.

Ps 71:19 Your righteousness reaches to the skies, O God, you who have done great things. Who, O God, is like you? (+Ps 89:14)

Ps 97:2 Clouds and thick darkness surround him; righteousness and justice are the foundation of his throne.

Ps 116:5 The LORD is gracious and righteous; our God is full of compassion.

Ps 145:7 They will celebrate your abundant goodness and joyfully sing of your righteousness.

Ps 145:17 The LORD is righteous in all his ways and loving toward all he has made.

Jer 12:1 You are always righteous, O LORD, when I bring a case before you. Yet I would speak with you about your justice: Why does the way of the wicked prosper? Why do all the faithless live at ease?

Da 9:7 "Lord, you are righteous, but this day we are covered with shame—the men of Judah and people of Jerusalem and all Israel, both near and far, in all the countries where you have scattered us because of our unfaithfulness to you.

Da 9:14 The LORD did not hesitate to bring the disaster upon us, for the LORD our God is righteous in everything he does; yet we have not obeyed him.

2Ti 4:8 Now there is in store for me the crown of righteousness, which the Lord, the righteous Judge, will award to me on that day—and not only to me, but also to all who have longed for his appearing.

Ascribed by Jesus—

Jn 17:25 "Righteous Father, though the world does not know you, I know you, and they know that you have sent me.

Ascribed by the angel—

Rev 16:5 Then I heard the angel in charge of the waters say: "You are just in these judgments, you who are and who were, the Holy One, because you have so judged;

Revealed in the heavens—

Ps 50:6 And the heavens proclaim his righteousness, for God himself is judge. *Selah*

Revealed in the gospel—

Ro 1:17 For in the gospel a righteousness from God is revealed, a righteousness that is by faith from first to last, just as it is written: "The righteous will live by faith."

Ro 3:4 Not at all! Let God be true, and every man a liar. As it is written: "So that you may be proved right when you speak and prevail when you judge." ⁵But if our unrighteousness brings out God's righteousness more clearly, what shall we say? That God is unjust in bringing his wrath on us? (I am using a human argument.) ⁶Certainly not! If that were so, how could God judge the world?

Ro 3:21 But now a righteousness from God, apart from law, has been made known, to which the Law and the Prophets testify. ²²This righteousness from God comes through faith in Jesus Christ to all who believe. There is no difference,

Ro 10:3 Since they did not know the righteousness that comes from God and sought to establish their own, they did not submit to God's righteousness. ⁴Christ is the end of the law so that there may be righteousness for everyone who believes.

2Pe 1:1 Simon Peter, a servant and apostle of Jesus Christ, To those who through the righteousness of our God and Savior Jesus Christ have received a faith as precious as ours:

Endures forever—

Ps 119:142 Your righteousness is everlasting and your law is true.

Ps 119:144 Your statutes are forever right; give me understanding that I may live.

Isa 51:8 For the moth will eat them up like a garment; the worm will devour them like wool. But my righteousness will last forever, my salvation through all generations."

See above, Holiness of, Perfection of.

Savior: (Ex 6:6-7)

Ps 3:8 From the LORD comes deliverance. May your blessing be on your people. *Selah*

Ps 18:30 As for God, his way is perfect; the word of the LORD is flawless. He is a shield for all who take refuge in him.

Ps 28:8 The LORD is the strength of his people, a fortress of salvation for his anointed one.

Ps 31:5 Into your hands I commit my spirit; redeem me, O LORD, the God of truth.

Ps 33:18 But the eyes of the LORD are on those who fear him, on those whose hope is in his unfailing love, [19]to deliver them from death and keep them alive in famine.

Ps 34:22 The LORD redeems his servants; no one will be condemned who takes refuge in him.

Ps 37:39 The salvation of the righteous comes from the LORD; he is their stronghold in time of trouble. [40]The LORD helps them and delivers them; he delivers them from the wicked and saves them, because they take refuge in him.

Ps 74:12 But you, O God, are my king from of old; you bring salvation upon the earth.

Ps 76:8 From heaven you pronounced judgment, and the land feared and was quiet— [9]when you, O God, rose up to judge, to save all the afflicted of the land. *Selah*

Ps 85:9 Surely his salvation is near those who fear him, that his glory may dwell in our land.

Ps 96:2 Sing to the LORD, praise his name; proclaim his salvation day after day.

Ps 98:2 The LORD has made his salvation known and revealed his righteousness to the nations. [3]He has remembered his love and his faithfulness to the house of Israel; all the ends of the earth have seen the salvation of our God.

Ps 111:9 He provided redemption for his people; he ordained his covenant forever—holy and awesome is his name.

Ps 118:14 The LORD is my strength and my song; he has become my salvation.

Ps 121:7 The LORD will keep you from all harm—he will watch over your life;

Ps 149:4 For the LORD takes delight in his people; he crowns the humble with salvation.

Isa 26:1 In that day this song will be sung in the land of Judah: We have a strong city; God makes salvation its walls and ramparts.

Isa 33:22 For the LORD is our judge, the LORD is our lawgiver, the LORD is our king; it is he who will save us.

Isa 35:4 say to those with fearful hearts, "Be strong, do not fear; your God will come, he will come with vengeance; with divine retribution he will come to save you."

Isa 43:3 For I am the LORD, your God, the Holy One of Israel, your Savior; I give Egypt for your ransom, Cush and Seba in your stead.

Isa 43:11 I, even I, am the LORD, and apart from me there is no savior. [12]I have revealed and saved and proclaimed— I, and not some foreign god among you. You are my witnesses," declares the LORD, "that I am God. (+Isa 43:14)

Isa 45:15 Truly you are a God who hides himself, O God and Savior of Israel.

Isa 45:17 But Israel will be saved by the LORD with an everlasting salvation; you will never be put to shame or disgraced, to ages everlasting.

Isa 45:21 Declare what is to be, present it—let them take counsel together. Who foretold this long ago, who declared it from the distant past? Was it not I, the LORD? And there is no God apart from me, a righteous God and a Savior; there is none but me.

[22]"Turn to me and be saved, all you ends of the earth; for I am God, and there is no other.

Isa 46:12 Listen to me, you stubborn-hearted, you who are far from righteousness. [13]I am bringing my righteousness near, it is not far away; and my salvation will not be

delayed. I will grant salvation to Zion, my splendor to Israel.

Isa 49:25 But this is what the LORD says: "Yes, captives will be taken from warriors, and plunder retrieved from the fierce; I will contend with those who contend with you, and your children I will save.

Isa 50:2 When I came, why was there no one? When I called, why was there no one to answer? Was my arm too short to ransom you? Do I lack the strength to rescue you? By a mere rebuke I dry up the sea, I turn rivers into a desert; their fish rot for lack of water and die of thirst.

Isa 59:1 Surely the arm of the LORD is not too short to save, nor his ear too dull to hear.

Isa 60:16 You will drink the milk of nations and be nursed at royal breasts. Then you will know that I, the LORD, am your Savior, your Redeemer, the Mighty One of Jacob.

Isa 63:8 He said, "Surely they are my people, sons who will not be false to me"; and so he became their Savior.

Isa 63:16 But you are our Father, though Abraham does not know us or Israel acknowledge us; you, O LORD, are our Father, our Redeemer from of old is your name.

Jer 3:23 Surely the [idolatrous] commotion on the hills and mountains is a deception; surely in the LORD our God is the salvation of Israel.

Jer 14:8 O Hope of Israel, its Savior in times of distress, why are you like a stranger in the land, like a traveler who stays only a night?

Jer 33:6 "'Nevertheless, I will bring health and healing to it; I will heal my people and will let them enjoy abundant peace and security.

Eze 37:23 They will no longer defile themselves with their idols and vile images or with any of their offenses, for I will save them from all their sinful backsliding, and I will cleanse them. They will be my people, and I will be their God.

Hos 1:7 Yet I will show love to the house of Judah; and I will save them—not by bow, sword or battle, or by horses and horsemen, but by the LORD their God."

Hos 13:4 "But I am the LORD your God, [who brought you] out of Egypt. You shall acknowledge no God but me, no Savior except me.

Joel 3:16 The LORD will roar from Zion and thunder from Jerusalem; the earth and the sky will tremble. But the LORD will be a refuge for his people, a stronghold for the people of Israel.

Jnh 2:9 But I, with a song of thanksgiving, will sacrifice to you. What I have vowed I will make good. Salvation comes from the LORD."

Lk 1:68 "Praise be to the Lord, the God of Israel, because he has come and has redeemed his people.

Jn 3:16 "For God so loved the world that he gave his one and only Son, that whoever believes in him shall not perish but have eternal life. [17]For God did not send his Son into the world to condemn the world, but to save the world through him.

Ro 8:30 And those he predestined, he also called; those he called, he also justified; those he justified, he also glorified.

[31]What, then, shall we say in response to this? If God is for us, who can be against us? [32]He who did not spare his own Son, but gave him up for us all—how will he not also, along with him, graciously give us all things?

1Ti 2:3 This is good, and pleases God our Savior, [4]who wants all men to be saved and to come to a knowledge of the truth.

1Ti 4:10 (and for this we labor and strive), that we have put our hope in the living God, who is the Savior of all men, and especially of those who believe.

Tit 1:2 a faith and knowledge resting on the hope of eternal life, which God, who does not lie, promised before the beginning of time, ³and at his appointed season he brought his word to light through the preaching entrusted to me by the command of God our Savior,

Tit 2:10 and not to steal from them, but to show that they can be fully trusted, so that in every way they will make the teaching about God our Savior attractive.

¹¹For the grace of God that brings salvation has appeared to all men.

Tit 3:4 But when the kindness and love of God our Savior appeared, ⁵he saved us, not because of righteous things we had done, but because of his mercy. He saved us through the washing of rebirth and renewal by the Holy Spirit,

1Jn 4:9 This is how God showed his love among us: He sent his one and only Son into the world that we might live through him. ¹⁰This is love: not that we loved God, but that he loved us and sent his Son as an atoning sacrifice for our sins.

Called Redeemer—

Ps 19:14 May the words of my mouth and the meditation of my heart be pleasing in your sight, O LORD, my Rock and my Redeemer.

Isa 41:14 Do not be afraid, O worm Jacob, O little Israel, for I myself will help you," declares the LORD, your Redeemer, the Holy One of Israel.

Isa 47:4 Our Redeemer—the LORD Almighty is his name—is the Holy One of Israel. (+Isa 48:17)

Jer 50:34 Yet their Redeemer is strong; the LORD Almighty is his name. He will vigorously defend their cause so that he may bring rest to their land, but unrest to those who live in Babylon.

Salvation—

Ps 27:1 The LORD is my light and my salvation—whom shall I fear? The LORD is the stronghold of my life—of whom shall I be afraid?

Ps 62:1 My soul finds rest in God alone; my salvation comes from him. (+Ps 62:2)

Ps 62:6 He alone is my rock and my salvation; he is my fortress, I will not be shaken. ⁷My salvation and my honor depend on God; he is my mighty rock, my refuge.

Isa 12:2 Surely God is my salvation; I will trust and not be afraid. The LORD, the LORD, is my strength and my song; he has become my salvation."

God of salvation—

Ps 25:5 guide me in your truth and teach me, for you are God my Savior, and my hope is in you all day long.

Ps 65:5 You answer us with awesome deeds of righteousness, O God our Savior, the hope of all the ends of the earth and of the farthest seas,

Ps 68:19 Praise be to the Lord, to God our Savior, who daily bears our burdens. Selah ²⁰Our God is a God who saves; from the Sovereign LORD comes escape from death.

Ps 88:1 O LORD, the God who saves me, day and night I cry out before you.

Rock of salvation—

Dt 32:15 Jeshurun grew fat and kicked; filled with food, he became heavy and sleek. He abandoned the God who made him and rejected the Rock his Savior.

Dt 32:31 For their rock is not like our Rock, as even our enemies concede.

Shield—

Dt 33:29 Blessed are you, O Israel! Who is like you, a

people saved by the LORD? He is your shield and helper and your glorious sword. Your enemies will cower before you, and you will trample down their high places."

Salvation from national adversity—

Ex 15:2 The LORD is my strength and my song; he has become my salvation. He is my God, and I will praise him, my father's God, and I will exalt him.

Isa 25:4 You have been a refuge for the poor, a refuge for the needy in his distress, a shelter from the storm and a shade from the heat. For the breath of the ruthless is like a storm driving against a wall

Isa 25:9 In that day they will say, "Surely this is our God; we trusted in him, and he saved us. This is the LORD, we trusted in him; let us rejoice and be glad in his salvation."

Isa 52:3 For this is what the LORD says: "You were sold for nothing, and without money you will be redeemed."

Isa 52:9 Burst into songs of joy together, you ruins of Jerusalem, for the LORD has comforted his people, he has redeemed Jerusalem. ¹⁰The LORD will lay bare his holy arm in the sight of all the nations, and all the ends of the earth will see the salvation of our God.

Salvation from sin—

Job 33:24 to be gracious to him and say, 'Spare him from going down to the pit; I have found a ransom for him'—

Job 33:27 Then he comes to men and says, 'I sinned, and perverted what was right, but I did not get what I deserved. ²⁸He redeemed my soul from going down to the pit, and I will live to enjoy the light.'

²⁹"God does all these things to a man—twice, even three times— ³⁰to turn back his soul from the pit, that the light of life may shine on him.

Isa 44:22 I have swept away your offenses like a cloud, your sins like the morning mist. Return to me, for I have redeemed you."

²³Sing for joy, O heavens, for the LORD has done this; shout aloud, O earth beneath. Burst into song, you mountains, you forests and all your trees, for the LORD has redeemed Jacob, he displays his glory in Israel.

²⁴"This is what the LORD says—your Redeemer, who formed you in the womb: I am the LORD, who has made all things, who alone stretched out the heavens, who spread out the earth by myself,

Ro 1:16 I am not ashamed of the gospel, because it is the power of God for the salvation of everyone who believes: first for the Jew, then for the Gentile.

Salvation through Christ—

2Ti 1:9 who has saved us and called us to a holy life—not because of anything we have done but because of his own purpose and grace. This grace was given us in Christ Jesus before the beginning of time,

Self-Existent:

Has life in himself—

Jn 5:26 For as the Father has life in himself, so he has granted the Son to have life in himself.

Is the I am that I am—

Ex 3:14 God said to Moses, "I AM WHO I AM. This is what you are to say to the Israelites: 'I AM has sent me to you.'"

Is the first and the last—

Isa 44:6 "This is what the LORD says—Israel's King and Redeemer, the LORD Almighty: I am the first and I am the last; apart from me there is no God.

Is the living God—

Jer 10:10 But the LORD is the true God; he is the living

God, the eternal King. When he is angry, the earth trembles; the nations cannot endure his wrath.

Lives forever—

Dt 32:40 I lift my hand to heaven and declare: As surely as I live forever,

Needs nothing—

Ac 17:24 "The God who made the world and everything in it is the Lord of heaven and earth and does not live in temples built by hands. ²⁵And he is not served by human hands, as if he needed anything, because he himself gives all men life and breath and everything else.

Sovereign: (Ex 20:3)

Job 25:2 "Dominion and awe belong to God; he establishes order in the heights of heaven.

Job 33:13 Why do you complain to him that he answers none of man's words?

Job 41:11 Who has a claim against me that I must pay? Everything under heaven belongs to me.

Ps 44:4 You are my King and my God, who decrees victories for Jacob. (+Ps 47:8)

Ps 59:13 consume them in wrath, consume them till they are no more. Then it will be known to the ends of the earth that God rules over Jacob. *Selah*

Ps 74:12 But you, O God, are my king from of old; you bring salvation upon the earth.

Ps 82:1 God presides in the great assembly; he gives judgment among the "gods":

Ps 82:8 Rise up, O God, judge the earth, for all the nations are your inheritance.

Ps 83:18 Let them know that you, whose name is the LORD—that you alone are the Most High over all the earth.

Ps 93:1 The LORD reigns, he is robed in majesty; the LORD is robed in majesty and is armed with strength. The world is firmly established; it cannot be moved. ²Your throne was established long ago; you are from all eternity.

Ps 95:3 For the LORD is the great God, the great King above all gods. ⁴In his hand are the depths of the earth, and the mountain peaks belong to him. ⁵The sea is his, for he made it, and his hands formed the dry land.

Ps 96:10 Say among the nations, "The LORD reigns." The world is firmly established, it cannot be moved; he will judge the peoples with equity.

Ps 97:1 The LORD reigns, let the earth be glad; let the distant shores rejoice. (+Ps 97:5)

Ps 97:9 For you, O LORD, are the Most High over all the earth; you are exalted far above all gods.

Ps 98:6 with trumpets and the blast of the ram's horn— shout for joy before the LORD, the King.

Ps 103:19 The LORD has established his throne in heaven, and his kingdom rules over all.

Ps 105:7 He is the LORD our God; his judgments are in all the earth.

Ps 113:4 The LORD is exalted over all the nations, his glory above the heavens.

Ps 115:3 Our God is in heaven; he does whatever pleases him.

Ps 115:16 The highest heavens belong to the LORD, but the earth he has given to man.

Ps 136:2 Give thanks to the God of gods. *His love endures forever.* ³Give thanks to the Lord of lords: *His love endures forever.*

Isa 24:23 The moon will be abashed, the sun ashamed; for the LORD Almighty will reign on Mount Zion and in Jerusalem, and before its elders, gloriously.

Isa 33:22 For the LORD is our judge, the LORD is our lawgiver, the LORD is our king; it is he who will save us.

Isa 40:22 He sits enthroned above the circle of the earth, and its people are like grasshoppers. He stretches out the heavens like a canopy, and spreads them out like a tent to live in. ²³He brings princes to naught and reduces the rulers of this world to nothing.

Isa 43:15 I am the LORD, your Holy One, Israel's Creator, your King."

Isa 44:6 "This is what the LORD says—Israel's King and Redeemer, the LORD Almighty: I am the first and I am the last; apart from me there is no God. (+Isa 52:7; 66:1)

La 3:37 Who can speak and have it happen if the Lord has not decreed it?

Mic 4:7 I will make the lame a remnant, those driven away a strong nation. The LORD will rule over them in Mount Zion from that day and forever.

Mic 4:13 "Rise and thresh, O Daughter of Zion, for I will give you horns of iron; I will give you hoofs of bronze and you will break to pieces many nations." You will devote their ill-gotten gains to the LORD, their wealth to the Lord of all the earth.

Mal 1:14 "Cursed is the cheat who has an acceptable male in his flock and vows to give it, but then sacrifices a blemished animal to the Lord. For I am a great king," says the LORD Almighty, "and my name is to be feared among the nations.

Jn 10:29 My Father, who has given them to me, is greater than all; no one can snatch them out of my Father's hand.

Jn 19:11 Jesus answered, "You would have no power over me if it were not given to you from above. Therefore the one who handed me over to you is guilty of a greater sin." (+Ac 7:49)

Ro 9:19 One of you will say to me: "Then why does God still blame us? For who resists his will?" (+Ro 11:36)

Eph 4:6 one God and Father of all, who is over all and through all and in all.

1Ti 6:15 which God will bring about in his own time— God, the blessed and only Ruler, the King of kings and Lord of lords, ¹⁶who alone is immortal and who lives in unapproachable light, whom no one has seen or can see. To him be honor and might forever. Amen.

Heb 1:3 The Son is the radiance of God's glory and the exact representation of his being, sustaining all things by his powerful word. After he had provided purification for sins, he sat down at the right hand of the Majesty in heaven.

Jas 4:12 There is only one Lawgiver and Judge, the one who is able to save and destroy. But you—who are you to judge your neighbor?

Rev 4:11 "You are worthy, our Lord and God, to receive glory and honor and power, for you created all things, and by your will they were created and have their being."

Rev 19:6 Then I heard what sounded like a great multitude, like the roar of rushing waters and like loud peals of thunder, shouting: "Hallelujah! For our Lord God Almighty reigns.

Over heaven—

2Ch 20:6 and said: "O LORD, God of our fathers, are you not the God who is in heaven? You rule over all the kingdoms of the nations. Power and might are in your hand, and no one can withstand you.

Over earth—

Ex 9:29 Moses replied, "When I have gone out of the city, I will spread out my hands in prayer to the LORD. The thunder will stop and there will be no more hail, so you may know that the earth is the LORD's.

Jos 3:11 See, the ark of the covenant of the Lord of all the earth will go into the Jordan ahead of you.

Ps 24:1 The earth is the LORD's, and everything in it, the world, and all who live in it;

Ps 24:10 Who is he, this King of glory? The LORD Almighty—he is the King of glory. *Selah*

Ps 47:2 How awesome is the LORD Most High, the great King over all the earth!

Ps 47:7 For God is the King of all the earth; sing to him a psalm of praise. ⁸God reigns over the nations; God is seated on his holy throne.

Ps 50:10 for every animal of the forest is mine, and the cattle on a thousand hills. ¹¹I know every bird in the mountains, and the creatures of the field are mine. ¹²If I were hungry I would not tell you, for the world is mine, and all that is in it.

Isa 54:5 For your Maker is your husband—the LORD Almighty is his name—the Holy One of Israel is your Redeemer; he is called the God of all the earth.

Jer 10:10 But the LORD is the true God; he is the living God, the eternal King. When he is angry, the earth trembles; the nations cannot endure his wrath. (+1Co 10:26)

Over heaven and earth—

Ge 14:18 Then Melchizedek king of Salem brought out bread and wine. He was priest of God Most High, ¹⁹and he blessed Abram, saying,

"Blessed be Abram by God Most High, Creator of heaven and earth. ²⁰And blessed be God Most High, who delivered your enemies into your hand."

Then Abram gave him a tenth of everything. (+Ge 14:22)

Ge 24:3 I want you to swear by the LORD, the God of heaven and the God of earth, that you will not get a wife for my son from the daughters of the Canaanites, among whom I am living, (+Ex 19:5)

Dt 4:39 Acknowledge and take to heart this day that the LORD is God in heaven above and on the earth below. There is no other.

Dt 10:14 To the LORD your God belong the heavens, even the highest heavens, the earth and everything in it.

Dt 10:17 For the LORD your God is God of gods and Lord of lords, the great God, mighty and awesome, who shows no partiality and accepts no bribes.

Jos 2:11 When we heard of it, our hearts melted and everyone's courage failed because of you, for the LORD your God is God in heaven above and on the earth below.

2Ki 19:15 And Hezekiah prayed to the LORD: "O LORD, God of Israel, enthroned between the cherubim, you alone are God over all the kingdoms of the earth. You have made heaven and earth.

1Ch 29:11 Yours, O LORD, is the greatness and the power and the glory and the majesty and the splendor, for everything in heaven and earth is yours. Yours, O LORD, is the kingdom; you are exalted as head over all. ¹²Wealth and honor come from you; you are the ruler of all things. In your hands are strength and power to exalt and give strength to all.

Ne 9:6 You alone are the LORD. You made the heavens, even the highest heavens, and all their starry host, the earth and all that is on it, the seas and all that is in them. You give life to everything, and the multitudes of heaven worship you.

Ps 89:11 The heavens are yours, and yours also the earth; you founded the world and all that is in it.

Ps 135:5 I know that the LORD is great, that our Lord is greater than all gods. ⁶The LORD does whatever pleases him, in the heavens and on the earth, in the seas and all their depths.

Mt 6:10 your kingdom come, your will be done on earth as it is in heaven.

Mt 11:25 At that time Jesus said, "I praise you, Father, Lord of heaven and earth, because you have hidden these things from the wise and learned, and revealed them to little children. (+Lk 10:21)

Ac 17:24 "The God who made the world and everything in it is the Lord of heaven and earth and does not live in temples built by hands. ²⁵And he is not served by human hands, as if he needed anything, because he himself gives all men life and breath and everything else. ²⁶From one man he made every nation of men, that they should inhabit the whole earth; and he determined the times set for them and the exact places where they should live.

Rev 11:4 These are the two olive trees and the two lampstands that stand before the Lord of the earth.

Rev 11:13 At that very hour there was a severe earthquake and a tenth of the city collapsed. Seven thousand people were killed in the earthquake, and the survivors were terrified and gave glory to the God of heaven.

Rev 11:17 saying: "We give thanks to you, Lord God Almighty, the One who is and who was, because you have taken your great power and have begun to reign.

Over the spirits of all mankind—

Nu 27:16 "May the LORD, the God of the spirits of all mankind, appoint a man over this community

Dt 32:39 "See now that I myself am He! There is no god besides me. I put to death and I bring to life, I have wounded and I will heal, and no one can deliver out of my hand.

Job 12:9 Which of all these does not know that the hand of the LORD has done this? ¹⁰In his hand is the life of every creature and the breath of all mankind.

Job 12:16 To him belong strength and victory; both deceived and deceiver are his. ¹⁷He leads counselors away stripped and makes fools of judges.

Ps 22:28 for dominion belongs to the LORD and he rules over the nations.

²⁹All the rich of the earth will feast and worship; all who go down to the dust will kneel before him—those who cannot keep themselves alive.

Ecc 9:1 So I reflected on all this and concluded that the righteous and the wise and what they do are in God's hands, but no man knows whether love or hate awaits him.

Isa 45:23 By myself I have sworn, my mouth has uttered in all integrity a word that will not be revoked: Before me every knee will bow; by me every tongue will swear. (+Jer 18:1-5)

Jer 18:6 "O house of Israel, can I not do with you as this potter does?" declares the LORD. "Like clay in the hand of the potter, so are you in my hand, O house of Israel. (+Jer 18:7-23)

Eze 18:4 For every living soul belongs to me, the father as well as the son—both alike belong to me. The soul who sins is the one who will die.

Ro 14:11 It is written: "'As surely as I live,' says the Lord, 'every knee will bow before me; every tongue will confess to God.'"

Sovereign in human affairs—

Ps 75:6 No one from the east or the west or from the desert can exalt a man. **⁷**But it is God who judges: He brings one down, he exalts another.

Jer 27:5 With my great power and outstretched arm I made the earth and its people and the animals that are on it, and I give it to anyone I please. **⁶**Now I will hand all your countries over to my servant Nebuchadnezzar king of Babylon; I will make even the wild animals subject to him. (+Jer 27:7; 32:27-28)

Eze 16:50 They were haughty and did detestable things before me. Therefore I did away with them as you have seen.

Eze 17:24 All the trees of the field will know that I the LORD bring down the tall tree and make the low tree grow tall. I dry up the green tree and make the dry tree flourish. "'I the LORD have spoken, and I will do it.'"

Da 2:20 and said: "Praise be to the name of God for ever and ever; wisdom and power are his. **²¹**He changes times and seasons; he sets up kings and deposes them. He gives wisdom to the wise and knowledge to the discerning.

Da 2:47 The king said to Daniel, "Surely your God is the God of gods and the Lord of kings and a revealer of mysteries, for you were able to reveal this mystery."

Da 4:3 How great are his signs, how mighty his wonders! His kingdom is an eternal kingdom; his dominion endures from generation to generation.

Da 4:17 "'The decision is announced by messengers, the holy ones declare the verdict, so that the living may know that the Most High is sovereign over the kingdoms of men and gives them to anyone he wishes and sets over them the lowliest of men.'

Da 4:25 You will be driven away from people and will live with the wild animals; you will eat grass like cattle and be drenched with the dew of heaven. Seven times will pass by for you until you acknowledge that the Most High is sovereign over the kingdoms of men and gives them to anyone he wishes. (+Da 4:34)

Da 4:35 All the peoples of the earth are regarded as nothing. He does as he pleases with the powers of heaven and the peoples of the earth. No one can hold back his hand or say to him: "What have you done?"

Da 4:37 Now I, Nebuchadnezzar, praise and exalt and glorify the King of heaven, because everything he does is right and all his ways are just. And those who walk in pride he is able to humble.

Da 5:18 "O king, the Most High God gave your father Nebuchadnezzar sovereignty and greatness and glory and splendor.

Da 5:26 "This is what these words mean: *Mene*: God has numbered the days of your reign and brought it to an end. **²⁷***Tekel*: You have been weighed on the scales and found wanting. **²⁸***Peres*: Your kingdom is divided and given to the Medes and Persians."

Everlasting—

Ex 15:18 The LORD will reign for ever and ever."

Ps 10:16 The LORD is King for ever and ever; the nations will perish from his land.

Ps 29:10 The LORD sits enthroned over the flood; the LORD is enthroned as King forever.

Ps 66:7 He rules forever by his power, his eyes watch the nations—let not the rebellious rise up against him. *Selah*

Ps 145:11 They will tell of the glory of your kingdom and speak of your might, **¹²**so that all men may know of your mighty acts and the glorious splendor of your kingdom. **¹³**Your kingdom is an everlasting kingdom, and your dominion endures through all generations. The LORD is

faithful to all his promises and loving toward all he has made.

Ps 146:10 The LORD reigns forever, your God, O Zion, for all generations. Praise the LORD.

La 5:19 You, O LORD, reign forever; your throne endures from generation to generation.

Da 6:26 "I issue a decree that in every part of my kingdom people must fear and reverence the God of Daniel. "For he is the living God and he endures forever; his kingdom will not be destroyed, his dominion will never end.

Spirit:

Jn 4:24 God is spirit, and his worshipers must worship in spirit and in truth." (+Ac 17:29) *See Holy Spirit.*

Teacher:

(Job 36:22; Ps 94:10,12; 119:135,171; Isa 28:26; 54:13; Jn 6:45; 1Th 4:9).

Truth: (Ge 24:27; Ex 34:6)

Nu 23:19 God is not a man, that he should lie, nor a son of man, that he should change his mind. Does he speak and then not act? Does he promise and not fulfill?

1Sa 15:29 He who is the Glory of Israel does not lie or change his mind; for he is not a man, that he should change his mind."

Ps 25:10 All the ways of the LORD are loving and faithful for those who keep the demands of his covenant.

Ps 31:5 Into your hands I commit my spirit; redeem me, O LORD, the God of truth.

Ps 33:4 For the word of the LORD is right and true; he is faithful in all he does.

Ps 43:3 Send forth your light and your truth, let them guide me; let them bring me to your holy mountain, to the place where you dwell.

Ps 57:3 He sends from heaven and saves me, rebuking those who hotly pursue me; *Selah* God sends his love and his faithfulness.

Ps 57:10 For great is your love, reaching to the heavens; your faithfulness reaches to the skies.

Ps 71:22 I will praise you with the harp for your faithfulness, O my God; I will sing praise to you with the lyre, O Holy One of Israel.

Ps 86:11 Teach me your way, O LORD, and I will walk in your truth; give me an undivided heart, that I may fear your name.

Ps 86:15 But you, O Lord, are a compassionate and gracious God, slow to anger, abounding in love and faithfulness.

Ps 89:14 Righteousness and justice are the foundation of your throne; love and faithfulness go before you.

Ps 108:4 For great is your love, higher than the heavens; your faithfulness reaches to the skies.

Ps 132:11 The LORD swore an oath to David, a sure oath that he will not revoke: "One of your own descendants I will place on your throne—

Ps 138:2 I will bow down toward your holy temple and will praise your name for your love and your faithfulness, for you have exalted above all things your name and your word.

Isa 25:1 O LORD, you are my God; I will exalt you and praise your name, for in perfect faithfulness you have done marvelous things, things planned long ago.

Isa 65:16 Whoever invokes a blessing in the land will do so by the God of truth; he who takes an oath in the land will swear by the God of truth. For the past troubles will be forgotten and hidden from my eyes.

Da 4:37 Now I, Nebuchadnezzar, praise and exalt and

glorify the King of heaven, because everything he does is right and all his ways are just. And those who walk in pride he is able to humble.

Jn 8:26 "I have much to say in judgment of you. But he who sent me is reliable, and what I have heard from him I tell the world."

Ro 3:4 Not at all! Let God be true, and every man a liar. As it is written: "So that you may be proved right when you speak and prevail when you judge."

Ro 3:7 Someone might argue, "If my falsehood enhances God's truthfulness and so increases his glory, why am I still condemned as a sinner?"

Tit 1:2 a faith and knowledge resting on the hope of eternal life, which God, who does not lie, promised before the beginning of time,

Rev 6:10 They called out in a loud voice, "How long, Sovereign Lord, holy and true, until you judge the inhabitants of the earth and avenge our blood?"

Rev 15:3 and sang the song of Moses the servant of God and the song of the Lamb: "Great and marvelous are your deeds, Lord God Almighty. Just and true are your ways, King of the ages.

Endures to all generations—

Ps 117:2 For great is his love toward us, and the faithfulness of the LORD endures forever. Praise the LORD.

Ps 146:6 the Maker of heaven and earth, the sea, and everything in them—the LORD, who remains faithful forever.

Ubiquitous: *See above, Omnipresent.*

Unchangeable: *See above, Immutable.*

Unity of: (Dt 4:35)

Dt 6:4 Hear, O Israel: The LORD our God, the LORD is one. (+2Sa 7:22)

Isa 42:8 "I am the LORD; that is my name! I will not give my glory to another or my praise to idols.

Taught by Jesus—

Mk 12:29 "The most important one," answered Jesus, "is this: 'Hear, O Israel, the Lord our God, the Lord is one.

Mk 12:32 "Well said, teacher," the man replied. "You are right in saying that God is one and there is no other but him.

Jn 17:3 Now this is eternal life: that they may know you, the only true God, and Jesus Christ, whom you have sent.

Taught by Paul—

1Co 8:4 So then, about eating food sacrificed to idols: We know that an idol is nothing at all in the world and that there is no God but one.

1Co 8:6 yet for us there is but one God, the Father, from whom all things came and for whom we live; and there is but one Lord, Jesus Christ, through whom all things came and through whom we live.

Gal 3:20 A mediator, however, does not represent just one party; but God is one. (+Eph 4:6)

1Ti 2:5 For there is one God and one mediator between God and men, the man Christ Jesus,

Disbelieved in by Syrians—

1Ki 20:28 The man of God came up and told the king of Israel, "This is what the LORD says: 'Because the Arameans think the LORD is a god of the hills and not a god of the valleys, I will deliver this vast army into your hands, and you will know that I am the LORD.'"

Believed in by demons—

Jas 2:19 You believe that there is one God. Good! Even the demons believe that—and shudder.

Unsearchable:

Dt 29:29 The secret things belong to the LORD our God, but the things revealed belong to us and to our children forever, that we may follow all the words of this law.

Job 5:8 "But if it were I, I would appeal to God; I would lay my cause before him. ⁹He performs wonders that cannot be fathomed, miracles that cannot be counted. (+Job 9:10)

Job 11:7 "Can you fathom the mysteries of God? Can you probe the limits of the Almighty? ⁸They are higher than the heavens—what can you do? They are deeper than the depths of the grave—what can you know? ⁹Their measure is longer than the earth and wider than the sea.

Job 26:9 He covers the face of the full moon, spreading his clouds over it.

Job 26:14 And these are but the outer fringe of his works; how faint the whisper we hear of him! Who then can understand the thunder of his power?"

Job 36:26 How great is God—beyond our understanding! The number of his years is past finding out.

Job 37:5 God's voice thunders in marvelous ways; he does great things beyond our understanding.

Job 37:23 The Almighty is beyond our reach and exalted in power; in his justice and great righteousness, he does not oppress.

Ps 77:19 Your path led through the sea, your way through the mighty waters, though your footprints were not seen.

Ps 139:6 Such knowledge is too wonderful for me, too lofty for me to attain.

Ps 145:3 Great is the LORD and most worthy of praise; his greatness no one can fathom.

Pr 30:4 Who has gone up to heaven and come down? Who has gathered up the wind in the hollow of his hands? Who has wrapped up the waters in his cloak? Who has established all the ends of the earth? What is his name, and the name of his son? Tell me if you know!

Ecc 3:11 He has made everything beautiful in its time. He has also set eternity in the hearts of men; yet they cannot fathom what God has done from beginning to end.

Ecc 11:5 As you do not know the path of the wind, or how the body is formed in a mother's womb, so you cannot understand the work of God, the Maker of all things.

Isa 40:28 Do you not know? Have you not heard? The LORD is the everlasting God, the Creator of the ends of the earth. He will not grow tired or weary, and his understanding no one can fathom.

Isa 45:15 Truly you are a God who hides himself, O God and Savior of Israel.

Isa 55:8 "For my thoughts are not your thoughts, neither are your ways my ways," declares the LORD. ⁹"As the heavens are higher than the earth, so are my ways higher than your ways and my thoughts than your thoughts.

Ro 11:33 Oh, the depth of the riches of the wisdom and knowledge of God! How unsearchable his judgments, and his paths beyond tracing out! ³⁴"Who has known the mind of the Lord? Or who has been his counselor?"

1Co 2:10 but God has revealed it to us by his Spirit. The Spirit searches all things, even the deep things of God.

¹¹For who among men knows the thoughts of a man except the man's spirit within him? In the same way no one knows the thoughts of God except the Spirit of God. (+1Co 2:16)

Symbolized by darkness (Ex 20:21; Dt 4:11; 5:22; 1Ki 8:12; Ps 18:11)—

Ps 97:2 Clouds and thick darkness surround him; righteousness and justice are the foundation of his throne.

By the cloud upon the atonement cover (Lev 16:2).

Name of, secret—

Jdg 13:18 He replied, "Why do you ask my name? It is beyond understanding."

Dwells in thick darkness—

1Ki 8:12 Then Solomon said, "The LORD has said that he would dwell in a dark cloud; (+Ps 97:2)

Known only to Christ, and to those to whom Christ reveals him—

Mt 11:27 "All things have been committed to me by my Father. No one knows the Son except the Father, and no one knows the Father except the Son and those to whom the Son chooses to reveal him.

See Mysteries.

Voice of: *See Anthropomorphisms.*

Wisdom of:

Ezr 7:25 And you, Ezra, in accordance with the wisdom of your God, which you possess, appoint magistrates and judges to administer justice to all the people of Trans-Euphrates—all who know the laws of your God. And you are to teach any who do not know them.

Job 9:4 His wisdom is profound, his power is vast. Who has resisted him and come out unscathed?

Job 12:13 "To God belong wisdom and power; counsel and understanding are his.

Job 12:16 To him belong strength and victory; both deceived and deceiver are his.

Isa 31:2 Yet he too is wise and can bring disaster; he does not take back his words. He will rise up against the house of the wicked, against those who help evildoers.

Da 2:20 and said: "Praise be to the name of God for ever and ever; wisdom and power are his. 21He changes times and seasons; he sets up kings and deposes them. He gives wisdom to the wise and knowledge to the discerning. 22He reveals deep and hidden things; he knows what lies in darkness, and light dwells with him.

Da 2:28 but there is a God in heaven who reveals mysteries. He has shown King Nebuchadnezzar what will happen in days to come. Your dream and the visions that passed through your mind as you lay on your bed are these: (+Ro 11:33)

Ro 16:27 to the only wise God be glory forever through Jesus Christ! Amen.

1Co 1:24 but to those whom God has called, both Jews and Greeks, Christ the power of God and the wisdom of God. 25For the foolishness of God is wiser than man's wisdom, and the weakness of God is stronger than man's strength.

Infinite—

Ps 147:5 Great is our Lord and mighty in power; his understanding has no limit.

Manifold—

Eph 3:10 His intent was that now, through the church, the manifold wisdom of God should be made known to the rulers and authorities in the heavenly realms,

Ascribed by angels—

Rev 7:12 saying: "Amen! Praise and glory and wisdom and thanks and honor and power and strength be to our God for ever and ever. Amen!"

Works made in—

Ps 104:24 How many are your works, O LORD! In wisdom you made them all; the earth is full of your creatures.

Ps 136:5 who by his understanding made the heavens, *His love endures forever.*

Pr 3:19 By wisdom the LORD laid the earth's foundations, by understanding he set the heavens in place; 20by his knowledge the deeps were divided, and the clouds let drop the dew.

Jer 10:12 But God made the earth by his power; he founded the world by his wisdom and stretched out the heavens by his understanding. *See above, Knowledge of.*

Works of:

In creation (Job 9:8-9; Ps 8:3-5; 89:11)—

Ps 136:5 who by his understanding made the heavens, *His love endures forever.* 6who spread out the earth upon the waters, *His love endures forever.* 7who made the great lights—*His love endures forever.* 8the sun to govern the day, *His love endures forever.* 9the moon and stars to govern the night; *His love endures forever.* (+Ps 139:13)

Ps 139:14 I praise you because I am fearfully and wonderfully made; your works are wonderful, I know that full well. (+Ps 148:4-5)

Ecc 3:11 He has made everything beautiful in its time. He has also set eternity in the hearts of men; yet they cannot fathom what God has done from beginning to end. (+Jer 10:12)

Good—

Ge 1:10 God called the dry ground "land," and the gathered waters he called "seas." And God saw that it was good. (+Ge 1:18,21,25)

Faithful—

Ps 33:4 For the word of the LORD is right and true; he is faithful in all he does.

Wonderful (Ps 26:7)—

Ps 40:5 Many, O LORD my God, are the wonders you have done. The things you planned for us no one can recount to you; were I to speak and tell of them, they would be too many to declare.

Incomparable—

Ps 86:8 Among the gods there is none like you, O Lord; no deeds can compare with yours.

In his overruling providence in the human affairs (Ps 26:7; 40:5)—

Ps 66:3 Say to God, "How awesome are your deeds! So great is your power that your enemies cringe before you.

Ps 75:1 We give thanks to you, O God, we give thanks, for your Name is near; men tell of your wonderful deeds.

Ps 111:2 Great are the works of the LORD; they are pondered by all who delight in them.

Ps 111:4 He has caused his wonders to be remembered; the LORD is gracious and compassionate.

Ps 111:6 He has shown his people the power of his works, giving them the lands of other nations.

Ps 118:17 I will not die but live, and will proclaim what the LORD has done. (+Ps 145:4-17) *See Creation.*

GODLESSNESS [2866, 2868, *813, 815, 1013*].
NIV+ See GOD

Described as:

Destitute of the love of God—

Jn 5:42 but I know you. I know that you do not have the love of God in your hearts.

Jn 5:44 How can you believe if you accept praise from one another, yet make no effort to obtain the praise that comes from the only God?

Forgetting God—

Job 8:11 Can papyrus grow tall where there is no marsh? Can reeds thrive without water? 12While still growing and uncut, they wither more quickly than grass. 13Such is the destiny of all who forget God; so perishes the hope of the godless. (+Ps 9:17; 50:22)

Isa 17:10 You have forgotten God your Savior; you have not remembered the Rock, your fortress. Therefore, though you set out the finest plants and plant imported vines,

Jer 2:32 Does a maiden forget her jewelry, a bride her wedding ornaments? Yet my people have forgotten me, days without number.

Ignoring God—

Job 35:10 But no one says, 'Where is God my Maker, who gives songs in the night, (+Ps 28:5; 52:7; 53:2-3; 54:3; 55:19)

Ps 86:14 The arrogant are attacking me, O God; a band of ruthless men seeks my life—men without regard for you. (+Isa 5:12)

Isa 22:11 You built a reservoir between the two walls for the water of the Old Pool, but you did not look to the One who made it, or have regard for the One who planned it long ago.

Isa 30:1 "Woe to the obstinate children," declares the LORD, "to those who carry out plans that are not mine, forming an alliance, but not by my Spirit, heaping sin upon sin;

Isa 31:1 Woe to those who go down to Egypt for help, who rely on horses, who trust in the multitude of their chariots and in the great strength of their horsemen, but do not look to the Holy One of Israel, or seek help from the LORD.

Hos 7:2 but they do not realize that I remember all their evil deeds. Their sins engulf them; they are always before me.

³"They delight the king with their wickedness, the princes with their lies. ⁴They are all adulterers, burning like an oven whose fire the baker need not stir from the kneading of the dough till it rises.

Forsaking God—

Dt 32:15 Jeshurun grew fat and kicked; filled with food, he became heavy and sleek. He abandoned the God who made him and rejected the Rock his Savior.

Despising God—

1Sa 2:30 "Therefore the LORD, the God of Israel, declares: 'I promised that your house and your father's house would minister before me forever.' But now the LORD declares: 'Far be it from me! Those who honor me I will honor, but those who despise me will be disdained. (+Ps 36:1)

Pr 14:2 He whose walk is upright fears the LORD, but he whose ways are devious despises him.

Jn 15:23 He who hates me hates my Father as well. ²⁴If I had not done among them what no one else did, they would not be guilty of sin. But now they have seen these miracles, and yet they have hated both me and my Father. ²⁵But this is to fulfill what is written in their Law: 'They hated me without reason.'

Loving deceit—

Isa 30:9 These are rebellious people, deceitful children, children unwilling to listen to the LORD's instruction. ¹⁰They say to the seers, "See no more visions!" and to the prophets, "Give us no more visions of what is right! Tell us pleasant things, prophesy illusions. ¹¹Leave this way, get off this path, and stop confronting us with the Holy One of Israel!"

Devoid of understanding (Ps 14:2-3; 53:4)—

Isa 1:3 The ox knows his master, the donkey his owner's manger, but Israel does not know, my people do not understand."

Ro 1:21 For although they knew God, they neither glorified him as God nor gave thanks to him, but their thinking became futile and their foolish hearts were darkened. ²²Although they claimed to be wise, they became fools (+Ro 3:11)

Eph 4:18 They are darkened in their understanding and separated from the life of God because of the ignorance that is in them due to the hardening of their hearts.

Rebellious—

Ps 2:2 The kings of the earth take their stand and the rulers gather together against the LORD and against his Anointed One. (+Isa 30:2)

Da 5:23 Instead, you have set yourself up against the Lord of heaven. You had the goblets from his temple brought to you, and you and your nobles, your wives and your concubines drank wine from them. You praised the gods of silver and gold, of bronze, iron, wood and stone, which cannot see or hear or understand. But you did not honor the God who holds in his hand your life and all your ways.

Haters of God—

Dt 7:10 But those who hate him he will repay to their face by destruction; he will not be slow to repay to their face those who hate him.

Enemies of God—

Col 1:21 Once you were alienated from God and were enemies in your minds because of your evil behavior.

Jas 4:4 You adulterous people, don't you know that friendship with the world is hatred toward God? Anyone who chooses to be a friend of the world becomes an enemy of God.

Sinfulness—

Ro 8:6 The mind of sinful man is death, but the mind controlled by the Spirit is life and peace; ⁷the sinful mind is hostile to God. It does not submit to God's law, nor can it do so. ⁸Those controlled by the sinful nature cannot please God.

Impugning God's justice (Eze 33:17-20)—

Mal 2:17 You have wearied the LORD with your words. "How have we wearied him?" you ask. By saying, "All who do evil are good in the eyes of the LORD, and he is pleased with them" or "Where is the God of justice?"

Atheistic; rejecting God (Ps 10:4; 14:1; 53:1)

Willfully sinning—

Heb 10:26 If we deliberately keep on sinning after we have received the knowledge of the truth, no sacrifice for sins is left, ²⁷but only a fearful expectation of judgment and of raging fire that will consume the enemies of God.

See Impenitence; Obduracy; Prayerlessness; Reprobacy; Unbelief; Wicked.

GODLINESS [466, 2883, *2327, 2354, 2356, 2357, 2536+2848, 2536, 2538*]. *See Holiness; Righteousness.*

GODLY *See Righteous.*

GODS [123, 337, 446, 466, 1425, 3942, 9214, 9572, 10033, *1228, 1483, 2536*]. *See Idol; Idolatry; Image.*

GOG [1573, *1223*] (*precious golden object*).

1. A Reubenite (1Ch 5:4).

2. A Scythian prince. Prophecy against (Eze 38; 39; Rev 20:8).

GOIIM [1582] (*nations, Gentiles*).

A people who, led by King Tidal, along with three Eastern kings, Amraphel king of Shinar, Arioch king of Ellasar, and Kedorlaomer king of Elam, went to war against Bera king of Sodom, Birsha king of Gomorrah, Shinab king of Admah, Shemeber king of Zeboiim, and the king of Bela (that is, Zoar) (Ge 14:1-2,9). This latter group of kings joined forces in the Valley of Siddim (the Salt Sea, which is the Dead Sea) (Ge 14:3).

The Goiim may have been non-Semitic tribes who lived to the N. They have been identified with the Hittites because of the resemblance of the name Tidal to the royal Hittite name Tudhaliash, and less reasonably to the Guti (in NE Mesopotamia). Goiim may be the generic Hebrew term for "nations." *See Goyim.*

GOLAN
[1584]. A town in Bashan. Given to Manasseh as a city of refuge (Dt 4:43; Jos 20:8). A Levitical city (Jos 21:27; 1Ch 6:71). *See Gaulanitis.*

GOLD
[234, 1309, 2298, 3021, 4188+, 6034, 7058, 10160, *5991, 5992, 5993, 5996*].

NIV+ GOLD-COVERED, GOLDEN, GOLDSMITH, GOLDSMITHS

Exported from Havilah (Ge 2:11-12). From Ophir (1Ki 9:28; 10:11; 1Ch 29:4; 2Ch 8:18; Job 22:24), Tarshish (1Ki 22:48), Parvaim (2Ch 3:6), Sheba (1Ki 10:10; 2Ch 9:9; Ps 72:15), Uphaz (Jer 10:9).

Refined (Job 28:19; 31:24; Pr 8:19; 17:3; 27:21; Zec 13:9; Mal 3:3).

Used in the Arts:

Beaten work (2Ch 9:15), made into wire threads and wrought into embroidered tapestry (Ex 39:3), apparel (Ps 45:9,13), in ornamenting the priests' garments (Ex 39), modeled into forms of fruits (Pr 25:11), into ornaments (Ge 24:22; Ex 3:22; 11:2; 28:11; Nu 31:50-51; SS 1:10; 5:14; Eze 16:17), crowns made of (Ex 25:25; 37:2-11; 39:30; Est 8:15; Ps 21:3; Zec 6:11), lampstands made of, for the tabernacle (Ex 25:31-38; 37:17-24), shields of (1Ki 10:16-17), overlaying with (Ex 25:11,13,24,28; 26:27,29; 30:5; 36:34,36,38; 37:2,4,11,15; 1Ki 6:20-22; 28,30,32,35), beds made of (Est 1:6). Wedge of (Jos 7:21; Isa 13:12).

Used as money (Ge 44:1,8; 1Ch 21:25; Ezr 8:25-28; Isa 13:17; 60:9; Eze 7:19; 28:4; Mt 2:11; 10:9; Ac 3:6; 20:33; 1Pe 1:18). Solomon rich in (1Ki 10:2,14,21).

Vessels and utensils made of, for the tabernacle (Ex 25:26,29,38-39; 37:16), for the temple (1Ch 18:11; 22:14,16; 29:2-7). Altar, lamps, and other articles made of (1Ki 7:49-51; 2Ki 25:15; Jer 52:19; Ezr 8:27; Da 5:3). *See above, Overlaying with.*

Belongs to God (Eze 16:17).

Figurative: (Ecc 12:6; Jer 51:7; La 4:1; 1Co 3:12).

Symbolic: (Da 2:32-45; Rev 21:18,21).

See Goldsmith.

GOLDEN CANDLESTICK *See Lampstand.*

GOLDEN RULE
Mt 7:12 So in everything, do to others what you would have them do to you, for this sums up the Law and the Prophets.

Lk 6:31 Do to others as you would have them do to you.
Lev 19:18 "'Do not seek revenge or bear a grudge against one of your people, but love your neighbor as yourself. I am the LORD. (+Ro 13:9; Gal 5:14)

See Love.

GOLDSMITH
[7671, 7672].

NIV+ See GOLD

(2Ch 2:7,14; Ne 3:8,31-32; Isa 40:19; 41:7; 46:6).

GOLGOTHA
[*1201*] (*skull*). The place of the crucifixion of Christ, located outside of Jerusalem (Mt 27:33; Mk 15:22) on the public road (Jn 19:20).

GOLIATH
[1669] (*exile*). A giant champion of Gath. Defied the armies of Israel and is slain by David (1Sa 17; 21:9; 22:10). His sons (2Sa 21:15-22; 1Ch 20:4-8).

GOMER
[1699, 1700] (*complete*).
1. Son of Japheth (Ge 10:2-3; 1Ch 1:5-6).
2. A people descended from Gomer (Eze 38:6).
3. Wife of Hosea (Hos 1:3).

GOMORRAH
[6686, *1202*] (*to overwhelm with water*). One of the "cities of the plain" (Ge 10:19; 13:10). Its king defeated by Kedorlaomer (Ge 14:2,8-11). Wickedness of (Ge 18:20). Destroyed (Ge 19:24-28; Dt 29:23; 32:32; Isa 1:9-10; 13:19; Jer 23:14; 49:18; 50:40; Am 4:11; Zep 2:9; Mt 10:14-15; Mk 6:11; Lk 9:5; Ro 9:29; 2Pe 2:6; Jude 7). *See Cities of the Plain.*

GONORRHEA
Possibly among the bodily discharges of Lev 15. *See Discharge, Bodily; Disease.*

GOOD AND EVIL
[*1413, 1415, 1694, 3202, 3206, 3208, 3512, 3603, 6694, 8273, 8934, 9459, 19, 16, 20, 604, 746, 2294, 2295, 2306, 2819, 2822, 3421, 4055, 5237, 5239, 5982, 6067; See also EVIL*]. Choice between, by Adam and Eve (Ge 3). Exhortation to choose between (Jos 24:15). Conflict between (Rev 16:13-21). Subjective conflict between (Ro 7:9-25).

GOOD FOR EVIL
Injunctions by Christ concerning—

Mt 5:44 But I tell you: Love your enemies and pray for those who persecute you, 45that you may be sons of your Father in heaven. He causes his sun to rise on the evil and the good, and sends rain on the righteous and the unrighteous. 46If you love those who love you, what reward will you get? Are not even the tax collectors doing that? 47And if you greet only your brothers, what are you doing more than others? Do not even pagans do that? 48Be perfect, therefore, as your heavenly Father is perfect.

Lk 6:27 "But I tell you who hear me: Love your enemies, do good to those who hate you, 28bless those who curse you, pray for those who mistreat you. 29If someone strikes you on one cheek, turn to him the other also. If someone takes your cloak, do not stop him from taking your tunic. 30Give to everyone who asks you, and if anyone takes what belongs to you, do not demand it back. 31Do to others as you would have them do to you.

32"If you love those who love you, what credit is that to you? Even 'sinners' love those who love them. 33And if you do good to those who are good to you, what credit is that to you? Even 'sinners' do that. 34And if you lend to those from whom you expect repayment, what credit is that to you? Even 'sinners' lend to 'sinners,' expecting to be repaid in full. 35But love your enemies, do good to them, and lend to them without expecting to get anything back. Then your reward will be great, and you will be sons of the Most High, because he is kind to the ungrateful and wicked. 36Be merciful, just as your Father is merciful.

Returning:

Instances of: Abraham, to Abimelech (Ge 20:14-18). David, to Saul (1Sa 24:17; 26). Elisha, to the Syrians (2Ki 6:22-23). David, to his enemies (Ps 35:12-14). Jesus, to his crucifiers (Lk 23:34). Stephen (Ac 7:60).

See Golden Rule; Evil for Good; Nonresistance.

GOOD NEWS [1413, 1415, *2294, 2295*]. (Pr 15:30; 25:25). *See Gospel.*

GOPHER WOOD *See Cypress Wood.*

GOSHEN [824+1777, 1777] (*mound of earth*).

1. A district in Egypt especially adapted to herds and flocks. Israelites dwelt in (Ge 45:10; 46:28; 47). Exempted from plagues (Ex 8:22; 9:26).

2. A town and district of Judah (Jos 10:41; 11:16; 15:51).

GOSPEL [*2294, 2295, 4603*] (*good news*). From God (Jn 17:7-8,14; 2Th 2:14). Contrasted with the law (Lk 16:16; Jn 1:16-17; Ac 12:24; 19:20; 2Co 3:6-11). Called the New Covenant (Jer 31:31-34; Heb 7:22; 8:6-13; 9:8-15; 10:9; 12:22-24).

Described as:

Dispensation of grace (Eph 3:2). Doctrine according to godliness (1Ti 6:3). Everlasting gospel or eternal good tidings (Rev 14:6). The faith (Jude 3). Glorious gospel (1Ti 1:11). Pattern of sound teaching (2Ti 1:13). gospel of the glory of Christ (2Co 4:4). Good tidings or good news (Isa 40:9; 41:27; 52:7; 61:1; Mt 11:5; Lk 7:22; Ac 13:32-33; 1Pe 1:25). Gospel, of Christ (Ro 1:16; 1Co 9:12,18; Gal 1:7; Php 1:27; 1Th 3:2), of God (Ro 1:1; 15:16; 1Th 2:8; 1Pe 4:17), of grace of God (Ac 20:24), of Jesus Christ (Mk 1:1), of the kingdom (Mt 4:23; 24:14), of peace (Eph 6:15), of salvation (Eph 1:13). The kingdom of God (Lk 16:16). The law of liberty (Jas 1:25). Ministration of the Spirit (2Co 3:8). Mystery, of Christ (Eph 3:4), of the gospel (Eph 6:19). Power of God (Ro 1:16; 1Co 1:18). Preaching of Jesus Christ (Ro 16:25). Word of Christ (Col 3:16), of faith (Ro 10:8), of God (1Th 2:13; 1Pe 1:23), of life (Php 2:16), of the Lord (1Pe 1:25), of reconciliation (2Co 5:19), of salvation (Ac 13:26), of truth (Eph 1:13). Words of this life (Ac 5:20).

Likened to:

A mustard seed (Mt 13:31-32; Mk 4:30-33; Lk 13:18-19), good seed (Mt 13:24-30,36-43), yeast (Mt 13:33), a pearl of great price (Mt 13:45-46; Lk 13:20-21), a treasure hidden in a field (Mt 13:44), a householder (Mt 20:1-16), a feast (Lk 14:16-24).

Dissemination of (Ac 14:3; 16:17; 20:24), commanded (Mt 24:14; 28:18-20; Mk 13:10; 16:15; Ac 5:20; Ro 10:15-18; 16:25-26; 1Co 1:18,21,24-25; 9:16-18; Eph 3:8-11). Desired by prophets, righteous, kings (Mt 13:17; Lk 23:34). Hid from the lost (2Co 4:3-4). Comes in power, word, assurance (1Th 1:5).

Proclaimed to Abraham (Gal 3:8), by angels (Lk 2:10-11; Rev 14:6). Preached by Jesus (Mt 4:23; Mk 1:14-15), by Peter (Ac 10:36), by Paul (Ac 13:32-33; 20:24; Ro 15:29; 1Co 9:16-18; Gal 2:2; Col 1:5-6,23), to the Gentiles (Gal 2:2; Eph 3:8; Col 1:23,26-29), to both Jews and Gentiles (Ro 1:16; 1Co 1:24), to the poor (Mt 11:4-6; Lk 7:22), to the dead (1Pe 3:19; 4:6), to every nation (Lk 2:10-11; Ro 16:26; Rev 14:6).

Life and immortality brought to light in (2Ti 1:10). Salvation through (Ro 1:16-17; 1Co 15:1-2; Eph 1:13-14; Jas 1:21; 1Pe 1:23).

Prophecies concerning:

Isa 2:3 Many peoples will come and say, "Come, let us go up to the mountain of the LORD, to the house of the God of Jacob. He will teach us his ways, so that we may walk in his paths." The law will go out from Zion, the word of the LORD from Jerusalem. ⁴He will judge between the nations and will settle disputes for many peoples. They will beat their swords into plowshares and their spears into pruning hooks. Nation will not take up sword against nation, nor will they train for war anymore.

⁵Come, O house of Jacob, let us walk in the light of the LORD.

Isa 4:2 In that day the Branch of the LORD will be beautiful and glorious, and the fruit of the land will be the pride and glory of the survivors in Israel. ³Those who are left in Zion, who remain in Jerusalem, will be called holy, all who are recorded among the living in Jerusalem. ⁴The Lord will wash away the filth of the women of Zion; he will cleanse the bloodstains from Jerusalem by a spirit of judgment and a spirit of fire. ⁵Then the LORD will create over all of Mount Zion and over those who assemble there a cloud of smoke by day and a glow of flaming fire by night; over all the glory will be a canopy. ⁶It will be a shelter and shade from the heat of the day, and a refuge and hiding place from the storm and rain.

Isa 9:2 The people walking in darkness have seen a great light; on those living in the land of the shadow of death a light has dawned.

Isa 9:6 For to us a child is born, to us a son is given, and the government will be on his shoulders. And he will be called Wonderful Counselor, Mighty God, Everlasting Father, Prince of Peace. ⁷Of the increase of his government and peace there will be no end. He will reign on David's throne and over his kingdom, establishing and upholding it with justice and righteousness from that time on and forever. The zeal of the LORD Almighty will accomplish this.

Isa 25:7 On this mountain he will destroy the shroud that enfolds all peoples, the sheet that covers all nations; (+Isa 25:8-9)

Isa 29:18 In that day the deaf will hear the words of the scroll, and out of gloom and darkness the eyes of the blind will see.

Isa 29:24 Those who are wayward in spirit will gain understanding; those who complain will accept instruction."

Isa 32:3 Then the eyes of those who see will no longer be closed, and the ears of those who hear will listen. (+Isa 32:4)

Isa 35:5 Then will the eyes of the blind be opened and the ears of the deaf unstopped. (+Isa 35:6-10)

Isa 40:9 You who bring good tidings to Zion, go up on a high mountain. You who bring good tidings to Jerusalem, lift up your voice with a shout, lift it up, do not be afraid; say to the towns of Judah, "Here is your God!"

Isa 41:27 I was the first to tell Zion, 'Look, here they are!' I gave to Jerusalem a messenger of good tidings.

Isa 42:6 "I, the LORD, have called you in righteousness; I will take hold of your hand. I will keep you and will make you to be a covenant for the people and a light for the Gentiles, ⁷to open eyes that are blind, to free captives from prison and to release from the dungeon those who sit in darkness.

Isa 46:13 I am bringing my righteousness near, it is not far away; and my salvation will not be delayed. I will grant salvation to Zion, my splendor to Israel.

Isa 49:13 Shout for joy, O heavens; rejoice, O earth; burst into song, O mountains! For the LORD comforts his people and will have compassion on his afflicted ones.

Isa 51:4 "Listen to me, my people; hear me, my nation: The law will go out from me; my justice will become a light to the nations. ⁵My righteousness draws near speedily, my salvation is on the way, and my arm will bring justice to the nations. The islands will look to me and wait in hope for my arm. **⁶**Lift up your eyes to the heavens, look at the earth beneath; the heavens will vanish like smoke, the earth will wear out like a garment and its inhabitants die like flies. But my salvation will last forever, my righteousness will never fail.

Isa 52:7 How beautiful on the mountains are the feet of those who bring good news, who proclaim peace, who bring good tidings, who proclaim salvation, who say to Zion, "Your God reigns!"

Isa 55:1 "Come, all you who are thirsty, come to the waters; and you who have no money, come, buy and eat! Come, buy wine and milk without money and without cost. **²**Why spend money on what is not bread, and your labor on what does not satisfy? Listen, listen to me, and eat what is good, and your soul will delight in the richest of fare. **³**Give ear and come to me; hear me, that your soul may live. I will make an everlasting covenant with you, my faithful love promised to David. **⁴**See, I have made him a witness to the peoples, a leader and commander of the peoples. **⁵**Surely you will summon nations you know not, and nations that do not know you will hasten to you, because of the LORD your God, the Holy One of Israel, for he has endowed you with splendor." (+Isa 60:1-22; 61:1-3; Jer 31:31-34)

Eze 34:23 I will place over them one shepherd, my servant David, and he will tend them; he will tend them and be their shepherd. **24**I the LORD will be their God, and my servant David will be prince among them. I the LORD have spoken.

25"'I will make a covenant of peace with them and rid the land of wild beasts so that they may live in the desert and sleep in the forests in safety. **26**I will bless them and the places surrounding my hill. I will send down showers in season; there will be showers of blessing. **27**The trees of the field will yield their fruit and the ground will yield its crops; the people will be secure in their land. They will know that I am the LORD, when I break the bars of their yoke and rescue them from the hands of those who enslaved them. **28**They will no longer be plundered by the nations, nor will wild animals devour them. They will live in safety, and no one will make them afraid. **29**I will provide for them a land renowned for its crops, and they will no longer be victims of famine in the land or bear the scorn of the nations. **30**Then they will know that I, the LORD their God, am with them and that they, the house of Israel, are my people, declares the Sovereign LORD. **31**You my sheep, the sheep of my pasture, are people, and I am your God, declares the Sovereign LORD.'" (+Eze 47:1-7)

Eze 47:8 He said to me, "This water flows toward the eastern region and goes down into the Arabah, where it enters the Sea. When it empties into the Sea, the water there becomes fresh. (+Eze 47:9-11)

Eze 47:12 Fruit trees of all kinds will grow on both banks of the river. Their leaves will not wither, nor will their fruit fail. Every month they will bear, because the water from the sanctuary flows to them. Their fruit will serve for food and their leaves for healing."

Joel 2:28 "And afterward, I will pour out my Spirit on all people. Your sons and daughters will prophesy, your old men will dream dreams, your young men will see visions. **29**Even on my servants, both men and women, I will pour out my Spirit in those days. **30**I will show wonders in the heavens and on the earth, blood and fire and billows of smoke. **31**The sun will be turned to darkness and the moon to blood before the coming of the great and dreadful day of

the LORD. **32**And everyone who calls on the name of the LORD will be saved; for on Mount Zion and in Jerusalem there will be deliverance, as the LORD has said, among the survivors whom the LORD calls.

Mic 4:1 In the last days the mountain of the LORD's temple will be established as chief among the mountains; it will be raised above the hills, and peoples will stream to it.

²Many nations will come and say, "Come, let us go up to the mountain of the LORD, to the house of the God of Jacob. He will teach us his ways, so that we may walk in his paths." The law will go out from Zion, the word of the LORD from Jerusalem. **³**He will judge between many peoples and will settle disputes for strong nations far and wide. They will beat their swords into plowshares and their spears into pruning hooks. Nation will not take up sword against nation, nor will they train for war anymore. **⁴**Every man will sit under his own vine and under his own fig tree, and no one will make them afraid, for the LORD Almighty has spoken. **⁵**All the nations may walk in the name of their gods; we will walk in the name of the LORD our God for ever and ever.

⁶"In that day," declares the LORD, "I will gather the lame; I will assemble the exiles and those I have brought to grief. **⁷**I will make the lame a remnant, those driven away a strong nation. The LORD will rule over them in Mount Zion from that day and forever.

Mt 24:14 And this gospel of the kingdom will be preached in the whole world as a testimony to all nations, and then the end will come. (+Lk 1:67-79; 2:12-14,34)

Fulfilled by Christ (Lk 4:18-19).

See Church, The Body of Believers, Prophecies Concerning; Jesus the Christ, Kingdom of, Mission of; Kingdom of God, of Heaven; Synoptic Gospels, The.

GOSSIP   [2143+8215, 8087, *5826, 5827, 6030, 6031*].

NIV+ GOSSIPING, GOSSIPS

Proverbs concerning—

Pr 11:13 A gossip betrays a confidence, but a trustworthy man keeps a secret.

Pr 16:28 A perverse man stirs up dissension, and a gossip separates close friends.

Pr 17:9 He who covers over an offense promotes love, but whoever repeats the matter separates close friends.

Pr 26:20 Without wood a fire goes out; without gossip a quarrel dies down.

Forbidden—

Lev 19:16 "'Do not go about spreading slander among your people. "'Do not do anything that endangers your neighbor's life. I am the LORD.

Ps 50:20 You speak continually against your brother and slander your own mother's son.

Pr 11:3 The integrity of the upright guides them, but the unfaithful are destroyed by their duplicity.

Pr 20:19 A gossip betrays a confidence; so avoid a man who talks too much.

Eze 22:9 In you are slanderous men bent on shedding blood; in you are those who eat at the mountain shrines and commit lewd acts.

See Slander; Speaking, Evil; Talebearer.

GOURD   [7225, 7226].

NIV+ GOURDS

Carvings of decorated the temple (1Ki 6:18) and its cast metal Sea (1Ki 7:24). Elisha purifies stew made with poisonous gourds (2Ki 4:38-41).

GOUT Perhaps Asa's disease in the feet (2Ch 16:12). *See Disease.*

GOVERNMENT [5385, 6269, 10424].

NIV+ GOVERN, GOVERNED, GOVERNING, GOVERNOR, GOVERNOR'S, GOVERNORS, GOVERNS

Paternal functions of (Ge 41:25-57). Civil service school provided by (Da 1:3-20). Maintains a system of public instruction (2Ch 17:7-9).

Constitutional:

It was provided in the law of Moses that in the event of the establishment of a monarchy a copy of the law of Moses should be made and the king should be required to study this law all the days of his life and conform his administration to it (Dt 17:18-20). This constituted the fundamental law and had its likeness to the constitution of modern governments. When David was crowned king of all Israel he made a league in the nature of a constitution which was a basis of good understanding between himself and the people (2Sa 5:3). When Joash was enthroned a covenant was made between him and the people (2Ch 23:3,11). This no doubt refers to the law of Moses (Dt 17:18-20), which had been preserved by Jehoiada, the priest. Zedekiah made a covenant with the people proclaiming liberty (Jer 34:8-11). That the king of the Medes and Persians was restricted by a constitution "which cannot be annulled," is evident from Da 6:12-15.

See Constitution; Israel, Israelites; Judge; Kings; Nation.

Corruption in:

1Ki 21:5 His wife Jezebel came in and asked him, "Why are you so sullen? Why won't you eat?"

[6]He answered her, "Because I said to Naboth the Jezreelite, 'Sell me your vineyard; or if you prefer, I will give you another vineyard in its place.' But he said, 'I will not give you my vineyard.'"

[7]Jezebel his wife said, "Is this how you act as king over Israel? Get up and eat! Cheer up. I'll get you the vineyard of Naboth the Jezreelite."

[8]So she wrote letters in Ahab's name, placed his seal on them, and sent them to the elders and nobles who lived in Naboth's city with him. [9]In those letters she wrote:

"Proclaim a day of fasting and seat Naboth in a prominent place among the people. [10]But seat two scoundrels opposite him and have them testify that he has cursed both God and the king. Then take him out and stone him to death."

[11]So the elders and nobles who lived in Naboth's city did as Jezebel directed in the letters she had written to them. [12]They proclaimed a fast and seated Naboth in a prominent place among the people. [13]Then two scoundrels came and sat opposite him and brought charges against Naboth before the people, saying, "Naboth has cursed both God and the king." So they took him outside the city and stoned him to death.

Pr 25:5 remove the wicked from the king's presence, and his throne will be established through righteousness.

Mic 3:1 Then I said, "Listen, you leaders of Jacob, you rulers of the house of Israel. Should you not know justice, [2]you who hate good and love evil; who tear the skin from my people and the flesh from their bones; [3]who eat my people's flesh, strip off their skin and break their bones in pieces; who chop them up like meat for the pan, like flesh for the pot?"

[4]Then they will cry out to the LORD, but he will not answer them. At that time he will hide his face from them because of the evil they have done.

Mic 3:9 Hear this, you leaders of the house of Jacob, you rulers of the house of Israel, who despise justice and distort all that is right; [10]who build Zion with bloodshed, and Jerusalem with wickedness. [11]Her leaders judge for a bribe, her priests teach for a price, and her prophets tell fortunes for money. Yet they lean upon the LORD and say, "Is not the LORD among us? No disaster will come upon us."

Instances of Corruption in:

Pilate, in delivering Jesus to death to please the noisy crowd (Mt 27:24; Jn 19:12-16). Felix, who hoped for money from Paul (Ac 24:26).

See Court, Of Law, Corrupt; Church, The Body of Believers, Evil Conditions of; Corrupt; Rulers, Wicked.

Duty of Citizens to:

To pay taxes—

Mt 22:17 Tell us then, what is your opinion? Is it right to pay taxes to Caesar or not?"

[18]But Jesus, knowing their evil intent, said, "You hypocrites, why are you trying to trap me? [19]Show me the coin used for paying the tax." They brought him a denarius, [20]and he asked them, "Whose portrait is this? And whose inscription?"

[21]"Caesar's," they replied.

Then he said to them, "Give to Caesar what is Caesar's, and to God what is God's." (+Lk 20:22-25)

To render obedience to civil authority—

Ro 13:1 Everyone must submit himself to the governing authorities, for there is no authority except that which God has established. The authorities that exist have been established by God. [2]Consequently, he who rebels against the authority is rebelling against what God has instituted, and those who do so will bring judgment on themselves. [3]For rulers hold no terror for those who do right, but for those who do wrong. Do you want to be free from fear of the one in authority? Then do what is right and he will commend you. [4]For he is God's servant to do you good. But if you do wrong, be afraid, for he does not bear the sword for nothing. He is God's servant, an agent of wrath to bring punishment on the wrongdoer. [5]Therefore, it is necessary to submit to the authorities, not only because of possible punishment but also because of conscience.

[6]This is also why you pay taxes, for the authorities are God's servants, who give their full time to governing. [7]Give everyone what you owe him: If you owe taxes, pay taxes; if revenue, then revenue; if respect, then respect; if honor, then honor.

Tit 3:1 Remind the people to be subject to rulers and authorities, to be obedient, to be ready to do whatever is good,

1Pe 2:13 Submit yourselves for the Lord's sake to every authority instituted among men: whether to the king, as the supreme authority, [14]or to governors, who are sent by him to punish those who do wrong and to commend those who do right. [15]For it is God's will that by doing good you should silence the ignorant talk of foolish men. [16]Live as free men, but do not use your freedom as a cover-up for evil; live as servants of God. [17]Show proper respect to everyone: Love the brotherhood of believers, fear God, honor the king.

God in:

(2Ch 22:7; Jer 18:6; Eze 21:25-27; 29:19-20). In appointment of Saul as king (1Sa 9:15-17; 10:1). In Saul's rejection (1Sa 15:26-28; Ac 13:22). In appointment of David (1Sa 16:1,7,13; 2Sa 7:13-16; Ps 89:19-37; Ac 13:22), of Solomon (1Ki 2:13-15). In counseling Solomon (1Ki 9:2-9). In magnifying Solomon (1Ch 29:25). In reproving Solomon's wickedness (1Ki 11:9-13). In raising adversaries against Solomon (1Ki 11:14,23). In tearing the nation of Israel in two (1Ki 11:13; 12:1-24; 2Ch 10:15; 11:4). In blotting out the house of Jeroboam (1Ki 14:7-16; 15:27-30). In appointment of kings (1Ki 14:14; 16:1-2; 1Ch 28:4-5; Da 2:20-21,37; 4:17; 5:18-23). In destruction of nations (Jer 25:12-17; Am 9:8; Hag 2:22).

Relation of God to—

Ps 22:28 for dominion belongs to the LORD and he rules over the nations.

Pr 8:15 By me kings reign and rulers make laws that are just; **16**by me princes govern, and all nobles who rule on earth.

Isa 9:6 For to us a child is born, to us a son is given, and the government will be on his shoulders. And he will be called Wonderful Counselor, Mighty God, Everlasting Father, Prince of Peace. **7**Of the increase of his government and peace there will be no end. He will reign on David's throne and over his kingdom, establishing and upholding it with justice and righteousness from that time on and forever. The zeal of the LORD Almighty will accomplish this.

Jer 1:9 Then the LORD reached out his hand and touched my mouth and said to me, "Now, I have put my words in your mouth. **10**See, today I appoint you over nations and kingdoms to uproot and tear down, to destroy and overthrow, to build and to plant."

Jer 18:6 "O house of Israel, can I not do with you as this potter does?" declares the LORD. "Like clay in the hand of the potter, so are you in my hand, O house of Israel. **7**If at any time I announce that a nation or kingdom is to be uprooted, torn down and destroyed, **8**and if that nation I warned repents of its evil, then I will relent and not inflict on it the disaster I had planned. **9**And if at another time I announce that a nation or kingdom is to be built up and planted, **10**and if it does evil in my sight and does not obey me, then I will reconsider the good I had intended to do for it.

Jer 25:12 "But when the seventy years are fulfilled, I will punish the king of Babylon and his nation, the land of the Babylonians, for their guilt," declares the LORD, "and will make it desolate forever. **13**I will bring upon that land all the things I have spoken against it, all that are written in this book and prophesied by Jeremiah against all the nations. **14**They themselves will be enslaved by many nations and great kings; I will repay them according to their deeds and the work of their hands."

15This is what the LORD, the God of Israel, said to me: "Take from my hand this cup filled with the wine of my wrath and make all the nations to whom I send you drink it. **16**When they drink it, they will stagger and go mad because of the sword I will send among them."

17So I took the cup from the LORD's hand and made all the nations to whom he sent me drink it:

Eze 21:25 "'O profane and wicked prince of Israel, whose day has come, whose time of punishment has reached its climax, **26**this is what the Sovereign LORD says: Take off the turban, remove the crown. It will not be as it was: The lowly will be exalted and the exalted will be brought low. **27**A ruin! A ruin! I will make it a ruin! It will not be restored until he comes to whom it rightfully belongs; to him I will give it.'

Eze 29:19 Therefore this is what the Sovereign LORD says: I am going to give Egypt to Nebuchadnezzar king of Babylon, and he will carry off its wealth. He will loot and plunder the land as pay for his army. **20**I have given him Egypt as a reward for his efforts because he and his army did it for me, declares the Sovereign LORD.

Da 2:20 and said: "Praise be to the name of God for ever and ever; wisdom and power are his. **21**He changes times and seasons; he sets up kings and deposes them. He gives wisdom to the wise and knowledge to the discerning.

Da 2:37 You, O king, are the king of kings. The God of heaven has given you dominion and power and might and glory;

Da 4:17 "'The decision is announced by messengers, the holy ones declare the verdict, so that the living may know that the Most High is sovereign over the kingdoms of men and gives them to anyone he wishes and sets over them the lowliest of men.'

Da 5:18 "O king, the Most High God gave your father Nebuchadnezzar sovereignty and greatness and glory and splendor. **19**Because of the high position he gave him, all the peoples and nations and men of every language dreaded and feared him. Those the king wanted to put to death, he put to death; those he wanted to spare, he spared; those he wanted to promote, he promoted; and those he wanted to humble, he humbled. **20**But when his heart became arrogant and hardened with pride, he was deposed from his royal throne and stripped of his glory. **21**He was driven away from people and given the mind of an animal; he lived with the wild donkeys and ate grass like cattle; and his body was drenched with the dew of heaven, until he acknowledged that the Most High God is sovereign over the kingdoms of men and sets over them anyone he wishes.

22"But you his son, O Belshazzar, have not humbled yourself, though you knew all this. **23**Instead, you have set yourself up against the Lord of heaven. You had the goblets from his temple brought to you, and you and your nobles, your wives and your concubines drank wine from them. You praised the gods of silver and gold, of bronze, iron, wood and stone, which cannot see or hear or understand. But you did not honor the God who holds in his hand your life and all your ways. **24**Therefore he sent the hand that wrote the inscription.

25"This is the inscription that was written: MENE, MENE, TEKEL, PARSIN

26"This is what these words mean: *Mene*: God has numbered the days of your reign and brought it to an end. **27***Tekel*: You have been weighed on the scales and found wanting. **28***Peres*: Your kingdom is divided and given to the Medes and Persians."

Da 10:13 But the prince of the Persian kingdom resisted me twenty-one days. Then Michael, one of the chief princes, came to help me, because I was detained there with the king of Persia.

Hos 8:4 They set up kings without my consent; they choose princes without my approval. With their silver and gold they make idols for themselves to their own destruction.

Am 9:8 "Surely the eyes of the Sovereign LORD are on the sinful kingdom. I will destroy it from the face of the earth—yet I will not totally destroy the house of Jacob," declares the LORD.

Hag 2:21 "Tell Zerubbabel governor of Judah that I will shake the heavens and the earth. **22**I will overturn royal thrones and shatter the power of the foreign kingdoms. I will overthrow chariots and their drivers; horses and their riders will fall, each by the sword of his brother.

Jn 19:10 "Do you refuse to speak to me?" Pilate said. "Don't you realize I have power either to free you or to crucify you?"

[11]Jesus answered, "You would have no power over me if it were not given to you from above. Therefore the one who handed me over to you is guilty of a greater sin."

See God, Sovereign; Jesus the Christ, Kingdom of.

Mosaic:

Administrative and judicial system—

Ex 18:13 The next day Moses took his seat to serve as judge for the people, and they stood around him from morning till evening. [14]When his father-in-law saw all that Moses was doing for the people, he said, "What is this you are doing for the people? Why do you alone sit as judge, while all these people stand around you from morning till evening?"

[15]Moses answered him, "Because the people come to me to seek God's will. [16]Whenever they have a dispute, it is brought to me, and I decide between the parties and inform them of God's decrees and laws."

[17]Moses' father-in-law replied, "What you are doing is not good. [18]You and these people who come to you will only wear yourselves out. The work is too heavy for you; you cannot handle it alone. [19]Listen now to me and I will give you some advice, and may God be with you. You must be the people's representative before God and bring their disputes to him. [20]Teach them the decrees and laws, and show them the way to live and the duties they are to perform. [21]But select capable men from all the people—men who fear God, trustworthy men who hate dishonest gain—and appoint them as officials over thousands, hundreds, fifties and tens. [22]Have them serve as judges for the people at all times, but have them bring every difficult case to you; the simple cases they can decide themselves. That will make your load lighter, because they will share it with you. [23]If you do this and God so commands, you will be able to stand the strain, and all these people will go home satisfied."

[24]Moses listened to his father-in-law and did everything he said. [25]He chose capable men from all Israel and made them leaders of the people, officials over thousands, hundreds, fifties and tens. [26]They served as judges for the people at all times. The difficult cases they brought to Moses, but the simple ones they decided themselves.

Nu 11:16 The LORD said to Moses: "Bring me seventy of Israel's elders who are known to you as leaders and officials among the people. Have them come to the Tent of Meeting, that they may stand there with you. [17]I will come down and speak with you there, and I will take of the Spirit that is on you and put the Spirit on them. They will help you carry the burden of the people so that you will not have to carry it alone.

Nu 11:24 So Moses went out and told the people what the LORD had said. He brought together seventy of their elders and had them stand around the Tent. [25]Then the LORD came down in the cloud and spoke with him, and he took of the Spirit that was on him and put the Spirit on the seventy elders. When the Spirit rested on them, they prophesied, but they did not do so again.

Dt 1:9 At that time I said to you, "You are too heavy a burden for me to carry alone. [10]The LORD your God has increased your numbers so that today you are as many as the stars in the sky. [11]May the LORD, the God of your fathers, increase you a thousand times and bless you as he

has promised! [12]But how can I bear your problems and your burdens and your disputes all by myself? [13]Choose some wise, understanding and respected men from each of your tribes, and I will set them over you."

[14]You answered me, "What you propose to do is good."

[15]So I took the leading men of your tribes, wise and respected men, and appointed them to have authority over you—as commanders of thousands, of hundreds, of fifties and of tens and as tribal officials. [16]And I charged your judges at that time: Hear the disputes between your brothers and judge fairly, whether the case is between brother Israelites or between one of them and an alien. [17]Do not show partiality in judging; hear both small and great alike. Do not be afraid of any man, for judgment belongs to God. Bring me any case too hard for you, and I will hear it.

Popular Government, by a National Assembly, or Its Representatives:

Accepted the law given by Moses (Ex 19:7-8; 24:3,7; Dt 29:10-15). Refused to make conquest of Canaan (Nu 14:1-10). Chose, or ratified, the chief ruler (1Sa 10:24; 8:4-22; 11:14-15; 2Sa 3:17-21; 5:1-3; 1Ch 29:22; 2Ch 23:3). Possessed veto power over king's purposes (1Sa 14:44-45). Constituted the court in certain capital cases (Nu 35:12,24-25).

Delegated, Council of Elders:

Closely associated with Moses and subsequent leaders—

Ex 3:16 "Go, assemble the elders of Israel and say to them, 'The LORD, the God of your fathers—the God of Abraham, Isaac and Jacob—appeared to me and said: I have watched over you and have seen what has been done to you in Egypt.

Ex 3:18 "The elders of Israel will listen to you. Then you and the elders are to go to the king of Egypt and say to him, 'The LORD, the God of the Hebrews, has met with us. Let us take a three-day journey into the desert to offer sacrifices to the LORD our God.'

Ex 4:29 Moses and Aaron brought together all the elders of the Israelites, [30]and Aaron told them everything the LORD had said to Moses. He also performed the signs before the people, [31]and they believed. And when they heard that the LORD was concerned about them and had seen their misery, they bowed down and worshiped. (+Ex 12:21; 17:5-6; 18:12)

Ex 19:7 So Moses went back and summoned the elders of the people and set before them all the words the LORD had commanded him to speak. [8]The people all responded together, "We will do everything the LORD has said." So Moses brought their answer back to the LORD.

Ex 24:1 Then he said to Moses, "Come up to the LORD, you and Aaron, Nadab and Abihu, and seventy of the elders of Israel. You are to worship at a distance,

Ex 24:14 He said to the elders, "Wait here for us until we come back to you. Aaron and Hur are with you, and anyone involved in a dispute can go to them."

Lev 4:15 The elders of the community are to lay their hands on the bull's head before the LORD, and the bull shall be slaughtered before the LORD. (+Lev 9:1)

Nu 11:16 The LORD said to Moses: "Bring me seventy of Israel's elders who are known to you as leaders and officials among the people. Have them come to the Tent of Meeting, that they may stand there with you. [17]I will come down and speak with you there, and I will take of the Spirit that is on you and put the Spirit on them. They will help you carry the burden of the people so that you will not have to carry it alone.

Nu 11:30 Then Moses and the elders of Israel returned to the camp. (+Nu 16:25)

Dt 1:13 Choose some wise, understanding and respected men from each of your tribes, and I will set them over you."

¹⁴You answered me, "What you propose to do is good."

¹⁵So I took the leading men of your tribes, wise and respected men, and appointed them to have authority over you—as commanders of thousands, of hundreds, of fifties and of tens and as tribal officials. (+Dt 5:23)

Dt 27:1 Moses and the elders of Israel commanded the people: "Keep all these commands that I give you today.

Dt 29:10 All of you are standing today in the presence of the LORD your God—your leaders and chief men, your elders and officials, and all the other men of Israel, ¹¹together with your children and your wives, and the aliens living in your camps who chop your wood and carry your water. ¹²You are standing here in order to enter into a covenant with the LORD your God, a covenant the LORD is making with you this day and sealing with an oath, ¹³to confirm you this day as his people, that he may be your God as he promised you and as he swore to your fathers, Abraham, Isaac and Jacob. ¹⁴I am making this covenant, with its oath, not only with you ¹⁵who are standing here with us today in the presence of the LORD our God but also with those who are not here today.

Dt 31:9 So Moses wrote down this law and gave it to the priests, the sons of Levi, who carried the ark of the covenant of the LORD, and to all the elders of Israel.

Dt 31:28 Assemble before me all the elders of your tribes and all your officials, so that I can speak these words in their hearing and call heaven and earth to testify against them.

Jos 7:6 Then Joshua tore his clothes and fell facedown to the ground before the ark of the LORD, remaining there till evening. The elders of Israel did the same, and sprinkled dust on their heads.

Jos 8:10 Early the next morning Joshua mustered his men, and he and the leaders of Israel marched before them to Ai.

Jos 8:32 There, in the presence of the Israelites, Joshua copied on stones the law of Moses, which he had written. ³³All Israel, aliens and citizens alike, with their elders, officials and judges, were standing on both sides of the ark of the covenant of the LORD, facing those who carried it—the priests, who were Levites. Half of the people stood in front of Mount Gerizim and half of them in front of Mount Ebal, as Moses the servant of the LORD had formerly commanded when he gave instructions to bless the people of Israel.

Jos 23:2 summoned all Israel—their elders, leaders, judges and officials—and said to them: "I am old and well advanced in years. ³You yourselves have seen everything the LORD your God has done to all these nations for your sake; it was the LORD your God who fought for you.

Jos 23:6 "Be very strong; be careful to obey all that is written in the Book of the Law of Moses, without turning aside to the right or to the left.

Jos 24:1 Then Joshua assembled all the tribes of Israel at Shechem. He summoned the elders, leaders, judges and officials of Israel, and they presented themselves before God.

Jos 24:24 And the people said to Joshua, "We will serve the LORD our God and obey him."

²⁵On that day Joshua made a covenant for the people,

and there at Shechem he drew up for them decrees and laws.

Jdg 21:16 And the elders of the assembly said, "With the women of Benjamin destroyed, how shall we provide wives for the men who are left? ¹⁷The Benjamite survivors must have heirs," they said, "so that a tribe of Israel will not be wiped out. (+Jdg 21:18-25)

Ac 5:17 Then the high priest and all his associates, who were members of the party of the Sadducees, were filled with jealousy. ¹⁸They arrested the apostles and put them in the public jail.

Ac 5:21 At daybreak they entered the temple courts, as they had been told, and began to teach the people. When the high priest and his associates arrived, they called together the Sanhedrin—the full assembly of the elders of Israel—and sent to the jail for the apostles. (+Ac 5:22-41)

Miscellaneous Facts Relating to the Council:

Demands a king (1Sa 8:4-10,19-22). Saul pleads to be honored before (1Sa 15:30). Chooses David as king (2Sa 5:3; 1Ch 11:3). Closely associated with David (2Sa 12:17; 1Ch 15:25; 21:16). Joins Absalom in his usurpation (2Sa 17:4). David rebukes (2Sa 19:11). Assists Solomon at the dedication of the temple (1Ki 8:1-3; 2Ch 5:2-4). Counsels King Rehoboam (1Ki 12:6-8,13). Counsels King Ahab (1Ki 20:7-8). Josiah assembles, to hear the law of the Lord (2Ki 23:1; 2Ch 34:29-30).

Legislates with Ezra in reforming certain marriages with the heathen (Ezr 9:1; 10:8-14). Legislates in later times (Mt 15:2,7-9; Mk 7:1-13). Sits as a court (Jer 26:10-24). Constitutes, with priests and scribes, a court for the trial of both civil and ecclesiastical causes (Mt 21:23; 26:3-5,57-68; 27:1-2; Mk 8:31; 14:43,53-65; 15:1; Lk 22:52-54,66-71; Ac 4:1-21; 6:9-15). Unfaithful to the city (La 1:19). Seeks counsel from prophets (Eze 8:1; 14:1; 20:1,3). Corrupt (1Ki 21:8-14; Eze 8:11-12; Mt 26:14-15, w Mt 27:3-4).

A similar council existed among the Egyptians (Ge 50:7) and among the Midianites and Moabites (Nu 22:4,7, and Gibeonites (Jos 9:11).

Executive officers of tribes and cities, called princes or nobles, members of the national assembly (Nu 1:4-16,44; 7:2-3,10-11,18,24,54,84; 10:4; 16:2; 17:2,6; 27:2; 31:13-14; 32:2; 34:18-29; 36:1; Jos 9:15-21; 17:4; 22:13-32; 1Ki 21:11-14; Ne 3:9,12,16,18-19).

The Mosaic judicial system. *See Court, Of Law; Judge; Levites; Priest; Rulers; Sanhedrin; Synagogue.*

Ecclesiastical: *See Church, The Body of Believers, Government of; Church, The Body of Believers, State; Priest.*

Imperial: (Ge 14:1; Jos 11:10; 1Ki 4:21; Est 1:1; Da 4:1; 6:1-3; Lk 2:1).

Monarchical:

Tyranny in: By Pharaoh (Ex 1:8-22; 2:23-24; 3:7; 5:1-10). By Saul (1Sa 22:6,12-19). By David (2Sa 11:14-17). By Solomon (1Ki 2:23-25,28-34,36-46). By Rehoboam (1Ki 12:1-16). By Ahab and Jezebel (1Ki 21:7-16). By Jehu (2Ki 10:1-14). By Xerxes (Est 1:11-12,19-22; 3:6-15; 8:8-13). By Nebuchadnezzar (Da 1:10; 2:5-13; 5:19). By Herod (Mk 6:27-28).

Municipal:

Based on a local council and executive officers (Dt 19:12; 21:2-8,18-21; 22:13-21; 25:7-9; Jos 20:4; Jdg 8:14-16; 11:5-11; Ru 4:2-11; 1Sa 11:3; 16:4; 30:26; 1Ki 21:8-14; 2Ki 10:1-7; Ezr 10:8,14; Ne 3:9,12,16,18-19; La 5:14).

Patriarchal: (Ge 27:29,37).

Provincial: (Ezr 4:8-9; 5:3,6; 6:6; 8:36; Ne 2:7,9; 5:14; Da 6:1-3; Mt 27:2; 28:14; Lk 2:2; 3:1; Ac 24:1).

Representative: (Dt 1:13-15; Jos 9:11).
See above, Delegated, Council of Elders.

Theocratic:

Ex 19:3 Then Moses went up to God, and the LORD called to him from the mountain and said, "This is what you are to say to the house of Jacob and what you are to tell the people of Israel: ⁴'You yourselves have seen what I did to Egypt, and how I carried you on eagles' wings and brought you to myself. ⁵Now if you obey me fully and keep my covenant, then out of all nations you will be my treasured possession. Although the whole earth is mine, ⁶you will be for me a kingdom of priests and a holy nation.' These are the words you are to speak to the Israelites."

⁷So Moses went back and summoned the elders of the people and set before them all the words the LORD had commanded him to speak. ⁸The people all responded together, "We will do everything the LORD has said." So Moses brought their answer back to the LORD. (+Dt 26:16-19)

Dt 29:1 These are the terms of the covenant the LORD commanded Moses to make with the Israelites in Moab, in addition to the covenant he had made with them at Horeb.

²Moses summoned all the Israelites and said to them: Your eyes have seen all that the LORD did in Egypt to Pharaoh, to all his officials and to all his land. ³With your own eyes you saw those great trials, those miraculous signs and great wonders. ⁴But to this day the LORD has not given you a mind that understands or eyes that see or ears that hear. ⁵During the forty years that I led you through the desert, your clothes did not wear out, nor did the sandals on your feet. ⁶You ate no bread and drank no wine or other fermented drink. I did this so that you might know that I am the LORD your God. ⁷When you reached this place, Sihon king of Heshbon and Og king of Bashan came out to fight against us, but we defeated them. ⁸We took their land and gave it as an inheritance to the Reubenites, the Gadites and the half-tribe of Manasseh.

⁹Carefully follow the terms of this covenant, so that you may prosper in everything you do. ¹⁰All of you are standing today in the presence of the LORD your God—your leaders and chief men, your elders and officials, and all the other men of Israel, ¹¹together with your children and your wives, and the aliens living in your camps who chop your wood and carry your water. ¹²You are standing here in order to enter into a covenant with the LORD your God, a covenant the LORD is making with you this day and sealing with an oath, ¹³to confirm you this day as his people, that he may be your God as he promised you and as he swore to your fathers, Abraham, Isaac and Jacob. (+Jdg 8:23)

1Sa 8:6 But when they said, "Give us a king to lead us," this displeased Samuel; so he prayed to the LORD. ⁷And the LORD told him: "Listen to all that the people are saying to you; it is not you they have rejected, but they have rejected me as their king. (+1Sa 10:19; 12:12; Isa 33:22)

See God, Sovereign; Jesus the Christ, Kingdom of.

GOVERNOR [5893, 5907, 7068, 7212, 7213, 8569, 8954, 9579, 10580, *1617, 2448, 2450*].

NIV+ GOVERNORS, GOVERNOR'S

A provincial or city ruler (1Ki 4:7; 10:15; Ezr 2:63; Jn 18:28). Joseph (Ge 42:6), Zebul (Jdg 9:30), Gedaliah (2Ki

25:23). Tattenai (Ezr 5:3,6). Sheshbazzar (Ezr 5:14). Nehemiah (Ne 7:65,70; 8:9; 10:1; 12:26).

GOYIM [1582] (*nations, Gentiles*). A people, where the king of Goyim in Gilgal, was among those defeated by Joshua (Jos 12:23). Goyim may be the generic Hebrew word for "nations." *See Goiim.*

GOZAN [1579]. A city located in NE Mesopotamia on the Habor River, to which the Israelites were deported by the Assyrians (2Ki 17:6; 18:11; 19:12; 1Ch 5:26).

GRACE [2834, 2858, 2876, *5919, 5921*].

NIV+ GRACIOUS, GRACIOUSLY

A term employed by the Biblical writers with a wide variety of meaning: charm, sweetness, loveliness (Ps 45:2), the attitude of God toward men (Tit 2:11), the method of salvation (Eph 2:5), the opposite of legalism (Gal 5:4), the impartation of spiritual power or gifts (1Co 2:6; 2Ti 2:1), the liberty which God gives to men (Jude 4).

Before meals. *See Prayer,Thanksgiving, and Before Taking Food.*

GRACE OF GOD

Unmerited favor—

Dt 7:7 The LORD did not set his affection on you and choose you because you were more numerous than other peoples, for you were the fewest of all peoples. ⁸But it was because the LORD loved you and kept the oath he swore to your forefathers that he brought you out with a mighty hand and redeemed you from the land of slavery, from the power of Pharaoh king of Egypt. (+2Ch 30:9; Eph 1:6; Tit 2:11; Heb 4:16)

Abundant—

1Ti 1:14 The grace of our Lord was poured out on me abundantly, along with the faith and love that are in Christ Jesus.

No warrant for sinful indulgence (Ro 6:1,15).

Divine help—

Ge 20:6 Then God said to him in the dream, "Yes, I know you did this with a clear conscience, and so I have kept you from sinning against me. That is why I did not let you touch her.

Job 10:12 You gave me life and showed me kindness, and in your providence watched over my spirit. (+Ps 84:11)

Ps 94:17 Unless the LORD had given me help, I would soon have dwelt in the silence of death. ¹⁸When I said, "My foot is slipping," your love, O LORD, supported me. ¹⁹When anxiety was great within me, your consolation brought joy to my soul.

Ps 138:3 When I called, you answered me; you made me bold and stouthearted.

1Co 10:13 No temptation has seized you except what is common to man. And God is faithful; he will not let you be tempted beyond what you can bear. But when you are tempted, he will also provide a way out so that you can stand up under it. (+2Co 1:12; 12:9)

1Pe 1:5 who through faith are shielded by God's power until the coming of the salvation that is ready to be revealed in the last time.

Growth in—

Ps 84:7 They go from strength to strength, till each appears before God in Zion.

Pr 4:18 The path of the righteous is like the first gleam of dawn, shining ever brighter till the full light of day.

Php 1:6 being confident of this, that he who began a good work in you will carry it on to completion until the day of Christ Jesus.

Php 1:9 And this is my prayer: that your love may abound more and more in knowledge and depth of insight, [10]so that you may be able to discern what is best and may be pure and blameless until the day of Christ, [11]filled with the fruit of righteousness that comes through Jesus Christ—to the glory and praise of God.

Php 3:12 Not that I have already obtained all this, or have already been made perfect, but I press on to take hold of that for which Christ Jesus took hold of me. [13]Brothers, I do not consider myself yet to have taken hold of it. But one thing I do: Forgetting what is behind and straining toward what is ahead, [14]I press on toward the goal to win the prize for which God has called me heavenward in Christ Jesus.

[15]All of us who are mature should take such a view of things. And if on some point you think differently, that too God will make clear to you.

Col 1:10 And we pray this in order that you may live a life worthy of the Lord and may please him in every way: bearing fruit in every good work, growing in the knowledge of God, [11]being strengthened with all power according to his glorious might so that you may have great endurance and patience, and joyfully

Col 2:19 He has lost connection with the Head, from whom the whole body, supported and held together by its ligaments and sinews, grows as God causes it to grow.

1Th 3:10 Night and day we pray most earnestly that we may see you again and supply what is lacking in your faith.

1Th 3:12 May the Lord make your love increase and overflow for each other and for everyone else, just as ours does for you. [13]May he strengthen your hearts so that you will be blameless and holy in the presence of our God and Father when our Lord Jesus comes with all his holy ones.

2Th 1:3 We ought always to thank God for you, brothers, and rightly so, because your faith is growing more and more, and the love every one of you has for each other is increasing.

Heb 6:1 Therefore let us leave the elementary teachings about Christ and go on to maturity, not laying again the foundation of repentance from acts that lead to death, and of faith in God, [3]And God permitting, we will do so.

1Pe 2:1 Therefore, rid yourselves of all malice and all deceit, hypocrisy, envy, and slander of every kind. [2]Like newborn babies, crave pure spiritual milk, so that by it you may grow up in your salvation, [3]now that you have tasted that the Lord is good.

2Pe 3:18 But grow in the grace and knowledge of our Lord and Savior Jesus Christ. To him be glory both now and forever! Amen.

Believers to be stewards of—

1Pe 4:10 Each one should use whatever gift he has received to serve others, faithfully administering God's grace in its various forms.

Intercessory prayer for—

Ps 143:11 For your name's sake, O LORD, preserve my life; in your righteousness, bring me out of trouble.

Da 9:18 Give ear, O God, and hear; open your eyes and see the desolation of the city that bears your Name. We do not make requests of you because we are righteous, but because of your great mercy.

Jn 17:11 I will remain in the world no longer, but they are still in the world, and I am coming to you. Holy Father, protect them by the power of your name—the name you gave me—so that they may be one as we are one. [12]While I was with them, I protected them and kept them safe by

that name you gave me. None has been lost except the one doomed to destruction so that Scripture would be fulfilled.

Jn 17:15 My prayer is not that you take them out of the world but that you protect them from the evil one.

1Th 1:1 Paul, Silas and Timothy, To the church of the Thessalonians in God the Father and the Lord Jesus Christ: Grace and peace to you. (+1Th 5:28; 2Pe 1:2)

Exhortation against rejecting (2Co 6:1-2).

With respect to Jacob and Esau—

Ro 9:10 Not only that, but Rebekah's children had one and the same father, our father Isaac. [11]Yet, before the twins were born or had done anything good or bad—in order that God's purpose in election might stand: [12]not by works but by him who calls—she was told, "The older will serve the younger." [13]Just as it is written: "Jacob I loved, but Esau I hated."

[14]What then shall we say? Is God unjust? Not at all! [15]For he says to Moses, "I will have mercy on whom I have mercy, and I will have compassion on whom I have compassion."

[16]It does not, therefore, depend on man's desire or effort, but on God's mercy.

Manifested:

In drawing people to Christ—

Jn 6:44 "No one can come to me unless the Father who sent me draws him, and I will raise him up at the last day. [45]It is written in the Prophets: 'They will all be taught by God.' Everyone who listens to the Father and learns from him comes to me.

In redemption—

Eph 1:5 he predestined us to be adopted as his sons through Jesus Christ, in accordance with his pleasure and will— [6]to the praise of his glorious grace, which he has freely given us in the One he loves. [7]In him we have redemption through his blood, the forgiveness of sins, in accordance with the riches of God's grace [8]that he lavished on us with all wisdom and understanding. [9]And he made known to us the mystery of his will according to his good pleasure, which he purposed in Christ,

Eph 1:11 In him we were also chosen, having been predestined according to the plan of him who works out everything in conformity with the purpose of his will, [12]in order that we, who were the first to hope in Christ, might be for the praise of his glory.

In justification—

Ge 15:6 Abram believed the LORD, and he credited it to him as righteousness.

Ro 3:22 This righteousness from God comes through faith in Jesus Christ to all who believe. There is no difference, [23]for all have sinned and fall short of the glory of God, [24]and are justified freely by his grace through the redemption that came by Christ Jesus.

Ro 4:4 Now when a man works, his wages are not credited to him as a gift, but as an obligation. [5]However, to the man who does not work but trusts God who justifies the wicked, his faith is credited as righteousness.

Ro 4:16 Therefore, the promise comes by faith, so that it may be by grace and may be guaranteed to all Abraham's offspring—not only to those who are of the law but also to those who are of the faith of Abraham. He is the father of us all.

Ro 5:2 through whom we have gained access by faith into this grace in which we now stand. And we rejoice in the hope of the glory of God.

Ro 5:6 You see, at just the right time, when we were still powerless, Christ died for the ungodly. [7]Very rarely will anyone die for a righteous man, though for a good man someone might possibly dare to die. [8]But God demonstrates his own love for us in this: While we were still sinners, Christ died for us.

Ro 5:15 But the gift is not like the trespass. For if the many died by the trespass of the one man, how much more did God's grace and the gift that came by the grace of the one man, Jesus Christ, overflow to the many! [16]Again, the gift of God is not like the result of the one man's sin: The judgment followed one sin and brought condemnation, but the gift followed many trespasses and brought justification. [17]For if, by the trespass of the one man, death reigned through that one man, how much more will those who receive God's abundant provision of grace and of the gift of righteousness reign in life through the one man, Jesus Christ.

[18]Consequently, just as the result of one trespass was condemnation for all men, so also the result of one act of righteousness was justification that brings life for all men. [19]For just as through the disobedience of the one man the many were made sinners, so also through the obedience of the one man the many will be made righteous.

[20]The law was added so that the trespass might increase. But where sin increased, grace increased all the more, [21]so that, just as sin reigned in death, so also grace might reign through righteousness to bring eternal life through Jesus Christ our Lord.

Tit 3:7 so that, having been justified by his grace, we might become heirs having the hope of eternal life.

Passing over transgressions (Nu 23:20-21; Ne 9:17; Ro 3:25)

In salvation—

Ro 11:5 So too, at the present time there is a remnant chosen by grace. [6]And if by grace, then it is no longer by works; if it were, grace would no longer be grace.

Eph 2:8 For it is by grace you have been saved, through faith—and this not from yourselves, it is the gift of God— [9]not by works, so that no one can boast.

2Ti 1:9 who has saved us and called us to a holy life—not because of anything we have done but because of his own purpose and grace. This grace was given us in Christ Jesus before the beginning of time,

In calling to service—

Gal 1:15 But when God, who set me apart from birth and called me by his grace, was pleased [16]to reveal his Son in me so that I might preach him among the Gentiles, I did not consult any man,

Spiritual growth—

Eph 3:16 I pray that out of his glorious riches he may strengthen you with power through his Spirit in your inner being,

In spiritual gifts—

1Co 1:4 I always thank God for you because of his grace given you in Christ Jesus. [5]For in him you have been enriched in every way—in all your speaking and in all your knowledge— [6]because our testimony about Christ was confirmed in you. [7]Therefore you do not lack any spiritual gift as you eagerly wait for our Lord Jesus Christ to be revealed. [8]He will keep you strong to the end, so that you will be blameless on the day of our Lord Jesus Christ.

Eph 4:7 But to each one of us grace has been given as Christ apportioned it. (+Eph 4:11)

Manifested:

In the character and conduct of the righteous—

1Co 15:10 But by the grace of God I am what I am, and his grace to me was not without effect. No, I worked harder than all of them—yet not I, but the grace of God that was with me.

2Co 1:12 Now this is our boast: Our conscience testifies that we have conducted ourselves in the world, and especially in our relations with you, in the holiness and sincerity that are from God. We have done so not according to worldly wisdom but according to God's grace. (+Php 2:13)

Php 2:13 for it is God who works in you to will and to act according to his good purpose.

In sustaining the righteous (1Ch 17:8)—

Da 10:18 Again the one who looked like a man touched me and gave me strength. [19]"Do not be afraid, O man highly esteemed," he said. "Peace! Be strong now; be strong."

When he spoke to me, I was strengthened and said, "Speak, my lord, since you have given me strength." (+2Co 12:9; 1Pe 1:5)

1Pe 5:10 And the God of all grace, who called you to his eternal glory in Christ, after you have suffered a little while, will himself restore you and make you strong, firm and steadfast.

Jude 24 To him who is able to keep you from falling and to present you before his glorious presence without fault and with great joy—

In sustaining in temptation (Ge 20:6; 1Co 10:13)—

Rev 3:10 Since you have kept my command to endure patiently, I will also keep you from the hour of trial that is going to come upon the whole world to test those who live on the earth.

Manifested to:

Enoch (Ge 5:24). Noah (Ge 6:8,17-18). Abraham (Ge 12:2; 21:22). Ishmael (Ge 21:20). Isaac (Ge 26:24). Jacob (Ge 46:3-4; 48:16). Joseph (Ge 39:2-3,23). Moses (Ex 3:12; 33:12-17). Israel (Dt 4:7). Naphtali (Dt 33:23). Joshua (Jos 1:5,9). Job (Job 10:12). David (1Sa 25:26,34; 2Sa 7:8-16). Daniel (Da 10:18-19). Jeremiah (Jer 15:20). The righteous (Ps 5:12; Ac 4:33).

See God, Grace of.

GRACES

NIV+ See GRACE

Christian—

Mt 5:3 "Blessed are the poor in spirit, for theirs is the kingdom of heaven. [4]Blessed are those who mourn, for they will be comforted. [5]Blessed are the meek, for they will inherit the earth. [6]Blessed are those who hunger and thirst for righteousness, for they will be filled. [7]Blessed are the merciful, for they will be shown mercy. [8]Blessed are the pure in heart, for they will see God. [9]Blessed are the peacemakers, for they will be called sons of God. [10]Blessed are those who are persecuted because of righteousness, for theirs is the kingdom of heaven.

[11]"Blessed are you when people insult you, persecute you and falsely say all kinds of evil against you because of me.

Ro 5:3 Not only so, but we also rejoice in our sufferings, because we know that suffering produces perseverance; [4]perseverance, character; and character, hope. [5]And hope does not disappoint us, because God has poured out his love into our hearts by the Holy Spirit, whom he has given us.

1Co 13:1 If I speak in the tongues of men and of angels, but have not love, I am only a resounding gong or a clanging cymbal. [2]If I have the gift of prophecy and can fathom all mysteries and all knowledge, and if I have a faith that can move mountains, but have not love, I am nothing. [3]If I give all I possess to the poor and surrender my body to the flames, but have not love, I gain nothing.

[4]Love is patient, love is kind. It does not envy, it does not boast, it is not proud. [5]It is not rude, it is not self-seeking, it is not easily angered, it keeps no record of wrongs. [6]Love does not delight in evil but rejoices with the truth. [7]It always protects, always trusts, always hopes, always perseveres.

[8]Love never fails. But where there are prophecies, they will cease; where there are tongues, they will be stilled; where there is knowledge, it will pass away.

1Co 13:13 And now these three remain: faith, hope and love. But the greatest of these is love.

Gal 5:22 But the fruit of the Spirit is love, joy, peace, patience, kindness, goodness, faithfulness, [23]gentleness and self-control. Against such things there is no law.

1Pe 1:5 who through faith are shielded by God's power until the coming of the salvation that is ready to be revealed in the last time. [6]In this you greatly rejoice, though now for a little while you may have had to suffer grief in all kinds of trials. [7]These have come so that your faith—of greater worth than gold, which perishes even though refined by fire—may be proved genuine and may result in praise, glory and honor when Jesus Christ is revealed. [8]Though you have not seen him, you love him; and even though you do not see him now, you believe in him and are filled with an inexpressible and glorious joy, [9]for you are receiving the goal of your faith, the salvation of your souls.

See Beatitudes; Character; Charitableness; Courage; Gentleness; Hope; Kindness; Knowledge; Longsuffering; Love; Meekness; Mercy; Patience; Peace; Perseverance; Purity; Righteousness, Fruits of; Stability; Temperance; Wisdom.

GRAFT [1596].

NIV+ GRAFTED

A horticultural process by which the branches of a cultivated tree may be inserted into the trunk of a wild tree. Figurative of Gentiles partaking of Israel's covenants and blessings (Ro 11:17ff.).

GRAIN [*1339, 1841, 1889, 2446, 2567, 4152, 4966, 6658, 6894, 7833, 7850, 8195, 8672, 8690, 8692, 262, 2843, 4992, 5092].

NIV+ GRAINS, GRANARIES

In valleys (Ps 65:13; Mk 4:28). A product of Egypt (Ge 41:47-49), Israel (Dt 33:28; Eze 27:17). Roasted (Ru 2:14; 1Sa 17:17; 25:18; 2Sa 17:28). Ground (2Sa 17:19). Eaten by the Israelites (Jos 5:11-12). Shocks of, burnt (Jdg 15:5). Mosaic laws concerning (Ex 22:6; Dt 23:25).

Individual heads of grain (Ge 41:5-7,22-27; Lev 23:14; Ru 2:2; Job 24:24; Isa 17:5; Mk 4:26-29). Grain that is ripe but soft, which is roasted and eaten (Lev 2:14). The poor may pick what they can eat on the spot; refers to grain rubbed between the hands (Dt 23:25). Picked by Christ's disciples (Mt 12:1; Mk 2:23; Lk 6:1). Newly ripened heads of grain (2Ki 4:42).

Figurative: (Ps 72:16; Hos 14:7; Jn 12:24).

Symbolic: (Ge 41:5).

See Barley; Barn; Bread; Firstfruits; Glean, Gleaning;

Harvest; Plants of the Bible; Reaping; Rye; Threshing; Tithes; Wheat.

GRANARY [4393, 4852, 4923].

NIV+ GRANARIES; See also GRAIN

A storehouse for grain and other dry crops (Ex 22:29; Jer 50:26; Joel 1:17).

See Barn; Storehouse.

GRANDFATHER [3].

NIV+ FATHER, GRANDCHILDREN, GRANDDAUGHTER, GRANDDAUGHTERS, GRANDFATHER'S, GRANDMOTHER, GRANDMOTHER'S, GRANDPARENTS, GRANDSON, GRANDSONS

Called Father (Ge 10:21).

GRAPE [112, 864, 1235, 1292, 1305, 3292, 4142, 6622, 6694, 7261, 8097, 9408, 306, 1084, 2843, 5091].

NIV+ GRAPES, GRAPEVINE, GRAPEVINES

Cultivated in vineyards, by Noah (Ge 9:20), Canaanites (Nu 13:24; Dt 6:11; Jos 24:13), Edomites (Nu 20:17), Amorites (Nu 21:22; Isa 16:8-9), Philistines (Jdg 15:5). Grown, at Baal Hamon (SS 8:11), Carmel (2Ch 26:10), En Gedi (SS 1:14), Jezreel (1Ki 21:1), Lebanon (Hos 14:7), Samaria (Jer 31:5), Shechem (Jdg 9:27), Shiloh (Jdg 21:20-21), Timnath (Jdg 14:5).

Culture of (Lev 25:3,11; Dt 28:39; 2Ch 26:10; SS 6:11; Isa 5:1; Jer 31:5).

Wine made of (Jer 25:30). Wine of, forbidden to Nazirites (Nu 6:4). *See Nazirite(s), Nazarite(s).*

See Vine; Vineyards; Wine.

Figurative:

(Dt 32:32; Ps 128:3; Jer 2:21; Eze 15; Hos 10:1; Rev 14:18-20).

Fable of (Jdg 9:12-13). Parables of the vine (Ps 80:8-14; Eze 17:6-10; 19:10-14; Jn 15:1-5). Proverb of (Eze 18:2).

See Vine; Vineyards; Wine.

GRASS [2013+4604, 2013, 2945, 3143, 3764, 6912, 10187, 10572, 5965]. Created on the third creative day (Ge 1:11). Mown (Ps 72:6). God's care of (Mt 6:30; Lk 12:28). On roofs of houses (Ps 129:6).

Figurative:

(Ps 90:5-6; Isa 40:6; 1Pe 1:24; Jas 1:10-11).

GRASSHOPPER [2506, 2885, 3540].

NIV+ GRASSHOPPERS

(Nu 13:33; Ecc 12:5; Isa 40:22; Na 3:17).
See Locust.

GRATE [4803].

NIV+ GRATING

A copper network, placed under the top of the great altar, to hold the sacrifice while burning (Ex 27:4; 35:16; 38:4-5).

GRATITUDE [2373, 2374, 5921].

NIV+ GRATEFUL, GRATIFY, GRATIFYING
See Thankfulness.

GRAVE [3243, 7690, 7700, 8619, 8827, 87, 3646, 5439].

NIV+ GRAVES

Prepared by Jacob (Ge 50:5). Defilement from touching (Nu 19:16,18). Weeping at (2Sa 3:32; Jn 11:31; 20:11). Of parents, honored (2Sa 19:37). Welcomed (Job 3:20-22).

Resurrection From:

Of Lazarus (Jn 11:43-44; 12:17), of Jesus (Mt 28:5-6; 1Co 15:12-20), of believers after Jesus' resurrection (Mt 27:52-53), of all the dead foretold (Jn 5:28; 1Co 15:22-54). *See Burial; Sheol; Tomb.*

GRAVE CLOTHES Preparatory to burial, the body was washed and anointed with spices, then wrapped in a winding sheet, bound with strips of cloth, and the head wrapped in a square cloth (Jn 11:44; 19:40).

GRAVEL [2953].

Figurative of food gained by fraud (Pr 20:17), of judgment (La 3:16).

GRAVEN IMAGE NIV "carved image" or "idol" of wood, stone, or metal (Dt 7:5; Isa 44:9-17; 45:20). *See Carving; Groves; High Places; Iconoclasm; Idol; Idolatry.*

GRAVING *See Engraving.*

GREAT OWL *See Birds.*

GREAT SEA *See Mediterranean Sea.*

GREATER SIDON *See Sidon.*

GREATNESS [1525, 1540, 1542, 5270, 8044, 10650, *3484, 5660*].

NIV+ GREAT, GREATER, GREATEST, GREATLY

Of God (Dt 3:24; Ps 77:13; 95:3; 104:1; 135:5; 145:3; Isa 12:6; Jer 32:18; Mal 1:11). Of Christ (Isa 53:12; 63:1; Mt 12:6; Lk 11:31; Php 2:9-10).

GREAVES [5196]. Leg armor worn below the knee (1Sa 17:6).

GREECE [3430, *1817*].

NIV+ GRECIAN, GREEK, GREEKS

Inhabitants of, called Gentiles (Mk 7:26; Jn 7:35; Ro 2:10; 3:9; 1Co 10:32; 12:13), desire to see Jesus (Jn 12:20-23), marry among the Jews (Ac 16:1), accept the Messiah (Ac 17:2-4,12,34), persecute the early Christians (Ac 6:9-14; 9:29; 18:17). Gentiles called Greeks (Ro 10:12; Gal 3:28; Col 3:11).

Schools of philosophy in Athens (Ac 19:9). Philosophy of (1Co 1:22-23). Poets of (Ac 17:28).

See Asceticism; Athens; Epicureans; Stoicism; Stoics.

GREED [1298, 1299, 5883, 8143, *154, 771, 4431, 4432*].

NIV+ GREEDY

Greed is idolatry (Col 3:5).

Insatiable—

Pr 1:19 Such is the end of all who go after ill-gotten gain; it takes away the lives of those who get it.

Pr 21:26 All day long he craves for more, but the righteous give without sparing.

Ecc 1:8 All things are wearisome, more than one can say. The eye never has enough of seeing, nor the ear its fill of hearing.

Ecc 4:8 There was a man all alone; he had neither son nor brother. There was no end to his toil, yet his eyes were not content with his wealth. "For whom am I toiling," he asked, "and why am I depriving myself of enjoyment?" This too is meaningless—a miserable business!

Ecc 5:10 Whoever loves money never has money enough; whoever loves wealth is never satisfied with his income. This too is meaningless.

[11]As goods increase, so do those who consume them. And what benefit are they to the owner except to feast his eyes on them?

Isa 56:11 They are dogs with mighty appetites; they never have enough. They are shepherds who lack understanding; they all turn to their own way, each seeks his own gain.

Root of evil—

1Ti 6:9 People who want to get rich fall into temptation and a trap and into many foolish and harmful desires that plunge men into ruin and destruction. [10]For the love of money is a root of all kinds of evil. Some people, eager for money, have wandered from the faith and pierced themselves with many griefs.

[11]But you, man of God, flee from all this, and pursue righteousness, godliness, faith, love, endurance and gentleness.

Tends to poverty—

Pr 11:24 One man gives freely, yet gains even more; another withholds unduly, but comes to poverty.

Pr 11:26 People curse the man who hoards grain, but blessing crowns him who is willing to sell.

Pr 22:16 He who oppresses the poor to increase his wealth and he who gives gifts to the rich—both come to poverty.

Gains of, unstable—

Job 20:15 He will spit out the riches he swallowed; God will make his stomach vomit them up.

Pr 23:4 Do not wear yourself out to get rich; have the wisdom to show restraint. [5]Cast but a glance at riches, and they are gone, for they will surely sprout wings and fly off to the sky like an eagle. (+Pr 23:6)

Jer 17:11 Like a partridge that hatches eggs it did not lay is the man who gains riches by unjust means. When his life is half gone, they will desert him, and in the end he will prove to be a fool.

Disqualifies from sacred office—

Ex 18:21 But select capable men from all the people—men who fear God, trustworthy men who hate dishonest gain—and appoint them as officials over thousands, hundreds, fifties and tens.

1Ti 3:3 not given to drunkenness, not violent but gentle, not quarrelsome, not a lover of money.

Tit 1:7 Since an overseer is entrusted with God's work, he must be blameless—not overbearing, not quick-tempered, not given to drunkenness, not violent, not pursuing dishonest gain. (+Tit 1:11)

1Pe 5:2 Be shepherds of God's flock that is under your care, serving as overseers—not because you must, but because you are willing, as God wants you to be; not greedy for money, but eager to serve;

Disqualifies from kingdom of God (Mt 19:23)—

Mt 19:24 Again I tell you, it is easier for a camel to go through the eye of a needle than for a rich man to enter the kingdom of God." (+Mt 22:25; Lk 18:24-25; 1Co 6:10)

Eph 5:3 But among you there must not be even a hint of sexual immorality, or of any kind of impurity, or of greed, because these are improper for God's holy people.

Eph 5:5 For of this you can be sure: No immoral, impure or greedy person—such a man is an idolater—has any inheritance in the kingdom of Christ and of God.

Php 3:18 For, as I have often told you before and now say again even with tears, many live as enemies of the cross of Christ. [19]Their destiny is destruction, their god is their stomach, and their glory is in their shame. Their mind is on earthly things.

Denounced—

Ps 10:3 He boasts of the cravings of his heart; he blesses the greedy and reviles the LORD. (+Pr 1:19)

Isa 5:8 Woe to you who add house to house and join field to field till no space is left and you live alone in the land.

Jude 11 Woe to them! They have taken the way of Cain; they have rushed for profit into Balaam's error; they have been destroyed in Korah's rebellion.

Warnings against (Dt 15:9-10; Pr 1:19)—

Pr 15:27 A greedy man brings trouble to his family, but he who hates bribes will live.

Hos 4:18 Even when their drinks are gone, they continue their prostitution; their rulers dearly love shameful ways.

Hab 2:5 indeed, wine betrays him; he is arrogant and never at rest. Because he is as greedy as the grave and like death is never satisfied, he gathers to himself all the nations and takes captive all the peoples.

⁶"Will not all of them taunt him with ridicule and scorn, saying,

"'Woe to him who piles up stolen goods and makes himself wealthy by extortion! How long must this go on?' ⁷Will not your debtors suddenly arise? Will they not wake up and make you tremble? Then you will become their victim. ⁸Because you have plundered many nations, the peoples who are left will plunder you. For you have shed man's blood; you have destroyed lands and cities and everyone in them.

⁹"Woe to him who builds his realm by unjust gain to set his nest on high, to escape the clutches of ruin!

Mt 6:19 "Do not store up for yourselves treasures on earth, where moth and rust destroy, and where thieves break in and steal. ²⁰But store up for yourselves treasures in heaven, where moth and rust do not destroy, and where thieves do not break in and steal. ²¹For where your treasure is, there your heart will be also.

Mt 6:24 "No one can serve two masters. Either he will hate the one and love the other, or he will be devoted to the one and despise the other. You cannot serve both God and Money.

²⁵"Therefore I tell you, do not worry about your life, what you will eat or drink; or about your body, what you will wear. Is not life more important than food, and the body more important than clothes?

Mt 6:31 So do not worry, saying, 'What shall we eat?' or 'What shall we drink?' or 'What shall we wear?' ³²For the pagans run after all these things, and your heavenly Father knows that you need them. ³³But seek first his kingdom and his righteousness, and all these things will be given to you as well.

Mt 13:22 The one who received the seed that fell among the thorns is the man who hears the word, but the worries of this life and the deceitfulness of wealth choke it, making it unfruitful.

Mt 16:26 What good will it be for a man if he gains the whole world, yet forfeits his soul? Or what can a man give in exchange for his soul? (+Mk 4:19)

Mk 7:21 For from within, out of men's hearts, come evil thoughts, sexual immorality, theft, murder, adultery, ²²greed, malice, deceit, lewdness, envy, slander, arrogance and folly. ²³All these evils come from inside and make a man 'unclean.'" (+Lk 8:14)

Lk 12:15 Then he said to them, "Watch out! Be on your guard against all kinds of greed; a man's life does not consist in the abundance of his possessions." (+Lk 12:16-21)

Jn 6:26 Jesus answered, "I tell you the truth, you are looking for me, not because you saw miraculous signs but because you ate the loaves and had your fill. ²⁷Do not work for food that spoils, but for food that endures to eternal life, which the Son of Man will give you. On him God the Father has placed his seal of approval."

1Co 5:11 But now I am writing you that you must not associate with anyone who calls himself a brother but is sexually immoral or greedy, an idolater or a slanderer, a drunkard or a swindler. With such a man do not even eat.

1Th 2:5 You know we never used flattery, nor did we put on a mask to cover up greed—God is our witness.

1Ti 6:5 and constant friction between men of corrupt mind, who have been robbed of the truth and who think that godliness is a means to financial gain.

⁶But godliness with contentment is great gain. ⁷For we brought nothing into the world, and we can take nothing out of it. ⁸But if we have food and clothing, we will be content with that.

2Ti 3:2 People will be lovers of themselves, lovers of money, boastful, proud, abusive, disobedient to their parents, ungrateful, unholy, (+2Ti 3:5)

Heb 13:5 Keep your lives free from the love of money and be content with what you have, because God has said, "Never will I leave you; never will I forsake you."

Jas 4:2 You want something but don't get it. You kill and covet, but you cannot have what you want. You quarrel and fight. You do not have, because you do not ask God.

1Jn 2:15 Do not love the world or anything in the world. If anyone loves the world, the love of the Father is not in him. (+1Jn 2:16-17)

Commandments against—

Ex 20:17 "You shall not covet your neighbor's house. You shall not covet your neighbor's wife, or his manservant or maidservant, his ox or donkey, or anything that belongs to your neighbor."

Dt 5:21 "You shall not covet your neighbor's wife. You shall not set your desire on your neighbor's house or land, his manservant or maidservant, his ox or donkey, or anything that belongs to your neighbor."

Ro 13:9 The commandments, "Do not commit adultery," "Do not murder," "Do not steal," "Do not covet," and whatever other commandment there may be, are summed up in this one rule: "Love your neighbor as yourself."

Col 3:2 Set your minds on things above, not on earthly things. (+1Ti 3:8)

Prayer against—

Ps 119:36 Turn my heart toward your statutes and not toward selfish gain.

Reproof for—

Ne 5:7 I pondered them in my mind and then accused the nobles and officials. I told them, "You are exacting usury from your own countrymen!" So I called together a large meeting to deal with them

Isa 1:23 Your rulers are rebels, companions of thieves; they all love bribes and chase after gifts. They do not defend the cause of the fatherless; the widow's case does not come before them.

Jer 6:13 "From the least to the greatest, all are greedy for gain; prophets and priests alike, all practice deceit.

Jer 22:17 "But your eyes and your heart are set only on dishonest gain, on shedding innocent blood and on oppression and extortion."

Eze 33:31 My people come to you, as they usually do, and sit before you to listen to your words, but they do not put them into practice. With their mouths they express devotion, but their hearts are greedy for unjust gain.

Hos 10:1 Israel was a spreading vine; he brought forth fruit for himself. As his fruit increased, he built more altars; as his land prospered, he adorned his sacred stones.

Mic 2:2 They covet fields and seize them, and houses, and take them. They defraud a man of his home, a fellowman of his inheritance.

Mic 3:11 Her leaders judge for a bribe, her priests teach for a price, and her prophets tell fortunes for money. Yet they lean upon the Lᴏʀᴅ and say, "Is not the Lᴏʀᴅ among us? No disaster will come upon us."

Mic 7:3 Both hands are skilled in doing evil; the ruler demands gifts, the judge accepts bribes, the powerful dictate what they desire—they all conspire together.

Hag 1:6 You have planted much, but have harvested little. You eat, but never have enough. You drink, but never have your fill. You put on clothes, but are not warm. You earn wages, only to put them in a purse with holes in it."

Ro 1:29 They have become filled with every kind of wickedness, evil, greed and depravity. They are full of envy, murder, strife, deceit and malice. They are gossips,

Punishment for (Ex 18:21)—

Job 31:24 "If I have put my trust in gold or said to pure gold, 'You are my security,' ²⁵if I have rejoiced over my great wealth, the fortune my hands had gained,

Job 31:28 then these also would be sins to be judged, for I would have been unfaithful to God on high.

Isa 57:17 I was enraged by his sinful greed; I punished him, and hid my face in anger, yet he kept on in his willful ways.

Jer 8:10 Therefore I will give their wives to other men and their fields to new owners. From the least to the greatest, all are greedy for gain; prophets and priests alike, all practice deceit.

Jer 51:13 You who live by many waters and are rich in treasures, your end has come, the time for you to be cut off.

Eze 22:12 In you men accept bribes to shed blood; you take usury and excessive interest and make unjust gain from your neighbors by extortion. And you have forgotten me, declares the Sovereign Lᴏʀᴅ.

¹³"'I will surely strike my hands together at the unjust gain you have made and at the blood you have shed in your midst.

Col 3:5 Put to death, therefore, whatever belongs to your earthly nature: sexual immorality, impurity, lust, evil desires and greed, which is idolatry. ⁶Because of these, the wrath of God is coming.

2Pe 2:3 In their greed these teachers will exploit you with stories they have made up. Their condemnation has long been hanging over them, and their destruction has not been sleeping.

2Pe 2:14 With eyes full of adultery, they never stop sinning; they seduce the unstable; they are experts in greed—an accursed brood! (+2Pe 2:15-17)

See Avarice; Greed; Rich, The; Riches; Worldliness.

Instances of:

Eve, in desiring the forbidden fruit (Ge 3:6). Lot, in choosing the plain of the Jordan (Ge 13:10-13). Laban, in giving Rebekah to be Isaac's wife (Ge 24:29-51), in deceiving Jacob when he served him seven years for Rachel (Ge 29:15-30), in deceiving Jacob in wages (Ge 31:7,15,41-42). Jacob, in defrauding Esau of his father's blessing (Ge 27:6-29), in defrauding Laban of his flocks and herds (Ge 30:35-43), in buying Esau's birthright (Ge 25:31). Balaam, in loving the wages of unrighteousness (2Pe 2:15, w Nu 22). Achan, in hiding the treasure (Jos 7:21). Eli's sons, in taking the flesh of the sacrifice (1Sa 2:13-17). Samuel's sons, in taking bribes (1Sa 8:3). Saul, in sparing Agag and the booty (1Sa 15:8-9). David, of Bathsheba (2Sa 11:2-5). Ahab, in desiring Naboth's vineyard (1Ki 21:2-16). Gehazi, in taking a gift from Naaman (2Ki 5:20-27). Jews, in exacting usury of their brothers (Ne 5:1-11), in keeping back the portion of the Levites (Ne 13:10), in building fine houses while the house of the Lord lay waste (Hag 1:4-9), in following Jesus for the loaves and fishes (Jn 6:26). Money changers in the temple (Mt 21:12-13; Lk 19:45-46; Jn 2:14-16). The rich young ruler (Mt 19:16-22). The rich fool (Lk 12:15-21). Judas, in betraying Jesus for thirty pieces of silver (Mt 26:15-16; Mk 14:10-11; Lk 22:3-6; Jn 12:6). The unjust steward (Lk 16:1-8). The Pharisees (Lk 16:14). Simon Magus, in trying to buy the gift of the Holy Spirit (Ac 8:18-23). The sorcerers, in filing complaint against Paul and Silas (Ac 16:19). Demetrius, in raising a riot against Paul and Silas (Ac 19:24,27). Felix, in hoping for a bribe from Paul (Ac 24:26). Demas, in forsaking Paul for love of the world (2Ti 4:10).

See Avarice; Bribery; Covetousness; Rich, The; Riches.

GREEK LANGUAGE Was a branch of the Indo-European family from which most of the languages of Europe are descended. The Attic dialect spoken in Athens and its colonies on the Ionian coast was combined with other dialects in the army of Alexander the Great and was spread by his conquests through the East. A kind of "Jewish Greek," influenced by semitic thought and culture, was widely spoken in Israel and became the chief language of the early church (Ac 21:37).

GREEK VERSIONS

There were several early translations of the Hebrew OT into Greek. Some of the major versions were:

1. The Septuagint, originating in Alexandria in the third and second centuries B.C.. This was the Bible of the early church.

2. The version of Aquila in the early second century A.D. 125) was a word-for-word rendering of the Hebrew produced for the Jewish people when Christians took over the Septuagint.

3. The version of Theodotion, a late second-century revision of the Septuagint.

4. The version of Symmachus, an idiomatic translation probably of the second century.

GREETINGS [606, 1385, 7925, 8626, 8934, 10147, 10720, *832, 833, 5897*].

NIV+ GREET, GREETED, GREETING, GREETS

Antiquity of (Ge 18:2; 19:1).

Given:

By brothers to each other (1Sa 17:22). By inferiors to their superiors (Ge 47:7). By superiors to inferiors (1Sa 30:21). By all passersby (1Sa 10:3-4; Ps 129:8). On entering a house (Jdg 18:15; Mt 10:12; Lk 1:40-41,44). Often sent through messengers (1Sa 25:5,14; 2Sa 8:10). Often sent by letter (Ro 16:21-23; 1Co 16:21; Col 4:18; 2Th 3:17). Denied to persons of bad character (2Jn 10). Persons in haste excused from giving or receiving (2Ki 4:29; Lk 10:24).

Expressions Used as:

"You are welcome at my house" (Jdg 19:20).

"Long life to you! Good health to you and your household! And good health to all that is yours" (1Sa 25:6).

"Peace to this house" (Lk 10:5).

"The LORD be with you! The LORD bless you!" (Ru 2:4).

"The blessing of the LORD be upon you; we bless you in the name of the LORD" (Ps 129:8).

"The LORD bless you! I have carried out the [LORD's] instructions" (1Sa 15:13).

"God be gracious to you my son" (Ge 43:29).

"How are you, my brother?" (2Sa 20:9).

"Greetings, Rabbi!" (Mt 26:49).

"Greetings, you who are highly favored! The Lord is with you" (Lk 1:28).

"Greetings" (Mt 28:9).

Sometimes insincere (2Sa 20:9; Mt 26:49). Given to Christ in derision (Mt 27:29, w Mk 15:18).

Often Accompanied by:

Embracing and kissing (Ge 33:4; 45:14-15; Lk 15:20). Taking hold of the beard with the right hand (2Sa 20:9). Bowing frequently to the ground (Ge 33:3). Embracing and kissing the feet (Mt 28:9; Lk 7:38,45). Touching the hem of the garment (Mt 14:36). Falling prostrate on the ground (Est 8:3; Mt 2:11; Lk 8:41). Kissing the dust (Ps 72:9; Isa 49:23). The Jews are condemned for giving only to their own countrymen (Mt 5:47). The Pharisees condemned for seeking, in public (Mt 23:7; Mk 12:38).

GREYHOUND NIV "strutting rooster" (Pr 30:31). *See Animals.*

GRIEF [*61, 63, 3324, 4088, 5352, 5714, 6772, 9342, *3382, 3383, 4291*].

NIV+ GRIEFS, GRIEVANCE, GRIEVANCES, GRIEVE, GRIEVED, GRIEVES, GRIEVING, GRIEVOUS

Attributed to the Holy Spirit (Eph 4:30; Heb 3:10,17). *See Affliction; Sorrow.*

GRIND [1990, 3221, 3222, 4197, 8835, *241*].

NIV+ GRINDERS, GRINDING

To pulverize grain between two millstones (Mt 24:41; Lk 17:35). *See Mill; Millstone.*

GROUND [*141, 824, 1990, 2750, 2754, 3000, 3317, 4793, 5776, 6641, 6760, 6881, 7536, 8187, 8441, 10075, *1178, 4838, 5912*].

NIV+ AGROUND, GROUNDS

Man made from (Ge 2:7; 3:19,23; Job 4:19; 33:6). Animals from (Ge 2:19). Vegetables from (Ge 2:9). Cursed (Ge 3:17; 5:29).

GROVES [1708, 2339, 3623, *3057*].

NIV+ GROVE

1. Groups of fruit trees (Dt 6:11; Ecc 2:6). *See Tree.*

2. NIV "Asherah [poles]"; an image of the Canaanite goddess Asherah. *See Asherah, 2; High Places; Idolatry.*

GROWTH *See Conformity; Discipleship; Grace of God, Growth in; Holiness; Sanctification.*

GUARD [*665, 1475, 2741, 3184, 4766, 4915, 5464, 5466, 5915, 6114, 7213, 7215, 8132, 9068, 9193, *1063, 1213, 3184, 4668, 5130, 5498, 5498, 5677, 5864, 5871, 5874, 5875*].

NIV+ BODYGUARD, GUARDED, GUARDIAN, GUARDIANS, GUARDING, GUARDROOM, GUARDS, SAFEGUARD

Imperial guard (Ge 37:36; 2Ki 25:8; Da 2:14), runner, trusted messengers of a king (1Ki 14:27-28), bodyguard

(2Sa 23:23), executioner (Mk 6:27), Roman guard (Mt 27:65).

GUDGODAH [1516] *(cleft).* A station of the Israelites in the wilderness (Dt 10:7), probably identical with Hor Haggidgad (Nu 33:32-33).

GUEST [448+995+1074, 6639, 7924, 9369, *367, 2813, 2906, 2907, 3825, 3826, 5263, 5626*].

NIV+ GUESTS

Greetings to (Ge 18:2). Abraham's hospitality to. *See Hospitality.*

Rules for the conduct of (Pr 23:1-3,6-8; 25:6-7,17; Lk 10:5-7; 14:7-11; 1Co 10:27). *See Hospitality.*

GUEST ROOM [*2906, 3825*]. According to Jewish custom an extra or upper room was offered to those who had come to Jerusalem to celebrate the Passover (Mk 14:14; Lk 22:11).

GUIDANCE *See God, Guidance of.*

GUILE *See Conspiracy; Deceit; Hypocrisy.*

GUILELESSNESS Truthfulness; without deceit. Commanded (Ps 34:13; 1Pe 2:1; 3:10). Of Jesus (1Pe 2:22). Of Nathanael (Jn 1:47). A grace of the righteous (Ps 32:2). *See Truthfulness.*

GUILT [870, 871, 873, 1947, 2628, 2631, 5927, 5929, 6404, 6411, 7322, *281, 1794*].

NIV+ BLOODGUILT, GUILTLESS, GUILTY, GUILTLESS

The deserving of punishment because of infraction of a law. Guilt could be the result of unconscious sin (Lev 5:17) or could be incurred by the group for the sin of an individual (Jos 7:10-15). There are degrees of guilt (Lk 12:47-48; Ac 17:30), but in the sight of God all people are guilty of sin (Ro 3:19).

See Conviction, of Sin.

GUILT OFFERING [871, 873]. Sacrifice of a ram for the purpose of expiation of sins against others; in addition to the sacrifice, restitution had to be made (Lev 5:16-19; 6:5-18; 7:1-10; Nu 5:7-8). Of the Servant's self-sacrifice (Isa 53:10 w Mt 20:28; Mk 10:45). *See Offerings.*

GULL [8830]. A bird. Forbidden as food (Lev 11:16; Dt 14:15).

GUM RESIN [5753]. Fragrant ingredient used in incense (Ex 30:34). *See Aromatic Resin; Incense.*

GUNI [1586, 1587] *(spotted sand grouse).*

1. Son of Naphtali (Ge 46:24; 1Ch 7:13) and his clan (Nu 26:48).

2. Father of Abdiel (1Ch 5:15).

GUR [1595].

NIV+ GUR BAAL

Place where Jehu slew Ahaziah (2Ki 9:27).

GUR BAAL [1597] *(sojourn of Baal).*

NIV+ BAAL, GUR

A town probably located S of Beersheba (2Ch 26:7).

GUTTER [2668]. Of the temple in Ezekiel's vision (Eze 43:13,14,17).

H

HAAHASHTARI [2028] (*the Ahashtarites*). Son of Naarah (1Ch 4:6).

HAARALOTH *See Gibeath Haaraloth.*

HABAIAH *See Hobaiah.*

HABAKKUK [2487] (*garden plant* KB). Prophet of the book which bears his name; wrote when the temple was still standing (Hab 2:20; 3:19), between c. 605-587 B.C., probably during the reign of the Judean king Jehoiakim.

HABAKKUK, BOOK OF (*garden plant* KB).

Author: Habakkuk

Date: Close to the battle of Carchemish (605 B.C.)

Outline:

I. Title (1:1).

II. Habakkuk's First Complaint: Why does the evil in Judah go unpunished? (1:2-4).

III. God's Answer: The Babylonians will punish Judah (1:5-11).

IV. Habakkuk's Second Complaint: How can a just God use wicked Babylon to punish a people more righteous than themselves? (1:12-2:1).

V. God's Answer: Babylon will be punished, and faith will be rewarded (2:2-20).

VI. Habakkuk's Prayer: After asking for manifestations of God's wrath and mercy (as in the past), he closes with confession of trust and joy in God (ch. 3).

See Prophets, The Minor.

HABAZZINIAH, HABAZINIAH [2484] (possibly *exuberant in Yahweh*). Head of the family of Recabites (Jer 35:3).

HABERGEON NIV "(coat of) armor," "javelin." *See Armor; Breastplate; Coat of Mail.*

HABIRU A people mentioned in Mari, Nuzi, and Amarna tablets; fundamental meaning seems to be "wanderers"; of mixed racial origin, including both Semites and non-Semites. Connection with Hebrews is obscure.

HABIT [4946+8997+9453, 6122, *1621*, *3443*]. (Ex 21:29,36; Nu 22:30; Jer 13:23; 22:21; Mic 2:1; 1Ti 5:13; Heb 10:25).

HABOR [2466]. A river of Mesopotamia (2Ki 17:6; 18:11; 1Ch 5:26).

HACALIAH [2678] (*dark*). Father of Nehemiah (Ne 1:1; 10:1).

HACHILAH *See Hakilah.*

HACMONI, HACMONITE; HACHMONI, HACHMONITE [1201+2685, 2685] (*wise*). Father of Jehiel and Jashobeam (2Sa 23:8, ftn; 1Ch 11:11; 27:32). *See Tahkemonite.*

HADAD [119, 2060, 2524] (*thunderer [Semitic storm god]*).

NIV+ BEN-HADAD, HADAD RIMMON

1. Grandson of Abraham (Ge 25:15).

2. A king of Edom (Ge 36:35-36; 1Ch 1:46-47).

3. Another king of Edom (Ge 36:39, ftn; 1Ch 1:50-51).

4. A member of the royal house of Edom who escaped to Egypt when David conquered Edom and then later returned to his homeland to revolt against Solomon (1Ki 11:14-25). The Hebrew actually reads "Adad" for the first "Hadad" in 1Ki 11:17, and it has been conjectured that 1Ki 11:14ff. combines two accounts, one of Hadad the Edomite and the other of Adad the Midianite. Convincing reasons have been given for identifying this Hadad with 3 above.

5. The ancient Semitic storm god who as the great Baal of the Ugaritic pantheon figured in the struggle of the religion of Israel against Canaanite religion.

HADAD RIMMON, HADAD-RIMMON [2062].

NIV+ HADAD, RIMMON

A place in the valley of Megiddo (Zec 12:11).

HADADEZER [2061] (*[pagan god] Hadad is a help*).

NIV+ HADADEZER'S

Son of Rehob, king of Zobah, vanquished by David (2Sa 8:3-13; 10:15-19; 1Ki 11:23; 1Ch 18:3-10; 19:6-19).

HADAR (*thunderer, Semitic storm god*).

1. Son of Ishmael (Ge 25:15, KJV). *See Hadad, 1.*

2. King of Edom (Ge 36:39, ftn.). *See Hadad, 3.*

HADAREZER *See Hadadezer.*

HADASHAH [2546] (*new*). A town in Judah (Jos 15:37).

HADASSAH [2073] (*myrtle* BDB and KB; possibly *myrtle* or *bride* IDB). The Hebrew name of Esther (Est 2:7). *See Esther.*

HADATTAH *See Hazor Hadattah.*

HADES [87] (*the underworld*). The unseen world (Mt 11:23; 16:18; Lk 10:15; 16:23; Ac 2:27,31; Rev 1:18; 6:8; 20:13-14).

Realm (or State) of the Dead:

Usually expressed in Hebrew by Sheol and in Greek by Hades—

2Sa 22:6 The cords of the grave coiled around me; the snares of death confronted me.

Job 26:5 "The dead are in deep anguish, those beneath the waters and all that live in them.

Ps 6:5 No one remembers you when he is dead. Who praises you from the grave?

Ps 17:15 And I—in righteousness I will see your face; when I awake, I will be satisfied with seeing your likeness.

Ps 30:9 "What gain is there in my destruction, in my going down into the pit? Will the dust praise you? Will it proclaim your faithfulness?

Ps 49:15 But God will redeem my life from the grave; he will surely take me to himself. *Selah*

Ps 86:13 For great is your love toward me; you have delivered me from the depths of the grave.

Ps 88:10 Do you show your wonders to the dead? Do those who are dead rise up and praise you? *Selah* [11]Is your love declared in the grave, your faithfulness in Destruction? [12]Are your wonders known in the place of darkness, or your righteous deeds in the land of oblivion?

Ps 115:17 It is not the dead who praise the LORD, those who go down to silence;

Ps 116:3 The cords of death entangled me, the anguish of the grave came upon me; I was overcome by trouble and sorrow.

Pr 15:24 The path of life leads upward for the wise to keep him from going down to the grave.

Pr 21:16 A man who strays from the path of understanding comes to rest in the company of the dead.

Pr 27:20 Death and Destruction are never satisfied, and neither are the eyes of man.

Ecc 9:4 Anyone who is among the living has hope—even a live dog is better off than a dead lion!

⁵For the living know that they will die, but the dead know nothing; they have no further reward, and even the memory of them is forgotten. ⁶Their love, their hate and their jealousy have long since vanished; never again will they have a part in anything that happens under the sun.

Isa 5:14 Therefore the grave enlarges its appetite and opens its mouth without limit; into it will descend their nobles and masses with all their brawlers and revelers.

Jnh 2:2 He said: "In my distress I called to the LORD, and he answered me. From the depths of the grave I called for help, and you listened to my cry.

Lk 23:42 Then he said, "Jesus, remember me when you come into your kingdom."

⁴³Jesus answered him, "I tell you the truth, today you will be with me in paradise."

Jn 8:22 This made the Jews ask, "Will he kill himself? Is that why he says, 'Where I go, you cannot come'?"

2Co 12:4 was caught up to paradise. He heard inexpressible things, things that man is not permitted to tell.

See Hell; Immortality; Paradise; Righteous, Promises to; Sheol; Spirit; Wicked, Punishment of.

HADID [2531] (*sharp*). A city of Benjamin. Captive of, returned from Babylon (Ezr 2:33; Ne 7:37; 11:34).

HADLAI [2536] (*resting* ISBE; *fat* IDB; *be stout* KB). Father of Amasa (2Ch 28:12).

HADORAM [2066, 2067] (*Hadad is exalted*).
1. Descendant of Shem (Ge 10:27; 1Ch 1:21).
2. Son of Tou (1Ch 18:10). Called Joram (2Sa 8:10).
3. Hebrew *Adoram* (2Sa 20:24, ftn) or *Hadoram* (2Ch 10:18, ftn), a variant of *Adoniram*. An officer in charge of forced labor during the reigns of David and then Solomon. He then held the same office under Rehoboam, Solomon's son. *See Adoniram.*

HADRACH [2541]. A district of Syria (Zec 9:1).

HAELEPH [2030]. A town of Benjamin, near Jerusalem (Jos 18:28).

HAGAB [2507] (*locust*). Ancestor of the temple servants who returned with Zerubbabel (Ezr 2:46).

HAGABA, HAGABAH [2509] (*locust*). One of the temple servants (Ezr 2:45; Ne 7:48).

HAGAR [2057, 29] (*emigration, flight*). A servant of Abraham and handmaid of Sarah. Given by Sarah to Abraham to be his wife (Ge 16). Descendants of (Ge 25:12-15; 1Ch 5:10,19-22; Ps 83:6, ftn). Allegorically identified with slavery to the law (Gal 4:24-25).

HAGARENES *See Hagar.*

HAGARITES, HAGERITES *See Hagrite(s).*

HAGGAI [2516, 10247] (*festal* BDB; *born on the feast day* KB). Haggai was a prophet who, with Zechariah, encouraged the returned exiles to rebuild the temple (Ezr

5:1-2; 6:14). The prophet's name ("festal,") may indicate he was born during one of the three pilgrimage feasts (Unleavened Bread, Pentecost or Weeks, and Tabernacles; cf. Dt 16:16). Based on 2:3 Haggai may have witnessed the destruction of Solomon's temple. If so, he must have been in his early 70s during his ministry.

HAGGAI, BOOK OF

Author: Haggai

Date:

The messages of Haggai were given during a four-month period in 520 B.C., the second year of King Darius. The first message was delivered on the first day of the sixth month (Aug. 29), the last on the 24th day of the ninth month (Dec. 18).

Outline:

I. First Message: The Call to Rebuild the Temple (1:1-11).
  A. The People's Lame Excuse (1:1-4).
  B. The Poverty of the People (1:5-6).
  C. The Reason God Has Cursed Them (1:7-11).
II. The Response of Zerubbabel and the People (1:12-15).
  A. The Leaders and Remnant Obey (1:12).
  B. The Lord Strengthens the Workers (1:13-15).
III. Second Message: The Temple to Be Filled with Glory (2:1-9).
  A. The People Encouraged (2:1-5).
  B. The Promise of Glory and Peace (2:6-9).
IV. Third Message: A Defiled People Purified and Blessed (2:10-19).
  A. The Rapid Spread of Sin (2:10-14).
  B. Poor Harvests Because of Disobedience (2:15-17).
  C. Blessing to Come as the Temple Is Rebuilt (2:18-19).
V. Fourth Message: The Promise to Zerubbabel (2:20-23).
  A. The Judgment of the Nations (2:20-22).
  B. The Significance of Zerubbabel (2:23).
  See Prophets, The Minor.

HAGGAN *See Beth Haggan.*

HAGGEDOLIM [2045] (*the great ones*). The father of Zabdiel, a priest (Ne 11:14).

HAGGI, HAGGITE [2515] (*festal* BDB; *born on the feast day* KB). Son of Gad (Ge 46:16) and his clan (Nu 26:15).

HAGGIAH [2517] (*feast of Yahweh*). A Levite (1Ch 6:30).

HAGGIDGAD *See Hor Haggidgad.*

HAGGITH [2518] (*festal* BDB; *born on the feast day* KB). Wife of David. Mother of Adonijah (2Sa 3:4; 1Ki 1:5,11; 2:13; 1Ch 3:2).

HAGGOYIM *See Harosheth Haggoyim.*

HAGIOGRAPHA (*holy writings*).

The third division of the Hebrew OT: Psalms, Proverbs, Job, Song of Solomon, Ruth, Lamentations, Ecclesiastes, Esther, Daniel, Ezra, Nehemiah, 1 and 2 Chronicles.

HAGRI [2058] (*wanderer*).
NIV+ HAGRITE, HAGRITES
Father of Mibhar (2Sa 23:36; 1Ch 11:38).

HAGRITE(S) [2058] (possibly *people from Hagar*).
NIV+ HAGRI

Descendants of Hagar, mother of Ishmael with whom Saul made war (1Ch 5:10,19-21; 27:31; Ps 83:6, ftn).

HAHIROTH *See Pi Hahiroth, Pi-Hahiroth.*

HAI *See Ai.*

HAIL [1351, 1352, 7943, *5897, 5898*].
NIV+ HAILSTONES, HAILSTORM

(Job 38:22; Hag 2:17). Plague of, in Egypt (Ex 9:18-29; Ps 78:48; 105:32). Destroys army of the Amorites (Jos 10:11).

Figurative:

(Isa 28:2; Rev 8:7; 11:19; 16:21).

HAIR [*6436, 8484, 8552, 8553, 8031, 10687, *2582*].
NIV+ GRAY-HAIRED, HAIRS, HAIRY

Numbered (Mt 10:30; Lk 12:7). Worn long by women (Isa 3:24; Lk 7:38; 1Co 11:5-6,15; 1Ti 2:9; 1Pe 3:3; Rev 9:8), by Absalom (2Sa 14:26). Worn short by men (1Co 11:14). Symbolic dividing of (Eze 5:1-2).

See Baldness; Leprosy; Mourning; Nazirite(s), Nazarite(s).

HAKILAH [2677]. A hill in Judah where David and his followers hid from Saul (1Sa 23:19; 26:3).

HAKKATAN [2214] (*the small one*). Father of Johanan (Ezr 8:12).

HAKKEREM *See Beth Hakkerem.*

HAKKORE *See En Hakkore.*

HAKKOZ [2212] (*the thorn*).

1. The eponym of a family of priests in David's time (1Ch 24:10). Members of this family were among those unable to document their claim to priestly rank after the Exile and so were suspended from office (Ezr 2:61; Ne 7:63).

2. Ancestor of Meremoth, who helped repair the wall of Jerusalem (Ne 3:4,21).

HAKUPHA [2979] (*crooked*). One of the temple servants (Ezr 2:51; Ne 7:53).

HALAH [2712]. A place to which Israelite captives were transported (2Ki 17:6; 18:11; 1Ch 5:26).

HALAK, MOUNT OF [2748] (*bare, bald*). A mountain, the southern limit of Joshua's conquests (Jos 11:17; 12:7).

HALF-HOMER *See Homer; Measure.*

HALF-TRIBE *See Manasseh, 2.*

HALHUL [2713]. A city in Judah (Jos 15:58).

HALI [2718] (*adornment*). A border town of Asher (Jos 19:25).

HALL [395, 1074+3516, 1074, 2121, 4384, 10103, *1141, 5391*].

1. Court of the high priest's palace (Lk 22:55).

2. Official residence of a Roman governor (Mt 27:27; Mk 15:16).

HALLEL (*praise*). Two liturgical collections of Psalms read at Passover. Psalms 113-118 called the "Egyptian Hallel"; Psalm 136, "the Hallel"; Psalms 120-136 are often called the "Great Hallel." *See Passover.*

HALLELUJAH [252] (*praise Yahweh*). Liturgical exclamation urging all to praise Yahweh. Occurs at the beginning of Psalms 106, 111-113, 117, 135, 146-150 and at the close of 104-106, 113, 115-117, 135, 146-150. *See Praise.*

HALLOHESH [2135] (*the whisperer*). Father of Shallum (Ne 3:12). Sealed the covenant with Nehemiah (Ne 10:24).

HALLOW, HALLOWED [39] (*to render as holy*).
NIV+ See HOLINESS

To set apart for sacred use; to hold sacred; to reverence as holy (Ex 20:11; Mt 6:9).

HAM [2154, 2769].
NIV+ HAMITES

1. Son of Noah (Ge 5:32; 9:18,24; 1Ch 1:4). Provokes his father's wrath (Ge 9:18-27). His children (Ge 10:6-20; 1Ch 1:8-16).

2. Family name of the descendants of Ham (1Ch 4:40; Ps 78:51; 105:23,27; 106:22).

3. Place where Kedorlaomer killed the Zuzites (Ge 14:5).

HAMAN [2172].
NIV+ HAMAN'S

Prime minister of Xerxes, king of Persia (Est 3:1,10; 7:7-10).

HAMATH, HAMATHITES [2828] (*fortress*).
NIV+ HAMATH ZOBAH, LEBO HAMATH

A city of upper Syria; the N border of the ideal limits of the Promised Land (Nu 13:21; 34:8; Jos 13:5; Eze 47:16). Solomon's kingdom extended from the Wadi of Egypt to the entrance of Hamath (1Ki 8:65), and the kingdom of Israel at the time of Jeroboam reached northward to the entrance of Hamath (2Ki 14:25; Am 6:14).

Inhabited by Canaanites (Ge 10:18). Prosperity of (Am 6:2). David receives gifts of gold and silver from Tou, king of (2Sa 8:9-10; 1Ch 18:3,9-10). Conquest of, by Jeroboam (2Ki 14:25,28), by the Chaldeans (2Ki 25:20-21). Israelites taken captive to (Isa 11:11). Prophecy concerning (Jer 49:23). Solomon builds store cities in (2Ch 8:4).

HAMATH ZOBAH, HAMATH-ZOBAH [2832] (*fortress of Zobah*).
NIV+ HAMATH, ZOBAH

A town on the border of Israel. Subdued by Solomon (2Ch 8:3).

HAMMAHLEKOTH *See Sela Hammahlekoth.*

HAMMATH [2829, 2830] (*hot springs*).

1. Fortified city of Naphtali, c. one mile S of Tiberias (Jos 19:35).

2. Founder of Recabites (1Ch 2:55).

HAMMEDATHA [2158] (*given by the moon [god]*). Father of Haman (Est 3:1,10; 8:5; 9:10,24).

HAMMELECH NIV "the king" (Jer 36:26; 38:6).

HAMMER [*2153, 5216, 7079, 8392, 8822*].
NIV+ HAMMERED, HAMMERS

A tool used for a variety of purposes:

Smoothing metals (Isa 41:7), driving tent pins (Jdg

4:21), forging (Isa 44:12). Sometimes used figuratively for any crushing power (Jer 23:29; 50:23).

HAMMOLEKETH, HAMMOLECHETH [2168]
(*the queen*). Daughter of Makir (1Ch 7:17-18).

HAMMON [2785] (*hot springs*).
1. A city of Asher (Jos 19:28).
2. A Levitical city of Naphtali (1Ch 6:76). Possibly identical with Hammath and Hammoth Dor.

HAMMOTH DOR, HAMMOTH-DOR [2831] (*hot spring of Dor*).
NIV+ DOR

Naphtali (Jos 21:32). Possibly identical with Hammath (Jos 19:35). Called Hammon (1Ch 6:76).

HAMMUEL [2781] (*God [El] of Ham* KB). A Simeonite (1Ch 4:26).

HAMMURABI King of Babylon (c. 1704-1662 B.C.).
Not the same as Amraphel (Ge 14:1-12). He was a great builder and lawgiver (Code of Hammurabi). *See Texts, Ancient Near Eastern Non-Biblical Texts Relating to the Old Testament.*

HAMON See *Baal Hamon; Hamon Gog*.

HAMON GOG, HAMON-GOG, VALLEY OF
[2163] (*multitude of Gog*).
NIV+ BAAL HAMON

Prophetic name for place E of Dead Sea where the "multitude of Gog" will be buried (Eze 39:11-15).

HAMONAH [2164] (*multitude*). Prophetic name of city near which Gog is defeated (Eze 39:16).

HAMOR [2791, 1846] (*male donkey*). Father of Shechem. Jacob buys ground from (Ge 33:19; Jos 24:32; Jdg 9:28). Murdered by the sons of Jacob (Ge 34:26; 49:6). Called Hamor (Ac 7:16).

HAMSTRING [6828].
NIV+ HAMSTRUNG

Disabling an animal by cutting the large tendon at the back of the knee, usually to render it useless for military service. Of horses (Jos 11:6,9; 2Sa 8:4; 1Ch 18:4). Of oxen (Ge 49:6).

HAMUL, HAMULITE [2783, 2784] (*pitied*). Son of Perez (Ge 46:12; 1Ch 2:5) and his clan (Nu 26:21).

HAMUTAL [2782] (*my husband's father is like dew*).
Wife of Josiah. Mother of Jehoahaz and Zedekiah (2Ki 23:31; 24:18; Jer 52:1).

HANAMEL [2856] (*God [El] is gracious*). Cousin of Jeremiah, to whom he sold a field in Anathoth (Jer 32:7-12).

HANAN [2860] (*gracious*).
1. Son of Shashak (1Ch 8:23).
2. Son of Azel (1Ch 8:38; 9:44).
3. One of David's mighty men (1Ch 11:43).
4. One of the temple servants (Ezr 2:46; Ne 7:49).
5. A Levite (Ne 8:7; 10:10). Probably identical with the one mentioned in Ne 13:13.
6. A chief who sealed the covenant with Nehemiah (Ne 10:22,26).
7. An officer in the temple (Jer 35:2-10).

HANANEL, HANANEEL, TOWER OF [2861]
(*God [El] is gracious*). Name of a tower forming part of the wall of Jerusalem (Ne 3:1; 12:39; Jer 31:38; Zec 14:10).

HANANI [2862] (*gracious*).
1. Son of Heman (1Ch 25:4,25).
2. A prophet who rebuked Asa, king of Judah (2Ch 16:7).
3. Father of Jehu the prophet (1Ki 16:1,7; 2Ch 19:2; 20:34). Possibly identical with 2.
4. A priest (Ezr 10:20).
5. A brother of Nehemiah and keeper of the gates of Jerusalem (Ne 1:2; 7:2).
6. A priest and musician (Ne 12:36).

HANANIAH [2863, 2864, 10275] (*Yahweh is gracious*).
1. Son of Heman (1Ch 25:4,23).
2. A captain of Uzziah's army (2Ch 26:11).
3. Father of Zedekiah (Jer 36:12).
4. A prophet of Gibeon who uttered false prophecies in the temple during the reign of Zedekiah (Jer 28).
5. Grandfather of Irijah (Jer 37:13).
6. Son of Shashak (1Ch 8:24).
7. Hebrew name of Shadrach. *See Shadrach.*
8. Son of Zerubbabel (1Ch 3:19,21).
9. Son of Bebai (Ezr 10:28).
10. A priest (Ne 3:8).
11. Son of Shelemiah (Ne 3:30).
12. A keeper of the gates of Jerusalem (Ne 7:2).
13. One who sealed the covenant (Ne 10:23).
14. A priest in time of Jehoiakim (Ne 12:12,41).

HAND [*2908, 3338, 4090, 10311, *1288, *942, *3638, *4140, *5931, *5935].
NIV+ HANDBREADTH, HANDED, HANDFUL, HANDFULS, HANDING, HANDS, LEFT-HANDED, OPENHANDED, RIGHT-HANDED

Laying on of hands (Heb 6:2), in consecration (Ge 48:14; Ex 29:10,15,19; Lev 1:4; 3:2,8,13; 4:15,24,33; 16:21), in ordaining the Levites (Nu 8:10-11), Joshua (Nu 27:18-23; Dt 34:9), Timothy (1Ti 4:14; 2Ti 1:6), in healing (Mk 6:5; 7:32; 16:18; Lk 4:40; Ac 28:8), in blessing children (Mt 19:13; Mk 10:16), in solemnizing testimony (Lev 24:14). Lifted up in benediction (Lev 9:22; Lk 24:50), in prayer. *See Prayer, Attitudes in.*

Ceremonial washing of (Mt 15:2; Mk 7:2-5). *See Washings; Cleanliness.*

Symbolic of righteousness (Job 17:9). Washing of, a symbol of innocence (Dt 21:6; Mt 27:24).

Clasping of, in token of contract (Ezr 10:19; Pr 6:1; 17:18; Eze 17:18), of friendship (2Ki 10:15; Job 17:3). Right hand lifted up in swearing (Ge 14:22; Ps 106:26; Isa 62:8), symbol of power (Isa 23:11; 41:10), place of honor (Ps 45:9; 80:17).

Figurative: (Mt 5:30; 18:8; Mk 9:43).

Anthropomorphic Use of:

Hand of the Lord considered limited in power (Nu 11:23), is mighty (Jos 4:24), was heavy (1Sa 5:6), against the Philistines (1Sa 5:7,13), on Elijah (1Ki 18:46), not limited in power (Isa 59:11), was with the early Christians (Ac 11:21). *See Anthropomorphisms.*

HANDBREADTH [3255, 3256, 3257].
NIV+ See HAND

A measure, about four inches (Ex 25:25; 1Ki 7:26; 2Ch

4:5; Ps 39:5; Isa 48:13; Eze 40:5,43; Jer 52:21). *See Fingers, Fingerbreadth; Span.*

HANDKERCHIEF [*5051*].

NIV+HANDKERCHIEFS

Sometimes translated "cloth," used for a variety of purposes (Lk 19:20-23; Jn 11:44; 20:7; Ac 19:12).

HANDLE [296, 2005, 5896, 5951, 6885, 6913, 8990, 9530, *721*].

NIV+HANDLED, HANDLES, HANDLING

Door knob (SS 5:5).

HANDMAID, HANDMAIDEN Female slave or servant. *See Maid(s), Maidservant(s); Servant.*

HANDS, LAYING ON OF

NIV+ See HAND

A ceremony having the idea of transference, identification, and devotion to God (Ex 29:10,15,19; Lev 16:21; Ac 8:14-17; 2Ti 1:6).

HANDSTAFF NIV "war clubs" (Eze 39:9). *See Club.*

HANES [2865]. A place in Egypt (Isa 30:4).

HANGING [*2871, 9434, *551*].

NIV+HANG, HANGED, HANGINGS, HANGS, HUNG, OVERHANG, OVERHANGING, OVERHANGS

Not a form of capital punishment in Bible times. Where used, except 2Sa 17:23; Mt 27:5, it refers to the suspension of a body from a tree or post after the criminal had been put to death (Ge 40:19,22; Dt 21:22).

HANGINGS [4158]. Material hung in the tabernacle so as to preserve the privacy and sacredness of that which was within (Ex 27:9-19; Mt 27:51).

HANIEL *See Hanniel, 2.*

HANNAH [2839] (*favor*). Mother of Samuel. Her trials, prayer, and promise (1Sa 1:1-18). Samuel born to, dedicates him to God, leaves him at the temple (1Sa 1:19-28). Her hymn of praise (1Sa 2:1-10). Visits Samuel at the temple from year to year (1Sa 2:18-19). Children of (1Sa 2:20-21).

HANNATHON [2872]. A city of Zebulun (Jos 19:14).

HANNIEL [2848] (*favor of God [El]*).

1. A son of Ephod, appointed by Moses to divide the land among the several tribes (Nu 34:23).

2. A son of Ulla (1Ch 7:39).

HANOCH, HANOCHITE [2840, 2854] (*initiation*).

1. Grandson of Abraham by Keturah (Ge 25:4; 1Ch 1:33).

2. Son of Reuben (Ge 46:9; Ex 6:14; 1Ch 5:3) and his clan (Nu 26:5).

HANUKKAH [*1589*] (*dedication*).

NIV+DEDICATION

The Feast of Rededication. After Judas Maccabeus had cleansed the temple from the pollution of pagan worship (c. 165 B.C.), the twenty-fifth of Kislev (December) was kept annually in memory of this.

See Dedication; Feasts; Kislev; Maccabees; Month, 9.

HANUN [2842] (*favored*).

1. King of Ammon who provoked David to war (2Sa 10:1-5; 1Ch 19:1-5).

---

2. Two men who helped repair wall of Jerusalem (Ne 3:13,30).

HAPHARAIM, HAPHRAIM [2921] (*place of two trenches*). A city of Issachar (Jos 19:19).

HAPPINESS [*245, 897, 3202, 8523, 8524, 8525, *5915*].

NIV+HAPPY, HAPPIER

Of the Wicked:

Limited to this life (Ps 17:14; Lk 16:25), short (Job 20:5), uncertain (Lk 12:20), vain (Ecc 2:1; 7:6).

Is derived from their wealth (Job 21:13; Ps 52:7), their power (Job 21:7; Ps 37:35), their worldly prosperity (Ps 17:14; 73:3-4,7), gluttony (Isa 22:13; Hab 1:16), drunkenness (Isa 5:11; 56:12), vain pleasure (Job 21:12; Isa 5:12), successful oppression (Hab 1:15). Marred by jealousy (Est 5:13), often interrupted by judgments (Nu 11:33; Job 15:21; Ps 73:18-20; Jer 25:10-11). Leads to sorrow (Pr 14:13). Leads to recklessness (Isa 22:12). Sometimes a stumbling-block to saints (Ps 73:3,16; Jer 12:1; Hab 1:13). Saints often permitted to see the end of (Ps 73:17-20), envy not (Ps 37:1). Woe against (Am 6:1; Lk 6:25).

Illustrated (Ps 37:35-36; Lk 12:16-20; 16:19-25).

Exemplified:

Israel (Nu 11:33). Haman (Est 5:9-11). Belshazzar (Da 5:1). Herod (Ac 12:21-23).

Of the Righteous:

In the Lord, through abundance—

Ps 36:8 They feast on the abundance of your house; you give them drink from your river of delights.

Ecc 2:24 A man can do nothing better than to eat and drink and find satisfaction in his work. This too, I see, is from the hand of God, [25]for without him, who can eat or find enjoyment? [26]To the man who pleases him, God gives wisdom, knowledge and happiness, but to the sinner he gives the task of gathering and storing up wealth to hand it over to the one who pleases God. This too is meaningless, a chasing after the wind.

Ecc 3:12 I know that there is nothing better for men than to be happy and do good while they live. [13]That everyone may eat and drink, and find satisfaction in all his toil—this is the gift of God.

Ecc 3:22 So I saw that there is nothing better for a man than to enjoy his work, because that is his lot. For who can bring him to see what will happen after him?

In chastisement—

Job 5:17 "Blessed is the man whom God corrects; so do not despise the discipline of the Almighty. [18]For he wounds, but he also binds up; he injures, but his hands also heal. [19]From six calamities he will rescue you; in seven no harm will befall you. [20]In famine he will ransom you from death, and in battle from the stroke of the sword. [21]You will be protected from the lash of the tongue, and need not fear when destruction comes. [22]You will laugh at destruction and famine, and need not fear the beasts of the earth. [23]For you will have a covenant with the stones of the field, and the wild animals will be at peace with you. [24]You will know that your tent is secure; you will take stock of your property and find nothing missing. [25]You will know that your children will be many, and your descendants like the grass of the earth. [26]You will come to the grave in full vigor, like sheaves gathered in season.

[27]"We have examined this, and it is true. So hear it and apply it to yourself."

In fellowship—
Ps 133:1 How good and pleasant it is when brothers live together in unity!

In good works—
Pr 14:21 He who despises his neighbor sins, but blessed is he who is kind to the needy. (+Ecc 3:12; Mt 5:3-9)

In hope—
Ro 5:2 through whom we have gained access by faith into this grace in which we now stand. And we rejoice in the hope of the glory of God.

In obedience—
Ps 40:8 I desire to do your will, O my God; your law is within my heart."

Ps 128:1 Blessed are all who fear the LORD, who walk in his ways. **²**You will eat the fruit of your labor; blessings and prosperity will be yours.

Ps 144:15 Blessed are the people of whom this is true; blessed are the people whose God is the LORD.

Ps 146:5 Blessed is he whose help is the God of Jacob, whose hope is in the LORD his God,

Pr 16:20 Whoever gives heed to instruction prospers, and blessed is he who trusts in the LORD.

Pr 28:14 Blessed is the man who always fears the LORD, but he who hardens his heart falls into trouble.

Pr 29:18 Where there is no revelation, the people cast off restraint; but blessed is he who keeps the law.

In peace—
Php 4:7 And the peace of God, which transcends all understanding, will guard your hearts and your minds in Christ Jesus.

In persecution (Mt 3:10-11)—
2Co 12:10 That is why, for Christ's sake, I delight in weaknesses, in insults, in hardships, in persecutions, in difficulties. For when I am weak, then I am strong.

1Pe 3:14 But even if you should suffer for what is right, you are blessed. "Do not fear what they fear; do not be frightened."

1Pe 4:12 Dear friends, do not be surprised at the painful trial you are suffering, as though something strange were happening to you.

In protection—
Dt 33:29 Blessed are you, O Israel! Who is like you, a people saved by the LORD? He is your shield and helper and your glorious sword. Your enemies will cower before you, and you will trample down their high places." (+Isa 12:2-3)

In satisfaction—
Ps 63:5 My soul will be satisfied as with the richest of foods; with singing lips my mouth will praise you.

Trust (Pr 16:20)

In wisdom—
Pr 3:13 Blessed is the man who finds wisdom, the man who gains understanding, **¹⁴**for she is more profitable than silver and yields better returns than gold. **¹⁵**She is more precious than rubies; nothing you desire can compare with her. **¹⁶**Long life is in her right hand; in her left hand are riches and honor. **¹⁷**Her ways are pleasant ways, and all her paths are peace. **¹⁸**She is a tree of life to those who embrace her; those who lay hold of her will be blessed.

Beatitudes—
Mt 5:3 "Blessed are the poor in spirit, for theirs is the kingdom of heaven. **⁴**Blessed are those who mourn, for they will be comforted. **⁵**Blessed are the meek, for they will inherit the earth. **⁶**Blessed are those who hunger and thirst for righteousness, for they will be filled. **⁷**Blessed are the merciful, for they will be shown mercy. **⁸**Blessed are the pure in heart, for they will see God. **⁹**Blessed are the peacemakers, for they will be called sons of God. **¹⁰**Blessed are those who are persecuted because of righteousness, for theirs is the kingdom of heaven.

¹¹"Blessed are you when people insult you, persecute you and falsely say all kinds of evil against you because of me. **¹²**Rejoice and be glad, because great is your reward in heaven, for in the same way they persecuted the prophets who were before you.

See Joy; Peace; Praise.

HAPPIZZEZ [2204]. A governor of the temple (1Ch 24:15).

HARA [2217] (*hill, highland*). Place in Assyria to which Israelites were exiled by Assyrians (1Ch 5:26).

HARADAH [3011] (*place of fear*). One of the camps of Israel (Nu 33:24-25).

HARAM *See Beth Haram.*

HARAN [2237, 3059, 3060, 5924] (earlier *mountaineer*, but perhaps *sanctuary*).

NIV+ BETH HARAN

1. Father of Lot and brother of Abraham (Ge 11:26-31).

2. Son of Caleb (1Ch 2:46).

3. A Levite (1Ch 23:9).

4. A place in Mesopotamia to which Terah and Abraham migrated (Ge 11:31; 12:4-5; Ac 7:2,4). Death of Terah at (Ge 11:32). Abraham leaves, by divine command (Ge 12:1-5). Jacob flees to (Ge 27:43; 28:7; 29), returns from, with Rachel and Leah (Ge 31:17-21). Conquest of, by king of Assyria (2Ki 19:12). Merchants of (Eze 27:23). Idolatry in (Jos 24:2,14; Isa 37:12).

HARARITE [2240] (*mountain dweller*). A place or family name (2Sa 23:11,33; 1Ch 11:34).

HARASHIM *See Ge Harashim.*

HARBONA, HARBONAH [3002, 3003] (*donkey driver*). Eunuch of Xerxes (Est 1:10; 7:9).

HARD, HARD-HEARTED *See Obduracy.*

HARDEST STONE The Lord makes Ezekiel's forehead harder than "the hardest stone" (Eze 3:9).

See Adamant; Diamond; Flint; Minerals of the Bible, 1; Stones.

HARE *See Animals; Rabbit.*

HAREM [851, 851+1074, 2256+8721+8721]. The wives and concubines of a king (Ecc 2:8; Est 2:3,13-14).

HAREPH [3073] (*autumn,* or *sharp* IDB; *scornful* ISBE). Son of Caleb (1Ch 2:51).

HARESETH *See Kir Hareseth.*

HARHAIAH [3015]. Father of Uzziel (Ne 3:8).

HARHAS [3030]. Grandfather of the husband of Huldah, the prophetess (2Ki 22:14). Called Hasrah (2Ch 34:22).

HARHUR [3028] (possibly *fever* BDB; possibly *raven* IDB; *one born during his mother's fever* KB). Head of a family that returned with Zerubbabel (Ezr 2:51; Ne 7:53).

HARIM [3053] (*consecrated [to Yahweh]*).

NIV+ HARIM'S

1. Priest (1Ch 24:8).

2. Family that returned with Zerubbabel (Ezr 2:39; Ne 7:35).

3. Family of priests (Ezr 2:39; 10:21; Ne 7:42; 12:15).

4. Family that married foreign wives (Ezr 10:31).

5. Father of a worker on the wall (Ne 3:11).

6. A man who sealed the covenant (Ne 10:27).

HARIPH [3040] (*one born at harvest time*).

1. One of the exiles (Ne 7:24). Probably the same as Jorah (Ezr 2:18).

2. One who sealed the covenant (Ne 10:19).

HARLOT [2390]. *See Adultery; Prostitute.*.

HARLOTRY *See Adultery; Prostitute.*

HARMON [2236]. Possibly a place name (Am 4:3, ftn.).

HARNEPHER [3062] (*[pagan god] Horus is merciful*). Asherite (1Ch 7:36).

HAROD, HARODITE [3008, 3012] (*trembling*). Spring beside which Gideon encamped (Jdg 7:1). Family name of Shammah and Elika (2Sa 23:25).

HAROEH [2218] (*the seer*). Grandson of Caleb (1Ch 2:52).

HARORITE [2229]. Shammoth, one of David's mighty men (1Ch 11:27).

HAROSHETH HAGGOYIM, HAROSHETH OF THE GENTILES [3099] (*Harosheth of the nations*). Town in N Israel c. sixteen miles NW of Megiddo; home of Sisera (Jdg 4:2,13,16).

HARP [4036, 5575, 5594, 10590, *3067, 3069*].

NIV+ HARPIST, HARPISTS, HARPS

A stringed instrument of music (Isa 38:20; Eze 33:32; Hab 3:19). With three strings (1Sa 18:6), ten strings (Ps 33:2; 92:3; 144:9; 150:4). Originated with Jubal (Ge 4:21). Made of almugwood (1Ki 10:12). David skillful in playing (1Sa 16:16,23). Used in worship (1Sa 10:5; 1Ch 16:5; 25:1-7; 2Ch 5:12-13; 29:25; Ps 33:2; 43:4; 49:4; 57:8; 71:22; 81:2; 93:3; 98:5; 108:2; 147:7; 149:3; 150:3). Used, in national jubilees, after the triumph over Goliath (1Sa 18:6), over the armies of Ammon and Moab (2Ch 20:20-29), when the new walls of Jerusalem were dedicated (Ne 12:27,36). Used in festivities (Ge 31:27; Job 21:11-12; Isa 5:12; 23:16; 24:8; 30:32; Eze 26:13; Rev 18:22), in mourning (Job 30:31). Discordant (1Co 14:7). Hung on the willows by the captive Israelites (Ps 137:2). Heard in heaven, in John's apocalyptic vision (Rev 5:8; 14:2; 15:2). The symbol used in the Psalms to indicate when the harp was to be introduced in the music was *neginah* or *neginoth. See titles of Pss 4; 6; 54; 55; 61; 67; 76.*

See Music, Instruments of, Symbols Used in.

HARROW [8440].

NIV+ HARROWING

Instrument for dragging or leveling off a field (Job 39:10), "breaking up the soil" (Isa 28:24; Hos 10:11). *See Picks, Iron.*

HARSHA [3095] (*deaf*).

NIV+ TEL HARSHA

One of the temple servants (Ezr 2:52; Ne 7:54).

HART *See Deer.*

HARUM [2227] (*consecrated*). A descendant of Judah (1Ch 4:8).

HARUMAPH [3018] (*disfigured nose*). Father of Jedaiah (Ne 3:10).

HARUPHITE [3020] (*sharp* or *autumn*). Designation of Shephatiah (1Ch 12:5).

HARUZ [3027] (perhaps *gold*, or *eager*). Father-in-law of King Manasseh (2Ki 21:19).

HARVEST [658, 665, 668, 1292, 1305, 3292, 3823+3824, 7811, 7907, 7917, 8040, 9311, *1163, 2545, 2546, 2843*].

NIV+ HARVESTED, HARVESTERS, HARVESTING, HARVESTS

Sabbath to be observed in (Ex 34:21). Sabbath desecrated in (Ne 13:15-22).

Of wheat at Pentecost, in Israel (Ex 34:22; Lev 23:15-17), and before vintage (Lev 26:5). Of barley, before wheat (Ex 9:31-32).

Celebrated with joy (Jdg 9:27; Isa 9:3; 16:10; Jer 48:33). Promises of plentiful (Ge 8:22; Jer 5:24; Joel 2:23-24).

Figurative:

(Job 24:5; Ps 10:5; Jer 8:20; Joel 3:13; Mt 9:37; 13:39; Lk 10:2; Rev 14:15).

See Pentecost, 1; Tabernacles, Feast of; Firstfruits; Reaping; Glean, Gleaning.

HASADIAH [2878] (*Yahweh is faithful*). Son of Zerubbabel (1Ch 3:20).

HASENUAH, HASSENUAH

1. Benjamite (1Ch 9:7).

2. Father of assistant overseer of Jerusalem (Ne 11:9).

HASHABIAH [3116, 3117] (*Yahweh has reckoned*).

1. Ancestor of Ethan (1Ch 6:45).

2. Ancestor of Shemaiah (1Ch 9:14; Ne 11:15).

3. Son of Jeduthun (1Ch 25:3).

4. Civil official in David's time (1Ch 26:30).

5. Overseer of tribe of Levi (1Ch 27:17).

6. Chief of Levites (2Ch 35:9).

7. Levite teacher (Ezr 8:19).

8. Chief priest (Ezr 8:24).

9. Worker on the wall (Ne 3:17).

10. Priest (Ne 12:21).

11. Ancestor of Uzzi (Ne 11:22).

12. Chief of Levites (Ne 3:17; 12:24).

HASHABNAH [3118] (probably *Yahweh has considered me*). Man who sealed covenant with Nehemiah (Ne 10:25).

HASHABNEIAH [3119] (probably *Yahweh has considered me*).

1. Father of Hattush (Ne 3:10).

2. A Levite (Ne 9:5).

HASHBADDANAH [3111] (probably *Yahweh has considered me*). A man who stood by Ezra as he read the law (Ne 8:4).

HASHEM [2244]. Father of several members of David's guard (1Ch 11:34).

HASHMONAH [3135]. A camp of the Israelites (Nu 33:29-30).

HASHUBAH [3112] (*consideration*). A descendant of King Jehoiakim (1Ch 3:20).

HASHUM [3130] (*broad-nosed*).

1. Family which returned from the Exile (Ezr 2:19; 10:33; Ne 7:22).

2. Priest who stood at side of Ezra when he read the law (Ne 8:4).

3. Chief of people who sealed the covenant (Ne 10:18). May be the same as 2.

HASHUPHA *See Hasupha, Hashupha.*

HASMONEANS *See Maccabees.*

HASRAH [2897]. Grandfather of Shallum (2Ch 34:22), "Harhas" (2Ki 22:14).

HASSENAAH [2189]. Father of sons who built fish gate in Jerusalem (Ne 3:3).

HASSENUAH [2190] (*the hated women*). A Benjamite and the father of Judah, a governor of Jerusalem (1Ch 9:7; Ne 11:9).

HASSHUB, HASHUB [3121] (*considerate*).

1. Son of Pahath-Moab (Ne 3:11).

2. One of the Captivity who assisted in repairing the wall of Jerusalem (Ne 3:23).

3. Head of a family (Ne 10:23).

4. A Levite (1Ch 9:14; Ne 11:15).

HASSOPHERETH [2191] (*the scribes*). May have once been an official title (Ezr 2:55).

HASTE [*237, 2590, 2906, 4960+5674, 5610].

NIV+ HASTEN, HASTILY, HASTY

In judgment, by Moses and the Israelites (Nu 32:1-19; Jos 22:10-34).

See Rashness.

HASUPHA, HASHUPHA [3102]. Family that returned from exile with Zerubbabel (Ezr 2:43; Ne 7:46).

HAT *See Dress; Headdress; Turbans.*

HATHACH [2251] (*good*). A eunuch in the court of Xerxes (Est 4:5-6,9-10).

HATHATH [3171] (possibly *terror* BDB and KB; possibly *weakness* IDB). A son of Othniel (1Ch 4:13).

HATIPHA [2640] (*taken captive*). One of the temple servants (Ezr 2:54; Ne 7:56).

HATITA [2638]. A gatekeeper of the temple (Ezr 2:42; Ne 7:45).

HATRED [*8533, 8534, *3631*].

NIV+ GOD-HATERS, HATE, HATED, HATES, HATING

Is blinding—

1Jn 2:9 Anyone who claims to be in the light but hates his brother is still in the darkness.

1Jn 2:11 But whoever hates his brother is in the darkness and walks around in the darkness; he does not know where he is going, because the darkness has blinded him.

Carnal—

Gal 5:19 The acts of the sinful nature are obvious: sexual immorality, impurity and debauchery; [20]idolatry and witchcraft; hatred, discord, jealousy, fits of rage, selfish ambition, dissensions, factions

Murderous—

1Jn 3:15 Anyone who hates his brother is a murderer, and you know that no murderer has eternal life in him.

Unforgiving—

Mt 6:15 But if you do not forgive men their sins, your Father will not forgive your sins.

Leads to deceit—

Pr 26:24 A malicious man disguises himself with his lips, but in his heart he harbors deceit. [25]Though his speech is charming, do not believe him, for seven abominations fill his heart. [26]His malice may be concealed by deception, but his wickedness will be exposed in the assembly.

Opposite of love—

Pr 15:17 Better a meal of vegetables where there is love than a fattened calf with hatred.

Prevents from loving God—

1Jn 4:20 If anyone says, "I love God," yet hates his brother, he is a liar. For anyone who does not love his brother, whom he has seen, cannot love God, whom he has not seen.

Produces strife—

Pr 10:12 Hatred stirs up dissension, but love covers over all wrongs.

Toward the righteous—

Ps 25:19 See how my enemies have increased and how fiercely they hate me!

Ps 35:19 Let not those gloat over me who are my enemies without cause; let not those who hate me without reason maliciously wink the eye.

Mt 10:22 All men will hate you because of me, but he who stands firm to the end will be saved.

Jn 15:18 "If the world hates you, keep in mind that it hated me first. [19]If you belonged to the world, it would love you as its own. As it is, you do not belong to the world, but I have chosen you out of the world. That is why the world hates you.

Jn 15:23 He who hates me hates my Father as well. [24]If I had not done among them what no one else did, they would not be guilty of sin. But now they have seen these miracles, and yet they have hated both me and my Father. [25]But this is to fulfill what is written in their Law: 'They hated me without reason.'

Jn 17:14 I have given them your word and the world has hated them, for they are not of the world any more than I am of the world.

Forbidden—

Eph 4:31 Get rid of all bitterness, rage and anger, brawling and slander, along with every form of malice.

Col 3:8 But now you must rid yourselves of all such things as these: anger, rage, malice, slander, and filthy language from your lips.

Toward a brother—

Lev 19:17 "'Do not hate your brother in your heart. Rebuke your neighbor frankly so you will not share in his guilt.

Toward an enemy—

Mt 5:43 "You have heard that it was said, 'Love your neighbor and hate your enemy.' [44]But I tell you: Love your enemies and pray for those who persecute you,

Justified against iniquity (Ps 97:10; 101:3; 119:104,

128,163; 139:21-22), of God (Ps 5:5; 45:7; Isa 61:8; Mal 2:16).

See Envy; Jealousy; Malice; Revenge.

HATTAAVAH *See Kibroth Hattaavah.*

HATTIL [2639] (*talkative*). A returned exile (Ezr 2:57; Ne 7:59).

HATTIN, HORNS OF (*hollows*). Hill near village of Hattin on which, tradition says, Christ delivered the Sermon on the Mount.

HATTUSH [2637].

1. Descendant of Zerubbabel (1Ch 3:22).
2. Man who returned from Babylon (Ezr 8:2).
3. Worker on the wall (Ne 3:10). May be the same as 2.
4. Man who sealed the covenant (Ne 10:4). May be the same as 2 or 3.
5. Priest who returned with Zerubbabel (Ne 12:2).

HAUGHTINESS [1467, 1468, 1469, 1470, 2294, 5294, 8123, 8124].

NIV+ HAUGHTY

See Pride.

HAURAN [2588] (*black*). Plateau E of Jordan and N of Gilead (Eze 47:16,18). Called Bashan in ancient times; in the time of the Romans, Auranitis.

HAVENS *See Fair Havens.*

HAVILAH [2564] (*stretch of sand*).

1. Son of Cush (Ge 10:7; 1Ch 1:9).
2. Son of Joktan (Ge 10:29; 1Ch 1:23).
3. Land encompassed by Pishon River (Ge 2:11-12).
4. One of the boundaries of the Ishmaelites (Ge 25:18; 1Sa 15:7).

HAVVOTH JAIR, HAVVOTH-JAIR [2596] (*villages of Jair*).

NIV+ JAIR

A group of unwalled towns in the NW part of Bashan (Nu 32:41; Dt 3:14; Jos 13:30; Jdg 10:4).

HAWK [5891]. A carnivorous and unclean bird (Lev 11:16; Dt 14:15; Job 39:26).

HAY [2945, 5965]. (Pr 27:25; Isa 15:6; 1Co 3:12).

HAZAEL [2599] (*God [El] sees*). King of Syria. Anointed king by Elijah (1Ki 19:15). Conquests by (2Ki 8:28-29; 9:14; 10:32-33; 12:17-18; 13:3,22; 2Ch 22:5-6). Conspires against, murders, and succeeds to the throne of Ben-Hadad (2Ki 8:8-15). Death of (2Ki 13:24).

HAZAIAH [2610] (*Yahweh sees*). A man of Judah (Ne 11:5).

HAZAR (*a settlement*). Often prefixed to descriptive place names. Also used for encampments of nomads.

HAZAR ADDAR, HAZAR-ADDAR [2960] (*settlement of Addar*). Also called Addar, a place on the southern boundary of Canaan (Nu 34:4; Jos 15:3).

HAZAR ENAN, HAZAR-ENAN [2965, 2966] (*settlement of Enan*). The NE boundary point of the promised land (Nu 34:9-10; Eze 47:17; 48:1).

HAZAR GADDAH, HAZAR-GADDAH [2961] (*settlement of [pagan god] Gad*). A town in the southern district of Judah (Jos 15:27).

HAZAR HATTICON, HAZAR-HATTICON *See Hazer Hatticon.*

HAZAR SHUAL, HAZAR-SHUAL [2967] (*settlement of Shual [jackal]*).

NIV+ SHUAL

Town in S Judah (Jos 15:28; 19:3; 1Ch 4:28; Ne 11:27).

HAZAR SUSAH, HAZAR SUSIM [2963, 2964] (*settlement of Susah [horse]*). Also called Hazar Susim, a city of Judah (Jos 19:5; 1Ch 4:31).

HAZARMAVETH [2975] (*village of [pagan god] Maveth*). Son and descendants of Joktan (Ge 10:26; 1Ch 1:20).

HAZAZON TAMAR, HAZAZON-TAMAR [2954] (*Hazazon of the palm trees*).

NIV+ EN GEDI, TAMAR

The ancient name of En Gedi, a town on W coast of Dead Sea (Ge 14:7; 2Ch 20:2).

HAZEL *See Almond.*

HAZER HATTICON, HAZAR-HATTICON [2962] (*place of Hatticon*). A place on the boundary of Hauran, probably E of Damascus (Eze 47:16).

HAZERIM (*unwalled settlements*). A district in the S of Canaan (Dt 2:23).

HAZEROTH [2972] (*settlements*). A station in the travels of the Israelites (Nu 11:35; 12:16; 33:17-18; Dt 1:1).

HAZEZON-TAMAR *See Hazazon Tamar, Hazazon-Tamar.*

HAZIEL [2609] (*vision of God [El]*). A Levite (1Ch 23:9).

HAZO [2605]. A son of Nahor (Ge 22:22).

HAZOR [2937] (*an enclosure*).

NIV+ BAAL HAZOR, EN HAZOR, HAZOR HADATTAH, KERIOTH HEZRON

1. City c. five miles W of waters of Merom, ruled by Jabin (Jos 11:1,10), conquered by Joshua and, later, by Deborah and Barak (Jdg 4; 1Sa 12:9), fortified by Solomon (1Ki 9:15), its inhabitants taken into exile by Assyria (2Ki 15:29).
2. Town in S of Judah (Jos 15:23).
3. Another town in S Judah (Jos 15:25).
4. Town N of Jerusalem (Ne 11:33).
5. Region in S Arabia (Jer 49:28-33).

HAZOR HADATTAH [2939] (*new Hazor*).

NIV+ HAZOR

Probably an adjective qualifying Hazor, making it equivalent to New Hazor. A city of Judah (Jos 15:25).

HAZZELELPONI, HAZELELPONI [2209]. Daughter of Etam (1Ch 4:3).

HAZZOBEBAH [2206]. Daughter of Koz (1Ch 4:8).

HAZZURIM *See Helkath Hazzurim.*

HEAD [*5265, 7721, 7949, 8031, 8484, 8553, 8569, 8672, 10646, *3051, *5092*].

NIV+ AHEAD, FIGUREHEAD, HEADED, HEADING, HEADS, HOTHEADED

Shaven when vows were taken (Ac 21:24). Diseases of (Isa 3:17). Anointed (Lev 14:18,29).

HEAD OF THE CHURCH Christ, who gives the church life, direction, strength (Eph 1:22; 5:23; Col 1:18).

HEADBANDS [710, 4457, 8667].

NIV+ HEADBAND, HEADDRESSES

Head coverings worn by priests (Ex 28:40; 29:9; Lev 8:13), by women (Isa 3:18,20). Used in disguise (1Ki 20:38-41). *See Dress; Turban.*

HEADSTONE *See Cornerstone.*

HEALING [*776, 5340, 8324, 9499, *1407, 2542, 2543, 2611, 2615, 2617, 5392*].

NIV+ HEAL, HEALED, HEALS, HEALTH, HEALTHIER, HEALTHY

The LORD the healer (Ge 20:17; Ex 15:26; Ps 6:2; 30:2; 103:3; Ac 4:30).

In answer to prayer (Jas 5:14-16), of Miriam (Nu 12:10-15), of Jeroboam (1Ki 13:1-6), of Hezekiah (2Ki 20:1-7).

By Elisha, of Naaman (2Ki 5:1-14).

By Jesus:

The nobleman's son (Jn 4:46-53). The disabled man (Jn 5:2-9). A leper (Mt 8:2-4; Mk 1:40-45; Lk 5:12-13). Peter's mother-in-law (Mt 8:14-15). Paralyzed man (Mt 9:2-8; Mk 2:1-12; Lk 5:17-26). The man with the withered hand (Mt 12:9-13; Mk 3:1-5; Lk 6:6-10). The centurion's servant (Mt 8:5-13; Lk 7:1-10). Demoniacs (Mt 8:28-34, w Mk 5:1-20, & Lk 8:26-36; Mt 12:22; 17:14-18; Mk 9:14-27; Lk 9:38-42; 11:14). Blind and mute (Mt 9:27-33; 12:22; 20:30-34; Mk 8:22-25; 10:46-52; Lk 18:35-43). Woman with issue of blood (Mt 9:20-22; Mk 5:25-34; Lk 8:43-48). Many sick (Mt 8:16; 9:35; 14:14,35-36; 15:30-31; 19:2; Mk 6:5,53-56; Lk 4:40; 9:11). Daughter of the Syrian Phoenician woman (Mt 15:22-28; Mk 7:25-30). Woman with an infirmity (Lk 13:10-13). Ten lepers (Lk 17:12-14). *See Miracles, of Jesus.*

Power of, given to the apostles (Mt 10:1,8; Mk 3:13-15; 6:7,13; Lk 9:1-2,6), to the Seventy (Lk 10:9,17), to all believers (Mk 16:18). Special gifts of (1Co 12:9,28,30).

By the Apostles:

The lame man, in Jerusalem (Ac 3:2-10), in Lystra (Ac 14:8-10). Sick, in Jerusalem (Ac 5:15-16), on the island of Malta (Ac 28:8-9). Aeneas (Ac 9:34).

Figurative:

Healing of disease a metaphor for forgiving of sins (Ps 103:3; Hos 7:1).

See Miracles.

HEALTH [776, 2014, 2730, 5340, 5507, 8326, 8934, *5617*].

NIV+ See HEALING

Health was a promised blessing of the Old Covenant (Ex 15:26; Dt 7:12-16), as diseases were part of its curse (Lev 26:14-16; Dt 28:20-29,58-63). Health can be affected by sin (Ps 38:3,7), but not all disease is the result of sin (Jn 9:1-3).

The wish for health and wholeness (Hebrew *shalom*) was part of standard greetings (Ge 29:6; 43:27,28; 1Sa 25:4-6; 3Jn 2). The fear of the LORD brings health (Pr

3:7-8), words of wisdom (Pr 4:20-22), good news (Pr 15:30).

See Healing.

HEAR *See Obedience.*

HEARERS [*263, 5583, 7754, 7992, 9048, 9051, 10725, *198, 201, 1653*].

NIV+ HEAR, HEARD, HEARING, HEARS, OVERHEARD

Heedless—

Eze 33:30 "As for you, son of man, your countrymen are talking together about you by the walls and at the doors of the houses, saying to each other, 'Come and hear the message that has come from the LORD.' [31]My people come to you, as they usually do, and sit before you to listen to your words, but they do not put them into practice. With their mouths they express devotion, but their hearts are greedy for unjust gain. [32]Indeed, to them you are nothing more than one who sings love songs with a beautiful voice and plays an instrument well, for they hear your words but do not put them into practice.

Mt 7:26 But everyone who hears these words of mine and does not put them into practice is like a foolish man who built his house on sand. [27]The rain came down, the streams rose, and the winds blew and beat against that house, and it fell with a great crash."

Mt 13:14 In them is fulfilled the prophecy of Isaiah: "'You will be ever hearing but never understanding; you will be ever seeing but never perceiving. [15]For this people's heart has become calloused; they hardly hear with their ears, and they have closed their eyes. Otherwise they might see with their eyes, hear with their ears, understand with their hearts and turn, and I would heal them.'

Mt 13:19 When anyone hears the message about the kingdom and does not understand it, the evil one comes and snatches away what was sown in his heart. This is the seed sown along the path. [20]The one who received the seed that fell on rocky places is the man who hears the word and at once receives it with joy. [21]But since he has no root, he lasts only a short time. When trouble or persecution comes because of the word, he quickly falls away. [22]The one who received the seed that fell among the thorns is the man who hears the word, but the worries of this life and the deceitfulness of wealth choke it, making it unfruitful. (+Lk 6:49; 8:11-14)

Ro 2:13 For it is not those who hear the law who are righteous in God's sight, but it is those who obey the law who will be declared righteous.

Jas 1:22 Do not merely listen to the word, and so deceive yourselves. Do what it says. [23]Anyone who listens to the word but does not do what it says is like a man who looks at his face in a mirror [24]and, after looking at himself, goes away and immediately forgets what he looks like.

Obedient—

Mt 7:24 "Therefore everyone who hears these words of mine and puts them into practice is like a wise man who built his house on the rock. [25]The rain came down, the streams rose, and the winds blew and beat against that house; yet it did not fall, because it had its foundation on the rock.

Mt 13:23 But the one who received the seed that fell on good soil is the man who hears the word and understands it. He produces a crop, yielding a hundred, sixty or thirty times what was sown." (+Lk 6:47-48; 8:15)

Jas 1:25 But the man who looks intently into the perfect law that gives freedom, and continues to do this, not forgetting what he has heard, but doing it—he will be blessed in what he does.

HEART [*1061, 789, 2668, 2693, 4000, 4213, 4220, 4222, 5055, 5570, 5883, 7931, 8120, 9348, 10381, *1571, 1591, 2426, 2510, 2840, 2841, 5016, 5073, 6034*].

NIV+BROKENHEARTED, DISHEARTENED, DOWNHEARTED, FAINTHEARTED, HARDHEARTED, HEART'S, HEARTACHE, HEARTLESS, HEARTS, HEARTS', KINDHEARTED, SIMPLEHEARTED, STOUTHEARTED, STUBBORN-HEARTED, WHOLEHEARTED, WHOLEHEARTEDLY

Seat of affection and source of action—

Dt 5:29 Oh, that their hearts would be inclined to fear me and keep all my commands always, so that it might go well with them and their children forever!

Dt 6:5 Love the LORD your God with all your heart and with all your soul and with all your strength. ⁶These commandments that I give you today are to be upon your hearts.

2Ch 12:14 He did evil because he had not set his heart on seeking the LORD.

Ps 57:7 My heart is steadfast, O God, my heart is steadfast; I will sing and make music. (+Ps 112:7)

Pr 4:23 Above all else, guard your heart, for it is the wellspring of life.

Pr 14:30 A heart at peace gives life to the body, but envy rots the bones.

Pr 15:13 A happy heart makes the face cheerful, but heartache crushes the spirit.

¹⁴The discerning heart seeks knowledge, but the mouth of a fool feeds on folly.

¹⁵All the days of the oppressed are wretched, but the cheerful heart has a continual feast.

Pr 16:1 To man belong the plans of the heart, but from the LORD comes the reply of the tongue.

Mt 9:4 Knowing their thoughts, Jesus said, "Why do you entertain evil thoughts in your hearts?

Mt 12:33 "Make a tree good and its fruit will be good, or make a tree bad and its fruit will be bad, for a tree is recognized by its fruit. (+Mt 12:35)

Mt 15:18 But the things that come out of the mouth come from the heart, and these make a man 'unclean.' ¹⁹For out of the heart come evil thoughts, murder, adultery, sexual immorality, theft, false testimony, slander. ²⁰These are what make a man 'unclean'; but eating with unwashed hands does not make him 'unclean.'"

Mt 23:26 Blind Pharisee! First clean the inside of the cup and dish, and then the outside also will be clean. (+Mk 7:21-23)

Lives forever (Ps 22:26).

Of the heathen, taught of God—

Ro 2:14 (Indeed, when Gentiles, who do not have the law, do by nature things required by the law, they are a law for themselves, even though they do not have the law, ¹⁵since they show that the requirements of the law are written on their hearts, their consciences also bearing witness, and their thoughts now accusing, now even defending them.) ¹⁶This will take place on the day when God will judge men's secrets through Jesus Christ, as my gospel declares.

Changed:

(Ps 51:10).

Instances of: Saul (1Sa 10:9), Solomon (1Ki 3:11-12), Paul (Ac 9:1-18).

Hardening of:

Forbidden (Heb 3:8,15; 4:7). Instances of: Pharaoh (Ex

4:21; 7:3,13,22; 8:15,32; 9:12,35; 10:1; 14:8), Sihon (Dt 2:30), king of Canaan (Jos 11:20), Philistines (1Sa 6:6).

Known to God:

Dt 31:21 And when many disasters and difficulties come upon them, this song will testify against them, because it will not be forgotten by their descendants. I know what they are disposed to do, even before I bring them into the land I promised them on oath."

1Sa 16:7 But the LORD said to Samuel, "Do not consider his appearance or his height, for I have rejected him. The LORD does not look at the things man looks at. Man looks at the outward appearance, but the LORD looks at the heart."

2Sa 7:20 "What more can David say to you? For you know your servant, O Sovereign LORD.

1Ki 8:39 then hear from heaven, your dwelling place. Forgive and act; deal with each man according to all he does, since you know his heart (for you alone know the hearts of all men),

1Ch 28:9 "And you, my son Solomon, acknowledge the God of your father, and serve him with wholehearted devotion and with a willing mind, for the LORD searches every heart and understands every motive behind the thoughts. If you seek him, he will be found by you; but if you forsake him, he will reject you forever. (+2Ch 6:30)

Job 11:11 Surely he recognizes deceitful men; and when he sees evil, does he not take note?

Job 16:19 Even now my witness is in heaven; my advocate is on high.

Job 31:4 Does he not see my ways and count my every step?

Ps 1:6 For the LORD watches over the way of the righteous, but the way of the wicked will perish.

Ps 44:21 would not God have discovered it, since he knows the secrets of the heart?

Ps 51:10 Create in me a pure heart, O God, and renew a steadfast spirit within me.

Ps 94:11 The LORD knows the thoughts of man; he knows that they are futile.

Ps 139:1 O LORD, you have searched me and you know me. ²You know when I sit and when I rise; you perceive my thoughts from afar. ³You discern my going out and my lying down; you are familiar with all my ways. ⁴Before a word is on my tongue you know it completely, O LORD.

⁵You hem me in—behind and before; you have laid your hand upon me. ⁶Such knowledge is too wonderful for me, too lofty for me to attain.

⁷Where can I go from your Spirit? Where can I flee from your presence? ⁸If I go up to the heavens, you are there; if I make my bed in the depths, you are there. ⁹If I rise on the wings of the dawn, if I settle on the far side of the sea, ¹⁰even there your hand will guide me, your right hand will hold me fast.

¹¹If I say, "Surely the darkness will hide me and the light become night around me," ¹²even the darkness will not be dark to you; the night will shine like the day, for darkness is as light to you.

Pr 5:21 For a man's ways are in full view of the LORD, and he examines all his paths.

Pr 16:2 All a man's ways seem innocent to him, but motives are weighed by the LORD.

Pr 21:2 All a man's ways seem right to him, but the LORD weighs the heart.

Isa 66:18 "And I, because of their actions and their imaginations, am about to come and gather all nations and tongues, and they will come and see my glory.

Jer 12:13 They will sow wheat but reap thorns; they will wear themselves out but gain nothing. So bear the shame of your harvest because of the LORD's fierce anger."

Jer 17:10 "I the LORD search the heart and examine the mind, to reward a man according to his conduct, according to what his deeds deserve."

Eze 11:5 Then the Spirit of the LORD came upon me, and he told me to say: "This is what the LORD says: That is what you are saying, O house of Israel, but I know what is going through your mind.

Eze 11:19 I will give them an undivided heart and put a new spirit in them; I will remove from them their heart of stone and give them a heart of flesh. **20**Then they will follow my decrees and be careful to keep my laws. They will be my people, and I will be their God. **21**But as for those whose hearts are devoted to their vile images and detestable idols, I will bring down on their own heads what they have done, declares the Sovereign LORD." (+Eze 36:25-26)

Lk 16:15 He said to them, "You are the ones who justify yourselves in the eyes of men, but God knows your hearts. What is highly valued among men is detestable in God's sight.

Ac 1:24 Then they prayed, "Lord, you know everyone's heart. Show us which of these two you have chosen

Ac 15:8 God, who knows the heart, showed that he accepted them by giving the Holy Spirit to them, just as he did to us.

Ro 8:27 And he who searches our hearts knows the mind of the Spirit, because the Spirit intercedes for the saints in accordance with God's will.

1Co 3:20 and again, "The Lord knows that the thoughts of the wise are futile."

Heb 4:12 For the word of God is living and active. Sharper than any double-edged sword, it penetrates even to dividing soul and spirit, joints and marrow; it judges the thoughts and attitudes of the heart.

Rev 2:23 I will strike her children dead. Then all the churches will know that I am he who searches hearts and minds, and I will repay each of you according to your deeds.

To Christ (Ro 8:27; Rev 2:23).

Regenerate:

Is penitent (Ps 34:18; 51:10,17; 147:3; Pr 15:3). Renewed (Dt 30:6; Ps 51:10; Eze 11:19; 18:31; 36:26; Jn 3:3,7; Ro 2:29; Eph 4:22-24; Col 3:9-10; Heb 10:22; Jas 4:8). Pure (Ps 24:4; 66:18; Pr 20:9; Mt 5:8; 2Ti 2:22; 1Pe 3:15). Enlightened (2Co 4:6). Established (Ps 57:7; 108:1; 112:7-8; 1Th 3:13). Refined by affliction (Pr 17:3). Tried or tested (1Ch 29:17; Ps 7:9; 26:2; Pr 17:3; Jer 11:20; 12:3; 20:12; 1Th 2:4; Heb 11:17; Rev 2:2,10). Strengthened (Ps 27:14; 112:8; 1Th 3:13). Graciously affected of God (1Sa 10:26; 1Ch 29:18; Ezr 6:22; 7:27; Pr 16:1; 21:1; Jer 20:9; Ac 16:14).

Should Render to God:

Obedience (Dt 10:12; 11:13; 26:16; 1Ki 2:4; Ps 119:1, 12; Eph 6:6). Faith (Ps 27:3; 112:7; Ac 8:37; Ro 6:17; 10:10). Trust (Pr 3:5). Love (Dt 6:5-6; Mt 22:37). Fear (Ps 119:161; Jer 32:40). Fidelity (Ne 9:8). Zeal (2Ch 17:16; Jer 20:9). Seek God (2Ch 19:3; 30:19; Ezr 7:10; Ps 10:17; 84:2).

Should Be:

Joyful (1Sa 2:1; Ps 4:7; 97:11; Isa 65:14; Zec 10:7). Perfect (1Ki 8:61; Ps 101:2). Upright (Ps 97:11; 125:4). Clean (Ps 51:10; 73:1). Pure (Ps 24:4; Pr 22:11; Mt 5:8;

1Ti 1:5; 2Ti 2:22; Jas 4:8; 1Pe 1:22). Sincere (Lk 8:15; Ac 2:46; Eph 6:5; Col 3:22; Heb 10:22). Repentant (Dt 30:2; Ps 34:18; 51:17). Devout (1Sa 1:13; Ps 4:4; 9:1; 27:8; 77:6; 119:10,69,145). Wise (1Ki 3:9,12; 4:29; Job 9:4; Pr 8:10; 10:8; 11:29; 14:33; 23:15). Tender (1Sa 24:5; 2Ki 22:19; Job 23:16; Ps 22:14; Eph 4:32). Holy (Ps 66:18; 1Pe 3:15). Compassionate (Jer 4:19; La 3:51). Lowly (Mt 11:29).

The Unregenerate Heart:

Is full of iniquity (Ge 6:5; 8:21; 1Sa 17:28; Pr 6:14,18; 11:20; Pr 20:9; Ecc 8:11; 9:3; Jer 4:14,18; 17:9; Ac 8:21-23; Ro 1:21). Loves evil (Dt 19:18; Ps 95:10; Jer 17:5). A fountain of evil (Mt 12:34-35; Mk 7:21). *See Depravity.* Wayward (2Ch 12:14; Ps 101:4; Pr 6:14; 11:20; 12:8; 17:20; Jer 5:23; Heb 3:10). Blind (Ro 1:21; Eph 4:18). *See Blindness, Spiritual.* Is double (1Ch 12:33; Ps 12:2; Pr 28:14; Isa 9:9; 10:12; 46:12; Hos 10:2; Jas 1:6,8). *See Instability.* Is hard (Ps 76:5; Eze 2:4; 3:7; 11:19; 36:26; Mk 6:52; 10:5; 16:14; Jn 12:40; Ro 1:21; 2:5). *See Impenitence; Obduracy.* Is deceitful (Jer 17:9). Proud (2Ki 14:10; 2Ch 25:19; Ps 101:5; Pr 18:12; 28:25; Jer 48:29; 49:16). *See Pride.* Is subtle (Pr 7:10). *See Hypocrisy.* Is sensual (Eze 6:9; Hos 13:6; Ro 8:7). *See Lasciviousness.* Is worldly (2Ch 26:16; Da 5:20; Ac 8:21-22). Judicially hardened (Ex 4:21; Jos 11:20; Isa 6:10; Ac 28:26-27). Malicious (Ps 28:3; 140:2; Pr 24:2; Ecc 7:26; Eze 25:15). *See Malice.* Is impenitent (Ro 2:5). *See Impenitence.* Is diabolical (Jn 13:2; Ac 5:3). Is covetous (Jer 22:17; 2Pe 2:14). *See Covetousness.* Is foolish (Pr 12:23; 22:15; Ecc 9:3). Under the wrath of God (Ro 1:18-19,31; 2:5-6).

See Regeneration; Sanctification.

HEARTH [789, 2219, 3683, 4612]. Of an altar (Lev 6:9; Isa 30:14; Eze 43:15-16). Figurative (Isa 29:2).

HEAT [2770, 2780, 2801, 2996, 3001, 3019, 3031, 3501, 3880, 9220, 9299, 9429, *2549, 3008, 3012, 3014*].

NIV+ HEATED, HOT, HOTLY, HOTTER

Jonah overcome with (Jnh 4:8). *See Sunstroke.*

HEATH *See Bush.*

HEATHEN [*1620*]. Under this head are grouped all who are not embraced under the Abrahamic covenant. Cast out of Canaan (Lev 18:24-25; Ps 44:2) and their land given to Israel (Ps 78:55; 105:44; 135:12; 136:21-22; Isa 54:1-3). Excluded from the temple (La 1:10).

Wicked practices of. *See Idolatry.*

Divine Revelations Given to:

Abimelech (Ge 20:3-7), Nebuchadnezzar (Da 4:1-18), Belshazzar (Da 5:5,24-29),+Cyrus (2Ch 36:23; Ezr 1:1-4), the Magi (Mt 1:1-11), the centurion (Mt 8:5-13; Lk 7:2-9), Cornelius (Ac 10:1-7).

Pious People Among (Isa 65:5; Ac 10:35):

Melchizedek (Ge 14:18-20). Abimelech (Ge 20). Balaam (Nu 22). Jethro (Ex 18). Cyrus (Ezr 1:1-3). Eliphaz (Job 4). Bildad (Job 8). Zophar (Job 11). Elihu (Job 32). Nebuchadnezzar, after his restoration (Da 4). The Ninevites (Jnh 3:5-10). The Magi (Mt 2:1-12). The centurion of Capernaum (Mt 8:5-13; Lk 7:2-9), of Caesarea (Ac 10). Believed in Christ (Mt 8:5-13; Lk 7:2-9).

See Gentiles.

HEAVE OFFERING *See Offerings.*

HEAVE SHOULDER *See Offerings.*

HEAVEN [5294, 9028, 10723, *1479, 2230, 4039, 4040, 4041, 5734, 5737*].

NIV+ HEAVEN'S, HEAVENLY, HEAVENS, HEAVENWARD

God's Dwelling Place:

Dt 26:15 Look down from heaven, your holy dwelling place, and bless your people Israel and the land you have given us as you promised on oath to our forefathers, a land flowing with milk and honey."

1Ki 8:30 Hear the supplication of your servant and of your people Israel when they pray toward this place. Hear from heaven, your dwelling place, and when you hear, forgive. (+1Ki 8:39,43,49)

1Ch 16:31 Let the heavens rejoice, let the earth be glad; let them say among the nations, "The LORD reigns!"

1Ch 21:26 David built an altar to the LORD there and sacrificed burnt offerings and fellowship offerings. He called on the LORD, and the LORD answered him with fire from heaven on the altar of burnt offering.

2Ch 2:6 But who is able to build a temple for him, since the heavens, even the highest heavens, cannot contain him? Who then am I to build a temple for him, except as a place to burn sacrifices before him? (+2Ch 6:21,27,30,33,35,39; 7:14)

2Ch 30:27 The priests and the Levites stood to bless the people, and God heard them, for their prayer reached heaven, his holy dwelling place. (+Ne 9:27)

Job 22:12 "Is not God in the heights of heaven? And see how lofty are the highest stars!

Job 22:14 Thick clouds veil him, so he does not see us as he goes about in the vaulted heavens.'

Ps 2:4 The One enthroned in heaven laughs; the Lord scoffs at them.

Ps 11:4 The LORD is in his holy temple; the LORD is on his heavenly throne. He observes the sons of men; his eyes examine them.

Ps 20:6 Now I know that the LORD saves his anointed; he answers him from his holy heaven with the saving power of his right hand.

Ps 33:13 From heaven the LORD looks down and sees all mankind;

Ps 102:19 "The LORD looked down from his sanctuary on high, from heaven he viewed the earth,

Ps 103:19 The LORD has established his throne in heaven, and his kingdom rules over all.

Ps 113:5 Who is like the LORD our God, the One who sits enthroned on high, (+Ps 113:6)

Ps 123:1 I lift up my eyes to you, to you whose throne is in heaven. (+Ps 135:6)

Ecc 5:2 Do not be quick with your mouth, do not be hasty in your heart to utter anything before God. God is in heaven and you are on earth, so let your words be few.

Isa 57:15 For this is what the high and lofty One says—he who lives forever, whose name is holy: "I live in a high and holy place, but also with him who is contrite and lowly in spirit, to revive the spirit of the lowly and to revive the heart of the contrite.

Isa 63:15 Look down from heaven and see from your lofty throne, holy and glorious. Where are your zeal and your might? Your tenderness and compassion are withheld from us.

Isa 66:1 This is what the LORD says: "Heaven is my throne, and the earth is my footstool. Where is the house you will build for me? Where will my resting place be? (+Jer 23:24)

La 3:41 Let us lift up our hearts and our hands to God in heaven, and say:

La 3:50 until the LORD looks down from heaven and sees.

Da 5:23 Instead, you have set yourself up against the Lord of heaven. You had the goblets from his temple brought to you, and you and your nobles, your wives and your concubines drank wine from them. You praised the gods of silver and gold, of bronze, iron, wood and stone, which cannot see or hear or understand. But you did not honor the God who holds in his hand your life and all your ways. (+Zec 2:13)

Mt 5:34 But I tell you, Do not swear at all: either by heaven, for it is God's throne;

Mt 5:45 that you may be sons of your Father in heaven. He causes his sun to rise on the evil and the good, and sends rain on the righteous and the unrighteous.

Mt 6:9 "This, then, is how you should pray: " 'Our Father in heaven, hallowed be your name,

Mt 10:32 "Whoever acknowledges me before men, I will also acknowledge him before my Father in heaven. [33]But whoever disowns me before men, I will disown him before my Father in heaven.

Mt 11:25 At that time Jesus said, "I praise you, Father, Lord of heaven and earth, because you have hidden these things from the wise and learned, and revealed them to little children.

Mt 12:50 For whoever does the will of my Father in heaven is my brother and sister and mother."

Mt 16:17 Jesus replied, "Blessed are you, Simon son of Jonah, for this was not revealed to you by man, but by my Father in heaven. (+Mt 18:10,14; Mk 11:25-26)

Mk 16:19 After the Lord Jesus had spoken to them, he was taken up into heaven and he sat at the right hand of God.

Ac 7:49 " 'Heaven is my throne, and the earth is my footstool. What kind of house will you build for me? says the Lord. Or where will my resting place be? (+Ac 7:55-56)

Ro 1:18 The wrath of God is being revealed from heaven against all the godlessness and wickedness of men who suppress the truth by their wickedness,

Heb 8:1 The point of what we are saying is this: We do have such a high priest, who sat down at the right hand of the throne of the Majesty in heaven,

Rev 8:1 When he opened the seventh seal, there was silence in heaven for about half an hour.

Rev 12:7 And there was war in heaven. Michael and his angels fought against the dragon, and the dragon and his angels fought back. [8]But he was not strong enough, and they lost their place in heaven. [9]The great dragon was hurled down—that ancient serpent called the devil, or Satan, who leads the whole world astray. He was hurled to the earth, and his angels with him.

Rev 21:22 I did not see a temple in the city, because the Lord God Almighty and the Lamb are its temple. [23]The city does not need the sun or the moon to shine on it, for the glory of God gives it light, and the Lamb is its lamp. [24]The nations will walk by its light, and the kings of the earth will bring their splendor into it. [25]On no day will its gates ever be shut, for there will be no night there. [26]The glory and honor of the nations will be brought into it. [27]Nothing impure will ever enter it, nor will anyone who does what is shameful or deceitful, but only those whose names are written in the Lamb's book of life.

Rev 22:1 Then the angel showed me the river of the water of life, as clear as crystal, flowing from the throne of God and of the Lamb [2]down the middle of the great street of the city. On each side of the river stood the tree of life, bearing twelve crops of fruit, yielding its fruit every month. And the leaves of the tree are for the healing of the nations. ³No longer will there be any curse. The throne of God and of the Lamb will be in the city, and his servants will serve him. ⁴They will see his face, and his name will be on their foreheads. ⁵There will be no more night. They will not need the light of a lamp or the light of the sun, for the Lord God will give them light. And they will reign for ever and ever.

Figurative:

Of divine government (Mt 16:19; 18:18; 23:22). Of God (Mt 21:25).

The Future Home of the Righteous:

(2Ki 2:11; Mt 5:12; 13:30,43; Lk 16:22; Jn 12:8,26; 13:36; 17:24; 2Co 5:1; Php 3:20; Col 1:5-6,12; 3:9; 1Th 4:17; Heb 10:34; 11:10,16; 12:22; 1Pe 1:4; Rev 2:7; 3:21).

Called:

A city (Heb 11:10,16), a garden (Mt 3:12), a house (Jn 14:2-3; 2Co 5:1), a kingdom (Mt 25:34; Lk 12:32; 22:29-30), the kingdom of Christ and of God (Eph 5:5), a heavenly country (Heb 11:16), a rest (Heb 4:9; Rev 14:13), glory (Col 3:4), paradise (Lk 23:43; 2Co 12:2,4; Rev 2:7).

Everlasting (2Co 5:1; Heb 10:34; 13:14; 1Pe 1:4; 2Pe 1:11). Allegorical representatives of (Rev 4:1-11; 5:1-14; 7:9-17; 14:1-3; 15:1-8; 21; 22:1-5). No marriage in (Mt 22:30; Lk 20:34-36). Names of the righteous written in (Lk 10:20; Heb 12:22-24). Treasures in (Mt 6:20; 19:21; Lk 12:33). Joy in (Ps 16:11; Lk 15:6-7,10). Righteousness dwells in (2Pe 3:13). No sorrow in (Rev 7:16-17; 21:4). The wicked excluded from (Gal 5:21; Eph 5:5; Rev 22:15).

See Righteous, Promises to.

HEAVEN OPENED (Mt 3:16; Ac 7:56; 10:11; Rev 19:11).

HEAVENLY PLACES [*2230*]. (Eph 1:3,20; 2:6; 3:10).

HEAVENS, NEW

To be created—

Isa 65:17 "Behold, I will create new heavens and a new earth. The former things will not be remembered, nor will they come to mind.

Isa 66:22 "As the new heavens and the new earth that I make will endure before me," declares the LORD, "so will your name and descendants endure.

2Pe 3:13 But in keeping with his promise we are looking forward to a new heaven and a new earth, the home of righteousness.

Rev 21:1 Then I saw a new heaven and a new earth, for the first heaven and the first earth had passed away, and there was no longer any sea. ²I saw the Holy City, the new Jerusalem, coming down out of heaven from God, prepared as a bride beautifully dressed for her husband. ³And I heard a loud voice from the throne saying, "Now the dwelling of God is with men, and he will live with them. They will be his people, and God himself will be with them and be their God. ⁴He will wipe every tear from their eyes. There will be no more death or mourning or crying or pain, for the old order of things has passed away."

HEAVENS, PHYSICAL

Ge 1:1 In the beginning God created the heavens and the earth. (+2Ch 2:6; 6:18; Job 38:31-33)

Ps 19:1 The heavens declare the glory of God; the skies proclaim the work of his hands.

Ps 50:6 And the heavens proclaim his righteousness, for God himself is judge. *Selah*

Ps 68:33 to him who rides the ancient skies above, who thunders with mighty voice.

Ps 89:29 I will establish his line forever, his throne as long as the heavens endure.

Ps 103:11 For as high as the heavens are above the earth, so great is his love for those who fear him;

Ps 113:4 The LORD is exalted over all the nations, his glory above the heavens.

Ps 115:16 The highest heavens belong to the LORD, but the earth he has given to man. (+Ps 136:5)

Jer 31:37 This is what the LORD says: "Only if the heavens above can be measured and the foundations of the earth below be searched out will I reject all the descendants of Israel because of all they have done," declares the LORD.

Eze 1:1 In the thirtieth year, in the fourth month on the fifth day, while I was among the exiles by the Kebar River, the heavens were opened and I saw visions of God.

Mt 24:29 "Immediately after the distress of those days " 'the sun will be darkened, and the moon will not give its light; the stars will fall from the sky, and the heavenly bodies will be shaken.'

³⁰"At that time the sign of the Son of Man will appear in the sky, and all the nations of the earth will mourn. They will see the Son of Man coming on the clouds of the sky, with power and great glory.

Ac 2:19 I will show wonders in the heaven above and signs on the earth below, blood and fire and billows of smoke. ²⁰The sun will be turned to darkness and the moon to blood before the coming of the great and glorious day of the Lord.

Created by God—

Ge 1:1 In the beginning God created the heavens and the earth.

Ge 2:1 Thus the heavens and the earth were completed in all their vast array. (+Ex 20:11; 1Ch 16:26)

2Ch 2:12 And Hiram added: "Praise be to the LORD, the God of Israel, who made heaven and earth! He has given King David a wise son, endowed with intelligence and discernment, who will build a temple for the LORD and a palace for himself.

Ne 9:6 You alone are the LORD. You made the heavens, even the highest heavens, and all their starry host, the earth and all that is on it, the seas and all that is in them. You give life to everything, and the multitudes of heaven worship you.

Job 9:8 He alone stretches out the heavens and treads on the waves of the sea.

Ps 8:3 When I consider your heavens, the work of your fingers, the moon and the stars, which you have set in place,

Ps 19:1 The heavens declare the glory of God; the skies proclaim the work of his hands.

Ps 33:6 By the word of the LORD were the heavens made, their starry host by the breath of his mouth.

Ps 33:9 For he spoke, and it came to be; he commanded, and it stood firm. (+Ps 102:25)

Ps 148:4 Praise him, you highest heavens and you waters above the skies. ⁵Let them praise the name of the LORD, for he commanded and they were created. ⁶He set them in place for ever and ever; he gave a decree that will never pass away.

Pr 8:27 I was there when he set the heavens in place, when he marked out the horizon on the face of the deep,

Isa 37:16 "O LORD Almighty, God of Israel, enthroned

between the cherubim, you alone are God over all the kingdoms of the earth. You have made heaven and earth.

Isa 40:22 He sits enthroned above the circle of the earth, and its people are like grasshoppers. He stretches out the heavens like a canopy, and spreads them out like a tent to live in.

Isa 42:5 This is what God the LORD says—he who created the heavens and stretched them out, who spread out the earth and all that comes out of it, who gives breath to its people, and life to those who walk on it:

Isa 45:12 It is I who made the earth and created mankind upon it. My own hands stretched out the heavens; I marshaled their starry hosts. (+Isa 45:18)

Jer 10:12 But God made the earth by his power; he founded the world by his wisdom and stretched out the heavens by his understanding.

Jer 32:17 "Ah, Sovereign LORD, you have made the heavens and the earth by your great power and outstretched arm. Nothing is too hard for you.

Jer 51:15 "He made the earth by his power; he founded the world by his wisdom and stretched out the heavens by his understanding.

Ac 4:24 When they heard this, they raised their voices together in prayer to God. "Sovereign Lord," they said, "you made the heaven and the earth and the sea, and everything in them. (+Ac 14:15)

Heb 1:10 He also says, "In the beginning, O Lord, you laid the foundations of the earth, and the heavens are the work of your hands.

Rev 10:6 And he swore by him who lives for ever and ever, who created the heavens and all that is in them, the earth and all that is in it, and the sea and all that is in it, and said, "There will be no more delay!

Rev 14:7 He said in a loud voice, "Fear God and give him glory, because the hour of his judgment has come. Worship him who made the heavens, the earth, the sea and the springs of water." *See Creation; God, Creator; Heavens, New.*

Destruction of—

Job 14:12 so man lies down and does not rise; till the heavens are no more, men will not awake or be roused from their sleep.

Ps 102:25 In the beginning you laid the foundations of the earth, and the heavens are the work of your hands. ²⁶They will perish, but you remain; they will all wear out like a garment. Like clothing you will change them and they will be discarded.

Isa 51:6 Lift up your eyes to the heavens, look at the earth beneath; the heavens will vanish like smoke, the earth will wear out like a garment and its inhabitants die like flies. But my salvation will last forever, my righteousness will never fail.

Mt 5:18 I tell you the truth, until heaven and earth disappear, not the smallest letter, not the least stroke of a pen, will by any means disappear from the Law until everything is accomplished.

Mt 24:35 Heaven and earth will pass away, but my words will never pass away.

Heb 1:10 He also says, "In the beginning, O Lord, you laid the foundations of the earth, and the heavens are the work of your hands. ¹¹They will perish, but you remain; they will all wear out like a garment. ¹²You will roll them up like a robe; like a garment they will be changed. But you remain the same, and your years will never end."

2Pe 3:10 But the day of the Lord will come like a thief. The heavens will disappear with a roar; the elements will be destroyed by fire, and the earth and everything in it will be laid bare. (+2Pe 3:11)

2Pe 3:12 as you look forward to the day of God and speed its coming. That day will bring about the destruction of the heavens by fire, and the elements will melt in the heat.

Rev 6:12 I watched as he opened the sixth seal. There was a great earthquake. The sun turned black like sackcloth made of goat hair, the whole moon turned blood red, ¹³and the stars in the sky fell to earth, as late figs drop from a fig tree when shaken by a strong wind. ¹⁴The sky receded like a scroll, rolling up, and every mountain and island was removed from its place.

Rev 20:11 Then I saw a great white throne and him who was seated on it. Earth and sky fled from his presence, and there was no place for them.

Rev 21:1 Then I saw a new heaven and a new earth, for the first heaven and the first earth had passed away, and there was no longer any sea.

Rev 21:4 He will wipe every tear from their eyes. There will be no more death or mourning or crying or pain, for the old order of things has passed away."

Figurative:

Of divine judgments (Isa 34:4).

See Sky.

HEAVING AND WAVING *See Offerings.*

HEBER, HEBERITE [2491, 2499] (*associate*).

NIV+ HEBER'S

1. An Asherite, the son of Beriah; great-grandson of Jacob (Ge 46:17; Nu 26:45; 1Ch 7:31-32).

2. Kenite whose wife Jael killed Sisera (Jdg 4:11-21; 5:24).

3. A Judahite, the father of Soco and son of Ezrah (1Ch 4:18).

4. A Benjamite and son of Elpaal (1Ch 8:17).

HEBREW [3376, 6303, 1578, 1580].

NIV+ HEBRAIC, HEBREWS

A word supposed to be a corruption of the name of Eber, who was an ancestor of Abraham (Ge 10:24; 11:14-26). *See Genealogy.* Applied to Abraham (Ge 14:13) and his descendants (Ge 39:14; 40:15; 43:32; Ex 2:6; Dt 15:12; 1Sa 4:9; 29:3; Jnh 1:9; Ac 6:1; 2Co 11:22; Php 3:5). Used to denote the language of the Jews (Jn 5:2; 19:20; Ac 21:40; 22:2; 26:14; Rev 9:11).

See Israel, Israelites; Jews.

HEBREW LANGUAGE The NW branch of the Semitic language family; has close affinity to Ugaritic, Phoenician, Moabitic, and the Canaanite dialects; sister languages include Arabic, Akkadian, and Aramaic. Except for a few Aramaic passages in Ezra, Daniel, and Jeremiah, it is the language of the OT.

HEBREW OF THE HEBREWS A Jew of pure blood, very strict in observing the law (Php 3:4-6).

HEBREWS, EPISTLE TO THE

Author: Anonymous. Historical speculations as to authorship include Paul, Barnabas, Apollos, and Priscilla.

Date: Before the destruction of Jerusalem and the temple in A.D. 70.

Outline:

I. Prologue: The Superiority of God's New Revelation (1:1-4).

II. The Superiority of Christ to Leaders of the Old Covenant (1:5-7:28).
A. Christ Is Superior to the Angels (1:5-2:18).
1. Scriptural proof of superiority (1:5-14).
2. Exhortation not to ignore the revelation of God in his Son (2:1-4).
3. Further Scriptural proof of superiority over the angels (2:5-18).
B. Christ Is Superior to Moses (3:1-4:13).
1. Demonstration of Christ's superiority (3:1-6).
2. Exhortation to enter salvation-rest (3:7-4:13).
C. Christ Is Superior to the Aaronic Priests (4:14-7:28).
1. Exhortation to hold fast (4:14-16).
2. Qualifications of a priest (5:1-10).
3. Exhortation to abandon spiritual lethargy (5:11-6:12).
4. Certainty of God's promise (6:13-20).
5. Christ's superior priestly order (ch. 7).
III. The Superior Sacrificial Work of Our High Priest (chs. 8-10).
A. A Better Covenant (ch. 8).
B. A Better Sanctuary (9:1-12).
C. A Better Sacrifice (9:13-10:18).
D. Exhortations (10:19-39).
IV. Final Plea for Persevering Faith (chs. 11-12).
A. Examples of Past Heroes of the Faith (ch. 11).
B. Encouragement for Persevering Faith (12:1-11).
C. Exhortations for Persevering Faith (12:12-17).
D. Motivation for Persevering Faith (12:18:29).
V. Conclusion (ch. 13).
A. Practical Rules for Christian Living (13:1-17).
B. Request for Prayer (13;18-19).
C. Benediction (13:20-21).
D. Personal Remarks (13:22-23).
E. Greetings and Final Benediction (13:24-25).

HEBRON [2496, 2497] (*association*).
NIV+ HEBRONITE, HEBRONITES, KIRIATH ARBA

1. For Jos 19:28 See *Abdon, 1*.
2. A city of Judah, S of Jerusalem. When built (Nu 13:22). Fortified (2Ch 11:10). Also called Kiriath Arba (Ge 23:2; 35:27; Jos 15:13). Abraham dwells and Sarah dies at (Ge 23:2). Hoham, king of, confederated with other kings of the Canaanites against Joshua (Jos 10:3-39). Children of Anakim dwell at (Nu 13:22; Jos 11:21). Conquest of, by Caleb (Jos 14:6-15; Jdg 1:10,20). A city of refuge (Jos 20:7; 21:11,13). David crowned king of Judah at (2Sa 2:1-11; 3), of Israel (2Sa 5:1-5). The burial place of Sarah (Ge 23:2), Abner (2Sa 3:32), Ish-Bosheth (2Sa 4:12). The conspirators against Ish-Bosheth hanged at (2Sa 4:12). Absalom made king at (2Sa 15:9-10). Jews of the Babylonian captivity dwell at (Ne 11:25). Pool of (2Sa 4:12).
3. Son of Kohath (Ex 6:18; Nu 3:19; 1Ch 6:2,18; 23:12,19).
4. The family name of Mareshah (1Ch 2:42-43; 15:9).

HEDGE [5004, 5372, 8455].
NIV+ HEDGED

Protecting a vineyard (Isa 5:5). Of thorns (Mic 7:4; Mk 12:1). Figurative of divine protection (Job 1:10), of divine entrapment (Job 3:23). *See Fence.*

HEEDFULNESS [1067, 7992, 8505, 9048, 9068].
NIV+ HEED, HEEDED, HEEDS

Commanded (Ex 23:13; Pr 4:25-27).

Necessary:

In the care of the soul (Dt 4:9). In the house and worship of God (Ecc 5:1). In what we hear (Mk 4:24). In how we hear (Lk 3:18). In keeping God's commandments (Jos 22:5). In conduct (Eph 5:15). In speech (Pr 13:3; Jas 1:19). In worldly company (Ps 39:1; Col 4:5). In giving judgment (2Ch 19:6-7). Against sin (Heb 12:15-16). Against unbelief (Heb 3:12). Against idolatry (Dt 4:15-16). Against false Christs, and false prophets (Mt 24:4-5,23-24). Against false teachers (Php 3:2; Col 2:8; 2Pe 3:16-17). Against presumption (1Co 10:12).

Promises to (1Ki 2:4; 1Ch 22:13).
See Obedience.

HEGAI, HEGE [2043, 2051]. Eunuch in charge of Xerxes' harem (Est 2:3,8,15).

HEIFER [6320, 7239, *1239*].
NIV+ HEIFER'S

When used as sacrifice, must be without blemish and must not have come under the yoke (Nu 19:2; Dt 21:3). An atonement for murder (Dt 21:1-9). The red heifer used for the water of separation (Nu 19; Heb 9:13).

Used for plowing (Jdg 14:18), for treading out wheat (Hos 10:11). Tractable (Hos 10:11). Intractable (Hos 4:16).
See Cattle; Offerings.

Figurative:

Of backsliders (Hos 4:16). Of the obedient (Hos 10:11).

HEIFER, RED *See Animals.*

HEIR [3769, 3772, *3101, 5169, 5626*].
NIV+ See INHERITANCE

Literal:

Mosaic law relating to inheritance of—

Nu 27:8 "Say to the Israelites, 'If a man dies and leaves no son, turn his inheritance over to his daughter. ⁹If he has no daughter, give his inheritance to his brothers. ¹⁰If he has no brothers, give his inheritance to his father's brothers. (+Nu 27:11)

Nu 36:1 The family heads of the clan of Gilead son of Makir, the son of Manasseh, who were from the clans of the descendants of Joseph, came and spoke before Moses and the leaders, the heads of the Israelite families. ²They said, "When the LORD commanded my lord to give the land as an inheritance to the Israelites by lot, he ordered you to give the inheritance of our brother Zelophehad to his daughters. ³Now suppose they marry men from other Israelite tribes; then their inheritance will be taken from our ancestral inheritance and added to that of the tribe they marry into. And so part of the inheritance allotted to us will be taken away. ⁴When the Year of Jubilee for the Israelites comes, their inheritance will be added to that of the tribe into which they marry, and their property will be taken from the tribal inheritance of our forefathers."

⁵Then at the LORD's command Moses gave this order to the Israelites: "What the tribe of the descendants of Joseph is saying is right. ⁶This is what the LORD commands for Zelophehad's daughters: They may marry anyone they please as long as they marry within the tribal clan of their father. ⁷No inheritance in Israel is to pass from tribe to tribe, for every Israelite shall keep the tribal land inherited from his forefathers. ⁸Every daughter who inherits land in any Israelite tribe must marry someone in her father's tribal clan, so that every Israelite will possess the inheritance of his fathers. (+Jos 17:3-6)

Prescribing right of, to redeem alienated land (Lev 25:25)—

Ru 4:1 Meanwhile Boaz went up to the town gate and sat there. When the kinsman-redeemer he had mentioned came along, Boaz said, "Come over here, my friend, and sit down." So he went over and sat down.

[2]Boaz took ten of the elders of the town and said, "Sit here," and they did so. [3]Then he said to the kinsman-redeemer, "Naomi, who has come back from Moab, is selling the piece of land that belonged to our brother Elimelech. [4]I thought I should bring the matter to your attention and suggest that you buy it in the presence of these seated here and in the presence of the elders of my people. If you will redeem it, do so. But if you will not, tell me, so I will know. For no one has the right to do it except you, and I am next in line."

"I will redeem it," he said.

[5]Then Boaz said, "On the day you buy the land from Naomi and from Ruth the Moabitess, you acquire the dead man's widow, in order to maintain the name of the dead with his property."

[6]At this, the kinsman-redeemer said, "Then I cannot redeem it because I might endanger my own estate. You redeem it yourself. I cannot do it."

[7](Now in earlier times in Israel, for the redemption and transfer of property to become final, one party took off his sandal and gave it to the other. This was the method of legalizing transactions in Israel.)

[8]So the kinsman-redeemer said to Boaz, "Buy it yourself." And he removed his sandal.

[9]Then Boaz announced to the elders and all the people, "Today you are witnesses that I have bought from Naomi all the property of Elimelech, Kilion and Mahlon. [10]I have also acquired Ruth the Moabitess, Mahlon's widow, as my wife, in order to maintain the name of the dead with his property, so that his name will not disappear from among his family or from the town records. Today you are witnesses!"

[11]Then the elders and all those at the gate said, "We are witnesses. May the LORD make the woman who is coming into your home like Rachel and Leah, who together built up the house of Israel. May you have standing in Ephrathah and be famous in Bethlehem. [12]Through the offspring the LORD gives you by this young woman, may your family be like that of Perez, whom Tamar bore to Judah."

To inherit slaves—

Lev 25:45 You may also buy some of the temporary residents living among you and members of their clans born in your country, and they will become your property. [46]You can will them to your children as inherited property and can make them slaves for life, but you must not rule over your fellow Israelites ruthlessly.

Firstborn son to have double portion—

Dt 21:15 If a man has two wives, and he loves one but not the other, and both bear him sons but the firstborn is the son of the wife he does not love, [16]when he wills his property to his sons, he must not give the rights of the firstborn to the son of the wife he loves in preference to his actual firstborn, the son of the wife he does not love. [17]He must acknowledge the son of his unloved wife as the firstborn by giving him a double share of all he has. That son is the first sign of his father's strength. The right of the firstborn belongs to him.

Children of wives and concubines are—

Ge 15:3 And Abram said, "You have given me no children; so a servant in my household will be my heir."

Ge 21:10 and she said to Abraham, "Get rid of that slave woman and her son, for that slave woman's son will never share in the inheritance with my son Isaac."

Ge 25:5 Abraham left everything he owned to Isaac. [6]But while he was still living, he gave gifts to the sons of his concubines and sent them away from his son Isaac to the land of the east. (+Gal 4:30)

All possessions left to—

Ecc 2:18 I hated all the things I had toiled for under the sun, because I must leave them to the one who comes after me. [19]And who knows whether he will be a wise man or a fool? Yet he will have control over all the work into which I have poured my effort and skill under the sun. This too is meaningless.

Minor, under guardians (Gal 4:1-2).

See Birthright; Firstborn; Inheritance; Orphan; Will.

Figurative:

Of spiritual adoption—

Ro 8:14 because those who are led by the Spirit of God are sons of God. [15]For you did not receive a spirit that makes you a slave again to fear, but you received the Spirit of sonship. And by him we cry, *"Abba, Father."* [16]The Spirit himself testifies with our spirit that we are God's children. [17]Now if we are children, then we are heirs—heirs of God and co-heirs with Christ, if indeed we share in his sufferings in order that we may also share in his glory.

Gal 3:29 If you belong to Christ, then you are Abraham's seed, and heirs according to the promise.

Gal 4:6 Because you are sons, God sent the Spirit of his Son into our hearts, the Spirit who calls out, *"Abba, Father."* [7]So you are no longer a slave, but a son; and since you are a son, God has made you also an heir.

Tit 3:7 so that, having been justified by his grace, we might become heirs having the hope of eternal life.

Jas 2:5 Listen, my dear brothers: Has not God chosen those who are poor in the eyes of the world to be rich in faith and to inherit the kingdom he promised those who love him? *See Adoption.*

HELAH [2690] (*necklace* IDB; *rust* KB). A wife of Asher (1Ch 4:5).

HELAM [2663]. Place in Syrian desert E of Jordan where David defeated forces of Hadadezer (2Sa 10:16-17).

HELBAH [2695] (*a fertile region*). A town of Asher (Jdg 1:31).

HELBON [2696] (*fertile*). A village near Damascus, noted for fine wines (Eze 27:18).

HELDAI [2702] (*mole*).

1. The Netophathite. One of David's heroes (1Ch 27:15). Heled is a variant spelling (2Sa 23:29; 1Ch 11:30).

2. A leader among those returned from the Exile (Zec 6:10,14).

HELECH [2662]. Possibly Cilicia, an area in SE (modern day) Turkey (Eze 27:11).

HELED [2699]. *See Heldai, 1.*

HELEK, HELEKITE [2751, 2757] (*portion, lot*). Son of Gilead (Jos 17:2) and his clan (Nu 26:30).

HELEM [2152] (*health*).

1. A descendant of Asher (1Ch 7:35).

2. Probably the same as Heldai (Zec 6:10,14).

HELEPH [2738] (possibly *sharp, cutting*). A town of Naphtali (Jos 19:33).

HELEZ [2742] (*vigor* BDB).

1. One of David's mighty men (2Sa 23:26; 1Ch 11:27; 27:10).

2. A man of Judah (1Ch 2:39).

HELI [*2459*] (*ascent [to God]*). Father of Joseph, the husband of Mary (Lk 3:23), or perhaps the father of Mary, the mother of Jesus.

HELIOPOLIS [225] (*sun [god] city*). City near S end of the Nile Delta called "On" in the Bible (Ge 41:45; 46:20; Isa 19:18, ftn).

See City of Destruction.

HELKAI [2758] (*Yahweh is [my] portion*). A priest (Ne 12:15).

HELKATH [2762] (*portion*).

NIV+ HELKATH HAZZURIM

A Levitical town (Jos 19:25; 21:31), also spelled Hukok (1Ch 6:75). *See Hukok.*

HELKATH HAZZURIM [2763] (possibly *portion [field] of rock*, or *swords* IDB; *portion [field] of snare* KB).

NIV+ HELKATH

Plain near pool of Gibeon where soldiers of Joab and Abner fought (2Sa 2:12-16).

HELL [*87, 1147, 5434*]. In the NIV, "hell" usually translates the Greek *geena* and *hades*, but is conceptually the same as the Hebrew *Sheol*, usually rendered "grave," the unseen world and abode of the dead (Ge 37:35; 42:38; 44:29,31; Dt 32:22; 1Sa 2:6; 2Sa 22:6; 1Ki 2:6,9; Job 7:9; 11:8; 14:13; 17:13; 21:13; 24:19; 26:6; Ps 9:17; 16:10; 18:5; 55:15; 86:13; 116:3; 139:8; Pr 5:5; 7:27; 9:18; 15:11, 24; 23:14; 27:20; Isa 5:14; 14:9,15; 28:15,18; 57:9; Eze 31:16-17; 32:21,27; Am 9:2; Jnh 2:2; Hab 2:5).

In the NT hell is the unseen world (Mt 11:23; 16:18; Lk 10:15; 16:23; Ac 2:27,31; Rev 1:18; 6:8; 20:13-14), a place of torment (Mt 5:22,29-30; 10:28; 18:9; 23:15,33; Lk 12:5; Jas 3:6) and of captivity for fallen angels (2Pe 2:4).

Figurative:

Of divine judgments (Dt 32:22; Eze 31:15-17).

The future state, or abode, of the wicked:

Ps 9:17 The wicked return to the grave, all the nations that forget God.

Pr 5:5 Her feet go down to death; her steps lead straight to the grave.

Pr 9:18 But little do they know that the dead are there, that her guests are in the depths of the grave.

Pr 15:24 The path of life leads upward for the wise to keep him from going down to the grave.

Pr 23:14 Punish him with the rod and save his soul from death.

Isa 30:33 Topheth has long been prepared; it has been made ready for the king. Its fire pit has been made deep and wide, with an abundance of fire and wood; the breath of the LORD, like a stream of burning sulfur, sets it ablaze.

Isa 33:14 The sinners in Zion are terrified; trembling grips the godless: "Who of us can dwell with the consuming fire? Who of us can dwell with everlasting burning?"

Mt 3:12 His winnowing fork is in his hand, and he will clear his threshing floor, gathering his wheat into the barn

and burning up the chaff with unquenchable fire." (+Mt 5:22)

Mt 5:29 If your right eye causes you to sin, gouge it out and throw it away. It is better for you to lose one part of your body than for your whole body to be thrown into hell. (+Mt 5:30)

Mt 7:13 "Enter through the narrow gate. For wide is the gate and broad is the road that leads to destruction, and many enter through it.

Mt 8:11 I say to you that many will come from the east and the west, and will take their places at the feast with Abraham, Isaac and Jacob in the kingdom of heaven. ¹²But the subjects of the kingdom will be thrown outside, into the darkness, where there will be weeping and gnashing of teeth."

Mt 10:28 Do not be afraid of those who kill the body but cannot kill the soul. Rather, be afraid of the One who can destroy both soul and body in hell.

Mt 13:30 Let both grow together until the harvest. At that time I will tell the harvesters: First collect the weeds and tie them in bundles to be burned; then gather the wheat and bring it into my barn.' "

Mt 13:38 The field is the world, and the good seed stands for the sons of the kingdom. The weeds are the sons of the evil one, ³⁹and the enemy who sows them is the devil. The harvest is the end of the age, and the harvesters are angels.

⁴⁰"As the weeds are pulled up and burned in the fire, so it will be at the end of the age. ⁴¹The Son of Man will send out his angels, and they will weed out of his kingdom everything that causes sin and all who do evil. ⁴²They will throw them into the fiery furnace, where there will be weeping and gnashing of teeth.

Mt 13:49 This is how it will be at the end of the age. The angels will come and separate the wicked from the righteous ⁵⁰and throw them into the fiery furnace, where there will be weeping and gnashing of teeth.

Mt 16:18 And I tell you that you are Peter, and on this rock I will build my church, and the gates of Hades will not overcome it.

Mt 18:8 If your hand or your foot causes you to sin cut it off and throw it away. It is better for you to enter life maimed or crippled than to have two hands or two feet and be thrown into eternal fire. ⁹And if your eye causes you to sin, gouge it out and throw it away. It is better for you to enter life with one eye than to have two eyes and be thrown into the fire of hell.

Mt 18:34 In anger his master turned him over to the jailers to be tortured, until he should pay back all he owed.

³⁵"This is how my heavenly Father will treat each of you unless you forgive your brother from your heart."

Mt 22:13 "Then the king told the attendants, 'Tie him hand and foot, and throw him outside, into the darkness, where there will be weeping and gnashing of teeth.'

Mt 25:30 And throw that worthless servant outside, into the darkness, where there will be weeping and gnashing of teeth.'

Mt 25:41 "Then he will say to those on his left, 'Depart from me, you who are cursed, into the eternal fire prepared for the devil and his angels.

Mt 25:46 "Then they will go away to eternal punishment, but the righteous to eternal life."

Mk 9:43 If your hand causes you to sin, cut it off. It is better for you to enter life maimed than with two hands to go into hell, where the fire never goes out. (+Mk 9:44-48)

Lk 3:17 His winnowing fork is in his hand to clear his

threshing floor and to gather the wheat into his barn, but he will burn up the chaff with unquenchable fire."

Lk 16:23 In hell, where he was in torment, he looked up and saw Abraham far away, with Lazarus by his side. ²⁴So he called to him, 'Father Abraham, have pity on me and send Lazarus to dip the tip of his finger in water and cool my tongue, because I am in agony in this fire.' (+Lk 16:25)

Lk 16:26 And besides all this, between us and you a great chasm has been fixed, so that those who want to go from here to you cannot, nor can anyone cross over from there to us.' (+Lk 16:27-28; Ac 1:25)

2Th 1:9 They will be punished with everlasting destruction and shut out from the presence of the Lord and from the majesty of his power

2Pe 2:4 For if God did not spare angels when they sinned, but sent them to hell, putting them into gloomy dungeons to be held for judgment;

Jude 6 And the angels who did not keep their positions of authority but abandoned their own home—these he has kept in darkness, bound with everlasting chains for judgment on the great Day.

Jude 23 snatch others from the fire and save them; to others show mercy, mixed with fear—hating even the clothing stained by corrupted flesh. (+Rev 2:11)

Rev 9:1 The fifth angel sounded his trumpet, and I saw a star that had fallen from the sky to the earth. The star was given the key to the shaft of the Abyss. ²When he opened the Abyss, smoke rose from it like the smoke from a gigantic furnace. The sun and sky were darkened by the smoke from the Abyss. (+Rev 11:7)

Rev 14:10 he, too, will drink of the wine of God's fury, which has been poured full strength into the cup of his wrath. He will be tormented with burning sulfur in the presence of the holy angels and of the Lamb. ¹¹And the smoke of their torment rises for ever and ever. There is no rest day or night for those who worship the beast and his image, or for anyone who receives the mark of his name."

Rev 19:20 But the beast was captured, and with him the false prophet who had performed the miraculous signs on his behalf. With these signs he had deluded those who had received the mark of the beast and worshiped his image. The two of them were thrown alive into the fiery lake of burning sulfur.

Rev 20:10 And the devil, who deceived them, was thrown into the lake of burning sulfur, where the beast and the false prophet had been thrown. They will be tormented day and night for ever and ever.

Rev 20:15 If anyone's name was not found written in the book of life, he was thrown into the lake of fire.

Rev 21:8 But the cowardly, the unbelieving, the vile, the murderers, the sexually immoral, those who practice magic arts, the idolaters and all liars—their place will be in the fiery lake of burning sulfur. This is the second death."

See Hades; Sheol; Wicked, Punishment of.

HELLENISTS NIV "Grecian Jews"; Jews of the Dispersion who spoke Greek and followed some aspects of Greek culture (Ac 6:1; 9:29).

HELM *See Rudder(s).*

HELMET [3916, 5057+8031, 7746, *4330*].
NIV+ HELMETS

A defensive headgear worn by soldiers (1Sa 17:5,38; 2Ch 26:14; Jer 46:4; Eze 23:24).
Figurative:
(Isa 59:17; Eph 6:17; 1Th 5:8).

HELON [2735] (*strength, power*). Father of Eliab (Nu 1:9; 2:7; 7:24,29; 10:16).

HELPER [5853, 6468, 6469, 6476, *1071, 5677*]. Woman created as a helper suitable for man (Ge 2:18,20). Yahweh is the helper of Israel (Dt 33:29; Hos 13:9), of the fatherless (Ps 10:14), of David (Ps 27:9). Eliezer means "God is my helper" (Ex 18:4, ftn.).

HELPMEET *See Helper.*

HELPS [6468, *2138, 5269*]. One of the gifts of the Spirit, probably the ability to perform helpful works in a gracious manner (1Co 12:7-11,28-31).

HEM OF A GARMENT [4053, 4193, 7443, 8767, *5309*]. Fringes or tassels on the borders of the Israelite outer garment (Nu 15:38-39).

HEMAM *See Homam.*

HEMAN [2124] (*faithful*).
NIV+ HEMAN'S
1. A man noted for wisdom, to whom Solomon is compared (1Ki 4:31; 1Ch 2:6).
2. "The Singer," a chief Levite, and musician (1Ch 6:33; 15:17,19; 16:41). The king's seer (1Ch 25:5). His sons and daughters temple musicians (1Ch 6:33; 25:1-6). "Maskil of," title of Psalm 88. *See Maskil.*

HEMATH
1. *See Hamath.*
2. *See Hammath, 2.*

HEMDAN [2777] (*desirable*). Son of Dishon (Ge 36:26).

HEMLOCK A poisonous and bitter plant (Hos 10:4; Am 6:12).
See Gall, 3; Plants of the Bible; Poison.

HEMORRHAGE Menstruation (Lev 15:19; Mt 9:20; Lk 8:43). A woman subject to bleeding for twelve years (Mk 5:25-29; Mk 5:24-34; Lk 8:). *See Bleeding, Subject to; Menstruation.*

HEMORRHOIDS NIV "tumors" (Dt 28:27); a disease with which the Philistines were afflicted (1Sa 5:6,12; 6:4; 5:11). *See Disease; Tumor.*

HEN [2835, *3998*] (as a proper name: *gracious*).
1. Son of Zephaniah (Zec 6:14).
2. Hen protecting her chicks figurative of Jesus' desire for Jerusalem (Mt 23:37; Lk 13:34).

HENA [2184] (*[pagan god] Anath*). A city on the Euphrates (2Ki 18:34; 19:13; Isa 37:13).

HENADAD [2836] (*favor of Hadad [pagan god]*). A Levite (Ezr 3:9; Ne 3:18,24; 10:9).

HENNA BLOSSOMS [4110]. A shrub of Israel (perhaps the cypress) with tightly clustered, aromatic blossoms (SS 1:14; 4:13).

HENOCH *See Enoch.*

HEPHER, HEPHERITE [2918, 2919, 2920] (perhaps *help*).
NIV+ GATH HEPHER
1. Son of Gilead, and ancestor of Zelophehad (Nu 26:32-33; 27:1; Jos 17:2-3).
2. Son of Naarah (1Ch 4:6).

3. One of David's heroes (1Ch 11:36).
4. A city W of the Jordan (Jos 12:17; 1Ki 4:10).

HEPHZIBAH [2915] (*my pleasure is in her*).
1. Wife of Hezekiah (2Ki 21:1).
2. Symbolic name given to Zion (Isa 62:4).

HERALD [7924, 10370, *3061*]. (Isa 40:3; Da 3:4). Signified by the word "preacher" (1Ti 2:7; 2Ti 1:11; 2Pe 2:5).

HERBS [246, 4865, 5353, *3303*]. Given for food (Ge 1:29-30; Pr 15:17). *See Vegetation.*

HERD [*546, 989, 1330, 6337, 6373, 8802, *36*, *2576*].
NIV+ HERDED, HERDING, HERDS, HERDSMEN

Herds of cattle were used in plowing, threshing, and sacrifice (Ge 18:7; Job 1:3; 42:12).

HERDSMAN [5238, 8286].
NIV+ See HERD

Person in charge of cattle (Ge 13:7) or pigs (Mt 8:33), despised in Egypt (Ge 46:34) but honored in Israel (Ge 47:6; 1Ch 27:29).

HEREDITY
Like gives birth to like—
Ge 5:3 When Adam had lived 130 years, he had a son in his own likeness, in his own image; and he named him Seth.
Job 14:4 Who can bring what is pure from the impure? No one!
Jn 3:6 Flesh gives birth to flesh, but the Spirit gives birth to spirit. [7]You should not be surprised at my saying, 'You must be born again.'

Results of:

Natural, depravity—
Job 21:19 [It is said,] 'God stores up a man's punishment for his sons.' Let him repay the man himself, so that he will know it!
Ps 51:5 Surely I was sinful at birth, sinful from the time my mother conceived me.
Ps 58:3 Even from birth the wicked go astray; from the womb they are wayward and speak lies.
Isa 48:8 You have neither heard nor understood; from of old your ear has not been open. Well do I know how treacherous you are; you were called a rebel from birth.
Jn 9:2 His disciples asked him, "Rabbi, who sinned, this man or his parents, that he was born blind?"
Ro 5:12 Therefore, just as sin entered the world through one man, and death through sin, and in this way death came to all men, because all sinned—
Eph 2:3 All of us also lived among them at one time, gratifying the cravings of our sinful nature and following its desires and thoughts. Like the rest, we were by nature objects of wrath.

Judicial, ordained consequences of parental conduct—
Ex 20:5 You shall not bow down to them or worship them; for I, the LORD your God, am a jealous God, punishing the children for the sin of the fathers to the third and fourth generation of those who hate me, [6]but showing love to a thousand [generations] of those who love me and keep my commandments. (+Ex 34:7; Nu 14:18)
Nu 14:33 Your children will be shepherds here for forty years, suffering for your unfaithfulness, until the last of your bodies lies in the desert. (+Dt 5:9)
Ps 37:28 For the LORD loves the just and will not forsake his faithful ones. They will be protected forever, but the offspring of the wicked will be cut off;

Isa 14:20 you will not join them in burial, for you have destroyed your land and killed your people. The offspring of the wicked will never be mentioned again.
[21]Prepare a place to slaughter his sons for the sins of their forefathers; they are not to rise to inherit the land and cover the earth with their cities.
Isa 65:6 "See, it stands written before me: I will not keep silent but will pay back in full; I will pay it back into their laps— [7]both your sins and the sins of your fathers," says the LORD. "Because they burned sacrifices on the mountains and defied me on the hills, I will measure into their laps the full payment for their former deeds."
Jer 32:18 You show love to thousands but bring the punishment for the fathers' sins into the laps of their children after them. O great and powerful God, whose name is the LORD Almighty, (+Ro 5:12)
1Co 15:22 For as in Adam all die, so in Christ all will be made alive.

Does not fix moral status—
Jer 31:29 "In those days people will no longer say, 'The fathers have eaten sour grapes, and the children's teeth are set on edge.' [30]Instead, everyone will die for his own sin; whoever eats sour grapes—his own teeth will be set on edge. (+Eze 18:1)
Eze 18:2 "What do you people mean by quoting this proverb about the land of Israel: "'The fathers eat sour grapes, and the children's teeth are set on edge'? (+Eze 18:3-18)
Eze 18:19 "Yet you ask, 'Why does the son not share the guilt of his father?' Since the son has done what is just and right and has been careful to keep all my decrees, he will surely live. [20]The soul who sins is the one who will die. The son will not share the guilt of the father, nor will the father share the guilt of the son. The righteousness of the righteous man will be credited to him, and the wickedness of the wicked will be charged against him. (+Eze 18:21-32)
Mt 3:9 And do not think you can say to yourselves, 'We have Abraham as our father.' I tell you that out of these stones God can raise up children for Abraham.

HERES [3065] (*sun*).
1. District around Aijalon (Jdg 1:35).
2. Place E of the Jordan (Jdg 8:13).
3. Egyptian city, translated "city of destruction" (Isa 19:18), undoubtedly Heliopolis.

HERESH [3090] (*deaf, silent*). A Levite (1Ch 9:15).

HERESY [*146*].
NIV+ HERESIES

Propagandism of, forbidden under severe penalties (Dt 13; Tit 3:10-11; 2Jn 10-11). Teachers of, among early Christians (Ac 15:24; 2Co 11:4; Gal 1:7; 2:4; 2Pe 2; Jude 3-16; Rev 2:2). Paul and Silas accused of (Ac 16:20-21,23). Paul accused of (Ac 18:13). Disavowed by Paul (Ac 24:13-17). *See Teachers, False.*

HERETH [3101]. A forest in which David found refuge from Saul (1Sa 22:5).

HERMAS [2254]. Friend of Paul in the church at Rome (Ro 16:14).

HERMES [2258] (possibly *rock, cairn*).
1. Greek god (messenger), the same as Mercury in Latin. Paul mistaken for (Ac 14:12).
2. Friend of Paul in the church at Rome (Ro 16:14).

HERMOGENES [2259] (*born of Hermes*). A Christian who deserted Paul (2Ti 1:15).

HERMON, MOUNT [3056] (*consecrated place*).

NIV+ BAAL HERMON, SENIR, SIRION, SIYON

Mountain marking S end of Anti-Lebanon range; thirty miles SW of Damascus; 9,000 ft. above sea level; marks N boundary of Israel; has three peaks. Has borne several names: the Amorites call it "Senir," (Dt 3:9), the Sidonians call it "Sirion" (Dt 3:9), "Siyon," (Dt 4:48). Probably the Mount of Transfiguration (Mt 17:1). Seat of Baal worship (Jdg 3:3). Modern Jebel es-Sheikh.

HEROD [2476].

NIV+ AGRIPPA, ANTIPAS, HEROD'S, HERODIANS

Idumean rulers of Israel (37 B.C. to A.D. 100). Line started with Antipater, whom Julius Caesar made procurator of Judea in 47 B.C.

1. Herod the Great, first procurator of Galilee, then king of the Jews (37- 4 B.C.); built Caesarea, temple at Jerusalem; slaughtered children at Bethlehem (Mt 2:1-18). At his death his kingdom was divided among his three sons: Archelaus, Herod Antipas, and Philip.

2. Archelaus ruled over Judea, Samaria, and Idumea (4 B.C. to A.D. 6), and was removed from office by the Romans (Mt 2:22).

3. Herod Antipas ruled over Galilee and Perea (4 B.C. to A.D. 39); killed John the Baptist (Mt 14:1-12); called "fox" by Jesus (Lk 13:32).

4. Philip, tetrarch of Batanaea, Trachonitis, Gaulanitis, and parts of Jamnia (4 B.C. to A.D. 34). Best of the Herods.

5. Herod Agrippa I; grandson of Herod the Great; tetrarch of Galilee; king of Israel (A.D. 37-44); killed James the apostle (Ac 12:1-23).

6. Herod Agrippa II. King of territory E of Galilee (A.D. 50-100); Paul appeared before him (Ac 25:13-26:32).

HERODIANS [2477].

NIV+ See HEROD

They are mentioned as enemies of Jesus once in Galilee, and again at Jerusalem (Mt 22:15-22; Mk 3:6; 12:13-17; Lk 20:20-26). The Pharisees were ardent nationalists, opposed to Roman rule, while the hated Herodians, as their name indicates, supported the Roman rule of the Herods. Now, however, the Pharisees enlisted the help of the Herodians to trap Jesus in his words. After trying to put him off guard with flattery, they sprang their question: "Is it right to pay taxes to Caesar or not?" (Mt 22:17). If he said "no," the Herodians would report him to the Roman governor and he would be executed for treason. If he said "yes," the Pharisees would denounce him to the people as disloyal to his nation.

HERODIAS [2478] (feminine form of Herod). Granddaughter of Herod the Great who had John the Baptist put to death (Mt 14:3-6; Mk 6:17; Lk 3:19).

HERODION [2479]. A Roman Christian (Ro 16:11).

HERON [649]. Large aquatic bird Israelites could not eat (Lev 11:19; Dt 14:18).

HESED *See Ben-Hesed.*

HESHBON [3114] (*reckoning*). A city of the Amorites (Nu 21:25-35; Dt 1:4). Built by Reuben (Nu 32:37). Allotted to Gad (Jos 21:38-39). Pools at (SS 7:4). Prophecy concerning (Isa 16:8; Jer 48:2,34-35; 49:1-3).

HESHMON [3132]. A town in the S of Judah (Jos 15:27).

HETH Son of Canaan and ancestor of the Hittites (Ge 10:15; 23:3, ftn,5,7,10,16,18; 27:46; 49:32; 1Ch 1:13). *See Hittite(s).*

HETHLON [3158]. A place on the northern frontier of Israel (Eze 47:15; 48:1).

HEXATEUCH (*six books*). A term referring to the Pentateuch and Joshua as though it were a literary unit.

HEZEKIAH [2624, 2625, 3490, 3491, *1614*] (*Yahweh is [my] strength*).

NIV+ HEZEKIAH'S

1. King of Judah (2Ki 16:20; 18:1-2; 1Ch 3:13; 2Ch 29:1; Mt 1:9). Religious zeal of (2Ch 29; 30; 31). Purges the nation of idolatry (2Ki 18:4; 2Ch 31:1; 33:3). Restores the true forms of worship (2Ch 31:2-21). His piety (2Ki 18:2,5-6; 2Ch 29:2; 31:20-21; 32:32; Jer 26:19). Military operations of (2Ki 18:19; 1Ch 4:39-43; 2Ch 32; Isa 36; 37). Sickness and restoration of (2Ki 20:1-11; 2Ch 32:24; Isa 38:1-8). His psalm of thanksgiving (Isa 38:9-22). His lack of wisdom in showing his resources to commissioners of Babylon (2Ki 20:12-19; 2Ch 32:25-26,31; Isa 39). Prospered of God (2Ki 18:7; 2Ch 32:27-30). Conducts the Brook Gihon into Jerusalem (2Ki 18:17; 20:20; 2Ch 32:4, 30; 33:14; Ne 2:13-15; 3:13,16; Isa 7:3; 22:9-11; 36:2). Scribes of (Pr 25:1). Death and burial of (2Ki 20:21; 2Ch 32:33). Prophecies concerning (2Ki 19:20-34; 20:5-6,16-18; Isa 38:5-8; 39:5-7; Jer 26:18-19).

2. One of the exiles (Ezr 2:16; Ne 7:21; 10:17).

3. An ancestor of the prophet Zephaniah (Zep 1:1).

4. *See Hizkiah, 1.*

HEZION [2611] (*vision* BDB; *one with floppy ears* IDB). Grandfather of Ben-Hadad (1Ki 15:18).

HEZIR [2615] (*boar*).

1. A Levite (1Ch 24:15).

2. A prince of Judah (Ne 10:20).

HEZRAI *See Hezro.*

HEZRO [2968]. Also called Hezrai. A Carmelite (2Sa 23:35; 1Ch 11:37).

HEZRON, HEZRONITE [2969, 2970, 2971, 2272] (*enclosure*).

1. A son of Perez (Ge 46:12). Ancestor of the Hezronites (Nu 26:6). An ancestor of Jesus (Mt 1:3; Lk 3:33).

2. A son of Reuben (Ge 46:9; Ex 6:14; 1Ch 4:1; 5:3). Ancestor of the Hezronites (Nu 26:21).

HIDDAI [2068]. One of David's heroes (2Sa 23:30). Called Hurai (1Ch 11:32).

HIDDEKEL *See Tigris.*

HIEL [2647] (*God [El] lives*). Rebuilder of Jericho (1Ki 16:34). In him was fulfilled the curse pronounced by Joshua (Jos 6:26).

HIERAPOLIS [2631] (*[pagan] sacred city*). Ancient Phrygian city near Colosse (Col 4:13).

HIEROGLYPHICS *See Writing.*

HIGGAION [2053].

A musical term probably meaning "solemn sound" or "meditation." It occurs in Ugaritic as with the meaning "to utter." According to Gesenius, it signifies the murmuring tone of a harp and therefore should be rendered in a melancholy manner (Ps 92:3). Combined with *Selah*, it may have been intended to indicate a pause in the vocal music while the instruments played an interlude (Ps 9:16, ftn). Mendelssohn translates it "meditation, thought" (Ps 19:14). Therefore, the music was to be rendered in a mode to promote devout meditation.

See Music, Symbols Used in.

HIGH PLACES [1195]. A term used to describe places of worship (Ge 12:8; 22:2,14; 31:54; 1Sa 9:12; 2Sa 24:25; 1Ki 3:2,4; 18:30,38; 1Ch 16:39; 2Ch 1:3; 33:17). Signify a place of idolatrous worship (Nu 22:41; 1Ki 11:7; 12:31; 14:23; 15:14; 22:43; 2Ki 17:9,29; Jer 7:31). Licentious practices at (Eze 16:24-43). The idolatrous, to be destroyed (Lev 26:30; Nu 33:52). Asa destroys (2Ch 14:3), Jehoshaphat (2Ch 17:6), Hezekiah (2Ki 18:4), Josiah (2Ki 23:8).

See Groves; Idolatry; Shrine.

HIGH PRIEST *See Priest.*

HIGHWAYS [2006, 5019, 5020, 6148] (*a built up road*).

NIV+ HIGHWAY

From, Gibeon to Beth Horon (Jos 10:10), Bethel to Shechem (Jdg 21:19), Judea to Galilee, by way of Samaria (Jn 4:3-5,43). To Bethel (Jdg 20:31), to Gibeah (Jdg 20:31), to cities of refuge (Dt 19:3). Built by rulers (Nu 20:17; 21:22).

Figurative:

Pr 16:17 The highway of the upright avoids evil; he who guards his way guards his life.

Isa 11:16 There will be a highway for the remnant of his people that is left from Assyria, as there was for Israel when they came up from Egypt.

Isa 35:8 And a highway will be there; it will be called the Way of Holiness. The unclean will not journey on it; it will be for those who walk in that Way; wicked fools will not go about on it. [9]No lion will be there, nor will any ferocious beast get up on it; they will not be found there. But only the redeemed will walk there, [10]and the ransomed of the LORD will return. They will enter Zion with singing; everlasting joy will crown their heads. Gladness and joy will overtake them, and sorrow and sighing will flee away.

Isa 40:3 A voice of one calling: "In the desert prepare the way for the LORD; make straight in the wilderness a highway for our God. [4]Every valley shall be raised up, every mountain and hill made low; the rough ground shall become level, the rugged places a plain. (+Mt 3:3)

Mt 7:13 "Enter through the narrow gate. For wide is the gate and broad is the road that leads to destruction, and many enter through it. [14]But small is the gate and narrow the road that leads to life, and only a few find it.

See Roads.

HILEN [2664]. A city of Judah. Assigned to the priests (1Ch 6:58). Called Holon (Jos 15:51; 21:15).

HILKIAH [2759, 2760] (*Yahweh is [my] portion*).

NIV+ HILKIAH'S

1. Father of Eliakim (2Ki 18:18).

2. Merarite Levite (1Ch 6:45).

3. Merarite Levite (1Ch 26:11).

4. High priest who found book of the Law and sent it to Josiah (2Ki 22-23; 2Ch 34:14).

5. Priest who returned with Zerubbabel (Ne 12:7).

6. Father of Jeremiah (Jer 1:1).

7. Father of Gemariah who stood by Ezra at Bible reading (Ne 8:4).

HILL COUNTRY [2215, *3978*].

NIV+ See HILLS

Any region of hills and valleys, but in Scripture generally the higher part of Judea (Lk 1:39,65).

HILLEL [2148] (*he has praises*). Father of Abdon (Jdg 12:13,15).

HILLS [1496, 2215, *1090*, *4001*].

NIV+ HILL, FOOTHILLS, HILLSIDE, HILLTOP, HILLTOPS

Perpetual (Ge 49:26; Hab 3:6).

HIN [2125]. A measure for liquids, and containing one-sixth or one-seventh of a bath. Probably equivalent to about four quarts (Ex 29:40; Lev 19:36; 23:13). *See Measure.*

HIND *See Deer.*

HINGE [6015, 7494].

NIV+ HINGED, HINGES

A fitting enabling a door or window to swing in its place (1Ki 7:50), often used figuratively for something of great importance.

HINNOM, VALLEY OF [2183].

NIV+ BEN HINNOM

A valley W and SW of Jerusalem (Jos 15:8; 18:16; 2Ki 23:10; Ne 11:30). Children offered in sacrifice in (2Ch 28:3; 33:6; Jer 7:31-32; 19:2,4,6; 32:35). Possibly valley of vision identical with (Isa 22:1,5).

See Ben Hinnom; Topheth, Tophet.

HIP AND THIGH Hebrew idiom denoting thoroughness with which Samson slew Philistines (Jdg 15:8, KJV).

HIPPOPOTAMUS *See Behemoth.*

HIRAH [2669]. An Adullamite (Ge 38:1,12).

HIRAM [2586, 2670, 2671] (*[my] brother is elevated*).

NIV+ HIRAM'S

Hiram (Hebrew *Huram*, a variant of *Hiram*), was a Phoenician king who was the first to accord the newly established King David international recognition. It was vital to him that he have good relations with the king of Israel since Israel dominated the inland trade routes to Tyre, and Tyre was dependent on Israelite agriculture for much of its food. A close relationship existed between these two realms until the Babylonian invasions. Builds a palace for David (2Sa 5:11; 1Ch 14:1; 2Ch 2:3). Aids Solomon in building the temple (1Ki 5; 2Ch 2:3-16). Dissatisfied with cities given by Solomon (1Ki 9:11-13). Makes presents of gold and seamen to Solomon (1Ki 9:14,26-28; 10:11).

HIRE [924, 8509, 8510, *3636*].

NIV+ HIRED, HIRES

Law concerning hired property (Ex 22:14-15).

See Employer; Master; Servant; Wages.

HIRED SERVANT [6128, 8502, 8509, *3140, 3634, 3636, 3638*]. Jacob (Ge 29:15; 30:26), re-employed (Ge 30:27-34; 31:6-7,41). Laborers for a vineyard (Mt 20:1-15). The prodigal (Lk 15:15-19).

Kindness to (Ru 2:4). Treatment of, more considerate than that accorded slaves (Lev 25:53).

Rights of:

To receive wages (Mt 10:10; Lk 10:7; Ro 4:4; 1Ti 5:18; Jas 5:4), daily (Lev 19:13; Dt 24:15). To share in spontaneous products of land in Sabbatic year (Lev 25:6). Wages of, paid in portion of flocks or products (Ge 30:31-32; 2Ch 2:10), or in money (Mt 20:2,9-10). Oppression of, forbidden (Dt 24:14; Col 4:1). Oppressors of, punished (Mal 3:5).

Mercenary (Job 7:2). Unfaithful (Jn 10:12-13).

See Employee; Master; Servant; Wages.

HIRELING *See Hired Servant.*

HISTORY

NIV+ HISTORIC

(Job 8:8-10).

See Genesis; Joshua; Judges; Ruth; Samuel, 1 and 2; Kings, 1 and 2; Chronicles, 1 and 2; Ezra; Nehemiah; Esther; Israel, Israelites; Jesus the Christ, History of.

HITTITE(S) [3147, 3153] (*descendants of Heth*). A tribe of Canaanites. Sons of Heth (Ge 10:15; 23:3, ftn, 5,7,10,16,18). Sell a burying-ground to Abraham (Ge 23). Esau intermarries with (Ge 26:34; 36:2). Dwelling place of (Ge 23:17-20; Nu 13:29; Jos 1:4; Jdg 1:26). Their land given to the Israelites (Ex 3:8; Dt 7:1; Jos 1:4). Conquered by Joshua (Jos 9:1-2; 10; 11; 12; 24:11). Intermarry with Israelites (Jdg 3:5-7; Ezr 9:1). Solomon intermarries with (1Ki 11:1; Ne 13:26). Pay tribute to Solomon (1Ki 9:20-21). Retain their own kings (1Ki 10:29; 2Ki 7:6; 2Ch 1:17). Officers from, in David's army (1Sa 26:6; 2Sa 11:3; 23:39).

HIVITE(S) [2563]. A tribe of Canaanites (Ge 10:17; 1Ch 1:15). Shechemites and Gibeonites were families of (Ge 34:2; Jos 9:7; 11:19). Esau intermarries with (Ge 26:34; 36:2). Dwelling place of (Jos 11:3; Jdg 3:3; 2Sa 24:7). Their land given to the Israelites (Ex 23:23,28; Dt 20:17; Jdg 3:5). Conquered by Joshua (Jos 9:1; 12:8; 24:11). Pay tribute to Solomon (1Ki 9:21; 2Ch 8:8).

HIZKI [2623] (*Yahweh is [my] strength,* or *my strength*). A Benjamite (1Ch 8:17).

HIZKIAH [2624] (*Yahweh is [my] strength*).

1. A son of Neariah (1Ch 3:23).

2. *See Hezekiah, 3.*

HIZKIJAH *See Hezekiah, 2.*

HOBAB [2463] (*beloved,* possibly *deceit*). Brother-in-law of Moses (Nu 10:29; Jdg 4:11).

HOBAH [2551]. A place N of Damascus (Ge 14:15).

HOBAIAH [2469] (*Yahweh has hidden*). Priest whose descendants were excluded from priesthood (Ezr 2:61; Ne 7:63).

HOD [2087] (*grandeur*). A son of Zophah (1Ch 7:37).

HODAVIAH, HODAIAH [2088, 2089, 2090] (*give thanks to Yahweh*).

1. Chief in Manasseh (1Ch 5:24).

2. Benjamite (1Ch 9:7).

3. Levite whose descendants returned with Zerubbabel (Ezr 2:40; 3:9; Ne 7:43).

4. Son of Elioenai (1Ch 3:24).

HODESH [2545] (*new moon*). Wife of Shaharaim (1Ch 8:9).

HODEVAH *See Hodaviah, Hodaiah, 3.*

HODIAH, HODIJAH [2091] (*grandeur is Yahweh*).

NIV+ HODIAH'S

1. Wife of Ezra (1Ch 4:19).

2. A Levite (Ne 8:7; 9:5; 10:10,13).

3. An Israelite chief (Ne 10:18).

HODSHI *See Tahtim Hodshi.*

HOGLAH [2519] (*partridge*).

NIV+ BETH HOGLAH

A daughter of Zelophehad (Nu 26:33; 27:1; 36:11; Jos 17:3).

HOHAM [2097]. Amorite king who entered a league against Joshua (Jos 10:3).

HOLIDAY [2182] (*a good day*). For rest. *See Sabbath.* One year in seven (Lev 25:2-7).

See Jubilee.

HOLINESS [*7705, 7727, 7731, 10620, 39, 40, 41, 42, 43, 605, 4008, 4009, 4949*].

NIV+ HOLY, HALLOWED, HOLIEST

Sin and holiness, sinful man and the holy Yahweh, were the dominant ideas in the Mosaic law. The supreme purpose of the system of Mosaic ordinances was to impress Israel as a separated people and through Israel to impress all people for all time that a holy God can be pleased by none but holy people. This is a central truth of the true religion. The student must, therefore, seek for this spiritual purpose through all the ordinances of the law. Defilement and uncleanness, exclusion of the unclean from the congregation atonements and atoning sacrifices, washings and purifications, whole burnt offerings, unblemished priests and unblemished offerings, typifying unblemished and uncorrupted motives in worship and service— all these were ordained as object lessons to teach that there is a difference between unholiness and holiness and thus to exalt holiness as the supreme lesson of life.

As in the books of the Mosaic law, so throughout the Holy Scriptures, the attainment of holiness is a dominant theme.

Attribute of God:

(Jos 24:19; 1Sa 6:20; Job 6:10; Ps 22:3; 47:8; 60:6; 89:35; 111:9; 145:17; Isa 5:16; 6:3; 29:19,23; 41:14; 43:14-15; 47:4; 49:7; 57:15; Eze 36:21-22; 39:7,25; Hos 11:9; Hab 1:12-13; Lk 1:49; Jn 17:11; Ro 1:23; Rev 4:8; 6:10; 15:4).

Described:

Ro 14:17 For the kingdom of God is not a matter of eating and drinking, but of righteousness, peace and joy in the Holy Spirit,

As walking in uprightness—

Isa 57:2 Those who walk uprightly enter into peace; they find rest as they lie in death.

As a highway—

Isa 35:8 And a highway will be there; it will be called the Way of Holiness. The unclean will not journey on it; it will be for those who walk in that Way; wicked fools will not go about on it.

As departing from evil (Ps 34:14)—

Ps 37:27 Turn from evil and do good; then you will dwell in the land forever.

As satisfying—

Jn 6:35 Then Jesus declared, "I am the bread of life. He who comes to me will never go hungry, and he who believes in me will never be thirsty.

As crucifying the sinful nature (Gal 5:24)

As a new creature—

Gal 6:15 Neither circumcision nor uncircumcision means anything; what counts is a new creation.

As a new self (Eph 4:24)—

Col 3:10 and have put on the new self, which is being renewed in knowledge in the image of its Creator.

As a rest—

Heb 4:3 Now we who have believed enter that rest, just as God has said, "So I declared on oath in my anger, 'They shall never enter my rest.'" And yet his work has been finished since the creation of the world.

Heb 4:9 There remains, then, a Sabbath-rest for the people of God;

As pure, peaceable, gentle—

Jas 3:17 But the wisdom that comes from heaven is first of all pure; then peace-loving, considerate, submissive, full of mercy and good fruit, impartial and sincere.

Commanded:

Ge 17:1 When Abram was ninety-nine years old, the LORD appeared to him and said, "I am God Almighty; walk before me and be blameless.

Ex 22:31 "You are to be my holy people. So do not eat the meat of an animal torn by wild beasts; throw it to the dogs.

Lev 10:8 Then the LORD said to Aaron, ⁹"You and your sons are not to drink wine or other fermented drink whenever you go into the Tent of Meeting, or you will die. This is a lasting ordinance for the generations to come. ¹⁰You must distinguish between the holy and the common, between the unclean and the clean,

Lev 11:44 I am the LORD your God; consecrate yourselves and be holy, because I am holy. Do not make yourselves unclean by any creature that moves about on the ground. ⁴⁵I am the LORD who brought you up out of Egypt to be your God; therefore be holy, because I am holy. (+Lev 19:2; 20:7,26; Nu 15:40)

Dt 13:17 None of those condemned things shall be found in your hands, so that the LORD will turn from his fierce anger; he will show you mercy, have compassion on you, and increase your numbers, as he promised on oath to your forefathers,

Dt 18:13 You must be blameless before the LORD your God.

Jos 7:13 "Go, consecrate the people. Tell them, 'Consecrate yourselves in preparation for tomorrow; for this is what the LORD, the God of Israel, says: That which is devoted is among you, O Israel. You cannot stand against your enemies until you remove it. (+2Ch 20:21)

Job 5:24 You will know that your tent is secure; you will take stock of your property and find nothing missing.

Ps 4:4 In your anger do not sin; when you are on your beds, search your hearts and be silent. *Selah*

Ps 97:10 Let those who love the LORD hate evil, for he guards the lives of his faithful ones and delivers them from the hand of the wicked.

Isa 52:1 Awake, awake, O Zion, clothe yourself with strength. Put on your garments of splendor, O Jerusalem, the holy city. The uncircumcised and defiled will not enter you again.

Isa 52:11 Depart, depart, go out from there! Touch no unclean thing! Come out from it and be pure, you who carry the vessels of the LORD.

Mic 6:8 He has showed you, O man, what is good. And what does the LORD require of you? To act justly and to love mercy and to walk humbly with your God.

Zep 2:3 Seek the LORD, all you humble of the land, you who do what he commands. Seek righteousness, seek humility; perhaps you will be sheltered on the day of the LORD's anger. (+Mt 5:19-28)

Mt 5:29 If your right eye causes you to sin, gouge it out and throw it away. It is better for you to lose one part of your body than for your whole body to be thrown into hell. ³⁰And if your right hand causes you to sin, cut it off and throw it away. It is better for you to lose one part of your body than for your whole body to go into hell.

Mt 5:48 Be perfect, therefore, as your heavenly Father is perfect. (+Mt 12:33)

Jn 5:14 Later Jesus found him at the temple and said to him, "See, you are well again. Stop sinning or something worse may happen to you."

Ro 6:1 What shall we say, then? Shall we go on sinning so that grace may increase? ²By no means! We died to sin; how can we live in it any longer? ³Or don't you know that all of us who were baptized into Christ Jesus were baptized into his death? ⁴We were therefore buried with him through baptism into death in order that, just as Christ was raised from the dead through the glory of the Father, we too may live a new life.

⁵If we have been united with him like this in his death, we will certainly also be united with him in his resurrection. ⁶For we know that our old self was crucified with him so that the body of sin might be done away with, that we should no longer be slaves to sin— ⁷because anyone who has died has been freed from sin.

⁸Now if we died with Christ, we believe that we will also live with him. ⁹For we know that since Christ was raised from the dead, he cannot die again; death no longer has mastery over him. ¹⁰The death he died, he died to sin once for all; but the life he lives, he lives to God.

¹¹In the same way, count yourselves dead to sin but alive to God in Christ Jesus. ¹²Therefore do not let sin reign in your mortal body so that you obey its evil desires. ¹³Do not offer the parts of your body to sin, as instruments of wickedness, but rather offer yourselves to God, as those who have been brought from death to life; and offer the parts of your body to him as instruments of righteousness. ¹⁴For sin shall not be your master, because you are not under law, but under grace.

¹⁵What then? Shall we sin because we are not under law but under grace? By no means! ¹⁶Don't you know that when you offer yourselves to someone to obey him as slaves, you are slaves to the one whom you obey— whether you are slaves to sin, which leads to death, or to obedience, which leads to righteousness? ¹⁷But thanks be to God that, though you used to be slaves to sin, you wholeheartedly obeyed the form of teaching to which you were entrusted. ¹⁸You have been set free from sin and have become slaves to righteousness.

¹⁹I put this in human terms because you are weak in your natural selves. Just as you used to offer the parts of your body in slavery to impurity and to ever-increasing wickedness, so now offer them in slavery to righteousness leading to holiness. ²⁰When you were slaves to sin, you were free

from the control of righteousness. [21]What benefit did you reap at that time from the things you are now ashamed of? Those things result in death! [22]But now that you have been set free from sin and have become slaves to God, the benefit you reap leads to holiness, and the result is eternal life. [23]For the wages of sin is death, but the gift of God is eternal life in Christ Jesus our Lord.

1Co 3:16 Don't you know that you yourselves are God's temple and that God's Spirit lives in you?

1Co 5:7 Get rid of the old yeast that you may be a new batch without yeast—as you really are. For Christ, our Passover lamb, has been sacrificed.

1Co 15:34 Come back to your senses as you ought, and stop sinning; for there are some who are ignorant of God— I say this to your shame.

2Co 6:14 Do not be yoked together with unbelievers. For what do righteousness and wickedness have in common? Or what fellowship can light have with darkness? [15]What harmony is there between Christ and Belial? What does a believer have in common with an unbeliever? [16]What agreement is there between the temple of God and idols? For we are the temple of the living God. As God has said: "I will live with them and walk among them, and I will be their God, and they will be my people."

[17]"Therefore come out from them and be separate, says the Lord. Touch no unclean thing, and I will receive you."

2Co 7:1 Since we have these promises, dear friends, let us purify ourselves from everything that contaminates body and spirit, perfecting holiness out of reverence for God. (+Eph 1:4; 5:1,3,8-11)

1Th 4:3 It is God's will that you should be sanctified: that you should avoid sexual immorality; [4]that each of you should learn to control his own body in a way that is holy and honorable,

1Th 4:7 For God did not call us to be impure, but to live a holy life.

1Th 5:22 Avoid every kind of evil.

[23]May God himself, the God of peace, sanctify you through and through. May your whole spirit, soul and body be kept blameless at the coming of our Lord Jesus Christ.

2Th 2:13 But we ought always to thank God for you, brothers loved by the Lord, because from the beginning God chose you to be saved through the sanctifying work of the Spirit and through belief in the truth.

1Ti 4:12 Don't let anyone look down on you because you are young, but set an example for the believers in speech, in life, in love, in faith and in purity. (+1Ti 5:22; 6:11-12)

2Ti 2:19 Nevertheless, God's solid foundation stands firm, sealed with this inscription: "The Lord knows those who are his," and, "Everyone who confesses the name of the Lord must turn away from wickedness."

2Ti 2:21 If a man cleanses himself from the latter, he will be an instrument for noble purposes, made holy, useful to the Master and prepared to do any good work.

[22]Flee the evil desires of youth, and pursue righteousness, faith, love and peace, along with those who call on the Lord out of a pure heart. (+1Pe 1:5)

2Pe 1:5 For this very reason, make every effort to add to your faith goodness; and to goodness, knowledge; [6]and to knowledge, self-control; and to self-control, perseverance; and to perseverance, godliness; [7]and to godliness, brotherly kindness; and to brotherly kindness, love. [8]For if you possess these qualities in increasing measure, they will keep you from being ineffective and unproductive in your knowledge of our Lord Jesus Christ.

1Jn 2:1 My dear children, I write this to you so that you will not sin. But if anybody does sin, we have one who speaks to the Father in our defense—Jesus Christ, the Righteous One.

1Jn 2:5 But if anyone obeys his word, God's love is truly made complete in him. This is how we know we are in him:

1Jn 2:29 If you know that he is righteous, you know that everyone who does what is right has been born of him.

2Jn 4 It has given me great joy to find some of your children walking in the truth, just as the Father commanded us.

Rev 18:4 Then I heard another voice from heaven say: "Come out of her, my people, so that you will not share in her sins, so that you will not receive any of her plagues;

Commanded upon Israel—

Ex 19:6 you will be for me a kingdom of priests and a holy nation.' These are the words you are to speak to the Israelites." (+Ex 22:31; Dt 7:6; 26:19)

Dt 28:9 The LORD will establish you as his holy people, as he promised you on oath, if you keep the commands of the LORD your God and walk in his ways.

Isa 4:3 Those who are left in Zion, who remain in Jerusalem, will be called holy, all who are recorded among the living in Jerusalem. (+Isa 52:1,11)

Isa 60:1 "Arise, shine, for your light has come, and the glory of the LORD rises upon you.

Isa 60:21 Then will all your people be righteous and they will possess the land forever. They are the shoot I have planted, the work of my hands, for the display of my splendor.

Zec 8:3 This is what the LORD says: "I will return to Zion and dwell in Jerusalem. Then Jerusalem will be called the City of Truth, and the mountain of the LORD Almighty will be called the Holy Mountain."

Zec 14:20 On that day HOLY TO THE LORD will be inscribed on the bells of the horses, and the cooking pots in the LORD's house will be like the sacred bowls in front of the altar. [21]Every pot in Jerusalem and Judah will be holy to the LORD Almighty, and all who come to sacrifice will take some of the pots and cook in them. And on that day there will no longer be a Canaanite in the house of the LORD Almighty.

Commanded upon the church—

2Co 11:2 I am jealous for you with a godly jealousy. I promised you to one husband, to Christ, so that I might present you as a pure virgin to him.

1Pe 2:5 you also, like living stones, are being built into a spiritual house to be a holy priesthood, offering spiritual sacrifices acceptable to God through Jesus Christ.

1Pe 2:9 But you are a chosen people, a royal priesthood, a holy nation, a people belonging to God, that you may declare the praises of him who called you out of darkness into his wonderful light.

Rev 19:8 Fine linen, bright and clean, was given her to wear." (Fine linen stands for the righteous acts of the saints.)

Exhortations to: (Mt 5:30; Jn 5:14; Ro 6:13,19; 12:1-2)

Ro 13:12 The night is nearly over; the day is almost here. So let us put aside the deeds of darkness and put on the armor of light. [13]Let us behave decently, as in the daytime, not in orgies and drunkenness, not in sexual immorality and debauchery, not in dissension and jealousy. [14]Rather, clothe yourselves with the Lord Jesus Christ, and do not think about how to gratify the desires of the sinful nature.

1Co 6:13 "Food for the stomach and the stomach for

food"—but God will destroy them both. The body is not meant for sexual immorality, but for the Lord, and the Lord for the body.

1Co 6:19 Do you not know that your body is a temple of the Holy Spirit, who is in you, whom you have received from God? You are not your own; [20]you were bought at a price. Therefore honor God with your body.

1Co 10:31 So whether you eat or drink or whatever you do, do it all for the glory of God.

2Co 13:7 Now we pray to God that you will not do anything wrong. Not that people will see that we have stood the test but that you will do what is right even though we may seem to have failed. [8]For we cannot do anything against the truth, but only for the truth. (+Eph 4:22-24)

Col 3:5 Put to death, therefore, whatever belongs to your earthly nature: sexual immorality, impurity, lust, evil desires and greed, which is idolatry.

Col 3:12 Therefore, as God's chosen people, holy and dearly loved, clothe yourselves with compassion, kindness, humility, gentleness and patience. [13]Bear with each other and forgive whatever grievances you may have against one another. Forgive as the Lord forgave you. [14]And over all these virtues put on love, which binds them all together in perfect unity.

[15]Let the peace of Christ rule in your hearts, since as members of one body you were called to peace. And be thankful.

1Th 2:12 encouraging, comforting and urging you to live lives worthy of God, who calls you into his kingdom and glory.

1Th 3:13 May he strengthen your hearts so that you will be blameless and holy in the presence of our God and Father when our Lord Jesus comes with all his holy ones. (+1Ti 4:12)

Tit 2:9 Teach slaves to be subject to their masters in everything, to try to please them, not to talk back to them, [10]and not to steal from them, but to show that they can be fully trusted, so that in every way they will make the teaching about God our Savior attractive.

Tit 2:12 It teaches us to say "No" to ungodliness and worldly passions, and to live self-controlled, upright and godly lives in this present age,

1Pe 4:1 Therefore, since Christ suffered in his body, arm yourselves also with the same attitude, because he who has suffered in his body is done with sin.

2Pe 3:11 Since everything will be destroyed in this way, what kind of people ought you to be? You ought to live holy and godly lives [12]as you look forward to the day of God and speed its coming. That day will bring about the destruction of the heavens by fire, and the elements will melt in the heat.

2Pe 3:14 So then, dear friends, since you are looking forward to this, make every effort to be found spotless, blameless and at peace with him. (+3Jn 11)

Motives to:

God's holiness (Ge 17:1; Lev 11:44-45; 19:2)—

Lev 20:26 You are to be holy to me because I, the LORD, am holy, and I have set you apart from the nations to be my own. (+Isa 6:1-8; Mt 5:48)

1Pe 1:15 But just as he who called you is holy, so be holy in all you do; [16]for it is written: "Be holy, because I am holy."

God's mercies (Ro 12:1).

A Condition of Eternal Salvation:

Heb 12:14 Make every effort to live in peace with all men and to be holy; without holiness no one will see the Lord.

Taught:

By figures—

Isa 61:9 Their descendants will be known among the nations and their offspring among the peoples. All who see them will acknowledge that they are a people the LORD has blessed."

[10]I delight greatly in the LORD; my soul rejoices in my God. For he has clothed me with garments of salvation and arrayed me in a robe of righteousness, as a bridegroom adorns his head like a priest, and as a bride adorns herself with her jewels. [11]For as the soil makes the sprout come up and a garden causes seeds to grow, so the Sovereign LORD will make righteousness and praise spring up before all nations.

Mt 12:33 "Make a tree good and its fruit will be good, or make a tree bad and its fruit will be bad, for a tree is recognized by its fruit.

1Co 3:17 If anyone destroys God's temple, God will destroy him; for God's temple is sacred, and you are that temple. (+Eph 2:21)

By inscriptions (Ex 28:36; Zec 14:20).

Lack of Holiness Leads to Disfellowship:

Of the uncircumcised (Ge 17:14). Of those who violated the law, of unleavened bread (Ex 12:15), of sacrifices (Lev 17:9; 19:5-7), of purification (Nu 19:20). Of those who were defiled (Lev 7:25,27; 13:5,21,26; 17:10; 18:29; 19:8; 20:3-6; Nu 5:2-3; 19:13). Of those who were guilty of blasphemy (Nu 15:31).

Typified:

In unblemished offerings (Ex 12:5; Lev 1:3,10; 3:1,6; 4:3,23; 5:15; 6:6; 9:2-3; 22:19,21; Nu 28:3,9,11,19,31; 29:2,8,13,17,20,23,26,29,32,36). In washing of offerings (Lev 1:9,13). In washing of priests (Ex 29:4; Lev 8:6; 1Ch 15:14). In washing of garments (Lev 11:28,40; 13:6,34; 14:8-9,47; 15:5-13; Nu 19:7-8,10,19,21). In purifications (Lev 12:4,6-8; 15:16-18,21-22,27; 16:4,24,26,28; 17:15-16).

By differentiating between clean and unclean animals (Lev 11:1-46)—

Lev 11:47 You must distinguish between the unclean and the clean, between living creatures that may be eaten and those that may not be eaten.'" (+Lev 20:25; Dt 14:3-20)

See God, Holiness of; Sanctification.

HOLM NIV "cypress" (Isa 44:14, RSV). *See Cypress Wood.*

HOLON [2708] (perhaps *sandy*).

1. Levitical city in hill country of Judah (Jos 15:51), called Hilen (1Ch 6:58).

2. Moabite town (Jer 48:21).

HOLY *See Sanctification.*

HOLY DAY *See Holiday.*

HOLY GHOST *See Holy Spirit.*

HOLY OF HOLIES Most holy place, in the tabernacle (Lev 4:6), in the temple (1Ki 6:16).

Separated from the holy place by the veil (Ex 26:33; Heb 9:3). Contained atonement cover and ark of the testimony (Ex 26:34; 40:20-21; 1Ki 8:6), the cherubim (Ex 25:18-20; 26:34; 37:7-9; Heb 9:3-5).

Divine dwelling place (Ex 25:8,21-22; 26:34; Lev 16:2). Entered by the high priest on the Day of Atonement (Ex 26:34; Lev 16:12-13; Heb 9:6-7). Atonement made for (Ex 26:34; Lev 16:15-17,33).

See Holy Place; Tabernacle.

HOLY PLACE
In the tabernacle and the temple. Separated from the most holy place by the veil (Ex 26:33).

Contents of:

Altar of incense (Ex 30:1-6; 40:5,26), the table of the bread of the Presence (Ex 40:4,24; Heb 9:2), the lampstand (Ex 26:35; 40:4,24; Heb 9:2). *See various items by name.*

Priests, ministered in (Ex 29:30; 39:1,41; Heb 9:6), required to eat sin offering in (Lev 6:25-26; 10:17).

See Sanctuary; Tabernacle; Temple.

HOLY SPIRIT

Ge 1:2 Now the earth was formless and empty, darkness was over the surface of the deep, and the Spirit of God was hovering over the waters.

Ps 51:11 Do not cast me from your presence or take your Holy Spirit from me.

Mt 1:18 This is how the birth of Jesus Christ came about: His mother Mary was pledged to be married to Joseph, but before they came together, she was found to be with child through the Holy Spirit. (+Mt 1:20)

Gal 3:2 I would like to learn just one thing from you: Did you receive the Spirit by observing the law, or by believing what you heard? ³Are you so foolish? After beginning with the Spirit, are you now trying to attain your goal by human effort?

Gal 3:14 He redeemed us in order that the blessing given to Abraham might come to the Gentiles through Christ Jesus, so that by faith we might receive the promise of the Spirit.

Gal 6:8 The one who sows to please his sinful nature, from that nature will reap destruction; the one who sows to please the Spirit, from the Spirit will reap eternal life.

Col 1:8 and who also told us of your love in the Spirit.

Heb 6:4 It is impossible for those who have once been enlightened, who have tasted the heavenly gift, who have shared in the Holy Spirit,

Convinces of sin—

Ge 6:3 Then the LORD said, "My Spirit will not contend with man forever, for he is mortal; his days will be a hundred and twenty years." (+Jn 16:8-11)

Comforts—

Jn 14:16 And I will ask the Father, and he will give you another Counselor to be with you forever— ¹⁷the Spirit of truth. The world cannot accept him, because it neither sees him nor knows him. But you know him, for he lives with you and will be in you.

Jn 14:26 But the Counselor, the Holy Spirit, whom the Father will send in my name, will teach you all things and will remind you of everything I have said to you.

Jn 15:26 "When the Counselor comes, whom I will send to you from the Father, the Spirit of truth who goes out from the Father, he will testify about me.

Jn 16:7 But I tell you the truth: It is for your good that I am going away. Unless I go away, the Counselor will not come to you; but if I go, I will send him to you. ⁸When he comes, he will convict the world of guilt in regard to sin and righteousness and judgment: ⁹in regard to sin, because men do not believe in me; ¹⁰in regard to righteousness, because I am going to the Father, where you can see me no

longer; ¹¹and in regard to judgment, because the prince of this world now stands condemned.

¹²"I have much more to say to you, more than you can now bear. ¹³But when he, the Spirit of truth, comes, he will guide you into all truth. He will not speak on his own; he will speak only what he hears, and he will tell you what is yet to come. ¹⁴He will bring glory to me by taking from what is mine and making it known to you.

Ac 9:31 Then the church throughout Judea, Galilee and Samaria enjoyed a time of peace. It was strengthened; and encouraged by the Holy Spirit, it grew in numbers, living in the fear of the Lord.

Guides (Jn 16:13)—

Ac 13:2 While they were worshiping the Lord and fasting, the Holy Spirit said, "Set apart for me Barnabas and Saul for the work to which I have called them." ³So after they had fasted and prayed, they placed their hands on them and sent them off.

⁴The two of them, sent on their way by the Holy Spirit, went down to Seleucia and sailed from there to Cyprus.

Ac 15:8 God, who knows the heart, showed that he accepted them by giving the Holy Spirit to them, just as he did to us.

Ac 15:28 It seemed good to the Holy Spirit and to us not to burden you with anything beyond the following requirements:

Ac 16:6 Paul and his companions traveled throughout the region of Phrygia and Galatia, having been kept by the Holy Spirit from preaching the word in the province of Asia. ⁷When they came to the border of Mysia, they tried to enter Bithynia, but the Spirit of Jesus would not allow them to.

Ro 8:4 in order that the righteous requirements of the law might be fully met in us, who do not live according to the sinful nature but according to the Spirit.

Ro 8:14 because those who are led by the Spirit of God are sons of God. (+Gal 5:16,18,25)

Helps our infirmities—

Ro 8:26 In the same way, the Spirit helps us in our weakness. We do not know what we ought to pray for, but the Spirit himself intercedes for us with groans that words cannot express.

Regenerates—

Jn 3:5 Jesus answered, "I tell you the truth, no one can enter the kingdom of God unless he is born of water and the Spirit. ⁶Flesh gives birth to flesh, but the Spirit gives birth to spirit.

2Co 3:3 You show that you are a letter from Christ, the result of our ministry, written not with ink but with the Spirit of the living God, not on tablets of stone but on tablets of human hearts.

2Co 3:18 And we, who with unveiled faces all reflect the Lord's glory, are being transformed into his likeness with ever-increasing glory, which comes from the Lord, who is the Spirit.

Tit 3:5 he saved us, not because of righteous things we had done, but because of his mercy. He saved us through the washing of rebirth and renewal by the Holy Spirit, ⁶whom he poured out on us generously through Jesus Christ our Savior,

Sanctifies—

Ro 15:16 to be a minister of Christ Jesus to the Gentiles with the priestly duty of proclaiming the gospel of God, so that the Gentiles might become an offering acceptable to God, sanctified by the Holy Spirit.

1Co 6:11 And that is what some of you were. But you

were washed, you were sanctified, you were justified in the name of the Lord Jesus Christ and by the Spirit of our God.

2Th 2:13 But we ought always to thank God for you, brothers loved by the Lord, because from the beginning God chose you to be saved through the sanctifying work of the Spirit and through belief in the truth.

1Pe 1:2 who have been chosen according to the foreknowledge of God the Father, through the sanctifying work of the Spirit, for obedience to Jesus Christ and sprinkling by his blood: Grace and peace be yours in abundance.

Dwells in believers—

Ro 8:11 And if the Spirit of him who raised Jesus from the dead is living in you, he who raised Christ from the dead will also give life to your mortal bodies through his Spirit, who lives in you.

Invites to salvation (Rev 22:17).

Communion with—

2Co 13:14 May the grace of the Lord Jesus Christ, and the love of God, and the fellowship of the Holy Spirit be with you all.

Php 2:1 If you have any encouragement from being united with Christ, if any comfort from his love, if any fellowship with the Spirit, if any tenderness and compassion,

Given to every Christian—

1Co 12:7 Now to each one the manifestation of the Spirit is given for the common good.

Given in answer to prayer—

Lk 11:13 If you then, though you are evil, know how to give good gifts to your children, how much more will your Father in heaven give the Holy Spirit to those who ask him!"

Ac 8:15 When they arrived, they prayed for them that they might receive the Holy Spirit,

Given through laying on of hands—

Ac 8:17 Then Peter and John placed their hands on them, and they received the Holy Spirit.

[18]When Simon saw that the Spirit was given at the laying on of the apostles' hands, he offered them money [19]and said, "Give me also this ability so that everyone on whom I lay my hands may receive the Holy Spirit."

Ac 19:6 When Paul placed his hands on them, the Holy Spirit came on them, and they spoke in tongues and prophesied.

Access to the Father by—

Eph 2:18 For through him we both have access to the Father by one Spirit.

Prayer in (Eph 6:18)—

Jude 20 But you, dear friends, build yourselves up in your most holy faith and pray in the Holy Spirit.

Wisdom and strength from—

Ne 9:20 You gave your good Spirit to instruct them. You did not withhold your manna from their mouths, and you gave them water for their thirst.

Zec 4:6 So he said to me, "This is the word of the LORD to Zerubbabel: 'Not by might nor by power, but by my Spirit,' says the LORD Almighty.

Eph 3:16 I pray that out of his glorious riches he may strengthen you with power through his Spirit in your inner being,

Liberty from—

2Co 3:17 Now the Lord is the Spirit, and where the Spirit of the Lord is, there is freedom.

Love of God given by—

Ro 5:5 And hope does not disappoint us, because God has poured out his love into our hearts by the Holy Spirit, whom he has given us.

Ministers commissioned by—

Ac 20:28 Keep watch over yourselves and all the flock of which the Holy Spirit has made you overseers. Be shepherds of the church of God, which he bought with his own blood.

Christian baptism in the name of, with the name of Father and son—

Mt 28:19 Therefore go and make disciples of all nations, baptizing them in the name of the Father and of the Son and of the Holy Spirit,

Gospel preached in power of—

1Co 2:4 My message and my preaching were not with wise and persuasive words, but with a demonstration of the Spirit's power, (+1Co 2:10)

1Th 1:5 because our gospel came to you not simply with words, but also with power, with the Holy Spirit and with deep conviction. You know how we lived among you for your sake.

1Pe 1:12 It was revealed to them that they were not serving themselves but you, when they spoke of the things that have now been told you by those who have preached the gospel to you by the Holy Spirit sent from heaven. Even angels long to look into these things.

Word of God, sword of—

Eph 6:17 Take the helmet of salvation and the sword of the Spirit, which is the word of God.

Water, a symbol of—

Jn 7:38 Whoever believes in me, as the Scripture has said, streams of living water will flow from within him." [39]By this he meant the Spirit, whom those who believed in him were later to receive. Up to that time the Spirit had not been given, since Jesus had not yet been glorified.

Demons cast out by—

Mt 12:28 But if I drive out demons by the Spirit of God, then the kingdom of God has come upon you.

Power to bestow, not for sale (Ac 8:18-20).

Poured Upon:

Israel—

Isa 32:15 till the Spirit is poured upon us from on high, and the desert becomes a fertile field, and the fertile field seems like a forest.

Eze 39:29 I will no longer hide my face from them, for I will pour out my Spirit on the house of Israel, declares the Sovereign LORD."

The Gentiles—

Ac 10:19 While Peter was still thinking about the vision, the Spirit said to him, "Simon, three men are looking for you. [20]So get up and go downstairs. Do not hesitate to go with them, for I have sent them."

Ac 10:44 While Peter was still speaking these words, the Holy Spirit came on all who heard the message. [45]The circumcised believers who had come with Peter were astonished that the gift of the Holy Spirit had been poured out even on the Gentiles. [46]For they heard them speaking in tongues and praising God. Then Peter said, [47]"Can anyone keep these people from being baptized with water? They have received the Holy Spirit just as we have."

Ac 11:15 "As I began to speak, the Holy Spirit came on them as he had come on us at the beginning. [16]Then I remembered what the Lord had said: 'John baptized with water, but you will be baptized with the Holy Spirit.'

All people—

Joel 2:28 "And afterward, I will pour out my Spirit on all people. Your sons and daughters will prophesy, your old men will dream dreams, your young men will see visions. [29]Even on my servants, both men and women, I will pour out my Spirit in those days. (+Ac 2:17)

Christians:

Are temples of—

1Co 3:16 Don't you know that you yourselves are God's temple and that God's Spirit lives in you?

1Co 6:19 Do you not know that your body is a temple of the Holy Spirit, who is in you, whom you have received from God? You are not your own;

Are filled with—

Ac 2:4 All of them were filled with the Holy Spirit and began to speak in other tongues as the Spirit enabled them.

Ac 2:33 Exalted to the right hand of God, he has received from the Father the promised Holy Spirit and has poured out what you now see and hear.

Ac 4:8 Then Peter, filled with the Holy Spirit, said to them: "Rulers and elders of the people!

Ac 4:31 After they prayed, the place where they were meeting was shaken. And they were all filled with the Holy Spirit and spoke the word of God boldly.

Ac 6:5 This proposal pleased the whole group. They chose Stephen, a man full of faith and of the Holy Spirit; also Philip, Procorus, Nicanor, Timon, Parmenas, and Nicolas from Antioch, a convert to Judaism. (+Ac 8:17)

Ac 11:24 He was a good man, full of the Holy Spirit and faith, and a great number of people were brought to the Lord.

Ac 13:9 Then Saul, who was also called Paul, filled with the Holy Spirit, looked straight at Elymas and said,

Ac 13:52 And the disciples were filled with joy and with the Holy Spirit. (+Eph 5:18)

2Ti 1:14 Guard the good deposit that was entrusted to you—guard it with the help of the Holy Spirit who lives in us.

Have fellowship with—

Ro 8:9 You, however, are controlled not by the sinful nature but by the Spirit, if the Spirit of God lives in you. And if anyone does not have the Spirit of Christ, he does not belong to Christ. (+Ro 8:11; 1Co 3:16; 6:19; 2Co 13:14; Php 2:1)

Receive deposit of—

2Co 1:22 set his seal of ownership on us, and put his Spirit in our hearts as a deposit, guaranteeing what is to come. (+2Co 5:5)

Eph 1:13 And you also were included in Christ when you heard the word of truth, the gospel of your salvation. Having believed, you were marked in him with a seal, the promised Holy Spirit, [14]who is a deposit guaranteeing our inheritance until the redemption of those who are God's possession—to the praise of his glory.

Are sealed with (2Co 1:22; Eph 1:13)—

Eph 4:30 And do not grieve the Holy Spirit of God, with whom you were sealed for the day of redemption.

Have righteousness, peace, and joy in—

Ro 14:17 For the kingdom of God is not a matter of eating and drinking, but of righteousness, peace and joy in the Holy Spirit,

Ro 15:13 May the God of hope fill you with all joy and peace as you trust in him, so that you may overflow with hope by the power of the Holy Spirit.

1Th 1:6 You became imitators of us and of the Lord; in spite of severe suffering, you welcomed the message with the joy given by the Holy Spirit.

Are unified by (1Co 12:13).

Testifiy that Jesus is Lord by (Jn 15:26; 16:14)—

1Co 12:3 Therefore I tell you that no one who is speaking by the Spirit of God says, "Jesus be cursed," and no one can say, "Jesus is Lord," except by the Holy Spirit.

Jesus and the Spirit:

Immaculate conception of Jesus by (Mt 1:20)—

Lk 1:35 The angel answered, "The Holy Spirit will come upon you, and the power of the Most High will overshadow you. So the holy one to be born will be called the Son of God.

Jesus anointed and led by—

Isa 61:1 The Spirit of the Sovereign LORD is on me, because the LORD has anointed me to preach good news to the poor. He has sent me to bind up the brokenhearted, to proclaim freedom for the captives and release from darkness for the prisoners,

Mt 3:16 As soon as Jesus was baptized, he went up out of the water. At that moment heaven was opened, and he saw the Spirit of God descending like a dove and lighting on him.

Mt 4:1 Then Jesus was led by the Spirit into the desert to be tempted by the devil. (+Mk 1:10; Lk 3:22; 4:18; Jn 1:32-33; Ac 10:38)

Heb 9:14 How much more, then, will the blood of Christ, who through the eternal Spirit offered himself unblemished to God, cleanse our consciences from acts that lead to death, so that we may serve the living God!

Sent in Jesus' name—

Jn 14:15 "If you love me, you will obey what I command. [16]And I will ask the Father, and he will give you another Counselor to be with you forever— [17]the Spirit of truth. The world cannot accept him, because it neither sees him nor knows him. But you know him, for he lives with you and will be in you.

Jn 15:26 "When the Counselor comes, whom I will send to you from the Father, the Spirit of truth who goes out from the Father, he will testify about me.

Baptism of:

Mt 3:11 "I baptize you with water for repentance. But after me will come one who is more powerful than I, whose sandals I am not fit to carry. He will baptize you with the Holy Spirit and with fire. (+Mk 1:8; Lk 3:16; Jn 1:33; 20:22)

Ac 1:5 For John baptized with water, but in a few days you will be baptized with the Holy Spirit." (+Ac 11:16)

Ac 19:2 and asked them, "Did you receive the Holy Spirit when you believed?"

They answered, "No, we have not even heard that there is a Holy Spirit."

[3]So Paul asked, "Then what baptism did you receive?"

"John's baptism," they replied.

[4]Paul said, "John's baptism was a baptism of repentance. He told the people to believe in the one coming after him, that is, in Jesus." [5]On hearing this, they were baptized into the name of the Lord Jesus. [6]When Paul placed his hands on them, the Holy Spirit came on them, and they spoke in tongues and prophesied. (+1Jn 2:20,27)

Fruit of:

Ro 8:23 Not only so, but we ourselves, who have the firstfruits of the Spirit, groan inwardly as we wait eagerly for our adoption as sons, the redemption of our bodies.

Gal 5:22 But the fruit of the Spirit is love, joy, peace, patience, kindness, goodness, faithfulness, [23]gentleness and self-control. Against such things there is no law.

Gifts of:

Foretold—

Isa 44:3 For I will pour water on the thirsty land, and streams on the dry ground; I will pour out my Spirit on your offspring, and my blessing on your descendants. (+Joel 2:28-29)

Of different kinds—

1Co 12:4 There are different kinds of gifts, but the same Spirit. [5]There are different kinds of service, but the same Lord. [6]There are different kinds of working, but the same God works all of them in all men.

1Co 12:8 To one there is given through the Spirit the message of wisdom, to another the message of knowledge by means of the same Spirit, [9]to another faith by the same Spirit, to another gifts of healing by that one Spirit, [10]to another miraculous powers, to another prophecy, to another distinguishing between spirits, to another speaking in different kinds of tongues, and to still another the interpretation of tongues. (+1Co 12:28)

Bestowed for the confirmation of the gospel—

Ro 15:19 by the power of signs and miracles, through the power of the Spirit. So from Jerusalem all the way around to Illyricum, I have fully proclaimed the gospel of Christ.

Heb 2:4 God also testified to it by signs, wonders and various miracles, and gifts of the Holy Spirit distributed according to his will.

Inspiration of:

Mt 10:20 for it will not be you speaking, but the Spirit of your Father speaking through you.

Mk 13:11 Whenever you are arrested and brought to trial, do not worry beforehand about what to say. Just say whatever is given you at the time, for it is not you speaking, but the Holy Spirit.

Lk 12:12 for the Holy Spirit will teach you at that time what you should say." (+1Co 2:4)

1Co 2:10 but God has revealed it to us by his Spirit. The Spirit searches all things, even the deep things of God.

[11]For who among men knows the thoughts of a man except the man's spirit within him? In the same way no one knows the thoughts of God except the Spirit of God. [12]We have not received the spirit of the world but the Spirit who is from God, that we may understand what God has freely given us. [13]This is what we speak, not in words taught us by human wisdom but in words taught by the Spirit, expressing spiritual truths in spiritual words. [14]The man without the Spirit does not accept the things that come from the Spirit of God, for they are foolishness to him, and he cannot understand them, because they are spiritually discerned.

1Ti 4:1 The Spirit clearly says that in later times some will abandon the faith and follow deceiving spirits and things taught by demons.

Instances of Inspiration of:

Joseph—

Ge 41:38 So Pharaoh asked them, "Can we find anyone like this man, one in whom is the spirit of God?"

Bezalel—

Ex 31:3 and I have filled him with the Spirit of God, with skill, ability and knowledge in all kinds of crafts— (+Ex 35:31)

The seventy elders (Nu 11:17). Balaam (Nu 24:2).

Judges Othniel (Jdg 3:10), Gideon (Jdg 6:34), Jephthah (Jdg 11:29).

King Saul (1Sa 11:6). King David (1Ch 28:11-12).

The prophets—

2Pe 1:21 For prophecy never had its origin in the will of man, but men spoke from God as they were carried along by the Holy Spirit.

Azariah (2Ch 15:1). Zechariah (2Ch 24:20).

Zechariah—

Lk 1:67 His father Zechariah was filled with the Holy Spirit and prophesied:

Elizabeth (Lk 1:41).

Simeon—

Lk 2:25 Now there was a man in Jerusalem called Simeon, who was righteous and devout. He was waiting for the consolation of Israel, and the Holy Spirit was upon him. [26]It had been revealed to him by the Holy Spirit that he would not die before he had seen the Lord's Christ.

John the Baptist—

Lk 1:15 for he will be great in the sight of the Lord. He is never to take wine or other fermented drink, and he will be filled with the Holy Spirit even from birth.

The disciples (Ac 6:3; 7:55; 8:29; 9:17; 10:45).

Intercession of: (Ro 8:26)

Ro 8:27 And he who searches our hearts knows the mind of the Spirit, because the Spirit intercedes for the saints in accordance with God's will.

Power of:

Promised—

Lk 24:49 I am going to send you what my Father has promised; but stay in the city until you have been clothed with power from on high."

Ac 1:8 But you will receive power when the Holy Spirit comes on you; and you will be my witnesses in Jerusalem, and in all Judea and Samaria, and to the ends of the earth."

Ac 2:38 Peter replied, "Repent and be baptized, every one of you, in the name of Jesus Christ for the forgiveness of your sins. And you will receive the gift of the Holy Spirit.

On Christ (Mt 12:28; Lk 4:14). On ministers (Ac 2:4; Ro 15:19). On the righteous (Ro 15:13; Eph 3:16).

Revelations from:

Mk 12:36 David himself, speaking by the Holy Spirit, declared: "'The Lord said to my Lord: "Sit at my right hand until I put your enemies under your feet."' (+Lk 2:26)

Lk 2:27 Moved by the Spirit, he went into the temple courts. When the parents brought in the child Jesus to do for him what the custom of the Law required, (+Jn 16:13; 1Co 2:10-11)

Eph 3:5 which was not made known to men in other generations as it has now been revealed by the Spirit to God's holy apostles and prophets. (+1Ti 4:1)

Heb 3:7 So, as the Holy Spirit says: "Today, if you hear his voice, (+2Pe 1:21)

Rev 2:7 He who has an ear, let him hear what the Spirit says to the churches. To him who overcomes, I will give the right to eat from the tree of life, which is in the paradise of God. (+Rev 2:11,29)

Rev 14:13 Then I heard a voice from heaven say, "Write: Blessed are the dead who die in the Lord from now on." "Yes," says the Spirit, "they will rest from their labor, for their deeds will follow them."

Sin Against:

Ac 8:18 When Simon saw that the Spirit was given at the laying on of the apostles' hands, he offered them money

[19]and said, "Give me also this ability so that everyone on whom I lay my hands may receive the Holy Spirit."

[20]Peter answered: "May your money perish with you, because you thought you could buy the gift of God with money! [21]You have no part or share in this ministry, because your heart is not right before God. [22]Repent of this wickedness and pray to the Lord. Perhaps he will forgive you for having such a thought in your heart. (+1Jn 5:16)

By grieving—

Isa 63:10 Yet they rebelled and grieved his Holy Spirit. So he turned and became their enemy and he himself fought against them.

[11]Then his people recalled the days of old, the days of Moses and his people—where is he who brought them through the sea, with the shepherd of his flock? Where is he who set his Holy Spirit among them,

Isa 63:14 like cattle that go down to the plain, they were given rest by the Spirit of the LORD. This is how you guided your people to make for yourself a glorious name.

Eph 4:30 And do not grieve the Holy Spirit of God, with whom you were sealed for the day of redemption.

By resisting—

Ac 5:9 Peter said to her, "How could you agree to test the Spirit of the Lord? Look! The feet of the men who buried your husband are at the door, and they will carry you out also."

Ac 7:51 "You stiff-necked people, with uncircumcised hearts and ears! You are just like your fathers: You always resist the Holy Spirit! (+Eph 4:30)

1Th 5:19 Do not put out the Spirit's fire;

Heb 10:29 How much more severely do you think a man deserves to be punished who has trampled the Son of God under foot, who has treated as an unholy thing the blood of the covenant that sanctified him, and who has insulted the Spirit of grace?

By blaspheming—

Mt 12:31 And so I tell you, every sin and blasphemy will be forgiven men, but the blasphemy against the Spirit will not be forgiven. [32]Anyone who speaks a word against the Son of Man will be forgiven, but anyone who speaks against the Holy Spirit will not be forgiven, either in this age or in the age to come.

Mk 3:29 But whoever blasphemes against the Holy Spirit will never be forgiven; he is guilty of an eternal sin." (+Lk 12:10)

By lying to—

Ac 5:3 Then Peter said, "Ananias, how is it that Satan has so filled your heart that you have lied to the Holy Spirit and have kept for yourself some of the money you received for the land?

Withdrawn From Unrepentant Sinners:

Ge 6:3 Then the LORD said, "My Spirit will not contend with man forever, for he is mortal; his days will be a hundred and twenty years."

Dt 32:30 How could one man chase a thousand, or two put ten thousand to flight, unless their Rock had sold them, unless the LORD had given them up?

Jer 7:29 Cut off your hair and throw it away; take up a lament on the barren heights, for the LORD has rejected and abandoned this generation that is under his wrath.

Hos 4:17 Ephraim is joined to idols; leave him alone! [18]Even when their drinks are gone, they continue their prostitution; their rulers dearly love shameful ways.

Hos 9:12 Even if they rear children, I will bereave them of every one. Woe to them when I turn away from them!

Ro 1:24 Therefore God gave them over in the sinful desires of their hearts to sexual impurity for the degrading of their bodies with one another.

Ro 1:26 Because of this, God gave them over to shameful lusts. Even their women exchanged natural relations for unnatural ones.

Ro 1:28 Furthermore, since they did not think it worthwhile to retain the knowledge of God, he gave them over to a depraved mind, to do what ought not to be done.

Instances of Withdrawal From Unrepentant Sinners:

Antediluvians (Ge 6:3-7). Israelites (Dt 1:42; 28:15-68; 31:17-18). Saul (1Sa 16:14; 18:12; 28:15-16; 2Sa 7:15).

Witness of:

Ac 5:32 We are witnesses of these things, and so is the Holy Spirit, whom God has given to those who obey him."

Ro 8:15 For you did not receive a spirit that makes you a slave again to fear, but you received the Spirit of sonship. And by him we cry, "Abba, Father." [16]The Spirit himself testifies with our spirit that we are God's children.

Ro 9:1 I speak the truth in Christ—I am not lying, my conscience confirms it in the Holy Spirit— (+2Co 1:22; 5:5)

Gal 4:6 Because you are sons, God sent the Spirit of his Son into our hearts, the Spirit who calls out, "Abba, Father." (+Eph 1:13-14)

Heb 10:15 The Holy Spirit also testifies to us about this. First he says:

1Jn 3:24 Those who obey his commands live in him, and he in them. And this is how we know that he lives in us: We know it by the Spirit he gave us.

1Jn 4:13 We know that we live in him and he in us, because he has given us of his Spirit.

1Jn 5:6 This is the one who came by water and blood—Jesus Christ. He did not come by water only, but by water and blood. And it is the Spirit who testifies, because the Spirit is the truth. [7]For there are three that testify: [8]the Spirit, the water and the blood; and the three are in agreement.

Emblems of:

Water—

(Jn 3:5; 7:38-39). Fertilizing (Ps 1:3; Isa 27:3; 44:3-4; 58:11). Refreshing (Ps 46:4; Isa 41:17-18). Freely given to those who are thirsty (Isa 55:1; Jn 4:14; Rev 22:17). Cleansing (Eze 16:9; 36:25; Eph 5:25-27; Heb 10:22). Abundant (Jn 7:37-38).

Fire—

As a guiding light as the Israelites traveled at night (Ex 13:21; Ps 78:14). Purifying (Isa 4:4; Mal 3:2-3). Searching (Zep 1:12, w 1Co 2:10).

Wind—

Powerful (1Ki 19:11, w Ac 2:2). Reviving (Eze 37:9-10,14). Independent (Jn 3:8). The coming of the promised Holy Spirit at Pentecost (Ac 2:2).

Oil—

Consecrating (Isa 61:1). Comforting (Isa 61:3; Heb 1:9). Illuminating (Mt 25:3-4; 1Jn 2:20,27). Healing (Lk 10:34; Jas 5:14).

Rain and Dew—

Blessing (Ps 133:3; Hos 14:5). Righteousness (Hos 10:12).

A Dove (Mt 3:16).

A Voice—

Guiding (Isa 30:21, w Jn 16:13). Speaking through the

Twelve as they were to go out (Mt 10:20). Warning (Heb 3:7-11).

A Seal—

(Rev 7:2). Authenticating (Jn 6:27; 2Co 1:22). Securing (Eph 1:13-14; 4:30).

Tongues of Fire (Ac 2:3-4,6-11).

See Titles and Names, Titles and Names of the Holy Spirit.

HOLY TRINITY *See God; Jesus the Christ; Holy Spirit; Trinity, Holy.*

HOMAGE [2556, 4200+5975+7023, *4686*]. Rendered, to Joseph (Ge 41:43), to kings (1Ki 1:16,23,31), to princes (Est 3:2,5), to Mordecai (Est 6:11), to Daniel (Da 2:46).

Refused, by Peter (Ac 10:25-26), by Paul and Barnabas (Ac 14:11-18), by the angel seen by John in his vision (Rev 10:10; 22:8-9).

See Worship.

HOMAM [2102, 2123]. An Edomite and a son of Lotan (Hebrew *Hemam,* a variant of *Homam*) (Ge 36:22, ftn; 1Ch 1:39).

HOME *See Family.*

HOMELESS [*841*].

NIV+ HOME, HOMELAND, HOMES

(Job 24:8; La 4:5; Lk 9:58; 1Co 4:11).

HOMER [2818] (*the load a donkey can carry*).

NIV+ HOMERS

A measure. *See Measure.*

HOMESTEAD Mortgaged (Ne 5:3). When alienable, and when inalienable (Lev 25:25-34). *See Land.*

HOMICIDE

NIV+ KILL, KILLED, KILLING, KILLS, See MURDER

Accidental:

Ex 21:13 However, if he does not do it intentionally, but God lets it happen, he is to flee to a place I will designate. **Nu 35:11** select some towns to be your cities of refuge, to which a person who has killed someone accidentally may flee. ¹²They will be places of refuge from the avenger, so that a person accused of murder may not die before he stands trial before the assembly. ¹³These six towns you give will be your cities of refuge. ¹⁴Give three on this side of the Jordan and three in Canaan as cities of refuge. ¹⁵These six towns will be a place of refuge for Israelites, aliens and any other people living among them, so that anyone who has killed another accidentally can flee there. **Nu 35:22** "'But if without hostility someone suddenly shoves another or throws something at him unintentionally ²³or, without seeing him, drops a stone on him that could kill him, and he dies, then since he was not his enemy and he did not intend to harm him, ²⁴the assembly must judge between him and the avenger of blood according to these regulations. ²⁵The assembly must protect the one accused of murder from the avenger of blood and send him back to the city of refuge to which he fled. He must stay there until the death of the high priest, who was anointed with the holy oil.

²⁶"'But if the accused ever goes outside the limits of the city of refuge to which he has fled ²⁷and the avenger of blood finds him outside the city, the avenger of blood may kill the accused without being guilty of murder. ²⁸The accused must stay in his city of refuge until the death of the

high priest; only after the death of the high priest may he return to his own property.

Nu 35:32 "'Do not accept a ransom for anyone who has fled to a city of refuge and so allow him to go back and live on his own land before the death of the high priest. (+Dt 4:41-43; 19:1-10)

Jos 20:1 Then the LORD said to Joshua: ²"Tell the Israelites to designate the cities of refuge, as I instructed you through Moses, ³so that anyone who kills a person accidentally and unintentionally may flee there and find protection from the avenger of blood.

⁴"When he flees to one of these cities, he is to stand in the entrance of the city gate and state his case before the elders of that city. Then they are to admit him into their city and give him a place to live with them. ⁵If the avenger of blood pursues him, they must not surrender the one accused, because he killed his neighbor unintentionally and without malice aforethought. ⁶He is to stay in that city until he has stood trial before the assembly and until the death of the high priest who is serving at that time. Then he may go back to his own home in the town from which he fled."

⁷So they set apart Kedesh in Galilee in the hill country of Naphtali, Shechem in the hill country of Ephraim, and Kiriath Arba (that is, Hebron) in the hill country of Judah. ⁸On the east side of the Jordan of Jericho they designated Bezer in the desert on the plateau in the tribe of Reuben, Ramoth in Gilead in the tribe of Gad, and Golan in Bashan in the tribe of Manasseh. ⁹Any of the Israelites or any alien living among them who killed someone accidentally could flee to these designated cities and not be killed by the avenger of blood prior to standing trial before the assembly.

See Cities of Refuge.

Murder:

Job 24:14 When daylight is gone, the murderer rises up and kills the poor and needy; in the night he steals forth like a thief.

Ps 10:8 He lies in wait near the villages; from ambush he murders the innocent, watching in secret for his victims.

Ps 38:12 Those who seek my life set their traps, those who would harm me talk of my ruin; all day long they plot deception.

Ps 94:3 How long will the wicked, O LORD, how long will the wicked be jubilant?

Ps 94:6 They slay the widow and the alien; they murder the fatherless.

Pr 12:6 The words of the wicked lie in wait for blood, but the speech of the upright rescues them.

Pr 28:17 A man tormented by the guilt of murder will be a fugitive till death; let no one support him.

Isa 59:3 For your hands are stained with blood, your fingers with guilt. Your lips have spoken lies, and your tongue mutters wicked things. (+Jer 2:34; 7:9-10; 19:4)

Eze 22:9 In you are slanderous men bent on shedding blood; in you are those who eat at the mountain shrines and commit lewd acts.

Hos 4:1 Hear the word of the LORD, you Israelites, because the LORD has a charge to bring against you who live in the land: "There is no faithfulness, no love, no acknowledgment of God in the land. ²There is only cursing, lying and murder, stealing and adultery; they break all bounds, and bloodshed follows bloodshed. ³Because of this the land mourns, and all who live in it waste away; the beasts of the field and the birds of the air and the fish of the sea are dying.

Hab 2:10 You have plotted the ruin of many peoples, shaming your own house and forfeiting your life.

Hab 2:12 "Woe to him who builds a city with bloodshed and establishes a town by crime!

God's abhorrence of—

Ps 5:6 You destroy those who tell lies; bloodthirsty and deceitful men the LORD abhors.

Ps 9:12 For he who avenges blood remembers; he does not ignore the cry of the afflicted.

Pr 6:16 There are six things the LORD hates, seven that are detestable to him: ¹⁷haughty eyes, a lying tongue, hands that shed innocent blood,

Forbidden—

Ex 20:13 "You shall not murder. (+Dt 5:17)

Pr 1:15 my son, do not go along with them, do not set foot on their paths; ¹⁶for their feet rush into sin, they are swift to shed blood.

Jer 22:3 This is what the LORD says: Do what is just and right. Rescue from the hand of his oppressor the one who has been robbed. Do no wrong or violence to the alien, the fatherless or the widow, and do not shed innocent blood in this place.

Mt 5:21 "You have heard that it was said to the people long ago, 'Do not murder, and anyone who murders will be subject to judgment.' (+Mt 19:18; Mk 10:19; Lk 18:20; Ro 13:9)

1Ti 1:9 We also know that law is made not for the righteous but for lawbreakers and rebels, the ungodly and sinful, the unholy and irreligious; for those who kill their fathers or mothers, for murderers,

Jas 2:11 For he who said, "Do not commit adultery," also said, "Do not murder." If you do not commit adultery but do commit murder, you have become a lawbreaker.

1Pe 4:15 If you suffer, it should not be as a murderer or thief or any other kind of criminal, or even as a meddler. (+1Jn 3:12)

1Jn 3:15 Anyone who hates his brother is a murderer, and you know that no murderer has eternal life in him.

Through conspiracy—

Ps 37:32 The wicked lie in wait for the righteous, seeking their very lives;

Pr 1:11 If they say, "Come along with us; let's lie in wait for someone's blood, let's waylay some harmless soul; ¹²let's swallow them alive, like the grave, and whole, like those who go down to the pit;

In hearts of the wicked—

Mt 15:19 For out of the heart come evil thoughts, murder, adultery, sexual immorality, theft, false testimony, slander. (+Mk 7:21)

Impenitence for—

Rev 9:21 Nor did they repent of their murders, their magic arts, their sexual immorality or their thefts.

Penitence for—

Ps 51:1 Have mercy on me, O God, according to your unfailing love; according to your great compassion blot out my transgressions. ²Wash away all my iniquity and cleanse me from my sin.

³For I know my transgressions, and my sin is always before me. ⁴Against you, you only, have I sinned and done what is evil in your sight, so that you are proved right when you speak and justified when you judge. ⁵Surely I was sinful at birth, sinful from the time my mother conceived me. ⁶Surely you desire truth in the inner parts; you teach me wisdom in the inmost place.

⁷Cleanse me with hyssop, and I will be clean; wash me,

and I will be whiter than snow. ⁸Let me hear joy and gladness; let the bones you have crushed rejoice. ⁹Hide your face from my sins and blot out all my iniquity.

¹⁰Create in me a pure heart, O God, and renew a steadfast spirit within me. ¹¹Do not cast me from your presence or take your Holy Spirit from me. ¹²Restore to me the joy of your salvation and grant me a willing spirit, to sustain me.

¹³Then I will teach transgressors your ways, and sinners will turn back to you. ¹⁴Save me from bloodguilt, O God, the God who saves me, and my tongue will sing of your righteousness. ¹⁵O Lord, open my lips, and my mouth will declare your praise. ¹⁶You do not delight in sacrifice, or I would bring it; you do not take pleasure in burnt offerings. ¹⁷The sacrifices of God are a broken spirit; a broken and contrite heart, O God, you will not despise.

Inquest over suspected—

Dt 21:1 If a man is found slain, lying in a field in the land the LORD your God is giving you to possess, and it is not known who killed him, ²your elders and judges shall go out and measure the distance from the body to the neighboring towns. ³Then the elders of the town nearest the body shall take a heifer that has never been worked and has never worn a yoke ⁴and lead her down to a valley that has not been plowed or planted and where there is a flowing stream. There in the valley they are to break the heifer's neck. ⁵The priests, the sons of Levi, shall step forward, for the LORD your God has chosen them to minister and to pronounce blessings in the name of the LORD and to decide all cases of dispute and assault. ⁶Then all the elders of the town nearest the body shall wash their hands over the heifer whose neck was broken in the valley, ⁷and they shall declare: "Our hands did not shed this blood, nor did our eyes see it done. ⁸Accept this atonement for your people Israel, whom you have redeemed, O LORD, and do not hold your people guilty of the blood of an innocent man." And the bloodshed will be atoned for. ⁹So you will purge from yourselves the guilt of shedding innocent blood, since you have done what is right in the eyes of the LORD.

Instances of:

By Cain (Ge 4:8), Lamech (Ge 4:23-24). Simeon and Levi (Ge 34:25-31). Pharaoh (Ex 1:16,22). Moses (Ex 2:12). Ehud (Jdg 3:16-23). Abimelech (Jdg 9:5,18,56). Joab (2Sa 3:24-27; 20:9-10; 1Ki 2:5). Solomon (1Ki 2:23-46). Recab and Baanah (2Sa 4:5-8). David (2Sa 11:14-17; 12:9). Absalom (2Sa 13:22-29). Baasha (1Ki 15:27-29). Zimri (1Ki 16:9-11). Ahab and Jezebel (1Ki 21:1024). Hazael (2Ki 8:15). Jehu (2Ki 9:24-37). Athaliah (2Ki 11:1). Of Joash by his servants (2Ki 12:20-21). Menahem (2Ki 15:16). Of Sennacherib, by his sons (2Ki 19:37; Isa 37:38). Manasseh (2Ki 21:16; 24:4). Of Amon, by his servants (2Ki 21:23). Jehoram (2Ch 21:4). Joash (2Ch 24:21). Amaziah's soldiers (2Ch 25:12). Nebuchadnezzar (Jer 39:6). Ishmael (Jer 41:1-7). Herod I (Mt 2:16). Herod (Mt 14:10; Mk 6:27). Barabbas (Mk 15:7; Ac 3:14).

Punishment for:

Lev 24:17 "'If anyone takes the life of a human being, he must be put to death.

Dt 19:11 But if a man hates his neighbor and lies in wait for him, assaults and kills him, and then flees to one of these cities, ¹²the elders of his town shall send for him, bring him back from the city, and hand him over to the avenger of blood to die. ¹³Show him no pity. You must purge from Israel the guilt of shedding innocent blood, so that it may go well with you.

Ps 55:23 But you, O God, will bring down the wicked into the pit of corruption; bloodthirsty and deceitful men will not live out half their days. But as for me, I trust in you.

By a curse—

Ge 4:9 Then the LORD said to Cain, "Where is your brother Abel?"

"I don't know," he replied. "Am I my brother's keeper?"

[10]The LORD said, "What have you done? Listen! Your brother's blood cries out to me from the ground. [11]Now you are under a curse and driven from the ground, which opened its mouth to receive your brother's blood from your hand. (+Ge 4:12; 49:7)

Dt 27:24 "Cursed is the man who kills his neighbor secretly."

Then all the people shall say, "Amen!"

[25]"Cursed is the man who accepts a bribe to kill an innocent person."

Then all the people shall say, "Amen!"

By death—

Ge 9:5 And for your lifeblood I will surely demand an accounting. I will demand an accounting from every animal. And from each man, too, I will demand an accounting for the life of his fellow man.

[6]"Whoever sheds the blood of man, by man shall his blood be shed; for in the image of God has God made man.

Ex 21:12 "Anyone who strikes a man and kills him shall surely be put to death.

Ex 21:14 But if a man schemes and kills another man deliberately, take him away from my altar and put him to death.

Nu 35:16 "'If a man strikes someone with an iron object so that he dies, he is a murderer; the murderer shall be put to death. [17]Or if anyone has a stone in his hand that could kill, and he strikes someone so that he dies, he is a murderer; the murderer shall be put to death. [18]Or if anyone has a wooden object in his hand that could kill, and he hits someone so that he dies, he is a murderer; the murderer shall be put to death. [19]The avenger of blood shall put the murderer to death; when he meets him, he shall put him to death. [20]If anyone with malice aforethought shoves another or throws something at him intentionally so that he dies [21]or if in hostility he hits him with his fist so that he dies, that person shall be put to death; he is a murderer. The avenger of blood shall put the murderer to death when he meets him.

Nu 35:30 "'Anyone who kills a person is to be put to death as a murderer only on the testimony of witnesses. But no one is to be put to death on the testimony of only one witness.

[31]"'Do not accept a ransom for the life of a murderer, who deserves to die. He must surely be put to death.

[32]"'Do not accept a ransom for anyone who has fled to a city of refuge and so allow him to go back and live on his own land before the death of the high priest.

[33]"'Do not pollute the land where you are. Bloodshed pollutes the land, and atonement cannot be made for the land on which blood has been shed, except by the blood of the one who shed it.

Dt 17:6 On the testimony of two or three witnesses a man shall be put to death, but no one shall be put to death on the testimony of only one witness. (+1Ki 21:19)

Eze 35:6 therefore as surely as I live, declares the Sovereign LORD, I will give you over to bloodshed and it will pursue you. Since you did not hate bloodshed, bloodshed will pursue you.

Hos 1:4 Then the LORD said to Hosea, "Call him Jezreel,

because I will soon punish the house of Jehu for the massacre at Jezreel, and I will put an end to the kingdom of Israel.

By everlasting punishment—

Rev 21:8 But the cowardly, the unbelieving, the vile, the murderers, the sexually immoral, those who practice magic arts, the idolaters and all liars—their place will be in the fiery lake of burning sulfur. This is the second death."

Rev 22:15 Outside are the dogs, those who practice magic arts, the sexually immoral, the murderers, the idolaters and everyone who loves and practices falsehood.

Instances Of Punishment For:

Cain (Ge 4:11-12)—

Ge 4:13 Cain said to the LORD, "My punishment is more than I can bear. [14]Today you are driving me from the land, and I will be hidden from your presence; I will be a restless wanderer on the earth, and whoever finds me will kill me." [15]But the LORD said to him, "Not so; if anyone kills Cain, he will suffer vengeance seven times over." Then the LORD put a mark on Cain so that no one who found him would kill him.

The murderer of Saul (2Sa 1:15-16).

David—

2Sa 12:9 Why did you despise the word of the LORD by doing what is evil in his eyes? You struck down Uriah the Hittite with the sword and took his wife to be your own. You killed him with the sword of the Ammonites. [10]Now, therefore, the sword will never depart from your house, because you despised me and took the wife of Uriah the Hittite to be your own.' [11]This is what the LORD says: 'Out of your own household I am going to bring calamity upon you. Before your very eyes I will take your wives and give them to one who is close to you, and he will lie with your wives in broad daylight. [12]You did it in secret, but I will do this thing in broad daylight before all Israel.'" (+2Sa 12:13-18)

Joab (1Ki 2:31-34). Haman (Est 7:10). The murderers of Ish-Bosheth (2Sa 4:11-12), of Joash (2Ki 14:5).

HOMOSEXUAL [3879, 780, 3434].

NIV+ MALE PROSTITUTES

Sexual activity between members of the same sex is universally condemned in Scripture. Male homosexuality forbidden by law and punished by death (Lev 18:22; 20:13). Male and female homosexuality condemned (Ro 1:26). With other sexually immoral persons excluded from the kingdom of God (1Co 6:9-11). Male shrine prostitution was practiced even in the temple (1Ki 14:24; 15:12; 2Ki 23:7). Male prostitutes also translates the derogatory term "dog" (Dt 23:17-18; possibly Rev 22:15).

Instances of: the men of Sodom (Ge 19:4-5; Jude 7) and Gibeah (Jdg 19:22).

HONESTY [575, 3841, 4026, 5477, 5791, 7404, 7406, 1465].

NIV+ HONEST, HONESTLY

Prayer of—

Ps 7:3 O LORD my God, if I have done this and there is guilt on my hands— [4]if I have done evil to him who is at peace with me or without cause have robbed my foe—

Promises for—

Ps 15:5 who lends his money without usury and does not accept a bribe against the innocent. He who does these things will never be shaken.

Ps 24:4 He who has clean hands and a pure heart, who does not lift up his soul to an idol or swear by what is false.

Pleases God—

Pr 11:1 The LORD abhors dishonest scales, but accurate weights are his delight.

Pr 12:22 The LORD detests lying lips, but he delights in men who are truthful.

Proceeds from God—

Pr 16:11 Honest scales and balances are from the LORD; all the weights in the bag are of his making.

Pr 20:10 Differing weights and differing measures—the LORD detests them both.

Golden rule of (Mt 7:12)—

Lk 6:31 Do to others as you would have them do to you.

Commanded:

Lev 19:35 " 'Do not use dishonest standards when measuring length, weight or quantity. ³⁶Use honest scales and honest weights, an honest ephah and an honest hin. I am the LORD your God, who brought you out of Egypt.

Dt 16:20 Follow justice and justice alone, so that you may live and possess the land the LORD your God is giving you.

Dt 25:13 Do not have two differing weights in your bag—one heavy, one light. ¹⁴Do not have two differing measures in your house—one large, one small. ¹⁵You must have accurate and honest weights and measures, so that you may live long in the land the LORD your God is giving you. ¹⁶For the LORD your God detests anyone who does these things, anyone who deals dishonestly.

Pr 4:25 Let your eyes look straight ahead, fix your gaze directly before you.

Eze 45:10 You are to use accurate scales, an accurate ephah and an accurate bath.

Mk 10:19 You know the commandments: 'Do not murder, do not commit adultery, do not steal, do not give false testimony, do not defraud, honor your father and mother.' "

Lk 3:12 Tax collectors also came to be baptized. "Teacher," they asked, "what should we do?"

¹³"Don't collect any more than you are required to," he told them. (+Ro 13:13)

Php 4:8 Finally, brothers, whatever is true, whatever is noble, whatever is right, whatever is pure, whatever is lovely, whatever is admirable—if anything is excellent or praiseworthy—think about such things.

Col 3:22 Slaves, obey your earthly masters in everything; and do it, not only when their eye is on you and to win their favor, but with sincerity of heart and reverence for the Lord.

1Th 4:11 Make it your ambition to lead a quiet life, to mind your own business and to work with your hands, just as we told you, ¹²so that your daily life may win the respect of outsiders and so that you will not be dependent on anybody. (+1Ti 2:2; 1Pe 2:11-12)

Instances of:

Jacob, returning money placed in sacks (Ge 43:12). Samuel, incorruptible in his judicial duties (1Sa 12:3-5). Overseers of temple repairs, with whom no reckoning was kept (2Ki 12:15; 22:4-7). Treasurers of the temple (Ne 13:13).

Paul, in all his actions—

Ac 24:16 So I strive always to keep my conscience clear before God and man.

2Co 4:1 Therefore, since through God's mercy we have this ministry, we do not lose heart. ²Rather, we have renounced secret and shameful ways; we do not use deception, nor do we distort the word of God. On the contrary,

by setting forth the truth plainly we commend ourselves to every man's conscience in the sight of God.

2Co 7:2 Make room for us in your hearts. We have wronged no one, we have corrupted no one, we have exploited no one.

2Co 8:21 For we are taking pains to do what is right, not only in the eyes of the Lord but also in the eyes of men.

The writer of Hebrews—

Heb 13:18 Pray for us. We are sure that we have a clear conscience and desire to live honorably in every way.

See Integrity; Righteousness; Dishonesty.

HONEY [1831, 3624, 5885, 3510].

NIV+ HONEYCOMB

(Ex 16:31; 2Sa 17:29; Pr 25:27; SS 4:11; Isa 7:15; Mt 3:4). Not to be offered with sacrifices (Lev 2:11). Found in rocks (Dt 32:13; Ps 81:16), upon the ground (1Sa 14:25). Samson's riddle concerning (Jdg 14:14). Sent as a present by Jacob to Egypt (Ge 43:11). Plentiful in Israel (Ex 3:8; Lev 20:24; Dt 8:8; Eze 20:6), in Assyria (2Ki 18:32). An article of merchandise from Israel (Eze 27:17).

HOOD NIV "tiaras" (Isa 3:23). *See Crown.*

HOOF [6811, 7271, 7274].

NIV+ HOOFS

Parting of, one of the physical marks used for distinguishing clean and unclean animals (Lev 11:3-8; Dt 14:3-8).

HOOKS [2260, 2560, 2626, 2676, 4661, 7553, 9191].

NIV+ FISHHOOK, FISHHOOKS, HOOK

For tabernacle, made of gold (Ex 26:32,37; 36:36), silver (Ex 27:10; 38:10-12,17,19). In the temple, seen in Ezekiel's vision (Eze 40:43). Used for catching fish (Eze 29:4). For pruning (Isa 2:4; 18:5; Joel 3:10). *See Meat Forks.*

Figurative: (Ex 38:4).

HOOPOE [1871]. A bird forbidden as food (Lev 11:19; Dt 14:18). *See Birds.*

HOPE [344, 1059, 2675, 3498, 4438, 4440, 5223, 7595, 7747, 8432, 8433, 9214, 9347, 9536, *1623, 1639+1827, 1827, 1828, 2671, 3607, 4054, 4598*].

NIV+ HOPED, HOPELESS, HOPES, HOPING

In God—

Ps 31:24 Be strong and take heart, all you who hope in the LORD.

Ps 33:22 May your unfailing love rest upon us, O LORD, even as we put our hope in you.

Ps 38:15 I wait for you, O LORD; you will answer, O Lord my God.

Ps 39:7 "But now, Lord, what do I look for? My hope is in you.

Ps 43:5 Why are you downcast, O my soul? Why so disturbed within me? Put your hope in God, for I will yet praise him, my Savior and my God.

Ps 71:5 For you have been my hope, O Sovereign LORD, my confidence since my youth.

Ps 71:14 But as for me, I will always have hope; I will praise you more and more.

Ps 78:7 Then they would put their trust in God and would not forget his deeds but would keep his commands.

Ps 130:7 O Israel, put your hope in the LORD, for with the LORD is unfailing love and with him is full redemption.

Ps 146:5 Blessed is he whose help is the God of Jacob, whose hope is in the LORD his God,

Jer 17:7 "But blessed is the man who trusts in the LORD, whose confidence is in him.

La 3:21 Yet this I call to mind and therefore I have hope:

La 3:24 I say to myself, "The LORD is my portion; therefore I will wait for him."

La 3:26 it is good to wait quietly for the salvation of the LORD.

1Pe 1:21 Through him you believe in God, who raised him from the dead and glorified him, and so your faith and hope are in God.

A helmet—

1Th 5:8 But since we belong to the day, let us be self-controlled, putting on faith and love as a breastplate, and the hope of salvation as a helmet.

An anchor—

Heb 6:18 God did this so that, by two unchangeable things in which it is impossible for God to lie, we who have fled to take hold of the hope offered to us may be greatly encouraged. [19]We have this hope as an anchor for the soul, firm and secure. It enters the inner sanctuary behind the curtain,

Joy in—

Pr 10:28 The prospect of the righteous is joy, but the hopes of the wicked come to nothing.

Ro 5:2 through whom we have gained access by faith into this grace in which we now stand. And we rejoice in the hope of the glory of God.

Ro 12:12 Be joyful in hope, patient in affliction, faithful in prayer.

Heb 3:6 But Christ is faithful as a son over God's house. And we are his house, if we hold on to our courage and the hope of which we boast.

Of God's calling—

Eph 1:18 I pray also that the eyes of your heart may be enlightened in order that you may know the hope to which he has called you, the riches of his glorious inheritance in the saints,

Eph 4:4 There is one body and one Spirit—just as you were called to one hope when you were called—

Of eternal life—

Col 1:5 the faith and love that spring from the hope that is stored up for you in heaven and that you have already heard about in the word of truth, the gospel (+Col 1:6)

Col 1:23 if you continue in your faith, established and firm, not moved from the hope held out in the gospel. This is the gospel that you heard and that has been proclaimed to every creature under heaven, and of which I, Paul, have become a servant.

Col 1:27 To them God has chosen to make known among the Gentiles the glorious riches of this mystery, which is Christ in you, the hope of glory.

Tit 1:2 a faith and knowledge resting on the hope of eternal life, which God, who does not lie, promised before the beginning of time,

Tit 2:13 while we wait for the blessed hope—the glorious appearing of our great God and Savior, Jesus Christ,

Tit 3:7 so that, having been justified by his grace, we might become heirs having the hope of eternal life.

1Pe 1:3 Praise be to the God and Father of our Lord Jesus Christ! In his great mercy he has given us new birth into a living hope through the resurrection of Jesus Christ from the dead,

1Pe 1:13 Therefore, prepare your minds for action; be self-controlled; set your hope fully on the grace to be given you when Jesus Christ is revealed.

1Jn 3:3 Everyone who has this hope in him purifies himself, just as he is pure.

Of the resurrection—

Ac 23:6 Then Paul, knowing that some of them were Sadducees and the others Pharisees, called out in the Sanhedrin, "My brothers, I am a Pharisee, the son of a Pharisee. I stand on trial because of my hope in the resurrection of the dead."

Ac 24:14 However, I admit that I worship the God of our fathers as a follower of the Way, which they call a sect. I believe everything that agrees with the Law and that is written in the Prophets, [15]and I have the same hope in God as these men, that there will be a resurrection of both the righteous and the wicked.

Ac 26:6 And now it is because of my hope in what God has promised our fathers that I am on trial today. [7]This is the promise our twelve tribes are hoping to see fulfilled as they earnestly serve God day and night. O king, it is because of this hope that the Jews are accusing me.

Ac 28:20 For this reason I have asked to see you and talk with you. It is because of the hope of Israel that I am bound with this chain."

Deferred—

Pr 13:12 Hope deferred makes the heart sick, but a longing fulfilled is a tree of life.

Of wicked shall perish—

Job 8:13 Such is the destiny of all who forget God; so perishes the hope of the godless.

Job 11:20 But the eyes of the wicked will fail, and escape will elude them; their hope will become a dying gasp."

Job 27:8 For what hope has the godless when he is cut off, when God takes away his life? (+Pr 10:28; 11:7,23)

Grounds of:

God's Word—

Ps 119:74 May those who fear you rejoice when they see me, for I have put my hope in your word.

Ps 119:81 My soul faints with longing for your salvation, but I have put my hope in your word.

Ro 15:4 For everything that was written in the past was written to teach us, so that through endurance and the encouragement of the Scriptures we might have hope.

God's mercy—

Ps 33:18 But the eyes of the LORD are on those who fear him, on those whose hope is in his unfailing love,

Jesus Christ—

1Th 1:3 We continually remember before our God and Father your work produced by faith, your labor prompted by love, and your endurance inspired by hope in our Lord Jesus Christ.

1Ti 1:1 Paul, an apostle of Christ Jesus by the command of God our Savior and of Christ Jesus our hope,

Instances of:

Job 31:24 "If I have put my trust in gold or said to pure gold, 'You are my security,'

Job 31:28 then these also would be sins to be judged, for I would have been unfaithful to God on high.

Ps 9:18 But the needy will not always be forgotten, nor the hope of the afflicted ever perish.

Ps 16:9 Therefore my heart is glad and my tongue rejoices; my body also will rest secure,

Ps 119:116 Sustain me according to your promise, and I will live; do not let my hopes be dashed.

Pr 14:32 When calamity comes, the wicked are brought down, but even in death the righteous have a refuge.

Pr 23:18 There is surely a future hope for you, and your hope will not be cut off. (+Pr 23:22)

Pr 24:14 Know also that wisdom is sweet to your soul; if you find it, there is a future hope for you, and your hope will not be cut off. (+Hos 2:15)

Zec 9:12 Return to your fortress, O prisoners of hope; even now I announce that I will restore twice as much to you.

Ro 4:18 Against all hope, Abraham in hope believed and so became the father of many nations, just as it had been said to him, "So shall your offspring be."

Ro 5:3 Not only so, but we also rejoice in our sufferings, because we know that suffering produces perseverance; ⁴perseverance, character; and character, hope. ⁵And hope does not disappoint us, because God has poured out his love into our hearts by the Holy Spirit, whom he has given us.

Ro 15:13 May the God of hope fill you with all joy and peace as you trust in him, so that you may overflow with hope by the power of the Holy Spirit.

1Co 13:13 And now these three remain: faith, hope and love. But the greatest of these is love.

2Co 3:12 Therefore, since we have such a hope, we are very bold.

Gal 5:5 But by faith we eagerly await through the Spirit the righteousness for which we hope.

Eph 2:12 remember that at that time you were separate from Christ, excluded from citizenship in Israel and foreigners to the covenants of the promise, without hope and without God in the world.

Php 1:20 I eagerly expect and hope that I will in no way be ashamed, but will have sufficient courage so that now as always Christ will be exalted in my body, whether by life or by death.

2Th 2:16 May our Lord Jesus Christ himself and God our Father, who loved us and by his grace gave us eternal encouragement and good hope,

Heb 6:11 We want each of you to show this same diligence to the very end, in order to make your hope sure.

1Pe 3:15 But in your hearts set apart Christ as Lord. Always be prepared to give an answer to everyone who asks you to give the reason for the hope that you have. But do this with gentleness and respect,

See Faith.

HOPHNI [2909] (*tadpole*). Son of Eli (1Sa 1:3). Sin of (1Sa 2:12-36; 3:11-14). Death of (1Sa 4:4,11,17).

HOPHRA [2922]. A pharoah who ruled Egypt from 589-570 B.C. (Jer 44:30).

HOR [2216] (perhaps *mountain*). Mountain on which Aaron died (Nu 20:22-29; 21:4; 33:38-39; 34:7-8; Dt 32:50).

HOR HAGGIDGAD [2988] (*cavern of the Gidgad*). Israelite encampment (Nu 33:32-33), called Gudgodah (Dt 10:7).

HORAM [2235] (*height* ISBE). King of Gezer (Jos 10:33).

HOREB [2998] (*dry, desolate*). A range of mountains of which Sinai is chief (Ex 3:1; 17:6; 33:6; Dt 1:2,6,19; 4:10,15; 5:2; 9:8; 29:1; 1Ki 8:9; 19:8; 2Ch 5:10; Ps 106:19; Mal 4:4). *See Sinai, Mount of, Desert of.*

HOREM [3054] (*consecrated*). A fortification in Naphtali (Jos 19:38).

HORESH [3092]. A stronghold in the Desert of Ziph (1Sa 23:15-19).

HORI [3036] (*cave-dweller*).
NIV+ HORITE, HORITES
1. Son of Lotan (Ge 36:22,30; 1Ch 1:39).
2. A Simeonite (Nu 13:5).

HORITE(S), HORIM [3037].
NIV+ HORI
People conquered by Kedorlaomer (Ge 14:6), may be the same as the Hivites (Ge 34:2; Jos 9:7), thought to be Hurrians, from highlands of Media.

HORMAH [3055] (*consecration*). A city SW of the Dead Sea (Nu 14:45; 21:1-3; Dt 1:44). Taken by Judah and Simeon (Jdg 1:17; Jos 12:14). Allotted to Simeon (Jos 19:4; 1Ch 4:30). Within the territory allotted to Judah (Jos 15:30; 1Sa 30:30).

HORN [2956, 3413, 7966, 7967, 8795, 10641, *3043*].
NIV+ HORNED, HORNS, TWO-HORNED
Used to hold the anointing oil (1Sa 16:1; 1Ki 1:39). Used for a trumpet. *See Trumpet.*

Figurative:
Of divine protection (2Sa 22:3). Of power (1Ki 22:11; Ps 89:24; 92:10; 132:17).

Symbolic:
(Da 7:7-24; 8:3-9,20; Am 6:13, ftn.; Mic 4:13; Zec 1:18-21; Rev 5:6; 12:3; 13:1,11; 17:3-16).

HORNET [7667] (*depression, discouragement*). A hornet or wasp (Ex 23:28; Dt 7:20; Jos 24:12).

HORON *See Beth Horon.*

HORONAIM [2589] (*twin hollows, twin caves*). A town of Moab (Isa 15:5; Jer 48:3,5,34).

HORONITE [3061] (*citizen of Horonaim*, or more probably *of Beth Horon*). Sanballat the Horonite, who opposed Nehemiah in the restoration of Jerusalem (Ne 2:10,19; 13:28).

HORSE [6061, 7304, 8207, 8224, *2691*].
NIV+ HORSE'S, HORSEBACK, HORSEMAN, HORSEMEN, HORSES, HORSES', WAR-HORSES

Description of:
Great strength (Job 39:19-25), swifter than eagles (Jer 4:13), snorting and neighing of (Isa 5:28; Jer 8:16), a vain thing for safety (Ps 33:17; Pr 21:31). Used by the Egyptians in war (Ex 14:9; 15:19), the Israelites (1Ki 22:4). Used for cavalry (2Ki 18:23; Jer 47:3; 51:21). Egypt famous for (Isa 31:1). Forbidden to kings of Israel (Dt 17:16). Hamstrung by Joshua (Jos 11:6,9), David (2Sa 8:4). Israel reproved for keeping (Isa 2:7; 3:1; Eze 17:15; Hos 14:3). Exported from Egypt (1Ki 10:28-29; 2Ch 9:25, 28), from Babylon (Ezr 2:66; Ne 7:68). Bits for (Jas 3:3), bells for (Zec 14:20), harness for (Jer 46:4). Color of (Zec 1:8). Commerce in (Rev 18:13). *See above, Exported.* Dedicated to religious uses (2Ki 23:11).

Symbolic:
(Zec 1:8; Rev 6:2-8; 9:17; 19:11-21).

HORSE GATE One of the gates of Jerusalem (Ne 3:28-32; Jer 31:38-40).

HORSE LEECH *See Leech.*

HORTICULTURE Encouraged (Lev 19:23-25; Dt 20:19-20). *See Agriculture; Graft; Pruning.*

HOSAH [2880, 2881] (*refuge*).
1. A city of Asher (Jos 19:29).
2. A Levite (1Ch 16:38; 26:10-11).

HOSANNA [6057] (*save now*). Originally a prayer, "O LORD, save us" (Ps 118:25), chanted when Jesus entered Jerusalem (Mt 21:9-15; Mk 11:9-10; Jn 12:13).

HOSEA [2107, 6060] (*salvation*).
Author: Hosea son of Beeri

Date: About the middle of the eighth century B.C.

Outline:
I. Superscription (1:1).
II. The Unfaithful Wife and the Faithful Husband (1:2-3:5).
  A. The Children as Signs (1:2-2:1).
  B. The Unfaithful Wife (2:2-23).
    1. The Lord's judgment of Israel (2:2-13).
    2. The Lord's restoration of Israel (2:14-23).
  C. The Faithful Husband (ch. 3).
III. The Unfaithful Nation and the Faithful God (chs. 4-14).
  A. Israel's Unfaithfulness (4:1-6:3).
    1. The general charge (4:1-3).
    2. The cause declared and the results described (4:4-19).
    3. A special message to the people and leaders (ch. 5).
    4. A sorrowful plea (6:1-3).
  B. Israel's Punishment (6:4-10:15).
    1. The case stated (6:4-7:16).
    2. The judgment pronounced (chs. 8-9).
    3. Summary and appeal (ch. 10).
  C. The Lord's Faithful Love (chs. 11-14).
    1. The Lord's fatherly love (11:1-11).
    2. Israel's punishment for unfaithfulness (11:12-13:16).
    3. Israel's restoration after repentance (ch. 14).
See Prophets, The Minor.

HOSHAIAH [2108] (*Yahweh has saved*).
1. One of the returned exiles (Ne 12:32).
2. A distinguished Israelite captive (Jer 42:1; 43:2).

HOSHAMA [2106] (*Yahweh has heard*). Son of Jehoiachin, king of Judah (1Ch 3:18).

HOSHEA [2107] (*salvation*).
NIV+JOSHUA
1. The original name of Joshua (Nu 13:8,16; Dt 32:44). *See Joshua.*
2. A chief of Ephraim (1Ch 27:20).
3. King of Israel. Assassinates Pekah and usurps the throne (2Ki 15:30). Evil reign of (2Ki 17:1-2). Becomes subject to Assyria (2Ki 17:3). Conspires against Assyria and is imprisoned (2Ki 17:4). Last king of Israel (2Ki 17:6; 18:9-12; Hos 10:3,7).
4. A Jewish exile (Ne 10:23).

HOSPITALITY [3827, 3828, 5696, 5810, 5811, 5819].
NIV+HOSPITABLE, HOSPITABLY

Unselfish—
Lk 14:12 Then Jesus said to his host, "When you give a luncheon or dinner, do not invite your friends, your brothers or relatives, or your rich neighbors; if you do, they may invite you back and so you will be repaid. [13]But when you give a banquet, invite the poor, the crippled, the lame, the blind, [14]and you will be blessed. Although they cannot repay you, you will be repaid at the resurrection of the righteous."

Deceitful guise of—
Pr 9:1 Wisdom has built her house; she has hewn out its seven pillars. [2]She has prepared her meat and mixed her wine; she has also set her table. [3]She has sent out her maids, and she calls from the highest point of the city. [4]"Let all who are simple come in here!" she says to those who lack judgment. [5]"Come, eat my food and drink the wine I have mixed.

Pr 23:6 Do not eat the food of a stingy man, do not crave his delicacies; [7]for he is the kind of man who is always thinking about the cost. "Eat and drink," he says to you, but his heart is not with you. [8]You will vomit up the little you have eaten and will have wasted your compliments.

Parable of (Mt 22:2-10).

Commanded:
Isa 58:6 "Is not this the kind of fasting I have chosen: to loose the chains of injustice and untie the cords of the yoke, to set the oppressed free and break every yoke? [7]Is it not to share your food with the hungry and to provide the poor wanderer with shelter—when you see the naked, to clothe him, and not to turn away from your own flesh and blood?

Mt 25:34 "Then the King will say to those on his right, 'Come, you who are blessed by my Father; take your inheritance, the kingdom prepared for you since the creation of the world. [35]For I was hungry and you gave me something to eat, I was thirsty and you gave me something to drink, I was a stranger and you invited me in, [36]I needed clothes and you clothed me, I was sick and you looked after me, I was in prison and you came to visit me.'
[37]"Then the righteous will answer him, 'Lord, when did we see you hungry and feed you, or thirsty and give you something to drink? [38]When did we see you a stranger and invite you in, or needing clothes and clothe you? [39]When did we see you sick or in prison and go to visit you?'

Ro 12:13 Share with God's people who are in need. Practice hospitality.

1Ti 3:2 Now the overseer must be above reproach, the husband of but one wife, temperate, self-controlled, respectable, hospitable, able to teach,

1Ti 5:10 and is well known for her good deeds, such as bringing up children, showing hospitality, washing the feet of the saints, helping those in trouble and devoting herself to all kinds of good deeds.

Tit 1:7 Since an overseer is entrusted with God's work, he must be blameless—not overbearing, not quick-tempered, not given to drunkenness, not violent, not pursuing dishonest gain. [8]Rather he must be hospitable, one who loves what is good, who is self-controlled, upright, holy and disciplined.

Heb 13:2 Do not forget to entertain strangers, for by so doing some people have entertained angels without knowing it.

1Pe 4:9 Offer hospitality to one another without grumbling. [10]Each one should use whatever gift he has received to serve others, faithfully administering God's grace in its various forms. [11]If anyone speaks, he should do it as one speaking the very words of God. If anyone serves, he should do it with the strength God provides, so that in all things God may be praised through Jesus Christ. To him be the glory and the power for ever and ever. Amen.

3Jn 5 Dear friend, you are faithful in what you are doing

for the brothers, even though they are strangers to you.
[6]They have told the church about your love. You will do
well to send them on their way in a manner worthy of God.
[7]It was for the sake of the Name that they went out,
receiving no help from the pagans. [8]We ought therefore to
show hospitality to such men so that we may work
together for the truth.

Toward strangers, enjoined—

Ex 22:11 the issue between them will be settled by the
taking of an oath before the LORD that the neighbor did not
lay hands on the other person's property. The owner is to
accept this, and no restitution is required.

Ex 23:9 "Do not oppress an alien; you yourselves know
how it feels to be aliens, because you were aliens in Egypt.

Lev 19:10 Do not go over your vineyard a second time or
pick up the grapes that have fallen. Leave them for the
poor and the alien. I am the LORD your God.

Lev 19:33 " 'When an alien lives with you in your land, do
not mistreat him. [34]The alien living with you must be
treated as one of your native-born. Love him as yourself,
for you were aliens in Egypt. I am the LORD your God.

Lev 24:22 You are to have the same law for the alien and
the native-born. I am the LORD your God.' "

Dt 10:18 He defends the cause of the fatherless and the
widow, and loves the alien, giving him food and clothing.
[19]And you are to love those who are aliens, for you yourselves were aliens in Egypt.

Dt 26:12 When you have finished setting aside a tenth of
all your produce in the third year, the year of the tithe, you
shall give it to the Levite, the alien, the fatherless and the
widow, so that they may eat in your towns and be satisfied.
[13]Then say to the LORD your God: "I have removed from
my house the sacred portion and have given it to the
Levite, the alien, the fatherless and the widow, according
to all you commanded. I have not turned aside from your
commands nor have I forgotten any of them.

Dt 27:19 "Cursed is the man who withholds justice from
the alien, the fatherless or the widow." Then all the people
shall say, "Amen!"

Instances of:

Pharaoh to Abraham (Ge 12:16). Melchizedek to
Abraham (Ge 14:18). Abraham to angels (Ge 18:1-8). Lot
to an angel (Ge 19:1-11). Abimelech to Abraham (Ge
20:14-15). Hittites, to Abraham (Ge 23:3, ftn, 6,11).
Laban, to Abraham's servant (Ge 24:31-33), to Jacob (Ge
29:13-14). Isaac to Abimelech (Ge 26:30). Joseph to his
brothers (Ge 43:31-34). Pharaoh to Jacob (Ge 45:16-20;
47:7-12). Jethro to Moses (Ex 2:20). Rahab to the spies
(Jos 2:1-16). Man of Gibeah to the Levite (Jdg 19:16-21).
Pharaoh to Hadad (1Ki 11:17,22). Jeroboam to the prophet
of Judah (1Ki 13:7). The widow of Zarephath to Elijah
(1Ki 17:10-24). The Shunammite to Elisha (2Ki 4:8).
Elisha to the Syrian spies (2Ki 6:22). Job to strangers (Job
31:32). David to Mephibosheth (2Sa 9:7-13). King of Babylon to Jehoiachin (2Ki 25:29-30). Nehemiah to rulers and
Jews (Ne 5:17-19).

Martha to Jesus (Lk 10:38; Jn 12:1-2). Pharisees to
Jesus (Lk 11:37-38). Zacchaeus to Jesus (Lk 19:1-10).
Disciples to Jesus (Lk 24:29). The tanner to Peter (Ac
10:6,23). Lydia to Paul and Silas (Ac 16:15). Barbarians to
Paul (Ac 28:2). Publius to Paul (Ac 28:7).

Phoebe to Paul—

Ro 16:2 I ask you to receive her in the Lord in a way
worthy of the saints and to give her any help she may need
from you, for she has been a great help to many people,
including me.

Onesiphorus to Paul (2Ti 1:16). Gaius (3Jn 5,8).

Rewarded, Instances of:

Rahab (Jos 6:17,22-25). Widow of Zarephath (1Ki
17:10-24).

See Feasts; Guest; Inhospitableness; Strangers.

HOST [*7372, 2813, 5131] (army).

NIV+ HOSTS

Army (Ge 21:22), angels (Ps 103:21; Jos 5:14), heavenly bodies (Dt 4:19), creation (Ge 2:1), God of hosts (1Sa
17:45), one who shows hospitality (Ro 16:23; Lk 10:35).

HOSTAGES [1201+9510]. (2Ki 14:14; 2Ch 25:24).

HOSTILITY [*368, 5286, 5378, 6584+7156, 7640, 7650, 7675, 7762, 7950, 8120, 8475, 1885, 2397].

NIV+ HOSTILE

To the Righteous (Mic 7:6; Mt 10:21,35-36; Mk 13:12;
Lk 12:53).

HOT SPRINGS (Ge 36:24).

HOTHAM [2598] (signet ring, seal).

1. Son of Heber an Asherite (1Ch 7:32).

2. An Aroerite and father of two of David's mighty men
(1Ch 11:44).

HOTHAN See Hotham, 2.

HOTHIR [2110] (one who remains). Son of Heman
(1Ch 25:4,28).

HOUGHING See Hamstring.

HOURS [6961, 2469, 4388, 6052].

NIV+ HOUR

A division of time. Twelve, in the day (Jn 11:9; Mt
20:3-12; 27:45-46), in the night (Ac 23:23).

Symbolic: (Rev 8:1; 9:15).

HOUSE [*185, 1074, 3998, 5659, 9572, 10103, 3836, 3864, 3865, 3867, 3875].

NIV+ HOUSEHOLD, HOUSEHOLDS, HOUSES, STOREHOUSE, STOREHOUSES

Built of stone (Lev 14:40-45; Isa 9:10; Am 5:11), brick
(Ge 11:3; Ex 1:11-14; Isa 9:10), wood (SS 1:17; Isa 9:10).
Built into city walls (Jos 2:15).

Used for worship (Ac 1:13-14; 12:12; Ro 16:5; 1Co
16:19; Col 4:15; Phm 2).

"A man's castle" (Dt 24:10-11).

Architecture of:

Foundations of stone (1Ki 5:17; 7:9; Ezr 6:3; Jer 51:26).
Figurative (Ps 87:1; Isa 28:16; 48:13; Ro 15:20; 1Co 3:11;
Eph 2:20; 1Ti 6:19; Heb 6:1; Rev 21:14). Cornerstone (Job
38:6; Ps 144:12). Figurative (Ps 118:22; Isa 28:16; Eph
2:20; 1Pe 2:6).

Porches (Jdg 3:23; 1Ki 7:6-7), courts (Est 1:5), summer
apartment (Jdg 3:20, w Am 3:15; 1Ki 17:19), inner chamber (1Ki 22:25), chambers (Ge 43:30; 2Sa 18:33; 2Ki 1:2;
4:10; Ac 1:13; 9:37; 20:8), guest chamber (Mk 14:14),
pillars (Pr 9:1), with courts (Ne 8:16), lattice (Jdg 5:28),
windows (Jdg 5:28; Pr 7:6), walls plastered (Da 5:5),
hinges (Pr 26:14).

Roofs, flat (Jos 2:6; Jdg 16:27; 1Sa 9:25; 2Sa 11:2;
16:22; Isa 15:3; 22:1; Mt 24:17; Lk 12:3), battlements
required in Mosaic law (Dt 22:8). Prayer on (Ac 10:9).
Altars on (2Ki 23:12; Jer 19:13; 32:29; Zep 1:5). Booths
on (Ne 8:16), used as place to sleep (Jos 2:8; Ac 10:9), as
dwelling place (Pr 21:9; 25:24).

Painted (Jer 22:14; Eze 8:10,12). Windows of (Hos 13:3). Laws regarding sale of (Lev 25:29-33; Ne 5:3). Dedicated (Dt 20:5; Ps 30 [title]).

Figurative:

(2Sa 7:18; Ps 23:6; 36:8; Jn 14:2; 2Co 5:1; 1Ti 3:15; Heb 3:2).

HOUSE OF GOD A place of prayer (Mt 21:13; Mk 11:17; Lk 19:46). Holy (Ecc 5:1; Isa 62:9; Eze 43:12; 1Co 3:17).

See Synagogue; Tabernacle; Temple.

HOUSEHOLD GODS [9572]. Used by Laban, stolen by Rachel (Ge 31:19,30-35), by Micah, stolen by the Danites (Jdg 17:5; 18:14,17-20). Condemned and disposed of by Jacob (Ge 35:2-4, w Ge 31:35-39). Destroyed by Josiah (2Ki 23:24). *See Idol.*

HOUSETOPS As places of resort (Jos 2:6; 1Sa 9:25; Ne 8:16; Pr 21:9; Mt 10:27; 24:17; Lk 5:19; Ac 10:9).

HUBBAH [2465] (*God has hidden [someone from danger]*). An Asherite (1Ch 7:34).

HUKKOK [2982]. A place on the boundary line of Naphtali (Jos 19:34).

HUKOK [2577]. The name of a Levitical city in Asher (1Ch 6:75), a variant spelling of Helkath (Jos 31:21). *See Helkath.*

HUL [2566]. Son of Aram (Ge 10:23; 1Ch 1:17).

HULDAH [2701] (*weasel*). A prophetess. Foretells the destruction of Jerusalem (2Ki 22:14-20; 2Ch 34:22-28).

HUMAN SACRIFICE *See Offerings, Human Sacrifices.*

HUMILIATION AND SELF-AFFLICTION

[1425+7156, 3075, 4009, *2875, 5428*].

NIV+ HUMILIATE, HUMILIATED, HUMILIATION

Commanded—

Lev 16:29 "This is to be a lasting ordinance for you: On the tenth day of the seventh month you must deny yourselves and not do any work—whether native-born or an alien living among you— [30]because on this day atonement will be made for you, to cleanse you. Then, before the LORD, you will be clean from all your sins. [31]It is a sabbath of rest, and you must deny yourselves; it is a lasting ordinance.

Lev 23:26 The LORD said to Moses, [27]"The tenth day of this seventh month is the Day of Atonement. Hold a sacred assembly and deny yourselves, and present an offering made to the LORD by fire. [28]Do no work on that day, because it is the Day of Atonement, when atonement is made for you before the LORD your God. [29]Anyone who does not deny himself on that day must be cut off from his people. [30]I will destroy from among his people anyone who does any work on that day. [31]You shall do no work at all. This is to be a lasting ordinance for the generations to come, wherever you live. [32]It is a sabbath of rest for you, and you must deny yourselves. From the evening of the ninth day of the month until the following evening you are to observe your sabbath."

Ezr 8:21 There, by the Ahava Canal, I proclaimed a fast, so that we might humble ourselves before our God and ask him for a safe journey for us and our children, with all our possessions. [22]I was ashamed to ask the king for soldiers and horsemen to protect us from enemies on the road,

because we had told the king, "The gracious hand of our God is on everyone who looks to him, but his great anger is against all who forsake him." [23]So we fasted and petitioned our God about this, and he answered our prayer.

2Ch 7:14 if my people, who are called by my name, will humble themselves and pray and seek my face and turn from their wicked ways, then will I hear from heaven and will forgive their sin and will heal their land.

See Fasting; Humility.

HUMILITY [6708, 7560, *4246+5425, 4559, 5425*].

NIV+ HUMBLE, HUMBLED, HUMBLES, HUMBLY, HUMILIATE, HUMILIATED, HUMILIATION

Ps 69:32 The poor will see and be glad—you who seek God, may your hearts live! (+Ps 51:17)

Ps 138:6 Though the LORD is on high, he looks upon the lowly, but the proud he knows from afar.

Pr 3:34 He mocks proud mockers but gives grace to the humble.

Pr 11:2 When pride comes, then comes disgrace, but with humility comes wisdom.

Pr 12:15 The way of a fool seems right to him, but a wise man listens to advice.

Pr 16:19 Better to be lowly in spirit and among the oppressed than to share plunder with the proud.

Isa 57:15 For this is what the high and lofty One says—he who lives forever, whose name is holy: "I live in a high and holy place, but also with him who is contrite and lowly in spirit, to revive the spirit of the lowly and to revive the heart of the contrite.

Isa 66:2 Has not my hand made all these things, and so they came into being?" declares the LORD. "This is the one I esteem: he who is humble and contrite in spirit, and trembles at my word.

Lk 10:21 At that time Jesus, full of joy through the Holy Spirit, said, "I praise you, Father, Lord of heaven and earth, because you have hidden these things from the wise and learned, and revealed them to little children. Yes, Father, for this was your good pleasure. (+2Co 7:6)

Gal 6:14 May I never boast except in the cross of our Lord Jesus Christ, through which the world has been crucified to me, and I to the world. (+Jas 4:6)

Commanded:

Dt 15:15 Remember that you were slaves in Egypt and the LORD your God redeemed you. That is why I give you this command today.

Pr 25:6 Do not exalt yourself in the king's presence, and do not claim a place among great men; [7a]it is better for him to say to you, "Come up here," than for him to humiliate you before a nobleman.

Pr 27:2 Let another praise you, and not your own mouth; someone else, and not your own lips.

Pr 30:32 "If you have played the fool and exalted yourself, or if you have planned evil, clap your hand over your mouth!

Ecc 5:2 Do not be quick with your mouth, do not be hasty in your heart to utter anything before God. God is in heaven and you are on earth, so let your words be few.

Jer 45:5 Should you then seek great things for yourself? Seek them not. For I will bring disaster on all people, declares the LORD, but wherever you go I will let you escape with your life.' " (+Mic 6:8)

Mt 18:2 He called a little child and had him stand among them. [3]And he said: "I tell you the truth, unless you change and become like little children, you will never enter the kingdom of heaven. ⁴Therefore, whoever humbles himself like this child is the greatest in the kingdom of heaven.

Mt 20:26 Not so with you. Instead, whoever wants to become great among you must be your servant, ²⁷and whoever wants to be first must be your slave— (+Mk 9:33-37; 10:43-44; Lk 9:46-48)

Lk 14:10 But when you are invited, take the lowest place, so that when your host comes, he will say to you, 'Friend, move up to a better place.' Then you will be honored in the presence of all your fellow guests.

Lk 17:10 So you also, when you have done everything you were told to do, should say, 'We are unworthy servants; we have only done our duty.'"

Lk 22:24 Also a dispute arose among them as to which of them was considered to be greatest. ²⁵Jesus said to them, "The kings of the Gentiles lord it over them; and those who exercise authority over them call themselves Benefactors. ²⁶But you are not to be like that. Instead, the greatest among you should be like the youngest, and the one who rules like the one who serves. ²⁷For who is greater, the one who is at the table or the one who serves? Is it not the one who is at the table? But I am among you as one who serves.

Jn 13:14 Now that I, your Lord and Teacher, have washed your feet, you also should wash one another's feet. ¹⁵I have set you an example that you should do as I have done for you. ¹⁶I tell you the truth, no servant is greater than his master, nor is a messenger greater than the one who sent him.

Ro 11:18 do not boast over those branches. If you do, consider this: You do not support the root, but the root supports you.

Ro 11:19 You will say then, "Branches were broken off so that I could be grafted in."

Ro 11:20 Granted. But they were broken off because of unbelief, and you stand by faith. Do not be arrogant, but be afraid.

Ro 11:25 I do not want you to be ignorant of this mystery, brothers, so that you may not be conceited: Israel has experienced a hardening in part until the full number of the Gentiles has come in.

Ro 12:3 For by the grace given me I say to every one of you: Do not think of yourself more highly than you ought, but rather think of yourself with sober judgment, in accordance with the measure of faith God has given you.

Ro 12:10 Be devoted to one another in brotherly love. Honor one another above yourselves.

Ro 12:16 Live in harmony with one another. Do not be proud, but be willing to associate with people of low position. Do not be conceited.

1Co 3:18 Do not deceive yourselves. If any one of you thinks he is wise by the standards of this age, he should become a "fool" so that he may become wise. (+1Co 4:6)

1Co 10:12 So, if you think you are standing firm, be careful that you don't fall!

Gal 5:26 Let us not become conceited, provoking and envying each other. (+Eph 4:1-2)

Eph 5:21 Submit to one another out of reverence for Christ.

Php 2:3 Do nothing out of selfish ambition or vain conceit, but in humility consider others better than yourselves. ⁴Each of you should look not only to your own interests, but also to the interests of others.

⁵Your attitude should be the same as that of Christ Jesus: ⁶Who, being in very nature God, did not consider equality with God something to be grasped, ⁷but made himself nothing, taking the very nature of a servant, being made in human likeness. ⁸And being found in appearance as a man, he humbled himself and became obedient to death—even death on a cross! ⁹Therefore God exalted him to the highest place and gave him the name that is above every name, ¹⁰that at the name of Jesus every knee should bow, in heaven and on earth and under the earth, ¹¹and every tongue confess that Jesus Christ is Lord, to the glory of God the Father.

Col 3:12 Therefore, as God's chosen people, holy and dearly loved, clothe yourselves with compassion, kindness, humility, gentleness and patience.

Jas 1:9 The brother in humble circumstances ought to take pride in his high position. ¹⁰But the one who is rich should take pride in his low position, because he will pass away like a wild flower.

Jas 4:10 Humble yourselves before the Lord, and he will lift you up. (+1Pe 5:3,5-6)

Feigned, forbidden (Col 2:18-23).

Rewards of:

Job 5:11 The lowly he sets on high, and those who mourn are lifted to safety.

Job 22:29 When men are brought low and you say, 'Lift them up!' then he will save the downcast. (+Ps 138:6)

Pr 15:33 The fear of the LORD teaches a man wisdom, and humility comes before honor. (+Pr 18:12)

Pr 22:4 Humility and the fear of the LORD bring wealth and honor and life.

Pr 29:23 A man's pride brings him low, but a man of lowly spirit gains honor.

Mt 5:3 "Blessed are the poor in spirit, for theirs is the kingdom of heaven.

Mt 23:12 For whoever exalts himself will be humbled, and whoever humbles himself will be exalted.

Lk 1:52 He has brought down rulers from their thrones but has lifted up the humble. (+Lk 14:11)

Lk 18:13 "But the tax collector stood at a distance. He would not even look up to heaven, but beat his breast and said, 'God, have mercy on me, a sinner.'

¹⁴"I tell you that this man, rather than the other, went home justified before God. For everyone who exalts himself will be humbled, and he who humbles himself will be exalted."

Exemplified in:

Abraham—

Ge 18:27 Then Abraham spoke up again: "Now that I have been so bold as to speak to the Lord, though I am nothing but dust and ashes, (+Ge 18:32)

Jacob—

Ge 32:10 I am unworthy of all the kindness and faithfulness you have shown your servant. I had only my staff when I crossed this Jordan, but now I have become two groups.

Joseph (Ge 41:16)

Moses—

Ex 3:11 But Moses said to God, "Who am I, that I should go to Pharaoh and bring the Israelites out of Egypt?"

Ex 4:10 Moses said to the LORD, "O Lord, I have never been eloquent, neither in the past nor since you have spoken to your servant. I am slow of speech and tongue."

David (1Sa 18:18-23; 23:14; 26:20)—

2Sa 7:18 Then King David went in and sat before the LORD, and he said: "Who am I, O Sovereign LORD, and what is my family, that you have brought me this far? ¹⁹And as if this were not enough in your sight, O Sovereign

LORD, you have also spoken about the future of the house of your servant. Is this your usual way of dealing with man, O Sovereign LORD? (+2Sa 7:20; 1Ch 17:16-18)

1Ch 29:14 "But who am I, and who are my people, that we should be able to give as generously as this? Everything comes from you, and we have given you only what comes from your hand.

The Psalmist—

Ps 8:3 When I consider your heavens, the work of your fingers, the moon and the stars, which you have set in place, ⁴what is man that you are mindful of him, the son of man that you care for him?

Ps 73:22 I was senseless and ignorant; I was a brute beast before you.

Ps 131:1 My heart is not proud, O LORD, my eyes are not haughty; I do not concern myself with great matters or things too wonderful for me. ²But I have stilled and quieted my soul; like a weaned child with its mother, like a weaned child is my soul within me.

Ps 141:5 Let a righteous man strike me—it is a kindness; let him rebuke me—it is oil on my head. My head will not refuse it. Yet my prayer is ever against the deeds of evildoers; (+Ps 144:3)

Solomon—

1Ki 3:7 "Now, O LORD my God, you have made your servant king in place of my father David. But I am only a little child and do not know how to carry out my duties. (+2Ch 1:10)

2Ch 2:6 But who is able to build a temple for him, since the heavens, even the highest heavens, cannot contain him? Who then am I to build a temple for him, except as a place to burn sacrifices before him?

Mephibosheth (2Sa 9:8), Ahab (1Ki 21:29), kings and princes of Israel (2Ch 12:6-7,12), Josiah (2Ki 22:18-19; 2Ch 34:26,27)

Job (Job 7:17-18)—

Job 9:14 "How then can I dispute with him? How can I find words to argue with him? ¹⁵Though I were innocent, I could not answer him; I could only plead with my Judge for mercy.

Job 40:4 "I am unworthy—how can I reply to you? I put my hand over my mouth. ⁵I spoke once, but I have no answer—twice, but I will say no more."

Job 42:2 "I know that you can do all things; no plan of yours can be thwarted. ³[You asked,] 'Who is this that obscures my counsel without knowledge?' Surely I spoke of things I did not understand, things too wonderful for me to know.

⁴["You said,] 'Listen now, and I will speak; I will question you, and you shall answer me.' ⁵My ears had heard of you but now my eyes have seen you. ⁶Therefore I despise myself and repent in dust and ashes."

Elihu (Job 32:4-7; 33:6)

Ezra—

Ezr 9:13 "What has happened to us is a result of our evil deeds and our great guilt, and yet, our God, you have punished us less than our sins have deserved and have given us a remnant like this. (+Ezr 9:15)

Agur—

Pr 30:2 "I am the most ignorant of men; I do not have a man's understanding. ³I have not learned wisdom, nor have I knowledge of the Holy One.

Isaiah (Isa 6:5), Hezekiah (Isa 38:15), Jeremiah (Jer 1:6; 10:23-24), Daniel (Da 2:30), Ezra and the Jews (Ezr 8:21, 23), Elizabeth (Lk 1:43)

John the Baptist (Mt 3:14; Mk 1:7; Lk 3:16)—

Jn 1:27 He is the one who comes after me, the thongs of whose sandals I am not worthy to untie."

Jn 3:29 The bride belongs to the bridegroom. The friend who attends the bridegroom waits and listens for him, and is full of joy when he hears the bridegroom's voice. That joy is mine, and it is now complete. ³⁰He must become greater; I must become less.

Jesus—

Mt 11:29 Take my yoke upon you and learn from me, for I am gentle and humble in heart, and you will find rest for your souls. (+Mt 13:4-16)

Woman of Canaan (Mt 15:27)

The righteous—

Mt 25:37 "Then the righteous will answer him, 'Lord, when did we see you hungry and feed you, or thirsty and give you something to drink? ³⁸When did we see you a stranger and invite you in, or needing clothes and clothe you? ³⁹When did we see you sick or in prison and go to visit you?'

⁴⁰'The King will reply, 'I tell you the truth, whatever you did for one of the least of these brothers of mine, you did for me.'

The tax collector (Lk 18:13)

Centurion (Mt 8:8)—

Lk 7:6 So Jesus went with them. He was not far from the house when the centurion sent friends to say to him: "Lord, don't trouble yourself, for I do not deserve to have you come under my roof. ⁷That is why I did not even consider myself worthy to come to you. But say the word, and my servant will be healed.

Peter (Ac 2:12)

Paul (Ac 20:19)—

Ro 7:18 I know that nothing good lives in me, that is, in my sinful nature. For I have the desire to do what is good, but I cannot carry it out.

1Co 2:1 When I came to you, brothers, I did not come with eloquence or superior wisdom as I proclaimed to you the testimony about God. ²For I resolved to know nothing while I was with you except Jesus Christ and him crucified. ³I came to you in weakness and fear, and with much trembling. (+1Co 15:9)

1Co 15:10 But by the grace of God I am what I am, and his grace to me was not without effect. No, I worked harder than all of them—yet not I, but the grace of God that was with me.

2Co 3:5 Not that we are competent in ourselves to claim anything for ourselves, but our competence comes from God.

2Co 11:30 If I must boast, I will boast of the things that show my weakness.

2Co 12:5 I will boast about a man like that, but I will not boast about myself, except about my weaknesses. ⁶Even if I should choose to boast, I would not be a fool, because I would be speaking the truth. But I refrain, so no one will think more of me than is warranted by what I do or say.

⁷To keep me from becoming conceited because of these surpassingly great revelations, there was given me a thorn in my flesh, a messenger of Satan, to torment me. ⁸Three times I pleaded with the Lord to take it away from me. ⁹But he said to me, "My grace is sufficient for you, for my power is made perfect in weakness." Therefore I will boast all the more gladly about my weaknesses, so that Christ's power may rest on me. ¹⁰That is why, for Christ's sake, I delight in weaknesses, in insults, in hardships, in

persecutions, in difficulties. For when I am weak, then I am strong.

[11]I have made a fool of myself, but you drove me to it. I ought to have been commended by you, for I am not in the least inferior to the "super-apostles," even though I am nothing. [12]The things that mark an apostle—signs, wonders and miracles—were done among you with great perseverance.

Eph 3:8 Although I am less than the least of all God's people, this grace was given me: to preach to the Gentiles the unsearchable riches of Christ,

Php 3:12 Not that I have already obtained all this, or have already been made perfect, but I press on to take hold of that for which Christ Jesus took hold of me. [13]Brothers, I do not consider myself yet to have taken hold of it. But one thing I do: Forgetting what is behind and straining toward what is ahead,

Php 4:12 I know what it is to be in need, and I know what it is to have plenty. I have learned the secret of being content in any and every situation, whether well fed or hungry, whether living in plenty or in want.

1Ti 1:15 Here is a trustworthy saying that deserves full acceptance: Christ Jesus came into the world to save sinners—of whom I am the worst.

HUMTAH [2794] (*an [unclean] reptile*). A city of Judah (Jos 15:54).

HUNGER [1061+4848, 1991, 2652, 4103, 5883, 7023, 8279, 8280, *3350, 3763, 4277*].

NIV+ HUNGRY

Man does not live by bread alone (Dt 8:3; Mt 4:4; Lk 4:3). Labor excites (Pr 16:26). Source of temptation (Ge 25:29-34; Ex 16:2-3; Heb 12:16). An occasion of the temptation of Jesus (Mt 4:3-4; Lk 4:2-3). Of an enemy, an opportunity for good works (Pr 25:21-22; Ro 12:20).

Experienced by Jesus (Mt 21:18; Mk 11:12). Endured, by Jesus during his temptation (Mt 4:2-4; Lk 4:2-4), by Paul for Christ's sake (1Co 4:11). Foretold as a judgment upon the Israelites (Isa 8:21; 9:20).

Figurative:

Of spiritual desire (Ps 107:9)—

Pr 2:3 and if you call out for insight and cry aloud for understanding, [4]and if you look for it as for silver and search for it as for hidden treasure, [5]then you will understand the fear of the LORD and find the knowledge of God.

Isa 55:1 "Come, all you who are thirsty, come to the waters; and you who have no money, come, buy and eat! Come, buy wine and milk without money and without cost. [2]Why spend money on what is not bread, and your labor on what does not satisfy? Listen, listen to me, and eat what is good, and your soul will delight in the richest of fare.

Am 8:11 "The days are coming," declares the Sovereign LORD, "when I will send a famine through the land—not a famine of food or a thirst for water, but a famine of hearing the words of the LORD. [12]Men will stagger from sea to sea and wander from north to east, searching for the word of the LORD, but they will not find it.

[13]"In that day "the lovely young women and strong young men will faint because of thirst.

Mt 5:6 Blessed are those who hunger and thirst for righteousness, for they will be filled. (+Lk 1:53)

Lk 6:21 Blessed are you who hunger now, for you will be satisfied. Blessed are you who weep now, for you will laugh. (+Jn 6:35)

1Pe 2:2 Like newborn babies, crave pure spiritual milk, so that by it you may grow up in your salvation,

See Appetite; Famine; Desire, Spiritual; Thirst.

HUNTING [1944, 2924, 7399, 7421, 7473, 8103].

NIV+ HUNT, HUNTED, HUNTER, HUNTERS, HUNTS

Authorized in the Mosaic law (Lev 17:13). By Nimrod (Ge 10:9). By Esau (Ge 27:3,5,30,33). By Ishmael (Ge 21:20). Of lion (Job 10:16). Fowling (1Sa 26:20; Ps 140:5; 141:9-10; Pr 1:17; Ecc 9:12; La 3:52; Am 3:5).

Figurative:

(Jer 16:16).

HUPHAM, HUPHAMITE [2573, 2574]. Son of Benjamin and his clan (Nu 26:39).

HUPPAH [2904] (*canopy,* hence *protection*). Priest in David's time (1Ch 24:13).

HUPPIM, HUPPITES [2907] (*coast people*). Descendants of Benjamin (Ge 46:21; 1Ch 7:12,15).

HUR [2581] (perhaps *child*).

NIV+ BEN-HUR

1. An Israelite who assisted in supporting Moses' hands during battle (Ex 17:10,12; 24:14).

2. A son of Caleb (Ex 31:2; 35:30; 38:22; 1Ch 2:19-20; 2Ch 1:5).

3. A king of Midian (Nu 31:8; Jos 13:21).

4. Called Ben-Hur, an officer of Solomon's commissary (1Ki 4:8).

5. Father of Caleb (1Ch 2:50; 4:4).

6. A son of Judah (1Ch 4:1).

7. A ruler (Ne 3:9).

HURAI [2584]. One of David's heroes (1Ch 11:32). Also called Hiddai (2Sa 23:30).

HURAM, HURAM-ABI [2586, 2587, 2671] (*brother of the exalted one*).

1. Benjamite (1Ch 8:5).

2. King of Tyre (2Ch 2:3, ftn, 11-12). Usually called Hiram (Hebrew *Huram,* a variant of *Hiram*). *See Hiram.*

3. Tyrian craftsman whose full name is Huram-Abi, is sent by King Hiram to execute the artistic work of the interior of the temple (1Ki 7:13-45; 2Ch 2:13; 4:11-16).

HURI [2585] (*linen weaver* ISBE). Father of Abihail (1Ch 5:14).

HURRIANS *See Horite(s), Horim.*

HUSBAND [408, 1249, 1251, 8276, *467, 476*].

NIV+ HUSBAND'S, HUSBANDS

Relation of, to wife—

Ge 2:23 The man said, "This is now bone of my bones and flesh of my flesh; she shall be called 'woman,' for she was taken out of man."

[24]For this reason a man will leave his father and mother and be united to his wife, and they will become one flesh. (+Mt 19:5-6; Mk 10:7; 1Co 7:3-5)

Eph 5:22 Wives, submit to your husbands as to the Lord. [23]For the husband is the head of the wife as Christ is the head of the church, his body, of which he is the Savior. [24]Now as the church submits to Christ, so also wives should submit to their husbands in everything.

[25]Husbands, love your wives, just as Christ loved the church and gave himself up for her [26]to make her holy, cleansing her by the washing with water through the word,

[27]and to present her to himself as a radiant church, without stain or wrinkle or any other blemish, but holy and blameless. [28]In this same way, husbands ought to love their wives as their own bodies. He who loves his wife loves himself. [29]After all, no one ever hated his own body, but he feeds and cares for it, just as Christ does the church— [30]for we are members of his body. [31]"For this reason a man will leave his father and mother and be united to his wife, and the two will become one flesh." [32]This is a profound mystery—but I am talking about Christ and the church. [33]However, each one of you also must love his wife as he loves himself, and the wife must respect her husband.

May give wife certificate of divorce (Dt 24:1-4).

Law relating to, in cases where wife's virtue is questioned (Nu 5:11-31)—

Dt 22:13 If a man takes a wife and, after lying with her, dislikes her [14]and slanders her and gives her a bad name, saying, "I married this woman, but when I approached her, I did not find proof of her virginity," [15]then the girl's father and mother shall bring proof that she was a virgin to the town elders at the gate. [16]The girl's father will say to the elders, "I gave my daughter in marriage to this man, but he dislikes her. [17]Now he has slandered her and said, 'I did not find your daughter to be a virgin.' But here is the proof of my daughter's virginity." Then her parents shall display the cloth before the elders of the town, [18]and the elders shall take the man and punish him. [19]They shall fine him a hundred shekels of silver and give them to the girl's father, because this man has given an Israelite virgin a bad name. She shall continue to be his wife; he must not divorce her as long as he lives.

[20]If, however, the charge is true and no proof of the girl's virginity can be found, [21]she shall be brought to the door of her father's house and there the men of her town shall stone her to death. She has done a disgraceful thing in Israel by being promiscuous while still in her father's house. You must purge the evil from among you.

Exemptions for—
Dt 24:5 If a man has recently married, he must not be sent to war or have any other duty laid on him. For one year he is to be free to stay at home and bring happiness to the wife he has married.

Chastity of—
Pr 5:15 Drink water from your own cistern, running water from your own well. [16]Should your springs overflow in the streets, your streams of water in the public squares? [17]Let them be yours alone, never to be shared with strangers. [18]May your fountain be blessed, and may you rejoice in the wife of your youth. [19]A loving doe, a graceful deer—may her breasts satisfy you always, may you ever be captivated by her love. (+Pr 5:20)

Mal 2:14 You ask, "Why?" It is because the LORD is acting as the witness between you and the wife of your youth, because you have broken faith with her, though she is your partner, the wife of your marriage covenant.

[15]Has not [the LORD] made them one? In flesh and spirit they are his. And why one? Because he was seeking godly offspring. So guard yourself in your spirit, and do not break faith with the wife of your youth.

[16]"I hate divorce," says the LORD God of Israel, "and I hate a man's covering himself with violence as well as with his garment," says the LORD Almighty.

So guard yourself in your spirit, and do not break faith.

Duties of—
Ecc 9:9 Enjoy life with your wife, whom you love, all the days of this meaningless life that God has given you under the sun—all your meaningless days. For this is your lot in life and in your toilsome labor under the sun.

Col 3:19 Husbands, love your wives and do not be harsh with them.

1Pe 3:7 Husbands, in the same way be considerate as you live with your wives, and treat them with respect as the weaker partner and as heirs with you of the gracious gift of life, so that nothing will hinder your prayers.

To provide for family (Ge 30:30)—
1Ti 5:8 If anyone does not provide for his relatives, and especially for his immediate family, he has denied the faith and is worse than an unbeliever.

Rights of—
1Co 7:3 The husband should fulfill his marital duty to his wife, and likewise the wife to her husband.

1Co 7:5 Do not deprive each other except by mutual consent and for a time, so that you may devote yourselves to prayer. Then come together again so that Satan will not tempt you because of your lack of self-control.

Sanctified in the wife—
1Co 7:14 For the unbelieving husband has been sanctified through his wife, and the unbelieving wife has been sanctified through her believing husband. Otherwise your children would be unclean, but as it is, they are holy.

1Co 7:16 How do you know, wife, whether you will save your husband? Or, how do you know, husband, whether you will save your wife?

Headship of—
1Co 11:3 Now I want you to realize that the head of every man is Christ, and the head of the woman is man, and the head of Christ is God.

Faithful:
Isaac (Ge 24:67), Joseph (Mt 1:19-20). Unreasonable and oppressive (Est 1:10-22).

Figurative:
(Isa 54:5-6; Jer 3:14; 31:32; Hos 2:19-20).
Family; Marriage.

HUSBANDMAN *See Agriculture; Farmer.*

HUSBANDRY *See Agriculture; Animals; Farmer.*

HUSHAH [2592] (perhaps *haste*). Son of Ezer (1Ch 4:4). Probably called Shuah (1Ch 4:11).

HUSHAI [2593]. An Arkite. A counselor of David who overthrew counsels of Ahithophel (2Sa 15:32,37; 16:16-18; 17:5-15; 1Ch 27:33).

HUSHAM [2595]. A Temanite (Ge 36:34-35; 1Ch 1:45-46).

HUSHATHITE [3144]. Family name of Sibbecai, one of David's heroes (2Sa 21:18; 1Ch 11:29; 20:4; 27:11).

HUSHIM [2594, 3123].
1. Son of Dan (Ge 46:23). Also called Shuham (Nu 26:42). *See Shuham, Shuhamite.*
2. Wife of Shaharaim (1Ch 8:8,11).

HUSHITES [3131]. Benjamites; descendants of Aher (1Ch 7:12).

HUSK The skin or heads of grain (Nu 6:4; 2Ki 4:42). *See Pods.*

HUZ Son of Nahor (Ge 22:21). *See Uz.*

HUZOTH *See Kiriath Huzoth.*

HYACINTH *See Colors, Figurative and Symbolic.*

HYBRIDIZING Forbidden (Lev 19:19).

HYENA [363].

NIV+ HYENAS

A scavenging wild dog that roams the desert (Isa 13:22; 34:14; Jer 50:39). *See Animals.*

HYGIENE (1Co 6:18; 9:25). *See Sanitation and Hygiene.*

HYKSOS A W Semitic people who ruled an Egyptian empire embracing Syria and Palestine; the core of their rule over Egypt was from 1648-1540.

HYMENAEUS [5628] (*of [pagan god] Hymen*). Apostate Christian excommunicated by Paul (1Ti 1:19-20; 2Ti 2:16-18).

HYMN [9335, 5630, 5631, 6010, 6011] *See Psalms; Song.*

HYPOCRISY [6623, 5347, 5694, 5695] (*pretender, pretentious*).

NIV+ HYPOCRITE, HYPOCRITES, HYPOCRITICAL

Described—

Job 31:33 if I have concealed my sin as men do, by hiding my guilt in my heart ³⁴because I so feared the crowd and so dreaded the contempt of the clans that I kept silent and would not go outside (+Ps 5:6)

Ps 5:9 Not a word from their mouth can be trusted; their heart is filled with destruction. Their throat is an open grave; with their tongue they speak deceit.

Ps 52:4 You love every harmful word, O you deceitful tongue!

Ps 78:34 Whenever God slew them, they would seek him; they eagerly turned to him again. ³⁵They remembered that God was their Rock, that God Most High was their Redeemer. ³⁶But then they would flatter him with their mouths, lying to him with their tongues; ³⁷their hearts were not loyal to him, they were not faithful to his covenant.

Isa 29:13 The Lord says: "These people come near to me with their mouth and honor me with their lips, but their hearts are far from me. Their worship of me is made up only of rules taught by men.

Isa 32:5 No longer will the fool be called noble nor the scoundrel be highly respected. ⁶For the fool speaks folly, his mind is busy with evil: He practices ungodliness and spreads error concerning the LORD; the hungry he leaves empty and from the thirsty he withholds water. (+Isa 48:1-2; 58:2-5)

Jer 12:2 You have planted them, and they have taken root; they grow and bear fruit. You are always on their lips but far from their hearts.

Jer 17:9 The heart is deceitful above all things and beyond cure. Who can understand it?

Eze 33:30 "As for you, son of man, your countrymen are talking together about you by the walls and at the doors of the houses, saying to each other, 'Come and hear the message that has come from the LORD.' ³¹My people come to you, as they usually do, and sit before you to listen to your words, but they do not put them into practice. With their mouths they express devotion, but their hearts are greedy for unjust gain. ³²Indeed, to them you are nothing more than one who sings love songs with a beautiful voice and plays an instrument well, for they hear your words but do not put them into practice.

Hos 6:4 "What can I do with you, Ephraim? What can I do

with you, Judah? Your love is like the morning mist, like the early dew that disappears.

Hos 10:1 Israel was a spreading vine; he brought forth fruit for himself. As his fruit increased, he built more altars; as his land prospered, he adorned his sacred stones.

Hos 10:4 They make many promises, take false oaths and make agreements; therefore lawsuits spring up like poisonous weeds in a plowed field.

Zec 7:5 "Ask all the people of the land and the priests, 'When you fasted and mourned in the fifth and seventh months for the past seventy years, was it really for me that you fasted? ⁶And when you were eating and drinking, were you not just feasting for yourselves? (+Mt 15:3-6)

Mt 15:7 You hypocrites! Isaiah was right when he prophesied about you: ⁸" 'These people honor me with their lips, but their hearts are far from me. ⁹They worship me in vain; their teachings are but rules taught by men.' " (+Mt 21:28-32; Mk 7:5-6)

Mk 7:7 They worship me in vain; their teachings are but rules taught by men.' ⁸You have let go of the commands of God and are holding on to the traditions of men." (+Mk 7:9-13; 9:50; 14:34-35; Lk 18:11-12)

Ro 9:6 It is not as though God's word had failed. For not all who are descended from Israel are Israel. ⁷Nor because they are his descendants are they all Abraham's children. On the contrary, "It is through Isaac that your offspring will be reckoned." (+1Co 5:8)

1Co 13:1 If I speak in the tongues of men and of angels, but have not love, I am only a resounding gong or a clanging cymbal.

2Co 4:2 Rather, we have renounced secret and shameful ways; we do not use deception, nor do we distort the word of God. On the contrary, by setting forth the truth plainly we commend ourselves to every man's conscience in the sight of God.

1Jn 1:6 If we claim to have fellowship with him yet walk in the darkness, we lie and do not live by the truth.

1Jn 1:10 If we claim we have not sinned, we make him out to be a liar and his word has no place in our lives.

1Jn 2:4 The man who says, "I know him," but does not do what he commands is a liar, and the truth is not in him.

1Jn 2:9 Anyone who claims to be in the light but hates his brother is still in the darkness.

1Jn 2:19 They went out from us, but they did not really belong to us. For if they had belonged to us, they would have remained with us; but their going showed that none of them belonged to us.

1Jn 4:20 If anyone says, "I love God," yet hates his brother, he is a liar. For anyone who does not love his brother, whom he has seen, cannot love God, whom he has not seen.

Rev 3:1 "To the angel of the church in Sardis write: These are the words of him who holds the seven spirits of God and the seven stars. I know your deeds; you have a reputation of being alive, but you are dead.

Abhorred by God—

Job 13:16 Indeed, this will turn out for my deliverance, for no godless man would dare come before him!

Ps 50:16 But to the wicked, God says: "What right have you to recite my laws or take my covenant on your lips? ¹⁷You hate my instruction and cast my words behind you.

Pr 15:8 The LORD detests the sacrifice of the wicked, but the prayer of the upright pleases him.

Pr 21:27 The sacrifice of the wicked is detestable—how much more so when brought with evil intent! (+Isa 1:9-12)

Isa 1:13 Stop bringing meaningless offerings! Your

incense is detestable to me. New Moons, Sabbaths and convocations—I cannot bear your evil assemblies. (+Isa 1:14)

Isa 1:15 When you spread out your hands in prayer, I will hide my eyes from you; even if you offer many prayers, I will not listen. Your hands are full of blood;

Isa 9:17 Therefore the Lord will take no pleasure in the young men, nor will he pity the fatherless and widows, for everyone is ungodly and wicked, every mouth speaks vileness. Yet for all this, his anger is not turned away, his hand is still upraised.

Isa 10:6 I send him against a godless nation, I dispatch him against a people who anger me, to seize loot and snatch plunder, and to trample them down like mud in the streets.

Isa 58:2 For day after day they seek me out; they seem eager to know my ways, as if they were a nation that does what is right and has not forsaken the commands of its God. They ask me for just decisions and seem eager for God to come near them. ³'Why have we fasted,' they say, 'and you have not seen it? Why have we humbled ourselves, and you have not noticed?' "Yet on the day of your fasting, you do as you please and exploit all your workers.

⁴Your fasting ends in quarreling and strife, and in striking each other with wicked fists. You cannot fast as you do today and expect your voice to be heard on high. ⁵Is this the kind of fast I have chosen, only a day for a man to humble himself? Is it only for bowing one's head like a reed and for lying on sackcloth and ashes? Is that what you call a fast, a day acceptable to the LORD?

Isa 61:8 "For I, the LORD, love justice; I hate robbery and iniquity. In my faithfulness I will reward them and make an everlasting covenant with them. (+Isa 65:2-4)

Isa 65:5 who say, 'Keep away; don't come near me, for I am too sacred for you!' Such people are smoke in my nostrils, a fire that keeps burning all day. (+Isa 66:3-5; Jer 5:2; 6:20; 7:4,8-10; Eze 5:11)

Eze 20:39 "'As for you, O house of Israel, this is what the Sovereign LORD says: Go and serve your idols, every one of you! But afterward you will surely listen to me and no longer profane my holy name with your gifts and idols. (+Hos 8:13; 9:4)

Hos 11:12 Ephraim has surrounded me with lies, the house of Israel with deceit. And Judah is unruly against God, even against the faithful Holy One.

Am 5:21 "I hate, I despise your religious feasts; I cannot stand your assemblies. (+Am 5:22)

Am 5:23 Away with the noise of your songs! I will not listen to the music of your harps. ²⁴But let justice roll on like a river, righteousness like a never-failing stream! (+Am 5:25-27; Zec 7:5-6)

Mal 1:6 "A son honors his father, and a servant his master. If I am a father, where is the honor due me? If I am a master, where is the respect due me?" says the LORD Almighty. "It is you, O priests, who show contempt for my name.

"But you ask, 'How have we shown contempt for your name?'

⁷"You place defiled food on my altar.

"But you ask, 'How have we defiled you?'

"By saying that the LORD's table is contemptible.

⁸When you bring blind animals for sacrifice, is that not wrong? When you sacrifice crippled or diseased animals, is that not wrong? Try offering them to your governor! Would he be pleased with you? Would he accept you?" says the LORD Almighty. (+Mal 1:9-12)

Mal 1:13 And you say, 'What a burden!' and you sniff at it contemptuously," says the LORD Almighty. "When you bring injured, crippled or diseased animals and offer them as sacrifices, should I accept them from your hands?" says the LORD. ¹⁴"Cursed is the cheat who has an acceptable male in his flock and vows to give it, but then sacrifices a blemished animal to the Lord. For I am a great king," says the LORD Almighty, "and my name is to be feared among the nations.

Mal 2:13 Another thing you do: You flood the LORD's altar with tears. You weep and wail because he no longer pays attention to your offerings or accepts them with pleasure from your hands.

Rebuked by Jesus—

Mt 3:7 But when he saw many of the Pharisees and Sadducees coming to where he was baptizing, he said to them: "You brood of vipers! Who warned you to flee from the coming wrath? ⁸Produce fruit in keeping with repentance. (+Mt 7:7-8)

Mt 9:13 But go and learn what this means: 'I desire mercy, not sacrifice.' For I have not come to call the righteous, but sinners." (+Mt 15:7-9)

Mt 16:3 and in the morning, 'Today it will be stormy, for the sky is red and overcast.' You know how to interpret the appearance of the sky, but you cannot interpret the signs of the times.

Mt 23:2 "The teachers of the law and the Pharisees sit in Moses' seat. ³So you must obey them and do everything they tell you. But do not do what they do, for they do not practice what they preach. ⁴They tie up heavy loads and put them on men's shoulders, but they themselves are not willing to lift a finger to move them.

⁵"Everything they do is done for men to see: They make their phylacteries wide and the tassels on their garments long; ⁶they love the place of honor at banquets and the most important seats in the synagogues; ⁷they love to be greeted in the marketplaces and to have men call them 'Rabbi.'

⁸"But you are not to be called 'Rabbi,' for you have only one Master and you are all brothers. ⁹And do not call anyone on earth 'father,' for you have one Father, and he is in heaven. ¹⁰Nor are you to be called 'teacher,' for you have one Teacher, the Christ. ¹¹The greatest among you will be your servant. ¹²For whoever exalts himself will be humbled, and whoever humbles himself will be exalted.

¹³"Woe to you, teachers of the law and Pharisees, you hypocrites! You shut the kingdom of heaven in men's faces. You yourselves do not enter, nor will you let those enter who are trying to.

Mt 23:15 "Woe to you, teachers of the law and Pharisees, you hypocrites! You travel over land and sea to win a single convert, and when he becomes one, you make him twice as much a son of hell as you are.

¹⁶"Woe to you, blind guides! You say, 'If anyone swears by the temple, it means nothing; but if anyone swears by the gold of the temple, he is bound by his oath.' ¹⁷You blind fools! Which is greater: the gold, or the temple that makes the gold sacred? ¹⁸You also say, 'If anyone swears by the altar, it means nothing; but if anyone swears by the gift on it, he is bound by his oath.' ¹⁹You blind men! Which is greater: the gift, or the altar that makes the gift sacred? ²⁰Therefore, he who swears by the altar swears by it and by everything on it. ²¹And he who swears by the temple swears by it and by the one who dwells in it. ²²And he who swears by heaven swears by God's throne and by the one who sits on it.

²³"Woe to you, teachers of the law and Pharisees, you hypocrites! You give a tenth of your spices—mint, dill and cummin. But you have neglected the more important matters of the law—justice, mercy and faithfulness. You should have practiced the latter, without neglecting the former. ²⁴You blind guides! You strain out a gnat but swallow a camel.

²⁵"Woe to you, teachers of the law and Pharisees, you hypocrites! You clean the outside of the cup and dish, but inside they are full of greed and self-indulgence. ²⁶Blind Pharisee! First clean the inside of the cup and dish, and then the outside also will be clean.

²⁷"Woe to you, teachers of the law and Pharisees, you hypocrites! You are like whitewashed tombs, which look beautiful on the outside but on the inside are full of dead men's bones and everything unclean. ²⁸In the same way, on the outside you appear to people as righteous but on the inside you are full of hypocrisy and wickedness.

²⁹"Woe to you, teachers of the law and Pharisees, you hypocrites! You build tombs for the prophets and decorate the graves of the righteous. ³⁰And you say, 'If we had lived in the days of our forefathers, we would not have taken part with them in shedding the blood of the prophets.' ³¹So you testify against yourselves that you are the descendants of those who murdered the prophets. ³²Fill up, then, the measure of the sin of your forefathers!

³³"You snakes! You brood of vipers! How will you escape being condemned to hell?

Lk 6:46 "Why do you call me, 'Lord, Lord,' and do not do what I say?

Lk 11:39 Then the Lord said to him, "Now then, you Pharisees clean the outside of the cup and dish, but inside you are full of greed and wickedness.

Lk 11:42 "Woe to you Pharisees, because you give God a tenth of your mint, rue and all other kinds of garden herbs, but you neglect justice and the love of God. You should have practiced the latter without leaving the former undone.

Lk 11:44 "Woe to you, because you are like unmarked graves, which men walk over without knowing it." (+Lk 12:54-56)

Lk 13:13 Then he put his hands on her, and immediately she straightened up and praised God.

¹⁴Indignant because Jesus had healed on the Sabbath, the synagogue ruler said to the people, "There are six days for work. So come and be healed on those days, not on the Sabbath."

¹⁵The Lord answered him, "You hypocrites! Doesn't each of you on the Sabbath untie his ox or donkey from the stall and lead it out to give it water? ¹⁶Then should not this woman, a daughter of Abraham, whom Satan has kept bound for eighteen long years, be set free on the Sabbath day from what bound her?"

¹⁷When he said this, all his opponents were humiliated, but the people were delighted with all the wonderful things he was doing.

Jn 6:26 Jesus answered, "I tell you the truth, you are looking for me, not because you saw miraculous signs but because you ate the loaves and had your fill.

Jn 6:70 Then Jesus replied, "Have I not chosen you, the Twelve? Yet one of you is a devil!"

Jn 7:19 Has not Moses given you the law? Yet not one of you keeps the law. Why are you trying to kill me?"

Jn 15:2 He cuts off every branch in me that bears no fruit, while every branch that does bear fruit he prunes so that it will be even more fruitful.

Jn 15:6 If anyone does not remain in me, he is like a branch that is thrown away and withers; such branches are picked up, thrown into the fire and burned.

Rev 2:9 I know your afflictions and your poverty—yet you are rich! I know the slander of those who say they are Jews and are not, but are a synagogue of Satan. (+Rev 3:9)

Exposed by Paul—

Ro 2:1 You, therefore, have no excuse, you who pass judgment on someone else, for at whatever point you judge the other, you are condemning yourself, because you who pass judgment do the same things.

Ro 2:3 So when you, a mere man, pass judgment on them and yet do the same things, do you think you will escape God's judgment?

Ro 2:17 Now you, if you call yourself a Jew; if you rely on the law and brag about your relationship to God; ¹⁸if you know his will and approve of what is superior because you are instructed by the law; ¹⁹if you are convinced that you are a guide for the blind, a light for those who are in the dark, ²⁰an instructor of the foolish, a teacher of infants, because you have in the law the embodiment of knowledge and truth— ²¹you, then, who teach others, do you not teach yourself? You who preach against stealing, do you steal? ²²You who say that people should not commit adultery, do you commit adultery? You who abhor idols, do you rob temples? ²³You who brag about the law, do you dishonor God by breaking the law? ²⁴As it is written: "God's name is blasphemed among the Gentiles because of you."

²⁵Circumcision has value if you observe the law, but if you break the law, you have become as though you had not been circumcised. ²⁶If those who are not circumcised keep the law's requirements, will they not be regarded as though they were circumcised? ²⁷The one who is not circumcised physically and yet obeys the law will condemn you who, even though you have the written code and circumcision, are a lawbreaker.

²⁸A man is not a Jew if he is only one outwardly, nor is circumcision merely outward and physical. ²⁹No, a man is a Jew if he is one inwardly; and circumcision is circumcision of the heart, by the Spirit, not by the written code. Such a man's praise is not from men, but from God.

2Co 5:12 We are not trying to commend ourselves to you again, but are giving you an opportunity to take pride in us, so that you can answer those who take pride in what is seen rather than in what is in the heart.

Gal 6:3 If anyone thinks he is something when he is nothing, he deceives himself.

Php 3:2 Watch out for those dogs, those men who do evil, those mutilators of the flesh.

Php 3:18 For, as I have often told you before and now say again even with tears, many live as enemies of the cross of Christ. ¹⁹Their destiny is destruction, their god is their stomach, and their glory is in their shame. Their mind is on earthly things.

1Ti 4:2 Such teachings come through hypocritical liars, whose consciences have been seared as with a hot iron.

2Ti 3:5 having a form of godliness but denying its power. Have nothing to do with them.

2Ti 3:13 while evil men and impostors will go from bad to worse, deceiving and being deceived.

Tit 1:16 They claim to know God, but by their actions they deny him. They are detestable, disobedient and unfit for doing anything good.

Betrays friends—

Ps 55:12 If an enemy were insulting me, I could endure it;

if a foe were raising himself against me, I could hide from him. ¹³But it is you, a man like myself, my companion, my close friend, ¹⁴with whom I once enjoyed sweet fellowship as we walked with the throng at the house of God.

Ps 55:20 My companion attacks his friends; he violates his covenant. (+Ps 55:21)

Ps 55:22 Cast your cares on the LORD and he will sustain you; he will never let the righteous fall. ²³But you, O God, will bring down the wicked into the pit of corruption; bloodthirsty and deceitful men will not live out half their days. But as for me, I trust in you.

Pr 11:9 With his mouth the godless destroys his neighbor, but through knowledge the righteous escape.

Pr 25:19 Like a bad tooth or a lame foot is reliance on the unfaithful in times of trouble.

Ob 7 All your allies will force you to the border; your friends will deceive and overpower you; those who eat your bread will set a trap for you, but you will not detect it.

Zec 13:6 If someone asks him, 'What are these wounds on your body?' he will answer, 'The wounds I was given at the house of my friends.'

Hypocrisy of prostitutes—

Pr 7:10 Then out came a woman to meet him, dressed like a prostitute and with crafty intent. ¹¹(She is loud and defiant, her feet never stay at home; ¹²now in the street, now in the squares, at every corner she lurks.) ¹³She took hold of him and kissed him and with a brazen face she said:

¹⁴"I have fellowship offerings at home; today I fulfilled my vows. ¹⁵So I came out to meet you; I looked for you and have found you! ¹⁶I have covered my bed with colored linens from Egypt. ¹⁷I have perfumed my bed with myrrh, aloes and cinnamon. ¹⁸Come, let's drink deep of love till morning; let's enjoy ourselves with love! ¹⁹My husband is not at home; he has gone on a long journey. ²⁰He took his purse filled with money and will not be home till full moon." ²¹With persuasive words she led him astray; she seduced him with her smooth talk.

Hypocrisy of false teachers—

Mic 3:11 Her leaders judge for a bribe, her priests teach for a price, and her prophets tell fortunes for money. Yet they lean upon the LORD and say, "Is not the LORD among us? No disaster will come upon us." (+Ro 16:17)

Ro 16:18 For such people are not serving our Lord Christ, but their own appetites. By smooth talk and flattery they deceive the minds of naive people.

2Pe 2:1 But there were also false prophets among the people, just as there will be false teachers among you. They will secretly introduce destructive heresies, even denying the sovereign Lord who bought them—bringing swift destruction on themselves. ²Many will follow their shameful ways and will bring the way of truth into disrepute. ³In their greed these teachers will exploit you with stories they have made up. Their condemnation has long been hanging over them, and their destruction has not been sleeping.

2Pe 2:17 These men are springs without water and mists driven by a storm. Blackest darkness is reserved for them.

2Pe 2:19 They promise them freedom, while they themselves are slaves of depravity—for a man is a slave to whatever has mastered him.

Hypocrisy of dishonest buyers—

Pr 20:14 "It's no good, it's no good!" says the buyer; then off he goes and boasts about his purchase.

Warning to—

Job 15:31 Let him not deceive himself by trusting what is worthless, for he will get nothing in return.

Job 15:33 He will be like a vine stripped of its unripe grapes, like an olive tree shedding its blossoms. ³⁴For the company of the godless will be barren, and fire will consume the tents of those who love bribes.

Job 17:8 Upright men are appalled at this; the innocent are aroused against the ungodly.

Job 20:4 "Surely you know how it has been from of old, ever since man was placed on the earth, ⁵that the mirth of the wicked is brief, the joy of the godless lasts but a moment.

Job 27:8 For what hope has the godless when he is cut off, when God takes away his life? ⁹Does God listen to his cry when distress comes upon him? ¹⁰Will he find delight in the Almighty? Will he call upon God at all times?

Job 34:30 to keep a godless man from ruling, from laying snares for the people.

Warning against—

Pr 23:6 Do not eat the food of a stingy man, do not crave his delicacies; ⁷for he is the kind of man who is always thinking about the cost. "Eat and drink," he says to you, but his heart is not with you. ⁸You will vomit up the little you have eaten and will have wasted your compliments.

Pr 26:18 Like a madman shooting firebrands or deadly arrows ¹⁹is a man who deceives his neighbor and says, "I was only joking!"

Pr 26:23 Like a coating of glaze over earthenware are fervent lips with an evil heart.

²⁴A malicious man disguises himself with his lips, but in his heart he harbors deceit. ²⁵Though his speech is charming, do not believe him, for seven abominations fill his heart. ²⁶His malice may be concealed by deception, but his wickedness will be exposed in the assembly.

Jer 9:8 Their tongue is a deadly arrow; it speaks with deceit. With his mouth each speaks cordially to his neighbor, but in his heart he sets a trap for him.

Mic 7:5 Do not trust a neighbor; put no confidence in a friend. Even with her who lies in your embrace be careful of your words. (+Mt 6:1-2,5,16,24; 7:5,15,21-23; 16:6; 23:14; Mk 8:15)

Mk 12:38 As he taught, Jesus said, "Watch out for the teachers of the law. They like to walk around in flowing robes and be greeted in the marketplaces, ³⁹and have the most important seats in the synagogues and the places of honor at banquets. ⁴⁰They devour widows' houses and for a show make lengthy prayers. Such men will be punished most severely."

Lk 12:1 Meanwhile, when a crowd of many thousands had gathered, so that they were trampling on one another, Jesus began to speak first to his disciples, saying: "Be on your guard against the yeast of the Pharisees, which is hypocrisy. ²There is nothing concealed that will not be disclosed, or hidden that will not be made known. (+Lk 13:26-27)

Lk 16:13 "No servant can serve two masters. Either he will hate the one and love the other, or he will be devoted to the one and despise the other. You cannot serve both God and Money."

Lk 16:15 He said to them, "You are the ones who justify yourselves in the eyes of men, but God knows your hearts. What is highly valued among men is detestable in God's sight.

Lk 20:46 "Beware of the teachers of the law. They like to walk around in flowing robes and love to be greeted in the marketplaces and have the most important seats in the synagogues and the places of honor at banquets. [47]They devour widows' houses and for a show make lengthy prayers. Such men will be punished most severely."

Jas 1:8 he is a double-minded man, unstable in all he does.

Jas 1:22 Do not merely listen to the word, and so deceive yourselves. Do what it says. [23]Anyone who listens to the word but does not do what it says is like a man who looks at his face in a mirror [24]and, after looking at himself, goes away and immediately forgets what he looks like.

Jas 1:26 If anyone considers himself religious and yet does not keep a tight rein on his tongue, he deceives himself and his religion is worthless.

Jas 3:17 But the wisdom that comes from heaven is first of all pure; then peace-loving, considerate, submissive, full of mercy and good fruit, impartial and sincere. (+Jas 4:8)

1Pe 2:1 Therefore, rid yourselves of all malice and all deceit, hypocrisy, envy, and slander of every kind.

1Pe 2:16 Live as free men, but do not use your freedom as a cover-up for evil; live as servants of God.

Jude 12 These men are blemishes at your love feasts, eating with you without the slightest qualm—shepherds who feed only themselves. They are clouds without rain, blown along by the wind; autumn trees, without fruit and uprooted—twice dead. [13]They are wild waves of the sea, foaming up their shame; wandering stars, for whom blackest darkness has been reserved forever.

Punishment for—

Job 8:13 Such is the destiny of all who forget God; so perishes the hope of the godless. [14]What he trusts in is fragile; what he relies on is a spider's web. [15]He leans on his web, but it gives way; he clings to it, but it does not hold.

Job 36:13 "The godless in heart harbor resentment; even when he fetters them, they do not cry for help. [14]They die in their youth, among male prostitutes of the shrines. (+Ps 55:23)

Ps 101:7 No one who practices deceit will dwell in my house; no one who speaks falsely will stand in my presence.

Isa 29:15 Woe to those who go to great depths to hide their plans from the LORD, who do their work in darkness and think, "Who sees us? Who will know?" [16]You turn things upside down, as if the potter were thought to be like the clay! Shall what is formed say to him who formed it, "He did not make me"? Can the pot say of the potter, "He knows nothing"?

Isa 33:14 The sinners in Zion are terrified; trembling grips the godless: "Who of us can dwell with the consuming fire? Who of us can dwell with everlasting burning?"

Jer 42:20 that you made a fatal mistake when you sent me to the LORD your God and said, 'Pray to the LORD our God for us; tell us everything he says and we will do it.' (+Jer 42:21-22; Eze 5:11; 14:3-4)

Eze 14:7 "'When any Israelite or any alien living in Israel separates himself from me and sets up idols in his heart and puts a wicked stumbling block before his face and then goes to a prophet to inquire of me, I the LORD will answer him myself. [8]I will set my face against that man and make him an example and a byword. I will cut him off from my people. Then you will know that I am the LORD. (+Hos 8:13; 9:4)

Mt 22:12 'Friend,' he asked, 'how did you get in here without wedding clothes?' The man was speechless.

[13]"Then the king told the attendants, 'Tie him hand and foot, and throw him outside, into the darkness, where there will be weeping and gnashing of teeth.'

Mt 24:50 The master of that servant will come on a day when he does not expect him and at an hour he is not aware of. [51]He will cut him to pieces and assign him a place with the hypocrites, where there will be weeping and gnashing of teeth. (+Mt 25:41-45)

Ro 1:18 The wrath of God is being revealed from heaven against all the godlessness and wickedness of men who suppress the truth by their wickedness,

See Deceit; Deception.

Instances of:

Jacob, in impersonating Esau and deceiving his father (Ge 27). Jacob's sons, in deception of their father concerning Joseph (Ge 37:29-35). Joseph's deception of his brothers (Ge 42-44). Pharaoh (Ex 8:15,28-29,32; 9:27-35; 10:8-29). Balaam (Jude 11, w Nu 22-24). Delilah, the wife of Samson (Jdg 16). Jael (Jdg 4:8-21). Ehud (Jdg 3:15-25). the Assyrian field commander (2Ki 18:17-37). Ahaz (Isa 7:12, w 17-25). Johanan (Jer 42:1-12,20,22). Ishmael (Jer 41:6-7). The false prophets (Eze 13:1-23). Herod (Mt 2:8). Judas (Mt 26:25,48; Jn 12:5-6). Pilate (Mt 27:24).

Pharisees (Mt 15:1-9)—

Mt 22:18 But Jesus, knowing their evil intent, said, "You hypocrites, why are you trying to trap me? (+Mk 12:13-14; Jn 8:4-9; 9:24; 19:15)

The ruler (Lk 13:14-17). Spies sent to entrap Jesus (Lk 20:21). Priests and Levites (Lk 10:31-32). Chief priests (Jn 18:28). Ananias and Sapphira (Ac 5:1-10). Simon (Ac 8:18-23). Peter and other Christians at Antioch (Gal 2:11-14). Judaizing Christians in Galatia (Gal 6:13). False teachers at Ephesus (Rev 2:2).

See Conspiracy; Treachery.

HYSSOP [257, 5727]. A plant indigenous to western Asia and northern Africa (1Ki 4:33). The Israelites used, in sprinkling the blood of the Passover lamb upon the frames of their doors (Ex 12:22), in sprinkling blood in purifications (Lev 14:4,6,51-52; Heb 9:19). Used in the sacrifices of separation (Nu 19:6). Used in giving Jesus vinegar on the cross (Jn 19:29).

Figurative:

Of spiritual cleansing (Ps 51:7).

I

I AM WHO I AM A name of God (Ex 3:14; Rev 1:4,11,17). *See God, Names of, Yahweh; Yahweh.*

IBEX [1913]. Probably a species of antelope (Dt 14:5).

IBHAR [3295] (*he chooses*). Son of David (2Sa 5:15; 1Ch 3:6; 14:5).

IBLEAM [3300]. A town given to the tribe of Manasseh (Jos 17:11). Ahaziah slain there (2Ki 9:27). Generally identified with Bileam (1Ch 6:70).

IBNEIAH, IBNIJAH [3307, 3308] (*Yahweh built*). A Benjamite (1Ch 9:8).

IBRI [6304] (*Hebrew*). A Levite (1Ch 24:27).

IBSAM [3311] (*fragrance*). Son of Tola (1Ch 7:2).

IBZAN [83] (*swift*). The tenth judge of Israel (Jdg 12:8-10), had thirty sons and thirty daughters.

ICE [7938, 7943].
NIV+ ICY
(Job 6:16; 37:10; 38:29; Ps 147:17; Eze 1:22).

ICHABOD [376] (*where is the glory?*).
NIV+ ICHABOD'S
Son of Phinehas, Eli's son (1Sa 4:18-22).

ICONIUM [*2658*]. A city of Asia Minor. Paul preaches in (Ac 13:51; 14:21-22; 16:2), is persecuted by the people of (Ac 14:1-6; 2Ti 3:11).

ICONOCLASM Idols to be destroyed (Ex 23:24; 34:13; Nu 33:52; Dt 7:5,25-26; 12:1-4; Jdg 2:2; Jer 50:2). Destroyed by, Jacob (Ge 35:2-4), Moses (Ex 32:19-20), Gideon (Jdg 6:28-32), David (2Sa 5:21; 1Ch 14:12), Jehu (2Ki 10:26-28), Jehoiada (2Ki 11:18), Hezekiah (2Ki 18:3-6), Josiah (2Ki 23:4-20), Asa (2Ch 14:3-5; 15:8-16), Jehoshaphat (2Ch 17:6; 19:3), Jews (2Ch 30:14), Manasseh (2Ch 33:15).
See Idolatry.

IDALAH [3339]. A town of Zebulun (Jos 19:15).

IDBASH [3340] (*honey*). A descendant of Judah (1Ch 4:3).

IDDO [120, 3346, 3587, 6333, 6341, 6342, 10529] (probably *Yahweh has adorned*).
NIV+ IDDO'S
1. Father of Ahinadab (1Ki 4:14).
2. A descendant of Gershom (1Ch 6:21).
3. A son of Zechariah (1Ch 27:21).
4. A prophet (2Ch 9:29; 12:15; 13:22).
5. Ancestor of Zechariah (Ezr 5:1; 6:14; Zec 1:1,7).
6. A priest (Ne 12:4,16).
7. The chief of the Jews established at Casiphia (Ezr 8:17).

IDENTIFICATION
With Jesus, price of—
Mt 4:19 "Come, follow me," Jesus said, "and I will make you fishers of men." (+Mt 8:22; 9:9)

Mt 16:24 Then Jesus said to his disciples, "If anyone would come after me, he must deny himself and take up his cross and follow me.

Mt 19:21 Jesus answered, "If you want to be perfect, go, sell your possessions and give to the poor, and you will have treasure in heaven. Then come, follow me." (+Mk 2:14; 8:34; 10:21; Lk 5:27; 9:23; 18:22)

Jn 15:14 You are my friends if you do what I command.

Jn 15:18 "If the world hates you, keep in mind that it hated me first. ¹⁹If you belonged to the world, it would love you as its own. As it is, you do not belong to the world, but I have chosen you out of the world. That is why the world hates you.

Jn 16:2 They will put you out of the synagogue; in fact, a time is coming when anyone who kills you will think he is offering a service to God.

Indication of—
Jn 10:27 My sheep listen to my voice; I know them, and they follow me.

Jn 12:26 Whoever serves me must follow me; and where I am, my servant also will be. My Father will honor the one who serves me.

Ac 11:26 and when he found him, he brought him to Antioch. So for a whole year Barnabas and Saul met with the church and taught great numbers of people. The disciples were called Christians first at Antioch.
See Discipleship.

IDLENESS [966, 5663, 6791, 8199, 9170, *734, 863, 864, 865, 1632*].
NIV+ IDLE, IDLERS
Comparisons regarding—
Pr 15:19 The way of the sluggard is blocked with thorns, but the path of the upright is a highway.

Pr 18:9 One who is slack in his work is brother to one who destroys. (+Pr 22:13)

Pr 26:13 The sluggard says, "There is a lion in the road, a fierce lion roaming the streets!"
¹⁴As a door turns on its hinges, so a sluggard turns on his bed.
¹⁵The sluggard buries his hand in the dish; he is too lazy to bring it back to his mouth.
¹⁶The sluggard is wiser in his own eyes than seven men who answer discreetly.

Ecc 4:5 The fool folds his hands and ruins himself.

Poverty from—
Pr 6:6 Go to the ant, you sluggard; consider its ways and be wise! (+Pr 6:7-8)

Pr 6:9 How long will you lie there, you sluggard? When will you get up from your sleep? ¹⁰A little sleep, a little slumber, a little folding of the hands to rest— ¹¹and poverty will come on you like a bandit and scarcity like an armed man.

Pr 10:4 Lazy hands make a man poor, but diligent hands bring wealth.
⁵He who gathers crops in summer is a wise son, but he who sleeps during harvest is a disgraceful son.

Pr 12:9 Better to be a nobody and yet have a servant than pretend to be somebody and have no food.

Pr 12:24 Diligent hands will rule, but laziness ends in slave labor.

Pr 12:27 The lazy man does not roast his game, but the diligent man prizes his possessions.

Pr 13:4 The sluggard craves and gets nothing, but the desires of the diligent are fully satisfied.

Pr 14:23 All hard work brings a profit, but mere talk leads only to poverty.

Pr 19:15 Laziness brings on deep sleep, and the shiftless man goes hungry.

Pr 20:4 A sluggard does not plow in season; so at harvest time he looks but finds nothing.

Pr 20:13 Do not love sleep or you will grow poor; stay awake and you will have food to spare.

Pr 23:21 for drunkards and gluttons become poor, and drowsiness clothes them in rags.

Pr 24:30 I went past the field of the sluggard, past the vineyard of the man who lacks judgment; [31]thorns had come up everywhere, the ground was covered with weeds, and the stone wall was in ruins. (+Pr 24:32)

Pr 24:33 A little sleep, a little slumber, a little folding of the hands to rest— [34]and poverty will come on you like a bandit and scarcity like an armed man.

Ecc 10:18 If a man is lazy, the rafters sag; if his hands are idle, the house leaks.

Denounced—

Pr 21:25 The sluggard's craving will be the death of him, because his hands refuse to work. [26]All day long he craves for more, but the righteous give without sparing.

Isa 56:10 Israel's watchmen are blind, they all lack knowledge; they are all mute dogs, they cannot bark; they lie around and dream, they love to sleep. (+Lk 19:20-24)

2Th 3:10 For even when we were with you, we gave you this rule: "If a man will not work, he shall not eat."

[11]We hear that some among you are idle. They are not busy; they are busybodies.

1Ti 5:13 Besides, they get into the habit of being idle and going about from house to house. And not only do they become idlers, but also gossips and busybodies, saying things they ought not to.

A sin of Sodom—

Eze 16:49 "'Now this was the sin of your sister Sodom: She and her daughters were arrogant, overfed and unconcerned; they did not help the poor and needy.

Other instances of—

Mt 20:6 About the eleventh hour he went out and found still others standing around. He asked them, 'Why have you been standing here all day long doing nothing?'

[7]"'Because no one has hired us,' they answered.

"He said to them, 'You also go and work in my vineyard.'

Ac 17:21 (All the Athenians and the foreigners who lived there spent their time doing nothing but talking about and listening to the latest ideas.)

See Laziness; Slothfulness; Industry.

IDOL [224, 1425, 5011, 5381, 6166, 6770, 7181, 8736, 9572, *1628, 1631*] (*image*).

NIV+ CALF-IDOL, CALF-IDOLS, IDOL'S, IDOLATER, IDOLATERS, IDOLATRIES, IDOLATROUS, IDOLATRY, IDOLS

Manufacture of (Ex 20:4; 32:4,20; Dt 4:23; Isa 40:19-20; 44:9-12,17; Hab 2:18; Ac 19:24-25). Manufacture of forbidden (Ex 20:4; 34:17). Made of gold (Ex 32:3-4; Ps 115:4-7; 135:15-17; Isa 2:20; 30:22; 31:7; Hos 8:4), silver (Isa 2:20; 30:22; 31:7; Hos 8:4), wood and stone (Lev 26:1; Dt 4:28; 2Ki 19:18; Isa 37:19; 41:6; 44:13-19; Eze 20:32). Coverings of (Isa 30:22).

Prayer to, unanswered (1Ki 18:25-29). Falls down before the ark of Yahweh (1Sa 5:1-5). Used by Michal to save the life of David (1Sa 19:13-17). Derided (Ps 115:4-8; 135:15-18; Isa 44:9-17). To be abandoned (Isa 2:20). To

be destroyed (Dt 12:3). Things offered to, not to be eaten (Ex 34:15). Paul's instructions concerning eating things offered to (1Co 8; 10:25-33).

See Iconoclasm; Idolatry.

IDOLATRY [496, 1658, 2393, 3913, 4024, 9572, *1629, 1630*] (*image*).

NIV+ See IDOL

Wicked Practices of:

Human sacrifices (Lev 18:21; 20:2-5; Dt 12:31; 18:10; 2Ki 3:26-27; 16:3; 17:17-18; 21:6; 23:10; 2Ch 28:3; 33:6; Ps 106:37-38; Isa 57:5; Jer 7:31; 19:4-7; 32:35; Eze 16:20-21; 20:26,31; 23:37,39; Mic 6:7), practices of, relating to the dead (Dt 14:1), licentiousness of (Ex 32:6,25; Nu 25:1-3; 1Ki 14:24; 15:12; 2Ki 17:30; 23:7; Eze 16:17; 23:1-44; Hos 4:12-14; Am 2:8; Mic 1:7; Ro 1:24,26-27; 1Co 10:7-8; 1Pe 4:3-4; Rev 2:14,20-22; 9:20-21; 14:8; 17:1-6).

Other Customs of:

Offered burnt offerings (Ex 32:6; 1Ki 18:26; Ac 14:13), libations (Isa 57:6; 65:11; Jer 7:18; 19:13; 32:29; 44:17, 19,25; Eze 20:28), of wine (Dt 32:38), of blood (Ps 16:4; Zec 9:7), meat offerings (Isa 57:6; Jer 7:18; 44:17; Eze 16:19), peace offerings (Ex 32:6).

Incense burned on altars (1Ki 12:33; 2Ch 30:14; 34:25; Isa 65:3; Jer 1:16; 11:12,17; 44:3; 48:35; Eze 16:18; 23:41; Hos 11:2). Prayers to idols (Jdg 10:14; Isa 44:17; 45:20; 46:7; Jnh 1:5). Praise (Jdg 16:24; Da 5:4).

Singing and dancing (Ex 32:18-19). Music (Da 3:5-7). Cutting the flesh (1Ki 18:28; Jer 41:5). Kissing (1Ki 19:18; Hos 13:2; Job 31:27). Bowing (1Ki 19:18; 2Ki 5:18). Tithes and gifts (2Ki 23:11; Da 11:38; Am 4:4-5).

Annual Feasts:

(1Ki 12:32; Eze 18:6,11-12,15; 22:9; Da 3:2-3).

Objects of:

Sun, moon, and stars (Dt 4:19; 2Ki 17:16; 21:3,5; 2Ch 33:3,5; Job 31:26-28; Jer 7:17-20; 8:2; Eze 8:15-16; Zep 1:4-5; Ac 7:42). Images of angels (Col 2:18), animals (Ro 1:23). Gods of Egypt (Ex 12:12). Golden calf (Ex 32:4). Bronze serpent (2Ki 18:4). Net and dragnet (Hab 1:16). Pictures (Nu 33:52; Isa 2:16). Pictures on walls (Eze 8:10). Earrings (Ge 35:4).

See Artemis; Shrine.

Folly of:

Dt 4:28 There you will worship man-made gods of wood and stone, which cannot see or hear or eat or smell. (+Dt 32:37-38; Jdg 6:31; 10:14; 1Sa 5:3-4; 12:21; 1Ki 18:25-26)

1Ki 18:27 At noon Elijah began to taunt them. "Shout louder!" he said. "Surely he is a god! Perhaps he is deep in thought, or busy, or traveling. Maybe he is sleeping and must be awakened." (+1Ki 18:28-29; 2Ki 19:18)

2Ch 25:15 The anger of the Lord burned against Amaziah, and he sent a prophet to him, who said, "Why do you consult this people's gods, which could not save their own people from your hand?" (+Ps 106:19-20)

Ps 115:4 But their idols are silver and gold, made by the hands of men. [5]They have mouths, but cannot speak, eyes, but they cannot see;

Ps 115:8 Those who make them will be like them, and so will all who trust in them. (+Ps 135:15-18; Isa 37:19; 44:9-18)

Isa 44:19 No one stops to think, no one has the knowledge or understanding to say, "Half of it I used for fuel; I even baked bread over its coals, I roasted meat and I ate. Shall I make a detestable thing from what is left? Shall I bow down to a block of wood?" (+Isa 44:20)

Isa 45:20 "Gather together and come; assemble, you fugitives from the nations. Ignorant are those who carry about idols of wood, who pray to gods that cannot save.

Isa 46:1 Bel bows down, Nebo stoops low; their idols are borne by beasts of burden. The images that are carried about are burdensome, a burden for the weary. ²They stoop and bow down together; unable to rescue the burden, they themselves go off into captivity.

Isa 46:6 Some pour out gold from their bags and weigh out silver on the scales; they hire a goldsmith to make it into a god, and they bow down and worship it. ⁷They lift it to their shoulders and carry it; they set it up in its place, and there it stands. From that spot it cannot move. Though one cries out to it, it does not answer; it cannot save him from his troubles.

Jer 2:28 Where then are the gods you made for yourselves? Let them come if they can save you when you are in trouble! For you have as many gods as you have towns, O Judah.

Jer 11:12 The towns of Judah and the people of Jerusalem will go and cry out to the gods to whom they burn incense, but they will not help them at all when disaster strikes.

Jer 16:19 O LORD, my strength and my fortress, my refuge in time of distress, to you the nations will come from the ends of the earth and say, "Our fathers possessed nothing but false gods, worthless idols that did them no good. ²⁰Do men make their own gods? Yes, but they are not gods!" (+Jer 48:13; 51:17)

Hos 8:5 Throw out your calf-idol, O Samaria! My anger burns against them. How long will they be incapable of purity? ⁶They are from Israel! This calf—a craftsman has made it; it is not God. It will be broken in pieces, that calf of Samaria. (+Zec 10:2; Ac 14:13)

Ac 14:15 "Men, why are you doing this? We too are only men, human like you. We are bringing you good news, telling you to turn from these worthless things to the living God, who made heaven and earth and sea and everything in them.

Ac 17:22 Paul then stood up in the meeting of the Areopagus and said: "Men of Athens! I see that in every way you are very religious. ²³For as I walked around and looked carefully at your objects of worship, I even found an altar with this inscription: TO AN UNKNOWN GOD. Now what you worship as something unknown I am going to proclaim to you.

Ac 17:29 "Therefore since we are God's offspring, we should not think that the divine being is like gold or silver or stone—an image made by man's design and skill.

Ro 1:22 Although they claimed to be wise, they became fools ²³and exchanged the glory of the immortal God for images made to look like mortal man and birds and animals and reptiles.

1Co 8:4 So then, about eating food sacrificed to idols: We know that an idol is nothing at all in the world and that there is no God but one. (+1Co 10:5)

1Co 12:2 You know that when you were pagans, somehow or other you were influenced and led astray to mute idols.

Gal 4:8 Formerly, when you did not know God, you were slaves to those who by nature are not gods.

Rev 9:20 The rest of mankind that were not killed by these plagues still did not repent of the work of their hands; they did not stop worshiping demons, and idols of gold, silver, bronze, stone and wood—idols that cannot see or hear or walk.

Folly of, illustrated by contrast of idols with the true God (Ps 96:5)—

Isa 40:12 Who has measured the waters in the hollow of his hand, or with the breadth of his hand marked off the heavens? Who has held the dust of the earth in a basket, or weighed the mountains on the scales and the hills in a balance? ¹³Who has understood the mind of the LORD, or instructed him as his counselor? ¹⁴Whom did the LORD consult to enlighten him, and who taught him the right way? Who was it that taught him knowledge or showed him the path of understanding?

¹⁵Surely the nations are like a drop in a bucket; they are regarded as dust on the scales; he weighs the islands as though they were fine dust. ¹⁶Lebanon is not sufficient for altar fires, nor its animals enough for burnt offerings. ¹⁷Before him all the nations are as nothing; they are regarded by him as worthless and less than nothing.

¹⁸To whom, then, will you compare God? What image will you compare him to? ¹⁹As for an idol, a craftsman casts it, and a goldsmith overlays it with gold and fashions silver chains for it. ²⁰A man too poor to present such an offering selects wood that will not rot. He looks for a skilled craftsman to set up an idol that will not topple.

²¹Do you not know? Have you not heard? Has it not been told you from the beginning? Have you not understood since the earth was founded? ²²He sits enthroned above the circle of the earth, and its people are like grasshoppers. He stretches out the heavens like a canopy, and spreads them out like a tent to live in. ²³He brings princes to naught and reduces the rulers of this world to nothing. ²⁴No sooner are they planted, no sooner are they sown, no sooner do they take root in the ground, than he blows on them and they wither, and a whirlwind sweeps them away like chaff.

²⁵"To whom will you compare me? Or who is my equal?" says the Holy One. ²⁶Lift your eyes and look to the heavens: Who created all these? He who brings out the starry host one by one, and calls them each by name. Because of his great power and mighty strength, not one of them is missing.

Isa 41:23 tell us what the future holds, so we may know that you are gods. Do something, whether good or bad, so that we will be dismayed and filled with fear. ²⁴But you are less than nothing and your works are utterly worthless; he who chooses you is detestable. (+Isa 41:24-29)

Jer 10:5 Like a scarecrow in a melon patch, their idols cannot speak; they must be carried because they cannot walk. Do not fear them; they can do no harm nor can they do any good." (+Jer 14:22; Da 5:23; Hab 2:18-20)

Folly of, exemplified in the ruin of Israel—

2Ch 28:22 In his time of trouble King Ahaz became even more unfaithful to the LORD. ²³He offered sacrifices to the gods of Damascus, who had defeated him; for he thought, "Since the gods of the kings of Aram have helped them, I will sacrifice to them so they will help me." But they were his downfall and the downfall of all Israel.

Denounced:

Dt 12:31 You must not worship the LORD your God in their way, because in worshiping their gods, they do all kinds of detestable things the LORD hates. They even burn their sons and daughters in the fire as sacrifices to their gods.

Dt 27:15 "Cursed is the man who carves an image or casts an idol—a thing detestable to the LORD, the work of the craftsman's hands—and sets it up in secret." Then all the people shall say, "Amen!"

Job 31:26 if I have regarded the sun in its radiance or the moon moving in splendor, [27]so that my heart was secretly enticed and my hand offered them a kiss of homage, [28]then these also would be sins to be judged, for I would have been unfaithful to God on high.

Ps 44:20 If we had forgotten the name of our God or spread out our hands to a foreign god, [21]would not God have discovered it, since he knows the secrets of the heart?

Ps 97:7 All who worship images are put to shame, those who boast in idols—worship him, all you gods!

Isa 42:17 But those who trust in idols, who say to images, 'You are our gods,' will be turned back in utter shame. (+Isa 45:16; Jer 3:1-11; 32:34-35; Eze 16:16-63; 43:7-9; Hos 1:2; 2:2-5; 4:12-19; 5:1-3; 9:10; 13:2-3)

Jnh 2:8 "Those who cling to worthless idols forfeit the grace that could be theirs. (+Am 4:4-5)

Hab 1:16 Therefore he sacrifices to his net and burns incense to his dragnet, for by his net he lives in luxury and enjoys the choicest food.

Ac 17:16 While Paul was waiting for them in Athens, he was greatly distressed to see that the city was full of idols. (+Ac 17:17-29)

Ro 1:25 They exchanged the truth of God for a lie, and worshiped and served created things rather than the Creator—who is forever praised. Amen.

1Co 6:9 Do you not know that the wicked will not inherit the kingdom of God? Do not be deceived: Neither the sexually immoral nor idolaters nor adulterers nor male prostitutes nor homosexual offenders [10]nor thieves nor the greedy nor drunkards nor slanderers nor swindlers will inherit the kingdom of God.

Forbidden:

Ge 35:2 So Jacob said to his household and to all who were with him, "Get rid of the foreign gods you have with you, and purify yourselves and change your clothes.

Ex 20:3 "You shall have no other gods before me. [4]"You shall not make for yourself an idol in the form of anything in heaven above or on the earth beneath or in the waters below. [5]You shall not bow down to them or worship them; for I, the LORD your God, am a jealous God, punishing the children for the sin of the fathers to the third and fourth generation of those who hate me, [6]but showing love to a thousand [generations] of those who love me and keep my commandments.

Ex 20:23 Do not make any gods to be alongside me; do not make for yourselves gods of silver or gods of gold.

Ex 23:13 "Be careful to do everything I have said to you. Do not invoke the names of other gods; do not let them be heard on your lips. (+Ex 23:24,32-33; 34:14,17)

Lev 19:4 "'Do not turn to idols or make gods of cast metal for yourselves. I am the LORD your God.

Lev 26:1 "'Do not make idols or set up an image or a sacred stone for yourselves, and do not place a carved stone in your land to bow down before it. I am the LORD your God.

Lev 26:30 I will destroy your high places, cut down your incense altars and pile your dead bodies on the lifeless forms of your idols, and I will abhor you.

Dt 4:15 You saw no form of any kind the day the LORD spoke to you at Horeb out of the fire. Therefore watch yourselves very carefully, [16]so that you do not become corrupt and make for yourselves an idol, an image of any shape, whether formed like a man or a woman, (+Dt 4:17-18)

Dt 4:19 And when you look up to the sky and see the sun, the moon and the stars—all the heavenly array—do not be enticed into bowing down to them and worshiping things the LORD your God has apportioned to all the nations under heaven. (+Dt 4:20-28; 5:7-9; 7:2-5,16; 11:16-17; 16:21-22)

Ps 81:9 You shall have no foreign god among you; you shall not bow down to an alien god. (+Eze 8:8-18; 14:1-8; 16:15-63; 20:7-8,16,18,24,27-32,39; 23:7-49; Ac 15:20-28)

Ac 15:29 You are to abstain from food sacrificed to idols, from blood, from the meat of strangled animals and from sexual immorality. You will do well to avoid these things. Farewell.

1Co 10:14 Therefore, my dear friends, flee from idolatry.

1Co 10:20 No, but the sacrifices of pagans are offered to demons, not to God, and I do not want you to be participants with demons. (+1Co 10:21-22)

1Jn 5:21 Dear children, keep yourselves from idols.

Prophecies Relating to:

(Isa 46:1-2). Its punishments (Nu 33:4; Dt 31:16-21,29; Isa 21:9; Jer 51:44,47,52).

Its end (Isa 2:8)—

Isa 2:18 and the idols will totally disappear.

Isa 2:20 In that day men will throw away to the rodents and bats their idols of silver and idols of gold, which they made to worship.

Isa 17:7 In that day men will look to their Maker and turn their eyes to the Holy One of Israel. [8]They will not look to the altars, the work of their hands, and they will have no regard for the Asherah poles and the incense altars their fingers have made.

Isa 27:9 By this, then, will Jacob's guilt be atoned for, and this will be the full fruitage of the removal of his sin: When he makes all the altar stones to be like chalk stones crushed to pieces, no Asherah poles or incense altars will be left standing.

Jer 10:11 "Tell them this: 'These gods, who did not make the heavens and the earth, will perish from the earth and from under the heavens.'"

Jer 10:15 They are worthless, the objects of mockery; when their judgment comes, they will perish.

Hos 10:2 Their heart is deceitful, and now they must bear their guilt. The LORD will demolish their altars and destroy their sacred stones. (+Hos 14:8)

Mic 5:13 I will destroy your carved images and your sacred stones from among you; you will no longer bow down to the work of your hands. (+Mic 5:14)

Zep 2:11 The LORD will be awesome to them when he destroys all the gods of the land. The nations on every shore will worship him, every one in its own land.

Zec 13:2 "On that day, I will banish the names of the idols from the land, and they will be remembered no more," declares the LORD Almighty. "I will remove both the prophets and the spirit of impurity from the land.

Punishment of:

(Dt 8:19; 11:28; 13:6-9; 17:2-5; 28:14-18; 30:17-18; 32:15-26; Jdg 2:3; 1Ki 9:6-9; Ne 9:27-37; Ps 16:4; 59:8; 78:58-64; 106:34-42; Isa 1:29-31; 2:6-22; 30:22; 65:3-7; Jer 1:15-16; 5:1-17; 7; 8:1-2,19; 13:9-27; 16; 17:1-6; 18:13-17; 19; 22:5-9; 44; Eze 6; 8:8-18; 9; 14:1-8; 16:15-63; 20:7-8,24-39; 22:4; 23:9-10,22-49; 44:10-12; Hos 8:5-14; 10; 13:14; 5:5; Mic 1:1-9; 5:12-14; 6:16; Zep 1; Mal 2:11-13; Rev 21:8; 22:15).

See Groves; High Places; Iconoclasm; Idol; Prostitute.

IDUMEA [2628] (*[land of] Edom*). Greek and Roman name for Edom (Mk 3:8).

IEZER, IEZERITE [404, 405] (*my [father] is help*). Chief in the tribe of Manasseh (Nu 26:30). Also called Abiezer (Jos 17:2). *See Abiezer, 1.*

IFS OF THE BIBLE *See Blessings, Spiritual, Contingent Upon Obedience.*

IGAL [3319] (*he redeems*).
1. Spy of Issachar (Nu 13:7).
2. One of David's heroes (2Sa 23:36).
3. Descendant of Jehoiachin (1Ch 3:22).

IGDALIAH [3323] (*Yahweh is great*). Father of Hanan (Jer 35:4).

IGEAL (*he redeems*). Son of Shemaiah (1Ch 3:22).

IGNORANCE [7344, *51, 52, 53*].
NIV+ IGNORE, IGNORANT, IGNORED, IGNORES, IGNORING

Characteristic of Mankind:
Job 8:9 for we were born only yesterday and know nothing, and our days on earth are but a shadow.
Job 28:12 "But where can wisdom be found? Where does understanding dwell? ¹³Man does not comprehend its worth; it cannot be found in the land of the living.
Job 28:20 "Where then does wisdom come from? Where does understanding dwell? ²¹It is hidden from the eyes of every living thing, concealed even from the birds of the air.
Pr 8:5 You who are simple, gain prudence; you who are foolish, gain understanding. (+Pr 19:2)
Ecc 7:23 All this I tested by wisdom and I said, "I am determined to be wise"—but this was beyond me. ²⁴Whatever wisdom may be, it is far off and most profound—who can discover it?
Jer 10:23 I know, O LORD, that a man's life is not his own; it is not for man to direct his steps. (+Jer 10:24,23; Hos 4:14)
Jn 13:7 Jesus replied, "You do not realize now what I am doing, but later you will understand."

Concerning God (1Sa 3:7)—
Job 11:7 "Can you fathom the mysteries of God? Can you probe the limits of the Almighty? ⁸They are higher than the heavens—what can you do? They are deeper than the depths of the grave—what can you know?
Job 11:12 But a witless man can no more become wise than a wild donkey's colt can be born a man.
Job 36:26 How great is God—beyond our understanding! The number of his years is past finding out.
Job 36:29 Who can understand how he spreads out the clouds, how he thunders from his pavilion?
Job 37:5 God's voice thunders in marvelous ways; he does great things beyond our understanding.
Job 37:15 Do you know how God controls the clouds and makes his lightning flash? ¹⁶Do you know how the clouds hang poised, those wonders of him who is perfect in knowledge?
Job 37:19 "Tell us what we should say to him; we cannot draw up our case because of our darkness.
Job 37:23 The Almighty is beyond our reach and exalted in power; in his justice and great righteousness, he does not oppress.
Ps 139:6 Such knowledge is too wonderful for me, too lofty for me to attain. (+Pr 30:3)

Pr 30:4 Who has gone up to heaven and come down? Who has gathered up the wind in the hollow of his hands? Who has wrapped up the waters in his cloak? Who has established all the ends of the earth? What is his name, and the name of his son? Tell me if you know!
Ac 17:23 For as I walked around and looked carefully at your objects of worship, I even found an altar with this inscription: TO AN UNKNOWN GOD. Now what you worship as something unknown I am going to proclaim to you.
Ac 17:30 In the past God overlooked such ignorance, but now he commands all people everywhere to repent.

Concerning God's works—
Ecc 3:11 He has made everything beautiful in its time. He has also set eternity in the hearts of men; yet they cannot fathom what God has done from beginning to end.
Ecc 8:17 then I saw all that God has done. No one can comprehend what goes on under the sun. Despite all his efforts to search it out, man cannot discover its meaning. Even if a wise man claims he knows, he cannot really comprehend it.
Ecc 11:5 As you do not know the path of the wind, or how the body is formed in a mother's womb, so you cannot understand the work of God, the Maker of all things.

Concerning God's wisdom—
1Co 2:7 No, we speak of God's secret wisdom, a wisdom that has been hidden and that God destined for our glory before time began. ⁸None of the rulers of this age understood it, for if they had, they would not have crucified the Lord of glory. ⁹However, as it is written:
"No eye has seen, no ear has heard, no mind has conceived what God has prepared for those who love him"—
¹⁰but God has revealed it to us by his Spirit.
The Spirit searches all things, even the deep things of God.

Concerning the future—
Pr 27:1 Do not boast about tomorrow, for you do not know what a day may bring forth.
Ecc 8:6 For there is a proper time and procedure for every matter, though a man's misery weighs heavily upon him.
⁷Since no man knows the future, who can tell him what is to come?
Ac 1:7 He said to them: "It is not for you to know the times or dates the Father has set by his own authority.
1Co 13:9 For we know in part and we prophesy in part,
1Co 13:12 Now we see but a poor reflection as in a mirror; then we shall see face to face. Now I know in part; then I shall know fully, even as I am fully known.
Concerning the Holy Spirit (Ac 19:2). Concerning Scripture (Mt 22:29; Mk 12:24; Jn 20:9; 1Ti 1:7).

Concerning snares of the wicked—
Pr 7:6 At the window of my house I looked out through the lattice. ⁷I saw among the simple, I noticed among the young men, a youth who lacked judgment. ⁸He was going down the street near her corner, walking along in the direction of her house ⁹at twilight, as the day was fading, as the dark of night set in.
¹⁰Then out came a woman to meet him, dressed like a prostitute and with crafty intent. ¹¹(She is loud and defiant, her feet never stay at home; ¹²now in the street, now in the squares, at every corner she lurks.) ¹³She took hold of him and kissed him and with a brazen face she said:
¹⁴"I have fellowship offerings at home; today I fulfilled my vows. ¹⁵So I came out to meet you; I looked for you and have found you! ¹⁶I have covered my bed with colored linens from Egypt. ¹⁷I have perfumed my bed with myrrh,

aloes and cinnamon. [18]Come, let's drink deep of love till morning; let's enjoy ourselves with love! [19]My husband is not at home; he has gone on a long journey. [20]He took his purse filled with money and will not be home till full moon."

[21]With persuasive words she led him astray; she seduced him with her smooth talk. [22]All at once he followed her like an ox going to the slaughter, like a deer stepping into a noose [23]till an arrow pierces his liver, like a bird darting into a snare, little knowing it will cost him his life.

Pr 9:14 She sits at the door of her house, on a seat at the highest point of the city, [15]calling out to those who pass by, who go straight on their way. (+Pr 9:16-17)

Pr 9:18 But little do they know that the dead are there, that her guests are in the depths of the grave.

Pr 22:3 A prudent man sees danger and takes refuge, but the simple keep going and suffer for it. (+Pr 27:12)

Remedy For:

Jas 1:5 If any of you lacks wisdom, he should ask God, who gives generously to all without finding fault, and it will be given to him. [6]But when he asks, he must believe and not doubt, because he who doubts is like a wave of the sea, blown and tossed by the wind.

Sins of:

Sacrifices for—

Unintentional sin by the anointed priest (Lev 4:1-12), by the whole community of Israel (Lev 4:13-21; Nu 15:22-26), by a leader (Lev 4:22-26), by a member of the community (Lev 4:27-35; 5:1-19; Nu 15:27-29; Eze 45:20)

Forgiven—

1Ti 1:12 I thank Christ Jesus our Lord, who has given me strength, that he considered me faithful, appointing me to his service. [13]Even though I was once a blasphemer and a persecutor and a violent man, I was shown mercy because I acted in ignorance and unbelief. (+Heb 5:2)

Forgiven on account of reparation—

Ge 20:1 Now Abraham moved on from there into the region of the Negev and lived between Kadesh and Shur. For a while he stayed in Gerar, [2]and there Abraham said of his wife Sarah, "She is my sister." Then Abimelech king of Gerar sent for Sarah and took her.

[3]But God came to Abimelech in a dream one night and said to him, "You are as good as dead because of the woman you have taken; she is a married woman."

[4]Now Abimelech had not gone near her, so he said, "Lord, will you destroy an innocent nation? [5]Did he not say to me, 'She is my sister,' and didn't she also say, 'He is my brother'? I have done this with a clear conscience and clean hands."

[6]Then God said to him in the dream, "Yes, I know you did this with a clear conscience, and so I have kept you from sinning against me. That is why I did not let you touch her. [7]Now return the man's wife, for he is a prophet, and he will pray for you and you will live. But if you do not return her, you may be sure that you and all yours will die."

Evil consequences of: (Isa 5:13)

Hos 4:6 my people are destroyed from lack of knowledge. "Because you have rejected knowledge, I also reject you as my priests; because you have ignored the law of your God, I also will ignore your children.

Alienates from God—

Eph 4:18 They are darkened in their understanding and separated from the life of God because of the ignorance that is in them due to the hardening of their hearts.

[19]Having lost all sensitivity, they have given themselves over to sensuality so as to indulge in every kind of impurity, with a continual lust for more.

Darkens understanding—

Lk 23:34 Jesus said, "Father, forgive them, for they do not know what they are doing." And they divided up his clothes by casting lots.

Jn 16:2 They will put you out of the synagogue; in fact, a time is coming when anyone who kills you will think he is offering a service to God. (+Jn 16:3)

1Co 2:8 None of the rulers of this age understood it, for if they had, they would not have crucified the Lord of glory.

Punishment of: (Eze 3:18)

Eze 33:6 But if the watchman sees the sword coming and does not blow the trumpet to warn the people and the sword comes and takes the life of one of them, that man will be taken away because of his sin, but I will hold the watchman accountable for his blood.'

Eze 33:8 When I say to the wicked, 'O wicked man, you will surely die,' and you do not speak out to dissuade him from his ways, that wicked man will die for his sin, and I will hold you accountable for his blood.

Lk 12:48 But the one who does not know and does things deserving punishment will be beaten with few blows. From everyone who has been given much, much will be demanded; and from the one who has been entrusted with much, much more will be asked.

By fines—

Lev 22:14 "'If anyone eats a sacred offering by mistake, he must make restitution to the priest for the offering and add a fifth of the value to it.

Instances of Punishment of Sins of:

Pharaoh (Ge 12:11-17). Abimelech (Ge 20:1-18). *See Knowledge; Wisdom.*

IIM [6517] (*heaps, ruins*).

1. For KJV Nu 33:45, *See Iyim.*

2. A town in the extreme S of Judah (Jos 15:29).

IJE-ABARIM *See Iye Abarim.*

IJON [6510] (*place of heaps [of stone]*). A town of Naphtali (1Ki 15:20; 2Ki 15:29; 2Ch 16:4).

IKKESH [6837] (*crooked, perverted*). Father of Iri (2Sa 23:26; 1Ch 11:28; 27:9).

ILAI [6519]. One of David's heroes (1Ch 11:29), called Zalmon (2Sa 23:28).

ILLEGITIMATE [2424, *3785*]. Excluded from the assembly of the Lord to the tenth generation (Dt 23:2). Had no claim to paternal care or the usual privileges and discipline of legitimate children.

Instances of:

Ishmael (Ge 16:3,15; Gal 4:22), Moab and Ammon (Ge 19:36-37), Jephthah (Jdg 11:1), David's child by Bathsheba (2Sa 11:2-5). Jesus slanderously accused of being (Jn 8:41).

Figurative: (Heb 12:8).

ILLYRICUM [2665]. Also called Dalmatia. Visited, by Paul (Ro 15:19), by Titus (2Ti 4:10). Now part of Yugoslavia.

IMAGE [1952, 5011, 6166, 6771, 7181, 7512, 9322, 9454, 10614, *1479*, *1635*, *5916*].

NIV+ IMAGES

Manufactured Images:

For idols. *See Idol; Idolatry.*

Figurative:

Mankind created in, of God (Ge 1:26-27; 5:1; 9:6; Jas 3:9). Regenerated into (Ps 17:15; Ro 8:29; 2Co 3:18; Eph 4:24; Col 3:10; 1Jn 3:1-3). Christ, of God (Col 1:15; Heb 1:3). *See Image of God.*

IMAGE, NEBUCHADNEZZAR'S Symbolic figure seen by Nebuchadnezzar in a dream the meaning of which was interpreted by Daniel (Da 2).

IMAGE OF GOD [7512, *1635*]. Mankind is created in God's image (Ge 1:26-27; 5:1,3; 9:6; 1Co 11:7; Eph 4:24; Col 3:10; Jas 3:9). The image is not corporeal but rational, spiritual, and social. The fall of man destroyed, but did not obliterate the image. Restoration of the image begins with regeneration.

IMAGE WORSHIP *See Idol.*

IMAGINATION [4213, 4742].

NIV+ IMAGINE, IMAGINATIONS

Of mankind, evil—

Ge 6:5 The LORD saw how great man's wickedness on the earth had become, and that every inclination of the thoughts of his heart was only evil all the time.

Ge 8:21 The LORD smelled the pleasing aroma and said in his heart: "Never again will I curse the ground because of man, even though every inclination of his heart is evil from childhood. And never again will I destroy all living creatures, as I have done.

Dt 29:19 When such a person hears the words of this oath, he invokes a blessing on himself and therefore thinks, "I will be safe, even though I persist in going my own way." This will bring disaster on the watered land as well as the dry. [20]The LORD will never be willing to forgive him; his wrath and zeal will burn against that man. All the curses written in this book will fall upon him, and the LORD will blot out his name from under heaven. (+Pr 6:16-18)

Vain—

Ro 1:21 For although they knew God, they neither glorified him as God nor gave thanks to him, but their thinking became futile and their foolish hearts were darkened.

An abomination to God—

Pr 6:16 There are six things the LORD hates, seven that are detestable to him: [17]haughty eyes, a lying tongue, hands that shed innocent blood, [18]a heart that devises wicked schemes, feet that are quick to rush into evil,

Condemned, as equal to act—

Mt 5:28 But I tell you that anyone who looks at a woman lustfully has already committed adultery with her in his heart.

Known of God—

1Ch 28:9 "And you, my son Solomon, acknowledge the God of your father, and serve him with wholehearted devotion and with a willing mind, for the LORD searches every heart and understands every motive behind the thoughts. If you seek him, he will be found by you; but if you forsake him, he will reject you forever.

To be subjected—

2Co 10:3 For though we live in the world, we do not wage war as the world does.

2Co 10:5 We demolish arguments and every pretension that sets itself up against the knowledge of God, and we take captive every thought to make it obedient to Christ.

IMLAH, IMLA [3550, 3551] (*fullness*). Father of Micaiah the prophet (1Ki 22:8-9; 2Ch 18:7-8).

IMMANENCE OF GOD *See Condescension of God.*

IMMANUEL [6672, *1842*] (*God with us*). Isaiah foretold the birth of this child, a sign to Ahaz that God would come near in judgment (Isa 7:14-25). Isaiah's son is called Immanuel (Isa 8:8,10) and might be the immediate fulfillment. The prophecy is applied to Jesus, whose name means "Yahweh is salvation." He is God come near to save (Mt 1:22-23). *See Jesus the Christ, Prophecies Concerning; Messianic Hope.*

IMMER [612, 613] (*lamb* KB).

1. A family of priests (1Ch 9:12; Ezr 2:37; 10:20; Ne 7:40; 11:13).

2. Head of a division of priests (1Ch 24:14).

3. Name of a man or town (Ezr 2:59; Ne 7:61).

4. Father of Zadok (Ne 3:29).

5. Father of Pashhur (Jer 20:1-2).

IMMORTALITY [440+4638, *114*, *914*, *915*].

NIV+ IMMORTAL

The biblical concept of immortality is not simply the survival of the soul after bodily death, but the self-conscious continuance of the whole person, body and soul together, in a state of blessedness, due to the redemption of Christ and the possession of "eternal life." The Bible nowhere attempts to prove this doctrine but everywhere assumes it as an undisputed postulate. The condition of believers in their state of immortality is not a bare endless existence but a communion with God in eternal satisfaction and blessedness.

Exemption from death and annihilation. *See Annihilation.*

Apparently understood:

By David (2Sa 12:23)—

Ps 21:4 He asked you for life, and you gave it to him— length of days, for ever and ever.

Ps 22:26 The poor will eat and be satisfied; they who seek the LORD will praise him—may your hearts live forever!

Ps 23:6 Surely goodness and love will follow me all the days of my life, and I will dwell in the house of the LORD forever.

Ps 37:18 The days of the blameless are known to the LORD, and their inheritance will endure forever.

Ps 37:27 Turn from evil and do good; then you will dwell in the land forever.

Ps 86:12 I will praise you, O Lord my God, with all my heart; I will glorify your name forever.

Ps 133:3 It is as if the dew of Hermon were falling on Mount Zion. For there the LORD bestows his blessing, even life forevermore.

Ps 145:1 I will exalt you, my God the King; I will praise your name for ever and ever. [2]Every day I will praise you and extol your name for ever and ever.

By Nehemiah—

Ne 9:5 And the Levites—Jeshua, Kadmiel, Bani, Hashabneiah, Sherebiah, Hodiah, Shebaniah and Pethahiah— said: "Stand up and praise the LORD your God, who is from everlasting to everlasting." "Blessed be your glorious name, and may it be exalted above all blessing and praise.

By Job—

Job 14:13 "If only you would hide me in the grave and conceal me till your anger has passed! If only you would set me a time and then remember me!

By the psalmists—

Ps 49:7 No man can redeem the life of another or give to God a ransom for him— ⁸the ransom for a life is costly, no payment is ever enough— ⁹that he should live on forever and not see decay.

Ps 73:26 My flesh and my heart may fail, but God is the strength of my heart and my portion forever.

Ps 121:8 the LORD will watch over your coming and going both now and forevermore.

By Moses (Ex 3:6; Mt 22:32)—

Mk 12:26 Now about the dead rising—have you not read in the book of Moses, in the account of the bush, how God said to him, 'I am the God of Abraham, the God of Isaac, and the God of Jacob'? ²⁷He is not the God of the dead, but of the living. You are badly mistaken!"

Lk 20:36 and they can no longer die; for they are like the angels. They are God's children, since they are children of the resurrection. ³⁷But in the account of the bush, even Moses showed that the dead rise, for he calls the Lord 'the God of Abraham, and the God of Isaac, and the God of Jacob.' ³⁸He is not the God of the dead, but of the living, for to him all are alive." (+Ac 7:32)

By Abraham—

Heb 11:10 For he was looking forward to the city with foundations, whose architect and builder is God.

Implied:

In the translation of Enoch—

Ge 5:24 Enoch walked with God; then he was no more, because God took him away.

Heb 11:5 By faith Enoch was taken from this life, so that he did not experience death; he could not be found, because God had taken him away. For before he was taken, he was commended as one who pleased God.

In the translation of Elijah—

2Ki 2:11 As they were walking along and talking together, suddenly a chariot of fire and horses of fire appeared and separated the two of them, and Elijah went up to heaven in a whirlwind.

In redemption from Sheol—

Ps 16:10 because you will not abandon me to the grave, nor will you let your Holy One see decay. ¹¹You have made known to me the path of life; you will fill me with joy in your presence, with eternal pleasures at your right hand.

In the spirit returning to God—

Ecc 3:21 Who knows if the spirit of man rises upward and if the spirit of the animal goes down into the earth?"

Ecc 12:7 and the dust returns to the ground it came from, and the spirit returns to God who gave it.

In the soul surviving the death of the body—

Mt 10:28 Do not be afraid of those who kill the body but cannot kill the soul. Rather, be afraid of the One who can destroy both soul and body in hell.

In the appearance of Moses and Elijah at the transfiguration of Jesus (Mt 17:2-9; Mk 9:2-10; Lk 9:29-36)

In the abolition of death—

Isa 25:8 he will swallow up death forever. The Sovereign LORD will wipe away the tears from all faces; he will remove the disgrace of his people from all the earth. The LORD has spoken.

In the Savior's promise to his disciples (Jn 14:2-3)

In the resurrection—

Isa 26:19 But your dead will live; their bodies will rise. You who dwell in the dust, wake up and shout for joy. Your dew is like the dew of the morning; the earth will give birth to her dead.

Da 12:2 Multitudes who sleep in the dust of the earth will awake: some to everlasting life, others to shame and everlasting contempt. ³Those who are wise will shine like the brightness of the heavens, and those who lead many to righteousness, like the stars for ever and ever.

Jn 6:40 For my Father's will is that everyone who looks to the Son and believes in him shall have eternal life, and I will raise him up at the last day." (+1Co 15:12-25)

1Th 4:13 Brothers, we do not want you to be ignorant about those who fall asleep, or to grieve like the rest of men, who have no hope. ¹⁴We believe that Jesus died and rose again and so we believe that God will bring with Jesus those who have fallen asleep in him. ¹⁵According to the Lord's own word, we tell you that we who are still alive, who are left till the coming of the Lord, will certainly not precede those who have fallen asleep. ¹⁶For the Lord himself will come down from heaven, with a loud command, with the voice of the archangel and with the trumpet call of God, and the dead in Christ will rise first. ¹⁷After that, we who are still alive and are left will be caught up together with them in the clouds to meet the Lord in the air. And so we will be with the Lord forever. ¹⁸Therefore encourage each other with these words.

1Th 5:10 He died for us so that, whether we are awake or asleep, we may live together with him.

In eternal inheritance—

Ac 20:32 "Now I commit you to God and to the word of his grace, which can build you up and give you an inheritance among all those who are sanctified.

Ac 26:18 to open their eyes and turn them from darkness to light, and from the power of Satan to God, so that they may receive forgiveness of sins and a place among those who are sanctified by faith in me.'

Heb 9:15 For this reason Christ is the mediator of a new covenant, that those who are called may receive the promised eternal inheritance—now that he has died as a ransom to set them free from the sins committed under the first covenant.

1Pe 1:3 Praise be to the God and Father of our Lord Jesus Christ! In his great mercy he has given us new birth into a living hope through the resurrection of Jesus Christ from the dead, ⁴and into an inheritance that can never perish, spoil or fade—kept in heaven for you, ⁵who through faith are shielded by God's power until the coming of the salvation that is ready to be revealed in the last time.

In the everlasting punishment of the wicked—

2Th 1:7 and give relief to you who are troubled, and to us as well. This will happen when the Lord Jesus is revealed from heaven in blazing fire with his powerful angels. ⁸He will punish those who do not know God and do not obey the gospel of our Lord Jesus. ⁹They will be punished with everlasting destruction and shut out from the presence of the Lord and from the majesty of his power

In the Judgment (2Pe 3:7).

Taught:

By Christ—

Mt 16:26 What good will it be for a man if he gains the

whole world, yet forfeits his soul? Or what can a man give in exchange for his soul?

Mt 19:16 Now a man came up to Jesus and asked, "Teacher, what good thing must I do to get eternal life?"

¹⁷"Why do you ask me about what is good?" Jesus replied. "There is only One who is good. If you want to enter life, obey the commandments."

Mt 25:46 "Then they will go away to eternal punishment, but the righteous to eternal life."

Mk 10:30 will fail to receive a hundred times as much in this present age (homes, brothers, sisters, mothers, children and fields—and with them, persecutions) and in the age to come, eternal life.

Lk 9:25 What good is it for a man to gain the whole world, and yet lose or forfeit his very self? (+Lk 10:25-28)

Jn 3:14 Just as Moses lifted up the snake in the desert, so the Son of Man must be lifted up, ¹⁵that everyone who believes in him may have eternal life.

¹⁶"For God so loved the world that he gave his one and only Son, that whoever believes in him shall not perish but have eternal life.

Jn 3:36 Whoever believes in the Son has eternal life, but whoever rejects the Son will not see life, for God's wrath remains on him."

Jn 5:39 You diligently study the Scriptures because you think that by them you possess eternal life. These are the Scriptures that testify about me, ⁴⁰yet you refuse to come to me to have life. (+Jn 6:39-40,44,47,50-58)

Jn 10:28 I give them eternal life, and they shall never perish; no one can snatch them out of my hand.

Jn 11:25 Jesus said to her, "I am the resurrection and the life. He who believes in me will live, even though he dies; ²⁶and whoever lives and believes in me will never die. Do you believe this?"

Jn 14:19 Before long, the world will not see me anymore, but you will see me. Because I live, you also will live.

Jn 17:2 For you granted him authority over all people that he might give eternal life to all those you have given him. ³Now this is eternal life: that they may know you, the only true God, and Jesus Christ, whom you have sent.

Rev 3:4 Yet you have a few people in Sardis who have not soiled their clothes. They will walk with me, dressed in white, for they are worthy.

By Paul—

Ro 2:7 To those who by persistence in doing good seek glory, honor and immortality, he will give eternal life.

Ro 6:22 But now that you have been set free from sin and have become slaves to God, the benefit you reap leads to holiness, and the result is eternal life. ²³For the wages of sin is death, but the gift of God is eternal life in Christ Jesus our Lord.

1Co 15:12 But if it is preached that Christ has been raised from the dead, how can some of you say that there is no resurrection of the dead? ¹³If there is no resurrection of the dead, then not even Christ has been raised. ¹⁴And if Christ has not been raised, our preaching is useless and so is your faith. ¹⁵More than that, we are then found to be false witnesses about God, for we have testified about God that he raised Christ from the dead. But he did not raise him if in fact the dead are not raised. ¹⁶For if the dead are not raised, then Christ has not been raised either. ¹⁷And if Christ has not been raised, your faith is futile; you are still in your sins. ¹⁸Then those also who have fallen asleep in Christ are lost. ¹⁹If only for this life we have hope in Christ, we are to be pitied more than all men.

²⁰But Christ has indeed been raised from the dead, the

firstfruits of those who have fallen asleep. ²¹For since death came through a man, the resurrection of the dead comes also through a man. ²²For as in Adam all die, so in Christ all will be made alive. ²³But each in his own turn: Christ, the firstfruits; then, when he comes, those who belong to him. ²⁴Then the end will come, when he hands over the kingdom to God the Father after he has destroyed all dominion, authority and power. ²⁵For he must reign until he has put all his enemies under his feet. (+2Co 5:1)

Gal 6:8 The one who sows to please his sinful nature, from that nature will reap destruction; the one who sows to please the Spirit, from the Spirit will reap eternal life.

Col 1:5 the faith and love that spring from the hope that is stored up for you in heaven and that you have already heard about in the word of truth, the gospel ⁶that has come to you. All over the world this gospel is bearing fruit and growing, just as it has been doing among you since the day you heard it and understood God's grace in all its truth.

2Th 2:16 May our Lord Jesus Christ himself and God our Father, who loved us and by his grace gave us eternal encouragement and good hope,

1Ti 4:8 For physical training is of some value, but godliness has value for all things, holding promise for both the present life and the life to come.

1Ti 6:12 Fight the good fight of the faith. Take hold of the eternal life to which you were called when you made your good confession in the presence of many witnesses.

1Ti 6:19 In this way they will lay up treasure for themselves as a firm foundation for the coming age, so that they may take hold of the life that is truly life.

2Ti 1:9 who has saved us and called us to a holy life—not because of anything we have done but because of his own purpose and grace. This grace was given us in Christ Jesus before the beginning of time, ¹⁰but it has now been revealed through the appearing of our Savior, Christ Jesus, who has destroyed death and has brought life and immortality to light through the gospel.

Tit 1:2 a faith and knowledge resting on the hope of eternal life, which God, who does not lie, promised before the beginning of time,

Tit 3:7 so that, having been justified by his grace, we might become heirs having the hope of eternal life.

By John—

1Jn 2:17 The world and its desires pass away, but the man who does the will of God lives forever.

1Jn 2:25 And this is what he promised us—even eternal life.

1Jn 5:13 I write these things to you who believe in the name of the Son of God so that you may know that you have eternal life.

Rev 1:7 Look, he is coming with the clouds, and every eye will see him, even those who pierced him; and all the peoples of the earth will mourn because of him. So shall it be! Amen.

Rev 22:5 There will be no more night. They will not need the light of a lamp or the light of the sun, for the Lord God will give them light. And they will reign for ever and ever.

By Jude—

Jude 21 Keep yourselves in God's love as you wait for the mercy of our Lord Jesus Christ to bring you to eternal life.

In Hebrews (Heb 9:15)—

Heb 10:34 You sympathized with those in prison and joyfully accepted the confiscation of your property, because you knew that you yourselves had better and lasting possessions. (+Heb 11:5,10)

Heb 11:13 All these people were still living by faith when they died. They did not receive the things promised; they only saw them and welcomed them from a distance. And they admitted that they were aliens and strangers on earth. ¹⁴People who say such things show that they are looking for a country of their own. ¹⁵If they had been thinking of the country they had left, they would have had opportunity to return. ¹⁶Instead, they were longing for a better country—a heavenly one. Therefore God is not ashamed to be called their God, for he has prepared a city for them. (+Heb 13:14)

See Eternal Life; Resurrection; Righteous, Promises to; Judgment; Wicked, Punishment of.

IMMUTABILITY (*not changeable*). The perfection of
God by which he is devoid of all change in essence, attributes, consciousness, will, and promises (Mal 3:6; Ps 33:11; 102:26).

IMNA [3557] (possibly *he is withheld* BDB; *luck, fortune* IDB). Son of Helem (1Ch 7:35).

IMNAH, IMNITE [3555] (*good fortune*).
1. Firstborn of Asher (Ge 46:17; Nu 26:44; 1Ch 7:30).
2. A Levite (2Ch 31:14).

IMPENITENCE
Admonitions Against:
Ps 95:8 do not harden your hearts as you did at Meribah, as you did that day at Massah in the desert,

Jer 6:16 This is what the LORD says: "Stand at the crossroads and look; ask for the ancient paths, ask where the good way is, and walk in it, and you will find rest for your souls. But you said, 'We will not walk in it.' ¹⁷I appointed watchmen over you and said, 'Listen to the sound of the trumpet!' But you said, 'We will not listen.' (+Jer 6:18)

Jer 6:19 Hear, O earth: I am bringing disaster on this people, the fruit of their schemes, because they have not listened to my words and have rejected my law.

2Co 12:21 I am afraid that when I come again my God will humble me before you, and I will be grieved over many who have sinned earlier and have not repented of the impurity, sexual sin and debauchery in which they have indulged. (+Heb 3:8)

Rev 2:5 Remember the height from which you have fallen! Repent and do the things you did at first. If you do not repent, I will come to you and remove your lampstand from its place.

Rev 2:16 Repent therefore! Otherwise, I will soon come to you and will fight against them with the sword of my mouth.

Rev 2:21 I have given her time to repent of her immorality, but she is unwilling. ²²So I will cast her on a bed of suffering, and I will make those who commit adultery with her suffer intensely, unless they repent of her ways.

Rev 3:3 Remember, therefore, what you have received and heard; obey it, and repent. But if you do not wake up, I will come like a thief, and you will not know at what time I will come to you.

Leads to Destruction:
Mt 24:38 For in the days before the flood, people were eating and drinking, marrying and giving in marriage, up to the day Noah entered the ark; ³⁹and they knew nothing about what would happen until the flood came and took them all away. That is how it will be at the coming of the Son of Man.

Mt 24:48 But suppose that servant is wicked and says to himself, 'My master is staying away a long time,' ⁴⁹and he then begins to beat his fellow servants and to eat and drink with drunkards. ⁵⁰The master of that servant will come on a day when he does not expect him and at an hour he is not aware of. ⁵¹He will cut him to pieces and assign him a place with the hypocrites, where there will be weeping and gnashing of teeth.

Lk 13:3 I tell you, no! But unless you repent, you too will all perish. (+Lk 13:5)

Rev 16:9 They were seared by the intense heat and they cursed the name of God, who had control over these plagues, but they refused to repent and glorify him.

¹⁰The fifth angel poured out his bowl on the throne of the beast, and his kingdom was plunged into darkness. Men gnawed their tongues in agony ¹¹and cursed the God of heaven because of their pains and their sores, but they refused to repent of what they had done.

¹²The sixth angel poured out his bowl on the great river Euphrates, and its water was dried up to prepare the way for the kings from the East. ¹³Then I saw three evil spirits that looked like frogs; they came out of the mouth of the dragon, out of the mouth of the beast and out of the mouth of the false prophet. ¹⁴They are spirits of demons performing miraculous signs, and they go out to the kings of the whole world, to gather them for the battle on the great day of God Almighty.

¹⁵"Behold, I come like a thief! Blessed is he who stays awake and keeps his clothes with him, so that he may not go naked and be shamefully exposed."

¹⁶Then they gathered the kings together to the place that in Hebrew is called Armageddon.

¹⁷The seventh angel poured out his bowl into the air, and out of the temple came a loud voice from the throne, saying, "It is done!" ¹⁸Then there came flashes of lightning, rumblings, peals of thunder and a severe earthquake. No earthquake like it has ever occurred since man has been on earth, so tremendous was the quake. ¹⁹The great city split into three parts, and the cities of the nations collapsed. God remembered Babylon the Great and gave her the cup filled with the wine of the fury of his wrath. ²⁰Every island fled away and the mountains could not be found.

Rev 16:21 From the sky huge hailstones of about a hundred pounds each fell upon men. And they cursed God on account of the plague of hail, because the plague was so terrible.

Judgments:
Denounced against—

Lev 23:29 Anyone who does not deny himself on that day must be cut off from his people.

Lev 26:21 "'If you remain hostile toward me and refuse to listen to me, I will multiply your afflictions seven times over, as your sins deserve. (+Lev 26:22-43)

Dt 29:19 When such a person hears the words of this oath, he invokes a blessing on himself and therefore thinks, "I will be safe, even though I persist in going my own way." This will bring disaster on the watered land as well as the dry. ²⁰The LORD will never be willing to forgive him; his wrath and zeal will burn against that man. All the curses written in this book will fall upon him, and the LORD will blot out his name from under heaven. ²¹The LORD will single him out from all the tribes of Israel for disaster, according to all the curses of the covenant written in this Book of the Law.

1Sa 15:23 For rebellion is like the sin of divination, and arrogance like the evil of idolatry. Because you have rejected the word of the LORD, he has rejected you as king."

Ps 7:11 God is a righteous judge, a God who expresses his wrath every day. [12]If he does not relent, he will sharpen his sword; he will bend and string his bow. (+Ps 7:13)

Ps 50:17 You hate my instruction and cast my words behind you.

Ps 50:21 These things you have done and I kept silent; you thought I was altogether like you. But I will rebuke you and accuse you to your face. (+Ps 68:21)

Ps 81:11 "But my people would not listen to me; Israel would not submit to me. [12]So I gave them over to their stubborn hearts to follow their own devices.

Ps 107:11 for they had rebelled against the words of God and despised the counsel of the Most High. [12]So he subjected them to bitter labor; they stumbled, and there was no one to help.

Pr 1:24 But since you rejected me when I called and no one gave heed when I stretched out my hand, [25]since you ignored all my advice and would not accept my rebuke, [26]I in turn will laugh at your disaster; I will mock when calamity overtakes you— [27]when calamity overtakes you like a storm, when disaster sweeps over you like a whirlwind, when distress and trouble overwhelm you.

[28]"Then they will call to me but I will not answer; they will look for me but will not find me. [29]Since they hated knowledge and did not choose to fear the LORD, [30]since they would not accept my advice and spurned my rebuke, [31]they will eat the fruit of their ways and be filled with the fruit of their schemes.

Pr 11:3 The integrity of the upright guides them, but the unfaithful are destroyed by their duplicity.

Pr 15:10 Stern discipline awaits him who leaves the path; he who hates correction will die.

Pr 15:32 He who ignores discipline despises himself, but whoever heeds correction gains understanding.

Pr 19:16 He who obeys instructions guards his life, but he who is contemptuous of his ways will die.

Pr 28:13 He who conceals his sins does not prosper, but whoever confesses and renounces them finds mercy.

[14]Blessed is the man who always fears the LORD, but he who hardens his heart falls into trouble.

Pr 29:1 A man who remains stiff-necked after many rebukes will suddenly be destroyed—without remedy.

Eze 3:19 But if you do warn the wicked man and he does not turn from his wickedness or from his evil ways, he will die for his sin; but you will have saved yourself.

Eze 3:26 I will make your tongue stick to the roof of your mouth so that you will be silent and unable to rebuke them, though they are a rebellious house.

Eze 33:4 then if anyone hears the trumpet but does not take warning and the sword comes and takes his life, his blood will be on his own head. [5]Since he heard the sound of the trumpet but did not take warning, his blood will be on his own head. If he had taken warning, he would have saved himself. (+Eze 33:9)

Hos 7:13 Woe to them, because they have strayed from me! Destruction to them, because they have rebelled against me! I long to redeem them but they speak lies against me. (+Hos 7:14)

Mt 11:16 "To what can I compare this generation? They are like children sitting in the marketplaces and calling out to others:

[17]"'We played the flute for you, and you did not dance; we sang a dirge, and you did not mourn.'

[18]For John came neither eating nor drinking, and they say, 'He has a demon.' [19]The Son of Man came eating and drinking, and they say, 'Here is a glutton and a drunkard, a friend of tax collectors and "sinners."' But wisdom is proved right by her actions."

[20]Then Jesus began to denounce the cities in which most of his miracles had been performed, because they did not repent. [21]"Woe to you, Korazin! Woe to you, Bethsaida! If the miracles that were performed in you had been performed in Tyre and Sidon, they would have repented long ago in sackcloth and ashes. (+Mt 12:41-42)

Mt 13:15 For this people's heart has become calloused; they hardly hear with their ears, and they have closed their eyes. Otherwise they might see with their eyes, hear with their ears, understand with their hearts and turn, and I would heal them.'

Mt 23:37 "O Jerusalem, Jerusalem, you who kill the prophets and stone those sent to you, how often I have longed to gather your children together, as a hen gathers her chicks under her wings, but you were not willing. [38]Look, your house is left to you desolate. (+Lk 7:35; 10:13; 13:34)

Ro 2:4 Or do you show contempt for the riches of his kindness, tolerance and patience, not realizing that God's kindness leads you toward repentance?

[5]But because of your stubbornness and your unrepentant heart, you are storing up wrath against yourself for the day of God's wrath, when his righteous judgment will be revealed.

Denounced against Israel's—

Isa 65:12 I will destine you for the sword, and you will all bend down for the slaughter; for I called but you did not answer, I spoke but you did not listen. You did evil in my sight and chose what displeases me."

Isa 65:15 You will leave your name to my chosen ones as a curse; the Sovereign LORD will put you to death, but to his servants he will give another name. (+Isa 66:4)

Jer 12:11 It will be made a wasteland, parched and desolate before me; the whole land will be laid waste because there is no one who cares.

Jer 13:17 But if you do not listen, I will weep in secret because of your pride; my eyes will weep bitterly, overflowing with tears, because the LORD's flock will be taken captive.

Jer 13:27 your adulteries and lustful neighings, your shameless prostitution! I have seen your detestable acts on the hills and in the fields. Woe to you, O Jerusalem! How long will you be unclean?"

Jer 14:10 This is what the LORD says about this people: "They greatly love to wander; they do not restrain their feet. So the LORD does not accept them; he will now remember their wickedness and punish them for their sins."

Jer 15:6 You have rejected me," declares the LORD. "You keep on backsliding. So I will lay hands on you and destroy you; I can no longer show compassion. [7]I will winnow them with a winnowing fork at the city gates of the land. I will bring bereavement and destruction on my people, for they have not changed their ways. (+Jer 19:15; 26:4-6; Eze 3:19,26)

Eze 20:8 "'But they rebelled against me and would not listen to me; they did not get rid of the vile images they had set their eyes on, nor did they forsake the idols of Egypt. So I said I would pour out my wrath on them and spend my anger against them in Egypt.

Eze 20:13 "'Yet the people of Israel rebelled against me in the desert. They did not follow my decrees but rejected my laws—although the man who obeys them will live by them—and they utterly desecrated my Sabbaths. So I said I would pour out my wrath on them and destroy them in the desert.

Eze 20:21 "'But the children rebelled against me: They did not follow my decrees, they were not careful to keep my laws—although the man who obeys them will live by them—and they desecrated my Sabbaths. So I said I would pour out my wrath on them and spend my anger against them in the desert.

Da 9:13 Just as it is written in the Law of Moses, all this disaster has come upon us, yet we have not sought the favor of the LORD our God by turning from our sins and giving attention to your truth.

Zec 7:11 "But they refused to pay attention; stubbornly they turned their backs and stopped up their ears. ¹²They made their hearts as hard as flint and would not listen to the law or to the words that the LORD Almighty had sent by his Spirit through the earlier prophets. So the LORD Almighty was very angry.

¹³"'When I called, they did not listen; so when they called, I would not listen,' says the LORD Almighty.

Mal 2:2 If you do not listen, and if you do not set your heart to honor my name," says the LORD Almighty, "I will send a curse upon you, and I will curse your blessings. Yes, I have already cursed them, because you have not set your heart to honor me.

Reason Given for Impenitence:

Evil company (Jer 2:25).

Hypocrisy—

Jer 3:10 In spite of all this, her unfaithful sister Judah did not return to me with all her heart, but only in pretense," declares the LORD.

Idolatry—

Isa 46:12 Listen to me, you stubborn-hearted, you who are far from righteousness. ¹³I am bringing my righteousness near, it is not far away; and my salvation will not be delayed. I will grant salvation to Zion, my splendor to Israel. (+Jer 44:17; Eze 20:8)

Hos 4:17 Ephraim is joined to idols; leave him alone!

Hos 11:2 But the more I called Israel, the further they went from me. They sacrificed to the Baals and they burned incense to images.

Hos 11:7 My people are determined to turn from me. Even if they call to the Most High, he will by no means exalt them.

Rev 9:20 The rest of mankind that were not killed by these plagues still did not repent of the work of their hands; they did not stop worshiping demons, and idols of gold, silver, bronze, stone and wood—idols that cannot see or hear or walk. ²¹Nor did they repent of their murders, their magic arts, their sexual immorality or their thefts.

Lack of understanding or spiritual blindness—

Job 33:14 For God does speak—now one way, now another—though man may not perceive it.

Ps 32:9 Do not be like the horse or the mule, which have no understanding but must be controlled by bit and bridle or they will not come to you.

Ps 82:5 "They know nothing, they understand nothing. They walk about in darkness; all the foundations of the earth are shaken.

Pr 26:11 As a dog returns to its vomit, so a fool repeats his folly.

Hos 5:4 "Their deeds do not permit them to return to their

God. A spirit of prostitution is in their heart; they do not acknowledge the LORD.

Leniency—

Ecc 8:11 When the sentence for a crime is not quickly carried out, the hearts of the people are filled with schemes to do wrong.

Isa 26:10 Though grace is shown to the wicked, they do not learn righteousness; even in a land of uprightness they go on doing evil and regard not the majesty of the LORD.

Material abundance—

Ps 52:1 Why do you boast of evil, you mighty man? Why do you boast all day long, you who are a disgrace in the eyes of God?

Isa 32:9 You women who are so complacent, rise up and listen to me; you daughters who feel secure, hear what I have to say! ¹⁰In little more than a year you who feel secure will tremble; the grape harvest will fail, and the harvest of fruit will not come. ¹¹Tremble, you complacent women; shudder, you daughters who feel secure! Strip off your clothes, put sackcloth around your waists.

Obstinacy—

Isa 48:4 For I knew how stubborn you were; the sinews of your neck were iron, your forehead was bronze.

Isa 48:8 You have neither heard nor understood; from of old your ear has not been open. Well do I know how treacherous you are; you were called a rebel from birth.

Jer 8:5 Why then have these people turned away? Why does Jerusalem always turn away? They cling to deceit; they refuse to return. ⁶I have listened attentively, but they do not say what is right. No one repents of his wickedness, saying, "What have I done?" Each pursues his own course like a horse charging into battle. ⁷Even the stork in the sky knows her appointed seasons, and the dove, the swift and the thrush observe the time of their migration. But my people do not know the requirements of the LORD. (+Eze 2:4)

Ac 7:51 "You stiff-necked people, with uncircumcised hearts and ears! You are just like your fathers: You always resist the Holy Spirit!

Rebellion—

Job 9:2 "Indeed, I know that this is true. But how can a mortal be righteous before God?

Job 9:4 His wisdom is profound, his power is vast. Who has resisted him and come out unscathed?

Job 24:13 "There are those who rebel against the light, who do not know its ways or stay in its paths.

Ps 10:3 He boasts of the cravings of his heart; he blesses the greedy and reviles the LORD.

Ps 50:7 "Hear, O my people, and I will speak, O Israel, and I will testify against you: I am God, your God. (+Ps 78:8)

Pr 21:29 A wicked man puts up a bold front, but an upright man gives thought to his ways.

Isa 57:11 "Whom have you so dreaded and feared that you have been false to me, and have neither remembered me nor pondered this in your hearts? Is it not because I have long been silent that you do not fear me?

Jer 5:21 Hear this, you foolish and senseless people, who have eyes but do not see, who have ears but do not hear: ²²Should you not fear me?" declares the LORD. "Should you not tremble in my presence? I made the sand a boundary for the sea, an everlasting barrier it cannot cross. The waves may roll, but they cannot prevail; they may roar, but they cannot cross it. ²³But these people have stubborn and rebellious hearts; they have turned aside and gone away. ²⁴They do not say to themselves, 'Let us fear the LORD our

God, who gives autumn and spring rains in season, who assures us of the regular weeks of harvest.'

Jer 6:10 To whom can I speak and give warning? Who will listen to me? Their ears are closed so they cannot hear. The word of the LORD is offensive to them; they find no pleasure in it. (+Jer 6:16-19)

Jer 44:10 To this day they have not humbled themselves or shown reverence, nor have they followed my law and the decrees I set before you and your fathers. (+Eze 2:4)

Eze 2:5 And whether they listen or fail to listen—for they are a rebellious house—they will know that a prophet has been among them.

Eze 12:2 "Son of man, you are living among a rebellious people. They have eyes to see but do not see and ears to hear but do not hear, for they are a rebellious people. (+Eze 22:8,13,21)

Refusal to listen—

Ps 58:3 Even from birth the wicked go astray; from the womb they are wayward and speak lies. ⁴Their venom is like the venom of a snake, like that of a cobra that has stopped its ears, ⁵that will not heed the tune of the charmer, however skillful the enchanter may be.

Ps 106:24 Then they despised the pleasant land; they did not believe his promise. ²⁵They grumbled in their tents and did not obey the LORD. (+Isa 28:12; 42:22-25; Jer 6:16-19)

Jer 7:13 While you were doing all these things, declares the LORD, I spoke to you again and again, but you did not listen; I called you, but you did not answer. ¹⁴Therefore, what I did to Shiloh I will now do to the house that bears my Name, the temple you trust in, the place I gave to you and your fathers.

Jer 7:24 But they did not listen or pay attention; instead, they followed the stubborn inclinations of their evil hearts. They went backward and not forward.

Jer 7:28 Therefore say to them, 'This is the nation that has not obeyed the LORD its God or responded to correction. Truth has perished; it has vanished from their lips. (+Jer 11:8)

Jer 16:12 But you have behaved more wickedly than your fathers. See how each of you is following the stubbornness of his evil heart instead of obeying me.

Jer 17:23 Yet they did not listen or pay attention; they were stiff-necked and would not listen or respond to discipline.

Jer 22:21 I warned you when you felt secure, but you said, 'I will not listen!' This has been your way from your youth; you have not obeyed me. (+Jer 25:4; 26:4-6)

Jer 29:19 For they have not listened to my words," declares the LORD, "words that I sent to them again and again by my servants the prophets. And you exiles have not listened either," declares the LORD. (+Jer 32:33; 35:14-17)

Jer 44:16 "We will not listen to the message you have spoken to us in the name of the LORD! ¹⁷We will certainly do everything we said we would: We will burn incense to the Queen of Heaven and will pour out drink offerings to her just as we and our fathers, our kings and our officials did in the towns of Judah and in the streets of Jerusalem. At that time we had plenty of food and were well off and suffered no harm.

Eze 3:5 You are not being sent to a people of obscure speech and difficult language, but to the house of Israel— ⁶not to many peoples of obscure speech and difficult language, whose words you cannot understand. Surely if I had sent you to them, they would have listened to you. ⁷But the house of Israel is not willing to listen to you because they are not willing to listen to me, for the whole house of Israel is hardened and obstinate. (+Eze 20:8; Zec 1:4; 7:11-13; Mt 13:15)

Lk 16:31 "He said to him, 'If they do not listen to Moses and the Prophets, they will not be convinced even if someone rises from the dead.'"

Seeming lack of hope (Jer 2:25)—

Jer 18:12 But they will reply, 'It's no use. We will continue with our own plans; each of us will follow the stubbornness of his evil heart.'"

Instances of:

Pharaoh (Ex 9:30,34; 10:27; 14:5-9). Israelites (Nu 14:22-23; 2Ki 17:14; 2Ch 24:19; 36:16-17; Ne 9:16-17, 29-30; Jer 36:31). Eli's sons (1Sa 2:25). Amaziah (2Ch 25:16). Manasseh (2Ch 33:10). Amon (2Ch 33:23). Zedekiah (2Ch 36:12-13; Jer 37:2). Jehoiakim and his servants (Jer 36:22-24). Belshazzar (Da 5:22-23). The rich young man (Mt 19:22).

Jews—

Mt 27:4 "I have sinned," he said, "for I have betrayed innocent blood." "What is that to us?" they replied. "That's your responsibility."

Mt 27:25 All the people answered, "Let his blood be on us and on our children!"

Mk 3:5 He looked around at them in anger and, deeply distressed at their stubborn hearts, said to the man, "Stretch out your hand." He stretched it out, and his hand was completely restored.

See Affliction, Of the Wicked; Backsliders; Blindness, Spiritual; Infidelity; Obduracy; Unbelief; Reprobates.

IMPORTS [995, 2256+3655+6590, 2424, 3655, 4604].

Of Israel:

From Egypt: Horses, chariots, and linen (1Ki 10:28-29; 2Ch 1:16).

From Gilead: Spices, balm, and myrrh (Ge 37:25).

From Ophir: Gold (1Ki 10:11; 22:48; 1Ch 29:4).

Tarshish: Gold, silver, ivory, apes, and baboons (1Ki 10:22; 2Ch 9:21), silver, iron, tin, lead, bronze, and slaves (Eze 27:12-13).

From Arabia: Sheep and goats (Eze 27:21).

Of Egypt:

From Gilead: Spices, balm, and myrrh (Ge 37:25).

Of Tyre:

All commodities from and of the trade world (Eze 27:12-25).

IMPORTUNITY *See Prayer.*

IMPOSITION OF HANDS *See Hands, Laying On of.*

IMPOSTORS [1200, 4418]. Deceivers who lead others astray (2Co 6:8); a general word for evil men, cheaters, who also lead others astray (2Ti 3:13).

IMPRECATION Instances of: Ruth (Ru 1:17). Samuel (1Sa 3:17). David (2Sa 1:21; 3:28-29). Shimei (2Sa 16:5,13).

IMPRECATORY PSALMS Especially 35, 58, 69, 70, 83, 109, 137, 140. These contain expressions of an apparent vengeful attitude towards enemies. For some people these psalms constitute one of the "moral difficulties" of the OT. In his covenant with Abraham, God promises to curse those who curse his people (Ge 12:3). *See Curse; Psalms.*

IMPRISONMENT [*5464+, 3973, 6037, 10054, *1301*, *5871*, *5872*].

NIV+ See PRISON

Of Joseph (Ge 39:20). Jeremiah (Jer 38:6). John the Baptist (Mt 11:2; 14:3). Apostles (Ac 5:18). Paul and Silas (Ac 16:24). Peter (Ac 12:4).

Debtors (Mt 5:26; 18:30).

See Prison; Prisoners; Punishment.

IMPUTATION *See Impute.*

IMPUTE To attribute something to a person, or reckon something to the account of another.

Aspects of the doctrine found in the NT:

1. The imputation of Adam's sin to his posterity.

2. The imputation of the sin of man to Christ.

3. The imputation of Christ's righteousness to the believer (Ge 2:3; Ro 3:24; 5:15; Gal 5:4; Tit 3:7; 1Pe 2:24).

IMRAH [3559] (*he rebels*). A chief of the tribe of Asher (1Ch 7:36).

IMRI [617] (*Yahweh spoke*).

1. A man of Judah (1Ch 9:4).

2. Father of Zaccur (Ne 3:2).

INCARNATION (*taking on flesh*). The doctrine that the eternal son of God became human, and that he did so without in any manner or degree diminishing his divine nature (Jn 1:4; Ro 8:3; 1Ti 3:16). *See Jesus the Christ, Incarnation of.*

INCENDIARISM *See Arson.*

INCENSE [2802, 4247, 5231, 5232, 5767+8194, 7777, 7787, 7789, 7792, 10478, *2592, 2593, 2594, 3337*].

NIV+ FRANKINCENSE, INCENSED

Formula for compounding (Ex 30:34-35). Uses of (Ex 30:36-38; Lev 16:12; Nu 16:17,40,46; Dt 33:10). Compounded by Bezalel (Ex 37:29), by priests (1Ch 9:30). Offered, morning and evening (Ex 30:7-8; 2Ch 13:11), on the golden altar (Ex 30:1-7; 40:5,27; 2Ch 2:4; 32:12), in making atonement (Lev 16:12-13; Nu 16:46-47; Lk 1:10). Unlawfully offered by Nadab and Abihu (Lev 10:1-2), Korah, Dathan, and Abiram (Nu 16:16-35), by Uzziah (2Ch 26:16-21). Offered in idolatrous worship (1Ki 12:33; Jer 41:5; Eze 8:11). Presented by the wise men to Jesus (Mt 2:11).

See Altar of Incense.

Figurative:

Of prayer (Ps 141:2). Of praise (Mal 1:11). Of an acceptable sacrifice (Eph 5:2).

Symbolic:

Of the prayers of saints (Rev 5:8; 8:3-4).

INCEST

Defined and forbidden—

Lev 18:6 "'No one is to approach any close relative to have sexual relations. I am the LORD.

7"'Do not dishonor your father by having sexual relations with your mother. She is your mother; do not have relations with her.

8"'Do not have sexual relations with your father's wife; that would dishonor your father.

9"'Do not have sexual relations with your sister, either your father's daughter or your mother's daughter, whether she was born in the same home or elsewhere.

10"'Do not have sexual relations with your son's daughter or your daughter's daughter; that would dishonor you.

11"'Do not have sexual relations with the daughter of your father's wife, born to your father; she is your sister.

12"'Do not have sexual relations with your father's sister; she is your father's close relative.

13"'Do not have sexual relations with your mother's sister, because she is your mother's close relative.

14"'Do not dishonor your father's brother by approaching his wife to have sexual relations; she is your aunt.

15"'Do not have sexual relations with your daughter-in-law. She is your son's wife; do not have relations with her.

16"'Do not have sexual relations with your brother's wife; that would dishonor your brother.

17"'Do not have sexual relations with both a woman and her daughter. Do not have sexual relations with either her son's daughter or her daughter's daughter; they are her close relatives. That is wickedness.

18"'Do not take your wife's sister as a rival wife and have sexual relations with her while your wife is living.

Lev 20:11 "'If a man sleeps with his father's wife, he has dishonored his father. Both the man and the woman must be put to death; their blood will be on their own heads.

12"'If a man sleeps with his daughter-in-law, both of them must be put to death. What they have done is a perversion; their blood will be on their own heads.

Lev 20:17 "'If a man marries his sister, the daughter of either his father or his mother, and they have sexual relations, it is a disgrace. They must be cut off before the eyes of their people. He has dishonored his sister and will be held responsible. (+Lev 20:18)

Lev 20:19 "'Do not have sexual relations with the sister of either your mother or your father, for that would dishonor a close relative; both of you would be held responsible.

20"'If a man sleeps with his aunt, he has dishonored his uncle. They will be held responsible; they will die childless.

21"'If a man marries his brother's wife, it is an act of impurity; he has dishonored his brother. They will be childless.

Dt 22:30 A man is not to marry his father's wife; he must not dishonor his father's bed.

Dt 27:20 "Cursed is the man who sleeps with his father's wife, for he dishonors his father's bed." Then all the people shall say, "Amen!" (+Dt 27:21)

Dt 27:22 "Cursed is the man who sleeps with his sister, the daughter of his father or the daughter of his mother."

Then all the people shall say, "Amen!"

23"Cursed is the man who sleeps with his mother-in-law."

Then all the people shall say, "Amen!"

Eze 22:11 In you one man commits a detestable offense with his neighbor's wife, another shamefully defiles his daughter-in-law, and another violates his sister, his own father's daughter.

1Co 5:1 It is actually reported that there is sexual immorality among you, and of a kind that does not occur even among pagans: A man has his father's wife.

Instances of:

Lot with his daughters (Ge 19:31-36). Abraham (Ge 20:12-13). Nahor (Ge 11:29). Reuben (Ge 35:22; 49:4). Amram (Ex 6:20). Judah (Ge 38:16-18; 1Ch 2:4). Amnon (2Sa 13:14). Absalom (2Sa 16:21-22). Israel (Am 2:7). Herod (Mt 14:3-4; Mk 6:17-18; Lk 3:19).

Instances of Marriage of Near Relatives:

Abraham with Sarah (Ge 20:11-13). Isaac with Rebekah (Ge 24:15,67). Jacob with Leah and Rachel (Ge 29:23,30). Rehoboam (2Ch 11:18).

INCINERATION *See Cremation.*

INCOMPARABILITY OF GOD *See God, Incomparable; None Like God.*

INCONSISTENCY

Hypocritical—

Mt 7:3 "Why do you look at the speck of sawdust in your brother's eye and pay no attention to the plank in your own eye? ⁴How can you say to your brother, 'Let me take the speck out of your eye,' when all the time there is a plank in your own eye? ⁵You hypocrite, first take the plank out of your own eye, and then you will see clearly to remove the speck from your brother's eye.

Mt 23:3 So you must obey them and do everything they tell you. But do not do what they do, for they do not practice what they preach. ⁴They tie up heavy loads and put them on men's shoulders, but they themselves are not willing to lift a finger to move them.

Inexcusable—

Ro 2:1 You, therefore, have no excuse, you who pass judgment on someone else, for at whatever point you judge the other, you are condemning yourself, because you who pass judgment do the same things. (+Ro 2:21)

Ro 2:22 You who say that people should not commit adultery, do you commit adultery? You who abhor idols, do you rob temples? ²³You who brag about the law, do you dishonor God by breaking the law?

Instances of:

Jehu (2Ki 10:16-31). The Jews, in oppressing the poor (Ne 5:8-9), in accusing Jesus of violating the Sabbath (Jn 7:22-23). Peter and the other disciples, in requiring of the Gentiles that which they did not require of themselves (Gal 2:11-14).

See Deceit; Deception; Hypocrisy.

INDECISION

About God—

1Ki 18:21 Elijah went before the people and said, "How long will you waver between two opinions? If the LORD is God, follow him; but if Baal is God, follow him." But the people said nothing.

Hos 10:2 Their heart is deceitful, and now they must bear their guilt. The LORD will demolish their altars and destroy their sacred stones.

Mt 6:24 "No one can serve two masters. Either he will hate the one and love the other, or he will be devoted to the one and despise the other. You cannot serve both God and Money.

About ethics—

Mt 26:41 "Watch and pray so that you will not fall into temptation. The spirit is willing, but the body is weak."

Jas 1:8 he is a double-minded man, unstable in all he does.

@T = Jas 4:17 Anyone, then, who knows the good he ought to do and doesn't do it, sins. (Rev 3:15)

See Decision; Instability; Lukewarmness.

Instances of:

Moses at the Red Sea (Ex 14:15). Joshua at Ai (Jos 7:10). Esther (Est 5:8). Rulers, who believed in Jesus (Jn 12:42). Felix (Ac 24:25).

INDIA [2064]. Probably the eastern limit of the kingdom of Xerxes (Est 1:1; 8:9).

INDICTMENTS [6219].

Instances of:

Naboth on charge of blasphemy (1Ki 21:13, w 21:1-16). Jeremiah of treasonable prophecy, but of which he was acquitted (Jer 26:1-24), a second indictment (Jer 37:13-15). Three Hebrew captives on the charge of resistance to authority (Da 3:12, w 3:1-28; 6:13, w 6:1-24). Jesus, under two charges, first, of blasphemy (Mt 26:61, w Mk 14:58; Mt 26:63-65, w Mk 14:61-64; Lk 22:67-71; Jn 19:7), second, of treason (Mt 27:11,37; Mk 15:2,26; Lk 23:2-3,38; Jn 18:30,33; 19:12,19-22).

Stephen for blasphemy (Ac 6:11,13). Paul (Ac 17:7; 18:13; 24:5; 25:18-19,26-27). Paul and Silas (Ac 16:20-21).

Indictment quashed (Ac 18:14-16).

INDIGESTION Of Timothy (1Ti 5:23). *See Disease.*

INDUSTRY

Brings prosperity—

Pr 10:4 Lazy hands make a man poor, but diligent hands bring wealth.

⁵He who gathers crops in summer is a wise son, but he who sleeps during harvest is a disgraceful son.

Pr 12:11 He who works his land will have abundant food, but he who chases fantasies lacks judgment.

Pr 12:24 Diligent hands will rule, but laziness ends in slave labor.

Pr 12:27 The lazy man does not roast his game, but the diligent man prizes his possessions.

Pr 13:4 The sluggard craves and gets nothing, but the desires of the diligent are fully satisfied.

Pr 13:11 Dishonest money dwindles away, but he who gathers money little by little makes it grow.

Pr 21:5 The plans of the diligent lead to profit as surely as haste leads to poverty.

Pr 22:29 Do you see a man skilled in his work? He will serve before kings; he will not serve before obscure men.

Pr 28:19 He who works his land will have abundant food, but the one who chases fantasies will have his fill of poverty.

Commanded—

Ge 2:15 The LORD God took the man and put him in the Garden of Eden to work it and take care of it.

Ex 23:12 "Six days do your work, but on the seventh day do not work, so that your ox and your donkey may rest and the slave born in your household, and the alien as well, may be refreshed.

Ex 35:2 For six days, work is to be done, but the seventh day shall be your holy day, a Sabbath of rest to the LORD. Whoever does any work on it must be put to death. (+Dt 5:13)

Pr 20:13 Do not love sleep or you will grow poor; stay awake and you will have food to spare.

Pr 27:23 Be sure you know the condition of your flocks, give careful attention to your herds; (+Pr 27:24-27)

Ecc 9:10 Whatever your hand finds to do, do it with all your might, for in the grave, where you are going, there is neither working nor planning nor knowledge nor wisdom.

Ecc 11:4 Whoever watches the wind will not plant; whoever looks at the clouds will not reap.

Ecc 11:6 Sow your seed in the morning, and at evening let not your hands be idle, for you do not know which will succeed, whether this or that, or whether both will do equally well.

Ro 12:11 Never be lacking in zeal, but keep your spiritual fervor, serving the Lord.

Eph 4:28 He who has been stealing must steal no longer, but must work, doing something useful with his own hands, that he may have something to share with those in need.

1Th 4:11 Make it your ambition to lead a quiet life, to mind your own business and to work with your hands, just as we told you, [12]so that your daily life may win the respect of outsiders and so that you will not be dependent on anybody.

2Th 3:10 For even when we were with you, we gave you this rule: "If a man will not work, he shall not eat."

[11]We hear that some among you are idle. They are not busy; they are busybodies. [12]Such people we command and urge in the Lord Jesus Christ to settle down and earn the bread they eo'.

1Ti 5:8 If anyone does not provide for his relatives, and especially for his immediate family, he has denied the faith and is worse than an unbeliever.

Instigated—

Pr 16:26 The laborer's appetite works for him; his hunger drives him on.

Profitable (Pr 14:4)—

Pr 14:23 All hard work brings a profit, but mere talk leads only to poverty.

Reflections concerning—

Ecc 1:3 What does man gain from all his labor at which he toils under the sun?

Ecc 2:10 I denied myself nothing my eyes desired; I refused my heart no pleasure. My heart took delight in all my work, and this was the reward for all my labor. [11]Yet when I surveyed all that my hands had done and what I had toiled to achieve, everything was meaningless, a chasing after the wind; nothing was gained under the sun.

Ecc 2:17 So I hated life, because the work that is done under the sun was grievous to me. All of it is meaningless, a chasing after the wind. [18]I hated all the things I had toiled for under the sun, because I must leave them to the one who comes after me. [19]And who knows whether he will be a wise man or a fool? Yet he will have control over all the work into which I have poured my effort and skill under the sun. This too is meaningless. [20]So my heart began to despair over all my toilsome labor under the sun. [21]For a man may do his work with wisdom, knowledge and skill, and then he must leave all he owns to someone who has not worked for it. This too is meaningless and a great misfortune. [22]What does a man get for all the toil and anxious striving with which he labors under the sun?

Exemplified:

By ants and conies—

Pr 30:25 Ants are creatures of little strength, yet they store up their food in the summer; [26]coneys are creatures of little power, yet they make their home in the crags;

By prudent wife—

Pr 31:27 She watches over the affairs of her household and does not eat the bread of idleness. (+Pr 31:13-26)

Instances of:

Jeroboam (1Ki 11:28). Paul (Ac 18:3; 20:33-34; 1Co 4:12; 1Th 2:9; 2Th 3:8).

See Frugality; Idleness; Labor; Slothfulness; Work.

INFANTICIDE The killing of children. Commanded by

Pharaoh (Ex 1:15-16; Ac 7:19); by God concerning Midianite boys (Nu 31:17); by Herod (Mt 2:16-18).

INFANTS *See Children.*

INFERTILITY *See Barrenness.*

INFIDELITY

Relating to God:

Disbelief in God—

Nu 15:30 "'But anyone who sins defiantly, whether native-born or alien, blasphemes the LORD, and that person must be cut off from his people. (+Nu 15:31; 2Ch 32:14)

2Ch 32:15 Now do not let Hezekiah deceive you and mislead you like this. Do not believe him, for no god of any nation or kingdom has been able to deliver his people from my hand or the hand of my fathers. How much less will your god deliver you from my hand!" (+2Ch 32:16-19)

Isa 29:16 You turn things upside down, as if the potter were thought to be like the clay! Shall what is formed say to him who formed it, "He did not make me"? Can the pot say of the potter, "He knows nothing"?

Prosperity tempts to—

Dt 32:15 Jeshurun grew fat and kicked; filled with food, he became heavy and sleek. He abandoned the God who made him and rejected the Rock his Savior.

Arguments against (Job 12:7-25)—

Ps 94:8 Take heed, you senseless ones among the people; you fools, when will you become wise? [9]Does he who implanted the ear not hear? Does he who formed the eye not see?

Isa 10:15 Does the ax raise itself above him who swings it, or the saw boast against him who uses it? As if a rod were to wield him who lifts it up, or a club brandish him who is not wood! (+Isa 19:16)

Isa 45:9 "Woe to him who quarrels with his Maker, to him who is but a potsherd among the potsherds on the ground. Does the clay say to the potter, 'What are you making?' Does your work say, 'He has no hands'? (+Isa 45:18; Ro 1:20)

Ro 9:20 But who are you, O man, to talk back to God? "Shall what is formed say to him who formed it, 'Why did you make me like this?'" [21]Does not the potter have the right to make out of the same lump of clay some pottery for noble purposes and some for common use?

Exemplified:

In mocking God—

Ps 14:1 The fool says in his heart, "There is no God." They are corrupt, their deeds are vile; there is no one who does good.

Ps 14:6 You evildoers frustrate the plans of the poor, but the LORD is their refuge.

Ps 50:21 These things you have done and I kept silent; you thought I was altogether like you. But I will rebuke you and accuse you to your face.

Isa 57:4 Whom are you mocking? At whom do you sneer and stick out your tongue? Are you not a brood of rebels, the offspring of liars? (+Isa 57:5-10)

Isa 57:11 "Whom have you so dreaded and feared that you have been false to me, and have neither remembered me nor pondered this in your hearts? Is it not because I have long been silent that you do not fear me?

Eze 36:2 This is what the Sovereign LORD says: The enemy said of you, 'Aha! The ancient heights have become our possession.'"

Da 3:15 Now when you hear the sound of the horn, flute,

zither, lyre, harp, pipes and all kinds of music, if you are ready to fall down and worship the image I made, very good. But if you do not worship it, you will be thrown immediately into a blazing furnace. Then what god will be able to rescue you from my hand?"

Ac 17:18 A group of Epicurean and Stoic philosophers began to dispute with him. Some of them asked, "What is this babbler trying to say?" Others remarked, "He seems to be advocating foreign gods." They said this because Paul was preaching the good news about Jesus and the resurrection.

2Pe 3:3 First of all, you must understand that in the last days scoffers will come, scoffing and following their own evil desires. **4**They will say, "Where is this 'coming' he promised? Ever since our fathers died, everything goes on as it has since the beginning of creation."

Jude 18 They said to you, "In the last times there will be scoffers who will follow their own ungodly desires." (+Jude 19)

In mocking God's servants—

1Ki 22:24 Then Zedekiah son of Kenaanah went up and slapped Micaiah in the face. "Which way did the spirit from the LORD go when he went from me to speak to you?" he asked.

2Ki 2:23 From there Elisha went up to Bethel. As he was walking along the road, some youths came out of the town and jeered at him. "Go on up, you baldhead!" they said. "Go on up, you baldhead!"

2Ch 30:6 At the king's command, couriers went throughout Israel and Judah with letters from the king and from his officials, which read: "People of Israel, return to the LORD, the God of Abraham, Isaac and Israel, that he may return to you who are left, who have escaped from the hand of the kings of Assyria.

2Ch 30:10 The couriers went from town to town in Ephraim and Manasseh, as far as Zebulun, but the people scorned and ridiculed them.

2Ch 36:16 But they mocked God's messengers, despised his words and scoffed at his prophets until the wrath of the LORD was aroused against his people and there was no remedy.

Jer 17:15 They keep saying to me, "Where is the word of the LORD? Let it now be fulfilled!" (+Jer 43:2)

Eze 20:49 Then I said, "Ah, Sovereign LORD! They are saying of me, 'Isn't he just telling parables?'"

Ac 2:13 Some, however, made fun of them and said, "They have had too much wine."

In rejecting God—

Ex 5:2 Pharaoh said, "Who is the LORD, that I should obey him and let Israel go? I do not know the LORD and I will not let Israel go."

Job 15:25 because he shakes his fist at God and vaunts himself against the Almighty, **26**defiantly charging against him with a thick, strong shield.

Job 21:14 Yet they say to God, 'Leave us alone! We have no desire to know your ways. **15**Who is the Almighty, that we should serve him? What would we gain by praying to him?' (+Ps 14:1; 53:1)

Ps 106:24 Then they despised the pleasant land; they did not believe his promise. **25**They grumbled in their tents and did not obey the LORD.

Jer 2:31 "You of this generation, consider the word of the LORD: "Have I been a desert to Israel or a land of great darkness? Why do my people say, 'We are free to roam; we will come to you no more'?"

In rejecting Christ—

Mt 12:24 But when the Pharisees heard this, they said, "It is only by Beelzebub, the prince of demons, that this fellow drives out demons."

Mt 27:39 Those who passed by hurled insults at him, shaking their heads **40**and saying, "You who are going to destroy the temple and build it in three days, save yourself! Come down from the cross, if you are the Son of God!"

41In the same way the chief priests, the teachers of the law and the elders mocked him. **42**"He saved others," they said, "but he can't save himself! He's the King of Israel! Let him come down now from the cross, and we will believe in him. **43**He trusts in God. Let God rescue him now if he wants him, for he said, 'I am the Son of God.'" **44**In the same way the robbers who were crucified with him also heaped insults on him. (+Mk 3:22; Lk 11:15)

Lk 19:14 "But his subjects hated him and sent a delegation after him to say, 'We don't want this man to be our king.'

Lk 19:27 But those enemies of mine who did not want me to be king over them—bring them here and kill them in front of me.'"

By Antichrist (Da 7:25)—

Da 8:25 He will cause deceit to prosper, and he will consider himself superior. When they feel secure, he will destroy many and take his stand against the Prince of princes. Yet he will be destroyed, but not by human power. (+Da 11:36-37)

In doubting God's help—

Ex 17:7 And he called the place Massah and Meribah because the Israelites quarreled and because they tested the LORD saying, "Is the LORD among us or not?"

Ps 3:2 Many are saying of me, "God will not deliver him." *Selah*

Ps 78:19 They spoke against God, saying, "Can God spread a table in the desert? (+Ps 78:20,22; 107:11-12)

In impugning God's holiness—

Job 35:3 Yet you ask him, 'What profit is it to me, and what do I gain by not sinning?'

Ps 10:11 He says to himself, "God has forgotten; he covers his face and never sees."

Ps 10:13 Why does the wicked man revile God? Why does he say to himself, "He won't call me to account"?

Eze 18:2 "What do you people mean by quoting this proverb about the land of Israel: "'The fathers eat sour grapes, and the children's teeth are set on edge'?

Eze 18:29 Yet the house of Israel says, 'The way of the Lord is not just.' Are my ways unjust, O house of Israel? Is it not your ways that are unjust?

Mal 1:7 "You place defiled food on my altar. "But you ask, 'How have we defiled you?' "By saying that the LORD's table is contemptible.

Mal 3:14 "You have said, 'It is futile to serve God. What did we gain by carrying out his requirements and going about like mourners before the LORD Almighty?

In impugning God's knowledge—

Job 22:13 Yet you say, 'What does God know? Does he judge through such darkness? **14**Thick clouds veil him, so he does not see us as he goes about in the vaulted heavens.'

Job 22:17 They said to God, 'Leave us alone! What can the Almighty do to us?'

Ps 59:7 See what they spew from their mouths—they spew out swords from their lips, and they say, "Who can hear us?"

Ps 64:5 They encourage each other in evil plans, they talk about hiding their snares; they say, "Who will see them?"

Ps 73:11 They say, "How can God know? Does the Most High have knowledge?"

Isa 29:15 Woe to those who go to great depths to hide their plans from the LORD, who do their work in darkness and think, "Who sees us? Who will know?" (+Eze 8:12)

In impugning God's mercy—

Ps 42:3 My tears have been my food day and night, while men say to me all day long, "Where is your God?"

God's righteousness (Eze 18:2,29).

Punishment for: (Nu 15:30-31)

Dt 29:19 When such a person hears the words of this oath, he invokes a blessing on himself and therefore thinks, "I will be safe, even though I persist in going my own way." This will bring disaster on the watered land as well as the dry. [20]The LORD will never be willing to forgive him; his wrath and zeal will burn against that man. All the curses written in this book will fall upon him, and the LORD will blot out his name from under heaven. (+Dt 29:21)

Ps 12:3 May the LORD cut off all flattering lips and every boastful tongue [4]that says, "We will triumph with our tongues; we own our lips—who is our master?"

Pr 3:34 He mocks proud mockers but gives grace to the humble.

Pr 9:12 If you are wise, your wisdom will reward you; if you are a mocker, you alone will suffer."

Pr 19:29 Penalties are prepared for mockers, and beatings for the backs of fools.

Pr 24:9 The schemes of folly are sin, and men detest a mocker.

Isa 3:8 Jerusalem staggers, Judah is falling; their words and deeds are against the LORD, defying his glorious presence.

Isa 5:18 Woe to those who draw sin along with cords of deceit, and wickedness as with cart ropes, [19]to those who say, "Let God hurry, let him hasten his work so we may see it. Let it approach, let the plan of the Holy One of Israel come, so we may know it."

Isa 5:24 Therefore, as tongues of fire lick up straw and as dry grass sinks down in the flames, so their roots will decay and their flowers blow away like dust; for they have rejected the law of the LORD Almighty and spurned the word of the Holy One of Israel. [25]Therefore the LORD's anger burns against his people; his hand is raised and he strikes them down. The mountains shake, and the dead bodies are like refuse in the streets. Yet for all this, his anger is not turned away, his hand is still upraised.

Isa 28:9 "Who is it he is trying to teach? To whom is he explaining his message? To children weaned from their milk, to those just taken from the breast? [10]For it is: Do and do, do and do, rule on rule, rule on rule; a little here, a little there."

Isa 28:14 Therefore hear the word of the LORD, you scoffers who rule this people in Jerusalem. [15]You boast, "We have entered into a covenant with death, with the grave we have made an agreement. When an overwhelming scourge sweeps by, it cannot touch us, for we have made a lie our refuge and falsehood our hiding place." (+Isa 28:16)

Isa 28:17 I will make justice the measuring line and righteousness the plumb line; hail will sweep away your refuge, the lie, and water will overflow your hiding place. [18]Your covenant with death will be annulled; your agreement with the grave will not stand. When the overwhelming scourge sweeps by, you will be beaten down by it. [19]As often as it comes it will carry you away; morning after morning, by day and by night, it will sweep through." The understanding of this message will bring sheer terror.

[20]The bed is too short to stretch out on, the blanket too narrow to wrap around you. [21]The LORD will rise up as he did at Mount Perazim, he will rouse himself as in the Valley of Gibeon—to do his work, his strange work, and perform his task, his alien task. [22]Now stop your mocking, or your chains will become heavier; the Lord, the LORD Almighty, has told me of the destruction decreed against the whole land.

Isa 47:10 You have trusted in your wickedness and have said, 'No one sees me.' Your wisdom and knowledge mislead you when you say to yourself, 'I am, and there is none besides me.' [11]Disaster will come upon you, and you will not know how to conjure it away. A calamity will fall upon you that you cannot ward off with a ransom; a catastrophe you cannot foresee will suddenly come upon you.

Jer 5:12 They have lied about the LORD; they said, "He will do nothing! No harm will come to us; we will never see sword or famine.

Jer 5:14 Therefore this is what the LORD God Almighty says: "Because the people have spoken these words, I will make my words in your mouth a fire and these people the wood it consumes.

Jer 48:42 Moab will be destroyed as a nation because she defied the LORD.

Jer 50:24 I set a trap for you, O Babylon, and you were caught before you knew it; you were found and captured because you opposed the LORD.

Jer 50:29 "Summon archers against Babylon, all those who draw the bow. Encamp all around her; let no one escape. Repay her for her deeds; do to her as she has done. For she has defied the LORD, the Holy One of Israel.

Eze 9:9 He answered me, "The sin of the house of Israel and Judah is exceedingly great; the land is full of bloodshed and the city is full of injustice. They say, 'The LORD has forsaken the land; the LORD does not see.' (+Eze 9:10; 32:20)

Hos 7:5 On the day of the festival of our king the princes become inflamed with wine, and he joins hands with the mockers.

Hos 7:13 Woe to them, because they have strayed from me! Destruction to them, because they have rebelled against me! I long to redeem them but they speak lies against me.

Hos 7:15 I trained them and strengthened them, but they plot evil against me.

Am 5:18 Woe to you who long for the day of the LORD! Why do you long for the day of the LORD? That day will be darkness, not light.

Am 7:16 Now then, hear the word of the LORD. You say, "'Do not prophesy against Israel, and stop preaching against the house of Isaac.'

[17]"Therefore this is what the LORD says:

"'Your wife will become a prostitute in the city, and your sons and daughters will fall by the sword. Your land will be measured and divided up, and you yourself will die in a pagan country. And Israel will certainly go into exile, away from their native land.'"

Mic 7:10 Then my enemy will see it and will be covered with shame, she who said to me, "Where is the LORD your God?" My eyes will see her downfall; even now she will be trampled underfoot like mire in the streets.

Zep 1:12 At that time I will search Jerusalem with lamps and punish those who are complacent, who are like wine left on its dregs, who think, 'The LORD will do nothing, either good or bad.' (+Lk 19:14,27; Heb 10:28)

Heb 10:29 How much more severely do you think a man deserves to be punished who has trampled the Son of God under foot, who has treated as an unholy thing the blood of the covenant that sanctified him, and who has insulted the Spirit of grace?

2Pe 2:1 But there were also false prophets among the people, just as there will be false teachers among you. They will secretly introduce destructive heresies, even denying the sovereign Lord who bought them—bringing swift destruction on themselves.

Relating to Friends:

(Ps 41:9; Mt 26:14-16,47-50; Mk 14:10-11,43-46; Lk 22:3-6,47-48; Jn 13:18; 18:2-5).

See Presumption; Skepticism; Unbelief.

INFINITY *See God, Infinite.*

INFIRMITY [2716, *819*].

NIV+ INFIRMITIES

Physical (Ecc 12:3). Of Isaac (Ge 27:1). Of Jacob (Ge 48:10). Moses exempt from (Dt 34:7). Caleb exempt from (Jos 14:11). Of Eli (1Sa 3:2). Of Barzillai (2Sa 19:32).

See Affliction; Blindness; Deafness; Lameness; Old Age; Taste.

INFLAMMATION [1945]. Disease brought as a curse for unfaithfulness to Yahweh (Dt 28:22). *See Disease.*

INFLUENCE [6476, *72, 1543*].

NIV+ INFLUENCED, INFLUENTIAL

Solicited, Bathsheba for Adonijah (1Ki 2:13-18).

Offered, Elisha for Shunammite woman (2Ki 4:12-13).

Intercession in Behalf of Friends:

Of Jonathan for David (1Sa 19:1-6; 20:4-9), of nobles of Judah in behalf of Tobiah (Ne 6:17-19), of mother of Zebedee's children for sons (Mt 20:20-24), of Blastus for Tyre and Sidon (Ac 12:20).

Good Influences:

Injunctions concerning—

Mt 5:13 "You are the salt of the earth. But if the salt loses its saltiness, how can it be made salty again? It is no longer good for anything, except to be thrown out and trampled by men.

[14]"You are the light of the world. A city on a hill cannot be hidden. [15]Neither do people light a lamp and put it under a bowl. Instead they put it on its stand, and it gives light to everyone in the house. [16]In the same way, let your light shine before men, that they may see your good deeds and praise your Father in heaven.

Mk 4:21 He said to them, "Do you bring in a lamp to put it under a bowl or a bed? Instead, don't you put it on its stand? [22]For whatever is hidden is meant to be disclosed, and whatever is concealed is meant to be brought out into the open. (+Lk 8:16)

Lk 11:33 "No one lights a lamp and puts it in a place where it will be hidden, or under a bowl. Instead he puts it on its stand, so that those who come in may see the light. [34]Your eye is the lamp of your body. When your eyes are good, your whole body also is full of light. But when they are bad, your body also is full of darkness. [35]See to it, then, that the light within you is not darkness. [36]Therefore, if your whole body is full of light, and no part of it dark, it will be completely lighted, as when the light of a lamp shines on you."

Jn 7:38 Whoever believes in me, as the Scripture has said,

streams of living water will flow from within him." (+1Co 7:14)

1Co 7:16 How do you know, wife, whether you will save your husband? Or, how do you know, husband, whether you will save your wife?

Php 2:15 so that you may become blameless and pure, children of God without fault in a crooked and depraved generation, in which you shine like stars in the universe

1Th 1:7 And so you became a model to all the believers in Macedonia and Achaia. [8]The Lord's message rang out from you not only in Macedonia and Achaia—your faith in God has become known everywhere. Therefore we do not need to say anything about it,

1Ti 6:1 All who are under the yoke of slavery should consider their masters worthy of full respect, so that God's name and our teaching may not be slandered.

Heb 11:4 By faith Abel offered God a better sacrifice than Cain did. By faith he was commended as a righteous man, when God spoke well of his offerings. And by faith he still speaks, even though he is dead.

1Pe 2:11 Dear friends, I urge you, as aliens and strangers in the world, to abstain from sinful desires, which war against your soul. [12]Live such good lives among the pagans that, though they accuse you of doing wrong, they may see your good deeds and glorify God on the day he visits us.

1Pe 3:1 Wives, in the same way be submissive to your husbands so that, if any of them do not believe the word, they may be won over without words by the behavior of their wives, [2]when they see the purity and reverence of your lives.

1Pe 3:15 But in your hearts set apart Christ as Lord. Always be prepared to give an answer to everyone who asks you to give the reason for the hope that you have. But do this with gentleness and respect, [16]keeping a clear conscience, so that those who speak maliciously against your good behavior in Christ may be ashamed of their slander.

Instances of: David over his successors (1Ki 3:3; 2Ki 18:3; 22:2; 2Ch 29:2; 34:2).

Asa over Jehoshaphat—

1Ki 22:42 Jehoshaphat was thirty-five years old when he became king, and he reigned in Jerusalem twenty-five years. His mother's name was Azubah daughter of Shilhi. [43]In everything he walked in the ways of his father Asa and did not stray from them; he did what was right in the eyes of the LORD. The high places, however, were not removed, and the people continued to offer sacrifices and burn incense there.

Joash over Amaziah (2Ki 14:3).

Amaziah over Azariah—

2Ki 15:1 In the twenty-seventh year of Jeroboam king of Israel, Azariah son of Amaziah king of Judah began to reign. [2]He was sixteen years old when he became king, and he reigned in Jerusalem fifty-two years. His mother's name was Jecoliah; she was from Jerusalem. [3]He did what was right in the eyes of the LORD, just as his father Amaziah had done.

Uzziah over Jotham—

2Ki 15:34 He did what was right in the eyes of the LORD, just as his father Uzziah had done.

Josiah, in religious zeal (2Ki 22; 23:1-5; 2Ch 34:33). Hezekiah, for religious reform (2Ch 29-31). Ezra, against marriage with idolaters (Ezr 10:1,9). Nehemiah, during the rebuilding of the walls of Jerusalem (Ne 4:7-23; 5).

Evil Influences:

Of ruler over servants (Pr 22:12).

Of wicked parents over children—

Jer 17:1 "Judah's sin is engraved with an iron tool, inscribed with a flint point, on the tablets of their hearts and on the horns of their altars. ²Even their children remember their altars and Asherah poles beside the spreading trees and on the high hills.

Of wicked priest and people—

Hos 4:9 And it will be: Like people, like priests. I will punish both of them for their ways and repay them for their deeds.

Warnings against—

Pr 22:24 Do not make friends with a hot-tempered man, do not associate with one easily angered, ²⁵or you may learn his ways and get yourself ensnared.

Lk 12:1 Meanwhile, when a crowd of many thousands had gathered, so that they were trampling on one another, Jesus began to speak first to his disciples, saying: "Be on your guard against the yeast of the Pharisees, which is hypocrisy.

1Co 5:6 Your boasting is not good. Don't you know that a little yeast works through the whole batch of dough? ⁷Get rid of the old yeast that you may be a new batch without yeast—as you really are. For Christ, our Passover lamb, has been sacrificed. ⁸Therefore let us keep the Festival, not with the old yeast, the yeast of malice and wickedness, but with bread without yeast, the bread of sincerity and truth.

Gal 5:7 You were running a good race. Who cut in on you and kept you from obeying the truth? ⁸That kind of persuasion does not come from the one who calls you. ⁹"A little yeast works through the whole batch of dough."

2Ti 2:14 Keep reminding them of these things. Warn them before God against quarreling about words; it is of no value, and only ruins those who listen.

2Ti 2:17 Their teaching will spread like gangrene. Among them are Hymenaeus and Philetus, ¹⁸who have wandered away from the truth. They say that the resurrection has already taken place, and they destroy the faith of some.

Heb 12:15 See to it that no one misses the grace of God and that no bitter root grows up to cause trouble and defile many.

Parable of—

Mt 13:24 Jesus told them another parable: "The kingdom of heaven is like a man who sowed good seed in his field. ²⁵But while everyone was sleeping, his enemy came and sowed weeds among the wheat, and went away.

Instances of Evil Influences:

Eve over Adam (Ge 3:6).

Solomon's wives—

1Ki 11:3 He had seven hundred wives of royal birth and three hundred concubines, and his wives led him astray. ⁴As Solomon grew old, his wives turned his heart after other gods, and his heart was not fully devoted to the LORD his God, as the heart of David his father had been.

The young men over Rehoboam (1Ki 12:8-14; 2Ch 10:8-14). Rehoboam over Abijah (1Ki 15:3).

Jeroboam over Nadab—

1Ki 15:25 Nadab son of Jeroboam became king of Israel in the second year of Asa king of Judah, and he reigned over Israel two years. ²⁶He did evil in the eyes of the LORD, walking in the ways of his father and in his sin, which he had caused Israel to commit.

Jezebel over Ahab (1Ki 21:4-16)—

1Ki 21:25 (There was never a man like Ahab, who sold himself to do evil in the eyes of the LORD, urged on by Jezebel his wife.

Ahab over Ahaziah—

1Ki 22:52 He did evil in the eyes of the LORD, because he walked in the ways of his father and mother and in the ways of Jeroboam son of Nebat, who caused Israel to sin. ⁵³He served and worshiped Baal and provoked the LORD, the God of Israel, to anger, just as his father had done.

2Ki 8:25 In the twelfth year of Joram son of Ahab king of Israel, Ahaziah son of Jehoram king of Judah began to reign. ²⁶Ahaziah was twenty-two years old when he became king, and he reigned in Jerusalem one year. His mother's name was Athaliah, a granddaughter of Omri king of Israel. ²⁷He walked in the ways of the house of Ahab and did evil in the eyes of the LORD, as the house of Ahab had done, for he was related by marriage to Ahab's family.

Ahab over Jehoram—

2Ki 8:16 In the fifth year of Joram son of Ahab king of Israel, when Jehoshaphat was king of Judah, Jehoram son of Jehoshaphat began his reign as king of Judah.

2Ki 8:18 He walked in the ways of the kings of Israel, as the house of Ahab had done, for he married a daughter of Ahab. He did evil in the eyes of the LORD.

2Ch 21:5 Jehoram was thirty-two years old when he became king, and he reigned in Jerusalem eight years. ⁶He walked in the ways of the kings of Israel, as the house of Ahab had done, for he married a daughter of Ahab. He did evil in the eyes of the LORD.

2Ch 22:3 He too walked in the ways of the house of Ahab, for his mother encouraged him in doing wrong. ⁴He did evil in the eyes of the LORD, as the house of Ahab had done, for after his father's death they became his advisers, to his undoing. ⁵He also followed their counsel when he went with Joram son of Ahab king of Israel to war against Hazael king of Aram at Ramoth Gilead. The Arameans wounded Joram;

Jeroboam over Israel—

2Ki 17:21 When he tore Israel away from the house of David, they made Jeroboam son of Nebat their king. Jeroboam enticed Israel away from following the LORD and caused them to commit a great sin. ²²The Israelites persisted in all the sins of Jeroboam and did not turn away from them

Manasseh over Judah—

2Ki 21:9 But the people did not listen. Manasseh led them astray, so that they did more evil than the nations the LORD had destroyed before the Israelites.

2Ch 33:9 But Manasseh led Judah and the people of Jerusalem astray, so that they did more evil than the nations the LORD had destroyed before the Israelites.

Manasseh over Amon (2Ki 21:20-21). Jehoiakim over Jehoiachin (2Ki 24:9).

Political:

1Ki 2:13 Now Adonijah, the son of Haggith, went to Bathsheba, Solomon's mother. Bathsheba asked him, "Do you come peacefully?"

He answered, "Yes, peacefully." ¹⁴Then he added, "I have something to say to you."

"You may say it," she replied.

¹⁵"As you know," he said, "the kingdom was mine. All Israel looked to me as their king. But things changed, and the kingdom has gone to my brother; for it has come to him from the LORD. ¹⁶Now I have one request to make of you. Do not refuse me."

"You may make it," she said.

¹⁷So he continued, "Please ask King Solomon—he will not refuse you—to give me Abishag the Shunammite as my wife."

¹⁸"Very well," Bathsheba replied, "I will speak to the king for you."

2Ki 4:12 He said to his servant Gehazi, "Call the Shunammite." So he called her, and she stood before him. ¹³Elisha said to him, "Tell her, 'You have gone to all this trouble for us. Now what can be done for you? Can we speak on your behalf to the king or the commander of the army?'"

She replied, "I have a home among my own people."

Ne 6:17 Also, in those days the nobles of Judah were sending many letters to Tobiah, and replies from Tobiah kept coming to them. ¹⁸For many in Judah were under oath to him, since he was son-in-law to Shecaniah son of Arah, and his son Jehohanan had married the daughter of Meshullam son of Berekiah. ¹⁹Moreover, they kept reporting to me his good deeds and then telling him what I said. And Tobiah sent letters to intimidate me.

Pr 19:6 Many curry favor with a ruler, and everyone is the friend of a man who gives gifts.

Pr 29:26 Many seek an audience with a ruler, but it is from the LORD that man gets justice.

Da 5:10 The queen, hearing the voices of the king and his nobles, came into the banquet hall. "O king, live forever!" she said. "Don't be alarmed! Don't look so pale! ¹¹There is a man in your kingdom who has the spirit of the holy gods in him. In the time of your father he was found to have insight and intelligence and wisdom like that of the gods. King Nebuchadnezzar your father—your father the king, I say—appointed him chief of the magicians, enchanters, astrologers and diviners. ¹²This man Daniel, whom the king called Belteshazzar, was found to have a keen mind and knowledge and understanding, and also the ability to interpret dreams, explain riddles and solve difficult problems. Call for Daniel, and he will tell you what the writing means."

Mt 20:20 Then the mother of Zebedee's sons came to Jesus with her sons and, kneeling down, asked a favor of him.

²¹"What is it you want?" he asked.

She said, "Grant that one of these two sons of mine may sit at your right and the other at your left in your kingdom."

²²"You don't know what you are asking," Jesus said to them. "Can you drink the cup I am going to drink?"

"We can," they answered.

²³Jesus said to them, "You will indeed drink from my cup, but to sit at my right or left is not for me to grant. These places belong to those for whom they have been prepared by my Father."

²⁴When the ten heard about this, they were indignant with the two brothers.

Ac 12:20 He had been quarreling with the people of Tyre and Sidon; they now joined together and sought an audience with him. Having secured the support of Blastus, a trusted personal servant of the king, they asked for peace, because they depended on the king's country for their food supply.

See Example; Politics.

INGATHERING, FEAST OF [658]. See

Tabernacles, Feast of.

INGRAFTING *See Graft.*

INGRATITUDE

To God:

Ro 1:21 For although they knew God, they neither glorified him as God nor gave thanks to him, but their thinking became futile and their foolish hearts were darkened.

2Ti 3:2 People will be lovers of themselves, lovers of money, boastful, proud, abusive, disobedient to their parents, ungrateful, unholy,

Prosperity tempts (Dt 6:10-12)—

Dt 8:12 Otherwise, when you eat and are satisfied, when you build fine houses and settle down, ¹³and when your herds and flocks grow large and your silver and gold increase and all you have is multiplied, ¹⁴then your heart will become proud and you will forget the LORD your God, who brought you out of Egypt, out of the land of slavery.

Dt 32:6 Is this the way you repay the LORD, O foolish and unwise people? Is he not your Father, your Creator, who made you and formed you? (+Dt 32:13)

Dt 32:15 Jeshurun grew fat and kicked; filled with food, he became heavy and sleek. He abandoned the God who made him and rejected the Rock his Savior.

Dt 32:18 You deserted the Rock, who fathered you; you forgot the God who gave you birth.

2Ch 26:15 In Jerusalem he made machines designed by skillful men for use on the towers and on the corner defenses to shoot arrows and hurl large stones. His fame spread far and wide, for he was greatly helped until he became powerful.

¹⁶But after Uzziah became powerful, his pride led to his downfall. He was unfaithful to the LORD his God, and entered the temple of the LORD to burn incense on the altar of incense.

Jer 5:7 "Why should I forgive you? Your children have forsaken me and sworn by gods that are not gods. I supplied all their needs, yet they committed adultery and thronged to the houses of prostitutes. ⁸They are well-fed, lusty stallions, each neighing for another man's wife. ⁹Should I not punish them for this?" declares the LORD. "Should I not avenge myself on such a nation as this?

Jer 5:24 They do not say to themselves, 'Let us fear the LORD our God, who gives autumn and spring rains in season, who assures us of the regular weeks of harvest.'

Hos 13:6 When I fed them, they were satisfied; when they were satisfied, they became proud; then they forgot me.

Punishment for—

Dt 28:47 Because you did not serve the LORD your God joyfully and gladly in the time of prosperity, ⁴⁸therefore in hunger and thirst, in nakedness and dire poverty, you will serve the enemies the LORD sends against you. He will put an iron yoke on your neck until he has destroyed you. (+1Ki 16:1-3)

2Ch 32:25 But Hezekiah's heart was proud and he did not respond to the kindness shown him; therefore the LORD's wrath was on him and on Judah and Jerusalem.

Ps 78:16 he brought streams out of a rocky crag and made water flow down like rivers.

¹⁷But they continued to sin against him, rebelling in the desert against the Most High.

Ps 78:27 He rained meat down on them like dust, flying birds like sand on the seashore. ²⁸He made them come down inside their camp, all around their tents. ²⁹They ate till they had more than enough, for he had given them what they craved. ³⁰But before they turned from the food they craved, even while it was still in their mouths, ³¹God's anger rose against them; he put to death the sturdiest among them, cutting down the young men of Israel.

[32]In spite of all this, they kept on sinning; in spite of his wonders, they did not believe. (+Ps 78:42-68)

Da 5:18 "O king, the Most High God gave your father Nebuchadnezzar sovereignty and greatness and glory and splendor.

Da 5:20 But when his heart became arrogant and hardened with pride, he was deposed from his royal throne and stripped of his glory. [21]He was driven away from people and given the mind of an animal; he lived with the wild donkeys and ate grass like cattle; and his body was drenched with the dew of heaven, until he acknowledged that the Most High God is sovereign over the kingdoms of men and sets over them anyone he wishes.

Instances of Ingratitude to God:

Nu 16:9 Isn't it enough for you that the God of Israel has separated you from the rest of the Israelite community and brought you near himself to do the work at the LORD's tabernacle and to stand before the community and minister to them? [10]He has brought you and all your fellow Levites near himself, but now you are trying to get the priesthood too.

Israel—

Dt 31:16 And the LORD said to Moses: "You are going to rest with your fathers, and these people will soon prostitute themselves to the foreign gods of the land they are entering. They will forsake me and break the covenant I made with them.

Jdg 2:10 After that whole generation had been gathered to their fathers, another generation grew up, who knew neither the LORD nor what he had done for Israel. [11]Then the Israelites did evil in the eyes of the LORD and served the Baals. [12]They forsook the LORD, the God of their fathers, who had brought them out of Egypt. They followed and worshiped various gods of the peoples around them. They provoked the LORD to anger

Jdg 8:34 did not remember the LORD their God, who had rescued them from the hands of all their enemies on every side. [35]They also failed to show kindness to the family of Jerub-Baal (that is, Gideon) for all the good things he had done for them.

Jdg 10:11 The LORD replied, "When the Egyptians, the Amorites, the Ammonites, the Philistines,

Jdg 10:13 But you have forsaken me and served other gods, so I will no longer save you. [14]Go and cry out to the gods you have chosen. Let them save you when you are in trouble!"

1Sa 8:7 And the LORD told him: "Listen to all that the people are saying to you; it is not you they have rejected, but they have rejected me as their king. [8]As they have done from the day I brought them up out of Egypt until this day, forsaking me and serving other gods, so they are doing to you.

1Sa 10:19 But you have now rejected your God, who saves you out of all your calamities and distresses. And you have said, 'No, set a king over us.' So now present yourselves before the LORD by your tribes and clans." (+Ne 9:25-26,35)

Ps 106:7 When our fathers were in Egypt, they gave no thought to your miracles; they did not remember your many kindnesses, and they rebelled by the sea, the Red Sea. (+Ps 106:21)

Isa 1:2 Hear, O heavens! Listen, O earth! For the LORD has spoken: "I reared children and brought them up, but they have rebelled against me. (+Jer 2:6-9)

Jer 2:17 Have you not brought this on yourselves by forsaking the LORD your God when he led you in the way?

Jer 2:31 "You of this generation, consider the word of the LORD: "Have I been a desert to Israel or a land of great darkness? Why do my people say, 'We are free to roam; we will come to you no more'? (+Jer 4:7; 7:13,19; 11:1,3)

Am 3:1 Hear this word the LORD has spoken against you, O people of Israel—against the whole family I brought up out of Egypt: [2]"You only have I chosen of all the families of the earth; therefore I will punish you for all your sins."

Mic 6:3 "My people, what have I done to you? How have I burdened you? Answer me. [4]I brought you up out of Egypt and redeemed you from the land of slavery. I sent Moses to lead you, also Aaron and Miriam.

Saul—

1Sa 15:17 Samuel said, "Although you were once small in your own eyes, did you not become the head of the tribes of Israel? The LORD anointed you king over Israel.

1Sa 15:19 Why did you not obey the LORD? Why did you pounce on the plunder and do evil in the eyes of the LORD?"

David—

2Sa 12:7 Then Nathan said to David, "You are the man! This is what the LORD, the God of Israel, says: 'I anointed you king over Israel, and I delivered you from the hand of Saul. [8]I gave your master's house to you, and your master's wives into your arms. I gave you the house of Israel and Judah. And if all this had been too little, I would have given you even more. [9]Why did you despise the word of the LORD by doing what is evil in his eyes? You struck down Uriah the Hittite with the sword and took his wife to be your own. You killed him with the sword of the Ammonites.

Baasha—

1Ki 16:1 Then the word of the LORD came to Jehu son of Hanani against Baasha: [2]"I lifted you up from the dust and made you leader of my people Israel, but you walked in the ways of Jeroboam and caused my people Israel to sin and to provoke me to anger by their sins.

Jerusalem—

Eze 16:17 You also took the fine jewelry I gave you, the jewelry made of my gold and silver, and you made for yourself male idols and engaged in prostitution with them.

Humanity (Ro 1:21; 2Ti 3:2).

Ingratitude to Jesus: The nine lepers (Lk 17:12-18). His own people (Jn 1:11).

Ingratitude of Person to Person: (Pr 17:13; 2Ti 3:2).

Instances of: Laban to Jacob (Ge 31). Pharaoh's cupbearer to Joseph (Ge 40:23). Israelites to Moses (Ex 16:3; 17:2-4; Nu 16:12-14), to Gideon (Jdg 8:35). Shechemites (Jdg 9:17-18). Men of Keilah to David (1Sa 23:5-12). Saul to David (1Sa 24). Nabal (1Sa 25:21). David to Joab (1Ki 2:5-6), with the history of Joab's services to David. *See Joab.* David to Uriah (2Sa 11:6-17). David's companions to David (Ps 35:11-16; 38:20; 41:9; 109:4-5). Citizens (Ecc 9:14-16). Joash (2Ch 24:22). Jeremiah's enemies (Jer 18:20).

INHERITANCE [1598, 2750, 3769, 3772, 4625, 5706, 5709, *2883, 3099, 3100, 3101, 3102, 4757*].

NIV+ CO-HEIRS, HEIR, HEIRS, HERITAGE, INHERIT, INHERITANCES, INHERITED, INHERITS

Of children—

Ge 24:36 My master's wife Sarah has borne him a son in her old age, and he has given him everything he owns.

Ge 25:5 Abraham left everything he owned to Isaac.

2Ch 21:3 Their father had given them many gifts of silver and gold and articles of value, as well as fortified cities in Judah, but he had given the kingdom to Jehoram because he was his firstborn son.

Of children of concubines—

Ge 15:3 And Abram said, "You have given me no children; so a servant in my household will be my heir."

Ge 21:9 But Sarah saw that the son whom Hagar the Egyptian had borne to Abraham was mocking, [10]and she said to Abraham, "Get rid of that slave woman and her son, for that slave woman's son will never share in the inheritance with my son Isaac."

[11]The matter distressed Abraham greatly because it concerned his son. (+Ge 25:6)

Of children of polygamous marriages—

Dt 21:15 If a man has two wives, and he loves one but not the other, and both bear him sons but the firstborn is the son of the wife he does not love,

Of daughters (Nu 27:8)—

Job 42:15 Nowhere in all the land were there found women as beautiful as Job's daughters, and their father granted them an inheritance along with their brothers.

Of all mankind—

Ecc 2:18 I hated all the things I had toiled for under the sun, because I must leave them to the one who comes after me. [19]And who knows whether he will be a wise man or a fool? Yet he will have control over all the work into which I have poured my effort and skill under the sun. This too is meaningless.

Of servants—

Pr 17:2 A wise servant will rule over a disgraceful son, and will share the inheritance as one of the brothers.

Of real estate inalienable—

1Ki 21:3 But Naboth replied, "The LORD forbid that I should give you the inheritance of my fathers."

Jer 32:6 Jeremiah said, "The word of the LORD came to me: [7]Hanamel son of Shallum your uncle is going to come to you and say, 'Buy my field at Anathoth, because as nearest relative it is your right and duty to buy it.'

[8]"Then, just as the LORD had said, my cousin Hanamel came to me in the courtyard of the guard and said, 'Buy my field at Anathoth in the territory of Benjamin. Since it is your right to redeem it and possess it, buy it for yourself.'

"I knew that this was the word of the LORD;

Eze 46:16 "'This is what the Sovereign LORD says: If the prince makes a gift from his inheritance to one of his sons, it will also belong to his descendants; it is to be their property by inheritance. [17]If, however, he makes a gift from his inheritance to one of his servants, the servant may keep it until the year of freedom; then it will revert to the prince. His inheritance belongs to his sons only; it is theirs. [18]The prince must not take any of the inheritance of the people, driving them off their property. He is to give his sons their inheritance out of his own property, so that none of my people will be separated from his property.'"

Law concerning—

Nu 27:6 and the LORD said to him, [7]"What Zelophehad's daughters are saying is right. You must certainly give them property as an inheritance among their father's relatives and turn their father's inheritance over to them.

[8]"Say to the Israelites, 'If a man dies and leaves no son, turn his inheritance over to his daughter. [9]If he has no daughter, give his inheritance to his brothers. [10]If he has no

brothers, give his inheritance to his father's brothers. [11]If his father had no brothers, give his inheritance to the nearest relative in his clan, that he may possess it. This is to be a legal requirement for the Israelites, as the LORD commanded Moses.'"

Lesson concerning, of prodigal—

Lk 15:12 The younger one said to his father, 'Father, give me my share of the estate.' So he divided his property between them.

Lk 15:25 "Meanwhile, the older son was in the field. When he came near the house, he heard music and dancing. [26]So he called one of the servants and asked him what was going on. [27]'Your brother has come,' he replied, 'and your father has killed the fattened calf because he has him back safe and sound.'

[28]"The older brother became angry and refused to go in. So his father went out and pleaded with him. [29]But he answered his father, 'Look! All these years I've been slaving for you and never disobeyed your orders. Yet you never gave me even a young goat so I could celebrate with my friends. [30]But when this son of yours who has squandered your property with prostitutes comes home, you kill the fattened calf for him!'

[31]"'My son,' the father said, 'you are always with me, and everything I have is yours.

Proverbs concerning (Pr 17:2)—

Pr 20:21 An inheritance quickly gained at the beginning will not be blessed at the end.

Instance of:

Israel to Joseph—

Ge 48:21 Then Israel said to Joseph, "I am about to die, but God will be with you and take you back to the land of your fathers. [22]And to you, as one who is over your brothers, I give the ridge of land I took from the Amorites with my sword and my bow."

Figurative:

Spiritual (Mt 25:34)—

Ac 20:32 "Now I commit you to God and to the word of his grace, which can build you up and give you an inheritance among all those who are sanctified.

Ac 26:18 to open their eyes and turn them from darkness to light, and from the power of Satan to God, so that they may receive forgiveness of sins and a place among those who are sanctified by faith in me.'

Ro 8:16 The Spirit himself testifies with our spirit that we are God's children. [17]Now if we are children, then we are heirs—heirs of God and co-heirs with Christ, if indeed we share in his sufferings in order that we may also share in his glory. (+Gal 4:7)

Eph 1:11 In him we were also chosen, having been predestined according to the plan of him who works out everything in conformity with the purpose of his will, [12]in order that we, who were the first to hope in Christ, might be for the praise of his glory. [13]And you also were included in Christ when you heard the word of truth, the gospel of your salvation. Having believed, you were marked in him with a seal, the promised Holy Spirit, [14]who is a deposit guaranteeing our inheritance until the redemption of those who are God's possession—to the praise of his glory. (+Col 3:24)

Tit 3:7 so that, having been justified by his grace, we might become heirs having the hope of eternal life.

Heb 1:14 Are not all angels ministering spirits sent to serve those who will inherit salvation? (+Heb 9:15-17)

See Firstborn; Heir; Testament; Will.

INHOSPITABLENESS

Instances of:

Toward the Israelites: Edom (Nu 20:1,18-21), Sihon (Nu 21:22-23), Ammonites and Moabites (Dt 23:3-6). Men of Gibeah toward a Levite (Jdg 19:15). Nabal toward David (1Sa 25:10-17). Samaritans toward Jesus (Lk 9:53). *See Hospitality.*

INIQUITIES, OUR [2633, 6411].

NIV+ INIQUITY

(Job 14:17; Ps 40:12; 90:8; 130:3; Isa 59:2; 64:6; Jer 2:22; Mic 7:10). *See Sin.*

INIQUITY [224, 6406, 6411].

NIV+ INIQUITIES

General references to (Job 15:16; Ps 41:6; 53:1; Isa 5:18; Jer 30:14; Eze 9:9; Hos 14:1; Mic 2:1; Mt 23:28; 24:12; Ro 6:19). *See Sin.*

INJUSTICE [224, 4202+5477, 4754, 6406, 6637, 8400].

An abomination to God—

Pr 17:15 Acquitting the guilty and condemning the innocent—the LORD detests them both.

An abomination to the righteous—

Pr 29:27 The righteous detest the dishonest; the wicked detest the upright.

In civil administration—

Ps 82:2 "How long will you defend the unjust and show partiality to the wicked? *Selah*

Ecc 5:8 If you see the poor oppressed in a district, and justice and rights denied, do not be surprised at such things; for one official is eyed by a higher one, and over them both are others higher still.

La 3:34 To crush underfoot all prisoners in the land, ³⁵to deny a man his rights before the Most High, ³⁶to deprive a man of justice—would not the Lord see such things?

In gains, unstable—

Pr 28:8 He who increases his wealth by exorbitant interest amasses it for another, who will be kind to the poor.

Am 5:11 You trample on the poor and force him to give you grain. Therefore, though you have built stone mansions, you will not live in them; though you have planted lush vineyards, you will not drink their wine. ¹²For I know how many are your offenses and how great your sins. You oppress the righteous and take bribes and you deprive the poor of justice in the courts.

Job innocent of—

Job 16:16 My face is red with weeping, deep shadows ring my eyes; ¹⁷yet my hands have been free of violence and my prayer is pure.

Job 31:13 "If I have denied justice to my menservants and maidservants when they had a grievance against me, ¹⁴what will I do when God confronts me? What will I answer when called to account? ¹⁵Did not he who made me in the womb make them? Did not the same one form us both within our mothers?

Judged—

Pr 11:7 When a wicked man dies, his hope perishes; all he expected from his power comes to nothing.

Ecc 3:16 And I saw something else under the sun: In the place of judgment—wickedness was there, in the place of justice—wickedness was there.

Lk 16:10 "Whoever can be trusted with very little can also be trusted with much, and whoever is dishonest with very little will also be dishonest with much.

1Th 4:7 For God did not call us to be impure, but to live a holy life.

Rev 22:11 Let him who does wrong continue to do wrong; let him who is vile continue to be vile; let him who does right continue to do right; and let him who is holy continue to be holy."

Practiced by the wicked—

Isa 26:10 Though grace is shown to the wicked, they do not learn righteousness; even in a land of uprightness they go on doing evil and regard not the majesty of the LORD.

Without shame—

Zep 3:5 The LORD within her is righteous; he does no wrong. Morning by morning he dispenses his justice, and every new day he does not fail, yet the unrighteous know no shame.

Protection from, given—

Ps 12:5 "Because of the oppression of the weak and the groaning of the needy, I will now arise," says the LORD. "I will protect them from those who malign them."

Interceded—

Ps 43:1 Vindicate me, O God, and plead my cause against an ungodly nation; rescue me from deceitful and wicked men.

INK [1902, 3506]. Any liquid used with pen or brush to form written characters (Jer 36:18; 2Co 3:3; 2Jn 12; 3Jn 13).

INKHORN *See Writing Kit.*

INN [2906, 4106].

NIV+ INNKEEPER

A lodging place for travelers. Inns in the modern sense were not very necessary in ancient times, since travelers found hospitality the rule (Ex 2:20; Jdg 19:15-21; 2Ki 4:8; Ac 28:7; Heb 13:2). Ancient inns were usually mere shelters for man and beast, although often strongly fortified.

INNOCENCE [5931, 7405, 7407].

NIV+ INNOCENT, INNOCENTLY

Signified by washing the hands (Dt 21:6; Ps 26:6; Mt 27:24). Found in Daniel (Da 6:22), Jeremiah (Jer 2:35). Professed by Pilate (Mt 27:24).

Contrasted with guilt (Ge 2:25; 3:7-11).

INNOCENT [870, 2341, 2855, 3838, 5927, 5929, 7404, 7405, 9447, 10229, *54, 127, 193, 360, 1465, 1467, 2754*].

NIV+ INNOCENCE, INNOCENTLY

Not to suffer for guilty (Dt 24:16; 2Ki 14:6; 2Ch 25:4; Jer 31:29-30; Eze 18:20).

INNOCENTS, SLAUGHTER OF The slaughter, by Herod the Great, of children in Bethlehem (Mt 2:16-18).

See Infanticide; Murder.

INNUENDO (Ps 35:19; Pr 6:13; 10:10). *See Accusation, False.*

INQUEST Into an unsolved murder (Dt 21:1-9).

I.N.R.I The initials of the Latin superscription on the cross of Jesus, standing for IESUS NAZARENUS, REX IUDAEORUM, "Jesus of Nazareth, King of the Jews" (Mt 27:37; Mk 15:26; Lk 23:38; Jn 19:19).

INSANITY [3248+9101, 8713, *3419, 3444*].

NIV+ MAD, MADDENING, MADMAN, MADMEN, MADNESS

(Pr 26:18). Feigned by David (1Sa 21:13-15). Sent as a

judgment from God (Dt 28:28; Zec 12:4). Nebuchadnezzar's (Da 4:32-34). Jesus accused of (Mk 3:21; Jn 10:20). Paul (Ac 26:24-25). Cured by Jesus (Mt 4:24; 17:15).

Demonic:

Saul (1Sa 16:14; 18:10).

False accusation of:

Against Jesus (Mk 3:21; Jn 10:20), against Paul (Ac 26:24-25; 2Co 5:13).

See Demons, Possession by.

INSCRIPTIONS
NIV+ INSCRIBE, INSCRIBED, INSCRIPTION

On gravestones (2Ki 23:17). On the turban of the high priest (Ex 28:36). On the sacred diadem (Ex 39:30). On the bells of horses (Zec 14:20).

Over Jesus at the Crucifixion (Mt 27:37; Mk 15:26; Lk 23:38; Jn 19:19). Precepts written on the doorframes and gates and worn on the hand and forehead (Dt 6:6-9; 11:18-20; Isa 57:8).

INSECTS [9238].
Created by God (Ge 1:24-25). Fed by God (Ps 104:25,27; Ps 145:9,15).

Divided Into:

Clean and fit for food (Lev 11:21-22). Unclean and abominable (Lev 11:23-24).

Mentioned in Scripture:

Ant (Pr 6:6; 30:25). Bee (Jdg 14:8; Ps 118:12; Isa 7:18). Cricket (Lev 11:22). Grasshopper (Ps 78:46; Isa 33:4; Na 3:15-16). Flea (1Sa 24:14). Fly (Ex 8:22; Ecc 10:1; Isa 7:18). Gnat (Ex 8:16; Ps 105:31; Mt 23:24).Grasshopper (Lev 11:22; Jdg 6:5; Job 39:20). Hornet (Dt 7:20). Katydid (Lev 11:22). Locust (Ex 10:12-13; Joel 1:4; 2:25). Maggot (Ex 16:20). Moth (Job 4:19; 27:18; Isa 50:9). Spider (Job 8:14; Isa 59:5). Worm (Job 25:6; Mic 7:17).

INSINCERITY *See Hypocrisy.*

INSINUATION *See Innuendo.*

INSOMNIA Instances of: Xerxes (Est 6:1). Nebuchadnezzar (Da 6:18).

INSPECTION GATE [5152]. Name of one of the gates of Jerusalem (Ne 3:31). *See Miphkad.*

INSPIRATION [8120] *(breathed into).*

Claims that the Scriptures are Inspired by God:

2Ti 3:16 All Scripture is God-breathed and is useful for teaching, rebuking, correcting and training in righteousness, (+1Ki 13:20; 2Ch 33:18; 36:15; Ne 9:30; Job 33:14-16; Isa 51:16; Jer 7:25; 17:16; Da 9:6,10; Hos 12:10; Joel 2:28; Am 3:7-8; Zec 7:12; Lk 1:70; Ac 3:18; Ro 1:1-2; 1Co 12:7-11; Heb 1:1; 2Pe 1:21; Rev 10:7; 22:6,8)

Instances of People Inspired by God:

Of Enoch (Jude 14). Joseph (Ge 40:8; 41:16,38-39).

Moses (Ex 3:14-15; 4:12,15,27; 6:13,29; 7:2; 19:9-19; 24:16)—

Ex 25:22 There, above the cover between the two cherubim that are over the ark of the Testimony, I will meet with you and give you all my commands for the Israelites. (+Ex 33:9,11; Lev 1:1; Nu 1:1; 7:8-9; 9:8-10; 11:17,25; 12:6-8; 16:28-29; Dt 1:5-6; 5:4-5,31; 34:10-11; Ps 103:7)

Aaron (Ex 6:13; 12:1). The tabernacle workmen (Ex 28:3; 31:3,6; 35:31; 36:1).

The seventy elders—

Nu 11:16 The LORD said to Moses: "Bring me seventy of Israel's elders who are known to you as leaders and officials among the people. Have them come to the Tent of Meeting, that they may stand there with you. [17]I will come down and speak with you there, and I will take of the Spirit that is on you and put the Spirit on them. They will help you carry the burden of the people so that you will not have to carry it alone.

Nu 11:24 So Moses went out and told the people what the LORD had said. He brought together seventy of their elders and had them stand around the Tent. [25]Then the LORD came down in the cloud and spoke with him, and he took of the Spirit that was on him and put the Spirit on the seventy elders. When the Spirit rested on them, they prophesied, but they did not do so again.

Eldad and Medad—

Nu 11:26 However, two men, whose names were Eldad and Medad, had remained in the camp. They were listed among the elders, but did not go out to the Tent. Yet the Spirit also rested on them, and they prophesied in the camp. [27]A young man ran and told Moses, "Eldad and Medad are prophesying in the camp."

[28]Joshua son of Nun, who had been Moses' aide since youth, spoke up and said, "Moses, my lord, stop them!"

[29]But Moses replied, "Are you jealous for my sake? I wish that all the LORD's people were prophets and that the LORD would put his Spirit on them!"

Balaam (Nu 23:5,16,20,26; 24:2-4,15-16). Joshua (Dt 34:9; Jos 4:15). Samuel (1Sa 3:1,4-10,19-21; 9:6,15-20; 15:16). Saul (1Sa 10:6-7,10-13; 19:23-24). Messengers of Saul (1Sa 19:20,23). David (2Sa 23:2-3; 1Ch 28:19; Mk 12:36). Nathan (1Ki 1:4-5). Elijah (1Ki 17:1,24; 19:15; 2Ki 10:10). Micaiah (1Ki 22:14,28; 2Ch 18:27). Elisha (2Ki 2:9; 3:11-12,15; 6:8-12,32; 15:8). Jahaziel (2Ch 20:14). Azariah (2Ch 15:1-2). Zechariah, the son of Jehoiada (2Ch 24:20; 26:5). Isaiah (2Ki 20:4; Isa 6:1-9; 8:11; 44:26; Ac 28:25). Jeremiah (2Ch 26:12; Jer 1:9; 2:1; 7:1; 11:1,18; 13:1-3; 16:1; 18:1; 20:9; 23:9; 24:4; 25:3; 26:1-2,12; 27:1-2; 29:30; 33:1; 34:1; 42:4,7; Da 9:2). Ezekiel (Eze 1:1,3; 2:1-2,4-5; 3:10-12,14,16-17,22,24,27; 8:1; 11:1,4-5,24; 33:22; 37:1; 40:1; 43:5-6). Daniel (Da 2:19; 7:16; 8:16; 9:22; 10:7-9). Hosea (Hos 1:1-2). Joel (Joel 1:1). Amos (Am 3:7-8; 7:14-15). Obadiah (Ob 1). Jonah (Jnh 1:1; 3:1-2). Micah (Mic 1:1; 3:8). Habakkuk (Hab 1:1). Haggai (Hag 1:13). Zechariah (Zec 2:9; 7:8). Elizabeth (Lk 1:41). Zechariah (Lk 1:67). Simeon (Lk 2:26-27).

Disciples (Mt 10:19; Mk 13:11; Lk 12:11)—

Lk 12:12 for the Holy Spirit will teach you at that time what you should say." (+Lk 21:14-15; Ac 21:4)

The apostles (Ac 2:4). Philip (Ac 8:29). Agabus (Ac 11:28; 21:10-11).

John the apostle—

Rev 1:10 On the Lord's Day I was in the Spirit, and I heard behind me a loud voice like a trumpet, [11]which said: "Write on a scroll what you see and send it to the seven churches: to Ephesus, Smyrna, Pergamum, Thyatira, Sardis, Philadelphia and Laodicea."

See Genius; Prophecy; Prophets; Revelation; Word of God, Inspiration of.

INSTABILITY
Warnings against—

Pr 24:21 Fear the LORD and the king, my son, and do not join with the rebellious, [22]for those two will send sudden destruction upon them, and who knows what calamities they can bring?

Pr 27:8 Like a bird that strays from its nest is a man who strays from his home.

Mt 6:24 "No one can serve two masters. Either he will hate the one and love the other, or he will be devoted to the one and despise the other. You cannot serve both God and Money. (+Mt 8:19-22)

Mt 12:25 Jesus knew their thoughts and said to them, "Every kingdom divided against itself will be ruined, and every city or household divided against itself will not stand. (+Mt 13:20-21)

Mk 4:16 Others, like seed sown on rocky places, hear the word and at once receive it with joy. ¹⁷But since they have no root, they last only a short time. When trouble or persecution comes because of the word, they quickly fall away. (+Lk 8:13)

Lk 9:57 As they were walking along the road, a man said to him, "I will follow you wherever you go."

⁵⁸Jesus replied, "Foxes have holes and birds of the air have nests, but the Son of Man has no place to lay his head."

⁵⁹He said to another man, "Follow me."

But the man replied, "Lord, first let me go and bury my father."

⁶⁰Jesus said to him, "Let the dead bury their own dead, but you go and proclaim the kingdom of God."

⁶¹Still another said, "I will follow you, Lord; but first let me go back and say good-by to my family."

⁶²Jesus replied, "No one who puts his hand to the plow and looks back is fit for service in the kingdom of God."

Eph 4:14 Then we will no longer be infants, tossed back and forth by the waves, and blown here and there by every wind of teaching and by the cunning and craftiness of men in their deceitful scheming.

Heb 13:9 Do not be carried away by all kinds of strange teachings. It is good for our hearts to be strengthened by grace, not by ceremonial foods, which are of no value to those who eat them.

Jas 1:6 But when he asks, he must believe and not doubt, because he who doubts is like a wave of the sea, blown and tossed by the wind. ⁷That man should not think he will receive anything from the Lord; ⁸he is a double-minded man, unstable in all he does.

Jas 4:8 Come near to God and he will come near to you. Wash your hands, you sinners, and purify your hearts, you double-minded.

2Pe 2:14 With eyes full of adultery, they never stop sinning; they seduce the unstable; they are experts in greed—an accursed brood!

Rev 2:4 Yet I hold this against you: You have forsaken your first love.

Rev 3:2 Wake up! Strengthen what remains and is about to die, for I have not found your deeds complete in the sight of my God.

Instances of:

Reuben—

Ge 49:4 Turbulent as the waters, you will no longer excel, for you went up onto your father's bed, onto my couch and defiled it.

Pharaoh—

Ex 8:15 But when Pharaoh saw that there was relief, he hardened his heart and would not listen to Moses and Aaron, just as the LORD had said. (+Ex 8:32)

Ex 9:34 When Pharaoh saw that the rain and hail and thunder had stopped, he sinned again: He and his officials hardened their hearts. (+Ex 10:8-11,16-20; 14:5)

Israel (Ex 19:8; 24:3,7)—

Ex 32:8 They have been quick to turn away from what I commanded them and have made themselves an idol cast in the shape of a calf. They have bowed down to it and sacrificed to it and have said, 'These are your gods, O Israel, who brought you up out of Egypt.'

⁹"I have seen these people," the LORD said to Moses, "and they are a stiff-necked people. (+Ex 32:10)

Jdg 2:17 Yet they would not listen to their judges but prostituted themselves to other gods and worshiped them. Unlike their fathers, they quickly turned from the way in which their fathers had walked, the way of obedience to the LORD's commands.

1Ki 18:21 Elijah went before the people and said, "How long will you waver between two opinions? If the LORD is God, follow him; but if Baal is God, follow him." But the people said nothing.

Ps 106:12 Then they believed his promises and sang his praise.

¹³But they soon forgot what he had done and did not wait for his counsel.

Jer 2:36 Why do you go about so much, changing your ways? You will be disappointed by Egypt as you were by Assyria.

Saul in his feelings toward David (1Sa 18:19). David, in yielding to lust (2Sa 11:2-4). Solomon, in yielding to his idolatrous wives (1Ki 11:1-8).

Ephraim and Judah—

Hos 6:4 "What can I do with you, Ephraim? What can I do with you, Judah? Your love is like the morning mist, like the early dew that disappears.

Jews (Hos 6:4-5)—

Jn 5:35 John was a lamp that burned and gave light, and you chose for a time to enjoy his light.

Lot's wife—

Lk 17:32 Remember Lot's wife!

Disciples (Jn 6:66). Mark (Ac 15:38).

Galatians—

Gal 1:6 I am astonished that you are so quickly deserting the one who called you by the grace of Christ and are turning to a different gospel—

Gal 4:9 But now that you know God—or rather are known by God—how is it that you are turning back to those weak and miserable principles? Do you wish to be enslaved by them all over again? ¹⁰You are observing special days and months and seasons and years! ¹¹I fear for you, that somehow I have wasted my efforts on you.

See Backsliding; Hypocrisy; Indecision.

INSTINCT [*5879, 5880, 6035*].

NIV+ INSTINCTS

Of animals (Pr 1:17; Isa 1:3). Of birds (Jer 8:7).

See Animals; Birds.

INSTRUCTION [*1067, 1819, 1821, 3579, 3723, 4375, 4592, 5184, 7422, 8505, 9368, 1439, 1948, 1953, 2994, 3364, 4132, 4133, 5204*].

NIV+ INSTRUCT, INSTRUCTED, INSTRUCTING, INSTRUCTIONS, INSTRUCTOR, INSTRUCTORS, INSTRUCTS

Provision for, made by the state—

2Ch 17:7 In the third year of his reign he sent his officials Ben-Hail, Obadiah, Zechariah, Nethanel and Micaiah to teach in the towns of Judah. ⁸With them were certain

Levites—Shemaiah, Nethaniah, Zebadiah, Asahel, Shemiramoth, Jehonathan, Adonijah, Tobijah and Tob-Adonijah—and the priests Elishama and Jehoram. ⁹They taught throughout Judah, taking with them the Book of the Law of the LORD; they went around to all the towns of Judah and taught the people.

Da 1:3 Then the king ordered Ashpenaz, chief of his court officials, to bring in some of the Israelites from the royal family and the nobility— ⁴young men without any physical defect, handsome, showing aptitude for every kind of learning, well informed, quick to understand, and qualified to serve in the king's palace. He was to teach them the language and literature of the Babylonians. ⁵The king assigned them a daily amount of food and wine from the king's table. They were to be trained for three years, and after that they were to enter the king's service.

Da 1:17 To these four young men God gave knowledge and understanding of all kinds of literature and learning. And Daniel could understand visions and dreams of all kinds.

¹⁸At the end of the time set by the king to bring them in, the chief official presented them to Nebuchadnezzar. ¹⁹The king talked with them, and he found none equal to Daniel, Hananiah, Mishael and Azariah; so they entered the king's service. ²⁰In every matter of wisdom and understanding about which the king questioned them, he found them ten times better than all the magicians and enchanters in his whole kingdom.

Sought (Ps 90:12)—

Ps 119:12 Praise be to you, O LORD; teach me your decrees.

Ps 143:8 Let the morning bring me word of your unfailing love, for I have put my trust in you. Show me the way I should go, for to you I lift up my soul.

Ps 143:10 Teach me to do your will, for you are my God; may your good Spirit lead me on level ground.

Paying attention to, commanded (Pr 4:1-2,10,13,20; 5:1-2)—

Pr 22:17 Pay attention and listen to the sayings of the wise; apply your heart to what I teach,

Pr 23:12 Apply your heart to instruction and your ears to words of knowledge.

Pr 23:23 Buy the truth and do not sell it; get wisdom, discipline and understanding.

Lack of—

2Ch 15:3 For a long time Israel was without the true God, without a priest to teach and without the law.

Pr 24:30 I went past the field of the sluggard, past the vineyard of the man who lacks judgment; ³¹thorns had come up everywhere, the ground was covered with weeds, and the stone wall was in ruins. ³²I applied my heart to what I observed and learned a lesson from what I saw: ³³A little sleep, a little slumber, a little folding of the hands to rest— (+Pr 24:34)

Hatred—

Ps 50:17 You hate my instruction and cast my words behind you. (+Pr 1:29-30; 5:12-13)

Jer 32:33 They turned their backs to me and not their faces; though I taught them again and again, they would not listen or respond to discipline.

Lk 20:1 One day as he was teaching the people in the temple courts and preaching the gospel, the chief priests and the teachers of the law, together with the elders, came up to him. ²"Tell us by what authority you are doing these things," they said. "Who gave you this authority?"

From nature (Pr 24:30-34; Ecc 1:13-18; 3; 4:1; Mt 6:25-30). From the study of human nature (Ecc 3-12).

In religion:

(Ex 24:12; Lev 10:11; Dt 24:8; 27:14-26; 31:9-13; 33:10)

2Ch 17:8 With them were certain Levites—Shemaiah, Nethaniah, Zebadiah, Asahel, Shemiramoth, Jehonathan, Adonijah, Tobijah and Tob-Adonijah—and the priests Elishama and Jehoram. ⁹They taught throughout Judah, taking with them the Book of the Law of the LORD; they went around to all the towns of Judah and taught the people. (+2Ch 35:3)

Ne 8:7 The Levites—Jeshua, Bani, Sherebiah, Jamin, Akkub, Shabbethai, Hodiah, Maaseiah, Kelita, Azariah, Jozabad, Hanan and Pelaiah—instructed the people in the Law while the people were standing there. ⁸They read from the Book of the Law of God, making it clear and giving the meaning so that the people could understand what was being read. (+Ne 8:9-13; Mal 2:6-7)

By means of the law—

Dt 27:1 Moses and the elders of Israel commanded the people: "Keep all these commands that I give you today. ²When you have crossed the Jordan into the land the LORD your God is giving you, set up some large stones and coat them with plaster. ³Write on them all the words of this law when you have crossed over to enter the land the LORD your God is giving you, a land flowing with milk and honey, just as the LORD, the God of your fathers, promised you. ⁴And when you have crossed the Jordan, set up these stones on Mount Ebal, as I command you today, and coat them with plaster. ⁵Build there an altar to the LORD your God, an altar of stones. Do not use any iron tool upon them. ⁶Build the altar of the LORD your God with fieldstones and offer burnt offerings on it to the LORD your God. ⁷Sacrifice fellowship offerings there, eating them and rejoicing in the presence of the LORD your God. ⁸And you shall write very clearly all the words of this law on these stones you have set up."

⁹Then Moses and the priests, who are Levites, said to all Israel, "Be silent, O Israel, and listen! You have now become the people of the LORD your God. ¹⁰Obey the LORD your God and follow his commands and decrees that I give you today."

¹¹On the same day Moses commanded the people:

¹²When you have crossed the Jordan, these tribes shall stand on Mount Gerizim to bless the people: Simeon, Levi, Judah, Issachar, Joseph and Benjamin. ¹³And these tribes shall stand on Mount Ebal to pronounce curses: Reuben, Gad, Asher, Zebulun, Dan and Naphtali.

¹⁴The Levites shall recite to all the people of Israel in a loud voice:

¹⁵"Cursed is the man who carves an image or casts an idol—a thing detestable to the LORD, the work of the craftsman's hands—and sets it up in secret."

Then all the people shall say, "Amen!"

¹⁶"Cursed is the man who dishonors his father or his mother."

Then all the people shall say, "Amen!"

¹⁷"Cursed is the man who moves his neighbor's boundary stone."

Then all the people shall say, "Amen!"

¹⁸"Cursed is the man who leads the blind astray on the road."

Then all the people shall say, "Amen!"

¹⁹"Cursed is the man who withholds justice from the alien, the fatherless or the widow."

Then all the people shall say, "Amen!"

[20]"Cursed is the man who sleeps with his father's wife, for he dishonors his father's bed."

Then all the people shall say, "Amen!"

[21]"Cursed is the man who has sexual relations with any animal."

Then all the people shall say, "Amen!"

[22]"Cursed is the man who sleeps with his sister, the daughter of his father or the daughter of his mother."

Then all the people shall say, "Amen!"

[23]"Cursed is the man who sleeps with his mother-in-law."

Then all the people shall say, "Amen!"

[24]"Cursed is the man who kills his neighbor secretly."

Then all the people shall say, "Amen!"

[25]"Cursed is the man who accepts a bribe to kill an innocent person."

Then all the people shall say, "Amen!"

[26]"Cursed is the man who does not uphold the words of this law by carrying them out."

Then all the people shall say, "Amen!"

Ro 2:18 if you know his will and approve of what is superior because you are instructed by the law;

Gal 3:24 So the law was put in charge to lead us to Christ that we might be justified by faith. [25]Now that faith has come, we are no longer under the supervision of the law.

By means of proverbs—

Pr 1:1 The proverbs of Solomon son of David, king of Israel: [2]for attaining wisdom and discipline; for understanding words of insight; [3]for acquiring a disciplined and prudent life, doing what is right and just and fair; [4]for giving prudence to the simple, knowledge and discretion to the young— [5]let the wise listen and add to their learning, and let the discerning get guidance— [6]for understanding proverbs and parables, the sayings and riddles of the wise.

Pr 1:20 Wisdom calls aloud in the street, she raises her voice in the public squares; [21]at the head of the noisy streets she cries out, in the gateways of the city she makes her speech:

[22]"How long will you simple ones love your simple ways? How long will mockers delight in mockery and fools hate knowledge? [23]If you had responded to my rebuke, I would have poured out my heart to you and made my thoughts known to you. [24]But since you rejected me when I called and no one gave heed when I stretched out my hand, [25]since you ignored all my advice and would not accept my rebuke, [26]I in turn will laugh at your disaster; I will mock when calamity overtakes you— [27]when calamity overtakes you like a storm, when disaster sweeps over you like a whirlwind, when distress and trouble overwhelm you.

[28]"Then they will call to me but I will not answer; they will look for me but will not find me. [29]Since they hated knowledge and did not choose to fear the LORD, [30]since they would not accept my advice and spurned my rebuke,

By means of the song of Moses—

Dt 31:19 "Now write down for yourselves this song and teach it to the Israelites and have them sing it, so that it may be a witness for me against them. (+Dt 32:1-44)

By priests—

Ezr 7:10 For Ezra had devoted himself to the study and observance of the Law of the LORD, and to teaching its decrees and laws in Israel. (+Mal 2:7)

By Jesus—

Mt 5:1 Now when he saw the crowds, he went up on a mountainside and sat down. His disciples came to him, [2]and he began to teach them, saying: (+Mk 6:2; 12:35)

Lk 4:16 He went to Nazareth, where he had been brought up, and on the Sabbath day he went into the synagogue, as was his custom. And he stood up to read. [17]The scroll of the prophet Isaiah was handed to him. Unrolling it, he found the place where it is written:

[18]"The Spirit of the Lord is on me, because he has anointed me to preach good news to the poor. He has sent me to proclaim freedom for the prisoners and recovery of sight for the blind, to release the oppressed, [19]to proclaim the year of the Lord's favor."

[20]Then he rolled up the scroll, gave it back to the attendant and sat down. The eyes of everyone in the synagogue were fastened on him, [21]and he began by saying to them, "Today this scripture is fulfilled in your hearing." (+Lk 19:47; 20:1-8)

Lk 21:37 Each day Jesus was teaching at the temple, and each evening he went out to spend the night on the hill called the Mount of Olives, [38]and all the people came early in the morning to hear him at the temple.

Lk 24:27 And beginning with Moses and all the Prophets, he explained to them what was said in all the Scriptures concerning himself.

Jn 7:14 Not until halfway through the Feast did Jesus go up to the temple courts and begin to teach. (+Jn 8:2)

By preachers (Ro 10:14)—

1Co 12:28 And in the church God has appointed first of all apostles, second prophets, third teachers, then workers of miracles, also those having gifts of healing, those able to help others, those with gifts of administration, and those speaking in different kinds of tongues. [29]Are all apostles? Are all prophets? Are all teachers? Do all work miracles?

Eph 4:11 It was he who gave some to be apostles, some to be prophets, some to be evangelists, and some to be pastors and teachers, (+Col 1:2,8)

Teachers (2Ki 23:2; Ne 8:7-8; 1Co 12:28-29; Eph 4:11). Symbols. *See Symbols and Similitudes.* Parables. *See Parable.* Inscriptions on doors and gates (Dt 11:20-21), on monuments (Jos 8:30-35). The public reading of the law (Dt 31:9-13; Jos 8:34-35; Ne 8:2-3).

By Object Lessons:

Passover feast (Ex 12:26-27).

Dedication of firstlings—

Ex 13:14 "In days to come, when your son asks you, 'What does this mean?' say to him, 'With a mighty hand the LORD brought us out of Egypt, out of the land of slavery. [15]When Pharaoh stubbornly refused to let us go, the LORD killed every firstborn in Egypt, both man and animal. This is why I sacrifice to the LORD the first male offspring of every womb and redeem each of my firstborn sons.' [16]And it will be like a sign on your hand and a symbol on your forehead that the LORD brought us out of Egypt with his mighty hand."

Phylacteries (Ex 13:9,16). Inscriptions (Ex 28:36; 39:30; Dt 6:6-9; 11:18-20; Zec 14:20; Mt 27:37). The pot of manna, a reminder of God's care (Ex 16:32). The sacred oil, a symbol of holiness (Ex 30:31). The pillar of twelve stones at the fords of the Jordan (Jos 4:7,19-24).

Tassels on the borders of garments—

Nu 15:38 "Speak to the Israelites and say to them: 'Throughout the generations to come you are to make tassels on the corners of your garments, with a blue cord on each tassel. [39]You will have these tassels to look at and so you will remember all the commands of the LORD, that you may obey them and not prostitute yourselves by going after the lusts of your own hearts and eyes.

The garment torn in pieces (1Ki 11:30-32). The symbolic wearing of sackcloth and going barefoot (Isa 20:2-3). The linen belt (Jer 13:1-11). Potter's vessel (Jer 19:1-12). Basket of figs (Jer 24). Bonds and yokes (Jer 27:2-11; 28). By stones being put in a brick pavement (Jer 43:8-13). Illustrations on a tile (Eze 4:1-3). Lying on one side in public view for a long period (Eze 4:4-8). Eating bread baked with dung (Eze 4:9-17). Shaving the head (Eze 5). Moving household goods (Eze 12:3-16). Eating and drinking sparingly (Eze 12:18-20). Sighing (Eze 21:6-7). The boiling pot (Eze 24:1-14). Widowhood (Eze 24:16-27). Two sticks joined together (Eze 37:16-22).

Of Children:

By parents, commanded—

Ex 10:2 that you may tell your children and grandchildren how I dealt harshly with the Egyptians and how I performed my signs among them, and that you may know that I am the LORD."

Ex 12:26 And when your children ask you, 'What does this ceremony mean to you?' ²⁷then tell them, 'It is the Passover sacrifice to the LORD, who passed over the houses of the Israelites in Egypt and spared our homes when he struck down the Egyptians.'" Then the people bowed down and worshiped.

Ex 13:8 On that day tell your son, 'I do this because of what the LORD did for me when I came out of Egypt.' ⁹This observance will be for you like a sign on your hand and a reminder on your forehead that the law of the LORD is to be on your lips. For the LORD brought you out of Egypt with his mighty hand. ¹⁰You must keep this ordinance at the appointed time year after year. (+Ex 13:14-16)

Dt 4:9 Only be careful, and watch yourselves closely so that you do not forget the things your eyes have seen or let them slip from your heart as long as you live. Teach them to your children and to their children after them. ¹⁰Remember the day you stood before the LORD your God at Horeb, when he said to me, "Assemble the people before me to hear my words so that they may learn to revere me as long as they live in the land and may teach them to their children."

Dt 6:6 These commandments that I give you today are to be upon your hearts. ⁷Impress them on your children. Talk about them when you sit at home and when you walk along the road, when you lie down and when you get up. ⁸Tie them as symbols on your hands and bind them on your foreheads. ⁹Write them on the doorframes of your houses and on your gates.

Dt 11:18 Fix these words of mine in your hearts and minds; tie them as symbols on your hands and bind them on your foreheads. ¹⁹Teach them to your children, talking about them when you sit at home and when you walk along the road, when you lie down and when you get up.

Ps 78:5 He decreed statutes for Jacob and established the law in Israel, which he commanded our forefathers to teach their children, ⁶so the next generation would know them, even the children yet to be born, and they in turn would tell their children. ⁷Then they would put their trust in God and would not forget his deeds but would keep his commands. ⁸They would not be like their forefathers—a stubborn and rebellious generation, whose hearts were not loyal to God, whose spirits were not faithful to him.

Pr 22:6 Train a child in the way he should go, and when he is old he will not turn from it.

Isa 38:19 The living, the living—they praise you, as I am doing today; fathers tell their children about your faithfulness.

Eph 6:4 Fathers, do not exasperate your children; instead, bring them up in the training and instruction of the Lord.

Law concerning—

Dt 31:9 So Moses wrote down this law and gave it to the priests, the sons of Levi, who carried the ark of the covenant of the LORD, and to all the elders of Israel. ¹⁰Then Moses commanded them: "At the end of every seven years, in the year for canceling debts, during the Feast of Tabernacles, ¹¹when all Israel comes to appear before the LORD your God at the place he will choose, you shall read this law before them in their hearing. ¹²Assemble the people—men, women and children, and the aliens living in your towns—so they can listen and learn to fear the LORD your God and follow carefully all the words of this law. ¹³Their children, who do not know this law, must hear it and learn to fear the LORD your God as long as you live in the land you are crossing the Jordan to possess." (+Jos 8:35)

Exemplified—

Ps 34:11 Come, my children, listen to me; I will teach you the fear of the LORD.

Pr 20:7 The righteous man leads a blameless life; blessed are his children after him.

Ac 22:3 "I am a Jew, born in Tarsus of Cilicia, but brought up in this city. Under Gamaliel I was thoroughly trained in the law of our fathers and was just as zealous for God as any of you are today.

2Ti 3:15 and how from infancy you have known the holy Scriptures, which are able to make you wise for salvation through faith in Christ Jesus.

See Children.

By Types:

See Washings; Blemish; Defilement; Disfellowship; Types.

See Firstborn; Holiness; Passover; Pillar; Purification.

INSTRUMENTALITY *See Agency.*

INSTRUMENTS, MUSICAL *See Music.*

INSURGENTS Army of, David's (1Sa 22:1-2).

INSURRECTION [5086, 5087].

NIV+INSURRECTIONISTS

(Ps 64:2). Described by David (Ps 55). Led by Bicri (2Sa 20), Absalom. *See Absalom.* Barabbas (Mk 15:7).

INTEGRITY [575, 622, 3841, 4797, 7406, 7407, 9447, 9448, 9450, *239, 917*].

Essential—

Ex 18:21 But select capable men from all the people—men who fear God, trustworthy men who hate dishonest gain—and appoint them as officials over thousands, hundreds, fifties and tens.

Lk 16:10 "Whoever can be trusted with very little can also be trusted with much, and whoever is dishonest with very little will also be dishonest with much.

2Co 8:21 For we are taking pains to do what is right, not only in the eyes of the Lord but also in the eyes of men.

Enjoined—

Dt 16:19 Do not pervert justice or show partiality. Do not accept a bribe, for a bribe blinds the eyes of the wise and twists the words of the righteous. ²⁰Follow justice and justice alone, so that you may live and possess the land the LORD your God is giving you.

Pr 4:25 Let your eyes look straight ahead, fix your gaze directly before you. ²⁶Make level paths for your feet and take only ways that are firm. ²⁷Do not swerve to the right or the left; keep your foot from evil.

Isa 56:1 This is what the LORD says: "Maintain justice and do what is right, for my salvation is close at hand and my righteousness will soon be revealed.

Mic 6:8 He has showed you, O man, what is good. And what does the LORD require of you? To act justly and to love mercy and to walk humbly with your God.

Zec 7:9 "This is what the LORD Almighty says: 'Administer true justice; show mercy and compassion to one another.

Lk 3:13 "Don't collect any more than you are required to," he told them.

¹⁴Then some soldiers asked him, "And what should we do?"

He replied, "Don't extort money and don't accuse people falsely—be content with your pay."

Lk 6:31 Do to others as you would have them do to you.

Lk 11:42 "Woe to you Pharisees, because you give God a tenth of your mint, rue and all other kinds of garden herbs, but you neglect justice and the love of God. You should have practiced the latter without leaving the former undone.

Ro 13:5 Therefore, it is necessary to submit to the authorities, not only because of possible punishment but also because of conscience.

Ro 14:5 One man considers one day more sacred than another; another man considers every day alike. Each one should be fully convinced in his own mind.

Ro 14:14 As one who is in the Lord Jesus, I am fully convinced that no food is unclean in itself. But if anyone regards something as unclean, then for him it is unclean.

Ro 14:22 So whatever you believe about these things keep between yourself and God. Blessed is the man who does not condemn himself by what he approves. (+Eph 6:6)

Php 4:8 Finally, brothers, whatever is true, whatever is noble, whatever is right, whatever is pure, whatever is lovely, whatever is admirable—if anything is excellent or praiseworthy—think about such things.

Col 3:22 Slaves, obey your earthly masters in everything; and do it, not only when their eye is on you and to win their favor, but with sincerity of heart and reverence for the Lord. ²³Whatever you do, work at it with all your heart, as working for the Lord, not for men,

1Ti 1:5 The goal of this command is love, which comes from a pure heart and a good conscience and a sincere faith.

1Ti 3:9 They must keep hold of the deep truths of the faith with a clear conscience.

Tit 1:7 Since an overseer is entrusted with God's work, he must be blameless—not overbearing, not quick-tempered, not given to drunkenness, not violent, not pursuing dishonest gain. ⁸Rather he must be hospitable, one who loves what is good, who is self-controlled, upright, holy and disciplined.

1Pe 2:12 Live such good lives among the pagans that, though they accuse you of doing wrong, they may see your good deeds and glorify God on the day he visits us.

1Pe 3:16 keeping a clear conscience, so that those who speak maliciously against your good behavior in Christ may be ashamed of their slander.

Rewards of (2Sa 22:21)—

Ps 15:1 LORD, who may dwell in your sanctuary? Who may live on your holy hill?

²He whose walk is blameless and who does what is righteous, who speaks the truth from his heart ³and has no slander on his tongue, who does his neighbor no wrong and casts no slur on his fellowman, ⁴who despises a vile man but honors those who fear the LORD, who keeps his oath even when it hurts, ⁵who lends his money without usury and does not accept a bribe against the innocent. He who does these things will never be shaken.

Ps 18:20 The LORD has dealt with me according to my righteousness; according to the cleanness of my hands he has rewarded me.

Ps 24:3 Who may ascend the hill of the LORD? Who may stand in his holy place? ⁴He who has clean hands and a pure heart, who does not lift up his soul to an idol or swear by what is false. ⁵He will receive blessing from the LORD and vindication from God his Savior.

Pr 10:9 The man of integrity walks securely, but he who takes crooked paths will be found out.

Pr 20:7 The righteous man leads a blameless life; blessed are his children after him.

Pr 28:20 A faithful man will be richly blessed, but one eager to get rich will not go unpunished.

Isa 26:7 The path of the righteous is level; O upright One, you make the way of the righteous smooth.

Isa 33:15 He who walks righteously and speaks what is right, who rejects gain from extortion and keeps his hand from accepting bribes, who stops his ears against plots of murder and shuts his eyes against contemplating evil— ¹⁶this is the man who will dwell on the heights, whose refuge will be the mountain fortress. His bread will be supplied, and water will not fail him.

Jer 7:5 If you really change your ways and your actions and deal with each other justly,

Jer 7:7 then I will let you live in this place, in the land I gave your forefathers for ever and ever.

Eze 18:5 "Suppose there is a righteous man who does what is just and right.

Eze 18:7 He does not oppress anyone, but returns what he took in pledge for a loan. He does not commit robbery but gives his food to the hungry and provides clothing for the naked. ⁸He does not lend at usury or take excessive interest. He withholds his hand from doing wrong and judges fairly between man and man. ⁹He follows my decrees and faithfully keeps my laws. That man is righteous; he will surely live, declares the Sovereign LORD.

Proverbs concerning—

Pr 2:2 turning your ear to wisdom and applying your heart to understanding,

Pr 2:5 then you will understand the fear of the LORD and find the knowledge of God.

Pr 2:9 Then you will understand what is right and just and fair—every good path.

Pr 3:3 Let love and faithfulness never leave you; bind them around your neck, write them on the tablet of your heart. ⁴Then you will win favor and a good name in the sight of God and man. (+Pr 4:25-27; 10:9)

Pr 11:3 The integrity of the upright guides them, but the unfaithful are destroyed by their duplicity.

Pr 11:5 The righteousness of the blameless makes a straight way for them, but the wicked are brought down by their own wickedness.

Pr 12:22 The LORD detests lying lips, but he delights in men who are truthful.

Pr 14:30 A heart at peace gives life to the body, but envy rots the bones.

Pr 15:21 Folly delights a man who lacks judgment, but a man of understanding keeps a straight course.

Pr 16:11 Honest scales and balances are from the LORD; all the weights in the bag are of his making.

Pr 19:1 Better a poor man whose walk is blameless than a fool whose lips are perverse. (+Pr 20:7)

Pr 21:3 To do what is right and just is more acceptable to the LORD than sacrifice.

Pr 21:15 When justice is done, it brings joy to the righteous but terror to evildoers.

Pr 22:11 He who loves a pure heart and whose speech is gracious will have the king for his friend. (+Pr 28:6,20)

Instances of:

Pharaoh, when he learned that Sarah was Abraham's wife (Ge 12:18-20).

Abraham, in instructing his family—

Ge 18:19 For I have chosen him, so that he will direct his children and his household after him to keep the way of the LORD by doing what is right and just, so that the LORD will bring about for Abraham what he has promised him."

Abimelech, when warned of God that the woman he had taken into his household was Isaac's wife (Ge 26:9-11). Jacob, in the care of Laban's property (Ge 31:39). Joseph, in resisting Potiphar's wife (Ge 39:8-12), in his innocence of the charge on which he was cast into the dungeon (Ge 40:15). Moses, in taking nothing from the Israelites in consideration of his services (Nu 16:15). Samuel, in exacting nothing from the people on account of services (1Sa 12:4-5). Workmen, who repaired the temple (1Ki 12:15; 22:7). Priests who received the offerings of gold and other gifts for the renewing of the temple under Ezra (Ezr 2:24-30,33-34). Nehemiah, in his reforms and in receiving no compensation for his own services (Ne 5:14-19).

Job (Job 1:8; 10:7)—

Job 13:15 Though he slay me, yet will I hope in him; I will surely defend my ways to his face.

Job 16:17 yet my hands have been free of violence and my prayer is pure.

Job 27:4 my lips will not speak wickedness, and my tongue will utter no deceit. [5]I will never admit you are in the right; till I die, I will not deny my integrity. [6]I will maintain my righteousness and never let go of it; my conscience will not reproach me as long as I live.

Job 29:14 I put on righteousness as my clothing; justice was my robe and my turban.

Job 31:1 "I made a covenant with my eyes not to look lustfully at a girl. [2]For what is man's lot from God above, his heritage from the Almighty on high? [3]Is it not ruin for the wicked, disaster for those who do wrong? [4]Does he not see my ways and count my every step?

[5]"If I have walked in falsehood or my foot has hurried after deceit— [6]let God weigh me in honest scales and he will know that I am blameless— [7]if my steps have turned from the path, if my heart has been led by my eyes, or if my hands have been defiled, [8]then may others eat what I have sown, and may my crops be uprooted.

[9]"If my heart has been enticed by a woman, or if I have lurked at my neighbor's door, [10]then may my wife grind another man's grain, and may other men sleep with her. [11]For that would have been shameful, a sin to be judged. [12]It is a fire that burns to Destruction; it would have uprooted my harvest.

[13]"If I have denied justice to my menservants and maidservants when they had a grievance against me, [14]what will I do when God confronts me? What will I answer when called to account? [15]Did not he who made me in the womb make them? Did not the same one form us both within our mothers?

[16]"If I have denied the desires of the poor or let the eyes of the widow grow weary, [17]if I have kept my bread to myself, not sharing it with the fatherless— [18]but from my youth I reared him as would a father, and from my birth I guided the widow— [19]if I have seen anyone perishing for lack of clothing, or a needy man without a garment, [20]and his heart did not bless me for warming him with the fleece from my sheep, [21]if I have raised my hand against the fatherless, knowing that I had influence in court, [22]then let my arm fall from the shoulder, let it be broken off at the joint. [23]For I dreaded destruction from God, and for fear of his splendor I could not do such things.

[24]"If I have put my trust in gold or said to pure gold, 'You are my security,' [25]if I have rejoiced over my great wealth, the fortune my hands had gained, [26]if I have regarded the sun in its radiance or the moon moving in splendor, [27]so that my heart was secretly enticed and my hand offered them a kiss of homage, [28]then these also would be sins to be judged, for I would have been unfaithful to God on high.

[29]"If I have rejoiced at my enemy's misfortune or gloated over the trouble that came to him— [30]I have not allowed my mouth to sin by invoking a curse against his life— [31]if the men of my household have never said, 'Who has not had his fill of Job's meat?'— [32]but no stranger had to spend the night in the street, for my door was always open to the traveler— [33]if I have concealed my sin as men do, by hiding my guilt in my heart [34]because I so feared the crowd and so dreaded the contempt of the clans that I kept silent and would not go outside

[35]("Oh, that I had someone to hear me! I sign now my defense—let the Almighty answer me; let my accuser put his indictment in writing. [36]Surely I would wear it on my shoulder, I would put it on like a crown. [37]I would give him an account of my every step; like a prince I would approach him.)—

[38]"if my land cries out against me and all its furrows are wet with tears, [39]if I have devoured its yield without payment or broken the spirit of its tenants, [40]then let briers come up instead of wheat and weeds instead of barley." The words of Job are ended.

The psalmist—

Ps 7:3 O LORD my God, if I have done this and there is guilt on my hands— [4]if I have done evil to him who is at peace with me or without cause have robbed my foe— [5]then let my enemy pursue and overtake me; let him trample my life to the ground and make me sleep in the dust. *Selah*

Ps 7:8 let the LORD judge the peoples. Judge me, O LORD, according to my righteousness, according to my integrity, O Most High.

Ps 17:3 Though you probe my heart and examine me at night, though you test me, you will find nothing; I have resolved that my mouth will not sin.

Ps 26:1 Vindicate me, O LORD, for I have led a blameless life; I have trusted in the LORD without wavering. [2]Test me, O LORD, and try me, examine my heart and my mind; [3]for your love is ever before me, and I walk continually in your truth.

Ps 69:4 Those who hate me without reason outnumber the hairs of my head; many are my enemies without cause, those who seek to destroy me. I am forced to restore what I did not steal.

Ps 73:15 If I had said, "I will speak thus," I would have betrayed your children.

Ps 119:121 I have done what is righteous and just; do not leave me to my oppressors.

The Recabites, in keeping the Nazirite vows (Jer 35:12-19). Daniel, in maintaining uprightness of character (Da 6:4). The three Hebrews, who refused to worship Nebuchadnezzar's idol (Da 3:16-21,28).

Levi, in his life and service—

Mal 2:6 True instruction was in his mouth and nothing false was found on his lips. He walked with me in peace and uprightness, and turned many from sin.

Joseph, the husband of Mary, in not jealously accusing her of immorality (Mt 1:19). Zacchaeus, in the administration of his wealth (Lk 19:8). Nathanael, in whom was no guile (Jn 1:47). Joseph, a counselor (Lk 23:50-51). Peter, when offered money by Simon (Ac 8:18-23). Paul and Barnabas (Ac 14:12-15).

Paul (Ac 23:1)—

Ac 24:16 So I strive always to keep my conscience clear before God and man. (+Ro 9:1)

2Co 4:2 Rather, we have renounced secret and shameful ways; we do not use deception, nor do we distort the word of God. On the contrary, by setting forth the truth plainly we commend ourselves to every man's conscience in the sight of God. (+2Co 5:11)

2Co 7:2 Make room for us in your hearts. We have wronged no one, we have corrupted no one, we have exploited no one.

1Th 2:4 On the contrary, we speak as men approved by God to be entrusted with the gospel. We are not trying to please men but God, who tests our hearts.

The author of Hebrews—

Heb 13:18 Pray for us. We are sure that we have a clear conscience and desire to live honorably in every way.

See Character; Dishonesty; Honesty; Justice; Righteousness.

INTEMPERANCE

See Abstinence; Drunkard; Drunkenness; Temperance; Wine.

INTERCESSION [4885, 7003, 7137, *1950, 1961, 5659*].

NIV+ INTERCEDE, INTERCEDED, INTERCEDES, INTERCEDING, INTERCESSOR

Of People With God: (Jer 27:18).

Priestly—

Ex 28:12 and fasten them on the shoulder pieces of the ephod as memorial stones for the sons of Israel. Aaron is to bear the names on his shoulders as a memorial before the LORD.

Ex 28:29 "Whenever Aaron enters the Holy Place, he will bear the names of the sons of Israel over his heart on the breastpiece of decision as a continuing memorial before the LORD. 30Also put the Urim and the Thummim in the breastpiece, so they may be over Aaron's heart whenever he enters the presence of the LORD. Thus Aaron will always bear the means of making decisions for the Israelites over his heart before the LORD.

Ex 28:38 It will be on Aaron's forehead, and he will bear the guilt involved in the sacred gifts the Israelites consecrate, whatever their gifts may be. It will be on Aaron's forehead continually so that they will be acceptable to the LORD. (+Lev 10:17)

For spiritual blessing—

Nu 6:23 "Tell Aaron and his sons, 'This is how you are to bless the Israelites. Say to them: 24"'"The LORD bless you and keep you; 25the LORD make his face shine upon you and be gracious to you; 26the LORD turn his face toward you and give you peace."'"

1Sa 12:23 As for me, far be it from me that I should sin against the LORD by failing to pray for you. And I will teach you the way that is good and right.

Job 1:5 When a period of feasting had run its course, Job would send and have them purified. Early in the morning he would sacrifice a burnt offering for each of them, thinking, "Perhaps my children have sinned and cursed God in their hearts." This was Job's regular custom.

Job 42:8 So now take seven bulls and seven rams and go to my servant Job and sacrifice a burnt offering for yourselves. My servant Job will pray for you, and I will accept his prayer and not deal with you according to your folly. You have not spoken of me what is right, as my servant Job has." 9So Eliphaz the Temanite, Bildad the Shuhite and Zophar the Naamathite did what the LORD told them; and the LORD accepted Job's prayer.

10After Job had prayed for his friends, the LORD made him prosperous again and gave him twice as much as he had before.

To avert judgment—

Ge 20:7 Now return the man's wife, for he is a prophet, and he will pray for you and you will live. But if you do not return her, you may be sure that you and all yours will die."

Ex 32:9 "I have seen these people," the LORD said to Moses, "and they are a stiff-necked people. 10Now leave me alone so that my anger may burn against them and that I may destroy them. Then I will make you into a great nation."

11But Moses sought the favor of the LORD his God. "O LORD," he said, "why should your anger burn against your people, whom you brought out of Egypt with great power and a mighty hand? 12Why should the Egyptians say, 'It was with evil intent that he brought them out, to kill them in the mountains and to wipe them off the face of the earth'? Turn from your fierce anger; relent and do not bring disaster on your people. 13Remember your servants Abraham, Isaac and Israel, to whom you swore by your own self: 'I will make your descendants as numerous as the stars in the sky and I will give your descendants all this land I promised them, and it will be their inheritance forever.'" 14Then the LORD relented and did not bring on his people the disaster he had threatened.

Nu 14:11 The LORD said to Moses, "How long will these people treat me with contempt? How long will they refuse to believe in me, in spite of all the miraculous signs I have performed among them? 12I will strike them down with a plague and destroy them, but I will make you into a nation greater and stronger than they."

13Moses said to the LORD, "Then the Egyptians will hear about it! By your power you brought these people up from among them. 14And they will tell the inhabitants of this land about it. They have already heard that you, O LORD, are with these people and that you, O LORD, have been seen face to face, that your cloud stays over them, and that you go before them in a pillar of cloud by day and a pillar of fire by night. 15If you put these people to death all at one time, the nations who have heard this report about you will say, 16'The LORD was not able to bring these people into the land he promised them on oath; so he slaughtered them in the desert.'

[17]"Now may the Lord's strength be displayed, just as you have declared: [18]'The LORD is slow to anger, abounding in love and forgiving sin and rebellion. Yet he does not leave the guilty unpunished; he punishes the children for the sin of the fathers to the third and fourth generation.' [19]In accordance with your great love, forgive the sin of these people, just as you have pardoned them from the time they left Egypt until now."

[20]The LORD replied, "I have forgiven them, as you asked. [21]Nevertheless, as surely as I live and as surely as the glory of the LORD fills the whole earth, (+Nu 16:45)

Nu 16:46 Then Moses said to Aaron, "Take your censer and put incense in it, along with fire from the altar, and hurry to the assembly to make atonement for them. Wrath has come out from the LORD; the plague has started." [47]So Aaron did as Moses said, and ran into the midst of the assembly. The plague had already started among the people, but Aaron offered the incense and made atonement for them. [48]He stood between the living and the dead, and the plague stopped. [49]But 14,700 people died from the plague, in addition to those who had died because of Korah. [50]Then Aaron returned to Moses at the entrance to the Tent of Meeting, for the plague had stopped.

Dt 9:18 Then once again I fell prostrate before the LORD for forty days and forty nights; I ate no bread and drank no water, because of all the sin you had committed, doing what was evil in the LORD's sight and so provoking him to anger. (+Dt 9:19)

Dt 9:20 And the LORD was angry enough with Aaron to destroy him, but at that time I prayed for Aaron too.

Dt 9:25 I lay prostrate before the LORD those forty days and forty nights because the LORD had said he would destroy you. [26]I prayed to the LORD and said, "O Sovereign LORD, do not destroy your people, your own inheritance that you redeemed by your great power and brought out of Egypt with a mighty hand. [27]Remember your servants Abraham, Isaac and Jacob. Overlook the stubbornness of this people, their wickedness and their sin. [28]Otherwise, the country from which you brought us will say, 'Because the LORD was not able to take them into the land he had promised them, and because he hated them, he brought them out to put them to death in the desert.' [29]But they are your people, your inheritance that you brought out by your great power and your outstretched arm."

Isa 65:8 This is what the LORD says: "As when juice is still found in a cluster of grapes and men say, 'Don't destroy it, there is yet some good in it,' so will I do in behalf of my servants; I will not destroy them all.

For deliverance from enemies—

1Sa 7:5 Then Samuel said, "Assemble all Israel at Mizpah and I will intercede with the LORD for you." [6]When they had assembled at Mizpah, they drew water and poured it out before the LORD. On that day they fasted and there they confessed, "We have sinned against the LORD." And Samuel was leader of Israel at Mizpah.

[7]When the Philistines heard that Israel had assembled at Mizpah, the rulers of the Philistines came up to attack them. And when the Israelites heard of it, they were afraid because of the Philistines. [8]They said to Samuel, "Do not stop crying out to the LORD our God for us, that he may rescue us from the hand of the Philistines." (+1Sa 7:9; Isa 37:4)

For healing of disease—

Jas 5:14 Is any one of you sick? He should call the elders of the church to pray over him and anoint him with oil in the name of the Lord. [15]And the prayer offered in faith will make the sick person well; the Lord will raise him up. If he has sinned, he will be forgiven. [16]Therefore confess your sins to each other and pray for each other so that you may be healed. The prayer of a righteous man is powerful and effective.

For stubborn sinners, unavailing—

Jer 7:16 "So do not pray for this people nor offer any plea or petition for them; do not plead with me, for I will not listen to you.

Jer 11:14 "Do not pray for this people nor offer any plea or petition for them, because I will not listen when they call to me in the time of their distress. (+Jer 14:11)

Commanded:

Jer 29:7 Also, seek the peace and prosperity of the city to which I have carried you into exile. Pray to the LORD for it, because if it prospers, you too will prosper." (+Joel 2:17; Mt 5:44)

Eph 6:18 And pray in the Spirit on all occasions with all kinds of prayers and requests. With this in mind, be alert and always keep on praying for all the saints.

1Ti 2:1 I urge, then, first of all, that requests, prayers, intercession and thanksgiving be made for everyone— [2]for kings and all those in authority, that we may live peaceful and quiet lives in all godliness and holiness.

1Jn 5:16 If anyone sees his brother commit a sin that does not lead to death, he should pray and God will give him life. I refer to those whose sin does not lead to death. There is a sin that leads to death. I am not saying that he should pray about that.

Examples of Intercessory Prayer:

Ge 48:16 the Angel who has delivered me from all harm— may he bless these boys. May they be called by my name and the names of my fathers Abraham and Isaac, and may they increase greatly upon the earth."

Ex 32:31 So Moses went back to the LORD and said, "Oh, what a great sin these people have committed! They have made themselves gods of gold. [32]But now, please forgive their sin—but if not, then blot me out of the book you have written."

Ex 34:9 "O Lord, if I have found favor in your eyes," he said, "then let the Lord go with us. Although this is a stiff-necked people, forgive our wickedness and our sin, and take us as your inheritance."

Nu 10:35 Whenever the ark set out, Moses said, "Rise up, O LORD! May your enemies be scattered; may your foes flee before you."

[36]Whenever it came to rest, he said, "Return, O LORD, to the countless thousands of Israel."

Nu 27:16 "May the LORD, the God of the spirits of all mankind, appoint a man over this community [17]to go out and come in before them, one who will lead them out and bring them in, so the LORD's people will not be like sheep without a shepherd."

Jos 7:8 O Lord, what can I say, now that Israel has been routed by its enemies? [9]The Canaanites and the other people of the country will hear about this and they will surround us and wipe out our name from the earth. What then will you do for your own great name?"

Jdg 5:31 "So may all your enemies perish, O LORD! But may they who love you be like the sun when it rises in its strength." Then the land had peace forty years.

Ru 2:12 May the LORD repay you for what you have done.

May you be richly rewarded by the LORD, the God of Israel, under whose wings you have come to take refuge."

1Sa 1:17 Eli answered, "Go in peace, and may the God of Israel grant you what you have asked of him."

1Sa 12:23 As for me, far be it from me that I should sin against the LORD by failing to pray for you. And I will teach you the way that is good and right.

2Sa 24:17 When David saw the angel who was striking down the people, he said to the LORD, "I am the one who has sinned and done wrong. These are but sheep. What have they done? Let your hand fall upon me and my family."

1Ki 8:29 May your eyes be open toward this temple night and day, this place of which you said, 'My Name shall be there,' so that you will hear the prayer your servant prays toward this place.

1Ki 8:38 and when a prayer or plea is made by any of your people Israel—each one aware of the afflictions of his own heart, and spreading out his hands toward this temple— [39]then hear from heaven, your dwelling place. Forgive and act; deal with each man according to all he does, since you know his heart (for you alone know the hearts of all men),

1Ki 8:44 "When your people go to war against their enemies, wherever you send them, and when they pray to the LORD toward the city you have chosen and the temple I have built for your Name, [45]then hear from heaven their prayer and their plea, and uphold their cause.

1Ch 29:18 O LORD, God of our fathers Abraham, Isaac and Israel, keep this desire in the hearts of your people forever, and keep their hearts loyal to you. [19]And give my son Solomon the wholehearted devotion to keep your commands, requirements and decrees and to do everything to build the palatial structure for which I have provided."

2Ch 6:40 "Now, my God, may your eyes be open and your ears attentive to the prayers offered in this place. [41]"Now arise, O LORD God, and come to your resting place, you and the ark of your might. May your priests, O LORD God, be clothed with salvation, may your saints rejoice in your goodness.

2Ch 30:18 Although most of the many people who came from Ephraim, Manasseh, Issachar and Zebulun had not purified themselves, yet they ate the Passover, contrary to what was written. But Hezekiah prayed for them, saying, "May the LORD, who is good, pardon everyone [19]who sets his heart on seeking God—the LORD, the God of his fathers—even if he is not clean according to the rules of the sanctuary."

Ps 7:9 O righteous God, who searches minds and hearts, bring to an end the violence of the wicked and make the righteous secure.

Ps 12:1 Help, LORD, for the godly are no more; the faithful have vanished from among men.

Ps 20:1 May the LORD answer you when you are in distress; may the name of the God of Jacob protect you. [2]May he send you help from the sanctuary and grant you support from Zion. [3]May he remember all your sacrifices and accept your burnt offerings. *Selah* [4]May he give you the desire of your heart and make all your plans succeed.

Ps 25:22 Redeem Israel, O God, from all their troubles!

Ps 28:9 Save your people and bless your inheritance; be their shepherd and carry them forever.

Ps 36:10 Continue your love to those who know you, your righteousness to the upright in heart.

Ps 51:18 In your good pleasure make Zion prosper; build up the walls of Jerusalem.

Ps 80:1 Hear us, O Shepherd of Israel, you who lead Joseph like a flock; you who sit enthroned between the cherubim, shine forth [2]before Ephraim, Benjamin and Manasseh. Awaken your might; come and save us.

Ps 80:14 Return to us, O God Almighty! Look down from heaven and see! Watch over this vine, [15]the root your right hand has planted, the son you have raised for yourself. (+Ps 80:16)

Ps 80:17 Let your hand rest on the man at your right hand, the son of man you have raised up for yourself. (+Ps 80:18)

Ps 80:19 Restore us, O LORD God Almighty; make your face shine upon us, that we may be saved.

Ps 122:7 May there be peace within your walls and security within your citadels." [8]For the sake of my brothers and friends, I will say, "Peace be within you."

Ps 125:4 Do good, O LORD, to those who are good, to those who are upright in heart.

Ps 132:9 May your priests be clothed with righteousness; may your saints sing for joy."

[10]For the sake of David your servant, do not reject your anointed one.

Ps 134:3 May the LORD, the Maker of heaven and earth, bless you from Zion.

Ps 141:5 Let a righteous man strike me—it is a kindness; let him rebuke me—it is oil on my head. My head will not refuse it. Yet my prayer is ever against the deeds of evildoers;

Isa 62:1 For Zion's sake I will not keep silent, for Jerusalem's sake I will not remain quiet, till her righteousness shines out like the dawn, her salvation like a blazing torch.

Isa 63:17 Why, O LORD, do you make us wander from your ways and harden our hearts so we do not revere you? Return for the sake of your servants, the tribes that are your inheritance. [18]For a little while your people possessed your holy place, but now our enemies have trampled down your sanctuary. [19]We are yours from of old; but you have not ruled over them, they have not been called by your name.

Isa 64:8 Yet, O LORD, you are our Father. We are the clay, you are the potter; we are all the work of your hand. [9]Do not be angry beyond measure, O LORD; do not remember our sins forever. Oh, look upon us, we pray, for we are all your people. [10]Your sacred cities have become a desert; even Zion is a desert, Jerusalem a desolation. [11]Our holy and glorious temple, where our fathers praised you, has been burned with fire, and all that we treasured lies in ruins. [12]After all this, O LORD, will you hold yourself back? Will you keep silent and punish us beyond measure?

Jer 18:20 Should good be repaid with evil? Yet they have dug a pit for me. Remember that I stood before you and spoke in their behalf to turn your wrath away from them.

Eze 9:8 While they were killing and I was left alone, I fell facedown, crying out, "Ah, Sovereign LORD! Are you going to destroy the entire remnant of Israel in this outpouring of your wrath on Jerusalem?" (+Eze 11:13)

Da 9:3 So I turned to the Lord God and pleaded with him in prayer and petition, in fasting, and in sackcloth and ashes.

[4]I prayed to the LORD my God and confessed:

"O Lord, the great and awesome God, who keeps his covenant of love with all who love him and obey his commands, [5]we have sinned and done wrong. We have been wicked and have rebelled; we have turned away from your commands and laws. [6]We have not listened to your servants the prophets, who spoke in your name to our kings, our princes and our fathers, and to all the people of the land.

7"Lord, you are righteous, but this day we are covered with shame—the men of Judah and people of Jerusalem and all Israel, both near and far, in all the countries where you have scattered us because of our unfaithfulness to you. 8O LORD, we and our kings, our princes and our fathers are covered with shame because we have sinned against you. 9The Lord our God is merciful and forgiving, even though we have rebelled against him; 10we have not obeyed the LORD our God or kept the laws he gave us through his servants the prophets. 11All Israel has transgressed your law and turned away, refusing to obey you.

"Therefore the curses and sworn judgments written in the Law of Moses, the servant of God, have been poured out on us, because we have sinned against you. 12You have fulfilled the words spoken against us and against our rulers by bringing upon us great disaster. Under the whole heaven nothing has ever been done like what has been done to Jerusalem. 13Just as it is written in the Law of Moses, all this disaster has come upon us, yet we have not sought the favor of the LORD our God by turning from our sins and giving attention to your truth. 14The LORD did not hesitate to bring the disaster upon us, for the LORD our God is righteous in everything he does; yet we have not obeyed him.

15"Now, O Lord our God, who brought your people out of Egypt with a mighty hand and who made for yourself a name that endures to this day, we have sinned, we have done wrong. 16O Lord, in keeping with all your righteous acts, turn away your anger and your wrath from Jerusalem, your city, your holy hill. Our sins and the iniquities of our fathers have made Jerusalem and your people an object of scorn to all those around us.

17"Now, our God, hear the prayers and petitions of your servant. For your sake, O Lord, look with favor on your desolate sanctuary. 18Give ear, O God, and hear; open your eyes and see the desolation of the city that bears your Name. We do not make requests of you because we are righteous, but because of your great mercy. 19O Lord, listen! O Lord, forgive! O Lord, hear and act! For your sake, O my God, do not delay, because your city and your people bear your Name."

Joel 2:17 Let the priests, who minister before the LORD, weep between the temple porch and the altar. Let them say, "Spare your people, O LORD. Do not make your inheritance an object of scorn, a byword among the nations. Why should they say among the peoples, 'Where is their God?'"

Mic 7:14 Shepherd your people with your staff, the flock of your inheritance, which lives by itself in a forest, in fertile pasturelands. Let them feed in Bashan and Gilead as in days long ago.

Mt 5:44 But I tell you: Love your enemies and pray for those who persecute you,

Mt 6:10 your kingdom come, your will be done on earth as it is in heaven.

Ac 7:60 Then he fell on his knees and cried out, "Lord, do not hold this sin against them." When he had said this, he fell asleep.

Ac 8:15 When they arrived, they prayed for them that they might receive the Holy Spirit, ·

Ro 1:9 God, whom I serve with my whole heart in preaching the gospel of his Son, is my witness how constantly I remember you

Ro 10:1 Brothers, my heart's desire and prayer to God for the Israelites is that they may be saved.

1Co 1:3 Grace and peace to you from God our Father and the Lord Jesus Christ.

2Co 9:10 Now he who supplies seed to the sower and bread for food will also supply and increase your store of seed and will enlarge the harvest of your righteousness.

2Co 9:14 And in their prayers for you their hearts will go out to you, because of the surpassing grace God has given you.

2Co 13:7 Now we pray to God that you will not do anything wrong. Not that people will see that we have stood the test but that you will do what is right even though we may seem to have failed. (+Gal 1:3)

Gal 6:16 Peace and mercy to all who follow this rule, even to the Israel of God.

Eph 1:15 For this reason, ever since I heard about your faith in the Lord Jesus and your love for all the saints, 16I have not stopped giving thanks for you, remembering you in my prayers. 17I keep asking that the God of our Lord Jesus Christ, the glorious Father, may give you the Spirit of wisdom and revelation, so that you may know him better. 18I pray also that the eyes of your heart may be enlightened in order that you may know the hope to which he has called you, the riches of his glorious inheritance in the saints, 19and his incomparably great power for us who believe. That power is like the working of his mighty strength,

Eph 3:14 For this reason I kneel before the Father, 15from whom his whole family in heaven and on earth derives its name. 16I pray that out of his glorious riches he may strengthen you with power through his Spirit in your inner being, 17so that Christ may dwell in your hearts through faith. And I pray that you, being rooted and established in love, 18may have power, together with all the saints, to grasp how wide and long and high and deep is the love of Christ, 19and to know this love that surpasses knowledge—that you may be filled to the measure of all the fullness of God.

Php 1:3 I thank my God every time I remember you. 4In all my prayers for all of you, I always pray with joy 5because of your partnership in the gospel from the first day until now,

Php 1:9 And this is my prayer: that your love may abound more and more in knowledge and depth of insight,

Col 1:3 We always thank God, the Father of our Lord Jesus Christ, when we pray for you, 4because we have heard of your faith in Christ Jesus and of the love you have for all the saints—

Col 1:9 For this reason, since the day we heard about you, we have not stopped praying for you and asking God to fill you with the knowledge of his will through all spiritual wisdom and understanding.

Col 2:1 I want you to know how much I am struggling for you and for those at Laodicea, and for all who have not met me personally. 2My purpose is that they may be encouraged in heart and united in love, so that they may have the full riches of complete understanding, in order that they may know the mystery of God, namely, Christ, (+Col 4:12; 1Th 1:2)

1Th 3:10 Night and day we pray most earnestly that we may see you again and supply what is lacking in your faith.

1Th 3:12 May the Lord make your love increase and overflow for each other and for everyone else, just as ours does for you. 13May he strengthen your hearts so that you will be blameless and holy in the presence of our God and Father when our Lord Jesus comes with all his holy ones.

1Th 5:23 May God himself, the God of peace, sanctify you through and through. May your whole spirit, soul and body be kept blameless at the coming of our Lord Jesus Christ.

2Th 1:11 With this in mind, we constantly pray for you, that our God may count you worthy of his calling, and that by his power he may fulfill every good purpose of yours and every act prompted by your faith.

2Th 2:16 May our Lord Jesus Christ himself and God our Father, who loved us and by his grace gave us eternal encouragement and good hope, [17]encourage your hearts and strengthen you in every good deed and word.

2Th 3:5 May the Lord direct your hearts into God's love and Christ's perseverance.

2Th 3:16 Now may the Lord of peace himself give you peace at all times and in every way. The Lord be with all of you. (+2Ti 1:3)

2Ti 4:16 At my first defense, no one came to my support, but everyone deserted me. May it not be held against them.

Phm 4 I always thank my God as I remember you in my prayers,

Phm 6 I pray that you may be active in sharing your faith, so that you will have a full understanding of every good thing we have in Christ.

Heb 13:20 May the God of peace, who through the blood of the eternal covenant brought back from the dead our Lord Jesus, that great Shepherd of the sheep, [21]equip you with everything good for doing his will, and may he work in us what is pleasing to him, through Jesus Christ, to whom be glory for ever and ever. Amen.

1Pe 5:10 And the God of all grace, who called you to his eternal glory in Christ, after you have suffered a little while, will himself restore you and make you strong, firm and steadfast.

Instances of:

Abraham, in behalf of Sodom (Ge 18:23-32), in behalf of Abimelech (Ge 20:17-18). Abraham's servant, in behalf of his master (Ge 24:12). Jacob, in behalf of his children (Ge 49). Moses, in behalf of Pharaoh (Ex 8:12-13,30-31; 9:33; 10:18-19). Moses for Israel (Nu 16:20-22; 21:7; Dt 33:6-17; Ps 106:23), for Miriam (Nu 12:13-15). David, for Israel (2Sa 24:17). Solomon, for Israel (1Ki 8:29-53). Ezra, for Israel (Ezr 9:5-15). Nehemiah, in behalf of Judah and Jerusalem (Ne 1:4-9). Asaph, for the church (Ps 80-83). The "Sons of Korah," for the church (Ps 85:1-7). Jeremiah, for Israel (Am 7:2-6). Syrian Phoenician woman, for her daughter (Mt 15:22). Disciples, in behalf of Peter's wife's mother (Lk 4:38-39). Parents, for demon-possessed son (Mt 17:15; Mk 9:17-27). Others, who sought Jesus in behalf of the afflicted (Mt 12:22; 15:22,30; 17:14-18; Mk 1:32; 2:3; Lk 5:18-20; Jn 4:47,49). Paul for the church (Ac 20:32). Onesiphorus (2Ti 1:16,18). For Paul, by the churches (Ac 14:26; 15:40).

Solicited:

Instances of: By Pharaoh, of Moses (Ex 8:8,28; 9:28; 10:17; 12:32), and by the Israelites (Nu 21:7). By Israel, of Samuel (1Sa 12:19). By Jeroboam, of a prophet (1Ki 13:6). By Hezekiah, of Isaiah (2Ki 19:1-4). By Zedekiah, of Jeremiah (Jer 37:3), and by Johanan (Jer 42:1-6). By Daniel, of Shadrach, Meshach and Abednego (Da 2:17-18). By Darius, of the Jews (Ezr 6:10). By Simon the sorcerer, of Peter (Ac 8:24).

By Paul, of the churches (Ro 15:30-32; 2Co 1:11; Eph 6:19-20; 1Th 5:25; 2Th 3:1)—

Heb 13:18 Pray for us. We are sure that we have a clear conscience and desire to live honorably in every way.

Answered:

Instances of: Of Moses in behalf of Pharaoh, for the plague of frogs to be ended (Ex 8:12,15); the plague of flies (Ex 8:30-32); the plague of rain, thunder, and hail (Ex 9:27-35); plague of locusts (Ex 10:16-20); plague of darkness (Ex 10:21-23). Of Moses, for the Israelites, during the battle with the Amalekites (Ex 17:11-14); after the Israelites had made the golden calf (Ex 32:11-14,31-34; Dt 9:18-29; 10:10; Ps 106:23); after the murmuring of the people (Ex 33:15-17); when the fire of the Lord consumed the people (Nu 11:1-2); when the people murmured on account of the report of the spies (Nu 14:11-20); that the fiery serpents might be taken away (Nu 21:4-9); that Miriam's leprosy might be healed (Nu 12:13); in behalf of Aaron, on account of his sin in making the golden calf (Dt 9:20). Of Samuel, for deliverance from the oppressions of the Philistines (1Sa 7:5-14). The prophet of Israel, for the restoration of Jeroboam's shriveled hand (1Ki 13:1-6). Of Elijah, for the raising from the dead the son of the hospitable widow (1Ki 17:20-23). Of Elisha, for the raising from the dead the son of the Shunammite woman (2Ki 4:33-36). Of Isaiah, in behalf of Hezekiah and the people, to be delivered from Sennacherib (2Ki 19).

Intercessional Influence of the Righteous:

Ge 18:26 The LORD said, "If I find fifty righteous people in the city of Sodom, I will spare the whole place for their sake." (+Ge 18:27-32)

Ge 19:22 But flee there quickly, because I cannot do anything until you reach it." (That is why the town was called Zoar.)

Ge 26:4 I will make your descendants as numerous as the stars in the sky and will give them all these lands, and through your offspring all nations on earth will be blessed, [5]because Abraham obeyed me and kept my requirements, my commands, my decrees and my laws."

Ge 26:24 That night the LORD appeared to him and said, "I am the God of your father Abraham. Do not be afraid, for I am with you; I will bless you and will increase the number of your descendants for the sake of my servant Abraham."

1Ki 11:12 Nevertheless, for the sake of David your father, I will not do it during your lifetime. I will tear it out of the hand of your son. [13]Yet I will not tear the whole kingdom from him, but will give him one tribe for the sake of David my servant and for the sake of Jerusalem, which I have chosen."

1Ki 11:34 " 'But I will not take the whole kingdom out of Solomon's hand; I have made him ruler all the days of his life for the sake of David my servant, whom I chose and who observed my commands and statutes.

1Ki 15:4 Nevertheless, for David's sake the LORD his God gave him a lamp in Jerusalem by raising up a son to succeed him and by making Jerusalem strong.

2Ki 8:19 Nevertheless, for the sake of his servant David, the LORD was not willing to destroy Judah. He had promised to maintain a lamp for David and his descendants forever. (+2Ch 21:7)

Ps 103:17 But from everlasting to everlasting the LORD's love is with those who fear him, and his righteousness with their children's children— [18]with those who keep his covenant and remember to obey his precepts.

Isa 37:35 "I will defend this city and save it, for my sake and for the sake of David my servant!"

Jer 5:1 "Go up and down the streets of Jerusalem, look around and consider, search through her squares. If you can find but one person who deals honestly and seeks the truth, I will forgive this city.

Eze 14:14 even if these three men—Noah, Daniel and Job—were in it, they could save only themselves by their righteousness, declares the Sovereign LORD.

Eze 14:16 as surely as I live, declares the Sovereign LORD, even if these three men were in it, they could not save their own sons or daughters. They alone would be saved, but the land would be desolate. (+Eze 14:18,20)

Mt 24:22 If those days had not been cut short, no one would survive, but for the sake of the elect those days will be shortened.

Ro 11:27 And this is my covenant with them when I take away their sins."

[28]As far as the gospel is concerned, they are enemies on your account; but as far as election is concerned, they are loved on account of the patriarchs,

Rev 5:8 And when he had taken it, the four living creatures and the twenty-four elders fell down before the Lamb. Each one had a harp and they were holding golden bowls full of incense, which are the prayers of the saints.

Rev 8:3 Another angel, who had a golden censer, came and stood at the altar. He was given much incense to offer, with the prayers of all the saints, on the golden altar before the throne. [4]The smoke of the incense, together with the prayers of the saints, went up before God from the angel's hand.

Intercession of People With Jesus: *See Mediation.*

Intercession of People with People:

Instances of: Reuben for Joseph (Ge 37:21-22). Judah for Joseph (Ge 37:26-27). Judah with Joseph (Ge 44:18-34). Pharaoh's chief baker for Joseph (Ge 41:9-14). Rahab for her people (Jos 2:12-13). Aaron for Miriam (Nu 12:12). Jonathan for David (1Sa 19:1-7). Abigail for Nabal (1Sa 25:23-35). Joab for Absalom (2Sa 14:1-24). Bathsheba, for Solomon (1Ki 1:11-22,28-31), for Adonijah (1Ki 2:13-25). Esther for her people (Est 7:2-6). Ebed-Melech for Jeremiah (Jer 38:7-13). Elisha offers to see the king for the Shunammite (2Ki 4:13). The king of Syria for Naaman (2Ki 5:6-8). Paul for Onesimus (Phm 10-21).

Intercession of Jesus:

(Lk 22:31-32; 23:33-34; Jn 14:16; 17:9,11,15-17,20-22; Ro 8:34; Heb 7:25; 9:24; 1Jn 2:1-2). *See Jesus the Christ, Mediation of.*

See Children, Of the Righteous, Blessed of God; Prayer, Intercessory.

INTEREST [5967, 5968, 8750, 9552, *3534, 4309, 5527*].

NIV+ INTERESTS

Income from lending money.

Charging of:

From poor Hebrew, forbidden—

Ex 22:25 "If you lend money to one of my people among you who is needy, do not be like a moneylender; charge him no interest.

Lev 25:36 Do not take interest of any kind from him, but fear your God, so that your countryman may continue to live among you. [37]You must not lend him money at interest or sell him food at a profit.

Dt 23:19 Do not charge your brother interest, whether on money or food or anything else that may earn interest.

From stranger, authorized—

Dt 23:20 You may charge a foreigner interest, but not a brother Israelite, so that the LORD your God may bless you in everything you put your hand to in the land you are entering to possess.

Unprofitable—

Pr 28:8 He who increases his wealth by exorbitant interest amasses it for another, who will be kind to the poor.

Rebuked—

Ne 5:1 Now the men and their wives raised a great outcry against their Jewish brothers. [2]Some were saying, "We and our sons and daughters are numerous; in order for us to eat and stay alive, we must get grain."

[3]Others were saying, "We are mortgaging our fields, our vineyards and our homes to get grain during the famine."

[4]Still others were saying, "We have had to borrow money to pay the king's tax on our fields and vineyards. [5]Although we are of the same flesh and blood as our countrymen and though our sons are as good as theirs, yet we have to subject our sons and daughters to slavery. Some of our daughters have already been enslaved, but we are powerless, because our fields and our vineyards belong to others."

[6]When I heard their outcry and these charges, I was very angry. [7]I pondered them in my mind and then accused the nobles and officials. I told them, "You are exacting usury from your own countrymen!" So I called together a large meeting to deal with them [8]and said: "As far as possible, we have bought back our Jewish brothers who were sold to the Gentiles. Now you are selling your brothers, only for them to be sold back to us!" They kept quiet, because they could find nothing to say.

[9]So I continued, "What you are doing is not right. Shouldn't you walk in the fear of our God to avoid the reproach of our Gentile enemies? [10]I and my brothers and my men are also lending the people money and grain. But let the exacting of usury stop! [11]Give back to them immediately their fields, vineyards, olive groves and houses, and also the usury you are charging them—the hundredth part of the money, grain, new wine and oil."

[12]"We will give it back," they said. "And we will not demand anything more from them. We will do as you say." Then I summoned the priests and made the nobles and officials take an oath to do what they had promised.

[13]I also shook out the folds of my robe and said, "In this way may God shake out of his house and possessions every man who does not keep this promise. So may such a man be shaken out and emptied!" At this the whole assembly said, "Amen," and praised the LORD. And the people did as they had promised.

Eze 22:12 In you men accept bribes to shed blood; you take usury and excessive interest and make unjust gain from your neighbors by extortion. And you have forgotten me, declares the Sovereign LORD.

Charging No Interest:

Rewarded—

Ps 15:5 who lends his money without usury and does not accept a bribe against the innocent. He who does these things will never be shaken.

Eze 18:8 He does not lend at usury or take excessive interest. He withholds his hand from doing wrong and judges fairly between man and man. [9]He follows my decrees and faithfully keeps my laws. That man is righteous; he will surely live, declares the Sovereign LORD.

Eze 18:17 He withholds his hand from sin and takes no usury or excessive interest. He keeps my laws and follows my decrees. He will not die for his father's sin; he will surely live.

Lender and borrower equal before God—

Isa 24:2 it will be the same for priest as for people, for master as for servant, for mistress as for maid, for seller as for buyer, for borrower as for lender, for debtor as for creditor.

See Borrowing; Debt; Debtor; Lending; Money; Usury.

INTERMARRY [995, 3161].

The patriarchs did not allow marriage outside their clan: Abraham (Ge 24:3), Jacob (Ge 28:1). Exceptions: Esau (Ge 26:34-35), Judah and his sons (Ge 38), Joseph (Ge 41:45,50), Moses (Nu 12:1). Aaron and Miriam judged for criticizing Moses' intermarriage (Nu 12:1-15).

Israel was forbidden to intermarry with the Canaanites for religious reasons, not racial (Dt 7:1-6; Jos 23:12-13). Negative results of (Jdg 3:6-7), Solomon (1Ki 11:1-6), returned exiles (Ezr 9:14-15).

There are no racial barriers in the church (Col 3:11). Even marriage between believers and unbelievers does not have to end in divorce (1Co 7:12-16), though is not recommended (2Co 6:14-18). *See Marriage.*

INTERMEDIATE STATE Period of time which elapses between death and the resurrection. For the righteous it is one of blessedness (2Co 5:8); for the wicked it is one of conscious suffering (Lk 16:19-31).

INTERPRETATION [7354, 7355, 8694, 10599, 10600+, *1359, 1450, 1507, 2146, 2255*].

NIV+ INTERPRET, INTERPRETATIONS, INTERPRETED, INTERPRETER, INTERPRETERS, INTERPRETS

Of dreams. *See Dream.* Of foreign tongues (1Co 14:9-19). *See Tongues, Gift of.*

INTERPRETER [2706, 4885, *1449*].

NIV+ See INTERPRETATION

Of dreams (Ge 40:8; 41:16; Da 2:18-30). Of languages (Ge 42:23; 2Ch 32:31; Ne 8:8; Job 33:23). In Christian churches (1Co 12:10,30; 14:5,13,26-28).

Figurative: (Job 33:23).

INTOLERANCE

Religious:

Exemplified by Cain (Ge 4:8), Joshua (Nu 11:24-28), James and John (Mk 9:38-39; Lk 9:49), the Jews, in persecuting Jesus. *See Jesus the Christ, Rejected.*

History of:

In persecuting the disciples (Ac 4:1-3,15-21; 17:13), Stephen (Ac 6:9-15; 7:57-59; 8:1-3), Paul (Ac 13:50; 17:5; 18:13; 21:28-31; 22:22-23; 23:2).

Of Idolatrous Religions:

Taught by Moses (Ex 22:20; Dt 13; 17:1-7).

Exemplified by: Elijah (1Ki 18:40), Jehu (2Ki 10:18-31), by the Jews, at the time of the religious revival under the leadership of Azariah (2Ch 15:12-13).

See Persecution.

INTOXICANTS *See Beer; Fermented Drink; Wine.*

INTOXICATION [*3499*].

NIV+ INTOXICATED. See DRINK

See Abstinence; Drunkenness.

INTRIGUE [744, 2648, 2761, 4600, 8222].

NIV+ INTRIGUES

See Conspiracy.

INVECTIVE *See Satire.*

INVENTION [*2388, 5054*].

NIV+ INVENT, INVENTED

Of Musical Instruments:

By Jubal (Ge 4:21), by David (1Ch 23:5; 2Ch 7:6; 29:26; Am 6:5).

The use of metals (Ge 4:22). Machines of war (2Ch 26:15).

INVESTIGATION [1335, 2011, 8626, 9365, *374, 2428, 4158*].

NIV+ INVESTIGATE, INVESTIGATED

By Solomon, into nature and design of things (Ecc 1:13-18; 2:1-12; 7:25; 8:17; 12:9-14).

INVITATIONS [*7924, *2813, 2263, 4151, 5251*].

NIV+ INVITE, INVITATION, INVITED, INVITES, INVITING

The "Comes" of God's Word (Ge 7:1; Nu 10:29; Isa 1:18; 55:1; Mt 11:28; 22:4; Lk 14:17; Rev 22:17). Divine pleading (Pr 1:24; Isa 1:18; 55:1; Eze 18:31; Mic 6:3; Mt 23:37; Ro 10:21; 2Co 5:20).

Divine Call:

To repentance (Jer 35:15; Eze 33:11; Hos 6:1; Mt 22:3; 2Co 5:20; Rev 3:20). To leadership (Ge 12:1; Ex 3:10; Jdg 6:14; 1Ki 19:19; Isa 6:8; Ac 26:16). Universality of (Isa 45:22; 55:1; Mt 22:9; Jn 7:37; Ro 10:12; 1Ti 2:4; Rev 22:17). Refused by people (Ps 81:11; Isa 65:12; Jer 7:13; Hos 9:17; Mt 22:3; Jn 5:40; Ro 10:21). Warnings (Ge 19:17; Dt 29:20; Jos 24:20; 1Sa 12:15; Isa 28:14; Jer 13:16; Jnh 3:4; Heb 12:25; 2Pe 3:17).

IPHDEIAH, IPHEDEIAH [3635] (*Yahweh redeems*). A Benjamite (1Ch 8:25).

IPHTAH [3652] (*he opens*).

NIV+ IPHTAH EL

A city of Judah (Jos 15:43).

IPHTAH EL [3654] (*God [El] opens*).

NIV+ IPHTAH

A valley in Zebulun (Jos 19:14,27).

IR [6553] (possibly *stallion donkey*). A Benjamite (1Ch 7:12).

IR NAHASH, IR-NAHASH [6560] (*city of Nahash*). Whether a man or a town is not clear (1Ch 4:12, ftn). *See Nahash.*

IR SHEMESH, IR-SHEMESH [6561] (*city of Shemesh*). A city of Dan (Jos 19:41).

IRA [6562] (possibly *stallion donkey*).

1. The Jairite, David's priest (2Sa 20:26).

2. The Ithrite, one of David's heroes (2Sa 23:38; 1Ch 11:40).

3. From Tekoa, one of David's heroes (2Sa 23:26; 1Ch 11:28; 27:9).

IRAD [6563]. Son of Enoch (Ge 4:18).

IRAM [6566]. A chief of Edom (Ge 36:43; 1Ch 1:54).

IRI [6565] (perhaps *donkey's colt*). A son of Bela (1Ch 7:7).

IRIJAH [3713] (*Yahweh sees*). A captain of the guard who imprisoned the prophet Jeremiah (Jer 37:13-14).

IRON [1366, 3712, 10591, *3013*, *4969*, *4970*].
NIV+ IRON-SMELTING, IRONS, NECK-IRONS

1. First recorded use of (Ge 4:22). Ore of (Dt 8:9; Job 28:2). Melted (Eze 22:20). Used in the temple (1Ch 22:3; 29:2,7).

Articles Made of:

Ax (2Ki 6:6; 2Ch 18:10; Ecc 10:10; Isa 10:34), bed (Dt 3:11), breastplate (Rev 9:9), chariot (Jos 17:16,18; Jdg 1:19; 4:3), fetters (Ps 105:18; 107:10,16; 149:8), file (Pr 27:17), furnace (Dt 4:20; 1Ki 8:51; Jer 11:4), gate (Ac 12:10), harrow (2Sa 12:31), horn (1Ki 22:11; 2Ch 18:10; Mic 4:13), idols (Da 2:33; 5:4,23), pans (Eze 4:3; 27:19), pen (Job 19:24; Jer 17:1), pillars (Jer 1:18), rods for scourging (Ps 2:9; Rev 2:27; 12:5; 19:15), threshing instruments (Am 1:3), tools (1Ki 6:7), vessels (Jos 6:24), weapons (Nu 35:16; 1Sa 17:7; Job 20:24; 41:7), yokes (Dt 28:48; Jer 28:13-14).

Stones of (Dt 8:9; Job 28:2; Isa 60:17).
See Steel.

Figurative: (2Sa 23:7; Jer 15:12; 1Ti 4:2).

2. A city of Naphtali (Jos 19:38).

IRONY

Instances of:

Michal to David (2Sa 6:20). Elijah to the priests of Baal (1Ki 18:27). Job to his accusers (Job 12:2). Ezekiel to the prince of Tyre (Eze 28:3-5). Micaiah (1Ki 22:15). Amos to the Samaritans (Am 4:4). Jesus to Pharisees (Mk 2:17). Pharisees and Herodians to Jesus (Mt 22:16). Roman soldiers to Jesus (Mt 27:29; Mk 15:17-19; Lk 23:11; Jn 19:2-3). Pilate, calling Jesus king (Mk 15:19; Jn 19:15). Superscription of Pilate over Jesus (Mt 27:37; Mk 15:26; Lk 23:38; Jn 19:19). Agrippa to Paul (Ac 26:28).

See Sarcasm; Satire.

IRPEEL [3761] (*God [El] heals*). A city of Benjamin (Jos 18:27).

IRRIGATION [9197].
NIV+ IRRIGATED

Of gardens (Dt 11:10; Pr 21:1; Ecc 2:6; Isa 58:11). Figurative (1Co 3:6,8).

IRU [6564]. Eldest son of Caleb (1Ch 4:15).

ISAAC [3663, 3773, *2693*] (*he laughs, he will laugh*, some contexts *mock;* other contexts *El [God] laughs*).
NIV+ ISAAC'S

1. Miraculous son of Abraham (Ge 17:15-19; 18:1-15; 21:1-8; Jos 24:3; 1Ch 1:28; Gal 4:28; Heb 11:11). Ancestor of Jesus (Mt 1:2). Offered in sacrifice by his father (Ge 22:1-19; Heb 11:17; Jas 2:21). Is provided a wife from among his kindred (Ge 24; 25:20). Abrahamic covenant confirmed in (Ge 26:2-5; 1Ch 16:15-19). Dwells in the south country at the well Beer Lahai Roi (Ge 24:62; 25:11). With Ishmael, buries his father in the cave of Machpelah (Ge 25:9). Esau and Jacob born to (Ge 25:19-26; 1Ch 1:34; Jos 24:4). Dwells in Gerar (Ge 26:7-11). Prospers (Ge 26:12-14). Possesses large flocks and herds (Ge 26:14). Digs wells, and is defrauded of them by the

herdsmen of Abimelech (Ge 26:15,21). Removes to the valley of Gerar, afterward called Beersheba (Ge 26:22-33). His old age, last blessing upon his sons (Ge 27:18-40). Death and burial of (Ge 35:27-29; 49:31). His filial obedience (Ge 22:9). His peaceableness (Ge 26:14-22). Was a prophet (Ge 27:28-29,39-40; Heb 11:20). Has devoutness (Ge 24:63; 25:21; 26:25; Mt 8:11; Lk 13:28). Prophecies concerning (Ge 17:16-21; 18:10-14; 21:12; 26:2-5,24; Ex 32:13; 1Ch 16:16; Ro 9:7).

2. A designation of the ten tribes (Am 7:9).

ISAIAH, BOOK OF

Author: Isaiah son of Amoz

Date: Between c. 701 and 681 B.C..

Outline:

Part 1: The Book of Judgment (chs. 1-39):

I. Messages of Rebuke and Promise (chs. 1-6).
   A. Introduction: Charges against Judah for Breaking the Covenant (ch. 1).
   B. The Future Discipline and Glory of Judah and Jerusalem (chs. 2-4).
      1. Jerusalem's future blessings (2:1-5).
      2. The discipline of Judah (2:6-4:11).
      3. The restoration of Zion (4:2-6).
   C. The Nation's Judgment and Exile (ch. 5).
   D. Isaiah's Unique Commission (ch. 6).
II. Prophecies Occasioned by the Aramean and Israelite Threat against Judah (chs. 7-12).
   A. Ahaz Warned Not to Fear the Aramean and Israelite Threat (chs. 7).
   B. Isaiah's Son and David's Son (8:1-9:7).
   C. Judgment against Israel (9:8-10:4).
   D. The Assyrian Empire and the Davidic Kingdom (10:5-12:6).
      1. The destruction of Assyria (10:5-34).
      2. The establishment of the Davidic king and his kingdom (ch. 11).
III. Judgment against the Nations (chs. 13-23).
   A. Against Assyria and Its Ruler (13:1-14:27).
   B. Against Philistia (14:28-32).
   C. Against Moab (chs. 15-16).
   D. Against Aram and Israel (ch. 17).
   E. Against Cush (ch. 18).
   F. Against Egypt and Cush (chs. 19-20).
   G. Against Babylon (21:1-10).
   H. Against Dumah (Edom) (21:11-12).
   I. Against Arabia (21:13-17).
   J. Against the Valley of Vision (Jerusalem) (ch. 22).
   K. Against Tyre (ch. 23).
IV. Judgment and Promise(the Lord's Kingdom) (chs. 24-27).
   A. Universal Judgments for Universal Sin (ch. 24).
   B. Deliverance and Blessing (ch. 25).
   C. Praise for the Lord's Sovereign Care (ch. 26).
   D. Israel's Enemies: Punished but Israel's Remnant Restored (ch. 27).
V. Six Woes: Five on the Unfaithful in Israel and One on Assyria (chs. 28-33).
   A. Woe to Ephraim (Samaria)—and to Judah (ch. 28).
   B. Woe to David's City, Jerusalem (29:1-14).
   C. Woe to Those Who Rely on Foreign Alliances (29:15-24).
   D. Woe to the Obstinate Nation (ch. 30).
   E. Woe to Those Who Rely on Egypt (chs. 31-32).
   F. Woe to Assyria—but Blessing for God's People (ch. 33).

VI. More Prophecies of Judgment and Promise (chs. 34-35).
  A. The Destruction of the Nations and the Avenging of God's People (ch. 34).
  B. The Future Blessings of Restored Zion (ch. 35).
VII. A Historical Transition from the Assyrian Threat to the Babylonian Exile (chs. 36-39).
  A. Jerusalem Preserved from the Assyrian Threat (chs. 36-37).
    1. The siege of Jerusalem by Sennacherib and the Assyrian army (ch. 36).
    2. The Lord's deliverance of Jerusalem (ch. 37).
  B. The Lord's Extension of Hezekiah's Life (ch. 38).
  C. The Babylonian Exile Predicted (ch. 39).

Part 2: The Book of Comfort (chs. 40-66):
VIII. The Deliverance and Restoration of Israel (chs. 40-48).
  A. The Coming of the Victorious God (40:1-26).
  B. Unfailing Strength for the Weary Exiles (40:27-31).
  C. The Lord of History (41:1-42:9).
  D. Praise and Exhortation (42:10-25).
  E. The Regathering and Renewal of Israel (43:1-44:5).
  F. The Only God (44:6-45:25).
  G. The Lord's Superiority over Babylon's Gods (ch. 46).
  H. The Fall of Babylon (ch. 47).
  I. The Lord's Exhortations to His People (ch. 48).
IX. The Servant's Ministry and Israel's Restoration (chs. 49-57).
  A. The Call and Mission of the Servant (49:1-13).
  B. The Repopulation of Zion (49:14-26).
  C. Israel's Sin and the Servant's Obedience (ch. 50).
  D. The Remnant Comforted Because of Their Glorious Prospect (51:1-52:12).
  E. The Sufferings and Glories of the Lord's Righteous Servant (52:13-53:12).
  F. The Future Glory of Zion (ch. 54).
  G. The Lord's Call to Salvation and Covenant Blessings (55:1-56:8).
  H. The Condemnation of the Wicked in Israel (56:9-57:21).
X. Everlasting Deliverance and Everlasting Judgment (chs. 58-66).
  A. False and True Worship (ch. 58).
  B. Zion's Confession and Redemption (ch. 59).
  C. Zion's Peace and Prosperity (ch. 60).
  D. The Lord's Favor (ch. 61).
  E. Zion's Restoration and Glory (62:1-63:6).
  F. Prayer for Divine Deliverance (63:7-64:12).
  G. The Lord's Answer: Mercy and Judgment (ch. 65).
  H. Judgment for False Worshipers and Blessing for True Worshipers (ch. 66).

ISAIAH, ISAIAS [3833, 2480] (*Yahweh saves*). Son of Amos (Isa 1:1). Prophecies in the days of Uzziah, Jotham, Ahaz, and Hezekiah, kings of Judah (Isa 1:1; 6:1; 7:1,3; 14:27; 20:1; 36:1; 38:1; 39:1), at the time of the invasion by the Assyrian supreme commander (Isa 20:1). Symbolically wears sackcloth, and walks barefoot, as a sign to Israel (Isa 20:2-3). Comforts and encourages Hezekiah and the people in the siege of Jerusalem by Sennacherib, king of Assyria (2Ki 18; 19; Isa 37:6-7). Comforts Hezekiah in his affliction (2Ki 20:1-11; Isa 38). Performs the miracle of the returning shadow to confirm Hezekiah's faith (2Ki 20:8-11). Reproves Hezekiah's folly in exhibiting his resources to the commissioners from Babylon (2Ki

20:12-19; Isa 39). Is chronicler of the times of Uzziah and Hezekiah (2Ch 26:22; 32:32).

Prophecies, Reproofs, and Exhortations of:
Foretells punishment of the Jews for idolatry, and reproves self-confidence and distrust of God (Isa 2:6-20). Foretells the destruction of the Jews (Isa 3). Promises to the remnant restoration of divine favor (Isa 4:2-6; 6). Delineates in the parable of the vineyard the ingratitude of the Jews, and reproves it (Isa 5:1-10). Denounces existing corruption (Isa 5:8-30). Foretells the ill success of the plot of the Israelites and Syrians against Judah (Isa 7:1-6). Pronounces calamities against Israel and Judah (Isa 7:16-25; 9:2-6). Foretells prosperity under Hezekiah, and the manifestation of the Messiah (Isa 9:1-7). Pronounces vengeance upon the enemies of Israel (Isa 9:8-12). Denounces the wickedness of Israel, and foretells the judgments of God (Isa 9:13-21). Pronounces judgments against false prophets (Isa 10:1-4). Foretells the destruction of Sennacherib's armies (Isa 10:5-34), the restoration of Israel and the triumph of the Messiah's kingdom (Isa 11). The burden of Babylon (Isa 13; 14:1-28). Denunciation against the Philistines (Isa 14:9-32). Burden of Moab (Isa 15-16). Burden of Damascus (Isa 17). Obscure prophecy, supposed by some authorities to be directed against the Assyrians, by others against the Egyptians, and by others against the Ethiopians (Isa 18). The burden of Egypt (Isa 19-20). Denunciations against Babylon (Isa 21:1-10). Prophecy concerning Seir (Isa 21:11-12), Arabia (Isa 21:13-17), concerning the conquest of Jerusalem, the captivity of Shebna, and the promotion of Eliakim (Isa 22:1-22), the overthrow of Tyre (Isa 23), the judgments upon the land, but that a remnant of the Jews would be saved (Isa 25-27). Reproves Ephraim for his wickedness, and foretells the destruction by Shalmaneser (Isa 28:1-5). Declares the glory of God upon the remnant who are saved (Isa 28:5-6). Exposes the corruption in Jerusalem and exhorts to repentance (Isa 28:7-29). Foretells the invasion of Sennacherib, the distress of the Jews and the destruction of the Assyrian army (Isa 29:1-8). Denounces the hypocrisy of the Jews (Isa 29:9-17). Promises a reformation (Isa 29:18-24). Reproves the people for their confidence in Egypt, and their contempt of God (Isa 30:1-17; 31:1-6). Declares the goodness and long-suffering of God toward them (Isa 30:18-26; 32-35). Reproves the Jews for their spiritual blindness and infidelity (Isa 42:18-25). Promises ultimate restoration of the Jews (Isa 43:1-13). Foretells the ultimate destruction of Babylon (Isa 43:14-17; 47). Exhorts the people to repent (Isa 43:22-28). Comforts the church with promises, exposes the folly of idolatry, and their future deliverance from captivity by Cyrus (Isa 44; 45:1-5; 48:20). Foretells the conversion of the Gentiles, and triumph of the gospel (Isa 45:5-25). Denounces the evils of idolatry (Isa 46). Reproves the Jews for their idolatries and other wickedness (Isa 48). Exhorts to sanctification (Isa 56:1-8). Foretells calamities to Judah (Isa 57-58; 59:9-12).

Foreshadows the person and the kingdom of the Messiah (Isa 32-35; 42; 45; 49-56; 59:15-21; 60-66).

ISCAH [3576]. Daughter of Haran and sister of Lot (Ge 11:29).

ISCARIOT [2697] (*man of Kerioth* or *of the assassins*). See Judas.

ISHBAH [3786] (*he boasts, congratulates*). Father of Eshtemoa (1Ch 4:17).

ISHBAK [3791]. Son of Abraham and Keturah (Ge 25:2; 1Ch 1:32).

ISHBI-BENOB [3787]. A giant warrior slain by Abishai (2Sa 21:16).

ISH-BOSHETH [410] (*man of shame*). Son of Saul. Called Esh-Baal (1Ch 8:33; 9:39). Made king by Abner (2Sa 2:8-10). Deserted by Abner (2Sa 3:6-12). Restores Michal, David's wife, to David (2Sa 3:14-16). Assassinated (2Sa 4:5-8). Avenged by David (2Sa 4:9-12).

ISHHOD [412] (*man of grandeur*). One of the tribe of Manasseh (1Ch 7:18).

ISHI [3831] (*God has saved*).
1. A play on the two Hebrew words for husband. In this verse the first is "husband"; the second is "master" which is identical with the name of the god Baal. There will be such a vigorous reaction against Baal worship that this Hebrew word for "master" will no longer be used of the Lord (Hos 2:16, ftn).
2. A son of Appaim (1Ch 2:31).
3. A descendant of Judah (1Ch 4:20).
4. A Simeonite (1Ch 4:42).
5. One of the heads of Manasseh (1Ch 5:24).

ISHIAH *See Isshiah.*

ISHIJAH [3807] (*Yahweh forget*). One of the sons of Harim (Ezr 10:31).

ISHMA [3816] (*desolate ISBE; God [El] he heard KB*). A descendant of Judah (1Ch 4:3).

ISHMACHIAH *See Ismakiah.*

ISHMAEL [3817] (*God [El] he heard*).
NIV+ ISHMAELITE, ISHMAELITES
1. Son of Abraham (Ge 16:11,15-16; 1Ch 1:28). Prayer of Abraham for (Ge 17:18,20). Circumcised (Ge 17:23-26). Promised to be the father of a nation (Ge 16:11-12; 17:20; 21:12-13,18). Sent away by Abraham (Ge 21:6-21). With Isaac buries his father (Ge 25:9). Children of (Ge 25:12-18; 1Ch 1:29-31). Daughter of, marries Esau (Ge 28:9; 36:2-3). Death of (Ge 25:17-18).
2. Father of Zebadiah (2Ch 19:11).
3. A son of Azel (1Ch 8:38; 9:44).
4. One of the captains of hundreds (2Ch 23:1).
5. A priest of the Exile (Ezr 10:22).
6. A son of Nethaniah. Assassinated Gedaliah, governor of Judah under king of Babylon, and takes captive many Jews (Jer 40:8-16; 41:1-11; 2Ki 25:23-25). Defeated by Johanan and put to flight (Jer 41:12-15).

ISHMAELITE(S), ISHMEELITE(S) [3818] (*one from Ishmael*).
NIV+ ISHMAEL
Descended from Abraham's son, Ishmael (Ge 16:15-16; 1Ch 1:28). Divided into twelve tribes (Ge 25:16). Heads of tribes of (Ge 25:13-15; 1Ch 1:29-31).

Called:
Hagrites, either Ishmaelites (descendants of Hagar; Ge 16) or a group mentioned in Assyrian inscriptions as an Aramean confederacy (1Ch 5:10,19-22; 27:31), are named among the enemies of Israel (Ps 83:6). Arabs (Isa 13:20). Original possessions of (Ge 25:18). Governed by kings (Jer 25:24). Dwelt in tents (Isa 13:20). Rich in cattle (1Ch 5:21). Wore ornaments of gold (Jdg 8:24). Were the merchants of the east (Ge 37:25; Eze 27:20-21). Traveled in large companies or caravans (Ge 37:25; Job 6:19). Waylaid and plundered travelers (Jer 3:2). Often confederate against Israel (Ps 83:6).

Overcome by:
Gideon (Jdg 8:10-24). Reubenites and Gadites (1Ch 5:10,18-20). Uzziah (2Ch 26:7). Sent presents to Solomon (1Ki 10:15; 2Ch 9:14). Sent flocks to Jehoshaphat (2Ch 17:11).

Prophecies Concerning:
To be numerous (Ge 16:10; 17:20). To be wild and savage (Ge 16:12). To be warlike and predatory (Ge 16:12). To be divided into twelve tribes (Ge 17:20). To continue independent (Ge 16:12). To be a great nation (Ge 21:13,18). To be judged with the nations (Ge 25:23-25). Their glory to be diminished (Isa 21:13-17). Their submission to Christ (Ps 72:10,15). Probably preached to by Paul (Gal 1:17).

ISHMAIAH [3819, 3820] (*Yahweh heard*).
1. Gibeonite (1Ch 12:4).
2. Chief of Zebulunites (1Ch 27:19).

ISHMEELITE *See Ishmaelite(s), Ishmeelite(s).*

ISHMERAI [3821] (*Yahweh guards*). A chief Benjamite (1Ch 8:18).

ISHOD *See Ishhod.*

ISHPAH [3834] (*he judged*). A Benjamite (1Ch 8:16).

ISHPAN [3836] (possibly *may God judge*). Son of Shashak (1Ch 8:22).

ISHTAR Semitic goddess worshiped in Phoenicia, Canaan, Assyria, and Babylonia, and sometimes even by the Israelites. Some identify her with Ashtoreth or Ashtaroth (Jdg 2:13; 10:6; 1Ki 11:5; 2Ki 23:13).

ISHTOB (*man of Tob*). See Tob, 2.

ISHUAH *See Ishvah.*

ISHUAI, ISHUI, ISUI *See Ishvi, Ishvite.*

ISHVAH [3796] (*he will level*). Son of Asher (Ge 46:17; 1Ch 7:30).

ISHVI, ISHVITE [3798, 3799].
1. Son of Asher (Ge 46:17; 1Ch 7:30) and his clan (Nu 26:44).
2. Son of Saul (1Sa 14:49).

ISLAND, ISLE [362, *3761, 3762*].
NIV+ ISLANDERS, ISLANDS
1. Dry land, as opposed to water (Isa 42:15).
2. Body of land surrounded by water (Jer 2:10).
3. Coastland (Ge 10:5; Isa 20:6).
4. The farthest regions of the earth (Isa 41:5; Zep 2:11).

ISMAIAH *See Ishmaiah.*

ISMAKIAH, ISMACHIAH [3577] (*Yahweh sustains*). Overseer of the temple (2Ch 31:13).

ISPAH *See Ishpah.*

ISRAEL, ISRAELITES [278, 3776+, 10335, *2702+, 2703+*] (*he struggles with God [El]*).
NIV+ ISRAEL'S, ISRAELITE, ISRAELITES', JACOB
1. A name given to Jacob (Ge 32:24-32; 2Ki 17:34; Hos 12:3-4).

2. A name of the Christ in prophecy (Isa 49:3).

3. A name given to the descendants of Jacob, a nation. Also called Israelites and Hebrews (Ge 43:32; Ex 1:15; 9:7; 10:3; 21:2; Lev 23:42; Jos 13:6; 1Sa 4:6; 13:3,19; 14:11,21; Php 3:5).

Tribes of:

Tribes of Israel were named after the sons of Jacob. In lists usually the names Levi and Joseph, two sons of Jacob, do not appear. The descendants of Levi were consecrated to the rites of religion, and the two sons of Joseph, Ephraim and Manasseh, were adopted by Jacob in Joseph's stead (Ge 48:5; Jos 14:4), and their names appear in the lists of tribes instead of those of Levi and Joseph, as follows: Asher, Benjamin, Dan, Ephraim, Gad, Issachar, Judah, Manasseh, Naphtali, Reuben, Simeon, Zebulun.

Names of, seen in John's vision, on the gates of the New Jerusalem (Rev 21:12).

Prophecies, concerning (Ge 15:5,13; 25:23; 26:4; 27:28-29,40; 48:19; 49; Dt 33), of the multitude of (Ge 13:16; 15:5; 22:17; 26:4; 28:14), of their captivity in Egypt (Ge 15:13-14; Ac 7:6-7).

Divided into families, each of which had a chief (Nu 25:14; 26; 36:1; Jos 7:14; 1Ch 4-8).

Number of, who went into Egypt (Ge 46:8-27; Ex 1:5; Dt 10:22; Ac 7:14). Number of, at the time of the Exodus (Ex 12:37-38, w Ge 47:27; Ex 1:7-20; Ps 105:24; Ac 7:17). Number of, fit for military service when they left Egypt (Ex 12:37), at Sinai, by tribes (Nu 1:1-50), after the plague (Nu 26), when David numbered (2Sa 24:1-9; 1Ch 21:5-6; 27:23-24), after the Captivity (Ezr 2:64; Ne 7:66-67), in John's apocalyptic vision (Rev 7:1-8).

Early History:

Dwelt in Goshen (Ge 46:28-34; 47:4-10,27-28). Dwelt in Egypt 430 years (Ge 15:13; Ex 12:40-41; Ac 7:6; Gal 3:17). Were enslaved and oppressed by the Egyptians (Ex 1-2; 5; Ac 7:18-36). Their groaning heard by God (Ex 2:23-25). Moses commissioned as deliverer (Ex 3:2-22; 4:1-17). The land of Egypt plagued on their account. *See Egypt.* Exempt from the plagues (Ex 8:22-23; 9:4-6,26; 10:23; 11:7; 12:13). Children were spared when the firstborn of the Egyptians were slain (Ex 12:13,23). Instituted the Passover (Ex 12:1-28). Borrowed jewels from the Egyptians (Ex 11:2-3; 12:35-36; Ps 105:37). Urged by the Egyptians to depart (Ex 12:31-39). Journey from Rameses to Succoth (Ex 12:37-39). Made the journey by night (Ex 12:42). The day of their deliverance to be a memorial (Ex 12:42; 13:3-16). Led of God (Ex 13:18,21-22). Providentially cared for (Dt 8:3-4; 29:5-6; 34:7; Ne 9:21; Ps 105:37). *See Manna; Cloud, Pillar of.*

Journey from Succoth, to Etham (Ex 13:20), to Pi Hahiroth (Ex 14:2; Nu 33:5-7). Pursued by the Egyptians (Ex 14:5-31). Pass through the Red Sea (Ex 14:19-22; Dt 11:4; Ps 78; 105-107; 136). Order of march (Nu 2). Journey to Marah (Ex 15:23; Nu 33:8). Murmur on account of the bitter water (Ex 15:23-25); water of sweetened (Ex 15:25). Journey to Elim (Ex 15:27; Nu 33:9). The itinerary (Nu 33).

Murmured for food (Ex 16:2-3). Provided with manna and quails (Ex 16:4-36). Murmured for want of water at Rephidim (Ex 17:2-7), water miraculously supplied from the rock at Meribah (Ex 17:5-7). Defeat the Amalekites (Ex 17:13; Dt 25:17-18). Arrive at Sinai (Ex 19:1; Nu 33:15). At the suggestion of Jethro, Moses' father-in-law, they organize a system of government (Ex 18:25; Dt 1:9-18). The message of God to them, requiring that they shall

be obedient to his commandments, and as a reward they would be to him a holy nation, and their reply (Ex 19:3-8). Sanctify themselves for receiving the law (Ex 19:10-15). The law delivered to (Ex 20-23; 24:1-4; 25-31; Lev 1-25; 27; Dt 5; 15:16). The people receive it and covenant obedience to it (Ex 24:3,7). Idolatry of (Ex 32; Dt 9:17-21). The anger of the Lord in consequence (Ex 32:9-14). Moses' indignation; breaks the tables of stone; enters the camp; commands the Levites; three thousand slain (Ex 32:19-35). Visited by a plague (Ex 32:35). Obduracy of (Ex 33:3; 34:9; Dt 9:12-29). God withdraws his presence (Ex 33:1-3). The mourning of, when God refused to lead them (Ex 33:4-10). Tablets renewed (Ex 34). Pattern for the tabernacle and its furnishings, and forms of worship to be observed (Ex 25-31). Gifts consecrated for the creation of the tabernacle (Ex 35; 36:1-7; Nu 7). The building of the tabernacle; the manufacture of its furnishings, including the garments of the priests; and their sanctification (Ex 36:8-38; 37-40). First sacrifice offered by under the law (Lev 8:14-36; 9:8-24). Second Passover observed (Nu 9:1-5).

March out of the wilderness (Nu 10:11-36). Itinerary (Nu 33). Order of camp and march (Nu 2). Arrive at the border of Canaan (Nu 12:16). Send twelve spies to view the land (Nu 13; 32:8; Dt 1:22,25; Jos 14:7). Return with a majority and minority report (Nu 13:26-33; 14:6-10). Murmuring over the report (Nu 14:1-5). The judgment of God upon them in consequence of their unbelief and murmuring (Nu 14:13-39). Reaction, and their purpose to enter the land; are defeated by the Amalekites (Nu 14:40-45; Dt 1:41-45). Stay at Kadesh (Nu 1:46). Return to the wilderness, where they remain thirty-eight years, and all die except Joshua and Caleb (Nu 14:20-39). Rebellion of Korah, Dathan, and Abiram (Nu 16:1-40; Dt 11:6). Murmur against Moses and Aaron; are plagued; 14,700 die; plague stayed (Nu 16:41-50). Murmur for want of water in Meribah; the rock is struck (Nu 20:1-13). Are refused passage through the country of Edom (Nu 20:14-21). The death of Aaron (Nu 20:22,29; 33:38-39; Dt 10:6). Defeat the Canaanites (Nu 21:1-3). Are scourged with serpents (Nu 21:4-9). Defeat Sihon, king of the Amorites (Nu 21:21-32; Dt 2:24-35), and Og, the king of Bashan (Nu 21:33-35; Dt 3:1-17). Arrive in the plains of Moab, at the fords of the Jordan (Nu 22:1; 33:48-49). Commit idolatry with the people of Moab (Nu 25:1-5). Visited by a plague in consequence; 24,000 die (Nu 25:6-15; 26:1). The people numbered for the allotment of the land (Nu 26). The daughters of Zelophehad sue for an inheritance (Nu 27:1-11; Jos 17:3-6). Conquest of the Midianites (Nu 31). Nations dread (Dt 2:25). Renew the covenant (Dt 29). Moses dies, and people mourn (Dt 34). Joshua appointed leader (Nu 27:18-23; Dt 31:23). *See Joshua, 1.*

All who were numbered at Sinai perished in the wilderness except Caleb and Joshua (Nu 26:63,65; Dt 2:14-16). Piety of those who entered Canaan (Jos 23:8; Jdg 2:7-10; Jer 2:2-3). Men chosen to allot the lands of Canaan among the tribes and families (Nu 34:17-29). Remove from Shittim to Jordan (Jos 3:1). Cross Jordan (Jos 4). Circumcision observed and Passover celebrated (Jos 5). Jericho taken (Jos 6). Ai taken (Jos 7-8). Make a covenant with the Gibeonites (Jos 9). Defeat the five Amorite kings (Jos 10). Conquest of the land (Jos 21:43-45, w Jdg 1). The land allotted (Jos 15-21).

Two and one-half tribes return from the west side of the Jordan; erect a memorial to signify the unity of the tribes; the memorial misunderstood; the controversy which followed; its amicable adjustment (Jos 22). Joshua's exhortation immediately before his death (Jos 23). Covenant renewed, death of Joshua (Jos 24; Jdg 2:8-9). Religious fidelity during the life of Joshua (Jos 24:31; Jdg 2:7).

Under the Judges:

Public affairs administered 450 years by the judges (Jdg 2:16-19; Ac 13:20). The original inhabitants not fully expelled (Jdg 1:27-36; 3:1-7). Reproved by an angel for not casting out the original inhabitants (Jdg 2:1-5). People turn to idolatry (Jdg 2:10-23). Delivered for their idolatry to the king of Mesopotamia during eight years; their repentance and deliverance (Jdg 3:8-11). Renew their idolatry, and are put under tribute to the king of Moab during eighteen years; repent and are delivered by Ehud; eighty years of peace follow (Jdg 3:12-30). Shamgar resists a foray of the Philistines and delivers Israel (Jdg 3:31). People again do evil and are put under bonds for twenty years to the king of Syria (Jdg 4:1-3). Delivered by Deborah, a prophetess, and judged (Jdg 4-5). Seven years of bondage to the Midianites; delivered by Gideon (Jdg 6-7; 8:1-28). *See Gideon.* Return to idolatry (Jdg 8:33-34). Abimelech foments an intertribal war (Jdg 9). Judged, by Tola twenty-three years (Jdg 10:1-2), by Jair twenty-two years (Jdg 10:3-4). People backslide, and are given over to the Philistines for discipline eighteen years; repent and turn to the Lord; delivered by Jephthah (Jdg 10:6-18; 11). Ephraimites go to war against other tribes; defeated by Jephthah (Jdg 12:1-7). Judged, by Ibzan seven years (Jdg 12:8-10), by Elon ten years (Jdg 12:11-12), by Abdon eight years (Jdg 12:13-15). Backslide again and are disciplined by the Philistines forty years (Jdg 13:1). Judged by Samson twenty years (Jdg 15:20, w Jdg 13-16). Scandal of the Bethlehemite's concubine, and the consequent war between the Benjamites and the other tribes (Jdg 19-21). Judged by Eli forty years (1Sa 4:18, w 1Sa 1-4). Smitten by the Philistines at Ebenezer (1Sa 4:1-2,10-11). Demand a king (1Sa 8:5-20; Hos 13:10).

The United Kingdom:

Saul anointed king (1Sa 10; 11:12-15; 12:13). Ammonites invade Israel, are defeated (1Sa 11). Philistines smitten (1Sa 14). Amalekites defeated (1Sa 15). David anointed king (1Sa 16:11-13). Goliath slain (1Sa 17). Israel defeated by the Philistines, and Saul and his sons killed (1Sa 31). *See Saul.* David defeats the Amalekites (1Sa 30; 2Sa 1:1), made king (2Sa 2:4,11). Ish-Bosheth made king (2Sa 2:8-10).

The conflict between the two political factions (2Sa 2:12-32; 3:1).

David made king over all Israel (2Sa 5:1-5). Conquests of David (2Sa 8), Absalom's rebellion (2Sa 15-18). *See David.*

Solomon anointed king (1Ki 1:32-40). Temple built (1Ki 6). Solomon's palace built (1Ki 7). Solomon's death (1Ki 11:41-43). *See Solomon.*

The Revolt of the Ten Tribes:

Foreshadowing circumstances indicating the separation: Disagreement after Saul's death (2Sa 2; 1Ch 12:23-40; 13). Lukewarmness of the ten tribes, and zeal of Judah for David in Absalom's rebellion (2Sa 19:41-43). The rebellion of Sheba (2Sa 20). The two factions are distinguished as Israel and Judah during David's reign (2Sa 21:2). Providential (Zec 11:14).

Revolt consummated under Rehoboam, son and successor of Solomon (1Ki 12).

The ten tribes that revolted from the house of David also called Ephraim (Hos 7:8,11), Jacob (Hos 12:2).

	The Kings of Israel		
	Names	Ruled	Dates
1.	Jeroboam I	22 years	930-909 B.C.
2.	Nadab	2 years	909-908
3.	Baasha	24 years	908-886
4.	Elah	2 years	886-885
5.	Zimri	7 days	885
6.	Omri	12 years	885-874
7.	Ahab	22 years	874-853
8.	Ahaziah	2 years	853-852
9.	Joram	12 years	852-841
10.	Jehu	28 years	841-814
11.	Jehoahaz	17 years	814-798
12.	Jehoash	16 years	798-782
13.	Jeroboam II	41 years	793-753
14.	Zechariah	6 months	753
15.	Shallum	1 month	752
16.	Menahem	10 years	752-742
17.	Pekahiah	2 years	742-740
18.	Pekah	20 years	752-732
19.	Hoshea	9 years	732-722

Note: Some kings, such as Jehoash and Jeroboam II, had overlapping reigns.

See also the chart at Kings; See each king by name.

History of: War continued between, the two kingdoms all the days of Rehoboam and Jeroboam (1Ki 14:30), and between Jeroboam and Abijah (1Ki 15:7), and between Baasha and Asa (1Ki 15:16,32). Famine prevails in the reign of Ahab (1Ki 18:1-6). Israel, also called Samaria, invaded by, but defeats, Ben-Hadad, king of Syria (1Ki 20). Moab rebels (2Ki 1:1; 3). Army of Syria invades Israel, but peacefully withdraws through the tact of the prophet Elisha (2Ki 6:8-23). Samaria besieged (2Ki 6:24-33; 7), city of, taken, and the people carried to Assyria (2Ki 17). The land repopulated (2Ki 17:24).

The remnant that remained after the able-bodied were carried into captivity associated with the kingdom of Judah (2Ch 30:18-26; 34:6; 35:18).

Prophecies Concerning: Of captivity, famine, and judgments (1Ki 14:15-16; 17:1; 20:13-28; 2Ki 7:1-2,17; 8:1; Isa 7:8; 8:4-7; 9:8-21; 17:3-11; 28:1-8; Hos 1:1-9; 2:1-13; 4-10; 11:5-6; 12:7-14; 13; Am 2:6-16; 3-9).

Of restoration (Hos 2:14-23; 11:9-11; 13:13-14; 14:8).

Of the reunion of the ten tribes and Judah (Jer 3:18; Eze 37:16-22).

Judah:

The nation composed of the tribes of Judah and Benjamin, called Judah (Isa 11:12-13; Jer 4:3), and Jews ruled by the descendants of David. *See Jews.*

In the historical books of the Kings and the Chronicles the nation is called Judah, but in the prophecies it is frequently referred to as Israel (Isa 8:14; 49:7).

The Kings (and Queen) of Judah			
	Name	Ruled	Dates
1.	Rehoboam	17 years	930-913 B.C.
2.	Abijah	3 years	913-910
3.	Asa	41 years	910-869
4.	Jehoshaphat	25 years	872-848
5.	Jehoram	8 years	848-841
6.	Ahaziah	1 year	841
7.	Queen Athaliah	6 years	841-835
8.	Joash	40 years	835-796
9.	Amaziah	29 years	796-767
10.	Uzziah / Azariah	52 years	792-740
11.	Jotham	16 years	750-735
12.	Ahaz	16 years	732-715
13.	Hezekiah	29 years	715-686
14.	Manasseh	55 years	697-642
15.	Amon	2 years	642-640
16.	Josiah	31 years	640-609
17.	Jehoahaz	3 months	609
18.	Jehoiakim	11 years	609-598
19.	Jehoiachin	3 months	598-597
20.	Zedekiah / Mattaniah	11 years	597-586

Note: Some kings, such as Uzziah and Jotham, had overlapping reigns.

See also the chart at Kings; See each king by name.

Rehoboam succeeds Solomon. In consequence of his arbitrary policy ten tribes rebel (1Ki 12). Other circumstances of his reign (1Ki 14:21-31; 2Ch 10-12). Death of Rehoboam (1Ki 14:31). Abijah's wicked reign (1Ki 15:1-8; 2Ch 13), Asa's good reign (1Ki 15:9-24; 2Ch 14-16). Asa makes a league with Ben-Hadad, king of Syria , to make war against Israel (1Ki 15:16-24). Jehoshaphat succeeds Asa (1Ki 15:24; 2Ch 17-20; 21:1), joins Ahab against the king of Syria (1Ki 22). *See Jehoshaphat.* Jehoram, also called Joram, reigns in the place of his father, Jehoshaphat (2Ki 8:16-24; 2Ch 21). Edom revolts (2Ki 8:20-22). Ahaziah also called Azariah (2Ch 22:6) and Jehoahaz (2Ch 21:17; 25:23), succeeds Jehoram (2Ki 8:24-29; 2Ch 22); slain by Jehu (2Ki 9:27-29; 2Ch 22:8-9); Athaliah, his mother, succeeds him (2Ki 11:1-16; 2Ch 22:10-12; 23:1-15). Jehoash, also called Joash, succeeds Athaliah (2Ki 11:21; 12:1-21; 2Ch 24). The temple repaired (2Ki 12). Amaziah reigns, and Judah is invaded by the king of Israel; Jerusalem is taken and the sacred things of the temple carried away (2Ki 14:1-20; 2Ch 25). Azariah, also called Uzziah, succeeds him (2Ki 14:21-22; 15:1-7; 2Ch 26). Jotham succeeds Uzziah (2Ki 15:7,32-38; 2Ch 27). Rezin, king of Syria, invades Judah (2Ki 15:37). Jotham is succeeded by Ahaz (2Ki 16:1; 2Ch 28). Judah is invaded by kings of Samaria and Syria; Ahaz hires the king of Assyria to make war on the king of Syria (2Ki 16:5-9). Ahaz changes the fashion of the altar in the temple (2Ki 16:10-18). Hezekiah succeeds Ahaz (2Ki 16:19-20; 2Ch 29-32). His good reign (2Ki 18:1-8). He revolts from the sovereignty of the king of Assyria (2Ki 18:7). King of Assyria invades Judah and blasphemes the

God of Judah; his army overthrown (2Ki 18:9-37; 19). Hezekiah's sickness and miraculous restoration (2Ki 20). Succeeded by Manasseh (2Ki 20:21; 2Ch 33:1-20). Manasseh's wicked reign (2Ki 21:1-18). Amon succeeds Manasseh on the throne (2Ki 21:18-26; 2Ch 33:20-25). Josiah succeeds Amon; the temple is repaired; the Book of the Law recovered; religious revival follows; and the king dies (2Ki 22; 23:1-30; 2Ch 34-35). Josiah is succeeded by Jehoahaz, who reigns three months, is dethroned by the king of Egypt, and the land put under tribute (2Ki 23:30-35; 2Ch 36:1-3). Jehoiakim is elevated to the throne; becomes tributary to Nebuchadnezzar for three years; rebels; is conquered and carried to Babylon (2Ki 24:1-6; 2Ch 36:4-8). Jehoiachin is made king, suffers invasion, and is carried to Babylon (2Ki 24:8-16; 2Ch 36:9-10). Zedekiah is made king by Nebuchadnezzar; rebels; Nebuchadnezzar invades Judah, takes Jerusalem, and carries the people to Babylon, despoiling the temple (2Ki 24:17-20; 25; 2Ch 36:11-21). The poorest of the people are left to occupy the country and are joined by fragments of the army of Judah, the dispersed Israelites in other lands, and the king's daughters (2Ki 25:12,22-23; Jer 39:10; 40:7-12; 52:16). Gedaliah appointed governor over (2Ki 25:22). His administration favorable to the people (2Ki 25:23-24; Jer 40:7-12). Conspired against and slain by Ishmael (2Ki 25:25; Jer 40:13-16; 41:1-3). Ishmael seeks to betray the people to the Ammonites (Jer 41:1-18). The people, in fear, take refuge in Egypt (2Ki 25:26; Jer 41:14-18; 42:13-18).

Captivity of Judah:

Great wickedness the cause of their adversity (Eze 5-7; 16; 23:22-44). Dwell in Babylon (Da 5:13; 6:13; Jer 52:28-30) by the Kebar River (Eze 1:1; 10:15). Patriotism of (Ps 137). Plotted against, by Haman (Est 3). Are saved by Esther (Est 4-9). Cyrus decrees their restoration (2Ch 36:22-23; Ezr 1:1-4). Cyrus directs the rebuilding of the temple and the restoration of the vessels that had been carried to Babylon (2Ch 36:23; Ezr 1:3-11). Proclamation renewed by Darius and Artaxerxes (Ezr 6:1-14). Ezra returns with 1,754 of the captives to Jerusalem (Ezr 2). Temple rebuilt and dedicated (Ezr 3-6). Artaxerxes issues proclamation to restore the temple service (Ezr 7). Priests and Levites authorized to return (Ezr 8). Corruption among the returned captives; their reform (Ezr 9-10).

Nehemiah leads 49,942 captives back to the land (Ne 2; 7:5-67; Ps 85; 87; 107; 126). Wall of Jerusalem rebuilt and dedicated (Ne 2-6; 12). The law read and expounded (Ne 8). Solemn feast is kept, priests are purified; and the covenant sealed (Ne 8-10). One-tenth of the people, to be determined by lot, volunteer to dwell in Jerusalem, and the remaining nine parts dwell in other cities (Ne 11). Catalog of the priests and Levites who came up with Zerubbabel (Ne 12). Nehemiah reforms various abuses (Ne 13). Expect a Messiah (Lk 3:15). Many accept Jesus as the Christ (Messiah) (Jn 2:23; 10:42; 11:45; 12:11; Ac 21:20). Reject Jesus. *See Jesus the Christ, Rejected.*

Rejected by God (Mt 21:43; Lk 20:16).

Prophecies Concerning Israel and Judah:

Of their rejection of the Messiah (Isa 8:14-15; 49:5,7; 52:14; 53:1-3; Zec 11; 13; Mt 21:33; 22:1).

Of war and other judgments (Dt 28:49-57; 2Ki 20:17-18; 21:12-15; 22:16-17; 23:26-27; Isa 1:1-24; 3; 4:1; 5; 6:9-13; 7:17-25; 8:14-22; 9; 10:12; 22:1-14; 28:14-22; 29:1-10; 30:1-17; 31:1-3; 32:9-14; Jer 1:11-16; 4:5-31; 6; 7:8-34; 8; 9:9-26; 10:17-22; 11:9-23; 13:9-27; 14:14-18;

15:1-14; 16; 17:1-4; 18:15-17; 19; 20:5; 21:4-7; 22:24-30; 25:8-38; 28; 34; 37; 38:1-3; 42:13-22; 43-45; La 5:6; Eze 4-5; 11:7-12; 12; 15-17; 19; 22:13-22; 23:22-35; 24; 33:21-29; Da 9:26-27; Joel 2:1-17; Am 2:4-5; Mic 2:10; 3; 4:8-10; Hab 1:6-11; Zep 1; Zec 11; 14:1-3; Mal 4:1; Mt 21:33-34; 23:35-38; 24:2,14-42; Mk 13:1-13; Lk 13:34-35; 19:43-44; 21:5-25; 23:28-31; Rev 1:7).

Dispersion of (Isa 24:1; Jer 9:16; Hos 9:17; Joel 3:6,20; Am 9:9; Eze 4:13; 5:10,12; 20:23; 36:19; Da 9:7; Jn 7:35; Ac 2:5).

Of blessing and restoration (Isa 1:25-27; 2:1-5; 4:2-6; 11:11-13; 25; 26:1-2,12-19; 27:13; 29:18-24; 30:18-26; 32:15-20; 33:13-24; 35; 37:31-32; 40:2,9; 41:27; 44; 49:13-23; 51; 52:1-12; 60; 61:4-9; 62; 66:5-22; Jer 3:14-18; 4:3-18; 12:14-16; 23:3; 24:1-7; 29:1-14; 30:3-22; 32:36-44; 33; 44:28; Eze 14:22-23; 16:60-63; 20:40-41; 36:1-38; 37:12,21; Da 11:30-45; 12:1; Joel 3; Am 9:9-15; Ob 17-21; Mic 2:12-13; 5:3; Zep 2:7; Zec 1:14-21; 2:8; 10:5-12; 12:1-14; 13; 14:3-21; Mal 3:4; Ro 11; 2Co 3:16; Rev 7:15).

ISRAELITES See Israel, Israelites.

ISSACHAR [1201+3779, 3779, 2704] (there is reward, Ge. 30:18; may [God] show mercy IDB; hired hand KB).

1. Fifth son of Jacob (Ge 30:18; Ex 1:3; 1Ch 2:1). Jacob's prophetic benedictions upon (Ge 49:14-15). In the time of David (1Ch 7:1-5).

2. Tribe of. Descended from Jacob's son (Ge 30:17-18). Prophecies concerning (Ge 49:14-15; Dt 33:18-19).

Persons selected from to number the people (Nu 1:8), to spy out the land (Nu 13:7). To divide the land (Nu 34:26). Strength of, on leaving Egypt (Nu 1:28-29; 2:6). Encamped under the standard of Judah east of the tabernacle (Nu 2:5). Next to and under the standard of Judah in the journeys of Israel (Nu 10:14-15). Offering of, at the dedication (Nu 7:18-23). Families of (Nu 26:23-24). Strength of, on entering Canaan (Nu 26:25). On Gerizim said amen to the blessings (Dt 27:12). Bounds of their inheritance (Jos 19:17-23). Assisted Deborah against Sisera (Jdg 5:15). Officers of, appointed by David (1Ch 27:18). Officers of, appointed by Solomon (1Ki 4:17). Some of, at David's coronation (1Ch 12:32). Number of warriors belonging to, in David's time (1Ch 7:2,5). Many of, at Hezekiah's Passover (2Ch 30:18). Remarkable persons of (Jdg 10:1; 1Ki 15:27).

ISSHIAH [3807, 3808] (Yahweh forgets).

1. Man of Issachar (1Ch 7:3).

2. A disaffected Israelite who joined David at Ziklag; one of David's heroes (1Ch 12:6).

3. A Kohathite Levite (1Ch 23:20).

4. A Levite (1Ch 24:21).

ISSUE OF BLOOD See Bleeding, Subject to; Hemorrhage.

ISUAH See Ishvah.

ISUI See Ishvi.

ITALIAN REGIMENT [2713]. Cohort of Italian soldiers stationed in Caesarea when Peter preached to Cornelius (Ac 10:1).

ITALY [2712].
NIV+ ITALIAN

(Ac 27:1; Heb 13:24). Aquila and Priscilla expelled from (Ac 18:2).

ITCH [3063, 5999, 3117].
NIV+ ITCHING

A skin disease (Lev 13:30-37; 14:54; Dt 28:27). See Disease; Scall.

ITHAI [416, 915]. Also called Ittai. One of David's valiant men (2Sa 23:29; 1Ch 11:31).

ITHAMAR [418] (possibly [is]land of palms BDB; [father] of Tamar KB).
NIV+ ITHAMAR'S

Son of Aaron (Ex 6:23; 28:1; 1Ch 6:3). Entrusted with money of the tabernacle (Ex 38:21). Charged with duties of the tabernacle (Nu 4:28; 7:8). Forbidden to lament the death of his brothers, Nadab and Abihu (Lev 10:6-7). Descendants of (1Ch 24:1-19).

ITHIEL [417] (God [El] is with me).

1. A Benjamite (Ne 11:7).

2. An unidentified person (Pr 30:1).

ITHLAH [3849] (hanging, lofty place). A city of Dan (Jos 19:42).

ITHMAH [3850] (fatherless KB; purity ISBE). A Moabite (1Ch 11:46).

ITHNAN [3854]. A town in the extreme S of Judah (Jos 15:23).

ITHRA (abundance BDB; what remained KB). Hebrew Ithra is a variant of Jether (2Sa 17:25, ftn). Father of Amasa (2Sa 17:25; 1Ch 2:17). See Jether, 3.

ITHRAN [3864] (what is over, profit KB; excellent ISBE).

1. Son of Dishon (Ge 36:26; 1Ch 1:41).

2. Son of Zophah (1Ch 7:37).

ITHREAM [3865] (remainder of the people). Son of David (2Sa 3:5; 1Ch 3:3).

ITHRITE(S) [3863] (excellence, or preeminence ISBE; remainder KB). Family from which two of David's heroes came (2Sa 23:38; 1Ch 11:40).

ITINERARY Of the Israelites (Nu 33; Dt 10:6-7). See Israel, Israelites.

ITTAH-KAZIN See Eth Kazin.

ITTAI [915] (possibly with me BDB).

1. One of David's heroes (2Sa 23:29; 1Ch 11:31).

2. Gittite who became a loyal follower of David (2Sa 15:18-22; 18:2,5).

ITUREA, ITURAEA [2714] (pertaining to Jetur). Region NE of Israel; its people descended from Jetur, son of Ishmael, and from whom the name Iturea is derived (Ge 25:15), ruled by Philip (Lk 3:1).

IVAH See Ivvah, Ivah.

IVORY [9094, 9105, 1804]. (SS 5:1,4; 7:4; Eze 27:15). Exported from, Tarshish (1Ki 10:22; 2Ch 9:21), the coasts of Cyprus, the Hebrew is Kittim (Eze 27:6).

Ahab's palace made of (1Ki 22:39). Other houses made of (Ps 45:8; Am 3:15). Other articles made of: Stringed instruments (Ps 45:8), thrones (1Ki 10:18; 2Ch 9:17), benches (Eze 27:6), beds (Am 6:4), vessels (Rev 18:12).

IVVAH, IVAH [6394]. A district in Babylon conquered by the Assyrians (2Ki 18:34; 19:13; Isa 37:13).

IYE ABARIM [6516] (*heaps of Abarim [regions beyond]*).

NIV+ ABARIM, IYIM

One of the places where Israel camped in the desert (Nu 21:11; 33:44). Also called Iyim (Nu 33:45, ftn).

IYIM [6517]. (Nu 33:45). *See Iye Abarim.*

IYYAR *See Month, 2; Ziv.*

IZHAR, IZHARITES [3659, 3660] (*the shining one*).

Son of Kohath (Ex 6:18,21; 1Ch 6:2,18,38; 23:12,18) and his descendants (Nu 3:27; 1Ch 24:22; 26:23,29).

IZLIAH [3468] (*long living, eternal* IDB; *Yahweh delivers* ISBE). A Benjamite son of Elpaal (1Ch 8:18).

IZRAHIAH [3474] (*Yahweh, he shines*). Grandson of Tola (1Ch 7:3).

IZRAHITE [3473] (*shining*). Family name of Shamhuth (1Ch 27:8).

IZRI [3673] (*Yahweh designs*). Perhaps the same as Zeri. Leader of the fourth division of Levitical singers (1Ch 25:11).

IZZIAH [3466] (*may Yahweh sprinkle [in atonement]* BDB; *Yahweh unites* ISBE). An Israelite of the Parosh family who marries an idolatrous wife (Ezr 10:25).

J

JAAKAN, JAAKANITES [1201+3622].

NIV+ BENE JAAKAN

Son of Ezer (Ge 36:20-21,27; Dt 10:6; 1Ch 1:42). A Horite (1Ch 1:42), and the same as Akan (Ge 36:27). *See Akan.*

See Bene Jaakan, Bene-Jaakan.

JAAKOBAH [3621] (*may [deity] protect* IDB). Descendant of Simeon (1Ch 4:36).

JAALA [3606, 3608]. One of the servants of Solomon returned from exile (Ezr 2:56; Ne 7:58).

JAALAM *See Jalam, Jaalam.*

JAAN *See Dan Jaan.*

JAANAI *See Janai, Jaanai.*

JAAR [3625]. An alternate name for Kiriath Jearim (Ps 132:6, ftn). *See Kiriath Jearim.*

JAARE-OREGIM [3629]. Father of Elhanan, who slew the giant brother of Goliath (2Sa 21:19). Spelled Jair (1Ch 20:5).

JAARESHIAH [3631] (*Yahweh plants*). Son of Jeroham (1Ch 8:27).

JAASAU *See Jaasu, Jaasau.*

JAASIEL, JASIEL [3634] (*God [El] does*). One of David's warriors (1Ch 11:47). Son of Abner (1Ch 27:21).

JAASU, JAASAU [3632]. Of the family of Bani (Ezr 10:37).

JAAZANIAH [3279, 3280, 3471] (*Yahweh listens*).

1. Also called Jezaniah (Jer 40:8, ftn). A Maacathite captain who joined Gedaliah at Mizpah (2Ki 25:23; Jer 42:1).

2. A Recabite (Jer 35:3).

3. An idolatrous zealot (Eze 8:11).

4. A wicked prince of Judah (Eze 11:1-13).

JAAZER *See Jazer, Jaazer.*

JAAZIAH [3596] (*may Yahweh nourish* IDB). A descendant of Merari (1Ch 24:26-27).

JAAZIEL [3595] (*God [El] strengthens* ISBE). A Levite musician (1Ch 15:18).

JABAL [3299]. Son of Lamech. A shepherd (Ge 4:20).

JABBOK [3309] (*flowing*). A stream on the E of the Jordan, the northern boundary of the possessions of the Ammonites (Nu 21:24; Jdg 11:13), of the Reubenites and the Gadites (Jos 12:2; Dt 3:16). The northern boundary of the Amorites (Jdg 11:22).

JABESH [3314, 3315] (*dry*).

NIV+ JABESH GILEAD

1. Father of King Shallum (2Ki 15:8-13).

2. Short term for Jabesh-Gilead (1Ch 10:12).

JABESH GILEAD, JABESH-GILEAD [3316]

(*dry Gilead*).

NIV+ GILEAD, JABESH

A city E of the Jordan (Jdg 21:8-15). Besieged by the Ammonites (1Sa 11:1-11). Saul and his sons buried at (1Sa 31:11-13; 2Sa 2:4; 1Ch 10:11-12). Bones of Saul and his son removed from, by David, and buried at Zela (2Sa 21:12-14).

JABEZ [3583, 3584] (*to grieve*).

1. A city of Judah (1Ch 2:55).

2. The head of a family (1Ch 4:9-10).

JABIN [3296] (*perceptive*).

NIV+ JABIN'S

1. King of Hazor, defeated and slain by Joshua (Jos 11).

2. Another king of Hazor, defeated by Barak (Jdg 4; 1Sa 12:9; Ps 83:9).

JABNEEL [3305] (*God [El] will build*).

1. Town in N border of Judah, just S of Joppa (Jos 15:11), modern Yebna. Called Jabneh (2Ch 26:6). Later called Jamnia.

2. Frontier town of Naphtali (Jos 19:33), modern Tell en-Naam.

JABNEH [3306]. A Philistine city (2Ch 26:6). *See Jabneel, 1.*

JACAN, JACHAN [3602]. A Gadite (1Ch 5:13).

JACHIN, JACHINITES *See Jakin.*

JACINTH [4385, 5611] (*hyacinth*).

A precious stone in the high priest's breastpiece (Ex 28:19; 39:12), in the foundation of New Jerusalem (Rev 21:20).

See Minerals of the Bible, 1; Stones.

JACKAL [280, 8785, 9478, 9490].

NIV+ JACKALS

A carnivorous scavenger, inhabiting the desert. Often translated "dragon" in the KJV (Job 30:29; Ps 44:19; Isa 13:21,22; Jer 9:11; Mal 1:3).

JACKAL WELL

Named only in Ne 2:13; possibly En Rogel or the Pool or Siloam. *See En Rogel; Siloam, Pool of.*

JACOB [3620, 2609] (*follower, replacer, one who follows the heel*).

NIV+ See ISRAEL, JACOB'S

Son of Isaac and twin brother of Esau (Ge 25:24-26; Jos 24:4; 1Ch 1:34; Ac 7:8). Ancestor of Jesus (Mt 1:2). Given in answer to prayer (Ge 25:21). Obtains Esau's birthright for a bowl of stew (Ge 25:29-34; Heb 12:16). Fraudulently obtains his father's blessing (Ge 27:1-29; Heb 11:20). Esau seeks to kill, escapes to Paddan Aram (Ge 27:41-46; 28:1-5; Hos 12:12). His vision of the stairway (Ge 28:10-22). God confirms the covenant of Abraham to (Ge 28:13-22; 35:9-15; 1Ch 16:13-18).

Lives in Haran with his uncle, Laban (Ge 29; 30; Hos 12:12). Serves fourteen years for Leah and Rachel (Ge 29:15-30; Hos 12:12). Sharp practice of, with the flocks and herds of Laban (Ge 30:32-43). Dissatisfied with Laban's treatment and returns to the land of Canaan (Ge 31). Meets angels of God on the journey and calls the place Mahanaim (Ge 32:1-2). Dreads to meet Esau; sends him presents; wrestles with an angel (Ge 32). Name of, changed to Israel (Ge 32:28; 35:10). *See Israel.* Reconciliation of, with Esau (Ge 33:4). Journeys to Succoth (Ge 33:17), to Shechem where he purchases a parcel of ground from Hamor, and erects an altar (Ge 33:18-20). His daughter, Dinah, humbled (Ge 34). Returns to Bethel, where he builds an altar and dedicates a pillar (Ge 35:1-7). Deborah, Rebekah's nurse, dies, and is buried at Bethel (Ge 35:8). Journeys to Ephrath; Benjamin is born to; Rachel dies, and is "buried on the way to Ephrath (that is, Bethlehem)" (Ge 35:16-19; 48:7). Erects a monument at Rachel's grave (Ge 35:20). The incest of his son, Reuben, and his concubine, Bilhah (Ge 35:22). List of the names of his twelve sons (Ge 35:23-26). Returns to Kiriath Arba, the city of his father (Ge 35:27). Lives in the land of Canaan (Ge 37:1). His partiality for his son, Joseph, and the consequent jealousy of his other sons (Ge 37:3-4). Joseph's prophetic dream concerning (Ge 37:9-11). His grief over the loss of Joseph (Ge 37:34-35). Sends into Egypt to buy grain (Ge 42:1-2; 43:1-14). His grief over the detention of Simeon and the demand for Benjamin to be taken into Egypt (Ge 42:36). His love for Benjamin (Ge 43:14; 44:29). Hears that Joseph still lives (Ge 45:26-28).

Moves to Egypt (Ge 46:1-7; 1Sa 12:8; Ps 105:23; Ac 7:14-15). List of his children and grandchildren who went down into Egypt (Ge 46:8-27). Meets Joseph (Ge 46:28-34). Pharaoh receives him and is blessed by Jacob (Ge 47:1-10). The land of Goshen assigned to (Ge 47:11-12,27). Lives in Egypt seventeen years (Ge 47:28). Exacts a promise from Joseph to bury him with his fathers (Ge 47:29-31). His benediction upon Joseph and his two sons (Ge 48:15-22). Gives the land of the two Amorites to Joseph (Ge 48:22; Jn 4:5).

His final prophetic benedictions upon his sons: Reuben (Ge 49:3-4), Simeon and Levi (Ge 49:5-7), Judah (Ge 49:8-12), Zebulun (Ge 49:13), Issachar (Ge 49:14-15), Dan (Ge 49:16-18), Gad (Ge 49:19), Asher (Ge 49:20), Naphtali (Ge 49:21), Joseph (Ge 49:22-26), Benjamin (Ge 49:27). Charges his sons to bury him in the field of Machpelah (Ge 49:29-30). Death of (Ge 49:33). Body of, embalmed (Ge 50:2). Forty days mourning for (Ge 50:3). Burial of (Ge 50:4-13). Descendants of (Ge 29:31-35; 30:1-24; 35:18,22-26; 46:8-27; Ex 1:1-5; 1Ch 2-9).

Prophecies concerning himself and descendants (Ge 25:23; 27:28-29; 28:10-15; Ge 31:3; 35:9-13; 46:3; Dt 1:8; Ps 105:10-11). His wealth (Ge 36:6-7). Well of (Jn 4:5-30).

JACOB'S WELL Well near base of Mt. Gerizim where Jesus talked with a Samaritan woman (Jn 4).

JADA [3360] (*shrewd one* BDB; *[God] has cared* IDB). A Judahite, son of Onam (1Ch 2:26,28).

JADAH [3586] (*honeycomb*).

Most Hebrew manuscripts have Jarah. Descendant of Gibeon (1Ch 9:42, ftn), Jehoaddah (1Ch 8:36).

JADAU *See Jaddai.*

JADDAI [3350]. An Israelite who married a foreign woman during the Captivity (Ezr 10:43).

JADDUA [3348] (*one known*).

1. Prince who sealed covenant (Ne 10:21).

2. Son of Jonathan; priest who returned from Babylon (Ne 12:11).

JADON [3347] (*frail one* or *Yahweh rules* IDB). One who helped in rebuilding of Jerusalem wall (Ne 3:7).

JAEL [3605] (*mountain goat*). Wife of Heber and killer of Sisera (Jdg 4:17-22; 5:6,24).

JAGUR [3327]. A town of Judah (Jos 15:21).

JAHATH [3511] (*snatch up*).

1. Grandson of Judah (1Ch 4:1-2).

2. Great-grandson of Levi (1Ch 6:16-20).

3. Levite (1Ch 23:10-11).

4. Levite (1Ch 24:22).

5. Merarite Levite (2Ch 34:8-12). *See Merari.*

JAHAZ [3403] (perhaps *a trodden* or *open place*). Also called Jahzah. A Levitical city in Reuben, taken from the Moabites (Jos 13:18; 21:36; Isa 15:4; Jer 48:21). Sihon defeated at (Nu 21:23; Dt 2:32; Jdg 11:20).

JAHAZIAH *See Jahzeiah.*

JAHAZIEL [3487] (*God [El] will see*).

1. A disaffected Israelite who joined David at Ziklag (1Ch 12:4).

2. A priest (1Ch 16:6).

3. Son of Hebron (1Ch 23:19; 24:23).

4. A Levite, and prophet (2Ch 20:14).

5. A chief, or the father of a chief, among the exiles, who returned from Babylon (Ezr 8:5).

JAHDAI [3367] (*Yahweh lead*). A descendant of Caleb (1Ch 2:47).

JAHDIEL [3484] (*God [El] gives joy*). Head of a family of Manasseh (1Ch 5:24).

JAHDO [3482] (*[God] gives joy*). Son of Buz (1Ch 5:14).

JAHLEEL, JAHLEELITE [3499, 3500] (*wait for God [El]* BDB; possibly *may God [El] show himself friendly* IDB). Son of Zebulun (Ge 46:14; Nu 26:26).

JAHMAI [3503] (*protect*). Son of Tola (1Ch 7:2).

JAHZAH [3404]. A city of Reuben (1Ch 6:78). *See Jahaz.*

JAHZEEL, JAHZEELITE [3505] (*God [El] apportions*). A son of Naphtali and his clan (Nu 26:48). Also spelled Jahziel (Ge 46:24; 1Ch 7:13).

JAHZEIAH [3488] (*Yahweh sees*). Israelite who opposed Ezra in the matter of divorcing wives (Ezr 10:15).

JAHZERAH [3492] (possibly *prudent*). A priest (1Ch 9:12).

JAHZIEL [3505, 3507]. *See Jahzeel.*

JAILER [991, 1302].
NIV+ JAIL, JAILERS
Of Philippi, converted (Ac 16:27-34).

JAIR, JAIRITE [3281, 3285, 3600] (*he gives light*).
NIV+ HAVVOTH JAIR

1. Son of Manasseh. Founder of twenty-three cities in Gilead (Nu 32:41; Dt 3:14; Jos 13:30; 1Ki 4:13; 1Ch 2:22-23).

2. A judge of Israel (Jdg 10:3-5).

3. A Benjamite (Est 2:5).

4. Father of Elhanan (1Ch 20:5).

JAIRUS [2608] (*he gives light*). A ruler of the

synagogue in Capernaum (Mt 9:18). Daughter of, restored to life (Mt 9:18,23-26; Mk 5:22-43; Lk 8:41-56).

JAKAN *See Akan; Jaakan, Jaakanites.*

JAKEH [3681] (*prudent*). Father of Agur, a writer of proverbs (Pr 30:1).

JAKIM [3691] (*he will establish*).
1. A Benjamite (1Ch 8:19).
2. Head of a priestly division in the tabernacle service (1Ch 24:12).

JAKIN, JAKINITE [3520, 3521, 3522] (*he establishes*).
1. Son of Simeon (Ge 46:10; Ex 6:15; Nu 26:12). Called Jarib (1Ch 4:24).
2. One of Solomon's brazen pillars erected at the temple. It stood on the right (south) side of the porch (1Ki 7:21; 2Ch 3:17).
　See Boaz, 2.
3. A priest who returned from exile to Jerusalem (1Ch 9:10; Ne 11:10).
4. A priest, head of one of the courses (1Ch 24:17).

JALAM, JAALAM [3609]. Son of Esau (Ge 36:5,14,18; 1Ch 1:35).

JALON [3534]. Son of Ezra (1Ch 4:17).

JAMBRES [*2612*]. An Egyptian magician (Ex 7:11; 2Ti 3:8).

JAMES [*2610*] (*follower, replacer, one who follows the heel*; same as Jacob).
1. An apostle. Son of Zebedee and Salome (Mt 4:21; 27:56). *See Salome.* Brother of John, and a fisherman (Lk 5:10). Called to be an apostle (Mt 4:21-22; 10:2; Mk 1:19-20; Lk 6:14; Ac 1:13). Surnamed Boanerges by Jesus (Mk 3:17).
An intimate companion of Jesus, and present at the large catch of fishes (Lk 5:10), the healing of Peter's mother-in-law (Mk 1:29), the raising of the daughter of Jairus (Mk 5:37; Lk 8:51), the transfiguration of Jesus (Mt 17:1; Mk 9:2; Lk 9:28), in Gethsemane (Mt 26:37; Mk 14:33). Asks Jesus concerning his second coming (Mk 13:3). Bigotry of (Lk 9:54). Civil ambitions of (Mt 20:20-23; Mk 10:35-41). Present at the sea of Tiberias when Jesus revealed himself to the disciples after his resurrection (Jn 21:2; 1Co 15:7). Martyred (Ac 12:2).
2. The younger, an apostle. Son of Alphaeus (Mt 10:3; Mk 3:18; 15:45; Lk 12:17).
3. Brother of Jesus (Mt 13:55; Mk 6:3; Gal 1:19; 2:9,12). The brother of Judas (Jude) and Joseph (Mt 13:55; Mk 6:3; Jude 1). A witness of Christ's resurrection (1Co 15:7). Addresses the council at Jerusalem in favor of liberty for the Gentile converts (Ac 15:13-21). Disciples sent by, to Antioch (Gal 2:12). Hears of the success attending Paul's ministry (Ac 21:18-19). Epistle of (Jas 1:1).
4. Father of apostle Judas (not Iscariot) (Lk 6:16; Ac 1:13).

JAMES, EPISTLE OF

Author: James, the brother of Jesus. *See James, 3.*

Date: In the early 60s, possibly before A.D. 50

Outline:

I. Greetings (1:1).
II. Trials and Temptations (1:2-18).
　A. The Testing of Faith (1:2-12).
　B. The Source of Temptation (1:13-18).
III. Listening and Doing (1:19-27).
IV. Favoritism Forbidden (2:1-13).
V. Faith and Deeds (2:14-26).
VI. Taming the Tongue (3:1-12).
VII. Two Kinds of Wisdom (3:13-18).
VIII. Warning against Worldliness (ch. 4).
　A. Quarrelsomeness (4:1-3).
　B. Spiritual Unfaithfulness (4:4).
　C. Pride (4:5-10).
　D. Slander (4:11-12).
　E. Boasting (4:13-17).
IX. Warning to Rich Oppressors (5:1-6).
X. Miscellaneous Exhortations (5:7-20).
　A. Concerning Patience in Suffering (5:7-11).
　B. Concerning Oaths (5:12).
　C. Concerning the Prayer of Faith (5:13-18).
　D. Concerning Those Who Wander from the Truth (5:19-20).
　See General Letters.

JAMES THE YOUNGER, THE LESS *See James, 2.*

JAMIN, JAMINITE [3546, 3547] (possibly *right hand* BDB; *south, an indication of [good] fortune* KB).
1. Son of Simeon (Ge 46:10; Ex 6:15; Nu 26:12; 1Ch 4:24).
2. Descendants of Hezron (1Ch 2:27).
3. A priest who expounded the law to the exiles who returned to Jerusalem (Ne 8:7).

JAMLECH [3552] (*he will reign*). Descendant of Simeon (1Ch 4:34).

JANAI, JAANAI [3614] (*he will answer*). A Gadite chief (1Ch 5:12).

JANIM [3565]. A city of Judah (Jos 15:53).

JANNAI, JANNA [*2613*] (*he will answer?*). Ancestor of Joseph (Lk 3:24).

JANNES [*2614*]. An Egyptian magician (Ex 7:11; 2Ti 3:8).

JANOAH, JANOHAH [3562] (*resting place*).
1. Town of Naphtali (2Ki 15:29).
2. Town on boundary of Ephraim (Jos 16:6-7).

JANUM *See Janim.*

JAPHETH [3651] (*enlarge*). Son of Noah (Ge 5:32; 6:10; 7:13; 10:21); had seven sons (Ge 10:2), descendants were maritime peoples (Ge 10:5); blessed by Noah (Ge 9:20-27).

JAPHIA [3643, 3644] (perhaps *may the deity shine*).
1. King of Lachish killed by Joshua (Jos 10:3).
2. Son David (2Sa 5:15; 1Ch 3:7).
3. City in E border of Zebulun (Jos 19:12).

JAPHLET [3646] (*he delivers* IDB; possibly *he escapes* ISBE).
　NIV+ JAPHLET'S, JAPHLETITES
　Grandson of Beriah (1Ch 7:33).

JAPHLETITES, JAPHLETI [3647] (*of Japhlet*).
　NIV+ JAPHLET
　Clan on W border of Ephraim (Jos 16:1-3).

JAPHO *See Joppa.*

JAR(S) [1318, 3902, 3998, 5532, 5574, *223, 3040, 5007, 5620*]. For holding water (Ge 24:14-26; Ru 2:9; Jn 2:6-7), flour (1Ki 17:10-16). Containing manna, kept in the ark (Ex 16:33; Heb 9:4). Figurative of fragile human body in which believers minister the New Covenant (2Co 4:7).

JARAH (*honeycomb*). *See Jadah.*

JAREB NIV "great king" of Assyria (Hos 5:13; 10:6).

JARED [3719, *2616*] (*servant* KB).
1. A descendant of Seth (Ge 5:15-16,18-20; 1Ch 1:2).
2. An ancestor of Jesus (Lk 3:37).
3. Son of Mahalalel (1Ch 1:2).

JARESIAH *See Jaareshiah.*

JARHA [3739]. Egyptian slave of Sheshan (1Ch 2:34-35).

JARIB [3743] (*Yahweh contends*).
1. Son of Simeon (1Ch 4:24).
2. A chief among the Captivity (Ezr 8:16).
3. A priest who married an idolatrous wife (Ezr 10:18).

JARKON *See Me Jarkon.*

JARMUTH [3754] (*height*).
1. City of Judah sixteen miles W by S of Jerusalem (Jos 15:35), modern Tell Yarmuk.
2. Levite city of Issachar (Jos 21:28-29). Ramoth (1Ch 6:73), Remeth (Jos 19:21).

JAROAH [3726] (*soft, delicate*). A descendant of Gad (1Ch 5:14).

JASHAR, JASHER, BOOK OF [3839] (*upright, straight*). Author of book quoted (Jos 10:13; 2Sa 1:18), in LXX version (1Ki 8:53).

JASHEN [3826] (possibly *asleep*). Father of some of David's heroes (2Sa 23:32), Hashem (1Ch 11:34).

JASHER, BOOK OF *See Jashar, Jasher, Book of.*

JASHOBEAM [3790] (*the people return*).
1. Hero who joined David at Ziklag (1Ch 12:6).
2. One of David's leaders (1Ch 11:11), Adino the Eznite in Hebrew and Septuagint (2Sa 23:8, ftn).
3. Hacmoni (1Ch 27:2-3). *See above, 2.* May be the same.

JASHUB, JASHUBITE [3793, 3795] (*he returns*).
1. Son of Issachar (Ge 46:13; Nu 26:24).
2. Shear-Jashub, a son of Isaiah (Isa 7:3).
3. Man who married foreign wife (Ezr 10:29).

JASHUBI LEHEM, JASHUBI-LEHEM [3788] (*[they] returned to Lehem*). A descendant of Shelah (1Ch 4:22).

JASIEL *See Jaasiel, Jasiel.*

JASON [2619] (*to heal*).
NIV+ JASON'S
A Christian at Thessalonica (Ac 17:5-7,9) and possibly Paul's relative (Ro 16:21).

JASPER [1486, 3835, *2618*]. A precious stone set in the high priest's breastplate (Ex 28:20; 39:13; Job 28:18; Eze 28:13; Rev 4:3; 21:11,18-19).
See Minerals of the Bible, 1; Stones.

JATHNIEL [3853] (*God [El] hires* BDB; *God [El] is forever* KB). Son of Meshelemiah (1Ch 26:2).

JATTIR [3848] (possibly *preeminence* IDB). A Levitical city (Jos 15:48; 21:14; 1Sa 30:27; 1Ch 6:57).

JAVAN [3430].
1. A son of Japheth. Father of Elishah, Tarshish, Kittim, and Rodanim (Ge 10:4; 1Ch 1:7). Javan is same as Greek Ionia, with whom the Hebrews traded (Isa 66:19; Joel 3:4-6).
2. A city in Arabia in which the Phoenicians traded (Eze 27:13,19).

JAVELIN [3959, 6038, 8657, 9233].
NIV+ JAVELINS
A heavy lance (Eze 39:9), used by Goliath (1Sa 17:6), by Saul (1Sa 18:11; 19:9-10).

JAZER, JAAZER [3597] (*he helps*).
1. Taken from the Amorites (Nu 21:32; 32:1,3,35). Ammonite stronghold E of the Jordan, probably c. fourteen miles N of Heshbon; assigned to Gad (Jos 13:24-25), later given to Levites; a city of refuge E of the Jordan (Jos 21:39).
2. Sea of (Jer 48:32).

JAZIZ [3467]. Overseer of David's flocks (1Ch 27:31).

JEALOUSY [6523, 7861, 7862, 7863+, 7868, *2419, 2420, 4143*].]
NIV+ JEALOUS
(Pr 6:34; 27:4; Ecc 4:4; SS 8:6). Law concerning, when husband is jealous of his wife (Nu 5:12-31). Image of (Eze 8:3-4). Forbidden (Ro 13:13).
Attributed to God (Ex 20:5; 34:13-14; Nu 25:11; Dt 29:20; 32:16,21; 1Ki 14:22; Ps 78:58; 79:5; Isa 30:1-2; 31:1,3; Eze 16:42; 23:25; 36:5-6; 38:19; Zep 1:18; 3:8; Zec 1:14; 8:2; 1Co 10:22).
See Anthropomorphisms.
A desire to emulate (Ro 10:19; 11:11).
See Emulation; Envy.

Figurative:
(2Co 11:2).

Instances of:
Cain, of Abel (Ge 4:5-6,8). Sarah, of Hagar (Ge 16:5). Joseph's brothers, of Joseph (Ge 37:4-11,18-28). Saul, of David (1Sa 18:8-30; 19:8-24; 20:24-34). Joab, of Abner (2Sa 3:24-27). Nathan, of Adonijah (1Ki 1:24-26). Ephraimites, of Gideon (Jdg 8:1), of Jephthah (Jdg 12:1). The brother of the prodigal son (Lk 15:25-32). Sectional, between Israel and the tribe of Judah (2Sa 19:41-43).

JEALOUSY, WATER OF *See Water of Bitterness.*

JEARIM [3630] (*timberlands*).
NIV+ KESALON, KIRIATH JEARIM
Hill on N border of Judah (Jos 15:10).

JEATHERAI, JEATERAI [3290]. Descendant of Gershom (1Ch 6:21).

JEBEREKIAH, JEBERECHIAH [3310] (*Yahweh blesses*). Father of Zechariah (Isa 8:2).

JEBUS [3293].
NIV+ JEBUSITE, JEBUSITES, JERUSALEM
Name of Jerusalem when in possession of Jebusites (Jos

15:63; Jdg 19:10), taken by Israelites (Jdg 1:8), but stronghold not captured until David's time (2Sa 5:7-8).

JEBUSITE(S), JEBUSI [3294] (*of Jebus*).

NIV+ JEBUS

One of the tribes of Canaan (Dt 7:1). Land of, given to
Abraham and his descendants (Ge 15:21; Ex 3:8,17;
23:23-24; Dt 20:17; Ex 33:2; 34:10-11). Conquered by
Joshua (Jos 10-12; 24:11), by David (2Sa 5:6-9). Jerusalem within the territory of (Jos 18:28). Not exterminated,
but intermarry with the Israelites (Jdg 3:5-6; Ezr 9:1-2;
10:18-44). Pay tribute to Solomon (1Ki 9:20-21).

JECAMIAH *See Jekamiah, Jecamiah.*

JECOLIAH, JECHOLIAH [3524, 3525] (*Yahweh is
able*). Mother of King Uzziah (2Ch 26:3; 2Ki 15:2).

JECONIAH, JECHONIAS [*2651*]. Variant of Jehoiachin (Jer 22:24,28; 37:1). *See Jehoiachin.* King of Judah,
captured by Nebuchadnezzar (2Ki 24:1-12).

JEDAIAH [3355, 3361] (*Yahweh has favored* IDB, or
Yahweh knows).

NIV+ JEDAIAH'S

1. Descendant of Simeon (1Ch 4:37).
2. A returned exile (Ne 3:10).
3. A priest of the Captivity (1Ch 9:10; 24:7; Ezr 2:36;
Ne 7:39).
4. A priest who lived at Jerusalem after the return of the
Captivity (Ne 11:10; 12:6,19; Zec 6:10,14).
5. Another priest, who returned from Babylon with
Nehemiah (Ne 12:7,21).

JEDIAEL [3356] (*known of God [El]*).

1. Son of Benjamin (1Ch 7:6,10-11).
2. Son of Shimri (1Ch 11:45).
3. A Manassite chief who joined David at Ziklag (1Ch
12:20).
4. Son of Meshelemiah (1Ch 26:2).

JEDIDAH [3352] (*beloved* BDB; *lovely, beloved* KB).
Mother of King Josiah (2Ki 22:1).

JEDIDIAH [3354] (*beloved of Yahweh*). Name that
Nathan gave to Solomon (2Sa 12:24-25).

JEDUTHUN [3349, 3357]. A musician of the temple
(1Ch 16:41; 25:1). Called Ethan (1Ch 6:44; 15:17). *See
titles of Psalms 39, 62, 77.*

JEEZER, JEEZERITES *See Abiezer, 1; Iezer.*

**JEGAR SAHADUTHA, JEGAR-
SAHADUTHA** [3337] (*witness heap*). Name given by
Laban to heap of stones set up as memorial of covenant
between him and Jacob; called Galeed by Jacob (Ge
31:47-48).

JEHALLELEL, JEHALELEEL, JEHALELEL
[3401] (*he shall praise God [El]* BDB; *God [El] shines
forth* IDB).

1. Descendant of Judah (1Ch 4:16).
2. Merarite Levite (2Ch 29:12).

JEHATH [3511]. A son of Gershon (1Ch. 6:20).

JEHDEIAH [3485] (*Yahweh rejoices [in his works]*).

1. Descendant of Moses (1Ch 24:20).
2. Man in charge of David's donkeys (1Ch 27:30).

JEHEZKEL, JEHEZEKEL [3489] (*God [El] gives
strength*). Priest in David's time (1Ch 24:16).

JEHIAH [3496] (*Yahweh lives*). A Levite, and
doorkeeper of the ark (1Ch 15:24).

JEHIEL [3493] (*God [El] lives*).

1. A Levite gatekeeper (1Ch 15:18). Probably identical
with Jehiah. *See Jehiah.*
2. A Gershonite Levite (1Ch 23:8; 29:8).
3. A companion of David's sons (1Ch 27:32).
4. Son of Jehoshaphat (2Ch 21:2).
5. Son of Heman (2Ch 29:14).
6. A Levite overseer in the temple (2Ch 31:13).
7. A priest who gave extraordinary offerings for the
Passover (2Ch 35:8).
8. Father of Obadiah (Ezr 8:9).
9. Father of Shecaniah (Ezr 10:2).
10. Name of two priests who married idolatrous wives
(Ezr 10:21,26).

JEHIELI [3494] (*of Jehiel*). Son of Ladan (1Ch 26:21-
22).

JEHIZKIAH [3491] (*Yahweh gives strength*). Israelite
chief in days of Ahaz, king of Judah (2Ch 28:12).

JEHOADDAH, JEHOADAH [3389]. Descendant
of King Saul (1Ch 8:36), Jadah (1Ch 9:42).

JEHOADDIN, JEHOADDAN [3390, 3391] (*probably Yahweh is delight*). Wife of King Joash of Judah
(2Ch 25:1), Jehoaddin (2Ki 14:2).

JEHOAHAZ [3370, 3407] (*Yahweh holds*).

1. Son of Jehu and king of Israel (2Ki 10:35; 13:1-9).
2. Son of Jehoram, king of Judah (2Ch 21:17). *See
Ahaziah.*
3. Also called Shallum. King of Judah and successor of
Josiah (2Ki 23:30-31; 1Ch 3:15; 2Ch 36:1; Jer 22:11).
Wicked reign of (2Ki 23:32). Pharaoh Neco, king of
Egypt, invades the kingdom of, defeats him, and takes him
captive to Egypt (2Ki 23:33-35; 2Ch 36:3-4). Prophecies
concerning (Jer 22:10-12).

JEHOASH, JOASH [3371, 3409] (*Yahweh bestows*
ISBE; *man of Yahweh* KB).

1. Grandson of Benjamin (1Ch 7:8).
2. Descendant of Judah (1Ch 4:22).
3. Father of Gideon (Jdg 6:12).
4. Keeper of David's supply of oil (1Ch 27:28).
5. Israelite who joined David at Ziklag (1Ch 12:3).
6. Son of King Ahab (1Ki 22:26).
7. King of Judah (2Ki 11-13; 2Ch 24-25).
8. King of Israel (2Ki 13:10-13; 14:8-16; 2Ch 25:17-
24).

JEHOHANAN [3380] (*Yahweh has been gracious*).

1. A gatekeeper of the tabernacle (1Ch 26:3).
2. A military chief under Jehoshaphat, whose corps
consisted of 280,000 men (2Ch 17:15). Probably identical
with a captain of a hundred (2Ch 23:1).
3. Son of Bebai (Ezr 10:28).
4. A priest among the exiles who returned from Babylon
(Ne 12:13).
5. A choir member in the temple (Ne 12:42).

JEHOIACHIN [3382, 3422, 3526, 3527, 4037₁ ‹Yahweh supports›].

NIV+JEHOIACHIN'S

(Jer 22:24; 37:1). King of Judah and successor to Jehoiakim (2Ki 24:6-8; 1Ch 3:16; 2Ch 36:8-9; Jer 24:1). Wicked reign of (2Ki 24:9; 2Ch 36:9). Nebuchadnezzar invades his kingdom, takes him captive to Babylon (2Ki 24:10-16; 2Ch 36:10; Est 2:6; Jer 27:20; 29:1-2; Eze 1:2). Confined in prison thirty-seven years (2Ki 25:27). Released from prison by Evil-Merodach and promoted above other kings, and honored until death (2Ki 25:27-30; Jer 52:31-34). Prophecies concerning (Jer 22:24-30; 28:4). Sons of (1Ch 3:17-18). Ancestor of Jesus, called Jeconiah (Mt 1:11,12).

JEHOIADA [3381] (Yahweh has known).

1. Father of Benaiah, one of David's officers (2Sa 8:18).

2. A high priest. Overthrows Athaliah, the usurping queen of Judah, and establishes Jehoash upon the throne (2Ki 11; 2Ch 23). Salutary influence of, over Joash (Hebrew Jehoash, a variant of Joash) (2Ki 12:2; 2Ch 24:2,22). Directs the repairs of the temple (2Ki 12:4-16; 2Ch 24:4-14). Death of (2Ch 24:15-16).

3. A priest who led 3,700 priests armed for war (1Ch 12:27).

4. Son of Benaiah (1Ch 27:34).

5. A returned exile (Ne 3:6).

6. A priest mentioned in Jeremiah's letter to the captive Israelites (Jer 29:26).

JEHOIAKIM [3383] (Yahweh lifts up, establishes).

NIV+JEHOIAKIM'S

Also called Eliakim. King of Judah (1Ch 3:15). Wicked reign and final overthrow of (2Ki 23:24-37; 24:1-6; 2Ch 36:4-8; Jer 22:13-19; 26:22-23; 36; Da 1:1-2). Dies and is succeeded by his son, Jehoiachin (2Ki 24:6).

JEHOIARIB [3384] (Yahweh argues [for me]).

1. Priest in days of David (1Ch 24:7).

2. Priest who returned from exile (1Ch 9:10). See Joiarib.

JEHONADAB [3386]. See Jonadab, 2.

JEHONATHAN [3387] (Yahweh has given).

1. Overseer of David's property (1Ch 27:25).

2. Levite (2Ch 17:8).

3. Priest (Ne 12:18).

JEHORAM [3393, 3456, 2732] (Yahweh exalts).

NIV+JEHORAM'S

1. King of Judah (1Ki 22:50; 2Ki 8:16; 1Ch 3:11; 2Ch 21:5). Ancestor of Jesus (Mt 1:8). Marries Athaliah, whose wicked counsels influence his reign for evil (2Ki 8:18-19; 2Ch 21:6-13).

Slays his brothers to strengthen himself in his sovereignty (2Ch 21:4,13). Edom revolts from (2Ki 8:20-22; 2Ch 21:8-10). Philistines and Arabs invade his territory (2Ch 21:16-17). Death of (2Ch 21:18-20; 2Ki 8:24). Prophecy concerning (2Ch 21:12-15).

2. A son of Ahab. See Joram.

3. A priest commissioned to go through Israel and instruct the people in the law (2Ch 17:8).

JEHOSHABEATH See Jehosheba.

JEHOSHAPHAT [3398, 3399, 2734] (Yahweh has judged).

NIV+JEHOSHAPHAT'S

1. David's recorder (2Sa 8:16; 20:24; 1Ki 4:3; 1Ch 18:15).

2. One of Solomon's district officers (1Ki 4:17).

3. King of Judah. Succeeds Asa (1Ki 15:24; 22:41; 1Ch 3:10; 2Ch 17:1; Mt 1:8). Strengthens himself against Israel (2Ch 17:2). Inaugurates a system of public instruction in the law (2Ch 17:7-9). His wise reign (1Ki 22:43; 2Ch 17:7-9; 19:3-11). His system of tribute (2Ch 17:11). His military forces and armament (2Ch 17:12-19). Joins Ahab in an invasion of Ramoth Gilead (1Ki 22; 2Ch 18). Rebuked by the prophet Jehu (2Ch 19:2). The allied forces of the Amorites, Moabites, and other tribes invade his territory and are defeated by (2Ch 20). Builds ships for commerce with Tarshish; ships are destroyed (1Ki 22:48-49; 2Ch 20:35-37). Joins Jehoram, king of Israel, in an invasion of the land of Moab, and defeats the Moabites (2Ki 3). Makes valuable gifts to the temple (2Ki 12:18). Death of (1Ki 22:50; 2Ch 21:1). Religious zeal of (1Ki 22:43,46; 2Ch 17:1-9; 19; 20:1-32; 22:9). Prosperity of (1Ki 22:45,48; 2Ch 17-20). Bequests of, to his children (2Ch 21:2-3).

4. Father of Jehu (2Ki 9:2,14).

5. A priest who assisted in bringing the ark from Obed-Edom (1Ch 15:24).

JEHOSHAPHAT, VALLEY OF (valley of Yahweh's judgment). Symbolic name for a valley where all nations will be gathered by Yahweh for judgment (Joel 3:2,12), also called "the valley of decision" (Joel 3:14).

JEHOSHEBA [3394, 3395] (Yahweh is an oath ISBE; Yahweh gives plenty, satisfies KB). Daughter of King Jehoram; wife of high priest Jehoiada; hid Joash from Athaliah (2Ki 11:2). Also spelled Jehoshabeath (1Ch 22:11, ftn).

JEHOSHUA, JEHOSHUAH See Joshua, 1.

JEHOVAH A misreading of the name of God, Yahweh. Hebrew was originally written using only consonants. The pronunciation (and vowels) of the Hebrew Bible was handed down orally. When the vowels were eventually added to the Hebrew text, the name Yahweh was no longer pronounced. Instead, out of reverence, the title Adonay (Lord) was substituted. In keeping with this oral tradition, the Jewish scribes inserted into Yahweh the vowels for Adonay, resulting in the spelling Yehowah, though the name was still pronounced Adonay in oral reading. In c. 1520 the Christian scholar Petrus Galatinus introduced the hybrid spelling Jehovah, which became widely used in English versions, literature, and hymns.

In the NIV, Yahweh is represented by LORD.
See God, Names of; Yahweh.

JEHOVAH-JIREH See God, Names of, Yahweh Yireh.

JEHOVAH-NISSI See God, Names of, Yahweh Nissi.

JEHOVAH-RAPAH See God, Names of, Yahweh Raphah.

JEHOVAH-SHALOM See God, Names of, Yahweh Shalom.

JEHOVAH-SHAMMAH See God, Names of, Yahweh Shammah.

JEHOVAH-TSIDKENU *See God, Names of, Yahweh Tsidkenu.*

JEHOZABAD [3379] (*Yahweh endows*).

1. Son of Shomer, and one of the assassins of King Jehoash (2Ki 12:21; 2Ch 24:26).

2. Son of Obed-Edom (1Ch 26:4).

3. A Benjamite chief who commanded 180,000 men (2Ch 17:18).

JEHOZADAK [3392] (*Yahweh is just*). Also called Jozadak. A priest of the Exile (1Ch 6:14-15; Hag 1:1,12,14; 2:2,4; Zec 6:11).

JEHU [3369] (*Yahweh is he*).

NIV+ JEHU'S

1. The prophet who announced the wrath of Yahweh against Baasha, king of Israel (1Ki 16:1,7,12; 2Ch 19:2; 20:34).

2. Son of Nimshi, king of Israel (1Ki 19:16; 2Ki 9:1-4). Religious zeal of, in killing idolaters (2Ki 9:14-37; 10:1-28; 2Ch 22:8-9). His territory invaded by Hazael, king of Syria (2Ki 10:32-33). Prophecies concerning (1Ki 19:17; 2Ki 10:30; 15:12; Hos 1:4). Death of (2Ki 10:35).

3. Son of Obed (1Ch 2:38).

4. Son of Joshibiah (1Ch 4:35).

5. A Benjamite (1Ch 12:3).

JEHUBBAH *See Hubbah.*

JEHUCAL [3385, 3426] (*Yahweh is capable*). Man sent by King Zedekiah to Jeremiah for prayers (Jer 37:3). Prince who put Jeremiah in prison (Hebrew *Jucal*, a variant of *Jehucal*) (Jer 38:1, ftn).

JEHUD [3372] (*declare*). Town in Dan, c. seven miles E of Joppa (Jos 19:45).

JEHUDI [3375] (*Jew*). Prince in Jehoiakim's court (Jer 36:14,21).

JEHUDIJAH NIV "Judean" wife of Mered (1Ch 4:18).

JEHUSH *See Jeush, 4.*

JEIEL [3599] (*God [El] has preserved* IDB; possibly *God [El] sweeps up* KB).

1. Also called Jehiel. A Reubenite (1Ch 5:7).

2. A Benjamite (1Ch 9:35).

3. One of David's heroes (1Ch 11:44).

4. A Levite and singer in the tabernacle service (1Ch 15:18,21; 16:5).

5. A Levite, ancestor of Jahaziel, who encouraged Judah against their enemies (2Ch 20:14).

6. A scribe during the reign of Uzziah (2Ch 26:11).

7. A Levite who cleansed the temple (2Ch 29:13).

8. A chief of the Levites who gave, with other chiefs, "five thousand Passover offerings and five hundred head of cattle for the Levites" for sacrifice (2Ch 35:9).

9. A son of Adonikam, an exile who returned to Jerusalem with Ezra (Ezr 8:13).

10. A priest who was defiled by marriage to an idolatrous woman (Ezr 10:43).

JEKABZEEL [3677] (*God [El] gathers*). A city in the S of Judah (Ne 11:25).

JEKAMEAM [3694] (*[my] kinsman establishes*). Son of Hebron (1Ch 23:19; 24:23).

JEKAMIAH, JECAMIAH [3693] (*Yahweh will establish*).

1. Judahite (1Ch 2:41).

2. Son of King Jehoiachin (Jehoiachin) (1Ch 3:18).

JEKUTHIEL [3688] (*God [El] will nourish*). Son of Ezra (1Ch 4:18).

JEMIMAH, JEMIMA [3544] (*dove*). Daughter of Job born after restoration from affliction (Job 42:14).

JEMUEL [3543]. Son of Simeon (Ge 46:10; Ex 6:15). Also called Nemuel (Nu 26:9,12; 1Ch 4:24). *See Nemuel, 1.*

JEPHTHAH [3653, 2650] (*Yahweh opens, frees*).

NIV+ JEPHTHAH'S

A judge of Israel. Illegitimate and therefore not entitled to inherit his father's property (Jdg 11:1-2). Escapes the violence of his half-brothers, lives in the land of Tob (Jdg 11:3). Recalled from the land of Tob by the elders of Gilead (Jdg 11:5). Made captain of the host (Jdg 11:5-11) and made head of the land of Gilead (Jdg 11:7-11). His message to the king of the Ammonites (Jdg 11:12-28). Leads the host of Israel against the Ammonites (Jdg 11:29-33). His rash vow concerning his daughter (Jdg 11:31,34-40). Falsely accused by the Ephraimites (Jdg 12:1). Leads the army of the Gileadites against the Ephraimites (Jdg 12:4). Judges Israel six years, dies, and is buried in Gilead (Jdg 12:7). Faith of (Heb 11:32).

JEPHUNNEH [3648] (perhaps *may he [God] turn* or *turned*).

1. Father of Caleb (Nu 13:6).

2. Son of Jether (1Ch 7:38).

JERAH [3733] (*moon [god?]*). Son of Joktan (Ge 10:26; 1Ch 1:20).

JERAHMEEL, JERAHMEELITE [3737, 3738] (*God [El] will have compassion*).

1. Son of Hezron (1Ch 2:9).

2. Son of Kish (1Ch 24:29).

3. An officer of Jehoiakim, king of Judah (Jer 36:26).

JERASH *See Gerasenes.*

JERED [3719] (*rose* IDB; *servant* KB). A Judahite (1Ch 4:18).

JEREMAI [3757] (possibly *fat*). Of the family of Hashum (Ezr 10:33).

JEREMIAH, BOOK OF

Author: Jeremiah, son of Berekiah

Date: Between 626 and 586 B.C.

Outline:

I. Call of the Prophet (ch. 1).

II. Warnings and Exhortations to Judah (chs. 2-35).

  A. Earliest Discourses (chs. 2-6).

  B. Temple Message (chs. 7-10).

  C. Covenant and Conspiracy (chs. 11-13).

  D. Messages concerning the Drought (chs. 14-15).

  E. Disaster and Comfort (16:1-17:18).

  F. Command to Keep the Sabbath Holy (17:19-27).

  G. Lessons from the Potter (chs. 18-20).

  H. Condemnation of Kings, Prophets and People (chs. 21-24).

  I. Foretelling the Babylonian Exile (chs. 25-29).

  J. Promises of Restoration (chs. 30-33).

K. Historical Appendix (chs. 34-35).

III. Suffering and Persecutions of the Prophet (chs. 36-38).

    A. Burning Jeremiah's Scroll (ch. 36).

    B. Imprisoning Jeremiah (chs. 37-38).

IV. The Fall of Jerusalem and Its Aftermath (chs. 39-45).

    A. The Fall Itself (ch. 39).

    B. Accession and Assassination of Gedaliah (40:1-41:15).

    C. Migration to Egypt (41:16-43:13).

    D. Prophecy against Those in Egypt (ch. 44).

    E. Historical Appendix: Promise to Baruch (ch. 45).

V. Judgment against the Nations (chs. 46-51).

    A. Against Egypt (ch. 46).

    B. Against Philistia (ch. 47).

    C. Against Moab (ch 48).

    D. Against Ammon (49:1-6).

    E. Against Edom (49:7-22).

    F. Against Damascus (49:23-27).

    G. Against Kedar and Hazor (Arabia) (49:28-33).

    H. Against Elam (49:34-39).

    I. Against Babylon (chs. 50-51).

VI. Historical Appendix (ch. 52).

JEREMIAH, JEREMIAS [3758, 3759, 2635] (*Yahweh loosens [the womb]* BDB; *Yahweh lifts up* IDB; possibly *Yahweh shoots, establishes* KB).

NIV+JEREMIAH'S

One of the greatest Hebrew prophets (c. 640-587 B.C.); born into priestly family of Anathoth, two-and-a-half miles NE of Jerusalem; called to prophetic office by a vision (Jer 1:4-10), and prophesied during last five kings of Judah (Josiah, Jehoahaz II, Jehoiakim, Jehoiachin, Zedekiah), probably helped Josiah in his reforms (2Ki 23), warned Jehoiakim against Egyptian alliance, prophetic roll destroyed by king (Jer 36), persecuted by nobility in days of the last king (Jer 36-37), Nebuchadnezzar kind to him after the destruction of Jerusalem (Jer 39:11-12), compelled to go to Egypt with Israelites who slew Gedaliah, and there he died (Jer 43:6-7).

Six other Jeremiahs are briefly mentioned in the OT:

1. Benjamite who came to David at Ziklag (1Ch 12:4).

2. A Gadite (1Ch 12:10).

3. A Gadite (1Ch 12:13).

4. A Manassite (1Ch 5:24).

5. Father of the wife of King Josiah (2Ki 23:30-31).

6. A Recabite (Jer 35:3).

JEREMOTH [3756] (*swollen* or *obese*).

1. A Benjamite (1Ch 7:8).

2. A Benjamite (1Ch 8:14).

3. Descendant of Elam who put away foreign wife (Ezr 10:26).

4. Descendant of Zattu who put away foreign wife (Ezr 10:27).

5. Descendant of Bani who put away foreign wife (Ezr 10:29).

JERIAH [3745, 3746] (*Yahweh founds*). A descendant of Hebron (1Ch 23:19; 24:23; 26:31).

JERIBAI [3744] (*Yahweh pleads*). A valiant man of David's guard (1Ch 11:46).

JERICHO [3735, 2637] (*moon city*).

1. A city E of Jerusalem and near the Jordan (Nu 22:1; 26:3; Dt 34:1). Called the City of Palm Trees (Dt 34:3). Situation of, pleasant (2Ki 2:19). Rahab the harlot lived in

(Jos 2; Heb 11:31). Joshua sees the "captain of the host" of the Lord near (Jos 5:13-15). Besieged by Joshua seven days; fall and destruction of (Jos 6; 24:11). Situated within the territory allotted to Benjamin (Jos 18:12,21). The Kenites lived at (Jdg 1:16). King of Moab makes conquest of, and establishes his capital at (Jdg 3:13). Rebuilt by Hiel (1Ki 16:34). Company of "the sons of the prophets," lived at (2Ki 2:4-5,15,18). Captives of Judah, taken by the king of Israel, released at, on account of the denunciation of the prophet Obed (2Ch 28:7-15). Inhabitants of, taken captive to Babylon, return to, with Ezra and Nehemiah (Ezr 2:34; Ne 7:36), assist in repairing the walls of Jerusalem (Ne 3:2). Blind men healed at, by Jesus (Mt 20:29-34; Mk 10:46; Lk 18:35). Zacchaeus lived at (Lk 19:1-10).

2. Plain of (2Ki 25:5; Jer 52:8).

3. Waters of (Jos 16:1). Purified by Elisha (2Ki 2:18-22).

JERIEL [3741] (*founded of God [El]* BDB; *God [El] will see* IDB). Son of Tola (1Ch 7:2).

JERIJAH *See Jeriah.*

JERIMOTH [3748, 3756] (*swollen* or *obese*). *See also Jeremoth.*

1. Son of Bela (1Ch 7:7).

2. A disaffected Israelite, who denounced Saul and joined David at Ziklag (1Ch 12:5).

3. Son of Mushi (1Ch 23:23; 24:30).

4. Son of Heman (1Ch 25:4,22).

5. A ruler of the tribe of Naphtali (1Ch 27:19).

6. A son of David (2Ch 11:18).

7. A Levite (2Ch 31:13).

JERIOTH [3750] (*tents*). Wife of Caleb. Probably identical with Azubah (1Ch 2:18).

JEROBOAM [3716] (*the people increase* BDB).

NIV+JEROBOAM'S

1. First king of Israel after the revolt. Promoted by Solomon (1Ki 11:28). Ahijah's prophecy concerning (1Ki 11:29-39; 14:5-16). Flees to Egypt to escape from Solomon (1Ki 11:26-40). Recalled from Egypt by the ten tribes on account of disaffection toward Rehoboam, and made king (1Ki 12:1-20; 2Ch 10:12-19). Subverts the religion of Moses (1Ki 12:25-33; 13:33-34; 14:9,16; 16:2,26,31; 2Ch 11:14; 13:8-9). Hand of, paralyzed (1Ki 13:1-10). His wife sent to consult the prophet Ahijah concerning her child (1Ki 14:1-18). His wars with Rehoboam (1Ki 14:19,30; 15:6; 2Ch 11:1-4). His war with Abijah (1Ki 15:7; 2Ch 13). Death of (1Ki 14:20; 2Ch 13:20).

2. King of Israel. Successor to Jehoash (2Ki 14:16,23). Makes conquest of Hamath and Damascus (2Ki 14:25-28). Wicked reign of (2Ki 14:24). Prophecies concerning (Am 7:7-13). Death of (2Ki 14:29). Genealogies written during his reign (1Ch 5:17).

JEROHAM [3736] (*he will be compassionate*).

1. A Levite, and grandfather of Samuel (1Sa 1:1; 1Ch 6:27,34).

2. A chief of the tribe of Benjamin (1Ch 8:27).

3. A descendant of Benjamin (1Ch 9:8).

4. A priest, and father of Adaiah, who lived in Jerusalem after the Exile (1Ch 9:12; Ne 11:12).

5. Father of two Israelites who joined David at Ziklag (1Ch 12:7).

6. The father of Azarel (1Ch 27:22).

7. Father of Azariah (2Ch 23:1).

JERUB-BAAL, JERUBBAAL [3715] (*Baal contends*). See Gideon.

JERUB-BESHETH, JERUBBESHETH [3717]
(*Shame [Baal] contends*). See Gideon.

JERUEL [3725] (*God [El] is a foundation*). A wilderness in the S of Judah (2Ch 20:16).

JERUSALEM [3731, 10332, 2643, 2647] (*foundation of Shalem [peace]*).

NIV+ JEBUS, JERUSALEM'S

Called:

Jebus (Jos 18:28; Jdg 19:10), Zion (1Ki 8:1; Zec 9:13), City of David (2Sa 5:7; Isa 22:9), Salem (Ge 14:18; Ps 76:2), Ariel (Isa 29:1), City of God (Ps 46:4), City of the Great King (Ps 48:2), City of Judah (2Ch 25:28), The Perfection of Beauty, The Joy of the Whole Earth (La 2:15), The Throne of the Lord (Jer 3:17), Holy Mountain (Da 9:16,20), Holy City (Ne 11:1,18; Mt 4:5), City of our festivals (Isa 33:20), City of Truth (Zec 8:3), to be called "The LORD Our Righteousness" (Jer 33:16), Yahweh Shammah (Eze 48:35), *See God, Names of: Yahweh Shammah*. New Jerusalem (Rev 21:2,10-27).

Situation and appearance of (Ps 122:3; 125:2; SS 6:4; Mic 4:8). Walls of (Jer 39:4).

Gates of:

Benjamin Gate (Jer 37:13; 38:7; Zec 14:10). Corner Gate (2Ki 14:13; 2Ch 25:23; 26:9; Jer 31:38; Zec 14:10). Dung Gate (Ne 2:13; 3:13,14; 12:31). East Gate (1Ch 26:14; 2Ch 31:14; Ne 3:29). Ephraim Gate (2Ki 14:13; 2Ch 25:23; Ne 8:16; 12:39). First Gate (Zec 14:10). Fish Gate (2Ch 33:14; Ne 3:3; 12:39; Zep 1:10). Fountain Gate (Ne 2:14; 3:15; 12:37). Foundation Gate (2Ch 23:5). Gate of Joshua (2Ki 23:8). gate of the guards (2Ki 11:19). Horse Gate (2Ch 23:15; Ne 3:28; Jer 31:40). Inspection Gate (Ne 3:31). Jeshanah [Old] Gate (Ne 3:6; 12:39). King's Gate (1Ch 9:18). Middle Gate (Jer 39:3). New Gate (Jer 26:10; 36:10). North Gate (1Ch 26:14). Potsherd Gate (Jer 19:2). Shalleketh Gate (1Ch 26:16). Sheep Gate (Ne 3:1,32; 12:39; Jn 5:2). South Gate (1Ch 26:15). Sur Gate (2Ki 11:6). Upper Gate (2Ki 15:35; 2Ch 23:20; 27:3). Upper Gate of Benjamin (Jer 20:2). Valley Gate (2Ch 26:9; Ne 2:13,15; 3:13). Water Gate (Ne 3:26; 8:1,3,16; 12:37). West Gate (1Ch 26:16).

Gates of the twelve tribes in Ezekiel's vision (Eze 48:31-34). Measurement of, in Ezekiel's vision (Eze 45:6).

Buildings:

High priest's palace (Jn 18:15). Barracks (Ac 21:34). Stairway of Ahaz (2Ki 20:11). Stairs (Ne 9:4).

Squares and Streets:

Square on the east side (2Ch 29:4). Square before the house of God (Ezr 10:9). Square before the Water Gate (Ne 8:1,3,16), by the Gate of Ephraim (Ne 8:16). Street of the bakers (Jer 37:21). Streets of Jerusalem (Jer 5:1; 7:17,34; 11:6,13; 14:16; 33:10; 44:6,9,17,21; Zec 8:4).

Towers:

See Beth Millo; Hananel, Hananeel, Tower of; Meah; Ophel; Siloam, Tower of.

Places in and Around:

Moriah (2Ch 3:1). The tomb of Jesus (Jn 19:41). *See Gethsemane; Golgotha; Jehoshaphat, Valley of; Olives, Mount of; Topheth, Topheth.*

History of:

Melchizedek ancient king and priest of (Ge 14:18). King of, confederated with the four other kings of the Amorites, against Joshua and the hosts of Israel (Jos 10:1-5). Confederated kings defeated, and the king of Jerusalem slain by Joshua (Jos 10:15-26). Fell to Benjamin in the allotment of the land of Canaan (Jos 18:28). Conquest of, made by David (2Sa 5:7). The inhabitants of, not expelled (Jos 15:63; Jdg 1:21). Conquest of Mount Zion in, made by David (1Ch 11:4-6). The citadel of Mount Zion, occupied by David, and called the City of David (2Sa 5:5-9; 1Ch 11:7). Ark brought to, by David (2Sa 6:12-19). The threshing floor of Araunah within the citadel of (2Sa 24:16). David purchased and built an altar upon it (2Sa 24:16-25). The city built around the citadel (1Ch 11:8). The capital of David's kingdom by divine appointment (1Ki 15:4; 2Ki 19:34; 2Ch 6:6; 12:13).

Fortified by Solomon (1Ki 3:1; 9:15). The temple built within the citadel. *See Temple.*

The chief Levites lived in (1Ch 9:34). The high priest lived at (Jn 18:15). Annual feasts kept at (Eze 36:38, w Dt 16:16, & Ps 122:3-5; Lk 2:41; Jn 4:20; 5:1; 7:1-14; 12:20; Ac 18:21). Prayers of the Israelites made toward (1Ki 8:38; Da 6:10). Beloved (Ps 122:6; 137:1-7; Isa 62:1-7). *See Country, Love of; Patriotism.* Oaths taken in the name of (Mt 5:35).

Captured and Pillaged by—

Shishak, king of Egypt (1Ki 14:25-26; 2Ch 12:9), Jehoash, king of Israel (2Ki 14:13-14; 2Ch 25:23-24), Nebuchadnezzar, king of Babylon (2Ki 24:8-16; 25:1-17; 2Ch 36:17-21; Jer 1:3; 32:2; 39; 52:4-7,12-24; La 1:5-8).

Walls of, Restored and Fortified—

By Uzziah (2Ch 26:9-10), Jotham (2Ch 27:3), Manasseh (2Ch 33:14).

Water Supply—

Brought in from the Gihon by Hezekiah (2Ki 18:17; 20:20; 2Ch 32:3-4,30; Ne 2:13-15; Isa 7:3; 22:9-11; 36:2).

Besieged—

By Pekah (2Ki 16:5), the Philistines (2Ch 21:16-17), Sennacherib (2Ki 18:13-37; 19:20-37; 2Ch 32).

Rebuilding of—

Ordered by proclamation of Cyrus (2Ch 36:23; Ezr 1:1-4). Rebuilt by Nehemiah under the direction of Artaxerxes (Ne 2-6). Wall of, dedicated (Ne 12:27-43). Temple restored. *See Temple.*

Roman Rulers Resided at—

Herod I (Mt 2:3), Pontius Pilate (Mt 27:2; Mk 15:1; Lk 23:1-7; Jn 18:28-29), Herod III (Ac 12:1-23).

Life and miracles of Jesus connected with—

See Jesus the Christ, History of.

Gospel preached—

First preached at (Mic 4:2; Lk 24:47; Ac 1:4; 2:14). Pentecostal revival occurs at (Ac 2). Stephen martyred at (Ac 6:8-7:60). Disciples persecuted and dispersed from (Ac 8:1-4; 11:19-21).

For Personal Incidents Occurring There:

See biographies of individuals; Israel, Israelites.

Sins of:

Wickedness (Lk 13:33-34). Catalog of abominations in (Eze 22:3-12,25-30; 23; 33:25-26). Led Judah to sin (Mic 1:5).

Prophecies Concerning:

Prophecies against (Isa 3:1-8; Jer 9:11; 19:6,15; 21:10; 26:9,11; Da 9:2,27; Mic 1:1; 3:12); of pestilence, famine, and war in (Jer 34:2; Eze 5:12; Joel 3:2-3; Am 2:5); of the destruction of (Jer 7:32-34; 26:18; 32:29,31-32; Da 9:24-27). Destruction of, foretold by Jesus (Mt 23:37-38; 24:15; Mk 13:14-23; Lk 13:35; 17:26-37; 19:41-44; 21:20-24).

Prophecies of the rebuilding of (Isa 44:28; Jer 31:38-40; Eze 48:15-22; Da 9:25; Zec 14:8-11). Of final restoration of (Joel 3:20-21; Zec 2:2-5; 8).

JERUSALEM, NEW City of God referred to as coming down out of heaven from God (Rev 3:12; 21:2). Described as the mother of believers (Gal 4:26).

JERUSHA, JERUSHAH [3729, 3730] (*possession*). Wife of King Uzziah and mother of King Jotham (2Ki 15:33; 2Ch 27:1).

JESARELAH, JESHARELAH [3777]. Ancestral head of a course of musicians (1Ch 25:14, ftn). Called Asarelah (1Ch 25:2).

JESHAIAH, JESAIAH [3832, 3833] (*Yahweh will save*).
1. Grandson of Zerubbabel (1Ch 3:21).
2. Son of Jeduthun (1Ch 25:3,15).
3. Grandson of Eliezer (1Ch 26:25).
4. A Jew of the family of Elam, who returned from exile (Ezr 8:7).
5. A Levite who joined Ezra to return to Jerusalem (Ezr 8:19).
6. A Benjamite, detailed by lot to live in Jerusalem after the Exile (Ne 11:7).

JESHANAH [3827] (*old*).
1. A city on the N of Benjamin (2Ch 13:19).
2. Gate in NW corner of Jerusalem in Nehemiah's time (Ne 3:6).

JESHEBEAB [3784] (*father lives*). A priest, and head of the fourteenth course (1Ch 24:13).

JESHER [3840] (perhaps *the deity shows himself just*). Son of Caleb (1Ch 2:18).

JESHIMON [3810] (*a waste, a desert*).
1. A place in the Sinai peninsula, E of the Jordan (Nu 21:20; 23:28).
2. A place in the desert of Judah (1Sa 23:24; 26:1).

JESHIMOTH *Beth Jeshimoth, Beth-Jeshimoth.*

JESHISHAI [3814] (*aged*). A Gadite (1Ch 5:14).

JESHOHAIAH [3797] (possibly *Yahweh humbles*). A descendant of Simeon (1Ch 4:36).

JESHUA [3800, 3801, 10336] (*Yahweh saves*).
1. A priest, head of the ninth course (1Ch 24:11). Nine hundred and seventy-three of his descendants returned from Babylon (Ezr 2:36; Ne 7:39).
2. A Levite, had charge of the tithes (2Ch 31:15). His descendants returned with Ezra from Babylon (Ezr 2:40; Ne 7:43).
3. Also called Joshua. A priest who accompanied Zerubbabel from Babylon (Ezr 2:2; Ne 7:7; 12:1). Descendants of (Ne 12:10). He rebuilt the altar (Ezr 3:2). Assisted Zerubbabel in restoring the temple (Ezr 3; 4:1-6; 5; Hag 1:1,12-14; 2:2). Contended with those who sought to defeat the rebuilding (Ezr 4:1-3; 5:1-2). Symbolic of the restoration of Israel (Zec 3; 6:9-15).
4. Father of Jozabad (Ezr 8:33).
5. Son of Pahath-Moab (Ezr 2:6; Ne 7:11).

6. Father of Ezer (Ne 3:19).
7. A Levite who explained the law to the people when Ezra read it (Ne 8:7; 12:8).
8. A Levite who sealed Nehemiah's covenant (Ne 10:9).
9. A city of Judah (Ne 11:26).

JESHURUN [3843] (*upright*). A name used poetically for Israel (Dt 32:15; 33:5,26; Isa 44:2).

JESIAH *See Isshiah, 2 & 3.*

JESIMIEL [3774] (*God [El] will establish*). A descendant of Simeon (1Ch 4:36).

JESSE [414, 3805, *2649*].
NIV+ JESSE'S

Father of David (Ru 4:17; 1Sa 17:12). Ancestor of Jesus (Mt 1:5-6). Samuel visits, under divine command, to select from his sons a successor to Saul (1Sa 16:1-13). Saul asks, to send David to become a member of his court (1Sa 16:19-23). Sons in Saul's army (1Sa 17:13-28). Lives with David in Moab (1Sa 22:3-4). Descendants of (1Ch 2:13-17).

JESTING Foolish, forbidden (Eph 5:4; Mt 12:36).

JESUI, JESUITES *See Ishvi, 1; Ishvites.*

JESUS THE CHRIST [2652] (*Yahweh Saves, Anointed One*).
NIV+ CHRIST'S, CHRISTIAN, CHRISTIANS, CHRISTS, JESUS', MESSIAH

History of:
Genealogy of (Mt 1:1-17; Lk 3:23-38).
The angel Gabriel appears to Mary (Lk 1:26-38). Mary visits Elizabeth (Lk 1:39-56). Mary's *magnificat* (Lk 1:46-55).
An angel appears to Joseph concerning Mary (Mt 1:18-25)
Birth of (Lk 2:1-7).
Angels appear to the shepherds (Lk 2:8-20).
Magi visit (Mt 2:1-12).
Circumcision of (Lk 2:21). Is presented in the temple (Lk 2:21-38).
Flight into, and return from, Egypt (Mt 2:13-23).
Disputes with the doctors in the temple (Lk 2:41-52).
Is baptized by John (Mt 3:13-17; Mk 1:9-11; Lk 3:21-23).
Temptation of (Mt 4:1-11; Mk 1:12-13; Lk 4:1-13)
John's testimony concerning him (Jn 1:1-18)
Testimony of John the Baptist concerning (Jn 1:19-34).
Disciples adhere to (Jn 1:35-51).
Miracles at Cana of Galilee (Jn 2:1-12).
Drives the money changers from the temple (Jn 2:13-25). Nicodemus comes to (Jn 3:1-21).
Baptizes (Jn 3:22; 4:2).
Returns to Galilee (Mt 4:12; Mk 1:14; Lk 4:14; Jn 4:1-3).
Visits Sychar, and teaches the Samaritan woman (Jn 4:4-42).
Teaches in Galilee (Mt 4:17; Mk 1:14-15; Lk 4:14-15; Jn 4:43-45).
Heals a nobleman's son of Capernaum (Jn 4:46-54).
Is rejected by the people of Nazareth, lives at Capernaum (Mt 4:13-16; Lk 4:16-31).
Chooses Peter, Andrew, James, and John as disciples, miracle of the catch of fishes (Mt 4:18-22; Mk 1:16-20; Lk 5:1-11).

Preaches throughout Galilee (Mt 4:23-25; Mk 1:35-39; Lk 4:42-44).

Heals a demoniac (Mk 1:21-28; Lk 4:31-37)

Heals Peter's mother-in-law (Mt 8:14-17; Mk 1:29-34; Lk 4:38-41).

Heals a leper in Galilee (Mt 8:2-4; Mk 1:40-45; Lk 5:12-16).

Heals a paralytic (Mt 9:2-8; Mk 2:1-12; Lk 5:17-26)

Calls Matthew (Mt 9:9; Mk 2:13-14; Lk 5:27-28).

Heals an invalid at the pool of Bethesda on the Sabbath day, is persecuted, and makes his defense (Jn 5:1-47)

Defines the law of the Sabbath on the occasion of his disciples picking the heads of grain (Mt 12:1-14; Mk 3:1-6; Lk 6:6-11).

Withdraws from Capernaum to the Sea of Galilee, where he heals many (Mt 12:15-21; Mk 3:7-12).

Goes up onto a mountain, and calls and ordains twelve disciples (Mt 10:2-4; Mk 3:13-19; Lk 6:12-19).

Delivers the "Sermon on the Mount" (Mt 5-7; Lk 6:20-49).

Heals the centurion's servant (Mt 8:5-13; Lk 7:1-10).

Raises from the dead the son of the widow of Nain (Lk 7:11-17).

Receives the message from John the Baptist (Mt 11:2-19; Lk 7:18-35).

Rebukes the unbelieving cities about Capernaum (Mt 11:20-30).

Anointed by a sinful woman (Lk 7:36-50).

Preaches in the cities of Galilee (Lk 8:1-3).

Heals a demoniac, and denounces the scribes and Pharisees (Mt 12:22-37; Mk 3:19-30; Lk 11:14-20).

Replies to the scribes and Pharisees who seek a sign from him (Mt 12:38-45; Lk 11:16-36).

Denounces the Pharisees and other hypocrites (Lk 11:37-54).

Discourses to his disciples (Lk 12:1-59).

Parable of the barren fig tree (Lk 13:6-9).

Parable of the sower (Mt 13:1-23; Mk 4:1-25; Lk 8:4-18).

Parable of the weeds, and other teachings (Mt 13:24-53; Mk 4:26-34).

Crosses the Sea of Galilee, and stills the tempest (Mt 8:18-27; Mk 4:35-41; Lk 8:22-25).

Casts out the legion of demons (Mt 8:28-33; Mk 5:1-21; Lk 8:26-40).

Returns to Capernaum (Mt 9:1; Mk 5:21; Lk 8:40).

Eats with tax collectors and sinners, and speaks on fasting (Mt 9:10-17; Mk 2:15-22; Lk 5:29-39).

Raises to life the daughter of Jairus, and heals the woman who has the issue of blood (Mt 9:18-26; Mk 5:22-43; Lk 8:41-56).

Heals two blind men and casts out a mute spirit (Mt 9:27-34).

Returns to Nazareth (Mt 13:53-58; Mk 6:1-6).

Teaches in various cities in Galilee (Mt 9:35-38).

Instructs his disciples and empowers them to heal diseases and cast out unclean spirits (Mt 10; Mk 6:6-13; Lk 9:1-6).

Herod falsely supposes him to be John, whom he had beheaded (Mt 14:1-2,6-12; Mk 6:14-16,21-29; Lk 9:7-9).

The Twelve return; he goes to the desert; multitudes follow him; he feeds five thousand (Mt 14:13-21; Mk 6:30-44; Lk 9:10-17; Jn 6:1-14).

Walks on the water (Mt 14:22-36; Mk 6:45-56; Jn 6:15-21).

Teaches in the synagogue in Capernaum (Jn 6:22-65).

Disciples forsake him (Jn 6:66-71).

He justifies his disciples in eating without washing their hands (Mt 15:1-20; Mk 7:1-23).

Heals the daughter of the Syrian Phoenician woman (Mt 15:21-28; Mk 7:24-30).

Heals a mute man (Mt 15:29-31; Mk 7:31-37).

Feeds four thousand (Mt 15:32-39; Mk 8:1-9).

Refuses to give a sign to the Pharisees (Mt 16:1-4; Mk 8:10-12).

Cautions his disciples against the yeast of hypocrisy (Mt 16:4-12; Mk 8:13-21).

Heals a blind man (Mk 8:22-26).

Foretells his death and resurrection (Mt 16:21-28; Mk 8:31-38; 9:1; Lk 9:21-27).

Is transfigured (Mt 17:1-13; Mk 9:2-13; Lk 9:28-36).

Heals a demoniac (Mt 17:14-21; Mk 9:14-29; Lk 9:37-43).

Foretells his death and resurrection (Mt 17:22-23; Mk 9:30-32; Lk 9:43-45)

Miracle of tribute money in the fish's mouth (Mt 17:24-27).

Reproves the ambition of his disciples (Mt 18:1-35; Mk 9:33-50; Lk 9:46-50).

Reproves the intolerance of his disciples (Mk 9:38-39; Lk 9:49-50).

Journeys to Jerusalem to attend the Feast of Tabernacles, passing through Samaria (Lk 9:51-62; Jn 7:2-11).

Commissions the Seventy (Lk 10:11-19).

Heals ten lepers (Lk 17:11-19).

Teaches in Jerusalem at the Feast of Tabernacles (Jn 7:14-53; 8).

Answers a lawyer, who tests his wisdom with the question, "What must I do to inherit eternal life?" by the parable of the good Samaritan (Lk 10:25-37).

Hears the report of the Seventy (Lk 10:17-24).

Teaches in the house of Mary, Martha, and Lazarus, in Bethany (Lk 10:38-42).

Teaches his disciples to pray (Lk 11:1-13).

Heals a blind man, who, because of his faith in Jesus, was excommunicated (Jn 9).

Teaches in Jerusalem (Jn 9:39-41; 10:1-21)

Teaches in the temple at Jerusalem, at the Feast of Dedication (Jn 10:22-39)

Goes across the Jordan to escape violence from the rulers (Jn 10:40-42; 11:3-16).

Returns to Bethany and raises Lazarus from the dead (Jn 11:1-46).

Escapes to the city of Ephraim from the conspiracy led by Caiaphas, the high priest (Jn 11:47-54).

Journeys toward Jerusalem to attend the Passover; heals many who are diseased and teaches the people (Mt 19:1-2; Mk 10:1; Lk 13:10-35).

Dines with a Pharisee on the Sabbath (Lk 14:1-24).

Teaches the multitude the conditions of discipleship (Lk 14:25-35).

Tells the parables of the lost sheep, the lost piece of silver, prodigal son, unjust steward (Lk 15:1-32; 16:1-13).

Reproves the hypocrisy of the Pharisees (Lk 16).

Tells the parable of the rich man and Lazarus (Lk 16:19-31).

Teaches his disciples concerning offenses, meekness, and humility (Lk 17:1-10).

Teaches the Pharisees concerning the coming of his kingdom (Lk 17:20-37).

Tells the parables of the unjust judge, and the Pharisee and tax collector praying in the temple (Lk 18:1-14).

Interprets the law concerning marriage and divorce (Mt 19:3-12; Mk 10:2-12).

Blesses little children (Mt 19:13-15; Mk 10:13-16; Lk 18:15-17).

Receives the rich young ruler, who asks what he must do to inherit eternal life (Mt 19:16-22; Mk 10:17-22; Lk 18:18-24).

Tells the parable of the vineyard (Mt 20:1-16).

Foretells his death and resurrection (Mt 20:17-19; Mk 10:32-34; Lk 18:31-34).

Listens to the mother of James and John in behalf of her sons (Mt 20:20-28; Mk 10:35-45).

Heals two blind men at Jericho (Mt 20:29-34; Mk 10:46-50; Lk 18:35-43).

Visits Zacchaeus (Lk 19:1-10).

Tells the parable of the pounds (Lk 19:11-28).

Goes to Bethany six days before the Passover (Jn 12:1-9).

Triumphal entry into Jerusalem, while the people throw palm branches in the way (Mt 21:1-11; Mk 11:1-11; Lk 19:29-44; Jn 12:12-19).

Enters the temple (Mt 21:12; Mk 11:11; Lk 19:45).

Drives the money changers out of the temple (Mt 21:12-13; Lk 19:45-46).

Heals the sick in the temple (Mt 21:14).

Teaches daily in the temple (Lk 19:47-48).

Performs the miracle of causing the barren fig tree to wither (Mt 21:17-22; Mk 11:12-14,20-22).

Tells the parable of the two sons (Mt 21:28-31), the parable of the wicked farmers (Mt 21:33-46; Mk 12:1-12; Lk 20:9-19), of the marriage (Mt 22:1-14; Lk 14:16-24).

Tested by the Pharisees and Herodians and enunciates the duty of the citizen to his government (Mt 22:15-22; Mk 12:13-17; Lk 20:20-26).

Tried by the Sadducees concerning the resurrection of the dead (Mt 22:23-33; Mk 12:18-27; Lk 20:27-40) and by a lawyer (Mt 22:34-40; Mk 12:28-34).

Exposes the hypocrisies of the scribes and Pharisees (Mt 23; Mk 12:38-40; Lk 20:45-47).

Extols the widow who casts two small copper coins into the treasury (Mk 12:41-44; Lk 21:1-4).

Verifies the prophecy of Isaiah concerning the un-believing Jews (Jn 12:37-50).

Foretells the destruction of the temple and of Jerusalem (Mt 24; Mk 13; Lk 21:5-36).

Laments over Jerusalem (Mt 23:37; Lk 19:41-44).

Tells the parables of the ten virgins and of the talents (Mt 25:1-30).

Foretells the scenes of the Day of Judgment (Mt 25:31-46).

Anointed with the box of precious ointment (Mt 26:6-13; Mk 14:3-9; Jn 12:1-8).

Last Passover, and institution of the Lord's Supper (Mt 26:17-30; Mk 14:12-25; Lk 22:7-20).

Washes the disciples' feet (Jn 13:1-17).

Foretells his betrayal (Mt 26:23; Mk 14:18-21; Lk 22:21; Jn 13:18).

Accuses Judas of his betrayal (Mt 26:21-25; Mk 14:18-21; Lk 22:21-23; Jn 13:21-30).

Teaches his disciples, and comforts them with promises, and promises the gift of the Holy Spirit (Jn 14-16).

Last prayer (Jn 17).

Moves to Gethsemane (Mt 26:30,36-46; Mk 14:26,32-42; Lk 22:39-46; Jn 18:1).

Is betrayed and apprehended (Mt 26:47-56; Mk 14:43-54,66-72; Lk 22:47-53; Jn 18:2-12).

Trial of, before Caiaphas (Mt 26:57-58,69-75; Mk 14:53-54,66-72; Lk 22:54-62; Jn 18:13-18,25-27).

Led by the council to Pilate (Mt 27:1-2,11-14; Mk 15:1-5; Lk 23:1-5; Jn 18:28-38).

Arraigned before Herod (Lk 23:6-12).

Tried before Pilate (Mt 27:15-26; Mk 15:6-15; Lk 23:13-25; Jn 18:39-40; 19:1-16).

Mocked by the soldiers (Mt 27:27-31; Mk 15:16-20).

Is led away to be crucified (Mt 27:31-34; Mk 15:20-23; Lk 23:26-32; Jn 19:16-17).

Crucified (Mt 27:35-56; Mk 15:24-41; Lk 23:33-49; Jn 19:18-30).

Taken from the cross and buried (Mt 27:57-66; Mk 15:42-47; Lk 23:50-56; Jn 19:31-42).

Arises from the dead (Mt 28:2-15; Mk 16:1-11; Lk 24:1-12; Jn 20:1-18).

Is seen by Mary Magdalene (Mt 28:1-10; Mk 16:9; Jn 20:11-17), by Peter (Lk 24:34; 1Co 15:5).

Appears to two disciples who journey to Emmaus (Mk 16:12-13; Lk 24:13-35).

Appears in the midst of the disciples, when Thomas is absent (Mk 16:14-18; Lk 24:36-49; Jn 20:19-23), when Thomas was present (Jn 20:26-29), at the Sea of Galilee (Mt 28:16; Jn 21:1-14), to the apostles and five hundred believers on a mountain in Galilee (Mt 28:16-20, w Ac 10:40-42; 13:31; 1Co 15:6-7).

Appears to James, and also to all the apostles (Ac 1:3-8; 1Co 15:7).

Ascends to heaven (Mk 16:19-20; Lk 24:50-53; Ac 1:9-12).

Appears to Paul (Ac 9:3-17; 18:9; 22:14,18; 23:11; 26:16; 1Co 9:1; 15:8).

Stephen's vision of (Ac 7:55-56).

Appears to John on Patmos (Rev 1:10-18)

Miscellaneous Facts Concerning:

Brothers of (Mt 13:55; Mk 6:3; 1Co 9:5; Gal 1:19). Sisters of (Mt 13:56; Mk 6:3).

Was with the Israelites in the wilderness (1Co 10:4,9; Heb 11:26; Jude 5).

Appearances of, After His Resurrection:

To Mary Magdalene and other women (Mt 28:1-10; Mk 16:9; Lk 24:1-10; Jn 20:11-17). To Peter (Lk 24:34; 1Co 15:5). To two disciples who journey to Emmaus (Mk 16:12-13; Lk 24:13-31). In the midst of the disciples, when Thomas is absent, in Jerusalem (Jn 20:19-23), when Thomas is present (Mk 16:14-18; Lk 24:36-49; Jn 20:26-29; 1Co 15:5). To certain disciples, Sea of Galilee (Jn 21:1-14). To the eleven disciples, mountain in Galilee (Mt 28:16). To upwards of five hundred, Galilee (1Co 15:6). To James, and also all the apostles, Jerusalem (Ac 1:3-8; 1Co 15:7). To Paul (Ac 9:3-6; 23:11; 26:13-18; 1Co 9:1; 15:8).

In Stephen's vision (Ac 7:55-56). To John, in a vision, on Patmos (Rev 1:10-18).

Ascension of:

Mk 16:19 After the Lord Jesus had spoken to them, he was taken up into heaven and he sat at the right hand of God.

Lk 24:50 When he had led them out to the vicinity of Bethany, he lifted up his hands and blessed them. [51]While he was blessing them, he left them and was taken up into heaven.

Jn 14:2 In my Father's house are many rooms; if it were not so, I would have told you. I am going there to prepare a place for you. [3]And if I go and prepare a place for you, I will come back and take you to be with me that you also may be where I am. **4**You know the way to the place where I am going."

Ac 1:9 After he said this, he was taken up before their very eyes, and a cloud hid him from their sight.

Ac 3:21 He must remain in heaven until the time comes for God to restore everything, as he promised long ago through his holy prophets.

Eph 1:20 which he exerted in Christ when he raised him from the dead and seated him at his right hand in the heavenly realms,

Eph 4:8 This is why it says: "When he ascended on high, he led captives in his train and gave gifts to men." **9**(What does "he ascended" mean except that he also descended to the lower, earthly regions? **10**He who descended is the very one who ascended higher than all the heavens, in order to fill the whole universe.)

1Ti 3:16 Beyond all question, the mystery of godliness is great: He appeared in a body, was vindicated by the Spirit, was seen by angels, was preached among the nations, was believed on in the world, was taken up in glory.

Heb 1:3 The Son is the radiance of God's glory and the exact representation of his being, sustaining all things by his powerful word. After he had provided purification for sins, he sat down at the right hand of the Majesty in heaven.

Heb 4:14 Therefore, since we have a great high priest who has gone through the heavens, Jesus the Son of God, let us hold firmly to the faith we profess.

Heb 9:24 For Christ did not enter a man-made sanctuary that was only a copy of the true one; he entered heaven itself, now to appear for us in God's presence.

Foretold—

Ps 47:5 God has ascended amid shouts of joy, the LORD amid the sounding of trumpets.

Ps 68:18 When you ascended on high, you led captives in your train; you received gifts from men, even from the rebellious—that you, O LORD God, might dwell there.

Lk 24:26 Did not the Christ have to suffer these things and then enter his glory?" (+Lk 24:50)

Jn 1:51 He then added, "I tell you the truth, you shall see heaven open, and the angels of God ascending and descending on the Son of Man."

Jn 6:62 What if you see the Son of Man ascend to where he was before!

Jn 7:33 Jesus said, "I am with you for only a short time, and then I go to the one who sent me. (+Jn 14:2-3)

Jn 14:12 I tell you the truth, anyone who has faith in me will do what I have been doing. He will do even greater things than these, because I am going to the Father.

Jn 14:28 "You heard me say, 'I am going away and I am coming back to you.' If you loved me, you would be glad that I am going to the Father, for the Father is greater than I.

Jn 16:5 "Now I am going to him who sent me, yet none of you asks me, 'Where are you going?'

Jn 16:7 But I tell you the truth: It is for your good that I am going away. Unless I go away, the Counselor will not come to you; but if I go, I will send him to you.

Jn 16:10 in regard to righteousness, because I am going to the Father, where you can see me no longer;

Jn 16:16 "In a little while you will see me no more, and then after a little while you will see me."

Jn 16:28 I came from the Father and entered the world; now I am leaving the world and going back to the Father."

Jn 17:13 "I am coming to you now, but I say these things while I am still in the world, so that they may have the full measure of my joy within them.

Jn 20:17 Jesus said, "Do not hold on to me, for I have not yet returned to the Father. Go instead to my brothers and tell them, 'I am returning to my Father and your Father, to my God and your God.'"

Atonement by:

(Ro 3:24-26; 5:11,15; 1Th 1:10; Heb 13:12; 1Jn 2:2; 3:5; 4:10; Rev 5:6,9; 13:8).

Made once for all (Heb 7:27; 9:24-28; 10:10,12,14; 1Pe 3:18).

Vicarious (Isa 53:4-12; Mt 20:28; Jn 6:51; 11:49-51; Gal 1:4; 3:13; Eph 5:2; 1Th 5:9-10; Heb 2:9; 1Pe 2:24).

Through his blood (Lk 22:20; 1Co 1:23; Eph 2:13-15; Heb 9:12-15,25-26; 12:24; 13:12,19-21; 1Jn 5:6; Rev 1:5; 5:9; 7:14; 12:11).

For reconciliation (Ro 5:1-21; 2Co 5:18-19,21; Eph 2:6-17; Col 1:20-22; Heb 2:17).

For remission of sins (Zec 13:1; Mt 26:28; Lk 24:46-47; Jn 1:29; Ro 4:25; 1Co 15:3; Gal 1:3-4; Eph 1:7; Col 1:14; Heb 1:3; 10:1-20; 1Jn 1:7; 3:5).

Atonement by, typified (Ex 29:36-37; 30:10,15-16; Lev 1:4; 5:6,16,18; 6:7; 8:34; 9:2-3,7; 10:17; 12:7-8; 14:18-20, 31,53; 15:14-15,29-30; 16:6,10-11,16-18,24,27,30,32-34; 17:11; 23:27-28; 25:9; Nu 8:19,21; 16:46; 25:13; 28:22; 30; 29:5; 31:50).

Atoning blood (Mt 26:28; Mk 14:24; Lk 22:20; Eph 1:7; 2:13; Heb 9:14; 10:19; 1Jn 1:7). Atoning blood of, typified (Ex 12:7,13,22-23; 24:6,8; 29:12,15,20-21; 30:10; Lev 1:5,10-11; 3:2,8,13; 4:5-7,17-18,25,30,34; 5:8-9; 6:30; 7:2; 8:2,15,19,23-24,30; 9:9,18; 14:6,14-15,25; 16:14-15, 18-19,27; 17:6,11; Nu 18:17; 19:2-4; Dt 12:27; 2Ki 16:13; 15; 2Ch 29:22; 30:16; 35:11; Eze 43:20; 45:19-20; 1Pe 1:19).

Benevolence of:

Manifested in his companionship with sinners (Mt 9:10-12; Mk 2:14-17; Lk 5:30; 15:2; 19:10-12).

See below, Compassion of; Love of.

Compassion of:

For those who were in spiritual distress—

Isa 42:3 A bruised reed he will not break, and a smoldering wick he will not snuff out. In faithfulness he will bring forth justice;

Mt 9:36 When he saw the crowds, he had compassion on them, because they were harassed and helpless, like sheep without a shepherd.

Mt 12:20 A bruised reed he will not break, and a smoldering wick he will not snuff out, till he leads justice to victory.

Mt 18:12 "What do you think? If a man owns a hundred sheep, and one of them wanders away, will he not leave the ninety-nine on the hills and go to look for the one that wandered off? **13**And if he finds it, I tell you the truth, he is happier about that one sheep than about the ninety-nine that did not wander off.

Mt 23:37 "O Jerusalem, Jerusalem, you who kill the prophets and stone those sent to you, how often I have longed to gather your children together, as a hen gathers her chicks under her wings, but you were not willing.

Mk 1:41 Filled with compassion, Jesus reached out his hand and touched the man. "I am willing," he said. "Be clean!"

Mk 6:34 When Jesus landed and saw a large crowd, he had compassion on them, because they were like sheep without a shepherd. So he began teaching them many things.

Lk 7:13 When the Lord saw her, his heart went out to her and he said, "Don't cry." (+Lk 13:34; 15:4-9,20-24)

Lk 19:41 As he approached Jerusalem and saw the city, he wept over it [42]and said, "If you, even you, had only known on this day what would bring you peace—but now it is hidden from your eyes.

Jn 11:33 When Jesus saw her weeping, and the Jews who had come along with her also weeping, he was deeply moved in spirit and troubled. [34]"Where have you laid him?" he asked. "Come and see, Lord," they replied. [35]Jesus wept. [36]Then the Jews said, "See how he loved him!" [37]But some of them said, "Could not he who opened the eyes of the blind man have kept this man from dying?" [38]Jesus, once more deeply moved, came to the tomb. It was a cave with a stone laid across the entrance.

Jn 18:8 "I told you that I am he," Jesus answered. "If you are looking for me, then let these men go." [9]This happened so that the words he had spoken would be fulfilled: "I have not lost one of those you gave me."

2Co 8:9 For you know the grace of our Lord Jesus Christ, that though he was rich, yet for your sakes he became poor, so that you through his poverty might become rich.

Heb 4:15 For we do not have a high priest who is unable to sympathize with our weaknesses, but we have one who has been tempted in every way, just as we are—yet was without sin.

Heb 5:2 He is able to deal gently with those who are ignorant and are going astray, since he himself is subject to weakness.

For those who were in temporal adversity—

Isa 53:4 Surely he took up our infirmities and carried our sorrows, yet we considered him stricken by God, smitten by him, and afflicted.

Isa 63:9 In all their distress he too was distressed, and the angel of his presence saved them. In his love and mercy he redeemed them; he lifted them up and carried them all the days of old.

Mt 8:3 Jesus reached out his hand and touched the man. "I am willing," he said. "Be clean!" Immediately he was cured of his leprosy.

Mt 8:16 When evening came, many who were demon-possessed were brought to him, and he drove out the spirits with a word and healed all the sick. [17]This was to fulfill what was spoken through the prophet Isaiah: "He took up our infirmities and carried our diseases."

Mt 14:14 When Jesus landed and saw a large crowd, he had compassion on them and healed their sick.

Mt 15:32 Jesus called his disciples to him and said, "I have compassion for these people; they have already been with me three days and have nothing to eat. I do not want to send them away hungry, or they may collapse on the way."

Mt 20:34 Jesus had compassion on them and touched their eyes. Immediately they received their sight and followed him.

Mk 8:2 "I have compassion for these people; they have already been with me three days and have nothing to eat. [3]If I send them home hungry, they will collapse on the way, because some of them have come a long distance."

For his sheep—

Isa 40:11 He tends his flock like a shepherd: He gathers the lambs in his arms and carries them close to his heart; he gently leads those that have young.

Mk 6:34 When Jesus landed and saw a large crowd, he had compassion on them, because they were like sheep without a shepherd. So he began teaching them many things.

Condescension of: (Lk 22:27; Jn 13:5,14)

2Co 8:9 For you know the grace of our Lord Jesus Christ, that though he was rich, yet for your sakes he became poor, so that you through his poverty might become rich.

Php 2:7 but made himself nothing, taking the very nature of a servant, being made in human likeness. [8]And being found in appearance as a man, he humbled himself and became obedient to death—even death on a cross! (+Heb 2:11)

Confessing:

See Confession, of Christ; Testimony, Religious.

Creator:

Jn 1:3 Through him all things were made; without him nothing was made that has been made.

Jn 1:10 He was in the world, and though the world was made through him, the world did not recognize him.

1Co 8:6 yet for us there is but one God, the Father, from whom all things came and for whom we live; and there is but one Lord, Jesus Christ, through whom all things came and through whom we live.

Eph 3:9 and to make plain to everyone the administration of this mystery, which for ages past was kept hidden in God, who created all things.

Col 1:16 For by him all things were created: things in heaven and on earth, visible and invisible, whether thrones or powers or rulers or authorities; all things were created by him and for him. [17]He is before all things, and in him all things hold together.

Heb 1:2 but in these last days he has spoken to us by his Son, whom he appointed heir of all things, and through whom he made the universe.

Heb 1:10 He also says, "In the beginning, O Lord, you laid the foundations of the earth, and the heavens are the work of your hands.

Rev 3:14 "To the angel of the church in Laodicea write: These are the words of the Amen, the faithful and true witness, the ruler of God's creation.

Death of: (Jn 12:32-33; Ac 5:30; 7:52; Heb 2:14)

Heb 12:2 Let us fix our eyes on Jesus, the author and perfecter of our faith, who for the joy set before him endured the cross, scorning its shame, and sat down at the right hand of the throne of God.

Heb 12:24 to Jesus the mediator of a new covenant, and to the sprinkled blood that speaks a better word than the blood of Abel.

Rev 5:12 In a loud voice they sang: "Worthy is the Lamb, who was slain, to receive power and wealth and wisdom and strength and honor and glory and praise!"

Rev 13:8 All inhabitants of the earth will worship the beast—all whose names have not been written in the book of life belonging to the Lamb that was slain from the creation of the world.

Death foretold by God—

Ge 3:15 And I will put enmity between you and the woman, and between your offspring and hers; he will crush your head, and you will strike his heel." (+Heb 2:14)

By the psalmist—

Ps 22:1 My God, my God, why have you forsaken me? Why are you so far from saving me, so far from the words of my groaning? (+Ps 22:17)

Ps 22:18 They divide my garments among them and cast lots for my clothing. (+Mt 27:46; Mk 15:34; Ps 22:17; Mt

27:36; Lk 23:35; Ps 22:18; Mt 27:35; Mk 15:24; Lk 23:34; Jn 19:23-24; Ps 34:20; Jn 19:36; Ps 69:21; Mt 27:34,48; Mk 15:36; Lk 23:36; Jn 19:28-30)

By Isaiah—

Isa 52:14 Just as there were many who were appalled at him—his appearance was so disfigured beyond that of any man and his form marred beyond human likeness—

Isa 53:7 He was oppressed and afflicted, yet he did not open his mouth; he was led like a lamb to the slaughter, and as a sheep before her shearers is silent, so he did not open his mouth. **8**By oppression and judgment he was taken away. And who can speak of his descendants? For he was cut off from the land of the living; for the transgression of my people he was stricken. **9**He was assigned a grave with the wicked, and with the rich in his death, though he had done no violence, nor was any deceit in his mouth.

10Yet it was the LORD's will to crush him and cause him to suffer, and though the LORD makes his life a guilt offering, he will see his offspring and prolong his days, and the will of the LORD will prosper in his hand. **11**After the suffering of his soul, he will see the light [of life] and be satisfied; by his knowledge my righteous servant will justify many, and he will bear their iniquities. **12**Therefore I will give him a portion among the great, and he will divide the spoils with the strong, because he poured out his life unto death, and was numbered with the transgressors. For he bore the sin of many, and made intercession for transgressors.

By Zechariah—

Zec 13:7 "Awake, O sword, against my shepherd, against the man who is close to me!" declares the LORD Almighty. "Strike the shepherd, and the sheep will be scattered, and I will turn my hand against the little ones.

By Jesus himself—

Mt 12:40 For as Jonah was three days and three nights in the belly of a huge fish, so the Son of Man will be three days and three nights in the heart of the earth.

Mt 16:4 A wicked and adulterous generation looks for a miraculous sign, but none will be given it except the sign of Jonah." Jesus then left them and went away.

Mt 16:21 From that time on Jesus began to explain to his disciples that he must go to Jerusalem and suffer many things at the hands of the elders, chief priests and teachers of the law, and that he must be killed and on the third day be raised to life.

Mt 17:12 But I tell you, Elijah has already come, and they did not recognize him, but have done to him everything they wished. In the same way the Son of Man is going to suffer at their hands." **13**Then the disciples understood that he was talking to them about John the Baptist.

Mt 17:22 When they came together in Galilee, he said to them, "The Son of Man is going to be betrayed into the hands of men. **23**They will kill him, and on the third day he will be raised to life." And the disciples were filled with grief.

Mt 20:17 Now as Jesus was going up to Jerusalem, he took the twelve disciples aside and said to them, **18**"We are going up to Jerusalem, and the Son of Man will be betrayed to the chief priests and the teachers of the law. They will condemn him to death **19**and will turn him over

to the Gentiles to be mocked and flogged and crucified. On the third day he will be raised to life!"

Mt 21:33 "Listen to another parable: There was a landowner who planted a vineyard. He put a wall around it, dug a winepress in it and built a watchtower. Then he rented the vineyard to some farmers and went away on a journey. **34**When the harvest time approached, he sent his servants to the tenants to collect his fruit.

35"The tenants seized his servants; they beat one, killed another, and stoned a third. **36**Then he sent other servants to them, more than the first time, and the tenants treated them the same way. **37**Last of all, he sent his son to them. 'They will respect my son,' he said.

38"But when the tenants saw the son, they said to each other, 'This is the heir. Come, let's kill him and take his inheritance.' **39**So they took him and threw him out of the vineyard and killed him.

Mt 26:2 "As you know, the Passover is two days away—and the Son of Man will be handed over to be crucified."

Mt 26:12 When she poured this perfume on my body, she did it to prepare me for burial.

Mt 26:18 He replied, "Go into the city to a certain man and tell him, 'The Teacher says: My appointed time is near. I am going to celebrate the Passover with my disciples at your house.'"

Mk 8:31 He then began to teach them that the Son of Man must suffer many things and be rejected by the elders, chief priests and teachers of the law, and that he must be killed and after three days rise again.

Mk 9:31 because he was teaching his disciples. He said to them, "The Son of Man is going to be betrayed into the hands of men. They will kill him, and after three days he will rise." (+Mk 10:32)

Mk 10:33 "We are going up to Jerusalem," he said, "and the Son of Man will be betrayed to the chief priests and teachers of the law. They will condemn him to death and will hand him over to the Gentiles, **34**who will mock him and spit on him, flog him and kill him. Three days later he will rise." (+Mk 14:8-9)

Lk 9:22 And he said, "The Son of Man must suffer many things and be rejected by the elders, chief priests and teachers of the law, and he must be killed and on the third day be raised to life."

Lk 9:44 "Listen carefully to what I am about to tell you: The Son of Man is going to be betrayed into the hands of men."

Lk 12:50 But I have a baptism to undergo, and how distressed I am until it is completed!

Lk 17:25 But first he must suffer many things and be rejected by this generation. (+Lk 18:31-33)

Lk 22:15 And he said to them, "I have eagerly desired to eat this Passover with you before I suffer. (+Lk 22:21)

Lk 22:37 It is written: 'And he was numbered with the transgressors'; and I tell you that this must be fulfilled in me. Yes, what is written about me is reaching its fulfillment."

Jn 2:19 Jesus answered them, "Destroy this temple, and I will raise it again in three days."

Jn 2:21 But the temple he had spoken of was his body.

Jn 10:11 "I am the good shepherd. The good shepherd lays down his life for the sheep.

Jn 10:15 just as the Father knows me and I know the Father—and I lay down my life for the sheep.

Jn 10:17 The reason my Father loves me is that I lay down my life—only to take it up again. **18**No one takes it from me, but I lay it down of my own accord. I have authority to

By Jesus himself—

Mt 26:31 Then Jesus told them, "This very night you will all fall away on account of me, for it is written: "'I will strike the shepherd, and the sheep of the flock will be scattered.'

lay it down and authority to take it up again. This command I received from my Father."

Jn 12:7 "Leave her alone," Jesus replied. "[It was intended] that she should save this perfume for the day of my burial. (+Jn 12:24)

Jn 12:32 But I, when I am lifted up from the earth, will draw all men to myself." [33]He said this to show the kind of death he was going to die.

[34]The crowd spoke up, "We have heard from the Law that the Christ will remain forever, so how can you say, 'The Son of Man must be lifted up'? Who is this 'Son of Man'?"

Jn 14:19 Before long, the world will not see me anymore, but you will see me. Because I live, you also will live.

Jn 18:11 Jesus commanded Peter, "Put your sword away! Shall I not drink the cup the Father has given me?"

Paul's testimony concerning Jesus' death—

Ac 17:3 explaining and proving that the Christ had to suffer and rise from the dead. "This Jesus I am proclaiming to you is the Christ," he said.

Ac 26:22 But I have had God's help to this very day, and so I stand here and testify to small and great alike. I am saying nothing beyond what the prophets and Moses said would happen— [23]that the Christ would suffer and, as the first to rise from the dead, would proclaim light to his own people and to the Gentiles."

1Co 1:17 For Christ did not send me to baptize, but to preach the gospel—not with words of human wisdom, lest the cross of Christ be emptied of its power.

[18]For the message of the cross is foolishness to those who are perishing, but to us who are being saved it is the power of God.

1Co 1:23 but we preach Christ crucified: a stumbling block to Jews and foolishness to Gentiles, [24]but to those whom God has called, both Jews and Greeks, Christ the power of God and the wisdom of God.

1Co 2:2 For I resolved to know nothing while I was with you except Jesus Christ and him crucified.

1Co 15:3 For what I received I passed on to you as of first importance: that Christ died for our sins according to the Scriptures, [4]that he was buried, that he was raised on the third day according to the Scriptures,

2Co 4:10 We always carry around in our body the death of Jesus, so that the life of Jesus may also be revealed in our body. [11]For we who are alive are always being given over to death for Jesus' sake, so that his life may be revealed in our mortal body.

2Co 13:4 For to be sure, he was crucified in weakness, yet he lives by God's power. Likewise, we are weak in him, yet by God's power we will live with him to serve you.

Gal 3:1 You foolish Galatians! Who has bewitched you? Before your very eyes Jesus Christ was clearly portrayed as crucified. (+1Th 2:15)

1Th 4:14 We believe that Jesus died and rose again and so we believe that God will bring with Jesus those who have fallen asleep in him.

See above, History of, for Circumstances of the Death of.

Purpose of His Death:

To make reconciliation—

Ro 5:6 You see, at just the right time, when we were still powerless, Christ died for the ungodly. [7]Very rarely will anyone die for a righteous man, though for a good man someone might possibly dare to die. [8]But God demonstrates his own love for us in this: While we were still sinners, Christ died for us.

[9]Since we have now been justified by his blood, how much more shall we be saved from God's wrath through him! [10]For if, when we were God's enemies, we were reconciled to him through the death of his Son, how much more, having been reconciled, shall we be saved through his life! [11]Not only is this so, but we also rejoice in God through our Lord Jesus Christ, through whom we have now received reconciliation.

Eph 2:13 But now in Christ Jesus you who once were far away have been brought near through the blood of Christ.

[14]For he himself is our peace, who has made the two one and has destroyed the barrier, the dividing wall of hostility, [15]by abolishing in his flesh the law with its commandments and regulations. His purpose was to create in himself one new man out of the two, thus making peace, [16]and in this one body to reconcile both of them to God through the cross, by which he put to death their hostility.

To redeem—

Isa 53:4 Surely he took up our infirmities and carried our sorrows, yet we considered him stricken by God, smitten by him, and afflicted. [5]But he was pierced for our transgressions, he was crushed for our iniquities; the punishment that brought us peace was upon him, and by his wounds we are healed. [6]We all, like sheep, have gone astray, each of us has turned to his own way; and the LORD has laid on him the iniquity of us all.

Isa 53:8 By oppression and judgment he was taken away. And who can speak of his descendants? For he was cut off from the land of the living; for the transgression of my people he was stricken.

Isa 53:10 Yet it was the LORD's will to crush him and cause him to suffer, and though the LORD makes his life a guilt offering, he will see his offspring and prolong his days, and the will of the LORD will prosper in his hand. [11]After the suffering of his soul, he will see the light [of life] and be satisfied; by his knowledge my righteous servant will justify many, and he will bear their iniquities. [12]Therefore I will give him a portion among the great, and he will divide the spoils with the strong, because he poured out his life unto death, and was numbered with the transgressors. For he bore the sin of many, and made intercession for the transgressors.

Mt 20:28 just as the Son of Man did not come to be served, but to serve, and to give his life as a ransom for many."

Mt 26:28 This is my blood of the covenant, which is poured out for many for the forgiveness of sins.

Mk 10:45 For even the Son of Man did not come to be served, but to serve, and to give his life as a ransom for many."

Mk 14:24 "This is my blood of the covenant, which is poured out for many," he said to them.

Jn 6:51 I am the living bread that came down from heaven. If anyone eats of this bread, he will live forever. This bread is my flesh, which I will give for the life of the world."

Jn 10:11 "I am the good shepherd. The good shepherd lays down his life for the sheep.

Jn 10:17 The reason my Father loves me is that I lay down my life—only to take it up again.

Jn 11:49 Then one of them, named Caiaphas, who was high priest that year, spoke up, "You know nothing at all! [50]You do not realize that it is better for you that one man die for the people than that the whole nation perish."

[51]He did not say this on his own, but as high priest that year he prophesied that Jesus would die for the Jewish nation, [52]and not only for that nation but also for the

scattered children of God, to bring them together and make them one.

Ac 20:28 Keep watch over yourselves and all the flock of which the Holy Spirit has made you overseers. Be shepherds of the church of God, which he bought with his own blood.

Ac 26:23 that the Christ would suffer and, as the first to rise from the dead, would proclaim light to his own people and to the Gentiles."

Ro 3:24 and are justified freely by his grace through the redemption that came by Christ Jesus. ²⁵God presented him as a sacrifice of atonement, through faith in his blood. He did this to demonstrate his justice, because in his forbearance he had left the sins committed beforehand unpunished—

Ro 8:3 For what the law was powerless to do in that it was weakened by the sinful nature, God did by sending his own Son in the likeness of sinful man to be a sin offering. And so he condemned sin in sinful man,

Ro 8:32 He who did not spare his own Son, but gave him up for us all—how will he not also, along with him, graciously give us all things?

1Co 5:7 Get rid of the old yeast that you may be a new batch without yeast—as you really are. For Christ, our Passover lamb, has been sacrificed.

1Co 6:20 you were bought at a price. Therefore honor God with your body.

1Co 8:11 So this weak brother, for whom Christ died, is destroyed by your knowledge.

1Co 15:3 For what I received I passed on to you as of first importance: that Christ died for our sins according to the Scriptures,

Gal 1:4 who gave himself for our sins to rescue us from the present evil age, according to the will of our God and Father,

Gal 3:13 Christ redeemed us from the curse of the law by becoming a curse for us, for it is written: "Cursed is everyone who is hung on a tree."

Gal 4:4 But when the time had fully come, God sent his Son, born of a woman, born under law, ⁵to redeem those under law, that we might receive the full rights of sons.

Eph 1:6 to the praise of his glorious grace, which he has freely given us in the One he loves. ⁷In him we have redemption through his blood, the forgiveness of sins, in accordance with the riches of God's grace

Eph 5:2 and live a life of love, just as Christ loved us and gave himself up for us as a fragrant offering and sacrifice to God.

Eph 5:25 Husbands, love your wives, just as Christ loved the church and gave himself up for her ²⁶to make her holy, cleansing her by the washing with water through the word, ²⁷and to present her to himself as a radiant church, without stain or wrinkle or any other blemish, but holy and blameless.

Col 1:14 in whom we have redemption, the forgiveness of sins.

Col 1:20 and through him to reconcile to himself all things, whether things on earth or things in heaven, by making peace through his blood, shed on the cross.

Col 1:22 But now he has reconciled you by Christ's physical body through death to present you holy in his sight, without blemish and free from accusation—

Col 2:14 having canceled the written code, with its regulations, that was against us and that stood opposed to us; he took it away, nailing it to the cross. ¹⁵And having disarmed

the powers and authorities, he made a public spectacle of them, triumphing over them by the cross.

1Th 1:10 and to wait for his Son from heaven, whom he raised from the dead—Jesus, who rescues us from the coming wrath.

1Ti 2:6 who gave himself as a ransom for all men—the testimony given in its proper time.

Tit 2:14 who gave himself for us to redeem us from all wickedness and to purify for himself a people that are his very own, eager to do what is good.

Heb 2:9 But we see Jesus, who was made a little lower than the angels, now crowned with glory and honor because he suffered death, so that by the grace of God he might taste death for everyone.

¹⁰In bringing many sons to glory, it was fitting that God, for whom and through whom everything exists, should make the author of their salvation perfect through suffering.

Heb 2:14 Since the children have flesh and blood, he too shared in their humanity so that by his death he might destroy him who holds the power of death—that is, the devil— ¹⁵and free those who all their lives were held in slavery by their fear of death.

Heb 2:18 Because he himself suffered when he was tempted, he is able to help those who are being tempted.

Heb 7:27 Unlike the other high priests, he does not need to offer sacrifices day after day, first for his own sins, and then for the sins of the people. He sacrificed for their sins once for all when he offered himself.

Heb 9:12 He did not enter by means of the blood of goats and calves; but he entered the Most Holy Place once for all by his own blood, having obtained eternal redemption. ¹³The blood of goats and bulls and the ashes of a heifer sprinkled on those who are ceremonially unclean sanctify them so that they are outwardly clean. ¹⁴How much more, then, will the blood of Christ, who through the eternal Spirit offered himself unblemished to God, cleanse our consciences from acts that lead to death, so that we may serve the living God!

¹⁵For this reason Christ is the mediator of a new covenant, that those who are called may receive the promised eternal inheritance—now that he has died as a ransom to set them free from the sins committed under the first covenant.

¹⁶In the case of a will, it is necessary to prove the death of the one who made it, ¹⁷because a will is in force only when somebody has died; it never takes effect while the one who made it is living.

Heb 9:25 Nor did he enter heaven to offer himself again and again, the way the high priest enters the Most Holy Place every year with blood that is not his own. ²⁶Then Christ would have had to suffer many times since the creation of the world. But now he has appeared once for all at the end of the ages to do away with sin by the sacrifice of himself.

Heb 9:28 so Christ was sacrificed once to take away the sins of many people; and he will appear a second time, not to bear sin, but to bring salvation to those who are waiting for him.

Heb 10:10 And by that will, we have been made holy through the sacrifice of the body of Jesus Christ once for all.

Heb 10:12 But when this priest had offered for all time one sacrifice for sins, he sat down at the right hand of God.

Heb 10:14 because by one sacrifice he has made perfect forever those who are being made holy.

Heb 10:17 Then he adds: "Their sins and lawless acts I will remember no more."

[18]And where these have been forgiven, there is no longer any sacrifice for sin.

[19]Therefore, brothers, since we have confidence to enter the Most Holy Place by the blood of Jesus, [20]by a new and living way opened for us through the curtain, that is, his body,

1Pe 1:18 For you know that it was not with perishable things such as silver or gold that you were redeemed from the empty way of life handed down to you from your forefathers, [19]but with the precious blood of Christ, a lamb without blemish or defect.

1Pe 2:21 To this you were called, because Christ suffered for you, leaving you an example, that you should follow in his steps.

1Pe 2:24 He himself bore our sins in his body on the tree, so that we might die to sins and live for righteousness; by his wounds you have been healed.

1Pe 3:18 For Christ died for sins once for all, the righteous for the unrighteous, to bring you to God. He was put to death in the body but made alive by the Spirit,

1Jn 2:2 He is the atoning sacrifice for our sins, and not only for ours but also for the sins of the whole world.

1Jn 3:16 This is how we know what love is: Jesus Christ laid down his life for us. And we ought to lay down our lives for our brothers.

1Jn 4:10 This is love: not that we loved God, but that he loved us and sent his Son as an atoning sacrifice for our sins.

Rev 1:5 and from Jesus Christ, who is the faithful witness, the firstborn from the dead, and the ruler of the kings of the earth.

To him who loves us and has freed us from our sins by his blood, [6]and has made us to be a kingdom and priests to serve his God and Father—to him be glory and power for ever and ever! Amen.

Rev 5:9 And they sang a new song: "You are worthy to take the scroll and to open its seals, because you were slain, and with your blood you purchased men for God from every tribe and language and people and nation. [10]You have made them to be a kingdom and priests to serve our God, and they will reign on the earth."

Rev 13:8 All inhabitants of the earth will worship the beast—all whose names have not been written in the book of life belonging to the Lamb that was slain from the creation of the world.

To purge sins—

Zec 13:1 "On that day a fountain will be opened to the house of David and the inhabitants of Jerusalem, to cleanse them from sin and impurity. (+Lk 24:46-47)

Jn 1:29 The next day John saw Jesus coming toward him and said, "Look, the Lamb of God, who takes away the sin of the world!

Heb 1:3 The Son is the radiance of God's glory and the exact representation of his being, sustaining all things by his powerful word. After he had provided purification for sins, he sat down at the right hand of the Majesty in heaven.

Heb 13:11 The high priest carries the blood of animals into the Most Holy Place as a sin offering, but the bodies are burned outside the camp. [12]And so Jesus also suffered outside the city gate to make the people holy through his own blood.

1Jn 1:7 But if we walk in the light, as he is in the light, we have fellowship with one another, and the blood of Jesus, his Son, purifies us from all sin.

Rev 7:14 I answered, "Sir, you know."

And he said, "These are they who have come out of the great tribulation; they have washed their robes and made them white in the blood of the Lamb. [15]Therefore,

"they are before the throne of God and serve him day and night in his temple; and he who sits on the throne will spread his tent over them.

To secure forgiveness—

Ac 5:30 The God of our fathers raised Jesus from the dead—whom you had killed by hanging him on a tree. [31]God exalted him to his own right hand as Prince and Savior that he might give repentance and forgiveness of sins to Israel.

Ro 4:25 He was delivered over to death for our sins and was raised to life for our justification.

To save—

Jn 3:14 Just as Moses lifted up the snake in the desert, so the Son of Man must be lifted up, [15]that everyone who believes in him may have eternal life.

[16]"For God so loved the world that he gave his one and only Son, that whoever believes in him shall not perish but have eternal life. [17]For God did not send his Son into the world to condemn the world, but to save the world through him.

Ro 6:3 Or don't you know that all of us who were baptized into Christ Jesus were baptized into his death? [4]We were therefore buried with him through baptism into death in order that, just as Christ was raised from the dead through the glory of the Father, we too may live a new life.

[5]If we have been united with him like this in his death, we will certainly also be united with him in his resurrection.

Ro 6:9 For we know that since Christ was raised from the dead, he cannot die again; death no longer has mastery over him. [10]The death he died, he died to sin once for all; but the life he lives, he lives to God.

Ro 14:9 For this very reason, Christ died and returned to life so that he might be the Lord of both the dead and the living.

Ro 14:15 If your brother is distressed because of what you eat, you are no longer acting in love. Do not by your eating destroy your brother for whom Christ died.

2Co 5:14 For Christ's love compels us, because we are convinced that one died for all, and therefore all died. [15]And he died for all, that those who live should no longer live for themselves but for him who died for them and was raised again.

2Co 5:19 that God was reconciling the world to himself in Christ, not counting men's sins against them. And he has committed to us the message of reconciliation.

2Co 5:21 God made him who had no sin to be sin for us, so that in him we might become the righteousness of God.

2Co 8:9 For you know the grace of our Lord Jesus Christ, that though he was rich, yet for your sakes he became poor, so that you through his poverty might become rich.

Gal 2:20 I have been crucified with Christ and I no longer live, but Christ lives in me. The life I live in the body, I live by faith in the Son of God, who loved me and gave himself for me.

1Th 5:9 For God did not appoint us to suffer wrath but to receive salvation through our Lord Jesus Christ. [10]He died for us so that, whether we are awake or asleep, we may live together with him.

Vicarious death of—

Isa 53:4 Surely he took up our infirmities and carried our sorrows, yet we considered him stricken by God, smitten by him, and afflicted. ⁵But he was pierced for our transgressions, he was crushed for our iniquities; the punishment that brought us peace was upon him, and by his wounds we are healed. ⁶We all, like sheep, have gone astray, each of us has turned to his own way; and the LORD has laid on him the iniquity of us all.

⁷He was oppressed and afflicted, yet he did not open his mouth; he was led like a lamb to the slaughter, and as a sheep before her shearers is silent, so he did not open his mouth. ⁸By oppression and judgment he was taken away. And who can speak of his descendants? For he was cut off from the land of the living; for the transgression of my people he was stricken. ⁹He was assigned a grave with the wicked, and with the rich in his death, though he had done no violence, nor was any deceit in his mouth.

¹⁰Yet it was the LORD's will to crush him and cause him to suffer, and though the LORD makes his life a guilt offering, he will see his offspring and prolong his days, and the will of the LORD will prosper in his hand. ¹¹After the suffering of his soul, he will see the light [of life] and be satisfied; by his knowledge my righteous servant will justify many, and he will bear their iniquities. ¹²Therefore I will give him a portion among the great, and he will divide the spoils with the strong, because he poured out his life unto death, and was numbered with the transgressors. For he bore the sin of many, and made intercession for the transgressors. (+Mt 20:28; Jn 6:51; 11:49,51; Gal 3:13; Eph 5:2; 1Th 5:9-10; Heb 2:9; 1Pe 2:24)

Vicarious death of, typified—

Ex 29:11 Slaughter it in the LORD's presence at the entrance to the Tent of Meeting.

Ex 29:15 "Take one of the rams, and Aaron and his sons shall lay their hands on its head. ¹⁶Slaughter it and take the blood and sprinkle it against the altar on all sides.

Ex 29:20 Slaughter it, take some of its blood and put it on the lobes of the right ears of Aaron and his sons, on the thumbs of their right hands, and on the big toes of their right feet. Then sprinkle blood against the altar on all sides.

Ex 29:38 "This is what you are to offer on the altar regularly each day: two lambs a year old. ³⁹Offer one in the morning and the other at twilight. ⁴⁰With the first lamb offer a tenth of an ephah of fine flour mixed with a quarter of a hin of oil from pressed olives, and a quarter of a hin of wine as a drink offering. ⁴¹Sacrifice the other lamb at twilight with the same grain offering and its drink offering as in the morning—a pleasing aroma, an offering made to the LORD by fire.

⁴²"For the generations to come this burnt offering is to be made regularly at the entrance to the Tent of Meeting before the LORD. There I will meet you and speak to you; (+Lev 1:5,11,15; 3:2,8,13; 4:4,15,24,29; 6:25; 7:2; 8:15,19; 9:8,15,18-19,23-24; 14:13,19,25; 2Ch 29:22,24; 30:15; 35:1)

See Atonement; Redemption.

Voluntary death of—

Isa 50:6 I offered my back to those who beat me, my cheeks to those who pulled out my beard; I did not hide my face from mocking and spitting.

Isa 53:12 Therefore I will give him a portion among the great, and he will divide the spoils with the strong, because he poured out his life unto death, and was numbered with the transgressors. For he bore the sin of many, and made

intercession for the transgressors. (+Lk 9:51; 12:50; 22:15,42)

Jn 10:17 The reason my Father loves me is that I lay down my life—only to take it up again. ¹⁸No one takes it from me, but I lay it down of my own accord. I have authority to lay it down and authority to take it up again. This command I received from my Father." (+Jn 18:5,8,11)

Php 2:8 And being found in appearance as a man, he humbled himself and became obedient to death—even death on a cross! (+Heb 7:27; 9:26; 1Jn 3:16)

Divine Sonship of:

Testified to: By God, at his baptism (Mt 3:17; Mk 1:11; Lk 3:22), at the transfiguration (Mt 17:5; Mk 9:7; Lk 9:35; 2Pe 1:17), in his commandment to believe in (1Jn 3:23).

Testified to: By himself (Mt 11:27; Lk 10:22; Mt 26:63-64; 27:43)—

Mk 14:61 But Jesus remained silent and gave no answer. Again the high priest asked him, "Are you the Christ, the Son of the Blessed One?"

⁶²"I am," said Jesus. "And you will see the Son of Man sitting at the right hand of the Mighty One and coming on the clouds of heaven." (+Lk 22:70)

Jn 3:16 "For God so loved the world that he gave his one and only Son, that whoever believes in him shall not perish but have eternal life. ¹⁷For God did not send his Son into the world to condemn the world, but to save the world through him. ¹⁸Whoever believes in him is not condemned, but whoever does not believe stands condemned already because he has not believed in the name of God's one and only Son.

Jn 3:34 For the one whom God has sent speaks the words of God, for God gives the Spirit without limit. ³⁵The Father loves the Son and has placed everything in his hands. ³⁶Whoever believes in the Son has eternal life, but whoever rejects the Son will not see life, for God's wrath remains on him." (+Jn 6:27,40,46,57)

Jn 9:35 Jesus heard that they had thrown him out, and when he found him, he said, "Do you believe in the Son of Man?"

³⁶"Who is he, sir?" the man asked. "Tell me so that I may believe in him."

³⁷Jesus said, "You have now seen him; in fact, he is the one speaking with you." (+Jn 11:4; 19:7)

Testified to: By the disciples (Mt 14:33; 1Jn 4:14), unclean spirits (Mt 8:29; Mk 3:11; 5:7, w Lk 8:28; Lk 4:41), Mark (Mk 1:1), John the Baptist (Jn 1:34), John the apostle (Jn 1:14,18; 1Jn 1:7; 2:22-24; 3:8,23; 4:9,10,14; 5:5,9-13,20; 2Jn 3; Rev 2:18), Nathanael (Jn 1:49), Martha (Jn 11:27), the centurion (Mt 27:54; Mk 15:39), Peter (Ac 3:13; 13:33), Paul (Ro 1:3-4,9; 8:3,29,32; 1Co 1:9; 15:24,27-28; 2Co 1:3,19; Gal 1:16; 4:4; Eph 1:3; Col 1:3; 1Th 1:10), the author of Hebrews (Heb 1:1-3,5; 4:14; 5:5,8; 6:6; 7:3; 10:29).

Declared God to be his Father (Mt 15:13; 18:10,19; 20:23; 26:53,63-64; Lk 10:22; 22:29; Jn 5:19-21,23,26-27, 30,36-37; 8:16,19,26-29,38,49,54; 10:15,17-18,29-30,36-38; 11:41; 12:49-50; 13:3; 14:7,9-11,13,16,20-21,23-24, 28,31; 15:1,8-10,15,23-24; 16:15,27-28,32; 17:1-26; 20:17,21).

Peter's confession of (Mt 16:15-17).

Prophecies concerning (Ps 2:7; Lk 1:32,35).

Worshiped by the disciples as the Son of God (Mt 14:33).

See below, Deity of; Relation of, to the Father; Son of God; Son of Man.

Deity of:

Indicated by the titles ascribed to him, as: Immanuel (Isa 7:14, w Mt 1:23)

First and Last (Rev 1:17)—

Rev 22:13 I am the Alpha and the Omega, the First and the Last, the Beginning and the End.

God (Ps 102:24-27, w Heb 1:10-13; Jn 1:1; 20:28; Ro 9:5; 1Jn 5:20-21), God and Savior Jesus Christ (2Pe 1:1)

God our Savior—

Tit 2:13 while we wait for the blessed hope—the glorious appearing of our great God and Savior, Jesus Christ,

Holy One (Ac 3:14)

Lord of lords and King of kings—

Rev 17:14 They will make war against the Lamb, but the Lamb will overcome them because he is Lord of lords and King of kings—and with him will be his called, chosen and faithful followers."

Lord (Ps 110:1; Mt 22:42-45)—

Isa 40:3 A voice of one calling: "In the desert prepare the way for the LORD; make straight in the wilderness a high-way for our God.

Mt 3:3 This is he who was spoken of through the prophet Isaiah: "A voice of one calling in the desert, 'Prepare the way for the Lord, make straight paths for him.'"

Ac 20:28 Keep watch over yourselves and all the flock of which the Holy Spirit has made you overseers. Be shep-herds of the church of God, which he bought with his own blood.

Lord Almighty—

Isa 8:13 The LORD Almighty is the one you are to regard as holy, he is the one you are to fear, he is the one you are to dread, [14]and he will be a sanctuary; but for both houses of Israel he will be a stone that causes men to stumble and a rock that makes them fall. And for the people of Jerusa-lem he will be a trap and a snare. (+1Pe 2:8)

My Lord and My God (Jn 20:28)

Lord of all—

Ac 10:36 You know the message God sent to the people of Israel, telling the good news of peace through Jesus Christ, who is Lord of all.

Ro 10:12 For there is no difference between Jew and Gentile—the same Lord is Lord of all and richly blesses all who call on him,

Mighty God—

Isa 9:6 For to us a child is born, to us a son is given, and the government will be on his shoulders. And he will be called Wonderful Counselor, Mighty God, Everlasting Father, Prince of Peace.

Only born of the Father (Jn 1:14,18; 3:16,18; 1Jn 4:9), Son of God (Mt 26:63-67; Mk 1:1; 15:39; 1Co 1:9; 2Co 1:19; Gal 2:20; Eph 4:13; Heb 1:2; 2Pe 1:17; 1Jn 1:2-3; 3:23; 5:10,12-13,20), Son of Man (Da 7:13-14; Mt 11:19; 12:8). *See above, Divine Sonship of; below, Son of God; Son of Man.*

Deity of, As Yahweh (Isa 40:3; Mt 3:3)

King or LORD of glory (Ps 24:7)—

Ps 24:10 Who is he, this King of glory? The LORD Al-mighty—he is the King of glory. *Selah* (+1Co 2:8; Jas 2:1)

The LORD our righteousness (Jer 23:5-6; 1Co 1:30), The LORD all (Ps 97:9; Jn 3:31), The First and the last, the Alpha and the Omega (Isa 44:6, w Rev 1:17; Isa 48:12-16, w Rev 22:13)

Yahweh's fellow and equal (Zec 13:7)—

Php 2:6 Who, being in very nature God, did not consider equality with God something to be grasped,

LORD Almighty—

Isa 6:1 In the year that King Uzziah died, I saw the Lord seated on a throne, high and exalted, and the train of his robe filled the temple. (+Isa 6:2-3 w Jn 12:41; Isa 8:13-14 w 1Pe 2:8)

LORD (Ps 110:1; Mt 22:42)—

Mt 22:43 He said to them, "How is it then that David, speaking by the Spirit, calls him 'Lord'? For he says,

[44]" 'The Lord said to my Lord:

"Sit at my right hand until I put your enemies under your feet." '

[45]If then David calls him 'Lord,' how can he be his son?"

Yahweh the Shepherd—

Isa 40:10 See, the Sovereign LORD comes with power, and his arm rules for him. See, his reward is with him, and his recompense accompanies him. [11]He tends his flock like a shepherd: He gathers the lambs in his arms and carries them close to his heart; he gently leads those that have young. (+Heb 13:20)

LORD, for whose glory all things were created (Pr 16:4; Col 1:16)

Lord the messenger of the covenant—

Mal 3:1 "See, I will send my messenger, who will prepare the way before me. Then suddenly the Lord you are seek-ing will come to his temple; the messenger of the cove-nant, whom you desire, will come," says the LORD Almighty. (+Lk 7:27)

Invoked as LORD (Joel 2:32; 1Co 1:2)

As the eternal God and Creator (Ps 102:24-27)—

Heb 1:8 But about the Son he says, "Your throne, O God, will last for ever and ever, and righteousness will be the scepter of your kingdom.

Heb 1:10 He also says, "In the beginning, O Lord, you laid the foundations of the earth, and the heavens are the work of your hands. (+Heb 1:11-12)

The Mighty God (Isa 9:6), the great God and Savior (Hos 1:7, w Tit 2:13), God over all (Ro 9:5), God the Judge (Ecc 12:14, w 1Co 4:5; 2Co 5:10; 2Ti 4:1), Im-manuel (Isa 7:14, w Mt 1:23), Lord of lords and King of kings (Da 10:17, w Rev 1:5; 17:14), the Holy and Right-eous One (1Sa 2:2, w Ac 3:14)

The Lord from heaven—

1Co 15:47 The first man was of the dust of the earth, the second man from heaven.

Lord of the Sabbath (Ge 2:3, w Mt 12:8), Lord of all (Ac 10:36; Ro 10:11-13). Son of God (Mt 26:63-67), the only born Son of the Father (Jn 1:14,18; 3:16,18; 1Jn 4:9). His blood is called the blood of God (Ac 20:28). One with the Father (Jn 10:30,38; 12:45; 14:7-10; 17:10). As sending the Spirit equally with the Father (Jn 14:16, w Jn 15:26). As unsearchable equally with the Father (Pr 30:4; Mt 11:27). As Creator of all things (Isa 40:28; Jn 1:3; Col 1:16), supporter and preserver of all things (Ne 9:6, w Col 1:17; Heb 1:3). Acknowledged by Old Testament saints (Ge 17:1, w 48:15-16; 32:24-30, w Hos 12:3-5; Jdg 6:22-24; 13:21-22; Job 19:25-27).

Is one with the Father (Jn 5:17-18,23; 10:30,33,38; 12:45; 14:7-11; 17:11,21-22).

Sends the Holy Spirit equally with the Father (Jn 14:16).

Identical with the Adonay (Lord) of the Old Testament (Jn 12:40-41, w Isa 6:8-11), and the Yahweh (LORD) of the Old Testament (Jn 19:37, w Zec 12:10).

Testimony concerning his deity: By the Father (Jn 5:32,34,37; 6:27; 8:18; Ac 13:33; 1Jn 5:9), at his baptism

(Mt 3:16-17; Mk 1:11; Lk 3:22), at his transfiguration (Mt 17:5; Mk 9:7; Lk 9:35; 2Pe 1:17).

By Jesus concerning himself (Jn 5:18,31,36; 8:18,42; 10:33,36,38; 12:45; 14:11-13; 16:27-28; 17:5,8,24-25; 19:7), to Peter and other disciples (Mt 16:16-17; Mk 8:29-30; Lk 9:20-21), to the Jews (Mt 22:43-44; Jn 5:23; 10:30,33,36,38; 12:45), to his disciples (Jn 16:27-28), to the restored blind man (Jn 9:35-37), to Philip (Jn 14:7-11,20), to Caiaphas (Mt 26:63-64; Mk 14:61-62; Lk 22:67-70), to Pilate (Jn 18:36-37; 1Ti 6:13).

By the angel, to Joseph (Mt 1:23), to Mary (Lk 1:32,35). John the Baptist (Jn 1:29-34; 5:33). John, the apostle (Jn 1:14,18; 13:3; 1Jn 2:22-24). The disciples (Jn 16:30). Paul (Ac 9:20). The author of the epistle to the Hebrews (Heb 11:26). The Scriptures (Jn 5:39). Thomas (Jn 20:28). Demons (Mt 8:29; Mk 1:23-24; 3:11; 5:6-7; Lk 4:34,41).

Has power to forgive sins (Mt 1:21; 9:6; Mk 2:5; Lk 5:20; Col 3:13).

Paul's apostleship from (Gal 1:1).

Invoked with the Father and the Spirit in benedictions—
Ro 1:7 To all in Rome who are loved by God and called to be saints: Grace and peace to you from God our Father and from the Lord Jesus Christ. (+1Co 1:3; 2Co 1:2)

Gal 1:3 Grace and peace to you from God our Father and the Lord Jesus Christ, (+Eph 1:2)

Eph 6:23 Peace to the brothers, and love with faith from God the Father and the Lord Jesus Christ. (+Eph 6:24; 1Th 1:1)

1Th 3:11 Now may our God and Father himself and our Lord Jesus clear the way for us to come to you. (+2Th 1:1-2)

2Th 2:16 May our Lord Jesus Christ himself and God our Father, who loved us and by his grace gave us eternal encouragement and good hope, ¹⁷encourage your hearts and strengthen you in every good deed and word. (+2Ti 1:2)

All power given to (Mt 28:17-18).

Eternity ascribed to (Jn 1:1-2; 1Jn 1:1). *See below, Eternity of.*

Is judge (2Co 5:10). *See below, Judge.*

Eternity of:

Called everlasting Father—
Isa 9:6 For to us a child is born, to us a son is given, and the government will be on his shoulders. And he will be called Wonderful Counselor, Mighty God, Everlasting Father, Prince of Peace.

Was before creation—
Jn 1:1 In the beginning was the Word, and the Word was with God, and the Word was God. ²He was with God in the beginning.

Jn 1:15 John testifies concerning him. He cries out, saying, "This was he of whom I said, 'He who comes after me has surpassed me because he was before me.'"

Jn 17:5 And now, Father, glorify me in your presence with the glory I had with you before the world began.

Jn 17:24 "Father, I want those you have given me to be with me where I am, and to see my glory, the glory you have given me because you loved me before the creation of the world.

Col 1:17 He is before all things, and in him all things hold together.

2Ti 1:9 who has saved us and called us to a holy life—not because of anything we have done but because of his own purpose and grace. This grace was given us in Christ Jesus before the beginning of time,

Was from the beginning—
1Jn 2:13 I write to you, fathers, because you have known him who is from the beginning. I write to you, young men, because you have overcome the evil one. I write to you, dear children, because you have known the Father.

Was from everlasting—
Mic 5:2 "But you, Bethlehem Ephrathah, though you are small among the clans of Judah, out of you will come for me one who will be ruler over Israel, whose origins are from of old, from ancient times."

Continues forever—
Ps 102:24 So I said: "Do not take me away, O my God, in the midst of my days; your years go on through all generations. ²⁵In the beginning you laid the foundations of the earth, and the heavens are the work of your hands. ²⁶They will perish, but you remain; they will all wear out like a garment. Like clothing you will change them and they will be discarded. ²⁷But you remain the same, and your years will never end.

Heb 1:10 He also says, "In the beginning, O Lord, you laid the foundations of the earth, and the heavens are the work of your hands. ¹¹They will perish, but you remain; they will all wear out like a garment. ¹²You will roll them up like a robe; like a garment they will be changed. But you remain the same, and your years will never end." (+Heb 1:13; Ps 110:4)

Eph 3:21 to him be glory in the church and in Christ Jesus throughout all generations, for ever and ever! Amen.

Heb 7:16 one who has become a priest not on the basis of a regulation as to his ancestry but on the basis of the power of an indestructible life.

Heb 7:24 but because Jesus lives forever, he has a permanent priesthood. ²⁵Therefore he is able to save completely those who come to God through him, because he always lives to intercede for them.

Rev 5:13 Then I heard every creature in heaven and on earth and under the earth and on the sea, and all that is in them, singing: "To him who sits on the throne and to the Lamb be praise and honor and glory and power, for ever and ever!"

¹⁴The four living creatures said, "Amen," and the elders fell down and worshiped.

The same yesterday and today and forever—
Heb 13:8 Jesus Christ is the same yesterday and today and forever.

Exaltation of:

Ps 2:8 Ask of me, and I will make the nations your inheritance, the ends of the earth your possession. ⁹You will rule them with an iron scepter; you will dash them to pieces like pottery."

Ps 68:18 When you ascended on high, you led captives in your train; you received gifts from men, even from the rebellious—that you, O LORD God, might dwell there.

Eph 4:8 This is why it says: "When he ascended on high, he led captives in his train and gave gifts to men."

In glory—
Mt 26:64 "Yes, it is as you say," Jesus replied. "But I say to all of you: In the future you will see the Son of Man sitting at the right hand of the Mighty One and coming on the clouds of heaven."

Mk 16:19 After the Lord Jesus had spoken to them, he was taken up into heaven and he sat at the right hand of God.

Lk 22:69 But from now on, the Son of Man will be seated at the right hand of the mighty God."

Lk 24:26 Did not the Christ have to suffer these things and then enter his glory?"

Jn 7:39 By this he meant the Spirit, whom those who believed in him were later to receive. Up to that time the Spirit had not been given, since Jesus had not yet been glorified.

Ac 2:33 Exalted to the right hand of God, he has received from the Father the promised Holy Spirit and has poured out what you now see and hear. [34]For David did not ascend to heaven, and yet he said, " 'The Lord said to my Lord: "Sit at my right hand

Ac 3:20 and that he may send the Christ, who has been appointed for you—even Jesus. [21]He must remain in heaven until the time comes for God to restore everything, as he promised long ago through his holy prophets.

Ac 7:55 But Stephen, full of the Holy Spirit, looked up to heaven and saw the glory of God, and Jesus standing at the right hand of God. [56]"Look," he said, "I see heaven open and the Son of Man standing at the right hand of God."

Ro 8:17 Now if we are children, then we are heirs—heirs of God and co-heirs with Christ, if indeed we share in his sufferings in order that we may also share in his glory. (+Ro 8:34)

Eph 1:20 which he exerted in Christ when he raised him from the dead and seated him at his right hand in the heavenly realms, (+Eph 1:21-22)

Eph 4:10 He who descended is the very one who ascended higher than all the heavens, in order to fill the whole universe.)

Col 3:1 Since, then, you have been raised with Christ, set your hearts on things above, where Christ is seated at the right hand of God.

1Ti 3:16 Beyond all question, the mystery of godliness is great: He appeared in a body, was vindicated by the Spirit, was seen by angels, was preached among the nations, was believed on in the world, was taken up in glory.

Heb 1:3 The Son is the radiance of God's glory and the exact representation of his being, sustaining all things by his powerful word. After he had provided purification for sins, he sat down at the right hand of the Majesty in heaven.

Heb 10:12 But when this priest had offered for all time one sacrifice for sins, he sat down at the right hand of God. [13]Since that time he waits for his enemies to be made his footstool,

Heb 12:2 Let us fix our eyes on Jesus, the author and perfecter of our faith, who for the joy set before him endured the cross, scorning its shame, and sat down at the right hand of the throne of God.

1Pe 3:22 who has gone into heaven and is at God's right hand—with angels, authorities and powers in submission to him.

Rev 3:21 To him who overcomes, I will give the right to sit with me on my throne, just as I overcame and sat down with my Father on his throne.

As Lord of heaven and earth—

Php 2:9 Therefore God exalted him to the highest place and gave him the name that is above every name, [10]that at the name of Jesus every knee should bow, in heaven and on earth and under the earth, [11]and every tongue confess that Jesus Christ is Lord, to the glory of God the Father.

Col 2:15 And having disarmed the powers and authorities, he made a public spectacle of them, triumphing over them by the cross.

As Savior—

Ac 5:31 God exalted him to his own right hand as Prince

and Savior that he might give repentance and forgiveness of sins to Israel.

As priestly mediator—

Heb 4:10 for anyone who enters God's rest also rests from his own work, just as God did from his.

Heb 4:14 Therefore, since we have a great high priest who has gone through the heavens, Jesus the Son of God, let us hold firmly to the faith we profess.

Heb 6:20 where Jesus, who went before us, has entered on our behalf. He has become a high priest forever, in the order of Melchizedek.

Heb 7:26 Such a high priest meets our need—one who is holy, blameless, pure, set apart from sinners, exalted above the heavens.

Heb 8:1 The point of what we are saying is this: We do have such a high priest, who sat down at the right hand of the throne of the Majesty in heaven,

Heb 9:24 For Christ did not enter a man-made sanctuary that was only a copy of the true one; he entered heaven itself, now to appear for us in God's presence.

An Example:

Claimed himself—

Mt 11:29 Take my yoke upon you and learn from me, for I am gentle and humble in heart, and you will find rest for your souls.

Mt 20:28 just as the Son of Man did not come to be served, but to serve, and to give his life as a ransom for many."

Mk 10:43 Not so with you. Instead, whoever wants to become great among you must be your servant, [44]and whoever wants to be first must be slave of all. [45]For even the Son of Man did not come to be served, but to serve, and to give his life as a ransom for many."

Lk 22:26 But you are not to be like that. Instead, the greatest among you should be like the youngest, and the one who rules like the one who serves. [27]For who is greater, the one who is at the table or the one who serves? Is it not the one who is at the table? But I am among you as one who serves.

Jn 10:4 When he has brought out all his own, he goes on ahead of them, and his sheep follow him because they know his voice.

Jn 13:13 "You call me 'Teacher' and 'Lord,' and rightly so, for that is what I am. [14]Now that I, your Lord and Teacher, have washed your feet, you also should wash one another's feet. [15]I have set you an example that you should do as I have done for you.

Jn 13:34 "A new command I give you: Love one another. As I have loved you, so you must love one another.

Jn 17:14 I have given them your word and the world has hated them, for they are not of the world any more than I am of the world.

Jn 17:18 As you sent me into the world, I have sent them into the world.

Jn 17:21 that all of them may be one, Father, just as you are in me and I am in you. May they also be in us so that the world may believe that you have sent me. [22]I have given them the glory that you gave me, that they may be one as we are one:

Rev 3:21 To him who overcomes, I will give the right to sit with me on my throne, just as I overcame and sat down with my Father on his throne.

Referred to by Paul—

Ro 8:29 For those God foreknew he also predestined to be conformed to the likeness of his Son, that he might be the firstborn among many brothers.

Ro 13:14 Rather, clothe yourselves with the Lord Jesus Christ, and do not think about how to gratify the desires of the sinful nature.

Ro 15:2 Each of us should please his neighbor for his good, to build him up. ³For even Christ did not please himself but, as it is written: "The insults of those who insult you have fallen on me." (+Ro 15:4)

Ro 15:5 May the God who gives endurance and encouragement give you a spirit of unity among yourselves as you follow Christ Jesus, ⁶so that with one heart and mouth you may glorify the God and Father of our Lord Jesus Christ. ⁷Accept one another, then, just as Christ accepted you, in order to bring praise to God.

2Co 4:10 We always carry around in our body the death of Jesus, so that the life of Jesus may also be revealed in our body.

2Co 8:9 For you know the grace of our Lord Jesus Christ, that though he was rich, yet for your sakes he became poor, so that you through his poverty might become rich.

2Co 10:1 By the meekness and gentleness of Christ, I appeal to you—I, Paul, who am "timid" when face to face with you, but "bold" when away!

Gal 3:27 for all of you who were baptized into Christ have clothed yourselves with Christ.

Gal 6:2 Carry each other's burdens, and in this way you will fulfill the law of Christ.

Eph 4:13 until we all reach unity in the faith and in the knowledge of the Son of God and become mature, attaining to the whole measure of the fullness of Christ.

Eph 4:15 Instead, speaking the truth in love, we will in all things grow up into him who is the Head, that is, Christ.

Eph 4:24 and to put on the new self, created to be like God in true righteousness and holiness.

Eph 5:2 and live a life of love, just as Christ loved us and gave himself up for us as a fragrant offering and sacrifice to God.

Eph 6:9 And masters, treat your slaves in the same way. Do not threaten them, since you know that he who is both their Master and yours is in heaven, and there is no favoritism with him.

Php 2:5 Your attitude should be the same as that of Christ Jesus: ⁶Who, being in very nature God, did not consider equality with God something to be grasped, ⁷but made himself nothing, taking the very nature of a servant, being made in human likeness. ⁸And being found in appearance as a man, he humbled himself and became obedient to death—even death on a cross!

Col 3:10 and have put on the new self, which is being renewed in knowledge in the image of its Creator. ¹¹Here there is no Greek or Jew, circumcised or uncircumcised, barbarian, Scythian, slave or free, but Christ is all, and is in all.

Col 3:13 Bear with each other and forgive whatever grievances you may have against one another. Forgive as the Lord forgave you.

1Th 1:6 You became imitators of us and of the Lord; in spite of severe suffering, you welcomed the message with the joy given by the Holy Spirit.

Referred to by other apostles—

Heb 3:1 Therefore, holy brothers, who share in the heavenly calling, fix your thoughts on Jesus, the apostle and high priest whom we confess.

Heb 12:2 Let us fix our eyes on Jesus, the author and perfecter of our faith, who for the joy set before him endured the cross, scorning its shame, and sat down at the right hand of the throne of God. ³Consider him who endured such opposition from sinful men, so that you will not grow weary and lose heart.

⁴In your struggle against sin, you have not yet resisted to the point of shedding your blood.

1Pe 1:15 But just as he who called you is holy, so be holy in all you do;

1Pe 2:21 To this you were called, because Christ suffered for you, leaving you an example, that you should follow in his steps.

²²"He committed no sin, and no deceit was found in his mouth."

²³When they hurled their insults at him, he did not retaliate; when he suffered, he made no threats. Instead, he entrusted himself to him who judges justly. ²⁴He himself bore our sins in his body on the tree, so that we might die to sins and live for righteousness; by his wounds you have been healed.

1Pe 3:17 It is better, if it is God's will, to suffer for doing good than for doing evil. ¹⁸For Christ died for sins once for all, the righteous for the unrighteous, to bring you to God. He was put to death in the body but made alive by the Spirit,

1Jn 2:6 Whoever claims to live in him must walk as Jesus did.

1Jn 3:1 How great is the love the Father has lavished on us, that we should be called children of God! And that is what we are! The reason the world does not know us is that it did not know him. ²Dear friends, now we are children of God, and what we will be has not yet been made known. But we know that when he appears, we shall be like him, for we shall see him as he is. ³Everyone who has this hope in him purifies himself, just as he is pure.

1Jn 3:16 This is how we know what love is: Jesus Christ laid down his life for us. And we ought to lay down our lives for our brothers.

1Jn 4:17 In this way, love is made complete among us so that we will have confidence on the day of judgment, because in this world we are like him.

Faith in:

See Faith in Christ; Salvation, Conditions of.

Faithfulness of:

(Isa 11:5; Lk 4:43; Jn 7:18; 8:29; 9:4; 14:3; 17:8; Heb 3:2; Rev 1:5; 3:14). In mediation (Heb 2:17).

Genealogy of:

See above, History of.

Glorification of:

(Jn 7:39; 12:16; 17:1; Ac 7:55-56; Heb 8:1).

Head of the Church:

(Ps 118:22-23, w Mt 21:42-43, & Mk 12:10; Isa 28:16, w Eph 2:2-22, & 1Pe 2:6; Lk 20:17-18, w 1Pe 2:7; Jn 15:1-8; 1Co 3:11; Eph 1:22-23; 4:15; 5:23-32; Col 1:18; 2:10,19; 3:11; Rev 2:2-28; 3:1,7; 22:16).

Holiness of:

Foretold—

Ps 45:7 You love righteousness and hate wickedness; therefore God, your God, has set you above your companions by anointing you with the oil of joy.

Isa 11:4 but with righteousness he will judge the needy, with justice he will give decisions for the poor of the earth. He will strike the earth with the rod of his mouth; with the breath of his lips he will slay the wicked. ⁵Righteousness will be his belt and faithfulness the sash around his waist.

Jer 23:5 "The days are coming," declares the LORD, "when I will raise up to David a righteous Branch, a King who will reign wisely and do what is just and right in the land.

Zec 9:9 Rejoice greatly, O Daughter of Zion! Shout, Daughter of Jerusalem! See, your king comes to you, righteous and having salvation, gentle and riding on a donkey, on a colt, the foal of a donkey.

Professed by himself—

Jn 5:30 By myself I can do nothing; I judge only as I hear, and my judgment is just, for I seek not to please myself but him who sent me.

Jn 7:18 He who speaks on his own does so to gain honor for himself, but he who works for the honor of the one who sent him is a man of truth; there is nothing false about him. (+Jn 8:46)

Jn 14:30 I will not speak with you much longer, for the prince of this world is coming. He has no hold on me,

Rev 3:7 "To the angel of the church in Philadelphia write: These are the words of him who is holy and true, who holds the key of David. What he opens no one can shut, and what he shuts no one can open.

Testified to by the angel to his mother—

Lk 1:35 The angel answered, "The Holy Spirit will come upon you, and the power of the Most High will overshadow you. So the holy one to be born will be called the Son of God.

Testified to by demons—

Mk 1:24 "What do you want with us, Jesus of Nazareth? Have you come to destroy us? I know who you are—the Holy One of God!"

Lk 4:34 "Ha! What do you want with us, Jesus of Nazareth? Have you come to destroy us? I know who you are—the Holy One of God!"

Testified to by the centurion at the Crucifixion—

Lk 23:47 The centurion, seeing what had happened, praised God and said, "Surely this was a righteous man."

Testified to by Stephen (Ac 7:52).

Testified to by Peter (Jn 6:69)—

Ac 3:14 You disowned the Holy and Righteous One and asked that a murderer be released to you.

Ac 4:27 Indeed Herod and Pontius Pilate met together with the Gentiles and the people of Israel in this city to conspire against your holy servant Jesus, whom you anointed. (+Ac 4:28-29)

Ac 4:30 Stretch out your hand to heal and perform miraculous signs and wonders through the name of your holy servant Jesus."

1Pe 1:19 but with the precious blood of Christ, a lamb without blemish or defect.

1Pe 2:22 "He committed no sin, and no deceit was found in his mouth."

Testified to by John (1Jn 2:1)—

1Jn 2:29 If you know that he is righteous, you know that everyone who does what is right has been born of him.

1Jn 3:5 But you know that he appeared so that he might take away our sins. And in him is no sin.

Testified to by Paul—

Ac 13:35 So it is stated elsewhere: "'You will not let your Holy One see decay.'

2Co 5:21 God made him who had no sin to be sin for us, so that in him we might become the righteousness of God.

Testified to by the author of Hebrews—

Heb 1:9 You have loved righteousness and hated wickedness; therefore God, your God, has set you above your companions by anointing you with the oil of joy."

Heb 4:15 For we do not have a high priest who is unable

to sympathize with our weaknesses, but we have one who has been tempted in every way, just as we are—yet was without sin.

Heb 7:26 Such a high priest meets our need—one who is holy, blameless, pure, set apart from sinners, exalted above the heavens. [27]Unlike the other high priests, he does not need to offer sacrifices day after day, first for his own sins, and then for the sins of the people. He sacrificed for their sins once for all when he offered himself. [28]For the law appoints as high priests men who are weak; but the oath, which came after the law, appointed the Son, who has been made perfect forever.

Heb 9:14 How much more, then, will the blood of Christ, who through the eternal Spirit offered himself unblemished to God, cleanse our consciences from acts that lead to death, so that we may serve the living God!

Humanity of:

Ps 22:22 I will declare your name to my brothers; in the congregation I will praise you.

Jn 1:14 The Word became flesh and made his dwelling among us. We have seen his glory, the glory of the One and Only, who came from the Father, full of grace and truth.

Took on himself human nature—

Php 2:7 but made himself nothing, taking the very nature of a servant, being made in human likeness. [8]And being found in appearance as a man, he humbled himself and became obedient to death—even death on a cross!

Heb 2:9 But we see Jesus, who was made a little lower than the angels, now crowned with glory and honor because he suffered death, so that by the grace of God he might taste death for everyone.

[10]In bringing many sons to glory, it was fitting that God, for whom and through whom everything exists, should make the author of their salvation perfect through suffering.

Heb 2:14 Since the children have flesh and blood, he too shared in their humanity so that by his death he might destroy him who holds the power of death—that is, the devil— [15]and free those who all their lives were held in slavery by their fear of death. [16]For surely it is not angels he helps, but Abraham's descendants. [17]For this reason he had to be made like his brothers in every way, in order that he might become a merciful and faithful high priest in service to God, and that he might make atonement for the sins of the people. [18]Because he himself suffered when he was tempted, he is able to help those who are being tempted.

Was born of flesh—

Isa 9:6 For to us a child is born, to us a son is given, and the government will be on his shoulders. And he will be called Wonderful Counselor, Mighty God, Everlasting Father, Prince of Peace.

Mt 1:18 This is how the birth of Jesus Christ came about: His mother Mary was pledged to be married to Joseph, but before they came together, she was found to be with child through the Holy Spirit. [19]Because Joseph her husband was a righteous man and did not want to expose her to public disgrace, he had in mind to divorce her quietly.

[20]But after he had considered this, an angel of the Lord appeared to him in a dream and said, "Joseph son of David, do not be afraid to take Mary home as your wife, because what is conceived in her is from the Holy Spirit. [21]She will give birth to a son, and you are to give him the name Jesus, because he will save his people from their sins." [22]All this took place to fulfill what the Lord had said

through the prophet: **23**"The virgin will be with child and will give birth to a son, and they will call him Immanuel"—which means, "God with us."

24When Joseph woke up, he did what the angel of the Lord had commanded him and took Mary home as his wife. **25**But he had no union with her until she gave birth to a son. And he gave him the name Jesus.

Lk 2:11 Today in the town of David a Savior has been born to you; he is Christ the Lord. **12**This will be a sign to you: You will find a baby wrapped in cloths and lying in a manger."

13Suddenly a great company of the heavenly host appeared with the angel, praising God and saying,

14"Glory to God in the highest, and on earth peace to men on whom his favor rests."

1Jn 4:2 This is how you can recognize the Spirit of God: Every spirit that acknowledges that Jesus Christ has come in the flesh is from God,

2Jn 7 Many deceivers, who do not acknowledge Jesus Christ as coming in the flesh, have gone out into the world. Any such person is the deceiver and the antichrist.

Called: Seed of the woman—

Ge 3:15 And I will put enmity between you and the woman, and between your offspring and hers; he will crush your head, and you will strike his heel."

Gal 4:4 But when the time had fully come, God sent his Son, born of a woman, born under law,

Called son of David—

Mt 20:30 Two blind men were sitting by the roadside, and when they heard that Jesus was going by, they shouted, "Lord, Son of David, have mercy on us!"

31The crowd rebuked them and told them to be quiet, but they shouted all the louder, "Lord, Son of David, have mercy on us!"

Mt 21:9 The crowds that went ahead of him and those that followed shouted,

"Hosanna to the Son of David!"

"Blessed is he who comes in the name of the Lord!"

"Hosanna in the highest!" (+Mt 22:42; Mk 12:35; Lk 18:38)

Called a prophet like Moses—

Dt 18:15 The LORD your God will raise up for you a prophet like me from among your own brothers. You must listen to him. **16**For this is what you asked of the LORD your God at Horeb on the day of the assembly when you said, "Let us not hear the voice of the LORD our God nor see this great fire anymore, or we will die."

17The LORD said to me: "What they say is good. **18**I will raise up for them a prophet like you from among their brothers; I will put my words in his mouth, and he will tell them everything I command him. **19**If anyone does not listen to my words that the prophet speaks in my name, I myself will call him to account. (+Ac 3:22-23)

Ac 7:37 "This is that Moses who told the Israelites, 'God will send you a prophet like me from your own people.'

Humility of:

2Co 8:9 For you know the grace of our Lord Jesus Christ, that though he was rich, yet for your sakes he became poor, so that you through his poverty might become rich.

Php 2:7 but made himself nothing, taking the very nature of a servant, being made in human likeness. **8**And being found in appearance as a man, he humbled himself and became obedient to death—even death on a cross!

Became a servant—

Lk 22:27 For who is greater, the one who is at the table or the one who serves? Is it not the one who is at the table? But I am among you as one who serves.

Jn 13:5 After that, he poured water into a basin and began to wash his disciples' feet, drying them with the towel that was wrapped around him.

Jn 13:14 Now that I, your Lord and Teacher, have washed your feet, you also should wash one another's feet.

See below, Meekness of.

Impeccability of:

See above, Holiness of; below, Temptation of.

Incarnation of: (Jn 16:28)

1Ti 3:16 Beyond all question, the mystery of godliness is great: He appeared in a body, was vindicated by the Spirit, was seen by angels, was preached among the nations, was believed on in the world, was taken up in glory.

Foretold—

Ge 3:15 And I will put enmity between you and the woman, and between your offspring and hers; he will crush your head, and you will strike his heel."

Dt 18:15 The LORD your God will raise up for you a prophet like me from among your own brothers. You must listen to him. **16**For this is what you asked of the LORD your God at Horeb on the day of the assembly when you said, "Let us not hear the voice of the LORD our God nor see this great fire anymore, or we will die."

17The LORD said to me: "What they say is good. **18**I will raise up for them a prophet like you from among their brothers; I will put my words in his mouth, and he will tell them everything I command him.

Ps 2:7 I will proclaim the decree of the LORD: He said to me, "You are my Son; today I have become your Father."

Isa 7:14 Therefore the Lord himself will give you a sign: The virgin will be with child and will give birth to a son, and will call him Immanuel. **15**He will eat curds and honey when he knows enough to reject the wrong and choose the right. **16**But before the boy knows enough to reject the wrong and choose the right, the land of the two kings you dread will be laid waste.

Isa 9:6 For to us a child is born, to us a son is given, and the government will be on his shoulders. And he will be called Wonderful Counselor, Mighty God, Everlasting Father, Prince of Peace.

Isa 11:1 A shoot will come up from the stump of Jesse; from his roots a Branch will bear fruit.

Jn 7:42 Does not the Scripture say that the Christ will come from David's family and from Bethlehem, the town where David lived?"

Ac 13:33 he has fulfilled for us, their children, by raising up Jesus. As it is written in the second Psalm: "'You are my Son; today I have become your Father.'

Heb 1:5 For to which of the angels did God ever say, "You are my Son; today I have become your Father"? Or again, "I will be his Father, and he will be my Son"?

Accomplished through the generation of the Holy Spirit—

Mt 1:1 A record of the genealogy of Jesus Christ the son of David, the son of Abraham:

Mt 1:16 and Jacob the father of Joseph, the husband of Mary, of whom was born Jesus, who is called Christ.

17Thus there were fourteen generations in all from Abraham to David, fourteen from David to the exile to Babylon, and fourteen from the exile to the Christ.

18This is how the birth of Jesus Christ came about: His mother Mary was pledged to be married to Joseph, but before they came together, she was found to be with child through the Holy Spirit.

Mt 1:23 "The virgin will be with child and will give birth to a son, and they will call him Immanuel"—which means, "God with us."

Lk 1:26 In the sixth month, God sent the angel Gabriel to Nazareth, a town in Galilee, [27]to a virgin pledged to be married to a man named Joseph, a descendant of David. The virgin's name was Mary. [28]The angel went to her and said, "Greetings, you who are highly favored! The Lord is with you."

[29]Mary was greatly troubled at his words and wondered what kind of greeting this might be. [30]But the angel said to her, "Do not be afraid, Mary, you have found favor with God. [31]You will be with child and give birth to a son, and you are to give him the name Jesus. [32]He will be great and will be called the Son of the Most High. The Lord God will give him the throne of his father David, [33]and he will reign over the house of Jacob forever; his kingdom will never end."

[34]"How will this be," Mary asked the angel, "since I am a virgin?"

[35]The angel answered, "The Holy Spirit will come upon you, and the power of the Most High will overshadow you. So the holy one to be born will be called the Son of God. (+Lk 1:36-37)

Lk 1:38 "I am the Lord's servant," Mary answered. "May it be to me as you have said." Then the angel left her.

[39]At that time Mary got ready and hurried to a town in the hill country of Judea, [40]where she entered Zechariah's home and greeted Elizabeth. [41]When Elizabeth heard Mary's greeting, the baby leaped in her womb, and Elizabeth was filled with the Holy Spirit. [42]In a loud voice she exclaimed: "Blessed are you among women, and blessed is the child you will bear! [43]But why am I so favored, that the mother of my Lord should come to me? [44]As soon as the sound of your greeting reached my ears, the baby in my womb leaped for joy. [45]Blessed is she who has believed that what the Lord has said to her will be accomplished!"

[46]And Mary said: "My soul glorifies the Lord [47]and my spirit rejoices in God my Savior, [48]for he has been mindful of the humble state of his servant. From now on all generations will call me blessed, [49]for the Mighty One has done great things for me—holy is his name. [50]His mercy extends to those who fear him, from generation to generation. [51]He has performed mighty deeds with his arm; he has scattered those who are proud in their inmost thoughts. [52]He has brought down rulers from their thrones but has lifted up the humble. [53]He has filled the hungry with good things but has sent the rich away empty. [54]He has helped his servant Israel, remembering to be merciful [55]to Abraham and his descendants forever, even as he said to our fathers."

[56]Mary stayed with Elizabeth for about three months and then returned home.

Was made a little lower than the angels (Heb 2:9,14).

Was made flesh—

Lk 24:39 Look at my hands and my feet. It is I myself! Touch me and see; a ghost does not have flesh and bones, as you see I have."

Jn 1:14 The Word became flesh and made his dwelling among us. We have seen his glory, the glory of the One and Only, who came from the Father, full of grace and truth.

Jn 20:27 Then he said to Thomas, "Put your finger here;

see my hands. Reach out your hand and put it into my side. Stop doubting and believe."

Ro 8:3 For what the law was powerless to do in that it was weakened by the sinful nature, God did by sending his own Son in the likeness of sinful man to be a sin offering. And so he condemned sin in sinful man,

1Co 15:47 The first man was of the dust of the earth, the second man from heaven.

2Co 5:16 So from now on we regard no one from a worldly point of view. Though we once regarded Christ in this way, we do so no longer.

Gal 4:4 But when the time had fully come, God sent his Son, born of a woman, born under law,

Php 2:7 but made himself nothing, taking the very nature of a servant, being made in human likeness. [8]And being found in appearance as a man, he humbled himself and became obedient to death—even death on a cross!

Heb 1:3 The Son is the radiance of God's glory and the exact representation of his being, sustaining all things by his powerful word. After he had provided purification for sins, he sat down at the right hand of the Majesty in heaven.

Heb 1:6 And again, when God brings his firstborn into the world, he says, "Let all God's angels worship him."

Heb 2:9 But we see Jesus, who was made a little lower than the angels, now crowned with glory and honor because he suffered death, so that by the grace of God he might taste death for everyone. (+Heb 2:10-13)

Heb 2:14 Since the children have flesh and blood, he too shared in their humanity so that by his death he might destroy him who holds the power of death—that is, the devil— (+Heb 2:15)

Heb 2:16 For surely it is not angels he helps, but Abraham's descendants. [17]For this reason he had to be made like his brothers in every way, in order that he might become a merciful and faithful high priest in service to God, and that he might make atonement for the sins of the people. [18]Because he himself suffered when he was tempted, he is able to help those who are being tempted.

Heb 10:5 Therefore, when Christ came into the world, he said: "Sacrifice and offering you did not desire, but a body you prepared for me;

1Jn 1:1 That which was from the beginning, which we have heard, which we have seen with our eyes, which we have looked at and our hands have touched—this we proclaim concerning the Word of life. (+1Jn 1:2)

1Jn 1:3 We proclaim to you what we have seen and heard, so that you also may have fellowship with us. And our fellowship is with the Father and with his Son, Jesus Christ.

1Jn 4:2 This is how you can recognize the Spirit of God: Every spirit that acknowledges that Jesus Christ has come in the flesh is from God,

2Jn 7 Many deceivers, who do not acknowledge Jesus Christ as coming in the flesh, have gone out into the world. Any such person is the deceiver and the antichrist.

Came in the lineage of Judah—

Heb 7:14 For it is clear that our Lord descended from Judah, and in regard to that tribe Moses said nothing about priests.

Was of the seed of David—

Mt 22:45 If then David calls him 'Lord,' how can he be his son?"

Ro 1:3 regarding his Son, who as to his human nature was a descendant of David,

Ro 9:5 Theirs are the patriarchs, and from them is traced the human ancestry of Christ, who is God over all, forever praised! Amen.

Rev 22:16 "I, Jesus, have sent my angel to give you this testimony for the churches. I am the Root and the Offspring of David, and the bright Morning Star."

Was the son of Mary—

Mt 13:55 "Isn't this the carpenter's son? Isn't his mother's name Mary, and aren't his brothers James, Joseph, Simon and Judas?

Lk 2:1 In those days Caesar Augustus issued a decree that a census should be taken of the entire Roman world. ²(This was the first census that took place while Quirinius was governor of Syria.) ³And everyone went to his own town to register.

⁴So Joseph also went up from the town of Nazareth in Galilee to Judea, to Bethlehem the town of David, because he belonged to the house and line of David. ⁵He went there to register with Mary, who was pledged to be married to him and was expecting a child. ⁶While they were there, the time came for the baby to be born, ⁷and she gave birth to her firstborn, a son. She wrapped him in cloths and placed him in a manger, because there was no room for them in the inn.

⁸And there were shepherds living out in the fields nearby, keeping watch over their flocks at night. ⁹An angel of the Lord appeared to them, and the glory of the Lord shone around them, and they were terrified. ¹⁰But the angel said to them, "Do not be afraid. I bring you good news of great joy that will be for all the people. ¹¹Today in the town of David a Savior has been born to you; he is Christ the Lord. ¹²This will be a sign to you: You will find a baby wrapped in cloths and lying in a manger."

¹³Suddenly a great company of the heavenly host appeared with the angel, praising God and saying,

¹⁴"Glory to God in the highest, and on earth peace to men on whom his favor rests."

¹⁵When the angels had left them and gone into heaven, the shepherds said to one another, "Let's go to Bethlehem and see this thing that has happened, which the Lord has told us about."

¹⁶So they hurried off and found Mary and Joseph, and the baby, who was lying in the manger. ¹⁷When they had seen him, they spread the word concerning what had been told them about this child, ¹⁸and all who heard it were amazed at what the shepherds said to them. ¹⁹But Mary treasured up all these things and pondered them in her heart. ²⁰The shepherds returned, glorifying and praising God for all the things they had heard and seen, which were just as they had been told.

²¹On the eighth day, when it was time to circumcise him, he was named Jesus, the name the angel had given him before he had been conceived.

See above, Humanity of; below, Relation of, to the Father.

Intercession of: *See below, Mediation of.*

Judge:

Mt 3:12 His winnowing fork is in his hand, and he will clear his threshing floor, gathering his wheat into the barn and burning up the chaff with unquenchable fire." (+Lk 3:17)

Mt 25:31 "When the Son of Man comes in his glory, and all the angels with him, he will sit on his throne in heavenly glory. ³²All the nations will be gathered before him, and he will separate the people one from another as a shepherd separates the sheep from the goats. ³³He will put the sheep on his right and the goats on his left.

³⁴"Then the King will say to those on his right, 'Come, you who are blessed by my Father; take your inheritance, the kingdom prepared for you since the creation of the world.

Ac 10:42 He commanded us to preach to the people and to testify that he is the one whom God appointed as judge of the living and the dead.

Ro 2:16 This will take place on the day when God will judge men's secrets through Jesus Christ, as my gospel declares.

1Co 4:4 My conscience is clear, but that does not make me innocent. It is the Lord who judges me. ⁵Therefore judge nothing before the appointed time; wait till the Lord comes. He will bring to light what is hidden in darkness and will expose the motives of men's hearts. At that time each will receive his praise from God.

2Co 5:10 For we must all appear before the judgment seat of Christ, that each one may receive what is due him for the things done while in the body, whether good or bad.

2Ti 4:1 In the presence of God and of Christ Jesus, who will judge the living and the dead, and in view of his appearing and his kingdom, I give you this charge:

2Ti 4:8 Now there is in store for me the crown of righteousness, which the Lord, the righteous Judge, will award to me on that day—and not only to me, but also to all who have longed for his appearing.

Rev 2:23 I will strike her children dead. Then all the churches will know that I am he who searches hearts and minds, and I will repay each of you according to your deeds.

Prophecy concerning—

Isa 2:4 He will judge between the nations and will settle disputes for many peoples. They will beat their swords into plowshares and their spears into pruning hooks. Nation will not take up sword against nation, nor will they train for war anymore.

Mic 4:3 He will judge between many peoples and will settle disputes for strong nations far and wide. They will beat their swords into plowshares and their spears into pruning hooks. Nation will not take up sword against nation, nor will they train for war anymore.

Isa 11:3 and he will delight in the fear of the LORD. He will not judge by what he sees with his eyes, or decide by what he hears with his ears; ⁴but with righteousness he will judge the needy, with justice he will give decisions for the poor of the earth. He will strike the earth with the rod of his mouth; with the breath of his lips he will slay the wicked.

Mic 5:1 Marshal your troops, O city of troops, for a siege is laid against us. They will strike Israel's ruler on the cheek with a rod.

Ordained of God—

Jn 5:22 Moreover, the Father judges no one, but has entrusted all judgment to the Son,

Ac 17:31 For he has set a day when he will judge the world with justice by the man he has appointed. He has given proof of this to all men by raising him from the dead."

Righteous—

2Ti 4:8 Now there is in store for me the crown of righteousness, which the Lord, the righteous Judge, will award to me on that day—and not only to me, but also to all who have longed for his appearing.

Justice of:

2Sa 23:3 The God of Israel spoke, the Rock of Israel said to me: 'When one rules over men in righteousness, when he rules in the fear of God,

Zec 9:9 Rejoice greatly, O Daughter of Zion! Shout, Daughter of Jerusalem! See, your king comes to you, righteous and having salvation, gentle and riding on a donkey, on a colt, the foal of a donkey.

Mt 27:19 While Pilate was sitting on the judge's seat, his wife sent him this message: "Don't have anything to do with that innocent man, for I have suffered a great deal today in a dream because of him."

Jn 5:30 By myself I can do nothing; I judge only as I hear, and my judgment is just, for I seek not to please myself but him who sent me.

Ac 3:14 You disowned the Holy and Righteous One and asked that a murderer be released to you.

Ac 22:14 "Then he said: 'The God of our fathers has chosen you to know his will and to see the Righteous One and to hear words from his mouth.

King:

Prophecies concerning—

Ge 49:10 The scepter will not depart from Judah, nor the ruler's staff from between his feet, until he comes to whom it belongs and the obedience of the nations is his.

1Sa 2:10 those who oppose the LORD will be shattered. He will thunder against them from heaven; the LORD will judge the ends of the earth. "He will give strength to his king and exalt the horn of his anointed."

2Sa 7:12 When your days are over and you rest with your fathers, I will raise up your offspring to succeed you, who will come from your own body, and I will establish his kingdom.

Ac 2:30 But he was a prophet and knew that God had promised him on oath that he would place one of his descendants on his throne.

Ps 2:6 "I have installed my King on Zion, my holy hill."

Ps 18:43 You have delivered me from the attacks of the people; you have made me the head of nations; people I did not know are subject to me. [44]As soon as they hear me, they obey me; foreigners cringe before me.

Ps 45:3 Gird your sword upon your side, O mighty one; clothe yourself with splendor and majesty. [4]In your majesty ride forth victoriously in behalf of truth, humility and righteousness; let your right hand display awesome deeds. [5]Let your sharp arrows pierce the hearts of the king's enemies; let the nations fall beneath your feet. [6]Your throne, O God, will last for ever and ever; a scepter of justice will be the scepter of your kingdom. [7]You love righteousness and hate wickedness; therefore God, your God, has set you above your companions by anointing you with the oil of joy.

Ps 72:5 He will endure as long as the sun, as long as the moon, through all generations.

Ps 72:8 He will rule from sea to sea and from the River to the ends of the earth.

Ps 72:11 All kings will bow down to him and all nations will serve him.

Ps 89:3 You said, "I have made a covenant with my chosen one, I have sworn to David my servant, [4]'I will establish your line forever and make your throne firm through all generations.' " *Selah*

Ps 89:19 Once you spoke in a vision, to your faithful people you said: "I have bestowed strength on a warrior; I have exalted a young man from among the people. [20]I have found David my servant; with my sacred oil I have anointed him. [21]My hand will sustain him; surely my arm will strengthen him.

Ps 89:23 I will crush his foes before him and strike down his adversaries.

Ps 89:27 I will also appoint him my firstborn, the most exalted of the kings of the earth.

Ps 89:29 I will establish his line forever, his throne as long as the heavens endure.

Ps 89:36 that his line will continue forever and his throne endure before me like the sun; [37]it will be established forever like the moon, the faithful witness in the sky."

Ps 110:1 The LORD says to my Lord: "Sit at my right hand until I make your enemies a footstool for your feet." [2]The LORD will extend your mighty scepter from Zion; you will rule in the midst of your enemies.

Ps 132:11 The LORD swore an oath to David, a sure oath that he will not revoke: "One of your own descendants I will place on your throne—

Ps 132:17 "Here I will make a horn grow for David and set up a lamp for my anointed one. [18]I will clothe his enemies with shame, but the crown on his head will be resplendent."

Isa 9:6 For to us a child is born, to us a son is given, and the government will be on his shoulders. And he will be called Wonderful Counselor, Mighty God, Everlasting Father, Prince of Peace. [7]Of the increase of his government and peace there will be no end. He will reign on David's throne and over his kingdom, establishing and upholding it with justice and righteousness from that time on and forever. The zeal of the LORD Almighty will accomplish this.

Isa 22:22 I will place on his shoulder the key to the house of David; what he opens no one can shut, and what he shuts no one can open.

Isa 32:1 See, a king will reign in righteousness and rulers will rule with justice.

Isa 52:7 How beautiful on the mountains are the feet of those who bring good news, who proclaim peace, who bring good tidings, who proclaim salvation, who say to Zion, "Your God reigns!"

Isa 52:13 See, my servant will act wisely; he will be raised and lifted up and highly exalted.

Jer 23:5 "The days are coming," declares the LORD, "when I will raise up to David a righteous Branch, a King who will reign wisely and do what is just and right in the land.

Jer 30:9 Instead, they will serve the LORD their God and David their king, whom I will raise up for them.

Jer 33:17 For this is what the LORD says: 'David will never fail to have a man to sit on the throne of the house of Israel,

Eze 37:24 " 'My servant David will be king over them, and they will all have one shepherd. They will follow my laws and be careful to keep my decrees. [25]They will live in the land I gave to my servant Jacob, the land where your fathers lived. They and their children and their children's children will live there forever, and David my servant will be their prince forever.

Da 2:35 Then the iron, the clay, the bronze, the silver and the gold were broken to pieces at the same time and became like chaff on a threshing floor in the summer. The wind swept them away without leaving a trace. But the rock that struck the statue became a huge mountain and filled the whole earth.

Da 2:44 "In the time of those kings, the God of heaven will set up a kingdom that will never be destroyed, nor will it be left to another people. It will crush all those kingdoms and bring them to an end, but it will itself endure forever.

Da 7:13 "In my vision at night I looked, and there before me was one like a son of man, coming with the clouds of heaven. He approached the Ancient of Days and was led into his presence. [14]He was given authority, glory and sovereign power; all peoples, nations and men of every language worshiped him. His dominion is an everlasting dominion that will not pass away, and his kingdom is one that will never be destroyed.

Hos 3:5 Afterward the Israelites will return and seek the LORD their God and David their king. They will come trembling to the LORD and to his blessings in the last days.

Mic 5:2 "But you, Bethlehem Ephrathah, though you are small among the clans of Judah, out of you will come for me one who will be ruler over Israel, whose origins are from of old, from ancient times."

Mic 5:4 He will stand and shepherd his flock in the strength of the LORD, in the majesty of the name of the LORD his God. And they will live securely, for then his greatness will reach to the ends of the earth. (+Zec 6:12)

Zec 6:13 It is he who will build the temple of the LORD, and he will be clothed with majesty and will sit and rule on his throne. And he will be a priest on his throne. And there will be harmony between the two.'

Zec 9:9 Rejoice greatly, O Daughter of Zion! Shout, Daughter of Jerusalem! See, your king comes to you, righteous and having salvation, gentle and riding on a donkey, on a colt, the foal of a donkey. [10]I will take away the chariots from Ephraim and the war-horses from Jerusalem, and the battle bow will be broken. He will proclaim peace to the nations. His rule will extend from sea to sea and from the River to the ends of the earth.

Mt 2:2 and asked, "Where is the one who has been born king of the Jews? We saw his star in the east and have come to worship him."

Mt 2:6 "'But you, Bethlehem, in the land of Judah, are by no means least among the rulers of Judah; for out of you will come a ruler who will be the shepherd of my people Israel.'"

Mt 21:5 "Say to the Daughter of Zion, 'See, your king comes to you, gentle and riding on a donkey, on a colt, the foal of a donkey.'"

Mt 22:42 "What do you think about the Christ? Whose son is he?"

"The son of David," they replied.

[43]He said to them, "How is it then that David, speaking by the Spirit, calls him 'Lord'? For he says,

[44]"'The Lord said to my Lord:

"Sit at my right hand until I put your enemies under your feet."'

[45]If then David calls him 'Lord,' how can he be his son?"

Lk 1:32 He will be great and will be called the Son of the Most High. The Lord God will give him the throne of his father David, [33]and he will reign over the house of Jacob forever; his kingdom will never end."

Ac 2:30 But he was a prophet and knew that God had promised him on oath that he would place one of his descendants on his throne.

Appointed by the Father as King—

Lk 22:29 And I confer on you a kingdom, just as my Father conferred one on me, [30]so that you may eat and drink at my table in my kingdom and sit on thrones, judging the twelve tribes of Israel.

Ac 2:30 But he was a prophet and knew that God had promised him on oath that he would place one of his descendants on his throne. (+Ac 2:36)

2Sa 7:12 When your days are over and you rest with your fathers, I will raise up your offspring to succeed you, who will come from your own body, and I will establish his kingdom.

Ac 5:31 God exalted him to his own right hand as Prince and Savior that he might give repentance and forgiveness of sins to Israel.

Eph 1:20 which he exerted in Christ when he raised him from the dead and seated him at his right hand in the heavenly realms, [21]far above all rule and authority, power and dominion, and every title that can be given, not only in the present age but also in the one to come. [22]And God placed all things under his feet and appointed him to be head over everything for the church,

Heb 2:7 You made him a little lower than the angels; you crowned him with glory and honor [8]and put everything under his feet."

In putting everything under him, God left nothing that is not subject to him. Yet at present we do not see everything subject to him.

Authority of Jesus as King—

Mk 2:28 So the Son of Man is Lord even of the Sabbath.

Jn 5:27 And he has given him authority to judge because he is the Son of Man.

Universal kingdom—

Mt 11:27 "All things have been committed to me by my Father. No one knows the Son except the Father, and no one knows the Father except the Son and those to whom the Son chooses to reveal him.

Lk 10:22 "All things have been committed to me by my Father. No one knows who the Son is except the Father, and no one knows who the Father is except the Son and those to whom the Son chooses to reveal him."

Mt 28:18 Then Jesus came to them and said, "All authority in heaven and on earth has been given to me.

Lk 19:27 But those enemies of mine who did not want me to be king over them—bring them here and kill them in front of me.'"

Jn 3:31 "The one who comes from above is above all; the one who is from the earth belongs to the earth, and speaks as one from the earth. The one who comes from heaven is above all. (+Jn 3:33)

Jn 13:3 Jesus knew that the Father had put all things under his power, and that he had come from God and was returning to God;

Jn 17:2 For you granted him authority over all people that he might give eternal life to all those you have given him.

Ro 9:5 Theirs are the patriarchs, and from them is traced the human ancestry of Christ, who is God over all, forever praised! Amen.

Ro 10:12 For there is no difference between Jew and Gentile—the same Lord is Lord of all and richly blesses all who call on him,

Ro 14:9 For this very reason, Christ died and returned to life so that he might be the Lord of both the dead and the living.

Col 2:10 and you have been given fullness in Christ, who is the head over every power and authority.

Heb 1:2 but in these last days he has spoken to us by his Son, whom he appointed heir of all things, and through whom he made the universe. [3]The Son is the radiance of God's glory and the exact representation of his being, sustaining all things by his powerful word. After he had provided purification for sins, he sat down at the right hand of the Majesty in heaven. [4]So he became as much superior to the angels as the name he has inherited is superior to theirs.

[5]For to which of the angels did God ever say,

"You are my Son; today I have become your Father"?

Or again, "I will be his Father, and he will be my Son"?

[6]And again, when God brings his firstborn into the world, he says, "Let all God's angels worship him." [7]In speaking of the angels he says,

"He makes his angels winds, his servants flames of fire."

[8]But about the Son he says,

"Your throne, O God, will last for ever and ever, and righteousness will be the scepter of your kingdom. [9]You have loved righteousness and hated wickedness; therefore God, your God, has set you above your companions by anointing you with the oil of joy."

[10]He also says, "In the beginning, O Lord, you laid the foundations of the earth, and the heavens are the work of your hands. [11]They will perish, but you remain; they will all wear out like a garment. [12]You will roll them up like a robe; like a garment they will be changed. But you remain the same, and your years will never end."

[13]To which of the angels did God ever say,

"Sit at my right hand until I make your enemies a footstool for your feet"?

Heb 2:7 You made him a little lower than the angels; you crowned him with glory and honor [8]and put everything under his feet."

In putting everything under him, God left nothing that is not subject to him. Yet at present we do not see everything subject to him.

1Pe 3:22 who has gone into heaven and is at God's right hand—with angels, authorities and powers in submission to him.

Rev 3:7 "To the angel of the church in Philadelphia write: These are the words of him who is holy and true, who holds the key of David. What he opens no one can shut, and what he shuts no one can open.

Rev 3:14 "To the angel of the church in Laodicea write: These are the words of the Amen, the faithful and true witness, the ruler of God's creation.

Rev 3:21 To him who overcomes, I will give the right to sit with me on my throne, just as I overcame and sat down with my Father on his throne.

Dominion of Jesus, universal—

Ac 10:36 You know the message God sent to the people of Israel, telling the good news of peace through Jesus Christ, who is Lord of all.

1Co 15:23 But each in his own turn: Christ, the firstfruits; then, when he comes, those who belong to him. [24]Then the end will come, when he hands over the kingdom to God the Father after he has destroyed all dominion, authority and power. [25]For he must reign until he has put all his enemies under his feet. [26]The last enemy to be destroyed is death. [27]For he "has put everything under his feet." Now when it says that "everything" has been put under him, it is clear that this does not include God himself, who put everything under Christ. [28]When he has done this, then the Son himself will be made subject to him who put everything under him, so that God may be all in all.

Eph 1:20 which he exerted in Christ when he raised him from the dead and seated him at his right hand in the heavenly realms, [21]far above all rule and authority, power and dominion, and every title that can be given, not only in the present age but also in the one to come. [22]And God

placed all things under his feet and appointed him to be head over everything for the church,

Php 2:9 Therefore God exalted him to the highest place and gave him the name that is above every name, [10]that at the name of Jesus every knee should bow, in heaven and on earth and under the earth, [11]and every tongue confess that Jesus Christ is Lord, to the glory of God the Father.

Rev 1:5 and from Jesus Christ, who is the faithful witness, the firstborn from the dead, and the ruler of the kings of the earth.

To him who loves us and has freed us from our sins by his blood, [6]and has made us to be a kingdom and priests to serve his God and Father—to him be glory and power for ever and ever! Amen.

[7]Look, he is coming with the clouds, and every eye will see him, even those who pierced him; and all the peoples of the earth will mourn because of him. So shall it be! Amen.

Rev 1:18 I am the Living One; I was dead, and behold I am alive for ever and ever! And I hold the keys of death and Hades.

Rev 11:15 The seventh angel sounded his trumpet, and there were loud voices in heaven, which said: "The kingdom of the world has become the kingdom of our Lord and of his Christ, and he will reign for ever and ever."

Future glory of Jesus as King—

Mt 19:28 Jesus said to them, "I tell you the truth, at the renewal of all things, when the Son of Man sits on his glorious throne, you who have followed me will also sit on twelve thrones, judging the twelve tribes of Israel.

Mt 25:31 "When the Son of Man comes in his glory, and all the angels with him, he will sit on his throne in heavenly glory. [32]All the nations will be gathered before him, and he will separate the people one from another as a shepherd separates the sheep from the goats. [33]He will put the sheep on his right and the goats on his left.

[34]"Then the King will say to those on his right, 'Come, you who are blessed by my Father; take your inheritance, the kingdom prepared for you since the creation of the world.

Mt 26:64 "Yes, it is as you say," Jesus replied. "But I say to all of you: In the future you will see the Son of Man sitting at the right hand of the Mighty One and coming on the clouds of heaven."

Mk 14:62 "I am," said Jesus. "And you will see the Son of Man sitting at the right hand of the Mighty One and coming on the clouds of heaven."

Lk 22:69 But from now on, the Son of Man will be seated at the right hand of the mighty God."

Heb 10:12 But when this priest had offered for all time one sacrifice for sins, he sat down at the right hand of God. [13]Since that time he waits for his enemies to be made his footstool,

Rev 5:13 Then I heard every creature in heaven and on earth and under the earth and on the sea, and all that is in them, singing: "To him who sits on the throne and to the Lamb be praise and honor and glory and power, for ever and ever!"

Kingship of: Avowed by himself (Mt 21:5; 27:11; Lk 23:2; Jn 18:36-37).

Ascribed, by disciples—

Lk 19:38 "Blessed is the king who comes in the name of the Lord!" "Peace in heaven and glory in the highest!"

Jn 1:49 Then Nathanael declared, "Rabbi, you are the Son of God; you are the King of Israel."

Jn 12:13 They took palm branches and went out to meet

him, shouting, "Hosanna!" "Blessed is he who comes in the name of the Lord!" "Blessed is the King of Israel!"

Jn 12:15 "Do not be afraid, O Daughter of Zion; see, your king is coming, seated on a donkey's colt." (+Ac 17:7)

In superscription on the cross (Jn 19:12,19).

Symbolic statements concerning—

Rev 5:5 Then one of the elders said to me, "Do not weep! See, the Lion of the tribe of Judah, the Root of David, has triumphed. He is able to open the scroll and its seven seals."

Rev 5:12 In a loud voice they sang: "Worthy is the Lamb, who was slain, to receive power and wealth and wisdom and strength and honor and glory and praise!"

Rev 6:2 I looked, and there before me was a white horse! Its rider held a bow, and he was given a crown, and he rode out as a conqueror bent on conquest.

Rev 6:15 Then the kings of the earth, the princes, the generals, the rich, the mighty, and every slave and every free man hid in caves and among the rocks of the mountains. [16]They called to the mountains and the rocks, "Fall on us and hide us from the face of him who sits on the throne and from the wrath of the Lamb! [17]For the great day of their wrath has come, and who can stand?"

Rev 14:14 I looked, and there before me was a white cloud, and seated on the cloud was one "like a son of man" with a crown of gold on his head and a sharp sickle in his hand.

Rev 17:14 They will make war against the Lamb, but the Lamb will overcome them because he is Lord of lords and King of kings—and with him will be his called, chosen and faithful followers."

Rev 19:11 I saw heaven standing open and there before me was a white horse, whose rider is called Faithful and True. With justice he judges and makes war. [12]His eyes are like blazing fire, and on his head are many crowns. He has a name written on him that no one knows but he himself.

Rev 19:15 Out of his mouth comes a sharp sword with which to strike down the nations. "He will rule them with an iron scepter." He treads the winepress of the fury of the wrath of God Almighty. [16]On his robe and on his thigh he has this name written: KING OF KINGS AND LORD OF LORDS.

See below, Lordship of.

Kingdom of:

Brings joy and gladness (Ps 46:4; Isa 25:6; 35; 52:9; 55:12). Brings peace (Ps 46:9; Isa 11:6-9).

Is within us—

Lk 17:21 nor will people say, 'Here it is,' or 'There it is,' because the kingdom of God is within you."

Truth—

Jn 18:37 "You are a king, then!" said Pilate. Jesus answered, "You are right in saying I am a king. In fact, for this reason I was born, and for this I came into the world, to testify to the truth. Everyone on the side of truth listens to me."

Is not of this world—

Jn 18:36 Jesus said, "My kingdom is not of this world. If it were, my servants would fight to prevent my arrest by the Jews. But now my kingdom is from another place."

Keys of (Mt 16:19). Glad tidings of (Lk 8:1). Mysteries of (Lk 8:10). Is not meat and drink (Ro 14:17).

Likened to a man who sowed good seed—

Mt 13:24 Jesus told them another parable: "The kingdom of heaven is like a man who sowed good seed in his field. [25]But while everyone was sleeping, his enemy came and

sowed weeds among the wheat, and went away. [26]When the wheat sprouted and formed heads, then the weeds also appeared.

[27]"The owner's servants came to him and said, 'Sir, didn't you sow good seed in your field? Where then did the weeds come from?'

[28]" 'An enemy did this,' he replied.

"The servants asked him, 'Do you want us to go and pull them up?'

[29]" 'No,' he answered, 'because while you are pulling the weeds, you may root up the wheat with them. [30]Let both grow together until the harvest. At that time I will tell the harvesters: First collect the weeds and tie them in bundles to be burned; then gather the wheat and bring it into my barn.' "

Mt 13:38 The field is the world, and the good seed stands for the sons of the kingdom. The weeds are the sons of the evil one, [39]and the enemy who sows them is the devil. The harvest is the end of the age, and the harvesters are angels.

[40]"As the weeds are pulled up and burned in the fire, so it will be at the end of the age. [41]The Son of Man will send out his angels, and they will weed out of his kingdom everything that causes sin and all who do evil. [42]They will throw them into the fiery furnace, where there will be weeping and gnashing of teeth. [43]Then the righteous will shine like the sun in the kingdom of their Father. He who has ears, let him hear. (+Mk 4:26-29)

Likened to a mustard seed—

Mt 13:31 He told them another parable: "The kingdom of heaven is like a mustard seed, which a man took and planted in his field. [32]Though it is the smallest of all your seeds, yet when it grows, it is the largest of garden plants and becomes a tree, so that the birds of the air come and perch in its branches."

Mk 4:30 Again he said, "What shall we say the kingdom of God is like, or what parable shall we use to describe it? [31]It is like a mustard seed, which is the smallest seed you plant in the ground.

Lk 13:18 Then Jesus asked, "What is the kingdom of God like? What shall I compare it to? [19]It is like a mustard seed, which a man took and planted in his garden. It grew and became a tree, and the birds of the air perched in its branches."

Likened to yeast—

Mt 13:33 He told them still another parable: "The kingdom of heaven is like yeast that a woman took and mixed into a large amount of flour until it worked all through the dough."

Lk 13:21 It is like yeast that a woman took and mixed into a large amount of flour until it worked all through the dough."

Likened to a treasure—

Mt 13:44 "The kingdom of heaven is like treasure hidden in a field. When a man found it, he hid it again, and then in his joy went and sold all he had and bought that field.

Likened to a pearl—

Mt 13:45 "Again, the kingdom of heaven is like a merchant looking for fine pearls.

Likened to a net—

Mt 13:47 "Once again, the kingdom of heaven is like a net that was let down into the lake and caught all kinds of fish. [48]When it was full, the fishermen pulled it up on the shore. Then they sat down and collected the good fish in baskets, but threw the bad away. [49]This is how it will be at the end of the age. The angels will come and separate the wicked from the righteous [50]and throw them into the fiery furnace, where there will be weeping and gnashing of teeth.

Likened to a king who called his servants to account— **Mt 18:23** "Therefore, the kingdom of heaven is like a king who wanted to settle accounts with his servants. [24]As he began the settlement, a man who owed him ten thousand talents was brought to him. [25]Since he was not able to pay, the master ordered that he and his wife and his children and all that he had be sold to repay the debt.

[26]"The servant fell on his knees before him. 'Be patient with me,' he begged, 'and I will pay back everything.' [27]The servant's master took pity on him, canceled the debt and let him go.

[28]"But when that servant went out, he found one of his fellow servants who owed him a hundred denarii. He grabbed him and began to choke him. 'Pay back what you owe me!' he demanded.

[29]"His fellow servant fell to his knees and begged him, 'Be patient with me, and I will pay you back.'

[30]"But he refused. Instead, he went off and had the man thrown into prison until he could pay the debt. [31]When the other servants saw what had happened, they were greatly distressed and went and told their master everything that had happened.

[32]"Then the master called the servant in. 'You wicked servant,' he said, 'I canceled all that debt of yours because you begged me to. [33]Shouldn't you have had mercy on your fellow servant just as I had on you?' [34]In anger his master turned him over to the jailers to be tortured, until he should pay back all he owed.

[35]"This is how my heavenly Father will treat each of you unless you forgive your brother from your heart."

Likened to a landowner— **Mt 20:1** "For the kingdom of heaven is like a landowner who went out early in the morning to hire men to work in his vineyard. [2]He agreed to pay them a denarius for the day and sent them into his vineyard.

[3]"About the third hour he went out and saw others standing in the marketplace doing nothing. [4]He told them, 'You also go and work in my vineyard, and I will pay you whatever is right.' [5]So they went. "He went out again about the sixth hour and the ninth hour and did the same thing.

[6]About the eleventh hour he went out and found still others standing around. He asked them, 'Why have you been standing here all day long doing nothing?'

[7]"'Because no one has hired us,' they answered. "He said to them, 'You also go and work in my vineyard.'

[8]"When evening came, the owner of the vineyard said to his foreman, 'Call the workers and pay them their wages, beginning with the last ones hired and going on to the first.'

[9]"The workers who were hired about the eleventh hour came and each received a denarius. [10]So when those came who were hired first, they expected to receive more. But each one of them also received a denarius. [11]When they received it, they began to grumble against the landowner. [12]'These men who were hired last worked only one hour,' they said, 'and you have made them equal to us who have borne the burden of the work and the heat of the day.'

[13]"But he answered one of them, 'Friend, I am not being unfair to you. Didn't you agree to work for a denarius? [14]Take your pay and go. I want to give the man who was hired last the same as I gave you. [15]Don't I have the right to do what I want with my own money? Or are you envious because I am generous?'

[16]"So the last will be first, and the first will be last."

Likened to a king who made a marriage feast for his son— **Mt 22:2** "The kingdom of heaven is like a king who prepared a wedding banquet for his son. [3]He sent his servants to those who had been invited to the banquet to tell them to come, but they refused to come.

[4]"Then he sent some more servants and said, 'Tell those who have been invited that I have prepared my dinner: My oxen and fattened cattle have been butchered, and everything is ready. Come to the wedding banquet.'

[5]"But they paid no attention and went off—one to his field, another to his business. [6]The rest seized his servants, mistreated them and killed them. [7]The king was enraged. He sent his army and destroyed those murderers and burned their city.

[8]"Then he said to his servants, 'The wedding banquet is ready, but those I invited did not deserve to come. [9]Go to the street corners and invite to the banquet anyone you find.' [10]So the servants went out into the streets and gathered all the people they could find, both good and bad, and the wedding hall was filled with guests.

[11]"But when the king came in to see the guests, he noticed a man there who was not wearing wedding clothes. [12]'Friend,' he asked, 'how did you get in here without wedding clothes?' The man was speechless.

[13]"Then the king told the attendants, 'Tie him hand and foot, and throw him outside, into the darkness, where there will be weeping and gnashing of teeth.'

[14]"For many are invited, but few are chosen." (+Lk 14:16-24)

Likened to ten virgins— **Mt 25:1** "At that time the kingdom of heaven will be like ten virgins who took their lamps and went out to meet the bridegroom. [2]Five of them were foolish and five were wise. [3]The foolish ones took their lamps but did not take any oil with them. [4]The wise, however, took oil in jars along with their lamps. [5]The bridegroom was a long time in coming, and they all became drowsy and fell asleep.

[6]"At midnight the cry rang out: 'Here's the bridegroom! Come out to meet him!'

[7]"Then all the virgins woke up and trimmed their lamps. [8]The foolish ones said to the wise, 'Give us some of your oil; our lamps are going out.'

[9]"'No,' they replied, 'there may not be enough for both us and you. Instead, go to those who sell oil and buy some for yourselves.'

[10]"But while they were on their way to buy the oil, the bridegroom arrived. The virgins who were ready went in with him to the wedding banquet. And the door was shut.

[11]"Later the others also came. 'Sir! Sir!' they said. 'Open the door for us!'

[12]"But he replied, 'I tell you the truth, I don't know you.'

[13]"Therefore keep watch, because you do not know the day or the hour.

Likened to a man who entrusted property to his servants— **Mt 25:14** "Again, it will be like a man going on a journey, who called his servants and entrusted his property to them. [15]To one he gave five talents of money, to another two talents, and to another one talent, each according to his ability. Then he went on his journey. [16]The man who had received the five talents went at once and put his money to work and gained five more. [17]So also, the one with the two talents gained two more. [18]But the man who had received the one talent went off, dug a hole in the ground and hid his master's money.

¹⁹"After a long time the master of those servants returned and settled accounts with them. ²⁰The man who had received the five talents brought the other five. 'Master,' he said, 'you entrusted me with five talents. See, I have gained five more.'

²¹"His master replied, 'Well done, good and faithful servant! You have been faithful with a few things; I will put you in charge of many things. Come and share your master's happiness!'

²²"The man with the two talents also came. 'Master,' he said, 'you entrusted me with two talents; see, I have gained two more.'

²³"His master replied, 'Well done, good and faithful servant! You have been faithful with a few things; I will put you in charge of many things. Come and share your master's happiness!'

²⁴"Then the man who had received the one talent came. 'Master,' he said, 'I knew that you are a hard man, harvesting where you have not sown and gathering where you have not scattered seed. ²⁵So I was afraid and went out and hid your talent in the ground. See, here is what belongs to you.'

²⁶"His master replied, 'You wicked, lazy servant! So you knew that I harvest where I have not sown and gather where I have not scattered seed? ²⁷Well then, you should have put my money on deposit with the bankers, so that when I returned I would have received it back with interest.

²⁸" 'Take the talent from him and give it to the one who has the ten talents. ²⁹For everyone who has will be given more, and he will have an abundance. Whoever does not have, even what he has will be taken from him. ³⁰And throw that worthless servant outside, into the darkness, where there will be weeping and gnashing of teeth.'

Lk 19:12 He said: "A man of noble birth went to a distant country to have himself appointed king and then to return. ¹³So he called ten of his servants and gave them ten minas. 'Put this money to work,' he said, 'until I come back.'

¹⁴"But his subjects hated him and sent a delegation after him to say, 'We don't want this man to be our king.'

¹⁵"He was made king, however, and returned home. Then he sent for the servants to whom he had given the money, in order to find out what they had gained with it.

¹⁶"The first one came and said, 'Sir, your mina has earned ten more.'

¹⁷" 'Well done, my good servant!' his master replied. 'Because you have been trustworthy in a very small matter, take charge of ten cities.'

¹⁸"The second came and said, 'Sir, your mina has earned five more.'

¹⁹"His master answered, 'You take charge of five cities.'

²⁰"Then another servant came and said, 'Sir, here is your mina; I have kept it laid away in a piece of cloth. ²¹I was afraid of you, because you are a hard man. You take out what you did not put in and reap what you did not sow.'

²²"His master replied, 'I will judge you by your own words, you wicked servant! You knew, did you, that I am a hard man, taking out what I did not put in, and reaping what I did not sow? ²³Why then didn't you put my money on deposit, so that when I came back, I could have collected it with interest?'

²⁴"Then he said to those standing by, 'Take his mina away from him and give it to the one who has ten minas.'

²⁵" 'Sir,' they said, 'he already has ten!'

²⁶"He replied, 'I tell you that to everyone who has, more will be given, but as for the one who has nothing, even what he has will be taken away. ²⁷But those enemies of mine who did not want me to be king over them—bring them here and kill them in front of me.' "

Prophecies concerning the kingdom of:

Its character: To enlighten—

Jer 31:34 No longer will a man teach his neighbor, or a man his brother, saying, 'Know the LORD,' because they will all know me, from the least of them to the greatest," declares the LORD. "For I will forgive their wickedness and will remember their sins no more."

Heb 8:11 No longer will a man teach his neighbor, or a man his brother, saying, 'Know the Lord,' because they will all know me, from the least of them to the greatest.

To bring peace—

Ps 46:9 He makes wars cease to the ends of the earth; he breaks the bow and shatters the spear, he burns the shields with fire.

Isa 65:25 The wolf and the lamb will feed together, and the lion will eat straw like the ox, but dust will be the serpent's food. They will neither harm nor destroy on all my holy mountain," says the LORD.

Mic 4:3 He will judge between many peoples and will settle disputes for strong nations far and wide. They will beat their swords into plowshares and their spears into pruning hooks. Nation will not take up sword against nation, nor will they train for war anymore. ⁴Every man will sit under his own vine and under his own fig tree, and no one will make them afraid, for the LORD Almighty has spoken. ⁵All the nations may walk in the name of their gods; we will walk in the name of the LORD our God for ever and ever.

⁶"In that day," declares the LORD, "I will gather the lame; I will assemble the exiles and those I have brought to grief. ⁷I will make the lame a remnant, those driven away a strong nation. The LORD will rule over them in Mount Zion from that day and forever.

To bring salvation—

Isa 62:11 The LORD has made proclamation to the ends of the earth: "Say to the Daughter of Zion, 'See, your Savior comes! See, his reward is with him, and his recompense accompanies him.' "

To bring joy—

Isa 25:6 On this mountain the LORD Almighty will prepare a feast of rich food for all peoples, a banquet of aged wine—the best of meats and the finest of wines.

Isa 35:1 The desert and the parched land will be glad; the wilderness will rejoice and blossom. Like the crocus, ²it will burst into bloom; it will rejoice greatly and shout for joy. The glory of Lebanon will be given to it, the splendor of Carmel and Sharon; they will see the glory of the LORD, the splendor of our God.

³Strengthen the feeble hands, steady the knees that give way; ⁴say to those with fearful hearts, "Be strong, do not fear; your God will come, he will come with vengeance; with divine retribution he will come to save you."

⁵Then will the eyes of the blind be opened and the ears of the deaf unstopped. ⁶Then will the lame leap like a deer, and the mute tongue shout for joy. Water will gush forth in the wilderness and streams in the desert. ⁷The burning sand will become a pool, the thirsty ground bubbling springs. In the haunts where jackals once lay, grass and reeds and papyrus will grow.

⁸And a highway will be there; it will be called the Way of Holiness. The unclean will not journey on it; it will be

for those who walk in that Way; wicked fools will not go about on it. ⁹No lion will be there, nor will any ferocious beast get up on it; they will not be found there. But only the redeemed will walk there, ¹⁰and the ransomed of the LORD will return. They will enter Zion with singing; everlasting joy will crown their heads. Gladness and joy will overtake them, and sorrow and sighing will flee away. (+Isa 42:1-7,18-21)

Lk 2:10 But the angel said to them, "Do not be afraid. I bring you good news of great joy that will be for all the people.

Shall be a river of salvation (Eze 47:1-2)—

Eze 47:3 As the man went eastward with a measuring line in his hand, he measured off a thousand cubits and then led me through water that was ankle-deep. ⁴He measured off another thousand cubits and led me through water that was knee-deep. He measured off another thousand and led me through water that was up to the waist. ⁵He measured off another thousand, but now it was a river that I could not cross, because the water had risen and was deep enough to swim in—a river that no one could cross. (+Eze 47:6)

Eze 47:7 When I arrived there, I saw a great number of trees on each side of the river. ⁸He said to me, "This water flows toward the eastern region and goes down into the Arabah, where it enters the Sea. When it empties into the Sea, the water there becomes fresh. ⁹Swarms of living creatures will live wherever the river flows. There will be large numbers of fish, because this water flows there and makes the salt water fresh; so where the river flows everything will live. (+Eze 47:10-11)

Eze 47:12 Fruit trees of all kinds will grow on both banks of the river. Their leaves will not wither, nor will their fruit fail. Every month they will bear, because the water from the sanctuary flows to them. Their fruit will serve for food and their leaves for healing."

Zec 14:8 On that day living water will flow out from Jerusalem, half to the eastern sea and half to the western sea, in summer and in winter.

⁹The LORD will be king over the whole earth. On that day there will be one LORD, and his name the only name.

Zec 14:16 Then the survivors from all the nations that have attacked Jerusalem will go up year after year to worship the King, the LORD Almighty, and to celebrate the Feast of Tabernacles.

Zec 14:20 On that day HOLY TO THE LORD will be inscribed on the bells of the horses, and the cooking pots in the LORD's house will be like the sacred bowls in front of the altar. ²¹Every pot in Jerusalem and Judah will be holy to the LORD Almighty, and all who come to sacrifice will take some of the pots and cook in them. And on that day there will no longer be a Canaanite in the house of the LORD Almighty.

Will be forever—

Isa 51:6 Lift up your eyes to the heavens, look at the earth beneath; the heavens will vanish like smoke, the earth will wear out like a garment and its inhabitants die like flies. But my salvation will last forever, my righteousness will never fail.

Isa 51:8 For the moth will eat them up like a garment; the worm will devour them like wool. But my righteousness will last forever, my salvation through all generations."

Lk 1:33 and he will reign over the house of Jacob forever; his kingdom will never end."

Heb 1:8 But about the Son he says, "Your throne, O God, will last for ever and ever, and righteousness will be the scepter of your kingdom.

2Pe 1:11 and you will receive a rich welcome into the eternal kingdom of our Lord and Savior Jesus Christ.

It transforms—

Isa 35:1 The desert and the parched land will be glad; the wilderness will rejoice and blossom. Like the crocus, ²it will burst into bloom; it will rejoice greatly and shout for joy. The glory of Lebanon will be given to it, the splendor of Carmel and Sharon; they will see the glory of the LORD, the splendor of our God. (+Isa 35:3-10)

Isa 55:12 You will go out in joy and be led forth in peace; the mountains and hills will burst into song before you, and all the trees of the field will clap their hands. ¹³Instead of the thornbush will grow the pine tree, and instead of briers the myrtle will grow. This will be for the LORD's renown, for an everlasting sign, which will not be destroyed."

Isa 65:17 "Behold, I will create new heavens and a new earth. The former things will not be remembered, nor will they come to mind. ¹⁸But be glad and rejoice forever in what I will create, for I will create Jerusalem to be a delight and its people a joy. ¹⁹I will rejoice over Jerusalem and take delight in my people; the sound of weeping and of crying will be heard in it no more.

²⁰"Never again will there be in it an infant who lives but a few days, or an old man who does not live out his years; he who dies at a hundred will be thought a mere youth; he who fails to reach a hundred will be considered accursed. ²¹They will build houses and dwell in them; they will plant vineyards and eat their fruit. ²²No longer will they build houses and others live in them, or plant and others eat. For as the days of a tree, so will be the days of my people; my chosen ones will long enjoy the works of their hands. ²³They will not toil in vain or bear children doomed to misfortune; for they will be a people blessed by the LORD, they and their descendants with them. ²⁴Before they call I will answer; while they are still speaking I will hear. ²⁵The wolf and the lamb will feed together, and the lion will eat straw like the ox, but dust will be the serpent's food. They will neither harm nor destroy on all my holy mountain," says the LORD.

Future glory and greatness of the kingdom (Isa 49:22-23)—

Hag 2:7 I will shake all nations, and the desired of all nations will come, and I will fill this house with glory,' says the LORD Almighty. ⁸'The silver is mine and the gold is mine,' declares the LORD Almighty. ⁹'The glory of this present house will be greater than the glory of the former house,' says the LORD Almighty. 'And in this place I will grant peace,' declares the LORD Almighty."

Rev 21:9 One of the seven angels who had the seven bowls full of the seven last plagues came and said to me, "Come, I will show you the bride, the wife of the Lamb." ¹⁰And he carried me away in the Spirit to a mountain great and high, and showed me the Holy City, Jerusalem, coming down out of heaven from God. ¹¹It shone with the glory of God, and its brilliance was like that of a very precious jewel, like a jasper, clear as crystal. ¹²It had a great, high wall with twelve gates, and with twelve angels at the gates. On the gates were written the names of the twelve tribes of Israel. ¹³There were three gates on the east, three on the north, three on the south and three on the west. ¹⁴The wall of the city had twelve foundations, and on them were the names of the twelve apostles of the Lamb.

¹⁵The angel who talked with me had a measuring rod of gold to measure the city, its gates and its walls. ¹⁶The city was laid out like a square, as long as it was wide. He

measured the city with the rod and found it to be 12,000 stadia in length, and as wide and high as it is long. [17]He measured its wall and it was 144 cubits thick, by man's measurement, which the angel was using. [18]The wall was made of jasper, and the city of pure gold, as pure as glass. [19]The foundations of the city walls were decorated with every kind of precious stone. The first foundation was jasper, the second sapphire, the third chalcedony, the fourth emerald, [20]the fifth sardonyx, the sixth carnelian, the seventh chrysolite, the eighth beryl, the ninth topaz, the tenth chrysoprase, the eleventh jacinth, and the twelfth amethyst. [21]The twelve gates were twelve pearls, each gate made of a single pearl. The great street of the city was of pure gold, like transparent glass.

[22]I did not see a temple in the city, because the Lord God Almighty and the Lamb are its temple. [23]The city does not need the sun or the moon to shine on it, for the glory of God gives it light, and the Lamb is its lamp. [24]The nations will walk by its light, and the kings of the earth will bring their splendor into it. [25]On no day will its gates ever be shut, for there will be no night there. [26]The glory and honor of the nations will be brought into it. [27]Nothing impure will ever enter it, nor will anyone who does what is shameful or deceitful, but only those whose names are written in the Lamb's book of life.

Universality of the kingdom—

Ge 12:3 I will bless those who bless you, and whoever curses you I will curse; and all peoples on earth will be blessed through you." (+Ge 22:18)

Ge 49:10 The scepter will not depart from Judah, nor the ruler's staff from between his feet, until he comes to whom it belongs and the obedience of the nations is his.

Ps 72:5 He will endure as long as the sun, as long as the moon, through all generations.

Ps 72:8 He will rule from sea to sea and from the River to the ends of the earth. [9]The desert tribes will bow before him and his enemies will lick the dust. [10]The kings of Tarshish and of distant shores will bring tribute to him; the kings of Sheba and Seba will present him gifts. [11]All kings will bow down to him and all nations will serve him.

Ps 72:16 Let grain abound throughout the land; on the tops of the hills may it sway. Let its fruit flourish like Lebanon; let it thrive like the grass of the field. [17]May his name endure forever; may it continue as long as the sun. All nations will be blessed through him, and they will call him blessed.

Ps 72:19 Praise be to his glorious name forever; may the whole earth be filled with his glory. Amen and Amen.

Ps 89:1 I will sing of the LORD's great love forever; with my mouth I will make your faithfulness known through all generations. [2]I will declare that your love stands firm forever, that you established your faithfulness in heaven itself.

[3]You said, "I have made a covenant with my chosen one, I have sworn to David my servant, [4]'I will establish your line forever and make your throne firm through all generations.'" *Selah*

[5]The heavens praise your wonders, O LORD, your faithfulness too, in the assembly of the holy ones. [6]For who in the skies above can compare with the LORD? Who is like the LORD among the heavenly beings? [7]In the council of the holy ones God is greatly feared; he is more awesome than all who surround him. [8]O LORD God Almighty, who is like you? You are mighty, O LORD, and your faithfulness surrounds you.

[9]You rule over the surging sea; when its waves mount up, you still them. [10]You crushed Rahab like one of the slain; with your strong arm you scattered your enemies. [11]The heavens are yours, and yours also the earth; you founded the world and all that is in it. [12]You created the north and the south; Tabor and Hermon sing for joy at your name. [13]Your arm is endued with power; your hand is strong, your right hand exalted.

[14]Righteousness and justice are the foundation of your throne; love and faithfulness go before you. [15]Blessed are those who have learned to acclaim you, who walk in the light of your presence, O LORD. [16]They rejoice in your name all day long; they exult in your righteousness. [17]For you are their glory and strength, and by your favor you exalt our horn. [18]Indeed, our shield belongs to the LORD, our king to the Holy One of Israel.

[19]Once you spoke in a vision, to your faithful people you said: "I have bestowed strength on a warrior; I have exalted a young man from among the people. [20]I have found David my servant; with my sacred oil I have anointed him. [21]My hand will sustain him; surely my arm will strengthen him. [22]No enemy will subject him to tribute; no wicked man will oppress him. [23]I will crush his foes before him and strike down his adversaries. [24]My faithful love will be with him, and through my name his horn will be exalted. [25]I will set his hand over the sea, his right hand over the rivers. [26]He will call out to me, 'You are my Father, my God, the Rock my Savior.' [27]I will also appoint him my firstborn, the most exalted of the kings of the earth. [28]I will maintain my love to him forever, and my covenant with him will never fail. [29]I will establish his line forever, his throne as long as the heavens endure.

[30]"If his sons forsake my law and do not follow my statutes, [31]if they violate my decrees and fail to keep my commands, [32]I will punish their sin with the rod, their iniquity with flogging; [33]but I will not take my love from him, nor will I ever betray my faithfulness. [34]I will not violate my covenant or alter what my lips have uttered. [35]Once for all, I have sworn by my holiness—and I will not lie to David— [36]that his line will continue forever and his throne endure before me like the sun; [37]it will be established forever like the moon, the faithful witness in the sky." *Selah*

Ps 113:3 From the rising of the sun to the place where it sets, the name of the LORD is to be praised. (+Isa 9:6)

Isa 9:7 Of the increase of his government and peace there will be no end. He will reign on David's throne and over his kingdom, establishing and upholding it with justice and righteousness from that time on and forever. The zeal of the LORD Almighty will accomplish this. (+Isa 40:4)

Isa 40:5 And the glory of the LORD will be revealed, and all mankind together will see it. For the mouth of the LORD has spoken." (+Isa 40:6-11; 42:1-2)

Isa 42:3 A bruised reed he will not break, and a smoldering wick he will not snuff out. In faithfulness he will bring forth justice; [4]he will not falter or be discouraged till he establishes justice on earth. In his law the islands will put their hope." (+Isa 42:5-7; 49:1-11)

Isa 49:12 See, they will come from afar—some from the north, some from the west, some from the region of Aswan." (+Isa 49:13-17)

Isa 49:18 Lift up your eyes and look around; all your sons gather and come to you. As surely as I live," declares the LORD, "you will wear them all as ornaments; you will put them on, like a bride. (+Isa 49:19-26; 52:10)

Isa 54:1 "Sing, O barren woman, you who never bore a child; burst into song, shout for joy, you who were never in labor; because more are the children of the desolate woman than of her who has a husband," says the LORD. [2]"Enlarge the place of your tent, stretch your tent curtains wide, do not hold back; lengthen your cords, strengthen your stakes. [3]For you will spread out to the right and to the left; your descendants will dispossess nations and settle in their desolate cities.

Isa 59:19 From the west, men will fear the name of the LORD, and from the rising of the sun, they will revere his glory. For he will come like a pent-up flood that the breath of the LORD drives along. (+Isa 59:20-21; Jer 3:14-19)

Da 2:35 Then the iron, the clay, the bronze, the silver and the gold were broken to pieces at the same time and became like chaff on a threshing floor in the summer. The wind swept them away without leaving a trace. But the rock that struck the statue became a huge mountain and filled the whole earth.

Da 2:44 "In the time of those kings, the God of heaven will set up a kingdom that will never be destroyed, nor will it be left to another people. It will crush all those kingdoms and bring them to an end, but it will itself endure forever.

Da 7:13 "In my vision at night I looked, and there before me was one like a son of man, coming with the clouds of heaven. He approached the Ancient of Days and was led into his presence. [14]He was given authority, glory and sovereign power; all peoples, nations and men of every language worshiped him. His dominion is an everlasting dominion that will not pass away, and his kingdom is one that will never be destroyed.

Da 7:18 But the saints of the Most High will receive the kingdom and will possess it forever—yes, for ever and ever.'

Da 7:22 until the Ancient of Days came and pronounced judgment in favor of the saints of the Most High, and the time came when they possessed the kingdom.

Da 7:27 Then the sovereignty, power and greatness of the kingdoms under the whole heaven will be handed over to the saints, the people of the Most High. His kingdom will be an everlasting kingdom, and all rulers will worship and obey him.'

Hab 2:14 For the earth will be filled with the knowledge of the glory of the LORD, as the waters cover the sea.

Zec 9:1 The word of the LORD is against the land of Hadrach and will rest upon Damascus—for the eyes of men and all the tribes of Israel are on the LORD—

Zec 9:10 I will take away the chariots from Ephraim and the war-horses from Jerusalem, and the battle bow will be broken. He will proclaim peace to the nations. His rule will extend from sea to sea and from the River to the ends of the earth. (+Mt 8:11; Lk 13:29-30)

Rev 14:6 Then I saw another angel flying in midair, and he had the eternal gospel to proclaim to those who live on the earth—to every nation, tribe, language and people.

Unity of the kingdom—

Jn 10:16 I have other sheep that are not of this sheep pen. I must bring them also. They too will listen to my voice, and there shall be one flock and one shepherd.

Growth of the kingdom—

Mt 13:31 He told them another parable: "The kingdom of heaven is like a mustard seed, which a man took and planted in his field. [32]Though it is the smallest of all your seeds, yet when it grows, it is the largest of garden plants and becomes a tree, so that the birds of the air come and perch in its branches."

[33]He told them still another parable: "The kingdom of heaven is like yeast that a woman took and mixed into a large amount of flour until it worked all through the dough." (+Lk 13:21)

Ends of earth shall turn to him—

Ps 66:4 All the earth bows down to you; they sing praise to you, they sing praise to your name." *Selah*

Ps 86:9 All the nations you have made will come and worship before you, O Lord; they will bring glory to your name.

Isa 2:2 In the last days the mountain of the LORD's temple will be established as chief among the mountains; it will be raised above the hills, and all nations will stream to it.

[3]Many peoples will come and say, "Come, let us go up to the mountain of the LORD, to the house of the God of Jacob. He will teach us his ways, so that we may walk in his paths." The law will go out from Zion, the word of the LORD from Jerusalem. [4]He will judge between the nations and will settle disputes for many peoples. They will beat their swords into plowshares and their spears into pruning hooks. Nation will not take up sword against nation, nor will they train for war anymore. (+Isa 45:14)

Isa 60:1 "Arise, shine, for your light has come, and the glory of the LORD rises upon you. [2]See, darkness covers the earth and thick darkness is over the peoples, but the LORD rises upon you and his glory appears over you. [3]Nations will come to your light, and kings to the brightness of your dawn.

[4]"Lift up your eyes and look about you: All assemble and come to you; your sons come from afar, and your daughters are carried on the arm. [5]Then you will look and be radiant, your heart will throb and swell with joy; the wealth on the seas will be brought to you, to you the riches of the nations will come. (+Isa 60:6)

Isa 60:7 All Kedar's flocks will be gathered to you, the rams of Nebaioth will serve you; they will be accepted as offerings on my altar, and I will adorn my glorious temple.

[8]"Who are these that fly along like clouds, like doves to their nests? [9]Surely the islands look to me; in the lead are the ships of Tarshish, bringing your sons from afar, with their silver and gold, to the honor of the LORD your God, the Holy One of Israel, for he has endowed you with splendor.

Jer 3:17 At that time they will call Jerusalem The Throne of the LORD, and all nations will gather in Jerusalem to honor the name of the LORD. No longer will they follow the stubbornness of their evil hearts.

Jer 16:19 O LORD, my strength and my fortress, my refuge in time of distress, to you the nations will come from the ends of the earth and say, "Our fathers possessed nothing but false gods, worthless idols that did them no good. [20]Do men make their own gods? Yes, but they are not gods!"

[21]"Therefore I will teach them—this time I will teach them my power and might. Then they will know that my name is the LORD. (+Jer 33:16)

Eze 17:22 "'This is what the Sovereign LORD says: I myself will take a shoot from the very top of a cedar and plant it; I will break off a tender sprig from its topmost shoots and plant it on a high and lofty mountain. [23]On the mountain heights of Israel I will plant it; it will produce branches and bear fruit and become a splendid cedar. Birds of every kind will nest in it; they will find shelter in the shade of its branches.

Mic 4:1 In the last days the mountain of the LORD's temple will be established as chief among the mountains; it will be raised above the hills, and peoples will stream to it.

[2]Many nations will come and say, "Come, let us go up to the mountain of the LORD, to the house of the God of

Jacob. He will teach us his ways, so that we may walk in his paths." The law will go out from Zion, the word of the LORD from Jerusalem. ³He will judge between many peoples and will settle disputes for strong nations far and wide. They will beat their swords into plowshares and their spears into pruning hooks. Nation will not take up sword against nation, nor will they train for war anymore. ⁴Every man will sit under his own vine and under his own fig tree, and no one will make them afraid, for the LORD Almighty has spoken.

Zep 2:11 The LORD will be awesome to them when he destroys all the gods of the land. The nations on every shore will worship him, every one in its own land.

Zec 2:10 "Shout and be glad, O Daughter of Zion. For I am coming, and I will live among you," declares the LORD. ¹¹"Many nations will be joined with the LORD in that day and will become my people. I will live among you and you will know that the LORD Almighty has sent me to you.

Zec 6:15 Those who are far away will come and help to build the temple of the LORD, and you will know that the LORD Almighty has sent me to you. This will happen if you diligently obey the LORD your God."

Zec 8:20 This is what the LORD Almighty says: "Many peoples and the inhabitants of many cities will yet come, ²¹and the inhabitants of one city will go to another and say, 'Let us go at once to entreat the LORD and seek the LORD Almighty. I myself am going.' ²²And many peoples and powerful nations will come to Jerusalem to seek the LORD Almighty and to entreat him."

²³This is what the LORD Almighty says: "In those days ten men from all languages and nations will take firm hold of one Jew by the hem of his robe and say, 'Let us go with you, because we have heard that God is with you.'"

Shall include all nations—

Ps 2:8 Ask of me, and I will make the nations your inheritance, the ends of the earth your possession.

Ps 68:31 Envoys will come from Egypt; Cush will submit herself to God.

³²Sing to God, O kingdoms of the earth, sing praise to the Lord, *Selah*

Ps 110:4 The LORD has sworn and will not change his mind: "You are a priest forever, in the order of Melchizedek."

⁵The Lord is at your right hand; he will crush kings on the day of his wrath. ⁶He will judge the nations, heaping up the dead and crushing the rulers of the whole earth. (+Hos 2:23; Am 9:11-12)

Mal 1:11 My name will be great among the nations, from the rising to the setting of the sun. In every place incense and pure offerings will be brought to my name, because my name will be great among the nations," says the LORD Almighty.

Final triumph of the kingdom (Ge 3:15; Ps 2:9; Isa 11:1-5)—

Isa 11:6 The wolf will live with the lamb, the leopard will lie down with the goat, the calf and the lion and the yearling together; and a little child will lead them. ⁷The cow will feed with the bear, their young will lie down together, and the lion will eat straw like the ox. ⁸The infant will play near the hole of the cobra, and the young child put his hand into the viper's nest. ⁹They will neither harm nor destroy on all my holy mountain, for the earth will be full of the knowledge of the LORD as the waters cover the sea. ¹⁰In that day the Root of Jesse will stand as a banner for the peoples; the nations will rally to him, and his place

of rest will be glorious. (+Isa 11:11-13; Da 2:44; 7:9-14,27; Mt 16:18)

Ac 2:34 For David did not ascend to heaven, and yet he said, "'The Lord said to my Lord: "Sit at my right hand ³⁵until I make your enemies a footstool for your feet."'

1Co 15:24 Then the end will come, when he hands over the kingdom to God the Father after he has destroyed all dominion, authority and power. ²⁵For he must reign until he has put all his enemies under his feet. ²⁶The last enemy to be destroyed is death. ²⁷For he "has put everything under his feet." Now when it says that "everything" has been put under him, it is clear that this does not include God himself, who put everything under Christ. ²⁸When he has done this, then the Son himself will be made subject to him who put everything under him, so that God may be all in all.

Eph 1:10 to be put into effect when the times will have reached their fulfillment—to bring all things in heaven and on earth together under one head, even Christ.

Php 2:10 that at the name of Jesus every knee should bow, in heaven and on earth and under the earth, ¹¹and every tongue confess that Jesus Christ is Lord, to the glory of God the Father.

Heb 10:13 Since that time he waits for his enemies to be made his footstool,

Heb 12:23 to the church of the firstborn, whose names are written in heaven. You have come to God, the judge of all men, to the spirits of righteous men made perfect, ²⁴to Jesus the mediator of a new covenant, and to the sprinkled blood that speaks a better word than the blood of Abel.

Heb 12:27 The words "once more" indicate the removing of what can be shaken—that is, created things—so that what cannot be shaken may remain.

²⁸Therefore, since we are receiving a kingdom that cannot be shaken, let us be thankful, and so worship God acceptably with reverence and awe,

Rev 5:9 And they sang a new song:

"You are worthy to take the scroll and to open its seals, because you were slain, and with your blood you purchased men for God from every tribe and language and people and nation. ¹⁰You have made them to be a kingdom and priests to serve our God, and they will reign on the earth."

Rev 5:13 Then I heard every creature in heaven and on earth and under the earth and on the sea, and all that is in them, singing:

"To him who sits on the throne and to the Lamb be praise and honor and glory and power, for ever and ever!"

¹⁴The four living creatures said, "Amen," and the elders fell down and worshiped.

Rev 6:2 I looked, and there before me was a white horse! Its rider held a bow, and he was given a crown, and he rode out as a conqueror bent on conquest.

Rev 11:15 The seventh angel sounded his trumpet, and there were loud voices in heaven, which said: "The kingdom of the world has become the kingdom of our Lord and of his Christ, and he will reign for ever and ever.

Rev 12:10 Then I heard a loud voice in heaven say: "Now have come the salvation and the power and the kingdom of our God, and the authority of his Christ. For the accuser of our brothers, who accuses them before our God day and night, has been hurled down.

Rev 19:11 I saw heaven standing open and there before me was a white horse, whose rider is called Faithful and True. With justice he judges and makes war. ¹²His eyes are like blazing fire, and on his head are many crowns. He has a name written on him that no one knows but he himself. [13]He is dressed in a robe dipped in blood, and his name is the Word of God. [14]The armies of heaven were following him, riding on white horses and dressed in fine linen, white and clean. [15]Out of his mouth comes a sharp sword with which to strike down the nations. "He will rule them with an iron scepter." He treads the winepress of the fury of the wrath of God Almighty. [16]On his robe and on his thigh he has this name written: KING OF KINGS AND LORD OF LORDS.

[17]And I saw an angel standing in the sun, who cried in a loud voice to all the birds flying in midair, "Come, gather together for the great supper of God, [18]so that you may eat the flesh of kings, generals, and mighty men, of horses and their riders, and the flesh of all people, free and slave, small and great."

[19]Then I saw the beast and the kings of the earth and their armies gathered together to make war against the rider on the horse and his army. [20]But the beast was captured, and with him the false prophet who had performed the miraculous signs on his behalf. With these signs he had deluded those who had received the mark of the beast and worshiped his image. The two of them were thrown alive into the fiery lake of burning sulfur. [21]The rest of them were killed with the sword that came out of the mouth of the rider on the horse, and all the birds gorged themselves on their flesh.

Rev 20:1 And I saw an angel coming down out of heaven, having the key to the Abyss and holding in his hand a great chain. [2]He seized the dragon, that ancient serpent, who is the devil, or Satan, and bound him for a thousand years. [3]He threw him into the Abyss, and locked and sealed it over him, to keep him from deceiving the nations anymore until the thousand years were ended. After that, he must be set free for a short time.

Secular notions concerning: To restore the kingdom of Israel—

Mk 11:9 Those who went ahead and those who followed shouted, "Hosanna!"

"Blessed is he who comes in the name of the Lord!"

[10]"Blessed is the coming kingdom of our father David!"

"Hosanna in the highest!"

Jn 6:14 After the people saw the miraculous sign that Jesus did, they began to say, "Surely this is the Prophet who is to come into the world." [15]Jesus, knowing that they intended to come and make him king by force, withdrew again to a mountain by himself.

Ac 1:6 So when they met together, they asked him, "Lord, are you at this time going to restore the kingdom to Israel?"

[7]He said to them: "It is not for you to know the times or dates the Father has set by his own authority.

Rank of princes in the kingdom of—

Mt 20:20 Then the mother of Zebedee's sons came to Jesus with her sons and, kneeling down, asked a favor of him.

[21]"What is it you want?" he asked.

She said, "Grant that one of these two sons of mine may sit at your right and the other at your left in your kingdom."

[22]"You don't know what you are asking," Jesus said to them. "Can you drink the cup I am going to drink?"

"We can," they answered.

[23]Jesus said to them, "You will indeed drink from my cup, but to sit at my right or left is not for me to grant.

These places belong to those for whom they have been prepared by my Father." (+Mk 10:35-40; Lk 9:46-48)

Love of:

Ps 69:9 for zeal for your house consumes me, and the insults of those who insult you fall on me.

Rev 3:9 I will make those who are of the synagogue of Satan, who claim to be Jews though they are not, but are liars—I will make them come and fall down at your feet and acknowledge that I have loved you.

Rev 3:19 Those whom I love I rebuke and discipline. So be earnest, and repent.

Jesus' love compels us—

2Co 5:13 If we are out of our mind, it is for the sake of God; if we are in our right mind, it is for you. [14]For Christ's love compels us, because we are convinced that one died for all, and therefore all died.

Jesus' love surpasses knowledge—

Eph 3:17 so that Christ may dwell in your hearts through faith. And I pray that you, being rooted and established in love, [18]may have power, together with all the saints, to grasp how wide and long and high and deep is the love of Christ, [19]and to know this love that surpasses knowledge— that you may be filled to the measure of all the fullness of God.

Jesus' love for his disciples—

Jn 10:3 The watchman opens the gate for him, and the sheep listen to his voice. He calls his own sheep by name and leads them out. [4]When he has brought out all his own, he goes on ahead of them, and his sheep follow him because they know his voice.

Jn 10:11 "I am the good shepherd. The good shepherd lays down his life for the sheep.

Jn 10:14 "I am the good shepherd; I know my sheep and my sheep know me— [15]just as the Father knows me and I know the Father—and I lay down my life for the sheep. [16]I have other sheep that are not of this sheep pen. I must bring them also. They too will listen to my voice, and there shall be one flock and one shepherd.

Jn 13:1 It was just before the Passover Feast. Jesus knew that the time had come for him to leave this world and go to the Father. Having loved his own who were in the world, he now showed them the full extent of his love.

Jn 13:23 One of them, the disciple whom Jesus loved, was reclining next to him.

Jn 14:1 "Do not let your hearts be troubled. Trust in God; trust also in me. [2]In my Father's house are many rooms; if it were not so, I would have told you. I am going there to prepare a place for you. [3]And if I go and prepare a place for you, I will come back and take you to be with me that you also may be where I am.

Jn 14:18 I will not leave you as orphans; I will come to you.

Jn 14:21 Whoever has my commands and obeys them, he is the one who loves me. He who loves me will be loved by my Father, and I too will love him and show myself to him."

Jn 14:27 Peace I leave with you; my peace I give you. I do not give to you as the world gives. Do not let your hearts be troubled and do not be afraid.

Jn 15:9 "As the Father has loved me, so have I loved you. Now remain in my love. [10]If you obey my commands, you will remain in my love, just as I have obeyed my Father's commands and remain in his love. [11]I have told you this so that my joy may be in you and that your joy may be complete. [12]My command is this: Love each other as I have loved you. [13]Greater love has no one than this, that he lay down his life for his friends.

Jn 15:15 I no longer call you servants, because a servant does not know his master's business. Instead, I have called you friends, for everything that I learned from my Father I have made known to you. (+Jn 17:6-11)

Jn 17:12 While I was with them, I protected them and kept them safe by that name you gave me. None has been lost except the one doomed to destruction so that Scripture would be fulfilled. (+Jn 17:13-14)

Jn 17:15 My prayer is not that you take them out of the world but that you protect them from the evil one. (+Jn 17:16-18)

Jn 17:19 For them I sanctify myself, that they too may be truly sanctified. (+Jn 17:20-26)

Ro 8:35 Who shall separate us from the love of Christ? Shall trouble or hardship or persecution or famine or nakedness or danger or sword?

Ro 8:37 No, in all these things we are more than conquerors through him who loved us. [38]For I am convinced that neither death nor life, neither angels nor demons, neither the present nor the future, nor any powers, [39]neither height nor depth, nor anything else in all creation, will be able to separate us from the love of God that is in Christ Jesus our Lord.

2Th 2:13 But we ought always to thank God for you, brothers loved by the Lord, because from the beginning God chose you to be saved through the sanctifying work of the Spirit and through belief in the truth.

Jesus' love for children (Mt 19:13-15)—

Mk 10:13 People were bringing little children to Jesus to have him touch them, but the disciples rebuked them. [14]When Jesus saw this, he was indignant. He said to them, "Let the little children come to me, and do not hinder them, for the kingdom of God belongs to such as these."

Mk 10:16 And he took the children in his arms, put his hands on them and blessed them. (+Lk 18:15-16)

Jesus' love for his mother—

Jn 19:26 When Jesus saw his mother there, and the disciple whom he loved standing nearby, he said to his mother, "Dear woman, here is your son," [27]and to the disciple, "Here is your mother." From that time on, this disciple took her into his home.

Jesus' love for the lost—

Isa 40:11 He tends his flock like a shepherd: He gathers the lambs in his arms and carries them close to his heart; he gently leads those that have young.

Mt 18:12 "What do you think? If a man owns a hundred sheep, and one of them wanders away, will he not leave the ninety-nine on the hills and go to look for the one that wandered off? [13]And if he finds it, I tell you the truth, he is happier about that one sheep than about the ninety-nine that did not wander off.

Mk 8:12 He sighed deeply and said, "Why does this generation ask for a miraculous sign? I tell you the truth, no sign will be given to it." (+Lk 13:34)

Jesus' love exemplified: In renunciation—

2Co 8:9 For you know the grace of our Lord Jesus Christ, that though he was rich, yet for your sakes he became poor, so that you through his poverty might become rich. (+Php 2:6-8)

In compassion—

Isa 42:3 A bruised reed he will not break, and a smoldering wick he will not snuff out. In faithfulness he will bring forth justice;

Mt 9:36 When he saw the crowds, he had compassion on them, because they were harassed and helpless, like sheep without a shepherd.

Mt 14:14 When Jesus landed and saw a large crowd, he had compassion on them and healed their sick.

Mt 15:32 Jesus called his disciples to him and said, "I have compassion for these people; they have already been with me three days and have nothing to eat. I do not want to send them away hungry, or they may collapse on the way."

Lk 7:13 When the Lord saw her, his heart went out to her and he said, "Don't cry."

Lk 22:31 "Simon, Simon, Satan has asked to sift you as wheat. [32]But I have prayed for you, Simon, that your faith may not fail. And when you have turned back, strengthen your brothers."

Jn 11:5 Jesus loved Martha and her sister and Lazarus.

Jn 11:33 When Jesus saw her weeping, and the Jews who had come along with her also weeping, he was deeply moved in spirit and troubled. [34]"Where have you laid him?" he asked.

"Come and see, Lord," they replied.

[35]Jesus wept.

[36]Then the Jews said, "See how he loved him!"

Ac 10:38 how God anointed Jesus of Nazareth with the Holy Spirit and power, and how he went around doing good and healing all who were under the power of the devil, because God was with him.

Heb 4:15 For we do not have a high priest who is unable to sympathize with our weaknesses, but we have one who has been tempted in every way, just as we are—yet was without sin.

In his heart for others—

Mt 23:37 "O Jerusalem, Jerusalem, you who kill the prophets and stone those sent to you, how often I have longed to gather your children together, as a hen gathers her chicks under her wings, but you were not willing.

Lk 23:28 Jesus turned and said to them, "Daughters of Jerusalem, do not weep for me; weep for yourselves and for your children. (+Lk 23:34)

Jn 18:8 "I told you that I am he," Jesus answered. "If you are looking for me, then let these men go." [9]This happened so that the words he had spoken would be fulfilled: "I have not lost one of those you gave me."

In his sacrifice—

Gal 2:20 I have been crucified with Christ and I no longer live, but Christ lives in me. The life I live in the body, I live by faith in the Son of God, who loved me and gave himself for me.

Eph 5:2 and live a life of love, just as Christ loved us and gave himself up for us as a fragrant offering and sacrifice to God.

Eph 5:25 Husbands, love your wives, just as Christ loved the church and gave himself up for her

Eph 5:29 After all, no one ever hated his own body, but he feeds and cares for it, just as Christ does the church— [30]for we are members of his body.

1Jn 3:16 This is how we know what love is: Jesus Christ laid down his life for us. And we ought to lay down our lives for our brothers.

Rev 1:5 and from Jesus Christ, who is the faithful witness, the firstborn from the dead, and the ruler of the kings of the earth. To him who loves us and has freed us from our sins by his blood,

In his vicarious suffering (Isa 53:4)—

Mt 8:17 This was to fulfill what was spoken through the

prophet Isaiah: "He took up our infirmities and carried our diseases."

Ro 15:3 For even Christ did not please himself but, as it is written: "The insults of those who insult you have fallen on me."

In redemption—

Ps 72:14 He will rescue them from oppression and violence, for precious is their blood in his sight.

Isa 63:9 In all their distress he too was distressed, and the angel of his presence saved them. In his love and mercy he redeemed them; he lifted them up and carried them all the days of old.

Lordship of:

The sovereignty of the Messiah, as conceived by Old Testament writers, seems best described by the word King; but New Testament writers use the word Lord. *See above, King.* Jesus said of himself, the son of man is Lord even of the Sabbath (Mt 12:8; Mk 2:28).

The student will find suggestions for profitable reflection in a study of the various forms of expression used by the authors of the epistles in which they attribute Lordship to our Savior (Mt 12:8; Ac 2:36; Ro 1:7; 5:1,11,21; 6:23; 7:25; 8:39; 10:9; 13:14; 14:14; 15:6,30; 16:20; 1Co 1:2-3,7-10; 5:4; 6:11)—

1Co 8:6 yet for us there is but one God, the Father, from whom all things came and for whom we live; and there is but one Lord, Jesus Christ, through whom all things came and through whom we live. (+1Co 9:1; 11:25; 12:3; 15:31,57; 16:23; 2Co 1:2-3,14; 4:5,14; 8:9; 11:31; 13:14; Gal 1:3; 6:14,18; Eph 1:2-3,17; 3:11; 5:20; 6:23-24; Php 1:2,11; 2:19; 3:20; 4:23; Col 1:3; 2:6; 3:17,24; 1Th 1:1,3; 4:1; 5:10,24,28; 2Th 1:1-2,7,12; 2:1,8,15-16; 3:6,12,18; 1Ti 1:2,12; 6:3,14; 2Ti 1:2; Phm 1,3,5,25; Jas 1:1; 2:1; 1Pe 1:3; 3:15; 2Pe 1:2,8,14,16; 2:20; 3:18; Jude 4,18,21,25)

Mediation of:

Jn 14:6 Jesus answered, "I am the way and the truth and the life. No one comes to the Father except through me.

Jn 14:14 You may ask me for anything in my name, and I will do it.

Jn 16:23 In that day you will no longer ask me anything. I tell you the truth, my Father will give you whatever you ask in my name. ²⁴Until now you have not asked for anything in my name. Ask and you will receive, and your joy will be complete.

Jn 16:26 In that day you will ask in my name. I am not saying that I will ask the Father on your behalf.

Jn 20:31 But these are written that you may believe that Jesus is the Christ, the Son of God, and that by believing you may have life in his name.

Ro 1:8 First, I thank my God through Jesus Christ for all of you, because your faith is being reported all over the world.

Ro 5:1 Therefore, since we have been justified through faith, we have peace with God through our Lord Jesus Christ, ²through whom we have gained access by faith into this grace in which we now stand. And we rejoice in the hope of the glory of God.

Ro 6:23 For the wages of sin is death, but the gift of God is eternal life in Christ Jesus our Lord.

1Co 6:11 And that is what some of you were. But you were washed, you were sanctified, you were justified in the name of the Lord Jesus Christ and by the Spirit of our God.

1Co 15:57 But thanks be to God! He gives us the victory through our Lord Jesus Christ.

2Co 1:20 For no matter how many promises God has made, they are "Yes" in Christ. And so through him the "Amen" is spoken by us to the glory of God.

Eph 3:12 In him and through faith in him we may approach God with freedom and confidence.

Eph 4:32 Be kind and compassionate to one another, forgiving each other, just as in Christ God forgave you.

Eph 5:20 always giving thanks to God the Father for everything, in the name of our Lord Jesus Christ.

Col 3:17 And whatever you do, whether in word or deed, do it all in the name of the Lord Jesus, giving thanks to God the Father through him.

1Ti 2:1 I urge, then, first of all, that requests, prayers, intercession and thanksgiving be made for everyone—

1Ti 2:3 This is good, and pleases God our Savior,

1Ti 2:5 For there is one God and one mediator between God and men, the man Christ Jesus,

Heb 9:11 When Christ came as high priest of the good things that are already here, he went through the greater and more perfect tabernacle that is not man-made, that is to say, not a part of this creation. ¹²He did not enter by means of the blood of goats and calves; but he entered the Most Holy Place once for all by his own blood, having obtained eternal redemption. (+Heb 9:13-14)

Heb 9:15 For this reason Christ is the mediator of a new covenant, that those who are called may receive the promised eternal inheritance—now that he has died as a ransom to set them free from the sins committed under the first covenant. (+Heb 9:16-23)

Heb 9:24 For Christ did not enter a man-made sanctuary that was only a copy of the true one; he entered heaven itself, now to appear for us in God's presence. (+Heb 9:25-28)

Heb 13:15 Through Jesus, therefore, let us continually offer to God a sacrifice of praise—the fruit of lips that confess his name.

1Pe 2:5 you also, like living stones, are being built into a spiritual house to be a holy priesthood, offering spiritual sacrifices acceptable to God through Jesus Christ.

1Jn 2:1 My dear children, I write this to you so that you will not sin. But if anybody does sin, we have one who speaks to the Father in our defense—Jesus Christ, the Righteous One. ²He is the atoning sacrifice for our sins, and not only for ours but also for the sins of the whole world.

1Jn 2:12 I write to you, dear children, because your sins have been forgiven on account of his name.

As a priest—

Ps 110:4 The LORD has sworn and will not change his mind: "You are a priest forever, in the order of Melchizedek."

Zec 6:13 It is he who will build the temple of the LORD, and he will be clothed with majesty and will sit and rule on his throne. And he will be a priest on his throne. And there will be harmony between the two.'

Heb 2:17 For this reason he had to be made like his brothers in every way, in order that he might become a merciful and faithful high priest in service to God, and that he might make atonement for the sins of the people.

Heb 3:1 Therefore, holy brothers, who share in the heavenly calling, fix your thoughts on Jesus, the apostle and high priest whom we confess. ²He was faithful to the one who appointed him, just as Moses was faithful in all God's house.

Heb 4:14 Therefore, since we have a great high priest who has gone through the heavens, Jesus the Son of God, let us hold firmly to the faith we profess. [15]For we do not have a high priest who is unable to sympathize with our weaknesses, but we have one who has been tempted in every way, just as we are—yet was without sin.

Heb 5:5 So Christ also did not take upon himself the glory of becoming a high priest. But God said to him,

"You are my Son; today I have become your Father."

[6]And he says in another place,

"You are a priest forever, in the order of Melchizedek."

Heb 5:10 and was designated by God to be high priest in the order of Melchizedek.

Heb 6:19 We have this hope as an anchor for the soul, firm and secure. It enters the inner sanctuary behind the curtain, [20]where Jesus, who went before us, has entered on our behalf. He has become a high priest forever, in the order of Melchizedek.

Heb 7:1 This Melchizedek was king of Salem and priest of God Most High. He met Abraham returning from the defeat of the kings and blessed him,

Heb 7:3 Without father or mother, without genealogy, without beginning of days or end of life, like the Son of God he remains a priest forever.

Heb 7:19 (for the law made nothing perfect), and a better hope is introduced, by which we draw near to God. (+Heb 7:21)

Heb 7:24 but because Jesus lives forever, he has a permanent priesthood. [25]Therefore he is able to save completely those who come to God through him, because he always lives to intercede for them. [26]Such a high priest meets our need—one who is holy, blameless, pure, set apart from sinners, exalted above the heavens. [27]Unlike the other high priests, he does not need to offer sacrifices day after day, first for his own sins, and then for the sins of the people. He sacrificed for their sins once for all when he offered himself. [28]For the law appoints as high priests men who are weak; but the oath, which came after the law, appointed the Son, who has been made perfect forever. (+Heb 8:1-2)

Heb 8:6 But the ministry Jesus has received is as superior to theirs as the covenant of which he is mediator is superior to the old one, and it is founded on better promises. (+Heb 9:11)

Heb 10:19 Therefore, brothers, since we have confidence to enter the Most Holy Place by the blood of Jesus, [20]by a new and living way opened for us through the curtain, that is, his body, [21]and since we have a great priest over the house of God,

Through his sacrifice—

Eph 2:13 But now in Christ Jesus you who once were far away have been brought near through the blood of Christ.

[14]For he himself is our peace, who has made the two one and has destroyed the barrier, the dividing wall of hostility, [15]by abolishing in his flesh the law with its commandments and regulations. His purpose was to create in himself one new man out of the two, thus making peace, [16]and in this one body to reconcile both of them to God through the cross, by which he put to death their hostility. [17]He came and preached peace to you who were far away and peace to those who were near. [18]For through him we both have access to the Father by one Spirit.

Heb 10:11 Day after day every priest stands and performs his religious duties; again and again he offers the same sacrifices, which can never take away sins. [12]But when this priest had offered for all time one sacrifice for sins, he sat down at the right hand of God.

Heb 12:24 to Jesus the mediator of a new covenant, and to the sprinkled blood that speaks a better word than the blood of Abel.

Exemplified in his intercession—

Isa 53:12 Therefore I will give him a portion among the great, and he will divide the spoils with the strong, because he poured out his life unto death, and was numbered with the transgressors. For he bore the sin of many, and made intercession for the transgressors. (+Lk 13:8-9)

Lk 22:31 "Simon, Simon, Satan has asked to sift you as wheat. [32]But I have prayed for you, Simon, that your faith may not fail. And when you have turned back, strengthen your brothers."

Lk 23:33 When they came to the place called the Skull, there they crucified him, along with the criminals—one on his right, the other on his left. [34]Jesus said, "Father, forgive them, for they do not know what they are doing." And they divided up his clothes by casting lots.

Jn 14:16 And I will ask the Father, and he will give you another Counselor to be with you forever—

Jn 17:9 I pray for them. I am not praying for the world, but for those you have given me, for they are yours.

Jn 17:11 I will remain in the world no longer, but they are still in the world, and I am coming to you. Holy Father, protect them by the power of your name—the name you gave me—so that they may be one as we are one.

Jn 17:15 My prayer is not that you take them out of the world but that you protect them from the evil one. [16]They are not of the world, even as I am not of it. [17]Sanctify them by the truth; your word is truth. (+Jn 17:19)

Jn 17:20 "My prayer is not for them alone. I pray also for those who will believe in me through their message, [21]that all of them may be one, Father, just as you are in me and I am in you. May they also be in us so that the world may believe that you have sent me. [22]I have given them the glory that you gave me, that they may be one as we are one:

Ro 8:34 Who is he that condemns? Christ Jesus, who died—more than that, who was raised to life—is at the right hand of God and is also interceding for us.

See below, Priesthood of.

Meekness of:

Mt 11:29 Take my yoke upon you and learn from me, for I am gentle and humble in heart, and you will find rest for your souls. (+Mk 14:60-61; 15:3-5)

2Co 10:1 By the meekness and gentleness of Christ, I appeal to you—I, Paul, who am "timid" when face to face with you, but "bold" when away!

Php 2:8 And being found in appearance as a man, he humbled himself and became obedient to death—even death on a cross!

Prophecies concerning—

Ps 45:4 In your majesty ride forth victoriously in behalf of truth, humility and righteousness; let your right hand display awesome deeds. (+Isa 42:1)

Isa 42:2 He will not shout or cry out, or raise his voice in the streets. (+Isa 42:3)

Isa 50:5 The Sovereign LORD has opened my ears, and I have not been rebellious; I have not drawn back. [6]I offered my back to those who beat me, my cheeks to those who pulled out my beard; I did not hide my face from mocking and spitting. (+Isa 52:1,14)

Isa 53:7 He was oppressed and afflicted, yet he did not open his mouth; he was led like a lamb to the slaughter, and as a sheep before her shearers is silent, so he did not open his mouth.

Mt 12:19 He will not quarrel or cry out; no one will hear his voice in the streets. [20]A bruised reed he will not break, and a smoldering wick he will not snuff out, till he leads justice to victory.

Mt 21:5 "Say to the Daughter of Zion, 'See, your king comes to you, gentle and riding on a donkey, on a colt, the foal of a donkey.'" (+Ac 8:32)

Exemplified in not resenting false accusation—

Mk 2:6 Now some teachers of the law were sitting there, thinking to themselves, [7]"Why does this fellow talk like that? He's blaspheming! Who can forgive sins but God alone?"

[8]Immediately Jesus knew in his spirit that this was what they were thinking in their hearts, and he said to them, "Why are you thinking these things? [9]Which is easier: to say to the paralytic, 'Your sins are forgiven,' or to say, 'Get up, take your mat and walk'? [10]But that you may know that the Son of Man has authority on earth to forgive sins . . . ." He said to the paralytic, [11]"I tell you, get up, take your mat and go home."

Exemplified in submitting to enemies (Mt 26:47-48)—

Mt 26:49 Going at once to Jesus, Judas said, "Greetings, Rabbi!" and kissed him.

[50]Jesus replied, "Friend, do what you came for."

Then the men stepped forward, seized Jesus and arrested him.

[51]With that, one of Jesus' companions reached for his sword, drew it out and struck the servant of the high priest, cutting off his ear.

[52]"Put your sword back in its place," Jesus said to him, "for all who draw the sword will die by the sword. [53]Do you think I cannot call on my Father, and he will at once put at my disposal more than twelve legions of angels? [54]But how then would the Scriptures be fulfilled that say it must happen in this way?"

[55]At that time Jesus said to the crowd, "Am I leading a rebellion, that you have come out with swords and clubs to capture me? Every day I sat in the temple courts teaching, and you did not arrest me. [56]But this has all taken place that the writings of the prophets might be fulfilled." Then all the disciples deserted him and fled.

[57]Those who had arrested Jesus took him to Caiaphas, the high priest, where the teachers of the law and the elders had assembled. [58]But Peter followed him at a distance, right up to the courtyard of the high priest. He entered and sat down with the guards to see the outcome.

[59]The chief priests and the whole Sanhedrin were looking for false evidence against Jesus so that they could put him to death. [60]But they did not find any, though many false witnesses came forward.

Finally two came forward [61]and declared, "This fellow said, 'I am able to destroy the temple of God and rebuild it in three days.'"

[62]Then the high priest stood up and said to Jesus, "Are you not going to answer? What is this testimony that these men are bringing against you?" [63]But Jesus remained silent.

The high priest said to him, "I charge you under oath by the living God: Tell us if you are the Christ, the Son of God."

Mt 27:12 When he was accused by the chief priests and the elders, he gave no answer. [13]Then Pilate asked him, "Don't you hear the testimony they are bringing against you?" [14]But Jesus made no reply, not even to a single charge—to the great amazement of the governor.

Jn 8:48 The Jews answered him, "Aren't we right in saying that you are a Samaritan and demon-possessed?"

[49]"I am not possessed by a demon," said Jesus, "but I honor my Father and you dishonor me. [50]I am not seeking glory for myself; but there is one who seeks it, and he is the judge.

Heb 12:2 Let us fix our eyes on Jesus, the author and perfecter of our faith, who for the joy set before him endured the cross, scorning its shame, and sat down at the right hand of the throne of God. [3]Consider him who endured such opposition from sinful men, so that you will not grow weary and lose heart.

1Pe 2:23 When they hurled their insults at him, he did not retaliate; when he suffered, he made no threats. Instead, he entrusted himself to him who judges justly.

Exemplified in praying for enemies—

Lk 23:34 Jesus said, "Father, forgive them, for they do not know what they are doing." And they divided up his clothes by casting lots.

Exemplified in becoming a servant—

Php 2:7 but made himself nothing, taking the very nature of a servant, being made in human likeness.

See above, Humility of; Meekness.

Messiah:

Messianic Psalms—

Ps 2:1 Why do the nations conspire and the peoples plot in vain? [2]The kings of the earth take their stand and the rulers gather together against the LORD and against his Anointed One. [3]"Let us break their chains," they say, "and throw off their fetters."

[4]The One enthroned in heaven laughs; the Lord scoffs at them. [5]Then he rebukes them in his anger and terrifies them in his wrath, saying, [6]"I have installed my King on Zion, my holy hill."

[7]I will proclaim the decree of the LORD: He said to me, "You are my Son; today I have become your Father. [8]Ask of me, and I will make the nations your inheritance, the ends of the earth your possession. [9]You will rule them with an iron scepter; you will dash them to pieces like pottery."

[10]Therefore, you kings, be wise; be warned, you rulers of the earth. [11]Serve the LORD with fear and rejoice with trembling. [12]Kiss the Son, lest he be angry and you be destroyed in your way, for his wrath can flare up in a moment. Blessed are all who take refuge in him.

Ps 67:1 May God be gracious to us and bless us and make his face shine upon us, *Selah* [2]that your ways may be known on earth, your salvation among all nations.

[3]May the peoples praise you, O God; may all the peoples praise you. [4]May the nations be glad and sing for joy, for you rule the peoples justly and guide the nations of the earth. *Selah* [5]May the peoples praise you, O God; may all the peoples praise you.

[6]Then the land will yield its harvest, and God, our God, will bless us. [7]God will bless us, and all the ends of the earth will fear him. (+Ps 68:1-27)

Ps 68:28 Summon your power, O God; show us your strength, O God, as you have done before. [29]Because of your temple at Jerusalem kings will bring you gifts. [30]Rebuke the beast among the reeds, the herd of bulls among the calves of the nations. Humbled, may it bring bars of silver. Scatter the nations who delight in war. [31]Envoys will come from Egypt; Cush will submit herself to God.

[32]Sing to God, O kingdoms of the earth, sing praise to the Lord, *Selah* [33]to him who rides the ancient skies above, who thunders with mighty voice. [34]Proclaim the power of God, whose majesty is over Israel, whose power is in the

skies. [35]You are awesome, O God, in your sanctuary; the God of Israel gives power and strength to his people. Praise be to God!

Ps 69:1 Save me, O God, for the waters have come up to my neck. [2]I sink in the miry depths, where there is no foothold. I have come into the deep waters; the floods engulf me. [3]I am worn out calling for help; my throat is parched. My eyes fail, looking for my God. [4]Those who hate me without reason outnumber the hairs of my head; many are my enemies without cause, those who seek to destroy me. I am forced to restore what I did not steal.

[5]You know my folly, O God; my guilt is not hidden from you.

[6]May those who hope in you not be disgraced because of me, O Lord, the LORD Almighty; may those who seek you not be put to shame because of me, O God of Israel. [7]For I endure scorn for your sake, and shame covers my face. [8]I am a stranger to my brothers, an alien to my own mother's sons; [9]for zeal for your house consumes me, and the insults of those who insult you fall on me. [10]When I weep and fast, I must endure scorn; [11]when I put on sackcloth, people make sport of me. [12]Those who sit at the gate mock me, and I am the song of the drunkards.

[13]But I pray to you, O LORD, in the time of your favor; in your great love, O God, answer me with your sure salvation. [14]Rescue me from the mire, do not let me sink; deliver me from those who hate me, from the deep waters. [15]Do not let the floodwaters engulf me or the depths swallow me up or the pit close its mouth over me. [16]Answer me, O LORD, out of the goodness of your love; in your great mercy turn to me. [17]Do not hide your face from your servant; answer me quickly, for I am in trouble. [18]Come near and rescue me; redeem me because of my foes.

[19]You know how I am scorned, disgraced and shamed; all my enemies are before you. [20]Scorn has broken my heart and has left me helpless; I looked for sympathy, but there was none, for comforters, but I found none. [21]They put gall in my food and gave me vinegar for my thirst.

[22]May the table set before them become a snare; may it become retribution and a trap. [23]May their eyes be darkened so they cannot see, and their backs be bent forever. [24]Pour out your wrath on them; let your fierce anger overtake them. [25]May their place be deserted; let there be no one to dwell in their tents. [26]For they persecute those you wound and talk about the pain of those you hurt. [27]Charge them with crime upon crime; do not let them share in your salvation. [28]May they be blotted out of the book of life and not be listed with the righteous.

[29]I am in pain and distress; may your salvation, O God, protect me.

[30]I will praise God's name in song and glorify him with thanksgiving. [31]This will please the LORD more than an ox, more than a bull with its horns and hoofs. [32]The poor will see and be glad—you who seek God, may your hearts live! [33]The LORD hears the needy and does not despise his captive people.

[34]Let heaven and earth praise him, the seas and all that move in them, [35]for God will save Zion and rebuild the cities of Judah. Then people will settle there and possess it; [36]the children of his servants will inherit it, and those who love his name will dwell there.

Ps 72:1 Endow the king with your justice, O God, the royal son with your righteousness. [2]He will judge your people in righteousness, your afflicted ones with justice. [3]The mountains will bring prosperity to the people, the hills the fruit of righteousness. [4]He will defend the

afflicted among the people and save the children of the needy; he will crush the oppressor.

[5]He will endure as long as the sun, as long as the moon, through all generations. [6]He will be like rain falling on a mown field, like showers watering the earth. [7]In his days the righteous will flourish; prosperity will abound till the moon is no more.

[8]He will rule from sea to sea and from the River to the ends of the earth. [9]The desert tribes will bow before him and his enemies will lick the dust. [10]The kings of Tarshish and of distant shores will bring tribute to him; the kings of Sheba and Seba will present him gifts. [11]All kings will bow down to him and all nations will serve him.

[12]For he will deliver the needy who cry out, the afflicted who have no one to help. [13]He will take pity on the weak and the needy and save the needy from death. [14]He will rescue them from oppression and violence, for precious is their blood in his sight.

[15]Long may he live! May gold from Sheba be given him. May people ever pray for him and bless him all day long. [16]Let grain abound throughout the land; on the tops of the hills may it sway. Let its fruit flourish like Lebanon; let it thrive like the grass of the field. [17]May his name endure forever; may it continue as long as the sun. All nations will be blessed through him, and they will call him blessed.

[18]Praise be to the LORD God, the God of Israel, who alone does marvelous deeds. [19]Praise be to his glorious name forever; may the whole earth be filled with his glory. Amen and Amen. (+Ps 72:20)

Ps 96:1 Sing to the LORD a new song; sing to the LORD, all the earth. [2]Sing to the LORD, praise his name; proclaim his salvation day after day. [3]Declare his glory among the nations, his marvelous deeds among all peoples.

[4]For great is the LORD and most worthy of praise; he is to be feared above all gods. [5]For all the gods of the nations are idols, but the LORD made the heavens. [6]Splendor and majesty are before him; strength and glory are in his sanctuary.

[7]Ascribe to the LORD, O families of nations, ascribe to the LORD glory and strength. [8]Ascribe to the LORD the glory due his name; bring an offering and come into his courts. [9]Worship the LORD in the splendor of his holiness; tremble before him, all the earth.

[10]Say among the nations, "The LORD reigns." The world is firmly established, it cannot be moved; he will judge the peoples with equity. [11]Let the heavens rejoice, let the earth be glad; let the sea resound, and all that is in it; [12]let the fields be jubilant, and everything in them. Then all the trees of the forest will sing for joy; [13]they will sing before the LORD, for he comes, he comes to judge the earth. He will judge the world in righteousness and the peoples in his truth.

Ps 98:1 Sing to the LORD a new song, for he has done marvelous things; his right hand and his holy arm have worked salvation for him. [2]The LORD has made his salvation known and revealed his righteousness to the nations. [3]He has remembered his love and his faithfulness to the house of Israel; all the ends of the earth have seen the salvation of our God.

[4]Shout for joy to the LORD, all the earth, burst into jubilant song with music; [5]make music to the LORD with the harp, with the harp and the sound of singing, [6]with trumpets and the blast of the ram's horn—shout for joy before the LORD, the King.

[7]Let the sea resound, and everything in it, the world, and all who live in it. [8]Let the rivers clap their hands, let the

mountains sing together for joy; ⁹let them sing before the LORD, for he comes to judge the earth. He will judge the world in righteousness and the peoples with equity.

Ps 110:1 The LORD says to my Lord: "Sit at my right hand until I make your enemies a footstool for your feet."

²The LORD will extend your mighty scepter from Zion; you will rule in the midst of your enemies. ³Your troops will be willing on your day of battle. Arrayed in holy majesty, from the womb of the dawn you will receive the dew of your youth.

⁴The LORD has sworn and will not change his mind: "You are a priest forever, in the order of Melchizedek."

⁵The Lord is at your right hand; he will crush kings on the day of his wrath. ⁶He will judge the nations, heaping up the dead and crushing the rulers of the whole earth. ⁷He will drink from a brook beside the way; therefore he will lift up his head.

Prophecies concerning the Messiah—

Da 9:25 "Know and understand this: From the issuing of the decree to restore and rebuild Jerusalem until the Anointed One, the ruler, comes, there will be seven 'sevens,' and sixty-two 'sevens.' It will be rebuilt with streets and a trench, but in times of trouble. ²⁶After the sixty-two 'sevens,' the Anointed One will be cut off and will have nothing. The people of the ruler who will come will destroy the city and the sanctuary. The end will come like a flood: War will continue until the end, and desolations have been decreed.

Ac 3:18 But this is how God fulfilled what he had foretold through all the prophets, saying that his Christ would suffer. (+Ac 3:19)

Ac 3:20 and that he may send the Christ, who has been appointed for you—even Jesus.

Simeon's testimony to the Messiah—

Lk 2:28 Simeon took him in his arms and praised God, saying:

²⁹"Sovereign Lord, as you have promised, you now dismiss your servant in peace. ³⁰For my eyes have seen your salvation, ³¹which you have prepared in the sight of all people, ³²a light for revelation to the Gentiles and for glory to your people Israel."

Andrew's belief in the Messiah—

Jn 1:41 The first thing Andrew did was to find his brother Simon and tell him, "We have found the Messiah" (that is, the Christ).

Jn 1:45 Philip found Nathanael and told him, "We have found the one Moses wrote about in the Law, and about whom the prophets also wrote—Jesus of Nazareth, the son of Joseph."

Peter's confession of the Messiah—

Mt 16:15 "But what about you?" he asked. "Who do you say I am?"

¹⁶Simon Peter answered, "You are the Christ, the Son of the living God." (+Mk 8:29; Lk 9:20; Jn 6:69)

His own testimony to his messiahship—

Mt 11:3 to ask him, "Are you the one who was to come, or should we expect someone else?"

⁴Jesus replied, "Go back and report to John what you hear and see: ⁵The blind receive sight, the lame walk, those who have leprosy are cured, the deaf hear, the dead are raised, and the good news is preached to the poor. ⁶Blessed is the man who does not fall away on account of me."

Mt 26:63 But Jesus remained silent.

The high priest said to him, "I charge you under oath by

the living God: Tell us if you are the Christ, the Son of God."

⁶⁴"Yes, it is as you say," Jesus replied. "But I say to all of you: In the future you will see the Son of Man sitting at the right hand of the Mighty One and coming on the clouds of heaven."

Lk 24:27 And beginning with Moses and all the Prophets, he explained to them what was said in all the Scriptures concerning himself.

Jn 4:25 The woman said, "I know that Messiah" (called Christ) "is coming. When he comes, he will explain everything to us."

²⁶Then Jesus declared, "I who speak to you am he."

Jn 4:29 "Come, see a man who told me everything I ever did. Could this be the Christ?"

Jn 4:42 They said to the woman, "We no longer believe just because of what you said; now we have heard for ourselves, and we know that this man really is the Savior of the world."

Jn 5:33 "You have sent to John and he has testified to the truth.

Jn 5:36 "I have testimony weightier than that of John. For the very work that the Father has given me to finish, and which I am doing, testifies that the Father has sent me. ³⁷And the Father who sent me has himself testified concerning me. You have never heard his voice nor seen his form,

Jn 5:39 You diligently study the Scriptures because you think that by them you possess eternal life. These are the Scriptures that testify about me,

Jn 5:46 If you believed Moses, you would believe me, for he wrote about me.

Jn 6:27 Do not work for food that spoils, but for food that endures to eternal life, which the Son of Man will give you. On him God the Father has placed his seal of approval."

Jn 8:14 Jesus answered, "Even if I testify on my own behalf, my testimony is valid, for I know where I came from and where I am going. But you have no idea where I come from or where I am going.

Jn 8:17 In your own Law it is written that the testimony of two men is valid. ¹⁸I am one who testifies for myself; my other witness is the Father, who sent me."

Jn 8:25 "Who are you?" they asked. "Just what I have been claiming all along," Jesus replied.

Jn 8:28 So Jesus said, "When you have lifted up the Son of Man, then you will know that I am [the one I claim to be] and that I do nothing on my own but speak just what the Father has taught me.

Jn 8:56 Your father Abraham rejoiced at the thought of seeing my day; he saw it and was glad."

Jn 13:19 "I am telling you now before it happens, so that when it does happen you will believe that I am He.

Was called David's son (Mt 22:42-45; Mk 12:35-37)—

Lk 20:41 Then Jesus said to them, "How is it that they say the Christ is the Son of David? ⁴²David himself declares in the Book of Psalms:

"'The Lord said to my Lord: "Sit at my right hand ⁴³until I make your enemies a footstool for your feet."'

⁴⁴David calls him 'Lord.' How then can he be his son?"

Is the anointed of God (Ps 2:2)—

Ac 4:26 The kings of the earth take their stand and the rulers gather together against the Lord and against his Anointed One.'

²⁷Indeed Herod and Pontius Pilate met together with the

Gentiles and the people of Israel in this city to conspire against your holy servant Jesus, whom you anointed.

Was proclaimed as Messiah by apostles—

Ac 9:22 Yet Saul grew more and more powerful and baffled the Jews living in Damascus by proving that Jesus is the Christ.

Ac 13:27 The people of Jerusalem and their rulers did not recognize Jesus, yet in condemning him they fulfilled the words of the prophets that are read every Sabbath.

Ac 17:2 As his custom was, Paul went into the synagogue, and on three Sabbath days he reasoned with them from the Scriptures, ³explaining and proving that the Christ had to suffer and rise from the dead. "This Jesus I am proclaiming to you is the Christ," he said.

Ac 26:6 And now it is because of my hope in what God has promised our fathers that I am on trial today. ⁷This is the promise our twelve tribes are hoping to see fulfilled as they earnestly serve God day and night. O king, it is because of this hope that the Jews are accusing me.

Ac 26:22 But I have had God's help to this very day, and so I stand here and testify to small and great alike. I am saying nothing beyond what the prophets and Moses said would happen— ²³that the Christ would suffer and, as the first to rise from the dead, would proclaim light to his own people and to the Gentiles." (+Ac 28:23)

Ro 1:1 Paul, a servant of Christ Jesus, called to be an apostle and set apart for the gospel of God— ²the gospel he promised beforehand through his prophets in the Holy Scriptures ³regarding his Son, who as to his human nature was a descendant of David,

1Co 15:3 For what I received I passed on to you as of first importance: that Christ died for our sins according to the Scriptures,

1Pe 1:10 Concerning this salvation, the prophets, who spoke of the grace that was to come to you, searched intently and with the greatest care, ¹¹trying to find out the time and circumstances to which the Spirit of Christ in them was pointing when he predicted the sufferings of Christ and the glories that would follow.

2Pe 1:16 We did not follow cleverly invented stories when we told you about the power and coming of our Lord Jesus Christ, but we were eyewitnesses of his majesty. ¹⁷For he received honor and glory from God the Father when the voice came to him from the Majestic Glory, saying, "This is my Son, whom I love; with him I am well pleased." ¹⁸We ourselves heard this voice that came from heaven when we were with him on the sacred mountain.

1Jn 5:6 This is the one who came by water and blood— Jesus Christ. He did not come by water only, but by water and blood. And it is the Spirit who testifies, because the Spirit is the truth. ⁷For there are three that testify: ⁸the Spirit, the water and the blood; and the three are in agreement. ⁹We accept man's testimony, but God's testimony is greater because it is the testimony of God, which he has given about his Son.

See above, King; Lordship of; below, Son of Man.
See also, Messianic Hope.

Miracles of:

Water made wine (Jn 2:1-11).

First miraculous catch of fishes (Lk 5:1-11).

Demoniac in the synagogue healed (Mk 1:23-26; Lk 4:33-36).

Heals Simon's wife's mother (Mt 8:14-15; Mk 1:29-31; Lk 4:38-39).

Heals diseases in Galilee (Mt 4:23-24; Mk 1:34).

Miracles at Jerusalem (Jn 2:23).

Cleanses the leper (Mt 8:1-4; Mk 1:40-45; Lk 5:12-16).

Heals the paralytic (Mt 9:1-8; Mk 2:1-12; Lk 5:17-26).

Heals the crippled man (Jn 5:1-16).

Restores the withered hand (Mt 12:9-13; Mk 3:1-5; Lk 6:6-11).

Heals multitudes from Judah, Jerusalem, and coasts of Tyre and Sidon (Lk 6:17-19).

Heals the centurion's servant (Mt 8:5-13; Lk 7:1-10).

Heals demoniacs (Mt 8:16-17; Lk 4:40-41).

Raises the widow's son (Lk 7:11-16).

Heals in Galilee (Lk 7:21-22).

Heals a demoniac (Mt 12:22-37; Mk 3:20-30; Lk 11:14-15,17-23).

Stills the tempest (Mt 8:23-27; Mk 4:35-41; Lk 8:22-25; Mt 14:32).

Healing of the diseased in the land of Gennesaret (Mt 14:34-36).

The demoniacs in Gadarenes healed (Mt 8:28-34; Mk 5:1-20; Lk 8:26-39).

Raises Jairus' daughter (Mt 9:18-19,23-26; Mk 5:22-24,35-43; Lk 8:41-42,49-56).

Heals the woman with the issue of blood (Mt 9:20-22; Mk 5:25-34; Lk 8:43-48).

Opens the eyes of two blind men in the house (Mt 9:27-31).

A demon cast out and a mute man cured (Mt 9:32-33).

Five thousand fed (Mt 14:15-21; Mk 6:35-44; Lk 9:12-17; Jn 6:5-14).

Heals sick in Galilee (Mt 14:14).

Walking on the sea (Mt 14:22-33; Mk 6:45-52; Jn 6:14-21).

The daughter of the Syrian Phoenician healed (Mt 15:21-28; Mk 7:24-30).

Healing of the lame, blind, mute, and maimed, near the Sea of Galilee (Mt 15:30).

Four thousand fed (Mt 15:32-39; Mk 8:1-9).

One deaf and mute cured (Mk 7:31-37).

One blind cured (Mk 8:22-36).

Child healed (Mt 17:14-21; Mk 9:14-29; Lk 9:37-43).

Piece of money in the fish's mouth (Mt 17:24-27).

The ten lepers cured (Lk 17:11-19).

Opening the eyes of one born blind (Jn 9).

Raising of Lazarus (Jn 11:1-54).

Woman with the spirit of infirmity cured (Lk 13:10-17).

The dropsy cured (Lk 14:1-6).

Two blind men cured near Jericho (Mt 20:29-34; Mk 10:46-52; Lk 18:35-43).

The fig tree blighted (Mt 21:17-22; Mk 11:12-14,20-24).

Healing of Malchus's ear (Lk 22:49-51).

Second catch of fishes (Jn 21:6).

Not particularly described (Mt 4:23-24; 14:14; 15:30; Mk 1:34; Lk 6:17-19; 7:21-22; Jn 2:23; 3:2). Resurrection (Mt 28:6; Mk 16:6; Lk 24:6; Jn 20:1-18). Holds the vision of his disciples, that they should not recognize him (Lk 24:16,31,35). His appearances and disappearances (Lk 24:15,31,36-45; Jn 20:19,26). Opening the understanding of his disciples (Lk 24:45). His Ascension (Lk 24:51; Ac 1:9).

See Miracles.

Mission of:

Isa 42:7 to open eyes that are blind, to free captives from prison and to release from the dungeon those who sit in darkness.

Mt 18:12 "What do you think? If a man owns a hundred sheep, and one of them wanders away, will he not leave the ninety-nine on the hills and go to look for the one that wandered off? [13]And if he finds it, I tell you the truth, he is happier about that one sheep than about the ninety-nine that did not wander off. [14]In the same way your Father in heaven is not willing that any of these little ones should be lost.

Lk 12:49 "I have come to bring fire on the earth, and how I wish it were already kindled! [50]But I have a baptism to undergo, and how distressed I am until it is completed! [51]Do you think I came to bring peace on earth? No, I tell you, but division. [52]From now on there will be five in one family divided against each other, three against two and two against three. [53]They will be divided, father against son and son against father, mother against daughter and daughter against mother, mother-in-law against daughter-in-law and daughter-in-law against mother-in-law." (+Jn 4:25)

Jn 4:34 "My food," said Jesus, "is to do the will of him who sent me and to finish his work.

Jn 18:37 "You are a king, then!" said Pilate. Jesus answered, "You are right in saying I am a king. In fact, for this reason I was born, and for this I came into the world, to testify to the truth. Everyone on the side of truth listens to me."

To fulfill the Law and the Prophets—

Mic 5:2 "But you, Bethlehem Ephrathah, though you are small among the clans of Judah, out of you will come for me one who will be ruler over Israel, whose origins are from of old, from ancient times."

Mt 5:17 "Do not think that I have come to abolish the Law or the Prophets; I have not come to abolish them but to fulfill them.

Ro 10:4 Christ is the end of the law so that there may be righteousness for everyone who believes.

To be Lord of all—

Ro 14:9 For this very reason, Christ died and returned to life so that he might be the Lord of both the dead and the living.

Ro 15:8 For I tell you that Christ has become a servant of the Jews on behalf of God's truth, to confirm the promises made to the patriarchs [9]so that the Gentiles may glorify God for his mercy, as it is written: "Therefore I will praise you among the Gentiles; I will sing hymns to your name."

2Co 5:15 And he died for all, that those who live should no longer live for themselves but for him who died for them and was raised again.

Eph 4:10 He who descended is the very one who ascended higher than all the heavens, in order to fill the whole universe.)

To glorify the Father (Jn 17:4).

To preach the gospel (Isa 61:1)—

Mt 4:23 Jesus went throughout Galilee, teaching in their synagogues, preaching the good news of the kingdom, and healing every disease and sickness among the people.

Mt 9:13 But go and learn what this means: 'I desire mercy, not sacrifice.' For I have not come to call the righteous, but sinners."

Mk 1:38 Jesus replied, "Let us go somewhere else—to the nearby villages—so I can preach there also. That is why I have come."

Lk 4:18 "The Spirit of the Lord is on me, because he has anointed me to preach good news to the poor. He has sent me to proclaim freedom for the prisoners and recovery of sight for the blind, to release the oppressed, [19]to proclaim the year of the Lord's favor."

Lk 4:43 But he said, "I must preach the good news of the

kingdom of God to the other towns also, because that is why I was sent." (+Lk 5:31-32)

Lk 8:1 After this, Jesus traveled about from one town and village to another, proclaiming the good news of the kingdom of God. The Twelve were with him,

To preach repentance (Lk 5:30-32)—

Lk 24:47 and repentance and forgiveness of sins will be preached in his name to all nations, beginning at Jerusalem. (+Ac 3:26)

Ac 5:31 God exalted him to his own right hand as Prince and Savior that he might give repentance and forgiveness of sins to Israel.

To bring life—

Jn 6:51 I am the living bread that came down from heaven. If anyone eats of this bread, he will live forever. This bread is my flesh, which I will give for the life of the world."

Jn 10:10 The thief comes only to steal and kill and destroy; I have come that they may have life, and have it to the full.

2Co 5:14 For Christ's love compels us, because we are convinced that one died for all, and therefore all died. (+2Co 5:21)

To give light (Isa 9:2)—

Isa 42:6 "I, the LORD, have called you in righteousness; I will take hold of your hand. I will keep you and will make you to be a covenant for the people and a light for the Gentiles,

Lk 1:78 because of the tender mercy of our God, by which the rising sun will come to us from heaven (+Lk 1:79; 2:30-32,34; Jn 1:1-9)

Jn 9:39 Jesus said, "For judgment I have come into this world, so that the blind will see and those who see will become blind."

Jn 12:46 I have come into the world as a light, so that no one who believes in me should stay in darkness.

[47]"As for the person who hears my words but does not keep them, I do not judge him. For I did not come to judge the world, but to save it.

To condemn sin—

Ro 8:3 For what the law was powerless to do in that it was weakened by the sinful nature, God did by sending his own Son in the likeness of sinful man to be a sin offering. And so he condemned sin in sinful man, (+Ro 8:4)

To die for sinners (Ro 5:6-8).

To be propitiation for sin—

Mt 20:28 just as the Son of Man did not come to be served, but to serve, and to give his life as a ransom for many." (+Mk 10:45)

Lk 24:26 Did not the Christ have to suffer these things and then enter his glory?"

Lk 24:46 He told them, "This is what is written: The Christ will suffer and rise from the dead on the third day, (+Jn 6:51)

Ac 26:23 that the Christ would suffer and, as the first to rise from the dead, would proclaim light to his own people and to the Gentiles." (+Ro 4:24-25)

Ro 5:6 You see, at just the right time, when we were still powerless, Christ died for the ungodly. [7]Very rarely will anyone die for a righteous man, though for a good man someone might possibly dare to die. [8]But God demonstrates his own love for us in this: While we were still sinners, Christ died for us. (+2Co 5:18)

Gal 1:3 Grace and peace to you from God our Father and the Lord Jesus Christ, [4]who gave himself for our sins to rescue us from the present evil age, according to the will of our God and Father,

Gal 4:4 But when the time had fully come, God sent his Son, born of a woman, born under law, **⁵**to redeem those under law, that we might receive the full rights of sons.

Heb 2:9 But we see Jesus, who was made a little lower than the angels, now crowned with glory and honor because he suffered death, so that by the grace of God he might taste death for everyone.

Heb 2:14 Since the children have flesh and blood, he too shared in their humanity so that by his death he might destroy him who holds the power of death—that is, the devil—

Heb 9:26 Then Christ would have had to suffer many times since the creation of the world. But now he has appeared once for all at the end of the ages to do away with sin by the sacrifice of himself.

1Jn 3:5 But you know that he appeared so that he might take away our sins. And in him is no sin.

1Jn 3:8 He who does what is sinful is of the devil, because the devil has been sinning from the beginning. The reason the Son of God appeared was to destroy the devil's work. (+1Jn 4:8)

1Jn 4:10 This is love: not that we loved God, but that he loved us and sent his Son as an atoning sacrifice for our sins.

To purge sins—

Zec 13:1 "On that day a fountain will be opened to the house of David and the inhabitants of Jerusalem, to cleanse them from sin and impurity.

Mal 3:2 But who can endure the day of his coming? Who can stand when he appears? For he will be like a refiner's fire or a launderer's soap. **³**He will sit as a refiner and purifier of silver; he will purify the Levites and refine them like gold and silver. Then the LORD will have men who will bring offerings in righteousness,

To give remission of sins—

Ac 10:43 All the prophets testify about him that everyone who believes in him receives forgiveness of sins through his name."

Ro 4:25 He was delivered over to death for our sins and was raised to life for our justification.

To destroy the works of the devil (Ge 3:15; Jn 3:8).

To bring salvation—

Mt 1:21 She will give birth to a son, and you are to give him the name Jesus, because he will save his people from their sins."

Mt 15:24 He answered, "I was sent only to the lost sheep of Israel."

Mt 18:12 "What do you think? If a man owns a hundred sheep, and one of them wanders away, will he not leave the ninety-nine on the hills and go to look for the one that wandered off? (+Mt 18:13-14; Lk 19:10)

Jn 3:13 No one has ever gone into heaven except the one who came from heaven—the Son of Man. **¹⁴**Just as Moses lifted up the snake in the desert, so the Son of Man must be lifted up, **¹⁵**that everyone who believes in him may have eternal life.

¹⁶"For God so loved the world that he gave his one and only Son, that whoever believes in him shall not perish but have eternal life. **¹⁷**For God did not send his Son into the world to condemn the world, but to save the world through him.

Ro 14:15 If your brother is distressed because of what you eat, you are no longer acting in love. Do not by your eating destroy your brother for whom Christ died.

1Ti 1:15 Here is a trustworthy saying that deserves full acceptance: Christ Jesus came into the world to save sinners—of whom I am the worst.

To deliver from fear of death—

Heb 2:15 and free those who all their lives were held in slavery by their fear of death.

To deliver from temptation—

Heb 2:18 Because he himself suffered when he was tempted, he is able to help those who are being tempted.

To comfort the contrite—

Isa 61:1 The Spirit of the Sovereign LORD is on me, because the LORD has anointed me to preach good news to the poor. He has sent me to bind up the brokenhearted, to proclaim freedom for the captives and release from darkness for the prisoners, **²**to proclaim the year of the LORD's favor and the day of vengeance of our God, to comfort all who mourn, **³**and provide for those who grieve in Zion—to bestow on them a crown of beauty instead of ashes, the oil of gladness instead of mourning, and a garment of praise instead of a spirit of despair. They will be called oaks of righteousness, a planting of the LORD for the display of his splendor.

To baptize with the Holy Spirit and with fire—

Mt 3:11 "I baptize you with water for repentance. But after me will come one who is more powerful than I, whose sandals I am not fit to carry. He will baptize you with the Holy Spirit and with fire. **¹²**His winnowing fork is in his hand, and he will clear his threshing floor, gathering his wheat into the barn and burning up the chaff with unquenchable fire." (+Lk 3:16)

To preach to spirits in prison (1Pe 3:19; 4:6, cf. Eph 4:9).

Names, Appellations, and Titles of:

Adam (1Co 15:45). Advocate (1Jn 2:1). Almighty (Rev 1:8). Alpha and Omega (Rev 22:13). Amen (Rev 3:14). Angel (Ge 48:16; Ex 23:20). Angel of his presence (Isa 63:9). Anointed (Ps 2:2). Apostle (Heb 3:1). Arm of the Lord (Isa 51:9-10). Atoning sacrifice (1Jn 2:2). Author of life (Ac 3:15). Author of salvation (Heb 2:10). Author and perfecter of our faith (Heb 12:2).

Banner for the peoples (Isa 11:10). Beginning and End (Rev 22:13). Blessed and only Ruler (1Ti 6:15). Branch (Jer 23:5; Zec 3:8). Bread of life (Jn 6:48). Bridegroom (Mt 9:15). Bright Morning Star (Rev 22:16).

Capstone (Mt 21:42). Carpenter (Mk 6:3). Carpenter's son (Mt 13:55). Chief Shepherd (1Pe 5:4). Child (Isa 9:6; Lk 2:27). Chosen one (Isa 42:1). Chosen by God (1Pe 2:4). Chosen and precious cornerstone (1Pe 2:6). Christ (Mt 1:16). The Christ (Mt 16:20; Mk 14:61,62; Lk 9:20). Christ, a king (Lk 23:2). Christ Jesus (Ro 3:24; 8:1; 1Co 1:2,30). Christ Jesus our Lord (1Ti 1:12; Ro 8:39). Christ of God (Lk 9:20). Christ of God, the Chosen One (Lk 23:35). Christ the Lord (Lk 2:11). Christ the power of God and the wisdom of God (1Co 1:24). Christ, the Son of God (Jn 11:27). Christ, the Son of the Blessed One (Mk 14:61). Commander (Isa 55:4). Commander of the LORD's army (Jos 5:14). Consolation of Israel (Lk 2:25). Cornerstone (Eph 2:20). Counselor (Isa 9:6). Covenant for the people (Isa 42:6).

David (Jer 30:9). Deliverer (Ro 11:26). Desired of all nations (Hag 2:7). Doctor (Mt 9:12).

Eternal life (1Jn 5:20). Everlasting Father (Isa 9:6). Exact representation of God's being (Heb 1:3).

Faithful and True (Rev 19:11). Faithful witness (Rev 1:5). Faithful and true witness (Rev 3:14). The First and the Last (Rev 1:17; 2:8; 22:13). Firstborn (Heb 1:6). First-born from the dead (Rev 1:5). Foundation (Isa 28:16). Fountain (Zec 13:1). Friend of tax collectors and sinners (Mt 11:19).

Gate (Jn 10:7). Gift of God (Jn 4:10). Glorious Lord Jesus Christ (Jas 2:1). Glory of Israel (Lk 2:32). God (Jn 20:28). God and Savior of Israel (Isa 45:15). God of all the earth (Isa 54:5). God over all, forever praised (Ro 9:5). God the One and Only (Jn 1:18). God with us (Mt 1:23). Good Shepherd (Jn 10:11,14). Good Teacher (Mk 10:17). Great God and Savior (Tit 2:13). Great high priest (Heb 4:14). Great Shepherd of the sheep (Heb 13:20). Guarantee (Heb 7:22).

Head of every man (1Co 11:3). Head of the body, the church (Col 1:18). Head of the church (Eph 5:23). Heir of all things (Heb 1:2). High priest (Heb 4:15). Holiness (1Co 1:30). Holy One (Ps 16:10). Holy One of God (Mk 1:24). Holy One of Israel (Isa 41:14; 54:5). Holy and Righteous One (Ac 3:14). Holy servant Jesus (Ac 4:30). Our Hope (1Ti 1:1). Horn of salvation (Lk 1:69).

I am (Jn 8:58). Immanuel (Isa 7:14; Mt 1:23). Indescribable gift (2Co 9:15). Innocent man (Mt 27:19). Israel (Isa 49:3).

Jesus (Mt 1:21). Jesus Christ (Mt 1:1; Jn 1:17; 17:3; Ac 2:38; 4:10; 9:34; 10:36; 16:18; Ro 1:6; 2:16; 5:15,17; 1Co 2:2; 2Co 1:19; 4:5; Gal 2:16; Php 1:11; 2:11; 2Ti 2:8; Heb 13:8; 1Jn 1:3; 2:1). Jesus Christ our Lord (Ro 5:21; 7:25; 1Co 1:9; Jude 25). Jesus Christ our Savior (Tit 3:6). Jesus of Nazareth (Mk 1:24; Lk 24:19). Jesus of Nazareth, King of the Jews (Jn 19:19). Jesus, the King of the Jews (Mt 27:37). Jesus the Son of God (Heb 4:14). Jesus, the Son of Joseph (Jn 6:42). Judge (Ac 10:42).

King (Mt 21:5). King of Israel (Jn 1:49). King of kings (1Ti 6:15; Rev 17:14). King of glory (Ps 24:7-10). King of the ages (Rev 15:3). King of the Jews (Mt 2:2). King over the whole earth (Zec 14:9).

Lamb (Rev 5:6,8; 6:16; 7:9-10,17; 12:11; 13:8; 14:1,4; 15:3; 17:14; 19:7,9; 21:9,14,22-23,27). Lamb of God (Jn 1:29). Lawgiver (Isa 33:22). Leader (Isa 55:4). Life (Jn 14:6). Light, everlasting (Isa 60:20). Light of the world (Jn 8:12). Light for the Gentiles (Isa 42:6). Light, true (Jn 1:9). Living bread (Jn 6:51). Living Stone (1Pe 2:4). Lion of the tribe of Judah (Rev 5:5). Lord (Jn 20:28). Lord Almighty (Jas 5:4). Lord of all (Ac 10:36; Ro 10:12). Lord of lords (Rev 17:14; 19:16). LORD Our Righteousness (Jer 23:6). Lord God Almighty (Rev 15:3). Lord and Savior Jesus Christ (2Pe 1:11; 3:18). Lord Christ (Col 3:24). Lord Jesus (Ac 7:59; Col 3:17; 1Th 4:2). Lord Jesus Christ (Ac 11:17; 15:26; 28:31; Ro 5:1,11; 13:14). LORD mighty in battle (Ps 24:8). Lord of the dead and the living (Ro 14:9). Lord of the Sabbath (Mk 2:28). Lord's Christ (Lk 2:26). LORD, your holy one (Isa 43:15). LORD, your redeemer (Isa 43:14).

Man Christ Jesus (1Ti 2:5). Man of sorrows (Isa 53:3). Man who is close to me [the LORD] (Zec 13:7). Master (Mt 23:8). Mediator (1Ti 2:5). Messenger of the covenant (Mal 3:1). Messiah (Jn 1:41). Mighty God (Isa 9:6). Mighty One of Israel (Isa 1:24). Mighty one of Jacob (Isa 49:26). Mighty to save (Isa 63:1). Morning star (2Pe 1:19; Rev 22:16).

Nazarene (Mt 2:23).

Offspring of David (Rev 22:16). Offspring of the woman (Ge 3:15). The One and Only (Jn 1:14). One and only Son (Jn 3:16,18). One he [the Father] loves (Eph 1:6). Only God our Savior (Jude 25). Overseer (1Pe 2:25).

Passover lamb (1Co 5:7). Perfecter of faith (Heb 12:2).

Power of God (1Co 1:24). Physician (Lk 4:23). Precious cornerstone (Isa 28:16). Priest (Heb 7:17). Prince (Ac 5:31). Prince of Peace (Isa 9:6). Prophet (Dt 18:15,18; Mt 21:11; Lk 24:19).

Rabbi (Jn 1:49). Rabboni (Jn 20:16). Radiance of God's glory (Heb 1:3). Ransom (1Ti 2:6). Redeemer (Isa 59:20). Resurrection and life (Jn 11:25). Redemption (1Co 1:30). Righteous Branch (Jer 23:5). Righteous Judge (2Ti 4:8). Righteous One (Ac 7:52; 22:14). Righteous servant (Isa 53:11). Righteousness (1Co 1:30). Rising sun (Lk 1:78). Rock (1Co 10:4). Rock that makes them fall (1Pe 2:8). Root of David (Rev 5:5; 22:16). Root of Jesse (Isa 11:10). Rose of Sharon (SS 2:1). Ruler (Mt 2:6; 1Ti 6:15). Ruler of God's creation (Rev 3:14). Ruler of the kings of the earth (Rev 1:5). Ruler over Israel (Mic 5:2).

Sacrifice (1Jn 2:2). Salvation (Lk 2:30). Sanctuary (Isa 8:14). Savior (Lk 2:11). Savior, Christ Jesus (2Ti 1:10). Savior Jesus Christ (Tit 2:13; 2Pe 1:1). Savior of the body (Eph 5:23). Savior of the world (1Jn 4:14). Scepter (Nu 24:17). Second man from heaven (1Co 15:47). Seed of Abraham (Gal 3:16). Servant (Isa 42:1). Servant of rulers (Isa 49:7). Serves in the sanctuary (Heb 8:2). Shepherd (Mk 14:27). Shepherd and Overseer of souls (1Pe 2:25). Shepherd, Chief (1Pe 5:4). Shepherd, good (Jn 10:11). Shepherd, great (Heb 13:20). Shepherd of Israel (Ps 80:1). Shiloh (Ge 49:10, ftn). Son he [God] loves (Col 1:13). Son of Abraham (Mt 1:1). Son of David (Mt 9:27). Son of the Father (2Jn 3). Son of God. *See Jesus the Christ, Son of God.* Son of Man. *See Jesus the Christ, Son of Man.* Son of the Blessed One (Mk 14:61). Son of the Most High (Lk 1:32). Star (Nu 24:17). Stone (Mt 21:42). Stone that causes men to stumble (1Pe 2:8). Sun of righteousness (Mal 4:2). Sure foundation (Isa 28:16).

Teacher (Jn 3:2). Tested stone (Isa 28:16). True God (1Jn 5:20). True vine (Jn 15:1). Truth (Jn 14:6).

Vine (Jn 15:1).

Way (Jn 14:6). Who is, who was, and who is to come (Rev 1:4). Wisdom (Pr 8:12). Wisdom of God (1Co 1:24). Witness (Isa 55:4; Rev 1:5). Wonderful Counselor (Isa 9:6). Word (Jn 1:1). Word of God (Rev 19:13). Word of life (1Jn 1:1).

Yahweh *See in list above: I am, Lord, and* LORD.

In His Name (1Co 6:11; Php 2:9; Col 3:17; Rev 19:16)—

Baptism (Mt 28:19; Ac 2:38). Life (Jn 20:31). Miracles performed (Ac 3:6; 4:10; 19:13). Prayer (Jn 14:13; 16:23-24,26; Eph 5:20; Col 3:17; Heb 13:15). Preaching (Lk 24:47). Faith (Mt 12:21; Jn 1:12; 2:23). Remission of sins (Lk 24:47; Ac 10:43; 1Jn 2:12). Salvation (Ac 4:12; 10:43). Those who use his name must turn away from wickedness (2Ti 2:19).

See above, Intercession of; below, Priesthood of.

Obedience of:

Foretold—

Ps 40:8 I desire to do your will, O my God; your law is within my heart."

Isa 11:5 Righteousness will be his belt and faithfulness the sash around his waist. (+Isa 11:6)

Heb 10:7 Then I said, 'Here I am—it is written about me in the scroll—I have come to do your will, O God.'"

[8]First he said, "Sacrifices and offerings, burnt offerings and sin offerings you did not desire, nor were you pleased with them" (although the law required them to be made). [9]Then he said, "Here I am, I have come to do your will." He sets aside the first to establish the second.

To his parents (Lk 2:51).

To God—

Lk 2:49 "Why were you searching for me?" he asked. "Didn't you know I had to be in my Father's house?"

Jn 4:34 "My food," said Jesus, "is to do the will of him who sent me and to finish his work.

Jn 5:30 By myself I can do nothing; I judge only as I hear, and my judgment is just, for I seek not to please myself but him who sent me.

Jn 5:36 "I have testimony weightier than that of John. For the very work that the Father has given me to finish, and which I am doing, testifies that the Father has sent me. (+Jn 6:38)

Jn 8:29 The one who sent me is with me; he has not left me alone, for I always do what pleases him."

Jn 8:46 Can any of you prove me guilty of sin? If I am telling the truth, why don't you believe me?

Jn 8:55 Though you do not know him, I know him. If I said I did not, I would be a liar like you, but I do know him and keep his word.

Jn 9:4 As long as it is day, we must do the work of him who sent me. Night is coming, when no one can work.

Jn 14:31 but the world must learn that I love the Father and that I do exactly what my Father has commanded me. "Come now; let us leave.

Jn 15:10 If you obey my commands, you will remain in my love, just as I have obeyed my Father's commands and remain in his love.

Jn 17:4 I have brought you glory on earth by completing the work you gave me to do.

Exemplified: In his baptism—

Mt 3:15 Jesus replied, "Let it be so now; it is proper for us to do this to fulfill all righteousness." Then John consented.

Sufferings—

Mt 26:39 Going a little farther, he fell with his face to the ground and prayed, "My Father, if it is possible, may this cup be taken from me. Yet not as I will, but as you will."

Mt 26:42 He went away a second time and prayed, "My Father, if it is not possible for this cup to be taken away unless I drink it, may your will be done." (+Mk 14:36; Lk 22:42)

Heb 5:8 Although he was a son, he learned obedience from what he suffered

Death—

Jn 19:30 When he had received the drink, Jesus said, "It is finished." With that, he bowed his head and gave up his spirit.

Php 2:8 And being found in appearance as a man, he humbled himself and became obedient to death—even death on a cross!

Omnipotence of:

Ps 45:3 Gird your sword upon your side, O mighty one; clothe yourself with splendor and majesty. 4In your majesty ride forth victoriously in behalf of truth, humility and righteousness; let your right hand display awesome deeds. 5Let your sharp arrows pierce the hearts of the king's enemies; let the nations fall beneath your feet.

Ps 110:3 Your troops will be willing on your day of battle. Arrayed in holy majesty, from the womb of the dawn you will receive the dew of your youth.

Isa 9:6 For to us a child is born, to us a son is given, and the government will be on his shoulders. And he will be called Wonderful Counselor, Mighty God, Everlasting Father, Prince of Peace.

Isa 40:10 See, the Sovereign LORD comes with power, and his arm rules for him. See, his reward is with him, and his recompense accompanies him.

Isa 50:2 When I came, why was there no one? When I called, why was there no one to answer? Was my arm too short to ransom you? Do I lack the strength to rescue you? By a mere rebuke I dry up the sea, I turn rivers into a desert; their fish rot for lack of water and die of thirst. 3I clothe the sky with darkness and make sackcloth its covering."

Isa 63:1 Who is this coming from Edom, from Bozrah, with his garments stained crimson? Who is this, robed in splendor, striding forward in the greatness of his strength? "It is I, speaking in righteousness, mighty to save." (+Mt 6:7)

Mt 28:18 Then Jesus came to them and said, "All authority in heaven and on earth has been given to me. (+Mt 12:13,28-29; Mk 3:27)

Lk 5:17 One day as he was teaching, Pharisees and teachers of the law, who had come from every village of Galilee and from Judea and Jerusalem, were sitting there. And the power of the Lord was present for him to heal the sick. (+Lk 9:1; 11:20-22; Jn 2:10)

Jn 5:21 For just as the Father raises the dead and gives them life, even so the Son gives life to whom he is pleased to give it.

Jn 5:28 "Do not be amazed at this, for a time is coming when all who are in their graves will hear his voice 29and come out—those who have done good will rise to live, and those who have done evil will rise to be condemned.

Jn 10:17 The reason my Father loves me is that I lay down my life—only to take it up again. 18No one takes it from me, but I lay it down of my own accord. I have authority to lay it down and authority to take it up again. This command I received from my Father."

Jn 10:28 I give them eternal life, and they shall never perish; no one can snatch them out of my hand.

Php 3:20 But our citizenship is in heaven. And we eagerly await a Savior from there, the Lord Jesus Christ, 21who, by the power that enables him to bring everything under his control, will transform our lowly bodies so that they will be like his glorious body.

Col 1:17 He is before all things, and in him all things hold together.

2Th 1:9 They will be punished with everlasting destruction and shut out from the presence of the Lord and from the majesty of his power

1Ti 6:16 who alone is immortal and who lives in unapproachable light, whom no one has seen or can see. To him be honor and might forever. Amen.

Heb 1:3 The Son is the radiance of God's glory and the exact representation of his being, sustaining all things by his powerful word. After he had provided purification for sins, he sat down at the right hand of the Majesty in heaven.

Heb 7:25 Therefore he is able to save completely those who come to God through him, because he always lives to intercede for them.

2Pe 1:16 We did not follow cleverly invented stories when we told you about the power and coming of our Lord Jesus Christ, but we were eyewitnesses of his majesty.

Rev 1:8 "I am the Alpha and the Omega," says the Lord God, "who is, and who was, and who is to come, the Almighty."

Rev 3:7 "To the angel of the church in Philadelphia write: These are the words of him who is holy and true, who holds the key of David. What he opens no one can shut, and what he shuts no one can open.

Rev 5:12 In a loud voice they sang: "Worthy is the Lamb, who was slain, to receive power and wealth and wisdom and strength and honor and glory and praise!"

Omnipresence of:

Mt 18:20 For where two or three come together in my name, there am I with them."

Mt 28:20 and teaching them to obey everything I have commanded you. And surely I am with you always, to the very end of the age."

Jn 3:13 No one has ever gone into heaven except the one who came from heaven—the Son of Man.

Eph 1:23 which is his body, the fullness of him who fills everything in every way.

Omniscience of:

Col 2:3 in whom are hidden all the treasures of wisdom and knowledge.

Rev 2:18 "To the angel of the church in Thyatira write: These are the words of the Son of God, whose eyes are like blazing fire and whose feet are like burnished bronze.

Rev 2:23 I will strike her children dead. Then all the churches will know that I am he who searches hearts and minds, and I will repay each of you according to your deeds.

Rev 5:5 Then one of the elders said to me, "Do not weep! See, the Lion of the tribe of Judah, the Root of David, has triumphed. He is able to open the scroll and its seven seals."

Rev 5:12 In a loud voice they sang: "Worthy is the Lamb, who was slain, to receive power and wealth and wisdom and strength and honor and glory and praise!"

Manifested in his knowledge, of the Father—

Mt 11:27 "All things have been committed to me by my Father. No one knows the Son except the Father, and no one knows the Father except the Son and those to whom the Son chooses to reveal him. (+Jn 7:29)

Knowledge of human hearts—

Mt 9:4 Knowing their thoughts, Jesus said, "Why do you entertain evil thoughts in your hearts?

Mt 12:25 Jesus knew their thoughts and said to them, "Every kingdom divided against itself will be ruined, and every city or household divided against itself will not stand. (+Mt 17:27)

Mt 22:18 But Jesus, knowing their evil intent, said, "You hypocrites, why are you trying to trap me?

Mk 2:8 Immediately Jesus knew in his spirit that this was what they were thinking in their hearts, and he said to them, "Why are you thinking these things?

Lk 5:22 Jesus knew what they were thinking and asked, "Why are you thinking these things in your hearts?

Lk 6:8 But Jesus knew what they were thinking and said to the man with the shriveled hand, "Get up and stand in front of everyone." So he got up and stood there.

Lk 9:46 An argument started among the disciples as to which of them would be the greatest. [47]Jesus, knowing their thoughts, took a little child and had him stand beside him. [48]Then he said to them, "Whoever welcomes this little child in my name welcomes me; and whoever welcomes me welcomes the one who sent me. For he who is least among you all—he is the greatest." (+Lk 11:17)

Lk 22:10 He replied, "As you enter the city, a man carrying a jar of water will meet you. Follow him to the house that he enters, [11]and say to the owner of the house, 'The Teacher asks: Where is the guest room, where I may eat

the Passover with my disciples?' [12]He will show you a large upper room, all furnished. Make preparations there." (+Mk 14:13-15)

Jn 1:48 "How do you know me?" Nathanael asked. Jesus answered, "I saw you while you were still under the fig tree before Philip called you."

Jn 2:24 But Jesus would not entrust himself to them, for he knew all men. [25]He did not need man's testimony about man, for he knew what was in a man.

Jn 4:16 He told her, "Go, call your husband and come back."

[17]"I have no husband," she replied.

Jesus said to her, "You are right when you say you have no husband. [18]The fact is, you have had five husbands, and the man you now have is not your husband. What you have just said is quite true."

[19]"Sir," the woman said, "I can see that you are a prophet.

Jn 4:28 Then, leaving her water jar, the woman went back to the town and said to the people, [29]"Come, see a man who told me everything I ever did. Could this be the Christ?"

Jn 5:42 but I know you. I know that you do not have the love of God in your hearts.

Jn 6:64 Yet there are some of you who do not believe." For Jesus had known from the beginning which of them did not believe and who would betray him.

Jn 13:11 For he knew who was going to betray him, and that was why he said not every one was clean.

Jn 21:17 The third time he said to him, "Simon son of John, do you love me?" Peter was hurt because Jesus asked him the third time, "Do you love me?" He said, "Lord, you know all things; you know that I love you." Jesus said, "Feed my sheep.

Knowledge of future events—

Mt 24:25 See, I have told you ahead of time.

Jn 13:1 It was just before the Passover Feast. Jesus knew that the time had come for him to leave this world and go to the Father. Having loved his own who were in the world, he now showed them the full extent of his love.

Jn 13:3 Jesus knew that the Father had put all things under his power, and that he had come from God and was returning to God;

Jn 13:10 Jesus answered, "A person who has had a bath needs only to wash his feet; his whole body is clean. And you are clean, though not every one of you."

Jn 16:30 Now we can see that you know all things and that you do not even need to have anyone ask you questions. This makes us believe that you came from God."

Jn 16:32 "But a time is coming, and has come, when you will be scattered, each to his own home. You will leave me all alone. Yet I am not alone, for my Father is with me.

Jn 18:4 Jesus, knowing all that was going to happen to him, went out and asked them, "Who is it you want?" (+Jn 21:6)

The coin in the fish's mouth (Mt 17:27), the presence of schools of fish (Lk 5:4-7; Jn 21:6).

Our example:

(Jn 10:4; Heb 3:1-2; 1Jn 2:6; Rev 14:4). In meekness (Mt 11:29; Heb 12:2-4; 1Pe 2:21-24). Humility (Lk 22:26-27; Jn 13:13-15,34; 2Co 10:1; Php 2:5-8). Ministering (Mt 20:28; Mk 10:43-45; 2Co 8:9, w 8:5-11; Gal 6:2). Loving others (Jn 13:34; Eph 5:2). Character (Ro 8:29; 15:2-3,5,7; 1Pe 1:15-16; 1Jn 3:1-3,16; 4:17). Enduring suffering (1Pe 3:17-18).

Parables of:

The wise and foolish builders (Mt 7:24-27; Lk 6:47,49).

Two debtors (Lk 7:41-47).

The rich fool (Lk 12:16-21).

The servants waiting for their lord (Lk 12:35-40).

Barren fig tree (Lk 13:6-9).

The sower (Mt 13:3-9,18-23; Mk 4:1-9,14-20; Lk 8:5-8,11-15).

The weeds (Mt 13:24-30,36-43).

Seed growing secretly (Mk 4:26-29).

Mustard seed (Mt 13:31-32; Mk 4:30-32; Lk 13:18-19).

Yeast (Mt 13:33; Lk 13:20-21).

Hid treasure (Mt 13:44).

Pearl of great price (Mt 13:45-46).

Fishing net (Mt 13:47-50).

Unmerciful servant (Mt 18:23-35).

Good Samaritan (Lk 10:30-37).

Friend at midnight (Lk 11:5-8).

Good shepherd (Jn 10:1-16).

Great supper (Lk 14:15-24).

Lost sheep (Mt 18:12-14; Lk 15:3-7).

Lost piece of money (Lk 15:8-10).

The prodigal and his brother (Lk 15:11-32).

The unjust steward (Lk 16:1-9).

Rich man and Lazarus (Lk 16:19-31).

Importunate widow (Lk 18:1-8).

Pharisee and tax collector (Lk 18:9-14).

Laborers in the vineyard (Mt 20:1-16).

The pounds (Lk 19:11-27).

The two sons (Mt 21:28-32).

Wicked farmers (Mt 21:33-44; Mk 12:1-12; Lk 20:9-18).

Marriage of the king's son (Mt 22:1-14).

Fig tree in leaf (Mt 24:32; Mk 13:28-29).

Man taking a far journey (Mk 13:34-37).

Ten virgins (Mt 25:1-13).

Talents (Mt 25:14-30).

The vine (Jn 15:1-5).

Passion of: *See below, Sufferings of.*

Possibility of Sinning: *See below, Temptation of.*

Perfections of: (Col 2:3).

Is the image of God—

2Co 4:4 The god of this age has blinded the minds of unbelievers, so that they cannot see the light of the gospel of the glory of Christ, who is the image of God. (+Col 1:15)

All the fullness of the Father lived in him—

Col 1:19 For God was pleased to have all his fullness dwell in him, (+Col 2:9)

Righteous—

Isa 11:5 Righteousness will be his belt and faithfulness the sash around his waist.

Jn 7:18 He who speaks on his own does so to gain honor for himself, but he who works for the honor of the one who sent him is a man of truth; there is nothing false about him.

2Co 1:19 For the Son of God, Jesus Christ, who was preached among you by me and Silas and Timothy, was not "Yes" and "No," but in him it has always been "Yes."

Without deceit—

Isa 53:9 He was assigned a grave with the wicked, and with the rich in his death, though he had done no violence, nor was any deceit in his mouth.

Sinless—

Mt 27:3 When Judas, who had betrayed him, saw that Jesus was condemned, he was seized with remorse and

returned the thirty silver coins to the chief priests and the elders. [4] "I have sinned," he said, "for I have betrayed innocent blood." "What is that to us?" they replied. "That's your responsibility."

Ac 13:28 Though they found no proper ground for a death sentence, they asked Pilate to have him executed.

2Co 5:21 God made him who had no sin to be sin for us, so that in him we might become the righteousness of God.

Faithful—

2Th 3:3 But the Lord is faithful, and he will strengthen and protect you from the evil one.

2Ti 2:13 if we are faithless, he will remain faithful, for he cannot disown himself.

Heb 3:2 He was faithful to the one who appointed him, just as Moses was faithful in all God's house.

Full of grace and truth—

Jn 1:14 The Word became flesh and made his dwelling among us. We have seen his glory, the glory of the One and Only, who came from the Father, full of grace and truth.

Jn 1:18 No one has ever seen God, but God the One and Only, who is at the Father's side, has made him known. (+Col 2:3)

Just in judgment—

Jn 5:30 By myself I can do nothing; I judge only as I hear, and my judgment is just, for I seek not to please myself but him who sent me.

Perfected through sufferings —

Heb 2:10 In bringing many sons to glory, it was fitting that God, for whom and through whom everything exists, should make the author of their salvation perfect through suffering

Perfections of typified (Lev 21:17-21).

Persecutions of: *See Persecution.*

Popularity of:

(Mt 4:24; 8:1; 13:2; 14:13,35; 19:1-2; 21:8-11; Mk 1:33; 2:2; 3:7,20; 5:21; 6:33,55-56; 10:1; 11:8-10; 12:37; Lk 4:14-15,42; 5:1; 9:11; 12:1; 19:35-38; Jn 6:15; 12:12-13,19).

Power of:

(Ps 110:3; 1Co 1:24).

Called Mighty God (Isa 9:6). Has all power (Mt 28:18; Jn 10:17-18,28; 17:2; Php 3:20-21; 2Th 1:9; 1Ti 6:16; 2Pe 1:16; Rev 3:7; 5:12).

Manifested: In creation (Jn 1:3,10; Col 1:16). Salvation of men (Heb 7:25). Upholding all things (Col 1:17; Heb 1:3).

In forgiving sins—

Mt 9:2 Some men brought to him a paralytic, lying on a mat. When Jesus saw their faith, he said to the paralytic, "Take heart, son; your sins are forgiven."

Mt 9:6 But so that you may know that the Son of Man has authority on earth to forgive sins. . . ." Then he said to the paralytic, "Get up, take your mat and go home." (+Mk 2:5,10; Lk 5:20,24)

Col 3:13 Bear with each other and forgive whatever grievances you may have against one another. Forgive as the Lord forgave you.

In healing diseases (Mt 8:3,16; 9:6-7; 12:13; Mk 5:27-34; Lk 5:17; 6:19; Ac 10:38). Casting out demons (Mt 8:16; 12:28-29; Mk 3:27; Lk 11:20-22). Stilling the tempest (Mt 8:27). Giving the apostles power to heal (Mt 10:1; Mk 6:7; Lk 9:11). Resurrection (Jn 2:19; 10:17-18).

Prayers of:

Mt 11:25 At that time Jesus said, "I praise you, Father, Lord of heaven and earth, because you have hidden these things from the wise and learned, and revealed them to little children. ²⁶Yes, Father, for this was your good pleasure.

Lk 3:21 When all the people were being baptized, Jesus was baptized too. And as he was praying, heaven was opened

Lk 11:1 One day Jesus was praying in a certain place. When he finished, one of his disciples said to him, "Lord, teach us to pray, just as John taught his disciples."

In secret—

Mt 14:23 After he had dismissed them, he went up on a mountainside by himself to pray. When evening came, he was there alone,

Mk 1:35 Very early in the morning, while it was still dark, Jesus got up, left the house and went off to a solitary place, where he prayed. (+Mk 6:46)

Lk 5:16 But Jesus often withdrew to lonely places and prayed.

Lk 6:12 One of those days Jesus went out to a mountainside to pray, and spent the night praying to God.

Lk 9:18 Once when Jesus was praying in private and his disciples were with him, he asked them, "Who do the crowds say I am?"

Lk 9:28 About eight days after Jesus said this, he took Peter, John and James with him and went up onto a mountain to pray. ²⁹As he was praying, the appearance of his face changed, and his clothes became as bright as a flash of lightning.

At the grave of Lazarus—

Jn 11:41 So they took away the stone. Then Jesus looked up and said, "Father, I thank you that you have heard me. ⁴²I knew that you always hear me, but I said this for the benefit of the people standing here, that they may believe that you sent me."

For Peter—

Lk 22:32 But I have prayed for you, Simon, that your faith may not fail. And when you have turned back, strengthen your brothers."

For believers (Jn 17:1-26)

In Gethsemane—

Mt 26:36 Then Jesus went with his disciples to a place called Gethsemane, and he said to them, "Sit here while I go over there and pray." ³⁷He took Peter and the two sons of Zebedee along with him, and he began to be sorrowful and troubled. ³⁸Then he said to them, "My soul is overwhelmed with sorrow to the point of death. Stay here and keep watch with me."

³⁹Going a little farther, he fell with his face to the ground and prayed, "My Father, if it is possible, may this cup be taken from me. Yet not as I will, but as you will." (+Mk 14:32-35; Lk 22:41)

Lk 22:42 "Father, if you are willing, take this cup from me; yet not my will, but yours be done." ⁴³An angel from heaven appeared to him and strengthened him. ⁴⁴And being in anguish, he prayed more earnestly, and his sweat was like drops of blood falling to the ground.

Heb 5:7 During the days of Jesus' life on earth, he offered up prayers and petitions with loud cries and tears to the one who could save him from death, and he was heard because of his reverent submission.

On the cross—

Mt 27:46 About the ninth hour Jesus cried out in a loud voice, "Eloi, Eloi, lama sabachthani?"—which means, "My God, my God, why have you forsaken me?"

Lk 23:34 Jesus said, "Father, forgive them, for they do not know what they are doing." And they divided up his clothes by casting lots.

Lk 23:46 Jesus called out with a loud voice, "Father, into your hands I commit my spirit." When he had said this, he breathed his last.

Preexistence of:

Was in the beginning—

Jn 1:1 In the beginning was the Word, and the Word was with God, and the Word was God. ²He was with God in the beginning.

³Through him all things were made; without him nothing was made that has been made. (+1Jn 2:13-14; Rev 3:14)

Came from heaven—

Jn 3:13 No one has ever gone into heaven except the one who came from heaven—the Son of Man.

Jn 6:62 What if you see the Son of Man ascend to where he was before!

Php 2:5 Your attitude should be the same as that of Christ Jesus: ⁶Who, being in very nature God, did not consider equality with God something to be grasped, ⁷but made himself nothing, taking the very nature of a servant, being made in human likeness.

Came from the Father (Jn 13:3; 16:28).

Was before creation—

Jn 17:5 And now, Father, glorify me in your presence with the glory I had with you before the world began. (+Jn 17:24; 2Ti 1:9; 1Jn 1:1-2; 1Pe 1:20)

Maker of all things (Jn 1:3)—

1Co 8:6 yet for us there is but one God, the Father, from whom all things came and for whom we live; and there is but one Lord, Jesus Christ, through whom all things came and through whom we live.

Col 1:15 He is the image of the invisible God, the firstborn over all creation. ¹⁶For by him all things were created: things in heaven and on earth, visible and invisible, whether thrones or powers or rulers or authorities; all things were created by him and for him. ¹⁷He is before all things, and in him all things hold together.

Heb 1:1 In the past God spoke to our forefathers through the prophets at many times and in various ways, ²but in these last days he has spoken to us by his Son, whom he appointed heir of all things, and through whom he made the universe. (+Heb 1:8-12)

Rev 4:11 "You are worthy, our Lord and God, to receive glory and honor and power, for you created all things, and by your will they were created and have their being."

Was before Abraham—

Jn 8:56 Your father Abraham rejoiced at the thought of seeing my day; he saw it and was glad."

⁵⁷"You are not yet fifty years old," the Jews said to him, "and you have seen Abraham!"

⁵⁸"I tell you the truth," Jesus answered, "before Abraham was born, I am!"

With the Israelites in the wilderness (1Co 10:4,9; Jude 5).

Prescience of: *See above, Omniscience of.*

Priesthood of:

Appointed and called by God (Heb 3:1-2; 5:4-5), after the order of Melchizedek (Ps 110:4; Heb 5:6; 6:20; 7:15-17), superior to Aaron and the Levitical priests (Heb 7:11, 16,22; 8:1-2,6). Consecrated with an oath (Heb 7:20-21).

Has an unchangeable priesthood (Heb 7:23,28). Is of unblemished purity (Heb 7:26,28), faithful (Heb 3:2). Needed no sacrifice for himself (Heb 7:27).

Offered himself as a sacrifice (Heb 9:14,26). His sacrifice superior to all others (Heb 9:13-14,23). Offered sacrifice but once (Heb 7:27). Made reconciliation (Heb 2:17). Obtained redemption for us (Heb 9:12). Entered into heaven (Heb 4:14; 10:12). Sympathizes with saints (Heb 2:18; 4:15). Intercedes (Heb 7:25; 9:24). Blesses (Nu 6:23-26; Ac 3:26). On his throne (Zec 6:13). Appointment of, an encouragement to steadfastness (Heb 4:14).

Typified: Melchizedek (Ge 14:18-20). Aaron and his sons (Ex 40:12-15).

Promises of, to his disciples:

Of everlasting life—

Mt 19:28 Jesus said to them, "I tell you the truth, at the renewal of all things, when the Son of Man sits on his glorious throne, you who have followed me will also sit on twelve thrones, judging the twelve tribes of Israel.
Mk 10:29 "I tell you the truth," Jesus replied, "no one who has left home or brothers or sisters or mother or father or children or fields for me and the gospel ³⁰will fail to receive a hundred times as much in this present age (homes, brothers, sisters, mothers, children and fields—and with them, persecutions) and in the age to come, eternal life. (+Lk 18:29-30)
Lk 23:43 Jesus answered him, "I tell you the truth, today you will be with me in paradise."
Jn 5:25 I tell you the truth, a time is coming and has now come when the dead will hear the voice of the Son of God and those who hear will live. ²⁶For as the Father has life in himself, so he has granted the Son to have life in himself. ²⁷And he has given him authority to judge because he is the Son of Man.

²⁸"Do not be amazed at this, for a time is coming when all who are in their graves will hear his voice ²⁹and come out—those who have done good will rise to live, and those who have done evil will rise to be condemned.
Jn 6:54 Whoever eats my flesh and drinks my blood has eternal life, and I will raise him up at the last day.
Jn 6:57 Just as the living Father sent me and I live because of the Father, so the one who feeds on me will live because of me. ⁵⁸This is the bread that came down from heaven. Your forefathers ate manna and died, but he who feeds on this bread will live forever."
Jn 12:25 The man who loves his life will lose it, while the man who hates his life in this world will keep it for eternal life. ²⁶Whoever serves me must follow me; and where I am, my servant also will be. My Father will honor the one who serves me.

Of power—

Lk 24:49 I am going to send you what my Father has promised; but stay in the city until you have been clothed with power from on high." (+Jn 7:38)
Jn 7:39 By this he meant the Spirit, whom those who believed in him were later to receive. Up to that time the Spirit had not been given, since Jesus had not yet been glorified.
Ac 1:4 On one occasion, while he was eating with them, he gave them this command: "Do not leave Jerusalem, but wait for the gift my Father promised, which you have heard me speak about. ⁵For John baptized with water, but in a few days you will be baptized with the Holy Spirit."

⁶So when they met together, they asked him, "Lord, are you at this time going to restore the kingdom to Israel?"
⁷He said to them: "It is not for you to know the times or

dates the Father has set by his own authority. ⁸But you will receive power when the Holy Spirit comes on you; and you will be my witnesses in Jerusalem, and in all Judea and Samaria, and to the ends of the earth."

Of the Counselor—

Jn 14:16 And I will ask the Father, and he will give you another Counselor to be with you forever—
Jn 14:26 But the Counselor, the Holy Spirit, whom the Father will send in my name, will teach you all things and will remind you of everything I have said to you.
Jn 15:26 "When the Counselor comes, whom I will send to you from the Father, the Spirit of truth who goes out from the Father, he will testify about me. ²⁷And you also must testify, for you have been with me from the beginning.
Jn 16:7 But I tell you the truth: It is for your good that I am going away. Unless I go away, the Counselor will not come to you; but if I go, I will send him to you. ⁸When he comes, he will convict the world of guilt in regard to sin and righteousness and judgment: ⁹in regard to sin, because men do not believe in me; ¹⁰in regard to righteousness, because I am going to the Father, where you can see me no longer; ¹¹and in regard to judgment, because the prince of this world now stands condemned.

¹²"I have much more to say to you, more than you can now bear. ¹³But when he, the Spirit of truth, comes, he will guide you into all truth. He will not speak on his own; he will speak only what he hears, and he will tell you what is yet to come. ¹⁴He will bring glory to me by taking from what is mine and making it known to you.

Of his mediatorship—

Jn 16:23 In that day you will no longer ask me anything. I tell you the truth, my Father will give you whatever you ask in my name. ²⁴Until now you have not asked for anything in my name. Ask and you will receive, and your joy will be complete.
Jn 16:26 In that day you will ask in my name. I am not saying that I will ask the Father on your behalf.

Prophecies Concerning:

(Ge 18:18; 22:18; 26:4; 28:14; Isa 53:2-12; Mt 8:17; Gal 3:8,16).

Described in prophecy as: The branch—

Isa 11:1 A shoot will come up from the stump of Jesse; from his roots a Branch will bear fruit.
Jer 23:5 "The days are coming," declares the LORD, "when I will raise up to David a righteous Branch, a King who will reign wisely and do what is just and right in the land. ⁶In his days Judah will be saved and Israel will live in safety. This is the name by which he will be called: The LORD Our Righteousness. (+Jer 33:15)
Zec 3:8 "'Listen, O high priest Joshua and your associates seated before you, who are men symbolic of things to come: I am going to bring my servant, the Branch. (+Ro 15:12)

Capstone and Cornerstone—

Ps 118:22 The stone the builders rejected has become the capstone;
Isa 28:16 So this is what the Sovereign LORD says: "See, I lay a stone in Zion, a tested stone, a precious cornerstone for a sure foundation; the one who trusts will never be dismayed.

Banner for the peoples—

Isa 11:10 In that day the Root of Jesse will stand as a banner for the peoples; the nations will rally to him, and his place of rest will be glorious.

Fountain for sin—

Zec 13:1 "On that day a fountain will be opened to the house of David and the inhabitants of Jerusalem, to cleanse them from sin and impurity.

King—

Zec 9:9 Rejoice greatly, O Daughter of Zion! Shout, Daughter of Jerusalem! See, your king comes to you, righteous and having salvation, gentle and riding on a donkey, on a colt, the foal of a donkey.

Leader and commander—

Isa 55:4 See, I have made him a witness to the peoples, a leader and commander of the peoples. [5]Surely you will summon nations you know not, and nations that do not know you will hasten to you, because of the LORD your God, the Holy One of Israel, for he has endowed you with splendor."

Light to the Gentiles (Isa 42:6-7)—

Isa 49:6 he says: "It is too small a thing for you to be my servant to restore the tribes of Jacob and bring back those of Israel I have kept. I will also make you a light for the Gentiles, that you may bring my salvation to the ends of the earth." (+Isa 52:10,15)

Lk 2:31 which you have prepared in the sight of all people, [32]a light for revelation to the Gentiles and for glory to your people Israel."

Lord—

Isa 40:3 A voice of one calling: "In the desert prepare the way for the LORD; make straight in the wilderness a highway for our God. (+Isa 40:5; 35:2; Jer 31:34)

Mal 3:1 "See, I will send my messenger, who will prepare the way before me. Then suddenly the Lord you are seeking will come to his temple; the messenger of the covenant, whom you desire, will come," says the LORD Almighty.

[2]But who can endure the day of his coming? Who can stand when he appears? For he will be like a refiner's fire or a launderer's soap. [3]He will sit as a refiner and purifier of silver; he will purify the Levites and refine them like gold and silver. Then the LORD will have men who will bring offerings in righteousness, (+Lk 3:4)

God's chosen one—

Isa 42:1 "Here is my servant, whom I uphold, my chosen one in whom I delight; I will put my Spirit on him and he will bring justice to the nations.

Priest (Ps 110:4)

Prophet (Dt 18:15,18)—

Ac 3:22 For Moses said, 'The Lord your God will raise up for you a prophet like me from among your own people; you must listen to everything he tells you. [23]Anyone who does not listen to him will be completely cut off from among his people.'

[24]"Indeed, all the prophets from Samuel on, as many as have spoken, have foretold these days.

Redeemer—

Isa 59:20 "The Redeemer will come to Zion, to those in Jacob who repent of their sins," declares the LORD.

Ruler over Israel (Mic 5:2)

Savior—

Isa 62:10 Pass through, pass through the gates! Prepare the way for the people. Build up, build up the highway! Remove the stones. Raise a banner for the nations.

[11]The LORD has made proclamation to the ends of the earth: "Say to the Daughter of Zion, 'See, your Savior comes! See, his reward is with him, and his recompense accompanies him.'"

Mt 1:21 She will give birth to a son, and you are to give him the name Jesus, because he will save his people from their sins."

Lk 1:31 You will be with child and give birth to a son, and you are to give him the name Jesus.

Seed of woman—

Ge 3:15 And I will put enmity between you and the woman, and between your offspring and hers; he will crush your head, and you will strike his heel."

Shepherd—

Isa 40:11 He tends his flock like a shepherd: He gathers the lambs in his arms and carries them close to his heart; he gently leads those that have young. (+Eze 34:23)

Son of man—

Da 7:13 "In my vision at night I looked, and there before me was one like a son of man, coming with the clouds of heaven. He approached the Ancient of Days and was led into his presence. [14]He was given authority, glory and sovereign power; all peoples, nations and men of every language worshiped him. His dominion is an everlasting dominion that will not pass away, and his kingdom is one that will never be destroyed.

Future glory and power—

Rev 19:11 I saw heaven standing open and there before me was a white horse, whose rider is called Faithful and True. With justice he judges and makes war. [12]His eyes are like blazing fire, and on his head are many crowns. He has a name written on him that no one knows but he himself.

Rev 19:15 Out of his mouth comes a sharp sword with which to strike down the nations. "He will rule them with an iron scepter." He treads the winepress of the fury of the wrath of God Almighty.

To have universal dominion (Ps 72:5,8-11,17,19; Isa 2:2-4; 9:6-7; 60:1-9; Da 2:35,44; 7:18,22,27; Mic 4:1-4).

To be King of kings (Ps 72:5,8-11,17,19)—

Rev 1:5 and from Jesus Christ, who is the faithful witness, the firstborn from the dead, and the ruler of the kings of the earth.

To him who loves us and has freed us from our sins by his blood, [6]and has made us to be a kingdom and priests to serve his God and Father—to him be glory and power for ever and ever! Amen.

[7]Look, he is coming with the clouds, and every eye will see him, even those who pierced him; and all the peoples of the earth will mourn because of him. So shall it be! Amen.

Rev 11:15 The seventh angel sounded his trumpet, and there were loud voices in heaven, which said: "The kingdom of the world has become the kingdom of our Lord and of his Christ, and he will reign for ever and ever."

Rev 12:10 Then I heard a loud voice in heaven say: "Now have come the salvation and the power and the kingdom of our God, and the authority of his Christ. For the accuser of our brothers, who accuses them before our God day and night, has been hurled down.

Rev 17:14 They will make war against the Lamb, but the Lamb will overcome them because he is Lord of lords and King of kings—and with him will be his called, chosen and faithful followers."

Rev 19:16 On his robe and on his thigh he has this name written: KING OF KINGS AND LORD OF LORDS.

Rev 20:4 I saw thrones on which were seated those who had been given authority to judge. And I saw the souls of those who had been beheaded because of their testimony for Jesus and because of the word of God. They had not worshiped the beast or his image and had not received his mark on their foreheads or their hands. They came to life and reigned with Christ a thousand years.

Rev 20:6 Blessed and holy are those who have part in the first resurrection. The second death has no power over them, but they will be priests of God and of Christ and will reign with him for a thousand years.

To sit at right hand of God—

Mk 14:62 "I am," said Jesus. "And you will see the Son of Man sitting at the right hand of the Mighty One and coming on the clouds of heaven."

1Pe 3:22 who has gone into heaven and is at God's right hand—with angels, authorities and powers in submission to him.

To be judge—

Jude 14 Enoch, the seventh from Adam, prophesied about these men: "See, the Lord is coming with thousands upon thousands of his holy ones [15]to judge everyone, and to convict all the ungodly of all the ungodly acts they have done in the ungodly way, and of all the harsh words ungodly sinners have spoken against him."

Rev 2:23 I will strike her children dead. Then all the churches will know that I am he who searches hearts and minds, and I will repay each of you according to your deeds.

Rev 6:16 They called to the mountains and the rocks, "Fall on us and hide us from the face of him who sits on the throne and from the wrath of the Lamb! [17]For the great day of their wrath has come, and who can stand?"

Rev 14:14 I looked, and there before me was a white cloud, and seated on the cloud was one "like a son of man" with a crown of gold on his head and a sharp sickle in his hand. (+Rev 14:15-16)

Prophet:

Dt 18:15 The LORD your God will raise up for you a prophet like me from among your own brothers. You must listen to him.

Dt 18:18 I will raise up for them a prophet like you from among their brothers; I will put my words in his mouth, and he will tell them everything I command him.

Mt 21:11 The crowds answered, "This is Jesus, the prophet from Nazareth in Galilee."

Mt 21:46 They looked for a way to arrest him, but they were afraid of the crowd because the people held that he was a prophet.

Lk 7:16 They were all filled with awe and praised God. "A great prophet has appeared among us," they said. "God has come to help his people."

Lk 13:33 In any case, I must keep going today and tomorrow and the next day—for surely no prophet can die outside Jerusalem!

Lk 24:19 "What things?" he asked. "About Jesus of Nazareth," they replied. "He was a prophet, powerful in word and deed before God and all the people.

Jn 4:19 "Sir," the woman said, "I can see that you are a prophet.

Jn 6:14 After the people saw the miraculous sign that Jesus did, they began to say, "Surely this is the Prophet who is to come into the world."

Jn 7:40 On hearing his words, some of the people said, "Surely this man is the Prophet."

Jn 9:17 Finally they turned again to the blind man, "What have you to say about him? It was your eyes he opened." The man replied, "He is a prophet." (+Ac 3:22-23; 7:37)

Foretold (Isa 52:7; Na 1:15). Anointed with the Holy Spirit (Isa 42:1; 61:1, w Lk 4:18; Jn 3:34).

Reveals God (Mt 11:27)—

Jn 3:2 He came to Jesus at night and said, "Rabbi, we know you are a teacher who has come from God. For no one could perform the miraculous signs you are doing if God were not with him." (+Jn 3:13,34; 17:6,14,26; Heb 1:1-2)

Declared his doctrine to be that of the Father (Jn 8:26,28; 12:49-50; 14:10,24; 15:15; 17:8,26). Foretold things to come (Mt 24:3-35; Lk 19:41-44). Faithful (Lk 4:43; Jn 17:8; Heb 3:2; Rev 1:5; 3:14). Abounded in wisdom (Lk 2:40,47,52; Col 2:3).

Mighty in deed and word—

Mt 13:54 Coming to his hometown, he began teaching the people in their synagogue, and they were amazed. "Where did this man get this wisdom and these miraculous powers?" they asked. (+Mk 1:27; Lk 4:32; Jn 7:46)

Humble in his teaching (Isa 42:2; Mt 12:17-20). God commands us to hear (Dt 18:15; Ac 3:22). God will severely visit neglect of (Dt 18:15,18-19; Ac 3:23; Heb 2:3).

Received:

Crowds attend his ministry (Mt 8:1)—

Mt 13:2 Such large crowds gathered around him that he got into a boat and sat in it, while all the people stood on the shore. (+Mt 14:13,35; 19:1-2)

Mk 1:37 and when they found him, they exclaimed: "Everyone is looking for you!"

Mk 1:45 Instead he went out and began to talk freely, spreading the news. As a result, Jesus could no longer enter a town openly but stayed outside in lonely places. Yet the people still came to him from everywhere.

Mk 2:2 So many gathered that there was no room left, not even outside the door, and he preached the word to them.

Mk 2:15 While Jesus was having dinner at Levi's house, many tax collectors and "sinners" were eating with him and his disciples, for there were many who followed him. (+Mk 3:7)

Mk 3:20 Then Jesus entered a house, and again a crowd gathered, so that he and his disciples were not even able to eat. [21]When his family heard about this, they went to take charge of him, for they said, "He is out of his mind." (+Mk 4:1; 5:21; 10:1; 11:18)

Mk 12:37 David himself calls him 'Lord.' How then can he be his son?" The large crowd listened to him with delight. (+Lk 9:11)

Lk 12:1 Meanwhile, when a crowd of many thousands had gathered, so that they were trampling on one another, Jesus began to speak first to his disciples, saying: "Be on your guard against the yeast of the Pharisees, which is hypocrisy. (+Lk 19:48)

Lk 21:38 and all the people came early in the morning to hear him at the temple. (+Jn 6:2; 8:2)

Many believe on him—

Mt 4:24 News about him spread all over Syria, and people brought to him all who were ill with various diseases, those suffering severe pain, the demon-possessed, those having seizures, and the paralyzed, and he healed them.

Mt 21:8 A very large crowd spread their cloaks on the road, while others cut branches from the trees and spread them on the road. [9]The crowds that went ahead of him and those that followed shouted,

"Hosanna to the Son of David!"

"Blessed is he who comes in the name of the Lord!"

"Hosanna in the highest!"

10When Jesus entered Jerusalem, the whole city was stirred and asked, "Who is this?"

11The crowds answered, "This is Jesus, the prophet from Nazareth in Galilee."

Mt 21:15 But when the chief priests and the teachers of the law saw the wonderful things he did and the children shouting in the temple area, "Hosanna to the Son of David," they were indignant.

Mk 2:12 He got up, took his mat and walked out in full view of them all. This amazed everyone and they praised God, saying, "We have never seen anything like this!"

Mk 6:55 They ran throughout that whole region and carried the sick on mats to wherever they heard he was. **56**And wherever he went—into villages, towns or countryside—they placed the sick in the marketplaces. They begged him to let them touch even the edge of his cloak, and all who touched him were healed. (+Mk 11:8-10)

Lk 6:17 He went down with them and stood on a level place. A large crowd of his disciples was there and a great number of people from all over Judea, from Jerusalem, and from the coast of Tyre and Sidon, **18**who had come to hear him and to be healed of their diseases. Those troubled by evil spirits were cured, **19**and the people all tried to touch him, because power was coming from him and healing them all.

Lk 7:16 They were all filled with awe and praised God. "A great prophet has appeared among us," they said. "God has come to help his people." **17**This news about Jesus spread throughout Judea and the surrounding country. (+Lk 19:36)

Lk 19:37 When he came near the place where the road goes down the Mount of Olives, the whole crowd of disciples began joyfully to praise God in loud voices for all the miracles they had seen: (+Lk 19:38)

Lk 19:47 Every day he was teaching at the temple. But the chief priests, the teachers of the law and the leaders among the people were trying to kill him. **48**Yet they could not find any way to do it, because all the people hung on his words.

Lk 23:27 A large number of people followed him, including women who mourned and wailed for him.

Jn 2:11 This, the first of his miraculous signs, Jesus performed at Cana in Galilee. He thus revealed his glory, and his disciples put their faith in him.

Jn 2:23 Now while he was in Jerusalem at the Passover Feast, many people saw the miraculous signs he was doing and believed in his name. (+Jn 4:45)

Jn 8:30 Even as he spoke, many put their faith in him.

Jn 10:41 and many people came to him. They said, "Though John never performed a miraculous sign, all that John said about this man was true." **42**And in that place many believed in Jesus.

Jn 11:45 Therefore many of the Jews who had come to visit Mary, and had seen what Jesus did, put their faith in him. **46**But some of them went to the Pharisees and told them what Jesus had done. **47**Then the chief priests and the Pharisees called a meeting of the Sanhedrin. "What are we accomplishing?" they asked. "Here is this man performing many miraculous signs.

48If we let him go on like this, everyone will believe in him, and then the Romans will come and take away both our place and our nation."

Jn 12:9 Meanwhile a large crowd of Jews found out that Jesus was there and came, not only because of him but also to see Lazarus, whom he had raised from the dead.

Jn 12:11 for on account of him many of the Jews were going over to Jesus and putting their faith in him. (+Jn 12:12-13)

Jn 12:18 Many people, because they had heard that he had given this miraculous sign, went out to meet him. **19**So the Pharisees said to one another, "See, this is getting us nowhere. Look how the whole world has gone after him!"

20Now there were some Greeks among those who went up to worship at the Feast. **21**They came to Philip, who was from Bethsaida in Galilee, with a request. "Sir," they said, "we would like to see Jesus."

Jn 12:42 Yet at the same time many even among the leaders believed in him. But because of the Pharisees they would not confess their faith for fear they would be put out of the synagogue;

Authority of his teaching confessed (Mk 1:22; Lk 4:32; Jn 3:2)—

Jn 7:46 "No one ever spoke the way this man does," the guards declared.

With astonishment and gladness (Mt 9:8,27-28,33; 13:54; 15:31; Mk 1:27; 2:12)—

Mk 5:42 Immediately the girl stood up and walked around (she was twelve years old). At this they were completely astonished.

Mk 7:37 People were overwhelmed with amazement. "He has done everything well," they said. "He even makes the deaf hear and the mute speak."

Lk 4:36 All the people were amazed and said to each other, "What is this teaching? With authority and power he gives orders to evil spirits and they come out!" **37**And the news about him spread throughout the surrounding area. (+Lk 4:42)

Lk 5:26 Everyone was amazed and gave praise to God. They were filled with awe and said, "We have seen remarkable things today."

Lk 13:17 When he said this, all his opponents were humiliated, but the people were delighted with all the wonderful things he was doing.

Lk 18:43 Immediately he received his sight and followed Jesus, praising God. When all the people saw it, they also praised God.

Jn 7:31 Still, many in the crowd put their faith in him. They said, "When the Christ comes, will he do more miraculous signs than this man?"

Jn 7:40 On hearing his words, some of the people said, "Surely this man is the Prophet."

41Others said, "He is the Christ."

Still others asked, "How can the Christ come from Galilee?

42Does not the Scripture say that the Christ will come from David's family and from Bethlehem, the town where David lived?" **43**Thus the people were divided because of Jesus. **44**Some wanted to seize him, but no one laid a hand on him.

Jn 9:17 Finally they turned again to the blind man, "What have you to say about him? It was your eyes he opened." The man replied, "He is a prophet."

Jn 9:24 A second time they summoned the man who had been blind. "Give glory to God," they said. "We know this man is a sinner."

25He replied, "Whether he is a sinner or not, I don't know. One thing I do know. I was blind but now I see!"

Jn 9:29 We know that God spoke to Moses, but as for this fellow, we don't even know where he comes from."

30The man answered, "Now that is remarkable! You don't know where he comes from, yet he opened my eyes.

Jn 9:33 If this man were not from God, he could do nothing."

Jn 11:37 But some of them said, "Could not he who opened the eyes of the blind man have kept this man from dying?"

Instances of his being received: By Matthew (Mt 9:9), by Peter and other fishermen (Mk 1:16-20; Lk 5:3-11), by Philip (Jn 1:43,45), by Nathanael (Jn 1:45-50), by Zacchaeus (Lk 19:1-10), by thief on the cross (Lk 23:40-42), by three thousand at Pentecost (Ac 2:41; 4:4).

Redeemer: *See below, Savior.*

See Redemption.

Rejected: (Lk 9:26)

Lk 10:16 "He who listens to you listens to me; he who rejects you rejects me; but he who rejects me rejects him who sent me."

Lk 11:23 "He who is not with me is against me, and he who does not gather with me, scatters. (+Heb 6:4-5)

Heb 6:6 if they fall away, to be brought back to repentance, because to their loss they are crucifying the Son of God all over again and subjecting him to public disgrace.

1Pe 2:4 As you come to him, the living Stone—rejected by men but chosen by God and precious to him—

1Pe 2:7 Now to you who believe, this stone is precious. But to those who do not believe,

"The stone the builders rejected has become the capstone,"

[8]and, "A stone that causes men to stumble and a rock that makes them fall."

They stumble because they disobey the message—which is also what they were destined for.

1Jn 2:22 Who is the liar? It is the man who denies that Jesus is the Christ. Such a man is the antichrist—he denies the Father and the Son. [23]No one who denies the Son has the Father; whoever acknowledges the Son has the Father also. (+1Jn 4:3)

2Jn 7 Many deceivers, who do not acknowledge Jesus Christ as coming in the flesh, have gone out into the world. Any such person is the deceiver and the antichrist.

Rejected by the Jews (Mt 13:54-57)—

Mt 13:58 And he did not do many miracles there because of their lack of faith. (+Isa 6:9-10; Mt 23:37)

Mk 6:3 Isn't this the carpenter? Isn't this Mary's son and the brother of James, Joseph, Judas and Simon? Aren't his sisters here with us?" And they took offense at him.

[4]Jesus said to them, "Only in his hometown, among his relatives and in his own house is a prophet without honor." [5]He could not do any miracles there, except lay his hands on a few sick people and heal them. [6]And he was amazed at their lack of faith.

Then Jesus went around teaching from village to village.

Lk 7:34 The Son of Man came eating and drinking, and you say, 'Here is a glutton and a drunkard, a friend of tax collectors and "sinners."'

Lk 13:34 "O Jerusalem, Jerusalem, you who kill the prophets and stone those sent to you, how often I have longed to gather your children together, as a hen gathers her chicks under her wings, but you were not willing! (+Lk 19:27)

Lk 19:42 and said, "If you, even you, had only known on this day what would bring you peace—but now it is hidden from your eyes.

Lk 22:67 "If you are the Christ," they said, "tell us." Jesus answered, "If I tell you, you will not believe me,

Jn 1:11 He came to that which was his own, but his own did not receive him.

Jn 5:38 nor does his word dwell in you, for you do not believe the one he sent.

Jn 5:40 yet you refuse to come to me to have life.

Jn 5:43 I have come in my Father's name, and you do not accept me; but if someone else comes in his own name, you will accept him.

Jn 7:3 Jesus' brothers said to him, "You ought to leave here and go to Judea, so that your disciples may see the miracles you do. [4]No one who wants to become a public figure acts in secret. Since you are doing these things, show yourself to the world." [5]For even his own brothers did not believe in him.

Jn 7:12 Among the crowds there was widespread whispering about him. Some said, "He is a good man."

Others replied, "No, he deceives the people." [13]But no one would say anything publicly about him for fear of the Jews.

Jn 7:15 The Jews were amazed and asked, "How did this man get such learning without having studied?"

Jn 7:25 At that point some of the people of Jerusalem began to ask, "Isn't this the man they are trying to kill? [26]Here he is, speaking publicly, and they are not saying a word to him. Have the authorities really concluded that he is the Christ? [27]But we know where this man is from; when the Christ comes, no one will know where he is from."

Jn 8:13 The Pharisees challenged him, "Here you are, appearing as your own witness; your testimony is not valid."

Jn 8:21 Once more Jesus said to them, "I am going away, and you will look for me, and you will die in your sin. Where I go, you cannot come."

[22]This made the Jews ask, "Will he kill himself? Is that why he says, 'Where I go, you cannot come'?"

Jn 8:24 I told you that you would die in your sins; if you do not believe that I am [the one I claim to be], you will indeed die in your sins."

Jn 8:45 Yet because I tell the truth, you do not believe me! [46]Can any of you prove me guilty of sin? If I am telling the truth, why don't you believe me? [47]He who belongs to God hears what God says. The reason you do not hear is that you do not belong to God."

Jn 8:53 Are you greater than our father Abraham? He died, and so did the prophets. Who do you think you are?"

Jn 9:16 Some of the Pharisees said, "This man is not from God, for he does not keep the Sabbath."

But others asked, "How can a sinner do such miraculous signs?" So they were divided.

[17]Finally they turned again to the blind man, "What have you to say about him? It was your eyes he opened."

The man replied, "He is a prophet."

Jn 9:24 A second time they summoned the man who had been blind. "Give glory to God," they said. "We know this man is a sinner."

Jn 10:20 Many of them said, "He is demon-possessed and raving mad. Why listen to him?"

[21]But others said, "These are not the sayings of a man possessed by a demon. Can a demon open the eyes of the blind?"

Jn 10:24 The Jews gathered around him, saying, "How long will you keep us in suspense? If you are the Christ, tell us plainly."

Jn 10:33 "We are not stoning you for any of these," replied the Jews, "but for blasphemy, because you, a mere man, claim to be God."

Jn 11:46 But some of them went to the Pharisees and told them what Jesus had done. **47**Then the chief priests and the Pharisees called a meeting of the Sanhedrin.

"What are we accomplishing?" they asked. "Here is this man performing many miraculous signs. **48**If we let him go on like this, everyone will believe in him, and then the Romans will come and take away both our place and our nation."

Jn 12:37 Even after Jesus had done all these miraculous signs in their presence, they still would not believe in him.

Jn 12:48 There is a judge for the one who rejects me and does not accept my words; that very word which I spoke will condemn him at the last day.

Ac 13:46 Then Paul and Barnabas answered them boldly: "We had to speak the word of God to you first. Since you reject it and do not consider yourselves worthy of eternal life, we now turn to the Gentiles.

Ac 18:5 When Silas and Timothy came from Macedonia, Paul devoted himself exclusively to preaching, testifying to the Jews that Jesus was the Christ. **6**But when the Jews opposed Paul and became abusive, he shook out his clothes in protest and said to them, "Your blood be on your own heads! I am clear of my responsibility. From now on I will go to the Gentiles."

Ac 22:18 and saw the Lord speaking. 'Quick!' he said to me. 'Leave Jerusalem immediately, because they will not accept your testimony about me.'

Ac 28:24 Some were convinced by what he said, but others would not believe. **25**They disagreed among themselves and began to leave after Paul had made this final statement: "The Holy Spirit spoke the truth to your forefathers when he said through Isaiah the prophet:

Ac 28:27 For this people's heart has become calloused; they hardly hear with their ears, and they have closed their eyes. Otherwise they might see with their eyes, hear with their ears, understand with their hearts and turn, and I would heal them.'

Ro 3:3 What if some did not have faith? Will their lack of faith nullify God's faithfulness?

Ro 9:31 but Israel, who pursued a law of righteousness, has not attained it. **32**Why not? Because they pursued it not by faith but as if it were by works. They stumbled over the "stumbling stone."

Ro 10:16 But not all the Israelites accepted the good news. For Isaiah says, "Lord, who has believed our message?"

Ro 10:21 But concerning Israel he says, "All day long I have held out my hands to a disobedient and obstinate people." (+1Co 1:8)

Rejected by Gadarenes or Gerasenes—
Mt 8:34 Then the whole town went out to meet Jesus. And when they saw him, they pleaded with him to leave their region. (+Mk 5:17; Lk 8:37)

Rejected by Gentiles—
1Co 1:23 but we preach Christ crucified: a stumbling block to Jews and foolishness to Gentiles,

Rejected by followers—
Jn 6:36 But as I told you, you have seen me and still you do not believe.

Jn 6:60 On hearing it, many of his disciples said, "This is a hard teaching. Who can accept it?"

61Aware that his disciples were grumbling about this, Jesus said to them, "Does this offend you? **62**What if you see the Son of Man ascend to where he was before! **63**The Spirit gives life; the flesh counts for nothing. The words I have spoken to you are spirit and they are life. **64**Yet there are some of you who do not believe." For Jesus had known

from the beginning which of them did not believe and who would betray him. **65**He went on to say, "This is why I told you that no one can come to me unless the Father has enabled him."

66From this time many of his disciples turned back and no longer followed him.

Prophecies concerning his rejection—
Ps 2:1 Why do the nations conspire and the peoples plot in vain? **2**The kings of the earth take their stand and the rulers gather together against the LORD and against his Anointed One. **3**"Let us break their chains," they say, "and throw off their fetters."

Ps 118:22 The stone the builders rejected has become the capstone;

Isa 53:1 Who has believed our message and to whom has the arm of the LORD been revealed? **2**He grew up before him like a tender shoot, and like a root out of dry ground. He had no beauty or majesty to attract us to him, nothing in his appearance that we should desire him. **3**He was despised and rejected by men, a man of sorrows, and familiar with suffering. Like one from whom men hide their faces he was despised, and we esteemed him not.

4Surely he took up our infirmities and carried our sorrows, yet we considered him stricken by God, smitten by him, and afflicted. (+Lk 9:44)

Foretold by himself—
Mt 11:16 "To what can I compare this generation? They are like children sitting in the marketplaces and calling out to others:

17"'We played the flute for you, and you did not dance; we sang a dirge, and you did not mourn.'

18For John came neither eating nor drinking, and they say, 'He has a demon.' **19**The Son of Man came eating and drinking, and they say, 'Here is a glutton and a drunkard, a friend of tax collectors and "sinners."' But wisdom is proved right by her actions." (+Mk 9:12; Lk 4:23-29; 7:31-35)

Lk 17:25 But first he must suffer many things and be rejected by this generation.

Jn 15:18 "If the world hates you, keep in mind that it hated me first.

Jn 15:20 Remember the words I spoke to you: 'No servant is greater than his master.' If they persecuted me, they will persecute you also. If they obeyed my teaching, they will obey yours also.

Jn 15:24 If I had not done among them what no one else did, they would not be guilty of sin. But now they have seen these miracles, and yet they have hated both me and my Father.

In the parable of the feast—
Lk 14:16 Jesus replied: "A certain man was preparing a great banquet and invited many guests. **17**At the time of the banquet he sent his servant to tell those who had been invited, 'Come, for everything is now ready.'

18"But they all alike began to make excuses. The first said, 'I have just bought a field, and I must go and see it. Please excuse me.'

19"Another said, 'I have just bought five yoke of oxen, and I'm on my way to try them out. Please excuse me.'

20"Still another said, 'I just got married, so I can't come.'

21"The servant came back and reported this to his master. Then the owner of the house became angry and ordered his servant, 'Go out quickly into the streets and alleys of the town and bring in the poor, the crippled, the blind and the lame.'

²²"'Sir,' the servant said, 'what you ordered has been done, but there is still room.'

²³"Then the master told his servant, 'Go out to the roads and country lanes and make them come in, so that my house will be full. ²⁴I tell you, not one of those men who were invited will get a taste of my banquet.'" (+Mt 22:2-14)

In the parable of the house built on the sand—

Mt 7:26 But everyone who hears these words of mine and does not put them into practice is like a foolish man who built his house on sand. (+Lk 6:46-49)

Punishment for rejection of, foretold—

Mt 8:12 But the subjects of the kingdom will be thrown outside, into the darkness, where there will be weeping and gnashing of teeth."

Mt 10:14 If anyone will not welcome you or listen to your words, shake the dust off your feet when you leave that home or town. ¹⁵I tell you the truth, it will be more bearable for Sodom and Gomorrah on the day of judgment than for that town.

Mt 10:33 But whoever disowns me before men, I will disown him before my Father in heaven.

Mt 12:38 Then some of the Pharisees and teachers of the law said to him, "Teacher, we want to see a miraculous sign from you."

³⁹He answered, "A wicked and adulterous generation asks for a miraculous sign! But none will be given it except the sign of the prophet Jonah. ⁴⁰For as Jonah was three days and three nights in the belly of a huge fish, so the Son of Man will be three days and three nights in the heart of the earth. ⁴¹The men of Nineveh will stand up at the judgment with this generation and condemn it; for they repented at the preaching of Jonah, and now one greater than Jonah is here. ⁴²The Queen of the South will rise at the judgment with this generation and condemn it; for she came from the ends of the earth to listen to Solomon's wisdom, and now one greater than Solomon is here.

⁴³"When an evil spirit comes out of a man, it goes through arid places seeking rest and does not find it. ⁴⁴Then it says, 'I will return to the house I left.' When it arrives, it finds the house unoccupied, swept clean and put in order. ⁴⁵Then it goes and takes with it seven other spirits more wicked than itself, and they go in and live there. And the final condition of that man is worse than the first. That is how it will be with this wicked generation." (+Mk 12:1-12)

Mk 16:16 Whoever believes and is baptized will be saved, but whoever does not believe will be condemned. (+Lk 20:9-18)

2Ti 2:12 if we endure, we will also reign with him. If we disown him, he will also disown us; (+Heb 6:6)

Heb 10:29 How much more severely do you think a man deserves to be punished who has trampled the Son of God under foot, who has treated as an unholy thing the blood of the covenant that sanctified him, and who has insulted the Spirit of grace?

2Pe 2:1 But there were also false prophets among the people, just as there will be false teachers among you. They will secretly introduce destructive heresies, even denying the sovereign Lord who bought them—bringing swift destruction on themselves.

Relation of, to the Father:

Ps 110:1 The LORD says to my Lord: "Sit at my right hand until I make your enemies a footstool for your feet." (+Mt 11:27)

1Th 5:18 give thanks in all circumstances, for this is God's will for you in Christ Jesus.

Heb 2:9 But we see Jesus, who was made a little lower than the angels, now crowned with glory and honor because he suffered death, so that by the grace of God he might taste death for everyone.

Called God his Father—

Mt 20:23 Jesus said to them, "You will indeed drink from my cup, but to sit at my right or left is not for me to grant. These places belong to those for whom they have been prepared by my Father."

Mt 26:39 Going a little farther, he fell with his face to the ground and prayed, "My Father, if it is possible, may this cup be taken from me. Yet not as I will, but as you will."

Mk 13:32 "No one knows about that day or hour, not even the angels in heaven, nor the Son, but only the Father.

Rev 2:27 'He will rule them with an iron scepter; he will dash them to pieces like pottery'—just as I have received authority from my Father.

With God in the beginning—

Jn 1:1 In the beginning was the Word, and the Word was with God, and the Word was God. ²He was with God in the beginning.

Jn 1:14 The Word became flesh and made his dwelling among us. We have seen his glory, the glory of the One and Only, who came from the Father, full of grace and truth.

Was sent by God—

Jn 3:34 For the one whom God has sent speaks the words of God, for God gives the Spirit without limit. ³⁵The Father loves the Son and has placed everything in his hands.

Jn 4:34 "My food," said Jesus, "is to do the will of him who sent me and to finish his work. (+Jn 6:27)

Jn 6:32 Jesus said to them, "I tell you the truth, it is not Moses who has given you the bread from heaven, but it is my Father who gives you the true bread from heaven. ³³For the bread of God is he who comes down from heaven and gives life to the world."

Jn 6:38 For I have come down from heaven not to do my will but to do the will of him who sent me. ³⁹And this is the will of him who sent me, that I shall lose none of all that he has given me, but raise them up at the last day. ⁴⁰For my Father's will is that everyone who looks to the Son and believes in him shall have eternal life, and I will raise him up at the last day."

Jn 6:44 "No one can come to me unless the Father who sent me draws him, and I will raise him up at the last day. ⁴⁵It is written in the Prophets: 'They will all be taught by God.' Everyone who listens to the Father and learns from him comes to me. ⁴⁶No one has seen the Father except the one who is from God; only he has seen the Father.

Jn 7:16 Jesus answered, "My teaching is not my own. It comes from him who sent me.

Jn 7:28 Then Jesus, still teaching in the temple courts, cried out, "Yes, you know me, and you know where I am from. I am not here on my own, but he who sent me is true. You do not know him, ²⁹but I know him because I am from him and he sent me."

Jn 7:33 Jesus said, "I am with you for only a short time, and then I go to the one who sent me.

Jn 8:16 But if I do judge, my decisions are right, because I am not alone. I stand with the Father, who sent me.

Jn 8:19 Then they asked him, "Where is your father?" "You do not know me or my Father," Jesus replied. "If you knew me, you would know my Father also."

Jn 8:28 So Jesus said, "When you have lifted up the Son

of Man, then you will know that I am [the one I claim to be] and that I do nothing on my own but speak just what the Father has taught me. ²⁹The one who sent me is with me; he has not left me alone, for I always do what pleases him."

Jn 8:38 I am telling you what I have seen in the Father's presence, and you do what you have heard from your father."

Jn 8:40 As it is, you are determined to kill me, a man who has told you the truth that I heard from God. Abraham did not do such things.

Jn 8:42 Jesus said to them, "If God were your Father, you would love me, for I came from God and now am here. I have not come on my own; but he sent me.

Jn 8:49 "I am not possessed by a demon," said Jesus, "but I honor my Father and you dishonor me.

Jn 8:54 Jesus replied, "If I glorify myself, my glory means nothing. My Father, whom you claim as your God, is the one who glorifies me. ⁵⁵Though you do not know him, I know him. If I said I did not, I would be a liar like you, but I do know him and keep his word.

Jn 9:4 As long as it is day, we must do the work of him who sent me. Night is coming, when no one can work.

Jn 11:41 So they took away the stone. Then Jesus looked up and said, "Father, I thank you that you have heard me. ⁴²I knew that you always hear me, but I said this for the benefit of the people standing here, that they may believe that you sent me."

Jn 12:44 Then Jesus cried out, "When a man believes in me, he does not believe in me only, but in the one who sent me.

Jn 12:49 For I did not speak of my own accord, but the Father who sent me commanded me what to say and how to say it. ⁵⁰I know that his command leads to eternal life. So whatever I say is just what the Father has told me to say."

Jn 17:1 After Jesus said this, he looked toward heaven and prayed:

"Father, the time has come. Glorify your Son, that your Son may glorify you. ²For you granted him authority over all people that he might give eternal life to all those you have given him. ³Now this is eternal life: that they may know you, the only true God, and Jesus Christ, whom you have sent. ⁴I have brought you glory on earth by completing the work you gave me to do. ⁵And now, Father, glorify me in your presence with the glory I had with you before the world began.

⁶"I have revealed you to those whom you gave me out of the world. They were yours; you gave them to me and they have obeyed your word. ⁷Now they know that everything you have given me comes from you. ⁸For I gave them the words you gave me and they accepted them. They knew with certainty that I came from you, and they believed that you sent me. ⁹I pray for them. I am not praying for the world, but for those you have given me, for they are yours. ¹⁰All I have is yours, and all you have is mine. And glory has come to me through them.

Jn 17:24 "Father, I want those you have given me to be with me where I am, and to see my glory, the glory you have given me because you loved me before the creation of the world.

²⁵"Righteous Father, though the world does not know you, I know you, and they know that you have sent me. ²⁶I have made you known to them, and will continue to make you known in order that the love you have for me may be in them and that I myself may be in them."

1Co 1:30 It is because of him that you are in Christ Jesus, who has become for us wisdom from God—that is, our righteousness, holiness and redemption.

Heb 3:2 He was faithful to the one who appointed him, just as Moses was faithful in all God's house.

1Pe 2:4 As you come to him, the living Stone—rejected by men but chosen by God and precious to him—

1Pe 2:23 When they hurled their insults at him, he did not retaliate; when he suffered, he made no threats. Instead, he entrusted himself to him who judges justly.

1Jn 4:9 This is how God showed his love among us: He sent his one and only Son into the world that we might live through him. ¹⁰This is love: not that we loved God, but that he loved us and sent his Son as an atoning sacrifice for our sins.

1Jn 4:14 And we have seen and testify that the Father has sent his Son to be the Savior of the world.

Endued with the Holy Spirit—

Isa 42:1 "Here is my servant, whom I uphold, my chosen one in whom I delight; I will put my Spirit on him and he will bring justice to the nations.

Isa 61:1 The Spirit of the Sovereign LORD is on me, because the LORD has anointed me to preach good news to the poor. He has sent me to bind up the brokenhearted, to proclaim freedom for the captives and release from darkness for the prisoners,

Mic 5:4 He will stand and shepherd his flock in the strength of the LORD, in the majesty of the name of the LORD his God. And they will live securely, for then his greatness will reach to the ends of the earth.

Ac 10:38 how God anointed Jesus of Nazareth with the Holy Spirit and power, and how he went around doing good and healing all who were under the power of the devil, because God was with him.

Is the Son of God—

Jn 5:19 Jesus gave them this answer: "I tell you the truth, the Son can do nothing by himself; he can do only what he sees his Father doing, because whatever the Father does the Son also does. ²⁰For the Father loves the Son and shows him all he does. Yes, to your amazement he will show him even greater things than these. ²¹For just as the Father raises the dead and gives them life, even so the Son gives life to whom he is pleased to give it. ²²Moreover, the Father judges no one, but has entrusted all judgment to the Son, ²³that all may honor the Son just as they honor the Father. He who does not honor the Son does not honor the Father, who sent him.

²⁴"I tell you the truth, whoever hears my word and believes him who sent me has eternal life and will not be condemned; he has crossed over from death to life. ²⁵I tell you the truth, a time is coming and has now come when the dead will hear the voice of the Son of God and those who hear will live. ²⁶For as the Father has life in himself, so he has granted the Son to have life in himself.

Jn 5:37 And the Father who sent me has himself testified concerning me. You have never heard his voice nor seen his form,

Jn 5:45 "But do not think I will accuse you before the Father. Your accuser is Moses, on whom your hopes are set.

Ro 8:32 He who did not spare his own Son, but gave him up for us all—how will he not also, along with him, graciously give us all things? (+Ro 15:6)

Heb 1:2 but in these last days he has spoken to us by his Son, whom he appointed heir of all things, and through whom he made the universe. ³The Son is the radiance of

God's glory and the exact representation of his being, sustaining all things by his powerful word. After he had provided purification for sins, he sat down at the right hand of the Majesty in heaven.

Heb 5:5 So Christ also did not take upon himself the glory of becoming a high priest. But God said to him,

"You are my Son; today I have become your Father."

6And he says in another place,

"You are a priest forever, in the order of Melchizedek."

7During the days of Jesus' life on earth, he offered up prayers and petitions with loud cries and tears to the one who could save him from death, and he was heard because of his reverent submission. **8**Although he was a son, he learned obedience from what he suffered **9**and, once made perfect, he became the source of eternal salvation for all who obey him **10**and was designated by God to be high priest in the order of Melchizedek.

2Pe 1:17 For he received honor and glory from God the Father when the voice came to him from the Majestic Glory, saying, "This is my Son, whom I love; with him I am well pleased."

Is one with the Father—

Jn 10:18 No one takes it from me, but I lay it down of my own accord. I have authority to lay it down and authority to take it up again. This command I received from my Father."

Jn 10:25 Jesus answered, "I did tell you, but you do not believe. The miracles I do in my Father's name speak for me,

Jn 10:30 I and the Father are one."

Jn 10:32 but Jesus said to them, "I have shown you many great miracles from the Father. For which of these do you stone me?"

33"We are not stoning you for any of these," replied the Jews, "but for blasphemy, because you, a mere man, claim to be God."

Jn 10:36 what about the one whom the Father set apart as his very own and sent into the world? Why then do you accuse me of blasphemy because I said, 'I am God's Son'? **37**Do not believe me unless I do what my Father does. **38**But if I do it, even though you do not believe me, believe the miracles, that you may know and understand that the Father is in me, and I in the Father."

Jn 14:7 If you really knew me, you would know my Father as well. From now on, you do know him and have seen him."

Jn 14:9 Jesus answered: "Don't you know me, Philip, even after I have been among you such a long time? Anyone who has seen me has seen the Father. How can you say, 'Show us the Father'? **10**Don't you believe that I am in the Father, and that the Father is in me? The words I say to you are not just my own. Rather, it is the Father, living in me, who is doing his work. **11**Believe me when I say that I am in the Father and the Father is in me; or at least believe on the evidence of the miracles themselves. **12**I tell you the truth, anyone who has faith in me will do what I have been doing. He will do even greater things than these, because I am going to the Father. **13**And I will do whatever you ask in my name, so that the Son may bring glory to the Father. (+Jn 14:14)

Jn 14:20 On that day you will realize that I am in my Father, and you are in me, and I am in you.

Jn 14:24 He who does not love me will not obey my teaching. These words you hear are not my own; they belong to the Father who sent me.

Jn 15:23 He who hates me hates my Father as well. **24**If I

had not done among them what no one else did, they would not be guilty of sin. But now they have seen these miracles, and yet they have hated both me and my Father. **25**But this is to fulfill what is written in their Law: 'They hated me without reason.'

26"When the Counselor comes, whom I will send to you from the Father, the Spirit of truth who goes out from the Father, he will testify about me.

Is subject to the Father (Ps 110:1)—

Mk 10:40 but to sit at my right or left is not for me to grant. These places belong to those for whom they have been prepared." (+Jn 20:17; Ac 2:22)

Ac 2:33 Exalted to the right hand of God, he has received from the Father the promised Holy Spirit and has poured out what you now see and hear.

Ac 2:36 "Therefore let all Israel be assured of this: God has made this Jesus, whom you crucified, both Lord and Christ." (+Ac 3:13,26; 4:27)

1Co 15:24 Then the end will come, when he hands over the kingdom to God the Father after he has destroyed all dominion, authority and power.

1Co 15:27 For he "has put everything under his feet." Now when it says that "everything" has been put under him, it is clear that this does not include God himself, who put everything under Christ. **28**When he has done this, then the Son himself will be made subject to him who put everything under him, so that God may be all in all.

Is the image of God—

2Co 4:4 The god of this age has blinded the minds of unbelievers, so that they cannot see the light of the gospel of the glory of Christ, who is the image of God.

2Co 4:6 For God, who said, "Let light shine out of darkness," made his light shine in our hearts to give us the light of the knowledge of the glory of God in the face of Christ.

Php 2:6 Who, being in very nature God, did not consider equality with God something to be grasped,

Col 1:15 He is the image of the invisible God, the firstborn over all creation.

Col 1:19 For God was pleased to have all his fullness dwell in him,

God raised him from the dead—

Ac 13:37 But the one whom God raised from the dead did not see decay.

Ro 1:4 and who through the Spirit of holiness was declared with power to be the Son of God by his resurrection from the dead: Jesus Christ our Lord.

Eph 1:17 I keep asking that the God of our Lord Jesus Christ, the glorious Father, may give you the Spirit of wisdom and revelation, so that you may know him better.

Eph 1:20 which he exerted in Christ when he raised him from the dead and seated him at his right hand in the heavenly realms, **21**far above all rule and authority, power and dominion, and every title that can be given, not only in the present age but also in the one to come. **22**And God placed all things under his feet and appointed him to be head over everything for the church,

1Pe 1:21 Through him you believe in God, who raised him from the dead and glorified him, and so your faith and hope are in God.

Ascended to the Father (Lk 24:51)—

Jn 16:5 "Now I am going to him who sent me, yet none of you asks me, 'Where are you going?'

Jn 16:10 in regard to righteousness, because I am going to the Father, where you can see me no longer;

Jn 16:28 I came from the Father and entered the world;

now I am leaving the world and going back to the Father."
(+Ac 1:9-11)

Rev 3:12 Him who overcomes I will make a pillar in the temple of my God. Never again will he leave it. I will write on him the name of my God and the name of the city of my God, the new Jerusalem, which is coming down out of heaven from my God; and I will also write on him my new name.

Rev 3:21 To him who overcomes, I will give the right to sit with me on my throne, just as I overcame and sat down with my Father on his throne.

See above, Deity of; Humanity of; Divine Sonship of.

Resurrection of:

Prophecies concerning—

Ps 2:7 I will proclaim the decree of the LORD: He said to me, "You are my Son; today I have become your Father.

Ps 16:9 Therefore my heart is glad and my tongue rejoices; my body also will rest secure, [10]because you will not abandon me to the grave, nor will you let your Holy One see decay. (+Isa 55:3; Ac 13:13-34)

Foretold by himself—

Mt 12:40 For as Jonah was three days and three nights in the belly of a huge fish, so the Son of Man will be three days and three nights in the heart of the earth.

Mt 16:4 A wicked and adulterous generation looks for a miraculous sign, but none will be given it except the sign of Jonah." Jesus then left them and went away.

Mt 16:21 From that time on Jesus began to explain to his disciples that he must go to Jerusalem and suffer many things at the hands of the elders, chief priests and teachers of the law, and that he must be killed and on the third day be raised to life. (+Mt 17:23)

Mt 20:19 and will turn him over to the Gentiles to be mocked and flogged and crucified. On the third day he will be raised to life!"

Mt 26:32 But after I have risen, I will go ahead of you into Galilee."

Mt 27:52 The tombs broke open and the bodies of many holy people who had died were raised to life. [53]They came out of the tombs, and after Jesus' resurrection they went into the holy city and appeared to many people.

Mt 27:63 "Sir," they said, "we remember that while he was still alive that deceiver said, 'After three days I will rise again.' (+Mk 8:31)

Mk 9:9 As they were coming down the mountain, Jesus gave them orders not to tell anyone what they had seen until the Son of Man had risen from the dead. [10]They kept the matter to themselves, discussing what "rising from the dead" meant. (+Mk 10:34; 14:58; Lk 9:22)

Lk 18:33 On the third day he will rise again." (+Lk 24:7)

Lk 24:46 He told them, "This is what is written: The Christ will suffer and rise from the dead on the third day,

Jn 2:19 Jesus answered them, "Destroy this temple, and I will raise it again in three days."

Jn 2:21 But the temple he had spoken of was his body. (+Jn 2:22)

Certified by angels—

Mt 28:6 He is not here; he has risen, just as he said. Come and see the place where he lay. [7]Then go quickly and tell his disciples: 'He has risen from the dead and is going ahead of you into Galilee. There you will see him.' Now I have told you." (+Mk 16:6-7; Lk 24:5-7)

Certified by Mary Magdalene (Mt 28:1-8; Mk 16:10; Lk 24:10; Jn 20:18), by Clopas and his fellow disciple on the road to Emmaus (Mk 16:12-13; Lk 24:13-35)

Certified by Luke—

Ac 1:3 After his suffering, he showed himself to these men and gave many convincing proofs that he was alive. He appeared to them over a period of forty days and spoke about the kingdom of God.

Ac 1:22 beginning from John's baptism to the time when Jesus was taken up from us. For one of these must become a witness with us of his resurrection."

Certified by Peter—

Ac 2:24 But God raised him from the dead, freeing him from the agony of death, because it was impossible for death to keep its hold on him.

Ac 2:31 Seeing what was ahead, he spoke of the resurrection of the Christ, that he was not abandoned to the grave, nor did his body see decay. [32]God has raised this Jesus to life, and we are all witnesses of the fact. (+Ps 16:9-10)

Ac 3:15 You killed the author of life, but God raised him from the dead. We are witnesses of this.

Ac 4:10 then know this, you and all the people of Israel: It is by the name of Jesus Christ of Nazareth, whom you crucified but whom God raised from the dead, that this man stands before you healed.

Ac 4:33 With great power the apostles continued to testify to the resurrection of the Lord Jesus, and much grace was upon them all.

Ac 5:30 The God of our fathers raised Jesus from the dead—whom you had killed by hanging him on a tree. [31]God exalted him to his own right hand as Prince and Savior that he might give repentance and forgiveness of sins to Israel. [32]We are witnesses of these things, and so is the Holy Spirit, whom God has given to those who obey him."

Ac 10:40 but God raised him from the dead on the third day and caused him to be seen. [41]He was not seen by all the people, but by witnesses whom God had already chosen— by us who ate and drank with him after he rose from the dead.

1Pe 1:3 Praise be to the God and Father of our Lord Jesus Christ! In his great mercy he has given us new birth into a living hope through the resurrection of Jesus Christ from the dead,

1Pe 1:21 Through him you believe in God, who raised him from the dead and glorified him, and so your faith and hope are in God.

1Pe 3:18 For Christ died for sins once for all, the righteous for the unrighteous, to bring you to God. He was put to death in the body but made alive by the Spirit,

1Pe 3:21 and this water symbolizes baptism that now saves you also—not the removal of dirt from the body but the pledge of a good conscience toward God. It saves you by the resurrection of Jesus Christ,

Certified by Paul—

Ac 13:30 But God raised him from the dead, [31]and for many days he was seen by those who had traveled with him from Galilee to Jerusalem. They are now his witnesses to our people.

[32]"We tell you the good news: What God promised our fathers [33]he has fulfilled for us, their children, by raising up Jesus. As it is written in the second Psalm:

"'You are my Son; today I have become your Father.'

[34]The fact that God raised him from the dead, never to decay, is stated in these words:

"'I will give you the holy and sure blessings promised to David.' (+Ps 2:7)

Ac 17:2 As his custom was, Paul went into the synagogue, and on three Sabbath days he reasoned with them from the

Scriptures, ³explaining and proving that the Christ had to suffer and rise from the dead. "This Jesus I am proclaiming to you is the Christ," he said.

Ac 17:31 For he has set a day when he will judge the world with justice by the man he has appointed. He has given proof of this to all men by raising him from the dead."

Ac 26:23 that the Christ would suffer and, as the first to rise from the dead, would proclaim light to his own people and to the Gentiles." (+Ac 26:26)

Ro 1:4 and who through the Spirit of holiness was declared with power to be the Son of God by his resurrection from the dead: Jesus Christ our Lord.

Ro 4:24 but also for us, to whom God will credit righteousness—for us who believe in him who raised Jesus our Lord from the dead. ²⁵He was delivered over to death for our sins and was raised to life for our justification.

Ro 5:10 For if, when we were God's enemies, we were reconciled to him through the death of his Son, how much more, having been reconciled, shall we be saved through his life!

Ro 6:4 We were therefore buried with him through baptism into death in order that, just as Christ was raised from the dead through the glory of the Father, we too may live a new life.

⁵If we have been united with him like this in his death, we will certainly also be united with him in his resurrection.

Ro 6:9 For we know that since Christ was raised from the dead, he cannot die again; death no longer has mastery over him. ¹⁰The death he died, he died to sin once for all; but the life he lives, he lives to God.

Ro 8:11 And if the Spirit of him who raised Jesus from the dead is living in you, he who raised Christ from the dead will also give life to your mortal bodies through his Spirit, who lives in you.

Ro 8:34 Who is he that condemns? Christ Jesus, who died—more than that, who was raised to life—is at the right hand of God and is also interceding for us. (+1Co 6:14)

1Co 15:3 For what I received I passed on to you as of first importance: that Christ died for our sins according to the Scriptures, ⁴that he was buried, that he was raised on the third day according to the Scriptures, (+1Co 15:5-8,12-19)

1Co 15:20 But Christ has indeed been raised from the dead, the firstfruits of those who have fallen asleep. ²¹For since death came through a man, the resurrection of the dead comes also through a man. ²²For as in Adam all die, so in Christ all will be made alive. ²³But each in his own turn: Christ, the firstfruits; then, when he comes, those who belong to him.

2Co 4:10 We always carry around in our body the death of Jesus, so that the life of Jesus may also be revealed in our body. ¹¹For we who are alive are always being given over to death for Jesus' sake, so that his life may be revealed in our mortal body.

2Co 4:14 because we know that the one who raised the Lord Jesus from the dead will also raise us with Jesus and present us with you in his presence.

2Co 5:15 And he died for all, that those who live should no longer live for themselves but for him who died for them and was raised again.

2Co 13:4 For to be sure, he was crucified in weakness, yet he lives by God's power. Likewise, we are weak in him, yet by God's power we will live with him to serve you.

Gal 1:1 Paul, an apostle—sent not from men nor by man,

but by Jesus Christ and God the Father, who raised him from the dead—

Eph 1:20 which he exerted in Christ when he raised him from the dead and seated him at his right hand in the heavenly realms,

Php 3:10 I want to know Christ and the power of his resurrection and the fellowship of sharing in his sufferings, becoming like him in his death,

Col 1:18 And he is the head of the body, the church; he is the beginning and the firstborn from among the dead, so that in everything he might have the supremacy.

Col 2:12 having been buried with him in baptism and raised with him through your faith in the power of God, who raised him from the dead.

1Th 1:10 and to wait for his Son from heaven, whom he raised from the dead—Jesus, who rescues us from the coming wrath.

1Th 4:14 We believe that Jesus died and rose again and so we believe that God will bring with Jesus those who have fallen asleep in him.

2Ti 2:8 Remember Jesus Christ, raised from the dead, descended from David. This is my gospel,

Certified by the author of Hebrews—

Heb 13:20 May the God of peace, who through the blood of the eternal covenant brought back from the dead our Lord Jesus, that great Shepherd of the sheep,

Certified by John—

Rev 1:5 and from Jesus Christ, who is the faithful witness, the firstborn from the dead, and the ruler of the kings of the earth. To him who loves us and has freed us from our sins by his blood,

Rev 1:18 I am the Living One; I was dead, and behold I am alive for ever and ever! And I hold the keys of death and Hades.

Appeared to the eleven apostles after his resurrection (Mk 16:14; Lk 24:36-51; Jn 20:19-29).

Rose for our justification (Ro 4:25).

Rose for our salvation (Ro 5:10)—

Ro 10:9 That if you confess with your mouth, "Jesus is Lord," and believe in your heart that God raised him from the dead, you will be saved.

An earnest of the general resurrection (Ro 6:5)—

1Co 6:14 By his power God raised the Lord from the dead, and he will raise us also. (+1Co 15:21-23; 2Co 4:14; 1Th 4:14; 1Pe 1:3)

The theme of apostolic preaching (Ac 2:24,31-32; 3:15; 4:10,33; 5:30-32; 10:40-41; 17:2-3).

See Resurrection.

Reticence of:

(Isa 53:7; Mt 26:63; 27:12,14; Mk 14:61; 15:4-5; Jn 19:9; 1Pe 2:23).

Revelation by:

Concerning his kingdom (Mt 8:11-12; 10:23,34; 13:24-50; 16:18,28; 21:43-44; 24:14; Mk 9:1; 16:17-18; Lk 9:27; 12:40-53; 13:24-35; 17:20-37; Jn 4:21,23; 5:25-29; 6:39, 54; 12:35; 13:19; 14:29; 16:4). His rejection by the Jews (Mt 21:33-44; Lk 17:25). His betrayal (Mt 26:21,23-25). His crucifixion (Jn 3:14; 8:28; 12:32, w Lk 24:6-7). Judgments upon the Jews (Mt 23:37-39). The destruction of the temple, and Jerusalem (Mt 24; Mk 13; Lk 19:41-44). The destruction of Capernaum (Mt 11:23; Lk 10:15).

Concerning persecutions of Christians (Mt 23:34-36). His being forsaken by his disciples (Jn 16:32). Lazarus (Jn 11:4,11,23,40). Peter (Jn 21:18-23). Fame of the woman who anointed his head (Mt 26:13; Mk 14:8-9). False

Christs (Mt 24:4-5,23-26; Mk 13:5-6,21-23; Lk 17:23-24; 21:8). Things to come (Rev 1:1).

Concerning his death and resurrection (Mt 12:39-40; 16:21; 17:12,22-23; 20:18-19; 21:33-39; 26:2,18,21,23-24,45-46; 27:63; Mk 8:31; 9:31; 10:32-34; Lk 9:22-24; 17:25; 18:31-33; 22:15,37; Jn 2:19; 10:15,17; 12:7,23,32; 13:18-27; 14:19; 16:20,32). His ascension (Jn 7:33-34; 8:21; 13:33; 16:10,16).

Righteousness of: *See above, Holiness of.*

Salvation by: *See Salvation.*

Savior:

Mt 1:21 She will give birth to a son, and you are to give him the name Jesus, because he will save his people from their sins."

Ac 5:31 God exalted him to his own right hand as Prince and Savior that he might give repentance and forgiveness of sins to Israel.

Ac 13:23 "From this man's descendants God has brought to Israel the Savior Jesus, as he promised.

Ac 13:38 "Therefore, my brothers, I want you to know that through Jesus the forgiveness of sins is proclaimed to you. ³⁹Through him everyone who believes is justified from everything you could not be justified from by the law of Moses. (+Ac 13:47)

Ac 15:11 No! We believe it is through the grace of our Lord Jesus that we are saved, just as they are."

Ac 16:31 They replied, "Believe in the Lord Jesus, and you will be saved—you and your household."

1Co 1:30 It is because of him that you are in Christ Jesus, who has become for us wisdom from God—that is, our righteousness, holiness and redemption.

1Co 15:57 But thanks be to God! He gives us the victory through our Lord Jesus Christ.

Eph 5:23 For the husband is the head of the wife as Christ is the head of the church, his body, of which he is the Savior.

Php 3:20 But our citizenship is in heaven. And we eagerly await a Savior from there, the Lord Jesus Christ,

1Ti 1:1 Paul, an apostle of Christ Jesus by the command of God our Savior and of Christ Jesus our hope,

1Ti 1:15 Here is a trustworthy saying that deserves full acceptance: Christ Jesus came into the world to save sinners—of whom I am the worst.

2Ti 1:9 who has saved us and called us to a holy life—not because of anything we have done but because of his own purpose and grace. This grace was given us in Christ Jesus before the beginning of time,

2Ti 1:10 but it has now been revealed through the appearing of our Savior, Christ Jesus, who has destroyed death and has brought life and immortality to light through the gospel.

2Ti 1:12 That is why I am suffering as I am. Yet I am not ashamed, because I know whom I have believed, and am convinced that he is able to guard what I have entrusted to him for that day.

2Ti 2:10 Therefore I endure everything for the sake of the elect, that they too may obtain the salvation that is in Christ Jesus, with eternal glory.

2Ti 3:15 and how from infancy you have known the holy Scriptures, which are able to make you wise for salvation through faith in Christ Jesus.

Tit 1:4 To Titus, my true son in our common faith: Grace and peace from God the Father and Christ Jesus our Savior.

Heb 2:3 how shall we escape if we ignore such a great salvation? This salvation, which was first announced by the Lord, was confirmed to us by those who heard him.

Heb 5:9 and, once made perfect, he became the source of eternal salvation for all who obey him

2Pe 1:11 and you will receive a rich welcome into the eternal kingdom of our Lord and Savior Jesus Christ.

2Pe 2:20 If they have escaped the corruption of the world by knowing our Lord and Savior Jesus Christ and are again entangled in it and overcome, they are worse off at the end than they were at the beginning.

1Jn 3:5 But you know that he appeared so that he might take away our sins. And in him is no sin.

1Jn 4:9 This is how God showed his love among us: He sent his one and only Son into the world that we might live through him.

1Jn 4:14 And we have seen and testify that the Father has sent his Son to be the Savior of the world.

1Jn 5:11 And this is the testimony: God has given us eternal life, and this life is in his Son. ¹²He who has the Son has life; he who does not have the Son of God does not have life.

¹³I write these things to you who believe in the name of the Son of God so that you may know that you have eternal life.

Savior through his death (Ro 3:25)—

Ro 4:25 He was delivered over to death for our sins and was raised to life for our justification.

Ro 5:1 Therefore, since we have been justified through faith, we have peace with God through our Lord Jesus Christ,

Ro 5:6 You see, at just the right time, when we were still powerless, Christ died for the ungodly.

Ro 5:8 But God demonstrates his own love for us in this: While we were still sinners, Christ died for us. (+Ro 5:9-10)

Gal 1:4 who gave himself for our sins to rescue us from the present evil age, according to the will of our God and Father,

Gal 2:20 I have been crucified with Christ and I no longer live, but Christ lives in me. The life I live in the body, I live by faith in the Son of God, who loved me and gave himself for me. (+Eph 2:13-18,20)

Eph 5:2 and live a life of love, just as Christ loved us and gave himself up for us as a fragrant offering and sacrifice to God.

Eph 5:25 Husbands, love your wives, just as Christ loved the church and gave himself up for her ²⁶to make her holy, cleansing her by the washing with water through the word,

Col 1:12 giving thanks to the Father, who has qualified you to share in the inheritance of the saints in the kingdom of light. ¹³For he has rescued us from the dominion of darkness and brought us into the kingdom of the Son he loves, ¹⁴in whom we have redemption, the forgiveness of sins.

1Th 1:10 and to wait for his Son from heaven, whom he raised from the dead—Jesus, who rescues us from the coming wrath.

1Th 5:9 For God did not appoint us to suffer wrath but to receive salvation through our Lord Jesus Christ. ¹⁰He died for us so that, whether we are awake or asleep, we may live together with him.

Tit 2:13 while we wait for the blessed hope—the glorious appearing of our great God and Savior, Jesus Christ, ¹⁴who gave himself for us to redeem us from all wickedness and to purify for himself a people that are his very own, eager to do what is good.

1Pe 1:18 For you know that it was not with perishable things such as silver or gold that you were redeemed from the empty way of life handed down to you from your forefathers, [19]but with the precious blood of Christ, a lamb without blemish or defect.

1Pe 3:18 For Christ died for sins once for all, the righteous for the unrighteous, to bring you to God. He was put to death in the body but made alive by the Spirit,

1Jn 4:10 This is love: not that we loved God, but that he loved us and sent his Son as an atoning sacrifice for our sins.

Savior through his resurrection—

Ac 3:26 When God raised up his servant, he sent him first to you to bless you by turning each of you from your wicked ways."

Ro 10:9 That if you confess with your mouth, "Jesus is Lord," and believe in your heart that God raised him from the dead, you will be saved.

1Co 15:17 And if Christ has not been raised, your faith is futile; you are still in your sins.

1Pe 3:21 and this water symbolizes baptism that now saves you also—not the removal of dirt from the body but the pledge of a good conscience toward God. It saves you by the resurrection of Jesus Christ,

Savior by his intercession—

Heb 7:22 Because of this oath, Jesus has become the guarantee of a better covenant.

Heb 7:25 Therefore he is able to save completely those who come to God through him, because he always lives to intercede for them.

Savior by redemption (Ro 3:24).

Savior by reconciliation—

Ro 5:15 But the gift is not like the trespass. For if the many died by the trespass of the one man, how much more did God's grace and the gift that came by the grace of the one man, Jesus Christ, overflow to the many!

Ro 5:17 For if, by the trespass of the one man, death reigned through that one man, how much more will those who receive God's abundant provision of grace and of the gift of righteousness reign in life through the one man, Jesus Christ.

[18]Consequently, just as the result of one trespass was condemnation for all men, so also the result of one act of righteousness was justification that brings life for all men. [19]For just as through the disobedience of the one man the many were made sinners, so also through the obedience of the one man the many will be made righteous.

Ro 5:21 so that, just as sin reigned in death, so also grace might reign through righteousness to bring eternal life through Jesus Christ our Lord.

2Co 5:18 All this is from God, who reconciled us to himself through Christ and gave us the ministry of reconciliation: [19]that God was reconciling the world to himself in Christ, not counting men's sins against them. And he has committed to us the message of reconciliation.

2Co 5:21 God made him who had no sin to be sin for us, so that in him we might become the righteousness of God.

Eph 2:7 in order that in the coming ages he might show the incomparable riches of his grace, expressed in his kindness to us in Christ Jesus.

Eph 2:13 But now in Christ Jesus you who once were far away have been brought near through the blood of Christ.

[14]For he himself is our peace, who has made the two one and has destroyed the barrier, the dividing wall of hostility, [15]by abolishing in his flesh the law with its commandments and regulations. His purpose was to create in himself one new man out of the two, thus making peace, [16]and in this one body to reconcile both of them to God through the cross, by which he put to death their hostility. [17]He came and preached peace to you who were far away and peace to those who were near. [18]For through him we both have access to the Father by one Spirit.

Eph 2:20 built on the foundation of the apostles and prophets, with Christ Jesus himself as the chief cornerstone.

Heb 2:17 For this reason he had to be made like his brothers in every way, in order that he might become a merciful and faithful high priest in service to God, and that he might make atonement for the sins of the people.

The only Savior—

Ac 4:12 Salvation is found in no one else, for there is no other name under heaven given to men by which we must be saved."

1Co 3:11 For no one can lay any foundation other than the one already laid, which is Jesus Christ.

Prophecies concerning him as Savior—

Ps 72:4 He will defend the afflicted among the people and save the children of the needy; he will crush the oppressor.

Ps 72:12 For he will deliver the needy who cry out, the afflicted who have no one to help. [13]He will take pity on the weak and the needy and save the needy from death. [14]He will rescue them from oppression and violence, for precious is their blood in his sight.

Ps 72:17 May his name endure forever; may it continue as long as the sun. All nations will be blessed through him, and they will call him blessed.

Isa 42:6 "I, the LORD, have called you in righteousness; I will take hold of your hand. I will keep you and will make you to be a covenant for the people and a light for the Gentiles, [7]to open eyes that are blind, to free captives from prison and to release from the dungeon those who sit in darkness.

Isa 49:6 he says: "It is too small a thing for you to be my servant to restore the tribes of Jacob and bring back those of Israel I have kept. I will also make you a light for the Gentiles, that you may bring my salvation to the ends of the earth."

Isa 49:8 This is what the LORD says: "In the time of my favor I will answer you, and in the day of salvation I will help you; I will keep you and will make you to be a covenant for the people, to restore the land and to reassign its desolate inheritances, [9]to say to the captives, 'Come out,' and to those in darkness, 'Be free!' "They will feed beside the roads and find pasture on every barren hill.

Isa 59:16 He saw that there was no one, he was appalled that there was no one to intervene; so his own arm worked salvation for him, and his own righteousness sustained him. [17]He put on righteousness as his breastplate, and the helmet of salvation on his head; he put on the garments of vengeance and wrapped himself in zeal as in a cloak.

Isa 59:20 "The Redeemer will come to Zion, to those in Jacob who repent of their sins," declares the LORD.

Isa 61:1 The Spirit of the Sovereign LORD is on me, because the LORD has anointed me to preach good news to the poor. He has sent me to bind up the brokenhearted, to proclaim freedom for the captives and release from darkness for the prisoners, [2]to proclaim the year of the LORD's favor and the day of vengeance of our God, to comfort all who mourn, [3]and provide for those who grieve in Zion—to bestow on them a crown of beauty instead of ashes, the oil of gladness instead of mourning, and a garment of praise instead of a spirit of despair. They will be called oaks of righteousness, a planting of the LORD for the display of his splendor.

Zec 9:9 Rejoice greatly, O Daughter of Zion! Shout, Daughter of Jerusalem! See, your king comes to you, righteous and having salvation, gentle and riding on a donkey, on a colt, the foal of a donkey.

Mal 4:2 But for you who revere my name, the sun of righteousness will rise with healing in its wings. And you will go out and leap like calves released from the stall.

Lk 1:68 "Praise be to the Lord, the God of Israel, because he has come and has redeemed his people. ⁶⁹He has raised up a horn of salvation for us in the house of his servant David ⁷⁰(as he said through his holy prophets of long ago), ⁷¹salvation from our enemies and from the hand of all who hate us— ⁷²to show mercy to our fathers and to remember his holy covenant, ⁷³the oath he swore to our father Abraham: ⁷⁴to rescue us from the hand of our enemies, and to enable us to serve him without fear ⁷⁵in holiness and righteousness before him all our days.

⁷⁶And you, my child, will be called a prophet of the Most High; for you will go on before the Lord to prepare the way for him, ⁷⁷to give his people the knowledge of salvation through the forgiveness of their sins, (+Lk 4:18-19)

Illustrated: By parables of lost sheep and lost coin—

Mt 18:12 "What do you think? If a man owns a hundred sheep, and one of them wanders away, will he not leave the ninety-nine on the hills and go to look for the one that wandered off? ¹³And if he finds it, I tell you the truth, he is happier about that one sheep than about the ninety-nine that did not wander off. (+Lk 15:1-10)

Testified to by angels—

Lk 2:11 Today in the town of David a Savior has been born to you; he is Christ the Lord.

Testified to by Simeon—

Lk 2:30 For my eyes have seen your salvation, ³¹which you have prepared in the sight of all people, ³²a light for revelation to the Gentiles and for glory to your people Israel."

Testified to by himself (Mt 9:12-13)—

Lk 5:31 Jesus answered them, "It is not the healthy who need a doctor, but the sick. ³²I have not come to call the righteous, but sinners to repentance."

Lk 19:10 For the Son of Man came to seek and to save what was lost."

Jn 5:33 "You have sent to John and he has testified to the truth. ³⁴Not that I accept human testimony; but I mention it that you may be saved.

Jn 5:40 yet you refuse to come to me to have life.

Jn 6:27 Do not work for food that spoils, but for food that endures to eternal life, which the Son of Man will give you. On him God the Father has placed his seal of approval."

Jn 6:32 Jesus said to them, "I tell you the truth, it is not Moses who has given you the bread from heaven, but it is my Father who gives you the true bread from heaven. ³³For the bread of God is he who comes down from heaven and gives life to the world."

Jn 6:35 Then Jesus declared, "I am the bread of life. He who comes to me will never go hungry, and he who believes in me will never be thirsty.

Jn 6:37 All that the Father gives me will come to me, and whoever comes to me I will never drive away.

Jn 6:39 And this is the will of him who sent me, that I shall lose none of all that he has given me, but raise them up at the last day.

Jn 6:51 I am the living bread that came down from heaven. If anyone eats of this bread, he will live forever. This bread is my flesh, which I will give for the life of the world."

Jn 6:53 Jesus said to them, "I tell you the truth, unless you eat the flesh of the Son of Man and drink his blood, you have no life in you. ⁵⁴Whoever eats my flesh and drinks my blood has eternal life, and I will raise him up at the last day. ⁵⁵For my flesh is real food and my blood is real drink. ⁵⁶Whoever eats my flesh and drinks my blood remains in me, and I in him. ⁵⁷Just as the living Father sent me and I live because of the Father, so the one who feeds on me will live because of me. ⁵⁸This is the bread that came down from heaven. Your forefathers ate manna and died, but he who feeds on this bread will live forever."

Jn 7:37 On the last and greatest day of the Feast, Jesus stood and said in a loud voice, "If anyone is thirsty, let him come to me and drink. ³⁸Whoever believes in me, as the Scripture has said, streams of living water will flow from within him." ³⁹By this he meant the Spirit, whom those who believed in him were later to receive. Up to that time the Spirit had not been given, since Jesus had not yet been glorified.

Jn 8:12 When Jesus spoke again to the people, he said, "I am the light of the world. Whoever follows me will never walk in darkness, but will have the light of life."

Jn 9:5 While I am in the world, I am the light of the world."

Jn 9:39 Jesus said, "For judgment I have come into this world, so that the blind will see and those who see will become blind."

Jn 10:7 Therefore Jesus said again, "I tell you the truth, I am the gate for the sheep.

Jn 10:9 I am the gate; whoever enters through me will be saved. He will come in and go out, and find pasture. (+Jn 10:10)

Jn 10:11 "I am the good shepherd. The good shepherd lays down his life for the sheep.

Jn 10:14 "I am the good shepherd; I know my sheep and my sheep know me— ¹⁵just as the Father knows me and I know the Father—and I lay down my life for the sheep. ¹⁶I have other sheep that are not of this sheep pen. I must bring them also. They too will listen to my voice, and there shall be one flock and one shepherd.

Jn 10:27 My sheep listen to my voice; I know them, and they follow me. ²⁸I give them eternal life, and they shall never perish; no one can snatch them out of my hand.

Jn 11:25 Jesus said to her, "I am the resurrection and the life. He who believes in me will live, even though he dies; ²⁶and whoever lives and believes in me will never die. Do you believe this?"

Jn 12:47 "As for the person who hears my words but does not keep them, I do not judge him. For I did not come to judge the world, but to save it.

Jn 14:6 Jesus answered, "I am the way and the truth and the life. No one comes to the Father except through me.

Jn 17:2 For you granted him authority over all people that he might give eternal life to all those you have given him. ³Now this is eternal life: that they may know you, the only true God, and Jesus Christ, whom you have sent. (+Jn 17:12)

Testified to by John—

Jn 1:29 The next day John saw Jesus coming toward him and said, "Look, the Lamb of God, who takes away the sin of the world!

Testified to by the people of Sychar—

Jn 4:42 They said to the woman, "We no longer believe just because of what you said; now we have heard for ourselves, and we know that this man really is the Savior of the world."

Testified to by the heavenly host—

Rev 5:5 Then one of the elders said to me, "Do not weep! See, the Lion of the tribe of Judah, the Root of David, has triumphed. He is able to open the scroll and its seven seals."

⁶Then I saw a Lamb, looking as if it had been slain, standing in the center of the throne, encircled by the four living creatures and the elders. He had seven horns and seven eyes, which are the seven spirits of God sent out into all the earth. **⁷**He came and took the scroll from the right hand of him who sat on the throne. **⁸**And when he had taken it, the four living creatures and the twenty-four elders fell down before the Lamb. Each one had a harp and they were holding golden bowls full of incense, which are the prayers of the saints. **⁹**And they sang a new song:

"You are worthy to take the scroll and to open its seals, because you were slain, and with your blood you purchased men for God from every tribe and language and people and nation. **¹⁰**You have made them to be a kingdom and priests to serve our God, and they will reign on the earth."

¹¹Then I looked and heard the voice of many angels, numbering thousands upon thousands, and ten thousand times ten thousand. They encircled the throne and the living creatures and the elders. **¹²**In a loud voice they sang:

"Worthy is the Lamb, who was slain, to receive power and wealth and wisdom and strength and honor and glory and praise!"

¹³Then I heard every creature in heaven and on earth and under the earth and on the sea, and all that is in them, singing:

"To him who sits on the throne and to the Lamb be praise and honor and glory and power, for ever and ever!"

¹⁴The four living creatures said, "Amen," and the elders fell down and worshiped.

See above, Death of; Purpose of His Death.

Second Coming:

Mt 26:64 "Yes, it is as you say," Jesus replied. "But I say to all of you: In the future you will see the Son of Man sitting at the right hand of the Mighty One and coming on the clouds of heaven."

Jn 14:28 "You heard me say, 'I am going away and I am coming back to you.' If you loved me, you would be glad that I am going to the Father, for the Father is greater than I. **²⁹**I have told you now before it happens, so that when it does happen you will believe. (+Jn 21:22)

Ac 1:11 "Men of Galilee," they said, "why do you stand here looking into the sky? This same Jesus, who has been taken from you into heaven, will come back in the same way you have seen him go into heaven."

Ac 3:20 and that he may send the Christ, who has been appointed for you—even Jesus. **²¹**He must remain in heaven until the time comes for God to restore everything, as he promised long ago through his holy prophets.

1Co 11:26 For whenever you eat this bread and drink this cup, you proclaim the Lord's death until he comes.

Php 3:20 But our citizenship is in heaven. And we eagerly await a Savior from there, the Lord Jesus Christ, **²¹**who, by the power that enables him to bring everything under his control, will transform our lowly bodies so that they will be like his glorious body.

1Th 1:10 and to wait for his Son from heaven, whom he raised from the dead—Jesus, who rescues us from the coming wrath.

1Th 2:19 For what is our hope, our joy, or the crown in which we will glory in the presence of our Lord Jesus when he comes? Is it not you?

1Th 3:13 May he strengthen your hearts so that you will be blameless and holy in the presence of our God and Father when our Lord Jesus comes with all his holy ones.

1Th 4:15 According to the Lord's own word, we tell you that we who are still alive, who are left till the coming of the Lord, will certainly not precede those who have fallen asleep. **¹⁶**For the Lord himself will come down from heaven, with a loud command, with the voice of the archangel and with the trumpet call of God, and the dead in Christ will rise first. **¹⁷**After that, we who are still alive and are left will be caught up together with them in the clouds to meet the Lord in the air. And so we will be with the Lord forever.

2Th 2:1 Concerning the coming of our Lord Jesus Christ and our being gathered to him, we ask you, brothers, **²**not to become easily unsettled or alarmed by some prophecy, report or letter supposed to have come from us, saying that the day of the Lord has already come. **³**Don't let anyone deceive you in any way, for that day will not come until the rebellion occurs and the man of lawlessness is revealed, the man doomed to destruction. (+2Th 2:4)

2Th 2:5 Don't you remember that when I was with you I used to tell you these things?

2Th 2:8 And then the lawless one will be revealed, whom the Lord Jesus will overthrow with the breath of his mouth and destroy by the splendor of his coming.

1Ti 6:14 to keep this command without spot or blame until the appearing of our Lord Jesus Christ, **¹⁵**which God will bring about in his own time—God, the blessed and only Ruler, the King of kings and Lord of lords,

Tit 2:13 while we wait for the blessed hope—the glorious appearing of our great God and Savior, Jesus Christ,

2Pe 3:3 First of all, you must understand that in the last days scoffers will come, scoffing and following their own evil desires. **⁴**They will say, "Where is this 'coming' he promised? Ever since our fathers died, everything goes on as it has since the beginning of creation."

At an unexpected time—

Mt 24:3 As Jesus was sitting on the Mount of Olives, the disciples came to him privately. "Tell us," they said, "when will this happen, and what will be the sign of your coming and of the end of the age?"

Mt 24:27 For as lightning that comes from the east is visible even in the west, so will be the coming of the Son of Man.

Mt 24:30 "At that time the sign of the Son of Man will appear in the sky, and all the nations of the earth will mourn. They will see the Son of Man coming on the clouds of the sky, with power and great glory. **³¹**And he will send his angels with a loud trumpet call, and they will gather his elect from the four winds, from one end of the heavens to the other.

Mt 24:37 As it was in the days of Noah, so it will be at the coming of the Son of Man. **³⁸**For in the days before the flood, people were eating and drinking, marrying and giving in marriage, up to the day Noah entered the ark; **³⁹**and they knew nothing about what would happen until the flood came and took them all away. That is how it will be at the coming of the Son of Man.

Mt 24:42 "Therefore keep watch, because you do not

know on what day your Lord will come. ⁴³But understand this: If the owner of the house had known at what time of night the thief was coming, he would have kept watch and would not have let his house be broken into. ⁴⁴So you also must be ready, because the Son of Man will come at an hour when you do not expect him. (+Mt 24:36)

Mt 25:6 "At midnight the cry rang out: 'Here's the bridegroom! Come out to meet him!'

Mt 25:10 "But while they were on their way to buy the oil, the bridegroom arrived. The virgins who were ready went in with him to the wedding banquet. And the door was shut.

Mt 25:13 "Therefore keep watch, because you do not know the day or the hour.

Mt 25:19 "After a long time the master of those servants returned and settled accounts with them. (+Mk 13:1-26)

Mk 13:27 And he will send his angels and gather his elect from the four winds, from the ends of the earth to the ends of the heavens. (+Mk 13:28-31)

Mk 13:32 "No one knows about that day or hour, not even the angels in heaven, nor the Son, but only the Father. (+Mk 13:33-34)

Mk 13:35 "Therefore keep watch because you do not know when the owner of the house will come back—whether in the evening, or at midnight, or when the rooster crows, or at dawn. ³⁶If he comes suddenly, do not let him find you sleeping. (+Mk 13:37)

Lk 12:37 It will be good for those servants whose master finds them watching when he comes. I tell you the truth, he will dress himself to serve, will have them recline at the table and will come and wait on them. ³⁸It will be good for those servants whose master finds them ready, even if he comes in the second or third watch of the night. ³⁹But understand this: If the owner of the house had known at what hour the thief was coming, he would not have let his house be broken into. ⁴⁰You also must be ready, because the Son of Man will come at an hour when you do not expect him." (+Lk 17:22-29)

Lk 17:30 "It will be just like this on the day the Son of Man is revealed. (+Lk 21:5-26)

Lk 21:27 At that time they will see the Son of Man coming in a cloud with power and great glory. ²⁸When these things begin to take place, stand up and lift up your heads, because your redemption is drawing near."

²⁹He told them this parable: "Look at the fig tree and all the trees. ³⁰When they sprout leaves, you can see for yourselves and know that summer is near. ³¹Even so, when you see these things happening, you know that the kingdom of God is near.

³²"I tell you the truth, this generation will certainly not pass away until all these things have happened. ³³Heaven and earth will pass away, but my words will never pass away.

³⁴"Be careful, or your hearts will be weighed down with dissipation, drunkenness and the anxieties of life, and that day will close on you unexpectedly like a trap. ³⁵For it will come upon all those who live on the face of the whole earth.

1Th 5:2 for you know very well that the day of the Lord will come like a thief in the night. ³While people are saying, "Peace and safety," destruction will come on them suddenly, as labor pains on a pregnant woman, and they will not escape.

1Th 5:23 May God himself, the God of peace, sanctify you through and through. May your whole spirit, soul and

body be kept blameless at the coming of our Lord Jesus Christ. (+2Pe 3:8-9)

2Pe 3:10 But the day of the Lord will come like a thief. The heavens will disappear with a roar; the elements will be destroyed by fire, and the earth and everything in it will be laid bare.

¹¹Since everything will be destroyed in this way, what kind of people ought you to be? You ought to live holy and godly lives ¹²as you look forward to the day of God and speed its coming. That day will bring about the destruction of the heavens by fire, and the elements will melt in the heat. (+2Pe 3:13-14)

Rev 16:15 "Behold, I come like a thief! Blessed is he who stays awake and keeps his clothes with him, so that he may not go naked and be shamefully exposed."

Rev 22:20 He who testifies to these things says, "Yes, I am coming soon." Amen. Come, Lord Jesus.

Coming in heavenly glory—

Mt 16:27 For the Son of Man is going to come in his Father's glory with his angels, and then he will reward each person according to what he has done.

Mt 25:31 "When the Son of Man comes in his glory, and all the angels with him, he will sit on his throne in heavenly glory. (+Mk 8:38; 13:26-27)

Mk 14:62 "I am," said Jesus. "And you will see the Son of Man sitting at the right hand of the Mighty One and coming on the clouds of heaven."

Lk 9:26 If anyone is ashamed of me and my words, the Son of Man will be ashamed of him when he comes in his glory and in the glory of the Father and of the holy angels. (+Lk 21:27)

Coming to judge the world (Mt 16:27; 25:31-46)—

Lk 19:12 He said: "A man of noble birth went to a distant country to have himself appointed king and then to return. ¹³So he called ten of his servants and gave them ten minas. 'Put this money to work,' he said, 'until I come back.'

Lk 19:15 "He was made king, however, and returned home. Then he sent for the servants to whom he had given the money, in order to find out what they had gained with it.

1Co 1:7 Therefore you do not lack any spiritual gift as you eagerly wait for our Lord Jesus Christ to be revealed. ⁸He will keep you strong to the end, so that you will be blameless on the day of our Lord Jesus Christ.

1Co 4:5 Therefore judge nothing before the appointed time; wait till the Lord comes. He will bring to light what is hidden in darkness and will expose the motives of men's hearts. At that time each will receive his praise from God.

2Th 1:7 and give relief to you who are troubled, and to us as well. This will happen when the Lord Jesus is revealed from heaven in blazing fire with his powerful angels. ⁸He will punish those who do not know God and do not obey the gospel of our Lord Jesus. ⁹They will be punished with everlasting destruction and shut out from the presence of the Lord and from the majesty of his power ¹⁰on the day he comes to be glorified in his holy people and to be marveled at among all those who have believed. This includes you, because you believed our testimony to you.

2Ti 4:1 In the presence of God and of Christ Jesus, who will judge the living and the dead, and in view of his appearing and his kingdom, I give you this charge:

Rev 22:12 "Behold, I am coming soon! My reward is with me, and I will give to everyone according to what he has done.

Coming to receive his saints—

Jn 14:3 And if I go and prepare a place for you, I will

come back and take you to be with me that you also may be where I am.

Jn 14:18 I will not leave you as orphans; I will come to you.

1Co 15:23 But each in his own turn: Christ, the firstfruits; then, when he comes, those who belong to him.

Col 3:4 When Christ, who is your life, appears, then you also will appear with him in glory. (+2Th 1:10)

2Ti 4:8 Now there is in store for me the crown of righteousness, which the Lord, the righteous Judge, will award to me on that day—and not only to me, but also to all who have longed for his appearing.

Heb 9:28 so Christ was sacrificed once to take away the sins of many people; and he will appear a second time, not to bear sin, but to bring salvation to those who are waiting for him.

1Pe 5:4 And when the Chief Shepherd appears, you will receive the crown of glory that will never fade away.

1Jn 3:2 Dear friends, now we are children of God, and what we will be has not yet been made known. But we know that when he appears, we shall be like him, for we shall see him as he is.

Exhortations in view of his coming—

Jas 5:7 Be patient, then, brothers, until the Lord's coming. See how the farmer waits for the land to yield its valuable crop and how patient he is for the autumn and spring rains. [8]You too, be patient and stand firm, because the Lord's coming is near. [9]Don't grumble against each other, brothers, or you will be judged. The Judge is standing at the door!

1Pe 1:7 These have come so that your faith—of greater worth than gold, which perishes even though refined by fire—may be proved genuine and may result in praise, glory and honor when Jesus Christ is revealed.

1Pe 1:13 Therefore, prepare your minds for action; be self-controlled; set your hope fully on the grace to be given you when Jesus Christ is revealed.

1Pe 4:13 But rejoice that you participate in the sufferings of Christ, so that you may be overjoyed when his glory is revealed.

1Jn 2:28 And now, dear children, continue in him, so that when he appears we may be confident and unashamed before him at his coming.

Rev 3:11 I am coming soon. Hold on to what you have, so that no one will take your crown.

Shepherd:

Jesus the true shepherd: Foretold (Ge 49:24; Isa 40:11; Eze 34:23; 37:24). The chief (1Pe 5:4). The good (Jn 10:11,14). The great (Mic 5:4; Heb 13:20).

His sheep he knows (Jn 10:14,27). He calls (Jn 10:3). He gathers (Isa 40:11; Jn 10:16). He guides (Ps 23:3; Jn 10:3-4). He feeds (Ps 23:1-2; Jn 10:9). He cherishes tenderly (Isa 40:11). He protects and preserves (Jer 31:10; Eze 34:10; Zec 9:16; Jn 10:28). He laid down his life for (Zec 13:7; Mt 26:31; Jn 10:11,15; Ac 20:28). He gives eternal life to (Jn 10:28).

Typified: David (1Sa 16:11).

Son of God:

Acclaimed by God (Ps 2:4; Ac 13:13; Ps 89:26-27)—

Mt 3:17 And a voice from heaven said, "This is my Son, whom I love; with him I am well pleased."

Mt 17:5 While he was still speaking, a bright cloud enveloped them, and a voice from the cloud said, "This is my Son, whom I love; with him I am well pleased. Listen to him!" (+Mk 1:11; 9:7; Lk 3:22)

Lk 9:35 A voice came from the cloud, saying, "This is my Son, whom I have chosen; listen to him." (+2Pe 1:17)

Proclaimed by angels—

Lk 1:32 He will be great and will be called the Son of the Most High. The Lord God will give him the throne of his father David,

Lk 1:35 The angel answered, "The Holy Spirit will come upon you, and the power of the Most High will overshadow you. So the holy one to be born will be called the Son of God.

Rev 2:18 "To the angel of the church in Thyatira write: These are the words of the Son of God, whose eyes are like blazing fire and whose feet are like burnished bronze.

Claimed by Christ—

Mt 10:40 "He who receives you receives me, and he who receives me receives the one who sent me.

Mt 11:27 "All things have been committed to me by my Father. No one knows the Son except the Father, and no one knows the Father except the Son and those to whom the Son chooses to reveal him.

Mt 15:13 He replied, "Every plant that my heavenly Father has not planted will be pulled up by the roots.

Mt 18:10 "See that you do not look down on one of these little ones. For I tell you that their angels in heaven always see the face of my Father in heaven.

Mt 18:19 "Again, I tell you that if two of you on earth agree about anything you ask for, it will be done for you by my Father in heaven.

Mt 20:23 Jesus said to them, "You will indeed drink from my cup, but to sit at my right or left is not for me to grant. These places belong to those for whom they have been prepared by my Father."

Mt 21:37 Last of all, he sent his son to them. 'They will respect my son,' he said.

Mt 26:53 Do you think I cannot call on my Father, and he will at once put at my disposal more than twelve legions of angels?

Mt 26:63 But Jesus remained silent.

The high priest said to him, "I charge you under oath by the living God: Tell us if you are the Christ, the Son of God."

[64]"Yes, it is as you say," Jesus replied. "But I say to all of you: In the future you will see the Son of Man sitting at the right hand of the Mighty One and coming on the clouds of heaven."

Mt 27:43 He trusts in God. Let God rescue him now if he wants him, for he said, 'I am the Son of God.'" (+Mk 14:61-62)

Lk 10:22 "All things have been committed to me by my Father. No one knows who the Son is except the Father, and no one knows who the Father is except the Son and those to whom the Son chooses to reveal him." (+Lk 20:13)

Lk 22:29 And I confer on you a kingdom, just as my Father conferred one on me,

Lk 22:70 They all asked, "Are you then the Son of God?" He replied, "You are right in saying I am." (+Jn 5:17)

Jn 5:19 Jesus gave them this answer: "I tell you the truth, the Son can do nothing by himself; he can do only what he sees his Father doing, because whatever the Father does the Son also does. [20]For the Father loves the Son and shows him all he does. Yes, to your amazement he will show him even greater things than these. [21]For just as the Father raises the dead and gives them life, even so the Son gives life to whom he is pleased to give it. [22]Moreover, the Father judges no one, but has entrusted all judgment to the

Son, ²³that all may honor the Son just as they honor the Father. He who does not honor the Son does not honor the Father, who sent him. (+Jn 5:24-25)

Jn 5:26 For as the Father has life in himself, so he has granted the Son to have life in himself. ²⁷And he has given him authority to judge because he is the Son of Man. (+Jn 5:28-29)

Jn 5:30 By myself I can do nothing; I judge only as I hear, and my judgment is just, for I seek not to please myself but him who sent me. (+Jn 5:31)

Jn 5:32 There is another who testifies in my favor, and I know that his testimony about me is valid. (+Jn 5:33-35)

Jn 5:36 "I have testimony weightier than that of John. For the very work that the Father has given me to finish, and which I am doing, testifies that the Father has sent me. ³⁷And the Father who sent me has himself testified concerning me. You have never heard his voice nor seen his form,

Jn 6:27 Do not work for food that spoils, but for food that endures to eternal life, which the Son of Man will give you. On him God the Father has placed his seal of approval."

Jn 6:38 For I have come down from heaven not to do my will but to do the will of him who sent me.

Jn 6:40 For my Father's will is that everyone who looks to the Son and believes in him shall have eternal life, and I will raise him up at the last day."

Jn 6:46 No one has seen the Father except the one who is from God; only he has seen the Father.

Jn 6:57 Just as the living Father sent me and I live because of the Father, so the one who feeds on me will live because of me.

Jn 6:69 We believe and know that you are the Holy One of God." (+Jn 7:17)

Jn 7:28 Then Jesus, still teaching in the temple courts, cried out, "Yes, you know me, and you know where I am from. I am not here on my own, but he who sent me is true. You do not know him, ²⁹but I know him because I am from him and he sent me."

Jn 8:16 But if I do judge, my decisions are right, because I am not alone. I stand with the Father, who sent me.

Jn 8:19 Then they asked him, "Where is your father?" "You do not know me or my Father," Jesus replied. "If you knew me, you would know my Father also."

Jn 8:26 "I have much to say in judgment of you. But he who sent me is reliable, and what I have heard from him I tell the world."

²⁷They did not understand that he was telling them about his Father. ²⁸So Jesus said, "When you have lifted up the Son of Man, then you will know that I am [the one I claim to be] and that I do nothing on my own but speak just what the Father has taught me. ²⁹The one who sent me is with me; he has not left me alone, for I always do what pleases him."

Jn 8:38 I am telling you what I have seen in the Father's presence, and you do what you have heard from your father." (+Jn 8:39-41)

Jn 8:42 Jesus said to them, "If God were your Father, you would love me, for I came from God and now am here. I have not come on my own; but he sent me.

Jn 8:49 "I am not possessed by a demon," said Jesus, "but I honor my Father and you dishonor me.

Jn 8:54 Jesus replied, "If I glorify myself, my glory means nothing. My Father, whom you claim as your God, is the one who glorifies me.

Jn 9:35 Jesus heard that they had thrown him out, and when he found him, he said, "Do you believe in the Son of Man?"

³⁶"Who is he, sir?" the man asked. "Tell me so that I may believe in him."

³⁷Jesus said, "You have now seen him; in fact, he is the one speaking with you."

Jn 10:15 just as the Father knows me and I know the Father—and I lay down my life for the sheep. ¹⁶I have other sheep that are not of this sheep pen. I must bring them also. They too will listen to my voice, and there shall be one flock and one shepherd.

Jn 10:17 The reason my Father loves me is that I lay down my life—only to take it up again. (+Jn 10:18)

Jn 10:29 My Father, who has given them to me, is greater than all; no one can snatch them out of my Father's hand. ³⁰I and the Father are one."

Jn 10:36 what about the one whom the Father set apart as his very own and sent into the world? Why then do you accuse me of blasphemy because I said, 'I am God's Son'? ³⁷Do not believe me unless I do what my Father does. ³⁸But if I do it, even though you do not believe me, believe the miracles, that you may know and understand that the Father is in me, and I in the Father."

Jn 11:4 When he heard this, Jesus said, "This sickness will not end in death. No, it is for God's glory so that God's Son may be glorified through it."

Jn 11:27 "Yes, Lord," she told him, "I believe that you are the Christ, the Son of God, who was to come into the world."

Jn 11:41 So they took away the stone. Then Jesus looked up and said, "Father, I thank you that you have heard me.

Jn 12:49 For I did not speak of my own accord, but the Father who sent me commanded me what to say and how to say it. ⁵⁰I know that his command leads to eternal life. So whatever I say is just what the Father has told me to say." (+Jn 14:7-13,16,20,24,28,31; 15:1,8-10,23-24; 16:5, 15,27-28,32; 17:1; 20:17,21,31)

As equality with the Father (Mt 10:40; 11:27; Lk 10:22; Jn 1:1-2; 8:16,19; 10:15-18,29-30,36-38; 14:7-13,16,20, 24,28,31; 15:23-24; 16:15).

Sonship recognized by the disciples—

Mt 14:33 Then those who were in the boat worshiped him, saying, "Truly you are the Son of God."

Mt 16:15 "But what about you?" he asked. "Who do you say I am?"

¹⁶Simon Peter answered, "You are the Christ, the Son of the living God."

¹⁷Jesus replied, "Blessed are you, Simon son of Jonah, for this was not revealed to you by man, but by my Father in heaven.

Sonship recognized by Peter (Mt 16:15-17)

Sonship recognized by the centurion—

Mt 27:54 When the centurion and those with him who were guarding Jesus saw the earthquake and all that had happened, they were terrified, and exclaimed, "Surely he was the Son of God!"

Mk 15:39 And when the centurion, who stood there in front of Jesus, heard his cry and saw how he died, he said, "Surely this man was the Son of God!"

Sonship recognized by Nathanael—

Jn 1:49 Then Nathanael declared, "Rabbi, you are the Son of God; you are the King of Israel."

⁵⁰Jesus said, "You believe because I told you I saw you under the fig tree. You shall see greater things than that."

Sonship recognized by Martha (Jn 11:27)

Sonship recognized by Satan, who tempted him—

Mt 4:3 The tempter came to him and said, "If you are the Son of God, tell these stones to become bread."

Mt 4:6 "If you are the Son of God," he said, "throw yourself down. For it is written: "'He will command his angels concerning you, and they will lift you up in their hands, so that you will not strike your foot against a stone.'"

Lk 4:3 The devil said to him, "If you are the Son of God, tell this stone to become bread."

Lk 4:9 The devil led him to Jerusalem and had him stand on the highest point of the temple. "If you are the Son of God," he said, "throw yourself down from here.

Sonship recognized by demons—

Mk 3:11 Whenever the evil spirits saw him, they fell down before him and cried out, "You are the Son of God."

Mk 5:7 He shouted at the top of his voice, "What do you want with me, Jesus, Son of the Most High God? Swear to God that you won't torture me!"

Lk 4:41 Moreover, demons came out of many people, shouting, "You are the Son of God!" But he rebuked them and would not allow them to speak, because they knew he was the Christ. (+Lk 8:28)

Claim to sonship recognized by the Jews (Mt 27:43; Jn 19:7)

Claim to sonship recognized by the high priest—

Mk 14:61 But Jesus remained silent and gave no answer. Again the high priest asked him, "Are you the Christ, the Son of the Blessed One?"

62"I am," said Jesus. "And you will see the Son of Man sitting at the right hand of the Mighty One and coming on the clouds of heaven."

Testified to by Mark—

Mk 1:1 The beginning of the gospel about Jesus Christ, the Son of God.

Testified to by Luke (Ac 3:13)

Testified to by John—

Jn 1:1 In the beginning was the Word, and the Word was with God, and the Word was God. **2**He was with God in the beginning.

Jn 1:14 The Word became flesh and made his dwelling among us. We have seen his glory, the glory of the One and Only, who came from the Father, full of grace and truth.

Jn 1:18 No one has ever seen God, but God the One and Only, who is at the Father's side, has made him known.

Jn 1:34 I have seen and I testify that this is the Son of God."

Jn 3:16 "For God so loved the world that he gave his one and only Son, that whoever believes in him shall not perish but have eternal life. **17**For God did not send his Son into the world to condemn the world, but to save the world through him. **18**Whoever believes in him is not condemned, but whoever does not believe stands condemned already because he has not believed in the name of God's one and only Son.

Jn 3:34 For the one whom God has sent speaks the words of God, for God gives the Spirit without limit. **35**The Father loves the Son and has placed everything in his hands. **36**Whoever believes in the Son has eternal life, but whoever rejects the Son will not see life, for God's wrath remains on him."

Jn 13:3 Jesus knew that the Father had put all things under his power, and that he had come from God and was returning to God; (+1Jn 1:7; 2:22-24)

1Jn 3:8 He who does what is sinful is of the devil, because

the devil has been sinning from the beginning. The reason the Son of God appeared was to destroy the devil's work.

1Jn 3:23 And this is his command: to believe in the name of his Son, Jesus Christ, and to love one another as he commanded us.

1Jn 4:9 This is how God showed his love among us: He sent his one and only Son into the world that we might live through him. **10**This is love: not that we loved God, but that he loved us and sent his Son as an atoning sacrifice for our sins.

1Jn 4:14 And we have seen and testify that the Father has sent his Son to be the Savior of the world.

1Jn 5:5 Who is it that overcomes the world? Only he who believes that Jesus is the Son of God.

1Jn 5:9 We accept man's testimony, but God's testimony is greater because it is the testimony of God, which he has given about his Son. **10**Anyone who believes in the Son of God has this testimony in his heart. Anyone who does not believe God has made him out to be a liar, because he has not believed the testimony God has given about his Son.

1Jn 5:13 I write these things to you who believe in the name of the Son of God so that you may know that you have eternal life.

1Jn 5:20 We know also that the Son of God has come and has given us understanding, so that we may know him who is true. And we are in him who is true—even in his Son Jesus Christ. He is the true God and eternal life.

2Jn 3 Grace, mercy and peace from God the Father and from Jesus Christ, the Father's Son, will be with us in truth and love.

Testified to by Paul (Ro 1:3-4,9; 8:3,29,32)—

1Co 1:9 God, who has called you into fellowship with his Son Jesus Christ our Lord, is faithful.

1Co 15:24 Then the end will come, when he hands over the kingdom to God the Father after he has destroyed all dominion, authority and power.

1Co 15:27 For he "has put everything under his feet." Now when it says that "everything" has been put under him, it is clear that this does not include God himself, who put everything under Christ. **28**When he has done this, then the Son himself will be made subject to him who put everything under him, so that God may be all in all.

2Co 1:3 Praise be to the God and Father of our Lord Jesus Christ, the Father of compassion and the God of all comfort,

2Co 1:19 For the Son of God, Jesus Christ, who was preached among you by me and Silas and Timothy, was not "Yes" and "No," but in him it has always been "Yes."

Gal 1:16 to reveal his Son in me so that I might preach him among the Gentiles, I did not consult any man,

Gal 4:4 But when the time had fully come, God sent his Son, born of a woman, born under law,

Eph 1:3 Praise be to the God and Father of our Lord Jesus Christ, who has blessed us in the heavenly realms with every spiritual blessing in Christ.

Eph 3:14 For this reason I kneel before the Father,

Col 1:3 We always thank God, the Father of our Lord Jesus Christ, when we pray for you,

Col 1:15 He is the image of the invisible God, the firstborn over all creation.

Col 1:19 For God was pleased to have all his fullness dwell in him,

Col 3:17 And whatever you do, whether in word or deed, do it all in the name of the Lord Jesus, giving thanks to God the Father through him.

1Th 1:10 and to wait for his Son from heaven, whom he

raised from the dead—Jesus, who rescues us from the coming wrath.

Testified to in Hebrews—

Heb 1:1 In the past God spoke to our forefathers through the prophets at many times and in various ways, ²but in these last days he has spoken to us by his Son, whom he appointed heir of all things, and through whom he made the universe. ³The Son is the radiance of God's glory and the exact representation of his being, sustaining all things by his powerful word. After he had provided purification for sins, he sat down at the right hand of the Majesty in heaven.

Heb 1:5 For to which of the angels did God ever say, "You are my Son; today I have become your Father"? Or again, "I will be his Father, and he will be my Son"?

Heb 4:14 Therefore, since we have a great high priest who has gone through the heavens, Jesus the Son of God, let us hold firmly to the faith we profess.

Heb 5:5 So Christ also did not take upon himself the glory of becoming a high priest. But God said to him, "You are my Son; today I have become your Father."

Heb 5:8 Although he was a son, he learned obedience from what he suffered

Heb 6:6 if they fall away, to be brought back to repentance, because to their loss they are crucifying the Son of God all over again and subjecting him to public disgrace.

Heb 7:3 Without father or mother, without genealogy, without beginning of days or end of life, like the Son of God he remains a priest forever.

Heb 10:29 How much more severely do you think a man deserves to be punished who has trampled the Son of God under foot, who has treated as an unholy thing the blood of the covenant that sanctified him, and who has insulted the Spirit of grace?

Belief in, basis of eternal life (Jn 1:1-2,12; 3:16-18,34-36; 6:40; 20:31; 1Jn 2:22-24; 3:23; 5:5,9-10,13,20)

Basis for growth and purity (Jn 15:1,8-10)—

1Jn 1:7 But if we walk in the light, as he is in the light, we have fellowship with one another, and the blood of Jesus, his Son, purifies us from all sin.

Denial of, basis of antichrist—

1Jn 2:22 Who is the liar? It is the man who denies that Jesus is the Christ. Such a man is the antichrist—he denies the Father and the Son. ²³No one who denies the Son has the Father; whoever acknowledges the Son has the Father also. ²⁴See that what you have heard from the beginning remains in you. If it does, you also will remain in the Son and in the Father.

See above, Deity of; Relation of, to the Father.
See Son of God.

Son of Man:

Used in a messianic sense (Da 7:13-14).

Used by Jesus: Of himself (Mt 11:19,27; 16:13; Mk 14:21,41; Lk 6:22; 7:34; 18:31; Jn 1:51; 3:13). In a messianic sense, of his coming (Mt 10:23; 16:27-28; 24:27, 30,37,44; 25:13,31; Mk 13:26; Lk 9:26; 12:40; 17:22,24, 26,30; 18:8; 21:27), his kingdom (Mt 16:28; 19:28; Mk 8:38; 14:62), his judgment (Mt 24:29-30; Mk 8:38; Lk 9:26; 12:8,10; 21:36), his lordship or deity (Mt 12:8; 13:37,41; 16:13, w 16:16,27-28; 19:28; 24:27; Mk 2:28; Lk 6:5; 12:8,10; 17:22,24; 21:36; 22:69; Jn 12:23; 13:31), his suffering and death (Mt 12:40; 17:9,12,22; 20:18,28; 26:2,24-25; Mk 8:31; 9:9,12,31; 10:33-34,45; 14:21,41; Lk 9:22,44; 11:30; 17:22-26; 18:31; 22:22,48; 24:7; Jn 3:14; 8:28; 12:23; 13:31), his resurrection (Mt 12:40; 17:9,

22-23; 20:18-19; Mk 8:31; 9:9,31; 10:33-34; Jn 6:62; 12:23; 13:31).

Of himself, as the supreme human (Mt 8:20; 12:32), a servant of mankind (Mt 20:28; Mk 10:45; Lk 9:56,58), the forgiver of sins (Mt 9:6; Mk 2:10; Lk 5:24; 12:10), the Redeemer (Mt 18:11; 20:28; Lk 12:8; 19:10; 6:27,53).

Used by the angel at the empty tomb, in quoting Christ (Lk 24:7); Stephen, in his vision of Jesus (Ac 7:56); John, in his vision of Jesus (Rev 1:13; 14:14).

Synonymous with *Christ*, as used by, Caiaphas the high priest (Mt 26:63, w 26:65; Mk 14:61-62), the religious leaders (Lk 22:70, w 22:66-71, & 23:35), the people in questioning him (Jn 12:34).

The title is a reference to the human nature of Jesus, designating him as the God-Man (Mt 8:20; 12:32).
See Son of Man.

Sovereignty of:

See above, King; Lordship of.

Sufferings of:

Foretold: By the psalmist (Ps 22:6-8,11-13,17-21, w Mt 27:35 & Mk 15:24 & Lk 23:34 & Jn 19:23-24; Ps 69:7-9,20), by prophets (Isa 50:6; 52:13-14; 53:1-12, w Mt 26:67 & 27:26 & Lk 22:37 & Jn 12:38; Mic 5:1; Zec 11:12-13; Lk 24:26,46; 1Pe 1:11), by himself (Mt 16:21; 17:12,22-23; 20:17-19; Mk 8:31; 9:12; 10:32-34; Lk 9:22; 18:31-33; Jn 3:14; 13:21).

Suffering in Gethsemane—

Mt 26:38 Then he said to them, "My soul is overwhelmed with sorrow to the point of death. Stay here and keep watch with me."

³⁹Going a little farther, he fell with his face to the ground and prayed, "My Father, if it is possible, may this cup be taken from me. Yet not as I will, but as you will."

⁴⁰Then he returned to his disciples and found them sleeping. "Could you men not keep watch with me for one hour?" he asked Peter. ⁴¹"Watch and pray so that you will not fall into temptation. The spirit is willing, but the body is weak."

⁴²He went away a second time and prayed, "My Father, if it is not possible for this cup to be taken away unless I drink it, may your will be done."

⁴³When he came back, he again found them sleeping, because their eyes were heavy. ⁴⁴So he left them and went away once more and prayed the third time, saying the same thing.

⁴⁵Then he returned to the disciples and said to them, "Are you still sleeping and resting? Look, the hour is near, and the Son of Man is betrayed into the hands of sinners. (+Mk 14:34-39; Lk 22:42-43)

Lk 22:44 And being in anguish, he prayed more earnestly, and his sweat was like drops of blood falling to the ground.

Jn 18:11 Jesus commanded Peter, "Put your sword away! Shall I not drink the cup the Father has given me?"

Suffering in Pilate's judgment hall—

Mt 27:24 When Pilate saw that he was getting nowhere, but that instead an uproar was starting, he took water and washed his hands in front of the crowd. "I am innocent of this man's blood," he said. "It is your responsibility!"

²⁵All the people answered, "Let his blood be on us and on our children!"

²⁶Then he released Barabbas to them. But he had Jesus flogged, and handed him over to be crucified.

²⁷Then the governor's soldiers took Jesus into the Praetorium and gathered the whole company of soldiers around him. ²⁸They stripped him and put a scarlet robe on

him, ²⁹and then twisted together a crown of thorns and set it on his head. They put a staff in his right hand and knelt in front of him and mocked him. "Hail, king of the Jews!" they said. ³⁰They spit on him, and took the staff and struck him on the head again and again. (+Mk 15:15-20; Jn 19:16-18)

Suffering at his crucifixion—

Mt 27:31 After they had mocked him, they took off the robe and put his own clothes on him. Then they led him away to crucify him.

³²As they were going out, they met a man from Cyrene, named Simon, and they forced him to carry the cross. ³³They came to a place called Golgotha (which means The Place of the Skull). ³⁴There they offered Jesus wine to drink, mixed with gall; but after tasting it, he refused to drink it. ³⁵When they had crucified him, they divided up his clothes by casting lots. ³⁶And sitting down, they kept watch over him there. ³⁷Above his head they placed the written charge against him: THIS IS JESUS, THE KING OF THE JEWS. ³⁸Two robbers were crucified with him, one on his right and one on his left. ³⁹Those who passed by hurled insults at him, shaking their heads ⁴⁰and saying, "You who are going to destroy the temple and build it in three days, save yourself! Come down from the cross, if you are the Son of God!"

⁴¹In the same way the chief priests, the teachers of the law and the elders mocked him. ⁴²"He saved others," they said, "but he can't save himself! He's the King of Israel! Let him come down now from the cross, and we will believe in him. ⁴³He trusts in God. Let God rescue him now if he wants him, for he said, 'I am the Son of God.'" ⁴⁴In the same way the robbers who were crucified with him also heaped insults on him.

⁴⁵From the sixth hour until the ninth hour darkness came over all the land. ⁴⁶About the ninth hour Jesus cried out in a loud voice, *"Eloi, Eloi, lama sabachthani?"*—which means, "My God, my God, why have you forsaken me?"

⁴⁷When some of those standing there heard this, they said, "He's calling Elijah."

⁴⁸Immediately one of them ran and got a sponge. He filled it with wine vinegar, put it on a stick, and offered it to Jesus to drink. ⁴⁹The rest said, "Now leave him alone. Let's see if Elijah comes to save him."

⁵⁰And when Jesus had cried out again in a loud voice, he gave up his spirit.

Mk 15:34 And at the ninth hour Jesus cried out in a loud voice, *"Eloi, Eloi, lama sabachthani?"*—which means, "My God, my God, why have you forsaken me?" (+Mk 15:36; Lk 23:33-46)

Jn 19:28 Later, knowing that all was now completed, and so that the Scripture would be fulfilled, Jesus said, "I am thirsty."

Apostolic teaching concerning his suffering—

Ac 3:18 But this is how God fulfilled what he had foretold through all the prophets, saying that his Christ would suffer.

Ac 17:3 explaining and proving that the Christ had to suffer and rise from the dead. "This Jesus I am proclaiming to you is the Christ," he said.

2Co 1:5 For just as the sufferings of Christ flow over into our lives, so also through Christ our comfort overflows.

Php 2:8 And being found in appearance as a man, he humbled himself and became obedient to death—even death on a cross!

Php 3:10 I want to know Christ and the power of his

resurrection and the fellowship of sharing in his sufferings, becoming like him in his death,

Heb 2:9 But we see Jesus, who was made a little lower than the angels, now crowned with glory and honor because he suffered death, so that by the grace of God he might taste death for everyone.

Heb 4:15 For we do not have a high priest who is unable to sympathize with our weaknesses, but we have one who has been tempted in every way, just as we are—yet was without sin.

Heb 5:7 During the days of Jesus' life on earth, he offered up prayers and petitions with loud cries and tears to the one who could save him from death, and he was heard because of his reverent submission. ⁸Although he was a son, he learned obedience from what he suffered

Heb 12:2 Let us fix our eyes on Jesus, the author and perfecter of our faith, who for the joy set before him endured the cross, scorning its shame, and sat down at the right hand of the throne of God. ³Consider him who endured such opposition from sinful men, so that you will not grow weary and lose heart.

1Pe 1:11 trying to find out the time and circumstances to which the Spirit of Christ in them was pointing when he predicted the sufferings of Christ and the glories that would follow.

1Pe 2:21 To this you were called, because Christ suffered for you, leaving you an example, that you should follow in his steps. ²²"He committed no sin, and no deceit was found in his mouth." ²³When they hurled their insults at him, he did not retaliate; when he suffered, he made no threats. Instead, he entrusted himself to him who judges justly. (+1Pe 3:18)

1Pe 4:1 Therefore, since Christ suffered in his body, arm yourselves also with the same attitude, because he who has suffered in his body is done with sin. (+1Pe 4:13)

Rev 5:6 Then I saw a Lamb, looking as if it had been slain, standing in the center of the throne, encircled by the four living creatures and the elders. He had seven horns and seven eyes, which are the seven spirits of God sent out into all the earth.

Rev 19:13 He is dressed in a robe dipped in blood, and his name is the Word of God.

See above, Death of.

Sympathy of: *See above, Compassion of, Love of.*

Teacher: (Mt 5:1-2; Jn 7:46)

Ac 1:1 In my former book, Theophilus, I wrote about all that Jesus began to do and to teach

From God—

Jn 3:2 He came to Jesus at night and said, "Rabbi, we know you are a teacher who has come from God. For no one could perform the miraculous signs you are doing if God were not with him."

Taught with authority—

Mt 7:29 because he taught as one who had authority, and not as their teachers of the law.

Mt 23:8 "But you are not to be called 'Rabbi,' for you have only one Master and you are all brothers. (+Mk 1:22)

Without respect of persons—

Mt 22:16 They sent their disciples to him along with the Herodians. "Teacher," they said, "we know you are a man of integrity and that you teach the way of God in accordance with the truth. You aren't swayed by men, because you pay no attention to who they are. (+Mk 12:14; Lk 20:21)

By the lake shore—

Mk 4:1 Again Jesus began to teach by the lake. The crowd that gathered around him was so large that he got into a boat and sat in it out on the lake, while all the people were along the shore at the water's edge.

In cities and villages—

Mt 11:1 After Jesus had finished instructing his twelve disciples, he went on from there to teach and preach in the towns of Galilee. (+Mk 6:6)

Lk 23:5 But they insisted, "He stirs up the people all over Judea by his teaching. He started in Galilee and has come all the way here."

In synagogues—

Mt 4:23 Jesus went throughout Galilee, teaching in their synagogues, preaching the good news of the kingdom, and healing every disease and sickness among the people. (+Mk 1:21)

Lk 4:15 He taught in their synagogues, and everyone praised him.

Lk 6:6 On another Sabbath he went into the synagogue and was teaching, and a man was there whose right hand was shriveled.

In the temple—

Mt 21:23 Jesus entered the temple courts, and, while he was teaching, the chief priests and the elders of the people came to him. "By what authority are you doing these things?" they asked. "And who gave you this authority?"

Mt 26:55 At that time Jesus said to the crowd, "Am I leading a rebellion, that you have come out with swords and clubs to capture me? Every day I sat in the temple courts teaching, and you did not arrest me. (+Mk 12:35; Lk 21:37; Jn 8:2)

In the wilderness (Mk 6:34).

Temptation of:

Lk 22:28 You are those who have stood by me in my trials.

In all points as we are—

Heb 4:15 For we do not have a high priest who is unable to sympathize with our weaknesses, but we have one who has been tempted in every way, just as we are—yet was without sin.

By the devil—

Mt 4:1 Then Jesus was led by the Spirit into the desert to be tempted by the devil. [2]After fasting forty days and forty nights, he was hungry. [3]The tempter came to him and said, "If you are the Son of God, tell these stones to become bread."

[4]Jesus answered, "It is written: 'Man does not live on bread alone, but on every word that comes from the mouth of God.'"

[5]Then the devil took him to the holy city and had him stand on the highest point of the temple. [6]"If you are the Son of God," he said, "throw yourself down. For it is written:

"'He will command his angels concerning you, and they will lift you up in their hands, so that you will not strike your foot against a stone.'"

[7]Jesus answered him, "It is also written: 'Do not put the Lord your God to the test.'"

[8]Again, the devil took him to a very high mountain and showed him all the kingdoms of the world and their splendor. [9]"All this I will give you," he said, "if you will bow down and worship me."

[10]Jesus said to him, "Away from me, Satan! For it is written: 'Worship the Lord your God, and serve him only.'"

[11]Then the devil left him, and angels came and attended him. (+Mk 1:12-13; Lk 4:1-13)

Typified:

In offerings (Ge 4:4; 8:20; 22:13; Ex 12:5-7; 24:5; 29:36-37; Lev 1:4,10-12; 3:6,12; 4:3-7,14-18,20,23-25, 28-30,32-34; 5:6-11,16,18; 6:6-7; 7:2; 8:14-15,18-19,22-24; 9:2,7-9,18; 12:6-8; 14:12-14,25,30-31; 15:15,29-30; 16:3, 5,9,11,14-16,21-22; 19:21-22; 22:18-19; 23:12,18-19,27-28; Nu 6:10-11,14,16-17; 8:8,12; 15:24-25,27; 28:3-4,9,11,15,19,22-23,27,30; 29:5,8,11,13,16-34,38; 1Ch 29:21; 2Ch 7:5; 29:21-24; Ezr 6:17,20; 8:35; Eze 43:18-27; 45:15,18-23).

In the Passover (Ex 12:3,5; Nu 28:16). In the cornerstone (Isa 28:16; Mk 12:10-11).

In David (Eze 34:23-24; 37:24-25; Hos 3:5). Solomon (Ps 72). Hezekiah (Isa 32:1).

Unchangeable:

(Heb 13:8).

Union of, with the righteous:

See Righteous, Union of, with Christ.

Wisdom of:

(Mk 6:2; Lk 2:40,46-47,52; Jn 7:15).
See above, Omniscience.

Worship of:

1Co 1:2 To the church of God in Corinth, to those sanctified in Christ Jesus and called to be holy, together with all those everywhere who call on the name of our Lord Jesus Christ—their Lord and ours:

2Co 12:8 Three times I pleaded with the Lord to take it away from me. [9]But he said to me, "My grace is sufficient for you, for my power is made perfect in weakness." Therefore I will boast all the more gladly about my weaknesses, so that Christ's power may rest on me.

Php 2:10 that at the name of Jesus every knee should bow, in heaven and on earth and under the earth, [11]and every tongue confess that Jesus Christ is Lord, to the glory of God the Father.

John's vision of—

Rev 5:8 And when he had taken it, the four living creatures and the twenty-four elders fell down before the Lamb. Each one had a harp and they were holding golden bowls full of incense, which are the prayers of the saints. [9]And they sang a new song:

"You are worthy to take the scroll and to open its seals, because you were slain, and with your blood you purchased men for God from every tribe and language and people and nation.

Rev 5:12 In a loud voice they sang:

"Worthy is the Lamb, who was slain, to receive power and wealth and wisdom and strength and honor and glory and praise!"

[13]Then I heard every creature in heaven and on earth and under the earth and on the sea, and all that is in them, singing:

"To him who sits on the throne and to the Lamb be praise and honor and glory and power, for ever and ever!"

[14]The four living creatures said, "Amen," and the elders fell down and worshiped. (+Rev 7:10)

Worship commanded—

Jn 5:23 that all may honor the Son just as they honor the Father. He who does not honor the Son does not honor the Father, who sent him.

Heb 1:6 And again, when God brings his firstborn into the world, he says, "Let all God's angels worship him."

Instances of: By the wise men—

Mt 2:2 and asked, "Where is the one who has been born king of the Jews? We saw his star in the east and have come to worship him."

By a certain ruler—

Mt 9:18 While he was saying this, a ruler came and knelt before him and said, "My daughter has just died. But come and put your hand on her, and she will live."

By the disciples—

Mt 14:33 Then those who were in the boat worshiped him, saying, "Truly you are the Son of God."

By the Canaanite woman—

Mt 15:25 The woman came and knelt before him. "Lord, help me!" she said.

By a leper (Mt 8:2).

By women after his resurrection—

Mt 28:9 Suddenly Jesus met them. "Greetings," he said. They came to him, clasped his feet and worshiped him.

By the eleven disciples after his resurrection—

Mt 28:17 When they saw him, they worshiped him; but some doubted.

Lk 24:52 Then they worshiped him and returned to Jerusalem with great joy.

By the multitudes—

Mk 11:9 Those who went ahead and those who followed shouted,

"Hosanna!"

"Blessed is he who comes in the name of the Lord!"

¹⁰"Blessed is the coming kingdom of our father David!"

"Hosanna in the highest!" (+Mt 21:9)

By Simon Peter—

Lk 5:8 When Simon Peter saw this, he fell at Jesus' knees and said, "Go away from me, Lord; I am a sinful man!"

By the blind man whom Jesus healed—

Jn 9:38 Then the man said, "Lord, I believe," and he worshiped him.

By evil spirits—

Mk 3:11 Whenever the evil spirits saw him, they fell down before him and cried out, "You are the Son of God."

By a demon-possessed man—

Mk 5:6 When he saw Jesus from a distance, he ran and fell on his knees in front of him. ⁷He shouted at the top of his voice, "What do you want with me, Jesus, Son of the Most High God? Swear to God that you won't torture me!"

By Stephen—

Ac 7:59 While they were stoning him, Stephen prayed, "Lord Jesus, receive my spirit." ⁶⁰Then he fell on his knees and cried out, "Lord, do not hold this sin against them." When he had said this, he fell asleep.

By Paul—

1Ti 1:12 I thank Christ Jesus our Lord, who has given me strength, that he considered me faithful, appointing me to his service.

2Pe 3:18 But grow in the grace and knowledge of our Lord and Savior Jesus Christ. To him be glory both now and forever! Amen.

Zeal of:

For God's house—

Lk 2:49 "Why were you searching for me?" he asked. "Didn't you know I had to be in my Father's house?"

Jn 2:17 His disciples remembered that it is written: "Zeal for your house will consume me."

Ps 69:9 for zeal for your house consumes me, and the insults of those who insult you fall on me.

In obedience to God—

Jn 4:32 But he said to them, "I have food to eat that you know nothing about."

Jn 4:34 "My food," said Jesus, "is to do the will of him who sent me and to finish his work.

Jn 9:4 As long as it is day, we must do the work of him who sent me. Night is coming, when no one can work.

Ro 15:3 For even Christ did not please himself but, as it is written: "The insults of those who insult you have fallen on me."

In doing good—

Ac 10:38 how God anointed Jesus of Nazareth with the Holy Spirit and power, and how he went around doing good and healing all who were under the power of the devil, because God was with him.

In preaching the gospel—

Mt 4:23 Jesus went throughout Galilee, teaching in their synagogues, preaching the good news of the kingdom, and healing every disease and sickness among the people. (+Mt 9:35; Mk 6:6; Lk 4:43; Mk 1:38; 8:1)

In giving himself as a sacrifice—

Lk 9:51 As the time approached for him to be taken up to heaven, Jesus resolutely set out for Jerusalem.

Lk 12:50 But I have a baptism to undergo, and how distressed I am until it is completed!

Lk 13:32 He replied, "Go tell that fox, 'I will drive out demons and heal people today and tomorrow, and on the third day I will reach my goal.' ³³In any case, I must keep going today and tomorrow and the next day—for surely no prophet can die outside Jerusalem!

1Ti 6:13 In the sight of God, who gives life to everything, and of Christ Jesus, who while testifying before Pontius Pilate made the good confession, I charge you

JESUS, JUSTUS *See Justus, 3.*

JETHER [3858, 3859] (*abundance*).

1. Jethro is the father-in-law of Moses (Ex 4:18).
2. Gideon's eldest son (Jdg 8:20-21).
3. Father of Amasa (2Sa 17:25; 1Ch 2:17).
4. Judahite (1Ch 2:32).
5. Judahite (1Ch 4:17).
6. Asherite, same as Ithran (1Ch 7:37, w 7:38).

JETHETH [3867]. Edomite chieftain (Ge 36:40; 1Ch 1:51).

JETHLAH *See Ithlah.*

JETHRO [3858, 3861] (*remainder* KB). A priest of Midian and father-in-law of Moses (Ex 3:1), personal name probably Reuel (Ex 2:18; 3:1), father of Zipporah, whom Moses married (Ex 3:1-2), advised Moses (Ex 18:14-24).

JETUR [3515]. Son of Ishmael and descendants (Ge 25:15; 1Ch 1:31), Itureans of NT times.

JEUEL [3590] (*God [El] has preserved*).

1. Judahite (1Ch 9:6).
2. Levite (2Ch 29:13).
3. Leader in Ezra's company (Ezr 8:13).

JEUSH [3593] (perhaps *may God aid*).

1. Son of Esau (Ge 36:5).
2. Benjamite (1Ch 7:10).
3. Gershonite Levite (1Ch 23:10-11).

4. Descendant of Jonathan (1Ch 8:39).

5. Son of Rehoboam (2Ch 11:19).

JEUZ [3591] (*he comes to help* BDB; possibly *encouraged* IDB). Head of a Benjamite family (1Ch 8:10).

JEWEL, JEWELRY [74, 2717, 2719, 3016, 3998, 6344+, 6736, 7382, *3345*, *5992*].

NIV+ JEWELS

Articles of jewelry in OT times: diadems, bracelets, necklaces, anklets, rings for fingers, gold nets for hair, pendants, amulets and pendants with magical meanings, jeweled perfume and ointment boxes, crescents for camels; used for personal adornment and utility and for religious festivals. Not much said about jewelry in NT; most condemnatory (1Ti 2:9; Jas 2:2). The New Jerusalem is adorned with jewels (Rev 21:19).

See Minerals of the Bible, 1; Stones.

JEWS [*3373, 3374, 10316, 2678, 2679, 2680, 2681+, 4364] (*from JUDAH*).

NIV+ JEW, JEWESS, JEWISH, JEWS', JUDAISM

A corrupted form of Judah, and applied to the people of the kingdom of Judah and Benjamin (2Ki 16:6; 25:25; 2Ch 32:18). After the dissolution of the kingdom of Israel, the name was applied to all Israelites as well as to those of the two tribes (Mt 27:11; Ac 2:5).

Sins that led to the Captivity of (Isa 1:4-25; 2:6-10; 3:9; 59:2-15; 65:2-7; Jer 5:1; 6:21-28; 44:1-3; Eze 5:6; 12:2; 16:2,15-47,57-63). See the book of Jeremiah, which deals chiefly with the sins of and the corrective judgments of God to be inflicted upon.

Captive in Babylon (2Ki 24:1-20; 25:1,21). Haman's plot against (Est 3:6-15). Feast of Purim instituted to commemorate their deliverance from Haman's plot (Est 9:26-32).

The proclamation of Cyrus authorizing their return to the land of Canaan (2Ch 36:22-23; Ezr 1:2-4), and of Artaxerxes (Ezr 7:11-26).

After the Captivity:

Return from Babylon (Ezr 7:1-9; 8:31-32). Lists of those who returned from Babylon (Ezr 2:1-67; 8:1-20; Ne 7:6-69; 12:1-21). Rebuild the temple (Ezr 3:8-13). Rebuilding suspended during the reign of Artaxerxes (Ezr 4:1-24). Resumption of the rebuilding interfered with by Tattenai, governor of the province, by protest followed by a letter to Darius (Ezr 5). Darius' reply to Tattenai authorizing the rebuilding of the temple; temple completed (Ezr 6:1-15).

Vessels of the temple, that were taken to Babylon by Nebuchadnezzar, returned by command of Cyrus (Ezr 1:7-11; 6:5). Liberality of Artaxerxes toward the temple (Ezr 7:14-23).

Made marriages among the Canaanites: Ezra instituted reforms (Ezr 10). Rebuilt the walls of Jerusalem under proclamation of Artaxerxes (Ne 2; 3; 4; 5; 6). Walls dedicated (Ne 12:27-43).

Mission of Jesus to (Mt 10:5-6; 15:24; Mk 7:27). Some accept Jesus (Jn 2:23; 10:42; 11:45; 12:11; Ac 21:20). Others disbelieve in Jesus (Mt 13:5-8; Jn 5:38,40,43; 6:36; 12:37). Reject Jesus (Lk 13:34; 17:25; Jn 1:11). Crucify Jesus. *See Crucifixion.* Devout, among them (Ac 2:5). Spurned Paul's preaching (Ac 13:46; 18:5-6; 28:24-27). Persecuted Paul (Ac 9:22-23; 13:50; 20:3,19; 23:12-30; 2Co 11:24). Entrusted with the oracles of God (Ac 7:38; Ro 3:1-2).

Prophecies Concerning:

Their rejection of the Messiah (Isa 49:5,7; 52:14; 53:1-3; Zec 13; Mt 21:33-39; 22:1-5).

War and other judgments (Isa 3; 4:1; 5; 6:9-13; 7:17-25; 8:14-22; 10:12; 22:1-14; 28:14-22; 29:1-10; 30:1-17; 31:1-3; 32:9-14; Jer 1:11-16; 4:5-31; 6; 7:8-34; 8; 9:9-26; 10:17-22; 11:9-23; 13:9-27; 14:14-18; 15:1-14; 16; 17:1-4; 18:15-17; 19; 20:5; 21:4-7; 22:24-30; 25:8-38; 28; 34; 37; 38:1-3; 42:13-22; 43-45; La 5:6; Eze 4; 5; 11:7-12; 12; 15-17; 19; 22:13-22; 23:22-35; 24; 33:21-29; Da 9:26-27; Joel 2:1-17; Am 2:4-5; Mic 3; 4:8-10; Hab 1:6-11; Zep 1; Zec 14:1-3; Mal 4:1; Mt 21:33-45; 23:35-38; 24:2,14-42; Mk 13:1-13; Lk 13:34-35; 19:43-44; 21:5-25; 23:28-31; Rev 1:7).

Dispersion of (Isa 24:1; Jer 9:16; Hos 9:17; Joel 3:6,20; Am 9:9; Eze 4:13; 5:10,12; 20:23; 36:19; Da 9:7).

Blessing and restoration of (Isa 1:25-27; 2:1-5; 4:2-6; 11:11-13; 25; 26:1-2,12-19; 27:13; 29:18-24; 30:18-26; 32:15-20; 33:13-24; 35; 37:31-32; 40:2,9; 41:27; 44; 49:13-23; 51; 52:1-12; 60; 61:4-9; 62; 66:5-22; Jer 3:14-18; 4:3-18; 12:14-16; 23:3; 24:1-7; 30:3-22; 32:36-44; 33; 44:28; Eze 14:22-23; 16:60-63; 20:40-41; 36:1-38; 37:12, 21; Da 11:30-45; 12:1; Joel 3; Am 9:9-15; Ob 17-21; Mic 2:12-13; 5:3; Zep 2:7; Zec 1:14-21; 2; 8; 10:5-12; 12:1-14; 13; 14:3-21; Mal 3:4; Ro 11).

See Israel, Israelites; Judah.

JEZANIAH [3470] (*Yahweh gives ear*). Also known as Azariah (Jer 42:1, ftn), as was King Uzziah (2Ki 14:21, ftn; 2Ch 26:1, ftn). *See also, Jaazaniah, 1.*

JEZEBEL [374, *2630*] (possibly *unexalted, unhusbanded* BDB).

NIV+ JEZEBEL'S

Daughter of Ethbaal, a Sidonian, and wife of Ahab (1Ki 16:31). Worshiped idols and persecuted the prophets of God (1Ki 18:4,13,19; 2Ki 3:2,13; 9:7,22). Vowed to kill Elijah (1Ki 19:1-3). Wickedly accomplishes the death of Naboth (1Ki 21:5-16). Death of, foretold (1Ki 21:23; 2Ki 9:10). Death of, at the hand of Jehu (2Ki 9:30-37).

Figurative: (Rev 2:20).

JEZER, JEZERITE [3672,   3673]   (*formed, fashioned*). Son of Naphtali (Ge 46:24; Nu 26:49; 1Ch 7:13).

JEZIAH See *Izziah.*

JEZIEL [3465]. A disaffected Israelite who joined David at Ziklag (1Ch 12:3).

JEZLIAH See *Izliah.*

JEZOAR See *Zohar, 3.*

JEZRAHIAH [3474] (*Yahweh will arise* or *shine*).

1. Descendant of Issachar called Izrahiah (1Ch 7:3).

2. Musician (Ne 12:42).

JEZREEL, JEZREELITE [3475, 3476, 3477] (*God [El] will sow*).

1. A city in the S of Judah (Jos 15:56; 1Sa 25:43; 27:3; 29:1,11).

2. A city of Issachar (Jos 19:18; 2Sa 2:9). Ahab's residence in (1Ki 18:45-46; 21:1). Naboth's vineyard in (1Ki 21:1). Joram's residence in (2Ki 8:29). Jehu kills King Ahab, his wife, and friends at (2Ki 9:15-37; 10:11). Prophecies concerning (Hos 1:4-5,11).

3. A valley (Jos 17:16). Place of Gideon's battle with

the Midianites (Jdg 6:33). Place of the defeat of the Israelites under Saul and Jonathan (1Sa 29:1,11; 31:1-6; 2Sa
4:4).

4. A descendant of Etam (1Ch 4:3).

5. Figurative of Israel (Hos 1:4-5,11).

JIBSAM *See Ibsam.*

JIDLAPH [3358] (*he weeps*). Son of Nahor (Ge 22:22).

JIMNA, JIMNAH *See Imnah.*

JIPHTAH *See Iphtah.*

JIPHTHAH-EL *See Iphtah El.*

JOAB [3405] (*Yahweh is father*).
NIV+ JOAB'S, ATROTH BETH JOAB

1. Son of David's sister (1Ch 2:16). Commander of
David's army (2Sa 8:16; 20:23; 1Ch 11:6; 18:15; 27:34).
Dedicated spoils of his battles (1Ch 26:28). Defeated the
Jebusites (1Ch 11:6). Defeats and slays Abner (2Sa 2:13-
32; 3:27; 1Ki 2:5). Destroys all the males in Edom (1Ki
11:16). *See Psalm 60, title.* Defeats the Ammonites (2Sa
10:7-14; 1Ch 19:6-15). Captures Rabbah (2Sa 11:1,15-25;
12:26-29; 1Ch 20:1-2).

Secures the return of Absalom to Jerusalem (2Sa 14:1-
24). Barley field of, burned by Absalom (2Sa 18). Rebukes
David for lamenting the death of Absalom (2Sa 19:1-8).
Replaced by Amasa as commander of David's army (2Sa
17:25; 19:13). Kills Amasa (2Sa 20:8-13; 1Ki 2:5). Causes
Sheba to be put to death (2Sa 20:16-22). Opposes the
numbering of the people (2Sa 24:3; 1Ch 21:3). Numbers
the people (2Sa 24:4-9; 1Ch 21:4-5; 27:23-24). Supports
Adonijah as successor to David (1Ki 1:7; 2:28). Slain by
Benaiah, under Solomon's order (1Ki 2:29-34).

2. A grandson of Kenaz (1Ch 4:14).

3. An Israelite (or the name of two Israelites) whose
descendants returned from Babylon to Jerusalem (Ezr 2:6;
8:9; Ne 7:11).

4. "House of Joab" (1Ch 2:54). Probably identical with
1. *See Atroth Beth Joab.*

JOAH [3406] (*Yahweh is brother*).

1. Son of Asaph (2Ki 18:18,26; Isa 36:3,11,22).

2. A descendant of Gershom (1Ch 6:21; 2Ch 29:12).

3. A son of Obed-Edom (1Ch 26:4).

4. A Levite, who repaired the temple (2Ch 34:8).

JOAHAZ [3407] (*Yahweh grips*). Father of Joah, recorder of King Josiah (2Ch 34:8).

JOANAN [2720]. An ancestor of Jesus (Lk 3:27).

JOANNA [2721] (probably feminine form of *John*).
Wife of Cuza, the steward of Herod Agrippa, and a
disciple of Jesus (Lk 8:3; 24:10).

JOASH [3371, 3409, 3447] (*Yahweh has bestowed*).

1. Son of Beker (1Ch 7:8).

2. Keeper of the stores of oil (1Ch 27:28).

3. Father of Gideon (Jdg 6:11,29,31; 7:14; 8:13,29-32).

4. Son of Ahab, king of Israel (1Ki 22:26; 2Ch 18:25).

5. Also called Jehoash. *See Jehoash, Joash.* Son of
Ahaziah and king of Judah. Saved from his grandmother
by Jehosheba, his aunt, and hidden for six years (2Ki
11:1-3; 2Ch 22:11-12). Anointed king by the priest,
Jehoiada (2Ki 11:12-21; 2Ch 23). Righteousness of, under
influence of Jehoiada (2Ki 12:2; 2Ch 24:2). Repaired the
temple (2Ki 12:4-16; 2Ch 24:4-14,27). Wickedness of,

after Jehoiada's death (2Ch 24:17-22). Secured peace
from Hazael, king of Syria, by gift of dedicated treasures
from the temple (2Ki 12:17-18; 2Ch 24:23-24). Prophecy
against (2Ch 24:19-20). Put Jehoiada's son to death (2Ch
24:20-22; Mt 23:35). Diseases of (2Ch 24:25). Conspired
against and slain (2Ki 12:20-21; 2Ch 24:25-26).

6. A king of Israel. *See Jehoash, Joash.*

7. A descendant of Shelah (1Ch 4:22).

8. One of David's officers (1Ch 12:3).

JOATHAM *See Jotham, 3.*

JOB [373, 6275, *3873*] (*where is my father,* or perhaps
where is my father, O God?).
NIV+ JOB'S

1. A man who lived in Uz (Job 1:1). Righteousness of
(Job 1:1,5,8; 2:3; Eze 14:14,20). Riches of (Job 1:3). Trial
of, by affliction of Satan (Job 1:13-19; 2:7-10). Fortitude
of (Job 1:20-22; 2:10; Jas 5:11). Visited by Eliphaz, Bildad, and Zophar as comforters (Job 2:11-13). Complaints
of, and replies by his three friends (Job 3-37). Replied to
by God (Job 38-41). Submission of, to God (Job 40:3-5;
42:1-6). Later blessings and riches of (Job 42:10-16).
Death of (Job 42:16-17).

2. *See Jashub.*

JOB, BOOK OF

Author: Anonymous

Date: Anytime from the reign of Solomon to the Exile.

Outline:

I. Prologue (chs. 1-2).
  A. Job's Happiness (1:1-5).
  B. Job's Testing (1:6-2:13).
    1. Satan's first accusation (1:6-12).
    2. Job's faith despite loss of family and property (1:13-
22).
    3. Satan's second accusation (2:1-6).
    4. Job's faith during personal sufferings (2:7-10).
    5. The coming of the three friends (2:11-13).
II. Dialogue-Dispute (chs. 3-27).
  A. Job's Opening Lament (ch. 3).
  B. First Cycle of Speeches (chs. 4-14).
    1. Eliphaz (chs. 4-5).
    2. Job's reply (chs. 6-7).
    3. Bildad (ch. 8).
    4. Job's reply (chs. 9-10).
    5. Zophar (ch. 11).
    6. Job's reply (chs. 12-14).
  C. Second Cycle of Speeches (chs. 15-21).
    1. Eliphaz (ch. 15).
    2. Job's reply (chs. 16-17).
    3. Bildad (ch. 18).
    4. Job's reply (ch. 19).
    5. Zophar (ch. 20).
    6. Job's reply (ch. 21).
  D. Third Cycle of Speeches (chs. 22-26).
    1. Eliphaz (ch. 22).
    2. Job's reply (chs. 23-24).
    3. Bildad (ch. 25).
    4. Job's reply (ch. 26).
  E. Job's Closing Discourse (ch. 27).
III. Interlude on Wisdom (ch. 28).
IV. Monologues (29:1-42:6).
  A. Job's Call for Vindication (chs. 29-31).
    1. His past honor and blessing (ch. 29).
    2. His present dishonor and suffering (ch. 30).

3. His protestations of innocence and final oath (ch. 31).
B. Elihu's Speeches (chs. 32-37).
  1. Introduction (32:1-5).
  2. The speeches themselves (32:6-37:24).
    a. First speech (32:6-33:33).
    b. Second speech (ch. 34).
    c. Third speech (ch. 35).
    d. Fourth speech (chs. 36-37).
C. Divine Discourses (38:1-42:6).
  1. God's first discourse (38:1-40:2).
  2. Job's response (40:3-5).
  3. God's second discourse (40:6-41:34).
  4. Job's repentance (42:1-6).
V. Epilogue (42:7-17).
A. God's Verdict (42:7-9).
B. Job's Restoration (42:10-17).

JOBAB [3411, 3412] (*howl*).
  1. Son of Joktan (Ge 10:29; 1Ch 1:23).
  2. Second king of Edom (Ge 36:33; 1Ch 1:44-45).
  3. King of Madon (Jos 11:1; 12:19).
  4. Benjamite (1Ch 8:9).
  5. Benjamite (1Ch 9:18).

JOCHEBED [3425] (*Yahweh is glorious*). Mother of Miriam, Aaron, and Moses (Ex 6:20; Nu 26:59). Nurses Moses when he is adopted by Pharaoh's daughter (Ex 2:1-9).

JODA [3511]. An ancestor of Joseph, the father (so it was thought) of Jesus (Lk 3:26).

JOED [3444] (*Yahweh is witness*). A Benjamite (Ne 11:7).

JOEL [3408, 2727] (*Yahweh is God [El]*).
  1. Son of Samuel (1Sa 8:2; 1Ch 6:33; 15:17).
  2. A Simeonite (1Ch 4:35).
  3. A Reubenite (1Ch 5:4,8).
  4. A Gadite (1Ch 5:12).
  5. A Kohathite Levite (1Ch 6:36).
  6. Descendant of Issachar (1Ch 7:3).
  7. One of David's valiant men (1Ch 11:38). Called "Igal son of Nathan" (2Sa 23:36).
  8. Name of two Gershonites (1Ch 15:7,11; 23:8; 26:22).
  9. Prince of Manasseh (1Ch 27:20).
  10. A Kohathite who assisted in the cleansing of the temple (2Ch 29:12).
  11. One of Nebo's family (Ezr 10:43).
  12. Son of Zicri (Ne 11:9).
  13. One of the twelve minor prophets, probably lived in the days of Uzziah (Joel 1:1; Ac 2:16).

JOEL, BOOK OF

Author: Joel

Date: As early as the ninth century B.C. to as late as the postexilic period (sixth century), after Haggai and Zechariah. In either case, its message is not significantly affected by its dating.

Outline:
I. Title (1:1).
II. Judah Experiences a Foretaste of the Day of the Lord (1:2-2:17).
A. A Call to Mourning and Prayer (1:2-14).
B. The Announcement of the Day of the Lord (1:15-2:11).
C. A Call to Repentance and Prayer (2:12-17).

III. Judah Is Assured of Salvation in the Day of the Lord (2:18-3:21).
A. The Lord's Restoration of Judah (2:18-27).
B. The Lord's Renewal of His People (2:28-32).
C. The Coming of the Day of the Lord (ch. 3).
  1. The nations judged (3:1-16).
  2. God's people blessed (3:17-21).
See Prophets, The Minor.

JOELAH [3443] (*let him help*). One of David's recruits at Ziklag (1Ch 12:7).

JOEZER [3445] (*Yahweh is help*). A Korahite, who joined David at Ziklag (1Ch 12:6).

JOGBEHAH [3322] (*height*). City in Gilead assigned to Gad (Nu 32:35; Jdg 8:11).

JOGLI [3332] (perhaps *may God reveal*). A prince of Dan (Nu 34:22).

JOHA [3418].
  1. A Benjamite (1Ch 8:16).
  2. One of David's valiant men (1Ch 11:45).

JOHANAN [3419] (*Yahweh is gracious*).
  1. Jewish leader who tried to save Gedaliah from plot to murder him (Jer 40:13-14), took Jews, including Jeremiah, to Egypt (Jer 40-43).
  2. Son of King Josiah (1Ch 3:15).
  3. Son of Elioenai (1Ch 3:24).
  4. Father of Azariah, high priest in Solomon's time (1Ch 6:9-10).
  5. Benjamite; joined David at Ziklag (1Ch 12:4).
  6. Gadite; captain in David's army (1Ch 28:12,14).
  7. Ephraimite chief (2Ch 28:12).
  8. One of those who left Babylon with Ezra (Ezr 8:12).
  9. Son of Tobiah, who married a Jewess in days of Nehemiah (Ne 6:18).
  10. Son of Eliashib (Ezr 10:6).
  11. High priest, grandson of Eliashib (Ne 12:22).

JOHN [2722] (*Yahweh is gracious*).
NIV+ JOHN'S
  1. John the Baptist. *See John the Baptist.*
  2. The apostle, the son of Zebedee, and brother of James. *See John, the Apostle.*
  3. John Mark. *See Mark.*
  4. Father of Simon Peter (Jn 1:42; 21:15,17).
  5. Jewish religious dignitary who called Peter and John to account for their preaching about Jesus (Ac 4:6).
  6. Father of Mattathias (1Mc 2:1).
  7. Eldest son of Mattathias (1Mc 9:36).
  8. Father of Eupolemus (2Mc 4:11).
  9. John Hyrcanus, son of Simon (1Mc 13:53; 16:1).
  10. Jewish envoy (2Mc 11:17).

JOHN, 1, 2 and 3

Author: The Apostle John, son of Zebedee

Date: Between A.D. 85 and 95

Outline of 1 John:
I. Introduction: The Reality of the Incarnation (1:1-4).
II. The Christian Life as Fellowship with the Father and the Son (1:5-2:28).
A. Ethical Tests of Fellowship (1:5-2:11).
  1. Moral likeness (1:5-7).
  2. Confession of sin (1:8-2:2).
  3. Obedience (2:3-6).
  4. Love for fellow believers (2:7-11).

B. Two Digressions (2:12-17).

C. Christological Test of Fellowship (2:18-28).

  1. Contrast: apostates versus believers (2:18-21).

  2. Person of Christ: the crux of the test (2:22-23).

  3. Persistent belief: key to continuing fellowship (2:24-28).

III. The Christian Life as Divine Sonship (2:29-4:6).

A. Ethical Tests of Sonship (2:29-3:24).

  1. Righteousness (2:29-3:10a).

  2. Love (3:10b-24).

B. Christological Tests of Sonship (4:1-6).

IV. The Christian Life as an Integration of the Ethical and the Christological (4:7-5:12).

A. The Ethical Test: Love (4:7-5:5).

  1. The source of love (4:7-16).

  2. The fruit of love (4:17-19).

  3. The relationship of love for God and love for one's spiritual brother (4:20-5:1).

  4. Obedience: the evidence of love for God's children (5:2-5).

B. The Christological Test (5:6-12).

V. Conclusion: Great Christian Certainties (5:13-21).

  See General Letters.

Outline of 2 John:

I. Salutation (1-3).

II. Commendation (4).

III. Exhortation and Warning (5-11).

IV. Conclusion (12-13).

  See General Letters.

Outline of 3 John:

I. Salutation (1-2).

II. Commendation of Gaius (3-8).

III. Condemnation of Diotrephes (9-10).

IV. Exhortation to Gaius (11).

V. Example of Demetrius (12).

VI. Conclusion (13-14).

  See General Letters.

JOHN MARK *See Mark, John.*

JOHN, THE APOSTLE Son of Zebedee and Salome, and brother of James (Mt 4:21; 27:56; Mk 15:40; Ac 12:1-2), lived in Galilee, probably in Bethsaida (Lk 5:10; Jn 1:44), fisherman (Mk 1:19-20), became disciple of Jesus through John the Baptist (Jn 1:35), called as an apostle (Mk 1:19-20; Lk 5:10), one of three apostles closest to Jesus (the others were Peter and James), at raising of Jairus' daughter (Mk 5:37; Lk 8:51), transfiguration (Mt 17:1; Mk 9:2; Lk 9:28), Gethsemane (Mt 26:37; Mk 14:33), asked Jesus to call fire down on Samaritans, and given name Boanerges (sons of thunder) (Mk 3:17; Lk 9:54), mother requested that John and James be given places of special honor in coming kingdom (Mk 10:35), helped Peter prepare Passover (Lk 22:8), lay close to Jesus' breast at Last Supper (Jn 13:25), present at trial of Jesus (Jn 18:15-16), witnessed crucifixion of Jesus (Jn 19:26-27), recognized Jesus at Sea of Galilee (Jn 21:1-7), active with Peter in apostolic church (Ac 3:1-4:22; 8:14-17). Lived to an old age; fourth Gospel and Revelation attributed to him. *See John, 1, 2 and 3; John, the Gospel of; Revelation.*

JOHN THE BAPTIST Forerunner of Jesus; son of Zechariah and Elizabeth, both of priestly descent (Lk 1:5-25,56-58), lived as Nazirite in desert (Lk 1:15; Mt 11:12-14,18), began ministry beyond Jordan in the fifteenth year of Tiberias Caesar (Lk 3:1-3), preached baptism of repen-

tance in preparation of coming of Messiah (Lk 3:4-14), baptized Jesus (Mt 3:13-17; Mk 1:9-10; Lk 3:21; Jn 1:32), bore witness to Jesus as Messiah (Jn 1:24-42), imprisoned and put to death by Herod Antipas (Mt 14:6-12; Mk 6:17-28), praised by Jesus (Mt 11:7-14; Lk 7:24-28), disciples loyal to him long after his death (Ac 18:25).

JOHN, THE GOSPEL OF

Author: The apostle John, son of Zebedee

Date: Traditionally toward the end of the first century, c. A.D. 85 or later. More recently, some scholars have suggested a date as early as the 50s and no later than 70.

Outline:

I. Prologue (1:1-18).

II. Beginnings of Jesus' Ministry (1:19-51).

A. The Ministry of His Forerunner (1:19-34).

B. Jesus' Introduction to Some Future Disciples (1:35-51).

III. Jesus' Public Ministry: Signs and Discourses (chs. 2-11).

A. Changing Water to Wine (2:1-11).

B. Cleansing the Temple (2:12-25).

C. Interview with Nicodemus (3:1-21).

D. Parallel Ministry with John the Baptist (3:22-4:3).

E. Journey through Samaria: The Woman at the Well (4:4-42).

F. Healing of the Official's Son (4:43-54).

G. Trip to Jerusalem for an Annual Feast (ch. 5).

H. The Feeding of the 5,000 and the Sermon on the Bread of Life (ch. 6).

I. Jesus at the Feast of Tabernacles (chs. 7-8).

J. Healing of the Man Born Blind (ch. 9).

K. Parable of the Good Shepherd (10:1-21).

L. Debating at the Feast of Dedication (10:22-39).

M. Ministry in Perea (10:40-42).

N. The Raising of Lazarus (ch. 11).

IV. The Passion Week (chs. 12-19).

A. The Anointing of Jesus' Feet (12:1-11).

B. The Triumphal Entry (12:12-19).

C. The Coming of the Greeks (12:20-36).

D. Continued Jewish Unbelief (12:37-50).

E. Farewell Discourses (chs. 13-17).

  1. Discourse at the Last Supper (chs. 13-14).

  2. Discourse on the way to Gethsemane (chs. 15-16).

  3. Jesus' prayer of intercession (ch. 17).

F. Jesus' Betrayal and Arrest (18:1-12).

G. The Trials of Jesus (18:13-19:15).

H. The Crucifixion and Burial (19:16-42).

V. The Resurrection (20:1-29).

VI. The Statement of Purpose (20:30-31).

VII. Epilogue (ch. 21).

  See Synoptic Gospels, The.

JOIADA [3421] (*Yahweh knows*).

  1. Repaired walls of Jerusalem (Ne 3:6).

  2. Son of Eliashib (Ne 12:10; 13:28).

JOIAKIM [3423] (*Yahweh lifts up*). Father of Eliashib (Ne 12:10,12,26).

JOIARIB [3424] (*Yahweh contends, pleads [your case]*).

  NIV+ JOIARIB'S

  1. A returned exile (Ezr 8:16).

  2. A descendant of Judah (Ne 11:5).

  3. A priest who returned from Babylon (Ne 12:6,19).

  See Jehoiarib.

JOKDEAM [3680]. A city of Judah (Jos 15:56).

JOKIM [3451] (*Yahweh lifts up*). A descendant of Shelah (1Ch 4:22).

JOKMEAM [3695] (*let the people arise*). A Levitical city of Ephraim (1Ch 6:68).

JOKNEAM [3696]. A Levitical city of Zebulun (Jos 12:22; 19:11; 21:34).

     See Jokmeam.

JOKSHAN [3705]. Son of Abraham, by Keturah (Ge 25:2-3,6; 1Ch 1:32).

JOKTAN [3690] (*smaller*). Son of Eber (Ge 10:25-26,29; 1Ch 1:19-20,23).

JOKTHEEL [3706].

     1. A city of Judah (Jos 15:38).

     2. A name given by Amaziah to Sela, a stronghold of Edom (2Ki 14:7; 2Ch 25:11-12). *See Sela.*

JONA *See Jonah.*

JONADAB [3386, 3432] (*Yahweh is generous, noble*).

     1. The son of Shimeah, David's brother (2Sa 13:3). His complicity with Amnon in his rape of Tamar (2Sa 13:3-5). Comforts David on death of Amnon (2Sa 13:32-35).

     2. A Kenite who helped Jehu abolish Baal worship (temporarily) in Samaria (2Ki 10:15-27). *Jonadab* is spelled "Jehonadab" in this passage (2Ki 10:15-23). He was also a leader of a conservative movement that was characterized by various practices of a settled agricultural society, including the building of houses, the sowing of crops, and the use of wine. *See Nazirite(s), Nazarite(s).*

     His followers still adhered to these principles nearly 250 years later and were known as Recabites (Jer 35:5-10,16-19). *See Recabite(s).*

JONAH [3434, *980, 2731*] (*dove*).

     NIV+ JONAH'S

     Prophet of Israel; son of Amittai; predicted victory over Syria through Jeroboam II, who reigned c. 793-753 B.C.; author of book of Jonah (2Ki 14:25; Jnh 1:1).

JONAH, BOOK OF

Author: Traditionally the prophet Jonah himself,

Date: Before the fall of Samaria in B.C. 722-721.

Outline:

I. Jonah Flees His Mission (chs. 1-2).

     A. Jonah's Commission and Flight (1:1-3).

     B. The Endangered Sailors' Cry to Their Gods (1:4-6).

     C. Jonah's Disobedience Exposed (1:7-10).

     D. Jonah's Punishment and Deliverance (1:11-2:1; 2:10).

     E. Jonah's Prayer of Thanksgiving (2:2-9).

II. Jonah Reluctantly Fulfills His Mission (chs. 3-4).

     A. Jonah's Renewed Commission and Obedience (3:1-4).

     B. The Endangered Ninevites' Repentant Appeal to the Lord (3:5-9).

     C. The Ninevites' Repentance Acknowledged (3:10-4:4).

     D. Jonah's Deliverance and Rebuke (4:5-11).

     See Prophets, The Minor.

JONAM [2729] (*Yahweh is gracious*). An ancestor of Christ (Lk 3:30).

JONAN *See Jonam.*

JONAS

     1. *See Jonah.*

     2. *See John, 4.*

JONATH-ELEM-RECHOKIM, UPON NIV "To [the tune of] A Dove on Distant Oaks" (Ps 56:T). Probably the melody to which Ps 56 was sung. *See Music, Symbols Used in.*

JONATHAN [3387, 3440] (*gift of Yahweh*).

     NIV+ JONATHAN'S

     1. A Levite of Bethlehem, who becomes a priest for Micah, accepts idolatry, joins the Danites (Jdg 17:7-13; 18:1-30).

     2. Son of Saul (1Sa 14:49). Victory of, over the Philistine garrison of Geba (1Sa 13:3-4,16), over Philistines at Micmash (1Sa 14:1-18). Under Saul's curse pronounced against any who might take food before he was avenged of his enemies (1Sa 14:24-30,43). Rescued by the people (1Sa 14:43-45). Love of, for David (1Sa 18:1-4; 19:1-7; 20; 23:16-18). Killed in battle with Philistines (1Sa 31:2,6; 2Sa 21:12-14; 1Ch 10:2). Buried by inhabitants of Jabesh Gilead (1Sa 31:11-13). Mourned by David (2Sa 1:12,17-27). Son of, cared for by David (2Sa 4:4; 9; 1Ch 8:34).

     3. Son of Abiathar (2Sa 15:27). Acts as spy for David (2Sa 15:27-28; 17:17-22). Informs Adonijah of Solomon's succession to David (1Ki 1:42-48).

     4. Nephew of David, slays a giant and becomes one of David's chief warriors (2Sa 21:21; 1Ch 20:7).

     5. One of David's heroes (2Sa 23:32; 1Ch 11:34).

     6. A son of Jada (1Ch 2:32-33).

     7. Secretary of the cabinet of David (1Ch 27:32).

     8. Father of Ebed (Ezr 8:6).

     9. Son of Asahel (Ezr 10:15).

     10. Also called Johanan. A descendant of Jeshua (Ne 12:11-12).

     11. Name of two priests (Ne 12:14,35).

     12. A scribe (Jer 37:15,20; 38:26).

     13. Son of Kareah (Jer 40:8).

JOPPA [3639, *2673*] (*beautiful*). An ancient walled town on coast of Israel, c. thirty-five miles NW of Jerusalem; assigned to Dan; mentioned in Amarna letters; seaport for Jerusalem.

     In NT times Peter raised Dorcas to life there (Ac 9:36ff) and received the vision of a sheet filled with animals (Ac 10:1ff; 11:5ff). Modern Jaffa.

JORAH [3454] (*one born during harvest*). Family which returned with Zerubbabel (Ezr 2:18). Also called Hariph (Ne 7:24).

JORAI [3455] (possibly *Yahweh sees* IDB; *whom Yahweh teaches* ISBE). A Gadite (1Ch 5:13).

JORAM [3393, 3456] (*Yahweh is exalted*). Same as longer form Jehoram.

     1. Son of king of Hamath (2Sa 8:10).

     2. Levite (1Ch 26:25).

     3. Son of Ahab, king of Israel (2Ki 8:29).

     4. King of Judah (2Ki 8:21-24; 11:2; 1Ch 3:11; Mt 1:8).

     5. Priest (2Ch 17:8).

JORDAN, VALLEY OF, PLAINS OF, RIVER OF [3720, *2674*] (*river of descent*).

     NIV+ JORDAN'S

     A river in Israel. Empties into the Dead Sea (Jos 15:5).

Fords of (Ge 32:10; Jos 2:7; Jdg 3:28; 7:24; 8:4; 10:9; 12:5-6; 2Sa 2:29; 17:22,24; 19:15,31; 1Ch 19:17). Swelling of, at harvest time (Jos 3:15; Jer 12:5), and in the early spring (1Ch 12:15). The waters of, miraculously separated for the passage of the Israelites (Jos 3; 4; 5:1; Ps 114:3), of Elijah (2Ki 2:6-8), of Elisha (2Ki 2:14). Crossed at a ford (2Sa 19:18). Naaman washes in, for the healing of his leprosy (2Ki 5:10-14). John the Baptist baptizes in (Mt 3:6; Mk 1:5), baptizes Jesus in (Mt 3:13; Mk 1:19).

Plain of:

(Ge 13:10-12). Israelites camped in (Nu 22:1; 26:3,63). Solomon's foundry in (1Ki 7:46; 2Ch 4:17).

JORIM [2733]. An ancestor of Jesus (Lk 3:29).

JORKEAM, JORKOAM [3767]. Descendant of Caleb (1Ch 2:44).

JOSABAD See Jozabad, 1.

JOSAPHAT See Jehoshaphat.

JOSE See Joshua, 5.

JOSECH [2738]. Father of Semein (Lk 3:26).

JOSEDECH See Jozadak.

JOSEPH [3388, 3441, 2736, 2737] (he will add).
NIV+ JOSEPH'S

1. Son of Jacob (Ge 30:24). Personal appearance of (Ge 39:6). His favorite child (Ge 33:2; 37:3-4,35; 48:22; 1Ch 5:2; Jn 4:5). His father's partiality for, excites the jealousy of his brothers (Ge 37:4,11,18-28; Ps 105:17; Ac 7:9). His prophetic dreams of his fortunes in Egypt (Ge 37:5-11). Sold into Egypt (Ge 37:27-28). Is falsely reported to his father as killed by wild beasts (Ge 37:29-35). Is bought by Potiphar, an officer of Pharaoh (Ge 37:36). Is prospered of God (Ge 39:2-5,21,23). Is falsely accused, and cast into prison; is delivered by the friendship of another prisoner (Ge 39; 40; Ps 105:18). Is an interpreter of dreams: of the two prisoners (Ge 40:5-23); of Pharaoh (Ge 41:1-37). His name is changed to Zaphenath-Paneah (Ge 41:45). Is promoted to authority next to Pharaoh at thirty years of age (Ge 41:37-46; Ps 105:19-22). Takes as his wife the daughter of the priest of On (Ge 41:45). Provides against the years of famine (Ge 41:46-57). Exports the produce of Egypt to other countries (Ge 41:57). Sells the stores of food to the people of Egypt, exacting of them all their money, flocks and herds, lands and lives (Ge 47:13-26). Exempts the priests from the exactions (Ge 47:22,26).

His father sends down into Egypt to buy grain (Ge 42-44). Reveals himself to his brothers, sends for his father, provides the land of Goshen for his people, and sustains them during the famine (Ge 45; 46; 47:1-12). His two sons (Ge 41:50,52; Dt 33:13-17). See Ephraim; Manasseh, 1. Mourns the death of his father (Ge 50:1-14). Exacts a pledge from his brothers to convey his remains to Canaan (Ge 50:24-25; Heb 11:22, w Ex 13:19; Jos 24:32; Ac 7:16). Death of (Ge 50:22-26).

Kindness of heart (Ge 40:7-8). His integrity (Ge 39:7-12), humility (Ge 41:16; 45:7-9), wisdom (Ge 41:33-57), piety (Ge 41:51-52), faith (Ge 45:5-8). Was a prophet (Ge 41:38-39; 50:25; Ex 13:19). God's providence with (Ge 39:2-5; Ps 105:17-22). Descendants of (Ge 46:20; Nu 26:28-37).

2. Father of Igal the spy (Nu 13:7).

3. Of the sons of Asaph (1Ch 25:2,9).

4. A returned exile (Ezr 10:42).

5. A priest (Ne 12:14).

6. Husband of Mary (Mt 13:55; Mk 6:3; Mt 1:18-25; Lk 1:27). His genealogy (Mt 1:1-16; Lk 3:23-38). An angel appears and testifies to the innocency of his betrothed (Mt 1:19-24). Lives at Nazareth (Lk 2:4). Belongs to the city of Bethlehem (Lk 2:4). Goes to Bethlehem to be enrolled (Lk 2:1-4). Jesus born to (Mt 1:25; Lk 2:7). Presents Jesus in the temple (Lk 2:22-39). Returns to Nazareth (Lk 2:39). Warned in a dream to escape to Egypt in order to save the child's life (Mt 2:13-15). Warned in a dream to return to Nazareth (Mt 2:19-23). Attends the annual feast at Jerusalem with his family (Lk 2:42-51).

7. Of Arimathea. Requests the body of Jesus for burial in his own tomb (Mt 27:57-60; Mk 15:42-47; Lk 23:50-56; Jn 19:38-42).

8. Three ancestors of Joseph, 6 (Lk 3:24,26,30).

9. One of the brothers of Jesus (Mt 13:55; Mk 6:3).

10. Also called Barsabbas and Justus. One of the two persons nominated in place of Judas (Ac 1:21-23).

11. A Levite, called Barnabas by the apostles (Ac 4:36). See Barnabas.

12. A designation of the ten tribes of Israel (Am 5:6).

JOSES [2736].

1. Son of Mary, 2; brother of the younger James (Mt 27:56; Mk 15:40,47).

2. See Joseph, 9.

3. See Joseph, 11.

JOSHAH [3459] (gift of Yahweh). A descendant of Simeon (1Ch 4:34).

JOSHAPHAT [3461] (Yahweh judges).

1. One of David's mighty men (1Ch 11:43).

2. Priest (1Ch 15:24).

JOSHAVIAH [3460] (Yahweh places). One of David's bodyguards (1Ch 11:46).

JOSHBEKASHAH, JOSHBAKASHAH [3792] (one sitting in request [prayer?]). Leader of the seventeenth course of musicians (1Ch 25:4,24).

JOSHEB-BASSHEBETH [3783] (one sitting in the seat). A Tahkemonite, who was the chief of the Three; one of David's mighty men (2Sa 23:8). This is probably a corruption of Jashobeam, a Hacmonite (1Ch 11:11).

JOSHIBIAH, JOSIBIAH [3458] (Yahweh places). A Simeonite (1Ch 4:35).

JOSHUA [2107, 3397, 3800, 2652] (Yahweh saves).
NIV+ HOSHEA

1. Also called Hoshea (Nu 13:8). Son of Nun (1Ch 7:27). Intimately associated with Moses (Ex 24:13; 32:17; 33:11). A religious zealot (Nu 11:28). Sent with others to view the promised land (Nu 13:8). Makes favorable report (Nu 14:6-10). Rewarded for his courage and fidelity (Nu 14:30,38; 32:12). Commissioned, ordained, and charged with the responsibilities of Moses' office (Nu 27:18-23; Dt 1:38; 3:28; 31:3,7,23; 34:9). Divinely inspired (Nu 27:18; Dt 34:9; Jos 1:5,9; 3:7; 8:8). His life miraculously preserved when he made a favorable report of the land (Nu 14:10). Promises to (Jos 1:5-9). Leads the people into the land of Canaan (Jos 1-4; Ac 7:45; Heb 4:8). Renews circumcision of the Israelites; reestablishes the Passover; has a vision of the angel of God (Jos 5). Besieges and takes Jericho (Jos 6). Takes Ai (Jos 7-8). Makes a league with the Gibeonites (Jos 9:3-27). The kings of the six nations of

the Canaanites confederate against him (Jos 9:1-2), make war upon the Gibeonites, are defeated and slain (Jos 10). Defeats seven other kings (Jos 10:28-43). Makes conquest of Hazor (Jos 11). Completes the conquest of the whole land (Jos 11:23). List of the kings whom Joshua killed (Jos 12). Allots the land (Jos 13-19). Sets the tabernacle up in Shiloh (Jos 18:1). Sets apart cities of refuge (Jos 20), forty-eight cities for the Levites (Jos 21). Exhortation of, before his death (Jos 23-24). Survives the Israelites who refused to enter Canaan (Nu 26:63-65). His portion of the land (Jos 19:49-50). Death and burial of (Jos 24:29-30). Esteem in which he was held (Jos 1:16-18). Faith of (Jos 6:16). Military genius of, as exhibited at the defeat of the Amalekites (Ex 17:13), at Ai (Jos 8), in Gibeon (Jos 10), at Hazor (Jos 11). Age of, at death (Jdg 2:8).

2. An Israelite (1Sa 6:14,18).

3. A governor of Jerusalem (2Ki 23:8).

4. The postexilic high priest. *See Jeshua, 3.*

5. An ancestor of Jesus (Lk 3:29).

JOSHUA, BOOK OF

Author: Traditionally Joshua the son of Nun

Date: Traditionally before 1375 B.C.

Outline:

I. The Entrance into the Land (1:1-5:12).
 A. The Exhortations to Conquer (ch. 1).
 B. The Reconnaissance of Jericho (ch. 2).
 C. The Crossing of the Jordan (chs. 3-4).
 D. The Consecration at Gilgal (5:1-12).
II. The Conquest of the Land (5:13-12:24).
 A. The Initial Battles (5:13-8:35).
  1. The victory at Jericho (5:13-6:27).
  2. The failure at Ai because of Achan's sin (ch. 7).
  3. The victory at Ai (8:1-29).
  4. The covenant renewed at Shechem (8:30-35).
 B. The Campaign in the South (chs. 9-10).
  1. The treaty with the Gibeonites (ch. 9).
  2. The long day of Joshua (10:1-15).
  3. The southern cities conquered (10:16-43).
 C. The Campaign in the North (ch. 11).
 D. The Defeated Kings of Canaan (ch. 12).
III. The Distribution of the Land (chs. 13-21).
 A. Areas Yet to Be Conquered (13:1-7).
 B. The Land East of the Jordan for Reuben, Gad and Half of Manasseh (13:8-33).
 C. The Lands Given to Judah and "Joseph" at Gilgal (chs. 14-17).
 D. The Lands Given to the Remaining Tribes at Shiloh (chs. 18-19).
  1. The tabernacle at Shiloh (18:1-10).
  2. The allotments for Benjamin, Simeon, Zebulun, Issachar, Asher, Naphtali, and Dan (18:1-10).
  3. The town given to Joshua (19:49-51).
 E. The Cities Assigned to the Levites (chs. 20-21).
  1. The six cities of refuge (ch. 20).
  2. The forty-eight cities of the priests (ch. 21).
IV. Epilogue: Tribal Unity and Loyalty to the Lord (chs. 22-24).
 A. The Altar of Witness by the Jordan (ch. 22).
 B. Joshua's Farewell Exhortation (ch. 23).
 C. The Renewal of the Covenant at Shechem (24:1-28).
 D. The Death and Burial of Joshua and Eleazar (24:29-33).

JOSIAH [3287, 3288, *2739*] (*let or may Yahweh give*).
NIV+ JOSIAH'S

1. King of Judah (2Ki 21:24-26; 22:1; 1Ch 3:14; 2Ch 33:25). Ancestor of Jesus (Mt 1:10-11). Slain in battle with Pharaoh Neco (2Ki 23:29-30; 2Ch 35:20-24). Lamentations for (2Ch 35:25). Piety of, exemplified in his repairing the temple (2Ki 22:3-7; 2Ch 34:1-4). Anxiety, when the copy of the law was discovered and read to him (2Ki 22:8-20; 2Ch 34:14-33), in keeping a solemn Passover (2Ki 23:21-23; 2Ch 35:1-19). Prophecies concerning (1Ki 13:1-3). Destroys the altar and high places of idolatry (2Ki 23:3-20,24-25).

2. Son of Zephaniah (Zec 6:10).

JOSIAS *See Josiah.*

JOSIPHIAH [3442] (*Yahweh will add*). Ancestor of family which returned with Ezra (Ezr 8:10).

JOT NIV "the smallest letter" of the Hebrew alphabet (Mt 5:17-18). Used figuratively to emphasize the importance of the smallest details of the law.

JOTBAH [3513] (*good, pleasant*). A place in Judah (2Ki 21:19). Possibly the same as Jotbathah (Dt 10:7).

JOTBATHAH, JOTBATH [3514] (*good, pleasant*). The twentieth encampment of Israel (Nu 33:33-34; Dt 10:7). Possibly the same as Jotbah (2Ki 21:19).

JOTHAM [3462, *2718*] (*Yahweh will complete*).
NIV+ JOTHAM'S

1. Son of Gideon; speaker of the first Bible parable (Jdg 9:5-57).

2. Judahite (1Ch 2:47).

3. Eleventh king of Judah; son of Uzziah, whose regent he was for a time; successful, righteous king (2Ki 15:5-38; 2Ch 27); contemporary of Isaiah (Isa 1:1), Hosea (Hos 1:1), Micah (Mic 1:1), ancestor of Jesus (Mt 1:9).

JOURNEY, SABBATH DAY'S [*2006, 5023, 6296, *623, 3847, 4636*].
NIV+ JOURNEYED, JOURNEYS

Three thousand feet (Ac 1:12).

JOY [*5375, 8131, 8523, 8525, 8262, 8264, 8607, 9558, *5897, 5915*].
NIV+ ENJOY, ENJOYED, ENJOYING, ENJOYMENT, ENJOYS, JOYFUL, JOYOUS, JOYFULLY, OVERJOYED, REJOICE, REJOICED, REJOICES, REJOICING

Ps 30:5 For his anger lasts only a moment, but his favor lasts a lifetime; weeping may remain for a night, but rejoicing comes in the morning.

Ps 30:11 You turned my wailing into dancing; you removed my sackcloth and clothed me with joy,

Ps 33:21 In him our hearts rejoice, for we trust in his holy name.

Ps 97:11 Light is shed upon the righteous and joy on the upright in heart.

Ps 132:16 I will clothe her priests with salvation, and her saints will ever sing for joy.

Pr 29:6 An evil man is snared by his own sin, but a righteous one can sing and be glad.

From God:

Ecc 2:26 To the man who pleases him, God gives wisdom, knowledge and happiness, but to the sinner he gives the task of gathering and storing up wealth to hand it over to the one who pleases God. This too is meaningless, a chasing after the wind.

Ro 15:13 May the God of hope fill you with all joy and peace as you trust in him, so that you may overflow with hope by the power of the Holy Spirit.

In the Lord—

Ps 9:2 I will be glad and rejoice in you; I will sing praise to your name, O Most High.

Ps 104:34 May my meditation be pleasing to him, as I rejoice in the LORD.

Isa 9:3 You have enlarged the nation and increased their joy; they rejoice before you as people rejoice at the harvest, as men rejoice when dividing the plunder.

Isa 29:19 Once more the humble will rejoice in the LORD; the needy will rejoice in the Holy One of Israel.

Isa 41:16 You will winnow them, the wind will pick them up, and a gale will blow them away. But you will rejoice in the LORD and glory in the Holy One of Israel.

Isa 61:10 I delight greatly in the LORD; my soul rejoices in my God. For he has clothed me with garments of salvation and arrayed me in a robe of righteousness, as a bridegroom adorns his head like a priest, and as a bride adorns herself with her jewels.

Lk 1:47 and my spirit rejoices in God my Savior,

Ro 5:11 Not only is this so, but we also rejoice in God through our Lord Jesus Christ, through whom we have now received reconciliation.

In Christ—

Php 3:3 For it is we who are the circumcision, we who worship by the Spirit of God, who glory in Christ Jesus, and who put no confidence in the flesh—

Php 4:4 Rejoice in the Lord always. I will say it again: Rejoice!

1Pe 1:8 Though you have not seen him, you love him; and even though you do not see him now, you believe in him and are filled with an inexpressible and glorious joy,

In the word of God—

Ps 19:8 The precepts of the LORD are right, giving joy to the heart. The commands of the LORD are radiant, giving light to the eyes.

Ps 119:14 I rejoice in following your statutes as one rejoices in great riches.

Ps 119:16 I delight in your decrees; I will not neglect your word.

Ps 119:111 Your statutes are my heritage forever; they are the joy of my heart.

Ps 119:162 I rejoice in your promise like one who finds great spoil.

Jer 15:16 When your words came, I ate them; they were my joy and my heart's delight, for I bear your name, O LORD God Almighty.

In worship—

2Ch 7:10 On the twenty-third day of the seventh month he sent the people to their homes, joyful and glad in heart for the good things the LORD had done for David and Solomon and for his people Israel.

Ezr 6:22 For seven days they celebrated with joy the Feast of Unleavened Bread, because the LORD had filled them with joy by changing the attitude of the king of Assyria, so that he assisted them in the work on the house of God, the God of Israel.

Ne 12:43 And on that day they offered great sacrifices, rejoicing because God had given them great joy. The women and children also rejoiced. The sound of rejoicing in Jerusalem could be heard far away.

Ps 42:4 These things I remember as I pour out my soul: how I used to go with the multitude, leading the procession to the house of God, with shouts of joy and thanksgiving among the festive throng.

Ps 43:4 Then will I go to the altar of God, to God, my joy and my delight. I will praise you with the harp, O God, my God.

Ps 71:23 My lips will shout for joy when I sing praise to you—I, whom you have redeemed. (+Isa 56:7)

Zep 3:14 Sing, O Daughter of Zion; shout aloud, O Israel! Be glad and rejoice with all your heart, O Daughter of Jerusalem!

Zec 2:10 "Shout and be glad, O Daughter of Zion. For I am coming, and I will live among you," declares the LORD.

Zec 9:9 Rejoice greatly, O Daughter of Zion! Shout, Daughter of Jerusalem! See, your king comes to you, righteous and having salvation, gentle and riding on a donkey, on a colt, the foal of a donkey.

A fruit of the Spirit—

Gal 5:22 But the fruit of the Spirit is love, joy, peace, patience, kindness, goodness, faithfulness,

Eph 5:18 Do not get drunk on wine, which leads to debauchery. Instead, be filled with the Spirit. ¹⁹Speak to one another with psalms, hymns and spiritual songs. Sing and make music in your heart to the Lord,

For salvation—

Ps 13:5 But I trust in your unfailing love; my heart rejoices in your salvation.

Ps 20:5 We will shout for joy when you are victorious and will lift up our banners in the name of our God. May the LORD grant all your requests.

Ps 21:1 O LORD, the king rejoices in your strength. How great is his joy in the victories you give!

Ps 21:6 Surely you have granted him eternal blessings and made him glad with the joy of your presence.

Ps 35:9 Then my soul will rejoice in the LORD and delight in his salvation.

Isa 12:2 Surely God is my salvation; I will trust and not be afraid. The LORD, the LORD, is my strength and my song; he has become my salvation." ³With joy you will draw water from the wells of salvation.

Isa 25:9 In that day they will say, "Surely this is our God; we trusted in him, and he saved us. This is the LORD, we trusted in him; let us rejoice and be glad in his salvation."

Isa 35:1 The desert and the parched land will be glad; the wilderness will rejoice and blossom. Like the crocus, ²it will burst into bloom; it will rejoice greatly and shout for joy. The glory of Lebanon will be given to it, the splendor of Carmel and Sharon; they will see the glory of the LORD, the splendor of our God.

Isa 35:10 and the ransomed of the LORD will return. They will enter Zion with singing; everlasting joy will crown their heads. Gladness and joy will overtake them, and sorrow and sighing will flee away.

Isa 55:12 You will go out in joy and be led forth in peace; the mountains and hills will burst into song before you, and all the trees of the field will clap their hands.

Ro 5:2 through whom we have gained access by faith into this grace in which we now stand. And we rejoice in the hope of the glory of God.

Ro 14:17 For the kingdom of God is not a matter of eating and drinking, but of righteousness, peace and joy in the Holy Spirit,

On account of a good conscience—

2Co 1:12 Now this is our boast: Our conscience testifies that we have conducted ourselves in the world, and especially in our relations with you, in the holiness and sincerity that are from God. We have done so not according to worldly wisdom but according to God's grace.

Over a sinner's repentance—

Lk 15:6 and goes home. Then he calls his friends and neighbors together and says, 'Rejoice with me; I have found my lost sheep.' [7]I tell you that in the same way there will be more rejoicing in heaven over one sinner who repents than over ninety-nine righteous persons who do not need to repent.

[8]"Or suppose a woman has ten silver coins and loses one. Does she not light a lamp, sweep the house and search carefully until she finds it? (+Lk 15:9)

Lk 15:10 In the same way, I tell you, there is rejoicing in the presence of the angels of God over one sinner who repents."

Lk 15:22 "But the father said to his servants, 'Quick! Bring the best robe and put it on him. Put a ring on his finger and sandals on his feet. [23]Bring the fattened calf and kill it. Let's have a feast and celebrate. [24]For this son of mine was dead and is alive again; he was lost and is found.' So they began to celebrate.

[25]"Meanwhile, the older son was in the field. When he came near the house, he heard music and dancing. [26]So he called one of the servants and asked him what was going on. [27]'Your brother has come,' he replied, 'and your father has killed the fattened calf because he has him back safe and sound.'

[28]"The older brother became angry and refused to go in. So his father went out and pleaded with him. [29]But he answered his father, 'Look! All these years I've been slaving for you and never disobeyed your orders. Yet you never gave me even a young goat so I could celebrate with my friends. [30]But when this son of yours who has squandered your property with prostitutes comes home, you kill the fattened calf for him!'

[31]"'My son,' the father said, 'you are always with me, and everything I have is yours. [32]But we had to celebrate and be glad, because this brother of yours was dead and is alive again; he was lost and is found.'"

Under adversity—

Ps 126:5 Those who sow in tears will reap with songs of joy. [6]He who goes out weeping, carrying seed to sow, will return with songs of joy, carrying sheaves with him.

Isa 61:3 and provide for those who grieve in Zion—to bestow on them a crown of beauty instead of ashes, the oil of gladness instead of mourning, and a garment of praise instead of a spirit of despair. They will be called oaks of righteousness, a planting of the LORD for the display of his splendor. (+Mt 5:12; Ac 5:41)

2Co 6:10 sorrowful, yet always rejoicing; poor, yet making many rich; having nothing, and yet possessing everything.

2Co 7:4 I have great confidence in you; I take great pride in you. I am greatly encouraged; in all our troubles my joy knows no bounds.

2Co 8:2 Out of the most severe trial, their overflowing joy and their extreme poverty welled up in rich generosity.

2Co 12:10 That is why, for Christ's sake, I delight in weaknesses, in insults, in hardships, in persecutions, in difficulties. For when I am weak, then I am strong.

Col 1:11 being strengthened with all power according to his glorious might so that you may have great endurance and patience, and joyfully

1Th 1:6 You became imitators of us and of the Lord; in spite of severe suffering, you welcomed the message with the joy given by the Holy Spirit.

Heb 10:34 You sympathized with those in prison and joyfully accepted the confiscation of your property, because you knew that you yourselves had better and lasting possessions.

Jas 1:2 Consider it pure joy, my brothers, whenever you face trials of many kinds,

1Pe 4:13 But rejoice that you participate in the sufferings of Christ, so that you may be overjoyed when his glory is revealed.

Fullness of—

Ps 16:11 You have made known to me the path of life; you will fill me with joy in your presence, with eternal pleasures at your right hand.

Ps 36:8 They feast on the abundance of your house; you give them drink from your river of delights.

Ps 63:5 My soul will be satisfied as with the richest of foods; with singing lips my mouth will praise you.

Jn 15:11 I have told you this so that my joy may be in you and that your joy may be complete.

Jn 16:24 Until now you have not asked for anything in my name. Ask and you will receive, and your joy will be complete.

Ac 2:28 You have made known to me the paths of life; you will fill me with joy in your presence.'

1Jn 1:4 We write this to make our joy complete.

Everlasting—

Isa 51:11 The ransomed of the LORD will return. They will enter Zion with singing; everlasting joy will crown their heads. Gladness and joy will overtake them, and sorrow and sighing will flee away.

Isa 61:7 Instead of their shame my people will receive a double portion, and instead of disgrace they will rejoice in their inheritance; and so they will inherit a double portion in their land, and everlasting joy will be theirs.

In heaven—

Mt 25:21 "His master replied, 'Well done, good and faithful servant! You have been faithful with a few things; I will put you in charge of many things. Come and share your master's happiness!' (+Lk 15:7,10)

Attributed to God (Dt 28:63; 30:9; Jer 32:41).

Commanded:

Dt 12:18 Instead, you are to eat them in the presence of the LORD your God at the place the LORD your God will choose—you, your sons and daughters, your menservants and maidservants, and the Levites from your towns—and you are to rejoice before the LORD your God in everything you put your hand to. (+Ne 8:10)

Ps 2:11 Serve the LORD with fear and rejoice with trembling.

Ps 5:11 But let all who take refuge in you be glad; let them ever sing for joy. Spread your protection over them, that those who love your name may rejoice in you.

Ps 32:11 Rejoice in the LORD and be glad, you righteous; sing, all you who are upright in heart!

Ps 68:3 But may the righteous be glad and rejoice before God; may they be happy and joyful.

Ps 97:12 Rejoice in the LORD, you who are righteous, and praise his holy name.

Ps 100:1 Shout for joy to the LORD, all the earth. [2]Worship the LORD with gladness; come before him with joyful songs.

Ps 105:3 Glory in his holy name; let the hearts of those who seek the LORD rejoice.

Ps 105:43 He brought out his people with rejoicing, his chosen ones with shouts of joy;

Ps 149:2 Let Israel rejoice in their Maker; let the people of Zion be glad in their King.

Ps 149:5 Let the saints rejoice in this honor and sing for joy on their beds.

Joel 2:23 Be glad, O people of Zion, rejoice in the LORD your God, for he has given you the autumn rains in righteousness. He sends you abundant showers, both autumn and spring rains, as before.

Lk 2:10 But the angel said to them, "Do not be afraid. I bring you good news of great joy that will be for all the people.

Lk 6:23 "Rejoice in that day and leap for joy, because great is your reward in heaven. For that is how their fathers treated the prophets.

Lk 10:20 However, do not rejoice that the spirits submit to you, but rejoice that your names are written in heaven."

Ro 12:12 Be joyful in hope, patient in affliction, faithful in prayer.

1Th 5:16 Be joyful always;

Instances of:

Of Moses and the Israelites, when Pharaoh and his army were destroyed (Ex 15:1-22). Of Deborah and the Israelites, when Sisera was overthrown (Jdg 5). Of Jephthah's daughter, when he returned from his victory over the Ammonites (Jdg 11:34).

Of Hannah, when Samuel was born—

1Sa 2:1 Then Hannah prayed and said: "My heart rejoices in the LORD; in the LORD my horn is lifted high. My mouth boasts over my enemies, for I delight in your deliverance. (+1Sa 2:2-11)

Of Naomi, when Boaz showed kindness to Ruth (Ru 2:20; 4:14).—

Of the Israelites: When Saul was presented as their king (1Sa 10:24), when David killed Goliath (1Sa 18:6-7), when they repaired to David to Hebron to make him king (1Ch 12:40), when they took the ark from Kiriath Jearim (1Ch 13:8), when they brought the ark from the house of Obed-Edom to Jerusalem (1Ch 15:16,25,28), when they made gifts to the house of God (1Ch 29:9), when they kept the dedication of the temple, and the feast of tabernacles under Ezra (Ezr 6:16,22).

Of the Jews, after hearing again the word of God (Ne 8:9)—

Ne 8:10 Nehemiah said, "Go and enjoy choice food and sweet drinks, and send some to those who have nothing prepared. This day is sacred to our Lord. Do not grieve, for the joy of the LORD is your strength." (+Ne 8:11)

Ne 8:12 Then all the people went away to eat and drink, to send portions of food and to celebrate with great joy, because they now understood the words that had been made known to them. (+Ne 8:13-18)

When they turned away from idolatry (2Ch 15:14-15; 23:18,21; 29:30,36; 30:21,23,26), when the wall of Jerusalem was dedicated (Ne 12:43), when the foundation of the second temple was laid (Ezr 3:11-13).

Of David, over the offerings of the princes and people for the house of God (1Ch 29:10-19). Jews, over the hanging of Haman (Est 8:15-16, w Est 7:10).

Of Elizabeth, when Mary visited he (Lk 1:5-44). Of Mary, when she visited Elizabeth (Lk 1:46-56). Of Zechariah, when John was born (Lk 1:67-79). Of angels, when Jesus was born (Lk 2:13-14). Of the shepherds when they saw the infant Jesus (Lk 2:20). Of the Magi (Mt 2:10). Of Simeon, when Jesus was presented in the temple (Lk 2:28-32). Of the disciples, because the demons were sub-

ject to them (Lk 10:17). Of the father, when his prodigal son returns (Lk 15:20-32). Of angels, when sinners repent (Lk 15:7,10). Of the disciples, when Jesus triumphantly entered Jerusalem (Mt 21:8-9; Mk 11:8-9; Mk 11:8-10). Of the women who returned from the Lord's tomb (Mt 28:8). The disciples, after the resurrection of Jesus (Lk 24:41).

Of the disciples in the temple after the Ascension of Jesus—

Lk 24:53 And they stayed continually at the temple, praising God.

Of the disciples in the temple because they had received the gift of the Holy Spirit (Ac 2:46-47). Of the crippled man, healed by Peter (Ac 3:8). Of Paul, when he went up to Jerusalem (Ac 20:22-24).

Of Paul and Silas, in the jail at Philippi—

Ac 16:25 About midnight Paul and Silas were praying and singing hymns to God, and the other prisoners were listening to them.

Of Rhoda, when she heard Peter at the gate (Ac 12:14). Of the disciples at Jerusalem, when Peter told them about the conversion of Cornelius and other Gentiles (Ac 11:18). Of Barnabas, when he saw the success of the gospel at Antioch (Ac 11:22-23).

Of Paul and the Corinthians, because the excommunicated member repented—

2Co 1:24 Not that we lord it over your faith, but we work with you for your joy, because it is by faith you stand firm. (+2Co 2:3)

Of Paul and Titus, because of the hospitality of the Corinthians (Ro 15:32; 1Co 16:18 2Co 7:13, w 2Co 8:6). Of the Macedonians, when he prayed for the Philippians (Php 1:4). Of Thessalonians, when they believed Paul's gospel (1Th 1:6). Of Paul, rejoicing over his converts (1Th 2:19-20; 3:9; Phm 7). Of early Christians, when they believed in Jesus (1Pe 1:8-9).

See Happiness; Praise; Thanksgiving.

Of the Wicked:

Short—

Job 20:5 that the mirth of the wicked is brief, the joy of the godless lasts but a moment.

Meaningless—

Ecc 2:10 I denied myself nothing my eyes desired; I refused my heart no pleasure. My heart took delight in all my work, and this was the reward for all my labor.

Ecc 7:6 Like the crackling of thorns under the pot, so is the laughter of fools. This too is meaningless.

Ecc 11:8 However many years a man may live, let him enjoy them all. But let him remember the days of darkness, for they will be many. Everything to come is meaningless.

⁹Be happy, young man, while you are young, and let your heart give you joy in the days of your youth. Follow the ways of your heart and whatever your eyes see, but know that for all these things God will bring you to judgment.

Shallow—

Pr 14:13 Even in laughter the heart may ache, and joy may end in grief.

Pr 15:21 Folly delights a man who lacks judgment, but a man of understanding keeps a straight course.

Overshadowed by impending judgment and sorrow (Pr 14:13; Ecc 11:8-9)—

Isa 16:10 Joy and gladness are taken away from the orchards; no one sings or shouts in the vineyards; no one treads out wine at the presses, for I have put an end to the shouting. (+Jas 4:10)

JOZABAD [3416] (*Yahweh bestowed*).

1. One of the two servants of Joash, who killed him in Millo (2Ki 12:21).
2. Gederathite; joined David at Ziklag (1Ch 12:4).
3. Two Manassites who also joined David (1Ch 12:20).
4. Levites (2Ch 31:13).
5. Chief Levite (2Ch 35:9).
6. Levite who assisted Ezra (Ezr 8:33).
7. Man who put foreign wife away (Ezr 10:22).
8. Another such man (Ezr 10:23).
9. Levite who helped Nehemiah (Ne 8:7).
10. Chief Levite in Nehemiah's time (Ne 11:16).

JOZACHAR (*Yahweh remembered*). *See Jehozabad, 1; Jozabad, 1; Zabad, 4.*

JOZADAK [3449, 10318] (*Yahweh is righteous*).
Father of Jeshua the high priest who returned with Zerubbabel (Ezr 3:2,8; 5:2; 10:18; Ne 12:26). Called Jehozadak in Haggai and Zechariah. *See Jehozadak.*

JUBAL [3415]. Son of Lamech. Inventor of harp and flute (Ge 4:21).

JUBILEE [3413].
Called:
Year of the Lord's favor (Isa 61:2). The year of freedom (Eze 46:17).

Laws concerning:
Lev 25:8 "'Count off seven sabbaths of years—seven times seven years—so that the seven sabbaths of years amount to a period of forty-nine years. 9Then have the trumpet sounded everywhere on the tenth day of the seventh month; on the Day of Atonement sound the trumpet throughout your land. 10Consecrate the fiftieth year and proclaim liberty throughout the land to all its inhabitants. It shall be a jubilee for you; each one of you is to return to his family property and each to his own clan. 11The fiftieth year shall be a jubilee for you; do not sow and do not reap what grows of itself or harvest the untended vines. 12For it is a jubilee and is to be holy for you; eat only what is taken directly from the fields.
13"'In this Year of Jubilee everyone is to return to his own property.
14"'If you sell land to one of your countrymen or buy any from him, do not take advantage of each other. 15You are to buy from your countryman on the basis of the number of years since the Jubilee. And he is to sell to you on the basis of the number of years left for harvesting crops. 16When the years are many, you are to increase the price, and when the years are few, you are to decrease the price, because what he is really selling you is the number of crops. 17Do not take advantage of each other, but fear your God. I am the LORD your God.
18"'Follow my decrees and be careful to obey my laws, and you will live safely in the land. 19Then the land will yield its fruit, and you will eat your fill and live there in safety. 20You may ask, "What will we eat in the seventh year if we do not plant or harvest our crops?" 21I will send you such a blessing in the sixth year that the land will yield enough for three years. 22While you plant during the eighth year, you will eat from the old crop and will continue to eat from it until the harvest of the ninth year comes in.
23"'The land must not be sold permanently, because the land is mine and you are but aliens and my tenants.

24Throughout the country that you hold as a possession, you must provide for the redemption of the land.
25"'If one of your countrymen becomes poor and sells some of his property, his nearest relative is to come and redeem what his countryman has sold. 26If, however, a man has no one to redeem it for him but he himself prospers and acquires sufficient means to redeem it, 27he is to determine the value for the years since he sold it and refund the balance to the man to whom he sold it; he can then go back to his own property. 28But if he does not acquire the means to repay him, what he sold will remain in the possession of the buyer until the Year of Jubilee. It will be returned in the Jubilee, and he can then go back to his property.
29"'If a man sells a house in a walled city, he retains the right of redemption a full year after its sale. During that time he may redeem it. 30If it is not redeemed before a full year has passed, the house in the walled city shall belong permanently to the buyer and his descendants. It is not to be returned in the Jubilee. 31But houses in villages without walls around them are to be considered as open country. They can be redeemed, and they are to be returned in the Jubilee.
32"'The Levites always have the right to redeem their houses in the Levitical towns, which they possess. 33So the property of the Levites is redeemable—that is, a house sold in any town they hold—and is to be returned in the Jubilee, because the houses in the towns of the Levites are their property among the Israelites. 34But the pastureland belonging to their towns must not be sold; it is their permanent possession.
35"'If one of your countrymen becomes poor and is unable to support himself among you, help him as you would an alien or a temporary resident, so he can continue to live among you. 36Do not take interest of any kind from him, but fear your God, so that your countryman may continue to live among you. 37You must not lend him money at interest or sell him food at a profit. 38I am the LORD your God, who brought you out of Egypt to give you the land of Canaan and to be your God.
39"'If one of your countrymen becomes poor among you and sells himself to you, do not make him work as a slave. 40He is to be treated as a hired worker or a temporary resident among you; he is to work for you until the Year of Jubilee. 41Then he and his children are to be released, and he will go back to his own clan and to the property of his forefathers. 42Because the Israelites are my servants, whom I brought out of Egypt, they must not be sold as slaves. 43Do not rule over them ruthlessly, but fear your God.
44"'Your male and female slaves are to come from the nations around you; from them you may buy slaves. 45You may also buy some of the temporary residents living among you and members of their clans born in your country, and they will become your property. 46You can will them to your children as inherited property and can make them slaves for life, but you must not rule over your fellow Israelites ruthlessly.
47"'If an alien or a temporary resident among you becomes rich and one of your countrymen becomes poor and sells himself to the alien living among you or to a member of the alien's clan, 48he retains the right of redemption after he has sold himself. One of his relatives may redeem him: 49An uncle or a cousin or any blood relative in his clan may redeem him. Or if he prospers, he may redeem himself. 50He and his buyer are to count the time from the year he

sold himself up to the Year of Jubilee. The price for his release is to be based on the rate paid to a hired man for that number of years. ⁵¹If many years remain, he must pay for his redemption a larger share of the price paid for him. ⁵²If only a few years remain until the Year of Jubilee, he is to compute that and pay for his redemption accordingly. ⁵³He is to be treated as a man hired from year to year; you must see to it that his owner does not rule over him ruthlessly.

⁵⁴"Even if he is not redeemed in any of these ways, he and his children are to be released in the Year of Jubilee, ⁵⁵for the Israelites belong to me as servants. They are my servants, whom I brought out of Egypt. I am the LORD your God.

Lev 27:17 If he dedicates his field during the Year of Jubilee, the value that has been set remains. ¹⁸But if he dedicates his field after the Jubilee, the priest will determine the value according to the number of years that remain until the next Year of Jubilee, and its set value will be reduced. ¹⁹If the man who dedicates the field wishes to redeem it, he must add a fifth to its value, and the field will again become his. ²⁰If, however, he does not redeem the field, or if he has sold it to someone else, it can never be redeemed. ²¹When the field is released in the Jubilee, it will become holy, like a field devoted to the LORD; it will become the property of the priests.

²²"If a man dedicates to the LORD a field he has bought, which is not part of his family land, ²³the priest will determine its value up to the Year of Jubilee, and the man must pay its value on that day as something holy to the LORD. ²⁴In the Year of Jubilee the field will revert to the person from whom he bought it, the one whose land it was.

Nu 36:4 When the Year of Jubilee for the Israelites comes, their inheritance will be added to that of the tribe into which they marry, and their property will be taken from the tribal inheritance of our forefathers."

See Emancipation; Sabbatic Year.

JUBILEES, BOOK OF Jewish apocalyptic book written in intertestamental period.

JUCAL *See Jehucal.*

JUDA *See Judah.*

JUDAEA *See Judea.*

JUDAH [3373+, 3374, 3376, 10315, 2683] (*praised*).
NIV+ JUDAH'S, JUDEA, JUDEAN

1. Son of Jacob (Ge 35:23). Intercedes for Joseph's life when his brothers were about to slay him, and proposes that they sell him to the Ishmaelites (Ge 37:26-27). Takes two wives (Ge 38:1-6). Lives at Kezib (Ge 38:5). His incest with his daughter-in-law (Ge 38:12-26). Goes down into Egypt for grain (Ge 43:1-10; 44:14-34; 46:28). Prophetic benediction of his father upon (Ge 49:8-12). The ancestor of Jesus (Mt 1:2-3; Rev 5:5).

2. Tribe of: Prophecies concerning (Ge 49:10). Enrollment of the military forces of, at Sinai (Nu 1:26-27; 2:4), at Bezek (1Sa 11:8; 2Sa 24:9), in the plain of Moab (Nu 26:22). Place of, in camp and march (Nu 2:3,9; 10:14). By whom commanded (Nu 2:3). Moses' benediction upon (Dt 33:7). Commissioned of God to lead in the conquest of the promised land (Jdg 1:1-3, w Jdg 1:4-21). Make David king (2Sa 2:1-11; 5:4-5). Rebuked by David for lukewarmness toward him after Absalom's defeat (2Sa 19:11-15). Accused by the other tribes of stealing the heart of David (2Sa 19:41-43). Loyal to David at the at the time of the

insurrection led by Sheba (2Sa 20:1-2). Is accorded the birthright forfeited by Reuben (1Ch 5:1-2; 28:4; Ps 60:7). Loyal to the house of David at the time of the revolt of the ten tribes (1Ki 12:20). Inheritance of (Jos 15; 18:5; 19:1,9).

3. Name of two exiled priests (Ezr 10:23; Ne 12:8).

4. A Benjamite (Ne 11:9).

5. A prince or priest who assisted in the dedication of the walls of Jerusalem (Ne 12:34,36).

JUDAISM [2682, 4670].
NIV+ See JEW

1. The religion of the Jews in NT times (Gal 1:13-14).

2. "Converts to Judaism" (Ac 2:11; 6:5; 13:43). Gentiles who adopted the religious beliefs and customs of the Jews.

JUDAS [2683] (Greek for *Judah*).

1. Surnamed Iscariot. Chosen as an apostle (Mt 10:4; Mk 3:19; Lk 6:16; Ac 1:17). Treasurer of the disciples (Jn 12:6; 13:29). His greed exemplified by his protest against the breaking of the box of ointment (Jn 12:4-6), by his bargain to betray Jesus for a sum of money (Mt 26:14-16; Mk 14:10-11; Lk 22:3-6; Jn 13:2). His apostasy (Jn 17:12). Betrays the Lord (Mt 26:47-50; Mk 14:43-45; Lk 22:47-49; Jn 18:2-5; Ac 1:16-25). Returns the money to the rulers of the Jews (Mt 27:3-10). Hangs himself (Mt 27:5; Ac 1:18). Prophecies concerning (Mt 26:21-25; Mk 14:18-21; Lk 22:21-23; Jn 13:18-26; 17:12; Ac 1:16,20, w Ps 41:9; 109:8; Zec 11:12-13).

2. One of the brothers of Jesus (Mt 13:55; Mk 6:3) and writer of the epistle of Jude (Jude 1).

3. Brother of James (Lk 6:16; Ac 1:13).

4. An apostle, probably identical with Lebbaeus, or Thaddaeus (Jn 14:22).

5. Of Galilee, who stirred up a sedition among the Jews soon after the birth of Jesus (Ac 5:37).

6. A disciple who entertained Paul (Ac 9:11).

7. Surnamed Barsabbas. A Christian sent to Antioch with Paul and Barnabas (Ac 15:22-32).

JUDE [2683] (*Judah*). The writer of the last of the NT epistles. The brother of James (Jude 1:1), probably brother of Jesus (Mk 6:3).

JUDE, EPISTLE OF

Author: Jude the brother of Jesus and James

Date: Probably c. A.D. 65

Outline:

I. Salutation (1-2).

II. Occasion for the Letter (3-4).
  A. The Change of Subject (3).
  B. The Reason for the Change: The Presence of Godless Apostates (4).

III. Warning against the False Teachers (5-16).
  A. Historical Examples of the Judgment of Apostates (5-7).
    1. Unbelieving Israel (5).
    2. Angels who fell (6).
    3. Sodom and Gomorrah (7).
  B. Description of the Apostates of Jude's Day (8-16).
    1. Their slanderous speech deplored (8-10).
    2. Their character graphically portrayed (11-13).
    3. Their destruction prophesied (14-16).

IV. Exhortation to Believers (17-23).

V. Concluding Doxology (24-25).
  See General Letters.

JUDEA [3373, 3374, *2677, 2681, 2683*] (*land of the Judahites, Jews*).

NIV+ See JUDAH

1. Also called Judah. The southern division of Israel. It extended from the Jordan and Dead Sea to the Mediterranean, and from Shiloh on the N to the wilderness on the S (Mt 4:25; Lk 5:17; Jn 4:47,54). The term is applied to all of Israel (Lk 1:5). The term is applied to the territory E of Jordan (Mt 19:1; Mk 10:1; Lk 23:5).

2. Wilderness of. Called Beth Arabah (Jos 18:22). John the Baptist preaches in (Mt 3:1; Lk 3:3).

JUDGE [*466, 1906, 1907, 3248, 3519, 4213, 5477, 6885, 7132, 7213, 9149, 9150, 9370, 10170, 10171, 10188, *373, 1037, 1191, 1359, 1471, 3210, 3212, 3213, 3216*].

NIV+ JUDGE'S, JUDGED, JUDGES, JUDGING, JUDGMENT, JUDGMENTS

Character of, and Precepts Relating to:

Must be righteous—

Ex 18:21 But select capable men from all the people—men who fear God, trustworthy men who hate dishonest gain—and appoint them as officials over thousands, hundreds, fifties and tens. [22]Have them serve as judges for the people at all times, but have them bring every difficult case to you; the simple cases they can decide themselves. That will make your load lighter, because they will share it with you.

Lev 19:15 "'Do not pervert justice; do not show partiality to the poor or favoritism to the great, but judge your neighbor fairly.

Dt 16:18 Appoint judges and officials for each of your tribes in every town the LORD your God is giving you, and they shall judge the people fairly. [19]Do not pervert justice or show partiality. Do not accept a bribe, for a bribe blinds the eyes of the wise and twists the words of the righteous. [20]Follow justice and justice alone, so that you may live and possess the land the LORD your God is giving you.

1Ki 3:9 So give your servant a discerning heart to govern your people and to distinguish between right and wrong. For who is able to govern this great people of yours?"

Ps 58:1 Do you rulers indeed speak justly? Do you judge uprightly among men? [2]No, in your heart you devise injustice, and your hands mete out violence on the earth.

Ps 72:1 Endow the king with your justice, O God, the royal son with your righteousness. [2]He will judge your people in righteousness, your afflicted ones with justice.

Ps 72:4 He will defend the afflicted among the people and save the children of the needy; he will crush the oppressor.

Must be intelligent—

Dt 1:12 But how can I bear your problems and your burdens and your disputes all by myself? [13]Choose some wise, understanding and respected men from each of your tribes, and I will set them over you."

Isa 28:6 He will be a spirit of justice to him who sits in judgment, a source of strength to those who turn back the battle at the gate.

Must judge righteously—

Dt 1:16 And I charged your judges at that time: Hear the disputes between your brothers and judge fairly, whether the case is between brother Israelites or between one of them and an alien. [17]Do not show partiality in judging; hear both small and great alike. Do not be afraid of any man, for judgment belongs to God. Bring me any case too hard for you, and I will hear it.

Jurisdiction of as judge—

1Sa 2:25 If a man sins against another man, God may mediate for him; but if a man sins against the LORD, who will intercede for him?" His sons, however, did not listen to their father's rebuke, for it was the LORD's will to put them to death.

Inferior and superior judges—

Dt 17:8 If cases come before your courts that are too difficult for you to judge—whether bloodshed, lawsuits or assaults—take them to the place the LORD your God will choose. [9]Go to the priests, who are Levites, and to the judge who is in office at that time. Inquire of them and they will give you the verdict. [10]You must act according to the decisions they give you at the place the LORD will choose. Be careful to do everything they direct you to do. [11]Act according to the law they teach you and the decisions they give you. Do not turn aside from what they tell you, to the right or to the left.

Held circuit courts (1Sa 7:16).

Rules for guidance of (Ex 18:22)—

Dt 19:16 If a malicious witness takes the stand to accuse a man of a crime, [17]the two men involved in the dispute must stand in the presence of the LORD before the priests and the judges who are in office at the time. [18]The judges must make a thorough investigation, and if the witness proves to be a liar, giving false testimony against his brother, [19]then do to him as he intended to do to his brother. You must purge the evil from among you.

Dt 25:1 When men have a dispute, they are to take it to court and the judges will decide the case, acquitting the innocent and condemning the guilty. [2]If the guilty man deserves to be beaten, the judge shall make him lie down and have him flogged in his presence with the number of lashes his crime deserves, [3]but he must not give him more than forty lashes. If he is flogged more than that, your brother will be degraded in your eyes.

2Ch 19:5 He appointed judges in the land, in each of the fortified cities of Judah. [6]He told them, "Consider carefully what you do, because you are not judging for man but for the LORD, who is with you whenever you give a verdict. [7]Now let the fear of the LORD be upon you. Judge carefully, for with the LORD our God there is no injustice or partiality or bribery."

[8]In Jerusalem also, Jehoshaphat appointed some of the Levites, priests and heads of Israelite families to administer the law of the LORD and to settle disputes. And they lived in Jerusalem. [9]He gave them these orders: "You must serve faithfully and wholeheartedly in the fear of the LORD. [10]In every case that comes before you from your fellow countrymen who live in the cities—whether bloodshed or other concerns of the law, commands, decrees or ordinances—you are to warn them not to sin against the LORD; otherwise his wrath will come on you and your brothers. Do this, and you will not sin.

Pr 24:23 These also are sayings of the wise: To show partiality in judging is not good:

Eze 44:24 "'In any dispute, the priests are to serve as judges and decide it according to my ordinances. They are to keep my laws and my decrees for all my appointed feasts, and they are to keep my Sabbaths holy.

Jn 7:24 Stop judging by mere appearances, and make a right judgment."

Kings and other rulers as (2Sa 8:15; 15:2; 1Ki 3:16-28; 10:9; 2Ki 8:1-6; Ps 72:1-4; Mt 27:11-26; Ac 23:34-35; 24; 25:11-12). Priests and Levites as (Dt 17:9; 1Ch 23:4; 2Ch

19:8; Eze 44:23-24; Mt 26:57-62). Women as: Deborah (Jdg 4:4).

Persian government provided (Ezr 7:25).

Corrupt:

1Sa 8:3 But his sons did not walk in his ways. They turned aside after dishonest gain and accepted bribes and perverted justice.

Ps 82:2 "How long will you defend the unjust and show partiality to the wicked? *Selah* ³Defend the cause of the weak and fatherless; maintain the rights of the poor and oppressed. ⁴Rescue the weak and needy; deliver them from the hand of the wicked.

Isa 5:22 Woe to those who are heroes at drinking wine and champions at mixing drinks, ²³who acquit the guilty for a bribe, but deny justice to the innocent.

Da 9:12 You have fulfilled the words spoken against us and against our rulers by bringing upon us great disaster. Under the whole heaven nothing has ever been done like what has been done to Jerusalem.

Mic 7:3 Both hands are skilled in doing evil; the ruler demands gifts, the judge accepts bribes, the powerful dictate what they desire—they all conspire together.

Zep 3:3 Her officials are roaring lions, her rulers are evening wolves, who leave nothing for the morning.

Instances of Corrupt: Eli's sons (1Sa 2:12-17,22-25). Samuel's sons (1Sa 8:1-5). The judges of Jezreel (1Ki 21:8-13). Pilate (Mt 27:24,26; Mk 15:15,19-24). Felix (Ac 24:26-27).

Of Israel:

Executives and leaders of the nation. During the time when the land was ruled by judges (Jdg 2:16-19; Ac 13:20).

Othniel (Jdg 3:9-11). Ehud (Jdg 3:15,30). Shamgar (Jdg 3:31). Deborah (Jdg 4:4-5). Gideon (Jdg 6:11-40; 7:8). Abimelech (Jdg 9:1-54). Tola (Jdg 10:1-2). Jair (Jdg 10:3-5). Jephthah (Jdg 12:7). Ibzan (Jdg 12:8-10). Elon (Jdg 12:11-12). Abdon (Jdg 12:13-14). Samson (Jdg 15:20; 16:31).

Eli (1Sa 4:18). Samuel (1Sa 7:6,15-17). The sons of Samuel (1Sa 8:1-5).

See Court, Of Law; God, Judge; Justice; Witness.

JUDGES, BOOK OF

Author: Anonymous; traditionally Samuel

Date: Possibly between 1040 and 1000 B.C.

Outline:

I. Prologue: Incomplete Conquest and Apostasy (1:1-3:6).
  A. First Episode: Israel's Failure to Purge the Land (1:1-2:5).
  B. Second Episode: God's Dealings with Israel's Rebellion (2:6-3:6).
II. Oppression and Deliverance (3:7-16:31).

Major Judges	*Minor Judges*

A. Othniel Defeats Aram Naharaim (3:7-11).
B. Ehud Defeats Moab (3:12-30).
  1. Shamgar (3:31).
C. Deborah Defeats Canaan (chs. 4-5).
D. Gideon Defeats Midian (chs. 6-8).
  (Abimelech, the anti-judge, ch. 9).
  2. Tola (10:1-2).
  3. Jair (10:3-5).
E. Jephthah Defeats Ammon (10:6-12:7).
  4. Ibzan (12:8-10).
  5. Elon (12:11-12).
  6. Abdon (12:13-15).

F. Samson Checks Philistia (chs. 17-21).
III. Epilogue: Religious and Moral Disorder (chs. 17-21).
  A. First Episode (chs. 17-18; see 17:6; 18:1).
    1. Micah's corruption of religion (ch 17).
    2. The Danites' departure from their tribal territory (ch. 18).
  B. Second Episode (chs. 19-21; see 19:1; 21:25).
    1. Gibeah's corruption of morals (ch. 19).
    2. The Benjamites' removal from their tribal territory (chs. 20-21).

JUDGING *See Uncharitableness.*

JUDGMENT [*466, 1906, 1907, 3248, 3519, 4213, 5477, 6885, 7132, 7213, 9149, 9150, 9370, 10170, 10171, 10188, *373, 1037, 1191, 1359, 1471, 3210, 3212, 3213, 3216*].

NIV+ See JUDGE

General:

Forewarned—

Ecc 11:9 Be happy, young man, while you are young, and let your heart give you joy in the days of your youth. Follow the ways of your heart and whatever your eyes see, but know that for all these things God will bring you to judgment.

Ecc 12:14 For God will bring every deed into judgment, including every hidden thing, whether it is good or evil.

Mt 8:29 "What do you want with us, Son of God?" they shouted. "Have you come here to torture us before the appointed time?" (+2Pe 2:4)

Jude 6 And the angels who did not keep their positions of authority but abandoned their own home—these he has kept in darkness, bound with everlasting chains for judgment on the great Day.

Mt 13:30 Let both grow together until the harvest. At that time I will tell the harvesters: First collect the weeds and tie them in bundles to be burned; then gather the wheat and bring it into my barn.' "

Mt 13:40 "As the weeds are pulled up and burned in the fire, so it will be at the end of the age. ⁴¹The Son of Man will send out his angels, and they will weed out of his kingdom everything that causes sin and all who do evil. ⁴²They will throw them into the fiery furnace, where there will be weeping and gnashing of teeth. ⁴³Then the righteous will shine like the sun in the kingdom of their Father. He who has ears, let him hear.

Mt 13:49 This is how it will be at the end of the age. The angels will come and separate the wicked from the righteous ⁵⁰and throw them into the fiery furnace, where there will be weeping and gnashing of teeth.

Mt 25:31 "When the Son of Man comes in his glory, and all the angels with him, he will sit on his throne in heavenly glory. ³²All the nations will be gathered before him, and he will separate the people one from another as a shepherd separates the sheep from the goats. ³³He will put the sheep on his right and the goats on his left. ³⁴"Then the King will say to those on his right, 'Come, you who are blessed by my Father; take your inheritance, the kingdom prepared for you since the creation of the world. ³⁵For I was hungry and you gave me something to eat, I was thirsty and you gave me something to drink, I was a stranger and you invited me in, ³⁶I needed clothes and you clothed me, I was sick and you looked after me, I was in prison and you came to visit me.' ³⁷"Then the righteous will answer him, 'Lord, when did we see you hungry and feed you, or thirsty and give you something to drink? ³⁸When did we see you a stranger and invite you in, or needing clothes and clothe you? ³⁹When did we see you sick or in prison and go to visit you?' ⁴⁰"The King will reply, 'I tell you the truth, whatever you did for one of the least of these brothers of mine, you did for me.' ⁴¹"Then he will say to those on his left, 'Depart from me, you who are cursed, into the eternal fire prepared for the devil and his angels. ⁴²For I was hungry and you gave me nothing to eat, I was thirsty and you gave me nothing to drink, ⁴³I was a stranger and you did not invite me in, I needed clothes and you did not clothe me, I was sick and in prison and you did not look after me.' ⁴⁴"They also will answer, 'Lord, when did we see you hungry or thirsty or a stranger or needing clothes or sick or in prison, and did not help you?' ⁴⁵"He will reply, 'I tell you the truth, whatever you did not do for one of the least of these, you did not do for me.' ⁴⁶"Then they will go away to eternal punishment, but the righteous to eternal life." (+Mk 8:38)

Ac 24:25 As Paul discoursed on righteousness, self-control and the judgment to come, Felix was afraid and said, "That's enough for now! You may leave. When I find it convenient, I will send for you."

2Th 1:7 and give relief to you who are troubled, and to us as well. This will happen when the Lord Jesus is revealed from heaven in blazing fire with his powerful angels. ⁸He will punish those who do not know God and do not obey the gospel of our Lord Jesus.

Heb 6:2 instruction about baptisms, the laying on of hands, the resurrection of the dead, and eternal judgment.

Fierce and fiery—

Mt 3:12 His winnowing fork is in his hand, and he will clear his threshing floor, gathering his wheat into the barn and burning up the chaff with unquenchable fire."

Mt 10:15 I tell you the truth, it will be more bearable for Sodom and Gomorrah on the day of judgment than for that town.

Mt 11:22 But I tell you, it will be more bearable for Tyre and Sidon on the day of judgment than for you.

Mt 12:36 But I tell you that men will have to give account on the day of judgment for every careless word they have spoken. ³⁷For by your words you will be acquitted, and by your words you will be condemned." (+Mt 12:38-40)

Mt 12:41 The men of Nineveh will stand up at the judgment with this generation and condemn it; for they repented at the preaching of Jonah, and now one greater than Jonah is here. ⁴²The Queen of the South will rise at the judgment with this generation and condemn it; for she came from the ends of the earth to listen to Solomon's wisdom, and now one greater than Solomon is here. (+Lk 3:17)

Lk 10:10 But when you enter a town and are not welcomed, go into its streets and say, ¹¹"Even the dust of your town that sticks to our feet we wipe off against you. Yet be sure of this: The kingdom of God is near.' ¹²I tell you, it will be more bearable on that day for Sodom than for that town.

¹³"Woe to you, Korazin! Woe to you, Bethsaida! For if the miracles that were performed in you had been performed in Tyre and Sidon, they would have repented long ago, sitting in sackcloth and ashes. ¹⁴But it will be more bearable for Tyre and Sidon at the judgment than for you. (+Lk 11:31-32)

Lk 13:24 "Make every effort to enter through the narrow door, because many, I tell you, will try to enter and will not be able to. ²⁵Once the owner of the house gets up and

closes the door, you will stand outside knocking and pleading, 'Sir, open the door for us.'

"But he will answer, 'I don't know you or where you come from.'

²⁶"Then you will say, 'We ate and drank with you, and you taught in our streets.'

²⁷"But he will reply, 'I don't know you or where you come from. Away from me, all you evildoers!'

²⁸"There will be weeping there, and gnashing of teeth, when you see Abraham, Isaac and Jacob and all the prophets in the kingdom of God, but you yourselves thrown out. ²⁹People will come from east and west and north and south, and will take their places at the feast in the kingdom of God.

Ac 2:19 I will show wonders in the heaven above and signs on the earth below, blood and fire and billows of smoke. ²⁰The sun will be turned to darkness and the moon to blood before the coming of the great and glorious day of the Lord.

According to opportunity and works—

Ge 4:7 If you do what is right, will you not be accepted? But if you do not do what is right, sin is crouching at your door; it desires to have you, but you must master it." (+1Sa 26:23)

Job 34:11 He repays a man for what he has done; he brings upon him what his conduct deserves. (+Job 34:12; Ps 62:12)

Pr 12:14 From the fruit of his lips a man is filled with good things as surely as the work of his hands rewards him.

Pr 24:11 Rescue those being led away to death; hold back those staggering toward slaughter. ¹²If you say, "But we knew nothing about this," does not he who weighs the heart perceive it? Does not he who guards your life know it? Will he not repay each person according to what he has done?

Isa 3:10 Tell the righteous it will be well with them, for they will enjoy the fruit of their deeds. ¹¹Woe to the wicked! Disaster is upon them! They will be paid back for what their hands have done.

Isa 59:18 According to what they have done, so will he repay wrath to his enemies and retribution to his foes; he will repay the islands their due.

Jer 17:10 "I the Lord search the heart and examine the mind, to reward a man according to his conduct, according to what his deeds deserve."

Jer 32:19 great are your purposes and mighty are your deeds. Your eyes are open to all the ways of men; you reward everyone according to his conduct and as his deeds deserve.

Eze 7:3 The end is now upon you and I will unleash my anger against you. I will judge you according to your conduct and repay you for all your detestable practices. ⁴I will not look on you with pity or spare you; I will surely repay you for your conduct and the detestable practices among you. Then you will know that I am the Lord.

Eze 7:27 The king will mourn, the prince will be clothed with despair, and the hands of the people of the land will tremble. I will deal with them according to their conduct, and by their own standards I will judge them. Then they will know that I am the Lord."

Eze 18:4 For every living soul belongs to me, the father as well as the son—both alike belong to me. The soul who sins is the one who will die. (+Eze 18:5-9)

Eze 18:19 "Yet you ask, 'Why does the son not share the guilt of his father?' Since the son has done what is just and right and has been careful to keep all my decrees, he will surely live. ²⁰The soul who sins is the one who will die. The son will not share the guilt of the father, nor will the father share the guilt of the son. The righteousness of the righteous man will be credited to him, and the wickedness of the wicked will be charged against him.

²¹"But if a wicked man turns away from all the sins he has committed and keeps all my decrees and does what is just and right, he will surely live; he will not die. ²²None of the offenses he has committed will be remembered against him. Because of the righteous things he has done, he will live. ²³Do I take any pleasure in the death of the wicked? declares the Sovereign LORD. Rather, am I not pleased when they turn from their ways and live?

²⁴"But if a righteous man turns from his righteousness and commits sin and does the same detestable things the wicked man does, will he live? None of the righteous things he has done will be remembered. Because of the unfaithfulness he is guilty of and because of the sins he has committed, he will die.

²⁵"Yet you say, 'The way of the Lord is not just.' Hear, O house of Israel: Is my way unjust? Is it not your ways that are unjust? ²⁶If a righteous man turns from his righteousness and commits sin, he will die for it; because of the sin he has committed he will die. ²⁷But if a wicked man turns away from the wickedness he has committed and does what is just and right, he will save his life. ²⁸Because he considers all the offenses he has committed and turns away from them, he will surely live; he will not die. ²⁹Yet the house of Israel says, 'The way of the Lord is not just.' Are my ways unjust, O house of Israel? Is it not your ways that are unjust?

³⁰"Therefore, O house of Israel, I will judge you, each one according to his ways, declares the Sovereign LORD. Repent! Turn away from all your offenses; then sin will not be your downfall. ³¹Rid yourselves of all the offenses you have committed, and get a new heart and a new spirit. Why will you die, O house of Israel? ³²For I take no pleasure in the death of anyone, declares the Sovereign LORD. Repent and live!

Eze 33:18 If a righteous man turns from his righteousness and does evil, he will die for it. ¹⁹And if a wicked man turns away from his wickedness and does what is just and right, he will live by doing so. ²⁰Yet, O house of Israel, you say, 'The way of the Lord is not just.' But I will judge each of you according to his own ways."

Hos 4:9 And it will be: Like people, like priests. I will punish both of them for their ways and repay them for their deeds. (+Hos 12:2)

Zec 1:6 But did not my words and my decrees, which I commanded my servants the prophets, overtake your forefathers? "Then they repented and said, 'The LORD Almighty has done to us what our ways and practices deserve, just as he determined to do.'"

Lk 12:47 "That servant who knows his master's will and does not get ready or does not do what his master wants will be beaten with many blows. ⁴⁸But the one who does not know and does things deserving punishment will be beaten with few blows. From everyone who has been given much, much will be demanded; and from the one who has been entrusted with much, much more will be asked.

Lk 13:6 Then he told this parable: "A man had a fig tree, planted in his vineyard, and he went to look for fruit on it, but did not find any. ⁷So he said to the man who took care of the vineyard, 'For three years now I've been coming to look for fruit on this fig tree and haven't found any. Cut it down! Why should it use up the soil?'

⁸"'Sir,' the man replied, 'leave it alone for one more year, and I'll dig around it and fertilize it. ⁹If it bears fruit next year, fine! If not, then cut it down.'"

Lk 19:12 He said: "A man of noble birth went to a distant country to have himself appointed king and then to return. ¹³So he called ten of his servants and gave them ten minas. 'Put this money to work,' he said, 'until I come back.'

¹⁴"But his subjects hated him and sent a delegation after him to say, 'We don't want this man to be our king.'

¹⁵"He was made king, however, and returned home. Then he sent for the servants to whom he had given the money, in order to find out what they had gained with it.

¹⁶"The first one came and said, 'Sir, your mina has earned ten more.'

¹⁷"'Well done, my good servant!' his master replied. 'Because you have been trustworthy in a very small matter, take charge of ten cities.'

¹⁸"The second came and said, 'Sir, your mina has earned five more.'

¹⁹"His master answered, 'You take charge of five cities.'

²⁰"Then another servant came and said, 'Sir, here is your mina; I have kept it laid away in a piece of cloth. ²¹I was afraid of you, because you are a hard man. You take out what you did not put in and reap what you did not sow.'

²²"His master replied, 'I will judge you by your own words, you wicked servant! You knew, did you, that I am a hard man, taking out what I did not put in, and reaping what I did not sow? ²³Why then didn't you put my money on deposit, so that when I came back, I could have collected it with interest?'

²⁴"Then he said to those standing by, 'Take his mina away from him and give it to the one who has ten minas.'

²⁵"'Sir,' they said, 'he already has ten!'

²⁶"He replied, 'I tell you that to everyone who has, more will be given, but as for the one who has nothing, even what he has will be taken away. ²⁷But those enemies of mine who did not want me to be king over them—bring them here and kill them in front of me.'" (+Mt 25:1-30)

Jn 3:19 This is the verdict: Light has come into the world, but men loved darkness instead of light because their deeds were evil. ²⁰Everyone who does evil hates the light, and will not come into the light for fear that his deeds will be exposed.

Ro 2:5 But because of your stubbornness and your unrepentant heart, you are storing up wrath against yourself for the day of God's wrath, when his righteous judgment will be revealed. ⁶God "will give to each person according to what he has done." ⁷To those who by persistence in doing good seek glory, honor and immortality, he will give eternal life. ⁸But for those who are self-seeking and who reject the truth and follow evil, there will be wrath and anger. ⁹There will be trouble and distress for every human being who does evil: first for the Jew, then for the Gentile; ¹⁰but glory, honor and peace for everyone who does good: first for the Jew, then for the Gentile. ¹¹For God does not show favoritism.

¹²All who sin apart from the law will also perish apart from the law, and all who sin under the law will be judged by the law.

1Co 3:8 The man who plants and the man who waters have one purpose, and each will be rewarded according to his own labor. (+1Co 3:12)

1Co 3:13 his work will be shown for what it is, because the Day will bring it to light. It will be revealed with fire, and the fire will test the quality of each man's work. [14]If what he has built survives, he will receive his reward. [15]If it is burned up, he will suffer loss; he himself will be saved, but only as one escaping through the flames.

2Co 11:15 It is not surprising, then, if his servants masquerade as servants of righteousness. Their end will be what their actions deserve.

Gal 6:7 Do not be deceived: God cannot be mocked. A man reaps what he sows. [8]The one who sows to please his sinful nature, from that nature will reap destruction; the one who sows to please the Spirit, from the Spirit will reap eternal life.

Eph 6:7 Serve wholeheartedly, as if you were serving the Lord, not men, [8]because you know that the Lord will reward everyone for whatever good he does, whether he is slave or free.

Col 3:25 Anyone who does wrong will be repaid for his wrong, and there is no favoritism.

Heb 10:26 If we deliberately keep on sinning after we have received the knowledge of the truth, no sacrifice for sins is left, [27]but only a fearful expectation of judgment and of raging fire that will consume the enemies of God. [28]Anyone who rejected the law of Moses died without mercy on the testimony of two or three witnesses. [29]How much more severely do you think a man deserves to be punished who has trampled the Son of God under foot, who has treated as an unholy thing the blood of the covenant that sanctified him, and who has insulted the Spirit of grace? [30]For we know him who said, "It is mine to avenge; I will repay," and again, "The Lord will judge his people."

Heb 12:25 See to it that you do not refuse him who speaks. If they did not escape when they refused him who warned them on earth, how much less will we, if we turn away from him who warns us from heaven?

Jas 2:13 because judgment without mercy will be shown to anyone who has not been merciful. Mercy triumphs over judgment!

1Pe 1:17 Since you call on a Father who judges each man's work impartially, live your lives as strangers here in reverent fear.

2Pe 2:20 If they have escaped the corruption of the world by knowing our Lord and Savior Jesus Christ and are again entangled in it and overcome, they are worse off at the end than they were at the beginning. [21]It would have been better for them not to have known the way of righteousness, than to have known it and then to turn their backs on the sacred command that was passed on to them.

Rev 2:23 I will strike her children dead. Then all the churches will know that I am he who searches hearts and minds, and I will repay each of you according to your deeds.

Rev 20:12 And I saw the dead, great and small, standing before the throne, and books were opened. Another book was opened, which is the book of life. The dead were judged according to what they had done as recorded in the books. [13]The sea gave up the dead that were in it, and death and Hades gave up the dead that were in them, and each person was judged according to what he had done.

Design of:

To exhibit a basis for rewards and punishments—

2Co 5:10 For we must all appear before the judgment seat of Christ, that each one may receive what is due him for the things done while in the body, whether good or bad.

2Ti 4:8 Now there is in store for me the crown of righteousness, which the Lord, the righteous Judge, will award

to me on that day—and not only to me, but also to all who have longed for his appearing.

Rev 11:18 The nations were angry; and your wrath has come. The time has come for judging the dead, and for rewarding your servants the prophets and your saints and those who reverence your name, both small and great—and for destroying those who destroy the earth."

Rev 22:12 "Behold, I am coming soon! My reward is with me, and I will give to everyone according to what he has done.

Revealing secrets (Ecc 12:14)—

Lk 12:2 There is nothing concealed that will not be disclosed, or hidden that will not be made known. [3]What you have said in the dark will be heard in the daylight, and what you have whispered in the ear in the inner rooms will be proclaimed from the roofs. (+Ro 2:16)

1Co 3:13 his work will be shown for what it is, because the Day will bring it to light. It will be revealed with fire, and the fire will test the quality of each man's work.

Who Will Be the Judge:

God as Judge—

1Ch 16:33 Then the trees of the forest will sing, they will sing for joy before the LORD, for he comes to judge the earth.

Ps 9:7 The LORD reigns forever; he has established his throne for judgment.

Ps 50:4 He summons the heavens above, and the earth, that he may judge his people:

Ps 50:6 And the heavens proclaim his righteousness, for God himself is judge. *Selah*

Ps 96:13 they will sing before the LORD, for he comes, he comes to judge the earth. He will judge the world in righteousness and the peoples in his truth. (+Ps 98:9; Ecc 12:14)

Da 7:9 "As I looked, "thrones were set in place, and the Ancient of Days took his seat. His clothing was as white as snow; the hair of his head was white like wool. His throne was flaming with fire, and its wheels were all ablaze. [10]A river of fire was flowing, coming out from before him. Thousands upon thousands attended him; ten thousand times ten thousand stood before him. The court was seated, and the books were opened. (+Ro 2:5,16; 3:6; 2Ti 4:8; Heb 10:30; 12:23; 13:4)

1Pe 4:5 But they will have to give account to him who is ready to judge the living and the dead.

Rev 20:11 Then I saw a great white throne and him who was seated on it. Earth and sky fled from his presence, and there was no place for them. [12]And I saw the dead, great and small, standing before the throne, and books were opened. Another book was opened, which is the book of life. The dead were judged according to what they had done as recorded in the books. [13]The sea gave up the dead that were in it, and death and Hades gave up the dead that were in them, and each person was judged according to what he had done. [14]Then death and Hades were thrown into the lake of fire. The lake of fire is the second death. [15]If anyone's name was not found written in the book of life, he was thrown into the lake of fire.

Jesus Christ as Judge—

Mt 7:22 Many will say to me on that day, 'Lord, Lord, did we not prophesy in your name, and in your name drive out demons and perform many miracles?' [23]Then I will tell them plainly, 'I never knew you. Away from me, you evildoers!' (+Mt 13:30,40-43,49-50; 16:25)

Mt 16:27 For the Son of Man is going to come in his

Father's glory with his angels, and then he will reward each person according to what he has done. (+Mt 25:31-46)

Mk 8:38 If anyone is ashamed of me and my words in this adulterous and sinful generation, the Son of Man will be ashamed of him when he comes in his Father's glory with the holy angels."

Jn 5:22 Moreover, the Father judges no one, but has entrusted all judgment to the Son,

Jn 12:48 There is a judge for the one who rejects me and does not accept my words; that very word which I spoke will condemn him at the last day.

Ac 10:42 He commanded us to preach to the people and to testify that he is the one whom God appointed as judge of the living and the dead.

Ac 17:31 For he has set a day when he will judge the world with justice by the man he has appointed. He has given proof of this to all men by raising him from the dead."

Ro 2:16 This will take place on the day when God will judge men's secrets through Jesus Christ, as my gospel declares.

Ro 14:10 You, then, why do you judge your brother? Or why do you look down on your brother? For we will all stand before God's judgment seat.

1Co 4:5 Therefore judge nothing before the appointed time; wait till the Lord comes. He will bring to light what is hidden in darkness and will expose the motives of men's hearts. At that time each will receive his praise from God. (+2Co 5:10; 2Th 1:7-8)

2Ti 4:1 In the presence of God and of Christ Jesus, who will judge the living and the dead, and in view of his appearing and his kingdom, I give you this charge:

2Pe 2:9 if this is so, then the Lord knows how to rescue godly men from trials and to hold the unrighteous for the day of judgment, while continuing their punishment. (+2Pe 3:10)

Rev 1:7 Look, he is coming with the clouds, and every eye will see him, even those who pierced him; and all the peoples of the earth will mourn because of him. So shall it be! Amen.

Rev 6:15 Then the kings of the earth, the princes, the generals, the rich, the mighty, and every slave and every free man hid in caves and among the rocks of the mountains. [16]They called to the mountains and the rocks, "Fall on us and hide us from the face of him who sits on the throne and from the wrath of the Lamb! [17]For the great day of their wrath has come, and who can stand?"

The saints as judges (Mt 19:28)—

1Co 6:2 Do you not know that the saints will judge the world? And if you are to judge the world, are you not competent to judge trivial cases? (+Jude 14)

Time of:

Appointed (Mt 13:30; Ac 17:31)—

Heb 9:27 Just as man is destined to die once, and after that to face judgment,

2Pe 3:7 By the same word the present heavens and earth are reserved for fire, being kept for the day of judgment and destruction of ungodly men.

2Pe 3:10 But the day of the Lord will come like a thief. The heavens will disappear with a roar; the elements will be destroyed by fire, and the earth and everything in it will be laid bare.

[11]Since everything will be destroyed in this way, what kind of people ought you to be? You ought to live holy and godly lives [12]as you look forward to the day of God and speed its coming. That day will bring about the destruction

of the heavens by fire, and the elements will melt in the heat.

Known to God only—

Mk 13:32 "No one knows about that day or hour, not even the angels in heaven, nor the Son, but only the Father.

Who Will Be Judged:

The righteous and wicked—

Ecc 3:17 I thought in my heart, "God will bring to judgment both the righteous and the wicked, for there will be a time for every activity, a time for every deed." (+Mt 25:31-46)

Jude 14 Enoch, the seventh from Adam, prophesied about these men: "See, the Lord is coming with thousands upon thousands of his holy ones [15]to judge everyone, and to convict all the ungodly of all the ungodly acts they have done in the ungodly way, and of all the harsh words ungodly sinners have spoken against him." (+Rev 11:18)

The wicked—

Job 21:30 that the evil man is spared from the day of calamity, that he is delivered from the day of wrath?

Eze 18:20 The soul who sins is the one who will die. The son will not share the guilt of the father, nor will the father share the guilt of the son. The righteousness of the righteous man will be credited to him, and the wickedness of the wicked will be charged against him.

[21]"But if a wicked man turns away from all the sins he has committed and keeps all my decrees and does what is just and right, he will surely live; he will not die. [22]None of the offenses he has committed will be remembered against him. Because of the righteous things he has done, he will live. [23]Do I take any pleasure in the death of the wicked? declares the Sovereign LORD. Rather, am I not pleased when they turn from their ways and live?

[24]"But if a righteous man turns from his righteousness and commits sin and does the same detestable things the wicked man does, will he live? None of the righteous things he has done will be remembered. Because of the unfaithfulness he is guilty of and because of the sins he has committed, he will die.

[25]"Yet you say, 'The way of the Lord is not just.' Hear, O house of Israel: Is my way unjust? Is it not your ways that are unjust? [26]If a righteous man turns from his righteousness and commits sin, he will die for it; because of the sin he has committed he will die. [27]But if a wicked man turns away from the wickedness he has committed and does what is just and right, he will save his life. [28]Because he considers all the offenses he has committed and turns away from them, he will surely live; he will not die. (+2Pe 2:9; 3:7)

The living and the dead (Ac 10:42; 2Ti 4:1; 1Pe 4:5).

All must be made manifest—

Mk 4:22 For whatever is hidden is meant to be disclosed, and whatever is concealed is meant to be brought out into the open. (+Ac 17:31; 2Co 5:10)

Kings and princes, slaves and freemen (Rev 6:15-16).

Fallen angels—

2Pe 2:4 For if God did not spare angels when they sinned, but sent them to hell, putting them into gloomy dungeons to be held for judgment; (+Jude 6)

See God, Judge; Jesus the Christ, Judge; Punishment, According to Deeds.

JUDGMENT, HALL OF *See Praetorium.*

JUDGMENT SEAT (Mt 27:19; Ac 18:12; 25:10). Of Christ (Ro 14:10).

JUDGMENTS [5477, 8652, 9150, *373, 3210, 3213*].

NIV+ See JUDGE

Denounced against Solomon (1Ki 11:9-14,23), Jeroboam (1Ki 14:7-15), Ahab and Jezebel (1Ki 21:19-24), Ahaziah (2Ch 22:7-9), Manasseh (2Ch 33:11).

Denounced against disobedience (Lev 26:14-39; Dt 28:15-68; 29:1-21)—

Dt 29:22 Your children who follow you in later generations and foreigners who come from distant lands will see the calamities that have fallen on the land and the diseases with which the LORD has afflicted it. ²³The whole land will be a burning waste of salt and sulfur—nothing planted, nothing sprouting, no vegetation growing on it. It will be like the destruction of Sodom and Gomorrah, Admah and Zeboiim, which the LORD overthrew in fierce anger. ²⁴All the nations will ask: "Why has the LORD done this to this land? Why this fierce, burning anger?"

²⁵And the answer will be: "It is because this people abandoned the covenant of the LORD, the God of their fathers, the covenant he made with them when he brought them out of Egypt. ²⁶They went off and worshiped other gods and bowed down to them, gods they did not know, gods he had not given them. ²⁷Therefore the LORD's anger burned against this land, so that he brought on it all the curses written in this book. ²⁸In furious anger and in great wrath the LORD uprooted them from their land and thrust them into another land, as it is now." (+Dt 29:29; 32:19-43)

Design of:

To correct (Dt 30:1-2; 1Ki 8:33-34; 2Ch 7:13; Job 5:17; 23:10; 34:31-32; Ps 94:12-13; 107:10-14,17; Pr 3:11; Isa 9:13-14)—

Isa 26:9 My soul yearns for you in the night; in the morning my spirit longs for you. When your judgments come upon the earth, the people of the world learn righteousness. (+Jer 24:5; 30:11; La 1:5,12; Eze 20:37,43; Hos 2:6-7; 5:15; 1Co 11:32; Heb 12:5-11)

To humble (2Co 12:7).

Misunderstood:

(Jer 16:10; Joel 2:17). No escape from (Ex 20:7; 34:7; Isa 2:10,12-19,21; Eze 14:13-14; Am 5:16-20; 9:1-4; Mt 23:33; Heb 2:1-3; 10:28-29; 12:25; Rev 6:16-17). *See Escape.* Executed by human instrumentality (Jer 51:2). Delayed (Ps 10:6; 50:21; 55:19). *See Punishment, Delayed.*

Instances of:

On the serpent (Ge 3:14-15), Eve (Ge 3:16), Adam (Ge 3:17-19), Cain (Ge 4:11-15), the Antediluvians (Ge 6-7), Sodomites (Ge 19:23-25)

Egyptians, the plagues and overthrow (Ex 7-13; 14:1-16)—

Ex 14:17 I will harden the hearts of the Egyptians so that they will go in after them. And I will gain glory through Pharaoh and all his army, through his chariots and his horsemen. ¹⁸The Egyptians will know that I am the LORD when I gain glory through Pharaoh, his chariots and his horsemen." (+Ex 14:19-30)

Ex 14:31 And when the Israelites saw the great power the LORD displayed against the Egyptians, the people feared the LORD and put their trust in him and in Moses his servant.

Nadab and Abihu (Lev 10:1-2)—

Lev 10:3 Moses then said to Aaron, "This is what the LORD spoke of when he said: "'Among those who

approach me I will show myself holy; in the sight of all the people I will be honored.'" Aaron remained silent.

Miriam (Nu 12:1-15).—

Upon the Israelites: For worshiping Aaron's calf (Ex 32:35), for murmuring (Nu 11:1,33-34; 14:22-23,32,35-37; 21:6; 25:4-5,9). The forty years wandering, a judgment (Nu 14:26-39; 26:63-65; Dt 2:14-17), delivered into the hands of the Assyrians (2Ki 17:6-41), Chaldeans (2Ch 36:14-21).

Upon the Canaanites: (Lev 18:25; Dt 7; 12:29-32), with the conquest of, by Joshua.

See Canaanite(s).

Upon Abimelech (Jdg 9:52-57), Uzzah (2Sa 6:7), Eli's house (1Sa 2:27-36, w 1Sa 4:10-22), the prophet of Judah, for disobedience (1Ki 13:1-24), Zimri (1Ki 16:18-19), Gehazi (2Ki 5:27), Sennacherib (2Ki 19:35-37), Hananiah, the false prophet (Jer 28:15,17).

See Chastisement, From God; Punishment; Sin, Punishment of.

JUDITH [3377] (*Jewess* or *Judahite*).

1. Wife of Esau (Ge 26:34).

2. Heroine of apocryphal book of Judith.

JULIA [2684] (*of Julian [the family of Julius Caesar]*). A Christian woman in Rome (Ro 16:15).

JULIUS [2685] (*of Julian [the family of Julius Caesar]*). Roman centurion to whom Paul was entrusted (Ac 27:1,3).

JUNIAS, JUNIA [2687]. A kinsman of Paul (Ro 16:7).

JUNIPER *See Broom Tree.*

JUPITER Latin for the god Zeus. *See Zeus.*

JURISDICTION *See Church, The Body of Believers, State.*

JURY Of ten elders (Ru 4:2). Of seventy elders (Nu 11:16-17,24-25).

JUSHAB-HESED [3457] (*loyal love will be returned*). Son of Zerubbabel (1Ch 3:20).

JUST, THE *See Righteous.*

JUST SHALL LIVE BY FAITH (Hab 2:4; Ro 1:17; Gal 3:11; Heb 10:38).

JUSTICE [1906, 1907, 2006, 4793, 4797, 5477, 5742, 7405, 7406, 7407, 8190, 9149, 10169, *1466, 1472, 1688, 1689, 3213*].

NIV+ JUST, JUSTIFICATION, JUSTIFIED, JUSTIFIES, JUSTIFY, JUSTIFYING, JUSTLY

From God—

Ps 72:1 Endow the king with your justice, O God, the royal son with your righteousness. ²He will judge your people in righteousness, your afflicted ones with justice.

Pr 29:26 Many seek an audience with a ruler, but it is from the LORD that man gets justice.

Commanded—

Ex 23:1 "Do not spread false reports. Do not help a wicked man by being a malicious witness.

²"Do not follow the crowd in doing wrong. When you give testimony in a lawsuit, do not pervert justice by siding with the crowd, ³and do not show favoritism to a poor man in his lawsuit.

Ex 23:6 "Do not deny justice to your poor people in their lawsuits. ⁷Have nothing to do with a false charge and do not put an innocent or honest person to death, for I will not acquit the guilty.

8"Do not accept a bribe, for a bribe blinds those who see and twists the words of the righteous.

Lev 19:13 "'Do not defraud your neighbor or rob him. "'Do not hold back the wages of a hired man overnight.

14"'Do not curse the deaf or put a stumbling block in front of the blind, but fear your God. I am the LORD.

15"'Do not pervert justice; do not show partiality to the poor or favoritism to the great, but judge your neighbor fairly.

Dt 16:18 Appoint judges and officials for each of your tribes in every town the LORD your God is giving you, and they shall judge the people fairly. **19**Do not pervert justice or show partiality. Do not accept a bribe, for a bribe blinds the eyes of the wise and twists the words of the righteous. **20**Follow justice and justice alone, so that you may live and possess the land the LORD your God is giving you.

Dt 25:1 When men have a dispute, they are to take it to court and the judges will decide the case, acquitting the innocent and condemning the guilty. **2**If the guilty man deserves to be beaten, the judge shall make him lie down and have him flogged in his presence with the number of lashes his crime deserves, **3**but he must not give him more than forty lashes. If he is flogged more than that, your brother will be degraded in your eyes.

4Do not muzzle an ox while it is treading out the grain.

Ps 82:3 Defend the cause of the weak and fatherless; maintain the rights of the poor and oppressed. **4**Rescue the weak and needy; deliver them from the hand of the wicked. (+Ps 106:3)

Pr 18:5 It is not good to be partial to the wicked or to deprive the innocent of justice.

Isa 1:17 learn to do right! Seek justice, encourage the oppressed. Defend the cause of the fatherless, plead the case of the widow. (+Jer 7:5,7)

La 3:35 to deny a man his rights before the Most High, **36**to deprive a man of justice—would not the Lord see such things? (+Mic 6:8; Zec 7:9)

Zec 8:16 These are the things you are to do: Speak the truth to each other, and render true and sound judgment in your courts;

Jn 7:24 Stop judging by mere appearances, and make a right judgment."

Jn 7:51 "Does our law condemn anyone without first hearing him to find out what he is doing?"

Must be impartial—

Pr 24:23 These also are sayings of the wise: To show partiality in judging is not good:

Pr 28:21 To show partiality is not good—yet a man will do wrong for a piece of bread.

Can be perverted—

Ecc 3:16 And I saw something else under the sun: In the place of judgment—wickedness was there, in the place of justice—wickedness was there.

Ecc 5:8 If you see the poor oppressed in a district, and justice and rights denied, do not be surprised at such things; for one official is eyed by a higher one, and over them both are others higher still.

Isa 59:14 So justice is driven back, and righteousness stands at a distance; truth has stumbled in the streets, honesty cannot enter. **15**Truth is nowhere to be found, and whoever shuns evil becomes a prey. The LORD looked and was displeased that there was no justice.

Jer 22:3 This is what the LORD says: Do what is just and right. Rescue from the hand of his oppressor the one who has been robbed. Do no wrong or violence to the alien, the fatherless or the widow, and do not shed innocent blood in this place.

Am 5:7 You who turn justice into bitterness and cast righteousness to the ground

Am 5:11 You trample on the poor and force him to give you grain. Therefore, though you have built stone mansions, you will not live in them; though you have planted lush vineyards, you will not drink their wine. **12**For I know how many are your offenses and how great your sins. You oppress the righteous and take bribes and you deprive the poor of justice in the courts.

Mic 7:3 Both hands are skilled in doing evil; the ruler demands gifts, the judge accepts bribes, the powerful dictate what they desire—they all conspire together.

Hab 1:4 Therefore the law is paralyzed, and justice never prevails. The wicked hem in the righteous, so that justice is perverted.

Mt 12:7 If you had known what these words mean, 'I desire mercy, not sacrifice,' you would not have condemned the innocent.

Will be rewarded—

Jer 22:4 For if you are careful to carry out these commands, then kings who sit on David's throne will come through the gates of this palace, riding in chariots and on horses, accompanied by their officials and their people. (+Jer 22:15-16; Eze 18:5-9)

Of God: *See God, Justice of.*

See Court, Of Law; Injustice; Judge.

JUSTIFICATION [*2342, 7136, 7405, 8750, *1466+ 1650, 1467, 1468, 1470*].

NIV+ See JUST

The act of divine grace which restores the sinner to the relationship with God that he would have had if he had not sinned; pardon of sin. The word is used also to denote the state of the sinner after he is restored to divine favor.

Not imputing guilt to the sinner—

Ps 32:2 Blessed is the man whose sin the LORD does not count against him and in whose spirit is no deceit.

Isa 53:11 After the suffering of his soul, he will see the light [of life] and be satisfied; by his knowledge my righteous servant will justify many, and he will bear their iniquities.

Zec 3:4 The angel said to those who were standing before him, "Take off his filthy clothes." Then he said to Joshua, "See, I have taken away your sin, and I will put rich garments on you."

Jn 5:24 "I tell you the truth, whoever hears my word and believes him who sent me has eternal life and will not be condemned; he has crossed over from death to life. (+Ro 4:6)

Ro 8:1 Therefore, there is now no condemnation for those who are in Christ Jesus,

Comes from God—

Isa 45:24 They will say of me, 'In the LORD alone are righteousness and strength.'" All who have raged against him will come to him and be put to shame. **25**But in the LORD all the descendants of Israel will be found righteous and will exult.

Isa 50:8 He who vindicates me is near. Who then will bring charges against me? Let us face each other! Who is my accuser? Let him confront me!

Isa 54:17 no weapon forged against you will prevail, and you will refute every tongue that accuses you. This is the heritage of the servants of the LORD, and this is their vindication from me," declares the LORD.

Isa 61:10 I delight greatly in the LORD; my soul rejoices in my God. For he has clothed me with garments of salvation and arrayed me in a robe of righteousness, as a bridegroom adorns his head like a priest, and as a bride adorns herself with her jewels. (+Ro 3:25)

Ro 8:30 And those he predestined, he also called; those he called, he also justified; those he justified, he also glorified.

Ro 8:33 Who will bring any charge against those whom God has chosen? It is God who justifies.

2Co 5:19 that God was reconciling the world to himself in Christ, not counting men's sins against them. And he has committed to us the message of reconciliation.

2Co 5:21 God made him who had no sin to be sin for us, so that in him we might become the righteousness of God.

Tit 3:7 so that, having been justified by his grace, we might become heirs having the hope of eternal life.

Is based on his righteousness—

Ps 71:16 I will come and proclaim your mighty acts, O Sovereign LORD; I will proclaim your righteousness, yours alone.

Ps 89:16 They rejoice in your name all day long; they exult in your righteousness.

Isa 42:21 It pleased the LORD for the sake of his righteousness to make his law great and glorious.

Isa 46:12 Listen to me, you stubborn-hearted, you who are far from righteousness. ¹³I am bringing my righteousness near, it is not far away; and my salvation will not be delayed. I will grant salvation to Zion, my splendor to Israel.

Isa 51:5 My righteousness draws near speedily, my salvation is on the way, and my arm will bring justice to the nations. The islands will look to me and wait in hope for my arm. ⁶Lift up your eyes to the heavens, look at the earth beneath; the heavens will vanish like smoke, the earth will wear out like a garment and its inhabitants die like flies. But my salvation will last forever, my righteousness will never fail.

Isa 56:1 This is what the LORD says: "Maintain justice and do what is right, for my salvation is close at hand and my righteousness will soon be revealed. (+Ro 1:16-17; Gal 5:4-6)

Is not by the law (Ro 3:20)—

Gal 2:16 know that a man is not justified by observing the law, but by faith in Jesus Christ. So we, too, have put our faith in Christ Jesus that we may be justified by faith in Christ and not by observing the law, because by observing the law no one will be justified. (+Gal 3:11; 5:4-6)

Is by faith—

Ge 15:6 Abram believed the LORD, and he credited it to him as righteousness. (+Hab 2:4)

Ro 1:16 I am not ashamed of the gospel, because it is the power of God for the salvation of everyone who believes: first for the Jew, then for the Gentile. ¹⁷For in the gospel a righteousness from God is revealed, a righteousness that is by faith from first to last, just as it is written: "The righteous will live by faith." (+Ro 3:20-22,24)

Ro 3:28 For we maintain that a man is justified by faith apart from observing the law.

Ro 3:30 since there is only one God, who will justify the circumcised by faith and the uncircumcised through that same faith. (+Ro 4:2-4)

Ro 4:5 However, to the man who does not work but trusts God who justifies the wicked, his faith is credited as righteousness. ⁶David says the same thing when he speaks of the blessedness of the man to whom God credits righteousness apart from works:

⁷"Blessed are they whose transgressions are forgiven, whose sins are covered. ⁸Blessed is the man whose sin the Lord will never count against him."

⁹Is this blessedness only for the circumcised, or also for the uncircumcised? We have been saying that Abraham's faith was credited to him as righteousness. ¹⁰Under what circumstances was it credited? Was it after he was circumcised, or before? It was not after, but before! ¹¹And he received the sign of circumcision, a seal of the righteousness that he had by faith while he was still uncircumcised. So then, he is the father of all who believe but have not been circumcised, in order that righteousness might be credited to them. ¹²And he is also the father of the circumcised who not only are circumcised but who also walk in the footsteps of the faith that our father Abraham had before he was circumcised.

¹³It was not through law that Abraham and his offspring received the promise that he would be heir of the world, but through the righteousness that comes by faith. ¹⁴For if those who live by law are heirs, faith has no value and the promise is worthless, ¹⁵because law brings wrath. And where there is no law there is no transgression.

¹⁶Therefore, the promise comes by faith, so that it may be by grace and may be guaranteed to all Abraham's offspring—not only to those who are of the law but also to those who are of the faith of Abraham. He is the father of us all. ¹⁷As it is written: "I have made you a father of many nations." He is our father in the sight of God, in whom he believed—the God who gives life to the dead and calls things that are not as though they were.

¹⁸Against all hope, Abraham in hope believed and so became the father of many nations, just as it had been said to him, "So shall your offspring be." ¹⁹Without weakening in his faith, he faced the fact that his body was as good as dead—since he was about a hundred years old—and that Sarah's womb was also dead. ²⁰Yet he did not waver through unbelief regarding the promise of God, but was strengthened in his faith and gave glory to God, ²¹being fully persuaded that God had power to do what he had promised. ²²This is why "it was credited to him as righteousness." ²³The words "it was credited to him" were written not for him alone, ²⁴but also for us, to whom God will credit righteousness—for us who believe in him who raised Jesus our Lord from the dead. ²⁵He was delivered over to death for our sins and was raised to life for our justification.

Ro 5:1 Therefore, since we have been justified through faith, we have peace with God through our Lord Jesus Christ,

Ro 9:30 What then shall we say? That the Gentiles, who did not pursue righteousness, have obtained it, a righteousness that is by faith; ³¹but Israel, who pursued a law of righteousness, has not attained it. ³²Why not? Because they pursued it not by faith but as if it were by works. They stumbled over the "stumbling stone."

Ro 10:4 Christ is the end of the law so that there may be righteousness for everyone who believes.

Ro 10:6 But the righteousness that is by faith says: "Do not say in your heart, 'Who will ascend into heaven?'" (that is, to bring Christ down)

Ro 10:8 But what does it say? "The word is near you; it is in your mouth and in your heart," that is, the word of faith we are proclaiming: ⁹That if you confess with your mouth,

"Jesus is Lord," and believe in your heart that God raised him from the dead, you will be saved. [10]For it is with your heart that you believe and are justified, and it is with your mouth that you confess and are saved. [11]As the Scripture says, "Anyone who trusts in him will never be put to shame." (+Gal 2:14-21; 3:6)

Gal 3:8 The Scripture foresaw that God would justify the Gentiles by faith, and announced the gospel in advance to Abraham: "All nations will be blessed through you." [9]So those who have faith are blessed along with Abraham, the man of faith.

Gal 3:21 Is the law, therefore, opposed to the promises of God? Absolutely not! For if a law had been given that could impart life, then righteousness would certainly have come by the law. [22]But the Scripture declares that the whole world is a prisoner of sin, so that what was promised, being given through faith in Jesus Christ, might be given to those who believe.

Gal 3:24 So the law was put in charge to lead us to Christ that we might be justified by faith.

Gal 5:4 You who are trying to be justified by law have been alienated from Christ; you have fallen away from grace. [5]But by faith we eagerly await through the Spirit the righteousness for which we hope. [6]For in Christ Jesus neither circumcision nor uncircumcision has any value. The only thing that counts is faith expressing itself through love.

Php 3:8 What is more, I consider everything a loss compared to the surpassing greatness of knowing Christ Jesus my Lord, for whose sake I have lost all things. I consider them rubbish, that I may gain Christ [9]and be found in him, not having a righteousness of my own that comes from the law, but that which is through faith in Christ—the righteousness that comes from God and is by faith.

Heb 11:4 By faith Abel offered God a better sacrifice than Cain did. By faith he was commended as a righteous man, when God spoke well of his offerings. And by faith he still speaks, even though he is dead.

Heb 11:7 By faith Noah, when warned about things not yet seen, in holy fear built an ark to save his family. By his faith he condemned the world and became heir of the righteousness that comes by faith.

Jas 2:20 You foolish man, do you want evidence that faith without deeds is useless? [21]Was not our ancestor Abraham considered righteous for what he did when he offered his son Isaac on the altar? [22]You see that his faith and his actions were working together, and his faith was made complete by what he did. [23]And the scripture was fulfilled that says, "Abraham believed God, and it was credited to him as righteousness," and he was called God's friend.

Jas 2:26 As the body without the spirit is dead, so faith without deeds is dead.

Achieved through Christ (Isa 53:11)—

Jer 23:6 In his days Judah will be saved and Israel will live in safety. This is the name by which he will be called: The Lord Our Righteousness.

Ac 13:39 Through him everyone who believes is justified from everything you could not be justified from by the law of Moses. (+Ro 3:20)

Ro 3:21 But now a righteousness from God, apart from law, has been made known, to which the Law and the Prophets testify. [22]This righteousness from God comes through faith in Jesus Christ to all who believe. There is no difference, (+Ro 3:23)

Ro 3:24 and are justified freely by his grace through the redemption that came by Christ Jesus. [25]God presented him as a sacrifice of atonement, through faith in his blood. He did this to demonstrate his justice, because in his forbearance he had left the sins committed beforehand unpunished—

Ro 5:9 Since we have now been justified by his blood, how much more shall we be saved from God's wrath through him!

Ro 5:11 Not only is this so, but we also rejoice in God through our Lord Jesus Christ, through whom we have now received reconciliation.

Ro 5:16 Again, the gift of God is not like the result of the one man's sin: The judgment followed one sin and brought condemnation, but the gift followed many trespasses and brought justification. [17]For if, by the trespass of the one man, death reigned through that one man, how much more will those who receive God's abundant provision of grace and of the gift of righteousness reign in life through the one man, Jesus Christ.

[18]Consequently, just as the result of one trespass was condemnation for all men, so also the result of one act of righteousness was justification that brings life for all men.

Ro 5:21 so that, just as sin reigned in death, so also grace might reign through righteousness to bring eternal life through Jesus Christ our Lord.

1Co 1:30 It is because of him that you are in Christ Jesus, who has become for us wisdom from God—that is, our righteousness, holiness and redemption.

1Co 6:11 And that is what some of you were. But you were washed, you were sanctified, you were justified in the name of the Lord Jesus Christ and by the Spirit of our God.

Col 2:13 When you were dead in your sins and in the uncircumcision of your sinful nature, God made you alive with Christ. He forgave us all our sins, [14]having canceled the written code, with its regulations, that was against us and that stood opposed to us; he took it away, nailing it to the cross.

Fruits of:

Peace (Ro 5:1).

Holiness—

Ro 6:22 But now that you have been set free from sin and have become slaves to God, the benefit you reap leads to holiness, and the result is eternal life.

Example of:

Abraham (Ge 15:6; Ro 4:3).

See Adoption; Forgiveness; Regeneration; Sanctification; Sin, Confession of, Forgiveness of.

JUSTUS [2688] (*just*).

NIV+ TITIUS

1. A disciple nominated with Matthias to succeed Judas Iscariot (Ac 1:23).

2. A believer in Corinth (Ac 18:7).

3. Also called Jesus. A disciple in Rome (Col 4:11).

JUTTAH [3420] (*extended, inclined*). A Levitical city in Judah (Jos 15:55; 21:16).

K

KAB *See Cab; Measure.*

KABZEEL [7696] (*God [El] collects*). A city of Judah (Jos 15:21; 2Sa 23:20; 1Ch 11:22).

KADESH [7729] (*sacred place*).

NIV+ EN MISHPAT, KADESH BARNEA, MERIBAH KADESH

Also known as En Mishpat (Ge 14:7). A place c. seventy miles S of Hebron, in the vicinity of which Israel wandered for thirty-seven years (Dt 1:46; Nu 33:37-38; Dt 2:14). Miriam died there (Nu 20:1), Moses sent spies to Israel from there (Nu 13:21-26; Dt 1:19-25), Moses displeased God there by striking the rock instead of speaking to it (Nu 20:2-13). Often called Kadesh Barnea (Nu 32:8; Dt 2:14).

KADESH BARNEA [7732] (*sacred place of Barnea*). *See Kadesh.*

KADMIEL [7718] (*[stand] before God [El]*).

1. A Levite (Ezr 2:40; 3:9; Ne 7:43; 12:8,24).
2. A Levite who assisted in leading the worship of the people (Ne 9:4-5; 10:9).

KADMONITES [7720] (*easterners*). Ancient Arab tribe between Egypt and Euphrates (Ge 15:18-21).

KAIN [7805] (*smith*).

1. Town in Judah (Jos 15:57).
2. Tribal name (Nu 24:22; Jdg 4:11). *See Kenite(s).*

KALLAI [7834] (*swift*). A priest (Ne 12:20).

KAMAI *See Leb Kamai.*

KAMON [7852]. Place where Jair was buried (Jdg 10:5).

KANAH [7867] (*reed*).

1. Brook flowing between Ephraim and Manasseh into the Mediterranean (Jos 16:8; 17:9).
2. City c. eight miles SE of Tyre, near boundary of Manasseh (Jos 19:28).

KAREAH [7945] (*bald head*). Father of Johanan, governor of Judah in the time of Gedaliah (2Ki 25:23; Jer 40:8,13; 41:11,13-14,16).

KARKA, KARKAA [7978] (*floor, ground*). A city of Judah (Jos 15:3).

KARKOR [7980]. Place E of Jordan where Gideon defeated Midianites (Jdg 8:10). Exact location unknown.

KARNAIM [7969]. (*horns*).

NIV+ Ashteroth Karnaim.

A city conquered by Israel (Am 6:13).

KARTAH [7985] (*city*). A city of Zebulun (Jos 21:34).

KARTAN [7986]. A Levitical city in Naphtali (Jos 21:32).

KATTATH [7793]. A city in Zebulun (Jos 19:15).

KATYDID [6155]. An insect permitted as food (Lev 11:22). *See Insects.*

KAZIN *See Eth Kazin.*

KEBAR [3894]. A river of Mesopotamia (Eze 1:1,3; 3:15,23; 10:15,22; 43:3).

KEDAR [7723] (*mighty*).

NIV+ KEDAR'S

1. Son of Ishmael (Ge 25:13; 1Ch 1:29).
2. A nomadic clan of the Ishmaelites (Ps 120:5; SS 1:5; Isa 21:16; 42:11; 60:7; Jer 49:28). Flocks of (Isa 60:7; Jer 49:28). Princes and commerce of (Eze 27:21).

KEDEMAH [7715] (*east*). Son of Ishmael (Ge 25:15; 1Ch 1:31).

KEDEMOTH [7717] (*east*). A city of Moab, allotted to Reuben and the Merarite Levites (Jos 13:18; 1Ch 6:79). Encircled by a wilderness of same name (Dt 2:26).

KEDESH [7730] (*sacred place*).

1. A city of Judah (Jos 15:23). Possibly identical with Kadesh Barnea.
2. Called also Kishion and Kishon. A Canaanite city taken by Joshua (Jos 12:22; 19:20; 21:28; 1Ch 6:72).
3. Called also Kedesh in Naphtali. A city of refuge (Jos 20:7; 21:32). Home of Barak and Heber (Jdg 4:6,9,11). Captured by Tiglath-Pileser (2Ki 15:29).

KEDESH NAPHTALI (*sacred place of Naphtali*). *See Kedesh, 3.*

KEDORLAOMER [3906] (*servant of [the deity] Lagamar*). King of Elam (Ge 14:1-16).

KEDRON *See Kidron.*

KEEPERS Of the prison (Ge 39:22; Ac 5:23; 12:6; 16:27,36).

KEHELATHAH [7739] (*assembly*). An encampment of Israel (Nu 33:22-23).

KEILAH [7881].

1. One of a group of nine cities in the southern part of Israel allotted to Judah (Jos 15:44). Philistines make a predatory excursion against, after harvest (1Sa 23:1). David rescues (1Sa 23:2-13). Rulers of, aid in restoring the wall of Jerusalem after the Captivity (Ne 3:17-18).
2. A descendant of Caleb (1Ch 4:19).

KELAIAH [7835] (perhaps *Yahweh has dishonored*).

NIV+ KELITA

Called also Kelita. A Levite who divorced his Gentile wife after the Captivity and assisted Ezra in expounding the law (Ezr 10:23; Ne 8:7; 10:10).

KELAL [4006] (*perfection, completeness*). Son of Pahath-Moab (Ezr 10:30).

KELITA *Kelaiah.*

KELUB [3991] (*basket*).

1. A descendant of Caleb (1Ch 4:11).
2. Father of Ezri (1Ch 27:26).

KELUBAI *See Caleb, 1.*

KELUHI [3988]. Son of Bani (Ezr 10:35).

KEMUEL [7851] (*God's [El's] mound* ISBE).

1. Son of Nahor; uncle of Laban and Rebekah (Ge 22:21).

2. Prince of Ephraim (Nu 34:24).

3. Father of Hashabiah, leading Levite (1Ch 27:17).

KENAANAH [4049] (*toward Canaan*).

1. Father of the false prophet Zedekiah (1Ki 22:11,24; 2Ch 18:10,23).

2. Brother of Ehud (1Ch 7:10).

KENAN [7809, *2783*]. Great-grandson of Adam (1Ch 1:2). Enosh is the father of Kenan (Ge 5:9-14).

KENANI [4039] (*Yahweh strengthens*). A Levite (Ne 9:4).

KENANIAH [4040, 4041] (*Yahweh strengthens*).

1. A Levite (1Ch 15:22,27).

2. An Izharite (1Ch 26:29).

KENATH [7875] (*possession*). Amorite city in region of Bashan in kingdom of Og (Nu 32:42; 1Ch 2:22-23).

KENAZ [7869] (*hunting*).

1. Grandson of Esau (Ge 36:11,15; 1Ch 1:36).

2. A chief of Edom (Ge 36:42; 1Ch 1:53).

3. Brother of Caleb (Jos 15:17; Jdg 1:13; 3:9,11; 1Ch 4:13).

4. Grandson of Caleb (1Ch 4:15).

KENITE(S) [7804, 7808] (*of the [copper] smiths*).

1. A Canaanite tribe whose country was given to Abraham (Ge 15:19; Nu 24:21-23).

2. The descendants of Jethro, a Midianite, father-in-law of Moses. Joined the Israelites and lived at Jericho (Jdg 1:16; 4:11; 1Ch 2:55), later in the wilderness of Judah (Jdg 1:16-17). Jael, one of the, betrayed and killed Sisera (Jdg 4:17-21).

KENIZZITE(S), KENEZITE(S) [7870]. Descendants of Kenaz (Ge 15:19). Caleb (Nu 32:12) and Othniel (Jos 15:17) were Kenizzites.

KENOSIS (*emptying*). A term applied to Christ's taking the form of a servant in the Incarnation (Php 2:7).

KEPHAR AMMONI [4112] (*village of Ammonites*). A town of Benjamin (Jos 18:24).

KEPHIRAH [4098] (*village*). A city of the Hivites (Jos 9:17; 18:26; Ezr 2:25; Ne 7:29).

KERAMIM *See Abel Keramim.*

KERAN [4154]. A Horite (Ge 36:26; 1Ch 1:41).

KERCHIEF *See Handkerchief.*

KEREN-HAPPUCH [7968] (*horn of [cosmetic] eyeshadow;* i.e., *cosmetic case*). Youngest daughter of Job (Job 42:14).

KERETHITE(S) [4165] (possibly *Cretans* BDB KB; *executioners* ISBE). A Philistine tribe, which allied with David and, with the Pelethites, formed his bodyguard (1Sa 30:14,16; 2Sa 8:18; 15:18; 20:7,23; 1Ki 1:38,44; 1Ch 18:17; Eze 25:16; Zep 2:5). Solomon's escort at his coronation (1Ki 1:38).

KERIOTH, KERIOTH HEZRON [7954, 7955] (*town of Hezron*).

NIV+ HAZOR, HEZRON

1. A city of Judah (Jos 15:25).

2. A city of Moab (Jer 48:24,41; Am 2:2).

KERITH [4134] (*cut off, perish*). A brook near Jericho (1Ki 17:3-7).

KEROS [7820]. Ancestor of the temple servants who returned with Zerubbabel (Ezr 2:44; Ne 7:47).

KERUB [4132]. Name of a place or person (Ezr 2:59; Ne 7:61).

KESALON [4076].

NIV+ JEARIM

A landmark in the N boundary of Judah (Jos 15:10).

KESED [4168] (*Chaldean [Babylonian]*). Son of Nahor (Ge 22:22).

KESIL [4069]. A town in the S of Israel (Jos 15:30). Probably identical with Bethul (Jos 19:4), and Bethuel (1Ch 4:30).

KESULLOTH [4063] (*loins or flanks [of Mt. Tabor]* BDB). A city of Issachar (Jos 19:18). Probably identical with Kisloth Tabor (Jos 19:12) and Tabor (1Ch 6:77).

KETTLE [1857, *5908*].

NIV+ KETTLES

Cooking vessel or basket (1Sa 2:14).

KETURAH [7778] (*incense, scented one*). Abraham's second wife. Mother of six sons, ancestors of Arabian tribes (Ge 25:1-6; 1Ch 1:33).

KEY [5158, *3090*].

NIV+ KEYS

(Jdg 3:25). A symbol of authority (Isa 22:22; Mt 16:19; Rev 1:18; 3:7; 9:1; 20:1). *See Binding and Loosing.*

Figurative: key of knowledge (Lk 11:52).

KEZIAH, KEZIA [7905] (*cassia [cinnamon]*). Second daughter of Job (Job 42:14).

KEZIB [3945] (*deceit*). Birthplace of Shelah (Ge 38:5), probably identical with Cozeba (1Ch 4:22), and Aczib (Jos 15:44).

KEZIZ *See Emek Keziz.*

KIBROTH HATTAAVAH, KIBROTH-HATTAAVAH [7701] (*graves of lust, greed*). A station where the Israelites were miraculously fed with quail (Nu 11:31-35; 33:16-17; Dt 9:22).

KIBZAIM [7698]. A Levitical city in Ephraim (Jos 21:22).

KID *See Animals; Goats.*

KIDNAPPING [1704+, 1705].

NIV+ KIDNAPPER, KIDNAPS

Forbidden (Ex 21:16; Dt 24:7).

Instance of:

(Jdg 21:20-23).

KIDNEY [4000].

NIV+ KIDNEYS

Used with surrounding fat as a burnt offering (Ex 29:13,

22; Lev 3:4,10,15; 4:9). Regarded as the seat of the emotions; usually translated "heart" (Ps 7:9; 16:7).

KIDON [3961]. Place where Uzzah was stricken to death because he had put his hand on the ark (1Ch 13:9-11). Called Nacon's threshing floor (2Sa 6:6).

KIDRON [7724, *3022*]. Brook of, running S under the eastern wall of Jerusalem between Jerusalem and the Mount of Olives (1Ki 2:37; Ne 2:15; Jer 31:40). David flees from Absalom across (2Sa 15:23). Destruction of idols at, by Asa, Josiah, and the Levites (1Ki 15:13; 2Ki 23:6,12; 2Ch 29:16). Source of, closed by Hezekiah (2Ch 32:1-4). Jesus crossed, on the night of his agony (Jn 18:1).

KILEAB [3976]. A son of David (2Sa 3:3). Also called Daniel (1Ch 3:1).

KILION [4002] (*annihilation*). Son of Elimelech and Naomi, married Orpah (Ru 1:2-5; 4:9-10).

KILLING *See Homicide.*

KILMAD [4008]. Merchants of (Eze 27:23).

KIMHAM [4016].
NIV+ GERUTH KIMHAM
A Gileadite (2Sa 19:37-38,40; Jer 41:17).

KINAH [7807] (*lament, dirge*). A city of Judah (Jos 15:22).

KINDNESS [1691, 2858, 2876, 3512, *14, 2307, 5789, 5792, 5982, 5983*].
NIV+ KIND, KINDEST, KINDHEARTED, KINDLY, KINDNESSES
Commanded—
Zec 7:9 "This is what the LORD Almighty says: 'Administer true justice; show mercy and compassion to one another. ¹⁰Do not oppress the widow or the fatherless, the alien or the poor. In your hearts do not think evil of each other.'
Mt 5:42 Give to the one who asks you, and do not turn away from the one who wants to borrow from you. (+Lk 6:30)
Lk 6:34 And if you lend to those from whom you expect repayment, what credit is that to you? Even 'sinners' lend to 'sinners,' expecting to be repaid in full. ³⁵But love your enemies, do good to them, and lend to them without expecting to get anything back. Then your reward will be great, and you will be sons of the Most High, because he is kind to the ungrateful and wicked.
Ac 20:35 In everything I did, I showed you that by this kind of hard work we must help the weak, remembering the words the Lord Jesus himself said: 'It is more blessed to give than to receive.'"
Ro 12:15 Rejoice with those who rejoice; mourn with those who mourn.
Ro 15:1 We who are strong ought to bear with the failings of the weak and not to please ourselves. ²Each of us should please his neighbor for his good, to build him up.
Gal 6:1 Brothers, if someone is caught in a sin, you who are spiritual should restore him gently. But watch yourself, or you also may be tempted. ²Carry each other's burdens, and in this way you will fulfill the law of Christ.
Gal 6:10 Therefore, as we have opportunity, let us do good to all people, especially to those who belong to the family of believers.
Eph 4:32 Be kind and compassionate to one another, forgiving each other, just as in Christ God forgave you.

Col 3:12 Therefore, as God's chosen people, holy and dearly loved, clothe yourselves with compassion, kindness, humility, gentleness and patience.
1Pe 3:8 Finally, all of you, live in harmony with one another; be sympathetic, love as brothers, be compassionate and humble. (+1Pe 3:9)
1Jn 3:17 If anyone has material possessions and sees his brother in need but has no pity on him, how can the love of God be in him? ¹⁸Dear children, let us not love with words or tongue but with actions and in truth.
    Commanded to enemies (Ex 23:4-5; Lk 6:34-35)
    Commanded to strangers—
Lev 19:34 The alien living with you must be treated as one of your native-born. Love him as yourself, for you were aliens in Egypt. I am the LORD your God.
    Commanded to a brother—
Dt 22:1 If you see your brother's ox or sheep straying, do not ignore it but be sure to take it back to him.
    Inspired by love—
1Co 13:4 Love is patient, love is kind. It does not envy, it does not boast, it is not proud. ⁵It is not rude, it is not self-seeking, it is not easily angered, it keeps no record of wrongs. ⁶Love does not delight in evil but rejoices with the truth. ⁷It always protects, always trusts, always hopes, always perseveres.
    Commends ministers (2Co 6:6).
    Rewards of—
Pr 14:21 He who despises his neighbor sins, but blessed is he who is kind to the needy.
Mt 5:7 Blessed are the merciful, for they will be shown mercy.
Mt 25:34 "Then the King will say to those on his right, 'Come, you who are blessed by my Father; take your inheritance, the kingdom prepared for you since the creation of the world. ³⁵For I was hungry and you gave me something to eat, I was thirsty and you gave me something to drink, I was a stranger and you invited me in,
    Of God (Lk 6:35).
    Kindness of good women—
Pr 31:26 She speaks with wisdom, and faithful instruction is on her tongue.
1Ti 5:9 No widow may be put on the list of widows unless she is over sixty, has been faithful to her husband, ¹⁰and is well known for her good deeds, such as bringing up children, showing hospitality, washing the feet of the saints, helping those in trouble and devoting herself to all kinds of good deeds.
    Kindness of good men—
Ps 112:5 Good will come to him who is generous and lends freely, who conducts his affairs with justice.
Heb 5:2 He is able to deal gently with those who are ignorant and are going astray, since he himself is subject to weakness.
    Of Jesus. *See Jesus the Christ, Compassion of.*

Instances of:
    Hittites to Abraham (Ge 23:6,11). Keeper of the prison to Joseph (Ge 39:21-23). Pharaoh to Jacob (Ge 45:16-20; 47:5-6). Pharaoh's daughter to Moses (Ex 2:6-10). Moses to Jethro's daughters (Ex 2:17,19). Jethro to Moses (Ex 2:20). Rahab to the spies (Jos 2:4-16). Boaz to Ruth (Ru 2:8-16; 3:15). David to Nabal (1Sa 25:15-16). Abigail to David (1Sa 25:14-35). David to Mephibosheth (2Sa 9:1-13). Joab to Absalom (2Sa 14:1-24). Obadiah to the prophets of the Lord (1Ki 18:4). Ahab to Ben-Hadad (1Ki 20:32-34). The Shunammite woman to Elisha (2Ki

4:8-10). Elisha to the Shunammite woman (2Ki 4:13-17, 28-37; 8:1). Evil-Merodach to Jehoiachin (2Ki 25:28-30). Jehosheba to Joash (2Ch 22:11). Nehemiah and the nobles to the people (Ne 5:8-19). Mordecai to Esther (Est 2:7). Ebed-Melech to Jeremiah (Jer 38:7-13). Nebuchadnezzar to Jeremiah (Jer 39:11-12).

Joseph to Mary (Mt 1:19,24). Centurion to his servant (Lk 7:2-6). Jews to Mary and Martha (Jn 11:19,33). John to Mary (Jn 19:27). Felix to Paul (Ac 24:23). Julius to Paul (Ac 27:3,43). Barbarians to Paul (Ac 28:2,7). Onesiphorus to Paul (2Ti 1:16-18).

KINE *See Cattle.*

KINGDOM OF GOD, OF HEAVEN [806, 4867, 4889, 4895, 4930, 4931, 4939, 10424, *993, 2026*]. The sovereign rule of God manifested in Christ to defeat His enemies, creating a people over whom He reigns, and issuing in a realm or realms in which the power of His reign is experienced. All they are members of the kingdom of God who voluntarily submit to the rule of God in their lives. Entrance into the kingdom is by the new birth (Jn 3:3-5); two stages in the kingdom of God; present and future in an eschatological sense; Jesus said that his ability to cast out demons was evidence that the kingdom of God had come among men (Mt 12:28). "Kingdom of heaven" is used exclusively in Matthew (33 times).

Likened to, a man who sowed good seed (Mt 13:24-30,38-43; Mk 4:26-29), a grain of mustard seed (Mt 13:31-32; Mk 4:30-31; Lk 13:18-19), leaven (Mt 13:33; Lk 13:21), a treasure (Mt 13:44), a pearl (Mt 13:45), a net (Mt 13:47-50), a king who called his servants to a reckoning (Mt 18:23-35), a house owner (Mt 20:1-16), a king who made a marriage feast for his son (Mt 22:2-14; Lk 14:16-24), ten virgins (Mt 25:1-13), a man traveling into a far country, who called his servants, and delivered to them his goods (Mt 25:14-30; Lk 19:12-27).

"My kingdom is not of this world" (Jn 18:36).

Children of the (Mt 18:3; 19:14; Mk 10:14; Lk 18:16). Rich cannot enter (Mt 19:23-24; Mk 10:23-25; Lk 18:24-25,29-30). Keys of (Mt 16:19). Glad tidings of (Lk 8:1). Mysteries of (Lk 8:10). Is not eating and drinking (Ro 14:17).

See Church, The Body of Believers; Jesus, Kingdom of.

KINGDOM OF ISRAEL *See Israel.*

KINGDOM OF JUDAH *See Judah.*

KINGDOM OF SATAN The realm of Satan's influence (Mt 12:26; Lk 11:18).

KINGS [3782, 4482, 4887, 4889, 4930, 10421, *995, 996, 5203*].

NIV+ KING, KING'S, KINGDOM, KINGDOMS, KINGS', KINGSHIP

Israel warned against seeking (1Sa 8:9-18). Sin of Israel in seeking (1Sa 12:17-20). Israel in seeking, rejected God as their king (1Sa 8:7; 10:19). Israel asked for, that they might be like the nations (1Sa 8:5,19-20). First given to Israel in anger (Hos 13:11). God reserved to himself the choice of (Dt 17:14-15; 1Sa 9:16-17; 16:12). When first established in Israel, not hereditary (Dt 17:20, w 1Sa 13:13-14; 15:28-29). Rendered hereditary in the family of David (2Sa 7:12-16; Ps 89:35-37). Of Israel not to be foreigners (Dt 17:15). Laws for the government of the kingdom by, written by Samuel (1Sa 10:25).

Forbidden to accumulate: Horses (Dt 17:16). Wives (Dt 17:17). Treasure (Dt 17:17).

Required to write and keep a copy of the divine law (Dt 17:18-20). Had power to make war and peace (1Sa 11:5-7). Often exercised power arbitrarily (1Sa 22:17-18; 2Sa 1:15; 4:9-12; 1Ki 2:23,25,31). Sometimes nominated their successors (1Ki 1:33-34; 2Ch 11:22-23). Punished for transgressing the divine law (2Sa 12:7-12; 1Ki 21:18-24). Called the Lord's anointed (1Sa 16:6; 24:6; 2Sa 19:21).

Ceremonies at Inauguration of:

Anointing (1Sa 10:1; 16:13; Ps 89:20). Crowning (2Ki 11:12; 2Ch 23:11; Ps 21:3). Proclaiming with trumpets (2Sa 15:10; 1Ki 1:34; 2Ki 9:13; 11:14). Enthroning (1Ki 1:35,46; 2Ki 11:19). Strapping on the sword (Ps 45:3). Putting into their hands the books of the law (2Ki 11:12; 2Ch 23:11). Covenanting to govern lawfully (2Sa 5:3). Receiving homage (1Sa 10:1; 1Ch 29:24). Shouting "Long live the King!" (1Sa 10:24; 2Sa 16:16; 2Ki 11:12). Offering sacrifice (1Sa 11:15). Feasting (1Ch 12:38-39; 29:22). Attended by a bodyguard (1Sa 13:2; 2Sa 8:18; 1Ch 11:25; 2Ch 12:10). Dwelt in royal palaces (2Ch 9:11; Ps 45:15). Arrayed in royal apparel (1Ki 22:30; Mt 6:29). Names of, often changed at their accession (2Ki 23:34; 24:17).

Officers of:

Prime minister (2Ch 19:11, w 2Ch 28:7). First Counselor (1Ch 27:33). Confident or king's special friend (1Ki 4:5; 1Ch 27:33). Comptroller of the household (1Ki 4:6; 2Ch 28:7). Scribe or secretary (2Sa 8:17; 1Ki 4:3). Captain of the host (2Sa 8:16; 1Ki 4:4). Captain of the guard (2Sa 8:18; 20:23). Recorder (2Sa 8:16; 1Ki 4:3). Providers for the king's table (1Ki 4:7-19). Master of the wardrobe (2Ki 22:14; 2Ch 34:22). Treasurer (1Ch 27:25). Storekeeper (1Ch 27:25). Overseer of, the tribute (1Ki 4:6; 12:18), royal farms (1Ch 27:26), royal vineyards (1Ch 27:27), royal plantations (1Ch 27:28), royal herds (1Sa 21:7; 1Ch 27:29), royal camels (1Ch 27:30), royal flocks (1Ch 27:31). Armor-bearer (1Sa 16:21). Cupbearer (1Ki 10:5; 2Ch 9:4). Approached with greatest reverence (1Sa 24:8; 2Sa 9:8; 14:22; 1Ki 1:23). Presented with gifts by strangers (1Ki 10:2,10,25; 2Ki 5:5; Mt 2:11). Right hand of, the place of honor (1Ki 2:19; Ps 45:9; 110:1). Attendants of, stood in their presence (1Ki 10:8; 2Ki 25:19). Exercised great hospitality (1Sa 20:25-27; 2Sa 9:7-13; 19:33; 1Ki 4:22-23,28).

Their Revenues Derived From:

Voluntary contributions (1Sa 10:27, w 1Sa 16:20; 1Ch 12:39-40). Tribute from foreign nations (1Ki 4:21,24-25; 2Ch 8:8; 17:11). Tax on produce of the land (1Ki 4:7-19). Tax on foreign merchandise (1Ki 10:15). Their own flocks and herds (2Ch 32:29). Produce of their own lands (2Ch 26:10).

Conspiracies Against:

Absalom against David (2Sa 15:10). Adonijah against Solomon (1Ki 1:5-7). Jeroboam against Rehoboam (1Ki 12:12,16). Baasha against Nadab (1Ki 15:27). Zimri against Elah (1Ki 16:9-10). Omri against Zimri (1Ki 16:17). Jehu against Joram (2Ki 9:14). Shallum against Zechariah (2Ki 15:10). Menahem against Shallum (2Ki 15:14). Pekah against Menahem (2Ki 15:25).

The Kings of Israel and Judah:

In chart on the facing page, some kings, such as Uzziah and Jotham, had overlapping reigns. *See also each king by name and the outlines of the books of Kings and Chronicles.*

	Name	Ruled	Dates B.C.	Biblical References
The Kings of the United Kingdom				
1.	Saul	40 years	1050-1010	1Sa 11:15,31; 1Ch 10
2.	David	40 years	1010-970	2Sa 2:4; 1Ki 2:11; 1Ch 11-29
3.	Solomon	40 years	970-930	1Ki 1:39; 11:43; 2Ch 1-9
The Kings (and Queen) of Judah				
1.	Rehoboam	17 years	930-913	1Ki 12:1-24; 14:21-31; 2Ch 10:1-17; 12
2.	Abijah	3 years	913-910	1Ki 15:1-8; 2Ch 13
3.	Asa	41 years	910-869	1Ki 15:9-24; 2Ch 14; 16:14
4.	Jehoshaphat	25 years	872-848	1Ki 22:41-50; 2Ch 17; 21:1
5.	Jehoram	8 years	848-841	2Ki 8:16-24; 21
6.	Ahaziah	1 year	841	2Ki 8:25-29; 9:16-29; 2Ch 22:1-9
7.	Queen Athaliah	6 years	841-835	2Ki 11:1-3; 2Ch 22:10-12
8.	Joash	40 years	835-796	2Ki 11:4; 12; 2Ch 23-24
9.	Amaziah	29 years	796-767	2Ki 14:1-20; 2Ch 25
10.	Uzziah / Azariah	52 years	792-740	2Ki 14:21-22; 15:1-7; 2Ch 26
11.	Jotham	16 years	750-735	2Ki 15:32-38; 2Ch 27
12.	Ahaz	16 years	732-715	2Ki 16; 2Ch 28
13.	Hezekiah	29 years	715-686	2Ki 18-20; 2Ch 29-32
14.	Manasseh	55 years	697-642	2Ki 21:1-18; 2Ch 33:1-20
15.	Amon	2 years	642-640	2Ki 21:19-26; 2Ch 33:21-25
16.	Josiah	31 years	640-609	2Ki 22; 23:1-30; 2Ch 34-35
17.	Jehoahaz	3 months	609	2Ki 23:31-33; 2Ch 36:1-4
18.	Jehoiakim	11 years	609-598	2Ki 23:34-37; 24:1-6; 2Ch 36:5-8
19.	Jehoiachin	3 months	598-597	2Ki 24:8-16; 2Ch 36:9-10
20.	Zedekiah / Mattaniah	11 years	597-586	2Ki 24:17-20; 25:1-7; 2Ch 36:11-21
The Kings of Israel				
1.	Jeroboam I	22 years	930-909 B.C.	1Ki 12:20,25; 14:20
2.	Nadab	2 years	909-908	1Ki 15:25-27,31
3.	Baasha	24 years	908-886	1Ki 15:28-34; 16:1-7
4.	Elah	2 years	886-885	1Ki 16:8-14
5.	Zimri	7 days	885	1Ki 16:11-12,15-20
6.	Omri	12 years	885-874	1Ki 16:23-28
7.	Ahab	22 years	874-853	1Ki 16:29-22:40
8.	Ahaziah	2 years	853-852	1Ki 22:51-53; 2Ki 1
9.	Joram	12 years	852-841	2Ki 3-9:26
10.	Jehu	28 years	841-814	2Ki 9:3-10; 36
11.	Jehoahaz	17 years	814-798	2Ki 13:1-9
12.	Jehoash	16 years	798-782	2Ki 13:10-25; 14:8-16
13.	Jeroboam II	41 years	793-753	2Ki 14:23-29
14.	Zechariah	6 months	753	2Ki 15:8-12
15.	Shallum	1 month	752	2Ki 15:13-15
16.	Menahem	10 years	752-742	2Ki 15:16-22
17.	Pekahiah	2 years	742-740	2Ki 15:23-26
18.	Pekah	20 years	752-732	2Ki 15:27-31; 16:5
19.	Hoshea	9 years	732-722	2Ki 17:1-6

Relation to God:

God chooses (Dt 17:15; 1Ch 28:4-6). God ordains (Ro 13:1). God anoints (1Sa 16:12; 2Sa 12:7). Set up by God (1Sa 12:13; Da 2:21). Removed by God (1Ki 11:11; Da 2:21). Christ is the Prince of (Rev 1:5). Christ is the King of (Rev 17:14). Reign by direction of Christ (Pr 8:15). Supreme judges of nations (1Sa 8:5). Resistance to, is resistance to the ordinance of God (Ro 13:2). Able to enforce their commands (Ecc 8:4). Numerous subjects the honor of (Pr 14:28). Not saved by their armies (Ps 33:16). Dependent on the earth (Ecc 5:9). Throne of, established by righteousness and justice (Pr 16:12; 29:14).

Should:

Fear God (Dt 17:19). Serve Christ (Ps 2:10-12). Keep the law of God (1Ki 2:3). Study the Scriptures (Dt 17:19). Promote the interests of the Church (Ezr 1:2-4; 6:1-12). Nourish the Church (Isa 49:23). Rule in the fear of God (2Sa 23:3). Maintain the cause of the poor and oppressed (Pr 31:8-9). Investigate all matters (Pr 25:2). Not pervert judgment (Pr 31:5). Prolong their reign by hating greed (Pr 28:16).

Specially Warned Against:

Impurity (Pr 31:3). Lying (Pr 17:7). Listening to lies (Pr 29:12). Intemperance (Pr 31:4-5). The gospel to be preached to (Ac 9:15; 26:27-28). Without understanding, are oppressors (Pr 28:16). Often reproved by God (1Ch 16:21). Judgments upon, when opposed to Christ (Ps 2:2, 5,9).

When Good:

Regard God as their strength (Ps 99:4). Speak righteously (Pr 16:10). Love righteous lips (Pr 16:13). Abhor wickedness (Pr 16:12). Reject evil (Pr 20:8). Punish the wicked (Pr 20:26). Favor the wise (Pr 14:35). Honor the diligent (Pr 22:29). Befriend the good (Pr 22:14). Are pacified by submission (Pr 16:14; 25:15). Evil counselors should be removed from (2Ch 22:3-4; Pr 25:5).

Good exemplified: David (2Sa 8:15). Asa (1Ki 15:11). Jehoshaphat (1Ki 22:43). Amaziah (2Ki 15:3). Uzziah (2Ki 15:34). Hezekiah (2Ki 18:3). Josiah (2Ki 22:2).

Should Be:

Honored (Ro 13:7; 1Pe 2:17). Feared (Pr 24:21). Revered (1Sa 24:8; 1Ki 1:23,31). Obeyed (Ro 13:1,5; 1Pe 2:13). Prayed for (1Ti 2:1-2). Folly of resisting (Pr 19:12; 20:2). Punishment for resisting the lawful authority of (Ro 13:2). Guilt and danger of stretching out the hand against (1Sa 26:9; 2Sa 1:14). Curse not, even in thought (Ex 22:28; Ecc 10:20). Speak no evil of (Job 34:18; 2Pe 2:10). Pay tribute to (Mt 22:21; Ro 13:6-7). Be not presumptuous before (Pr 25:6). Wicked despise (2Pe 2:10; Jude 8).

KING'S GARDEN Near the Pool of Siloam (2Ki 25:4; Jer 39:4; 52:7; Ne 3:15).

KING'S HIGHWAY Ancient N and S route E of the Jordan through Edom and Moab (Nu 20:17; 21:22). The road is still in use.

KING'S VALLEY, KING'S DALE Valley of Shaveh E of Jerusalem (Ge 14:17; 2Sa 18:18).

KINGS, 1 and 2

Author: Anonymous; Jewish tradition credits Jeremiah.

Date: Between 562 B.C. and 538.

Outline:

I. The Solomonic Era (1:1-12:24).
  A. Solomon's Succession to the Throne (1:1-2:12).

  B. Solomon's Throne Consolidated (2:13-46).
  C. Solomon's Wisdom (ch. 3).
  D. Solomon's Reign Characterized (ch. 4).
  E. Solomon's Building Projects (5:1-9:9).
    1. Preparation for building the temple (ch. 5).
    2. Building the temple (ch. 6).
    3. Building the palace (7:1-12).
    4. The temple furnishings (7:13-51).
    5. Dedication of the temple (ch. 8).
    6. The Lord's response and warning (9:1-9).
  F. Solomon's Reign Characterized (9:10-10:29).
  G. Solomon's Folly (11:1-13).
  H. Solomon's Throne Threatened (11:14-43).
  I. Rehoboam's Succession to the Throne (12:1-24).
II. Israel and Judah from Jeroboam I/Rehoboam to Ahab/Asa (12:25-16:34).
  A. Jeroboam I of Israel (12:25-14:20).
  B. Rehoboam of Judah (14:21-31).
  C. Abijah of Judah (15:1-8).
  D. Asa of Judah (15:9-24).
  E. Nadab of Israel (15:25-32).
  F. Baasha of Israel (15:33-16:7).
  G. Elah of Israel (16:8-14).
  H. Zimri of Israel (16:15-20).
  I. Omri of Israel (16:21-28).
  J. Ahab of Israel (16:29-34).
III. The Ministries of Elijah and Elisha and Other Prophets from Ahab/Asa to Joram/Jehoshaphat (17:1-2Ki 8:15).
  A. Elijah (and Other Prophets) in the Reign of Ahab (17:1-22:40).
    1. Elijah and the drought (ch. 17).
    2. Elijah on Mount Carmel (ch. 18).
    3. Elijah's flight to Horeb (ch. 19).
    4. A prophet condemns Ahab for sparing Ben-Hadad (ch. 20).
    5. Elijah condemns Ahab for seizing Naboth's vineyard (ch. 21).
    6. Micaiah prophesies Ahab's death; its fulfillment (22:1-40).
  B. Jehoshaphat of Judah (22:41-50).
  C. Ahaziah of Israel; Elijah's Last Prophecy (22:51-2Ki 1:18).
  D. Elijah's Translation; Elisha's Inauguration (2Ki 2:1-18).
  E. Elisha in the Reign of Joram (2:19-8:15).
    1. Elisha's initial miraculous signs (2:19-25).
    2. Elisha during the campaign against Moab (ch. 3).
    3. Elisha's ministry to needy ones in Israel (ch. 4).
    4. Elisha heals Naaman (ch. 5).
    5. Elisha's deliverance of one of the prophets (6:1-7).
    6. Elisha's deliverance of Joram from Aramean raiders (6:8-23).
    7. Aramean siege of Samaria lifted, as Elisha prophesied (6:24-7:20).
    8. The Shunammite's land restored (8:1-6).
    9. Elisha prophesies Hazael's oppression of Israel (8:7-15).
IV. Israel and Judah from Joram/Jehoram to the Exile of Israel (2Ki 8:16-17:41).
  A. Jehoram of Judah (8:16-24).
  B. Ahaziah of Judah (8:25-29).
  C. Jehu's Revolt and Reign (chs. 9-10).
    1. Elisha orders Jehu's anointing (9:1-13).
    2. Jehu's assassination of Joram and Ahaziah (9:14-29).
    3. Jehu's execution of Jezebel (9:30-37).

4. Jehu's slaughter of Ahab's family (10:1-17).

5. Jehu's eradication of Baal worship (10:18-36).

D. Athaliah and Joash of Judah; Repair of the Temple (chs. 11-12).

E. Jehoahaz of Israel (13:1-9).

F. Jehoash of Israel; Elisha's Last Prophecy (13:10-25).

G. Amaziah of Judah (14:1-22).

H. Jeroboam II of Israel (14:23-29).

I. Azariah of Judah (15:1-7).

J. Zechariah of Israel (15:8-12).

K. Shallum of Israel (15:13-16).

L. Menahem of Israel (15:17-22).

M. Pekahiah of Israel (15:23-26).

N. Pekah of Israel (15:27-31).

O. Jotham of Judah (15:32-38).

P. Ahaz of Judah (ch. 16).

Q. Hoshea of Israel (17:1-6).

R. Exile of Israel; Resettlement of the Land (17:7-41).

V. Judah from Hezekiah to the Babylonian Exile (2Ki 18-25).

A. Hezekiah (chs. 18-20).

1. Hezekiah's good reign (18:1-8).

2. The Assyrian threat and deliverance (18:9-19:37).

3. Hezekiah's illness; alliance with Babylon (ch. 20).

B. Manasseh (21:1-18).

C. Amon (21:19-26).

D. Josiah (22:1-23:30).

1. Repair of the temple; discovery of the Book of the Law (ch. 22).

2. Renewal of the covenant; end of Josiah's reign (23:1-30).

E. Jehoahaz Exiled to Egypt (23:31-35).

F. Jehoiakim: First Babylonian Invasion (23:36-24:7).

G. Jehoiachin: Second Babylonian Invasion (24:8-17).

H. Zedekiah (24:18-20).

I. Babylonian Exile of Judah (25:1-21).

J. Removal of the Remnant to Egypt (25:22-26).

K. Elevation of Jehoiachin in Babylon (25:27-30).

KINNERETH [4054, 4055] (zithers, lyres).

1. A district in the N of Israel (Jos 11:2; 1Ki 15:20).

2. A city in Naphtali (Jos 19:35).

3. The sea of (Nu 34:11; Jos 12:3; 13:27). See Galilee, Sea of.

KINSMAN [278, 1457, 4530, 4531, 7940].
NIV+ KIN, KINSMAN-REDEEMER, KINSMAN-REDEEMERS, KINSMEN

Family or friends (Job 19:14), of same tribe (1Ch 12:2, 29; 2Ch 29:34; Ezr 8:17), fellow Israelites (2Ch 28:8). Figurative of wisdom (Pr 7:4). See Kinsman-Redeemer.

KINSMAN-REDEEMER [1457].
NIV+ KIN, KINSMAN, KINSMAN-REDEEMERS, KINSMEN

A close relative responsible for protecting the interests of needy members of the extended family. To provide an heir for a brother who had died (Ge 38:6-11; Dt 25:5-10; Ru 3-4). See Levirite Marriage. To redeem land that a poor relative had sold outside the family (Lev 25:25-28). To redeem a relative who had been sold into slavery (Lev 25:47-49). To avenge the killing of a relative (Nu 35:19-21). See Avenger of Blood.

KIOS [5944]. An island W of Smyrna (Ac 20:15).

KIR [7816, 7817] (walled enclosure).
NIV+ KIR HARESETH

The inhabitants of Damascus carried into captivity to,

by the king of Assyria (2Ki 16:9). Prophecies concerning (Isa 22:6; Am 1:5; 9:7).

KIR HARESETH, KIR-HARASETH [7818, 7819] (walled [city] of pottery fragments).
NIV+ KIR

A city of Moab (2Ki 3:25; Isa 16:7,11; Jer 48:31,36). Called Kir of Moab (Isa 15:1).

KIR OF MOAB See Kir.

KIRIATH ARBA, KIRJATH-ARBA [7957, 7959] (city of four).
NIV+ ARBA, HEBRON

Ancient name for Hebron (Ge 23:2; Jos 14:15; 15:54; 20:7).

KIRIATH BAAL See Kiriath Jearim.

KIRIATH HUZOTH, KIRJATH-HUZOTH [7960] (city of Huzoth [outside spaces]).
NIV+ HUZOTH

A residence of Balak (Nu 22:39).

KIRIATH JEARIM, KIRJATH-JEARIM [7961] (city of timberlands).
NIV+ BAALAH, JEARIM, KIRIATH BAAL

Called also Baalah, one of the four cities of the Gibeonites. Inhabitants of, not destroyed, on account of the covenant made by the Israelites with the Gibeonites, but put under servitude (Jos 9:17, w Jos 9:3-27).

In the territory allotted to Judah (Jos 15:9,60; 18:14). The Philistines bring the ark to (1Sa 6:21, w 1Sa 6:1-21), ark remains twenty years at (1Sa 7:1-2; 1Ch 13:5-6). David brings the ark from (2Sa 6:1-11; 1Ch 13:5-8; 2Ch 1:4). Inhabitants of, who were taken into captivity to Babylon, returned (Ezr 2:25; Ne 7:29). Uriah, the prophet, an inhabitant of (Jer 26:20).

KIRIATH, KIRJATH (city of). City of Benjamin (Jos 18:28).

KIRIATH SANNAH, KIRJATH-SANNAH [7962] (city of Sannah).
NIV+ DEBIR, SANNAH

A city of Judah (Jos 15:49); also called Kiriath Sepher and Debir. See Debir; Kiriath Sepher.

KIRIATH SEPHER, KIRJATH-SEPHER [7963] (city of scribe).
NIV+ DEBIR, SEPHER

A city of Judah (Jos 15:15-16); also called Kiriath Sannah and Debir. See Debir; Kiriath Sannah.

KIRIATHAIM, KIRJATHAIM [7964] (two cities).
NIV+ SHAVEH KIRIATHAIM

1. Town in Moab N of Arnon. Assigned to Reuben (Nu 32:37; Jos 13:19).

2. City of Gershonite Levites in Naphtali (1Ch 6:76). Called Kartan (Jos 21:32).

KIRIOTH See Kerioth, Kerioth Hezron.

KIRJATH-ARIM See Kiriath Jearim, Kirjath-Jearim.

KISH [7821, 3078] (bow, power).

1. Father of Saul (1Sa 9:1-3; 10:21; 2Sa 21:14). Called Kish (Ac 13:21).

2. A Benjamite (1Ch 8:30; 9:36).

3. A Levite (1Ch 23:21-22; 24:29).

4. A Levite (2Ch 29:12).

5. Great-grandfather of Mordecai (Est 2:5).

KISHI [7823] (possibly *gift* IDB; *snarer* ISBE). Also called Kushaiah. Father of Ethan, a chief assistant in the temple music (1Ch 6:44; 15:17).

KISHION [8002]. City of Issachar (Jos 19:20). Also called Kedesh (1Ch 6:72).

KISHON [7822] (*cunning*). A river of Israel emptying into the Mediterranean near the northern base of Mount Carmel. Sisera defeated here, and his army destroyed (Jdg 4:7,13; 5:21; Ps 83:9). Prophets of Baal destroyed by Elijah at (1Ki 18:40).

KISLEV [4075]. Month nine in sacred sequence, month three in civil sequence (Ezr 10:9; Jer 36:9,22; Zec 7:1). The rainy season (November-December); the season for planting. The Feast of Dedication (Jn 10:22).

See Dedication; Feasts; Hanukkah; Maccabees; Month, 9.

KISLON [4077] (*slow* IDB; *strength* ISBE). Father of Eldad (Nu 34:21).

KISLOTH TABOR [4079].

NIV+ TABOR

A place on the border of Zebulun (Jos 19:12). Called Tabor (1Ch 6:77). Probably the same as Kesulloth (Jos 19:18).

KISS [5965, 5975, *2968*, *5797*, *5799*].

NIV+ KISSED, KISSES, KISSING

Of affection (Ge 27:26-27; 31:55; 33:4; 48:10; 50:1; Ex 18:7; Ru 1:14; 2Sa 14:33; 19:39; Lk 15:20; Ac 20:37). The feet of Jesus kissed by the penitent woman (Lk 7:38).

Deceitful (Pr 27:6), of Joab, when he killed Amasa (2Sa 20:9-10), of Judas, when he betrayed Jesus (Mt 26:48; Lk 22:48).

Holy (Ro 16:16; 2Co 13:12; 1Th 5:26; 1Pe 5:14).

KITE [370, 1798, 8012]. A bird forbidden as food (Lev 11:14; Dt 14:13).

KITLISH, KITHLISH [4186]. Town in lowlands of Judah (Jos 15:40), site unknown.

KITRON [7790] (*incense, [sacrificial] smoke*). A city of Zebulun (Jdg 1:30).

KITTIM [4183].

1. Descendants of Javan (Ge 10:4; 1Ch 1:7).

2. The Hebrew name for Cyprus; probably inhabited islands of the Mediterranean (Isa 23:1,12; Jer 2:10; Eze 27:6).

3. Prophecies concerning (Nu 24:24; Da 11:30).

KNEADING TROUGH [4297, 5400].

NIV+ KNEAD, KNEADED, KNEADING, WELL-KNEADED

Shallow vessel for kneading dough with hands (Ex 8:3; 12:34).

KNEE [1386, 4156, 10072, 10123, *1205*, *1206*, *4686*].]

NIV+ KNEE-DEEP, KNEES

Bowing the knee or kneeling regarding as an act of reverence (Ge 41:43; 2Ki 1:13), and subjection (Isa 45:23; Php 2:10).

KNIFE [2995, 4408, 4661, 7644, 8501, 9509].

NIV+ KNIVES

An edged tool used by Abraham in offering Isaac (Ge 22:6,10). Of flint, used in circumcision (Ex 4:25; Jos 5:2,3). Used for pruning (Isa 18:5), by scribes (Jer 36:23).

KNOB *See Capital.*

KNOWLEDGE [*1978, 1981, 3359, 4529, 5795, 7924, 8011, 10313, 10430, *1182*, *1192*, *1194*, *1196*, *2105*, *2106*, *2179*, *2813*, *3857*].

NIV+ FOREKNEW, FOREKNOWLEDGE, KNEW, KNOW, KNOWING, KNOWN, KNOWS, WELL-KNOWN

Of good and evil (Ge 2:9,17; 3:22). Is power (Pr 3:20; 24:5). Desire for (1Ki 3:9; Ps 119:66; Pr 2; 3; 12:1; 15:14; 18:15). Rejected (Hos 4:6). Those who reject are destroyed (Hos 4:6). Fools hate (Pr 1:22,29). A divine gift (1Co 12:8). Is pleasant (Pr 2:10). Shall be increased (Da 12:4).

The earth shall be full of (Isa 11:9). Fear of the Lord is the beginning of (Pr 1:7). Of more value than gold (Pr 8:10). The priest's lips should keep (Mal 2:7).

Of salvation (Lk 1:77). Key of (Lk 11:52). Now we know in part (1Co 13:9-12). Of God more than burnt offering (Hos 6:6). Of Christ (Php 3:8).

See God, Knowledge of; Jesus the Christ, Omniscience of; Wisdom.

KOA [7760]. People E of Tigris, between Elam and Media (Eze 23:23).

KOHATH [7740, 7741].

NIV+ KOHATH'S, KOHATHITE, KOHATHITES

Second son of Levi (Ge 46:11; Ex 6:16). Grandfather of Moses, Aaron, and Miriam (Nu 26:58-59). Father of the Kohathites, one of the divisions of the Levites (Ex 6:18; Nu 3:19,27).

See Levites.

KOLAIAH [7755] (*Yahweh's voice*).

1. A Benjamite and ancestor of Sallu (Ne 11:7).

2. Father of the false prophet Ahab (Jer 29:21).

KORAH, KORAHITE(S) [7946, 7948, *3169*] (*shaven, bald*).

NIV+ KORAH'S

1. Son of Esau (Ge 36:5,14,18; 1Ch 1:35).

2. Grandson of Esau (Ge 36:16).

3. Descendant of Caleb (1Ch 2:43).

4. Levite from whom the Korahites were descended (Ex 6:24; 1Ch 6:22).

KORAZIN [*5960*]. Denunciation against (Mt 11:21; Lk 10:13).

KORE [7927] (*proclaimer*).

1. A Korahite (1Ch 9:19; 26:1).

2. A Levite, keeper of the East Gate (2Ch 31:14).

KORHITE(S) *See Korah, Korahite(s), 4; Levites.*

KOZ [7766] (*thorn*). The father of Anub and Hazzobebah (1Ch 4:8).

KUE [7745, 7750]. Probably Cilicia in SE Asia Minor (1Ki 10:28; 2Ch 1:16).

KUSHAIAH [7773]. Merarite Levite (1Ch 15:17). Also called Kishi (1Ch 6:44).

L

LAADAH [4355] (perhaps *having a fat neck or throat*). Son of Shelah (1Ch 4:21).

LAADAN *See Ladan.*

LABAN [4238, 4239] (*white*).

NIV+ LABAN'S

1. Son of Bethuel (Ge 28:5). Brother of Rebekah (Ge 22:23; 24:15,29). Receives the servant of Abraham (Ge 24:29-33). Receives Jacob and gives him his daughters in marriage (Ge 29:12-30). Jacob becomes his servant (Ge 29:15-20,27; 30:27-43). Outwitted by Jacob (Ge 30:37-43; 31:1-21). Pursues Jacob, overtakes him in hill country of Gilead, and covenants with him (Ge 31:22-55).

2. Place in Plains of Moab (Dt 1:1).

LABOR [*2655, 3330, 3333, 4989, 5126, 6025, 6026, 6268, 6275, 6661, 6662, 7189, 7674, 8492, *3159, 3160*].

NIV+ LABORED, LABORER, LABORER'S, LABORERS, LABORING, LABORS

Honorable (Ps 128:2; Pr 21:25; 1Th 4:11). Laborers protected by laws (Dt 24:14). Creative work of God described as labor (Ge 2:2).

Difficult labor the result of the curse (Ge 3:17-18)—

Ge 3:19 By the sweat of your brow you will eat your food until you return to the ground, since from it you were taken; for dust you are and to dust you will return."

Sleep of labor sweet—

Ecc 5:12 The sleep of a laborer is sweet, whether he eats little or much, but the abundance of a rich man permits him no sleep.

Labor commanded (Ge 3:19)—

Ex 20:9 Six days you shall labor and do all your work, [10]but the seventh day is a Sabbath to the LORD your God. On it you shall not do any work, neither you, nor your son or daughter, nor your manservant or maidservant, nor your animals, nor the alien within your gates. [11]For in six days the LORD made the heavens and the earth, the sea, and all that is in them, but he rested on the seventh day. Therefore the LORD blessed the Sabbath day and made it holy.

Ex 23:12 "Six days do your work, but on the seventh day do not work, so that your ox and your donkey may rest and the slave born in your household, and the alien as well, may be refreshed.

Ex 34:21 "Six days you shall labor, but on the seventh day you shall rest; even during the plowing season and harvest you must rest. (+Lev 23:3; Lk 13:14)

Ac 20:35 In everything I did, I showed you that by this kind of hard work we must help the weak, remembering the words the Lord Jesus himself said: 'It is more blessed to give than to receive.'"

Eph 4:28 He who has been stealing must steal no longer, but must work, doing something useful with his own hands, that he may have something to share with those in need.

1Th 4:11 Make it your ambition to lead a quiet life, to mind your own business and to work with your hands, just as we told you, (+2Th 3:10-12)

Compensation for—

Lev 19:13 "'Do not defraud your neighbor or rob him. "'Do not hold back the wages of a hired man overnight.

Dt 25:4 Do not muzzle an ox while it is treading out the grain. (+1Co 9:9; 1Ti 5:18)

Jer 22:13 "Woe to him who builds his palace by unrighteousness, his upper rooms by injustice, making his countrymen work for nothing, not paying them for their labor.

Mal 3:5 "So I will come near to you for judgment. I will be quick to testify against sorcerers, adulterers and perjurers, against those who defraud laborers of their wages, who oppress the widows and the fatherless, and deprive aliens of justice, but do not fear me," says the LORD Almighty.

Mt 20:1 "For the kingdom of heaven is like a landowner who went out early in the morning to hire men to work in his vineyard. [2]He agreed to pay them a denarius for the day and sent them into his vineyard.

[3]"About the third hour he went out and saw others standing in the marketplace doing nothing. [4]He told them, 'You also go and work in my vineyard, and I will pay you whatever is right.' [5]So they went. "He went out again about the sixth hour and the ninth hour and did the same thing.

[6]About the eleventh hour he went out and found still others standing around. He asked them, 'Why have you been standing here all day long doing nothing?'

[7]"'Because no one has hired us,' they answered.

"He said to them, 'You also go and work in my vineyard.'

[8]"When evening came, the owner of the vineyard said to his foreman, 'Call the workers and pay them their wages, beginning with the last ones hired and going on to the first.'

[9]"The workers who were hired about the eleventh hour came and each received a denarius. [10]So when those came who were hired first, they expected to receive more. But each one of them also received a denarius. [11]When they received it, they began to grumble against the landowner. [12]'These men who were hired last worked only one hour,' they said, 'and you have made them equal to us who have borne the burden of the work and the heat of the day.'

[13]"But he answered one of them, 'Friend, I am not being unfair to you. Didn't you agree to work for a denarius? [14]Take your pay and go. I want to give the man who was hired last the same as I gave you. [15]Don't I have the right to do what I want with my own money? Or are you envious because I am generous?'

Lk 10:7 Stay in that house, eating and drinking whatever they give you, for the worker deserves his wages. Do not move around from house to house.

Jas 5:4 Look! The wages you failed to pay the workmen who mowed your fields are crying out against you. The cries of the harvesters have reached the ears of the Lord Almighty.

Of servants must not be oppressive—

Dt 24:14 Do not take advantage of a hired man who is poor and needy, whether he is a brother Israelite or an alien living in one of your towns. [15]Pay him his wages each day before sunset, because he is poor and is counting on it. Otherwise he may cry to the LORD against you, and you will be guilty of sin.

Paul, an example—

2Th 3:8 nor did we eat anyone's food without paying for it. On the contrary, we worked night and day, laboring and toiling so that we would not be a burden to any of you. [9]We did this, not because we do not have the right to such help, but in order to make ourselves a model for you to follow. [10]For even when we were with you, we gave you this rule: "If a man will not work, he shall not eat." [11]We hear that some among you are idle. They are not busy; they are busybodies. [12]Such people we command and urge in the Lord Jesus Christ to settle down and earn the bread they eat. [13]And as for you, brothers, never tire of doing what is right.

See Capital and Labor; Employee; Employer; Idleness; Industry; Master; Servant.

LACE Cord used to bind high priest's breastplate to the ephod (Ex 28:28,37; 39:21,31).

LACHISH [4337]. Canaanite royal city and Judean border fortress, occupying a strategic valley twenty-five miles SW of Jerusalem. It is identified with Tell ed-Duweir (Tell Lakhish). Joshua captured it (Jos 10:31-33); destroyed by Nebuchadnezzar along with Jerusalem (2Ki 24-25; Jer 34:7), resettled after the Exile (Ne 11:30). Lachish Letters (ostraca) from the time of Jeremiah reveal much about the city.

LACHRYMATORY A container for holding the tears of mourners (Ps 56:8, ftn).

LADAN [4356].
1. A descendant of Ephraim (1Ch 7:26).
2. A Levite, called also Libni (1Ch 6:17; 23:7-9; 26:21).

LADDER (Ge 28:12, ftn). *See Stairs.*

LAEL [4210] (*[belonging] to God [El]*). Father of Eliasaph (Nu 3:24).

LAHAD [4262] (perhaps *slow, indolent*). A descendant of Judah (1Ch 4:2).

LAHAI-ROI *See Beer Lahai Roi, Beer-La-Hai-Roi.*

LAHMAS, LAHMAM [4314]. Town in Judean Shephelah (Jos 15:40). Probably modern Khirbet el-Lahm.

LAHMI [4313]. Brother of Goliath. Slain by Elhanan (2Sa 21:19; 1Ch 20:5).

LAISH [4331, 4332] (*lion*).
1. A Sidonian city at the N. extremity of Israel (Jdg 18:7,14,27,29). Called also Leshem (Jos 19:47), and afterwards Dan. *See Dan, 3; Leshem.*
2. A native of Gallim; a Benjamite, whose son became the husband of Michal, David's wife (1Sa 25:44; 2Sa 3:15).
3. *See Laishah.*

LAISHAH [4333] (*lion*). A town near Jerusalem (Isa 10:30).

LAKE OF FIRE [3349]. (Rev 19:20; 20:10,14-15; 21:8).

LAKKUM, LAKUM [4373]. Town of Naphtali (Jos 19:33), location unknown.

LAMA SABACHTHANI *See Eloi, Eloi, Lama Sabachthani.*

LAMB [3231, 3897, 3898, 4166, 4167, 7175, 8445+, 303, 768, 4247].

NIV+ LAMB'S, LAMBS

Used, for food (Dt 32:14; Am 6:4), for sacrifices (Ge

4:4; 22:7), especially at Passover (Ex 12:3-5). Sacrificial lambs typical of Christ (Jn 1:29; Rev 5:6,8).

Offering of (Lev 3:7; 5:6; 22:23; 23:12; Nu 7:15,21; 28:3-8), at the daily morning and evening sacrifices (Ex 29:38-42). Offering of, at the Feast of Passover (Ex 12:15), Pentecost (Lev 23:18-20), Tabernacles (Nu 29:13-40), the New Moon (Nu 28:11), trumpets (Nu 29:2). Offering of, on the Sabbath day (Nu 28:9), at purifications (Lev 12:6; 14:10-25), by the Nazirite (Nu 6:12), for sin of ignorance (Lev 4:32).

Figurative:

The wolf living with, a figure of Messiah's reign (Isa 11:6; 65:25). A type of young believers (Jn 21:15).

A name given to Christ (Jn 1:29,36; Rev 5:6,8,12-13; 6:1,16; 7:9-10,14; 12:11; 13:8; 14:4,10; 17:14; 19:7,9; 21:9,14,22-23,27; 22:1,3). Jesus compared to (Isa 53:7; Ac 8:32; 1Pe 1:19).

LAMB OF GOD A title of Jesus (Jn 1:29; Rev 6:16; 7:9-10,14,17; 12:11; 13:8; 14:1,4; 15:3; 17:14; 19:7; 21:9,14,22-23,27; 22:1,3).

LAME *See Disease.*

LAMECH [4347, *3285*].
1. Father of Jabal, Jubal, and Tubal-Cain (Ge 4:18-24).
2. Son of Methuselah, and father of Noah, lived 777 years (Ge 5:25-31; 1Ch 1:3). Ancestor of Jesus (Lk 3:36).

LAMENESS [5048, 5783, 7177, 7519, *6000*].

NIV+ LAME

Disqualified priest from exercising the priestly office (Lev 21:18). Disqualified animals for sacrificial uses (Dt 15:21). Hated by David (2Sa 5:8). Healed by Jesus (Mt 11:5; 15:31; 21:14; Lk 7:22), by Peter (Ac 3:2-11).

LAMENTATIONS [61, 627, 640, 650, 2047, 3538, 2411, 5654, 6199, 7801, 7806, 8490].

NIV+ LAMENT, LAMENTATION, LAMENTED, LAMENTS

Of David (Ps 60:1-3). Of Jeremiah (La 1-5). Of Ezekiel (Eze 19; 28:12-19).

See Elegy.

LAMENTATIONS, BOOK OF

Author: Anonymous, traditionally Jeremiah

Date: Shortly after the fall of Jerusalem in 586 B.C.

Outline:

I. Jerusalem's Misery and Desolation (ch. 1).
II. The Lord's Anger against His People (ch. 2).
III. Judah's Complaint—and Basis of Consolation (ch. 3).
IV. The Contrast between Zion's Past and Present (ch. 4).
V. Judah's Appeal for God's Forgiveness (ch. 5).

LAMP [240, 4963, 5775, 5944, *3286, 3394*].

NIV+ LAMPS, LAMPSTAND, LAMPSTANDS

Figurative—

Of joy (Jer 25:10). Life (Job 18:5-6; 21:17; Pr 13:9; 20:20). The word of God (Ps 119:105; Pr 6:23; 2Pe 1:19). Spiritual illumination (Mt 6:22). Religious influence (Mt 5:15; Mk 4:21; Lk 8:16; 11:33). Jesus is the lamp of the New Jerusalem (Rev 21:23).

Symbolic (Rev 4:5; 8:10).

See Lampstand.

LAMPSTAND [4963, 10456, *3393*]

NIV+ LAMP, LAMPS, LAMPSTANDS

Of the tabernacle: Made of gold after divine pattern (Ex 25:31-40; 37:17-24; Nu 8:4), burned olive oil (Ex 27:20).

Place of (Ex 26:35; 40:24-25; Heb 9:2). Furniture of (Ex 25:38; 37:23; Nu 4:9-10). Burned every night (Ex 27:20-21). Trimmed every morning (Ex 30:7). Carried by Kohathites (Nu 4:4,15). Called the lamp of God (1Sa 3:3).

Of the temple: Ten branches of (1Ki 7:49-50). Of gold (1Ch 28:15; 2Ch 4:20). Taken with other spoils to Babylon (Jer 52:19).

Symbolic: (Zec 4:2,11; Rev 1:12-13,20; 2:5; 11:4).

LANCE [3959]. *See Javelin; Spear.*

LAND [*141, 824, 1074, 1473, 2475, 3000, 3317, 5226, 5659, 5709, 8441, 10075, *1178, 2982, 6001, 6005*].

NIV+ BORDERLAND, GRASSLANDS, LAND'S, LANDED, LANDOWNER, LANDS, MAINLAND, SHORELANDS, WASTELAND, WASTELANDS

Appeared on third creative day (Ge 1:9). Original title to, from God (Ge 13:14-17; 15:7; Ex 23:31; Lev 25:33). Bought and sold (Ge 23:3-18; 33:19; Ac 4:34; 5:1-8).

Sale and redemption of, laws concerning (Lev 25:15-16,23-33; 27:17-24; Nu 36:4; Jer 32:7-16,25,44; Eze 46:18). Conveyance of, by written deeds and other forms (Ge 23:3-20; Ru 4:3-8,11; Jer 32:9-14), witnessed (Ge 23:10-11; Ru 4:9-11; Jer 32:9-14).

Sold for debt (Ne 5:3-5). Rights in, alienated (2Ki 8:1-6). Leased (Lk 20:9-16; Mt 21:33-41).

Priest's part in (Ge 47:22; Eze 48:10). King's part in (Eze 48:21). Widow's share in (Ru 4:3-9). Unmarried woman's rights in (Nu 27:1-11; 36:1-11).

To rest every seventh year for the benefit of the poor (Ex 23:11). Products of, for all (Ecc 5:9). Monopoly of (Ge 47:20-26; Isa 5:8; Mic 2:1-2). *See Mortgage.*

Rules for apportioning Canaan among the tribes (Eze 47:22). *See Canaan.*

LANDMARKS (*border*). Protected from fraudulent removal (Dt 19:14; 27:17; Job 24:2; Pr 22:28; 23:10; Hos 5:10).
See Boundary Stones.

LANES [5850]. Country lanes (Lk 14:21). *See Streets.*

LANGUAGE [848, 1821, 3376, 4383, 8557, 9553, 10392, *155, 1185, 1365, 3281, 3282, 3378, 5889*].

NIV+ LANGUAGES

Unity of (Ge 11:1,6). Confusion of (Ge 11:1-9; 10:5,20,31). Dialects of the Jews (Jdg 12:6; Mt 26:73). Many spoken at Jerusalem (Jn 19:20; Ac 2:8-11).

Gift of (Mk 16:17; Ac 2:7-8; 10:46; 19:6; 1Co 12:10; 14). *See Tongues, Gift of.*

Mentioned in Scripture:

Aramaic (2Ki 18:26; Ezr 4:7; Da 2:4). Of Ashdod (Ne 13:24). Babylonian [or Chaldean] (Da 1:4). Canaanite (Isa 19:18). Egyptian (Ac 2:10; Ps 81:5). Greek (Jn 19:20; Ac 21:37). Hebrew (Rev 9:11; 16:16). Of Judah (Ne 13:24). Latin (Jn 19:20). Lycaonia (Ac 14:11). Parthia and other lands (Ac 2:9-11).

LANTERN [3286]. (Jn 18:3).

LAODICEA [3293].

NIV+ LAODICEANS

A Phrygian city. Paul's concern for (Col 2:1). Epaphras' zeal for (Col 4:13). Epistle to the Colossians to be read in (Col 4:15-16). Message to, through John (Rev 1:11; 3:14-22).

LAODICEA, CHURCH AT *See Laodicea.*

LAODICEANS, EPISTLE TO Letter mentioned by Paul (Col 4:16). This is probably a letter of Paul that was not preserved for the canon. Some theorize it may be the letter to the Ephesians as a circular letter. An apocryphal epistle to the Laodiceans exists in Latin.

LAPIDARY One who cuts precious stones (Ex 31:5; 35:33).

LAPPED, LAPPETH [4379].

NIV+ LAP, LAPS

A Hebrew verb used to indicate alertness (Jdg 7:5-7) and disgust (1Ki 21:19; 22:38).

LAPPIDOTH, LAPIDOTH [4366] (*flames*). Husband of Deborah (Jdg 4:4).

LAPWING *See Hoopoe.*

LARCENY *See Theft.*

LASCIVIOUSNESS Unbridled lust, licentiousness, wantonness.

Forbidden—

Col 3:5 Put to death, therefore, whatever belongs to your earthly nature: sexual immorality, impurity, lust, evil desires and greed, which is idolatry. (+1Th 4:3-4)

1Th 4:5 not in passionate lust like the heathen, who do not know God; (+1Th 4:6)

Warnings against—

Pr 2:16 It will save you also from the adulteress, from the wayward wife with her seductive words, **¹⁷**who has left the partner of her youth and ignored the covenant she made before God.

¹⁸For her house leads down to death and her paths to the spirits of the dead.

Pr 5:3 For the lips of an adulteress drip honey, and her speech is smoother than oil; **⁴**but in the end she is bitter as gall, sharp as a double-edged sword. **⁵**Her feet go down to death; her steps lead straight to the grave.

Pr 5:8 Keep to a path far from her, do not go near the door of her house, **⁹**lest you give your best strength to others and your years to one who is cruel, **¹⁰**lest strangers feast on your wealth and your toil enrich another man's house. **¹¹**At the end of your life you will groan, when your flesh and body are spent. **¹²**You will say, "How I hated discipline! How my heart spurned correction! **¹³**I would not obey my teachers or listen to my instructors. (+Pr 7:6-27)

Pr 9:13 The woman Folly is loud; she is undisciplined and without knowledge. **¹⁴**She sits at the door of her house, on a seat at the highest point of the city, **¹⁵**calling out to those who pass by, who go straight on their way. **¹⁶**"Let all who are simple come in here!" she says to those who lack judgment. **¹⁷**"Stolen water is sweet; food eaten in secret is delicious!" **¹⁸**But little do they know that the dead are there, that her guests are in the depths of the grave.

Pr 30:18 "There are three things that are too amazing for me, four that I do not understand: **¹⁹**the way of an eagle in the sky, the way of a snake on a rock, the way of a ship on the high seas, and the way of a man with a maiden.

²⁰"This is the way of an adulteress: She eats and wipes her mouth and says, 'I've done nothing wrong.' (+Pr 31:3)

Ro 13:13 Let us behave decently, as in the daytime, not in orgies and drunkenness, not in sexual immorality and debauchery, not in dissension and jealousy. (+1Co 6:13,15-18)

1Pe 4:2 As a result, he does not live the rest of his earthly life for evil human desires, but rather for the will of God.

3For you have spent enough time in the past doing what pagans choose to do—living in debauchery, lust, drunkenness, orgies, carousing and detestable idolatry.

Jude 4 For certain men whose condemnation was written about long ago have secretly slipped in among you. They are godless men, who change the grace of our God into a license for immorality and deny Jesus Christ our only Sovereign and Lord.

Jude 7 In a similar way, Sodom and Gomorrah and the surrounding towns gave themselves up to sexual immorality and perversion. They serve as an example of those who suffer the punishment of eternal fire.

Sinful practices in—

Joel 3:3 They cast lots for my people and traded boys for prostitutes; they sold girls for wine that they might drink.

Ro 1:22 Although they claimed to be wise, they became fools **23**and exchanged the glory of the immortal God for images made to look like mortal man and birds and animals and reptiles.

24Therefore God gave them over in the sinful desires of their hearts to sexual impurity for the degrading of their bodies with one another. **25**They exchanged the truth of God for a lie, and worshiped and served created things rather than the Creator—who is forever praised. Amen.

26Because of this, God gave them over to shameful lusts. Even their women exchanged natural relations for unnatural ones. **27**In the same way the men also abandoned natural relations with women and were inflamed with lust for one another. Men committed indecent acts with other men, and received in themselves the due penalty for their perversion.

28Furthermore, since they did not think it worthwhile to retain the knowledge of God, he gave them over to a depraved mind, to do what ought not to be done. **29**They have become filled with every kind of wickedness, evil, greed and depravity. They are full of envy, murder, strife, deceit and malice. They are gossips,

Proceeds from unregenerate heart—

Mk 7:21 For from within, out of men's hearts, come evil thoughts, sexual immorality, theft, murder, adultery, **22**greed, malice, deceit, lewdness, envy, slander, arrogance and folly. **23**All these evils come from inside and make a man 'unclean.'" (+Gal 5:19)

Eph 4:17 So I tell you this, and insist on it in the Lord, that you must no longer live as the Gentiles do, in the futility of their thinking.

18They are darkened in their understanding and separated from the life of God because of the ignorance that is in them due to the hardening of their hearts. **19**Having lost all sensitivity, they have given themselves over to sensuality so as to indulge in every kind of impurity, with a continual lust for more.

Impenitence in—

2Co 12:21 I am afraid that when I come again my God will humble me before you, and I will be grieved over many who have sinned earlier and have not repented of the impurity, sexual sin and debauchery in which they have indulged.

Excludes from the kingdom of God—

1Co 6:9 Do you not know that the wicked will not inherit the kingdom of God? Do not be deceived: Neither the sexually immoral nor idolaters nor adulterers nor male prostitutes nor homosexual offenders **10**nor thieves nor the greedy nor drunkards nor slanderers nor swindlers will inherit the kingdom of God.

1Co 6:13 "Food for the stomach and the stomach for food"—but God will destroy them both. The body is not meant for sexual immorality, but for the Lord, and the Lord for the body.

1Co 6:15 Do you not know that your bodies are members of Christ himself? Shall I then take the members of Christ and unite them with a prostitute? Never! **16**Do you not know that he who unites himself with a prostitute is one with her in body? For it is said, "The two will become one flesh." **17**But he who unites himself with the Lord is one with him in spirit. **18**Flee from sexual immorality. All other sins a man commits are outside his body, but he who sins sexually sins against his own body.

1Co 9:27 No, I beat my body and make it my slave so that after I have preached to others, I myself will not be disqualified for the prize.

Gal 5:19 The acts of the sinful nature are obvious: sexual immorality, impurity and debauchery;

Gal 5:21 and envy; drunkenness, orgies, and the like. I warn you, as I did before, that those who live like this will not inherit the kingdom of God.

Eph 5:5 For of this you can be sure: No immoral, impure or greedy person—such a man is an idolater—has any inheritance in the kingdom of Christ and of God.

Lascivious practices in idolatrous worship. *See Idolatry, Wicked practices of.*

See Adultery; Homosexual; Incest; Lust; Prostitute; Rape; Sensuality.

Figurative: (Eze 16:15-59). *See Prostitute.*

Instances of:

Sodomites (Ge 19:5). Lot's daughters (Ge 19:30-38). Judah (Ge 38:15-16). The Gibeahites (Jdg 19:22-25). Eli's sons (1Sa 2:22). David (2Sa 5:13; 11:2-27). Amnon (2Sa 13:1-14). Solomon (1Ki 11:1-3). Rehoboam (2Ch 11:21-23). Persian kings (Est 2:3,13-14,19).

LASEA [*3297*]. Seaport on S coast of Crete. Visited by Paul (Ac 27:8).

LASHA [*4388*]. Place near Sodom and Gomorrah (Ge 10:19). Site not identified.

LASHARON [*4389*] (*[belonging to] Sharon*). King of, killed by Joshua (Jos 12:18).

LASHES [*5782, 6424, 8765*].

NIV+ LASH, LASHED

1. Beating could subject the culprit to abuse, so the law kept the punishment from becoming inhumane (Dt 25:2-3). Solomon uses hyperbole to illustrate that a rebuke has greater influence on a wise man than a hundred lashes will have on a fool (Pr 17:10). Compare Paul's experience (2Co 11:24). *See Stripes.*

2. A figurative description of Jerusalem experiencing the wrath of God finally being rebuilt into the Holy City, the New Jerusalem (Isa 54:11-12, w Rev 21:10,18-21).

See Assault and Battery; Bruise, Bruises; Flog, Flogging; Scourging; Stoning.

LAST [**340, 2274*].

First and last: a title of Yahweh (Isa 44:6; 48:12), of Jesus (Rev 1:17; 2:8; 22:13). *See Titles and Names.*

The first will be last and the last first (Nu 24:20; Mt 19:30; 20:16; Mk 9:35; 10:31; Lk 13:30).

LAST DAYS [*344, 2274*].

The days before the final judgment (Jn 12:48), when God's kingdom is established on earth (Isa 2:2-4; Mic 4:1-8), and Israel is restored to her God (Hos 3:5). Began with the coming of Jesus and of the Spirit (Ac 2:16-21; Heb 1:2; 1Pe 1:20). The time of the resurrection (Jn 6:39-44,54; 11:24). A time of great trouble and deception (1Ti 3:1-17; 2Pe 3:3-17; Jude 18-19), culminating in the Second Coming of Christ (1Pe 1:5). *See Day of the Lord; Eschatology.*

LATCHET *See Thong.*

LATIN [*4872*]. The language of the Roman Empire, used in Israel in NT times (Jn 19:20).

LATRINE [*4738*]. Temple of Baal used as (2Ki 10:27).

LATTICE [*876, 3048, 8422*]. Latticework used for privacy, ventilation, decoration (Jdg 5:28; 2Ki 1:2; Pr 7:6).

LAUGHTER [*6600, 7464, 7465, 8468, 8471, 1151, 1152, 2860*].

NIV+ LAUGH, LAUGHED, LAUGHINGSTOCK, LAUGHS

Used to express joy (Ge 21:6; Lk 6:21), derision (Ps 2:4), disbelief (Ge 18:13).

LAUNDERER [*3891*].

NIV+ LAUNDERER'S

See Fuller.

LAVER *See Bronze Basin; Bronze Sea.*

LAW [**2017, 2976, 2978, 5477, 9368, 10186, 492, 491, 1208, 2003, 3788, 3791, 3795*].

NIV+ LAW'S, LAWFUL, LAWGIVER, LAWS, LAWYER

1. Ten Commandments given to Moses (Ex 20:3-17; Dt 5:6-21), summarizing God's requirements of mankind.

2. The Torah, first five books of OT (Mt 5:17; Lk 16:16).

3. The whole OT (Jn 10:34; 12:34).

4. God's will in words, acts, precepts (Ex 20:1-17; Ps 19:1-6)

Ps 19:7 The law of the LORD is perfect, reviving the soul. The statutes of the LORD are trustworthy, making wise the simple. **8**The precepts of the LORD are right, giving joy to the heart. The commands of the LORD are radiant, giving light to the eyes. **9**The fear of the LORD is pure, enduring forever. The ordinances of the LORD are sure and altogether righteous. (+Ps 19:10-14)

The Purpose of the Law:

Under the old covenant, believers manifested their faith in Yahweh by observing the law for their own good (Dt 6:4-9; 10:12-13; 30:1-16). Christ fulfilled the law; respected, loved it, and showed its deeper significance (Mt 5:17-48). The law prepared the way for the coming of Christ (Gal 3:24). The law could not bring victory over sin (Ro 3-8; Gal).

Jesus' summary of the law: It demands perfect love for God, and love for one's neighbor comparable to that which one has for oneself (Mt 22:35-40).

Made for the lawless—

1Ti 1:8 We know that the law is good if one uses it properly. **9**We also know that law is made not for the righteous but for lawbreakers and rebels, the ungodly and sinful, the unholy and irreligious; for those who kill their fathers or mothers, for murderers, **10**for adulterers and perverts, for slave traders and liars and perjurers—and for whatever else is contrary to the sound doctrine

Must be obeyed—

Mt 22:21 "Caesar's," they replied. Then he said to them,

"Give to Caesar what is Caesar's, and to God what is God's." (+Lk 20:22-25)

Law of God:

Ps 119:1 Blessed are they whose ways are blameless, who walk according to the law of the LORD. **2**Blessed are they who keep his statutes and seek him with all their heart. **3**They do nothing wrong; they walk in his ways. **4**You have laid down precepts that are to be fully obeyed. **5**Oh, that my ways were steadfast in obeying your decrees! **6**Then I would not be put to shame when I consider all your commands. **7**I will praise you with an upright heart as I learn your righteous laws. **8**I will obey your decrees; do not utterly forsake me.

Jas 1:25 But the man who looks intently into the perfect law that gives freedom, and continues to do this, not forgetting what he has heard, but doing it—he will be blessed in what he does.

Spiritual—

Ro 7:14 We know that the law is spiritual; but I am unspiritual, sold as a slave to sin.

Must be obeyed—

1Jn 5:3 This is love for God: to obey his commands. And his commands are not burdensome,

Love, the fulfilling of—

Ro 13:10 Love does no harm to its neighbor. Therefore love is the fulfillment of the law.

1Ti 1:5 The goal of this command is love, which comes from a pure heart and a good conscience and a sincere faith.

See Litigation; Commandments and Statutes, Of God; Duty, Of People to God.

Law of Moses:

Contained in the books of Exodus, Leviticus, Numbers, and Deuteronomy. Divine authority for (Ex 19:16-24; 20:1-2; 24:12-18; 32:15-16; 34:1-4,27-28; Lev 26:46; Dt 4:10-13,36; 5:1-22; 9:10; 10:1-5; 33:2-4; 1Ki 8:9; Ezr 7:6; Ne 1:7; 8:1; 9:14; Ps 78:5; 103:7; Isa 33:22; Mal 4:4; Ac 7:38,53; Gal 3:19; Heb 9:18-21).

Given at Sinai (Ex 19; Dt 1:1; 4:10-13,44-46; 32:2; Hab 3:3). Received by the disposition of angels (Dt 32:2; Ps 68:17; Ac 7:53; Gal 3:19; Heb 2:2). Was given because of transgression until the Messiah came (Gal 3:19). Engraved on stone (Ex 20:3-17; 24:12; 31:18; 32:16; 34:29; 40:20; Dt 4:13; 5:4-22; 9:10), on monuments (Dt 27:2-8; Jos 8:30-35),

See Tablets of the Law; Commandments and Statutes, Of God.

Preserved in the ark of the covenant (Ex 25:16; Dt 31:9,26). To be written on doorframes (Dt 6:9; 11:20) and as a symbol on the forehead and a sign on the hand (Ex 13:9,16; Dt 6:4-9; 11:18-21), meaning the law was to govern society, home, personal thoughts and actions. Children instructed in. *See Children; Instruction.*

Expounded by priests and Levites (Lev 10:11; Dt 33:10; 2Ch 35:3), by princes, priests, and Levites (Ezr 7:10; Ne 8:1-18), from city to city (2Ch 17:7-10), in synagogues (Lk 4:16; Ac 13:14-52; 15:21, w Ac 9:20, & 14:1; 17:1-3; 18:4,26). Expounded to the assembled nation at the feast of tabernacles in the sabbatic year (Dt 31:10-13). Rehearsed by Moses, with many admonitions (Dt 4:44-46; 5-34).

Obedience to, commanded (Dt 4:40; 5:32; 6:17; 7:11; 8:1,6; 10:12-13; 11:1,8,32; 13:4; 16:12; 27:1; 30:16; 32:46; Jos 1:7; 22:5; 1Ki 2:3; 8:61; 2Ki 17:37). Found by Hilkiah in the house of the Lord (2Ki 22:8; 2Ch 34:14).

Blessings and curses of, responsively read by Levites and people at Ebal and Gerizim (Dt 27:12-26; Jos 8:33-35).

Formed a constitution on which the civil government of the Israelites was founded, and according to which rulers were required to rule (Dt 17:18-20; 2Ki 11:12; 2Ch 23:11). *See Constitution; Government.*

Was given because of transgressions until the coming of the Messiah (Gal 3:19). Was committed to the Jews (Ro 3:1-2).

Brings the knowledge of sin (Ro 3:20)—

Ro 7:7 What shall we say, then? Is the law sin? Certainly not! Indeed I would not have known what sin was except through the law. For I would not have known what coveting really was if the law had not said, "Do not covet."

Prophecies in, of the Messiah (Lk 24:44; Jn 1:45; 5:46; 12:34; Ac 26:22-23; 28:23; Ro 3:21-22). *See Jesus the Christ, Prophecies Concerning.*

Epitomized by Jesus (Mt 22:40; Mk 12:29-33; Lk 10:27).

Temporary:

Jer 3:16 In those days, when your numbers have increased greatly in the land," declares the LORD, "men will no longer say, 'The ark of the covenant of the LORD.' It will never enter their minds or be remembered; it will not be missed, nor will another one be made.

Da 9:27 He will confirm a covenant with many for one 'seven.' In the middle of the 'seven' he will put an end to sacrifice and offering. And on a wing [of the temple] he will set up an abomination that causes desolation, until the end that is decreed is poured out on him."

Heb 10:1 The law is only a shadow of the good things that are coming—not the realities themselves. For this reason it can never, by the same sacrifices repeated endlessly year after year, make perfect those who draw near to worship. [2]If it could, would they not have stopped being offered? For the worshipers would have been cleansed once for all, and would no longer have felt guilty for their sins. [3]But those sacrifices are an annual reminder of sins, [4]because it is impossible for the blood of bulls and goats to take away sins.

[5]Therefore, when Christ came into the world, he said:

"Sacrifice and offering you did not desire, but a body you prepared for me; [6]with burnt offerings and sin offerings you were not pleased. [7]Then I said, 'Here I am—it is written about me in the scroll—I have come to do your will, O God.' "

[8]First he said, "Sacrifices and offerings, burnt offerings and sin offerings you did not desire, nor were you pleased with them" (although the law required them to be made). [9]Then he said, "Here I am, I have come to do your will." He sets aside the first to establish the second. [10]And by that will, we have been made holy through the sacrifice of the body of Jesus Christ once for all.

[11]Day after day every priest stands and performs his religious duties; again and again he offers the same sacrifices, which can never take away sins. [12]But when this priest had offered for all time one sacrifice for sins, he sat down at the right hand of God. [13]Since that time he waits for his enemies to be made his footstool, [14]because by one sacrifice he has made perfect forever those who are being made holy.

[15]The Holy Spirit also testifies to us about this. First he says:

[16]"This is the covenant I will make with them after that time, says the Lord. I will put my laws in their hearts, and I will write them on their minds."

[17]Then he adds: "Their sins and lawless acts I will remember no more."

[18]And where these have been forgiven, there is no longer any sacrifice for sin.

Weakness of the law—

Ro 8:3 For what the law was powerless to do in that it was weakened by the sinful nature, God did by sending his own Son in the likeness of sinful man to be a sin offering. And so he condemned sin in sinful man, (+Ro 8:6)

Law fulfilled by Christ—

Mt 5:17 "Do not think that I have come to abolish the Law or the Prophets; I have not come to abolish them but to fulfill them. [18]I tell you the truth, until heaven and earth disappear, not the smallest letter, not the least stroke of a pen, will by any means disappear from the Law until everything is accomplished. [19]Anyone who breaks one of the least of these commandments and teaches others to do the same will be called least in the kingdom of heaven, but whoever practices and teaches these commands will be called great in the kingdom of heaven. [20]For I tell you that unless your righteousness surpasses that of the Pharisees and the teachers of the law, you will certainly not enter the kingdom of heaven. (+Mt 5:21-45)

Ac 6:14 For we have heard him say that this Jesus of Nazareth will destroy this place and change the customs Moses handed down to us."

Ac 13:39 Through him everyone who believes is justified from everything you could not be justified from by the law of Moses. (+Ro 10:3)

Ro 10:4 Christ is the end of the law so that there may be righteousness for everyone who believes.

Eph 2:15 by abolishing in his flesh the law with its commandments and regulations. His purpose was to create in himself one new man out of the two, thus making peace,

Heb 8:4 If he were on earth, he would not be a priest, for there are already men who offer the gifts prescribed by the law. [5]They serve at a sanctuary that is a copy and shadow of what is in heaven. This is why Moses was warned when he was about to build the tabernacle: "See to it that you make everything according to the pattern shown you on the mountain." [6]But the ministry Jesus has received is as superior to theirs as the covenant of which he is mediator is superior to the old one, and it is founded on better promises.

[7]For if there had been nothing wrong with that first covenant, no place would have been sought for another. [8]But God found fault with the people and said: "The time is coming, declares the Lord, when I will make a new covenant with the house of Israel and with the house of Judah. [9]It will not be like the covenant I made with their forefathers when I took them by the hand to lead them out of Egypt, because they did not remain faithful to my covenant, and I turned away from them, declares the Lord. [10]This is the covenant I will make with the house of Israel after that time, declares the Lord. I will put my laws in their minds and write them on their hearts. I will be their God, and they will be my people. [11]No longer will a man teach his neighbor, or a man his brother, saying, 'Know the Lord,' because they will all know me, from the least of them to the greatest. [12]For I will forgive their wickedness and will remember their sins no more."

[13]By calling this covenant "new," he has made the first one obsolete; and what is obsolete and aging will soon disappear.

Heb 9:8 The Holy Spirit was showing by this that the way into the Most Holy Place had not yet been disclosed as long as the first tabernacle was still standing. ⁹This is an illustration for the present time, indicating that the gifts and sacrifices being offered were not able to clear the conscience of the worshiper. ¹⁰They are only a matter of food and drink and various ceremonial washings—external regulations applying until the time of the new order.

¹¹When Christ came as high priest of the good things that are already here, he went through the greater and more perfect tabernacle that is not man-made, that is to say, not a part of this creation. ¹²He did not enter by means of the blood of goats and calves; but he entered the Most Holy Place once for all by his own blood, having obtained eternal redemption. ¹³The blood of goats and bulls and the ashes of a heifer sprinkled on those who are ceremonially unclean sanctify them so that they are outwardly clean. ¹⁴How much more, then, will the blood of Christ, who through the eternal Spirit offered himself unblemished to God, cleanse our consciences from acts that lead to death, so that we may serve the living God!

¹⁵For this reason Christ is the mediator of a new covenant, that those who are called may receive the promised eternal inheritance—now that he has died as a ransom to set them free from the sins committed under the first covenant.

¹⁶In the case of a will, it is necessary to prove the death of the one who made it, ¹⁷because a will is in force only when somebody has died; it never takes effect while the one who made it is living. ¹⁸This is why even the first covenant was not put into effect without blood. ¹⁹When Moses had proclaimed every commandment of the law to all the people, he took the blood of calves, together with water, scarlet wool and branches of hyssop, and sprinkled the scroll and all the people. ²⁰He said, "This is the blood of the covenant, which God has commanded you to keep." ²¹In the same way, he sprinkled with the blood both the tabernacle and everything used in its ceremonies. ²²In fact, the law requires that nearly everything be cleansed with blood, and without the shedding of blood there is no forgiveness.

²³It was necessary, then, for the copies of the heavenly things to be purified with these sacrifices, but the heavenly things themselves with better sacrifices than these. ²⁴For Christ did not enter a man-made sanctuary that was only a copy of the true one; he entered heaven itself, now to appear for us in God's presence. (+Heb 10:3-9)

Superseded by the gospel—

Lk 16:16 "The Law and the Prophets were proclaimed until John. Since that time, the good news of the kingdom of God is being preached, and everyone is forcing his way into it. ¹⁷It is easier for heaven and earth to disappear than for the least stroke of a pen to drop out of the Law.

Jn 1:17 For the law was given through Moses; grace and truth came through Jesus Christ.

Jn 4:20 Our fathers worshiped on this mountain, but you Jews claim that the place where we must worship is in Jerusalem."

²¹Jesus declared, "Believe me, woman, a time is coming when you will worship the Father neither on this mountain nor in Jerusalem. ²²You Samaritans worship what you do not know; we worship what we do know, for salvation is from the Jews. ²³Yet a time is coming and has now come when the true worshipers will worship the Father in spirit and truth, for they are the kind of worshipers the Father

seeks. ²⁴God is spirit, and his worshipers must worship in spirit and in truth."

Jn 8:35 Now a slave has no permanent place in the family, but a son belongs to it forever. (+Gal 4:30-31)

Ac 10:28 He said to them: "You are well aware that it is against our law for a Jew to associate with a Gentile or visit him. But God has shown me that I should not call any man impure or unclean.

Ac 15:1 Some men came down from Judea to Antioch and were teaching the brothers: "Unless you are circumcised, according to the custom taught by Moses, you cannot be saved." ²This brought Paul and Barnabas into sharp dispute and debate with them. So Paul and Barnabas were appointed, along with some other believers, to go up to Jerusalem to see the apostles and elders about this question. ³The church sent them on their way, and as they traveled through Phoenicia and Samaria, they told how the Gentiles had been converted. This news made all the brothers very glad. ⁴When they came to Jerusalem, they were welcomed by the church and the apostles and elders, to whom they reported everything God had done through them.

⁵Then some of the believers who belonged to the party of the Pharisees stood up and said, "The Gentiles must be circumcised and required to obey the law of Moses."

⁶The apostles and elders met to consider this question. ⁷After much discussion, Peter got up and addressed them: "Brothers, you know that some time ago God made a choice among you that the Gentiles might hear from my lips the message of the gospel and believe. ⁸God, who knows the heart, showed that he accepted them by giving the Holy Spirit to them, just as he did to us. ⁹He made no distinction between us and them, for he purified their hearts by faith. ¹⁰Now then, why do you try to test God by putting on the necks of the disciples a yoke that neither we nor our fathers have been able to bear? ¹¹No! We believe it is through the grace of our Lord Jesus that we are saved, just as they are."

¹²The whole assembly became silent as they listened to Barnabas and Paul telling about the miraculous signs and wonders God had done among the Gentiles through them. ¹³When they finished, James spoke up: "Brothers, listen to me. ¹⁴Simon has described to us how God at first showed his concern by taking from the Gentiles a people for himself. ¹⁵The words of the prophets are in agreement with this, as it is written:

¹⁶"'After this I will return and rebuild David's fallen tent. Its ruins I will rebuild, and I will restore it, ¹⁷that the remnant of men may seek the Lord, and all the Gentiles who bear my name, says the Lord, who does these things' ¹⁸that have been known for ages.

¹⁹"It is my judgment, therefore, that we should not make it difficult for the Gentiles who are turning to God. ²⁰Instead we should write to them, telling them to abstain from food polluted by idols, from sexual immorality, from the meat of strangled animals and from blood.

Ac 21:20 When they heard this, they praised God. Then they said to Paul: "You see, brother, how many thousands of Jews have believed, and all of them are zealous for the law. ²¹They have been informed that you teach all the Jews who live among the Gentiles to turn away from Moses, telling them not to circumcise their children or live according to our customs. ²²What shall we do? They will certainly hear that you have come, ²³so do what we tell you. There are four men with us who have made a vow. ²⁴Take these men, join in their purification rites and pay their expenses, so that they can have their heads shaved. Then everybody will know there is no truth in these reports about you, but that you yourself are living in obedience to the law. ²⁵As for the Gentile believers, we have written to them our decision that they should abstain from food sacrificed to idols, from blood, from the meat of strangled animals and from sexual immorality."

Ro 7:1 Do you not know, brothers—for I am speaking to men who know the law—that the law has authority over a man only as long as he lives? ²For example, by law a married woman is bound to her husband as long as he is alive, but if her husband dies, she is released from the law of marriage. ³So then, if she marries another man while her husband is still alive, she is called an adulteress. But if her husband dies, she is released from that law and is not an adulteress, even though she marries another man.

⁴So, my brothers, you also died to the law through the body of Christ, that you might belong to another, to him who was raised from the dead, in order that we might bear fruit to God. ⁵For when we were controlled by the sinful nature, the sinful passions aroused by the law were at work in our bodies, so that we bore fruit for death. ⁶But now, by dying to what once bound us, we have been released from the law so that we serve in the new way of the Spirit, and not in the old way of the written code.

2Co 3:7 Now if the ministry that brought death, which was engraved in letters on stone, came with glory, so that the Israelites could not look steadily at the face of Moses because of its glory, fading though it was, ⁸will not the ministry of the Spirit be even more glorious? ⁹If the ministry that condemns men is glorious, how much more glorious is the ministry that brings righteousness! ¹⁰For what was glorious has no glory now in comparison with the surpassing glory. ¹¹And if what was fading away came with glory, how much greater is the glory of that which lasts!

¹²Therefore, since we have such a hope, we are very bold. ¹³We are not like Moses, who would put a veil over his face to keep the Israelites from gazing at it while the radiance was fading away. ¹⁴But their minds were made dull, for to this day the same veil remains when the old covenant is read. It has not been removed, because only in Christ is it taken away.

Gal 2:3 Yet not even Titus, who was with me, was compelled to be circumcised, even though he was a Greek. ⁴[This matter arose] because some false brothers had infiltrated our ranks to spy on the freedom we have in Christ Jesus and to make us slaves. ⁵We did not give in to them for a moment, so that the truth of the gospel might remain with you.

⁶As for those who seemed to be important—whatever they were makes no difference to me; God does not judge by external appearance—those men added nothing to my message. ⁷On the contrary, they saw that I had been entrusted with the task of preaching the gospel to the Gentiles, just as Peter had been to the Jews. ⁸For God, who was at work in the ministry of Peter as an apostle to the Jews, was also at work in my ministry as an apostle to the Gentiles. ⁹James, Peter and John, those reputed to be pillars, gave me and Barnabas the right hand of fellowship when they recognized the grace given to me. They agreed that we should go to the Gentiles, and they to the Jews. (+Gal 2:19; 4:4-29)

Gal 4:30 But what does the Scripture say? "Get rid of the slave woman and her son, for the slave woman's son will never share in the inheritance with the free woman's son."

³¹Therefore, brothers, we are not children of the slave woman, but of the free woman. (+Gal 5:1-18)

Col 2:14 having canceled the written code, with its regulations, that was against us and that stood opposed to us; he took it away, nailing it to the cross. ¹⁵And having disarmed the powers and authorities, he made a public spectacle of them, triumphing over them by the cross.

¹⁶Therefore do not let anyone judge you by what you eat or drink, or with regard to a religious festival, a New Moon celebration or a Sabbath day. ¹⁷These are a shadow of the things that were to come; the reality, however, is found in Christ. ¹⁸Do not let anyone who delights in false humility and the worship of angels disqualify you for the prize. Such a person goes into great detail about what he has seen, and his unspiritual mind puffs him up with idle notions. ¹⁹He has lost connection with the Head, from whom the whole body, supported and held together by its ligaments and sinews, grows as God causes it to grow.

²⁰Since you died with Christ to the basic principles of this world, why, as though you still belonged to it, do you submit to its rules: ²¹"Do not handle! Do not taste! Do not touch!"? ²²These are all destined to perish with use, because they are based on human commands and teachings. ²³Such regulations indeed have an appearance of wisdom, with their self-imposed worship, their false humility and their harsh treatment of the body, but they lack any value in restraining sensual indulgence. (+Heb 7:5-9)

LAW OF MOSES *See Law.*

LAWGIVER [2980, 3794].
NIV+ See LAW

God is the only absolute lawgiver (Jas 4:12), instrumentally, Moses bears this description (Jn 1:17; 7:19).

LAWSUITS [1907+1907+4200, 5477, 8190, 3210].
NIV+ LAWSUIT

To be avoided (Pr 25:8-10; Mt 5:25-26; 1Co 6:1-8).

See Actions at Law; Adjudication at Law; Arbitration; Compromise; Court, Of Law; Justice.

LAWYER [3788, 4842].
NIV+ See LAW

One versed in the law of Moses. Test Jesus with questions (Mt 22:35; Lk 10:25-37). Jesus' satire against (Lk 11:45-52). Tertullus presents case against Paul (Ac 24:1-2). Zenas (Tit 3:13). *See Litigation.*

LAYING ON OF HANDS Symbolic act signifying impartation of inheritance rights (Ge 48:14-20), gifts and rights of an office (Nu 27:18,23), dedication of animals (Lev 1:4), priests (Nu 8:10), people for special service (Ac 6:6; 13:3).

LAZARUS [3276] (*one whom God helps*).

1. Brother of Martha and Mary; raised from the dead by Jesus (Jn 11:1-12:19).

2. Beggar who died and went to Abraham's side (Lk 16:19-31). *See Abraham's Side.*

LAZINESS [4206, 6790, 6792, 8244, 8332, 734, 3821, 3891].
NIV+ LAZY

(Pr 12:27; 18:9; 19:24; 21:25; 22:13; 26:13-16).

Brings adversity (Pr 12:24; Ecc 10:18), destruction (Pr 13:4; 19:15; 20:4; 23:21; 24:30-34).

Admonitions against (Pr 6:6-11; 10:4-5,26; 15:19).

Denounced (Mt 25:26-27). Of ministers, denounced (Isa 56:10). Forbidden (Ro 12:11; Heb 6:12).

See Idleness; Slothfulness.

LEAD [6769]. A mineral (Ex 15:10). Purified by fire (Nu 31:22; Jer 6:29; Eze 22:18,20). Used in making inscriptions on stone (Job 19:24). Refining (Jer 6:29; Eze 22:18,20). Trade in (Eze 27:12). Used for weighing (Zec 5:7-8).

LEADERSHIP [3338, 7213, *2175*, *4613*].
NIV+ LEAD, LEADER, LEADER'S, LEADERS, LEADERS', LEADERSHIP, LEADING, LEADS, LED, RINGLEADER

Instances of: Abraham, Moses, Joshua, Gideon, Deborah. *See each under its own entry.*

LEAF [6290, 6591, 6997, *2400+5877*].
NIV+ LEAFY, LEAVES

Leaf of a tree, page of a book, leaf of a door. Metaphorically, green leaves symbolize prosperity, and dry leaves ruin and decay (Ps 1:3; Pr 11:28; Job 13:25; Isa 1:30).

LEAGUE *See Alliances; Treaty.*

LEAH [4207] (possibly *wild-cow* BDB; *wild cow, gazelle* IDB; *cow* KB [cf. Rachel = *ewe*]).
NIV+ LEAH'S

Daughter of Laban (Ge 29:16). Married to Jacob (Ge 29:23-26). Children of (Ge 29:31-35; 30:9-13,17-21). Flees with Jacob (Ge 31:4,14,17; 33:2-7). "... built up the house of Israel" (Ru 4:11).

LEANNOTH [4361] (*the suffering of affliction, NIV; sickness or suffering poem, JB*). *See Music, Symbols Used in.*

LEARNING [1067, 1981, 2683, 3359, 4375, *1207, 3443*, *4785*].
NIV+ LEARN, LEARNED, LEARNS
See Instruction; Knowledge.

LEASE *See Land; Renting.*

LEASING An obsolete word for falsehood (Ps 4:2; 5:6).

LEATHER [6425, 9391, *1294*] (*skin*). Designates the tanned hide of animals. Skins were used for rough clothing as well as for armor, bags, sandals, and writing materials (Lev 13:48; Eze 16:10; Mt 3:4; Heb 11:37).

LEAVEN [2809] (*piece of fermented dough*).
NIV+ LEAVENED, UNLEAVENED, YEAST

For bread (Ex 12:34,39; Hos 7:4; Mt 13:33). Leavened bread used with peace offering (Lev 7:13; Am 4:5), with wave offering (Lev 23:15-17). Leavened bread forbidden with meat offerings (Lev 2:11; 6:17; 10:12; Ex 23:18; 34:25), at the Passover (Ex 12:19-20; 13:3-4,7; 23:18; 34:25), with blood (Ex 23:18; 34:25).

A type of sin (1Co 5:6-8).

Figurative:
Of the hypocrisy of the Pharisees (Mt 16:6-12; Mk 8:15; Lk 12:1). Of other evils (1Co 5:6-8; Gal 5:9). Parable of (Mt 13:33; Lk 13:21).

LEB KAMAI [4214] (*the heart of my attackers*). A cryptogram (hidden code) for Babylon (Jer 51:1 ftn). *See Babylon.*

LEBANA, LEBANAH [4245] (*white*). Ancestor of a family which returned from the Exile (Ezr 2:45; Ne 7:48).

LEBANON [4248] (*white, snow*). A mountain range. Northern boundary of the land of Canaan (Dt 1:7; 3:25; 11:24; Jos 1:4; 9:1). Early inhabitants of (Jdg 3:3). Snow of (Jer 18:14). Streams of (SS 4:15). Cedars of (Jdg 9:15; 2Ki 19:23; 2Ch 2:8; Ps 29:5; 104:16; Isa 2:13; 14:8; Eze 27:5). Other trees (2Ki 19:23; 2Ch 2:8). Flower of (Na 1:4). Beasts of (Isa 40:16). Fertility and productiveness of (Hos 14:5-7). "Palace of the Forest of," (1Ki 7:2-5). Valley of (Jos 11:17; 12:7). Tower of (SS 7:4). Solomon had store cities (1Ki 9:19).

Figurative: (Isa 29:17; Jer 22:6).

LEBAOTH [4219] (*lionesses*).
NIV+ BETH LEBAOTH

Town in S Judah (Jos 15:32), also called Beth-Lebaoth (Jos 19:6), and probably Beth Biri (1Ch 4:31).

LEBBAEUS (*[one near to] my heart*). An alternate reading in some mss for Thaddaeus, one of Christ's apostles (Mt 10:3). *See Thaddaeus.*

LEBO HAMATH [4217] (*the entrance to Hamath*).
NIV+ HAMATH

A city located on the Orontes River of Northern Syria, though it might be "the entrance to Hamath" rather than a named city (Nu 13:21; 34:8 and ftns). *See Hamath.*

LEBONAH [4228] (*frankincense*). A city on the highway from Bethel to Shechem (Jdg 21:19).

LECAH [4336] (*to you*). A town or person in Judah (1Ch 4:21).

LEECH [6598]. Bloodsucking parasite, personifying greed (Pr 30:15). *See Animals.*

LEEK [2946].
NIV+ LEEKS

A herb of the lily family, similar in flavor to the onion (Nu 11:5).

LEES (*something preserved*). Sediment of wine (Isa 25:6). Also used figuratively to describe blessings of messianic times, spiritual lethargy, inevitability of God's judgment (Jer 48:11; Ps 75:8).

LEFT [*8520, 8521*].
NIV+ LEFT-HANDED, LEFTOVER

Used with a variety of meanings. Simple direction; North (Ge 14:15). Lesser blessing (Ge 48:13-19). Characteristic of Benjamites (Jdg 3:15,21; 20:16).

LEFT-HANDED [360+3338+3545, 8521].
NIV+ HAND, LEFT

Characteristic of Benjamites (Jdg 3:15; 20:16; 1Ch 12:2).

LEGALISTIC [*1877+3795*].
NIV+ LEGAL, LEGALIZING

Seeking God's favor by keeping the letter of the law without keeping its spirit (Mt 23:23-24). Legalists in the early church required circumcision for salvation (Ac 15:1-29). Paul's first letter, Galatians, was written to combat legalistic teaching about the Christian life (Gal 3:2,10-14; 4:9-11).

The Christian lives a life of grace, not works (Eph 2:8-9) and is not judged by ritual observance of special diet or holy days (Ro 14:1-18; Col 2:16-19; Heb 13:9). *See Commandments and Statutes, Of Men; Grace.*

LEGENDS *See Inscriptions.*

LEGION [*3305*] (*military company*).
NIV+ LEGIONS

1. Largest unit in the Roman army, including infantry and cavalry.

2. Vast number (Mt 26:53; Mk 5:9).

LEGISLATION Class, forbidden (Ex 12:49; Lev 24:22; Nu 9:14; 15:15,29; Gal 3:28).

Supplemental, concerning Sabbath-breaking (Nu 15:32-35), inheritance (Nu 27:1-11). *See Government; Law.*

LEGS [3751, 4157, 5274, 8079, 8797, 9393, 10284+10626, 10741, *4546, 5003*].
NIV+ LEG

Of the crucified broken (Jn 19:31-32).

LEHABITES, LEHABIM [4260]. Descendants of Mizraim (Ge 10:13; 1Ch 1:11).

LEHEM *See Jashubi Lehem.*

LEHI [4306] (*jawbone*).
NIV+ RAMATH LEHI

Place where Samson killed a thousand Philistines with a jawbone of a donkey (Jdg 15:9,14).

LEMUEL [4345] (*[belonging] to God [El]*). A king, otherwise unknown, to whom his mother taught the maxims in Pr 31:1-9.

LENDING [2118, 4278, 5957, 5989, 6292, *1247, 3079*].
NIV+ LEND, LENDER, LENDS, LENT, MONEYLENDER

To the poor, commanded:

Lev 25:35 "'If one of your countrymen becomes poor and is unable to support himself among you, help him as you would an alien or a temporary resident, so he can continue to live among you.

Dt 15:7 If there is a poor man among your brothers in any of the towns of the land that the LORD your God is giving you, do not be hardhearted or tightfisted toward your poor brother.

Dt 15:11 There will always be poor people in the land. Therefore I command you to be openhanded toward your brothers and toward the poor and needy in your land.

Commanded by Christ—

Mt 5:42 Give to the one who asks you, and do not turn away from the one who wants to borrow from you.

Lk 6:34 And if you lend to those from whom you expect repayment, what credit is that to you? Even 'sinners' lend to 'sinners,' expecting to be repaid in full. **35**But love your enemies, do good to them, and lend to them without expecting to get anything back. Then your reward will be great, and you will be sons of the Most High, because he is kind to the ungrateful and wicked.

Encouraged—

Ps 112:5 Good will come to him who is generous and lends freely, who conducts his affairs with justice.

Pr 19:17 He who is kind to the poor lends to the LORD, and he will reward him for what he has done.

God, the merciful Lender—

Ps 37:25 I was young and now I am old, yet I have never seen the righteous forsaken or their children begging bread. **26**They are always generous and lend freely; their children will be blessed.

Borrower to be released in the year of release—

Dt 15:1 At the end of every seven years you must cancel debts. **2**This is how it is to be done: Every creditor shall cancel the loan he has made to his fellow Israelite. He shall not require payment from his fellow Israelite or brother, because the LORD's time for canceling debts has been proclaimed. **3**You may require payment from a foreigner, but you must cancel any debt your brother owes you. **4**However, there should be no poor among you, for in the land the LORD your God is giving you to possess as your inheritance, he will richly bless you, **5**if only you fully obey the LORD your God and are careful to follow all these commands I am giving you today. **6**For the LORD your God will bless you as he has promised, and you will lend to many nations but will borrow from none. You will rule over many nations but none will rule over you.

Things Forbidden as Security of Loans:
Millstones—

Dt 24:6 Do not take a pair of millstones—not even the upper one—as security for a debt, because that would be taking a man's livelihood as security.

Widow's cloak—

Dt 24:17 Do not deprive the alien or the fatherless of justice, or take the cloak of the widow as a pledge.

Lender:

Forbidden to take interest from poor Hebrews—

Ex 22:25 "If you lend money to one of my people among you who is needy, do not be like a moneylender; charge him no interest. **26**If you take your neighbor's cloak as a pledge, return it to him by sunset, **27**because his cloak is the only covering he has for his body. What else will he sleep in? When he cries out to me, I will hear, for I am compassionate.

Lev 25:36 Do not take interest of any kind from him, but fear your God, so that your countryman may continue to live among you. **37**You must not lend him money at interest or sell him food at a profit.

Dt 23:19 Do not charge your brother interest, whether on money or food or anything else that may earn interest. **20**You may charge a foreigner interest, but not a brother Israelite, so that the LORD your God may bless you in everything you put your hand to in the land you are entering to possess.

Forbidden to enter debtor's house for security—

Dt 24:10 When you make a loan of any kind to your neighbor, do not go into his house to get what he is offering as a pledge. **11**Stay outside and let the man to whom you are making the loan bring the pledge out to you.

Forbidden to keep overnight clothing left in pledge—

Dt 24:12 If the man is poor, do not go to sleep with his pledge in your possession. **13**Return his cloak to him by sunset so that he may sleep in it. Then he will thank you, and it will be regarded as a righteous act in the sight of the LORD your God.

Oppression of borrower—

Ne 5:1 Now the men and their wives raised a great outcry against their Jewish brothers. **2**Some were saying, "We and our sons and daughters are numerous; in order for us to eat and stay alive, we must get grain."

3Others were saying, "We are mortgaging our fields, our vineyards and our homes to get grain during the famine."

4Still others were saying, "We have had to borrow money to pay the king's tax on our fields and vineyards. **5**Although we are of the same flesh and blood as our countrymen and though our sons are as good as theirs, yet we have to subject our sons and daughters to slavery. Some of our daughters have already been enslaved, but we are powerless, because our fields and our vineyards belong to others."

⁶When I heard their outcry and these charges, I was very angry. ⁷I pondered them in my mind and then accused the nobles and officials. I told them, "You are exacting usury from your own countrymen!" So I called together a large meeting to deal with them ⁸and said: "As far as possible, we have bought back our Jewish brothers who were sold to the Gentiles. Now you are selling your brothers, only for them to be sold back to us!" They kept quiet, because they could find nothing to say.

⁹So I continued, "What you are doing is not right. Shouldn't you walk in the fear of our God to avoid the reproach of our Gentile enemies? ¹⁰I and my brothers and my men are also lending the people money and grain. But let the exacting of usury stop! ¹¹Give back to them immediately their fields, vineyards, olive groves and houses, and also the usury you are charging them—the hundredth part of the money, grain, new wine and oil."

¹²"We will give it back," they said. "And we will not demand anything more from them. We will do as you say." Then I summoned the priests and made the nobles and officials take an oath to do what they had promised. ¹³I also shook out the folds of my robe and said, "In this way may God shake out of his house and possessions every man who does not keep this promise. So may such a man be shaken out and emptied!" At this the whole assembly said, "Amen," and praised the LORD. And the people did as they had promised.

Is master of borrower—

Pr 22:7 The rich rule over the poor, and the borrower is servant to the lender.

Lender and borrower will be equal—

Isa 24:1 See, the LORD is going to lay waste the earth and devastate it; he will ruin its face and scatter its inhabitants— ²it will be the same for priest as for people, for master as for servant, for mistress as for maid, for seller as for buyer, for borrower as for lender, for debtor as for creditor.

Wicked, punished—

Pr 28:8 He who increases his wealth by exorbitant interest amasses it for another, who will be kind to the poor.

Eze 18:13 He lends at usury and takes excessive interest. Will such a man live? He will not! Because he has done all these detestable things, he will surely be put to death and his blood will be on his own head.

See Borrowing; Interest; Money.

LENTIL(S), LENTILES [6378]. (Ge 25:34; 2Sa 17:28; 23:11; Eze 4:9).

LEOPARD [5807, 10480, *4203*].

NIV+ LEOPARDS

A carnivorous animal (SS 4:8). Fierceness of (Jer 5:6; 13:23; Hos 13:7; Hab 1:8).

Figurative:

(Da 7:6). Taming of, the triumph of the gospel (Isa 11:6).

LEPROSY [7665, 7669, *3319, 3320*].

NIV+ LEPER, LEPROUS

Law concerning (Lev 13-14; 22:4; Nu 5:1-3; 12:14; Dt 24:8; Mt 8:4; Lk 5:14; 17:14). Sent as a judgment. On Miriam (Nu 12:1-10), Gehazi (2Ki 5:27), Uzziah (2Ch

26:20-21). Entailed (2Ki 5:27). Isolation of lepers (Lev 13:46; Nu 5:2; 12:14; 2Ki 15:5; 2Ch 26:21). Separate burial (2Ch 26:23).

Instances of leprosy not mentioned above: Four lepers outside Samaria (2Ki 7:3), Azariah (2Ki 15:5), Simon (Mk 14:3).

Healed:

Miriam (Nu 12:13-14), Naaman (2Ki 5:8-14), by Jesus (Mt 8:3; Mk 1:40-42; Lk 5:13; 17:12-14).

Disciples empowered to heal (Mt 10:8).

LESBIAN Sexual activity between females is condemned (Ro 1:26). *See Homosexual.*

LESHEM [4386] (*lion*). City renamed Dan, at extreme N of Israel (Jos 19:47), variant of Laish. *See Dan, 3; Laish.*

LETHEK [4390]. About 10 bushels (330 liters) (Hos 3:2). *See Measure.*

LETTER [115, 4181, 4844, 6219, 10007, 10496, *1207, 1211, 2186, 2740*].

NIV+ LETTERS

Designates an alphabetical symbol, rudimentary education (Jn 7:15), written communication, the external (Ro 2:27,29), Jewish legalism (Ro 7:6; 2Co 3:6). In ancient times correspondence was privately delivered. Archaeology has uncovered many different kinds of letters. *See Writing.*

LETTERS [115, 6219, *1207, 2186*].

NIV+ LETTER

Written by David to Joab (2Sa 11:14), king of Syria to king of Israel (2Ki 5:5-6), the field commander to Hezekiah (Isa 37:9-14), king of Babylon to Hezekiah (Isa 39:1), Sennacherib to Hezekiah (2Ki 19:14). Of Artaxerxes to Nehemiah (Ne 2:7-9). Open letter from Sanballat to Nehemiah (Ne 6:5). Luke to Theophilus, the books of Luke and Acts (Ac 1:1). Claudius Lysias to Felix (Ac 23:25-30). Letter of intercession by Paul to Philemon in behalf of Onesimus (Phm 1), of recommendation (2Co 3:1). In the NT, the books of Romans through Jude and Rev 1-3. *See Writing.*

LETUSHITES, LETUSHIM [4322] (*sharpened*). Descendants of Dedan, grandson of Abraham (Ge 25:3).

LEUMMITES, LEUMMIM [4212] (perhaps *peoples* or *hordes*). Descendants of Dedan (Ge 25:3).

LEVI [4290, 4291, *3322*] (perhaps *wild cow* or *person pledged for a debt or vow*).

NIV+ LEVI'S, LEVITE, LEVITES, LEVITICAL

Son of Jacob (Ge 29:34; 35:23; 1Ch 2:1). Avenges the seduction of Dinah (Ge 34; 49:5-7). Jacob's prophecy regarding (Ge 49:5-7). His age at death (Ex 6:16). Descendants of, made ministers of religion. *See Levites.*

LEVIATHAN [4293] (*coiled one [like a serpent]*). Possibly a crocodile (Job 41; Ps 104:26). A sea monster figurative of forces of chaos opposed to Yahweh (Job 3:8; Ps 74:14; Isa 27:1). *See Dragon; Serpent.*

LEVIRATE MARRIAGE Jewish custom according to which when an Israelite died without male heirs, his nearest relative married the widow, and their firstborn son became the heir of the first husband (Dt 25:5-10; Ru 3-4). *See Kinsman-Redeemer.*

LEVITES [278, 4290+, 4291+, 10387, *3324, 3325*] (*of Levi*).

NIV+ LEVI, LEVITE, LEVITICAL

The descendants of Levi. Set apart as ministers of religion (Nu 1:47-54; 3:6-16; 16:9; 26:57-62; Dt 10:8; 1Ch 15:2). Substituted in the place of the firstborn (Nu 3:12,41-45; 8:14,16-18; 18:6). Religious zeal of (Ex 32:23-28; Dt 33:9-10; Mal 2:4-5). Consecration of (Nu 8:6-21). Sedition among, led by Korah, Dathan, Abiram, and On, on account of jealousy toward Moses and Aaron (Nu 16, w 4:19-20).

Three Divisions of:

Each having the name of one of its progenitors. Gershon, Kohath, and Merari (Nu 3:17). Gershonites and their duties (Nu 3:18-26; 4:23-26; 10:17). Ruling chief over the Gershonites was the second son of the ruling high priest (Nu 4:28). Kohathites, consisting of the families of the Amramites, Izharites, Hebronites, Uzzielites (Nu 3:27; 4:18-20). Of the Amramites, Aaron, and his family were set apart as priests (Ex 28:1; 29:9; Nu 3:38; 8:1-14; 17; 18:1), the remaining families appointed to take charge of the ark, table, lampstand, altars and vessels of the sanctuary, the hangings, and all the service (Nu 3:27-32; 4:2-15). The chief over the Kohathite was the oldest son of the ruling high priest (Nu 3:32; 1Ch 9:20). Merarites (Nu 3:20,33-37; 4:31-33; 7:8; 10:17; 1Ch 6:19,29-30; 23:21-23). The chief over the Merarites was the second son of the ruling high priest (Nu 4:33).

Place of, in camp and march (Nu 1:50-53; 2:17; 3:23-35). Cities assigned to, in the land of Canaan (Jos 21). Lodged in the chambers of the temple (1Ch 9:27,33; Eze 40:44). Resided also in villages outside of Jerusalem (Ne 12:29).

Age of, when inducted into office (Nu 4:3,30,47; 8:23-26; 1Ch 23:3,24,27; Ezr 3:8), when retired from office (Nu 4:3,47; 8:25-26).

Functions of:

Had charge of the tabernacle in camp and on the march (Nu 1:50-53; 3:6-9,21-37; 4:1-15,17-49; 8:19,22; 18:3-6), and of the temple (1Ch 9:27-29; 23:2-32; Ezr 8:24-34).

Bore the ark of the covenant (Dt 10:8; 1Ch 15:2,26-27). Ministered before the ark (1Ch 16:4). Custodians and administrators of the tithes and other offerings (1Ch 9:26-29; 26:28; 29:8; 2Ch 24:5,11; 31:11-19; 34:9; Ezr 8:29-30,33; Ne 12:44). Prepared the bread of the Presence (1Ch 23:28-29). Assisted the priests in preparing the sacrifice (2Ch 29:12-36; 2Ch 35:1-18). Killed the Passover for the children of the Captivity (Ezr 6:20-21). Teachers of the law (Dt 33:10; 2Ch 17:8-9; 30:22; 35:3; Ne 8:7-13; Mal 2:6-7). Were judges (Dt 17:9; 1Ch 23:4; 26:29; 2Ch 19:8-11; Ne 11:16). *See Judge.*

Were scribes of the sacred books. *See Scribe.* Pronounced the blessings of the law in the responsive service at Mount Gerizim (Dt 27:12; Jos 8:33). Were gatekeepers of the temple. *See Gatekeepers.* Were overseers in building and the repairs of the temple (1Ch 23:2-4; Ezr 3:8-9). Were musicians of the temple service. *See Music.* Supervised weights and measures (1Ch 23:29).

List of those who returned from the Captivity (Ezr 2:40-63; 7:7; 8:16-20; Ne 7:43-73; 12). Sealed the covenant with Nehemiah (Ne 10:9-28).

Privileges of:

In lieu of landed inheritance, forty-eight cities with suburbs were assigned to them (Nu 35:2-8, w 18:24 & 26:62; Dt 10:9; 12:12,18-19; 14:27-29; 18:1-8; Jos 13:14;

14:3; 18:7; 1Ch 6:54-81; 13:2; 2Ch 23:2; Eze 34:1-5). Assigned to, by families (Jos 21:4-40). Suburbs of their cities were inalienable for debt (Lev 25:32-34). Tithes and other offerings (Nu 18:24,26-32; Dt 18:1-8; 26:11-13; Jos 13:14; Ne 10:38-39; 12:44,47). Firstfruits (Ne 12:44,47). Spoils of war, including captives (Nu 31:30,42-47). *See Tithes.* Tithes withheld from (Ne 13:10-13; Mal 3:10). Pensioned (2Ch 31:16-18). Owned lands (Dt 18:8, w 1Ki 2:26). Land allotted to, by Ezekiel (Eze 48:13-14).

Enrollment of, at Sinai (Nu 1:47-49; 2:33; 3:14-39; 4:2-3; 26:57-62; 1Ch 23:3-5). Degraded from the Levitical office by Jeroboam (2Ch 11:13-17; 13:9-11). Loyal to the ruler (2Ki 11:7-11; 2Ch 23:7).

Intermarry with Canaanites (Ezr 9:1-2; 10:23-24). Exempt from enrollment for military duty (Nu 1:47-54, w 1Ch 12:26). Subordinate to the sons of Aaron (Nu 3:9; 8:19; 18:6).

Prophecies Concerning:

(Jer 33:18; Eze 44:10-14; Mal 3:3), of their repentance of the crucifixion of the Messiah (Zec 12:10-13). John's vision concerning (Rev 7:7).

LEVITICUS (*relating to the Levites*).

Author: Moses

Date: Between 1445 and 1406 B.C.

Outline:

I. The Five Main Offerings (chs. 1-7).
   A. Their Content, Purpose and Manner of Offering (1:1-6:7).
   B. Additional Regulations (6:8-7:38).
II. The Ordination, Installation and Work of Aaron and His Sons (chs. 8-10).
III. Laws of Cleanness—Food, Childbirth, Infections, etc. (chs. 11-15).
IV. The Day of Atonement and the Centrality of Worship at the Tabernacle (chs. 18-20).
V. Moral Laws Covering Incest, Honesty, Thievery, Idolatry, etc. (chs. 18-20).
VI. Regulations for the Priests, the Offerings and the Annual Feasts (21:1-24:9).
VII. Punishment for Blasphemy, Murder, etc. (24:10-23).
VIII. The Sabbath Year, Jubilee, Land Tenure and Reform of Slavery (ch. 25).
IX. Blessings and Curses for Covenant Obedience and Disobedience (ch. 26).
X. Regulations for Offerings Vowed to the Lord (ch. 27).

LEVY [6740, 6741] A tribute imposed by a conquering king (2Ki 23:33; 2Ch 36:3).

LEX TALIONIS *See Retaliation.*

LIARS [*3941, 3942, 3950, 3951, 5327, 8736, 9214, 6014, 6016, 6017, 6022, 6026*].

NIV+ LIAR, LIE, LIED, LIES, LYING

All people are liars (Ps 116:11). Satan the father of lies (Jn 8:44,55). Ungodly (1Ti 1:10). Characterisitc of Cretans (Tit 1:12). Eternally punished (Rev 21:8).

God cannot lie (Nu 23:19; Tit 1:2; Heb 6:18).

See Deceit; Deception; False Witness; Falsehood; Hypocrisy.

LIBATION [5821] (*pour [as an offering]*).

NIV+ LIBATIONS

Pouring out of wine or some other liquid as an offering to a deity as an act of worship (Ex 29:40-41; Jer 44:17-25). *See Offerings, Drink.*

LIBERALITY [3338].

NIV+ LIBERAL, LIBERALLY

Commanded:

Ex 22:29 "Do not hold back offerings from your granaries or your vats. "You must give me the firstborn of your sons.
[30]Do the same with your cattle and your sheep. Let them stay with their mothers for seven days, but give them to me on the eighth day.

Ex 23:15 "Celebrate the Feast of Unleavened Bread; for seven days eat bread made without yeast, as I commanded you. Do this at the appointed time in the month of Abib, for in that month you came out of Egypt. "No one is to appear before me empty-handed. (+Ex 34:20; Lev 23:22; 25:35-43)

Dt 12:11 Then to the place the Lord your God will choose as a dwelling for his Name—there you are to bring everything I command you: your burnt offerings and sacrifices, your tithes and special gifts, and all the choice possessions you have vowed to the Lord. [12]And there rejoice before the Lord your God, you, your sons and daughters, your menservants and maidservants, and the Levites from your towns, who have no allotment or inheritance of their own.

Dt 12:17 You must not eat in your own towns the tithe of your grain and new wine and oil, or the firstborn of your herds and flocks, or whatever you have vowed to give, or your freewill offerings or special gifts. [18]Instead, you are to eat them in the presence of the Lord your God at the place the Lord your God will choose—you, your sons and daughters, your menservants and maidservants, and the Levites from your towns—and you are to rejoice before the Lord your God in everything you put your hand to. [19]Be careful not to neglect the Levites as long as you live in your land. (+Pr 3:27-28; Mt 5:42)

Ac 20:35 In everything I did, I showed you that by this kind of hard work we must help the weak, remembering the words the Lord Jesus himself said: 'It is more blessed to give than to receive.'"

Ro 12:8 if it is encouraging, let him encourage; if it is contributing to the needs of others, let him give generously; if it is leadership, let him govern diligently; if it is showing mercy, let him do it cheerfully.

2Co 8:7 But just as you excel in everything—in faith, in speech, in knowledge, in complete earnestness and in your love for us—see that you also excel in this grace of giving.

2Co 8:9 For you know the grace of our Lord Jesus Christ, that though he was rich, yet for your sakes he became poor, so that you through his poverty might become rich.

2Co 8:11 Now finish the work, so that your eager willingness to do it may be matched by your completion of it, according to your means. [12]For if the willingness is there, the gift is acceptable according to what one has, not according to what he does not have.

[13]Our desire is not that others might be relieved while you are hard pressed, but that there might be equality. [14]At the present time your plenty will supply what they need, so that in turn their plenty will supply what you need. Then there will be equality,

2Co 8:24 Therefore show these men the proof of your love and the reason for our pride in you, so that the churches can see it. (+1Ti 6:18)

Heb 13:16 And do not forget to do good and to share with others, for with such sacrifices God is pleased.

In offerings, for tabernacle—

Ex 25:1 The Lord said to Moses, [2]"Tell the Israelites to bring me an offering. You are to receive the offering for me from each man whose heart prompts him to give. [3]These are the offerings you are to receive from them: gold, silver and bronze; [4]blue, purple and scarlet yarn and fine linen; goat hair; [5]ram skins dyed red and hides of sea cows; acacia wood; [6]olive oil for the light; spices for the anointing oil and for the fragrant incense; [7]and onyx stones and other gems to be mounted on the ephod and breastpiece. [8]"Then have them make a sanctuary for me, and I will dwell among them.

Ex 35:4 Moses said to the whole Israelite community, "This is what the Lord has commanded: [5]From what you have, take an offering for the Lord. Everyone who is willing is to bring to the Lord an offering of gold, silver and bronze; [6]blue, purple and scarlet yarn and fine linen; goat hair; [7]ram skins dyed red and hides of sea cows; acacia wood;

[8]olive oil for the light; spices for the anointing oil and for the fragrant incense; [9]and onyx stones and other gems to be mounted on the ephod and breastpiece.

[10]"All who are skilled among you are to come and make everything the Lord has commanded: [11]the tabernacle with its tent and its covering, clasps, frames, crossbars, posts and bases; [12]the ark with its poles and the atonement cover and the curtain that shields it; [13]the table with its poles and all its articles and the bread of the Presence; [14]the lampstand that is for light with its accessories, lamps and oil for the light; [15]the altar of incense with its poles, the anointing oil and the fragrant incense; the curtain for the doorway at the entrance to the tabernacle; [16]the altar of burnt offering with its bronze grating, its poles and all its utensils; the bronze basin with its stand; [17]the curtains of the courtyard with its posts and bases, and the curtain for the entrance to the courtyard; [18]the tent pegs for the tabernacle and for the courtyard, and their ropes; [19]the woven garments worn for ministering in the sanctuary—both the sacred garments for Aaron the priest and the garments for his sons when they serve as priests."

[20]Then the whole Israelite community withdrew from Moses' presence, [21]and everyone who was willing and whose heart moved him came and brought an offering to the Lord for the work on the Tent of Meeting, for all its service, and for the sacred garments. [22]All who were willing, men and women alike, came and brought gold jewelry of all kinds: brooches, earrings, rings and ornaments. They all presented their gold as a wave offering to the Lord. [23]Everyone who had blue, purple or scarlet yarn or fine linen, or goat hair, ram skins dyed red or hides of sea cows brought them. [24]Those presenting an offering of silver or bronze brought it as an offering to the Lord, and everyone who had acacia wood for any part of the work brought it. [25]Every skilled woman spun with her hands and brought what she had spun—blue, purple or scarlet yarn or fine linen. [26]And all the women who were willing and had the skill spun the goat hair. [27]The leaders brought onyx stones and other gems to be mounted on the ephod and breastpiece. [28]They also brought spices and olive oil for the light and for the anointing oil and for the fragrant incense. [29]All the Israelite men and women who were willing brought to the Lord freewill offerings for all the work the Lord through Moses had commanded them to do.

Ex 36:3 They received from Moses all the offerings the Israelites had brought to carry out the work of constructing the sanctuary. And the people continued to bring freewill offerings morning after morning. [4]So all the skilled craftsmen who were doing all the work on the sanctuary left their work ⁵and said to Moses, "The people are bringing more than enough for doing the work the LORD commanded to be done."

⁶Then Moses gave an order and they sent this word throughout the camp: "No man or woman is to make anything else as an offering for the sanctuary." And so the people were restrained from bringing more,

Ex 38:8 They made the bronze basin and its bronze stand from the mirrors of the women who served at the entrance to the Tent of Meeting.

For the temple—

Hag 1:8 Go up into the mountains and bring down timber and build the house, so that I may take pleasure in it and be honored," says the LORD.

With the Levites (Dt 12:11-12,17-19)—

Dt 18:1 The priests, who are Levites—indeed the whole tribe of Levi—are to have no allotment or inheritance with Israel. They shall live on the offerings made to the LORD by fire, for that is their inheritance. ²They shall have no inheritance among their brothers; the LORD is their inheritance, as he promised them.

³This is the share due the priests from the people who sacrifice a bull or a sheep: the shoulder, the jowls and the inner parts. ⁴You are to give them the firstfruits of your grain, new wine and oil, and the first wool from the shearing of your sheep, ⁵for the LORD your God has chosen them and their descendants out of all your tribes to stand and minister in the LORD's name always.

⁶If a Levite moves from one of your towns anywhere in Israel where he is living, and comes in all earnestness to the place the LORD will choose, ⁷he may minister in the name of the LORD his God like all his fellow Levites who serve there in the presence of the LORD. ⁸He is to share equally in their benefits, even though he has received money from the sale of family possessions.

For the temple commanded by Cyrus—

Ezr 1:2 "This is what Cyrus king of Persia says: "'The LORD, the God of heaven, has given me all the kingdoms of the earth and he has appointed me to build a temple for him at Jerusalem in Judah. ³Anyone of his people among you—may his God be with him, and let him go up to Jerusalem in Judah and build the temple of the LORD, the God of Israel, the God who is in Jerusalem. ⁴And the people of any place where survivors may now be living are to provide him with silver and gold, with goods and livestock, and with freewill offerings for the temple of God in Jerusalem.'"

In offerings for sacrifice—

2Sa 24:24 But the king replied to Araunah, "No, I insist on paying you for it. I will not sacrifice to the LORD my God burnt offerings that cost me nothing." So David bought the threshing floor and the oxen and paid fifty shekels of silver for them.

In paying tithes—

Dt 14:27 And do not neglect the Levites living in your towns, for they have no allotment or inheritance of their own.

²⁸At the end of every three years, bring all the tithes of that year's produce and store it in your towns, ²⁹so that the Levites (who have no allotment or inheritance of their own) and the aliens, the fatherless and the widows who live in your towns may come and eat and be satisfied, and so that the LORD your God may bless you in all the work of your hands.

In gifts to God—

Ps 76:11 Make vows to the LORD your God and fulfill them; let all the neighboring lands bring gifts to the One to be feared.

In gifts to the poor—

Dt 15:7 If there is a poor man among your brothers in any of the towns of the land that the LORD your God is giving you, do not be hardhearted or tightfisted toward your poor brother. ⁸Rather be openhanded and freely lend him whatever he needs. ⁹Be careful not to harbor this wicked thought: "The seventh year, the year for canceling debts, is near," so that you do not show ill will toward your needy brother and give him nothing. He may then appeal to the LORD against you, and you will be found guilty of sin. ¹⁰Give generously to him and do so without a grudging heart; then because of this the LORD your God will bless you in all your work and in everything you put your hand to. ¹¹There will always be poor people in the land. Therefore I command you to be openhanded toward your brothers and toward the poor and needy in your land.

Dt 24:19 When you are harvesting in your field and you overlook a sheaf, do not go back to get it. Leave it for the alien, the fatherless and the widow, so that the LORD your God may bless you in all the work of your hands. ²⁰When you beat the olives from your trees, do not go over the branches a second time. Leave what remains for the alien, the fatherless and the widow. ²¹When you harvest the grapes in your vineyard, do not go over the vines again. Leave what remains for the alien, the fatherless and the widow. ²²Remember that you were slaves in Egypt. That is why I command you to do this. (+Ne 8:10)

Ps 41:1 Blessed is he who has regard for the weak; the LORD delivers him in times of trouble. ²The LORD will protect him and preserve his life; he will bless him in the land and not surrender him to the desire of his foes. ³The LORD will sustain him on his sickbed and restore him from his bed of illness. (+Isa 58:6-7)

Mt 19:21 Jesus answered, "If you want to be perfect, go, sell your possessions and give to the poor, and you will have treasure in heaven. Then come, follow me."

²²When the young man heard this, he went away sad, because he had great wealth. (+Mk 10:21)

Lk 3:10 "What should we do then?" the crowd asked.

¹¹John answered, "The man with two tunics should share with him who has none, and the one who has food should do the same."

Ro 12:13 Share with God's people who are in need. Practice hospitality.

Ro 15:27 They were pleased to do it, and indeed they owe it to them. For if the Gentiles have shared in the Jews' spiritual blessings, they owe it to the Jews to share with them their material blessings.

2Co 9:6 Remember this: Whoever sows sparingly will also reap sparingly, and whoever sows generously will also reap generously. ⁷Each man should give what he has decided in his heart to give, not reluctantly or under compulsion, for God loves a cheerful giver. ⁸And God is able to make all grace abound to you, so that in all things at all times, having all that you need, you will abound in every good work. ⁹As it is written:

"He has scattered abroad his gifts to the poor; his righteousness endures forever."

¹⁰Now he who supplies seed to the sower and bread for food will also supply and increase your store of seed and will enlarge the harvest of your righteousness. ¹¹You will be made rich in every way so that you can be generous on

every occasion, and through us your generosity will result in thanksgiving to God.

[12]This service that you perform is not only supplying the needs of God's people but is also overflowing in many expressions of thanks to God. (+2Co 9:13-15; Gal 2:10)

Eph 4:28 He who has been stealing must steal no longer, but must work, doing something useful with his own hands, that he may have something to share with those in need.

1Ti 5:16 If any woman who is a believer has widows in her family, she should help them and not let the church be burdened with them, so that the church can help those widows who are really in need.

1Ti 6:17 Command those who are rich in this present world not to be arrogant nor to put their hope in wealth, which is so uncertain, but to put their hope in God, who richly provides us with everything for our enjoyment. [18]Command them to do good, to be rich in good deeds, and to be generous and willing to share. [19]In this way they will lay up treasure for themselves as a firm foundation for the coming age, so that they may take hold of the life that is truly life. (+Jas 2:15-16)

1Jn 3:17 If anyone has material possessions and sees his brother in need but has no pity on him, how can the love of God be in him? [18]Dear children, let us not love with words or tongue but with actions and in truth.

By the noble woman (Pr 31:20).

In gifts to liberated Hebrew slaves—

Dt 15:12 If a fellow Hebrew, a man or a woman, sells himself to you and serves you six years, in the seventh year you must let him go free. [13]And when you release him, do not send him away empty-handed. [14]Supply him liberally from your flock, your threshing floor and your winepress. Give to him as the LORD your God has blessed you. [15]Remember that you were slaves in Egypt and the LORD your God redeemed you. That is why I give you this command today.

[16]But if your servant says to you, "I do not want to leave you," because he loves you and your family and is well off with you, [17]then take an awl and push it through his ear lobe into the door, and he will become your servant for life. Do the same for your maidservant.

[18]Do not consider it a hardship to set your servant free, because his service to you these six years has been worth twice as much as that of a hired hand. And the LORD your God will bless you in everything you do.

Giving according to ability (Nu 35:8)—

Dt 16:10 Then celebrate the Feast of Weeks to the LORD your God by giving a freewill offering in proportion to the blessings the LORD your God has given you.

Dt 16:17 Each of you must bring a gift in proportion to the way the LORD your God has blessed you.

1Co 16:1 Now about the collection for God's people: Do what I told the Galatian churches to do. [2]On the first day of every week, each one of you should set aside a sum of money in keeping with his income, saving it up, so that when I come no collections will have to be made. [3]Then, when I arrive, I will give letters of introduction to the men you approve and send them with your gift to Jerusalem. (+2Co 8:12)

Giving without a show—

Mt 6:1 "Be careful not to do your 'acts of righteousness' before men, to be seen by them. If you do, you will have no reward from your Father in heaven.

[2]"So when you give to the needy, do not announce it with trumpets, as the hypocrites do in the synagogues and on the streets, to be honored by men. I tell you the truth, they have received their reward in full. [3]But when you give to the needy, do not let your left hand know what your right hand is doing, [4]so that your giving may be in secret. Then your Father, who sees what is done in secret, will reward you.

Giving of freewill—

Lev 19:5 "'When you sacrifice a fellowship offering to the LORD, sacrifice it in such a way that it will be accepted on your behalf. (+Lev 22:9)

1Ch 29:5 for the gold work and the silver work, and for all the work to be done by the craftsmen. Now, who is willing to consecrate himself today to the LORD?"

Pr 21:26 All day long he craves for more, but the righteous give without sparing. (+2Co 8:12; 9:1-6)

Phm 14 But I did not want to do anything without your consent, so that any favor you do will be spontaneous and not forced.

Giving with love—

1Co 13:3 If I give all I possess to the poor and surrender my body to the flames, but have not love, I gain nothing.

Rewards for giving—

Ps 112:5 Good will come to him who is generous and lends freely, who conducts his affairs with justice.

Ps 112:9 He has scattered abroad his gifts to the poor, his righteousness endures forever; his horn will be lifted high in honor.

Pr 3:9 Honor the LORD with your wealth, with the firstfruits of all your crops; [10]then your barns will be filled to overflowing, and your vats will brim over with new wine.

Pr 11:24 One man gives freely, yet gains even more; another withholds unduly, but comes to poverty.

[25]A generous man will prosper; he who refreshes others will himself be refreshed.

Pr 13:7 One man pretends to be rich, yet has nothing; another pretends to be poor, yet has great wealth.

Pr 14:21 He who despises his neighbor sins, but blessed is he who is kind to the needy.

Pr 19:6 Many curry favor with a ruler, and everyone is the friend of a man who gives gifts.

Pr 19:17 He who is kind to the poor lends to the LORD, and he will reward him for what he has done.

Pr 22:9 A generous man will himself be blessed, for he shares his food with the poor.

Pr 28:27 He who gives to the poor will lack nothing, but he who closes his eyes to them receives many curses.

Ecc 11:1 Cast your bread upon the waters, for after many days you will find it again. [2]Give portions to seven, yes to eight, for you do not know what disaster may come upon the land.

Isa 32:8 But the noble man makes noble plans, and by noble deeds he stands. (+Isa 58:10-12; Eze 18:7-16)

Mal 3:10 Bring the whole tithe into the storehouse, that there may be food in my house. Test me in this," says the LORD Almighty, "and see if I will not throw open the floodgates of heaven and pour out so much blessing that you will not have room enough for it. [11]I will prevent pests from devouring your crops, and the vines in your fields will not cast their fruit," says the LORD Almighty. [12]"Then all the nations will call you blessed, for yours will be a delightful land," says the LORD Almighty. (+Mt 5:42)

Mt 25:34 "Then the King will say to those on his right, 'Come, you who are blessed by my Father; take your inheritance, the kingdom prepared for you since the creation of the world. [35]For I was hungry and you gave me something to eat, I was thirsty and you gave me something to drink, I was a stranger and you invited me in, ³⁶I needed clothes and you clothed me, I was sick and you looked after me, I was in prison and you came to visit me.'

³⁷"Then the righteous will answer him, 'Lord, when did we see you hungry and feed you, or thirsty and give you something to drink? ³⁸When did we see you a stranger and invite you in, or needing clothes and clothe you? ³⁹When did we see you sick or in prison and go to visit you?'

⁴⁰"The King will reply, 'I tell you the truth, whatever you did for one of the least of these brothers of mine, you did for me.' (+Mt 25:46; Lk 6:30-37)

Lk 6:38 Give, and it will be given to you. A good measure, pressed down, shaken together and running over, will be poured into your lap. For with the measure you use, it will be measured to you."

Lk 12:33 Sell your possessions and give to the poor. Provide purses for yourselves that will not wear out, a treasure in heaven that will not be exhausted, where no thief comes near and no moth destroys. ³⁴For where your treasure is, there your heart will be also.

Heb 6:10 God is not unjust; he will not forget your work and the love you have shown him as you have helped his people and continue to help them.

See *Alms; Beneficence; Charitableness; Giving; Minister; Poor, Duty to; Rich, The; Riches; Tithes.*

Instances of:

King of Sodom to Abraham (Ge 14:21). Jacob, consecrating the tenth of his income (Ge 28:22). Pharaoh to Joseph's people (Ge 45:18-20). Israelites at the building of the tabernacle (Ex 35:21-29; 36:3-7; 38:8; Nu 7; 31:48-54; Jos 18:1). Reubenites (Jos 22:24-29).

David—

Ps 132:1 O LORD, remember David and all the hardships he endured.

²He swore an oath to the LORD and made a vow to the Mighty One of Jacob: ³"I will not enter my house or go to my bed— ⁴I will allow no sleep to my eyes, no slumber to my eyelids, ⁵till I find a place for the LORD, a dwelling for the Mighty One of Jacob." (+2Sa 7:2; 1Ch 17:1; 2Sa 8:11; 1Ki 7:51; 8:17-18; 1Ch 21:24; 22; 26:26; 28:2; 29:2-5,17)

Barzillai and others to David (2Sa 17:27-29; 19:32). Araunah for sacrifice (2Sa 24:22-23). Joab to David (2Sa 12:26-28).

Israelites' offerings for the temple 1Ch 29:6-9,16-17). Samuel (1Ch 26:27-28). Solomon (1Ki 4:29; 5:4-5; 2Ch 2:1-6; 1Ki 6; 7:51; 8:13). Queen of Sheba to Solomon (1Ki 10:10). Asa and Abijah (1Ki 15:15). Elisha toward Elijah (1Ki 19:21). Jehoshaphat (2Ki 12:18). Joash and his people (2Ki 12:4-14; 2Ch 24:4-14). David (1Ch 16:3). Hezekiah (2Ch 29; 30:1-12; 31:1-10,21). Manasseh (2Ch 33:16). Josiah (2Ki 22:3-6; 2Ch 34:8-13; 35:1-19).

Jews after the Captivity (Ezr 1:5-6; 2:68-69; 3:2-9; 5:2-6; 6:14-22; 8:25-35; Ne 3; 4:6; 6:3; 7:70-72; 10:32-39; 13:12,31; Hag 1:12-19).

Cyrus (Ezr 1:2-4,7-11; 3:7; 5:13-15; 6:3). Darius (Ezr 6:7-12). Artaxerxes (Ezr 7:13-27; 8:24-36). The Magi (Mt 2:11). Centurion (Lk 7:4-5). Mary Magdalene (Lk 8:2-3). The good Samaritan (Lk 10:33-35). Poor widow (Lk 21:2-4). Christians in Jerusalem (Ac 2:44-45; 4:32-37), in Antioch (Ac 11:29), at Philippi (Php 4:18), Corinth (2Co 8:19; 9:1-13), Macedonia (2Co 8:1-4). People of Malta to Paul (Ac 28:10).

LIBERTINES *See Freedman.*

LIBERTY [2002].
NIV+ LIBERATED

Freedom, whether physical, moral, or spiritual. Israelites who had becomes slaves were freed in the Year of Jubilee (Lev 25:8-17). Through Christ's death and resurrection the believer is free from sin's dominion (Jn 1:29; 8:36; Ro 6-7), Satan's control (Ac 26:18), the law (Gal 3), fear, the second death, future judgment.

Of Hebrew servants:

In the seventh year (Ex 21:2; Dt 15:12; Jer 34:14), in Year of Jubilee (Lev 25:10,40).

Political: (Ac 22:28).

Religious: In Rome (Ac 28:31).

Spiritual: (Ps 119:45; Isa 61:1; Lk 4:18; Jn 8:32-33,36; Ro 6:6,22; 8:1-2; 1Co 7:22; 2Co 3:17; Gal 2:4; 1Pe 2:16).

Figurative: Of the gospel (Jas 1:25; 2:12).

LIBNAH [4243] (*white*).
NIV+ LIBNITE, LIBNITES

1. A station of the Israelites in the desert (Nu 33:20).

2. A city of Judah, captured by Joshua (Jos 10:29-32,39; 12:15). Allotted to the priests (Jos 21:13; 1Ch 6:57). Sennacherib besieged; his army defeated near (2Ki 19:8,35; Isa 37:8-36).

LIBNATH *See Shihor Libnath.*

LIBNI, LIBNITE(S) [4249, 4250] (*[descendant of] Libni* or *white*).
NIV+ LIBNAH

1. Son of Gershon (Ex 6:17; Nu 3:18; 1Ch 6:17,20). Descendants called Libnites (Nu 3:21; 26:58).

2. Grandson of Merari (1Ch 6:29).

LIBRARIES Libraries, both public and private, were
not uncommon in ancient times in the Oriental, Greek, and Roman worlds. The Dead Sea Scrolls are one example of an ancient library that has survived to modern times.

LIBYA, LIBYANS [4275, 3340].

A people of N Africa, W of Egypt, who were allies of Egypt (2Ch 12:3; 16:8; Eze 30:5; 38:5; Da 11:43; Ac 2:10). Also called Put. *See Put, 2.*

LICE *See Gnat.*

LICENTIOUSNESS *See Adultery; Lasciviousness.*

LIEUTENANTS *See Satrap; Secretary.*

LIFE [*344, 1414, 2006, 2644, 2649, 2652, 3427, 5883, 6409, 419, 482, 1053, 1586, 2409, 2437, 2443, 2461, 4344, 6034].
NIV+ ALIVE, LIFE'S, LIFELESS, LIFETIME, LIVED, LIVES, LIVING, OUTLIVED

Breath of (Ge 2:7). Called breath of God (Job 27:3). Tree of (Ge 2:9; 3:22,24; Pr 3:18; 13:12; Rev 2:7). Sacredness of, an inference from what is taught in the law concerning murder. *See Homicide.* Meaninglessness of (Ecc 1-7).

Weary of:

Job (Job 3; 7:1-3; 10:18-19). Jeremiah (Jer 20:14-18), Elijah (1Ki 19:1-4), Jonah (Jnh 4:8), Paul (Php 1:21-24). *See Suicide.*

Hated (Ecc 2:17). To be hated for Christ's sake (Lk 14:26). What shall a man give in exchange for (Mt 16:26; Mk 8:37). He that loses it for Christ's sake shall save it (Mt 10:39; 16:25-26; Lk 9:24; Jn 12:25).

Long life promised (Ge 6:3; Ps 91:16), to Solomon (1Ki 3:11-14), to the wise (Pr 3:16; 9:11), to the obedient (Dt 4:40; 22:7; Pr 3:1-2), to those who honor parents (Ex 20:12; Dt 5:16), to those who show kindness to animals (Dt 22:7), given to those who fear God (Pr 10:27; Isa 65:20).

See Longevity.

Brevity of:

Ge 47:9 And Jacob said to Pharaoh, "The years of my pilgrimage are a hundred and thirty. My years have been few and difficult, and they do not equal the years of the pilgrimage of my fathers."

Job 10:9 Remember that you molded me like clay. Will you now turn me to dust again?

Job 10:20 Are not my few days almost over? Turn away from me so I can have a moment's joy ²¹before I go to the place of no return, to the land of gloom and deep shadow,

Job 13:12 Your maxims are proverbs of ashes; your defenses are defenses of clay.

Job 13:25 Will you torment a windblown leaf? Will you chase after dry chaff?

Job 13:28 "So man wastes away like something rotten, like a garment eaten by moths.

Ps 89:47 Remember how fleeting is my life. For what futility you have created all men! ⁴⁸What man can live and not see death, or save himself from the power of the grave? *Selah* (+Ps 90:10)

Ps 146:4 When their spirit departs, they return to the ground; on that very day their plans come to nothing.

Isa 2:22 Stop trusting in man, who has but a breath in his nostrils. Of what account is he?

Compared, to a shadow—

1Ch 29:15 We are aliens and strangers in your sight, as were all our forefathers. Our days on earth are like a shadow, without hope.

Job 8:9 for we were born only yesterday and know nothing, and our days on earth are but a shadow.

Job 14:1 "Man born of woman is of few days and full of trouble. ²He springs up like a flower and withers away; like a fleeting shadow, he does not endure. (+Ps 102:11; 144:3)

Ps 144:4 Man is like a breath; his days are like a fleeting shadow.

Ecc 6:12 For who knows what is good for a man in life, during the few and meaningless days he passes through like a shadow? Who can tell him what will happen under the sun after he is gone?

To a weaver's shuttle—

Job 7:6 "My days are swifter than a weaver's shuttle, and they come to an end without hope. ⁷Remember, O God, that my life is but a breath; my eyes will never see happiness again. ⁸The eye that now sees me will see me no longer; you will look for me, but I will be no more. ⁹As a cloud vanishes and is gone, so he who goes down to the grave does not return. ¹⁰He will never come to his house again; his place will know him no more.

To a courier—

Job 9:25 "My days are swifter than a runner; they fly away without a glimpse of joy. ²⁶They skim past like boats of papyrus, like eagles swooping down on their prey.

To a handbreadth—

Ps 39:4 "Show me, O LORD, my life's end and the number of my days; let me know how fleeting is my life. ⁵You have made my days a mere handbreadth; the span of my

years is as nothing before you. Each man's life is but a breath. *Selah*

Ps 39:11 You rebuke and discipline men for their sin; you consume their wealth like a moth—each man is but a breath. *Selah*

To a wind—

Ps 78:39 He remembered that they were but flesh, a passing breeze that does not return.

To grass—

Ps 90:3 You turn men back to dust, saying, "Return to dust, O sons of men."

Ps 90:5 You sweep men away in the sleep of death; they are like the new grass of the morning— ⁶though in the morning it springs up new, by evening it is dry and withered.

Ps 90:9 All our days pass away under your wrath; we finish our years with a moan. ¹⁰The length of our days is seventy years—or eighty, if we have the strength; yet their span is but trouble and sorrow, for they quickly pass, and we fly away.

Ps 102:11 My days are like the evening shadow; I wither away like grass.

Ps 103:14 for he knows how we are formed, he remembers that we are dust. ¹⁵As for man, his days are like grass, he flourishes like a flower of the field; ¹⁶the wind blows over it and it is gone, and its place remembers it no more.

Isa 40:6 A voice says, "Cry out." And I said, "What shall I cry?" "All men are like grass, and all their glory is like the flowers of the field.

⁷The grass withers and the flowers fall, because the breath of the LORD blows on them. Surely the people are grass. (+Isa 40:8)

Isa 40:24 No sooner are they planted, no sooner are they sown, no sooner do they take root in the ground, than he blows on them and they wither, and a whirlwind sweeps them away like chaff.

Isa 51:12 "I, even I, am he who comforts you. Who are you that you fear mortal men, the sons of men, who are but grass,

Jas 1:10 But the one who is rich should take pride in his low position, because he will pass away like a wild flower. ¹¹For the sun rises with scorching heat and withers the plant; its blossom falls and its beauty is destroyed. In the same way, the rich man will fade away even while he goes about his business. (+1Pe 1:24)

To a leaf—

Isa 64:6 All of us have become like one who is unclean, and all our righteous acts are like filthy rags; we all shrivel up like a leaf, and like the wind our sins sweep us away.

To a vapor—

Jas 4:14 Why, you do not even know what will happen tomorrow. What is your life? You are a mist that appears for a little while and then vanishes.

Uncertainty of:

1Sa 20:3 But David took an oath and said, "Your father knows very well that I have found favor in your eyes, and he has said to himself, 'Jonathan must not know this or he will be grieved.' Yet as surely as the LORD lives and as you live, there is only a step between me and death."

Job 4:19 how much more those who live in houses of clay, whose foundations are in the dust, who are crushed more readily than a moth! ²⁰Between dawn and dusk they are broken to pieces; unnoticed, they perish forever. ²¹Are not the cords of their tent pulled up, so that they die without wisdom?'

Job 17:1 My spirit is broken, my days are cut short, the grave awaits me.

Pr 27:1 Do not boast about tomorrow, for you do not know what a day may bring forth.

Lk 12:20 "But God said to him, 'You fool! This very night your life will be demanded from you. Then who will get what you have prepared for yourself?'

End of, certain—

2Sa 14:14 Like water spilled on the ground, which cannot be recovered, so we must die. But God does not take away life; instead, he devises ways so that a banished person may not remain estranged from him.

Ps 22:29 All the rich of the earth will feast and worship; all who go down to the dust will kneel before him—those who cannot keep themselves alive.

Ecc 1:4 Generations come and generations go, but the earth remains forever.

Isa 38:12 Like a shepherd's tent my house has been pulled down and taken from me. Like a weaver I have rolled up my life, and he has cut me off from the loom; day and night you made an end of me.

See Death, Physical.

Comes From God:

Ge 2:7 the LORD God formed the man from the dust of the ground and breathed into his nostrils the breath of life, and the man became a living being.

Dt 8:3 He humbled you, causing you to hunger and then feeding you with manna, which neither you nor your fathers had known, to teach you that man does not live on bread alone but on every word that comes from the mouth of the LORD.

Dt 30:20 and that you may love the LORD your God, listen to his voice, and hold fast to him. For the LORD is your life, and he will give you many years in the land he swore to give to your fathers, Abraham, Isaac and Jacob.

Dt 32:39 "See now that I myself am He! There is no god besides me. I put to death and I bring to life, I have wounded and I will heal, and no one can deliver out of my hand.

1Sa 2:6 "The LORD brings death and makes alive; he brings down to the grave and raises up.

Job 27:3 as long as I have life within me, the breath of God in my nostrils,

Ps 30:3 O LORD, you brought me up from the grave; you spared me from going down into the pit.

Ps 104:30 When you send your Spirit, they are created, and you renew the face of the earth.

Ecc 12:7 and the dust returns to the ground it came from, and the spirit returns to God who gave it.

Isa 38:16 Lord, by such things men live; and my spirit finds life in them too. You restored me to health and let me live.

Ac 17:25 And he is not served by human hands, as if he needed anything, because he himself gives all men life and breath and everything else.

Ac 17:28 'For in him we live and move and have our being.' As some of your own poets have said, 'We are his offspring.'

Ro 4:17 As it is written: "I have made you a father of many nations." He is our father in the sight of God, in whom he believed—the God who gives life to the dead and calls things that are not as though they were.

1Ti 6:13 In the sight of God, who gives life to everything, and of Christ Jesus, who while testifying before Pontius Pilate made the good confession, I charge you

Jas 4:15 Instead, you ought to say, "If it is the Lord's will, we will live and do this or that."

Spiritual Life: (Dt 8:3).

From Christ (Jn 1:4)—

Jn 6:27 Do not work for food that spoils, but for food that endures to eternal life, which the Son of Man will give you. On him God the Father has placed his seal of approval."

Jn 6:33 For the bread of God is he who comes down from heaven and gives life to the world."

Jn 6:35 Then Jesus declared, "I am the bread of life. He who comes to me will never go hungry, and he who believes in me will never be thirsty.

Jn 10:10 The thief comes only to steal and kill and destroy; I have come that they may have life, and have it to the full.

Jn 17:2 For you granted him authority over all people that he might give eternal life to all those you have given him. ³Now this is eternal life: that they may know you, the only true God, and Jesus Christ, whom you have sent.

Ro 6:11 In the same way, count yourselves dead to sin but alive to God in Christ Jesus.

Ro 8:10 But if Christ is in you, your body is dead because of sin, yet your spirit is alive because of righteousness. (+Col 3:4)

Through faith—

Jn 3:14 Just as Moses lifted up the snake in the desert, so the Son of Man must be lifted up, ¹⁵that everyone who believes in him may have eternal life.

¹⁶"For God so loved the world that he gave his one and only Son, that whoever believes in him shall not perish but have eternal life.

Jn 5:24 "I tell you the truth, whoever hears my word and believes him who sent me has eternal life and will not be condemned; he has crossed over from death to life. ²⁵I tell you the truth, a time is coming and has now come when the dead will hear the voice of the Son of God and those who hear will live. ²⁶For as the Father has life in himself, so he has granted the Son to have life in himself.

Jn 5:40 yet you refuse to come to me to have life.

Jn 6:40 For my Father's will is that everyone who looks to the Son and believes in him shall have eternal life, and I will raise him up at the last day."

Jn 6:47 I tell you the truth, he who believes has everlasting life.

Jn 11:25 Jesus said to her, "I am the resurrection and the life. He who believes in me will live, even though he dies; ²⁶and whoever lives and believes in me will never die. Do you believe this?"

Jn 20:31 But these are written that you may believe that Jesus is the Christ, the Son of God, and that by believing you may have life in his name. (+Gal 2:19-20)

Signified, in figure of new birth—

Jn 3:3 In reply Jesus declared, "I tell you the truth, no one can see the kingdom of God unless he is born again."

⁴"How can a man be born when he is old?" Nicodemus asked. "Surely he cannot enter a second time into his mother's womb to be born!"

⁵Jesus answered, "I tell you the truth, no one can enter the kingdom of God unless he is born of water and the Spirit. ⁶Flesh gives birth to flesh, but the Spirit gives birth to spirit. ⁷You should not be surprised at my saying, 'You must be born again.' ⁸The wind blows wherever it pleases. You hear its sound, but you cannot tell where it comes

from or where it is going. So it is with everyone born of the Spirit." (+Tit 3:5)

In figure of death, burial, and resurrection—

Ro 6:4 We were therefore buried with him through baptism into death in order that, just as Christ was raised from the dead through the glory of the Father, we too may live a new life.

[5]If we have been united with him like this in his death, we will certainly also be united with him in his resurrection. (+Ro 6:6-7)

Ro 6:8 Now if we died with Christ, we believe that we will also live with him.

Everlasting:

Ps 21:4 He asked you for life, and you gave it to him—length of days, for ever and ever.

Ps 121:8 the LORD will watch over your coming and going both now and forevermore.

Ps 133:3 It is as if the dew of Hermon were falling on Mount Zion. For there the LORD bestows his blessing, even life forevermore.

Isa 25:8 he will swallow up death forever. The Sovereign LORD will wipe away the tears from all faces; he will remove the disgrace of his people from all the earth. The LORD has spoken.

Da 12:2 Multitudes who sleep in the dust of the earth will awake: some to everlasting life, others to shame and everlasting contempt.

Mt 19:16 Now a man came up to Jesus and asked, "Teacher, what good thing must I do to get eternal life?"

[17]"Why do you ask me about what is good?" Jesus replied. "There is only One who is good. If you want to enter life, obey the commandments."

[18]"Which ones?" the man inquired.

Jesus replied, "'Do not murder, do not commit adultery, do not steal, do not give false testimony, [19]honor your father and mother,' and 'love your neighbor as yourself.'"

[20]"All these I have kept," the young man said. "What do I still lack?"

[21]Jesus answered, "If you want to be perfect, go, sell your possessions and give to the poor, and you will have treasure in heaven. Then come, follow me."

Mt 19:29 And everyone who has left houses or brothers or sisters or father or mother or children or fields for my sake will receive a hundred times as much and will inherit eternal life.

Mt 25:46 "Then they will go away to eternal punishment, but the righteous to eternal life." (+Mk 10:17-21,29-30; Lk 18:18-22,29)

Lk 18:30 will fail to receive many times as much in this age and, in the age to come, eternal life."

Lk 20:36 and they can no longer die; for they are like the angels. They are God's children, since they are children of the resurrection.

Jn 3:14 Just as Moses lifted up the snake in the desert, so the Son of Man must be lifted up, [15]that everyone who believes in him may have eternal life.

[16]"For God so loved the world that he gave his one and only Son, that whoever believes in him shall not perish but have eternal life. (+Jn 3:36)

Jn 4:14 but whoever drinks the water I give him will never thirst. Indeed, the water I give him will become in him a spring of water welling up to eternal life."

Jn 5:24 "I tell you the truth, whoever hears my word and believes him who sent me has eternal life and will not be condemned; he has crossed over from death to life. [25]I tell you the truth, a time is coming and has now come when the dead will hear the voice of the Son of God and those who hear will live.

Jn 5:29 and come out—those who have done good will rise to live, and those who have done evil will rise to be condemned.

Jn 5:39 You diligently study the Scriptures because you think that by them you possess eternal life. These are the Scriptures that testify about me,

Jn 6:27 Do not work for food that spoils, but for food that endures to eternal life, which the Son of Man will give you. On him God the Father has placed his seal of approval."

Jn 6:40 For my Father's will is that everyone who looks to the Son and believes in him shall have eternal life, and I will raise him up at the last day."

Jn 6:47 I tell you the truth, he who believes has everlasting life.

Jn 6:50 But here is the bread that comes down from heaven, which a man may eat and not die. [51]I am the living bread that came down from heaven. If anyone eats of this bread, he will live forever. This bread is my flesh, which I will give for the life of the world."

[52]Then the Jews began to argue sharply among themselves, "How can this man give us his flesh to eat?"

[53]Jesus said to them, "I tell you the truth, unless you eat the flesh of the Son of Man and drink his blood, you have no life in you. [54]Whoever eats my flesh and drinks my blood has eternal life, and I will raise him up at the last day. [55]For my flesh is real food and my blood is real drink. [56]Whoever eats my flesh and drinks my blood remains in me, and I in him. [57]Just as the living Father sent me and I live because of the Father, so the one who feeds on me will live because of me. [58]This is the bread that came down from heaven. Your forefathers ate manna and died, but he who feeds on this bread will live forever."

Jn 6:68 Simon Peter answered him, "Lord, to whom shall we go? You have the words of eternal life.

Jn 10:10 The thief comes only to steal and kill and destroy; I have come that they may have life, and have it to the full.

Jn 10:27 My sheep listen to my voice; I know them, and they follow me. [28]I give them eternal life, and they shall never perish; no one can snatch them out of my hand.

Jn 12:25 The man who loves his life will lose it, while the man who hates his life in this world will keep it for eternal life.

Jn 12:50 I know that his command leads to eternal life. So whatever I say is just what the Father has told me to say."

Jn 17:2 For you granted him authority over all people that he might give eternal life to all those you have given him. [3]Now this is eternal life: that they may know you, the only true God, and Jesus Christ, whom you have sent.

Ac 13:46 Then Paul and Barnabas answered them boldly: "We had to speak the word of God to you first. Since you reject it and do not consider yourselves worthy of eternal life, we now turn to the Gentiles.

Ac 13:48 When the Gentiles heard this, they were glad and honored the word of the Lord; and all who were appointed for eternal life believed.

Ro 2:7 To those who by persistence in doing good seek glory, honor and immortality, he will give eternal life.

Ro 5:21 so that, just as sin reigned in death, so also grace might reign through righteousness to bring eternal life through Jesus Christ our Lord.

Ro 6:22 But now that you have been set free from sin and have become slaves to God, the benefit you reap leads to holiness, and the result is eternal life. ²³For the wages of sin is death, but the gift of God is eternal life in Christ Jesus our Lord.

1Co 15:53 For the perishable must clothe itself with the imperishable, and the mortal with immortality. ⁵⁴When the perishable has been clothed with the imperishable, and the mortal with immortality, then the saying that is written will come true: "Death has been swallowed up in victory."

2Co 5:1 Now we know that if the earthly tent we live in is destroyed, we have a building from God, an eternal house in heaven, not built by human hands.

Gal 6:8 The one who sows to please his sinful nature, from that nature will reap destruction; the one who sows to please the Spirit, from the Spirit will reap eternal life.

1Ti 1:16 But for that very reason I was shown mercy so that in me, the worst of sinners, Christ Jesus might display his unlimited patience as an example for those who would believe on him and receive eternal life.

1Ti 4:8 For physical training is of some value, but godliness has value for all things, holding promise for both the present life and the life to come.

1Ti 6:12 Fight the good fight of the faith. Take hold of the eternal life to which you were called when you made your good confession in the presence of many witnesses. (+1Ti 6:19)

2Ti 1:10 but it has now been revealed through the appearing of our Savior, Christ Jesus, who has destroyed death and has brought life and immortality to light through the gospel.

Tit 1:2 a faith and knowledge resting on the hope of eternal life, which God, who does not lie, promised before the beginning of time,

Tit 3:7 so that, having been justified by his grace, we might become heirs having the hope of eternal life.

1Jn 2:25 And this is what he promised us—even eternal life.

1Jn 3:15 Anyone who hates his brother is a murderer, and you know that no murderer has eternal life in him.

1Jn 5:11 And this is the testimony: God has given us eternal life, and this life is in his Son. ¹²He who has the Son has life; he who does not have the Son of God does not have life.

¹³I write these things to you who believe in the name of the Son of God so that you may know that you have eternal life.

1Jn 5:20 We know also that the Son of God has come and has given us understanding, so that we may know him who is true. And we are in him who is true—even in his Son Jesus Christ. He is the true God and eternal life.

Jude 21 Keep yourselves in God's love as you wait for the mercy of our Lord Jesus Christ to bring you to eternal life.

Rev 1:18 I am the Living One; I was dead, and behold I am alive for ever and ever! And I hold the keys of death and Hades.

See Immortality.

LIFE, THE BOOK OF Figurative expression denoting God's record of those who inherit eternal life (Php 4:3; Rev 3:5; 21:27).

LIGHT [*239, 240, 4401, 5585, 5586, 5944, *847, 3290, 5766, 5890, 5894, 5895*].

NIV+ DAYLIGHT, ENLIGHTEN, ENLIGHTENED, LIGHTED, LIGHTEN, LIGHTENED, LIGHTER, LIGHTING, LIGHTLY, LIGHTS, LIT, SUNLIGHT, TWILIGHT

Physical:

Created (Ge 1:3-5; Ps 74:16; Isa 45:7; 2Co 4:6).

Miraculous (Ex 13:21; Dt 1:33; Mt 17:2; Mk 9:3; Lk 9:29; Ac 9:3; 12:7; 26:13).

Figurative:

1Ki 11:36 I will give one tribe to his son so that David my servant may always have a lamp before me in Jerusalem, the city where I chose to put my Name.

Of the Lord—

Ps 27:1 The LORD is my light and my salvation—whom shall I fear? The LORD is the stronghold of my life—of whom shall I be afraid?

Isa 60:19 The sun will no more be your light by day, nor will the brightness of the moon shine on you, for the LORD will be your everlasting light, and your God will be your glory. ²⁰Your sun will never set again, and your moon will wane no more; the LORD will be your everlasting light, and your days of sorrow will end. (+Jas 1:17)

1Jn 1:5 This is the message we have heard from him and declare to you: God is light; in him there is no darkness at all.

1Jn 1:7 But if we walk in the light, as he is in the light, we have fellowship with one another, and the blood of Jesus, his Son, purifies us from all sin. (+1Jn 2:8-10)

Of the Lord's word—

Ps 119:105 Your word is a lamp to my feet and a light for my path.

Pr 6:23 For these commands are a lamp, this teaching is a light, and the corrections of discipline are the way to life,

Of personal influence for righteousness—

Mt 5:14 "You are the light of the world. A city on a hill cannot be hidden. (+Mt 5:15)

Mt 5:16 In the same way, let your light shine before men, that they may see your good deeds and praise your Father in heaven. (+Mk 4:21; Lk 8:16)

Of the righteous—

Lk 16:8 "The master commended the dishonest manager because he had acted shrewdly. For the people of this world are more shrewd in dealing with their own kind than are the people of the light.

Eph 5:8 For you were once darkness, but now you are light in the Lord. Live as children of light

Eph 5:14 for it is light that makes everything visible. This is why it is said: "Wake up, O sleeper, rise from the dead, and Christ will shine on you."

Php 2:15 so that you may become blameless and pure, children of God without fault in a crooked and depraved generation, in which you shine like stars in the universe

1Th 5:5 You are all sons of the light and sons of the day. We do not belong to the night or to the darkness.

Of John the Baptist—

Jn 5:35 John was a lamp that burned and gave light, and you chose for a time to enjoy his light.

Of spiritual understanding—

Isa 8:20 To the law and to the testimony! If they do not speak according to this word, they have no light of dawn. (+Lk 1:33-36; 2Co 4:6)

Of the gospel (2Co 4:4,6).

Of spiritual wisdom—

Ps 119:130 The unfolding of your words gives light; it gives understanding to the simple. (+Isa 2:5)

2Pe 1:19 And we have the word of the prophets made more certain, and you will do well to pay attention to it, as to a light shining in a dark place, until the day dawns and the morning star rises in your hearts.

Of righteousness (Mt 5:16)—

Ac 26:18 to open their eyes and turn them from darkness

to light, and from the power of Satan to God, so that they may receive forgiveness of sins and a place among those who are sanctified by faith in me.'

1Pe 2:9 But you are a chosen people, a royal priesthood, a holy nation, a people belonging to God, that you may declare the praises of him who called you out of darkness into his wonderful light.

Of heavenly glory—

Rev 21:23 The city does not need the sun or the moon to shine on it, for the glory of God gives it light, and the Lamb is its lamp.

Of Christ's heavenly glory—

1Ti 6:16 who alone is immortal and who lives in unapproachable light, whom no one has seen or can see. To him be honor and might forever. Amen.

Of Christ's kingdom—

Isa 58:8 Then your light will break forth like the dawn, and your healing will quickly appear; then your righteousness will go before you, and the glory of the LORD will be your rear guard.

Of the Savior—

Isa 49:6 he says: "It is too small a thing for you to be my servant to restore the tribes of Jacob and bring back those of Israel I have kept. I will also make you a light for the Gentiles, that you may bring my salvation to the ends of the earth." (+Mal 4:2)

Mt 4:16 the people living in darkness have seen a great light; on those living in the land of the shadow of death a light has dawned."

Lk 2:32 a light for revelation to the Gentiles and for glory to your people Israel."

Jn 1:4 In him was life, and that life was the light of men. **5**The light shines in the darkness, but the darkness has not understood it.

Jn 1:7 He came as a witness to testify concerning that light, so that through him all men might believe. **8**He himself was not the light; he came only as a witness to the light. **9**The true light that gives light to every man was coming into the world.

Jn 3:19 This is the verdict: Light has come into the world, but men loved darkness instead of light because their deeds were evil. **20**Everyone who does evil hates the light, and will not come into the light for fear that his deeds will be exposed. **21**But whoever lives by the truth comes into the light, so that it may be seen plainly that what he has done has been done through God."

Jn 8:12 When Jesus spoke again to the people, he said, "I am the light of the world. Whoever follows me will never walk in darkness, but will have the light of life."

Jn 9:5 While I am in the world, I am the light of the world."

Jn 12:35 Then Jesus told them, "You are going to have the light just a little while longer. Walk while you have the light, before darkness overtakes you. The man who walks in the dark does not know where he is going. **36**Put your trust in the light while you have it, so that you may become sons of light." When he had finished speaking, Jesus left and hid himself from them. (+Jn 12:46; Rev 21:23)

LIGHTNING [240, 836, 1027, 1397+1398, 1398, 4365, 8404, *847, 848, 1993*]. (Job 28:26; 37:3; 38:25,35; Ps 18:14; 77:18; 78:48; 97:4; 135:7; 144:6; Jer 10:13; 51:16; Eze 1:13-14; Da 10:6; Na 2:4; Zec 9:14; 10:1; Mt 24:27; 28:3; Lk 10:18; Rev 4:5; 8:5; 11:19; 16:18).

Plague of, sent upon Egypt (Ex 9:23; Ps 77:18; 78:48; 105:32).

LIGN ALOES *See Aloes.*

LIGURE *See Jacinth.*

LIKHI [4376] (*take, marry*). Manassite (1Ch 7:19).

LILY [8808, *3211*].

NIV+ LILIES

The principal capitals of the temple ornamented with carvings of (1Ki 7:19,22,26). Molded on the rim of the bronze Sea in the temple (1Ki 7:26; 2Ch 4:5). Lessons of trust gathered from (Mt 6:28-30; Lk 12:27).

Figurative:

Of the lips of the beloved (SS 5:13).

LIME [8487]. (Isa 33:12; Am 2:1).

LINE [74, 204, 339, 448+4578+7156, 643, 1074, 1201, 1858, 2006, 2446, 2475, 2562, 5055, 5120, 5487, 5916+9247, 6885, 7742, 9292, 9352, *45, 3980, 4255*].

NIV+ LINED, LINES

Usually a measuring line (2Sa 8:2; Ps 78:55), a portion (Ps 16:6), sound made by a musical chord (Ps 19:4).

LINE OF JUDGMENT The divine (2Ki 21:13; Isa 28:17; 34:11; La 2:8; Am 7:8).

LINEN [355, 965, 1009, 2583, 4158, 6041, 7324, 9254, *1115, 1116, 3024, 3351, 3856, 4984*].

NIV+ LINENS

Exported from Egypt (1Ki 10:38; Eze 27:7), from Syria (Eze 27:16). Curtains of the tabernacle made of (Ex 26:1; 27:9). Robes of priests made of (Ex 28:5-8,15,39-42), of royal households made of (Ge 41:42; Est 8:15). Garments for men made of (Ge 41:42; Eze 9:2; Lk 16:19), for women (Isa 3:23; Eze 16:10-13). Bedding made of (Pr 7:16). Mosaic law forbade its being mingled with wool (Lev 19:19; Dt 22:11). The body of Jesus wrapped in (Mk 15:46; Jn 20:5).

Figurative:

Pure and white, of righteousness (Rev 15:6; 19:8,14).

LINTEL Horizontal beam forming the upper part of the doorway (Ex 12:22-23).

LINUS [*3352*]. A Christian at Rome (2Ti 4:21).

LION [787, 793, 4097, 4216, 4233, 4234, 4330, 8828, 10069, *3329*].

NIV+ LION'S, LIONESS, LIONESSES, LIONS, LIONS'

King of beasts (Mic 5:8). Fierceness of (Job 4:10; 28:8; Ps 7:2; Pr 22:13; Jer 2:15; 49:19; 50:44; Hos 13:8). The roaring of (Ps 22:13; Pr 20:2). Strength of (Pr 30:30; Isa 38:13; Joel 1:6). Instincts of, in taking prey (Ps 10:9; 17:12; La 3:10; Am 3:4; Na 2:12). Lair of, in the jungles (Jer 4:7; 25:38). Lair of in the temple ornamented by moldings of (1Ki 7:29,36). Twelve statues of, on the stairs leading to Solomon's throne (1Ki 10:19-20). Samson's riddle concerning (Jdg 14:14,18). Proverb of (Ecc 9:4). Parable of (Eze 19:1-9). Kept in captivity (Da 6). Sent as judgment upon the Samaritans (2Ki 17:25-26). Slain by Samson (Jdg 14:5-9), David (1Sa 17:34,36), Benaiah (2Sa 23:20), saints (Heb 11:33). Disobedient prophet slain by (1Ki 13:24-28), an unnamed person slain by (1Ki 20:36). Used for the torture of criminals (Da 6:16-24; 7:12; 2Ti 4:17).

Figurative:

Of a ruler's wrath (Pr 19:12; Jer 5:6; 50:17; Hos 5:14), of Satan (1Pe 5:8), of divine judgments (Isa 15:9).

Symbolic:

(Ge 49:9; Isa 29:1; Eze 1:10; 10:14; Da 7:4; Rev 4:7; 5:5; 9:8,17; 13:2).

LITIGATION To be avoided (Mt 5:25; Lk 12:58; 1Co 6:1-8).

See Actions at Law; Adjudication at Law; Arbitration; Compromise.

LITTER *See Wagon.*

LITTLE EVILS So called (Pr 6:10; Ecc 10:1; SS 2:15; 1Co 5:6).

LITTLE OWL *See Birds.*

LIVER [3879, 5355]. Considered center of life and feeling (Pr 7:23), used especially for sacrifice (Ex 29:13) and divination (Eze 21:21).

LIVERY *See Dress; Land, Conveyance of.*

LIVING CREATURES [2651, *2442*]. Possibly identical with cherubim (Eze 1:5-22; 3:13; Rev 4:6-9).

LIVING GOD [2645, 10261, *2409*]. Title emphasizing the reality and existence of the true God (Dt 5:26; Jos 3:10; 1Sa 17:26; Ps 42:2; 84:2; Isa 37:17; Jer 23:36; Da 6:26; Mt 26:63; Ac 14:15; 1Th 1:9; Heb 10:31; Rev 7:2).

LIZARD [3947, 4321, 7370, 8532]. Unclean; not permitted as food (Lev 11:29-30; Pr 30:28).

LO-AMMI [4204] (*not my people*). Symbolic naming for Hosea's third child to represent a break in the covenant relationship between the Lord and Israel (Ex 6:7; Jer 7:23). This break would later be restored (Hos 1:9-10, ftn; 2:1,23). The warnings became more severe in moving from the first to the third child.

See Lo-Ruhamah; Ruhamah.

LO DEBAR, LO-DEBAR [4203, 4274] (*no pasture*). A city in Manasseh (2Sa 9:4-5; 17:27). Home of Mephibosheth, the lame son of Jonathan (2Sa 9:3-5).

LOAVES [2705, 3971, 4312, *788*].

NIV+ LOAF

Miracle of the five (Mt 14:15-21; 16:9; Mk 6:37-44; Lk 9:12-17; Jn 6:5-13), of the seven (Mt 15:34-38; 16:10; Mk 8:1-10).

See Bread.

LOBBYING To frustrate rebuilding the temple (Ezr 4:4-5).

LOCK [4980, 5835, 6037, *2881, 3091, 5168*].

NIV+ LOCKED

Beams of wood or iron used for fastening gates or doors (SS 5:5; Lk 11:7).

LOCUST [746, 1466, 1479, 1612, 2506, 2885, 3540, 7526, *210*].

NIV+ LOCUSTS

Authorized as food (Lev 11:22), used as (Mt 3:4; Mk 1:6). Plague of (Ex 10:1-19; Ps 105:34-35). Devastation by (Dt 28:38; 1Ki 8:37; 2Ch 7:13; Isa 33:4; Joel 1:4-7; Rev 9:7-10). Sun obscured by (Joel 2:2,10). Instincts of (Pr 30:27).

See Grasshopper.

Figurative: (Jer 46:23).

Symbolic: (Rev 9:3-10).

LOD [4254]. A city in Benjamin (1Ch 8:12; Ezr 2:33; Ne 7:37; 11:35). Called Lydda (Ac 9:38).

LODGE [3519, 4180, 4472, 4869, *2907, 5685*].

NIV+ LODGED, LODGING

Temporary shelter built in a garden for a watchman guarding ripening fruit (Isa 1:8).

LOFT *See Upper Chamber, Upper Room.*

LOG [4253].

NIV+ LOGS

A measure for liquids, holding about a pint (Lev 14:10,12,15,24).

LOGIA Greek word for the nonbiblical sayings of Christ, such as those in the so-called Gospel of Thomas discovered in 1945.

LOGOS Usually rendered "word," in the Johannine writings it also appears as a title of Jesus: "The Word" (Jn 1:1ff; 1Jn 1:1; Rev 19:13). In the OT God creates by the word (Ge 1:3; Ps 33:9). In the Judaism of NT times, "word" was used as a way of referring to God himself. In Greek philosophy, "word" refers to the dynamic principle of reason operating in the world and forming a medium of communion between God and man. *See Jesus the Christ, Names, Appellations, and Titles of; Logos.*

LOIN [4072, 5516].

NIV+ LOINCLOTH, LOINS

Part of the body between the ribs and thighs (Lev 3:4,10,15), vulnerable (Dt 33:11), a seat of strength (Job 40:16).

LOIS [*3396*] (perhaps *more desirable, better*). Grandmother of Timothy, commended by Paul for her faith (2Ti 1:5).

LONGEVITY

Ge 6:3 Then the LORD said, "My Spirit will not contend with man forever, for he is mortal; his days will be a hundred and twenty years."

Ps 90:10 The length of our days is seventy years—or eighty, if we have the strength; yet their span is but trouble and sorrow, for they quickly pass, and we fly away.

Promised to the obedient under the old covenant—

Ex 20:12 "Honor your father and your mother, so that you may live long in the land the LORD your God is giving you. (+Dt 4:40; 22:7)

To the righteous—

Job 5:26 You will come to the grave in full vigor, like sheaves gathered in season.

Ps 21:4 He asked you for life, and you gave it to him—length of days, for ever and ever.

Ps 34:11 Come, my children, listen to me; I will teach you the fear of the LORD. [12]Whoever of you loves life and desires to see many good days, [13]keep your tongue from evil and your lips from speaking lies.

Ps 91:16 With long life will I satisfy him and show him my salvation."

Pr 3:2 for they will prolong your life many years and bring you prosperity.

Pr 3:16 Long life is in her right hand; in her left hand are riches and honor.

Pr 9:11 For through me your days will be many, and years will be added to your life.

Pr 10:27 The fear of the LORD adds length to life, but the years of the wicked are cut short.

Isa 65:20 "Never again will there be in it an infant who lives but a few days, or an old man who does not live out his years; he who dies at a hundred will be thought a mere youth; he who fails to reach a hundred will be considered accursed.

1Pe 3:10 For, "Whoever would love life and see good days must keep his tongue from evil and his lips from deceitful speech. ¹¹He must turn from evil and do good; he must seek peace and pursue it.

To Solomon (1Ki 3:11-14).

Instances of:

Adam, 930 years (Ge 5:5). Seth, 912 years (Ge 5:8). Enos, 905 years (Ge 5:11). Kenan, 910 years (Ge 5:14). Mahalalel, 895 years (Ge 5:17). Jared, 962 years (Ge 5:20). Enoch, 365 years (Ge 5:23). Methuselah, 969 years (Ge 5:27). Lamech, 777 years (Ge 5:31). Noah, 950 years (Ge 9:29). Shem (Ge 11:11). Arphaxad (Ge 11:13). Shelah (Ge 11:15). Eber (Ge 11:17). Peleg (Ge 11:19). Reu (Ge 11:21). Serug (Ge 11:23). Nahor (Ge 11:25). Terah, 205 years (Ge 11:32). Sarah, 127 years (Ge 23:1). Abraham, 175 years (Ge 25:7). Isaac, 180 years (Ge 35:28). Jacob, 147 years (Ge 47:28). Joseph, 110 years (Ge 50:26). Amram, 173 years (Ex 6:20). Aaron, 123 years (Nu 33:39). Moses, 120 years (Dt 31:2; 34:7). Joshua, 110 years (Jos 24:29). Eli, 98 years (1Sa 4:15). Barzillai, 80 years (2Sa 19:32). Job, 140 years (Job 42:16). Jehoiada, 130 years (2Ch 24:15). Anna, 84 years (Lk 2:36-37). Paul (Phm 9).

See Old Age.

LONGSUFFERING [678+800].

NIV+ LONG-SUFFERING, SLOW TO ANGER

1Ti 1:16 But for that very reason I was shown mercy so that in me, the worst of sinners, Christ Jesus might display his unlimited patience as an example for those who would believe on him and receive eternal life.

A Christian grace—

1Co 13:4 Love is patient, love is kind. It does not envy, it does not boast, it is not proud.

1Co 13:7 It always protects, always trusts, always hopes, always perseveres.

2Co 6:4 Rather, as servants of God we commend ourselves in every way: in great endurance; in troubles, hardships and distresses; ⁵in beatings, imprisonments and riots; in hard work, sleepless nights and hunger; ⁶in purity, understanding, patience and kindness; in the Holy Spirit and in sincere love;

Gal 5:22 But the fruit of the Spirit is love, joy, peace, patience, kindness, goodness, faithfulness,

Col 1:11 being strengthened with all power according to his glorious might so that you may have great endurance and patience, and joyfully

2Ti 3:10 You, however, know all about my teaching, my way of life, my purpose, faith, patience, love, endurance,

2Ti 4:2 Preach the Word; be prepared in season and out of season; correct, rebuke and encourage—with great patience and careful instruction.

Commanded—

Eph 4:2 Be completely humble and gentle; be patient, bearing with one another in love.

Col 3:12 Therefore, as God's chosen people, holy and dearly loved, clothe yourselves with compassion, kindness, humility, gentleness and patience. ¹³Bear with each other and forgive whatever grievances you may have against one another. Forgive as the Lord forgave you.

See Charitableness; God, Longsuffering of; Patience.

LOOKING BACKWARD Toward the old life (Ge 19:17,26; Nu 11:5; 14:4; Lk 9:62).

LOOKING GLASS *See Mirror.*

LORD [(Yahweh: 3051, 3363, 3378) 123, 151, 1484, 8606, 10437, *1305, 2894, 3258, 3259, 3261, 3448*].

NIV+ LORD, LORD'S, LORDED, LORDING, LORDS

A term applied to both men and God, expressing varied degrees of honor, dignity, and majesty; applied also to idols (Ex 22:8; Jdg 2:11,13), used of Jesus as Messiah (Ac 2:36; Php 2:9-11; Ro 1:4; 14:8). *See God, Names of; Titles and Names; Yahweh.*

LORD'S DAY (*day belonging to the master [Jesus]*). The day especially associated with the Lord Jesus Christ; a day consecrated to the Lord; the first day of the week, commemorating the resurrection of Jesus (Jn 20:1-25; Rev 1:10) and the pouring out of the Spirit (Ac 2:1-41), set aside for worship (Ac 20:7).

LORD'S PRAYER, THE Prayer taught by Jesus as a model of how his disciples should pray (Mt 6:9-13; Lk 11:2-4).

LORD'S SUPPER Instituted by Christ on the night of his betrayal immediately after the Passover Feast to be a memorial of his death and a visible sign of the blessings of the new covenant.

Variously Called:

Body and blood of Christ (Mt 26:26,28), communion of the body and blood of Christ (1Co 10:16), bread and cup of the Lord (1Co 11:27), breaking of bread (Ac 2:42; 20:7), Lord's Supper (1Co 11:20).

Not to be observed unworthily (1Co 11:27-32).

See Eucharist.

LO-RUHAMAH [4205] (*no compassion*). Symbolic name given to Hosea's daughter (Hos 1:6,8; 2:4,23). The naming represents a reversal of the love (compassion) that God had earlier shown to Israel (Ex 33:19; Dt 7:6-8) but was later promised again (Hos 2:23).

See Lo-Ammi; Ruhamah.

LOST SHEEP Parable of (Mt 18:12-13; Lk 15:4-7).

LOST, THE *See Wicked, Punishment of.*

LOT [4288, *3397*].

NIV+ LOT'S

The son of Haran. Accompanies Terah from Ur of the Chaldeans to Haran (Ge 11:31). Migrates with Abraham to the land of Canaan (Ge 12:4). Accompanies Abraham to Egypt: returns with him to Bethel (Ge 13:1-3). Rich in flocks, herds, and servants; separates from Abraham and locates in Sodom (Ge 13:5-14). Taken captive by Kedorlaomer; rescued by Abraham (Ge 14:1-16). Providentially saved from destruction in Sodom (Ge 19; Lk 17:28-29). Righteous (2Pe 2:7-8). Disobediently protests against going to the mountains, and chooses Zoar (Ge 19:17-22). His wife disobediently longs after Sodom, and becomes a pillar of salt (Ge 19:26; Lk 17:32). Commits incest with his daughters (Ge 19:30-38). Descendants of. *See Ammonite(s); Moabite(s).*

LOT, THE [1598, 2750, 3926+4987, 5162, 7877, *3102*, *3275*].

NIV+ LOTS, PUR

(Pr 16:33; 18:18; Isa 34:17; Joel 3:3). The scapegoat chosen by (Lev 16:8-10).

The land of Canaan divided among the tribes by (Nu 26:55; Jos 15; 18:10; 19:51; 21; 1Ch 6:61,65; Eze 45:1; 47:22; 48:29; Mic 2:5; Ac 13:19). Saul chosen king by (1Sa 10:20-21). Priests and Levites designated by, for sanctuary service (1Ch 24:5-31; 26:13; Ne 10:34; Lk 1:9). Used after the Captivity (Ne 11:1). An apostle chosen by (Ac 1:26). Achan's guilt discovered by (Jos 7:14-18), Jonathan's (1Sa 14:41-42), Jonah's (Jnh 1:7). Used to fix the time for the execution of condemned persons (Est 3:7; 9:24). The garments of Jesus divided by (Ps 22:18; Mt 27:35; Mk 15:24; Jn 19:23-24).

For Feast of, *See Casting Lots; Purim.*

LOTAN [4289] (*of Lot*).

NIV+ LOTAN'S

Son of Seir (Ge 36:20,22,29).

LOTS, CASTING *See Casting Lots; Lot, The.*

LOTUS [7365].

NIV+ LOTUSES

A water plant (Job 40:21-22). *See Plants of the Bible.*

LOVE [*170, 171, 172, 173, 1856, 2668, 2876, 2883, 3137, 3351, 8163, 8533, *26, 27, 28, 921, 5789, 5797*].

NIV+ BELOVED, LOVED, LOVELY, LOVER, LOVER'S, LOVERS, LOVES, LOVING, LOVING-KINDNESS, LOVINGLY

(1Co 13; 14:1; Col 1:8; 2:2; 1Th 1:3; 5:8; 1Ti 6:11; 2Ti 1:7; Phm 5; Heb 10:24; 1Jn 4:7,16-18).

The theme of the Song of Solomon, and often allegorized representing the love of the Messiah for the church and of his church for the Messiah (SS 1-8). *See Church, Loved.*

Love of Person For Person: (Ro 5:7; Jas 1:27).

Defined—

1Co 13:1 If I speak in the tongues of men and of angels, but have not love, I am only a resounding gong or a clanging cymbal. [2]If I have the gift of prophecy and can fathom all mysteries and all knowledge, and if I have a faith that can move mountains, but have not love, I am nothing. [3]If I give all I possess to the poor and surrender my body to the flames, but have not love, I gain nothing.

[4]Love is patient, love is kind. It does not envy, it does not boast, it is not proud. [5]It is not rude, it is not self-seeking, it is not easily angered, it keeps no record of wrongs. [6]Love does not delight in evil but rejoices with the truth. [7]It always protects, always trusts, always hopes, always perseveres.

[8]Love never fails. But where there are prophecies, they will cease; where there are tongues, they will be stilled; where there is knowledge, it will pass away. [9]For we know in part and we prophesy in part, [10]but when perfection comes, the imperfect disappears. [11]When I was a child, I talked like a child, I thought like a child, I reasoned like a child. When I became a man, I put childish ways behind me. [12]Now we see but a poor reflection as in a mirror; then we shall see face to face. Now I know in part; then I shall know fully, even as I am fully known.

[13]And now these three remain: faith, hope and love. But the greatest of these is love.

In the parable of the good Samaritan (Lk 10:25-37).

Is edifying—

1Co 8:1 Now about food sacrificed to idols: We know that we all possess knowledge. Knowledge puffs up, but love builds up.

Is precious—

Pr 15:17 Better a meal of vegetables where there is love than a fattened calf with hatred.

Is unquenchable—

Pr 17:17 A friend loves at all times, and a brother is born for adversity.

SS 8:6 Place me like a seal over your heart, like a seal on your arm; for love is as strong as death, its jealousy unyielding as the grave. It burns like blazing fire, like a mighty flame. [7]Many waters cannot quench love; rivers cannot wash it away. If one were to give all the wealth of his house for love, it would be utterly scorned.

Is a fruit of the Spirit—

Gal 5:22 But the fruit of the Spirit is love, joy, peace, patience, kindness, goodness, faithfulness,

Promotes peace—

Pr 10:12 Hatred stirs up dissension, but love covers over all wrongs.

Pr 17:9 He who covers over an offense promotes love, but whoever repeats the matter separates close friends.

A proof, of discipleship of Jesus (Jn 13:34-35), of regeneration (1Jn 3:14,19).

Commanded—

Lev 19:18 " 'Do not seek revenge or bear a grudge against one of your people, but love your neighbor as yourself. I am the LORD. (+Mt 5:40)

Mt 5:41 If someone forces you to go one mile, go with him two miles. [42]Give to the one who asks you, and do not turn away from the one who wants to borrow from you. (+Mt 7:12)

Mt 19:19 honor your father and mother,' and 'love your neighbor as yourself.' " (+Mt 22:39-40)

Mk 12:30 Love the Lord your God with all your heart and with all your soul and with all your mind and with all your strength.' [31]The second is this: 'Love your neighbor as yourself.' There is no commandment greater than these."

[32]"Well said, teacher," the man replied. "You are right in saying that God is one and there is no other but him. [33]To love him with all your heart, with all your understanding and with all your strength, and to love your neighbor as yourself is more important than all burnt offerings and sacrifices." (+Lk 6:30)

Lk 6:31 Do to others as you would have them do to you.

[32]"If you love those who love you, what credit is that to you? Even 'sinners' love those who love them. [33]And if you do good to those who are good to you, what credit is that to you? Even 'sinners' do that. [34]And if you lend to those from whom you expect repayment, what credit is that to you? Even 'sinners' lend to 'sinners,' expecting to be repaid in full. [35]But love your enemies, do good to them, and lend to them without expecting to get anything back. Then your reward will be great, and you will be sons of the Most High, because he is kind to the ungrateful and wicked. (+Lk 6:36-38)

Ro 12:9 Love must be sincere. Hate what is evil; cling to what is good. (+Ro 12:15)

Ro 13:8 Let no debt remain outstanding, except the continuing debt to love one another, for he who loves his fellowman has fulfilled the law. [9]The commandments, "Do not commit adultery," "Do not murder," "Do not steal," "Do not covet," and whatever other commandment there may be, are summed up in this one rule: "Love your neighbor as yourself." [10]Love does no harm to its neighbor. Therefore love is the fulfillment of the law. (+1Co 10:24)

1Co 16:14 Do everything in love. (+Gal 6:1-2,10; Eph 4:2,32)

Eph 5:2 and live a life of love, just as Christ loved us and gave himself up for us as a fragrant offering and sacrifice to God.

Php 1:9 And this is my prayer: that your love may abound more and more in knowledge and depth of insight, (+Col 3:14)

1Th 3:12 May the Lord make your love increase and overflow for each other and for everyone else, just as ours does for you.

1Ti 1:5 The goal of this command is love, which comes from a pure heart and a good conscience and a sincere faith.

1Ti 4:12 Don't let anyone look down on you because you are young, but set an example for the believers in speech, in life, in love, in faith and in purity.

1Ti 6:11 But you, man of God, flee from all this, and pursue righteousness, godliness, faith, love, endurance and gentleness.

2Ti 2:22 Flee the evil desires of youth, and pursue righteousness, faith, love and peace, along with those who call on the Lord out of a pure heart.

Jas 2:8 If you really keep the royal law found in Scripture, "Love your neighbor as yourself," you are doing right.

2Pe 1:7 and to godliness, brotherly kindness; and to brotherly kindness, love. (+1Jn 4:20-21)

Commanded toward strangers—

Lev 19:34 The alien living with you must be treated as one of your native-born. Love him as yourself, for you were aliens in Egypt. I am the LORD your God.

Dt 10:19 And you are to love those who are aliens, for you yourselves were aliens in Egypt.

Commandments toward enemies (Pr 24:17; Mt 5:43-48; Lk 6:35; Ro 12:14,20)

Commanded toward fellow Christians—

Jn 13:14 Now that I, your Lord and Teacher, have washed your feet, you also should wash one another's feet. [15]I have set you an example that you should do as I have done for you.

Jn 13:34 "A new command I give you: Love one another. As I have loved you, so you must love one another. [35]By this all men will know that you are my disciples, if you love one another."

Jn 15:12 My command is this: Love each other as I have loved you. [13]Greater love has no one than this, that he lay down his life for his friends. (+Jn 15:17)

Ro 12:9 Love must be sincere. Hate what is evil; cling to what is good. [10]Be devoted to one another in brotherly love. Honor one another above yourselves. (+Ro 12:15-16; 14:19,21; 15:1-2,5,7; 16:1-2)

1Co 14:1 Follow the way of love and eagerly desire spiritual gifts, especially the gift of prophecy.

2Co 8:7 But just as you excel in everything—in faith, in speech, in knowledge, in complete earnestness and in your love for us—see that you also excel in this grace of giving. [8]I am not commanding you, but I want to test the sincerity of your love by comparing it with the earnestness of others.

Gal 5:13 You, my brothers, were called to be free. But do not use your freedom to indulge the sinful nature; rather, serve one another in love. (+Gal 5:14; 6:1-2,10; Eph 4:2,32)

Php 2:2 then make my joy complete by being like-minded, having the same love, being one in spirit and purpose.

Col 2:2 My purpose is that they may be encouraged in heart and united in love, so that they may have the full riches of complete understanding, in order that they may know the mystery of God, namely, Christ,

Col 3:12 Therefore, as God's chosen people, holy and dearly loved, clothe yourselves with compassion, kindness, humility, gentleness and patience. [13]Bear with each other and forgive whatever grievances you may have against one another. Forgive as the Lord forgave you. [14]And over all these virtues put on love, which binds them all together in perfect unity. (+1Th 3:12; 5:8,11,14)

1Ti 6:2 Those who have believing masters are not to show less respect for them because they are brothers. Instead, they are to serve them even better, because those who benefit from their service are believers, and dear to them. These are the things you are to teach and urge on them. (+Phm 16)

Heb 10:24 And let us consider how we may spur one another on toward love and good deeds. (+Heb 13:13)

1Pe 1:22 Now that you have purified yourselves by obeying the truth so that you have sincere love for your brothers, love one another deeply, from the heart.

1Pe 2:17 Show proper respect to everyone: Love the brotherhood of believers, fear God, honor the king. (+1Pe 3:8-9; 4:8; 2Pe 1:7)

1Jn 3:11 This is the message you heard from the beginning: We should love one another.

1Jn 3:14 We know that we have passed from death to life, because we love our brothers. Anyone who does not love remains in death.

1Jn 3:16 This is how we know what love is: Jesus Christ laid down his life for us. And we ought to lay down our lives for our brothers. [17]If anyone has material possessions and sees his brother in need but has no pity on him, how can the love of God be in him? [18]Dear children, let us not love with words or tongue but with actions and in truth. (+1Jn 3:19)

1Jn 3:23 And this is his command: to believe in the name of his Son, Jesus Christ, and to love one another as he commanded us.

1Jn 4:7 Dear friends, let us love one another, for love comes from God. Everyone who loves has been born of God and knows God.

1Jn 4:11 Dear friends, since God so loved us, we also ought to love one another. [12]No one has ever seen God; but if we love one another, God lives in us and his love is made complete in us.

1Jn 4:20 If anyone says, "I love God," yet hates his brother, he is a liar. For anyone who does not love his brother, whom he has seen, cannot love God, whom he has not seen. [21]And he has given us this command: Whoever loves God must also love his brother.

2Jn 5 And now, dear lady, I am not writing you a new command but one we have had from the beginning. I ask that we love one another.

Demonstrated by obedience—

1Jn 5:1 Everyone who believes that Jesus is the Christ is born of God, and everyone who loves the father loves his child as well. [2]This is how we know that we love the children of God: by loving God and carrying out his commands.

Rewards of—

Mt 10:41 Anyone who receives a prophet because he is a

prophet will receive a prophet's reward, and anyone who receives a righteous man because he is a righteous man will receive a righteous man's reward. [42]And if anyone gives even a cup of cold water to one of these little ones because he is my disciple, I tell you the truth, he will certainly not lose his reward."

Mt 25:34 "Then the King will say to those on his right, 'Come, you who are blessed by my Father; take your inheritance, the kingdom prepared for you since the creation of the world. [35]For I was hungry and you gave me something to eat, I was thirsty and you gave me something to drink, I was a stranger and you invited me in, [36]I needed clothes and you clothed me, I was sick and you looked after me, I was in prison and you came to visit me.'

[37]"Then the righteous will answer him, 'Lord, when did we see you hungry and feed you, or thirsty and give you something to drink? [38]When did we see you a stranger and invite you in, or needing clothes and clothe you? [39]When did we see you sick or in prison and go to visit you?'

[40]"The King will reply, 'I tell you the truth, whatever you did for one of the least of these brothers of mine, you did for me.' (+Mt 25:46)

Mk 9:41 I tell you the truth, anyone who gives you a cup of water in my name because you belong to Christ will certainly not lose his reward.

1Jn 2:10 Whoever loves his brother lives in the light, and there is nothing in him to make him stumble.

Exemplified:

By Paul—

Ac 26:29 Paul replied, "Short time or long—I pray God that not only you but all who are listening to me today may become what I am, except for these chains." (+Ro 1:11)

Ro 1:12 that is, that you and I may be mutually encouraged by each other's faith. (+Ro 9:1-2)

Ro 9:3 For I could wish that I myself were cursed and cut off from Christ for the sake of my brothers, those of my own race, (+1Co 4:9-13)

1Co 4:14 I am not writing this to shame you, but to warn you, as my dear children. [15]Even though you have ten thousand guardians in Christ, you do not have many fathers, for in Christ Jesus I became your father through the gospel. [16]Therefore I urge you to imitate me.

1Co 8:13 Therefore, if what I eat causes my brother to fall into sin, I will never eat meat again, so that I will not cause him to fall.

2Co 1:3 Praise be to the God and Father of our Lord Jesus Christ, the Father of compassion and the God of all comfort, [4]who comforts us in all our troubles, so that we can comfort those in any trouble with the comfort we ourselves have received from God. [5]For just as the sufferings of Christ flow over into our lives, so also through Christ our comfort overflows. [6]If we are distressed, it is for your comfort and salvation; if we are comforted, it is for your comfort, which produces in you patient endurance of the same sufferings we suffer.

2Co 1:14 as you have understood us in part, you will come to understand fully that you can boast of us just as we will boast of you in the day of the Lord Jesus. (+2Co 1:23-24)

2Co 2:4 For I wrote you out of great distress and anguish of heart and with many tears, not to grieve you but to let you know the depth of my love for you.

2Co 3:2 You yourselves are our letter, written on our hearts, known and read by everybody.

2Co 4:5 For we do not preach ourselves, but Jesus Christ as Lord, and ourselves as your servants for Jesus' sake.

2Co 6:4 Rather, as servants of God we commend our-

selves in every way: in great endurance; in troubles, hardships and distresses; [5]in beatings, imprisonments and riots; in hard work, sleepless nights and hunger; [6]in purity, understanding, patience and kindness; in the Holy Spirit and in sincere love;

2Co 6:11 We have spoken freely to you, Corinthians, and opened wide our hearts to you. [12]We are not withholding our affection from you, but you are withholding yours from us. [13]As a fair exchange—I speak as to my children—open wide your hearts also.

2Co 7:1 Since we have these promises, dear friends, let us purify ourselves from everything that contaminates body and spirit, perfecting holiness out of reverence for God.

[2]Make room for us in your hearts. We have wronged no one, we have corrupted no one, we have exploited no one. [3]I do not say this to condemn you; I have said before that you have such a place in our hearts that we would live or die with you. [4]I have great confidence in you; I take great pride in you. I am greatly encouraged; in all our troubles my joy knows no bounds.

2Co 11:2 I am jealous for you with a godly jealousy. I promised you to one husband, to Christ, so that I might present you as a pure virgin to him.

2Co 12:14 Now I am ready to visit you for the third time, and I will not be a burden to you, because what I want is not your possessions but you. After all, children should not have to save up for their parents, but parents for their children. [15]So I will very gladly spend for you everything I have and expend myself as well. If I love you more, will you love me less? [16]Be that as it may, I have not been a burden to you. Yet, crafty fellow that I am, I caught you by trickery!

2Co 12:19 Have you been thinking all along that we have been defending ourselves to you? We have been speaking in the sight of God as those in Christ; and everything we do, dear friends, is for your strengthening. [20]For I am afraid that when I come I may not find you as I want you to be, and you may not find me as you want me to be. I fear that there may be quarreling, jealousy, outbursts of anger, factions, slander, gossip, arrogance and disorder. [21]I am afraid that when I come again my God will humble me before you, and I will be grieved over many who have sinned earlier and have not repented of the impurity, sexual sin and debauchery in which they have indulged.

2Co 13:9 We are glad whenever we are weak but you are strong; and our prayer is for your perfection.

Gal 4:19 My dear children, for whom I am again in the pains of childbirth until Christ is formed in you, [20]how I wish I could be with you now and change my tone, because I am perplexed about you!

Eph 3:13 I ask you, therefore, not to be discouraged because of my sufferings for you, which are your glory.

Php 1:3 I thank my God every time I remember you. [4]In all my prayers for all of you, I always pray with joy [5]because of your partnership in the gospel from the first day until now,

Php 1:7 It is right for me to feel this way about all of you, since I have you in my heart; for whether I am in chains or defending and confirming the gospel, all of you share in God's grace with me. [8]God can testify how I long for all of you with the affection of Christ Jesus.

Php 1:23 I am torn between the two: I desire to depart and be with Christ, which is better by far; [24]but it is more necessary for you that I remain in the body. [25]Convinced of this, I know that I will remain, and I will continue with all of you for your progress and joy in the faith, [26]so that through my being with you again your joy in Christ Jesus will overflow on account of me.

Php 2:19 I hope in the Lord Jesus to send Timothy to you soon, that I also may be cheered when I receive news about you.

Php 4:1 Therefore, my brothers, you whom I love and long for, my joy and crown, that is how you should stand firm in the Lord, dear friends!

Col 1:3 We always thank God, the Father of our Lord Jesus Christ, when we pray for you, [4]because we have heard of your faith in Christ Jesus and of the love you have for all the saints—

Col 1:24 Now I rejoice in what was suffered for you, and I fill up in my flesh what is still lacking in regard to Christ's afflictions, for the sake of his body, which is the church.

Col 1:28 We proclaim him, admonishing and teaching everyone with all wisdom, so that we may present everyone perfect in Christ. [29]To this end I labor, struggling with all his energy, which so powerfully works in me.

Col 2:1 I want you to know how much I am struggling for you and for those at Laodicea, and for all who have not met me personally.

Col 2:5 For though I am absent from you in body, I am present with you in spirit and delight to see how orderly you are and how firm your faith in Christ is. (+Col 4:7)

1Th 2:7 but we were gentle among you, like a mother caring for her little children. [8]We loved you so much that we were delighted to share with you not only the gospel of God but our lives as well, because you had become so dear to us.

1Th 2:11 For you know that we dealt with each of you as a father deals with his own children, [12]encouraging, comforting and urging you to live lives worthy of God, who calls you into his kingdom and glory.

1Th 2:17 But, brothers, when we were torn away from you for a short time (in person, not in thought), out of our intense longing we made every effort to see you. [18]For we wanted to come to you—certainly I, Paul, did, again and again—but Satan stopped us. [19]For what is our hope, our joy, or the crown in which we will glory in the presence of our Lord Jesus when he comes? Is it not you? [20]Indeed, you are our glory and joy.

1Th 3:5 For this reason, when I could stand it no longer, I sent to find out about your faith. I was afraid that in some way the tempter might have tempted you and our efforts might have been useless.

1Th 3:7 Therefore, brothers, in all our distress and persecution we were encouraged about you because of your faith. [8]For now we really live, since you are standing firm in the Lord. [9]How can we thank God enough for you in return for all the joy we have in the presence of our God because of you? [10]Night and day we pray most earnestly that we may see you again and supply what is lacking in your faith.

1Th 3:12 May the Lord make your love increase and overflow for each other and for everyone else, just as ours does for you.

2Th 1:4 Therefore, among God's churches we boast about your perseverance and faith in all the persecutions and trials you are enduring.

2Ti 1:3 I thank God, whom I serve, as my forefathers did, with a clear conscience, as night and day I constantly remember you in my prayers. [4]Recalling your tears, I long to see you, so that I may be filled with joy.

2Ti 1:8 So do not be ashamed to testify about our Lord, or

ashamed of me his prisoner. But join with me in suffering for the gospel, by the power of God,

2Ti 2:10 Therefore I endure everything for the sake of the elect, that they too may obtain the salvation that is in Christ Jesus, with eternal glory. (+Tit 3:15)

Phm 9 yet I appeal to you on the basis of love. I then, as Paul—an old man and now also a prisoner of Christ Jesus—

Phm 12 I am sending him—who is my very heart—back to you.

Phm 16 no longer as a slave, but better than a slave, as a dear brother. He is very dear to me but even dearer to you, both as a man and as a brother in the Lord.

Instances of:

Abraham for Lot (Ge 14:14-16).

Moses for Israel—

Ex 32:31 So Moses went back to the LORD and said, "Oh, what a great sin these people have committed! They have made themselves gods of gold. [32]But now, please forgive their sin—but if not, then blot me out of the book you have written."

David and Jonathan (1Sa 18:1; 20:17). Israel and Judah for David (1Sa 18:16). David's subjects for David (2Sa 15:30; 17:27-29). Hiram for David (1Ki 5:1). Obadiah for the prophets (1Ki 18:4). Nehemiah for Israelites (Ne 5:10-18). Job's friends (Job 42:11). Centurion for his servant (Lk 7:2-6).

Good Samaritan—

Lk 10:29 But he wanted to justify himself, so he asked Jesus, "And who is my neighbor?"

[30]In reply Jesus said: "A man was going down from Jerusalem to Jericho, when he fell into the hands of robbers. They stripped him of his clothes, beat him and went away, leaving him half dead. [31]A priest happened to be going down the same road, and when he saw the man, he passed by on the other side. [32]So too, a Levite, when he came to the place and saw him, passed by on the other side. [33]But a Samaritan, as he traveled, came where the man was; and when he saw him, he took pity on him. [34]He went to him and bandaged his wounds, pouring on oil and wine. Then he put the man on his own donkey, took him to an inn and took care of him. [35]The next day he took out two silver coins and gave them to the innkeeper. 'Look after him,' he said, 'and when I return, I will reimburse you for any extra expense you may have.'

[36]"Which of these three do you think was a neighbor to the man who fell into the hands of robbers?"

[37]The expert in the law replied, "The one who had mercy on him."

Jesus told him, "Go and do likewise."

Stephen (Ac 7:60). Roman Christians for Paul (Ac 28:15). Priscilla and Aquila for Paul (Ro 16:3-4).

See Brother; Fraternity; Friendship; Golden Rule.

Love of Man for Woman:

Isaac for Rebekah (Ge 24:67). Jacob for Rachel (Ge 29:20,30). Shechem for Dinah (Ge 34:3,12). Boaz for Ruth (Ru 2-4).

Love of People for God:

Defined—

1Jn 5:3 This is love for God: to obey his commands. And his commands are not burdensome, (+2Jn 6)

Incompatible with love of the world—

1Jn 2:15 Do not love the world or anything in the world. If anyone loves the world, the love of the Father is not in him.

Incompatible with hatred of brother—

1Jn 4:20 If anyone says, "I love God," yet hates his brother, he is a liar. For anyone who does not love his brother, whom he has seen, cannot love God, whom he has not seen. [21]And he has given us this command: Whoever loves God must also love his brother.

Incompatible with guilty fear—

2Ti 1:7 For God did not give us a spirit of timidity, but a spirit of power, of love and of self-discipline.

1Jn 4:18 There is no fear in love. But perfect love drives out fear, because fear has to do with punishment. The one who fears is not made perfect in love.

Reasons for—

Ps 116:1 I love the LORD, for he heard my voice; he heard my cry for mercy.

1Jn 4:19 We love because he first loved us.

The gift of God—

Dt 30:6 The LORD your God will circumcise your hearts and the hearts of your descendants, so that you may love him with all your heart and with all your soul, and live. (+2Ti 1:7)

Through the Holy Spirit—

Ro 5:5 And hope does not disappoint us, because God has poured out his love into our hearts by the Holy Spirit, whom he has given us.

Commanded—

Dt 6:5 Love the LORD your God with all your heart and with all your soul and with all your strength.

Dt 10:12 And now, O Israel, what does the LORD your God ask of you but to fear the LORD your God, to walk in all his ways, to love him, to serve the LORD your God with all your heart and with all your soul,

Dt 11:1 Love the LORD your God and keep his requirements, his decrees, his laws and his commands always. (+Dt 11:13,22; 19:9; 30:16,19-20)

Jos 22:5 But be very careful to keep the commandment and the law that Moses the servant of the LORD gave you: to love the LORD your God, to walk in all his ways, to obey his commands, to hold fast to him and to serve him with all your heart and all your soul."

Jos 23:11 So be very careful to love the LORD your God.

Ps 31:23 Love the LORD, all his saints! The LORD preserves the faithful, but the proud he pays back in full.

Pr 23:26 My son, give me your heart and let your eyes keep to my ways, (+Mt 22:37-38)

Mk 12:29 "The most important one," answered Jesus, "is this: 'Hear, O Israel, the Lord our God, the Lord is one. [30]Love the Lord your God with all your heart and with all your soul and with all your mind and with all your strength.'

Mk 12:32 "Well said, teacher," the man replied. "You are right in saying that God is one and there is no other but him. [33]To love him with all your heart, with all your understanding and with all your strength, and to love your neighbor as yourself is more important than all burnt offerings and sacrifices."

Lk 11:42 "Woe to you Pharisees, because you give God a tenth of your mint, rue and all other kinds of garden herbs, but you neglect justice and the love of God. You should have practiced the latter without leaving the former undone.

2Th 3:5 May the Lord direct your hearts into God's love and Christ's perseverance.

Jude 21 Keep yourselves in God's love as you wait for the mercy of our Lord Jesus Christ to bring you to eternal life.

Tested—

Dt 13:3 you must not listen to the words of that prophet or dreamer. The LORD your God is testing you to find out whether you love him with all your heart and with all your soul.

Obedience proof of—

1Jn 2:5 But if anyone obeys his word, God's love is truly made complete in him. This is how we know we are in him:

1Jn 5:1 Everyone who believes that Jesus is the Christ is born of God, and everyone who loves the father loves his child as well. [2]This is how we know that we love the children of God: by loving God and carrying out his commands.

2Jn 6 And this is love: that we walk in obedience to his commands. As you have heard from the beginning, his command is that you walk in love.

Leads to liberality (1Jn 3:17-18)

Hate of evil—

Ps 97:10 Let those who love the LORD hate evil, for he guards the lives of his faithful ones and delivers them from the hand of the wicked.

Love from God (Ps 8:1-8).

Rewards of—

Ex 20:6 but showing love to a thousand [generations] of those who love me and keep my commandments. (+Dt 5:10)

Dt 7:9 Know therefore that the LORD your God is God; he is the faithful God, keeping his covenant of love to a thousand generations of those who love him and keep his commands.

Ps 37:4 Delight yourself in the LORD and he will give you the desires of your heart.

Ps 69:35 for God will save Zion and rebuild the cities of Judah. Then people will settle there and possess it; [36]the children of his servants will inherit it, and those who love his name will dwell there.

Ps 91:14 "Because he loves me," says the LORD, "I will rescue him; I will protect him, for he acknowledges my name.

Ps 145:20 The LORD watches over all who love him, but all the wicked he will destroy.

Isa 56:6 And foreigners who bind themselves to the LORD to serve him, to love the name of the LORD, and to worship him, all who keep the Sabbath without desecrating it and who hold fast to my covenant— [7]these I will bring to my holy mountain and give them joy in my house of prayer. Their burnt offerings and sacrifices will be accepted on my altar; for my house will be called a house of prayer for all nations."

Jer 2:2 "Go and proclaim in the hearing of Jerusalem: "'I remember the devotion of your youth, how as a bride you loved me and followed me through the desert, through a land not sown. [3]Israel was holy to the LORD, the firstfruits of his harvest; all who devoured her were held guilty, and disaster overtook them,'" declares the LORD.

Ro 8:28 And we know that in all things God works for the good of those who love him, who have been called according to his purpose.

1Co 8:3 But the man who loves God is known by God.

Exemplified—

Ps 18:1 I love you, O LORD, my strength.

Ps 63:5 My soul will be satisfied as with the richest of foods; with singing lips my mouth will praise you.

[6]On my bed I remember you; I think of you through the watches of the night.

Ps 73:25 Whom have I in heaven but you? And earth has nothing I desire besides you. [26]My flesh and my heart may fail, but God is the strength of my heart and my portion forever. (+Ps 103)

Love of People for Jesus:

Commanded—

Mt 10:37 "Anyone who loves his father or mother more than me is not worthy of me; anyone who loves his son or daughter more than me is not worthy of me; (+Mt 10:38)

Jn 15:9 "As the Father has loved me, so have I loved you. Now remain in my love.

1Co 16:22 If anyone does not love the Lord—a curse be on him. Come, O Lord!

Love of God produces—

Jn 8:42 Jesus said to them, "If God were your Father, you would love me, for I came from God and now am here. I have not come on my own; but he sent me.

Obedience results from—

Jn 14:15 "If you love me, you will obey what I command.

Jn 14:21 Whoever has my commands and obeys them, he is the one who loves me. He who loves me will be loved by my Father, and I too will love him and show myself to him."

Jn 14:23 Jesus replied, "If anyone loves me, he will obey my teaching. My Father will love him, and we will come to him and make our home with him. (+2Co 5:6)

2Co 5:8 We are confident, I say, and would prefer to be away from the body and at home with the Lord.

2Co 5:14 For Christ's love compels us, because we are convinced that one died for all, and therefore all died. [15]And he died for all, that those who live should no longer live for themselves but for him who died for them and was raised again.

Rewards of—

Mt 25:34 "Then the King will say to those on his right, 'Come, you who are blessed by my Father; take your inheritance, the kingdom prepared for you since the creation of the world. [35]For I was hungry and you gave me something to eat, I was thirsty and you gave me something to drink, I was a stranger and you invited me in, [36]I needed clothes and you clothed me, I was sick and you looked after me, I was in prison and you came to visit me.'

[37]"Then the righteous will answer him, 'Lord, when did we see you hungry and feed you, or thirsty and give you something to drink? [38]When did we see you a stranger and invite you in, or needing clothes and clothe you? [39]When did we see you sick or in prison and go to visit you?'

[40]"The King will reply, 'I tell you the truth, whatever you did for one of the least of these brothers of mine, you did for me.' (+Mt 25:46)

Mk 9:41 I tell you the truth, anyone who gives you a cup of water in my name because you belong to Christ will certainly not lose his reward. (+Lk 7:37-46)

Lk 7:47 Therefore, I tell you, her many sins have been forgiven—for she loved much. But he who has been forgiven little loves little." (+Lk 7:48-50)

Jn 16:27 No, the Father himself loves you because you have loved me and have believed that I came from God. (+Eph 6:24)

2Ti 4:8 Now there is in store for me the crown of righteousness, which the Lord, the righteous Judge, will award to me on that day—and not only to me, but also to all who have longed for his appearing.

Heb 6:10 God is not unjust; he will not forget your work

and the love you have shown him as you have helped his people and continue to help them.

Jas 1:12 Blessed is the man who perseveres under trial, because when he has stood the test, he will receive the crown of life that God has promised to those who love him.

Jas 2:5 Listen, my dear brothers: Has not God chosen those who are poor in the eyes of the world to be rich in faith and to inherit the kingdom he promised those who love him?

Instances of Love for Jesus:

Mary (Mt 26:6-13; Lk 10:39; Jn 12:3-8).

Peter (Mt 17:4; Jn 13:37; 18:10; 20:3-6; 21:15-16)—

Jn 21:17 The third time he said to him, "Simon son of John, do you love me?" Peter was hurt because Jesus asked him the third time, "Do you love me?" He said, "Lord, you know all things; you know that I love you." Jesus said, "Feed my sheep.

The healed demoniac (Mk 5:18; Lk 8:38). Thomas (Jn 11:16). The disciples (Mk 16:10; Lk 24:17-41; Jn 16:27; 20:20).

Mary Magdalene and other disciples—

Mt 27:55 Many women were there, watching from a distance. They had followed Jesus from Galilee to care for his needs. [56]Among them were Mary Magdalene, Mary the mother of James and Joses, and the mother of Zebedee's sons.

Mt 27:61 Mary Magdalene and the other Mary were sitting there opposite the tomb. (+Mt 28:1-9; Lk 8:2-3; 23:27,55-56; 24:1-10; Jn 20:1-2,11-18)

Joseph of Arimathea—

Mt 27:57 As evening approached, there came a rich man from Arimathea, named Joseph, who had himself become a disciple of Jesus. [58]Going to Pilate, he asked for Jesus' body, and Pilate ordered that it be given to him. [59]Joseph took the body, wrapped it in a clean linen cloth, [60]and placed it in his own new tomb that he had cut out of the rock. He rolled a big stone in front of the entrance to the tomb and went away.

Nicodemus (Jn 19:39-40). Women of Jerusalem (Lk 23:27).

Paul—

Ac 21:13 Then Paul answered, "Why are you weeping and breaking my heart? I am ready not only to be bound, but also to die in Jerusalem for the name of the Lord Jesus." (+Php 1:20-21)

Php 1:23 I am torn between the two: I desire to depart and be with Christ, which is better by far;

Php 3:7 But whatever was to my profit I now consider loss for the sake of Christ. [8]What is more, I consider everything a loss compared to the surpassing greatness of knowing Christ Jesus my Lord, for whose sake I have lost all things. I consider them rubbish, that I may gain Christ (+2Ti 4:8)

Philemon—

Phm 5 because I hear about your faith in the Lord Jesus and your love for all the saints.

Early Christians—

1Pe 1:8 Though you have not seen him, you love him; and even though you do not see him now, you believe in him and are filled with an inexpressible and glorious joy,

1Pe 2:7 Now to you who believe, this stone is precious. But to those who do not believe, "The stone the builders rejected has become the capstone,"

Lost that love—

Rev 2:4 Yet I hold this against you: You have forsaken your first love.

Of Children for Parents: *See Children.*

Of God: *See God, Love of.*

Of Jesus: *See Jesus the Christ, Love of.*

Of Money:

A root of all kinds of evil (1Ti 6:10). *See Avarice; Riches.*

Of Parents for Children: *See Parents.*

LOVE FEAST [27] (*agape feast*).
A common meal eaten by early Christians in connection with the Lord's Supper to express and deepen brotherly love (1Co 11:18-22,33-34; Jude 12).

LOVERS [170, 172, 1856, 6311, 7108, 8276, *920, 921, 5795, 5796, 5798, 5806*].
NIV+ See LOVE

Instances Within or Resulting in Marriage:

Isaac and Rebekah (Ge 24:67). Jacob and Rachel (Ge 29:20,30). Boaz and Ruth (Ru 2-4). The beloved and her lover (SS 1-8).

Instances Outside of Marriage:

Shechem and Dinah (Ge 34:3,12). Gomer and her lovers (Hos 1-3).

Figurative of Disloyalty to Yahweh:

Israel and pagan gods (Jer 3:1-2; Hos 2). Jerusalem and political allies (La 1:2; Eze 16:33-42; 23).

LOVING-KINDNESS [2876].
NIV+ See LOVE

The kindness and mercy of God toward man (Ps 17:7; 26:3).

LOYALTY [339, 586, 2876, 3922, 5466+9068, *1188*].
NIV+ LOYAL

Commanded (Ex 22:28; Nu 27:20; Ezr 6:10; 7:26; Job 34:18; Pr 24:21; Ecc 8:2; 10:4; Ro 13:1; Tit 3:1). Enforced (Ezr 10:8; Pr 17:11). Disloyalty (2Pe 2:10).

See Patriotism.

Instances of:

Israelites (Jos 1:16-18; 2Sa 3:36-37; 15:23,30; 18:3; 21:17; 1Ch 12:38). David (1Sa 24:6-10; 26:6-16; 2Sa 1:14). Uriah (2Sa 11:9). Ittai (2Sa 15:21). Hushai (2Sa 17:15-16). David's soldiers (2Sa 18:12-13; 23:15-16). Joab (2Sa 19:5-6). Barzillai (2Sa 19:32). Jehoiada (2Ki 11:4-12). Mordecai (Est 2:21-23).

LUBIM(S) *See Libya, Libyans; Put, 2.*

LUCAS *See Luke.*

LUCIFER
Latin for "morning star" (Isa 14:12); a title of the king of Babylon, often understood as a reference to the devil. *See Devil; Satan.*

LUCIUS [*3372*].
1. A Christian at Antioch (Ac 13:1).
2. A relative of Paul (Ro 16:21).

LUD [4276].
A son of Shem (Ge 10:22; 1Ch 1:17).

LUDITES, LUDIM [4276].
Descendants of Mizraim (Ge 10:13; 1Ch 1:11). Perhaps the same as the Lydians. *See Lydia, Lydians.*

LUHITH [4284].
A city of Moab (Isa 15:5; Jer 48:5).

LUKE [*3371*].
A disciple. A physician (Col 4:14). Wrote to Theophilus (Lk 1:1-4; Ac 1:1-2). Accompanies Paul in his tour of Asia and Macedonia (Ac 16:10-13; 20:5-6), to Jerusalem (Ac 21:1-18), to Rome (Ac 27:28; 2Ti 4:1; Phm 24).

LUKE, GOSPEL OF

Author: Traditionally Luke, the companion of Paul

Date: The two most commonly suggested periods for dating the Gospel of Luke are: (1) A.D. 59-63, and (2) the 70s or the 80s.

Outline:

I. The Preface (1:1-4).
II. The Coming of Jesus (1:5-2:52).
  A. The Annunciations (1:5-56).
  B. The Birth of John the Baptist (1:57-80).
  C. The Birth and Childhood of Jesus (ch. 2).
III. The Preparation of Jesus for His Public Ministry (3:1-4:13).
  A. His Forerunner (3:1-20).
  B. His Baptism (3:21-22).
  C. His Genealogy (3:23-38).
  D. His Temptation (4:1-13).
IV. His Ministry in Galilee (4:14-9:9).
  A. The Beginning of the Ministry in Galilee (4:14-41).
  B. The First Tour of Galilee (4:42-5:39).
  C. A Sabbath Controversy (6:1-11).
  D. The Choice of the Twelve Apostles (6:12-16).
  E. The Sermon on the Plain (6:17-49).
  F. Miracles in Capernaum and Nain (7:1-18).
  G. The Inquiry of John the Baptist (7:19-29).
  H. Jesus and the Pharisees (7:30-50).
  I. The Second Tour of Galilee (8:1-3).
  J. The Parables of the Kingdom (8:4-21).
  K. The Trip across the Sea of Galilee (8:22-39).
  L. The Third Tour of Galilee (8:40-9:9).
V. His Withdrawal to Regions around Galilee (9:10-50).
  A. To the Eastern Shore of the Sea of Galilee (9:10-17).
  B. To Caesarea Philippi (9:18-50).
VI. His Ministry in Judea (9:51-13:21).
  A. Journey through Samaria to Judea (9:51-62).
  B. The Mission to the Seventy (10:1-24).
  C. The Lawyer and the Parable of the Good Samaritan (10:25-37).
  D. Jesus at Bethany with Mary and Martha (10:38-42).
  E. Teachings in Judea (11:1-13:21).
VII. His Ministry in and around Perea (13:22-19:27).
  A. The Narrow Door (13:22-30).
  B. Warning concerning Herod (13:31-35).
  C. At a Pharisee's House (14:1-23).
  D. The Cost of Discipleship (14:24-35).
  E. The Parables of the Lost Sheep, the Lost Coin and the Prodigal Son (ch. 15).
  F. The Parable of the Shrewd Manager (16:1-18).
  G. The Rich Man and Lazarus (16:19-31).
  H. Miscellaneous Teachings (17:1-10).
  I. Ten Healed of Leprosy (17:11-19).
  J. The Coming of the Kingdom (17:20-37).
  K. The Persistent Widow (18:1-8).
  L. The Pharisee and the Tax Collector (18:9-14).
  M. Jesus and the Children (18:15-17).
  N. The Rich Young Ruler (18:18-30).
  O. Christ Foretells His Death (18:31-34).
  P. A Blind Beggar Given His Sight (18:35-43).
  Q. Jesus and Zacchaeus (19:1-10).
  R. The Parable of the Ten Minas (19:11-27).

VIII. His Last Days: Sacrifice and Triumph (19:28-24:53).

A. The Triumph Entry (19:28-44).

B. The Cleansing of the Temple (19:45-48).

C. The Last Controversies with the Jewish Leaders (ch. 20).

D. The Olivet Discourse (ch. 21).

E. The Last Supper (22:1-38).

F. Jesus Praying in Gethsemane (22:39-46).

G. Jesus' Arrest (22:47-65).

H. Jesus on Trial (22:66-23:25).

I. The Crucifixion (23:26-56).

J. The Resurrection (24:1-12).

K. The Post-Resurrection Ministry (24:13-49).

L. The Ascension (24:50-53).

See Acts of the Apostles; Synoptic Gospels, The.

LUKEWARMNESS [5950].

NIV+ LUKEWARM

Rev 3:2 Wake up! Strengthen what remains and is about to die, for I have not found your deeds complete in the sight of my God.

Rev 3:5 He who overcomes will, like them, be dressed in white. I will never blot out his name from the book of life, but will acknowledge his name before my Father and his angels.

Rev 3:16 So, because you are lukewarm—neither hot nor cold—I am about to spit you out of my mouth.

Instances of:

The Reubenites and other tribes, when Deborah called on them to assist Sisera (Jdg 5:16-17).

Israel—

Hos 10:2 Their heart is deceitful, and now they must bear their guilt. The LORD will demolish their altars and destroy their sacred stones.

The Jews (Ne 3:5; 13:11)—

Hag 1:2 This is what the LORD Almighty says: "These people say, 'The time has not yet come for the LORD's house to be built.'" (+Hag 1:3-11)

The church, at Pergamum (Rev 2:14-16), Thyatira (Rev 2:20-24), Sardis (Rev 3:1-3), Laodicea (Rev 3:14-16).

See Backsliding; Blindness, Spiritual; Complacency.

LUNACY *See Insanity; Demons.*

LUST [2388+, 2393, 2773, 2801, 6311, 6312, 9373, *2123, 3979, 4079, 4432*] (*evil desires*).

NIV+ LUSTED, LUSTFUL, LUSTFULLY, LUSTS, LUSTY

Sinful—

Job 31:9 "If my heart has been enticed by a woman, or if I have lurked at my neighbor's door, ¹⁰then may my wife grind another man's grain, and may other men sleep with her. ¹¹For that would have been shameful, a sin to be judged. ¹²It is a fire that burns to Destruction; it would have uprooted my harvest.

Mt 5:28 But I tell you that anyone who looks at a woman lustfully has already committed adultery with her in his heart.

Worldly—

1Jn 2:16 For everything in the world—the cravings of sinful man, the lust of his eyes and the boasting of what he has and does—comes not from the Father but from the world. ¹⁷The world and its desires pass away, but the man who does the will of God lives forever.

Chokes the word—

Mk 4:19 but the worries of this life, the deceitfulness of wealth and the desires for other things come in and choke the word, making it unfruitful.

Tempts to sin—

Ge 3:6 When the woman saw that the fruit of the tree was good for food and pleasing to the eye, and also desirable for gaining wisdom, she took some and ate it. She also gave some to her husband, who was with her, and he ate it.

Jas 1:14 but each one is tempted when, by his own evil desire, he is dragged away and enticed. ¹⁵Then, after desire has conceived, it gives birth to sin; and sin, when it is full-grown, gives birth to death.

2Pe 2:18 For they mouth empty, boastful words and, by appealing to the lustful desires of sinful human nature, they entice people who are just escaping from those who live in error.

Forbidden—

Ex 20:17 "You shall not covet your neighbor's house. You shall not covet your neighbor's wife, or his manservant or maidservant, his ox or donkey, or anything that belongs to your neighbor."

Pr 6:24 keeping you from the immoral woman, from the smooth tongue of the wayward wife. ²⁵Do not lust in your heart after her beauty or let her captivate you with her eyes, (+Ro 13:14)

Eph 4:22 You were taught, with regard to your former way of life, to put off your old self, which is being corrupted by its deceitful desires; (+Col 3:5; 1Th 4:5)

Tit 2:12 It teaches us to say "No" to ungodliness and worldly passions, and to live self-controlled, upright and godly lives in this present age,

1Pe 2:11 Dear friends, I urge you, as aliens and strangers in the world, to abstain from sinful desires, which war against your soul.

The righteous restrain—

1Co 9:27 No, I beat my body and make it my slave so that after I have preached to others, I myself will not be disqualified for the prize.

Wicked under power of—

Jn 8:44 You belong to your father, the devil, and you want to carry out your father's desire. He was a murderer from the beginning, not holding to the truth, for there is no truth in him. When he lies, he speaks his native language, for he is a liar and the father of lies. (+Ro 1:24,26-27)

1Ti 6:9 People who want to get rich fall into temptation and a trap and into many foolish and harmful desires that plunge men into ruin and destruction.

Jas 4:1 What causes fights and quarrels among you? Don't they come from your desires that battle within you? ²You want something but don't get it. You kill and covet, but you cannot have what you want. You quarrel and fight. You do not have, because you do not ask God. ³When you ask, you do not receive, because you ask with wrong motives, that you may spend what you get on your pleasures.

1Pe 4:3 For you have spent enough time in the past doing what pagans choose to do—living in debauchery, lust, drunkenness, orgies, carousing and detestable idolatry.

2Pe 3:3 First of all, you must understand that in the last days scoffers will come, scoffing and following their own evil desires.

Jude 16 These men are grumblers and faultfinders; they follow their own evil desires; they boast about themselves and flatter others for their own advantage.

Jude 18 They said to you, "In the last times there will be scoffers who will follow their own ungodly desires."

Warnings against—

1Co 10:6 Now these things occurred as examples to keep us from setting our hearts on evil things as they did. **7**Do not be idolaters, as some of them were; as it is written: "The people sat down to eat and drink and got up to indulge in pagan revelry."

2Ti 2:22 Flee the evil desires of youth, and pursue righteousness, faith, love and peace, along with those who call on the Lord out of a pure heart.

Of Israelites (Ps 106:13-14).

See Adultery; Covetousness; Homosexual; Incest; Lasciviousness; Sensuality.

LUTE [4036, 8956].

NIV+ LUTES

Stringed instrument used to accompany songs of praise (1Sa 18:6; 2Ch 20:28). *See Music, Instruments of.*

LUZ [4281] (*almond tree*).

NIV+ BETHEL

1. Town on N boundary of Benjamin (Jos 16:2; 18:13).
2. Hittite town (Jdg 1:26).

LYCAONIA [*3377, 3378*].

NIV+ LYCAONIAN

A province of Asia Minor. Paul visits towns of (Ac 14:6-21; 16:1-2).

LYCIA [*3379*]. A province of Asia Minor. Paul visits (Ac 27:5).

LYDDA [*3375*]. Called also Lod. A city of Benjamin (1Ch 8:12; Ezr 2:33; Ne 11:35). Peter heals Aeneas in (Ac 9:32-35).

LYDIA, LYDIANS [*4276, 3376*].

NIV+ LYDIA'S, LYDIANS

1. A woman of Thyatira, who with her household, was converted through the preaching of Paul (Ac 16:14-15). Entertains Paul and Silas (Ac 16:15,40).

2. A country and people in the N Africa or Asia Minor; mercenary warriors (Isa 66:19; Jer 46:9; Eze 27:10; 30:5). Perhaps the same as the Ludites. *See Ludites, Ludim.*

LYING [*3941, 3942, 3950, 3951, 5327, 8736, 9214, 6014, 6016, 6017, 6022, 6026*].

NIV+ LIAR, LIE, LIED, LIES

Lying spirit from God (1Ki 22:21-23; 2Ch 18:20-22). *See Falsehood; Hypocrisy; Liars.*

LYRE [4036, 5575, 10676]. Used in religious services (2Sa 6:5; 1Ch 13:8; 16:5; 25:1,5-6; 2Ch 29:25; Ps 33:2; 57:8; 71:22; 81:2; 92:3; 108:2; 144:9; 150:3). At the dedication of the new wall when the captives returned (Ne 12:27). Used in idolatrous worship (Da 3:5,7,10,15).

See Music, Instruments of.

LYSANIAS [*3384*]. A tetrarch (Lk 3:1).

LYSIAS [*3385*]. Chief captain of Roman troops in Jerusalem (Ac 24:7, ftn; 24:22). *See Claudius Lysias.*

LYSTRA [*3388*]. One of two cities of Lycaonia to which Paul and Barnabas fled from persecutions in Iconium (Ac 14:6-23; 2Ti 3:11). Church of, elders ordained for, by Paul and Barnabas (Ac 14:23). Timothy a resident of (Ac 16:1-4).

M

MAACAH, MAACHAH [5081, 5082, 5084] (perhaps *dull, stupid*).

NIV+ MAACATHITE, MAACATHITES, ABEL BETH MAACAH, ARAM MAACAH

1. Son of Nahor (Ge 22:24).
2. Mother of Absalom (2Sa 3:3; 1Ch 3:2).
3. Father of Achish, king of Gath (1Sa 27:2). Possibly the same as Maoch. (1Ki 2:39).
4. Mother of Abijah and grandmother of Asa (1Ki 15:2, 10-13; 2Ch 11:20-23; 15:16). Also called Micaiah (2Ch 13:2, ftn).
5. Wife of Makir (1Ch 7:15-16).
6. Concubine of Caleb (1Ch 2:48).
7. Wife of Jeiel (1Ch 8:29; 9:35).
8. Father of Hanan (1Ch 11:43).
9. Father of Shephatiah (1Ch 27:16).
10. A small kingdom E of Bashan. *See Maacathite(s).*

MAACATHITE(S), MAACHATHI, MAACHATHITE(S) [5084].

NIV+ MAACAH

People of the nation of Maacah, in the region of Bashan (Dt 3:14; Jos 12:5; 13:11; 2Sa 10:6,8; 23:34; 1Ch 4:19; 19:6-7).

MAADAI [5049] (*ornaments*). Israelite who married a foreign woman (Ezr 10:34).

MAADIAH *See Moadiah.*

MAAI [5076] (*to be compassionate*). Priest who blew trumpet at dedication of wall (Ne 12:36).

MAALEH-ACRABBIM *See Scorpion Pass.*

MAARATH [5125] (*barren*). A city of Judah (Jos 15:59).

MAASAI, MAASIAI [5127] (*work of Yahweh*). Priestly family after the Exile (1Ch 9:12).

MAASEIAH, MAHSEIAH [5128, 5129] (*Yahweh is a refuge*).

1. Levite musician (1Ch 15:18,20).
2. Army captain who assisted Jehoiada in overthrowing Athaliah (2Ch 23:1).
3. Officer of Uzziah (2Ch 26:11).
4. Son Ahaz, king of Judah (2Ch 28:7).
5. Governor of Jerusalem in Josiah's reign (2Ch 34:8).
6. A priest who married foreign woman (Ezr 10:18).
7. A priest who married foreign woman (Ezr 10:21).
8. A priest who married foreign woman (Ezr 10:22).
9. Israelite who married foreign woman (Ezr 10:30).
10. Father of Azariah (Ne 3:23).
11. Priest; assistant of Ezra (Ne 8:4).
12. Man who explained law to people (Ne 8:7).
13. Chief who sealed covenant with Nehemiah (Ne 10:25).
14. Descendant of son of Baruch (Ne 11:5).
15. Benjamite (Ne 11:7).
16. Priest who blew trumpet at dedication of temple (Ne 12:41).

MAATH [3399] (*to be small*). An ancestor of Jesus (Lk 3:26).

MAAZ [5106] (perhaps *angry* or *wrath*). A son of Ram (1Ch 2:27).

MAAZIAH [5068, 5069] (*Yahweh is a refuge*).

1. A priest (1Ch 24:18).
2. A priest who sealed the covenant with Nehemiah (Ne 10:8).

MACBANNAI, MACHBANAI [4801] (*clad with a cloak*). A Gadite warrior (1Ch 12:13).

MACBENAH, MACHBENAH [4800] (*bond*). A descendant of Caleb (1Ch 2:49). "Father of" may mean "founder of" or "leader of" a city.

MACCABEES (*hammer*). Hasmonean Jewish family of Modein (or Modin) that led revolt against Antiochus Epiphanes, king of Syria, and won freedom for the Jews.

The family consisted of the father, Mattathias, an aged priest, and his five sons: Johanan, Simon, Judas, Eleazar, and Jonathan. The name Maccabee was first given to Judas, perhaps because he inflicted sledgehammer blows against the Syrian armies, and later was also used for his brothers. The revolt began in 168 B.C. The temple was recaptured and sacrifices were resumed in 165 B.C. The cleansing of the temple and resumption of sacrifices have been celebrated annually ever since in the Feast of Dedication. The Maccabees served as both high priests and kings. The story of Maccabees is told in two books of the Apocrypha, I and II Maccabees.

The following were the most prominent of the Maccabees: Judas (166-160 B.C.), Jonathan (160-142 B.C.), Simon (142-134 B.C.), John Hyrcanus (134-104 B.C.), Aristobulus (104-103 B.C.), Alexander Jannaeus (103-76 B.C.), Alexandra (76-67 B.C.), Aristobulus II (66-63 B.C.). In 63 B.C. the Romans took over when Pompey conquered the Israelites.

See Dedication; Feasts; Hanukkah; Kislev; Month, 9; Testaments, Time Between.

MACEDONIA [3423, 3424].

NIV+ MACEDONIAN, MACEDONIANS

A province in N Greece. Paul has a vision concerning (Ac 16:9), preaches in, at Philippi (Ac 16:12), revisits (Ac 20:1-6; 2Co 2:13; 7:5). Church at, sends contributions to the poor in Jerusalem (Ro 15:26; 2Co 8:1-5). Timothy visits (Ac 19:22). Disciples in (Ac 19:22; 27:2).

MACEDONIAN EMPIRE, THE Called the kingdom of Greece (Da 11:2).

Illustrated by the:

Bronze part of the image in Nebuchadnezzar's dream (Da 2:32,39). Leopard with four wings and four heads (Da 7:6,17). Shaggy goat with notable horn (Da 8:5-8,21). Philippi the chief city of (Ac 16:12).

Predictions Respecting:

Conquest of the Medo-Persian kingdom (Da 8:6-7; 11:2-3). Power and greatness of Alexander its last king (Da 8:8; 11:3). Division of it into four kingdoms (Da 8:8,22). Divisions of it ruled by strangers (Da 11:4). History of its four divisions (Da 11:4-29). The little horn to arise out of one of its divisions (Da 8:8-12). Gospel preached in, by God's desire (Ac 16:9-10). Liberality of the churches of (2Co 8:1-5).

MACHAERUS Fortress stronghold built by Alexander

Janneus (c. 90 B.C.) and used as a citadel by Herod Antipas; located on E of Dead Sea; John the Baptist was put to death there (Mt 14:3ff).

MACHI *See Maki.*

MACHIR *See Makir.*

MACHPELAH [4834] (*double [cave]*). The burying place of Sarah, Abraham, Isaac, Rebekah, Leah, and Jacob (Ge 23:9,17-20; 25:9; 49:30-31; 50:13; Ac 7:16).

MACNADEBAI, MACHNADEBAI [4827] (possibly *possession of Nebo*). Israelite who divorced foreign wife (Ezr 10:40).

MADAI [4512] (*Medes*). People descended from Japheth (Ge 10:2; 1Ch 1:5).

MADMANNAH [4525, 4526] (*dung place*).
1. Town in S Judah eight miles S of Kiriath Sepher (Jos 15:31).
2. Grandson of Caleb (1Ch 2:48-49).

MADMEN [2099, 2100, 2147, 4522, 8713, 8714, *3419, 4197*] ((*sounds like) be silenced*).
NIV+ MADMAN
1. A place (Jer 48:2).
2. A maniac, of insane persons (1Sa 21:15). *See Insanity.*

MADMENAH [4524] (*dunghill*). City of Benjamin (Isa 10:31).

MADNESS *See Insanity; Madmen.*

MADON [4507] (*contention*). Canaanite city near modern Qarn Hattin (Jos 11:1; 12:19).

MAGADAN [*3400*]. A town on the NW shore of Sea of Galilee, three miles N of Tiberias. Also called Magdala, the home of Mary Magdalene (Mt 15:39). Mark (8:10) has "Dalmanutha." *See Dalmanutha.*

MAGBISH [4455] (perhaps *thick*). Name of man or place (Ezr 2:30).

MAGDALA *See Dalmanutha; Magadan.*

MAGDALENE [*3402*] (*of Magdala*). *See Mary, 3.*

MAGDIEL [4462] (*choice gift of God [El]*). Chief of Edom (Ge 36:43; 1Ch 1:54).

MAGGOT [8231, 9357]
NIV+ MAGGOTS
Infested leftover manna (Ex 16:20,24). Synonymous with "worm" (Job 25:6). *See Animals.*

MAGI [*3407*]. Originally a religious caste among the Persians; devoted to astrology, divination, and interpretation of dreams. Later the word came to be applied generally to fortune-tellers and exponents of esoteric religious cults throughout the Mediterranean world (Ac 8:9; 13:6, 8). Nothing is known of the Magi of the Nativity story (Mt 2); they may have come from S Arabia.

MAGIC [2490, 3033, 4086, 10282, *3404, 5758, 5760, 5761*].
NIV+ MAGICIAN, MAGICIANS
The art or science of influencing or controlling the course of nature, events, and supernatural powers through occult science of mysterious arts (Ge 41:8; Ex 7:11,22;

8:7,18; Ac 19:19). Includes necromancy, exorcism, dreams, shaking arrows, inspecting entrails of animals, divination, sorcery, astrology, soothsaying, divining by rods, witchcraft (1Sa 28:8; Eze 21:21; Ac 16:16).

MAGICIAN [3033, 10282].
NIV+ MAGIC, MAGICIANS
A person who claims to understand and explain mysteries by magic (Da 1:20). Failed to interpret Pharaoh's dreams (Ge 41:8,24), Nebuchadnezzar's (Da 2:2-13; 4:7). Wrought apparent miracles (Ex 7:11-12,22; 8:7,18).

MAGISTRATE(S) [10735, 10767, *807, 5130*]. An officer of civil law (Jdg 18:7; Ezr 7:25; Lk 12:11,58; Ac 16:20,22,35,38). Obedience to, commanded (Tit 3:1).
See Government; Rulers.

MAGNA CARTA *See Constitution.*

MAGNANIMITY
Instances of:
Joshua and the elders of Israel to the Gibeonites who had deceived the Israelites (Jos 9:3-27). Of Moses. *See Moses.* David to Saul (1Sa 24:3-11). Ahab to Ben-Hadad (1Ki 20:32-34).
See Charitableness.

MAGNIFICAT Song of praise by Mary (Lk 1:46-55).

MAGOG [4470, *3408*] (perhaps *land of Gog*).
1. Son of Japheth (Ge 10:2; 1Ch 1:5).
2. Land of God.
Various identifications: Scythians, Lydians, Tartars of Russia. Used symbolically for forces of evil (Rev 20:7-9).

MAGOR-MISSABIB [4474] (*terror on every side*). A symbolic name given by Jeremiah to Pashhur (Jer 20:3-6).

MAGPIASH [4488] (*moth killer*). Israelite who sealed covenant with Nehemiah (Ne 10:20).

MAGUS, SIMON *See Simon, 8.*

MAHALAH *See Mahlah, 2.*

MAHALALEL, MAHALALEEL [4546, *3435*] (*praise of God [El]*).
1. Son of Kenan (Ge 5:12-17; 1Ch 1:2; Lk 3:37).
2. A man of Judah (Ne 11:4).

MAHALATH [4714, 4715] (*the suffering of affliction* NIV; *sickness or suffering poem, JB*).
1. Daughter of Ishmael (Ge 28:9).
2. Wife of Rehoboam (2Ch 11:18).
3. Musical term in the titles of Pss 53 and 88. Possibly the name of a tune. The Hebrew appears to be the word for "suffering" or "sickness." Perhaps the Hebrew phrase indicates here that the psalm is to be used in a time of affliction, when the godless mock. *See Music, Symbols Used in.*

MAHALI *See Mahli, 1.*

MAHANAIM [4724] (*double camp*). The place where Jacob had the vision of angels (Ge 32:2). The town of, allotted to Gad (Jos 13:26,30). One of the Levitical cities (Jos 21:38). Ish-Bosheth establishes himself at, when made king over Israel (2Sa 2:8-12). David lodges at, at the time of Absalom's rebellion (2Sa 17:27-29; 1Ki 2:8).

MAHANEH DAN, MAHANEH-DAN [4723]

(*camp of Dan*).

NIV+ DAN

1. Place between Zorah and Eshtaol (Jdg 13:25).
2. Place W of Kiriath Jearim (Jdg 18:12).

MAHARAI [4560] (*impetuous* ISBE). One of David's warriors (2Sa 23:28; 1Ch 11:30; 27:13).

MAHATH [4744] (perhaps *tough*).

1. Kohathite; ancestor of Heman the singer (1Ch 6:35).
2. Levite who helped Hezekiah (2Ch 29:12; 31:13).

MAHAVITE [4687] (*villagers*). Family name of Eliel, one of David's warriors (1Ch 11:46).

MAHAZIOTH [4692] (*visions*). Son of Heman (1Ch 25:4,30).

MAHER-SHALAL-HASH-BAZ [4561] (*quick to the plunder, swift to the spoil*). The symbolic name Isaiah gave his son (Isa 8:1,3).

MAHLAH [4702] (perhaps *weak one*).

1. Daughter of Zelophehad (Nu 26:33; 27:1ff; 36; Jos 17:3ff).
2. Grandson of Manasseh (1Ch 7:18).

MAHLI [4706] (perhaps *shrewd, cunning*).

NIV+ MAHLITE, MAHLITES

1. Son of Merari (Ex 6:19; 1Ch 6:19; Ezr 8:18).
2. Son of Mushi (1Ch 6:47; 23:23; 24:30).

MAHLITE(S) [4707].

NIV+ MAHLAH

Descendant of Mahli, son of Merari (Nu 3:33; 26:58; 1Ch 23:22).

MAHLON [4705] (*sick*).

NIV+ MAHLON'S

Son of Naomi and first husband of Ruth (Ru 1:2,5; 4:9-10).

MAHOL [4689] (*place of round-dancing*). Father of Heman, Calcol, and Darda (1Ki 4:31).

MAID(S), MAIDSERVANT(S) [563, 5855, 9148, 4087]

1. Female slave or servant (Ge 12:16; 16:1; Lk 12:45).
2. Female personal servant or attendant (Ge 24:61; 1Sa 25:42; Est 2:9).

See Servant.

MAIDEN(S) [1426, 1435, 6625].

1. Young woman (Ps 68:25; 148:12).
2. Young woman of marriageable age, probably a virgin (Ge 24:43; Ps 78:63; Isa 62:5; Jer 2:32).

MAIL

1. Sending of letters (2Sa 11:14-15; 1Ki 21:8-11; 2Ki 5:5-7; Est 3:13; 8:10; 2Pe 3:16). *See Letter; Letters.*
2. Armor (1Sa 17:5). *See Armor.*

MAIMED [3024, *3245*]. Not acceptable as sacrifices (Lev 22:22). *See Disease.*

MAJESTY [129, 158, 398, 466, 1452, 1454, 1455, 1525, 1542, 2077, 2086, 3636, 4889, 5905, 10199, *1518*, *3261*, *3484*, *3485*, *3488*].

NIV+ MAJESTIC

Name of God (Heb 1:3; 8:1). *See God.*

MAJORITY AND MINORITY REPORTS Of the spies (Nu 13:26-33; 14:6-10).

MAKAZ [5242]. A place in Judah (1Ki 4:9).

MAKHELOTH [5221] (*assemblies*). An encampment of Israel (Nu 33:25-26).

MAKI [4809] (perhaps *reduced* or *bought*). Gadite; father of Geuel, one of 12 spies (Nu 13:15).

MAKIR, MAKIRITE [4810, 4811] (*bought*).

NIV+ MAKIR'S, MAKIRITES

1. One of the sons of Manasseh (Ge 50:23). Father of the Makirites (Nu 26:29; 36:1). The land of Gilead allotted to (Nu 32:39-40; Dt 3:15; Jos 13:31). Certain cities of Bashan given to (Jos 13:31; 17:1).
2. A man of Lo Debar who took care of Jonathan's lame son, Mephibosheth (2Sa 9:4-5; 17:27).

MAKKEDAH [5218] (*locality of shepherds*). A city in Judah, conquered by Joshua (Jos 10:28; 12:16). Five kings of the Amorites hide in a cave of, and are slain by Joshua (Jos 10:5,16-27).

MAKTESH (*mortar*). A district where merchants traded (Zep 1:11, ftn). *See Agora; Market.*

MALACHI [4858] (*my messenger* or *messenger of Yahweh*). Prophet of Judah who lived c. 450-400 B.C.; author of OT book which bears his name; nothing known of him beyond what is said in his book; contemporary of Nehemiah (Mal 2:11-17; Ne 13:23-31).

MALACHI, BOOK OF

Author: The prophet Malachi

Date: c. 433 to 400 B.C.

Outline:

I. Title (1:1).
II. Introduction: God's Covenant Love for Israel Affirmed (1:2-5).
III. Israel's Unfaithfulness Rebuked (1:6-2:16).
  A. The Unfaithfulness of the Priests (1:6-2:9).
    1. They dishonor God in their sacrifices (1:6-14).
    2. They do not faithfully teach the law (2:1-9).
  B. The Unfaithfulness of the People (2:10-16).
IV. The Lord's Coming Announced (2:17-4:6).
  A. The Lord Will Come to Purify the Priests and Judge the People (2:17-3:5).
  B. A Call to Repentance in View of the Lord's Coming (3:6-18).
    1. An exhortation to faithful giving (3:6-12).
    2. An exhortation to faithful service (3:13-18).
  C. The Day of the Lord Announced (ch. 4).
  See Prophets, The Minor.

MALCAM, MALCHAM [4903] (*their king* ISBE KB; or [*servant of*] *Malk* [*pagan god*]).

1. A Benjamite (1Ch 8:9).
2. Either Molech, a god of the Moabites and Ammonites (Jer 49:1,3; Am 1:15; Zep 1:5, ftns) or their king; maybe both. *See Molech.*

MALCHIAH, MALCHIJAH *See Malkijah.*

MALCHIEL *See Malkiel.*

MALCHIJAH *See Malkijah, 2,3,4,7,11,12.*

MALCHIRAM *See Malkiram.*

MALCHI-SHUA *See Malki-Shua.*

MALCHUS [*3438*] (*king*). Servant of the high priest; Peter assaults in Gethsemane; healed by Jesus (Mt 26:51; Mk 14:47; Lk 22:50-51; Jn 18:10).

MALEFACTOR *See Criminals.*

MALELEEL *See Mahalalel, 1.*

MALFEASANCE IN OFFICE Illustrated in the Parables of Jesus: The tenants of the vineyard (Mk 12:1-8; Lk 20:9-15). The rich man's manager (Lk 16:1-7).

MALICE [224, 2095, 8273, 8288, 8534, 8624, *2798, 2799, 4504*].

NIV+ MALICIOUS, MALICIOUSLY

Characteristics:

Outgrowth of original sin—

Ge 3:15 And I will put enmity between you and the woman, and between your offspring and hers; he will crush your head, and you will strike his heel."

Is hated by God (Pr 6:16-17)—

Pr 6:18 a heart that devises wicked schemes, feet that are quick to rush into evil, [19]a false witness who pours out lies and a man who stirs up dissension among brothers.

Reacts (Job 15:35)—

Ps 7:15 He who digs a hole and scoops it out falls into the pit he has made. [16]The trouble he causes recoils on himself; his violence comes down on his own head. (+Ps 10:7,14)

Jer 20:10 I hear many whispering, "Terror on every side! Report him! Let's report him!" All my friends are waiting for me to slip, saying, "Perhaps he will be deceived; then we will prevail over him and take our revenge on him."

Blinds those possessed of—

1Jn 2:9 Anyone who claims to be in the light but hates his brother is still in the darkness. (+1Jn 2:10)

1Jn 2:11 But whoever hates his brother is in the darkness and walks around in the darkness; he does not know where he is going, because the darkness has blinded him.

1Jn 4:20 If anyone says, "I love God," yet hates his brother, he is a liar. For anyone who does not love his brother, whom he has seen, cannot love God, whom he has not seen.

Is murderous—

1Jn 3:13 Do not be surprised, my brothers, if the world hates you. [14]We know that we have passed from death to life, because we love our brothers. Anyone who does not love remains in death. [15]Anyone who hates his brother is a murderer, and you know that no murderer has eternal life in him.

Preludes divine forgiveness—

Mt 6:15 But if you do not forgive men their sins, your Father will not forgive your sins.

Mt 18:28 "But when that servant went out, he found one of his fellow servants who owed him a hundred denarii. He grabbed him and began to choke him. 'Pay back what you owe me!' he demanded.

[29]"His fellow servant fell to his knees and begged him, 'Be patient with me, and I will pay you back.'

[30]"But he refused. Instead, he went off and had the man thrown into prison until he could pay the debt. [31]When the other servants saw what had happened, they were greatly distressed and went and told their master everything that had happened.

[32]"Then the master called the servant in. 'You wicked servant,' he said, 'I canceled all that debt of yours because you begged me to. [33]Shouldn't you have had mercy on your fellow servant just as I had on you?' [34]In anger his master turned him over to the jailers to be tortured, until he should pay back all he owed.

[35]"This is how my heavenly Father will treat each of you unless you forgive your brother from your heart."

Is forbidden—

Lev 19:14 "'Do not curse the deaf or put a stumbling block in front of the blind, but fear your God. I am the LORD.

Lev 19:17 "'Do not hate your brother in your heart. Rebuke your neighbor frankly so you will not share in his guilt.

[18]"'Do not seek revenge or bear a grudge against one of your people, but love your neighbor as yourself. I am the LORD.

2Ki 6:21 When the king of Israel saw them, he asked Elisha, "Shall I kill them, my father? Shall I kill them?"

[22]"Do not kill them," he answered. "Would you kill men you have captured with your own sword or bow? Set food and water before them so that they may eat and drink and then go back to their master."

Pr 20:22 Do not say, "I'll pay you back for this wrong!" Wait for the LORD, and he will deliver you.

Pr 24:17 Do not gloat when your enemy falls; when he stumbles, do not let your heart rejoice, [18]or the LORD will see and disapprove and turn his wrath away from him.

Pr 24:29 Do not say, "I'll do to him as he has done to me; I'll pay that man back for what he did." (+Zec 7:10)

Zec 8:17 do not plot evil against your neighbor, and do not love to swear falsely. I hate all this," declares the LORD.

Mt 5:38 "You have heard that it was said, 'Eye for eye, and tooth for tooth.' [39]But I tell you, Do not resist an evil person. If someone strikes you on the right cheek, turn to him the other also. [40]And if someone wants to sue you and take your tunic, let him have your cloak as well. [41]If someone forces you to go one mile, go with him two miles. (+Lk 6:29)

Ro 12:19 Do not take revenge, my friends, but leave room for God's wrath, for it is written: "It is mine to avenge; I will repay," says the Lord.

1Co 5:8 Therefore let us keep the Festival, not with the old yeast, the yeast of malice and wickedness, but with bread without yeast, the bread of sincerity and truth.

1Co 14:20 Brothers, stop thinking like children. In regard to evil be infants, but in your thinking be adults.

Eph 4:31 Get rid of all bitterness, rage and anger, brawling and slander, along with every form of malice.

Col 3:8 But now you must rid yourselves of all such things as these: anger, rage, malice, slander, and filthy language from your lips.

1Th 5:15 Make sure that nobody pays back wrong for wrong, but always try to be kind to each other and to everyone else.

1Pe 2:1 Therefore, rid yourselves of all malice and all deceit, hypocrisy, envy, and slander of every kind.

1Pe 3:9 Do not repay evil with evil or insult with insult, but with blessing, because to this you were called so that you may inherit a blessing.

The wicked filled with—

Dt 32:32 Their vine comes from the vine of Sodom and from the fields of Gomorrah. Their grapes are filled with poison, and their clusters with bitterness. [33]Their wine is the venom of serpents, the deadly poison of cobras.

Ps 10:7 His mouth is full of curses and lies and threats;

trouble and evil are under his tongue. [8]He lies in wait near the villages; from ambush he murders the innocent, watching in secret for his victims. [9]He lies in wait like a lion in cover; he lies in wait to catch the helpless; he catches the helpless and drags them off in his net. [10]His victims are crushed, they collapse; they fall under his strength.

Ps 10:14 But you, O God, do see trouble and grief; you consider it to take it in hand. The victim commits himself to you; you are the helper of the fatherless.

Pr 4:16 For they cannot sleep till they do evil; they are robbed of slumber till they make someone fall. [17]They eat the bread of wickedness and drink the wine of violence. (+Pr 6:14)

Pr 21:10 The wicked man craves evil; his neighbor gets no mercy from him.

Pr 30:14 those whose teeth are swords and whose jaws are set with knives to devour the poor from the earth, the needy from among mankind.

Isa 59:4 No one calls for justice; no one pleads his case with integrity. They rely on empty arguments and speak lies; they conceive trouble and give birth to evil. [5]They hatch the eggs of vipers and spin a spider's web. Whoever eats their eggs will die, and when one is broken, an adder is hatched. [6]Their cobwebs are useless for clothing; they cannot cover themselves with what they make. Their deeds are evil deeds, and acts of violence are in their hands. (+Mt 13:25,28)

Jn 8:44 You belong to your father, the devil, and you want to carry out your father's desire. He was a murderer from the beginning, not holding to the truth, for there is no truth in him. When he lies, he speaks his native language, for he is a liar and the father of lies.

Ro 1:29 They have become filled with every kind of wickedness, evil, greed and depravity. They are full of envy, murder, strife, deceit and malice. They are gossips, [30]slanderers, God-haters, insolent, arrogant and boastful; they invent ways of doing evil; they disobey their parents; [31]they are senseless, faithless, heartless, ruthless. [32]Although they know God's righteous decree that those who do such things deserve death, they not only continue to do these very things but also approve of those who practice them.

Gal 5:19 The acts of the sinful nature are obvious: sexual immorality, impurity and debauchery; [20]idolatry and witchcraft; hatred, discord, jealousy, fits of rage, selfish ambition, dissensions, factions [21]and envy; drunkenness, orgies, and the like. I warn you, as I did before, that those who live like this will not inherit the kingdom of God.

Tit 3:3 At one time we too were foolish, disobedient, deceived and enslaved by all kinds of passions and pleasures. We lived in malice and envy, being hated and hating one another.

3Jn 10 So if I come, I will call attention to what he is doing, gossiping maliciously about us. Not satisfied with that, he refuses to welcome the brothers. He also stops those who want to do so and puts them out of the church.

Punishment for:

Dt 27:17 "Cursed is the man who moves his neighbor's boundary stone."

Then all the people shall say, "Amen!"

[18]"Cursed is the man who leads the blind astray on the road."

Then all the people shall say, "Amen!"

Pr 6:14 who plots evil with deceit in his heart—he always stirs up dissension. [15]Therefore disaster will overtake him

in an instant; he will suddenly be destroyed—without remedy.

Pr 17:5 He who mocks the poor shows contempt for their Maker; whoever gloats over disaster will not go unpunished.

Pr 28:10 He who leads the upright along an evil path will fall into his own trap, but the blameless will receive a good inheritance.

Isa 29:20 The ruthless will vanish, the mockers will disappear, and all who have an eye for evil will be cut down— [21]those who with a word make a man out to be guilty, who ensnare the defender in court and with false testimony deprive the innocent of justice.

Isa 32:6 For the fool speaks folly, his mind is busy with evil: He practices ungodliness and spreads error concerning the LORD; the hungry he leaves empty and from the thirsty he withholds water.

Eze 18:18 But his father will die for his own sin, because he practiced extortion, robbed his brother and did what was wrong among his people.

Eze 26:2 "Son of man, because Tyre has said of Jerusalem, 'Aha! The gate to the nations is broken, and its doors have swung open to me; now that she lies in ruins I will prosper,' [3]therefore this is what the Sovereign LORD says: I am against you, O Tyre, and I will bring many nations against you, like the sea casting up its waves. (+Eze 28:3,6-7,12-17)

Am 1:11 This is what the LORD says: "For three sins of Edom, even for four, I will not turn back [my wrath]. Because he pursued his brother with a sword, stifling all compassion, because his anger raged continually and his fury flamed unchecked,

Mic 2:1 Woe to those who plan iniquity, to those who plot evil on their beds! At morning's light they carry it out because it is in their power to do it.

Mt 26:52 "Put your sword back in its place," Jesus said to him, "for all who draw the sword will die by the sword.

Jas 2:13 because judgment without mercy will be shown to anyone who has not been merciful. Mercy triumphs over judgment!

Not practiced by Job—

Job 31:29 "If I have rejoiced at my enemy's misfortune or gloated over the trouble that came to him— [30]I have not allowed my mouth to sin by invoking a curse against his life—

Psalmist demands retribution (Ps 10:7-10,14)—

Ps 70:2 May those who seek my life be put to shame and confusion; may all who desire my ruin be turned back in disgrace. [3]May those who say to me, "Aha! Aha!" turn back because of their shame.

Ps 71:10 For my enemies speak against me; those who wait to kill me conspire together. [11]They say, "God has forsaken him; pursue him and seize him, for no one will rescue him." (+Ps 71:12-13,24)

Proverbs concerning (Pr 4:16-17; 6:14-16,18-19; 10:6, 12; 11:17; 12:10; 14:17,22; 15:17; 16:30; 17:5; 20:22; 21:10; 24:8,17-18,29; 26:2,27; 28:10; 30:14).

Instances of:

Cain toward Abel (Ge 4:8; 1Jn 3:12). Ishmael toward Sarah (Ge 21:9). Sarah toward Hagar (Ge 21:10). Philistines toward Isaac (Ge 26:12-15,18-21). Esau toward Jacob (Ge 27:41-42). Joseph's brothers toward Joseph (Ge 37:2-28; 42:21; Ac 7:9-10). Potiphar's wife toward Joseph (Ge 39:14-20). Ammonites toward the Israelites (Dt 23:3-4). Saul toward David (1Sa 18:8-29; 19; 20:30-33; 22:6-23; 23:7-28; 26:1-2,18). David toward Michal (2Sa

6:21-23), toward Joab (1Ki 2:5-6), toward Shimei (1Ki 2:8-9). Shimei toward David (2Sa 16:5-8). Ahithophel toward David (2Sa 17:1-3). Jezebel toward Elijah (1Ki 19:1-2). Ahaziah toward Elijah (2Ki 1:7-15). Jehoram toward Elisha (2Ki 6:31). Samaritans toward the Jews (Ezr 4; Ne 2:10; 4:6). Haman toward Mordecai (Est 3:5-15; 5:9-14).

The psalmist's enemies—

Ps 22:7 All who see me mock me; they hurl insults, shaking their heads: **8**"He trusts in the LORD; let the LORD rescue him. Let him deliver him, since he delights in him."
Ps 35:15 But when I stumbled, they gathered in glee; attackers gathered against me when I was unaware. They slandered me without ceasing. **16**Like the ungodly they maliciously mocked; they gnashed their teeth at me.
Ps 35:19 Let not those gloat over me who are my enemies without cause; let not those who hate me without reason maliciously wink the eye. **20**They do not speak peaceably, but devise false accusations against those who live quietly in the land. **21**They gape at me and say, "Aha! Aha! With our own eyes we have seen it."
Ps 38:16 For I said, "Do not let them gloat or exalt themselves over me when my foot slips."
Ps 38:19 Many are those who are my vigorous enemies; those who hate me without reason are numerous.
Ps 41:5 My enemies say of me in malice, "When will he die and his name perish?" **6**Whenever one comes to see me, he speaks falsely, while his heart gathers slander; then he goes out and spreads it abroad.
7All my enemies whisper together against me; they imagine the worst for me, saying, **8**"A vile disease has beset him; he will never get up from the place where he lies."
Ps 55:3 at the voice of the enemy, at the stares of the wicked; for they bring down suffering upon me and revile me in their anger.
Ps 56:5 All day long they twist my words; they are always plotting to harm me. **6**They conspire, they lurk, they watch my steps, eager to take my life.
Ps 57:4 I am in the midst of lions; I lie among ravenous beasts—men whose teeth are spears and arrows, whose tongues are sharp swords.
Ps 57:6 They spread a net for my feet—I was bowed down in distress. They dug a pit in my path—but they have fallen into it themselves. *Selah*
Ps 59:3 See how they lie in wait for me! Fierce men conspire against me for no offense or sin of mine, O LORD. **4**I have done no wrong, yet they are ready to attack me. Arise to help me; look on my plight!
Ps 59:7 See what they spew from their mouths—they spew out swords from their lips, and they say, "Who can hear us?"
Ps 62:3 How long will you assault a man? Would all of you throw him down—this leaning wall, this tottering fence? **4**They fully intend to topple him from his lofty place; they take delight in lies. With their mouths they bless, but in their hearts they curse. *Selah*
Ps 64:2 Hide me from the conspiracy of the wicked, from that noisy crowd of evildoers.
3They sharpen their tongues like swords and aim their words like deadly arrows. **4**They shoot from ambush at the innocent man; they shoot at him suddenly, without fear.
5They encourage each other in evil plans, they talk about hiding their snares; they say, "Who will see them?" **6**They plot injustice and say, "We have devised a perfect plan!" Surely the mind and heart of man are cunning.
Ps 69:4 Those who hate me without reason outnumber the hairs of my head; many are my enemies without cause, those who seek to destroy me. I am forced to restore what I did not steal.
Ps 69:10 When I weep and fast, I must endure scorn; **11**when I put on sackcloth, people make sport of me. **12**Those who sit at the gate mock me, and I am the song of the drunkards.
Ps 69:26 For they persecute those you wound and talk about the pain of those you hurt.
Ps 86:14 The arrogant are attacking me, O God; a band of ruthless men seeks my life—men without regard for you.
Ps 102:8 All day long my enemies taunt me; those who rail against me use my name as a curse.
Ps 109:2 for wicked and deceitful men have opened their mouths against me; they have spoken against me with lying tongues. **3**With words of hatred they surround me; they attack me without cause. **4**In return for my friendship they accuse me, but I am a man of prayer. **5**They repay me evil for good, and hatred for my friendship.
Ps 109:16 For he never thought of doing a kindness, but hounded to death the poor and the needy and the brokenhearted. **17**He loved to pronounce a curse—may it come on him; he found no pleasure in blessing—may it be far from him. **18**He wore cursing as his garment; it entered into his body like water, into his bones like oil.
Ps 140:1 Rescue me, O LORD, from evil men; protect me from men of violence, **2**who devise evil plans in their hearts and stir up war every day. **3**They make their tongues as sharp as a serpent's; the poison of vipers is on their lips. *Selah*
4Keep me, O LORD, from the hands of the wicked; protect me from men of violence who plan to trip my feet.

Jeremiah's enemies (Jer 26:8-11; 38:1-6). Nebuchadnezzar toward Zedekiah (Jer 52:10-11). Daniel's enemies (Da 6:4-15). Herodias toward John (Mt 14:3-11; Mk 6:24-28). James and John toward the Samaritans (Lk 9:54).

Enemies of Jesus (Ps 22:11; Mt 27:18,27-30,39-43; Mk 12:13)—

Mk 15:10 knowing it was out of envy that the chief priests had handed Jesus over to him. (+Mk 15:11,16-19,29-32; Lk 11:53-54; 23:10-11,39)
Jn 18:22 When Jesus said this, one of the officials nearby struck him in the face. "Is this the way you answer the high priest?" he demanded.
23"If I said something wrong," Jesus replied, "testify as to what is wrong. But if I spoke the truth, why did you strike me?"

Paul's enemies (Ac 14:5,19; 16:19-24; 17:5; 19:24-35; 21:27-31,36; 22:22-23)—

Ac 23:12 The next morning the Jews formed a conspiracy and bound themselves with an oath not to eat or drink until they had killed Paul. **13**More than forty men were involved in this plot. **14**They went to the chief priests and elders and said, "We have taken a solemn oath not to eat anything until we have killed Paul. (+Ac 153)

Php 1:15 It is true that some preach Christ out of envy and rivalry, but others out of goodwill. **16**The latter do so in love, knowing that I am put here for the defense of the gospel. (+Php 1:17)

See Conspiracy; Hatred; Homicide; Jealousy; Persecution; Retaliation; Revenge.

MALINGERING Instances of: David feigning madness (1Sa 21:13-15), the sluggard (Pr 6:9-11).

MALKIEL, MALKIELITE [4896, 4897] (*God [El] is*

[my] king). An Asherite; son of Beriah (Ge 46:17; Nu 26:45; 1Ch 7:31).

MALKIJAH, MALCHIJAH, MALCHIAH [4898, 4899] *(Yahweh is [my] king).*

1. Gershonite (1Ch 6:40).
2. Ancestor of Adaiah (1Ch 9:12; Ne 11:12).
3. Priest (1Ch 24:9).
4. Israelite who married foreign woman (Ezr 10:25).
5. Another who did same thing (Ezr 10:25).
6. Another who did same thing (Ezr 10:31).
7. Son of Harim (Ne 3:11).
8. Son of Recab (Ne 3:14).
9. Goldsmith (Ne 3:31).
10. Man who assisted Ezra (Ne 8:4).
11. Israelite who sealed covenant with Nehemiah (Ne 10:3).
12. Priest (Ne 12:42). May be same as 11.
13. Father of Pashhur who helped arrest Jeremiah (Jer 21:1; 38:1).

MALKIRAM [4901] *([my] king is exalted).* Son of Jehoiachin (1Ch 3:18).

MALKI-SHUA [4902] *([my] king saves).* Son of King Saul (1Sa 14:49; 31:2; 1Ch 8:33; 9:39; 10:2).

MALLOTHI, MALOTHI [4871] *(my expression).* Son of Heman, a singer (1Ch 25:4,26).

MALLOWS *See Salt Herbs.*

MALLUCH, MALLUCHI [4866] *(counselor* ISBE; *king* KB).

NIV+ MALLUCH'S
1. Levite; ancestor of Ethan (1Ch 6:44).
2. Man who married foreign woman (Ezr 10:29).
3. Another such man (Ezr 10:32).
4. Priest who came with Zerubbabel (Ne 10:4; 12:2).
5. Chief of people who sealed covenant (Ne 10:27).
6. Head of a priestly family (Ne 12:14).

MALTA [3514]. An island in the Mediterranean. Paul shipwrecked on the coast of (Ac 28:1-10).

MAMMON *(wealth).* Aramaic word for riches (Mt 6:24; Lk 16:11,13).

MAMRE [4934, 4935] *(strength).*

1. A plain near Hebron. Abraham resides in (Ge 13:18; 14:13), entertains three angels and is promised a son (Ge 18:1-15). Isaac lives in (Ge 35:27).
2. An Amorite and confederate of Abraham (Ge 14:13,24).

MAN *See Mankind.*

MAN OF SIN *See Antichrist(s).*

MAN, SON OF A phrase used by God in addressing Daniel (Da 8:17) and Ezekiel (over eighty times), by Daniel in describing a person he saw in a night vision (Da 7:13-14), and many times by Jesus when referring to himself, undoubtedly identifying himself with the Son of Man of Daniel's prophecy and emphasizing his union with mankind (Lk 9:26; 19:10; 22:48; Jn 6:62).

See Jesus the Christ, Son of Man; Son of Man.

MANAEN [3441] *(comforter).* An associate of Herod in his youth, and a Christian teacher (Ac 13:1).

MANAHATH [4969, 4970] *(resting place).*

NIV+ MANAHATHITES
1. Son of Shobal (Ge 36:23; 1Ch 1:40).
2. A city in Benjamin (1Ch 8:6).

MANAHATHITES, MANAHETHITES [4971] *(of Manahath).*

NIV+ MANAHATH
1. Descendants of Shobal, son of Caleb (1Ch 2:52).
2. Descendants of Salma, son of Caleb (1Ch 2:54).

MANASSEH [4985, 4986, *3442*] *(one that makes to forget).*

NIV+ MANASSEH'S, MANASSITES
1. Son of Joseph and Asenath (Ge 41:50-51; 46:20), adopted by Jacob on his deathbed (Ge 48:1,5-20).
2. Tribe of. Descendants of Joseph. The two sons of Joseph, Ephraim and Manasseh, were reckoned among the primogenitors of the twelve tribes, taking the places of Joseph and Levi.

Adopted by Jacob (Ge 48:5). Prophecy concerning (Ge 49:25-26). Enumeration of (Nu 1:34-35; 26:29-34). Place of in camp and march (Nu 2:18,20; 10:22-23). Blessing of Moses on (Dt 33:13-17). Inheritance of one-half of the tribe E of the Jordan (Nu 32:33,39-42). One-half of the tribe W of the Jordan (Jos 16:9; 17:5-11). The eastern half assist in the conquest of the country W of the Jordan (Dt 3:18-20; Jos 1:12-15; 4:12-13). Join the other eastern tribes in erecting a monument to testify to the unity of all Israel; misunderstood; makes satisfactory explanation (Jos 22). Join Gideon in war with the Midianites (Jdg 6-7). Malcontents of, join David (1Ch 12:19,31). Smitten by Hazael (2Ki 10:33). Return from the Captivity (1Ch 9:3). Reallotment of territory to, by Ezekiel (Eze 48:4). Affiliate with the Israelites in the reign of Hezekiah (2Ch 30). Incorporated into kingdom of Judah (2Ch 15:9; 34:6-7). 144,000 from (Rev 7:6).

See Israel, Tribes of.
3. The father of Gershom (Jdg 18:30).
4. King of Judah. History of (2Ki 21:1-18; 2Ch 33:1-20; Mt 1:10).
5. Two Jews who put away their Gentile wives after the Captivity (Ezr 10:30,33).

MANASSES *See Manasseh.*

MANASSITES [1201+4985, 4986] *(forgetting).*

NIV+ MANASSEH
Descendants of Joseph's son Manasseh (Ge 41:51).

MANDRAKE [1859].

NIV+ MANDRAKES
(Ge 30:14-16; SS 7:13).

MANEH *See Mina, Minas.*

MANGER [17, *5764*]. Stall or trough for feeding livestock (Job 39:9; Pr 14:4; Isa 1:3; Lk 2:7-16).

MANKIND [*132, 408, 632, 1033, 1201, 1414, 1475, 1505, 2344, 2351, 3529, 3782, 3813, 4855, 5493, 5883, 6269, 6639, 8502, 10050, 10131, 10392, *81, 467, 474, 476, 1651, 3734, 4922*].

NIV+ COUNTRYMAN, COUNTRYMEN, FELLOWMAN, FEMALE, HORSEMAN, HORSEMEN, HUMAN, HUMANITY, MALE, MAN'S, MAN-MADE, MANHOOD, MANKIND, MANNED, MEN, MEN'S, SPOKESMAN, SPOKESMEN, WOODSMAN, WOODSMEN, WOMAN,

WOMAN'S, WOMEN, WOMEN'S, WORKMAN,
WORKMAN'S, WORKMEN

Created as Male and Female:

Ge 1:26 Then God said, "Let us make man in our image, in our likeness, and let them rule over the fish of the sea and the birds of the air, over the livestock, over all the earth, and over all the creatures that move along the ground." [27]So God created man in his own image, in the image of God he created him; male and female he created them.

Ge 2:7 the LORD God formed the man from the dust of the ground and breathed into his nostrils the breath of life, and the man became a living being.

Ge 5:1 This is the written account of Adam's line. When God created man, he made him in the likeness of God.

[2]He created them male and female and blessed them. And when they were created, he called them "man."

Dt 4:32 Ask now about the former days, long before your time, from the day God created man on the earth; ask from one end of the heavens to the other. Has anything so great as this ever happened, or has anything like it ever been heard of?

Job 4:17 'Can a mortal be more righteous than God? Can a man be more pure than his Maker?

Job 10:2 I will say to God: Do not condemn me, but tell me what charges you have against me. [3]Does it please you to oppress me, to spurn the work of your hands, while you smile on the schemes of the wicked?

Job 10:8 "Your hands shaped me and made me. Will you now turn and destroy me? [9]Remember that you molded me like clay. Will you now turn me to dust again?

Job 31:15 Did not he who made me in the womb make them? Did not the same one form us both within our mothers?

Job 33:4 The Spirit of God has made me; the breath of the Almighty gives me life.

Job 34:19 who shows no partiality to princes and does not favor the rich over the poor, for they are all the work of his hands?

Job 35:10 But no one says, 'Where is God my Maker, who gives songs in the night, (+Job 36:3)

Ps 8:5 You made him a little lower than the heavenly beings and crowned him with glory and honor.

Ps 100:3 Know that the LORD is God. It is he who made us, and we are his; we are his people, the sheep of his pasture.

Ps 119:73 Your hands made me and formed me; give me understanding to learn your commands.

Ps 138:8 The LORD will fulfill [his purpose] for me; your love, O LORD, endures forever—do not abandon the works of your hands.

Ps 139:14 I praise you because I am fearfully and wonderfully made; your works are wonderful, I know that full well. (+Ps 139:15)

Ecc 7:29 This only have I found: God made mankind upright, but men have gone in search of many schemes."

Isa 17:7 In that day men will look to their Maker and turn their eyes to the Holy One of Israel.

Isa 42:5 This is what God the LORD says—he who created the heavens and stretched them out, who spread out the earth and all that comes out of it, who gives breath to its people, and life to those who walk on it:

Isa 43:7 everyone who is called by my name, whom I created for my glory, whom I formed and made."

Isa 45:12 It is I who made the earth and created mankind upon it. My own hands stretched out the heavens; I marshaled their starry hosts.

Isa 64:8 Yet, O LORD, you are our Father. We are the clay, you are the potter; we are all the work of your hand.

Jer 27:5 With my great power and outstretched arm I made the earth and its people and the animals that are on it, and I give it to anyone I please.

Zec 12:1 This is the word of the LORD concerning Israel. The LORD, who stretches out the heavens, who lays the foundation of the earth, and who forms the spirit of man within him, declares:

Mal 2:10 Have we not all one Father? Did not one God create us? Why do we profane the covenant of our fathers by breaking faith with one another? (+Mt 19:4)

Mk 10:6 "But at the beginning of creation God 'made them male and female.'

Heb 2:7 You made him a little lower than the angels; you crowned him with glory and honor

A little lower than the angels—

Job 4:18 If God places no trust in his servants, if he charges his angels with error, [19]how much more those who live in houses of clay, whose foundations are in the dust, who are crushed more readily than a moth! [20]Between dawn and dusk they are broken to pieces; unnoticed, they perish forever. [21]Are not the cords of their tent pulled up, so that they die without wisdom?'

Ps 8:5 You made him a little lower than the heavenly beings and crowned him with glory and honor.

Heb 2:7 You made him a little lower than the angels; you crowned him with glory and honor [8]and put everything under his feet."

In putting everything under him, God left nothing that is not subject to him. Yet at present we do not see everything subject to him.

Than God (Ps 8:5), above other creatures (Mt 10:31; 12:12).

Design of:

To have dominion over all creation—

Ge 1:26 Then God said, "Let us make man in our image, in our likeness, and let them rule over the fish of the sea and the birds of the air, over the livestock, over all the earth, and over all the creatures that move along the ground."

Ge 1:28 God blessed them and said to them, "Be fruitful and increase in number; fill the earth and subdue it. Rule over the fish of the sea and the birds of the air and over every living creature that moves on the ground."

Ge 2:19 Now the LORD God had formed out of the ground all the beasts of the field and all the birds of the air. He brought them to the man to see what he would name them; and whatever the man called each living creature, that was its name. [20]So the man gave names to all the livestock, the birds of the air and all the beasts of the field. But for Adam no suitable helper was found.

Ge 9:2 The fear and dread of you will fall upon all the beasts of the earth and all the birds of the air, upon every creature that moves along the ground, and upon all the fish of the sea; they are given into your hands. [3]Everything that lives and moves will be food for you. Just as I gave you the green plants, I now give you everything.

Ps 8:6 You made him ruler over the works of your hands; you put everything under his feet: [7]all flocks and herds, and the beasts of the field, [8]the birds of the air, and the fish of the sea, all that swim the paths of the seas.

Jer 27:6 Now I will hand all your countries over to my servant Nebuchadnezzar king of Babylon; I will make even the wild animals subject to him. (+Jer 28:14)

Da 2:38 in your hands he has placed mankind and the

beasts of the field and the birds of the air. Wherever they live, he has made you ruler over them all. You are that head of gold.

Heb 2:7 You made him a little lower than the angels; you crowned him with glory and honor **8**and put everything under his feet."

In putting everything under him, God left nothing that is not subject to him. Yet at present we do not see everything subject to him. (+Jas 3:7)

For the glory and pleasure of God—

Pr 16:4 The LORD works out everything for his own ends—even the wicked for a day of disaster.

Isa 43:7 everyone who is called by my name, whom I created for my glory, whom I formed and made."

Equality of all people (Job 21:26)—

Job 31:13 "If I have denied justice to my menservants and maidservants when they had a grievance against me, **14**what will I do when God confronts me? What will I answer when called to account? **15**Did not he who made me in the womb make them? Did not the same one form us both within our mothers?

Ps 33:13 From heaven the LORD looks down and sees all mankind; **14**from his dwelling place he watches all who live on earth— **15**he who forms the hearts of all, who considers everything they do.

Pr 22:2 Rich and poor have this in common: The LORD is the Maker of them all.

Mt 20:25 Jesus called them together and said, "You know that the rulers of the Gentiles lord it over them, and their high officials exercise authority over them. **26**Not so with you. Instead, whoever wants to become great among you must be your servant, **27**and whoever wants to be first must be your slave— **28**just as the Son of Man did not come to be served, but to serve, and to give his life as a ransom for many."

Mt 23:8 "But you are not to be called 'Rabbi,' for you have only one Master and you are all brothers. (+Mt 23:9-10)

Mt 23:11 The greatest among you will be your servant.

Mk 10:42 Jesus called them together and said, "You know that those who are regarded as rulers of the Gentiles lord it over them, and their high officials exercise authority over them. **43**Not so with you. Instead, whoever wants to become great among you must be your servant, **44**and whoever wants to be first must be slave of all.

Ac 10:28 He said to them: "You are well aware that it is against our law for a Jew to associate with a Gentile or visit him. But God has shown me that I should not call any man impure or unclean. (+Ac 10:34-35)

Ac 17:26 From one man he made every nation of men, that they should inhabit the whole earth; and he determined the times set for them and the exact places where they should live.

Equality under the gospel—

Gal 3:28 There is neither Jew nor Greek, slave nor free, male nor female, for you are all one in Christ Jesus.

See Race, 1.

Mortal—

Job 4:17 'Can a mortal be more righteous than God? Can a man be more pure than his Maker?

Ecc 2:14 The wise man has eyes in his head, while the fool walks in the darkness; but I came to realize that the same fate overtakes them both.

15Then I thought in my heart, "The fate of the fool will overtake me also. What then do I gain by being wise?" I said in my heart, "This too is meaningless."

Ecc 3:20 All go to the same place; all come from dust, and to dust all return.

1Co 15:21 For since death came through a man, the resurrection of the dead comes also through a man. **22**For as in Adam all die, so in Christ all will be made alive.

Heb 9:27 Just as man is destined to die once, and after that to face judgment, *See Immortality.*

Insignificance of (Ge 6:3; 18:27)—

Job 4:18 If God places no trust in his servants, if he charges his angels with error, **19**how much more those who live in houses of clay, whose foundations are in the dust, who are crushed more readily than a moth! (+Job 7:17)

Job 15:14 "What is man, that he could be pure, or one born of woman, that he could be righteous?

Job 22:2 "Can a man be of benefit to God? Can even a wise man benefit him? **3**What pleasure would it give the Almighty if you were righteous? What would he gain if your ways were blameless?

4"Is it for your piety that he rebukes you and brings charges against you? **5**Is not your wickedness great? Are not your sins endless? (+Job 25:2-3)

Job 25:4 How then can a man be righteous before God? How can one born of woman be pure? **5**If even the moon is not bright and the stars are not pure in his eyes, **6**how much less man, who is but a maggot—a son of man, who is only a worm!"

Job 35:2 "Do you think this is just? You say, 'I will be cleared by God.' **3**Yet you ask him, 'What profit is it to me, and what do I gain by not sinning?'

4"I would like to reply to you and to your friends with you. **5**Look up at the heavens and see; gaze at the clouds so high above you. **6**If you sin, how does that affect him? If your sins are many, what does that do to him? **7**If you are righteous, what do you give to him, or what does he receive from your hand? **8**Your wickedness affects only a man like yourself, and your righteousness only the sons of men.

Job 38:4 "Where were you when I laid the earth's foundation? Tell me, if you understand.

Job 38:12 "Have you ever given orders to the morning, or shown the dawn its place, **13**that it might take the earth by the edges and shake the wicked out of it?

Ps 8:3 When I consider your heavens, the work of your fingers, the moon and the stars, which you have set in place, **4**what is man that you are mindful of him, the son of man that you care for him? (+Ps 78:39)

Ps 144:3 O LORD, what is man that you care for him, the son of man that you think of him? **4**Man is like a breath; his days are like a fleeting shadow.

A spirit—

Job 4:19 how much more those who live in houses of clay, whose foundations are in the dust, who are crushed more readily than a moth! (+Job 14:10)

Job 32:8 But it is the spirit in a man, the breath of the Almighty, that gives him understanding.

Ps 31:5 Into your hands I commit my spirit; redeem me, O LORD, the God of truth.

Pr 20:27 The lamp of the LORD searches the spirit of a man; it searches out his inmost being.

Ecc 1:8 All things are wearisome, more than one can say. The eye never has enough of seeing, nor the ear its fill of hearing.

Ecc 3:21 Who knows if the spirit of man rises upward and if the spirit of the animal goes down into the earth?"

Ecc 12:7 and the dust returns to the ground it came from, and the spirit returns to God who gave it.

Isa 26:9 My soul yearns for you in the night; in the morning my spirit longs for you. When your judgments come upon the earth, the people of the world learn righteousness.

Zec 12:1 This is the word of the LORD concerning Israel. The LORD, who stretches out the heavens, who lays the foundation of the earth, and who forms the spirit of man within him, declares:

Mt 4:4 Jesus answered, "It is written: 'Man does not live on bread alone, but on every word that comes from the mouth of God.'"

Mt 10:28 Do not be afraid of those who kill the body but cannot kill the soul. Rather, be afraid of the One who can destroy both soul and body in hell.

Mt 26:41 "Watch and pray so that you will not fall into temptation. The spirit is willing, but the body is weak." (+Mk 14:38; Lk 22:40)

Lk 23:46 Jesus called out with a loud voice, "Father, into your hands I commit my spirit." When he had said this, he breathed his last.

Lk 24:39 Look at my hands and my feet. It is I myself! Touch me and see; a ghost does not have flesh and bones, as you see I have."

Jn 3:3 In reply Jesus declared, "I tell you the truth, no one can see the kingdom of God unless he is born again."

⁴"How can a man be born when he is old?" Nicodemus asked. "Surely he cannot enter a second time into his mother's womb to be born!"

⁵Jesus answered, "I tell you the truth, no one can enter the kingdom of God unless he is born of water and the Spirit. ⁶Flesh gives birth to flesh, but the Spirit gives birth to spirit. ⁷You should not be surprised at my saying, 'You must be born again.' ⁸The wind blows wherever it pleases. You hear its sound, but you cannot tell where it comes from or where it is going. So it is with everyone born of the Spirit."

Jn 4:24 God is spirit, and his worshipers must worship in spirit and in truth."

Ac 7:59 While they were stoning him, Stephen prayed, "Lord Jesus, receive my spirit."

Ro 1:9 God, whom I serve with my whole heart in preaching the gospel of his Son, is my witness how constantly I remember you

Ro 2:29 No, a man is a Jew if he is one inwardly; and circumcision is circumcision of the heart, by the Spirit, not by the written code. Such a man's praise is not from men, but from God.

Ro 7:14 We know that the law is spiritual; but I am unspiritual, sold as a slave to sin. ¹⁵I do not understand what I do. For what I want to do I do not do, but what I hate I do. ¹⁶And if I do what I do not want to do, I agree that the law is good. ¹⁷As it is, it is no longer I myself who do it, but it is sin living in me. ¹⁸I know that nothing good lives in me, that is, in my sinful nature. For I have the desire to do what is good, but I cannot carry it out. ¹⁹For what I do is not the good I want to do; no, the evil I do not want to do—this I keep on doing. ²⁰Now if I do what I do not want to do, it is no longer I who do it, but it is sin living in me that does it.

²¹So I find this law at work: When I want to do good, evil is right there with me. ²²For in my inner being I delight in God's law; ²³but I see another law at work in the members of my body, waging war against the law of my mind and making me a prisoner of the law of sin at work within my members. ²⁴What a wretched man I am! Who will rescue me from this body of death? ²⁵Thanks be to God—through Jesus Christ our Lord!

So then, I myself in my mind am a slave to God's law, but in the sinful nature a slave to the law of sin.

1Co 2:11 For who among men knows the thoughts of a man except the man's spirit within him? In the same way no one knows the thoughts of God except the Spirit of God.

1Co 6:20 you were bought at a price. Therefore honor God with your body.

1Co 7:34 and his interests are divided. An unmarried woman or virgin is concerned about the Lord's affairs: Her aim is to be devoted to the Lord in both body and spirit. But a married woman is concerned about the affairs of this world—how she can please her husband.

1Co 14:14 For if I pray in a tongue, my spirit prays, but my mind is unfruitful.

2Co 4:6 For God, who said, "Let light shine out of darkness," made his light shine in our hearts to give us the light of the knowledge of the glory of God in the face of Christ.

⁷But we have this treasure in jars of clay to show that this all-surpassing power is from God and not from us.

2Co 4:16 Therefore we do not lose heart. Though outwardly we are wasting away, yet inwardly we are being renewed day by day.

2Co 5:1 Now we know that if the earthly tent we live in is destroyed, we have a building from God, an eternal house in heaven, not built by human hands. ²Meanwhile we groan, longing to be clothed with our heavenly dwelling, ³because when we are clothed, we will not be found naked. ⁴For while we are in this tent, we groan and are burdened, because we do not wish to be unclothed but to be clothed with our heavenly dwelling, so that what is mortal may be swallowed up by life. ⁵Now it is God who has made us for this very purpose and has given us the Spirit as a deposit, guaranteeing what is to come.

⁶Therefore we are always confident and know that as long as we are at home in the body we are away from the Lord. ⁷We live by faith, not by sight. ⁸We are confident, I say, and would prefer to be away from the body and at home with the Lord. ⁹So we make it our goal to please him, whether we are at home in the body or away from it.

Eph 3:16 I pray that out of his glorious riches he may strengthen you with power through his Spirit in your inner being,

Eph 4:4 There is one body and one Spirit—just as you were called to one hope when you were called—

1Th 5:23 May God himself, the God of peace, sanctify you through and through. May your whole spirit, soul and body be kept blameless at the coming of our Lord Jesus Christ.

Heb 4:12 For the word of God is living and active. Sharper than any double-edged sword, it penetrates even to dividing soul and spirit, joints and marrow; it judges the thoughts and attitudes of the heart.

Jas 2:26 As the body without the spirit is dead, so faith without deeds is dead.

See Duty; Ignorance; Neighbor; Young Men.

MANNA [4942, 3445] (*What is it?;* possibly *food*).
Miraculously given to Israel for food in the wilderness (Ex 16:4,15; Ne 9:15).

Called:

God's manna (Ne 9:20). Bread of heaven (Ps 105:40). Bread from heaven (Ps 78:24). Angel's food (Ps 78:25).

Spiritual food (1Co 10:3). Previously unknown (Dt 8:3,16).

Described as:

Like coriander seed (Ex 16:31; Nu 11:7). White (Ex 16:31). Like in, color to resin (Nu 11:7), taste to wafers made with honey (Ex 16:31), taste to oil (Nu 11:8). Like frost (Ex 16:14). Fell after the evening dew (Nu 11:9). None fell on the Sabbath (Ex 16:26-27). Gathered every morning (Ex 16:21). An omer of, gathered for each person (Ex 16:16). Two portions of, gathered the sixth day on account of the Sabbath (Ex 16:5,22-26). He that gathered much or little had sufficient and nothing left over (Ex 16:18). Melted away by the sun (Ex 16:21).

Given:

When Israel murmured for bread (Ex 16:2-3). In answer to prayer (Ps 105:40). Through Moses (Jn 6:31-32). To exhibit God's glory (Ex 16:7). As a sign of Moses' divine mission (Jn 6:30-31). For forty years (Ne 9:21). As a test of obedience (Ex 16:4). To teach that man does not live by bread only (Dt 8:3, w Mt 4:4). To humble and prove Israel (Dt 8:16). If kept longer than a day (except on the Sabbath) began to spoil (Ex 16:19-20).

The Israelites:

At first covetous of (Ex 16:17). Ground, made into cakes and baked in pans (Nu 11:8). Counted, inferior to food of Egypt (Nu 11:4-6). Loathed (Nu 21:5). Punished for despising (Nu 11:10-20). Punished for loathing (Nu 21:6). Ceased when Israel entered Canaan (Ex 16:35; Jos 5:12).

Illustrative of:

Christ (Jn 6:32-35). Blessedness given to saints (Rev 2:17). A golden pot of, laid up in the holiest for a memorial (Ex 16:32-34; Heb 9:4).

MANNERS Social customs. Obeisance to strangers (Ge 18:2; 19:1). Standing while guests eat (Ge 18:8), in presence of superiors (Ge 31:35; Job 29:8), of the aged (Lev 19:32). Courteousness commanded (1Pe 3:8). Rule for guests (Pr 23:1-2; 1Co 10:27).

See Salutations.

MANOAH [4956] (*rest*). A Danite of Zorah and father of Samson (Jdg 13:2-24).

MANSERVANT [6269]. *See Servant.*

MANSIONS [1074, 2292]. Spacious homes of the rich that offer no protection from God's judgment (Ps 49:14; Isa 5:9; Am 3:15; 5:11).

MANSLAUGHTER *See Fratricide; Homicide; Infanticide; Regicide.*

MANSLAYER A person who has killed another human being accidentally; the manslayer could find asylum in cities of refuge (Nu 35; Dt 4:42; 19:3-10; Jos 20:3). *See Cities of Refuge.*

MANTLE [6486]. Rent in token of grief (Ezr 9:3; Job 1:20; 2:12). Of Elijah (1Ki 19:19; 2Ki 2:8,13-14).

See Dress.

MANURE [4523, 7616, *3161*]. Used as fertilizer (Isa 25:10; Lk 13:8; 14:34-35).

MANUSCRIPTS, DEAD SEA *See Dead Sea Scrolls.*

MAOCH [5059] (*a poor one*). The father of Achish,

king of Gath, who protected David (1Sa 27:2; 29:1-11). Possibly the same as Maacah, 2. *See Maacah, 2.*

MAON [5062, 5063] (*dwelling*).

NIV+ MAONITES

1. Descendant of Caleb (1Ch 2:42-45).
2. Town S of Hebron (1Sa 23:24-28; 25:1-3).

MAONITES [5062].

NIV+ MAON

Enemies of Israel (Jdg 10:11-12), possibly from Maon 2, also called Meunim or Meunites. *See Meunim, Meunites.*

MARA [5259] (*bitter*). Name Naomi called herself (Ru 1:20).

MARAH [5288] (*bitter*). The first station of the Israelites, where Moses made the bitter waters sweet (Ex 15:22-25; Nu 33:8-9).

MARALAH [5339]. A landmark on the boundary of Zebulun (Jos 19:11).

MARANATHA, MARAN-ATHA (*our Lord has come* or *our Lord, come!*). An expression of greeting and encouragement, marking the desire of Christians for the Lord's return (1Co 16:22).

MARBLE [74+8880, 9253, *3454*] (*marble* or *alabaster*). In the temple (1Ch 29:2). Pillars of (Est 1:6; SS 5:15). Merchandise of (Rev 18:12). Mosaics of (Est 1:6).

MARCABOTH *See Beth Marcaboth.*

MARCHESHVAN *See Bul; Month, 8.*

MARCUS *See Mark, John.,*

MARDUK [5281]. Marduk, the chief god of the Babylonians (Jer 50:2).

MARESHAH [5358, 5359] (perhaps *head place*).

1. A city of Judah (Jos 15:44; 2Ch 11:8; 14:9-10). Birthplace of Eliezer the prophet (2Ch 20:37). Prophecy concerning (Mic 1:15).
2. Father of Hebron (1Ch 2:42).
3. A son of, or possibly a city founded by, Laadah (1Ch 4:21).

MARI Ancient city of Euphrates Valley, discovered in 1933 and subsequently excavated. Twenty thousand cuneiform tablets have been found, throwing much light upon ancient Syrian civilization. Mari kingdom was contemporary with Hammurabi of Babylon and the Amorite tribes of Canaan, ancestors of the Hebrews.

MARINER [362, 4876].

NIV+ MARINERS, MARITIME

(1Ki 9:27; 2Ch 8:18; Isa 42:10; Eze 27:27). Perils of (Ps 107:23-30; Jnh 1:5; Ac 27:17-44). Cowardice of (Ac 27:30). *See Commerce; Ship.*

MARK [*2980, 4182, 7483, 8574, 9306, 9338, 9344, 9419, *4956*, *5116*, *5596*, *5916*].

NIV+ MARKED, MARKER, MARKS

A word with various meanings: a special sign of ownership (Eze 9:4,6; Rev 7:2-8), signature (Job 31:35), a target (1Sa 20:20), a form of tattooing banned by the Lord (Lev 19:28), a goal to be attained (Php 3:14), a particular brand denoting the nature or rank of men (Rev 13:16).

MARK, GOSPEL OF

Author: Anonymous, traditionally John Mark

Date : Possibly in the 50s or early 60s A.D.

Outline:

I. The Beginnings of Jesus' Ministry (1:1-13).
  A. His Forerunner (1:1-8).
  B. His Baptism (1:9-11).
  C. His Temptation (1:12-13).
II. Jesus' Ministry in Galilee (1:14-6:29).
  A. Early Galilean Ministry (1:14-3:12).
    1. Call of the first disciples (1:14-20).
    2. Miracles in Capernaum (1:21-34).
    3. A tour of Galilee (1:21-34).
    4. Ministry in Capernaum (2:1-22).
    5. Sabbath controversy (2:23-3:12).
  B. Later Galilean Ministry (3:13-6:29).
    1. Selection of the twelve apostles (3:13-19).
    2. Teachings in Capernaum (3:20-35).
    3. Parables of the kingdom (4:1-34).
    4. Trip across the Sea of Galilee (4:35-5:20).
    5. More Galilee miracles (5:21-43).
    6. Unbelief in Jesus' hometown (6:1-6).
    7. Six apostolic teams tour Galilee (6:7-13).
    8. King Herod's reaction to Jesus' ministry (6:14-29).
III. Withdrawals from Galilee (6:30-9:32).
  A. To the Eastern Shore of the Sea of Galilee (6:30-52).
  B. To the Western Shore of the Sea of Galilee (6:53-7:23)
  C. To Phoenicia (7:24-30).
  D. To the Region of the Decapolis (7:31-8:10).
  E. To the Vicinity of Caesarea Philippi (8:11-9:32).
IV. Final Ministry in Galilee (9:33-50).
V. Jesus' Ministry in Judea and Perea (ch. 10).
  A. Teaching concerning Divorce (10:1-12).
  B. Teaching concerning Divorce (10:13-16).
  C. The Rich Young Man (10:17-31).
  D. Prediction of Jesus' Death (10:32-34).
  E. A Request of Two Brothers (10:35-45).
  F. Restoration of Bartimaeus's Sight (10:46-52).
  VI. The Passion of Jesus (chs. 11-15).
  A. The Triumphal Entry (11:12-19).
  B. The Cleansing of the Temple (11:12-19).
  C. Concluding Controversies with Jewish Leaders (11:20-12:44).
  D. The Olivet Discourse concerning the End of the Age (ch. 13).
  E. The Anointing of Jesus (14:1-11).
  F. The Arrest, Trial and Death of Jesus (14:12-15:47).
VII. The Resurrection of Jesus (ch. 16).
  See Synoptic Gospels, The.

MARK, JOHN [3453] (Mark [Latin] *a large hammer*;

John [Hebrew] *Yahweh is gracious*). Author of the second Gospel. John was his Jewish name, Mark (Marcus) his Roman; called John (Ac 13:5,13), Mark (Ac 15:39), "John, also called Mark" (Ac 12:12), relative of Barnabas (Col 4:10), accompanied and then deserted Paul on first missionary journey (Ac 12:25; 13:13), went with Barnabas to Cyprus after Paul refused to take him on his second missionary journey (Ac 15:36-39), fellow-worker with Paul (Phm 24), recommended by Paul to church at Colosse (Col 4:10), may have been the young man of Mark 14:51-52. Early tradition makes him the "interpreter" of Peter in Rome and founder of the church in Alexandria.

MARKET [2575, 4847, 5326, 6087, 7337, *59, 61, 1866+3875, 3425*].

NIV+ MARKETPLACE, MARKETPLACES

A place for general merchandise. Held at gates. *See Gates.* Judgment seat at (Ac 16:19). Trade of, in Tyre, consisted of horses, horsemen, mules, horns, ivory, and ebony, emeralds, purple, embroidered wares, linen, coral, agate, honey, balm, wine, wool, oil, cassia, calamus, charioteers' clothing, lambs, rams, goats, precious stones, and gold, spices, and costly apparel (Eze 27:13-25). *See Agora.*

MAROTH [5300] (*bitterness*). A city of Judah (Mic 1:12).

MARRIAGE [*829, 851+, 1249+, 1436, 2118+4200, 3782, 4374, 4374, 5951, 5989, 9393, *1138, 1139, 1140, 1141, 1181, 1222+, 2400, 3284, 3650*].

NIV+ INTERMARRY, MARITAL, MARRIAGES, MARRIED, MARRIES, MARRY, MARRYING

Divine institution of (Ge 2:18,20-22)—

Ge 2:23 The man said, "This is now bone of my bones and flesh of my flesh; she shall be called 'woman,' for she was taken out of man."

²⁴For this reason a man will leave his father and mother and be united to his wife, and they will become one flesh. (+Mt 19:4-6; Mk 10:7-8; 1Co 6:16; Eph 5:31)

Based on principle of creation—

1Co 11:11 In the Lord, however, woman is not independent of man, nor is man independent of woman. ¹²For as woman came from man, so also man is born of woman. But everything comes from God. (+Ge 2:18)

Unity of husband and wife in (Ge 2:23-24; Mt 19:5-6)—

Mk 10:2 Some Pharisees came and tested him by asking, "Is it lawful for a man to divorce his wife?"

³"What did Moses command you?" he replied.

⁴They said, "Moses permitted a man to write a certificate of divorce and send her away."

⁵"It was because your hearts were hard that Moses wrote you this law," Jesus replied. ⁶"But at the beginning of creation God 'made them male and female.' ⁷'For this reason a man will leave his father and mother and be united to his wife, ⁸and the two will become one flesh.' So they are no longer two, but one. ⁹Therefore what God has joined together, let man not separate."

¹⁰When they were in the house again, the disciples asked Jesus about this. (+1Co 6:16; Eph 5:31,33)

Commended—

Pr 18:22 He who finds a wife finds what is good and receives favor from the LORD.

Heb 13:4 Marriage should be honored by all, and the marriage bed kept pure, for God will judge the adulterer and all the sexually immoral.

Obligations under, inferior to duty to God (Dt 13:6-10; Mt 19:29; Lk 14:26).

Indissoluble except for adultery—

Mal 2:13 Another thing you do: You flood the LORD's altar with tears. You weep and wail because he no longer pays attention to your offerings or accepts them with pleasure from your hands. ¹⁴You ask, "Why?" It is because the LORD is acting as the witness between you and the wife of your youth, because you have broken faith with her, though she is your partner, the wife of your marriage covenant.

¹⁵Has not [the LORD] made them one? In flesh and spirit

they are his. And why one? Because he was seeking godly offspring. So guard yourself in your spirit, and do not break faith with the wife of your youth.

¹⁶"I hate divorce," says the LORD God of Israel, "and I hate a man's covering himself with violence as well as with his garment," says the LORD Almighty.

So guard yourself in your spirit, and do not break faith.

Mt 5:31 "It has been said, 'Anyone who divorces his wife must give her a certificate of divorce.' ³²But I tell you that anyone who divorces his wife, except for marital unfaithfulness, causes her to become an adulteress, and anyone who marries the divorced woman commits adultery.

Mk 10:11 He answered, "Anyone who divorces his wife and marries another woman commits adultery against her. ¹²And if she divorces her husband and marries another man, she commits adultery."

Lk 16:18 "Anyone who divorces his wife and marries another woman commits adultery, and the man who marries a divorced woman commits adultery.

Ro 7:1 Do you not know, brothers—for I am speaking to men who know the law—that the law has authority over a man only as long as he lives? ²For example, by law a married woman is bound to her husband as long as he is alive, but if her husband dies, she is released from the law of marriage. ³So then, if she marries another man while her husband is still alive, she is called an adulteress. But if her husband dies, she is released from that law and is not an adulteress, even though she marries another man. (+1Co 7:39-40)

Dissolved by death (Mt 22:29-30; Mk 12:24-25; Ro 7:1-3).

Commanded of exiled Israelites—

Jer 29:6 Marry and have sons and daughters; find wives for your sons and give your daughters in marriage, so that they too may have sons and daughters. Increase in number there; do not decrease.

Commanded because of immorality—

1Co 7:1 Now for the matters you wrote about: It is good for a man not to marry. ²But since there is so much immorality, each man should have his own wife, and each woman her own husband. ³The husband should fulfill his marital duty to his wife, and likewise the wife to her husband. ⁴The wife's body does not belong to her alone but also to her husband. In the same way, the husband's body does not belong to him alone but also to his wife. ⁵Do not deprive each other except by mutual consent and for a time, so that you may devote yourselves to prayer. Then come together again so that Satan will not tempt you because of your lack of self-control. ⁶I say this as a concession, not as a command. ⁷I wish that all men were as I am. But each man has his own gift from God; one has this gift, another has that.

None in the resurrection state (Mt 22:29-30; Mk 12:24-25). Levirate (the brother required to marry a brother's widow) (Ge 38:8,11; Dt 25:5-10; Ru 4:5; Mt 22:24-27; Mk 12:19-23; Lk 20:28-33).

Mosaic Laws Concerning:

Of priest—

Lev 21:1 The LORD said to Moses, "Speak to the priests, the sons of Aaron, and say to them: 'A priest must not make himself ceremonially unclean for any of his people who die,

Lev 21:7 "'They must not marry women defiled by prostitution or divorced from their husbands, because priests are holy to their God.

Lev 21:13 "'The woman he marries must be a virgin. ¹⁴He must not marry a widow, a divorced woman, or a woman defiled by prostitution, but only a virgin from his own people, ¹⁵so he will not defile his offspring among his people. I am the LORD, who makes him holy.'"

Captives—

Dt 21:10 When you go to war against your enemies and the LORD your God delivers them into your hands and you take captives, ¹¹if you notice among the captives a beautiful woman and are attracted to her, you may take her as your wife. ¹²Bring her into your home and have her shave her head, trim her nails ¹³and put aside the clothes she was wearing when captured. After she has lived in your house and mourned her father and mother for a full month, then you may go to her and be her husband and she shall be your wife. ¹⁴If you are not pleased with her, let her go wherever she wishes. You must not sell her or treat her as a slave, since you have dishonored her.

Divorced persons—

Dt 24:1 If a man marries a woman who becomes displeasing to him because he finds something indecent about her, and he writes her a certificate of divorce, gives it to her and sends her from his house, ²and if after she leaves his house she becomes the wife of another man, ³and her second husband dislikes her and writes her a certificate of divorce, gives it to her and sends her from his house, or if he dies, ⁴then her first husband, who divorced her, is not allowed to marry her again after she has been defiled. That would be detestable in the eyes of the LORD. Do not bring sin upon the land the LORD your God is giving you as an inheritance.

⁵If a man has recently married, he must not be sent to war or have any other duty laid on him. For one year he is to be free to stay at home and bring happiness to the wife he has married.

A virgin, not pledged to be married, who has been seduced—

Ex 22:16 "If a man seduces a virgin who is not pledged to be married and sleeps with her, he must pay the bride-price, and she shall be his wife. ¹⁷If her father absolutely refuses to give her to him, he must still pay the bride-price for virgins.

Within tribes—

Nu 36:8 Every daughter who inherits land in any Israelite tribe must marry someone in her father's tribal clan, so that every Israelite will possess the inheritance of his fathers.

Incestuous, forbidden—

Lev 18:6 "'No one is to approach any close relative to have sexual relations. I am the LORD.

⁷"'Do not dishonor your father by having sexual relations with your mother. She is your mother; do not have relations with her.

⁸"'Do not have sexual relations with your father's wife; that would dishonor your father.

⁹"'Do not have sexual relations with your sister, either your father's daughter or your mother's daughter, whether she was born in the same home or elsewhere.

¹⁰"'Do not have sexual relations with your son's daughter or your daughter's daughter; that would dishonor you.

¹¹"'Do not have sexual relations with the daughter of your father's wife, born to your father; she is your sister.

¹²"'Do not have sexual relations with your father's sister; she is your father's close relative.

[13]"'Do not have sexual relations with your mother's sister, because she is your mother's close relative.

[14]"'Do not dishonor your father's brother by approaching his wife to have sexual relations; she is your aunt.

[15]"'Do not have sexual relations with your daughter-in-law. She is your son's wife; do not have relations with her.

[16]"'Do not have sexual relations with your brother's wife; that would dishonor your brother.

[17]"'Do not have sexual relations with both a woman and her daughter. Do not have sexual relations with either her son's daughter or her daughter's daughter; they are her close relatives. That is wickedness.

[18]"'Do not take your wife's sister as a rival wife and have sexual relations with her while your wife is living. (+Dt 22:30)

Lev 20:14 "'If a man marries both a woman and her mother, it is wicked. Both he and they must be burned in the fire, so that no wickedness will be among you.

Lev 20:17 "'If a man marries his sister, the daughter of either his father or his mother, and they have sexual relations, it is a disgrace. They must be cut off before the eyes of their people. He has dishonored his sister and will be held responsible.

Lev 20:19 "'Do not have sexual relations with the sister of either your mother or your father, for that would dishonor a close relative; both of you would be held responsible.

[20]"'If a man sleeps with his aunt, he has dishonored his uncle. They will be held responsible; they will die childless.

[21]"'If a man marries his brother's wife, it is an act of impurity; he has dishonored his brother. They will be childless.

Mk 6:17 For Herod himself had given orders to have John arrested, and he had him bound and put in prison. He did this because of Herodias, his brother Philip's wife, whom he had married. [18]For John had been saying to Herod, "It is not lawful for you to have your brother's wife."

Among antediluvians (Ge 6:2). Among relatives, Abraham and Sarah (Ge 11:29; 12:13; 20:2,9-16), Isaac and Rebekah (Ge 24:3-4,67), Jacob and his wives (Ge 28:2; 29:15-30). Levirate (the brother required to marry a brother's widow) (Ge 38:8,11; Dt 25:5-10; Ru 4:5; Mt 22:24-27; Mk 12:19-23; Lk 20:28-33).

Intermarriage. *See Intermarry.*

Various Principles:

Parents contract for their children—

Hagar selects a wife for Ishmael (Ge 21:21). Abraham for Isaac (Ge 24). Laban arranges for his daughters' marriage (Ge 29). Samson asks his parents to procure him a wife (Jdg 14:2). Parents' consent required in the Mosaic law (Ex 22:17). Presents given to parents to secure their favor (Ge 24:53; 34:12; 1Sa 18:25). Nuptial feasts (Ge 29:22; Jdg 14:12; Est 2:18; Mt 22:11-12). Jesus present at (Jn 2:1-5). Ceremony attested by witnesses (Ru 4:1-11; Isa 8:1-3). Bridegroom exempt one year from military duty (Dt 24:5). Bridal ornaments (Isa 49:18; Jer 2:32). Bridal presents (Ge 24:53). Herald preceded the bridegroom (Mt 25:6). Wedding robes adorned with jewels (Isa 61:10). Festivities attending (Jer 7:34; 16:9; 25:10; Rev 18:23).

Wives obtained by purchase (Ge 29:20,27-29; 31:41; Ru 4:10; 2Sa 3:14; Hos 3:2; 12:12), by kidnapping (Jdg 21:21-23). Given by kings (1Sa 17:25; 18:17,27). Daughters given in, as rewards of valor (Jdg 1:12; 1Sa 17:25; 18:27).

Wives taken by edict (Est 2:2-4,8-14). David gave 100 foreskins for a wife (2Sa 3:14).

Wives among the Israelites must be Israelites (Ex 34:16; Dt 7:3-4; Ezr 9:1-2,12; Ne 10:30; 13:26-27; Mal 2:11). Betrothal a quasi-marriage (Mt 1:18; Lk 1:27).

Discouraged among the Corinthians (1Co 7:1)—

1Co 7:8 Now to the unmarried and the widows I say: It is good for them to stay unmarried, as I am. [9]But if they cannot control themselves, they should marry, for it is better to marry than to burn with passion.

1Co 7:25 Now about virgins: I have no command from the Lord, but I give a judgment as one who by the Lord's mercy is trustworthy. [26]Because of the present crisis, I think that it is good for you to remain as you are. [27]Are you married? Do not seek a divorce. Are you unmarried? Do not look for a wife. [28]But if you do marry, you have not sinned; and if a virgin marries, she has not sinned. But those who marry will face many troubles in this life, and I want to spare you this.

[29]What I mean, brothers, is that the time is short. From now on those who have wives should live as if they had none; [30]those who mourn, as if they did not; those who are happy, as if they were not; those who buy something, as if it were not theirs to keep; [31]those who use the things of the world, as if not engrossed in them. For this world in its present form is passing away.

[32]I would like you to be free from concern. An unmarried man is concerned about the Lord's affairs—how he can please the Lord. [33]But a married man is concerned about the affairs of this world—how he can please his wife— [34]and his interests are divided. An unmarried woman or virgin is concerned about the Lord's affairs: Her aim is to be devoted to the Lord in both body and spirit. But a married woman is concerned about the affairs of this world—how she can please her husband. [35]I am saying this for your own good, not to restrict you, but that you may live in a right way in undivided devotion to the Lord.

[36]If anyone thinks he is acting improperly toward the virgin he is engaged to, and if she is getting along in years and he feels he ought to marry, he should do as he wants. He is not sinning. They should get married. [37]But the man who has settled the matter in his own mind, who is under no compulsion but has control over his own will, and who has made up his mind not to marry the virgin—this man also does the right thing. [38]So then, he who marries the virgin does right, but he who does not marry her does even better.

[39]A woman is bound to her husband as long as he lives. But if her husband dies, she is free to marry anyone she wishes, but he must belong to the Lord. [40]In my judgment, she is happier if she stays as she is—and I think that I too have the Spirit of God.

Celibacy deplored (Jdg 11:38; Isa 4:1).

Unhappiness in—

Pr 21:9 Better to live on a corner of the roof than share a house with a quarrelsome wife.

Pr 21:19 Better to live in a desert than with a quarrelsome and ill-tempered wife.

Marriage of widows (Ro 7:1-3; 1Co 7:39-40)—

1Ti 5:14 So I counsel younger widows to marry, to have children, to manage their homes and to give the enemy no opportunity for slander.

Marriage of ministers (Lev 21:7-8,13-14; Eze 44:22)—

1Co 9:5 Don't we have the right to take a believing wife along with us, as do the other apostles and the Lord's brothers and Cephas?

1Ti 3:2 Now the overseer must be above reproach, the

husband of but one wife, temperate, self-controlled, re-spectable, hospitable, able to teach,

1Ti 3:12 A deacon must be the husband of but one wife and must manage his children and his household well.

Prophecies concerning the forbidding of—

1Ti 4:1 The Spirit clearly says that in later times some will abandon the faith and follow deceiving spirits and things taught by demons.

1Ti 4:3 They forbid people to marry and order them to abstain from certain foods, which God created to be received with thanksgiving by those who believe and who know the truth.

Figurative: (Isa 54:5; 62:4-5; Jer 3:14; 31:32; Eze 16:8)

Hos 2:19 I will betroth you to me forever; I will betroth you in righteousness and justice, in love and compassion. ²⁰I will betroth you in faithfulness, and you will acknowledge the LORD. (+Eph 5:23-32; Rev 19:7-9)

Parables of (Mt 22:2-10; 25:1-10; Mk 2:19-20; Jn 3:29; 2Co 11:2). ·

See Bride; Bridegroom; Divorce; Husband; Intermarry; Wife.

MARROW [4672, 3678]. Heart of the bone (Job 21:24), used figuratively of good things (Ps 63:5; Isa 25:6).

MARS HILL *See Areopagus.*

MARSENA [5333]. Counselor of King Xerxes (Est 1:10-14).

MARSH [106, 1289, 1465]. Swamp lands (Eze 47:11).

MARTHA [*3450*] (*a lady, [female] lord*). Sister of Mary and Lazarus (Jn 11:1). Ministers to Jesus (Lk 10:38-42; Jn 12:2). Beloved by Jesus (Jn 11:5).

See Lazarus; Mary, 4.

MARTYR [*3459*] (*witness*). One who dies to bear witness to a cause (Ac 22:20; Rev 17:6).

MARTYRDOM

Of prophets—

Mt 23:34 Therefore I am sending you prophets and wise men and teachers. Some of them you will kill and crucify; others you will flog in your synagogues and pursue from town to town. (+Lk 11:50)

Rev 16:6 for they have shed the blood of your saints and prophets, and you have given them blood to drink as they deserve."

Followers of Jesus exposed to—

Mt 10:21 "Brother will betray brother to death, and a father his child; children will rebel against their parents and have them put to death. ²²All men will hate you because of me, but he who stands firm to the end will be saved.

Mt 10:39 Whoever finds his life will lose it, and whoever loses his life for my sake will find it. (+Mt 23:34)

Mt 24:9 "Then you will be handed over to be persecuted and put to death, and you will be hated by all nations because of me. (+Mk 13:12; Lk 21:16-17)

Must be based on love—

1Co 13:3 If I give all I possess to the poor and surrender my body to the flames, but have not love, I gain nothing.

Prophetic reference to—

Rev 6:9 When he opened the fifth seal, I saw under the altar the souls of those who had been slain because of the word of God and the testimony they had maintained. ¹⁰They called out in a loud voice, "How long, Sovereign

Lord, holy and true, until you judge the inhabitants of the earth and avenge our blood?" ¹¹Then each of them was given a white robe, and they were told to wait a little longer, until the number of their fellow servants and brothers who were to be killed as they had been was completed.

Rev 11:7 Now when they have finished their testimony, the beast that comes up from the Abyss will attack them, and overpower and kill them. ⁸Their bodies will lie in the street of the great city, which is figuratively called Sodom and Egypt, where also their Lord was crucified. ⁹For three and a half days men from every people, tribe, language and nation will gaze on their bodies and refuse them burial. ¹⁰The inhabitants of the earth will gloat over them and will celebrate by sending each other gifts, because these two prophets had tormented those who live on the earth. ¹¹But after the three and a half days a breath of life from God entered them, and they stood on their feet, and terror struck those who saw them. ¹²Then they heard a loud voice from heaven saying to them, "Come up here." And they went up to heaven in a cloud, while their enemies looked on.

Rev 17:6 I saw that the woman was drunk with the blood of the saints, the blood of those who bore testimony to Jesus. When I saw her, I was greatly astonished.

Spirit of, required by Jesus (Mt 16:25)—

Lk 9:24 For whoever wants to save his life will lose it, but whoever loses his life for me will save it. (+Jn 12:25)

Possessed by the righteous—

Ps 44:22 Yet for your sake we face death all day long; we are considered as sheep to be slaughtered. (+Ro 8:36)

Rev 12:11 They overcame him by the blood of the Lamb and by the word of their testimony; they did not love their lives so much as to shrink from death.

See Persecution.

Instances of:

Abel (Ge 4:3-8). Prophets slain by Jezebel (1Ki 18:4,13). Zechariah (2Ch 24:21-22). John the Baptist (Mk 6:18-28). Jesus. *See Jesus the Christ, Death of.* Stephen (Ac 7:58-60). James the apostle (Ac 12:2).

The prophets (Mt 22:6)—

Mt 23:35 And so upon you will come all the righteous blood that has been shed on earth, from the blood of righteous Abel to the blood of Zechariah son of Berekiah, whom you murdered between the temple and the altar. (+Ro 11:3; 1Th 2:15; Heb 11:32-37)

MARY [*3451*] (perhaps *fat one; See Miriam*).

NIV+ MARY'S

1. *See Mary, The Virgin.*

2. Mother of James and Joses (Mt 27:56; Mk 15:40; Lk 24:10), probably the wife of Clopas (Jn 19:25), witnessed Crucifixion and visited grave on resurrection morning (Mt 27:56; 28:1).

3. Mary Magdalene; Jesus cast seven demons out of her (Mk 16:9; Lk 8:2), appears at Jesus' crucifixion (Mt 27:55-56; Mk 15:40-41; Jn 19:25), followed body of Jesus to grave (Mt 27:61) and was first to learn of the Resurrection (Mt 28:1-8; Mk 16:9; Lk 24:1-12; Jn 20:1-9,18). *See Dalmanutha; Magadan.*

4. Mary of Bethany; sister of Lazarus and Martha; lived in Bethany (Jn 11:1), commended by Jesus (Lk 10:42), anointed feet of Jesus (Jn 12:3).

5. Mother of John Mark; sister of Barnabas (Col 4:10), home in Jerusalem meeting place of Christians (Ac 12:12).

6. Christian at Rome (Ro 16:6).

MARY, THE VIRGIN [*3451*] (perhaps *fat one; See Miriam*).

Wife of Joseph (Mt 1:18-25), relative of Elizabeth, the mother of John the Baptist (Lk 1:36), of the seed of David (Ac 2:30; Ro 1:3; 2Ti 2:8), mother of Jesus (Mt 1:18,20; Lk 2:1-20), attended to ceremonial purification (Lk 2:22-38), fled to Egypt with Joseph and Jesus (Mt 2:13-15), lived in Nazareth (Mt 2:19-23), took twelve-year-old Jesus to temple (Lk 2:41-50), at wedding in Cana of Galilee (Jn 2:1-11), concerned for Jesus' safety (Mt 12:46; Mk 3:21,31ff; Lk 8:19-21), at the cross of Jesus (Jn 19:25ff) where she was entrusted by Jesus to the care of John (Jn 19:25-27), in the Upper Room (Ac 1:14).

Distinctive Roman Catholic doctrines about Mary: Perpetual Virginity, Intercession, Immaculate Conception (1854), and Assumption of Mary (1950).

MASCHIL *See Maskil.*

MASH Variant spelling of Meshech, son of Aram (Ge 10:22-23, ftn). *See Meshech.*

MASHAL [*5443*]. Also called Mishal and Misheal (Jos 19:26; 21:30). *See Mishal, Misheal.* A Levitical city in Asher (1Ch 6:74).

MASKIL [*5380*]. Occurs in the titles of several psalms (Pss 32; 42; 44-45; 52-55; 74; 78; 88-89; 142). The Hebrew word perhaps indicates that these psalms contain instruction in godliness (14:2; 53:2, "any who understand"; 41:1, "he who has regard"; 47:7, ftn).

See Music, Symbols Used in.

MASKING *See Disguises.*

MASON [*74+3093, 1553, 2935*].

NIV+ MASONS

A trade in the time of David (2Sa 5:11), of later times (2Ki 12:12; 22:6; 1Ch 14:1; Ezr 3:7).

MASREKAH [*5388*] (perhaps *vineyard*). Royal city of King Samlah, in Edom (Ge 36:31,36-37; 1Ch 1:47-48).

MASSA [*5364*] (*burden, oracle*). Tribe descended from Ishmael near Persian Gulf (Ge 25:14; 1Ch 1:30).

MASSACRE [*1947*]. Authorized by Moses (Dt 20:13, 16). Decree to destroy the Jews (Est 3).

Instances of:

Inhabitants of Heshbon (Dt 2:34), of Bashan (Dt 3:6), of Ai (Jos 8:24-26), of Hazor (Jos 11:11-12), of the cities of the seven kings (Jos 10:28-40). Midianites (Nu 31:7-8). Prophets of Baal (1Ki 18:40). Worshipers of Baal (2Ki 10:18-28). Sons of Ahab (2Ki 10:1-8). Royal family of Athaliah (2Ki 11:1). Inhabitants of Tiphsah (2Ki 15:16). Edomites (2Ki 14:7).

See Captive.

MASSAH [*5001*] (*test, try*). Site of rock in Horeb from which Moses drew water (Ex 17:1-7; Dt 6:16; 9:22), connected with Meribah (Dt 33:8).

MASTER [*123, 1067, 1251, 4856+6913, 5440, 7864, 804, 1305, 1437, 2181, 3259, 3261*].

NIV+ MASTER'S, MASTERED, MASTERS, MASTERS', MASTERY

Yahweh called (Jer 31:32, ftn; Hos 2:16). *See Baali.* Jesus called (Mt 8:19; 10:25; 23:8; 26:18,25,49; Mk 14:45; Lk 8:24; Jn 13:13-14). Jesus spoke against abuse of the title (Mt 23:8). *See Lord.*

MASTER, OF SERVANTS

Duties to Servants:

Must allow Sabbath rest—

Dt 5:14 but the seventh day is a Sabbath to the LORD your God. On it you shall not do any work, neither you, nor your son or daughter, nor your manservant or maidservant, nor your ox, your donkey or any of your animals, nor the alien within your gates, so that your manservant and maidservant may rest, as you do.

Compensate—

Jer 22:13 "Woe to him who builds his palace by unrighteousness, his upper rooms by injustice, making his countrymen work for nothing, not paying them for their labor.

Ro 4:4 Now when a man works, his wages are not credited to him as a gift, but as an obligation.

Col 4:1 Masters, provide your slaves with what is right and fair, because you know that you also have a Master in heaven.

1Ti 5:18 For the Scripture says, "Do not muzzle the ox while it is treading out the grain," and "The worker deserves his wages."

Pay promptly—

Lev 19:13 "'Do not defraud your neighbor or rob him. "'Do not hold back the wages of a hired man overnight.

Dt 24:15 Pay him his wages each day before sunset, because he is poor and is counting on it. Otherwise he may cry to the LORD against you, and you will be guilty of sin.

Jas 5:4 Look! The wages you failed to pay the workmen who mowed your fields are crying out against you. The cries of the harvesters have reached the ears of the Lord Almighty.

Forbidden to oppress (Lev 19:13)—

Lev 25:43 Do not rule over them ruthlessly, but fear your God.

Dt 24:14 Do not take advantage of a hired man who is poor and needy, whether he is a brother Israelite or an alien living in one of your towns. (+Job 31:13-14)

Pr 22:16 He who oppresses the poor to increase his wealth and he who gives gifts to the rich—both come to poverty.

Mal 3:5 "So I will come near to you for judgment. I will be quick to testify against sorcerers, adulterers and perjurers, against those who defraud laborers of their wages, who oppress the widows and the fatherless, and deprive aliens of justice, but do not fear me," says the LORD Almighty.

Forbidden to threaten—

Eph 6:9 And masters, treat your slaves in the same way. Do not threaten them, since you know that he who is both their Master and yours is in heaven, and there is no favoritism with him.

Exhorted to show kindness—

Phm 10 I appeal to you for my son Onesimus, who became my son while I was in chains. [11]Formerly he was useless to you, but now he has become useful both to you and to me.

[12]I am sending him—who is my very heart—back to you. [13]I would have liked to keep him with me so that he could take your place in helping me while I am in chains for the gospel. [14]But I did not want to do anything without your consent, so that any favor you do will be spontaneous and not forced. [15]Perhaps the reason he was separated from you for a little while was that you might have him back for good— [16]no longer as a slave, but better than a slave, as a

dear brother. He is very dear to me but even dearer to you, both as a man and as a brother in the Lord.

Exhorted to show wisdom—

Pr 29:12 If a ruler listens to lies, all his officials become wicked.

Pr 29:21 If a man pampers his servant from youth, he will bring grief in the end.

See Employer; Employee; Hired Servant; Servant.

Good Masters:

Abraham (Ge 18:19)

Job—

Job 31:13 "If I have denied justice to my menservants and maidservants when they had a grievance against me, ¹⁴what will I do when God confronts me? What will I answer when called to account? ¹⁵Did not he who made me in the womb make them? Did not the same one form us both within our mothers?

The centurion (Lk 7:2).

Unjust Masters:

Instances of: Sarah to Hagar (Ge 16:6). Laban to Jacob (Ge 31:7). Potiphar's wife to Joseph (Ge 39:7-20).

Violent, to be punished—

Ex 21:20 "If a man beats his male or female slave with a rod and the slave dies as a direct result, he must be punished, ²¹but he is not to be punished if the slave gets up after a day or two, since the slave is his property.

Ex 21:26 "If a man hits a manservant or maidservant in the eye and destroys it, he must let the servant go free to compensate for the eye. ²⁷And if he knocks out the tooth of a manservant or maidservant, he must let the servant go free to compensate for the tooth.

MASTER CRAFTSMAN

Instances of:

Tubal-Cain (Ge 4:22), Bezalel (Ex 31:2-11; 35:30-35), Huram or Huram-Abi (1Ki 7:13-50; 2Ch 2:13-14; 4:11-18), Wisdom (Pr 8:30), Paul (1Co 3:10). *See Art.*

MATERIALISM Love of things, possessions.

Love of money:

A root of all kinds of evil—

1Ti 6:10 For the love of money is a root of all kinds of evil. Some people, eager for money, have wandered from the faith and pierced themselves with many griefs.

Insatiable—

Ecc 4:7 Again I saw something meaningless under the sun: ⁸There was a man all alone; he had neither son nor brother. There was no end to his toil, yet his eyes were not content with his wealth. "For whom am I toiling," he asked, "and why am I depriving myself of enjoyment?" This too is meaningless—a miserable business!

Ecc 5:10 Whoever loves money never has money enough; whoever loves wealth is never satisfied with his income. This too is meaningless.

¹¹As goods increase, so do those who consume them. And what benefit are they to the owner except to feast his eyes on them?

Forbidden in overseer—

1Ti 3:2 Now the overseer must be above reproach, the husband of but one wife, temperate, self-controlled, respectable, hospitable, able to teach, ³not given to drunkenness, not violent but gentle, not quarrelsome, not a lover of money.

Tit 1:7 Since an overseer is entrusted with God's work, he must be blameless—not overbearing, not quick-tempered, not given to drunkenness, not violent, not pursuing dishonest gain.

Materialists Do Not Love God:

Mt 6:24 —No one can serve two masters. Either he will hate the one and love the other, or he will be devoted to the one and despise the other. You cannot serve both God and Money.

1Jn 2:15 Do not love the world or anything in the world. If anyone loves the world, the love of the Father is not in him. ¹⁶For everything in the world— the cravings of sinful man, the lust of his eyes and the boasting of what he has and does— comes not from the Father but from the world. ¹⁷The world and its desires pass away, but the man who does the will of God lives forever.

1Jn 3:17 If anyone has material possessions and sees his brother in need but has no pity on him, how can the love of God be in him?

Treasures in Heaven Versus Materialism:

Mt 6:19 "Do not store up for yourselves treasures on earth, where moth and rust destroy, and where thieves break in and steal. ²⁰But store up for yourselves treasures in heaven, where moth and rust do not destroy, and where thieves do not break in and steal. ²¹For where your treasure is, there your heart will be also.

1Ti 6:17 Command those who are rich in this present world not to be arrogant nor to put their hope in wealth, which is so uncertain, but to put their hope in God, who richly provides us with everything for our enjoyment. ¹⁸Command them to do good, to be rich in good deeds, and to be generous and willing to share. ¹⁹In this way they will lay up treasure for themselves as a firm foundation for the coming age, so that they may take hold of the life that is truly life.

See Avarice; Greed; Love, Of Money; Rich, The; Riches.

MATHUSALA *See Methuselah.*

MATRED [4765] (perhaps *spear*). Mother of Mehetabel, wife of Hadad (Ge 36:39), who is called "Hadad" (1Ch 1:50).

MATRI [4767] (*rainy*). Head of Benjamite family (1Sa 10:21).

MATTAN [5509] (*gift*).

1. A priest of Baal slain in the idol temple at Jerusalem (2Ki 11:18; 2Ch 23:17).
2. Father of Shephatiah (Jer 38:1).

MATTANAH [5511] (*gift*). Encampment of Israel in wilderness (Nu 21:18-19).

MATTANIAH [5514, 5515] (*gift of Yahweh*).

1. Original name of King Zedekiah (2Ki 24:17).
2. Chief choir leader and watchman (Ne 11:17; 12:8,25).
3. Levite (2Ch 20:14).
4. Son of Elam (Ezr 10:26).
5. Son of Zattu (Ezr 10:27).
6. Son of Pahath-Moab (Ezr 10:30).
7. Son of Bani (Ezr 10:37).
8. Grandfather of Hanan (Ne 13:13).
9. Son of Heman; head musician (1Ch 25:4-5,7,16).
10. Levite who assisted Hezekiah (2Ch 29:13).

MATTATHA [3477]. An ancestor of Jesus (Lk 3:31).

MATTATHAH *See Mattattah.*

MATTATHIAS [3478] (gift of Yahweh).

1. Assistant of Ezra, spelled Mattithiah (Ne 8:4).

2. Name borne by two ancestors of Christ (Lk 3:25-26).

3. Priest; founder of Maccabee family (1Mc 2). *See also, 1Mc 11:70; 16:14-16; 2Mc 14:19.*

MATTATTAH [5523] (gift). One of the family of Hashum (Ezr 10:33).

MATTENAI [5513] (gift).

1. Two Israelites who put away their Gentile wives after the Captivity (Ezr 10:33,37).

2. A priest in the time of Joiakim (Ne 12:19).

MATTHAN [3474] (gift). Grandfather of Joseph, Mary's husband (Mt 1:15).

MATTHAT [3415] (gift of God).

1. Father of Heli, ancestor of Joseph (Lk 3:23).

2. Father of Jorim, and ancestor of Joseph (Lk 3:29).

MATTHEW [3414] (gift of Yahweh).

NIV+ MATTHEW'S

Son of Alphaeus (Mk 2:14), tax collector, also called Levi (Mk 2:14; Lk 5:27), called by Jesus to become disciple (Mt 9:9; Mk 2:14; Lk 5:27) and gave feast for Jesus; appointed apostle (Mt 10:3; Mk 3:18; Lk 6:15; Ac 1:13).

MATTHEW, GOSPEL OF

Author: Anonymous, traditionally The Apostle Matthew

Date: Probably in the late 60s A.D.

Outline:

I. The Birth and Early Years of Jesus (chs. 1-2).
   A. His Genealogy (1:1-17).
   B. His Birth (1:18-2:12).
   C. His Sojourn in Egypt (2:13-23).
II. The Beginnings of Jesus' Ministry (3:1-4:11).
   A. His Forerunner (3:1-12).
   B. His Baptism (3:13-17).
   C. His Temptation (4:1-11).
III. Jesus' Ministry in Galilee (4:12-14:12).
   A. The Beginning of the Galilean Campaign (4:12-25).
   B. The Sermon on the Mount (chs. 5-7).
   C. A Collection of Miracles (chs. 8-9).
   D. The Commissioning of the twelve Apostles (ch. 10).
   E. Ministry throughout Galilee (chs. 11-12).
   F. The Parables of the Kingdom (ch. 13).
   G. Herod's Reaction to Jesus' Ministry (14:1-12).
IV. Jesus' Withdrawals from Galilee (14:13-17:20).
   A. To the Eastern Shore of the Sea of Galilee (14:13-15:20).
   B. To Phoenicia (15:21-28).
   C. To the Decapolis (15:29-16:12).
   D. To Caesarea Philippi (16:13-17:20).
V. Jesus' Last Ministry in Galilee (17:22-18:35).
   A. Prediction of Jesus' Death (17:22-23).
   B. Temple Tax (17:24-27).
   C. Discourse on Life in the Kingdom (ch. 18).
VI. Jesus' Ministry in Judea and Perea (chs. 19-20).
   A. Teaching concerning Divorce (19:1-12).
   B. Teaching concerning Little Children (19:13-15).
   C. The Rich Young Man (19:16-30).
   D. The Parable of the Workers in the Vineyard (20:1-16).
   E. Prediction of Jesus' Death (20:17-19).
   F. A Mother's Request (20:20-28).
   G. Restoration of Sight at Jericho (20:29-34).

VII. Passion Week (chs. 21-27).
   A. The Triumphal Entry (21:1-11).
   B. The Cleansing of the Temple (21:12-17).
   C. The Last Controversies with the Jewish Leaders (21:18-23:39).
   D. The Olivet Discourse concerning the End of the Age (chs. 24-25).
   E. The Anointing of Jesus' Feet (26:1-13).
   F. The Arrest, Trials and Death of Jesus (26:14-27:66).
VIII. The Resurrection (ch. 28).
   See Synoptic Gospels, The.

MATTHIAS [3416] (gift of Yahweh). Apostle chosen by lot to take place of Judas (Ac 1:15-26), had been follower of Christ (Ac 1:21-22).

MATTITHIAH [5524, 5525] (gift of Yahweh).

1. A Levite who had charge of the baked offerings (1Ch 9:31).

2. A Levite musician (1Ch 15:18,21; 16:5).

3. A chief of the fourteenth division of temple musicians (1Ch 25:3,21).

4. An Israelite who divorced his Gentile wife after the Captivity (Ezr 10:43).

5. A prince who stood by Ezra when he read the law to the people (Ne 8:4).

MATTOCK [908] (cut in, plow).

NIV+ MATTOCKS

Single-headed farming tool with point on one side and broad edge on other side (1Sa 13:20-21; Isa 7:25).

MAUL See Club.

MAW One of the stomachs of a ruminating animal (Dt 18:3).

MAZZAROTH See Constellations.

ME JARKON, ME-JARKON (waters of Jarkon [greenish?]). A city in Dan (Jos 19:46).

MEADOW [4120, 5303, 5661].

NIV+ MEADOWS

1. Place where reeds grow (Ge 41:2,18).

2. Pastureland (Jdg 20:33).

MEAH NIV "Hundred" (Ne 3:1; 12:38). See Tower, Of the Hundred.

MEAL See Grain.

MEAL OFFERING See Offerings.

MEANINGLESS See Vanity, 1.

MEARAH (cave). See Arah, 4.

MEASURE [*406, 4394+6330, 4499, 4500, 5374, 6015+6017, 7742, 3582, 3586].

NIV+ IMMEASURABLY, MEASURED, MEASURELESS, MEASUREMENT, MEASUREMENTS, MEASURES, MEASURING

False and Just:

Just required—

Lev 19:35 "'Do not use dishonest standards when measuring length, weight or quantity. 36Use honest scales and honest weights, an honest ephah and an honest hin. I am the LORD your God, who brought you out of Egypt.

Dt 25:13 Do not have two differing weights in your bag—one heavy, one light. 14Do not have two differing measures in your house—one large, one small. ¹⁵You must have accurate and honest weights and measures, so that you may live long in the land the LORD your God is giving you. ¹⁶For the LORD your God detests anyone who does these things, anyone who deals dishonestly.

Pr 16:11 Honest scales and balances are from the LORD; all the weights in the bag are of his making.

False—

Hos 12:7 The merchant uses dishonest scales; he loves to defraud. ⁸Ephraim boasts, "I am very rich; I have become wealthy. With all my wealth they will not find in me any iniquity or sin."

⁹"I am the LORD your God, [who brought you] out of Egypt; I will make you live in tents again, as in the days of your appointed feasts.

An abomination—

Pr 11:1 The LORD abhors dishonest scales, but accurate weights are his delight.

Pr 20:10 Differing weights and differing measures—the LORD detests them both.

Pr 20:23 The LORD detests differing weights, and dishonest scales do not please him.

Mic 6:10 Am I still to forget, O wicked house, your ill-gotten treasures and the short ephah, which is accursed? ¹¹Shall I acquit a man with dishonest scales, with a bag of false weights? ¹²Her rich men are violent; her people are liars and their tongues speak deceitfully.

See Dishonesty; Integrity.

MEAT [1414, 3181, 3186, 4657, 4950, 5984, 7002, 7507, 8638, *3200, 3425, 4465*]. *See Food.*

MEAT FORKS Used in the tabernacle (Ex 27:3; 38:3; Nu 4:14; 1Sa 2:13-14). Made of gold (1Ch 28:17), of bronze (2Ch 4:16).

MEAT OFFERING *See Offerings, Meat.*

MEBUNNAI [4446] (*well built*). One of David's bodyguards (2Sa 23:27), called Sibbecai (2Sa 21:18).

MECHANIC *See Art; Master Craftsman.*

MECHERATHITE *See Mekerathite.*

MECONAH [4828] (*foundation*). A city in Judah (Ne 11:28).

MEDAD [4773] (*beloved*). One of the seventy elders who did not go to the tabernacle with Moses, but prophesied in the camp (Nu 11:26-29).

MEDAN [4527] (*dissension*). Son of Abraham and Keturah (Ge 25:2; 1Ch 1:32).

MEDDLING [6297, 258].

NIV+ MEDDLER, MEDDLES

See Busybody; Talebearer.

MEDEBA [4772]. A city of Moab (Nu 21:30). An idolatrous high place (Isa 15:2). Allotted to Reuben (Jos

Biblical Weights and Measures and Approximate Equivalents

Dry Capacity:					
1.	Cor or homer	10 ephahs	6 bushels	220 liters	1Ki 4:22; 5:11; 2Ch 2:10; 27:5; Ezr 7:22
2.	Lethek	5 ephahs	3 bushels	110 liters	Hos 3:2
3.	Ephah	10 omers	3/5 bushel	22 liters	Ex 16:36; Lev 5:11; Nu 5:15; Jdg 6:19; Ru 2:17; 1Sa 1:24; Isa 5:10; Eze 45:10-11,13,24; Am 8:5
4.	Seah	1/3 ephah	7 quarts	7.3 liters	Ge 18:6; 1Sa 25:18; 1Ki 18:32; 2Ki 7:1,16,18
5.	Omer	1/10 ephah	2 quarts	2 liters	Ex 16:16,18,22,32-33,36
6.	Cab	1/18 ephah	1 quart	1 liter	2Ki 6:25
Liquid Capacity:					
1.	Bath	1 ephah	6 gallons	22 liters	1Ki 7:26,38; 2Ch 2:10; 4:5; Ezr 7:22; Isa 5:10; Eze 45:10-11,14; Lk 16:6
2.	Hin	1/6 bath	4 quarts	4 liters	Ex 29:40; 30:24; Lev 19:36; 23:13; Nu 15:4-10; 28:5,7,14; Eze 4:11; 45:24; 46:5,7,11,14
3.	Log	1/72 bath	1/3 quart	0.3 liter	Lev 14:10,12,14,21,24
Weight:					
1.	Talent	60 minas	75 pounds	34 kilograms	Ex 25:39; 38:27
2.	Mina	50 shekels	1.25 pounds	0.6 kilogram	1Ki 10:17; Ezr 2:69; Da 5:26-28
3.	Shekel	2 bekas	2/5 ounce	11.5 grams	Ge 20:16; Eze 45:12
4.	Pim	2/3 shekel	1/3 ounce	7.6 grams	1Sa 13:21, ftn
5.	Beka	10 gerahs	1/5 ounce	5.5 grams	Ge 24:22; Ex 38:26
6.	Gerah	1/20 shekel	1/50 ounce	0.6 gram	Ex 30:13; Lev 27:25
Length:					
1.	Cubit		18 inches	0.5 meter	Ge 6:15-16; Rev 21:17
2.	Span		9 inches	23 cm.	Ex 28:16; 1Sa 17:4; Isa 40:12; La 2:20; Eze 43:13
3.	Handbreadth		3 inches	8 centimeters	Ex 25:25; 1Ki 7:26; 2Ch 4:5; Ps 39:5; Eze 43:13
4.	Finger		0.75 inch	1.85 cm.	Jer 52:21

13:9,16). David defeats army and the Ammonites at (1Ch 19:7-15).

MEDES [4512, 4513, 10404, *3597*].

NIV+ MEDE, MEDIA

Inhabitants of Media. Israelites distributed among, when carried to Assyria (2Ki 17:6; 18:11). Palace in the Babylonian province of (Ezr 6:2). An essential part of the Medo-Persian Empire (Est 1:1-19). Supremacy over the Babylonian Empire (Da 5:28,31; 9:1; 11:1).

MEDIA [4512, 10404]. *See Medes.*

MEDIATION [4885, 7136, *3542*].

NIV+ MEDIATE, MEDIATOR

Between People and God:

(Ex 18:19; Job 9:33; Gal 3:19). Solicited by Israel (Ex 20:19-20; Dt 5:27).

Instances of: By Moses (Ex 32:11-13; 34:9; Nu 14:13-19; 27:5; Dt 5:5; 9:18-20,25-29). Aaron (Nu 16:47-48). Joshua (Jos 7:6-9). Samuel (1Sa 8:10,21). David (2Sa 24:17).

Between People and Jesus:

In behalf of the afflicted (Mt 12:22; 15:30; Mk 1:32). The four friends for the paralytic (Mt 2:3-12; 9:2-8; Lk 5:18-20). Jairus (Mt 9:18; Mk 5:23; Lk 8:41). The nobleman for his son (Jn 4:47,49). The father of the demoniac for his son (Mt 17:15; Mk 9:17-18). The Syrian Phoenician woman for her daughter (Mt 15:22; Mk 7:24-26). The disciples for Peter's mother-in-law (Mk 1:30; Lk 4:38-39).

Between Persons:

Reuben for Joseph (Ge 37:21-22). Judah for Joseph (Ge 37:26-27). Pharaoh's chief baker for Joseph (Ge 41:9-13, w 40:14). Jonathan for David (1Sa 19:1-7). Abigail for Nabal (1Sa 25:23-35). Joab for Absalom (2Sa 14:1-24). Bathsheba for Solomon (1Ki 1:15-31), for Adonijah (1Ki 2:13-25). Ebed-Melech for Jeremiah (Jer 38:7-13). Elisha offers to see the king for the Shunammite (2Ki 4:13). The king of Syria for Naaman (2Ki 5:6-8). Paul for Onesimus (Phm 10-21).

See Intercession; Jesus, Mediation of.

MEDICINE [1565].

Used—

Isa 38:21 Isaiah had said, "Prepare a poultice of figs and apply it to the boil, and he will recover."

Lk 10:34 He went to him and bandaged his wounds, pouring on oil and wine. Then he put the man on his own donkey, took him to an inn and took care of him. *See Disease; Physician.*

Figurative:

Pr 17:22 A cheerful heart is good medicine, but a crushed spirit dries up the bones.

Isa 1:6 From the sole of your foot to the top of your head there is no soundness—only wounds and welts and open sores, not cleansed or bandaged or soothed with oil.

Jer 8:22 Is there no balm in Gilead? Is there no physician there? Why then is there no healing for the wound of my people?

Jer 30:13 There is no one to plead your cause, no remedy for your sore, no healing for you.

Jer 46:11 "Go up to Gilead and get balm, O Virgin Daughter of Egypt. But you multiply remedies in vain; there is no healing for you.

Jer 51:8 Babylon will suddenly fall and be broken. Wail over her! Get balm for her pain; perhaps she can be healed.

⁹"'We would have healed Babylon, but she cannot be healed; let us leave her and each go to his own land, for her judgment reaches to the skies, it rises as high as the clouds.'

Allegorical—

Eze 47:12 Fruit trees of all kinds will grow on both banks of the river. Their leaves will not wither, nor will their fruit fail. Every month they will bear, because the water from the sanctuary flows to them. Their fruit will serve for food and their leaves for healing."

Rev 22:2 down the middle of the great street of the city. On each side of the river stood the tree of life, bearing twelve crops of fruit, yielding its fruit every month. And the leaves of the tree are for the healing of the nations.

MEDITATION [1948, 2047, 2052, 2053, 8452, 8488, 8490, 8491].

NIV+ MEDITATE, MEDITATED, MEDITATES

On the Lord—

Ps 63:5 My soul will be satisfied as with the richest of foods; with singing lips my mouth will praise you.

⁶On my bed I remember you; I think of you through the watches of the night.

Ps 104:34 May my meditation be pleasing to him, as I rejoice in the LORD.

Ps 139:17 How precious to me are your thoughts, O God! How vast is the sum of them! ¹⁸Were I to count them, they would outnumber the grains of sand. When I awake, I am still with you.

On the law of the Lord—

Ps 1:2 But his delight is in the law of the LORD, and on his law he meditates day and night.

Ps 19:14 May the words of my mouth and the meditation of my heart be pleasing in your sight, O LORD, my Rock and my Redeemer.

Ps 49:3 My mouth will speak words of wisdom; the utterance from my heart will give understanding.

Ps 119:11 I have hidden your word in my heart that I might not sin against you.

Ps 119:15 I meditate on your precepts and consider your ways. ¹⁶I delight in your decrees; I will not neglect your word.

Ps 119:23 Though rulers sit together and slander me, your servant will meditate on your decrees.

Ps 119:48 I lift up my hands to your commands, which I love, and I meditate on your decrees.

Ps 119:55 In the night I remember your name, O LORD, and I will keep your law.

Ps 119:59 I have considered my ways and have turned my steps to your statutes.

Ps 119:78 May the arrogant be put to shame for wronging me without cause; but I will meditate on your precepts.

Ps 119:97 Oh, how I love your law! I meditate on it all day long. (+Ps 119:98)

Ps 119:99 I have more insight than all my teachers, for I meditate on your statutes.

Ps 119:148 My eyes stay open through the watches of the night, that I may meditate on your promises.

Commanded—

Jos 1:8 Do not let this Book of the Law depart from your mouth; meditate on it day and night, so that you may be careful to do everything written in it. Then you will be prosperous and successful.

On the works of the Lord—

Ps 77:10 Then I thought, "To this I will appeal: the years of the right hand of the Most High." [11]I will remember the deeds of the LORD; yes, I will remember your miracles of long ago. [12]I will meditate on all your works and consider all your mighty deeds.

Ps 143:5 I remember the days of long ago; I meditate on all your works and consider what your hands have done.

Instances of:

Isaac (Ge 24:63).

David—

Ps 4:4 In your anger do not sin; when you are on your beds, search your hearts and be silent. *Selah*

Ps 39:3 My heart grew hot within me, and as I meditated, the fire burned; then I spoke with my tongue:

MEDITERRANEAN SEA

Mentioned in Scripture as: The Sea (Nu 34:5; Ps 80:11). The Great Sea (Nu 34:6-7; Jos 1:4; 9:1; 15:12,47; 23:4; Eze 47:10,15,20; 48:28). Sea of the Philistines (Ex 23:31). The western sea (Dt 11:24; Joel 2:20; Zec 14:8).

MEDIUM [200+, 6726].

NIV+ MEDIUMS

A spiritist; one who consults the dead (Lev 19:31; 20:6; Dt 18:9-13; Isa 8:19-22). Punished by death in the law (Lev 20:27). Saul and the medium at Endor (1Sa 28:3-25; 1Ch 10:13-14). *See Necromancer, Necromancy; Sorcery; Spiritists.*

MEEKNESS [6705, 6714, *4558*, *4559*].

NIV+ MEEK, MEEKLY

Advantageous—

Ps 25:9 He guides the humble in what is right and teaches them his way.

Pr 14:29 A patient man has great understanding, but a quick-tempered man displays folly.

Pr 17:1 Better a dry crust with peace and quiet than a house full of feasting, with strife.

Pr 19:11 A man's wisdom gives him patience; it is to his glory to overlook an offense.

Ecc 7:8 The end of a matter is better than its beginning, and patience is better than pride.

Ecc 10:4 If a ruler's anger rises against you, do not leave your post; calmness can lay great errors to rest.

Am 3:3 Do two walk together unless they have agreed to do so?

1Co 13:4 Love is patient, love is kind. It does not envy, it does not boast, it is not proud. [5]It is not rude, it is not self-seeking, it is not easily angered, it keeps no record of wrongs.

1Co 13:7 It always protects, always trusts, always hopes, always perseveres.

Honorable—

Pr 20:3 It is to a man's honor to avoid strife, but every fool is quick to quarrel.

Potent—

Pr 15:1 A gentle answer turns away wrath, but a harsh word stirs up anger.

Pr 15:18 A hot-tempered man stirs up dissension, but a patient man calms a quarrel.

Pr 16:32 Better a patient man than a warrior, a man who controls his temper than one who takes a city.

Pr 25:15 Through patience a ruler can be persuaded, and a gentle tongue can break a bone.

Pr 29:8 Mockers stir up a city, but wise men turn away anger.

Commanded—

Zep 2:3 Seek the LORD, all you humble of the land, you who do what he commands. Seek righteousness, seek humility; perhaps you will be sheltered on the day of the LORD's anger.

Mt 5:38 "You have heard that it was said, 'Eye for eye, and tooth for tooth.' [39]But I tell you, Do not resist an evil person. If someone strikes you on the right cheek, turn to him the other also. [40]And if someone wants to sue you and take your tunic, let him have your cloak as well. [41]If someone forces you to go one mile, go with him two miles. (+Lk 6:29)

Mt 11:29 Take my yoke upon you and learn from me, for I am gentle and humble in heart, and you will find rest for your souls.

Mk 9:50 "Salt is good, but if it loses its saltiness, how can you make it salty again? Have salt in yourselves, and be at peace with each other."

Ro 12:14 Bless those who persecute you; bless and do not curse.

Ro 12:18 If it is possible, as far as it depends on you, live at peace with everyone.

Ro 14:19 Let us therefore make every effort to do what leads to peace and to mutual edification.

1Co 6:7 The very fact that you have lawsuits among you means you have been completely defeated already. Why not rather be wronged? Why not rather be cheated?

1Co 7:15 But if the unbeliever leaves, let him do so. A believing man or woman is not bound in such circumstances; God has called us to live in peace.

1Co 10:32 Do not cause anyone to stumble, whether Jews, Greeks or the church of God—

2Co 13:11 Finally, brothers, good-by. Aim for perfection, listen to my appeal, be of one mind, live in peace. And the God of love and peace will be with you.

Gal 6:1 Brothers, if someone is caught in a sin, you who are spiritual should restore him gently. But watch yourself, or you also may be tempted.

Eph 4:1 As a prisoner for the Lord, then, I urge you to live a life worthy of the calling you have received. [2]Be completely humble and gentle; be patient, bearing with one another in love.

Php 2:14 Do everything without complaining or arguing, [15]so that you may become blameless and pure, children of God without fault in a crooked and depraved generation, in which you shine like stars in the universe

Col 3:12 Therefore, as God's chosen people, holy and dearly loved, clothe yourselves with compassion, kindness, humility, gentleness and patience. [13]Bear with each other and forgive whatever grievances you may have against one another. Forgive as the Lord forgave you.

1Th 5:14 And we urge you, brothers, warn those who are idle, encourage the timid, help the weak, be patient with everyone. [15]Make sure that nobody pays back wrong for wrong, but always try to be kind to each other and to everyone else.

1Ti 3:3 not given to drunkenness, not violent but gentle, not quarrelsome, not a lover of money.

1Ti 6:11 But you, man of God, flee from all this, and pursue righteousness, godliness, faith, love, endurance and gentleness.

2Ti 2:24 And the Lord's servant must not quarrel; instead, he must be kind to everyone, able to teach, not resentful. [25]Those who oppose him he must gently instruct, in the hope that God will grant them repentance leading them to a knowledge of the truth,

Tit 2:2 Teach the older men to be temperate, worthy of respect, self-controlled, and sound in faith, in love and in endurance.

Tit 2:9 Teach slaves to be subject to their masters in everything, to try to please them, not to talk back to them,

Tit 3:2 to slander no one, to be peaceable and considerate, and to show true humility toward all men.

Heb 10:36 You need to persevere so that when you have done the will of God, you will receive what he has promised.

Heb 12:14 Make every effort to live in peace with all men and to be holy; without holiness no one will see the Lord.

Jas 1:4 Perseverance must finish its work so that you may be mature and complete, not lacking anything.

Jas 1:19 My dear brothers, take note of this: Everyone should be quick to listen, slow to speak and slow to become angry,

Jas 1:21 Therefore, get rid of all moral filth and the evil that is so prevalent and humbly accept the word planted in you, which can save you.

Jas 3:13 Who is wise and understanding among you? Let him show it by his good life, by deeds done in the humility that comes from wisdom.

1Pe 2:18 Slaves, submit yourselves to your masters with all respect, not only to those who are good and considerate, but also to those who are harsh. [19]For it is commendable if a man bears up under the pain of unjust suffering because he is conscious of God. [20]But how is it to your credit if you receive a beating for doing wrong and endure it? But if you suffer for doing good and you endure it, this is commendable before God. [21]To this you were called, because Christ suffered for you, leaving you an example, that you should follow in his steps.

[22]"He committed no sin, and no deceit was found in his mouth."

[23]When they hurled their insults at him, he did not retaliate; when he suffered, he made no threats. Instead, he entrusted himself to him who judges justly.

1Pe 3:4 Instead, it should be that of your inner self, the unfading beauty of a gentle and quiet spirit, which is of great worth in God's sight.

1Pe 3:11 He must turn from evil and do good; he must seek peace and pursue it.

1Pe 3:15 But in your hearts set apart Christ as Lord. Always be prepared to give an answer to everyone who asks you to give the reason for the hope that you have. But do this with gentleness and respect,

2Pe 1:5 For this very reason, make every effort to add to your faith goodness; and to goodness, knowledge; [6]and to knowledge, self-control; and to self-control, perseverance; and to perseverance, godliness; [7]and to godliness, brotherly kindness; and to brotherly kindness, love.

A fruit of the Spirit—

Gal 5:22 But the fruit of the Spirit is love, joy, peace, patience, kindness, goodness, faithfulness, [23]gentleness and self-control. Against such things there is no law.

Gal 5:26 Let us not become conceited, provoking and envying each other.

Rewards of—

Ps 22:26 The poor will eat and be satisfied; they who seek the LORD will praise him—may your hearts live forever!

Ps 37:11 But the meek will inherit the land and enjoy great peace.

Ps 76:8 From heaven you pronounced judgment, and the

land feared and was quiet— [9]when you, O God, rose up to judge, to save all the afflicted of the land. *Selah*

Ps 147:6 The LORD sustains the humble but casts the wicked to the ground.

Ps 149:4 For the LORD takes delight in his people; he crowns the humble with salvation.

Isa 29:19 Once more the humble will rejoice in the LORD; the needy will rejoice in the Holy One of Israel.

Mt 5:5 Blessed are the meek, for they will inherit the earth. (+Mt 11:29)

Instances of:

Abraham (Ge 13:8-9). Isaac (Ge 26:20-22). Moses (Ex 16:7-8; 17:2-7; Nu 12:3; 16:4-11). Gideon (Jdg 8:2-3). Hannah (1Sa 1:13-16). Saul (1Sa 10:27). David (1Sa 17:29; 2Sa 16:9-14; Ps 38:13-14). Psalmist (Ps 120:5-7).

Jesus—

Isa 11:4 but with righteousness he will judge the needy, with justice he will give decisions for the poor of the earth. He will strike the earth with the rod of his mouth; with the breath of his lips he will slay the wicked.

Isa 42:1 "Here is my servant, whom I uphold, my chosen one in whom I delight; I will put my Spirit on him and he will bring justice to the nations. [2]He will not shout or cry out, or raise his voice in the streets. [3]A bruised reed he will not break, and a smoldering wick he will not snuff out. In faithfulness he will bring forth justice; [4]he will not falter or be discouraged till he establishes justice on earth. In his law the islands will put their hope."

Isa 53:7 He was oppressed and afflicted, yet he did not open his mouth; he was led like a lamb to the slaughter, and as a sheep before her shearers is silent, so he did not open his mouth.

La 3:28 Let him sit alone in silence, for the LORD has laid it on him. [29]Let him bury his face in the dust—there may yet be hope. [30]Let him offer his cheek to one who would strike him, and let him be filled with disgrace. (+Mt 11:29; 12:19-20)

Mt 26:47 While he was still speaking, Judas, one of the Twelve, arrived. With him was a large crowd armed with swords and clubs, sent from the chief priests and the elders of the people. [48]Now the betrayer had arranged a signal with them: "The one I kiss is the man; arrest him." [49]Going at once to Jesus, Judas said, "Greetings, Rabbi!" and kissed him.

[50]Jesus replied, "Friend, do what you came for."

Then the men stepped forward, seized Jesus and arrested him. [51]With that, one of Jesus' companions reached for his sword, drew it out and struck the servant of the high priest, cutting off his ear.

[52]"Put your sword back in its place," Jesus said to him, "for all who draw the sword will die by the sword. [53]Do you think I cannot call on my Father, and he will at once put at my disposal more than twelve legions of angels? [54]But how then would the Scriptures be fulfilled that say it must happen in this way?"

Mt 27:13 Then Pilate asked him, "Don't you hear the testimony they are bringing against you?" [14]But Jesus made no reply, not even to a single charge—to the great amazement of the governor. (+Mk 15:4-5; Lk 23:34)

2Co 10:1 By the meekness and gentleness of Christ, I appeal to you—I, Paul, who am "timid" when face to face with you, but "bold" when away! (+1Pe 2:21-23) *See Jesus the Christ, Humility of; Meekness of.*

Stephen (Ac 7:60). Paul (Ac 21:20-26; 1Co 4:12-13; 2Co 12:10; 1Th 2:7; 2Ti 4:16). The Thessalonians (2Th 1:4). Job (Jas 5:11).

The archangel—
Jude 9 But even the archangel Michael, when he was disputing with the devil about the body of Moses, did not dare to bring a slanderous accusation against him, but said, "The Lord rebuke you!"

Of God (La 3:22,28-30).
See Humility; Kindness; Patience.

MEGIDDO [4459, 4461] (*place of troops*). City on the Great Road linking Gaza and Damascus, connecting the coastal plain and the Plain of Esdraelon or Megiddo (Jos 12:21; 17:11; Jdg 1:27; 5:19), fortified by Solomon (1Ki 9:15), wounded Ahaziah died there (2Ki 9:27), Josiah lost life there in battle with Pharaoh Neco (2Ki 23:29-30; 2Ch 35:20-27). Large-scale excavations have revealed a great deal of material of great archaeological value.

MEGIDDON *See Megiddo.*

MEHETABEEL *See Mehetabel, 2.*

MEHETABEL, MEHETABEEL [4541] (*God [El] does good*).
1. Wife of Hadad (Ge 36:39; 1Ch 1:50).
2. A person whose grandson tried to intimidate Nehemiah (Ne 6:10).

MEHIDA [4694] (possibly *bought as slave*). A person whose descendants returned from Babylon (Ezr 2:52; Ne 7:54).

MEHIR [4698] (*hired hand*). Son of Kelub (1Ch 4:11).

MEHOLAH, MEHOLATHITE [4716].
NIV+ ABEL MEHOLAH
A city in Issachar, probably the same as Abel Meholah. Barzillai and his son Adriel lived there (1Sa 18:19; 2Sa 21:8). *See Abel Meholah.*

MEHUJAEL [4686]. Descendant of Cain; father of Methushael (Ge 4:18).

MEHUMAN [4540]. Eunuch of Xerxes, king of Persia (Est 1:10).

MEHUNIM *See Maonites; Meunim, Meunites, 2.*

MEKERATHITE [4841] (*one of Mekerath*). Description of Hepher (1Ch 11:36).

MEKONAH *See Meconah.*

MELAH *See Tel Melah.*

MELATIAH [4882] (*Yahweh sets free*). A Gibeonite who assisted in repairing the wall of Jerusalem (Ne 3:7).

MELCHESEDEC *See Melchizedek.*

MELCHI *See Melki.*

MELCHIAH *See Malkijah.*

MELCHISHUA, MELCHI-SHUA *See Malki-Shua.*

MELCHIZEDEK, MELCHISEDEC [4900, 3519] (*[my] king is Zedek [just]*). Priest and king of Salem (Jerusalem); blessed Abram in the name of Most High God and received tithes from him (Ge 14:18-20), type of Christ, the Priest-King (Ps 110:4; Heb 5:6-10; 6:20; 7).

MELEA [3507]. Ancestor of Jesus (Lk 3:31).

MELECH [4890] (*king*). Son of Micah (1Ch 8:35; 9:41).

MELICU *See Malluch, 6.*

MELITA *See Malta.*

MELKI [3518] (*my king*).
1. Ancestor of Jesus (Lk 3:24).
2. Remote ancestor of Jesus (Lk 3:28).

MELODY [2053, 5834].
NIV+ MELODIOUS
See Music.

MELON [19, 5252].
NIV+ MELONS
(Nu 11:5).

MELZAR NIV "guard" (Da 1:11,16). *See Guard.*

MEMBER [408, 1201, 4632, 4946, 5883, 6830, *741, 1085, 2363, 3517, 3858, 3865, 3875, 5362*].
NIV+ MEMBERS
Any feature or part of the body (Job 17:7; Jas 3:5).

MEMORIAL [260, 2349, 2355, 3338, *3649*].
NIV+ MEMORY, MEMORABLE, MEMORIES
Passover (Ex 12:14). *See Passover.*
Firstborn set apart as a (Ex 13:12-16). Pot of manna (Ex 16:32-34). Feast of Tabernacles (Lev 23:43). Shoulder stones of the ephod (Ex 28:12). Atonement money (Ex 30:16). The twelve stones of Jordan (Jos 4:1-9).
The Lord's Supper (Lk 22:19; 1Co 11:24-26).
See Pillar.

MEMPHIS [5132, 5862]. Capital city of Egypt, on W bank of Nile, c. twenty miles S of modern Cairo; its destruction foretold by prophets (Isa 19:13; Jer 2:16; 44:1; 46:14,19; Eze 30:13,16).

MEMUCAN [4925]. One of the seven princes of Xerxes who counsels the king to divorce Queen Vashti (Est 1:14-21).

MENAHEM [4968] (*comforter*).
NIV+ MENAHEM'S
Sixteenth king of Israel; evil; slew his predecessor, Shallum (2Ki 15:13-22).

MENAN *See Menna.*

MENE, MENE, TEKEL, PARSIN
[10428+10593+10770]. Four Aramaic words, probably meaning "numbered, numbered, weighed, and divided," which suddenly appeared on the walls of Belshazzar's banquet hall (Da 5:25-28).

MENI *See Destiny, 2.*

MENNA [3527]. An ancestor of Jesus (Lk 3:31).

MENSES *See Menstruation.*

MENSTRUATION [1865].
NIV+ MENSTRUAL
Law relating to (Lev 15:19-30; 20:18; Eze 18:6). Cessation of, in old age (Ge 18:11). Immunities of women during (Ge 31:35). Uncleanness of (Isa 30:22).
Figurative:
(Isa 30:22; La 1:17; Eze 36:17).
See Bleeding, Subject to.

MEON *See Baal Meon; Beth Baal Meon; Beth Meon.*

MEONENIM *See Soothsayers' Tree.*

MEONOTHAI [5065] (*my dwellings*). Father of Ophrah (1Ch 4:14).

MEPHAATH [4789] (*splendor*). A Levitical city in Reuben (Jos 13:18; 21:37; 1Ch 6:79; Jer 48:21).

MEPHIBOSHETH [5136] (*from the mouth of shame* [a derogatory term for Baal]).

1. Son of Saul by Rizpah, whom David surrendered to the Gibeonites to be slain (2Sa 21:8-9).

2. Son of Jonathan (2Sa 4:4). Also called Merib-Baal (1Ch 8:34; 9:40). Was lame (2Sa 4:4). David entertains him at his table (2Sa 9:1-7; 21:7). Property restored to (2Sa 9:9-10). His ingratitude to David at the time of Absalom's usurpation (2Sa 16:1-4; 19:24-30). Property of, confiscated (2Sa 16:4; 19:29-30).

MERAB [5266] (*abundant*). Daughter of King Saul (1Sa 14:49). Betrothed to David by Saul (1Sa 18:17-18), but given to Adriel as his wife (1Sa 18:19).

MERAIAH [5316] (*loved by Yahweh*). A priest (Ne 12:12).

MERAIOTH [5318] (*rebellious*).

1. High priest (1Ch 6:6-7).

2. Priest; ancestor of Hilkiah (1Ch 9:11).

3. Another priestly ancestor of Helkai (Ne 12:15). May be same as "Meremoth" (Ne 12:3).

MERARI, MERARITE(S) [5356, 5357] (*bitter*). Youngest son of Levi; progenitor of Merarites (Nu 3:17,33-37; Jos 21:7,34-40).

MERATHAIM [5361] (*double rebellion*). Symbolic name for Babylon (Jer 50:21).

MERCENARIES [8502]. *See Soldiers.*

MERCHANDISE [4836, 5229, 6087, 6442, 8219, *5007*]. *See Commerce.*

MERCHANT [*2142, 4047, 4051, 6086, 8217, *1867*].
NIV+ MERCHANTS

(Ge 23:16; 37:28; 1Ki 10:15,28; 2Ch 9:14; Ne 3:32; 13:20; Job 41:6; SS 3:6; Isa 23:2; 47:15; Eze 17:4; 27:13,17,21-36; 38:13; Hos 12:7; Na 3:16; Mt 13:45; Rev 18:3,11,23). *See Commerce.*

MERCURIUS, MERCURY *See Hermes, 1.*

MERCY [2571, 2798, 2799, 2858, 2876, 8163, 8171, 9382, 9384, 10664, *447, 1796, 1799, 1799+5073, 2661, 3880, 3881*].
NIV+ MERCIFUL, MERCILESS, MERCILESSLY

Ps 85:10 Love and faithfulness meet together; righteousness and peace kiss each other.

Pr 20:28 Love and faithfulness keep a king safe; through love his throne is made secure.

Hos 4:1 Hear the word of the LORD, you Israelites, because the LORD has a charge to bring against you who live in the land: "There is no faithfulness, no love, no acknowledgment of God in the land.

Jas 2:13 because judgment without mercy will be shown to anyone who has not been merciful. Mercy triumphs over judgment!

A grace of the godly (Ps 37:25-26)—

Pr 11:17 A kind man benefits himself, but a cruel man brings trouble on himself.

Pr 12:10 A righteous man cares for the needs of his animal, but the kindest acts of the wicked are cruel.

Pr 14:22 Do not those who plot evil go astray? But those who plan what is good find love and faithfulness.

Pr 14:31 He who oppresses the poor shows contempt for their Maker, but whoever is kind to the needy honors God.

Ro 12:8 if it is encouraging, let him encourage; if it is contributing to the needs of others, let him give generously; if it is leadership, let him govern diligently; if it is showing mercy, let him do it cheerfully.

Of the wicked, cruel (Pr 12:10). Iniquity atoned by (Pr 16:6).

Commanded—

Pr 3:3 Let love and faithfulness never leave you; bind them around your neck, write them on the tablet of your heart.

Hos 12:6 But you must return to your God; maintain love and justice, and wait for your God always.

Mic 6:8 He has showed you, O man, what is good. And what does the LORD require of you? To act justly and to love mercy and to walk humbly with your God. (+Mt 9:13; 12:7)

Mt 23:23 "Woe to you, teachers of the law and Pharisees, you hypocrites! You give a tenth of your spices—mint, dill and cummin. But you have neglected the more important matters of the law—justice, mercy and faithfulness. You should have practiced the latter, without neglecting the former.

Lk 6:36 Be merciful, just as your Father is merciful.

Col 3:12 Therefore, as God's chosen people, holy and dearly loved, clothe yourselves with compassion, kindness, humility, gentleness and patience. [13]Bear with each other and forgive whatever grievances you may have against one another. Forgive as the Lord forgave you.

To be shown with cheerfulness (Ro 12:8).

Rewards of—

2Sa 22:26 "To the faithful you show yourself faithful, to the blameless you show yourself blameless,

Ps 18:25 To the faithful you show yourself faithful, to the blameless you show yourself blameless,

Ps 37:25 I was young and now I am old, yet I have never seen the righteous forsaken or their children begging bread. [26]They are always generous and lend freely; their children will be blessed.

Pr 14:21 He who despises his neighbor sins, but blessed is he who is kind to the needy.

Pr 21:21 He who pursues righteousness and love finds life, prosperity and honor.

Mt 5:7 Blessed are the merciful, for they will be shown mercy.

See God, Mercy of; Kindness.

Instances of:

The prison keeper, to Joseph (Ge 39:21-23). Joshua to Rahab (Jos 6:25). The Israelites to the man of Bethel (Jdg 1:23-26). David to Saul (1Sa 24:10-13,17).

MERCY SEAT *See Atonement Cover; Tabernacle.*

MERED [5279] (*rebel*).
NIV+ MERED'S

Son of Ezra (1Ch 4:17-18).

MEREMOTH [5329] (*elevations*).
NIV+ MEREMOTH'S

1. Priest who returned from the Exile (Ne 12:3).

2. Another priest who returned from the Exile (Ezr 8:33; Ne 3:4,21).

3. Man who divorced foreign wife (Ezr 10:36).

4. Priest who signed covenant with Nehemiah (Ne 10:5).

MERES [5332] (*worthy*). One of the princes of Persia (Est 1:14).

MERIBAH [5313] (*to strive, contend*).

NIV+ MERIBAH KADESH

1. Place NW of Sinai where God gave Israelites water from a rock (Ex 17:1-7).

2. Place near Kadesh Barnea where God also gave Israelites water from a rock. Because of Moses' loss of temper God did not permit him to enter the Promised Land (Nu 20:1-13). Also called Meribah Kadesh (Nu 27:14; Dt 32:51).

MERIBAH KADESH, MERIBAH-KADESH
[5315]. *See Meribah, 2.*

MERIB-BAAL [5311] (*Baal contends*). Son of Jonathan (1Ch 8:34; 9:40). *See Mephibosheth, 2.*

MERIT Personal. *See Grace.*

MERODACH *See Marduk.*

MERODACH-BALADAN, MERODACH BALADAN [5282] (*Marduk has given a son*). Twice king of Babylon (722-710; 703-702 B.C.), invited Hezekiah to join conspiracy against Assyria (2Ki 20:12-19; Isa 39:1-8).

MEROM [5295] (*high place*). Place near headwaters of Jordan river where Joshua defeated N coalition (Jos 11:5,7). Possibly identified with Tell el-Khirba.

MERON *See Shimron Meron.*

MERONOTH, MERONOTHITE [5331]. A place near Gibeon (Ne 3:7) and its inhabitants (1Ch 27:30).

MEROZ [5292]. A place N of Mount Tabor. Deborah and Barak curse the inhabitants of, in their song of triumph (Jdg 5:23).

MESECH *See Meshech.*

MESHA [4791, 4795, 4796, 5392].

1. Place in S Arabia (Ge 10:30).

2. Benjamite (1Ch 8:9).

3. Descendant of Judah (1Ch 2:42).

4. King of Moab in days of Ahab, Ahaziah, and Jehoram (2Ki 3:4).

MESHACH [4794, 10415] (perhaps *I have become weak*).

His Hebrew name was Mishael. He was taken as a captive to Babylon with Daniel, Hananiah, and Azariah, where each one was given a Babylonian name (Da 1:6-20; 2:17,49; 3:12-30). Mishael was given the Akkadian name Meshach.

Shadrach, Meshach, and Abednego were chosen to learn the language and the ways of the Babylonians so that they could enter the king's service (Da 1:3-5,17-20), c. 605 B.C. These three were eventually thrown into Nebuchadnezzar's furnace because they refused to bow down and worship the huge golden image that he had made (Da 3:1,4-6,8-30).

MESHECH [5434].

1. Son of Japheth (Ge 10:2; 1Ch 1:5).

2. Son of Shem (Ge 10:23; 1Ch 1:17).

3. A tribe (Ps 120:5; Eze 27:13; 32:26; 38:2-3); descendants of 1.

MESHELEMIAH [5452, 5453] (*Yahweh repays*). Father of Zechariah (1Ch 9:21; 26:1-2,9), "Shelemiah" (1Ch 26:14).

MESHEZABEL, MESHEZABEEL [5430] (*God [El] delivers*).

1. Ancestor of Meshullam (Ne 3:4).

2. Covenanter with Nehemiah (Ne 10:21).

3. Judahite (Ne 11:24).

MESHILLEMITH [5454] (*restitution*). A priest (1Ch 9:12).

MESHILLEMOTH [5451] (*restitution*).

1. Father of an Ephraimite who protested against the attempt of the Israelites to enslave their captive brothers (2Ch 28:12-13).

2. A priest (Ne 11:13).

MESHOBAB [5411]. A Simeonite (1Ch 4:34).

MESHULLAM [5450] (*restitution* KB).

1. Grandfather of Shaphan (2Ki 22:3).

2. Son of Zerubbabel (1Ch 3:19).

3. Leading Gadite (1Ch 5:13).

4. Chief Benjamite (1Ch 8:17).

5. Father of Sallu (1Ch 9:7).

6. Benjamite of Jerusalem (1Ch 9:8).

7. Priest (1Ch 9:11; Ne 11:11).

8. Ancestor of priest (1Ch 9:12).

9. Kohathite (2Ch 34:12).

10. Israelite who returned with Ezra (Ezr 8:16).

11. Man active in matter of putting away foreign wives (Ezr 10:15).

12. Divorced foreign wife (Ezr 10:29).

13. Son of Berekiah; helped rebuild Jerusalem wall (Ne 3:4,30; 6:18).

14. Another repairer of wall (Ne 3:6).

15. Helper of Ezra (Ne 8:4).

16. Priest (Ne 10:7).

17. Priest who sealed covenant (Ne 10:20).

18. Benjamite (Ne 11:7).

19. Priest (Ne 12:13).

20. Possibly the same man (Ne 12:33).

21. Another priest (Ne 12:16).

22. Levite (Ne 12:25).

MESHULLEMETH [5455] (*restitution*). Wife of Manasseh and mother of Amon (2Ki 21:19).

MESOBAITE *See Mezobaite.*

MESOPOTAMIA [3544] (*[land] between rivers*). The country between the Tigris and the Euphrates. Abraham a native of (Ac 7:2). Nahor lived in (Ge 24:10). People who lived in, called Syrians (Ge 25:20). Balaam from (Dt 23:4). The Israelites subjected to, eight years under the judgments of God (Jdg 3:8), delivered from, by Othniel (Jdg 3:9-10). Chariots hired from, by the Ammonites (1Ch 19:6-7). People of, present at Pentecost (Ac 2:9).

See Babylon; Chaldea.

MESS Any dish of food sent to the table (Ge 43:34; 2Sa 11:8; Heb 12:16).

MESSENGER [1413, 2296, 4637, 4855, 5583, 7495, 6269, 8078, 8938, 10541, *34*, *693*] (*send*).

NIV+ MESSAGE, MESSENGERS

Figurative:

(Hag 1:13; Mal 2:7; 3:1; 4:5-6; Mt 11:10; Mk 1:2; Lk 7:27). Of Satan (2Co 12:7).

MESSIAH [5431, *3549*] (*anointed*).

NIV+ CHRIST

The basic meaning of the Hebrew *mashiah* and the Greek *christos* is "anointed one." In the OT the word is used of prophets, priests, and kings who were consecrated to their office with oil. The expression "the Lord's anointed" and its equivalent is not used as a technical designation of the Messiah, but refers to the king of the line of David ruling in Jerusalem and anointed by the Lord through the priest. With the possible exception of Da 9:25-26, the title "Messiah" as a reference to Israel's eschatological king does not occur in the OT. It appears in this sense later in the NT, where he is almost always called "the Christ." The OT pictures the Messiah as one who will put an end to sin and war and usher in universal righteousness and through his death will make vicarious atonement for the salvation of sinful people. The NT concept of the Messiah is developed directly from the teaching of the OT. Jesus of Nazareth claimed to be the Messiah (Mt 23:63-64; Mk 14:61-62; Lk 22:67-70; Jn 4:25-26) and the claim was acknowledged by his disciples (Mt 16:16; Mk 8:29; Lk 9:20; Ac 4:27; 10:38).

See Jesus the Christ, Messiah.

MESSIANIC HOPE (Mt 13:17; Jn 8:56; Ac 9:22; Heb 11:13; 1Pe 1:10-12). Created by prophecy (Ge 49:10; Nu 24:17; 1Sa 1:10; 2Sa 7:12-13; Isa 9:6-7; 11:1-9; 33:17; 40:3-5; 55:3-5; 62:10-11; Jer 23:5-6; 33:15-17; Da 2:44; 7:13-14; 9:24-27; Mic 5:2; Zec 9:9; Mal 3:1-3; Ac 13:27), by the covenant with David to establish his throne forever (2Sa 7:12-16; 1Ch 17:11-14; 22:10; 28:7), by the messianic psalms (Pss 2; 16; 21; 22; 45; 72; 87; 89; 96; 110; 132:11,17-18). Confirmed in the vision of Mary (Lk 1:30-33).

Exemplified, by the priest Zechariah (Lk 1:68-79), by the prophet Simeon (Lk 2:25,29-32), by the prophetess Anna (Lk 2:36-38), by the wise men of the East (Mt 2:1-12), by John the Baptist (Mt 11:3), by the people (Jn 7:31,40-42; 12:34), by Caiaphas (Mt 26:63; Mk 14:61), by Joseph of Arimathea (Mk 15:43; Lk 23:51), by the disciples on the way to Emmaus (Lk 24:21), by Paul (Ac 26:6-7).

See Jesus the Christ, Prophecies Concerning.

MESSIAS *See Messiah.*

METAL [1031, 3133, 4607, 5011, 5816, 5822, 7110].

NIV+ METALS, METALWORKER

See Bronze; Copper; Gold; Iron; Lead; Silver; Tin.

METAPHOR A figure of speech that describes by comparison without using the word "like" or "as." Used extensively in the Song of Songs, for example "How beautiful you are, my darling! Oh, how beautiful! Your eyes are doves" (SS 1:15). Jesus spoke in metaphors (Mt 5:13-16). *See Parable.*

METEOROLOGY

Controlled by God—

Ge 2:5 and no shrub of the field had yet appeared on the earth and no plant of the field had yet sprung up, for the LORD God had not sent rain on the earth and there was no man to work the ground, **6**but streams came up from the earth and watered the whole surface of the ground—

Ge 27:39 His father Isaac answered him, "Your dwelling will be away from the earth's richness, away from the dew of heaven above.

Job 9:7 He speaks to the sun and it does not shine; he seals off the light of the stars.

Job 26:7 He spreads out the northern [skies] over empty space; he suspends the earth over nothing. **8**He wraps up the waters in his clouds, yet the clouds do not burst under their weight.

Job 26:11 The pillars of the heavens quake, aghast at his rebuke.

Ps 19:2 Day after day they pour forth speech; night after night they display knowledge. **3**There is no speech or language where their voice is not heard. **4**Their voice goes out into all the earth, their words to the ends of the world.

In the heavens he has pitched a tent for the sun, **5**which is like a bridegroom coming forth from his pavilion, like a champion rejoicing to run his course. **6**It rises at one end of the heavens and makes its circuit to the other; nothing is hidden from its heat.

Ps 104:2 He wraps himself in light as with a garment; he stretches out the heavens like a tent **3**and lays the beams of his upper chambers on their waters. He makes the clouds his chariot and rides on the wings of the wind.

Ps 104:7 But at your rebuke the waters fled, at the sound of your thunder they took to flight;

Ps 104:13 He waters the mountains from his upper chambers; the earth is satisfied by the fruit of his work. (+Ps 104:19)

Ps 104:20 You bring darkness, it becomes night, and all the beasts of the forest prowl. (+Ps 107:25)

Ecc 11:3 If clouds are full of water, they pour rain upon the earth. Whether a tree falls to the south or to the north, in the place where it falls, there will it lie.

Isa 13:13 Therefore I will make the heavens tremble; and the earth will shake from its place at the wrath of the LORD Almighty, in the day of his burning anger.

Isa 24:18 Whoever flees at the sound of terror will fall into a pit; whoever climbs out of the pit will be caught in a snare. The floodgates of the heavens are opened, the foundations of the earth shake.

Isa 50:3 I clothe the sky with darkness and make sackcloth its covering."

Jer 4:11 At that time this people and Jerusalem will be told, "A scorching wind from the barren heights in the desert blows toward my people, but not to winnow or cleanse; **12**a wind too strong for that comes from me. Now I pronounce my judgments against them."

Jer 10:13 When he thunders, the waters in the heavens roar; he makes clouds rise from the ends of the earth. He sends lightning with the rain and brings out the wind from his storehouses.

Jer 51:16 When he thunders, the waters in the heavens roar; he makes clouds rise from the ends of the earth. He sends lightning with the rain and brings out the wind from his storehouses.

Da 2:21 He changes times and seasons; he sets up kings and deposes them. He gives wisdom to the wise and knowledge to the discerning.

Hos 8:7 "They sow the wind and reap the whirlwind. The stalk has no head; it will produce no flour. Were it to yield grain, foreigners would swallow it up.

Joel 2:30 I will show wonders in the heavens and on the

earth, blood and fire and billows of smoke. [31]The sun will be turned to darkness and the moon to blood before the coming of the great and dreadful day of the LORD.

Am 9:6 he who builds his lofty palace in the heavens and sets its foundation on the earth, who calls for the waters of the sea and pours them out over the face of the land—the LORD is his name.

Na 1:3 The LORD is slow to anger and great in power; the LORD will not leave the guilty unpunished. His way is in the whirlwind and the storm, and clouds are the dust of his feet.

Mt 24:27 For as lightning that comes from the east is visible even in the west, so will be the coming of the Son of Man.

Mt 24:29 "Immediately after the distress of those days "'the sun will be darkened, and the moon will not give its light; the stars will fall from the sky, and the heavenly bodies will be shaken.'

Lk 21:25 "There will be signs in the sun, moon and stars. On the earth, nations will be in anguish and perplexity at the roaring and tossing of the sea.

Jn 3:8 The wind blows wherever it pleases. You hear its sound, but you cannot tell where it comes from or where it is going. So it is with everyone born of the Spirit."

Ac 2:19 I will show wonders in the heaven above and signs on the earth below, blood and fire and billows of smoke. [20]The sun will be turned to darkness and the moon to blood before the coming of the great and glorious day of the Lord.

2Pe 2:17 These men are springs without water and mists driven by a storm. Blackest darkness is reserved for them.

Jude 12 These men are blemishes at your love feasts, eating with you without the slightest qualm—shepherds who feed only themselves. They are clouds without rain, blown along by the wind; autumn trees, without fruit and uprooted—twice dead.

Tempest stilled by Jesus—

Mt 8:24 Without warning, a furious storm came up on the lake, so that the waves swept over the boat. But Jesus was sleeping. [25]The disciples went and woke him, saying, "Lord, save us! We're going to drown!"

[26]He replied, "You of little faith, why are you so afraid?" Then he got up and rebuked the winds and the waves, and it was completely calm.

[27]The men were amazed and asked, "What kind of man is this? Even the winds and the waves obey him!" (+Lk 8:22-25)

Weather, affected by godly prayers (1Sa 12:16-18; 1Ki 18:41-45)—

Isa 5:5 Now I will tell you what I am going to do to my vineyard: I will take away its hedge, and it will be destroyed; I will break down its wall, and it will be trampled. [6]I will make it a wasteland, neither pruned nor cultivated, and briers and thorns will grow there. I will command the clouds not to rain on it."

Jas 5:17 Elijah was a man just like us. He prayed earnestly that it would not rain, and it did not rain on the land for three and a half years. [18]Again he prayed, and the heavens gave rain, and the earth produced its crops.

Forecast of weather—

Mt 16:2 He replied, "When evening comes, you say, 'It will be fair weather, for the sky is red,' [3]and in the morning, 'Today it will be stormy, for the sky is red and overcast.' You know how to interpret the appearance of the sky, but you cannot interpret the signs of the times.

Lk 12:54 He said to the crowd: "When you see a cloud rising in the west, immediately you say, 'It's going to rain,' and it does. [55]And when the south wind blows, you say, 'It's going to be hot,' and it is. [56]Hypocrites! You know how to interpret the appearance of the earth and the sky. How is it that you don't know how to interpret this present time?

Weather in the land of Uz—

Job 27:20 Terrors overtake him like a flood; a tempest snatches him away in the night. [21]The east wind carries him off, and he is gone; it sweeps him out of his place.

Job 28:24 for he views the ends of the earth and sees everything under the heavens. [25]When he established the force of the wind and measured out the waters, [26]when he made a decree for the rain and a path for the thunderstorm, [27]then he looked at wisdom and appraised it; he confirmed it and tested it.

Job 29:19 My roots will reach to the water, and the dew will lie all night on my branches.

Job 36:27 "He draws up the drops of water, which distill as rain to the streams; [28]the clouds pour down their moisture and abundant showers fall on mankind. [29]Who can understand how he spreads out the clouds, how he thunders from his pavilion? [30]See how he scatters his lightning about him, bathing the depths of the sea. [31]This is the way he governs the nations and provides food in abundance. [32]He fills his hands with lightning and commands it to strike its mark. [33]His thunder announces the coming storm; even the cattle make known its approach.

Job 37:6 He says to the snow, 'Fall on the earth,' and to the rain shower, 'Be a mighty downpour.' [7]So that all men he has made may know his work, he stops every man from his labor. [8]The animals take cover; they remain in their dens. [9]The tempest comes out from its chamber, the cold from the driving winds. [10]The breath of God produces ice, and the broad waters become frozen. [11]He loads the clouds with moisture; he scatters his lightning through them. [12]At his direction they swirl around over the face of the whole earth to do whatever he commands them. [13]He brings the clouds to punish men, or to water his earth and show his love.

[14]"Listen to this, Job; stop and consider God's wonders. [15]Do you know how God controls the clouds and makes his lightning flash? [16]Do you know how the clouds hang poised, those wonders of him who is perfect in knowledge? [17]You who swelter in your clothes when the land lies hushed under the south wind, [18]can you join him in spreading out the skies, hard as a mirror of cast bronze?

[19]"Tell us what we should say to him; we cannot draw up our case because of our darkness. [20]Should he be told that I want to speak? Would any man ask to be swallowed up? [21]Now no one can look at the sun, bright as it is in the skies after the wind has swept them clean. [22]Out of the north he comes in golden splendor; God comes in awesome majesty. (+Job 38:8)

Job 38:9 when I made the clouds its garment and wrapped it in thick darkness, (+Job 38:10-11)

Job 38:22 "Have you entered the storehouses of the snow or seen the storehouses of the hail,

Job 38:24 What is the way to the place where the lightning is dispersed, or the place where the east winds are scattered over the earth? [25]Who cuts a channel for the torrents of rain, and a path for the thunderstorm, [26]to water a land where no man lives, a desert with no one in it, [27]to satisfy a desolate wasteland and make it sprout with grass? [28]Does the rain have a father? Who fathers the drops of dew?

²⁹From whose womb comes the ice? Who gives birth to the frost from the heavens (+Job 38:30)

Job 38:31 "Can you bind the beautiful Pleiades? Can you loose the cords of Orion? ³²Can you bring forth the constellations in their seasons or lead out the Bear with its cubs? ³³Do you know the laws of the heavens? Can you set up [God's] dominion over the earth?

³⁴"Can you raise your voice to the clouds and cover yourself with a flood of water? ³⁵Do you send the lightning bolts on their way? Do they report to you, 'Here we are'? (+Job 38:36)

Job 38:37 Who has the wisdom to count the clouds? Who can tip over the water jars of the heavens

Weather in Israel—

Ps 18:10 He mounted the cherubim and flew; he soared on the wings of the wind. ¹¹He made darkness his covering, his canopy around him—the dark rain clouds of the sky. ¹²Out of the brightness of his presence clouds advanced, with hailstones and bolts of lightning. ¹³The LORD thundered from heaven; the voice of the Most High resounded. ¹⁴He shot his arrows and scattered [the enemies], great bolts of lightning and routed them. ¹⁵The valleys of the sea were exposed and the foundations of the earth laid bare at your rebuke, O LORD, at the blast of breath from your nostrils.

Ps 29:3 The voice of the LORD is over the waters; the God of glory thunders, the LORD thunders over the mighty waters. ⁴The voice of the LORD is powerful; the voice of the LORD is majestic. ⁵The voice of the LORD breaks the cedars; the LORD breaks in pieces the cedars of Lebanon. ⁶He makes Lebanon skip like a calf, Sirion like a young wild ox. ⁷The voice of the LORD strikes with flashes of lightning. ⁸The voice of the LORD shakes the desert; the LORD shakes the Desert of Kadesh. ⁹The voice of the LORD twists the oaks and strips the forests bare. And in his temple all cry, "Glory!" ¹⁰The LORD sits enthroned over the flood; the LORD is enthroned as King forever. (+Ps 48:7)

Ps 65:8 Those living far away fear your wonders; where morning dawns and evening fades you call forth songs of joy.

⁹You care for the land and water it; you enrich it abundantly. The streams of God are filled with water to provide the people with grain, for so you have ordained it. ¹⁰You drench its furrows and level its ridges; you soften it with showers and bless its crops. ¹¹You crown the year with your bounty, and your carts overflow with abundance. ¹²The grasslands of the desert overflow; the hills are clothed with gladness. (+Ps 133:3; 135:6-7)

Ps 147:7 Sing to the LORD with thanksgiving; make music to our God on the harp. ⁸He covers the sky with clouds; he supplies the earth with rain and makes grass grow on the hills.

Ps 148:7 Praise the LORD from the earth, you great sea creatures and all ocean depths, ⁸lightning and hail, snow and clouds, stormy winds that do his bidding,

Pr 25:23 As a north wind brings rain, so a sly tongue brings angry looks.

Pr 26:1 Like snow in summer or rain in harvest, honor is not fitting for a fool. (+Pr 30:4)

Ecc 1:6 The wind blows to the south and turns to the north; round and round it goes, ever returning on its course. ⁷All streams flow into the sea, yet the sea is never full. To the place the streams come from, there they return again.

Hos 6:4 "What can I do with you, Ephraim? What can I do with you, Judah? Your love is like the morning mist, like the early dew that disappears.

Hos 13:15 even though he thrives among his brothers. An east wind from the LORD will come, blowing in from the desert; his spring will fail and his well dry up. His storehouse will be plundered of all its treasures.

The autumnal storms of the Mediterranean (Ac 27:9-20,27).

Phenomena of:

The deluge (Ge 7:8). Fire from heaven on the cities of the plain (Ge 19:24-25). Plagues of hail, thunder, and lightning in Egypt (Ex 9:22-29; Ps 78:17-23), of darkness (Ex 10:22-23). East wind that divided the Red Sea (Ex 14:21), that brought the quails (Nu 11:31-32; Ps 78:26-28). Pillar of cloud and fire. *See Pillar.* Sun stood still (Jos 10:12-13). Dew on Gideon's fleece (Jdg 6:36-40). Stars in their courses fought against Sisera (Jdg 5:20). Stones from heaven (Jos 10:11). Fire from heaven at Elijah's command (2Ki 1:10-14). The whirlwind which carried Elijah to heaven (2Ki 2:1,11).

Wind under God's control (Ps 107:25). East wind (Ps 48:7). Rain, formation of (Ps 135:6-7). Dew, copious (Ps 133:3). Rain in answer to Samuel's prayer (1Sa 12:16-18), Elijah's prayer (1Ki 18:41-45). Rain discomfits the Philistine army (1Sa 7:10). Wind destroyed Job's children (Job 1:18-19).

Darkness at the Crucifixion—

Mt 27:45 From the sixth hour until the ninth hour darkness came over all the land. (+Lk 23:44-45)

See Astronomy; Celestial Phenomena; Dew; Hail; Rain; Weather.

Symbolic:

Used in the Revelation of John—

Rev 6:12 I watched as he opened the sixth seal. There was a great earthquake. The sun turned black like sackcloth made of goat hair, the whole moon turned blood red, ¹³and the stars in the sky fell to earth, as late figs drop from a fig tree when shaken by a strong wind. ¹⁴The sky receded like a scroll, rolling up, and every mountain and island was removed from its place.

Rev 7:1 After this I saw four angels standing at the four corners of the earth, holding back the four winds of the earth to prevent any wind from blowing on the land or on the sea or on any tree. (+Rev 8:3-4)

Rev 8:5 Then the angel took the censer, filled it with fire from the altar, and hurled it on the earth; and there came peals of thunder, rumblings, flashes of lightning and an earthquake. (+Rev 8:6)

Rev 8:7 The first angel sounded his trumpet, and there came hail and fire mixed with blood, and it was hurled down upon the earth. A third of the earth was burned up, a third of the trees were burned up, and all the green grass was burned up. (+Rev 8:8-9)

Rev 8:10 The third angel sounded his trumpet, and a great star, blazing like a torch, fell from the sky on a third of the rivers and on the springs of water— (+Rev 8:11)

Rev 8:12 The fourth angel sounded his trumpet, and a third of the sun was struck, a third of the moon, and a third of the stars, so that a third of them turned dark. A third of the day was without light, and also a third of the night.

Rev 9:1 The fifth angel sounded his trumpet, and I saw a star that had fallen from the sky to the earth. The star was given the key to the shaft of the Abyss. ²When he opened the Abyss, smoke rose from it like the smoke from a gigantic furnace. The sun and sky were darkened by the smoke from the Abyss. (+Rev 9:17-19; 10:1-6)

Rev 11:6 These men have power to shut up the sky so that it will not rain during the time they are prophesying; and they have power to turn the waters into blood and to strike the earth with every kind of plague as often as they want. (+Rev 12:1-4,7-9; 14; 15:1-4; 16:8,17-20)

Rev 16:21 From the sky huge hailstones of about a hundred pounds each fell upon men. And they cursed God on account of the plague of hail, because the plague was so terrible. (+Rev 19:11-18; 20:11; 21:1)

METEYARD Archaic word for "measures of length" (Lev 19:35).

METHEG AMMAH, METHEG-AMMAH [5497] *(the bridle of the metropolis)*. A town David took from the Philistines (2Sa 8:1).

METHUSAEL *See Methushael.*

METHUSELAH [5500, *3417*] *(man of the javelin)*. Son of Enoch and grandfather of Noah (Ge 5:21-27; 1Ch 1:3).

METHUSHAEL [5499] (questionable, but perhaps *man of God*). Father of Lamech (Ge 4:18).

MEUNIM, MEUNITES [5064] *(the people of Maon)*.
1. People conquered by the Simeonites (1Ch 4:41); fought against Jehoshaphat (2Ch 20:1) and Uzziah (2Ch 26:7).
2. Counted among the temple servants (Ezr 2:50; Ne 7:52). May be the descendants of 1.
See Maonites.

ME-ZAHAB, MEZAHAB [4771] *(waters of gold)*. Grandfather of Mehetabel (Ge 36:39; 1Ch 1:50).

MEZOBAITE [5168]. Name of place otherwise unknown (1Ch 11:47).

MIAMIN *See Mijamin.*

MIBHAR [4437] *(choice)*. One of David's valiant men (1Ch 11:38).

MIBSAM [4452] *(sweet odor)*.
1. Son of Ishmael (Ge 25:13; 1Ch 1:29).
2. Son of Shallum (1Ch 4:25).

MIBZAR [4449] *(bastion)*. Chief of Edom (Ge 36:42; 1Ch 1:53).

MICA, MICHA [4775, 4777] *(who is like Yahweh?)*.
1. Grandson of Jonathan (2Sa 9:12). *See Micah, 3.*
2. A Levite; descendant of Asaph (1Ch 9:15; Ne 11:17,22).
3. A Levite covenanter (Ne 10:11), possibly the same as 2.

MICAH [4777, 4781] *(who is like Yahweh?)*.
NIV+ MICAH'S
1. Ephraimite whose mother made an image for which he secured a priest; both image and priest were later stolen by the tribe of Dan (Jdg 17-18).
2. Reubenite (1Ch 5:5).
3. Grandson of Jonathan (1Ch 8:34; 9:40). *See Mica, 1.*
4. Levite (1Ch 23:20).
5. Father of Abdon, one of Josiah's officers (2Ch 34:20). *See Micaiah, 2.*
6. Prophet Micah, the Moreshethite; prophesied in the

reigns of Jotham, Ahaz, and Hezekiah (Mic 1:1; Jer 26:18).

MICAH, BOOK OF
Author: The prophet Micah of Moresheth
Date: Sometime between 750 and 686 B.C.
Outline:
I. Superscription (1:1).
II. Judgment against Israel and Judah (1:2-3:12).
  A. Introduction (1:2).
  B. The Predicted Destruction (1:3-7).
  C. Lamentation for the Destruction (1:8-16).
  D. Corruption in Micah's Society (2:1-11).
  E. Hope in the Midst of Gloom (2:12-13).
  F. The Leaders Condemned (ch. 3).
III. Hope for Israel and Judah (chs. 4-5).
  A. The Coming Kingdom (ch. 4).
  B. The Coming King (5:1-5a).
  C. Victory for the People of God (5:5b-15).
IV. The Lord's Case against Israel (ch. 6).
  A. The Lord's Accusation (6:1-8).
  B. The Coming Judgment (6:9-16).
V. Gloom Turns to Triumph (ch. 7).
  A. Micah Laments the Corruption of His Society (7:1-6).
  B. Micah's Assurance of Hope (7:7).
  C. A Bright Future for God's People (7:8-13).
  D. Victory for God's Kingdom (7:14-20).
  See Prophets, The Minor.

MICAIAH, MICHAIAH [4777, 4779, 4780, 4781] *(who is like Yahweh?)*.
1. A prophet living in Samaria who predicted the death of King Ahab (1Ki 22; 2Ch 18).
2. Father of Acbor, one of Josiah's officers (2Ki 22:12-14). *See Micah, 5.*
3. Daughter of Uriel of Gibeah (2Ch 13:2).
4. Offical of Jehoshaphat; a teacher (2Ch 17:7).
5. Ancestor of priest in Nehemiah's time (Ne 12:35).
6. Priest (Ne 12:41).
7. Grandson of Shaphan the secretary (Jer 36:11-13).
8. *See Maacah, 4.*

MICE *See Rat(s).*

MICHA *See Mica, Micha.*

MICHAEL [4776, *3640*] *(who is like God [El]?)*.
1. An Asherite (Nu 13:13).
2. Two Gadites (1Ch 5:13-14).
3. A Gershonite Levite (1Ch 6:40).
4. A descendant of Issachar (1Ch 7:3).
5. A Benjamite (1Ch 8:16).
6. A captain of the thousands of Manasseh who joined David at Ziklag (1Ch 12:20).
7. Father of Omri (1Ch 27:18).
8. Son of Jehoshaphat. Slain by his brother, Jehoram (2Ch 21:2-4).
9. Father of Zebadiah (Ezr 8:8).
10. The archangel. His message to Daniel (Da 10:13,21; 12:1). Contention with the devil (Jude 9). Fights with the dragon (Rev 12:7).

MICHAH *See Micah.*

MICHAIAH *See Micaiah, Michaiah.*

MICHAL [4783] *(who is like God [El]?)*. Daughter of Saul. Given to David as a reward for slaying Goliath (1Sa

18:22-28). Rescues David from death (1Sa 19:9-17). Saul forcibly separates them, and she is given in marriage to Paltiel (1Sa 25:44). David recovers her to himself (2Sa 3:13-16). Ridicules David on account of his religious zeal (2Sa 6:16,20-23).

MICHMAS, MICHMASH *See Micmash.*

MICHRI *See Micri, Michri.*

MICHTAM *See Miktam.*

MICMASH [4820, 4825] (perhaps *hidden place*). A place in Benjamin c. eight miles NE of Jerusalem; Jonathan led Israelites to victory over Philistines there (1Sa 14:31; Ne 11:31).

MICMETHATH, MICHMETHAH [4826] A city between Ephraim and Manasseh (Jos 16:6; 17:7).

MICRI, MICHRI [4840]. A Benjamite (1Ch 9:8).

MIDDIN [4516]. A city in Judah in the wilderness just W of the Dead Sea (Jos 15:61).

MIDDLE WALL *See Dividing Wall.*

MIDIAN [824+4518, 4518, *1178+3409*].
NIV+ MIDIAN'S, MIDIANITE, MIDIANITES

A son of Abraham by Keturah (Ge 25:2,4; 1Ch 1:32-33).

MIDIANITE(S) [4518, 4520].
NIV+ MIDIAN

Descendants of Midian, son of Abraham by Keturah (Ge 25:1-2,4; 1Ch 1:32-33). Called Ishmaelites (Ge 37:25,28; Jdg 8:24). Were merchants (Ge 37:28). Buy Joseph and sell him to Potiphar (Ge 37:28,36). Defeated by the Israelites under Phinehas; five of their kings slain, the women taken captives, their cities burned, and rich spoils taken (Nu 31). Defeated by Gideon (Jdg 6-8). Owned multitudes of camels and large quantities of gold (Isa 60:6). A snare to the Israelites (Nu 25:16-18). Prophecies concerning (Isa 60:6; Hab 3:7).

MIDNIGHT [2021+2942+4326, 2940+4326, *3543, 3545+3816*].
NIV+ See NIGHT

Scenes at (Ex 11:4; Mt 25:6; Ac 16:25; 20:7).

MIDWIVES [3528].
NIV+ MIDWIFE

Assist in childbirth (Ge 35:17; 38:28). Save Israelite boys in Egypt (Ex 1:15-21).

MIGDAL EDER [4468]. *See Eder, 1.*

MIGDAL EL, MIGDAL-EL [4466] (*tower of God [El]*). A city of Naphtali (Jos 19:38).

MIGDAL GAD, MIGDAL-GAD [4467] (*tower of Gad*).
NIV+ GAD

A city of Judah (Jos 15:37).

MIGDOL [4465] (*tower*).
1. A place near the Red Sea where the Israelites encamped (Ex 14:2; Nu 33:7-8).
2. A city on the NE border of lower Egypt (Jer 44:1; 46:14).

MIGRON [4491] (*precipice*). A city in Benjamin. Saul encamps near, under a pomegranate tree (1Sa 14:2). Prophesy concerning (Isa 10:28).

MIJAMIN [4785] (*from the right hand*).
1. Priest in David's time (1Ch 24:9).
2. A man who divorced his foreign wife (Ezr 10:25).
3. Covenanter priest (Ne 10:7).
4. Priest who returned from the Exile (Ne 12:5).

MIKLOTH [5235] (*rods*).
1. A Benjamite of Jerusalem (1Ch 8:32; 9:37-38).
2. A ruler in the reign of David (1Ch 27:4).

MIKNEIAH [5240] (*Yahweh acquires*). A doorkeeper of the temple and musician (1Ch 15:18,21).

MIKTAM [4846]. The term always stands in the superscription of Davidic prayers occasioned by great danger (Ps 16,56-60). Variously related to words for "golden," "inscription," and "atonement."
See Music, Symbols Used in.

MILALAI [4912]. A priest who took part in the dedication of the walls of Jerusalem (Ne 12:36).

MILCAH [4894] (*queen*).
1. Wife of Nahor and mother of Bethuel (Ge 11:29; 22:20-23; 24:15,24,47).
2. Daughter of Zelophehad. Special legislation in regard to the inheritance of (Nu 26:33; 27:1-7; 36:1-12; Jos 17:3-4).

MILCOM *See Molech.*

MILDEW [3766, 5596, 7076, 7669] (*yellow, pale*). Fungus growth destructive of grains and fruits (Dt 28:22; 1Ki 8:37; Am 4:9; Hag 2:17).

MILE [*3627, 5084*].
NIV+ MILES

Equal to about 3,500 cubits or 8.6 stadia (Eze 45:3; Mt 5:41; Lk 24:13).

MILETUS [*3626*]. A seaport in Asia Minor. Paul visits (Ac 20:15), and sends to Ephesus for the elders of the church, and addresses them here (Ac 20:17-38). Trophimus left sick at (2Ti 4:20).

MILITARY INSTRUCTION Of children (2Sa 1:18).
See Armies.

MILK [2692, 2772, *1128*]. Used for food (Ge 18:8; Jdg 4:19; SS 5:1; Eze 25:4; 1Co 9:7). Of goats (Pr 27:27), sheep (Dt 32:14; Isa 7:21-22), camels (Ge 32:15), cows (Dt 32:14; 1Sa 6:7,10). Churned (Pr 30:33). Kid not to be cooked in its mother's milk (Ex 23:19; Dt 14:21).
Figurative:
(Ex 3:8,17; 13:5; 33:3; Nu 13:27; Dt 26:9,15; Isa 55:1; 60:16; Jer 11:5; 32:22; Eze 20:6; Joel 3:18; 1Co 3:2; Heb 5:12-13; 1Pe 2:2).

MILL [1003, 8160, *3685*].
NIV+ HANDMILL

(Jer 25:10). Upper and lower stones of (Dt 24:6; Job 41:24; Isa 47:2). Used in Egypt (Ex 11:5). Operated by women (Mt 24:41), and captives (Jdg 16:21; La 5:13). Manna ground in (Nu 11:8). Sound of, to cease (Rev 18:22). *See Grind; Millstone.*

MILLENNIUM The Latin for a thousand years.

It comes from—

Rev 20:1 And I saw an angel coming down out of heaven, having the key to the Abyss and holding in his hand a great chain. ²He seized the dragon, that ancient serpent, who is the devil, or Satan, and bound him for a thousand years. ³He threw him into the Abyss, and locked and sealed it over him, to keep him from deceiving the nations anymore until the thousand years were ended. After that, he must be set free for a short time.

⁴I saw thrones on which were seated those who had been given authority to judge. And I saw the souls of those who had been beheaded because of their testimony for Jesus and because of the word of God. They had not worshiped the beast or his image and had not received his mark on their foreheads or their hands. They came to life and reigned with Christ a thousand years. ⁵(The rest of the dead did not come to life until the thousand years were ended.) This is the first resurrection. ⁶Blessed and holy are those who have part in the first resurrection. The second death has no power over them, but they will be priests of God and of Christ and will reign with him for a thousand years. (+Rev 20:7-15)

It refers to a period when Christ rules and Satan is bound; when Jesus shall have triumphed over all forms of evil (1Co 15:24-28; 2Th 2:8; Rev 14:6-18; 19:11-16). At the restoration of all things (Ac 3:21). When the creation shall be delivered from the corruption of evil (Ro 8:19-21). When the Son of Man shall sit on the throne of his glory (Mt 19:28; Lk 22:28-30), and the righteous shall be clothed with authority (Da 7:22; Mt 19:28; Lk 22:28-30; 1Co 6:2; Rev 2:5), and possess the kingdom (Mt 25:34; Lk 12:32; 22:29). *Amillenialists* believe Jesus is reigning now. *Premillenialists* believe Jesus will literally reign on earth for a thousand years after his second coming. *Postmillenialists* believe the Church will Christianize the world for a long period of time after which Christ will return.

Christ rules from his throne in Zion or Jerusalem—

Isa 65:17 "Behold, I will create new heavens and a new earth. The former things will not be remembered, nor will they come to mind. ¹⁸But be glad and rejoice forever in what I will create, for I will create Jerusalem to be a delight and its people a joy. ¹⁹I will rejoice over Jerusalem and take delight in my people; the sound of weeping and of crying will be heard in it no more.

²⁰"Never again will there be in it an infant who lives but a few days, or an old man who does not live out his years; he who dies at a hundred will be thought a mere youth; he who fails to reach a hundred will be considered accursed. ²¹They will build houses and dwell in them; they will plant vineyards and eat their fruit. ²²No longer will they build houses and others live in them, or plant and others eat. For as the days of a tree, so will be the days of my people; my chosen ones will long enjoy the works of their hands. ²³They will not toil in vain or bear children doomed to misfortune; for they will be a people blessed by the LORD, they and their descendants with them. ²⁴Before they call I will answer; while they are still speaking I will hear. ²⁵The wolf and the lamb will feed together, and the lion will eat straw like the ox, but dust will be the serpent's food. They will neither harm nor destroy on all my holy mountain," says the LORD.

Zep 3:11 On that day you will not be put to shame for all the wrongs you have done to me, because I will remove from this city those who rejoice in their pride. Never again will you be haughty on my holy hill. ¹²But I will leave

within you the meek and humble, who trust in the name of the LORD. ¹³The remnant of Israel will do no wrong; they will speak no lies, nor will deceit be found in their mouths. They will eat and lie down and no one will make them afraid."

Zec 9:9 Rejoice greatly, O Daughter of Zion! Shout, Daughter of Jerusalem! See, your king comes to you, righteous and having salvation, gentle and riding on a donkey, on a colt, the foal of a donkey. ¹⁰I will take away the chariots from Ephraim and the war-horses from Jerusalem, and the battle bow will be broken. He will proclaim peace to the nations. His rule will extend from sea to sea and from the River to the ends of the earth.

Zec 14:16 Then the survivors from all the nations that have attacked Jerusalem will go up year after year to worship the King, the LORD Almighty, and to celebrate the Feast of Tabernacles. ¹⁷If any of the peoples of the earth do not go up to Jerusalem to worship the King, the LORD Almighty, they will have no rain. ¹⁸If the Egyptian people do not go up and take part, they will have no rain. The LORD will bring on them the plague he inflicts on the nations that do not go up to celebrate the Feast of Tabernacles. ¹⁹This will be the punishment of Egypt and the punishment of all the nations that do not go up to celebrate the Feast of Tabernacles.

²⁰On that day HOLY TO THE LORD will be inscribed on the bells of the horses, and the cooking pots in the LORD's house will be like the sacred bowls in front of the altar. ²¹Every pot in Jerusalem and Judah will be holy to the LORD Almighty, and all who come to sacrifice will take some of the pots and cook in them. And on that day there will no longer be a Canaanite in the house of the LORD Almighty.

Christ fulfills the promise of the kingdom of God on earth—

Mt 16:18 And I tell you that you are Peter, and on this rock I will build my church, and the gates of Hades will not overcome it. ¹⁹I will give you the keys of the kingdom of heaven; whatever you bind on earth will be bound in heaven, and whatever you loose on earth will be loosed in heaven."

Mt 26:29 I tell you, I will not drink of this fruit of the vine from now on until that day when I drink it anew with you in my Father's kingdom." (+Mk 14:25)

Heb 8:11 No longer will a man teach his neighbor, or a man his brother, saying, 'Know the Lord,' because they will all know me, from the least of them to the greatest.

See Church, The Body of Believers, Prophecies Concerning; Jesus the Christ, Kingdom of; Second Coming of.

MILLET [1893]. (Eze 4:9).

MILLO *See Beth Millo.*

MILLSTONE [3218, 7115, 8160, *3684+, 3685+*].
NIV+ MILLSTONES, STONE

Not to be taken in pledge (Dt 24:6). Probably used in executions by drowning (Mt 18:6; Mk 9:42; Lk 17:2). Abimelech killed by one being hurled upon him (Jdg 9:53). Figurative of the hard heart (Job 41:24). *See Grind; Mill.*

MINA, MINAS [4949, *3641*]. In the sexagesimal system (based on the number 60) that originated in Mesopotamia, there were 60 shekels in a mina and 60 minas in a talent. A shekel, which was about two-fifths of an ounce of silver, was the average wage for a month's work. Thus a mina would be the equivalent of five years' wages, and a talent would be 300 years' wages (1Ki 10:17, ftn, w 2Ch 9:16, ftn; Ezr 2:69; Ne 7:71-72, ftn). *See Measure.*

MINCING [2143+2256+3262] (*to go like a little child, i.e., to trip along*). To speak, walk, or behave in an affectedly elegant, dainty, or nice manner. Used of the haughty women of Zion (Isa 3:16).

MIND [*2349, 4000, 4213, 4222, 5714, 5883, 8120, 10381, 10646, 1379, 2014, 2840, 3212, 3419, 3564, 3784, 3808, 5404, 5858, 5859, 6034].

NIV+ DOUBLE-MINDED, LIKE-MINDED, MINDED, MINDFUL, MINDS

In Scripture it often means "heart" or "soul." In the NT it is often used in an ethical sense (Ro 7:25; Col 2:18).

MINERALS OF THE BIBLE The science of mineralogy is a recent one, and did not exist in ancient times. It is often impossible to be certain that when a mineral name is used in the Bible, it is used with the same meaning as that attached in modern mineralogy.

The following minerals are mentioned in the Bible:

1. Precious stones: Agate (Ex 28:19; 39:12), amethyst (Ex 28:19; 39:12; Rev 21:20), aromatic resin or resin (Ge 2:12; Nu 11:7), beryl (Ex 28:17; 39:10; Eze 28:13; Rev 21:20), carnelian (Rev 4:3; 21:20), chalcedony (Rev 21:19), chrysolite (Da 10:6; Rev 21:20), chrysoprase (Rev 21:20), coral (Job 28:18; Eze 27:16), crystal (Job 28:17; Rev 4:6; 21:11; 22:1), emerald (Ex 28:18; 39:11), glowing metal (Eze 1:4,27; 8:2; Rev 1:15), hardest stone (Eze 3:9; Zec 7:12), jacinth (Ex 28:19; 39:12; Rev 9:17), jasper (Ex 28:20; 39:13; Job 28:18; Eze 28:13; Rev 4:3; 21:11,18,19), onyx (Ge 2:12; Ex 25:7; 28:9,20; 35:9,27; 39:6,13; 1Ch 29:2; Job 28:16; Eze 28:13), pearl (Rev 21:21), ruby (Ex 28:17; 39:10; Job 28:18; Eze 28:13,16), sapphire (Ex 24:10; 28:18; 39:11; Eze 1:26; 10:1; 28:13; Rev 21:19), sardonyx (Rev 21:20), sparkling jewels (Isa 54:12), topaz (Ex 28:17; 39:10; Job 28:19; Eze 28:13; Rev 21:20), turquoise (Ex 28:18; Eze 27:16).

2. Metals: Gold (Ge 2:11-12), silver (Mt 10:9), iron (Nu 31:22), bronze (Ge 4:22; Ezr 8:27), lead (Ex 15:10), tin (Nu 31:22), glowing metal (Eze 1:4,27; 8:2), dross (Ps 119:119; Pr 25:4; Isa 1:22,25; Eze 22:18-19).

3. The common minerals: Alabaster (Mt 26:7; Mk 14:3; Lk 7:37), flint (Isa 5:28; 50:7; Jer 17:1; Eze 3:9; Zec 7:12), marble (1Ch 29:2; Est 1:6; SS 5:15; Rev 18:12), soda (Pr 25:20; Jer 2:22), sulfur (Ge 19:24; Dt 29:23; Job 18:15; Ps 11:6; Isa 30:33; 34:9; Eze 38:22; Lk 17:29; Rev 9:17-18; 14:10; 19:20; 20:10; 21:8), water.

See Stones.

MINES, MINING [4604].

NIV+ MINE

An ancient occupation; described in (Job 28:1-11; Dt 8:9; 1Ki 7:13-50).

MINGLED PEOPLE Non-Israelite people who left Egypt with the Israelites (Ex 12:38). The term is also used for the mixed blood of certain of Israel's enemies (Jer 25:20; 50:37).

MINIAMIN, MINJAMIN [4975] (*from the right, good fortune*).

NIV+ MINIAMIN'S

1. Levite (2Ch 31:15).
2. Head of a family of priests (Ne 12:17).
3. A priest in Nehemiah's time (Ne 12:41).

MINISTER [2143, 6268, 6275, 6641, 9250, 692, 1354, 1355, 1356, 3302, 3311, 3313, 3364] (*servant*).

NIV+ MINISTERED, MINISTERING, MINISTERS, MINISTRY

1. An officer in civil government. Joseph (Ge 41:40-44), Iri (2Sa 20:26), Zabud (1Ki 4:5), Ahithophel (1Ch 27:33), Zebadiah (2Ch 19:11), Elkanah (2Ch 28:7), Haman (Est 3:1), Mordecai (Est 10:3, w Est 8; 9), Daniel (Da 2:48; 6:1-3).

See Cabinet.

2. A sacred teacher. Likened to sowers (Ps 126:6; Mt 13:3-8; Mk 4:3-8; Lk 8:5-8). Teachers of schools (1Sa 19:20; 2Ki 2:3,5,15; 4:38; 2Ch 15:3; 17:7-9; Ac 13:1).

Hired (Jdg 17:10; 18:4). Exempt from taxation (Ezr 7:24). In politics (2Sa 15:24-27). In war (2Ch 13:12-14).

Influential in public affairs (1Sa 12:6-10), designate kings (1Sa 9:15-16; 10:1; 16:1-13), recommend civil and military appointments (2Ki 4:13).

In vigorous opposition with rulers: Samuel with Saul (1Sa 13:11-14; 15:10-31), Nathan with David (2Sa 12:1-4), Elijah with Ahab (1Ki 18:17-18).

Recreation for (Mk 6:31-32). Take leave of congregations (Ac 20:17-38). Personal bearing of (Tit 2:7-8). Preach with ecclesiastical authority (Gal 1:15-24; 2:1-9). Work of, will be tried (1Co 3:12-15). Responsibility of (Eze 3:17-21; 33:8; Mt 10:14-40; Ac 18:6; 20:26-27; 1Co 1:23; 2Co 2:15-17; 5:11,18-19; 1Ti 6:20). Speaking evil of, forbidden (Jude 8,10). Clothed with authority (1Th 5:12; Tit 1:13-14; 2:15; 3:1-2,8-9; Heb 13:6-7,17). *See the epistles to Timothy and Titus in their entirety.* Clothed with salvation (2Ch 6:41). Exhorted to grow in grace (1Ti 6:11; 2Ti 2:22).

Marriage of (Lev 21:7-15; Mt 8:14; Mk 1:30; 1Co 9:5; 1Ti 3:2,12; Tit 1:5-7).

Incorruptible: Balaam (Nu 22:18,37-38; 23:8,12; 24:12-14, w 2Pe 2:15-16), Micaiah (1Ki 22:13-14), Peter (Ac 8:18-23). Patience of (Jas 5:10). Inconsistent (Mt 27:3-7). Love of, for the church, exemplified by Paul (Php 1:7; 1Th 1:2-4; 2:8,11). Kindness to, Ebed-Melech to Jeremiah (Jer 38:7-13). Fear of (1Sa 16:4). Example to the flock (Php 3:17; 2Th 3:9; 1Ti 4:12; Tit 2:1,7-8; 1Pe 5:3). Intolerance of (Mt 15:23; 19:13; Mk 10:13; Lk 18:15). Message of, rejected (Jer 7:27; Eze 33:30-33). God's care of (1Ki 17:1-16; 19:1-8; Mt 10:29-31; Lk 12:6-7). Their calling, glorious (2Co 3:7-11). Discouragements of (Isa 30:10-11; 53:1; Eze 3:8-9,14; Hab 1:2-3; Mt 13:57; Mk 6:3-4; Lk 4:24; Jn 4:44).

Defended (Jer 26:16-24; Ac 23:9). Beloved (Ac 20:37-38; 21:5-6).

Sent out in teams of two: Disciples (Mk 6:7), Paul and Barnabas (Ac 13:2-3), Judas and Silas (Ac 15:27), Barnabas and Mark (Ac 15:37,39), Paul and Silas (Ac 15:40), Paul and Titus (2Co 8:19,23), Timothy and Erastus (Ac 19:22), Titus and a companion (2Co 12:18).

Call of:

Am 2:11 I also raised up prophets from among your sons and Nazirites from among your young men. Is this not true, people of Israel?" declares the LORD. (+Mt 9:38)

Ro 10:14 How, then, can they call on the one they have not believed in? And how can they believe in the one of whom they have not heard? And how can they hear without someone preaching to them? [15]And how can they preach unless they are sent? As it is written, "How beautiful are the feet of those who bring good news!"

Eph 4:11 It was he who gave some to be apostles, some to be prophets, some to be evangelists, and some to be pastors and teachers, [12]to prepare God's people for works of service, so that the body of Christ may be built up

Heb 5:4 No one takes this honor upon himself; he must be called by God, just as Aaron was.

Aaron and his sons—

Ex 28:1 "Have Aaron your brother brought to you from among the Israelites, along with his sons Nadab and Abihu, Eleazar and Ithamar, so they may serve me as priests.

1Ch 23:13 The sons of Amram: Aaron and Moses. Aaron was set apart, he and his descendants forever, to consecrate the most holy things, to offer sacrifices before the LORD, to minister before him and to pronounce blessings in his name forever. (+Heb 5:4)

Levites—

Nu 3:5 The LORD said to Moses, [6]"Bring the tribe of Levi and present them to Aaron the priest to assist him. [7]They are to perform duties for him and for the whole community at the Tent of Meeting by doing the work of the tabernacle. [8]They are to take care of all the furnishings of the Tent of Meeting, fulfilling the obligations of the Israelites by doing the work of the tabernacle. [9]Give the Levites to Aaron and his sons; they are the Israelites who are to be given wholly to him. [10]Appoint Aaron and his sons to serve as priests; anyone else who approaches the sanctuary must be put to death."

[11]The LORD also said to Moses, [12]"I have taken the Levites from among the Israelites in place of the first male offspring of every Israelite woman. The Levites are mine, [13]for all the firstborn are mine. When I struck down all the firstborn in Egypt, I set apart for myself every firstborn in Israel, whether man or animal. They are to be mine. I am the LORD." (+Nu 16:5,9)

Samuel—

1Sa 3:4 Then the LORD called Samuel.

Samuel answered, "Here I am." [5]And he ran to Eli and said, "Here I am; you called me."

But Eli said, "I did not call; go back and lie down." So he went and lay down.

[6]Again the LORD called, "Samuel!" And Samuel got up and went to Eli and said, "Here I am; you called me."

"My son," Eli said, "I did not call; go back and lie down." [7]Now Samuel did not yet know the LORD: The word of the LORD had not yet been revealed to him.

[8]The LORD called Samuel a third time, and Samuel got up and went to Eli and said, "Here I am; you called me."

Then Eli realized that the LORD was calling the boy. [9]So Eli told Samuel, "Go and lie down, and if he calls you, say, 'Speak, LORD, for your servant is listening.'" So Samuel went and lay down in his place.

[10]The LORD came and stood there, calling as at the other times, "Samuel! Samuel!"

Then Samuel said, "Speak, for your servant is listening."

Elisha—

1Ki 19:16 Also, anoint Jehu son of Nimshi king over Israel, and anoint Elisha son of Shaphat from Abel Meholah to succeed you as prophet.

1Ki 19:19 So Elijah went from there and found Elisha son of Shaphat. He was plowing with twelve yoke of oxen, and he himself was driving the twelfth pair. Elijah went up to him and threw his cloak around him.

Isaiah—

Isa 6:8 Then I heard the voice of the Lord saying, "Whom shall I send? And who will go for us?" And I said, "Here am I. Send me!"

[9]He said, "Go and tell this people:

"'Be ever hearing, but never understanding; be ever seeing, but never perceiving.' [10]Make the heart of this people calloused; make their ears dull and close their eyes. Otherwise they might see with their eyes, hear with their ears, understand with their hearts, and turn and be healed."

Jeremiah—

Jer 1:5 "Before I formed you in the womb I knew you, before you were born I set you apart; I appointed you as a prophet to the nations."

Jonah—

Jnh 1:1 The word of the LORD came to Jonah son of Amittai: [2]"Go to the great city of Nineveh and preach against it, because its wickedness has come up before me." (+Jnh 3:1-2)

The twelve apostles—

Mt 4:18 As Jesus was walking beside the Sea of Galilee, he saw two brothers, Simon called Peter and his brother Andrew. They were casting a net into the lake, for they were fishermen. [19]"Come, follow me," Jesus said, "and I will make you fishers of men." [20]At once they left their nets and followed him.

[21]Going on from there, he saw two other brothers, James son of Zebedee and his brother John. They were in a boat with their father Zebedee, preparing their nets. Jesus called them, [22]and immediately they left the boat and their father and followed him. (+Mk 1:17-20)

Mt 9:9 As Jesus went on from there, he saw a man named Matthew sitting at the tax collector's booth. "Follow me," he told him, and Matthew got up and followed him. (+Mk 2:14; Lk 5:27; Mt 10:1-5)

Jn 1:43 The next day Jesus decided to leave for Galilee. Finding Philip, he said to him, "Follow me."

The seventy-two disciples—

Lk 10:1 After this the Lord appointed seventy-two others and sent them two by two ahead of him to every town and place where he was about to go. [2]He told them, "The harvest is plentiful, but the workers are few. Ask the Lord of the harvest, therefore, to send out workers into his harvest field.

Paul—

Ac 13:2 While they were worshiping the Lord and fasting, the Holy Spirit said, "Set apart for me Barnabas and Saul for the work to which I have called them." [3]So after they had fasted and prayed, they placed their hands on them and sent them off.

Ac 20:24 However, I consider my life worth nothing to me, if only I may finish the race and complete the task the Lord Jesus has given me—the task of testifying to the gospel of God's grace.

Ac 22:12 "A man named Ananias came to see me. He was a devout observer of the law and highly respected by all the Jews living there. [13]He stood beside me and said, 'Brother Saul, receive your sight!' And at that very moment I was able to see him.

[14]"Then he said: 'The God of our fathers has chosen you to know his will and to see the Righteous One and to hear words from his mouth. [15]You will be his witness to all men of what you have seen and heard.

Ac 26:14 We all fell to the ground, and I heard a voice saying to me in Aramaic, 'Saul, Saul, why do you persecute me? It is hard for you to kick against the goads.'

[15]"Then I asked, 'Who are you, Lord?'

"'I am Jesus, whom you are persecuting,' the Lord replied. [16]'Now get up and stand on your feet. I have appeared to you to appoint you as a servant and as a witness of what you have seen of me and what I will show you. [17]I will rescue you from your own people and from the Gentiles. I am sending you to them [18]to open their eyes and turn them from darkness to light, and from the power of Satan to God, so that they may receive forgiveness of sins and a place among those who are sanctified by faith in me.'

Ro 1:1 Paul, a servant of Christ Jesus, called to be an apostle and set apart for the gospel of God—

1Co 1:1 Paul, called to be an apostle of Christ Jesus by the will of God, and our brother Sosthenes,

1Co 1:27 But God chose the foolish things of the world to shame the wise; God chose the weak things of the world to shame the strong. [28]He chose the lowly things of this world and the despised things—and the things that are not—to nullify the things that are, (+2Co 1:1; Col 1:1)

1Co 9:16 Yet when I preach the gospel, I cannot boast, for I am compelled to preach. Woe to me if I do not preach the gospel! [17]If I preach voluntarily, I have a reward; if not voluntarily, I am simply discharging the trust committed to me. [18]What then is my reward? Just this: that in preaching the gospel I may offer it free of charge, and so not make use of my rights in preaching it.

[19]Though I am free and belong to no man, I make myself a slave to everyone, to win as many as possible.

2Co 5:18 All this is from God, who reconciled us to himself through Christ and gave us the ministry of reconciliation: [19]that God was reconciling the world to himself in Christ, not counting men's sins against them. And he has committed to us the message of reconciliation. [20]We are therefore Christ's ambassadors, as though God were making his appeal through us. We implore you on Christ's behalf: Be reconciled to God.

Gal 1:15 But when God, who set me apart from birth and called me by his grace, was pleased [16]to reveal his Son in me so that I might preach him among the Gentiles, I did not consult any man,

Eph 3:7 I became a servant of this gospel by the gift of God's grace given me through the working of his power. [8]Although I am less than the least of all God's people, this grace was given me: to preach to the Gentiles the unsearchable riches of Christ,

Col 1:25 I have become its servant by the commission God gave me to present to you the word of God in its fullness— [26]the mystery that has been kept hidden for ages and generations, but is now disclosed to the saints. [27]To them God has chosen to make known among the Gentiles the glorious riches of this mystery, which is Christ in you, the hope of glory.

[28]We proclaim him, admonishing and teaching everyone with all wisdom, so that we may present everyone perfect in Christ. [29]To this end I labor, struggling with all his energy, which so powerfully works in me. (+1Ti 1:11; Tit 1:5)

Barnabas (Ac 13:2-3).

Archippus—

Col 4:17 Tell Archippus: "See to it that you complete the work you have received in the Lord."

See Call, Personal; Excuses.

Character and Qualifications of:

Lev 10:3 Moses then said to Aaron, "This is what the LORD spoke of when he said:

"'Among those who approach me I will show myself holy; in the sight of all the people I will be honored.'"

Aaron remained silent.

[4]Moses summoned Mishael and Elzaphan, sons of Aaron's uncle Uzziel, and said to them, "Come here; carry your cousins outside the camp, away from the front of the sanctuary." [5]So they came and carried them, still in their tunics, outside the camp, as Moses ordered.

[6]Then Moses said to Aaron and his sons Eleazar and Ithamar, "Do not let your hair become unkempt, and do not tear your clothes, or you will die and the LORD will be angry with the whole community. But your relatives, all the house of Israel, may mourn for those the LORD has destroyed by fire. [7]Do not leave the entrance to the Tent of Meeting or you will die, because the LORD's anointing oil is on you." So they did as Moses said.

[8]Then the LORD said to Aaron, [9]"You and your sons are not to drink wine or other fermented drink whenever you go into the Tent of Meeting, or you will die. This is a lasting ordinance for the generations to come. [10]You must distinguish between the holy and the common, between the unclean and the clean, [11]and you must teach the Israelites all the decrees the LORD has given them through Moses."

Blameless—

1Ti 3:2 Now the overseer must be above reproach, the husband of but one wife, temperate, self-controlled, respectable, hospitable, able to teach, [3]not given to drunkenness, not violent but gentle, not quarrelsome, not a lover of money. [4]He must manage his own family well and see that his children obey him with proper respect.

1Ti 3:7 He must also have a good reputation with outsiders, so that he will not fall into disgrace and into the devil's trap.

[8]Deacons, likewise, are to be men worthy of respect, sincere, not indulging in much wine, and not pursuing dishonest gain. [9]They must keep hold of the deep truths of the faith with a clear conscience. [10]They must first be tested; and then if there is nothing against them, let them serve as deacons.

[11]In the same way, their wives are to be women worthy of respect, not malicious talkers but temperate and trustworthy in everything.

[12]A deacon must be the husband of but one wife and must manage his children and his household well. [13]Those who have served well gain an excellent standing and great assurance in their faith in Christ Jesus.

Tit 1:5 The reason I left you in Crete was that you might straighten out what was left unfinished and appoint elders in every town, as I directed you. [6]An elder must be blameless, the husband of but one wife, a man whose children believe and are not open to the charge of being wild and disobedient. [7]Since an overseer is entrusted with God's work, he must be blameless—not overbearing, not quick-tempered, not given to drunkenness, not violent, not pursuing dishonest gain. [8]Rather he must be hospitable, one who loves what is good, who is self-controlled, upright, holy and disciplined. [9]He must hold firmly to the trustworthy message as it has been taught, so that he can encourage others by sound doctrine and refute those who oppose it.

Compassionate—

Heb 5:2 He is able to deal gently with those who are ignorant and are going astray, since he himself is subject to weakness.

Consecrated—

Nu 16:9 Isn't it enough for you that the God of Israel has separated you from the rest of the Israelite community and brought you near himself to do the work at the LORD's tabernacle and to stand before the community and minister to them? ¹⁰He has brought you and all your fellow Levites near himself, but now you are trying to get the priesthood too.

Consistent—

Ro 2:21 you, then, who teach others, do you not teach yourself? You who preach against stealing, do you steal? ²²You who say that people should not commit adultery, do you commit adultery? You who abhor idols, do you rob temples? ²³You who brag about the law, do you dishonor God by breaking the law?

Courageous—

Jer 1:7 But the LORD said to me, "Do not say, 'I am only a child.' You must go to everyone I send you to and say whatever I command you. ⁸Do not be afraid of them, for I am with you and will rescue you," declares the LORD. (+Jer 1:17-19)

Ac 20:22 "And now, compelled by the Spirit, I am going to Jerusalem, not knowing what will happen to me there.

Ac 20:24 However, I consider my life worth nothing to me, if only I may finish the race and complete the task the Lord Jesus has given me—the task of testifying to the gospel of God's grace. (+2Ti 1:7)

Diligent (2Ch 29:11)—

1Co 15:10 But by the grace of God I am what I am, and his grace to me was not without effect. No, I worked harder than all of them—yet not I, but the grace of God that was with me.

Eager to serve—

Isa 6:8 Then I heard the voice of the Lord saying, "Whom shall I send? And who will go for us?" And I said, "Here am I. Send me!"

Endued with power—

Lk 24:49 I am going to send you what my Father has promised; but stay in the city until you have been clothed with power from on high."

Ac 1:8 But you will receive power when the Holy Spirit comes on you; and you will be my witnesses in Jerusalem, and in all Judea and Samaria, and to the ends of the earth."

Ac 4:8 Then Peter, filled with the Holy Spirit, said to them: "Rulers and elders of the people!

Ac 4:31 After they prayed, the place where they were meeting was shaken. And they were all filled with the Holy Spirit and spoke the word of God boldly.

Gal 2:8 For God, who was at work in the ministry of Peter as an apostle to the Jews, was also at work in my ministry as an apostle to the Gentiles.

Gentle (2Ti 2:24-25).

A good example—

Tit 2:1 You must teach what is in accord with sound doctrine.

Tit 2:7 In everything set them an example by doing what is good. In your teaching show integrity, seriousness ⁸and soundness of speech that cannot be condemned, so that those who oppose you may be ashamed because they have nothing bad to say about us.

Tit 2:15 These, then, are the things you should teach. Encourage and rebuke with all authority. Do not let anyone despise you.

Jas 3:1 Not many of you should presume to be teachers, my brothers, because you know that we who teach will be judged more strictly.

Jas 3:13 Who is wise and understanding among you? Let him show it by his good life, by deeds done in the humility that comes from wisdom.

Jas 3:16 For where you have envy and selfish ambition, there you find disorder and every evil practice.

¹⁷But the wisdom that comes from heaven is first of all pure; then peace-loving, considerate, submissive, full of mercy and good fruit, impartial and sincere. ¹⁸Peacemakers who sow in peace raise a harvest of righteousness.

Holy—

Lev 21:6 They must be holy to their God and must not profane the name of their God. Because they present the offerings made to the LORD by fire, the food of their God, they are to be holy.

Isa 6:7 With it he touched my mouth and said, "See, this has touched your lips; your guilt is taken away and your sin atoned for."

Isa 52:11 Depart, depart, go out from there! Touch no unclean thing! Come out from it and be pure, you who carry the vessels of the LORD.

Mal 2:6 True instruction was in his mouth and nothing false was found on his lips. He walked with me in peace and uprightness, and turned many from sin.

Jn 17:17 Sanctify them by the truth; your word is truth.

1Co 9:27 No, I beat my body and make it my slave so that after I have preached to others, I myself will not be disqualified for the prize. (+2Ti 2:21; Tit 1:5-9)

Humble—

Mt 20:25 Jesus called them together and said, "You know that the rulers of the Gentiles lord it over them, and their high officials exercise authority over them. ²⁶Not so with you. Instead, whoever wants to become great among you must be your servant, ²⁷and whoever wants to be first must be your slave— ²⁸just as the Son of Man did not come to be served, but to serve, and to give his life as a ransom for many."

Mt 23:8 "But you are not to be called 'Rabbi,' for you have only one Master and you are all brothers. (+Mt 23:10-11; Lk 22:27)

Jn 13:13 "You call me 'Teacher' and 'Lord,' and rightly so, for that is what I am. ¹⁴Now that I, your Lord and Teacher, have washed your feet, you also should wash one another's feet. ¹⁵I have set you an example that you should do as I have done for you. ¹⁶I tell you the truth, no servant is greater than his master, nor is a messenger greater than the one who sent him. ¹⁷Now that you know these things, you will be blessed if you do them.

Jn 15:20 Remember the words I spoke to you: 'No servant is greater than his master.' If they persecuted me, they will persecute you also. If they obeyed my teaching, they will obey yours also.

2Co 4:5 For we do not preach ourselves, but Jesus Christ as Lord, and ourselves as your servants for Jesus' sake.

Meek—

1Co 4:12 We work hard with our own hands. When we are cursed, we bless; when we are persecuted, we endure it; ¹³when we are slandered, we answer kindly. Up to this moment we have become the scum of the earth, the refuse of the world.

2Co 10:1 By the meekness and gentleness of Christ, I appeal to you—I, Paul, who am "timid" when face to face with you, but "bold" when away!

Patient (Jas 5:10).

Persevering—

Mt 10:22 All men will hate you because of me, but he who stands firm to the end will be saved. ²³When you are persecuted in one place, flee to another. I tell you the truth, you will not finish going through the cities of Israel before the Son of Man comes.

[24]"A student is not above his teacher, nor a servant above his master. (+2Co 4:1)

2Co 4:8 We are hard pressed on every side, but not crushed; perplexed, but not in despair; [9]persecuted, but not abandoned; struck down, but not destroyed. [10]We always carry around in our body the death of Jesus, so that the life of Jesus may also be revealed in our body.

Prepared—

Ezr 7:10 For Ezra had devoted himself to the study and observance of the Law of the LORD, and to teaching its decrees and laws in Israel.

Responsible—

1Pe 4:10 Each one should use whatever gift he has received to serve others, faithfully administering God's grace in its various forms. [11]If anyone speaks, he should do it as one speaking the very words of God. If anyone serves, he should do it with the strength God provides, so that in all things God may be praised through Jesus Christ. To him be the glory and the power for ever and ever. Amen.

Saved—

2Ch 6:41 "Now arise, O LORD God, and come to your resting place, you and the ark of your might. May your priests, O LORD God, be clothed with salvation, may your saints rejoice in your goodness.

Sincere—

2Co 4:1 Therefore, since through God's mercy we have this ministry, we do not lose heart. [2]Rather, we have renounced secret and shameful ways; we do not use deception, nor do we distort the word of God. On the contrary, by setting forth the truth plainly we commend ourselves to every man's conscience in the sight of God.

Strong (2Ti 2:1).

Tactful—

1Co 9:18 What then is my reward? Just this: that in preaching the gospel I may offer it free of charge, and so not make use of my rights in preaching it.

[19]Though I am free and belong to no man, I make myself a slave to everyone, to win as many as possible. [20]To the Jews I became like a Jew, to win the Jews. To those under the law I became like one under the law (though I myself am not under the law), so as to win those under the law. [21]To those not having the law I became like one not having the law (though I am not free from God's law but am under Christ's law), so as to win those not having the law. [22]To the weak I became weak, to win the weak. I have become all things to all men so that by all possible means I might save some. [23]I do all this for the sake of the gospel, that I may share in its blessings. (+1Co 10:23,28-33)

2Co 6:3 We put no stumbling block in anyone's path, so that our ministry will not be discredited. (+2Co 12:16)

Willing to suffer hardship (2Ti 2:3; 4:5).

Wise—

Mal 2:7 "For the lips of a priest ought to preserve knowledge, and from his mouth men should seek instruction—because he is the messenger of the LORD Almighty. (+Pr 11:30)

Mt 10:16 I am sending you out like sheep among wolves. Therefore be as shrewd as snakes and as innocent as doves.

Lk 6:39 He also told them this parable: "Can a blind man lead a blind man? Will they not both fall into a pit?

2Co 4:6 For God, who said, "Let light shine out of darkness," made his light shine in our hearts to give us the light

of the knowledge of the glory of God in the face of Christ. (+2Ti 2:7)

2Ti 3:14 But as for you, continue in what you have learned and have become convinced of, because you know those from whom you learned it,

2Ti 3:16 All Scripture is God-breathed and is useful for teaching, rebuking, correcting and training in righteousness, [17]so that the man of God may be thoroughly equipped for every good work.

Not quarrelsome (2Ti 2:14,23-24)—

Tit 3:9 But avoid foolish controversies and genealogies and arguments and quarrels about the law, because these are unprofitable and useless.

Not of the world (Jn 15:19)—

Jn 17:16 They are not of the world, even as I am not of it.

Not entangled with the world (2Ti 2:4-5).

Zealous—

Jer 20:9 But if I say, "I will not mention him or speak any more in his name," his word is in my heart like a fire, a fire shut up in my bones. I am weary of holding it in; indeed, I cannot. (+Eze 34:1)

Eze 34:2 "Son of man, prophesy against the shepherds of Israel; prophesy and say to them: 'This is what the Sovereign LORD says: Woe to the shepherds of Israel who only take care of themselves! Should not shepherds take care of the flock? (+Eze 34:3-31)

2Ti 1:6 For this reason I remind you to fan into flame the gift of God, which is in you through the laying on of my hands. [7]For God did not give us a spirit of timidity, but a spirit of power, of love and of self-discipline.

[8]So do not be ashamed to testify about our Lord, or ashamed of me his prisoner. But join with me in suffering for the gospel, by the power of God, (+2Ti 4:2) *See Zeal.*

Instances of zealousness: Titus (2Co 8:16-17), Epaphroditus (Php 2:25-30), Epaphras (Col 4:12-13), John, in his vision (Rev 5:4-5).

Faithful—

1Sa 2:35 I will raise up for myself a faithful priest, who will do according to what is in my heart and mind. I will firmly establish his house, and he will minister before my anointed one always. (+Mt 24:45)

Lk 12:42 The Lord answered, "Who then is the faithful and wise manager, whom the master puts in charge of his servants to give them their food allowance at the proper time? [43]It will be good for that servant whom the master finds doing so when he returns. [44]I tell you the truth, he will put him in charge of all his possessions. (+Ac 20:22,24)

1Co 2:2 For I resolved to know nothing while I was with you except Jesus Christ and him crucified.

2Co 6:4 Rather, as servants of God we commend ourselves in every way: in great endurance; in troubles, hardships and distresses; [5]in beatings, imprisonments and riots; in hard work, sleepless nights and hunger; [6]in purity, understanding, patience and kindness; in the Holy Spirit and in sincere love; [7]in truthful speech and in the power of God; with weapons of righteousness in the right hand and in the left;

Instances of faithfulness: Moses (Dt 4:26; 30:19; Heb 3:2,5), Micaiah (2Ch 18:12-13), Azariah (2Ch 26:16-20), Balaam (Nu 22:18,38; 23:8,12; 24:12-14), Nathan (2Sa 12:1-14), Isaiah (Isa 22:4-5; 39:3-7), Jeremiah (Jer 17:16; 26:1-15; 28; 37:9-10,16-18), John the Baptist (Mt 3:2-12; Mk 6:18; Lk 3:7-19), the apostles (Ac 4:19-20,31; 5:21,29-32), Peter (Ac 2:14-40; 3:12-26; 4:8-12; 8:18-23),

Paul (Ac 15:25-26; 17:16-17; 19:8; 20:26-27), Tychicus (Col 4:7).

See the epistles to Timothy and Titus in their entirety.

Described as:

Administering God's grace (1Pe 4:10). Ambassadors for Christ (2Co 5:20; Eph 6:20). Angels of the church (Rev 1:20; 2:1,8,12,18; 3:1,7,14). Apostles (Lk 6:13; Rev 18:20). Apostles of Jesus Christ (Tit 1:1). Defenders of the gospel (Php 1:7). Elders (1Ti 5:17; 1Pe 5:1). Entrusted with God's work (Tit 1:7), with the secret things of God (1Co 4:1). Evangelists (Eph 4:11; 2Ti 4:5). Fishers of men (Mt 4:19; Mk 1:17). God's fellow workers (1Th 3:2). Lights (Jn 5:35). Men of God (Dt 33:1; 1Ti 6:11). Messengers of the Church (2Co 8:23), of the LORD Almighty (Mal 2:7). Ministers of God (Isa 61:6), before the LORD (Joel 2:17), of Christ (Ro 15:16; 1Ti 4:6), of a new covenant (2Co 3:6), in the Sanctuary (Eze 45:4).

Overseers (Ac 20:28). Pastors (Eph 4:11). Preachers (Ro 10:14; 1Ti 2:7), of righteousness (2Pe 2:5). Servants of the Church (2Co 4:5), of God (Tit 1:1; Jas 1:1), of the Gospel (Eph 3:7; Col 1:23), of Jesus Christ (Php 1:1; Jude 1), of the Lord (2Ti 2:24), of the Word (Lk 1:2). Shepherds (Jer 23:4). Soldiers of Christ (Php 2:25; 2Ti 2:3-4). Stars (Rev 1:20; 2:1). Teachers (Isa 30:20; Eph 4:11). Watchmen (Isa 62:6; Eze 33:7). Witnesses (Ac 1:8; 5:32; 26:16). Workers (Mt 9:38; Phm 1), together with God (2Co 6:1).

Charges delivered to:

Nu 18:1 The LORD said to Aaron, "You, your sons and your father's family are to bear the responsibility for offenses against the sanctuary, and you and your sons alone are to bear the responsibility for offenses against the priesthood. ²Bring your fellow Levites from your ancestral tribe to join you and assist you when you and your sons minister before the Tent of the Testimony. ³They are to be responsible to you and are to perform all the duties of the Tent, but they must not go near the furnishings of the sanctuary or the altar, or both they and you will die. ⁴They are to join you and be responsible for the care of the Tent of Meeting—all the work at the Tent—and no one else may come near where you are.

⁵"You are to be responsible for the care of the sanctuary and the altar, so that wrath will not fall on the Israelites again. ⁶I myself have selected your fellow Levites from among the Israelites as a gift to you, dedicated to the LORD to do the work at the Tent of Meeting. ⁷But only you and your sons may serve as priests in connection with everything at the altar and inside the curtain. I am giving you the service of the priesthood as a gift. Anyone else who comes near the sanctuary must be put to death."

Nu 27:18 So the LORD said to Moses, "Take Joshua son of Nun, a man in whom is the spirit, and lay your hand on him. ¹⁹Have him stand before Eleazar the priest and the entire assembly and commission him in their presence. ²⁰Give him some of your authority so the whole Israelite community will obey him. ²¹He is to stand before Eleazar the priest, who will obtain decisions for him by inquiring of the Urim before the LORD. At his command he and the entire community of the Israelites will go out, and at his command they will come in."

²²Moses did as the LORD commanded him. He took Joshua and had him stand before Eleazar the priest and the whole assembly. ²³Then he laid his hands on him and commissioned him, as the LORD instructed through Moses. (+Dt 31:7-8,14-23)

Jos 1:1 After the death of Moses the servant of the LORD, the LORD said to Joshua son of Nun, Moses' aide: ²"Moses my servant is dead. Now then, you and all these people, get ready to cross the Jordan River into the land I am about to give to them—to the Israelites. ³I will give you every place where you set your foot, as I promised Moses. ⁴Your territory will extend from the desert to Lebanon, and from the great river, the Euphrates—all the Hittite country—to the Great Sea on the west. ⁵No one will be able to stand up against you all the days of your life. As I was with Moses, so I will be with you; I will never leave you nor forsake you.

⁶"Be strong and courageous, because you will lead these people to inherit the land I swore to their forefathers to give them. ⁷Be strong and very courageous. Be careful to obey all the law my servant Moses gave you; do not turn from it to the right or to the left, that you may be successful wherever you go. ⁸Do not let this Book of the Law depart from your mouth; meditate on it day and night, so that you may be careful to do everything written in it. Then you will be prosperous and successful. ⁹Have I not commanded you? Be strong and courageous. Do not be terrified; do not be discouraged, for the LORD your God will be with you wherever you go." (+Jer 1:18-19)

Eze 3:4 He then said to me: "Son of man, go now to the house of Israel and speak my words to them.

Jesus to the twelve (Mt 10:5-42), to the seventy-two (Lk 10:1-16).

Paul charges Timothy—

1Ti 1:18 Timothy, my son, I give you this instruction in keeping with the prophecies once made about you, so that by following them you may fight the good fight, ¹⁹holding on to faith and a good conscience. Some have rejected these and so have shipwrecked their faith. ²⁰Among them are Hymenaeus and Alexander, whom I have handed over to Satan to be taught not to blaspheme. (+1Ti 2; 3; 4; 5; 6)

2Ti 1:6 For this reason I remind you to fan into flame the gift of God, which is in you through the laying on of my hands. ⁷For God did not give us a spirit of timidity, but a spirit of power, of love and of self-discipline.

⁸So do not be ashamed to testify about our Lord, or ashamed of me his prisoner. But join with me in suffering for the gospel, by the power of God, ⁹who has saved us and called us to a holy life—not because of anything we have done but because of his own purpose and grace. This grace was given us in Christ Jesus before the beginning of time, ¹⁰but it has now been revealed through the appearing of our Savior, Christ Jesus, who has destroyed death and has brought life and immortality to light through the gospel. ¹¹And of this gospel I was appointed a herald and an apostle and a teacher. ¹²That is why I am suffering as I am. Yet I am not ashamed, because I know whom I have believed, and am convinced that he is able to guard what I have entrusted to him for that day.

¹³What you heard from me, keep as the pattern of sound teaching, with faith and love in Christ Jesus. (+ 2Ti 2; 3; 4)

Duties of:

Eph 4:11 It was he who gave some to be apostles, some to be prophets, some to be evangelists, and some to be pastors and teachers, ¹²to prepare God's people for works of service, so that the body of Christ may be built up

To preach—

Mt 10:7 As you go, preach this message: 'The kingdom of heaven is near.'

Ro 1:14 I am obligated both to Greeks and non-Greeks,

both to the wise and the foolish. [15]That is why I am so eager to preach the gospel also to you who are at Rome.

To preach the unsearchable riches of Christ—

Eph 3:8 Although I am less than the least of all God's people, this grace was given me: to preach to the Gentiles the unsearchable riches of Christ, [9]and to make plain to everyone the administration of this mystery, which for ages past was kept hidden in God, who created all things. [10]His intent was that now, through the church, the manifold wisdom of God should be made known to the rulers and authorities in the heavenly realms, (+Eph 3:11-12)

To admonish—

Isa 58:1 "Shout it aloud, do not hold back. Raise your voice like a trumpet. Declare to my people their rebellion and to the house of Jacob their sins.

Isa 62:6 I have posted watchmen on your walls, O Jerusalem; they will never be silent day or night. You who call on the LORD, give yourselves no rest, [7]and give him no rest till he establishes Jerusalem and makes her the praise of the earth.

To exhort—

2Co 5:20 We are therefore Christ's ambassadors, as though God were making his appeal through us. We implore you on Christ's behalf: Be reconciled to God. (+1Ti 4:13)

1Ti 6:17 Command those who are rich in this present world not to be arrogant nor to put their hope in wealth, which is so uncertain, but to put their hope in God, who richly provides us with everything for our enjoyment. [18]Command them to do good, to be rich in good deeds, and to be generous and willing to share.

2Pe 1:12 So I will always remind you of these things, even though you know them and are firmly established in the truth you now have. [13]I think it is right to refresh your memory as long as I live in the tent of this body, [14]because I know that I will soon put it aside, as our Lord Jesus Christ has made clear to me. [15]And I will make every effort to see that after my departure you will always be able to remember these things.

[16]We did not follow cleverly invented stories when we told you about the power and coming of our Lord Jesus Christ, but we were eyewitnesses of his majesty.

To warn (Jer 7:25)—

Eze 33:1 The word of the LORD came to me: [2]"Son of man, speak to your countrymen and say to them: 'When I bring the sword against a land, and the people of the land choose one of their men and make him their watchman, [3]and he sees the sword coming against the land and blows the trumpet to warn the people, [4]then if anyone hears the trumpet but does not take warning and the sword comes and takes his life, his blood will be on his own head. [5]Since he heard the sound of the trumpet but did not take warning, his blood will be on his own head. If he had taken warning, he would have saved himself. [6]But if the watchman sees the sword coming and does not blow the trumpet to warn the people and the sword comes and takes the life of one of them, that man will be taken away because of his sin, but I will hold the watchman accountable for his blood.'

[7]"Son of man, I have made you a watchman for the house of Israel; so hear the word I speak and give them warning from me. [8]When I say to the wicked, 'O wicked man, you will surely die,' and you do not speak out to dissuade him from his ways, that wicked man will die for his sin, and I will hold you accountable for his blood. [9]But if you do warn the wicked man to turn from his ways and he does

not do so, he will die for his sin, but you will have saved yourself.

To reprove—

Eze 6:11 "'This is what the Sovereign LORD says: Strike your hands together and stamp your feet and cry out "Alas!" because of all the wicked and detestable practices of the house of Israel, for they will fall by the sword, famine and plague. (+ Eze 34)

Jnh 1:2 "Go to the great city of Nineveh and preach against it, because its wickedness has come up before me."

2Co 7:8 Even if I caused you sorrow by my letter, I do not regret it. Though I did regret it—I see that my letter hurt you, but only for a little while— *See Reproof.*

To teach—

Lev 10:11 and you must teach the Israelites all the decrees the LORD has given them through Moses."

2Ki 17:27 Then the king of Assyria gave this order: "Have one of the priests you took captive from Samaria go back to live there and teach the people what the god of the land requires." [28]So one of the priests who had been exiled from Samaria came to live in Bethel and taught them how to worship the LORD. (+2Ch 15:3; Ezr 7:10)

Jer 26:2 "This is what the LORD says: Stand in the courtyard of the LORD's house and speak to all the people of the towns of Judah who come to worship in the house of the LORD. Tell them everything I command you; do not omit a word.

Eze 44:23 They are to teach my people the difference between the holy and the common and show them how to distinguish between the unclean and the clean. (+Mt 10:7)

Mt 10:27 What I tell you in the dark, speak in the daylight; what is whispered in your ear, proclaim from the roofs.

Mt 28:19 Therefore go and make disciples of all nations, baptizing them in the name of the Father and of the Son and of the Holy Spirit, [20]and teaching them to obey everything I have commanded you. And surely I am with you always, to the very end of the age." (+Mk 10:43-45)

Ac 5:20 "Go, stand in the temple courts," he said, "and tell the people the full message of this new life."

Ac 6:4 and will give our attention to prayer and the ministry of the word."

Ac 16:4 As they traveled from town to town, they delivered the decisions reached by the apostles and elders in Jerusalem for the people to obey.

Ac 18:9 One night the Lord spoke to Paul in a vision: "Do not be afraid; keep on speaking, do not be silent. [10]For I am with you, and no one is going to attack and harm you, because I have many people in this city."

Ac 26:16 'Now get up and stand on your feet. I have appeared to you to appoint you as a servant and as a witness of what you have seen of me and what I will show you. [17]I will rescue you from your own people and from the Gentiles. I am sending you to them [18]to open their eyes and turn them from darkness to light, and from the power of Satan to God, so that they may receive forgiveness of sins and a place among those who are sanctified by faith in me.' (+Ro 1:15)

Ro 12:6 We have different gifts, according to the grace given us. If a man's gift is prophesying, let him use it in proportion to his faith. [7]If it is serving, let him serve; if it is teaching, let him teach;

2Co 10:8 For even if I boast somewhat freely about the authority the Lord gave us for building you up rather than pulling you down, I will not be ashamed of it. (+Eph 3:8-10; 4:11-12)

1Ti 2:7 And for this purpose I was appointed a herald and an apostle—I am telling the truth, I am not lying—and a teacher of the true faith to the Gentiles.

1Ti 4:13 Until I come, devote yourself to the public reading of Scripture, to preaching and to teaching. [14]Do not neglect your gift, which was given you through a prophetic message when the body of elders laid their hands on you.

[15]Be diligent in these matters; give yourself wholly to them, so that everyone may see your progress. [16]Watch your life and doctrine closely. Persevere in them, because if you do, you will save both yourself and your hearers.

2Ti 2:2 And the things you have heard me say in the presence of many witnesses entrust to reliable men who will also be qualified to teach others.

2Ti 2:14 Keep reminding them of these things. Warn them before God against quarreling about words; it is of no value, and only ruins those who listen. [15]Do your best to present yourself to God as one approved, a workman who does not need to be ashamed and who correctly handles the word of truth.

2Ti 2:24 And the Lord's servant must not quarrel; instead, he must be kind to everyone, able to teach, not resentful. [25]Those who oppose him he must gently instruct, in the hope that God will grant them repentance leading them to a knowledge of the truth,

2Ti 4:1 In the presence of God and of Christ Jesus, who will judge the living and the dead, and in view of his appearing and his kingdom, I give you this charge: [2]Preach the Word; be prepared in season and out of season; correct, rebuke and encourage—with great patience and careful instruction.

2Ti 4:5 But you, keep your head in all situations, endure hardship, do the work of an evangelist, discharge all the duties of your ministry.

To teach the lordship of Jesus—

2Co 4:5 For we do not preach ourselves, but Jesus Christ as Lord, and ourselves as your servants for Jesus' sake.

To serve—

Mt 20:25 Jesus called them together and said, "You know that the rulers of the Gentiles lord it over them, and their high officials exercise authority over them. [26]Not so with you. Instead, whoever wants to become great among you must be your servant, [27]and whoever wants to be first must be your slave— [28]just as the Son of Man did not come to be served, but to serve, and to give his life as a ransom for many." (+Mk 10:43-45; 2Co 4:5)

To make disciples of Christ (Mt 28:19-20).

To win souls (Pr 11:30)—

Jn 4:35 Do you not say, 'Four months more and then the harvest'? I tell you, open your eyes and look at the fields! They are ripe for harvest. [36]Even now the reaper draws his wages, even now he harvests the crop for eternal life, so that the sower and the reaper may be glad together. [37]Thus the saying 'One sows and another reaps' is true. [38]I sent you to reap what you have not worked for. Others have done the hard work, and you have reaped the benefits of their labor."

2Co 5:18 All this is from God, who reconciled us to himself through Christ and gave us the ministry of reconciliation: (+2Co 5:20)

To witness for Christ—

Lk 24:48 You are witnesses of these things.

Jn 15:27 And you also must testify, for you have been with me from the beginning.

Ac 1:22 beginning from John's baptism to the time when Jesus was taken up from us. For one of these must become a witness with us of his resurrection."

Ac 10:42 He commanded us to preach to the people and to testify that he is the one whom God appointed as judge of the living and the dead.

Ac 22:15 You will be his witness to all men of what you have seen and heard.

To do the work of an evangelist (2Ti 4:5). To give himself continually to prayer (Ac 6:4). To lament over the worldliness and sins of the church (Joel 1:13-15; 2:17).

To speak boldly—

Eph 6:20 for which I am an ambassador in chains. Pray that I may declare it fearlessly, as I should.

To minister to all without respect of persons or races (Ro 1:14-15).

To exercise authority in the church (Mt 16:19)—

Mt 18:18 "I tell you the truth, whatever you bind on earth will be bound in heaven, and whatever you loose on earth will be loosed in heaven. (+1Co 4:19-20)

1Co 4:21 What do you prefer? Shall I come to you with a whip, or in love and with a gentle spirit? (+2Co 7:8-9,12,15)

2Co 13:2 I already gave you a warning when I was with you the second time. I now repeat it while absent: On my return I will not spare those who sinned earlier or any of the others, (+2Co 13:3)

2Co 13:10 This is why I write these things when I am absent, that when I come I may not have to be harsh in my use of authority—the authority the Lord gave me for building you up, not for tearing you down.

2Th 3:4 We have confidence in the Lord that you are doing and will continue to do the things we command.

1Ti 1:3 As I urged you when I went into Macedonia, stay there in Ephesus so that you may command certain men not to teach false doctrines any longer [4]nor to devote themselves to myths and endless genealogies. These promote controversies rather than God's work—which is by faith.

1Ti 1:11 that conforms to the glorious gospel of the blessed God, which he entrusted to me.

1Ti 1:18 Timothy, my son, I give you this instruction in keeping with the prophecies once made about you, so that by following them you may fight the good fight,

1Ti 5:19 Do not entertain an accusation against an elder unless it is brought by two or three witnesses. [20]Those who sin are to be rebuked publicly, so that the others may take warning.

[21]I charge you, in the sight of God and Christ Jesus and the elect angels, to keep these instructions without partiality, and to do nothing out of favoritism.

[22]Do not be hasty in the laying on of hands, and do not share in the sins of others. Keep yourself pure.

1Pe 5:1 To the elders among you, I appeal as a fellow elder, a witness of Christ's sufferings and one who also will share in the glory to be revealed: [2]Be shepherds of God's flock that is under your care, serving as overseers—not because you must, but because you are willing, as God wants you to be; not greedy for money, but eager to serve; [3]not lording it over those entrusted to you, but being examples to the flock.

To feed the flock (Jer 3:15)—

Jer 23:4 I will place shepherds over them who will tend them, and they will no longer be afraid or terrified, nor will any be missing," declares the LORD.

Jer 23:22 But if they had stood in my council, they would have proclaimed my words to my people and would have turned them from their evil ways and from their evil deeds.

Jer 23:28 Let the prophet who has a dream tell his dream, but let the one who has my word speak it faithfully. For what has straw to do with grain?" declares the LORD.

Jn 21:15 When they had finished eating, Jesus said to Simon Peter, "Simon son of John, do you truly love me more than these?"

"Yes, Lord," he said, "you know that I love you."

Jesus said, "Feed my lambs."

[16]Again Jesus said, "Simon son of John, do you truly love me?"

He answered, "Yes, Lord, you know that I love you."

Jesus said, "Take care of my sheep."

[17]The third time he said to him, "Simon son of John, do you love me?"

Peter was hurt because Jesus asked him the third time, "Do you love me?" He said, "Lord, you know all things; you know that I love you."

Jesus said, "Feed my sheep.

Ac 20:28 Keep watch over yourselves and all the flock of which the Holy Spirit has made you overseers. Be shepherds of the church of God, which he bought with his own blood. (+1Co 14:1-33; 1Pe 5:2-3)

1Pe 5:4 And when the Chief Shepherd appears, you will receive the crown of glory that will never fade away.

To strengthen the discouraged—

Lk 22:32 But I have prayed for you, Simon, that your faith may not fail. And when you have turned back, strengthen your brothers."

To comfort the people—

Isa 40:1 Comfort, comfort my people, says your God. [2]Speak tenderly to Jerusalem, and proclaim to her that her hard service has been completed, that her sin has been paid for, that she has received from the LORD's hand double for all her sins.

Isa 40:9 You who bring good tidings to Zion, go up on a high mountain. You who bring good tidings to Jerusalem, lift up your voice with a shout, lift it up, do not be afraid; say to the towns of Judah, "Here is your God!"

Isa 40:11 He tends his flock like a shepherd: He gathers the lambs in his arms and carries them close to his heart; he gently leads those that have young.

1Th 3:2 We sent Timothy, who is our brother and God's fellow worker in spreading the gospel of Christ, to strengthen and encourage you in your faith,

Duty of the Church to:

To esteem—

1Th 5:12 Now we ask you, brothers, to respect those who work hard among you, who are over you in the Lord and who admonish you. [13]Hold them in the highest regard in love because of their work. Live in peace with each other.

To pray for—

Heb 13:18 Pray for us. We are sure that we have a clear conscience and desire to live honorably in every way. (+2Ch 6:41; Ps 132:9; Mt 9:37-38; Ac 4:29; 12:5; Ro 15:30-32; 2Co 1:11; Eph 6:18-20; Php 1:19; Col 4:2-4; 1Th 5:25; 2Th 3:1-2; Phm 22; Heb 13:19)

To imitate the example of—

1Co 11:1 Follow my example, as I follow the example of Christ.

Php 3:17 Join with others in following my example, brothers, and take note of those who live according to the pattern we gave you. (+2Th 3:7; Heb 13:7)

To submit to the authority of—

1Co 11:2 I praise you for remembering me in everything and for holding to the teachings, just as I passed them on to you.

1Co 16:16 to submit to such as these and to everyone who joins in the work, and labors at it. (+1Th 5:12-13; 2Th 3:4)

Heb 13:7 Remember your leaders, who spoke the word of God to you. Consider the outcome of their way of life and imitate their faith.

Heb 13:17 Obey your leaders and submit to their authority. They keep watch over you as men who must give an account. Obey them so that their work will be a joy, not a burden, for that would be of no advantage to you.

To provide for the support, of priest and Levite (Nu 18:20-21; Dt 10:9; 14:27; 18:1-4; Jos 13:14; 18:7; Jer 31:14; Eze 44:28), of the twelve apostles (Mt 10:9-10; Mk 6:8; Lk 22:35), of the seventy-two disciples (Lk 10:7-8), of Christian preachers (1Co 9:3-4,7-14; Gal 6:6; Php 4:10-18; 1Ti 5:18).

Right of support, waived by Paul (Ac 20:33-35; 1Co 9:15)—

1Co 9:16 Yet when I preach the gospel, I cannot boast, for I am compelled to preach. Woe to me if I do not preach the gospel! [17]If I preach voluntarily, I have a reward; if not voluntarily, I am simply discharging the trust committed to me. (+1Co 9:18; 2Co 11:7-10; 12:13-14)

2Co 12:15 So I will very gladly spend for you everything I have and expend myself as well. If I love you more, will you love me less? (+2Co 12:16-18)

1Th 2:5 You know we never used flattery, nor did we put on a mask to cover up greed—God is our witness. [6]We were not looking for praise from men, not from you or anyone else.

As apostles of Christ we could have been a burden to you, (+1Th 2:9; 2Th 3:7-9)

See Church, The Body of Believers, Responsibilities and Duties.

Hospitality to:

Woman of Zarephath to Elijah (1Ki 17:10-16). The Shunammite to Elisha (2Ki 4:8-10). The barbarians to Paul (Ac 28:1-10). Simon the tanner to Peter (Ac 9:43). The Philippian jailer (Ac 16:33-34). Aquila and Priscilla to Paul (Ac 18:3), to Apollos (Ac 18:26). Justus to Paul (Ac 18:7). Philip the evangelist to Paul (Ac 21:8-10).

Joys of:

(Jn 4:36-38; 2Co 2:14; 7:6-7; Php 2:16; 1Th 2:13,19-20; 3:8-9; 2Jn 4; 3Jn 4).

Ordination of:

Matthias (Ac 1:26), seven deacons (Ac 6:5-6), Paul and Barnabas (Ac 13:3), Timothy (1Ti 4:14).

See Levites; Priest.

Prayer for:

Commanded—

Mt 9:37 Then he said to his disciples, "The harvest is plentiful but the workers are few. [38]Ask the Lord of the harvest, therefore, to send out workers into his harvest field." (+Lk 10:2)

Ro 15:30 I urge you, brothers, by our Lord Jesus Christ and by the love of the Spirit, to join me in my struggle by praying to God for me. [31]Pray that I may be rescued from the unbelievers in Judea and that my service in Jerusalem may be acceptable to the saints there, [32]so that by God's will I may come to you with joy and together with you be refreshed.

2Co 1:11 as you help us by your prayers. Then many will give thanks on our behalf for the gracious favor granted us in answer to the prayers of many.

Eph 6:18 And pray in the Spirit on all occasions with all kinds of prayers and requests. With this in mind, be alert and always keep on praying for all the saints.

19Pray also for me, that whenever I open my mouth, words may be given me so that I will fearlessly make known the mystery of the gospel, **20**for which I am an ambassador in chains. Pray that I may declare it fearlessly, as I should.

Php 1:19 for I know that through your prayers and the help given by the Spirit of Jesus Christ, what has happened to me will turn out for my deliverance.

Col 4:2 Devote yourselves to prayer, being watchful and thankful. **3**And pray for us, too, that God may open a door for our message, so that we may proclaim the mystery of Christ, for which I am in chains. **4**Pray that I may proclaim it clearly, as I should.

1Th 5:25 Brothers, pray for us.

2Th 3:1 Finally, brothers, pray for us that the message of the Lord may spread rapidly and be honored, just as it was with you. **2**And pray that we may be delivered from wicked and evil men, for not everyone has faith.

Phm 22 And one thing more: Prepare a guest room for me, because I hope to be restored to you in answer to your prayers.

Heb 13:18 Pray for us. We are sure that we have a clear conscience and desire to live honorably in every way. **19**I particularly urge you to pray so that I may be restored to you soon.

Exemplified—

2Ch 6:41 "Now arise, O LORD God, and come to your resting place, you and the ark of your might. May your priests, O LORD God, be clothed with salvation, may your saints rejoice in your goodness.

Ps 132:9 May your priests be clothed with righteousness; may your saints sing for joy.

Ac 1:24 Then they prayed, "Lord, you know everyone's heart. Show us which of these two you have chosen **25**to take over this apostolic ministry, which Judas left to go where he belongs."

Ac 4:29 Now, Lord, consider their threats and enable your servants to speak your word with great boldness.

Ac 6:6 They presented these men to the apostles, who prayed and laid their hands on them.

Ac 12:5 So Peter was kept in prison, but the church was earnestly praying to God for him.

Ac 14:23 Paul and Barnabas appointed elders for them in each church and, with prayer and fasting, committed them to the Lord, in whom they had put their trust.

Precepts for Guidance of:

(Jer 1:7-8,17-19; Eze 2:6-8; Mt 7:6; 10:7-8,11-13,16, 25-28; Lk 10:1-11; Col 4:17; 1Ti 1:3-4,11,18-19; 4:6-7, 12-16; 5:1-3,7-11,19-22; 6:3-4,10-14,17-21; 2Ti 1:6-8; 2:2-7,14-16,23-25; 4:1-2,5; 1Pe 5:1-4; 2Pe 1:12-16).

Promises to:

2Sa 23:6 But evil men are all to be cast aside like thorns, which are not gathered with the hand. **7**Whoever touches thorns uses a tool of iron or the shaft of a spear; they are burned up where they lie."

Ps 126:5 Those who sow in tears will reap with songs of joy. **6**He who goes out weeping, carrying seed to sow, will return with songs of joy, carrying sheaves with him.

Jer 1:7 But the LORD said to me, "Do not say, 'I am only a child.' You must go to everyone I send you to and say whatever I command you. **8**Do not be afraid of them, for I am with you and will rescue you," declares the LORD.

9Then the LORD reached out his hand and touched my

mouth and said to me, "Now, I have put my words in your mouth. **10**See, today I appoint you over nations and kingdoms to uproot and tear down, to destroy and overthrow, to build and to plant."

Jer 1:17 "Get yourself ready! Stand up and say to them whatever I command you. Do not be terrified by them, or I will terrify you before them. **18**Today I have made you a fortified city, an iron pillar and a bronze wall to stand against the whole land—against the kings of Judah, its officials, its priests and the people of the land. **19**They will fight against you but will not overcome you, for I am with you and will rescue you," declares the LORD. (+Jer 15:20-21)

Jer 20:11 But the LORD is with me like a mighty warrior; so my persecutors will stumble and not prevail. They will fail and be thoroughly disgraced; their dishonor will never be forgotten.

Da 12:3 Those who are wise will shine like the brightness of the heavens, and those who lead many to righteousness, like the stars for ever and ever.

Mt 10:28 Do not be afraid of those who kill the body but cannot kill the soul. Rather, be afraid of the One who can destroy both soul and body in hell. **29**Are not two sparrows sold for a penny? Yet not one of them will fall to the ground apart from the will of your Father. **30**And even the very hairs of your head are all numbered. **31**So don't be afraid; you are worth more than many sparrows.

Mt 28:20 and teaching them to obey everything I have commanded you. And surely I am with you always, to the very end of the age." (+Lk 10:19)

Lk 12:11 "When you are brought before synagogues, rulers and authorities, do not worry about how you will defend yourselves or what you will say, **12**for the Holy Spirit will teach you at that time what you should say."

Lk 24:49 I am going to send you what my Father has promised; but stay in the city until you have been clothed with power from on high."

Jn 4:36 Even now the reaper draws his wages, even now he harvests the crop for eternal life, so that the sower and the reaper may be glad together. **37**Thus the saying 'One sows and another reaps' is true. **38**I sent you to reap what you have not worked for. Others have done the hard work, and you have reaped the benefits of their labor."

Ac 1:4 On one occasion, while he was eating with them, he gave them this command: "Do not leave Jerusalem, but wait for the gift my Father promised, which you have heard me speak about. **5**For John baptized with water, but in a few days you will be baptized with the Holy Spirit."

Ac 1:8 But you will receive power when the Holy Spirit comes on you; and you will be my witnesses in Jerusalem and in all Judea and Samaria, and to the ends of the earth.' (+Ac 18:9-10; 1Co 3:8)

1Co 9:9 For it is written in the Law of Moses: "Do not muzzle an ox while it is treading out the grain." Is it about oxen that God is concerned? **10**Surely he says this for us, doesn't he? Yes, this was written for us, because when the plowman plows and the thresher threshes, they ought to do so in the hope of sharing in the harvest.

2Co 2:14 But thanks be to God, who always leads us in triumphal procession in Christ and through us spreads everywhere the fragrance of the knowledge of him. **15**For we are to God the aroma of Christ among those who are being saved and those who are perishing. **16**To the one we are the smell of death; to the other, the fragrance of life. And who is equal to such a task?

2Co 7:6 But God, who comforts the downcast, comforted

us by the coming of Titus, [7]and not only by his coming but also by the comfort you had given him. He told us about your longing for me, your deep sorrow, your ardent concern for me, so that my joy was greater than ever.

Php 2:16 as you hold out the word of life—in order that I may boast on the day of Christ that I did not run or labor for nothing.

1Th 2:13 And we also thank God continually because, when you received the word of God, which you heard from us, you accepted it not as the word of men, but as it actually is, the word of God, which is at work in you who believe.

1Th 2:19 For what is our hope, our joy, or the crown in which we will glory in the presence of our Lord Jesus when he comes? Is it not you? [20]Indeed, you are our glory and joy.

1Th 3:8 For now we really live, since you are standing firm in the Lord. [9]How can we thank God enough for you in return for all the joy we have in the presence of our God because of you? (+1Pe 5:4)

3Jn 4 I have no greater joy than to hear that my children are walking in the truth.

See Righteous, Promises to.

Success Attending:

Jonah (Jnh 1:5-6,9,14,16; 3:4-9). Apostles (Ac 2:1-4,41). Philip (Ac 8:6,8,12). Peter (Ac 9:32-35). Paul (Ac 13:16-43; 1Co 4:15; 9:2; 15:11; 2Co 3:2-3; 12:12; 13:4; Php 2:16; 1Th 1:5). Apollos (Ac 18:24-28).

See Revivals.

Trials and Persecutions of:

Foretold—

Mt 10:16 I am sending you out like sheep among wolves. Therefore be as shrewd as snakes and as innocent as doves.

[17]"Be on your guard against men; they will hand you over to the local councils and flog you in their synagogues. [18]On my account you will be brought before governors and kings as witnesses to them and to the Gentiles. [19]But when they arrest you, do not worry about what to say or how to say it. At that time you will be given what to say, [20]for it will not be you speaking, but the Spirit of your Father speaking through you.

[21]"Brother will betray brother to death, and a father his child; children will rebel against their parents and have them put to death. [22]All men will hate you because of me, but he who stands firm to the end will be saved. [23]When you are persecuted in one place, flee to another. I tell you the truth, you will not finish going through the cities of Israel before the Son of Man comes.

[24]"A student is not above his teacher, nor a servant above his master. [25]It is enough for the student to be like his teacher, and the servant like his master. If the head of the house has been called Beelzebub, how much more the members of his household!

[26]"So do not be afraid of them. There is nothing concealed that will not be disclosed, or hidden that will not be made known. [27]What I tell you in the dark, speak in the daylight; what is whispered in your ear, proclaim from the roofs. (+Jn 13:16; Mt 23:34)

Rehearsed—

Mt 23:34 Therefore I am sending you prophets and wise men and teachers. Some of them you will kill and crucify; others you will flog in your synagogues and pursue from town to town.

Instances of trials and persecutions of: Elijah (1Ki 22:24-27; 2Ch 18:23-26). Hanani (2Ch 16:10). Zechariah (2Ch 24:20-22,25; Mt 23:35; Lk 11:51).

Isaiah—

Isa 20:2 at that time the LORD spoke through Isaiah son of Amoz. He said to him, "Take off the sackcloth from your body and the sandals from your feet." And he did so, going around stripped and barefoot.

[3]Then the LORD said, "Just as my servant Isaiah has gone stripped and barefoot for three years, as a sign and portent against Egypt and Cush,

Jeremiah (Jer 11:19-21; 15:10,15; 17:15-18; 18:18-23; 20:1-3,7-18; 32:2-3; 33:1; 37:15-21; 38:6-13; 39:15; 43:1-7; La 3:53-55).

Ezekiel (Eze 3:24-25)—

Eze 24:15 The word of the LORD came to me: [16]"Son of man, with one blow I am about to take away from you the delight of your eyes. Yet do not lament or weep or shed any tears. [17]Groan quietly; do not mourn for the dead. Keep your turban fastened and your sandals on your feet; do not cover the lower part of your face or eat the customary food [of mourners]."

[18]So I spoke to the people in the morning, and in the evening my wife died. The next morning I did as I had been commanded.

Hosea—

Hos 1:2 When the LORD began to speak through Hosea, the LORD said to him, "Go, take to yourself an adulterous wife and children of unfaithfulness, because the land is guilty of the vilest adultery in departing from the LORD."

Amos—

Am 5:10 you hate the one who reproves in court and despise him who tells the truth.

Am 7:10 Then Amaziah the priest of Bethel sent a message to Jeroboam king of Israel: "Amos is raising a conspiracy against you in the very heart of Israel. The land cannot bear all his words. [11]For this is what Amos is saying:

"'Jeroboam will die by the sword, and Israel will surely go into exile, away from their native land.'"

[12]Then Amaziah said to Amos, "Get out, you seer! Go back to the land of Judah. Earn your bread there and do your prophesying there. [13]Don't prophesy anymore at Bethel, because this is the king's sanctuary and the temple of the kingdom."

[14]Amos answered Amaziah, "I was neither a prophet nor a prophet's son, but I was a shepherd, and I also took care of sycamore-fig trees. [15]But the LORD took me from tending the flock and said to me, 'Go, prophesy to my people Israel.' [16]Now then, hear the word of the LORD. You say,

"'Do not prophesy against Israel, and stop preaching against the house of Isaac.'

[17]"Therefore this is what the LORD says:

"'Your wife will become a prostitute in the city, and your sons and daughters will fall by the sword. Your land will be measured and divided up, and you yourself will die in a pagan country. And Israel will certainly go into exile, away from their native land.'"

The apostles (Ac 5:17-42). Peter (Ac 12:3-19).

Paul (Ac 9:23-25,29-30; 14:4-6,11-20; 16:16-24; 17:5-10,13-14; 18:12-13; 20:3; 21:27-40; 22:22-30; 23:10-35; 24:26-27; 27:9-44)—

1Co 2:1 When I came to you, brothers, I did not come with eloquence or superior wisdom as I proclaimed to you the testimony about God. [2]For I resolved to know nothing while I was with you except Jesus Christ and him crucified. [3]I came to you in weakness and fear, and with much trembling. [4]My message and my preaching were not with wise and persuasive words, but with a demonstration of the Spirit's power,

1Co 4:9 For it seems to me that God has put us apostles on display at the end of the procession, like men condemned to die in the arena. We have been made a spectacle to the whole universe, to angels as well as to men. [10]We are fools for Christ, but you are so wise in Christ! We are weak, but you are strong! You are honored, we are dishonored! [11]To this very hour we go hungry and thirsty, we are in rags, we are brutally treated, we are homeless. [12]We work hard with our own hands. When we are cursed, we bless; when we are persecuted, we endure it; [13]when we are slandered, we answer kindly. Up to this moment we have become the scum of the earth, the refuse of the world.

2Co 6:4 Rather, as servants of God we commend ourselves in every way: in great endurance; in troubles, hardships and distresses; [5]in beatings, imprisonments and riots; in hard work, sleepless nights and hunger; [6]in purity, understanding, patience and kindness; in the Holy Spirit and in sincere love; [7]in truthful speech and in the power of God; with weapons of righteousness in the right hand and in the left; [8]through glory and dishonor, bad report and good report; genuine, yet regarded as impostors; [9]known, yet regarded as unknown; dying, and yet we live on; beaten, and yet not killed; [10]sorrowful, yet always rejoicing; poor, yet making many rich; having nothing, and yet possessing everything.

2Co 7:5 For when we came into Macedonia, this body of ours had no rest, but we were harassed at every turn—conflicts on the outside, fears within.

2Co 11:23 Are they servants of Christ? (I am out of my mind to talk like this.) I am more. I have worked much harder, been in prison more frequently, been flogged more severely, and been exposed to death again and again. [24]Five times I received from the Jews the forty lashes minus one. [25]Three times I was beaten with rods, once I was stoned, three times I was shipwrecked, I spent a night and a day in the open sea, [26]I have been constantly on the move. I have been in danger from rivers, in danger from bandits, in danger from my own countrymen, in danger from Gentiles; in danger in the city, in danger in the country, in danger at sea; and in danger from false brothers. [27]I have labored and toiled and have often gone without sleep; I have known hunger and thirst and have often gone without food; I have been cold and naked. [28]Besides everything else, I face daily the pressure of my concern for all the churches. [29]Who is weak, and I do not feel weak? Who is led into sin, and I do not inwardly burn? [30]If I must boast, I will boast of the things that show my weakness. [31]The God and Father of the Lord Jesus, who is to be praised forever, knows that I am not lying. [32]In Damascus the governor under King Aretas had the city of the Damascenes guarded in order to arrest me. [33]But I was lowered in a basket from a window in the wall and slipped through his hands.

2Co 12:7 To keep me from becoming conceited because of these surpassingly great revelations, there was given me a thorn in my flesh, a messenger of Satan, to torment me. [8]Three times I pleaded with the Lord to take it away from me. [9]But he said to me, "My grace is sufficient for you, for my power is made perfect in weakness." Therefore I will boast all the more gladly about my weaknesses, so that Christ's power may rest on me. [10]That is why, for Christ's sake, I delight in weaknesses, in insults, in hardships, in persecutions, in difficulties. For when I am weak, then I am strong.

Eph 3:1 For this reason I, Paul, the prisoner of Christ Jesus for the sake of you Gentiles—

Eph 3:13 I ask you, therefore, not to be discouraged because of my sufferings for you, which are your glory. (+2Ti 1:8,16; 2:9; 4:16-17)

See Paul, Persecutions of; also, Accusation, False; Persecution.

Zealous:

Titus (2Co 8:16-17). Epaphroditus (Php 2:25-30). Epaphras (Col 4:12-13). Tychicus (Col 4:7). John, in his vision (Rev 5:4-5). *See Zeal.*

False and Corrupt:

1Ki 12:31 Jeroboam built shrines on high places and appointed priests from all sorts of people, even though they were not Levites.

Ne 13:29 Remember them, O my God, because they defiled the priestly office and the covenant of the priesthood and of the Levites.

Jer 2:8 The priests did not ask, 'Where is the LORD?' Those who deal with the law did not know me; the leaders rebelled against me. The prophets prophesied by Baal, following worthless idols.

Jer 6:13 "From the least to the greatest, all are greedy for gain; prophets and priests alike, all practice deceit. [14]They dress the wound of my people as though it were not serious. 'Peace, peace,' they say, when there is no peace. (+Jer 8:10-11)

Jer 12:10 Many shepherds will ruin my vineyard and trample down my field; they will turn my pleasant field into a desolate wasteland.

La 2:14 The visions of your prophets were false and worthless; they did not expose your sin to ward off your captivity. The oracles they gave you were false and misleading.

Eze 22:25 There is a conspiracy of her princes within her like a roaring lion tearing its prey; they devour people, take treasures and precious things and make many widows within her.

Eze 22:28 Her prophets whitewash these deeds for them by false visions and lying divinations. They say, 'This is what the Sovereign LORD says'—when the LORD has not spoken.

Eze 44:8 Instead of carrying out your duty in regard to my holy things, you put others in charge of my sanctuary.

Eze 44:10 "'The Levites who went far from me when Israel went astray and who wandered from me after their idols must bear the consequences of their sin. (+Hos 9:7)

Hos 9:8 The prophet, along with my God, is the watchman over Ephraim, yet snares await him on all his paths, and hostility in the house of his God.

Zep 3:4 Her prophets are arrogant; they are treacherous men. Her priests profane the sanctuary and do violence to the law.

Mal 1:6 "A son honors his father, and a servant his master. If I am a father, where is the honor due me? If I am a master, where is the respect due me?" says the LORD Almighty. "It is you, O priests, who show contempt for my name. "But you ask, 'How have we shown contempt for your name?' (+Mal 1:7-10; 2Ti 4:3)

Mercenary (1Sa 8:3)—

Isa 56:11 They are dogs with mighty appetites; they never have enough. They are shepherds who lack understanding; they all turn to their own way, each seeks his own gain.

Mic 3:11 Her leaders judge for a bribe, her priests teach for a price, and her prophets tell fortunes for money. Yet they lean upon the LORD and say, "Is not the LORD among us? No disaster will come upon us."

Presumptuous—

Dt 18:20 But a prophet who presumes to speak in my name anything I have not commanded him to say, or a prophet who speaks in the name of other gods, must be put to death."

²¹You may say to yourselves, "How can we know when a message has not been spoken by the LORD?" ²²If what a prophet proclaims in the name of the LORD does not take place or come true, that is a message the LORD has not spoken. That prophet has spoken presumptuously. Do not be afraid of him.

Jn 5:43 I have come in my Father's name, and you do not accept me; but if someone else comes in his own name, you will accept him.

Insincere—

Php 1:15 It is true that some preach Christ out of envy and rivalry, but others out of goodwill. ¹⁶The latter do so in love, knowing that I am put here for the defense of the gospel.

Senseless—

Jer 10:21 The shepherds are senseless and do not inquire of the LORD; so they do not prosper and all their flock is scattered.

Adulterous (1Sa 2:22; Jer 23:14)—

Hos 6:9 As marauders lie in ambush for a man, so do bands of priests; they murder on the road to Shechem, committing shameful crimes.

Murderous (Hos 6:9).

Pervert the truth—

2Co 2:17 Unlike so many, we do not peddle the word of God for profit. On the contrary, in Christ we speak before God with sincerity, like men sent from God.

2Co 11:3 But I am afraid that just as Eve was deceived by the serpent's cunning, your minds may somehow be led astray from your sincere and pure devotion to Christ. ⁴For if someone comes to you and preaches a Jesus other than the Jesus we preached, or if you receive a different spirit from the one you received, or a different gospel from the one you accepted, you put up with it easily enough.

2Co 11:13 For such men are false apostles, deceitful workmen, masquerading as apostles of Christ. ¹⁴And no wonder, for Satan himself masquerades as an angel of light. ¹⁵It is not surprising, then, if his servants masquerade as servants of righteousness. Their end will be what their actions deserve.

Gal 1:6 I am astonished that you are so quickly deserting the one who called you by the grace of Christ and are turning to a different gospel— ⁷which is really no gospel at all. Evidently some people are throwing you into confusion and are trying to pervert the gospel of Christ. ⁸But even if we or an angel from heaven should preach a gospel other than the one we preached to you, let him be eternally condemned!

1Ti 4:1 The Spirit clearly says that in later times some will abandon the faith and follow deceiving spirits and things taught by demons. ²Such teachings come through hypocritical liars, whose consciences have been seared as with a hot iron. ³They forbid people to marry and order them to abstain from certain foods, which God created to be received with thanksgiving by those who believe and who know the truth.

1Ti 4:7 Have nothing to do with godless myths and old wives' tales; rather, train yourself to be godly.

Lead the people astray (Isa 3:12)—

Jer 50:6 "My people have been lost sheep; their shepherds have led them astray and caused them to roam on the mountains. They wandered over mountain and hill and forgot their own resting place.

Addicted to alcohol—

Isa 28:7 And these also stagger from wine and reel from beer: Priests and prophets stagger from beer and are befuddled with wine; they reel from beer, they stagger when seeing visions, they stumble when rendering decisions.

Isa 56:12 "Come," each one cries, "let me get wine! Let us drink our fill of beer! And tomorrow will be like today, or even far better."

Indifferent to good and evil—

Isa 56:10 Israel's watchmen are blind, they all lack knowledge; they are all mute dogs, they cannot bark; they lie around and dream, they love to sleep.

Eze 22:26 Her priests do violence to my law and profane my holy things; they do not distinguish between the holy and the common; they teach that there is no difference between the unclean and the clean; and they shut their eyes to the keeping of my Sabbaths, so that I am profaned among them.

Desired by the wicked—

Isa 30:10 They say to the seers, "See no more visions!" and to the prophets, "Give us no more visions of what is right! Tell us pleasant things, prophesy illusions. (+Isa 30:11; Jer 5:13-14,30-31)

Am 2:11 I also raised up prophets from among your sons and Nazirites from among your young men. Is this not true, people of Israel?" declares the LORD. ¹²"But you made the Nazirites drink wine and commanded the prophets not to prophesy.

Mic 2:11 If a liar and deceiver comes and says, 'I will prophesy for you plenty of wine and beer,' he would be just the prophet for this people!

Denunciations against false ministers—

Isa 5:20 Woe to those who call evil good and good evil, who put darkness for light and light for darkness, who put bitter for sweet and sweet for bitter.

Jer 23:11 "Both prophet and priest are godless; even in my temple I find their wickedness," declares the LORD. (+Jer 23:12)

Jer 23:14 And among the prophets of Jerusalem I have seen something horrible: They commit adultery and live a lie. They strengthen the hands of evildoers, so that no one turns from his wickedness. They are all like Sodom to me; the people of Jerusalem are like Gomorrah."

¹⁵Therefore, this is what the LORD Almighty says concerning the prophets:

"I will make them eat bitter food and drink poisoned water, because from the prophets of Jerusalem ungodliness has spread throughout the land."

¹⁶This is what the LORD Almighty says:

"Do not listen to what the prophets are prophesying to you; they fill you with false hopes. They speak visions from their own minds, not from the mouth of the LORD. (+Jer 23:17-20)

Jer 23:21 I did not send these prophets, yet they have run with their message; I did not speak to them, yet they have prophesied. (+Jer 23:22-30)

Jer 23:31 Yes," declares the LORD, "I am against the prophets who wag their own tongues and yet declare, 'The

LORD declares.' [32]Indeed, I am against those who prophesy false dreams," declares the LORD. "They tell them and lead my people astray with their reckless lies, yet I did not send or appoint them. They do not benefit these people in the least," declares the LORD. (+Jer 23:33-35)

Jer 23:36 But you must not mention 'the oracle of the LORD' again, because every man's own word becomes his oracle and so you distort the words of the living God, the LORD Almighty, our God. (+Jer 23:37-40)

La 4:13 But it happened because of the sins of her prophets and the iniquities of her priests, who shed within her the blood of the righteous.

[14]Now they grope through the streets like men who are blind. They are so defiled with blood that no one dares to touch their garments. (+Eze 13:1)

Eze 13:2 "Son of man, prophesy against the prophets of Israel who are now prophesying. Say to those who prophesy out of their own imagination: 'Hear the word of the LORD! [3]This is what the Sovereign LORD says: Woe to the foolish prophets who follow their own spirit and have seen nothing! [4]Your prophets, O Israel, are like jackals among ruins. [5]You have not gone up to the breaks in the wall to repair it for the house of Israel so that it will stand firm in the battle on the day of the LORD. (+Eze 13:6-9)

Eze 13:10 "'Because they lead my people astray, saying, "Peace," when there is no peace, and because, when a flimsy wall is built, they cover it with whitewash, [11]therefore tell those who cover it with whitewash that it is going to fall. Rain will come in torrents, and I will send hailstones hurtling down, and violent winds will burst forth. (+Eze 13:12-15)

Eze 13:16 those prophets of Israel who prophesied to Jerusalem and saw visions of peace for her when there was no peace, declares the Sovereign LORD."'

[17]"Now, son of man, set your face against the daughters of your people who prophesy out of their own imagination. Prophesy against them [18]and say, 'This is what the Sovereign LORD says: Woe to the women who sew magic charms on all their wrists and make veils of various lengths for their heads in order to ensnare people. Will you ensnare the lives of my people but preserve your own? [19]You have profaned me among my people for a few handfuls of barley and scraps of bread. By lying to my people, who listen to lies, you have killed those who should not have died and have spared those who should not live. (+Eze 13:20-21)

Eze 13:22 Because you disheartened the righteous with your lies, when I had brought them no grief, and because you encouraged the wicked not to turn from their evil ways and so save their lives, (+Eze 13:23; 34:1-10,16-22; Mt 23:4-7,13-14,36)

2Pe 2:1 But there were also false prophets among the people, just as there will be false teachers among you. They will secretly introduce destructive heresies, even denying the sovereign Lord who bought them—bringing swift destruction on themselves. [2]Many will follow their shameful ways and will bring the way of truth into disrepute. [3]In their greed these teachers will exploit you with stories they have made up. Their condemnation has long been hanging over them, and their destruction has not been sleeping. (+2Pe 2:4-12)

2Pe 2:13 They will be paid back with harm for the harm they have done. Their idea of pleasure is to carouse in broad daylight. They are blots and blemishes, reveling in their pleasures while they feast with you. [14]With eyes full of adultery, they never stop sinning; they seduce the un-

stable; they are experts in greed—an accursed brood! [15]They have left the straight way and wandered off to follow the way of Balaam son of Beor, who loved the wages of wickedness. [16]But he was rebuked for his wrongdoing by a donkey—a beast without speech—who spoke with a man's voice and restrained the prophet's madness. [17]These men are springs without water and mists driven by a storm. Blackest darkness is reserved for them. [18]For they mouth empty, boastful words and, by appealing to the lustful desires of sinful human nature, they entice people who are just escaping from those who live in error. [19]They promise them freedom, while they themselves are slaves of depravity—for a man is a slave to whatever has mastered him. (+2Pe 2:20-22)

Warnings against false ministers—

Dt 13:1 If a prophet, or one who foretells by dreams, appears among you and announces to you a miraculous sign or wonder, [2]and if the sign or wonder of which he has spoken takes place, and he says, "Let us follow other gods" (gods you have not known) "and let us worship them," [3]you must not listen to the words of that prophet or dreamer. The LORD your God is testing you to find out whether you love him with all your heart and with all your soul. [4]It is the LORD your God you must follow, and him you must revere. Keep his commands and obey him; serve him and hold fast to him.

Isa 8:19 When men tell you to consult mediums and spiritists, who whisper and mutter, should not a people inquire of their God? Why consult the dead on behalf of the living? [20]To the law and to the testimony! If they do not speak according to this word, they have no light of dawn.

Jer 14:13 But I said, "Ah, Sovereign LORD, the prophets keep telling them, 'You will not see the sword or suffer famine. Indeed, I will give you lasting peace in this place.'"

[14]Then the LORD said to me, "The prophets are prophesying lies in my name. I have not sent them or appointed them or spoken to them. They are prophesying to you false visions, divinations, idolatries and the delusions of their own minds. [15]Therefore, this is what the LORD says about the prophets who are prophesying in my name: I did not send them, yet they are saying, 'No sword or famine will touch this land.' Those same prophets will perish by sword and famine. [16]And the people they are prophesying to will be thrown out into the streets of Jerusalem because of the famine and sword. There will be no one to bury them or their wives, their sons or their daughters. I will pour out on them the calamity they deserve. (+Jer 27:9-18)

Mt 5:19 Anyone who breaks one of the least of these commandments and teaches others to do the same will be called least in the kingdom of heaven, but whoever practices and teaches these commands will be called great in the kingdom of heaven.

Mt 7:15 "Watch out for false prophets. They come to you in sheep's clothing, but inwardly they are ferocious wolves. (+Mt 7:16-21)

Mt 7:22 Many will say to me on that day, 'Lord, Lord, did we not prophesy in your name, and in your name drive out demons and perform many miracles?' [23]Then I will tell them plainly, 'I never knew you. Away from me, you evildoers!'

Mt 15:9 They worship me in vain; their teachings are but rules taught by men.'"

Mt 15:13 He replied, "Every plant that my heavenly Father has not planted will be pulled up by the roots.

[14]Leave them; they are blind guides. If a blind man leads a blind man, both will fall into a pit." (+Lk 6:39)

Mt 23:3 So you must obey them and do everything they tell you. But do not do what they do, for they do not practice what they preach. [4]They tie up heavy loads and put them on men's shoulders, but they themselves are not willing to lift a finger to move them.

Mt 23:13 "Woe to you, teachers of the law and Pharisees, you hypocrites! You shut the kingdom of heaven in men's faces. You yourselves do not enter, nor will you let those enter who are trying to.

Mt 24:4 Jesus answered: "Watch out that no one deceives you. [5]For many will come in my name, claiming, 'I am the Christ,' and will deceive many. (+Mt 24:11)

Mt 24:24 For false Christs and false prophets will appear and perform great signs and miracles to deceive even the elect—if that were possible. (+Mt 24:26,48-51)

Mk 13:21 At that time if anyone says to you, 'Look, here is the Christ!' or, 'Look, there he is!' do not believe it. [22]For false Christs and false prophets will appear and perform signs and miracles to deceive the elect—if that were possible. (+Lk 21:8)

Jn 10:1 "I tell you the truth, the man who does not enter the sheep pen by the gate, but climbs in by some other way, is a thief and a robber.

Jn 10:5 But they will never follow a stranger; in fact, they will run away from him because they do not recognize a stranger's voice."

Jn 10:8 All who ever came before me were thieves and robbers, but the sheep did not listen to them.

Jn 10:10 The thief comes only to steal and kill and destroy; I have come that they may have life, and have it to the full.

Jn 10:12 The hired hand is not the shepherd who owns the sheep. So when he sees the wolf coming, he abandons the sheep and runs away. Then the wolf attacks the flock and scatters it. [13]The man runs away because he is a hired hand and cares nothing for the sheep. (+Ac 20:20)

Ac 20:30 Even from your own number men will arise and distort the truth in order to draw away disciples after them.

Eph 4:14 Then we will no longer be infants, tossed back and forth by the waves, and blown here and there by every wind of teaching and by the cunning and craftiness of men in their deceitful scheming.

Php 3:2 Watch out for those dogs, those men who do evil, those mutilators of the flesh.

Col 2:4 I tell you this so that no one may deceive you by fine-sounding arguments.

Col 2:8 See to it that no one takes you captive through hollow and deceptive philosophy, which depends on human tradition and the basic principles of this world rather than on Christ.

Col 2:18 Do not let anyone who delights in false humility and the worship of angels disqualify you for the prize. Such a person goes into great detail about what he has seen, and his unspiritual mind puffs him up with idle notions. [19]He has lost connection with the Head, from whom the whole body, supported and held together by its ligaments and sinews, grows as God causes it to grow.

1Ti 1:3 As I urged you when I went into Macedonia, stay there in Ephesus so that you may command certain men not to teach false doctrines any longer [4]nor to devote themselves to myths and endless genealogies. These promote controversies rather than God's work—which is by faith. [5]The goal of this command is love, which comes from a pure heart and a good conscience and a sincere

faith. [6]Some have wandered away from these and turned to meaningless talk. [7]They want to be teachers of the law, but they do not know what they are talking about or what they so confidently affirm.

1Ti 6:3 If anyone teaches false doctrines and does not agree to the sound instruction of our Lord Jesus Christ and to godly teaching, [4]he is conceited and understands nothing. He has an unhealthy interest in controversies and quarrels about words that result in envy, strife, malicious talk, evil suspicions [5]and constant friction between men of corrupt mind, who have been robbed of the truth and who think that godliness is a means to financial gain.

2Ti 2:17 Their teaching will spread like gangrene. Among them are Hymenaeus and Philetus, [18]who have wandered away from the truth. They say that the resurrection has already taken place, and they destroy the faith of some.

Tit 1:10 For there are many rebellious people, mere talkers and deceivers, especially those of the circumcision group. [11]They must be silenced, because they are ruining whole households by teaching things they ought not to teach—and that for the sake of dishonest gain. [12]Even one of their own prophets has said, "Cretans are always liars, evil brutes, lazy gluttons." [13]This testimony is true. Therefore, rebuke them sharply, so that they will be sound in the faith [14]and will pay no attention to Jewish myths or to the commands of those who reject the truth.

1Jn 2:18 Dear children, this is the last hour; and as you have heard that the antichrist is coming, even now many antichrists have come. This is how we know it is the last hour. (+1Jn 2:19,22-23)

1Jn 2:26 I am writing these things to you about those who are trying to lead you astray.

1Jn 4:1 Dear friends, do not believe every spirit, but test the spirits to see whether they are from God, because many false prophets have gone out into the world. [2]This is how you can recognize the Spirit of God: Every spirit that acknowledges that Jesus Christ has come in the flesh is from God, [3]but every spirit that does not acknowledge Jesus is not from God. This is the spirit of the antichrist, which you have heard is coming and even now is already in the world.

1Jn 4:5 They are from the world and therefore speak from the viewpoint of the world, and the world listens to them.

2Jn 7 Many deceivers, who do not acknowledge Jesus Christ as coming in the flesh, have gone out into the world. Any such person is the deceiver and the antichrist.

2Jn 10 If anyone comes to you and does not bring this teaching, do not take him into your house or welcome him. [11]Anyone who welcomes him shares in his wicked work.

Rev 2:12 "To the angel of the church in Pergamum write: These are the words of him who has the sharp, double-edged sword.

Rev 2:14 Nevertheless, I have a few things against you: You have people there who hold to the teaching of Balaam, who taught Balak to entice the Israelites to sin by eating food sacrificed to idols and by committing sexual immorality. [15]Likewise you also have those who hold to the teaching of the Nicolaitans.

Rev 2:18 "To the angel of the church in Thyatira write: These are the words of the Son of God, whose eyes are like blazing fire and whose feet are like burnished bronze. (+Rev 2:20)

Rev 2:21 I have given her time to repent of her immorality, but she is unwilling. [22]So I will cast her on a bed of suffering, and I will make those who commit adultery with her suffer intensely, unless they repent of her ways.

²³I will strike her children dead. Then all the churches will know that I am he who searches hearts and minds, and I will repay each of you according to your deeds.

Judgments upon false ministers—

Isa 29:10 The LORD has brought over you a deep sleep: He has sealed your eyes (the prophets); he has covered your heads (the seers).

¹¹For you this whole vision is nothing but words sealed in a scroll. And if you give the scroll to someone who can read, and say to him, "Read this, please," he will answer, "I can't; it is sealed." (+Hos 5:1)

Gal 5:10 I am confident in the Lord that you will take no other view. The one who is throwing you into confusion will pay the penalty, whoever he may be.

Punishment of false ministers (Dt 13:1)—

Dt 13:5 That prophet or dreamer must be put to death, because he preached rebellion against the LORD your God, who brought you out of Egypt and redeemed you from the land of slavery; he has tried to turn you from the way the LORD your God commanded you to follow. You must purge the evil from among you.

Dt 18:20 But a prophet who presumes to speak in my name anything I have not commanded him to say, or a prophet who speaks in the name of other gods, must be put to death."

Isa 43:27 Your first father sinned; your spokesmen rebelled against me. ²⁸So I will disgrace the dignitaries of your temple, and I will consign Jacob to destruction and Israel to scorn. (+Jer 14:15)

Jer 23:1 "Woe to the shepherds who are destroying and scattering the sheep of my pasture!" declares the LORD. ²Therefore this is what the LORD, the God of Israel, says to the shepherds who tend my people: "Because you have scattered my flock and driven them away and have not bestowed care on them, I will bestow punishment on you for the evil you have done," declares the LORD. (+Jer 23:11,15,21; 27:9-18; La 4:13-14)

Eze 14:9 "'And if the prophet is enticed to utter a prophecy, I the LORD have enticed that prophet, and I will stretch out my hand against him and destroy him from among my people Israel. ¹⁰They will bear their guilt—the prophet will be as guilty as the one who consults him. (+Hos 4:5-6,8-13)

Mic 3:5 This is what the LORD says: "As for the prophets who lead my people astray, if one feeds them, they proclaim 'peace'; if he does not, they prepare to wage war against him. ⁶Therefore night will come over you, without visions, and darkness, without divination. The sun will set for the prophets, and the day will go dark for them. ⁷The seers will be ashamed and the diviners disgraced. They will all cover their faces because there is no answer from God."

Zec 10:3 "My anger burns against the shepherds, and I will punish the leaders; for the LORD Almighty will care for his flock, the house of Judah, and make them like a proud horse in battle.

Zec 13:2 "On that day, I will banish the names of the idols from the land, and they will be remembered no more," declares the LORD Almighty. "I will remove both the prophets and the spirit of impurity from the land. ³And if anyone still prophesies, his father and mother, to whom he was born, will say to him, 'You must die, because you have told lies in the LORD's name.' When he prophesies, his own parents will stab him.

⁴"On that day every prophet will be ashamed of his prophetic vision. He will not put on a prophet's garment of hair in order to deceive. ⁵He will say, 'I am not a prophet. I am a farmer; the land has been my livelihood since my youth.' (+Mal 2:1-3,8-9; Lk 12:45-46; 2Pe 2:3)

Jude 4 For certain men whose condemnation was written about long ago have secretly slipped in among you. They are godless men, who change the grace of our God into a license for immorality and deny Jesus Christ our only Sovereign and Lord.

Jude 11 Woe to them! They have taken the way of Cain; they have rushed for profit into Balaam's error; they have been destroyed in Korah's rebellion.

Instances of false and corrupt: Nadab and Abihu (Lev 10:1-2). Korah, Dathan, and Abiram (Nu 16:1-40). Eli's sons (1Sa 2:12-17,22,25,29,34; 3:13; 4:11). Samuel's sons (1Sa 8:1-3). The old prophet of Bethel (1Ki 13:11-32). Jonathan (Jdg 17:7-13; 18). Noadiah (Ne 6:14). Priests under, Jehoash (2Ki 12:7; 2Ch 24:5-6). Hezekiah (2Ch 30:3,5). Priests and Levites (Ezr 2:61-62; 9:1-2; 10:18-24; Ne 13:4-9,28-29; Zec 7:5-6). Hananiah (Jer 28). Jonah (Jnh 1:1-6). Scribes and Pharisees (Mt 23:15-16), Caiaphas (Mt 26:2-3,57,63-65; Jn 11:49-51; 18:14). Judas (Mt 26:14-16,21-25,47-50; 27:3-5; Jn 12:4-6; Ac 1:18). Judaizing Christians (Gal 3:1-2; 4:17; 6:12-13). Hymenaeus (1Ti 1:20; 2Ti 2:17-18). Alexander (1Ti 1:20). Philetus (2Ti 2:17-18).

MINNI [4973]. A district of Armenia (Jer 51:27).

MINNITH [4976]. A place E of the Jordan (Jdg 11:33; Eze 27:17).

MINOR PROPHETS, THE See Prophets, The Minor.

MINORITY REPORT See Reports.

MINORS Legal status of (Gal 4:1-2).
See Orphan; Young Men.

MINSTREL NIV "harpist" (1Sa 16:23); "flute players" (Mt 9:23). See Flute; Harp.

MINT [2455] (sweet odor). (Mt 23:23; Lk 11:42).

MIPHKAD See Gate, Inspection.

MIRACLES [4603, 7098, 7099, 1539, 2240, 4956, 5469].

NIV+ MIRACLE, MIRACULOUS, MIRACULOUSLY

Called: Marvelous things (Ps 78:12), marvelous works (Ps 105:5; Isa 29:14), signs and wonders (Jer 32:21; Jn 4:48; 2Co 12:12).

Performed through the power of God (Jn 3:2; Ac 14:3; 15:12; 19:11), of the Holy Spirit (Mt 12:28; Ro 15:19; 1Co 12:9-10,28-30), in the name of Christ (Mk 16:17; Ac 3:16; 4:30). Faith required in those who perform (Mt 17:20; 21:21; Jn 14:12; Ac 3:16; 6:8). Faith required in those for whom they were performed (Mt 9:28; Mk 9:22-24; Ac 14:9). Power to work, given the disciples (Mk 3:14-15; 16:17-18,20). Demanded by unbelievers (Mt 12:38-39; 16:1; Lk 11:16,29; 23:8).

Alleged miracles performed by magicians (Ex 7:10-12,22; 8:7), by other impostors (Mt 7:22). Performed through the powers of evil (2Th 2:9; Rev 16:14). Done in support of false religions (Dt 13:1-2), by false Christs (Mt 24:24), by false prophets (Mt 24:24; Rev 19:20), by the medium of Endor (1Sa 28:7-14), by Simon (Ac 8:9-11). Not to be regarded (Dt 13:3). Deceive the ungodly (2Th 2:10-12; Rev 13:14; 19:20). A mark of apostasy (2Th 2:3,9; Rev 13:13).

Catalog of, and Supernatural Events:

Creation (Ge 1). Flood (Ge 7-8). Confusion of tongues (Ge 11:1-9). Fire on Abraham's sacrifice (Ge 15:17). Conception of Isaac (Ge 17:17; 18:12; 21:2). Destruction of Sodom (Ge 19). Lot's wife turned to salt (Ge 19:26). Closing of the wombs of Abimelech's household (Ge 20:17-18). Opening of Hagar's eyes (Ge 21:19). Conception of Jacob and Esau (Ge 25:21). Opening of Rachel's womb (Ge 30:22).

Burning bush (Ex 3:2). Transformation of Moses' rod into a serpent (Ex 4:3-4,30; 7:10,12). Moses' leprosy (Ex 4:6-7,30). Plagues in Egypt. *See Plague.* Pillar of cloud and fire (Ex 13:21-22; 14:19-20). Passage of the Red Sea (Ex 14:22). Destruction of Pharaoh and his army (Ex 4:23-30). Sweetening the waters of Marah (Ex 15:25). Manna (Ex 16:4-31). Quail (Ex 16:13). Defeat of Amalek (Ex 17:9-13). Transfiguration of the face of Moses (Ex 34:29-35). Water from the rock (Ex 17:5,7). Thundering and lightning on Sinai (Ex 19:16-20; 24:10,15-17; Dt 4:33). Miriam's leprosy (Nu 12:10-15). Judgments by fire (Nu 11:1-3). Destruction of Korah (Nu 16:31-35; Dt 11:6-7). Plague (Nu 16:46-50). Aaron's rod buds (Nu 17:1-9). Waters from the rock in Kadesh (Nu 20:8-11). Plague of serpents (Nu 21:6-9). Destruction of Nadab and Abihu (Lev 10:1-2). Balaam's donkey speaks (Nu 22:23-30). Preservation of Moses (Dt 34:7).

Jordan divided (Jos 3:14-17; 4:16-18). Fall of Jericho (Jos 6:20). Midianites destroyed (Jdg 7:16-22). Hail on the confederated kings (Jos 10:11). Sun and moon stand still (Jos 10:12-14).

Dew on Gideon's fleece (Jdg 6:37-40). Samson's strength (Jdg 14:6; 16:3,29-30). Samson supplied with water (Jdg 15:19).

Fall of Dagon (1Sa 6:7-14). Tumors (1Sa 5:9-12; 6:1-18). Destruction of the people of Beth Shemesh (1Sa 6:19-20). Thunder (1Sa 12:16-18). Destruction of Uzzah (2Sa 6:1-8). Plague in Israel (1Ch 21:14-26).

Fire on the sacrifices of Aaron (Lev 9:24), of Gideon (Jdg 6:21), of Manoah (Jdg 13:19-20), of Solomon (2Ch 7:1), of Elijah (1Ki 18:38).

Jeroboam's hand withered (1Ki 13:3-6). Appearance of blood (2Ki 3:20-22). Panic of the Syrians (2Ki 7:6-7). Elijah is fed by ravens (1Ki 17:6), by an angel (1Ki 19:1-8), increases the widow's meal and oil (1Ki 17:9-16; Lk 4:26), raises the widow's son (1Ki 17:17-24). Rain in answer to Elijah's prayer (1Ki 18:41-45). Elijah brings fire on Ahaziah's army (2Ki 1:10-12), divides Jordan (2Ki 2:8). Elijah's translation (2Ki 2:11).

Elisha divides Jordan (2Ki 2:14), sweetens the waters of Jericho (2Ki 2:19-22), increases a widow's oil (2Ki 4:1-7), raises the Shunammite's child (2Ki 4:18-37), renders the poisoned stew harmless (2Ki 4:38-41), feeds one hundred men (2Ki 4:42-44), cures Naaman (2Ki 5:1-19), strikes Gehazi with leprosy (2Ki 5:26-27), causes the ax to float (2Ki 6:6), reveals the counsel of the king of Syria (2Ki 6:12), causes the eyes of his servant to be opened (2Ki 6:17), strikes with blindness the army of the king of Syria (2Ki 6:18), the dead man restored to life (2Ki 13:21).

Destruction of Sennacherib's army (2Ki 19:35; Isa 37:36), return of the shadow on the stairway (2Ki 20:9-11), Hezekiah's cure (Isa 38:21), deliverance of Shadrach, Meshach, and Abednego (Da 3:23-27), of Daniel (Da 6:22), the sea calmed on Jonah being cast into it (Jnh 1:15), Jonah in the fish's belly (Jnh 1:17; 2:10), his plant (Jnh 4:6-7).

Conception by Elizabeth (Lk 1:18,24-25). The incarna-tion of Jesus (Mt 1:18-25; Lk 1:26-80). The appearance of the star of Bethlehem (Mt 2:1-9). The deliverance of Jesus (Mt 2:13-23).

Of Jesus, in Chronological Order:

Water changed into wine (Jn 2:1-11). Heals the nobleman's son (Jn 4:46-54). Catch of fish (Lk 5:1-11). Heals the demoniac (Mk 1:23-26; Lk 4:33-36). Heals Peter's mother-in-law (Mt 8:14-17; Mk 1:29-31; Lk 4:38-39). Cleanses the leper (Mt 8:1-4; Mk 1:40-45; Lk 5:12-16). Heals the paralytic (Mt 9:1-8; Mk 2:1-12; Lk 5:17-26). Heals the crippled man (Jn 5:1-16). Restores the withered hand (Mt 12:9-13; Mk 3:1-5; Lk 6:6-11). Restores the centurion's servant (Mt 8:5-13; Lk 7:1-10). Raises the widow's son to life (Lk 7:11-16). Heals a demoniac (Mt 12:22-37; Mk 3:11; Lk 11:14-15). Stills the tempest (Mt 8:23-27; 14:32; Mk 4:35-41; Lk 8:22-25). Casts demons out of two men of Gadara (Mt 8:28-34; Mk 5:1-20; Lk 8:26-39). Raises from the dead the daughter of Jairus (Mt 9:18-19,23-26; Mk 5:22-24,35-43; Lk 8:41-42,49-56). Cures the woman with the issue of blood (Mt 9:20-22; Mk 5:25-34; Lk 8:43-48). Restores two blind men to sight (Mt 9:27-31). Heals a demoniac (Mt 9:32-33). Feeds five thousand people (Mt 14:15-21; Mk 6:35-44; Lk 9:12-17; Jn 6:5-14). Walks on the sea (Mt 14:22-33; Mk 6:45-52; Jn 6:16-21). Heals the daughter of the Syrian Phoenician woman (Mt 15:21-28; Mk 7:24-30). Feeds four thousand people (Mt 15:32-39; Mk 8:1-9). Restores one deaf and mute (Mk 7:31-37). Restores a blind man (Mk 8:22-26). Restores a possessed child (Mt 17:14-21; Mk 9:14-29; Lk 9:37-43). Tribute money obtained from a fish's mouth (Mt 17:24-27). Restores ten lepers (Lk 17:11-19). Opens the eyes of a man born blind (Jn 9). Raises Lazarus from the dead (Jn 11:1-46). Heals the woman with the spirit of infirmity (Lk 13:10-17). Cures a man with dropsy (Lk 14:1-6). Restores two blind men near Jericho (Mt 20:29-34; Mk 10:46-52; Lk 18:35-43). Curses a fig tree (Mt 21:17-22; Mk 11:12-14,20-24). Heals the ear of Malchus (Lk 22:49-51). Second catch of fish (Jn 21:6).

Of the Disciples of Jesus:

By the seventy-two (Lk 10:17-20), by other disciples (Mk 9:39; Jn 14:12), by the apostles (Ac 3:6,12-13,16; 4:10,30; 9:34-35; 16:18). Peter cures the sick (Ac 5:15-16), Aeneas (Ac 9:34), raises Dorcas (Ac 9:40), announces the death of Ananias and Sapphira (Ac 5:5,10). Peter and John cure a lame man (Ac 3:2-11). Peter and other apostles delivered from prison (Ac 5:19-23; 12:6-11; 16:26). Philip carried away by the Spirit (Ac 8:39). Paul strikes Elymas with blindness (Ac 13:11), heals a cripple (Ac 14:10), casts out evil spirits and cures sick (Ac 16:18; 19:11-12; 28:8-9), raises Eutychus to life (Ac 20:9-12), shakes a viper off of his hand (Ac 28:5). Paul cured of blindness (Ac 9:3-6,17-18).

Convincing Effect of, on:

The Israelites—

Ex 4:28 Then Moses told Aaron everything the Lord had sent him to say, and also about all the miraculous signs he had commanded him to perform.

[29]Moses and Aaron brought together all the elders of the Israelites, [30]and Aaron told them everything the Lord had said to Moses. He also performed the signs before the people, [31]and they believed. And when they heard that the Lord was concerned about them and had seen their misery, they bowed down and worshiped.

Ex 14:31 And when the Israelites saw the great power the Lord displayed against the Egyptians, the people feared the LORD and put their trust in him and in Moses his servant. (+Nu 17:1-13)

Pharaoh's servants—

Ex 10:7 Pharaoh's officials said to him, "How long will this man be a snare to us? Let the people go, so that they may worship the LORD their God. Do you not yet realize that Egypt is ruined?"

Pharaoh—

Ex 10:16 Pharaoh quickly summoned Moses and Aaron and said, "I have sinned against the LORD your God and against you. [17]Now forgive my sin once more and pray to the LORD your God to take this deadly plague away from me."

Ex 12:31 During the night Pharaoh summoned Moses and Aaron and said, "Up! Leave my people, you and the Israelites! Go, worship the LORD as you have requested. [32]Take your flocks and herds, as you have said, and go. And also bless me."

Egyptians—

Ex 12:33 The Egyptians urged the people to hurry and leave the country. "For otherwise," they said, "we will all die!" (+1Sa 6:6)

The Canaanites (Jos 2:9-11; 5:1).

Gideon—

Jdg 6:17 Gideon replied, "If now I have found favor in your eyes, give me a sign that it is really you talking to me. [18]Please do not go away until I come back and bring my offering and set it before you." And the LORD said, "I will wait until you return."

[19]Gideon went in, prepared a young goat, and from an ephah of flour he made bread without yeast. Putting the meat in a basket and its broth in a pot, he brought them out and offered them to him under the oak.

[20]The angel of God said to him, "Take the meat and the unleavened bread, place them on this rock, and pour out the broth." And Gideon did so. [21]With the tip of the staff that was in his hand, the angel of the LORD touched the meat and the unleavened bread. Fire flared from the rock, consuming the meat and the bread. And the angel of the LORD disappeared. [22]When Gideon realized that it was the angel of the LORD, he exclaimed, "Ah, Sovereign LORD! I have seen the angel of the LORD face to face!"

Jdg 6:36 Gideon said to God, "If you will save Israel by my hand as you have promised— [37]look, I will place a wool fleece on the threshing floor. If there is dew only on the fleece and all the ground is dry, then I will know that you will save Israel by my hand, as you said." [38]And that is what happened. Gideon rose early the next day; he squeezed the fleece and wrung out the dew—a bowlful of water.

[39]Then Gideon said to God, "Do not be angry with me. Let me make just one more request. Allow me one more test with the fleece. This time make the fleece dry and the ground covered with dew." [40]That night God did so. Only the fleece was dry; all the ground was covered with dew.

Jdg 7:1 Early in the morning, Jerub-Baal (that is, Gideon) and all his men camped at the spring of Harod. The camp of Midian was north of them in the valley near the hill of Moreh.

People who witnessed Elijah's (1Ki 18:24,37-39). Naaman (2Ki 5:14-15).

Nebuchadnezzar (Da 2:47)—

Da 3:28 Then Nebuchadnezzar said, "Praise be to the God of Shadrach, Meshach and Abednego, who has sent his angel and rescued his servants! They trusted in him and

defied the king's command and were willing to give up their lives rather than serve or worship any god except their own God. [29]Therefore I decree that the people of any nation or language who say anything against the God of Shadrach, Meshach and Abednego be cut into pieces and their houses be turned into piles of rubble, for no other god can save in this way."

Da 4:2 It is my pleasure to tell you about the miraculous signs and wonders that the Most High God has performed for me. [3]How great are his signs, how mighty his wonders! His kingdom is an eternal kingdom; his dominion endures from generation to generation.

Darius (Da 6:20-27).

Simon Peter—

Lk 5:4 When he had finished speaking, he said to Simon, "Put out into deep water, and let down the nets for a catch."

[5]Simon answered, "Master, we've worked hard all night and haven't caught anything. But because you say so, I will let down the nets."

[6]When they had done so, they caught such a large number of fish that their nets began to break. [7]So they signaled their partners in the other boat to come and help them, and they came and filled both boats so full that they began to sink.

[8]When Simon Peter saw this, he fell at Jesus' knees and said, "Go away from me, Lord; I am a sinful man!" [9]For he and all his companions were astonished at the catch of fish they had taken, [10]and so were James and John, the sons of Zebedee, Simon's partners.

Then Jesus said to Simon, "Don't be afraid; from now on you will catch men."

[11]So they pulled their boats up on shore, left everything and followed him.

Disciples of Jesus—

Jn 2:11 This, the first of his miraculous signs, Jesus performed at Cana in Galilee. He thus revealed his glory, and his disciples put their faith in him.

Jn 2:22 After he was raised from the dead, his disciples recalled what he had said. Then they believed the Scripture and the words that Jesus had spoken.

[23]Now while he was in Jerusalem at the Passover Feast, many people saw the miraculous signs he was doing and believed in his name.

Jn 20:30 Jesus did many other miraculous signs in the presence of his disciples, which are not recorded in this book. [31]But these are written that you may believe that Jesus is the Christ, the Son of God, and that by believing you may have life in his name.

The nobleman whose child Jesus healed—

Jn 4:48 "Unless you people see miraculous signs and wonders," Jesus told him, "you will never believe."

[49]The royal official said, "Sir, come down before my child dies."

[50]Jesus replied, "You may go. Your son will live."

The man took Jesus at his word and departed. [51]While he was still on the way, his servants met him with the news that his boy was living. [52]When he inquired as to the time when his son got better, they said to him, "The fever left him yesterday at the seventh hour."

[53]Then the father realized that this was the exact time at which Jesus had said to him, "Your son will live." So he and all his household believed.

People who witnessed Christ's—

Jn 7:31 Still, many in the crowd put their faith in him.

They said, "When the Christ comes, will he do more miraculous signs than this man?"

Jn 11:43 When he had said this, Jesus called in a loud voice, "Lazarus, come out!" **44**The dead man came out, his hands and feet wrapped with strips of linen, and a cloth around his face. Jesus said to them, "Take off the grave clothes and let him go."

45Therefore many of the Jews who had come to visit Mary, and had seen what Jesus did, put their faith in him.

Jn 12:10 So the chief priests made plans to kill Lazarus as well, **11**for on account of him many of the Jews were going over to Jesus and putting their faith in him.

People who witnessed Philip's—

Ac 8:6 When the crowds heard Philip and saw the miraculous signs he did, they all paid close attention to what he said.

People who witnessed Peter's—

Ac 9:32 As Peter traveled about the country, he went to visit the saints in Lydda. **33**There he found a man named Aeneas, a paralytic who had been bedridden for eight years. **34**"Aeneas," Peter said to him, "Jesus Christ heals you. Get up and take care of your mat." Immediately Aeneas got up. **35**All those who lived in Lydda and Sharon saw him and turned to the Lord.

36In Joppa there was a disciple named Tabitha (which, when translated, is Dorcas), who was always doing good and helping the poor. **37**About that time she became sick and died, and her body was washed and placed in an upstairs room. **38**Lydda was near Joppa; so when the disciples heard that Peter was in Lydda, they sent two men to him and urged him, "Please come at once!"

39Peter went with them, and when he arrived he was taken upstairs to the room. All the widows stood around him, crying and showing him the robes and other clothing that Dorcas had made while she was still with them.

40Peter sent them all out of the room; then he got down on his knees and prayed. Turning toward the dead woman, he said, "Tabitha, get up." She opened her eyes, and seeing Peter she sat up. **41**He took her by the hand and helped her to her feet. Then he called the believers and the widows and presented her to them alive. **42**This became known all over Joppa, and many people believed in the Lord.

Sergius Paulus, the deputy—

Ac 13:8 But Elymas the sorcerer (for that is what his name means) opposed them and tried to turn the proconsul from the faith. **9**Then Saul, who was also called Paul, filled with the Holy Spirit, looked straight at Elymas and said, **10**"You are a child of the devil and an enemy of everything that is right! You are full of all kinds of deceit and trickery. Will you never stop perverting the right ways of the Lord? **11**Now the hand of the Lord is against you. You are going to be blind, and for a time you will be unable to see the light of the sun." Immediately mist and darkness came over him, and he groped about, seeking someone to lead him by the hand.

12When the proconsul saw what had happened, he believed, for he was amazed at the teaching about the Lord.

Gentiles—

Ro 15:18 I will not venture to speak of anything except what Christ has accomplished through me in leading the Gentiles to obey God by what I have said and done— **19**by the power of signs and miracles, through the power of the Spirit. So from Jerusalem all the way around to Illyricum, I have fully proclaimed the gospel of Christ.

Resisted by the obdurate (Ne 9:17; Ps 78:10-32; Jn 9:24-28; 15:24-25).

Design of, to:

Reveal God—

Ex 7:5 And the Egyptians will know that I am the LORD when I stretch out my hand against Egypt and bring the Israelites out of it."

Ex 7:17 This is what the LORD says: By this you will know that I am the LORD: With the staff that is in my hand I will strike the water of the Nile, and it will be changed into blood.

Ex 8:8 Pharaoh summoned Moses and Aaron and said, "Pray to the LORD to take the frogs away from me and my people, and I will let your people go to offer sacrifices to the LORD."

9Moses said to Pharaoh, "I leave to you the honor of setting the time for me to pray for you and your officials and your people that you and your houses may be rid of the frogs, except for those that remain in the Nile."

10"Tomorrow," Pharaoh said.

Moses replied, "It will be as you say, so that you may know there is no one like the LORD our God.

Ex 8:22 "'But on that day I will deal differently with the land of Goshen, where my people live; no swarms of flies will be there, so that you will know that I, the LORD, am in this land.

5The LORD set a time and said, "Tomorrow the LORD will do this in the land." **6**And the next day the LORD did it: All the livestock of the Egyptians died, but not one animal belonging to the Israelites died. **7**Pharaoh sent men to investigate and found that not even one of the animals of the Israelites had died. Yet his heart was unyielding and he would not let the people go.

8Then the LORD said to Moses and Aaron, "Take handfuls of soot from a furnace and have Moses toss it into the air in the presence of Pharaoh. **9**It will become fine dust over the whole land of Egypt, and festering boils will break out on men and animals throughout the land."

10So they took soot from a furnace and stood before Pharaoh. Moses tossed it into the air, and festering boils broke out on men and animals. **11**The magicians could not stand before Moses because of the boils that were on them and on all the Egyptians. **12**But the LORD hardened Pharaoh's heart and he would not listen to Moses and Aaron, just as the LORD had said to Moses.

13Then the LORD said to Moses, "Get up early in the morning, confront Pharaoh and say to him, 'This is what the LORD, the God of the Hebrews, says: Let my people go, so that they may worship me, **14**or this time I will send the full force of my plagues against you and against your officials and your people, so you may know that there is no one like me in all the earth. **15**For by now I could have stretched out my hand and struck you and your people with a plague that would have wiped you off the earth. **16**But I have raised you up for this very purpose, that I might show you my power and that my name might be proclaimed in all the earth.

Ex 9:29 Moses replied, "When I have gone out of the city, I will spread out my hands in prayer to the LORD. The thunder will stop and there will be no more hail, so you may know that the earth is the LORD's.

Ex 10:1 Then the LORD said to Moses, "Go to Pharaoh, for I have hardened his heart and the hearts of his officials so that I may perform these miraculous signs of mine among them [2]that you may tell your children and grandchildren how I dealt harshly with the Egyptians and how I performed my signs among them, and that you may know that I am the LORD."

Ex 14:4 And I will harden Pharaoh's heart, and he will pursue them. But I will gain glory for myself through Pharaoh and all his army, and the Egyptians will know that I am the LORD." So the Israelites did this.

Ex 14:18 The Egyptians will know that I am the LORD when I gain glory through Pharaoh, his chariots and his horsemen."

Dt 4:33 Has any other people heard the voice of God speaking out of fire, as you have, and lived? [34]Has any god ever tried to take for himself one nation out of another nation, by testings, by miraculous signs and wonders, by war, by a mighty hand and an outstretched arm, or by great and awesome deeds, like all the things the LORD your God did for you in Egypt before your very eyes?

[35]You were shown these things so that you might know that the LORD is God; besides him there is no other. (+Dt 4:36-39)

Jos 4:23 For the LORD your God dried up the Jordan before you until you had crossed over. The LORD your God did to the Jordan just what he had done to the Red Sea when he dried it up before us until we had crossed over. [24]He did this so that all the peoples of the earth might know that the hand of the LORD is powerful and so that you might always fear the LORD your God."

1Ki 18:24 Then you call on the name of your god, and I will call on the name of the LORD. The god who answers by fire—he is God." Then all the people said, "What you say is good."

1Ki 18:37 Answer me, O LORD, answer me, so these people will know that you, O LORD, are God, and that you are turning their hearts back again." [38]Then the fire of the LORD fell and burned up the sacrifice, the wood, the stones and the soil, and also licked up the water in the trench. [39]When all the people saw this, they fell prostrate and cried, "The LORD—he is God! The LORD—he is God!"

Jer 32:20 You performed miraculous signs and wonders in Egypt and have continued them to this day, both in Israel and among all mankind, and have gained the renown that is still yours.

Produce faith in God—

Ex 14:31 And when the Israelites saw the great power the LORD displayed against the Egyptians, the people feared the LORD and put their trust in him and in Moses his servant.

Nu 14:11 The LORD said to Moses, "How long will these people treat me with contempt? How long will they refuse to believe in me, in spite of all the miraculous signs I have performed among them? (+Jos 3:7-9)

Jos 3:10 This is how you will know that the living God is among you and that he will certainly drive out before you the Canaanites, Hittites, Hivites, Perizzites, Girgashites, Amorites and Jebusites. [11]See, the ark of the covenant of the Lord of all the earth will go into the Jordan ahead of you. (+Jos 3:12-17)

2Ch 7:1 When Solomon finished praying, fire came down from heaven and consumed the burnt offering and the sacrifices, and the glory of the LORD filled the temple. [2]The priests could not enter the temple of the LORD because the glory of the LORD filled it. [3]When all the Israelites saw the fire coming down and the glory of the LORD above the temple, they knelt on the pavement with their faces to the

ground, and they worshiped and gave thanks to the LORD, saying, "He is good; his love endures forever."

Ps 106:9 He rebuked the Red Sea, and it dried up; he led them through the depths as through a desert. [10]He saved them from the hand of the foe; from the hand of the enemy he redeemed them. [11]The waters covered their adversaries; not one of them survived. [12]Then they believed his promises and sang his praise.

Produce the fear of God—

1Sa 12:17 Is it not wheat harvest now? I will call upon the LORD to send thunder and rain. And you will realize what an evil thing you did in the eyes of the LORD when you asked for a king."

[18]Then Samuel called upon the LORD, and that same day the LORD sent thunder and rain. So all the people stood in awe of the LORD and of Samuel.

Da 6:20 When he came near the den, he called to Daniel in an anguished voice, "Daniel, servant of the living God, has your God, whom you serve continually, been able to rescue you from the lions?"

[21]Daniel answered, "O king, live forever! [22]My God sent his angel, and he shut the mouths of the lions. They have not hurt me, because I was found innocent in his sight. Nor have I ever done any wrong before you, O king."

[23]The king was overjoyed and gave orders to lift Daniel out of the den. And when Daniel was lifted from the den, no wound was found on him, because he had trusted in his God.

[24]At the king's command, the men who had falsely accused Daniel were brought in and thrown into the lions' den, along with their wives and children. And before they reached the floor of the den, the lions overpowered them and crushed all their bones.

[25]Then King Darius wrote to all the peoples, nations and men of every language throughout the land:

"May you prosper greatly!

[26]"I issue a decree that in every part of my kingdom people must fear and reverence the God of Daniel.

"For he is the living God and he endures forever; his kingdom will not be destroyed, his dominion will never end. [27]He rescues and he saves; he performs signs and wonders in the heavens and on the earth. He has rescued Daniel from the power of the lions."

Jnh 1:14 Then they cried to the LORD, "O LORD, please do not let us die for taking this man's life. Do not hold us accountable for killing an innocent man, for you, O LORD, have done as you pleased." [15]Then they took Jonah and threw him overboard, and the raging sea grew calm. [16]At this the men greatly feared the LORD, and they offered a sacrifice to the LORD and made vows to him.

Encourage obedience—

Ex 16:4 Then the LORD said to Moses, "I will rain down bread from heaven for you. The people are to go out each day and gather enough for that day. In this way I will test them and see whether they will follow my instructions. [5]On the sixth day they are to prepare what they bring in, and that is to be twice as much as they gather on the other days."

[6]So Moses and Aaron said to all the Israelites, "In the evening you will know that it was the LORD who brought you out of Egypt,

Ex 19:4 'You yourselves have seen what I did to Egypt, and how I carried you on eagles' wings and brought you to myself. [5]Now if you obey me fully and keep my covenant, then out of all nations you will be my treasured possession. Although the whole earth is mine,

Dt 11:1 Love the LORD your God and keep his requirements, his decrees, his laws and his commands always. [2]Remember today that your children were not the ones who saw and experienced the discipline of the LORD your God: his majesty, his mighty hand, his outstretched arm; [3]the signs he performed and the things he did in the heart of Egypt, both to Pharaoh king of Egypt and to his whole country; [4]what he did to the Egyptian army, to its horses and chariots, how he overwhelmed them with the waters of the Red Sea as they were pursuing you, and how the LORD brought lasting ruin on them. [5]It was not your children who saw what he did for you in the desert until you arrived at this place, [6]and what he did to Dathan and Abiram, sons of Eliab the Reubenite, when the earth opened its mouth right in the middle of all Israel and swallowed them up with their households, their tents and every living thing that belonged to them. [7]But it was your own eyes that saw all these great things the LORD has done.

[8]Observe therefore all the commands I am giving you today, so that you may have the strength to go in and take over the land that you are crossing the Jordan to possess, (+Dt 29:1-4)

Dt 29:5 During the forty years that I led you through the desert, your clothes did not wear out, nor did the sandals on your feet. [6]You ate no bread and drank no wine or other fermented drink. I did this so that you might know that I am the LORD your God. (+Dt 29:7-9)

Jdg 2:7 The people served the LORD throughout the lifetime of Joshua and of the elders who outlived him and who had seen all the great things the LORD had done for Israel.

Ps 78:10 they did not keep God's covenant and refused to live by his law. [11]They forgot what he had done, the wonders he had shown them. [12]He did miracles in the sight of their fathers in the land of Egypt, in the region of Zoan. [13]He divided the sea and led them through; he made the water stand firm like a wall. [14]He guided them with the cloud by day and with light from the fire all night. [15]He split the rocks in the desert and gave them water as abundant as the seas; [16]he brought streams out of a rocky crag and made water flow down like rivers.

[17]But they continued to sin against him, rebelling in the desert against the Most High. [18]They willfully put God to the test by demanding the food they craved. [19]They spoke against God, saying, "Can God spread a table in the desert? [20]When he struck the rock, water gushed out, and streams flowed abundantly. But can he also give us food? Can he supply meat for his people?" [21]When the LORD heard them, he was very angry; his fire broke out against Jacob, and his wrath rose against Israel, [22]for they did not believe in God or trust in his deliverance. [23]Yet he gave a command to the skies above and opened the doors of the heavens; [24]he rained down manna for the people to eat, he gave them the grain of heaven. [25]Men ate the bread of angels; he sent them all the food they could eat. [26]He let loose the east wind from the heavens and led forth the south wind by his power. [27]He rained meat down on them like dust, flying birds like sand on the seashore. [28]He made them come down inside their camp, all around their tents. [29]They ate till they had more than enough, for he had given them what they craved. [30]But before they turned from the food they craved, even while it was still in their mouths, [31]God's anger rose against them; he put to death the sturdiest among them, cutting down the young men of Israel.

[32]In spite of all this, they kept on sinning; in spite of his wonders, they did not believe.

Glorify God (Lk 5:26; Jn 11:4)—
Ac 4:21 After further threats they let them go. They could not decide how to punish them, because all the people were praising God for what had happened. [22]For the man who was miraculously healed was over forty years old.

Testify to the messiahship of Jesus (Mt 11:2)—
Mt 11:3 to ask him, "Are you the one who was to come, or should we expect someone else?"

[4]Jesus replied, "Go back and report to John what you hear and see: [5]The blind receive sight, the lame walk, those who have leprosy are cured, the deaf hear, the dead are raised, and the good news is preached to the poor. (+Lk 7:19-22)
Mk 2:9 Which is easier: to say to the paralytic, 'Your sins are forgiven,' or to say, 'Get up, take your mat and walk'? [10]But that you may know that the Son of Man has authority on earth to forgive sins . . . ." He said to the paralytic, [11]"I tell you, get up, take your mat and go home." [12]He got up, took his mat and walked out in full view of them all. This amazed everyone and they praised God, saying, "We have never seen anything like this!" (+Lk 5:24-26)
Lk 18:42 Jesus said to him, "Receive your sight; your faith has healed you." [43]Immediately he received his sight and followed Jesus, praising God. When all the people saw it, they also praised God.
Jn 2:11 This, the first of his miraculous signs, Jesus performed at Cana in Galilee. He thus revealed his glory, and his disciples put their faith in him.
Jn 4:48 "Unless you people see miraculous signs and wonders," Jesus told him, "you will never believe."
Jn 5:36 "I have testimony weightier than that of John. For the very work that the Father has given me to finish, and which I am doing, testifies that the Father has sent me.
Jn 11:4 When he heard this, Jesus said, "This sickness will not end in death. No, it is for God's glory so that God's Son may be glorified through it."
Jn 11:40 Then Jesus said, "Did I not tell you that if you believed, you would see the glory of God?" [41]So they took away the stone. Then Jesus looked up and said, "Father, I thank you that you have heard me. [42]I knew that you always hear me, but I said this for the benefit of the people standing here, that they may believe that you sent me." (+Jn 14:11; 15:24)

Glorify Jesus—
Ac 3:1 One day Peter and John were going up to the temple at the time of prayer—at three in the afternoon. [2]Now a man crippled from birth was being carried to the temple gate called Beautiful, where he was put every day to beg from those going into the temple courts. [3]When he saw Peter and John about to enter, he asked them for money. [4]Peter looked straight at him, as did John. Then Peter said, "Look at us!" [5]So the man gave them his attention, expecting to get something from them.

[6]Then Peter said, "Silver or gold I do not have, but what I have I give you. In the name of Jesus Christ of Nazareth, walk." [7]Taking him by the right hand, he helped him up, and instantly the man's feet and ankles became strong. [8]He jumped to his feet and began to walk. Then he went with them into the temple courts, walking and jumping, and praising God. [9]When all the people saw him walking and praising God, [10]they recognized him as the same man who used to sit begging at the temple gate called Beautiful, and they were filled with wonder and amazement at what had happened to him. (+Ac 3:12-13)

Testify to God's servants—
Ex 4:2 Then the LORD said to him, "What is that in your hand?"

"A staff," he replied.

[3]The LORD said, "Throw it on the ground." Moses threw it on the ground and it became a snake, and he ran from it. [4]Then the LORD said to him, "Reach out your hand and take it by the tail." So Moses reached out and took hold of the snake and it turned back into a staff in his hand. [5]"This," said the LORD, "is so that they may believe that the LORD, the God of their fathers—the God of Abraham, the God of Isaac and the God of Jacob—has appeared to you."

[6]Then the LORD said, "Put your hand inside your cloak." So Moses put his hand into his cloak, and when he took it out, it was leprous, like snow.

[7]"Now put it back into your cloak," he said. So Moses put his hand back into his cloak, and when he took it out, it was restored, like the rest of his flesh.

[8]Then the LORD said, "If they do not believe you or pay attention to the first miraculous sign, they may believe the second. [9]But if they do not believe these two signs or listen to you, take some water from the Nile and pour it on the dry ground. The water you take from the river will become blood on the ground."

Ex 19:9 The LORD said to Moses, "I am going to come to you in a dense cloud, so that the people will hear me speaking with you and will always put their trust in you." Then Moses told the LORD what the people had said.

Nu 16:28 Then Moses said, "This is how you will know that the LORD has sent me to do all these things and that it was not my idea: [29]If these men die a natural death and experience only what usually happens to men, then the LORD has not sent me. [30]But if the LORD brings about something totally new, and the earth opens its mouth and swallows them, with everything that belongs to them, and they go down alive into the grave, then you will know that these men have treated the LORD with contempt."

[31]As soon as he finished saying all this, the ground under them split apart [32]and the earth opened its mouth and swallowed them, with their households and all Korah's men and all their possessions. [33]They went down alive into the grave, with everything they owned; the earth closed over them, and they perished and were gone from the community. [34]At their cries, all the Israelites around them fled, shouting, "The earth is going to swallow us too!"

[35]And fire came out from the LORD and consumed the 250 men who were offering the incense. (+1Sa 12:17-18)

Zec 2:9 I will surely raise my hand against them so that their slaves will plunder them. Then you will know that the LORD Almighty has sent me.

Ac 2:22 "Men of Israel, listen to this: Jesus of Nazareth was a man accredited by God to you by miracles, wonders and signs, which God did among you through him, as you yourselves know. (+Heb 2:4)

Preserve the righteous—

Da 3:28 Then Nebuchadnezzar said, "Praise be to the God of Shadrach, Meshach and Abednego, who has sent his angel and rescued his servants! They trusted in him and defied the king's command and were willing to give up their lives rather than serve or worship any god except their own God. [29]Therefore I decree that the people of any nation or language who say anything against the God of Shadrach, Meshach and Abednego be cut into pieces and their houses be turned into piles of rubble, for no other god can save in this way." (+Da 6:20-27)

Change wicked purposes—

Ex 3:19 But I know that the king of Egypt will not let you go unless a mighty hand compels him. [20]So I will stretch out my hand and strike the Egyptians with all the wonders that I will perform among them. After that, he will let you go. (+Ex 9:16-17)

Ex 10:16 Pharaoh quickly summoned Moses and Aaron and said, "I have sinned against the LORD your God and against you. [17]Now forgive my sin once more and pray to the LORD your God to take this deadly plague away from me."

Ex 11:1 Now the LORD had said to Moses, "I will bring one more plague on Pharaoh and on Egypt. After that, he will let you go from here, and when he does, he will drive you out completely. (+Ex 11:2-6)

Ex 11:7 But among the Israelites not a dog will bark at any man or animal.' Then you will know that the LORD makes a distinction between Egypt and Israel. [8]All these officials of yours will come to me, bowing down before me and saying, 'Go, you and all the people who follow you!' After that I will leave." Then Moses, hot with anger, left Pharaoh.

[9]The LORD had said to Moses, "Pharaoh will refuse to listen to you—so that my wonders may be multiplied in Egypt." (+Ex 11:10)

Ex 12:29 At midnight the LORD struck down all the first-born in Egypt, from the firstborn of Pharaoh, who sat on the throne, to the firstborn of the prisoner, who was in the dungeon, and the firstborn of all the livestock as well. [30]Pharaoh and all his officials and all the Egyptians got up during the night, and there was loud wailing in Egypt, for there was not a house without someone dead.

[31]During the night Pharaoh summoned Moses and Aaron and said, "Up! Leave my people, you and the Israelites! Go, worship the LORD as you have requested. [32]Take your flocks and herds, as you have said, and go. And also bless me."

[33]The Egyptians urged the people to hurry and leave the country. "For otherwise," they said, "we will all die!"

Ex 14:24 During the last watch of the night the LORD looked down from the pillar of fire and cloud at the Egyptian army and threw it into confusion. [25]He made the wheels of their chariots come off so that they had difficulty driving. And the Egyptians said, "Let's get away from the Israelites! The LORD is fighting for them against Egypt."

Miraculous Gifts of the Holy Spirit:

Foretold (Isa 35:4-6; Joel 2:28-29). Of different kinds (1Co 12:4-6). Enumerated (1Co 12:8-10,28). Christ was endued with (Mt 12:28). Poured out on Pentecost (Ac 2:1-4). Communicated on preaching the gospel (Ac 10:44-46), by laying on of the apostles' hands (Ac 8:17-18; 19:6), for the confirmation of the gospel (Mk 16:20; Ac 14:3; Ro 15:19; Heb 2:4), for the edification of the church (1Co 12:7; 14:12-13). To be sought after (1Co 12:31; 14:1). Temporary nature of (1Co 13:8). Not to be neglected (1Ti 4:14; 2Ti 1:6), or despised (1Th 5:20), or purchased (Ac 8:20).

MIRE [3226, 3431, 8347].

NIV+ MIRY

Figurative of distress (Ps 40:2; 69:2).

MIRIAM [5319] (variously *bitterness, plump one, the wished-for child, one who loves* or *is loved*).

1. Sister of Aaron and Moses; saved life of the baby Moses (Ex 2:4,7-8), prophetess (Ex 15:20), criticized Moses for his marriage (Nu 12), buried at Kadesh (Nu 20:1).

2. Judahite (1Ch 4:17).

MIRMAH, MIRMA [5328] (*deceit*). A Benjamite (1Ch 8:10).

MIRROR [1663, 5262, 8023, *2269*].
NIV+ MIRRORS
Ancient mirrors were made of polished metal (Ex 38:8; Job 37:18; 1Co 13:12; 2Co 3:18; Jas 1:23). *See Glass.*

MISCARRY [8897].
NIV+ MISCARRIED
Of people, a judgment of God (Hos 9:14). Lack of in people and in animals, a sign of God's blessing (Ge 31:38; Ex 23:25-26; Job 21:10). *See Abortion.*

MISCEGENATION *See Intermarry.*

MISER (Ecc 4:7-8).

MISGAB NIV "stronghold"; An unknown place mentioned (Jer 48:1).

MISHAEL [4792, 10414] (*who belongs to God [El]?*).
1. A son of Uzziel, helps carry the bodies of Nadab and Abihu out of the camp (Ex 6:22; Lev 10:4).
2. A Jew who stood by Ezra when he read the law to the people (Ne 8:4).
3. Also called Meshach. *See Meshach.*

MISHAL, MISHEAL [5398]. Levitical city in Asher (Jos 19:26; 21:30), also called Mashal (1Ch 6:74). *See Mashal.*

MISHAM [5471]. Son of Elpaal (1Ch 8:12).

MISHMA [5462] (*rumor*).
1. Son of Ishmael (Ge 25:14; 1Ch 1:30).
2. Of the tribe of Simeon (1Ch 4:25-26).

MISHMANNAH [5459] (*fatness*). A Gadite who joined David at Ziklag (1Ch 12:10).

MISHPAT *See En Mishpat.*

MISHRAITES [5490]. Clan of Kiriath Jearim in Judah (1Ch 2:53).

MISJUDGMENT
Instances of:
Of the Reubenites and Gadites (Nu 32:1-33; Jos 22:11-31). Of Hannah (1Sa 1:14-17).
See Accusation, False; Uncharitableness.

MISPAR [5032] (*number*). Coworker of Zerubbabel (Ezr 2:2). "Mispereth" (Ne 7:7).

MISPERETH [5033]. Also called Mizpar. A Jew who returned with Zerubbabel from Babylon (Ezr 2:2; Ne 7:7).

MISREPHOTH MAIM, MISREPHOTH-MAIM
[5387] (*waters of Misrephoth [lime burning]*). Place near Sidon and Tyre (Jos 11:8; 13:6).

MISSIONARY JOURNEYS OF PAUL [*1355*].
I. The First Missionary Journey, c. A.D. 46-48 (Ac 13:1-14:28).
A. Barnabas and Saul are Sent From Antioch (13:1-3).
B. Ministry at Cyprus (13:4-13).
  1. Preaching in the synagogues (13:4-5).
  2. Controversy with Bar-Jesus (13:6-13).
C. Ministry at Antioch (13:14-50).
  1. Paul preaches on first Sabbath (13:14-43).
  2. Paul preaches on second Sabbath (13:44-50).
D. Ministry at Iconium (13:51-14:5).

E. Ministry at Lystra (14:6-20).
  1. A lame man is healed (14:6-10).
  2. Paul and Barnabas are deified (14:11-18).
  3. Paul is stoned (14:19-20).
F. Ministry on the Return Trip (14:21-25).
G. Report on the First Missionary Journey (14:26-28).
II. The Jerusalem Council (15:1-35).
A. Debate Over Gentiles Keeping the Law (15:1-5).
B. Peter Preaches Salvation Through Grace (15:6-11).
C. Paul and Barnabas Testify (15:12).
D. James Proves Gentiles are Free From the Law (15:13-21).
E. The Council Sends an Official Letter (15:22-29).
F. Report to Antioch (15:30-35).
III. The Second Missionary Journey, c. A.D. 49-52 (Ac 15:36-18:22).
A. Contention Over John Mark (15:36-41).
B. Derbe and Lystra: Timothy is Circumcised (16:1-5).
C. Troas: Macedonian Call (16:6-10).
D. Philippi: Extensive Ministry (16:11-40).
  1. Lydia is converted (16:11-15).
  2. Spirit of divination is cast out (16:16-24).
  3. Philippian jailer is converted (16:25-34).
  4. Paul is released from prison (16:35-40).
E. Thessalonica: "Turn the World Upside Down" (17:1-9).
F. Berea: Many Receive the Word (17:10-15).
G. Athens: Paul's Sermon on Mars' Hill (17:16-34).
H. Corinth: One-and-a-Half Years of Ministry (18:1-17).
  1. Paul works with Aquila and Priscilla (18:1-3).
  2. Jews reject Paul (18:4-6).
  3. Crispus, the Gentile, is converted (18:7-11).
  4. Gallio will not try Paul (18:12-17).
I. Return Trip to Antioch (18:18-22).
IV. The Third Missionary Journey, c. A.D. 53-57 (Ac 18:23-21:16).
A. Galatia and Phrygia: Strengthening the Disciples (18:23).
B. Ephesus: Three Years of Ministry (18:24-19:41).
  1. Apollos teaches effectively (18:24-28).
  2. Disciples of John receive the Holy Spirit (19:1-7).
  3. Paul teaches in Tyrannus' school (19:8-10).
  4. Miracles are performed at Ephesus (19:11-20).
  5. Timothy and Erastus are sent to Macedonia (19:21-22).
  6. Demetrius causes uproar at Ephesus (19:23-41).
C. Macedonia: Three Months of Ministry (20:1-5).
D. Troas: Eutychus Falls From Loft (20:6-12).
E. Miletus: Paul Bids Farewell to Ephesian Elders (20:13-38).
F. Tyre: Paul is Warned About Jerusalem (21:1-6).
G. Caesarea: Agabus's Prediction (21:7-16).
V. The Trip to Rome, c. A.D. 57-59 (Ac 21:17-28:31).
A. Paul Witnesses in Jerusalem (21:17-23:33).
  1. Paul conforms to Jewish customs (21:17-26).
  2. Paul's arrest (21:27-39).
  3. Paul's defense before the crowd (21:40-22:23).
  4. Paul's defense before the centurion (22:24-29).
  5. Paul's defense before the Sanhedrin (22:30-23:11).
  6. Jews' plan to kill Paul (23:12-22).
  7. Paul's rescue (23:23-33).
B. Paul's Witnesses in Caesarea (23:34-28:31).
  1. Paul is tried before Felix (23:34-24:27).
  2. Paul is tried before Festus (25:1-22).
  3. Paul is tried before Agrippa (25:23-26:32).

C. Paul Witnesses in Rome (27:1-28:31).
  1. Paul's witness during the shipwreck (27:1-44).
  2. Paul's witness on Malta (28:1-15).
  3. Paul's witness in Rome (28:16-31).
VI. The Fourth Missionary Journey, c. A.D. 62-68.

It is clear from Ac 13:1-21:17 that Paul went on three missionary journeys. There is also reason to believe that he made a fourth journey after his release from the Roman imprisonment recorded in Ac 28. The conclusion that such a journey did indeed take place is based on: (1) Paul's declared intention to go to Spain (Ro 15:24,28), (2) Eusebius's implication that Paul was released following his first Roman imprisonment (*Ecclesiastical History*, 2.22.2-3) and (3) statements in early Christian literature that he took the Gospel as far as Spain (Clement of Rome, *Epistle to the Corinthians*, ch. 5; *Actus Petri Vercellenses*, chs. 1-3; Muratorian Canon, lines 34-39).

The places Paul may have visited after his release from prison are indicated by statements of intention in his earlier writings and by subsequent mention in the Pastoral Letters. The order of his travel cannot be determined with certainty, but the itinerary that follows seems likely.

  1. Rome: released from prison in c. A.D. 62.
  2. Spain: c. A.D. 62-64 (Ro 15:24,28).
  3. Crete: c. A.D. 64-65 (Tit 1:5).
  4. Miletus: c. A.D. 65 (2Ti 4:20).
  5. Colosse: c. A.D. 66 (Phm 22).
  6. Ephesus: c. A.D. 66 (1Ti 1:3).
  7. Philippi: c. A.D. 66 (Php 2:23-24; 1Ti 1:3).
  8. Nicopolis: c. A.D. 66-67 (Tit 3:12).
  9. Rome: c. A.D. 67.
  10. Martyrdom: c. A.D. 67/68.
  See Paul; Pastoral Epistles.

MISSIONS [*1355*].

NIV+ MISSION

Religious propagandism—

2Ki 17:27 Then the king of Assyria gave this order: "Have one of the priests you took captive from Samaria go back to live there and teach the people what the god of the land requires." **28**So one of the priests who had been exiled from Samaria came to live in Bethel and taught them how to worship the LORD.

1Ch 16:23 Sing to the LORD, all the earth; proclaim his salvation day after day. **24**Declare his glory among the nations, his marvelous deeds among all peoples.

Commanded—

Ps 96:3 Declare his glory among the nations, his marvelous deeds among all peoples.

Ps 96:10 Say among the nations, "The LORD reigns." The world is firmly established, it cannot be moved; he will judge the peoples with equity.

Mt 28:19 Therefore go and make disciples of all nations, baptizing them in the name of the Father and of the Son and of the Holy Spirit,

Mk 16:15 He said to them, "Go into all the world and preach the good news to all creation.

Lk 24:47 and repentance and forgiveness of sins will be preached in his name to all nations, beginning at Jerusalem. **48**You are witnesses of these things.

Prophecy concerning—

Mt 24:14 And this gospel of the kingdom will be preached in the whole world as a testimony to all nations, and then the end will come.

Mk 13:10 And the gospel must first be preached to all nations.

Peter's vision concerning—

Ac 10:9 About noon the following day as they were on their journey and approaching the city, Peter went up on the roof to pray. **10**He became hungry and wanted something to eat, and while the meal was being prepared, he fell into a trance. **11**He saw heaven opened and something like a large sheet being let down to earth by its four corners. **12**It contained all kinds of four-footed animals, as well as reptiles of the earth and birds of the air. **13**Then a voice told him, "Get up, Peter. Kill and eat."

14"Surely not, Lord!" Peter replied. "I have never eaten anything impure or unclean."

15The voice spoke to him a second time, "Do not call anything impure that God has made clean."

16This happened three times, and immediately the sheet was taken back to heaven.

17While Peter was wondering about the meaning of the vision, the men sent by Cornelius found out where Simon's house was and stopped at the gate. **18**They called out, asking if Simon who was known as Peter was staying there.

19While Peter was still thinking about the vision, the Spirit said to him, "Simon, three men are looking for you. **20**So get up and go downstairs. Do not hesitate to go with them, for I have sent them."

Ordained by Jesus (Mt 24:14; 28:19; Mt 16:15-16; Lk 24:47-49).

Saul and Barnabas ordained for—

Ac 13:2 While they were worshiping the Lord and fasting, the Holy Spirit said, "Set apart for me Barnabas and Saul for the work to which I have called them." **3**So after they had fasted and prayed, they placed their hands on them and sent them off.

4The two of them, sent on their way by the Holy Spirit, went down to Seleucia and sailed from there to Cyprus.

Ac 13:47 For this is what the Lord has commanded us: "'I have made you a light for the Gentiles, that you may bring salvation to the ends of the earth.'"

Paul appointed to—

Ac 26:14 We all fell to the ground, and I heard a voice saying to me in Aramaic, 'Saul, Saul, why do you persecute me? It is hard for you to kick against the goads.'

15"Then I asked, 'Who are you, Lord?'

"'I am Jesus, whom you are persecuting,' the Lord replied. **16**'Now get up and stand on your feet. I have appeared to you to appoint you as a servant and as a witness of what you have seen of me and what I will show you. **17**I will rescue you from your own people and from the Gentiles. I am sending you to them **18**to open their eyes and turn them from darkness to light, and from the power of Satan to God, so that they may receive forgiveness of sins and a place among those who are sanctified by faith in me.'

1Co 16:9 because a great door for effective work has opened to me, and there are many who oppose me.

Practiced by the psalmist—

Ps 18:49 Therefore I will praise you among the nations, O LORD; I will sing praises to your name.

Practiced by Jonah—

Jnh 3:1 Then the word of the LORD came to Jonah a second time: **2**"Go to the great city of Nineveh and proclaim to it the message I give you."

3Jonah obeyed the word of the LORD and went to Nineveh. Now Nineveh was a very important city—a visit required three days. **4**On the first day, Jonah started into the city. He proclaimed: "Forty more days and Nineveh will be overturned." ⁵The Ninevites believed God. They declared a fast, and all of them, from the greatest to the least, put on sackcloth.

⁶When the news reached the king of Nineveh, he rose from his throne, took off his royal robes, covered himself with sackcloth and sat down in the dust. ⁷Then he issued a proclamation in Nineveh: "By the decree of the king and his nobles: Do not let any man or beast, herd or flock, taste anything; do not let them eat or drink.

⁸But let man and beast be covered with sackcloth. Let everyone call urgently on God. Let them give up their evil ways and their violence. ⁹Who knows? God may yet relent and with compassion turn from his fierce anger so that we will not perish."

Symbolized by the flying angel—

Rev 14:6 Then I saw another angel flying in midair, and he had the eternal gospel to proclaim to those who live on the earth—to every nation, tribe, language and people. ⁷He said in a loud voice, "Fear God and give him glory, because the hour of his judgment has come. Worship him who made the heavens, the earth, the sea and the springs of water."

Missionary Hymn (Ps 96).

The first to do homage to the Messiah were heathen (Mt 2:11).

See Gentiles, Conversion of; Heathen; Jesus the Christ, King; Jesus the Christ, Kingdom of.

Missionaries, All Christians Should Be As:

After the example of Christ (Ac 10:38). Women and children as well as men (Ps 8:2; Pr 31:26; Mt 21:15-16; Php 4:3; 1Ti 5:10; Tit 2:3-5; 1Pe 3:1). The zeal of idolaters should provoke to (Jer 7:18). The zeal of hypocrites should provoke to (Mt 23:15). An imperative duty (Jdg 5:23; Lk 19:40). The principle on which (2Co 5:14-15). However weak they may be (1Co 1:27). From their calling as saints (Ex 19:6; 1Pe 2:9). As faithful stewards (1Pe 4:10-11). In youth (Ps 71:17; 148:12-13). In old age (Dt 32:7; Ps 71:18). In the family (Dt 6:7; Ps 78:5-8; Isa 38:19; 1Co 7:16; 1Pe 2:12). In first giving their own selves to the Lord (2Co 8:5). In declaring what God has done for them (Ps 66:16; 116:16-19). In hating one's life for Christ (Lk 14:26). In openly confessing Christ (Mt 10:32). In following Christ (Lk 14:27; 18:22). In preferring Christ above all relations (Lk 14:26; 1Co 2:2). In joyfully suffering for Christ (Heb 10:34). In forsaking all for Christ (Heb 10:34). In a holy example (Mt 5:16; Php 2:15; 1Th 1:7). In holy conduct (1Pe 2:12). In holy boldness (Ps 119:46). In dedicating themselves to the service of God (Jos 24:15; Ps 27:4). In devoting all property to God (1Ch 29:2-3,14,16; Ecc 11:1; Mt 6:19-20; Mk 12:44; Lk 12:33; 18:22,28; Ac 2:45; 4:32-34). In holy conversation (Ps 37:30, w Pr 10:31; Pr 15:7; Eph 4:29; Col 4:6). In talking of God and his works (Ps 71:24; 77:12; 119:27; 145:11-12). In showing forth God's praises (Isa 43:21). In inviting others to embrace the Gospel (Ps 34:8; Isa 2:3; Jn 1:46; 4:29). In seeking the edification of others (Ro 14:19; 15:2; 1Th 5:11). In admonishing others (1Th 5:14; 2Th 3:15). In reproving others (Lev 19:17; Eph 5:11). In teaching and exhorting (Ps 34:11; 51:13; Col 3:16; Heb 3:13; 10:25). In interceding for others (Col 4:3; Heb 13:18; Jas 5:16). In aiding ministers in their labors (Ro 16:3,9; 2Co 11:9; Php 4:14-16; 3Jn 6). In giving a reason for their faith (Ex 12:26-27; Dt 6:20-21; 1Pe 3:15). In encouraging the weak (Isa 35:3-4; Ro 14:1; 15:1; 1Th 5:14). In visiting and relieving the poor and sick (Lev 25:35; Ps 112:9, w 2Co 9:9; Mt 25:36; Ac 20:35; Jas 1:27). With a willing heart

(Ex 35:29; 1Ch 29:9,14). With a superabundant liberality (Ex 36:5-7; 2Co 8:3). Encouragement to (Pr 11:25,30; 1Co 1:27; Jas 5:19-20). Blessedness of (Da 12:3). Illustrated (Mt 25:14; Lk 19:13).

See Minister.

MIST [6727, *874, 944, 3920*].

NIV+ MISTS

1. Steamy vapor rising from the ground (Ge 2:6).

2. Dimness of vision (Ac 13:11).

3. Description of false teachers (2Pe 2:17).

MITE(S) *See Money; Penny.*

MITHCAH, MITHKAH [5520] (*sweetness*). An encampment of the Israelites (Nu 33:28-29).

MITHNITE [5512]. Family name of Joshaphat (1Ch 11:43).

MITHRAISM Cult of Mithras, Persian sun-god, widely disseminated in the Roman Empire in the first century A.D.

MITHREDATH [5521] (*gift to [pagan deity] Mithra*).

1. Treasurer of Cyrus (Ezr 1:8).

2. A Persian officer who joined in writing a letter hostile to the Jews (Ezr 4:7).

MITRE *See Turban.*

MITYLENE [*3639*]. Capital of Lesbos. Paul visits (Ac 20:14-15).

MIXED MARRIAGE *See Intermarry.*

MIXED MULTITUDE Non-Israelites who traveled and associated with the Israelites (Nu 11:4-6; Ne 13:3).

MIZAR [5204] (*small*). A hill near Mt. Hermon (Ps 42:6).

MIZPAH [5206, 5207] (*lookout point*).

NIV+ RAMATH MIZPAH

1. A city allotted to Benjamin (Jos 18:26). The Israelites assemble at (Jdg 20:1-3), and decree the penalty to be executed upon the Benjamites for their mistreatment of the Levite's concubine (Jdg 20:10). Assembled by Samuel that he might reprove them for their idolatry (1Sa 7:5). Crown Saul king of Israel at (1Sa 10:17-25). A judgment seat of Samuel (1Sa 7:16). Walled by Asa (1Ki 15:22; 2Ch 16:6). Temporarily the capital of the country after the Israelites had been carried away captive (2Ki 25:23,25; Jer 40:6-15; 41:1-14). Captivity returned to (Ne 3:7,15,19).

2. A valley near Lebanon (Jos 11:3,8).

3. A city in Moab. David gives his parents to the care of the king of (1Sa 22:3-4).

4. A city in the lowland of Judah (Jos 15:38).

5. A town in Gilead (Jos 10:17; Jdg 11:34). May be the location of a treaty between Jacob and Laban (Ge 31:48-49).

MIZPAR *See Mispar.*

MIZPEH *See Mizpah.*

MIZRAIM [5213] (Hebrew word for *Egypt*).

NIV+ ABEL MIZRAIM

Son of Ham (Ge 10:6,13; 1Ch 1:8,11), progenitor of the Egyptians, a people of N Africa, Hamitic people of Canaan.

MIZZAH [4645] (*terror*). Son of Reuel (Ge 36:13,17; 1Ch 1:37).

MNASON [*3643*]. A native and Christian of Cyprus who entertained Paul (Ac 21:16).

MOAB [824+4566, 4565, 4566, 4566+8441, 4567] (*seed*).

NIV+ MOAB'S, MOABITE, MOABITES, MOABITESS

1. Son of Lot (Ge 19:37).

2. Plains of. Israelites come in (Dt 2:17-18). Military forces numbered in (Nu 26:3,63). The law rehearsed in, by Moses (Nu 35-36; Dt 29-33). The Israelites renew their covenant in (Dt 29:1). The land of promise allotted in (Jos 13:32).

MOABITE STONE, THE Black basalt stele, two by four feet., inscribed by Mesha king of Moab, with thirty-four lines in the Moabite language (practically a dialect of Hebrew), giving his side of the story (2Ki 3).

MOABITE(S) [408+4566, 1201+4566, 4566, 4567].

NIV+ MOAB

Descendants of Lot through his son Moab (Ge 19:37). Called the people of Chemosh (Nu 21:29). The territory E of Jordan, bounded on the N by the Arnon River (Nu 21:13; Jdg 11:18). Israelites commanded not to distress the Moabites (Dt 2:9). Refuse passage of Jephthah's army through their territory (Jdg 11:17-18). Balak was king of (Nu 22:4), calls for Balaam to curse Israel (Nu 22-24; Jos 24:9; Mic 6:5). Are a snare to the Israelites (Nu 25:1-3; Ru 1:4; 1Ki 11:1; 1Ch 8:8; Ezr 9:1-2; Ne 13:23). Land of, not given to the Israelites as a possession (Dt 2:9,29). David takes refuge among, from Saul (1Sa 22:3-4). David conquers (2Sa 8:2; 23:20; 1Ch 11:22; 18:2-11). Israelites had war with (2Ki 3:5-27; 13:20; 24:2; 2Ch 20). Prophecies concerning judgments upon (Jer 48).

MOADIAH [4598, 5050] (perhaps *Yahweh assembles* or *Yahweh promises*).

NIV+ MOADIAH'S

A chief priest who returned from the Exile with Zerubbabel at the time of Joiakim (Ne 12:5,17).

MOB [7736, *4062, 4063*]. At Thessalonica (Ac 17:5), Jerusalem (Ac 21:28,30), Ephesus (Ac 19:29-40).

MOCKING [*3070, 3075, 4329, 4352, 4370, 5593, 9511, *1850*].

NIV+ MOCK, MOCKED, MOCKER, MOCKERS, MOCKERY, MOCKS

Ishmael mocks Sarah (Ge 21:9). Elijah mocks the priests of Baal (1Ki 18:27). Zedekiah mocks Micaiah (1Ki 22:24). Children mock Elisha (2Ki 2:23). The tormentors of Job mock (Job 15:12; 30:1). The persecutors of Jesus mock him (Mt 26:67-68; 27:28-31,39-44; Mk 10:34; 14:65; 15:17-20,29-32; Lk 23:11; Jn 19:2-3,5; 1Pe 2:23). The Ammonites mock God (Eze 25:3). Tyre mocks Jerusalem (Eze 26:2). The wicked mock (Isa 28:15,22; 2Pe 3:3).

See Scoffing.

Figurative: (Ecc 7:16; 1Co 7:31).

MODESTY [*2362*].

NIV+ MODESTLY

Of women (1Ti 2:9).

Instances of:

Moses (Nu 12:3). Saul (1Sa 9:21). Vashti (Est 1:11-12). Elihu (Job 32:4-7).

See Humility.

MOLADAH [4579] (*generation*). Town c. ten miles E of Beersheba (Ne 11:26).

MOLDING [2425] (*wreath* or *border*).

NIV+ MOLDS, MOLDED

(Job 28:2; Eze 24:11). The decorative ledge of gold around the ark of the covenant (Ex 25:11; 37:2), the table (Ex 25:24-25; 37:11-12), and the incense altar (Ex 30:3-4; 37:26-27). Of images (Ex 32:4,8; 34:17; Lev 19:4; Dt 9:12), pillars (1Ki 7:15), bronze Sea (1Ki 7:23), done in the plain of Jordan (1Ki 7:46; 2Ch 4:17), mirrors (Job 37:18).

MOLECH [4891, 4903, 4904, *3661*] (*"shameful" king*) Molech is the deliberate misvocalization of the name of a pagan god. The consonants for the word king, *melek*, are combined with the vowels for shame, *bosheth*. An idol of the Ammonites (Ac 7:43). Worshiped by the wives of Solomon, and by Solomon (1Ki 11:1-8). Children sacrificed to (2Ki 23:10, w Jer 32:35; 2Ki 16:3; 21:6; 2Ch 28:3; Isa 57:5; Jer 7:31; Eze 16:20-21; 20:26,31; 23:37,39, w Lev 18:21; 20:2-5). *See Malcam, 2.*

MOLE(S) NIV "chameleon" (Lev 11:30), "rodent" (Isa 2:20). *See Animals; Chameleon.*

MOLID [4582] (*descendant*). A descendant of Judah, the son of Abishur and his wife Abihail (1Ch 2:29).

MOLTEN IMAGE *See Tabernacle.*

MONARCHY Described by Samuel (1Sa 8:11-18).

See Government; Kings.

MONEY [*4084, 10362, *736, 921, 2238, 3142, 3440, 5507, 5910, 5975*].

NIV+ COIN, COINS, DENARII, DENARIUS, DRACHMA, DRACHMAS, FOUR-DRACHMA, TWO-DRACHMA

Silver used as (Ge 17:12-13,23,27; 20:16; 23:9,13; 31:15; 37:28; 42:25-35; 43:12-23; 44:1-8; 47:14-18; Ex 12:44; 21:11,21,34-35; 22:7,17,25; 30:16; Lev 22:11; 25:37,51; 27:15,18; Nu 3:48-51; 18:16; Dt 2:6,28; 14:25-26; 21:14; 23:19; Jdg 5:19; 16:18; 17:4; 1Ki 21:2,6,15; 2Ki 5:26; 12:4,7-16; 15:20; 22:7,9; 23:35; 2Ch 24:5,11,14; 34:9,14,17; Ezr 3:7; 7:7; Ne 5:4,10-11; Est 4:7; Job 31:39; Ps 15:5; Pr 7:20; Ecc 7:12; 10:19; Isa 43:24; 52:3; 55:1-2; Jer 32:9-10,25,44; La 5:4; Mic 3:11; Mt 25:18,27; 28:12, 15; Mk 14:11; Lk 9:3; 19:15,23; 22:5; Ac 7:16; 8:20).

Gold used as (Ge 13:2; 24:35; 44:8, w 44:1; 1Ch 21:25; Ezr 8:25-27; Isa 13:17; 46:6; 60:9; Eze 7:19; 28:4; Mt 2:11; 10:9; Ac 3:6; 20:33; 1Pe 1:18).

Copper used as (Mt 10:9; Mk 6:8; 12:42; Lk 21:2).

Weighed (Ge 23:16; 43:21; Job 28:15; Jer 32:9-10; Zec 11:12). Image on (Mt 22:20-21). Conscience (Mt 17:2; Mt 27:3,5). Ransom atonement (Ex 30:12-16; Lev 5:15-16). Sin offering (2Ki 12:16). Value of, varied corruptly (Am 8:5). Love of, the root of evil (1Ti 6:10). *See Materialism.*

See Daric; Drachma; Gerah; Penny; Pound; Shekel; Silver; Talent.

MONEY CHANGERS [*3142*]Those who changed foreign currency into sanctuary money at a profit (Mt 21:12; Mk 11:15; Jn 2:14-15).

MONITOR LIZARD [3947]. Unclean for food (Lev 11:30). *See Animals.*

MONOPOLY Of lands (Isa 5:8; Mic 2:2), by Pharaoh (Ge 47:19-26), of food (Pr 11:26).

MONOTHEISM (*one God*). Belief that there is but one God.

MONSTERS [9490]. *See Animals; Behemoth; Leviathan; Serpent.*

MONTH [2544, 3732, 10333, *3604, 5485, 5564*].

NIV+ MONTHLY, MONTHS, MONTHS'

Sun and moon for signs and seasons (Ge 1:14). The beginning and ending of the Flood (Ge 7:11; 8:4).

Twelve months reckoned to a year (1Ki 4:7; 1Ch 27:1-15; Est 2:12). Time computed by months (Ge 29:14; Nu 10:10; Jdg 11:37; 1Sa 6:1; Ps 81:3; Rev 22:2). Months in prophecy (Rev 11:2).

1. Abib (Post-Exilic name: Nisan) March-April

Month 7 in civil sequence. The Jewish calendar began with (Ex 12:2; 13:4; Dt 16:1). Passover instituted and celebrated in (Ex 12:1-28; 23:15). Israelites left Egypt in (Ex 13:4). Tabernacle set up in (Ex 40:2,17). Israelites arrive at Zin in (Nu 20:1). Cross Jordan in (Jos 4:19). Jordan overflows in (1Ch 12:15). After the Captivity called Nisan (Ne 2:1; Est 3:7). Decree to put the Jews to death in (Est 3:12). The death of Jesus in (Mt 26:27).

Season: Spring; Later rains.

Agriculture: Barley and flax harvest begin.

Feasts: 14th, Passover (Ex 12:18; Lev 23:5); 15-21st, Unleavened Bread (Lev 23:6); 16th, Firstfruits (Lev 23:10f).

2. Ziv (Post-Exilic name: Iyyar) April-May

Month 8 in civil sequence. Israel numbered in (Nu 1:1,18). Passover to be observed in, by the unclean and others who could not observe it in the first month (Nu 9:10-11). Israel departed from the wilderness of Zin in (Nu 10:11). Temple begun in (1Ki 6:1; 2Ch 3:2). An irregular Passover celebrated in (2Ch 30:1-27). Rebuilding of the temple begun in (Ezr 3:8).

Season: Dry season begins.

Agriculture: Barley harvest.

Feasts: 14th, Later Passover (Nu 9:10-11).

3. Sivan (A Post-Exilic name) May-June

Month 9 in civil sequence. Asa renews the covenant of himself and people in (2Ch 15:10).

Agriculture: Early figs ripen; Wheat harvest.

Feasts: 6th, Pentecost or Feast of Weeks (Lev 23:15ff); Harvest.

4. Tammuz (Post-Exilic name) June-July

Month 10 in civil sequence. The number only appears in the Bible. Jerusalem taken by Nebuchadnezzar in (Jer 39:2; 52:6-7).

Agriculture: Tending vines.

Feasts: None.

5. Ab (Post-Exilic name) July-August

Month 11 in civil sequence. Number only mentioned. Aaron died on the first day of (Nu 33:38). Temple destroyed in (2Ki 25:8-10; Jer 1:3; 52:12-30). Ezra arrived at Jerusalem in (Ezr 7:8-9).

Agriculture: Ripening of grapes, figs, and olives.

Feasts: None.

6. Elul (Post-Exilic name) August-September

Month 12 in civil sequence. Wall of Jerusalem finished in (Ne 6:15). Temple built in (Hag 1:14-15).

Agriculture: Processing grapes, dates, summer figs, and olives.

Feasts: None.

7. Ethanim (Post-Exilic name: Tishri) September-October

Month 1 in civil sequence. Feasts held in (Lev 23:24,27; Ne 8:13-15). Jubilee proclaimed in (Lev 25:9). Solomon's temple dedicated in (1Ki 8:2). Altar rebuilt and offerings renewed in (Ezr 3:1,6).

Season: Autumn (early) rains begin.

Agriculture: Plowing.

Feasts: 1st, Trumpets (Nu 29:1; Lev 23:24); 10th, Atonement (Lev 16:29ff; 23:27ff); 15-21st, Tabernacles or Booths (Lev 23:34ff); 22nd, Solemn assembly (Lev 23:36).

8. Bul (Post-Exilic name: Marcheshvan) October-November

Month 2 in civil sequence. The temple finished in (1Ki 6:38). Jeroboam's idolatrous feast in (1Ki 12:32-33; 1Ch 27:11).

Season: Plowing.

Agriculture: Winter figs; sowing of wheat and barley.

Feasts: None.

9. Kislev (Post-Exilic name) November-December

Month 3 in civil sequence.

Agriculture: Sowing.

Feasts: 25th, Hanukkah or Dedication (1Mc 4:52f; Jn 10:22).

10. Tebeth (Post-Exilic name) December-January

Month 4 in civil sequence. Nebuchadnezzar besieges Jerusalem in (2Ki 25:1; Jer 52:4). Esther chosen queen (Est 2:16).

Season: Winter rains begin (snow on high ground).

Agriculture: None.

Feasts: None.

11. Shebat (Post-Exilic name) January-February

Month 5 in civil sequence. Moses probably died in (Dt 1:3).

Agriculture: None.

Feasts: None.

12. Adar (Post-Exilic name) February-March

Month 6 in civil sequence. Second temple finished in (Ezr 6:15). Feast of Purim in (Est 9:1-26).

Agriculture: Almond trees bloom; citrus fruit harvest.

Feasts: Purim.

13. Adar Sheni (not in Bible)

Second Adar is an intercalary month added about every three years so the lunar calendar would correspond to the solar year.

See Calendar; Time. See also each month by name.

MONUMENT [3338, 5167, 5893]. *See Pillar.*

MOON [2544, 3732, 3734, 4057, 4244, 4401, *3741, 4943*].

NIV+ MOONS

Created by God (Ge 1:16; Ps 8:3; 136:7-9). Its light (Job 31:26; Ecc 12:2; SS 6:10; Jer 31:35; 1Co 15:41). Its influences (Dt 33:14; Ps 121:6). Seasons of (months) (Ps 104:19). Joseph's dream concerning (Ge 37:9). Stand still (Jos 10:12-13; Hab 3:11). Worship of, forbidden (Dt 4:19; 17:3). Worshiped (2Ki 23:5; Job 31:26-27; Jer 7:18; 8:2;

44:17-19,25). No light of, in heaven (Rev 21:23). Darkening of (Job 25:5; Isa 13:10; 24:23; Eze 32:7; Joel 2:10,31; 3:15; Mt 24:29; Mk 13:24; Lk 21:25; Ac 2:20; Rev 6:12; 8:12).

Figurative:

Shining of (Isa 30:26; 60:19; Rev 21:23).

Symbolic: (Rev 12:1).

Feast of the New Moon:

(Nu 10:10; 28:11-15; 1Ch 23:31; 2Ch 31:3; Ezr 3:5). Trade at time of, prohibited (Am 8:5).

MORAL AGENCY See Contingencies.

MORAL LAW See Law.

MORALITY See Duty of People to People; Integrity; Neighbor.

MORASTHITE See Moresheth.

MORDECAI [5283] (pagan Babylonian god Marduk).
NIV+ MORDECAI'S

A Jewish captive in Persia (Est 2:5-6). Foster father of Esther (Est 2:7). Informs Xerxes of a conspiracy against his life, and is rewarded (Est 2:21-23; 6:1-11). Promoted in Haman's place (Est 8:1-2,15; 10:1-3). Intercedes with Xerxes for the Jews; establishes the festival of Purim in commemoration of their deliverance (Est 8-9).

MOREH [4622] ([place of] instructor).

1. A plain near Shechem and Gilgal (Ge 12:6; Dt 11:30).

2. A hill in the plain of Jezreel where the Midianites encamped (Jdg 7:1,12).

MORESHETH [4629] (possession of Gath).
NIV+ MORESHETH GATH

Hometown of Micah; probably Moresheth Gath (Jer 26:18; Mic 1:1).

MORESHETH GATH, MORESHETH-GATH
[4628] (possession of Gath).
NIV+ MORESHETH

Town c. five miles W of Gath in the Shephelah (Mic 1:14). See Moresheth.

MORIAH [5317]. Place to which Abraham to offer up Isaac (Ge 22:2). Solomon built temple on Mt. Moriah (2Ch 3:1), but it is not certain whether it is the same place.

MORNING [*1332, 5974, 6727, 8840, 8899, 4745, 4746, 4748, 5892].
NIV+ MORNING'S, MORNINGS

The second part of the day at the Creation (Ge 1:5,8,13,19,23,31). The first part of the natural day (Mk 16:2). Ordained by God (Job 38:12). Began with first dawn (Jos 6:15; Ps 119:147). Continued until noon (1Ki 18:26; Ne 8:3). Dawning of calls for rejoicing (Ps 65:8).

The Jews:

Generally rose early in (Ge 28:18; Jdg 6:28). Eat but little in (Ecc 10:16). Went to the temple in (Lk 21:38; Jn 8:2). Offered a part of the daily sacrifice in (Ex 29:38-39; Nu 28:4-7). Devoted a part of to prayer and praise (Ps 5:3; 59:16; 88:13). Gathered the manna in (Ex 16:21). Began their journeys in (Ge 22:3). Held courts of justice in (Jer 21:12; Mt 27:1). Contracted covenants in (Ge 26:31). Transacted business in (Ecc 11:6; Mt 20:1). Was frequent-

ly cloudless (2Sa 23:4). A red sky in, a sign of bad weather (Mt 16:3). Ushered in by the morning stars (Job 38:7).

Illustrative:

Of the resurrection day (Ps 49:14). Breaking forth, of the glory of the church (SS 6:10; Isa 58:8). Star of, of the glory of Christ (Rev 22:16). Star of, of reward of saints (Rev 2:28). Clouds in, of the short-lived profession of hypocrites (Hos 6:4). Wings of, of rapid movements (Ps 139:9). Spread upon the mountains, of heavy calamities (Joel 2:2).

MORNING SACRIFICE See Offerings.

MORNING STAR [2122, 843, 5892]. Figurative of the glory of the king of Babylon (Isa 14:12). Of Jesus (2Pe 1:19; Rev 2:26; 22:16).

MORSEL [4269].
NIV+ MORSELS

A choice bit of food (Pr 18:8; 26:22).

MORTAL, MORTALITY [132, 632, 928+5883, 1414, 4637, 8358, 2570, 5778].
NIV+ MORTALLY, MORTALS

A mortal is a being subject to death (Ro 8:11; 1Co 15:53-54).

MORTAR [2817, 4521, 4847].

1. An instrument for crushing grain (Nu 11:8; Pr 27:22). See Grinding; Mill.

2. A cement (Ex 1:14). Tar used as, in building tower of Babel (Ge 11:3). Used to plaster houses (Lev 14:42-45). Untempered, not enduring (Eze 13:10-15; 22:28). To be trodden to make firm (Na 3:14).

Figurative: (Isa 41:25).

MORTGAGE (take on pledge, give in pledge, exchange). On land (Ne 5:3). See Land.

MORTIFICATION (self-denial). Instances of: David's ambassadors, sent to Hanun (2Sa 10:1-5). Judas (Mt 27:3-5). See Humility.

MOSAIC [8367]. Picture or design made by setting tiny squares or cones of varicolored marble, limestone, or semiprecious stones in some medium such as plaster to tell a story or to form a decoration (Est 1:6).

MOSERAH, MOSERA [4594] (possession). An encampment of the Israelites where Aaron died (Dt 10:6). Probably identical with Moseroth, below.

MOSEROTH [5035] (possession). An encampment of the Israelites (Nu 33:30-31).

MOSES [5407, 10441, 3707] (drawn out Ex 2:10; Egyptian for son).
NIV+ MOSES'

A Levite and son of Amram (Ex 2:1-4; 6:20; Ac 7:20; Heb 11:23). Hidden in an basket (Ex 2:3). Discovered and adopted by the daughter of Pharaoh (Ex 2:5-10). Learned in all the wisdom of Egypt (Ac 7:22). His loyalty to his race (Heb 11:24-26). Takes the life of an Egyptian; flees from Egypt; finds refuge among the Midianites (Ex 2:11-22; Ac 7:24-29). Joins himself to Jethro, priest of Midian; marries Jethro's daughter Zipporah; has two sons (Ex 2:15-22; 18:3-4). Is herdsman for Jethro in the desert of Horeb (Ex 3:1). Has the vision of the burning bush (Ex 3:2-6). God reveals to him his purpose to deliver the Israelites and bring them into the land of Canaan (Ex

3:7-10). Commissioned as a leader of the Israelites (Ex 3:10-22; 6:13). His rod miraculously turned into a serpent, his hand made leprous, and each restored (Ex 4:1-9,28). With his wife and sons leaves Jethro to perform his mission (Ex 4:18-20). His controversy with his wife on account of circumcision (Ex 4:20-26). Meets Aaron in the wilderness (Ex 4:27-28).

With Aaron assembles the leaders of Israel (Ex 4:29-31). With Aaron goes before Pharaoh, in the name of Yahweh demands the liberties of his people (Ex 5:1). Rejected by Pharaoh; hardships of the Israelites increased (Ex 5). People murmur against Moses and Aaron (Ex 5:20-21; 15:24; 16:2-3; 17:2-3; Nu 14:2-4; 16:41; 20:2-5; 21:4-6; Dt 1:12,26-28). *See Israel.* Receives comfort and assurance from the land (Ex 6:1-8). Unbelief of the people (Ex 6:9). Renews his appeal to Pharaoh (Ex 6:11). Under divine direction brings plagues upon the land of Egypt (Ex 7-12). Secures the deliverance of the people and leads them out of Egypt (Ex 13). Crosses the Red Sea; Pharaoh and his army are destroyed (Ex 14). Composes a song for the Israelites on their deliverance from Pharaoh (Ex 15). Joined by his family in the wilderness (Ex 18:1-12).

Institutes a system of government (Ex 18:13-26; Nu 11:16-30; Dt 1:9-18). Receives the law and ordains various statutes. *See Law of Moses.* Face of, transfigured (Ex 34:29-35; 2Co 3:13). Sets up the tabernacle. *See Tabernacle.* Reproves Aaron for making the golden calf (Ex 32:22-23), for irregularity in the offerings (Lev 10:16-20). Jealousy of Aaron and Miriam toward (Nu 12). Rebellion of Korah, Dathan, and Abiram against (Nu 16). Appoints Joshua as his successor (Nu 27:22-23; Dt 31:7-8,14,23; 34:9).

Not permitted to enter Canaan, but views the land from the top of Pisgah (Nu 27:12-14; Dt 3:17; 3:23-29; 32:48-52; 34:1-8). Death and burial of (Nu 31:2; Dt 32:50; 34:1-6). Body of, disputed over (Jude 9). 120 years old at death (Dt 31:2). Mourning for, thirty days in the plains of Moab (Dt 34:8). His virility (Dt 31:2; 34:7).

Present with Jesus on the Mount of Transfiguration (Mt 17:3-4; Mk 9:4; Lk 9:30).

Type of Christ (Dt 18:15-18; Ac 3:22; 7:37).

Benedictions of:

Upon the people (Lev 9:23; Nu 10:35-36; Dt 1:11). Last benediction upon the twelve tribes (Dt 33).

Character of:

Murmurings of (Ex 5:22-23; Nu 11:10-15). Impatience of (Ex 5:22-23; 6:12; 32:19; Nu 11:10-15; 16:15; 20:10; 31:14). Respected and feared (Ex 33:8). Faith of (Nu 10:29; Dt 9:1-3; Heb 11:23-28). Called the man of God (Dt 33:1). God spoke to, as a man to his friend (Ex 33:11). Magnified of God (Ex 19:9; Nu 14:12-20; Dt 9:13-29, w Ex 32:30). Magnanimity of, toward Eldad and Medad (Nu 11:29). Meekness of (Ex 14:13-14; 15:24-25; 16:2-3,7-8; Nu 12:3; 16:4-11). Obedience of (Ex 7:6; 40:16,19,21). Unaspiring (Nu 14:12-20; Dt 9:13-29, w Ex 32:30).

Intercessory Prayers of: *See Intercession, Instances of; Intercession, Solicited; Intercession, Answered,.*

Miracles of: *See Miracles.*

Prophecies of:

(Ex 3:10; 4:5,11-12; 6:13; 7:2; 17:16; 19:3-9; 33:11; Nu 11:17; 12:7-8; 36:13; Dt 1:3; 5:31; 18:15,18; 34:10,12; Hos 12:13; Mk 7:9-10; Ac 7:37-38).

MOSES, ASSUMPTION OF Pseudonymous

Jewish apocalyptic book, probably written early in the early first century A.D.; gives prophecy of future of Israel. Possibly quoted in Jude 9

MOSES, LAW OF *See Law.*

MOST HIGH [6583, 6604, 6610, 10546, 10548, *5736*].

Title of God (Ge 14:18-19,20,22; Ps 7:17). *See God, Names of, Elyon.*

MOST HOLY PLACE *See Holy of Holies.*

MOTE *See Speck.*

MOTH [6931, *1181+4963, 4962*]. An insect (Job 4:19; 27:18; Ps 39:11). Destructive of garments (Job 13:28; Isa 50:9; 51:8; Hos 5:12).

Figurative (Mt 6:19-20; Jas 5:2).

MOTHER [562, 851, 1485, 3528, *298, 1222, 1666, 3120, 3613, 3836, 5577*].

NIV+ GRANDMOTHER, GRANDMOTHER'S, MOTHER-IN-LAW, MOTHER'S, MOTHERS, MOTHERS'

Reverence for, commanded (Ex 20:12)—

Lev 19:3 "'Each of you must respect his mother and father, and you must observe my Sabbaths. I am the Lord your God. (+Dt 5:16)

Pr 23:22 Listen to your father, who gave you life, and do not despise your mother when she is old. (+Mt 15:4; 19:19; Mk 7:10; 10:19; Lk 18:20; Eph 6:2)

To be obeyed (Dt 21:18)—

Pr 1:8 Listen, my son, to your father's instruction and do not forsake your mother's teaching.

Pr 6:20 My son, keep your father's commands and do not forsake your mother's teaching.

Love for—

1Ki 19:20 Elisha then left his oxen and ran after Elijah. "Let me kiss my father and mother good-by," he said, "and then I will come with you." "Go back," Elijah replied. "What have I done to you?"

Must be subordinate to love for Christ (Mt 10:37).—
Sanctifying influence of (1Co 7:14; 2Ti 1:5).

Dishonoring of, to be punished—

Ex 21:15 "Anyone who attacks his father or his mother must be put to death.

Lev 20:9 "'If anyone curses his father or mother, he must be put to death. He has cursed his father or his mother, and his blood will be on his own head.

Pr 20:20 If a man curses his father or mother, his lamp will be snuffed out in pitch darkness.

Pr 28:24 He who robs his father or mother and says, "It's not wrong"—he is partner to him who destroys.

Pr 30:11 "There are those who curse their fathers and do not bless their mothers;

Pr 30:17 "The eye that mocks a father, that scorns obedience to a mother, will be pecked out by the ravens of the valley, will be eaten by the vultures. (+Mt 15:4-6; Mk 7:10-12)

Incest with, forbidden—

Lev 18:7 "'Do not dishonor your father by having sexual relations with your mother. She is your mother; do not have relations with her.

Wicked (Ge 27:6-17; 2Ki 11:1-3).

Love of: (Isa 49:15; 66:13).

Exemplified by: Hagar (Ge 21:14-16). The mother of Moses (Ex 2:1-3). Hannah (1Sa 1:20-28). Rizpah (2Sa 21:8-11). Bathsheba (1Ki 1:16-21). The mother whose child was brought to Solomon (1Ki 3:16-26). The woman whose sons were to be taken for debt (2Ki 4:1-7). The

Shunammite (2Ki 4:18-37). Mary the mother of Jesus (Lk 2:41-50). The bereaved mothers of Bethlehem (Mt 2:16-18). The Syrian Phoenician woman (Mt 15:21-28; Mk 7:24-30).

Grieves over wayward children—

Pr 10:1 The proverbs of Solomon: A wise son brings joy to his father, but a foolish son grief to his mother.

Pr 19:26 He who robs his father and drives out his mother is a son who brings shame and disgrace.

Pr 29:15 The rod of correction imparts wisdom, but a child left to himself disgraces his mother.

Rejoices over good children—

Pr 23:23 Buy the truth and do not sell it; get wisdom, discipline and understanding. [24]The father of a righteous man has great joy; he who has a wise son delights in him. [25]May your father and mother be glad; may she who gave you birth rejoice! (+Pr 23:26-35)

MOTHER-IN-LAW [2792, 3165, *4289*].

NIV+ See MOTHER

Not to be defiled (Lev 18:17; 20:14; Dt 27:23). Conflict with (Mic 7:6; Mt 10:35). Beloved by Ruth (Ru 1:14-17). Peter's, healed by Jesus (Mk 1:30-31).

MOTIVE [3671, 8120, *1087*, *4733*].

NIV+ MOTIVES

Ascribed to God (Ps 106:8; Eze 36:21-22,32). Right, required (Mt 6:1-18). Sinful, illustrated by Cain (Ge 4:7; 1Jn 3:12).

Misunderstood:

The tribes of Reuben and Gad, in asking inheritance E of Jordan (Nu 32:1-33), when they built the memorial (Jos 22:9-34). David's, by King Hanun (2Sa 10:2-3; 1Ch 19:3-4). The king of Syria's, in sending presents to the king of Israel by Naaman (2Ki 5:5-7). Job's in his righteousness (Job 1:9-11; 2:4-5).

MOTTO *See Inscriptions.*

MOUNT EPHRAIM *See Ephraim.*

MOUNT OF BEATITUDES Site of the Sermon on the Mount (Mt 5-7), exact location unknown. *See Beatitudes; Hattin, Horns of; Sermon on the Mount.*

MOUNTAIN [844, 850, 2065, 2215, 2378, 6152, 7600, 10296, *4001*].

NIV+ MOUNT, MOUNTAINS, MOUNTAINSIDE, MOUNTAINTOP, MOUNTAINTOPS, MOUNTS

Melted (Ps 97:5; Dt 4:11; 5:23; Jdg 5:5; Isa 64:1-3; Mic 1:4; Na 1:5). Overturning and removing of (Job 9:5; 14:18; 28:9; Eze 38:20). Abraham offers Isaac upon Mount Zion, the site of the temple (Ge 22:2). *See Zion.* Used for idolatrous worship (Dt 12:2; 1Sa 10:5; 1Ki 14:23; Jer 3:6; Hos 4:13). Jesus tempted upon (Mt 4:8; Lk 4:5). Jesus preaches from (Mt 5:1). Jesus goes up into, for prayer (Mt 14:23; Lk 6:12; 9:28), is transfigured upon (Mt 17:1-9; Mk 9:2-10; Lk 9:28-36), meets his disciples on, after his resurrection (Mt 28:16-17). Signals from (Isa 13:2; 18:3; 30:17). Removed by faith (Mt 17:20; 21:21; Mk 11:23). Burning mountains. *See Volcanoes.*

MOURNING [*61, 63, 65, 1134, 5027, 5631, 5653, 6199, 7722, 9302, *4292*, *4291*, *3081*, *3164*].

NIV+ MOURN, MOURNED, MOURNERS, MOURNFUL, MOURNFULLY, MOURNS

For the Dead:

Head uncovered (Lev 10:6; 21:10), lying on the ground (2Sa 12:16), personal appearance neglected (2Sa 14:2), cutting the flesh (Lev 19:28; 21:1-5; Dt 14:1; Jer 16:6-7; 41:5), lamentations (Ge 50:10; Ex 12:30; 1Sa 30:4; Jer 22:18; Mt 2:17-18), fasting (1Sa 31:13; 2Sa 1:12; 3:35). Priests prohibited, except for nearest of kin (Lev 21:1-11). For Nadab and Abihu forbidden (Lev 10:6). Sexes separated in (Zec 12:12,14).

Hired mourners (2Ch 35:25; Ecc 12:5; Jer 9:17; Mt 9:23).

Abraham mourned for Sarah (Ge 23:2), Egyptians, for Jacob seventy days (Ge 50:1-3), Israelites, for Aaron thirty days (Nu 20:29).

David's lamentations over the death of Saul and his sons (2Sa 1:17-27), the death of Abner (2Sa 3:33-34), the death of Absalom (2Sa 18:33).

Jeremiah and the singing men and singing women lament for Josiah (2Ch 35:25).

For Calamities and Other Sorrows:

Tearing the garments (Ge 37:29,34; 44:13; Nu 14:6; Jdg 11:35; 2Sa 1:2,11; 3:31; 13:19,31; 15:32; 2Ki 2:12; 5:8; 6:30; 11:14; 19:1; 22:11,19; Ezr 9:3,5; Job 1:20; 2:12; Isa 37:1; Jer 41:5; Mt 26:65; Ac 14:14). Wearing mourning dress (Ge 38:14; 2Sa 14:2). *See Sackcloth.* Cutting or plucking off the hair and beard (Ezr 9:3; Jer 7:29). *See Baldness.* Covering the head and face (2Sa 15:30; 19:4; Est 6:12; Jer 14:3-4), and the upper lip (Lev 13:45; Eze 24:17,22; Mic 3:7). Laying aside ornaments (Ex 33:4,6). Walking barefoot (2Sa 15:30; Isa 20:2). Laying the hand on the head (2Sa 13:19; Jer 2:37). Ashes put on the head (Eze 27:30). Dust on the head (Jos 7:6). Dressing in black (Jer 14:2). Sitting on the ground (Isa 3:26).

Caused ceremonial defilement (Nu 19:11-16; 31:19; Lev 21:1). Prevented offerings from being accepted (Dt 26:14; Hos 9:4).

See Elegy.

MOUSE *See Rat(s).*

MOUTH [1744, 2674, 4498, 4918, 7023, 7156, 7339, 7895, 8557, 10588, *930*, *931*, *3364*, *5125*, *5779*].

NIV+ MOUTHS

Has various connotations: literal mouth, language, opening; sometimes personified (Ps 119:108; Pr 15:14; Rev 19:15).

MOWING [1600, *286*].

NIV+ MOWED, MOWN

This was done by hand with a short sickle—originally of flint, later of metal (Ps 72:6; Jas 5:4). The king's share were the portion of the harvest taken as taxes (Am 7:1).

MOZA [4605] *(sunrise)*.

1. A son of Caleb (1Ch 2:46).
2. A Benjamite (1Ch 8:36-37; 9:42-43).

MOZAH [5173]. A city of Benjamin (Jos 18:26).

MUFFLER *See Veil.*

MULBERRY TREE [*5189*]. (Lk 17:6).

MULE [7234, 7235].
NIV+ MULES

Uses of:

For royal riders (2Sa 13:29; 18:9; 1Ki 1:33,38), by saints in Isaiah's prophetic vision of the kingdom of Christ (Isa 66:20), as pack animals (2Ki 5:17; 1Ch 12:40). Tribute paid in (1Ki 10:25). Used in barter (Eze 27:14), by the exiles returning from Babylon (Ezr 2:66; Ne 7:68), in war (Zec 14:15).

MULTITUDE FED Miraculously (Ex 16:13; Nu 11:31; 2Ki 4:43; Mt 14:21; 15:38).

MUMMIFICATION *See Embalming.*

MUNITIONS Fortifications (Na 2:1).

MUPPIM [5137]. Son or descendant of Benjamin (Ge 46:21). Called Shupham (Nu 26:39) and Shuppim (1Ch 7:12,15). Shephuphan may be the same person (1Ch 8:5).

MURDER [1947, 2222, 4637, 5782, 8357, *5377, 5838, 5839, 5840*].
NIV+ MURDERED, MURDERER, MURDERERS, MURDERING, MURDEROUS, MURDERS

Forbidden on penalty of death (Ge 9:4-6; Ex 21:14; Lev 24:17; Dt 19:11-13), a murdered man's nearest relative had the duty to pursue the slayer and kill him (Nu 35:19), but the slayer could flee to a city of refuge, where he would be tried and then either turned over to the avenger or be protected (Nu 35:9-34; Dt 19:1-10). *See Homicide; Infanticide; Regicide.*

MURMURING
NIV+ MUTTER, MUTTERED, MUTTERS

Forbidden (1Co 10:10)—
Php 2:14 Do everything without complaining or arguing,
Jas 5:9 Don't grumble against each other, brothers, or you will be judged. The Judge is standing at the door!

Rebuked—
Job 15:11 Are God's consolations not enough for you, words spoken gently to you? [12]Why has your heart carried you away, and why do your eyes flash, [13]so that you vent your rage against God and pour out such words from your mouth?
Ecc 7:10 Do not say, "Why were the old days better than these?" For it is not wise to ask such questions.
La 3:39 Why should any living man complain when punished for his sins?
Ro 9:19 One of you will say to me: "Then why does God still blame us? For who resists his will?" [20]But who are you, O man, to talk back to God? "Shall what is formed say to him who formed it, 'Why did you make me like this?'"

Punishment for—
Nu 14:26 The LORD said to Moses and Aaron: [27]"How long will this wicked community grumble against me? I have heard the complaints of these grumbling Israelites. [28]So tell them, 'As surely as I live, declares the LORD, I will do to you the very things I heard you say: [29]In this desert your bodies will fall—every one of you twenty years old or more who was counted in the census and who has grumbled against me. [30]Not one of you will enter the land I swore with uplifted hand to make your home, except Caleb son of Jephunneh and Joshua son of Nun. [31]As for your children that you said would be taken as plunder, I will bring them in to enjoy the land you have rejected. [32]But you—your bodies will fall in this desert. [33]Your

children will be shepherds here for forty years, suffering for your unfaithfulness, until the last of your bodies lies in the desert. [34]For forty years—one year for each of the forty days you explored the land—you will suffer for your sins and know what it is like to have me against you.' [35]I, the LORD, have spoken, and I will surely do these things to this whole wicked community, which has banded together against me. They will meet their end in this desert; here they will die."

[36]So the men Moses had sent to explore the land, who returned and made the whole community grumble against him by spreading a bad report about it— [37]these men responsible for spreading the bad report about the land were struck down and died of a plague before the LORD. (+Nu 17:10-11)

Foolish—
Pr 19:3 A man's own folly ruins his life, yet his heart rages against the LORD.

Murmuring Against God:
Cain (Ge 4:13-14).

Moses—
Ex 5:22 Moses returned to the LORD and said, "O Lord, why have you brought trouble upon this people? Is this why you sent me? [23]Ever since I went to Pharaoh to speak in your name, he has brought trouble upon this people, and you have not rescued your people at all." (+Nu 11:11-15)

Israelites—
Ex 16:8 Moses also said, "You will know that it was the LORD when he gives you meat to eat in the evening and all the bread you want in the morning, because he has heard your grumbling against him. Who are we? You are not grumbling against us, but against the LORD."
Ex 16:12 "I have heard the grumbling of the Israelites. Tell them, 'At twilight you will eat meat, and in the morning you will be filled with bread. Then you will know that I am the LORD your God.'" (+Ex 17:2-3; Nu 11:1-10; 14; 16:41; 20:2-5; 21:5-6; Dt 1:26-28)

Ps 44:9 But now you have rejected and humbled us; you no longer go out with our armies. [10]You made us retreat before the enemy, and our adversaries have plundered us. [11]You gave us up to be devoured like sheep and have scattered us among the nations. [12]You sold your people for a pittance, gaining nothing from their sale.

[13]You have made us a reproach to our neighbors, the scorn and derision of those around us. [14]You have made us a byword among the nations; the peoples shake their heads at us. [15]My disgrace is before me all day long, and my face is covered with shame [16]at the taunts of those who reproach and revile me, because of the enemy, who is bent on revenge.

[17]All this happened to us, though we had not forgotten you or been false to your covenant. [18]Our hearts had not turned back; our feet had not strayed from your path. [19]But you crushed us and made us a haunt for jackals and covered us over with deep darkness.

[20]If we had forgotten the name of our God or spread out our hands to a foreign god, [21]would not God have discovered it, since he knows the secrets of the heart? [22]Yet for your sake we face death all day long; we are considered as sheep to be slaughtered.

[23]Awake, O Lord! Why do you sleep? Rouse yourself! Do not reject us forever. [24]Why do you hide your face and forget our misery and oppression?

[25]We are brought down to the dust; our bodies cling to the

ground. [26]Rise up and help us; redeem us because of your unfailing love. (+Ps 106:24-26)

Mal 3:14 "You have said, 'It is futile to serve God. What did we gain by carrying out his requirements and going about like mourners before the LORD Almighty?

Korah (Nu 16:8-11).

Job (Job 3; 6; 7; 9:10; 13; 16:6-14; 19:7-20; 30)—

Job 33:12 "But I tell you, in this you are not right, for God is greater than man. [13]Why do you complain to him that he answers none of man's words?

David (2Sa 6:8; Ps 116:10-11).

The psalmist—

Ps 73:13 Surely in vain have I kept my heart pure; in vain have I washed my hands in innocence. [14]All day long I have been plagued; I have been punished every morning.

[15]If I had said, "I will speak thus," I would have betrayed your children. [16]When I tried to understand all this, it was oppressive to me [17]till I entered the sanctuary of God; then I understood their final destiny.

[18]Surely you place them on slippery ground; you cast them down to ruin. [19]How suddenly are they destroyed, completely swept away by terrors! [20]As a dream when one awakes, so when you arise, O Lord, you will despise them as fantasies.

[21]When my heart was grieved and my spirit embittered, (+Ps 73:22)

Elijah (1Ki 19:4,10). Jonah (Jnh 4). Jews, against Jesus (Jn 6:41-43,52).

Murmuring Against Moses:

By the Israelites (Ex 5:21; 14:11-12; 15:24; 16:2-3; 17:2-3; Nu 14; 16:2-3,14,41; 20:2-5).

Instances of:

Rachel (Ge 30:1). Asaph (Ps 73:3). Solomon (Ecc 2:17-18). Hezekiah (Isa 38:10-18). Jeremiah (Jer 20:14-18; La 3).

Martha—

Lk 10:40 But Martha was distracted by all the preparations that had to be made. She came to him and asked, "Lord, don't you care that my sister has left me to do the work by myself? Tell her to help me!"

Prodigal's brother (Lk 15:29-30).

See Doubt; Envy; Ingratitude; also Contentment; Resignation.

MURRAIN A plague of Egypt (Ex 9:3,6; Ps 78:50).

MUSHI, MUSHITE(S) [4633, 4634]. Merarite Levite; progenitor of Mushites (Ex 6:19; Nu 3:20; 26:58; 1Ch 6:19,47; 23:21,23).

MUSIC [2369, 2376, 2379, 2727, 4944, 5593, 5904, 7754, 8877, 9512, 10233, *5246, 5889, 6010*].

NIV+ MELODIOUS, MELODY, MUSICAL, MUSICIAN, MUSICIANS

Used at the crowning of kings (1Ki 1:39)—

1Ki 1:40 And all the people went up after him, playing flutes and rejoicing greatly, so that the ground shook with the sound.

2Ch 23:13 She looked, and there was the king, standing by his pillar at the entrance. The officers and the trumpeters were beside the king, and all the people of the land were rejoicing and blowing trumpets, and singers with musical instruments were leading the praises. Then Athaliah tore her robes and shouted, "Treason! Treason!"

2Ch 23:18 Then Jehoiada placed the oversight of the temple of the LORD in the hands of the priests, who were

Levites, to whom David had made assignments in the temple, to present the burnt offerings of the LORD as written in the Law of Moses, with rejoicing and singing, as David had ordered.

In national triumphs—

Ex 15:1 Then Moses and the Israelites sang this song to the LORD: "I will sing to the LORD, for he is highly exalted. The horse and its rider he has hurled into the sea. (+Ex 15:2-19)

Ex 15:20 Then Miriam the prophetess, Aaron's sister, took a tambourine in her hand, and all the women followed her, with tambourines and dancing. [21]Miriam sang to them: "Sing to the LORD, for he is highly exalted. The horse and its rider he has hurled into the sea."

Nu 21:17 Then Israel sang this song: "Spring up, O well! Sing about it, [18]about the well that the princes dug, that the nobles of the people sank—the nobles with scepters and staffs." Then they went from the desert to Mattanah,

Jdg 5:1 On that day Deborah and Barak son of Abinoam sang this song:

[2]"When the princes in Israel take the lead, when the people willingly offer themselves— praise the LORD!

[3]"Hear this, you kings! Listen, you rulers! I will sing to the LORD, I will sing; I will make music to the LORD, the God of Israel. (+Jdg 5:4-31)

Jdg 11:34 When Jephthah returned to his home in Mizpah, who should come out to meet him but his daughter, dancing to the sound of tambourines! She was an only child. Except for her he had neither son nor daughter.

1Sa 18:6 When the men were returning home after David had killed the Philistine, the women came out from all the towns of Israel to meet King Saul with singing and dancing, with joyful songs and with tambourines and lutes. [7]As they danced, they sang: "Saul has slain his thousands, and David his tens of thousands."

In worship—

1Ch 6:31 These are the men David put in charge of the music in the house of the LORD after the ark came to rest there. [32]They ministered with music before the tabernacle, the Tent of Meeting, until Solomon built the temple of the LORD in Jerusalem. They performed their duties according to the regulations laid down for them.

1Ch 15:16 David told the leaders of the Levites to appoint their brothers as singers to sing joyful songs, accompanied by musical instruments: lyres, harps and cymbals.

[17]So the Levites appointed Heman son of Joel; from his brothers, Asaph son of Berekiah; and from their brothers the Merarites, Ethan son of Kushaiah; [18]and with them their brothers next in rank: Zechariah, Jaaziel, Shemiramoth, Jehiel, Unni, Eliab, Benaiah, Maaseiah, Mattithiah, Eliphelehu, Mikneiah, Obed-Edom and Jeiel, the gatekeepers.

[19]The musicians Heman, Asaph and Ethan were to sound the bronze cymbals; [20]Zechariah, Aziel, Shemiramoth, Jehiel, Unni, Eliab, Maaseiah and Benaiah were to play the lyres according to *alamoth,* [21]and Mattithiah, Eliphelehu, Mikneiah, Obed-Edom, Jeiel and Azaziah were to play the harps, directing according to *sheminith.* [22]Kenaniah the head Levite was in charge of the singing; that was his responsibility because he was skillful at it.

1Ch 15:24 Shebaniah, Joshaphat, Nethanel, Amasai, Zechariah, Benaiah and Eliezer the priests were to blow trumpets before the ark of God. Obed-Edom and Jehiah were also to be doorkeepers for the ark.

1Ch 15:27 Now David was clothed in a robe of fine linen, as were all the Levites who were carrying the ark, and as were the singers, and Kenaniah, who was in charge of the singing of the choirs. David also wore a linen ephod. **²⁸**So all Israel brought up the ark of the covenant of the LORD with shouts, with the sounding of rams' horns and trumpets, and of cymbals, and the playing of lyres and harps.

1Ch 16:4 He appointed some of the Levites to minister before the ark of the LORD, to make petition, to give thanks, and to praise the LORD, the God of Israel: **⁵**Asaph was the chief, Zechariah second, then Jeiel, Shemiramoth, Jehiel, Mattithiah, Eliab, Benaiah, Obed-Edom and Jeiel. They were to play the lyres and harps, Asaph was to sound the cymbals, **⁶**and Benaiah and Jahaziel the priests were to blow the trumpets regularly before the ark of the covenant of God. (+1Ch 16:7-36)

1Ch 16:42 Heman and Jeduthun were responsible for the sounding of the trumpets and cymbals and for the playing of the other instruments for sacred song. The sons of Jeduthun were stationed at the gate.

1Ch 23:5 Four thousand are to be gatekeepers and four thousand are to praise the LORD with the musical instruments I have provided for that purpose."

1Ch 25:1 David, together with the commanders of the army, set apart some of the sons of Asaph, Heman and Jeduthun for the ministry of prophesying, accompanied by harps, lyres and cymbals. Here is the list of the men who performed this service: (+1Ch 25:2-4)

1Ch 25:5 All these were sons of Heman the king's seer. They were given him through the promises of God to exalt him. God gave Heman fourteen sons and three daughters.

⁶All these men were under the supervision of their fathers for the music of the temple of the LORD, with cymbals, lyres and harps, for the ministry at the house of God. Asaph, Jeduthun and Heman were under the supervision of the king. **⁷**Along with their relatives—all of them trained and skilled in music for the LORD—they numbered 288.

2Ch 5:12 All the Levites who were musicians—Asaph, Heman, Jeduthun and their sons and relatives—stood on the east side of the altar, dressed in fine linen and playing cymbals, harps and lyres. They were accompanied by 120 priests sounding trumpets. **¹³**The trumpeters and singers joined in unison, as with one voice, to give praise and thanks to the LORD. Accompanied by trumpets, cymbals and other instruments, they raised their voices in praise to the LORD and sang: "He is good; his love endures forever." Then the temple of the LORD was filled with a cloud,

2Ch 20:19 Then some Levites from the Kohathites and Korahites stood up and praised the LORD, the God of Israel, with very loud voice.

2Ch 20:21 After consulting the people, Jehoshaphat appointed men to sing to the LORD and to praise him for the splendor of his holiness as they went out at the head of the army, saying: "Give thanks to the LORD, for his love endures forever."

²²As they began to sing and praise, the LORD set ambushes against the men of Ammon and Moab and Mount Seir who were invading Judah, and they were defeated.

2Ch 20:28 They entered Jerusalem and went to the temple of the LORD with harps and lutes and trumpets.

2Ch 29:25 He stationed the Levites in the temple of the LORD with cymbals, harps and lyres in the way prescribed by David and Gad the king's seer and Nathan the prophet; this was commanded by the LORD through his prophets. **²⁶**So the Levites stood ready with David's instruments, and the priests with their trumpets.

²⁷Hezekiah gave the order to sacrifice the burnt offering on the altar. As the offering began, singing to the LORD

began also, accompanied by trumpets and the instruments of David king of Israel. **²⁸**The whole assembly bowed in worship, while the singers sang and the trumpeters played. All this continued until the sacrifice of the burnt offering was completed. (+2Ch 29:29-30)

2Ch 35:15 The musicians, the descendants of Asaph, were in the places prescribed by David, Asaph, Heman and Jeduthun the king's seer. The gatekeepers at each gate did not need to leave their posts, because their fellow Levites made the preparations for them.

Ezr 2:64 The whole company numbered 42,360, **⁶⁵**besides their 7,337 menservants and maidservants; and they also had 200 men and women singers.

Ezr 3:10 When the builders laid the foundation of the temple of the LORD, the priests in their vestments and with trumpets, and the Levites (the sons of Asaph) with cymbals, took their places to praise the LORD, as prescribed by David king of Israel. **¹¹**With praise and thanksgiving they sang to the LORD: "He is good; his love to Israel endures forever."

And all the people gave a great shout of praise to the LORD, because the foundation of the house of the LORD was laid.

Ne 12:27 At the dedication of the wall of Jerusalem, the Levites were sought out from where they lived and were brought to Jerusalem to celebrate joyfully the dedication with songs of thanksgiving and with the music of cymbals, harps and lyres. **²⁸**The singers also were brought together from the region around Jerusalem—from the villages of the Netophathites, **²⁹**from Beth Gilgal, and from the area of Geba and Azmaveth, for the singers had built villages for themselves around Jerusalem. **³⁰**When the priests and Levites had purified themselves ceremonially, they purified the people, the gates and the wall.

³¹I had the leaders of Judah go up on top of the wall. I also assigned two large choirs to give thanks. One was to proceed on top of the wall to the right, toward the Dung Gate. (+Ne 12:32-47)

Ps 33:1 Sing joyfully to the LORD, you righteous; it is fitting for the upright to praise him. **²**Praise the LORD with the harp; make music to him on the ten-stringed lyre. **³**Sing to him a new song; play skillfully, and shout for joy. (+Ps 68:4)

Ps 68:25 In front are the singers, after them the musicians; with them are the maidens playing tambourines. **²⁶**Praise God in the great congregation; praise the LORD in the assembly of Israel.

Ps 68:32 Sing to God, O kingdoms of the earth, sing praise to the Lord, *Selah*

Ps 81:1 Sing for joy to God our strength; shout aloud to the God of Jacob! **²**Begin the music, strike the tambourine, play the melodious harp and lyre.

³Sound the ram's horn at the New Moon, and when the moon is full, on the day of our Feast;

Ps 87:7 As they make music they will sing, "All my fountains are in you."

Ps 92:1 It is good to praise the LORD and make music to your name, O Most High, **²**to proclaim your love in the morning and your faithfulness at night, **³**to the music of the ten-stringed lyre and the melody of the harp.

Ps 95:1 Come, let us sing for joy to the LORD; let us shout aloud to the Rock of our salvation. **²**Let us come before him with thanksgiving and extol him with music and song.

Ps 98:1 Sing to the LORD a new song, for he has done marvelous things; his right hand and his holy arm have worked salvation for him. **²**The LORD has made his salvation known and revealed his righteousness to the nations. ³He has remembered his love and his faithfulness to the house of Israel; all the ends of the earth have seen the salvation of our God.

⁴Shout for joy to the LORD, all the earth, burst into jubilant song with music; ⁵make music to the LORD with the harp, with the harp and the sound of singing, ⁶with trumpets and the blast of the ram's horn—shout for joy before the LORD, the King.

⁷Let the sea resound, and everything in it, the world, and all who live in it. ⁸Let the rivers clap their hands, let the mountains sing together for joy;

Ps 104:33 I will sing to the LORD all my life; I will sing praise to my God as long as I live.

Ps 105:2 Sing to him, sing praise to him; tell of all his wonderful acts.

Ps 135:1 Praise the LORD.

Praise the name of the LORD; praise him, you servants of the LORD, ²you who minister in the house of the LORD, in the courts of the house of our God.

³Praise the LORD, for the LORD is good; sing praise to his name, for that is pleasant.

Ps 144:9 I will sing a new song to you, O God; on the ten-stringed lyre I will make music to you,

Ps 149:1 Praise the LORD.

Sing to the LORD a new song, his praise in the assembly of the saints.

²Let Israel rejoice in their Maker; let the people of Zion be glad in their King. ³Let them praise his name with dancing and make music to him with tambourine and harp.

Ps 149:6 May the praise of God be in their mouths and a double-edged sword in their hands,

Ps 150:1 Praise the LORD.

Praise God in his sanctuary; praise him in his mighty heavens.

²Praise him for his acts of power; praise him for his surpassing greatness. ³Praise him with the sounding of the trumpet, praise him with the harp and lyre, ⁴praise him with tambourine and dancing, praise him with the strings and flute, ⁵praise him with the clash of cymbals, praise him with resounding cymbals.

⁶Let everything that has breath praise the LORD. Praise the LORD.

Mk 14:26 When they had sung a hymn, they went out to the Mount of Olives.

1Co 14:15 So what shall I do? I will pray with my spirit, but I will also pray with my mind; I will sing with my spirit, but I will also sing with my mind.

Eph 5:19 Speak to one another with psalms, hymns and spiritual songs. Sing and make music in your heart to the Lord,

Col 3:16 Let the word of Christ dwell in you richly as you teach and admonish one another with all wisdom, and as you sing psalms, hymns and spiritual songs with gratitude in your hearts to God.

Heb 2:12 He says, "I will declare your name to my brothers; in the presence of the congregation I will sing your praises."

At the offering of sacrifices (2Ch 29:27-28)

In idolatrous worship—

Da 3:4 Then the herald loudly proclaimed, "This is what you are commanded to do, O peoples, nations and men of every language: ⁵As soon as you hear the sound of the horn, flute, zither, lyre, harp, pipes and all kinds of music, you must fall down and worship the image of gold that King Nebuchadnezzar has set up. ⁶Whoever does not fall

down and worship will immediately be thrown into a blazing furnace."

⁷Therefore, as soon as they heard the sound of the horn, flute, zither, lyre, harp and all kinds of music, all the peoples, nations and men of every language fell down and worshiped the image of gold that King Nebuchadnezzar had set up. (+Da 3:10,15)

For dancing (Mt 11:17)

In joy—

Ge 31:27 Why did you run off secretly and deceive me? Why didn't you tell me, so I could send you away with joy and singing to the music of tambourines and harps?

2Sa 19:35 I am now eighty years old. Can I tell the difference between what is good and what is not? Can your servant taste what he eats and drinks? Can I still hear the voices of men and women singers? Why should your servant be an added burden to my lord the king?

Job 21:12 They sing to the music of tambourine and harp; they make merry to the sound of the flute.

Ecc 2:8 I amassed silver and gold for myself, and the treasure of kings and provinces. I acquired men and women singers, and a harem as well—the delights of the heart of man.

Isa 5:12 They have harps and lyres at their banquets, tambourines and flutes and wine, but they have no regard for the deeds of the LORD, no respect for the work of his hands.

In revelry (Am 5:12; 6:5)

In mourning—

2Ch 35:25 Jeremiah composed laments for Josiah, and to this day all the men and women singers commemorate Josiah in the laments. These became a tradition in Israel and are written in the Laments.

In preparing for funerals—

Mt 9:23 When Jesus entered the ruler's house and saw the flute players and the noisy crowd,

Refrained from in sorrow—

Job 30:31 My harp is tuned to mourning, and my flute to the sound of wailing.

Pr 25:20 Like one who takes away a garment on a cold day, or like vinegar poured on soda, is one who sings songs to a heavy heart.

Isa 16:10 Joy and gladness are taken away from the orchards; no one sings or shouts in the vineyards; no one treads out wine at the presses, for I have put an end to the shouting.

Isa 24:8 The gaiety of the tambourines is stilled, the noise of the revelers has stopped, the joyful harp is silent. ⁹No longer do they drink wine with a song; the beer is bitter to its drinkers.

Eze 26:13 I will put an end to your noisy songs, and the music of your harps will be heard no more.

Rev 18:22 The music of harpists and musicians, flute players and trumpeters, will never be heard in you again. No workman of any trade will ever be found in you again. The sound of a millstone will never be heard in you again.

Captive Jews refrained from—

Ps 137:1 By the rivers of Babylon we sat and wept when we remembered Zion. ²There on the poplars we hung our harps, ³for there our captors asked us for songs, our tormentors demanded songs of joy; they said, "Sing us one of the songs of Zion!"

⁴How can we sing the songs of the LORD while in a foreign land?

Teachers of (1Ch 15:22; 25:7)—

1Ch 25:8 Young and old alike, teacher as well as student, cast lots for their duties. (+2Ch 23:13)

Physical effect of, on people (1Sa 16:15-16,23)—

Eze 33:32 Indeed, to them you are nothing more than one who sings love songs with a beautiful voice and plays an instrument well, for they hear your words but do not put them into practice.

Choir director (Ne 12:42). Chief musician (Ne 12:42; Hab 3:19). Chambers for musicians in the temple (Eze 40:44).

In heaven (Rev 5:8-9)—

Rev 14:2 And I heard a sound from heaven like the roar of rushing waters and like a loud peal of thunder. The sound I heard was like that of harpists playing their harps. ³And they sang a new song before the throne and before the four living creatures and the elders. No one could learn the song except the 144,000 who had been redeemed from the earth. (+Rev 15:2-3)

Allegorical (Rev 5:8-9; 14:2-3; 15:2-3; 18:22).

Symbolic of judgment—

Isa 23:16 "Take up a harp, walk through the city, O prostitute forgotten; play the harp well, sing many a song, so that you will be remembered."

Of God's emotions—

Isa 30:29 And you will sing as on the night you celebrate a holy festival; your hearts will rejoice as when people go up with flutes to the mountain of the LORD, to the Rock of Israel.

Isa 30:32 Every stroke the LORD lays on them with his punishing rod will be to the music of tambourines and harps, as he fights them in battle with the blows of his arm. (+Jer 31:4)

Instruments of:

Invented by Jubal (Ge 4:21), David (1Ch 23:5; 2Ch 7:6; 29:26; Am 6:5). Made by Solomon (1Ki 10:12; 2Ch 9:11; Ecc 2:8), Tyrians (Eze 28:13).

Kinds—

Horn (Da 3:5,7,10). *See Trumpet.* Cymbal (1Ch 15:19,28; 1Co 13:1). *See Cymbal.* Flute (Ge 4:21; Da 3:5,7,10,15). Gittith, possibly a stringed instrument (Ps 8; 81; 84, T). Harp (1Sa 10:5; 16:16,23; 1Ch 16:5). *See Harp.* Lyre (1Ch 16:5). *See Lyre.* Pipe (1Sa 10:5; Isa 30:20; Da 3:5,10,15). *See Pipe.* Sistrum (2Sa 6:5). Tambourine (Ex 15:20). *See Tambourine.* Trumpet (Jos 6:4). *See Trumpet.* Zither (Da 3:5,7,10,15).

Symbols Used in:

Many of psalm titles contain terms that may indicate the tunes of songs popular at the time of the psalmists. This practice of setting new words to an old tune is common to the hymnology of every age.

Aijeleth Shahar, NIV "To [the tune of] The Doe of the Morning" (Ps 22:T). This is probably a tune designation.

Alamoth (1Ch 15:20; Ps 46:T). The Hebrew word means "maidens." It may refer to "maidens playing tambourines" to accompany the music.

Al-taschith, NIV "[To the tune of] Do Not Destroy" (Titles of Ps 57-59; 75). The phrase also occurs in Isa 65:8, leading some to deduce it is the name of a vintage or wine-making song.

Gittith (Titles of Pss 8; 81; 84). This may mean a Gittite lyre or the name of a tune.

Higgaion (Ps 9:16). The word is also translated "meditation" (Ps 19:14), "melody" (Ps 92:3), and "mutter" (La 3:62). Combined with "Selah," it may have been in-

tended to indicate a pause in the vocal music while the instruments played an interlude, a time for devout meditation.

Jonath-elem-rechokim, NIV "To [the tune of] A Dove on Distant Oaks" (Ps 56:T). This is probably a tune designation.

Mahalath (Ps 53:T), *Mahalath Leannoth* (Ps 88:T). The Hebrew appears to be the word for "suffering" or "sickness." Perhaps it indicates that the psalms are to be used in a time of affliction, such as when the godless mock.

Maskil (Titles of Pss 32; 42; 44; 45; 52; 53; 54; 55; 74; 79; 88; 89; 142). Related to a word meaning "to instruct" or "to become wise by instruction," it may indicate a psalm that instructs or that is skillfully made.

Miktam (Titles of Pss 16; 56-60). Variously related to words for "golden," "inscription," and "atonement."

Muth-Labben, NIV "To [the tune of] The Death of the Son" (Ps 9:T). This may be a variant of *alamoth* or a funeral song.

Neginah and *Neginoth,* NIV "stringed instruments" (Titles of Pss 4; 54-55; 61; 67; Hab 3:19). This seems to indicate that the song should be accompanied (perhaps exclusively) by stringed instruments.

Nehiloth, NIV "flutes" (Ps 5:T). This seems to indicate accompaniment (perhaps exclusively) by wind instruments (Ps 5).

Selah. This term appears seventy-one times in the Psalms and in Hab 3:3,9,13. Its meaning is not clear. Possibly it signified a pause in the vocal music while an instrumental interlude played.

Sheminith. (1Ch 15:21; Ps 6:T; 12:T). Related to the word for "eighth," this may have indicated an octave or accompaniment by a eight-stringed instrument.

Shiggaion (Ps 7:T) and *Shigionoth* (Hab 3:1). These could be tune designations or literary categories.

Shoshannim NIV "To [the tune of] Lilies" (Ps 45; 69:T) and *Shushan-eduth,* NIV "To [the tune of] The Lily of the Covenant" (Ps 60:T; 80:T). Again, these are probably tune designations.

MUSTARD SEED [4983]. Kingdom of heaven compared to (Mt 13:31-32; Mk 4:31-32; Lk 13:19). Faith compared to (Mt 17:20).

MUSTER [599, 665, 6641, 7212, 7213, 7695, 7735]. NIV+ MUSTERED, MUSTERING

Of troops (1Sa 14:17; 2Sa 20:4; 1Ki 20:26; 2Ki 25:29; Isa 13:4).

See Armies.

MUTE [522, *228, 936, 3273*]. Stricken of God (Ex 4:11; Lk 1:20,64), miraculous healing of, by Jesus (Mt 9:32-33; 12:22; 15:30-31; Mk 7:37; 9:17,25-26).

See Deafness.

MUTH-LABBEN NIV "To [the tune of] The Death of the Son" (Ps 9:T). Probably name of the tune to which the psalm was sung. *See Music, Symbols Used in.*

MUTILATORS [*2961*]. Sarcastic term for Judaizers who required circumcision for salvation (Php 3:2). *See Circumcision.*

MUTINY Israelites against Moses (Nu 14:4). *See Conspiracy; Rebellion.*

MUZZLE [2888, 4727, *3055, 5821*]. Mosaic law forbade muzzling of oxen when they were treading out the grain (Dt 25:4).

MYRA [*3688*]. A city of Lycia. Paul visits (Ac 27:5-6).

MYRRH [4320, 5255, *3693, 5043, 5046*]. A fragrant gum. A product of the land of Canaan (SS 4:6,14; 5:1). One of the compounds in the sacred anointing oil (Ex 30:23). Used as a perfume (Est 2:12; Ps 45:8; Pr 7:17; SS 3:6; 5:13). Brought by wise men as a present to Jesus (Mt 2:11). Offered to Jesus on the cross (Mk 15:23). Used for embalming (Jn 19:39). Trade in (Ge 37:25; 43:11).

MYRTLE [2072].
NIV+ MYRTLES

(Ne 8:15; Isa 41:19; 55:13; Zec 1:8).

MYSIA [*3695*]. District occupying NW end of Asia Minor bounded by the Aegean, the Hellespont, the Propontis, Bithynia, Phrygia, and Lydia. In 133 B.C. it fell to the Romans and they made it a part of the province of Asia. Traversed by Paul (Ac 16:7-8).

MYSTERIES [2984, 10661, *3696*].
NIV+ MYSTERY

Of God—

Dt 29:29 The secret things belong to the LORD our God, but the things revealed belong to us and to our children forever, that we may follow all the words of this law.

Job 15:8 Do you listen in on God's council? Do you limit wisdom to yourself? (+Ps 25:14; Pr 3:32; Am 3:5)

Heb 5:11 We have much to say about this, but it is hard to explain because you are slow to learn.

Of iniquity—

2Th 2:7 For the secret power of lawlessness is already at work; but the one who now holds it back will continue to do so till he is taken out of the way.

Of redemption—

Mt 11:25 At that time Jesus said, "I praise you, Father, Lord of heaven and earth, because you have hidden these things from the wise and learned, and revealed them to little children.

Mt 13:11 He replied, "The knowledge of the secrets of the kingdom of heaven has been given to you, but not to them.

Mt 13:35 So was fulfilled what was spoken through the prophet: "I will open my mouth in parables, I will utter things hidden since the creation of the world."

Mk 4:11 He told them, "The secret of the kingdom of God has been given to you. But to those on the outside everything is said in parables

Lk 8:10 He said, "The knowledge of the secrets of the kingdom of God has been given to you, but to others I speak in parables, so that, "'though seeing, they may not see; though hearing, they may not understand.'

Ro 16:25 Now to him who is able to establish you by my gospel and the proclamation of Jesus Christ, according to the revelation of the mystery hidden for long ages past, [26]but now revealed and made known through the prophetic writings by the command of the eternal God, so that all nations might believe and obey him—

1Co 2:7 No, we speak of God's secret wisdom, a wisdom that has been hidden and that God destined for our glory before time began. [8]None of the rulers of this age understood it, for if they had, they would not have crucified the Lord of glory. [9]However, as it is written: "No eye has seen, no ear has heard, no mind has conceived what God has prepared for those who love him"—

[10]but God has revealed it to us by his Spirit. The Spirit searches all things, even the deep things of God.

2Co 3:12 Therefore, since we have such a hope, we are very bold. [13]We are not like Moses, who would put a veil over his face to keep the Israelites from gazing at it while the radiance was fading away. [14]But their minds were made dull, for to this day the same veil remains when the old covenant is read. It has not been removed, because only in Christ is it taken away. [15]Even to this day when Moses is read, a veil covers their hearts. [16]But whenever anyone turns to the Lord, the veil is taken away. [17]Now the Lord is the Spirit, and where the Spirit of the Lord is, there is freedom. [18]And we, who with unveiled faces all reflect the Lord's glory, are being transformed into his likeness with ever-increasing glory, which comes from the Lord, who is the Spirit.

Eph 1:9 And he made known to us the mystery of his will according to his good pleasure, which he purposed in Christ, [10]to be put into effect when the times will have reached their fulfillment—to bring all things in heaven and on earth together under one head, even Christ.

Eph 3:3 that is, the mystery made known to me by revelation, as I have already written briefly. [4]In reading this, then, you will be able to understand my insight into the mystery of Christ, [5]which was not made known to men in other generations as it has now been revealed by the Spirit to God's holy apostles and prophets.

Eph 3:9 and to make plain to everyone the administration of this mystery, which for ages past was kept hidden in God, who created all things.

Eph 3:18 may have power, together with all the saints, to grasp how wide and long and high and deep is the love of Christ, (+Eph 3:19)

Eph 6:19 Pray also for me, that whenever I open my mouth, words may be given me so that I will fearlessly make known the mystery of the gospel,

Col 1:25 I have become its servant by the commission God gave me to present to you the word of God in its fullness— [26]the mystery that has been kept hidden for ages and generations, but is now disclosed to the saints. [27]To them God has chosen to make known among the Gentiles the glorious riches of this mystery, which is Christ in you, the hope of glory.

Col 2:2 My purpose is that they may be encouraged in heart and united in love, so that they may have the full riches of complete understanding, in order that they may know the mystery of God, namely, Christ,

Col 4:3 And pray for us, too, that God may open a door for our message, so that we may proclaim the mystery of Christ, for which I am in chains.

1Ti 3:9 They must keep hold of the deep truths of the faith with a clear conscience.

1Ti 3:16 Beyond all question, the mystery of godliness is great: He appeared in a body, was vindicated by the Spirit, was seen by angels, was preached among the nations, was believed on in the world, was taken up in glory.

1Pe 1:10 Concerning this salvation, the prophets, who spoke of the grace that was to come to you, searched intently and with the greatest care, [11]trying to find out the time and circumstances to which the Spirit of Christ in them was pointing when he predicted the sufferings of Christ and the glories that would follow. [12]It was revealed to them that they were not serving themselves but you, when they spoke of the things that have now been told you by those who have preached the gospel to you by the Holy Spirit sent from heaven. Even angels long to look into these things.

Rev 10:7 But in the days when the seventh angel is about to sound his trumpet, the mystery of God will be accomplished, just as he announced to his servants the prophets."

Of regeneration—

Jn 3:8 The wind blows wherever it pleases. You hear its sound, but you cannot tell where it comes from or where it is going. So it is with everyone born of the Spirit."

⁹"How can this be?" Nicodemus asked.

¹⁰"You are Israel's teacher," said Jesus, "and do you not understand these things? ¹¹I tell you the truth, we speak of what we know, and we testify to what we have seen, but still you people do not accept our testimony. ¹²I have spoken to you of earthly things and you do not believe; how then will you believe if I speak of heavenly things?

MYSTERY RELIGIONS Greek religious movement that thrived from c. 700 B.C. to A.D. 400. To gain access to the divine mysteries, specially appointed priests carefully prepared individuals through stages of initiation, instruction, and secret revelation. The enlightened were then joined with the divine and could receive healing, success, and immortality. Though the word "mystery" is used in the NT (Ro 11:25; 16:25; 1Co 15:51; Eph 3:3-9), the openness of the preaching of the Gospel makes it clear that Christianity is not a mystery religion. *See Mysteries.*

MYTHS [*3680*]. Untrue stories or speculations about religion that are contrary to sound doctrine and godliness (1Ti 1:4; 4:7; 2Ti 4:4; Tit 1:14).

N

NAAM [5839] (*pleasant*). Son of Caleb (1Ch 4:15).

NAAMAH [5841, 5842] (*pleasant*).

1. Daughter of Lamech and Zillah (Ge 4:22).
2. Wife of Solomon; mother of Rehoboam (1Ki 14:21, 31).
3. Town in Judah (Jos 15:41), site unknown.

NAAMAN, NAAMITE [5844, 5845, 3722] (*pleasantness*).

NIV+ NAAMAN'S

1. Son of Benjamin (Ge 46:21).
2. Son of Bela and his clan (Nu 26:40; 1Ch 8:4).
3. Son of Ehud (1Ch 8:7).
4. A Syrian general healed of leprosy by Elisha (2Ki 5:1-23; Lk 4:27).

NAAMATHITE [5847] (*of Naamath*). Designation of Zophar (Job 2:11; 11:1; 20:1; 42:9).

NAARAH [5856, 5857] (*[young] woman*).

1. Wife of Ashhur (1Ch 4:5f).
2. Place on border of Ephraim (Jos 16:7).

NAARAI [5858] (*young man of Yahweh*). Called also Paarai. One of David's heroes (1Ch 11:37).

NAARAN [5860]. A city in the eastern limits of Ephraim (1Ch 7:28).

NAARATH See Naarah, 2.

NAASHON, NAASSON See Nahshon.

NABAL [5573] (*fool*).

NIV+ NABAL'S

Rich shepherd of Maon in Judah who insulted David and was saved from vengeance by his wife Abigail, who after Nabal's death became David's wife (1Sa 25:1-42).

NABATEA, NABATEANS Arabian tribe named in the Apocrypha but not in Bible. Their king, Aretas IV, controlled Damascus when Paul was there (2Co 11:32). Capital was Petra.

See Petra; Sela.

NABONIDAS, NABONIDUS (*[pagan god] Nabu is wonderful*). Last ruler of Neo-Babylonian Empire (556-539 B.C.), his son Belshazzar (Da 5; 7:1; 8:1) was coregent with him from the third year of his reign.

NABOPOLASSAR (*[pagan god] Nabu protect the son!*). First ruler of the Neo-Babylonian Empire (626-605 B.C.). Allied with Medes and Scythians, he overthrew the Assyrian Empire, destroying Nineveh in 612 B.C., as prophesied (Zep 2:13-15).

NABOTH [5559] (*a sprout*).

NIV+ NABOTH'S

A Jezreelite. His vineyard forcibly taken by Ahab; stoned at the instigation of Jezebel (1Ki 21:1-19). His murder avenged (2Ki 9:21-36).

NACHOR See Nahor, 1.

NACON, NACHON [5789] (*established*). Benjamite at whose threshing floor Uzzah was killed for touching the ark (2Sa 6:6). Also called Kidon (1Ch 13:9, ftn). The place was subsequently called Perez Uzzah. *See Perez Uzzah*.

NADAB [5606] (*volunteer, free will offering*).

NIV+ NADAB'S

1. Son of Aaron (Ex 6:23). Called to Mount Sinai with Moses and Aaron to worship (Ex 24:1,9-10). Set apart to priesthood (Ex 28:1,4,40-43). Offers unauthorized fire to God and is destroyed (Lev 10:1-2; Nu 3:4; 26:61). Is buried (Lev 10:4-5). His father and brothers forbidden to mourn (Lev 10:6-7).
2. Son and successor of Jeroboam (1Ki 14:20). His wicked reign; murdered by Baasha (1Ki 15:25-31).
3. Great-grandson of Jerahmeel (1Ch 2:28,30).
4. A Benjamite (1Ch 8:30; 9:36).

NAGGAI, NAGGE [*3710*]. Ancestor of Christ (Lk 3:25).

NAGGING [7439]. Proverbs concerning (Pr 19:13; 21:9,19; 25:24; 26:21; 27:15). Jezebel's destroys Samson (Jdg 16:16).

NAHALAL, NAHALLAL [5634] (*watering place*). Also spelled Nahalol (Jdg 1:30). A Levitical city within Zebulun's territory (Jos 19:15; 21:35; Jdg 1:30).

NAHALIEL [5712] (*wadi of God [El]*). A station of the Israelites (Nu 21:19).

NAHALOL, NAHALLAL [5636]. See Nahalal.

NAHAM [5715] (*repent, console*). Descendant of Judah through Caleb (1Ch 4:19).

NAHAMANI [5720] (*Yahweh has consoled*). A Jewish exile (Ne 7:7).

NAHARAI, NAHARI [5726]. Beerothite, Joab's armor-bearer (2Sa 23:37).

NAHARAIM See Aram Naharaim.

NAHASH [5731] (*viper* or *copper*).

NIV+ IR NAHASH

1. Ammonite king defeated by Saul (1Sa 11:1-2; 12:12).
2. Ammonite king whose son insulted David's messengers, and David avenged the insult (2Sa 10; 1Ch 19).
3. Father of Abigail and Zeruiah (2Sa 17:25).

See also Ir Nahash, Ir-Nahash.

NAHATH [5740] (*descent; possibly rest*).

1. Son of Reuel (Ge 36:13,17; 1Ch 1:37).
2. A Levite, grandson of the Kohathite Elkanah (1Ch 6:26); probably the same as Tohu (1Sa 1:1), and Toah (1Ch 6:34).
3. A Levite and overseer of the sacred offerings in the time of Hezekiah (2Ch 31:13).

NAHBI [5696] (perhaps *hidden* or *timid*). A leader of Naphtali and one of the twelve spies (Nu 13:14).

NAHOR [5701, *3732*] (apparently from Assyrian place name Til-Nahiri, *the mound of Nahuru*).

NIV+ NAHOR'S

1. Grandfather of Abraham (Ge 11:22-26; 1Ch 1:26). In the lineage of Christ (Lk 3:34).
2. Brother of Abraham (Ge 11:26; Jos 24:2). Marriage and descendants of (Ge 11:27,29; 22:20-24; 24:15,24).

NAHSHON [5732, *3709*] (*small viper*). A captain of Judah's host (Ex 6:23; Nu 1:7; 2:3; 7:12,17; 10:14). In the lineage of Christ (Mt 1:4; Lk 3:32).

NAHUM [5699, *3725*] (*comfort*).

1. Author of book of Nahum; native of Elkosh; prophesied 663-612 B.C. (Na 1:1; 3:8-11).

2. An ancestor of Jesus (Lk 3:25).

NAHUM, BOOK OF

Author: The prophet Nahum

Date: Between 663 and 612 B.C.

Outline:

I. Title (1:1).

II. Nineveh's Judge (1:2-15).
   A. The Lord's Kindness and Sternness (1:2-8).
   B. Nineveh's Overthrow and Judah's Joy (1:9-15).

III. Nineveh's Judgment (ch. 2).
   A. Nineveh Besieged (2:1-10).
   B. Nineveh's Desolation Contrasted with Her Former Glory (2:11-13).

IV. Nineveh's Total Destruction (ch. 3).
   A. Nineveh's Sins (3:1-4).
   B. Nineveh's Doom (3:5-19).
   See Prophets, The Minor.

NAIL [5021, 5383, 7632, 10303, *2464*, *4669*, *4699*].

NIV+ NAILING, NAILS

1. Fingernail (Dt 21:12; Da 4:33; 7:19).

2. Tent peg (Jdg 4:21-22; 5:26), peg driven into wall to hang things on (Ezr 9:8; Isa 22:23-25).

3. Nails of metal: iron, bronze, gold (1Ch 22:3; 2Ch 3:9).

NAIN [*3723*] (*pleasant, delightful*). A city in Galilee. Jesus restores to life a widow's son in (Lk 7:11).

NAIOTH [5766] (*dwellings*). Place in or near Ramah of Benjamin where Samuel lived with a band of prophets (1Sa 19:18-20:1).

NAKED [3338, 5067, 5113, 5122, 6567, 6867, 6872, 6873, 6880, *1218*, *1219*].]

NIV+ NAKEDNESS

1. Without any clothing (Ge 2:25; 3:7-11).

2. Poorly clad (Job 22:6).

3. Without an outer garment (Jn 21:7). Often used figuratively for spiritual poverty (Rev 3:17) and a lack of power (Ge 42:9).

NAME [*606, 2352, 9005, 10721, *3306*, *3950*, *3951*].

NIV+ NAME'S, NAMED, NAMELESS, NAMELY, NAMES

Value of a good (Pr 22:1; Ecc 7:1). A new name given, to persons who have spiritual adoption (Isa 62:2), to Abraham (Ge 17:5), Sarah (Ge 17:15), Jacob (Ge 32:28), Peter (Mt 16:18), Paul (Ac 13:9). Intercessional influence of the name of Jesus. *See Jesus the Christ, In His Name.*

Symbolic (Hos 1:3-4,6,9; 2:1), of prestige (1Ki 1:47).

NAMES OF GOD *See God, Names of; Titles and Names.*

NAMES OF JESUS *See Jesus the Christ, Names, Appellations, and Titles of; Titles and Names.*

NANNAR (*lightgiver*). Name given at Ur to Babylonian moon-god Sin.

NAOMI [5843] (*my joy*).

NIV+ NAOMI'S

Wife of Elimelech; mother-in-law of Ruth; lived in Moab; returns to Bethlehem; kinswoman of Boaz (Ru 1-4).

NAPHISH [5874] (*refreshed*). The eleventh son of Ishmael; progenitor of a tribe, probably the Nephussim (Ge 25:15; 1Ch 1:31; 5:19).

NAPHOTH [5868] (*heights*).

NIV+ DOR, NAPHOTH DOR

A town assigned to Manasseh, also called Dor and Naphoth Dor (Jos 17:11, ftn). Conquered by Joshua (Jos 11:2; 12:23). *See Dor; Naphoth Dor.*

NAPHOTH DOR [5869] (*heights of Dor*).

A town assigned to Manasseh, also called Dor and Naphoth (Jos 17:11, ftn). *See Dor; Naphoth.*

NAPHTALI, NAPHTALITES [824+5889, 1201+5889, 5889, *3750*] (*wrestling*).

1. Son of Jacob and Bilhah (Ge 30:7-8; 35:25). Jacob blesses (Ge 49:21). Sons of (Ge 46:24; 1Ch 7:13).

2. Tribe of. Census of (Nu 1:42-43; 26:48-50). Position assigned to, in camp and march (Nu 2:25-31; 10:25-27). Moses' benediction on (Dt 33:23). Inheritance of (Jos 19:32-39; Jdg 1:33; Eze 48:3).

Defeat Sisera (Jdg 4:6,10; 5:18). Follow Gideon (Jdg 6:35; 7:23). Aid in conveying the ark to Jerusalem (Ps 68:27). Military operations of (1Ch 12:34,40), against (1Ki 15:20; 2Ki 15:29; 2Ch 16:4).

Prophecies concerning (Isa 9:1-2; Rev 7:6).

NAPHTUHITES, NAPHTUHIM [5888]. The inhabitants of central Egypt (Ge 10:13; 1Ch 1:11).

NAPKIN Cloth for wiping perspiration off (Lk 19:20; Jn 11:44; 20:7).

NARCISSUS [*3727*]. A believer at Rome (Ro 16:11).

NARD [5948, *3726*]. An aromatic plant (SS 4:13-14). *See Perfume; Plants of the Bible.*

NATHAN [5990, *3718*] (*gift*).

1. Prophet during reigns of David and Solomon; told David that not he but Solomon was to build the temple (2Sa 7; 1Ch 17), rebuked David for sin with Bathsheba (2Sa 12:1-25), helped get throne for Solomon (1Ki 1:8-53), wrote chronicles of reign of David (1Ch 29:29) and Solomon (2Ch 9:29), associated with David in arranging musical services for house of God (2Ch 29:25).

2. Son of David (2Sa 5:14; 1Ch 14:4).

3. Father of Igal (2Sa 23:36).

4. Judahite (1Ch 2:36).

5. Israelite who returned from the Exile (Ezr 8:16).

6. Man who put away his foreign wife (Ezr 10:39).

NATHANAEL [*3720*] (*gift of God [El]*). Disciple of Jesus (Jn 1:45-51), identified commonly with Bartholomew. Church Fathers use the two names interchangeably.

NATHAN-MELECH [5994] (*gift of king* or *gift of Melek, Molech, Malk [pagan god]*). Officer of Josiah (2Ki 23:11).

NATION [824, 1580, 4211, 5476, 6639, 10040, *1620, 5876*].

NIV+ NATIONAL, NATIONALITIES, NATIONALITY, NATIONS, NATIONS'

People divided into nations after the Flood (Ge 10:1-32). Ordained of God (Ac 17:26). Righteousness exalts (Pr 14:34).

Peace of: (Job 34:29; Ps 33:12; 89:15-18).

Promises of peace to (Lev 26:6; 1Ki 2:33; 2Ki 20:19; 1Ch 22:9; Ps 29:11; 46:9; 72:3,7; 128:6; Isa 2:4; 14:4-7; 60:17-18; 65:25; Jer 30:10; 50:34; Eze 34:25-28; Hos 2:18; Mic 4:3-4; Zec 1:11; 3:10; 8:4-5; 9:10; 14:11). Prayer for peace (Jer 29:7; 1Ti 2:1-2). Peace given by God (Jos 21:44; 1Ch 22:18; 23:25; Ps 147:13-14; Ecc 3:8; Isa 45:7). Instances of national peace (Jos 14:15; Jdg 3:11,30; 1Ki 4:24-25). *See War.*

Sins of:

Involved in sins, of rulers (Ge 20:4,9; 2Sa 24:10-17; 1Ki 15:26,30,34; 2Ki 24:3; 1Ch 21:7-17; Jer 15:4), of other individuals, as Achan (Jos 7:1,11-26).

Atonement made for (2Ch 29:21). Penitent, promises to (Lev 26:40-42; Dt 4:29-31; 5:29; 30:1-10; 2Ch 7:13-14; Jer 3:22).

In adversity, prayer of (Jdg 6:7; 10:10; 21:2-4; 2Ch 7:13-14; Ps 74; Jer 3:21; 31:18; Joel 2:12), prayer for (Ezr 9:6-15; Ne 1:4-11; Ps 74; 84:1-7; Isa 63:7-19; Jer 6:14; 8:11,20-21; 9:1-2; 14:7,20; La 2:20-22; Da 9:3-21). *See Sin, National.*

Judgments Against:

Chastisement of (Lev 18:24-30; 26:28; Dt 11:2; 2Ch 6:24,26,28; 7:13-14; Ps 106:43; Isa 14:26-27; Jer 2:30; 5:29; 18:6-10; 25:12-33; 30:14; 31:18-20; 46:28; Eze 2:3-5; 39:23-24; Da 7:9-12; 9:3-16; La 1:5; Hos 7:12; 10:10; Joel 1:1-20; Am 9:9; Zep 3:6,8; Hag 2:17). Perish (Ps 9:17; Isa 60:12).

Judgments denounced against, on account of its unrighteousness (Dt 9:5; Ps 9:17; Isa 3:4-8; 14:24-27; 19:4; 59:1-15; 60:12; Jer 2:19,35-37; 5:6-29; 6; 9:7-26; 12:14, 17; 18:6-10; 25:12-33; 50:45-46; 51; Eze 2:9-10; 7; 22:12-31; 24:6-24; 33:25-29; Hos 4:1-10; 7:12-13,16; 13; Am 2; 3; 5; 9:8-10; Mic 6:13-16; Zep 3:8).

Instances of punishment of: The Canaanites (Dt 9:5). The Sodomites (Ge 19:24-25,28-29; La 4:6). The Egyptians (Ex 7-11; 12:1-36; 14). The Israelites (2Sa 21:1; 24:14-16; 2Ki 24:2-4,20; 2Ch 28:1,5-8,16-19; 29:8-9; 30:7; 36:16-20; Ezr 9:7; Ne 9:36-37; Jer 2:15-16; 30:11-15; La 1:3,8,14; Eze 36:16-20; 39:17-24; Joel 1:1-20; Am 4:6-11).

See Government; Kings; Rulers.

NATIONAL RELIGION Supported by taxes (Ex 30:11-16; 38:26). Ministers of, supported by state (1Ki 18:19; 2Ch 11:13-15). Subverted by Jeroboam (1Ki 12:26-33; 2Ch 11:13-15). Idolatrous, established by Jeroboam (1Ki 12:26-33).

NATIONS BLESSED BY ABRAHAM (Ge 12:2; 18:18; 22:18; 26:4; Ac 3:25; Gal 3:8).

NATURAL

NIV+ NATURE

Natural death (Nu 16:29; 19:16,18), sleep (Jn 11:13), physical relations (Ro 1:26-27), body (1Co 15:44,46), instincts (Jude 1:19).

NATURAL RELIGION *See Religion, Natural.*

NATURALIZATION Giving rights of citizenship to aliens (Ac 22:28).

Figurative: (Eph 2:12-13,19).

NATURE [*2522, 3517, 3671, 4922, 5882*].

NIV+ NATURAL

The entire compass of one's life (Jas 3:6). The inherent character of a person or thing (Ro 1:26; 2:14; 11:21-24). Disposition (2Pe 1:4). Sinful nature (Ro 7:18,25; 1Co 5:5; Gal 5:13).

Laws of, uniform in operation: In the vegetable kingdom (Ge 1:11,12; Mt 7:16-18; Lk 6:43-44; 1Co 15:36-38; Gal 6:7; Jas 3:12), animal kingdom (Ge 1:21,24-25; Jer 13:23), succession of seasons (Ge 8:22), succession of day and night (Ge 8:22; Jer 33:20).

NAUGHTINESS *See Sin.*

NAUM *See Nahum.*

NAVE *See Rim.*

NAVEL [9219]. "Belly button" (SS 7:2).

NAVIGATION Sounding in (Ac 27:28).

See Commerce; Mariner; Navy.

NAVY Solomon's (1Ki 9:26), Hiram's (1Ki 10:11), of Kittim (Da 11:30, ftn, 40).

See Commerce; Mariner.

NAZARENE [*3716, 3717*] (possibly *sprout, branch*).

NIV+ NAZARETH

1. Inhabitant of Nazareth (Mt 2:23); possibly a wordplay on the Hebrew *nezer*, "branch," a messianic title (cf. Isa 11:1). *See Branch.*

2. A Christian (Ac 24:5).

NAZARETH [*3714, 3716, 3717*] (possibly *sprout, branch* or *watchtower*).

NIV+ NAZARENE

A village in Galilee. Joseph and Mary live at (Mt 2:23; Lk 1:26-27,56; 2:4,39,51). Jesus from (Mt 21:11; Mk 1:24; 10:47; Lk 4:34; 18:37; 24:19). People of, reject Jesus (Lk 4:16-30). Its name infamous (Jn 1:46).

NAZARETH DECREE An inscription on a slab of white marble, dating c. A.D. 40-50, by Claudius Caesar, found in Nazareth, decreeing capital punishment for anyone disturbing graves and tombs.

NAZIRITE(S), NAZARITE [5687, 5693, 5694] (*one under sacred vow*). An Israelite who consecrated himself or herself and took a vow of separation and self-imposed abstinence for the purpose of some special service. The Nazirite vow included a renunciation of wine, prohibition of the use of the razor, and avoidance of contact with a dead body. The period of time for the vow was anywhere from 30 days to a lifetime (Nu 6:1-21; Jdg 13:5-7; Am 2:11,12).

Instances of:

Samson (Jdg 13:5,7; 16:17). Samuel (1Sa 1:11). Recabites (Jer 35). John the Baptist (Mt 11:18; Lk 1:15; 7:33).

See Abstinence; Wine.

NEAH [5828]. A border town in Zebulun (Jos 19:13). The site is unknown.

NEAPOLIS [*3735*] (*new city*). A seaport of Macedonia. Paul visits (Ac 16:11).

NEARIAH [5859] (*[young] man of Yahweh*).
1. Son of Shemaiah (1Ch 3:22-23).
2. A Simeonite leader (1Ch 4:42).

NEBAI [5763] (*thrive*). Signer of the covenant with Nehemiah (Ne 10:19).

NEBAIOTH [5568]. Son of Ishmael (Ge 25:13; 28:9; 36:3; 1Ch 1:29). Prophecies concerning (Isa 60:7).

NEBALLAT [5579]. A town occupied by the Benjamites after the Captivity (Ne 11:34).

NEBAT [5565] (*look to, regard [approvingly]*). Father of Jeroboam (1Ki 11:26; 12:2).

NEBO [5549, 5550, 5551] (*height* or *Mount of Nabu [Nebo]*).
NIV+ NEBO-SARSEKIM
1. A city allotted to Reuben (Nu 32:3,38; 1Ch 5:8). Prophecies concerning (Isa 15:2; Jer 48:1,22).
2. A mountain range E of the Jordan. Moses views Canaan from (Dt 32:49-50), dies on (Dt 34:1).
3. A city in Judah (Ezr 2:29; Ne 7:33).
4. The ancestor of certain Jews (Ezr 10:43).
5. A Babylonian idol (Isa 46:1).

NEBO-SARSEKIM [5552].
NIV+ NEBO
A prince of Nebuchadnezzar who entered Jerusalem when it fell (Jer 39:3, ftn).

NEBUCHADNEZZAR, NEBUCHADREZZAR
[5556, 5557, 10453] (*Nebo protect my boundary stone* BDB and IDB; *Nebo protect my son!* KB).
NIV+ NEBUCHADNEZZAR'S
1. The fourth Dynasty ruler of the Old Babylonian Empire (c. 1140 B.C.).
2. Ruler of the Neo-Babylonian Empire (605-562 B.C.); son of Nabopolassar; conquered Pharaoh Neco at Carchemish (605 B.C.); destroyed Jerusalem and carried Israelites into captivity (587 B.C.) (2Ki 25:1-21); succeeded by son Evil-Merodach. Often mentioned in OT (1Ch 6:15; 2Ch 36; Ezr 1:7; 2:1; 5:12,14; 6:5; Ne 7:6; Est 2:6; Jer 21:2; 52:4; Da 1-5).

NEBUSHAZBAN, NEBUSHASBAN [5558]
(*Nebo [Nabu] save me!*). Chief officer of Nebuchadnezzar (Jer 39:11-14).

NEBUZARADAN [5555] (*Nebo [Nabu] has given seed [offspring]*). Nebuchadnezzar's general when the Babylonians besieged Jerusalem (2Ki 25:1,11-12,20; Jer 52:12ff), conducted captives to Babylon.

NECK [1738, 1744, 4305, 5154, 5883, 6902, 6904, 7023, 7418, 10611, *5549*].
NIV+ NECKS, STIFF-NECKED
Term often used in Bible with literal and figurative meanings (Ex 32:9; Dt 9:13; Ps 75:5; Ac 7:51).

NECKLACE [3921, 6735, 7454, 8054, 8448].
NIV+ NECKLACES
Ornamental chain worn around the neck (Isa 3:19).

NECO, NECCO, NECHO, NECHOH [5785, 5786]. Pharaoh of Egypt (609-595 B.C.); defeated Josiah at battle of Megiddo (2Ki 23:29; 2Ch 35:20ff); defeated by Nebuchadnezzar at battle of Carchemish (2Ki 24:7; Isa 10:9; Jer 46:2).

NECROMANCER, NECROMANCY Consulting with the dead; forbidden by Mosaic law (Dt 18:10-11), King Saul consulted with the medium of Endor (1Sa 28:7-25). Judgment upon (Isa 8:19; 29:4).
See Medium; Sorcery; Witchcraft.

NEDABIAH [5608] (*Yahweh volunteers*). A son of Jehoiachin (1Ch 3:18).

NEEDLE'S EYE [*1017, 4827*]. Expression used by Jesus (Mt 19:24; Mk 10:25; Lk 18:25). Jesus does not say that salvation is threatened by possessing riches but that those who are wealthy will have great difficulty subordinating their riches to the will of God; in addition, a wealthy man will not enter the kingdom of God based on his riches, but only on the saving grace of God and the finished work of Jesus Christ (Mt 19:25-26).

NEEDLEWORK Art of working in with the needle various kinds of colored threads in cloth (Jdg 5:30; Ps 45:14).

NEESING NIV "snorting" (Job 41:18).

NEGEV, NEGEB [824+5582, 5582] (*dry [land]*, hence *south country*).
NIV+ RAMOTH NEGEV
The desert region lying to the S of Judea, sometimes translated "the south" (Ge 12:9; 13:1; 20:1; Nu 13:29; 1Sa 27:5-6).

NEGINAH *See Music, Symbols Used in.*

NEGINOTH *See Music, Symbols Used in.*

NEHELAMITE [5713] (perhaps *of Nehelam* or a play on the word for *dream*). Designation of Shemaiah, a false prophet (Jer 29:24,31-32).

NEHEMIAH [5718] (*Yahweh has comforted*).
1. Leader of Jews who returned with Zerubbabel (Ezr 2:2; Ne 7:7).
2. Son of Azbuk; helped rebuild walls of Jerusalem (Ne 3:16).
3. Son of Hacaliah; governor of Persian province of Judah after 444 B.C.; cupbearer to King Artaxerxes of Persia (Ne 1:11; 2:1); rebuilt walls of Jerusalem (Ne 1:4-6); cooperated with Ezra in numerous reforms (Ne 8); nothing known of the end of his life.

NEHEMIAH, BOOK OF
Author: Nehemiah
Date: c. 430 B.C.
Outline:
I. Nehemiah's First Administration (chs. 1-12).
A. Nehemiah's Response to the Situation in Jerusalem (ch. 1).
1. News of the plight of Jerusalem (1:1-4).
2. Nehemiah's prayer (1:5-11).
B. Nehemiah's Journey to Jerusalem (ch. 2).
1. The king response (2:1-8).
2. The journey itself (2:9-10).
3. Nehemiah's nocturnal inspection of the walls (2:11-16).
4. His exhortation to rebuild (2:17-18).
5. The opposition of Sanballat, Tobiah and Geshem (2:19-20).

C. List of the Builders of the Wall (ch. 3).
   1. The northern section (3:1-7).
   2. The western section (3:8-13).
   3. The southern section (3:14).
   4. The eastern section (3:15-32).
D. Opposition to Rebuilding the Wall (ch. 4).
   1. The derision of Sanballat and Tobiah (4:1-5).
   2. The threat of attack (4:6-15).
   3. Rebuilding the wall (4:16-23).
E. Social and Economic Problems (ch. 5).
   1. The complaints of the poor (5:1-5).
   2. The cancellation of debts (5:6-13).
   3. Nehemiah's unselfish example (5:14-19).
F. The Wall Rebuilt Despite Opposition (ch. 6).
   1. Attempts to snare Nehemiah (6:1-9).
   2. The hiring of false prophets (6:10-14).
   3. The completion of the wall (6:15-19).
G. List of Exiles (7:1-73a).
   1. Provisions for the protection of Jerusalem (7:1-3).
   2. Nehemiah's discovery of the list of returnees (7:4-5).
   3. The returnees delineated (7:6-72).
   4. Settlement of the exiles (7:73a).
H. Ezra's Preaching and the Outbreak of Revival
   (7:73b-10:39).
   1. The public exposition of the Scriptures (7:73b-8:12).
   2. The Feast of Tabernacles (8:13-18).
   3. A day of fasting, confession and prayer (9:1-5a).
   4. A recital of God's dealings with Israel (9:5b-31).
   5. Confession of sins (9:32-37).
   6. A binding agreement (9:38).
   7. A list of those who sealed it (10:1-29).
   8. Provisions of the agreement (10:30-39).
I. New Residents of Judah and Jerusalem (ch. 11).
   1. New residents for Jerusalem (11:1-24).
     a. Introductory remarks (11:1-4a).
     b. Residents from Judah (11:4b-6).
     c. From Benjamin (11:7-9).
     d. From the priests (11:10-14).
     e. From the Levites (11:15-18).
     f. From the temple staff (11:25-36).
   2. New residents for Judah (11:25-36).
     a. Places settled by those from Judah (11:25-30).
     b. Places settled by those from Benjamin (11:31-35).
     c. Transfer of Levites from Judah to Benjamin (11:36).
J. Lists of Priests and the Dedication of the Wall (ch. 12).
   1. Priests and Levites from the first return (12:1-9).
   2. High priests and Levites since Joiakim (12:10-26).
   3. Dedication of the wall of Jerusalem (12:27-43).
   4. Regulation of the temple offerings and services
   (12:44-47).
II. Nehemiah's Second Administration (ch. 13).
A. Abuses During His Absence (13:1-5).
   1. Mixed marriages (13:1-3).
   2. Tobiah's occupation of the temple quarters (13:4-5).
B. Nehemiah's Return (13:6-9).
   1. His arrival (13:6-7).
   2. His expulsion of Tobiah (13:8-9).
C. Reorganization and Reforms (13:10-31).
   1. Offerings for the temple staff (13:10-14).
   2. The abuse of the Sabbath (13:15-22).
   3. Mixed marriages (13:23-29).
   4. Provisions of wood and firstfruits (13:30-31).

NEHILOTH *See Music, Symbols Used in.*

NEHUM [5700] (*comfort*). Chief of Judah who returned with Zerubbabel; also called "Rehum" (Ezr 2:2; Ne 7:7).

NEHUSHTA [5735] (*[strong as or color of] bronze*). Wife of Jehoiakim, king of Judah, and mother of Jehoiachin (2Ki 24:6,8).

NEHUSHTAN [5736] (combination of *bronze* and *viper*). The bronze serpent (2Ki 18:4).

NEIEL [5832]. A landmark on the boundary of Asher (Jos 19:27).

NEIGHBOR [408, 824, 6017, 6660, 7940, 8276, 8907, *1150, 4340, 4341, 4446, 4489*].
NIV+ NEIGHBOR'S, NEIGHBORING, NEIGHBORS, NEIGHBORS'

Defined—
Lk 10:25 On one occasion an expert in the law stood up to test Jesus. "Teacher," he asked, "what must I do to inherit eternal life?"
[26]"What is written in the Law?" he replied. "How do you read it?"
[27]He answered: "'Love the Lord your God with all your heart and with all your soul and with all your strength and with all your mind'; and, 'Love your neighbor as yourself.'"
[28]"You have answered correctly," Jesus replied. "Do this and you will live."
[29]But he wanted to justify himself, so he asked Jesus, "And who is my neighbor?" [30]In reply Jesus said: "A man was going down from Jerusalem to Jericho, when he fell into the hands of robbers. They stripped him of his clothes, beat him and went away, leaving him half dead. [31]A priest happened to be going down the same road, and when he saw the man, he passed by on the other side. [32]So too, a Levite, when he came to the place and saw him, passed by on the other side. [33]But a Samaritan, as he traveled, came where the man was; and when he saw him, he took pity on him. [34]He went to him and bandaged his wounds, pouring on oil and wine. Then he put the man on his own donkey, took him to an inn and took care of him. [35]The next day he took out two silver coins and gave them to the innkeeper. 'Look after him,' he said, 'and when I return, I will reimburse you for any extra expense you may have.'
[36]"Which of these three do you think was a neighbor to the man who fell into the hands of robbers?"
[37]The expert in the law replied, "The one who had mercy on him."
Jesus told him, "Go and do likewise."

Duty to, defined in the Golden Rule—
Mt 7:12 So in everything, do to others what you would have them do to you, for this sums up the Law and the Prophets.

Love does no harm to—
Ro 13:10 Love does no harm to its neighbor. Therefore love is the fulfillment of the law.

Love for, commanded—
Lev 19:18 "'Do not seek revenge or bear a grudge against one of your people, but love your neighbor as yourself. I am the LORD. (+Mt 19:19; 22:39; Mk 12:31-33; Lk 10:25-37; Ro 13:9-10; Gal 5:14)
Jas 2:8 If you really keep the royal law found in Scripture, "Love your neighbor as yourself," you are doing right. [9]But if you show favoritism, you sin and are convicted by the law as lawbreakers.

Kindness to, commanded—
Ex 23:4 "If you come across your enemy's ox or donkey wandering off, be sure to take it back to him. [5]If you see

the donkey of someone who hates you fallen down under its load, do not leave it there; be sure you help him with it.
Dt 22:1 If you see your brother's ox or sheep straying, do not ignore it but be sure to take it back to him. [2]If the brother does not live near you or if you do not know who he is, take it home with you and keep it until he comes looking for it. Then give it back to him. [3]Do the same if you find your brother's donkey or his cloak or anything he loses. Do not ignore it.

[4]If you see your brother's donkey or his ox fallen on the road, do not ignore it. Help him get it to its feet.

Isa 58:6 "Is not this the kind of fasting I have chosen: to loose the chains of injustice and untie the cords of the yoke, to set the oppressed free and break every yoke? [7]Is it not to share your food with the hungry and to provide the poor wanderer with shelter—when you see the naked, to clothe him, and not to turn away from your own flesh and blood?

Gal 6:10 Therefore, as we have opportunity, let us do good to all people, especially to those who belong to the family of believers.

Charitableness toward, commanded—

Ro 15:2 Each of us should please his neighbor for his good, to build him up.

Benevolence toward, commanded—

Pr 3:28 Do not say to your neighbor, "Come back later; I'll give it tomorrow"—when you now have it with you.

[29]Do not plot harm against your neighbor, who lives trustfully near you.

Righteous treatment of, commanded—

Zec 8:16 These are the things you are to do: Speak the truth to each other, and render true and sound judgment in your courts; [17]do not plot evil against your neighbor, and do not love to swear falsely. I hate all this," declares the LORD.

Honesty toward, commanded—

Lev 19:13 "'Do not defraud your neighbor or rob him. "'Do not hold back the wages of a hired man overnight.

Kindness to, rewarded—

Isa 58:8 Then your light will break forth like the dawn, and your healing will quickly appear; then your righteousness will go before you, and the glory of the LORD will be your rear guard. [9]Then you will call, and the LORD will answer; you will cry for help, and he will say: Here am I.

"If you do away with the yoke of oppression, with the pointing finger and malicious talk, [10]and if you spend yourselves in behalf of the hungry and satisfy the needs of the oppressed, then your light will rise in the darkness, and your night will become like the noonday. [11]The LORD will guide you always; he will satisfy your needs in a sun-scorched land and will strengthen your frame. You will be like a well-watered garden, like a spring whose waters never fail. [12]Your people will rebuild the ancient ruins and will raise up the age-old foundations; you will be called Repairer of Broken Walls, Restorer of Streets with Dwellings.

[13]"If you keep your feet from breaking the Sabbath and from doing as you please on my holy day, if you call the Sabbath a delight and the LORD's holy day honorable, and if you honor it by not going your own way and not doing as you please or speaking idle words, [14]then you will find your joy in the LORD, and I will cause you to ride on the heights of the land and to feast on the inheritance of your father Jacob." The mouth of the LORD has spoken.

Mt 25:34 "Then the King will say to those on his right,

'Come, you who are blessed by my Father; take your inheritance, the kingdom prepared for you since the creation of the world. [35]For I was hungry and you gave me something to eat, I was thirsty and you gave me something to drink, I was a stranger and you invited me in, [36]I needed clothes and you clothed me, I was sick and you looked after me, I was in prison and you came to visit me.'

[37]"Then the righteous will answer him, 'Lord, when did we see you hungry and feed you, or thirsty and give you something to drink? [38]When did we see you a stranger and invite you in, or needing clothes and clothe you? [39]When did we see you sick or in prison and go to visit you?'

[40]"The King will reply, 'I tell you the truth, whatever you did for one of the least of these brothers of mine, you did for me.'

[41]"Then he will say to those on his left, 'Depart from me, you who are cursed, into the eternal fire prepared for the devil and his angels. [42]For I was hungry and you gave me nothing to eat, I was thirsty and you gave me nothing to drink, [43]I was a stranger and you did not invite me in, I needed clothes and you did not clothe me, I was sick and in prison and you did not look after me.'

[44]"They also will answer, 'Lord, when did we see you hungry or thirsty or a stranger or needing clothes or sick or in prison, and did not help you?'

[45]"He will reply, 'I tell you the truth, whatever you did not do for one of the least of these, you did not do for me.'

[46]"Then they will go away to eternal punishment, but the righteous to eternal life."

Righteous treatment of, rewarded—

Ps 15:1 LORD, who may dwell in your sanctuary? Who may live on your holy hill? [2]He whose walk is blameless and who does what is righteous, who speaks the truth from his heart [3]and has no slander on his tongue, who does his neighbor no wrong and casts no slur on his fellowman,

False witness against, forbidden (Ex 20:16)—

Lev 19:16 "'Do not go about spreading slander among your people. "'Do not do anything that endangers your neighbor's life. I am the LORD.

Hatred of, forbidden—

Lev 19:17 "'Do not hate your brother in your heart. Rebuke your neighbor frankly so you will not share in his guilt.

Oppression of, denounced—

Jer 22:13 "Woe to him who builds his palace by unrighteousness, his upper rooms by injustice, making his countrymen work for nothing, not paying them for their labor.

Penalty for violation of the rights of (Lev 6:2-5).
See Duty; Mankind.

NEKEB *See Adami Nekeb.*

NEKODA [5928]. Head of a family of temple servants who could not prove Israelite descent (Ne 7:50,62; Ezr 2:60).

NEMUEL, NEMUELITE [5803, 5804].

1. Brother of Dathan and Abiram (Nu 26:9).

2. Son of Simeon (Nu 26:12; 1Ch 4:24). Also called Jemuel (Ge 46:10; Ex 6:15). *See Jemuel.*

NEPHEG [5863] (*sprout, shoot*).

1. Brother of Korah, Dathan, and Abiram (Ex 6:21).

2. Son of David (2Sa 5:15; 1Ch 3:7; 14:6).

NEPHEW [278+1201, 1201+2157].

NIV+ NEPHEWS

Grandson (Jdg 12:14), descendant (Job 18:19; Isa 14:22), grandchild (1Ti 5:4).

NEPHILIM [5872] (*ones falling [upon]*, hence *violent ones*, possibly *giants*). Antediluvians (Ge 6:4), aboriginal dwellers in Canaan (Nu 13:32-33), not angelic fallen beings (Dt 1:28).

NEPHISH *See Naphish.*

NEPHISHESIM, NEPHUSSIM *See Nephussim.*

NEPHTHALIM, NEPTHALIM *See Naphtali.*

NEPHTOAH [5886] (*an opening*). Spring and town on the border of Judah and Benjamin (Jos 15:9; 18:15), two miles NW of Jerusalem; modern Lifta.

NEPHUSSIM [5866, 5867]. A family of the temple servants (Ezr 2:50; Ne 7:52).

NEPOTISM Of Joseph (Ge 47:11-12). Of Saul (1Sa 14:50). Of David (2Sa 8:16; 19:13). Of Nehemiah (Ne 7:2).

NER [5945] (*lamp*).

1. Father of Abner (1Sa 14:50; 26:14).
2. Grandfather of King Saul (1Ch 8:33).

NEREUS [3759] (*pagan Greek deity*). A Christian at Rome (Ro 16:15).

NERGAL [5946] (*pagan deity*). Babylonian deity of destruction (2Ki 17:30).

NERGAL-SHAREZER [5947] (*Nergal protect the prince!*). The name of princes of Babylon (Jer 39:3,13).

NERI [3760] (*lamp of Yahweh*). An ancestor of Jesus (Lk 3:27).

NERIAH [5949, 5950] (*lamp of Yahweh*). Father of Baruch (Jer 32:12).

NERIGLISSAR *See Nergal-Sharezer.*

NERO (*family name*).

The fifth Roman emperor (A.D. 54-68); killed many Christians when Rome burned in A.D. 64; called "Caesar" (Ac 25:11; Php 4:22).

NEST [748, 4402, 7860, 7873, 8905, 10709, *2943*].

NIV+ NESTED, NESTING, NESTS

Bird's (Nu 24:21; Mt 8:20). Birds stir up (Dt 32:11).

NET [3052, 4821, 5178, 5182, 8407, *311*, *312*, *1473*, *4880*].

NIV+ DRAGNET, FISHNETS, NETS

Of interwoven chains (1Ki 7:17). Hidden in a pit (Ps 35:7-8). Set for birds (Pr 1:17), wild animals (Isa 51:20). Fish caught in (Mt 4:18-21; 13:47; Lk 5:4; Jn 21:6-11).

See Snare.

Figurative:

(Job 18:8; 19:6; Ps 9:15; 10:9; 25:15; 31:4; 35:7-8; 57:6; 66:11; 140:5; 141:10; Pr 12:12; 29:5; Ecc 7:26; 9:12; Isa 19:8; Eze 26:5,14; 47:10; Hos 7:12).

NETAIM [5751]. Residence of Judahite potters (1Ch 4:23).

NETHANEL, NETHANEEL [5991] (*God [El] has given*).

1. The prince of Issachar. Numbers the tribe (Nu 1:8). Captain of the host of Issachar (Nu 2:5; 10:15). Liberality of, for the tabernacle (Nu 7:18-23).
2. A priest and doorkeeper for the ark (1Ch 15:24).
3. A Levite (1Ch 24:6).
4. Son of Obed-Edom and gatekeeper of the temple (1Ch 26:4).
5. A prince sent by Jehoshaphat to teach the law in the cities of Judah (2Ch 17:7).
6. A Levite (2Ch 35:9).
7. A priest who divorced his Gentile wife (Ezr 10:22).
8. A priest (Ne 12:21).
9. A Levite and musician (Ne 12:36).

NETHANIAH [5992, 5993] (*Yahweh has given*).

1. Father of Ishmael (2Ki 25:23,25; Jer 40:8,14-15; 41:1-2,6-7,9-12).
2. A singer and chief of the temple musicians (1Ch 25:2,12).
3. A Levite appointed by Jehoshaphat to accompany the princes who were to teach the law in Judah (2Ch 17:8).
4. Father of Jehudi (Jer 36:14).

NETHINIM *See Temple Servants.*

NETOPHAH, NETOPHATHITE(S), NETOPHATHI [5743, 5756] (*trickle, drip*). Village of Judah and its inhabitants; c. three miles S of Jerusalem (2Sa 23:28-29; 1Ch 2:54; 9:16; Ne 12:28).

NETTLES [7853]. An stinging plant (Pr 24:31; Isa 34:13).

Figurative: (Job 30:7; Hos 9:6; Zep 2:9).

NETWORK [8407, 8422]. White cloth (Isa 19:9), or-namental carving upon pillars of Solomon's temple (1Ki 7:18,42), a grate for the great altar of burnt offerings at the tabernacle (Ex 27:4; 38:4).

NEW BIRTH The corruption of human nature requires (Jn 3:6; Ro 8:7-8). None can enter heaven without (Jn 3:3). Is of the will of God (Jas 1:18). Is of the mercy of God (Tit 3:5). Is for the glory of God (Isa 43:7).

Effected by:

God (Jn 1:13; 1Pe 1:3). Christ (1Jn 2:29). The Holy Spirit (Jn 3:6; Tit 3:5). By means of: The word of God (Jas 1:18; 1Pe 1:23). The resurrection of Christ (1Pe 1:3). The ministry of the Gospel (1Co 4:15).

Described as:

A new creation (2Co 5:17; Gal 6:15; Eph 2:10). New-ness of life (Ro 6:4). A spiritual resurrection (Ro 6:4-6; Eph 2:1,5; Col 2:12; 3:1). A new heart (Eze 36:26). A new spirit (Eze 11:19; Ro 7:6). Putting on the new man (Eph 4:24). The inward man (Ro 7:22; 2Co 4:16). Circumcision of the heart (Dt 30:6, w Ro 2:29; Col 2:11). Partaking of the divine nature (2Pe 1:4). The washing of regeneration (Tit 3:5). All saints partake of (Ro 8:16-17; 1Pe 2:2; 1Jn 5:1).

Produces:

Likeness to God (Eph 4:24; Col 3:10). Likeness to Christ (Ro 8:29; 2Co 3:18; 1Jn 3:2). Knowledge of God (Jer 24:7; Col 3:10). Hatred of sin (1Jn 3:9; 5:18). Victory over the world (1Jn 5:4). Delight in God's law (Ro 7:22).

Evidenced by:

Faith in Christ (1Jn 5:1). Righteousness (1Jn 2:29).

Brotherly love (1Jn 4:7). Connected with adoption (Isa 43:6-7; Jn 1:12-13). Literalistic objection to (Jn 3:4). Manner of effecting illustrated (Jn 3:8). Preserves from Satan's devices (1Jn 5:18).

NEW COVENANT See Covenants, Major in the Old Testament.

NEW CREATION See Regeneration.

NEW MOON Feast of (Nu 10:10; 28:11-15; 1Ch 23:31; 2Ch 31:3). Commerce at time of, suspended (Am 8:5).

NEW TESTAMENT A collection of twenty-seven documents regarded by the church as inspired and authoritative, consisting of four Gospels, the Acts of the Apostles, twenty-one letters, and the book of Revelation. All were written during the apostolic period, either by apostles or by men closely associated with the apostles. The Gospels tell the story of the coming of the Messiah, God in the flesh, to become the Savior of the world. Acts describes the beginnings and growth of the church. The letters set forth the significance of the person and work of Christ and rules for the Church. Revelation tells of the consummation of all things in Jesus Christ. The formation of the NT canon was a gradual process, the Holy Spirit working in the church and guiding it to recognize and choose those Christian books God wanted brought together to form the Christian counterpart of the Jewish OT. By the end of the fourth century, the NT canon was basically settled.

NEW THINGS (Isa 42:9; 43:19; 48:6; 65:17; 2Co 5:17; Rev 21:5).

NEW YEAR See Feasts; Trumpets, Feast of.

NEZIAH [5909] (director [of worship]). One of the temple servants (Ezr 2:54; Ne 7:56).

NEZIB [5908] (pillar, garrison). A city in Judah (Jos 15:43).

NIBHAZ [5563]. An idol (2Ki 17:31).

NIBSHAN [5581]. A city of Judah (Jos 15:62).

NICANOR [3770] (victor). A deacon of the church at Jerusalem (Ac 6:5).

NICODEMUS [3773] (victor over people). Pharisee; member of the Sanhedrin; came to Jesus at night for conversation (Jn 3); spoke up for Jesus before the Sanhedrin (Jn 7:25-44); brought spices for burial of Jesus (Jn 19:39-42).

NICOLAITANS [3774] (follower of Nicolas). A heretical sect with immoral practices (Rev 2:6,15).

NICOLAS [3775] (victor over people). A proselyte of Antioch and deacon of the church at Jerusalem (Ac 6:5-6).

NICOPOLIS [3776] (victory city). City in Epirus in NW Greece, founded by Augustus Caesar (Tit 3:12).

NIGER [3769] (black). Surname of Simeon, leader of the church at Antioch (Ac 13:1-3).

NIGHT [*621, 874, 4325, 4326, 4328, 4869, 6847, 10391, 887, 3816, 5871].

NIV+ ALL-NIGHT, MIDNIGHT, NIGHTFALL, NIGHTS, NIGHTTIME, OVERNIGHT

(Ge 1:5,16,18). Meditations in (Ps 19:2; 77:6; 119:148; 139:11). Worship in (Ps 134:1). Jesus prays all night (Lk 6:12). No night in heaven (Rev 21:25; 22:5). Divided into hours (Ac 23:23). Used figuratively (Isa 15:1; 21:11-12; Jn 9:4; Ro 13:12; 1Th 5:5).

NIGHT HAWK See Screech Owl.

NILE [3284]. The main river of Egypt and of Africa, 4,050 miles long; it begins at Lake Victoria and flows northward to the Mediterranean; the annual overflow deposits sediment which makes N Egypt one of the most fertile regions in the world. Moses was placed on the Nile in a basket of papyrus (Ex 2:3); the turning of the Nile into blood was one of the ten plagues (Ex 7:20-21); on its bank grows the reed from which the famous papyrus writing material is made. See River of Egypt.

NIMRAH [5809] (spotted leopard BDB; basin of limpid [clear] water KB).

NIV+ BETH NIMRAH

A city of Gad (Nu 32:3).

NIMRIM, WATERS OF [5810] (limpid [clear] waters KB; wholesome waters BDB; possibly waters of leopards IDB). Waters on the borders of Gad and Moab (Isa 15:6; Jer 48:34).

NIMROD [5808] (perhaps to rebel, or the Arrow, the mighty hero). Son of Cush. "A mighty hunter before the LORD" (Ge 10:8-9; 1Ch 1:10). Founder of Babylon. See Babylon.

NIMRUD Ancient Calah in Assyria, founded by Nimrod (Ge 10:11,12).

NIMSHI [5811]. Father of Jehu (2Ki 9:2,20).

NINEVEH [5770, 3780].

NIV+ NINEVITES

A capital of the Assyrian Empire (Ge 10:11-12). Nineveh and its surrounding region had a population of upwards of 120,000 when Jonah preached (Jnh 4:11). Extent of (Jnh 3:4). Sennacherib in (2Ki 19:36-37; Isa 37:37-38). Jonah preaches to (Jnh 1:1-2; 3). Nahum prophesies against (Na 1-3). Zephaniah foretells the desolation of (Zep 2:13-15).

NISAN [5772].

Babylonian name for Abib (Ne 2:1; Est 3:7). See Abib; Month, 1.

NISROCH [5827]. An idol (2Ki 19:36-37; Isa 37:37-38).

NITRE See Soda.

NO See Thebes.

NOADIAH [5676] (meet with Yahweh).

1. Levite who returned to Jerusalem after the Exile (Ezr 8:33).

2. False prophetess who tried to terrorize Nehemiah (Ne 6:14).

NOAH [5695, 5829, *3820*] (*rest, comfort*).

NIV+ NOAH'S

1. Son of Lamech (Ge 5:28-29), righteous in a corrupt age (Ge 6:8-9; 7:1; Eze 14:14), warned people of the Flood 120 years (Ge 6:3), built an ark (Ge 6:12-22), saved from the Flood with wife and family, together with beasts and fowl of every kind (Ge 7:8), repopulated earth (Ge 9:10), lived 950 years.

God establishes a covenant with (Ge 9:8-17). *See Covenants, Major in the Old Testament.*

2. Daughter of Zelophehad (Nu 26:33; 27:1; 36:11; Jos 17:3).

NOB [5546]. A city of Benjamin (Ne 11:31-32). Called "the town of the priests" (1Sa 22:19). Home of Ahimelech the priest (1Sa 21:1; 22:11). Probable seat of the tabernacle in Saul's time (1Sa 21:4,6,9). David flees to, and is aided by Ahimelech (1Sa 21:1-9; 22:9-10). Destroyed by Saul (2Sa 22:19). Prophecy concerning (Isa 10:32).

NOBAH [5561, 5562] (*barking*).

1. Manassite; took Kenath from Amorites (Nu 32:42).

2. Town near which Gideon defeated the Midianites (Jdg 8:11).

NOBAI *See Nebai.*

NOBLE [2657, 2985, 3202, 5618, 5619, 7312, *2302*, *2819*, *4948*, *5507*].

NIV+ NOBILITY, NOBLEMAN, NOBLES, NOBLEST

A word which is used to describe people who were renowned for deeds performed or in some other way were distinguished for skills or genius; people of high rank, position, title, or one well born (Jdg 5:13; Ezr 4:10; Est 6:9; Pr 17:26; Lk 19:12-27; 1Co 1:26), persons who possess high moral qualities or ideals (Ps 16:3; Isa 32:5; Ac 17:11), anything having qualities of a very high order (Eze 17:8,23; 1Ti 3:1; Lk 21:5).

A nobleman supports and defends his community. He has a generous heart (Ex 35:5,22; 2Ch 29:31; Nu 21:18; 1Ch 28:21). He is one belonging to a king (Jn 4:46-53). The noble wife is praised in Pr 31:10-31.

NOD [5655] (*wandering*). Region E of Eden to which Cain went (Ge 4:16).

NODAB [5656]. Tribe of Arabs, probably Ishmaelites E of the Jordan (1Ch 5:19).

NOE *See Noah.*

NOGAH [5587] (*joy, splendor*). Son of David (1Ch 3:7; 14:6).

NOHAH [5666] (*rest*). Son of Benjamin (1Ch 8:2).

NOLLE PROSEQUI The complaint against Paul (Ac 18:12-17).

NON *See Nun.*

NONCONFORMITY *See Church, The Body of Believers; State; Form; Formalism.*

NONE LIKE GOD (Ex 8:10; 15:11; Dt 33:26; 2Sa 7:22; 1Ki 8:23; 1Ch 17:20; Ps 89:6; Isa 40:18; Mk 12:32).

NONRESISTANCE Commanded (Mt 5:38-41; Ro 12:17-21; 1Th 5:15; 1Pe 2:19-23). Forgive those who wrong you (Mt 18:15,21-35; Lk 6:36-37; Eph 4:32; Jas 2:13; 1Pe 3:9). Love your enemies (Ex 23:4-5; Job 31:29-30; Pr 25:21-22; Mt 5:43-48; 6:14-15; Lk 6:27-36; 10:30-

37; Ro 12:17-21; 13:10; 1Jn 3:10-11). Return good for evil (Pr 15:1; 25:21-22; Mt 5:38-41; 6:14-15; Ro 12:17-21; 1Th 5:15; 1Pe 3:9). Seek peace (Ps 34:14; 133:1-3; Mt 5:9; 18:15; 2Co 13:11; Gal 5:22; Col 3:12-13; Heb 12:14; Jas 3:17-18; 1Pe 3:11). Suffer gladly for Christ (Mt 5:10-12; Lk 6:22-23; Jn 15:20; Ac 5:41; Ro 12:14; 1Co 4:12-13; 13:7; Gal 5:22; Col 3:12-13; 1Pe 2:19-23; 3:14).

Christ, our example (Lk 23:34; 1Pe 2:19-23; 1Jn 2:6). Exemplified by Stephen (Ac 7:60).

See Revenge; Good for Evil; Evil for Good.

NOON [2021+3427+4734, 7416, *1761+6052, 2465+ 3545, 3540*].

NIV+ AFTERNOON, NOONDAY

(Dt 28:29; Job 11:17; Ps 55:17; 91:6; Isa 58:10; Ac 22:6).

NOPH *See Memphis.*

NOPHAH [5871]. A city of Sihon (Nu 21:30).

NORTH [7600+, 8520, 8522, *1080*].

NIV+ NORTHERN, NORTHWARD

Often merely as a point of the compass; but sometimes a particular country, usually Assyria or Babylonia (Jer 3:18; 46:6; Eze 26:7; Zep 2:13).

NORTHEASTER [*2350*] An hurricane-force E wind the Mediterranean; shipwrecked Paul (Ac 27:14).

NOSE [678, 5690, 5705].

NIV+ NOSES, NOSTRILS

Jewels for (Pr 11:22; Isa 3:21; Eze 16:12). Mutilated (Eze 23:25).

NUBIANS [3934]. An African people (Da 11:43).

NUCLEAR WAR Some see a reference to nuclear war in predictions of the fiery destruction of the earth (Zep 1:18; 2Pe 3:7,10) and in the seven trumpets of Revelation (Rev 8:5-9:19).

NUMBERS [*2118, 4848, 4948, 5031, 5070, 6369, 7023, 7212, 8041, 8044, 8049, 749, 750, 2653, 4436, 4498*].

NIV+ NUMBER, NUMBERED, NUMBERING,
NUMBERLESS, NUMEROUS

Hebrews did not use figures to denote numbers. They spelled numbers out in full; from second century B.C. they used Hebrew letters of the alphabet for numbers. Numbers were often used symbolically; some had special religious significance (Ge 2:2; Ex 20:3-17; Dt 6:4), especially 1, 3, 7, 10, 12, 40, 70, 666, 1,000.

NUMBERS, BOOK OF

Author: Traditionally ascribed to Moses

Date: 1445 to 1406 B.C.

Outline:

I. Israel at Sinai, Preparing to Depart for the Promised Land (1:1-10:10).

A. The Commands for the Census of the People (chs. 1-4).

1. The numbers of men from each tribe mustered for war (ch. 1).

2. The placement of the tribes around the tabernacle and their order for march (ch. 2).

3. The placement of the Levites around the tabernacle, and the numbers of the Levites and the firstborn of Israel (ch. 3).

4. The numbers of the Levites in their tabernacle service for the Lord (ch. 4).
B. The Commands for Purity of the People (5:1-10:10).
1. The test for purity in the law of jealousy (ch. 5).
2. The Nazirite vow and the Aaronic benediction (ch. 6).
3. The offerings of the twelve leaders at the dedication of the tabernacle (ch. 7).
4. The setting up of the lamps and the separation of the Levites (ch. 8).
5. The observance of the Passover (9:1-14).
6. The covering cloud and the silver trumpets (9:15-10:10).
II. The Journey from Sinai to Kadesh (10:11-12:16).
A. The Beginning of the Journey (10:11-36).
B. The Beginning of the Sorrows: Fire and Quail (ch. 11).
C. The Opposition of Miriam and Aaron (ch. 12).
III. Israel at Kadesh, the Delay Resulting from Rebellion (14:1-20:13).
A. The Twelve Spies and Their Mixed Report of the Good Land (ch. 13).
B. The People's Rebellion against God's Commission, and Their Defeat (ch. 14).
C. A Collection of Laws on Offerings, the Sabbath and Tassels on Garments (ch. 15).
D. The Rebellion of Korah and His Allies (ch. 16).
E. The Budding of Aaron's Staff: A Sign for Rebels (ch. 17).
F. Concerning Priests, Their Duties and Their Support (ch. 18).
G. The Red Heifer and the Cleansing Water (ch. 19).
H. The Sin of Moses (20:1-13).
IV. The Journey from Kadesh to the Plains of Moab (20:14-22:1).
A. The Resistance of Edom (20:14-21).
B. The Death of Aaron (20:22-29).
C. The Destruction of Arad (21:1-3).
D. The Bronze Snake (21:4-9).
E. The Song of the Well (21:10-20).

F. The Defeat of Sihon and Og (21:21-30).
G. Israel Enters Moab (21:31-22:1).
V. Israel on the Plains of Moab, in Anticipation of Taking the Promised Land (22:2-32:42).
A. Balak of Moab Hires Balaam to Curse Israel (22:2-41).
B. Balaam Blesses Israel in Seven Oracles (chs. 23-24).
C. The Baal of Peor and Israel's Apostasy (ch. 25).
D. The Second Census (ch. 26).
E. Instructions for the New Generation (chs. 27-30).
1. The inheritance for women (27:1-11).
2. The successor to Moses (27:12-23).
3. Commands regarding offerings (28:1-15).
4. Commands regarding festivals (28:16-29:40).
5. Commands regarding vows (ch. 30).
F. The War against Midian (ch. 31).
G. The Settlement of the Transjordan Tribes (ch. 32).
VI. Appendixes Dealing with Various Matters (chs. 33-36).
A. The Stages of the Journey (ch. 33).
B. The Land of Inheritance (chs. 34-35).
C. The Inheritance for Women (ch. 36).

NUN [5673] (*fish* hence *fertile, productive*). Father of Joshua (Ex 33:11).

NURSE [587, 3437, 3567, 4787, 6402, *1923, 2558, 5555*].

NIV+ NURSED, NURSING

(Ge 24:59; 35:8; Ex 2:7; Ru 4:16; 2Ki 11:2; Isa 60:4; 1Th 2:7). Careless (2Sa 4:4).

NUT [100, 1063].

NIV+ NUTS

Pistachio and almond (Ge 43:11), perhaps walnut (SS 6:11).

NYMPHA, NYMPHAS [*3809*]. A Christian of Laodicea. House of, used as a place of worship (Col 4:15).

O

OAK [381, 461, 464, 473].

NIV+ OAKS

A tree. Grew in Israel (Ge 35:4). Absalom hung in the boughs of (2Sa 18:9,14). Deborah buried under (Ge 35:8). Oars made of (Eze 27:6).

Figurative: (Am 2:9).

OAR [5414, 5415, 8868, *1785*].

NIV+ OARS, OARSMEN

For propelling boats (Isa 33:21; Eze 27:6,29).

OATH [457, 460, 8123, 8652+, 8678, *354, 2019, 2155, 3923, 3992, 3993, 4053*].

NIV+ OATHS

A solemn and binding promise.

Used in solemnizing covenants:

Between Abraham and the king of Sodom (Ge 14:22-23), and Abimelech (Ge 21:22-23), between Isaac and Abimelech (Ge 26:26-29,31). Abraham requires oath of his servant Eliezer (Ge 24:2-3,9). Esau confirms the sale of his birthright by (Ge 25:33). Jacob confirms the covenant between him and Laban by (Ge 31:53), requires Joseph to swear that he would bury Jacob with his fathers (Ge 47:28-31). Joseph requires a like oath (Ge 50:25). Rahab requires an oath from the spies (Jos 2:12-14; 6:14). The Israelites confirm the covenant with the Hivites (Jos 9:3-20). Moses covenants with Caleb by (Jos 14:9). The elders of Gilead confirm their pledge to Jephthah by (Jdg 11:10). The Israelites swear in Mizpah (Jdg 21:5). Ruth swears to Naomi (Ru 1:17). Boaz swears to Ruth (Ru 3:13). Saul swears to Jonathan (1Sa 19:6). Jonathan and David confirm a covenant by (1Sa 20:3,13-17). David swears to Saul (1Sa 24:21-22; 2Sa 21:7). Saul swears to the medium of Endor (1Sa 28:10). David swears not to eat until the sun goes down (2Sa 3:35). Joab confirms his word by (2Sa 19:7). David swears to Bathsheba that Solomon confirms his word by (1Ki 2:23), so also does Shimei (1Ki 2:42). Elisha seals his vow to follow Elijah by (2Ki 2:2). King of Samaria confirms his word with an (2Ki 6:31). Gehazi confirms his lie by (2Ki 5:20). Jehoiada requires an oath from the rulers (2Ki 11:4). Zedekiah violates (2Ch 36:13). Ezra requires, of the priests and Levites (Ezr 10:5,19), so also does Nehemiah (Ne 5:12-13). Zedekiah swears to Jeremiah (Jer 38:16). Gedaliah confirms his word by (Jer 40:9). Peter confirms his denial of Jesus by (Mk 14:71). Used to cast out demons (Ac 19:13); used by Gadarene demoniac in an attempt to keep Jesus from casting out the legion (Mk 5:7).

Attributed to God:

(Ge 22:16; Ps 89:35; 95:11; 105:9; 132:11; Isa 14:24; 45:23; Jer 11:5; 22:5; 49:13; 51:14; Lk 1:73; Heb 3:11,18; 4:3; 6:13-14,17; 7:21,28; Rev 10:6).

Required of Christ—

Mt 26:63 But Jesus remained silent. The high priest said to him, "I charge you under oath by the living God: Tell us if you are the Christ, the Son of God."

Christ's teachings concerning—

Mt 23:18 You also say, 'If anyone swears by the altar, it means nothing; but if anyone swears by the gift on it, he is bound by his oath.' [19]You blind men! Which is greater: the gift, or the altar that makes the gift sacred? [20]Therefore, he who swears by the altar swears by it and by everything on it. [21]And he who swears by the temple swears by it and by the one who dwells in it. [22]And he who swears by heaven swears by God's throne and by the one who sits on it.

Paul confirms certain statements by—

2Co 1:23 I call God as my witness that it was in order to spare you that I did not return to Corinth.

Gal 1:20 I assure you before God that what I am writing you is no lie.

Samuel affirms his honesty of administration by (1Sa 12:5).

Written in the law of Moses—

Da 9:11 All Israel has transgressed your law and turned away, refusing to obey you. "Therefore the curses and sworn judgments written in the Law of Moses, the servant of God, have been poured out on us, because we have sinned against you.

Mosaic law concerning—

Ex 23:1 "Do not spread false reports. Do not help a wicked man by being a malicious witness.

Used in solemnizing testimony—

Ex 22:10 "If a man gives a donkey, an ox, a sheep or any other animal to his neighbor for safekeeping and it dies or is injured or is taken away while no one is looking, [11]the issue between them will be settled by the taking of an oath before the LORD that the neighbor did not lay hands on the other person's property. The owner is to accept this, and no restitution is required.

Nu 5:19 Then the priest shall put the woman under oath and say to her, "If no other man has slept with you and you have not gone astray and become impure while married to your husband, may this bitter water that brings a curse not harm you. [20]But if you have gone astray while married to your husband and you have defiled yourself by sleeping with a man other than your husband"— [21]here the priest is to put the woman under this curse of the oath—"may the LORD cause your people to curse and denounce you when he causes your thigh to waste away and your abdomen to swell. [22]May this water that brings a curse enter your body so that your abdomen swells and your thigh wastes away."

"'Then the woman is to say, "Amen. So be it."

[23]"'The priest is to write these curses on a scroll and then wash them off into the bitter water. [24]He shall have the woman drink the bitter water that brings a curse, and this water will enter her and cause bitter suffering.

Dt 6:13 Fear the LORD your God, serve him only and take your oaths in his name. (+Dt 10:20)

1Ki 8:31 "When a man wrongs his neighbor and is required to take an oath and he comes and swears the oath before your altar in this temple, [32]then hear from heaven and act. Judge between your servants, condemning the guilty and bringing down on his own head what he has done. Declare the innocent not guilty, and so establish his innocence.

Ps 15:1 LORD, who may dwell in your sanctuary? Who may live on your holy hill?

[2]He whose walk is blameless and who does what is righteous, who speaks the truth from his heart (+Ps 15:3)

Ps 15:4 who despises a vile man but honors those who fear the LORD, who keeps his oath even when it hurts,

Heb 6:16 Men swear by someone greater than themselves, and the oath confirms what is said and puts an end to all argument.

Used in confirming allegiance to sovereigns—

Ecc 8:2 Obey the king's command, I say, because you took an oath before God.

Used as a result of returning to God—

Jer 4:2 and if in a truthful, just and righteous way you swear, 'As surely as the LORD lives,' then the nations will be blessed by him and in him they will glory."

Heard, in Daniel's vision—

Da 12:7 The man clothed in linen, who was above the waters of the river, lifted his right hand and his left hand toward heaven, and I heard him swear by him who lives forever, saying, "It will be for a time, times and half a time. When the power of the holy people has been finally broken, all these things will be completed."

In John's vision—

Rev 10:5 Then the angel I had seen standing on the sea and on the land raised his right hand to heaven. ⁶And he swore by him who lives for ever and ever, who created the heavens and all that is in them, the earth and all that is in it, and the sea and all that is in it, and said, "There will be no more delay!

Profane and Wicked:

Forbidden—

Ex 20:7 "You shall not misuse the name of the LORD your God, for the LORD will not hold anyone guiltless who misuses his name.

Lev 19:12 "'Do not swear falsely by my name and so profane the name of your God. I am the LORD. (+Dt 5:11)

Mt 5:33 "Again, you have heard that it was said to the people long ago, 'Do not break your oath, but keep the oaths you have made to the Lord.' ³⁴But I tell you, Do not swear at all: either by heaven, for it is God's throne; ³⁵or by the earth, for it is his footstool; or by Jerusalem, for it is the city of the Great King. ³⁶And do not swear by your head, for you cannot make even one hair white or black. ³⁷Simply let your 'Yes' be 'Yes,' and your 'No,' 'No'; anything beyond this comes from the evil one.

Jas 5:12 Above all, my brothers, do not swear—not by heaven or by earth or by anything else. Let your "Yes" be yes, and your "No," no, or you will be condemned.

Unrighteous, forbidden (Lev 19:12)—

Hos 4:15 "Though you commit adultery, O Israel, let not Judah become guilty. "Do not go to Gilgal; do not go up to Beth Aven. And do not swear, 'As surely as the LORD lives!'

Punishment for—

Lev 6:2 "If anyone sins and is unfaithful to the LORD by deceiving his neighbor about something entrusted to him or left in his care or stolen, or if he cheats him, ³or if he finds lost property and lies about it, or if he swears falsely, or if he commits any such sin that people may do— ⁴when he thus sins and becomes guilty, he must return what he has stolen or taken by extortion, or what was entrusted to him, or the lost property he found, ⁵or whatever it was he swore falsely about. He must make restitution in full, add a fifth of the value to it and give it all to the owner on the day he presents his guilt offering.

Made by Israelites—

Isa 48:1 "Listen to this, O house of Jacob, you who are called by the name of Israel and come from the line of Judah, you who take oaths in the name of the LORD and invoke the God of Israel—but not in truth or righteousness—

Jer 5:2 Although they say, 'As surely as the LORD lives,' still they are swearing falsely."

Jer 5:7 "Why should I forgive you? Your children have forsaken me and sworn by gods that are not gods. I supplied all their needs, yet they committed adultery and thronged to the houses of prostitutes.

Jer 7:8 But look, you are trusting in deceptive words that are worthless.

⁹"'Will you steal and murder, commit adultery and perjury, burn incense to Baal and follow other gods you have not known,

Made by Herod—

Mt 14:7 that he promised with an oath to give her whatever she asked.

Mt 14:9 The king was distressed, but because of his oaths and his dinner guests, he ordered that her request be granted (+Mk 6:23,26)

Made by enemies of Paul—

Ac 23:12 The next morning the Jews formed a conspiracy and bound themselves with an oath not to eat or drink until they had killed Paul. ¹³More than forty men were involved in this plot. ¹⁴They went to the chief priests and elders and said, "We have taken a solemn oath not to eat anything until we have killed Paul.

Idolatrous:

Jer 12:16 And if they learn well the ways of my people and swear by my name, saying, 'As surely as the LORD lives'—even as they once taught my people to swear by Baal—then they will be established among my people.

See Covenant; False Witness; God, Name of; Perjury.

OBADIAH [6281, 6282] *(servant [worshiper] of Yahweh).*

1. Governor of Ahab's household (1Ki 18:3-16).
2. Judahite (1Ch 3:21).
3. Chief of Issachar (1Ch 7:3).
4. Son of Azel (1Ch 8:38).
5. Levite who returned from captivity (1Ch 9:16). Also called Abda (Ne 11:17).
6. Gadite soldier (1Ch 12:9).
7. Father of Ishmaiah, prince of Zebulun (1Ch 27:19).
8. Prince of Judah (2Ch 17:7).
9. Merarite Levite (2Ch 34:12).
10. Jew who returned from captivity (Ezr 8:9).
11. Priestly covenanter with Nehemiah (Ne 10:5).
12. Gatekeeper in Jerusalem (Ne 12:25).
13. A prophet who wrote the book of Obadiah.

OBADIAH, BOOK OF

Author: The prophet Obadiah

Date:

If Obadiah relates to the invasion of Jerusalem by Philistines and Arabs during the reign of Jehoram (853-841 B.C.) (2Ki 8:20-22; 2Ch 21:8-20), the prophet would be a contemporary of Elisha.

If Obadiah relates to the Babylonian attacks on Jerusalem (605-586), the prophet would be a contemporary of Jeremiah. This alternative seems more likely.

Outline:

I. Title and Introduction (1).

II. Judgment on Edom (2-14).

  A. Edom's Destruction Announced (2-7).

    1. The humbling of her pride (2-4).

    2. The completeness of her destruction (5-7).

  B. Edom's Destruction Reaffirmed (8-14).

    1. Her shame and destruction (8-10).

    2. Her crimes against Israel (11-14).

III. The Day of the Lord (15-21).

A. Judgment on the Nations but Deliverance for Zion (15-18).

B. The Lord's Kingdom Established (19-21).

See Prophets, The Minor.

OBAL [6382]. Called also Ebal. A son of Joktan (Ge 10:28; 1Ch 1:22).

OBDURACY Callousness, hardness.

Angers God (Ps 78:31; Isa 57:17).

Warnings against—

Ps 95:8 do not harden your hearts as you did at Meribah, as you did that day at Massah in the desert, **9**where your fathers tested and tried me, though they had seen what I did. **10**For forty years I was angry with that generation; I said, "They are a people whose hearts go astray, and they have not known my ways." **11**So I declared on oath in my anger, "They shall never enter my rest." (+Heb 3:8,15; 4:7)

Punishment for (Lev 26:23-25; Ps 78:31-32)—

Pr 1:24 But since you rejected me when I called and no one gave heed when I stretched out my hand, **25**since you ignored all my advice and would not accept my rebuke, **26**I in turn will laugh at your disaster; I will mock when calamity overtakes you— **27**when calamity overtakes you like a storm, when disaster sweeps over you like a whirlwind, when distress and trouble overwhelm you. **28**"Then they will call to me but I will not answer; they will look for me but will not find me. **29**Since they hated knowledge and did not choose to fear the LORD, **30**since they would not accept my advice and spurned my rebuke, **31**they will eat the fruit of their ways and be filled with the fruit of their schemes.

Pr 29:1 A man who remains stiff-necked after many rebukes will suddenly be destroyed—without remedy. (+Jer 3:2; Am 4:6-11)

Instances of:

The antediluvians (Ge 6:3,5,7). Sodomites (Ge 19:14). Pharaoh (Ex 7:14,22-23; 8:15,19,32; 9:7,12,35; 10:20,28; 11:10; 14:5-8). Israelites (Nu 14:22; Ne 9:28-29; Ps 78:32; Isa 9:13-14; Jer 2:20; 5:3; Am 4:6-12; Zec 7:11-12). Sons of Eli (1Sa 2:22-25). Brothers of a rich man (Lk 16:31).

Mankind in the last days—

Rev 9:20 The rest of mankind that were not killed by these plagues still did not repent of the work of their hands; they did not stop worshiping demons, and idols of gold, silver, bronze, stone and wood—idols that cannot see or hear or walk. **21**Nor did they repent of their murders, their magic arts, their sexual immorality or their thefts.

See Afflictions, Of the Wicked; Impenitence; Reprobacy.

OBED [6381, 2725] (*servant [worshiper]*).

1. Son of Boaz and grandfather of David (Ru 4:17-22; 1Ch 2:12; Mt 1:5; Lk 3:32).

2. Son of Ephlal and grandson of Zabad (1Ch 2:37-38).

3. One of David's heroes (1Ch 11:47).

4. Son of Shemaiah. A gatekeeper of the temple (1Ch 26:7).

5. Father of Azariah (2Ch 23:1).

OBED-EDOM [6273] (*servant [worshiper] of Edom*).

1. A Korahite Levite. Doorkeeper of the ark (1Ch 15:18, 24; 26:4-8). David leaves the ark with (2Sa 6:10; 1Ch 13:13-14). Ark removed from (2Sa 6:12; 1Ch 15:25). Appointed to sound with harps (1Ch 15:21). Appointed to minister the ark (1Ch 16:4-5,37-38).

2. A doorkeeper of the temple (1Ch 16:38).

3. A caretaker of the vessels of the temple in time of Amaziah (2Ch 25:24).

OBEDIENCE [*3682, 5915, 6913, 9048, 9068, *2848, 4272, 4275, 5498, 5633, 5634, 5675, 5875*].

NIV+ OBEY, OBEDIENT, OBEYED, OBEYING, OBEYS

Better than sacrifice (1Sa 15:22; Ps 40:6-9; Pr 21:3; Jer 7:22-23; Hos 6:6; Mic 6:6-8; Mt 9:13; 12:7; Mk 12:33; Heb 10:8-9).

Commanded—

Ge 17:9 Then God said to Abraham, "As for you, you must keep my covenant, you and your descendants after you for the generations to come.

Ex 23:22 If you listen carefully to what he says and do all that I say, I will be an enemy to your enemies and will oppose those who oppose you. (+Lev 19:19)

Lev 19:36 Use honest scales and honest weights, an honest ephah and an honest hin. I am the LORD your God, who brought you out of Egypt.

37"'Keep all my decrees and all my laws and follow them. I am the LORD.'"

Lev 20:8 Keep my decrees and follow them. I am the LORD, who makes you holy.

Lev 20:22 "'Keep all my decrees and laws and follow them, so that the land where I am bringing you to live may not vomit you out. (+Lev 22:31)

Nu 15:38 "Speak to the Israelites and say to them: 'Throughout the generations to come you are to make tassels on the corners of your garments, with a blue cord on each tassel. **39**You will have these tassels to look at and so you will remember all the commands of the LORD, that you may obey them and not prostitute yourselves by going after the lusts of your own hearts and eyes. **40**Then you will remember to obey all my commands and will be consecrated to your God. (+Nu 30:2)

Dt 4:1 Hear now, O Israel, the decrees and laws I am about to teach you. Follow them so that you may live and may go in and take possession of the land that the LORD, the God of your fathers, is giving you. **2**Do not add to what I command you and do not subtract from it, but keep the commands of the LORD your God that I give you. (+Dt 4:3-4)

Dt 4:5 See, I have taught you decrees and laws as the LORD my God commanded me, so that you may follow them in the land you are entering to take possession of it. **6**Observe them carefully, for this will show your wisdom and understanding to the nations, who will hear about all these decrees and say, "Surely this great nation is a wise and understanding people." (+Dt 4:7-8)

Dt 4:9 Only be careful, and watch yourselves closely so that you do not forget the things your eyes have seen or let them slip from your heart as long as you live. Teach them to your children and to their children after them. **10**Remember the day you stood before the LORD your God at Horeb, when he said to me, "Assemble the people before me to hear my words so that they may learn to revere me as long as they live in the land and may teach them to their children." (+Dt 4:11-38)

Dt 4:39 Acknowledge and take to heart this day that the LORD is God in heaven above and on the earth below. There is no other. **40**Keep his decrees and commands, which I am giving you today, so that it may go well with you and your children after you and that you may live long in the land the LORD your God gives you for all time.

Dt 5:1 Moses summoned all Israel and said: Hear, O

Israel, the decrees and laws I declare in your hearing today. Learn them and be sure to follow them. (+Dt 5:2-31)

Dt 5:32 So be careful to do what the LORD your God has commanded you; do not turn aside to the right or to the left. ³³Walk in all the way that the LORD your God has commanded you, so that you may live and prosper and prolong your days in the land that you will possess.

Dt 6:1 These are the commands, decrees and laws the LORD your God directed me to teach you to observe in the land that you are crossing the Jordan to possess, ²so that you, your children and their children after them may fear the LORD your God as long as you live by keeping all his decrees and commands that I give you, and so that you may enjoy long life. ³Hear, O Israel, and be careful to obey so that it may go well with you and that you may increase greatly in a land flowing with milk and honey, just as the LORD, the God of your fathers, promised you.

⁴Hear, O Israel: The LORD our God, the LORD is one. ⁵Love the LORD your God with all your heart and with all your soul and with all your strength. ⁶These commandments that I give you today are to be upon your hearts. ⁷Impress them on your children. Talk about them when you sit at home and when you walk along the road, when you lie down and when you get up. ⁸Tie them as symbols on your hands and bind them on your foreheads. ⁹Write them on the doorframes of your houses and on your gates. (+Dt 6:10-25)

Dt 8:1 Be careful to follow every command I am giving you today, so that you may live and increase and may enter and possess the land that the LORD promised on oath to your forefathers. ²Remember how the LORD your God led you all the way in the desert these forty years, to humble you and to test you in order to know what was in your heart, whether or not you would keep his commands. ³He humbled you, causing you to hunger and then feeding you with manna, which neither you nor your fathers had known, to teach you that man does not live on bread alone but on every word that comes from the mouth of the LORD. ⁴Your clothes did not wear out and your feet did not swell during these forty years. ⁵Know then in your heart that as a man disciplines his son, so the LORD your God disciplines you.

⁶Observe the commands of the LORD your God, walking in his ways and revering him.

Dt 8:11 Be careful that you do not forget the LORD your God, failing to observe his commands, his laws and his decrees that I am giving you this day. ¹²Otherwise, when you eat and are satisfied, when you build fine houses and settle down, ¹³and when your herds and flocks grow large and your silver and gold increase and all you have is multiplied, ¹⁴then your heart will become proud and you will forget the LORD your God, who brought you out of Egypt, out of the land of slavery. (+Dt 8:15)

Dt 8:16 He gave you manna to eat in the desert, something your fathers had never known, to humble and to test you so that in the end it might go well with you. ¹⁷You may say to yourself, "My power and the strength of my hands have produced this wealth for me." ¹⁸But remember the LORD your God, for it is he who gives you the ability to produce wealth, and so confirms his covenant, which he swore to your forefathers, as it is today.

¹⁹If you ever forget the LORD your God and follow other gods and worship and bow down to them, I testify against you today that you will surely be destroyed. ²⁰Like the nations the LORD destroyed before you, so you will be destroyed for not obeying the LORD your God.

Dt 10:12 And now, O Israel, what does the LORD your God ask of you but to fear the LORD your God, to walk in all his ways, to love him, to serve the LORD your God with all your heart and with all your soul, ¹³and to observe the LORD's commands and decrees that I am giving you today for your own good?

Dt 11:1 Love the LORD your God and keep his requirements, his decrees, his laws and his commands always. ²Remember today that your children were not the ones who saw and experienced the discipline of the LORD your God: his majesty, his mighty hand, his outstretched arm; ³the signs he performed and the things he did in the heart of Egypt, both to Pharaoh king of Egypt and to his whole country;

Dt 11:8 Observe therefore all the commands I am giving you today, so that you may have the strength to go in and take over the land that you are crossing the Jordan to possess, ⁹and so that you may live long in the land that the LORD swore to your forefathers to give to them and their descendants, a land flowing with milk and honey.

Dt 11:13 So if you faithfully obey the commands I am giving you today—to love the LORD your God and to serve him with all your heart and with all your soul— ¹⁴then I will send rain on your land in its season, both autumn and spring rains, so that you may gather in your grain, new wine and oil. ¹⁵I will provide grass in the fields for your cattle, and you will eat and be satisfied.

¹⁶Be careful, or you will be enticed to turn away and worship other gods and bow down to them. ¹⁷Then the LORD's anger will burn against you, and he will shut the heavens so that it will not rain and the ground will yield no produce, and you will soon perish from the good land the LORD is giving you. ¹⁸Fix these words of mine in your hearts and minds; tie them as symbols on your hands and bind them on your foreheads. ¹⁹Teach them to your children, talking about them when you sit at home and when you walk along the road, when you lie down and when you get up. ²⁰Write them on the doorframes of your houses and on your gates, ²¹so that your days and the days of your children may be many in the land that the LORD swore to give your forefathers, as many as the days that the heavens are above the earth.

²²If you carefully observe all these commands I am giving you to follow—to love the LORD your God, to walk in all his ways and to hold fast to him— ²³then the LORD will drive out all these nations before you, and you will dispossess nations larger and stronger than you. ²⁴Every place where you set your foot will be yours: Your territory will extend from the desert to Lebanon, and from the Euphrates River to the western sea. ²⁵No man will be able to stand against you. The LORD your God, as he promised you, will put the terror and fear of you on the whole land, wherever you go.

²⁶See, I am setting before you today a blessing and a curse— ²⁷the blessing if you obey the commands of the LORD your God that I am giving you today; ²⁸the curse if you disobey the commands of the LORD your God and turn from the way that I command you today by following other gods, which you have not known. (+Dt 11:32)

Dt 13:4 It is the LORD your God you must follow, and him you must revere. Keep his commands and obey him; serve him and hold fast to him.

Dt 26:16 The LORD your God commands you this day to follow these decrees and laws; carefully observe them with all your heart and with all your soul. [17]You have declared this day that the LORD is your God and that you will walk in his ways, that you will keep his decrees, commands and laws, and that you will obey him. [18]And the LORD has declared this day that you are his people, his treasured possession as he promised, and that you are to keep all his commands.

Dt 27:1 Moses and the elders of Israel commanded the people: "Keep all these commands that I give you today. [2]When you have crossed the Jordan into the land the LORD your God is giving you, set up some large stones and coat them with plaster. [3]Write on them all the words of this law when you have crossed over to enter the land the LORD your God is giving you, a land flowing with milk and honey, just as the LORD, the God of your fathers, promised you. [4]And when you have crossed the Jordan, set up these stones on Mount Ebal, as I command you today, and coat them with plaster. [5]Build there an altar to the LORD your God, an altar of stones. Do not use any iron tool upon them. [6]Build the altar of the LORD your God with fieldstones and offer burnt offerings on it to the LORD your God. [7]Sacrifice fellowship offerings there, eating them and rejoicing in the presence of the LORD your God. [8]And you shall write very clearly all the words of this law on these stones you have set up."

[9]Then Moses and the priests, who are Levites, said to all Israel, "Be silent, O Israel, and listen! You have now become the people of the LORD your God. [10]Obey the LORD your God and follow his commands and decrees that I give you today."

Dt 32:46 he said to them, "Take to heart all the words I have solemnly declared to you this day, so that you may command your children to obey carefully all the words of this law.

Jos 22:5 But be very careful to keep the commandment and the law that Moses the servant of the LORD gave you: to love the LORD your God, to walk in all his ways, to obey his commands, to hold fast to him and to serve him with all your heart and all your soul."

Jos 23:6 "Be very strong; be careful to obey all that is written in the Book of the Law of Moses, without turning aside to the right or to the left. [7]Do not associate with these nations that remain among you; do not invoke the names of their gods or swear by them. You must not serve them or bow down to them.

Jos 24:14 "Now fear the LORD and serve him with all faithfulness. Throw away the gods your forefathers worshiped beyond the River and in Egypt, and serve the LORD. [15]But if serving the LORD seems undesirable to you, then choose for yourselves this day whom you will serve, whether the gods your forefathers served beyond the River, or the gods of the Amorites, in whose land you are living. But as for me and my household, we will serve the LORD." (+1Sa 12:14,20)

1Sa 12:24 But be sure to fear the LORD and serve him faithfully with all your heart; consider what great things he has done for you.

1Sa 15:22 But Samuel replied: "Does the LORD delight in burnt offerings and sacrifices as much as in obeying the voice of the LORD? To obey is better than sacrifice, and to heed is better than the fat of rams.

2Ki 17:37 You must always be careful to keep the decrees and ordinances, the laws and commands he wrote for you. Do not worship other gods. [38]Do not forget the covenant I have made with you, and do not worship other gods.

1Ch 16:15 He remembers his covenant forever, the word he commanded, for a thousand generations,

1Ch 28:9 "And you, my son Solomon, acknowledge the God of your father, and serve him with wholehearted devotion and with a willing mind, for the LORD searches every heart and understands every motive behind the thoughts. If you seek him, he will be found by you; but if you forsake him, he will reject you forever. [10]Consider now, for the LORD has chosen you to build a temple as a sanctuary. Be strong and do the work."

1Ch 28:20 David also said to Solomon his son, "Be strong and courageous, and do the work. Do not be afraid or discouraged, for the LORD God, my God, is with you. He will not fail you or forsake you until all the work for the service of the temple of the LORD is finished.

Ezr 7:23 Whatever the God of heaven has prescribed, let it be done with diligence for the temple of the God of heaven. Why should there be wrath against the realm of the king and of his sons?

Ps 76:11 Make vows to the LORD your God and fulfill them; let all the neighboring lands bring gifts to the One to be feared. (+Pr 7:1)

Ecc 12:13 Now all has been heard; here is the conclusion of the matter: Fear God and keep his commandments, for this is the whole [duty] of man.

Jer 26:13 Now reform your ways and your actions and obey the LORD your God. Then the LORD will relent and not bring the disaster he has pronounced against you.

Jer 38:20 "They will not hand you over," Jeremiah replied. "Obey the LORD by doing what I tell you. Then it will go well with you, and your life will be spared.

Da 7:27 Then the sovereignty, power and greatness of the kingdoms under the whole heaven will be handed over to the saints, the people of the Most High. His kingdom will be an everlasting kingdom, and all rulers will worship and obey him.'

Mal 4:4 "Remember the law of my servant Moses, the decrees and laws I gave him at Horeb for all Israel.

Eph 6:6 Obey them not only to win their favor when their eye is on you, but like slaves of Christ, doing the will of God from your heart. [7]Serve wholeheartedly, as if you were serving the Lord, not men, [8]because you know that the Lord will reward everyone for whatever good he does, whether he is slave or free.

Php 2:12 Therefore, my dear friends, as you have always obeyed—not only in my presence, but now much more in my absence—continue to work out your salvation with fear and trembling,

1Ti 6:14 to keep this command without spot or blame until the appearing of our Lord Jesus Christ,

1Ti 6:18 Command them to do good, to be rich in good deeds, and to be generous and willing to share.

Jas 1:22 Do not merely listen to the word, and so deceive yourselves. Do what it says. [23]Anyone who listens to the word but does not do what it says is like a man who looks at his face in a mirror [24]and, after looking at himself, goes away and immediately forgets what he looks like. [25]But the man who looks intently into the perfect law that gives freedom, and continues to do this, not forgetting what he has heard, but doing it—he will be blessed in what he does.

Jas 2:10 For whoever keeps the whole law and yet stumbles at just one point is guilty of breaking all of it. [11]For he who said, "Do not commit adultery," also said, "Do not murder." If you do not commit adultery but do commit murder, you have become a lawbreaker.

¹²Speak and act as those who are going to be judged by the law that gives freedom,

1Pe 1:2 who have been chosen according to the foreknowledge of God the Father, through the sanctifying work of the Spirit, for obedience to Jesus Christ and sprinkling by his blood: Grace and peace be yours in abundance.

1Pe 1:14 As obedient children, do not conform to the evil desires you had when you lived in ignorance.

Proof of love—

Jn 14:15 "If you love me, you will obey what I command.

Jn 14:21 Whoever has my commands and obeys them, he is the one who loves me. He who loves me will be loved by my Father, and I too will love him and show myself to him."

1Jn 2:5 But if anyone obeys his word, God's love is truly made complete in him. This is how we know we are in him: ⁶Whoever claims to live in him must walk as Jesus did. (+1Jn 5:2-3)

2Jn 6 And this is love: that we walk in obedience to his commands. As you have heard from the beginning, his command is that you walk in love.

2Jn 9 Anyone who runs ahead and does not continue in the teaching of Christ does not have God; whoever continues in the teaching has both the Father and the Son.

Proof that we know God—

1Jn 2:3 We know that we have come to know him if we obey his commands. ⁴The man who says, "I know him," but does not do what he commands is a liar, and the truth is not in him.

Vows of—

Ex 24:7 Then he took the Book of the Covenant and read it to the people. They responded, "We will do everything the LORD has said; we will obey." (+Jos 24:24)

Ps 119:15 I meditate on your precepts and consider your ways. (+Ps 119:106)

Ps 119:109 Though I constantly take my life in my hands, I will not forget your law.

Justification by, under Mosaic law (Lev 18:5; Eze 20:11,13,21; Lk 10:28; Ro 10:5)—

Gal 3:10 All who rely on observing the law are under a curse, for it is written: "Cursed is everyone who does not continue to do everything written in the Book of the Law."

Gal 3:12 The law is not based on faith; on the contrary, "The man who does these things will live by them."

Prayer for guidance in—

Ps 143:10 Teach me to do your will, for you are my God; may your good Spirit lead me on level ground.

Cannot be rendered to two masters—

Mt 6:24 "No one can serve two masters. Either he will hate the one and love the other, or he will be devoted to the one and despise the other. You cannot serve both God and Money.

Rewards:

Ge 18:19 For I have chosen him, so that he will direct his children and his household after him to keep the way of the LORD by doing what is right and just, so that the LORD will bring about for Abraham what he has promised him."

Lev 26:3 "'If you follow my decrees and are careful to obey my commands, ⁴I will send you rain in its season, and the ground will yield its crops and the trees of the field their fruit. ⁵Your threshing will continue until grape harvest and the grape harvest will continue until planting, and you will eat all the food you want and live in safety in your land.

⁶"'I will grant peace in the land, and you will lie down and no one will make you afraid. I will remove savage beasts from the land, and the sword will not pass through your country. ⁷You will pursue your enemies, and they will fall by the sword before you. ⁸Five of you will chase a hundred, and a hundred of you will chase ten thousand, and your enemies will fall by the sword before you.

⁹"'I will look on you with favor and make you fruitful and increase your numbers, and I will keep my covenant with you. ¹⁰You will still be eating last year's harvest when you will have to move it out to make room for the new. ¹¹I will put my dwelling place among you, and I will not abhor you. ¹²I will walk among you and be your God, and you will be my people. ¹³I am the LORD your God, who brought you out of Egypt so that you would no longer be slaves to the Egyptians; I broke the bars of your yoke and enabled you to walk with heads held high.

Nu 14:24 But because my servant Caleb has a different spirit and follows me wholeheartedly, I will bring him into the land he went to, and his descendants will inherit it. (+Dt 7:12-15)

Dt 28:1 If you fully obey the LORD your God and carefully follow all his commands I give you today, the LORD your God will set you high above all the nations on earth. ²All these blessings will come upon you and accompany you if you obey the LORD your God:

³You will be blessed in the city and blessed in the country.

⁴The fruit of your womb will be blessed, and the crops of your land and the young of your livestock—the calves of your herds and the lambs of your flocks.

⁵Your basket and your kneading trough will be blessed.

⁶You will be blessed when you come in and blessed when you go out.

⁷The LORD will grant that the enemies who rise up against you will be defeated before you. They will come at you from one direction but flee from you in seven.

⁸The LORD will send a blessing on your barns and on everything you put your hand to. The LORD your God will bless you in the land he is giving you.

⁹The LORD will establish you as his holy people, as he promised you on oath, if you keep the commands of the LORD your God and walk in his ways. ¹⁰Then all the peoples on earth will see that you are called by the name of the LORD, and they will fear you. ¹¹The LORD will grant you abundant prosperity—in the fruit of your womb, the young of your livestock and the crops of your ground—in the land he swore to your forefathers to give you.

¹²The LORD will open the heavens, the storehouse of his bounty, to send rain on your land in season and to bless all the work of your hands. You will lend to many nations but will borrow from none. ¹³The LORD will make you the head, not the tail. If you pay attention to the commands of the LORD your God that I give you this day and carefully follow them, you will always be at the top, never at the bottom. ¹⁴Do not turn aside from any of the commands I give you today, to the right or to the left, following other gods and serving them.

¹⁵However, if you do not obey the LORD your God and do not carefully follow all his commands and decrees I am giving you today, all these curses will come upon you and overtake you: (+Jos 14:6-14)

2Ki 21:8 I will not again make the feet of the Israelites wander from the land I gave their forefathers, if only they will be careful to do everything I commanded them and will keep the whole Law that my servant Moses gave them."

Isa 1:19 If you are willing and obedient, you will eat the best from the land;

Rewarded by: Prosperity (Dt 7:9,12-15; 15:4; Jos 1:8; 1Ki 2:3-4; 9:3-5; 1Ch 22:13; 28:7-8; 2Ch 26:5; 27:6; Job 36:11)

Pr 28:7 He who keeps the law is a discerning son, but a companion of gluttons disgraces his father. (+Jer 7:3-7; 11:1-5; 22:16; Mal 3:10-12)

1Jn 3:22 and receive from him anything we ask, because we obey his commands and do what pleases him.

Long life (Dt 4:1,40; 32:47)—

1Ki 3:14 And if you walk in my ways and obey my statutes and commands as David your father did, I will give you a long life." (+Pr 3:1-2)

Pr 19:16 He who obeys instructions guards his life, but he who is contemptuous of his ways will die.

Victory over enemies (Ex 23:22; Pr 16:7)

Triumph over adversities (Mt 7:24-25)—

Lk 6:46 "Why do you call me, 'Lord, Lord,' and do not do what I say? ⁴⁷I will show you what he is like who comes to me and hears my words and puts them into practice. ⁴⁸He is like a man building a house, who dug down deep and laid the foundation on rock. When a flood came, the torrent struck that house but could not shake it, because it was well built.

Divine favor—

Ex 19:5 Now if you obey me fully and keep my covenant, then out of all nations you will be my treasured possession. Although the whole earth is mine,

Ex 20:6 but showing love to a thousand [generations] of those who love me and keep my commandments. (+Dt 5:10; 11:26-27; 12:28; 1Ki 8:23)

Ne 1:5 Then I said: "O LORD, God of heaven, the great and awesome God, who keeps his covenant of love with those who love him and obey his commands,

Ps 25:10 All the ways of the LORD are loving and faithful for those who keep the demands of his covenant.

Ps 103:17 But from everlasting to everlasting the LORD's love is with those who fear him, and his righteousness with their children's children— ¹⁸with those who keep his covenant and remember to obey his precepts.

Ps 103:20 Praise the LORD, you his angels, you mighty ones who do his bidding, who obey his word.

Ps 112:1 Praise the LORD. Blessed is the man who fears the LORD, who finds great delight in his commands.

Ps 119:2 Blessed are they who keep his statutes and seek him with all their heart.

Pr 1:33 but whoever listens to me will live in safety and be at ease, without fear of harm." (+Jer 7:23; 11:4)

Mt 5:19 Anyone who breaks one of the least of these commandments and teaches others to do the same will be called least in the kingdom of heaven, but whoever practices and teaches these commands will be called great in the kingdom of heaven.

Mt 25:20 The man who had received the five talents brought the other five. 'Master,' he said, 'you entrusted me with five talents. See, I have gained five more.'

²¹"His master replied, 'Well done, good and faithful servant! You have been faithful with a few things; I will put you in charge of many things. Come and share your master's happiness!'

²²"The man with the two talents also came. 'Master,' he said, 'you entrusted me with two talents; see, I have gained two more.'

²³"His master replied, 'Well done, good and faithful servant! You have been faithful with a few things; I will put you in charge of many things. Come and share your master's happiness!'

Lk 11:28 He replied, "Blessed rather are those who hear the word of God and obey it."

Lk 12:37 It will be good for those servants whose master finds them watching when he comes. I tell you the truth, he will dress himself to serve, will have them recline at the table and will come and wait on them. ³⁸It will be good for those servants whose master finds them ready, even if he comes in the second or third watch of the night.

Jn 12:26 Whoever serves me must follow me; and where I am, my servant also will be. My Father will honor the one who serves me.

Jn 13:17 Now that you know these things, you will be blessed if you do them. (+Jas 1:25)

Rev 22:7 "Behold, I am coming soon! Blessed is he who keeps the words of the prophecy in this book."

Fellowship with Christ—

Mt 12:50 For whoever does the will of my Father in heaven is my brother and sister and mother."

Mk 3:35 Whoever does God's will is my brother and sister and mother."

Lk 8:21 He replied, "My mother and brothers are those who hear God's word and put it into practice."

Jn 14:23 Jesus replied, "If anyone loves me, he will obey my teaching. My Father will love him, and we will come to him and make our home with him.

Jn 15:10 If you obey my commands, you will remain in my love, just as I have obeyed my Father's commands and remain in his love.

Jn 15:14 You are my friends if you do what I command.

1Jn 3:24 Those who obey his commands live in him, and he in them. And this is how we know that he lives in us: We know it by the Spirit he gave us.

Everlasting life—

Mt 19:17 "Why do you ask me about what is good?" Jesus replied. "There is only One who is good. If you want to enter life, obey the commandments."

Mt 19:29 And everyone who has left houses or brothers or sisters or father or mother or children or fields for my sake will receive a hundred times as much and will inherit eternal life.

Jn 8:51 I tell you the truth, if anyone keeps my word, he will never see death."

1Jn 2:17 The world and its desires pass away, but the man who does the will of God lives forever. (+Rev 2:10)

Exemplified: (Dt 33:9)

Ps 1:2 But his delight is in the law of the LORD, and on his law he meditates day and night. (+Ps 103:1-20)

Ps 103:21 Praise the LORD, all his heavenly hosts, you his servants who do his will. (+Ps 103:22)

1Th 1:9 for they themselves report what kind of reception you gave us. They tell how you turned to God from idols to serve the living and true God,

Rev 2:19 I know your deeds, your love and faith, your service and perseverance, and that you are now doing more than you did at first.

Noah—

Ge 6:9 This is the account of Noah. Noah was a righteous man, blameless among the people of his time, and he walked with God. (+Ge 6:22; 7:5; Heb 11:7)

Abraham (Ge 12:1-4; 17:23; 18:19; 21:4; 22:12,18; 26:3-5; Ne 9:8; Ac 7:3-8; Heb 11:8-17; Jas 2:21). Bethuel and Laban (Ge 24:50), Jacob (Ge 35:1,7), Laban (Ge 31:29), Moses (Nu 27:12-22; Heb 3:2-3), Moses and Aaron (Ex 7:6; 40:16,21,23,32)

Israelites (Ex 12:28; 32:25-29; 39:42-43; Nu 9:20-21)—

Nu 9:23 At the LORD's command they encamped, and at the LORD's command they set out. They obeyed the LORD's order, in accordance with his command through Moses. (+Dt 33:9)

Jos 22:2 and said to them, "You have done all that Moses the servant of the LORD commanded, and you have obeyed me in everything I commanded. (+Jdg 2:7)

Ps 99:7 He spoke to them from the pillar of cloud; they kept his statutes and the decrees he gave them.

Israelites under the preaching of Haggai (Hag 1:12).

Caleb—

Nu 14:24 But because my servant Caleb has a different spirit and follows me wholeheartedly, I will bring him into the land he went to, and his descendants will inherit it. (+Dt 1:36; Jos 14:6-14)

Joshua (Jos 10:40; 11:15), Reubenites (Jos 22:2-3), Gibeon (Jdg 6:25-28), David (1Ki 11:6,34; 15:5; 2Ch 29:2; Ac 13:22), Elijah (1Ki 17:5).

The psalmist—

Ps 17:3 Though you probe my heart and examine me at night, though you test me, you will find nothing; I have resolved that my mouth will not sin.

Ps 26:3 for your love is ever before me, and I walk continually in your truth. **4**I do not sit with deceitful men, nor do I consort with hypocrites; **5**I abhor the assembly of evildoers and refuse to sit with the wicked. **6**I wash my hands in innocence, and go about your altar, O LORD,

Ps 119:30 I have chosen the way of truth; I have set my heart on your laws. **31**I hold fast to your statutes, O LORD; do not let me be put to shame.

Ps 119:40 How I long for your precepts! Preserve my life in your righteousness.

Ps 119:44 I will always obey your law, for ever and ever.

Ps 119:47 for I delight in your commands because I love them. **48**I lift up my hands to your commands, which I love, and I meditate on your decrees.

Ps 119:51 The arrogant mock me without restraint, but I do not turn from your law.

Ps 119:55 In the night I remember your name, O LORD, and I will keep your law. **56**This has been my practice: I obey your precepts.

Ps 119:59 I have considered my ways and have turned my steps to your statutes. **60**I will hasten and not delay to obey your commands.

Ps 119:67 Before I was afflicted I went astray, but now I obey your word.

Ps 119:69 Though the arrogant have smeared me with lies, I keep your precepts with all my heart.

Ps 119:100 I have more understanding than the elders, for I obey your precepts.

Ps 119:102 I have not departed from your laws, for you yourself have taught me.

Ps 119:105 Your word is a lamp to my feet and a light for my path. **106**I have taken an oath and confirmed it, that I will follow your righteous laws.

Ps 119:110 The wicked have set a snare for me, but I have not strayed from your precepts.

Ps 119:112 My heart is set on keeping your decrees to the very end. (+Ps 119:119)

Ps 119:166 I wait for your salvation, O LORD, and I follow your commands. **167**I obey your statutes, for I love them

greatly. **168**I obey your precepts and your statutes, for all my ways are known to you.

Elisha (1Ki 19:19-21)

Hezekiah—

2Ki 18:6 He held fast to the LORD and did not cease to follow him; he kept the commands the LORD had given Moses.

2Ki 20:3 "Remember, O LORD, how I have walked before you faithfully and with wholehearted devotion and have done what is good in your eyes." And Hezekiah wept bitterly. (+2Ch 31:20-21; Isa 38:3)

Josiah (2Ki 22:2; 23:24-25), Asa (2Ch 14:2), Jehoshaphat (2Ch 17:3-6; 20:32; 22:9), Uzziah (2Ch 26:4-5), Jotham (2Ch 27:2), Levites (2Ch 29:34), Cyrus (Ezr 1:1-4)

Ezra—

Ezr 7:10 For Ezra had devoted himself to the study and observance of the Law of the LORD, and to teaching its decrees and laws in Israel.

Hanani—

Ne 7:2 I put in charge of Jerusalem my brother Hanani, along with Hananiah the commander of the citadel, because he was a man of integrity and feared God more than most men do.

Job—

Job 1:8 Then the LORD said to Satan, "Have you considered my servant Job? There is no one on earth like him; he is blameless and upright, a man who fears God and shuns evil."

By, the three Hebrews (Da 3), Jonah (Jnh 3:3), Ninevites (Jnh 3:5-10)

Zechariah—

Lk 1:6 Both of them were upright in the sight of God, observing all the Lord's commandments and regulations blamelessly.

Simeon (Lk 2:25), Joseph (Mt 1:24; 2:14), Mary (Lk 1:38).

Jesus (Mt 3:15; 26:39,42; Lk 22:42; Jn 4:32,34; 5:30; 6:38)—

Jn 8:28 So Jesus said, "When you have lifted up the Son of Man, then you will know that I am [the one I claim to be] and that I do nothing on my own but speak just what the Father has taught me. (+Jn 8:29)

Jn 9:4 As long as it is day, we must do the work of him who sent me. Night is coming, when no one can work. (+Jn 12:49-50)

Jn 14:31 but the world must learn that I love the Father and that I do exactly what my Father has commanded me. "Come now; let us leave. (+Jn 17:4; Php 2:8; Heb 3:2)

By, John the Baptist (Mt 3:15), John and James (Mk 1:19-20)

Matthew—

Mt 9:9 As Jesus went on from there, he saw a man named Matthew sitting at the tax collector's booth. "Follow me," he told him, and Matthew got up and followed him.

Simon and Andrew (Mk 1:16-18), Levi (Mk 2:14), the rich young man (Mt 19:20; Mk 10:20; Lk 18:21)

The disciples (Jn 17:6)—

Ac 4:19 But Peter and John replied, "Judge for yourselves whether it is right in God's sight to obey you rather than God. (+Ac 4:20)

Ac 5:29 Peter and the other apostles replied: "We must obey God rather than men!

Cornelius (Ac 10:2)

Paul—

Ac 23:1 Paul looked straight at the Sanhedrin and said,

"My brothers, I have fulfilled my duty to God in all good conscience to this day." (+Ac 24:17; 26:4-5)

Php 3:7 But whatever was to my profit I now consider loss for the sake of Christ. **8**What is more, I consider everything a loss compared to the surpassing greatness of knowing Christ Jesus my Lord, for whose sake I have lost all things. I consider them rubbish, that I may gain Christ **9**and be found in him, not having a righteousness of my own that comes from the law, but that which is through faith in Christ—the righteousness that comes from God and is by faith. **10**I want to know Christ and the power of his resurrection and the fellowship of sharing in his sufferings, becoming like him in his death, **11**and so, somehow, to attain to the resurrection from the dead. **12**Not that I have already obtained all this, or have already been made perfect, but I press on to take hold of that for which Christ Jesus took hold of me. **13**Brothers, I do not consider myself yet to have taken hold of it. But one thing I do: Forgetting what is behind and straining toward what is ahead, **14**I press on toward the goal to win the prize for which God has called me heavenward in Christ Jesus.

2Ti 1:3 I thank God, whom I serve, as my forefathers did, with a clear conscience, as night and day I constantly remember you in my prayers.

Paul and Timothy—

2Co 1:12 Now this is our boast: Our conscience testifies that we have conducted ourselves in the world, and especially in our relations with you, in the holiness and sincerity that are from God. We have done so not according to worldly wisdom but according to God's grace.

2Co 6:3 We put no stumbling block in anyone's path, so that our ministry will not be discredited.

Paul, Timothy, and Silas—

1Th 2:1 You know, brothers, that our visit to you was not a failure.

The Christians at Rome—

Ro 6:17 But thanks be to God that, though you used to be slaves to sin, you wholeheartedly obeyed the form of teaching to which you were entrusted.

To Civil Law. *See Citizens.*

Filial. *See Children.*

See Blessings, Spiritual, Contingent Upon Obedience; Commandments and Statutes, Of God; Duty; Faithfulness; Law.

OBEISANCE The act of bowing low or of prostrating oneself in token of respect or submission (Ge 43:28; Ex 18:7; 2Sa 1:2). *See Worship, Attitudes in.*

OBIL [201] (*camel driver*). An Ishmaelite. Camel keeper for David (1Ch 27:30).

OBJECT TEACHING *See Instruction.*

OBLATION *See Offerings.*

OBLIGATION [673, 5466, 5929, 8966, 10419+10420, *4050, 4052*].

NIV+ OBLIGATE, OBLIGATED, OBLIGATES, OBLIGATIONS

A motive of obedience (Dt 4:32-40; 6-11; 26:16; 32:6; 1Sa 12:24; 1Ch 16:12; Ro 2:4; 2Co 5:15). Acknowledgment of (Ps 116:12-14,17). *See Duty.*

OBLIQUITY *See Depravity.*

OBOTH [95] (*fathers*). A camping place of Israel in the forty years' wandering (Nu 21:10-11; 33:43-44).

OBSEQUIOUSNESS *See Tact.*

OBSTETRICS (Eze 16:4). *See Midwives.*

OCCULTISM *See Sorcery.*

OCCUPATIONS AND PROFESSIONS

Artisan—a worker with any materials, as carpenter, smith, engraver, etc.—author; baker; barber; beggar; carpenter; clerk; coppersmith; counselor; cupbearer; doctor; diviner, dyer; farmer; fisherman; gatekeeper; herdsman; hunter; judge; launderer; lawyer; magician; mason; medium; musician; nurse; perfumer; physician; plowman; potter; preacher; priest; prophet; rabbi; recorder; robber; ruler; sailor; scribe; seer; servant; sheep-shearer; shepherd; silversmith; singer; slave; smith; soldier; sorcerer; spinner; steward; tanner; taskmaster; tax collector; teacher; tentmaker; tiller; town clerk; treasurer; watchman; weaver; witch; writer.

OCRAN, OCHRAN [6581] (*trouble*). An Asherite and the father of Pagiel who numbered Israel (Nu 1:13; 2:27; 10:26).

ODED [6389] (*restorer*).

1. A prophet in Samaria (2Ch 28:9).
2. Father of the prophet Azariah (2Ch 15:1).

ODOR [*3853*]. Pleasant or unpleasant smell (Ge 8:21; Lev 1:9-17; Jn 11:39). Also used figuratively (Ro 5:8).

OFFENSE [*6411, 7321, 7322, *4997, 4998*].

NIV+ OFFEND, OFFENDED, OFFENDER, OFFENDERS, OFFENSES, OFFENSIVE

Used in a variety of ways: Injury, hurt, damage, occasion of sin, stumbling block, infraction of the law, sin, transgression, state of being offended.

OFFERINGS [*852, 871, 2284, 2285, 2627, 2633, 2853, 4003, 4854, 4966, 5605, 5607, 5818, 5821, 6590, 6592, 7175, 7731, 7787, 7928, 7933, 8968, 9343, 9485, 9556, 10432, *1126, 3906, 4712, 4714, 5064*].

NIV+ OFFER, OFFERED, OFFERING, OFFERS

Holy (Lev 2:3; 6:17,25,27,29; 7:1,6; 10:12; Nu 18:9-10). Offered at door of the tabernacle (Lev 1:3; 3:2; 17:4,8-9), of the temple (1Ki 8:62; 12:27; 2Ch 7:12).

All animal sacrifices, must be eight days old or over (Lev 22:27), must be without blemish (Ex 12:5; 29:1; Lev 1:3,10; 22:18-25; Dt 15:21; 17:1; Eze 43:23; Mal 1:8,14; Heb 9:14; 1Pe 1:19), *See Bruise, Bruises, 2*, must be salted (Lev 2:13; Eze 43:24; Mk 9:49), accompanied with leaven (Lev 7:13; Am 4:5), without leaven (Ex 23:18; 34:25), eaten (1Sa 9:13). Ordinance relating to scapegoat (Lev 16:7-26). Atonement for sin made by. *See Atonement.*

Figurative:

(Ps 51:17; Jer 33:11; Ro 12:1; Php 4:18; Heb 13:15).

Animal Sacrifices:

A type of Christ (Ps 40:6-8, w Heb 10:1-14; Isa 53:11-12, w Lev 16:21; Jn 1:29; 1Co 5:7; 2Co 5:21; Eph 5:2; Heb 9:19-28; 10:1,11-12; 13:11-13; Rev 5:6).

Burnt:

(Lev 9:2). Its purpose was to make an atonement for sin (Lev 1:4; 7). Ordinances concerning (Ex 29:15-18; Lev 1; 5:7-13; 6:9-13; 17:8-9; 23:18,26-37; Nu 15:24-25; 19:9; 28:26-31; 29). Accompanied by other offerings (Nu 15:3-16). Skins of, belonged to priests (Lev 7:8). Offered daily, morning and evening (Ge 15:17; Ex 29:38-42; Lev 6:20;

Nu 28; 29:6; 1Ch 16:40; 2Ch 2:4; 13:11; Ezr 3:3; Eze 46:13-15). Music with (Nu 10:10).

Offered, by Noah (Ge 8:20), in idolatrous worship (Ex 32:6; 1Ki 18:26; 2Ki 10:25; Ac 14:13). For cleansing leprosy (Lev 14).

Daily:

Sacrificial (Ex 29:38-42; Lev 6:20; Nu 28:3-8; 29:6; 1Ki 18:29; 1Ch 16:40; 2Ch 2:4; 13:11; Ezr 3:3-6; 9:4-5; Ps 141:2; Eze 46:13-15; Da 9:21,27; 11:31).

Drink:

Libations of wine offered with the sacrifices (Ge 35:14; Ex 29:40-41; 30:9; Lev 23:13,18; Nu 6:17; 15:24; 28:5-15,24-31; 29:6-11,18-40; 2Ki 16:13; 1Ch 29:21; 2Ch 29:35; Ezr 7:17).

Fellowship:

Laws concerning (Ex 20:24; 24:5; Lev 3:6; 7:11-18; 9:3-4,18-22; 19:5; 23:10; Nu 6:14; 10:10). Offered, by the tribal leaders (Nu 7:17,23,29,35,41,47,53,59,65,71,77,83, 88), by Joshua (Jos 8:31), by David (2Sa 6:17; 24:25).

Offered in idolatrous worship (Ex 32:6). Offered by harlots (Pr 7:14).

Free Will:

(Lev 23:38; Nu 29:39; Dt 12:6; 2Ch 31:14; Ezr 3:5). Must be perfect (Lev 22:17-25). To be eaten, at tabernacle (Dt 12:17-18), by priests (Lev 7:16-17). With meat and drink offerings (Nu 15:1-16). Obligatory (Dt 16:10), when signified in a vow (Dt 23:23).

Guilt: Ordinances concerning (Lev 5; 6:1-7; 7:1-7; 14:10-22; 15:15,29-30; 19:21-22; Nu 6:12; Ezr 10:19). To be eaten by the priests (Lev 7:6-7; 14:13; Nu 18:9-10). Offered by idolaters (1Sa 6:3,8,17-18). *See below, Sin.*

Heave: *See below, Presentation or Wave.*

Human Sacrifices:

Forbidden (Lev 18:21; 20:2-5; Dt 12:31). Offered by Abraham (Ge 22:1-19; Heb 11:17-19), by Canaanites (Dt 12:31), Moabites (2Ki 3:27), Israelites (2Ki 16:3; 2Ch 28:3; 2Ki 23:10; Isa 57:5; Jer 7:31; 19:5; 32:35; Eze 16:20-21; 20:26,31; 23:37,39), by the Sepharvites to idols (2Ki 17:31). To demons (Ps 106:37-38), and to Baal (Jer 19:5-6).

Meat:

Ordinances concerning (Ex 29:40-41; 30:9; 40:29; Lev 2; 5:11-12; 6:14-23; 7:9-13,37; 9:17; 23:13,16-17; Nu 4:16; 5:15,18,25-26; 8:8; 15:3-16,24; 18:9; 28:5,9,12-13, 20-21,26-31; 29:3-4,14). To be eaten in the Holy Place (Lev 10:13; Nu 18:9-10). Offered with animal sacrifices (Nu 15:3-16). Not mixed with leaven (Lev 2:4,11; 6:14-18; 10:12-13; Nu 6:15,17). Storerooms for, in the temple (Ne 12:44; 13:5-6), provided for in the vision of Ezekiel (Eze 42:12).

Peace: *See above, Fellowship.*

Presentation or Wave:

Given to the priests' families as part of their share (Lev 10:14; Nu 5:9; 18:10-19,24). Consecrated by being elevated by the priest (Ex 29:27). Consisted of the right thigh or hindquarter (Ex 29:27-28; Lev 7:12-14,32,34; 10:15), spoils, including captives and other articles of war (Nu 31:29,41). When offered (Lev 7:12-14; Nu 6:20; 15:19-21). In certain instances this offering was brought to the tabernacle, or temple (Dt 12:6,11,17-18). To be offered on taking possession of the land of Canaan (Nu 15:18-21).

Sin:

Ordinances concerning (Ex 29:10-14, w Heb 13:11-13;

Lev 4; 5; 6:1-7,26-30; 9:1-21; 12:6-8; 14:19,22,31; 15:30; 23:19; Nu 6:10-11,14,16; 8:8,12; 15:27; 28:15,22-24,30; 29:5-6,11,16-38). Temporary (Da 11:31; Heb 9-10).

Special Sacrifices:

In consecration of the altar. *See Altar.* Of priests. *See Priest.* Of the temple. *See Temple, Solomon's.* For leprosy. *See Leprosy.* For defilement. *See Defilement.*

Thank:

Ordinances concerning (Lev 7:11-15; 22:29; Dt 12:11-12).

Trespass: *See above, Guilt.*

Vow:

(Lev 7:16-17; 22:17-25; Dt 23:21-23).

Wave:

Ordinances concerning (Ex 29:22,26-28; Lev 7:29-34; 8:25-29; 9:19-21; 10:14-15; 23:10-11,17,20; Nu 5:25; 6:19-20). Belonged to the priests (Ex 29:26-28; Lev 7:31, 34; 8:29; 9:21; 23:20; Nu 18:11,18). To be eaten (Lev 10:14-15; Nu 18:11,18-19,31).

Wood:

Fuel for the temple (Ne 10:34; 13:31).

Insufficiency of:

Heb 8:7 For if there had been nothing wrong with that first covenant, no place would have been sought for another. [8]But God found fault with the people and said:

"The time is coming, declares the Lord, when I will make a new covenant with the house of Israel and with the house of Judah. [9]It will not be like the covenant I made with their forefathers when I took them by the hand to lead them out of Egypt, because they did not remain faithful to my covenant, and I turned away from them, declares the Lord. [10]This is the covenant I will make with the house of Israel after that time, declares the Lord. I will put my laws in their minds and write them on their hearts. I will be their God, and they will be my people. [11]No longer will a man teach his neighbor, or a man his brother, saying, 'Know the Lord,' because they will all know me, from the least of them to the greatest. [12]For I will forgive their wickedness and will remember their sins no more."

[13]By calling this covenant "new," he has made the first one obsolete; and what is obsolete and aging will soon disappear.

Heb 9:1 Now the first covenant had regulations for worship and also an earthly sanctuary. [2]A tabernacle was set up. In its first room were the lampstand, the table and the consecrated bread; this was called the Holy Place. [3]Behind the second curtain was a room called the Most Holy Place, [4]which had the golden altar of incense and the gold-covered ark of the covenant. This ark contained the gold jar of manna, Aaron's staff that had budded, and the stone tablets of the covenant. [5]Above the ark were the cherubim of the Glory, overshadowing the atonement cover. But we cannot discuss these things in detail now.

[6]When everything had been arranged like this, the priests entered regularly into the outer room to carry on their ministry. [7]But only the high priest entered the inner room, and that only once a year, and never without blood, which he offered for himself and for the sins the people had committed in ignorance. [8]The Holy Spirit was showing by this that the way into the Most Holy Place had not yet been disclosed as long as the first tabernacle was still standing. [9]This is an illustration for the present time, indicating that the gifts and sacrifices being offered were not able to clear the conscience of the worshiper. [10]They are only a matter

of food and drink and various ceremonial washings—external regulations applying until the time of the new order.

[11]When Christ came as high priest of the good things that are already here, he went through the greater and more perfect tabernacle that is not man-made, that is to say, not a part of this creation. [12]He did not enter by means of the blood of goats and calves; but he entered the Most Holy Place once for all by his own blood, having obtained eternal redemption. [13]The blood of goats and bulls and the ashes of a heifer sprinkled on those who are ceremonially unclean sanctify them so that they are outwardly clean. [14]How much more, then, will the blood of Christ, who through the eternal Spirit offered himself unblemished to God, cleanse our consciences from acts that lead to death, so that we may serve the living God!

[15]For this reason Christ is the mediator of a new covenant, that those who are called may receive the promised eternal inheritance—now that he has died as a ransom to set them free from the sins committed under the first covenant.

Heb 10:1 The law is only a shadow of the good things that are coming—not the realities themselves. For this reason it can never, by the same sacrifices repeated endlessly year after year, make perfect those who draw near to worship. [2]If it could, would they not have stopped being offered? For the worshipers would have been cleansed once for all, and would no longer have felt guilty for their sins. [3]But those sacrifices are an annual reminder of sins, [4]because it is impossible for the blood of bulls and goats to take away sins.

[5]Therefore, when Christ came into the world, he said:

"Sacrifice and offering you did not desire, but a body you prepared for me; [6]with burnt offerings and sin offerings you were not pleased. [7]Then I said, 'Here I am—it is written about me in the scroll—I have come to do your will, O God.'"

[8]First he said, "Sacrifices and offerings, burnt offerings and sin offerings you did not desire, nor were you pleased with them" (although the law required them to be made). [9]Then he said, "Here I am, I have come to do your will." He sets aside the first to establish the second. [10]And by that will, we have been made holy through the sacrifice of the body of Jesus Christ once for all.

[11]Day after day every priest stands and performs his religious duties; again and again he offers the same sacrifices, which can never take away sins. [12]But when this priest had offered for all time one sacrifice for sins, he sat down at the right hand of God.

Heb 10:18 And where these have been forgiven, there is no longer any sacrifice for sin.

[19]Therefore, brothers, since we have confidence to enter the Most Holy Place by the blood of Jesus, [20]by a new and living way opened for us through the curtain, that is, his body,

Unavailing, when not accompanied by piety—

1Sa 15:22 But Samuel replied: "Does the LORD delight in burnt offerings and sacrifices as much as in obeying the voice of the LORD? To obey is better than sacrifice, and to heed is better than the fat of rams.

Ps 40:6 Sacrifice and offering you did not desire, but my ears you have pierced; burnt offerings and sin offerings you did not require.

Ps 50:8 I do not rebuke you for your sacrifices or your burnt offerings, which are ever before me. [9]I have no need of a bull from your stall or of goats from your pens, [10]for every animal of the forest is mine, and the cattle on a

thousand hills. [11]I know every bird in the mountains, and the creatures of the field are mine. [12]If I were hungry I would not tell you, for the world is mine, and all that is in it. [13]Do I eat the flesh of bulls or drink the blood of goats? [14]Sacrifice thank offerings to God, fulfill your vows to the Most High,

Ps 51:16 You do not delight in sacrifice, or I would bring it; you do not take pleasure in burnt offerings. [17]The sacrifices of God are a broken spirit; a broken and contrite heart, O God, you will not despise.

Pr 21:3 To do what is right and just is more acceptable to the LORD than sacrifice.

Pr 21:27 The sacrifice of the wicked is detestable—how much more so when brought with evil intent!

Isa 1:11 "The multitude of your sacrifices—what are they to me?" says the LORD. "I have more than enough of burnt offerings, of rams and the fat of fattened animals; I have no pleasure in the blood of bulls and lambs and goats. [12]When you come to appear before me, who has asked this of you, this trampling of my courts? [13]Stop bringing meaningless offerings! Your incense is detestable to me. New Moons, Sabbaths and convocations—I cannot bear your evil assemblies. [14]Your New Moon festivals and your appointed feasts my soul hates. They have become a burden to me; I am weary of bearing them.

Isa 66:3 But whoever sacrifices a bull is like one who kills a man, and whoever offers a lamb, like one who breaks a dog's neck; whoever makes a grain offering is like one who presents pig's blood, and whoever burns memorial incense, like one who worships an idol. They have chosen their own ways, and their souls delight in their abominations;

Jer 6:20 What do I care about incense from Sheba or sweet calamus from a distant land? Your burnt offerings are not acceptable; your sacrifices do not please me."

Jer 7:21 "'This is what the LORD Almighty, the God of Israel, says: Go ahead, add your burnt offerings to your other sacrifices and eat the meat yourselves! [22]For when I brought your forefathers out of Egypt and spoke to them, I did not just give them commands about burnt offerings and sacrifices, [23]but I gave them this command: Obey me, and I will be your God and you will be my people. Walk in all the ways I command you, that it may go well with you.

Jer 14:12 Although they fast, I will not listen to their cry; though they offer burnt offerings and grain offerings, I will not accept them. Instead, I will destroy them with the sword, famine and plague."

Hos 6:6 For I desire mercy, not sacrifice, and acknowledgment of God rather than burnt offerings.

Hos 8:13 They offer sacrifices given to me and they eat the meat, but the LORD is not pleased with them. Now he will remember their wickedness and punish their sins: They will return to Egypt.

Am 5:21 "I hate, I despise your religious feasts; I cannot stand your assemblies. [22]Even though you bring me burnt offerings and grain offerings, I will not accept them. Though you bring choice fellowship offerings, I will have no regard for them. [23]Away with the noise of your songs! I will not listen to the music of your harps. [24]But let justice roll on like a river, righteousness like a never-failing stream!

Mic 6:6 With what shall I come before the LORD and bow down before the exalted God? Shall I come before him with burnt offerings, with calves a year old? [7]Will the LORD be pleased with thousands of rams, with ten thousand rivers of oil? Shall I offer my firstborn for my transgression, the fruit of my body for the sin of my soul? ⁸He has showed you, O man, what is good. And what does the LORD require of you? To act justly and to love mercy and to walk humbly with your God. (+Mt 9:13; 12:7)

Mk 12:33 To love him with all your heart, with all your understanding and with all your strength, and to love your neighbor as yourself is more important than all burnt offerings and sacrifices."

OFFICER [*5592, 5853, 5893, 6036, 6247, 6269, 7068, 7212, 7224, 8042, 8097, 8569, 8853, 8957, 10061, 10716, *1672, 3489, 4485, 4551, 4812, 5130, 5677*].

NIV+ OFFICE, OFFICERS, OFFICIAL, OFFICIALS, OFFICIATE

Civil:
Chosen by the people (Dt 1:13-16), appointed by kings (2Sa 8:16-18; 20:23-26; 1Ki 4:1-19; 9:22; Ezr 7:25).
See Government; Judge; Rulers.

Ecclesiastical: *See Priest; Levites; Apostle; Elders; Deacon; Minister.*

OFFSCOURING Contemptuous word; NIV "scum" (La 3:45; 1Co 4:13).

OG [6384].

NIV+ OG'S

King of Bashan. A man of gigantic stature (Nu 21:33; Dt 3:11; Jos 12:4; 13:12). Defeated and slain by Moses (Nu 21:33-35; Dt 1:4; 3:1-7; 29:7; 31:4; Jos 2:10; 9:10; Ps 135:10-11; 136:18-20). Land of, given to Gad, Reuben, and Manasseh (Nu 32:33; Dt 3:8-17; 4:47-49; 29:7-8; Jos 12:4-6; 13:12,30-31; 1Ki 4:19; Ne 9:22; Ps 136:20-21).

OHAD [176]. Son of Simeon (Ge 46:10; Ex 6:15).

OHEL [186] (*[skin] tent*). Son of Zerubbabel (1Ch 3:20).

OHOLAH [188] (*she who has a tent*). In God's parable to Ezekiel (ch. 23), Oholah is a woman representing Samaria, who with her sister Oholibah (Jerusalem) was accused of being unfaithful to Yahweh. Imaginary characters, figurative of idolatry (Eze 23:4-5,36,44).

OHOLIAB [190] (*tent of [my] Father*). A craftsman of the tabernacle (Ex 31:6; 35:34; 36:1-2; 38:23).

OHOLIBAH [191] (*my tent is in her*). See Oholah.

OHOLIBAMAH [192] (*[my] tent is a high-place*).
1. One of Esau's three wives (Ge 36:2,18,25). Also called Judith the daughter of Beeri (Ge 26:34).
2. An Edomite chief (Ge 36:41; 1Ch 1:52), probably so named from the district of his possession.

OIL [2016, 3658, 5417, 9043, 10442, *230, 1778*].

NIV+ OILS

Sacred (Ex 30:23-25; 31:11; 35:8,15,28; 37:29; 39:38; Nu 4:16; 1Ch 9:30). Compounded by Bezalel (Ex 37:1, 29). Punishment for profaning (Ex 30:31-33). Used for idols (Eze 23:41). Illuminating, for tabernacle (Ex 25:6; 27:20; Lev 24:2-4). Of olives (Ex 25:6).
For domestic use (Mt 25:3). Used for food (Lev 2:4-5; 14:10,21; Dt 12:17; 1Ki 17:12-16; Job 29:6; Pr 21:17; Eze 16:13; Hos 2:5). For the head (Ps 23:5; 105:15; Lk 7:46). For anointing kings (1Sa 10:1; 16:1,13; 1Ki 1:39).
Tribute paid in (Hos 12:1). Commerce in (2Ki 4:1-7).
See Anointing; Ointment.

OIL TREE See *Plants of the Bible.*

OINTMENT [5350, 9043].

NIV+ OINTMENTS

(Job 41:31). Used in care of newborns (Eze 16:9).

OLD AGE [*1201, 2416, 2418, 2419, 2420, 2421, 3427, 3813, 6409, 8484, *1179*].

Wise (1Ki 12:6-8; 2Ch 10:6-8)—

Job 12:12 Is not wisdom found among the aged? Does not long life bring understanding?

Devout—

Lk 2:37 and then was a widow until she was eighty-four. She never left the temple but worshiped night and day, fasting and praying.

Exemplary, commanded—

Tit 2:2 Teach the older men to be temperate, worthy of respect, self-controlled, and sound in faith, in love and in endurance.

³Likewise, teach the older women to be reverent in the way they live, not to be slanderers or addicted to much wine, but to teach what is good.

Deference toward (Lev 19:32)—

Job 32:4 Now Elihu had waited before speaking to Job because they were older than he. ⁵But when he saw that the three men had nothing more to say, his anger was aroused. ⁶So Elihu son of Barakel the Buzite said: "I am young in years, and you are old; that is why I was fearful, not daring to tell you what I know. ⁷I thought, 'Age should speak; advanced years should teach wisdom.' ⁸But it is the spirit in a man, the breath of the Almighty, that gives him understanding. ⁹It is not only the old who are wise, not only the aged who understand what is right.

Righteous, is glorious—

Pr 16:31 Gray hair is a crown of splendor; it is attained by a righteous life.

Wasted, is bitter—

Ge 47:9 And Jacob said to Pharaoh, "The years of my pilgrimage are a hundred and thirty. My years have been few and difficult, and they do not equal the years of the pilgrimage of my fathers."

Ecc 6:3 A man may have a hundred children and live many years; yet no matter how long he lives, if he cannot enjoy his prosperity and does not receive proper burial, I say that a stillborn child is better off than he.

Ecc 6:6 even if he lives a thousand years twice over but fails to enjoy his prosperity. Do not all go to the same place?

Ecc 12:1 Remember your Creator in the days of your youth, before the days of trouble come and the years approach when you will say, "I find no pleasure in them"— ²before the sun and the light and the moon and the stars grow dark, and the clouds return after the rain; ³when the keepers of the house tremble, and the strong men stoop, when the grinders cease because they are few, and those looking through the windows grow dim; ⁴when the doors to the street are closed and the sound of grinding fades; when men rise up at the sound of birds, but all their songs grow faint; ⁵when men are afraid of heights and of dangers in the streets; when the almond tree blossoms and the grasshopper drags himself along and desire no longer is stirred. Then man goes to his eternal home and mourners go about the streets. ⁶Remember him—before the silver cord is severed, or the golden bowl is broken; before the pitcher is shattered at the spring, or the wheel broken at the well, ⁷and the dust returns to the ground it came from, and the spirit returns to God who gave it.

Promised to the righteous—

Ge 15:15 You, however, will go to your fathers in peace and be buried at a good old age.

Job 5:26 You will come to the grave in full vigor, like sheaves gathered in season. (+Ps 34:12-14; 91:14,16; Pr 3:1-2)

God's care in—

Isa 46:4 Even to your old age and gray hairs I am he, I am he who will sustain you. I have made you and I will carry you; I will sustain you and I will rescue you.

Psalmist prays not to be forsaken in—

Ps 71:9 Do not cast me away when I am old; do not forsake me when my strength is gone.

Ps 71:18 Even when I am old and gray, do not forsake me, O God, till I declare your power to the next generation, your might to all who are to come.

David enjoys—

1Ch 29:28 He died at a good old age, having enjoyed long life, wealth and honor. His son Solomon succeeded him as king.

Infirmities in—

2Sa 19:34 But Barzillai answered the king, "How many more years will I live, that I should go up to Jerusalem with the king? [35]I am now eighty years old. Can I tell the difference between what is good and what is not? Can your servant taste what he eats and drinks? Can I still hear the voices of men and women singers? Why should your servant be an added burden to my lord the king? [36]Your servant will cross over the Jordan with the king for a short distance, but why should the king reward me in this way? [37]Let your servant return, that I may die in my own town near the tomb of my father and mother. But here is your servant Kimham. Let him cross over with my lord the king. Do for him whatever pleases you."

Ps 90:10 The length of our days is seventy years—or eighty, if we have the strength; yet their span is but trouble and sorrow, for they quickly pass, and we fly away.

Vigor in—

Dt 34:7 Moses was a hundred and twenty years old when he died, yet his eyes were not weak nor his strength gone. (+Ps 92:12-13)

Ps 92:14 They will still bear fruit in old age, they will stay fresh and green,

Join in praise to the Lord—

Ps 148:12 young men and maidens, old men and children.
[13]Let them praise the name of the LORD, for his name alone is exalted; his splendor is above the earth and the heavens.

Paul, the aged—

Phm 9 yet I appeal to you on the basis of love. I then, as Paul—an old man and now also a prisoner of Christ Jesus—

See Longevity; Infirmity.

OLD GATE *See Jeshanah, 2.*

OLD TESTAMENT In Protestant Bibles, thirty-nine books from Genesis to Malachi: Five of law, twelve of history, five of poetry, five of major prophets, and twelve of minor prophets. In the Hebrew Bible, the same contents are organized into twenty-four books from Genesis to Chronicles: Five of law, eight of the prophets, and eleven of miscellaneous writings. All of these books were regarded by Israelites as Scripture, inspired and authoritative, before the first century A.D. (Mt 5:17-20; Lk 24:44; Jn

17:17; 2Ti 3:16). They appeared over a period of c. 1000 years. The authors of many of them are unknown.

OLIVE [1737, 2339, 3658, 4184, 7414, 9043, 10442, 66, 1777, 1778, 2814].
NIV+ OLIVES

A fruit tree. Branch of, brought by the dove to Noah's ark (Ge 8:11). Common to the land of Canaan (Ex 23:11; Dt 6:11; 8:8), Israelites commanded to cultivate in the land of promise (Dt 28:40). Branches of, used for booths (Ne 8:15). Produces blooms (Job 15:33). Precepts concerning gleaning the fruit of (Dt 24:20; Isa 17:6). Cherubim made of the wood of (1Ki 6:23,31-33). Fable of (Jdg 9:8).

Figurative:

Of prosperity (Ps 128:3). The wild, a figure of the Gentiles; the cultivated, of the Jews (Ro 11:17-21,24).

Symbolic: (Zec 4:2-12; Rev 11:4).

Fruit of:

Oil extracted from, used as illuminating oil in the tabernacle (Ex 39:37; Lev 24:2; Zec 4:12).
See Oil.

OLIVES, MOUNT OF [2339, 1777, 1779]. A ridge, c. one mile long, with four identifiable summits, E of Jerusalem, beyond the Valley of Jehoshaphat, through which flows the Kidron stream. Gethsemane, Bethphage, and Bethany are on its slopes (2Sa 15:30; Zec 14:4; Mt 21:1; 24:3; 26:30; Mk 11:1; 13:3; 14:26; Lk 19:29,37; 22:39; Jn 8:1; Ac 1:12).

OLIVET *See Olives, Mount of.*

OLYMPAS [3912]. A believer at Rome (Ro 16:15).

OMAR [223] (*speaker*). Son of Eliphaz, grandson of Esau (Ge 36:11,15; 1Ch 1:36).

OMEGA [6042]. Alpha and Omega, a title of Christ, meaning he is the beginning and end of all things (Rev 1:8,11; 21:6; 22:13). *See Jesus the Christ, Names of; Titles and Names.*

OMER [6685].
NIV+ OMERS

One-tenth part of an ephah. A dry measure containing, according to the Rabbis, two quarts, but according to Josephus, three and one-half quarts (Ex 16:16-18,36).

OMNIPOTENCE (*all power*). The attribute of God which describes his ability to do whatever he wills. He cannot do anything contrary to his nature as God, such as to ignore sin, to sin, or to do something absurd or self-contradictory. God is not controlled by his power, but has complete control over it; otherwise he would not be a free being. Although the word "omnipotence" is not found in the Bible, the Scriptures clearly teach the omnipotence of God (Job 42:2; Jer 32:17; Mt 19:26; Lk 1:37; Rev 19:6).

See God, Omnipotent; Jesus the Christ, Power of.

OMNIPRESENCE (*all presence*). The attribute of God by virtue of which he fills the universe in all its parts and is present everywhere at once. Not a part, but the whole of God is present in every place. The Bible teaches the omnipresence of God (Ps 139:7-12; Jer 23:23-24; Ac 17:27-28). This is true of all three members of the Trinity.

See God, Omnipresent.

OMNISCIENCE (*all knowing*). The attribute by which God perfectly and eternally knows all things which can be

known, past, present, and future. God's omniscience is clearly taught in Scripture (Ps 147:5; Pr 15:11; Isa 46:1).

See God, Knowledge of; Jesus the Christ, Omniscience of.

OMRI [6687] *(thrive, live long* ISBE).

NIV+ OMRI'S

1. King of Israel. Was commander of the army of Israel, and was proclaimed king by the army upon news of the assassination of King Elah (1Ki 16:16). Defeats his rival, Tibni, and establishes himself (1Ki 16:17-22). Surrendered cities to the king of Syria (1Ki 20:34). Wicked reign and death of (1Ki 16:23-28). Denounced by Micah (Mic 6:16).

2. Son of Beker, grandson of Benjamin (1Ch 7:8).

3. A descendant of Perez (1Ch 9:4).

4. Son of Michael, and ruler of tribe of Issachar in time of David (1Ch 27:18).

ON [227, 228] *(sun [god] city).*

1. Capital of lower Egypt (Ge 41:45; 46:20).

2. A leader of the Reubenites who rebelled against Moses (Nu 16:1).

ONAM [231] *(intense, strong).* A son of Shobal (Ge 36:23; 1Ch 1:40).

ONAN [232] *(powerful, intense).* Son of Judah. Slain for his refusal to raise seed to his brother (Ge 38:4,8-10; 46:12; Nu 26:19; 1Ch 2:3).

ONE AND ONLY [3666]. A title applied to Jesus by John (Jn 1:14,18; 3:16,18; 1Jn 4:9), and once in Hebrews (Heb 11:17). It emphasizes the unique relationship of Jesus to God the Father. In ancient mss of Jn 1:18, Jesus is called God the One and Only, a clear reference to his deity.

ONE ANOTHER Responsibilities of fellow believers to (1Pe 4:7-10). All believers members of (Ro 12:5; Eph 4:25).

Commanded to:

Admonish (Ro 15:14; Col 3:16, w 2Th 3:15). Assemble together with (Heb 10:24). Bear burdens of (Gal 6:2). Comfort (1Th 4:18; 5:11, w 14). Confess faults to (Jas 5:16). Consider above self (Heb 10:24). Be courteous (1Pe 3:8). Edify (Ro 14:18; 1Th 5:11). Encourage (Heb 10:24). Equality with (Ro 12:16; 15:5,7; 1Co 11:33; 12:25; Php 2:3). Exhort daily (Heb 3:13). Have fellowship with (1Jn 1:7). Forgive (Eph 4:32; Col 3:13). Do good to (1Th 5:15). Be hospitable to (1Pe 4:9), in greeting (Ro 16:16; 1Co 16:20; 2Co 13:12; 1Pe 5:5). Be kind to (Eph 4:32). Love (Jn 13:34-35; 15:12,17; Ro 12:10; 13:8; 1Co 12:25; Gal 5:13; Eph 4:2,32; 1Th 3:12; 4:9; 1Pe 1:22; 2:17; 3:8; 1Jn 3:11,23; 4:7,11-12; 2Jn 5). Minister to (1Pe 4:10). Be patient with (Eph 4:2; Col 3:13). Be at peace with (Mk 9:50; 1Th 5:13). Pray for (Jas 5:16). Prefer (Ro 12:10; Php 2:3; 1Ti 5:21). Provoke to love and good works (Heb 10:24). Serve (Gal 5:13; 1Pe 4:10), by washing feet of (Jn 13:14). Be subject to (1Pe 5:5), husband and wife, each to be subject to (Eph 5:21). Teach (Col 3:16). Wait for (1Co 11:33).

Not to: Deceive (1Co 7:5), devour and consume (Gal 5:15), do evil to (1Th 5:5), envy (Gal 5:26), grudge (Jas 5:9), judge (Ro 14:13), lie to (Lev 19:11; Col 3:9), owe anything to (Ro 13:8), provoke (Gal 5:26), speak evil of (Jas 4:11).

Love of, exemplified (2Th 1:3).

ONE GOD (Dt 4:35; 6:4; 32:39; 2Sa 7:22; 1Ch 17:20; Ps 83:18; 86:10; Isa 43:10; 44:6; 45:18; Mk 12:29; 1Co 8:4; Eph 4:6; 1Ti 2:5; 1Jn 5:7). That God is one (Dt 6:4) does not deny the doctrine of the Trinity, for the same word is used of husband and wife as "one flesh" (Ge 2:24).

ONESIMUS [3946] *(useful).* Runaway slave of Philemon of Colosse; converted through Paul, who wrote the letter to Philemon in his behalf (Col 4:9; Phm).

See Philemon, Epistle to.

ONESIPHORUS [3947] *(one bringing usefulness).* A Christian of Ephesus (2Ti 1:16-17; 4:19).

ONION [1294].

NIV+ ONIONS

Enjoyed by Israel in Egypt (Nu 11:5).

ONLY-BEGOTTEN *See One and Only.*

ONO [229] *(strong).* Town in Benjamin, c. six miles SE of Joppa (1Ch 8:12; Ne 6:2; 11:35).

ONYCHA [8829]. A component of the sacred perfume, made from the shells of a species of mussel, possessing an odor (Ex 30:34).

ONYX [8732]. Exported from Havilah (Ge 2:12). Contributed by Israelites for the priests' garments (Ex 25:7; 35:9). Used in the breastplate (Ex 28:9-12,20; 39:6,13). Used in building the temple (1Ch 29:2). Precious stone (Job 28:16; Eze 28:13). Seen in the foundations of the city of the New Jerusalem in John's apocalyptic vision (Rev 21:20).

See Minerals of the Bible, 1; Stones.

OPHEL [6755] *(mound, hill).* A gate in the wall of the city and the temple (2Ch 27:3; 33:14; Ne 3:26-27).

OPHIR [234].

1. Son of Joktan (Ge 10:29; 1Ch 1:23).

2. A country celebrated for its gold and other valuable merchandise. Products of, used by Solomon and Hiram (1Ki 9:28; 10:11; 2Ch 8:18; 9:10). Jehoshaphat sends ships to, which are wrecked (1Ki 22:48). Gold of, proverbial for its fineness (1Ch 29:4; Job 22:24; 28:16; Ps 45:9; Isa 13:12).

OPHNI [6756]. A town of the Benjamites (Jos 18:24).

OPHRAH [6763, 6764] *(young gazelle).*

NIV+ BETH OPHRAH

1. A city in Benjamin (Jos 18:23; 1Sa 13:17). Possibly identical with Ephron (2Ch 13:19) and Ephraim (Jn 11:54).

2. A city in Manasseh, home of Gideon (Jdg 6:11,24; 8:27,32; 9:5).

3. Son of Meonothai and descendant of Judah through Kenaz and Othniel (1Ch 4:14).

OPINION [1819, 4213, 6191, *1506*].

NIV+ OPINIONS

Public:

Kings influenced by. *See Kings.* Jesus inquires about (Mt 16:13; Lk 9:18). Feared by Nicodemus (Jn 3:2), Joseph of Arimathea (Jn 19:38), the parents of the man who was born blind (Jn 9:21-22), rulers who believed in Jesus but feared the Pharisees (Jn 12:42-43), chief priests who feared to answer the questions of Jesus (Mt 21:26; Mk

11:18,32; 12:12), and to further persecute the disciples (Ac 4:21; 5:26).

Concessions to:

By Paul in circumcising Timothy (Ac 16:3). James and the Christian elders who required Paul to observe certain rites (Ac 21:18-26). Disciples who urged circumcision (Gal 6:12). Peter and Barnabas with others (Gal 2:11-14).

See Prudence.

Corrupt Yielding to:

By Herod, in the case of John the Baptist (Mk 6:26), of Peter (Ac 12:3), by Peter, concerning Jesus (Mt 26:69-75), by Pilate (Mt 27:23-27; Mk 15:15; Lk 23:13-25; Jn 18:38-39; 19:4-16), by Felix and Festus, concerning Paul (Ac 24:27; 25:9).

OPPORTUNITY [4595, *177, 929, 2320, 2321, 2323, 2789, 5536*].

NIV+ OPPORTUNE

Providential (1Co 16:9; 2Co 2:12). Neglected (Lk 12:47). Spurned (Pr 1:24-25; Mt 23:34-38; Lk 14:16-24).

Lost (Nu 14:40-43; Pr 1:28)—

Jer 8:20 "The harvest is past, the summer has ended, and we are not saved."

Hos 5:6 When they go with their flocks and herds to seek the Lord, they will not find him; he has withdrawn himself from them. (+Mt 24:50-51; 25:1-10,24-28; Lk 19:20-24; 13:25-28)

Terrible consequences of neglecting—

Eze 3:19 But if you do warn the wicked man and he does not turn from his wickedness or from his evil ways, he will die for his sin; but you will have saved yourself. (+Mt 25:3-13,24-30,41-46)

Terrible consequences of spurning—

Pr 1:24 But since you rejected me when I called and no one gave heed when I stretched out my hand, [25]since you ignored all my advice and would not accept my rebuke, [26]I in turn will laugh at your disaster; I will mock when calamity overtakes you— [27]when calamity overtakes you like a storm, when disaster sweeps over you like a whirlwind, when distress and trouble overwhelm you.

[28]"Then they will call to me but I will not answer; they will look for me but will not find me. [29]Since they hated knowledge and did not choose to fear the Lord, [30]since they would not accept my advice and spurned my rebuke, [31]they will eat the fruit of their ways and be filled with the fruit of their schemes. [32]For the waywardness of the simple will kill them, and the complacency of fools will destroy them;

Mt 10:14 If anyone will not welcome you or listen to your words, shake the dust off your feet when you leave that home or town. [15]I tell you the truth, it will be more bearable for Sodom and Gomorrah on the day of judgment than for that town.

Mt 11:20 Then Jesus began to denounce the cities in which most of his miracles had been performed, because they did not repent. [21]"Woe to you, Korazin! Woe to you, Bethsaida! If the miracles that were performed in you had been performed in Tyre and Sidon, they would have repented long ago in sackcloth and ashes. [22]But I tell you, it will be more bearable for Tyre and Sidon on the day of judgment than for you. [23]And you, Capernaum, will you be lifted up to the skies? No, you will go down to the depths. If the miracles that were performed in you had been performed in Sodom, it would have remained to this day.

[24]But I tell you that it will be more bearable for Sodom on the day of judgment than for you."

The measure of responsibility (Pr 1:24-30; Jer 8:20; Eze 3:19; 33:1-17; Hos 5:6; Mt 10:14-15; 11:20-24)—

Mt 23:34 Therefore I am sending you prophets and wise men and teachers. Some of them you will kill and crucify; others you will flog in your synagogues and pursue from town to town. [35]And so upon you will come all the righteous blood that has been shed on earth, from the blood of righteous Abel to the blood of Zechariah son of Berekiah, whom you murdered between the temple and the altar. [36]I tell you the truth, all this will come upon this generation.

[37]"O Jerusalem, Jerusalem, you who kill the prophets and stone those sent to you, how often I have longed to gather your children together, as a hen gathers her chicks under her wings, but you were not willing. [38]Look, your house is left to you desolate.

Mt 25:1 "At that time the kingdom of heaven will be like ten virgins who took their lamps and went out to meet the bridegroom. [2]Five of them were foolish and five were wise. [3]The foolish ones took their lamps but did not take any oil with them. [4]The wise, however, took oil in jars along with their lamps. [5]The bridegroom was a long time in coming, and they all became drowsy and fell asleep.

[6]"At midnight the cry rang out: 'Here's the bridegroom! Come out to meet him!'

[7]"Then all the virgins woke up and trimmed their lamps. [8]The foolish ones said to the wise, 'Give us some of your oil; our lamps are going out.'

[9]"No,' they replied, 'there may not be enough for both us and you. Instead, go to those who sell oil and buy some for yourselves.'

[10]"But while they were on their way to buy the oil, the bridegroom arrived. The virgins who were ready went in with him to the wedding banquet. And the door was shut.

[11]"Later the others also came. 'Sir! Sir!' they said. 'Open the door for us!'

[12]"But he replied, 'I tell you the truth, I don't know you.'

[13]"Therefore keep watch, because you do not know the day or the hour.

[14]"Again, it will be like a man going on a journey, who called his servants and entrusted his property to them. [15]To one he gave five talents of money, to another two talents, and to another one talent, each according to his ability. Then he went on his journey. [16]The man who had received the five talents went at once and put his money to work and gained five more. [17]So also, the one with the two talents gained two more. [18]But the man who had received the one talent went off, dug a hole in the ground and hid his master's money.

[19]"After a long time the master of those servants returned and settled accounts with them. [20]The man who had received the five talents brought the other five. 'Master,' he said, 'you entrusted me with five talents. See, I have gained five more.'

[21]"His master replied, 'Well done, good and faithful servant! You have been faithful with a few things; I will put you in charge of many things. Come and share your master's happiness!'

[22]"The man with the two talents also came. 'Master,' he said, 'you entrusted me with two talents; see, I have gained two more.'

[23]"His master replied, 'Well done, good and faithful servant! You have been faithful with a few things; I will put you in charge of many things. Come and share your master's happiness!'

²⁴"Then the man who had received the one talent came. 'Master,' he said, 'I knew that you are a hard man, harvesting where you have not sown and gathering where you have not scattered seed. ²⁵So I was afraid and went out and hid your talent in the ground. See, here is what belongs to you.'

²⁶"His master replied, 'You wicked, lazy servant! So you knew that I harvest where I have not sown and gather where I have not scattered seed? ²⁷Well then, you should have put my money on deposit with the bankers, so that when I returned I would have received it back with interest.

²⁸"'Take the talent from him and give it to the one who has the ten talents. ²⁹For everyone who has will be given more, and he will have an abundance. Whoever does not have, even what he has will be taken from him. ³⁰And throw that worthless servant outside, into the darkness, where there will be weeping and gnashing of teeth.'

³¹"When the Son of Man comes in his glory, and all the angels with him, he will sit on his throne in heavenly glory. ³²All the nations will be gathered before him, and he will separate the people one from another as a shepherd separates the sheep from the goats. ³³He will put the sheep on his right and the goats on his left.

³⁴"Then the King will say to those on his right, 'Come, you who are blessed by my Father; take your inheritance, the kingdom prepared for you since the creation of the world. ³⁵For I was hungry and you gave me something to eat, I was thirsty and you gave me something to drink, I was a stranger and you invited me in, ³⁶I needed clothes and you clothed me, I was sick and you looked after me, I was in prison and you came to visit me.'

³⁷"Then the righteous will answer him, 'Lord, when did we see you hungry and feed you, or thirsty and give you something to drink? ³⁸When did we see you a stranger and invite you in, or needing clothes and clothe you? ³⁹When did we see you sick or in prison and go to visit you?'

⁴⁰"The King will reply, 'I tell you the truth, whatever you did for one of the least of these brothers of mine, you did for me.'

⁴¹"Then he will say to those on his left, 'Depart from me, you who are cursed, into the eternal fire prepared for the devil and his angels. ⁴²For I was hungry and you gave me nothing to eat, I was thirsty and you gave me nothing to drink, ⁴³I was a stranger and you did not invite me in, I needed clothes and you did not clothe me, I was sick and in prison and you did not look after me.'

⁴⁴"They also will answer, 'Lord, when did we see you hungry or thirsty or a stranger or needing clothes or sick or in prison, and did not help you?'

⁴⁵"He will reply, 'I tell you the truth, whatever you did not do for one of the least of these, you did not do for me.'

⁴⁶"Then they will go away to eternal punishment, but the righteous to eternal life." (+Lk 19:20-24)

Lk 12:47 That servant who knows his master's will and does not get ready or does not do what his master wants will be beaten with many blows.

Lk 13:25 Once the owner of the house gets up and closes the door, you will stand outside knocking and pleading, 'Sir, open the door for us.'

"But he will answer, 'I don't know you or where you come from.'

²⁶"Then you will say, 'We ate and drank with you, and you taught in our streets.'

²⁷"But he will reply, 'I don't know you or where you come from. Away from me, all you evildoers!'

²⁸"There will be weeping there, and gnashing of teeth, when you see Abraham, Isaac and Jacob and all the prophets in the kingdom of God, but you yourselves thrown out.

Lk 14:16 Jesus replied: "A certain man was preparing a great banquet and invited many guests. ¹⁷At the time of the banquet he sent his servant to tell those who had been invited, 'Come, for everything is now ready.'

¹⁸"But they all alike began to make excuses. The first said, 'I have just bought a field, and I must go and see it. Please excuse me.'

¹⁹"Another said, 'I have just bought five yoke of oxen, and I'm on my way to try them out. Please excuse me.'

²⁰"Still another said, 'I just got married, so I can't come.'

²¹"The servant came back and reported this to his master. Then the owner of the house became angry and ordered his servant, 'Go out quickly into the streets and alleys of the town and bring in the poor, the crippled, the blind and the lame.'

²²"'Sir,' the servant said, 'what you ordered has been done, but there is still room.'

²³"Then the master told his servant, 'Go out to the roads and country lanes and make them come in, so that my house will be full. ²⁴I tell you, not one of those men who were invited will get a taste of my banquet.'"

See Judgment, According to Opportunity and Works; Responsibility.

OPPRESSION [*1916, 3561, 4315, 4316, 5601, 6662, 6700, 6705, 6714, 6808, 6935, 6943, 6945, 7439, 7674, 7675, 8368, 8719].

NIV+ OPPRESS, OPPRESSED, OPPRESSES, OPPRESSING, OPPRESSIVE, OPPRESSOR, OPPRESSORS

Seeming hopelessness under (Ecc 4:1).

God:

A refuge from—

Ps 9:9 The LORD is a refuge for the oppressed, a stronghold in times of trouble. (+Ps 12:5)

Promises aid against—

Ps 12:5 "Because of the oppression of the weak and the groaning of the needy, I will now arise," says the LORD. "I will protect them from those who malign them." (+Ps 72:4,14)

Isa 58:6 "Is not this the kind of fasting I have chosen: to loose the chains of injustice and untie the cords of the yoke, to set the oppressed free and break every yoke? (+Jer 50:34)

God will judge—

Ps 10:17 You hear, O LORD, the desire of the afflicted; you encourage them, and you listen to their cry, ¹⁸defending the fatherless and the oppressed, in order that man, who is of the earth, may terrify no more. (+Ps 103:6; Ecc 5:8; Isa 10)

Jer 21:12 O house of David, this is what the LORD says: "'Administer justice every morning; rescue from the hand of his oppressor the one who has been robbed, or my wrath will break out and burn like fire because of the evil you have done—burn with no one to quench it. (+Jer 22:17; Eze 22:7; Am 4:1)

Mic 2:2 They covet fields and seize them, and houses, and take them. They defraud a man of his home, a fellowman of his inheritance.

Hab 2:5 indeed, wine betrays him; he is arrogant and never at rest. Because he is as greedy as the grave and like death is never satisfied, he gathers to himself all the nations and takes captive all the peoples.

⁶"Will not all of them taunt him with ridicule and scorn, saying, "'Woe to him who piles up stolen goods and makes himself wealthy by extortion! How long must this go on?' ⁷Will not your debtors suddenly arise? Will they not wake up and make you tremble? Then you will become their victim. ⁸Because you have plundered many nations, the peoples who are left will plunder you. For you have shed man's blood; you have destroyed lands and cities and everyone in them.

⁹"Woe to him who builds his realm by unjust gain to set his nest on high, to escape the clutches of ruin! ¹⁰You have plotted the ruin of many peoples, shaming your own house and forfeiting your life. ¹¹The stones of the wall will cry out, and the beams of the woodwork will echo it. (+Mal 3:5; Jas 5:4)

God will reward those who fight against—

Isa 33:15 He who walks righteously and speaks what is right, who rejects gain from extortion and keeps his hand from accepting bribes, who stops his ears against plots of murder and shuts his eyes against contemplating evil— ¹⁶this is the man who will dwell on the heights, whose refuge will be the mountain fortress. His bread will be supplied, and water will not fail him.

National: God judges (Ac 7:7), relieved (Ex 3:9; 12:30-39; Dt 26:7-8; Jdg 2:14; 6-8; 10-11; 2Ki 13; Isa 52:4).

Prayer for deliverance from (Ps 17:8-9; 44:24)—

Ps 74:21 Do not let the oppressed retreat in disgrace; may the poor and needy praise your name. (+Ps 119:121)

Ps 119:134 Redeem me from the oppression of men, that I may obey your precepts. (+Isa 38:14)

Oppressors:

Punished—

Job 27:13 "Here is the fate God allots to the wicked, the heritage a ruthless man receives from the Almighty: ¹⁴However many his children, their fate is the sword; his offspring will never have enough to eat. ¹⁵The plague will bury those who survive him, and their widows will not weep for them. ¹⁶Though he heaps up silver like dust and clothes like piles of clay, ¹⁷what he lays up the righteous will wear, and the innocent will divide his silver. ¹⁸The house he builds is like a moth's cocoon, like a hut made by a watchman. ¹⁹He lies down wealthy, but will do so no more; when he opens his eyes, all is gone. ²⁰Terrors overtake him like a flood; a tempest snatches him away in the night. ²¹The east wind carries him off, and he is gone; it sweeps him out of his place. ²²It hurls itself against him without mercy as he flees headlong from its power. ²³It claps its hands in derision and hisses him out of his place. (+Ps 72:4; 103:6; Isa 10)

Oppression forbidden—

Ex 22:21 "Do not mistreat an alien or oppress him, for you were aliens in Egypt.

²²"Do not take advantage of a widow or an orphan. ²³If you do and they cry out to me, I will certainly hear their cry. ²⁴My anger will be aroused, and I will kill you with the sword; your wives will become widows and your children fatherless.

Dt 23:15 If a slave has taken refuge with you, do not hand him over to his master. ¹⁶Let him live among you wherever he likes and in whatever town he chooses. Do not oppress him.

Dt 24:14 Do not take advantage of a hired man who is poor and needy, whether he is a brother Israelite or an alien living in one of your towns. ¹⁵Pay him his wages each day before sunset, because he is poor and is counting on it. Otherwise he may cry to the LORD against you, and you will be guilty of sin.

Pr 22:22 Do not exploit the poor because they are poor and do not crush the needy in court,

Zec 7:10 Do not oppress the widow or the fatherless, the alien or the poor. In your hearts do not think evil of each other.'

Oppression warned against—

Ps 62:10 Do not trust in extortion or take pride in stolen goods; though your riches increase, do not set your heart on them.

Eze 45:9 "'This is what the Sovereign LORD says: You have gone far enough, O princes of Israel! Give up your violence and oppression and do what is just and right. Stop dispossessing my people, declares the Sovereign LORD. (+Jas 2:6)

Command to relieve the oppressed—

Isa 1:17 learn to do right! Seek justice, encourage the oppressed. Defend the cause of the fatherless, plead the case of the widow.

Proverbs concerning—

Pr 3:31 Do not envy a violent man or choose any of his ways,

Pr 14:31 He who oppresses the poor shows contempt for their Maker, but whoever is kind to the needy honors God. (+Pr 22:16,22)

Pr 28:3 A ruler who oppresses the poor is like a driving rain that leaves no crops.

Pr 30:14 those whose teeth are swords and whose jaws are set with knives to devour the poor from the earth, the needy from among mankind.

Ecc 4:1 Again I looked and saw all the oppression that was taking place under the sun: I saw the tears of the oppressed—and they have no comforter; power was on the side of their oppressors—and they have no comforter.

Ecc 5:8 If you see the poor oppressed in a district, and justice and rights denied, do not be surprised at such things; for one official is eyed by a higher one, and over them both are others higher still.

Ecc 7:7 Extortion turns a wise man into a fool, and a bribe corrupts the heart.

Instances of:

Hagar, by Sarah (Ge 16:6). Jacob, by Laban (Ge 31:39). Israelites, by Egyptians (Ex 1:10-22; 5), by Assyrians (Isa 52:4). Rehoboam resolves to oppress the Israelites (1Ki 12:14).

Strangers and the poor and needy, by Israelites—

Eze 22:29 The people of the land practice extortion and commit robbery; they oppress the poor and needy and mistreat the alien, denying them justice.

Am 5:11 You trample on the poor and force him to give you grain. Therefore, though you have built stone mansions, you will not live in them; though you have planted lush vineyards, you will not drink their wine. ¹²For I know how many are your offenses and how great your sins. You oppress the righteous and take bribes and you deprive the poor of justice in the courts.

Am 8:4 Hear this, you who trample the needy and do away with the poor of the land, ⁵saying, "When will the New Moon be over that we may sell grain, and the Sabbath be ended that we may market wheat?"—skimping the measure, boosting the price and cheating with dishonest scales, ⁶buying the poor with silver and the needy for a pair of sandals, selling even the sweepings with the wheat.

Of people, by the scribes and Pharisees—

Mt 23:2 "The teachers of the law and the Pharisees sit in Moses' seat. ³So you must obey them and do everything they tell you. But do not do what they do, for they do not practice what they preach. ⁴They tie up heavy loads and put them on men's shoulders, but they themselves are not willing to lift a finger to move them.

ORACLE [5363, 5442, 5536, 7877] (speak).

NIV+ ORACLES

Utterance of prophecy. KJV "burden," (Isa 14:28; 15:1; Eze 12:10; Na 1:1) or "parable" (Nu 23:7,18; 24:3,4,15,16, 20,21,23) or "prophecy" (Pr 30:1; 31:1).

ORACLES [5363].

NIV+ ORACLE

NIV "words" of God. Scriptures called (Ac 7:38; Ro 3:2; Heb 5:12; 1Pe 4:11).

ORATOR A public speaker.

Instances of: Judah (Ge 44:18-34). Aaron (Ex 4:14-16). Moses (Dt 1-4:40). Jonah (Jnh 3:4-10). Peter (Ac 2:14-40; 3:12-26; 4:8-12; 10:34-48; 11:4-17). Stephen (Ac 7:2-60). Paul and Barnabas (Ac 14:14-17). Paul (Ac 13:16-41; 17:22-31; 22:1-21; 24:10-21; 26:1-29; 27:21-25). James (Ac 15:13-21). Apollos (Ac 18:24-28). Herod (Ac 12:21). The city clerk (Ac 19:35-41). Tertullus (Ac 24:1).

ORDAIN, ORDINATION [3338+4848, 3569, 3670, 3922, 4854, 5989, 6913, 7422, 2936].

NIV+ ORDAINED

An act of conferring a sacred office upon someone, as: Deacons (Ac 6:6), missionaries (Ac 13:3), elders (Ac 14:23). OT priests were ordained to office (Ex 28:41; 29:9).

Instances of:

Priests (Ex 29:1-9,19-35; 40:12-16; Lev 8:6-35; Heb 7:21). Apostles (Mk 3:14). Ministers: the seven (Ac 6:5-6), Paul and Barnabas (Ac 13:2-3), Timothy (1Ti 4:14).

ORDINANCE [2976, 2978, 5477].

NIV+ ORDINANCES

A decree (Ex 12:14,24,43; 13:10; 15:25; Nu 9:14; 10:8; 15:15; 18:8; Isa 24:5; Mal 4:4; Ro 13:2; 1Pe 2:13).

Insufficiency, in salvation—

Isa 1:10 Hear the word of the LORD, you rulers of Sodom; listen to the law of our God, you people of Gomorrah! ¹¹"The multitude of your sacrifices—what are they to me?" says the LORD. "I have more than enough of burnt offerings, of rams and the fat of fattened animals; I have no pleasure in the blood of bulls and lambs and goats. ¹²When you come to appear before me, who has asked this of you, this trampling of my courts? ¹³Stop bringing meaningless offerings! Your incense is detestable to me. New Moons, Sabbaths and convocations—I cannot bear your evil assemblies. ¹⁴Your New Moon festivals and your appointed feasts my soul hates. They have become a burden to me; I am weary of bearing them. ¹⁵When you spread out your hands in prayer, I will hide my eyes from you; even if you offer many prayers, I will not listen. Your hands are full of blood; ¹⁶wash and make yourselves clean. Take your evil deeds out of my sight! Stop doing wrong, ¹⁷learn to do right! Seek justice, encourage the oppressed. Defend the cause of the fatherless, plead the case of the widow.

Gal 5:6 For in Christ Jesus neither circumcision nor uncir-

cumcision has any value. The only thing that counts is faith expressing itself through love.

Gal 6:15 Neither circumcision nor uncircumcision means anything; what counts is a new creation.

Eph 2:15 by abolishing in his flesh the law with its commandments and regulations. His purpose was to create in himself one new man out of the two, thus making peace,

Col 2:14 having canceled the written code, with its regulations, that was against us and that stood opposed to us; he took it away, nailing it to the cross.

Col 2:20 Since you died with Christ to the basic principles of this world, why, as though you still belonged to it, do you submit to its rules: ²¹"Do not handle! Do not taste! Do not touch!"? ²²These are all destined to perish with use, because they are based on human commands and teachings. ²³Such regulations indeed have an appearance of wisdom, with their self-imposed worship, their false humility and their harsh treatment of the body, but they lack any value in restraining sensual indulgence.

Heb 9:1 Now the first covenant had regulations for worship and also an earthly sanctuary.

Heb 9:8 The Holy Spirit was showing by this that the way into the Most Holy Place had not yet been disclosed as long as the first tabernacle was still standing. ⁹This is an illustration for the present time, indicating that the gifts and sacrifices being offered were not able to clear the conscience of the worshiper. ¹⁰They are only a matter of food and drink and various ceremonial washings—external regulations applying until the time of the new order.

See Form; Formalism.

OREB [6855]·(raven).

1. A prince of Midian, overcome by Gideon and killed by the Ephraimites (Jdg 7:25; 8:3; Ps 83:11).

2. A rock E of the Jordan, where Oreb was slain (Jdg 7:25; Isa 10:26).

OREN [816] (fir or cedar BDB IDB; laurel KB). Son of Jerahmeel (1Ch 2:25).

ORGAN See Flute; Music, Instruments of.

ORION [4068]. The constellation of (Job 9:9; 38:31; Isa 13:10; Am 5:8).

ORNAN See Araunah.

ORONTES The chief river of Syria, c. 400 miles long, rises in Anti-Lebanon range and flows N for most of its course.

ORPAH [6905] (neck, the girl with a full mane[?], or rain cloud). Daughter-in-law of Naomi (Ru 1:4,14).

ORPHAN [3846, 4003].

NIV+ ORPHAN'S, ORPHANS

To be visited—

Jas 1:27 Religion that God our Father accepts as pure and faultless is this: to look after orphans and widows in their distress and to keep oneself from being polluted by the world.

Beneficent provision for—

Dt 14:28 At the end of every three years, bring all the tithes of that year's produce and store it in your towns, ²⁹so that the Levites (who have no allotment or inheritance of their own) and the aliens, the fatherless and the widows who live in your towns may come and eat and be satisfied, and so that the LORD your God may bless you in all the work of your hands. (+Dt 16:10)

Dt 16:11 And rejoice before the LORD your God at the place he will choose as a dwelling for his Name—you, your sons and daughters, your menservants and maidservants, the Levites in your towns, and the aliens, the fatherless and the widows living among you.

Dt 16:14 Be joyful at your Feast—you, your sons and daughters, your menservants and maidservants, and the Levites, the aliens, the fatherless and the widows who live in your towns. (+Dt 24:19-22)

Dt 26:12 When you have finished setting aside a tenth of all your produce in the third year, the year of the tithe, you shall give it to the Levite, the alien, the fatherless and the widow, so that they may eat in your towns and be satisfied. [13]Then say to the LORD your God: "I have removed from my house the sacred portion and have given it to the Levite, the alien, the fatherless and the widow, according to all you commanded. I have not turned aside from your commands nor have I forgotten any of them.

Kindness toward—

Job 29:12 because I rescued the poor who cried for help, and the fatherless who had none to assist him. [13]The man who was dying blessed me; I made the widow's heart sing.

Job 31:16 "If I have denied the desires of the poor or let the eyes of the widow grow weary, [17]if I have kept my bread to myself, not sharing it with the fatherless— [18]but from my youth I reared him as would a father, and from my birth I guided the widow—

Job 31:21 if I have raised my hand against the fatherless, knowing that I had influence in court,

God the friend of—

Ex 22:22 "Do not take advantage of a widow or an orphan. [23]If you do and they cry out to me, I will certainly hear their cry. [24]My anger will be aroused, and I will kill you with the sword; your wives will become widows and your children fatherless.

Dt 10:18 He defends the cause of the fatherless and the widow, and loves the alien, giving him food and clothing.

Ps 10:14 But you, O God, do see trouble and grief; you consider it to take it in hand. The victim commits himself to you; you are the helper of the fatherless.

Ps 10:17 You hear, O LORD, the desire of the afflicted; you encourage them, and you listen to their cry, [18]defending the fatherless and the oppressed, in order that man, who is of the earth, may terrify no more.

Ps 27:10 Though my father and mother forsake me, the LORD will receive me.

Ps 68:5 A father to the fatherless, a defender of widows, is God in his holy dwelling.

Ps 146:9 The LORD watches over the alien and sustains the fatherless and the widow, but he frustrates the ways of the wicked.

Pr 23:10 Do not move an ancient boundary stone or encroach on the fields of the fatherless, (+Pr 23:11)

Jer 49:11 Leave your orphans; I will protect their lives. Your widows too can trust in me."

Hos 14:3 Assyria cannot save us; we will not mount war-horses. We will never again say 'Our gods' to what our own hands have made, for in you the fatherless find compassion."

Mal 3:5 "So I will come near to you for judgment. I will be quick to testify against sorcerers, adulterers and perjurers, against those who defraud laborers of their wages, who oppress the widows and the fatherless, and deprive aliens of justice, but do not fear me," says the LORD Almighty.

Justice to, required—

Dt 24:17 Do not deprive the alien or the fatherless of justice, or take the cloak of the widow as a pledge. [18]Remember that you were slaves in Egypt and the LORD your God redeemed you from there. That is why I command you to do this.

[19]When you are harvesting in your field and you overlook a sheaf, do not go back to get it. Leave it for the alien, the fatherless and the widow, so that the LORD your God may bless you in all the work of your hands. [20]When you beat the olives from your trees, do not go over the branches a second time. Leave what remains for the alien, the fatherless and the widow. [21]When you harvest the grapes in your vineyard, do not go over the vines again. Leave what remains for the alien, the fatherless and the widow. [22]Remember that you were slaves in Egypt. That is why I command you to do this.

Dt 27:19 "Cursed is the man who withholds justice from the alien, the fatherless or the widow." Then all the people shall say, "Amen!"

Ps 82:3 Defend the cause of the weak and fatherless; maintain the rights of the poor and oppressed.

Isa 1:17 learn to do right! Seek justice, encourage the oppressed. Defend the cause of the fatherless, plead the case of the widow.

Isa 1:23 Your rulers are rebels, companions of thieves; they all love bribes and chase after gifts. They do not defend the cause of the fatherless; the widow's case does not come before them.

Jer 7:6 if you do not oppress the alien, the fatherless or the widow and do not shed innocent blood in this place, and if you do not follow other gods to your own harm, [7]then I will let you live in this place, in the land I gave your forefathers for ever and ever.

Jer 22:3 This is what the LORD says: Do what is just and right. Rescue from the hand of his oppressor the one who has been robbed. Do no wrong or violence to the alien, the fatherless or the widow, and do not shed innocent blood in this place.

Oppressed—

Job 6:27 You would even cast lots for the fatherless and barter away your friend.

Job 22:9 And you sent widows away empty-handed and broke the strength of the fatherless.

Job 24:3 They drive away the orphan's donkey and take the widow's ox in pledge.

Job 24:9 The fatherless child is snatched from the breast; the infant of the poor is seized for a debt.

Isa 10:1 Woe to those who make unjust laws, to those who issue oppressive decrees, [2]to deprive the poor of their rights and withhold justice from the oppressed of my people, making widows their prey and robbing the fatherless.

Jer 5:28 and have grown fat and sleek. Their evil deeds have no limit; they do not plead the case of the fatherless to win it, they do not defend the rights of the poor.

See Adoption; Children; Widow.

Instances of:

Lot (Ge 11:27-28). Daughters of Zelophehad (Nu 27:1-5). Jotham (Jdg 9:16-21). Mephibosheth (2Sa 9:3). Joash (2Ki 11:1-12). Esther (Est 2:7). A type of Zion in affliction (La 5:3).

OSEE *See Hosea.*

OSHEA *See Joshua.*

OSNAPPAR *See Ashurbanipal.*

OSPRAY *See Vulture.*

OSPREY [8164, 8168]. A carnivorous bird. Forbidden as food (Lev 11:13; Dt 14:12).

OSSIFRAGE *See Vulture.*

OSTENTATION In prayer and almsgiving (Mt 6:1; Pr 25:14; 27:2). *See Boasting.*

OSTIA The port of Rome on the Tiber, some sixteen miles from the city.

OSTRACA Inscribed fragments of pottery, or potsherds. Some important ancient documents have come down to us in this form, i.e., the Lachish Letters.

OSTRICH [3612, 8266].
NIV+ OSTRICHES
A large, flightless bird that does not take care of its young well (Job 39:13-18; La 4:3).

OTHNI [6978]. Son of Shemaiah (1Ch 26:7).

OTHNIEL [6979]. Son of Kenaz and nephew of Caleb. Conquers Kiriath Sepher, and as reward secures Caleb's daughter as his wife (Jos 15:16-20; Jdg 1:12-13). Becomes deliverer and judge of Israel (Jdg 3:8-11). Death of (Jdg 3:11). Descendants of (1Ch 4:13-14).

OUCHES *See Filigree.*

OUTCASTS [5615].
NIV+ CAST, OUTCAST
General references to (Isa 11:12; 16:3; 27:13; Jer 30:17).

OVEN [9486].
NIV+ OVENS
Ancient ovens were primitive, often a hole in the ground coated with clay and in which a fire was made. The dough was spread on the inside and baked. Sometimes ovens were made of stone, from which the fire was raked when the oven was very hot and into which the unbaked loaves

were placed (Ex 8:3; Lev 2:4; 7:9; 11:35; 26:26; Hos 7:4-7).

Figurative: (Ps 21:9; Mal 4:1; Mt 6:30; Lk 12:28).

OVERCOMING [2200, 3523, 3899, 3983, 5162, 6296, *2093, 2487, 2952, 2996, 3771, 5309*].
NIV+ OVERCOME, OVERCAME, OVERCOMES
See Perseverance.

OVERSEER [8853, *2175, 2176*].
NIV+ OVERSEERS, OVERSIGHT
Ruler (Pr 6:7). Office of church leadership, traditionally "bishop," (Ac 20:28; Php 1:1; 1Ti 3:1-7) same as an elder (Tit 1:5-9; 1Pe 5:1-4). A title of Christ (1Pe 2:25). *See Elders.*

OVERWEIGHT *See Corpulency.*

OWL [1426+3613, 3568, 3927, 7684, 7887, 7889, 9379, 9492].
NIV+ OWLS
Several kinds of carnivorous bird (Isa 14:23; 34:11; Zep 2:14). Unclean for food (Lev 11:16-18; Dt 14:15-17). Lives in the desert (Job 30:29; Ps 102:6; Isa 13:21; 34:11-15; 43:20; Jer 50:39; Mic 1:8).

OWNER OF A SHIP Usually captained his ship or contracted to state service (Ac 27:11).

OX [476, 546, 1330, 7228, 7538, 8028, 8802, *1091, 3675, 5436*].
NIV+ OXEN
See Bull; Cattle; Wild Ox.

OXGOAD [1330+4913]. A pointed stick used to prod the ox on to further effort. Used by Shamgar to kill six hundred Philistines (Jdg 3:31).

OZEM [730].
1. Son of Jesse (1Ch 2:15).
2. Son of Jerahmeel (1Ch 2:25).

OZIAS *See Uzziah, 1.*

OZNI, OZNITE [269, 270] (*my ear, my hearing*). Son of Gad and his clan (Nu 26:16).

P

PAARAI [7197] (*devotee of Peor*). One of David's valiant men (2Sa 23:35). Called Naarai (1Ch 11:37).

PACK ANIMALS Used for transporting army supplies (1Ch 12:40).

PADDAN ARAM, PADAN-ARAM [7019, 7020] (*plain of Aram*).

NIV+ ARAM, PADDAN

1. Region near the head of the fertile crescent; sometimes called simply "Paddan," (Ge 48:7, ftn). Another name for Aram Naharaim (Ge 24:10). Literally "Aram of the two rivers"—the Euphrates and the Tigris. Naharaim was the northern part of the area called later by the Greeks "Mesopotamia"—literally "between the rivers." It was located NE of Canaan, the area known today as Syria.

2. A town near Shechem (Ge 33:18, ftn).

PADON [7013] (*ransom*). One of the temple servants (Ezr 2:44; Ne 7:47).

PAGIEL [7005] (perhaps *fortune of God* or *God is entreated*, less probably *God has met his worshiper*). Son of Ocran and leader of the tribe of Asher at the time of the Exodus (Nu 1:13; 2:27; 7:72,77; 10:26).

PAHATH-MOAB [7075] (*supervisor of Moab*). The ancestor of an influential family of Judah, which returned to Jerusalem from the Captivity (Ezr 2:6; 10:30; Ne 3:11; 7:11).

PAI *See Pau.*

PAIN [2477, 2655, 2659, 2660, 2714, 3872, 3873, 4799, 6772, 6776, 6778, 7496, 7828, 9377, *989, 992, 3383, 4506*].

NIV+ PAINFUL, PAINS

Experienced on earth (Job 14:22; 30:17-18; La 3:5; Rev 16:10). Chastens (Job 33:19). None in Heaven (Rev 21:4).
See Afflictions.

PAINTING [3949, 7037].

NIV+ PAINT, PAINTED

Around the eyes, to enhance their appearance (2Ki 9:30; Jer 4:30; Eze 23:40). Of rooms (Jer 22:14). Of portraits (Eze 23:14).

PALACE [810, 1074, 1131, 2121, 5092, 5249, 6247, 10206, *885, 994, 3875, 4550*].

NIV+ PALACES, PALATIAL

For kings (1Ki 21:1; 2Ki 15:25; Jer 49:27; Am 1:12; Na 2:6). Of David (2Sa 7:2). Of Solomon (1Ki 7:1-12). At Babylon (Da 4:29; 5:5; 6:18). At Susa (Ne 1:1; Est 1:2; 7:7; Da 8:2). Archives kept in (Ezr 6:2). Proclamations issued from (Am 3:9).

Figurative:
Of a government (Am 1:12; 2:2; Na 2:6).

PALAL [7138] (*he has judged*). Son of Uzai. One of the workmen in rebuilding the walls of Jerusalem (Ne 3:25).

PALE HORSE Symbol of death (Rev 6:8).

PALESTINE The name is derived from Philistia, an area along the S seacoast occupied by the Philistines (Ps 60:8). The original name was Canaan (Ge 12:5); after the Conquest it came to be known as Israel (1Sa 13:19), and in the Greco-Roman period, Judea, Samaria, and Galilee.

The land was c. seventy miles wide and 150 miles long, from the Lebanon mountains in the N to Beersheba in the S. The area W of the Jordan was 6,000 miles; E of the Jordan, 4,000 miles. In the N, from Acco to the Sea of Galilee was twenty-eight miles. From Gaza to the Dead Sea in the S, fifty-four miles.

Physically, the land is divided into five parts: the Plain of Sharon and the Philistine Plain along the coast; adjoining it, the Shephelah, or foothills region; then the central mountain range; after that the Jordan valley; and E of the Jordan the Transjordan plateau.

The varied configuration of Palestine produces a great variety of climate. The Maritime Plain has an annual average temperature of 57 degrees at Joppa; Jerusalem averages 63 degrees; while Jericho and the Dead Sea area have a tropical climate. As a result, plants and animals of varied latitudes may be found.

Before the Conquest the land was inhabited by Canaanites, Amorites, Hittites, Horites, and Amalekites. These were conquered by Joshua, the judges, and the kings. The kingdom was split in 931 B.C.; the N kingdom was taken into captivity by the Assyrians in 722 B.C.; the S kingdom by the Babylonians in 587 B.C. From 587 B.C. to the time of the Maccabees the land was under foreign rule by the Babylonians, Persians, Alexander the Great, Egyptians, and Syrians. In 63 B.C. the Maccabees lost control of the land to the Romans, who held it until the time of Mohammed.

In NT times Palestine W of the Jordan was divided into Galilee, Samaria, and Judea; and E of the Jordan into the Decapolis and Perea.
See Philistia; Philistines.

PALLU, PALLUITE [7101, 7112] (*wonderful*). Son of Reuben (Ge 46:9; Ex 6:14; Nu 26:5,8; 1Ch 5:3).

PALM SUNDAY *See Triumphal Entry of Jesus.*

PALM TREE [4093, 9469, 9472, 9474, *5836*].

NIV+ PALMS

Deborah judged Israel under (Jdg 4:5). Wood of, used in the temple (1Ki 6:29,32,35; 2Ch 3:5). In the temple seen in the vision of Ezekiel (Eze 40:16; 41:18). Branches of, thrown in the way when Jesus made his triumphal entry into Jerusalem (Jn 12:13). Jericho was called the City of Palm Trees (Dt 34:3).

Figurative:
Of the prosperity of the righteous (Ps 92:12). Used as a symbol of victory (Rev 7:9).

PALMER WORM *See Locust.*

PALMS, CITY OF *See Jericho.*

PALSY *See Paralysis.*

PALTI [7120] (*[God (El)] is [my] deliverance*).
1. Spy from Benjamin (Nu 13:9),
2. *See Paltiel, 2.*

PALTIEL [7120, 7123] (*God [El] is [my] deliverance*).
1. Prince of Issachar (Nu 34:26).
2. Son-in-law of Saul (1Sa 25:44; 2Sa 3:15).

PALTITE [7121] (*delivered*). One of David's mighty men (2Sa 23:26), "Pelonite" (1Ch 11:27; 27:10).

PAMPHYLIA [*4103*]. A province in Asia Minor. Men of, in Jerusalem (Ac 2:10). Paul goes to (Ac 13:13-14; 14:24). John, surnamed Mark, in (Ac 13:13; 15:38). Sea of (Ac 27:5).

PAN(S) [3963, 4679, 4709, 5306, 5389, 6105, 7505]. Clay pan for cooking the grain offering (Lev 2:7; 7:9). For baking bread (2Sa 13:9). Silver pans of the temple (Ezr 1:9). Iron (Eze 4:3).

PANIC [2169, 3010, 3169, 4539, 6907, 8185, 9451]. In armies (Lev 26:17; Dt 32:30; Jos 23:10; Ps 35:5). From God (Ge 35:5; Ex 15:14-16; Jdg 7:22; 1Sa 14:15-20; 2Ki 7:6-7; 2Ch 20:22-23).

See Armies.

PANNAG *See Confection.*

PANTOMIME By Isaiah (Isa 20:2-3). By Ezekiel (Eze 4:1-8; 12:18). Agabus (Ac 21:11).

PAPER [*5925*]. (2Jn 12). *See Parchment.*

PAPHOS [*4265*]. A city of Cyprus. Paul blinds a sorcerer in (Ac 13:6-13).

PAPS NIV "breasts" (Lk 23:28) or "chest" (Rev 1:13). *See Breast.*

PAPYRUS [15, 1687] (*reed plant*). A reed which grows in swamps and along rivers or lakes, especially along the Nile; from eight to twelve feet tall; used to make baskets, sandals, boats, and especially paper, the most common writing material of antiquity (Job 8:11; Isa 18:2). The NT books were undoubtedly all written on papyrus. Moses' basket of (Ex 2:3).

PARABLE [1948, 4886, 5442, *4130*] (*to be similar, to be comparable*).

NIV+ PARABLES

Defined:

1. Proverbial saying used in wisdom and prophetic discourse (Ps 78:2; Pr 1:6).

2. A story in which things in the spiritual realm are compared with events that could happen in the temporal realm; or, an earthly story with a heavenly meaning (Eze 17; 24; Mt 13; Lk 15). Differs from a fable, myth, allegory, or proverb. A characteristic teaching method of Jesus.

Listing of:

Of the trees (Jdg 9:8-15). Of the lamb (2Sa 12:1-6). Of the woman of Tekoa (2Sa 14:5-12). Of the garment torn to pieces (1Ki 11:30-32). Of the prisoner of war (1Ki 20:39-42). Of the thistle and cedar (2Ki 14:9). Of a vine of Egypt (Ps 80:8-16). Of the vineyard (Isa 5:1-7; 27:2-3). Of the farmer (Isa 28:23-29). Of the skins filled with wine (Jer 13:12-14). Of the two eagles (Eze 17). Of lions' cubs (Eze 19:1-9). Of Oholah and Oholibah (Eze 23). The boiling pot (Eze 24:3-5). The plant (Jnh 4:10-11). The sheet let down from heaven in Peter's vision (Ac 10:10-16). The two covenants (Gal 4:22-31). The mercenary soldier (2Ti 2:3-4). Husbandman (2Ti 2:6). Furnished house (2Ti 2:20-21). The athlete (2Ti 2:5). Mirror (Jas 1:23-25).

See Jesus the Christ, Parables of; Symbols and Similitudes; Types.

PARACLETE (*comforter, exhorter*). One who pleads another's cause. Used by Christ of the Holy Spirit in John's Gospel (Jn 14:16,26; 15:26; 16:7), and of Christ (1Jn 2:1).

PARADISE [*4137*] (*park* or *garden*). Park (Ecc 2:5), forest (Ne 2:8), orchard (SS 4:13), home of those who die in Christ (Lk 23:43). Exact location uncertain.

PARADOX Of wealth (Pr 13:7). Wisdom (1Co 3:18). Life (Mt 10:39; 16:25; Mk 8:35; Lk 17:33; Jn 12:25). Christian life (2Co 6:4,8-10; 12:4,10-11; Eph 3:17-19; Php 3:7). New Jerusalem (Rev 21:18,21).

PARAH [7240] (*cow*). A city in Benjamin (Jos 18:23).

PARALLELISM A characteristic of OT Hebrew poetry. Rather that rhyming words as in English poetry, Hebrew poetry rhymes thoughts by comparison and contrast of two or three lines. Two major categories of parallelism are "synonymous," in which the parallel lines echo similar ideas, and "antithetical," in which the parallel lines contrast. In the NIV, parallelism is shown by identation: the indented line is parallel to the preceding line.

Examples of synonymous parallelism—

Ps 2:1 Why do the nations conspire
and the peoples plot in vain?

²The kings of the earth take their stand
and the rulers gather together
against the LORD
and against his Anointed One.

³"Let us break their chains," they say,
"and throw off their fetters."

⁴The One enthroned in heaven laughs;
the Lord scoffs at them.

Examples of antithetical parallelism—

Ps 1:6 The LORD watches over the way of the righteous,
but the way of the wicked will perish.

Pr 1:7 The fear of the LORD is the beginning of knowledge,
but fools despise wisdom and discipline.

See Poetry; Psalms.

PARALYSIS [7028, *3831*, *4166*, *4168*] (*lame*).

NIV+ PARALYTIC, PARALYTICS, PARALYZED

Cured by Jesus (Mt 4:24; 8:6,13; 9:2,6), by Philip (Ac 8:7), by Peter (Ac 9:33-34).

PARAMOUR *See Lovers.*

PARAN, MOUNT PARAN, DESERT OF PARAN [7000] (*plain*). Desert or wilderness of (Ge 21:21; Nu 10:12; 12:16; 13:3,26; Dt 1:1). Mountains of (Dt 33:2; Hab 3:3). Israelites encamp in (Nu 12:16). David takes refuge in (1Sa 25:1). Hadad flees to (1Ki 11:17-18).

PARBAR NIV "the court to the west" of the temple (1Ch 26:18).

PARCHED LAND [62, 2990, 3081, 3083, 3312, 5980, 6546, 7457, 7480, 7533]. Symbolic of loss of strength or blessing (Job 30:1; Ps 143:6). Changed to flowing springs, symbolic of blessing (Ps 107:35; Isa 35:1).

PARCHMENT [*3521*].

NIV+ PARCHMENTS

Writing material made of animals skins, probably copies of books of the OT in 2Ti 4:13.

PARDON [4105, 5927, 5951, 6142].

NIV+ PARDONED, PARDONS

Forgiveness. God demands a righteous ground for pardoning the sinner—the atoning work of Christ (Ex 34:9; 1Sa 15:25-26; Isa 55:7). *See Atonement; Forgiveness.*

PARENTAL BLESSINGS Very important in OT times; often prophetic of a child's future (Ge 27:4,12,27-29).

PARENTS [3, 3+562+2256, *1204, 4252, 4591*].

NIV+ See FATHER, GRANDPARENTS, MOTHER

To be revered (Ex 20:12; Lev 19:3; Dt 5:16; Mt 15:4; 19:19; Mk 7:10; 10:19; Lk 18:20). Obeyed (Pr 1:8; 6:20; 23:22; Eph 6:1; Col 3:20). Covenant blessings of, entailed upon children (Ge 6:18; Ex 20:6; Ps 103:17).

Curses upon, entailed upon children—

Ex 20:5 You shall not bow down to them or worship them; for I, the LORD your God, am a jealous God, punishing the children for the sin of the fathers to the third and fourth generation of those who hate me, (+Lev 20:5; Isa 14:20; Jer 9:14; La 5:7)

Involved in children's wickedness (1Sa 2:27-36; 4:10-18).

Mother, beloved—

Pr 31:28 Her children arise and call her blessed; her husband also, and he praises her:

Cursing of, to be punished—

Ex 21:17 "Anyone who curses his father or mother must be put to death. (+Lev 20:9)

Beloved:

By Joseph (Ge 46:29). Rahab (Jos 2:12-13). Ruth (Ru 1:16-17). Elisha (1Ki 19:20).

Duties of:

Fathers to direct household—

Ge 18:19 For I have chosen him, so that he will direct his children and his household after him to keep the way of the LORD by doing what is right and just, so that the LORD will bring about for Abraham what he has promised him."

Lev 20:9 "'If anyone curses his father or mother, he must be put to death. He has cursed his father or his mother, and his blood will be on his own head. (+Pr 3:12)

Pr 13:24 He who spares the rod hates his son, but he who loves him is careful to discipline him.

Pr 19:18 Discipline your son, for in that there is hope; do not be a willing party to his death.

1Ti 3:4 He must manage his own family well and see that his children obey him with proper respect. **5**(If anyone does not know how to manage his own family, how can he take care of God's church?)

1Ti 3:12 A deacon must be the husband of but one wife and must manage his children and his household well.

Tit 1:6 An elder must be blameless, the husband of but one wife, a man whose children believe and are not open to the charge of being wild and disobedient.

Heb 12:7 Endure hardship as discipline; God is treating you as sons. For what son is not disciplined by his father?

To govern with kindness—

Eph 6:4 Fathers, do not exasperate your children; instead, bring them up in the training and instruction of the Lord.

Col 3:21 Fathers, do not embitter your children, or they will become discouraged.

A prerequisite to church leadership (1Ti 3:4-5,12).

To provide for children—

2Co 12:14 Now I am ready to visit you for the third time, and I will not be a burden to you, because what I want is not your possessions but you. After all, children should not have to save up for their parents, but parents for their children.

1Ti 5:8 If anyone does not provide for his relatives, and especially for his immediate family, he has denied the faith and is worse than an unbeliever.

To instruct children in righteousness—

Ex 10:2 that you may tell your children and grandchildren how I dealt harshly with the Egyptians and how I performed my signs among them, and that you may know that I am the LORD."

Ex 12:27 then tell them, 'It is the Passover sacrifice to the LORD, who passed over the houses of the Israelites in Egypt and spared our homes when he struck down the Egyptians.'" Then the people bowed down and worshiped.

Ex 13:8 On that day tell your son, 'I do this because of what the LORD did for me when I came out of Egypt.'

Ex 13:14 "In days to come, when your son asks you, 'What does this mean?' say to him, 'With a mighty hand the LORD brought us out of Egypt, out of the land of slavery.

Dt 4:9 Only be careful, and watch yourselves closely so that you do not forget the things your eyes have seen or let them slip from your heart as long as you live. Teach them to your children and to their children after them. **10**Remember the day you stood before the LORD your God at Horeb, when he said to me, "Assemble the people before me to hear my words so that they may learn to revere me as long as they live in the land and may teach them to their children."

Dt 6:7 Impress them on your children. Talk about them when you sit at home and when you walk along the road, when you lie down and when you get up.

Dt 6:20 In the future, when your son asks you, "What is the meaning of the stipulations, decrees and laws the LORD our God has commanded you?" **21**tell him: "We were slaves of Pharaoh in Egypt, but the LORD brought us out of Egypt with a mighty hand. **22**Before our eyes the LORD sent miraculous signs and wonders—great and terrible—upon Egypt and Pharaoh and his whole household. **23**But he brought us out from there to bring us in and give us the land that he promised on oath to our forefathers. **24**The LORD commanded us to obey all these decrees and to fear the LORD our God, so that we might always prosper and be kept alive, as is the case today. (+Dt 6:25)

Dt 11:18 Fix these words of mine in your hearts and minds; tie them as symbols on your hands and bind them on your foreheads. **19**Teach them to your children, talking about them when you sit at home and when you walk along the road, when you lie down and when you get up. **20**Write them on the doorframes of your houses and on your gates, **21**so that your days and the days of your children may be many in the land that the LORD swore to give your forefathers, as many as the days that the heavens are above the earth.

Dt 32:46 he said to them, "Take to heart all the words I have solemnly declared to you this day, so that you may command your children to obey carefully all the words of this law.

Ps 78:5 He decreed statutes for Jacob and established the law in Israel, which he commanded our forefathers to teach their children, **6**so the next generation would know them, even the children yet to be born, and they in turn would tell their children.

Pr 22:6 Train a child in the way he should go, and when he is old he will not turn from it.

Pr 22:15 Folly is bound up in the heart of a child, but the rod of discipline will drive it far from him.

Pr 27:11 Be wise, my son, and bring joy to my heart; then I can answer anyone who treats me with contempt.

Isa 38:19 The living, the living—they praise you, as I am doing today; fathers tell their children about your faithfulness.

Joel 1:3 Tell it to your children, and let your children tell it to their children, and their children to the next generation. (+Eph 6:4)

1Th 2:11 For you know that we dealt with each of you as a father deals with his own children,

To discipline children (Pr 19:8; 22:6,15)—

Pr 23:13 Do not withhold discipline from a child; if you punish him with the rod, he will not die. ¹⁴Punish him with the rod and save his soul from death.

Pr 29:15 The rod of correction imparts wisdom, but a child left to himself disgraces his mother.

Pr 29:17 Discipline your son, and he will give you peace; he will bring delight to your soul.

Indulgent:

Eli (1Sa 2:27-36; 3:13-14), David (1Ki 1:6).

Influence of:

Evil (1Ki 15:26; 22:52-53; 2Ki 8:27; 21:20; 2Ch 21:6; 22:3). Good (1Ki 22:43; 2Ki 15:3,34). *See Influence.*

Love of:

Reflection of God's love—

Ps 103:13 As a father has compassion on his children, so the LORD has compassion on those who fear him;

Pr 3:12 because the LORD disciplines those he loves, as a father the son he delights in.

Isa 66:13 As a mother comforts her child, so will I comfort you; and you will be comforted over Jerusalem."

Isa 49:15 "Can a mother forget the baby at her breast and have no compassion on the child she has borne? Though she may forget, I will not forget you! (+Mt 7:9-11)

Lk 11:11 "Which of you fathers, if your son asks for a fish, will give him a snake instead? ¹²Or if he asks for an egg, will give him a scorpion? ¹³If you then, though you are evil, know how to give good gifts to your children, how much more will your Father in heaven give the Holy Spirit to those who ask him!"

Must be exceeded by love for Christ—

Mt 10:37 "Anyone who loves his father or mother more than me is not worthy of me; anyone who loves his son or daughter more than me is not worthy of me;

To be taught—

Tit 2:4 Then they can train the younger women to love their husbands and children,

Parental affection exemplified:

By Hagar (Ge 21:15-16), Rebekah's mother (Ge 24:55), Isaac and Rebekah (Ge 25:28), Isaac (Ge 27:26-27), Laban (Ge 31:26-28), Jacob (Ge 37:3-4; 42:4,38; 43:13-14; 45:26-28; 48:10-11), Moses' mother (Ex 2), Naomi (Ru 1:8-9), Hannah (1Sa 2:19), David (2Sa 12:18-23; 13:38-39; 14:1,33; 18:5,12-13,33; 19:1-6), Rizpah (2Sa 21:10), the mother of the infant brought to Solomon by the harlots (1Ki 3:22-28), Mary (Mt 12:46; Lk 2:48; Jn 2:5; 19:25), Jairus (Mk 5:23), father of the demoniac (Mk 9:24), nobleman (Jn 4:49).

Paternal blessings:

Of Noah (Ge 9:24-27), Abraham (Ge 17:18), Isaac (Ge

27:10-40; 28:3-4), Laban (Ge 31:55), Jacob (Ge 48:15-20; 49:1-28), reproaches (Ge 9:24-25; 49:3-7).

Partiality of:

Isaac for Esau (Ge 25:28), Rebekah for Jacob (Ge 25:28; 27:6-17), Jacob for Joseph (Ge 33:2; 37:3; 48:22), for Benjamin (Ge 42:4). *See Partiality.*

Prayers in behalf of children:

Of Hannah (1Sa 1:27), David (2Sa 7:25-29; 1Ch 17:16-27; 2Sa 12:16; 1Ch 22:12; 29:19), Job (Job 1:5). *See Children, Instruction of.*

PARLOR *See Upper Room.*

PARMASHTA [7269] *(the very first).* Son of Haman (Est 9:9).

PARMENAS [4226] *(steady, reliable).* One of seven men chosen for daily ministration to the poor (Ac 6:5).

PARNACH [7270]. Father of Elizaphan (Nu 34:25).

PAROSH [7283] *(flea).* The ancestor of one of the families which returned to Jerusalem from captivity in Babylon (Ezr 2:3; 8:3; Ne 7:8; 10:14).

PAROUSIA *(presence, coming).* A Greek word frequently used in NT of our Lord's return (Mt 24:3; 1Co 15:23; 1Th 3:13; 4:15; 2Pe 1:16).

PARRICIDE One who murders his father, mother, or a close relative (2Ki 19:37; 2Ch 32:21; Isa 37:38).

PARSHANDATHA [7309]. One of the ten sons of Haman (Est 9:7).

PARSIMONY Stinginess with money or resources. Of the Jews toward the temple (Hag 1:2,4,6,9), toward God (Mal 3:8-9). Punishment of (Hag 1:9-11). *See Liberality.*

PARSIN [10593]. Aramaic for "divided," symbolic of the division of Babylon between the Medes and Persians (Da 5:24-28).

PARTHIANS [4222]. The inhabitants of Parthia, a country NW of Persia (Ac 2:9).

PARTIALITY [5365+7156, 5795+7156, 5951+7156, 3284+4725, 4622].

NIV+ PARTIAL

Forbidden, among Christians (1Ti 5:21), by parents (Dt 21:15-17). Effects upon children (Ge 37:4). *See Parents.*

Instances of:

Of Brothers: Joseph for Benjamin (Ge 43:30,34).

Of parents: Isaac for Esau (Ge 25:25), Rebekah for Jacob (Ge 25:28; 27:6-17), Jacob, for Joseph (Ge 33:2; 37:3-4; 48:22), for Benjamin (Ge 42:4).

Of husbands: Jacob for Rachel (Ge 29:30), Elkanah for Hannah (1Sa 1:4-5).

See Respect of Persons.

PARTICEPS CRIMINIS Participating in evil (2Jn 11). *See Collusion.*

PARTITION, MIDDLE WALL OF *See Dividing Wall.*

PARTNERSHIP [476, 2492, 2500, 3126, 3128, 3581, 5007, 5212].

NIV+ PARTNER, PARTNERS

With God (1Co 3:7,9; 2Co 6:1; Php 2:13).

PARTRIDGE [7926]. (1Sa 26:20; Jer 17:11).

PARUAH [7245] (*blooming* ISBE; *cheerful* KB). Father of Jehoshaphat (1Ki 4:17).

PARVAIM [7246]. An unknown gold region (2Ch 3:6).

PAS DAMMIM, PAS-DAMMIM [7169] (*place of blood*). A battle between David and the Philistines, fought at (1Ch 11:13). Called Ephes Dammim (1Sa 17:1).

PASACH [7179] (*to divide*). Son of Japhlet (1Ch 7:33).

PASCHAL LAMB *See Passover.*

PASEAH [7176] (*hobbling one*).
1. A son of Eshton (1Ch 4:12).
2. Ancestor of a family which returned to Jerusalem from captivity in Babylon (Ezr 2:49; Ne 7:51).
3. Father of Jehoiada, probably identical with preceding (Ne 3:6).

PASHHUR, PASHUR [7319] (perhaps *be quiet, and round about*).
1. A priest, son of Malkijah (1Ch 9:12). An influential man and ancestor of an influential family (Jer 21:1; 38:1; Ezr 2:38; 10:22; Ne 7:41; 10:3; 11:12).
2. Son of Immer and governor of the temple. Beats and imprisons Jeremiah (Jer 20:1-6).
3. Father of Gedaliah, who persecuted Jeremiah (Jer 38:1).

PASSAGE [2006, 4544, *4047*, *4343*].
NIV+ PASSAGEWAY
Ford of a river (Ge 32:23), mountain pass (1Sa 13:23), a crossing (Jos 22:11).

PASSENGERS *See Commerce.*

PASSION [678, *2123*, *4077*, *4792*].
NIV+ PASSIONATE, PASSIONS
1. Lust or desire (Hos 7:6; 1Co 7:9).
2. Often used as a technical term of the suffering of Jesus. *See Jesus the Christ, Sufferings of.*

PASSIVITY *See Nonresistance.*

PASSOVER [7175, *2038*, *4247*] (*pass over, spare*). Institution of (Ex 12:3-49; 23:15-18; 34:18; Lev 23:4-8; Nu 9:2-5,13-14; 28:16-25; Dt 16:1-8,16; Ps 81:3,5). Design of (Ex 12:21-28).
Special Passover, for those who were unclean, or on a journey, to be held in the second month (Nu 9:6-12; 2Ch 30:2-4). Lamb killed by Levites, for those who were ceremonially unclean (2Ch 30:17; 35:3-11; Ezr 6:20). Strangers authorized to celebrate (Ex 12:48-49; Nu 9:14).
Observed at place designated by God (Dt 16:5-7), with unleavened bread (Ex 12:8,15-20; 13:3,6; 23:15; Lev 23:6; Nu 9:11; 29:17; Dt 16:3-4; Mk 14:12; Lk 22:7; Ac 12:3; 1Co 5:8). Penalty for neglecting to observe (Nu 9:13).
Reinstituted by Ezekiel (Eze 45:21-24).
Observation of, renewed by the Israelites on entering Canaan (Jos 5:10-11), by Hezekiah (2Ch 30:1), by Josiah (2Ki 23:22-23; 2Ch 35:1,18), after return from captivity (Ezr 6:19-20). Observed by Jesus (Mt 26:17-20; Lk 22:15; Jn 2:13,23; 13). Jesus in the temple at the time of (Lk 2:41-50). Jesus crucified at the time of (Mt 26:2; Mk 14:1-2; Jn 18:28). The lamb of, a type of Christ (1Co 5:7). Lord's supper ordained at (Mt 26:26-28; Mk 14:12-25; Lk 22:7-20).
Prisoner released at, by the Romans (Mt 27:15; Mk

15:6; Lk 23:16-17; Jn 18:39). Peter imprisoned at the time of (Ac 12:3).
Christ called our Passover (1Co 5:7).
See Feasts; Hallel.

PASSPORTS *See Safe-conduct.*

PASTOR [*4478*] A leader of the church (Eph 4:11), possibly the same as elder and overseer. *See Elders; Overseer.*

PASTORAL EPISTLES A common title for 1 and 2 Timothy and Titus, which were written by the apostle Paul to his special envoys sent on specific missions in accordance with the needs of the hour. They give instruction to Timothy and Titus concerning the pastoral care of churches. Though some date the Pastorals within the framework of Acts, most scholars believe all three were written not long after the events of Ac 28.
After his imprisonment in Rome (c. A.D. 60-62), Paul most likely began his fourth missionary journey. *See Missionary Journeys of Paul.*
1 Timothy was written to Timothy at Ephesus while Paul was still traveling in the coastal regions of the Aegean Sea. Titus was written to Titus in Crete (c. A.D. 63-65), probably from Nicopolis or some other city in Macedonia. 2 Timothy was written from Rome toward the end of Paul's second imprisonment shortly before he was executed (A.D. 67 or 68).
The epistles concern church organization and discipline, including such matters as the appointment of bishops and deacons, the opposition of heretical or rebellious members, and the provision for maintenance of doctrinal purity.
Certain themes and phrases recur throughout the Pastoral Letters: (1) *God the Savior.* Three times in 1 Timothy and three times in Titus God the Father is called Savior (1Ti 1:1; 2:3; 4:10; Tit 1:3; 2:10; 3:4). Once in 2 Timothy and three times in Titus Jesus is also called Savior (2Ti 1:10; Tit 1:4; 2:13; 3:6). (2) *Sound doctrine, faith, and teaching.* Correct teaching, in keeping with that of the apostles (1Ti 1:10; 6:3; 2Ti 1:13; 4:3; Tit 1:9). The teaching is called "sound" not only because it builds up in the faith, but because it protects against the corrupting influence of false teachers. (3) *Godliness.* A key word (along with "godly") in the Pastorals, occurring eight times in 1 Timothy (2:2; 3:16; 4:7-8; 6:3,5-6,11), once in 2 Timothy (3:5) and once in Titus (1:1), but nowhere else in the writings of Paul. (4) *Controversies.* Appearing in (1Ti 1:4; 6:4; 2Ti 2:23; Tit 3:9); (5) *Trustworthy sayings.* A clause found nowhere else in the NT but used five times in the Pastorals (1Ti 1:15; 3:1; 4:9; 2Ti 2:11; Tit 3:8).
The authorship of these letters has been disputed because of differences in vocabulary and style from the other epistles ascribed to Paul, and because their references to his travels do not accord with the itineraries described in Acts. The differences though real, have been exaggerated, and can be explained on the basis of a change of time, subject-matter, scribes, and destination.
See also Church, New Testament Church, Qualifications for Elders/Overseers and Deacons; Timothy, 1 and 2; Titus.

PASTURE [*1824, 4494, 5337, 5338, 5659, 5661, 8286, 3786*].
NIV+ PASTURED, PASTURELAND, PASTURELANDS, PASTURES
A place to graze sheep (Jn 10:9; Ge 29:7); essential for

survival of flocks (Ge 47:4; 1Ch 4:39-41; Job 39:8; Isa 14:30; Jer 14:6); where David worked (2Sa 7:8; 1Ch 17:7); for cattle (1Ki 4:23); a figure of peace (Ps 23:2; Ps 37:3); a figure of God's flock (Ps 74:1; 79:13; 83:12; 95:7; 100:3; Jer 23:1-3; 50:7, 19; Eze 34:14); for camels (Eze 25:5). Pasturelands were the environs around towns and villages (Nu 35).

PATARA [4249]. A Lycian city in Asia Minor. Visited by Paul (Ac 21:1-2).

PATHROS See Upper Egypt.

PATHRUSITES, PATHRUSIM [7357] (of Pathros). A descendant of Mizraim and ancestor of the Philistines (Ge 10:14; 1Ch 1:12).

PATHS, RIGHT (Ps 16:11; 23:3; 25:10; 119:35; Pr 2:9; 4:11,18; Isa 2:3; 26:7; Heb 12:13).

PATHWAY OF SIN General references to (Pr 2:15; 12:15; 13:15; 14:12; 15:9; Isa 49:8; Mt 7:13). Walking in (Dt 29:19; Jer 7:24; Eph 2:2; Php 3:18; 1Pe 4:3; 2Pe 2:10; 3:3; Jude 18).

PATIENCE [*4206, 3428, 3429, 5705].

NIV+ PATIENT, PATIENTLY

Commended—

Ecc 7:8 The end of a matter is better than its beginning, and patience is better than pride. **9**Do not be quickly provoked in your spirit, for anger resides in the lap of fools.

La 3:26 it is good to wait quietly for the salvation of the LORD. **27**It is good for a man to bear the yoke while he is young.

Commended—

Ps 37:7 Be still before the LORD and wait patiently for him; do not fret when men succeed in their ways, when they carry out their wicked schemes.

8Refrain from anger and turn from wrath; do not fret—it leads only to evil. **9**For evil men will be cut off, but those who hope in the LORD will inherit the land.

Eph 4:2 Be completely humble and gentle; be patient, bearing with one another in love.

Col 3:12 Therefore, as God's chosen people, holy and dearly loved, clothe yourselves with compassion, kindness, humility, gentleness and patience. **13**Bear with each other and forgive whatever grievances you may have against one another. Forgive as the Lord forgave you.

1Th 5:14 And we urge you, brothers, warn those who are idle, encourage the timid, help the weak, be patient with everyone.

1Ti 6:11 But you, man of God, flee from all this, and pursue righteousness, godliness, faith, love, endurance and gentleness.

2Ti 2:24 And the Lord's servant must not quarrel; instead, he must be kind to everyone, able to teach, not resentful. **25**Those who oppose him he must gently instruct, in the hope that God will grant them repentance leading them to a knowledge of the truth,

Tit 2:2 Teach the older men to be temperate, worthy of respect, self-controlled, and sound in faith, in love and in endurance.

Heb 12:1 Therefore, since we are surrounded by such a great cloud of witnesses, let us throw off everything that hinders and the sin that so easily entangles, and let us run with perseverance the race marked out for us.

Jas 5:7 Be patient, then, brothers, until the Lord's coming.

See how the farmer waits for the land to yield its valuable crop and how patient he is for the autumn and spring rains. **8**You too, be patient and stand firm, because the Lord's coming is near.

2Pe 1:5 For this very reason, make every effort to add to your faith goodness; and to goodness, knowledge; **6**and to knowledge, self-control; and to self-control, perseverance; and to perseverance, godliness;

A fruit of tribulation—

Ro 5:3 Not only so, but we also rejoice in our sufferings, because we know that suffering produces perseverance; **4**perseverance, character; and character, hope.

Rev 1:9 I, John, your brother and companion in the suffering and kingdom and patient endurance that are ours in Jesus, was on the island of Patmos because of the word of God and the testimony of Jesus.

A grace of the righteous—

Lk 8:15 But the seed on good soil stands for those with a noble and good heart, who hear the word, retain it, and by persevering produce a crop.

Lk 21:19 By standing firm you will gain life.

Ro 2:7 To those who by persistence in doing good seek glory, honor and immortality, he will give eternal life.

Ro 8:25 But if we hope for what we do not yet have, we wait for it patiently.

Ro 12:12 Be joyful in hope, patient in affliction, faithful in prayer.

Ro 15:4 For everything that was written in the past was written to teach us, so that through endurance and the encouragement of the Scriptures we might have hope.

5May the God who gives endurance and encouragement give you a spirit of unity among yourselves as you follow Christ Jesus,

1Co 13:4 Love is patient, love is kind. It does not envy, it does not boast, it is not proud. **5**It is not rude, it is not self-seeking, it is not easily angered, it keeps no record of wrongs.

2Co 6:4 Rather, as servants of God we commend ourselves in every way: in great endurance; in troubles, hardships and distresses; **5**in beatings, imprisonments and riots; in hard work, sleepless nights and hunger; **6**in purity, understanding, patience and kindness; in the Holy Spirit and in sincere love;

2Co 12:12 The things that mark an apostle—signs, wonders and miracles—were done among you with great perseverance.

Col 1:10 And we pray this in order that you may live a life worthy of the Lord and may please him in every way: bearing fruit in every good work, growing in the knowledge of God, **11**being strengthened with all power according to his glorious might so that you may have great endurance and patience, and joyfully

1Th 1:3 We continually remember before our God and Father your work produced by faith, your labor prompted by love, and your endurance inspired by hope in our Lord Jesus Christ.

2Th 3:5 May the Lord direct your hearts into God's love and Christ's perseverance.

Heb 6:12 We do not want you to become lazy, but to imitate those who through faith and patience inherit what has been promised.

Heb 10:36 You need to persevere so that when you have done the will of God, you will receive what he has promised.

Jas 1:3 because you know that the testing of your faith develops perseverance. **4**Perseverance must finish its work so that you may be mature and complete, not lacking anything.

Jas 1:19 My dear brothers, take note of this: Everyone should be quick to listen, slow to speak and slow to become angry,

1Pe 2:19 For it is commendable if a man bears up under the pain of unjust suffering because he is conscious of God. **20**But how is it to your credit if you receive a beating for doing wrong and endure it? But if you suffer for doing good and you endure it, this is commendable before God. **21**To this you were called, because Christ suffered for you, leaving you an example, that you should follow in his steps. **22**"He committed no sin, and no deceit was found in his mouth."

23When they hurled their insults at him, he did not retaliate; when he suffered, he made no threats. Instead, he entrusted himself to him who judges justly.

Rev 14:12 This calls for patient endurance on the part of the saints who obey God's commandments and remain faithful to Jesus.

Prerequisite of a overseer—

1Ti 3:2 Now the overseer must be above reproach, the husband of but one wife, temperate, self-controlled, respectable, hospitable, able to teach,

Propagates peace—

Pr 15:18 A hot-tempered man stirs up dissension, but a patient man calms a quarrel.

Possible because of God's righteousness—

Rev 13:10 If anyone is to go into captivity, into captivity he will go. If anyone is to be killed with the sword, with the sword he will be killed. This calls for patient endurance and faithfulness on the part of the saints.

Instances of:

Isaac toward the people of Gerar (Ge 26:15-22). Moses (Ex 16:7-8). Job (Job 1:21; Jas 5:11). David (Ps 40:1). Simeon (Lk 2:25). Paul (2Ti 3:10). Prophets (Jas 5:10). The Thessalonians (2Th 1:4). The church at Ephesus (Rev 2:2-3) and Thyatira (Rev 2:19). John (Rev 1:9).

Of Jesus (1Pe 2:21-23; Rev 1:9). *See Jesus the Christ.*

See Longsuffering; Meekness.

PATMOS [4253]. An island in the Aegean Sea. John an exile on (Rev 1:9).

PATRIARCHAL GOVERNMENT *See Government.*

PATRIARCHS, PATRIARCHAL AGE [4252, 4256] (*first father [of a nation, tribe]*).

NIV+PATRIARCH

Name given in NT to those who founded the Hebrew race and nation: Abraham (Heb 7:4), sons of Jacob (Ac 7:8-9), David (Ac 2:29). The term is now commonly used to refer to the persons whose names appear in the genealogies and covenant-histories before the time of Moses (Ge 5,11).

PATRICIDE Killing one's father. Of Sennacherib (2Ki 19:37; Isa 37:38; 1Ti 1:9).

PATRIOTISM

Commanded—

Ps 51:18 In your good pleasure make Zion prosper; build up the walls of Jerusalem.

Ps 122:6 Pray for the peace of Jerusalem: "May those who

love you be secure. **7**May there be peace within your walls and security within your citadels."

Exhortation concerning (2Sa 10:12).

Religious ceremony for the fostering of, commanded —

Dt 26:1 When you have entered the land the LORD your God is giving you as an inheritance and have taken possession of it and settled in it, **2**take some of the firstfruits of all that you produce from the soil of the land the LORD your God is giving you and put them in a basket. Then go to the place the LORD your God will choose as a dwelling for his Name **3**and say to the priest in office at the time, "I declare today to the LORD your God that I have come to the land the LORD swore to our forefathers to give us." **4**The priest shall take the basket from your hands and set it down in front of the altar of the LORD your God. **5**Then you shall declare before the LORD your God: "My father was a wandering Aramean, and he went down into Egypt with a few people and lived there and became a great nation, powerful and numerous. **6**But the Egyptians mistreated us and made us suffer, putting us to hard labor. **7**Then we cried out to the LORD, the God of our fathers, and the LORD heard our voice and saw our misery, toil and oppression. **8**So the LORD brought us out of Egypt with a mighty hand and an outstretched arm, with great terror and with miraculous signs and wonders. **9**He brought us to this place and gave us this land, a land flowing with milk and honey; **10**and now I bring the firstfruits of the soil that you, O LORD, have given me." Place the basket before the LORD your God and bow down before him. **11**And you and the Levites and the aliens among you shall rejoice in all the good things the LORD your God has given to you and your household.

Appealed to in battle (2Sa 10:12).

Songs of—

The song of Deborah (Jdg 5:1-31).

Ps 85:1 You showed favor to your land, O LORD; you restored the fortunes of Jacob. **2**You forgave the iniquity of your people and covered all their sins. *Selah* **3**You set aside all your wrath and turned from your fierce anger.

4Restore us again, O God our Savior, and put away your displeasure toward us. **5**Will you be angry with us forever? Will you prolong your anger through all generations? **6**Will you not revive us again, that your people may rejoice in you? **7**Show us your unfailing love, O LORD, and grant us your salvation.

8I will listen to what God the LORD will say; he promises peace to his people, his saints—but let them not return to folly. **9**Surely his salvation is near those who fear him, that his glory may dwell in our land.

10Love and faithfulness meet together; righteousness and peace kiss each other. **11**Faithfulness springs forth from the earth, and righteousness looks down from heaven. **12**The LORD will indeed give what is good, and our land will yield its harvest. **13**Righteousness goes before him and prepares the way for his steps.

Ps 137:1 By the rivers of Babylon we sat and wept when we remembered Zion. **2**There on the poplars we hung our harps, **3**for there our captors asked us for songs, our tormentors demanded songs of joy; they said, "Sing us one of the songs of Zion!"

4How can we sing the songs of the LORD while in a foreign land? **5**If I forget you, O Jerusalem, may my right hand forget [its skill]. **6**May my tongue cling to the roof of my mouth if I do not remember you, if I do not consider Jerusalem my highest joy.

Lack of, lamented (La 5:1-22).

Instances of:

Moses (Heb 11:24-26). Deborah and Barak (Jdg 4:5). The tribes of Zebulun and Naphtali (Jdg 5:18-20). Eli (1Sa 4:17-18). Phinehas' wife (1Sa 4:19-22). Joab (2Sa 10:12). Uriah (2Sa 11:11). The Psalmist (Ps 51:18; 85:1-13). Hadad (1Ki 11:21-22). The lepers of Samaria (2Ki 7:9). Israelite exiles (Ne 1:1-11; 2:1-20; Ps 137:1-6). Nehemiah (Ne 1:2,4-11; 2:3). The Jews in public defense (Ne 2:3; 4:1-23).

Isaiah—

Isa 62:1 For Zion's sake I will not keep silent, for Jerusalem's sake I will not remain quiet, till her righteousness shines out like the dawn, her salvation like a blazing torch.

Jeremiah—

Jer 8:11 They dress the wound of my people as though it were not serious. "Peace, peace," they say, when there is no peace.

Jer 8:21 Since my people are crushed, I am crushed; I mourn, and horror grips me. ²²Is there no balm in Gilead? Is there no physician there? Why then is there no healing for the wound of my people?

Jer 9:1 Oh, that my head were a spring of water and my eyes a fountain of tears! I would weep day and night for the slain of my people. ²Oh, that I had in the desert a lodging place for travelers, so that I might leave my people and go away from them; for they are all adulterers, a crowd of unfaithful people.

La 5:1 Remember, O LORD, what has happened to us; look, and see our disgrace. ²Our inheritance has been turned over to aliens, our homes to foreigners. ³We have become orphans and fatherless, our mothers like widows. ⁴We must buy the water we drink; our wood can be had only at a price. ⁵Those who pursue us are at our heels; we are weary and find no rest. ⁶We submitted to Egypt and Assyria to get enough bread. ⁷Our fathers sinned and are no more, and we bear their punishment. ⁸Slaves rule over us, and there is none to free us from their hands. ⁹We get our bread at the risk of our lives because of the sword in the desert. ¹⁰Our skin is hot as an oven, feverish from hunger. ¹¹Women have been ravished in Zion, and virgins in the towns of Judah. ¹²Princes have been hung up by their hands; elders are shown no respect. ¹³Young men toil at the millstones; boys stagger under loads of wood. ¹⁴The elders are gone from the city gate; the young men have stopped their music. ¹⁵Joy is gone from our hearts; our dancing has turned to mourning. ¹⁶The crown has fallen from our head. Woe to us, for we have sinned! ¹⁷Because of this our hearts are faint, because of these things our eyes grow dim ¹⁸for Mount Zion, which lies desolate, with jackals prowling over it.

¹⁹You, O LORD, reign forever; your throne endures from generation to generation. ²⁰Why do you always forget us? Why do you forsake us so long? ²¹Restore us to yourself, O LORD, that we may return; renew our days as of old ²²unless you have utterly rejected us and are angry with us beyond measure.

Lacking in:

The tribes of Reuben, Asher, and Dan (Jdg 5:15-17). Inhabitants, of Meroz (Jdg 5:23), of Succoth and Peniel (Jdg 8:4-17).

See Country, Love of.

PATROBAS [4259] (*father of existence*). A believer at Rome (Ro 16:14).

PATTERN Of the tabernacle (Heb 8:5-9:23). *See Tabernacle.*

PAU [7185] (*groaning, bleating*). A city of Edom (Ge 36:39; 1Ch 1:50).

PAUL [4263] (*little*).

NIV+ PAUL'S, SAUL

Background and conversion:

Also called Saul (Ac 8:1; 9:1; 13:9). Of the tribe of Benjamin (Ro 11:1; Php 3:5). Personal appearance of (2Co 10:1,10; 11:6). Born in Tarsus (Ac 9:11; 21:39; 22:3). Educated at Jerusalem in the school of Gamaliel (Ac 22:3; 26:4). A zealous Pharisee (Ac 22:3; 23:6; 26:5; 2Co 11:22; Gal 1:14; Php 3:5). A Roman (Ac 16:37; 22:25-28). Persecutes the Christians; present at and gives consent to the stoning of Stephen (Ac 7:58; 8:1,3; 9:1; 22:4). Sent to Damascus with letters for the arrest and return to Jerusalem of Christians (Ac 9:1-2). His vision and conversion (Ac 9:3-22; 22:4-19; 26:9-15; 1Co 9:11; 15:8; Gal 1:13; 1Ti 1:12-13). Is baptized (Ac 9:18; 22:16). Called to be an apostle (Ac 22:14-21; 26:14-21; 26:16-18; Ro 1:1; 1Co 1:1; 9:1-2; 15:9; Gal 1:1,15-16; Eph 1:1; Col 1:1; 1Ti 1:1; 2:7; 2Ti 1:1,11; Tit 1:1,3). Preaches in Damascus (Ac 9:20,22). Is persecuted by the Jews (Ac 9:23-24). Escapes by being let down from the wall in a basket; goes to Arabia (Gal 1:17), Jerusalem (Ac 9:25-26; Gal 1:18-19). Received by the disciples in Jerusalem (Ac 9:26-29). Goes to Caesarea and returns to Tarsus (Ac 9:30; 18:22).

Brought to Antioch by Barnabas (Ac 11:25-26). Teaches at Antioch one year (Ac 11:26). Brings the contributions of the Christians in Antioch to the Christians in Jerusalem (Ac 11:27-30). Returns with John to Antioch (Ac 12:25).

First Missionary Journey:

See Missionary Journeys of Paul. Sent to the Gentiles (Ac 13:2-3,47-48; 22:17;21; Ro 11:13; 15:16; Gal 1:15-24). Visits Seleucia (Ac 13:4), Cyprus (Ac 13:4). Preaches at Salamis (Ac 13:5), at Paphos (Ac 13:6). Sergius Paulus the proconsul is converted (Ac 13:7-12). Contends with Elymas the sorcerer (Ac 13:6-12). Visits Perga in Pamphylia (Ac 13:13). John, a companion of, departs for Jerusalem (Ac 13:13). Visits Antioch in Pisidia and preaches in the synagogue (Ac 13:14-41). His message received gladly by the Gentiles (Ac 13:42,49). Persecuted and expelled (Ac 13:50-51). Visits Iconium and preaches to the Jews and Greeks; is persecuted; escapes to Lystra; goes to Derbe (Ac 14:1-6). Heals an crippled man (Ac 14:8-10). The people attempt to worship him (Ac 14:11-18). Is persecuted by Jews from Antioch and Iconium and is stoned (Ac 14:19; 2Co 11:25; 2Ti 3:11). Escapes to Derbe, where he preaches the Gospel, and returns to Lystra, Iconium, and to Antioch, encourages the disciples, and ordains elders (Ac 14:19-23). Revisits Pisidia, Pamphylia, Perga, Attalia, and returns to Antioch (Ac 14:24-28). Contends with the Judaizing Christians against circumcision (Ac 15:1-2). Refers the question of circumcision to the apostles and elders at Jerusalem (Ac 15:2,4). He declares to the apostles at Jerusalem the miracles and wonders God had done among the Gentiles by them (Ac 15:12). Returns to Antioch, accompanied by Barnabas, Judas, and Silas, with letters to the Gentiles (Ac 15:22,25).

Second Missionary Journey:

See Missionary Journeys of Paul. Makes his second tour of the churches (Ac 15:36). Chooses Silas as his companion, and passes through Syria and Cilicia, confirming the churches (Ac 15:36-41). Visits Lystra; circumcises Timothy (Ac 16:1-5). Goes through Phrygia and Galatia; is forbidden by the Holy Spirit to preach in Asia; visits Mysia; desires to go to Bithynia, but is restrained by the Spirit; goes to Troas, where he has a vision of a man saying, "Come over into Macedonia, and help us"; he immediately proceeds to Macedonia (Ac 16:6-10). Visits Samothrace and Neapolis; comes to Philippi, the chief city of Macedonia; visits a place of prayer at the riverside; preaches the Word; the merchant, Lydia of Thyatira, is converted and baptized (Ac 16:11-15). Exorcizes a demon from a fortune-teller (Ac 16:16-18). Persecuted, beaten, and cast into prison with Silas; sings songs of praise in the prison; an earthquake shakes the prison; he preaches to the alarmed jailer, who believes and is baptized with his household (Ac 16:19-34). Is released by the civil authorities on the ground of his being a Roman citizen (Ac 16:35-39; 2Co 6:5; 11:25; 1Th 2:2). Is received at the house of Lydia (Ac 16:40). Visits Amphipolis, Apollonia, and Thessalonica; preaches in the synagogue (Ac 17:1-4). Is persecuted (Ac 17:5-9; 2Th 1:1-4). Escapes to Berea by night; preaches in the synagogue; many honorable women and men believe (Ac 17:10-12). Persecuted by the Jews who come from Thessalonica; is conducted by the brothers to Athens (Ac 17:13-15). Disputes on Mars' Hill with philosophers (Ac 17:16-34). Visits Corinth; lives with Aquila and his wife, Priscilla, who were tentmakers; joins in their trade; reasons in the synagogue every Sabbath; is rejected by the Jews; turns to the Gentiles; stays there one year and six months, teaching the word of God (Ac 18:1-11). Persecuted by Jews, taken before the proconsul; accusation dismissed; takes his leave after many days, and sails to Syria, accompanied by Aquila and Priscilla (Ac 18:12-18). Visits Ephesus, where he leaves Aquila and Priscilla; enters into a synagogue, where he reasons with the Jews; starts on his return journey to Jerusalem; visits Caesarea, and returns to Antioch (Ac 18:19-22).

Third Missionary Journey:

See Missionary Journeys of Paul. Returning to Ephesus, passes through Galatia and Phrygia, strengthening the disciples (Ac 18:18-23). Baptizes disciples of John in the name of the Lord Jesus; preaches in the synagogue, remains in Ephesus for two years; heals the sick (Ac 19:1-12). Jewish exorcists are beaten by a demon and many Ephesians believe, bringing their books of sorcery to be burned (Ac 19:13-20; 1Co 16:8-9). Sends Timothy and Erastus into Macedonia, but he himself remains in Asia for a period of time (Ac 19:21-22). The spread of the gospel through his preaching interferes with the idol-makers; he is persecuted, and a great uproar of the city is created; the city clerk appeases the people; dismisses the accusation against Paul, and disperses the people (Ac 19:23-41; 2Co 1:8; 2Ti 4:14). Proceeds to Macedonia after encouraging the churches in those parts; comes into Greece and stays three months; returns through Macedonia, accompanied by Sopater, Aristarchus, Secundus, Gaius, Timothy, Tychicus, and Trophimus (Ac 20:1-6). Visits Troas; preaches until the break of day; restores to life Eutychus, who fell from the window (Ac 20:6-12). Visits Assos, Mitylene, Kios, Samos, and Miletus, hurrying to Jerusalem, to be there at Pentecost (Ac 20:13-16). Sends for the elders of the church of Ephesus; tells them of how he had preached in Asia, and of his tests and afflictions testifying repentance toward God; declares he was compelled by the Spirit to go to Jerusalem; exhorts them to watch over themselves and their flock; kneels down, prays, and

departs (Ac 20:17-38). Visits Cos, Rhodes, Patara; takes a ship for Tyre; stays seven days; is brought on his way by the disciples to the outskirts of the city; kneels, prays, and leaves; comes to Ptolemais; greets the brothers and stays one day (Ac 21:1-7). Departs for Caesarea; enters the house of Philip the evangelist; is warned by Agabus not to go to Jerusalem; proceeds to Jerusalem (Ac 21:8-16).

Arrest and Trials:

See Missionary Journeys of Paul. Is received warmly by the brothers; talks of the things that had been done among the Gentiles by his ministry; enters the temple; the people are stirred against him by the Jews from Asia; an uproar is created; he is thrown out of the temple; the commander of the troops interposes and arrests him (Ac 21:17-33). His defense (Ac 21:33-40; 22:1-21). Is confined in the barracks (Ac 22:24-30). Is brought before the Sanhedrin; his defense (Ac 22:30; 23:1-5). Is returned to the barracks (Ac 23:10). Is encouraged by a vision, promising him that he must testify in Rome (Ac 23:11). Jews conspire against his life (Ac 23:12-15). Thwarted by his nephew (Ac 23:16-22). Is escorted to Caesarea by a military guard (Ac 23:23-33). Is confined in Herod's palace in Caesarea (Ac 23:35). His trial before Felix (Ac 24). Remains in custody for two years (Ac 24:27). His trial before Festus (Ac 25:1-12). Appeals to Caesar (Ac 25:10-12). His examination before Agrippa (Ac 25:13-27; 26).

Is taken to Rome in custody of Julius, a centurion, and guard of soldiers; boards the ship, accompanied by other prisoners, and sails along the coast of Asia; stops at Sidon and Myra (Ac 27:1-5). Transferred to a ship of Alexandria; sails past Cnidus, Crete, and Salmone to Fair Havens (Ac 27:6-8). Predicts loss of the ship; his advice not heeded, and the voyage resumed (Ac 27:9-13). The ship encounters a hurricane; Paul encourages and comforts the officers and crew; the soldiers advise putting the prisoners to death; the centurion interferes, and all 276 on board are saved (Ac 27:14-44). The ship is wrecked, and all on board take refuge on the island of Malta (Ac 27:14-44). Kind treatment by the inhabitants of the island (Ac 28:1-2). Is bitten by a viper and miraculously preserved (Ac 28:3-6). Heals the chief official's father and others (Ac 28:7-10). Is delayed in Malta three months; proceeds on the voyage; delays at Syracuse; sails by Rhegium and Puteoli; meets brothers who accompany him to Rome from the Forum of Appius; arrives at Rome and is permitted to live by himself in custody of a soldier (Ac 28:11-16). Calls the chief Jews together; states his situation; is kindly received; expounds the gospel; testifies to the kingdom of heaven (Ac 28:17-29). Lives two years in his own hired house, preaching and teaching (Ac 28:30-31).

Sickness in Asia (2Co 1:8-11). Caught up to the third heavens (2Co 12:1-4). Has "a thorn in the flesh" (2Co 12:7-9; Gal 4:13-14). His independence of character (1Th 2:9; 2Th 3:8).

Persecutions of:

Ac 9:16 I will show him how much he must suffer for my name."

Ac 9:23 After many days had gone by, the Jews conspired to kill him, [24]but Saul learned of their plan. Day and night they kept close watch on the city gates in order to kill him. [25]But his followers took him by night and lowered him in a basket through an opening in the wall.

Ac 9:29 He talked and debated with the Grecian Jews, but they tried to kill him. (+Ac 14:19)

Ac 16:19 When the owners of the slave girl realized that their hope of making money was gone, they seized Paul and Silas and dragged them into the marketplace to face the authorities. ²⁰They brought them before the magistrates and said, "These men are Jews, and are throwing our city into an uproar ²¹by advocating customs unlawful for us Romans to accept or practice."

²²The crowd joined in the attack against Paul and Silas, and the magistrates ordered them to be stripped and beaten. ²³After they had been severely flogged, they were thrown into prison, and the jailer was commanded to guard them carefully. ²⁴Upon receiving such orders, he put them in the inner cell and fastened their feet in the stocks.

²⁵About midnight Paul and Silas were praying and singing hymns to God, and the other prisoners were listening to them.

Ac 20:22 "And now, compelled by the Spirit, I am going to Jerusalem, not knowing what will happen to me there. ²³I only know that in every city the Holy Spirit warns me that prison and hardships are facing me. ²⁴However, I consider my life worth nothing to me, if only I may finish the race and complete the task the Lord Jesus has given me—the task of testifying to the gospel of God's grace.

Ac 21:13 Then Paul answered, "Why are you weeping and breaking my heart? I am ready not only to be bound, but also to die in Jerusalem for the name of the Lord Jesus."

Ac 21:27 When the seven days were nearly over, some Jews from the province of Asia saw Paul at the temple. They stirred up the whole crowd and seized him, ²⁸shouting, "Men of Israel, help us! This is the man who teaches all men everywhere against our people and our law and this place. And besides, he has brought Greeks into the temple area and defiled this holy place." ²⁹(They had previously seen Trophimus the Ephesian in the city with Paul and assumed that Paul had brought him into the temple area.)

³⁰The whole city was aroused, and the people came running from all directions. Seizing Paul, they dragged him from the temple, and immediately the gates were shut. ³¹While they were trying to kill him, news reached the commander of the Roman troops that the whole city of Jerusalem was in an uproar. ³²He at once took some officers and soldiers and ran down to the crowd. When the rioters saw the commander and his soldiers, they stopped beating Paul.

³³The commander came up and arrested him and ordered him to be bound with two chains. Then he asked who he was and what he had done.

Ac 22:22 The crowd listened to Paul until he said this. Then they raised their voices and shouted, "Rid the earth of him! He's not fit to live!"

²³As they were shouting and throwing off their cloaks and flinging dust into the air, ²⁴the commander ordered Paul to be taken into the barracks. He directed that he be flogged and questioned in order to find out why the people were shouting at him like this.

Ac 23:10 The dispute became so violent that the commander was afraid Paul would be torn to pieces by them. He ordered the troops to go down and take him away from them by force and bring him into the barracks.

Ac 23:12 The next morning the Jews formed a conspiracy and bound themselves with an oath not to eat or drink until they had killed Paul. ¹³More than forty men were involved in this plot. ¹⁴They went to the chief priests and elders and said, "We have taken a solemn oath not to eat anything until we have killed Paul. ¹⁵Now then, you and the Sanhedrin petition the commander to bring him before you on the pretext of wanting more accurate information about his case. We are ready to kill him before he gets here."

Ro 8:35 Who shall separate us from the love of Christ? Shall trouble or hardship or persecution or famine or nakedness or danger or sword? ³⁶As it is written: "For your sake we face death all day long; we are considered as sheep to be slaughtered."

³⁷No, in all these things we are more than conquerors through him who loved us.

1Co 4:9 For it seems to me that God has put us apostles on display at the end of the procession, like men condemned to die in the arena. We have been made a spectacle to the whole universe, to angels as well as to men.

1Co 4:11 To this very hour we go hungry and thirsty, we are in rags, we are brutally treated, we are homeless. ¹²We work hard with our own hands. When we are cursed, we bless; when we are persecuted, we endure it; ¹³when we are slandered, we answer kindly. Up to this moment we have become the scum of the earth, the refuse of the world.

2Co 1:8 We do not want you to be uninformed, brothers, about the hardships we suffered in the province of Asia. We were under great pressure, far beyond our ability to endure, so that we despaired even of life. ⁹Indeed, in our hearts we felt the sentence of death. But this happened that we might not rely on ourselves but on God, who raises the dead. ¹⁰He has delivered us from such a deadly peril, and he will deliver us. On him we have set our hope that he will continue to deliver us,

2Co 4:8 We are hard pressed on every side, but not crushed; perplexed, but not in despair; ⁹persecuted, but not abandoned; struck down, but not destroyed.

2Co 6:4 Rather, as servants of God we commend ourselves in every way: in great endurance; in troubles, hardships and distresses; ⁵in beatings, imprisonments and riots; in hard work, sleepless nights and hunger;

2Co 6:8 through glory and dishonor, bad report and good report; genuine, yet regarded as impostors; ⁹known, yet regarded as unknown; dying, and yet we live on; beaten, and yet not killed; ¹⁰sorrowful, yet always rejoicing; poor, yet making many rich; having nothing, and yet possessing everything.

2Co 11:23 Are they servants of Christ? (I am out of my mind to talk like this.) I am more. I have worked much harder, been in prison more frequently, been flogged more severely, and been exposed to death again and again. ²⁴Five times I received from the Jews the forty lashes minus one. ²⁵Three times I was beaten with rods, once I was stoned, three times I was shipwrecked, I spent a night and a day in the open sea, ²⁶I have been constantly on the move. I have been in danger from rivers, in danger from bandits, in danger from my own countrymen, in danger from Gentiles; in danger in the city, in danger in the country, in danger at sea; and in danger from false brothers. ²⁷I have labored and toiled and have often gone without sleep; I have known hunger and thirst and have often gone without food; I have been cold and naked.

2Co 11:32 In Damascus the governor under King Aretas had the city of the Damascenes guarded in order to arrest me. ³³But I was lowered in a basket from a window in the wall and slipped through his hands.

2Co 12:10 That is why, for Christ's sake, I delight in weaknesses, in insults, in hardships, in persecutions, in difficulties. For when I am weak, then I am strong.

Gal 5:11 Brothers, if I am still preaching circumcision, why am I still being persecuted? In that case the offense of the cross has been abolished.

Gal 6:17 Finally, let no one cause me trouble, for I bear on my body the marks of Jesus.

Php 1:30 since you are going through the same struggle you saw I had, and now hear that I still have.

Col 1:24 Now I rejoice in what was suffered for you, and I fill up in my flesh what is still lacking in regard to Christ's afflictions, for the sake of his body, which is the church.

1Th 2:2 We had previously suffered and been insulted in Philippi, as you know, but with the help of our God we dared to tell you his gospel in spite of strong opposition.

1Th 2:14 For you, brothers, became imitators of God's churches in Judea, which are in Christ Jesus: You suffered from your own countrymen the same things those churches suffered from the Jews, ¹⁵who killed the Lord Jesus and the prophets and also drove us out. They displease God and are hostile to all men (+1Th 3:4)

2Ti 1:12 That is why I am suffering as I am. Yet I am not ashamed, because I know whom I have believed, and am convinced that he is able to guard what I have entrusted to him for that day.

2Ti 2:9 for which I am suffering even to the point of being chained like a criminal. But God's word is not chained. ¹⁰Therefore I endure everything for the sake of the elect, that they too may obtain the salvation that is in Christ Jesus, with eternal glory.

2Ti 3:11 persecutions, sufferings—what kinds of things happened to me in Antioch, Iconium and Lystra, the persecutions I endured. Yet the Lord rescued me from all of them. ¹²In fact, everyone who wants to live a godly life in Christ Jesus will be persecuted,

2Ti 4:16 At my first defense, no one came to my support, but everyone deserted me. May it not be held against them. ¹⁷But the Lord stood at my side and gave me strength, so that through me the message might be fully proclaimed and all the Gentiles might hear it. And I was delivered from the lion's mouth.

Character of:

(2Co 10:1,10; 11:6; Gal 4:13). Cheerful in adversity (Ac 10:25; Ro 8:35-37; 2Co 4:8-10; 12:10; 2Ti 2:10; 3:11-12; 4:16-17). Courageous (Ac 9:29; 20:22-24; 21:13; Eph 6:20; 1Th 2:2). Purposeful, even when the Holy Spirit warns him not to go to Jerusalem (Ac 20:22-23; 21:4,10-14). Indomitable (Ro 8:35-37; 1Co 4:9-13; 2Co 4:8-12; 6:4-10; 11:23-33; 12:10; 1Th 2:2; 2Ti 1:12; 3:11; 4:17). Joyous in suffering (Ac 16:25; Php 2:17; Col 1:24; 2Ti 2:9). Meek (1Co 4:12-13; 2Ti 4:16). Self-forgetful (1Co 4:9,11-13). Self-supporting (Ac 18:3; 20:33-35; 2Co 11:7,9; 1Th 2:9; 2Th 3:8). Tactful (1Co 9:19-22; 10:33; Phm 8-21). Zealous (Ro 9:3; 2Co 5:11-14; 6:4-10; 11:22-33; 12:10,14-15; Php 3:6-16; Col 1:29). Ready for death (2Ti 4:6-8).

PAULUS, SERGIUS [4263]. Roman proconsul of Cyprus; became a Christian through Paul (Ac 13:6-12).

PAVEMENT, STONE [4246, 4861, 8367, *3346*]. The courtyard outside the palace in Jerusalem where Pilate passed public sentence on Jesus (Jn 19:13).

PAVILION [2903, 6109] (*booth, tent*). Movable tent or canopy (1Ki 20:12; Jer 43:10). Figuratively of God's protection (Ps 27:5) or majesty (Job 36:29).

PAWN *See Surety.*

PAZZEZ *See Beth Pazzez.*

PEACE [1388, 4957, 5341, 5663, 5739, 8092, 8922, 8932, 8934, 8966, 9200, *457, 1644, 1645, 1646, 1647*].
NIV+ PACIFIES, PACIFY, PEACE-LOVING, PEACEABLE, PEACEABLY, PEACEFUL, PEACEFULLY, PEACEMAKERS, PEACETIME

From God:

Nu 6:26 the LORD turn his face toward you and give you peace." ' (+Ps 29:11; 85:8; Isa 26:12; 57:19)

1Co 14:33 For God is not a God of disorder but of peace. As in all the congregations of the saints,

Social:

Beneficence of—

Ps 133:1 How good and pleasant it is when brothers live together in unity!

Pr 15:17 Better a meal of vegetables where there is love than a fattened calf with hatred.

Pr 17:1 Better a dry crust with peace and quiet than a house full of feasting, with strife.

Pr 17:14 Starting a quarrel is like breaching a dam; so drop the matter before a dispute breaks out.

Ecc 4:6 Better one handful with tranquillity than two handfuls with toil and chasing after the wind.

Honorable—

Pr 20:3 It is to a man's honor to avoid strife, but every fool is quick to quarrel.

Commanded—

Ge 45:24 Then he sent his brothers away, and as they were leaving he said to them, "Don't quarrel on the way!"

Ps 34:14 Turn from evil and do good; seek peace and pursue it.

Jer 29:7 Also, seek the peace and prosperity of the city to which I have carried you into exile. Pray to the LORD for it, because if it prospers, you too will prosper."

Mk 9:50 "Salt is good, but if it loses its saltiness, how can you make it salty again? Have salt in yourselves, and be at peace with each other."

Ro 12:18 If it is possible, as far as it depends on you, live at peace with everyone.

Ro 14:19 Let us therefore make every effort to do what leads to peace and to mutual edification.

2Co 13:11 Finally, brothers, good-by. Aim for perfection, listen to my appeal, be of one mind, live in peace. And the God of love and peace will be with you.

Eph 4:3 Make every effort to keep the unity of the Spirit through the bond of peace. (+Eph 4:31-32)

1Th 5:13 Hold them in the highest regard in love because of their work. Live in peace with each other.

1Ti 2:2 for kings and all those in authority, that we may live peaceful and quiet lives in all godliness and holiness.

2Ti 2:22 Flee the evil desires of youth, and pursue righteousness, faith, love and peace, along with those who call on the Lord out of a pure heart.

Heb 12:14 Make every effort to live in peace with all men and to be holy; without holiness no one will see the Lord.

1Pe 3:10 For, "Whoever would love life and see good days must keep his tongue from evil and his lips from deceitful speech. ¹¹He must turn from evil and do good; he must seek peace and pursue it.

Love of, commanded—

Zec 8:19 This is what the LORD Almighty says: "The fasts of the fourth, fifth, seventh and tenth months will become joyful and glad occasions and happy festivals for Judah. Therefore love truth and peace."

Promised—

Lev 26:6 " 'I will grant peace in the land, and you will lie down and no one will make you afraid. I will remove savage beasts from the land, and the sword will not pass through your country.

Job 5:23 For you will have a covenant with the stones of the field, and the wild animals will be at peace with you. ²⁴You will know that your tent is secure; you will take stock of your property and find nothing missing.

Isa 2:4 He will judge between the nations and will settle disputes for many peoples. They will beat their swords into plowshares and their spears into pruning hooks. Nation will not take up sword against nation, nor will they train for war anymore. (+Isa 11:6-9,13; 60:17-18)

Hos 2:18 In that day I will make a covenant for them with the beasts of the field and the birds of the air and the creatures that move along the ground. Bow and sword and battle I will abolish from the land, so that all may lie down in safety.

The righteous assured of—
Pr 16:7 When a man's ways are pleasing to the LORD, he makes even his enemies live at peace with him.

Broken by the gospel—
Mt 10:21 "Brother will betray brother to death, and a father his child; children will rebel against their parents and have them put to death. ²²All men will hate you because of me, but he who stands firm to the end will be saved.

Mt 10:34 "Do not suppose that I have come to bring peace to the earth. I did not come to bring peace, but a sword. ³⁵For I have come to turn

"'a man against his father, a daughter against her mother, a daughter-in-law against her mother-in-law— ³⁶a man's enemies will be the members of his own household.' (+Lk 12:51-53)

Moses' efforts in behalf of, resented (Ex 2:13-14)—
Ac 7:26 The next day Moses came upon two Israelites who were fighting. He tried to reconcile them by saying, 'Men, you are brothers; why do you want to hurt each other?'

²⁷"But the man who was mistreating the other pushed Moses aside and said, 'Who made you ruler and judge over us? ²⁸Do you want to kill me as you killed the Egyptian yesterday?' ²⁹When Moses heard this, he fled to Midian, where he settled as a foreigner and had two sons.

Promoters of Peace Promised:

Joy—
Pr 12:20 There is deceit in the hearts of those who plot evil, but joy for those who promote peace.

Adoption—
Mt 5:9 Blessed are the peacemakers, for they will be called sons of God.

Fruit of righteousness—
Jas 3:17 But the wisdom that comes from heaven is first of all pure; then peace-loving, considerate, submissive, full of mercy and good fruit, impartial and sincere. ¹⁸Peacemakers who sow in peace raise a harvest of righteousness.

God's favor—
Lk 2:14 "Glory to God in the highest, and on earth peace to men on whom his favor rests."

Instances of Promoters of Peace:

Abraham (Ge 13:8-9), Abimelech (Ge 26:29), Mordecai (Est 10:3)

David—
Ps 120:6 Too long have I lived among those who hate peace. ⁷I am a man of peace; but when I speak, they are for war.

See Charitableness; Nation, Peace of.

Spiritual:

Through Christ (Isa 2:4)—
Isa 9:6 For to us a child is born, to us a son is given, and the government will be on his shoulders. And he will be called Wonderful Counselor, Mighty God, Everlasting Father, Prince of Peace. (+Isa 9:7; 11:6)

Isa 11:13 Ephraim's jealousy will vanish, and Judah's enemies will be cut off; Ephraim will not be jealous of Judah, nor Judah hostile toward Ephraim. (+Mic 4:3,5)

Lk 1:79 to shine on those living in darkness and in the shadow of death, to guide our feet into the path of peace." (+Jn 7:38; 14:27)

Ac 10:36 You know the message God sent to the people of Israel, telling the good news of peace through Jesus Christ, who is Lord of all.

Ro 5:1 Therefore, since we have been justified through faith, we have peace with God through our Lord Jesus Christ,

Ro 10:15 And how can they preach unless they are sent? As it is written, "How beautiful are the feet of those who bring good news!"

To the world (Isa 2:4)—
Isa 11:6 The wolf will live with the lamb, the leopard will lie down with the goat, the calf and the lion and the yearling together; and a little child will lead them. ⁷The cow will feed with the bear, their young will lie down together, and the lion will eat straw like the ox. ⁸The infant will play near the hole of the cobra, and the young child put his hand into the viper's nest. ⁹They will neither harm nor destroy on all my holy mountain, for the earth will be full of the knowledge of the LORD as the waters cover the sea.

Lk 2:14 "Glory to God in the highest, and on earth peace to men on whom his favor rests."

To God's children—
Isa 54:10 Though the mountains be shaken and the hills be removed, yet my unfailing love for you will not be shaken nor my covenant of peace be removed," says the LORD, who has compassion on you.

Isa 54:13 All your sons will be taught by the LORD, and great will be your children's peace.

From God—
Job 34:29 But if he remains silent, who can condemn him? If he hides his face, who can see him? Yet he is over man and nation alike,

Ps 29:11 The LORD gives strength to his people; the LORD blesses his people with peace. (+Ps 72:3,7)

Ps 85:8 I will listen to what God the LORD will say; he promises peace to his people, his saints—but let them not return to folly.

Jer 33:6 "'Nevertheless, I will bring health and healing to it; I will heal my people and will let them enjoy abundant peace and security.

Eze 34:25 "'I will make a covenant of peace with them and rid the land of wild beasts so that they may live in the desert and sleep in the forests in safety.

Hag 2:9 'The glory of this present house will be greater than the glory of the former house,' says the LORD Almighty. 'And in this place I will grant peace,' declares the LORD Almighty."

Mal 2:5 "My covenant was with him, a covenant of life and peace, and I gave them to him; this called for reverence and he revered me and stood in awe of my name.

Ro 15:13 May the God of hope fill you with all joy and

peace as you trust in him, so that you may overflow with hope by the power of the Holy Spirit.

Ro 15:33 The God of peace be with you all. Amen. (+Ro 16:20; 1Co 1:3; 14:33; 2Co 1:2)

Gal 1:3 Grace and peace to you from God our Father and the Lord Jesus Christ,

Php 4:7 And the peace of God, which transcends all understanding, will guard your hearts and your minds in Christ Jesus.

Php 4:9 Whatever you have learned or received or heard from me, or seen in me—put it into practice. And the God of peace will be with you. (+1Th 1:1; 5:23)

2Th 3:16 Now may the Lord of peace himself give you peace at all times and in every way. The Lord be with all of you. (+1Ti 1:2; 2Ti 1:2; Tit 1:4; Phm ; Heb 13:20; Rev 1:4)

From Christ (Mt 11:29)—

Jn 14:27 Peace I leave with you; my peace I give you. I do not give to you as the world gives. Do not let your hearts be troubled and do not be afraid.

Jn 16:33 "I have told you these things, so that in me you may have peace. In this world you will have trouble. But take heart! I have overcome the world."

Jn 20:19 On the evening of that first day of the week, when the disciples were together, with the doors locked for fear of the Jews, Jesus came and stood among them and said, "Peace be with you!"

Eph 2:14 For he himself is our peace, who has made the two one and has destroyed the barrier, the dividing wall of hostility, [15]by abolishing in his flesh the law with its commandments and regulations. His purpose was to create in himself one new man out of the two, thus making peace, [16]and in this one body to reconcile both of them to God through the cross, by which he put to death their hostility. [17]He came and preached peace to you who were far away and peace to those who were near.

Col 3:15 Let the peace of Christ rule in your hearts, since as members of one body you were called to peace. And be thankful. (+Rev 1:4-5)

A fruit of the Spirit—

Ro 14:17 For the kingdom of God is not a matter of eating and drinking, but of righteousness, peace and joy in the Holy Spirit,

Gal 5:22 But the fruit of the Spirit is love, joy, peace, patience, kindness, goodness, faithfulness,

A fruit of righteousness—

Ro 2:10 but glory, honor and peace for everyone who does good: first for the Jew, then for the Gentile.

Assured to the righteous—

Ps 37:4 Delight yourself in the LORD and he will give you the desires of your heart.

Ps 37:11 But the meek will inherit the land and enjoy great peace.

Ps 37:37 Consider the blameless, observe the upright; there is a future for the man of peace.

Ps 125:1 Those who trust in the LORD are like Mount Zion, which cannot be shaken but endures forever.

Ps 125:5 But those who turn to crooked ways the LORD will banish with the evildoers. Peace be upon Israel.

Pr 3:17 Her ways are pleasant ways, and all her paths are peace.

Pr 3:24 when you lie down, you will not be afraid; when you lie down, your sleep will be sweet.

Isa 26:3 You will keep in perfect peace him whose mind is steadfast, because he trusts in you.

Isa 26:12 LORD, you establish peace for us; all that we have accomplished you have done for us.

Isa 32:2 Each man will be like a shelter from the wind and a refuge from the storm, like streams of water in the desert and the shadow of a great rock in a thirsty land.

Isa 32:17 The fruit of righteousness will be peace; the effect of righteousness will be quietness and confidence forever. [18]My people will live in peaceful dwelling places, in secure homes, in undisturbed places of rest.

Isa 55:2 Why spend money on what is not bread, and your labor on what does not satisfy? Listen, listen to me, and eat what is good, and your soul will delight in the richest of fare.

Isa 55:12 You will go out in joy and be led forth in peace; the mountains and hills will burst into song before you, and all the trees of the field will clap their hands.

Isa 57:1 The righteous perish, and no one ponders it in his heart; devout men are taken away, and no one understands that the righteous are taken away to be spared from evil. [2]Those who walk uprightly enter into peace; they find rest as they lie in death.

Isa 57:19 creating praise on the lips of the mourners in Israel. Peace, peace, to those far and near," says the LORD. "And I will heal them."

Ro 8:6 The mind of sinful man is death, but the mind controlled by the Spirit is life and peace;

Through the reconciliation of Christ—

Isa 53:5 But he was pierced for our transgressions, he was crushed for our iniquities; the punishment that brought us peace was upon him, and by his wounds we are healed.

Jn 7:38 Whoever believes in me, as the Scripture has said, streams of living water will flow from within him." (+Ro 5:1)

Col 1:20 and through him to reconcile to himself all things, whether things on earth or things in heaven, by making peace through his blood, shed on the cross.

Through acquaintance with God—

Job 22:21 "Submit to God and be at peace with him; in this way prosperity will come to you.

Job 22:26 Surely then you will find delight in the Almighty and will lift up your face to God.

Ps 4:8 I will lie down and sleep in peace, for you alone, O LORD, make me dwell in safety.

Ps 17:15 And I—in righteousness I will see your face; when I awake, I will be satisfied with seeing your likeness.

Ps 73:25 Whom have I in heaven but you? And earth has nothing I desire besides you. [26]My flesh and my heart may fail, but God is the strength of my heart and my portion forever.

Isa 12:1 In that day you will say: "I will praise you, O LORD. Although you were angry with me, your anger has turned away and you have comforted me. [2]Surely God is my salvation; I will trust and not be afraid. The LORD, the LORD, is my strength and my song; he has become my salvation."

Isa 25:7 On this mountain he will destroy the shroud that enfolds all peoples, the sheet that covers all nations; [8]he will swallow up death forever. The Sovereign LORD will wipe away the tears from all faces; he will remove the disgrace of his people from all the earth. The LORD has spoken.

Isa 28:12 to whom he said, "This is the resting place, let the weary rest"; and, "This is the place of repose"—but they would not listen.

Lk 2:29 "Sovereign Lord, as you have promised, you now dismiss your servant in peace.

Through loving God's law—

Ps 1:1 Blessed is the man who does not walk in the counsel of the wicked or stand in the way of sinners or sit in the seat of mockers. ²But his delight is in the law of the LORD, and on his law he meditates day and night.

Ps 119:165 Great peace have they who love your law, and nothing can make them stumble.

Through obedience—

Ps 25:12 Who, then, is the man that fears the LORD? He will instruct him in the way chosen for him. ¹³He will spend his days in prosperity, and his descendants will inherit the land.

Isa 48:18 If only you had paid attention to my commands, your peace would have been like a river, your righteousness like the waves of the sea. (+Jer 6:16)

No peace to the wicked (Isa 48:22; 57:21).

To be made with God—

Isa 27:5 Or else let them come to me for refuge; let them make peace with me, yes, let them make peace with me."

See Charitableness; Joy; Praise.

PEACE OFFERINGS *See Fellowship Offerings; Offerings.*

PEACOCK *See Baboons; Ostrich.*

PEARL [*3449*].

NIV+ MOTHER-OF-PEARL, PEARLS

(Rev 17:4; 18:12,16). "Pearl of great price" (Mt 13:45-46). Ornaments made of (1Ti 2:9).

Figurative:

Teaching should be given in accordance with the spiritual capacity of the learners (Mt 7:6).

Symbolic:

The twelve gates of the Holy City, the New Jerusalem, are each made of a single pearl (Rev 21:21).

See Minerals of the Bible, 1; Stones.

PECULIAR PEOPLE *See Saints.*

PEDAHEL [7010] (*God [El] ransoms*). Chief of Naphtali (Nu 34:28).

PEDAHZUR [7011] (*the Rock ransoms*). Father of Gamaliel (Nu 1:10; 2:20; 7:54,59; 10:23).

PEDAIAH [7015, 7016] (*Yahweh ransoms*).

1. Grandfather of Jehoiakim (2Ki 23:36).
2. Father of Zerubbabel (1Ch 3:18).
3. Father of Joel, chief of Manasseh (1Ch 27:20).
4. Man who helped build the wall of Jerusalem (Ne 3:25).
5. A Benjamite, the father of Joed (Ne 11:7).
6. Levite; temple treasurer (Ne 13:13).

PEEP NIV "chirp" of a bird (Isa 10:14); "whisper" of a medium supposed to come from the dead (Isa 8:19).

PEKAH [7220] (*he has opened*).

NIV+ PEKAH'S

The son of Remaliah the eighteenth king of Israel; murdered Pekahiah; reigned from 752-732 B.C. (2Ki 15:27); made a league with Damascus against Judah (2Ki 15:37-38); became subject to Assyria (2Ki 15:29); murdered by Hoshea (2Ki 15:25-31; 2Ch 28:5-15).

PEKAHIAH [7222] (*Yahweh opens*).

NIV+ PEKAHIAH'S

Israel's seventeenth king; son of Menahem; wicked and idolatrous (2Ki 15:24); murdered by Pekah (2Ki 15:22-25).

PEKOD [7216] (*visitation*). Aramean tribe living to the E and near the mouth of the Tigris (Jer 50:21; Eze 23:23).

PELAIAH [7102, 7126] (*Yahweh is spectacular*).

1. Son of Elioenai (1Ch 3:24).
2. A Levite who assisted Ezra in instructing the people in the law (Ne 8:7; 10:10).

PELALIAH [7139] (*Yahweh intercedes in arbitration*). A priest; the father of Jeroham and Amzi (Ne 11:12).

PELATIAH [7124, 7125] (*Yahweh rescues*).

1. Grandson of Zerubbabel (1Ch 3:21).
2. A Simeonite military leader (1Ch 4:42).
3. A man who sealed a covenant with Nehemiah (Ne 10:22).
4. A prince of Israel; Ezekiel prophesied against him (Eze 11:2,13).

PELEG [7105, *5744*] (*water canal*). The son of Eber (Ge 10:25; 11:16-19; 1Ch 1:19,25; Lk 3:35).

PELET [7118] (*rescue*).

NIV+ BETH PELET

1. Son of Jahdai (1Ch 2:47).
2. Son of Azmaveth (1Ch 12:3).

PELETH [7150] (perhaps *swift*, or *swiftness*).

NIV+ PELETHITES

1. A Reubenite (Nu 16:1).
2. Son of Jonathan (1Ch 2:33).

PELETHITES [7152] (*courier*).

NIV+ PELETH

A part of David's bodyguard (1Ki 1:38; 2Sa 8:18; 20:7, 23; 1Ch 18:17). Absalom's escort (2Sa 15:18).

PELICAN *See Owl.*

PELLA A city E of the Sea of Galilee; one of the cities forming the Decapolis.

PELONITE(S) [7113] (*separates*). Designation of two of David's mighty men: Helez (1Ch 11:27; 27:10) and Ahijah (1Ch 11:36).

PELUSIUM [6096]. An Egyptian city on the E arm of the Nile, KJV "Sin" (Eze 30:15-16).

PEN [1074+2025, 1312, 3032, 4813, 6485, *885, 2812, 3037*].

NIV+ PENNED, PENS, PENT-UP

(Jdg 5:14; Ps 45:1; Isa 8:1; Jer 8:8; 3Jn 13). Made of iron (Job 19:24; Jer 17:1).

PENALTY [871, 2365, 6741, 7322, 9150, 10186, *165+2505, 521, 3210*].

NIV+ PENALTIES

Vicariously assumed:

By Rebekah (Ge 27:13), Abigail (1Sa 25:24), the woman of Tekoa (2Sa 14:9), the persecutors of the Jews (Mt 27:25), Jesus for the human race (Gal 3:13). Paul desires to assume for Israel (Ro 9:3). *See Suffering, Vicarious.*

See Fine; Judgments; Punishment; Sin, Punishment of; Wicked, Punishment of. See also penalties under various crimes, such as Murder.

PENCE *See Money; Penny.*

PENDANTS [5755]. Articles of jewelry (Jdg 8:26).
See Dress.

PENIEL [7159, 7161] (*face of God [El]*).

NIV+ PENUEL

The place where Jacob wrestled with the angel of Yahweh (Ge 32:24-32), not far from Succoth (Jdg 8:8-9,17). Also spelled Penuel (Ge 32:31; Jdg 8:8; 1Ki 12:25, ftns).

PENINNAH [7166] (possibly *pearls, coral branches* BDB; *woman with rich hair* KB). One of the wives of Elkanah (1Sa 1:2).

PENITENCE *See Repentance; Sin, Confession of.*

PENITENT [8740].

NIV+ See REPENTANCE

Promises to:

Of mercy—

Lev 26:40 "'But if they will confess their sins and the sins of their fathers—their treachery against me and their hostility toward me, **41**which made me hostile toward them so that I sent them into the land of their enemies—then when their uncircumcised hearts are humbled and they pay for their sin, **42**I will remember my covenant with Jacob and my covenant with Isaac and my covenant with Abraham, and I will remember the land.

Dt 4:29 But if from there you seek the LORD your God, you will find him if you look for him with all your heart and with all your soul. **30**When you are in distress and all these things have happened to you, then in later days you will return to the LORD your God and obey him. **31**For the LORD your God is a merciful God; he will not abandon or destroy you or forget the covenant with your forefathers, which he confirmed to them by oath.

Dt 30:1 When all these blessings and curses I have set before you come upon you and you take them to heart wherever the LORD your God disperses you among the nations, **2**and when you and your children return to the LORD your God and obey him with all your heart and with all your soul according to everything I command you today, **3**then the LORD your God will restore your fortunes and have compassion on you and gather you again from all the nations where he scattered you. **4**Even if you have been banished to the most distant land under the heavens, from there the LORD your God will gather you and bring you back. **5**He will bring you to the land that belonged to your fathers, and you will take possession of it. He will make you more prosperous and numerous than your fathers. **6**The LORD your God will circumcise your hearts and the hearts of your descendants, so that you may love him with all your heart and with all your soul, and live. **7**The LORD your God will put all these curses on your enemies who hate and persecute you. **8**You will again obey the LORD and follow all his commands I am giving you today. **9**Then the LORD your God will make you most prosperous in all the work of your hands and in the fruit of your womb, the young of your livestock and the crops of your land. The LORD will again delight in you and make you prosperous, just as he delighted in your fathers, **10**if you obey the LORD your God and keep his commands and decrees that are written in this Book of the Law and turn to the LORD your God with all your heart and with all your soul.

2Ki 22:19 Because your heart was responsive and you humbled yourself before the LORD when you heard what I

have spoken against this place and its people, that they would become accursed and laid waste, and because you tore your robes and wept in my presence, I have heard you, declares the LORD.

1Ch 28:9 "And you, my son Solomon, acknowledge the God of your father, and serve him with wholehearted devotion and with a willing mind, for the LORD searches every heart and understands every motive behind the thoughts. If you seek him, he will be found by you; but if you forsake him, he will reject you forever.

Job 22:23 If you return to the Almighty, you will be restored: If you remove wickedness far from your tent **24**and assign your nuggets to the dust, your gold of Ophir to the rocks in the ravines, **25**then the Almighty will be your gold, the choicest silver for you. **26**Surely then you will find delight in the Almighty and will lift up your face to God. **27**You will pray to him, and he will hear you, and you will fulfill your vows. **28**What you decide on will be done, and light will shine on your ways. **29**When men are brought low and you say, 'Lift them up!' then he will save the downcast.

Job 33:26 He prays to God and finds favor with him, he sees God's face and shouts for joy; he is restored by God to his righteous state. **27**Then he comes to men and says, 'I sinned, and perverted what was right, but I did not get what I deserved. **28**He redeemed my soul from going down to the pit, and I will live to enjoy the light.'

Ps 6:8 Away from me, all you who do evil, for the LORD has heard my weeping. **9**The LORD has heard my cry for mercy; the LORD accepts my prayer.

Ps 9:10 Those who know your name will trust in you, for you, LORD, have never forsaken those who seek you.

Ps 22:26 The poor will eat and be satisfied; they who seek the LORD will praise him—may your hearts live forever!

Ps 90:14 Satisfy us in the morning with your unfailing love, that we may sing for joy and be glad all our days. **15**Make us glad for as many days as you have afflicted us, for as many years as we have seen trouble.

Ps 145:18 The LORD is near to all who call on him, to all who call on him in truth. **19**He fulfills the desires of those who fear him; he hears their cry and saves them.

Ps 147:3 He heals the brokenhearted and binds up their wounds.

Isa 27:5 Or else let them come to me for refuge; let them make peace with me, yes, let them make peace with me."

Mt 5:4 Blessed are those who mourn, for they will be comforted.

Mt 7:7 "Ask and it will be given to you; seek and you will find; knock and the door will be opened to you. **8**For everyone who asks receives; he who seeks finds; and to him who knocks, the door will be opened.

9"Which of you, if his son asks for bread, will give him a stone? **10**Or if he asks for a fish, will give him a snake? **11**If you, then, though you are evil, know how to give good gifts to your children, how much more will your Father in heaven give good gifts to those who ask him! (+Lk 11:9-13)

Mt 12:20 A bruised reed he will not break, and a smoldering wick he will not snuff out, till he leads justice to victory.

Mt 12:31 And so I tell you, every sin and blasphemy will be forgiven men, but the blasphemy against the Spirit will not be forgiven. (+Lk 12:10)

Of forgiveness—

Ps 32:5 Then I acknowledged my sin to you and did not

cover up my iniquity. I said, "I will confess my transgressions to the LORD"—and you forgave the guilt of my sin.

⁶Therefore let everyone who is godly pray to you while you may be found; surely when the mighty waters rise, they will not reach him.

Ps 34:18 The LORD is close to the brokenhearted and saves those who are crushed in spirit.

Ps 51:17 The sacrifices of God are a broken spirit; a broken and contrite heart, O God, you will not despise. (+Ps 86:5; Isa 55:7)

Eze 18:21 "But if a wicked man turns away from all the sins he has committed and keeps all my decrees and does what is just and right, he will surely live; he will not die. ²²None of the offenses he has committed will be remembered against him. Because of the righteous things he has done, he will live. ²³Do I take any pleasure in the death of the wicked? declares the Sovereign LORD. Rather, am I not pleased when they turn from their ways and live? (+Eze 33:10-16)

Mt 6:14 For if you forgive men when they sin against you, your heavenly Father will also forgive you. ¹⁵But if you do not forgive men their sins, your Father will not forgive your sins.

Mt 11:28 "Come to me, all you who are weary and burdened, and I will give you rest. ²⁹Take my yoke upon you and learn from me, for I am gentle and humble in heart, and you will find rest for your souls. ³⁰For my yoke is easy and my burden is light."

Lk 6:37 "Do not judge, and you will not be judged. Do not condemn, and you will not be condemned. Forgive, and you will be forgiven.

Lk 15:4 "Suppose one of you has a hundred sheep and loses one of them. Does he not leave the ninety-nine in the open country and go after the lost sheep until he finds it? ⁵And when he finds it, he joyfully puts it on his shoulders ⁶and goes home. Then he calls his friends and neighbors together and says, 'Rejoice with me; I have found my lost sheep.' ⁷I tell you that in the same way there will be more rejoicing in heaven over one sinner who repents than over ninety-nine righteous persons who do not need to repent.

⁸"Or suppose a woman has ten silver coins and loses one. Does she not light a lamp, sweep the house and search carefully until she finds it? ⁹And when she finds it, she calls her friends and neighbors together and says, 'Rejoice with me; I have found my lost coin.' ¹⁰In the same way, I tell you, there is rejoicing in the presence of the angels of God over one sinner who repents."

¹¹Jesus continued: "There was a man who had two sons. ¹²The younger one said to his father, 'Father, give me my share of the estate.' So he divided his property between them.

¹³"Not long after that, the younger son got together all he had, set off for a distant country and there squandered his wealth in wild living. ¹⁴After he had spent everything, there was a severe famine in that whole country, and he began to be in need. ¹⁵So he went and hired himself out to a citizen of that country, who sent him to his fields to feed pigs. ¹⁶He longed to fill his stomach with the pods that the pigs were eating, but no one gave him anything.

¹⁷"When he came to his senses, he said, 'How many of my father's hired men have food to spare, and here I am starving to death! ¹⁸I will set out and go back to my father and say to him: Father, I have sinned against heaven and against you. ¹⁹I am no longer worthy to be called your son; make me like one of your hired men.' ²⁰So he got up and went to his father.

"But while he was still a long way off, his father saw him and was filled with compassion for him; he ran to his son, threw his arms around him and kissed him.

²¹"The son said to him, 'Father, I have sinned against heaven and against you. I am no longer worthy to be called your son.'

²²"But the father said to his servants, 'Quick! Bring the best robe and put it on him. Put a ring on his finger and sandals on his feet. ²³Bring the fattened calf and kill it. Let's have a feast and celebrate. ²⁴For this son of mine was dead and is alive again; he was lost and is found.' So they began to celebrate.

²⁵"Meanwhile, the older son was in the field. When he came near the house, he heard music and dancing. ²⁶So he called one of the servants and asked him what was going on. ²⁷'Your brother has come,' he replied, 'and your father has killed the fattened calf because he has him back safe and sound.'

²⁸"The older brother became angry and refused to go in. So his father went out and pleaded with him. ²⁹But he answered his father, 'Look! All these years I've been slaving for you and never disobeyed your orders. Yet you never gave me even a young goat so I could celebrate with my friends. ³⁰But when this son of yours who has squandered your property with prostitutes comes home, you kill the fattened calf for him!'

³¹"'My son,' the father said, 'you are always with me, and everything I have is yours. ³²But we had to celebrate and be glad, because this brother of yours was dead and is alive again; he was lost and is found.'" (+Mt 18:12-14)

Lk 18:10 "Two men went up to the temple to pray, one a Pharisee and the other a tax collector. ¹¹The Pharisee stood up and prayed about himself: 'God, I thank you that I am not like other men—robbers, evildoers, adulterers—or even like this tax collector. ¹²I fast twice a week and give a tenth of all I get.'

¹³"But the tax collector stood at a distance. He would not even look up to heaven, but beat his breast and said, 'God, have mercy on me, a sinner.'

¹⁴"I tell you that this man, rather than the other, went home justified before God. For everyone who exalts himself will be humbled, and he who humbles himself will be exalted."

Jn 6:37 All that the Father gives me will come to me, and whoever comes to me I will never drive away.

Ac 13:38 "Therefore, my brothers, I want you to know that through Jesus the forgiveness of sins is proclaimed to you. ³⁹Through him everyone who believes is justified from everything you could not be justified from by the law of Moses.

1Jn 1:9 If we confess our sins, he is faithful and just and will forgive us our sins and purify us from all unrighteousness.

Of salvation (Ps 145:18-19)—

Lk 4:18 "The Spirit of the Lord is on me, because he has anointed me to preach good news to the poor. He has sent me to proclaim freedom for the prisoners and recovery of sight for the blind, to release the oppressed,

Lk 19:10 For the Son of Man came to seek and to save what was lost."

Ro 10:9 That if you confess with your mouth, "Jesus is Lord," and believe in your heart that God raised him from the dead, you will be saved. ¹⁰For it is with your heart that you believe and are justified, and it is with your mouth that you confess and are saved. ¹¹As the Scripture says, "Anyone who trusts in him will never be put to shame."

[12]For there is no difference between Jew and Gentile—the same Lord is Lord of all and richly blesses all who call on him, [13]for, "Everyone who calls on the name of the Lord will be saved." (+Heb 7:25)

Of divine favor—

Nu 5:6 "Say to the Israelites: 'When a man or woman wrongs another in any way and so is unfaithful to the LORD, that person is guilty [7]and must confess the sin he has committed. He must make full restitution for his wrong, add one fifth to it and give it all to the person he has wronged. (+Isa 66:2)

See Forgiveness; Repentance; Sin, Confession of.
See also, Obduracy; Reprobacy.

PENKNIFE *See Knife.*

PENNY [*837, 3119, 3321*].
NIV+ PENNIES

The smallest Roman copper coin (Mt 5:26; Mk 12:42; Lk 12:6,59). *See Money.*

PENS [774, 1556, 1556+7366, 4813].
NIV+ See PEN

1. Walled enclosure for livestock (Nu 32:16,24,36; Jn 10:1,16).
2. Instrument for writing (Ps 45:1; Isa 8:1; Jer 8:8; 3Jn 13).

PENSION Of Levites (2Ch 31:16-18).

PENTATEUCH, THE *(five books, i.e., the torah or law).* The first five books of the Bible; covers the period of time from the creation to the end of the Mosaic era; authorship is attributed to Moses in Scripture.

Outline:
1. Era of beginnings (Ge 1:1-11:32).
2. Patriarchal period (Ge 12:1-50:26).
3. Emancipation of Israel (Ex 1:1-19:2).
4. Religion of Israel (Ex 19:3-Lev 27:34).
5. Organization of Israel (Nu 1:1-10:10).
6. Wilderness wanderings (Nu 10:11-22:1).
7. Preparations for entering Canaan (Nu 22:2-36:13).
8. Retrospect and prospect (Dt 1-34).

PENTECOST [*4300*] *(fiftieth [day]).*
1. The Israelite Feast of Weeks (Ex 34:22; Dt 16:9-11), also called the Feast of Harvest (Ex 23:16) and the day of firstfruits (Nu 28:26), which fell on the fiftieth day after Passover. The feast originally celebrated the dedication of the firstfruits of the wheat harvest, the last crop to ripen. The ritual of the feast is described (Lev 23:15-21). Institution of (Ex 23:16; 34:22; Lev 23:15-21; Nu 28:26-31; Dt 16:9-12,16). Called in the NT the Day of Pentecost (Ac 2:1; 20:16; 1Co 16:8). *See Annual Feasts; Feasts.*
2. The Christian Pentecost fell on the same day as the Israelite Feast of Weeks. The coming of the Holy Spirit (Ac 2) transformed the Israelite festival into a Christian anniversary, marking the beginning of the Christian church.

PENUEL [7158] *(face of God [El]).*
NIV+ PENIEL

1. Son of Hur and chief of Gedor (1Ch 4:4).
2. Son of Shashak (1Ch 8:25).
3. Variant spelling of Peniel. *See Peniel.*

PENURIOUSNESS *See Parsimony.*

PEOPLE [*132, 278, 408, 1074, 1201, 1414, 1580,

2446, 3782, 4211, 5476, 5883, 6337, 6638, 6639, 10050, 10553, *41, 81, 476, 1620, 3295, 3836, 4063, 5626*].
NIV+ PEOPLE'S, PEOPLED, PEOPLES

Common. Heard Jesus gladly (Mt 7:28; 9:8,33; 13:54; Mk 6:2).

PEOR [7186] *(opening).*
NIV+ BAAL PEOR, BETH PEOR

1. A mountain in Moab near the town of Beth Peor (Dt 3:29).
2. Contraction for Baal Peor (Nu 25:18; 31:16; Jos 22:17). *See Baal Peor.*

PERAEA *See Perea.*

PERATH [7310]. In Hebrew it has the same spelling as Euphrates (Jer 13:4-7, ftn). Some identify it with Wadi Farah (Parah, Jos 18:23) near Anathoth.

PERAZIM, MOUNT [7292] *(breaking out).*
NIV+ BAAL PERAZIM

Usually identified with Baal Perazim, where David obtained a victory over the Philistines (2Sa 5:20; 1Ch 14:11).

PERDITION *(ruin, destruction).* In the NT the word refers to the final state of the wicked, one of loss or destruction (Jn 17:12; Php 1:28; 2Th 2:3; 1Ti 6:9).

PERDITION, SON OF A phrase used to designate Judas Iscariot (Jn 17:12) and the "man of lawlessness" who is the Antichrist (2Th 2:3).

PEREA *(beyond the Jordan).* The name given by Josephus to the region E of the Jordan; known in the Gospels as "across the Jordan" (Mt 4:15,25; Mk 3:7-8).

PERES [10593] *(divided).* One of the words written on a wall for Belshazzar and interpreted by Daniel (Da 5:1-29).

PERESH [7303] *(offal eviscerated* BDB; *dung* ISBE; *contents of stomach [not intestine]* KB). Son of Makir (1Ch 7:16).

PEREZ, PEREZITE [7289, 7291, 5756] *(breaking out).*
NIV+ PEREZ UZZAH, RIMMON PEREZ

A son of Judah by Tamar (Ge 38:29; 1Ch 2:4), descendants of (Ge 46:12; Nu 26:20-21; 1Ch 2:5; 9:4), return from the Captivity (Ne 11:4,6). In the lineage of David and Jesus (Ru 4:12; Mt 1:3; Lk 3:33).

PEREZ UZZAH, PEREZ-UZZAH [7290] *(breaking out of Uzzah).*
NIV+ PEREZ

The name of the place where Uzzah was struck dead for touching the ark of God (2Sa 6:8, ftn). Perez Uzzah means *outbreak against Uzzah;* the place-name memorialized a divine warning that was not soon forgotten.

See Nacon, Nachon.

PERFECTION [*4003, 4005, 9459, 5455, 5457*].
NIV+ PERFECT, PERFECTER, PERFECTION, PERFECTLY

Major idea: complete or whole, rather than without fault or shortcoming.

None without sin—

2Ch 6:36 "When they sin against you—for there is no one who does not sin—and you become angry with them and give them over to the enemy, who takes them captive to a land far away or near;

Ecc 7:20 There is not a righteous man on earth who does what is right and never sins.

From God:

Ps 18:32 It is God who arms me with strength and makes my way perfect.

1Pe 5:10 And the God of all grace, who called you to his eternal glory in Christ, after you have suffered a little while, will himself restore you and make you strong, firm and steadfast.

Through Christ—

Col 1:21 Once you were alienated from God and were enemies in your minds because of your evil behavior. ²²But now he has reconciled you by Christ's physical body through death to present you holy in his sight, without blemish and free from accusation—

Col 1:28 We proclaim him, admonishing and teaching everyone with all wisdom, so that we may present everyone perfect in Christ.

Col 2:9 For in Christ all the fullness of the Deity lives in bodily form, ¹⁰and you have been given fullness in Christ, who is the head over every power and authority. ¹¹In him you were also circumcised, in the putting off of the sinful nature, not with a circumcision done by the hands of men but with the circumcision done by Christ,

Heb 10:14 because by one sacrifice he has made perfect forever those who are being made holy.

Heb 13:20 May the God of peace, who through the blood of the eternal covenant brought back from the dead our Lord Jesus, that great Shepherd of the sheep, ²¹equip you with everything good for doing his will, and may he work in us what is pleasing to him, through Jesus Christ, to whom be glory for ever and ever. Amen. (+1Pe 5:10)

1Jn 3:6 No one who lives in him keeps on sinning. No one who continues to sin has either seen him or known him.

⁷Dear children, do not let anyone lead you astray. He who does what is right is righteous, just as he is righteous. ⁸He who does what is sinful is of the devil, because the devil has been sinning from the beginning. The reason the Son of God appeared was to destroy the devil's work. ⁹No one who is born of God will continue to sin, because God's seed remains in him; he cannot go on sinning, because he has been born of God. ¹⁰This is how we know who the children of God are and who the children of the devil are: Anyone who does not do what is right is not a child of God; nor is anyone who does not love his brother.

Through God's love—

1Jn 4:12 No one has ever seen God; but if we love one another, God lives in us and his love is made complete in us.

Ascribed to:

Noah (Ge 6:8-9), Jacob (Nu 23:21), David (1Ki 11:4,6), Asa (1Ki 15:14), Job (Job 1:1), Zechariah and Elizabeth (Lk 1:6), Nathanael (Jn 1:47)

The peaceful—

Ps 37:31 The law of his God is in his heart; his feet do not slip.

Ps 37:37 Consider the blameless, observe the upright; there is a future for the man of peace.

The wise—

1Co 2:6 We do, however, speak a message of wisdom among the mature, but not the wisdom of this age or of the rulers of this age, who are coming to nothing.

Man of God (2Ti 3:17)

The self-controlled—

Jas 3:2 We all stumble in many ways. If anyone is never at fault in what he says, he is a perfect man, able to keep his whole body in check.

Those who obey God's word—

1Jn 2:5 But if anyone obeys his word, God's love is truly made complete in him. This is how we know we are in him:

Blessings of—

Ps 106:3 Blessed are they who maintain justice, who constantly do what is right.

Ps 119:1 Blessed are they whose ways are blameless, who walk according to the law of the LORD. ²Blessed are they who keep his statutes and seek him with all their heart. ³They do nothing wrong; they walk in his ways.

Ps 119:6 Then I would not be put to shame when I consider all your commands. (+Mt 5:6)

Desire for:

Mt 5:6 Blessed are those who hunger and thirst for righteousness, for they will be filled.

2Ti 3:17 so that the man of God may be thoroughly equipped for every good work.

In Job—

Job 9:20 Even if I were innocent, my mouth would condemn me; if I were blameless, it would pronounce me guilty.

²¹"Although I am blameless, I have no concern for myself; I despise my own life.

In David—

Ps 101:2 I will be careful to lead a blameless life—when will you come to me? I will walk in my house with blameless heart.

In Paul—

Php 3:12 Not that I have already obtained all this, or have already been made perfect, but I press on to take hold of that for which Christ Jesus took hold of me. ¹³Brothers, I do not consider myself yet to have taken hold of it. But one thing I do: Forgetting what is behind and straining toward what is ahead, ¹⁴I press on toward the goal to win the prize for which God has called me heavenward in Christ Jesus.

¹⁵All of us who are mature should take such a view of things. And if on some point you think differently, that too God will make clear to you.

Commanded:

Ge 17:1 When Abram was ninety-nine years old, the LORD appeared to him and said, "I am God Almighty; walk before me and be blameless.

Dt 5:32 So be careful to do what the LORD your God has commanded you; do not turn aside to the right or to the left.

Dt 18:13 You must be blameless before the LORD your God.

Jos 23:6 "Be very strong; be careful to obey all that is written in the Book of the Law of Moses, without turning aside to the right or to the left.

1Ki 8:61 But your hearts must be fully committed to the LORD our God, to live by his decrees and obey his commands, as at this time."

1Ch 28:9 "And you, my son Solomon, acknowledge the God of your father, and serve him with wholehearted devotion and with a willing mind, for the LORD searches every heart and understands every motive behind the thoughts. If you seek him, he will be found by you; but if you forsake him, he will reject you forever.

Mt 5:48 Be perfect, therefore, as your heavenly Father is perfect.

2Co 7:1 Since we have these promises, dear friends, let us purify ourselves from everything that contaminates body and spirit, perfecting holiness out of reverence for God.

2Co 13:11 Finally, brothers, good-by. Aim for perfection, listen to my appeal, be of one mind, live in peace. And the God of love and peace will be with you.

Php 1:10 so that you may be able to discern what is best and may be pure and blameless until the day of Christ,

Php 2:15 so that you may become blameless and pure, children of God without fault in a crooked and depraved generation, in which you shine like stars in the universe

Col 3:14 And over all these virtues put on love, which binds them all together in perfect unity.

Jas 1:4 Perseverance must finish its work so that you may be mature and complete, not lacking anything.

Prayer for:

1Ch 29:19 And give my son Solomon the wholehearted devotion to keep your commands, requirements and decrees and to do everything to build the palatial structure for which I have provided."

2Co 13:9 We are glad whenever we are weak but you are strong; and our prayer is for your perfection.

Col 4:12 Epaphras, who is one of you and a servant of Christ Jesus, sends greetings. He is always wrestling in prayer for you, that you may stand firm in all the will of God, mature and fully assured.

1Th 3:10 Night and day we pray most earnestly that we may see you again and supply what is lacking in your faith.

1Th 3:13 May he strengthen your hearts so that you will be blameless and holy in the presence of our God and Father when our Lord Jesus comes with all his holy ones. (+Heb 13:20-21)

Program for:

Eph 4:11 It was he who gave some to be apostles, some to be prophets, some to be evangelists, and some to be pastors and teachers, ¹²to prepare God's people for works of service, so that the body of Christ may be built up ¹³until we all reach unity in the faith and in the knowledge of the Son of God and become mature, attaining to the whole measure of the fullness of Christ.

Heb 6:1 Therefore let us leave the elementary teachings about Christ and go on to maturity, not laying again the foundation of repentance from acts that lead to death, and of faith in God, (+1Jn 2:5)

Requirements for (Dt 5:32; Jos 23:6; 1Ki 8:61; 1Ch 29:19)—

Mt 19:21 Jesus answered, "If you want to be perfect, go, sell your possessions and give to the poor, and you will have treasure in heaven. Then come, follow me." (+2Co 7:1)

Reward of (Ps 37:31,37)—

Pr 2:21 For the upright will live in the land, and the blameless will remain in it;

Lk 6:40 A student is not above his teacher, but everyone who is fully trained will be like his teacher.

1Jn 5:18 We know that anyone born of God does not continue to sin; the one who was born of God keeps him safe, and the evil one cannot harm him.

See God, Perfection of; Holiness; Sanctification.

PERFIDY *See Conspiracy; Hypocrisy; Treachery.*

PERFUME, PERFUMER [1411, 5349, 5678, 5883, 5948, 6057, 7787, 8379, 8384, 9043, *3690, 3693*].

NIV+ PERFUME-MAKERS, PERFUMED, PERFUMERS, PERFUMES

1. For personal use (Pr 7:17; 27:9; SS 1:12; 3:6; Isa 3:20,24), burial (2Ch 16:14).

2. For sacred incense (Ex 30:34-38; 37:29).

See Nard.

PERGA [*4308*]. The capital of Pamphylia. Paul preaches in (Ac 13:13-14; 14:25).

PERGAMUM, PERGAMOS [*4307*]. A city of Mysia. One of the "seven churches" (Rev 1:11; 2:12-17).

PERIDA [7263] (*single, unique*). One of the servants of Solomon. Descendants of, returned to Jerusalem, from captivity in Babylon (Ne 7:57). Called Peruda (Ezr 2:55).

PERIZZITES [7254] (*villager*). One of the seven nations in the land of Canaan (Ge 13:7). Territory of, given to Abraham (Ge 15:20; Ex 3:8; 23:23). Doomed to destruction (Dt 20:17). Not all destroyed; Israelites marry among (Jdg 3:5-7; Ezr 9:1-2).

See Canaanite(s).

PERJURY [2021+4200+8678+9214, *2156*].

NIV+ PERJURERS

Isa 48:1 "Listen to this, O house of Jacob, you who are called by the name of Israel and come from the line of Judah, you who take oaths in the name of the Lᴏʀᴅ and invoke the God of Israel—but not in truth or righteousness—

Jer 5:2 Although they say, 'As surely as the Lᴏʀᴅ lives,' still they are swearing falsely."

Jer 7:9 "'Will you steal and murder, commit adultery and perjury, burn incense to Baal and follow other gods you have not known,

1Ti 1:9 We also know that law is made not for the righteous but for lawbreakers and rebels, the ungodly and sinful, the unholy and irreligious; for those who kill their fathers or mothers, for murderers, ¹⁰for adulterers and perverts, for slave traders and liars and perjurers—and for whatever else is contrary to the sound doctrine

Forbidden—

Lev 19:12 "'Do not swear falsely by my name and so profane the name of your God. I am the Lᴏʀᴅ.

Zec 8:17 do not plot evil against your neighbor, and do not love to swear falsely. I hate all this," declares the Lᴏʀᴅ.

Mt 5:33 "Again, you have heard that it was said to the people long ago, 'Do not break your oath, but keep the oaths you have made to the Lord.'

Penalty for—

Lev 6:2 "If anyone sins and is unfaithful to the Lᴏʀᴅ by deceiving his neighbor about something entrusted to him or left in his care or stolen, or if he cheats him, ³or if he finds lost property and lies about it, or if he swears falsely, or if he commits any such sin that people may do— ⁴when he thus sins and becomes guilty, he must return what he has stolen or taken by extortion, or what was entrusted to him, or the lost property he found, ⁵or whatever it was he swore falsely about. He must make restitution in full, add a fifth of the value to it and give it all to the owner on the day he presents his guilt offering. ⁶And as a penalty he must bring to the priest, that is, to the Lᴏʀᴅ, his guilt offering, a ram from the flock, one without defect and of the proper value. ⁷In this way the priest will make atonement for him before the LORD, and he will be forgiven for any of these things he did that made him guilty."

Judgments upon perjurers—

Hos 10:4 They make many promises, take false oaths and make agreements; therefore lawsuits spring up like poisonous weeds in a plowed field. (+Zec 5:3)

Zec 5:4 The LORD Almighty declares, 'I will send it out, and it will enter the house of the thief and the house of him who swears falsely by my name. It will remain in his house and destroy it, both its timbers and its stones.'"

Mal 3:5 "So I will come near to you for judgment. I will be quick to testify against sorcerers, adulterers and perjurers, against those who defraud laborers of their wages, who oppress the widows and the fatherless, and deprive aliens of justice, but do not fear me," says the LORD Almighty.

Instances of:

Zedekiah (2Ch 36:13). Witnesses against Naboth (1Ki 21:8-13), against David (Ps 35:11), against Jesus (Mt 26:59-61; Mk 14:56-59), against Stephen (Ac 6:11,13-14). Peter, when he denied Jesus with an oath (Mt 26:74; Mk 14:71).

See Falsehood; False Witness; Oath.

PERSECUTION [6715, 8103, *1502, 1503, 2567, 2568, 2808*].

NIV+ PERSECUTE, PERSECUTED, PERSECUTING, PERSECUTIONS, PERSECUTOR, PERSECUTORS

Of Jesus:

Ac 4:27 Indeed Herod and Pontius Pilate met together with the Gentiles and the people of Israel in this city to conspire against your holy servant Jesus, whom you anointed.

Heb 12:2 Let us fix our eyes on Jesus, the author and perfecter of our faith, who for the joy set before him endured the cross, scorning its shame, and sat down at the right hand of the throne of God. ³Consider him who endured such opposition from sinful men, so that you will not grow weary and lose heart.

1Pe 4:1 Therefore, since Christ suffered in his body, arm yourselves also with the same attitude, because he who has suffered in his body is done with sin.

Meekly endured (Isa 50:6).

Foretold—

Ge 3:15 And I will put enmity between you and the woman, and between your offspring and hers; he will crush your head, and you will strike his heel."

Isa 49:7 This is what the LORD says—the Redeemer and Holy One of Israel—to him who was despised and abhorred by the nation, to the servant of rulers: "Kings will see you and rise up, princes will see and bow down, because of the LORD, who is faithful, the Holy One of Israel, who has chosen you."

Isa 50:6 I offered my back to those who beat me, my cheeks to those who pulled out my beard; I did not hide my face from mocking and spitting.

Isa 52:14 Just as there were many who were appalled at him—his appearance was so disfigured beyond that of any man and his form marred beyond human likeness—

Isa 53:2 He grew up before him like a tender shoot, and like a root out of dry ground. He had no beauty or majesty to attract us to him, nothing in his appearance that we should desire him. ³He was despised and rejected by men, a man of sorrows, and familiar with suffering. Like one from whom men hide their faces he was despised, and we esteemed him not.

⁴Surely he took up our infirmities and carried our sorrows, yet we considered him stricken by God, smitten by him, and afflicted. ⁵But he was pierced for our transgressions, he was crushed for our iniquities; the punishment that brought us peace was upon him, and by his wounds we are healed. (+Isa 53:6)

Isa 53:7 He was oppressed and afflicted, yet he did not open his mouth; he was led like a lamb to the slaughter, and as a sheep before her shearers is silent, so he did not open his mouth. ⁸By oppression and judgment he was taken away. And who can speak of his descendants? For he was cut off from the land of the living; for the transgression of my people he was stricken. ⁹He was assigned a grave with the wicked, and with the rich in his death, though he had done no violence, nor was any deceit in his mouth.

¹⁰Yet it was the LORD's will to crush him and cause him to suffer, and though the LORD makes his life a guilt offering, he will see his offspring and prolong his days, and the will of the LORD will prosper in his hand.

Mic 5:1 Marshal your troops, O city of troops, for a siege is laid against us. They will strike Israel's ruler on the cheek with a rod. (+Zec 12:10)

Mt 2:13 When they had gone, an angel of the Lord appeared to Joseph in a dream. "Get up," he said, "take the child and his mother and escape to Egypt. Stay there until I tell you, for Herod is going to search for the child to kill him."

Typified, in the persecutions of Israel's kings—

Ps 2:1 Why do the nations conspire and the peoples plot in vain? ²The kings of the earth take their stand and the rulers gather together against the LORD and against his Anointed One. ³"Let us break their chains," they say, "and throw off their fetters." ⁴The One enthroned in heaven laughs; the Lord scoffs at them. ⁵Then he rebukes them in his anger and terrifies them in his wrath, saying,

Ps 22:1 My God, my God, why have you forsaken me? Why are you so far from saving me, so far from the words of my groaning? ²O my God, I cry out by day, but you do not answer, by night, and am not silent.

Ps 22:6 But I am a worm and not a man, scorned by men and despised by the people. ⁷All who see me mock me; they hurl insults, shaking their heads: ⁸"He trusts in the LORD; let the LORD rescue him. Let him deliver him, since he delights in him."

Ps 22:11 Do not be far from me, for trouble is near and there is no one to help. ¹²Many bulls surround me; strong bulls of Bashan encircle me. ¹³Roaring lions tearing their prey open their mouths wide against me. ¹⁴I am poured out like water, and all my bones are out of joint. My heart has turned to wax; it has melted away within me. ¹⁵My strength is dried up like a potsherd, and my tongue sticks to the roof of my mouth; you lay me in the dust of death. ¹⁶Dogs have surrounded me; a band of evil men has encircled me, they have pierced my hands and my feet. ¹⁷I can count all my bones; people stare and gloat over me. ¹⁸They divide my garments among them and cast lots for my clothing. ¹⁹But you, O LORD, be not far off; O my Strength, come quickly to help me. ²⁰Deliver my life from the sword, my precious life from the power of the dogs. ²¹Rescue me from the mouth of the lions; save me from the horns of the wild oxen. (+Ps 69:1-6)

Ps 69:7 For I endure scorn for your sake, and shame covers my face. ⁸I am a stranger to my brothers, an alien to my own mother's sons; ⁹for zeal for your house consumes me, and the insults of those who insult you fall on me.

¹⁰When I weep and fast, I must endure scorn; ¹¹when I put on sackcloth, people make sport of me. ¹²Those who sit at the gate mock me, and I am the song of the drunkards. (+Ps 69:13-21)

Ps 109:25 I am an object of scorn to my accusers; when they see me, they shake their heads. (+Ro 15:3)

Persecution by the Jews—

Mt 12:14 But the Pharisees went out and plotted how they might kill Jesus. (+Mt 22:15)

Mt 26:3 Then the chief priests and the elders of the people assembled in the palace of the high priest, whose name was Caiaphas, ⁴and they plotted to arrest Jesus in some sly way and kill him. (+Mk 12:13; 15:14; Lk 6:11)

Lk 11:53 When Jesus left there, the Pharisees and the teachers of the law began to oppose him fiercely and to besiege him with questions, ⁵⁴waiting to catch him in something he might say. (+Lk 20:20; 22:2-5,52-53; 23:23)

Jn 5:16 So, because Jesus was doing these things on the Sabbath, the Jews persecuted him.

Jn 7:1 After this, Jesus went around in Galilee, purposely staying away from Judea because the Jews there were waiting to take his life.

Jn 7:7 The world cannot hate you, but it hates me because I testify that what it does is evil.

Jn 7:19 Has not Moses given you the law? Yet not one of you keeps the law. Why are you trying to kill me?"

Jn 11:57 But the chief priests and Pharisees had given orders that if anyone found out where Jesus was, he should report it so that they might arrest him.

Jn 15:18 "If the world hates you, keep in mind that it hated me first.

Jn 15:20 Remember the words I spoke to you: 'No servant is greater than his master.' If they persecuted me, they will persecute you also. If they obeyed my teaching, they will obey yours also. ²¹They will treat you this way because of my name, for they do not know the One who sent me.

Jn 18:22 When Jesus said this, one of the officials nearby struck him in the face. "Is this the way you answer the high priest?" he demanded.

²³"If I said something wrong," Jesus replied, "testify as to what is wrong. But if I spoke the truth, why did you strike me?"

Jn 19:6 As soon as the chief priests and their officials saw him, they shouted, "Crucify! Crucify!" But Pilate answered, "You take him and crucify him. As for me, I find no basis for a charge against him."

Jn 19:15 But they shouted, "Take him away! Take him away! Crucify him!" "Shall I crucify your king?" Pilate asked. "We have no king but Caesar," the chief priests answered.

Ac 2:23 This man was handed over to you by God's set purpose and foreknowledge; and you, with the help of wicked men, put him to death by nailing him to the cross.

In making false imputation—

Mt 12:24 But when the Pharisees heard this, they said, "It is only by Beelzebub, the prince of demons, that this fellow drives out demons." (+Mk 3:22; Lk 11:15)

Jn 10:20 Many of them said, "He is demon-possessed and raving mad. Why listen to him?"

In bringing false accusation (Mt 11:19)—

Lk 7:34 The Son of Man came eating and drinking, and you say, 'Here is a glutton and a drunkard, a friend of tax collectors and "sinners." ' (+Jn 8:29-30)

In acts of violence—

Lk 4:28 All the people in the synagogue were furious when they heard this. ²⁹They got up, drove him out of the town, and took him to the brow of the hill on which the town was built, in order to throw him down the cliff. (+Lk 22:63-65; Mt 26:67; Mk 14:65)

In seeking false testimony—

Mt 26:59 The chief priests and the whole Sanhedrin were looking for false evidence against Jesus so that they could put him to death.

In seeking his death—

Mt 26:14 Then one of the Twelve—the one called Judas Iscariot—went to the chief priests ¹⁵and asked, "What are you willing to give me if I hand him over to you?" So they counted out for him thirty silver coins. ¹⁶From then on Judas watched for an opportunity to hand him over.

Mk 3:6 Then the Pharisees went out and began to plot with the Herodians how they might kill Jesus.

Mk 3:21 When his family heard about this, they went to take charge of him, for they said, "He is out of his mind." (+Mk 14:1,48; 11:18)

Lk 19:47 Every day he was teaching at the temple. But the chief priests, the teachers of the law and the leaders among the people were trying to kill him.

Jn 7:20 "You are demon-possessed," the crowd answered. "Who is trying to kill you?"

Jn 7:30 At this they tried to seize him, but no one laid a hand on him, because his time had not yet come.

Jn 7:32 The Pharisees heard the crowd whispering such things about him. Then the chief priests and the Pharisees sent temple guards to arrest him.

Jn 8:37 I know you are Abraham's descendants. Yet you are ready to kill me, because you have no room for my word.

Jn 8:40 As it is, you are determined to kill me, a man who has told you the truth that I heard from God. Abraham did not do such things.

Jn 8:48 The Jews answered him, "Aren't we right in saying that you are a Samaritan and demon-possessed?"

Jn 8:52 At this the Jews exclaimed, "Now we know that you are demon-possessed! Abraham died and so did the prophets, yet you say that if anyone keeps your word, he will never taste death.

Jn 8:59 At this, they picked up stones to stone him, but Jesus hid himself, slipping away from the temple grounds. (+Jn 10:31)

In crucifying him—

Ac 3:13 The God of Abraham, Isaac and Jacob, the God of our fathers, has glorified his servant Jesus. You handed him over to be killed, and you disowned him before Pilate, though he had decided to let him go. ¹⁴You disowned the Holy and Righteous One and asked that a murderer be released to you. ¹⁵You killed the author of life, but God raised him from the dead. We are witnesses of this.

Ac 7:52 Was there ever a prophet your fathers did not persecute? They even killed those who predicted the coming of the Righteous One. And now you have betrayed and murdered him—

Ac 13:27 The people of Jerusalem and their rulers did not recognize Jesus, yet in condemning him they fulfilled the words of the prophets that are read every Sabbath. ²⁸Though they found no proper ground for a death sentence, they asked Pilate to have him executed. ²⁹When they had carried out all that was written about him, they took him down from the tree and laid him in a tomb. (+1Co 2:8)

Persecution by Herod—

Lk 13:31 At that time some Pharisees came to Jesus and said to him, "Leave this place and go somewhere else. Herod wants to kill you."

Lk 23:11 Then Herod and his soldiers ridiculed and mocked him. Dressing him in an elegant robe, they sent him back to Pilate.

Persecution by the Roman soldiers—

Mt 27:25 All the people answered, "Let his blood be on us and on our children!"

²⁶Then he released Barabbas to them. But he had Jesus flogged, and handed him over to be crucified.

²⁷Then the governor's soldiers took Jesus into the Praetorium and gathered the whole company of soldiers around him. ²⁸They stripped him and put a scarlet robe on him, ²⁹and then twisted together a crown of thorns and set it on his head. They put a staff in his right hand and knelt in front of him and mocked him. "Hail, king of the Jews!" they said. ³⁰They spit on him, and took the staff and struck him on the head again and again. (+Mk 15:15-20; Jn 19:2-3)

Forsaken by God—

Mk 15:34 And at the ninth hour Jesus cried out in a loud voice, *"Eloi, Eloi, lama sabachthani?"*—which means, "My God, my God, why have you forsaken me?"

Of the righteous:

Ge 49:23 With bitterness archers attacked him; they shot at him with hostility.

Ps 11:2 For look, the wicked bend their bows; they set their arrows against the strings to shoot from the shadows at the upright in heart.

Ps 37:32 The wicked lie in wait for the righteous, seeking their very lives;

Ps 38:20 Those who repay my good with evil slander me when I pursue what is good.

Ps 74:7 They burned your sanctuary to the ground; they defiled the dwelling place of your Name. ⁸They said in their hearts, "We will crush them completely!" They burned every place where God was worshiped in the land.

Ps 119:51 The arrogant mock me without restraint, but I do not turn from your law.

Ps 119:61 Though the wicked bind me with ropes, I will not forget your law.

Ps 119:69 Though the arrogant have smeared me with lies, I keep your precepts with all my heart.

Ps 119:78 May the arrogant be put to shame for wronging me without cause; but I will meditate on your precepts.

Ps 119:85 The arrogant dig pitfalls for me, contrary to your law. ⁸⁶All your commands are trustworthy; help me, for men persecute me without cause. ⁸⁷They almost wiped me from the earth, but I have not forsaken your precepts.

Ps 119:95 The wicked are waiting to destroy me, but I will ponder your statutes.

Ps 119:110 The wicked have set a snare for me, but I have not strayed from your precepts.

Ps 119:157 Many are the foes who persecute me, but I have not turned from your statutes.

Ps 119:161 Rulers persecute me without cause, but my heart trembles at your word.

Pr 29:10 Bloodthirsty men hate a man of integrity and seek to kill the upright.

Pr 29:27 The righteous detest the dishonest; the wicked detest the upright.

Isa 26:20 Go, my people, enter your rooms and shut the doors behind you; hide yourselves for a little while until his wrath has passed by.

Isa 29:20 The ruthless will vanish, the mockers will disappear, and all who have an eye for evil will be cut down— ²¹those who with a word make a man out to be guilty, who

ensnare the defender in court and with false testimony deprive the innocent of justice.

Isa 59:15 Truth is nowhere to be found, and whoever shuns evil becomes a prey. The LORD looked and was displeased that there was no justice.

Jer 11:19 I had been like a gentle lamb led to the slaughter; I did not realize that they had plotted against me, saying, "Let us destroy the tree and its fruit; let us cut him off from the land of the living, that his name be remembered no more."

Jer 15:10 Alas, my mother, that you gave me birth, a man with whom the whole land strives and contends! I have neither lent nor borrowed, yet everyone curses me.

Jer 18:18 They said, "Come, let's make plans against Jeremiah; for the teaching of the law by the priest will not be lost, nor will counsel from the wise, nor the word from the prophets. So come, let's attack him with our tongues and pay no attention to anything he says."

Am 5:10 you hate the one who reproves in court and despise him who tells the truth. (+Ro 8:35)

2Co 12:10 That is why, for Christ's sake, I delight in weaknesses, in insults, in hardships, in persecutions, in difficulties. For when I am weak, then I am strong.

Gal 4:29 At that time the son born in the ordinary way persecuted the son born by the power of the Spirit. It is the same now. (+Gal 6:17)

By mocking—

Ps 42:3 My tears have been my food day and night, while men say to me all day long, "Where is your God?"

Ps 42:10 My bones suffer mortal agony as my foes taunt me, saying to me all day long, "Where is your God?" (+Ps 69:9)

Ps 69:10 When I weep and fast, I must endure scorn; (+Ps 69:11)

Ps 69:12 Those who sit at the gate mock me, and I am the song of the drunkards. (+Ps 119:51; Jer 20:7)

Jer 20:8 Whenever I speak, I cry out proclaiming violence and destruction. So the word of the LORD has brought me insult and reproach all day long.

By violence—

Ps 94:5 They crush your people, O LORD; they oppress your inheritance.

Jer 2:30 "In vain I punished your people; they did not respond to correction. Your sword has devoured your prophets like a ravening lion.

Jer 50:7 Whoever found them devoured them; their enemies said, 'We are not guilty, for they sinned against the LORD, their true pasture, the LORD, the hope of their fathers.'

Ac 5:29 Peter and the other apostles replied: "We must obey God rather than men!

Ac 5:40 His speech persuaded them. They called the apostles in and had them flogged. Then they ordered them not to speak in the name of Jesus, and let them go.

⁴¹The apostles left the Sanhedrin, rejoicing because they had been counted worthy of suffering disgrace for the Name. ⁴²Day after day, in the temple courts and from house to house, they never stopped teaching and proclaiming the good news that Jesus is the Christ. (+Ac 7:52)

Gal 6:12 Those who want to make a good impression outwardly are trying to compel you to be circumcised. The only reason they do this is to avoid being persecuted for the cross of Christ.

Gal 6:17 Finally, let no one cause me trouble, for I bear on my body the marks of Jesus.

1Th 2:2 We had previously suffered and been insulted in

Philippi, as you know, but with the help of our God we dared to tell you his gospel in spite of strong opposition.

1Th 2:14 For you, brothers, became imitators of God's churches in Judea, which are in Christ Jesus: You suffered from your own countrymen the same things those churches suffered from the Jews, [15]who killed the Lord Jesus and the prophets and also drove us out. They displease God and are hostile to all men

Jas 2:6 But you have insulted the poor. Is it not the rich who are exploiting you? Are they not the ones who are dragging you into court?

By ecclesiastical censure (Jn 9:22,34)—

Jn 12:42 Yet at the same time many even among the leaders believed in him. But because of the Pharisees they would not confess their faith for fear they would be put out of the synagogue;

2Ti 4:16 At my first defense, no one came to my support, but everyone deserted me. May it not be held against them. [17]But the Lord stood at my side and gave me strength, so that through me the message might be fully proclaimed and all the Gentiles might hear it. And I was delivered from the lion's mouth.

Divine permissions of, mysterious—

Hab 1:13 Your eyes are too pure to look on evil; you cannot tolerate wrong. Why then do you tolerate the treacherous? Why are you silent while the wicked swallow up those more righteous than themselves?

The mode of divine chastisement (La 1:3).

Done to church members (Ac 8:1)—

Ac 8:4 Those who had been scattered preached the word wherever they went. (+Ac 11:19-21)

Php 1:12 Now I want you to know, brothers, that what has happened to me has really served to advance the gospel. [13]As a result, it has become clear throughout the whole palace guard and to everyone else that I am in chains for Christ. [14]Because of my chains, most of the brothers in the Lord have been encouraged to speak the word of God more courageously and fearlessly. (+Php 1:18)

Powerless to separate from the love of Christ—

Ro 8:17 Now if we are children, then we are heirs—heirs of God and co-heirs with Christ, if indeed we share in his sufferings in order that we may also share in his glory.

Ro 8:35 Who shall separate us from the love of Christ? Shall trouble or hardship or persecution or famine or nakedness or danger or sword? [36]As it is written: "For your sake we face death all day long; we are considered as sheep to be slaughtered."

[37]No, in all these things we are more than conquerors through him who loved us. [38]For I am convinced that neither death nor life, neither angels nor demons, neither the present nor the future, nor any powers, [39]neither height nor depth, nor anything else in all creation, will be able to separate us from the love of God that is in Christ Jesus our Lord.

Exhortations to courage under—

Isa 51:12 "I, even I, am he who comforts you. Who are you that you fear mortal men, the sons of men, who are but grass, (+Isa 51:16)

Heb 12:3 Consider him who endured such opposition from sinful men, so that you will not grow weary and lose heart.

[4]In your struggle against sin, you have not yet resisted to the point of shedding your blood.

Heb 13:13 Let us, then, go to him outside the camp, bearing the disgrace he bore.

1Pe 3:14 But even if you should suffer for what is right, you are blessed. "Do not fear what they fear; do not be frightened."

1Pe 3:16 keeping a clear conscience, so that those who speak maliciously against your good behavior in Christ may be ashamed of their slander. [17]It is better, if it is God's will, to suffer for doing good than for doing evil.

1Pe 4:12 Dear friends, do not be surprised at the painful trial you are suffering, as though something strange were happening to you. [13]But rejoice that you participate in the sufferings of Christ, so that you may be overjoyed when his glory is revealed. [14]If you are insulted because of the name of Christ, you are blessed, for the Spirit of glory and of God rests on you.

1Pe 4:16 However, if you suffer as a Christian, do not be ashamed, but praise God that you bear that name.

1Pe 4:19 So then, those who suffer according to God's will should commit themselves to their faithful Creator and continue to do good.

Courageously endured—

Jer 26:11 Then the priests and the prophets said to the officials and all the people, "This man should be sentenced to death because he has prophesied against this city. You have heard it with your own ears!"

[12]Then Jeremiah said to all the officials and all the people: "The LORD sent me to prophesy against this house and this city all the things you have heard. [13]Now reform your ways and your actions and obey the LORD your God. Then the LORD will relent and not bring the disaster he has pronounced against you. [14]As for me, I am in your hands; do with me whatever you think is good and right.

1Co 4:9 For it seems to me that God has put us apostles on display at the end of the procession, like men condemned to die in the arena. We have been made a spectacle to the whole universe, to angels as well as to men. [10]We are fools for Christ, but you are so wise in Christ! We are weak, but you are strong! You are honored, we are dishonored! [11]To this very hour we go hungry and thirsty, we are in rags, we are brutally treated, we are homeless. [12]We work hard with our own hands. When we are cursed, we bless; when we are persecuted, we endure it; [13]when we are slandered, we answer kindly. Up to this moment we have become the scum of the earth, the refuse of the world.

2Co 4:8 We are hard pressed on every side, but not crushed; perplexed, but not in despair; [9]persecuted, but not abandoned; struck down, but not destroyed. [10]We always carry around in our body the death of Jesus, so that the life of Jesus may also be revealed in our body. [11]For we who are alive are always being given over to death for Jesus' sake, so that his life may be revealed in our mortal body. [12]So then, death is at work in us, but life is at work in you.

2Co 6:4 Rather, as servants of God we commend ourselves in every way: in great endurance; in troubles, hardships and distresses; [5]in beatings, imprisonments and riots; in hard work, sleepless nights and hunger;

2Co 6:8 through glory and dishonor, bad report and good report; genuine, yet regarded as impostors; [9]known, yet regarded as unknown; dying, and yet we live on; beaten, and yet not killed; [10]sorrowful, yet always rejoicing; poor, yet making many rich; having nothing, and yet possessing everything.

2Co 11:23 Are they servants of Christ? (I am out of my mind to talk like this.) I am more. I have worked much harder, been in prison more frequently, been flogged more severely, and been exposed to death again and again. [24]Five times I received from the Jews the forty lashes minus one. [25]Three times I was beaten with rods, once I was stoned, three times I was shipwrecked, I spent a night and a day in the open sea, [26]I have been constantly on the move. I have been in danger from rivers, in danger from bandits, in danger from my own countrymen, in danger from Gentiles; in danger in the city, in danger in the country, in danger at sea; and in danger from false brothers. [27]I have labored and toiled and have often gone without sleep; I have known hunger and thirst and have often gone without food; I have been cold and naked. (+2Co 12:10)

2Th 1:4 Therefore, among God's churches we boast about your perseverance and faith in all the persecutions and trials you are enduring.

2Ti 1:8 So do not be ashamed to testify about our Lord, or ashamed of me his prisoner. But join with me in suffering for the gospel, by the power of God,

2Ti 1:12 That is why I am suffering as I am. Yet I am not ashamed, because I know whom I have believed, and am convinced that he is able to guard what I have entrusted to him for that day.

2Ti 2:9 for which I am suffering even to the point of being chained like a criminal. But God's word is not chained. [10]Therefore I endure everything for the sake of the elect, that they too may obtain the salvation that is in Christ Jesus, with eternal glory.

Heb 11:25 He chose to be mistreated along with the people of God rather than to enjoy the pleasures of sin for a short time. [26]He regarded disgrace for the sake of Christ as of greater value than the treasures of Egypt, because he was looking ahead to his reward. [27]By faith he left Egypt, not fearing the king's anger; he persevered because he saw him who is invisible.

Heb 11:33 who through faith conquered kingdoms, administered justice, and gained what was promised; who shut the mouths of lions, [34]quenched the fury of the flames, and escaped the edge of the sword; whose weakness was turned to strength; and who became powerful in battle and routed foreign armies. [35]Women received back their dead, raised to life again. Others were tortured and refused to be released, so that they might gain a better resurrection. [36]Some faced jeers and flogging, while still others were chained and put in prison. [37]They were stoned; they were sawed in two; they were put to death by the sword. They went about in sheepskins and goatskins, destitute, persecuted and mistreated— [38]the world was not worthy of them. They wandered in deserts and mountains, and in caves and holes in the ground.

Jas 5:6 You have condemned and murdered innocent men, who were not opposing you.

Jas 5:10 Brothers, as an example of patience in the face of suffering, take the prophets who spoke in the name of the Lord.

Rejoicing under (Ro 5:3)—

Col 1:24 Now I rejoice in what was suffered for you, and I fill up in my flesh what is still lacking in regard to Christ's afflictions, for the sake of his body, which is the church.

1Th 1:6 You became imitators of us and of the Lord; in spite of severe suffering, you welcomed the message with the joy given by the Holy Spirit.

Heb 10:32 Remember those earlier days after you had received the light, when you stood your ground in a great contest in the face of suffering. [33]Sometimes you were publicly exposed to insult and persecution; at other times you stood side by side with those who were so treated.

[34]You sympathized with those in prison and joyfully accepted the confiscation of your property, because you knew that you yourselves had better and lasting possessions.

Perseverance under—

Ps 44:15 My disgrace is before me all day long, and my face is covered with shame [16]at the taunts of those who reproach and revile me, because of the enemy, who is bent on revenge.

[17]All this happened to us, though we had not forgotten you or been false to your covenant. [18]Our hearts had not turned back; our feet had not strayed from your path.

Ps 44:22 Yet for your sake we face death all day long; we are considered as sheep to be slaughtered.

Prayer for deliverance from (Ps 70:1-5; 83:1; 140:1,4; 142:6). Deliverance from (Ps 124; 129:1-2).

John's vision concerning—

Rev 2:3 You have persevered and have endured hardships for my name, and have not grown weary.

Rev 2:10 Do not be afraid of what you are about to suffer. I tell you, the devil will put some of you in prison to test you, and you will suffer persecution for ten days. Be faithful, even to the point of death, and I will give you the crown of life.

Rev 2:13 I know where you live—where Satan has his throne. Yet you remain true to my name. You did not renounce your faith in me, even in the days of Antipas, my faithful witness, who was put to death in your city—where Satan lives.

Rev 6:9 When he opened the fifth seal, I saw under the altar the souls of those who had been slain because of the word of God and the testimony they had maintained. [10]They called out in a loud voice, "How long, Sovereign Lord, holy and true, until you judge the inhabitants of the earth and avenge our blood?" [11]Then each of them was given a white robe, and they were told to wait a little longer, until the number of their fellow servants and brothers who were to be killed as they had been was completed.

Rev 7:13 Then one of the elders asked me, "These in white robes—who are they, and where did they come from?"

[14]I answered, "Sir, you know."

And he said, "These are they who have come out of the great tribulation; they have washed their robes and made them white in the blood of the Lamb.

[15]Therefore, "they are before the throne of God and serve him day and night in his temple; and he who sits on the throne will spread his tent over them. [16]Never again will they hunger; never again will they thirst. The sun will not beat upon them, nor any scorching heat. [17]For the Lamb at the center of the throne will be their shepherd; he will lead them to springs of living water. And God will wipe away every tear from their eyes." (+Rev 12:10)

Rev 12:11 They overcame him by the blood of the Lamb and by the word of their testimony; they did not love their lives so much as to shrink from death.

Rev 17:6 I saw that the woman was drunk with the blood of the saints, the blood of those who bore testimony to Jesus. When I saw her, I was greatly astonished.

Rev 20:4 I saw thrones on which were seated those who had been given authority to judge. And I saw the souls of those who had been beheaded because of their testimony for Jesus and because of the word of God. They had not worshiped the beast or his image and had not received his mark on their foreheads or their hands. They came to life and reigned with Christ a thousand years.

Of Christians, foretold—

Mt 20:22 "You don't know what you are asking," Jesus said to them. "Can you drink the cup I am going to drink?"

"We can," they answered.

Mt 23:34 Therefore I am sending you prophets and wise men and teachers. Some of them you will kill and crucify; others you will flog in your synagogues and pursue from town to town. [35]And so upon you will come all the righteous blood that has been shed on earth, from the blood of righteous Abel to the blood of Zechariah son of Berekiah, whom you murdered between the temple and the altar.

Mt 24:8 All these are the beginning of birth pains.

[9]"Then you will be handed over to be persecuted and put to death, and you will be hated by all nations because of me. [10]At that time many will turn away from the faith and will betray and hate each other,

Mk 13:9 "You must be on your guard. You will be handed over to the local councils and flogged in the synagogues. On account of me you will stand before governors and kings as witnesses to them. [10]And the gospel must first be preached to all nations. [11]Whenever you are arrested and brought to trial, do not worry beforehand about what to say. Just say whatever is given you at the time, for it is not you speaking, but the Holy Spirit. [12]"Brother will betray brother to death, and a father his child. Children will rebel against their parents and have them put to death. [13]All men will hate you because of me, but he who stands firm to the end will be saved.

Lk 21:12 "But before all this, they will lay hands on you and persecute you. They will deliver you to synagogues and prisons, and you will be brought before kings and governors, and all on account of my name. [13]This will result in your being witnesses to them. [14]But make up your mind not to worry beforehand how you will defend yourselves. [15]For I will give you words and wisdom that none of your adversaries will be able to resist or contradict. [16]You will be betrayed even by parents, brothers, relatives and friends, and they will put some of you to death. [17]All men will hate you because of me. [18]But not a hair of your head will perish. [19]By standing firm you will gain life.

Jn 15:18 "If the world hates you, keep in mind that it hated me first. [19]If you belonged to the world, it would love you as its own. As it is, you do not belong to the world, but I have chosen you out of the world. That is why the world hates you. (+Jn 15:20-21)

Jn 16:1 "All this I have told you so that you will not go astray. [2]They will put you out of the synagogue; in fact, a time is coming when anyone who kills you will think he is offering a service to God.

2Ti 3:2 People will be lovers of themselves, lovers of money, boastful, proud, abusive, disobedient to their parents, ungrateful, unholy, [3]without love, unforgiving, slanderous, without self-control, brutal, not lovers of the good, (+2Ti 3:12)

2Ti 3:13 while evil men and impostors will go from bad to worse, deceiving and being deceived.

1Jn 3:1 How great is the love the Father has lavished on us, that we should be called children of God! And that is what we are! The reason the world does not know us is that it did not know him.

1Jn 3:13 Do not be surprised, my brothers, if the world hates you.

Christ offers consolation (Mk 8:38; 9:42)—

Lk 6:22 Blessed are you when men hate you, when they exclude you and insult you and reject your name as evil, because of the Son of Man.

[23]"Rejoice in that day and leap for joy, because great is your reward in heaven. For that is how their fathers treated the prophets. (+Lk 17:33)

Jn 17:14 I have given them your word and the world has hated them, for they are not of the world any more than I am of the world.

Promises to those who endure—

Mt 5:10 Blessed are those who are persecuted because of righteousness, for theirs is the kingdom of heaven.

[11]"Blessed are you when people insult you, persecute you and falsely say all kinds of evil against you because of me. [12]Rejoice and be glad, because great is your reward in heaven, for in the same way they persecuted the prophets who were before you.

Mt 10:16 I am sending you out like sheep among wolves. Therefore be as shrewd as snakes and as innocent as doves.

[17]"Be on your guard against men; they will hand you over to the local councils and flog you in their synagogues. [18]On my account you will be brought before governors and kings as witnesses to them and to the Gentiles.

Mt 10:21 "Brother will betray brother to death, and a father his child; children will rebel against their parents and have them put to death. [22]All men will hate you because of me, but he who stands firm to the end will be saved. [23]When you are persecuted in one place, flee to another. I tell you the truth, you will not finish going through the cities of Israel before the Son of Man comes.

Mt 10:28 Do not be afraid of those who kill the body but cannot kill the soul. Rather, be afraid of the One who can destroy both soul and body in hell. (+Mt 10:29-31; Lk 6:22-23)

Should provoke love—

1Co 13:3 If I give all I possess to the poor and surrender my body to the flames, but have not love, I gain nothing.

Instances of:

Abel (Ge 4:8; Mt 23:35; 1Jn 3:12). Lot (Ge 19:9). Moses (Ex 2:15; 17:4).

David (Ps 31:13)—

Ps 56:5 All day long they twist my words; they are always plotting to harm me. (+Ps 59:1-2)

Prophets martyred by Jezebel (1Ki 18:4). Gideon (Jdg 6:28-32). Elijah (1Ki 18:10; 19; 2Ki 1:9; 2:23). Micaiah (1Ki 22:26; 2Ch 18:26). Elisha (2Ki 6:31). Hanani (2Ch 16:10). Zechariah (2Ch 24:21; Mt 23:35).

Job—

Job 1:9 "Does Job fear God for nothing?" Satan replied.

Job 2:4 "Skin for skin!" Satan replied. "A man will give all he has for his own life. [5]But stretch out your hand and strike his flesh and bones, and he will surely curse you to your face."

Job 12:4 "I have become a laughingstock to my friends, though I called upon God and he answered—a mere laughingstock, though righteous and blameless! [5]Men at ease have contempt for misfortune as the fate of those whose feet are slipping. (+Job 13:4-13; 16:1-4; 17:2; 19:1-5; 30:1-10)

Jeremiah (Jer 11:19; 15:10,15; 17:15-18; 18:18-23; 26; 32:2; 33:1; 36:26; 37; 38:1-6). Uriah (Jer 26:23). The prophets (2Ch 36:16; Mt 21:35-36; 1Th 2:15). The three Hebrews of the Captivity (Da 3:8-23). Daniel (Da 6). The Jews (Ezr 4; Ne 4).

John the Baptist (Mt 14:3-12). James (Ac 12:2). Simon (Mk 15:21). The disciples (Jn 9:22,34; 20:19). Lazarus (Jn 9:22,34; 12:10; 20:19).

The apostles (Ac 4:3-15)—

Ac 4:16 "What are we going to do with these men?" they asked. "Everybody living in Jerusalem knows they have done an outstanding miracle, and we cannot deny it. (+Ac 4:18; 5:18-42; 12:1-19; Rev 1:9)

Stephen (Ac 6:9-15; 7:1-51)—

Ac 7:52 Was there ever a prophet your fathers did not persecute? They even killed those who predicted the coming of the Righteous One. And now you have betrayed and murdered him— (+Ac 7:53-60)

The church (Ac 8:1; 9:1-14; Gal 1:13). Timothy (Heb 13:23). John (Rev 1:9). Antipas (Rev 2:13). The church of Smyrna (Rev 2:8-10).

Paul—

2Ti 2:9 for which I am suffering even to the point of being chained like a criminal. But God's word is not chained. [10]Therefore I endure everything for the sake of the elect, that they too may obtain the salvation that is in Christ Jesus, with eternal glory.

2Ti 4:16 At my first defense, no one came to my support, but everyone deserted me. May it not be held against them. [17]But the Lord stood at my side and gave me strength, so that through me the message might be fully proclaimed and all the Gentiles might hear it. And I was delivered from the lion's mouth. (+Ac 9:16,23-25,29; 16:19-25; 21:2-33; 22:22-24; 23:10,12-15; 1Co 4:9,11-13; 2Co 1:8-10; 4:8-12; 6:4-5,8-10; 11:23-27,32-33; Col 1:24; 1Th 2:2,14-15; 2Ti 1:8,12; 3:11-12)

See Paul.

PERSEPOLIS Capital of Persia, thirty miles NE of modern Shiraz; founded by Darius I (521-486 B.C.); destroyed by Alexander the Great in 331 B.C.

PERSEVERANCE [2846, 2152, 5702, 5705].

NIV+ PERSEVERE, PERSEVERED, PERSEVERES, PERSEVERING

From the Lord:

Ps 37:24 though he stumble, he will not fall, for the LORD upholds him with his hand.

Ps 37:28 For the LORD loves the just and will not forsake his faithful ones. They will be protected forever, but the offspring of the wicked will be cut off;

Ro 8:30 And those he predestined, he also called; those he called, he also justified; those he justified, he also glorified.

Ro 8:33 Who will bring any charge against those whom God has chosen? It is God who justifies. [34]Who is he that condemns? Christ Jesus, who died—more than that, who was raised to life—is at the right hand of God and is also interceding for us. [35]Who shall separate us from the love of Christ? Shall trouble or hardship or persecution or famine or nakedness or danger or sword?

1Co 1:8 He will keep you strong to the end, so that you will be blameless on the day of our Lord Jesus Christ. [9]God, who has called you into fellowship with his Son Jesus Christ our Lord, is faithful.

2Co 1:21 Now it is God who makes both us and you stand firm in Christ. He anointed us, [22]set his seal of ownership on us, and put his Spirit in our hearts as a deposit, guaranteeing what is to come.

Acknowledged—

Ps 73:24 You guide me with your counsel, and afterward you will take me into glory.

Ps 138:8 The LORD will fulfill [his purpose] for me; your

love, O LORD, endures forever—do not abandon the works of your hands.

Ro 8:37 No, in all these things we are more than conquerors through him who loved us. [38]For I am convinced that neither death nor life, neither angels nor demons, neither the present nor the future, nor any powers, [39]neither height nor depth, nor anything else in all creation, will be able to separate us from the love of God that is in Christ Jesus our Lord.

Col 2:7 rooted and built up in him, strengthened in the faith as you were taught, and overflowing with thankfulness.

2Ti 4:18 The Lord will rescue me from every evil attack and will bring me safely to his heavenly kingdom. To him be glory for ever and ever. Amen.

Promised—

Jer 32:40 I will make an everlasting covenant with them: I will never stop doing good to them, and I will inspire them to fear me, so that they will never turn away from me. (+Jn 6:34-36)

Jn 6:37 All that the Father gives me will come to me, and whoever comes to me I will never drive away. (+Jn 6:38)

Jn 6:39 And this is the will of him who sent me, that I shall lose none of all that he has given me, but raise them up at the last day. [40]For my Father's will is that everyone who looks to the Son and believes in him shall have eternal life, and I will raise him up at the last day."

Jn 10:28 I give them eternal life, and they shall never perish; no one can snatch them out of my hand. [29]My Father, who has given them to me, is greater than all; no one can snatch them out of my Father's hand.

Commanded—

1Ch 16:11 Look to the LORD and his strength; seek his face always.

Hos 12:6 But you must return to your God; maintain love and justice, and wait for your God always.

1Th 5:21 Test everything. Hold on to the good.

2Th 2:15 So then, brothers, stand firm and hold to the teachings we passed on to you, whether by word of mouth or by letter.

[16]May our Lord Jesus Christ himself and God our Father, who loved us and by his grace gave us eternal encouragement and good hope, [17]encourage your hearts and strengthen you in every good deed and word.

2Ti 2:1 You then, my son, be strong in the grace that is in Christ Jesus.

2Ti 2:3 Endure hardship with us like a good soldier of Christ Jesus.

2Ti 2:12 if we endure, we will also reign with him. If we disown him, he will also disown us;

2Ti 3:14 But as for you, continue in what you have learned and have become convinced of, because you know those from whom you learned it,

Tit 1:9 He must hold firmly to the trustworthy message as it has been taught, so that he can encourage others by sound doctrine and refute those who oppose it.

Jas 1:4 Perseverance must finish its work so that you may be mature and complete, not lacking anything.

Jas 1:25 But the man who looks intently into the perfect law that gives freedom, and continues to do this, not forgetting what he has heard, but doing it—he will be blessed in what he does. (+1Pe 4:16)

1Pe 5:8 Be self-controlled and alert. Your enemy the devil prowls around like a roaring lion looking for someone to devour. (+1Pe 5:9)

Rev 22:11 Let him who does wrong continue to do wrong;

let him who is vile continue to be vile; let him who does right continue to do right; and let him who is holy continue to be holy."

Exhortations to—

Ac 11:23 When he arrived and saw the evidence of the grace of God, he was glad and encouraged them all to remain true to the Lord with all their hearts.

Ac 13:43 When the congregation was dismissed, many of the Jews and devout converts to Judaism followed Paul and Barnabas, who talked with them and urged them to continue in the grace of God.

Ac 14:21 They preached the good news in that city and won a large number of disciples. Then they returned to Lystra, Iconium and Antioch, [22]strengthening the disciples and encouraging them to remain true to the faith. "We must go through many hardships to enter the kingdom of God," they said.

1Co 15:58 Therefore, my dear brothers, stand firm. Let nothing move you. Always give yourselves fully to the work of the Lord, because you know that your labor in the Lord is not in vain.

1Co 16:13 Be on your guard; stand firm in the faith; be men of courage; be strong.

Gal 5:1 It is for freedom that Christ has set us free. Stand firm, then, and do not let yourselves be burdened again by a yoke of slavery.

Gal 5:10 I am confident in the Lord that you will take no other view. The one who is throwing you into confusion will pay the penalty, whoever he may be.

Eph 4:14 Then we will no longer be infants, tossed back and forth by the waves, and blown here and there by every wind of teaching and by the cunning and craftiness of men in their deceitful scheming. (+Eph 4:15)

Eph 6:13 Therefore put on the full armor of God, so that when the day of evil comes, you may be able to stand your ground, and after you have done everything, to stand.

Eph 6:18 And pray in the Spirit on all occasions with all kinds of prayers and requests. With this in mind, be alert and always keep on praying for all the saints.

Php 1:27 Whatever happens, conduct yourselves in a manner worthy of the gospel of Christ. Then, whether I come and see you or only hear about you in my absence, I will know that you stand firm in one spirit, contending as one man for the faith of the gospel

Php 3:16 Only let us live up to what we have already attained.

Php 4:1 Therefore, my brothers, you whom I love and long for, my joy and crown, that is how you should stand firm in the Lord, dear friends!

Col 1:10 And we pray this in order that you may live a life worthy of the Lord and may please him in every way: bearing fruit in every good work, growing in the knowledge of God,

Col 1:22 But now he has reconciled you by Christ's physical body through death to present you holy in his sight, without blemish and free from accusation— [23]if you continue in your faith, established and firm, not moved from the hope held out in the gospel. This is the gospel that you heard and that has been proclaimed to every creature under heaven, and of which I, Paul, have become a servant.

1Th 3:8 For now we really live, since you are standing firm in the Lord. (+2Th 3:15)

2Ti 1:13 What you heard from me, keep as the pattern of sound teaching, with faith and love in Christ Jesus.

Heb 2:1 We must pay more careful attention, therefore, to what we have heard, so that we do not drift away.

Heb 6:1 Therefore let us leave the elementary teachings about Christ and go on to maturity, not laying again the foundation of repentance from acts that lead to death, and of faith in God,

Heb 6:11 We want each of you to show this same diligence to the very end, in order to make your hope sure. [12]We do not want you to become lazy, but to imitate those who through faith and patience inherit what has been promised.

Heb 6:15 And so after waiting patiently, Abraham received what was promised.

Heb 10:23 Let us hold unswervingly to the hope we profess, for he who promised is faithful.

Heb 10:35 So do not throw away your confidence; it will be richly rewarded. [36]You need to persevere so that when you have done the will of God, you will receive what he has promised.

Heb 12:5 And you have forgotten that word of encouragement that addresses you as sons:

"My son, do not make light of the Lord's discipline, and do not lose heart when he rebukes you, [6]because the Lord disciplines those he loves, and he punishes everyone he accepts as a son."

[7]Endure hardship as discipline; God is treating you as sons. For what son is not disciplined by his father? [8]If you are not disciplined (and everyone undergoes discipline), then you are illegitimate children and not true sons. [9]Moreover, we have all had human fathers who disciplined us and we respected them for it. How much more should we submit to the Father of our spirits and live! [10]Our fathers disciplined us for a little while as they thought best; but God disciplines us for our good, that we may share in his holiness. [11]No discipline seems pleasant at the time, but painful. Later on, however, it produces a harvest of righteousness and peace for those who have been trained by it.

[12]Therefore, strengthen your feeble arms and weak knees. [13]"Make level paths for your feet," so that the lame may not be disabled, but rather healed.

Heb 12:15 See to it that no one misses the grace of God and that no bitter root grows up to cause trouble and defile many.

Heb 13:9 Do not be carried away by all kinds of strange teachings. It is good for our hearts to be strengthened by grace, not by ceremonial foods, which are of no value to those who eat them.

Heb 13:13 Let us, then, go to him outside the camp, bearing the disgrace he bore.

2Pe 3:17 Therefore, dear friends, since you already know this, be on your guard so that you may not be carried away by the error of lawless men and fall from your secure position. [18]But grow in the grace and knowledge of our Lord and Savior Jesus Christ. To him be glory both now and forever! Amen.

Rev 16:15 "Behold, I come like a thief! Blessed is he who stays awake and keeps his clothes with him, so that he may not go naked and be shamefully exposed."

A proof of discipleship—

Jn 8:31 To the Jews who had believed him, Jesus said, "If you hold to my teaching, you are really my disciples. [32]Then you will know the truth, and the truth will set you free."

A condition of fruitfulness—

Jn 15:4 Remain in me, and I will remain in you. No branch can bear fruit by itself; it must remain in the vine. Neither can you bear fruit unless you remain in me.

[5]"I am the vine; you are the branches. If a man remains in

me and I in him, he will bear much fruit; apart from me you can do nothing.

Jn 15:7 If you remain in me and my words remain in you, ask whatever you wish, and it will be given you.

Jn 15:9 "As the Father has loved me, so have I loved you. Now remain in my love.

Intercessory prayer for—

Lk 22:31 "Simon, Simon, Satan has asked to sift you as wheat. ³²But I have prayed for you, Simon, that your faith may not fail. And when you have turned back, strengthen your brothers."

Motives to:

The example, of Moses—

Heb 3:5 Moses was faithful as a servant in all God's house, testifying to what would be said in the future.

Of the prophets—

Jas 5:10 Brothers, as an example of patience in the face of suffering, take the prophets who spoke in the name of the Lord. ¹¹As you know, we consider blessed those who have persevered. You have heard of Job's perseverance and have seen what the Lord finally brought about. The Lord is full of compassion and mercy.

Of Christ—

Heb 3:6 But Christ is faithful as a son over God's house. And we are his house, if we hold on to our courage and the hope of which we boast.

Heb 3:14 We have come to share in Christ if we hold firmly till the end the confidence we had at first.

Heb 12:2 Let us fix our eyes on Jesus, the author and perfecter of our faith, who for the joy set before him endured the cross, scorning its shame, and sat down at the right hand of the throne of God. ³Consider him who endured such opposition from sinful men, so that you will not grow weary and lose heart.

⁴In your struggle against sin, you have not yet resisted to the point of shedding your blood.

The intercession of Christ—

Heb 4:14 Therefore, since we have a great high priest who has gone through the heavens, Jesus the Son of God, let us hold firmly to the faith we profess.

The heavenly witnesses—

Heb 12:1 Therefore, since we are surrounded by such a great cloud of witnesses, let us throw off everything that hinders and the sin that so easily entangles, and let us run with perseverance the race marked out for us.

Acceptance by Christ—

2Co 5:9 So we make it our goal to please him, whether we are at home in the body or away from it.

2Co 5:15 And he died for all, that those who live should no longer live for themselves but for him who died for them and was raised again.

1Pe 1:4 and into an inheritance that can never perish, spoil or fade—kept in heaven for you, ⁵who through faith are shielded by God's power until the coming of the salvation that is ready to be revealed in the last time. ⁶In this you greatly rejoice, though now for a little while you may have had to suffer grief in all kinds of trials. ⁷These have come so that your faith—of greater worth than gold, which perishes even though refined by fire—may be proved genuine and may result in praise, glory and honor when Jesus Christ is revealed.

Rewards contingent upon—

Gal 6:9 Let us not become weary in doing good, for at the proper time we will reap a harvest if we do not give up.

Jas 1:12 Blessed is the man who perseveres under trial,

because when he has stood the test, he will receive the crown of life that God has promised to those who love him.

Rev 2:7 He who has an ear, let him hear what the Spirit says to the churches. To him who overcomes, I will give the right to eat from the tree of life, which is in the paradise of God.

Rev 2:10 Do not be afraid of what you are about to suffer. I tell you, the devil will put some of you in prison to test you, and you will suffer persecution for ten days. Be faithful, even to the point of death, and I will give you the crown of life.

¹¹He who has an ear, let him hear what the Spirit says to the churches. He who overcomes will not be hurt at all by the second death.

Rev 2:17 He who has an ear, let him hear what the Spirit says to the churches. To him who overcomes, I will give some of the hidden manna. I will also give him a white stone with a new name written on it, known only to him who receives it.

Rev 2:25 Only hold on to what you have until I come.

²⁶To him who overcomes and does my will to the end, I will give authority over the nations—

²⁷'He will rule them with an iron scepter; he will dash them to pieces like pottery'—

just as I have received authority from my Father. ²⁸I will also give him the morning star.

Rev 3:5 He who overcomes will, like them, be dressed in white. I will never blot out his name from the book of life, but will acknowledge his name before my Father and his angels.

Rev 3:11 I am coming soon. Hold on to what you have, so that no one will take your crown.

Rev 3:21 To him who overcomes, I will give the right to sit with me on my throne, just as I overcame and sat down with my Father on his throne.

Rev 14:12 This calls for patient endurance on the part of the saints who obey God's commandments and remain faithful to Jesus.

Rev 21:7 He who overcomes will inherit all this, and I will be his God and he will be my son.

Eternal life contingent upon (Mt 10:22)—

Mt 24:13 but he who stands firm to the end will be saved. (+Mk 13:13)

Ro 2:6 God "will give to each person according to what he has done."

⁷To those who by persistence in doing good seek glory, honor and immortality, he will give eternal life.

2Pe 1:10 Therefore, my brothers, be all the more eager to make your calling and election sure. For if you do these things, you will never fall, ¹¹and you will receive a rich welcome into the eternal kingdom of our Lord and Savior Jesus Christ.

Lacking in:

The wayside and other hearers—

Mk 4:3 "Listen! A farmer went out to sow his seed. ⁴As he was scattering the seed, some fell along the path, and the birds came and ate it up. ⁵Some fell on rocky places, where it did not have much soil. It sprang up quickly, because the soil was shallow. ⁶But when the sun came up, the plants were scorched, and they withered because they had no root. ⁷Other seed fell among thorns, which grew up and choked the plants, so that they did not bear grain. ⁸Still other seed fell on good soil. It came up, grew and produced a crop, multiplying thirty, sixty, or even a hundred times."

Churches of Asia (Rev 2:5; 3:1-3,14-18).

Instances of:

Caleb and Joshua, in representing the land of promise (Nu 14:24,38).

The righteous—

Job 17:9 Nevertheless, the righteous will hold to their ways, and those with clean hands will grow stronger.

Pr 4:18 The path of the righteous is like the first gleam of dawn, shining ever brighter till the full light of day.

In prayer, Abraham in interceding for Sodom (Ge 18:23-32), Jacob (Ge 32:24-26), Elijah for rain (1Ki 18:42-45), Paul for the removal of the thorn in his flesh (2Co 12:7-9).

See Character; Instability; Stability.

PERSIA [7273, 7275, 10060, 10594, 10595].

NIV+ PERSIAN, PERSIANS

An empire which extended from India to Ethiopia, comprising 127 provinces (Est 1:1; Da 6:1). Government of, restricted by constitutional limitations (Est 8:8; Da 6:8-12). Municipal governments in, provided with dual governors (Ne 3:9,12,16-18). The princes advisory in matters of administration (Da 6:1-7). Status of women in, queen sat on the throne with the king (Ne 2:6). Vashti divorced for refusing to appear before the king's courtiers (Est 1:10-22; 2:4).

Israel captive in (2Ch 36:20), captivity foretold (Hos 13:16). Men of in the Syrian army (Eze 27:10).

Rulers of:

Xerxes (Est 1:3). Darius (Da 5:31; 6; 9:1). Artaxerxes I (Ezr 4:7-24). Artaxerxes II (Ezr 7; Ne 2; 5:1). Cyrus (2Ch 36:22-23; Ezr 1; 3:7; 4:3; 5:13-14,17; 6:3; Isa 41:2-3; 44:28; 45:1-4,13; 46:11; 48:14-15). Princes of (Est 1:14).

System of justice (Ezr 7:25). Prophecies concerning (Isa 13:17; 21:1-10; Jer 49:34-39; 51:11-64; Eze 32:24-25; 38:5; Da 2:31-45; 5:28; 7; 8; 11:1-4).

See Babylon; Chaldea.

PERSIS [4372] (female Persian). A Christian woman in Rome (Ro 16:12).

PERSONAL CALL *See Call, Personal; Minister, Call of.*

PERSONIFICATION Of wisdom (Pr 1; 2:1-19; 8-9). Of the Israel and/or the Church, in allegorical interpretation (SS 1-8). *See Pantomime.*

PERUDA [7243] (single, unique). One of the servants of Solomon. Descendants of, return to Jerusalem from captivity in Babylon (Ezr 2:55). Called Perida (Ne 7:57).

PERVERSENESS [4279, 6390, 6835, 6836, 6838, 9316, 9337, 1406, 4415].

NIV+ PERVERSE, PERVERSION, PERVERSITY, PERVERT, PERVERTED, PERVERTING, PERVERTS

(Pr 11:3; 12:8; 15:4; 28:6; Eze 9:9; Mt 17:17; 1Ti 6:5).

PESHITTA (simple, i.e., no marginal notes). Ancient Syriac translation of the Bible.

PESTILENCE [1822, 8404, 3369].

NIV+ PESTILENCES

Sent as a judgment (Lev 26:16,25). Sent upon the Egyptians. *See Egypt; Plague.*

PESTLE [6605]. An instrument used to grind in a mortar (Pr 27:22).

PETER, 1 and 2

1 Peter:

Author: The Apostle Peter

Date: In the early 60s A.D.

Outline:

I. Salutation (1:1-2).
II. Praise to God for His Grace and Salvation (1:3-12).
III. Exhortations to Holiness of Life (1:13-5:11).
  A. The Requirement of Holiness (2:4-12).
  B. The Position of Believers (2:4-12).
    1. A spiritual house (2:4-8).
    2. A chosen people (2:9-10).
    3. Aliens and strangers (2:11-12).
  C. Submission to Authority (2:13-3:7).
    1. Submission to rulers (2:13-17).
    2. Submission to masters (2:18-20).
    3. Christ's example of submission (2:21-25).
    4. Submission of wives to husbands (3:1-6).
    5. The corresponding duty of husbands (3:7).
  D. Duties of All (3:8-17).
  E. Christ's Example (3:18-4:6).
  F. Conduct in View of the End of All Things (4:7-11).
  G. Conduct of Those Who Suffer for Christ (4:12-19).
  H. Conduct of Elders (5:1-4).
  I. Conduct of Young Men (5:5-11).
IV. The Purpose of the Letter (5:12).
V. Closing Greetings (5:13-14).
  See General Letters.

2 Peter:

Author: The apostle (Simon) Peter

Date: Probably between 65 and 68.

Outline:

I. Introduction (1:1-2).
II. Exhortation to Growth in Christian Virtues (1:3-11).
  A. The Divine Enablement (1:3-4).
  B. The Call for Growth (1:5-7).
  C. The Value of Such Growth (1:8-11).
III. The Purpose and Authentication of Peter's Message (1:12-21).
  A. His Aim in Writing (1:12-15).
  B. The Basis of His Authority (1:16-21).
IV. Warning against False Teachers (ch. 2).
  A. Their Coming Predicted (2:1-3a).
  B. Their Judgment Assured (2:3b-9).
  C. Their Characteristics Set Forth (2:10-22).
V. The Fact of Christ's Return (3:1-16).
  A. Peter's Purpose in Writing Restated (3:1-2).
  B. The Coming of Scoffers (3:3-7).
  C. The Certainty of Christ's Return (3:8-10).
  D. Exhortations Based on the Fact of Christ's Return (3:11-16).
VI. Concluding Remarks (3:17-18).
  See General Letters.

PETER, SIMON [3064, 4377] (rock, stone).

NIV+ CEPHAS, PETER'S, SIMON

Also called Simon and Cephas (Mt 16:16-19; Mk 3:16; Jn 1:42). Simeon (Ac 15:14, ftn). A fisherman (Mt 4:18; Lk 5:1-7; Jn 21:3). Call of (Mt 4:18-20; Mk 1:16-18; Lk 5:1-11). His wife's mother healed (Mt 8:14; Mk 1:29-30; Lk 4:38). An apostle (Mt 10:2; 16:18-19; Mk 3:16; Lk 6:14; Ac 1:13). An evangelist (Mk 1:36-37). Confesses Jesus as Christ (Mt 16:16-19; Mk 8:29; Lk 9:20; Jn 6:68-69). His presumption in rebuking Jesus (Mt 16:22-23; Mk

8:32-33), when the throng was pressing Jesus and the woman touched him (Lk 8:45), when Jesus foretold his persecution and death (Mt 16:21-23; Mk 8:31-33), in refusing to let Jesus wash his feet (Jn 13:6-11). Present at the healing of Jairus's daughter (Mk 5:37; Lk 8:51), at the transfiguration (Mt 17:1-4; Mk 9:2-6; Lk 9:28-33; 2Pe 1:16-18), in Gethsemane (Mt 26:36-46; Mk 14:33-42; Lk 22:40-46). Seeks the interpretation of the parable of the manager (Lk 12:41), of the law of forgiveness (Mt 18:21), of the law of defilement (Mt 15:15), of the prophecy of Jesus concerning his second coming (Mk 13:34). Walks upon the water of the Sea of Galilee (Mt 14:28-31). Sent with John to prepare the Passover (Lk 22:8). Calls attention to the withered fig tree (Mk 11:21). His failure foretold by Jesus, and his profession of fidelity (Mt 26:33-35; Mk 14:29-31; Lk 22:31-34; Jn 13:36-38). Cuts off the ear of Malchus (Mt 26:51; Mk 14:47; Lk 22:50). Follows Jesus to the high priest's palace (Mt 26:58; Mk 14:54; Lk 22:54; Jn 18:15). His denial of Jesus and his repentance (Mt 26:69-75; Mk 14:66-72; Lk 22:55-62; Jn 18:17-18,25-27). Visits the tomb (Lk 24:12; Jn 20:2-6). Jesus sends message to, after the Resurrection (Mk 16:7). Jesus appears to (Lk 24:34; 1Co 15:4-5). Present at the Sea of Tiberias when Jesus appeared to his disciples; leaps into the sea, and comes to land when Jesus is recognized, is commissioned to feed the flock of Christ (Jn 21:1-23).

Remains in Jerusalem (Ac 1:13). His statement before the disciples concerning the death of Judas, and his recommendation that the vacancy in the apostleship be filled (Ac 1:15-22). Preaches at Pentecost (Ac 2:14-40). Heals the crippled man in the portico of the temple (Ac 3). Accused by the council; his defense (Ac 4:1-23). Foretells the death of Ananias and Sapphira (Ac 5:1-11). Imprisoned and scourged; his defense before the council (Ac 5:17-42). Goes to Samaria (Ac 8:14). Prays for the baptism of the Holy Spirit (Ac 8:15-18). Rebukes Simon, the sorcerer, who desires to purchase like power (Ac 8:18-24). Returns to Jerusalem (Ac 8:25). Receives Paul (Gal 1:18; 2:9). Visits Lydda; heals Aeneas (Ac 9:32-34). Visits Joppa; stays with Simon the tanner; raises Dorcas from the dead (Ac 9:36-43). Has a vision of a sheet containing clean and unclean animals (Ac 10:9-16). Receives the servant of the centurion; goes to Caesarea; preaches and baptizes the centurion and his household (Ac 10). Advocates, in the council of the apostles and elders, the preaching of the Gospel to the Gentiles (Ac 11:1-18; 15:7-11). Imprisoned and delivered by an angel (Ac 12:3-19). Writes two letters (1Pe 1:1; 2Pe 1:1).

Miracles of. *See Miracles, Of the Disciples of Jesus.*

PETHAHIAH [7342] (*Yahweh opens*).

1. A priest in the reign of David (1Ch 24:16).

2. A Levite who divorced his Gentile wife (Ezr 10:23). Probably identical with the one mentioned (Ne 9:5).

3. A counselor of Artaxerxes (Ne 11:24).

PETHOR [7335]. A city in Mesopotamia. Home of the prophet Balaam (Nu 22:5; Dt 23:4).

PETHUEL [7333] (*God's opening*). Father of the prophet Joel (Joel 1:1).

PETITION [1335, 2349, 8629, 9382, 9384, 9525, *1255, 1872, 1961, 2656*].

NIV+ PETITIONED, PETITIONS

Right of, recognized by Pharaoh (Ex 5:15-18), Israel (Nu 27:1-5; 32:1-5; 36:1-5; Jos 17:4,14,16; 21:1-2), David

(1Ki 1:15-21), Rehoboam (1Ki 12:1-17; 2Ch 10), Jehoram (2Ki 8:3,6).

PETRA (*rock, cliff, rock grotto*). OT Sela (Jdg 1:36; 2Ki 14:7; Isa 16:1). Capital city of the Nabateans. *See Nabatea, Nabateans; Sela.*

PEULLETHAI, PEULTHAI [7191] (*worker, wage earner*). A gatekeeper of the tabernacle (1Ch 26:5).

PHALEC *See Peleg.*

PHALLU *See Pallu.*

PHALTI *See Palti.*

PHALTIEL *See Paltiel.*

PHANUEL [5750] (*face of God [El]*). Father of Anna the prophetess (Lk 2:36).

PHARAOH [7281, 5755] (*the great house*).

NIV+ PHARAOH'S

1. King of Egypt at the time of Abraham (Ge 12:14-20; Ps 105:14).

2. Ruler of Egypt at the time of the famine. *See Egypt; Israel, Israelites.*

3. Ruler of Egypt at the time of the deliverance and exodus of the Israelites. *See Israel, Israelites.*

4. Father-in-law of Mered (1Ch 4:18).

5. Ruler of Egypt at the time of David (1Ki 11:17-22).

6. Father-in-law of Solomon (1Ki 3:1; 9:16).

7. At the time of Hezekiah (2Ki 18:21).

8. Pharaoh Neco. His invasion of Assyria, Josiah's death (2Ki 23:29-35; 24:7; 2Ch 35:20-24; 36:3-4; Jer 46:2; 47:1).

9. Pharaoh. (Jer 37:4-7; 44; Eze 17:15-17). Prophecies concerning (Jer 44:30; 46:25-26; Eze 29; 30:21-26).

PHARES, PHAREZ *See Perez.*

PHARISEES [5757] (*separate ones*).

NIV+ PHARISEE, PHARISEE'S

A sect of the Jews (Ac 15:5). Doctrines of (Mt 15:9), concerning the Resurrection (Ac 23:6,8), association with tax collectors and sinners (Mt 9:11-13).

Traditions of, in regard to fasting (Mt 9:14; Lk 18:12), the washing of hands (Mt 15:1-3; Mk 7:1-15), the duties of children to parents (Mt 15:4-9), the Sabbath (Mt 12:2-8). Denounced by Jesus (Mt 23:2-36; Lk 11:39-44). Hypocrisy of, reproved by John (Mt 3:7-10), by Jesus (Mt 6:2-8,16-18; 15:1-9; 16:1-12; 21:33-46; 23:2-33; Lk 11:14-54; 12:1; 15:1-9). Reject John (Lk 7:30), Christ (Mt 12:38-39; 15:12; Jn 7:48). Come to Jesus with questions (Mt 19:3; 22:15-22).

Minister to Jesus (Lk 7:36; 11:37; 14:1). Become disciples of Jesus (Jn 3:1; Ac 15:5; 22:5).

Paul a Pharisee (Ac 23:6; 26:5).

See Herodians; Sadducees; Testaments, Time Between.

PHAROSH *See Parosh.*

PHARPAR [7286]. A river of Damascus. Referred to by Naaman (2Ki 5:12).

PHARZITES *See Perez, Perezite.*

PHASEAH *See Paseah.*

PHASELIS Rhodian colony in Lycia (1Mc 15:23).

PHASELUS Latinization of Phasael, the son of Antipater the Idumean, and brother of Herod the Great.

PHEBE *See Phoebe.*

PHENICE *See Phoenicia; Phoenix.*

PHENICIA *See Phoenicia, Phenicia.*

PHICOL, PHICHOL [7087]. Chief captain of the Philistines (Ge 21:22,32; 26:26).

PHILADELPHIA [5788] (*love of brother, sister*). A city of Lydia. One of the seven churches (Rev 1:11; 3:7-13).

PHILANTHROPY *See Alms; Beneficence; Charitableness; Giving; Liberality; Neighbor; Poor.*

PHILEMON [5800] (*beloved*). Convert of Paul at Colosse; Epistle to Philemon written to him.

PHILEMON, EPISTLE TO
Author: The Apostle Paul
Date: c. A.D. 60
Outline:
I. Greetings (1-3).
II. Thanksgiving and Prayer (4-7).
III. Paul's Plea for Onesimus (8-21).
IV. Final Request, Greetings and Benedictions (22-25).

PHILETUS [5801] (*beloved*). False teacher in the church at Ephesus (2Ti 2:17).

PHILIP [5805] (*horse lover*).
NIV+ PHILIP'S
1. King of Macedonia; father of Alexander the Great; founder of city of Philippi in Macedonia (1Mc 1:1).
2. Philip V, king of Macedonia (1Mc 8:5).
3. Governor of Jerusalem under Antiochus, regent of Syria (2Mc 5:22).
4. Herod Philip. Married Herodias (Mt 14:3; Mk 6:17; Lk 3:19).
5. Herod Philip II, tetrarch of Batanaea, Trachonitis, Gaulanitis, and parts of Jamnia. Best of Herods (Lk 3:1).

PHILIP THE APOSTLE Native of Bethsaida, the same town as Andrew and Peter (Jn 1:44), undoubtedly first a disciple of John the Baptist (Jn 1:43), brought his friend Nathanael to Jesus (Jn 1:45), called to apostleship (Mt 10:3; Mk 3:18; Lk 6:14), faith tested by Jesus before feeding of the 5,000 (Jn 6:5-6), brought Greeks to Jesus (Jn 12:20-23), asked to see the Father (Jn 14:8-12), in the Upper Room with 120 (Ac 1:13).

PHILIP THE EVANGELIST Chosen one of the seven (Ac 6:5). A Hellenist, or Greek-speaking Jew, preached in Samaria (Ac 8). Ethiopian eunuch converted through him (Ac 8:26-40). Paul stayed at his home in Caesarea, where he lived with his four unmarried daughters who were prophetesses (Ac 21:8-9).

PHILIPPI [5803, 5804, 5805].
NIV+ PHILIPPIANS
A city of Macedonia. Paul preaches in (Ac 16:12-40; 20:1-6; 1Th 2:1-2). Contributes to the maintenance of Paul (Php 4:10-18). Paul sends Epaphroditus to (Php 2:25). Paul writes a letter to the Christians of (Php 1:1).

PHILIPPIANS, EPISTLE TO THE
Author: The Apostle Paul
Date: c. A.D. 61

Outline:
I. Salutation (1:1-2).
II. Thanksgiving and Prayer for the Philippians (1:3-11).
III. Paul's Personal Circumstances (1:12-26).
IV. Exhortations (1:27-2:18).
  A. Living a Life Worthy of the Gospel (1:27-30).
  B. Following the Servant Attitude of Christ (2:1-18).
V. Paul's Associates in the Gospel (2:19-30).
  A. Timothy (2:19-24).
  B. Epaphroditus (2:25-30).
VI. Warnings against Judaizers and Antinomians (3:1-4:1).
  A. Against Judaizers or Legalists (3:1-16).
  B. Against Antinomians or Libertines (3:17-4:1).
VII. Final Exhortations, Thanks and Conclusion (4:2-23).
  A. Exhortations concerning Various Aspects of the Christian Life (4:2-9).
  B. Concluding Testimony and Repeated Thanks (4:10-20).
  C. Greetings and Benediction (4:21-23).

PHILISTIA [7148, 7149].
NIV+ PHILISTINE, PHILISTINE'S, PHILISTINES
The seacoast in the W of Dan and Simeon (Ps 60:8; 87:4; 108:9).

PHILISTINES [7148, 7149].
NIV+ PHILISTIA, PHILISTINE, PHILISTINE'S
Descendants of Mizraim (Ge 10:14; 1Ch 1:12; Jer 47:4; Am 9:7). Called Kerethites (1Sa 30:14-16; Eze 25:16; Zep 2:5), Casluhites (Ge 10:14; 1Ch 1:12), Caphtor (Jer 47:4; Am 9:7). Territory of (Ex 13:17; 23:31; Dt 2:23; Jos 13:3; 15:47). Rulers of (Jos 13:3; Jdg 3:3; 16:5,30; 1Sa 5:8,11; 6:4,12; 7:7; 29:2,6-7). Kings of: Abimelech I (Ge 20), Abimelech II (Ge 26), Achish (1Sa 21:10-15; 27:2-12; 28:1-2; 29:1).

Relations with Israel—
Allowed to remain in Canaan (Jdg 3:3-4). Shamgar slays six hundred with an oxgoad (Jdg 3:31). For their history during the leadership of Samson (Jdg 13-16). Defeat the Israelites; take the ark; suffer plagues, and return the ark (1Sa 4-6). Army of (1Sa 13:5). Defeated by Samuel (1Sa 7), by Saul and Jonathan (1Sa 9:16; 13-14). Their champion, Goliath, slain by David (1Sa 17). David slays two hundred (1Sa 18:22-30). David finds refuge among (1Sa 27). Defeat the Israelites and slay Saul and his sons (1Sa 31; 1Ch 10:1). Defeated by David (2Sa 5:17-25; 23:9-16; 1Ch 14:8-16). Pay tribute to Jehoshaphat (2Ch 17:11). Defeated by Hezekiah (2Ki 18:8). Prophecies against (Isa 9:11-12; 14:29-31; Jer 25:17-20; 47; Eze 25:15-17; Am 1:6-8; Zep 2:4-7; Zec 9:5-7).

PHILOLOGUS [5807] (*lover of words [education]*). Christian in Rome to whom Paul sent a salutation (Ro 16:15).

PHILOSOPHY [5814, 5815, 5186] (*lover of discernment, lover of wisdom*).
NIV+ PHILOSOPHER, PHILOSOPHERS
The nature of things (Ecc 1-7). A philosophical discourse on wisdom (Job 28). Philosophical inductions and deductions relating to God and his providence (Job 5:8-20; 9; 10:2-21; 12:6-24; 33:12-30; 37). Reveals the mysteries of providence (Pr 25:2; Ro 1:19-20). Is not sufficient for an adequate knowledge of God (1Co 1:21-22), or of salvation through the atonement of Jesus Christ (1Co 2:6-10). Employment of, was not Paul's method of preaching the

Gospel (1Co 1:17,19,21; 2:1-5,13). Greek schools of (Ac 17:18). Rabbinical (Col 2:8,16-19; 1Ti 6:20).

See Aratus; Asceticism; Epicureans; Gnosticism; Stoicism; Stoics; Reasoning; Wisdom.

PHINEHAS [7090] (*the Negro*).

1. Son of Eleazar and grandson of Aaron (Ex 6:25; 1Ch 6:4,50; 9:20; Ezr 7:5; 8:2), who slew Zimri and Cozbi at God's command (Nu 25:6-15; Ps 106:30).

God establishes a covenant with (Nu 25:10-13). *See Covenants, Major in the Old Testament.*

2. Son of Eli; sinful priest (1Sa 1:3; 2:12-17,22-25,27-36; 3:11-13). He and his brother were killed by Philistines (1Sa 4).

3. Father of Eleazar who returned from exile (Ezr 8:33).

PHLEGON [5823] (*burning*). A disciple in Rome (Ro 16:14).

PHOEBE [5833] (*radiant*). A deaconess of the church at Cenchrea (Ro 16:1).

PHOENICIA, PHENICIA [4046, 5834] (*land of purple [dye for trading]*, possibly *land of date palms*).

NIV+ SYRIAN PHOENICIA

Country along Mediterranean coast, c. 120 miles long, extending from Arvad (Arados, 1Mc 15:23) to Dor, just S of Carmel. The Semitic name for the land was Canaan. The term Phoenicia is from a Greek word meaning "purple-red," perhaps because the Phoenicians were the discoverers of the crimson-purple dye derived form the murex shellfish. The people were Semites who came in a migration from the Mesopotamian region during the second millennium B.C. They became great seafarers, establishing colonies at Carthage and Spain, and perhaps even reached England. Inhabitants of, descended from Canaan (Ge 10:15,18-19). Called Sidonians (Jdg 18:7; Eze 32:30). They were famous shipbuilders (Eze 27:9) and carpenters (1Ki 16:31; 18:19). Hiram, one of their kings was friendly with David and Solomon (2Sa 5:11; 1Ki 5:1-12; 2Ch 2:3-16), and another Hiram helped Solomon in the building of the temple in Jerusalem (1Ki 7:13-47; 2Ch 2:13-14). Jews from, hear Jesus (Mk 3:8). Jesus healed a Syrian Phoenician woman's daughter in its regions (Mk 7:24-30). Paul visited Christians there (Ac 15:3; 21:2-7; 27:3).

PHOENIX [5837]. Town on the S coast of Crete (Ac 27:12).

PHRYGIA [5867]. An inland province of Asia Minor. People from, in Jerusalem (Ac 2:10). Paul in (Ac 16:6; 18:23).

PHURAH *See Purah, Pura.*

PHUT *See Put.*

PHUVAH *See Puah, Pua.*

PHYGELUS, PHYGELLUS [5869] (*fugitive*). A Christian in Asia. Turns from Paul (2Ti 1:15).

PHYLACTERY [5873] (*safeguard, means of protection*).

NIV+ PHYLACTERIES

A small box containing slips of parchment on which were written portions of the law (Ex 13:9,16; Dt 6:4-9; 11:18). Worn ostentatiously on the forehead and left arm (Mt 23:5).

PHYSICIAN [8324, *2620*].

NIV+ PHYSICIANS

(2Ch 16:12; Mt 9:12; Mk 5:26; Lk 8:43). Proverbs about (Mk 2:17; Lk 4:23). Luke a physician (Col 4:14).

Figurative: (Job 13:4; Jer 8:22; Lk 5:31).

PHYSIOGNOMY The art of discovering temperament and character from outward appearance. Character revealed in (Isa 3:9). *See Countenance; Face.*

PHYSIOLOGY The human body (Job 10:11; Ps 139:14-16; Pr 14:30). *See Hygiene.* Figurative of the Church (Eph 4:16; Col 2:19).

PI-BESETH, PI BESETH (*temple [house] of Bastet [pagan goddess]*). *See Bubastis.*

PI HAHIROTH, PI-HAHIROTH [7084] (*temple [house] of Hathor [pagan goddess]*; possibly *mouth of canals*). The place on the W shore of the Red Sea where Pharaoh overtook the Israelites (Ex 14:2,9; Nu 33:7-8).

PICKS, IRON [3044]. An instrument of iron used by prisoners of war (2Sa 12:31; 1Ch 20:3), who were used by victorious kings as menial laborers in royal building projects (1Ki 9:20-21; cf. also Ex 1:11).

PICTURES *See Idol; Idolatry.*

PIECE OF SILVER *See Silver.*

PIERCING THE EAR [4125, 8361]. A token of servitude for life (Ex 21:6; Dt 15:17; Ps 40:6).

PIETY [3711]. Religious duty.

PIG [2614, *5956*].

NIV+ PIGS, PIGS'

An unclean animal (Lev 11:7; Dt 14:8; Isa 65:4; 66:3,17). Possessed by demons (Mt 8:30-33). *See Animals.*

PIGEON [1578, 3433, *4361*] (*young bird*).

NIV+ PIGEONS

Used as sacrifice (Ge 15:9; Lev 1:14; 5:7; 12:8; 14:22; Lk 2:24). *See Dove.*

PILATE, PONTIUS [*4397*] (*family name*).

NIV+ PILATE'S

Roman governor of Judea (Mt 27:2; Lk 3:1). Causes slaughter of certain Galileans (Lk 13:1). Tries Jesus and orders his crucifixion (Mt 27; Mk 15; Lk 23; Jn 18:28-40; 19; Ac 3:13; 4:27; 13:28; 1Ti 6:13). Allows Joseph of Arimathea to take Jesus' body (Mt 27:57-58; Mk 15:43-45; Lk 23:52; Jn 19:38).

PILDASH [7109] (*steely* ISBE; *spider* KB). Son of Nahor (Ge 22:22).

PILEHA *See Pilha.*

PILGRIM *See Sojourners.*

PILGRIMAGE [4472, 5019].

1. Jews were expected to make pilgrimages to the temple in Jerusalem for the great feasts (Ps 120-134; Ac 2:5-11).

2. The NT describes Christians as pilgrims or aliens (Heb 11:13; 1Pe 2:11).

PILHA [7116] (*millstone* IDB; *plowman* ISBE; *harelip* KB). One of those who sealed the covenant with Nehemiah (Ne 10:24).

PILLAR [2312, 4117, 5164, 5167, 5170, 5907, 6641, 6647, *5146*].

NIV+ PILLARS

Of Solomon's temple (1Ki 7:13-22; 2Ki 25:17). Broken and carried to Babylon (2Ki 25:13; Jer 52:17,20-21). Of Solomon's palaces (1Ki 7:6).

Used to mark roads (Jer 31:21). Pillar of salt, Lot's wife turned to (Ge 19:26; Lk 17:32).

Monuments Erected to Commemorate Events:

By Jacob, his vision of angels (Ge 28:18, w 31:13; 35:14), his covenant with Laban (Ge 31:45); by Moses, the covenant between Yahweh and Israel (Ex 24:4); by Joshua, the passing over Jordan (Jos 4:1-9, w Dt 27:2-6; Jos 8:30), at Shechem (Jos 24:25-27, w Jdg 9:6); by Samuel, the discomfiture of the Philistines (1Sa 7:12); by Absalom, to keep his name in remembrance (2Sa 18:18). As a boundary (Jos 15:6, w 18:17), a marker (1Sa 20:19), a landmark (2Sa 20:8; 1Ki 1:9). Prophecy of one in Egypt (Isa 19:19). Monuments of idolatry, to be destroyed (Dt 12:3).

Figurative: (Rev 3:12).

PILLAR OF CLOUD AND FIRE God guided Israel out of Egypt and through the wilderness by a pillar of cloud by day and fire by night (Ex 13:21-22). The pillar of cloud rested over the tent of meeting outside the camp whenever the Lord met Moses there (Ex 33:7-11). The cloud and fire were divine manifestations. *See Celestial Phenomena.*

PILLOW

1. A support for the head (Ge 28:11,18; 1Sa 26:7,11,16).
2. NIV "magic charms" (Eze 13:18,20).

PILOT [*3237, 3995*] Captain or operator of a ship (Ac 27:11; Jas 3:4).

PILTAI [7122] (*Yahweh rescues*). A priest who returned to Jerusalem from captivity in Babylon (Ne 12:17).

PIM *See Measure.*

PIN [3845, 5782]. Tent peg (Jdg 4:21; 5:26), stick for beating up wool in the loom (Jdg 16:13-14). KJV "crisping pins" (Isa 3:22) are NIV "purses."

PINE [581, 815, 1360].

NIV+ PINES

A tree (Ne 8:15; Isa 41:19; 60:13).

PINING AWAY (Lev 26:39; La 4:9; Eze 4:17; 24:23; 33:10).

PINNACLE (*sun,* or *a little wing*). On a building, a turret, battlement, pointed roof or peak. Satan tried to get Jesus to throw himself down from the pinnacle of the temple (Mt 4:5-6; Lk 4:9).

PINON [89, 7091] (*darkness* ISBE; name related to *famous copper mines* KB). Chief of Edom of the family of Esau (Ge 36:40-41; 1Ch 1:52).

PIPE [7574, 10507].

NIV+ PIPES

A wind instrument of music. Used in religious services (1Sa 10:5; Isa 30:29). *See Music, Instruments of.*

PIRAM [7231] (possibly *wild donkey* IDB; *indomitable* ISBE; possibly *zebra* KB). A king of the Amorites. Overcome and slain by Joshua (Jos 10:3,16-18,24-27).

PIRATHON, PIRATHONITE [7284, 7285]. A place in the land of Ephraim (Jdg 12:15). Men of (Jdg 12:13; 2Sa 23:30; 1Ch 11:31; 27:14).

PISGAH [7171]. A ridge or mountain E of the Jordan, opposite to Jericho. The Israelites come to (Nu 21:20). The water courses flowing from Mount Pisgah were a boundary of the country assigned to the Reubenites and Gadites (Dt 3:17; 4:49; Jos 12:3). Balaam prophesies on (Nu 23:14-24). Moses views Israel from (Dt 3:27; 34:1-4).

PISHON [7093]. One of the rivers of Eden (Ge 2:11).

PISIDIA [*4407, 4408*]. A province in Asia Minor. Paul visits (Ac 13:14; 14:24).

PISIDIAN ANTIOCH *See Antioch, 2; Pisidia.*

PISON *See Pishon.*

PISPAH [7183]. An Asherite (1Ch 7:38).

PISTACHIO [1063]. Nuts, in a gift sent by Jacob to Joseph (Ge 43:11). *See Plants of the Bible; Tree.*

PIT [931, 1014, 1585, 4509, 7074, 8757, 8846, 8864, *1073, 5700*].

NIV+ PITS

Bitumen deposit "tar pits" (Ge 14:10), deep place (Ge 37:20-29; Mt 12:11), well or cistern (Jer 14:3; Lk 14:5), earthen vessel (Lev 11:33), death, grave, or Sheol (Job 33:18; Isa 14:15; Nu 16:30,33).

PITCH [182, 854+3125, 2413, 4109, 5742, 5749, 5989, 9546].

NIV+ PITCHED

1. Pitch or tar (Ge 14:10; Ex 2:3). *See Caulkers; Tar.*
2. To encamp (Ge 12:8; 31:25; Ex 17:1; Nu 1:51; Jos 8:11).

PITCHER [3902, 7987, *3829*].

NIV+ PITCHERS

Jars for temple service and personal use (Ex 25:29; 37:16; 1Ch 28:17; Ecc 12:6; Mk 7:4).

PITHOM [7351] (*temple [house] of [pagan god] Atum*). Egyptian store city in a valley between the Nile and Lake Timsah; dedicated to the sun god Atum (Ex 1:11).

PITHON [7094]. Son of Micah (1Ch 8:35; 9:41).

PITY [365, 2571, 2798, 2858, 5714, 8163, 8171, *1796, 3091+3836+5073, 5072*].

NIV+ PITIED, PITIFUL

Tender, considerate, compassionate feeling for others.

Commanded (Job 6:14; 1Pe 3:8). For the poor (Pr 19:17; 28:8). Forbidden, to Canaanites (Dt 7:16), to idolatrous proselytizers (Dt 13:8), to murderers (Dt 19:13), to false witnesses (Dt 19:21), to wife in certain situations (Dt 25:12).

Withholding of, from Jesus, prefigured in David (Ps 69:20). Of God (Ps 103:13; Isa 63:9; Joel 2:18; Jnh 4:11; Jas 5:11), withheld from reprobates (Jer 13:14; 21:7; Eze 5:11; 7:4; 8:18; 9:5,10; Zec 11:6).

Required of believers (Isa 1:17; Mt 18:28-35).

See God, Mercy of; Jesus the Christ, Compassion of; Mercy.

PLACE OF ATONEMENT *See Atonement Cover.*

PLAGUE [1815, 1822, 4487, 4638, 4804, 5595, 5596, 5597, 5598, 7776, 8103, *2505*, *4435*].

NIV+ PLAGUED, PLAGUES

As a judgment on the Egyptians (Ps 105; 135:8-9; Ac 7:36). The plague of blood (Ex 7:14-25), frogs (Ex 8:1,15), lice (Ex 8:16-19), flies (Ex 8:20). On cattle (Ex 9:1-7). Of boils and blains (Ex 9:8-12), hail (Ex 9:18-34), locusts (Ex 10:1-20), darkness (Ex 10:21-23). Death of the firstborn (Ex 11:4-7; 12:17,29-30).

On the Israelites:

On account of idolatry (Ex 32:35), after eating quail (Nu 11:33), after refusing to enter the promised land (Nu 14:37), after murmuring on account of the destruction of Korah (Nu 16:41-50), of serpents (Nu 21:6), for the sin of Peor (Jos 22:17), on account of David's sin (2Sa 24:10-25).

On the Philistines (1Sa 6:4-5).

Denounced as a judgment (Lev 26:21; Dt 28:59). Foretold (Rev 11:6; 15:1,6-8; 16; 22:18-19).

See Judgments; Pestilence.

PLAIN [930, 1326, 3971, 4793, 6677, 10117, *5745, 5746, 5894*].

NIV+ PLAINLY, PLAINS

Broad stretch of level land (Ge 11:2; Eze 3:22).

PLAN OF SALVATION See *Jesus the Christ, Mission of; Redemption; Salvation.*

PLANE [6895]. A tool (Isa 44:13). See *Tools.*

PLANE TREE Possibly a chestnut tree (Ge 30:37; Eze 31:8).

PLANET See *Astronomy; Stars.*

PLANTS OF THE BIBLE [*2445, 4760, 5749, 6912, 9278, *3303, 5062, 5885*].

NIV+ IMPLANTED, PLANT, PLANTED, PLANTER, PLANTING, REPLANTED, TRANSPLANTED

The following plants are mentioned in the Bible. Some of them are not identifiable with certainty.

Acacia tree (Ex 25:10ff), algum tree (2Ch 2:8; 9:11), almond (tree) (Ge 30:37; Ex 25:33-36; Ecc 12:5; Jer 1:11), almugwood (1Ki 10:11,12; 2Ch. 2:8, 9:10 ftn.), aloes (Nu 24:6; Ps 45:8; Pr 7:17; SS 4:14; Jn 19:39), apple tree (SS 2:3; 8:5; Joel 1:12).

Balm (Ge 37:25; 43:11; 2Ch 28:15; Jer 8:22; 46:11; Eze 27:17), barley (Hos 3:2), beans (2Sa 17:28; Eze 4:9), brambles (Isa 34:13; Jdg 9:14-15), briers (Jdg 8:7, 16; Job 31:40; Isa 5:6, 7:23; Eze 28:24), broom tree (1Ki 19:3-4; Job 30:4; Ps 120:4), bush (burning bush) (Ex 3:2-3).

Calamus (SS 4:14; Isa 43:24; Jer 6:20; Eze 27:19), caraway (Isa 28:25-27), cassia (Ex 30:22-25; Ps 45:8; Eze 27:19), cedar (Lev 14:4, 6, 49; Nu 19:6; 2Sa 5:11; 1Ki 5:8), cedars of Lebanon (1Ki 4:33; Eze 31:3,5), cinnamon (Ex 30:23; Pr 7:17; SS 4:14; Rev 18:13), citron wood (Rev 18:12), coriander (Ex 16:31; Nu 11:7), crocus (Isa 35:1), cucumber (Nu 11:5), cummin (Isa 28:26-27; Mt 23:23), cypress (Ge 6:14; Isa 41:19, 44:14, 60:13; Eze 27:6).

Date (Nu 33:9), dill (Mt 23:23), ebony (Eze 27:15), fig (Ge 3:6-7; Dt 8:8; Jdg 9:10-11; 1Ki 4:25; Isa 41:19; 60:13), flax (Ex 9:31; Jos 2:6; Jdg 15:14), frankincense (Ex 30:34; Rev 18:13), galbanum (Ex 30:34-36), garlic (Nu 11:5), gourd (1Ki 6:18; 7:24; 2Ki 4:39), grain (Lev 23:14), grape (Ge 40:10-11), green tree (Ps 37:35), gum resin (Ex 30:34).

Henna blossoms (SS 1:14; 4:13), herbs, bitter herbs (Ex

12:8), hyssop (Ex 12:22; Lev 14:4; Ps 51:7; 1Ki 4:33), leeks (Nu 11:5), lentils (Ge 25:29-30,34; 2Sa 17:28), lilies (1Ki 7:19,22,26; SS 5:13; Mt 6:28; Lk 12:27), linen (Est 1:5-6).

Mandrakes (Ge 30:14-16; SS 7:13), melon (Nu 11:5; Isa 1:8; Jer 10:5), millet (Eze 4:9; 27:17), mint (Mt 23:23; Lk 11:42), mulberry tree (Lk 17:6), mustard (Mt 13:31-32; 17:20; Mk 4:31; Lk 13:19), myrrh (Ge 37:25-27, 43:11; Est 2:12; Pr 7:17; SS 1:13; Mt 2:11), myrtle (Isa 41:19, 55:13; Zec 1:7-10), nettles (Isa 34:13), nut trees (SS 6:11), nuts [pistachio] (Ge 43:11).

Oak (Ge 35:4; Zec 11:2), olive tree (Jdg 9:8; Job 15:33; Ps 52:8; Isa 17:6; Isa 41:19), onion (Nu 11:5), onycha (Ex 30:34-35), palm (Nu 33:9), pine tree (1Ki 5:10; Isa 60:13), plane tree (Ge 30:37; Eze 31:8), poisonous weeds (Hos 10:4), pomegranate (Dt 8:8; 1Sa 14:2), poplars (Ge 30:37; Lev 23:40; Job 40:22; Ps 137:2; Isa 15:7, 44:4), reed (Job 40:15,20-22), reeds (Ex 2:3; Job 8:11), resin (Ge 2:12; Nu 11:6-7), rose of Sharon (SS 2:1-2), rue (Lk 11:42), rush (Isa 9:6).

Saffron (SS 4:14), salt herbs (Job 30:1,3-4), seaweed (Jnh 2:5), seed pods (2Ki 6:25, ftn.), spelt (Ex 9:32; Isa 28:5; Ezr 4:9), spices (Ge 37:25; 43:11; Ex 25:6; Mt 23:23), sycamore (1Ki 10:27; 1Ch 27:28; 2Ch 1:15; Am 7:14; Lk 19:4), terebinth (Isa 6:13; Hos 4:13), thistles (Ge 3:18; 2Ki 14:9; Heb 6:8), thorns (Isa 7:19; Mt 27:29; Mk 15:17; Jn 19:5), tumbleweed (Ps 83:13; Isa 17:13), vine (Ge 9:20, 40:9-11; Jnh 4:5-7), weeds (Job 31:40; Pr 24:31; Mt 13:25), wheat (Ge 30:14; Dt 8:8), wild vine (2Ki 4:39; Jer 2:21), willow (Eze 17:5), wormwood (Rev 8:11).

See Tree.

PLASTER [3212, 3220, 6760, 8487, 10142].

NIV+ PLASTERED

In Egypt stone buildings, even the finest granite, were plastered, inside and out, to make a smooth surface for decoration (Dt 27:2,4). The poor used a mixture of clay and straw. In Israel an outside clay coating would have to be renewed after the rainy season.

PLASTER, MEDICINAL A cake of figs applied to a boil (Isa 38:21).

PLATE, PLATTER [7488, 7883, *4402*]

NIV+ PLATES

Dedicated to the tabernacle (Nu 7:13,19,25,31,37,43, 49,55,61,67,73,79,84-85). John Baptist's head carried on (Mt 14:8,11).

PLEADING [*1335, 1819, 1906, 2858, 7003, 7754, 8189, 8262, 9382, *1289, 3306, 4151*].

NIV+ PLEA, PLEAD, PLEADED, PLEADS, PLEAS

(Dt 17:8). Of the guilty (Jos 7:19-21). Jesus declined to plead (Mt 26:62; Mk 15:2; Lk 23:3; Jn 18:33-34). Prisoners required to plead (Ac 7:1). See *Defense.*

PLEASANT LAND [2275]. The land of Israel (Ps 106:24; Zec 7:14; cf. Jer 3:19; 12:10; Dt 8:7-9). See *Israel.*

PLEASING AROMA [5767, *2298, 2380*]. Of sacrifices (Ge 8:21; Ex 29:18,25,41; Lev 1:9,13,17; 2:2,9,12; 3:5,16; 4:31; 6:15,21; 8:21,28; 17:6; 23:13,18; 26:31; Nu 15:3,7,10,13,14,24; 18:17; 28:2,6,8,13,24,27; 29:2,6,8,13, 36; Eze 6:13; 16:19; 20:28,41). Of Christian service (2Co 2:15; Eph 5:2; Php 4:18). See *Offerings.*

PLEASURE, WORLDLY

Unfulfilling—

Job 21:12 They sing to the music of tambourine and harp;

they make merry to the sound of the flute. ¹³They spend their years in prosperity and go down to the grave in peace.
Ecc 1:17 Then I applied myself to the understanding of wisdom, and also of madness and folly, but I learned that this, too, is a chasing after the wind.
Ecc 2:1 I thought in my heart, "Come now, I will test you with pleasure to find out what is good." But that also proved to be meaningless. ²"Laughter," I said, "is foolish. And what does pleasure accomplish?" ³I tried cheering myself with wine, and embracing folly—my mind still guiding me with wisdom. I wanted to see what was worthwhile for men to do under heaven during the few days of their lives.
⁴I undertook great projects: I built houses for myself and planted vineyards. ⁵I made gardens and parks and planted all kinds of fruit trees in them. ⁶I made reservoirs to water groves of flourishing trees. ⁷I bought male and female slaves and had other slaves who were born in my house. I also owned more herds and flocks than anyone in Jerusalem before me. ⁸I amassed silver and gold for myself, and the treasure of kings and provinces. I acquired men and women singers, and a harem as well—the delights of the heart of man. ⁹I became greater by far than anyone in Jerusalem before me. In all this my wisdom stayed with me.
¹⁰I denied myself nothing my eyes desired; I refused my heart no pleasure. My heart took delight in all my work, and this was the reward for all my labor. ¹¹Yet when I surveyed all that my hands had done and what I had toiled to achieve, everything was meaningless, a chasing after the wind; nothing was gained under the sun.
¹²Then I turned my thoughts to consider wisdom, and also madness and folly. What more can the king's successor do than what has already been done? ¹³I saw that wisdom is better than folly, just as light is better than darkness.
1Ti 5:6 But the widow who lives for pleasure is dead even while she lives.

Proverbs and parables concerning—
Pr 9:17 "Stolen water is sweet; food eaten in secret is delicious!"
Pr 15:21 Folly delights a man who lacks judgment, but a man of understanding keeps a straight course.
Pr 21:17 He who loves pleasure will become poor; whoever loves wine and oil will never be rich.
Lk 8:14 The seed that fell among thorns stands for those who hear, but as they go on their way they are choked by life's worries, riches and pleasures, and they do not mature.

Rejected and judged by God—
Job 20:12 "Though evil is sweet in his mouth and he hides it under his tongue, ¹³though he cannot bear to let it go and keeps it in his mouth, ¹⁴yet his food will turn sour in his stomach; it will become the venom of serpents within him. ¹⁵He will spit out the riches he swallowed; God will make his stomach vomit them up. ¹⁶He will suck the poison of serpents; the fangs of an adder will kill him.
Isa 5:11 Woe to those who rise early in the morning to run after their drinks, who stay up late at night till they are inflamed with wine. ¹²They have harps and lyres at their banquets, tambourines and flutes and wine, but they have no regard for the deeds of the LORD, no respect for the work of his hands.
Isa 22:12 The Lord, the LORD Almighty, called you on that day to weep and to wail, to tear out your hair and put on sackcloth. ¹³But see, there is joy and revelry, slaughtering of cattle and killing of sheep, eating of meat and

drinking of wine! "Let us eat and drink," you say, "for tomorrow we die!"
Isa 47:8 "Now then, listen, you wanton creature, lounging in your security and saying to yourself, 'I am, and there is none besides me. I will never be a widow or suffer the loss of children.' ⁹Both of these will overtake you in a moment, on a single day: loss of children and widowhood. They will come upon you in full measure, in spite of your many sorceries and all your potent spells.
Am 6:1 Woe to you who are complacent in Zion, and to you who feel secure on Mount Samaria, you notable men of the foremost nation, to whom the people of Israel come!
Ro 1:32 Although they know God's righteous decree that those who do such things deserve death, they not only continue to do these very things but also approve of those who practice them.
2Th 2:12 and so that all will be condemned who have not believed the truth but have delighted in wickedness.

Rejected by Moses—
Heb 11:25 He chose to be mistreated along with the people of God rather than to enjoy the pleasures of sin for a short time. ²⁶He regarded disgrace for the sake of Christ as of greater value than the treasures of Egypt, because he was looking ahead to his reward.

Rejected by Paul—
2Ti 3:4 treacherous, rash, conceited, lovers of pleasure rather than lovers of God—
Tit 3:3 At one time we too were foolish, disobedient, deceived and enslaved by all kinds of passions and pleasures. We lived in malice and envy, being hated and hating one another.

Rejected by Peter—
2Pe 2:13 They will be paid back with harm for the harm they have done. Their idea of pleasure is to carouse in broad daylight. They are blots and blemishes, reveling in their pleasures while they feast with you.
See Gluttony; Happiness; Joy; Worldliness.

PLEDGE [674, 829, 2471, 2478, 2481, 5989, 6287, 6641, 6842, 6860, 9364, 9546, *2090, 4411*].

NIV+ PLEDGED, PLEDGES

1. Personal property of a debtor held to secure a payment (Ge 38:17-18). Law of Moses was concerned with protection of the poor. A pledged outer garment had to be restored at sunset for a bed covering (Ex 22:26-27), a widow's clothing could not be taken (Dt 24:17), a handmill or its upper millstone could not be taken (Dt 24:6).

2. In marriage *See Betrothal.*

PLEIADES [3966] (*heap, group [of stars]*). Stars in the constellation Taurus (Job 9:9; 38:31).

PLINY Gaius Plinius Caecilius Secundus, called "the Younger," Roman governmental official, famous as the author of literary letters covering all types of subjects, one of which contains a description of the Christian church in Bithynia, a province which Pliny governed in A.D. 112. The letter, together with the reply of the emperor Trajan are important evidence for the official attitude towards the Christians.

PLOTTING [*2047, 2372, 2750, 2754, 3086, 3108, 3619, 4742, 6783, 6870, 8003, *2101*].

NIV+ PLOT, PLOTS, PLOTTED

General References to:
(Est 3:9; Ps 36:4; 37:12; Pr 6:14; Isa 32:7; Mic 2:1).

Against Christ (Mt 12:14; 26:4; 27:1; Lk 6:11; 19:47; 22:4; Jn 5:16; 11:47,53).

General Examples of:
(Ge 37:18; Nu 16:3; Jdg 9:1; 2Ki 12:20; 14:19; Da 6:4; Mt 12:14; Ac 23:13).

PLOW, PLOUGH [1330, 3045, 3086, 6268, 7114, 9439, *769, 770*].

NIV+ PLOWED, PLOWING, PLOWMAN, PLOWMEN, PLOWS, PLOWSHARES

The ancient plow consisted of a forked stick, the trunk hitched to the animals which drew it, the branch braced and terminating in the share, which was at first the sharpened end of the branch, later a metal point. It was ordinarily drawn by a yoke of oxen (Job 1:14; Am 6:12). Such a plow did not turn over the soil; it did little more than scratch the surface.

Figurative: Of afflictions (Ps 129:3).

PLOWSHARE [908, 4739] (*the blade of a plow*).

NIV+ See PLOW

To beat swords into plowshares was symbolic of an age of peace (Isa 2:4), to beat plowshares into swords portended coming war (Joel 3:10).

PLUMB LINE [74, 74+974, 643, 5487]. A cord with a weight, the plummet, tied to one end; used in testing whether a wall is perpendicular (Am 7:7-9; 2Ki 21:13; Isa 28:17).

PLUMMET See *Plumb Line.*

POCHERETH See *Pokereth-Hazzebaim.*

PODS [1807, 3044]. Seed pods eaten in famine (2Ki 6:24). Perhaps carob, eaten by the prodigal son and the pigs (Lk 15:16). See *Plants of the Bible.*

POET [5439, 4475] (*doer,* or *a maker*).

NIV+ POETS

Paul quotes from pagan poets (Ac 17:28; 1Co 15:32; Tit 1:12). A great deal of the OT is written in the form of poetry.

POETRY

Acrostic:
(Ps 25; 34; 37; 111; 112; 119; 145; Pr 31:10-31; La 1-5).

Didactic:
Moses' song (Dt 32). The book of Job, the Proverbs, the Song of Songs, much of the books of prophecy. *See Psalms, Topically Arranged.*

Elegy:
On the death of Saul (2Sa 1:19-27). Of Abner (2Sa 3:33-34). *See Elegy.*

Epic:
Moses' song (Ex 15:1-19). Miriam's song (Ex 15:21). Deborah's song (Jdg 5) David's song of praise (2Sa 22).

Lyrics, Sacred:
Moses' and Miriam's songs (Ex 15). Hannah's song (1Sa 2:1-10). The song of Elizabeth (Lk 1:42-45). Of Mary (Lk 1:46-55). Of Zechariah (Lk 1:68-79). The Psalms. *See Psalms.*

See Parallelism

POETS, PAGAN, QUOTATIONS FROM

Paul quotes pagan poets in arguments. Examples include: Cleanthes (Ac 17:28), Epimenides (Tit 1:12), Menander (1Co 15:33).

POISON [2779, 7301, 8032, *2503+5516, 2675, 2808*].

NIV+ POISONED, POISONOUS, POISONS

A substance producing a deadly effect, like the venom of reptiles (Dt 32:24,33; Job 20:16; Ps 58:4). Vegetable poisons were known in antiquity: poisonous weeds (Hos 10:4), wild gourd (2Ki 4:39-40). A poisoned drink is referred to in Mark (Mk 16:18).

POKERETH-HAZZEBAIM, POCHERETH OF ZEBAIM [7097] (*pitfall of gazelles,* i.e., *gazelle hunter*). The ancestor of a family which returned to Jerusalem from captivity in Babylon (Ezr 2:57; Ne 7:59).

POLE [895, 964, 4573, 4574, 5812, 7771].

NIV+ POLES

Used to carry the ark (Ex 24:13-15), the table of the bread of the Presence (Ex 25:27-28), the bronze altar (Ex 27:6-7), the incense altar (Ex 30:4-5). Standard on which the bronze serpent was displayed (Nu 21:8-9),

POLICY See *Diplomacy.*

POLITARCH City magistrate of Thessalonica (Ac 17:6,8). Sixteen epigraphical inscriptions with the word have been discovered.

POLITICS Statecraft.

Corruption in:
(Ps 12:8), in the court of Xerxes (Est 3), of Darius (Da 6:4-15).

Instances of:
Absalom, electioneering for the throne (2Sa 15:2-6). Pilate, condemning Jesus to gratify popular clamor (Mt 27:23-27; Mk 15:15; Lk 23:13-25; Jn 18:38-39; 19:4-13).

Ministers:
Zadok the priest, a partisan of David (2Sa 15:24-29). Nathan the prophet influences the selection of David's successor (1Ki 1:11-40).

Women in:
The wise woman of Abel, who saved the city through diplomacy (2Sa 20:16-22). Bathsheba, in securing the crown for Solomon (1Ki 1:15-21). Herodias, in influencing the administration of Herod (Mt 14:3-11; Mk 6:17-28). Mother of Zebedee's children, in seeking favor for her sons (Mt 20:20-23).
Influence in. *See Influence, Political.*
See Diplomacy; Government.

POLL TAX See *Tax.*

POLLUTION [2866, 5614, 8845, *246, 834, 3620*].

NIV+ POLLUTE, POLLUTED, POLLUTES

Ceremonial or moral defilement, profanation, and uncleanness (Ex 20:25; 2Pe 2:20). *See Corruption; Defilement; Unclean, Uncleanness; Sanitation and Hygiene.*

POLLUX [*1483*]. With Castor, one of the twin gods, sons of Zeus and patrons of sailors (Ac 28:11).

POLYGAMY (*many marriages*). Forbidden (Dt 17:17; Lev 18:18; Mal 2:14-15; Mt 19:4-5; Mk 10:2-8; 1Ti 3:2, 12; Tit 1:6). Authorized (2Sa 12:8).

Examples of:
Tolerated (Ex 21:10; 1Sa 1:2; 2Ch 24:3). Practiced by, (Job 27:15), Lamech (Ge 4:19), Abraham (Ge 16), Esau (Ge 26:34; 28:9), Jacob (Ge 29:30), Ashhur (1Ch 4:5), Gideon (Jdg 8:30), Elkanah (1Sa 1:2), David (1Sa 25:39-44; 2Sa 3:2-5; 5:13; 1Ch 14:3), Solomon (1Ki 11:1-8),

Rehoboam (2Ch 11:18-23), Abijah (2Ch 13:21), Jehoram (2Ch 21:14), Joash (2Ch 24:3), Ahab (2Ki 10:1), Jehoiachin (2Ki 24:15), Belshazzar (Da 5:2, w 1Ch 2-8), Hosea (Hos 3:1-2). Mosaic law respecting the firstborn in (Dt 21:15-17).

Sought by women [polyandry] (Isa 4:1).

The Evil Effects of:

Husband's favoritism in (Dt 21:15-17), Jacob's (Ge 29:30; 30:15), Elkanah's (1Sa 1:5), Rehoboam's (2Ch 11:21). Domestic infelicity, in Abraham's family (Ge 16; 21:9-16), Jacob's (Ge 29:30-34; 30:1-23), Elkanah's (1Sa 1:4-7). Upon Solomon (1Ki 11:4-8).

See Concubinage; Marriage.

POLYTHEISM (Ge 31:19; 35:2,4; Jos 24:2,23; Jdg 2:13; 3:7; 10:16; 17:5; Jer 2:28; 11:13; Da 4:8; 1Co 8:5).

POMEGRANATE [8232].

NIV+ POMEGRANATES

A fruit. Abounded in the land of Canaan (1Sa 14:2). Brought by the spies to show the fruitfulness of the land of Canaan (Nu 13:23). Figures of the fruits of, were embroidered on the ephod (Ex 28:33-34; 39:24), carved on the pillars of the temple (1Ki 7:18,20,42; Jer 52:22-23). Wine made of (SS 8:2).

POMMEL *See Capital.*

PONTIUS PILATE [4508]. *See Pilate, Pontius.*

PONTUS [4507, 4509] (*sea*). A province of Asia Minor (Ac 2:9; 1Pe 1:1). Aquila lived in (Ac 18:2).

POOL [106, 1391, 4784, 6524, *3148*].

NIV+ POOLS

Of Gibeon (2Sa 2:13; Jer 41:12). Of Hebron (2Sa 4:12). Of Samaria (1Ki 22:38). Of Heshbon (SS 7:4).

Of Jerusalem:

Upper pool (2Ki 18:17; Isa 36:2), lower pool (Isa 22:9), Siloam (Jn 9:7,11), called Siloam (Ne 3:15, ftn), and probably identical with the king's pool (Ne 2:14).

POOR [*36, 1924, 1930, 3769, 4575, 4728, 5014, 6705, 8133, 8203, 8273, *1797, 4775, 4777*].

NIV+ IMPOVERISHED, POOREST, POVERTY

Proverbs concerning—

Ps 37:16 Better the little that the righteous have than the wealth of many wicked; (+Isa 29:19)

Pr 10:15 The wealth of the rich is their fortified city, but poverty is the ruin of the poor.

Pr 13:7 One man pretends to be rich, yet has nothing; another pretends to be poor, yet has great wealth.

8A man's riches may ransom his life, but a poor man hears no threat.

Pr 13:23 A poor man's field may produce abundant food, but injustice sweeps it away.

Pr 18:23 A poor man pleads for mercy, but a rich man answers harshly.

Pr 19:1 Better a poor man whose walk is blameless than a fool whose lips are perverse.

Pr 19:4 Wealth brings many friends, but a poor man's friend deserts him.

Pr 19:7 A poor man is shunned by all his relatives—how much more do his friends avoid him! Though he pursues them with pleading, they are nowhere to be found.

Pr 19:17 He who is kind to the poor lends to the LORD, and he will reward him for what he has done.

Pr 19:22 What a man desires is unfailing love; better to be poor than a liar.

Pr 20:13 Do not love sleep or you will grow poor; stay awake and you will have food to spare.

Pr 21:13 If a man shuts his ears to the cry of the poor, he too will cry out and not be answered.

Pr 22:2 Rich and poor have this in common: The LORD is the Maker of them all.

Pr 22:9 A generous man will himself be blessed, for he shares his food with the poor.

Pr 23:21 for drunkards and gluttons become poor, and drowsiness clothes them in rags. (+Pr 24:20-21,31)

Pr 28:6 Better a poor man whose walk is blameless than a rich man whose ways are perverse.

Pr 28:8 He who increases his wealth by exorbitant interest amasses it for another, who will be kind to the poor.

Pr 28:11 A rich man may be wise in his own eyes, but a poor man who has discernment sees through him.

Pr 28:19 He who works his land will have abundant food, but the one who chases fantasies will have his fill of poverty.

Pr 29:14 If a king judges the poor with fairness, his throne will always be secure.

Ecc 4:6 Better one handful with tranquillity than two handfuls with toil and chasing after the wind.

Ecc 4:13 Better a poor but wise youth than an old but foolish king who no longer knows how to take warning.

Ecc 6:8 What advantage has a wise man over a fool? What does a poor man gain by knowing how to conduct himself before others?

Ecc 9:15 Now there lived in that city a man poor but wise, and he saved the city by his wisdom. But nobody remembered that poor man. **16**So I said, "Wisdom is better than strength." But the poor man's wisdom is despised, and his words are no longer heeded.

Always part of the society—

Mt 26:11 The poor you will always have with you, but you will not always have me. (+Mk 14:7; Jn 12:8)

Attitudes toward:

Job—

Job 30:25 Have I not wept for those in trouble? Has not my soul grieved for the poor?

Jesus and the poor widow—

Mk 12:43 Calling his disciples to him, Jesus said, "I tell you the truth, this poor widow has put more into the treasury than all the others. **44**They all gave out of their wealth; but she, out of her poverty, put in everything—all she had to live on."

Lazarus—

Lk 16:20 At his gate was laid a beggar named Lazarus, covered with sores **21**and longing to eat what fell from the rich man's table. Even the dogs came and licked his sores.

Judas—

Jn 12:6 He did not say this because he cared about the poor but because he was a thief; as keeper of the money bag, he used to help himself to what was put into it.

James—

Jas 1:9 The brother in humble circumstances ought to take pride in his high position. **10**But the one who is rich should take pride in his low position, because he will pass away like a wild flower.

Duty to:

Ex 22:25 "If you lend money to one of my people among you who is needy, do not be like a moneylender; charge him no interest. **26**If you take your neighbor's cloak as a pledge, return it to him by sunset, [27]because his cloak is the only covering he has for his body. What else will he sleep in? When he cries out to me, I will hear, for I am compassionate.

Ex 23:11 but during the seventh year let the land lie unplowed and unused. Then the poor among your people may get food from it, and the wild animals may eat what they leave. Do the same with your vineyard and your olive grove.

Lev 19:9 " 'When you reap the harvest of your land, do not reap to the very edges of your field or gather the gleanings of your harvest. [10]Do not go over your vineyard a second time or pick up the grapes that have fallen. Leave them for the poor and the alien. I am the LORD your God.

Lev 25:25 " 'If one of your countrymen becomes poor and sells some of his property, his nearest relative is to come and redeem what his countryman has sold. [26]If, however, a man has no one to redeem it for him but he himself prospers and acquires sufficient means to redeem it, [27]he is to determine the value for the years since he sold it and refund the balance to the man to whom he sold it; he can then go back to his own property. [28]But if he does not acquire the means to repay him, what he sold will remain in the possession of the buyer until the Year of Jubilee. It will be returned in the Jubilee, and he can then go back to his property.

Lev 25:35 " 'If one of your countrymen becomes poor and is unable to support himself among you, help him as you would an alien or a temporary resident, so he can continue to live among you. [36]Do not take interest of any kind from him, but fear your God, so that your countryman may continue to live among you. [37]You must not lend him money at interest or sell him food at a profit. (+Lev 25:38)

Lev 25:39 " 'If one of your countrymen becomes poor among you and sells himself to you, do not make him work as a slave. [40]He is to be treated as a hired worker or a temporary resident among you; he is to work for you until the Year of Jubilee. [41]Then he and his children are to be released, and he will go back to his own clan and to the property of his forefathers. [42]Because the Israelites are my servants, whom I brought out of Egypt, they must not be sold as slaves. [43]Do not rule over them ruthlessly, but fear your God.

Dt 14:28 At the end of every three years, bring all the tithes of that year's produce and store it in your towns, [29]so that the Levites (who have no allotment or inheritance of their own) and the aliens, the fatherless and the widows who live in your towns may come and eat and be satisfied, and so that the LORD your God may bless you in all the work of your hands.

Dt 15:2 This is how it is to be done: Every creditor shall cancel the loan he has made to his fellow Israelite. He shall not require payment from his fellow Israelite or brother, because the LORD's time for canceling debts has been proclaimed. [3]You may require payment from a foreigner, but you must cancel any debt your brother owes you. [4]However, there should be no poor among you, for in the land the LORD your God is giving you to possess as your inheritance, he will richly bless you, [5]if only you fully obey the LORD your God and are careful to follow all these commands I am giving you today. [6]For the LORD your God will bless you as he has promised, and you will lend to many nations but will borrow from none. You will rule over many nations but none will rule over you.

[7]If there is a poor man among your brothers in any of the towns of the land that the LORD your God is giving you, do not be hardhearted or tightfisted toward your poor brother. [8]Rather be openhanded and freely lend him whatever he needs. [9]Be careful not to harbor this wicked thought: "The seventh year, the year for canceling debts, is near," so that you do not show ill will toward your needy brother and give him nothing. He may then appeal to the LORD against you, and you will be found guilty of sin. [10]Give generously to him and do so without a grudging heart; then because of this the LORD your God will bless you in all your work and in everything you put your hand to. [11]There will always be poor people in the land. Therefore I command you to be openhanded toward your brothers and toward the poor and needy in your land.

[12]If a fellow Hebrew, a man or a woman, sells himself to you and serves you six years, in the seventh year you must let him go free. [13]And when you release him, do not send him away empty-handed. [14]Supply him liberally from your flock, your threshing floor and your winepress. Give to him as the LORD your God has blessed you.

Dt 24:12 If the man is poor, do not go to sleep with his pledge in your possession. [13]Return his cloak to him by sunset so that he may sleep in it. Then he will thank you, and it will be regarded as a righteous act in the sight of the LORD your God.

[14]Do not take advantage of a hired man who is poor and needy, whether he is a brother Israelite or an alien living in one of your towns. [15]Pay him his wages each day before sunset, because he is poor and is counting on it. Otherwise he may cry to the LORD against you, and you will be guilty of sin.

[16]Fathers shall not be put to death for their children, nor children put to death for their fathers; each is to die for his own sin.

[17]Do not deprive the alien or the fatherless of justice, or take the cloak of the widow as a pledge. [18]Remember that you were slaves in Egypt and the LORD your God redeemed you from there. That is why I command you to do this.

[19]When you are harvesting in your field and you overlook a sheaf, do not go back to get it. Leave it for the alien, the fatherless and the widow, so that the LORD your God may bless you in all the work of your hands. [20]When you beat the olives from your trees, do not go over the branches a second time. Leave what remains for the alien, the fatherless and the widow. [21]When you harvest the grapes in your vineyard, do not go over the vines again. Leave what remains for the alien, the fatherless and the widow.

Dt 26:12 When you have finished setting aside a tenth of all your produce in the third year, the year of the tithe, you shall give it to the Levite, the alien, the fatherless and the widow, so that they may eat in your towns and be satisfied. [13]Then say to the LORD your God: "I have removed from my house the sacred portion and have given it to the Levite, the alien, the fatherless and the widow, according to all you commanded. I have not turned aside from your commands nor have I forgotten any of them.

Ne 8:10 Nehemiah said, "Go and enjoy choice food and sweet drinks, and send some to those who have nothing prepared. This day is sacred to our Lord. Do not grieve, for the joy of the LORD is your strength."

Ps 37:21 The wicked borrow and do not repay, but the righteous give generously;

Ps 37:26 They are always generous and lend freely; their children will be blessed.

Ps 41:1 Blessed is he who has regard for the weak; the LORD delivers him in times of trouble. [2]The LORD will protect him and preserve his life; he will bless him in the land and not surrender him to the desire of his foes. ³The LORD will sustain him on his sickbed and restore him from his bed of illness.

Ps 112:4 Even in darkness light dawns for the upright, for the gracious and compassionate and righteous man. ⁵Good will come to him who is generous and lends freely, who conducts his affairs with justice.

Ps 112:9 He has scattered abroad his gifts to the poor, his righteousness endures forever; his horn will be lifted high in honor. (+Pr 28:27; 29:7; 31:9,20)

Isa 1:7 Your country is desolate, your cities burned with fire; your fields are being stripped by foreigners right before you, laid waste as when overthrown by strangers.

Isa 16:3 "Give us counsel, render a decision. Make your shadow like night—at high noon. Hide the fugitives, do not betray the refugees. ⁴Let the Moabite fugitives stay with you; be their shelter from the destroyer." The oppressor will come to an end, and destruction will cease; the aggressor will vanish from the land.

Isa 58:7 Is it not to share your food with the hungry and to provide the poor wanderer with shelter—when you see the naked, to clothe him, and not to turn away from your own flesh and blood?

Isa 58:10 and if you spend yourselves in behalf of the hungry and satisfy the needs of the oppressed, then your light will rise in the darkness, and your night will become like the noonday.

Eze 18:7 He does not oppress anyone, but returns what he took in pledge for a loan. He does not commit robbery but gives his food to the hungry and provides clothing for the naked.

Da 4:27 Therefore, O king, be pleased to accept my advice: Renounce your sins by doing what is right, and your wickedness by being kind to the oppressed. It may be that then your prosperity will continue."

Zec 7:10 Do not oppress the widow or the fatherless, the alien or the poor. In your hearts do not think evil of each other.'

Mt 5:42 Give to the one who asks you, and do not turn away from the one who wants to borrow from you.

Mt 19:21 Jesus answered, "If you want to be perfect, go, sell your possessions and give to the poor, and you will have treasure in heaven. Then come, follow me."

Mt 25:35 For I was hungry and you gave me something to eat, I was thirsty and you gave me something to drink, I was a stranger and you invited me in, ³⁶I needed clothes and you clothed me, I was sick and you looked after me, I was in prison and you came to visit me.'

Mk 14:7 The poor you will always have with you, and you can help them any time you want. But you will not always have me.

Lk 3:11 John answered, "The man with two tunics should share with him who has none, and the one who has food should do the same." (+Lk 6:30)

Lk 11:41 But give what is inside [the dish] to the poor, and everything will be clean for you.

Lk 12:33 Sell your possessions and give to the poor. Provide purses for yourselves that will not wear out, a treasure in heaven that will not be exhausted, where no thief comes near and no moth destroys.

Lk 14:12 Then Jesus said to his host, "When you give a luncheon or dinner, do not invite your friends, your brothers or relatives, or your rich neighbors; if you do, they may invite you back and so you will be repaid. ¹³But when you give a banquet, invite the poor, the crippled, the

lame, the blind, ¹⁴and you will be blessed. Although they cannot repay you, you will be repaid at the resurrection of the righteous."

Lk 18:22 When Jesus heard this, he said to him, "You still lack one thing. Sell everything you have and give to the poor, and you will have treasure in heaven. Then come, follow me."

Lk 19:8 But Zacchaeus stood up and said to the Lord, "Look, Lord! Here and now I give half of my possessions to the poor, and if I have cheated anybody out of anything, I will pay back four times the amount."

Ac 20:35 In everything I did, I showed you that by this kind of hard work we must help the weak, remembering the words the Lord Jesus himself said: 'It is more blessed to give than to receive.'"

Ro 12:8 if it is encouraging, let him encourage; if it is contributing to the needs of others, let him give generously; if it is leadership, let him govern diligently; if it is showing mercy, let him do it cheerfully.

Ro 12:13 Share with God's people who are in need. Practice hospitality.

Ro 12:20 On the contrary: "If your enemy is hungry, feed him; if he is thirsty, give him something to drink. In doing this, you will heap burning coals on his head."

1Co 13:3 If I give all I possess to the poor and surrender my body to the flames, but have not love, I gain nothing.

1Co 16:1 Now about the collection for God's people: Do what I told the Galatian churches to do. ²On the first day of every week, each one of you should set aside a sum of money in keeping with his income, saving it up, so that when I come no collections will have to be made.

2Co 6:10 sorrowful, yet always rejoicing; poor, yet making many rich; having nothing, and yet possessing everything. (+2Co 8:9)

2Co 9:5 So I thought it necessary to urge the brothers to visit you in advance and finish the arrangements for the generous gift you had promised. Then it will be ready as a generous gift, not as one grudgingly given.

⁶Remember this: Whoever sows sparingly will also reap sparingly, and whoever sows generously will also reap generously. ⁷Each man should give what he has decided in his heart to give, not reluctantly or under compulsion, for God loves a cheerful giver.

Gal 2:10 All they asked was that we should continue to remember the poor, the very thing I was eager to do.

Gal 6:10 Therefore, as we have opportunity, let us do good to all people, especially to those who belong to the family of believers.

Eph 4:28 He who has been stealing must steal no longer, but must work, doing something useful with his own hands, that he may have something to share with those in need.

1Ti 5:9 No widow may be put on the list of widows unless she is over sixty, has been faithful to her husband, ¹⁰and is well known for her good deeds, such as bringing up children, showing hospitality, washing the feet of the saints, helping those in trouble and devoting herself to all kinds of good deeds.

1Ti 5:16 If any woman who is a believer has widows in her family, she should help them and not let the church be burdened with them, so that the church can help those widows who are really in need.

Heb 13:3 Remember those in prison as if you were their fellow prisoners, and those who are mistreated as if you yourselves were suffering.

Jas 1:27 Religion that God our Father accepts as pure and faultless is this: to look after orphans and widows in their distress and to keep oneself from being polluted by the world.

Jas 2:2 Suppose a man comes into your meeting wearing a gold ring and fine clothes, and a poor man in shabby clothes also comes in. ³If you show special attention to the man wearing fine clothes and say, "Here's a good seat for you," but say to the poor man, "You stand there" or "Sit on the floor by my feet," ⁴have you not discriminated among yourselves and become judges with evil thoughts?

⁵Listen, my dear brothers: Has not God chosen those who are poor in the eyes of the world to be rich in faith and to inherit the kingdom he promised those who love him? ⁶But you have insulted the poor. Is it not the rich who are exploiting you? Are they not the ones who are dragging you into court? ⁷Are they not the ones who are slandering the noble name of him to whom you belong?

⁸If you really keep the royal law found in Scripture, "Love your neighbor as yourself," you are doing right. ⁹But if you show favoritism, you sin and are convicted by the law as lawbreakers.

Jas 2:15 Suppose a brother or sister is without clothes and daily food. ¹⁶If one of you says to him, "Go, I wish you well; keep warm and well fed," but does nothing about his physical needs, what good is it?

Jas 5:4 Look! The wages you failed to pay the workmen who mowed your fields are crying out against you. The cries of the harvesters have reached the ears of the Lord Almighty.

1Jn 3:17 If anyone has material possessions and sees his brother in need but has no pity on him, how can the love of God be in him? ¹⁸Dear children, let us not love with words or tongue but with actions and in truth. ¹⁹This then is how we know that we belong to the truth, and how we set our hearts at rest in his presence

God's care of:

1Sa 2:7 The LORD sends poverty and wealth; he humbles and he exalts. (+1Sa 2:8)

Job 5:15 He saves the needy from the sword in their mouth; he saves them from the clutches of the powerful. ¹⁶So the poor have hope, and injustice shuts its mouth.

Job 31:15 Did not he who made me in the womb make them? Did not the same one form us both within our mothers?

Job 34:18 Is he not the One who says to kings, 'You are worthless,' and to nobles, 'You are wicked,' ¹⁹who shows no partiality to princes and does not favor the rich over the poor, for they are all the work of his hands?

Job 34:28 They caused the cry of the poor to come before him, so that he heard the cry of the needy.

Job 36:6 He does not keep the wicked alive but gives the afflicted their rights.

Job 36:15 But those who suffer he delivers in their suffering; he speaks to them in their affliction.

Ps 9:18 But the needy will not always be forgotten, nor the hope of the afflicted ever perish.

Ps 10:14 But you, O God, do see trouble and grief; you consider it to take it in hand. The victim commits himself to you; you are the helper of the fatherless.

Ps 12:5 "Because of the oppression of the weak and the groaning of the needy, I will now arise," says the LORD. "I will protect them from those who malign them."

Ps 14:6 You evildoers frustrate the plans of the poor, but the LORD is their refuge.

Ps 34:6 This poor man called, and the LORD heard him; he saved him out of all his troubles.

Ps 35:10 My whole being will exclaim, "Who is like you, O LORD? You rescue the poor from those too strong for them, the poor and needy from those who rob them."

Ps 68:10 Your people settled in it, and from your bounty, O God, you provided for the poor.

Ps 69:33 The LORD hears the needy and does not despise his captive people.

Ps 72:2 He will judge your people in righteousness, your afflicted ones with justice.

Ps 72:4 He will defend the afflicted among the people and save the children of the needy; he will crush the oppressor.

Ps 72:12 For he will deliver the needy who cry out, the afflicted who have no one to help. ¹³He will take pity on the weak and the needy and save the needy from death. ¹⁴He will rescue them from oppression and violence, for precious is their blood in his sight.

Ps 74:21 Do not let the oppressed retreat in disgrace; may the poor and needy praise your name.

Ps 102:17 He will respond to the prayer of the destitute; he will not despise their plea.

Ps 107:9 for he satisfies the thirsty and fills the hungry with good things.

Ps 107:36 there he brought the hungry to live, and they founded a city where they could settle.

Ps 107:41 But he lifted the needy out of their affliction and increased their families like flocks.

Ps 109:31 For he stands at the right hand of the needy one, to save his life from those who condemn him.

Ps 113:7 He raises the poor from the dust and lifts the needy from the ash heap; ⁸he seats them with princes, with the princes of their people.

Ps 132:15 I will bless her with abundant provisions; her poor will I satisfy with food.

Ps 140:12 I know that the LORD secures justice for the poor and upholds the cause of the needy.

Ps 146:5 Blessed is he whose help is the God of Jacob, whose hope is in the LORD his God,

Ps 146:7 He upholds the cause of the oppressed and gives food to the hungry. The LORD sets prisoners free,

Pr 22:2 Rich and poor have this in common: The LORD is the Maker of them all.

Pr 22:22 Do not exploit the poor because they are poor and do not crush the needy in court, ²³for the LORD will take up their case and will plunder those who plunder them.

Pr 29:13 The poor man and the oppressor have this in common: The LORD gives sight to the eyes of both.

Ecc 5:8 If you see the poor oppressed in a district, and justice and rights denied, do not be surprised at such things; for one official is eyed by a higher one, and over them both are others higher still.

Isa 11:4 but with righteousness he will judge the needy, with justice he will give decisions for the poor of the earth. He will strike the earth with the rod of his mouth; with the breath of his lips he will slay the wicked.

Isa 14:30 The poorest of the poor will find pasture, and the needy will lie down in safety. But your root I will destroy by famine; it will slay your survivors.

Isa 14:32 What answer shall be given to the envoys of that nation? "The LORD has established Zion, and in her his afflicted people will find refuge."

Isa 25:4 You have been a refuge for the poor, a refuge for the needy in his distress, a shelter from the storm and a shade from the heat. For the breath of the ruthless is like a storm driving against a wall

Isa 29:19 Once more the humble will rejoice in the LORD; the needy will rejoice in the Holy One of Israel.

Isa 41:17 "The poor and needy search for water, but there is none; their tongues are parched with thirst. But I the LORD will answer them; I, the God of Israel, will not forsake them.

Jer 20:13 Sing to the LORD! Give praise to the LORD! He rescues the life of the needy from the hands of the wicked.

Zep 3:12 But I will leave within you the meek and humble, who trust in the name of the LORD.

Zec 11:7 So I pastured the flock marked for slaughter, particularly the oppressed of the flock. Then I took two staffs and called one Favor and the other Union, and I pastured the flock.

Mt 11:5 The blind receive sight, the lame walk, those who have leprosy are cured, the deaf hear, the dead are raised, and the good news is preached to the poor.

Lk 4:18 "The Spirit of the Lord is on me, because he has anointed me to preach good news to the poor. He has sent me to proclaim freedom for the prisoners and recovery of sight for the blind, to release the oppressed, (+Lk 7:22)

Lk 16:22 "The time came when the beggar died and the angels carried him to Abraham's side. The rich man also died and was buried.

Jas 2:5 Listen, my dear brothers: Has not God chosen those who are poor in the eyes of the world to be rich in faith and to inherit the kingdom he promised those who love him?

See God, Goodness of, Providence of.

The Poor, Without Friends:

Pr 14:20 The poor are shunned even by their neighbors, but the rich have many friends. (+Pr 19:4,7)

Wisdom of, despised (Ecc 9:15-16).

Warning against neglect of (Pr 20:13; 21:13; 22:16)—

Eze 16:49 "'Now this was the sin of your sister Sodom: She and her daughters were arrogant, overfed and unconcerned; they did not help the poor and needy.

Neglect of, by the disciples (Ac 6:1-6).

Neglect of, denounced—

Mt 25:42 For I was hungry and you gave me nothing to eat, I was thirsty and you gave me nothing to drink,

Mt 25:45 "He will reply, 'I tell you the truth, whatever you did not do for one of the least of these, you did not do for me.'

Righteous treatment of, required—

Ps 82:3 Defend the cause of the weak and fatherless; maintain the rights of the poor and oppressed. ⁴Rescue the weak and needy; deliver them from the hand of the wicked. (+Pr 22:22; 31:9; Isa 1:17)

Rewarded (Pr 29:14)—

Jer 22:16 He defended the cause of the poor and needy, and so all went well. Is that not what it means to know me?" declares the LORD. (+Eze 18:7,16-17; Da 4:27)

Compassion toward (Job 30:25)—

Pr 14:21 He who despises his neighbor sins, but blessed is he who is kind to the needy. (+Pr 29:7; Heb 13:3; Jas 1:27)

Liberality to (Pr 31:20; Isa 58:7; Mt 5:42, w Lk 6:30; Lk 3:11; 19:8; Ro 12:8,13,20; 1Co 13:3; 16:1-2; 2Co 9:1-15; Gal 2:10; Eph 4:28; 1Ti 5:9-10,16; Jas 2:15-16; 1Jn 3:17).

Liberality to, rewarded (Pr 19:17; 22:9; 28:27; Ps 112:9; Mt 19:21; 25:34-36)—

Lk 6:35 But love your enemies, do good to them, and lend to them without expecting to get anything back. Then your reward will be great, and you will be sons of the Most

High, because he is kind to the ungrateful and wicked. (+Lk 12:33; 18:22; Ac 20:35)

Kindness to:

Commanded—

Ne 8:10 Nehemiah said, "Go and enjoy choice food and sweet drinks, and send some to those who have nothing prepared. This day is sacred to our Lord. Do not grieve, for the joy of the LORD is your strength."

Ne 8:12 Then all the people went away to eat and drink, to send portions of food and to celebrate with great joy, because they now understood the words that had been made known to them.

Rewarded (Ps 41:1-3; Isa 58:10; Lk 14:12-14).—

Instances of kindness to: By Ruth, to Naomi (Ru 2:2,11). Boaz, to Ruth (Ru 2:8-16; 3:15). Elijah, to the widow of Zarephath (1Ki 17:12-24). Elisha, to the prophet's widow (2Ki 4:1-7). The Jews (Est 9:22).

Job—

Job 29:11 Whoever heard me spoke well of me, and those who saw me commended me, ¹²because I rescued the poor who cried for help, and the fatherless who had none to assist him. ¹³The man who was dying blessed me; I made the widow's heart sing. (+Job 29:14)

Job 29:15 I was eyes to the blind and feet to the lame. ¹⁶I was a father to the needy; I took up the case of the stranger. (+Job 29:17)

Job 31:16 "If I have denied the desires of the poor or let the eyes of the widow grow weary, ¹⁷if I have kept my bread to myself, not sharing it with the fatherless— ¹⁸but from my youth I reared him as would a father, and from my birth I guided the widow— ¹⁹if I have seen anyone perishing for lack of clothing, or a needy man without a garment, ²⁰and his heart did not bless me for warming him with the fleece from my sheep, ²¹if I have raised my hand against the fatherless, knowing that I had influence in court, ²²then let my arm fall from the shoulder, let it be broken off at the joint. (+Job 31:38-40)

The Temanites (Isa 21:14). Nebuzaradan (Jer 39:10). The good Samaritan (Lk 10:33-35). Zacchaeus (Lk 19:8). Dorcas (Ac 9:36). Cornelius (Ac 10:2,4). Christian church, at Jerusalem (Ac 6:1), at Antioch (Ac 11:29-30). Churches of Macedonia and Achaia (Ro 15:25-26; 2Co 8:1-5). By Paul (Ro 15:25).

Oppression of:

Ne 5:1 Now the men and their wives raised a great outcry against their Jewish brothers. ²Some were saying, "We and our sons and daughters are numerous; in order for us to eat and stay alive, we must get grain."

³Others were saying, "We are mortgaging our fields, our vineyards and our homes to get grain during the famine."

⁴Still others were saying, "We have had to borrow money to pay the king's tax on our fields and vineyards. ⁵Although we are of the same flesh and blood as our countrymen and though our sons are as good as theirs, yet we have to subject our sons and daughters to slavery. Some of our daughters have already been enslaved, but we are powerless, because our fields and our vineyards belong to others."

⁶When I heard their outcry and these charges, I was very angry. ⁷I pondered them in my mind and then accused the nobles and officials. I told them, "You are exacting usury from your own countrymen!" So I called together a large meeting to deal with them ⁸and said: "As far as possible, we have bought back our Jewish brothers who were sold to the Gentiles. Now you are selling your brothers, only for

them to be sold back to us!" They kept quiet, because they could find nothing to say.

⁹So I continued, "What you are doing is not right. Shouldn't you walk in the fear of our God to avoid the reproach of our Gentile enemies? ¹⁰I and my brothers and my men are also lending the people money and grain. But let the exacting of usury stop! ¹¹Give back to them immediately their fields, vineyards, olive groves and houses, and also the usury you are charging them—the hundredth part of the money, grain, new wine and oil."

¹²"We will give it back," they said. "And we will not demand anything more from them. We will do as you say." Then I summoned the priests and made the nobles and officials take an oath to do what they had promised.

¹³I also shook out the folds of my robe and said, "In this way may God shake out of his house and possessions every man who does not keep this promise. So may such a man be shaken out and emptied!" At this the whole assembly said, "Amen," and praised the LORD. And the people did as they had promised.

Job 20:19 For he has oppressed the poor and left them destitute; he has seized houses he did not build.

²⁰"Surely he will have no respite from his craving; he cannot save himself by his treasure. ²¹Nothing is left for him to devour; his prosperity will not endure.

Job 22:6 You demanded security from your brothers for no reason; you stripped men of their clothing, leaving them naked. ⁷You gave no water to the weary and you withheld food from the hungry,

Job 22:9 And you sent widows away empty-handed and broke the strength of the fatherless. ¹⁰That is why snares are all around you, why sudden peril terrifies you, ¹¹why it is so dark you cannot see, and why a flood of water covers you.

Job 24:4 They thrust the needy from the path and force all the poor of the land into hiding.

Job 24:7 Lacking clothes, they spend the night naked; they have nothing to cover themselves in the cold. ⁸They are drenched by mountain rains and hug the rocks for lack of shelter. ⁹The fatherless child is snatched from the breast; the infant of the poor is seized for a debt. ¹⁰Lacking clothes, they go about naked; they carry the sheaves, but still go hungry. (+Job 24:11-12)

Ps 10:2 In his arrogance the wicked man hunts down the weak, who are caught in the schemes he devises.

Ps 10:8 He lies in wait near the villages; from ambush he murders the innocent, watching in secret for his victims. ⁹He lies in wait like a lion in cover; he lies in wait to catch the helpless; he catches the helpless and drags them off in his net. ¹⁰His victims are crushed, they collapse; they fall under his strength.

Ps 37:14 The wicked draw the sword and bend the bow to bring down the poor and needy, to slay those whose ways are upright.

Ps 109:16 For he never thought of doing a kindness, but hounded to death the poor and the needy and the brokenhearted.

Pr 14:31 He who oppresses the poor shows contempt for their Maker, but whoever is kind to the needy honors God.

Pr 17:5 He who mocks the poor shows contempt for their Maker; whoever gloats over disaster will not go unpunished.

Pr 19:7 A poor man is shunned by all his relatives—how much more do his friends avoid him! Though he pursues them with pleading, they are nowhere to be found.

Pr 22:7 The rich rule over the poor, and the borrower is servant to the lender. (+Pr 22:16)

Pr 28:3 A ruler who oppresses the poor is like a driving rain that leaves no crops.

Pr 28:15 Like a roaring lion or a charging bear is a wicked man ruling over a helpless people.

Pr 30:14 those whose teeth are swords and whose jaws are set with knives to devour the poor from the earth, the needy from among mankind.

Ecc 5:8 If you see the poor oppressed in a district, and justice and rights denied, do not be surprised at such things; for one official is eyed by a higher one, and over them both are others higher still.

Isa 3:14 The LORD enters into judgment against the elders and leaders of his people: "It is you who have ruined my vineyard; the plunder from the poor is in your houses. ¹⁵What do you mean by crushing my people and grinding the faces of the poor?" declares the Lord, the LORD Almighty.

Isa 10:1 Woe to those who make unjust laws, to those who issue oppressive decrees, ²to deprive the poor of their rights and withhold justice from the oppressed of my people, making widows their prey and robbing the fatherless.

Isa 32:6 For the fool speaks folly, his mind is busy with evil: He practices ungodliness and spreads error concerning the LORD; the hungry he leaves empty and from the thirsty he withholds water. ⁷The scoundrel's methods are wicked, he makes up evil schemes to destroy the poor with lies, even when the plea of the needy is just.

Eze 18:12 He oppresses the poor and needy. He commits robbery. He does not return what he took in pledge. He looks to the idols. He does detestable things.

Eze 22:29 The people of the land practice extortion and commit robbery; they oppress the poor and needy and mistreat the alien, denying them justice.

Am 2:6 This is what the LORD says: "For three sins of Israel, even for four, I will not turn back [my wrath]. They sell the righteous for silver, and the needy for a pair of sandals.

Am 4:1 Hear this word, you cows of Bashan on Mount Samaria, you women who oppress the poor and crush the needy and say to your husbands, "Bring us some drinks!"

Am 5:11 You trample on the poor and force him to give you grain. Therefore, though you have built stone mansions, you will not live in them; though you have planted lush vineyards, you will not drink their wine. ¹²For I know how many are your offenses and how great your sins. You oppress the righteous and take bribes and you deprive the poor of justice in the courts.

Am 8:4 Hear this, you who trample the needy and do away with the poor of the land, (+Am 8:5)

Am 8:6 buying the poor with silver and the needy for a pair of sandals, selling even the sweepings with the wheat.

Hab 3:14 With his own spear you pierced his head when his warriors stormed out to scatter us, gloating as though about to devour the wretched who were in hiding. (+Jas 2:6; 5:4)

Oppression forbidden (Dt 24:14; Zec 7:10).

Instances of oppression of: (2Ki 4:1; Ne 5:1-5).

Mosaic laws concerning:

Atonement money of, must be uniform with that of the rich (Ex 30:15). Inexpensive offerings authorized for (Lev 5:7; 12:8; 14:21-22).

Discrimination, in favor of, forbidden—

Ex 23:3 and do not show favoritism to a poor man in his lawsuit.

Lev 19:15 "'Do not pervert justice; do not show partiality to the poor or favoritism to the great, but judge your neighbor fairly.

Against, forbidden—

Ex 23:6 "Do not deny justice to your poor people in their lawsuits. (+Jas 2:2-9)

Exactions of interest from, forbidden (Ex 22:25; Lev 25:35-37). Garments of, taken in pledge, to be restored (Ex 22:26; Dt 24:12-13). To participate triennially in the tithes (Dt 14:28-29; 26:12-13). Gleanings reserved for (Lev 19:9-10; 23:22; Dt 24:19-21). To share the products of the land in the seventh year (Ex 23:11). To be released from servitude, in seventh year (Dt 15:12), in Jubilee (Lev 25:39-43). Alienated lands of, to be restored in Jubilee (Lev 25:25-28).

Figurative:

Poor in spirit (Isa 66:2; Mt 5:3; Lk 6:20).

See Alms; Beneficence; Creditor; Debtor; Employee; Employer; Liberality; Orphans; Poverty; Rich, The; Riches; Servants; Wages; Widow.

POPLAR [4242, 6857] (*white*).

NIV+ POPLARS

A tree (Ge 30:37; Hos 4:13).

POPLARS, RAVINE OF A brook, probably on the boundary between Moab and Edom (Isa 15:7).

POPULARITY Instances of: David (2Sa 3:36). Absalom (2Sa 15:2-6,13). Job (Job 29).

POPULARITY OF JESUS (Mt 4:24; 8:1; 13:2; 14:13,35; 19:1-2; 21:8-9; Mk 1:33; 2:2; 3:7,20; 5:21; 6:33, 55-56; 10:1; 11:8-10; 12:37; Lk 4:14-15,42; 5:1; 9:11; 12:1; 19:35-38; Jn 6:2,15; 12:12-13,19).

PORATHA [7054]. Son of Haman (Est 9:8).

PORCH [395, 4997].

NIV+ PORTICO, PORTICOES

An area with a roof supported by columns: colonnade (1Ki 7:6ff), porch (Jdg 3:23, ftn), place before a court (Mk 14:68), gateway (Mt 26:71).

PORCIUS [*4517*]. *See Festus, Porcius.*

PORPHYRY [985]. A purple stone used in mosaics (Est 1:6).

PORPOISE *See Sea Cow.*

PORTERS *See Gatekeepers.*

PORTION [260, 2475, 2745, 2750, 2754, 2976, 3338, 4595, 4950, 4987, 5368, 5419, 5421, 5467, 7023, 7731, 8123, 9556].

NIV+ APPORTIONED, PORTIONS

A part; less than the whole of anything; share (Nu 31:30,47; Ne 8:10,12).

POST [4647, 5226, 5466, 6641, 7212, 8492, *2653*].

NIV+ POSTED, POSTING, POSTS

1. Of the tabernacle (Ex 26:32,37; 27:1-17). Of a city gate (Jdg 16:3).

2. Of a watchman (Ne 7:3; 13:11; Ecc 10:4; Isa 62:6).

POSTERITY PROMISED [2446]. (Ge 15:5,18; 17:20; 22:17; 26:14; Lev 26:9; Dt 7:13; Ro 4:18).

POT [1857, 3671, 3968, 3998, 5350, 5574, 6105, 6775, 7248, 7831].

NIV+ POTS, POTSHERD, POTSHERDS, POTTER, POTTER'S, POTTERS, POTTERY

Utensil of metal of clay for holding liquids or other substances (2Ki 4:38).

POTENTATE *See Rulers.*

POTIPHAR [7035] (*he whom [pagan god] Ra gives*). An officer of Pharaoh. Joseph's master (Ge 37:36; 39:1).

POTIPHERA, POTI-PHERAH [7036] (*he whom [pagan god] Ra gives*). A priest of On. Joseph's father-in-law (Ge 41:45,50; 46:20).

POTSHERD [3068, 3084].

NIV+ See POT

A fragment of earthenware (Job 2:8; Isa 45:9).

POTTAGE *See Stew.*

POTTER [3450, *3038*]. *See Occupations and Professions.*

POTTER'S FIELD Piece of ground which the priests bought with the money Judas received for betraying our Lord (Mt 27:7).

POTTER'S GATE Of Jerusalem (Jer 19:2).

POTTERY [3084, 3450+, 3998, *5007*].

NIV+ See POT

One of the oldest crafts in the Bible lands. The place where potter's clay was dug was called "potter's field" (Mt 27:7). Pottery was shaped by hand on a potter's wheel, powered by foot or by an apprentice (Jer 18:3-6), then dried and baked in a kiln.

Many different items were made: basins, bowls, cups, dishes, flasks, jars, lamps, ovens, pots. Thousands of objects have been found by the archaeologists. Careful study has been made of the historical development of pottery styles, so that experts can date and place pottery with considerable accuracy.

POUND

NIV+ POUNDS

[*1669+3354, 5418*]. A talent equaled about seventy-five pounds (Ex 25:39, ftn), a mina about 1.25 pounds (1Ki 10:17, ftn), forty shekels about one pound (Ge 3:15, ftn). *See Measure.*

POVERTY [2895, 2896, 3769, 4728, 8133, 8203, *4775, 5729, 5730*].

NIV+ See POOR

(1Sa 2:7). Destructive (Pr 10:15). A source of temptation (Pr 30:8-9). To be preferred over wealth, with trouble (Pr 15:16), without right (Pr 16:8; Ecc 4:6). *See Poor.*

Caused:

By laziness (Pr 6:11; 20:13; 24:33-34), by drunkenness (Pr 23:21), by evil associations (Pr 28:19).

POWER [*226, 600, 1475, 1476, 1524, 2432, 2616, 2617, 3338, 3946, 6434, 6437, 6786, 6793, 7502, 7756, 10130, 10717, 10768, 794, 1539, 1543, 1918, 2026, 2708, 3197*].

NIV+ OVERPOWER, OVERPOWERED,

OVERPOWERING, OVERPOWERS, POWERFUL, POWERFULLY, POWERLESS, POWERS

Of Christ:

As the Son of God, is the power of God (Jn 5:17-19; 10:28-30), as man, is from the Father (Ac 10:38).

Described as supreme (Eph 1:20-21; 1Pe 3:22), unlimited (Mt 28:18), over all flesh (Jn 17:2), over all things (Jn 3:35; Eph 1:22), glorious (2Th 1:9), everlasting (1Ti 6:16). Is able to subdue all things (Php 3:21).

Exemplified in, creation (Jn 1:3,10; Col 1:16), upholding all things (Col 1:17; Heb 1:3), salvation (Isa 63:1; Heb 7:25), His teaching (Mt 7:28-29; Lk 4:32), working miracles (Mt 8:27; Lk 5:17), enabling others to work miracles (Mt 10:1; Ac 5:31), giving spiritual life (Jn 5:21,25-26), giving eternal life (Jn 17:2), raising the dead (Jn 5:28-29), rising from the dead (Jn 2:19; 10:18), overcoming the world (Jn 16:33), overcoming Satan (Col 2:15; Heb 2:14), destroying the works of Satan (1Jn 3:8), ministers should make known (2Pe 1:16).

Saints made willing by (Ps 110:3), aided by (Heb 2:18), strengthened by (Php 4:13; 2Ti 4:17), preserved by (2Ti 1:12; 4:18), bodies of, shall be changed by (Php 3:21), rests upon saints (2Co 12:9). Present in the assembly of saints (1Co 5:4). Shall be specially manifested at his second coming (Mk 13:26; 2Pe 1:16). Shall subdue all power (1Co 15:24). The wicked shall be destroyed by (Ps 2:9; Isa 11:4; 63:3; 2Th 1:9).

See Jesus the Christ, Omnipotence of; Power of.

Of God:

One of his attributes (Ps 62:11).

Expressed by the voice of God (Ps 29:3,5; 68:33), finger of God (Ex 9:3,15; Isa 48:13), arm of God (Job 40:9; Isa 52:10), thunder of his power (Job 26:14).

Described as, great (Ps 79:11; Na 1:3), strong (Ps 89:13; 136:12), glorious (Ex 15:6; Isa 63:12), mighty (Job 9:4; Ps 89:13), everlasting (Isa 26:4; Ro 1:20), sovereign (Ro 9:21), effectual (Isa 43:13; Eph 3:7), irresistible (Dt 32:39; Da 4:35), incomparable (Ex 15:11-12; Dt 3:24; Job 40:9; Ps 89:8), unsearchable (Job 5:9; 9:10), incomprehensible (Job 26:14; Ecc 3:11).

All things possible to (Mt 19:26). Nothing too hard for (Ge 18:14; Jer 32:27). Can save by many or by few (1Sa 14:6). Is the source of all strength (1Ch 29:12; Ps 68:35).

Exemplified, in the creation (Ps 102:25; Jer 10:12), in establishing and governing all things (Ps 65:6; 66:7), in the miracles of Christ (Lk 11:20), in the resurrection of Christ (2Co 13:4; Col 2:12), in the resurrection of saints (1Co 6:14), in making the gospel effectual (Ro 1:16; 1Co 1:18, 24), in delivering his people (Ps 106:8), in the destruction of the wicked (Ex 9:16; Ro 9:22).

Saints, long for exhibitions of (Ps 63:1-2), have confidence in (Jer 20:11), receive increase of grace by (2Co 9:8), strengthened by (Eph 6:10; Col 1:11), upheld by (Ps 37:17; Isa 41:10), supported in affliction by (2Co 6:7; 2Ti 1:8), delivered by (Nu 1:10; Da 3:17), exalted by (Job 36:22), kept by, for salvation (1Pe 1:5). Exerted in behalf of saints (1Ch 16:9). Works in and for saints (2Co 13:4; Eph 1:19; 3:20). The faith of saints stands in (1Co 2:5).

Should be acknowledged (1Ch 29:11; Isa 33:13), pleaded in prayer (Ps 79:11; Mt 6:13), feared (Jer 5:22; Mt 10:28), magnified (Ps 21:13; Jude 25). Efficiency of ministers is through (1Co 3:6-8; Gal 2:8; Eph 3:7). Is a ground of trust (Isa 26:4; Ro 4:21).

The wicked know not (Mt 22:29), have against them

(Ezr 8:22), shall be destroyed by (Lk 12:5). The heavenly host magnified (Rev 4:11; 5:13; 11:17).

See God, Omnipotent, Power of.

Of the Holy Spirit:

Is the power of God (Mt 12:28, w Lk 11:20). Christ worked his miracles (Mt 12:28).

Exemplified in creation (Ge 1:2; Job 26:13; Ps 104:30), the conception of Christ (Lk 1:35), raising Christ from the dead (1Pe 3:18), giving spiritual life (Eze 37:11-14, w Ro 8:11), working miracles (Ro 15:19), making the Gospel efficacious (1Co 2:4; 1Th 1:5), overcoming all difficulties (Zec 4:6-7). Promised by the Father (Lk 24:49). Promised by Christ (Ac 1:8).

Saints upheld by (Ps 51:12), strengthened by (Eph 3:16), enabled to speak the truth boldly by (Mic 3:8; Ac 6:5,10; 2Ti 1:7-8), helped in prayer by (Ro 8:26), abound in hope by (Ro 15:13). Qualifies ministers (Lk 24:49; Ac 1:8-9). God's word the instrument of (Eph 6:17).

See Holy Spirit.

Spiritual:

From God—

Isa 40:29 He gives strength to the weary and increases the power of the weak. [30]Even youths grow tired and weary, and young men stumble and fall; [31]but those who hope in the LORD will renew their strength. They will soar on wings like eagles; they will run and not grow weary, they will walk and not be faint. (+Lk 24:49)

1Co 1:24 but to those whom God has called, both Jews and Greeks, Christ the power of God and the wisdom of God. [25]For the foolishness of God is wiser than man's wisdom, and the weakness of God is stronger than man's strength.

[26]Brothers, think of what you were when you were called. Not many of you were wise by human standards; not many were influential; not many were of noble birth. [27]But God chose the foolish things of the world to shame the wise; God chose the weak things of the world to shame the strong. [28]He chose the lowly things of this world and the despised things—and the things that are not—to nullify the things that are, (+Php 2:13)

2Ti 1:7 For God did not give us a spirit of timidity, but a spirit of power, of love and of self-discipline.

From Christ—

2Co 12:9 But he said to me, "My grace is sufficient for you, for my power is made perfect in weakness." Therefore I will boast all the more gladly about my weaknesses, so that Christ's power may rest on me.

Eph 1:19 and his incomparably great power for us who believe. That power is like the working of his mighty strength, [20]which he exerted in Christ when he raised him from the dead and seated him at his right hand in the heavenly realms,

From the Holy Spirit—

Jn 7:38 Whoever believes in me, as the Scripture has said, streams of living water will flow from within him." [39]By this he meant the Spirit, whom those who believed in him were later to receive. Up to that time the Spirit had not been given, since Jesus had not yet been glorified.

Ac 1:8 But you will receive power when the Holy Spirit comes on you; and you will be my witnesses in Jerusalem, and in all Judea and Samaria, and to the ends of the earth." (+Ac 2:2-4)

On believers—

Ac 6:8 Now Stephen, a man full of God's grace and

power, did great wonders and miraculous signs among the people. (+Ac 6:10)

1Co 4:19 But I will come to you very soon, if the Lord is willing, and then I will find out not only how these arrogant people are talking, but what power they have. **20**For the kingdom of God is not a matter of talk but of power.

Heb 6:5 who have tasted the goodness of the word of God and the powers of the coming age,

In the spirit of Elijah—

Lk 1:17 And he will go on before the Lord, in the spirit and power of Elijah, to turn the hearts of the fathers to their children and the disobedient to the wisdom of the righteous—to make ready a people prepared for the Lord."

In preaching (Ac 4:33; 6:10)—

1Th 1:5 because our gospel came to you not simply with words, but also with power, with the Holy Spirit and with deep conviction. You know how we lived among you for your sake.

Of Christ—

Lk 4:32 They were amazed at his teaching, because his message had authority.

Through prayer—

Ge 32:28 Then the man said, "Your name will no longer be Jacob, but Israel, because you have struggled with God and with men and have overcome." (+Ge 9:29)

Lk 24:49 I am going to send you what my Father has promised; but stay in the city until you have been clothed with power from on high." (+Ac 1:14; 2:1)

Ac 2:2 Suddenly a sound like the blowing of a violent wind came from heaven and filled the whole house where they were sitting. **3**They saw what seemed to be tongues of fire that separated and came to rest on each of them. **4**All of them were filled with the Holy Spirit and began to speak in other tongues as the Spirit enabled them.

PRAETOR Originally the highest Roman magistrate; later, officials elected to administer justice; under the principate the office declined in prestige, power, and functions.

PRAETORIAN GUARD (*residence of the Praetor [leader]*). Guard of imperial palace or provincial governor; NIV "palace guard" (Php 1:13) and "Caesar's household" (Php 4:22).

PRAETORIUM [*4550*] (*residence of the Praetor [leader]*). In the Gospels it refers to the temporary palace or headquarters of the Roman governor while in Jerusalem (Mt 27:27; Mk 15:16), the palace of Herod at Caesarea (Ac 23:35).

PRAISE [*1385, 2146, 2376, 3344, 9335, 10122, 10693, *140, 1518, 1519, 2018, 2046, 2047, 2328, 2329, 2330*].
NIV+ PRAISED, PRAISES, PRAISEWORTHY, PRAISING

Exemplified:

Ps 7:17 I will give thanks to the LORD because of his righteousness and will sing praise to the name of the LORD Most High.

Ps 22:22 I will declare your name to my brothers; in the congregation I will praise you. **23**You who fear the LORD, praise him! All you descendants of Jacob, honor him! Revere him, all you descendants of Israel!

Ps 28:6 Praise be to the LORD, for he has heard my cry for mercy. **7**The LORD is my strength and my shield; my heart trusts in him, and I am helped. My heart leaps for joy and I will give thanks to him in song.

Ps 32:11 Rejoice in the LORD and be glad, you righteous; sing, all you who are upright in heart!

Ps 34:1 I will extol the LORD at all times; his praise will always be on my lips. **2**My soul will boast in the LORD; let the afflicted hear and rejoice. **3**Glorify the LORD with me; let us exalt his name together.

Ps 41:13 Praise be to the LORD, the God of Israel, from everlasting to everlasting. Amen and Amen.

Ps 42:4 These things I remember as I pour out my soul: how I used to go with the multitude, leading the procession to the house of God, with shouts of joy and thanksgiving among the festive throng.

Ps 51:15 O Lord, open my lips, and my mouth will declare your praise.

Ps 65:1 Praise awaits you, O God, in Zion; to you our vows will be fulfilled. (+Ps 71:8,14-15)

Ps 75:1 We give thanks to you, O God, we give thanks, for your Name is near; men tell of your wonderful deeds.

Ps 79:13 Then we your people, the sheep of your pasture, will praise you forever; from generation to generation we will recount your praise.

Ps 81:1 Sing for joy to God our strength; shout aloud to the God of Jacob!

Ps 84:4 Blessed are those who dwell in your house; they are ever praising you. *Selah*

Ps 86:12 I will praise you, O Lord my God, with all my heart; I will glorify your name forever. (+Ps 89:95)

Ps 104:33 I will sing to the LORD all my life; I will sing praise to my God as long as I live. **34**May my meditation be pleasing to him, as I rejoice in the LORD.

Ps 109:30 With my mouth I will greatly extol the LORD; in the great throng I will praise him.

Ps 113:1 Praise the LORD. Praise, O servants of the LORD, praise the name of the LORD.

2Let the name of the LORD be praised, both now and forevermore.

Ps 115:18 it is we who extol the LORD, both now and forevermore. Praise the LORD.

Ps 118:15 Shouts of joy and victory resound in the tents of the righteous: "The LORD's right hand has done mighty things!

Ps 140:13 Surely the righteous will praise your name and the upright will live before you.

Ps 145:1 I will exalt you, my God the King; I will praise your name for ever and ever. **2**Every day I will praise you and extol your name for ever and ever.

3Great is the LORD and most worthy of praise; his greatness no one can fathom. **4**One generation will commend your works to another; they will tell of your mighty acts. **5**They will speak of the glorious splendor of your majesty, and I will meditate on your wonderful works. **6**They will tell of the power of your awesome works, and I will proclaim your great deeds. **7**They will celebrate your abundant goodness and joyfully sing of your righteousness.

8The LORD is gracious and compassionate, slow to anger and rich in love. **9**The LORD is good to all; he has compassion on all he has made. **10**All you have made will praise you, O LORD; your saints will extol you. **11**They will tell of the glory of your kingdom and speak of your might, **12**so that all men may know of your mighty acts and the glorious splendor of your kingdom. **13**Your kingdom is an everlasting kingdom, and your dominion endures through all generations. The LORD is faithful to all his promises and loving toward all he has made.

14The LORD upholds all those who fall and lifts up all who are bowed down. **15**The eyes of all look to you, and you give them their food at the proper time. ¹⁶You open your hand and satisfy the desires of every living thing.

¹⁷The LORD is righteous in all his ways and loving toward all he has made. ¹⁸The LORD is near to all who call on him, to all who call on him in truth. ¹⁹He fulfills the desires of those who fear him; he hears their cry and saves them. ²⁰The LORD watches over all who love him, but all the wicked he will destroy.

²¹My mouth will speak in praise of the LORD. Let every creature praise his holy name for ever and ever.

Ps 146:1 Praise the LORD.

Praise the LORD, O my soul.

²I will praise the LORD all my life; I will sing praise to my God as long as I live.

³Do not put your trust in princes, in mortal men, who cannot save. ⁴When their spirit departs, they return to the ground; on that very day their plans come to nothing.

⁵Blessed is he whose help is the God of Jacob, whose hope is in the LORD his God, ⁶the Maker of heaven and earth, the sea, and everything in them—the LORD, who remains faithful forever. ⁷He upholds the cause of the oppressed and gives food to the hungry. The LORD sets prisoners free, ⁸the LORD gives sight to the blind, the LORD lifts up those who are bowed down, the LORD loves the righteous. ⁹The LORD watches over the alien and sustains the fatherless and the widow, but he frustrates the ways of the wicked.

¹⁰The LORD reigns forever, your God, O Zion, for all generations.

Praise the LORD.

Ps 148:1 Praise the LORD.

Praise the LORD from the heavens, praise him in the heights above.

²Praise him, all his angels, praise him, all his heavenly hosts. ³Praise him, sun and moon, praise him, all you shining stars. ⁴Praise him, you highest heavens and you waters above the skies. ⁵Let them praise the name of the LORD, for he commanded and they were created.

⁶He set them in place for ever and ever; he gave a decree that will never pass away. ⁷Praise the LORD from the earth, you great sea creatures and all ocean depths, ⁸lightning and hail, snow and clouds, stormy winds that do his bidding, ⁹you mountains and all hills, fruit trees and all cedars, ¹⁰wild animals and all cattle, small creatures and flying birds, ¹¹kings of the earth and all nations, you princes and all rulers on earth, ¹²young men and maidens, old men and children. ¹³Let them praise the name of the LORD, for his name alone is exalted; his splendor is above the earth and the heavens. ¹⁴He has raised up for his people a horn, the praise of all his saints, of Israel, the people close to his heart.

Praise the LORD.

Ps 149:1 Praise the LORD.

Sing to the LORD a new song, his praise in the assembly of the saints.

²Let Israel rejoice in their Maker; let the people of Zion be glad in their King. ³Let them praise his name with dancing and make music to him with tambourine and harp. ⁴For the LORD takes delight in his people; he crowns the humble with salvation. ⁵Let the saints rejoice in this honor and sing for joy on their beds.

⁶May the praise of God be in their mouths and a double-edged sword in their hands, ⁷to inflict vengeance on the nations and punishment on the peoples, ⁸to bind their kings with fetters, their nobles with shackles of iron, ⁹to carry

out the sentence written against them. This is the glory of all his saints.

Praise the LORD.

Ps 150:1 Praise the LORD.

Praise God in his sanctuary; praise him in his mighty heavens. ²Praise him for his acts of power; praise him for his surpassing greatness. ³Praise him with the sounding of the trumpet, praise him with the harp and lyre, ⁴praise him with tambourine and dancing, praise him with the strings and flute, ⁵praise him with the clash of cymbals, praise him with resounding cymbals. ⁶Let everything that has breath praise the LORD.

Praise the LORD.

Isa 24:15 Therefore in the east give glory to the LORD; exalt the name of the LORD, the God of Israel, in the islands of the sea. ¹⁶From the ends of the earth we hear singing: "Glory to the Righteous One." But I said, "I waste away, I waste away! Woe to me! The treacherous betray! With treachery the treacherous betray!"

Isa 25:1 O LORD, you are my God; I will exalt you and praise your name, for in perfect faithfulness you have done marvelous things, things planned long ago.

Isa 35:10 and the ransomed of the LORD will return. They will enter Zion with singing; everlasting joy will crown their heads. Gladness and joy will overtake them, and sorrow and sighing will flee away.

Isa 38:19 The living, the living—they praise you, as I am doing today; fathers tell their children about your faithfulness.

Isa 43:21 the people I formed for myself that they may proclaim my praise.

Isa 49:13 Shout for joy, O heavens; rejoice, O earth; burst into song, O mountains! For the LORD comforts his people and will have compassion on his afflicted ones.

Isa 51:3 The LORD will surely comfort Zion and will look with compassion on all her ruins; he will make her deserts like Eden, her wastelands like the garden of the LORD. Joy and gladness will be found in her, thanksgiving and the sound of singing.

Isa 52:7 How beautiful on the mountains are the feet of those who bring good news, who proclaim peace, who bring good tidings, who proclaim salvation, who say to Zion, "Your God reigns!" ⁸Listen! Your watchmen lift up their voices; together they shout for joy. When the LORD returns to Zion, they will see it with their own eyes. ⁹Burst into songs of joy together, you ruins of Jerusalem, for the LORD has comforted his people, he has redeemed Jerusalem. ¹⁰The LORD will lay bare his holy arm in the sight of all the nations, and all the ends of the earth will see the salvation of our God.

Jer 31:7 This is what the LORD says: "Sing with joy for Jacob; shout for the foremost of the nations. Make your praises heard, and say, 'O LORD, save your people, the remnant of Israel.' (+Ro 11:36)

Ro 16:27 to the only wise God be glory forever through Jesus Christ! Amen.

1Co 15:57 But thanks be to God! He gives us the victory through our Lord Jesus Christ.

Eph 3:20 Now to him who is able to do immeasurably more than all we ask or imagine, according to his power that is at work within us, ²¹to him be glory in the church and in Christ Jesus throughout all generations, for ever and ever! Amen.

Heb 2:12 He says, "I will declare your name to my brothers; in the presence of the congregation I will sing your praises."

Jude 25 to the only God our Savior be glory, majesty, power and authority, through Jesus Christ our Lord, before all ages, now and forevermore! Amen.

Rev 1:6 and has made us to be a kingdom and priests to serve his God and Father—to him be glory and power for ever and ever! Amen.

Rev 14:7 He said in a loud voice, "Fear God and give him glory, because the hour of his judgment has come. Worship him who made the heavens, the earth, the sea and the springs of water."

With music—

Ps 33:2 Praise the LORD with the harp; make music to him on the ten-stringed lyre. ³Sing to him a new song; play skillfully, and shout for joy.

Ps 43:3 Send forth your light and your truth, let them guide me; let them bring me to your holy mountain, to the place where you dwell. ⁴Then will I go to the altar of God, to God, my joy and my delight. I will praise you with the harp, O God, my God.

Ps 47:1 Clap your hands, all you nations; shout to God with cries of joy.

Ps 47:6 Sing praises to God, sing praises; sing praises to our King, sing praises.

⁷For God is the King of all the earth; sing to him a psalm of praise.

Ps 57:7 My heart is steadfast, O God, my heart is steadfast; I will sing and make music. ⁸Awake, my soul! Awake, harp and lyre! I will awaken the dawn.

⁹I will praise you, O Lord, among the nations; I will sing of you among the peoples. (+Ps 108:1-3)

Ps 66:1 Shout with joy to God, all the earth! ²Sing the glory of his name; make his praise glorious!

Ps 66:4 All the earth bows down to you; they sing praise to you, they sing praise to your name." Selah

Ps 67:4 May the nations be glad and sing for joy, for you rule the peoples justly and guide the nations of the earth. Selah

Ps 68:4 Sing to God, sing praise to his name, extol him who rides on the clouds—his name is the LORD—and rejoice before him.

Ps 68:32 Sing to God, O kingdoms of the earth, sing praise to the Lord, Selah ³³to him who rides the ancient skies above, who thunders with mighty voice. ³⁴Proclaim the power of God, whose majesty is over Israel, whose power is in the skies.

Ps 69:30 I will praise God's name in song and glorify him with thanksgiving.

Ps 71:22 I will praise you with the harp for your faithfulness, O my God; I will sing praise to you with the lyre, O Holy One of Israel. (+Ps 81:1)

Ps 92:1 It is good to praise the LORD and make music to your name, O Most High, ²to proclaim your love in the morning and your faithfulness at night, ³to the music of the ten-stringed lyre and the melody of the harp.

Ps 95:1 Come, let us sing for joy to the LORD; let us shout aloud to the Rock of our salvation. ²Let us come before him with thanksgiving and extol him with music and song.

Ps 98:4 Shout for joy to the LORD, all the earth, burst into jubilant song with music; ⁵make music to the LORD with the harp, with the harp and the sound of singing, ⁶with trumpets and the blast of the ram's horn—shout for joy before the LORD, the King. (+Ps 104:33)

Ps 144:9 I will sing a new song to you, O God; on the ten-stringed lyre I will make music to you, (+Ps 149:2-3; 150:3-5)

Jas 5:13 Is any one of you in trouble? He should pray. Is anyone happy? Let him sing songs of praise.

Daily—

1Ch 23:30 They were also to stand every morning to thank and praise the LORD. They were to do the same in the evening (+Ps 92:1-2; 145:2)

In the night (Ps 42:8; 63:5-6; 77:6; 92:1-3)—

Ps 119:62 At midnight I rise to give you thanks for your righteous laws. (+Ps 134:1; 149:5)

Ac 16:25 About midnight Paul and Silas were praying and singing hymns to God, and the other prisoners were listening to them.

Seven times a day—

Ps 119:164 Seven times a day I praise you for your righteous laws.

Congregational (Ps 22:22)—

Ps 26:12 My feet stand on level ground; in the great assembly I will praise the LORD. (+Ps 68:26)

Ps 111:1 Praise the LORD. I will extol the LORD with all my heart in the council of the upright and in the assembly.

Ps 116:18 I will fulfill my vows to the LORD in the presence of all his people, ¹⁹in the courts of the house of the LORD—in your midst, O Jerusalem.

Praise the LORD.

Ps 134:1 Praise the LORD, all you servants of the LORD who minister by night in the house of the LORD. ²Lift up your hands in the sanctuary and praise the LORD.

Ps 135:2 you who minister in the house of the LORD, in the courts of the house of our God. (+Ps 149:1)

For God's goodness and mercy (Ps 13:6)—

Ps 63:3 Because your love is better than life, my lips will glorify you. ⁴I will praise you as long as I live, and in your name I will lift up my hands. ⁵My soul will be satisfied as with the richest of foods; with singing lips my mouth will praise you.

⁶On my bed I remember you; I think of you through the watches of the night.

Ps 100:5 For the LORD is good and his love endures forever; his faithfulness continues through all generations.

Ps 101:1 I will sing of your love and justice; to you, O LORD, I will sing praise.

Ps 106:1 Praise the LORD. Give thanks to the LORD, for he is good; his love endures forever.

Ps 106:48 Praise be to the LORD, the God of Israel, from everlasting to everlasting. Let all the people say, "Amen!" Praise the LORD.

Ps 107:8 Let them give thanks to the LORD for his unfailing love and his wonderful deeds for men, ⁹for he satisfies the thirsty and fills the hungry with good things. (+Ps 107:15,21,31)

Ps 117:2 For great is his love toward us, and the faithfulness of the LORD endures forever. Praise the LORD.

Ps 118:29 Give thanks to the LORD, for he is good; his love endures forever. (+Ps 136:1)

Ps 136:2 Give thanks to the God of gods. His love endures forever. (+Ps 136:3-26)

Ps 138:2 I will bow down toward your holy temple and will praise your name for your love and your faithfulness, for you have exalted above all things your name and your word.

Ps 144:1 Praise be to the LORD my Rock, who trains my hands for war, my fingers for battle. ²He is my loving God and my fortress, my stronghold and my deliverer, my shield, in whom I take refuge, who subdues peoples under me. (+Ps 145:7-9,14-21; 146:7-9)

Isa 12:1 In that day you will say: "I will praise you, O Lord. Although you were angry with me, your anger has turned away and you have comforted me. ²Surely God is my salvation; I will trust and not be afraid. The Lord, the Lord, is my strength and my song; he has become my salvation." ³With joy you will draw water from the wells of salvation.

⁴In that day you will say: "Give thanks to the Lord, call on his name; make known among the nations what he has done, and proclaim that his name is exalted. ⁵Sing to the Lord, for he has done glorious things; let this be known to all the world. ⁶Shout aloud and sing for joy, people of Zion, for great is the Holy One of Israel among you."

Jer 33:11 the sounds of joy and gladness, the voices of bride and bridegroom, and the voices of those who bring thank offerings to the house of the Lord, saying, "Give thanks to the Lord Almighty, for the Lord is good; his love endures forever." For I will restore the fortunes of the land as they were before,' says the Lord.

For God's greatness—

Ps 48:1 Great is the Lord, and most worthy of praise, in the city of our God, his holy mountain. (+Ps 145:3,10-12; 147:1-20)

Isa 24:14 They raise their voices, they shout for joy; from the west they acclaim the Lord's majesty.

For God's holiness—

Ps 99:2 Great is the Lord in Zion; he is exalted over all the nations.

Ps 99:5 Exalt the Lord our God and worship at his footstool; he is holy.

Ps 99:9 Exalt the Lord our God and worship at his holy mountain, for the Lord our God is holy.

For God's works (Ps 9:1-2; 107:8-9,15,21,31-32; 145:4-6,10-13; 147:12-18; 150:2).

For deliverance from enemies—

Ge 14:20 And blessed be God Most High, who delivered your enemies into your hand." Then Abram gave him a tenth of everything. (+Ps 44:7-8; 54:6-7; 69:16)

For salvation—

Isa 61:3 and provide for those who grieve in Zion—to bestow on them a crown of beauty instead of ashes, the oil of gladness instead of mourning, and a garment of praise instead of a spirit of despair. They will be called oaks of righteousness, a planting of the Lord for the display of his splendor.

Commanded: (Dt 8:10)

Ps 9:11 Sing praises to the Lord, enthroned in Zion; proclaim among the nations what he has done.

Ps 30:4 Sing to the Lord, you saints of his; praise his holy name. (+Ps 32:11; 33:1-3; 69:34)

Ps 70:4 But may all who seek you rejoice and be glad in you; may those who love your salvation always say, "Let God be exalted!" (+Ps 95:1-2)

Ps 95:6 Come, let us bow down in worship, let us kneel before the Lord our Maker; ⁷ªfor he is our God and we are the people of his pasture, the flock under his care.

Ps 96:1 Sing to the Lord a new song; sing to the Lord, all the earth. ²Sing to the Lord, praise his name; proclaim his salvation day after day. ³Declare his glory among the nations, his marvelous deeds among all peoples.

⁴For great is the Lord and most worthy of praise; he is to be feared above all gods.

Ps 96:7 Ascribe to the Lord, O families of nations, ascribe to the Lord glory and strength. ⁸Ascribe to the Lord the glory due his name; bring an offering and come into his courts. ⁹Worship the Lord in the splendor of his holiness; tremble before him, all the earth. (+Ps 97:12)

Ps 100:1 Shout for joy to the Lord, all the earth. ²Worship the Lord with gladness; come before him with joyful songs. ³Know that the Lord is God. It is he who made us, and we are his; we are his people, the sheep of his pasture.

⁴Enter his gates with thanksgiving and his courts with praise; give thanks to him and praise his name. ⁵For the Lord is good and his love endures forever; his faithfulness continues through all generations.

Ps 105:1 Give thanks to the Lord, call on his name; make known among the nations what he has done. ²Sing to him, sing praise to him; tell of all his wonderful acts. ³Glory in his holy name; let the hearts of those who seek the Lord rejoice. ⁴Look to the Lord and his strength; seek his face always.

⁵Remember the wonders he has done, his miracles, and the judgments he pronounced, (+Ps 117:1; 134:1-2)

Ps 135:1 Praise the Lord.

Praise the name of the Lord; praise him, you servants of the Lord, ²you who minister in the house of the Lord, in the courts of the house of our God.

³Praise the Lord, for the Lord is good; sing praise to his name, for that is pleasant.

Ps 135:19 O house of Israel, praise the Lord; O house of Aaron, praise the Lord; ²⁰O house of Levi, praise the Lord; you who fear him, praise the Lord. ²¹Praise be to the Lord from Zion, to him who dwells in Jerusalem. Praise the Lord.

Isa 42:10 Sing to the Lord a new song, his praise from the ends of the earth, you who go down to the sea, and all that is in it, you islands, and all who live in them. ¹¹Let the desert and its towns raise their voices; let the settlements where Kedar lives rejoice. Let the people of Sela sing for joy; let them shout from the mountaintops. ¹²Let them give glory to the Lord and proclaim his praise in the islands.

Eph 5:19 Speak to one another with psalms, hymns and spiritual songs. Sing and make music in your heart to the Lord,

Heb 13:15 Through Jesus, therefore, let us continually offer to God a sacrifice of praise—the fruit of lips that confess his name.

1Pe 4:11 If anyone speaks, he should do it as one speaking the very words of God. If anyone serves, he should do it with the strength God provides, so that in all things God may be praised through Jesus Christ. To him be the glory and the power for ever and ever. Amen.

1Pe 5:11 To him be the power for ever and ever. Amen.

All nations to praise God (Ps 69:34)—

Ps 103:22 Praise the Lord, all his works everywhere in his dominion. Praise the Lord, O my soul. (+Ps 148:1-14)

Angels exhorted to—

Ps 103:20 Praise the Lord, you his angels, you mighty ones who do his bidding, who obey his word. ²¹Praise the Lord, all his heavenly hosts, you his servants who do his will. (+Ps 148:2)

In Heaven:

Ne 9:6 You alone are the Lord. You made the heavens, even the highest heavens, and all their starry host, the earth and all that is on it, the seas and all that is in them. You give life to everything, and the multitudes of heaven worship you.

Job 38:7 while the morning stars sang together and all the angels shouted for joy?

Ps 103:20 Praise the Lord, you his angels, you mighty ones who do his bidding, who obey his word. ²¹Praise the

Lord, all his heavenly hosts, you his servants who do his will.

Ps 148:2 Praise him, all his angels, praise him, all his heavenly hosts. [3]Praise him, sun and moon, praise him, all you shining stars. [4]Praise him, you highest heavens and you waters above the skies.

Isa 6:3 And they were calling to one another: "Holy, holy, holy is the Lord Almighty; the whole earth is full of his glory."

Eze 3:12 Then the Spirit lifted me up, and I heard behind me a loud rumbling sound—May the glory of the Lord be praised in his dwelling place!—

Lk 2:13 Suddenly a great company of the heavenly host appeared with the angel, praising God and saying,

[14]"Glory to God in the highest, and on earth peace to men on whom his favor rests." (+Lk 15:7)

Lk 15:10 In the same way, I tell you, there is rejoicing in the presence of the angels of God over one sinner who repents."

Rev 1:6 and has made us to be a kingdom and priests to serve his God and Father—to him be glory and power for ever and ever! Amen.

Rev 4:8 Each of the four living creatures had six wings and was covered with eyes all around, even under his wings. Day and night they never stop saying:

"Holy, holy, holy is the Lord God Almighty, who was, and is, and is to come."

[9]Whenever the living creatures give glory, honor and thanks to him who sits on the throne and who lives for ever and ever, [10]the twenty-four elders fall down before him who sits on the throne, and worship him who lives for ever and ever. They lay their crowns before the throne and say:

[11]"You are worthy, our Lord and God, to receive glory and honor and power, for you created all things, and by your will they were created and have their being."

Rev 5:9 And they sang a new song:

"You are worthy to take the scroll and to open its seals, because you were slain, and with your blood you purchased men for God from every tribe and language and people and nation. [10]You have made them to be a kingdom and priests to serve our God, and they will reign on the earth."

[11]Then I looked and heard the voice of many angels, numbering thousands upon thousands, and ten thousand times ten thousand. They encircled the throne and the living creatures and the elders. [12]In a loud voice they sang:

"Worthy is the Lamb, who was slain, to receive power and wealth and wisdom and strength and honor and glory and praise!"

[13]Then I heard every creature in heaven and on earth and under the earth and on the sea, and all that is in them, singing:

"To him who sits on the throne and to the Lamb be praise and honor and glory and power, for ever and ever!"

[14]The four living creatures said, "Amen," and the elders fell down and worshiped.

Rev 7:9 After this I looked and there before me was a great multitude that no one could count, from every nation, tribe, people and language, standing before the throne and in front of the Lamb. They were wearing white robes and were holding palm branches in their hands. [10]And they cried out in a loud voice:

"Salvation belongs to our God, who sits on the throne, and to the Lamb."

[11]All the angels were standing around the throne and around the elders and the four living creatures. They fell down on their faces before the throne and worshiped God, [12]saying:

"Amen! Praise and glory and wisdom and thanks and honor and power and strength be to our God for ever and ever. Amen!"

Rev 11:16 And the twenty-four elders, who were seated on their thrones before God, fell on their faces and worshiped God, [17]saying:

"We give thanks to you, Lord God Almighty, the One who is and who was, because you have taken your great power and have begun to reign."

Rev 14:2 And I heard a sound from heaven like the roar of rushing waters and like a loud peal of thunder. The sound I heard was like that of harpists playing their harps. [3]And they sang a new song before the throne and before the four living creatures and the elders. No one could learn the song except the 144,000 who had been redeemed from the earth.

Rev 15:3 and sang the song of Moses the servant of God and the song of the Lamb:

"Great and marvelous are your deeds, Lord God Almighty. Just and true are your ways, King of the ages. [4]Who will not fear you, O Lord, and bring glory to your name? For you alone are holy. All nations will come and worship before you, for your righteous acts have been revealed."

Rev 19:1 After this I heard what sounded like the roar of a great multitude in heaven shouting:

"Hallelujah! Salvation and glory and power belong to our God, [2]for true and just are his judgments. He has condemned the great prostitute who corrupted the earth by her adulteries. He has avenged on her the blood of his servants."

[3]And again they shouted:

"Hallelujah! The smoke from her goes up for ever and ever."

[4]The twenty-four elders and the four living creatures fell down and worshiped God, who was seated on the throne. And they cried:

"Amen, Hallelujah!"

[5]Then a voice came from the throne, saying:

"Praise our God, all you his servants, you who fear him, both small and great!"

[6]Then I heard what sounded like a great multitude, like the roar of rushing waters and like loud peals of thunder, shouting:

"Hallelujah! For our Lord God Almighty reigns. [7]Let us rejoice and be glad and give him glory! For the wedding of the Lamb has come, and his bride has made herself ready.

Instances of:

Song of Moses, after the passage of the Red Sea—

Ex 15:1 Then Moses and the Israelites sang this song to the Lord:

"I will sing to the Lord, for he is highly exalted. The horse and its rider he has hurled into the sea. [2]The Lord is my strength and my song; he has become my salvation. He is my God, and I will praise him, my father's God, and I will exalt him. (+Ex 15:3-19)

Miriam (Ex 15:21).

Deborah, after defeating the Canaanites (Jdg 5:1-2)—

Jdg 5:3 "Hear this, you kings! Listen, you rulers! I will sing to the Lord, I will sing; I will make music to the Lord, the God of Israel. (+Jdg 5:4-31)

Hannah (1Sa 2:1-10).

David, celebrating his deliverance from the hand of Saul (2Sa 22:1-3)—

2Sa 22:4 I call to the LORD, who is worthy of praise, and I am saved from my enemies. (+2Sa 22:5-51)

On bringing the ark to Zion (1Ch 16:8-30)—

1Ch 16:31 Let the heavens rejoice, let the earth be glad; let them say among the nations, "The LORD reigns!" (+1Ch 16:32)

1Ch 16:33 Then the trees of the forest will sing, they will sing for joy before the LORD, for he comes to judge the earth.

³⁴Give thanks to the LORD, for he is good; his love endures forever. (+1Ch 16:35)

1Ch 16:36 Praise be to the LORD, the God of Israel, from everlasting to everlasting. Then all the people said "Amen" and "Praise the LORD."

At the close of his reign (1Ch 29:10-19).—

The choir when Solomon brought the ark into the temple (2Ch 5:13).

Psalms of, for God's goodness to Israel—

(Pss 46; 48; 65:66; 68; 76; 81; 85; 98; 105; 124; 126; 129)

Ps 135:1 Praise the LORD.

Praise the name of the LORD; praise him, you servants of the LORD, ²you who minister in the house of the LORD, in the courts of the house of our God.

³Praise the LORD, for the LORD is good; sing praise to his name, for that is pleasant. (+Ps 135:4-18)

Ps 135:19 O house of Israel, praise the LORD; O house of Aaron, praise the LORD; ²⁰O house of Levi, praise the LORD; you who fear him, praise the LORD. ²¹Praise be to the LORD from Zion, to him who dwells in Jerusalem.

Praise the LORD. (+Ps 136)

For God's goodness to righteous men (Ps 23; 34; 36; 91; 100; 103; 107; 117; 121).

For God's goodness to individuals (Ps 9; 18; 22; 30; 40; 75; 103; 108; 116:1-11)—

Ps 116:12 How can I repay the LORD for all his goodness to me? ¹³I will lift up the cup of salvation and call on the name of the LORD. ¹⁴I will fulfill my vows to the LORD in the presence of all his people. (+Ps 116:15-19; 118:1-27)

Ps 118:28 You are my God, and I will give you thanks; you are my God, and I will exalt you. (+Ps 118:29; 138; 144)

For God's attributes (Ps 8:1)—

Ps 8:2 From the lips of children and infants you have ordained praise because of your enemies, to silence the foe and the avenger. (+Ps 8:3-9; 19; 22; 24:1-6)

Ps 24:7 Lift up your heads, O you gates; be lifted up, you ancient doors, that the King of glory may come in. ⁸Who is this King of glory? The LORD strong and mighty, the LORD mighty in battle. ⁹Lift up your heads, O you gates; lift them up, you ancient doors, that the King of glory may come in. ¹⁰Who is he, this King of glory? The LORD Almighty—he is the King of glory. *Selah* (+Ps 29; 33; 47; 50:1-22)

Ps 50:23 He who sacrifices thank offerings honors me, and he prepares the way so that I may show him the salvation of God." (+Ps 65; 66:1-7)

Ps 66:8 Praise our God, O peoples, let the sound of his praise be heard; (+Ps 66:9-20; 76:77; 92:93; 95:99; 104; 111; 113:115; 134; 139; 147:148; 150)

Israelites (2Ch 7:2)—

2Ch 7:3 When all the Israelites saw the fire coming down and the glory of the LORD above the temple, they knelt on the pavement with their faces to the ground, and they worshiped and gave thanks to the LORD, saying, "He is good; his love endures forever."

Ne 9:5 And the Levites—Jeshua, Kadmiel, Bani, Hashab-neiah, Sherebiah, Hodiah, Shebaniah and Pethahiah—said: "Stand up and praise the LORD your God, who is from everlasting to everlasting."

"Blessed be your glorious name, and may it be exalted above all blessing and praise. ⁶You alone are the LORD. You made the heavens, even the highest heavens, and all their starry host, the earth and all that is on it, the seas and all that is in them. You give life to everything, and the multitudes of heaven worship you.

The choir when Solomon brought the ark into the temple (2Ch 5:13).

Daniel—

Da 2:20 and said: "Praise be to the name of God for ever and ever; wisdom and power are his.

Da 2:23 I thank and praise you, O God of my fathers: You have given me wisdom and power, you have made known to me what we asked of you, you have made known to us the dream of the king."

Nebuchadnezzar—

Da 4:37 Now I, Nebuchadnezzar, praise and exalt and glorify the King of heaven, because everything he does is right and all his ways are just. And those who walk in pride he is able to humble.

Jonah—

Jnh 2:9 But I, with a song of thanksgiving, will sacrifice to you. What I have vowed I will make good. Salvation comes from the LORD."

Mary—

Lk 1:46 And Mary said: "My soul glorifies the Lord ⁴⁷and my spirit rejoices in God my Savior, ⁴⁸for he has been mindful of the humble state of his servant. From now on all generations will call me blessed, ⁴⁹for the Mighty One has done great things for me—holy is his name. ⁵⁰His mercy extends to those who fear him, from generation to generation. ⁵¹He has performed mighty deeds with his arm; he has scattered those who are proud in their inmost thoughts. ⁵²He has brought down rulers from their thrones but has lifted up the humble. ⁵³He has filled the hungry with good things but has sent the rich away empty. ⁵⁴He has helped his servant Israel, remembering to be merciful ⁵⁵to Abraham and his descendants forever, even as he said to our fathers."

Shepherds—

Lk 2:20 The shepherds returned, glorifying and praising God for all the things they had heard and seen, which were just as they had been told.

The leper—

Lk 17:15 One of them, when he saw he was healed, came back, praising God in a loud voice.

Jesus and his disciples—

Mt 26:30 When they had sung a hymn, they went out to the Mount of Olives. (+Mk 14:26)

Disciples—

Ac 2:46 Every day they continued to meet together in the temple courts. They broke bread in their homes and ate together with glad and sincere hearts, ⁴⁷praising God and enjoying the favor of all the people. And the Lord added to their number daily those who were being saved.

Ac 4:24 When they heard this, they raised their voices together in prayer to God. "Sovereign Lord," they said, "you made the heaven and the earth and the sea, and everything in them.

Paul and Silas, in prison (Ac 16:25).

See Glorifying God; Hallelujah; Prayer; Thankfulness.

PRAYER [*606, 1819, 6983, 7137, 9525, 10114, 10612, *1255, 1289, 2263, 2377, 4666, 4667*].

NIV+ PRAY, PRAYED, PRAYERS, PRAYING, PRAYS

(Ps 17:1,6; 22:1-2,19; 28:1-2; 35:22; 55:1-2,16-17; 57:2; 61:1-2; 70:5; 102:1-2; 130:1-2; 141:1-2; 142:1-2).

Attitudes in: *See Worship.*

Boldness in:

Commanded (Heb 4:16). Exemplified by Abraham in his inquiry concerning Sodom (Ge 18:23-32), by Moses, supplicating for assistance in delivering Israel (Ex 33:12, 18). Secret (Ge 24:63; Mt 6:6). Silent (Ps 5:1). Weeping in (Ezr 10:1). In a loud voice, satirized by Elijah (1Ki 18:27).

Long: Of Pharisees (Mt 23:14), scribes (Mk 12:40; Lk 20:47). Profuse, to be avoided (Ecc 5:2; Mt 6:7). Vain repetitions of, to be avoided (Mt 6:7).

Daily:

In the morning (Ps 5:3; 88:13; 143:8; Isa 32:2). Morning and evening (Ps 92:2). Twice daily (Ps 88:1). Three times a day (Ps 55:17; Da 6:10). In the night (Ps 119:55,62). All night (Lk 6:12). Without ceasing (1Th 5:17).

Disbelief in: (Job 21:15).

Family:

By Abraham (Ge 12:7-8; 13:4,8). By Jacob (Ge 35:3,7). Cornelius (Ac 10:2).

Hypocritical:

Forbidden (Mt 6:5).

Discreet—

Ecc 5:2 Do not be quick with your mouth, do not be hasty in your heart to utter anything before God. God is in heaven and you are on earth, so let your words be few. (+Mt 6:6)

"Lord's prayer":

A model taught to the disciples (Mt 6:9-12; Lk 11:2-4) *See below, Of Jesus.*

Of the righteous, acceptable:

Pr 15:8 The LORD detests the sacrifice of the wicked, but the prayer of the upright pleases him. (+Pr 15:29)

Spirit of, from God—

Zec 12:10 "And I will pour out on the house of David and the inhabitants of Jerusalem a spirit of grace and supplication. They will look on me, the one they have pierced, and they will mourn for him as one mourns for an only child, and grieve bitterly for him as one grieves for a firstborn son.

Divine help in—

Ro 8:26 In the same way, the Spirit helps us in our weakness. We do not know what we ought to pray for, but the Spirit himself intercedes for us with groans that words cannot express.

Postures in:

Bowing (Ge 24:26,48,52; Ex 4:31; 34:8-9; 2Ch 29:29). Kneeling (1Ki 8:54; 2Ch 6:13; Ezr 9:5; Ps 95:6; Da 6:10; Lk 22:41; Ac 20:36; 21:5).

Hands uplifted (1Ki 8:22; 2Ch 6:12-13; Ezr 9:5; Isa 1:15)—

La 3:41 Let us lift up our hearts and our hands to God in heaven, and say: (+1Ti 2:8)

Standing (Lk 18:11,13).

Power of:

Mk 9:28 After Jesus had gone indoors, his disciples asked him privately, "Why couldn't we drive it out?"

[29]He replied, "This kind can come out only by prayer." (+Jas 5:16-18)

Accompanied by works—

Ne 4:9 But we prayed to our God and posted a guard day and night to meet this threat.

Kept in divine remembrance—

Rev 5:8 And when he had taken it, the four living creatures and the twenty-four elders fell down before the Lamb. Each one had a harp and they were holding golden bowls full of incense, which are the prayers of the saints.

Rev 8:3 Another angel, who had a golden censer, came and stood at the altar. He was given much incense to offer, with the prayers of all the saints, on the golden altar before the throne. [4]The smoke of the incense, together with the prayers of the saints, went up before God from the angel's hand.

Public and Private:

Prayer contest: Proposed by Elijah (1Ki 18:24-39). Public, should edify (1Co 14:14-15). Social (Mt 18:19; Ac 1:13-14; 16:16,25; 20:36; 21:5). Held in private houses (Ac 1:13-14; 12:12), in the temple (Ac 2:46; 3:1). Perseverance in (Ro 12:12; Eph 6:18). Evils averted by (Jer 26:19).

Private commanded (Mt 6:6). Exemplified by Lot (Ge 19:20), Eliezer (Ge 24:12), Jacob (Ge 32:9-12), Gideon (Jdg 6:22,36,39), Hannah (1Sa 1:10), David (2Sa 7:18-29), Hezekiah (2Ki 20:2), Isaiah (2Ki 20:11), Manasseh (2Ch 33:18-19), Ezra (Ezr 9:5-6), Nehemiah (Ne 2:4), Jeremiah (Jer 32:16-25), Daniel (Da 9:3,19), Jonah (Jnh 2:1), Habakkuk (Hab 1:2), Anna (Lk 2:37), Jesus (Mt 14:23; 26:36,39; Mk 1:35; Lk 9:18,29), Paul (Ac 9:11), Peter (Ac 9:40; 10:9), Cornelius (Ac 10:30).

Rebuked:

Of Moses, at the Red Sea (Ex 14:15), when he prayed to see Canaan (Dt 3:23-27). Of Joshua (Jos 7:10).

Submissiveness in:

Exemplified by Jesus (Mt 26:39; Mk 14:36; Lk 22:42), David (2Sa 12:22-23), Job (Job 1:20-21).

Tokens asked for, as assurance of answer:

By Abraham's servant (Ge 24:14,42-44). By Gideon (Jdg 6:36-40).

Answer to:

Promised:—

Ex 33:17 And the LORD said to Moses, "I will do the very thing you have asked, because I am pleased with you and I know you by name."

[18]Then Moses said, "Now show me your glory."

[19]And the LORD said, "I will cause all my goodness to pass in front of you, and I will proclaim my name, the LORD, in your presence. I will have mercy on whom I will have mercy, and I will have compassion on whom I will have compassion. [20]But," he said, "you cannot see my face, for no one may see me and live." (+1Ki 8:22-53)

1Ch 28:9 "And you, my son Solomon, acknowledge the God of your father, and serve him with wholehearted devotion and with a willing mind, for the LORD searches every heart and understands every motive behind the thoughts. If you seek him, he will be found by you; but if you forsake him, he will reject you forever. (+2Ch 6)

Job 8:5 But if you will look to God and plead with the Almighty, [6]if you are pure and upright, even now he will rouse himself on your behalf and restore you to your rightful place.

Job 12:4 "I have become a laughingstock to my friends, though I called upon God and he answered—a mere laughingstock, though righteous and blameless!

Job 22:27 You will pray to him, and he will hear you, and you will fulfill your vows.

Job 33:26 He prays to God and finds favor with him, he sees God's face and shouts for joy; he is restored by God to his righteous state.

Ps 10:17 You hear, O LORD, the desire of the afflicted; you encourage them, and you listen to their cry,

Ps 81:10 I am the LORD your God, who brought you up out of Egypt. Open wide your mouth and I will fill it.

Pr 10:24 What the wicked dreads will overtake him; what the righteous desire will be granted.

Pr 15:8 The LORD detests the sacrifice of the wicked, but the prayer of the upright pleases him.

Pr 15:29 The LORD is far from the wicked but he hears the prayer of the righteous.

Pr 16:1 To man belong the plans of the heart, but from the LORD comes the reply of the tongue.

Isa 58:9 Then you will call, and the LORD will answer; you will cry for help, and he will say: Here am I. "If you do away with the yoke of oppression, with the pointing finger and malicious talk,

Isa 65:24 Before they call I will answer; while they are still speaking I will hear.

Eze 36:37 "This is what the Sovereign LORD says: Once again I will yield to the plea of the house of Israel and do this for them: I will make their people as numerous as sheep,

Mt 6:5 "And when you pray, do not be like the hypocrites, for they love to pray standing in the synagogues and on the street corners to be seen by men. I tell you the truth, they have received their reward in full. ⁶But when you pray, go into your room, close the door and pray to your Father, who is unseen. Then your Father, who sees what is done in secret, will reward you. ⁷And when you pray, do not keep on babbling like pagans, for they think they will be heard because of their many words. ⁸Do not be like them, for your Father knows what you need before you ask him.

Mt 18:19 "Again, I tell you that if two of you on earth agree about anything you ask for, it will be done for you by my Father in heaven. ²⁰For where two or three come together in my name, there am I with them."

Mt 21:22 If you believe, you will receive whatever you ask for in prayer."

Mk 11:24 Therefore I tell you, whatever you ask for in prayer, believe that you have received it, and it will be yours. ²⁵And when you stand praying, if you hold anything against anyone, forgive him, so that your Father in heaven may forgive you your sins." (+Lk 11:9-12)

Lk 11:13 If you then, though you are evil, know how to give good gifts to your children, how much more will your Father in heaven give the Holy Spirit to those who ask him!"

Lk 18:6 And the Lord said, "Listen to what the unjust judge says. ⁷And will not God bring about justice for his chosen ones, who cry out to him day and night? Will he keep putting them off? ⁸I tell you, he will see that they get justice, and quickly. However, when the Son of Man comes, will he find faith on the earth?"

Lk 21:36 Be always on the watch, and pray that you may be able to escape all that is about to happen, and that you may be able to stand before the Son of Man."

Lk 4:10 For it is written: "'He will command his angels concerning you to guard you carefully;

Lk 4:23 Jesus said to them, "Surely you will quote this proverb to me: 'Physician, heal yourself! Do here in your hometown what we have heard that you did in Capernaum.'"

²⁴"I tell you the truth," he continued, "no prophet is accepted in his hometown.

Jn 16:23 In that day you will no longer ask me anything. I tell you the truth, my Father will give you whatever you ask in my name. ²⁴Until now you have not asked for anything in my name. Ask and you will receive, and your joy will be complete.

²⁵"Though I have been speaking figuratively, a time is coming when I will no longer use this kind of language but will tell you plainly about my Father. ²⁶In that day you will ask in my name. I am not saying that I will ask the Father on your behalf. ²⁷No, the Father himself loves you because you have loved me and have believed that I came from God.

Ro 8:26 In the same way, the Spirit helps us in our weakness. We do not know what we ought to pray for, but the Spirit himself intercedes for us with groans that words cannot express.

Ro 10:12 For there is no difference between Jew and Gentile—the same Lord is Lord of all and richly blesses all who call on him, ¹³for, "Everyone who calls on the name of the Lord will be saved."

Eph 2:18 For through him we both have access to the Father by one Spirit.

Eph 3:20 Now to him who is able to do immeasurably more than all we ask or imagine, according to his power that is at work within us,

Heb 4:16 Let us then approach the throne of grace with confidence, so that we may receive mercy and find grace to help us in our time of need.

Heb 10:22 let us draw near to God with a sincere heart in full assurance of faith, having our hearts sprinkled to cleanse us from a guilty conscience and having our bodies washed with pure water. ²³Let us hold unswervingly to the hope we profess, for he who promised is faithful.

Jas 1:5 If any of you lacks wisdom, he should ask God, who gives generously to all without finding fault, and it will be given to him. ⁶But when he asks, he must believe and not doubt, because he who doubts is like a wave of the sea, blown and tossed by the wind. ⁷That man should not think he will receive anything from the Lord;

1Jn 3:22 and receive from him anything we ask, because we obey his commands and do what pleases him.

1Jn 5:14 This is the confidence we have in approaching God: that if we ask anything according to his will, he hears us. ¹⁵And if we know that he hears us—whatever we ask—we know that we have what we asked of him.

Promised to those in adversity—

Ex 6:5 Moreover, I have heard the groaning of the Israelites, whom the Egyptians are enslaving, and I have remembered my covenant. (+Ex 6:6; Ac 7:34)

Ex 22:23 If you do and they cry out to me, I will certainly hear their cry.

Ex 22:27 because his cloak is the only covering he has for his body. What else will he sleep in? When he cries out to me, I will hear, for I am compassionate.

Ps 9:10 Those who know your name will trust in you, for you, LORD, have never forsaken those who seek you.

Ps 9:12 For he who avenges blood remembers; he does not ignore the cry of the afflicted.

Ps 18:3 I call to the LORD, who is worthy of praise, and I am saved from my enemies.

Ps 32:6 Therefore let everyone who is godly pray to you while you may be found; surely when the mighty waters rise, they will not reach him.

Ps 34:15 The eyes of the LORD are on the righteous and his ears are attentive to their cry;

Ps 34:17 The righteous cry out, and the LORD hears them; he delivers them from all their troubles.

Ps 37:4 Delight yourself in the LORD and he will give you the desires of your heart.

5Commit your way to the LORD; trust in him and he will do this:

Ps 38:15 I wait for you, O LORD; you will answer, O Lord my God.

Ps 50:15 and call upon me in the day of trouble; I will deliver you, and you will honor me."

Ps 55:16 But I call to God, and the LORD saves me. 17Evening, morning and noon I cry out in distress, and he hears my voice.

Ps 56:9 Then my enemies will turn back when I call for help. By this I will know that God is for me.

Ps 65:2 O you who hear prayer, to you all men will come.

Ps 65:5 You answer us with awesome deeds of righteousness, O God our Savior, the hope of all the ends of the earth and of the farthest seas, (+Ps 69:32)

Ps 69:33 The LORD hears the needy and does not despise his captive people.

Ps 86:7 In the day of my trouble I will call to you, for you will answer me.

Ps 91:15 He will call upon me, and I will answer him; I will be with him in trouble, I will deliver him and honor him.

Ps 102:17 He will respond to the prayer of the destitute; he will not despise their plea.

18Let this be written for a future generation, that a people not yet created may praise the LORD: 19"The LORD looked down from his sanctuary on high, from heaven he viewed the earth, 20to hear the groans of the prisoners and release those condemned to death."

Isa 19:20 It will be a sign and witness to the LORD Almighty in the land of Egypt. When they cry out to the LORD because of their oppressors, he will send them a savior and defender, and he will rescue them.

Isa 30:19 O people of Zion, who live in Jerusalem, you will weep no more. How gracious he will be when you cry for help! As soon as he hears, he will answer you. (+Isa 31:9)

Joel 2:18 Then the LORD will be jealous for his land and take pity on his people.

19The LORD will reply to them:

"I am sending you grain, new wine and oil, enough to satisfy you fully; never again will I make you an object of scorn to the nations.

Joel 2:32 And everyone who calls on the name of the LORD will be saved; for on Mount Zion and in Jerusalem there will be deliverance, as the LORD has said, among the survivors whom the LORD calls.

Zec 10:1 Ask the LORD for rain in the springtime; it is the LORD who makes the storm clouds. He gives showers of rain to men, and plants of the field to everyone.

Zec 10:6 "I will strengthen the house of Judah and save the house of Joseph. I will restore them because I have compassion on them. They will be as though I had not rejected them, for I am the LORD their God and I will answer them. (+Zec 13:9)

Promised to those who diligently seek God—

2Ch 7:14 if my people, who are called by my name, will humble themselves and pray and seek my face and turn from their wicked ways, then will I hear from heaven and will forgive their sin and will heal their land.

Ps 145:18 The LORD is near to all who call on him, to all who call on him in truth. 19He fulfills the desires of those who fear him; he hears their cry and saves them.

Pr 2:3 and if you call out for insight and cry aloud for understanding,

Pr 2:5 then you will understand the fear of the LORD and find the knowledge of God.

Pr 3:6 in all your ways acknowledge him, and he will make your paths straight.

Isa 55:6 Seek the LORD while he may be found; call on him while he is near.

Jer 29:12 Then you will call upon me and come and pray to me, and I will listen to you. 13You will seek me and find me when you seek me with all your heart.

Jer 33:3 'Call to me and I will answer you and tell you great and unsearchable things you do not know.'

La 3:25 The LORD is good to those whose hope is in him, to the one who seeks him;

Am 5:4 This is what the LORD says to the house of Israel: "Seek me and live; 5do not seek Bethel, do not go to Gilgal, do not journey to Beersheba. For Gilgal will surely go into exile, and Bethel will be reduced to nothing." 6Seek the LORD and live, or he will sweep through the house of Joseph like a fire; it will devour, and Bethel will have no one to quench it.

Zep 2:3 Seek the LORD, all you humble of the land, you who do what he commands. Seek righteousness, seek humility; perhaps you will be sheltered on the day of the LORD's anger.

Zec 13:9 This third I will bring into the fire; I will refine them like silver and test them like gold. They will call on my name and I will answer them; I will say, 'They are my people,' and they will say, 'The LORD is our God.'"

Mt 7:7 "Ask and it will be given to you; seek and you will find; knock, and the door will be opened to you. 8For everyone who asks receives; he who seeks finds; and to him who knocks, the door will be opened.

9"Which of you, if his son asks for bread, will give him a stone? 10Or if he asks for a fish, will give him a snake? 11If you, then, though you are evil, know how to give good gifts to your children, how much more will your Father in heaven give good gifts to those who ask him!

Jn 9:31 We know that God does not listen to sinners. He listens to the godly man who does his will.

Jn 15:7 If you remain in me and my words remain in you, ask whatever you wish, and it will be given you.

Jn 15:16 You did not choose me, but I chose you and appointed you to go and bear fruit—fruit that will last. Then the Father will give you whatever you ask in my name.

Heb 11:6 And without faith it is impossible to please God, because anyone who comes to him must believe that he exists and that he rewards those who earnestly seek him.

Jas 4:8 Come near to God and he will come near to you. Wash your hands, you sinners, and purify your hearts, you double-minded.

Jas 4:10 Humble yourselves before the Lord, and he will lift you up.

Jas 5:16 Therefore confess your sins to each other and pray for each other so that you may be healed. The prayer of a righteous man is powerful and effective.

Promised to the meek (Mk 11:25)

Promised to the penitent—

Dt 4:30 When you are in distress and all these things have happened to you, then in later days you will return to the LORD your God and obey him. [31]For the LORD your God is a merciful God; he will not abandon or destroy you or forget the covenant with your forefathers, which he confirmed to them by oath.

2Ch 7:13 "When I shut up the heavens so that there is no rain, or command locusts to devour the land or send a plague among my people, [14]if my people, who are called by my name, will humble themselves and pray and seek my face and turn from their wicked ways, then will I hear from heaven and will forgive their sin and will heal their land. [15]Now my eyes will be open and my ears attentive to the prayers offered in this place.

Delayed (Ps 22:1-2; 40:1; 80:4; 88:14; Jer 42:2-7; Hab 1:2; Lk 18:7).

Withheld: Of Balaam (Dt 23:5; Jos 24:10). Of Job (Job 30:20, w 42:12). Of the Israelites, when attacked by the Amorites (Dt 1:45). The prayer of Jesus, "Let this cup pass" (Mt 26:39,42,44, w 45-75 & Mt 27).

Exceeds petition (Eph 3:20). Solomon asked wisdom; the answer included wisdom, riches, honor and long life (1Ki 3:7-14; 2Ch 1:7-12). Disciples prayed for Peter, the answer included Peter's deliverance (Ac 12:15, w v.5).

Different from request: Moses asked to see God's face; God revealed his goodness (Ex 33:18-20). Moses asked to be permitted to cross the Jordan; the answer was permission to view the land of promise (Dt 3:23-27). Martha and Mary asked Jesus to come and heal their brother Jesus to come and heal their brother Lazarus; Jesus delayed, but raised Lazarus from the dead (Jn 11). Paul asked that the thorn in the flesh be removed; the answer was a promise of grace to endure it (2Co 12:8-9).

Answer given—

Job 34:28 They caused the cry of the poor to come before him, so that he heard the cry of the needy.

Ps 3:4 To the LORD I cry aloud, and he answers me from his holy hill. *Selah*

Ps 4:1 Answer me when I call to you, O my righteous God. Give me relief from my distress; be merciful to me and hear my prayer.

Ps 6:8 Away from me, all you who do evil, for the LORD has heard my weeping. [9]The LORD has heard my cry for mercy; the LORD accepts my prayer.

Ps 18:6 In my distress I called to the LORD; I cried to my God for help. From his temple he heard my voice; my cry came before him, into his ears.

Ps 21:2 You have granted him the desire of his heart and have not withheld the request of his lips. *Selah*

Ps 21:4 He asked you for life, and you gave it to him— length of days, for ever and ever.

Ps 22:4 In you our fathers put their trust; they trusted and you delivered them. [5]They cried to you and were saved; in you they trusted and were not disappointed.

Ps 22:24 For he has not despised or disdained the suffering of the afflicted one; he has not hidden his face from him but has listened to his cry for help.

Ps 28:6 Praise be to the LORD, for he has heard my cry for mercy.

Ps 30:2 O LORD my God, I called to you for help and you healed me. [3]O LORD, you brought me up from the grave; you spared me from going down into the pit.

Ps 31:22 In my alarm I said, "I am cut off from your

sight!" Yet you heard my cry for mercy when I called to you for help.

Ps 34:4 I sought the LORD, and he answered me; he delivered me from all my fears. [5]Those who look to him are radiant; their faces are never covered with shame. [6]This poor man called, and the LORD heard him; he saved him out of all his troubles.

Ps 40:1 I waited patiently for the LORD; he turned to me and heard my cry.

Ps 66:19 but God has surely listened and heard my voice in prayer. [20]Praise be to God, who has not rejected my prayer or withheld his love from me!

Ps 77:1 I cried out to God for help; I cried out to God to hear me. [2]When I was in distress, I sought the Lord; at night I stretched out untiring hands and my soul refused to be comforted.

Ps 81:7 In your distress you called and I rescued you, I answered you out of a thundercloud; I tested you at the waters of Meribah. *Selah*

Ps 99:6 Moses and Aaron were among his priests, Samuel was among those who called on his name; they called on the LORD and he answered them. [7]He spoke to them from the pillar of cloud; they kept his statutes and the decrees he gave them.

[8]O LORD our God, you answered them; you were to Israel a forgiving God, though you punished their misdeeds.

Ps 106:44 But he took note of their distress when he heard their cry;

Ps 107:6 Then they cried out to the LORD in their trouble, and he delivered them from their distress. (+Ps 107:13)

Ps 116:1 I love the LORD, for he heard my voice; he heard my cry for mercy. [2]Because he turned his ear to me, I will call on him as long as I live. (+Ps 116:3-8)

Ps 118:5 In my anguish I cried to the LORD, and he answered by setting me free.

Ps 118:21 I will give you thanks, for you answered me; you have become my salvation.

Ps 119:26 I recounted my ways and you answered me; teach me your decrees. (+Ps 120:1)

Ps 138:3 When I called, you answered me; you made me bold and stouthearted.

La 3:57 You came near when I called you, and you said, "Do not fear."

[58]O Lord, you took up my case; you redeemed my life.

Hos 12:4 He struggled with the angel and overcame him; he wept and begged for his favor. He found him at Bethel and talked with him there—

Jnh 2:1 From inside the fish Jonah prayed to the LORD his God. [2]He said: "In my distress I called to the LORD, and he answered me. From the depths of the grave I called for help, and you listened to my cry.

Jnh 2:7 "When my life was ebbing away, I remembered you, LORD, and my prayer rose to you, to your holy temple.

Lk 23:42 Then he said, "Jesus, remember me when you come into your kingdom."

[43]Jesus answered him, "I tell you the truth, today you will be with me in paradise."

Ac 4:31 After they prayed, the place where they were meeting was shaken. And they were all filled with the Holy Spirit and spoke the word of God boldly.

2Co 12:8 Three times I pleaded with the Lord to take it away from me. [9]But he said to me, "My grace is sufficient for you, for my power is made perfect in weakness." Therefore I will boast all the more gladly about my weaknesses, so that Christ's power may rest on me.

Jas 5:17 Elijah was a man just like us. He prayed earnestly that it would not rain, and it did not rain on the land for three and a half years. ¹⁸Again he prayed, and the heavens gave rain, and the earth produced its crops.

Instances of answered: Cain (Ge 4:13-15). Abraham, for a son (Ge 15), entreating for Sodom (Ge 18:23-33), for Ishmael (Ge 17:20), for Abimelech (Ge 20:17). Hagar, for deliverance (Ge 16:7-13). Abraham's servant, for guidance (Ge 24:12-52). Rebekah, concerning her pains in pregnancy (Ge 25:22-23).

Jacob, for deliverance from Esau (Ge 32:9-23)—

Ge 32:24 So Jacob was left alone, and a man wrestled with him till daybreak. ²⁵When the man saw that he could not overpower him, he touched the socket of Jacob's hip so that his hip was wrenched as he wrestled with the man. ²⁶Then the man said, "Let me go, for it is daybreak."

But Jacob replied, "I will not let you go unless you bless me."

²⁷The man asked him, "What is your name?"

"Jacob," he answered.

²⁸Then the man said, "Your name will no longer be Jacob, but Israel, because you have struggled with God and with men and have overcome."

²⁹Jacob said, "Please tell me your name."

But he replied, "Why do you ask my name?" Then he blessed him there. (+Ge 32:30-32; 33:1-17)

Moses, for help at the Red Sea (Ex 14:15-16), at the waters of Marah (Ex 15:25), at Horeb (Ex 17:4-6), in the battle with the Amalekites (Ex 17:8-14), concerning the murmuring of the Israelites for flesh (Nu 11:11-35), in behalf of Miriam's leprosy (Nu 12:13-15). Moses, Aaron, and Samuel (Ps 99:6).

Israelites: For deliverance from bondage (Ex 2:23-25; 3:7-10; Ac 7:34), from Pharaoh's army (Ex 14:10-30), from the king of Mesopotamia (Jdg 3:9,15), Sisera (Jdg 4:3,23-24; 1Sa 12:9-11), Ammon (Jdg 10:6-18; 11:1-33), for God's favor under the reproofs of Azariah (2Ch 15:1-15), from Babylonian bondage (Ne 9:27).

Gideon, asking the token of dew (Jdg 6:36-40). Manoah, asking about Samson (Jdg 13:8-9). Samson, asking for strength (Jdg 16:28-30). Hannah, asking for a child (1Sa 1:10-17,19-20). David, asking whether Keilah would be delivered into his hands (1Sa 23:10-12), and Ziklag (1Sa 30:8), whether he should go into Judah after Saul's death (2Sa 2:1), whether he should go against the Philistines (2Sa 5:19-25). David, in adversity (Ps 118:5; 138:3). Solomon, asking wisdom (1Ki 3:1-13; 9:2-3). Elijah, raising the widow's son (1Ki 17:22), asking fire on his sacrifice (1Ki 18:36-38), rain (1Ki 17:1; 18:1,42-45; Jas 5:17). Elisha, leading the Syrian army (2Ki 6:17-20). Jabez, asking for prosperity (1Ch 4:10). Abijah, for victory over Jeroboam (2Ch 13:14-18). Asa, for victory over Zerah (2Ch 14:11-15). The people of Judah (2Ch 15:15). Jehoshaphat, for victory over the Canaanites (2Ch 18:31; 20:6-7). Jehoahaz, for victory over Hazael (2Ki 13:4). Priests and Levites, when blessing the people (2Ch 30:27). Hezekiah and Isaiah, for deliverance from Sennacherib (2Ki 19:14-20; 2Ch 32:20-23), to save Hezekiah's life (2Ki 20:1-7,11; 2Ch 32:24). Manasseh, for deliverance from the king of Babylon (2Ch 33:13,19). Reubenites, for deliverance from the Hagrites (1Ch 5:20). The Jews, returning from the Captivity (Ezr 8:21,23). Ezekiel, to have the baking of his bread of affliction changed (Eze 4:12-15). Daniel, for the interpretation of Nebuchadnezzar's dream (Da 2:19-23), interceding for the people (Da 9:20-23), in a vision (Da 10:12). Zechariah, for a son (Lk 1:13). The leper, for healing (Mt 8:2-3; Mk 1:40-43;

Lk 5:12-13). Centurion, for his servant (Mt 8:5-13; Lk 7:3-10; Jn 4:50-51). Peter, asking that Tabitha be restored (Ac 9:40). The disciples, for Peter (Ac 12:5-17). Paul, to be restored to health (2Co 1:9-11).

Confession in: (Lev 26:40; Ezr 10:1; Lk 15:21; 16:13).

Commanded—

Lev 5:5 "'When anyone is guilty in any of these ways, he must confess in what way he has sinned

Nu 5:6 "Say to the Israelites: 'When a man or woman wrongs another in any way and so is unfaithful to the LORD, that person is guilty ⁷and must confess the sin he has committed. He must make full restitution for his wrong, add one fifth to it and give it all to the person he has wronged.

Jer 3:13 Only acknowledge your guilt—you have rebelled against the LORD your God, you have scattered your favors to foreign gods under every spreading tree, and have not obeyed me,'" declares the LORD.

Jer 3:25 Let us lie down in our shame, and let our disgrace cover us. We have sinned against the LORD our God, both we and our fathers; from our youth till this day we have not obeyed the LORD our God."

A condition of forgiveness—

1Ki 8:47 and if they have a change of heart in the land where they are held captive, and repent and plead with you in the land of their conquerors and say, 'We have sinned, we have done wrong, we have acted wickedly'; (+1Ki 8:49-50)

Pr 28:13 He who conceals his sins does not prosper, but whoever confesses and renounces them finds mercy. (+1Jn 1:9)

Instances of Confession in:—

Jdg 10:10 Then the Israelites cried out to the LORD, "We have sinned against you, forsaking our God and serving the Baals."

Jdg 10:15 But the Israelites said to the LORD, "We have sinned. Do with us whatever you think best, but please rescue us now."

1Sa 12:10 They cried out to the LORD and said, 'We have sinned; we have forsaken the LORD and served the Baals and the Ashtoreths. But now deliver us from the hands of our enemies, and we will serve you.'

Ne 9:2 Those of Israelite descent had separated themselves from all foreigners. They stood in their places and confessed their sins and the wickedness of their fathers. (+Ne 9:3)

Ne 9:33 In all that has happened to us, you have been just; you have acted faithfully, while we did wrong. ³⁴Our kings, our leaders, our priests and our fathers did not follow your law; they did not pay attention to your commands or the warnings you gave them. ³⁵Even while they were in their kingdom, enjoying your great goodness to them in the spacious and fertile land you gave them, they did not serve you or turn from their evil ways.

Ps 31:10 My life is consumed by anguish and my years by groaning; my strength fails because of my affliction, and my bones grow weak.

Ps 32:5 Then I acknowledged my sin to you and did not cover up my iniquity. I said, "I will confess my transgressions to the LORD"—and you forgave the guilt of my sin. *Selah*

Ps 38:4 My guilt has overwhelmed me like a burden too heavy to bear.

Ps 38:18 I confess my iniquity; I am troubled by my sin. (+Ps 40:11)

Ps 40:12 For troubles without number surround me; my sins have overtaken me, and I cannot see. They are more than the hairs of my head, and my heart fails within me. (+Ps 41:4; 51:2)

Ps 51:3 For I know my transgressions, and my sin is always before me. ⁴Against you, you only, have I sinned and done what is evil in your sight, so that you are proved right when you speak and justified when you judge. (+Ps 51:5)

Ps 69:5 You know my folly, O God; my guilt is not hidden from you.

Ps 106:6 We have sinned, even as our fathers did; we have done wrong and acted wickedly.

Ps 119:176 I have strayed like a lost sheep. Seek your servant, for I have not forgotten your commands.

Ps 130:3 If you, O LORD, kept a record of sins, O Lord, who could stand?

Moses for Israel (Ex 32:31-32; 34:9).

Ezra confesses for Judah—

Ezr 9:6 and prayed: "O my God, I am too ashamed and disgraced to lift up my face to you, my God, because our sins are higher than our heads and our guilt has reached to the heavens. (+Ezr 9:7-14)

Ezr 9:15 O LORD, God of Israel, you are righteous! We are left this day as a remnant. Here we are before you in our guilt, though because of it not one of us can stand in your presence."

Nehemiah confesses for Judah (Ne 1:4-5)—

Ne 1:6 let your ear be attentive and your eyes open to hear the prayer your servant is praying before you day and night for your servants, the people of Israel. I confess the sins we Israelites, including myself and my father's house, have committed against you. ⁷We have acted very wickedly toward you. We have not obeyed the commands, decrees and laws you gave your servant Moses. (+Ne 1:8-11)

Isaiah confesses for Judah (Isa 14:20-21)—

Isa 59:12 For our offenses are many in your sight, and our sins testify against us. Our offenses are ever with us, and we acknowledge our iniquities: ¹³rebellion and treachery against the LORD, turning our backs on our God, fomenting oppression and revolt, uttering lies our hearts have conceived. (+Isa 59:14-15; 64:5-7)

Jeremiah confesses for Judah—

Jer 14:7 Although our sins testify against us, O LORD, do something for the sake of your name. For our backsliding is great; we have sinned against you.

Jer 14:20 O LORD, we acknowledge our wickedness and the guilt of our fathers; we have indeed sinned against you. (+La 1:18,20)

La 3:42 "We have sinned and rebelled and you have not forgiven.

Daniel confesses for Judah—

Da 9:5 we have sinned and done wrong. We have been wicked and have rebelled; we have turned away from your commands and laws. ⁶We have not listened to your servants the prophets, who spoke in your name to our kings, our princes and our fathers, and to all the people of the land.

⁷"Lord, you are righteous, but this day we are covered with shame—the men of Judah and people of Jerusalem and all Israel, both near and far, in all the countries where you have scattered us because of our unfaithfulness to you. ⁸O LORD, we and our kings, our princes and our fathers are covered with shame because we have sinned against you. ⁹The Lord our God is merciful and forgiving, even though

we have rebelled against him; ¹⁰we have not obeyed the LORD our God or kept the laws he gave us through his servants the prophets. ¹¹All Israel has transgressed your law and turned away, refusing to obey you. "Therefore the curses and sworn judgments written in the Law of Moses, the servant of God, have been poured out on us, because we have sinned against you.

¹²You have fulfilled the words spoken against us and against our rulers by bringing upon us great disaster. Under the whole heaven nothing has ever been done like what has been done to Jerusalem. ¹³Just as it is written in the Law of Moses, all this disaster has come upon us, yet we have not sought the favor of the LORD our God by turning from our sins and giving attention to your truth. ¹⁴The LORD did not hesitate to bring the disaster upon us, for the LORD our God is righteous in everything he does; yet we have not obeyed him.

¹⁵"Now, O Lord our God, who brought your people out of Egypt with a mighty hand and who made for yourself a name that endures to this day, we have sinned, we have done wrong.

Commanded:

1Ch 16:11 Look to the LORD and his strength; seek his face always.

1Ch 16:35 Cry out, "Save us, O God our Savior; gather us and deliver us from the nations, that we may give thanks to your holy name, that we may glory in your praise."

Ps 105:3 Glory in his holy name; let the hearts of those who seek the LORD rejoice. ⁴Look to the LORD and his strength; seek his face always. (+Isa 55:6; La 3:1; Lk 18:1; Eph 1:18)

Php 4:6 Do not be anxious about anything, but in everything, by prayer and petition, with thanksgiving, present your requests to God.

Col 4:2 Devote yourselves to prayer, being watchful and thankful.

1Th 5:17 pray continually; ¹⁸give thanks in all circumstances, for this is God's will for you in Christ Jesus.

1Ti 2:8 I want men everywhere to lift up holy hands in prayer, without anger or disputing.

Heb 4:16 Let us then approach the throne of grace with confidence, so that we may receive mercy and find grace to help us in our time of need.

Exemplified:

By Eliezer (Ge 24:12). Jacob (Ge 32:9-12). Gideon (Jdg 6:22,36,39). Hannah (1Sa 1:10,13). David (2Sa 7:18-29). Solomon at the dedication of the temple (1Ki 8:23-53; 2Ch 6:14-42). Hezekiah (2Ki 20:2). Isaiah (2Ki 20:11). Manasseh (2Ch 33:18-19). Ezra (Ezr 9:5-15). Nehemiah (Ne 2:4). Jeremiah (Jer 32:16-25). Daniel (Da 9:3-19). Jonah (Jnh 2:1-9). Habakkuk (Hab 1:2). Anna (Lk 2:37). Jesus (Mt 14:23; 26:36,39; Mk 1:35; 6:46; Lk 5:16; 6:12; 9:18, 28-29). Paul (Ac 9:11). Peter (Ac 9:40; 10:9). Cornelius (Ac 10:30).

Persistence in:

Ps 17:1 Hear, O LORD, my righteous plea; listen to my cry. Give ear to my prayer—it does not rise from deceitful lips. ²May my vindication come from you; may your eyes see what is right.

³Though you probe my heart and examine me at night, though you test me, you will find nothing; I have resolved that my mouth will not sin. ⁴As for the deeds of men—by the word of your lips I have kept myself from the ways of the violent. ⁵My steps have held to your paths; my feet have not slipped.

⁶I call on you, O God, for you will answer me; give ear to me and hear my prayer.

Ps 22:1 My God, my God, why have you forsaken me? Why are you so far from saving me, so far from the words of my groaning? ²O my God, I cry out by day, but you do not answer, by night, and am not silent.

Ps 22:19 But you, O LORD, be not far off; O my Strength, come quickly to help me.

Ps 28:1 To you I call, O LORD my Rock; do not turn a deaf ear to me. For if you remain silent, I will be like those who have gone down to the pit. ²Hear my cry for mercy as I call to you for help, as I lift up my hands toward your Most Holy Place.

Ps 35:22 O LORD, you have seen this; be not silent. Do not be far from me, O Lord. ²³Awake, and rise to my defense! Contend for me, my God and Lord.

Ps 55:1 Listen to my prayer, O God, do not ignore my plea; ²hear me and answer me. My thoughts trouble me and I am distraught

Ps 55:16 But I call to God, and the LORD saves me. ¹⁷Evening, morning and noon I cry out in distress, and he hears my voice.

Ps 57:2 I cry out to God Most High, to God, who fulfills [his purpose] for me.

Ps 61:1 Hear my cry, O God; listen to my prayer.

²From the ends of the earth I call to you, I call as my heart grows faint; lead me to the rock that is higher than I.

Ps 70:5 Yet I am poor and needy; come quickly to me, O God. You are my help and my deliverer; O LORD, do not delay.

Ps 86:3 Have mercy on me, O Lord, for I call to you all day long.

Ps 86:6 Hear my prayer, O LORD; listen to my cry for mercy.

Ps 88:1 O LORD, the God who saves me, day and night I cry out before you. ²May my prayer come before you; turn your ear to my cry.

Ps 88:9 my eyes are dim with grief. I call to you, O LORD, every day; I spread out my hands to you.

Ps 88:13 But I cry to you for help, O LORD; in the morning my prayer comes before you.

Ps 102:1 Hear my prayer, O LORD; let my cry for help come to you. ²Do not hide your face from me when I am in distress. Turn your ear to me; when I call, answer me quickly. (+Ps 102:3-28)

Ps 119:145 I call with all my heart; answer me, O LORD, and I will obey your decrees. ¹⁴⁶I call out to you; save me and I will keep your statutes. ¹⁴⁷I rise before dawn and cry for help; I have put my hope in your word.

Ps 130:1 Out of the depths I cry to you, O LORD; ²O Lord, hear my voice. Let your ears be attentive to my cry for mercy.

Ps 141:1 O LORD, I call to you; come quickly to me. Hear my voice when I call to you. ²May my prayer be set before you like incense; may the lifting up of my hands be like the evening sacrifice.

Ps 142:1 I cry aloud to the LORD; I lift up my voice to the LORD for mercy. ²I pour out my complaint before him; before him I tell my trouble.

Isa 62:7 and give him no rest till he establishes Jerusalem and makes her the praise of the earth. (+Hos 12:4)

Lk 11:5 Then he said to them, "Suppose one of you has a friend, and he goes to him at midnight and says, 'Friend, lend me three loaves of bread, ⁶because a friend of mine on a journey has come to me, and I have nothing to set before him.'

⁷"Then the one inside answers, 'Don't bother me. The door is already locked, and my children are with me in bed. I can't get up and give you anything.' ⁸I tell you, though he will not get up and give him the bread because he is his friend, yet because of the man's boldness he will get up and give him as much as he needs.

Lk 18:1 Then Jesus told his disciples a parable to show them that they should always pray and not give up. ²He said: "In a certain town there was a judge who neither feared God nor cared about men. ³And there was a widow in that town who kept coming to him with the plea, 'Grant me justice against my adversary.'

⁴"For some time he refused. But finally he said to himself, 'Even though I don't fear God or care about men, ⁵yet because this widow keeps bothering me, I will see that she gets justice, so that she won't eventually wear me out with her coming!'"

⁶And the Lord said, "Listen to what the unjust judge says. ⁷And will not God bring about justice for his chosen ones, who cry out to him day and night? Will he keep putting them off?

Instances of persistence in: Abraham—

Ge 18:23 Then Abraham approached him and said: "Will you sweep away the righteous with the wicked? ²⁴What if there are fifty righteous people in the city? Will you really sweep it away and not spare the place for the sake of the fifty righteous people in it? ²⁵Far be it from you to do such a thing—to kill the righteous with the wicked, treating the righteous and the wicked alike. Far be it from you! Will not the Judge of all the earth do right?"

²⁶The LORD said, "If I find fifty righteous people in the city of Sodom, I will spare the whole place for their sake."

²⁷Then Abraham spoke up again: "Now that I have been so bold as to speak to the Lord, though I am nothing but dust and ashes, ²⁸what if the number of the righteous is five less than fifty? Will you destroy the whole city because of five people?"

"If I find forty-five there," he said, "I will not destroy it."

²⁹Once again he spoke to him, "What if only forty are found there?"

He said, "For the sake of forty, I will not do it."

³⁰Then he said, "May the Lord not be angry, but let me speak. What if only thirty can be found there?"

He answered, "I will not do it if I find thirty there."

³¹Abraham said, "Now that I have been so bold as to speak to the Lord, what if only twenty can be found there?"

He said, "For the sake of twenty, I will not destroy it."

³²Then he said, "May the Lord not be angry, but let me speak just once more. What if only ten can be found there?"

He answered, "For the sake of ten, I will not destroy it."

Jacob—

Ge 32:24 So Jacob was left alone, and a man wrestled with him till daybreak. ²⁵When the man saw that he could not overpower him, he touched the socket of Jacob's hip so that his hip was wrenched as he wrestled with the man. ²⁶Then the man said, "Let me go, for it is daybreak." But Jacob replied, "I will not let you go unless you bless me."

²⁷The man asked him, "What is your name?"

"Jacob," he answered.

²⁸Then the man said, "Your name will no longer be Jacob, but Israel, because you have struggled with God and with men and have overcome."

²⁹Jacob said, "Please tell me your name."

But he replied, "Why do you ask my name?" Then he blessed him there. (+Ge 32:30)

Moses—

Ex 32:32 But now, please forgive their sin—but if not, then blot me out of the book you have written." (+Ex 33:12-16; 34:9; Dt 9:18)

Dt 9:25 I lay prostrate before the LORD those forty days and forty nights because the LORD had said he would destroy you.

Gideon—

Jdg 6:36 Gideon said to God, "If you will save Israel by my hand as you have promised— ³⁷look, I will place a wool fleece on the threshing floor. If there is dew only on the fleece and all the ground is dry, then I will know that you will save Israel by my hand, as you said." ³⁸And that is what happened. Gideon rose early the next day; he squeezed the fleece and wrung out the dew—a bowlful of water.

³⁹Then Gideon said to God, "Do not be angry with me. Let me make just one more request. Allow me one more test with the fleece. This time make the fleece dry and the ground covered with dew." ⁴⁰That night God did so. Only the fleece was dry; all the ground was covered with dew.

Samson—

Jdg 16:28 Then Samson prayed to the LORD, "O Sovereign LORD, remember me. O God, please strengthen me just once more, and let me with one blow get revenge on the Philistines for my two eyes."

Hannah—

1Sa 1:10 In bitterness of soul Hannah wept much and prayed to the LORD. ¹¹And she made a vow, saying, "O LORD Almighty, if you will only look upon your servant's misery and remember me, and not forget your servant but give her a son, then I will give him to the LORD for all the days of his life, and no razor will ever be used on his head."

Elijah—

1Ki 18:24 Then you call on the name of your god, and I will call on the name of the LORD. The god who answers by fire—he is God."

Then all the people said, "What you say is good."

²⁵Elijah said to the prophets of Baal, "Choose one of the bulls and prepare it first, since there are so many of you. Call on the name of your god, but do not light the fire." ²⁶So they took the bull given them and prepared it.

Then they called on the name of Baal from morning till noon. "O Baal, answer us!" they shouted. But there was no response; no one answered. And they danced around the altar they had made.

²⁷At noon Elijah began to taunt them. "Shout louder!" he said. "Surely he is a god! Perhaps he is deep in thought, or busy, or traveling. Maybe he is sleeping and must be awakened." ²⁸So they shouted louder and slashed themselves with swords and spears, as was their custom, until their blood flowed. ²⁹Midday passed, and they continued their frantic prophesying until the time for the evening sacrifice. But there was no response, no one answered, no one paid attention.

³⁰Then Elijah said to all the people, "Come here to me." They came to him, and he repaired the altar of the LORD, which was in ruins. (+1Ki 18:31-44; Jas 5:17-18)

Hezekiah (2Ki 19:15-19)—

Isa 38:2 Hezekiah turned his face to the wall and prayed to the LORD, ³"Remember, O LORD, how I have walked before you faithfully and with wholehearted devotion and

have done what is good in your eyes." And Hezekiah wept bitterly.

Asa (2Ch 14:11).

Ezra—

Ezr 9:5 Then, at the evening sacrifice, I rose from my self-abasement, with my tunic and cloak torn, and fell on my knees with my hands spread out to the LORD my God

Nehemiah—

Ne 1:4 When I heard these things, I sat down and wept. For some days I mourned and fasted and prayed before the God of heaven. ⁵Then I said: "O LORD, God of heaven, the great and awesome God, who keeps his covenant of love with those who love him and obey his commands, ⁶let your ear be attentive and your eyes open to hear the prayer your servant is praying before you day and night for your servants, the people of Israel. I confess the sins we Israelites, including myself and my father's house, have committed against you. (+Ne 1:7-11; 9:32)

Isaiah—

Isa 64:12 After all this, O LORD, will you hold yourself back? Will you keep silent and punish us beyond measure?

Daniel—

Da 9:3 So I turned to the Lord God and pleaded with him in prayer and petition, in fasting, and in sackcloth and ashes.

Da 9:17 "Now, our God, hear the prayers and petitions of your servant. For your sake, O Lord, look with favor on your desolate sanctuary. ¹⁸Give ear, O God, and hear; open your eyes and see the desolation of the city that bears your Name. We do not make requests of you because we are righteous, but because of your great mercy. ¹⁹O Lord, listen! O Lord, forgive! O Lord, hear and act! For your sake, O my God, do not delay, because your city and your people bear your Name."

Mariners—

Jnh 1:14 Then they cried to the LORD, "O LORD, please do not let us die for taking this man's life. Do not hold us accountable for killing an innocent man, for you, O LORD, have done as you pleased."

Habakkuk—

Hab 1:2 How long, O LORD, must I call for help, but you do not listen? Or cry out to you, "Violence!" but you do not save?

Two blind men of Jericho (Mt 20:30-31; Mk 10:48; Lk 18:39).

The Syrian Phoenician woman—

Mt 15:22 A Canaanite woman from that vicinity came to him, crying out, "Lord, Son of David, have mercy on me! My daughter is suffering terribly from demon-possession."

²³Jesus did not answer a word. So his disciples came to him and urged him, "Send her away, for she keeps crying out after us."

²⁴He answered, "I was sent only to the lost sheep of Israel."

²⁵The woman came and knelt before him. "Lord, help me!" she said.

²⁶He replied, "It is not right to take the children's bread and toss it to their dogs."

²⁷"Yes, Lord," she said, "but even the dogs eat the crumbs that fall from their masters' table."

²⁸Then Jesus answered, "Woman, you have great faith! Your request is granted." And her daughter was healed from that very hour. (+Mk 7:25-30)

The centurion (Mt 8:5)—

Lk 7:3 The centurion heard of Jesus and sent some elders of the Jews to him, asking him to come and heal his servant. (+Lk 7:4)

Jesus (Mt 26:39,42; Mk 14:36,39; Lk 22:42-43)—

Lk 22:44 And being in anguish, he prayed more earnestly, and his sweat was like drops of blood falling to the ground.

Heb 5:7 During the days of Jesus' life on earth, he offered up prayers and petitions with loud cries and tears to the one who could save him from death, and he was heard because of his reverent submission.

Paul—

2Co 12:8 Three times I pleaded with the Lord to take it away from me.

Believers—

Ro 8:26 In the same way, the Spirit helps us in our weakness. We do not know what we ought to pray for, but the Spirit himself intercedes for us with groans that words cannot express.

Eph 6:18 And pray in the Spirit on all occasions with all kinds of prayers and requests. With this in mind, be alert and always keep on praying for all the saints.

Imprecatory:

Asking for vengeance against enemies (Nu 16:15; 22:6-11; 23:7-8; 24:9-10; Dt 11:29-30; 27:11-13; 33:11; Jos 8:33-34; Jdg 16:28; 2Sa 16:10-12; Ne 4:4-5; 5:13; Job 3:1-10; 27:7; Ps 5:10; 6:10; 9:20; 10:2,15; 25:3; 28:4; 31:17-18; 35:4,8,26; 40:14-15; 54:5; 55:9,15; 56:7; 58:7; 59:5,11,15; 68:1-2; 69:23-24,27-28; 70:2-3; 71:13; 79:10, 12; 83:13-17; 94:2; 109:7,9-20,28-29; 119:78,84; 129:5; 140:9-10; 143:12; 144:6; Jer 11:20; 12:3; 15:15; 17:18; 18:21-23; 20:12; La 1:22; 3:64-66; Gal 1:8-9; 2Ti 4:14-15). *See Imprecation.*

In Adversity:

By Jacob (Ge 43:14). Moses (Ex 32:32). The Israelites (Nu 20:16; Dt 26:7; Jdg 3:9). David (2Sa 22:7). Hezekiah (2Ki 19:16,19). Jehoshaphat (2Ch 20:4-13). Manasseh (2Ch 33:12-13). The Psalmist (Ps 5:1-12; 7:1-2,6-7; 13:1-4; 22:1-21; 25:2,16-19,22; 27:11-12; 28:1; 31:1-4,9,14-18; 35:1-28; 38:1-22; 43:1-5; 44:4,23-26; 54:1-3; 55:1-17; 56:1-13; 57:1-2; 59:1-17; 64:1-2; 69:1-36; 70:1-5; 71:1-24; 74:1-23; 79:1-13; 94:1-23; 102; 108:6,12; 109:1-2,21, 26-28; 120:2; 140:1-13; 142:1-2,5-7; 143:1-12). Jeremiah (Jer 15:15). Jonah (Jnh 2:1-9). Stephen (Ac 7:59-60). Paul and Silas (Ac 16:25).

In Behalf of the Nations: *See Nation, Sin of.*

Intercessory:

(Ge 20:7; Jer 27:18; 29:7; Mt 5:44; Eph 6:18-19; 1Ti 2:1; Heb 13:20-21; Jas 5:14-16)

Priestly (Ex 28:12,29-30,38; Lev 10:17). For spiritual blessing (Nu 6:23-26; 1Sa 12:23; Job 1:5; 42:8-10). To avert judgments (Ge 20:7; Ex 32:9-14; Nu 14:11-21; 16:45-50; Dt 9:18-20,25-29; Isa 65:8). For deliverance from enemies (1Sa 7:5-9; Isa 37:4). For healing disease (Jas 5:14-16).

For the unrepentant, unavailing (Jer 7:16; 11:14; 14:11). Of Moses for Israel (Ex 32:11-14,31-32; 34:9; Nu 14:19; 21:7; Dt 9:18,20,24-29). Of Joshua for Israel (Jos 7:6-7). Of Boaz for Ruth (Ru 2:12). Of Eli for Hannah (1Sa 1:17). Of Samuel for Israel (1Sa 7:9; 12:23). Of David, for Israel (2Sa 24:17; 1Ch 29:18), for Solomon (1Ch 29:19). Of Solomon (1Ki 8:31-53; 2Ch 6:22-42). Of Hezekiah for transgressors (2Ch 30:18-19). Of Job for his three friends (Job 42:8-10). Of the Psalmist for the righteous (Ps 7:9; 28:9; 36:10; 80:14-15). Of Daniel for Israel

(Da 9:3-19). Of Jesus for his murderers (Lk 23:34). Of Stephen for his murderers (Ac 7:60). Of Peter and John for Samaritan believers (Ac 8:15). Of the recipients of bounty for Corinthian donors (2Co 9:14).

Of Paul, for unbelieving Jews (Ro 10:1), for Roman Christians (Ro 1:9), for Ephesian Christians (Eph 1:15-19; 3:14-19), for Philippian Christians (Php 1:3-5,9), for Colossian Christians (Col 1:3,9), for Thessalonian Christians (1Th 1:2; 3:10,12-13; 5:23; 2Th 1:11-12; 2:16-17; 3:5,16), for Onesiphorus (2Ti 1:16,18), for Philemon (Phm 4). Of Philemon for Paul (Phm 22).

See Intercession; Jesus the Christ, Mediation of; Mediation.

Requested (Nu 21:7; Ro 15:30-32; 2Co 1:11; Eph 6:19; Col 4:3; 1Th 5:25; 2Th 3:1; Heb 13:18). *See Intercession, Solicited.*

Of Jesus:

Mt 6:9 "This, then, is how you should pray: " 'Our Father in heaven, hallowed be your name, ¹⁰your kingdom come, your will be done on earth as it is in heaven. ¹¹Give us today our daily bread. ¹²Forgive us our debts, as we also have forgiven our debtors. ¹³And lead us not into temptation, but deliver us from the evil one.' (+Mt 11:25-26; Lk 3:21; Lk 11:1-4; Jn 12:27-28)

Before day (Mk 1:35). In secret (Mt 14:23; Mk 1:35; 6:46; Lk 5:16; 6:12; 9:18,28-29). In a mountain (Mt 14:23; Mk 6:46; Lk 6:12; 9:28). In the wilderness (Lk 5:16). Thanksgiving before eating (Mt 14:19; 15:36; 26:26-27; Mk 6:41; 8:6; 1Co 11:24). In distress (Jn 12:27; Heb 5:7). In blessing children (Mt 19:13,15; Mk 10:16). At the grave of Lazarus (Jn 11:41-42). For Peter (Lk 22:31-32). For believers (Jn 17:1-26). For the Comforter, the Holy Spirit (Jn 14:16). In Gethsemane (Mt 26:36-44; Mk 14:32-35; Lk 22:41-44; Heb 5:7). On the cross (Mt 27:46; Lk 23:34,46). Present ministry, at the right hand of the Father (Heb 7:25), Of his apostles (Ac 1:24-25).

See Jesus the Christ, Prayers of.

Of the Wicked, Not Heard:

(Dt 1:45; 2Sa 22:42; Job 35:12-13; Ps 18:41; 66:18; Pr 1:24-28; 15:8,29; 21:13,27; 28:9; Isa 1:15; 45:19; 59:2; Jer 11:11; 14:12; 15:1; 18:17; La 3:8,44; Eze 8:18; 20:8,31; Hos 5:6; Mic 3:4; Zec 7:12-13; Mal 2:11-13; Jn 9:31; Jas 1:6-7; 4:3). *See Wicked, Prayers of.*

To idols (1Ki 18:26-29). *See Idolatry.*

Penitential:

Of David (Ps 51:1-17), the tax collector (Lk 18:13). *See above, Confession in; See Sin, Confession of.*

Pleas Offered in:

Ex 33:13 If you are pleased with me, teach me your ways so I may know you and continue to find favor with you. Remember that this nation is your people."

Nu 14:13 Moses said to the LORD, "Then the Egyptians will hear about it! By your power you brought these people up from among them. ¹⁴And they will tell the inhabitants of this land about it. They have already heard that you, O LORD, are with these people and that you, O LORD, have been seen face to face, that your cloud stays over them, and that you go before them in a pillar of cloud by day and a pillar of fire by night. ¹⁵If you put these people to death all at one time, the nations who have heard this report about you will say, ¹⁶'The LORD was not able to bring these people into the land he promised them on oath; so he slaughtered them in the desert.'

¹⁷"Now may the Lord's strength be displayed, just as you have declared: ¹⁸'The LORD is slow to anger, abounding in

love and forgiving sin and rebellion. Yet he does not leave the guilty unpunished; he punishes the children for the sin of the fathers to the third and fourth generation.' (+Nu 14:19)

Nu 16:22 But Moses and Aaron fell facedown and cried out, "O God, God of the spirits of all mankind, will you be angry with the entire assembly when only one man sins?"

Dt 3:24 "O Sovereign LORD, you have begun to show to your servant your greatness and your strong hand. For what god is there in heaven or on earth who can do the deeds and mighty works you do? ²⁵Let me go over and see the good land beyond the Jordan—that fine hill country and Lebanon."

Dt 9:26 I prayed to the LORD and said, "O Sovereign LORD, do not destroy your people, your own inheritance that you redeemed by your great power and brought out of Egypt with a mighty hand. ²⁷Remember your servants Abraham, Isaac and Jacob. Overlook the stubbornness of this people, their wickedness and their sin. ²⁸Otherwise, the country from which you brought us will say, 'Because the LORD was not able to take them into the land he had promised them, and because he hated them, he brought them out to put them to death in the desert.' ²⁹But they are your people, your inheritance that you brought out by your great power and your outstretched arm." (+Jos 7:7)

Jos 7:8 O Lord, what can I say, now that Israel has been routed by its enemies? ⁹The Canaanites and the other people of the country will hear about this and they will surround us and wipe out our name from the earth. What then will you do for your own great name?"

2Sa 7:25 "And now, LORD God, keep forever the promise you have made concerning your servant and his house. Do as you promised, ²⁶so that your name will be great forever. Then men will say, 'The LORD Almighty is God over Israel!' And the house of your servant David will be established before you.

²⁷"O LORD Almighty, God of Israel, you have revealed this to your servant, saying, 'I will build a house for you.' So your servant has found courage to offer you this prayer. ²⁸O Sovereign LORD, you are God! Your words are trustworthy, and you have promised these good things to your servant. ²⁹Now be pleased to bless the house of your servant, that it may continue forever in your sight; for you, O Sovereign LORD, have spoken, and with your blessing the house of your servant will be blessed forever."

2Ki 19:15 And Hezekiah prayed to the LORD: "O LORD, God of Israel, enthroned between the cherubim, you alone are God over all the kingdoms of the earth. You have made heaven and earth. ¹⁶Give ear, O LORD, and hear; open your eyes, O LORD, and see; listen to the words Sennacherib has sent to insult the living God.

¹⁷"It is true, O LORD, that the Assyrian kings have laid waste these nations and their lands. ¹⁸They have thrown their gods into the fire and destroyed them, for they were not gods but only wood and stone, fashioned by men's hands. ¹⁹Now, O LORD our God, deliver us from his hand, so that all kingdoms on earth may know that you alone, O LORD, are God."

2Ch 14:11 Then Asa called to the LORD his God and said, "LORD, there is no one like you to help the powerless against the mighty. Help us, O LORD our God, for we rely on you, and in your name we have come against this vast army. O LORD, you are our God; do not let man prevail against you."

Ne 9:32 "Now therefore, O our God, the great, mighty and awesome God, who keeps his covenant of love, do not let

all this hardship seem trifling in your eyes—the hardship that has come upon us, upon our kings and leaders, upon our priests and prophets, upon our fathers and all your people, from the days of the kings of Assyria until today.

Ps 9:19 Arise, O LORD, let not man triumph; let the nations be judged in your presence. ²⁰Strike them with terror, O LORD; let the nations know they are but men. *Selah*

Ps 38:16 For I said, "Do not let them gloat or exalt themselves over me when my foot slips."

Ps 71:18 Even when I am old and gray, do not forsake me, O God, till I declare your power to the next generation, your might to all who are to come.

Ps 74:10 How long will the enemy mock you, O God? Will the foe revile your name forever? ¹¹Why do you hold back your hand, your right hand? Take it from the folds of your garment and destroy them!

Ps 74:18 Remember how the enemy has mocked you, O LORD, how foolish people have reviled your name.

Ps 74:20 Have regard for your covenant, because haunts of violence fill the dark places of the land. ²¹Do not let the oppressed retreat in disgrace; may the poor and needy praise your name.

²²Rise up, O God, and defend your cause; remember how fools mock you all day long. ²³Do not ignore the clamor of your adversaries, the uproar of your enemies, which rises continually.

Ps 79:10 Why should the nations say, "Where is their God?" Before our eyes, make known among the nations that you avenge the outpoured blood of your servants. ¹¹May the groans of the prisoners come before you; by the strength of your arm preserve those condemned to die.

¹²Pay back into the laps of our neighbors seven times the reproach they have hurled at you, O Lord.

Ps 83:1 O God, do not keep silent; be not quiet, O God, be not still. ²See how your enemies are astir, how your foes rear their heads.

Ps 83:18 Let them know that you, whose name is the LORD—that you alone are the Most High over all the earth.

Ps 119:42 then I will answer the one who taunts me, for I trust in your word.

Ps 119:73 Your hands made me and formed me; give me understanding to learn your commands.

Ps 119:146 I call out to you; save me and I will keep your statutes.

Ps 119:149 Hear my voice in accordance with your love; preserve my life, O LORD, according to your laws.

Ps 119:153 Look upon my suffering and deliver me, for I have not forgotten your law.

Ps 143:11 For your name's sake, O LORD, preserve my life; in your righteousness, bring me out of trouble. ¹²In your unfailing love, silence my enemies; destroy all my foes, for I am your servant. (+Isa 37:15-20)

Isa 63:17 Why, O LORD, do you make us wander from your ways and harden our hearts so we do not revere you? Return for the sake of your servants, the tribes that are your inheritance. ¹⁸For a little while your people possessed your holy place, but now our enemies have trampled down your sanctuary. ¹⁹We are yours from of old; but you have not ruled over them, they have not been called by your name.

La 3:56 You heard my plea: "Do not close your ears to my cry for relief." ⁵⁷You came near when I called you, and you said, "Do not fear."

⁵⁸O Lord, you took up my case; you redeemed my life. ⁵⁹You have seen, O LORD, the wrong done to me. Uphold

my cause! **⁶⁰**You have seen the depth of their vengeance, all their plots against me.

⁶¹O LORD, you have heard their insults, all their plots against me— **⁶²**what my enemies whisper and mutter against me all day long. **⁶³**Look at them! Sitting or standing, they mock me in their songs.

Joel 2:17 Let the priests, who minister before the LORD, weep between the temple porch and the altar. Let them say, "Spare your people, O LORD. Do not make your inheritance an object of scorn, a byword among the nations. Why should they say among the peoples, 'Where is their God?'"

Pleas Based on:

God's mercy—

Ps 69:13 But I pray to you, O LORD, in the time of your favor; in your great love, O God, answer me with your sure salvation.

Ps 69:16 Answer me, O LORD, out of the goodness of your love; in your great mercy turn to me.

Ps 109:21 But you, O Sovereign LORD, deal well with me for your name's sake; out of the goodness of your love, deliver me.

Ps 109:26 Help me, O LORD my God; save me in accordance with your love. **²⁷**Let them know that it is your hand, that you, O LORD, have done it.

Ps 115:1 Not to us, O LORD, not to us but to your name be the glory, because of your love and faithfulness. (+Ps 119:124)

God's providence—

Ps 4:1 Answer me when I call to you, O my righteous God. Give me relief from my distress; be merciful to me and hear my prayer.

Ps 27:8 My heart says of you, "Seek his face!" Your face, LORD, I will seek.

God's promises—

Ge 32:9 Then Jacob prayed, "O God of my father Abraham, God of my father Isaac, O LORD, who said to me, 'Go back to your country and your relatives, and I will make you prosper,' **¹⁰**I am unworthy of all the kindness and faithfulness you have shown your servant. I had only my staff when I crossed this Jordan, but now I have become two groups. **¹¹**Save me, I pray, from the hand of my brother Esau, for I am afraid he will come and attack me, and also the mothers with their children. **¹²**But you have said, 'I will surely make you prosper and will make your descendants like the sand of the sea, which cannot be counted.'"

Ex 32:13 Remember your servants Abraham, Isaac and Israel, to whom you swore by your own self: 'I will make your descendants as numerous as the stars in the sky and I will give your descendants all this land I promised them, and it will be their inheritance forever.'"

1Ki 8:25 "Now LORD, God of Israel, keep for your servant David my father the promises you made to him when you said, 'You shall never fail to have a man to sit before me on the throne of Israel, if only your sons are careful in all they do to walk before me as you have done.' **²⁶**And now, O God of Israel, let your word that you promised your servant David my father come true.

1Ki 8:59 And may these words of mine, which I have prayed before the LORD, be near to the LORD our God day and night, that he may uphold the cause of his servant and the cause of his people Israel according to each day's need, **⁶⁰**so that all the peoples of the earth may know that the LORD is God and that there is no other.

Ne 1:8 "Remember the instruction you gave your servant

Moses, saying, 'If you are unfaithful, I will scatter you among the nations, **⁹**but if you return to me and obey my commands, then even if your exiled people are at the farthest horizon, I will gather them from there and bring them to the place I have chosen as a dwelling for my Name.'

Ps 89:49 O Lord, where is your former great love, which in your faithfulness you swore to David? **⁵⁰**Remember, Lord, how your servant has been mocked, how I bear in my heart the taunts of all the nations, **⁵¹**the taunts with which your enemies have mocked, O LORD, with which they have mocked every step of your anointed one.

Ps 119:43 Do not snatch the word of truth from my mouth, for I have put my hope in your laws.

Ps 119:49 Remember your word to your servant, for you have given me hope.

Ps 119:116 Sustain me according to your promise, and I will live; do not let my hopes be dashed.

Jer 14:21 For the sake of your name do not despise us; do not dishonor your glorious throne. Remember your covenant with us and do not break it.

Personal consecration—

Ps 119:94 Save me, for I am yours; I have sought out your precepts.

Personal righteousness—

Ps 86:1 Hear, O LORD, and answer me, for I am poor and needy. **²**Guard my life, for I am devoted to you. You are my God; save your servant who trusts in you.

Ps 86:4 Bring joy to your servant, for to you, O Lord, I lift up my soul.

⁵You are forgiving and good, O Lord, abounding in love to all who call to you.

Ps 86:17 Give me a sign of your goodness, that my enemies may see it and be put to shame, for you, O LORD, have helped me and comforted me.

Ps 119:38 Fulfill your promise to your servant, so that you may be feared.

Ps 119:145 I call with all my heart; answer me, O LORD, and I will obey your decrees.

Ps 119:173 May your hand be ready to help me, for I have chosen your precepts. **¹⁷⁴**I long for your salvation, O LORD, and your law is my delight. **¹⁷⁵**Let me live that I may praise you, and may your laws sustain me. **¹⁷⁶**I have strayed like a lost sheep. Seek your servant, for I have not forgotten your commands.

Jer 18:20 Should good be repaid with evil? Yet they have dug a pit for me. Remember that I stood before you and spoke in their behalf to turn your wrath away from them.

Thanksgiving, and Before Taking Food:

Jos 9:14 The men of Israel sampled their provisions but did not inquire of the LORD.

1Sa 9:13 As soon as you enter the town, you will find him before he goes up to the high place to eat. The people will not begin eating until he comes, because he must bless the sacrifice; afterward, those who are invited will eat. Go up now; you should find him about this time."

Ro 14:6 He who regards one day as special, does so to the Lord. He who eats meat, eats to the Lord, for he gives thanks to God; and he who abstains, does so to the Lord and gives thanks to God.

1Co 10:30 If I take part in the meal with thankfulness, why am I denounced because of something I thank God for?

³¹So whether you eat or drink or whatever you do, do it all for the glory of God.

1Ti 4:3 They forbid people to marry and order them to abstain from certain foods, which God created to be received with thanksgiving by those who believe and who know the truth. [4]For everything God created is good, and nothing is to be rejected if it is received with thanksgiving, [5]because it is consecrated by the word of God and prayer.

See Praise; Thankfulness.

Exemplified: By Jesus—

Mt 14:19 And he directed the people to sit down on the grass. Taking the five loaves and the two fish and looking up to heaven, he gave thanks and broke the loaves. Then he gave them to the disciples, and the disciples gave them to the people. (+Mt 15:36)

Mt 26:26 While they were eating, Jesus took bread, gave thanks and broke it, and gave it to his disciples, saying, "Take and eat; this is my body."

[27]Then he took the cup, gave thanks and offered it to them, saying, "Drink from it, all of you. (+Mk 6:41)

Mk 8:6 He told the crowd to sit down on the ground. When he had taken the seven loaves and given thanks, he broke them and gave them to his disciples to set before the people, and they did so. [7]They had a few small fish as well; he gave thanks for them also and told the disciples to distribute them. (+Mk 14:22-23; Lk 9:16; 22:19; Jn 6:11, 23; 1Co 11:24)

By Paul—

Ac 27:35 After he said this, he took some bread and gave thanks to God in front of them all. Then he broke it and began to eat.

PRAYERFULNESS

Commanded—

Ro 12:12 Be joyful in hope, patient in affliction, faithful in prayer. (+Col 4:2)

1Th 5:17 pray continually;

Spirit of, from God (Zec 12:10).

Exemplified by:

The psalmist—

Ps 5:1 Give ear to my words, O LORD, consider my sighing. [2]Listen to my cry for help, my King and my God, for to you I pray. [3]In the morning, O LORD, you hear my voice; in the morning I lay my requests before you and wait in expectation.

Ps 42:8 By day the LORD directs his love, at night his song is with me—a prayer to the God of my life.

Ps 109:4 In return for my friendship they accuse me, but I am a man of prayer.

Ps 116:2 Because he turned his ear to me, I will call on him as long as I live.

Daniel—

Da 6:10 Now when Daniel learned that the decree had been published, he went home to his upstairs room where the windows opened toward Jerusalem. Three times a day he got down on his knees and prayed, giving thanks to his God, just as he had done before.

Anna—

Lk 2:37 and then was a widow until she was eighty-four. She never left the temple but worshiped night and day, fasting and praying.

The apostles—

Ac 6:4 and will give our attention to prayer and the ministry of the word."

Cornelius—

Ac 10:2 He and all his family were devout and God-fearing; he gave generously to those in need and prayed to God regularly.

Peter—

Ac 10:9 About noon the following day as they were on their journey and approaching the city, Peter went up on the roof to pray.

Paul—

Ro 1:9 God, whom I serve with my whole heart in preaching the gospel of his Son, is my witness how constantly I remember you

Eph 1:15 For this reason, ever since I heard about your faith in the Lord Jesus and your love for all the saints, [16]I have not stopped giving thanks for you, remembering you in my prayers.

Col 1:9 For this reason, since the day we heard about you, we have not stopped praying for you and asking God to fill you with the knowledge of his will through all spiritual wisdom and understanding.

1Th 3:10 Night and day we pray most earnestly that we may see you again and supply what is lacking in your faith.

2Ti 1:3 I thank God, whom I serve, as my forefathers did, with a clear conscience, as night and day I constantly remember you in my prayers.

Widows—

1Ti 5:5 The widow who is really in need and left all alone puts her hope in God and continues night and day to pray and to ask God for help.

See Prayer; Prayerlessness.

PRAYERLESSNESS

Jos 9:14 The men of Israel sampled their provisions but did not inquire of the LORD.

Job 15:4 But you even undermine piety and hinder devotion to God.

Job 21:14 Yet they say to God, 'Leave us alone! We have no desire to know your ways. [15]Who is the Almighty, that we should serve him? What would we gain by praying to him?'

Ps 14:4 Will evildoers never learn—those who devour my people as men eat bread and who do not call on the LORD? (+Ps 53:4)

Ps 79:6 Pour out your wrath on the nations that do not acknowledge you, on the kingdoms that do not call on your name;

Isa 43:22 "Yet you have not called upon me, O Jacob, you have not wearied yourselves for me, O Israel.

Isa 64:7 No one calls on your name or strives to lay hold of you; for you have hidden your face from us and made us waste away because of our sins.

Jer 10:21 The shepherds are senseless and do not inquire of the LORD; so they do not prosper and all their flock is scattered.

Jer 10:25 Pour out your wrath on the nations that do not acknowledge you, on the peoples who do not call on your name. For they have devoured Jacob; they have devoured him completely and destroyed his homeland.

Da 9:13 Just as it is written in the Law of Moses, all this disaster has come upon us, yet we have not sought the favor of the LORD our God by turning from our sins and giving attention to your truth.

Hos 7:7 All of them are hot as an oven; they devour their rulers. All their kings fall, and none of them calls on me.

Jnh 1:6 The captain went to him and said, "How can you sleep? Get up and call on your god! Maybe he will take notice of us, and we will not perish."

Zep 1:6 those who turn back from following the LORD and neither seek the LORD nor inquire of him.

See Prayer.

PREACHING [5752, 10452, *1877+3364, 2294, 2294+ 2295, 2295, 2859, 3060, 3062, 3281, 3364+3836, 4155*].

NIV+ PREACH, PREACHED, PREACHER, PREACHES

The act of exhorting, prophesying, reproving, teaching. Noah called preacher (2Pe 2:5). Solomon called preacher (Ecc 1:1,12). Sitting while (Mt 5:1; Lk 4:20; 5:3). Moses slow to (Ex 4:10-12).

Appointed and practiced by Jesus as the method of promulgating the Gospel (Mt 4:17; 11:1; Mk 16:15,20; Lk 4:18-19,43).

Attested to by Paul—

Tit 1:3 and at his appointed season he brought his word to light through the preaching entrusted to me by the command of God our Savior,

Grave responsibility of—

2Co 2:14 But thanks be to God, who always leads us in triumphal procession in Christ and through us spreads everywhere the fragrance of the knowledge of him. ¹⁵For we are to God the aroma of Christ among those who are being saved and those who are perishing. (+2Co 2:16-17)

Repentance, the subject, of John the Baptist's (Mt 3:2; Mk 1:4,15; Lk 3:3), of Christ's (Mt 4:17; Mk 1:15), the apostle's (Mk 6:12). The gospel of the kingdom of God, the subject of Christ's (Mk 1:14-15; 2:2; Lk 8:1). Christ crucified and risen, the burden of Paul's (Ac 17:3).

Jesus preaches to the spirits in prison (1Pe 3:19; 4:9, w Eph 4:9).

Preaching Should:

Edify—

1Co 14:1 Follow the way of love and eagerly desire spiritual gifts, especially the gift of prophecy. ²For anyone who speaks in a tongue does not speak to men but to God. Indeed, no one understands him; he utters mysteries with his spirit. ³But everyone who prophesies speaks to men for their strengthening, encouragement and comfort. ⁴He who speaks in a tongue edifies himself, but he who prophesies edifies the church. ⁵I would like every one of you to speak in tongues, but I would rather have you prophesy. He who prophesies is greater than one who speaks in tongues, unless he interprets, so that the church may be edified.

⁶Now, brothers, if I come to you and speak in tongues, what good will I be to you, unless I bring you some revelation or knowledge or prophecy or word of instruction? ⁷Even in the case of lifeless things that make sounds, such as the flute or harp, how will anyone know what tune is being played unless there is a distinction in the notes? ⁸Again, if the trumpet does not sound a clear call, who will get ready for battle? ⁹So it is with you. Unless you speak intelligible words with your tongue, how will anyone know what you are saying? You will just be speaking into the air. ¹⁰Undoubtedly there are all sorts of languages in the world, yet none of them is without meaning. ¹¹If then I do not grasp the meaning of what someone is saying, I am a foreigner to the speaker, and he is a foreigner to me. ¹²So it is with you. Since you are eager to have spiritual gifts, try to excel in gifts that build up the church.

¹³For this reason anyone who speaks in a tongue should pray that he may interpret what he says. ¹⁴For if I pray in a tongue, my spirit prays, but my mind is unfruitful. ¹⁵So what shall I do? I will pray with my spirit, but I will also pray with my mind; I will sing with my spirit, but I will also sing with my mind. ¹⁶If you are praising God with your spirit, how can one who finds himself among those who do not understand say "Amen" to your thanksgiving, since he does not know what you are saying? ¹⁷You may

be giving thanks well enough, but the other man is not edified.

¹⁸I thank God that I speak in tongues more than all of you. ¹⁹But in the church I would rather speak five intelligible words to instruct others than ten thousand words in a tongue.

²⁰Brothers, stop thinking like children. In regard to evil be infants, but in your thinking be adults. (+1Co 14:21-23)

1Co 14:24 But if an unbeliever or someone who does not understand comes in while everybody is prophesying, he will be convinced by all that he is a sinner and will be judged by all, ²⁵and the secrets of his heart will be laid bare. So he will fall down and worship God, exclaiming, "God is really among you!"

Be skillful—

2Ti 2:15 Do your best to present yourself to God as one approved, a workman who does not need to be ashamed and who correctly handles the word of truth. ¹⁶Avoid godless chatter, because those who indulge in it will become more and more ungodly.

Be in power—

1Th 1:5 because our gospel came to you not simply with words, but also with power, with the Holy Spirit and with deep conviction. You know how we lived among you for your sake.

Be with boldness (Ac 13:46)—

2Co 3:12 Therefore, since we have such a hope, we are very bold. ¹³We are not like Moses, who would put a veil over his face to keep the Israelites from gazing at it while the radiance was fading away.

Not be, with mere human strategy (Mt 26) with deceit or flattery—

1Th 2:3 For the appeal we make does not spring from error or impure motives, nor are we trying to trick you. ⁴On the contrary, we speak as men approved by God to be entrusted with the gospel. We are not trying to please men but God, who tests our hearts. ⁵You know we never used flattery, nor did we put on a mask to cover up greed—God is our witness. ⁶We were not looking for praise from men, not from you or anyone else. As apostles of Christ we could have been a burden to you,

Is Effective:

By Azariah (2Ch 15:1-15), Jonah (Jnh 3), Haggai (Hag 1:7-12), Peter (Ac 2:14-41), Philip (Ac 8:5-12,27-38), Paul (Ac 9:20-22; 13:16-43). *See Revivals.*

Impenitence Under:

Asa (2Ch 16:7-10), Ahab (2Ch 18:7-26), the Jews (Ac 13:46). *See Obduracy.*

See Minister; Call, Personal.

PRECEPTS [2976, 5477, 7218]. *See Commandments and Statutes, Of God; Law.*

PRECIOUS STONES In the breastpiece of the high priest the stones were set, probably, in the order of the tribes of the Israelites. The first stone, ruby, was probably the tribal stone for Reuben; topaz for Simeon; beryl for Levi; turquoise for Judah; sapphire for Issachar; emerald for Zebulun; jacinth for Dan; agate for Naphtali; amethyst for Asher; chrysolite for Gad; onyx for Joseph; jasper for Benjamin (Ex 28:9-21; 39:6-14).

Voluntary offerings of, by the Israelites for the breastpiece and ephod (Ex 35:27). Exported, from Sheba (1Ki 10:2,10; 2Ch 9:1,9; Eze 27:22), from Ophir (1Ki 10:11; 2Ch 9:10).

Partial catalog of (Eze 28:13). Seen in the foundation of

the New Jerusalem in John's apocalyptic vision (Rev 21:19-21). In kings' crowns (2Sa 12:30; 1Ch 20:2).

Figurative: (Isa 54:11-12).

See Stones; Agate; Amethyst; Beryl, 1; Carbuncle; Crystal; Diamond; Emerald; Jasper; Ruby; Sapphire; Sardis; Topaz.

PREDESTINATION [4633].

NIV+ DESTINE, PREDESTINED

According to the purpose of grace—

Ex 33:19 And the LORD said, "I will cause all my goodness to pass in front of you, and I will proclaim my name, the LORD, in your presence. I will have mercy on whom I will have mercy, and I will have compassion on whom I will have compassion.

Isa 44:1 "But now listen, O Jacob, my servant, Israel, whom I have chosen. ²This is what the LORD says—he who made you, who formed you in the womb, and who will help you: Do not be afraid, O Jacob, my servant, Jeshurun, whom I have chosen.

Isa 44:7 Who then is like me? Let him proclaim it. Let him declare and lay out before me what has happened since I established my ancient people, and what is yet to come— yes, let him foretell what will come.

Mal 1:2 "I have loved you," says the LORD.

"But you ask, 'How have you loved us?'

"Was not Esau Jacob's brother?" the LORD says. "Yet I have loved Jacob, ³but Esau I have hated, and I have turned his mountains into a wasteland and left his inheritance to the desert jackals."

Ac 13:48 When the Gentiles heard this, they were glad and honored the word of the Lord; and all who were appointed for eternal life believed. (+Ro 8:28-30,33)

Ro 9:11 Yet, before the twins were born or had done anything good or bad—in order that God's purpose in election might stand: ¹²not by works but by him who calls—she was told, "The older will serve the younger." ¹³Just as it is written: "Jacob I loved, but Esau I hated."

¹⁴What then shall we say? Is God unjust? Not at all! ¹⁵For he says to Moses, "I will have mercy on whom I have mercy, and I will have compassion on whom I have compassion."

¹⁶It does not, therefore, depend on man's desire or effort, but on God's mercy. ¹⁷For the Scripture says to Pharaoh: "I raised you up for this very purpose, that I might display my power in you and that my name might be proclaimed in all the earth." ¹⁸Therefore God has mercy on whom he wants to have mercy, and he hardens whom he wants to harden. (+Ro 9:19-22)

Ro 9:23 What if he did this to make the riches of his glory known to the objects of his mercy, whom he prepared in advance for glory— ²⁴even us, whom he also called, not only from the Jews but also from the Gentiles? (+Ro 9:25-26)

Ro 9:27 Isaiah cries out concerning Israel:

"Though the number of the Israelites be like the sand by the sea, only the remnant will be saved. ²⁸For the Lord will carry out his sentence on earth with speed and finality."

²⁹It is just as Isaiah said previously:

"Unless the Lord Almighty had left us descendants, we would have become like Sodom, we would have been like Gomorrah."

Ro 11:5 So too, at the present time there is a remnant chosen by grace.

Ro 11:7 What then? What Israel sought so earnestly it did not obtain, but the elect did. The others were hardened, ⁸as

it is written: "God gave them a spirit of stupor, eyes so that they could not see and ears so that they could not hear, to this very day."

1Co 1:26 Brothers, think of what you were when you were called. Not many of you were wise by human standards; not many were influential; not many were of noble birth. ²⁷But God chose the foolish things of the world to shame the wise; God chose the weak things of the world to shame the strong. ²⁸He chose the lowly things of this world and the despised things—and the things that are not—to nullify the things that are, ²⁹so that no one may boast before him.

Eph 1:4 For he chose us in him before the creation of the world to be holy and blameless in his sight. In love ⁵he predestined us to be adopted as his sons through Jesus Christ, in accordance with his pleasure and will—

Eph 1:9 And he made known to us the mystery of his will according to his good pleasure, which he purposed in Christ, ¹⁰to be put into effect when the times will have reached their fulfillment—to bring all things in heaven and on earth together under one head, even Christ.

¹¹In him we were also chosen, having been predestined according to the plan of him who works out everything in conformity with the purpose of his will,

Eph 3:11 according to his eternal purpose which he accomplished in Christ Jesus our Lord. (+2Th 2:13; 2Ti 1:9; Tit 1:1-2; 1Pe 1:2,20)

Of prosperity to Abraham (Ge 21:12; Ne 9:7-8).

Of Joseph's mission to Egypt (Ge 45:5-7)—

Ps 105:17 and he sent a man before them—Joseph, sold as a slave. ¹⁸They bruised his feet with shackles, his neck was put in irons, ¹⁹till what he foretold came to pass, till the word of the LORD proved him true. ²⁰The king sent and released him, the ruler of peoples set him free. ²¹He made him master of his household, ruler over all he possessed, ²²to instruct his princes as he pleased and teach his elders wisdom.

Of Israel as a nation (Ge 21:12; Dt 4:37)—

Dt 7:7 The LORD did not set his affection on you and choose you because you were more numerous than other peoples, for you were the fewest of all peoples. ⁸But it was because the LORD loved you and kept the oath he swore to your forefathers that he brought you out with a mighty hand and redeemed you from the land of slavery, from the power of Pharaoh king of Egypt.

Dt 10:15 Yet the LORD set his affection on your forefathers and loved them, and he chose you, their descendants, above all the nations, as it is today.

Dt 32:8 When the Most High gave the nations their inheritance, when he divided all mankind, he set up boundaries for the peoples according to the number of the sons of Israel.

1Sa 12:22 For the sake of his great name the LORD will not reject his people, because the LORD was pleased to make you his own.

Ps 33:12 Blessed is the nation whose God is the LORD, the people he chose for his inheritance.

Ps 135:4 For the LORD has chosen Jacob to be his own, Israel to be his treasured possession.

Of Ishmael as a nation—

Ge 21:12 But God said to him, "Do not be so distressed about the boy and your maidservant. Listen to whatever Sarah tells you, because it is through Isaac that your offspring will be reckoned. ¹³I will make the son of the maidservant into a nation also, because he is your offspring." (+Ge 25:12-18)

Of famine in Egypt (Ge 41:30-32).

Of judgment to Pharaoh—

Ex 9:16 But I have raised you up for this very purpose, that I might show you my power and that my name might be proclaimed in all the earth.

Of David as king—

2Ch 6:6 But now I have chosen Jerusalem for my Name to be there, and I have chosen David to rule my people Israel.'

Ps 78:67 Then he rejected the tents of Joseph, he did not choose the tribe of Ephraim; **68**but he chose the tribe of Judah, Mount Zion, which he loved.

Ps 78:70 He chose David his servant and took him from the sheep pens; **71**from tending the sheep he brought him to be the shepherd of his people Jacob, of Israel his inheritance. **72**And David shepherded them with integrity of heart; with skillful hands he led them.

Of Jehu's dynasty (2Ki 10:30; 15:12).

Of the dividing of Solomon's kingdom (1Ki 11:11-12,31-39)—

1Ki 12:15 So the king did not listen to the people, for this turn of events was from the LORD, to fulfill the word the LORD had spoken to Jeroboam son of Nebat through Ahijah the Shilonite.

Of mercy to the widow at Sidon—

Lk 4:25 I assure you that there were many widows in Israel in Elijah's time, when the sky was shut for three and a half years and there was a severe famine throughout the land. **26**Yet Elijah was not sent to any of them, but to a widow in Zarephath in the region of Sidon. **27**And there were many in Israel with leprosy in the time of Elisha the prophet, yet not one of them was cleansed—only Naaman the Syrian."

Of the destruction of the Canaanites—

Jos 11:20 For it was the LORD himself who hardened their hearts to wage war against Israel, so that he might destroy them totally, exterminating them without mercy, as the LORD had commanded Moses.

Of Ben-Hadad—

1Ki 20:42 He said to the king, "This is what the LORD says: 'You have set free a man I had determined should die. Therefore it is your life for his life, your people for his people.'"

Of Ahaziah (2Ch 22:7), of Amaziah and the idolatrous Israelites (2Ch 25:20).

Acknowledged by Job—

Job 23:13 "But he stands alone, and who can oppose him? He does whatever he pleases. **14**He carries out his decree against me, and many such plans he still has in store.

Of agent to execute divine judgments—

2Ki 19:25 "'Have you not heard? Long ago I ordained it. In days of old I planned it; now I have brought it to pass, that you have turned fortified cities into piles of stone. (+2Ch 22:7; Hab 1:12)

Of Jeremiah as prophet—

Jer 1:4 The word of the LORD came to me, saying, **5**"Before I formed you in the womb I knew you, before you were born I set you apart; I appointed you as a prophet to the nations."

Of revelation to a chosen people—

Mt 11:25 At that time Jesus said, "I praise you, Father, Lord of heaven and earth, because you have hidden these things from the wise and learned, and revealed them to little children. **26**Yes, Father, for this was your good pleasure.

Lk 8:10 He said, "The knowledge of the secrets of the kingdom of God has been given to you, but to others I speak in parables, so that, "'though seeing, they may not see; though hearing, they may not understand.'

1Co 2:7 No, we speak of God's secret wisdom, a wisdom that has been hidden and that God destined for our glory before time began.

Of the death of Jesus (Mt 26:24; Mk 14:21)—

Lk 22:22 The Son of Man will go as it has been decreed, but woe to that man who betrays him." (+Lk 24:26-27)

Ac 2:23 This man was handed over to you by God's set purpose and foreknowledge; and you, with the help of wicked men, put him to death by nailing him to the cross.

Ac 3:18 But this is how God fulfilled what he had foretold through all the prophets, saying that his Christ would suffer.

Ac 4:28 They did what your power and will had decided beforehand should happen.

Rev 13:8 All inhabitants of the earth will worship the beast—all whose names have not been written in the book of life belonging to the Lamb that was slain from the creation of the world.

Of Paul to the ministry (Ac 9:15)—

Gal 1:15 But when God, who set me apart from birth and called me by his grace, was pleased (+Gal 1:16; 1Ti 2:7)

Of the times and bounds of nations—

Ac 17:26 From one man he made every nation of men, that they should inhabit the whole earth; and he determined the times set for them and the exact places where they should live.

Of times and seasons—

Ac 1:7 He said to them: "It is not for you to know the times or dates the Father has set by his own authority.

Of the standard of righteousness—

Eph 2:10 For we are God's workmanship, created in Christ Jesus to do good works, which God prepared in advance for us to do.

Of the kingdom prepared for the righteous—

Mt 25:34 "Then the King will say to those on his right, 'Come, you who are blessed by my Father; take your inheritance, the kingdom prepared for you since the creation of the world.

Of salvation and election—

Mt 20:16 "So the last will be first, and the first will be last."

Mt 20:23 Jesus said to them, "You will indeed drink from my cup, but to sit at my right or left is not for me to grant. These places belong to those for whom they have been prepared by my Father."

Mt 24:22 If those days had not been cut short, no one would survive, but for the sake of the elect those days will be shortened.

Mt 24:40 Two men will be in the field; one will be taken and the other left.

Mk 13:20 If the Lord had not cut short those days, no one would survive. But for the sake of the elect, whom he has chosen, he has shortened them.

Mk 13:22 For false Christs and false prophets will appear and perform signs and miracles to deceive the elect—if that were possible.

Lk 10:20 However, do not rejoice that the spirits submit to you, but rejoice that your names are written in heaven." (+Lk 17:34-36)

Lk 18:7 And will not God bring about justice for his

chosen ones, who cry out to him day and night? Will he keep putting them off?

Jn 6:37 All that the Father gives me will come to me, and whoever comes to me I will never drive away.

Jn 6:39 And this is the will of him who sent me, that I shall lose none of all that he has given me, but raise them up at the last day.

Jn 6:44 "No one can come to me unless the Father who sent me draws him, and I will raise him up at the last day. ⁴⁵It is written in the Prophets: 'They will all be taught by God.' Everyone who listens to the Father and learns from him comes to me.

Jn 15:16 You did not choose me, but I chose you and appointed you to go and bear fruit—fruit that will last. Then the Father will give you whatever you ask in my name.

Jn 15:19 If you belonged to the world, it would love you as its own. As it is, you do not belong to the world, but I have chosen you out of the world. That is why the world hates you.

Jn 17:2 For you granted him authority over all people that he might give eternal life to all those you have given him.

Jn 17:6 "I have revealed you to those whom you gave me out of the world. They were yours; you gave them to me and they have obeyed your word.

Jn 17:9 I pray for them. I am not praying for the world, but for those you have given me, for they are yours. (+Ac 2:39,47; 13:48)

Ac 22:14 "Then he said: 'The God of our fathers has chosen you to know his will and to see the Righteous One and to hear words from his mouth.

Ro 1:6 And you also are among those who are called to belong to Jesus Christ.

Ro 8:28 And we know that in all things God works for the good of those who love him, who have been called according to his purpose. ²⁹For those God foreknew he also predestined to be conformed to the likeness of his Son, that he might be the firstborn among many brothers. ³⁰And those he predestined, he also called; those he called, he also justified; those he justified, he also glorified.

Ro 8:33 Who will bring any charge against those whom God has chosen? It is God who justifies. (+Ro 11:5,7-8; 1Co 1:26-29; Eph 1:9-11)

Col 3:12 Therefore, as God's chosen people, holy and dearly loved, clothe yourselves with compassion, kindness, humility, gentleness and patience.

1Th 1:4 For we know, brothers loved by God, that he has chosen you,

1Th 2:12 encouraging, comforting and urging you to live lives worthy of God, who calls you into his kingdom and glory.

2Th 2:13 But we ought always to thank God for you, brothers loved by the Lord, because from the beginning God chose you to be saved through the sanctifying work of the Spirit and through belief in the truth.

2Ti 1:9 who has saved us and called us to a holy life—not because of anything we have done but because of his own purpose and grace. This grace was given us in Christ Jesus before the beginning of time,

Tit 1:1 Paul, a servant of God and an apostle of Jesus Christ for the faith of God's elect and the knowledge of the truth that leads to godliness— ²a faith and knowledge resting on the hope of eternal life, which God, who does not lie, promised before the beginning of time,

Jas 1:18 He chose to give us birth through the word of truth, that we might be a kind of firstfruits of all he created.

1Pe 1:2 who have been chosen according to the foreknowledge of God the Father, through the sanctifying work of the Spirit, for obedience to Jesus Christ and sprinkling by his blood: Grace and peace be yours in abundance.

1Pe 1:20 He was chosen before the creation of the world, but was revealed in these last times for your sake.

2Pe 1:10 Therefore, my brothers, be all the more eager to make your calling and election sure. For if you do these things, you will never fall,

Of the wicked, to the day of evil—

Pr 16:4 The LORD works out everything for his own ends—even the wicked for a day of disaster.

Of the wicked, to condemnation—

Jude 4 For certain men whose condemnation was written about long ago have secretly slipped in among you. They are godless men, who change the grace of our God into a license for immorality and deny Jesus Christ our only Sovereign and Lord.

Of the day of judgment (Ac 17:31).

See Election.

PREJUDICE *See Respect of Persons.*

PREPAREDNESS [*273, 430, 2284, 3670, 3922, 6885, 6913, 7155, 7727, 7756, 8492, *2286, 2936, 2941, 4187, 4472, 4602*].

NIV+ PREPARE, PREPARATION, PREPARATIONS, PREPARED, PREPARES, PREPARING

(Mt 24:44; 25:1-13; Mk 13:32-37; Lk 12:35-48; 19:41-44). *See Faithfulness.*

PRESBYTERY *See Elders.*

PRESCIENCE *See God, Foreknowledge of.*

PRESENTS [*1388, 4950, 5989, 9556; See also GIFTS].

NIV+ PRESENT, PRESENTED, PRESENTING

To Abraham, by Pharaoh (Ge 12:16), by Abimelech (Ge 20:14). To Rebekah (Ge 24:22). To Esau (Ge 32:13-15). To prophets (1Ki 14:3; 2Ki 4:42). To those in adversity (Job 42:10-11).

Betrothal (Ge 24:53). Marriage (Est 2:18). Propitiatory (Ge 32:20; 33:8-11; 1Sa 25:27-35; Pr 21:14). To confirm covenants (Ge 21:28-30; 1Sa 18:3-4). Rewards of service (Da 5:7). Kings to kings (2Sa 8:10; 1Ki 10:10,13; 15:18-19).

To corrupt courts, forbidden (Ex 23:8; Dt 16:19; 27:25; Isa 5:23). *See Bribery; Liberality.*

PRESIDENTS *See Administrators.*

PRESS [2005, 2616, 4315, 7439, 8103, 8104, 8492, *1503, 1592, 2989, 3332*].

NIV+ PRESSED, PRESSES, PRESSING, PRESSURE

Crowd (Mk 2:4; Lk 8:19).

PRESSVAT NIV "wine vat" (Hag 2:16). *See Wine.*

PRESUMPTION [928+2295, 2326, 6753].

NIV+ PRESUME, PRESUMES, PRESUMPTUOUSLY

Dt 29:19 When such a person hears the words of this oath, he invokes a blessing on himself and therefore thinks, "I will be safe, even though I persist in going my own way." This will bring disaster on the watered land as well as the dry. ²⁰The LORD will never be willing to forgive him; his wrath and zeal will burn against that man. All the curses written in this book will fall upon him, and the LORD will blot out his name from under heaven. (+Ps 10:6)

Ps 19:13 Keep your servant also from willful sins; may they not rule over me. Then will I be blameless, innocent of great transgression. (+Ps 73:8-9)

Admonitions against (Pr 25:6-7)—

Lk 14:7 When he noticed how the guests picked the places of honor at the table, he told them this parable: [8]"When someone invites you to a wedding feast, do not take the place of honor, for a person more distinguished than you may have been invited. [9]If so, the host who invited both of you will come and say to you, 'Give this man your seat.' Then, humiliated, you will have to take the least important place. [10]But when you are invited, take the lowest place, so that when your host comes, he will say to you, 'Friend, move up to a better place.' Then you will be honored in the presence of all your fellow guests. [11]For everyone who exalts himself will be humbled, and he who humbles himself will be exalted."

Sins of:

The self-righteous—

Isa 65:5 who say, 'Keep away; don't come near me, for I am too sacred for you!' Such people are smoke in my nostrils, a fire that keeps burning all day.

Lk 18:11 The Pharisee stood up and prayed about himself: 'God, I thank you that I am not like other men—robbers, evildoers, adulterers—or even like this tax collector. [12]I fast twice a week and give a tenth of all I get.'

The selfish rich, in forgetting God—

Lk 12:18 "Then he said, 'This is what I'll do. I will tear down my barns and build bigger ones, and there I will store all my grain and my goods. [19]And I'll say to myself, "You have plenty of good things laid up for many years. Take life easy; eat, drink and be merry."'

[20]"But God said to him, 'You fool! This very night your life will be demanded from you. Then who will get what you have prepared for yourself?'

Temptation to (Dt 6:16)—

Mt 4:5 Then the devil took him to the holy city and had him stand on the highest point of the temple. [6]"If you are the Son of God," he said, "throw yourself down. For it is written:

"'He will command his angels concerning you, and they will lift you up in their hands, so that you will not strike your foot against a stone.'"

[7]Jesus answered him, "It is also written: 'Do not put the Lord your God to the test.'" (+Lk 4:9-11)

In ignoring God—

Isa 10:15 Does the ax raise itself above him who swings it, or the saw boast against him who uses it? As if a rod were to wield him who lifts it up, or a club brandish him who is not wood! (+Isa 29:16; 37:23-25; Ro 9:23-25,20-21)

Jas 4:13 Now listen, you who say, "Today or tomorrow we will go to this or that city, spend a year there, carry on business and make money." [14]Why, you do not even know what will happen tomorrow. What is your life? You are a mist that appears for a little while and then vanishes. [15]Instead, you ought to say, "If it is the Lord's will, we will live and do this or that."

Questioning God's righteousness—

Isa 58:3 'Why have we fasted,' they say, 'and you have not seen it? Why have we humbled ourselves, and you have not noticed?' "Yet on the day of your fasting, you do as you please and exploit all your workers. (+Ro 9:20-21)

Defying God—

Job 15:25 because he shakes his fist at God and vaunts himself against the Almighty, (+Ps 94:7)

Isa 5:18 Woe to those who draw sin along with cords of deceit, and wickedness as with cart ropes, [19]to those who say, "Let God hurry, let him hasten his work so we may see it. Let it approach, let the plan of the Holy One of Israel come, so we may know it."

[20]Woe to those who call evil good and good evil, who put darkness for light and light for darkness, who put bitter for sweet and sweet for bitter.

[21]Woe to those who are wise in their own eyes and clever in their own sight.

[22]Woe to those who are heroes at drinking wine and champions at mixing drinks, [23]who acquit the guilty for a bribe, but deny justice to the innocent. [24]Therefore, as tongues of fire lick up straw and as dry grass sinks down in the flames, so their roots will decay and their flowers blow away like dust; for they have rejected the law of the LORD Almighty and spurned the word of the Holy One of Israel. [25]Therefore the LORD's anger burns against his people; his hand is raised and he strikes them down. The mountains shake, and the dead bodies are like refuse in the streets. Yet for all this, his anger is not turned away, his hand is still upraised.

Isa 14:13 You said in your heart, "I will ascend to heaven; I will raise my throne above the stars of God; I will sit enthroned on the mount of assembly, on the utmost heights of the sacred mountain. [14]I will ascend above the tops of the clouds; I will make myself like the Most High."

Isa 28:14 Therefore hear the word of the LORD, you scoffers who rule this people in Jerusalem. [15]You boast, "We have entered into a covenant with death, with the grave we have made an agreement. When an overwhelming scourge sweeps by, it cannot touch us, for we have made a lie our refuge and falsehood our hiding place."

[16]So this is what the Sovereign LORD says: "See, I lay a stone in Zion, a tested stone, a precious cornerstone for a sure foundation; the one who trusts will never be dismayed. [17]I will make justice the measuring line and righteousness the plumb line; hail will sweep away your refuge, the lie, and water will overflow your hiding place. [18]Your covenant with death will be annulled; your agreement with the grave will not stand. When the overwhelming scourge sweeps by, you will be beaten down by it.

Isa 28:22 Now stop your mocking, or your chains will become heavier; the Lord, the LORD Almighty, has told me of the destruction decreed against the whole land.

Isa 29:15 Woe to those who go to great depths to hide their plans from the LORD, who do their work in darkness and think, "Who sees us? Who will know?" [16]You turn things upside down, as if the potter were thought to be like the clay! Shall what is formed say to him who formed it, "He did not make me"? Can the pot say of the potter, "He knows nothing"?

Isa 29:20 The ruthless will vanish, the mockers will disappear, and all who have an eye for evil will be cut down— (+Isa 40:27)

Isa 45:9 "Woe to him who quarrels with his Maker, to him who is but a potsherd among the potsherds on the ground. Does the clay say to the potter, 'What are you making?' Does your work say, 'He has no hands'? [10]Woe to him who says to his father, 'What have you begotten?' or to his mother, 'What have you brought to birth?'

Ro 1:32 Although they know God's righteous decree that those who do such things deserve death, they not only continue to do these very things but also approve of those who practice them.

Ro 9:20 But who are you, O man, to talk back to God? "Shall what is formed say to him who formed it, 'Why did you make me like this?'" [21]Does not the potter have the right to make out of the same lump of clay some pottery for noble purposes and some for common use?

2Th 2:3 Don't let anyone deceive you in any way, for that day will not come until the rebellion occurs and the man of lawlessness is revealed, the man doomed to destruction.

Reviling God's prophet (1Ki 22:24).

Despising the lordship of Christ, and the authority of the Church—

2Pe 2:10 This is especially true of those who follow the corrupt desire of the sinful nature and despise authority. Bold and arrogant, these men are not afraid to slander celestial beings; [11]yet even angels, although they are stronger and more powerful, do not bring slanderous accusations against such beings in the presence of the Lord.

Warning against—

1Co 10:9 We should not test the Lord, as some of them did—and were killed by snakes. [10]And do not grumble, as some of them did—and were killed by the destroying angel. [11]These things happened to them as examples and were written down as warnings for us, on whom the fulfillment of the ages has come. [12]So, if you think you are standing firm, be careful that you don't fall!

Excommunication for—

Nu 15:30 "'But anyone who sins defiantly, whether native-born or alien, blasphemes the LORD, and that person must be cut off from his people.

Proverbs concerning—

Pr 18:12 Before his downfall a man's heart is proud, but humility comes before honor. [13]He who answers before listening—that is his folly and his shame.

Pr 25:6 Do not exalt yourself in the king's presence, and do not claim a place among great men; [7a]it is better for him to say to you, "Come up here," than for him to humiliate you before a nobleman.

Punishment for—

Jer 23:34 If a prophet or a priest or anyone else claims, 'This is the oracle of the LORD,' I will punish that man and his household.

Instances of:

Satan, when he said to Eve, "You will not surely die" (Ge 3:1-5). Builders of Babel (Ge 11:4). Abraham, in questioning about Sodom (Ge 18:23-32).

Pharaoh—

Ex 5:2 Pharaoh said, "Who is the LORD, that I should obey him and let Israel go? I do not know the LORD and I will not let Israel go."

Moses, in scolding Yahweh (Nu 11:11-15,22). Nadab and Abihu (Lev 10:1-2). Israelites, in ascending to the top of the hill against the Amalekites (Nu 14:44-45, w Dt 1:43),

Murmuring—

Ex 14:11 They said to Moses, "Was it because there were no graves in Egypt that you brought us to the desert to die? What have you done to us by bringing us out of Egypt? [12]Didn't we say to you in Egypt, 'Leave us alone; let us serve the Egyptians'? It would have been better for us to serve the Egyptians than to die in the desert!" (+Ex 17:2)

Ex 17:7 And he called the place Massah and Meribah because the Israelites quarreled and because they tested the LORD saying, "Is the LORD among us or not?"

Nu 16:41 The next day the whole Israelite community grumbled against Moses and Aaron. "You have killed the LORD's people," they said.

Nu 21:5 they spoke against God and against Moses, and said, "Why have you brought us up out of Egypt to die in the desert? There is no bread! There is no water! And we detest this miserable food!" (+1Co 10:9-12)

In reviling God (Mal 1:6-7,12; 3:7-8,13). Korah, Dathan, and Abiram (Nu 16:3). Saul, in sacrificing (1Sa 13:8-14), sparing the Amalekites (1Sa 15:3,9-23). Men of Beth Shemesh (1Sa 6:19). Uzzah, in steadying the ark (2Sa 6:6-7). David's anger at Uzzah's death (2Sa 6:8). David, in numbering Israel (2Sa 24:1-17). Jeroboam (1Ki 13:4). Ben-Hadad (1Ki 20:10).

The Syrians, in limiting the sovereignty of God (1Ki 20:23)—

1Ki 20:28 The man of God came up and told the king of Israel, "This is what the LORD says: 'Because the Arameans think the LORD is a god of the hills and not a god of the valleys, I will deliver this vast army into your hands, and you will know that I am the LORD.'"

Zedekiah—

1Ki 22:24 Then Zedekiah son of Kenaanah went up and slapped Micaiah in the face. "Which way did the spirit from the LORD go when he went from me to speak to you?" he asked. (+1Ki 22:25; 2Ch 18:23-24)

Uzziah (2Ch 26:16). Sennacherib (2Ki 19:22; 2Ch 32:13-14; Isa 37:23-25). Job, in cursing the day of his birth (Job 3), reproved by Eliphaz (Job 4:5). Jonah (Jnh 4:1-8).

Peter, in objecting to Jesus' statement that he must be killed (Mt 16:21-23; Mk 8:32), in reflecting on his knowledge when he asked, amid a throng, who touched him (Lk 8:45), in objecting to Jesus washing his feet (Jn 13:8), in asking Jesus, "What shall this man do?" (Jn 21:20-22). The disciples, in rebuking those who brought little children to Jesus (Mt 19:13; Mk 10:13-14; Lk 18:15), in their indignation at the anointing of Jesus (Mt 26:8-9; Mk 14:4-5; Jn 12:5), reproving Jesus (Jn 7:3-5). The brothers of Jesus (Jn 7:3-5). James and John, in desiring to call down fire on the Samaritans (Lk 9:54). Those who reviled Jesus (Mt 27:42-43; Mk 15:29-32). Theudas (Ac 5:36). Sons of Sceva (Ac 19:13-14). Diotrephes (3Jn 9).

See Blasphemy; Mocking; Pride.

PRETORIUM *See Praetorium.*

PRICK *See Goad; Thorn.*

PRIDE [*1450, 1452, 1454, 1455, 1467, 1469, 1575, 2086, 2295, 5294, 8123, 8124, 8146, *3016, 3017, 3018, 5662, 5881*].

NIV+ PROUD, PROUDLY

Admonitions against—

Dt 8:11 Be careful that you do not forget the LORD your God, failing to observe his commands, his laws and his decrees that I am giving you this day. [12]Otherwise, when you eat and are satisfied, when you build fine houses and settle down, [13]and when your herds and flocks grow large and your silver and gold increase and all you have is multiplied, [14]then your heart will become proud and you will forget the LORD your God, who brought you out of Egypt, out of the land of slavery.

Dt 8:17 You may say to yourself, "My power and the strength of my hands have produced this wealth for me." [18]But remember the LORD your God, for it is he who gives you the ability to produce wealth, and so confirms his covenant, which he swore to your forefathers, as it is today.

¹⁹If you ever forget the LORD your God and follow other gods and worship and bow down to them, I testify against you today that you will surely be destroyed. ²⁰Like the nations the LORD destroyed before you, so you will be destroyed for not obeying the LORD your God.

Ps 49:11 Their tombs will remain their houses forever, their dwellings for endless generations, though they had named lands after themselves.

Ps 75:4 To the arrogant I say, 'Boast no more,' and to the wicked, 'Do not lift up your horns. ⁵Do not lift your horns against heaven; do not speak with outstretched neck.'"

⁶No one from the east or the west or from the desert can exalt a man.

Jer 9:23 This is what the LORD says: "Let not the wise man boast of his wisdom or the strong man boast of his strength or the rich man boast of his riches, (+Mt 23:5-7)

Lk 14:8 "When someone invites you to a wedding feast, do not take the place of honor, for a person more distinguished than you may have been invited. ⁹If so, the host who invited both of you will come and say to you, 'Give this man your seat.' Then, humiliated, you will have to take the least important place.

Lk 20:46 "Beware of the teachers of the law. They like to walk around in flowing robes and love to be greeted in the marketplaces and have the most important seats in the synagogues and the places of honor at banquets. ⁴⁷They devour widows' houses and for a show make lengthy prayers. Such men will be punished most severely."

Ro 11:17 If some of the branches have been broken off, and you, though a wild olive shoot, have been grafted in among the others and now share in the nourishing sap from the olive root, ¹⁸do not boast over those branches. If you do, consider this: You do not support the root, but the root supports you. ¹⁹You will say then, "Branches were broken off so that I could be grafted in." ²⁰Granted. But they were broken off because of unbelief, and you stand by faith. Do not be arrogant, but be afraid. ²¹For if God did not spare the natural branches, he will not spare you either.

Ro 11:25 I do not want you to be ignorant of this mystery, brothers, so that you may not be conceited: Israel has experienced a hardening in part until the full number of the Gentiles has come in.

Ro 12:3 For by the grace given me I say to every one of you: Do not think of yourself more highly than you ought, but rather think of yourself with sober judgment, in accordance with the measure of faith God has given you.

Ro 12:16 Live in harmony with one another. Do not be proud, but be willing to associate with people of low position. Do not be conceited.

1Co 4:6 Now, brothers, I have applied these things to myself and Apollos for your benefit, so that you may learn from us the meaning of the saying, "Do not go beyond what is written." Then you will not take pride in one man over against another. ⁷For who makes you different from anyone else? What do you have that you did not receive? And if you did receive it, why do you boast as though you did not?

⁸Already you have all you want! Already you have become rich! You have become kings—and that without us! How I wish that you really had become kings so that we might be kings with you!

1Co 4:10 We are fools for Christ, but you are so wise in Christ! We are weak, but you are strong! You are honored, we are dishonored!

1Co 5:2 And you are proud! Shouldn't you rather have been filled with grief and have put out of your fellowship the man who did this?

1Co 5:6 Your boasting is not good. Don't you know that a little yeast works through the whole batch of dough?

1Co 8:1 Now about food sacrificed to idols: We know that we all possess knowledge. Knowledge puffs up, but love builds up. ²The man who thinks he knows something does not yet know as he ought to know.

1Co 10:12 So, if you think you are standing firm, be careful that you don't fall!

1Co 13:4 Love is patient, love is kind. It does not envy, it does not boast, it is not proud.

1Co 14:38 If he ignores this, he himself will be ignored.

2Co 10:5 We demolish arguments and every pretension that sets itself up against the knowledge of God, and we take captive every thought to make it obedient to Christ.

2Co 10:12 We do not dare to classify or compare ourselves with some who commend themselves. When they measure themselves by themselves and compare themselves with themselves, they are not wise.

2Co 10:18 For it is not the one who commends himself who is approved, but the one whom the Lord commends.

Gal 6:3 If anyone thinks he is something when he is nothing, he deceives himself.

Eph 4:17 So I tell you this, and insist on it in the Lord, that you must no longer live as the Gentiles do, in the futility of their thinking.

Php 2:3 Do nothing out of selfish ambition or vain conceit, but in humility consider others better than yourselves.

1Ti 2:9 I also want women to dress modestly, with decency and propriety, not with braided hair or gold or pearls or expensive clothes,

1Ti 6:3 If anyone teaches false doctrines and does not agree to the sound instruction of our Lord Jesus Christ and to godly teaching, ⁴he is conceited and understands nothing. He has an unhealthy interest in controversies and quarrels about words that result in envy, strife, malicious talk, evil suspicions

1Ti 6:17 Command those who are rich in this present world not to be arrogant nor to put their hope in wealth, which is so uncertain, but to put their hope in God, who richly provides us with everything for our enjoyment.

2Ti 3:2 People will be lovers of themselves, lovers of money, boastful, proud, abusive, disobedient to their parents, ungrateful, unholy,

2Ti 3:4 treacherous, rash, conceited, lovers of pleasure rather than lovers of God—

1Pe 5:3 not lording it over those entrusted to you, but being examples to the flock.

Rev 3:17 You say, 'I am rich; I have acquired wealth and do not need a thing.' But you do not realize that you are wretched, pitiful, poor, blind and naked. ¹⁸I counsel you to buy from me gold refined in the fire, so you can become rich; and white clothes to wear, so you can cover your shameful nakedness; and salve to put on your eyes, so you can see.

Prayer regarding—

Ps 9:20 Strike them with terror, O LORD; let the nations know they are but men. *Selah*

Ps 10:2 In his arrogance the wicked man hunts down the weak, who are caught in the schemes he devises. ³He boasts of the cravings of his heart; he blesses the greedy and reviles the LORD. ⁴In his pride the wicked does not seek him; in all his thoughts there is no room for God. [5]His ways are always prosperous; he is haughty and your laws are far from him; he sneers at all his enemies. [6]He says to himself, "Nothing will shake me; I'll always be happy and never have trouble."

Ps 10:11 He says to himself, "God has forgotten; he covers his face and never sees."

Prevented by divine discipline—

2Co 12:7 To keep me from becoming conceited because of these surpassingly great revelations, there was given me a thorn in my flesh, a messenger of Satan, to torment me.

Proceeds from the carnal mind—

Mk 7:21 For from within, out of men's hearts, come evil thoughts, sexual immorality, theft, murder, adultery, [22]greed, malice, deceit, lewdness, envy, slander, arrogance and folly.

1Jn 2:16 For everything in the world—the cravings of sinful man, the lust of his eyes and the boasting of what he has and does—comes not from the Father but from the world.

Leads, to strife (Pr 13:10; 28:25)

To destruction (Pr 15:25; 16:18; 17:19; 18:11-12)—

Isa 14:12 How you have fallen from heaven, O morning star, son of the dawn! You have been cast down to the earth, you who once laid low the nations! [13]You said in your heart, "I will ascend to heaven; I will raise my throne above the stars of God; I will sit enthroned on the mount of assembly, on the utmost heights of the sacred mountain. [14]I will ascend above the tops of the clouds; I will make myself like the Most High." [15]But you are brought down to the grave, to the depths of the pit.

[16]Those who see you stare at you, they ponder your fate: "Is this the man who shook the earth and made kingdoms tremble,

Isa 26:5 He humbles those who dwell on high, he lays the lofty city low; he levels it to the ground and casts it down to the dust. (+Isa 28:3)

Da 11:45 He will pitch his royal tents between the seas at the beautiful holy mountain. Yet he will come to his end, and no one will help him.

Zep 3:11 On that day you will not be put to shame for all the wrongs you have done to me, because I will remove from this city those who rejoice in their pride. Never again will you be haughty on my holy hill.

Mal 4:1 "Surely the day is coming; it will burn like a furnace. All the arrogant and every evildoer will be stubble, and that day that is coming will set them on fire," says the LORD Almighty. "Not a root or a branch will be left to them.

1Ti 3:6 He must not be a recent convert, or he may become conceited and fall under the same judgment as the devil.

Rev 18:7 Give her as much torture and grief as the glory and luxury she gave herself. In her heart she boasts, 'I sit as queen; I am not a widow, and I will never mourn.' [8]Therefore in one day her plagues will overtake her: death, mourning and famine. She will be consumed by fire, for mighty is the Lord God who judges her.

Rebuked—

1Sa 2:3 "Do not keep talking so proudly or let your mouth speak such arrogance, for the LORD is a God who knows, and by him deeds are weighed.

[4]"The bows of the warriors are broken, but those who stumbled are armed with strength. [5]Those who were full hire themselves out for food, but those who were hungry hunger no more. She who was barren has borne seven children, but she who has had many sons pines away.

2Ki 14:9 But Jehoash king of Israel replied to Amaziah king of Judah: "A thistle in Lebanon sent a message to a cedar in Lebanon, 'Give your daughter to my son in marriage.' Then a wild beast in Lebanon came along and trampled the thistle underfoot. [10]You have indeed defeated Edom and now you are arrogant. Glory in your victory, but stay at home! Why ask for trouble and cause your own downfall and that of Judah also?" (+2Ch 25:18-19; Job 12:2)

Jer 13:9 "This is what the LORD says: 'In the same way I will ruin the pride of Judah and the great pride of Jerusalem.

Jer 13:15 Hear and pay attention, do not be arrogant, for the LORD has spoken.

Jer 13:17 But if you do not listen, I will weep in secret because of your pride; my eyes will weep bitterly, overflowing with tears, because the LORD's flock will be taken captive.

Hab 2:4 "See, he is puffed up; his desires are not upright—but the righteous will live by his faith— [5]indeed, wine betrays him; he is arrogant and never at rest. Because he is as greedy as the grave and like death is never satisfied, he gathers to himself all the nations and takes captive all the peoples.

Hab 2:9 "Woe to him who builds his realm by unjust gain to set his nest on high, to escape the clutches of ruin!

Repugnant to God (Job 37:24)—

Ps 12:3 May the LORD cut off all flattering lips and every boastful tongue

Ps 18:27 You save the humble but bring low those whose eyes are haughty.

Ps 31:23 Love the LORD, all his saints! The LORD preserves the faithful, but the proud he pays back in full.

Ps 101:5 Whoever slanders his neighbor in secret, him will I put to silence; whoever has haughty eyes and a proud heart, him will I not endure.

Ps 138:6 Though the LORD is on high, he looks upon the lowly, but the proud he knows from afar. (+Pr 6:16-17; 8:13; 16:5)

Jer 50:31 "See, I am against you, O arrogant one," declares the Lord, the LORD Almighty, "for your day has come, the time for you to be punished. [32]The arrogant one will stumble and fall and no one will help her up; I will kindle a fire in her towns that will consume all who are around her."

Lk 1:51 He has performed mighty deeds with his arm; he has scattered those who are proud in their inmost thoughts.

Jas 4:6 But he gives us more grace. That is why Scripture says: "God opposes the proud but gives grace to the humble."

The proud shall be humbled—

Lev 26:19 I will break down your stubborn pride and make the sky above you like iron and the ground beneath you like bronze. (+Ps 52:6-7; Pr 11:2)

Isa 2:11 The eyes of the arrogant man will be humbled and the pride of men brought low; the LORD alone will be exalted in that day.

[12]The LORD Almighty has a day in store for all the proud and lofty, for all that is exalted (and they will be humbled), [13]for all the cedars of Lebanon, tall and lofty, and all the oaks of Bashan, [14]for all the towering mountains and all the high hills, [15]for every lofty tower and every fortified wall, [16]for every trading ship and every stately vessel. [17]The arrogance of man will be brought low and the pride

of men humbled; the LORD alone will be exalted in that day,

Isa 3:16 The LORD says, "The women of Zion are haughty, walking along with outstretched necks, flirting with their eyes, tripping along with mincing steps, with ornaments jingling on their ankles. [17]Therefore the Lord will bring sores on the heads of the women of Zion; the LORD will make their scalps bald."

[18]In that day the Lord will snatch away their finery: the bangles and headbands and crescent necklaces, [19]the earrings and bracelets and veils, [20]the headdresses and ankle chains and sashes, the perfume bottles and charms, [21]the signet rings and nose rings, [22]the fine robes and the capes and cloaks, the purses [23]and mirrors, and the linen garments and tiaras and shawls.

[24]Instead of fragrance there will be a stench; instead of a sash, a rope; instead of well-dressed hair, baldness; instead of fine clothing, sackcloth; instead of beauty, branding. [25]Your men will fall by the sword, your warriors in battle. [26]The gates of Zion will lament and mourn; destitute, she will sit on the ground. (+Isa 5:13)

Isa 13:11 I will punish the world for its evil, the wicked for their sins. I will put an end to the arrogance of the haughty and will humble the pride of the ruthless.

Isa 22:16 What are you doing here and who gave you permission to cut out a grave for yourself here, hewing your grave on the height and chiseling your resting place in the rock?

Isa 22:19 I will depose you from your office, and you will be ousted from your position.

Isa 23:7 Is this your city of revelry, the old, old city, whose feet have taken her to settle in far-off lands?

Isa 23:9 The LORD Almighty planned it, to bring low the pride of all glory and to humble all who are renowned on the earth.

Isa 24:4 The earth dries up and withers, the world languishes and withers, the exalted of the earth languish.

Isa 24:21 In that day the LORD will punish the powers in the heavens above and the kings on the earth below.

Jer 49:4 Why do you boast of your valleys, boast of your valleys so fruitful? O unfaithful daughter, you trust in your riches and say, 'Who will attack me?'

Jer 49:16 The terror you inspire and the pride of your heart have deceived you, you who live in the clefts of the rocks, who occupy the heights of the hill. Though you build your nest as high as the eagle's, from there I will bring you down," declares the LORD.

Da 4:37 Now I, Nebuchadnezzar, praise and exalt and glorify the King of heaven, because everything he does is right and all his ways are just. And those who walk in pride he is able to humble.

Ob 3 The pride of your heart has deceived you, you who live in the clefts of the rocks and make your home on the heights, you who say to yourself, 'Who can bring me down to the ground?' [4]Though you soar like the eagle and make your nest among the stars, from there I will bring you down," declares the LORD. (+Mt 23:12; Mk 10:43)

Lk 1:52 He has brought down rulers from their thrones but has lifted up the humble. (+Lk 9:46; 18:14; Rev 18:7-8)

Pride discussed with Job—

Job 11:12 But a witless man can no more become wise than a wild donkey's colt can be born a man.

Job 12:2 "Doubtless you are the people, and wisdom will die with you! [3]But I have a mind as well as you; I am not inferior to you. Who does not know all these things?

Job 13:2 What you know, I also know; I am not inferior to you.

Job 13:5 If only you would be altogether silent! For you, that would be wisdom.

Job 15:1 Then Eliphaz the Temanite replied: [2]"Would a wise man answer with empty notions or fill his belly with the hot east wind? [3]Would he argue with useless words, with speeches that have no value? [4]But you even undermine piety and hinder devotion to God. [5]Your sin prompts your mouth; you adopt the tongue of the crafty. [6]Your own mouth condemns you, not mine; your own lips testify against you. [7]"Are you the first man ever born? Were you brought forth before the hills? [8]Do you listen in on God's council? Do you limit wisdom to yourself? [9]What do you know that we do not know? What insights do you have that we do not have? [10]The gray-haired and the aged are on our side, men even older than your father. [11]Are God's consolations not enough for you, words spoken gently to you? [12]Why has your heart carried you away, and why do your eyes flash, [13]so that you vent your rage against God and pour out such words from your mouth?

Job 18:3 Why are we regarded as cattle and considered stupid in your sight? [4]You who tear yourself to pieces in your anger, is the earth to be abandoned for your sake? Or must the rocks be moved from their place?

Job 21:31 Who denounces his conduct to his face? Who repays him for what he has done? [32]He is carried to the grave, and watch is kept over his tomb.

Job 32:9 It is not only the old who are wise, not only the aged who understand what is right.

[10]"Therefore I say: Listen to me; I too will tell you what I know. [11]I waited while you spoke, I listened to your reasoning; while you were searching for words, [12]I gave you my full attention. But not one of you has proved Job wrong; none of you has answered his arguments. [13]Do not say, 'We have found wisdom; let God refute him, not man.'

Job 37:24 Therefore, men revere him, for does he not have regard for all the wise in heart?"

Proverbs concerning—

Pr 3:34 He mocks proud mockers but gives grace to the humble.

Pr 6:16 There are six things the LORD hates, seven that are detestable to him: [17]haughty eyes, a lying tongue, hands that shed innocent blood,

Pr 8:13 To fear the LORD is to hate evil; I hate pride and arrogance, evil behavior and perverse speech.

Pr 10:17 He who heeds discipline shows the way to life, but whoever ignores correction leads others astray.

Pr 11:2 When pride comes, then comes disgrace, but with humility comes wisdom.

Pr 11:12 A man who lacks judgment derides his neighbor, but a man of understanding holds his tongue.

Pr 12:9 Better to be a nobody and yet have a servant than pretend to be somebody and have no food.

Pr 12:15 The way of a fool seems right to him, but a wise man listens to advice.

Pr 13:10 Pride only breeds quarrels, but wisdom is found in those who take advice.

Pr 14:21 He who despises his neighbor sins, but blessed is he who is kind to the needy.

Pr 15:5 A fool spurns his father's discipline, but whoever heeds correction shows prudence.

Pr 15:10 Stern discipline awaits him who leaves the path; he who hates correction will die.

Pr 15:12 A mocker resents correction; he will not consult the wise.

Pr 15:25 The LORD tears down the proud man's house but he keeps the widow's boundaries intact.

Pr 15:32 He who ignores discipline despises himself, but whoever heeds correction gains understanding.

Pr 16:5 The LORD detests all the proud of heart. Be sure of this: They will not go unpunished.

Pr 16:18 Pride goes before destruction, a haughty spirit before a fall.

¹⁹Better to be lowly in spirit and among the oppressed than to share plunder with the proud.

Pr 17:19 He who loves a quarrel loves sin; he who builds a high gate invites destruction.

Pr 18:11 The wealth of the rich is their fortified city; they imagine it an unscalable wall.

¹²Before his downfall a man's heart is proud, but humility comes before honor.

Pr 21:4 Haughty eyes and a proud heart, the lamp of the wicked, are sin!

Pr 21:24 The proud and arrogant man—"Mocker" is his name; he behaves with overweening pride.

Pr 25:14 Like clouds and wind without rain is a man who boasts of gifts he does not give.

Pr 25:27 It is not good to eat too much honey, nor is it honorable to seek one's own honor.

Pr 26:5 Answer a fool according to his folly, or he will be wise in his own eyes.

Pr 26:12 Do you see a man wise in his own eyes? There is more hope for a fool than for him.

Pr 26:16 The sluggard is wiser in his own eyes than seven men who answer discreetly.

Pr 27:2 Let another praise you, and not your own mouth; someone else, and not your own lips.

Pr 28:11 A rich man may be wise in his own eyes, but a poor man who has discernment sees through him.

Pr 28:25 A greedy man stirs up dissension, but he who trusts in the LORD will prosper.

Pr 29:8 Mockers stir up a city, but wise men turn away anger.

Pr 29:23 A man's pride brings him low, but a man of lowly spirit gains honor.

Pr 30:12 those who are pure in their own eyes and yet are not cleansed of their filth; ¹³those whose eyes are ever so haughty, whose glances are so disdainful;

Cited by the psalmists (Ps 10:2-6,11; 49:11)—

Ps 52:7 "Here now is the man who did not make God his stronghold but trusted in his great wealth and grew strong by destroying others!"

Ps 73:6 Therefore pride is their necklace; they clothe themselves with violence.

Ps 73:8 They scoff, and speak with malice; in their arrogance they threaten oppression. ⁹Their mouths lay claim to heaven, and their tongues take possession of the earth.

Ps 119:21 You rebuke the arrogant, who are cursed and who stray from your commands.

Ps 119:69 Though the arrogant have smeared me with lies, I keep your precepts with all my heart. ⁷⁰Their hearts are callous and unfeeling, but I delight in your law.

Ps 119:78 May the arrogant be put to shame for wronging me without cause; but I will meditate on your precepts.

See Rich, The.

Instances of:

Pharaoh (Ex 7-11; 12:29-36; 14). Ahithophel (2Sa 17:23). Naaman (2Ki 5:11-13). Hezekiah (2Ki 20:13; 2Ch

32:25-26,31; Isa 39:2). Uzziah (2Ch 26:16-19). Haman (Est 3:5; 5:11,13; 6:6; 7:10).

Moab (Isa 16:6-7)—

Jer 48:7 Since you trust in your deeds and riches, you too will be taken captive, and Chemosh will go into exile, together with his priests and officials.

Jer 48:14 "How can you say, 'We are warriors, men valiant in battle'? ¹⁵Moab will be destroyed and her towns invaded; her finest young men will go down in the slaughter," declares the King, whose name is the LORD Almighty. (+Jer 48:16-28)

Jer 48:29 "We have heard of Moab's pride—her overweening pride and conceit, her pride and arrogance and the haughtiness of her heart. (+Zep 2:9)

Israel—

Isa 9:9 All the people will know it—Ephraim and the inhabitants of Samaria—who say with pride and arrogance of heart, ¹⁰"The bricks have fallen down, but we will rebuild with dressed stone; the fig trees have been felled, but we will replace them with cedars." (+Hos 5:5; 7:10)

Assyria—

Isa 10:5 "Woe to the Assyrian, the rod of my anger, in whose hand is the club of my wrath! ⁶I send him against a godless nation, I dispatch him against a people who anger me, to seize loot and snatch plunder, and to trample them down like mud in the streets. ⁷But this is not what he intends, this is not what he has in mind; his purpose is to destroy, to put an end to many nations. ⁸'Are not my commanders all kings?' he says. ⁹'Has not Calno fared like Carchemish? Is not Hamath like Arpad, and Samaria like Damascus? ¹⁰As my hand seized the kingdoms of the idols, kingdoms whose images excelled those of Jerusalem and Samaria— ¹¹shall I not deal with Jerusalem and her images as I dealt with Samaria and her idols?'"

¹²When the Lord has finished all his work against Mount Zion and Jerusalem, he will say, "I will punish the king of Assyria for the willful pride of his heart and the haughty look in his eyes. ¹³For he says:

"'By the strength of my hand I have done this, and by my wisdom, because I have understanding. I removed the boundaries of nations, I plundered their treasures; like a mighty one I subdued their kings. ¹⁴As one reaches into a nest, so my hand reached for the wealth of the nations; as men gather abandoned eggs, so I gathered all the countries; not one flapped a wing, or opened its mouth to chirp.'"

¹⁵Does the ax raise itself above him who swings it, or the saw boast against him who uses it? As if a rod were to wield him who lifts it up, or a club brandish him who is not wood! ¹⁶Therefore, the Lord, the LORD Almighty, will send a wasting disease upon his sturdy warriors; under his pomp a fire will be kindled like a blazing flame.

Eze 31:10 "'Therefore this is what the Sovereign LORD says: Because it towered on high, lifting its top above the thick foliage, and because it was proud of its height, ¹¹I handed it over to the ruler of the nations, for him to deal with according to its wickedness. I cast it aside,

Jerusalem—

Eze 16:56 You would not even mention your sister Sodom in the day of your pride,

Tyre—

Eze 28:2 "Son of man, say to the ruler of Tyre, 'This is what the Sovereign LORD says:

"'In the pride of your heart you say, "I am a god; I sit on the throne of a god in the heart of the seas." But you are a man and not a god, though you think you are as wise as a god. ³Are you wiser than Daniel? Is no secret hidden from you? ⁴By your wisdom and understanding you have gained wealth for yourself and amassed gold and silver in your treasuries. ⁵By your great skill in trading you have increased your wealth, and because of your wealth your heart has grown proud.

⁶" 'Therefore this is what the Sovereign LORD says: " 'Because you think you are wise, as wise as a god, ⁷I am going to bring foreigners against you, the most ruthless of nations; they will draw their swords against your beauty and wisdom and pierce your shining splendor. ⁸They will bring you down to the pit, and you will die a violent death in the heart of the seas. ⁹Will you then say, "I am a god," in the presence of those who kill you? You will be but a man, not a god, in the hands of those who slay you.

Eze 28:17 Your heart became proud on account of your beauty, and you corrupted your wisdom because of your splendor. So I threw you to the earth; I made a spectacle of you before kings.

Egypt—

Eze 30:6 " 'This is what the LORD says: " 'The allies of Egypt will fall and her proud strength will fail. From Migdol to Aswan they will fall by the sword within her, declares the Sovereign LORD.

Nebuchadnezzar (Da 4:30-34; 5:20). Moab and Ammon (Zep 2:9).

Nineveh—

Zep 2:15 This is the carefree city that lived in safety. She said to herself, "I am, and there is none besides me." What a ruin she has become, a lair for wild beasts! All who pass by her scoff and shake their fists.

The Scribes and Pharisees (Mt 20:6)—

Mt 23:6 they love the place of honor at banquets and the most important seats in the synagogues; ⁷they love to be greeted in the marketplaces and to have men call them 'Rabbi.'

⁸"But you are not to be called 'Rabbi,' for you have only one Master and you are all brothers.

Mt 23:11 The greatest among you will be your servant. ¹²For whoever exalts himself will be humbled, and whoever humbles himself will be exalted. (+Mk 10:43)

Mk 12:38 As he taught, Jesus said, "Watch out for the teachers of the law. They like to walk around in flowing robes and be greeted in the marketplaces, ³⁹and have the most important seats in the synagogues and the places of honor at banquets. (+Lk 9:46)

Lk 11:43 "Woe to you Pharisees, because you love the most important seats in the synagogues and greetings in the marketplaces. (+Lk 18:14; 20:45-47)

Herod (Ac 12:21-23).

See Ambition.

PRIEST [2424, 3912, 3913, 3914, 10347, *797, 2634, 2632, 2633, 2636*].

NIV+ PRIEST'S, PRIESTHOOD, PRIESTLY, PRIESTS, PRIESTS'

Before the Mosaic Covenant:

Melchizedek (Ge 14:18; Heb 5:6,10-11; 6:20; 7:1-21). Jethro (Ex 2:16). Priests in Israel before the giving of the law (Ex 19:22,24).

Mosaic:

(Ex 28:1-4; 29:9,44; Nu 3:10; 18:7; 1Ch 23:13). Hereditary descent of office (Ex 27:21; 28:43; 29:9). Consecration of (Ex 29:1-9,19-35; 40:12-16; Lev 6:20-23; 8:6-35; Heb 7:21). Is holy (Lev 21:6-7; 22:9,16). Washings of

(Ex 40:30-32; Lev 16:24). Must be without blemish (Lev 21:17-23). Vestments of (Ex 28:2-43; 39:1-29; Lev 6:10-11; 8:13; Eze 44:17-19). Put on vestments in the temple (Eze 42:14; 44:19). Atonement for (Lev 16:6,24; Eze 44:27). Defilement and purification of (Eze 44:25-26). Marriage of (Lev 21:7-15; Eze 44:22). Chambers for, in the temple (Eze 40:45-46). Exempt from tax (Ezr 7:24). Armed and organized for war at the time of the disaffection toward Saul (1Ch 12:27-28). Beard and hair of (Eze 44:20).

Twenty-four courses of (1Ch 24:1-19; 28:13,21; 2Ch 8:14; 31:2; 35:4-5; Ezr 2:36-39; Ne 13:30). Chosen by lot (Lk 1:8-9,23),

Usurpations of the office of (Nu 3:10; 16; 18:7; 2Ch 26:18). Jeroboam appointed priests who were not of the sons of Levi (1Ki 12:31; 13:33).

See Levites; Minister.

Compensation for—

No part of the land of Canaan allowed to (Nu 18:20; Dt 10:9; 14:27; 18:1-2; Jos 13:14,33; 14:3; 18:7; Eze 44:28). Provided with cities and suburbs (Lev 25:32-34; Nu 35:2-8; Jos 21:1-4,13-19,41-42; 1Ch 6:57-60; Ne 11:3,20; Eze 45:1-6; 48:8-20). Own lands sanctified to the Lord (Lev 27:21). Tithes of the tithes (Nu 18:8-18,26-32; Ne 10:38). Part of the spoils of war, including captives (Nu 31:25-29). Firstfruits (Lev 23:20; 24:9; Nu 18:12-13,17-18; Dt 18:3-5; Ne 10:36). Redemption money (Lev 27:23), of the firstborn (Nu 3:46-51; 18:15-16). Things devoted (Lev 27:21; Nu 5:9-10; 18:14). Fines (Lev 5:16; 22:14; Nu 5:8). Trespass money and other trespass offerings (Lev 5:15,18; Nu 5:5-10; 18:9; 2Ki 12:16). The bread of the Presence (Ex 25:30; Lev 24:5-9; 2Ch 2:4; 13:11; Ne 10:33; Mt 12:4; Heb 9:2). *See Bread, Consecrated.* Portions of sacrifices and offerings (Ex 29:27-34; Lev 2:2-3,9-10; 5:12-13,16; 6:15-18,26; 7:6-10,31-34; 10:12-14; 14:12-13; Nu 6:19-20; 18:8-19; Dt 18:3-5; 1Sa 2:13-14; Eze 44:28-31; 45:1-4; 1Co 9:13; 10:18).

Regulations by Hezekiah concerning compensation (2Ch 31:4-19). Portion of the land allotted to, in redistribution in Ezekiel's vision (Eze 48:8-14). For sustenance of their families (Lev 22:11-13; Nu 18:11,19).

Duties of—

To offer sacrifices (Lev 1:4-17; 2:2,16; 3:5,11,13,16; 4:5-12,17,25-26,30-35; 1Ch 16:40; 2Ch 13:11; 29:34; 35:11-14; Ezr 6:20; Heb 10:11). *See Offerings.* To offer the first fruits (Lev 23:10-11; Dt 26:3-4). To pronounce benedictions (Nu 6:22-27; Dt 21:5; 2Ch 30:27). Teach the law (Lev 10:11; Dt 24:8; 27:14; 31:9-13; 33:10; Jer 2:8; Mal 2:7). Light the lamps in the tabernacle (Ex 27:20-21; 2Ch 13:11; Lev 24:3-4). Keep the sacred fire always burning (Lev 6:12-13). To furnish a quota of wood for the sanctuary (Ne 10:34). Responsible for the sanctuary (Nu 4:5-15; 18:1,5,7). To act as scribes (Ezr 7:1-6; Ne 8:9). Be present at and supervise the tithing (Ne 10:38). Sound the trumpet in calling assemblies and in battle (Nu 10:2-10; 31:6; Jos 6; 2Ch 13:12). Examine lepers. *See Leprosy.* Purify the unclean (Lev 15:31). *See Defilement.* Value things devoted (Lev 27:8,12). Officiated in the holy place (Heb 9:6). Chiefs of Levites (Nu 3:9,32; 4:19,28,33; 1Ch 9:20). To act as magistrates (Nu 5:14-31; Dt 17:8-13; 19:17; 21:5; 2Ch 19:8; Eze 44:23-24). To encourage the army on the eve of battle (Dt 20:2-4). Bear the ark through the Jordan (Jos 3; 4:15-18), in battle (1Sa 4:3-5).

Figurative (Ex 19:6; Isa 61:6; 1Pe 2:9; Rev 1:6; 5:10; 20:6).

High Priest:

Moses did not designate Aaron chief or high priest. The function he served was superior to that of other priests. The title appears after the institution of the office (Lev 21:10-15; Nu 3:32). Qualifications of, consecration of, etc. *See above, Mosaic.*

Clothing of (Ex 28:2-43; 39:1-31; Lev 8:7-9). Respect due to (Ac 23:5).

Duties of—

Had charge of the sanctuary and altar (Nu 18:2,5,7). To offer sacrifices (Heb 5:1; 8:3). To designate subordinate priests for duty (Nu 4:19; 1Sa 2:36). To officiate in consecrations of the Levites (Nu 8:11-21). To have charge of the treasury (2Ki 12:10; 22:4; 2Ch 24:6-14; 34:9). To light the lamps of the tabernacle (Ex 27:20-21; 30:8; Lev 24:3-4; Nu 8:3). To burn incense (Ex 30:7-8; 1Sa 2:28; 1Ch 23:13). To place bread of the Presence on the table every Sabbath (Lev 24:8). To offer for his own sins of ignorance (Lev 4:3-12).

On the Day of Atonement (Ex 30:10; Lev 16; Heb 5:3; 9:7,22-23).

Judicial (Nu 5:15; Dt 17:8-13; 1Sa 4:18; Hos 4:4; Mt 26:3,50,57,62; Ac 5:21-28; 23:1-5). To number the people (Nu 1:3). Officiate at the choice of the ruler (Nu 27:18-19,21). To distribute the spoils of war (Nu 31:26-29).

Compensation of. *See above, Compensation for.*

A second priest, under the high priest (Nu 3:32; 4:16; 31:6; 1Ch 9:20; 2Sa 15:24; 2Ki 25:18; Lk 3:2).

Miscellaneous Facts Concerning:

Priestly office performed by prophets (1Sa 16:5). Loyal to Rehoboam at the time of the revolt of the ten tribes (2Ch 11:13). Zeal of (1Ch 9:10-13), in purging the temple (2Ch 29:4-17). Wickedness of (2Ch 36:14). Taken with the captives to Babylon (Jer 29:1). Return from the Captivity (Ezr 1:5; 2:36-39,61,70; 3:8; 7:7; 8:24-30; Ne 7:39-42,63-73; 10:1-8; 12:1-7). Polluted by marrying idolatrous wives (Ezr 9:1-2; 10:5,18-19; Ne 10:28). Restore the altar and offer sacrifices (Ezr 3:1-7). Supervise the building of the temple (Ezr 3:8-13). Inquire of John the Baptist whether he was the Christ (Jn 1:19). Conspire to destroy Jesus (Mt 26:3-5,14-15,47,51; Mk 14:10-11,43-47,53-66; 15:1; Lk 22:1-6,50,54,66-71; 23:1-2; Jn 11:47; 19:15-16,18). Try and condemn Jesus (Mt 26:57-68; 27:1-2; Mk 14:53-65; Lk 22:54-71; 23:13-24; Jn 18:15-32). Incite the people to ask that Barabbas be released and Jesus destroyed (Mt 27:20; Mk 15:11; Lk 23:18). Persecute the disciples (Ac 22:5). Reprove and threaten Peter and John (Ac 4:6-21; 5:17-41). Try, condemn, and stone Stephen (Ac 6:12-15; 7). Paul brought before (Ac 22:30; 23:1-5). Many converts among (Ac 6:7).

Corrupt: (Jer 23:11-12; Eze 22:26; Lk 10:31).

Instances of: Eli's sons (1Sa 2:12-17,22), of the returned exiles (Ezr 9:1-2; 10:18-22; Ne 13:4-9,13,28-29).

Idolatrous (1Ki 12:32; 2Ki 10:19; 11:18; 23:5; 2Ch 23:17; 34:4-5; Jer 48:35; Hos 10:5; Zep 1:4).

PRIMOGENITURE *See Birthright; Firstborn.*

PRINCE OF PEACE *See Jesus.*

PRINCE, PRINCESS [1201+, 2980, 5592, 5618, 5687, 5954, 7278, 7312, 8138, 8569, *795*, *807*].

NIV+ PRINCE'S, PRINCELY, PRINCES

A prince is a leader, an exalted person clothed with authority. A princess is the daughter or wife of a chief or king. The prince may be the head of a family or tribe, a ruler, governor, magistrate, satrap, or royal descendant (Nu 22:8; 1Sa 18:30). He may also be a spiritual ruler (Isa 9:6) or the ruler of demons (Mt 9:34).

PRINCIPALITIES

1. Rule; ruler (Eph 1:21; Tit 3:1).

2. Order of powerful angels and demons (Ro 8:38; Eph 3:10; 6:12). *See Demons.*

PRINT A mark made by pressure (Lev 19:28; Jn 20:25).

PRISCILLA, PRISCA [*4571*]. Priscilla (diminutive of Prisca) was the wife of the Jewish Christian Aquila, with whom she is always mentioned in the NT; tentmakers; had a church in their house; taught Apollos; assisted Paul (Ac 18:2,26; Ro 16:3; 1Co 16:19; 2Ti 4:19).

PRISON [*1074+, 3975, 4993, *1300, 1303, 1313, 4140, 5871*].

NIV+ IMPRISON, IMPRISONED, IMPRISONMENT, IMPRISONMENTS, IMPRISONS, PRISONER, PRISONERS, PRISONS

Prisoners were often put in dry wells or cisterns (Ge 37:24; Jer 38:6-13), or dungeons which were part of a palace (1Ki 22:27). The Herods and the Romans had royal prisons (Lk 3:20; Ac 12:4; 23:10,35). Jesus foretells imprisonment for his disciples (Lk 21:12). Disobedient spirits are now in prison (1Pe 3:19). Satan will be imprisoned (Rev 20:7).

PRISONERS [*659, 673, 4374, 8660, 8664, *170, 1300, 1304, 1313, 5257*].

NIV+ See PRISON

Joseph (Ge 39:20-23; 40; 41:44). Jeremiah (Jer 38:6-28; 39:14). John the Baptist (Mt 11:2; 14:3-12; Mk 6:17; Lk 3:20). Jesus (Mt 26:47-75; 27; Mk 14:43-72; 15; Lk 22:47-71; 23; Jn 18:3-40; 19). Apostles (Ac 5:17-42). Peter (Ac 12:3-19). Paul (Ac 16:19-40; 21:27-40; 22-28). Silas (Ac 16:19-40).

Required to labor (Jdg 16:21). Kept on bread and water of affliction (1Ki 22:27; 2Ch 18:26; Isa 30:20), in chains (Ac 12:6), in stocks (Pr 7:22; Jer 29:26; Ac 16:24).

Confined in the court of the palace (Jer 32:2), house of the scribe (Jer 37:15), house of captain of the guard (Ge 40:3). Visited by friends (Mt 11:2; Ac 24:23). Bound to soldiers (Ac 12:6-7).

Severe hardships of, mitigated (Jer 37:20-21). Cruelty to (Jer 38:6; La 3:53-54). *See Captive.* Keepers responsible for (Ac 12:18-19). Tortured to extort self-incriminating testimony (Ac 22:24). Flogged (Mt 27:26; Mk 15:15; Ac 16:23,33; 2Co 6:5; 11:23-24). *See Flog, Flogging; Scourging.* Permitted to make defense (Ac 24:10; 25:8,16; 26:1; 2Ti 4:16).

Kindness to: By the prison keeper to Jeremiah (Jer 38:7-28), by Philippian jailer to Paul (Ac 16:33), by Felix (Ac 24:23), by Julius, the centurion (Ac 27:1,3; 28:16,30-31). To be visited and ministered to (Mt 25:35-46). Released at feasts (Mt 27:15-17; Mk 15:6; Lk 23:17; Jn 18:39).

Of War:

Put to death (Jos 10:16-27; 1Sa 15:33; 27:11; 2Sa 12:31; 2Ki 25:7; 1Ch 20:3; Hos 13:16; Am 1:13; La 3:34), by divine command (Nu 31:9,17). Thumbs and toes cut off (Jdg 1:6-7). Blinded (2Ki 25:7).

See Captive.

Consolations for (Ps 69:33; 79:11; 102:19-20; 146:7).

See Captive; Imprisonment.

Figurative:

(Isa 61:1; Lk 4:18).

PRIVILEGE *See Judgment, According to Opportunity and Works; Responsibility.*

PRIZE [3701, *1092, 2857, 2898*].

NIV+ PRIZES

A reward of competition according to the rules (1Co 9:24-27), figurative of living the Christian life by faith (Php 3:14; Col 2:18).

PROBATION

A period of critical examination and evaluation (Ro 5:3-4).

Adam on (Ge 2:15-17; 3:3). Amorites (Ge 15:16). Solomon (1Ki 3:14; 9:4-9, w 11:9-12). Taught in parables of the talents and minas (Mt 25:14-30; Lk 19:12-27), the fig tree (Lk 13:6-9), embezzling steward (Lk 16:1-12). Taught by the author of Hebrews (Heb 6).

None after death (Mt 12:32; 25:10-13; 26:4).

See Perseverance.

PROCHORUS *See Procorus.*

PROCLAMATION [*1413, 1819, 2349, 4887, 5583, 5989, 6218, 7754, 7924, 9048, *550, 1334, 2294, 2859, 3062, 3281*].

NIV+ PROCLAIM, PROCLAIMED, PROCLAIMING, PROCLAIMS

Imperial (2Ch 30:1-10; Est 1:22; 6:9; 8:10-14; Isa 40:3,9; Da 3:4-7; 4:1; 5:29). Emancipation (2Ch 36:23; Ezr 1:1-4).

PROCONSUL [*478*] (*for the consul*).

NIV+ PROCONSULS

Roman official who served as deputy consul in a Roman province; term of the office was usually one year; Sergius Paulus and Gallio were proconsuls (Ac 13:7; 18:12).

PROCORUS [*4743*]. An early Christian deacon (Ac 6:5).

PROCRASTINATION

Eze 11:2 The LORD said to me, "Son of man, these are the men who are plotting evil and giving wicked advice in this city. ³They say, 'Will it not soon be time to build houses? This city is a cooking pot, and we are the meat.'

Eze 12:22 "Son of man, what is this proverb you have in the land of Israel: 'The days go by and every vision comes to nothing'?

Eze 12:27 "Son of man, the house of Israel is saying, 'The vision he sees is for many years from now, and he prophesies about the distant future.'

²⁸"Therefore say to them, 'This is what the Sovereign LORD says: None of my words will be delayed any longer; whatever I say will be fulfilled, declares the Sovereign LORD.'"

Rebuked—

Mt 8:21 Another disciple said to him, "Lord, first let me go and bury my father." (+Mt 8:22; Lk 9:59,61)

Admonition against—

1Th 5:2 for you know very well that the day of the Lord will come like a thief in the night. ³While people are saying, "Peace and safety," destruction will come on them suddenly, as labor pains on a pregnant woman, and they will not escape.

Forbidden—

Ex 22:29 "Do not hold back offerings from your granaries or your vats. "You must give me the firstborn of your sons.

Warning against—

Heb 3:7 So, as the Holy Spirit says:

"Today, if you hear his voice, ⁸do not harden your hearts as you did in the rebellion, during the time of testing in the desert, ⁹where your fathers tested and tried me and for forty years saw what I did. ¹⁰That is why I was angry with that generation, and I said, 'Their hearts are always going astray, and they have not known my ways.' ¹¹So I declared on oath in my anger, 'They shall never enter my rest.'"

¹²See to it, brothers, that none of you has a sinful, unbelieving heart that turns away from the living God. ¹³But encourage one another daily, as long as it is called Today, so that none of you may be hardened by sin's deceitfulness. ¹⁴We have come to share in Christ if we hold firmly till the end the confidence we had at first. ¹⁵As has just been said:

"Today, if you hear his voice, do not harden your hearts as you did in the rebellion."

¹⁶Who were they who heard and rebelled? Were they not all those Moses led out of Egypt? ¹⁷And with whom was he angry for forty years? Was it not with those who sinned, whose bodies fell in the desert? ¹⁸And to whom did God swear that they would never enter his rest if not to those who disobeyed? ¹⁹So we see that they were not able to enter, because of their unbelief.

Parables of:

Evil servant—

Mt 24:48 But suppose that servant is wicked and says to himself, 'My master is staying away a long time,' ⁴⁹and he then begins to beat his fellow servants and to eat and drink with drunkards. ⁵⁰The master of that servant will come on a day when he does not expect him and at an hour he is not aware of. ⁵¹He will cut him to pieces and assign him a place with the hypocrites, where there will be weeping and gnashing of teeth.

The five foolish virgins—

Mt 25:2 Five of them were foolish and five were wise. ³The foolish ones took their lamps but did not take any oil with them. ⁴The wise, however, took oil in jars along with their lamps. ⁵The bridegroom was a long time in coming, and they all became drowsy and fell asleep.

⁶"At midnight the cry rang out: 'Here's the bridegroom! Come out to meet him!'

⁷"Then all the virgins woke up and trimmed their lamps. ⁸The foolish ones said to the wise, 'Give us some of your oil; our lamps are going out.'

⁹"'No,' they replied, 'there may not be enough for both us and you. Instead, go to those who sell oil and buy some for yourselves.'

¹⁰"But while they were on their way to buy the oil, the bridegroom arrived. The virgins who were ready went in with him to the wedding banquet. And the door was shut.

¹¹"Later the others also came. 'Sir! Sir!' they said. 'Open the door for us!'

¹²"But he replied, 'I tell you the truth, I don't know you.'

¹³"Therefore keep watch, because you do not know the day or the hour.

See Excuses.

Instances of:

Pharaoh (Ex 8:10). Elisha (1Ki 19:20-21). Esther (Est 5:8). Disciple of Christ whose father died (Mt 8:21; Lk 9:59,61).

Felix—

Ac 24:25 As Paul discoursed on righteousness, self-control and the judgment to come, Felix was afraid and said, "That's enough for now! You may leave. When I find it convenient, I will send for you."

PROCURATOR The governor of a Roman province appointed by the emperor; often subject to the imperial legate of a larger political area. Pilate, Felix, and Festus were procurators (Mt 27:2; Ac 23:24; 26:30).

PRODIGAL SON Parable of (Lk 15:11-32).

PRODIGALITY *See Extravagance; Frugality; Industry.*

PROFANATION Of God's name (Lev 20:3; Pr 30:9), forbidden (Ex 20:7; 18:21; 19:12; 21:6; 22:2-3; Dt 5:11).

Instances of:

(Ps 139:20; Isa 52:5; Ro 2:24).

Of the Sabbath (Ne 13:15-22; Eze 20:12-13,16; 22:8; 23:38).

Of the house of God (2Ch 33:7; Ne 13:7; Jer 7:11; Mt 21:13; Mk 11:17; Lk 19:46).

Of holy things: Forbidden (Lev 22:15).

See Profane; Profanity.

PROFANE [2725, 2729] (*unloose, set free*).

NIV+ PROFANED

To desecrate or defile (Ex 31:14; Lev 19:8,12; Eze 22:26; Mt 12:5), common as opposed to holy (Eze 28:16; 42:20), godless, unholy (Heb 12:16). *See Sacrilege.*

PROFANITY Of the name of God. *See God, Name of.* Of the Sabbath. *See Sabbath.*

See Blasphemy; Oath.

PROFESSION [2040, 3934].

NIV+ PROFESS, PROFESSED

False (Pr 20:6; Hos 8:2). Of faith in Jesus. *See Confession; Testimony, Religious.*

PROGNOSTICATION By astrologers (Isa 47:13).

See Prophecy; Prophets.

PROHIBITION Of the use of intoxicating liquors. To priests on duty (Lev 10:9). To Nazirites (Nu 6:3-4).

See Abstinence; Commandments and Statutes, Of God; Drunkenness.

PROMISCUITY [2388, 9373].

Punished by death under the law (Dt 22:20-21).

Figurative of Israel's alliances with the nations and their gods (Eze 16; 23).

See Adultery; Bestiality; Fornication; Homosexual; Prostitute.

PROMISE [*606, 614, 1819, 1821, 4439, 8678, *2039, 2040, 3923, 4600*].

NIV+ PROMISED, PROMISES

First promise of the Redeemer (Ge 3:15), promise repeated to Abraham (Ge 12:2,7), promise made to David that his house would continue forever (2Sa 7:12-13,28). Jesus' promise of the Spirit fulfilled at Pentecost. There are hundreds of promises made to believers (Jas 2:5; 1Ti 4:8; 2Pe 3:9).

PROMISES [*606, 614, 1819, 1821, 4439, 8678, *2039, 2040, 3923, 4600*].

NIV+ PROMISE, PROMISED

To the afflicted. *See Afflictions, Consolation Under.* To backsliders. *See Backsliders.* To children. *See Children.* To orphans. *See Orphans.* To the righteous. *See Righteous.* To seekers. *See Seekers.*

PROMISES, OR GROUND OF ASSURANCE

(Heb 6:12; Jas 2:5; 2Pe 1:4; 3:13). Against the recurrence of universal flood (Ge 9:11). Of answer to prayer (2Ch 7:14; Job 22:27; Ps 2:8; 145:19; Isa 58:9; 65:24; Jer 29:12; 33:3; Mt 6:6; 7:7-8,11; 17:20; 18:19; 21:22; Mk 11:24; Lk 11:13; Jn 14:13-14; 15:7,16; 16:23-24; Jas 1:5; 5:15-16; 1Jn 5:14-15). Of blessings upon worshipers (Ex 20:24; Isa 40:31). Of comfort in sorrow (Ps 46:1; 50:15; 146:8; 147:3; Isa 43:2; Lk 6:21; 2Co 1:3-4; 7:6). Of spiritual enlightenment (Isa 29:18,24; 35:5-6; 42:16; Mt 10:19; Lk 21:14-15; Jn 7:17; 8:12,32; Heb 8:10). Of God's presence (Ex 3:12; Dt 31:8; 1Sa 10:7). Of Christ's presence with believers (Mt 18:20; 28:20). Of forgiveness (Ps 130:4; Isa 1:18; 43:25; 55:7; Jer 31:34; 33:8; Mt 6:14; 12:31-32; Mk 3:28; Lk 12:10; Ac 10:43; 13:38-39; Jas 5:15-16; 1Jn 1:9). Of healing (Jas 5:15). Of the Holy Spirit (Joel 2:28; Lk 11:13; 24:49; Jn 7:38-39; 14:16-17,26; 15:26; 16:7; Ac 2:38). Of spiritual adoption (Lev 26:12; 2Co 6:17-18; Heb 8:10). Of victory of the Messiah over Satan (Ge 3:15).

Given:

To believers (Jer 17:7-8; Mk 16:16-18; Jn 3:15-16; 5:24; 6:35,40,47; 7:38; 11:25; 14:12-14; Ro 9:33; 10:9, 11). Backsliders (Lev 26:40-42; Dt 30:1-3; 2Ch 30:9; Jer 3:12-15; Hos 14:4; Mal 3:7). Children (Ex 20:12; Dt 5:16; Mt 19:14; Mk 10:14; Lk 18:15-16; Eph 6:3).

To the burdened (Mt 11:28-29). The afflicted (Job 33:24-28; 36:15; Ps 9:9; 12:5; 18:27; 41:3; La 3:31). Orphans and widows (Dt 10:18; Ps 68:5; 146:9; Pr 15:25; Jer 49:11).

To seekers (Dt 4:29; 1Ch 28:9; 2Ch 15:2; Ezr 8:22; Ps 34:10; 145:18; Jer 29:13; Mt 5:6; 6:33; Lk 6:21; Jn 6:37; Ro 10:13; Heb 11:6).

To the faithful (Mt 25:21,23; Lk 12:42-44; 19:16-19; Ro 2:7,10; Rev 2:10). The forgiving, of divine forgiveness (Mt 6:14; Mk 11:25; Lk 6:37). The humble (Isa 57:15; Mt 5:3; 18:4; 23:12; Lk 6:20; 14:11; 18:14; Jas 4:6; 1Pe 5:5-6). The compassionate giver (Ps 41:1-3; 112:9; Pr 3:9-10; 11:25; 22:9; 28:27; Ecc 11:1; Isa 58:10-11; Mt 6:4; Lk 6:38; 2Co 9:6,8). The meek (Ps 10:17; 22:26; 25:9; 37:11; 147:6; 149:4; Pr 29:23; Isa 29:19; Mt 5:5). The merciful (2Sa 22:26; Ps 18:25; 41:1-3; Mt 5:7). Ministers (Ps 126:5-6; Jer 1:8; 20:11; Da 12:3; Mt 28:20; Jn 4:36-37; 1Pe 5:4).

To the obedient (Ex 15:26; 19:5-6; 20:6, w Dt 5:11; Ex 23:22,25-26; Dt 4:40; 6:2-3; 12:28; 28:1-6; 30:2-10; 1Ki 3:14; Ne 1:5; Ps 1:1,3; 25:10; 103:17-18; 119:1-2; Pr 1:33; Isa 1:19; Jer 7:23; Eze 18:19; Mal 3:10-11; Mt 5:19; 12:50; Mk 3:35; Lk 8:21; 11:28; Jn 8:51; 12:26; 14:21,23; 15:10; 1Jn 2:5,17; 3:24).

To those who fear the Lord (Ps 34:7; 103:11-13,17; 112:1; 115:13; 128:1-6; 145:19; Pr 10:27; 19:23; Ecc 7:18; 8:12). Those who have spiritual desire (Isa 55:1; Mt 5:6; Lk 6:21). Those who endure to the end (Mt 10:22; 24:13; Mk 13:13; Rev 2:7,11,17,26-28; 3:5,12,21; 21:7). Those who love their enemies (Mt 5:44-45). Those who rebuke the wicked (Pr 24:25). Those who confess Christ (Mt 10:32; Ro 10:9; 1Jn 2:23; 4:15). Peacemakers, of sonship

(Mt 5:9). Penitents (Lev 26:40-42; Dt 4:20-31; 2Ch 7:14; 30:9; Ps 34:18; 147:3; Isa 1:18; 55:7; Mt 5:4). The poor (Ex 22:27; Job 36:15; Ps 12:5; 35:10; 69:33; 72:2,4,12-14; 109:31; 132:15; Pr 22:22-23; Isa 41:17). The pure in heart (Mt 5:8). Persecuted saints (Mt 5:10-11; Lk 6:22-23; 21:12-18; 1Pe 4:14).

To the righteous (Job 17:9; 36:11; Ps 1:1-3; 34:7,22; 37:4-5; 55:22; 119:1,105; 138:8; 145:20; 146:8; Pr 25:22; Isa 58:8; Jer 17:7; Mt 6:30,33; 10:22,42; 24:13; Lk 6:35; 18:6-8; Ro 5:9; 8:30-31; 1Co 2:9; 3:21-22; Gal 6:9; Php 4:7; 2Th 3:3; Rev 2:17,26,28; 3:5; 14:13). The wise of heart (Pr 2:10-21).

Concerning:

Answer to prayer (Pr 15:29; Mk 11:23-24; Jn 14:13-14; Ac 10:4; 1Pe 3:12; 1Jn 3:22).

Blessings upon their children (Ps 103:17; 112:2-3; Isa 59:21).

Comfort (Isa 25:8; 66:13-14; Mt 5:4; Jn 14:16-18; Rev 21:4).

Deliverance, from temptation (1Co 10:13; Jas 4:7; 2Pe 2:9), from trouble (Job 5:19-24; Ps 33:18-19; 34:15,17; 50:15; 97:10-11; Pr 3:25-26; Isa 41:10-13; 43:2).

Divine help (Ps 55:22; Isa 41:10-11,13; 2Co 12:9; Php 4:19; Heb 13:5-6). Divine guidance (Ps 25:12; 32:8; 37:23-24; 48:14; 73:24; Pr 3:5-6; 58:11). Divine mercy (Ps 32:10; 103:17-18; Mal 3:17). Divine presence (Ge 26:3,24; 28:15; 31:3; Ex 33:14; Dt 31:6,8; Jos 1:5; 1Ki 6:13; Hag 1:13; 2:4-5; Mt 18:20; 28:20; Jn 14:17,23; 2Co 6:16; 13:11; Php 4:9; Heb 13:5; Jas 4:8; Rev 21:3). Divine likeness (1Jn 3:2). The ministry of angels (Heb 1:14).

Peace (Isa 26:3; Jn 16:33; Ro 2:10). Providential care (Ge 15:1; Ex 23:22; Lev 26:5-6,10; Dt 33:27; 1Sa 2:9; 2Ch 16:9; Ezr 8:22; Job 5:15; Ps 34:9-10; 37:23-26; 121:2-8; 125:1-3; 145:19-20; Pr 1:33; 2:7; 3:6; 10:3; 16:7; Isa 49:9-11; 65:13-14; Eze 34:11-17,22-31; Lk 12:7; 21:18; 1Pe 5:7). Overruling providence (Ro 8:28; 2Co 4:17). Spiritual enlightenment (Isa 2:3; Jn 8:12). Seeing God (Mt 5:8). Spiritual blessings (Isa 64:4; 1Co 2:9).

Refuge in adversity (Ps 33:18-19; 62:8; 91:1,3-7,9-12; Pr 14:26; Na 1:7). Strength in adversity (Ps 29:11). Security (Ps 32:6-7; 84:11; 121:3-8; Isa 33:16).

Temporal blessings (Lev 25:18-19; 26:5; Dt 28:1-13; Ps 37:9; 128:1-6; Pr 2:21; 3:1-4,7-10; Mt 6:26-33; Mk 10:30; Lk 18:29-30). Wisdom (Jas 1:5).

The rest of faith (Heb 4:9). Heavenly rest (Heb 4:9). Eternal life (Da 12:2-3; Mt 19:29; 25:46; Mk 10:29-30; Lk 18:29-30; Jn 3:15-16,36; 4:14; 5:24,29; 6:40; 10:28; 12:25; 17:2; Ro 2:7; 6:22-23; Gal 6:8; 1Th 4:15-17; 1Ti 1:16; 4:8; Tit 1:2; 1Jn 2:25; 5:13; Rev 22:5). Living with Christ (Jn 14:2-3; 17:24; Col 3:4; 1Th 4:17; 5:10). Everlasting remembrance (Ps 112:6). Names written in heaven (Lk 10:20). Resurrection (Jn 5:29; 1Co 15:48-57; 2Co 4:14; 1Th 4:16). Future glory (Mt 13:43; Ro 8:18; Col 3:4; 2Ti 2:10; 1Pe 1:5; 5:4; Rev 7:14-17). Treasure in heaven (Mt 10:21; Lk 18:22). Inheritance (Mt 25:34; Ac 20:32; 26:18; Col 1:12; 3:24; Tit 3:7; Heb 9:15; Jas 2:5; 1Pe 1:4). Heavenly reward (Mt 5:12; 13:43; 2Ti 4:8; Heb 11:16; Jas 1:12; 2Pe 1:11; Rev 2:7,10; 22:5,12,14). Reigning forever (Rev 22:5, w 1Co 4:8; Rev 5:10; 11:15).

See Blessings, Spiritual; God, Goodness of; Jesus the Christ, Compassion of, Love of.

PROMOTION (Ps 75:6-7; 78:70-71; 113:7-8). As a reward of merit (1Ch 11:6).

Instances of:

Abraham (Ge 12:2). Joseph, from imprisoned slave to prince (Ge 41:1-45). Moses, from exile to lawgiver. *See Moses.* Aaron, from slave to high priest. *See Aaron.* Saul, from obscurity to a scepter. *See Saul.* David, from shepherd to throne. *See David.* Jeroboam, from slave to the throne (1Ki 11:26-35). Baasha, "out of dust" to the throne (1Ki 16:1-2). Daniel, from captive to premier (Da 2:48). *See Daniel.* Shadrach, Meshach, and Abednego (Da 3:30).

PROPAGATION Of species, commanded (Ge 1:11-12,21-25,28; 9:1,7). *See Barrenness.*

PROPERTY [8, 296, 299, 1821+3972+9455, 2745, 3769, 4084, 4856, 5126, 5239, 5659, 5709, 7871, 8214, 8965, 10479, *1050, 3228, 5639*].

In Real Estate:

(Ge 23:17-18; 26:20). Rights in, violated (Ge 21:25-32; 26:18-22). Dedicated (Lev 27:16-25). *See Land.*

Dwellings:

Alienated for debt (Lev 25:14-15).

Confiscation of Naboth's vineyard (1Ki 21:15-16). Priests exempt from taxes (Ge 47:22). Restriction of to lineal descendants (Nu 27:1-11; 36:1-9). Inherited (Ecc 2:21). Landmarks of, not to be removed (Dt 19:14; 27:17).

Personal:

Rights in, sacred (Ex 20:17; Dt 5:21). Laws concerning trespass of, and violence to (Ex 21:28-36; 22:9; Dt 23:25). Strayed, to be returned to owner (Lev 6:3-4; Dt 22:1-3). Hired (Ex 22:14-15), or loaned (Ex 22:10-15). Sold for debt (Pr 22:26-27), rights of redemption of (Jer 32:7). Dedicated to God, redemption of (Lev 27:9-13,26-33). In slaves (Ex 21:4).

PROPHECY [1821, 5547, 5363, 5553, 5566, 5752, 10451, *4460, 4735, 4736*] (*speak before*).

NIV+ PROPHECIES, PROPHECY, PROPHESIED, PROPHESIES, PROPHESY, PROPHESYING, PROPHET, PROPHET'S, PROPHETESS, PROPHETIC, PROPHETS

Concerning Jesus. *See Jesus the Christ, Prophecies Concerning.* Concerning the Church. *See Church, The Body of Believers, Prophecies Concerning.* Relating to various countries, nations, and cities. *See under their respective names.* Respecting individuals. *See individuals by name.*

Inspired (Isa 28:22; Lk 1:70; 2Ti 3:16; 2Pe 1:21). "The word of the Lord came to," Elijah (1Ki 17:8; 21:17,28), Isaiah (Isa 2:1; 8:5; 13:1; 14:28; 38:4), Jeremiah (Jer 1:4; 7:1; 11:1; 13:8; 16:1; 18:1; 25:1-2; 26:1; 27:1; 29:30; 30:1,4; 32:1,6,26; 33:1,19,23; 34:12; 35:12; 36:1; 37:6; 40:1; 43:8; 44:1; 46:1; 49:34; 50:1), Ezekiel (Eze 3:16; 6:1; 7:1; 11:14; 12:1,8,17,21; 13:1; 14:12; 15:1; 16:1; 17:1,11; 18:1; 20:45; 21:1,8,18; 22:1,17,23; 23:1; 24:1,5, 20; 25:1; 26:1; 27:1; 28:1,11,20; 29:1,17; 30:1,20; 31:1; 32:1,17; 33:1,23; 34:1; 35:1; 36:16; 37:15; 38:1), Amos (Am 7:14-15), Jonah (Jnh 3:1), Haggai (Hag 2:1,10,20), Zechariah (Zec 1:7; 4:8; 6:9; 7:1,4,8; 8:1,18).

Publicly proclaimed (Jer 11:6). Exemplified in pantomime (Eze 4; 5:1-4; Ac 21:11). Written, by an amanuensis (Jer 45:1), in books (Jer 45:1; 51:60).

Proof of God's foreknowledge (Isa 43:9). Sure fulfillment of (Eze 12:22-25,28; Hab 2:3; Mt 5:18; 24:35; Ac 13:27,29). Cessation of (La 2:9).

Of apostasy (1Jn 2:18; Jude 17-18), false teachers (2Pe 2:3). Tribulations of the righteous (Rev 2:10).

Concerning Jesus the Messiah, With Their Fulfillment:

The first messianic prophecy (Ge 3:15), concerns the

prophetic announcement of the victor over Satan, the victor described as "the seed of the woman."

Messianic Prophecies and Fulfillments	
Ge 12:3; 18:18; 22:18	Ac 3:25; Gal 3:8
Ge 17:7,19; 22:16-17	Lk 1:55,72-74
Dt 18:15,18	Ac 3:22-23
Ps 2:1-2	Ac 4:25-26
Ps 2:7	Ac 13:33; Heb 1:5; 5:5
Ps 8:2	Mt 21:16
Ps 8:4-6	Heb 2:6-8
Ps 16:8-11	Ac 2:25-28,31
Ps 16:10	Ac 13:35
Ps 22:1	Mt 27:46; Mk 15:34
Ps 22:18	Mt 27:35; Mk 15:24; Lk 23:34; Jn 19:24
Ps 22:22	Heb 2:12
Ps 31:5	Lk 23:46
Ps 41:9	Jn 13:18; Ac 1:16
Ps 45:6-7	Heb 1:8-9
Ps 68:18	Eph 4:8-13
Ps 69:21	Mt 27:34,48; Mk 15:23,36; Lk 23:36; Jn 19:28-29
Ps 69:25; 109:8	Ac 1:20
Ps 78:2	Mt 13:35
Ps 95:7-11	Heb 3:7-11; 4:3,5-7
Ps 102:25-27	Heb 1:10-12
Ps 110:1	Mt 22:43-44; Mk 12:36-37; Lk 20:42-44; Ac 2:34-36; Heb 1:13
Ps 110:4	Heb 5:6; 7:15-17,21
Ps 118:22-23	Mt 21:42; Mk 12:10-11; Lk 20:17; Ac 4:11; Eph 2:20; 1Pe 2:7
Ps 118:25-26	Mt 21:9; Mk 11:9; Lk 13:35; Jn 12:13
Ps 132:11,17	Lk 1:69; Ac 2:30
Isa 7:14	Mt 1:23
Isa 9:1-2	Mt 4:15-16
Isa 9:7; Da 7:14,27	Lk 1:32-33
Isa 11:10	Ro 15:12
Isa 25:8	1Co 15:54-55
Isa 28:16	Ro 9:33; 10:11; 1Pe 2:6
Isa 40:3-5	Mt 3:3; Mk 1:3; Lk 3:4-6; Jn 1:23
Isa 42:1-4	Mt 12:17-21
Isa 49:6	Lk 2:32; Ac 13:47-48; 26:23
Isa 53:1	Jn 12:38; Ro 10:16
Isa 53:3-6	Ac 26:22-23
Isa 53:4-6,11	1Pe 2:24-25
Isa 53:4	Mt 8:17
Isa 53:9	1Pe 2:22
Isa 53:12	Mk 15:27-28; Lk 22:37
Isa 54:13	Jn 6:45
Isa 55:3	Ac 13:34
Isa 59:20-21	Ro 11:26-27
Jer 31:31-34	Heb 8:8-12; 10:16-17
Hos 1:10	Ro 9:26
Hos 2:23	Ro 9:25; 1Pe 2:10
Joel 2:28-32	Ac 2:16-21; Ro 10:13
Am 9:11-12	Ac 15:16-17
Mic 5:2	Mt 2:5-6; Jn 7:42
Hab 1:5	Ac 13:40-41
Hag 2:6	Heb 12:26
Zec 9:9	Mt 21:4-5; Jn 12:14-15
Zec 11:13	Mt 27:9-10
Zec 12:10	Jn 19:34,37
Zec 13:7	Mt 26:31,56; Mk 14:27,50
Mal 3:1	Mt 11:10; Mk 1:2; Lk 7:27
Mal 4:5-6	Mt 11:13-14; 17:10-13; Mk 9:11-13; Lk 1:16-17

See Jesus the Christ, Prophecies Concerning; Jesus the Christ, King, Prophecies Concerning.

Miscellaneous, Fulfilled:

The birth and zeal of Josiah (1Ki 13:2; 2Ki 23:1-20). Death of the prophet of Judah (1Ki 13:21-22,24-30). Extinction of Jeroboam's house (1Ki 14:5-17), of Baasha's house (1Ki 16:2-3,9-13). Concerning the rebuilding of Jericho (Jos 6:26; 1Ki 16:34). The drought, foretold by Elijah (1Ki 17:14). Destruction of Ben-Hadad's army (1Ki 20:13-30). The death of a man who refused to kill a prophet (1Ki 20:35-36). The death of Ahab (1Ki 20:42; 21:18-24; 22:31-38). The death of Ahaziah (2Ki 1:3-17). Elijah's translation (2Ki 2:3-11). Cannibalism among the Israelites (Lev 26:29; Dt 28:53; 2Ki 6:28-29; Jer 19:9; La 4:10). The death of the Samaritan lord (2Ki 7:2,19-20). The end of the famine in Samaria (2Ki 7:1-18). Jezebel's tragic death (1Ki 21:23; 2Ki 9:10,33-37). The killing of Syria by Joash (2Ki 13:16-25). Conquests of Jeroboam (2Ki 14:25-28). Four generations of Jehu to sit upon the throne of Israel (2Ki 10:30, w 15:12). Destruction of Sennacherib's army, and his death (2Ki 19:6-7,20-37). The captivity of Judah (2Ki 20:17-18; 24:10-16; 25:11-21). Concerning Christ. *See Jesus the Christ, Prophecies Concerning. See above, Concerning Jesus the Messiah.* Concerning John (Mt 3:3). Rachel weeping for her children (Jer 31:15; Mt 2:17-18). Deliverance of Jeremiah (Jer 39:15-18). Invasion of Judah by the Chaldeans (Hab 1:6-11), fulfilled (2Ki 25; 2Ch 36:17-21), betrayal of Jesus by Judas, prophecy (Ps 41:9), fulfillment (Jn 13:18; 18:1-9), Judas' self-destruction (Ps 69:25; Ac 1:16,20), fulfilled (Mt 27:5; Ac 1:16-20). Outpouring of the Holy Spirit (Joel 2:28-29), fulfilled (Ac 2:16-21). Spiritual blindness of the Israelites (Isa 6:9; 29:13), fulfilled (Mk 7:6-7; Ac 28:25-27). Mission of Jesus (Ps 68:18), fulfilled (Eph 4:8,10). *See Jesus the Christ, Mission of.* Captivity of the Israelites (Jer 25:11-12; 29:10,14; 32:3-5; Da 9:2, w 2Ki 25:1-8; Ezr 1). Of the destruction of the ship in which Paul sailed (Ac 27:10, 18-44). *See Prophetesses; Prophets.*

PROPHETESSES [5567, 4739] (*speak before*).

NIV+ See PROPHESY

Miriam (Ex 15:20). Deborah (Jdg 4:4). Huldah (2Ki 22:14). False (Eze 13:17-19). Isaiah's wife (Isa 8:3). All the daughters of Israel (Joel 2:28-29). Noadiah (Ne 6:14). Elizabeth (Lk 1:41-45). Anna (Lk 2:36-38). Daughters of Philip (Ac 21:9). Jezebel (Rev 2:20).

See Women.

PROPHETS [967, 2602, 5547, 5566, 5567, 5752, 10455, 4737, 4739, 6021] (*speak before*).

NIV+ See PROPHESY

Called seers (1Sa 9:19; 2Sa 15:27; 24:11; 2Ki 17:13; 1Ch 9:22; 29:29; 2Ch 9:29; 12:15; 29:30; Isa 30:10; Mic 3:7). Schools of (1Ki 20:35; 2Ki 2:3-15; 4:1,38; 9:1). Kept the chronicles or records (1Ch 29:29; 2Ch 9:29; 12:15). Not honored in their own country (Mt 13:57; Lk 4:24-27; Jn 4:44). Officiate at installation of kings (1Ki 1:32-35). Counselors to kings (1Ki 22:6-28; 2Ki 6:9-12; Isa 37:2-3; Jer 27:12-15).

Inspired by angels (Zec 1:9,13-14,19; Ac 7:53; Gal 3:19; Heb 2:2). Persecutions of (2Ch 36:16; Am 2:12). Martyrs (Jer 2:30; Mt 23:37; Mk 12:5; Lk 13:34; 1Th 2:15; Heb 11:37; Rev 16:6).

Compensation of:

Presents (1Sa 9:7-8; 1Ki 14:3; 2Ki 4:42; 8:8-9; Eze 13:19). Presents refused by (Nu 22:18; 1Ki 13:7-8; 2Ki 5:5,16).

Inspiration of:

1Ki 13:20 While they were sitting at the table, the word of the LORD came to the old prophet who had brought him back.

2Ch 33:18 The other events of Manasseh's reign, including his prayer to his God and the words the seers spoke to him in the name of the LORD, the God of Israel, are written in the annals of the kings of Israel. (+2Ch 36:15)

Ne 9:30 For many years you were patient with them. By your Spirit you admonished them through your prophets. Yet they paid no attention, so you handed them over to the neighboring peoples.

Job 33:14 For God does speak—now one way, now another—though man may not perceive it. ¹⁵In a dream, in a vision of the night, when deep sleep falls on men as they slumber in their beds, ¹⁶he may speak in their ears and terrify them with warnings,

Jer 7:25 From the time your forefathers left Egypt until now, day after day, again and again I sent you my servants the prophets.

Da 9:6 We have not listened to your servants the prophets, who spoke in your name to our kings, our princes and our fathers, and to all the people of the land.

Da 9:10 we have not obeyed the LORD our God or kept the laws he gave us through his servants the prophets.

Hos 12:10 I spoke to the prophets, gave them many visions and told parables through them."

Joel 2:28 "And afterward, I will pour out my Spirit on all people. Your sons and daughters will prophesy, your old men will dream dreams, your young men will see visions.

Am 3:7 Surely the Sovereign LORD does nothing without revealing his plan to his servants the prophets. ⁸The lion has roared—who will not fear? The Sovereign LORD has spoken—who can but prophesy?

Zec 7:12 They made their hearts as hard as flint and would

not listen to the law or to the words that the LORD Almighty had sent by his Spirit through the earlier prophets. So the LORD Almighty was very angry.

Lk 1:70 (as he said through his holy prophets of long ago),

Ac 3:18 But this is how God fulfilled what he had foretold through all the prophets, saying that his Christ would suffer.

Ro 1:1 Paul, a servant of Christ Jesus, called to be an apostle and set apart for the gospel of God— ²the gospel he promised beforehand through his prophets in the Holy Scriptures

1Co 12:7 Now to each one the manifestation of the Spirit is given for the common good. ⁸To one there is given through the Spirit the message of wisdom, to another the message of knowledge by means of the same Spirit, ⁹to another faith by the same Spirit, to another gifts of healing by that one Spirit, ¹⁰to another miraculous powers, to another prophecy, to another distinguishing between spirits, to another speaking in different kinds of tongues, and to still another the interpretation of tongues. ¹¹All these are the work of one and the same Spirit, and he gives them to each one, just as he determines.

Heb 1:1 In the past God spoke to our forefathers through the prophets at many times and in various ways,

2Pe 1:21 For prophecy never had its origin in the will of man, but men spoke from God as they were carried along by the Holy Spirit.

Rev 10:7 But in the days when the seventh angel is about to sound his trumpet, the mystery of God will be accomplished, just as he announced to his servants the prophets."

Rev 22:6 The angel said to me, "These words are trustworthy and true. The Lord, the God of the spirits of the prophets, sent his angel to show his servants the things that must soon take place."

Rev 22:8 I, John, am the one who heard and saw these things. And when I had heard and seen them, I fell down to worship at the feet of the angel who had been showing them to me.

Examples of Prophets:

Enoch—

Jude 14 Enoch, the seventh from Adam, prophesied about these men: "See, the Lord is coming with thousands upon thousands of his holy ones

Joseph—

Ge 40:8 "We both had dreams," they answered, "but there is no one to interpret them." Then Joseph said to them, "Do not interpretations belong to God? Tell me your dreams."

Ge 41:16 "I cannot do it," Joseph replied to Pharaoh, "but God will give Pharaoh the answer he desires."

Ge 41:38 So Pharaoh asked them, "Can we find anyone like this man, one in whom is the spirit of God?"

³⁹Then Pharaoh said to Joseph, "Since God has made all this known to you, there is no one so discerning and wise as you.

Moses—

Ex 3:14 God said to Moses, "I AM WHO I AM. This is what you are to say to the Israelites: 'I AM has sent me to you.'"

¹⁵God also said to Moses, "Say to the Israelites, 'The LORD, the God of your fathers—the God of Abraham, the God of Isaac and the God of Jacob—has sent me to you.' This is my name forever, the name by which I am to be remembered from generation to generation.

Ex 4:12 Now go; I will help you speak and will teach you what to say."

Ex 4:15 You shall speak to him and put words in his mouth; I will help both of you speak and will teach you what to do.

Ex 4:27 The LORD said to Aaron, "Go into the desert to meet Moses." So he met Moses at the mountain of God and kissed him.

Ex 6:13 Now the LORD spoke to Moses and Aaron about the Israelites and Pharaoh king of Egypt, and he commanded them to bring the Israelites out of Egypt.

Ex 6:29 he said to him, "I am the LORD. Tell Pharaoh king of Egypt everything I tell you." (+Ex 7:2)

Ex 19:9 The LORD said to Moses, "I am going to come to you in a dense cloud, so that the people will hear me speaking with you and will always put their trust in you." Then Moses told the LORD what the people had said. (+Ex 19:10-18)

Ex 19:19 and the sound of the trumpet grew louder and louder. Then Moses spoke and the voice of God answered him.

Ex 24:16 and the glory of the LORD settled on Mount Sinai. For six days the cloud covered the mountain, and on the seventh day the LORD called to Moses from within the cloud.

Ex 25:22 There, above the cover between the two cherubim that are over the ark of the Testimony, I will meet with you and give you all my commands for the Israelites.

Ex 33:9 As Moses went into the tent, the pillar of cloud would come down and stay at the entrance, while the LORD spoke with Moses.

Ex 33:11 The LORD would speak to Moses face to face, as a man speaks with his friend. Then Moses would return to the camp, but his young aide Joshua son of Nun did not leave the tent. (+Lev 1:1; Nu 1:1)

Nu 7:89 When Moses entered the Tent of Meeting to speak with the LORD, he heard the voice speaking to him from between the two cherubim above the atonement cover on the ark of the Testimony. And he spoke with him.

Nu 9:8 Moses answered them, "Wait until I find out what the LORD commands concerning you." (+Nu 9:9-10)

Nu 11:17 I will come down and speak with you there, and I will take of the Spirit that is on you and put the Spirit on them. They will help you carry the burden of the people so that you will not have to carry it alone.

Nu 11:25 Then the LORD came down in the cloud and spoke with him, and he took of the Spirit that was on him and put the Spirit on the seventy elders. When the Spirit rested on them, they prophesied, but they did not do so again.

Nu 12:6 he said, "Listen to my words: "When a prophet of the LORD is among you, I reveal myself to him in visions, I speak to him in dreams. [7]But this is not true of my servant Moses; he is faithful in all my house. [8]With him I speak face to face, clearly and not in riddles; he sees the form of the LORD. Why then were you not afraid to speak against my servant Moses?"

Nu 16:28 Then Moses said, "This is how you will know that the LORD has sent me to do all these things and that it was not my idea: [29]If these men die a natural death and experience only what usually happens to men, then the LORD has not sent me.

Dt 1:5 East of the Jordan in the territory of Moab, Moses began to expound this law, saying:

[6]The LORD our God said to us at Horeb, "You have stayed long enough at this mountain.

Dt 5:4 The LORD spoke to you face to face out of the fire on the mountain. [5](At that time I stood between the LORD and you to declare to you the word of the LORD, because you were afraid of the fire and did not go up the mountain.) And he said:

Dt 5:31 But you stay here with me so that I may give you all the commands, decrees and laws you are to teach them to follow in the land I am giving them to possess."

Dt 34:10 Since then, no prophet has risen in Israel like Moses, whom the LORD knew face to face, [11]who did all those miraculous signs and wonders the LORD sent him to do in Egypt—to Pharaoh and to all his officials and to his whole land.

Ps 103:7 He made known his ways to Moses, his deeds to the people of Israel:

Aaron (Ex 6:13; 12:1), Eleazar (Nu 26:1)

Balaam—

Nu 23:5 The LORD put a message in Balaam's mouth and said, "Go back to Balak and give him this message." (+Nu 23:16)

Nu 23:20 I have received a command to bless; he has blessed, and I cannot change it.

Nu 23:26 Balaam answered, "Did I not tell you I must do whatever the LORD says?"

Nu 24:2 When Balaam looked out and saw Israel encamped tribe by tribe, the Spirit of God came upon him [3]and he uttered his oracle:

"The oracle of Balaam son of Beor, the oracle of one whose eye sees clearly, [4]the oracle of one who hears the words of God, who sees a vision from the Almighty, who falls prostrate, and whose eyes are opened: (+Nu 24:15-16)

Joshua (Jos 4:15)

Samuel—

1Sa 3:1 The boy Samuel ministered before the LORD under Eli. In those days the word of the LORD was rare; there were not many visions. (+1Sa 3:4-6)

1Sa 3:7 Now Samuel did not yet know the LORD: The word of the LORD had not yet been revealed to him. (+1Sa 3:8-10)

1Sa 3:19 The LORD was with Samuel as he grew up, and he let none of his words fall to the ground. [20]And all Israel from Dan to Beersheba recognized that Samuel was attested as a prophet of the LORD. [21]The LORD continued to appear at Shiloh, and there he revealed himself to Samuel through his word.

1Sa 9:6 But the servant replied, "Look, in this town there is a man of God; he is highly respected, and everything he says comes true. Let's go there now. Perhaps he will tell us what way to take."

1Sa 9:15 Now the day before Saul came, the LORD had revealed this to Samuel: (+1Sa 9:16-20; 15:16)

Saul—

1Sa 10:6 The Spirit of the LORD will come upon you in power, and you will prophesy with them; and you will be changed into a different person. [7]Once these signs are fulfilled, do whatever your hand finds to do, for God is with you.

1Sa 10:10 When they arrived at Gibeah, a procession of prophets met him; the Spirit of God came upon him in power, and he joined in their prophesying. (+1Sa 10:11-13)

1Sa 19:23 So Saul went to Naioth at Ramah. But the Spirit of God came even upon him, and he walked along prophesying until he came to Naioth.

Saul's men—

1Sa 19:20 so he sent men to capture him. But when they saw a group of prophets prophesying, with Samuel standing there as their leader, the Spirit of God came upon Saul's men and they also prophesied.

David—

2Sa 23:2 "The Spirit of the LORD spoke through me; his word was on my tongue. ³The God of Israel spoke, the Rock of Israel said to me: 'When one rules over men in righteousness, when he rules in the fear of God,

Mk 12:36 David himself, speaking by the Holy Spirit, declared: "'The Lord said to my Lord: "Sit at my right hand until I put your enemies under your feet."'

Nathan (2Sa 7:3)—

2Sa 7:4 That night the word of the LORD came to Nathan, saying: (+2Sa 7:8)

Gad (2Sa 24:11)

Ahijah—

1Ki 14:5 But the LORD had told Ahijah, "Jeroboam's wife is coming to ask you about her son, for he is ill, and you are to give her such and such an answer. When she arrives, she will pretend to be someone else."

Elijah—

1Ki 17:1 Now Elijah the Tishbite, from Tishbe in Gilead, said to Ahab, "As the LORD, the God of Israel, lives, whom I serve, there will be neither dew nor rain in the next few years except at my word."

1Ki 17:24 Then the woman said to Elijah, "Now I know that you are a man of God and that the word of the LORD from your mouth is the truth." (+1Ki 19:15)

2Ki 10:10 Know then, that not a word the LORD has spoken against the house of Ahab will fail. The LORD has done what he promised through his servant Elijah."

Micaiah—

1Ki 22:14 But Micaiah said, "As surely as the LORD lives, I can tell him only what the LORD tells me."

1Ki 22:28 Micaiah declared, "If you ever return safely, the LORD has not spoken through me." Then he added, "Mark my words, all you people!" (+2Ch 18:27)

Elisha—

2Ki 2:9 When they had crossed, Elijah said to Elisha, "Tell me, what can I do for you before I am taken from you?" "Let me inherit a double portion of your spirit," Elisha replied.

2Ki 3:11 But Jehoshaphat asked, "Is there no prophet of the LORD here, that we may inquire of the LORD through him?"

An officer of the king of Israel answered, "Elisha son of Shaphat is here. He used to pour water on the hands of Elijah."

¹²Jehoshaphat said, "The word of the LORD is with him." So the king of Israel and Jehoshaphat and the king of Edom went down to him.

2Ki 3:15 But now bring me a harpist." While the harpist was playing, the hand of the LORD came upon Elisha

2Ki 5:8 When Elisha the man of God heard that the king of Israel had torn his robes, he sent him this message: "Why have you torn your robes? Have the man come to me and he will know that there is a prophet in Israel."

2Ki 6:8 Now the king of Aram was at war with Israel. After conferring with his officers, he said, "I will set up my camp in such and such a place."

⁹The man of God sent word to the king of Israel: "Beware

of passing that place, because the Arameans are going down there." ¹⁰So the king of Israel checked on the place indicated by the man of God. Time and again Elisha warned the king, so that he was on his guard in such places.

¹¹This enraged the king of Aram. He summoned his officers and demanded of them, "Will you not tell me which of us is on the side of the king of Israel?"

¹²"None of us, my lord the king," said one of his officers, "but Elisha, the prophet who is in Israel, tells the king of Israel the very words you speak in your bedroom."

2Ki 6:32 Now Elisha was sitting in his house, and the elders were sitting with him. The king sent a messenger ahead, but before he arrived, Elisha said to the elders, "Don't you see how this murderer is sending someone to cut off my head? Look, when the messenger comes, shut the door and hold it shut against him. Is not the sound of his master's footsteps behind him?"

Jahaziel—

2Ch 20:14 Then the Spirit of the LORD came upon Jahaziel son of Zechariah, the son of Benaiah, the son of Jeiel, the son of Mattaniah, a Levite and descendant of Asaph, as he stood in the assembly.

Azariah (2Ch 15:1-2)

Zechariah, the son of Jehoiada (2Ch 24:20)—

2Ch 26:5 He sought God during the days of Zechariah, who instructed him in the fear of God. As long as he sought the LORD, God gave him success.

Isaiah (2Ki 20:4)—

Isa 6:1 In the year that King Uzziah died, I saw the Lord seated on a throne, high and exalted, and the train of his robe filled the temple. (+Isa 6:2-7)

Isa 6:8 Then I heard the voice of the Lord saying, "Whom shall I send? And who will go for us?"

And I said, "Here am I. Send me!"

⁹He said, "Go and tell this people: "'Be ever hearing, but never understanding; be ever seeing, but never perceiving.'

Isa 8:11 The LORD spoke to me with his strong hand upon me, warning me not to follow the way of this people. He said:

Isa 44:26 who carries out the words of his servants and fulfills the predictions of his messengers, who says of Jerusalem, 'It shall be inhabited,' of the towns of Judah, 'They shall be built,' and of their ruins, 'I will restore them,'

Ac 28:25 They disagreed among themselves and began to leave after Paul had made this final statement: "The Holy Spirit spoke the truth to your forefathers when he said through Isaiah the prophet:

Jeremiah—

2Ch 36:12 He did evil in the eyes of the LORD his God and did not humble himself before Jeremiah the prophet, who spoke the word of the LORD.

Jer 1:1 The words of Jeremiah son of Hilkiah, one of the priests at Anathoth in the territory of Benjamin. ²The word of the LORD came to him in the thirteenth year of the reign of Josiah son of Amon king of Judah, (+Jer 1:3)

Jer 1:4 The word of the LORD came to me, saying, ⁵"Before I formed you in the womb I knew you, before you were born I set you apart; I appointed you as a prophet to the nations."

⁶"Ah, Sovereign LORD," I said, "I do not know how to speak; I am only a child."

⁷But the LORD said to me, "Do not say, 'I am only a child.' You must go to everyone I send you to and say

whatever I command you. **8**Do not be afraid of them, for I am with you and will rescue you," declares the LORD.

9Then the LORD reached out his hand and touched my mouth and said to me, "Now, I have put my words in your mouth. **10**See, today I appoint you over nations and kingdoms to uproot and tear down, to destroy and overthrow, to build and to plant." (+Jer 1:11-19; 2:1; 7:1; 11:1)

Jer 11:18 Because the LORD revealed their plot to me, I knew it, for at that time he showed me what they were doing. (+Jer 13:1-3; 16:1; 18:1)

Jer 20:9 But if I say, "I will not mention him or speak any more in his name," his word is in my heart like a fire, a fire shut up in my bones. I am weary of holding it in; indeed, I cannot.

Jer 23:9 Concerning the prophets: My heart is broken within me; all my bones tremble. I am like a drunken man, like a man overcome by wine, because of the LORD and his holy words. (+Jer 24:4; 25:3; 26:1)

Jer 26:2 "This is what the LORD says: Stand in the courtyard of the LORD's house and speak to all the people of the towns of Judah who come to worship in the house of the LORD. Tell them everything I command you; do not omit a word. (+Jer 26:12; 27:1-2; 29:30; 33:1; 34:1)

Jer 42:4 "I have heard you," replied Jeremiah the prophet. "I will certainly pray to the LORD your God as you have requested; I will tell you everything the LORD says and will keep nothing back from you."

Jer 42:7 Ten days later the word of the LORD came to Jeremiah.

Da 9:2 in the first year of his reign, I, Daniel, understood from the Scriptures, according to the word of the LORD given to Jeremiah the prophet, that the desolation of Jerusalem would last seventy years.

Ezekiel—

Eze 1:1 In the thirtieth year, in the fourth month on the fifth day, while I was among the exiles by the Kebar River, the heavens were opened and I saw visions of God.

Eze 1:3 the word of the LORD came to Ezekiel the priest, the son of Buzi, by the Kebar River in the land of the Babylonians. There the hand of the LORD was upon him.

Eze 2:1 He said to me, "Son of man, stand up on your feet and I will speak to you." **2**As he spoke, the Spirit came into me and raised me to my feet, and I heard him speaking to me.

Eze 2:4 The people to whom I am sending you are obstinate and stubborn. Say to them, 'This is what the Sovereign LORD says.' **5**And whether they listen or fail to listen—for they are a rebellious house—they will know that a prophet has been among them.

Eze 3:10 And he said to me, "Son of man, listen carefully and take to heart all the words I speak to you. **11**Go now to your countrymen in exile and speak to them. Say to them, 'This is what the Sovereign LORD says,' whether they listen or fail to listen."

12Then the Spirit lifted me up, and I heard behind me a loud rumbling sound—May the glory of the LORD be praised in his dwelling place!—

Eze 3:14 The Spirit then lifted me up and took me away, and I went in bitterness and in the anger of my spirit, with the strong hand of the LORD upon me.

Eze 3:16 At the end of seven days the word of the LORD came to me: **17**"Son of man, I have made you a watchman for the house of Israel; so hear the word I speak and give them warning from me.

Eze 3:22 The hand of the LORD was upon me there, and he

said to me, "Get up and go out to the plain, and there I will speak to you."

Eze 3:24 Then the Spirit came into me and raised me to my feet. He spoke to me and said: "Go, shut yourself inside your house.

Eze 3:27 But when I speak to you, I will open your mouth and you shall say to them, 'This is what the Sovereign LORD says.' Whoever will listen let him listen, and whoever will refuse let him refuse; for they are a rebellious house.

Eze 8:1 In the sixth year, in the sixth month on the fifth day, while I was sitting in my house and the elders of Judah were sitting before me, the hand of the Sovereign LORD came upon me there.

Eze 11:1 Then the Spirit lifted me up and brought me to the gate of the house of the LORD that faces east. There at the entrance to the gate were twenty-five men, and I saw among them Jaazaniah son of Azzur and Pelatiah son of Benaiah, leaders of the people.

Eze 11:4 Therefore prophesy against them; prophesy, son of man."

5Then the Spirit of the LORD came upon me, and he told me to say: "This is what the LORD says: That is what you are saying, O house of Israel, but I know what is going through your mind.

Eze 11:24 The Spirit lifted me up and brought me to the exiles in Babylonia in the vision given by the Spirit of God. Then the vision I had seen went up from me,

Eze 33:22 Now the evening before the man arrived, the hand of the LORD was upon me, and he opened my mouth before the man came to me in the morning. So my mouth was opened and I was no longer silent.

Eze 37:1 The hand of the LORD was upon me, and he brought me out by the Spirit of the LORD and set me in the middle of a valley; it was full of bones.

Eze 40:1 In the twenty-fifth year of our exile, at the beginning of the year, on the tenth of the month, in the fourteenth year after the fall of the city—on that very day the hand of the LORD was upon me and he took me there.

Eze 43:5 Then the Spirit lifted me up and brought me into the inner court, and the glory of the LORD filled the temple. (+Eze 43:6)

Daniel—

Da 2:19 During the night the mystery was revealed to Daniel in a vision. Then Daniel praised the God of heaven

Da 7:16 I approached one of those standing there and asked him the true meaning of all this. "So he told me and gave me the interpretation of these things:

Da 8:16 And I heard a man's voice from the Ulai calling, "Gabriel, tell this man the meaning of the vision."

Da 9:22 He instructed me and said to me, "Daniel, I have now come to give you insight and understanding.

Da 10:7 I, Daniel, was the only one who saw the vision; the men with me did not see it, but such terror overwhelmed them that they fled and hid themselves. **8**So I was left alone, gazing at this great vision; I had no strength left, my face turned deathly pale and I was helpless. **9**Then I heard him speaking, and as I listened to him, I fell into a deep sleep, my face to the ground.

Hosea—

Hos 1:1 The word of the LORD that came to Hosea son of Beeri during the reigns of Uzziah, Jotham, Ahaz and Hezekiah, kings of Judah, and during the reign of Jeroboam son of Jehoash king of Israel: (+Hos 1:2)

Joel (Joel 1:1)

Amos (Am 3:7-8)—

Am 7:14 Amos answered Amaziah, "I was neither a prophet nor a prophet's son, but I was a shepherd, and I also took care of sycamore-fig trees. [15]But the LORD took me from tending the flock and said to me, 'Go, prophesy to my people Israel.'

Obadiah (Ob 1)

Jonah (Jnh 1:1)—

Jnh 3:1 Then the word of the LORD came to Jonah a second time: [2]"Go to the great city of Nineveh and proclaim to it the message I give you."

Micah (Mic 1:1)—

Mic 3:8 But as for me, I am filled with power, with the Spirit of the LORD, and with justice and might, to declare to Jacob his transgression, to Israel his sin.

Habakkuk (Hab 1:1)

Haggai—

Hag 1:13 Then Haggai, the LORD's messenger, gave this message of the LORD to the people: "I am with you," declares the LORD.

Zechariah, the son of Berekiah—

Zec 2:9 I will surely raise my hand against them so that their slaves will plunder them. Then you will know that the LORD Almighty has sent me. (+Zec 7:8)

Elizabeth—

Lk 1:41 When Elizabeth heard Mary's greeting, the baby leaped in her womb, and Elizabeth was filled with the Holy Spirit.

Zechariah—

Lk 1:67 His father Zechariah was filled with the Holy Spirit and prophesied:

Simeon—

Lk 2:26 It had been revealed to him by the Holy Spirit that he would not die before he had seen the Lord's Christ. [27]Moved by the Spirit, he went into the temple courts. When the parents brought in the child Jesus to do for him what the custom of the Law required,

John the Baptist—

Lk 3:2 during the high priesthood of Annas and Caiaphas, the word of God came to John son of Zechariah in the desert.

The apostles—

Ac 2:4 All of them were filled with the Holy Spirit and began to speak in other tongues as the Spirit enabled them.

Philip—

Ac 8:29 The Spirit told Philip, "Go to that chariot and stay near it."

Agabus—

Ac 11:28 One of them, named Agabus, stood up and through the Spirit predicted that a severe famine would spread over the entire Roman world. (This happened during the reign of Claudius.)

Ac 21:10 After we had been there a number of days, a prophet named Agabus came down from Judea. [11]Coming over to us, he took Paul's belt, tied his own hands and feet with it and said, "The Holy Spirit says, 'In this way the Jews of Jerusalem will bind the owner of this belt and will hand him over to the Gentiles.'"

Disciple at Tyre (Ac 21:4), John, the apostle (Rev 1:10-11).

See Revelation; Word of God, Inspiration of.

False:

(Dt 18:21-22; 1Ki 13:18; Ne 6:12; Jer 23:16-27,30-32; La 2:14). Warnings against (Dt 13:1-3; Mt 24:5,23-24,26; Mk 13:6,21-22; Lk 21:8). Denunciations against (Dt

18:20; Jer 14:15). Punishment of (Dt 18:20; Jer 14:13-16; 20:6; 28:16-17; 29:32; Zec 13:3). Drunken (Isa 28:7).

Instances of False:

Noadiah (Ne 6:14), four hundred in Samaria (1Ki 22:6-12; 2Ch 18:5), Pashhur (Jer 20:6), Hanani (Jer 28; Ro 15:16).

Idolatrous: (1Ki 18:19,22,25-28,40).

See Minister, False and Corrupt.

PROPHETS, THE MINOR

Also known as "The Book of the Twelve." In Ecclesiasticus (an Apocryphal book written c. 190 B.C.), Jesus ben Sirach spoke of "the twelve prophets" (Sir 49:10) as a unit parallel to Isaiah, Jeremiah and Ezekiel. He thus indicated that these twelve prophecies were at that time thought of as a unit and were probably already written together on one scroll, as is the case in later times. Josephus (*Against Apion*, 1.8.3) also was aware of this grouping. Augustine (*The City of God*, 18.25) called them the "Minor Prophets," referring to the small size of these books by comparison with the major prophetic books and not at all suggesting that they are of minor importance.

In the tradition of Jewish canon these works are arranged in what was thought to be their chronological order:

(1) the books that came from the period of Assyrian power (Hosea, Joel, Amos, Obadiah, Jonah, Micah),

(2) those written about the time of the decline of Assyria (Nahum, Habakkuk, Zephaniah) and

(3) those dating from the postexilic era (Haggai, Zechariah, Malachi).

On the other hand, their order in the Septuagint (the earliest Greek translation of the OT) is: Hosea, Amos, Micah, Joel, Obadiah, Jonah, Nahum, Habakkuk, Zephaniah, Haggai, Zechariah, Malachi (the order of the first six was probably determined by length, except for Jonah, which is placed last among them because of its different character).

In any event, it appears that within a century after the composition of Malachi the Jews had brought together the twelve shorter prophecies to form a book (scroll) of prophetic writings, which was received as canonical and paralleled the three major prophetic books of Isaiah, Jeremiah and Ezekiel. The great Greek manuscripts Alexandrinus and Vaticanus place the minor prophets before the major prophets, but in the traditional Jewish canon and in all modern versions they appear after them.

PROPITIATION *(to cover)*. To appease the wrath of God so that his justice and holiness will be satisfied and he can forgive sin. Propitiation does not make God merciful; it makes divine forgiveness possible. An atonement must be provided; in OT times, animal sacrifices; now, the death of Christ for man's sin. Through Christ's death propitiation is made for man's sin (Ro 3:25; 5:1,10-11; 2Co 5:18-19; Col 1:20-22; 1Jn 2:2; 4:10; Heb 9:5).

See Atonement.

PROSELYTE A person of Gentile origin who had accepted the Jewish religion, whether living in Israel or elsewhere (Mt 23:15; Ac 2:10; 6:5; 13:43). A distinction was apparently made between uncircumcised proselytes, i.e., those who had not fully identified themselves with the Jewish nation and religion; and circumcised proselytes, those who identified themselves fully with Judaism.

See Converts.

PROSPERITY [*2014, 3201, 3202, 3206, 3208, 3512, 7407, 7503, 8505, 8934, 10613, 10713, 10720].

NIV+ PROSPER, PROSPERED, PROSPEROUS, PROSPERS

From God (Ge 33:11; 49:24-26; Ps 127:1; 128:1-2). Design of (Ecc 7:14).

Evil Effects of—

Pride in (2Ch 32:25). Forgetfulness of God in (2Ch 12:1; 26:16; Hos 4:7). The prosperous despise the unfortunate (Job 12:5). Dangers of (Dt 8:10-18; 31:20; 32:15; Jer 5:7; Hos 13:6).

Promised to the righteous (Job 22:23-27).

Instances of wisdom in—

Joseph and Daniel as deduced from their general conduct. *See Joseph, 1; Daniel.*

See Blessings, Temporal; Rich, The; Riches.

PROSTITUTE [924, 2388, 2390, 3978, 7728, 9373, *3434, 4520*].

NIV+ PROSTITUTE'S, PROSTITUTED, PROSTITUTES, PROSTITUTING, PROSTITUTION

Forbidden (Lev 19:29; Dt 23:17). Punishment of (Lev 21:9). Shamelessness of (Pr 2:16; 7:11-27; 9:13-18). Schemes of (Pr 7:10; 9:14-17; Isa 23:15-16; Hos 2:13). To be shunned (Pr 5:3-20; 7:25-27).

In ancient heathen worship a special class of prostitutes was connected with shrines and temples (Ge 38:15,21,22), male (1Ki 14:24; 15:12). *See Shrine.* Their earnings were not to be received at the temple (Dt 23:17-18). The term is often used in the OT to refer to religious unfaithfulness (Ex 34:15-16; Isa 1:21; Jer 2:20; Eze 23).

Rahab (Jos 2:3-6; 6:17,23,25; Heb 11:31). Jephthah, the son of (Jdg 11:1). Gomer (Hos 1:2-3; 3:3). Babylon (Rev 17).

PROSTRATION *See Obeisance; Worship, Attitude in.*

PROTRACTED MEETINGS (1Ki 8:65; 2Ch 7:8-10; 30:23).

See Revivals.

PROUD [*1450, 1452, 1454, 1455, 1467, 1469, 1575, 2086, 2295, 5294, 8123, 8124, 8146, *3016, 3017, 3018, 5662, 5881*]. *See Pride.*

PROVENDER *See Fodder.*

PROVERB [5439, 5442, *4130, 4231*].

NIV+ PROVERBS

Pithy saying, comparison or question expressing a familiar or useful truth (Ge 10:9; 1Sa 10:12; Proverbs). Design of (Pr 1:1-4). Written and compiled by Solomon (Pr 1:1; 25:1).

Miscellany of:

(1Sa 10:12; 24:13-14; 2Sa 3:8; 20:18; 1Ki 20:11; Pr 1:17; Eze 12:22-23; 16:44; 18:2-4, w Jer 31:29; Hos 4:9; Mt 12:33, w Lk 6:44; Lk 4:23; 14:34; Jn 1:46; 1Co 15:33; Gal 6:7).

See Proverbs, The Book of Proverbs Arranged Topically.

PROVERBS, BOOK OF

Authors: Although the book begins with a title ascribing the proverbs to Solomon, it is clear from later chapters that he was not the only author of the book. Pr 22:17 and 24:23 refer to the "sayings of the wise." Ch. 30 is attributed to Agur son of Jakeh and 31:1-9 to King Lemuel.

Date: If Solomon is granted a prominent role in the book,

most of Proverbs would stem from the tenth century B.C. The role of Hezekiah's men (25:1) indicates that important sections of Proverbs were compiled and edited from 715 to 686 B.C. Perhaps it was also at this time that the sayings of Agur (ch. 30) and Lemuel (31:1-9) and the other "sayings of the wise" (22:17-24:22; 24:23-34) were added to the Solomonic collections.

Outline:

I. Prologue: Purpose and Theme (1:1-7).
II. The Superiority of the Way of Wisdom (1:8-9:18).
  A. Appeals and Warnings Confronting Youth (1:8-33).
    1. Enticements to secure happiness by violence (1:8-19).
    2. Warnings against rejecting wisdom (1:20-33).
  B. Commendation of Wisdom (chs. 2-4).
    1. Benefits of accepting wisdom's instructions (ch. 2).
    2. Wisdom's instructions and benefits (3:1-20).
    3. Wisdom's instructions and benefits (3:21-35).
    4. Challenge to hold on to wisdom (ch. 4).
  C. Warnings against Folly (chs. 5-7).
    1. Warning against adultery (ch. 5).
    2. Warning against perverse ways (6:1-19).
    3. Cost of committing adultery (6:20-35).
    4. Warning against the enticements of an adulteress (ch. 7).
  D. Appeals Addressed to Youth (chs. 8-9).
    1. Wisdom's appeal (ch. 8).
    2. Invitations of wisdom and folly (ch. 9).
III. The Main Collection of Solomon's Proverbs (10:1-22:16).
IV. The Thirty Sayings of the Wise (22:17-24:22).
V. Additional Sayings of the Wise (24:23-34).
VI. Hezekiah's Collection of Solomon's Proverbs (chs. 25-29).
VII. The Words of Agur (ch. 30).
VIII. The Words of King Lemuel (31:1-9).
IX. Epilogue: The Ideal Wife (31:10-31).

The Book of Proverbs Arranged Topically:

Introduction to Wisdom—

The call of Wisdom (8:1-36; 9:1-6). Benefits of following Wisdom (2:1-22; 3:13-24). Dangers of rejecting Wisdom (1:20-33; 9:13-18). Solomon' personal plea (4:1-27).

Proverbs of Solomon and Sayings of the Wise—

Value of wise sayings (22:17-21). Purpose of the Proverbs (1:1-7).

Preeminence of God: Fear of the Lord (9:10-12; 10:27; 14:2,26-27; 15:33; 19:23; 28:14). Trust in God or self (3:5-8; 14:12, & 16:25; 16:3,20; 18:2,4,10; 19:3; 20:24; 21:22; 26:12; 28:26; 29:25). Divine providence (15:3; 16:1,4,9,33; 19:21; 21:30-31; 22:12; 27:1).

Insight and Ignorance: Wisdom and folly (13:14; 14:24; 15:24; 16:22; 17:12; 24:7,13-14). Dealing with fools (26:4-11; 27:22; 29:9). Discernment and understanding (10:13,23; 13:15; 14:6,8,15,33; 15:21; 16:16; 17:24; 19:8; 20:5; 20:12). Knowledge (10:14; 13:16; 14:18; 15:14; 18:15; 19:2; 20:15; 21:11-12; 23:3-4).

Sharing and Responding to Wisdom: Advice and rebuke (3:1-2; 9:7-9; 10:8; 12:15; 13:1; 13:13; 15:31; 17:10; 19:16,20,25,27; 23:9; 25:12; 27:5-6; 27:17; 29:1). Value of Advisors (11:14; 15:22; 20:18; 24:5-6). Discipline (3:11-12; 10:17; 12:1; 13:18,24; 15:5,10,12,32; 19:18; 20:30; 22:6,15; 23:13-14; 29:15,17,19,21). Lawkeeping (28:4,7,9; 29:18). Repentance (14:9; 28:13).

Good and Evil: Righteousness and wickedness (10:6-7,16,28-30; 11:5-10,18-20,23; 12:2-3,5-8,12,21,28; 13:9,

21,25; 14:11,19,23; 15:6,9; 20:7; 21:18; 24:15-16; 28:12, 28; 29:2,16,27). Integrity and perversion (10:9; 13:6; 15:26; 21:8; 24:8-9; 28:18; 29:10). Appropriate consequences (3:33-35; 10:3,22; 10:24-25; 11:21,27,30-31; 14:14,22; 16:7; 17:13; 18:3; 19:29; 21:12,16,21; 22:8; 26:1,3,27).

Sincere Motivation: Motive and the heart (15:11; 16:2; 17:3; 20:11,27; 21:2; 27:19). False worship (15:8,29; 21:3, 27). Duplicity (6:12-15; 10:10-11; 11:3; 16:30; 20:14; 23:6-8; 26:23-26).

Concern for others: Love and faithfulness (3:3-4; 16:6; 20:6; 25:19). Love, hatred, and compassion (10:12; 15:17; 17:5; 24:17-18; 25:21-22). Kindness and mercy (11:16-17; 12:10,25; 21:10). Overstaying welcome (25:16-17).

Concern for Self: Pride and humility (11:2; 12:9; 13:7, 10; 15:25; 16:5,18-19; 18:12; 19:10; 20:9; 21:4,24; 22:4; 25:27; 26:16; 27:2; 27:21; 29:23). Selfishness (18:1). Jealousy (27:4). Envy (14:30; 24:19-20). Greed (28:25).

Control of Self: Self-control (25:28; 29:11). Rashness (20:25; 21:5; 25:8; 29:20). Temper and patience (12:16; 14:16-17,29; 15:18; 16:32; 19:11,19; 22:24-25; 29:8,22). Drunkenness and gluttony (20:1; 23:19-21; 23:29-35). Adultery (5:1-23; 6:20-35; 7:1-27; 22:14). Prostitution (23:26-28; 29:3).

Control of the Tongue: Wise and foolish talk (14:3; 15:2,7; 16:23; 18:6-7; 19:1; 23:15-16). Righteous and wicked talk (10:20-21,31-32; 11:11; 12:13-14; 13:2; 15:28; 17:4). Appropriate speech (15:23; 16:21,24; 25:11; 27:14). Maintaining silence (10:19; 12:23; 13:3; 17:28; 18:13; 21:23). Controlled speech (15:1; 17:27; 25:15). Flattery (26:28; 28:23; 29:5). Slander and gossip (10:18; 11:13; 16:28; 17:9; 18:8, & 26:22; 20:19; 26:20). Hurtful talk (11:12; 12:18; 15:4; 16:27; 25:23; 26:2). Quarreling (17:14,19; 20:3; 22:10; 26:21). Lying (12:19,22; 17:20; 19:5,22; 21:6). Power of tongue (18:20-21).

Disharmony and Strife: Solicitation to evil (1:10-19; 16:29; 25:26; 27:3; 28:10). Violence (3:31-32; 21:7; 21:29). Murderers (28:17). Causing others harm (3:29-30). Revenge (20:22; 24:28-29). Dissension and strife (6:16-19; 17:1; 18:18-19). Meddling (26:17).

Honesty: Truthfulness (12:20; 13:5; 24:26; 26:18-19). Accurate weights (11:1; 16:11; 20:10,23). Boundary stones (22:28; 23:10-11). Wrongfully obtained gains (10:2; 13:11; 20:17,21). Bribery (15:27; 17:8,23; 21:14).

Justice: False witnesses (12:17; 14:5,25; 19:9,28; 21:28; 25:18). Open-mindedness (18:17). Judicial justice (17:15,26; 18:5; 21:15; 24:11-12,23-25; 28:5; 29:26).

Economic Well-Being: Wealth and poverty (3:9-10; 10:15; 11:4,28; 13:8; 14:20; 15:16; 17:16; 18:11,23; 19:4, 6-7; 22:2,7; 23:4-5; 27:7; 28:6,8,11,20-22). Bene-volence and generosity (3:27-28; 11:24-26; 13:22; 14:21; 18:16; 19:17; 21:13; 22:9; 25:14; 28:27). Oppression of the poor (13:23; 14:31; 15:15; 16:8; 22:16,22-23; 29:7,13). Industriousness (6:6-11; 10:4-5,26; 12:11,24,27; 13:4; 14:4,23; 15:19; 16:26; 18:9; 19:15; 19:24, & 26:15; 20:4,13,17; 21:25-26; 22:29; 24:27,30-34; 26:14; 27:18,23-27; 28:19). Conservation (21:20). Surety for another (6:1-5; 11:15; 17:18; 20:16, & 27:13; 22:26-27).

Persons and Attributes: Parents and children (1:8-9; 10:1; 11:29; 15:20; 17:2,6,21,25; 19:26; 20:20; 23:22-25; 28:24). The elderly (16:31; 20:29). Women and wives (11:22; 12:4; 14:1; 18:22; 19:13-14; 21:9, & 25:24; 21:19; 27:15-16). Kings and rulers (14:28,35; 16:10,12-15; 17:7, 11; 19:12; 20:2,8,26,28; 21:1; 22:11; 23:1-3; 24:21-22; 25:2-7; 28:2-3; 28:15-16; 29:4,12,14). Messengers (13:17;

25:13). Companions (12:26; 13:20; 14:7; 17:17; 18:24; 24:1-2; 27:8-10; 29:24).

Various Concerns: Caution (16:17; 22:3, & 27:12; 22:5). Reputation (22:1; 25:9-10). Courage (3:25-26; 14:32; 22:13; 24:10; 26:13; 28:1). Hope (13:12; 13:19; 23:17-18).

Various Observations: Joy and grief (14:10,13; 15:13; 17:22; 18:14; 25:20; 27:11; 29:6). Good news (15:30; 25:25). Curiosity (27:20).

The sayings of Agur son of Jakeh (30:1-33).

The sayings of King Lemuel (31:1-9).

A wife of noble character (31:10-31).

PROVIDENCE [7213].

NIV+ PROVIDE, PROVIDED, PROVIDES, PROVIDING, PROVISION, PROVISIONS

The universal sovereign reign of God; God's preserving and governing all his creatures, and all their actions (Job 9:5-6; 28:25; Ps 104:10-25; 145:15; 147:9; Mt 4:4; 6:26-28; Lk 12:6-7; Ac 17:25-28). General providence includes the government of the entire universe, especially the affairs of men. Special providence is God's particular care over the life and activity of the believer (Ro 8:28).

See God, Providence of.

PROVINCE [4519, 10406, *823, 824, 825, 2065, 3070*].

NIV+ PROVINCES, PROVINCIAL

Unit of an empire, like those of the Roman Empire. In Persia they were called satrapies. Rome's provinces were divided into two categories: imperial, those requiring a frontier army, and ruled by a legate appointed by the emperor; senatorial, those presenting no major problems and ruled by someone appointed by the Senate—a proconsul (Ac 13:7).

PROVOCATION [1741, 4087, 4088+, 7861, 7911, 8074, *4614*].

NIV+ PROVOKE, PROVOKED, PROVOKES, PROVOKING

Any cause of God's anger at sin (1Ki 15:30; 21:22; Eze 20:28; Ne 9:18,26).

PROXY In priest's service (2Ch 30:17).

See Substitution; Suffering, Vicarious.

PRUDENCE [1067, 6874, 6891, 6893, 8505].

NIV+ PRUDENT

Job 34:3 For the ear tests words as the tongue tastes food. [4]Let us discern for ourselves what is right; let us learn together what is good.

Ps 112:5 Good will come to him who is generous and lends freely, who conducts his affairs with justice.

Hos 14:9 Who is wise? He will realize these things. Who is discerning? He will understand them. The ways of the LORD are right; the righteous walk in them, but the rebellious stumble in them.

Mt 7:6 "Do not give dogs what is sacred; do not throw your pearls to pigs. If you do, they may trample them under their feet, and then turn and tear you to pieces.

In restraining speech—

Ps 39:1 I said, "I will watch my ways and keep my tongue from sin; I will put a muzzle on my mouth as long as the wicked are in my presence." (+Pr 12:8; 21:23; 23:9; 26:4; 29:11)

Am 5:13 Therefore the prudent man keeps quiet in such times, for the times are evil.

In heeding counsel (Pr 15:5; 20:18). In restraining appetite (Pr 23:1-2). In avoiding strife (Pr 25:8-10; 29:8).

In refraining from making a guarantee—

Pr 6:1 My son, if you have put up security for your neighbor, if you have struck hands in pledge for another, [2]if you have been trapped by what you said, ensnared by the words of your mouth,

Proverbs concerning—

Pr 8:12 "I, wisdom, dwell together with prudence; I possess knowledge and discretion.

Pr 11:13 A gossip betrays a confidence, but a trustworthy man keeps a secret.

Pr 11:15 He who puts up security for another will surely suffer, but whoever refuses to strike hands in pledge is safe.

Pr 11:29 He who brings trouble on his family will inherit only wind, and the fool will be servant to the wise.

Pr 12:8 A man is praised according to his wisdom, but men with warped minds are despised.

Pr 12:16 A fool shows his annoyance at once, but a prudent man overlooks an insult.

Pr 12:23 A prudent man keeps his knowledge to himself, but the heart of fools blurts out folly.

Pr 13:16 Every prudent man acts out of knowledge, but a fool exposes his folly.

Pr 14:8 The wisdom of the prudent is to give thought to their ways, but the folly of fools is deception.

Pr 14:15 A simple man believes anything, but a prudent man gives thought to his steps.

[16]A wise man fears the LORD and shuns evil, but a fool is hotheaded and reckless.

Pr 14:18 The simple inherit folly, but the prudent are crowned with knowledge.

Pr 15:5 A fool spurns his father's discipline, but whoever heeds correction shows prudence.

Pr 15:22 Plans fail for lack of counsel, but with many advisers they succeed.

Pr 16:20 Whoever gives heed to instruction prospers, and blessed is he who trusts in the LORD.

[21]The wise in heart are called discerning, and pleasant words promote instruction.

Pr 17:2 A wise servant will rule over a disgraceful son, and will share the inheritance as one of the brothers.

Pr 17:18 A man lacking in judgment strikes hands in pledge and puts up security for his neighbor.

Pr 18:15 The heart of the discerning acquires knowledge; the ears of the wise seek it out.

[16]A gift opens the way for the giver and ushers him into the presence of the great.

Pr 19:2 It is not good to have zeal without knowledge, nor to be hasty and miss the way.

Pr 20:5 The purposes of a man's heart are deep waters, but a man of understanding draws them out.

Pr 20:16 Take the garment of one who puts up security for a stranger; hold it in pledge if he does it for a wayward woman.

Pr 20:18 Make plans by seeking advice; if you wage war, obtain guidance.

Pr 21:5 The plans of the diligent lead to profit as surely as haste leads to poverty.

Pr 21:20 In the house of the wise are stores of choice food and oil, but a foolish man devours all he has.

Pr 21:23 He who guards his mouth and his tongue keeps himself from calamity.

Pr 22:3 A prudent man sees danger and takes refuge, but the simple keep going and suffer for it.

Pr 22:7 The rich rule over the poor, and the borrower is servant to the lender.

Pr 22:26 Do not be a man who strikes hands in pledge or puts up security for debts; [27]if you lack the means to pay, your very bed will be snatched from under you.

Pr 23:1 When you sit to dine with a ruler, note well what is before you, [2]and put a knife to your throat if you are given to gluttony. [3]Do not crave his delicacies, for that food is deceptive.

Pr 23:9 Do not speak to a fool, for he will scorn the wisdom of your words.

Pr 24:6 for waging war you need guidance, and for victory many advisers.

Pr 24:27 Finish your outdoor work and get your fields ready; after that, build your house.

Pr 25:8 do not bring hastily to court, for what will you do in the end if your neighbor puts you to shame?

[9]If you argue your case with a neighbor, do not betray another man's confidence, [10]or he who hears it may shame you and you will never lose your bad reputation.

Pr 26:4 Do not answer a fool according to his folly, or you will be like him yourself.

[5]Answer a fool according to his folly, or he will be wise in his own eyes.

Pr 27:12 The prudent see danger and take refuge, but the simple keep going and suffer for it.

Pr 29:8 Mockers stir up a city, but wise men turn away anger.

Pr 29:11 A fool gives full vent to his anger, but a wise man keeps himself under control.

Ecc 7:16 Do not be overrighteous, neither be overwise—why destroy yourself? [17]Do not be overwicked, and do not be a fool—why die before your time?

Ecc 8:2 Obey the king's command, I say, because you took an oath before God. [3]Do not be in a hurry to leave the king's presence. Do not stand up for a bad cause, for he will do whatever he pleases.

Ecc 10:1 As dead flies give perfume a bad smell, so a little folly outweighs wisdom and honor. (+Ecc 10:10)

Illustration of—

Lk 14:28 "Suppose one of you wants to build a tower. Will he not first sit down and estimate the cost to see if he has enough money to complete it? [29]For if he lays the foundation and is not able to finish it, everyone who sees it will ridicule him, [30]saying, 'This fellow began to build and was not able to finish.'

[31]"Or suppose a king is about to go to war against another king. Will he not first sit down and consider whether he is able with ten thousand men to oppose the one coming against him with twenty thousand? [32]If he is not able, he will send a delegation while the other is still a long way off and will ask for terms of peace.

Injunctions concerning—

Ro 14:16 Do not allow what you consider good to be spoken of as evil.

1Co 6:12 "Everything is permissible for me"—but not everything is beneficial. "Everything is permissible for me"—but I will not be mastered by anything.

1Co 8:8 But food does not bring us near to God; we are no worse if we do not eat, and no better if we do.

[9]Be careful, however, that the exercise of your freedom does not become a stumbling block to the weak. [10]For if anyone with a weak conscience sees you who have this knowledge eating in an idol's temple, won't he be emboldened to eat what has been sacrificed to idols? [11]So this weak brother, for whom Christ died, is destroyed by your knowledge. [12]When you sin against your brothers in this way and wound their weak conscience, you sin against

Christ. [13]Therefore, if what I eat causes my brother to fall into sin, I will never eat meat again, so that I will not cause him to fall.

1Co 10:25 Eat anything sold in the meat market without raising questions of conscience, [26]for, "The earth is the Lord's, and everything in it."

[27]If some unbeliever invites you to a meal and you want to go, eat whatever is put before you without raising questions of conscience. [28]But if anyone says to you, "This has been offered in sacrifice," then do not eat it, both for the sake of the man who told you and for conscience' sake— [29]the other man's conscience, I mean, not yours. For why should my freedom be judged by another's conscience? [30]If I take part in the meal with thankfulness, why am I denounced because of something I thank God for?

[31]So whether you eat or drink or whatever you do, do it all for the glory of God. [32]Do not cause anyone to stumble, whether Jews, Greeks or the church of God— [33]even as I try to please everybody in every way. For I am not seeking my own good but the good of many, so that they may be saved.

Col 4:5 Be wise in the way you act toward outsiders; make the most of every opportunity.

Jas 1:19 My dear brothers, take note of this: Everyone should be quick to listen, slow to speak and slow to become angry,

See Diplomacy; Gentleness; Wisdom.

Instances of:

Jacob, in his conduct toward Esau (Ge 32:3-21), toward his sons, after Dinah's defilement (Ge 34:5,30). Joseph, in the affairs of Egypt (Ge 41:33-57). Jethro's advice to Moses (Ex 18:17-23). The Israelites, in the threatened war with the two and one-half tribes (Jos 22:10-34). Saul, in not slaying the Jabesh Gileadites (1Sa 11:13). David, in his overthrowing Ahithophel's counsel (2Sa 15:33-37). Abigail, in averting David's wrath (1Sa 25:18-31). Achish, in dismissing David (1Sa 29). Elijah, in his flight from Jezebel (1Ki 19:3-4). Rehoboam's counselors (1Ki 12:7). Jehoram, in suspecting a Syrian stratagem (2Ki 7:12-13). Nehemiah, in conduct of affairs at Jerusalem (Ne 2:12-16; 4:13-23). Daniel (Da 1:8-14). Certain elders of Israel (Jer 26:17-23). Of Jesus, in charging those who were healed not to advertise his miracles (Mt 9:30; 16:20; Mk 3:12; 5:43; 7:36; 8:30; 9:9), going to the feast secretly (Jn 7:10), in restricting his public appearances (Jn 11:54; 12:36), in avoiding his enemies (Mt 12:14-16; Mk 3:7; Jn 11:47-54). Joseph, in his conduct toward Mary (Mt 1:19). Peter, in escaping Herod (Ac 12:17). Paul, in circumcising Timothy (Ac 16:3), in performing temple rites (Ac 21:20-26), in setting the Jewish sects on each other (Ac 23:6), avoiding suspicion in administering the gifts of the churches (2Co 8:20), his lack of, in his persistence in going to Jerusalem despite the warnings of the Spirit and his friends (Ac 20:22-25,37-38; 21:10-14), Paul and Barnabas, in escaping persecution (Ac 14:6), Paul and Silas, in escaping from Berea (Ac 17:10-15). The town clerk of Ephesus, in averting a riot (Ac 19:29-41).

See Diplomacy; Tact.

PRUNING [2377, 4661, *2748*].

NIV+ PRUNE, PRUNED, PRUNES

To care for and increase productivity of vines (Lev 25:3-4; Isa 5:6; 18:5). Pruning hook (Isa 2:4; 18:5; Joel 3:10; Mic 4:3). Figurative of discipline (Jn 15:2-6).

PSALMODY *See Music.*

PSALMS [3344, 4660, 5380, 9335, *6011*].

NIV+ PSALM

Psalms Outside the Book of:

Of Moses celebrating the deliverance at the Red Sea (Ex 15:1-19). Didactic songs composed by Moses, celebrating the providence, righteousness, and judgments of God (Dt 32:1-43; Ps 90). Song of Deborah, celebrating Israel's victory over Sisera (Jdg 5). Of Hannah, in thankfulness for a son (1Sa 2:1-10). Of David, celebrating his deliverance (2Sa 22), on the occasion of removing the ark (1Ch 16:7-36), at the close of his reign (2Sa 23:2-7; 1Ch 29:10-19). Of Isaiah (Isa 12; 25-26). Of Hezekiah, celebrating deliverance from death (Isa 38:9-20). Of Mary (Lk 1:46-55). Elizabeth (Lk 1:42-45). Zechariah (Lk 1:68-79).

Book of Psalms:

Collection and Structure—
The Hebrew Psalter is divided into five books:
1. Psalms 1-41.
2. Psalms 42-72.
3. Psalms 73-89.
4. Psalms 90-106.
5. Psalms 107-150.

The formation of psalters probably goes back to the early days of the first (Solomon's) temple or even to the time of David. The Psalter was put into its final form by postexilic temple personnel, who completed it probably in the third century B.C.

Topically Arranged—
Psalms of affliction (Ps 3-5; 11; 13; 16-17; 22; 26-28; 31; 35; 41-42; 44; 54-57; 59-64; 69-71; 74; 77; 79-80; 83-84; 86; 88-89; 102; 109; 120; 123; 129; 137; 140-143). Didactic psalms (Ps 1; 5; 7; 9-12; 14-15; 17; 24-25; 32; 34; 36-37; 39; 49; 50; 52-53; 58; 73; 75; 82; 84; 90-92; 94; 101; 112; 119; 121; 125; 127-128; 131; 133). Historical psalms (Ps 78; 105-106). Imprecatory psalms. *See Prayer, Imprecatory.* Intercessional psalms (Ps 20; 67; 122; 132; 144). Messianic Psalms. *See Jesus the Christ, Messiah, Messianic Psalms.* Penitential psalms (Ps 6; 25; 32; 38; 51; 102; 130; 143). Psalms of praise (Ps 8; 19; 24; 29; 33; 47; 50; 65-66; 76-77; 93; 95-97; 99; 104; 111; 113-115; 134; 139; 147-148; 150). Prophetic psalms (Ps 2; 16; 22; 40; 68-69; 72; 87; 97; 110; 118).

Psalms of thanksgiving: For God's goodness to Israel (Ps 21; 46; 48; 65-66; 76; 81; 85; 98; 105; 124; 126; 129; 135-136; 149). For God's goodness to good people (Ps 23; 34; 36; 91; 100; 103; 107; 117; 121; 145-146). For God's mercies to individuals (Ps 9; 18; 30; 34; 40; 75; 103; 108; 118; 138; 144).

Superscriptions and authorship—
Of the 150 psalms, only 34 lack superscriptions of any kind (only 17 in the Septuagint). If the superscriptions refer to authorship, authors include Moses (Ps 90), David (Ps 3-9; 11-32; 34-41; 51-65; 68-70; 86; 101; 103; 108-110; 122; 124; 131; 133; 138-145), Solomon (Ps 72; 127), Asaph (Ps 50; 73-83), sons of Korah (Ps 42; 44-49; 84-85; 87-88), Heman (Ps 88), Ethan (Ps 89). Many of the psalm titles include musical terms in Hebrew, some designating ancient melodies, others preserving musical instructions. The meaning of some of these terms is uncertain or unknown. *See Music, Symbols Used in.*

PSALMS OF SOLOMON One of the pseudepigrapha, consisting of 18 psalms in imitation of the canonical psalms, probably written between 64 and 46 B.C.

PSALTERY *See Harp; Lyre.*

PSEUDEPIGRAPHA (*writing under a false name*). Books not in the Hebrew canon or the Apocrypha, ascribed to earlier biblical authors. They were written chiefly during the intertestamental, apostolic, and post-apostolic periods.

PTOLEMAIS [*4767*]. A seaport in Asher, formerly called Accho. Paul visits (Ac 21:7).

See Acco, Accho.

PTOLEMY Common name of the fifteen Macedonian kings of Egypt whose dynasty extended from the death of Alexander the Great in 323 B.C. to the murder of Ptolemy XV, son of Julius Caesar and Cleopatra in 30 B.C.; Ptolemy I, Soter (323-285 B.C.); Ptolemy II, Philadelphus (285-246 B.C.); LXX translated, Golden Age of Ptolemaic Egypt; Ptolemy III (c. 246-221 B.C.); Ptolemy IV, Philopator (221-203 B.C.); Ptolemy V, Epiphanes (203-181 B.C.); Ptolemy VI, Philometor (181-146 B.C.); Ptolemy VII, Neos Philopator (146-117 B.C.); Ptolemy XI was the last of the male line of Ptolemy I, killed by Alexandrians; Ptolemy XII (51-47 B.C.) fled to Rome; Ptolemy XIII had Cleopatra as his wife. *See Testaments, Time Between.*

PUAH, PUA [*7025, 7026, 7045*] (perhaps from the Ugaritic meaning *girl*).

NIV+ PUITE

1. Son of Issachar (Ge 46:13; Nu 26:23, ftn; 1Ch 7:1).

2. A Hebrew midwife (Ex 1:15).

3. Father of Tola (Jdg 10:1).

PUBLIC OPINION

Kings influenced by: Saul (1Sa 14:45; 15:24), David (2Ch 20:21), Hezekiah (2Ch 30:2), Zedekiah (Jer 38:19,24-27), Herod (Mt 14:5; Ac 12:2-3), Pilate (Jn 19:6-13).

Jesus inquires about (Mt 16:13; Mk 8:27; Lk 9:18). Feared by Nicodemus (Jn 3:2), by Joseph of Arimathea (Jn 19:38), by the parents of the man who was born blind (Jn 9:21-22), by rulers who believed in Jesus but feared the Pharisees (Jn 12:42-43), by Herod (Mt 14:5), by chief priests (Mt 21:26; Mk 11:18,32; Lk 12:12; 20:6), by those who feared to further persecute the disciples (Ac 4:21; 5:26).

Concessions to:

By Paul in circumcising Timothy (Ac 16:3). By James and the Christian elders who required Paul to observe certain rites (Ac 21:18-26). By disciples who urged circumcision (Gal 6:12). By Peter and Barnabas with others (Gal 2:11-14).

Corrupt Yielding to:

By Herod in the case of John the Baptist (Mk 6:26), Peter (Ac 12:3). By Peter concerning Jesus (Mt 26:69-75; Mk 14:66-72; Lk 22:54-62). By Pilate (Mt 27:23-27; Mk 15:15; Lk 23:13-25; Jn 18:38-39; 19:4-16). By Felix and Festus concerning Paul (Ac 24:27; 25:9).

PUBLICANS *See Tax Collectors.*

PUBLIUS [*4511*] (*first*). Chief man in the island of Malta. Father of, healed by Paul (Ac 28:7-8).

PUDENS [*4545*] (*modest*). A Christian in Rome (2Ti 4:21).

PUHITES *See Puthites.*

PUITE [*7027*].

NIV+ PUAH

The descendants of Puah, of the tribe of Issachar (Nu 26:23, ftn; 1Ch 7:1). *See Puah, Pua.* The Masoretic Text has "through Puvah, the Punite."

PUL [*7040*].

NIV+ TIGLATH-PILESER

1. King of Assyria. Forced tribute from Menahem, king of Israel (2Ki 15:19; 1Ch 5:26).

2. A place or tribe in Africa (Isa 66:19).

PULPIT NIV "platform" used primarily as a position from which to speak (Ne 8:4).

PULSE NIV "lentils" (2Sa 17:28) and "vegetables" (Da 1:12,16). *See Vegetarians; Vegetation.*

PUNISHMENT [**2633, 3519, 3579, 4592, 5477, 5782, 5933, 6411, 6740, 7212, 7213, 9150, 9350, 1472, 1689, 1690, 3136, 4084, 5512*].

NIV+ PUNISH, PUNISHED, PUNISHES, PUNISHING, PUNISHMENTS

Assumed for others (Ge 27:13; 1Sa 25:24; 2Sa 14:9; Mt 27:25).

See Affliction; Afflictions; Chastisement, From God; Fine; Judgments; Penalty; Retaliation; Wicked, Punishment of.

Death Penalty:

Shall not be remitted (Nu 35:31). In the Mosaic law the death penalty was inflicted for murder (Ge 9:5-6; Nu 35:16-21,30-33; Dt 17:6), adultery (Lev 20:10; Dt 22:24), incest (Lev 20:11-12,14), bestiality (Ex 22:19; Lev 20:15-16), sodomy (Lev 18:22; 20:13), promiscuity (Dt 22:21-24), rape of an engaged virgin (Dt 22:25), perjury (Zec 5:4), kidnapping (Ex 21:16; Dt 24:7), a priest's daughter who became a prostitute (Lev 21:9), witchcraft (Ex 22:18), offering human sacrifice (Lev 20:2-5), striking or cursing father or mother (Ex 21:15,17; Lev 20:9), disobedience to parents (Dt 21:18-21), theft (Zec 5:3-4), blasphemy (Lev 24:11-14,16,23), Sabbath desecration (Ex 35:2; Nu 15:32-36), prophesying falsely or propagating false doctrines (Dt 13:1-10), sacrificing to false gods (Ex 22:20), refusing to abide by the decision of a court (Dt 17:12), treason (1Ki 2:25; Est 2:23), sedition (Ac 5:36-37).

Modes of execution of Death Penalty—

Burning (Ge 38:24; Lev 20:14; 21:9; Jer 29:22; Eze 23:25; Da 3:19-23), stoning (Lev 20:2,27; 24:14; Nu 14:10; 15:33-36; Dt 13:10; 17:5; 22:21,24; Jos 7:25; 1Ki 21:10; Eze 16:40), hanging (Ge 40:22; Dt 21:22-23; Jos 8:29), beheading (Mt 14:10; Mk 6:16,27-28), crucifixion (Mt 27:35,38; Mk 15:24,27; Lk 23:33), the sword (Ex 32:27-28; 1Ki 2:25,34,46; Ac 12:2). Executed by the witnesses (Dt 13:9; 17:7; Ac 7:58), by the congregation (Nu 15:35-36; Dt 13:9).

Not inflicted on testimony of less than two witnesses (Nu 35:30; Dt 17:6; 19:15).

Minor Offenses:

Punishable by scourging (Lev 19:20; Dt 22:18; 25:2-3; Pr 17:10; 19:29; 20:30; Mt 27:26; Mk 15:15; Lk 23:16; Jn 19:1; Ac 22:24,29), imprisonment (Ge 39:20; 40). *See Prison.* Confinement within limits (1Ki 2:26,36-38).

By God:

According to deeds—

Job 34:11 He repays a man for what he has done; he brings upon him what his conduct deserves.

Ps 62:12 and that you, O Lord, are loving. Surely you will reward each person according to what he has done.

Pr 12:14 From the fruit of his lips a man is filled with good things as surely as the work of his hands rewards him.

Pr 24:12 If you say, "But we knew nothing about this," does not he who weighs the heart perceive it? Does not he who guards your life know it? Will he not repay each person according to what he has done?

Isa 59:13 rebellion and treachery against the LORD, turning our backs on our God, fomenting oppression and revolt, uttering lies our hearts have conceived.

Jer 17:10 "I the LORD search the heart and examine the mind, to reward a man according to his conduct, according to what his deeds deserve."

Eze 7:3 The end is now upon you and I will unleash my anger against you. I will judge you according to your conduct and repay you for all your detestable practices. (+Eze 7:27)

Eze 16:59 "'This is what the Sovereign LORD says: I will deal with you as you deserve, because you have despised my oath by breaking the covenant.

Eze 39:24 I dealt with them according to their uncleanness and their offenses, and I hid my face from them.

Zec 1:6 But did not my words and my decrees, which I commanded my servants the prophets, overtake your forefathers? "Then they repented and said, 'The LORD Almighty has done to us what our ways and practices deserve, just as he determined to do.'"

Mt 5:22 But I tell you that anyone who is angry with his brother will be subject to judgment. Again, anyone who says to his brother, 'Raca,' is answerable to the Sanhedrin. But anyone who says, 'You fool!' will be in danger of the fire of hell.

Mt 16:27 For the Son of Man is going to come in his Father's glory with his angels, and then he will reward each person according to what he has done. (+Mt 25:14-30)

Mk 12:40 They devour widows' houses and for a show make lengthy prayers. Such men will be punished most severely."

Lk 12:47 "That servant who knows his master's will and does not get ready or does not do what his master wants will be beaten with many blows. 48But the one who does not know and does things deserving punishment will be beaten with few blows. From everyone who has been given much, much will be demanded; and from the one who has been entrusted with much, much more will be asked. (+2Pe 3:7)

See Judgment, According to Opportunity and Works.

See parables of the vineyard (Isa 5:1-7), landowner (Mt 21:33-41), talents (Mt 25:14-30), servants (Lk 12:47-48).

To impose on children (Ex 34:7; Jer 31:29; La 5:7). Not imposed on children (Dt 24:16; 2Ch 25:4).

Delayed—

Ps 50:21 These things you have done and I kept silent; you thought I was altogether like you. But I will rebuke you and accuse you to your face.

Ps 55:19 God, who is enthroned forever, will hear them and afflict them—*Selah* men who never change their ways and have no fear of God.

Pr 1:24 But since you rejected me when I called and no one gave heed when I stretched out my hand, 25since you ignored all my advice and would not accept my rebuke, 26I in turn will laugh at your disaster; I will mock when calamity overtakes you— 27when calamity overtakes you

like a storm, when disaster sweeps over you like a whirlwind, when distress and trouble overwhelm you.

28"Then they will call to me but I will not answer; they will look for me but will not find me. 29Since they hated knowledge and did not choose to fear the LORD, 30since they would not accept my advice and spurned my rebuke, 31they will eat the fruit of their ways and be filled with the fruit of their schemes.

Ecc 8:11 When the sentence for a crime is not quickly carried out, the hearts of the people are filled with schemes to do wrong. 12Although a wicked man commits a hundred crimes and still lives a long time, I know that it will go better with God-fearing men, who are reverent before God. 13Yet because the wicked do not fear God, it will not go well with them, and their days will not lengthen like a shadow.

Hab 1:2 How long, O LORD, must I call for help, but you do not listen? Or cry out to you, "Violence!" but you do not save? 3Why do you make me look at injustice? Why do you tolerate wrong? Destruction and violence are before me; there is strife, and conflict abounds. 4Therefore the law is paralyzed, and justice never prevails. The wicked hem in the righteous, so that justice is perverted.

Design of, to secure obedience—

Ge 2:17 but you must not eat from the tree of the knowledge of good and evil, for when you eat of it you will surely die."

Ex 20:3 "You shall have no other gods before me. 4"You shall not make for yourself an idol in the form of anything in heaven above or on the earth beneath or in the waters below. 5You shall not bow down to them or worship them; for I, the LORD your God, am a jealous God, punishing the children for the sin of the fathers to the third and fourth generation of those who hate me,

Lev 26:14 "'But if you will not listen to me and carry out all these commands, 15and if you reject my decrees and abhor my laws and fail to carry out all my commands and so violate my covenant, 16then I will do this to you: I will bring upon you sudden terror, wasting diseases and fever that will destroy your sight and drain away your life. You will plant seed in vain, because your enemies will eat it. 17I will set my face against you so that you will be defeated by your enemies; those who hate you will rule over you, and you will flee even when no one is pursuing you.

18"'If after all this you will not listen to me, I will punish you for your sins seven times over. 19I will break down your stubborn pride and make the sky above you like iron and the ground beneath you like bronze. 20Your strength will be spent in vain, because your soil will not yield its crops, nor will the trees of the land yield their fruit.

21"'If you remain hostile toward me and refuse to listen to me, I will multiply your afflictions seven times over, as your sins deserve. 22I will send wild animals against you, and they will rob you of your children, destroy your cattle and make you so few in number that your roads will be deserted.

23"'If in spite of these things you do not accept my correction but continue to be hostile toward me, 24I myself will be hostile toward you and will afflict you for your sins seven times over. 25And I will bring the sword upon you to avenge the breaking of the covenant. When you withdraw into your cities, I will send a plague among you, and you will be given into enemy hands. 26When I cut off your supply of bread, ten women will be able to bake your bread in one oven, and they will dole out the bread by weight. You will eat, but you will not be satisfied.

²⁷"'If in spite of this you still do not listen to me but continue to be hostile toward me, ²⁸then in my anger I will be hostile toward you, and I myself will punish you for your sins seven times over. ²⁹You will eat the flesh of your sons and the flesh of your daughters. ³⁰I will destroy your high places, cut down your incense altars and pile your dead bodies on the lifeless forms of your idols, and I will abhor you. ³¹I will turn your cities into ruins and lay waste your sanctuaries, and I will take no delight in the pleasing aroma of your offerings. ³²I will lay waste the land, so that your enemies who live there will be appalled. ³³I will scatter you among the nations and will draw out my sword and pursue you. Your land will be laid waste, and your cities will lie in ruins. ³⁴Then the land will enjoy its sabbath years all the time that it lies desolate and you are in the country of your enemies; then the land will rest and enjoy its sabbaths. ³⁵All the time that it lies desolate, the land will have the rest it did not have during the sabbaths you lived in it.

³⁶"'As for those of you who are left, I will make their hearts so fearful in the lands of their enemies that the sound of a windblown leaf will put them to flight. They will run as though fleeing from the sword, and they will fall, even though no one is pursuing them. ³⁷They will stumble over one another as though fleeing from the sword, even though no one is pursuing them. So you will not be able to stand before your enemies. ³⁸You will perish among the nations; the land of your enemies will devour you. ³⁹Those of you who are left will waste away in the lands of their enemies because of their sins; also because of their fathers' sins they will waste away.

Dt 13:10 Stone him to death, because he tried to turn you away from the LORD your God, who brought you out of Egypt, out of the land of slavery. ¹¹Then all Israel will hear and be afraid, and no one among you will do such an evil thing again. (+Dt 17:13; 19:19-20)

Dt 21:21 Then all the men of his town shall stone him to death. You must purge the evil from among you. All Israel will hear of it and be afraid. (+Dt 21:22)

Pr 19:25 Flog a mocker, and the simple will learn prudence; rebuke a discerning man, and he will gain knowledge.

Pr 21:11 When a mocker is punished, the simple gain wisdom; when a wise man is instructed, he gets knowledge.

Pr 26:3 A whip for the horse, a halter for the donkey, and a rod for the backs of fools!

See Judgments, Design of.

No escape from (Ge 3:7-19; 4:9-11)—

Job 11:20 But the eyes of the wicked will fail, and escape will elude them; their hope will become a dying gasp." (+Job 34:21-22)

Pr 1:24 But since you rejected me when I called and no one gave heed when I stretched out my hand, ²⁵since you ignored all my advice and would not accept my rebuke, ²⁶I in turn will laugh at your disaster; I will mock when calamity overtakes you— ²⁷when calamity overtakes you like a storm, when disaster sweeps over you like a whirlwind, when distress and trouble overwhelm you.

²⁸"Then they will call to me but I will not answer; they will look for me but will not find me. ²⁹Since they hated knowledge and did not choose to fear the LORD, ³⁰since they would not accept my advice and spurned my rebuke, ³¹they will eat the fruit of their ways and be filled with the fruit of their schemes.

Pr 11:21 Be sure of this: The wicked will not go unpunished, but those who are righteous will go free.

Pr 16:5 The LORD detests all the proud of heart. Be sure of this: They will not go unpunished.

Pr 29:1 A man who remains stiff-necked after many rebukes will suddenly be destroyed—without remedy. (+Isa 10:3)

Jer 11:11 Therefore this is what the LORD says: 'I will bring on them a disaster they cannot escape. Although they cry out to me, I will not listen to them.

Jer 15:1 Then the LORD said to me: "Even if Moses and Samuel were to stand before me, my heart would not go out to this people. Send them away from my presence! Let them go!

Jer 25:28 But if they refuse to take the cup from your hand and drink, tell them, 'This is what the LORD Almighty says: You must drink it! ²⁹See, I am beginning to bring disaster on the city that bears my Name, and will you indeed go unpunished? You will not go unpunished, for I am calling down a sword upon all who live on the earth, declares the LORD Almighty.' (+Eze 7:19)

Am 2:14 The swift will not escape, the strong will not muster their strength, and the warrior will not save his life. ¹⁵The archer will not stand his ground, the fleet-footed soldier will not get away, and the horseman will not save his life. ¹⁶Even the bravest warriors will flee naked on that day," declares the LORD. (+Am 9:1-4)

Zep 1:18 Neither their silver nor their gold will be able to save them on the day of the LORD's wrath. In the fire of his jealousy the whole world will be consumed, for he will make a sudden end of all who live in the earth."

Mt 10:28 Do not be afraid of those who kill the body but cannot kill the soul. Rather, be afraid of the One who can destroy both soul and body in hell.

Mt 23:33 "You snakes! You brood of vipers! How will you escape being condemned to hell?

Ro 2:3 So when you, a mere man, pass judgment on them and yet do the same things, do you think you will escape God's judgment? (+1Th 5:2-3)

Col 3:25 Anyone who does wrong will be repaid for his wrong, and there is no favoritism.

Heb 2:3 how shall we escape if we ignore such a great salvation? This salvation, which was first announced by the Lord, was confirmed to us by those who heard him.

Heb 12:25 See to it that you do not refuse him who speaks. If they did not escape when they refused him who warned them on earth, how much less will we, if we turn away from him who warns us from heaven? (+Heb 12:26; Rev 6:15-17)

Eternal—

Isa 34:8 For the LORD has a day of vengeance, a year of retribution, to uphold Zion's cause. ⁹Edom's streams will be turned into pitch, her dust into burning sulfur; her land will become blazing pitch! ¹⁰It will not be quenched night and day; its smoke will rise forever. From generation to generation it will lie desolate; no one will ever pass through it again.

Da 12:2 Multitudes who sleep in the dust of the earth will awake: some to everlasting life, others to shame and everlasting contempt.

Mt 3:12 His winnowing fork is in his hand, and he will clear his threshing floor, gathering his wheat into the barn and burning up the chaff with unquenchable fire."

Mt 10:28 Do not be afraid of those who kill the body but cannot kill the soul. Rather, be afraid of the One who can destroy both soul and body in hell.

Mt 18:8 If your hand or your foot causes you to sin cut it off and throw it away. It is better for you to enter life maimed or crippled than to have two hands or two feet and be thrown into eternal fire.

Mt 25:41 "Then he will say to those on his left, 'Depart from me, you who are cursed, into the eternal fire prepared for the devil and his angels.

Mt 25:46 "Then they will go away to eternal punishment, but the righteous to eternal life."

Mk 3:29 But whoever blasphemes against the Holy Spirit will never be forgiven; he is guilty of an eternal sin."

Lk 3:17 His winnowing fork is in his hand to clear his threshing floor and to gather the wheat into his barn, but he will burn up the chaff with unquenchable fire."

Jn 5:29 and come out—those who have done good will rise to live, and those who have done evil will rise to be condemned.

Heb 6:2 instruction about baptisms, the laying on of hands, the resurrection of the dead, and eternal judgment.

Heb 10:28 Anyone who rejected the law of Moses died without mercy on the testimony of two or three witnesses. [29] How much more severely do you think a man deserves to be punished who has trampled the Son of God under foot, who has treated as an unholy thing the blood of the covenant that sanctified him, and who has insulted the Spirit of grace? [30] For we know him who said, "It is mine to avenge; I will repay," and again, "The Lord will judge his people." [31] It is a dreadful thing to fall into the hands of the living God.

Rev 14:10 he, too, will drink of the wine of God's fury, which has been poured full strength into the cup of his wrath. He will be tormented with burning sulfur in the presence of the holy angels and of the Lamb. [11] And the smoke of their torment rises for ever and ever. There is no rest day or night for those who worship the beast and his image, or for anyone who receives the mark of his name."

Rev 19:3 And again they shouted: "Hallelujah! The smoke from her goes up for ever and ever."

Rev 20:10 And the devil, who deceived them, was thrown into the lake of burning sulfur, where the beast and the false prophet had been thrown. They will be tormented day and night for ever and ever.

See Wicked, Punishment of.

PUNISHMENT, EVERLASTING

Is taught in Scripture for those who reject God's love revealed in Christ (Mt 25:46; Da 12:2). The final place of everlasting punishment is called the "lake of fire" (Rev 19:20; 20:10,14-15), also called "the second death" (Rev 14:9-11; 20:6). "Hell" in Scripture translates the word *Hades*, the unseen realm where the souls of all the dead are. *Gehenna* is the place of punishment of *Hades; paradise* is the place of blessing of *Hades* (Lk 16:19-31). The reason for eternal punishment is man's rejection of God's provision for the forgiveness of sin through the life and work of Jesus Christ, God's Son (Jn 3:16-18).

PUNITE *See Puite.*

PUNON
[7044]. A city of Edom. A camping ground of the Israelites in their forty years' wandering (Nu 33:42-43).

PUR
[7052] (*lots*).

NIV+ LOT

Lot cast to destroy Jews in the time of Esther (Est 3:7; 9:24,26). Feast of Purim is a Jewish festival commemorat-

ing the deliverance of the Jews from mass murder by Haman. *See Lot, The; Purim.*

PURAH, PURA
[7242] (*branch* ISBE; *imposing* KB). A servant of Gideon (Jdg 7:10-11).

PURIFICATION
[2633, 3198, 3200, *49, 50, 2752*].

NIV+ See PURITY

In studying the Mosaic law relating to purifications, it must be kept in mind that sin defiles. To keep this great truth constantly before the mind of the Israelites, specific ordinances concerning purifications were given to Moses; the purpose being, by this object lesson, to teach that sin defiles and only the pure in heart can see God. Therefore, certain incidents, such as eating that which had died of itself, touching the dead, etc., were signified as defiling, and definite ceremonies were prescribed for persons who were defiled. During the period of defilement, and when performing the ceremonies required of them, the defiled were expected to contemplate the defilement of sin and the need of purification of the heart.

Required:

Sanitary and symbolic (Ex 19:10,14; Heb 9:10). For women after childbirth (Lev 12:6-8; Lk 2:22)

After menstruation—

Lev 15:19 " 'When a woman has her regular flow of blood, the impurity of her monthly period will last seven days, and anyone who touches her will be unclean till evening. [20] " 'Anything she lies on during her period will be unclean, and anything she sits on will be unclean. [21] Whoever touches her bed must wash his clothes and bathe with water, and he will be unclean till evening. [22] Whoever touches anything she sits on must wash his clothes and bathe with water, and he will be unclean till evening. [23] Whether it is the bed or anything she was sitting on, when anyone touches it, he will be unclean till evening. [24] " 'If a man lies with her and her monthly flow touches him, he will be unclean for seven days; any bed he lies on will be unclean. [25] " 'When a woman has a discharge of blood for many days at a time other than her monthly period or has a discharge that continues beyond her period, she will be unclean as long as she has the discharge, just as in the days of her period. [26] Any bed she lies on while her discharge continues will be unclean, as is her bed during her monthly period, and anything she sits on will be unclean, as during her period. [27] Whoever touches them will be unclean; he must wash his clothes and bathe with water, and he will be unclean till evening. (+Lev 15:28-33; 2Sa 11:4)

After intercourse—

Lev 15:16 " 'When a man has an emission of semen, he must bathe his whole body with water, and he will be unclean till evening. [17] Any clothing or leather that has semen on it must be washed with water, and it will be unclean till evening. [18] When a man lies with a woman and there is an emission of semen, both must bathe with water, and they will be unclean till evening.

For a discharge—

Lev 15:4 " 'Any bed the man with a discharge lies on will be unclean, and anything he sits on will be unclean. [5] Anyone who touches his bed must wash his clothes and bathe with water, and he will be unclean till evening. [6] Whoever sits on anything that the man with a discharge sat on must wash his clothes and bathe with water, and he will be unclean till evening. [7] " 'Whoever touches the man who has a discharge must wash his clothes and bathe with water, and he will be unclean till evening.

⁸"'If the man with the discharge spits on someone who is clean, that person must wash his clothes and bathe with water, and he will be unclean till evening.

⁹"'Everything the man sits on when riding will be unclean, ¹⁰and whoever touches any of the things that were under him will be unclean till evening; whoever picks up those things must wash his clothes and bathe with water, and he will be unclean till evening.

¹¹"'Anyone the man with a discharge touches without rinsing his hands with water must wash his clothes and bathe with water, and he will be unclean till evening.

¹²"'A clay pot that the man touches must be broken, and any wooden article is to be rinsed with water.

¹³"'When a man is cleansed from his discharge, he is to count off seven days for his ceremonial cleansing; he must wash his clothes and bathe himself with fresh water, and he will be clean. (+Lev 15:14-18)

For those cleansed of leprosy—

Lev 14:8 "The person to be cleansed must wash his clothes, shave off all his hair and bathe with water; then he will be ceremonially clean. After this he may come into the camp, but he must stay outside his tent for seven days. ⁹On the seventh day he must shave off all his hair; he must shave his head, his beard, his eyebrows and the rest of his hair. He must wash his clothes and bathe himself with water, and he will be clean.

For eating that which died of itself—

Lev 17:15 "'Anyone, whether native-born or alien, who eats anything found dead or torn by wild animals must wash his clothes and bathe with water, and he will be ceremonially unclean till evening; then he will be clean.

For those who had slain in battle (Nu 31:19-24).

Of priests (Ex 29:4; 30:18-21; 40:12,30-32; Lev 8:6)—

Lev 16:4 He is to put on the sacred linen tunic, with linen undergarments next to his body; he is to tie the linen sash around him and put on the linen turban. These are sacred garments; so he must bathe himself with water before he puts them on.

Lev 16:24 He shall bathe himself with water in a holy place and put on his regular garments. Then he shall come out and sacrifice the burnt offering for himself and the burnt offering for the people, to make atonement for himself and for the people.

Lev 16:26 "The man who releases the goat as a scapegoat must wash his clothes and bathe himself with water; afterward he may come into the camp.

Lev 16:28 The man who burns them must wash his clothes and bathe himself with water; afterward he may come into the camp.

Lev 22:3 "Say to them: 'For the generations to come, if any of your descendants is ceremonially unclean and yet comes near the sacred offerings that the Israelites consecrate to the LORD, that person must be cut off from my presence. I am the LORD.

Nu 19:7 After that, the priest must wash his clothes and bathe himself with water. He may then come into the camp, but he will be ceremonially unclean till evening. ⁸The man who burns it must also wash his clothes and bathe with water, and he too will be unclean till evening.

2Ch 4:6 He then made ten basins for washing and placed five on the south side and five on the north. In them the things to be used for the burnt offerings were rinsed, but the Sea was to be used by the priests for washing.

Of Levites—

Nu 8:6 "Take the Levites from among the other Israelites and make them ceremonially clean. ⁷To purify them, do this: Sprinkle the water of cleansing on them; then have them shave their whole bodies and wash their clothes, and so purify themselves.

Nu 8:21 The Levites purified themselves and washed their clothes. Then Aaron presented them as a wave offering before the LORD and made atonement for them to purify them.

Of lepers. *See Leprosy.* Of the Jews before the Passover (Jn 11:55). By fire, for things that resist fire (Nu 31:23). By blood (Ex 24:5-8; Lev 14:6-7; Heb 9:12-14,19-22). By abstaining from sexual intercourse (Ex 19:15). By washing in water, parts of animal sacrifices (Lev 1:9,13; 9:14; 2Ch 4:6). Penalty to be imposed upon those who do not observe the ordinances concerning (Lev 7:20-21; 22:3; Nu 19:13,20).

Water of (Nu 19:17-21; 31:23). Washing hands in water, symbolic of innocence (Dt 21:6; Ps 26:6).

Traditions of the elders concerning (Mt 15:2)—

Mk 7:2 saw some of his disciples eating food with hands that were "unclean," that is, unwashed. ³(The Pharisees and all the Jews do not eat unless they give their hands a ceremonial washing, holding to the tradition of the elders. ⁴When they come from the marketplace they do not eat unless they wash. And they observe many other traditions, such as the washing of cups, pitchers and kettles.)

⁵So the Pharisees and teachers of the law asked Jesus, "Why don't your disciples live according to the tradition of the elders instead of eating their food with 'unclean' hands?"

Mk 7:8 You have let go of the commands of God and are holding on to the traditions of men."

⁹And he said to them: "You have a fine way of setting aside the commands of God in order to observe your own traditions! (+Lk 11:38)

Of Paul, to show his fidelity to the law (Ac 21:24,26).

See Washing; Defilement; Sanitation and Hygiene; Spiritual Purification.

Practiced by:

Jacob—

Ge 35:2 So Jacob said to his household and to all who were with him, "Get rid of the foreign gods you have with you, and purify yourselves and change your clothes.

Moses—

Ex 19:10 And the LORD said to Moses, "Go to the people and consecrate them today and tomorrow. Have them wash their clothes

Ex 19:14 After Moses had gone down the mountain to the people, he consecrated them, and they washed their clothes.

Aaron—

Ex 29:4 Then bring Aaron and his sons to the entrance to the Tent of Meeting and wash them with water.

Ex 30:18 "Make a bronze basin, with its bronze stand, for washing. Place it between the Tent of Meeting and the altar, and put water in it. ¹⁹Aaron and his sons are to wash their hands and feet with water from it. ²⁰Whenever they enter the Tent of Meeting, they shall wash with water so that they will not die. Also, when they approach the altar to minister by presenting an offering made to the LORD by fire, ²¹they shall wash their hands and feet so that they will not die. This is to be a lasting ordinance for Aaron and his descendants for the generations to come."

Ex 40:12 "Bring Aaron and his sons to the entrance to the Tent of Meeting and wash them with water.

Ex 40:30 He placed the basin between the Tent of Meeting and the altar and put water in it for washing, ³¹and Moses and Aaron and his sons used it to wash their hands and feet. ³²They washed whenever they entered the Tent of Meeting or approached the altar, as the LORD commanded Moses.

Lev 8:6 Then Moses brought Aaron and his sons forward and washed them with water.

Figurative:

(Ps 26:6; 51:7; Eze 36:25). *See Spiritual Purification.*

PURIM [7052] (*lots*). A feast instituted to commemorate the deliverance of the Jews from the plot of Haman (Est 9:20-32). *See Annual Feasts; Lot, The; Pur.*

PURITY [*1338, 1405, 2341, 2342, 2348, 2627, 2633, 3196, 3197, 3198, 3200, 6034, 7058, 7727, *48, 49, 54, 55, 299, 2751, 2751, 2752, 2754, 4410*].

NIV+ PURE, PUREST, PURIFICATION, PURIFIED, PURIFIER, PURIFIES, PURIFY, PURIFYING, PURITY

A Christian virtue (1Ti 4:12; 5:22)—

Tit 1:15 To the pure, all things are pure, but to those who are corrupted and do not believe, nothing is pure. In fact, both their minds and consciences are corrupted.

Jesus our pattern in—

1Jn 3:3 Everyone who has this hope in him purifies himself, just as he is pure.

Word of God pure—

Ps 19:8 The precepts of the LORD are right, giving joy to the heart. The commands of the LORD are radiant, giving light to the eyes. (+Ps 12:6)

Ps 119:140 Your promises have been thoroughly tested, and your servant loves them.

Of the Human Heart:

Ps 24:3 Who may ascend the hill of the LORD? Who may stand in his holy place? ⁴He who has clean hands and a pure heart, who does not lift up his soul to an idol or swear by what is false. ⁵He will receive blessing from the LORD and vindication from God his Savior.

Ps 65:3 When we were overwhelmed by sins, you forgave our transgressions.

Pr 15:26 The LORD detests the thoughts of the wicked, but those of the pure are pleasing to him.

Pr 20:9 Who can say, "I have kept my heart pure; I am clean and without sin"?

Pr 21:8 The way of the guilty is devious, but the conduct of the innocent is upright.

Pr 30:12 those who are pure in their own eyes and yet are not cleansed of their filth;

Isa 1:18 "Come now, let us reason together," says the LORD. "Though your sins are like scarlet, they shall be as white as snow; though they are red as crimson, they shall be like wool.

Isa 1:25 I will turn my hand against you; I will thoroughly purge away your dross and remove all your impurities.

Isa 6:7 With it he touched my mouth and said, "See, this has touched your lips; your guilt is taken away and your sin atoned for."

Mic 6:11 Shall I acquit a man with dishonest scales, with a bag of false weights?

1Ti 1:5 The goal of this command is love, which comes from a pure heart and a good conscience and a sincere faith. (+2Ti 2:21-22)

Heb 10:2 If it could, would they not have stopped being offered? For the worshipers would have been cleansed once for all, and would no longer have felt guilty for their sins.

Blessedness of—

Mt 5:8 Blessed are the pure in heart, for they will see God.

Prayer for—

Ps 51:7 Cleanse me with hyssop, and I will be clean; wash me, and I will be whiter than snow.

Da 12:10 Many will be purified, made spotless and refined, but the wicked will continue to be wicked. None of the wicked will understand, but those who are wise will understand.

Heb 9:13 The blood of goats and bulls and the ashes of a heifer sprinkled on those who are ceremonially unclean sanctify them so that they are outwardly clean. ¹⁴How much more, then, will the blood of Christ, who through the eternal Spirit offered himself unblemished to God, cleanse our consciences from acts that lead to death, so that we may serve the living God!

Through divine discipline—

Mal 3:2 But who can endure the day of his coming? Who can stand when he appears? For he will be like a refiner's fire or a launderer's soap. ³He will sit as a refiner and purifier of silver; he will purify the Levites and refine them like gold and silver. Then the LORD will have men who will bring offerings in righteousness,

Jn 15:2 He cuts off every branch in me that bears no fruit, while every branch that does bear fruit he prunes so that it will be even more fruitful.

The blood of Christ (Heb 9:13-14).

Commanded—

1Ti 3:9 They must keep hold of the deep truths of the faith with a clear conscience.

1Ti 5:22 Do not be hasty in the laying on of hands, and do not share in the sins of others. Keep yourself pure. (+2Ti 1:3)

2Ti 2:21 If a man cleanses himself from the latter, he will be an instrument for noble purposes, made holy, useful to the Master and prepared to do any good work.

²²Flee the evil desires of youth, and pursue righteousness, faith, love and peace, along with those who call on the Lord out of a pure heart.

Jas 4:8 Come near to God and he will come near to you. Wash your hands, you sinners, and purify your hearts, you double-minded.

1Pe 1:22 Now that you have purified yourselves by obeying the truth so that you have sincere love for your brothers, love one another deeply, from the heart.

Meditation upon, commanded—

Php 4:8 Finally, brothers, whatever is true, whatever is noble, whatever is right, whatever is pure, whatever is lovely, whatever is admirable—if anything is excellent or praiseworthy—think about such things.

Exemplified by Paul (2Ti 1:3).

See Holiness; Sanitation and Hygiene; Spiritual Purification.

For symbolisms of purity, *See Colors, Figurative and Symbolic, White; Defilement; Purification; Washings.*

PURPLE [760, 763, 9355, 10066, *4525, 4526, 4527*]. A color highly esteemed in ancient times; because of its costliness, it became a mark of distinction to wear robes of purple. Royalty was so dressed. The color included various shades between crimson and violet (Ex 25:4; 26:36; 28:15; 35:6; Jdg 8:26; 2Ch 2:14).

See Colors, Figurative and Symbolic.

PURSE [3038, 3967, 7655, 7975, *964*].

NIV+ PURSES

A bag for holding money (Pr 1:14; 7:20; Hag 1:6; Lk 10:4).

PURTENANCE Entrails (Lev 1:9).

PURVEYOR Those providing supplies to Solomon (1Ki 4:7-19,27).

PUT [*7033].

1. Son of Ham (Ge 10:6; 1Ch 1:8).

2. The descendants of Put, or the country inhabited by them; Put has also been taken to signify Egypt and is often associated with the Libyans (Isa 66:19, ftn; Eze 27:10; 30:5; 38:5; Jer 46:9; Na 3:9). *See Libya.*

PUTEOLI [*4541*] (Latin *rotten [sulfur] smell* or *well,* *spring*). Seaport of Italy, eight miles W of Naples; nearest harbor to Rome (Ac 28:13-14).

PUTHITES [7057] (*simple*). Family descended from Caleb (1Ch 2:50,53).

PUTIEL [7034] (*he whom God [El] gives*). The father-in-law of Eleazar the priest (Ex 6:25).

PUVAH *See Puah, Pua.*

PYGARG *See Ibex.*

PYRAMIDS (possibly *pointed* [like a flame tongue, or a wheat tip]). Tombs with superstructures of triangular form made for the interment of royalty in Egypt. About eighty survive. *See Ziggurat.*

PYRRHUS [*4795*] (*fiery-red*). Father of Sopater (Ac 20:4).

Q

QUAIL [8513]. Miracle of, in the wilderness of Sin (Ex 16:13), Kibroth Hattaavah (Nu 11:31-32; Ps 105:40).

QUARANTANIA The mountain where according to tradition Satan tempted Jesus to worship him (Mt 4:8-10), Tell el-Sultan, a short distance W of OT Jericho.

QUARANTINE For prevention of the spread of disease. *See Sanitation and Hygiene.*

QUARRIES [1014+5217, 5024, 5825, 8696].
NIV+ QUARRY

A place to remove building stone (Jos 7:5; 1Ki 5:17, 6:7; Ecc 10:9; Isa 51:1).

QUARTUS [*3181*] *(fourth [born])*. A Christian in Corinth (Ro 16:23).

QUATERNION *(four)*. A squad of four soldiers (Ac 12:4).

QUEEN [1485, 1509, 4867, 4887, 4893, 4906, 8576, 8712, 10423, *999*].
NIV+ QUEEN'S, QUEENS

The wife of a king (1Ki 11:19). Crowned (Est 1:11; 2:17). Divorced (Est 1:10-22). Sits on the throne with the king (Ne 2:6). Makes feasts for the women of the royal household (Est 1:9). Exerts an evil influence in public affairs. *See Jezebel.* Counsels the king (Da 5:10-12). Queen of Sheba visits Solomon (1Ki 10:1-13). Candace, of Ethiopia (Ac 8:27).

Queen Athaliah was the only independent female ruler of Israel or Judah. *See Athaliah.*

Queen of Heaven (Jer 7:18; 44:7-19,25). *See Idolatry; Queen of Heaven.*

QUEEN OF HEAVEN Ishtar, Babylonian female deity (Jer 7:18; 44:17-25). *See Idolatry.*

QUICKENING Coming to life. Of the church: By the Father (Ps 71:20; 80:18; Ro 4:17; 8:11; Eph 2:1; 1Ti 6:13), by the Holy Spirit (Jn 6:63; Ro 8:11; 2Co 3:6; 1Pe 3:18). *See Life; Regeneration; Resurrection.*

QUICKSANDS NIV "sandbars" (Ac 27:17). *See Sandbars.*

QUIRINIUS [*3256*]. Governor of Syria A.D. 6-9. His census of A.D. 6 at the request of the emperor Augustus is referred to in Ac 5:37. Another census, in which Joseph and Mary were registered, is mentioned in Lk 2:2. This may indicate Quirinius served an earlier term as governor of Syria and Luke mentions his "first" (NIV) and otherwise unknown census. Or the verse may be translated "This was *before* the census that took place while Quirinius was governor of Syria."

QUIVER [880, 9437] (from a root meaning *to hang, suspend*).
NIV+ QUIVERED, QUIVERS

For arrows (Ge 27:3; Isa 22:6).

R

RA Egyptian sun-god. Joseph married a daughter of the priest of On, center of the cult of Ra (Ge 41:45,50). The plague of darkness was an insult against (Ex 10:21-23).

RAAMAH [8309, 8311].

1. Son of Cush (Ge 10:7; 1Ch 1:9).

2. A place in Arabia (Eze 27:22).

RAAMIAH [8313] (*Yahweh has thundered*). An Israelite who returned from captivity with Zerubbabel (Ne 7:7).

RAAMSES *See Rameses.*

RABBAH, RABBATH [8051] (*chief, capital [city]*).

1. A town in Judah (Jos 15:60), not now identifiable.

2. Capital of Ammon, represented today by Amman, the capital of Jordan, twenty-two miles E of Jordan (Jos 13:25; 2Sa 11:1; 12:27-29; 1Ch 20:1; Jer 49:2-3). Subsequently captured by Ptolemy Philadelphus (285-247 B.C.), who changed its name to Philadelphia; became one of the cities of the Decapolis. Twice spelled "Rabbath" (Dt 3:11; Eze 21:20).

RABBATH-AMMON (*chief city of Ammon*). *See Rabbah.*

RABBI, RABBONI [4806, 4808] (*[my] great one, [my] master*). The title of a teacher (Mt 23:7-8; Jn 3:2). Ostentatiously used by the Pharisees (Mt 23:7). Used in addressing John the Baptist (Jn 3:26), in addressing Jesus (Mt 26:25,49; Mk 9:5; 10:51; 11:21; 14:45; Jn 4:31; 9:2; 11:8 Jn 1:38,49; 3:2; 6:25). Jesus called "Rabboni" (Jn 20:16). Forbidden by Jesus as a title to his disciples (Mt 23:8).

RABBIM *See Bath Rabbim.*

RABBIT [817]. Forbidden as food (Lev 11:6; Dt 14:7). *See Animals.*

RABBITH [8056] (*great*). A city in Issachar (Jos 19:20).

RABBLE, THE [132+8044, 671]. (Ex 12:38; Nu 11:4; Mt 26:47; Ac 16:22; 17:5).

RABBONI [4808] (*[my] great one, [my] master*).

NIV+ RABBI

Variant of Rabbi, the Aramaic word for Teacher (Jn 20:16).

RABMAG, RAB-MAG NIV "high official"; the Babylonian title of Nergal-Sharezer (Jer 39:3,13).

RABSARIS, RAB-SARIS NIV "chief officer"; a title used of Assyrian (2Ki 18:17) and Babylonian officials (Jer 39:3,13).

RABSHAKEH, RAB-SHAKEH NIV "field commander"; a title of a Assyrian officer sent by Sennacherib against Jerusalem. He speaks publicly in Hebrew to cause disloyalty to Hezekiah and a surrender of the city (2Ki 18:17-37; 19:4,8; Isa 36; 37:4,8).

RACA [4819] (*empty [headed]*). A term of contempt and scorn (Mt 5:22).

RACAL, RACHAL [8218] (*trade*). A city in Judah (1Sa 30:29).

RACE

NIV+ RACED

1. Human. Unity of (Ge 3:20; Mal 2:10; Ac 17:26). *See Mankind.*

2. Foot race. Figurative: (Ps 19:5; Ecc 9:11; 1Co 9:24; Gal 5:7; Php 2:16; Heb 12:1-2).

RACHAB *See Rahab.*

RACHAL *See Racal, Rachal.*

RACHEL [8162, 4830] (*ewe*).

NIV+ RACHEL'S

Daughter of Laban and wife of Jacob. Meets Jacob at the well (Ge 29:9-12). Jacob serves Laban fourteen years to secure her for his wife (Ge 29:15-30). Sterility of (Ge 29:31). Her grief in consequence of her sterility; gives her maid to Jacob in order to secure children in her own name (Ge 30:1-8,15,22-34). Later fertility of; becomes the mother of Joseph (Ge 30:22-25), of Benjamin (Ge 35:16-18,24). Steals the household images of her father (Ge 31:4,14-19,33-35). Her death and burial (Ge 35:18-20; 48:7; 1Sa 10:2).

RADDAI [8099] (possibly *beating down* ISBE; *Yahweh rules* KB). Son of Jesse (1Ch 2:14).

RAGAU *See Reu.*

RAGUEL *See Jethro; Reuel, 2.*

RAHAB [8105, 8147, 4805, 4829] (*spacious, broad*).

1. A harlot of Jericho who hid Israelites spies (Jos 2:1), mother of Boaz; great-grandmother of King David (Mt 1:5; Ru 4:18-21), shining example of faith (Heb 11:31).

2. Mythical monster of the deep; enemy of Yahweh (Job 9:13; Ps 89:10), applied to Egypt (Ps 87:4; Isa 30:7; 51:9).

RAHAM [8165] (*compassion*). Son of Shema (1Ch 2:44).

RAHEL *See Rachel.*

RAIL [2147]. Taunts of the enemy (Ps 102:6). *See Slander; Speaking or Speech, Evil.*

RAIMENT *See Cloth; Clothing; Dress; Garment; Robe.*

RAIMENT, CHANGES OF *See Dress.*

RAIN [1772, 1773, 4763, 4764, 4784, 4919, 5752, 8053, 8319, 8852, *536, 1101, 1104, 2262+3915, 5624*].

NIV+ RAINBOW, RAINED, RAINING, RAINS, RAINY

Forty days of, at the time of the Flood (Ge 7:4,10-12,17-24). The plague of, upon Egypt (Ex 9:22-26,33-34). Miraculously caused by Samuel (1Sa 12:16-19), by Elijah (1Ki 18:41-45). David delivered by (2Sa 5:17-21; Isa 28:21). North wind unfavorable to (Pr 25:23). Withheld as judgment (Dt 11:17; 28:24; 1Ki 8:35; 2Ch 7:13; Jer 3:3; Am 4:7; Zec 14:17). Sent by God (Dt 11:13-14; Job 37:6; Isa 30:23; Jer 5:24; 14:22). Contingent upon obedience (Lev 26:3-4; Dt 11:13-14). Prayer for (1Ki 8:35-36; 2Ch 6:26-27). Answer to prayer for, promised (2Ch 7:13-14; Zec 10:1). Withheld, in answer to prayer (Jas 5:17-18).

In Israel the rainy season extends from October to April; the dry season, from May to September. The early rain occurs in October and November (Ps 84:6; Isa 30:23; Jer 5:24), the latter rain in March and April (Job 29:23; Pr 16:15; Jer 3:3; 5:24; Zec 10:1). Crops are therefore planted so that they will grow during the rainy season.

"Rain" is often used in the OT in a figurative sense. An abundance of rain denotes the rich blessing of Yahweh upon his people (Dt 28:12), lack of rain is a sign of God's displeasure (Dt 28:23-24). In Canaanite religion, Baal was conceived of as the god of rain, and was therefore ardently worshiped.

RAINBOW [8008, 2692].

NIV+ See RAIN

A token that the earth shall never again be destroyed by flooding (Ge 9:8-16; Eze 1:28). See Meteorology.

Symbolic: (Rev 4:3; 10:1).

RAISIN [862, 6694, 7540].

NIV+ RAISINS

Preserved grapes. Given by Abigail to David (1Sa 25:18). Given to the famished Egyptian to revive him (1Sa 30:12). Given by Ziba to David (2Sa 16:1). Given to David at Ziklag (1Ch 12:40).

RAISING From the dead. See Dead; Resurrection.

RAKEM [8388] (weaver, embroider). A descendant of Makir, son of Manasseh (1Ch 7:16).

RAKKATH [8395] (narrow place). A fortified city in Naphtali (Jos 19:35), probably near the Sea of Galilee on the site of Tiberias.

RAKKON [8378] (narrow place). A city in Dan (Jos 19:46).

RAM [380, 4854, 8226, 730] (As a proper name high, exalted).

NIV+ RAM'S, RAMS, RAMS'

1. The son of Hezron and an ancestor of Jesus (Ru 4:19; 1Ch 2:9-10). Called Aram (Mt 1:3-4; Lk 3:33).

2. The son of Jerahmeel (1Ch 2:25,27).

3. An ancestor, probably of Elihu (Job 32:2).

4. A sheep. Skins of, used for the roof of the tabernacle (Ex 26:14; 39:34). Seen in Daniel's vision (Da 8:3,20). Used in sacrifice. See Offerings.

Trumpets made of the horns of. See Horn; Trumpet.

5. A weapon used to break down doors and gates. See Battering Ram.

RAMAH, RAMA [8230, 4821] (elevated spot).

1. A city allotted to Benjamin (Jos 18:25; Jdg 19:13). Attempted fortification of, by King Baasha; destruction of, by Asa (1Ki 15:17-22; 2Ch 16:1-6). People of, return from the Babylonian Captivity (Ezr 2:26; Ne 7:30; 11:33). Jeremiah imprisoned in (Jer 40:1). Prophecies concerning (Isa 10:29; Jer 31:15; Hos 5:8; Mt 2:18).

2. A city of S Judah allotted to the tribe of Simeon (Jos 19:8).

3. A city of Asher (Jos 19:29).

4. A city of Naphtali (Jos 19:36).

5. Also called Ramathaim. A city in the hill country of Ephraim (Jdg 4:5; 1Sa 1:1). Home of Elkanah (1Sa 1:1,19; 2:11), and of Samuel (1Sa 1:19-20; 7:17; 8:4; 15:34; 16:13). David flees to (1Sa 19:18). Samuel dies and is buried in (1Sa 25:1; 28:3).

See Ramoth Gilead, Ramoth-Gilead.

RAMATH See Ramah, 2.

RAMATH LEHI, RAMATH-LEHI [8257] (height [hill] of Lehi).

NIV+ LEHI

The place where Samson killed a thousand Philistines with the jawbone of a donkey (Jdg 15:17).

RAMATH MIZPAH, RAMATH-MIZPEH [8256] (height [hill] of Mizpah [watch tower]).

NIV+ MIZPAH

N boundary line of Gad (Jos 13:26). Also called Mizpah, Galeed, and Jegar Sahadutha (Ge 31:47-49).

RAMATHAIM-ZOPHIM, RAMATHAIM ZUPHIM (two heights of Zophim). See Ramah, 5.

RAMATHITE [8258] (of Ramah).

NIV+ RAMATH

Designation of Shimei, King David's overseer in charge of the vineyards (1Ch 27:27).

RAMESES [8314]. (Ra [pagan sun god] created him).

1. Egyptian store city built by Israelites (Ex 1:11), possibly the modern San el-Habar in the NE part of the Delta.

2. The name of eleven Egyptian pharaohs, of whom Rameses II (c. 1301-1234 B.C.) was the most famous, many scholars holding that he was the pharaoh of the Exodus. Some of these pharaohs must have had at least an indirect influence on Israelite life, but none of them is mentioned in the OT.

RAMIAH [8243] (Yahweh is exalted). An Israelite in the time of Ezra who married a foreign wife (Ezr 10:25).

RAMOTH [8030, 8230] (height).

NIV+ RAMOTH GILEAD, RAMOTH NEGEV

1. Ramoth in Gilead. See Ramoth Gilead, Ramoth-Gilead.

2. Ramoth Negev. A place probably in the south of Simeon (Jos 19:8; 1Sa 30:27). See Ramah, 2.

3. A city of Issachar, allotted to the Levites (1Ch 6:73).

4. See Jeremoth, 6.

RAMOTH GILEAD, RAMOTH-GILEAD [8240] (heights in Gilead).

NIV+ GILEAD, RAMOTH

A city of Gad, and a city of refuge (Dt 4:43; Jos 20:8; 1Ch 6:80). One of Solomon's district governors at (1Ki 4:13). In the possession of the Syrians (1Ki 22:3). Besieged by Israel and Judah; Ahab slain at (1Ki 22:29-36; 2Ch 18). Recovered by Joram; Joram wounded at (2Ki 8:28-29; 9:14-15; 2Ch 22:5-6). Elisha anoints Jehu king at (2Ki 9:1-6).

RAMS' HORNS [3413, 8795]. See Shofar; Trumpet.

RAMS' SKINS

NIV+ See RAM

Skins of sheep; used for clothing of shepherds and covering for the tabernacle (Ex 25:5).

RANSOM [4105, 4111, 7009, 7014, 7018, 8815, 519, 667, 3389].

NIV+ RANSOMED, RANSOMS

Of a human life (Ex 21:30; 30:12; Job 36:18; Ps 49:7-8; Pr 6:35; 13:8; Hos 13:14).

Jesus as:

Mt 20:28 just as the Son of Man did not come to be served,

but to serve, and to give his life as a ransom for many." (+Mk 10:45)

1Ti 2:5 For there is one God and one mediator between God and men, the man Christ Jesus, ⁶who gave himself as a ransom for all men— the testimony given in its proper time. (+Heb 9:15)

Figurative: (Job 33:24; Isa 35:10; 51:10).

See Jesus the Christ, Redeemer; Savior, Saviour; Redemption.

RAPACITY
Of the wicked (Lk 11:39; 20:14,47; Jn 10:12; Ac 20:29; Gal 5:15; Jas 4:2; 1Pe 5:8). *See Greed; Wicked.*

RAPE
[2256+6700+8886, 3359, 6700, 8711].

NIV+ RAPED, RAPES, RAVISH, RAVISHED

Law imposes death penalty for (Dt 22:25-27). Captives afflicted with (Isa 13:16; La 5:11; Zec 14:2).

Instances of:

Dinah by Shechem (Ge 34:1-2). The servant of a Levite by Benjamites; tribe of Benjamin nearly exterminated by the army of the other tribes as punishment for (Jdg 19:22-30; 20:35). Tamar by Amnon; avenged in the death of Amnon at the hand of Absalom, Tamar's brother (2Sa 13:6-29,32-33).

RAPHA, RAPHAH
[8325, 8334, 8335] (possibly *one healed*).

NIV+ BETH RAPHA

1. Son of Benjamin (1Ch 8:2).
2. A descendant of Jonathan also called Rephaiah (1Ch 9:43) and Raphah (1Ch 8:37). *See Rephaiah, 4.*
3. An ancestor of certain Philistine warriors (2Sa 21:16,20,22; 1Ch 20:4,6,8). *See Rephaites.*

RAPHU
[8336] (*healed*). The father of Palti, who was sent from the tribe of Benjamin to spy out the land of Canaan (Nu 13:9).

RAPTURE
The imminent translation or removal from earth of the Church at the second coming of Christ (Mt 24:36-42; Mk 13:32; Ac 1:7,11; 1Co 15:50-52; 1Th 4:14-18; Tit 2:13; 1Pe 3:12; Rev 1:7).

Includes both living and dead (1Co 15:50-52; Php 3:20-21; 1Th 4:13-17; 1Jn 3:2). Followed by the marriage of the Church to Christ (Mt 25:1-10; 2Co 11:2; Eph 5:23,32; Rev 19:6-9), believers being rewarded (Mt 25:19; 1Co 3:12-15; 2Co 5:10; 2Ti 4:8; 1Pe 5:2).

See Second Coming of Christ, The.

RAS SHAMRA
(*fennel mound*). The modern name of the mound marking the site of the ancient city of Ugarit, located on the Syrian coast opposite the island of Cyprus; an important commercial center; destroyed by Sea Peoples who overran the area c. 1200 B.C.; reached the peak of prosperity in 1500-1200 B.C. Several hundred clay tablets, forming part of a scribal library, were found from 1929 through 1936; personal and diplomatic correspondence; business, legal, and governmental records; veterinary texts, and most importantly, religious literature. These throw a great deal of light upon Canaanite religion and culture, and Hebrew literary style; they show striking similarities between Canaanite and Hebrew systems of worship. They clarify our knowledge of the world in which Israel developed. *See Texts, Ancient Near Eastern Non-Biblical Texts Relating to the Old Testament.*

RASH
[993, 5030, 6204]. Regulations for determining whether clean or unclean (Lev 13-14). *See Disease.*

RASHNESS
[1051, 4362, 4439, 4554, *4637*].

NIV+ RASH, RASHLY

Ps 116:11 And in my dismay I said, "All men are liars."

Pr 19:2 It is not good to have zeal without knowledge, nor to be hasty and miss the way.

Admonitions against—

Pr 25:8 do not bring hastily to court, for what will you do in the end if your neighbor puts you to shame?

Ecc 5:2 Do not be quick with your mouth, do not be hasty in your heart to utter anything before God. God is in heaven and you are on earth, so let your words be few.

Ecc 7:9 Do not be quickly provoked in your spirit, for anger resides in the lap of fools.

Folly of—

Pr 14:29 A patient man has great understanding, but a quick-tempered man displays folly.

Pr 29:20 Do you see a man who speaks in haste? There is more hope for a fool than for him.

Tends to want—

Pr 21:5 The plans of the diligent lead to profit as surely as haste leads to poverty.

Instances of:

Moses, in slaying the Egyptian (Ex 2:11-12; Ac 7:24-25), when he struck the rock (Nu 20:10-12). Jephthah's vow (Jdg 11:31-39). Israel's vow to destroy the Benjamites (Jdg 21:1-23). Uzzah, in steadying the ark (2Sa 6:6-7). David, in his generosity to Ziba (2Sa 16:4, w 19:26-29). Rehoboam, in forsaking the counsel of the old men (1Ki 12:8-15). Josiah, in fighting against Neco (2Ch 35:20-24). Naaman, in refusing to wash in the Jordan (2Ki 5:11-12). Peter, in cutting off the ear of Malchus (Mt 26:51; Mk 14:47; Lk 22:50). James and John, in desiring to call down fire on the Samaritans (Lk 9:54). Paul, in persisting to go to Jerusalem against the repeated admonitions of the Holy Spirit (Ac 21:4,10-15). The centurion, in rejecting Paul's counsel (Ac 27:11).

RAT(S)
[6572]. Forbidden as food (Lev 11:29), used as food (Isa 66:17). Images of (1Sa 6:4-5,11,18).

RAVEN
[6854, *3165*] (*crow, raven*).

NIV+ RAVENS

A black carnivorous bird (Pr 30:17; SS 5:11). Forbidden as food (Lev 11:15; Dt 14:14). Preserved by Noah in the ark (Ge 8:7). Fed Elijah (1Ki 17:4-6). Cared for by divine providence (Lk 12:24).

RAVISHMENT
See Rape.

RAZOR
[4623, 9509] (*any instrument of iron*). Priests of Israel were not permitted to cut their beard (Lev 21:5). Nazirites could not use the razor as long as their vows were upon them (Nu 6:5).

RE
See Ra.

READING
[*606, 7924, 10637, *336, 342*].

NIV+ READ, READER, READS

Taught (Dt 6:9; 11:20).

READINGS

Select:

Judah's Defense (Ge 44:18-34). Joseph Revealing His Identity (Ge 45:1-15). The Deliverance of the Israelites From Pharaoh (Ex 14:5-30). Song of Moses When

Pharaoh and His Army Were Overthrown (Ex 15:1-19). David's Lament Over Absalom (2Sa 18:19-33). Lights and Shadows (Ru 1:1-22). Elijah's Miraculous Preservation (1Ki 17:1-16). Elisha and the Widow's Oil (2Ki 4:1-7). Naaman the Leper (2Ki 5:1-14). Esther's Triumph (Est 4:1-17; 7:1-10). The Brevity of Life (Job 14:1-10). Nature's Testimony (Job 28:1-28). God's Challenge to Job (Job 38). The Beasts of the Field (Job 39). The Righteous and the Wicked in Contrast (Ps 1). The Triumphant King (Ps 2). Man in Nature (Ps 8). Man in Extremity (Ps 18:1-19). Confidence in God (Ps 23). The King of Glory (Ps 24). The Glory of God (Ps 29). Our Refuge (Ps 46). The Majesty of God (Ps 77:13-20). The Joy of the Righteous (Ps 84). The State of the Glory (Ps 91). The New Song (Ps 98). The Majesty and Providence of God (Ps 104). In Captivity (Ps 137). The Omnipresence of God (Ps 139). Old Age (Ecc 12:1-7). Christ's Kingdom Foreshadowed (Isa 35:1-10). The Omnipotence and Incomparableness of God (Isa 40:1-30). The Wrath of God (Am 9:1-6). The Majesty of God (Hab 3:3-13). Mary's Magnificat (Lk 1:46-56). The Prophetic Blessing of Zechariah (Lk 1:67-80). The Beatitudes (Mt 5:1-16). God's Providence (Mt 6:26-34). Wise and Foolish Builders (Mt 7:21-27). The Good Samaritan (Lk 10:25-37). The Prodigal Son (Lk 15:11-32). The Raising of Lazarus (Jn 11:1-45). The Betrayal (Lk 22:47-62). The Resurrection (Lk 24:1-12). Peter at Pentecost (Ac 2:1-36). Stephen's Defense (Ac 7). Paul and Silas in Prison (Ac 16:16-40). Paul on Mars' Hill (Ac 17:22-31). Paul Before Felix (Ac 24:1-27). Paul Before Agrippa (Ac 26:1-32). Love (1Co 13). The New Heaven and the New Earth (Rev 21:1-7). The River of Life (Rev 22:1-21).

REAIA See Reaiah, Reaia, 2.

REAIAH, REAIA [8025] (Yahweh has seen).

1. A man of Judah, son of Shobal (1Ch 4:2). Apparently called Haroeh (1Ch 2:52).

2. Son of Micah, a Reubenite (1Ch 5:5).

3. Ancestor of a family which returned to Jerusalem from captivity in Babylon (Ezr 2:47; Ne 7:50).

REAPING [5162, 7907, 7917, 9530, 2400, 2545].

NIV+ REAP, REAPED, REAPER, REAPERS, REAPS, REAPS'

In ancient times done either by pulling up grain by roots or cutting with a sickle. The stalks are then bound into bundles and taken to threshing floor (Ps 129:7).

Laws concerning gleaning at the time of reaping (Lev 19:9-10; 23:22; Dt 24:19-20).

Figurative:

(Ps 126:6; Hos 10:12-13; Jn 4:35-38), of deeds that produce own harvest (Pr 22:8; Hos 8:7; 1Co 9:11; Gal 6:7-8).

REASONING [*9312, 1363, 3357].

NIV+ REASON, REASONABLE, REASONED, REASONS

With God (Job 13:3,17-28). God reasons with people (Ex 4:11; 20:5,11; Isa 1:18; 5:3-4; 43:26; Hos 4:1; Mic 6:2).

Natural understanding (Da 4:36). To be applied to religion (1Co 10:15; 1Pe 3:15). Not a sufficient guide in human affairs (Dt 12:8; Pr 3:5; 14:12). Of the Pharisees (Lk 5:21-22; 20:5). Of Paul from the Scriptures (Ac 17:2; 18:4,19; 24:25). The Gospel cannot be explained by human wisdom (1Co 1:18-2:14).

See Investigation; Philosophy; Wisdom.

REBA [8064] (fourth part). A king of Midian. Slain by the Israelites (Nu 31:8; Jos 13:21).

REBECCA See Rebekah.

REBEKAH [8071, 4831] (possibly choice calf).

NIV+ REBEKAH'S

Daughter of Bethuel, grand-niece of Abraham (Ge 22:20-23). Becomes Isaac's wife (Ge 24:15-67; 25:20). Mother of Esau and Jacob (Ge 25:21-28; Ro 9:10). Passes as Isaac's sister (Ge 26:6-11). Displeased with Esau's wives (Ge 26:34-35). Prompts Jacob to deceive Isaac (Ge 27:5-29). Sends Jacob to Laban (Ge 27:42-46). Burial place of (Ge 49:31).

REBELLION [*5277, 5286, 5308, 5897, 6240, 6253, 7321, 7322, 10439, 538, 2060, 3334, 4177].

NIV+ REBEL, REBELLED, REBELLING, REBELLIOUS, REBELS

Treasonable (Pr 17:11).

Instances of:

Absalom (2Sa 15-18). Sheba (2Sa 20). Revolt of the ten tribes (1Ki 12:16-20; 2Ch 10; 13:5-12).

See Sin.

REBUKE [*1721, 1722, 3519, 8189, 9349, 9350, 1791, 1794, 2203].

NIV+ REBUKED, REBUKES, REBUKING

Cain rebukes God (Ge 4:13-14). Pharaoh rebukes Abraham for calling his wife his sister (Ge 12:18-19). Abimelech rebukes Abraham for a like offense (Ge 20:9-10). Abimelech rebukes Isaac for similar conduct (Ge 26:9-10). Isaac and Laban rebuke each other (Ge 31:26-42). Jacob rebukes Simeon and Levi for killing Hamor and Shechem (Ge 34:30). Reuben rebukes his brothers for their treatment of Joseph (Ge 42:22). Israelites rebuke Moses and tempt God (Ex 17:7). Deborah rebukes Israel in her poem (Jdg 5:16-23). David rebukes Joab for killing Abner (2Sa 3:28-31). Joab rebukes David for lamenting the death of Absalom (2Sa 19:5-7).

Jesus rebukes his disciples because of their unbelief (Mt 8:26; 14:31; 16:8-11; 17:17; Mk 4:40; Lk 8:25), for slowness of heart (Mt 15:16; 16:8-9,11; Mk 7:18; Lk 24:25; Jn 14:9), for sleeping in Gethsemane (Mt 26:40; Mk 14:27), for forbidding children to be brought to him (Mt 19:14; Mk 10:14; Lk 18:16).

David prays to escape Yahweh's rebuke (Ps 6:1; 38:1). Do not rebuke a mocker (Pr 9:8), an older man (1Ti 5:1).

RECAB [8209] (probably rider or horseman, from to mount, ride).

1. Son of Rimmon. Murders Ish-Bosheth, son of Saul; put to death by David (2Sa 4:5-12).

2. Father of Jehonadab (2Ki 10:15,23; 1Ch 2:55; Jer 35:6,8,16,19). Ancestor of the Recabites (Jer 35).

3. Father of Malkijah (Ne 3:14).

RECABITE(S) [8211].

NIV+ RECAB

A family of Kenites descended from Recab, through Jonadab (1Ch 2:55; Jer 35:6). Commanded by Jonadab to drink no wine (Jer 35:6); perpetuation of the family promised as a reward (Jer 35).

See Abstinence; Nazirite(s), Nazarite(s).

RECAH [8212]. Unknown place in tribe of Judah (1Ch 4:12).

RECHAB *See Recab.*

RECHABITE(S) *See Recabite(s).*

RECHAH *See Recah.*

RECIPROCITY Returning good for good (Ro 15:27; 1Co 9:11; Gal 6:6). *See One Another.*

RECONCILIATION [557, 639, 1367, 2903, 2904].
NIV+ RECONCILE, RECONCILED, RECONCILING

Between People (Mt 5:23-26).

Between Esau and Jacob (Ge 33:4,11). Between Saul and David (1Sa 19:7). Between Pilate and Herod (Lk 23:12).

Between God and People:

Through atonement of animal sacrifices—

Lev 8:15 Moses slaughtered the bull and took some of the blood, and with his finger he put it on all the horns of the altar to purify the altar. He poured out the rest of the blood at the base of the altar. So he consecrated it to make atonement for it.

Eze 45:15 Also one sheep is to be taken from every flock of two hundred from the well-watered pastures of Israel. These will be used for the grain offerings, burnt offerings and fellowship offerings to make atonement for the people, declares the Sovereign LORD.

After the seventy weeks of Daniel's vision—

Da 9:24 "Seventy 'sevens' are decreed for your people and your holy city to finish transgression, to put an end to sin, to atone for wickedness, to bring in everlasting righteousness, to seal up vision and prophecy and to anoint the most holy.

Through Christ—

Ro 5:1 Therefore, since we have been justified through faith, we have peace with God through our Lord Jesus Christ,

Ro 5:10 For if, when we were God's enemies, we were reconciled to him through the death of his Son, how much more, having been reconciled, shall we be saved through his life!

Ro 11:15 For if their rejection is the reconciliation of the world, what will their acceptance be but life from the dead?

2Co 5:18 All this is from God, who reconciled us to himself through Christ and gave us the ministry of reconciliation: ¹⁹that God was reconciling the world to himself in Christ, not counting men's sins against them. And he has committed to us the message of reconciliation. ²⁰We are therefore Christ's ambassadors, as though God were making his appeal through us. We implore you on Christ's behalf: Be reconciled to God. ²¹God made him who had no sin to be sin for us, so that in him we might become the righteousness of God.

Eph 2:15 by abolishing in his flesh the law with its commandments and regulations. His purpose was to create in himself one new man out of the two, thus making peace, ¹⁶and in this one body to reconcile both of them to God through the cross, by which he put to death their hostility. ¹⁷He came and preached peace to you who were far away and peace to those who were near. ¹⁸For through him we both have access to the Father by one Spirit.

Col 1:20 and through him to reconcile to himself all things, whether things on earth or things in heaven, by making peace through his blood, shed on the cross. ²¹Once you were alienated from God and were enemies in your minds because of your evil behavior. ²²But now he

has reconciled you by Christ's physical body through death to present you holy in his sight, without blemish and free from accusation—

Heb 2:17 For this reason he had to be made like his brothers in every way, in order that he might become a merciful and faithful high priest in service to God, and that he might make atonement for the sins of the people.

See Atonement; Jesus the Christ, Mission of; Propitiation; Redemption.

RECONNAISSANCE Of Jericho (Jos 2:1-24), Bethel (Jdg 1:23), Laish (Jdg 18:2-10). *See Spies.*

RECORDER [4654]. *See Occupations and Professions.*

RECREATION *See Rest.*

RED [131, 137, 145, 1798, 2813, 6068, 8012, 9266, 135+6055, 2261, 4791, 4793, 4794].
NIV+ REDDISH

Bloodlike or blood-red color (Ex 25:5; 26:14; 35:7; Zec 1:8; Rev 6:4).

RED HEIFER Ashes of red heifer were used for removal of certain types of ceremonial uncleanness (Nu 19:9).

RED KITE A carnivorous bird, unclean for food (Dt 14:13).

RED SEA [3542+6068, 2261+2498]. "Sea of Reeds" in NIV ftns. The locusts that devastated Egypt destroyed in (Ex 10:19). Israelites cross; Pharaoh and his army drowned in (Ex 14; 15:1,4,11,19; Nu 33:8; Dt 11:4; Jos 2:10; 4:23; 24:6-7; Jdg 11:16; 2Sa 22:16; Ne 9:9-11; Ps 66:6; 78:13,53; 106:7-11,22; 136:13-15; Isa 43:16-17; Ac 7:36; 1Co 10:1-2; Heb 11:29). Israelites camp by (Ex 14:2,9; Nu 14:25; 21:4; 33:10-11; Dt 1:40; 2:1-3). Boundary of the promised land (Ex 23:31). Solomon builds ships on (1Ki 9:26).

REDEEMED, THE [1457, 1460, 7009, 60, 1973, 3390, 3391+4472].
NIV+ See REDEEM

(Isa 35:9; 51:11; Mt 8:11; Rev 5:9; 7:9; 14:4; 19:6).

REDEEMER [1457].
NIV+ See REDEEM

See Jesus the Christ, Savior; Redemption.

REDEMPTION [1453, 1460, 7009, 7012, 7014, 7017, 667, 3391] (*to tear loose; a ransom*).
NIV+ REDEEM, KINSMAN-REDEEMER, KINSMAN-REDEEMERS, REDEEMABLE, REDEEMED, REDEEMER, REDEEMS

Deliverance from the enslavement of sin and release to a new freedom by the sacrifice of the Redeemer, Jesus Christ. The death of Christ is the redemptive price. The word contains both the ideas of deliverance and the price of that deliverance, or ransom (Ro 3:24; Gal 3:13; Eph 1:7; 1Pe 1:18-19).

Of Person or Property:

(Ex 13:13; Lev 25:25-34; 27:2-33; Ro 4:3-10). Redemption money paid to priests (Nu 3:46-51). Of the firstborn (Ex 13:13; 34:20; Lev 27:27; Nu 3:40-51; 18:15-17).

Of Land:

(Lev 27:19-20; Jer 32:7). In Hebrew society, any land

that was forfeited through economic distress could be redeemed by the nearest of kin. If not so redeemed, it returned to its original owner in the Year of Jubilee (Lev 25:24-34).

Of Our Souls:

Ps 111:9 He provided redemption for his people; he ordained his covenant forever—holy and awesome is his name.

Ps 130:7 O Israel, put your hope in the LORD, for with the LORD is unfailing love and with him is full redemption.

Through Christ (Mt 20:28)—

Mk 10:45 For even the Son of Man did not come to be served, but to serve, and to give his life as a ransom for many."

Lk 2:38 Coming up to them at that very moment, she gave thanks to God and spoke about the child to all who were looking forward to the redemption of Jerusalem.

Ac 20:28 Keep watch over yourselves and all the flock of which the Holy Spirit has made you overseers. Be shepherds of the church of God, which he bought with his own blood.

Ro 3:24 and are justified freely by his grace through the redemption that came by Christ Jesus. ²⁵God presented him as a sacrifice of atonement, through faith in his blood. He did this to demonstrate his justice, because in his forbearance he had left the sins committed beforehand unpunished— ²⁶he did it to demonstrate his justice at the present time, so as to be just and the one who justifies those who have faith in Jesus.

1Co 1:30 It is because of him that you are in Christ Jesus, who has become for us wisdom from God—that is, our righteousness, holiness and redemption.

1Co 6:20 you were bought at a price. Therefore honor God with your body.

1Co 7:23 You were bought at a price; do not become slaves of men.

Gal 1:4 who gave himself for our sins to rescue us from the present evil age, according to the will of our God and Father,

Gal 2:20 I have been crucified with Christ and I no longer live, but Christ lives in me. The life I live in the body, I live by faith in the Son of God, who loved me and gave himself for me.

Gal 4:4 But when the time had fully come, God sent his Son, born of a woman, born under law, ⁵to redeem those under law, that we might receive the full rights of sons.

Eph 1:7 In him we have redemption through his blood, the forgiveness of sins, in accordance with the riches of God's grace

Eph 5:2 and live a life of love, just as Christ loved us and gave himself up for us as a fragrant offering and sacrifice to God.

Col 1:14 in whom we have redemption, the forgiveness of sins.

Col 1:20 and through him to reconcile to himself all things, whether things on earth or things in heaven, by making peace through his blood, shed on the cross.

²¹Once you were alienated from God and were enemies in your minds because of your evil behavior. ²²But now he has reconciled you by Christ's physical body through death to present you holy in his sight, without blemish and free from accusation—

1Ti 2:6 who gave himself as a ransom for all men—the testimony given in its proper time.

Tit 2:14 who gave himself for us to redeem us from all

wickedness and to purify for himself a people that are his very own, eager to do what is good.

Heb 9:12 He did not enter by means of the blood of goats and calves; but he entered the Most Holy Place once for all by his own blood, having obtained eternal redemption.

Heb 9:15 For this reason Christ is the mediator of a new covenant, that those who are called may receive the promised eternal inheritance—now that he has died as a ransom to set them free from the sins committed under the first covenant.

1Pe 1:18 For you know that it was not with perishable things such as silver or gold that you were redeemed from the empty way of life handed down to you from your forefathers, ¹⁹but with the precious blood of Christ, a lamb without blemish or defect.

Rev 5:9 And they sang a new song: "You are worthy to take the scroll and to open its seals, because you were slain, and with your blood you purchased men for God from every tribe and language and people and nation. ¹⁰You have made them to be a kingdom and priests to serve our God, and they will reign on the earth."

See Atonement; Ransom; Redeemer.

REED [109, 286, 6068, 7866, *2812*].

NIV+ REEDS

A water plant (Isa 19:6-7; 35:7; Jer 51:32). Used as a measuring device of six cubits (Eze 40:3-8; 41:8; 42:16-19; 45:1; Rev 11:1; 21:15-16). Mockingly given to Jesus as a symbol of royalty (Mt 27:29). Jesus struck with (Mt 27:30; Mk 15:19).

Figurative:

Of weakness (1Ki 14:15; 2Ki 18:21; Isa 36:6; 42:3; Eze 29:6; Mt 11:7; 12:20).

REEDS, SEA OF *See Red Sea.*

REELAIAH [8305]. A returned captive from Babylon (Ezr 2:2).

REFINING [2423, 7671, *1507*, *4792*].

NIV+ REFINE, REFINED, REFINER, REFINER'S

The process of eliminating by fire the dross of metals. Of gold (1Ch 28:18). Of silver (1Ch 29:4). Of wine (Isa 25:6).

Figurative:

Of the corrective judgments of God (Isa 1:25; 48:10; Jer 9:7; Zec 13:9; Mal 3:2-3). Of the purity of the word of God (Ps 18:30; 119:140).

REFUGE, CITIES OF [*5236]. *See Cities of Refuge.*

REFUGEE SLAVES

NIV+ REFUGE

Laws concerning (Dt 23:15-16). Onesimus (Phm 1). *See Servant.*

REGEM [8084] (*friend*). Son of Jahdai (1Ch 2:47).

REGEM-MELECH [8085] (*friend of king*, possibly *chief of troops of the king*). A captive sent as a messenger from the Jews in Babylon to Jerusalem (Zec 7:2).

REGENCY *See Deputy.*

REGENERATION The new birth, the inner recreating of fallen human nature by the gracious working of the Holy Spirit. It changes human disposition from godlessness, lawlessness, rebellion, self-seeking, and unbelief to a desire to love and serve God.

Also Called:

Born again or born from above—

Jn 3:3 In reply Jesus declared, "I tell you the truth, no one can see the kingdom of God unless he is born again."

4"How can a man be born when he is old?" Nicodemus asked. "Surely he cannot enter a second time into his mother's womb to be born!"

5Jesus answered, "I tell you the truth, no one can enter the kingdom of God unless he is born of water and the Spirit. **6**Flesh gives birth to flesh, but the Spirit gives birth to spirit. **7**You should not be surprised at my saying, 'You must be born again.' **8**The wind blows wherever it pleases. You hear its sound, but you cannot tell where it comes from or where it is going. So it is with everyone born of the Spirit." (+1Pe 1:2-3,22-23)

Born of God—

Jn 1:12 Yet to all who received him, to those who believed in his name, he gave the right to become children of God— **13**children born not of natural descent, nor of human decision or a husband's will, but born of God.

Jn 1:16 From the fullness of his grace we have all received one blessing after another.

Jas 1:18 He chose to give us birth through the word of truth, that we might be a kind of firstfruits of all he created.

1Jn 2:27 As for you, the anointing you received from him remains in you, and you do not need anyone to teach you. But as his anointing teaches you about all things and as that anointing is real, not counterfeit—just as it has taught you, remain in him.

1Jn 2:29 If you know that he is righteous, you know that everyone who does what is right has been born of him.

1Jn 3:9 No one who is born of God will continue to sin, because God's seed remains in him; he cannot go on sinning, because he has been born of God.

1Jn 3:14 We know that we have passed from death to life, because we love our brothers. Anyone who does not love remains in death.

1Jn 4:7 Dear friends, let us love one another, for love comes from God. Everyone who loves has been born of God and knows God.

1Jn 5:1 Everyone who believes that Jesus is the Christ is born of God, and everyone who loves the father loves his child as well.

1Jn 5:4 for everyone born of God overcomes the world. This is the victory that has overcome the world, even our faith. **5**Who is it that overcomes the world? Only he who believes that Jesus is the Son of God.

1Jn 5:11 And this is the testimony: God has given us eternal life, and this life is in his Son. **12**He who has the Son has life; he who does not have the Son of God does not have life.

1Jn 5:18 We know that anyone born of God does not continue to sin; the one who was born of God keeps him safe, and the evil one cannot harm him.

Born by the Spirit (Jn 3:5-6)—

Gal 4:29 At that time the son born in the ordinary way persecuted the son born by the power of the Spirit. It is the same now.

Through the Holy Spirit (Eze 12:10; Jn 3:5-8)—

1Co 12:13 For we were all baptized by one Spirit into one body—whether Jews or Greeks, slave or free—and we were all given the one Spirit to drink.

2Th 2:13 But we ought always to thank God for you, brothers loved by the Lord, because from the beginning God chose you to be saved through the sanctifying work of the Spirit and through belief in the truth.

1Pe 1:2 who have been chosen according to the foreknowledge of God the Father, through the sanctifying work of the Spirit, for obedience to Jesus Christ and sprinkling by his blood: Grace and peace be yours in abundance.

3Praise be to the God and Father of our Lord Jesus Christ! In his great mercy he has given us new birth into a living hope through the resurrection of Jesus Christ from the dead,

1Pe 1:22 Now that you have purified yourselves by obeying the truth so that you have sincere love for your brothers, love one another deeply, from the heart. **23**For you have been born again, not of perishable seed, but of imperishable, through the living and enduring word of God.

Necessity of:

Jer 13:23 Can the Ethiopian change his skin or the leopard its spots? Neither can you do good who are accustomed to doing evil.

Mt 12:33 "Make a tree good and its fruit will be good, or make a tree bad and its fruit will be bad, for a tree is recognized by its fruit. **34**You brood of vipers, how can you who are evil say anything good? For out of the overflow of the heart the mouth speaks. **35**The good man brings good things out of the good stored up in him, and the evil man brings evil things out of the evil stored up in him.

Mt 18:3 And he said: "I tell you the truth, unless you change and become like little children, you will never enter the kingdom of heaven. (+Mk 10:15; Lk 18:17; Jn 3:3,5)

Tit 3:5 he saved us, not because of righteous things we had done, but because of his mercy. He saved us through the washing of rebirth and renewal by the Holy Spirit, **6**whom he poured out on us generously through Jesus Christ our Savior,

Parables of:

Mt 13:23 But the one who received the seed that fell on good soil is the man who hears the word and understands it. He produces a crop, yielding a hundred, sixty or thirty times what was sown."

Mt 13:33 He told them still another parable: "The kingdom of heaven is like yeast that a woman took and mixed into a large amount of flour until it worked all through the dough." (+Mk 4:20)

Mk 4:26 He also said, "This is what the kingdom of God is like. A man scatters seed on the ground. **27**Night and day, whether he sleeps or gets up, the seed sprouts and grows, though he does not know how. **28**All by itself the soil produces grain—first the stalk, then the head, then the full kernel in the head. **29**As soon as the grain is ripe, he puts the sickle to it, because the harvest has come." (+Lk 13:21)

Other terms related to the beginning of spiritual life:

Circumcision of the heart (Dt 29:4)—

Dt 30:6 The LORD your God will circumcise your hearts and the hearts of your descendants, so that you may love him with all your heart and with all your soul, and live.

Eze 44:7 In addition to all your other detestable practices, you brought foreigners uncircumcised in heart and flesh into my sanctuary, desecrating my temple while you offered me food, fat and blood, and you broke my covenant.

Eze 44:9 This is what the Sovereign LORD says: No foreigner uncircumcised in heart and flesh is to enter my sanctuary, not even the foreigners who live among the Israelites.

Ro 2:28 A man is not a Jew if he is only one outwardly, nor is circumcision merely outward and physical.

Col 2:11 In him you were also circumcised, in the putting off of the sinful nature, not with a circumcision done by the hands of men but with the circumcision done by Christ, [12]having been buried with him in baptism and raised with him through your faith in the power of God, who raised him from the dead.

[13]When you were dead in your sins and in the uncircumcision of your sinful nature, God made you alive with Christ. He forgave us all our sins,

Change of heart—

Ps 51:2 Wash away all my iniquity and cleanse me from my sin.

Ps 51:7 Cleanse me with hyssop, and I will be clean; wash me, and I will be whiter than snow.

Ps 51:10 Create in me a pure heart, O God, and renew a steadfast spirit within me. (+Jer 24:7)

Jer 31:33 "This is the covenant I will make with the house of Israel after that time," declares the LORD. "I will put my law in their minds and write it on their hearts. I will be their God, and they will be my people. [34]No longer will a man teach his neighbor, or a man his brother, saying, 'Know the LORD,' because they will all know me, from the least of them to the greatest," declares the LORD. "For I will forgive their wickedness and will remember their sins no more." (+Heb 8:10-11; Jer 32:28-40)

Eze 11:19 I will give them an undivided heart and put a new spirit in them; I will remove from them their heart of stone and give them a heart of flesh. [20]Then they will follow my decrees and be careful to keep my laws. They will be my people, and I will be their God.

Eze 18:31 Rid yourselves of all the offenses you have committed, and get a new heart and a new spirit. Why will you die, O house of Israel?

Eze 36:26 I will give you a new heart and put a new spirit in you; I will remove from you your heart of stone and give you a heart of flesh. [27]And I will put my Spirit in you and move you to follow my decrees and be careful to keep my laws.

Eze 36:29 I will save you from all your uncleanness. I will call for the grain and make it plentiful and will not bring famine upon you.

Ro 12:2 Do not conform any longer to the pattern of this world, but be transformed by the renewing of your mind. Then you will be able to test and approve what God's will is—his good, pleasing and perfect will.

New creature—

2Co 5:17 Therefore, if anyone is in Christ, he is a new creation; the old has gone, the new has come!

Gal 6:15 Neither circumcision nor uncircumcision means anything; what counts is a new creation.

Eph 4:22 You were taught, with regard to your former way of life, to put off your old self, which is being corrupted by its deceitful desires; [23]to be made new in the attitude of your minds; [24]and to put on the new self, created to be like God in true righteousness and holiness.

Col 3:9 Do not lie to each other, since you have taken off your old self with its practices [10]and have put on the new self, which is being renewed in knowledge in the image of its Creator.

Spiritual cleansing (Jn 15:3)—

Ac 15:9 He made no distinction between us and them, for he purified their hearts by faith.

1Co 6:11 And that is what some of you were. But you were washed, you were sanctified, you were justified in the name of the Lord Jesus Christ and by the Spirit of our God.

Spiritual illumination—

Jn 6:44 "No one can come to me unless the Father who sent me draws him, and I will raise him up at the last day. [45]It is written in the Prophets: 'They will all be taught by God.' Everyone who listens to the Father and learns from him comes to me.

Jn 8:12 When Jesus spoke again to the people, he said, "I am the light of the world. Whoever follows me will never walk in darkness, but will have the light of life."

Ac 26:18 to open their eyes and turn them from darkness to light, and from the power of Satan to God, so that they may receive forgiveness of sins and a place among those who are sanctified by faith in me.' (+1Co 2:11)

1Co 2:12 We have not received the spirit of the world but the Spirit who is from God, that we may understand what God has freely given us.

1Co 2:14 The man without the Spirit does not accept the things that come from the Spirit of God, for they are foolishness to him, and he cannot understand them, because they are spiritually discerned. [15]The spiritual man makes judgments about all things, but he himself is not subject to any man's judgment:

[16]"For who has known the mind of the Lord that he may instruct him?" But we have the mind of Christ.

2Co 4:6 For God, who said, "Let light shine out of darkness," made his light shine in our hearts to give us the light of the knowledge of the glory of God in the face of Christ.

Eph 5:14 for it is light that makes everything visible. This is why it is said: "Wake up, O sleeper, rise from the dead, and Christ will shine on you."

Heb 10:16 "This is the covenant I will make with them after that time, says the Lord. I will put my laws in their hearts, and I will write them on their minds."

To make spiritually alive (Heb 6:21)

Spiritual resurrection—

Jn 5:24 "I tell you the truth, whoever hears my word and believes him who sent me has eternal life and will not be condemned; he has crossed over from death to life.

Ro 6:3 Or don't you know that all of us who were baptized into Christ Jesus were baptized into his death? [4]We were therefore buried with him through baptism into death in order that, just as Christ was raised from the dead through the glory of the Father, we too may live a new life.

[5]If we have been united with him like this in his death, we will certainly also be united with him in his resurrection. [6]For we know that our old self was crucified with him so that the body of sin might be done away with, that we should no longer be slaves to sin— [7]because anyone who has died has been freed from sin.

[8]Now if we died with Christ, we believe that we will also live with him. [9]For we know that since Christ was raised from the dead, he cannot die again; death no longer has mastery over him. [10]The death he died, he died to sin once for all; but the life he lives, he lives to God.

[11]In the same way, count yourselves dead to sin but alive to God in Christ Jesus. [12]Therefore do not let sin reign in your mortal body so that you obey its evil desires. [13]Do not offer the parts of your body to sin, as instruments of wickedness, but rather offer yourselves to God, as those who have been brought from death to life; and offer the parts of your body to him as instruments of righteousness. [14]For sin shall not be your master, because you are not under law, but under grace.

[15]What then? Shall we sin because we are not under law

but under grace? By no means! ¹⁶Don't you know that when you offer yourselves to someone to obey him as slaves, you are slaves to the one whom you obey— whether you are slaves to sin, which leads to death, or to obedience, which leads to righteousness? ¹⁷But thanks be to God that, though you used to be slaves to sin, you wholeheartedly obeyed the form of teaching to which you were entrusted. ¹⁸You have been set free from sin and have become slaves to righteousness.

¹⁹I put this in human terms because you are weak in your natural selves. Just as you used to offer the parts of your body in slavery to impurity and to ever-increasing wickedness, so now offer them in slavery to righteousness leading to holiness. ²⁰When you were slaves to sin, you were free from the control of righteousness. ²¹What benefit did you reap at that time from the things you are now ashamed of? Those things result in death! ²²But now that you have been set free from sin and have become slaves to God, the benefit you reap leads to holiness, and the result is eternal life. ²³For the wages of sin is death, but the gift of God is eternal life in Christ Jesus our Lord.

Ro 8:2 because through Christ Jesus the law of the Spirit of life set me free from the law of sin and death. ³For what the law was powerless to do in that it was weakened by the sinful nature, God did by sending his own Son in the likeness of sinful man to be a sin offering. And so he condemned sin in sinful man, ⁴in order that the righteous requirements of the law might be fully met in us, who do not live according to the sinful nature but according to the Spirit.

Gal 2:20 I have been crucified with Christ and I no longer live, but Christ lives in me. The life I live in the body, I live by faith in the Son of God, who loved me and gave himself for me.

Other Scriptures related to—

1Ki 8:58 May he turn our hearts to him, to walk in all his ways and to keep the commands, decrees and regulations he gave our fathers.

Ps 36:9 For with you is the fountain of life; in your light we see light.

Ps 65:3 When we were overwhelmed by sins, you forgave our transgressions.

Ps 68:18 When you ascended on high, you led captives in your train; you received gifts from men, even from the rebellious—that you, O LORD God, might dwell there.

Ps 110:3 Your troops will be willing on your day of battle. Arrayed in holy majesty, from the womb of the dawn you will receive the dew of your youth.

Pr 4:23 Above all else, guard your heart, for it is the wellspring of life.

Pr 12:28 In the way of righteousness there is life; along that path is immortality.

Pr 14:27 The fear of the LORD is a fountain of life, turning a man from the snares of death.

Isa 1:16 wash and make yourselves clean. Take your evil deeds out of my sight! Stop doing wrong, ¹⁷learn to do right! Seek justice, encourage the oppressed. Defend the cause of the fatherless, plead the case of the widow.

Isa 1:25 I will turn my hand against you; I will thoroughly purge away your dross and remove all your impurities.

Isa 4:4 The Lord will wash away the filth of the women of Zion; he will cleanse the bloodstains from Jerusalem by a spirit of judgment and a spirit of fire.

Isa 12:3 With joy you will draw water from the wells of salvation.

Isa 26:12 LORD, you establish peace for us; all that we have accomplished you have done for us.

Isa 32:3 Then the eyes of those who see will no longer be closed, and the ears of those who hear will listen. ⁴The mind of the rash will know and understand, and the stammering tongue will be fluent and clear.

Isa 32:15 till the Spirit is poured upon us from on high, and the desert becomes a fertile field, and the fertile field seems like a forest.

Isa 32:17 The fruit of righteousness will be peace; the effect of righteousness will be quietness and confidence forever.

Isa 35:5 Then will the eyes of the blind be opened and the ears of the deaf unstopped. ⁶Then will the lame leap like a deer, and the mute tongue shout for joy. Water will gush forth in the wilderness and streams in the desert.

Isa 42:16 I will lead the blind by ways they have not known, along unfamiliar paths I will guide them; I will turn the darkness into light before them and make the rough places smooth. These are the things I will do; I will not forsake them.

Isa 43:7 everyone who is called by my name, whom I created for my glory, whom I formed and made."

Isa 44:3 For I will pour water on the thirsty land, and streams on the dry ground; I will pour out my Spirit on your offspring, and my blessing on your descendants. ⁴They will spring up like grass in a meadow, like poplar trees by flowing streams. ⁵One will say, 'I belong to the LORD'; another will call himself by the name of Jacob; still another will write on his hand, 'The LORD's,' and will take the name Israel.

Isa 55:1 "Come, all you who are thirsty, come to the waters; and you who have no money, come, buy and eat! Come, buy wine and milk without money and without cost. ²Why spend money on what is not bread, and your labor on what does not satisfy? Listen, listen to me, and eat what is good, and your soul will delight in the richest of fare. ³Give ear and come to me; hear me, that your soul may live. I will make an everlasting covenant with you, my faithful love promised to David.

Jer 17:13 O LORD, the hope of Israel, all who forsake you will be put to shame. Those who turn away from you will be written in the dust because they have forsaken the LORD, the spring of living water.

¹⁴Heal me, O LORD, and I will be healed; save me and I will be saved, for you are the one I praise.

Jer 24:7 I will give them a heart to know me, that I am the LORD. They will be my people, and I will be their God, for they will return to me with all their heart.

Jer 31:3 The LORD appeared to us in the past, saying: "I have loved you with an everlasting love; I have drawn you with loving-kindness.

Jer 33:6 "'Nevertheless, I will bring health and healing to it; I will heal my people and will let them enjoy abundant peace and security.

Eze 16:9 "'I bathed you with water and washed the blood from you and put ointments on you.

Lk 1:16 Many of the people of Israel will he bring back to the Lord their God. ¹⁷And he will go on before the Lord, in the spirit and power of Elijah, to turn the hearts of the fathers to their children and the disobedient to the wisdom of the righteous—to make ready a people prepared for the Lord."

Jn 4:10 Jesus answered her, "If you knew the gift of God and who it is that asks you for a drink, you would have asked him and he would have given you living water."

Jn 4:14 but whoever drinks the water I give him will never thirst. Indeed, the water I give him will become in him a spring of water welling up to eternal life."

Jn 10:9 I am the gate; whoever enters through me will be saved. He will come in and go out, and find pasture. [10]The thief comes only to steal and kill and destroy; I have come that they may have life, and have it to the full.

Jn 13:8 "No," said Peter, "you shall never wash my feet." Jesus answered, "Unless I wash you, you have no part with me."

Jn 17:2 For you granted him authority over all people that he might give eternal life to all those you have given him.

Ac 2:38 Peter replied, "Repent and be baptized, every one of you, in the name of Jesus Christ for the forgiveness of your sins. And you will receive the gift of the Holy Spirit.

Ac 2:47 praising God and enjoying the favor of all the people. And the Lord added to their number daily those who were being saved.

Ac 3:26 When God raised up his servant, he sent him first to you to bless you by turning each of you from your wicked ways."

Ac 11:17 So if God gave them the same gift as he gave us, who believed in the Lord Jesus Christ, who was I to think that I could oppose God?"

Ac 11:21 The Lord's hand was with them, and a great number of people believed and turned to the Lord.

Ac 16:14 One of those listening was a woman named Lydia, a dealer in purple cloth from the city of Thyatira, who was a worshiper of God. The Lord opened her heart to respond to Paul's message.

Ro 7:6 But now, by dying to what once bound us, we have been released from the law so that we serve in the new way of the Spirit, and not in the old way of the written code.

Ro 7:24 What a wretched man I am! Who will rescue me from this body of death?

Ro 15:16 to be a minister of Christ Jesus to the Gentiles with the priestly duty of proclaiming the gospel of God, so that the Gentiles might become an offering acceptable to God, sanctified by the Holy Spirit.

1Co 1:9 God, who has called you into fellowship with his Son Jesus Christ our Lord, is faithful.

1Co 1:24 but to those whom God has called, both Jews and Greeks, Christ the power of God and the wisdom of God.

1Co 1:30 It is because of him that you are in Christ Jesus, who has become for us wisdom from God—that is, our righteousness, holiness and redemption.

1Co 3:6 I planted the seed, Apollos watered it, but God made it grow. [7]So neither he who plants nor he who waters is anything, but only God, who makes things grow.

1Co 3:9 For we are God's fellow workers; you are God's field, God's building.

1Co 15:10 But by the grace of God I am what I am, and his grace to me was not without effect. No, I worked harder than all of them—yet not I, but the grace of God that was with me.

2Co 1:21 Now it is God who makes both us and you stand firm in Christ. He anointed us, [22]set his seal of ownership on us, and put his Spirit in our hearts as a deposit, guaranteeing what is to come.

2Co 3:3 You show that you are a letter from Christ, the result of our ministry, written not with ink but with the Spirit of the living God, not on tablets of stone but on tablets of human hearts.

2Co 3:18 And we, who with unveiled faces all reflect the Lord's glory, are being transformed into his likeness with

ever-increasing glory, which comes from the Lord, who is the Spirit. (+Php 1:6)

Heb 4:12 For the word of God is living and active. Sharper than any double-edged sword, it penetrates even to dividing soul and spirit, joints and marrow; it judges the thoughts and attitudes of the heart.

Jas 5:19 My brothers, if one of you should wander from the truth and someone should bring him back, [20]remember this: Whoever turns a sinner from the error of his way will save him from death and cover over a multitude of sins.

1Pe 2:3 now that you have tasted that the Lord is good.

1Pe 2:9 But you are a chosen people, a royal priesthood, a holy nation, a people belonging to God, that you may declare the praises of him who called you out of darkness into his wonderful light.

2Pe 1:3 His divine power has given us everything we need for life and godliness through our knowledge of him who called us by his own glory and goodness. [4]Through these he has given us his very great and precious promises, so that through them you may participate in the divine nature and escape the corruption in the world caused by evil desires.

See Atonement; Conversion; Reconciliation; Redemption; Righteous; Salvation; Sanctification; Sin, Forgiveness of.

REGICIDE *(murder of a king.)* Of Ehud (Jdg 3:16-23). Of Saul (2Sa 1:16). Of Ish-Bosheth (2Sa 4:5-8). Of Nadab (1Ki 15:27-29). Of Elah (1Ki 16:9-11). Of Joram (2Ki 9:24). Of Ahaziah (2Ki 9:27). Of Joash (2Ki 12:20-21). Of Amaziah (2Ki 14:19-20). Of Zechariah (2Ki 15:10). Of Shallum (2Ki 15:14). Of Pekahiah (2Ki 15:25). Of Pekah (2Ki 15:30). Of Sennacherib (2Ki 19:36-37; Isa 37:37-38).

See Homicide.

REGISTRATION [3509, 4180, 5918, 7212, *616*].

NIV+ REGISTER, REGISTERED

Of citizens (Isa 4:3). *See Census.*

REHABIAH [8152, 8153] (*Yahweh has enlarged*). Son of Eliezer (1Ch 23:17; 24:21; 26:25).

REHOB [8149, 8150] (*broad, wide [place, market]*).

NIV+ BETH REHOB

1. Father of Hadadezer, king of Zobah (2Sa 8:3,12).

2. A Levite who sealed the covenant with Nehemiah (Ne 10:11).

3. A town in northern Israel. The limit of the investigation made by the twelve spies (Nu 13:21). Possessed by the Syrians (2Sa 10:6,8). Called Beth Rehob (2Sa 10:6).

4. A town of Asher (Jos 19:28).

5. A Levitical city of Asher (Jos 19:30; 21:31; 1Ch 6:75). Canaanites not driven from (Jdg 1:31).

REHOBOAM [8154, *4850*] (*[my] people will enlarge, expand*).

NIV+ REHOBOAM'S

Successor to Solomon as king (1Ki 11:43; 2Ch 9:31). Refuses to reform abuses (1Ki 12:1-15; 2Ch 10:1-15). Ten tribes, under the leadership of Jeroboam, who successfully revolt from (1Ki 12:16-24; 2Ch 10:16-19; 11:1-4). Builds fortified cities; is temporarily prosperous (2Ch 11:5-23). Invaded by the king of Egypt and despoiled (1Ki 14:25-28; 2Ch 12:1-12). Death of (1Ki 14:31; 2Ch 12:16). Genealogy and descendants of (1Ch 3; Mt 1:7).

REHOBOTH [8151] (*broad, wide [places, markets]*).
NIV+ REHOBOTH IR

1. A city built by Asshur (Ge 10:11).
2. A city of the Edomites (Ge 36:37; 1Ch 1:48).
3. The name given to a well dug by Isaac (Ge 26:22).

REHUM [8156, 10662] (*[he] is compassionate*).

1. A captive who returned to Jerusalem from Babylon (Ezr 2:2). Called Nehum (Ne 7:7).
2. An official who wrote a letter to Artaxerxes, influencing him against the Jews (Ezr 4:8-9,17,23).
3. A Levite who repaired part of the wall of Jerusalem (Ne 3:17).
4. A Jew of the Exile who signed the covenant with Nehemiah (Ne 10:25).
5. A priest who returned to Jerusalem from the Captivity in Babylon (Ne 12:3).

REI [8298] (*friendly* or *[my] friend*). An Israelite loyal to David at the time of the usurpation of Adonijah (1Ki 1:8).

REINS KJV word for internal parts; kidneys as the seat of the emotions (Ps 7:9; 26:2; Jer 17:10; Job 19:27). *See Heart; Kidney.*

REJECTION [*2396, 4415, 5540, 5759, 6073, 6136, 6440, *119*, *578*, *627*, *723*].
NIV+ REJECT, REJECTED, REJECTING, REJECTS

Of God (1Sa 8:7; 10:19; 2Ki 17:15; Lk 7:30). *See God, Rejected.*

Of Israel by God (Nu 14:12,26-37; 2Ki 17:20; Jer 6:30; 7:29; 14:19; La 5:22). Of Saul by God (1Sa 15:23,26).

Of Jesus. *See Jesus the Christ, Rejected.*

REKEM [8389, 8390] (*friendship*).

1. A king of the Midianites, slain by the Israelites (Nu 31:8; Jos 13:21).
2. A son of Hebron (1Ch 2:43-44).
3. A city in Benjamin (Jos 18:27).

RELEASE [*3655, 5927, 5929, 6142, 7337, 8938, *668*, *2934*, *3395*].
NIV+ RELEASED, RELEASES

Year of: *See Jubilee; Sabbatic Year.*

RELENT [5714, 8740].
NIV+ RELENTED, RELENTS

God relents, or changes his mind, in response to change in his people—

Jer 18:5 Then the word of the LORD came to me: **6**"O house of Israel, can I not do with you as this potter does?" declares the LORD. "Like clay in the hand of the potter, so are you in my hand, O house of Israel. **7**If at any time I announce that a nation or kingdom is to be uprooted, torn down and destroyed, **8**and if that nation I warned repents of its evil, then I will relent and not inflict on it the disaster I had planned. **9**And if at another time I announce that a nation or kingdom is to be built up and planted, **10**and if it does evil in my sight and does not obey me, then I will reconsider the good I had intended to do for it. (+Jer 26:1-6,12-13,17-19)

In response to the intercession of Moses, when Israel sinned with the golden calf (Ex 32:11-14); of Amos (Am 7:1-6).

Because of his covenant love—

Ps 106:44 But he took note of their distress when he heard their cry; **45**for their sake he remembered his covenant and

out of his great love he relented. (+Joel 2:13-14; Jnh 3:8-4:2)

Requests for God to relent (Job 6:29; Ps 90:13-16).

God will not relent when his people deserve his judgment (Jer 4:27-28)—

Eze 24:14 "'I the LORD have spoken. The time has come for me to act. I will not hold back; I will not have pity, nor will I relent. You will be judged according to your conduct and your actions, declares the Sovereign LORD.'"

See Repentance.

RELIGION [*1272*, *2355*, *2579*].
NIV+ RELIGIOUS

False: (Dt 32:31-33).
See Idolatry; Intolerance; Teachers, False.

Family: *See Family.*

National:

Supported by taxes (Ex 30:11-16; 38:26). Priests supported by the state (1Ki 18:19; 2Ch 11:13-15). Subverted by Jeroboam (1Ki 12:26-33; 2Ch 11:13-15). Idolatrous established by Jeroboam (1Ki 12:26-33).

Natural:

Job 12:7 "But ask the animals, and they will teach you, or the birds of the air, and they will tell you; **8**or speak to the earth, and it will teach you, or let the fish of the sea inform you. **9**Which of all these does not know that the hand of the LORD has done this? **10**In his hand is the life of every creature and the breath of all mankind. **11**Does not the ear test words as the tongue tastes food? **12**Is not wisdom found among the aged? Does not long life bring understanding?

13"To God belong wisdom and power; counsel and understanding are his. **14**What he tears down cannot be rebuilt; the man he imprisons cannot be released. **15**If he holds back the waters, there is drought; if he lets them loose, they devastate the land. **16**To him belong strength and victory; both deceived and deceiver are his.

Job 37:1 "At this my heart pounds and leaps from its place. **2**Listen! Listen to the roar of his voice, to the rumbling that comes from his mouth. **3**He unleashes his lightning beneath the whole heaven and sends it to the ends of the earth. **4**After that comes the sound of his roar; he thunders with his majestic voice. When his voice resounds, he holds nothing back. **5**God's voice thunders in marvelous ways; he does great things beyond our understanding. **6**He says to the snow, 'Fall on the earth,' and to the rain shower, 'Be a mighty downpour.' **7**So that all men he has made may know his work, he stops every man from his labor. **8**The animals take cover; they remain in their dens. **9**The tempest comes out from its chamber, the cold from the driving winds. **10**The breath of God produces ice, and the broad waters become frozen. **11**He loads the clouds with moisture; he scatters his lightning through them. **12**At his direction they swirl around over the face of the whole earth to do whatever he commands them. **13**He brings the clouds to punish men, or to water his earth and show his love.

14"Listen to this, Job; stop and consider God's wonders. **15**Do you know how God controls the clouds and makes his lightning flash? **16**Do you know how the clouds hang poised, those wonders of him who is perfect in knowledge? **17**You who swelter in your clothes when the land lies hushed under the south wind, **18**can you join him in spreading out the skies, hard as a mirror of cast bronze?

19"Tell us what we should say to him; we cannot draw up our case because of our darkness. **20**Should he be told that I want to speak? Would any man ask to be swallowed up? ²¹Now no one can look at the sun, bright as it is in the skies after the wind has swept them clean. ²²Out of the north he comes in golden splendor; God comes in awesome majesty. ²³The Almighty is beyond our reach and exalted in power; in his justice and great righteousness, he does not oppress. ²⁴Therefore, men revere him, for does he not have regard for all the wise in heart?"

Ps 8:1 O LORD, our Lord, how majestic is your name in all the earth! You have set your glory above the heavens.

²From the lips of children and infants you have ordained praise because of your enemies, to silence the foe and the avenger.

³When I consider your heavens, the work of your fingers, the moon and the stars, which you have set in place, ⁴what is man that you are mindful of him, the son of man that you care for him? ⁵You made him a little lower than the heavenly beings and crowned him with glory and honor.

⁶You made him ruler over the works of your hands; you put everything under his feet: ⁷all flocks and herds, and the beasts of the field, ⁸the birds of the air, and the fish of the sea, all that swim the paths of the seas.

⁹O LORD, our Lord, how majestic is your name in all the earth!

Ps 19:1 The heavens declare the glory of God; the skies proclaim the work of his hands. ²Day after day they pour forth speech; night after night they display knowledge. ³There is no speech or language where their voice is not heard. ⁴Their voice goes out into all the earth, their words to the ends of the world.

In the heavens he has pitched a tent for the sun, ⁵which is like a bridegroom coming forth from his pavilion, like a champion rejoicing to run his course. ⁶It rises at one end of the heavens and makes its circuit to the other; nothing is hidden from its heat.

Ac 14:17 Yet he has not left himself without testimony: He has shown kindness by giving you rain from heaven and crops in their seasons; he provides you with plenty of food and fills your hearts with joy."

Ac 17:23 For as I walked around and looked carefully at your objects of worship, I even found an altar with this inscription: TO AN UNKNOWN GOD. Now what you worship as something unknown I am going to proclaim to you.

²⁴"The God who made the world and everything in it is the Lord of heaven and earth and does not live in temples built by hands. ²⁵And he is not served by human hands, as if he needed anything, because he himself gives all men life and breath and everything else. ²⁶From one man he made every nation of men, that they should inhabit the whole earth; and he determined the times set for them and the exact places where they should live. ²⁷God did this so that men would seek him and perhaps reach out for him and find him, though he is not far from each one of us. ²⁸'For in him we live and move and have our being.' As some of your own poets have said, 'We are his offspring.'

Ro 1:18 The wrath of God is being revealed from heaven against all the godlessness and wickedness of men who suppress the truth by their wickedness, ¹⁹since what may be known about God is plain to them, because God has made it plain to them. ²⁰For since the creation of the world God's invisible qualities—his eternal power and divine nature—have been clearly seen, being understood from what has been made, so that men are without excuse.

Ro 10:16 But not all the Israelites accepted the good news.

For Isaiah says, "Lord, who has believed our message?" ¹⁷Consequently, faith comes from hearing the message, and the message is heard through the word of Christ. ¹⁸But I ask: Did they not hear? Of course they did: "Their voice has gone out into all the earth, their words to the ends of the world."

See Revivals.

True, As Presented By:

Jesus—

Mt 22:36 "Teacher, which is the greatest commandment in the Law?" ³⁷Jesus replied: "'Love the Lord your God with all your heart and with all your soul and with all your mind.' ³⁸This is the first and greatest commandment. ³⁹And the second is like it: 'Love your neighbor as yourself.' ⁴⁰All the Law and the Prophets hang on these two commandments."

In the "Sermon on the Mount": True blessedness (Mt 5:2-16), fulfillment of the law (Mt 5:17-48), "acts of righteousness" (Mt 6:1-18), service and treasure (Mt 6:19-21), judgment (Mt 7:1-6), asking (Mt 7:7-11), the "golden rule" (Mt 7:12), wholehearted commitment to God (Mt 7:13-29; Mt 22:26-35)

Paul—

Ro 8:18 I consider that our present sufferings are not worth comparing with the glory that will be revealed in us.
Ro 10:1 Brothers, my heart's desire and prayer to God for the Israelites is that they may be saved. ²For I can testify about them that they are zealous for God, but their zeal is not based on knowledge. ³Since they did not know the righteousness that comes from God and sought to establish their own, they did not submit to God's righteousness. ⁴Christ is the end of the law so that there may be righteousness for everyone who believes.

⁵Moses describes in this way the righteousness that is by the law: "The man who does these things will live by them." ⁶But the righteousness that is by faith says: "Do not say in your heart, 'Who will ascend into heaven?'" (that is, to bring Christ down) ⁷"or 'Who will descend into the deep?'" (that is, to bring Christ up from the dead). ⁸But what does it say? "The word is near you; it is in your mouth and in your heart," that is, the word of faith we are proclaiming: ⁹That if you confess with your mouth, "Jesus is Lord," and believe in your heart that God raised him from the dead, you will be saved. ¹⁰For it is with your heart that you believe and are justified, and it is with your mouth that you confess and are saved. ¹¹As the Scripture says, "Anyone who trusts in him will never be put to shame." ¹²For there is no difference between Jew and Gentile—the same Lord is Lord of all and richly blesses all who call on him, ¹³for, "Everyone who calls on the name of the Lord will be saved."

Ro 12:1 Therefore, I urge you, brothers, in view of God's mercy, to offer your bodies as living sacrifices, holy and pleasing to God—this is your spiritual act of worship. ²Do not conform any longer to the pattern of this world, but be transformed by the renewing of your mind. Then you will be able to test and approve what God's will is—his good, pleasing and perfect will.

³For by the grace given me I say to every one of you: Do not think of yourself more highly than you ought, but rather think of yourself with sober judgment, in accordance with the measure of faith God has given you. ⁴Just as each of us has one body with many members, and these members do not all have the same function, ⁵so in Christ we who are many form one body, and each member belongs to all the others. ⁶We have different gifts, according

to the grace given us. If a man's gift is prophesying, let him use it in proportion to his faith. [7]If it is serving, let him serve; if it is teaching, let him teach; [8]if it is encouraging, let him encourage; if it is contributing to the needs of others, let him give generously; if it is leadership, let him govern diligently; if it is showing mercy, let him do it cheerfully.

[9]Love must be sincere. Hate what is evil; cling to what is good. [10]Be devoted to one another in brotherly love. Honor one another above yourselves. [11]Never be lacking in zeal, but keep your spiritual fervor, serving the Lord. [12]Be joyful in hope, patient in affliction, faithful in prayer. [13]Share with God's people who are in need. Practice hospitality.

[14]Bless those who persecute you; bless and do not curse. [15]Rejoice with those who rejoice; mourn with those who mourn. [16]Live in harmony with one another. Do not be proud, but be willing to associate with people of low position. Do not be conceited.

[17]Do not repay anyone evil for evil. Be careful to do what is right in the eyes of everybody. [18]If it is possible, as far as it depends on you, live at peace with everyone. [19]Do not take revenge, my friends, but leave room for God's wrath, for it is written: "It is mine to avenge; I will repay," says the Lord. [20]On the contrary:

"If your enemy is hungry, feed him; if he is thirsty, give him something to drink. In doing this, you will heap burning coals on his head."

[21]Do not be overcome by evil, but overcome evil with good.

1Co 13:1 If I speak in the tongues of men and of angels, but have not love, I am only a resounding gong or a clanging cymbal. [2]If I have the gift of prophecy and can fathom all mysteries and all knowledge, and if I have a faith that can move mountains, but have not love, I am nothing. [3]If I give all I possess to the poor and surrender my body to the flames, but have not love, I gain nothing.

[4]Love is patient, love is kind. It does not envy, it does not boast, it is not proud. [5]It is not rude, it is not self-seeking, it is not easily angered, it keeps no record of wrongs. [6]Love does not delight in evil but rejoices with the truth. [7]It always protects, always trusts, always hopes, always perseveres.

[8]Love never fails. But where there are prophecies, they will cease; where there are tongues, they will be stilled; where there is knowledge, it will pass away. [9]For we know in part and we prophesy in part, [10]but when perfection comes, the imperfect disappears. [11]When I was a child, I talked like a child, I thought like a child, I reasoned like a child. When I became a man, I put childish ways behind me. [12]Now we see but a poor reflection as in a mirror; then we shall see face to face. Now I know in part; then I shall know fully, even as I am fully known.

[13]And now these three remain: faith, hope and love. But the greatest of these is love.

Gal 5:22 But the fruit of the Spirit is love, joy, peace, patience, kindness, goodness, faithfulness, [23]gentleness and self-control. Against such things there is no law. [24]Those who belong to Christ Jesus have crucified the sinful nature with its passions and desires. [25]Since we live by the Spirit, let us keep in step with the Spirit.

1Th 5:15 Make sure that nobody pays back wrong for wrong, but always try to be kind to each other and to everyone else.

[16]Be joyful always; [17]pray continually; [18]give thanks in all circumstances, for this is God's will for you in Christ Jesus.

[19]Do not put out the Spirit's fire; [20]do not treat prophecies with contempt. [21]Test everything. Hold on to the good. [22]Avoid every kind of evil.

[23]May God himself, the God of peace, sanctify you through and through. May your whole spirit, soul and body be kept blameless at the coming of our Lord Jesus Christ.

James—

Jas 1:27 Religion that God our Father accepts as pure and faultless is this: to look after orphans and widows in their distress and to keep oneself from being polluted by the world.

Jas 2:8 If you really keep the royal law found in Scripture, "Love your neighbor as yourself," you are doing right. [9]But if you show favoritism, you sin and are convicted by the law as lawbreakers. [10]For whoever keeps the whole law and yet stumbles at just one point is guilty of breaking all of it. [11]For he who said, "Do not commit adultery," also said, "Do not murder." If you do not commit adultery but do commit murder, you have become a lawbreaker.

[12]Speak and act as those who are going to be judged by the law that gives freedom, [13]because judgment without mercy will be shown to anyone who has not been merciful. Mercy triumphs over judgment!

[14]What good is it, my brothers, if a man claims to have faith but has no deeds? Can such faith save him? [15]Suppose a brother or sister is without clothes and daily food. [16]If one of you says to him, "Go, I wish you well; keep warm and well fed," but does nothing about his physical needs, what good is it? [17]In the same way, faith by itself, if it is not accompanied by action, is dead.

[18]But someone will say, "You have faith; I have deeds." Show me your faith without deeds, and I will show you my faith by what I do.

[19]You believe that there is one God. Good! Even the demons believe that—and shudder.

[20]You foolish man, do you want evidence that faith without deeds is useless? [21]Was not our ancestor Abraham considered righteous for what he did when he offered his son Isaac on the altar? [22]You see that his faith and his actions were working together, and his faith was made complete by what he did. [23]And the scripture was fulfilled that says, "Abraham believed God, and it was credited to him as righteousness," and he was called God's friend. [24]You see that a person is justified by what he does and not by faith alone.

[25]In the same way, was not even Rahab the prostitute considered righteous for what she did when she gave lodging to the spies and sent them off in a different direction? [26]As the body without the spirit is dead, so faith without deeds is dead.

Peter—

1Pe 2:5 you also, like living stones, are being built into a spiritual house to be a holy priesthood, offering spiritual sacrifices acceptable to God through Jesus Christ. [6]For in Scripture it says:

"See, I lay a stone in Zion, a chosen and precious cornerstone, and the one who trusts in him will never be put to shame."

[7]Now to you who believe, this stone is precious. But to those who do not believe,

"The stone the builders rejected has become the capstone," [8]and,

"A stone that causes men to stumble and a rock that makes them fall."

They stumble because they disobey the message—which is also what they were destined for.

⁹But you are a chosen people, a royal priesthood, a holy nation, a people belonging to God, that you may declare the praises of him who called you out of darkness into his wonderful light.

Jude—

Jude 20 But you, dear friends, build yourselves up in your most holy faith and pray in the Holy Spirit. ²¹Keep yourselves in God's love as you wait for the mercy of our Lord Jesus Christ to bring you to eternal life. *See Blessings, Spiritual; Commandments and Statutes, Of God; Duty; Graces; Regeneration; Repentance; Sanctification; Sin, Forgiveness of.*

Instances of Properly Religious Persons:

Abel (Ge 4:4-8; Heb 11:4). Noah (Ge 6-9). Abraham (Ge 12:1-8; 15; 17; 18:22-33). Jacob (Ge 28:10-22; 32:24-32). Moses (Ex 3:2-22; Dt 32-32). Jethro (Ex 18:12). Joshua (Jos 1). Gideon (Jdg 6-7). Samuel (1Sa 3). David. *See Psalms.* Solomon (1Ki 5:3-5; 2Ch 6). Jehu (2Ki 10:16-30). Hezekiah (2Ki 18:3-7; 19:14-19). Jehoshaphat (2Ch 17:3-9; 19-20). Jabez (1Ch 4:9-10). Asa (2Ch 14-15). Josiah (2Ki 22-23). Daniel (Da 6:4-22). The three Hebrews (Da 3). Zechariah (Lk 1:13,67-79). Simeon (Lk 2:25-35). Anna the prophetess (Lk 2:36-37). The centurion (Lk 7:1-10). Cornelius (Ac 10). Eunice and Lois (2Ti 1:5).

See for additional instances John, Paul, Peter, Simon, Stephen, and other apostles and disciples, also each of the prophets.

RELIGIOUS [2504, 1273, 2038, 2580, 3310].

NIV+ RELIGION

Coercion:

(Ex 22:20; 2Ch 15:12-15; Da 3:2-6; 6:26-27). *See Intolerance.*

Revivals:

(Zec 8:20-23). Prayer for (Hab 3:2). Prophecies concerning (Isa 32:15; Joel 2:28; Mic 4:1-8). *See Revivals.*

Testimony:

(Ps 18:49; 22:22; 26:12; 34:8-9; Isa 45:24; 1Co 13:1; Rev 12:11). *See Testimony, Religious.*

REMALIAH [8248] (*Yahweh has adorned*).

NIV+ REMALIAH'S

Father of Pekah, king of Israel (2Ki 15:25,27,30; 16:1,5; 2Ch 28:6; Isa 7:1,4; 8:6).

REMETH [8255] (*heights*). A city in Issachar (Jos 19:17-21), probably, Ramoth (1Ch 6:73), and Jarmuth (Jos 21:29).

REMMON *See Rimmon, 2.*

REMMON-METHOAR *See Rimmon, 3.*

REMNANT [3856, 7129, 8636, 8637, 8642, 2905, 3307, 5698].

1. People who survived political or military crises (Jos 12:4; 13:12).

2. Spiritual core of Israel who would survive God's judgment and become the seed of the new people of God (Isa 10:20-23; 11:11-12; Jer 32:38-39; Zep 3:13; Zec 8:12).

REMORSE [3564].

Pr 1:25 since you ignored all my advice and would not accept my rebuke, ²⁶I in turn will laugh at your disaster; I

will mock when calamity overtakes you— ²⁷when calamity overtakes you like a storm, when disaster sweeps over you like a whirlwind, when distress and trouble overwhelm you.

Of the promiscuous—

Pr 5:7 Now then, my sons, listen to me; do not turn aside from what I say. ⁸Keep to a path far from her, do not go near the door of her house, ⁹lest you give your best strength to others and your years to one who is cruel, ¹⁰lest strangers feast on your wealth and your toil enrich another man's house. ¹¹At the end of your life you will groan, when your flesh and body are spent. ¹²You will say, "How I hated discipline! How my heart spurned correction! ¹³I would not obey my teachers or listen to my instructors.

Of the lost—

Lk 13:28 "There will be weeping there, and gnashing of teeth, when you see Abraham, Isaac and Jacob and all the prophets in the kingdom of God, but you yourselves thrown out.

Of the wicked—

Pr 28:1 The wicked man flees though no one pursues, but the righteous are as bold as a lion.

Isa 2:19 Men will flee to caves in the rocks and to holes in the ground from dread of the LORD and the splendor of his majesty, when he rises to shake the earth.

Isa 57:20 But the wicked are like the tossing sea, which cannot rest, whose waves cast up mire and mud. ²¹"There is no peace," says my God, "for the wicked."

Eze 7:16 All who survive and escape will be in the mountains, moaning like doves of the valleys, each because of his sins. ¹⁷Every hand will go limp, and every knee will become as weak as water. ¹⁸They will put on sackcloth and be clothed with terror. Their faces will be covered with shame and their heads will be shaved.

Eze 7:25 When terror comes, they will seek peace, but there will be none. ²⁶Calamity upon calamity will come, and rumor upon rumor. They will try to get a vision from the prophet; the teaching of the law by the priest will be lost, as will the counsel of the elders.

Of Israelites—

Eze 33:10 "Son of man, say to the house of Israel, 'This is what you are saying: "Our offenses and sins weigh us down, and we are wasting away because of them. How then can we live?"'

Of believers—

1Jn 3:20 whenever our hearts condemn us. For God is greater than our hearts, and he knows everything.

Instances of:

David—

Ps 31:10 My life is consumed by anguish and my years by groaning; my strength fails because of my affliction, and my bones grow weak.

Ps 38:2 For your arrows have pierced me, and your hand has come down upon me. ³Because of your wrath there is no health in my body; my bones have no soundness because of my sin. ⁴My guilt has overwhelmed me like a burden too heavy to bear.

⁵My wounds fester and are loathsome because of my sinful folly. ⁶I am bowed down and brought very low; all day long I go about mourning.

Ps 51:1 Have mercy on me, O God, according to your unfailing love; according to your great compassion blot out my transgressions. ²Wash away all my iniquity and cleanse me from my sin.

³For I know my transgressions, and my sin is always

before me. ⁴Against you, you only, have I sinned and done what is evil in your sight, so that you are proved right when you speak and justified when you judge. (+Ps 51:5-6)

Ps 51:7 Cleanse me with hyssop, and I will be clean; wash me, and I will be whiter than snow. ⁸Let me hear joy and gladness; let the bones you have crushed rejoice. ⁹Hide your face from my sins and blot out all my iniquity.

¹⁰Create in me a pure heart, O God, and renew a steadfast spirit within me. ¹¹Do not cast me from your presence or take your Holy Spirit from me. ¹²Restore to me the joy of your salvation and grant me a willing spirit, to sustain me.

¹³Then I will teach transgressors your ways, and sinners will turn back to you. ¹⁴Save me from bloodguilt, O God, the God who saves me, and my tongue will sing of your righteousness. ¹⁵O Lord, open my lips, and my mouth will declare your praise. ¹⁶You do not delight in sacrifice, or I would bring it; you do not take pleasure in burnt offerings. ¹⁷The sacrifices of God are a broken spirit; a broken and contrite heart, O God, you will not despise. (+Ps 51:18-19)

Isaiah—

Isa 6:5 "Woe to me!" I cried. "I am ruined! For I am a man of unclean lips, and I live among a people of unclean lips, and my eyes have seen the King, the LORD Almighty."

Jeremiah—

La 1:20 "See, O LORD, how distressed I am! I am in torment within, and in my heart I am disturbed, for I have been most rebellious. Outside, the sword bereaves; inside, there is only death.

Peter (Mt 26:75). Judas (Mt 27:3-5).

The Jews—

Ac 2:37 When the people heard this, they were cut to the heart and said to Peter and the other apostles, "Brothers, what shall we do?"

Paul—

Ac 9:6 "Now get up and go into the city, and you will be told what you must do."

See Conviction, of Sin; Penitent; Repentance; Sin, Confession of.

REMPHAN *See Rephan.*

RENDING [7973].

NIV+ REND

Of garments, a token of affliction (Ge 37:29,34; 44:13; Nu 14:6; Jdg 11:35; 2Sa 1:2,11; 3:31; 13:19,31; 15:32; 2Ki 2:12; 5:8; 6:30; 11:14; 19:1; 22:11,19; Ezr 9:3,5; Job 1:20; 2:12; Isa 36:22; 37:1; Jer 41:5; Mt 26:65; Ac 14:14).

Figurative (Joel 2:13). Symbol of dividing of a kingdom (1Sa 15:27-28).

RENTING [*1686, 3637*].

NIV+ RENT, RENTED

Land (Mt 21:33-41; Lk 20:9-16). Houses (Ac 28:30).

RENUNCIATION (Php 3:7-8). Of self for others, exemplified, by Moses (Ex 32:32), Jesus (Php 2:7), Paul (Ro 9:3; 2Co 13:7).

Of self for Christ (Mt 16:25; Lk 14:26-33; 17:33; Jn 12:25). Of business for Christ (Mt 4:20; 9:9; Mk 1:18-20; 2:14; Lk 5:27-28). Of possessions for Christ (Mt 19:21-29; Mk 10:21-30; Lk 18:22-30). Of one's all for Christ, illustrated by parable (Mt 13:44-46).

Of the will, to the Father, exemplified by Jesus (Mk 14:36; Lk 22:42; Jn 5:30; 6:38).

See Self-Denial.

REPENTANCE [4044, 5714, 8740, 8746, *3564, 3566, 3567*].

NIV+ PENITENT, REPENT, REPENTED, REPENTS

Ps 34:14 Turn from evil and do good; seek peace and pursue it.

Ps 34:18 The LORD is close to the brokenhearted and saves those who are crushed in spirit.

Isa 22:12 The Lord, the LORD Almighty, called you on that day to weep and to wail, to tear out your hair and put on sackcloth.

Exhortations to:

Pr 1:22 "How long will you simple ones love your simple ways? How long will mockers delight in mockery and fools hate knowledge? ²³If you had responded to my rebuke, I would have poured out my heart to you and made my thoughts known to you.

Jer 6:16 This is what the LORD says: "Stand at the crossroads and look; ask for the ancient paths, ask where the good way is, and walk in it, and you will find rest for your souls. But you said, 'We will not walk in it.' (+Jer 6:17-18; 7:3)

Jer 26:3 Perhaps they will listen and each will turn from his evil way. Then I will relent and not bring on them the disaster I was planning because of the evil they have done. (+Hos 6:1)

Hos 14:1 Return, O Israel, to the LORD your God. Your sins have been your downfall! ²Take words with you and return to the LORD. Say to him: "Forgive all our sins and receive us graciously, that we may offer the fruit of our lips. (+Hos 14:3; Am 5:4-6; Mt 3:2)

Commanded—

Dt 32:29 If only they were wise and would understand this and discern what their end will be!

2Ch 30:6 At the king's command, couriers went throughout Israel and Judah with letters from the king and from his officials, which read:

"People of Israel, return to the LORD, the God of Abraham, Isaac and Israel, that he may return to you who are left, who have escaped from the hand of the kings of Assyria. ⁷Do not be like your fathers and brothers, who were unfaithful to the LORD, the God of their fathers, so that he made them an object of horror, as you see. ⁸Do not be stiff-necked, as your fathers were; submit to the LORD. Come to the sanctuary, which he has consecrated forever. Serve the LORD your God, so that his fierce anger will turn away from you. ⁹If you return to the LORD, then your brothers and your children will be shown compassion by their captors and will come back to this land, for the LORD your God is gracious and compassionate. He will not turn his face from you if you return to him."

Job 36:10 He makes them listen to correction and commands them to repent of their evil. (+Isa 22:12)

Isa 31:6 Return to him you have so greatly revolted against, O Israelites.

Isa 44:22 I have swept away your offenses like a cloud, your sins like the morning mist. Return to me, for I have redeemed you."

Isa 55:6 Seek the LORD while he may be found; call on him while he is near. ⁷Let the wicked forsake his way and the evil man his thoughts. Let him turn to the LORD, and he will have mercy on him, and to our God, for he will freely pardon.

Jer 3:4 Have you not just called to me: 'My Father, my friend from my youth,

Jer 3:12 Go, proclaim this message toward the north:

" 'Return, faithless Israel,' declares the LORD, 'I will frown on you no longer, for I am merciful,' declares the LORD, 'I will not be angry forever. ¹³Only acknowledge your guilt—you have rebelled against the LORD your God, you have scattered your favors to foreign gods under every spreading tree, and have not obeyed me,'" declares the LORD.

¹⁴"Return, faithless people," declares the LORD, "for I am your husband. I will choose you—one from a town and two from a clan—and bring you to Zion.

Jer 3:19 "I myself said, " 'How gladly would I treat you like sons and give you a desirable land, the most beautiful inheritance of any nation.' I thought you would call me 'Father' and not turn away from following me. (+Jer 3:22; 18:11)

Jer 25:5 They said, "Turn now, each of you, from your evil ways and your evil practices, and you can stay in the land the LORD gave to you and your fathers for ever and ever. (+Jer 25:6)

Jer 26:13 Now reform your ways and your actions and obey the LORD your God. Then the LORD will relent and not bring the disaster he has pronounced against you. (+Jer 35:15; Eze 12:1-2)

Eze 12:3 "Therefore, son of man, pack your belongings for exile and in the daytime, as they watch, set out and go from where you are to another place. Perhaps they will understand, though they are a rebellious house. (+Eze 12:4-5)

Eze 14:6 "Therefore say to the house of Israel, 'This is what the Sovereign LORD says: Repent! Turn from your idols and renounce all your detestable practices! (+Eze 18:30-32)

Eze 33:10 "Son of man, say to the house of Israel, 'This is what you are saying: "Our offenses and sins weigh us down, and we are wasting away because of them. How then can we live?"' ¹¹Say to them, 'As surely as I live, declares the Sovereign LORD, I take no pleasure in the death of the wicked, but rather that they turn from their ways and live. Turn! Turn from your evil ways! Why will you die, O house of Israel?'

¹²"Therefore, son of man, say to your countrymen, 'The righteousness of the righteous man will not save him when he disobeys, and the wickedness of the wicked man will not cause him to fall when he turns from it. The righteous man, if he sins, will not be allowed to live because of his former righteousness.'

Eze 33:14 And if I say to the wicked man, 'You will surely die,' but he then turns away from his sin and does what is just and right— ¹⁵if he gives back what he took in pledge for a loan, returns what he has stolen, follows the decrees that give life, and does no evil, he will surely live; he will not die. ¹⁶None of the sins he has committed will be remembered against him. He has done what is just and right; he will surely live.

Eze 33:19 And if a wicked man turns away from his wickedness and does what is just and right, he will live by doing so.

Da 4:27 Therefore, O king, be pleased to accept my advice: Renounce your sins by doing what is right, and your wickedness by being kind to the oppressed. It may be that then your prosperity will continue."

Hos 10:12 Sow for yourselves righteousness, reap the fruit of unfailing love, and break up your unplowed ground; for it is time to seek the LORD, until he comes and showers righteousness on you. (+Hos 14:1-2)

Joel 1:14 Declare a holy fast; call a sacred assembly. Summon the elders and all who live in the land to the house of the LORD your God, and cry out to the LORD.

Joel 2:12 "Even now," declares the LORD, "return to me with all your heart, with fasting and weeping and mourning."

¹³Rend your heart and not your garments. Return to the LORD your God, for he is gracious and compassionate, slow to anger and abounding in love, and he relents from sending calamity.

Joel 2:15 Blow the trumpet in Zion, declare a holy fast, call a sacred assembly. ¹⁶Gather the people, consecrate the assembly; bring together the elders, gather the children, those nursing at the breast. Let the bridegroom leave his room and the bride her chamber. ¹⁷Let the priests, who minister before the LORD, weep between the temple porch and the altar. Let them say, "Spare your people, O LORD. Do not make your inheritance an object of scorn, a byword among the nations. Why should they say among the peoples, 'Where is their God?' "

Am 4:12 "Therefore this is what I will do to you, Israel, and because I will do this to you, prepare to meet your God, O Israel."

Jnh 3:8 But let man and beast be covered with sackcloth. Let everyone call urgently on God. Let them give up their evil ways and their violence. ⁹Who knows? God may yet relent and with compassion turn from his fierce anger so that we will not perish."

Hag 1:7 This is what the LORD Almighty says: "Give careful thought to your ways.

Zec 1:3 Therefore tell the people: This is what the LORD Almighty says: 'Return to me,' declares the LORD Almighty, 'and I will return to you,' says the LORD Almighty.

Mt 4:17 From that time on Jesus began to preach, "Repent, for the kingdom of heaven is near."

Mk 1:4 And so John came, baptizing in the desert region and preaching a baptism of repentance for the forgiveness of sins.

Mk 1:15 "The time has come," he said. "The kingdom of God is near. Repent and believe the good news!"

Mk 6:12 They went out and preached that people should repent. (+Lk 3:3; Ac 2:38)

Ac 3:19 Repent, then, and turn to God, so that your sins may be wiped out, that times of refreshing may come from the Lord,

Ac 8:22 Repent of this wickedness and pray to the Lord. Perhaps he will forgive you for having such a thought in your heart.

Ac 17:30 In the past God overlooked such ignorance, but now he commands all people everywhere to repent.

Rev 2:5 Remember the height from which you have fallen! Repent and do the things you did at first. If you do not repent, I will come to you and remove your lampstand from its place.

Rev 2:16 Repent therefore! Otherwise, I will soon come to you and will fight against them with the sword of my mouth.

Rev 3:2 Wake up! Strengthen what remains and is about to die, for I have not found your deeds complete in the sight of my God. ³Remember, therefore, what you have received and heard; obey it, and repent. But if you do not wake up, I will come like a thief, and you will not know at what time I will come to you.

Rev 3:19 Those whom I love I rebuke and discipline. So be earnest, and repent.

Source:

Gift of God—

2Ti 2:25 Those who oppose him he must gently instruct, in the hope that God will grant them repentance leading them to a knowledge of the truth,

Gift of Christ—

Ac 5:31 God exalted him to his own right hand as Prince and Savior that he might give repentance and forgiveness of sins to Israel.

Goodness of God leads to—

Ro 2:4 Or do you show contempt for the riches of his kindness, tolerance and patience, not realizing that God's kindness leads you toward repentance?

Tribulation leads to (Dt 4:30; 30:1-3)—

1Ki 8:33 "When your people Israel have been defeated by an enemy because they have sinned against you, and when they turn back to you and confess your name, praying and making supplication to you in this temple, ³⁴then hear from heaven and forgive the sin of your people Israel and bring them back to the land you gave to their fathers.

³⁵"When the heavens are shut up and there is no rain because your people have sinned against you, and when they pray toward this place and confess your name and turn from their sin because you have afflicted them, ³⁶then hear from heaven and forgive the sin of your servants, your people Israel. Teach them the right way to live, and send rain on the land you gave your people for an inheritance.

³⁷"When famine or plague comes to the land, or blight or mildew, locusts or grasshoppers, or when an enemy besieges them in any of their cities, whatever disaster or disease may come, ³⁸and when a prayer or plea is made by any of your people Israel—each one aware of the afflictions of his own heart, and spreading out his hands toward this temple— ³⁹then hear from heaven, your dwelling place. Forgive and act; deal with each man according to all he does, since you know his heart (for you alone know the hearts of all men), ⁴⁰so that they will fear you all the time they live in the land you gave our fathers.

⁴¹"As for the foreigner who does not belong to your people Israel but has come from a distant land because of your name— ⁴²for men will hear of your great name and your mighty hand and your outstretched arm—when he comes and prays toward this temple, ⁴³then hear from heaven, your dwelling place, and do whatever the foreigner asks of you, so that all the peoples of the earth may know your name and fear you, as do your own people Israel, and may know that this house I have built bears your Name.

⁴⁴"When your people go to war against their enemies, wherever you send them, and when they pray to the LORD toward the city you have chosen and the temple I have built for your Name, ⁴⁵then hear from heaven their prayer and their plea, and uphold their cause.

⁴⁶"When they sin against you—for there is no one who does not sin—and you become angry with them and give them over to the enemy, who takes them captive to his own land, far away or near; ⁴⁷and if they have a change of heart in the land where they are held captive, and repent and plead with you in the land of their conquerors and say, 'We have sinned, we have done wrong, we have acted wickedly'; ⁴⁸and if they turn back to you with all their heart and soul in the land of their enemies who took them captive, and pray to you toward the land you gave their fathers, toward the city you have chosen and the temple I have built for your Name; ⁴⁹then from heaven, your dwelling place, hear their prayer and their plea, and uphold their

cause. ⁵⁰And forgive your people, who have sinned against you; forgive all the offenses they have committed against you, and cause their conquerors to show them mercy; (+2Ch 6:36-39)

Job 34:31 "Suppose a man says to God, 'I am guilty but will offend no more. ³²Teach me what I cannot see; if I have done wrong, I will not do so again.'

Condition, of Forgiveness:

Lev 26:40 "'But if they will confess their sins and the sins of their fathers—their treachery against me and their hostility toward me, ⁴¹which made me hostile toward them so that I sent them into the land of their enemies—then when their uncircumcised hearts are humbled and they pay for their sin, ⁴²I will remember my covenant with Jacob and my covenant with Isaac and my covenant with Abraham, and I will remember the land.

Dt 4:29 But if from there you seek the LORD your God, you will find him if you look for him with all your heart and with all your soul. ³⁰When you are in distress and all these things have happened to you, then in later days you will return to the LORD your God and obey him. ³¹For the LORD your God is a merciful God; he will not abandon or destroy you or forget the covenant with your forefathers, which he confirmed to them by oath.

Dt 30:1 When all these blessings and curses I have set before you come upon you and you take them to heart wherever the LORD your God disperses you among the nations, ²and when you and your children return to the LORD your God and obey him with all your heart and with all your soul according to everything I command you today, ³then the LORD your God will restore your fortunes and have compassion on you and gather you again from all the nations where he scattered you.

Dt 30:8 You will again obey the LORD and follow all his commands I am giving you today. (+1Ki 8:33-50; 2Ch 6:36-39)

2Ch 7:14 if my people, who are called by my name, will humble themselves and pray and seek my face and turn from their wicked ways, then will I hear from heaven and will forgive their sin and will heal their land.

Ne 1:9 but if you return to me and obey my commands, then even if your exiled people are at the farthest horizon, I will gather them from there and bring them to the place I have chosen as a dwelling for my Name.'

Job 11:13 "Yet if you devote your heart to him and stretch out your hands to him, ¹⁴if you put away the sin that is in your hand and allow no evil to dwell in your tent, ¹⁵then you will lift up your face without shame; you will stand firm and without fear.

Job 22:23 If you return to the Almighty, you will be restored: If you remove wickedness far from your tent (+Ps 34:18)

Pr 28:13 He who conceals his sins does not prosper, but whoever confesses and renounces them finds mercy. (+Isa 55:7; Jer 3:4,12-14,19)

Jer 7:5 If you really change your ways and your actions and deal with each other justly, (+Jer 7:6)

Jer 7:7 then I will let you live in this place, in the land I gave your forefathers for ever and ever. (+Jer 18:7-8)

Jer 36:3 Perhaps when the people of Judah hear about every disaster I plan to inflict on them, each of them will turn from his wicked way; then I will forgive their wickedness and their sin."

Eze 18:21 "But if a wicked man turns away from all the sins he has committed and keeps all my decrees and does what is just and right, he will surely live; he will not die.

²²None of the offenses he has committed will be remembered against him. Because of the righteous things he has done, he will live. ²³Do I take any pleasure in the death of the wicked? declares the Sovereign LORD. Rather, am I not pleased when they turn from their ways and live?

Eze 18:27 But if a wicked man turns away from the wickedness he has committed and does what is just and right, he will save his life. ²⁸Because he considers all the offenses he has committed and turns away from them, he will surely live; he will not die.

Eze 18:30 "Therefore, O house of Israel, I will judge you, each one according to his ways, declares the Sovereign LORD. Repent! Turn away from all your offenses; then sin will not be your downfall. ³¹Rid yourselves of all the offenses you have committed, and get a new heart and a new spirit. Why will you die, O house of Israel?

Am 5:6 Seek the LORD and live, or he will sweep through the house of Joseph like a fire; it will devour, and Bethel will have no one to quench it.

Mal 3:7 Ever since the time of your forefathers you have turned away from my decrees and have not kept them. Return to me, and I will return to you," says the LORD Almighty. "But you ask, 'How are we to return?'

Mt 5:4 Blessed are those who mourn, for they will be comforted.

Lk 13:1 Now there were some present at that time who told Jesus about the Galileans whose blood Pilate had mixed with their sacrifices. ²Jesus answered, "Do you think that these Galileans were worse sinners than all the other Galileans because they suffered this way? ³I tell you, no! But unless you repent, you too will all perish. ⁴Or those eighteen who died when the tower in Siloam fell on them—do you think they were more guilty than all the others living in Jerusalem? ⁵I tell you, no! But unless you repent, you too will all perish."

1Jn 1:9 If we confess our sins, he is faithful and just and will forgive us our sins and purify us from all unrighteousness.

Of divine favor (Lev 26:40-42; 2Ch 7:14)—

Isa 57:15 For this is what the high and lofty One says—he who lives forever, whose name is holy: "I live in a high and holy place, but also with him who is contrite and lowly in spirit, to revive the spirit of the lowly and to revive the heart of the contrite.

To be Preached to All Nations—

Lk 24:47 and repentance and forgiveness of sins will be preached in his name to all nations, beginning at Jerusalem.

Joy in heaven over (Lk 15:1-6)—

Lk 15:7 I tell you that in the same way there will be more rejoicing in heaven over one sinner who repents than over ninety-nine righteous persons who do not need to repent. (+Lk 15:8-10)

Foretold:

Of Israel—

Jer 50:4 "In those days, at that time," declares the LORD, "the people of Israel and the people of Judah together will go in tears to seek the LORD their God. ⁵They will ask the way to Zion and turn their faces toward it. They will come and bind themselves to the LORD in an everlasting covenant that will not be forgotten.

Eze 11:18 "They will return to it and remove all its vile images and detestable idols. ¹⁹I will give them an undivided heart and put a new spirit in them; I will remove from their heart of stone and give them a heart of

flesh. ²⁰Then they will follow my decrees and be careful to keep my laws. They will be my people, and I will be their God.

Hos 3:5 Afterward the Israelites will return and seek the LORD their God and David their king. They will come trembling to the LORD and to his blessings in the last days.

Zec 12:10 "And I will pour out on the house of David and the inhabitants of Jerusalem a spirit of grace and supplication. They will look on me, the one they have pierced, and they will mourn for him as one mourns for an only child, and grieve bitterly for him as one grieves for a firstborn son.

Universal—

Ps 22:27 All the ends of the earth will remember and turn to the LORD, and all the families of the nations will bow down before him,

Ro 14:11 It is written: "'As surely as I live,' says the Lord, 'every knee will bow before me; every tongue will confess to God.'"

Rewards of:

Isa 59:20 "The Redeemer will come to Zion, to those in Jacob who repent of their sins," declares the LORD. (+Pr 1:23; Jer 7:3,5,7)

Jer 24:7 I will give them a heart to know me, that I am the LORD. They will be my people, and I will be their God, for they will return to me with all their heart. (+Eze 18:21-23,27-28)

Preached by:

John the Baptist—

Mt 3:2 and saying, "Repent, for the kingdom of heaven is near."

Mt 3:7 But when he saw many of the Pharisees and Sadducees coming to where he was baptizing, he said to them: "You brood of vipers! Who warned you to flee from the coming wrath? ⁸Produce fruit in keeping with repentance. (+Mk 1:4,15; Lk 3:3)

Jesus (Mt 4:17; Mk 1:15)—

Lk 5:32 I have not come to call the righteous, but sinners to repentance."

Peter—

Ac 2:38 Peter replied, "Repent and be baptized, every one of you, in the name of Jesus Christ for the forgiveness of your sins. And you will receive the gift of the Holy Spirit.

Ac 2:40 With many other words he warned them; and he pleaded with them, "Save yourselves from this corrupt generation." (+Ac 3:19; 8:22)

Paul (Ac 17:30)—

Ac 20:21 I have declared to both Jews and Greeks that they must turn to God in repentance and have faith in our Lord Jesus.

Ac 26:20 First to those in Damascus, then to those in Jerusalem and in all Judea, and to the Gentiles also, I preached that they should repent and turn to God and prove their repentance by their deeds.

The apostles (Mk 6:12).—

Unavailing, to Israel (Nu 14:39-45), to Esau (Heb 12:16-17).

Attributed to God:

God relents, or changes his mind, in response to change in his people (Ge 6:6-7; Ex 32:14; Dt 32:36; Jdg 2:18; 1Sa 15:11,35; 2Sa 24:16; 1Ch 21:15; Ps 106:45; 110:4; 135:14; Jer 15:6; 18:1-10; 26:3; 42:10; Joel 2:13; Am 7:3,6; Jnh 3:9-10). *See Relent.*

God will not repent (Nu 23:19; 1Sa 15:29; Ps 110:4; Ro 11:29).

Exemplified:

By Job—

Job 7:20 If I have sinned, what have I done to you, O watcher of men? Why have you made me your target? Have I become a burden to you? (+Job 7:21)

Job 9:20 Even if I were innocent, my mouth would condemn me; if I were blameless, it would pronounce me guilty.

Job 13:23 How many wrongs and sins have I committed? Show me my offense and my sin.

Job 40:4 "I am unworthy—how can I reply to you? I put my hand over my mouth.

Job 42:5 My ears had heard of you but now my eyes have seen you. ⁶Therefore I despise myself and repent in dust and ashes."

By David—

Ps 32:5 Then I acknowledged my sin to you and did not cover up my iniquity. I said, "I will confess my transgressions to the LORD"—and you forgave the guilt of my sin. *Selah*

Ps 38:3 Because of your wrath there is no health in my body; my bones have no soundness because of my sin. ⁴My guilt has overwhelmed me like a burden too heavy to bear.

Ps 38:18 I confess my iniquity; I am troubled by my sin.

Ps 40:12 For troubles without number surround me; my sins have overtaken me, and I cannot see. They are more than the hairs of my head, and my heart fails within me.

Ps 41:4 I said, "O LORD, have mercy on me; heal me, for I have sinned against you."

Ps 51:1 Have mercy on me, O God, according to your unfailing love; according to your great compassion blot out my transgressions. ²Wash away all my iniquity and cleanse me from my sin.

³For I know my transgressions, and my sin is always before me. ⁴Against you, you only, have I sinned and done what is evil in your sight, so that you are proved right when you speak and justified when you judge.

Ps 51:7 Cleanse me with hyssop, and I will be clean; wash me, and I will be whiter than snow. ⁸Let me hear joy and gladness; let the bones you have crushed rejoice. ⁹Hide your face from my sins and blot out all my iniquity.

¹⁰Create in me a pure heart, O God, and renew a steadfast spirit within me. ¹¹Do not cast me from your presence or take your Holy Spirit from me. ¹²Restore to me the joy of your salvation and grant me a willing spirit, to sustain me.

¹³Then I will teach transgressors your ways, and sinners will turn back to you. ¹⁴Save me from bloodguilt, O God, the God who saves me, and my tongue will sing of your righteousness. ¹⁵O Lord, open my lips, and my mouth will declare your praise. ¹⁶You do not delight in sacrifice, or I would bring it; you do not take pleasure in burnt offerings. ¹⁷The sacrifices of God are a broken spirit; a broken and contrite heart, O God, you will not despise.

By the Israelites—

Nu 21:7 The people came to Moses and said, "We sinned when we spoke against the LORD and against you. Pray that the LORD will take the snakes away from us." So Moses prayed for the people.

2Ch 29:6 Our fathers were unfaithful; they did evil in the eyes of the LORD our God and forsook him. They turned their faces away from the LORD's dwelling place and turned their backs on him.

Jer 3:21 A cry is heard on the barren heights, the weeping and pleading of the people of Israel, because they have perverted their ways and have forgotten the LORD their God.

²²"Return, faithless people; I will cure you of backsliding." "Yes, we will come to you, for you are the LORD our God.

Jer 3:25 Let us lie down in our shame, and let our disgrace cover us. We have sinned against the LORD our God, both we and our fathers; from our youth till this day we have not obeyed the LORD our God."

Jer 14:7 Although our sins testify against us, O LORD, do something for the sake of your name. For our backsliding is great; we have sinned against you. (+Jer 14:8-9)

Jer 14:20 O LORD, we acknowledge our wickedness and the guilt of our fathers; we have indeed sinned against you.

Jer 31:18 "I have surely heard Ephraim's moaning: 'You disciplined me like an unruly calf, and I have been disciplined. Restore me, and I will return, because you are the LORD my God. ¹⁹After I strayed, I repented; after I came to understand, I beat my breast. I was ashamed and humiliated because I bore the disgrace of my youth.'

La 3:40 Let us examine our ways and test them, and let us return to the LORD. ⁴¹Let us lift up our hearts and our hands to God in heaven, and say:

By Daniel for the Jews—

Da 9:5 we have sinned and done wrong. We have been wicked and have rebelled; we have turned away from your commands and laws. ⁶We have not listened to your servants the prophets, who spoke in your name to our kings, our princes and our fathers, and to all the people of the land.

⁷"Lord, you are righteous, but this day we are covered with shame—the men of Judah and people of Jerusalem and all Israel, both near and far, in all the countries where you have scattered us because of our unfaithfulness to you.

Da 10:12 Then he continued, "Do not be afraid, Daniel. Since the first day that you set your mind to gain understanding and to humble yourself before your God, your words were heard, and I have come in response to them.

By the prodigal son—

Lk 15:17 "When he came to his senses, he said, 'How many of my father's hired men have food to spare, and here I am starving to death! ¹⁸I will set out and go back to my father and say to him: Father, I have sinned against heaven and against you. ¹⁹I am no longer worthy to be called your son; make me like one of your hired men.' ²⁰So he got up and went to his father.

"But while he was still a long way off, his father saw him and was filled with compassion for him; he ran to his son, threw his arms around him and kissed him.

Instances of:

Joseph's brothers, for their ill treatment of Joseph (Ge 42:21; 50:17-18). Pharaoh, for his hardness of heart (Ex 9:27; 10:16-17). Balaam, for his spiritual blindness (Nu 22:34, w 22:24-35). Israelites, for worshiping the golden calf (Ex 33:3-4), for their murmuring on account of the lack of bread and water, when the plague of fiery serpents came upon them (Nu 21:4-7), when rebuked by an angel for not expelling the Canaanites (Jdg 2:1-5), for their idolatry, when afflicted by the Philistines (Jdg 10:6-16; 1Sa 7:3-6), for asking for a king (1Sa 12:16-20), in the time of Asa, under the preaching of Azariah (2Ch 15:1-15), under the preaching of Oded (2Ch 28:9-15), under the influence of Hezekiah (2Ch 30:11). Achan, for his theft (Jos 7:19-21). Saul, at the reproof of Samuel for not destroying the Amalekites (1Sa 15:24, w 15:6-11). Job (Job 42:6). David, at the rebuke of Nathan, the prophet

(2Sa 12:11,13, w 12:7-14; Ps 32:5; 38:3-4,18; 40:12; 41:4; 51:1-4,7-17)

David for numbering Israel—

2Sa 24:10 David was conscience-stricken after he had counted the fighting men, and he said to the LORD, "I have sinned greatly in what I have done. Now, O LORD, I beg you, take away the guilt of your servant. I have done a very foolish thing."

2Sa 24:17 When David saw the angel who was striking down the people, he said to the LORD, "I am the one who has sinned and done wrong. These are but sheep. What have they done? Let your hand fall upon me and my family."

The psalmist (Ps 106:6)—

Ps 119:59 I have considered my ways and have turned my steps to your statutes. **60**I will hasten and not delay to obey your commands.

Ps 119:176 I have strayed like a lost sheep. Seek your servant, for I have not forgotten your commands.

Ps 130:1 Out of the depths I cry to you, O LORD; **2**O Lord, hear my voice. Let your ears be attentive to my cry for mercy.

3If you, O LORD, kept a record of sins, O Lord, who could stand?

See Psalms, Topically Arranged.

Rehoboam, when his kingdom was invaded, and Jerusalem besieged (2Ch 12:1-12)

Isaiah—

Isa 6:5 "Woe to me!" I cried. "I am ruined! For I am a man of unclean lips, and I live among a people of unclean lips, and my eyes have seen the King, the LORD Almighty."

Hezekiah, for his pride—

Isa 38:15 But what can I say? He has spoken to me, and he himself has done this. I will walk humbly all my years because of this anguish of my soul.

At the time of his sickness (2Ch 32:26), when reproved by the prophet Micah (Jer 26:18-19). Ahab, when reproved by Elijah for his idolatry (1Ki 21:27). Jehoahaz (2Ki 13:4). Josiah, when he heard the law which had been discovered in the temple, by Hilkiah (2Ki 22:11-20). Manasseh, when he was carried captive to Babylon by the king of Assyria (2Ch 33:12-13).

The Jews of the Captivity, at the dedication of the temple (Ezr 6:21)—

Ezr 9:4 Then everyone who trembled at the words of the God of Israel gathered around me because of this unfaithfulness of the exiles. And I sat there appalled until the evening sacrifice.

Ezr 9:6 and prayed: "O my God, I am too ashamed and disgraced to lift up my face to you, my God, because our sins are higher than our heads and our guilt has reached to the heavens.

Ezr 9:10 "But now, O our God, what can we say after this? For we have disregarded the commands

Ezr 9:13 "What has happened to us is a result of our evil deeds and our great guilt, and yet, our God, you have punished us less than our sins have deserved and have given us a remnant like this. **14**Shall we again break your commands and intermarry with the peoples who commit such detestable practices? Would you not be angry enough with us to destroy us, leaving us no remnant or survivor?

For their idolatrous marriages (Ezr 10), for their oppressive usury (Ne 5:1-13), after hearing the law which had been expounded by Ezra (Ne 9:1-3), under the preaching of Haggai (Hag 1). Jonah, after his punishment (Jnh 2:2-9).

The Ninevites, at the preaching of Jonah (Jnh 3:5,9)—

Jnh 3:10 When God saw what they did and how they turned from their evil ways, he had compassion and did not bring upon them the destruction he had threatened.

The Jews under the preaching of John the Baptist (Mt 3:6). The woman who anointed Jesus with oil (Lk 7:37-48). The disobedient son (Mt 21:29). The prodigal son (Lk 15:17-21).

The tax collector—

Lk 18:13 "But the tax collector stood at a distance. He would not even look up to heaven, but beat his breast and said, 'God, have mercy on me, a sinner.'

Peter, of his denial of Jesus (Mt 26:75; Mk 14:72; Lk 22:62). The Ephesians, under the preaching of Paul (Ac 19:18).

See Conviction, of Sin; Penitence; Remorse; Sin, Confession of; Sin, Forgiveness of.

REPETITION [*606, 1819, 6218, 8049, 9101, *4625*].
NIV+ REPEAT, REPEATED, REPEATEDLY, REPEATS
In Prayers: *See Babbling; Prayer, Persistence in.*

REPHAEL [8330] (*God [El] heals*). A gatekeeper of the temple in the time of David (1Ch 26:7).

REPHAH [8338] (possibly *rich* IDB; *easy [life]* KB). A grandson of Ephraim (1Ch 7:25).

REPHAIAH [8341] (*Yahweh heals*).
1. A descendant of David (1Ch 3:21).
2. A Simeonite captain (1Ch 4:42).
3. Son of Tola, of the tribe of Issachar (1Ch 7:2).
4. A descendant of Jonathan (1Ch 9:43). Also called Raphah (1Ch 8:37).
5. Governor over half of Jerusalem in the time of Nehemiah (Ne 3:9).

REPHAIM *See Rephaites.*

REPHAIM, VALLEY OF [8329] (*sunken, powerless ones [giants]* BDB; possibly *shades, ghosts of the dead [giants]* KB). Fertile plain S of Jerusalem, three miles from Bethlehem (Jos 15:8; 18:16; 2Sa 5:18,22; 23:13; 1Ch 11:15; 14:9; Isa 17:4-5).

REPHAITES [8328] (*mighty*). Giant people who lived in Canaan even before Abraham's time (Ge 14:5; 15:20; Dt 2:11,20; 3:11,13; Jos 12:4; 13:12; 17:15; 1Ch 20:4). *See Giants.*

REPHAN [*4818*]. A pagan god noted in Ac 7:43 quoting the LXX (Am 5:26, ftn). In Am 5:26, the NIV translates the Hebrew word "pedestal," though the ftn offers the proper name "Kaiwan." The Egyptian *repa* and the Assyrian "Kaiwan" both refer to the planet Saturn, which may harmonize the two texts. *See Chiun.*

REPHIDIM [8340] (possibly *supports, rests* BDB; *resting place* KB). Encampment of Israelites in the wilderness; there Moses struck a rock to secure water (Ex 17:1-7; 19:2), battle with Amalekites took place there (Ex 17:8-16).

REPORTS [*606, 995, 1804, 1819, 1821, 5583, 5989, 9019, 9048, 9051, 9053, *334, 550, 3364*].
NIV+ REPORT

Majority and Minority:
Of spies (Nu 13:26-33; 14:6-10).

REPROBACY

Admonitions against—

2Co 13:5 Examine yourselves to see whether you are in the faith; test yourselves. Do you not realize that Christ Jesus is in you—unless, of course, you fail the test? **6**And I trust that you will discover that we have not failed the test. **7**Now we pray to God that you will not do anything wrong. Not that people will see that we have stood the test but that you will do what is right even though we may seem to have failed.

Heb 3:10 That is why I was angry with that generation, and I said, 'Their hearts are always going astray, and they have not known my ways.' **11**So I declared on oath in my anger, 'They shall never enter my rest.'"

12See to it, brothers, that none of you has a sinful, unbelieving heart that turns away from the living God.

Heb 3:17 And with whom was he angry for forty years? Was it not with those who sinned, whose bodies fell in the desert? **18**And to whom did God swear that they would never enter his rest if not to those who disobeyed? **19**So we see that they were not able to enter, because of their unbelief.

Heb 6:4 It is impossible for those who have once been enlightened, who have tasted the heavenly gift, who have shared in the Holy Spirit, **5**who have tasted the goodness of the word of God and the powers of the coming age, **6**if they fall away, to be brought back to repentance, because to their loss they are crucifying the Son of God all over again and subjecting him to public disgrace.

7Land that drinks in the rain often falling on it and that produces a crop useful to those for whom it is farmed receives the blessing of God. **8**But land that produces thorns and thistles is worthless and is in danger of being cursed. In the end it will be burned.

9Even though we speak like this, dear friends, we are confident of better things in your case—things that accompany salvation.

Heb 12:15 See to it that no one misses the grace of God and that no bitter root grows up to cause trouble and defile many. **16**See that no one is sexually immoral, or is godless like Esau, who for a single meal sold his inheritance rights as the oldest son. **17**Afterward, as you know, when he wanted to inherit this blessing, he was rejected. He could bring about no change of mind, though he sought the blessing with tears.

Curses denounced against—

Dt 28:15 However, if you do not obey the LORD your God and do not carefully follow all his commands and decrees I am giving you today, all these curses will come upon you and overtake you:

16You will be cursed in the city and cursed in the country.

17Your basket and your kneading trough will be cursed.

18The fruit of your womb will be cursed, and the crops of your land, and the calves of your herds and the lambs of your flocks.

19You will be cursed when you come in and cursed when you go out.

20The LORD will send on you curses, confusion and rebuke in everything you put your hand to, until you are destroyed and come to sudden ruin because of the evil you have done in forsaking him. **21**The LORD will plague you with diseases until he has destroyed you from the land you are entering to possess. **22**The LORD will strike you with wasting disease, with fever and inflammation, with scorching heat and drought, with blight and mildew, which will plague you until you perish. **23**The sky over your head will be bronze, the ground beneath you iron. **24**The LORD will turn the rain of your country into dust and powder; it will come down from the skies until you are destroyed.

25The LORD will cause you to be defeated before your enemies. You will come at them from one direction but flee from them in seven, and you will become a thing of horror to all the kingdoms on earth. **26**Your carcasses will be food for all the birds of the air and the beasts of the earth, and there will be no one to frighten them away. **27**The LORD will afflict you with the boils of Egypt and with tumors, festering sores and the itch, from which you cannot be cured. **28**The LORD will afflict you with madness, blindness and confusion of mind. **29**At midday you will grope about like a blind man in the dark. You will be unsuccessful in everything you do; day after day you will be oppressed and robbed, with no one to rescue you.

30You will be pledged to be married to a woman, but another will take her and ravish her. You will build a house, but you will not live in it. You will plant a vineyard, but you will not even begin to enjoy its fruit. **31**Your ox will be slaughtered before your eyes, but you will eat none of it. Your donkey will be forcibly taken from you and will not be returned. Your sheep will be given to your enemies, and no one will rescue them. **32**Your sons and daughters will be given to another nation, and you will wear out your eyes watching for them day after day, powerless to lift a hand. **33**A people that you do not know will eat what your land and labor produce, and you will have nothing but cruel oppression all your days. **34**The sights you see will drive you mad. **35**The LORD will afflict your knees and legs with painful boils that cannot be cured, spreading from the soles of your feet to the top of your head.

36The LORD will drive you and the king you set over you to a nation unknown to you or your fathers. There you will worship other gods, gods of wood and stone. **37**You will become a thing of horror and an object of scorn and ridicule to all the nations where the LORD will drive you.

38You will sow much seed in the field but you will harvest little, because locusts will devour it. **39**You will plant vineyards and cultivate them but you will not drink the wine or gather the grapes, because worms will eat them. **40**You will have olive trees throughout your country but you will not use the oil, because the olives will drop off. **41**You will have sons and daughters but you will not keep them, because they will go into captivity. **42**Swarms of locusts will take over all your trees and the crops of your land.

43The alien who lives among you will rise above you higher and higher, but you will sink lower and lower. **44**He will lend to you, but you will not lend to him. He will be the head, but you will be the tail.

45All these curses will come upon you. They will pursue you and overtake you until you are destroyed, because you did not obey the LORD your God and observe the commands and decrees he gave you. **46**They will be a sign and a wonder to you and your descendants forever. **47**Because you did not serve the LORD your God joyfully and gladly in the time of prosperity, **48**therefore in hunger and thirst, in nakedness and dire poverty, you will serve the enemies the LORD sends against you. He will put an iron yoke on your neck until he has destroyed you.

49The LORD will bring a nation against you from far away, from the ends of the earth, like an eagle swooping down, a nation whose language you will not understand, **50**a fierce-looking nation without respect for the old or pity for the young. [51]They will devour the young of your livestock and the crops of your land until you are destroyed. They will leave you no grain, new wine or oil, nor any calves of your herds or lambs of your flocks until you are ruined. [52]They will lay siege to all the cities throughout your land until the high fortified walls in which you trust fall down. They will besiege all the cities throughout the land the LORD your God is giving you.

[53]Because of the suffering that your enemy will inflict on you during the siege, you will eat the fruit of the womb, the flesh of the sons and daughters the LORD your God has given you. [54]Even the most gentle and sensitive man among you will have no compassion on his own brother or the wife he loves or his surviving children, [55]and he will not give to one of them any of the flesh of his children that he is eating. It will be all he has left because of the suffering your enemy will inflict on you during the siege of all your cities. [56]The most gentle and sensitive woman among you—so sensitive and gentle that she would not venture to touch the ground with the sole of her foot—will begrudge the husband she loves and her own son or daughter [57]the afterbirth from her womb and the children she bears. For she intends to eat them secretly during the siege and in the distress that your enemy will inflict on you in your cities.

[58]If you do not carefully follow all the words of this law, which are written in this book, and do not revere this glorious and awesome name—the LORD your God— [59]the LORD will send fearful plagues on you and your descendants, harsh and prolonged disasters, and severe and lingering illnesses. [60]He will bring upon you all the diseases of Egypt that you dreaded, and they will cling to you. [61]The LORD will also bring on you every kind of sickness and disaster not recorded in this Book of the Law, until you are destroyed. [62]You who were as numerous as the stars in the sky will be left but few in number, because you did not obey the LORD your God. [63]Just as it pleased the LORD to make you prosper and increase in number, so it will please him to ruin and destroy you. You will be uprooted from the land you are entering to possess.

[64]Then the LORD will scatter you among all nations, from one end of the earth to the other. There you will worship other gods—gods of wood and stone, which neither you nor your fathers have known. [65]Among those nations you will find no repose, no resting place for the sole of your foot. There the LORD will give you an anxious mind, eyes weary with longing, and a despairing heart. [66]You will live in constant suspense, filled with dread both night and day, never sure of your life. [67]In the morning you will say, "If only it were evening!" and in the evening, "If only it were morning!"—because of the terror that will fill your hearts and the sights that your eyes will see. [68]The LORD will send you back in ships to Egypt on a journey I said you should never make again. There you will offer yourselves for sale to your enemies as male and female slaves, but no one will buy you.

Dt 31:17 On that day I will become angry with them and forsake them; I will hide my face from them, and they will be destroyed. Many disasters and difficulties will come upon them, and on that day they will ask, 'Have not these disasters come upon us because our God is not with us?' [18]And I will certainly hide my face on that day because of all their wickedness in turning to other gods.

Isa 65:12 I will destine you for the sword, and you will all bend down for the slaughter; for I called but you did not

answer, I spoke but you did not listen. You did evil in my sight and chose what displeases me." (+Hos 9:12)

Mk 3:29 But whoever blasphemes against the Holy Spirit will never be forgiven; he is guilty of an eternal sin."

Heb 10:26 If we deliberately keep on sinning after we have received the knowledge of the truth, no sacrifice for sins is left, [27]but only a fearful expectation of judgment and of raging fire that will consume the enemies of God. [28]Anyone who rejected the law of Moses died without mercy on the testimony of two or three witnesses. [29]How much more severely do you think a man deserves to be punished who has trampled the Son of God under foot, who has treated as an unholy thing the blood of the covenant that sanctified him, and who has insulted the Spirit of grace? [30]For we know him who said, "It is mine to avenge; I will repay," and again, "The Lord will judge his people." [31]It is a dreadful thing to fall into the hands of the living God.

See Reprobates.

REPROBATE Moral corruption, unfitness, disqualification, disapproved (Ro 1:28; 1Co 9:27).

See Reprobacy; Reprobates.

REPROBATES (Jer 6:30; Ro 1:21-32; 2Ti 3:8; 1Jn 5:16; Jude 4-13; Rev 22:4). Called, men of corrupt minds (2Ti 3:8), vessels of wrath (Ro 9:22).

Moral insensibility of (Isa 22:12-14; 28:13; 29:9-12; Mt 13:14-15; 15:14; Ro 11:7-8). Rejected of God (Ps 81:11-12; Pr 1:24-28; Jer 6:30; 7:16; 15:1; Hos 5:6; Mt 15:14; 25:8-13; Lk 13:24-28; 14:24; Jn 10:26; Ro 1:21-26,28; 2Th 2:10-11; Heb 3:10-12,17-19; 6:4-8; 10:26-31). Admonitions against (Heb 12:15-17).

In Israel (Nu 14:26-48; Dt 1:42; Isa 6:9-10; Heb 3:10-12,17-19; Jude 5). In the Church (2Co 13:5-7; Heb 3:10-12,17-19; 6:4-9; Jude 4-13).

Instances of:

Antediluvians (Ge 6:5-7), Sodomites (Ge 13:13; 19:13; Jude 7), Jannes and Jambres (2Ti 3:8), Eli's house (1Sa 3:14), Saul (1Sa 15:23; 16:14; 18:12; 28:15), Judas (Jn 17:12), Angels (Jude 6), Antichrist (2Th 2:7-12).

See Obduracy; Reprobacy.

REPRODUCTION *See Propagation.*

REPROOF, REPROVE [3519].

NIV+ REPROVES

Commanded:

Lev 19:17 "'Do not hate your brother in your heart. Rebuke your neighbor frankly so you will not share in his guilt.

Ps 141:5 Let a righteous man strike me—it is a kindness; let him rebuke me—it is oil on my head. My head will not refuse it. Yet my prayer is ever against the deeds of evildoers;

Pr 9:7 "Whoever corrects a mocker invites insult; whoever rebukes a wicked man incurs abuse. [8]Do not rebuke a mocker or he will hate you; rebuke a wise man and he will love you.

Pr 10:17 He who heeds discipline shows the way to life, but whoever ignores correction leads others astray.

Pr 26:5 Answer a fool according to his folly, or he will be wise in his own eyes.

Mt 18:15 "If your brother sins against you, go and show him his fault, just between the two of you. If he listens to you, you have won your brother over. [16]But if he will not listen, take one or two others along, so that 'every matter may be established by the testimony of two or three witnesses.' [17]If he refuses to listen to them, tell it to the church; and if he refuses to listen even to the church, treat him as you would a pagan or a tax collector.

Lk 17:3 So watch yourselves.

"If your brother sins, rebuke him, and if he repents, forgive him. [4]If he sins against you seven times in a day, and seven times comes back to you and says, 'I repent,' forgive him."

Eph 5:11 Have nothing to do with the fruitless deeds of darkness, but rather expose them. (+1Th 5:14,20; 2Ti 4:2; Tit 1:13; Heb 3:13)

Of seniors, forbidden (1Ti 5:1-2).

Profitable:

Pr 13:18 He who ignores discipline comes to poverty and shame, but whoever heeds correction is honored.

Pr 15:5 A fool spurns his father's discipline, but whoever heeds correction shows prudence.

Pr 15:31 He who listens to a life-giving rebuke will be at home among the wise.

[32]He who ignores discipline despises himself, but whoever heeds correction gains understanding.

Pr 27:5 Better is open rebuke than hidden love.

[6]Wounds from a friend can be trusted, but an enemy multiplies kisses.

Pr 28:23 He who rebukes a man will in the end gain more favor than he who has a flattering tongue.

Ecc 7:5 It is better to heed a wise man's rebuke than to listen to the song of fools.

Wise profit by—

Pr 17:10 A rebuke impresses a man of discernment more than a hundred lashes a fool.

Pr 19:25 Flog a mocker, and the simple will learn prudence; rebuke a discerning man, and he will gain knowledge.

Pr 21:11 When a mocker is punished, the simple gain wisdom; when a wise man is instructed, he gets knowledge.

Pr 25:12 Like an earring of gold or an ornament of fine gold is a wise man's rebuke to a listening ear.

Needed in the Church:

Eph 4:15 Instead, speaking the truth in love, we will in all things grow up into him who is the Head, that is, Christ.

Php 3:1 Finally, my brothers, rejoice in the Lord! It is no trouble for me to write the same things to you again, and it is a safeguard for you.

1Th 5:14 And we urge you, brothers, warn those who are idle, encourage the timid, help the weak, be patient with everyone.

1Ti 5:1 Do not rebuke an older man harshly, but exhort him as if he were your father. Treat younger men as brothers, [2]older women as mothers, and younger women as sisters, with absolute purity.

1Ti 5:20 Those who sin are to be rebuked publicly, so that the others may take warning.

2Ti 4:2 Preach the Word; be prepared in season and out of season; correct, rebuke and encourage—with great patience and careful instruction.

Tit 1:13 This testimony is true. Therefore, rebuke them sharply, so that they will be sound in the faith

Heb 3:13 But encourage one another daily, as long as it is called Today, so that none of you may be hardened by sin's deceitfulness.

Hated:

Pr 12:1 Whoever loves discipline loves knowledge, but he who hates correction is stupid. (+Pr 10:17)

Pr 15:10 Stern discipline awaits him who leaves the path; he who hates correction will die.

Pr 15:12 A mocker resents correction; he will not consult the wise.

Am 5:10 you hate the one who reproves in court and despise him who tells the truth.

Jn 7:7 The world cannot hate you, but it hates me because I testify that what it does is evil.

Gal 4:16 Have I now become your enemy by telling you the truth? *See below, Despised.*

Faithfulness in:

Instances of: Moses, of Pharaoh (Ex 10:29; 11:8), of the Israelites (Ex 16:6-7; 32:19-30; Nu 14:41; 20:10; 32:14; Dt 1:12,26-43; 9:16-24; 29:2-4; 31:27-29; 32:15-18), of Eleazar (Lev 10:16-18), of Korah (Nu 16:9-11). Israelites, of the two and one-half tribes (Jos 22:15-20), of the tribe of Benjamin (Jdg 20:12-13). Samuel, of Saul (1Sa 15:14-35). Jonathan, of Saul (1Sa 19:4-5). Nathan, of David (2Sa 12:1-9). Joab, of David (2Sa 19:1-7; 24:3; 1Ch 21:3). The prophet Gad, of David (2Sa 24:13). Shemaiah, of Rehoboam (2Ch 12:5). A prophet of Judah, of Jeroboam (1Ki 13:1-10; 2Ch 13:8-11). Elijah, of Ahab (1Ki 18:18-21; 21:20-24), of Ahaziah (2Ki 1). Micaiah, of Ahab (1Ki 22:14-28). Elisha, of Jehoram (2Ki 3:13-14), of Gehazi (2Ki 5:26), of Hazael (2Ki 8:11-13), of Jeroboam (2Ki 13:19). Isaiah, of Hezekiah (2Ki 20:17). Jehoash, of Jehoiada (2Ki 12:7). Azariah, of Asa (2Ch 15:2), of Uzziah (2Ch 26:17-18). Hanani, of Asa (2Ch 16:7-9). Jehu, of Jehoshaphat (2Ch 19:2). Zechariah, of the princes of Judah (2Ch 24:20). Oded, of the people of Samaria (2Ch 28:9-11). Jeremiah, of the cities of Judah (Jer 26:8-11). Ezra, of the men of Judah and Benjamin (Ezr 10:10). Nehemiah, of the Jews (Ne 5:6-13), of the corruptions in the temple, and of the violation of the Sabbath (Ne 13). Daniel, of Nebuchadnezzar (Da 4:27), of Belshazzar (Da 5:17-24). Amos, of the Israelites (Am 7:12-17).

Jesus, of the Jews—

When Pharisees and Sadducees came to him desiring a sign (Mt 16:1-4; Mk 8:11-12), of the scribes and Pharisees (Mt 23; Lk 11:37-54), of the Pharisees (Lk 16), when they brought the woman to him who was caught in adultery (Jn 8:7).

In his parables: Of the king's feast (Lk 14:16-24), of the two sons (Mt 21:28-32), of the vineyard (Mt 21:33-46; Mk 12:1-12; Lk 20:9-20), of the barren fig tree (Lk 13:6-9), the withering of the fig tree (Mt 21:17-20; Mk 11:12-14).

John the Baptist, of the Jews (Mt 3:7-12; Lk 3:7-9), of Herod (Mt 14:3; Mk 6:17; Lk 3:19-20). Peter, of Simon, the sorcerer (Ac 8:20-23). Stephen, of the high priest (Ac 7:51-53). Paul, of Elymas, the sorcerer (Ac 13:9-11), of Ananias, the high priest (Ac 23:3). Paul and Silas, of the magistrates of Philippi (Ac 16:37-40).

Despised:

By the Israelites (Nu 14:9-10; Jer 26:11). By Ahab (1Ki 18:17; 21:20; 22:8). By Asa (2Ch 16:10). By Herodias (Mk 6:18-19). By people of Nazareth (Lk 4:28-29). Jews (Ac 5:33; 7:54).

See One Another; Reprobacy.

REPTILES [8254, *2260*]. (1Ki 4:33; Ac 10:12; 11:6; Ro 1:23). Adder (Job 20:16). Cobra (Isa 11:8). Chameleon (Lev 11:30). Frog (Ex 8:2). Gecko (Lev 11:30). Lizards (Lev 11:29-30). Serpent (Job 20:14,16). Skink (Lev

11:30). Snake (Ex 7:9-12). Viper (Ge 49:17; Isa 59:5). *See Animals.*

REPUTATION, GOOD [1804, 9053, *3456, 3950*].
NIV+ REPUTED

(Pr 3:4; 22:1; Ecc 7:1). Of Mordecai (Est 9:4). Of overseers (1Ti 3:7). *See Character; Name.*

RESEN [8271]. A town founded by Nimrod (Ge 10:8-12), between Nineveh and Calah.

RESERVOIR [1391+4784, 4784+5224, 5225].
NIV+ RESERVOIRS

A place where water is collected and kept for use when wanted, chiefly in large quantities. Because most of W Asia was subject to periodic droughts, and because of frequent sieges, reservoirs and cisterns were a necessity (2Ch 26:10; 18:31; Ecc 2:6).

RESHEPH [8405] (*flame, flash of fire*). Grandson of Ephraim (1Ch 7:25).

RESIGNATION

Commanded:

Ps 4:4 In your anger do not sin; when you are on your beds, search your hearts and be silent. *Selah*
Ps 46:10 "Be still, and know that I am God; I will be exalted among the nations, I will be exalted in the earth."
Lk 21:19 By standing firm you will gain life.
Ro 12:12 Be joyful in hope, patient in affliction, faithful in prayer.
Php 2:14 Do everything without complaining or arguing, (+Col 1:10)
Col 1:11 being strengthened with all power according to his glorious might so that you may have great endurance and patience, and joyfully
Jas 1:9 The brother in humble circumstances ought to take pride in his high position. ¹⁰But the one who is rich should take pride in his low position, because he will pass away like a wild flower.
Jas 4:7 Submit yourselves, then, to God. Resist the devil, and he will flee from you.
1Pe 4:12 Dear friends, do not be surprised at the painful trial you are suffering, as though something strange were happening to you. ¹³But rejoice that you participate in the sufferings of Christ, so that you may be overjoyed when his glory is revealed.
1Pe 4:19 So then, those who suffer according to God's will should commit themselves to their faithful Creator and continue to do good.

Under chastisement and afflictions—
Job 5:17 "Blessed is the man whom God corrects; so do not despise the discipline of the Almighty.
Pr 3:11 My son, do not despise the LORD's discipline and do not resent his rebuke,
Pr 18:14 A man's spirit sustains him in sickness, but a crushed spirit who can bear?
Jer 51:50 You who have escaped the sword, leave and do not linger! Remember the LORD in a distant land, and think on Jerusalem."
La 3:39 Why should any living man complain when punished for his sins?
Mic 6:9 Listen! The LORD is calling to the city—and to fear your name is wisdom—"Heed the rod and the One who appointed it.
1Th 3:3 so that no one would be unsettled by these trials. You know quite well that we were destined for them.

2Ti 2:3 Endure hardship with us like a good soldier of Christ Jesus.
2Ti 4:5 But you, keep your head in all situations, endure hardship, do the work of an evangelist, discharge all the duties of your ministry. (+Heb 2:6-12)
Heb 12:5 And you have forgotten that word of encouragement that addresses you as sons: "My son, do not make light of the Lord's discipline, and do not lose heart when he rebukes you,
Heb 12:9 Moreover, we have all had human fathers who disciplined us and we respected them for it. How much more should we submit to the Father of our spirits and live! (+Jas 5:11)
Jas 5:13 Is any one of you in trouble? He should pray. Is anyone happy? Let him sing songs of praise.
1Pe 1:6 In this you greatly rejoice, though now for a little while you may have had to suffer grief in all kinds of trials.

Under bereavement (1Th 4:13-18).

Exemplified by:

Aaron—
Lev 10:1 Aaron's sons Nadab and Abihu took their censers, put fire in them and added incense; and they offered unauthorized fire before the LORD, contrary to his command. ²So fire came out from the presence of the LORD and consumed them, and they died before the LORD. ³Moses then said to Aaron, "This is what the LORD spoke of when he said:
"'Among those who approach me I will show myself holy; in the sight of all the people I will be honored.'"
Aaron remained silent.

The Israelites—
Jdg 10:15 But the Israelites said to the LORD, "We have sinned. Do with us whatever you think best, but please rescue us now."

Eli—
1Sa 3:18 So Samuel told him everything, hiding nothing from him. Then Eli said, "He is the LORD; let him do what is good in his eyes."

David—
2Sa 12:23 But now that he is dead, why should I fast? Can I bring him back again? I will go to him, but he will not return to me."
2Sa 15:26 But if he says, 'I am not pleased with you,' then I am ready; let him do to me whatever seems good to him."
2Sa 16:10 But the king said, "What do you and I have in common, you sons of Zeruiah? If he is cursing because the LORD said to him, 'Curse David,' who can ask, 'Why do you do this?'"
¹¹David then said to Abishai and all his officials, "My son, who is of my own flesh, is trying to take my life. How much more, then, this Benjamite! Leave him alone; let him curse, for the LORD has told him to.
2Sa 24:14 David said to Gad, "I am in deep distress. Let us fall into the hands of the LORD, for his mercy is great; but do not let me fall into the hands of men."

The Shunammite—
2Ki 4:26 Run to meet her and ask her, 'Are you all right? Is your husband all right? Is your child all right?'" "Everything is all right," she said.

Hezekiah—
2Ki 20:19 "The word of the LORD you have spoken is good," Hezekiah replied. For he thought, "Will there not be peace and security in my lifetime?" (+Isa 39:8)

Nehemiah—

Ne 9:33 In all that has happened to us, you have been just; you have acted faithfully, while we did wrong.

By Esther—

Est 4:16 "Go, gather together all the Jews who are in Susa, and fast for me. Do not eat or drink for three days, night or day. I and my maids will fast as you do. When this is done, I will go to the king, even though it is against the law. And if I perish, I perish."

Job—

Job 1:13 One day when Job's sons and daughters were feasting and drinking wine at the oldest brother's house, [14]a messenger came to Job and said, "The oxen were plowing and the donkeys were grazing nearby, [15]and the Sabeans attacked and carried them off. They put the servants to the sword, and I am the only one who has escaped to tell you!"

[16]While he was still speaking, another messenger came and said, "The fire of God fell from the sky and burned up the sheep and the servants, and I am the only one who has escaped to tell you!"

[17]While he was still speaking, another messenger came and said, "The Chaldeans formed three raiding parties and swept down on your camels and carried them off. They put the servants to the sword, and I am the only one who has escaped to tell you!"

[18]While he was still speaking, yet another messenger came and said, "Your sons and daughters were feasting and drinking wine at the oldest brother's house, [19]when suddenly a mighty wind swept in from the desert and struck the four corners of the house. It collapsed on them and they are dead, and I am the only one who has escaped to tell you!"

[20]At this, Job got up and tore his robe and shaved his head. Then he fell to the ground in worship [21]and said:

"Naked I came from my mother's womb, and naked I will depart. The LORD gave and the LORD has taken away; may the name of the LORD be praised."

[22]In all this, Job did not sin by charging God with wrongdoing.

Job 2:9 His wife said to him, "Are you still holding on to your integrity? Curse God and die!"

[10]He replied, "You are talking like a foolish woman. Shall we accept good from God, and not trouble?"

In all this, Job did not sin in what he said.

Job 34:31 "Suppose a man says to God, 'I am guilty but will offend no more.

Jas 5:11 As you know, we consider blessed those who have persevered. You have heard of Job's perseverance and have seen what the Lord finally brought about. The Lord is full of compassion and mercy.

The psalmists—

Ps 39:9 I was silent; I would not open my mouth, for you are the one who has done this.

Ps 103:10 he does not treat us as our sins deserve or repay us according to our iniquities.

Ps 119:75 I know, O LORD, that your laws are righteous, and in faithfulness you have afflicted me.

Jeremiah—

Jer 10:19 Woe to me because of my injury! My wound is incurable! Yet I said to myself, "This is my sickness, and I must endure it."

La 1:18 "The LORD is righteous, yet I rebelled against his command. Listen, all you peoples; look upon my suffering. My young men and maidens have gone into exile.

Daniel—

Da 9:14 The LORD did not hesitate to bring the disaster upon us, for the LORD our God is righteous in everything he does; yet we have not obeyed him.

Micah—

Mic 7:9 Because I have sinned against him, I will bear the LORD's wrath, until he pleads my case and establishes my right. He will bring me out into the light; I will see his righteousness.

Jesus—

Mt 26:39 Going a little farther, he fell with his face to the ground and prayed, "My Father, if it is possible, may this cup be taken from me. Yet not as I will, but as you will." (+Mk 14:36; Lk 22:42)

Jn 18:11 Jesus commanded Peter, "Put your sword away! Shall I not drink the cup the Father has given me?"

The thief on the cross—

Lk 23:40 But the other criminal rebuked him. "Don't you fear God," he said, "since you are under the same sentence? [41]We are punished justly, for we are getting what our deeds deserve. But this man has done nothing wrong."

Stephen—

Ac 7:59 While they were stoning him, Stephen prayed, "Lord Jesus, receive my spirit." [60]Then he fell on his knees and cried out, "Lord, do not hold this sin against them." When he had said this, he fell asleep.

Agabus, Luke, and others when Paul insisted on going to Jerusalem—

Ac 21:14 When he would not be dissuaded, we gave up and said, "The Lord's will be done."

Paul—

Ro 5:3 Not only so, but we also rejoice in our sufferings, because we know that suffering produces perseverance; [4]perseverance, character; and character, hope. [5]And hope does not disappoint us, because God has poured out his love into our hearts by the Holy Spirit, whom he has given us. (+2Co 6:4-8)

2Co 6:9 known, yet regarded as unknown; dying, and yet we live on; beaten, and yet not killed; [10]sorrowful, yet always rejoicing; poor, yet making many rich; having nothing, and yet possessing everything.

2Co 7:4 I have great confidence in you; I take great pride in you. I am greatly encouraged; in all our troubles my joy knows no bounds.

Php 1:20 I eagerly expect and hope that I will in no way be ashamed, but will have sufficient courage so that now as always Christ will be exalted in my body, whether by life or by death. [21]For to me, to live is Christ and to die is gain. [22]If I am to go on living in the body, this will mean fruitful labor for me. Yet what shall I choose? I do not know! [23]I am torn between the two: I desire to depart and be with Christ, which is better by far; [24]but it is more necessary for you that I remain in the body.

Php 4:11 I am not saying this because I am in need, for I have learned to be content whatever the circumstances. [12]I know what it is to be in need, and I know what it is to have plenty. I have learned the secret of being content in any and every situation, whether well fed or hungry, whether living in plenty or in want.

2Ti 4:6 For I am already being poured out like a drink offering, and the time has come for my departure.

Paul and Silas (Ac 16:25).

Thessalonian believers—

2Th 1:4 Therefore, among God's churches we boast about

your perseverance and faith in all the persecutions and trials you are enduring.

Hebrew believers—

Heb 10:34 You sympathized with those in prison and joyfully accepted the confiscation of your property, because you knew that you yourselves had better and lasting possessions.

See Afflicted Believers; Affliction; Afflictions, Made Beneficial.

RESIN [978, 5753]. *See Aromatic Resin; Gum Resin.*

RESPECT [*3359, 3707, 3877, *1956*, 3455, 4948, 5507, *5832*].

NIV+ RESPECTABLE, RESPECTED, RESPECTS

To the aged (Lev 19:32). To rulers (Pr 25:6). To a host (Lk 14:10). To one another (Ro 12:10; Php 2:3; 1Pe 2:17).

RESPECT OF PERSONS (Pr 24:23; 28:21; Jas 2:1-9). God does not have (Dt 10:17; 2Ch 19:7; Job 31:13-15; 34:19; Ac 10:34; 15:9; Ro 2:11-12; 10:12; Eph 6:8-9; Col 3:25; 1Pe 1:17).

See God, Justice of; Justice.

RESPONSIBILITY [5466, 6411, 6584, *3972+5148, 5970*].

NIV+ RESPONSIBLE, RESPONSIBILITIES

Attempts to shift: Adam (Ge 3:12-13), Eve (Ge 3:13), Sarah (Ge 16:5, w 16:2), Esau (Ge 27:36, w Ge 25:29-34), Aaron (Ex 32:22-24), Saul (1Sa 15:20-21), Pilate (Mt 27:24). Assumed by the Jews for the death of Jesus (Mt 27:25).

Personal (Eze 14:14-20; 18:20,30; Mt 12:37; Jn 9:41; 15:22-24; Ro 14:12; 1Co 3:8,13-15; Gal 6:5; 1Pe 4:5; Rev 2:23).

According to privilege—

Eze 18:1 The word of the LORD came to me: ²"What do you people mean by quoting this proverb about the land of Israel:

"'The fathers eat sour grapes, and the children's teeth are set on edge'?

³"As surely as I live, declares the Sovereign LORD, you will no longer quote this proverb in Israel. ⁴For every living soul belongs to me, the father as well as the son— both alike belong to me. The soul who sins is the one who will die.

⁵"Suppose there is a righteous man who does what is just and right. ⁶He does not eat at the mountain shrines or look to the idols of the house of Israel. He does not defile his neighbor's wife or lie with a woman during her period. ⁷He does not oppress anyone, but returns what he took in pledge for a loan. He does not commit robbery but gives his food to the hungry and provides clothing for the naked. ⁸He does not lend at usury or take excessive interest. He withholds his hand from doing wrong and judges fairly between man and man. ⁹He follows my decrees and faithfully keeps my laws. That man is righteous; he will surely live, declares the Sovereign LORD.

¹⁰"Suppose he has a violent son, who sheds blood or does any of these other things ¹¹(though the father has done none of them):

"He eats at the mountain shrines. He defiles his neighbor's wife. ¹²He oppresses the poor and needy. He commits robbery. He does not return what he took in pledge. He looks to the idols. He does detestable things. ¹³He lends at usury and takes excessive interest.

Will such a man live? He will not! Because he has done all these detestable things, he will surely be put to death and his blood will be on his own head.

¹⁴"But suppose this son has a son who sees all the sins his father commits, and though he sees them, he does not do such things:

¹⁵"He does not eat at the mountain shrines or look to the idols of the house of Israel. He does not defile his neighbor's wife. ¹⁶He does not oppress anyone or require a pledge for a loan. He does not commit robbery but gives his food to the hungry and provides clothing for the naked. ¹⁷He withholds his hand from sin and takes no usury or excessive interest. He keeps my laws and follows my decrees.

He will not die for his father's sin; he will surely live. ¹⁸But his father will die for his own sin, because he practiced extortion, robbed his brother and did what was wrong among his people.

¹⁹"Yet you ask, 'Why does the son not share the guilt of his father?' Since the son has done what is just and right and has been careful to keep all my decrees, he will surely live. ²⁰The soul who sins is the one who will die. The son will not share the guilt of the father, nor will the father share the guilt of the son. The righteousness of the righteous man will be credited to him, and the wickedness of the wicked will be charged against him.

²¹"But if a wicked man turns away from all the sins he has committed and keeps all my decrees and does what is just and right, he will surely live; he will not die. ²²None of the offenses he has committed will be remembered against him. Because of the righteous things he has done, he will live. ²³Do I take any pleasure in the death of the wicked? declares the Sovereign LORD. Rather, am I not pleased when they turn from their ways and live?

²⁴"But if a righteous man turns from his righteousness and commits sin and does the same detestable things the wicked man does, will he live? None of the righteous things he has done will be remembered. Because of the unfaithfulness he is guilty of and because of the sins he has committed, he will die.

²⁵"Yet you say, 'The way of the Lord is not just.' Hear, O house of Israel: Is my way unjust? Is it not your ways that are unjust? ²⁶If a righteous man turns from his righteousness and commits sin, he will die for it; because of the sin he has committed he will die. ²⁷But if a wicked man turns away from the wickedness he has committed and does what is just and right, he will save his life. ²⁸Because he considers all the offenses he has committed and turns away from them, he will surely live; he will not die. ²⁹Yet the house of Israel says, 'The way of the Lord is not just.' Are my ways unjust, O house of Israel? Is it not your ways that are unjust?

³⁰"Therefore, O house of Israel, I will judge you, each one according to his ways, declares the Sovereign LORD. Repent! Turn away from all your offenses; then sin will not be your downfall.

Eze 33:1 The word of the LORD came to me: ²"Son of man, speak to your countrymen and say to them: 'When I bring the sword against a land, and the people of the land choose one of their men and make him their watchman, ³and he sees the sword coming against the land and blows the trumpet to warn the people, ⁴then if anyone hears the trumpet but does not take warning and the sword comes and takes his life, his blood will be on his own head. ⁵Since he heard the sound of the trumpet but did not take warning, his blood will be on his own head. If he had taken warning, he would have saved himself. ⁶But if the watchman sees the sword coming and does not blow the trumpet to warn the people and the sword comes and takes the life of one of them, that man will be taken away because of his sin, but I will hold the watchman accountable for his blood.'

⁷"Son of man, I have made you a watchman for the house of Israel; so hear the word I speak and give them warning from me. ⁸When I say to the wicked, 'O wicked man, you will surely die,' and you do not speak out to dissuade him from his ways, that wicked man will die for his sin, and I will hold you accountable for his blood. ⁹But if you do warn the wicked man to turn from his ways and he does not do so, he will die for his sin, but you will have saved yourself.

¹⁰"Son of man, say to the house of Israel, 'This is what you are saying: "Our offenses and sins weigh us down, and we are wasting away because of them. How then can we live?"' ¹¹Say to them, 'As surely as I live, declares the Sovereign LORD, I take no pleasure in the death of the wicked, but rather that they turn from their ways and live. Turn! Turn from your evil ways! Why will you die, O house of Israel?'

¹²"Therefore, son of man, say to your countrymen, 'The righteousness of the righteous man will not save him when he disobeys, and the wickedness of the wicked man will not cause him to fall when he turns from it. The righteous man, if he sins, will not be allowed to live because of his former righteousness.' ¹³If I tell the righteous man that he will surely live, but then he trusts in his righteousness and does evil, none of the righteous things he has done will be remembered; he will die for the evil he has done. ¹⁴And if I say to the wicked man, 'You will surely die,' but he then turns away from his sin and does what is just and right— ¹⁵if he gives back what he took in pledge for a loan, returns what he has stolen, follows the decrees that give life, and does no evil, he will surely live; he will not die. ¹⁶None of the sins he has committed will be remembered against him. He has done what is just and right; he will surely live.

¹⁷"Yet your countrymen say, 'The way of the Lord is not just.' But it is their way that is not just. ¹⁸If a righteous man turns from his righteousness and does evil, he will die for it. ¹⁹And if a wicked man turns away from his wickedness and does what is just and right, he will live by doing so.

Mt 10:11 "Whatever town or village you enter, search for some worthy person there and stay at his house until you leave. ¹²As you enter the home, give it your greeting. ¹³If the home is deserving, let your peace rest on it; if it is not, let your peace return to you. ¹⁴If anyone will not welcome you or listen to your words, shake the dust off your feet when you leave that home or town. ¹⁵I tell you the truth, it will be more bearable for Sodom and Gomorrah on the day of judgment than for that town.

Mt 11:20 Then Jesus began to denounce the cities in which most of his miracles had been performed, because they did not repent. ²¹"Woe to you, Korazin! Woe to you, Bethsaida! If the miracles that were performed in you had been performed in Tyre and Sidon, they would have repented long ago in sackcloth and ashes. ²²But I tell you, it will be more bearable for Tyre and Sidon on the day of judgment than for you. ²³And you, Capernaum, will you be lifted up to the skies? No, you will go down to the depths. If the miracles that were performed in you had been performed in Sodom, it would have remained to this day. ²⁴But I tell you that it will be more bearable for Sodom on the day of judgment than for you."

Mt 12:41 The men of Nineveh will stand up at the judgment with this generation and condemn it; for they

repented at the preaching of Jonah, and now one greater than Jonah is here. ⁴²The Queen of the South will rise at the judgment with this generation and condemn it; for she came from the ends of the earth to listen to Solomon's wisdom, and now one greater than Solomon is here.

Mt 23:31 So you testify against yourselves that you are the descendants of those who murdered the prophets. ³²Fill up, then, the measure of the sin of your forefathers!

³³"You snakes! You brood of vipers! How will you escape being condemned to hell? ³⁴Therefore I am sending you prophets and wise men and teachers. Some of them you will kill and crucify; others you will flog in your synagogues and pursue from town to town. ³⁵And so upon you will come all the righteous blood that has been shed on earth, from the blood of righteous Abel to the blood of Zechariah son of Berekiah, whom you murdered between the temple and the altar.

Mt 25:14 "Again, it will be like a man going on a journey, who called his servants and entrusted his property to them. ¹⁵To one he gave five talents of money, to another two talents, and to another one talent, each according to his ability. Then he went on his journey. ¹⁶The man who had received the five talents went at once and put his money to work and gained five more. ¹⁷So also, the one with the two talents gained two more. ¹⁸But the man who had received the one talent went off, dug a hole in the ground and hid his master's money.

¹⁹"After a long time the master of those servants returned and settled accounts with them. ²⁰The man who had received the five talents brought the other five. 'Master,' he said, 'you entrusted me with five talents. See, I have gained five more.'

²¹"His master replied, 'Well done, good and faithful servant! You have been faithful with a few things; I will put you in charge of many things. Come and share your master's happiness!'

²²"The man with the two talents also came. 'Master,' he said, 'you entrusted me with two talents; see, I have gained two more.'

²³"His master replied, 'Well done, good and faithful servant! You have been faithful with a few things; I will put you in charge of many things. Come and share your master's happiness!'

²⁴"Then the man who had received the one talent came. 'Master,' he said, 'I knew that you are a hard man, harvesting where you have not sown and gathering where you have not scattered seed. ²⁵So I was afraid and went out and hid your talent in the ground. See, here is what belongs to you.'

²⁶"His master replied, 'You wicked, lazy servant! So you knew that I harvest where I have not sown and gather where I have not scattered seed? ²⁷Well then, you should have put my money on deposit with the bankers, so that when I returned I would have received it back with interest.

²⁸"'Take the talent from him and give it to the one who has the ten talents. ²⁹For everyone who has will be given more, and he will have an abundance. Whoever does not have, even what he has will be taken from him. ³⁰And throw that worthless servant outside, into the darkness, where there will be weeping and gnashing of teeth.'

Mk 6:11 And if any place will not welcome you or listen to you, shake the dust off your feet when you leave, as a testimony against them." (+Lk 9:5; 10:10-15; 11:31-32, 49-51)

Lk 13:6 Then he told this parable: "A man had a fig tree, planted in his vineyard, and he went to look for fruit on it, but did not find any. ⁷So he said to the man who took care of the vineyard, 'For three years now I've been coming to look for fruit on this fig tree and haven't found any. Cut it down! Why should it use up the soil?'

⁸"'Sir,' the man replied, 'leave it alone for one more year, and I'll dig around it and fertilize it. ⁹If it bears fruit next year, fine! If not, then cut it down.'" (+Lk 19:12-27)

Lk 21:1 As he looked up, Jesus saw the rich putting their gifts into the temple treasury. ²He also saw a poor widow put in two very small copper coins. ³"I tell you the truth," he said, "this poor widow has put in more than all the others. ⁴All these people gave their gifts out of their wealth; but she out of her poverty put in all she had to live on."

Jn 3:18 Whoever believes in him is not condemned, but whoever does not believe stands condemned already because he has not believed in the name of God's one and only Son. ¹⁹This is the verdict: Light has come into the world, but men loved darkness instead of light because their deeds were evil.

Jn 12:48 There is a judge for the one who rejects me and does not accept my words; that very word which I spoke will condemn him at the last day.

Jn 15:22 If I had not come and spoken to them, they would not be guilty of sin. Now, however, they have no excuse for their sin.

Jn 15:24 If I had not done among them what no one else did, they would not be guilty of sin. But now they have seen these miracles, and yet they have hated both me and my Father.

Ac 17:30 In the past God overlooked such ignorance, but now he commands all people everywhere to repent. ³¹For he has set a day when he will judge the world with justice by the man he has appointed. He has given proof of this to all men by raising him from the dead."

Ro 12:3 For by the grace given me I say to every one of you: Do not think of yourself more highly than you ought, but rather think of yourself with sober judgment, in accordance with the measure of faith God has given you.

Ro 12:6 We have different gifts, according to the grace given us. If a man's gift is prophesying, let him use it in proportion to his faith. ⁷If it is serving, let him serve; if it is teaching, let him teach; ⁸if it is encouraging, let him encourage; if it is contributing to the needs of others, let him give generously; if it is leadership, let him govern diligently; if it is showing mercy, let him do it cheerfully.

Eph 4:7 But to each one of us grace has been given as Christ apportioned it.

1Ti 6:20 Timothy, guard what has been entrusted to your care. Turn away from godless chatter and the opposing ideas of what is falsely called knowledge,

See Judgment, According to Opportunity and Works.

RESPONSIVE RELIGIOUS SERVICE

Reciting the curses of the covenant (Dt 27:14-26). In worship (Ps 48; 118:2-4; 124:1; 129:1). At the dedication of the wall of Jerusalem (Ne 12).

REST [*1954, 1957, 3782, 4328, 4955, 4957, 5663, 8069, 8070, 8089, 8697, 8702, 8886, 8905, 9200, *398, 399, 2923, 2924*].

NIV+ RESTED, RESTING, RESTLESS, RESTS, SABBATH-REST

Divine institution for. *See Sabbath.* Commanded (Ex 16:23; 20:10; 23:12; 31:15; 34:21; 35:2; Dt 5:12,14).

The annual feasts added rest days: First and last days of feasts of Passover and Tabernacles (Ex 12:16; Lev 23:5-8,39-40; Nu 28:18,25; 29:12,35), Pentecost (Nu 28:26), trumpets (Lev 23:24-25; Nu 29:1), Atonement (Lev 16:29-31; 23:27-28; Nu 29:7). In seventh year (Ex 23:11; Lev 25:1-4). In the Year of Jubilee (Lev 25:11-12).

Recommended by Jesus (Mk 6:31-32; 7:24, w Mt 8:18, 24). Heavenly (2Th 1:7). Spiritual (Mt 11:29; Heb 4:1-11).

See Peace, Spiritual; Resignation.

RESTITUTION [5989, 8740, 8966]. To be made for injury to life, limb, or property (Ex 21:30-36; Lev 24:18), for theft (Ex 22:1-4; Pr 6:30-31; Eze 33:15), for dishonesty (Lev 6:2-5; Nu 5:7; Job 20:18; Eze 33:15; Lk 19:8).

RESTORATION [*1215, 2542, 2616, 2649, 6441, 7756, 8740, 8966, 10354, 10754, *635, 2936*].

NIV+ RESTORE, RESTORED, RESTORER, RESTORES, RESTORING

Of the Jews. *See Israel; Israelites.* Of all things (Ac 3:21; Rev 21:1-5).

RESURRECTION [414, 1587, 1983].

In the Old Testament:

As understood by Job—

Job 14:12 so man lies down and does not rise; till the heavens are no more, men will not awake or be roused from their sleep.

¹³"If only you would hide me in the grave and conceal me till your anger has passed! If only you would set me a time and then remember me! ¹⁴If a man dies, will he live again? All the days of my hard service I will wait for my renewal to come. ¹⁵You will call and I will answer you; you will long for the creature your hands have made.

Job 19:25 I know that my Redeemer lives, and that in the end he will stand upon the earth. ²⁶And after my skin has been destroyed, yet in my flesh I will see God; ²⁷I myself will see him with my own eyes—I, and not another. How my heart yearns within me!

By the psalmists—

Ps 16:9 Therefore my heart is glad and my tongue rejoices; my body also will rest secure, ¹⁰because you will not abandon me to the grave, nor will you let your Holy One see decay.

Ps 17:15 And I—in righteousness I will see your face; when I awake, I will be satisfied with seeing your likeness.

Ps 49:15 But God will redeem my life from the grave; he will surely take me to himself. *Selah*

By the prophets—

Isa 25:8 he will swallow up death forever. The Sovereign LORD will wipe away the tears from all faces; he will remove the disgrace of his people from all the earth. The LORD has spoken.

Isa 26:19 But your dead will live; their bodies will rise. You who dwell in the dust, wake up and shout for joy. Your dew is like the dew of the morning; the earth will give birth to her dead.

Da 12:2 Multitudes who sleep in the dust of the earth will awake: some to everlasting life, others to shame and everlasting contempt. ³Those who are wise will shine like the brightness of the heavens, and those who lead many to righteousness, like the stars for ever and ever.

Da 12:13 "As for you, go your way till the end. You will rest, and then at the end of the days you will rise to receive your allotted inheritance."

Hos 13:14 "I will ransom them from the power of the grave; I will redeem them from death. Where, O death, are your plagues? Where, O grave, is your destruction? "I will have no compassion,

In the New Testament:

Debated by the Pharisees and Sadducees (Ac 23:6,8; 24:14-15; 26:6-8)—

Mt 22:23 That same day the Sadducees, who say there is no resurrection, came to him with a question. ²⁴"Teacher," they said, "Moses told us that if a man dies without having children, his brother must marry the widow and have children for him. ²⁵Now there were seven brothers among us. The first one married and died, and since he had no children, he left his wife to his brother. ²⁶The same thing happened to the second and third brother, right on down to the seventh. ²⁷Finally, the woman died. ²⁸Now then, at the resurrection, whose wife will she be of the seven, since all of them were married to her?"

²⁹Jesus replied, "You are in error because you do not know the Scriptures or the power of God. ³⁰At the resurrection people will neither marry nor be given in marriage; they will be like the angels in heaven. ³¹But about the resurrection of the dead—have you not read what God said to you, ³²'I am the God of Abraham, the God of Isaac, and the God of Jacob'? He is not the God of the dead but of the living."

Taught by Jesus (Mt 22:30-32)—

Mt 24:31 And he will send his angels with a loud trumpet call, and they will gather his elect from the four winds, from one end of the heavens to the other. (+Mk 12:25-27)

Lk 14:14 and you will be blessed. Although they cannot repay you, you will be repaid at the resurrection of the righteous." (+Lk 20:27-34)

Lk 20:35 But those who are considered worthy of taking part in that age and in the resurrection from the dead will neither marry nor be given in marriage, ³⁶and they can no longer die; for they are like the angels. They are God's children, since they are children of the resurrection. ³⁷But in the account of the bush, even Moses showed that the dead rise, for he calls the Lord 'the God of Abraham, and the God of Isaac, and the God of Jacob.' ³⁸He is not the God of the dead, but of the living, for to him all are alive."

Jn 5:21 For just as the Father raises the dead and gives them life, even so the Son gives life to whom he is pleased to give it.

Jn 5:25 I tell you the truth, a time is coming and has now come when the dead will hear the voice of the Son of God and those who hear will live.

Jn 5:28 "Do not be amazed at this, for a time is coming when all who are in their graves will hear his voice ²⁹and come out—those who have done good will rise to live, and those who have done evil will rise to be condemned.

Jn 6:39 And this is the will of him who sent me, that I shall lose none of all that he has given me, but raise them up at the last day. ⁴⁰For my Father's will is that everyone who looks to the Son and believes in him shall have eternal life, and I will raise him up at the last day."

Jn 6:44 "No one can come to me unless the Father who sent me draws him, and I will raise him up at the last day.

Jn 6:54 Whoever eats my flesh and drinks my blood has eternal life, and I will raise him up at the last day.

Jn 11:23 Jesus said to her, "Your brother will rise again."

²⁴Martha answered, "I know he will rise again in the resurrection at the last day."

²⁵Jesus said to her, "I am the resurrection and the life. He who believes in me will live, even though he dies;

By the apostles—

Ac 4:1 The priests and the captain of the temple guard and the Sadducees came up to Peter and John while they were speaking to the people. ²They were greatly disturbed because the apostles were teaching the people and proclaiming in Jesus the resurrection of the dead.

Ac 17:18 A group of Epicurean and Stoic philosophers began to dispute with him. Some of them asked, "What is this babbler trying to say?" Others remarked, "He seems to be advocating foreign gods." They said this because Paul was preaching the good news about Jesus and the resurrection. (+Ac 17:31)

Ac 17:32 When they heard about the resurrection of the dead, some of them sneered, but others said, "We want to hear you again on this subject."

Ac 23:6 Then Paul, knowing that some of them were Sadducees and the others Pharisees, called out in the Sanhedrin, "My brothers, I am a Pharisee, the son of a Pharisee. I stand on trial because of my hope in the resurrection of the dead." (+Ac 23:7)

Ac 23:8 (The Sadducees say that there is no resurrection, and that there are neither angels nor spirits, but the Pharisees acknowledge them all.)

Ac 24:14 However, I admit that I worship the God of our fathers as a follower of the Way, which they call a sect. I believe everything that agrees with the Law and that is written in the Prophets, ¹⁵and I have the same hope in God as these men, that there will be a resurrection of both the righteous and the wicked.

Ac 26:6 And now it is because of my hope in what God has promised our fathers that I am on trial today. ⁷This is the promise our twelve tribes are hoping to see fulfilled as they earnestly serve God day and night. O king, it is because of this hope that the Jews are accusing me. ⁸Why should any of you consider it incredible that God raises the dead?

Ro 4:16 Therefore, the promise comes by faith, so that it may be by grace and may be guaranteed to all Abraham's offspring—not only to those who are of the law but also to those who are of the faith of Abraham. He is the father of us all. ¹⁷As it is written: "I have made you a father of many nations." He is our father in the sight of God, in whom he believed—the God who gives life to the dead and calls things that are not as though they were.

¹⁸Against all hope, Abraham in hope believed and so became the father of many nations, just as it had been said to him, "So shall your offspring be." ¹⁹Without weakening in his faith, he faced the fact that his body was as good as dead—since he was about a hundred years old—and that Sarah's womb was also dead. ²⁰Yet he did not waver through unbelief regarding the promise of God, but was strengthened in his faith and gave glory to God, ²¹being fully persuaded that God had power to do what he had promised.

Ro 8:10 But if Christ is in you, your body is dead because of sin, yet your spirit is alive because of righteousness. ¹¹And if the Spirit of him who raised Jesus from the dead is living in you, he who raised Christ from the dead will also give life to your mortal bodies through his Spirit, who lives in you.

Ro 8:19 The creation waits in eager expectation for the sons of God to be revealed.

Ro 8:21 that the creation itself will be liberated from its bondage to decay and brought into the glorious freedom of the children of God.

²²We know that the whole creation has been groaning as

in the pains of childbirth right up to the present time. [23]Not only so, but we ourselves, who have the firstfruits of the Spirit, groan inwardly as we wait eagerly for our adoption as sons, the redemption of our bodies.

1Co 6:14 By his power God raised the Lord from the dead, and he will raise us also.

1Co 15:12 But if it is preached that Christ has been raised from the dead, how can some of you say that there is no resurrection of the dead? [13]If there is no resurrection of the dead, then not even Christ has been raised. [14]And if Christ has not been raised, our preaching is useless and so is your faith. [15]More than that, we are then found to be false witnesses about God, for we have testified about God that he raised Christ from the dead. But he did not raise him if in fact the dead are not raised. [16]For if the dead are not raised, then Christ has not been raised either. [17]And if Christ has not been raised, your faith is futile; you are still in your sins. [18]Then those also who have fallen asleep in Christ are lost. [19]If only for this life we have hope in Christ, we are to be pitied more than all men.

[20]But Christ has indeed been raised from the dead, the firstfruits of those who have fallen asleep. [21]For since death came through a man, the resurrection of the dead comes also through a man. [22]For as in Adam all die, so in Christ all will be made alive. [23]But each in his own turn: Christ, the firstfruits; then, when he comes, those who belong to him. [24]Then the end will come, when he hands over the kingdom to God the Father after he has destroyed all dominion, authority and power. [25]For he must reign until he has put all his enemies under his feet. [26]The last enemy to be destroyed is death. [27]For he "has put everything under his feet." Now when it says that "everything" has been put under him, it is clear that this does not include God himself, who put everything under Christ. [28]When he has done this, then the Son himself will be made subject to him who put everything under him, so that God may be all in all.

[29]Now if there is no resurrection, what will those do who are baptized for the dead? If the dead are not raised at all, why are people baptized for them? [30]And as for us, why do we endanger ourselves every hour? [31]I die every day—I mean that, brothers—just as surely as I glory over you in Christ Jesus our Lord. [32]If I fought wild beasts in Ephesus for merely human reasons, what have I gained? If the dead are not raised,

"Let us eat and drink, for tomorrow we die." (+1Co 15:33-34)

1Co 15:35 But someone may ask, "How are the dead raised? With what kind of body will they come?" [36]How foolish! What you sow does not come to life unless it dies. [37]When you sow, you do not plant the body that will be, but just a seed, perhaps of wheat or of something else. [38]But God gives it a body as he has determined, and to each kind of seed he gives its own body. [39]All flesh is not the same: Men have one kind of flesh, animals another, birds another and fish another. [40]There are also heavenly bodies and there are earthly bodies; but the splendor of the heavenly bodies is one kind, and the splendor of the earthly bodies is another. [41]The sun has one kind of splendor, the moon another and the stars another; and star differs from star in splendor.

[42]So will it be with the resurrection of the dead. The body that is sown is perishable, it is raised imperishable; [43]it is sown in dishonor, it is raised in glory; it is sown in weakness, it is raised in power; [44]it is sown a natural body, it is raised a spiritual body. If there is a natural body, there is also a spiritual body.

[45]So it is written: "The first man Adam became a living being"; the last Adam, a life-giving spirit. [46]The spiritual did not come first, but the natural, and after that the spiritual. [47]The first man was of the dust of the earth, the second man from heaven. [48]As was the earthly man, so are those who are of the earth; and as is the man from heaven, so also are those who are of heaven. [49]And just as we have borne the likeness of the earthly man, so shall we bear the likeness of the man from heaven.

[50]I declare to you, brothers, that flesh and blood cannot inherit the kingdom of God, nor does the perishable inherit the imperishable. [51]Listen, I tell you a mystery: We will not all sleep, but we will all be changed— [52]in a flash, in the twinkling of an eye, at the last trumpet. For the trumpet will sound, the dead will be raised imperishable, and we will be changed. [53]For the perishable must clothe itself with the imperishable, and the mortal with immortality. [54]When the perishable has been clothed with the imperishable, and the mortal with immortality, then the saying that is written will come true: "Death has been swallowed up in victory."

[55]"Where, O death, is your victory? Where, O death, is your sting?"

[56]The sting of death is sin, and the power of sin is the law. [57]But thanks be to God! He gives us the victory through our Lord Jesus Christ.

2Co 4:14 because we know that the one who raised the Lord Jesus from the dead will also raise us with Jesus and present us with you in his presence.

2Co 5:1 Now we know that if the earthly tent we live in is destroyed, we have a building from God, an eternal house in heaven, not built by human hands. [2]Meanwhile we groan, longing to be clothed with our heavenly dwelling, [3]because when we are clothed, we will not be found naked. [4]For while we are in this tent, we groan and are burdened, because we do not wish to be unclothed but to be clothed with our heavenly dwelling, so that what is mortal may be swallowed up by life. [5]Now it is God who has made us for this very purpose and has given us the Spirit as a deposit, guaranteeing what is to come.

Php 3:10 I want to know Christ and the power of his resurrection and the fellowship of sharing in his sufferings, becoming like him in his death, [11]and so, somehow, to attain to the resurrection from the dead.

Php 3:21 who, by the power that enables him to bring everything under his control, will transform our lowly bodies so that they will be like his glorious body. (+Rev 20:5-6)

Heb 6:2 instruction about baptisms, the laying on of hands, the resurrection of the dead, and eternal judgment.

Heb 11:35 Women received back their dead, raised to life again. Others were tortured and refused to be released, so that they might gain a better resurrection.

Error in the early church—

2Ti 2:18 who have wandered away from the truth. They say that the resurrection has already taken place, and they destroy the faith of some. (+1Co 15:12-58)

Of Jesus:

Typified by Isaac (Ge 22:13; Heb 11:19), by Jonah (Jnh 2:10, w Mt 12:40). Foretold (Ps 16:9-10), by himself (Mt 16:21; 17:9,23; 20:19; 26:61; 27:63; Mk 8:31; 9:9-10,31; 10:34; Lk 9:22; 18:33; 24:7,46; Jn 2:19-21; 10:17-18; 14:19).

Appearances after the resurrection (Mt 27:53; 28:2-15;

Mk 16:1-11; Lk 24:1-12; Jn 20:1-18; Rev 1:18). Denied by the Jews (Mt 28:12-15).

Raised by the power of God (Ac 2:24,32; 3:15,26; 4:10; 5:30; 10:40; 15:20,30,33-34,37; 17:31; Ro 4:24; 8:11; 10:9; 1Co 6:14; 15:15; 2Co 4:14; Gal 1:4; Eph 1:20; Col 2:12; 2Ti 1:10; 1Pe 1:21)

For our justification (Ro 4:25; 1Pe 3:21). Guarantee of general resurrection (1Co 15:12-15; 1Pe 1:3).

The theme of apostolic preaching (Ac 2:24,31-32; 3:15; 4:10,33; 5:30-32; 10:40-41; 17:2-3,18).

See Grave; Jesus the Christ, Resurrection of.

Special Resurrections:

Of saints after Christ's resurrection—
Mt 27:52 The tombs broke open and the bodies of many holy people who had died were raised to life. **⁵³**They came out of the tombs, and after Jesus' resurrection they went into the holy city and appeared to many people.

The two witnesses (Rev 11:11).
See Dead, Raised to Life.

At Christ's Second Coming:

1Th 4:14 We believe that Jesus died and rose again and so we believe that God will bring with Jesus those who have fallen asleep in him.
1Th 4:16 For the Lord himself will come down from heaven, with a loud command, with the voice of the archangel and with the trumpet call of God, and the dead in Christ will rise first.

The first resurrection—
Rev 20:4 I saw thrones on which were seated those who had been given authority to judge. And I saw the souls of those who had been beheaded because of their testimony for Jesus and because of the word of God. They had not worshiped the beast or his image and had not received his mark on their foreheads or their hands. They came to life and reigned with Christ a thousand years. **⁵**(The rest of the dead did not come to life until the thousand years were ended.) This is the first resurrection. **⁶**Blessed and holy are those who have part in the first resurrection. The second death has no power over them, but they will be priests of God and of Christ and will reign with him for a thousand years.

Of all the dead (Jn 5:28-29; Ac 24:15; 1Co 15:20-21)—
Rev 20:13 The sea gave up the dead that were in it, and death and Hades gave up the dead that were in them, and each person was judged according to what he had done.

Figurative:

Of the restoration of Israel—
Eze 37:1 The hand of the LORD was upon me, and he brought me out by the Spirit of the LORD and set me in the middle of a valley; it was full of bones. **²**He led me back and forth among them, and I saw a great many bones on the floor of the valley, bones that were very dry. **³**He asked me, "Son of man, can these bones live?"

I said, "O Sovereign LORD, you alone know."

⁴Then he said to me, "Prophesy to these bones and say to them, 'Dry bones, hear the word of the LORD! **⁵**This is what the Sovereign LORD says to these bones: I will make breath enter you, and you will come to life. **⁶**I will attach tendons to you and make flesh come upon you and cover you with skin; I will put breath in you, and you will come to life. Then you will know that I am the LORD.'"

⁷So I prophesied as I was commanded. And as I was prophesying, there was a noise, a rattling sound, and the bones came together, bone to bone. **⁸**I looked, and tendons and flesh appeared on them and skin covered them, but there was no breath in them.

⁹Then he said to me, "Prophesy to the breath; prophesy, son of man, and say to it, 'This is what the Sovereign LORD says: Come from the four winds, O breath, and breathe into these slain, that they may live.'" **¹⁰**So I prophesied as he commanded me, and breath entered them; they came to life and stood up on their feet—a vast army.

¹¹Then he said to me: "Son of man, these bones are the whole house of Israel. They say, 'Our bones are dried up and our hope is gone; we are cut off.' **¹²**Therefore prophesy and say to them: 'This is what the Sovereign LORD says: O my people, I am going to open your graves and bring you up from them; I will bring you back to the land of Israel. **¹³**Then you, my people, will know that I am the LORD, when I open your graves and bring you up from them. **¹⁴**I will put my Spirit in you and you will live, and I will settle you in your own land. Then you will know that I the LORD have spoken, and I have done it, declares the LORD.'"

Of regeneration (Ro 6:4; Eph 2:1,5-6; Col 2:12; 3:1).

RETALIATION [5/8].
NIV+ RETALIATE

Ps 10:2 In his arrogance the wicked man hunts down the weak, who are caught in the schemes he devises.

Judicial, ordained in Mosaic law:

Ex 21:23 But if there is serious injury, you are to take life for life, **²⁴**eye for eye, tooth for tooth, hand for hand, foot for foot, **²⁵**burn for burn, wound for wound, bruise for bruise.

Lev 24:17 "'If anyone takes the life of a human being, he must be put to death. **¹⁸**Anyone who takes the life of someone's animal must make restitution—life for life. **¹⁹**If anyone injures his neighbor, whatever he has done must be done to him: **²⁰**fracture for fracture, eye for eye, tooth for tooth. As he has injured the other, so he is to be injured. **²¹**Whoever kills an animal must make restitution, but whoever kills a man must be put to death. **²²**You are to have the same law for the alien and the native-born. I am the LORD your God.'"

Dt 19:19 then do to him as he intended to do to his brother. You must purge the evil from among you. **²⁰**The rest of the people will hear of this and be afraid, and never again will such an evil thing be done among you. **²¹**Show no pity: life for life, eye for eye, tooth for tooth, hand for hand, foot for foot.

Malicious, forbidden:

Lev 19:18 "'Do not seek revenge or bear a grudge against one of your people, but love your neighbor as yourself. I am the LORD.

Pr 20:22 Do not say, "I'll pay you back for this wrong!" Wait for the LORD, and he will deliver you.

Pr 24:29 Do not say, "I'll do to him as he has done to me; I'll pay that man back for what he did."

Mt 5:38 "You have heard that it was said, 'Eye for eye, and tooth for tooth.' **³⁹**But I tell you, Do not resist an evil person. If someone strikes you on the right cheek, turn to him the other also. **⁴⁰**And if someone wants to sue you and take your tunic, let him have your cloak as well. **⁴¹**If someone forces you to go one mile, go with him two miles. **⁴²**Give to the one who asks you, and do not turn away from the one who wants to borrow from you.

⁴³"You have heard that it was said, 'Love your neighbor and hate your enemy.' **⁴⁴**But I tell you: Love your enemies and pray for those who persecute you,

Mt 7:1 "Do not judge, or you too will be judged. **²**For in the same way you judge others, you will be judged, and with the measure you use, it will be measured to you.

Lk 9:54 When the disciples James and John saw this, they asked, "Lord, do you want us to call fire down from heaven to destroy them?"

Ro 12:17 Do not repay anyone evil for evil. Be careful to do what is right in the eyes of everybody.

Ro 12:19 Do not take revenge, my friends, but leave room for God's wrath, for it is written: "It is mine to avenge; I will repay," says the Lord.

1Co 6:7 The very fact that you have lawsuits among you means that you have been completely defeated already. Why not rather be wronged? Why not rather be cheated? **8**Instead, you yourselves cheat and do wrong, and you do this to your brothers.

1Th 5:15 Make sure that nobody pays back wrong for wrong, but always try to be kind to each other and to everyone else.

1Pe 3:9 Do not repay evil with evil or insult with insult, but with blessing, because to this you were called so that you may inherit a blessing.

Warning against—

Pr 26:27 If a man digs a pit, he will fall into it; if a man rolls a stone, it will roll back on him.

Isa 33:1 Woe to you, O destroyer, you who have not been destroyed! Woe to you, O traitor, you who have not been betrayed! When you stop destroying, you will be destroyed; when you stop betraying, you will be betrayed. (+Mt 7:1-2)

See Avenger of Blood; Hatred; Malice; Revenge.

Instances of:

Israelites on the Amalekites (Dt 25:17-19, w 1Sa 15:1-9). Gideon on the princes of Succoth (Jdg 8:7,13-16), kings of Midian (Jdg 8:18-21), Peniel (Jdg 8:8,17). Joab on Abner (2Sa 3:27,30). David upon Michal (2Sa 6:21-23), on Joab (1Ki 2:5-6), Shimei (1Ki 2:8-9). Jews on the Chaldeans (Est 9).

RETICENCE OF JESUS (Isa 53:7; Mt 26:63; 27:12, 14; Mk 14:61; 15:4-5; Jn 19:9; 1Pe 2:23). *See Jesus the Christ, Reticence of.*

RETRIBUTION [1691, 1692, 8936, *501*]. *See Sin, Punishment of.*

REU [8293, *4814*] *(friend [of God])*. Son of Peleg and ancestor of Abraham and of Jesus (Ge 11:18-21; 1Ch 1:25; Lk 3:35).

REUBEN [1201+8017, 1201+8018, 8017, 8018, *4857*] *(see, a son! [Ge. 29:32]; substitute a son IDB).*

NIV+ REUBENITE, REUBENITES

Son of Jacob (Ge 29:32; 1Ch 2:1). Brings mandrakes to his mother (Ge 30:14). Commits incest with one of his father's concubines, and, in consequence, forfeits the birthright (Ge 35:22; 49:4; 1Ch 5:1). Tactfully seeks to save Joseph from the conspiracy of his brothers (Ge 37:21-30; 42:22). Offers to become surety for Benjamin (Ge 42:37). Jacob's prophetic benediction upon (Ge 49:3-4). His children (Ge 46:9; Ex 6:14; 1Ch 5:3-6; Nu 16:1).

REUBENITE(S) [1201+8017, 8018] *(of Reuben).*

NIV+ REUBEN

The descendants of Reuben. Military enrollment of, at Sinai (Nu 1:20-21), in Moab (Nu 26:7). Place of, in camp and march (Nu 2:10). Standard of (Nu 10:18). Have their inheritance east of the Jordan (Nu 32; Dt 3:1-20; Jos

13:15-23; 18:7). Assist the other tribes in conquest of the region west of the Jordan (Jos 1:12-18; 22:1-6). Unite with the other tribes in building a monument to signify the unity of the tribes on the east of the Jordan with the tribes on the west of the river; monument misunderstood; the explanation and reconciliation (Jos 22:10-34). Reproached by Deborah (Jdg 5:15-16). Taken captive into Assyria (2Ki 15:29; 1Ch 5:26).

See Israel.

REUEL [8294] *(friend of God [El]).*

1. Son of Esau (Ge 36:4,10).

2. Father-in-law of Moses (Ex 2:16-22), probably the same as Jethro (Ex 3:1). *See Jethro.*

3. The father of Eliasaph (Nu 2:14). Called Deuel (Nu 1:14).

4. Benjamite (1Ch 9:8).

REUMAH [8020]. A concubine of Nahor (Ge 22:24).

REVELATION [1821, 2606, 2612, *636*, *637*].

NIV+ REVEAL, REVEALED, REVEALER, REVEALING, REVEALS, REVELATIONS

The doctrine of God's making himself and relevant truths known to mankind. Revelation is of two kinds: general and special. General revelation is available to all people, and is communicated through nature, conscience, and history. Special revelation is revelation given to particular people at particular times (although it may be intended for others as well), and comes chiefly through the Bible and Jesus Christ. God reveals himself to Moses (Ex 3:1-6,14; 6:1-3). The law is revealed (Ex 20-35; Lev 1-7) The pattern of the temple (1Ch 28:11-19). The sonship of Jesus (Mt 3:17; 16:17; 17:5). The nature of the Father through the Son (Jn 1:18; 14:8).

See Inspiration; Prophecy; Prophets; Word of God, Inspiration of.

REVELATION, BOOK OF THE

Author: the Apostle John.

Date: Probably in the latter part of Nero's reign (A.D. 54-68) or the latter part of Domitian's reign (81-96)

Outline:

I. Introduction (1:1-8).
   A. Prologue (1:1-3).
   B. Greetings and Doxology (1:4-8).
II. Jesus among the Seven Churches (1:9-20).
III. The Letters to the Seven Churches (chs. 2-3).
   A. Ephesus (2:1-7).
   B. Smyrna (2:8-11).
   C. Pergamum (2:12-17).
   D. Thyatira (2:18-29).
   E. Sardis (3:1-6).
   F. Philadelphia (3:7-13).
   G. Laodicea (3:14-22).
IV. The Throne, the Scroll and the Lamb (chs. 4-5).
   A. The Throne in Heaven (ch. 4).
   B. The Seven-Sealed Scroll (5:1-5).
   C. The Lamb Slain (5:6-14).
V. The Seven Seals (6:1-8:1).
   A. First Seal: The White Horse (6:1-2).
   B. Second Seal: The Red Horse (6:3-4).
   C. Third Seal: The Black Horse (6:5-6).
   D. Fourth Seal: The Pale Horse (6:7-8).
   E. Fifth Seal: The Souls under the Altar (6:9-11).
   F. Sixth Seal: The Great Earthquake (6:12-17).
   G. The Sealing of the 144,000 (7:1-8).

H. The Great Multitude (7:9-17).
I. Seventh Seal: Silence in Heaven (8:1).
VI. The Seven Trumpets (8:2-11:19).
  A. Introduction (8:2-5).
  B. First Trumpet: Hail and Fire Mixed with Blood (8:6-7).
  C. Second Trumpet: A Mountain Thrown in the Sea (8:8-9).
  D. Third Trumpet: The Star Wormwood (8:10-11).
  E. Fourth Trumpet: A Third of the Sun, Moon and Stars Struck (8:12-13).
  F. Fifth Trumpet: The Plague of Locusts (9:1-12).
  G. Sixth Trumpet: Release of the Four Angels (9:13-21).
  H. The Angel and the Little Scroll (ch. 10).
  I. The Two Witnesses (11:1-14).
  J. Seventh Trumpet: Judgments and Rewards (11:15-19).
VII. Various Personages and Events (chs. 12-14).
  A. The Woman and the Dragon (ch. 12).
  B. The Two Beasts (ch. 13).
  C. The Lamb and the 144,000 (14:1-5).
  D. The Harvest of the Earth (14:6-20).
VIII. The Seven Bowls (chs. 15-16).
  A. Introduction: The Song of Moses and the Seven Angels with the Seven Plagues (ch. 15).
  B. First Bowl: Ugly and Painful Sores (16:1-2).
  C. Second Bowl: Sea Turns to Blood (16:3).
  D. Third Bowl: Rivers and Springs of Water Become Blood (16:4-7).
  E. Fourth Bowl: Sun Scorches People with Fire (16:8-9).
  F. Fifth Bowl: Darkness (16:10-11).
  G. Sixth Bowl: Euphrates River Dries Up (16:12-16).
  H. Seventh Bowl: Tremendous Earthquake (16:17-21).
IX. Babylon: The Great Prostitute (17:1-19:5).
  A. Babylon Described (ch. 17).
  B. The Fall of Babylon (ch. 18).
  C. Praise for Babylon's Fall (19:1-5).
X. Praise for the Wedding of the Lamb (19:6-10).
XI. The Return of Christ (19:11-21).
XII. The Thousand Years (20:1-6).
XIII. Satan's Doom (20:7-10).
XIV. Great White Throne Judgment (20:11-15).
XV. New Heaven, New Earth, New Jerusalem (21:1-22:5).
XVI. Conclusion (22:6-21).

REVELING [2510, 6357, 6600, 6601, 6611, 7464, 8471, 8525, *1960, 4089*].
NIV+ REVELED, REVELERS, REVELRY

Any extreme intemperance and lustful indulgence, usually accompanying pagan worship (Gal 5:21; 1Pe 4:3).

REVENGE [5933, 5934, 5935, *1688+4932*].
NIV+ AVENGE, AVENGED, AVENGER, AVENGES, AVENGING, VENGEANCE

Forbidden (Lev 19:18; Pr 24:29; Ro 12:17,19; 1Th 5:15; 1Pe 3:9). Jesus an example of forbearing (1Pe 2:23). Rebuked by Jesus (Lk 9:54-55). Inconsistent with a Christian spirit (Lk 9:55). Proceeds from a spiteful heart (Eze 25:15). Punishment for (Eze 25:15-17; Am 1:11-12).

Exemplified:

By Simeon and Levi (Ge 34:25). By Samson (Jdg 15:7-8; 16:28-30). By Joab (2Sa 3:27). By Absalom (2Sa 13:23-29). By Jezebel (1Ki 19:2). By Ahab (1Ki 22:27). By

Haman (Est 3:8-15). By the Edomites (Eze 25:12). By the Philistines (Eze 25:15). By Herodias (Mk 6:19-24). By James and John (Lk 9:54). By the chief priests (Ac 5:33). By the Jews (Ac 7:54-59; 23:12).

See Retaliation; Vengeance.

REVENUE [5006, 9202, 9311, 10063, 10402, *5465*].
NIV+ REVENUES

Solomon's (2Ch 9:13-14).
See Tax.

REVERENCE [*1593, 3707, 3711, 10167, *2325, 5828, 5832*].
NIV+ REVERE, REVERED, REVERENT, REVERING

For God (Ge 17:3; Ex 3:5; 19:16-24; 34:29-35; Isa 45:9). *See Fear of God.* For God's house (Lev 19:30; 26:2). For ministers (1Sa 16:4; Ac 28:10; 1Co 16:18; Php 2:29; 1Th 5:12-13; 1Ti 5:17; Heb 13:7,17). *See Minister.* For Kings (1Sa 24:6; 26:9,11; 2Sa 1:14; 16:21; Ecc 10:20; 1Pe 2:17). *See Rulers.* For magistrates (Ex 22:28; 2Pe 2:10; Jude 8). *See Rulers.* For parents (Ex 20:12; Lev 19:3; Isa 45:10). *See Parents.* For the aged (Lev 19:32; Job 32:4-7).

REVILE, REVILING [1552, 5540, 7837, 8475].
NIV+ REVILED, REVILES

To revile is to address or speak of someone abusively; to reproach (Ex 21:17; Zep 2:8; Mk 15:32; 1Co 6:10).

REVIVALS
Religious:

(Zec 8:20-23). Prayer for (Hab 3:2). Prophecies concerning (Isa 32:15; Joel 2:28; Mic 4:1-8; Hab 3:2).

Instances of:

Under Joshua (Jos 5:2-9), Samuel (1Sa 7:1-6), Elijah (1Ki 18:17-40), Jehoash and Jehoiada (2Ki 11-12; 2Ch 23-24), Hezekiah (2Ki 18:1-7; 2Ch 29-31), Josiah (2Ki 22-23; 2Ch 34-35), Asa (2Ch 14:2-5; 15:1-14), Manasseh (2Ch 33:12-19). In Nineveh (Jnh 3:4-10). At Pentecost and post-Pentecostal times (Ac 2:1-42,46-47; 4:4; 5:14; 6:7; 9:35; 11:20-21; 12:24; 14:1; 19:17-20).

See Religion.

REVOLT [5277, 6240, 7321, 7756, 10492, *189, 415, 923*].
NIV+ REVOLTED, REVOLUTIONS

Of the ten tribes (1Ki 12:1-24).

REWARD [*2750, 3877, 5989, 7190, 8510, 8740, 8966, 10454, *625, 3632, 3635*].
NIV+ REWARDED, REWARDING, REWARDS

Isa 40:10 See, the Sovereign LORD comes with power, and his arm rules for him. See, his reward is with him, and his recompense accompanies him. [11]He tends his flock like a shepherd: He gathers the lambs in his arms and carries them close to his heart; he gently leads those that have young.

In Moses' choice—

Heb 11:26 He regarded disgrace for the sake of Christ as of greater value than the treasures of Egypt, because he was looking ahead to his reward.

For bravery (1Sa 17:25; Jdg 1:13).

A Motive:

To repentance—

Lev 26:40 " 'But if they will confess their sins and the sins of their fathers—their treachery against me and their hostility toward me, [41]which made me hostile toward them so that I sent them into the land of their enemies—then when their uncircumcised hearts are humbled and they pay for their sin, ⁴²I will remember my covenant with Jacob and my covenant with Isaac and my covenant with Abraham, and I will remember the land. ⁴³For the land will be deserted by them and will enjoy its sabbaths while it lies desolate without them. They will pay for their sins because they rejected my laws and abhorred my decrees. ⁴⁴Yet in spite of this, when they are in the land of their enemies, I will not reject them or abhor them so as to destroy them completely, breaking my covenant with them. I am the LORD their God. ⁴⁵But for their sake I will remember the covenant with their ancestors whom I brought out of Egypt in the sight of the nations to be their God. I am the LORD.'"

Isa 1:16 wash and make yourselves clean. Take your evil deeds out of my sight! Stop doing wrong, ¹⁷learn to do right! Seek justice, encourage the oppressed. Defend the cause of the fatherless, plead the case of the widow.

¹⁸"Come now, let us reason together," says the LORD. "Though your sins are like scarlet, they shall be as white as snow; though they are red as crimson, they shall be like wool. ¹⁹If you are willing and obedient, you will eat the best from the land; ²⁰but if you resist and rebel, you will be devoured by the sword." For the mouth of the LORD has spoken.

Ac 26:18 to open their eyes and turn them from darkness to light, and from the power of Satan to God, so that they may receive forgiveness of sins and a place among those who are sanctified by faith in me.'

To obedience—

Ex 20:6 but showing love to a thousand [generations] of those who love me and keep my commandments.

Lev 25:18 "'Follow my decrees and be careful to obey my laws, and you will live safely in the land. ¹⁹Then the land will yield its fruit, and you will eat your fill and live there in safety.

Lev 26:3 "'If you follow my decrees and are careful to obey my commands, ⁴I will send you rain in its season, and the ground will yield its crops and the trees of the field their fruit. ⁵Your threshing will continue until grape harvest and the grape harvest will continue until planting, and you will eat all the food you want and live in safety in your land.

⁶"'I will grant peace in the land, and you will lie down and no one will make you afraid. I will remove savage beasts from the land, and the sword will not pass through your country. ⁷You will pursue your enemies, and they will fall by the sword before you. ⁸Five of you will chase a hundred, and a hundred of you will chase ten thousand, and your enemies will fall by the sword before you.

⁹"'I will look on you with favor and make you fruitful and increase your numbers, and I will keep my covenant with you. ¹⁰You will still be eating last year's harvest when you will have to move it out to make room for the new. ¹¹I will put my dwelling place among you, and I will not abhor you. ¹²I will walk among you and be your God, and you will be my people. ¹³I am the LORD your God, who brought you out of Egypt so that you would no longer be slaves to the Egyptians; I broke the bars of your yoke and enabled you to walk with heads held high.

Dt 4:40 Keep his decrees and commands, which I am giving you today, so that it may go well with you and your children after you and that you may live long in the land the LORD your God gives you for all time.

Dt 6:3 Hear, O Israel, and be careful to obey so that it may go well with you and that you may increase greatly in a land flowing with milk and honey, just as the LORD, the God of your fathers, promised you. (+Dt 6:18)

Dt 11:13 So if you faithfully obey the commands I am giving you today—to love the LORD your God and to serve him with all your heart and with all your soul— ¹⁴then I will send rain on your land in its season, both autumn and spring rains, so that you may gather in your grain, new wine and oil. ¹⁵I will provide grass in the fields for your cattle, and you will eat and be satisfied.

¹⁶Be careful, or you will be enticed to turn away and worship other gods and bow down to them.

Dt 11:18 Fix these words of mine in your hearts and minds; tie them as symbols on your hands and bind them on your foreheads. ¹⁹Teach them to your children, talking about them when you sit at home and when you walk along the road, when you lie down and when you get up. ²⁰Write them on the doorframes of your houses and on your gates, ²¹so that your days and the days of your children may be many in the land that the LORD swore to give your forefathers, as many as the days that the heavens are above the earth.

Dt 11:26 See, I am setting before you today a blessing and a curse— ²⁷the blessing if you obey the commands of the LORD your God that I am giving you today; ²⁸the curse if you disobey the commands of the LORD your God and turn from the way that I command you today by following other gods, which you have not known. ²⁹When the LORD your God has brought you into the land you are entering to possess, you are to proclaim on Mount Gerizim the blessings, and on Mount Ebal the curses. (+Dt 27:12-26; Jos 8:33; Isa 1:16-20)

Isa 3:10 Tell the righteous it will be well with them, for they will enjoy the fruit of their deeds. (+Eph 6:1-3)

Heb 12:28 Therefore, since we are receiving a kingdom that cannot be shaken, let us be thankful, and so worship God acceptably with reverence and awe,

To faithfulness (Mt 24:45-47; 25:14-33; Lk 12:42-44; 19:12-27)—

1Co 3:8 The man who plants and the man who waters have one purpose, and each will be rewarded according to his own labor.

Rev 2:10 Do not be afraid of what you are about to suffer. I tell you, the devil will put some of you in prison to test you, and you will suffer persecution for ten days. Be faithful, even to the point of death, and I will give you the crown of life.

Rev 22:12 "Behold, I am coming soon! My reward is with me, and I will give to everyone according to what he has done.

To righteous conduct—

Ro 2:10 but glory, honor and peace for everyone who does good: first for the Jew, then for the Gentile.

1Pe 3:9 Do not repay evil with evil or insult with insult, but with blessing, because to this you were called so that you may inherit a blessing. ¹⁰For, "Whoever would love life and see good days must keep his tongue from evil and his lips from deceitful speech. ¹¹He must turn from evil and do good; he must seek peace and pursue it. ¹²For the eyes of the Lord are on the righteous and his ears are attentive to their prayer, but the face of the Lord is against those who do evil."

To patience—

Heb 10:36 You need to persevere so that when you have done the will of God, you will receive what he has promised.

To perseverance (Mt 10:22; 24:13)—

Mk 13:13 All men will hate you because of me, but he who stands firm to the end will be saved. (+Ro 2:6-7; Gal 6:9)

Rev 2:17 He who has an ear, let him hear what the Spirit says to the churches. To him who overcomes, I will give some of the hidden manna. I will also give him a white stone with a new name written on it, known only to him who receives it.

Rev 2:25 Only hold on to what you have until I come.

²⁶To him who overcomes and does my will to the end, I will give authority over the nations—

²⁷'He will rule them with an iron scepter; he will dash them to pieces like pottery'—

just as I have received authority from my Father. ²⁸I will also give him the morning star. (+Rev 3:5,11-12,21; 21:7)

To honesty—

Dt 25:15 You must have accurate and honest weights and measures, so that you may live long in the land the LORD your God is giving you.

To follow Christ—

Mt 10:32 "Whoever acknowledges me before men, I will also acknowledge him before my Father in heaven.

Mt 16:24 Then Jesus said to his disciples, "If anyone would come after me, he must deny himself and take up his cross and follow me. ²⁵For whoever wants to save his life will lose it, but whoever loses his life for me will find it. ²⁶What good will it be for a man if he gains the whole world, yet forfeits his soul? Or what can a man give in exchange for his soul? ²⁷For the Son of Man is going to come in his Father's glory with his angels, and then he will reward each person according to what he has done.

Mt 20:1 "For the kingdom of heaven is like a landowner who went out early in the morning to hire men to work in his vineyard. ²He agreed to pay them a denarius for the day and sent them into his vineyard.

³"About the third hour he went out and saw others standing in the marketplace doing nothing. ⁴He told them, 'You also go and work in my vineyard, and I will pay you whatever is right.' ⁵So they went.

"He went out again about the sixth hour and the ninth hour and did the same thing. ⁶About the eleventh hour he went out and found still others standing around. He asked them, 'Why have you been standing here all day long doing nothing?'

⁷"'Because no one has hired us,' they answered.

"He said to them, 'You also go and work in my vineyard.'

⁸"When evening came, the owner of the vineyard said to his foreman, 'Call the workers and pay them their wages, beginning with the last ones hired and going on to the first.'

⁹"The workers who were hired about the eleventh hour came and each received a denarius. ¹⁰So when those came who were hired first, they expected to receive more. But each one of them also received a denarius. ¹¹When they received it, they began to grumble against the landowner. ¹²'These men who were hired last worked only one hour,' they said, 'and you have made them equal to us who have borne the burden of the work and the heat of the day.'

¹³"But he answered one of them, 'Friend, I am not being unfair to you. Didn't you agree to work for a denarius? ¹⁴Take your pay and go. I want to give the man who was hired last the same as I gave you. ¹⁵Don't I have the right to do what I want with my own money? Or are you envious

because I am generous?' ¹⁶"So the last will be first, and the first will be last."

Mt 25:34 "Then the King will say to those on his right, 'Come, you who are blessed by my Father; take your inheritance, the kingdom prepared for you since the creation of the world. ³⁵For I was hungry and you gave me something to eat, I was thirsty and you gave me something to drink, I was a stranger and you invited me in, ³⁶I needed clothes and you clothed me, I was sick and you looked after me, I was in prison and you came to visit me.'

³⁷"Then the righteous will answer him, 'Lord, when did we see you hungry and feed you, or thirsty and give you something to drink? ³⁸When did we see you a stranger and invite you in, or needing clothes and clothe you? ³⁹When did we see you sick or in prison and go to visit you?'

⁴⁰"The King will reply, 'I tell you the truth, whatever you did for one of the least of these brothers of mine, you did for me.'

⁴¹"Then he will say to those on his left, 'Depart from me, you who are cursed, into the eternal fire prepared for the devil and his angels. ⁴²For I was hungry and you gave me nothing to eat, I was thirsty and you gave me nothing to drink, ⁴³I was a stranger and you did not invite me in, I needed clothes and you did not clothe me, I was sick and in prison and you did not look after me.'

⁴⁴"They also will answer, 'Lord, when did we see you hungry or thirsty or a stranger or needing clothes or sick or in prison, and did not help you?'

⁴⁵"He will reply, 'I tell you the truth, whatever you did not do for one of the least of these, you did not do for me.'

⁴⁶"Then they will go away to eternal punishment, but the righteous to eternal life."

Mk 10:21 Jesus looked at him and loved him. "One thing you lack," he said. "Go, sell everything you have and give to the poor, and you will have treasure in heaven. Then come, follow me." (+Lk 12:8)

2Pe 1:10 Therefore, my brothers, be all the more eager to make your calling and election sure. For if you do these things, you will never fall, ¹¹and you will receive a rich welcome into the eternal kingdom of our Lord and Savior Jesus Christ.

To endure persecution—

Lk 6:22 Blessed are you when men hate you, when they exclude you and insult you and reject your name as evil, because of the Son of Man.

²³"Rejoice in that day and leap for joy, because great is your reward in heaven. For that is how their fathers treated the prophets.

Heb 10:34 You sympathized with those in prison and joyfully accepted the confiscation of your property, because you knew that you yourselves had better and lasting possessions.

To endure tribulation (Rev 2:7,10)—

Rev 7:14 I answered, "Sir, you know."

And he said, "These are they who have come out of the great tribulation; they have washed their robes and made them white in the blood of the Lamb.

¹⁵Therefore, "they are before the throne of God and serve him day and night in his temple; and he who sits on the throne will spread his tent over them. ¹⁶Never again will they hunger; never again will they thirst. The sun will not beat upon them, nor any scorching heat. ¹⁷For the Lamb at the center of the throne will be their shepherd; he will lead them to springs of living water. And God will wipe away every tear from their eyes."

To love enemies—

Lk 6:35 But love your enemies, do good to them, and lend to them without expecting to get anything back. Then your reward will be great, and you will be sons of the Most High, because he is kind to the ungrateful and wicked.

To deliver the oppressed—

Jer 22:3 This is what the LORD says: Do what is just and right. Rescue from the hand of his oppressor the one who has been robbed. Do no wrong or violence to the alien, the fatherless or the widow, and do not shed innocent blood in this place. [4]For if you are careful to carry out these commands, then kings who sit on David's throne will come through the gates of this palace, riding in chariots and on horses, accompanied by their officials and their people. (+Jer 17:24-26)

To honor parents—

Ex 20:12 "Honor your father and your mother, so that you may live long in the land the LORD your God is giving you. (+Eph 6:1-3)

To honor the Sabbath (Jer 17:24-26).

To give generously—

Dt 15:9 Be careful not to harbor this wicked thought: "The seventh year, the year for canceling debts, is near," so that you do not show ill will toward your needy brother and give him nothing. He may then appeal to the LORD against you, and you will be found guilty of sin. [10]Give generously to him and do so without a grudging heart; then because of this the LORD your God will bless you in all your work and in everything you put your hand to. [11]There will always be poor people in the land. Therefore I command you to be openhanded toward your brothers and toward the poor and needy in your land.

Dt 24:19 When you are harvesting in your field and you overlook a sheaf, do not go back to get it. Leave it for the alien, the fatherless and the widow, so that the LORD your God may bless you in all the work of your hands.

To show kindness to animals (Dt 24:7).

See Blessings, Spiritual, Contingent Upon Obedience; Punishment; Righteous, Promises to; Sin, Separates From God; Wicked, Punishment of.

REZEPH [8364] (*heated stones, live coals*). A city destroyed by the Assyrians (2Ki 19:12; Isa 37:12).

REZIA *See Rizia.*

REZIN [8360].

NIV+ REZIN'S

1. A king of Syria who harassed the kingdom of Judah (2Ki 15:37; 16:5-9). Prophecy against (Isa 7:1-9; 8:4-8; 9:11).

2. A returned Babylonian captive (Ezr 2:48; Ne 7:50).

REZON [8139] (*prince* IDB; *high official* KB). King of Damascus. An adversary of Solomon (1Ki 11:23-25).

RHEGIUM [4836]. A city of Italy. Touched by Paul on the way to Rome (Ac 28:13).

RHESA [4840]. An ancestor of Jesus (Lk 3:27).

RHODA [4851] (*rose*). A servant or slave girl in the home of Mary, John Mark's mother (Ac 12:13).

RHODES [8102, 4852] (*rose*). An island on the SW tip of Asia Minor; commercial center until crippled by Rome is 166 B.C.; famous for Colossus, a statue of Helios; Paul stopped off there (Ac 21:1).

RIBAI [8192] (*opponent*). A Benjamite. The father of Ittai (2Sa 23:29; 1Ch 11:31).

RIBBON, RIBBAND [2562]. Ribbon used in poetic imagery (SS 4:3). Tassels of thread on the corners of garments; NIV "cord" (Nu 15:38).

RIBLAH [8058].

1. A city on the boundary of Canaan and Israel, N of the Sea of Galilee (Nu 34:11).

2. An important town on the E bank of the Orontes River fifty miles S of Hamath. There Pharaoh Neco (609 B.C.) put King Jehoahaz II of Judah in chains. Also in this place, Nebuchadnezzar killed the sons of King Zedekiah of Judah (587 B.C.) and put out his eyes. Following this, Zedekiah was carried off in chains to Babylon (2Ki 25:6f; Jer 39:5-7). It is possible that the two Riblahs may be the same.

RICH, THE [*238, 419, 2016, 2104, 2657, 2890, 3202, 3702, 3883, 5794, 6938, 6947, 6948, 9045, *4454, 4456, 4457, 4458*].

NIV+ ENRICH, ENRICHED, RICHER, RICHES, RICHEST, RICHLY, RICHNESS

Admonitions to the Rich:

Jer 9:23 This is what the LORD says: "Let not the wise man boast of his wisdom or the strong man boast of his strength or the rich man boast of his riches,

1Ti 6:17 Command those who are rich in this present world not to be arrogant nor to put their hope in wealth, which is so uncertain, but to put their hope in God, who richly provides us with everything for our enjoyment. [18]Command them to do good, to be rich in good deeds, and to be generous and willing to share. [19]In this way they will lay up treasure for themselves as a firm foundation for the coming age, so that they may take hold of the life that is truly life.

Jas 1:9 The brother in humble circumstances ought to take pride in his high position. [10]But the one who is rich should take pride in his low position, because he will pass away like a wild flower. [11]For the sun rises with scorching heat and withers the plant; its blossom falls and its beauty is destroyed. In the same way, the rich man will fade away even while he goes about his business.

Not to trust riches for divine favor—

Ps 49:16 Do not be overawed when a man grows rich, when the splendor of his house increases; [17]for he will take nothing with him when he dies, his splendor will not descend with him. [18]Though while he lived he counted himself blessed—and men praise you when you prosper—

Ecc 7:19 Wisdom makes one wise man more powerful than ten rulers in a city.

Zep 1:18 Neither their silver nor their gold will be able to save them on the day of the LORD's wrath. In the fire of his jealousy the whole world will be consumed, for he will make a sudden end of all who live in the earth."

Characteristics of:

Have many friends—

Pr 14:20 The poor are shunned even by their neighbors, but the rich have many friends. (+Pr 19:9)

Made so by God—

Ecc 5:19 Moreover, when God gives any man wealth and possessions, and enables him to enjoy them, to accept his lot and be happy in his work—this is a gift of God. [20]He seldom reflects on the days of his life, because God keeps him occupied with gladness of heart.

Difficult to enter the kingdom—

Mt 19:24 Again I tell you, it is easier for a camel to go through the eye of a needle than for a rich man to enter the kingdom of God."

Mk 10:17 As Jesus started on his way, a man ran up to him and fell on his knees before him. "Good teacher," he asked, "what must I do to inherit eternal life?"

[18]"Why do you call me good?" Jesus answered. "No one is good—except God alone. [19]You know the commandments: 'Do not murder, do not commit adultery, do not steal, do not give false testimony, do not defraud, honor your father and mother.' "

[20]"Teacher," he declared, "all these I have kept since I was a boy."

[21]Jesus looked at him and loved him. "One thing you lack," he said. "Go, sell everything you have and give to the poor, and you will have treasure in heaven. Then come, follow me."

[22]At this the man's face fell. He went away sad, because he had great wealth.

[23]Jesus looked around and said to his disciples, "How hard it is for the rich to enter the kingdom of God!"

[24]The disciples were amazed at his words. But Jesus said again, "Children, how hard it is to enter the kingdom of God! [25]It is easier for a camel to go through the eye of a needle than for a rich man to enter the kingdom of God."

[26]The disciples were even more amazed, and said to each other, "Who then can be saved?"

[27]Jesus looked at them and said, "With man this is impossible, but not with God; all things are possible with God." (+Lk 18:24-25)

Wicked—

Job 21:7 Why do the wicked live on, growing old and increasing in power? [8]They see their children established around them, their offspring before their eyes. [9]Their homes are safe and free from fear; the rod of God is not upon them. [10]Their bulls never fail to breed; their cows calve and do not miscarry. [11]They send forth their children as a flock; their little ones dance about. [12]They sing to the music of tambourine and harp; they make merry to the sound of the flute. [13]They spend their years in prosperity and go down to the grave in peace. [14]Yet they say to God, 'Leave us alone! We have no desire to know your ways. [15]Who is the Almighty, that we should serve him? What would we gain by praying to him?' (+Ps 73:3-9; Pr 28:8,20,22; Jer 5:27-28)

Lk 12:15 Then he said to them, "Watch out! Be on your guard against all kinds of greed; a man's life does not consist in the abundance of his possessions."

[16]And he told them this parable: "The ground of a certain rich man produced a good crop. [17]He thought to himself, 'What shall I do? I have no place to store my crops.'

[18]"Then he said, 'This is what I'll do. I will tear down my barns and build bigger ones, and there I will store all my grain and my goods. [19]And I'll say to myself, "You have plenty of good things laid up for many years. Take life easy; eat, drink and be merry." '

[20]"But God said to him, 'You fool! This very night your life will be demanded from you. Then who will get what you have prepared for yourself?'

[21]"This is how it will be with anyone who stores up things for himself but is not rich toward God."

Lk 16:19 "There was a rich man who was dressed in purple and fine linen and lived in luxury every day. [20]At his gate was laid a beggar named Lazarus, covered with sores [21]and longing to eat what fell from the rich man's table. Even the dogs came and licked his sores.

[22]"The time came when the beggar died and the angels carried him to Abraham's side. The rich man also died and was buried. [23]In hell, where he was in torment, he looked up and saw Abraham far away, with Lazarus by his side. [24]So he called to him, 'Father Abraham, have pity on me and send Lazarus to dip the tip of his finger in water and cool my tongue, because I am in agony in this fire.'

[25]"But Abraham replied, 'Son, remember that in your lifetime you received your good things, while Lazarus received bad things, but now he is comforted here and you are in agony. [26]And besides all this, between us and you a great chasm has been fixed, so that those who want to go from here to you cannot, nor can anyone cross over from there to us.' (+Lk 16:27-31; Jas 2:6-7)

Immoral—

Jer 5:7 "Why should I forgive you? Your children have forsaken me and sworn by gods that are not gods. I supplied all their needs, yet they committed adultery and thronged to the houses of prostitutes. [8]They are well-fed, lusty stallions, each neighing for another man's wife.

Deluded (Pr 11:28; 13:7)—

Pr 18:11 The wealth of the rich is their fortified city; they imagine it an unscalable wall.

Conceited—

Pr 28:11 A rich man may be wise in his own eyes, but a poor man who has discernment sees through him.

Proud (Ps 73:3,6,8-9)—

Eze 28:5 By your great skill in trading you have increased your wealth, and because of your wealth your heart has grown proud.

Arrogant (Ps 73:8).

Oppressive—

Ne 5:1 Now the men and their wives raised a great outcry against their Jewish brothers. [2]Some were saying, "We and our sons and daughters are numerous; in order for us to eat and stay alive, we must get grain."

[3]Others were saying, "We are mortgaging our fields, our vineyards and our homes to get grain during the famine."

[4]Still others were saying, "We have had to borrow money to pay the king's tax on our fields and vineyards. [5]Although we are of the same flesh and blood as our countrymen and though our sons are as good as theirs, yet we have to subject our sons and daughters to slavery. Some of our daughters have already been enslaved, but we are powerless, because our fields and our vineyards belong to others."

[6]When I heard their outcry and these charges, I was very angry. [7]I pondered them in my mind and then accused the nobles and officials. I told them, "You are exacting usury from your own countrymen!" So I called together a large meeting to deal with them [8]and said: "As far as possible, we have bought back our Jewish brothers who were sold to the Gentiles. Now you are selling your brothers, only for them to be sold back to us!" They kept quiet, because they could find nothing to say.

[9]So I continued, "What you are doing is not right. Shouldn't you walk in the fear of our God to avoid the reproach of our Gentile enemies? [10]I and my brothers and my men are also lending the people money and grain. But let the exacting of usury stop! [11]Give back to them immediately their fields, vineyards, olive groves and houses, and also the usury you are charging them—the hundredth part of the money, grain, new wine and oil."

¹²"We will give it back," they said. "And we will not demand anything more from them. We will do as you say." Then I summoned the priests and made the nobles and officials take an oath to do what they had promised.

¹³I also shook out the folds of my robe and said, "In this way may God shake out of his house and possessions every man who does not keep this promise. So may such a man be shaken out and emptied!" At this the whole assembly said, "Amen," and praised the LORD. And the people did as they had promised. (+Mic 6:10-11)

Mic 6:12 Her rich men are violent; her people are liars and their tongues speak deceitfully. (+Mic 6:13; Jas 2:6)

Cruel to the poor—

Pr 18:23 A poor man pleads for mercy, but a rich man answers harshly.

Envied—

Ps 73:3 For I envied the arrogant when I saw the prosperity of the wicked.

⁴They have no struggles; their bodies are healthy and strong. ⁵They are free from the burdens common to man; they are not plagued by human ills. ⁶Therefore pride is their necklace; they clothe themselves with violence. ⁷From their callous hearts comes iniquity; the evil conceits of their minds know no limits. ⁸They scoff, and speak with malice; in their arrogance they threaten oppression. ⁹Their mouths lay claim to heaven, and their tongues take possession of the earth. ¹⁰Therefore their people turn to them and drink up waters in abundance. ¹¹They say, "How can God know? Does the Most High have knowledge?"

¹²This is what the wicked are like—always carefree, they increase in wealth.

¹³Surely in vain have I kept my heart pure; in vain have I washed my hands in innocence. ¹⁴All day long I have been plagued; I have been punished every morning.

¹⁵If I had said, "I will speak thus," I would have betrayed your children. ¹⁶When I tried to understand all this, it was oppressive to me ¹⁷till I entered the sanctuary of God; then I understood their final destiny.

¹⁸Surely you place them on slippery ground; you cast them down to ruin. ¹⁹How suddenly are they destroyed, completely swept away by terrors! ²⁰As a dream when one awakes, so when you arise, O Lord, you will despise them as fantasies.

²¹When my heart was grieved and my spirit embittered, ²²I was senseless and ignorant; I was a brute beast before you.

Hated (Job 27:19,23).

Denounced (Isa 5:8)—

Jer 17:11 Like a partridge that hatches eggs it did not lay is the man who gains riches by unjust means. When his life is half gone, they will desert him, and in the end he will prove to be a fool.

Jer 22:13 "Woe to him who builds his palace by unrighteousness, his upper rooms by injustice, making his countrymen work for nothing, not paying them for their labor. ¹⁴He says, 'I will build myself a great palace with spacious upper rooms.' So he makes large windows in it, panels it with cedar and decorates it in red.

¹⁵"Does it make you a king to have more and more cedar? Did not your father have food and drink? He did what was right and just, so all went well with him.

Am 6:1 Woe to you who are complacent in Zion, and to you who feel secure on Mount Samaria, you notable men of the foremost nation, to whom the people of Israel come! ²Go to Calneh and look at it; go from there to great Hamath, and then go down to Gath in Philistia. Are they

better off than your two kingdoms? Is their land larger than yours? ³You put off the evil day and bring near a reign of terror. ⁴You lie on beds inlaid with ivory and lounge on your couches. You dine on choice lambs and fattened calves. ⁵You strum away on your harps like David and improvise on musical instruments. ⁶You drink wine by the bowlful and use the finest lotions, but you do not grieve over the ruin of Joseph.

Lk 6:24 "But woe to you who are rich, for you have already received your comfort. ²⁵Woe to you who are well fed now, for you will go hungry. Woe to you who laugh now, for you will mourn and weep.

Jas 5:1 Now listen, you rich people, weep and wail because of the misery that is coming upon you. ²Your wealth has rotted, and moths have eaten your clothes. ³Your gold and silver are corroded. Their corrosion will testify against you and eat your flesh like fire. You have hoarded wealth in the last days. (+Jas 5:4)

Unscrupulous methods of (Jer 5:26)—

Jer 5:27 Like cages full of birds, their houses are full of deceit; they have become rich and powerful ²⁸and have grown fat and sleek. Their evil deeds have no limit; they do not plead the case of the fatherless to win it, they do not defend the rights of the poor.

Discrimination in favor of, in the church, forbidden (Jas 2:1-9).

Divine judgments against—

Job 27:13 "Here is the fate God allots to the wicked, the heritage a ruthless man receives from the Almighty: ¹⁴However many his children, their fate is the sword; his offspring will never have enough to eat. ¹⁵The plague will bury those who survive him, and their widows will not weep for them. ¹⁶Though he heaps up silver like dust and clothes like piles of clay, ¹⁷what he lays up the righteous will wear, and the innocent will divide his silver. ¹⁸The house he builds is like a moth's cocoon, like a hut made by a watchman. ¹⁹He lies down wealthy, but will do so no more; when he opens his eyes, all is gone. ²⁰Terrors overtake him like a flood; a tempest snatches him away in the night. ²¹The east wind carries him off, and he is gone; it sweeps him out of his place. ²²It hurls itself against him without mercy as he flees headlong from its power. ²³It claps its hands in derision and hisses him out of his place. (+Ps 52:1-7; 73:18-20)

Instances of Righteous Rich:

Abraham (Ge 13:2; 24:35). Isaac (Ge 26:12-14). Solomon (1Ki 10:23; 2Ch 9:22). Jehoshaphat (2Ch 18:1). Hezekiah (2Ki 20:12-13).

Job (Job 1:3)—

Job 31:24 "If I have put my trust in gold or said to pure gold, 'You are my security,' ²⁵if I have rejoiced over my great wealth, the fortune my hands had gained,

Job 31:28 then these also would be sins to be judged, for I would have been unfaithful to God on high.

Joseph of Arimathea (Mt 27:57). Zacchaeus (Lk 19:2). *See Riches.*

RICHES [238, 2104, 2657, 2776, 2890, 3702, 3883, 4759, 5794, 6217, 6948, 8214, *3353*, *4458*].

NIV+ See RICH

1Sa 2:7 The LORD sends poverty and wealth; he humbles and he exalts.

Ps 37:16 Better the little that the righteous have than the wealth of many wicked; (+Ps 52:7)

Pr 11:4 Wealth is worthless in the day of wrath, but righteousness delivers from death.

Pr 14:24 The wealth of the wise is their crown, but the folly of fools yields folly.

Pr 15:6 The house of the righteous contains great treasure, but the income of the wicked brings them trouble.

Pr 15:16 Better a little with the fear of the LORD than great wealth with turmoil.

[17]Better a meal of vegetables where there is love than a fattened calf with hatred.

Pr 16:8 Better a little with righteousness than much gain with injustice.

Pr 19:4 Wealth brings many friends, but a poor man's friend deserts him. (+Ecc 4:8)

Ecc 5:11 As goods increase, so do those who consume them. And what benefit are they to the owner except to feast his eyes on them?

[12]The sleep of a laborer is sweet, whether he eats little or much, but the abundance of a rich man permits him no sleep.

[13]I have seen a grievous evil under the sun: wealth hoarded to the harm of its owner, [14]or wealth lost through some misfortune, so that when he has a son there is nothing left for him.

Ecc 6:1 I have seen another evil under the sun, and it weighs heavily on men: [2]God gives a man wealth, possessions and honor, so that he lacks nothing his heart desires, but God does not enable him to enjoy them, and a stranger enjoys them instead. This is meaningless, a grievous evil.

Ecc 7:11 Wisdom, like an inheritance, is a good thing and benefits those who see the sun. [12]Wisdom is a shelter as money is a shelter, but the advantage of knowledge is this: that wisdom preserves the life of its possessor. (+Ecc 10:19)

Isa 5:8 Woe to you who add house to house and join field to field till no space is left and you live alone in the land.

Jer 48:36 "So my heart laments for Moab like a flute; it laments like a flute for the men of Kir Hareseth. The wealth they acquired is gone.

Delusive—

Pr 11:28 Whoever trusts in his riches will fall, but the righteous will thrive like a green leaf. (+Lk 12:16-21)

Unstable (Pr 23:5)—

Pr 27:24 for riches do not endure forever, and a crown is not secure for all generations.

Unsatisfying to the covetous (Ecc 5:10-12).

A snare—

Dt 6:10 When the LORD your God brings you into the land he swore to your fathers, to Abraham, Isaac and Jacob, to give you—a land with large, flourishing cities you did not build, [11]houses filled with all kinds of good things you did not provide, wells you did not dig, and vineyards and olive groves you did not plant—then when you eat and are satisfied, [12]be careful that you do not forget the LORD, who brought you out of Egypt, out of the land of slavery. (+Dt 8:7-9)

Dt 8:10 When you have eaten and are satisfied, praise the LORD your God for the good land he has given you. [11]Be careful that you do not forget the LORD your God, failing to observe his commands, his laws and his decrees that I am giving you this day. [12]Otherwise, when you eat and are satisfied, when you build fine houses and settle down, [13]and when your herds and flocks grow large and your silver and gold increase and all you have is multiplied, [14]then your heart will become proud and you will forget the LORD your God, who brought you out of Egypt, out of the land of slavery. [15]He led you through the vast and dreadful desert, that thirsty and waterless land, with its venomous snakes and scorpions. He brought you water out of hard rock. [16]He gave you manna to eat in the desert, something your fathers had never known, to humble and to test you so that in the end it might go well with you. [17]You may say to yourself, "My power and the strength of my hands have produced this wealth for me."

Dt 31:20 When I have brought them into the land flowing with milk and honey, the land I promised on oath to their forefathers, and when they eat their fill and thrive, they will turn to other gods and worship them, rejecting me and breaking my covenant.

Dt 32:15 Jeshurun grew fat and kicked; filled with food, he became heavy and sleek. He abandoned the God who made him and rejected the Rock his Savior.

Pr 30:8 Keep falsehood and lies far from me; give me neither poverty nor riches, but give me only my daily bread. [9]Otherwise, I may have too much and disown you and say, 'Who is the LORD?' Or I may become poor and steal, and so dishonor the name of my God. (+Jer 5:7-8)

Hos 12:8 Ephraim boasts, "I am very rich; I have become wealthy. With all my wealth they will not find in me any iniquity or sin."

Mt 13:22 The one who received the seed that fell among the thorns is the man who hears the word, but the worries of this life and the deceitfulness of wealth choke it, making it unfruitful.

Mt 19:16 Now a man came up to Jesus and asked, "Teacher, what good thing must I do to get eternal life?"

[17]"Why do you ask me about what is good?" Jesus replied. "There is only One who is good. If you want to enter life, obey the commandments."

[18]"Which ones?" the man inquired.

Jesus replied, "'Do not murder, do not commit adultery, do not steal, do not give false testimony, [19]honor your father and mother,' and 'love your neighbor as yourself.'"

[20]"All these I have kept," the young man said. "What do I still lack?"

[21]Jesus answered, "If you want to be perfect, go, sell your possessions and give to the poor, and you will have treasure in heaven. Then come, follow me."

[22]When the young man heard this, he went away sad, because he had great wealth.

[23]Then Jesus said to his disciples, "I tell you the truth, it is hard for a rich man to enter the kingdom of heaven. [24]Again I tell you, it is easier for a camel to go through the eye of a needle than for a rich man to enter the kingdom of God."

Mk 4:19 but the worries of this life, the deceitfulness of wealth and the desires for other things come in and choke the word, making it unfruitful. (+Mk 10:17-25; Lk 16:19-26; 18:18-25)

1Ti 6:9 People who want to get rich fall into temptation and a trap and into many foolish and harmful desires that plunge men into ruin and destruction. [10]For the love of money is a root of all kinds of evil. Some people, eager for money, have wandered from the faith and pierced themselves with many griefs.

[11]But you, man of God, flee from all this, and pursue righteousness, godliness, faith, love, endurance and gentleness.

1Ti 6:17 Command those who are rich in this present world not to be arrogant nor to put their hope in wealth, which is so uncertain, but to put their hope in God, who richly provides us with everything for our enjoyment.

Worthless in the day of calamity (Eze 7:17,19; Zep 1:18).

Fraudulently gotten, unprofitable—

Pr 10:2 Ill-gotten treasures are of no value, but righteousness delivers from death.

Pr 21:6 A fortune made by a lying tongue is a fleeting vapor and a deadly snare.

Pr 28:8 He who increases his wealth by exorbitant interest amasses it for another, who will be kind to the poor. (+Jer 17:11)

Admonitions against the desire for—

Pr 23:4 Do not wear yourself out to get rich; have the wisdom to show restraint.

Pr 28:20 A faithful man will be richly blessed, but one eager to get rich will not go unpunished.

Pr 28:22 A stingy man is eager to get rich and is unaware that poverty awaits him. (+1Ti 6:9-11,17)

The heart not to be set upon (Ps 62:10)—

Mt 6:19 "Do not store up for yourselves treasures on earth, where moth and rust destroy, and where thieves break in and steal. **20**But store up for yourselves treasures in heaven, where moth and rust do not destroy, and where thieves do not break in and steal. **21**For where your treasure is, there your heart will be also.

Liberality with—

Pr 13:7 One man pretends to be rich, yet has nothing; another pretends to be poor, yet has great wealth.

8A man's riches may ransom his life, but a poor man hears no threat.

Benevolent use of, required—

1Jn 3:17 If anyone has material possessions and sees his brother in need but has no pity on him, how can the love of God be in him?

Figurative (Rev 3:17-18).

See Covetousness; Rich, The.

RIDDLE [2648, 10019] (*hidden saying, proverb*).

NIV+ RIDDLES

Any "dark saying" of which the meaning is not immediately clear and must be found by shrewd thought (Nu 12:8; Pr 1:6). It may be a parable (Ps 49:4), or something for men to guess (Jdg 14:12-19), or just a hard question (1Ki 10:1; 2Ch 9:1).

RIGHTEOUS [3838, 7404, 7405, 7406, 7407, 9448, *1464, 1465, 1466, 1467, 1468, 1469*].

NIV+ See RIGHTEOUSNESS

Compared with:

The sun (Jdg 5:31; Mt 13:43), stars (Da 12:3)

Lights—

Mt 5:14 "You are the light of the world. A city on a hill cannot be hidden.

Php 2:15 so that you may become blameless and pure, children of God without fault in a crooked and depraved generation, in which you shine like stars in the universe

Mount Zion (Ps 125:1-2), Lebanon (Hos 14:5-7), treasure (Ex 19:5; Ps 135:4), treasured possession (Mal 3:17), gold (Job 23:10; La 4:2), vessels of gold and silver (2Ti 2:20), stones of a crown (Zec 9:16)

Living stones—

1Pe 2:5 you also, like living stones, are being built into a spiritual house to be a holy priesthood, offering spiritual sacrifices acceptable to God through Jesus Christ.

Babes (Mt 11:25; 1Pe 2:2), little children (Mt 18:3; 1Co 14:20), obedient children (1Pe 1:14), members of the body (1Co 12:20,27), soldiers (2Ti 2:3-4), runners in a race (1Co 9:24; Heb 12:1), wrestlers (2Ti 2:5), good servants (Mt 25:21), strangers and pilgrims (1Pe 2:11), sheep (Ps

78:52; Mt 25:33; Jn 10), lambs (Isa 40:11; Jn 21:15), calves of the stall (Mal 4:2), lions (Pr 28:1; Mic 5:8), eagles (Ps 103:5; Isa 40:31), doves (Ps 68:13; Isa 60:8), thirsty deer (Ps 42:1), good fish (Mt 13:48), dew and showers (Mic 5:7), watered gardens (Isa 58:11), unfailing springs (Isa 58:11), vines (SS 6:11; Hos 14:7), branches of a vine (Jn 15:2,4-5), pomegranates (SS 4:13), good figs (Jer 24:2-7), lilies (SS 2:2; Hos 14:5), poplars by flowing streams (Isa 44:4), trees planted by rivers (Ps 1:3), cedars in Lebanon (Ps 92:12), palm trees (Ps 92:12), green olive trees (Ps 52:8; Hos 14:6), fruitful trees (Ps 1:3; Jer 17:8), grain (Hos 14:7), wheat (Mt 3:12; 13:29-30)

Salt—

Mt 5:13 "You are the salt of the earth. But if the salt loses its saltiness, how can it be made salty again? It is no longer good for anything, except to be thrown out and trampled by men.

Access of, to God (Ps 31:19-20; Isa 12:6). Few (Mt 7:14; 22:14). Relation of, to God (Lev 20:24-26). Righteous and wicked, circumstances of, contrasted (Job 8; Ps 17:14-15). *See below, Contrasted with the wicked.*

At the judgment. *See Judgment.*

Fellowship of. *See Fellowship.*

Hatred toward. *See Persecution.*

Joy of. *See Joy.*

Perseverance of. *See Perseverance.*

Contrasted with the wicked—

(Ps 1:1-6; 11:5; 17:14-15; 32:10; 37:17-22,37-38; 73:1-28; 75:10; 91:7-8; Pr 2:21-22; 3:32-33; 4:16-17)

Pr 4:18 The path of the righteous is like the first gleam of dawn, shining ever brighter till the full light of day. (+Pr 4:19; 10:3,6,9,11,16,20-21,23-25,28-32; 11:3,5-6,8-11, 18-21,23,31; 12:3,5-7,10,12-13,21,26)

Pr 13:5 The righteous hate what is false, but the wicked bring shame and disgrace. (+Pr 13:6,9,17,21-22,25; 14:2, 11,19,22-32; 15:6,8-9,28-29; 22:5,8-9; 24:16; 28:1,4-5, 13-14,18; 29:2,6-7,27; Isa 32:1-8; 65:13-14; Ro 2:7-10; Eph 2:12-14; Php 2:15; 1Th 5:5-8; Tit 1:15; 1Pe 4:17-18)

1Jn 3:3 Everyone who has this hope in him purifies himself, just as he is pure. (+1Jn 3:4-5)

1Jn 3:6 No one who lives in him keeps on sinning. No one who continues to sin has either seen him or known him.

7Dear children, do not let anyone lead you astray. He who does what is right is righteous, just as he is righteous. (+1Jn 3:8)

1Jn 3:9 No one who is born of God will continue to sin, because God's seed remains in him; he cannot go on sinning, because he has been born of God. (+1Jn 3:10-13)

1Jn 3:14 We know that we have passed from death to life, because we love our brothers. Anyone who does not love remains in death. (+1Jn 3:15-17)

See Wicked, Contrasted with the Righteous; Described as.

Described:

Ps 1:1 Blessed is the man who does not walk in the counsel of the wicked or stand in the way of sinners or sit in the seat of mockers.

2But his delight is in the law of the LORD, and on his law he meditates day and night. **3**He is like a tree planted by streams of water, which yields its fruit in season and whose leaf does not wither. Whatever he does prospers.

Ps 15:1 LORD, who may dwell in your sanctuary? Who may live on your holy hill? **2**He whose walk is blameless and who does what is righteous, who speaks the truth from his heart **3**and has no slander on his tongue, who does his neighbor no wrong and casts no slur on his fellowman,

[4]who despises a vile man but honors those who fear the LORD, who keeps his oath even when it hurts, [5]who lends his money without usury and does not accept a bribe against the innocent. He who does these things will never be shaken.

Ps 24:3 Who may ascend the hill of the LORD? Who may stand in his holy place? [4]He who has clean hands and a pure heart, who does not lift up his soul to an idol or swear by what is false. [5]He will receive blessing from the LORD and vindication from God his Savior.

Ps 37:26 They are always generous and lend freely; their children will be blessed.

Ps 37:30 The mouth of the righteous man utters wisdom, and his tongue speaks what is just. [31]The law of his God is in his heart; his feet do not slip.

Ps 84:7 They go from strength to strength, till each appears before God in Zion.

Ps 112:1 Praise the LORD. Blessed is the man who fears the LORD, who finds great delight in his commands.

[2]His children will be mighty in the land; the generation of the upright will be blessed. [3]Wealth and riches are in his house, and his righteousness endures forever. [4]Even in darkness light dawns for the upright, for the gracious and compassionate and righteous man. [5]Good will come to him who is generous and lends freely, who conducts his affairs with justice. [6]Surely he will never be shaken; a righteous man will be remembered forever. [7]He will have no fear of bad news; his heart is steadfast, trusting in the LORD. [8]His heart is secure, he will have no fear; in the end he will look in triumph on his foes. [9]He has scattered abroad his gifts to the poor, his righteousness endures forever; his horn will be lifted high in honor.

[10]The wicked man will see and be vexed, he will gnash his teeth and waste away; the longings of the wicked will come to nothing.

Ps 119:1 Blessed are they whose ways are blameless, who walk according to the law of the LORD. [2]Blessed are they who keep his statutes and seek him with all their heart. [3]They do nothing wrong; they walk in his ways.

Isa 33:15 He who walks righteously and speaks what is right, who rejects gain from extortion and keeps his hand from accepting bribes, who stops his ears against plots of murder and shuts his eyes against contemplating evil— [16]this is the man who will dwell on the heights, whose refuge will be the mountain fortress. His bread will be supplied, and water will not fail him.

Isa 51:1 "Listen to me, you who pursue righteousness and who seek the LORD: Look to the rock from which you were cut and to the quarry from which you were hewn;

Isa 62:12 They will be called the Holy People, the Redeemed of the LORD; and you will be called Sought After, the City No Longer Deserted.

Isa 63:8 He said, "Surely they are my people, sons who will not be false to me"; and so he became their Savior. (+Jer 17:7-8)

Jer 31:12 They will come and shout for joy on the heights of Zion; they will rejoice in the bounty of the LORD—the grain, the new wine and the oil, the young of the flocks and herds. They will be like a well-watered garden, and they will sorrow no more. [13]Then maidens will dance and be glad, young men and old as well. I will turn their mourning into gladness; I will give them comfort and joy instead of sorrow. [14]I will satisfy the priests with abundance, and my people will be filled with my bounty," declares the LORD.

Jer 31:33 "This is the covenant I will make with the house of Israel after that time," declares the LORD. "I will put my law in their minds and write it on their hearts. I will be their God, and they will be my people. [34]No longer will a man teach his neighbor, or a man his brother, saying, 'Know the LORD,' because they will all know me, from the least of them to the greatest," declares the LORD. "For I will forgive their wickedness and will remember their sins no more."

Eze 18:5 "Suppose there is a righteous man who does what is just and right. [6]He does not eat at the mountain shrines or look to the idols of the house of Israel. He does not defile his neighbor's wife or lie with a woman during her period. [7]He does not oppress anyone, but returns what he took in pledge for a loan. He does not commit robbery but gives his food to the hungry and provides clothing for the naked. [8]He does not lend at usury or take excessive interest. He withholds his hand from doing wrong and judges fairly between man and man. [9]He follows my decrees and faithfully keeps my laws. That man is righteous; he will surely live, declares the Sovereign LORD.

Zec 3:2 The LORD said to Satan, "The LORD rebuke you, Satan! The LORD, who has chosen Jerusalem, rebuke you! Is not this man a burning stick snatched from the fire?"

Zec 3:7 "This is what the LORD Almighty says: 'If you will walk in my ways and keep my requirements, then you will govern my house and have charge of my courts, and I will give you a place among these standing here.

[8]"'Listen, O high priest Joshua and your associates seated before you, who are men symbolic of things to come: I am going to bring my servant, the Branch.

As dead to sin—

Ro 6:2 By no means! We died to sin; how can we live in it any longer?

Ro 6:11 In the same way, count yourselves dead to sin but alive to God in Christ Jesus.

Col 3:3 For you died, and your life is now hidden with Christ in God.

Freed from sin—

Ro 6:7 because anyone who has died has been freed from sin.

Ro 6:18 You have been set free from sin and have become slaves to righteousness. (+Ro 6:22; 1Jn 3:6,9)

Good—

Lk 6:45 The good man brings good things out of the good stored up in his heart, and the evil man brings evil things out of the evil stored up in his heart. For out of the overflow of his heart his mouth speaks.

Pure—

Mt 5:8 Blessed are the pure in heart, for they will see God. (+1Jn 3:3; 2Ti 2:21-22)

Holy (Dt 7:6; Eph 1:4; 4:24; Col 1:22; 3:12; 1Pe 1:15)—

2Ti 2:19 Nevertheless, God's solid foundation stands firm, sealed with this inscription: "The Lord knows those who are his," and, "Everyone who confesses the name of the Lord must turn away from wickedness." (+Heb 3:1)

Sanctified—

1Co 1:2 To the church of God in Corinth, to those sanctified in Christ Jesus and called to be holy, together with all those everywhere who call on the name of our Lord Jesus Christ—their Lord and ours:

1Co 6:11 And that is what some of you were. But you were washed, you were sanctified, you were justified in the name of the Lord Jesus Christ and by the Spirit of our God.

Godly—

Ps 4:3 Know that the LORD has set apart the godly for himself; the LORD will hear when I call to him. (+2Pe 2:9)

Wise (Ps 37:30)—

Pr 2:9 Then you will understand what is right and just and fair—every good path. [10]For wisdom will enter your heart, and knowledge will be pleasant to your soul. [11]Discretion will protect you, and understanding will guard you.

[12]Wisdom will save you from the ways of wicked men, from men whose words are perverse,

Faithful (Mt 24:45; 25:21,23; Lk 19:17; Eph 1:1; Col 1:2; Rev 17:14)

Merciful—

Mt 5:7 Blessed are the merciful, for they will be shown mercy.

Meek—

Mt 5:5 Blessed are the meek, for they will inherit the earth. (+2Ti 2:25)

Industrious—

Eph 4:28 He who has been stealing must steal no longer, but must work, doing something useful with his own hands, that he may have something to share with those in need.

2Jn 9 Anyone who runs ahead and does not continue in the teaching of Christ does not have God; whoever continues in the teaching has both the Father and the Son.

Stable—

Mt 7:24 "Therefore everyone who hears these words of mine and puts them into practice is like a wise man who built his house on the rock. [25]The rain came down, the streams rose, and the winds blew and beat against that house; yet it did not fall, because it had its foundation on the rock. [26]But everyone who hears these words of mine and does not put them into practice is like a foolish man who built his house on sand. [27]The rain came down, the streams rose, and the winds blew and beat against that house, and it fell with a great crash."

Eph 4:14 Then we will no longer be infants, tossed back and forth by the waves, and blown here and there by every wind of teaching and by the cunning and craftiness of men in their deceitful scheming.

Saved—

Ac 2:47 praising God and enjoying the favor of all the people. And the Lord added to their number daily those who were being saved.

Saints—

Ro 1:7 To all in Rome who are loved by God and called to be saints: Grace and peace to you from God our Father and from the Lord Jesus Christ. (+1Co 1:2; Eph 1:1)

Chosen—

1Pe 2:9 But you are a chosen people, a royal priesthood, a holy nation, a people belonging to God, that you may declare the praises of him who called you out of darkness into his wonderful light.

Rev 17:14 They will make war against the Lamb, but the Lamb will overcome them because he is Lord of lords and King of kings—and with him will be his called, chosen and faithful followers."

Spotless (Jas 1:27)

Separate—

Ex 33:16 How will anyone know that you are pleased with me and with your people unless you go with us? What else will distinguish me and your people from all the other people on the face of the earth?"

Obedient—

Mt 12:50 For whoever does the will of my Father in heaven is my brother and sister and mother."

Jn 15:14 You are my friends if you do what I command.

1Jn 2:3 We know that we have come to know him if we obey his commands.

1Jn 2:5 But if anyone obeys his word, God's love is truly made complete in him. This is how we know we are in him:

New creature (2Co 5:17; Eph 2:10)—

Eph 4:23 to be made new in the attitude of your minds; [24]and to put on the new self, created to be like God in true righteousness and holiness. (+Col 3:9-10)

Spiritually minded (Ro 8:4)—

Ro 8:6 The mind of sinful man is death, but the mind controlled by the Spirit is life and peace;

Servants of Christ (Eph 6:6)

Servants of righteousness—

Ro 6:19 I put this in human terms because you are weak in your natural selves. Just as you used to offer the parts of your body in slavery to impurity and to ever-increasing wickedness, so now offer them in slavery to righteousness leading to holiness.

Children of light—

1Th 5:5 You are all sons of the light and sons of the day. We do not belong to the night or to the darkness.

Sons of God—

Ro 8:14 because those who are led by the Spirit of God are sons of God.

Ro 8:16 The Spirit himself testifies with our spirit that we are God's children. (+Jn 3:2)

A temple of God (2Co 6:16), beloved of God (Ro 1:7)

Poor in spirit—

Mt 5:3 "Blessed are the poor in spirit, for theirs is the kingdom of heaven.

Hungering and thirsting after righteousness—

Mt 5:6 Blessed are those who hunger and thirst for righteousness, for they will be filled.

Growing in grace (Ps 84:7)—

Eph 4:13 until we all reach unity in the faith and in the knowledge of the Son of God and become mature, attaining to the whole measure of the fullness of Christ.

Imitators of Christ—

1Pe 4:1 Therefore, since Christ suffered in his body, arm yourselves also with the same attitude, because he who has suffered in his body is done with sin. [2]As a result, he does not live the rest of his earthly life for evil human desires, but rather for the will of God.

1Jn 2:6 Whoever claims to live in him must walk as Jesus did.

Salt of the earth (Mt 5:13)

City set on a hill—

Mt 5:14 "You are the light of the world. A city on a hill cannot be hidden.

Led by the spirit (Ro 8:14; Gal 5:18)

Filled with goodness and knowledge—

Ro 15:14 I myself am convinced, my brothers, that you yourselves are full of goodness, complete in knowledge and competent to instruct one another.

Col 1:9 For this reason, since the day we heard about you, we have not stopped praying for you and asking God to fill you with the knowledge of his will through all spiritual wisdom and understanding. [10]And we pray this in order that you may live a life worthy of the Lord and may please him in every way: bearing fruit in every good work, growing in the knowledge of God, [11]being strengthened with all power according to his glorious might so that you may have great endurance and patience, and joyfully [12]giving thanks to the Father, who has qualified you to share in the inheritance of the saints in the kingdom of light. [13]For he has rescued us from the dominion of darkness and brought us into the kingdom of the Son he loves,

Grounded in love (Eph 3:17), following Christ (Mt 10:38; 16:24; Mk 8:34; Lk 9:23)

Rooted in Christ—

Col 2:7 rooted and built up in him, strengthened in the faith as you were taught, and overflowing with thankfulness.

Patient, long-suffering, joyful (Col 1:11)—

1Th 1:3 We continually remember before our God and Father your work produced by faith, your labor prompted by love, and your endurance inspired by hope in our Lord Jesus Christ.

Peaceful, meek, gentle, patient—

2Ti 2:21 If a man cleanses himself from the latter, he will be an instrument for noble purposes, made holy, useful to the Master and prepared to do any good work.

[22]Flee the evil desires of youth, and pursue righteousness, faith, love and peace, along with those who call on the Lord out of a pure heart. [23]Don't have anything to do with foolish and stupid arguments, because you know they produce quarrels. [24]And the Lord's servant must not quarrel; instead, he must be kind to everyone, able to teach, not resentful. [25]Those who oppose him he must gently instruct, in the hope that God will grant them repentance leading them to a knowledge of the truth,

Blameless, harmless, and without blemish (Eph 1:4; Php 2:15)

Kind, tender-hearted, forgiving—

Eph 4:32 Be kind and compassionate to one another, forgiving each other, just as in Christ God forgave you.

Hating falsehood (Pr 13:5), abhorring wickedness (Ps 101:3-4), having renounced dishonesty (2Co 4:2)

Without bitterness, wrath, anger, clamor, evil speaking, malice—

Eph 4:31 Get rid of all bitterness, rage and anger, brawling and slander, along with every form of malice.

Grieved by the wickedness of the wicked (Ps 119:158; Ac 17:16; 2Pe 2:7-8).

Happiness of:

(Job 5:17-27; Pr 3:13-18; 16:20; Mt 4:3-12). Satisfying (Ps 36:8; 63:5).

Under fiery trials (1Pe 4:12-13).

Under persecution—

Mt 5:10 Blessed are those who are persecuted because of righteousness, for theirs is the kingdom of heaven. (+Mt 5:11-12)

Promises to and Grounds of Assurance and Comfort of:

Deliverance from temptation (1Co 10:13)—

2Pe 2:9 if this is so, then the Lord knows how to rescue godly men from trials and to hold the unrighteous for the day of judgment, while continuing their punishment.

Deliverance from trouble—

Job 5:19 From six calamities he will rescue you; in seven no harm will befall you. [20]In famine he will ransom you from death, and in battle from the stroke of the sword. [21]You will be protected from the lash of the tongue, and need not fear when destruction comes. [22]You will laugh at destruction and famine, and need not fear the beasts of the earth. [23]For you will have a covenant with the stones of the field, and the wild animals will be at peace with you. [24]You will know that your tent is secure; you will take stock of your property and find nothing missing.

Ps 34:15 The eyes of the LORD are on the righteous and his ears are attentive to their cry;

Ps 34:17 The righteous cry out, and the LORD hears them; he delivers them from all their troubles.

Ps 50:15 and call upon me in the day of trouble; I will deliver you, and you will honor me." (+Ps 91:15)

Ps 97:10 Let those who love the LORD hate evil, for he guards the lives of his faithful ones and delivers them from the hand of the wicked. [11]Light is shed upon the righteous and joy on the upright in heart.

Pr 3:25 Have no fear of sudden disaster or of the ruin that overtakes the wicked, [26]for the LORD will be your confidence and will keep your foot from being snared. (+Isa 41:10-13)

Isa 43:2 When you pass through the waters, I will be with you; and when you pass through the rivers, they will not sweep over you. When you walk through the fire, you will not be burned; the flames will not set you ablaze.

Refuge in adversity—

Ps 33:18 But the eyes of the LORD are on those who fear him, on those whose hope is in his unfailing love, [19]to deliver them from death and keep them alive in famine.

Ps 62:8 Trust in him at all times, O people; pour out your hearts to him, for God is our refuge. *Selah*

Ps 91:1 He who dwells in the shelter of the Most High will rest in the shadow of the Almighty. (+Ps 91:2)

Ps 91:3 Surely he will save you from the fowler's snare and from the deadly pestilence. [4]He will cover you with his feathers, and under his wings you will find refuge; his faithfulness will be your shield and rampart. [5]You will not fear the terror of night, nor the arrow that flies by day, [6]nor the pestilence that stalks in the darkness, nor the plague that destroys at midday. [7]A thousand may fall at your side, ten thousand at your right hand, but it will not come near you. (+Ps 91:8)

Ps 91:9 If you make the Most High your dwelling—even the LORD, who is my refuge— [10]then no harm will befall you, no disaster will come near your tent. [11]For he will command his angels concerning you to guard you in all your ways; (+Ps 91:12-15)

Pr 14:26 He who fears the LORD has a secure fortress, and for his children it will be a refuge.

Na 1:7 The LORD is good, a refuge in times of trouble. He cares for those who trust in him,

Strength in adversity—

Ps 29:11 The LORD gives strength to his people; the LORD blesses his people with peace.

Security—

Ps 32:6 Therefore let everyone who is godly pray to you while you may be found; surely when the mighty waters rise, they will not reach him. [7]You are my hiding place; you will protect me from trouble and surround me with songs of deliverance. *Selah*

Ps 84:11 For the LORD God is a sun and shield; the LORD bestows favor and honor; no good thing does he withhold from those whose walk is blameless.

Ps 121:3 He will not let your foot slip—he who watches over you will not slumber; [4]indeed, he who watches over Israel will neither slumber nor sleep.

[5]The LORD watches over you—the LORD is your shade at your right hand; [6]the sun will not harm you by day, nor the moon by night.

[7]The LORD will keep you from all harm—he will watch over your life; [8]the LORD will watch over your coming and going both now and forevermore.

Isa 33:16 this is the man who will dwell on the heights, whose refuge will be the mountain fortress. His bread will be supplied, and water will not fail him.

Providential care—

Ge 15:1 After this, the word of the LORD came to Abram in a vision: "Do not be afraid, Abram. I am your shield, your very great reward."

Ex 23:22 If you listen carefully to what he says and do all that I say, I will be an enemy to your enemies and will oppose those who oppose you.

Lev 26:5 Your threshing will continue until grape harvest and the grape harvest will continue until planting, and you will eat all the food you want and live in safety in your land.

[6]"'I will grant peace in the land, and you will lie down and no one will make you afraid. I will remove savage beasts from the land, and the sword will not pass through your country.

Lev 26:10 You will still be eating last year's harvest when you will have to move it out to make room for the new.

Dt 33:27 The eternal God is your refuge, and underneath are the everlasting arms. He will drive out your enemy before you, saying, 'Destroy him!' (+1Sa 2:9)

2Ch 16:9 For the eyes of the LORD range throughout the earth to strengthen those whose hearts are fully committed to him. You have done a foolish thing, and from now on you will be at war."

Ezr 8:22 I was ashamed to ask the king for soldiers and horsemen to protect us from enemies on the road, because we had told the king, "The gracious hand of our God is on everyone who looks to him, but his great anger is against all who forsake him."

Job 5:15 He saves the needy from the sword in their mouth; he saves them from the clutches of the powerful.

Ps 34:9 Fear the LORD, you his saints, for those who fear him lack nothing. [10]The lions may grow weak and hungry, but those who seek the LORD lack no good thing.

Ps 125:1 Those who trust in the LORD are like Mount Zion, which cannot be shaken but endures forever. [2]As the mountains surround Jerusalem, so the LORD surrounds his people both now and forevermore.

[3]The scepter of the wicked will not remain over the land allotted to the righteous, for then the righteous might use their hands to do evil.

Ps 145:19 He fulfills the desires of those who fear him; he hears their cry and saves them. [20]The LORD watches over all who love him, but all the wicked he will destroy.

Pr 1:33 but whoever listens to me will live in safety and be at ease, without fear of harm." (+Pr 2:7; 3:6)

Pr 10:3 The LORD does not let the righteous go hungry but he thwarts the craving of the wicked.

Pr 16:7 When a man's ways are pleasing to the LORD, he makes even his enemies live at peace with him.

Isa 49:9 to say to the captives, 'Come out,' and to those in darkness, 'Be free!'

"They will feed beside the roads and find pasture on every barren hill. [10]They will neither hunger nor thirst, nor will the desert heat or the sun beat upon them. He who has compassion on them will guide them and lead them beside springs of water. [11]I will turn all my mountains into roads, and my highways will be raised up.

Isa 65:13 Therefore this is what the Sovereign LORD says: "My servants will eat, but you will go hungry; my servants

will drink, but you will go thirsty; my servants will rejoice, but you will be put to shame. [14]My servants will sing out of the joy of their hearts, but you will cry out from anguish of heart and wail in brokenness of spirit.

Eze 34:11 "'For this is what the Sovereign LORD says: I myself will search for my sheep and look after them. [12]As a shepherd looks after his scattered flock when he is with them, so will I look after my sheep. I will rescue them from all the places where they were scattered on a day of clouds and darkness. [13]I will bring them out from the nations and gather them from the countries, and I will bring them into their own land. I will pasture them on the mountains of Israel, in the ravines and in all the settlements in the land. [14]I will tend them in a good pasture, and the mountain heights of Israel will be their grazing land. There they will lie down in good grazing land, and there they will feed in a rich pasture on the mountains of Israel. [15]I myself will tend my sheep and have them lie down, declares the Sovereign LORD. [16]I will search for the lost and bring back the strays. I will bind up the injured and strengthen the weak, but the sleek and the strong I will destroy. I will shepherd the flock with justice.

[17]"'As for you, my flock, this is what the Sovereign LORD says: I will judge between one sheep and another, and between rams and goats.

Eze 34:22 I will save my flock, and they will no longer be plundered. I will judge between one sheep and another. [23]I will place over them one shepherd, my servant David, and he will tend them; he will tend them and be their shepherd. [24]I the LORD will be their God, and my servant David will be prince among them. I the LORD have spoken.

[25]"'I will make a covenant of peace with them and rid the land of wild beasts so that they may live in the desert and sleep in the forests in safety. [26]I will bless them and the places surrounding my hill. I will send down showers in season; there will be showers of blessing. [27]The trees of the field will yield their fruit and the ground will yield its crops; the people will be secure in their land. They will know that I am the LORD, when I break the bars of their yoke and rescue them from the hands of those who enslaved them. [28]They will no longer be plundered by the nations, nor will wild animals devour them. They will live in safety, and no one will make them afraid. [29]I will provide for them a land renowned for its crops, and they will no longer be victims of famine in the land or bear the scorn of the nations. [30]Then they will know that I, the LORD their God, am with them and that they, the house of Israel, are my people, declares the Sovereign LORD. [31]You my sheep, the sheep of my pasture, are people, and I am your God, declares the Sovereign LORD.'"

Lk 12:7 Indeed, the very hairs of your head are all numbered. Don't be afraid; you are worth more than many sparrows.

Lk 12:32 "Do not be afraid, little flock, for your Father has been pleased to give you the kingdom.

Lk 21:18 But not a hair of your head will perish.

1Pe 5:7 Cast all your anxiety on him because he cares for you.

Overruling providence—

Ro 8:28 And we know that in all things God works for the good of those who love him, who have been called according to his purpose.

2Co 4:17 For our light and momentary troubles are achieving for us an eternal glory that far outweighs them all.

Answer to prayer—

Pr 15:29 The LORD is far from the wicked but he hears the prayer of the righteous.

Mk 11:23 "I tell you the truth, if anyone says to this mountain, 'Go, throw yourself into the sea,' and does not doubt in his heart but believes that what he says will happen, it will be done for him. [24]Therefore I tell you, whatever you ask for in prayer, believe that you have received it, and it will be yours.

Jn 14:13 And I will do whatever you ask in my name, so that the Son may bring glory to the Father. [14]You may ask me for anything in my name, and I will do it.

Ac 10:4 Cornelius stared at him in fear. "What is it, Lord?" he asked. The angel answered, "Your prayers and gifts to the poor have come up as a memorial offering before God.

1Pe 3:12 For the eyes of the Lord are on the righteous and his ears are attentive to their prayer, but the face of the Lord is against those who do evil."

1Jn 3:22 and receive from him anything we ask, because we obey his commands and do what pleases him.

Temporal blessings (Lev 25:18-19; 26:5)—

Dt 28:1 If you fully obey the LORD your God and carefully follow all his commands I give you today, the LORD your God will set you high above all the nations on earth. [2]All these blessings will come upon you and accompany you if you obey the LORD your God:

[3]You will be blessed in the city and blessed in the country.

[4]The fruit of your womb will be blessed, and the crops of your land and the young of your livestock—the calves of your herds and the lambs of your flocks.

[5]Your basket and your kneading trough will be blessed.

[6]You will be blessed when you come in and blessed when you go out.

[7]The LORD will grant that the enemies who rise up against you will be defeated before you. They will come at you from one direction but flee from you in seven.

[8]The LORD will send a blessing on your barns and on everything you put your hand to. The LORD your God will bless you in the land he is giving you.

[9]The LORD will establish you as his holy people, as he promised you on oath, if you keep the commands of the LORD your God and walk in his ways. [10]Then all the peoples on earth will see that you are called by the name of the LORD, and they will fear you. [11]The LORD will grant you abundant prosperity—in the fruit of your womb, the young of your livestock and the crops of your ground—in the land he swore to your forefathers to give you.

[12]The LORD will open the heavens, the storehouse of his bounty, to send rain on your land in season and to bless all the work of your hands. You will lend to many nations but will borrow from none. [13]The LORD will make you the head, not the tail. If you pay attention to the commands of the LORD your God that I give you this day and carefully follow them, you will always be at the top, never at the bottom.

Ps 37:9 For evil men will be cut off, but those who hope in the LORD will inherit the land.

Ps 128:1 Blessed are all who fear the LORD, who walk in his ways. [2]You will eat the fruit of your labor; blessings and prosperity will be yours. [3]Your wife will be like a fruitful vine within your house; your sons will be like olive shoots around your table. [4]Thus is the man blessed who fears the LORD.

[5]May the LORD bless you from Zion all the days of your life; may you see the prosperity of Jerusalem, [6]and may you live to see your children's children. Peace be upon Israel.

Pr 2:21 For the upright will live in the land, and the blameless will remain in it;

Pr 3:1 My son, do not forget my teaching, but keep my commands in your heart, [2]for they will prolong your life many years and bring you prosperity.

[3]Let love and faithfulness never leave you; bind them around your neck, write them on the tablet of your heart. [4]Then you will win favor and a good name in the sight of God and man.

Pr 3:7 Do not be wise in your own eyes; fear the LORD and shun evil. [8]This will bring health to your body and nourishment to your bones.

[9]Honor the LORD with your wealth, with the firstfruits of all your crops; [10]then your barns will be filled to overflowing, and your vats will brim over with new wine. (+Mt 6:26-33; Mk 10:30; Lk 18:29-30)

Blessings upon their children (Ps 103:17; 112:2-3).

Receive: Comfort in tribulation—

Isa 25:8 he will swallow up death forever. The Sovereign LORD will wipe away the tears from all faces; he will remove the disgrace of his people from all the earth. The LORD has spoken.

Isa 66:13 As a mother comforts her child, so will I comfort you; and you will be comforted over Jerusalem."

[14]When you see this, your heart will rejoice and you will flourish like grass; the hand of the LORD will be made known to his servants, but his fury will be shown to his foes.

Mt 5:4 Blessed are those who mourn, for they will be comforted.

Jn 14:16 And I will ask the Father, and he will give you another Counselor to be with you forever— [17]the Spirit of truth. The world cannot accept him, because it neither sees him nor knows him. But you know him, for he lives with you and will be in you. [18]I will not leave you as orphans; I will come to you.

Rev 21:4 He will wipe every tear from their eyes. There will be no more death or mourning or crying or pain, for the old order of things has passed away."

Joy—

Isa 35:10 and the ransomed of the LORD will return. They will enter Zion with singing; everlasting joy will crown their heads. Gladness and joy will overtake them, and sorrow and sighing will flee away.

Isa 51:11 The ransomed of the LORD will return. They will enter Zion with singing; everlasting joy will crown their heads. Gladness and joy will overtake them, and sorrow and sighing will flee away.

Spiritual enlightenment (Isa 2:3)—

Jn 8:12 When Jesus spoke again to the people, he said, "I am the light of the world. Whoever follows me will never walk in darkness, but will have the light of life."

Peace—

Isa 26:3 You will keep in perfect peace him whose mind is steadfast, because he trusts in you.

Ro 2:10 but glory, honor and peace for everyone who does good: first for the Jew, then for the Gentile.

Seeing God—

Mt 5:8 Blessed are the pure in heart, for they will see God.

Inconceivable spiritual blessings—

Isa 64:4 Since ancient times no one has heard, no ear has perceived, no eye has seen any God besides you, who acts on behalf of those who wait for him.

1Co 2:9 However, as it is written: "No eye has seen, no ear has heard, no mind has conceived what God has prepared for those who love him"—

The rest of faith—

Heb 4:9 There remains, then, a Sabbath-rest for the people of God;

Wisdom—

Jas 1:5 If any of you lacks wisdom, he should ask God, who gives generously to all without finding fault, and it will be given to him.

Divine help—

Ps 55:22 Cast your cares on the LORD and he will sustain you; he will never let the righteous fall. (+Isa 41:10-13)

Heb 13:5 Keep your lives free from the love of money and be content with what you have, because God has said, "Never will I leave you; never will I forsake you."

⁶So we say with confidence, "The Lord is my helper; I will not be afraid. What can man do to me?"

Divine guidance—

Ps 25:12 Who, then, is the man that fears the LORD? He will instruct him in the way chosen for him.

Ps 32:8 I will instruct you and teach you in the way you should go; I will counsel you and watch over you.

Ps 37:23 If the LORD delights in a man's way, he makes his steps firm; ²⁴though he stumble, he will not fall, for the LORD upholds him with his hand. (+Ps 48:14)

Ps 73:24 You guide me with your counsel, and afterward you will take me into glory.

Pr 3:5 Trust in the LORD with all your heart and lean not on your own understanding; ⁶in all your ways acknowledge him, and he will make your paths straight.

Divine mercy—

Ps 32:10 Many are the woes of the wicked, but the LORD's unfailing love surrounds the man who trusts in him. (+Ps 103:17-18)

Mal 3:17 "They will be mine," says the LORD Almighty, "in the day when I make up my treasured possession. I will spare them, just as in compassion a man spares his son who serves him.

The divine presence (Ge 26:3,24; 28:15; 31:3; Ex 33:14; Dt 31:6,8; Jos 1:5; 1Ki 6:13)—

Hag 1:13 Then Haggai, the LORD's messenger, gave this message of the LORD to the people: "I am with you," declares the LORD.

Hag 2:4 But now be strong, O Zerubbabel,' declares the LORD. 'Be strong, O Joshua son of Jehozadak, the high priest. Be strong, all you people of the land,' declares the LORD, 'and work. For I am with you,' declares the LORD Almighty. ⁵'This is what I covenanted with you when you came out of Egypt. And my Spirit remains among you. Do not fear.'

Mt 28:20 and teaching them to obey everything I have commanded you. And surely I am with you always, to the very end of the age." (+Jn 14:17)

Jn 14:23 Jesus replied, "If anyone loves me, he will obey my teaching. My Father will love him, and we will come to him and make our home with him. (+2Co 6:16; 13:11; Php 4:9; Heb 13:5)

Jas 4:8 Come near to God and he will come near to you. Wash your hands, you sinners, and purify your hearts, you double-minded.

Rev 21:3 And I heard a loud voice from the throne saying, "Now the dwelling of God is with men, and he will live

with them. They will be his people, and God himself will be with them and be their God.

The divine likeness—

1Jn 3:2 Dear friends, now we are children of God, and what we will be has not yet been made known. But we know that when he appears, we shall be like him, for we shall see him as he is.

The ministry of angels—

Heb 1:14 Are not all angels ministering spirits sent to serve those who will inherit salvation?

Dwelling with Christ—

Jn 14:2 In my Father's house are many rooms; if it were not so, I would have told you. I am going there to prepare a place for you. ³And if I go and prepare a place for you, I will come back and take you to be with me that you also may be where I am.

Col 3:4 When Christ, who is your life, appears, then you also will appear with him in glory. (+1Th 4:17)

1Th 5:10 He died for us so that, whether we are awake or asleep, we may live together with him.

Everlasting remembrance—

Ps 112:6 Surely he will never be shaken; a righteous man will be remembered forever.

Having names written in heaven—

Lk 10:20 However, do not rejoice that the spirits submit to you, but rejoice that your names are written in heaven."

Resurrection (Jn 5:29)—

1Co 15:48 As was the earthly man, so are those who are of the earth; and as is the man from heaven, so also are those who are of heaven. ⁴⁹And just as we have borne the likeness of the earthly man, so shall we bear the likeness of the man from heaven.

⁵⁰I declare to you, brothers, that flesh and blood cannot inherit the kingdom of God, nor does the perishable inherit the imperishable. ⁵¹Listen, I tell you a mystery: We will not all sleep, but we will all be changed— (+1Co 15:52-57)

2Co 4:14 because we know that the one who raised the Lord Jesus from the dead will also raise us with Jesus and present us with you in his presence. (+1Th 4:16)

Future glory—

Ro 8:18 I consider that our present sufferings are not worth comparing with the glory that will be revealed in us. (+Col 3:4)

2Ti 2:10 Therefore I endure everything for the sake of the elect, that they too may obtain the salvation that is in Christ Jesus, with eternal glory.

1Pe 5:4 And when the Chief Shepherd appears, you will receive the crown of glory that will never fade away.

Inheritance (Mt 25:34)—

Ac 20:32 "Now I commit you to God and to the word of his grace, which can build you up and give you an inheritance among all those who are sanctified.

Ac 26:18 to open their eyes and turn them from darkness to light, and from the power of Satan to God, so that they may receive forgiveness of sins and a place among those who are sanctified by faith in me.'

Col 1:12 giving thanks to the Father, who has qualified you to share in the inheritance of the saints in the kingdom of light.

Col 3:24 since you know that you will receive an inheritance from the Lord as a reward. It is the Lord Christ you are serving.

Tit 3:7 so that, having been justified by his grace, we might become heirs having the hope of eternal life.

Heb 9:15 For this reason Christ is the mediator of a new covenant, that those who are called may receive the promised eternal inheritance—now that he has died as a ransom to set them free from the sins committed under the first covenant.

Jas 2:5 Listen, my dear brothers: Has not God chosen those who are poor in the eyes of the world to be rich in faith and to inherit the kingdom he promised those who love him?

1Pe 1:4 and into an inheritance that can never perish, spoil or fade—kept in heaven for you,

Heavenly reward—

Mt 5:12 Rejoice and be glad, because great is your reward in heaven, for in the same way they persecuted the prophets who were before you.

Mt 13:43 Then the righteous will shine like the sun in the kingdom of their Father. He who has ears, let him hear.

2Ti 4:8 Now there is in store for me the crown of righteousness, which the Lord, the righteous Judge, will award to me on that day—and not only to me, but also to all who have longed for his appearing.

Heb 11:16 Instead, they were longing for a better country—a heavenly one. Therefore God is not ashamed to be called their God, for he has prepared a city for them.

Jas 1:12 Blessed is the man who perseveres under trial, because when he has stood the test, he will receive the crown of life that God has promised to those who love him.

2Pe 1:11 and you will receive a rich welcome into the eternal kingdom of our Lord and Savior Jesus Christ. (+Rev 2:7,10; 22:5)

Rev 22:12 "Behold, I am coming soon! My reward is with me, and I will give to everyone according to what he has done.

Rev 22:14 "Blessed are those who wash their robes, that they may have the right to the tree of life and may go through the gates into the city.

Eternal life—

Da 12:2 Multitudes who sleep in the dust of the earth will awake: some to everlasting life, others to shame and everlasting contempt. [3]Those who are wise will shine like the brightness of the heavens, and those who lead many to righteousness, like the stars for ever and ever. (+Mt 19:29; 25:46)

Mk 10:29 "I tell you the truth," Jesus replied, "no one who has left home or brothers or sisters or mother or father or children or fields for me and the gospel [30]will fail to receive a hundred times as much in this present age (homes, brothers, sisters, mothers, children and fields—and with them, persecutions) and in the age to come, eternal life.

Lk 18:29 "I tell you the truth," Jesus said to them, "no one who has left home or wife or brothers or parents or children for the sake of the kingdom of God [30]will fail to receive many times as much in this age and, in the age to come, eternal life."

Jn 3:15 that everyone who believes in him may have eternal life.

[16]"For God so loved the world that he gave his one and only Son, that whoever believes in him shall not perish but have eternal life. [17]For God did not send his Son into the world to condemn the world, but to save the world through him. [18]Whoever believes in him is not condemned, but whoever does not believe stands condemned already because he has not believed in the name of God's one and only Son.

Jn 3:36 Whoever believes in the Son has eternal life, but whoever rejects the Son will not see life, for God's wrath remains on him."

Jn 4:14 but whoever drinks the water I give him will never thirst. Indeed, the water I give him will become in him a spring of water welling up to eternal life."

Jn 5:24 "I tell you the truth, whoever hears my word and believes him who sent me has eternal life and will not be condemned; he has crossed over from death to life.

Jn 5:29 and come out—those who have done good will rise to live, and those who have done evil will rise to be condemned.

Jn 6:39 And this is the will of him who sent me, that I shall lose none of all that he has given me, but raise them up at the last day. [40]For my Father's will is that everyone who looks to the Son and believes in him shall have eternal life, and I will raise him up at the last day."

Jn 10:28 I give them eternal life, and they shall never perish; no one can snatch them out of my hand.

Jn 12:25 The man who loves his life will lose it, while the man who hates his life in this world will keep it for eternal life. [26]Whoever serves me must follow me; and where I am, my servant also will be. My Father will honor the one who serves me.

Ro 2:7 To those who by persistence in doing good seek glory, honor and immortality, he will give eternal life.

Ro 6:22 But now that you have been set free from sin and have become slaves to God, the benefit you reap leads to holiness, and the result is eternal life. [23]For the wages of sin is death, but the gift of God is eternal life in Christ Jesus our Lord.

Gal 6:8 The one who sows to please his sinful nature, from that nature will reap destruction; the one who sows to please the Spirit, from the Spirit will reap eternal life.

1Th 4:15 According to the Lord's own word, we tell you that we who are still alive, who are left till the coming of the Lord, will certainly not precede those who have fallen asleep. [16]For the Lord himself will come down from heaven, with a loud command, with the voice of the archangel and with the trumpet call of God, and the dead in Christ will rise first. [17]After that, we who are still alive and are left will be caught up together with them in the clouds to meet the Lord in the air. And so we will be with the Lord forever.

1Ti 1:16 But for that very reason I was shown mercy so that in me, the worst of sinners, Christ Jesus might display his unlimited patience as an example for those who would believe on him and receive eternal life.

1Ti 4:8 For physical training is of some value, but godliness has value for all things, holding promise for both the present life and the life to come. (+Tit 1:2)

1Jn 2:25 And this is what he promised us—even eternal life.

1Jn 5:13 I write these things to you who believe in the name of the Son of God so that you may know that you have eternal life.

Rev 7:14 I answered, "Sir, you know."

And he said, "These are they who have come out of the great tribulation; they have washed their robes and made them white in the blood of the Lamb.

[15]Therefore, "they are before the throne of God and serve him day and night in his temple; and he who sits on the throne will spread his tent over them. [16]Never again will they hunger; never again will they thirst. The sun will not beat upon them, nor any scorching heat. [17]For the Lamb at the center of the throne will be their shepherd; he

will lead them to springs of living water. And God will wipe away every tear from their eyes."

Contingent upon perseverance—

Heb 10:36 You need to persevere so that when you have done the will of God, you will receive what he has promised.

Rev 2:7 He who has an ear, let him hear what the Spirit says to the churches. To him who overcomes, I will give the right to eat from the tree of life, which is in the paradise of God.

Rev 2:10 Do not be afraid of what you are about to suffer. I tell you, the devil will put some of you in prison to test you, and you will suffer persecution for ten days. Be faithful, even to the point of death, and I will give you the crown of life.

[11]He who has an ear, let him hear what the Spirit says to the churches. He who overcomes will not be hurt at all by the second death.

Rev 2:17 He who has an ear, let him hear what the Spirit says to the churches. To him who overcomes, I will give some of the hidden manna. I will also give him a white stone with a new name written on it, known only to him who receives it.

Rev 2:26 To him who overcomes and does my will to the end, I will give authority over the nations—

[27]'He will rule them with an iron scepter; he will dash them to pieces like pottery'—

just as I have received authority from my Father. [28]I will also give him the morning star. (+Rev 3:4-5,10,12,21)

Rev 21:7 He who overcomes will inherit all this, and I will be his God and he will be my son.

See Adoption; Affliction, Comfort in; God, Preserver, Providence of.

Promises in specific areas. *See the specific topic.*

Union of, with God: (1Jn 3:24; 4:13,15-16; 2Jn 9).

Union of, with Christ: (Jn 6:51-58; 14:20)

Jn 15:1 "I am the true vine, and my Father is the gardener. [2]He cuts off every branch in me that bears no fruit, while every branch that does bear fruit he prunes so that it will be even more fruitful. [3]You are already clean because of the word I have spoken to you. [4]Remain in me, and I will remain in you. No branch can bear fruit by itself; it must remain in the vine. Neither can you bear fruit unless you remain in me.

[5]"I am the vine; you are the branches. If a man remains in me and I in him, he will bear much fruit; apart from me you can do nothing. [6]If anyone does not remain in me, he is like a branch that is thrown away and withers; such branches are picked up, thrown into the fire and burned. [7]If you remain in me and my words remain in you, ask whatever you wish, and it will be given you. [8]This is to my Father's glory, that you bear much fruit, showing yourselves to be my disciples.

[9]"As the Father has loved me, so have I loved you. Now remain in my love. [10]If you obey my commands, you will remain in my love, just as I have obeyed my Father's commands and remain in his love. [11]I have told you this so that my joy may be in you and that your joy may be complete.

Jn 17:21 that all of them may be one, Father, just as you are in me and I am in you. May they also be in us so that the world may believe that you have sent me. [22]I have given them the glory that you gave me, that they may be one as we are one: [23]I in them and you in me. May they be brought to complete unity to let the world know that you sent me and have loved them even as you have loved me.

Jn 17:26 I have made you known to them, and will continue to make you known in order that the love you have for me may be in them and that I myself may be in them."

Ro 8:1 Therefore, there is now no condemnation for those who are in Christ Jesus,

Ro 12:5 so in Christ we who are many form one body, and each member belongs to all the others.

1Co 6:13 "Food for the stomach and the stomach for food"—but God will destroy them both. The body is not meant for sexual immorality, but for the Lord, and the Lord for the body. [14]By his power God raised the Lord from the dead, and he will raise us also. [15]Do you not know that your bodies are members of Christ himself? Shall I then take the members of Christ and unite them with a prostitute? Never! [16]Do you not know that he who unites himself with a prostitute is one with her in body? For it is said, "The two will become one flesh." [17]But he who unites himself with the Lord is one with him in spirit.

[18]Flee from sexual immorality. All other sins a man commits are outside his body, but he who sins sexually sins against his own body. [19]Do you not know that your body is a temple of the Holy Spirit, who is in you, whom you have received from God? You are not your own; [20]you were bought at a price. Therefore honor God with your body.

1Co 10:16 Is not the cup of thanksgiving for which we give thanks a participation in the blood of Christ? And is not the bread that we break a participation in the body of Christ?

2Co 13:5 Examine yourselves to see whether you are in the faith; test yourselves. Do you not realize that Christ Jesus is in you—unless, of course, you fail the test?

Gal 2:20 I have been crucified with Christ and I no longer live, but Christ lives in me. The life I live in the body, I live by faith in the Son of God, who loved me and gave himself for me.

Col 1:27 To them God has chosen to make known among the Gentiles the glorious riches of this mystery, which is Christ in you, the hope of glory.

Col 2:6 So then, just as you received Christ Jesus as Lord, continue to live in him, [7]rooted and built up in him, strengthened in the faith as you were taught, and overflowing with thankfulness.

1Jn 2:6 Whoever claims to live in him must walk as Jesus did.

1Jn 2:24 See that what you have heard from the beginning remains in you. If it does, you also will remain in the Son and in the Father.

1Jn 2:28 And now, dear children, continue in him, so that when he appears we may be confident and unashamed before him at his coming.

1Jn 3:6 No one who lives in him keeps on sinning. No one who continues to sin has either seen him or known him.

1Jn 3:24 Those who obey his commands live in him, and he in them. And this is how we know that he lives in us: We know it by the Spirit he gave us.

1Jn 5:12 He who has the Son has life; he who does not have the Son of God does not have life.

1Jn 5:20 We know also that the Son of God has come and has given us understanding, so that we may know him who is true. And we are in him who is true—even in his Son Jesus Christ. He is the true God and eternal life.

2Jn 9 Anyone who runs ahead and does not continue in the teaching of Christ does not have God; whoever continues in the teaching has both the Father and the Son.

See Adoption; Communion; Fellowship, with Christ.

RIGHTEOUSNESS [7404, 7405, 7406, 7407, *1465, 1466, 1468, 2319*].

NIV+ OVERRIGHTEOUS, RIGHTEOUS, RIGHTEOUSLY, RIGHTEOUSNESS'

(Ps 15:1-5; 24:3-5; 106:3; Pr 11:5-6,18,30; Hos 10:12; Mt 5:20; Lk 1:75; Jn 16:8,10; Ro 6:19-22; 8:4; Eph 4:24; Jas 1:27). Figuratively described as a garment (Job 29:14; Isa 61:10; Zec 3:4; Mt 22:11-14; Rev 6:11; 7:9; 19:8). Required (Isa 28:17; Hos 10:12; Mic 6:8; Zec 7:9-10; 8:16-17; Mal 3:3; Mt 5:20; 23:23; Lk 3:10-14; 13:6-9; Ro 6:19-22; 7:4-6; 8:4; 14:17-19; 2Ti 2:22; 1Jn 3:10). Commanded in official administration (Jer 22:3,6).

Imputed, on account of obedience (Rev 6:25; Ps 106:31; Eze 18:9), on account of faith (Ge 15:6; Ro 4:3,5,9,11, 13,20,22,24; Gal 3:6; Jas 2:23). Proof of regeneration (1Jn 2:29). Exalts a nation (Pr 14:34). Safeguards life (Pr 10:2, 16; 11:19; 12:28; 13:6). Winning others to, rewarded (Da 12:3).

Fruits of:

Ps 1:3 He is like a tree planted by streams of water, which yields its fruit in season and whose leaf does not wither. Whatever he does prospers. (+Mt 7:16-18)

Mt 12:35 The good man brings good things out of the good stored up in him, and the evil man brings evil things out of the evil stored up in him. (+Lk 6:43)

Jn 15:4 Remain in me, and I will remain in you. No branch can bear fruit by itself; it must remain in the vine. Neither can you bear fruit unless you remain in me.

⁵"I am the vine; you are the branches. If a man remains in me and I in him, he will bear much fruit; apart from me you can do nothing. (+Jn 15:6-7)

Jn 15:8 This is to my Father's glory, that you bear much fruit, showing yourselves to be my disciples.

2Co 9:10 Now he who supplies seed to the sower and bread for food will also supply and increase your store of seed and will enlarge the harvest of your righteousness.

Gal 5:22 But the fruit of the Spirit is love, joy, peace, patience, kindness, goodness, faithfulness, ²³gentleness and self-control. Against such things there is no law.

Php 1:11 filled with the fruit of righteousness that comes through Jesus Christ—to the glory and praise of God.

Col 3:12 Therefore, as God's chosen people, holy and dearly loved, clothe yourselves with compassion, kindness, humility, gentleness and patience. ¹³Bear with each other and forgive whatever grievances you may have against one another. Forgive as the Lord forgave you. ¹⁴And over all these virtues put on love, which binds them all together in perfect unity.

¹⁵Let the peace of Christ rule in your hearts, since as members of one body you were called to peace. And be thankful.

1Th 1:3 We continually remember before our God and Father your work produced by faith, your labor prompted by love, and your endurance inspired by hope in our Lord Jesus Christ.

Tit 2:2 Teach the older men to be temperate, worthy of respect, self-controlled, and sound in faith, in love and in endurance. (+Tit 2:3-6)

Tit 2:11 For the grace of God that brings salvation has appeared to all men. ¹²It teaches us to say "No" to ungodliness and worldly passions, and to live self-controlled, upright and godly lives in this present age,

1Pe 3:8 Finally, all of you, live in harmony with one another; be sympathetic, love as brothers, be compassionate and humble. ⁹Do not repay evil with evil or insult with insult, but with blessing, because to this you were called so that you may inherit a blessing. ¹⁰For, "Whoever would love life and see good days must keep his tongue from evil and his lips from deceitful speech. ¹¹He must turn from evil and do good; he must seek peace and pursue it. (+1Pe 3:12-13)

1Pe 3:14 But even if you should suffer for what is right, you are blessed. "Do not fear what they fear; do not be frightened."

2Pe 1:5 For this very reason, make every effort to add to your faith goodness; and to goodness, knowledge; ⁶and to knowledge, self-control; and to self-control, perseverance; and to perseverance, godliness; ⁷and to godliness, brotherly kindness; and to brotherly kindness, love. ⁸For if you possess these qualities in increasing measure, they will keep you from being ineffective and unproductive in your knowledge of our Lord Jesus Christ.

1Jn 3:7 Dear children, do not let anyone lead you astray. He who does what is right is righteous, just as he is righteous.

Generousity (Ac 11:29).

Peace—

Isa 32:17 The fruit of righteousness will be peace; the effect of righteousness will be quietness and confidence forever. (+Jas 3:8)

Symbolized: (Eze 47:12; Rev 22:2).

Of God: *See God, Righteousness of.*

Of Jesus: *See Jesus the Christ, Holiness of, Righteousness of.*

See also, Sin, Fruits of; Works, Good.

RIM [1473, 4995, 8557].

NIV+ RIMS

The rim of a wheel (1Ki 7:33; Eze 1:18).

RIMMON [8233, 8234, 8235] (*pomegranate,* or *Rimmon [pagan thunder, storm god]*).

NIV+ EN RIMMON, GATH RIMMON, HADAD RIMMON, RIMMON PEREZ

1. Father of the murderers of Ish-Bosheth (2Sa 4:2,5,9).

2. A city S of Jerusalem (Zec 14:10). Allotted to Judah (Jos 15:32; Ne 11:29), afterward to Simeon (Jos 19:7; 1Ch 4:32). Also called En Rimmon (Ne 11:29).

3. A city of Zebulun (Jos 19:13). Also called Rimmono (1Ch 6:77).

4. A rock in Benjamin (Jdg 20:45,47; 21:13).

5. A Syrian idol (2Ki 5:18).

RIMMON-METHOAR *See Rimmon, 3.*

RIMMON PEREZ, RIMMON-PAREZ [8236] (*pomegranate pass [breach]*).

NIV+ PEREZ, RIMMON

A camping place of the Israelites (Nu 33:19-20).

RIMMON, ROCK OF (*pomegranate rock*). The fortress to which 600 Benjamites fled after escaping slaughter (Jdg 20:45,47; 21:13), near Gibeah.

RIMMONO [8237]. *See Rimmon, 3.*

RING [2597, 3192, 5690, 6584, 10536, *1234, 5993*].

NIV+ RANG, RINGED, RINGS

Of gold (Nu 31:50). Worn as a sign of office (Ge 41:42).

Given as a token (Est 3:10,12; 8:2-10). Worn in the nose (Pr 11:22; Isa 3:21). Offerings of, to the tabernacle (Ex 35:22; Nu 31:50).

RINGSTRAKED See Streaked.

RINNAH [8263] (ringing cry [of joy] to Yahweh). A son of Shimon (1Ch 4:20).

RIOT [189, 2572, 2573, 5087].
NIV+ RIOTERS, RIOTING, RIOTS

To squander in evil ways (Pr 23:20; 28:7), waste (Tit 1:6; 1Pe 4:4), revelry (Ro 13:13), luxury (2Pe 2:13).

RIPHATH [8196]. A son of Gomer (Ge 10:3; 1Ch 1:6).

RISING [*2436, 3655, 4667, 5951, 6590, 6590, 6641, 7756, 8123, 10624, 414, 422, 424, 482, 1586].
NIV+ ARISE, ARISEN, ARISES, AROSE, RAISE, RAISED, RAISES, RAISING, RISE, RISEN, RISES, ROSE, UPRAISED, UPRISING

Early:
(Pr 31:15). For devotions (Ps 5:3; 59:16; 63:1; 88:13; SS 7:12; Isa 26:9). Practiced by the wicked (Pr 27:14; Mic 2:1; Zep 3:7), by drunkards (Isa 5:11). Illustrates spiritual diligence (Ro 13:11-12).

Instances of:
Lot (Ge 19:23). Abraham (Ge 19:27; 21:14; 22:3). Isaac (Ge 26:31). Abimelech (Ge 20:8). Jacob (Ge 28:18; 32:31). Laban (Ge 31:55). Moses (Ex 8:20; 9:13). Joshua (Jos 3:1; 6:12,15; 7:16). Gideon (Jdg 6:38). Elkanah (1Sa 1:19). Samuel (1Sa 15:12). David (1Sa 17:20). Mary (Mk 16:2; Lk 24:1). Apostles (Ac 5:21).
See Industry.

Late:
Consequences of (Pr 6:9-11; 24:33-34).
See Idleness; Slothfulness.

RISSAH [8267] (dew ISBE). Encampment of Israelites in the wilderness (Nu 33:21-22), site unknown.

RITHMAH [8414] ([place of] broom plants). A camping place of the Israelites (Nu 33:18-19).

RIVER [3284, 3542, 3720, 4784, 5045, 5643, 5707, 10468, 4532].
NIV+ RIVERBANK, RIVERBED, RIVERS

May refer to large streams (Ge 2:10-14), the Nile (Ge 41:1; 2Ki 19:24), a winter torrent, the bed of which is dry during summer (Am 6:14), fountain stream (Ps 119:136).

Figurative:
Of salvation (Ps 36:8; 46:4; Isa 32:2; Eze 47:1-12; Rev 22:1-2). Of grief (Ps 119:136; La 3:48).

RIVER OF EGYPT [3284, 5643, 5707].
1. The Brook or Wadi of Egypt on the SW border of Israel, flowing into the Mediterranean Sea (Ge 15:18; Nu 34:5; 2Ki 24:7; Isa 27:12), probably modern Wadi el-Arish, though some identify it with the Nile.
2. The Nile (Am 8:8; 9:5).
See Egypt; Nile.

RIVERS [3284, 5643, 5707, 4532].
NIV+ See RIVER

Names of: Abana (2Ki 5:12). Arnon (Dt 2:36). Kebar (Eze 1:1). Euphrates (Ge 2:14). Gozan (2Ki 17:6; 1Ch 5:26). Jordan. See Jordan. Kanah (Jos 16:8). Kishon (Jdg 5:21). Of Egypt (Ex 1:22). Pharpar (2Ki 5:12). Pishon (Ge 2:11). Tigris (Ge 2:14). Ulai (Da 8:16).

RIZIA [8359] (possibly pleasant one KB). An Asherite (1Ch 7:39).

RIZPAH [8366] (heated stones, live coals). Concubine of Saul (2Sa 3:7). Guards the bodies of her sons hanged by command of David (2Sa 21:8-11).

ROADS [784, 2006, 3718, 4618, 5019, 5986, 7483, 1451, 2853, 3847].
NIV+ CROSSROADS, ROAD, ROADSIDE

May refer to paths or highways; hundreds of allusions to roads in the Bible; road robbers quite common (Mt 11:10; Lk 10:30), Romans built highways throughout the empire, some of which are still in use; used by traders, travelers, and armies; Paul used Roman roads on his missionary journeys; the statement "All roads lead to Rome" shows how well provided the Roman empire was with roads. *See Highways.*

ROBBERS [7265, 8720, 774, 3334].
NIV+ See ROB

(Pr 1:11-16). Dens of (Jer 7:11). Bands of (Hos 6:9; 7:1).

ROBBERY [1024, 1608+1611, 1608+1610, 1610, 7693].
NIV+ ROB, ROBBED, ROBBER, ROBBERS, ROBBING, ROBS

Illegal seizure of another's property; forbidden by law (Lev 19:13); highways unsafe (Jdg 5:6; Lk 10:30; 2Co 11:26); houses built to resist robbers; even priests sometimes turned to pillage (Hos 6:9); denounced by prophets (Isa 61:8; Eze 22:29); withholding tithes and offerings from God's storehouse regarded as robbery (Mal 3:8). *See Theft.*

ROBE [*168, 955, 4189, 4230, 4252, 4860, 5077, 8515, 10517, 2264, 2668, 4525, 5124, 5948].
NIV+ ROBED, ROBES

Of righteousness (2Ch 6:41; Isa 61:10; Rev 6:11; 7:9,13). Parable of the man who was not dressed in a wedding garment (Mt 22:11).
See Dress.

ROBINSON'S ARCH The remains of ancient Jerusalem masonry, named for the American archaeologist Edward Robinson, who discovered it in 1838. Giant stones, projecting from the SW wall of the temple enclosure are evidently part of an arch that in Herod's time supported a monumental stairway.

ROBOAM See Rehoboam, 2.

ROCK [74, 1643, 2734, 4091, 6152, 7446, 10006, 3292, 4376, 5536+5550].
NIV+ ROCKS, ROCKY

Struck by Moses for water (Dt 8:15; Ps 78:15-16,20). Houses in (Jer 49:16; Ob 3; Mt 7:24-25). Oil from (Job 29:6; Dt 32:13). Name of deity (Dt 32:4).

Figurative:
(2Sa 22:32,47; 23:3; Ps 18:2; 31:2; 40:2; Isa 17:10; 32:2; Mt 16:18; 1Co 10:4).

ROD [2643, 4751, 4962, 7866, 8657, 2812, 4811].
NIV+ RODS

Branch, stick, staff; symbol of authority (Ex 4:2,17,20; 9:23; 14:16), discipline symbolized by rod (Mic 5:1), messianic ruler (Isa 11:1), affliction (Job 9:34).

ROD OF AARON (Ex 7:9-10,12,15,19-20; 8:5,16-17; Nu 17:6,8,10; Heb 9:4).

ROD OF CORRECTION (Ps 89:32; Pr 10:13; 13:24; 22:15; 23:14; 26:3; 29:15; La 3:1).

ROD OF MOSES (Ex 4:2,17,20; 7:19; 8:16; 9:23; 10:13; 14:16; 17:5,9).

RODANIM [8102] (*people of Rhodes*). The son of Javan; most manuscripts of the Masoretic Text have *Dodanim* (Ge 10:4, ftn). Tribe descended from Javan, son of Japheth (1Ch 1:7).

RODENTS [2923]. (Isa 2:20). *See Animals; Rat(s).*

ROE DEER [3502].
NIV+ DEER, ROEBUCKS
Permitted as food (Dt 14:5). *See Deer.*

ROGELIM [8082] (*[place of] treaders, fullers [one who cleans clothes by kneading with no soap]*). A town near Mahanaim whose citizens assisted David (2Sa 17:27, 29; 19:31).

ROHGAH [8108]. Son of Shomer (1Ch 7:34).

ROI *See Beer Lahai Roi.*

ROLL [1670, 1676, 1723, 6015, 7147, 7571+7572, 7886, 8740, *653, 1813, 3244, 4685, 4771*].
NIV+ ROLLED, ROLLING, ROLLS
Sheets of papyrus or parchment (made of skin) sewn together to make a long sheet of writing material which was wound around a stick to make a scroll (Isa 34:4; Jer 36; Eze 3:1-3; Rev 5; 10:1-10).

ROLLER NIV "splint" (Eze 30:21).

ROMAMTI-EZER [8251] (*[he is my] highest help*). Son of Heman (1Ch 25:4,31).

ROMAN EMPIRE
NIV+ ROME
A city of Rome founded in 753 B.C.; a monarchy until 509 B.C.; a republic from 509 to 31 B.C.; the empire began in 31 B.C., fell in the fifth century A.D. Rome extended its hold over all Italy and eventually over the whole Mediterranean world, Gaul, half of Britain, the Rhine-Danube rivers, and as far as Parthia. Augustus, the first Roman emperor, divided the Roman provinces into senatorial districts, which were ruled by proconsuls (Ac 13:7; 18:12; 19:38), and imperial districts ruled by governors (Mt 27:2; Lk 2:2; Ac 23:24). Moral corruption was among the causes of the decline and fall of the Roman Empire. Roman reservoirs, aqueducts, roads, public buildings, statues survive. Many Roman officials are referred to in the NT, including the emperors Augustus (Lk 2:1), Tiberius (Lk 3:1), Claudius (Ac 11:28), and Nero (Ac 25:11-12).

ROMANS, EPISTLE TO THE
Author: The Apostle Paul
Date: Probably written in the early spring of A.D. 57
Outline:
I. Introduction (1:1-15).
II. Theme: Righteousness from God (1:16-17).
III. The Unrighteousness of All Mankind (1:18-3:20).
 A. Gentiles (1:18-32).
 B. Jews (2:1-3:8).
 C. Summary: All People (3:9-20).
IV. Righteousness Imputed: Justification (3:21-5:21).
 A. Through Christ (3:21-26).
 B. Received by Faith (3:27-4:25).
  1. The principle established (3:27-31).
  2. The principle illustrated (ch. 4).
 C. The Fruits of Righteousness (5:1-11).
 D. Summary: Man's Unrighteousness Contrasted with God's Gift of Righteousness (5:12-21).
V. Righteousness Imparted: Sanctification (chs. 6-8).
 A. Freedom from Sin's Tyranny (ch. 6).
 B. Freedom from the Law's Condemnation (ch. 7).
 C. Life in the Power of the Holy Spirit (ch. 8).
VI. God's Righteousness Vindicated: The Problem of the Rejection of Israel (chs. 9-11).
 A. The Justice of the Rejection (9:1-29).
 B. The Cause of the Rejection (9:30-10:21).
 C. Facts That Lessen the Difficulty (ch. 11).
  1. The rejection is not total (11:1-10).
  2. The rejection is not final (11:11-24).
  3. God's ultimate purpose is mercy (11:25-36).
VII. Righteousness Practiced (12:1-15:13).
 A. In the Body—the Church (ch. 12).
 B. In the World (ch. 13).
 C. Among Weak and Strong Christians (14:1-15:13).
VIII. Conclusion (15:14-33).
IX. Commendation and Greetings (ch. 16).

ROME [*4871, 4873*].
NIV+ ROMAN, ROMANS
The capital of the Roman Empire. The Jews were excluded from Rome by Claudius (Ac 18:2). Paul's visit to Rome. *See Paul.* Visited by Onesiphorus (2Ti 1:16-17). Paul desires to preach in (Ro 1:15). Abominations in (Ro 1:18-32). Christians in (Ro 16:5-17; Php 1:12-18; 4:22; 2Ti 4:21).

ROOF [1511, 2674, 4918, 6264, 7415, 7771, 7815, *1560, 5094*].
NIV+ ROOFED, ROOFING, ROOFS
See House, Architecture of.

ROOM [*1074, 2540, 4384, 5226, 6608, 7521, *333, 2906, 5008, 5421, 5536, 5673, 6003*].
NIV+ ROOMS, STOREROOM, STOREROOMS
1. Chamber in a house (Ac 1:13). Used as a place for private prayer (Mt 6:6).
2. Place or position in society (Mt 23:6; Lk 14:7-8; 20:46).

ROOSTER [2435+5516, *232*]. Stately in its stride (Pr 30:31). Its crowing a sign of Peter's denial of Jesus (Mt 26:34,74-75; Mk 13:35; 14:30,68,72).

ROOT [4035, 9245+, 9247, 10743, *1748, 4844, 4845*].
NIV+ ROOTED, ROOTS
Usually used in a figurative sense.
1. Essential cause of something (1Ti 6:10).
2. Foundation or support of something (2Ki 19:20; Job 5:3).
3. Injured roots means loss of life or vitality (Job 31:12; Isa 5:24).
4. Root of Jesse and Root of David, messianic titles (Isa 11:10; Ro 15:12; Rev 5:5; 22:16). *See Titles and Names, Of Jesus.*

ROPE [2475, 4593, 4798, 5940, 6310, *1069, 2415, 5389*].

NIV+ ROPES

Threefold (Ecc 4:12). Worn on the head as an emblem of servitude (1Ki 20:31-32). Used in casting lots (Mic 2:5).

Figurative:

Of love (Hos 11:4). Of affliction (Job 36:8). Of temptations (Ps 140:5; Pr 5:22).

ROSE [*2483]. Or "crocus" (SS 2:1; Isa 35:1).

ROSETTA STONE Inscribed basalt slab, found on Rosetta branch of the Nile in 1799, with text in hieroglyphics, demotic (a cursive Egyptian language), and Greek. It furnished the key for the decipherment of Egyptian hieroglyphics.

ROSH [8033] (*head, leader*).

1. Son of Benjamin (Ge 46:21).
2. Chief of three nations that are to invade Israel during the latter days (Eze 38:2; 39:1).

ROW, ROWERS

NIV+ ROWED, ROWS

See Ship.

RUBY [138, 3905, 7165].

NIV+ RUBIES

A precious stone (Job 28:18; Pr 20:15; 31:10; La 4:7; Eze 27:16). In the priestly breastplate (Ex 28:17; 39:10). In the Garden of Eden (Eze 28:13).

See Minerals of the Bible, 1; Sardius; Stones.

RUDDER(S) [4382]. Used to steer a ship (Ac 27:40; Jas 3:4).

RUDDY [131, 137, 145]. Red or fair complexion (1Sa 16:12).

RUDE [858] (*untrained, ignorant of rules*). Technically not trained (2Co 11:6).

RUDIMENTS (*first principles or elements of anything*). Elements (Gal 4:3,9; 2Pe 3:10,12), first principles (Heb 5:12), physical elements of the world (2Pe 3:10,12).

RUE [4379]. (Lk 11:42).

RUFUS [4859] (*red haired*).

1. Brother of Alexander and son of Simon of Cyrene who bore the cross (Mk 15:21).
2. Friend of Paul (Ro 16:13).

RUHAMAH (*pitied*). A symbolic name of Israel used to indicate the return of God's mercy (Hos 2:1; cf Ro 9:25-26; 1Pe 2:10). A play on words is involved, for the second child of Gomer, wife of Hosea, was called Lo-Ruhamah, denoting a time when God had turned his back on Israel because of her apostasy. The NT references apply to Gentiles coming into the Church (Ro 9:25-26; 1Pe 2:10).

See Lo-Ammi; Lo-Ruhamah.

RULERS [*380, 5440, 5592, 5601, 5618, 5954, 6249, 7903, 8142, 8569, 8954, 9149, 10715, *794, 801, 807, 1541, 2451*].

NIV+ RULE, RULED, RULER, RULER'S, RULES, RULING

Appointed and removed by God. *See Government, God in.*

Chastised (Da 4). *See Nation.*

Monarchical. *See Kings.*

Patriarchal (Ge 27:29,37). Instances of: Nimrod (Ge 10:8-10). Abraham (Ge 14:13-24; 17:6; 21:21-32). Melchizedek (Ge 14:18). Isaac (Ge 26:26-31). Judah (Ge 38:24). Heads of families (Ex 6:14). Ishmael (Ge 17:20). Esau and the chiefs of Edom (Ge 36).

Theocratic. *See Government.*

Ordained of God (2Ch 9:8; Ro 13:1-2,4; 1Pe 2:14). Appointed by God (1Sa 9:15-17; 10:1; 15:17; 16:1,7,13; 2Sa 7:13-16; 1Ki 14:14; 16:1-4; 1Ch 28:4-5; 29:25; Ps 89:19-37; Da 2:21,37; 5:21; Ac 13:22). Accountable to God (2Ch 19:6-7).

Servants of the people (1Ki 12:7; 2Ch 10:7; Eze 34:2-4). Loyalty to, commanded (Eze 7:26). Must not be reviled (Ex 22:28; 2Sa 16:9; 19:21; Ecc 10:20; Ac 23:5; 2Pe 2:10-11; Jude 8).

Righteous, beloved (Pr 29:2,14). Incompetent, oppress (Pr 28:16). Corrupted, by evil counselors (Pr 25:5), by gifts (Pr 29:4; Isa 1:23; Am 5:11-12; Mic 7:3).

Should not drink wine (Pr 31:4-5). Forbidden to take bribes (Ex 23:8; Dt 16:19), to show partiality (Lev 19:15; Dt 1:17; 16:19; Pr 24:23).

Required to judge justly (Ex 18:16,20-21; 23:3,6-7,9; Lev 19:15; 24:22; Dt 1:16-17; 25:1; 2Ch 9:8; Ps 82:2-4; Pr 31:9; Isa 16:5; 58:6; Jer 22:2-3; Zec 7:9-10; 8:16). A terror to evildoers (Pr 14:35; Ro 13:3).

Mosaic law concerning atonement for sins of (Lev 4:22-26).

Character and Qualifications of:

(Nu 27:16-17; 2Sa 23:4)

Pr 20:8 When a king sits on his throne to judge, he winnows out all evil with his eyes.

Pr 20:26 A wise king winnows out the wicked; he drives the threshing wheel over them.

Pr 20:28 Love and faithfulness keep a king safe; through love his throne is made secure.

Diligent—

Ro 12:8 if it is encouraging, let him encourage; if it is contributing to the needs of others, let him give generously; if it is leadership, let him govern diligently; if it is showing mercy, let him do it cheerfully.

Wise—

Ge 41:33 "And now let Pharaoh look for a discerning and wise man and put him in charge of the land of Egypt.

Dt 1:13 Choose some wise, understanding and respected men from each of your tribes, and I will set them over you."

Ps 2:10 Therefore, you kings, be wise; be warned, you rulers of the earth. (+Pr 20:26)

Pr 28:2 When a country is rebellious, it has many rulers, but a man of understanding and knowledge maintains order.

Merciful—

Isa 16:5 In love a throne will be established; in faithfulness a man will sit on it—one from the house of David—one who in judging seeks justice and speeds the cause of righteousness. (+Zec 7:9)

Required to know the law (Jos 1:8)—

Ezr 7:25 And you, Ezra, in accordance with the wisdom of your God, which you possess, appoint magistrates and judges to administer justice to all the people of Trans-Euphrates—all who know the laws of your God. And you are to teach any who do not know them.

Required to fear the Lord—

Ps 2:11 Serve the LORD with fear and rejoice with trembling.

Required to be truthful—

Pr 17:7 Arrogant lips are unsuited to a fool—how much worse lying lips to a ruler!

Required to be righteous—

Ex 18:21 But select capable men from all the people—men who fear God, trustworthy men who hate dishonest gain—and appoint them as officials over thousands, hundreds, fifties and tens.

Dt 16:19 Do not pervert justice or show partiality. Do not accept a bribe, for a bribe blinds the eyes of the wise and twists the words of the righteous.

Dt 27:19 "Cursed is the man who withholds justice from the alien, the fatherless or the widow." Then all the people shall say, "Amen!"

2Sa 23:3 The God of Israel spoke, the Rock of Israel said to me: 'When one rules over men in righteousness, when he rules in the fear of God, ⁴he is like the light of morning at sunrise on a cloudless morning, like the brightness after rain that brings the grass from the earth.'

Pr 16:10 The lips of a king speak as an oracle, and his mouth should not betray justice.

Pr 16:12 Kings detest wrongdoing, for a throne is established through righteousness.

Duties of:

To rule in righteousness—

Isa 58:6 "Is not this the kind of fasting I have chosen: to loose the chains of injustice and untie the cords of the yoke, to set the oppressed free and break every yoke?

Jer 22:1 This is what the LORD says: "Go down to the palace of the king of Judah and proclaim this message there: ²'Hear the word of the LORD, O king of Judah, you who sit on David's throne—you, your officials and your people who come through these gates. ³This is what the LORD says: Do what is just and right. Rescue from the hand of his oppressor the one who has been robbed. Do no wrong or violence to the alien, the fatherless or the widow, and do not shed innocent blood in this place.

To be judges—

2Ch 9:8 Praise be to the LORD your God, who has delighted in you and placed you on his throne as king to rule for the LORD your God. Because of the love of your God for Israel and his desire to uphold them forever, he has made you king over them, to maintain justice and righteousness."

To judge according to law—

Dt 17:18 When he takes the throne of his kingdom, he is to write for himself on a scroll a copy of this law, taken from that of the priests, who are Levites. ¹⁹It is to be with him, and he is to read it all the days of his life so that he may learn to revere the LORD his God and follow carefully all the words of this law and these decrees

Jos 1:7 Be strong and very courageous. Be careful to obey all the law my servant Moses gave you; do not turn from it to the right or to the left, that you may be successful wherever you go. ⁸Do not let this Book of the Law depart from your mouth; meditate on it day and night, so that you may be careful to do everything written in it. Then you will be prosperous and successful.

In judicial functions to make thorough investigations—

Dt 19:18 The judges must make a thorough investigation, and if the witness proves to be a liar, giving false testimony against his brother, ¹⁹then do to him as he intended to do to his brother. You must purge the evil from among you.

Righteous:

Instances of: Pharaoh, in his treatment of Abraham (Ge 12:15-20). Abimelech, in his treatment of Abraham (Ge 20), of Isaac (Ge 26:6-11). Joseph, in his conduct of the affairs of Egypt (Ge 41:37-57). Pharaoh, in his treatment of Jacob and his family (Ge 47:5-10; 50:1-6). Moses, in his administration of the affairs of the Israelites (Nu 16:15). *See Government, Mosaic.* Samuel, in not taking reward for judgment (1Sa 12:3-4). Saul, after the defeat of the Ammonites (1Sa 11:12-13). Solomon, in his judgment between the two women who claimed the same child (1Ki 3:16-28), according to the testimony of the queen of Sheba (1Ki 10:6-9). Asa, in abolishing sodomy and other abominations of idolatry (1Ki 15:11-15; 2Ch 14:2-5). Jehoshaphat, in walking in the ways of the Lord (1Ki 22:41-46; 2Ch 17:3-10; 19; 20:3-30). Hezekiah, in his fear of the Lord (2Ki 18:3; 20:1-11; 2Ch 30; 31). Josiah, in repairing the temple and in other good works (2Ki 22; 23; 2Ch 34; 35). Cyrus, in emancipating the Jews (Ezr 1). Darius, in advancing the rebuilding of the temple (Ezr 6:1-12). Artaxerxes, in commissioning Ezra to restore the forms of worship at Jerusalem (Ezr 7; Ne 2; 5:14). Nehemiah (Ne 4; 5). Daniel. *See Daniel.* King of Nineveh, in repenting and proclaiming a fast (Jnh 3:6-9).

Wicked:

Ne 9:34 Our kings, our leaders, our priests and our fathers did not follow your law; they did not pay attention to your commands or the warnings you gave them. ³⁵Even while they were in their kingdom, enjoying your great goodness to them in the spacious and fertile land you gave them, they did not serve you or turn from their evil ways.

³⁶"But see, we are slaves today, slaves in the land you gave our forefathers so they could eat its fruit and the other good things it produces. ³⁷Because of our sins, its abundant harvest goes to the kings you have placed over us. They rule over our bodies and our cattle as they please. We are in great distress.

Ps 58:1 Do you rulers indeed speak justly? Do you judge uprightly among men? ²No, in your heart you devise injustice, and your hands mete out violence on the earth.

Ps 82:2 "How long will you defend the unjust and show partiality to the wicked? *Selah*

Ps 94:20 Can a corrupt throne be allied with you—one that brings on misery by its decrees? ²¹They band together against the righteous and condemn the innocent to death.

Ecc 3:16 And I saw something else under the sun:

In the place of judgment—wickedness was there, in the place of justice—wickedness was there.

¹⁷I thought in my heart, "God will bring to judgment both the righteous and the wicked, for there will be a time for every activity, a time for every deed."

Ecc 5:8 If you see the poor oppressed in a district, and justice and rights denied, do not be surprised at such things; for one official is eyed by a higher one, and over them both are others higher still.

Isa 5:7 The vineyard of the LORD Almighty is the house of Israel, and the men of Judah are the garden of his delight. And he looked for justice, but saw bloodshed; for righteousness, but heard cries of distress.

Isa 28:14 Therefore hear the word of the LORD, you scoffers who rule this people in Jerusalem. ¹⁵You boast, "We have entered into a covenant with death, with the grave we have made an agreement. When an overwhelming scourge sweeps by, it cannot touch us, for we have made a lie our refuge and falsehood our hiding place."

Hos 7:3 "They delight the king with their wickedness, the princes with their lies."

Oppress the people—

Ex 3:9 And now the cry of the Israelites has reached me, and I have seen the way the Egyptians are oppressing them.

1Sa 8:10 Samuel told all the words of the LORD to the people who were asking him for a king. ¹¹He said, "This is what the king who will reign over you will do: He will take your sons and make them serve with his chariots and horses, and they will run in front of his chariots. ¹²Some he will assign to be commanders of thousands and commanders of fifties, and others to plow his ground and reap his harvest, and still others to make weapons of war and equipment for his chariots. ¹³He will take your daughters to be perfumers and cooks and bakers. ¹⁴He will take the best of your fields and vineyards and olive groves and give them to his attendants. ¹⁵He will take a tenth of your grain and of your vintage and give it to his officials and attendants. ¹⁶Your menservants and maidservants and the best of your cattle and donkeys he will take for his own use. ¹⁷He will take a tenth of your flocks, and you yourselves will become his slaves. ¹⁸When that day comes, you will cry out for relief from the king you have chosen, and the LORD will not answer you in that day."

Job 35:9 "Men cry out under a load of oppression; they plead for relief from the arm of the powerful.

Pr 28:15 Like a roaring lion or a charging bear is a wicked man ruling over a helpless people.

¹⁶A tyrannical ruler lacks judgment, but he who hates ill-gotten gain will enjoy a long life. (+Am 4:1; 5:11-12)

Pervert justice—

Dt 27:19 "Cursed is the man who withholds justice from the alien, the fatherless or the widow." Then all the people shall say, "Amen!"

Cause people to mourn (Pr 29:2)—

Ecc 4:1 Again I looked and saw all the oppression that was taking place under the sun: I saw the tears of the oppressed—and they have no comforter; power was on the side of their oppressors—and they have no comforter.

A public calamity—

Ecc 10:16 Woe to you, O land whose king was a servant and whose princes feast in the morning. (+Isa 5:22-23)

An abomination to God—

Pr 17:15 Acquitting the guilty and condemning the innocent—the LORD detests them both.

Abhorred by men (Pr 21:24)—

Pr 29:2 When the righteous thrive, the people rejoice; when the wicked rule, the people groan.

Admonitions to—

Eze 34:2 "Son of man, prophesy against the shepherds of Israel; prophesy and say to them: 'This is what the Sovereign LORD says: Woe to the shepherds of Israel who only take care of themselves! Should not shepherds take care of the flock? ³You eat the curds, clothe yourselves with the wool and slaughter the choice animals, but you do not take care of the flock. ⁴You have not strengthened the weak or healed the sick or bound up the injured. You have not brought back the strays or searched for the lost. You have ruled them harshly and brutally.

Eze 34:7 " 'Therefore, you shepherds, hear the word of the LORD: ⁸As surely as I live, declares the Sovereign LORD, because my flock lacks a shepherd and so has been plundered and has become food for all the wild animals, and because my shepherds did not search for my flock but

cared for themselves rather than for my flock, ⁹therefore, O shepherds, hear the word of the LORD: ¹⁰This is what the Sovereign LORD says: I am against the shepherds and will hold them accountable for my flock. I will remove them from tending the flock so that the shepherds can no longer feed themselves. I will rescue my flock from their mouths, and it will no longer be food for them.

Eze 45:9 " 'This is what the Sovereign LORD says: You have gone far enough, O princes of Israel! Give up your violence and oppression and do what is just and right. Stop dispossessing my people, declares the Sovereign LORD.

Denounced (Eze 34:2-4,7-10)—

Am 4:1 Hear this word, you cows of Bashan on Mount Samaria, you women who oppress the poor and crush the needy and say to your husbands, "Bring us some drinks!" ²The Sovereign LORD has sworn by his holiness: "The time will surely come when you will be taken away with hooks, the last of you with fishhooks.

Mic 3:1 Then I said, "Listen, you leaders of Jacob, you rulers of the house of Israel. Should you not know justice, ²you who hate good and love evil; who tear the skin from my people and the flesh from their bones; ³who eat my people's flesh, strip off their skin and break their bones in pieces; who chop them up like meat for the pan, like flesh for the pot?"

Mic 3:9 Hear this, you leaders of the house of Jacob, you rulers of the house of Israel, who despise justice and distort all that is right; ¹⁰who build Zion with bloodshed, and Jerusalem with wickedness. ¹¹Her leaders judge for a bribe, her priests teach for a price, and her prophets tell fortunes for money. Yet they lean upon the LORD and say, "Is not the LORD among us? No disaster will come upon us."

Zep 3:3 Her officials are roaring lions, her rulers are evening wolves, who leave nothing for the morning.

Divine judgment upon—

Isa 3:14 The LORD enters into judgment against the elders and leaders of his people: "It is you who have ruined my vineyard; the plunder from the poor is in your houses. ¹⁵What do you mean by crushing my people and grinding the faces of the poor?" declares the Lord, the LORD Almighty.

Isa 10:1 Woe to those who make unjust laws, to those who issue oppressive decrees, ²to deprive the poor of their rights and withhold justice from the oppressed of my people, making widows their prey and robbing the fatherless. ³What will you do on the day of reckoning, when disaster comes from afar? To whom will you run for help? Where will you leave your riches?

Isa 30:33 Topheth has long been prepared; it has been made ready for the king. Its fire pit has been made deep and wide, with an abundance of fire and wood; the breath of the LORD, like a stream of burning sulfur, sets it ablaze.

Isa 40:23 He brings princes to naught and reduces the rulers of this world to nothing.

Jer 5:28 and have grown fat and sleek. Their evil deeds have no limit; they do not plead the case of the fatherless to win it, they do not defend the rights of the poor. ²⁹Should I not punish them for this?" declares the LORD. "Should I not avenge myself on such a nation as this?

Eze 21:25 " 'O profane and wicked prince of Israel, whose day has come, whose time of punishment has reached its climax, ²⁶this is what the Sovereign LORD says: Take off the turban, remove the crown. It will not be as it was: The lowly will be exalted and the exalted will be brought low.

Hos 5:10 Judah's leaders are like those who move

boundary stones. I will pour out my wrath on them like a flood of water.

Am 5:11 You trample on the poor and force him to give you grain. Therefore, though you have built stone mansions, you will not live in them; though you have planted lush vineyards, you will not drink their wine. ¹²For I know how many are your offenses and how great your sins. You oppress the righteous and take bribes and you deprive the poor of justice in the courts.

Zep 1:8 On the day of the LORD's sacrifice I will punish the princes and the king's sons and all those clad in foreign clothes.

Instances of—

Potiphar, putting Joseph into prison (Ge 39:20, w 40:15). Pharaoh, oppressing the Israelites (Ex 1-11). Adoni-Bezek, torturing seventy kings (Jdg 1:7). Abimelech, slaying his seventy brothers (Jdg 9:1-5). Eli's sons, desecrating the sacrifices (1Sa 2:12-17), debauching themselves and the worshipers (1Sa 2:22). Samuel's sons, taking bribes (1Sa 8:1-5).

Saul, sparing Agag and the best of the booty (1Sa 15:8-35), in jealousy plotting against David (1Sa 18:8-29), seeking to slay David (1Sa 19), slaying Ahimelech and the priests (1Sa 22:7-19), Hanun, mistreating David's servants (2Sa 10:4; 1Ch 19:2-5). David, numbering Israel and Judah (2Sa 24:1-9; 1Ch 21:1-7; 27:23-24). Solomon, luxurious and idolatrous (1Ki 11:1-13), oppressing the people (1Ki 12:4; 4:7-23). Rehoboam, making the yoke heavy (1Ki 12:8-11; 2Ch 10:1-15).

Jeroboam, perverting the true worship (1Ki 12:26-33; 13:1-5; 14:16), exalting wicked persons to the priesthood (1Ki 12:31; 13:33; 2Ki 17:32; 2Ch 11:14-15; Eze 44:7, w Nu 3:10). Abijah, walking in the sins of Rehoboam (1Ki 15:3). Nadab, walking in the ways of Jeroboam (1Ki 15:26). Baasha, walking in the ways of Jeroboam (1Ki 15:33-34). Asa, imprisoning the seer and oppressing the people (2Ch 16:10). Zimri, walking in the ways of Jeroboam (1Ki 16:19). Omri, walking in the ways of Jeroboam (1Ki 16:25-29). Ahab, serving Baal (1Ki 16:30-33; 21:21-26), confiscating Naboth's vineyard (1Ki 21, w 1Sa 8:14; 1Ki 22:38; 2Ki 9:26). Jehoram, following the sins of Jeroboam (2Ki 3:2-3). Hazael, committing atrocities (2Ki 8:12; 10:32; 12:17; 13:3-7). Jehoram, walking in the ways of the kings of Israel (2Ki 8:18; 2Ch 21:13). Jehu, did not depart from the sins of Jeroboam (2Ki 10:29). Jehoahaz, in following the sins of Jeroboam (2Ki 13:1-2). Jehoash, in following the wicked example of Jeroboam (2Ki 13:10-11). Jeroboam II, not departing from the sins of Jeroboam (2Ki 14:23-24). Zechariah, Menahem, Pekahiah, and Pekah, following the sins of Jeroboam (2Ki 15:9,18,24,28), conspiring against and slaying Pekahiah (2Ki 15:25). Hoshea, who conspired against Pekah (2Ki 15:30), in permitting Baal worship (2Ki 17:1-2,7-18). Ahaz, burning his children in idolatrous sacrifice (2Ki 16:3; 2Ch 28:2-4).

Manasseh, who committed the abominations of the heathen (2Ki 21:1-17; 2Ch 33:2-7). Amon, who followed the evil example of Manasseh (2Ki 21:19-22). Jehoahaz, who followed in the ways of his fathers (2Ki 23:32). Jehoiakim, in walking in the ways of his fathers (2Ki 23:37), and Jehoiachin (2Ki 24:9). Zedekiah, following the evil example of Jehoiakim (2Ki 24:19; 2Ch 36:12-13) and persecuting Jeremiah (Jer 38:5-6). Joash, killing

Zechariah (2Ch 24:2,17-25). Ahaziah, doing evil like the house of Ahab (2Ch 22:1-9). Amaziah, worshiping the gods of Seir (2Ch 25:14). Uzziah, invading the priest's office (2Ch 26:16).

Xerxes and Haman, decreeing the death of the Jews (Est 3). Nebuchadnezzar, commanding to destroy the wise men (Da 2:1-13), and committing the three Hebrews to the furnace (Da 3:1-23). Belshazzar, in drunkenness and committing sacrilege (Da 5:22-23). Darius, in deifying himself (Da 6:7,9). The princes, conspiring against Daniel (Da 6:1-9).

Herod the Great, slaying the children in Bethlehem (Mt 2:16-18). Herod Antipas, in beheading John the Baptist (Mt 14:1-11), in craftiness and tyranny (Lk 13:31-32; 23:6-15). Herod Agrippa, persecuting the church (Ac 12:1-19). Pilate, delivering Jesus for crucifixion (Mt 27:11-26; Mk 15:15). Chief priests, elders, and all the council, seeking false witness against Jesus (Mt 26:59). Ananias, commanding that Paul be struck (Ac 23:2).

See Government; Judge; Kings.

RUMAH [8126] (*height*). Home of Pedaiah, whose daughter Zebidah bore Jehoiakim to Josiah, king of Judah (2Ki 23:36), perhaps Arumah near Shechem, or Rumah in Galilee.

RUNNER [*5938, 8132, 5556]. A bodyguard running before kings and princes (1Sa 8:11; 2Sa 15:1; 1Ki 1:5). An athlete (Job 9:25; 1Co 9:24). *See Army; Games.*

RUSH [*6068]. A water plant (Isa 19:6). *See Plants of the Bible; Reed.*

RUTH [8134, 4858] (*friendship* BDB; *refreshed [as with water]* IDB; possibly *comrade, companion* ISBE). A Moabitess who married a son of Elimelech and Naomi of Bethlehem (Ru 1:1-4), ancestor of Christ (Mt 1:5), the Book of Ruth is about her.

RUTH, BOOK OF

Author: Anonymous, Jewish tradition points to Samuel

Date: During the period of the monarchy.

Outline:

I. Introduction: Naomi Emptied (1:1-5).

II. Naomi Returns from Moab (1:6-22).

  A. Ruth Clings to Naomi (1:6-18).

  B. Ruth and Naomi Return to Bethlehem (1:19-22).

III. Ruth and Boaz Meet in the Harvest Fields (ch. 2).

  A. Ruth Begins Work (2:1-7).

  B. Boaz Shows Kindness to Ruth (2:8-16).

  C. Ruth Returns to Naomi (2:17-23).

IV. Ruth Goes to Boaz at the Threshing Floor (ch. 3).

  A. Naomi Instructs Ruth (3:1-5).

  B. Boaz Pledges to Secure Redemption (3:6-15).

  C. Ruth Returns to Naomi (3:16-18).

V. Boaz Arranges to Marry Ruth (4:1-12).

  A. Boaz Confronts the Unnamed Kinsman (4:1-8).

  B. Boaz Buys Naomi's Property and Announces His Marriage to Ruth (4:9-12).

VI. Conclusion: Naomi Filled (4:13-17).

VII. Epilogue: Genealogy of David (4:18-22).

RYE *See Spelt.*

S

SABACHTHANI [4876] *See Eloi, Eloi, Lama Sabach-thani.*

SABAEANS *See Sabeans; Seba.*

SABAOTH, LORD OF [7372, 4877] (*Yahweh of [angelic] armies*). Regularly translated "LORD Almighty" in the NIV. *See Almighty; God, Names of, Yahweh Tsabbaoth.*

SABBATH [*8701, 4640, 4878, 4879] (*cease, rest*).
NIV+ SABBATHS, SABBATH-REST

A Time of Rest:
Ge 2:2 By the seventh day God had finished the work he had been doing; so on the seventh day he rested from all his work. ³And God blessed the seventh day and made it holy, because on it he rested from all the work of creating that he had done. (+Lev 23:25)
Lev 26:34 Then the land will enjoy its sabbath years all the time that it lies desolate and you are in the country of your enemies; then the land will rest and enjoy its sabbaths. ³⁵All the time that it lies desolate, the land will have the rest it did not have during the sabbaths you lived in it.

Holy (Ex 16:23)—
Ex 20:8 "Remember the Sabbath day by keeping it holy.
Ex 20:11 For in six days the LORD made the heavens and the earth, the sea, and all that is in them, but he rested on the seventh day. Therefore the LORD blessed the Sabbath day and made it holy.
Ex 31:14 "'Observe the Sabbath, because it is holy to you. Anyone who desecrates it must be put to death; whoever does any work on that day must be cut off from his people. (+Ex 35:2; Dt 5:12)
Ne 9:14 You made known to them your holy Sabbath and gave them commands, decrees and laws through your servant Moses. (+Isa 58:13-14)
Eze 44:24 "'In any dispute, the priests are to serve as judges and decide it according to my ordinances. They are to keep my laws and my decrees for all my appointed feasts, and they are to keep my Sabbaths holy.

A sign—
Ex 31:13 "Say to the Israelites, 'You must observe my Sabbaths. This will be a sign between me and you for the generations to come, so you may know that I am the LORD, who makes you holy.
Ex 31:16 The Israelites are to observe the Sabbath, celebrating it for the generations to come as a lasting covenant. ¹⁷It will be a sign between me and the Israelites forever, for in six days the LORD made the heavens and the earth, and on the seventh day he abstained from work and rested.'" (+Eze 20:12-13,16,20-21,24)

The Lord is represented as resting on (Ge 2:2-3; Ex 31:17)—
Heb 4:4 For somewhere he has spoken about the seventh day in these words: "And on the seventh day God rested from all his work."

Rest on, commanded (Ex 16:28-30)—
Ex 23:12 "Six days do your work, but on the seventh day do not work, so that your ox and your donkey may rest and the slave born in your household, and the alien as well, may be refreshed.

Ex 31:15 For six days, work is to be done, but the seventh day is a Sabbath of rest, holy to the LORD. Whoever does any work on the Sabbath day must be put to death.
Ex 34:21 "Six days you shall labor, but on the seventh day you shall rest; even during the plowing season and harvest you must rest.
Ex 35:2 For six days, work is to be done, but the seventh day shall be your holy day, a Sabbath of rest to the LORD. Whoever does any work on it must be put to death. ³Do not light a fire in any of your dwellings on the Sabbath day." (+Lev 6:29-31)
Lev 19:3 "'Each of you must respect his mother and father, and you must observe my Sabbaths. I am the LORD your God.
Lev 19:30 "'Observe my Sabbaths and have reverence for my sanctuary. I am the LORD.
Lev 23:1 The LORD said to Moses, ²"Speak to the Israelites and say to them: 'These are my appointed feasts, the appointed feasts of the LORD, which you are to proclaim as sacred assemblies.
³"'There are six days when you may work, but the seventh day is a Sabbath of rest, a day of sacred assembly. You are not to do any work; wherever you live, it is a Sabbath to the LORD.
Lev 23:27 "The tenth day of this seventh month is the Day of Atonement. Hold a sacred assembly and deny yourselves, and present an offering made to the LORD by fire. ²⁸Do no work on that day, because it is the Day of Atonement, when atonement is made for you before the LORD your God. ²⁹Anyone who does not deny himself on that day must be cut off from his people. ³⁰I will destroy from among my people anyone who does any work on that day. ³¹You shall do no work at all. This is to be a lasting ordinance for the generations to come, wherever you live. ³²It is a sabbath of rest for you, and you must deny yourselves. From the evening of the ninth day of the month until the following evening you are to observe your sabbath."
Lev 26:2 "'Observe my Sabbaths and have reverence for my sanctuary. I am the LORD.
Dt 5:12 "Observe the Sabbath day by keeping it holy, as the LORD your God has commanded you. ¹³Six days you shall labor and do all your work, ¹⁴but the seventh day is a Sabbath to the LORD your God. On it you shall not do any work, neither you, nor your son or daughter, nor your manservant or maidservant, nor your ox, your donkey or any of your animals, nor the alien within your gates, so that your manservant and maidservant may rest, as you do. ¹⁵Remember that you were slaves in Egypt and that the LORD your God brought you out of there with a mighty hand and an outstretched arm. Therefore the LORD your God has commanded you to observe the Sabbath day.
2Ch 36:21 The land enjoyed its sabbath rests; all the time of its desolation it rested, until the seventy years were completed in fulfillment of the word of the LORD spoken by Jeremiah.
Jer 17:21 This is what the LORD says: Be careful not to carry a load on the Sabbath day or bring it through the gates of Jerusalem. ²²Do not bring a load out of your houses or do any work on the Sabbath, but keep the Sabbath day holy, as I commanded your forefathers.
Jer 17:24 But if you are careful to obey me, declares the LORD, and bring no load through the gates of this city on the Sabbath, but keep the Sabbath day holy by not doing any work on it, ²⁵then kings who sit on David's throne will come through the gates of this city with their officials.

They and their officials will come riding in chariots and on horses, accompanied by the men of Judah and those living in Jerusalem, and this city will be inhabited forever.

Jer 17:27 But if you do not obey me to keep the Sabbath day holy by not carrying any load as you come through the gates of Jerusalem on the Sabbath day, then I will kindle an unquenchable fire in the gates of Jerusalem that will consume her fortresses.'" (+Lk 23:56)

Rest on, of servants and animals commanded—

Ex 16:5 On the sixth day they are to prepare what they bring in, and that is to be twice as much as they gather on the other days."

Ex 16:23 He said to them, "This is what the LORD commanded: 'Tomorrow is to be a day of rest, a holy Sabbath to the LORD. So bake what you want to bake and boil what you want to boil. Save whatever is left and keep it until morning.'"

²⁴So they saved it until morning, as Moses commanded, and it did not stink or get maggots in it. ²⁵"Eat it today," Moses said, "because today is a Sabbath to the LORD. You will not find any of it on the ground today. ²⁶Six days you are to gather it, but on the seventh day, the Sabbath, there will not be any."

²⁷Nevertheless, some of the people went out on the seventh day to gather it, but they found none. ²⁸Then the LORD said to Moses, "How long will you refuse to keep my commands and my instructions? ²⁹Bear in mind that the LORD has given you the Sabbath; that is why on the sixth day he gives you bread for two days. Everyone is to stay where he is on the seventh day; no one is to go out." ³⁰So the people rested on the seventh day.

Ex 20:10 but the seventh day is a Sabbath to the LORD your God. On it you shall not do any work, neither you, nor your son or daughter, nor your manservant or maidservant, nor your animals, nor the alien within your gates.

Mk 16:1 When the Sabbath was over, Mary Magdalene, Mary the mother of James, and Salome bought spices so that they might go to anoint Jesus' body. (+Lk 23:56)

Observation of:

Offerings prescribed for—

Lev 24:8 This bread is to be set out before the LORD regularly, Sabbath after Sabbath, on behalf of the Israelites, as a lasting covenant.

Nu 28:9 "'On the Sabbath day, make an offering of two lambs a year old without defect, together with its drink offering and a grain offering of two-tenths of an ephah of fine flour mixed with oil. ¹⁰This is the burnt offering for every Sabbath, in addition to the regular burnt offering and its drink offering. (+1Ch 9:32; 23:31; 2Ch 2:4; Eze 46:4-5)

Song for—

Ps 92:1 It is good to praise the LORD and make music to your name, O Most High, ²to proclaim your love in the morning and your faithfulness at night, ³to the music of the ten-stringed lyre and the melody of the harp.

⁴For you make me glad by your deeds, O LORD; I sing for joy at the works of your hands. ⁵How great are your works, O LORD, how profound your thoughts! ⁶The senseless man does not know, fools do not understand, ⁷that though the wicked spring up like grass and all evildoers flourish, they will be forever destroyed.

⁸But you, O LORD, are exalted forever.

⁹For surely your enemies, O LORD, surely your enemies will perish; all evildoers will be scattered. ¹⁰You have exalted my horn like that of a wild ox; fine oils have been poured upon me. ¹¹My eyes have seen the defeat of my adversaries; my ears have heard the rout of my wicked foes.

¹²The righteous will flourish like a palm tree, they will grow like a cedar of Lebanon; ¹³planted in the house of the LORD, they will flourish in the courts of our God. ¹⁴They will still bear fruit in old age, they will stay fresh and green, ¹⁵proclaiming, "The LORD is upright; he is my Rock, and there is no wickedness in him."

Ps 118:24 This is the day the LORD has made; let us rejoice and be glad in it.

Preparation for (Ex 16:5,22; Mt 27:62; Mk 15:42)—

Lk 23:54 It was Preparation Day, and the Sabbath was about to begin.

Jn 19:31 Now it was the day of Preparation, and the next day was to be a special Sabbath. Because the Jews did not want the bodies left on the crosses during the Sabbath, they asked Pilate to have the legs broken and the bodies taken down.

Religious usages on (Ge 2:3; Mk 6:2)—

Lk 4:16 He went to Nazareth, where he had been brought up, and on the Sabbath day he went into the synagogue, as was his custom. And he stood up to read.

Lk 4:31 Then he went down to Capernaum, a town in Galilee, and on the Sabbath began to teach the people.

Lk 6:6 On another Sabbath he went into the synagogue and was teaching, and a man was there whose right hand was shriveled. (+Lk 13:10; Ac 13:14)

Worship on—

Eze 46:1 "'This is what the Sovereign LORD says: The gate of the inner court facing east is to be shut on the six working days, but on the Sabbath day and on the day of the New Moon it is to be opened.

Eze 46:3 On the Sabbaths and New Moons the people of the land are to worship in the presence of the LORD at the entrance to that gateway. (+Ac 15:21)

Ac 16:13 On the Sabbath we went outside the city gate to the river, where we expected to find a place of prayer. We sat down and began to speak to the women who had gathered there.

Commanded (Eze 46:1,3).

Religious instruction on (Mk 6:2; Lk 4:16,31; 6:6; 13:10)—

Ac 13:14 From Perga they went on to Pisidian Antioch. On the Sabbath they entered the synagogue and sat down.

Ac 13:27 The people of Jerusalem and their rulers did not recognize Jesus, yet in condemning him they fulfilled the words of the prophets that are read every Sabbath.

Ac 13:42 As Paul and Barnabas were leaving the synagogue, the people invited them to speak further about these things on the next Sabbath.

Ac 13:44 On the next Sabbath almost the whole city gathered to hear the word of the Lord.

Ac 15:21 For Moses has been preached in every city from the earliest times and is read in the synagogues on every Sabbath."

Ac 17:2 As his custom was, Paul went into the synagogue, and on three Sabbath days he reasoned with them from the Scriptures,

Ac 18:4 Every Sabbath he reasoned in the synagogue, trying to persuade Jews and Greeks.

Apostles taught on (Ac 13:14-43,44-48; 17:2; 18:4).

Hypocritical observance, provokes divine displeasure—

Isa 1:13 Stop bringing meaningless offerings! Your incense is detestable to me. New Moons, Sabbaths and convocations—I cannot bear your evil assemblies.

La 2:6 He has laid waste his dwelling like a garden; he has destroyed his place of meeting. The LORD has made Zion forget her appointed feasts and her Sabbaths; in his fierce anger he has spurned both king and priest.

Eze 20:12 Also I gave them my Sabbaths as a sign between us, so they would know that I the LORD made them holy.

¹³"'Yet the people of Israel rebelled against me in the desert. They did not follow my decrees but rejected my laws—although the man who obeys them will live by them—and they utterly desecrated my Sabbaths. So I said I would pour out my wrath on them and destroy them in the desert.

Eze 20:16 because they rejected my laws and did not follow my decrees and desecrated my Sabbaths. For their hearts were devoted to their idols. (+Eze 20:21,24)

Am 8:5 saying, "When will the New Moon be over that we may sell grain, and the Sabbath be ended that we may market wheat?"—skimping the measure, boosting the price and cheating with dishonest scales,

Rewards for observance of—

Isa 56:2 Blessed is the man who does this, the man who holds it fast, who keeps the Sabbath without desecrating it, and keeps his hand from doing any evil."

Isa 56:4 For this is what the LORD says: "To the eunuchs who keep my Sabbaths, who choose what pleases me and hold fast to my covenant— ⁵to them I will give within my temple and its walls a memorial and a name better than sons and daughters; I will give them an everlasting name that will not be cut off. ⁶And foreigners who bind themselves to the LORD to serve him, to love the name of the LORD, and to worship him, all who keep the Sabbath without desecrating it and who hold fast to my covenant— ⁷these I will bring to my holy mountain and give them joy in my house of prayer. Their burnt offerings and sacrifices will be accepted on my altar; for my house will be called a house of prayer for all nations."

Isa 58:13 "If you keep your feet from breaking the Sabbath and from doing as you please on my holy day, if you call the Sabbath a delight and the LORD's holy day honorable, and if you honor it by not going your own way and not doing as you please or speaking idle words, ¹⁴then you will find your joy in the LORD, and I will cause you to ride on the heights of the land and to feast on the inheritance of your father Jacob." The mouth of the LORD has spoken. (+Jer 17:21-22,24-25)

Observed by—

Moses (Nu 15:32-34). Nehemiah (Ne 13:15,21).

The women preparing to embalm the body of Jesus—

Lk 23:56 Then they went home and prepared spices and perfumes. But they rested on the Sabbath in obedience to the commandment.

Paul (Ac 13:14). The disciples (Ac 16:13). John (Rev 1:10).

Violations of:

Punished, by death (Ex 35:2; Nu 15:32-36), by judgments (Jer 17:27).

Instances of: Gathering manna (Ex 16:27). Gathering sticks (Nu 15:32).

By men from Tyre—

Ne 13:16 Men from Tyre who lived in Jerusalem were bringing in fish and all kinds of merchandise and selling them in Jerusalem on the Sabbath to the people of Judah.

Inhabitants of Jerusalem (Jer 17:21-23).

Profanation of (Ex 16:27-28)—

Nu 15:32 While the Israelites were in the desert, a man was found gathering wood on the Sabbath day. ³³Those who found him gathering wood brought him to Moses and Aaron and the whole assembly, ³⁴and they kept him in custody, because it was not clear what should be done to him. ³⁵Then the LORD said to Moses, "The man must die. The whole assembly must stone him outside the camp." ³⁶So the assembly took him outside the camp and stoned him to death, as the LORD commanded Moses.

Ne 10:31 "When the neighboring peoples bring merchandise or grain to sell on the Sabbath, we will not buy from them on the Sabbath or on any holy day. Every seventh year we will forgo working the land and will cancel all debts.

Ne 13:15 In those days I saw men in Judah treading winepresses on the Sabbath and bringing in grain and loading it on donkeys, together with wine, grapes, figs and all other kinds of loads. And they were bringing all this into Jerusalem on the Sabbath. Therefore I warned them against selling food on that day.

Ne 13:21 But I warned them and said, "Why do you spend the night by the wall? If you do this again, I will lay hands on you." From that time on they no longer came on the Sabbath. (+Jer 17:21-23)

Eze 22:8 You have despised my holy things and desecrated my Sabbaths.

Eze 23:38 They have also done this to me: At that same time they defiled my sanctuary and desecrated my Sabbaths.

Christ's interpretation of:

Mt 12:1 At that time Jesus went through the grainfields on the Sabbath. His disciples were hungry and began to pick some heads of grain and eat them. ²When the Pharisees saw this, they said to him, "Look! Your disciples are doing what is unlawful on the Sabbath."

³He answered, "Haven't you read what David did when he and his companions were hungry? ⁴He entered the house of God, and he and his companions ate the consecrated bread—which was not lawful for them to do, but only for the priests. ⁵Or haven't you read in the Law that on the Sabbath the priests in the temple desecrate the day and yet are innocent? ⁶I tell you that one greater than the temple is here. ⁷If you had known what these words mean, 'I desire mercy, not sacrifice,' you would not have condemned the innocent. ⁸For the Son of Man is Lord of the Sabbath."

Mt 12:10 and a man with a shriveled hand was there. Looking for a reason to accuse Jesus, they asked him, "Is it lawful to heal on the Sabbath?"

¹¹He said to them, "If any of you has a sheep and it falls into a pit on the Sabbath, will you not take hold of it and lift it out? ¹²How much more valuable is a man than a sheep! Therefore it is lawful to do good on the Sabbath."

¹³Then he said to the man, "Stretch out your hand." So he stretched it out and it was completely restored, just as sound as the other. (+Lk 6:1-10; Mk 2:23-28; 13:10-17)

Mk 14:1 Now the Passover and the Feast of Unleavened Bread were only two days away, and the chief priests and the teachers of the law were looking for some sly way to arrest Jesus and kill him. ²"But not during the Feast," they said, "or the people may riot."

³While he was in Bethany, reclining at the table in the home of a man known as Simon the Leper, a woman came with an alabaster jar of very expensive perfume, made of

pure nard. She broke the jar and poured the perfume on his head.

[4]Some of those present were saying indignantly to one another, "Why this waste of perfume? [5]It could have been sold for more than a year's wages and the money given to the poor." And they rebuked her harshly. (+Jn 7:21-24; 9:14)

Christ is Lord of (Mt 12:8; Mk 2:28; Lk 6:5).

Christ performed miracles on (Mt 12:10-13; Mk 3:1-5; Lk 6:1-10)—

Lk 13:10 On a Sabbath Jesus was teaching in one of the synagogues, [11]and a woman was there who had been crippled by a spirit for eighteen years. She was bent over and could not straighten up at all. [12]When Jesus saw her, he called her forward and said to her, "Woman, you are set free from your infirmity." [13]Then he put his hands on her, and immediately she straightened up and praised God.

[14]Indignant because Jesus had healed on the Sabbath, the synagogue ruler said to the people, "There are six days for work. So come and be healed on those days, not on the Sabbath."

[15]The Lord answered him, "You hypocrites! Doesn't each of you on the Sabbath untie his ox or donkey from the stall and lead it out to give it water? [16]Then should not this woman, a daughter of Abraham, whom Satan has kept bound for eighteen long years, be set free on the Sabbath day from what bound her?"

[17]When he said this, all his opponents were humiliated, but the people were delighted with all the wonderful things he was doing.

Jn 5:5 One who was there had been an invalid for thirty-eight years. [6]When Jesus saw him lying there and learned that he had been in this condition for a long time, he asked him, "Do you want to get well?"

[7]"Sir," the invalid replied, "I have no one to help me into the pool when the water is stirred. While I am trying to get in, someone else goes down ahead of me."

[8]Then Jesus said to him, "Get up! Pick up your mat and walk." [9]At once the man was cured; he picked up his mat and walked.

The day on which this took place was a Sabbath, [10]and so the Jews said to the man who had been healed, "It is the Sabbath; the law forbids you to carry your mat."

[11]But he replied, "The man who made me well said to me, 'Pick up your mat and walk.'"

[12]So they asked him, "Who is this fellow who told you to pick it up and walk?"

[13]The man who was healed had no idea who it was, for Jesus had slipped away into the crowd that was there.

[14]Later Jesus found him at the temple and said to him, "See, you are well again. Stop sinning or something worse may happen to you."

Jn 7:21 Jesus said to them, "I did one miracle, and you are all astonished. [22]Yet, because Moses gave you circumcision (though actually it did not come from Moses, but from the patriarchs), you circumcise a child on the Sabbath. [23]Now if a child can be circumcised on the Sabbath so that the law of Moses may not be broken, why are you angry with me for healing the whole man on the Sabbath? [24]Stop judging by mere appearances, and make a right judgment."

Christ taught on (Mk 1:21-22; 6:2; Lk 4:16,31; 6:6; 13:10-17).

The Christian and the Sabbath:

Christian not to be judged regarding—
Col 2:16 Therefore do not let anyone judge you by what

you eat or drink, or with regard to a religious festival, a New Moon celebration or a Sabbath day. (+Ro 1:1-12)

The first day of the week is called the Lord's day (Mt 28:1,5-7)—

Mk 16:9 When Jesus rose early on the first day of the week, he appeared first to Mary Magdalene, out of whom he had driven seven demons. (+Jn 20:1,11-16)

Jn 20:19 On the evening of that first day of the week, when the disciples were together, with the doors locked for fear of the Jews, Jesus came and stood among them and said, "Peace be with you!"

Jn 20:26 A week later his disciples were in the house again, and Thomas was with them. Though the doors were locked, Jesus came and stood among them and said, "Peace be with you!"

Ac 20:7 On the first day of the week we came together to break bread. Paul spoke to the people and, because he intended to leave the next day, kept on talking until midnight.

1Co 16:2 On the first day of every week, each one of you should set aside a sum of money in keeping with his income, saving it up, so that when I come no collections will have to be made.

Rev 1:10 On the Lord's Day I was in the Spirit, and I heard behind me a loud voice like a trumpet,

SABBATH, COVERT FOR THE NIV "Sabbath canopy" (2Ki 16:18).

SABBATH, DAY AFTER THE The waving of the sheaf in Lev 23:11 may be on the day after the ordinary weekly Sabbath or after the first day of the Passover.

SABBATH DAY'S JOURNEY A limited journey (c. 3,000 feet) which Rabbinic scholars thought a Jew might travel on the Sabbath without breaking the law (Ac 1:12; cf. Ex 16:29; Nu 35:5; Jos 3:4).

SABBATIC YEAR A rest recurring every seventh year. Called the Year of Release (Dt 15:9; 31:10). Ordinances concerning (Ex 23:9-11; Lev 25). Israelite servants set free in (Ex 21:2; Dt 15:12; Jer 34:14). Creditors required to release debtors in (Dt 15:1-6,12-18; Ne 10:31). Ordinances concerning instruction in the law during (Dt 31:10-13; Ne 8:18). Punishment to follow a violation of the ordinances concerning (Lev 26:34-35, w 32-41; Jer 34:12-22).

See Jubilee.

SABBEUS *See Shemaiah, 17.*

SABEANS [6014, 8644, 8645]. One of the Sabean monarchs was the famous Queen of Sheba (1Ki 10:1,4,10,13; 2Ch 9:1,3,9,12). *See Sheba, 7.* The Sabeans were a merchant people from Sheba who in early times lived in SW Arabia (modern Yemen) in a region bordering Ophir and Havilah (Isa 45:14; Eze 23:42 cf. Eze 27:20-22). Romans called it *Arabia Felix.* Sabean raiders invaded the land of Uz and killed Job's flocks and servants (Job 1:15; Isa 43:3). Prophecies concerning (Isa 43:3; Joel 3:8). Giants among (Isa 45:14). Proverbial drunkards (Eze 23:42, ftn). They were slave traders (Joel 3:8).

See Seba.

SABTA, SABTAH [6029, 6030]. A son of Cush (Ge 10:7; 1Ch 1:9), perhaps also a place in S Arabia.

SABTECA, SABTECAH, SABTECHA [6031]. A son of Cush (Ge 10:7; 1Ch 1:9).

SACAR [8511] (*reward [given by God], possibly hired hand*).

1. Father of Ahiam (1Ch 11:35), "Sharar" (2Sa 23:33, ftn). *See Sharar.*

2. Son of Obed-Edom (1Ch 26:4).

SACKBUT *See Lyre.*

SACKCLOTH [2520, 8566, *4884*]. A symbol of mourning (1Ki 20:31-32; Job 16:15; Isa 15:3; Jer 4:8; 6:26; 49:3; La 2:10; Eze 7:18; Da 9:3; Joel 1:8). Worn by Jacob when it was reported to him that Joseph had been devoured by wild beasts (Ge 37:34). Animals covered with, at the time of national mourning (Jnh 3:8).

See Mourning.

SACRAMENT (*something obligated [to do]*). A symbolic rite instituted by Christ setting forth the central truths of the Christian faith: death and resurrection with Christ and participation in the redemptive benefits of Christ's mediatorial death. The Roman Catholic Church has seven sacraments; the Protestant Church has two, often called ordinances: baptism and the Lord's Supper.

SACRED PLACES (Dt 12:5,11; 14:23; 15:20; 16:2; 17:8; Jos 9:27; 18:1; 1Ch 22:1; 2Ch 7:15; Ps 78:68). *See Tabernacle; Temple.*

SACRIFICES [*852, 2284, 2285, 4966, 6296, 6590, 6592, 6592, 6913, 7787, 7928, 8596, 8821, 9458, 10638, 1628, 2602, 2604, 2662, 4712, 4714*].

NIV+ SACRIFICE, SACRIFICED, SACRIFICING

Figurative:

(Isa 34:6; Eze 39:17; Zep 1:7-8; Ro 12:1; Php 2:17; 4:18). Of self-denial (Php 3:7-8). Of praise (Ps 116:17; Jer 33:11; Hos 14:2; Heb 13:15). "Fruit of the lips" signifies praise (Hos 14:2).

See Bruise, Bruises, 2; Offerings.

SACRILEGE (*stealing,* hence, *profaning something sacred*). Profaning holy things. Forbidden (Lev 19:8; 1Co 3:17; Tit 1:11; 1Pe 5:2).

Instances of:

Esau sells his birthright (Ge 25:33). Nadab and Abihu offer unauthorized fire (Lev 10:1-7; Nu 3:4). Of Uzzah (2Sa 6:6-7). Of Uzziah (2Ch 26:16-21). Of Korah and his company (Nu 16:40). Of the people of Beth Shemesh (1Sa 6:19). Of Ahaz (2Ch 28:24). Of money changers in the temple (Mt 21:12-13; Lk 19:45; Jn 2:14-16). Of those who profaned the Lord's Supper (1Co 11:29).

SADDLE [2502, 4121, 4496, 8210] (*to ride, riding seat*).

NIV+ SADDLEBAGS, SADDLED

Getting a beast ready for riding (Ge 22:3; Nu 22:21; Jdg 19:10; 2Sa 16:1; 17:23). Donkeys were not ridden with saddles; when carrying heavy burdens they had a thick cushion on their backs.

SADDUCEES [*4881*] (*followers of Zadok;* possibly *righteous*). A Jewish religious sect in the time of Christ.

Beliefs: Acceptance only of the Law and rejection of oral tradition; denial of the Resurrection, immortality of the soul, and the spirit world (Mk 12:18; Lk 20:27; Ac 23:8); they supported the Maccabeans; a relatively small group, but generally held the high priesthood; they were denounced by John the Baptist (Mt 3:7-8) and Jesus (Mt 16:6,11-12); they opposed Christ (Mt 21:12f; Mk 11:15f;

Lk 19:47) and the apostles (Ac 5:17,33). *See Testaments, Time Between.*

SADOC *See Zadok.*

SAFE-CONDUCT [6296]. Letters or passports provided to Nehemiah (Ne 2:7).

SAFFRON [4137]. *See Plants of the Bible.*

SAHADUTHA *See Jegar Sahadutha.*

SAIL

NIV+ FORESAIL, SAILED, SAILING, SAILORS

See Ship.

SAILORS [408+641, 4876, *3731*]. *See Mariner; Occupations and Professions.*

SAINTS [2883, 7705, 10620, *41*] (*unique, consecrated, holy ones*).

1. A member of God's covenant people Israel, whether a layman (Ps 34:9; 79:1; 85:8), or a leader (2Ch 6:41; Ps 16:3).

2. A NT believer (Ac 9:13; 2Co 1:1). The saints are the Church (2Co 1:1), people called out of the world to be God's own people. Throughout the Bible the saints are urged to live lives befitting their position (Eph 4:1; Col 1:10), for even saints can sin (1Jn 1:10-2:2). *See Sanctification; Holiness.*

SAKIA [8499] (possibly *one who looks to Yahweh* KB). Son of Shaharaim (1Ch 8:10).

SALAH, SALA (*missile* or *petition* ISBE; possibly *javelin* KB). *See Shelah, 1.*

SALAMIS [4887] (*peace*). A city of Cyprus. Paul and Barnabas preach in (Ac 13:4-5).

SALATHIEL *See Shealtiel, 2.*

SALECAH, SALCAH [6146] A city on the NE boundary of Bashan (Dt 3:10; Jos 12:5; 13:11; 1Ch 5:11); possibly identified with Salkhad.

SALEM [8970, *4889*] (*peace*). Name of a city of which Melchizedek was king (Ge 14:18; Ps 76:2; Heb 7:1-2), probably Jerusalem.

SALIM [*4890*]. A place near Aenon W of Jordan (Jn 1:28; 3:23,26; 10:40).

SALLAI [6144] (possibly *God had restored*).

1. A Benjamite dwelling in Jerusalem (Ne 11:8).

2. *See Sallu.*

SALLU [6132, 6139] (possibly *he restores*).

NIV+ SALLU'S

1. A Benjamite dwelling in Jerusalem (1Ch 9:7; Ne 11:7).

2. A priest who returned to Jerusalem with Zerubbabel (Ne 12:20).

SALMA [8514] (*little spark* KB).

1. A son of Caleb (1Ch 2:51,54).

2. *See Salmon.*

SALMON [8517, *4885*, *4891*] (*little spark* KB). The father of Boaz, the husband of Ruth (Ru 4:20-21; 1Ch 2:11). In the lineage of Joseph (Mt 1:4-5; Lk 3:32). Also spelled Salma (Ru 4:20, ftn).

SALMONE [*4892*]. A promontory of Crete (Ac 27:7).

SALOME [4897] (peaceful, prosperous one).

1. The wife of Zebedee and the mother of James and John (Mt 27:56; Mk 15:40; 16:1), ministered to Jesus (Mk 15:40-41), present at the crucifixion of Jesus (Mt 27:56), came to the tomb to anoint the body of Jesus (Mk 16:1).

2. The daughter of Herodias; as a reward for her dancing she obtained the head of John the Baptist (Mt 14:3-11; Mk 6:17-28). Her name is not given in the Gospels, but in Josephus.

SALT [4865, 4873, 4875, 4877, 7490, 10420, 229, 266, 4395].

NIV+ SALTED, SALTINESS, SALTY

Lot's wife turned into a pillar of (Ge 19:26). The city of Salt (Jos 15:62). The valley of salt (2Sa 8:13; 2Ki 14:7). Salt sea (Ge 14:3; Nu 34:12; Dt 3:17; Jos 3:16; 12:3; 15:2). Salt pits (Zep 2:9). All animal sacrifices were required to be seasoned with (Lev 2:13; Ezr 6:9; Eze 43:24; Mk 9:49). Used in ratifying covenants (Nu 18:19; 2Ch 13:5). Elisha casts, into the pool of Jericho, to purify it (2Ki 2:20-21).

Symbolic:

Of fidelity (Nu 18:19; 2Ch 13:5), of barrenness and desolation (Dt 29:23; Jdg 9:45; Jer 17:6; Zep 2:7).

Figurative:

Of the saving efficacy of the church (Mt 5:13; Mk 9:49-50; Lk 14:34). Of wise conversation (Col 4:6).

SALT, CITY OF A city in the wilderness of Judah, between Nibshan and En Gedi (Jos 15:62), the site of which is uncertain; possibly Qumran.

SALT, COVENANT OF A covenant confirmed with sacrificial meals at which salt was used (Lev 2:13; Nu 18:19).

SALT HERBS [4865]. A plant that grows in harsh terrain (Job 30:4).

SALT SEA See Dead Sea.

SALT, VALLEY OF A valley between Jerusalem and Edom in which great victories were won over the Edomites (2Sa 8:13; 2Ki 14:7; 2Ch 25:11).

SALU [6140] (restored IDB). Father of Zimri (Nu 25:14).

SALUTATIONS See Greetings.

SALVATION [3802, 3828, 3829, 7407, 9591, 5401, 5403].

NIV+ SAFE, SAFELY, SAFETY, SAVE, SAVED, SAVES, SAVING, SAVIOR

Call to:

Dt 30:19 This day I call heaven and earth as witnesses against you that I have set before you life and death, blessings and curses. Now choose life, so that you and your children may live [20]and that you may love the LORD your God, listen to his voice, and hold fast to him. For the LORD is your life, and he will give you many years in the land he swore to give to your fathers, Abraham, Isaac and Jacob.

Isa 55:1 "Come, all you who are thirsty, come to the waters; and you who have no money, come, buy and eat! Come, buy wine and milk without money and without cost. [2]Why spend money on what is not bread, and your labor on what does not satisfy? Listen, listen to me, and eat what is good, and your soul will delight in the richest of fare. [3]Give ear and come to me; hear me, that your soul

may live. I will make an everlasting covenant with you, my faithful love promised to David.

Isa 55:6 Seek the LORD while he may be found; call on him while he is near. [7]Let the wicked forsake his way and the evil man his thoughts. Let him turn to the LORD, and he will have mercy on him, and to our God, for he will freely pardon. (+Lk 3:6; Ac 16:31; Heb 2:3)

Signifying:

Gracious providence—

Dt 32:15 Jeshurun grew fat and kicked; filled with food, he became heavy and sleek. He abandoned the God who made him and rejected the Rock his Savior. (+Ps 68:19-20)

Ps 91:16 With long life will I satisfy him and show him my salvation." (+Ps 95:1; 116:13; 149:4; Isa 12:2-3)

Personal deliverance from enemies (2Sa 22:36)—

Ps 3:8 From the LORD comes deliverance. May your blessing be on your people. Selah (+Ps 18:2; 37:39)

Isa 1:18 "Come now, let us reason together," says the LORD. "Though your sins are like scarlet, they shall be as white as snow; though they are red as crimson, they shall be like wool.

Isa 32:1 See, a king will reign in righteousness and rulers will rule with justice. [2]Each man will be like a shelter from the wind and a refuge from the storm, like streams of water in the desert and the shadow of a great rock in a thirsty land.

[3]Then the eyes of those who see will no longer be closed, and the ears of those who hear will listen. [4]The mind of the rash will know and understand, and the stammering tongue will be fluent and clear.

National deliverance from enemies—

Ex 15:2 The LORD is my strength and my song; he has become my salvation. He is my God, and I will praise him, my father's God, and I will exalt him.

1Ch 16:35 Cry out, "Save us, O God our Savior; gather us and deliver us from the nations, that we may give thanks to your holy name, that we may glory in your praise."

Ps 98:2 The LORD has made his salvation known and revealed his righteousness to the nations. [3]He has remembered his love and his faithfulness to the house of Israel; all the ends of the earth have seen the salvation of our God.

Ps 106:8 Yet he saved them for his name's sake, to make his mighty power known. (+Isa 46:12-13; Jer 3:23)

A divine standard of righteousness (Isa 56:1), the saving power of divine truth (Isa 45:17), the light and glory of Zion (Isa 62:1)

The promised Messiah—

Jn 4:22 You Samaritans worship what you do not know; we worship what we do know, for salvation is from the Jews.

Personal righteousness—

2Ch 6:41 "Now arise, O LORD God, and come to your resting place, you and the ark of your might. May your priests, O LORD God, be clothed with salvation, may your saints rejoice in your goodness.

Ps 132:16 I will clothe her priests with salvation, and her saints will ever sing for joy.

Eternal life (1Th 5:8-9)—

1Pe 1:5 who through faith are shielded by God's power until the coming of the salvation that is ready to be revealed in the last time.

1Pe 1:9 for you are receiving the goal of your faith, the salvation of your souls. (+1Jn 5:11)

Everlasting (Isa 45:17; 52:10)

Liberty—

Isa 61:1 The Spirit of the Sovereign LORD is on me, because the LORD has anointed me to preach good news to the poor. He has sent me to bind up the brokenhearted, to proclaim freedom for the captives and release from darkness for the prisoners, ²to proclaim the year of the LORD's favor and the day of vengeance of our God, to comfort all who mourn, ³and provide for those who grieve in Zion—to bestow on them a crown of beauty instead of ashes, the oil of gladness instead of mourning, and a garment of praise instead of a spirit of despair. They will be called oaks of righteousness, a planting of the LORD for the display of his splendor.

Mt 11:28 "Come to me, all you who are weary and burdened, and I will give you rest. ²⁹Take my yoke upon you and learn from me, for I am gentle and humble in heart, and you will find rest for your souls. ³⁰For my yoke is easy and my burden is light."

To be developed:

Php 2:12 Therefore, my dear friends, as you have always obeyed—not only in my presence, but now much more in my absence—continue to work out your salvation with fear and trembling,

1Th 5:8 But since we belong to the day, let us be self-controlled, putting on faith and love as a breastplate, and the hope of salvation as a helmet. ⁹For God did not appoint us to suffer wrath but to receive salvation through our Lord Jesus Christ. ¹⁰He died for us so that, whether we are awake or asleep, we may live together with him. (+Jude 3)

From God: (Ps 3:8)

Ps 36:8 They feast on the abundance of your house; you give them drink from your river of delights. ⁹For with you is the fountain of life; in your light we see light. (+Ps 37:39)

Ps 68:18 When you ascended on high, you led captives in your train; you received gifts from men, even from the rebellious—that you, O LORD God, might dwell there.

¹⁹Praise be to the Lord, to God our Savior, who daily bears our burdens. *Selah* ²⁰Our God is a God who saves; from the Sovereign LORD comes escape from death. (+Ps 91:16; 98:2-3; 106:8)

Ps 121:1 I lift up my eyes to the hills—where does my help come from? ²My help comes from the LORD, the Maker of heaven and earth.

³He will not let your foot slip—he who watches over you will not slumber; ⁴indeed, he who watches over Israel will neither slumber nor sleep.

⁵The LORD watches over you—the LORD is your shade at your right hand; ⁶the sun will not harm you by day, nor the moon by night.

⁷The LORD will keep you from all harm—he will watch over your life; ⁸the LORD will watch over your coming and going both now and forevermore. (+Isa 46:12-13)

Isa 51:4 "Listen to me, my people; hear me, my nation: The law will go out from me; my justice will become a light to the nations. ⁵My righteousness draws near speedily, my salvation is on the way, and my arm will bring justice to the nations. The islands will look to me and wait in hope for my arm.

Isa 63:9 In all their distress he too was distressed, and the angel of his presence saved them; in his love and mercy he redeemed them; he lifted them up and carried them all the days of old.

Jer 3:23 Surely the [idolatrous] commotion on the hills and mountains is a deception; surely in the LORD our God is the salvation of Israel.

Jer 21:8 "Furthermore, tell the people, 'This is what the LORD says: See, I am setting before you the way of life and the way of death.

Eze 18:32 For I take no pleasure in the death of anyone, declares the Sovereign LORD. Repent and live!

Joel 2:32 And everyone who calls on the name of the LORD will be saved; for on Mount Zion and in Jerusalem there will be deliverance, as the LORD has said, among the survivors whom the LORD calls. (+1Pe 1:5)

1Jn 2:25 And this is what he promised us—even eternal life.

Through Christ: (Isa 61:10; Mt 1:21; Lk 19:10; 24:46)

Lk 24:47 and repentance and forgiveness of sins will be preached in his name to all nations, beginning at Jerusalem. (+Jn 3:14-17)

Jn 11:51 He did not say this on his own, but as high priest that year he prophesied that Jesus would die for the Jewish nation, ⁵²and not only for that nation but also for the scattered children of God, to bring them together and make them one.

Ac 4:12 Salvation is found in no one else, for there is no other name under heaven given to men by which we must be saved." (+Ac 13:26,38-39,47; 16:30-31; Ro 5:15-21)

Ro 7:24 What a wretched man I am! Who will rescue me from this body of death? ²⁵Thanks be to God—through Jesus Christ our Lord! So then, I myself in my mind am a slave to God's law, but in the sinful nature a slave to the law of sin.

Ro 9:30 What then shall we say? That the Gentiles, who did not pursue righteousness, have obtained it, a righteousness that is by faith; ³¹but Israel, who pursued a law of righteousness, has not attained it. ³²Why not? Because they pursued it not by faith but as if it were by works. They stumbled over the "stumbling stone." ³³As it is written: "See, I lay in Zion a stone that causes men to stumble and a rock that makes them fall, and the one who trusts in him will never be put to shame."

1Co 6:11 And that is what some of you were. But you were washed, you were sanctified, you were justified in the name of the Lord Jesus Christ and by the Spirit of our God. (+Gal 1:4; 3:13-14)

Eph 1:9 And he made known to us the mystery of his will according to his good pleasure, which he purposed in Christ, ¹⁰to be put into effect when the times will have reached their fulfillment—to bring all things in heaven and on earth together under one head, even Christ.

Eph 1:13 And you also were included in Christ when you heard the word of truth, the gospel of your salvation. Having believed, you were marked in him with a seal, the promised Holy Spirit,

2Ti 1:9 who has saved us and called us to a holy life—not because of anything we have done but because of his own purpose and grace. This grace was given us in Christ Jesus before the beginning of time, ¹⁰but it has now been revealed through the appearing of our Savior, Christ Jesus, who has destroyed death and has brought life and immortality to light through the gospel.

2Ti 2:10 Therefore I endure everything for the sake of the elect, that they too may obtain the salvation that is in Christ Jesus, with eternal glory.

Tit 3:5 he saved us, not because of righteous things we had done, but because of his mercy. He saved us through the washing of rebirth and renewal by the Holy Spirit, ⁶whom he poured out on us generously through Jesus Christ our

Savior, [7]so that, having been justified by his grace, we might become heirs having the hope of eternal life.

Heb 2:3 how shall we escape if we ignore such a great salvation? This salvation, which was first announced by the Lord, was confirmed to us by those who heard him.

Heb 2:10 In bringing many sons to glory, it was fitting that God, for whom and through whom everything exists, should make the author of their salvation perfect through suffering.

Heb 5:9 and, once made perfect, he became the source of eternal salvation for all who obey him

Heb 7:25 Therefore he is able to save completely those who come to God through him, because he always lives to intercede for them.

1Jn 4:9 This is how God showed his love among us: He sent his one and only Son into the world that we might live through him. [10]This is love: not that we loved God, but that he loved us and sent his Son as an atoning sacrifice for our sins.

1Jn 5:11 And this is the testimony: God has given us eternal life, and this life is in his Son.

Jude 3 Dear friends, although I was very eager to write to you about the salvation we share, I felt I had to write and urge you to contend for the faith that was once for all entrusted to the saints.

Rev 3:20 Here I am! I stand at the door and knock. If anyone hears my voice and opens the door, I will come in and eat with him, and he with me. (+Rev 5:9)

By the atonement (1Co 1:18,21,24-25)—

Gal 1:4 who gave himself for our sins to rescue us from the present evil age, according to the will of our God and Father,

Gal 3:8 The Scripture foresaw that God would justify the Gentiles by faith, and announced the gospel in advance to Abraham: "All nations will be blessed through you."

Gal 3:13 Christ redeemed us from the curse of the law by becoming a curse for us, for it is written: "Cursed is everyone who is hung on a tree." [14]He redeemed us in order that the blessing given to Abraham might come to the Gentiles through Christ Jesus, so that by faith we might receive the promise of the Spirit.

Gal 3:21 Is the law, therefore, opposed to the promises of God? Absolutely not! For if a law had been given that could impart life, then righteousness would certainly have come by the law.

Gal 3:26 You are all sons of God through faith in Christ Jesus, [27]for all of you who were baptized into Christ have clothed yourselves with Christ. [28]There is neither Jew nor Greek, slave nor free, male nor female, for you are all one in Christ Jesus.

Col 1:20 and through him to reconcile to himself all things, whether things on earth or things in heaven, by making peace through his blood, shed on the cross.

[21]Once you were alienated from God and were enemies in your minds because of your evil behavior. [22]But now he has reconciled you by Christ's physical body through death to present you holy in his sight, without blemish and free from accusation— [23]if you continue in your faith, established and firm, not moved from the hope held out in the gospel. This is the gospel that you heard and that has been proclaimed to every creature under heaven, and of which I, Paul, have become a servant.

Col 1:26 the mystery that has been kept hidden for ages and generations, but is now disclosed to the saints. [27]To them God has chosen to make known among the Gentiles

the glorious riches of this mystery, which is Christ in you, the hope of glory.

1Ti 2:6 who gave himself as a ransom for all men—the testimony given in its proper time. (+Rev 5:9)

By the Resurrection (Ro 5:10).

By the gospel (Ro 1:16)—

Jas 1:21 Therefore, get rid of all moral filth and the evil that is so prevalent and humbly accept the word planted in you, which can save you.

By the grace of God (Eph 2:8-9)—

Tit 2:11 For the grace of God that brings salvation has appeared to all men.

2Pe 3:15 Bear in mind that our Lord's patience means salvation, just as our dear brother Paul also wrote you with the wisdom that God gave him.

By the word of God (Jas 1:21).

By the power of God—

1Co 1:18 For the message of the cross is foolishness to those who are perishing, but to us who are being saved it is the power of God.

Message of:

Foretold by the prophets—

Isa 29:18 In that day the deaf will hear the words of the scroll, and out of gloom and darkness the eyes of the blind will see. [19]Once more the humble will rejoice in the LORD; the needy will rejoice in the Holy One of Israel.

Isa 29:24 Those who are wayward in spirit will gain understanding; those who complain will accept instruction."

Isa 35:8 And a highway will be there; it will be called the Way of Holiness. The unclean will not journey on it; it will be for those who walk in that Way; wicked fools will not go about on it. (+Lk 2:31-32)

1Pe 1:10 Concerning this salvation, the prophets, who spoke of the grace that was to come to you, searched intently and with the greatest care,

By angels (Lk 2:9-14). From the seed of Abraham (Ge 12:13).

Proclaimed by Christ—

Lk 19:10 For the Son of Man came to seek and to save what was lost."

Jn 12:32 But I, when I am lifted up from the earth, will draw all men to myself."

Preached by the apostles (Ac 11:17-18)—

Ac 16:17 This girl followed Paul and the rest of us, shouting, "These men are servants of the Most High God, who are telling you the way to be saved."

Wisdom for, derived from the Scriptures—

2Ti 3:15 and how from infancy you have known the holy Scriptures, which are able to make you wise for salvation through faith in Christ Jesus.

Praise for, ascribed to God and the Lamb (Rev 7:9-10).

For:

For Israel—

Isa 45:17 But Israel will be saved by the LORD with an everlasting salvation; you will never be put to shame or disgraced, to ages everlasting.

Isa 46:12 Listen to me, you stubborn-hearted, you who are far from righteousness. [13]I am bringing my righteousness near, it is not far away; and my salvation will not be delayed. I will grant salvation to Zion, my splendor to Israel.

Ac 13:26 "Brothers, children of Abraham, and you God-fearing Gentiles, it is to us that this message of salvation has been sent.

Ac 13:38 "Therefore, my brothers, I want you to know that through Jesus the forgiveness of sins is proclaimed to you. [39]Through him everyone who believes is justified from everything you could not be justified from by the law of Moses.

Ac 13:47 For this is what the Lord has commanded us: "'I have made you a light for the Gentiles, that you may bring salvation to the ends of the earth.'" (+Ro 1:16)

For the Gentiles—

1Ki 8:41 "As for the foreigner who does not belong to your people Israel but has come from a distant land because of your name— [42]for men will hear of your great name and your mighty hand and your outstretched arm— when he comes and prays toward this temple, [43]then hear from heaven, your dwelling place, and do whatever the foreigner asks of you, so that all the peoples of the earth may know your name and fear you, as do your own people Israel, and may know that this house I have built bears your Name.

Isa 52:10 The LORD will lay bare his holy arm in the sight of all the nations, and all the ends of the earth will see the salvation of our God.

Isa 52:15 so will he sprinkle many nations, and kings will shut their mouths because of him. For what they were not told, they will see, and what they have not heard, they will understand.

Isa 56:1 This is what the LORD says: "Maintain justice and do what is right, for my salvation is close at hand and my righteousness will soon be revealed.

Isa 56:6 And foreigners who bind themselves to the LORD to serve him, to love the name of the LORD, and to worship him, all who keep the Sabbath without desecrating it and who hold fast to my covenant— [7]these I will bring to my holy mountain and give them joy in my house of prayer. Their burnt offerings and sacrifices will be accepted on my altar; for my house will be called a house of prayer for all nations." [8]The Sovereign LORD declares—he who gathers the exiles of Israel: "I will gather still others to them besides those already gathered."

Mt 21:31 "Which of the two did what his father wanted?" "The first," they answered. Jesus said to them, "I tell you the truth, the tax collectors and the prostitutes are entering the kingdom of God ahead of you.

Mt 24:14 And this gospel of the kingdom will be preached in the whole world as a testimony to all nations, and then the end will come.

Jn 10:16 I have other sheep that are not of this sheep pen. I must bring them also. They too will listen to my voice, and there shall be one flock and one shepherd.

Ac 11:17 So if God gave them the same gift as he gave us, who believed in the Lord Jesus Christ, who was I to think that I could oppose God?"

[18]When they heard this, they had no further objections and praised God, saying, "So then, God has granted even the Gentiles repentance unto life."

Ac 15:7 After much discussion, Peter got up and addressed them: "Brothers, you know that some time ago God made a choice among you that the Gentiles might hear from my lips the message of the gospel and believe. [8]God, who knows the heart, showed that he accepted them by giving the Holy Spirit to them, just as he did to us. [9]He made no distinction between us and them, for he purified their hearts by faith.

Ac 15:11 No! We believe it is through the grace of our Lord Jesus that we are saved, just as they are."

Ac 28:28 "Therefore I want you to know that God's salvation has been sent to the Gentiles, and they will listen!"

Ro 11:11 Again I ask: Did they stumble so as to fall beyond recovery? Not at all! Rather, because of their transgression, salvation has come to the Gentiles to make Israel envious. [12]But if their transgression means riches for the world, and their loss means riches for the Gentiles, how much greater riches will their fullness bring!

Ro 15:9 so that the Gentiles may glorify God for his mercy, as it is written: "Therefore I will praise you among the Gentiles; I will sing hymns to your name."

Ro 15:16 to be a minister of Christ Jesus to the Gentiles with the priestly duty of proclaiming the gospel of God, so that the Gentiles might become an offering acceptable to God, sanctified by the Holy Spirit. (+Gal 3:8,14)

Eph 3:6 This mystery is that through the gospel the Gentiles are heirs together with Israel, members together of one body, and sharers together in the promise in Christ Jesus.

Eph 3:9 and to make plain to everyone the administration of this mystery, which for ages past was kept hidden in God, who created all things.

For all people—

Mt 18:14 In the same way your Father in heaven is not willing that any of these little ones should be lost.

Mt 22:9 Go to the street corners and invite to the banquet anyone you find.' [10]So the servants went out into the streets and gathered all the people they could find, both good and bad, and the wedding hall was filled with guests.

Mt 22:14 "For many are invited, but few are chosen."

Lk 2:10 But the angel said to them, "Do not be afraid. I bring you good news of great joy that will be for all the people.

Lk 2:31 which you have prepared in the sight of all people, [32]a light for revelation to the Gentiles and for glory to your people Israel."

Lk 3:6 And all mankind will see God's salvation.'"

Lk 13:29 People will come from east and west and north and south, and will take their places at the feast in the kingdom of God. (+Gal 3:28)

Eph 2:14 For he himself is our peace, who has made the two one and has destroyed the barrier, the dividing wall of hostility,

Eph 2:17 He came and preached peace to you who were far away and peace to those who were near.

Col 3:11 Here there is no Greek or Jew, circumcised or uncircumcised, barbarian, Scythian, slave or free, but Christ is all, and is in all.

1Ti 2:3 This is good, and pleases God our Savior, [4]who wants all men to be saved and to come to a knowledge of the truth.

1Ti 4:10 (and for this we labor and strive), that we have put our hope in the living God, who is the Savior of all men, and especially of those who believe.

2Pe 3:9 The Lord is not slow in keeping his promise, as some understand slowness. He is patient with you, not wanting anyone to perish, but everyone to come to repentance.

Rev 5:9 And they sang a new song: "You are worthy to take the scroll and to open its seals, because you were slain, and with your blood you purchased men for God from every tribe and language and people and nation.

Rev 7:9 After this I looked and there before me was a great multitude that no one could count, from every nation, tribe, people and language, standing before the throne and in front of the Lamb. They were wearing white robes and were holding palm branches in their hands. ¹⁰And they cried out in a loud voice: "Salvation belongs to our God, who sits on the throne, and to the Lamb."

Rev 14:6 Then I saw another angel flying in midair, and he had the eternal gospel to proclaim to those who live on the earth—to every nation, tribe, language and people. (+Rev 22:17)

From:

From sin—

Mt 1:21 She will give birth to a son, and you are to give him the name Jesus, because he will save his people from their sins."

Mk 2:17 On hearing this, Jesus said to them, "It is not the healthy who need a doctor, but the sick. I have not come to call the righteous, but sinners." (+Lk 5:31-32)

From spiritual hunger and thirst—

Jn 4:14 but whoever drinks the water I give him will never thirst. Indeed, the water I give him will become in him a spring of water welling up to eternal life."

Jn 6:35 Then Jesus declared, "I am the bread of life. He who comes to me will never go hungry, and he who believes in me will never be thirsty.

Jn 7:37 On the last and greatest day of the Feast, Jesus stood and said in a loud voice, "If anyone is thirsty, let him come to me and drink. ³⁸Whoever believes in me, as the Scripture has said, streams of living water will flow from within him."

See Adoption; Redemption; Regeneration; Sanctification.

Conditions of:

Repentance—

Mt 3:2 and saying, "Repent, for the kingdom of heaven is near."

Mk 1:4 And so John came, baptizing in the desert region and preaching a baptism of repentance for the forgiveness of sins.

Lk 3:8 Produce fruit in keeping with repentance. And do not begin to say to yourselves, 'We have Abraham as our father.' For I tell you that out of these stones God can raise up children for Abraham.

Ac 2:38 Peter replied, "Repent and be baptized, every one of you, in the name of Jesus Christ for the forgiveness of your sins. And you will receive the gift of the Holy Spirit.

Ac 3:19 Repent, then, and turn to God, so that your sins may be wiped out, that times of refreshing may come from the Lord,

2Co 7:10 Godly sorrow brings repentance that leads to salvation and leaves no regret, but worldly sorrow brings death.

Faith in Christ—

Mk 16:15 He said to them, "Go into all the world and preach the good news to all creation. ¹⁶Whoever believes and is baptized will be saved, but whoever does not believe will be condemned.

Jn 3:14 Just as Moses lifted up the snake in the desert, so the Son of Man must be lifted up, ¹⁵that everyone who believes in him may have eternal life.

¹⁶"For God so loved the world that he gave his one and only Son, that whoever believes in him shall not perish but have eternal life. ¹⁷For God did not send his Son into the world to condemn the world, but to save the world through him. ¹⁸Whoever believes in him is not condemned, but whoever does not believe stands condemned already because he has not believed in the name of God's one and only Son.

Jn 5:24 "I tell you the truth, whoever hears my word and believes him who sent me has eternal life and will not be condemned; he has crossed over from death to life.

Jn 6:47 I tell you the truth, he who believes has everlasting life.

Jn 9:35 Jesus heard that they had thrown him out, and when he found him, he said, "Do you believe in the Son of Man?"

Jn 11:25 Jesus said to her, "I am the resurrection and the life. He who believes in me will live, even though he dies; ²⁶and whoever lives and believes in me will never die. Do you believe this?"

Jn 12:36 Put your trust in the light while you have it, so that you may become sons of light." When he had finished speaking, Jesus left and hid himself from them.

Jn 20:31 But these are written that you may believe that Jesus is the Christ, the Son of God, and that by believing you may have life in his name. (+Ac 2:21)

Ac 16:30 He then brought them out and asked, "Sirs, what must I do to be saved?"

³¹They replied, "Believe in the Lord Jesus, and you will be saved—you and your household."

Ac 20:21 I have declared to both Jews and Greeks that they must turn to God in repentance and have faith in our Lord Jesus.

Ro 1:16 I am not ashamed of the gospel, because it is the power of God for the salvation of everyone who believes: first for the Jew, then for the Gentile. ¹⁷For in the gospel a righteousness from God is revealed, a righteousness that is by faith from first to last, just as it is written: "The righteous will live by faith."

Ro 3:21 But now a righteousness from God, apart from law, has been made known, to which the Law and the Prophets testify. ²²This righteousness from God comes through faith in Jesus Christ to all who believe. There is no difference, ²³for all have sinned and fall short of the glory of God, ²⁴and are justified freely by his grace through the redemption that came by Christ Jesus. ²⁵God presented him as a sacrifice of atonement, through faith in his blood. He did this to demonstrate his justice, because in his forbearance he had left the sins committed beforehand unpunished— ²⁶he did it to demonstrate his justice at the present time, so as to be just and the one who justifies those who have faith in Jesus. (+Ro 3:27-28)

Ro 3:29 Is God the God of Jews only? Is he not the God of Gentiles too? Yes, of Gentiles too, ³⁰since there is only one God, who will justify the circumcised by faith and the uncircumcised through that same faith.

Ro 4:1 What then shall we say that Abraham, our forefather, discovered in this matter? ²If, in fact, Abraham was justified by works, he had something to boast about—but not before God. ³What does the Scripture say? "Abraham believed God, and it was credited to him as righteousness."

⁴Now when a man works, his wages are not credited to him as a gift, but as an obligation. ⁵However, to the man who does not work but trusts God who justifies the wicked, his faith is credited as righteousness. ⁶David says the same thing when he speaks of the blessedness of the man to whom God credits righteousness apart from works:

⁷"Blessed are they whose transgressions are forgiven, whose sins are covered. ⁸Blessed is the man whose sin the Lord will never count against him."

⁹Is this blessedness only for the circumcised, or also for the uncircumcised? We have been saying that Abraham's faith was credited to him as righteousness. ¹⁰Under what

circumstances was it credited? Was it after he was circumcised, or before? It was not after, but before! ¹¹And he received the sign of circumcision, a seal of the righteousness that he had by faith while he was still uncircumcised. So then, he is the father of all who believe but have not been circumcised, in order that righteousness might be credited to them. ¹²And he is also the father of the circumcised who not only are circumcised but who also walk in the footsteps of the faith that our father Abraham had before he was circumcised.

¹³It was not through law that Abraham and his offspring received the promise that he would be heir of the world, but through the righteousness that comes by faith. ¹⁴For if those who live by law are heirs, faith has no value and the promise is worthless, ¹⁵because law brings wrath. And where there is no law there is no transgression.

¹⁶Therefore, the promise comes by faith, so that it may be by grace and may be guaranteed to all Abraham's offspring—not only to those who are of the law but also to those who are of the faith of Abraham. He is the father of us all. ¹⁷As it is written: "I have made you a father of many nations." He is our father in the sight of God, in whom he believed—the God who gives life to the dead and calls things that are not as though they were.

¹⁸Against all hope, Abraham in hope believed and so became the father of many nations, just as it had been said to him, "So shall your offspring be." ¹⁹Without weakening in his faith, he faced the fact that his body was as good as dead—since he was about a hundred years old—and that Sarah's womb was also dead. ²⁰Yet he did not waver through unbelief regarding the promise of God, but was strengthened in his faith and gave glory to God, ²¹being fully persuaded that God had power to do what he had promised. ²²This is why "it was credited to him as righteousness." ²³The words "it was credited to him" were written not for him alone, ²⁴but also for us, to whom God will credit righteousness—for us who believe in him who raised Jesus our Lord from the dead. ²⁵He was delivered over to death for our sins and was raised to life for our justification.

Ro 5:1 Therefore, since we have been justified through faith, we have peace with God through our Lord Jesus Christ, ²through whom we have gained access by faith into this grace in which we now stand. And we rejoice in the hope of the glory of God.

Ro 10:4 Christ is the end of the law so that there may be righteousness for everyone who believes. (+Ro 10:8-13; Gal 2:16; 3:8,26-28; Eph 2:8)

Php 3:9 and be found in him, not having a righteousness of my own that comes from the law, but that which is through faith in Christ—the righteousness that comes from God and is by faith. (+2Th 2:13)

1Ti 1:15 Here is a trustworthy saying that deserves full acceptance: Christ Jesus came into the world to save sinners—of whom I am the worst. ¹⁶But for that very reason I was shown mercy so that in me, the worst of sinners, Christ Jesus might display his unlimited patience as an example for those who would believe on him and receive eternal life.

Heb 4:1 Therefore, since the promise of entering his rest still stands, let us be careful that none of you be found to have fallen short of it. ²For we also have had the gospel preached to us, just as they did; but the message they heard was of no value to them, because those who heard did not combine it with faith. (+1Pe 1:9)

Supreme love to Christ—

Lk 14:25 Large crowds were traveling with Jesus, and turning to them he said: ²⁶"If anyone comes to me and does not hate his father and mother, his wife and children, his brothers and sisters—yes, even his own life—he cannot be my disciple. ²⁷And anyone who does not carry his cross and follow me cannot be my disciple.

Renunciation of the world—

Mt 19:16 Now a man came up to Jesus and asked, "Teacher, what good thing must I do to get eternal life?"

¹⁷"Why do you ask me about what is good?" Jesus replied. "There is only One who is good. If you want to enter life, obey the commandments."

¹⁸"Which ones?" the man inquired.

Jesus replied, "'Do not murder, do not commit adultery, do not steal, do not give false testimony, ¹⁹honor your father and mother,' and 'love your neighbor as yourself.'"

²⁰"All these I have kept," the young man said. "What do I still lack?"

²¹Jesus answered, "If you want to be perfect, go, sell your possessions and give to the poor, and you will have treasure in heaven. Then come, follow me."

Lk 14:33 In the same way, any of you who does not give up everything he has cannot be my disciple. (+Lk 18:18-26)

Choice—

Dt 30:19 This day I call heaven and earth as witnesses against you that I have set before you life and death, blessings and curses. Now choose life, so that you and your children may live ²⁰and that you may love the LORD your God, listen to his voice, and hold fast to him. For the LORD is your life, and he will give you many years in the land he swore to give to your fathers, Abraham, Isaac and Jacob. (+Ps 65:4)

Eph 1:4 For he chose us in him before the creation of the world to be holy and blameless in his sight. In love ⁵he predestined us to be adopted as his sons through Jesus Christ, in accordance with his pleasure and will—

Seeking God—

Am 5:4 This is what the LORD says to the house of Israel: "Seek me and live;

Fear of God (Pr 14:27; 15:23; 16:6)—

Mal 4:2 But for you who revere my name, the sun of righteousness will rise with healing in its wings. And you will go out and leap like calves released from the stall.

Not by works (Ro 3:28; 4:1-25; 9:30-33)—

Ro 11:6 And if by grace, then it is no longer by works; if it were, grace would no longer be grace.

Gal 2:16 know that a man is not justified by observing the law, but by faith in Jesus Christ. So we, too, have put our faith in Christ Jesus that we may be justified by faith in Christ and not by observing the law, because by observing the law no one will be justified.

Eph 2:8 For it is by grace you have been saved, through faith—and this not from yourselves, it is the gift of God—⁹not by works, so that no one can boast. (+2Ti 1:9-10; Tit 3:5-7)

See Blessings, Spiritual, Contingent Upon Obedience; Faith; Obedience; Perseverance; Repentance.

Plan of:

Jn 17:4 I have brought you glory on earth by completing the work you gave me to do.

Heb 6:17 Because God wanted to make the unchanging nature of his purpose very clear to the heirs of what was promised, he confirmed it with an oath. ¹⁸God did this so that, by two unchangeable things in which it is impossible for God to lie, we who have fled to take hold of the hope offered to us may be greatly encouraged. [19]We have this hope as an anchor for the soul, firm and secure. It enters the inner sanctuary behind the curtain, [20]where Jesus, who went before us, has entered on our behalf. He has become a high priest forever, in the order of Melchizedek.

Foreordained—

Eph 1:4 For he chose us in him before the creation of the world to be holy and blameless in his sight. In love [5]he predestined us to be adopted as his sons through Jesus Christ, in accordance with his pleasure and will— [6]to the praise of his glorious grace, which he has freely given us in the One he loves. (+Eph 3:11)

Described as a mystery (Mt 13:11)—

Mk 4:11 He told them, "The secret of the kingdom of God has been given to you. But to those on the outside everything is said in parables (+Lk 8:10; Ro 16:25-26; 1Co 2:7-9; Eph 1:9-10)

Eph 1:13 And you also were included in Christ when you heard the word of truth, the gospel of your salvation. Having believed, you were marked in him with a seal, the promised Holy Spirit,

Eph 3:9 and to make plain to everyone the administration of this mystery, which for ages past was kept hidden in God, who created all things. [10]His intent was that now, through the church, the manifold wisdom of God should be made known to the rulers and authorities in the heavenly realms,

Eph 6:19 Pray also for me, that whenever I open my mouth, words may be given me so that I will fearlessly make known the mystery of the gospel, (+Col 1:26-27; 1Ti 3:16)

Rev 10:7 But in the days when the seventh angel is about to sound his trumpet, the mystery of God will be accomplished, just as he announced to his servants the prophets."

Includes:

The incarnation of Christ—

Gal 4:4 But when the time had fully come, God sent his Son, born of a woman, born under law, [5]to redeem those under law, that we might receive the full rights of sons.

The atonement by Christ—

Jn 18:11 Jesus commanded Peter, "Put your sword away! Shall I not drink the cup the Father has given me?"

Jn 19:28 Later, knowing that all was now completed, and so that the Scripture would be fulfilled, Jesus said, "I am thirsty." [29]A jar of wine vinegar was there, so they soaked a sponge in it, put the sponge on a stalk of the hyssop plant, and lifted it to Jesus' lips. [30]When he had received the drink, Jesus said, "It is finished." With that, he bowed his head and gave up his spirit.

Ac 3:18 But this is how God fulfilled what he had foretold through all the prophets, saying that his Christ would suffer.

Ac 17:3 explaining and proving that the Christ had to suffer and rise from the dead. "This Jesus I am proclaiming to you is the Christ," he said. (+Ro 16:25-26)

1Co 1:21 For since in the wisdom of God the world through its wisdom did not know him, God was pleased through the foolishness of what was preached to save those who believe. [22]Jews demand miraculous signs and Greeks look for wisdom, [23]but we preach Christ crucified: a stumbling block to Jews and foolishness to Gentiles, [24]but to those whom God has called, both Jews and Greeks, Christ the power of God and the wisdom of God. [25]For the foolishness of God is wiser than man's wisdom, and the weakness of God is stronger than man's strength.

1Co 2:7 No, we speak of God's secret wisdom, a wisdom that has been hidden and that God destined for our glory before time began. [8]None of the rulers of this age understood it, for if they had, they would not have crucified the Lord of glory. [9]However, as it is written: "No eye has seen, no ear has heard, no mind has conceived what God has prepared for those who love him"—

Eph 1:7 In him we have redemption through his blood, the forgiveness of sins, in accordance with the riches of God's grace [8]that he lavished on us with all wisdom and understanding. [9]And he made known to us the mystery of his will according to his good pleasure, which he purposed in Christ, [10]to be put into effect when the times will have reached their fulfillment—to bring all things in heaven and on earth together under one head, even Christ.

[11]In him we were also chosen, having been predestined according to the plan of him who works out everything in conformity with the purpose of his will, (+Eph 3:18; 6:19; Col 1:26-27)

Heb 2:9 But we see Jesus, who was made a little lower than the angels, now crowned with glory and honor because he suffered death, so that by the grace of God he might taste death for everyone.

[10]In bringing many sons to glory, it was fitting that God, for whom and through whom everything exists, should make the author of their salvation perfect through suffering. (+Heb 2:11-13)

Heb 2:14 Since the children have flesh and blood, he too shared in their humanity so that by his death he might destroy him who holds the power of death—that is, the devil— [15]and free those who all their lives were held in slavery by their fear of death. [16]For surely it is not angels he helps, but Abraham's descendants. [17]For this reason he had to be made like his brothers in every way, in order that he might become a merciful and faithful high priest in service to God, and that he might make atonement for the sins of the people. [18]Because he himself suffered when he was tempted, he is able to help those who are being tempted. (+Heb 10:10)

Initial grace—

Jn 6:37 All that the Father gives me will come to me, and whoever comes to me I will never drive away.

Jn 6:44 "No one can come to me unless the Father who sent me draws him, and I will raise him up at the last day. [45]It is written in the Prophets: 'They will all be taught by God.' Everyone who listens to the Father and learns from him comes to me. (+Jn 6:65)

Eph 2:5 made us alive with Christ even when we were dead in transgressions—it is by grace you have been saved. (+Tit 2:11)

The election of grace—

2Th 2:13 But we ought always to thank God for you, brothers loved by the Lord, because from the beginning God chose you to be saved through the sanctifying work of the Spirit and through belief in the truth. [14]He called you to this through our gospel, that you might share in the glory of our Lord Jesus Christ.

2Ti 1:9 who has saved us and called us to a holy life—not because of anything we have done but because of his own purpose and grace. This grace was given us in Christ Jesus before the beginning of time, [10]but it has now been revealed through the appearing of our Savior, Christ Jesus, who has destroyed death and has brought life and immortality to light through the gospel.

Inheritance—
Heb 1:14 Are not all angels ministering spirits sent to serve those who will inherit salvation?

Regeneration (Jn 3:3-12).

Sets Forth:

Reconciliation to God through Christ—
2Co 5:18 All this is from God, who reconciled us to himself through Christ and gave us the ministry of reconciliation: [19]that God was reconciling the world to himself in Christ, not counting men's sins against them. And he has committed to us the message of reconciliation. (+Col 1:9,19-23; Heb 2:14-18)

Righteousness by faith in the atonement of Christ, as opposed to righteousness by works—
Ro 10:3 Since they did not know the righteousness that comes from God and sought to establish their own, they did not submit to God's righteousness. [4]Christ is the end of the law so that there may be righteousness for everyone who believes.

[5]Moses describes in this way the righteousness that is by the law: "The man who does these things will live by them." [6]But the righteousness that is by faith says: "Do not say in your heart, 'Who will ascend into heaven?'" (that is, to bring Christ down) [7]"or 'Who will descend into the deep?'" (that is, to bring Christ up from the dead). [8]But what does it say? "The word is near you; it is in your mouth and in your heart," that is, the word of faith we are proclaiming: [9]That if you confess with your mouth, "Jesus is Lord," and believe in your heart that God raised him from the dead, you will be saved.

Ro 16:25 Now to him who is able to establish you by my gospel and the proclamation of Jesus Christ, according to the revelation of the mystery hidden for long ages past, [26]but now revealed and made known through the prophetic writings by the command of the eternal God, so that all nations might believe and obey him—

Eph 2:6 And God raised us up with Christ and seated us with him in the heavenly realms in Christ Jesus, [7]in order that in the coming ages he might show the incomparable riches of his grace, expressed in his kindness to us in Christ Jesus. [8]For it is by grace you have been saved, through faith—and this not from yourselves, it is the gift of God— [9]not by works, so that no one can boast. [10]For we are God's workmanship, created in Christ Jesus to do good works, which God prepared in advance for us to do.

Experienced by Moses (Ex 15:2). Priests clothed with (2Ch 6:41; Ps 132:16).

Offered and Rejected: (Dt 32:15; Mt 22:3-13)

Mt 23:37 "O Jerusalem, Jerusalem, you who kill the prophets and stone those sent to you, how often I have longed to gather your children together, as a hen gathers her chicks under her wings, but you were not willing.

Lk 14:16 Jesus replied: "A certain man was preparing a great banquet and invited many guests. [17]At the time of the banquet he sent his servant to tell those who had been invited, 'Come, for everything is now ready.'

[18]"But they all alike began to make excuses. The first said, 'I have just bought a field, and I must go and see it. Please excuse me.'

[19]"Another said, 'I have just bought five yoke of oxen, and I'm on my way to try them out. Please excuse me.'

[20]"Still another said, 'I just got married, so I can't come.'

[21]"The servant came back and reported this to his master. Then the owner of the house became angry and ordered his servant, 'Go out quickly into the streets and alleys of the town and bring in the poor, the crippled, the blind and the lame.'

[22]"'Sir,' the servant said, 'what you ordered has been done, but there is still room.'

[23]"Then the master told his servant, 'Go out to the roads and country lanes and make them come in, so that my house will be full. [24]I tell you, not one of those men who were invited will get a taste of my banquet.'"

Jn 5:40 yet you refuse to come to me to have life.

Parables of:

Lk 15:2 But the Pharisees and the teachers of the law muttered, "This man welcomes sinners and eats with them."

Lk 15:4 "Suppose one of you has a hundred sheep and loses one of them. Does he not leave the ninety-nine in the open country and go after the lost sheep until he finds it? [5]And when he finds it, he joyfully puts it on his shoulders [6]and goes home. Then he calls his friends and neighbors together and says, 'Rejoice with me; I have found my lost sheep.' [7]I tell you that in the same way there will be more rejoicing in heaven over one sinner who repents than over ninety-nine righteous persons who do not need to repent.

[8]"Or suppose a woman has ten silver coins and loses one. Does she not light a lamp, sweep the house and search carefully until she finds it? [9]And when she finds it, she calls her friends and neighbors together and says, 'Rejoice with me; I have found my lost coin.' [10]In the same way, I tell you, there is rejoicing in the presence of the angels of God over one sinner who repents."

[11]Jesus continued: "There was a man who had two sons. [12]The younger one said to his father, 'Father, give me my share of the estate.' So he divided his property between them.

[13]"Not long after that, the younger son got together all he had, set off for a distant country and there squandered his wealth in wild living. [14]After he had spent everything, there was a severe famine in that whole country, and he began to be in need. [15]So he went and hired himself out to a citizen of that country, who sent him to his fields to feed pigs. [16]He longed to fill his stomach with the pods that the pigs were eating, but no one gave him anything.

[17]"When he came to his senses, he said, 'How many of my father's hired men have food to spare, and here I am starving to death! [18]I will set out and go back to my father and say to him: Father, I have sinned against heaven and against you. [19]I am no longer worthy to be called your son; make me like one of your hired men.' [20]So he got up and went to his father.

"But while he was still a long way off, his father saw him and was filled with compassion for him; he ran to his son, threw his arms around him and kissed him.

[21]"The son said to him, 'Father, I have sinned against heaven and against you. I am no longer worthy to be called your son.'

[22]"But the father said to his servants, 'Quick! Bring the best robe and put it on him. Put a ring on his finger and sandals on his feet. [23]Bring the fattened calf and kill it. Let's have a feast and celebrate. [24]For this son of mine was dead and is alive again; he was lost and is found.' So they began to celebrate.

[25]"Meanwhile, the older son was in the field. When he came near the house, he heard music and dancing. [26]So he called one of the servants and asked him what was going on. [27]'Your brother has come,' he replied, 'and your father has killed the fattened calf because he has him back safe and sound.'

²⁸"The older brother became angry and refused to go in. So his father went out and pleaded with him. ²⁹But he answered his father, 'Look! All these years I've been slaving for you and never disobeyed your orders. Yet you never gave me even a young goat so I could celebrate with my friends. ³⁰But when this son of yours who has squandered your property with prostitutes comes home, you kill the fattened calf for him!'

³¹"'My son,' the father said, 'you are always with me, and everything I have is yours. ³²But we had to celebrate and be glad, because this brother of yours was dead and is alive again; he was lost and is found.'"

Illustrated by:

A horn (Ps 18:2; Lk 1:69), a tower (2Sa 22:51), a helmet (Isa 59:17; Eph 6:17), a shield (2Sa 22:36), a lamp (Isa 62:1), a cup (Ps 116:13), clothing (2Ch 6:41; Ps 132:16; 149:4; Isa 61:10), wells (Isa 12:3), walls and bulwarks (Isa 26:1; 60:18), chariots (Hab 3:8), a victory (1Co 15:57).

Typified by the brazen serpent (Nu 21:4-9, w Jn 3:14-15).

See Atonement; Jesus the Christ, Mission of; Redemption; Regeneration; Sanctification; Sin, Forgiveness of.

SAMARIA [9076, 9085, 10726, 4899] *(belonging to clan of Shemer, 1Ki. 16:24, [BDB])*.

NIV+ SAMARITAN, SAMARITANS

1. City of, built by Omri (1Ki 16:24). Capital of the kingdom of the ten tribes (1Ki 16:29; 22:51; 2Ki 13:1,10; 15:8). Besieged by Ben-Hadad (1Ki 20; 2Ki 6:24-33; 7). The king of Syria is led into, by Elisha, who miraculously blinds him and his army (2Ki 6:8-23). Ahab ruled in. *See Ahab; Jezebel.* Besieged by Shalmaneser, king of Assyria, three years; taken; the people carried away to Halah and Habor, cities of the Medes (2Ki 17:5-6; 18:9-11). Idolatry of (1Ki 16:32; 2Ki 13:6). Temple of, destroyed (2Ki 10:17-28; 23:19). Paul and Barnabas preach in (Ac 15:3). Visited by Philip, Peter, and John (Ac 8:5-25).

2. Country of (Isa 7:9). Foreign colonies distributed among the cities of, by the king of Assyria (2Ki 17:24-41; Ezr 4:9-10). Roads through, from Judea into Galilee (Lk 17:11; Jn 4:3-8). Jesus journeys through (Jn 4:1-42), heals lepers in (Lk 17:11-19). The good Samaritan from (Lk 10:33-35). No dealings between the Jews and the inhabitants of (Jn 4:9). Expect the Messiah (Jn 4:25). Disciples made from the inhabitants of (Jn 4:39-42; Ac 8:5-8,4-17, 25). Jesus forbids the apostles to preach in the cities of (Mt 10:5).

SAMARITAN PENTATEUCH *See Samaritan(s), 2.*

SAMARITAN(S) [4899, 4901, 4902] *(of Samaria).*

NIV+ SAMARIA

1. The inhabitants of the region of Samaria (2Ki 17:26; Mt 10:5; Lk 9:52; 10:33; Jn 4:9,30,40; Ac 8:25). After the captivity of the N kingdom colonists from Babylonia, Syria, Elam, and other Assyrian territories (2Ki 17:24-34), intermarried with remnants of Jews in Samaria; held in contempt by the Jews (Ne 4:1-3; Mt 10:5; Jn 4:9-26).

2. The sect which derived its name from Samaria, a term of contempt with the Jews (Jn 8:48). Religion of the Samaritans was based on the Pentateuch alone.

SAMGAR, SAMGAR-NEBO [6161]. Depending on word division, Samgar is the city of Nergal-Sharezer, a Babylonian official at the siege of Jerusalem, or Samgar-Nebo is himself an official (Jer 39:3 and ftn).

See Nebo-Sarsekim.

SAMLAH [8528] *(a garment).* One of the ancient kings of Edom (Ge 36:36-37; 1Ch 1:47-48).

SAMOS [4904] *(heights, lofty place).* An island in the Aegean Sea. Visited by Paul (Ac 20:15).

SAMOTHRACE, SAMOTHRACIA [4903] *(Thracian Samos).* An island in the Aegean Sea. Visited by Paul (Ac 16:11).

SAMSON [9088, 4907] *(little one of Shemesh [pagan sun god] or sunny IDB KB; strong, Josephus Antiq. 5.8.4).*

NIV+ SAMSON'S

A judge of Israel (Jdg 16:31). A Danite, son of Manoah; miraculous birth of; a Nazirite from his mother's womb; the mother forbidden to drink wine or strong drink, or to eat any unclean thing during gestation (Jdg 13:2-7,24-25). Desires a Philistine woman for his wife; slays a lion (Jdg 14:1-7). His marriage feast and the riddle propounded (Jdg 14:8-19). Wife of, estranged (Jdg 14:20; 15:1-2). Is avenged for the estrangement of his wife (Jdg 15:3-8). His great strength (Jdg 15:7-14; Heb 11:32). Slays a thousand Philistines with the jawbone of a donkey (Jdg 15:13-17). Miraculously supplied with water (Jdg 15:18-19). Consorts with Delilah, a harlot; her plots with the Philistines to overcome him (Jdg 16:4-20). Is blinded by the Philistines and confined to hard labor in prison; pulls down the pillars of the temple, killing himself and many Philistines (Jdg 16:21-31; Heb 11:32).

SAMUEL [9017, 4905] *(his name is God [El] BDB IDB ISBE; heard of God, KD; the unnamed god is El KB).*

NIV+ SAMUEL'S

1. Last of the judges (1Sa 7:15), and first of the prophets after Moses (2Ch 25:18; Jer 15:1). A seer (1Sa 9:9) and priest (1Sa 2:18,27,35). The son of Elkanah and Hannah (1Sa 1:19-20), birth the result of special providence. Brought up by Eli (1Sa 3), anointed Saul (1Sa 10) and David (1Sa 16:13). Traditional author of biblical books which bear his name, died at Ramah (1Sa 25:1).

2. Descendant of Issachar (1Ch 7:2).

SAMUEL, 1 and 2

Author: Anonymous, some have suggested Zabud, son of Nathan the prophet, who is referred to in 1Ki 4:5 as the "personal adviser" to King Solomon.

Date: Probably shortly after Solomon's death (930 B.C.)

Chronology of the Books of Samuel (all dates B.C.):

1105: Birth of Samuel (1Sa 1:20).

1080: Birth of Saul.

1050: Saul anointed to be king (1Sa 10:1).

1040: Birth of David.

1025: David anointed to be Saul's successor (1Sa 16:1-13).

1010: Death of Saul and beginning of David's reign over Judah in Hebron (2Sa 1:1; 2:1,4,11).

1003: Beginning of David's reign over all Israel and capture of Jerusalem (2Sa 5).

997-992: David's wars (2Sa 8:1-14).

991: Birth of Solomon (2Sa 12:24; 1Ki 3:7; 11:42).

980: David's census (2Sa 24:1).

970: End of David's reign (2Sa 5:4-5; 1Ki 2:10-11).

Outline:

I. Historical Setting for the Establishment of Kingship in Israel (1Sa 1-7).

　A. Samuel's Birth, Youth and Calling to Be a Prophet; Judgment on the House of Eli (1Sa 1-3).

B. Israel Defeated by the Philistines, the Ark of God Taken and the Ark Restored; Samuel's Role as Judge and Deliverer (1Sa 4-7).

II. The Establishment of Kingship in Israel under the Guidance of Samuel the Prophet (1Sa 8-12).

A. The People's Sinful Request for a King and God's Intent to Give Them a King (1Sa 8).

B. Samuel Anoints Saul Privately to Be King (1Sa 9:1-10:16).

C. Saul Chosen to Be King Publicly by Lot at Mizpah (1Sa 10:17-27).

D. The Choice of Saul as King Confirmed by Victory over the Ammonites (1Sa 11:1-13).

E. Saul's Reign Inaugurated at a Covenant Renewal Ceremony Convened by Samuel at Gilgal (1Sa 11:14-12:25).

III. Saul's Kingship a Failure (1Sa 13-15).

IV. David's Rise to the Throne; Progressive Deterioration and End of Saul's Reign (1Sa 16:1-2Sa 5:5).

A. David Is Anointed Privately, Enters the Service of King Saul and Flees for His Life (1Sa 16-26).

B. David Seeks Refuge in Philistia, and Saul and His Sons Are Killed in Battle (1Sa 27-31).

C. David Becomes King over Judah (2Sa 1-4).

D. David Becomes King over All Israel (2Sa 5:1-5).

V. David's Kingship in Its Accomplishments and Glory (2Sa 5:6-9:12).

A. David Conquers Jerusalem and Defeats the Philistines (2Sa 5:6-25).

B. David Brings the Ark to Jerusalem (2Sa 6).

C. God Promises David and Everlasting Dynasty (2Sa 7).

D. The Extension of David's Kingdom Externally and the Justice of His Rule Internally (2Sa 8).

E. David's Faithfulness to His Covenant with Jonathan (2Sa 9).

VI. David's Kingship in Its Weaknesses and Failures (2Sa 10-20).

A. David Commits Adultery and Murder (2Sa 10-12).

B. David Loses His Sons Amnon and Absalom (2Sa 13-20).

VII. Final Reflections on David's Reign (2Sa 21-24).

SANBALLAT [6172] (*Sin [pagan moon god] has given life*). A very influential Samaritan who tried unsuccessfully to defeat Nehemiah's plans for rebuilding the walls of Jerusalem (Ne 4:1ff; 6:1-14; 13:28).

SANCTIFICATION [39, 40].

NIV+ SANCTIFIED, SANCTIFY, SANCTIFYING

Separated, Set Apart, Made Holy:

For God—

Ex 33:16 How will anyone know that you are pleased with me and with your people unless you go with us? What else will distinguish me and your people from all the other people on the face of the earth?"

Dt 7:6 For you are a people holy to the LORD your God. The LORD your God has chosen you out of all the peoples on the face of the earth to be his people, his treasured possession.

From iniquity—

2Ti 2:21 If a man cleanses himself from the latter, he will be an instrument for noble purposes, made holy, useful to the Master and prepared to do any good work.

By God (Ex 29:44)—

Ex 31:13 "Say to the Israelites, 'You must observe my

Sabbaths. This will be a sign between me and you for the generations to come, so you may know that I am the LORD, who makes you holy. (+Lev 20:8)

Lev 21:8 Regard them as holy, because they offer up the food of your God. Consider them holy, because I the LORD am holy—I who make you holy.

Lev 21:15 so he will not defile his offspring among his people. I am the LORD, who makes him holy.'"

Lev 21:23 yet because of his defect, he must not go near the curtain or approach the altar, and so desecrate my sanctuary. I am the LORD, who makes them holy.'" (+Lev 22:9,16)

Jer 1:5 "Before I formed you in the womb I knew you, before you were born I set you apart; I appointed you as a prophet to the nations." (+Eze 20:12)

Eze 37:28 Then the nations will know that I the LORD make Israel holy, when my sanctuary is among them forever.'"

In Christ—

1Co 1:2 To the church of God in Corinth, to those sanctified in Christ Jesus and called to be holy, together with all those everywhere who call on the name of our Lord Jesus Christ—their Lord and ours:

1Co 1:30 It is because of him that you are in Christ Jesus, who has become for us wisdom from God—that is, our righteousness, holiness and redemption.

1Co 6:11 And that is what some of you were. But you were washed, you were sanctified, you were justified in the name of the Lord Jesus Christ and by the Spirit of our God.

Eph 5:25 Husbands, love your wives, just as Christ loved the church and gave himself up for her [26]to make her holy, cleansing her by the washing with water through the word, [27]and to present her to himself as a radiant church, without stain or wrinkle or any other blemish, but holy and blameless.

Heb 2:11 Both the one who makes men holy and those who are made holy are of the same family. So Jesus is not ashamed to call them brothers.

Heb 10:10 And by that will, we have been made holy through the sacrifice of the body of Jesus Christ once for all.

Heb 10:14 because by one sacrifice he has made perfect forever those who are being made holy.

Heb 13:12 And so Jesus also suffered outside the city gate to make the people holy through his own blood.

By the Holy Spirit—

Ro 15:16 to be a minister of Christ Jesus to the Gentiles with the priestly duty of proclaiming the gospel of God, so that the Gentiles might become an offering acceptable to God, sanctified by the Holy Spirit.

2Th 2:13 But we ought always to thank God for you, brothers loved by the Lord, because from the beginning God chose you to be saved through the sanctifying work of the Spirit and through belief in the truth. [14]He called you to this through our gospel, that you might share in the glory of our Lord Jesus Christ.

1Pe 1:2 who have been chosen according to the foreknowledge of God the Father, through the sanctifying work of the Spirit, for obedience to Jesus Christ and sprinkling by his blood: Grace and peace be yours in abundance.

By the blood of Christ—

Heb 9:14 How much more, then, will the blood of Christ, who through the eternal Spirit offered himself unblemished to God, cleanse our consciences from acts that lead to death, so that we may serve the living God! (+Heb 13:12)

By faith in Christ—

Ac 26:17 I will rescue you from your own people and from the Gentiles. I am sending you to them [18]to open their eyes and turn them from darkness to light, and from the power of Satan to God, so that they may receive forgiveness of sins and a place among those who are sanctified by faith in me.'

By the truth—

Jn 17:17 Sanctify them by the truth; your word is truth.

Jn 17:19 For them I sanctify myself, that they too may be truly sanctified.

By confession of sin—

1Jn 1:9 If we confess our sins, he is faithful and just and will forgive us our sins and purify us from all unrighteousness.

By intercessory prayer for—

1Th 5:23 May God himself, the God of peace, sanctify you through and through. May your whole spirit, soul and body be kept blameless at the coming of our Lord Jesus Christ.

Sanctification is the will of God—

1Th 4:3 It is God's will that you should be sanctified: that you should avoid sexual immorality; [4]that each of you should learn to control his own body in a way that is holy and honorable.

Instances of:

The altar sanctifies the gift (Ex 29:37; 30:29; Mt 23:19). Of The Sabbath (Ge 2:3; Dt 5:12; Ne 13:22). Mount Sinai (Ex 19:23). The tabernacle (Ex 29:43-44; 30:26,29; 40:34-35; Lev 8:10; Nu 7:1). The furniture of the tabernacle (Ex 30:26-29; Nu 7:1). The altar of burnt offerings (Ex 29:36-37; 40:10-11; Lev 8:11,15; Nu 7:1). The basin (Ex 30:23; Lev 8:11). The temple (2Ch 29:5,17,19).

Of Houses (Lev 27:14-15). Land (Lev 27:16-19,22). Offerings (Ex 29:27). Material things by anointing (Ex 40:9-11).

Of the firstborn of Israelites (Ex 13:2; Lev 27:26; Nu 8:17; Dt 15:19). Eleazar to fetch the ark (1Sa 7:1). Jesse to offer a sacrifice (1Sa 16:5). Of Levites (1Ch 15:12,14; 2Ch 29:34; 30:15). Of Levites, commanded (1Ch 15:12; 2Ch 29:5). Of priests (1Ch 15:14; 2Ch 5:11; 30:24). Of priests, commanded (Ex 19:22). Of Aaron and his sons (Ex 28:41; 29:33,44; 40:13; Lev 8:12,30). Of Israel (Ex 29:10,14). Of Israel, commanded (Ex 19:10; Lev 11:44; 20:7; Nu 11:18; Jos 3:5; 7:13; Joel 2:16). Job's children, by Job (Job 1:5).

Of the Corinthian Christians (1Co 1:2; 6:11; 7:14).

Of the church (Eph 5:26; 1Th 5:23)—

Jude 24 To him who is able to keep you from falling and to present you before his glorious presence without fault and with great joy—

See Holiness; Purity; Sin, Forgiveness of; Spiritual Purification.

SANCTUARY [185, 1074, 1808, 2121, 5219, 7163, 7164, 7731, 41, 3302, 3875] (*sacredness, apartness, place apart, sacred place, holy place*).

NIV+SANCTUARIES

1. The tabernacle or temple, where God established his earthly abode.

2. Judah (Ps 114:2).

3. Place of asylum (1Ki 2:28f).

4. In plural, idolatrous shrines (Am 7:9).

5. Earthly sanctuary a type of the heavenly sanctuary, in which Christ is high priest and sacrifice (Heb 10:1-18).

SAND [2567, 6760, 9220, 302].

NIV+SANDY

Found in the desert and on the shores of large bodies of water; symbolic of numberlessness, vastness (Ge 22:17; Jer 33:22; 1Ki 4:29), weight (Job 6:3), and instability (Mt 7:26).

SANDAL [5836, 5837, 4908, 5687].

NIV+SANDALED, SANDALS

Taken off on holy ground (Ex 3:5; Jos 5:15; Ac 7:33), in mourning (Eze 24:17), in token of refusal to observe the Levirate marriage (Dt 25:9; Ru 4:7-8). Of the Israelites did not wear out (Dt 29:5). Poor sold for a pair of (Am 2:6; 8:6). Made of leather (Eze 16:10), thong of (Ge 14:23; Isa 5:27; Mk 1:7), untying of, a humble service (Lk 3:16).

See Dress.

SANDBARS [1458+5536, 5358]. Off the shores of N Africa S of Crete; site of Paul's shipwreck (Ac 27:17,41).

SANHEDRIN [5284] (*sit together*). Highest Jewish tribunal during Greek and Roman periods; its origin is unknown; lost its authority when Jerusalem fell to the Romans in A.D. 70; in the time of Jesus it had authority only in Judea, but its influence was recognized even in the Diaspora (Ac 9:2; 22:5; 26:12). Composed of seventy members, plus the president, who was the high priest; members drawn from chief priests, scribes, and elders (Mt 16:21; 27:41; Mk 8:31; 11:27; 14:43,53; Lk 9:22); the secular nobility of Jerusalem; final court of appeal for all questions connected with the Mosaic law; could order arrests by its own officers of justice (Mt 26:47; Mk 14:43; Ac 4:3; 5:17f; 9:2); did not have the right of capital punishment in the time of Christ (Jn 18:31-32). *See Elders, Council of.*

SANITATION AND HYGIENE

Relating to:

Carcasses—

Lev 5:2 "'Or if a person touches anything ceremonially unclean—whether the carcasses of unclean wild animals or of unclean livestock or of unclean creatures that move along the ground—even though he is unaware of it, he has become unclean and is guilty.

Lev 10:4 Moses summoned Mishael and Elzaphan, sons of Aaron's uncle Uzziel, and said to them, "Come here; carry your cousins outside the camp, away from the front of the sanctuary." [5]So they came and carried them, still in their tunics, outside the camp, as Moses ordered.

Lev 11:24 "'You will make yourselves unclean by these; whoever touches their carcasses will be unclean till evening. [25]Whoever picks up one of their carcasses must wash his clothes, and he will be unclean till evening.

[26]"'Every animal that has a split hoof not completely divided or that does not chew the cud is unclean for you; whoever touches [the carcass of] any of them will be unclean. [27]Of all the animals that walk on all fours, those that walk on their paws are unclean for you; whoever touches their carcasses will be unclean till evening. [28]Anyone who picks up their carcasses must wash their clothes, and he will be unclean till evening. They are unclean for you. (+Lev 11:29-30)

Lev 11:31 Of all those that move along the ground, these are unclean for you. Whoever touches them when they are dead will be unclean till evening. [32]When one of them dies and falls on something, that article, whatever its use, will be unclean, whether it is made of wood, cloth, hide or sackcloth. Put it in water; it will be unclean till evening, and then it will be clean. ³³If one of them falls into a clay pot, everything in it will be unclean, and you must break the pot. ³⁴Any food that could be eaten but has water on it from such a pot is unclean, and any liquid that could be drunk from it is unclean. ³⁵Anything that one of their carcasses falls on becomes unclean; an oven or cooking pot must be broken up. They are unclean, and you are to regard them as unclean. ³⁶A spring, however, or a cistern for collecting water remains clean, but anyone who touches one of these carcasses is unclean. ³⁷If a carcass falls on any seeds that are to be planted, they remain clean. ³⁸But if water has been put on the seed and a carcass falls on it, it is unclean for you.

³⁹" 'If an animal that you are allowed to eat dies, anyone who touches the carcass will be unclean till evening. ⁴⁰Anyone who eats some of the carcass must wash his clothes, and he will be unclean till evening. Anyone who picks up the carcass must wash his clothes, and he will be unclean till evening.

Lev 22:4 " 'If a descendant of Aaron has an infectious skin disease or a bodily discharge, he may not eat the sacred offerings until he is cleansed. He will also be unclean if he touches something defiled by a corpse or by anyone who has an emission of semen,

Lev 22:6 The one who touches any such thing will be unclean till evening. He must not eat any of the sacred offerings unless he has bathed himself with water.

Nu 9:6 But some of them could not celebrate the Passover on that day because they were ceremonially unclean on account of a dead body. So they came to Moses and Aaron that same day

Nu 9:10 "Tell the Israelites: 'When any of you or your descendants are unclean because of a dead body or are away on a journey, they may still celebrate the LORD's Passover.

Nu 19:11 "Whoever touches the dead body of anyone will be unclean for seven days. ¹²He must purify himself with the water on the third day and on the seventh day; then he will be clean. But if he does not purify himself on the third and seventh days, he will not be clean. ¹³Whoever touches the dead body of anyone and fails to purify himself defiles the LORD's tabernacle. That person must be cut off from Israel. Because the water of cleansing has not been sprinkled on him, he is unclean; his uncleanness remains on him.

¹⁴"This is the law that applies when a person dies in a tent: Anyone who enters the tent and anyone who is in it will be unclean for seven days, ¹⁵and every open container without a lid fastened on it will be unclean.

¹⁶"Anyone out in the open who touches someone who has been killed with a sword or someone who has died a natural death, or anyone who touches a human bone or a grave, will be unclean for seven days.

Nu 31:19 "All of you who have killed anyone or touched anyone who was killed must stay outside the camp seven days. On the third and seventh days you must purify yourselves and your captives.

Dt 21:22 If a man guilty of a capital offense is put to death and his body is hung on a tree, ²³you must not leave his body on the tree overnight. Be sure to bury him that same day, because anyone who is hung on a tree is under God's curse. You must not desecrate the land the LORD your God is giving you as an inheritance.

Childbirth—

Lev 12:3 On the eighth day the boy is to be circumcised.

Eze 16:4 On the day you were born your cord was not cut, nor were you washed with water to make you clean, nor were you rubbed with salt or wrapped in cloths.

Circumcision. *See Circumcision.*

Contagion—

Lev 5:2 " 'Or if a person touches anything ceremonially unclean—whether the carcasses of unclean wild animals or of unclean livestock or of unclean creatures that move along the ground—even though he is unaware of it, he has become unclean and is guilty.

³" 'Or if he touches human uncleanness—anything that would make him unclean—even though he is unaware of it, when he learns of it he will be guilty.

Lev 7:19 " 'Meat that touches anything ceremonially unclean must not be eaten; it must be burned up. As for other meat, anyone ceremonially clean may eat it.

Lev 7:21 If anyone touches something unclean—whether human uncleanness or an unclean animal or any unclean, detestable thing—and then eats any of the meat of the fellowship offering belonging to the LORD, that person must be cut off from his people.' ". (+Lev 11:24-40)

Nu 9:6 But some of them could not celebrate the Passover on that day because they were ceremonially unclean on account of a dead body. So they came to Moses and Aaron that same day

Nu 9:10 "Tell the Israelites: 'When any of you or your descendants are unclean because of a dead body or are away on a journey, they may still celebrate the LORD's Passover. (+Nu 19:11-16)

Nu 19:22 Anything that an unclean person touches becomes unclean, and anyone who touches it becomes unclean till evening."

Nu 31:19 "All of you who have killed anyone or touched anyone who was killed must stay outside the camp seven days. On the third and seventh days you must purify yourselves and your captives. ²⁰Purify every garment as well as everything made of leather, goat hair or wood."

Infectious skin diseases (Lev 13-14)—

Nu 5:2 "Command the Israelites to send away from the camp anyone who has an infectious skin disease or a discharge of any kind, or who is ceremonially unclean because of a dead body. ³Send away male and female alike; send them outside the camp so they will not defile their camp, where I dwell among them." ⁴The Israelites did this; they sent them outside the camp. They did just as the LORD had instructed Moses.

Dt 24:8 In cases of leprous diseases be very careful to do exactly as the priests, who are Levites, instruct you. You must follow carefully what I have commanded them.

Bodily discharges (Lev 15:2-33)—

Lev 22:4 " 'If a descendant of Aaron has an infectious skin disease or a bodily discharge, he may not eat the sacred offerings until he is cleansed. He will also be unclean if he touches something defiled by a corpse or by anyone who has an emission of semen, ⁵or if he touches any crawling thing that makes him unclean, or any person who makes him unclean, whatever the uncleanness may be. ⁶The one who touches any such thing will be unclean till evening. He must not eat any of the sacred offerings unless he has bathed himself with water. ⁷When the sun goes down, he will be clean, and after that he may eat the sacred offerings, for they are his food. ⁸He must not eat anything found dead or torn by wild animals, and so become unclean through it. I am the LORD.

For Prevention of the Spread of Disease:

By washing—

Lev 13:6 On the seventh day the priest is to examine him again, and if the sore has faded and has not spread in the skin, the priest shall pronounce him clean; it is only a rash. The man must wash his clothes, and he will be clean.

Lev 13:34 On the seventh day the priest is to examine the itch, and if it has not spread in the skin and appears to be no more than skin deep, the priest shall pronounce him clean. He must wash his clothes, and he will be clean.

Lev 13:53 "But if, when the priest examines it, the mildew has not spread in the clothing, or the woven or knitted material, or the leather article, ⁵⁴he shall order that the contaminated article be washed. Then he is to isolate it for another seven days.

Lev 13:58 The clothing, or the woven or knitted material, or any leather article that has been washed and is rid of the mildew, must be washed again, and it will be clean."

⁵⁹These are the regulations concerning contamination by mildew in woolen or linen clothing, woven or knitted material, or any leather article, for pronouncing them clean or unclean.

Lev 14:8 "The person to be cleansed must wash his clothes, shave off all his hair and bathe with water; then he will be ceremonially clean. After this he may come into the camp, but he must stay outside his tent for seven days. ⁹On the seventh day he must shave off all his hair; he must shave his head, his beard, his eyebrows and the rest of his hair. He must wash his clothes and bathe himself with water, and he will be clean. (+Lev 14:46,48,54-57; 15:2-28)

Nu 31:19 "All of you who have killed anyone or touched anyone who was killed must stay outside the camp seven days. On the third and seventh days you must purify yourselves and your captives. ²⁰Purify every garment as well as everything made of leather, goat hair or wood."

Nu 31:22 Gold, silver, bronze, iron, tin, lead ²³and anything else that can withstand fire must be put through the fire, and then it will be clean. But it must also be purified with the water of cleansing. And whatever cannot withstand fire must be put through that water. ²⁴On the seventh day wash your clothes and you will be clean. Then you may come into the camp." (+Dt 23:10-11)

By burning—

Lev 7:19 "'Meat that touches anything ceremonially unclean must not be eaten; it must be burned up. As for other meat, anyone ceremonially clean may eat it.

Lev 13:51 On the seventh day he is to examine it, and if the mildew has spread in the clothing, or the woven or knitted material, or the leather, whatever its use, it is a destructive mildew; the article is unclean. ⁵²He must burn up the clothing, or the woven or knitted material of wool or linen, or any leather article that has the contamination in it, because the mildew is destructive; the article must be burned up.

Lev 13:55 After the affected article has been washed, the priest is to examine it, and if the mildew has not changed its appearance, even though it has not spread, it is unclean. Burn it with fire, whether the mildew has affected one side or the other. ⁵⁶If, when the priest examines it, the mildew has faded after the article has been washed, he is to tear the contaminated part out of the clothing, or the leather, or the woven or knitted material. ⁵⁷But if it reappears in the clothing, or in the woven or knitted material, or in the leather article, it is spreading, and whatever has the mildew must be burned with fire. (+Nu 31:19-20,22-23)

By isolation, *i.e.*, quarantine—

Lev 13:2 "When anyone has a swelling or a rash or a bright spot on his skin that may become an infectious skin disease, he must be brought to Aaron the priest or to one of his sons who is a priest. ³The priest is to examine the sore on his skin, and if the hair in the sore has turned white and the sore appears to be more than skin deep, it is an infectious skin disease. When the priest examines him, he shall pronounce him ceremonially unclean. ⁴If the spot on his skin is white but does not appear to be more than skin deep and the hair in it has not turned white, the priest is to put the infected person in isolation for seven days. ⁵On the seventh day the priest is to examine him, and if he sees that the sore is unchanged and has not spread in the skin, he is to keep him in isolation another seven days.

Lev 13:31 But if, when the priest examines this kind of sore, it does not seem to be more than skin deep and there is no black hair in it, then the priest is to put the infected person in isolation for seven days. ³²On the seventh day the priest is to examine the sore, and if the itch has not spread and there is no yellow hair in it and it does not appear to be more than skin deep, ³³he must be shaved except for the diseased area, and the priest is to keep him in isolation another seven days.

Lev 13:45 "The person with such an infectious disease must wear torn clothes, let his hair be unkempt, cover the lower part of his face and cry out, 'Unclean! Unclean!' ⁴⁶As long as he has the infection he remains unclean. He must live alone; he must live outside the camp.

Lev 13:47 "If any clothing is contaminated with mildew— any woolen or linen clothing, ⁴⁸any woven or knitted material of linen or wool, any leather or anything made of leather— ⁴⁹and if the contamination in the clothing, or leather, or woven or knitted material, or any leather article, is greenish or reddish, it is a spreading mildew and must be shown to the priest. ⁵⁰The priest is to examine the mildew and isolate the affected article for seven days.

Lev 14:34 "When you enter the land of Canaan, which I am giving you as your possession, and I put a spreading mildew in a house in that land, ³⁵the owner of the house must go and tell the priest, 'I have seen something that looks like mildew in my house.' ³⁶The priest is to order the house to be emptied before he goes in to examine the mildew, so that nothing in the house will be pronounced unclean. After this the priest is to go in and inspect the house. ³⁷He is to examine the mildew on the walls, and if it has greenish or reddish depressions that appear to be deeper than the surface of the wall, ³⁸the priest shall go out the doorway of the house and close it up for seven days.

Lev 15:19 "'When a woman has her regular flow of blood, the impurity of her monthly period will last seven days, and anyone who touches her will be unclean till evening.

Nu 5:2 "Command the Israelites to send away from the camp anyone who has an infectious skin disease or a discharge of any kind, or who is ceremonially unclean because of a dead body. ³Send away male and female alike; send them outside the camp so they will not defile their camp, where I dwell among them."

Nu 12:10 When the cloud lifted from above the Tent, there stood Miriam—leprous, like snow. Aaron turned toward her and saw that she had leprosy;

Nu 12:14 The LORD replied to Moses, "If her father had spit in her face, would she not have been in disgrace for seven days? Confine her outside the camp for seven days; after that she can be brought back." ¹⁵So Miriam was confined outside the camp for seven days, and the people did not move on till she was brought back.

2Ki 7:3 Now there were four men with leprosy at the entrance of the city gate. They said to each other, "Why stay here until we die?

2Ki 15:5 The LORD afflicted the king with leprosy until the day he died, and he lived in a separate house. Jotham the king's son had charge of the palace and governed the people of the land. (+2Ch 26:21)

Lk 17:12 As he was going into a village, ten men who had leprosy met him. They stood at a distance

By demolishing infected houses—

Lev 14:39 On the seventh day the priest shall return to inspect the house. If the mildew has spread on the walls, [40]he is to order that the contaminated stones be torn out and thrown into an unclean place outside the town. [41]He must have all the inside walls of the house scraped and the material that is scraped off dumped into an unclean place outside the town. [42]Then they are to take other stones to replace these and take new clay and plaster the house.

[43]"If the mildew reappears in the house after the stones have been torn out and the house scraped and plastered, [44]the priest is to go and examine it and, if the mildew has spread in the house, it is a destructive mildew; the house is unclean. [45]It must be torn down—its stones, timbers and all the plaster—and taken out of the town to an unclean place.

Food:

Acceptable: Animals with split hoof that chew cud—

Lev 11:2 "Say to the Israelites: 'Of all the animals that live on land, these are the ones you may eat: [3]You may eat any animal that has a split hoof completely divided and that chews the cud.

Dt 14:6 You may eat any animal that has a split hoof divided in two and that chews the cud.

Acceptable: Aquatic animals having fins and scales—

Lev 11:9 "'Of all the creatures living in the water of the seas and the streams, you may eat any that have fins and scales.

Dt 14:9 Of all the creatures living in the water, you may eat any that has fins and scales.

Acceptable: Certain insects—

Lev 11:22 Of these you may eat any kind of locust, katydid, cricket or grasshopper.

Forbidden: Fat—

Lev 3:17 "'This is a lasting ordinance for the generations to come, wherever you live: You must not eat any fat or any blood.'"

Lev 7:23 "Say to the Israelites: 'Do not eat any of the fat of cattle, sheep or goats. [24]The fat of an animal found dead or torn by wild animals may be used for any other purpose, but you must not eat it. [25]Anyone who eats the fat of an animal from which an offering by fire may be made to the LORD must be cut off from his people.

Forbidden: Blood (Lev 3:17)—

Lev 7:26 And wherever you live, you must not eat the blood of any bird or animal. [27]If anyone eats blood, that person must be cut off from his people.'"

Lev 17:10 "'Any Israelite or any alien living among them who eats any blood—I will set my face against that person who eats blood and will cut him off from his people. [11]For the life of a creature is in the blood, and I have given it to you to make atonement for yourselves on the altar; it is the blood that makes atonement for one's life. [12]Therefore I

say to the Israelites, "None of you may eat blood, nor may an alien living among you eat blood."

[13]"'Any Israelite or any alien living among you who hunts any animal or bird that may be eaten must drain out the blood and cover it with earth, [14]because the life of every creature is its blood. That is why I have said to the Israelites, "You must not eat the blood of any creature, because the life of every creature is its blood; anyone who eats it must be cut off." (+Lev 19:26)

Dt 12:16 But you must not eat the blood; pour it out on the ground like water.

Dt 12:20 When the LORD your God has enlarged your territory as he promised you, and you crave meat and say, "I would like some meat," then you may eat as much of it as you want. [21]If the place where the LORD your God chooses to put his Name is too far away from you, you may slaughter animals from the herds and flocks the LORD has given you, as I have commanded you, and in your own towns you may eat as much of them as you want. [22]Eat them as you would gazelle or deer. Both the ceremonially unclean and the clean may eat. [23]But be sure you do not eat the blood, because the blood is the life, and you must not eat the life with the meat. [24]You must not eat the blood; pour it out on the ground like water. [25]Do not eat it, so that it may go well with you and your children after you, because you will be doing what is right in the eyes of the LORD. (+Dt 15:22-23)

Forbidden: Meat that touched anything unclean—

Lev 7:19 "'Meat that touches anything ceremonially unclean must not be eaten; it must be burned up. As for other meat, anyone ceremonially clean may eat it.

Meat of fellowship and thank offerings remaining until the second day—

Lev 7:15 The meat of his fellowship offering of thanksgiving must be eaten on the day it is offered; he must leave none of it till morning. (+Lev 22:30)

Forbidden: Meat of vow or voluntary offerings left until the third day—

Lev 7:16 "'If, however, his offering is the result of a vow or is a freewill offering, the sacrifice shall be eaten on the day he offers it, but anything left over may be eaten on the next day.

Lev 7:18 If any meat of the fellowship offering is eaten on the third day, it will not be accepted. It will not be credited to the one who offered it, for it is impure; the person who eats any of it will be held responsible.

Lev 19:5 "'When you sacrifice a fellowship offering to the LORD, sacrifice it in such a way that it will be accepted on your behalf. [6]It shall be eaten on the day you sacrifice it or on the next day; anything left over until the third day must be burned up. [7]If any of it is eaten on the third day, it is impure and will not be accepted. [8]Whoever eats it will be held responsible because he has desecrated what is holy to the LORD; that person must be cut off from his people.

Forbidden: Animals that only chew cud or only have a split hoof—

Lev 11:4 "'There are some that only chew the cud or only have a split hoof, but you must not eat them. The camel, though it chews the cud, does not have a split hoof; it is ceremonially unclean for you.

Lev 11:8 You must not eat their meat or touch their carcasses; they are unclean for you.

Lev 11:26 "'Every animal that has a split hoof not completely divided or that does not chew the cud is unclean for you; whoever touches [the carcass of] any of them will be unclean.

Dt 14:7 However, of those that chew the cud or that have a split hoof completely divided you may not eat the camel, the rabbit or the coney. Although they chew the cud, they do not have a split hoof; they are ceremonially unclean for you. **8**The pig is also unclean; although it has a split hoof, it does not chew the cud. You are not to eat their meat or touch their carcasses.

Forbidden: Aquatic animals without fins and scales—
Lev 11:10 But all creatures in the seas or streams that do not have fins and scales—whether among all the swarming things or among all the other living creatures in the water—you are to detest. **11**And since you are to detest them, you must not eat their meat and you must detest their carcasses. **12**Anything living in the water that does not have fins and scales is to be detestable to you.
Dt 14:10 But anything that does not have fins and scales you may not eat; for you it is unclean.

Forbidden: Animals dying of themselves or torn by beasts (Ex 22:31)—
Lev 17:15 "'Anyone, whether native-born or alien, who eats anything found dead or torn by wild animals must wash his clothes and bathe with water, and he will be ceremonially unclean till evening; then he will be clean.
Lev 22:8 He must not eat anything found dead or torn by wild animals, and so become unclean through it. I am the LORD.
Dt 14:21 Do not eat anything you find already dead. You may give it to an alien living in any of your towns, and he may eat it, or you may sell it to a foreigner. But you are a people holy to the LORD your God. Do not cook a young goat in its mother's milk.

Forbidden: Certain insects—
Lev 11:23 But all other winged creatures that have four legs you are to detest.

Forbidden: Certain creatures that move on the ground—
Lev 11:20 "'All flying insects that walk on all fours are to be detestable to you. **21**There are, however, some winged creatures that walk on all fours that you may eat: those that have jointed legs for hopping on the ground.
Lev 11:28 Anyone who picks up their carcasses must wash his clothes, and he will be unclean till evening. They are unclean for you.
29"'Of the animals that move about on the ground, these are unclean for you: the weasel, the rat, any kind of great lizard, **30**the gecko, the monitor lizard, the wall lizard, the skink and the chameleon. **31**Of all those that move along the ground, these are unclean for you. Whoever touches them when they are dead will be unclean till evening.
Lev 11:41 "'Every creature that moves about on the ground is detestable; it is not to be eaten.

Forbidden: Certain birds—
Lev 11:13 "'These are the birds you are to detest and not eat because they are detestable: the eagle, the vulture, the black vulture, **14**the red kite, any kind of black kite, **15**any kind of raven, **16**the horned owl, the screech owl, the gull, any kind of hawk, **17**the little owl, the cormorant, the great owl, **18**the white owl, the desert owl, the osprey,

Waste Products:

Disposition—
Ex 29:14 But burn the bull's flesh and its hide and its offal outside the camp. It is a sin offering.
Ex 29:34 And if any of the meat of the ordination ram or any bread is left over till morning, burn it up. It must not be eaten, because it is sacred.
Lev 4:11 But the hide of the bull and all its flesh, as well

as the head and legs, the inner parts and offal— **12**that is, all the rest of the bull—he must take outside the camp to a place ceremonially clean, where the ashes are thrown, and burn it in a wood fire on the ash heap. (+Lev 4:21; 6:30; 7:17)
Lev 7:19 "'Meat that touches anything ceremonially unclean must not be eaten; it must be burned up. As for other meat, anyone ceremonially clean may eat it.
Lev 8:17 But the bull with its hide and its flesh and its offal he burned up outside the camp, as the LORD commanded Moses.
Lev 8:32 Then burn up the rest of the meat and the bread.
Lev 9:11 the flesh and the hide he burned up outside the camp.
Lev 16:27 The bull and the goat for the sin offerings, whose blood was brought into the Most Holy Place to make atonement, must be taken outside the camp; their hides, flesh and offal are to be burned up. **28**The man who burns them must wash his clothes and bathe himself with water; afterward he may come into the camp. (+Lev 19:6)
Dt 23:12 Designate a place outside the camp where you can go to relieve yourself. **13**As part of your equipment have something to dig with, and when you relieve yourself, dig a hole and cover up your excrement.
Heb 13:11 The high priest carries the blood of animals into the Most Holy Place as a sin offering, but the bodies are burned outside the camp.

Women in childbirth: (Lev 12:2,4-5).

Penalties Concerning:

Dt 28:15 However, if you do not obey the LORD your God and do not carefully follow all his commands and decrees I am giving you today, all these curses will come upon you and overtake you:
Dt 28:21 The LORD will plague you with diseases until he has destroyed you from the land you are entering to possess. **22**The LORD will strike you with wasting disease, with fever and inflammation, with scorching heat and drought, with blight and mildew, which will plague you until you perish.
Dt 28:27 The LORD will afflict you with the boils of Egypt and with tumors, festering sores and the itch, from which you cannot be cured.
Dt 28:35 The LORD will afflict your knees and legs with painful boils that cannot be cured, spreading from the soles of your feet to the top of your head.
Dt 28:45 All these curses will come upon you. They will pursue you and overtake you until you are destroyed, because you did not obey the LORD your God and observe the commands and decrees he gave you.
Dt 28:59 the LORD will send fearful plagues on you and your descendants, harsh and prolonged disasters, and severe and lingering illnesses. **60**He will bring upon you all the diseases of Egypt that you dreaded, and they will cling to you. **61**The LORD will also bring on you every kind of sickness and disaster not recorded in this Book of the Law, until you are destroyed. **62**You who were as numerous as the stars in the sky will be left but few in number, because you did not obey the LORD your God.

See Defilement; Leprosy; Purification; Unclean, Uncleanness; Washings.

SANNAH *See Kiriath Sannah.*

SANSANNAH [6179] (*a palm branch*). A city of Judah (Jos 15:31).

SAPH [6198] (*a basin, threshold*). A Philistine giant, slain by one of David's heroes (2Sa 21:18; 1Ch 20:4).

SAPHIR See *Shaphir.*

SAPPHIRA [4912] (*beautiful*). The wife of Ananias; struck dead at Peter's feet because she lied (Ac 5:1-10).

SAPPHIRE [6209, 4913].

NIV+ SAPPHIRES

1. A precious stone (Ex 24:10; Eze 28:13).
2. Set in the priestly breastplate (Ex 28:18; 39:11).

Symbolic:

Throne of God (Ex 24:10; Eze 1:26; 10:1). Seen in the foundation of the Holy City, the New Jerusalem in John's apocalyptic vision (Rev 21:19).

Figurative:

Ezekiel uses imagery of the Creation and the Fall to picture the career of the king of Tyre; unlike Adam, who was naked, the king is pictured as a fully clothed priest, ordained to guard God's holy place; the nine stones listed are among the twelve worn by the priest (Eze 28:13).

See *Minerals of the Bible, 1; Stones.*

SARAH, SARA, SARAI [8577, 8584, 4925] (*princess*).

NIV+ SARAH'S

1. .The wife of Abraham (Ge 11:29-31; 12:5). Near of kin to Abraham (Ge 12:10-20; 20:12). Abraham represents her as his sister, and Abimelech, king of Gerar, takes her; she is restored to Abraham by means of a dream (Ge 20:1-14). Is sterile; gives her maid, Hagar, to Abraham as a wife to bear his child (Ge 16:1-3). Her jealousy of Hagar (Ge 16:4-6; 21:9-14). Her miraculous conception of Isaac (Ge 17:15-21; 18:9-15). Name changed from Sarai to Sarah (Ge 17:15). Gives birth to Isaac (Ge 21:3,6-8). Death and burial of (Ge 23; 25:10). Character of (Heb 11:11; 1Pe 3:5-6).
2. The daughter of Asher (Ge 46:17; Nu 26:46; 1Ch 7:30).

SARAPH [8598] (*burning one, serpent*). A descendant of Shelah (1Ch 4:22).

SARCASM

Instances of:

Cain's self-justifying argument when God asked him where Abel was (Ge 4:9). Israelites reproaching Israel (Nu 11:20; Jdg 10:14). Balak reproaching Balaam (Nu 24:11). Joshua to descendants of Joseph (Jos 17:15). By Jotham (Jdg 9:7-19), Samson (Jdg 14:18). The men of Jabesh to Nahash (1Sa 11:10). Eliab to David (1Sa 17:28). Elijah to the priests of Baal (1Ki 18:27). David's reply to Michal's irony (2Sa 6:21). Ahab's reply to Ben-Hadad (1Ki 20:11). Jehoash to Amaziah (2Ki 14:9-10; 2Ch 25:18-19). The field commander to Hezekiah (2Ki 18:23-24). Sanballat's address to the army of Samaria (Ne 4:2-3). Zophar to Job (Job 11:12). Job to Zophar (Job 12:2-3). Of Solomon (Pr 26:16). The persecutors of Jesus (Mt 27:28-29; Lk 23:11; Jn 19:2-3,5,15). Paul (1Ti 4:7). Agrippa to Paul (Ac 26:28).

See *Irony; Satire.*

SARDINE See *Carnelian; Minerals of the Bible.*

SARDIS [4915]. Chief city of Lydia; famous for arts and crafts; patron of mystery cults (Rev 1:11; 3:1-6).

SARDITE See *Sered, Seredite.*

SARDIUS See *Carnelian; Minerals of the Bible, 1; Ruby; Stones.*

SARDONYX [4918]. A precious stone seen in the foundation of the Holy City, the New Jerusalem (Rev 21:20). See *Minerals of the Bible, 1; Stones.*

SAREPTA See *Zarephath.*

SARGON [6236] (*firm, faithful king* BDB; *the king is legitimate* IDB).

1. Sargon I, king and founder of early Babylonian Empire (2400 B.C.). Not referred to in the Bible.
2. Sargon II (722-705 B.C.), an Assyrian king (Isa 20:1), successor of Shalmaneser who captured Samaria (2Ki 17:1-6), defeated Egyptian ruler So (2Ki 17:4), destroyed the Hittite Empire; succeeded by his son Sennacherib.

SARID [8587] (*survivor*). A village on the boundary of Zebulun (Jos 19:10,12); modern Tel Shadud, N of Megiddo.

SARON See *Sharon.*

SARSECHIM See *Nebo-Sarsekim.*

SARUCH See *Serug.*

SASH [77, 258, 2512, 2514, 8005, 2438].

NIV+ SASHES

A belt or waistband. Worn by the high priest (Ex 28:4, 39; 39:29; Lev 8:7; 16:4), by other priests (Ex 28:40; 29:9; Lev 8:13), by women (Isa 3:18-24), by Jesus in John's vision (Rev 1:13). Commerce in (Pr 31:24). See *Belt; Dress.*

SATAN [8477, 4928] (*hostile opponent*).

NIV+ SATAN'S

1. As a common noun; enemy or adversary (1Sa 29:4; 1Ki 5:4; 11:14; Ps 38:20; 109:6).
2. As a proper noun; the chief of the fallen spirits, the grand adversary of God and man (Jn 1:6,12; 2:1; Zec 3:1), hostile to everything good. Not an independent rival of God, but is able to go only as far as God permits (Job 1:12; 2:6; Lk 22:31). Basically evil; story of his origin not told, but he was originally good; fell as a star out of heaven because of pride (possibly Isa 14:12; Eze 29:12-19; Lk 10:18; 1Ti 3:6). Ruler of a powerful kingdom standing in opposition to God (Mt 12:26; Lk 11:18); continually seeks to defeat the divine plans of grace toward mankind (1Pe 5:8); defeated by Christ at Calvary (Ge 3:15; Jn 3:8).

Sterilizes the heart (Mt 13:19,38-39; Mk 4:15; Lk 8:12). Causes spiritual blindness (2Co 4:4), physical infirmities (Lk 13:16).

Devices of (2Co 2:11; 12:7; Eph 6:11-12,16; 1Th 2:18; 1Ti 3:6-7).

Hymenaeus and Alexander delivered to (1Ti 1:20). Contends with Michael (Jude 9). Ministers of, masquerade as apostles of Christ (2Co 11:15).

To be resisted (Eph 4:27; Jas 4:7; 1Pe 5:8-9). Resistance of, effectual (1Jn 2:13; 5:18). Gracious deliverance from the power of (Ac 27:18; Col 1:13). Persecutes the church (Rev 2:10,13-14).

Christ accused of being (Mt 9:34; Mk 2:22-26; Lk 11:15,18). Paul accuses Elymas the sorcerer of being (Ac 13:10).

Called:

Beelzebub (Mt 12:24; Mk 3:22; Lk 11:15). Belial (2Co 6:15). The devil (Mt 4:1; 13:39; Lk 4:2-6; Rev 20:2). Satan

(1Ch 21:1; Job 1:6; Zec 3:1; Lk 22:31; Jn 13:27; Ac 5:3; 26:18; Ro 16:20). Possibly Apollyon (Rev 9:11) and Lucifer (Isa 14:12, KJV). *See Titles and Names, Of the Devil.*

Character of:

Accuser (Job 1:6-7,9-12; 2:3-7), Adversary (Lk 22:31, 53; 1Pe 5:8). Deceiver of the whole world (Rev 12:9). Murderer and liar (Jn 8:44; Ac 5:3). Sinned from the beginning (1Jn 3:8). Subtle (Ge 3:1; 2Co 11:3). Tempter (Mt 4:3; 1Co 7:5; 1Th 3:5; 1Ti 5:15). Transforms himself into an angel of light (2Co 11:14).

Described as:

Accuser of our brothers (Rev 12:10). Ancient serpent (Rev 12:9; 20:2). Angel of the bottomless pit (Rev 9:11). Enemy (Mt 13:29). Father of lies (Jn 8:44). Great dragon (Rev 12:9). Evil one (Mt 13:19,38). Power of darkness (Col 1:13). Prince of this world (Jn 12:31; 14:30; 16:11), of demons (Mt 12:24), of the power of the air (Eph 2:2). Ruler of the darkness of this world (Eph 6:12). Spirit that works in the children of disobedience (Eph 2:2). The god of this world (2Co 4:4).

Instances of Temptations of:

Eve (Ge 3:1,4-5,14-15; 2Co 11:3). Job (Job 1:13-22; 2:7-10). David (1Ch 21:1). Jesus (Mt 4:1-11; Mk 1:13; Lk 4:1-13; Jn 14:30). Judas (Jn 13:2,27).

Kingdom of:

Called gates of hell (Mt 16:18). To be destroyed (Ge 3:15; Mt 13:30; Ro 16:20; 1Jn 3:8).

Symbolized:

By the serpent (Ge 3:13; 2Co 11:3). By the dragon (Rev 12:3-4).

Synagogue of: (Rev 2:9; 3:9).

See Demons.

Destiny of:

A conquered enemy of believers (Jn 12:31; 16:9-10; 1Jn 3:8; Col 2:15). Judged already (Jn 16:11). Under perpetual curse (Ge 3:14; Isa 65:25). To be cast out of this world (Jn 12:31), bound (Rev 20:1-3), cast into the lake of fire (Mt 25:41; Rev 20:10).

SATIRE Hannah's song of exultation over Peninnah (1Sa 2:1-10, w 1:5-10). Of Jesus against hypocrites (Mt 23:2-33; Mk 12:13-40; Lk 11:39-54).

See Irony; Sarcasm.

SATRAP [346, 10026] (*protector of the land*).

NIV+ SATRAPS

An official in the Persian Empire who ruled several small provinces (satraps), each having its own governor. (Ezr 8:36; Est 3:12; 8:9; 9:3; Da 3:2-3,27; 6:1-7).

SATYR NIV "goat idols" (Lev 17:7; 2Ch 11:15); "wild goats" (Isa 34:14).

SAUL [8620, *4910, 4930*] (*asked,* possibly *dedicated to God*).

NIV+ SAUL'S

1. Also called Shaul. King of Edom (Ge 36:37-38; 1Ch 1:48-49).

2. King of Israel. A Benjamite, son of Kish (1Sa 9:1-2). Sons of (1Ch 8:33). His personal appearance (1Sa 9:2; 10:23). Made king of Israel (1Sa 9; 10; 11:12-15; Hos 13:11). Dwells at Gibeah of Saul (1Sa 14:2; 15:34; Isa 10:29). Defeats the Philistines (1Sa 13; 14:46,52). Kills the Amalekites (1Sa 15). Is reproved by Samuel for usurp-

ing the priestly functions (1Sa 13:11-14), for disobedience in not slaying the Amalekites; the loss of his kingdom foretold (1Sa 15). Dedicates the spoils of war (1Sa 15:21-25; 1Ch 26:28). Sends messengers to Jesse, asking that David be sent to him as musician and armor-bearer (1Sa 16:17-23). Defeats the Philistines after Goliath is slain by David (1Sa 17). His jealousy of David; gives his daughter, Michal, to David to be his wife; becomes David's enemy (1Sa 18). Tries to slay David; Jonathan intercedes and incurs his father's displeasure; David's loyalty to him; Saul's repentance; prophesies (1Sa 19). Hears Doeg against Ahimelech and slays the priest and his family (1Sa 22:9-19). Pursues David to the wilderness of Ziph; the Ziphites betray David to (1Sa 23). Pursues David to En Gedi (1Sa 24:1-6). His life saved by David (1Sa 24:5-8). Saul's contribution for his bad faith (1Sa 24:16-22). David is again betrayed to, by the Ziphites; Saul pursues him to the hill of Hakilah; his life spared again by David; his confession and his blessing upon David (1Sa 26). Slays the Gibeonites; crime avenged by the death of seven of his sons (2Sa 21:1-9). His kingdom invaded by Philistines; seeks counsel of the medium of Endor, who foretells his death (1Sa 28:3-25; 29:1). Is defeated and with his sons is slain (1Sa 31), their bodies exposed in Beth Shan; rescued by the people of Jabesh and burned; bones of, buried under a tree at Jabesh (1Sa 31, w 2Sa 1; 2; 1Ch 10). His death a judgment on account of his sins (1Ch 10:13).

3. Of Tarsus. *See Paul.*

SAVIOR, SAVIOUR [3802, 3829, 4635, 9591, *5400*] (*deliverer*).

NIV+ See SALVATION

One who saves, delivers, or preserves from any evil or danger, whether physical or spiritual, temporal or eternal; term applied both to people (Jdg 3:9,15; 2Ki 13:5; Ne 9:27; Ob 21) and to God (Ps 44:3,7; Isa 43:11; 45:21; 60:16; Jer 14:8; Hos 13:4). In NT it is never applied to people, but only to God and Christ (Lk 1:47; 1Ti 1:1; 2:3; 4:10; Tit 1:3). Savior is preeminently the title of the Son (2Ti 1:10; Tit 1:4; 2:13; 3:6; 2Pe 1:1; 1Jn 4:10).

See God, Savior; Jesus the Christ, Savior.

SAVOR, SAVOUR Taste (Mt 5:13; Lk 14:34), smell (Joel 2:20). Also used metaphorically (2Co 2:14; Eph 5:2; Php 4:18).

SAVORY MEAT NIV "tasty food." Meals made by Jacob and Esau for their father Isaac prior to receiving his blessings (Ge 27:4,9,14,17,31).

SAW [4490, *4569*].

NIV+ SAWED, SAWS

Used as an instrument of torture (Heb 11:37), for cutting stone (2Sa 12:31; 1Ki 7:9).

Figurative (Isa 10:15).

SCAB [1599+6760]. Disease of the skin (Lev 13:2,6-8; 14:56; 21:20; 22:22; Dt 28:27; Isa 3:17).

See Disease; Sanitation and Hygiene.

SCAFFOLD NIV "platform" (2Ch 6:13).

SCALE [1925, 4404, 6590, 7144, 7866, 7989, 10396, *2433, 3318*].

NIV+ SCALES

1. Only fish having fins and scales were permitted as food for Hebrews (Lev 11:9-12).

2. Instrument for weighing (Isa 40:12; Pr 16:11; 20:23).

SCALL NIV "itch," an infectious skin disease (Lev 13:30-37; 14:54; Dt 28:27). *See Disease; Leprosy; Sore.*

SCAPEBIRD (Lev 14:4-7,53).

SCAPEGOAT [6439].

NIV+ GOAT

The second of two goats for which lots were cast on the Day of Atonement (Lev 16:8,10,26). The first was sacrificed as a sin offering, but the second had the people's sins transferred to it by prayer and was then taken into the wilderness and released.

See Azazel.

SCARLET [9106, 9443, *3132*]. Probably a bright rich crimson. Scarlet cloth was used for the hangings of the tabernacle (Ex 25:4), high priest's vestments (Ex 39:1), royal or expensive apparel (2Sa 1:24). Sins are "as scarlet" (Isa 1:18).

See Colors, Figurative and Symbolic.

SCEPTER [2980, 4751, 8657, 9222, *4811*] (*royal staff*).

NIV+ SCEPTERS

A staff used by kings to signify favor or disfavor to those who desired audience (Est 5:2; 8:4). A symbol of authority (Nu 24:17; Isa 14:5). Made of gold (Est 4:11), of iron (Ps 2:9; Rev 2:27; 12:5).

Figurative: (Ge 49:10; Nu 24:17; Isa 9:4).

SCEVA [*5005*]. Chief priest living in Ephesus whose seven sons were exorcists (Ac 19:14-17).

SCHISM (*division*). A formal division inside a religious group (1Co 12:25). *See Divisions.*

SCHOOL Company of the prophets at Naioth (1Sa 19:20), Bethel (2Ki 2:3), Jericho (2Ki 2:5,15), Gilgal (2Ki 4:38), Jerusalem, probably (2Ki 22:14; 2Ch 34:22). Crowded attendance at (2Ki 6:1).

In the home (Dt 4:9-10; 6:7,9; 11:19-20; Ps 78:5-8). Assembly to hear public reading of the law (Dt 31:10-13). State (2Ch 17:7-9; Da 1:3-21). Of Gamaliel (Ac 5:34; 22:3). Of Tyrannus (Ac 19:9).

See Instruction; Psalms, Topically Arranged; Sons of the Prophets.

SCIENCE Observations of, and deductions from, facts (Job 26:7-14; 28; Ecc 1:13-17). The key of knowledge (Lk 11:52; Ro 2:20). *See Astronomy; Geology; Philosophy.*

SCOFFER [408+4371, *1851, 2970*].

NIV+ See SCOFFING

One who derides, mocks (2Pe 3:3).

SCOFFING [4352, 4610, 5377, 8471, 9239, 9506, *1848*].

NIV+ SCOFF, SCOFFED, SCOFFERS, SCOFFS

By the People of Israel:

2Ch 30:6 At the king's command, couriers went throughout Israel and Judah with letters from the king and from his officials, which read: "People of Israel, return to the LORD, the God of Abraham, Isaac and Israel, that he may return to you who are left, who have escaped from the hand of the kings of Assyria.

[7]Do not be like your fathers and brothers, who were unfaithful to the LORD, the God of their fathers, so that he made them an object of horror, as you see. [8]Do not be stiff-necked, as your fathers were; submit to the LORD.

Come to the sanctuary, which he has consecrated forever. Serve the LORD your God, so that his fierce anger will turn away from you. [9]If you return to the LORD, then your brothers and your children will be shown compassion by their captors and will come back to this land, for the LORD your God is gracious and compassionate. He will not turn his face from you if you return to him."

[10]The couriers went from town to town in Ephraim and Manasseh, as far as Zebulun, but the people scorned and ridiculed them.

2Ch 36:16 But they mocked God's messengers, despised his words and scoffed at his prophets until the wrath of the LORD was aroused against his people and there was no remedy. (+Ps 78:19-20)

Ps 107:11 for they had rebelled against the words of God and despised the counsel of the Most High. [12]So he subjected them to bitter labor; they stumbled, and there was no one to help.

Hos 7:5 On the day of the festival of our king the princes become inflamed with wine, and he joins hands with the mockers.

By Unbelievers:

Ps 42:3 My tears have been my food day and night, while men say to me all day long, "Where is your God?" (+Ps 42:10; 73:8-9)

Ps 73:11 They say, "How can God know? Does the Most High have knowledge?" (+Ps 73:12)

Pr 1:22 "How long will you simple ones love your simple ways? How long will mockers delight in mockery and fools hate knowledge?

Pr 1:25 since you ignored all my advice and would not accept my rebuke,

Jer 17:15 They keep saying to me, "Where is the word of the LORD? Let it now be fulfilled!"

Jer 43:2 Azariah son of Hoshaiah and Johanan son of Kareah and all the arrogant men said to Jeremiah, "You are lying! The LORD our God has not sent you to say, 'You must not go to Egypt to settle there.'

La 1:7 In the days of her affliction and wandering Jerusalem remembers all the treasures that were hers in days of old. When her people fell into enemy hands, there was no one to help her. Her enemies looked at her and laughed at her destruction.

Eze 8:12 He said to me, "Son of man, have you seen what the elders of the house of Israel are doing in the darkness, each at the shrine of his own idol? They say, 'The LORD does not see us; the LORD has forsaken the land.'"

Eze 9:9 He answered me, "The sin of the house of Israel and Judah is exceedingly great; the land is full of bloodshed and the city is full of injustice. They say, 'The LORD has forsaken the land; the LORD does not see.'

Eze 12:22 "Son of man, what is this proverb you have in the land of Israel: 'The days go by and every vision comes to nothing'?

2Pe 3:3 First of all, you must understand that in the last days scoffers will come, scoffing and following their own evil desires. [4]They will say, "Where is this 'coming' he promised? Ever since our fathers died, everything goes on as it has since the beginning of creation."

By the Wicked at God's Requirements:

Job 21:14 Yet they say to God, 'Leave us alone! We have no desire to know your ways. [15]Who is the Almighty, that we should serve him? What would we gain by praying to him?'

Isa 10:15 Does the ax raise itself above him who swings it, or the saw boast against him who uses it? As if a rod were to wield him who lifts it up, or a club brandish him who is not wool!

Isa 57:4 Whom are you mocking? At whom do you sneer and stick out your tongue? Are you not a brood of rebels, the offspring of liars?

Eze 11:2 The LORD said to me, "Son of man, these are the men who are plotting evil and giving wicked advice in this city. ³They say, 'Will it not soon be time to build houses? This city is a cooking pot, and we are the meat.'

Eze 33:20 Yet, O house of Israel, you say, 'The way of the Lord is not just.' But I will judge each of you according to his own ways."

Against Christ:

Mt 12:24 But when the Pharisees heard this, they said, "It is only by Beelzebub, the prince of demons, that this fellow drives out demons." (+Mk 3:22)

Lk 4:23 Jesus said to them, "Surely you will quote this proverb to me: 'Physician, heal yourself! Do here in your hometown what we have heard that you did in Capernaum.'" (+Lk 11:15)

Lk 16:14 The Pharisees, who loved money, heard all this and were sneering at Jesus.

Against the First Christians:

Ac 2:13 Some, however, made fun of them and said, "They have had too much wine."

Against Paul:

Ac 13:45 When the Jews saw the crowds, they were filled with jealousy and talked abusively against what Paul was saying.

Ac 17:18 A group of Epicurean and Stoic philosophers began to dispute with him. Some of them asked, "What is this babbler trying to say?" Others remarked, "He seems to be advocating foreign gods." They said this because Paul was preaching the good news about Jesus and the resurrection.

Ac 17:32 When they heard about the resurrection of the dead, some of them sneered, but others said, "We want to hear you again on this subject."

Proverbs Concerning: (Pr 1:22,25)

Pr 3:34 He mocks proud mockers but gives grace to the humble.

Pr 9:12 If you are wise, your wisdom will reward you; if you are a mocker, you alone will suffer."

Pr 13:1 A wise son heeds his father's instruction, but a mocker does not listen to rebuke.

Pr 14:6 The mocker seeks wisdom and finds none, but knowledge comes easily to the discerning.

Pr 14:9 Fools mock at making amends for sin, but goodwill is found among the upright.

Pr 19:29 Penalties are prepared for mockers, and beatings for the backs of fools.

Pr 21:11 When a mocker is punished, the simple gain wisdom; when a wise man is instructed, he gets knowledge.

Pr 21:24 The proud and arrogant man—"Mocker" is his name; he behaves with overweening pride.

Pr 22:10 Drive out the mocker, and out goes strife; quarrels and insults are ended.

Pr 24:9 The schemes of folly are sin, and men detest a mocker.

Punishment for: (Pr 3:24; 9:12; 19:29)

Isa 5:18 Woe to those who draw sin along with cords of deceit, and wickedness as with cart ropes, ¹⁹to those who say, "Let God hurry, let him hasten his work so we may

see it. Let it approach, let the plan of the Holy One of Israel come, so we may know it."

Isa 5:24 Therefore, as tongues of fire lick up straw and as dry grass sinks down in the flames, so their roots will decay and their flowers blow away like dust; for they have rejected the law of the LORD Almighty and spurned the word of the Holy One of Israel. ²⁵Therefore the LORD's anger burns against his people; his hand is raised and he strikes them down. The mountains shake, and the dead bodies are like refuse in the streets. Yet for all this, his anger is not turned away, his hand is still upraised.

Isa 29:20 The ruthless will vanish, the mockers will disappear, and all who have an eye for evil will be cut down—

Heb 10:29 How much more severely do you think a man deserves to be punished who has trampled the Son of God under foot, who has treated as an unholy thing the blood of the covenant that sanctified him, and who has insulted the Spirit of grace?

See Hatred; Malice; Unbelief.

Instances of:

Ishmael (Ge 21:9). Children at Bethel (2Ki 2:23). Ephraim and Manasseh (2Ch 30:10). Chiefs of Judah (2Ch 36:16). Sanballat (Ne 4:1). Enemies of Job (Job 30:1,9). Enemies of David (Ps 35:15-16). Rulers of Israel (Isa 28:14). Ammonites (Eze 25:3). Tyrians (Eze 26:2). Heathen (Eze 36:2-3). Soldiers (Mt 27:28-30; Lk 23:36). Chief priests (Mt 27:41). Pharisees (Lk 16:14). The men who held Jesus (Lk 22:63-64). Herod (Lk 23:11). People and rulers (Lk 23:35). Some of the multitude (Ac 2:13). Athenians (Ac 17:32).

SCORNERS [*996, 3075, 4009, 4353, 5653, 9240].
NIV+ SCORN, SCORNED, SCORNFULLY, SCORNING, SCORNS

(Ps 1:1; Pr 9:12; 21:11,24). An abomination (Pr 24:9). Admonitions to (Pr 1:22-23). Punishment of (Pr 19:29; Isa 29:20). Warnings against (Pr 3:34; 13:1; 14:6; 19:29; 22:10; 29:8).

See Mocking; Scoffing.

SCORPION [6832, 5026].
NIV+ SCORPIONS

A venomous insect common in the wilderness through which the Israelites journeyed (Dt 8:15). Power over, given to the seventy-two (Lk 10:19). Unfit for food (Lk 11:12). Sting of in the tail (Rev 9:10).

Symbolic: (Rev 9:3,5,10).

Figurative:

Of enemies (Eze 2:6). Of cruelty (1Ki 12:11,14).

SCORPION PASS A chain of hills in the south of Israel (Nu 34:4; Jdg 1:36). Area assigned to tribe of Judah (Jos 15:3).

SCOURGING [3579, 5596, 8765].
NIV+ SCOURGE, SCOURGED

Corporal punishment by stripes. Prescribed in the Mosaic law for fornication (Lev 19:20; Dt 22:18), for other offenses (Dt 25:2). Forty stripes the maximum limit (Dt 25:3). Fatal (Job 9:23), of servants avenged (Ex 21:20). Foretold by Jesus as a persecution of the Christians (Mt 10:17).

Of children. *See Children, Correction and Punishment; Punishment.*

Instances of:

Of Jesus (Mt 20:19; 27:26; Mk 15:15; Jn 19:1). Of Paul

and Silas (Ac 16:23). Of Paul (Ac 21:32; 22:24; 2Co 11:24-25). Of Sosthenes (Ac 18:17).

Figurative:

Of the oppressions of rulers (1Ki 12:11). Of the evil tongue (Job 5:21).

See Assault and Battery; Bruise, Bruises; Lashes; Stoning; Stripes.

SCREECH OWL [7887, 9379]. Forbidden as food (Lev 11:16; Dt 14:15). *See Birds.*

SCRIBE [6221, 8853] (*write, copy*).

NIV+ SCRIBE'S, SCRIBES

A writer and transcriber of the law (2Sa 8:17; 20:25; 1Ki 4:3; 2Ki 12:10; 18:37; 19:2; 1Ch 24:6; 27:32; Ne 13:13; Jer 36:12). King's secretary (2Ki 12:10-12; 22:1-14; Est 3:12; 8:9). Mustering officer of the army (2Ki 25:19; 2Ch 26:11). Instructors in the law (Mt 7:29; 13:52; 17:10; 23:2-3). *See Levites.* Test Jesus with questions, bringing to Jesus a woman taken in adultery (Jn 8:3). Members of the council (Mt 2:4). Conspire against Jesus (Mt 26:3,57; 27:41; Mk 14:1; Lk 22:66). Hypocrisy of, reproved by Jesus (Mt 15:20; 9:3; 12:38; 15:1; 16:21; 20:18; 21:15).

SCRIPTURES [6219, *1207, 1210*] (*writing*).

NIV+ SCRIPTURE

The Word of God (Jer 30:2). Interpreted by doctors (Jn 3:10; 7:52). Inspired (2Ti 3:16).

See Word of God.

SCROLL [1663, 4479, 5532, 6219, 10399, *1044, 1046, 1047*].

NIV+ SCROLLS

A document made of papyrus or smoothed skins of animals sewn together to make a long strip which was wound around sticks at both ends (Isa 34:4; Jer 36; Eze 3:1-3; Rev 5; 10:1-10). They varied in length from a few feet to thirty-five feet. The codex form of a book was not used until the second century A.D.

SCROLLS, DEAD SEA *See Dead Sea Scrolls.*

SCULPTURE *See Art.*

SCURVY *See Disease; Scab; Sore.*

SCYTHIAN [*5033*]. A nomadic people, savage and uncivilized, living N and E of the Black Sea (Col 3:11).

SEA [3542, 4784, 8254, 9391, 9490, 10322, *102, 343, 1113, 1879, 2498, 3237, 4283, 5007*].

NIV+ SEAFARERS, SEAMEN, SEAS, SEASHORE

Creation of (Ge 1:9-10; Ps 95:5; 148:4-5). Limits of established by God (Ge 1:9; Job 26:10; 38:8; Ps 33:7; Jer 5:22). Calmed by Jesus (Mt 8:24-26; Mk 4:37-39). Jesus walked on (Mt 14:25-31). Dead, to be given up by, at the Resurrection (Rev 20:13).

Symbolic:

In Daniel's vision (Da 7:2-3). In John's apocalyptic vision (Rev 4:6; 8:8-9; 10:2,5-6,8; 13:1; 15:2; 16:3; 21:1).

Waves of:

Reuben is as turbulent as (Ge 49:3-4). God walks on (Job 9:8). God controls (Job 38:8,11; Ps 65:7; 89:9; 93:3-4; Jer 5:22). The wicked are like (Isa 57:20-21; Jude 13). Jesus controls (Mt 8:23-26; 14:32; Mk 4:35-41). Jesus walks through on the surface of the sea of Galilee (Mt 14:22-33). When God's people are built up and become

mature, attaining to the whole measure of the fullness of Christ, they will no longer be tossed back and forth by every deceitful doctrine and scheme like the waves of the sea (Eph 4:14). Doubters are like (Jas 1:6).

SEA, BRONZE The great basin in Solomon's temple where the priests washed their hands and feet preparatory to temple ministry (1Ki 7:23-26; 2Ch 4:2-6).

SEA COW [9391]. Native to the Red Sea. Skins of, used for covering of tabernacle (Ex 25:5; 26:14; 35:7,23; 36:19; 39:34; Nu 4:6,8,10-12,14,25). For sandals (Eze 16:10).

SEA MEW *See Birds.*

SEA MONSTER [9490]. Figurative of forces of chaos opposed to God (Job 7:12; Ps 74:13; Isa 27:1; Eze 32:2) *See Dragon; Leviathan.*

SEA OF GALILEE Called Sea of Kinnereth (Nu 34:11; Dt 3:17; Jos 12:3; 13:27). Lake of Gennesaret (Lk 5:1). Sea of Tiberias (Jn 21:1).

Jesus calls disciples on the shore of (Mt 4:18-22; Lk 5:1-11). Jesus teaches from a boat on (Mt 13:13). Miracles of Jesus on (Mt 8:24-32; 14:22-33; 17:27; Mk 4:37-39; Lk 5:1-9; 8:22-24; Jn 12:1-11).

SEA OF GLASS A crystalline pavement or basin before the throne of God (Rev 4:6; 15:2).

SEA OF JAZER Perhaps the Dead Sea (Jer 48:32).

SEAL [2597, 3159, 3160, 3973, 6258, *5381, 5382*].

NIV+ SEALED, SEALING, SEALS

1. A stamp used for signifying documents. Given as a pledge (Ge 38:18). Engraved (Ex 28:11,21,36; 39:6,14,30; 2Ti 2:19). Decrees signified by (1Ki 21:8; Est 8:8).

Documents sealed with: Ahab's letter, under false pretenses (1Ki 21:8), covenants (Ne 9:38; 10:1; Isa 8:16), decrees (Est 8:8; Da 6:9), deeds (Jer 32:10). Treasures secured by (Dt 32:34). Lion's den made sure by (Da 6:17; tomb of Jesus (Mt 27:66).

Circumcision a seal of righteousness (Ro 4:11).

Figurative:

Of secrecy (Da 12:9; Rev 5:1). Of certainty of divine approval (Jn 6:27; 2Co 1:22; Eph 1:13; 4:30; Rev 7:3-4). In John's vision (Rev 6; 8:1; 10:4).

2. An amphibious animal. Skins of were used as a covering of the tabernacle (Ex 25:5; 26:14; 35:7,23; 36:19; 39:34; Nu 4:25).

SEAMEN [2480]. *See Mariner.*

SEASONS [3045, 3074, 3427, 4595, 4873, 6961, 10232, *178, 2323, 2789*].

NIV+ SEASON

(Ge 1:14; 8:22; Ps 104:19; Jer 33:20; Da 2:21; Mt 21:41; 24:32; Mk 12:2; Ac 1:7; 1Th 5:1).

SEAT [*3782, 4058, 4632, 10338, *1037, 2757, 2764, 2767, 4751*].

NIV+ SEATED, SEATING, SEATS

Chair, stool, throne (1Sa 20:18; Lk 1:52).

SEBA [6013].

1. Son of Cush (Ge 10:7; 1Ch 1:9).

2. A region in Ethiopia (Ps 72:10; Isa 43:3).

See Sabeans; Sheba.

SEBAM [8423] (*sweet smell*). A town in Reuben (Nu

32:3), also called Sibmah (Nu 32:38), E of the Dead Sea, but the exact location is unknown.

SEBAT *See Shebat.*

SECACAH [6117] (*thicket, cover*). A village in the wilderness of Judah (Jos 15:61), location unknown.

SECHU *See Secu.*

SECOND ADAR This intercalary month (not in the Bible) was added about every three years so the lunar calendar would correspond to the solar year.

See Adar Sheni; Month, 13.

SECOND COMING OF CHRIST, THE The time of, unknown (Mt 24:36; Mk 13:32).

Called the:
Times of refreshing from the presence of the Lord (Ac 3:19). Times of restitution of all things (Ac 3:21, w Ro 8:21). Last time (1Pe 1:5). Appearing of Jesus Christ (1Pe 1:7). Revelation of Jesus Christ (1Pe 1:13). Glorious appearing of the great God and our Savior (Tit 2:13). Coming of the day of God (2Pe 3:12). Day of our Lord Jesus Christ (1Co 1:8).

Foretold by:
Prophets (Da 7:13; Jude 14). Jesus (Mt 25:31; Jn 14:3). Apostles (Ac 3:20; 1Ti 6:14). Angels (Ac 1:10-11). Signs preceding (Mt 24:3).

The Manner of:
In clouds (Mt 24:30; 26:64; Rev 1:7). In the glory of his Father (Mt 16:27). In his own glory (Mt 25:31). In flaming fire (2Th 1:8). With power and great glory (Mt 24:30). As he ascended (Ac 1:9,11). With a shout and the voice of the archangel (1Th 4:16). Accompanied by angels (Mt 16:27; 25:31; Mk 8:38; 2Th 1:7). With his saints (1Th 3:13; Jude 14). Suddenly (Mk 13:36). Unexpectedly (Mt 24:44; Lk 12:40). As a thief in the night (1Th 5:2; 2Pe 3:10; Rev 16:15). As the lightning (Mt 24:27). The heavens and earth shall be dissolved (2Pe 3:10,12). They who shall have died in Christ shall rise first at (1Th 4:16). The saints alive at, shall be caught up to meet him (1Th 4:17). Is not to make atonement (Heb 9:28, w Ro 6:9-10; Heb 10:14).

The Purposes of:
To complete the salvation of saints (Heb 9:28; 1Pe 1:5). Be glorified in his saints (2Th 1:10). Be marveled at among those who believe (2Th 1:10). Bring to light the hidden things of darkness (1Co 4:5). Judge (Ps 50:3-4, w Jn 5:22; 2Ti 4:1; Jude 15; Rev 20:11-13). Reign (Isa 24:23; Da 7:14; Rev 11:15). Destroy death (1Co 15:25-26). Every eye shall see him at (Rev 1:7). Should be always considered as at hand (Ro 13:12; Php 4:5; 1Pe 4:7). Blessedness of being prepared for (Mt 24:46; Lk 12:37-38).

The Saints:
Assured of (Job 19:25-26). Love (2Ti 4:8). Look for (Php 3:20; Tit 2:13). Wait for (1Co 1:7; 1Th 1:10). Speed its coming (2Pe 3:12). Pray for (Rev 22:20). Should be ready for (Mt 24:44; Lk 12:40). Should watch for (Mt 24:42; Mk 13:35-37; Lk 21:36). Should be patient unto (2Th 3:5; Jas 5:7-8). Shall be preserved unto (Php 1:6; 2Ti 4:18; 1Pe 1:5; Jude 24). Shall not be ashamed at (1Jn 2:28; 1Jn 4:17). Shall be blameless at (1Co 1:8; 1Th 3:13; 5:23; Jude 24). Shall be like him at (Php 3:21; 1Jn 3:2). Shall see him as he is (1Jn 3:2). Shall appear with him in glory at (Col 3:4). Shall receive a crown of glory at (2Ti 4:8; 1Pe 5:4). Shall reign with him at (Da 7:27; 2Ti 2:12; Rev 5:10; 20:6; 22:5). Faith of, will be praised at (1Pe 1:7).

The Wicked:
Scoff at (2Pe 3:3-4). Presume upon the delay of (Mt 24:48). Shall be surprised by (Mt 24:37-39; 1Th 5:3; 2Pe 3:10). Shall be punished at (2Th 1:8-9). The man of sin to be destroyed at (2Th 2:8). Illustrated (Mt 25:6; Lk 12:36,39; 19:12,15).

See Jesus the Christ, Second Coming.

SECOND DEATH (Rev 19:20; 20:14; 21:8). Righteous exempt from (Rev 2:11).

See Punishment, Eternal; Wicked, Punishment of.

SECRET [401+5583, 928+4537, 1821, 2668, 4268, 4319, 5041, 5915, 6259, 6260, 6623, 7621, 8078, 9502, 3220, 3224, 3225, 3291, 3679, 3696].

NIV+ SECRETLY, SECRETS

Alms to be given in (Mt 6:4). Prayer to be offered in (Mt 6:6). Of others not to be divulged (Pr 25:9; Mt 18:15).

Belong to God:
Dt 29:29 The secret things belong to the LORD our God, but the things revealed belong to us and to our children forever, that we may follow all the words of this law.
Ps 25:14 The LORD confides in those who fear him; he makes his covenant known to them.

God Knows Secrets of the Heart:
Dt 31:21 And when many disasters and difficulties come upon them, this song will testify against them, because it will not be forgotten by their descendants. I know what they are disposed to do, even before I bring them into the land I promised them on oath."
1Sa 16:7 But the LORD said to Samuel, "Do not consider his appearance or his height, for I have rejected him. The LORD does not look at the things man looks at. Man looks at the outward appearance, but the LORD looks at the heart."
2Sa 7:20 "What more can David say to you? For you know your servant, O Sovereign LORD.
2Ki 19:27 "'But I know where you stay and when you come and go and how you rage against me.
Ps 44:21 would not God have discovered it, since he knows the secrets of the heart?
Ps 90:8 You have set our iniquities before you, our secret sins in the light of your presence.
Heb 4:12 For the word of God is living and active. Sharper than any double-edged sword, it penetrates even to dividing soul and spirit, joints and marrow; it judges the thoughts and attitudes of the heart. [13]Nothing in all creation is hidden from God's sight Everything is uncovered and laid bare before the eyes of him to whom we must give account.

Shall be Revealed and Judged:
Ecc 12:14 For God will bring every deed into judgment, including every hidden thing, whether it is good or evil.
Da 2:28 but there is a God in heaven who reveals mysteries. He has shown King Nebuchadnezzar what will happen in days to come. Your dream and the visions that passed through your mind as you lay on your bed are these:
Da 2:47 The king said to Daniel, "Surely your God is the God of gods and the Lord of kings and a revealer of mysteries, for you were able to reveal this mystery."
Am 3:7 Surely the Sovereign LORD does nothing without revealing his plan to his servants the prophets.
Mk 4:22 For whatever is hidden is meant to be disclosed, and whatever is concealed is meant to be brought out into the open.
Lk 8:16 "No one lights a lamp and hides it in a jar or puts

it under a bed. Instead, he puts it on a stand, so that those who come in can see the light. ¹⁷For there is nothing hidden that will not be disclosed, and nothing concealed that will not be known or brought out into the open.

Ro 2:16 This will take place on the day when God will judge men's secrets through Jesus Christ, as my gospel declares.

1Co 4:5 Therefore judge nothing before the appointed time; wait till the Lord comes. He will bring to light what is hidden in darkness and will expose the motives of men's hearts. At that time each will receive his praise from God.

See Mysteries.

SECRETARY [6221, 10516].

NIV+ SECRETARIES, SECRETARY'S

(2Sa 8:17; 20:24; 1Ki 4:3; 2Ki 12:10-12; 18:18,37; 22:1-14; 1Ch 27:32; Est 3:12; 8:9). Military (2Ki 25:19; 2Ch 26:11). *See Amanuensis; Scribe.*

SECT [*146, 899*] (*sect, party, school*).

Religious group with distinctive doctrine: Sadducees (Ac 5:17), Pharisees (Ac 15:5; 26:5), Christians (Ac 24:5; 28:22).

SECU [8497] (*lookout point*). Village near Ramah (1Sa 19:22).

SECUNDUS [*4941*] (*second*). A Thessalonian Christian. Accompanies Paul from Corinth (Ac 20:4-6).

SECURITY [*622, 1053, 1055, 2471, 3782, 3922, 4440, 6184, 6842, 8631, 8932, *856*].

NIV+ SECURE, SECURED, SECURELY, SECURES

In Salvation:

The theological teaching which maintains the certain continuation of the salvation of those who are saved; also known as the perseverance of the saints (Jn 10:28; Ro 8:38-39; Php 1:6; 2Th 3:3; 1Pe 1:5).

False:

From the evils of sin. Promises peace and long life (Job 29:18). Is ignorant of God and truth (Ps 10:4; 50:21). Trusts in lies (Isa 28:15; Rev 3:17). Is inconsiderate and forgetful (Isa 47:7). Relies on earthly treasures (Jer 49:4, 16). Is deceived by pride (Ob 3; Rev 18:7). Puts off the evil day (Am 6:3). Leads to increased guilt (Ecc 8:11). Its refuge will be swept away (Isa 28:17). Ruin shall overtake it (Isa 47:9; Am 9:10). God is against it (Jer 21:13; Eze 39:6; Am 6:1).

See Confidence, False; Self-Deception; Self-Delusion.

For Debt:

A guarantee to pay: not to be taken if essential to life (garments) or livelihood (millstones) (Ex 22:26; Dt 24:6,6, 17); not to be used as unreasonable leverage upon the disadvantaged (Job 22:6; 24:3,9; Eze 18:16; Am 2:8).

Instances of: Judah (Ge 43:9; 44:32); fields and vineyards (Ne 5:3).

Warnings against: (Pr 6:1; 11:15; 17:18; 20:16).

See Debt.

SEDITION [10083]. Charged against Paul (Ac 24:5). How punished (Ac 5:36-37).

SEDUCER *See Impostors.*

SEDUCTION [2744, 5615, 7331, *1284*].

NIV+ SEDUCE, SEDUCED, SEDUCES, SEDUCTIVE

(2Ti 3:6,13). Laws concerning (Ex 22:16-17; Dt 22:23-29). *See Rape.*

Instances of:

Of Dinah (Ge 34:2). Tamar (2Sa 13:1-14).

SEED [1807, 2433, 2445, 2446, 3079, 7237, *1399, 2843, 3133, 5062, 5065, 5076, 5078*].

NIV+ SEED-BEARING, SEEDS, SEEDTIME

Every herb, tree, and grass, yields its own (Ge 1:11-12,29). Each kind has its own body (1Co 15:38). Not to be mingled in sowing (Lev 19:19; Dt 22:9).

Parables concerning (Mt 13; Lk 8).

Illustrative (Ecc 11:6; Hos 10:12; 2Co 9:6; Gal 6:7-8).

Sowing of, type of burial of the body (1Co 15:36-38).

SEEDTIME [2446]. *See Agriculture.*

SEEKERS [*1329, 1335, 2011, 2704+, 8838, *1699, 2426*].

NIV+ SEEK, SEEKING, SEEKS, SELF-SEEKING, SOUGHT

Must:

Have faith—

Heb 11:6 And without faith it is impossible to please God, because anyone who comes to him must believe that he exists and that he rewards those who earnestly seek him.

Remember God's mercies—

Isa 51:1 "Listen to me, you who pursue righteousness and who seek the LORD: Look to the rock from which you were cut and to the quarry from which you were hewn;

Count the cost—

Lk 14:26 "If anyone comes to me and does not hate his father and mother, his wife and children, his brothers and sisters—yes, even his own life—he cannot be my disciple. ²⁷And anyone who does not carry his cross and follow me cannot be my disciple.

²⁸"Suppose one of you wants to build a tower. Will he not first sit down and estimate the cost to see if he has enough money to complete it? ²⁹For if he lays the foundation and is not able to finish it, everyone who sees it will ridicule him, ³⁰saying, 'This fellow began to build and was not able to finish.'

³¹"Or suppose a king is about to go to war against another king. Will he not first sit down and consider whether he is able with ten thousand men to oppose the one coming against him with twenty thousand? ³²If he is not able, he will send a delegation while the other is still a long way off and will ask for terms of peace. ³³In the same way, any of you who does not give up everything he has cannot be my disciple.

Seeking God:

Commanded—

1Ch 16:11 Look to the LORD and his strength; seek his face always.

1Ch 22:19 Now devote your heart and soul to seeking the LORD your God. Begin to build the sanctuary of the LORD God, so that you may bring the ark of the covenant of the LORD and the sacred articles belonging to God into the temple that will be built for the Name of the LORD."

Ps 105:4 Look to the LORD and his strength; seek his face always.

Isa 26:8 Yes, LORD, walking in the way of your laws, we wait for you; your name and renown are the desire of our hearts. ⁹My soul yearns for you in the night; in the morning my spirit longs for you. When your judgments come upon the earth, the people of the world learn righteousness.

Hos 10:12 Sow for yourselves righteousness, reap the fruit of unfailing love, and break up your unplowed ground; for it is time to seek the Lord, until he comes and showers righteousness on you.

Joel 2:12 "Even now," declares the Lord, "return to me with all your heart, with fasting and weeping and mourning."

[13]Rend your heart and not your garments. Return to the Lord your God, for he is gracious and compassionate, slow to anger and abounding in love, and he relents from sending calamity.

Am 5:4 This is what the Lord says to the house of Israel: "Seek me and live; [5]do not seek Bethel, do not go to Gilgal, do not journey to Beersheba. For Gilgal will surely go into exile, and Bethel will be reduced to nothing." [6]Seek the Lord and live, or he will sweep through the house of Joseph like a fire; it will devour, and Bethel will have no one to quench it.

Am 5:8 (he who made the Pleiades and Orion, who turns blackness into dawn and darkens day into night, who calls for the waters of the sea and pours them out over the face of the land—the Lord is his name—

Am 5:14 Seek good, not evil, that you may live. Then the Lord God Almighty will be with you, just as you say he is.

Zep 2:3 Seek the Lord, all you humble of the land, you who do what he commands. Seek righteousness, seek humility; perhaps you will be sheltered on the day of the Lord's anger. (+Mt 6:33)

Jas 4:8 Come near to God and he will come near to you. Wash your hands, you sinners, and purify your hearts, you double-minded.

Rev 22:17 The Spirit and the bride say, "Come!" And let him who hears say, "Come!" Whoever is thirsty, let him come; and whoever wishes, let him take the free gift of the water of life.

For salvation—

Ge 49:18 "I look for your deliverance, O Lord.

To sacrifice—

2Ch 11:16 Those from every tribe of Israel who set their hearts on seeking the Lord, the God of Israel, followed the Levites to Jerusalem to offer sacrifices to the Lord, the God of their fathers.

The result of adversity—

Ps 78:34 Whenever God slew them, they would seek him; they eagerly turned to him again.

Ps 83:16 Cover their faces with shame so that men will seek your name, O Lord.

Hos 5:15 Then I will go back to my place until they admit their guilt. And they will seek my face; in their misery they will earnestly seek me."

Prophesied—

Jer 50:4 "In those days, at that time," declares the Lord, "the people of Israel and the people of Judah together will go in tears to seek the Lord their God.

Hos 3:5 Afterward the Israelites will return and seek the Lord their God and David their king. They will come trembling to the Lord and to his blessings in the last days.

Zec 8:20 This is what the Lord Almighty says: "Many peoples and the inhabitants of many cities will yet come, [21]and the inhabitants of one city will go to another and say, 'Let us go at once to entreat the Lord and seek the Lord Almighty. I myself am going.' [22]And many peoples and powerful nations will come to Jerusalem to seek the Lord Almighty and to entreat him."

[23]This is what the Lord Almighty says: "In those days ten men from all languages and nations will take firm hold of one Jew by the hem of his robe and say, 'Let us go with you, because we have heard that God is with you.'"

Punishment for not seeking—

2Ch 15:13 All who would not seek the Lord, the God of Israel, were to be put to death, whether small or great, man or woman.

Isa 8:19 When men tell you to consult mediums and spiritists, who whisper and mutter, should not a people inquire of their God? Why consult the dead on behalf of the living?

Not of self—

Ro 3:11 there is no one who understands, no one who seeks God.

By unrepentant sinners, vain—

Am 8:12 Men will stagger from sea to sea and wander from north to east, searching for the word of the Lord, but they will not find it.

Lk 13:24 "Make every effort to enter through the narrow door, because many, I tell you, will try to enter and will not be able to.

See Seeking God.

Promises:

Jn 6:37 All that the Father gives me will come to me, and whoever comes to me I will never drive away.

Of finding God—

Dt 4:29 But if from there you seek the Lord your God, you will find him if you look for him with all your heart and with all your soul.

1Ch 28:9 "And you, my son Solomon, acknowledge the God of your father, and serve him with wholehearted devotion and with a willing mind, for the Lord searches every heart and understands every motive behind the thoughts. If you seek him, he will be found by you; but if you forsake him, he will reject you forever.

2Ch 15:2 He went out to meet Asa and said to him, "Listen to me, Asa and all Judah and Benjamin. The Lord is with you when you are with him. If you seek him, he will be found by you, but if you forsake him, he will forsake you.

2Ch 15:12 They entered into a covenant to seek the Lord, the God of their fathers, with all their heart and soul.

Pr 8:17 I love those who love me, and those who seek me find me.

Pr 8:34 Blessed is the man who listens to me, watching daily at my doors, waiting at my doorway. (+Pr 8:35; Isa 45:19,22)

Jer 29:13 You will seek me and find me when you seek me with all your heart.

Ac 17:27 God did this so that men would seek him and perhaps reach out for him and find him, though he is not far from each one of us.

Of pardon—

2Ch 30:18 Although most of the many people who came from Ephraim, Manasseh, Issachar and Zebulun had not purified themselves, yet they ate the Passover, contrary to what was written. But Hezekiah prayed for them, saying, "May the Lord, who is good, pardon everyone [19]who sets his heart on seeking God—the Lord, the God of his fathers—even if he is not clean according to the rules of the sanctuary."

Ps 69:32 The poor will see and be glad—you who seek God, may your hearts live!

Isa 55:6 Seek the Lord while he may be found; call on him while he is near. [7]Let the wicked forsake his way and the evil man his thoughts. Let him turn to the Lord, and he will have mercy on him, and to our God, for he will freely pardon.

Eze 18:21 "But if a wicked man turns away from all the sins he has committed and keeps all my decrees and does what is just and right, he will surely live; he will not die. ²²None of the offenses he has committed will be remembered against him. Because of the righteous things he has done, he will live. ²³Do I take any pleasure in the death of the wicked? declares the Sovereign LORD. Rather, am I not pleased when they turn from their ways and live?

Ac 2:21 And everyone who calls on the name of the Lord will be saved.'

Of salvation—

Heb 9:28 so Christ was sacrificed once to take away the sins of many people; and he will appear a second time, not to bear sin, but to bring salvation to those who are waiting for him.

Of providential care—

2Ch 26:5 He sought God during the days of Zechariah, who instructed him in the fear of God. As long as he sought the LORD, God gave him success.

Ezr 8:22 I was ashamed to ask the king for soldiers and horsemen to protect us from enemies on the road, because we had told the king, "The gracious hand of our God is on everyone who looks to him, but his great anger is against all who forsake him."

Ps 34:4 I sought the LORD, and he answered me; he delivered me from all my fears.

Ps 81:10 I am the LORD your God, who brought you up out of Egypt. Open wide your mouth and I will fill it. (+Ps 145:19)

Isa 49:9 to say to the captives, 'Come out,' and to those in darkness, 'Be free!' "They will feed beside the roads and find pasture on every barren hill.

¹⁰They will neither hunger nor thirst, nor will the desert heat or the sun beat upon them. He who has compassion on them will guide them and lead them beside springs of water. ¹¹I will turn all my mountains into roads, and my highways will be raised up. ¹²See, they will come from afar—some from the north, some from the west, some from the region of Aswan."

Isa 49:23 Kings will be your foster fathers, and their queens your nursing mothers. They will bow down before you with their faces to the ground; they will lick the dust at your feet. Then you will know that I am the LORD; those who hope in me will not be disappointed." (+Mt 6:33)

Of spiritual blessings—

Job 8:5 But if you will look to God and plead with the Almighty, ⁶if you are pure and upright, even now he will rouse himself on your behalf and restore you to your rightful place.

Ps 9:10 Those who know your name will trust in you, for you, LORD, have never forsaken those who seek you.

Ps 22:26 The poor will eat and be satisfied; they who seek the LORD will praise him—may your hearts live forever!

Ps 24:3 Who may ascend the hill of the LORD? Who may stand in his holy place? ⁴He who has clean hands and a pure heart, who does not lift up his soul to an idol or swear by what is false. ⁵He will receive blessing from the LORD and vindication from God his Savior. ⁶Such is the generation of those who seek him, who seek your face, O God of Jacob. *Selah*

Ps 40:1 I waited patiently for the LORD; he turned to me and heard my cry. ²He lifted me out of the slimy pit, out of the mud and mire; he set my feet on a rock and gave me a firm place to stand. ³He put a new song in my mouth, a hymn of praise to our God. Many will see and fear and put their trust in the LORD.

⁴Blessed is the man who makes the LORD his trust, who does not look to the proud, to those who turn aside to false gods.

Ps 63:1 O God, you are my God, earnestly I seek you; my soul thirsts for you, my body longs for you, in a dry and weary land where there is no water.

²I have seen you in the sanctuary and beheld your power and your glory. ³Because your love is better than life, my lips will glorify you. ⁴I will praise you as long as I live, and in your name I will lift up my hands. ⁵My soul will be satisfied as with the richest of foods; with singing lips my mouth will praise you.

⁶On my bed I remember you; I think of you through the watches of the night. ⁷Because you are my help, I sing in the shadow of your wings. ⁸My soul clings to you; your right hand upholds me.

Ps 70:4 But may all who seek you rejoice and be glad in you; may those who love your salvation always say, "Let God be exalted!"

⁵Yet I am poor and needy; come quickly to me, O God. You are my help and my deliverer; O LORD, do not delay.

Ps 119:2 Blessed are they who keep his statutes and seek him with all their heart.

Ps 145:18 The LORD is near to all who call on him, to all who call on him in truth. ¹⁹He fulfills the desires of those who fear him; he hears their cry and saves them.

Pr 2:3 and if you call out for insight and cry aloud for understanding, ⁴and if you look for it as for silver and search for it as for hidden treasure, ⁵then you will understand the fear of the LORD and find the knowledge of God.

Pr 28:5 Evil men do not understand justice, but those who seek the LORD understand it fully.

Isa 44:3 For I will pour water on the thirsty land, and streams on the dry ground; I will pour out my Spirit on your offspring, and my blessing on your descendants. ⁴They will spring up like grass in a meadow, like poplar trees by flowing streams.

Isa 45:19 I have not spoken in secret, from somewhere in a land of darkness; I have not said to Jacob's descendants, 'Seek me in vain.' I, the LORD, speak the truth; I declare what is right.

Isa 45:22 "Turn to me and be saved, all you ends of the earth; for I am God, and there is no other. (+Isa 55:6-7)

Isa 61:1 The Spirit of the Sovereign LORD is on me, because the LORD has anointed me to preach good news to the poor. He has sent me to bind up the brokenhearted, to proclaim freedom for the captives and release from darkness for the prisoners, ²to proclaim the year of the LORD's favor and the day of vengeance of our God, to comfort all who mourn, ³and provide for those who grieve in Zion—to bestow on them a crown of beauty instead of ashes, the oil of gladness instead of mourning, and a garment of praise instead of a spirit of despair. They will be called oaks of righteousness, a planting of the LORD for the display of his splendor.

La 3:25 The LORD is good to those whose hope is in him, to the one who seeks him; ²⁶it is good to wait quietly for the salvation of the LORD.

La 3:41 Let us lift up our hearts and our hands to God in heaven, and say:

Mt 5:6 Blessed are those who hunger and thirst for righteousness, for they will be filled.

Mt 6:33 But seek first his kingdom and his righteousness, and all these things will be given to you as well. (+Mt 7:7-11)

Lk 6:21 Blessed are you who hunger now, for you will be

satisfied. Blessed are you who weep now, for you will laugh.

Lk 11:9 "So I say to you: Ask and it will be given to you; seek and you will find; knock and the door will be opened to you. ¹⁰For everyone who asks receives; he who seeks finds; and to him who knocks, the door will be opened.

¹¹"Which of you fathers, if your son asks for a fish, will give him a snake instead? ¹²Or if he asks for an egg, will give him a scorpion? ¹³If you then, though you are evil, know how to give good gifts to your children, how much more will your Father in heaven give the Holy Spirit to those who ask him!" (+Ac 2:21; Ro 10:12)

Ro 10:13 for, "Everyone who calls on the name of the Lord will be saved."

Heb 7:25 Therefore he is able to save completely those who come to God through him, because he always lives to intercede for them.

Rev 3:20 Here I am! I stand at the door and knock. If anyone hears my voice and opens the door, I will come in and eat with him, and he with me.

Rev 21:6 He said to me: "It is done. I am the Alpha and the Omega, the Beginning and the End. To him who is thirsty I will give to drink without cost from the spring of the water of life.

Instances of:

Asa (2Ch 14:7). Jehoshaphat (2Ch 17:3-4). Uzziah (2Ch 26:5).

Hezekiah—

2Ch 31:21 In everything that he undertook in the service of God's temple and in obedience to the law and the commands, he sought his God and worked wholehearted-ly. And so he prospered.

Josiah (2Ch 34:4). Ezra (Ezr 7:10).

Job—

Job 5:8 "But if it were I, I would appeal to God; I would lay my cause before him.

David—

Ps 17:1 Hear, O Lord, my righteous plea; listen to my cry. Give ear to my prayer—it does not rise from deceitful lips. ²May my vindication come from you; may your eyes see what is right.

Ps 25:5 guide me in your truth and teach me, for you are God my Savior, and my hope is in you all day long.

Ps 25:15 My eyes are ever on the Lord, for only he will release my feet from the snare.

Ps 27:4 One thing I ask of the Lord, this is what I seek: that I may dwell in the house of the Lord all the days of my life, to gaze upon the beauty of the Lord and to seek him in his temple.

Ps 27:8 My heart says of you, "Seek his face!" Your face, Lord, I will seek. (+Ps 34:4; 40:1-2; 63:1-8)

Ps 143:6 I spread out my hands to you; my soul thirsts for you like a parched land. *Selah*

The psalmists—

Ps 33:20 We wait in hope for the Lord; he is our help and our shield.

Ps 42:1 As the deer pants for streams of water, so my soul pants for you, O God. ²My soul thirsts for God, for the living God. When can I go and meet with God? ³My tears have been my food day and night, while men say to me all day long, "Where is your God?" ⁴These things I remember as I pour out my soul: how I used to go with the multitude, leading the procession to the house of God, with shouts of joy and thanksgiving among the festive throng.

Ps 77:1 I cried out to God for help; I cried out to God to

hear me. ²When I was in distress, I sought the Lord; at night I stretched out untiring hands and my soul refused to be comforted.

³I remembered you, O God, and I groaned; I mused, and my spirit grew faint. *Selah*

⁴You kept my eyes from closing; I was too troubled to speak. ⁵I thought about the former days, the years of long ago; ⁶I remembered my songs in the night. My heart mused and my spirit inquired:

⁷"Will the Lord reject forever? Will he never show his favor again? ⁸Has his unfailing love vanished forever? Has his promise failed for all time? ⁹Has God forgotten to be merciful? Has he in anger withheld his compassion?"

Ps 84:2 My soul yearns, even faints, for the courts of the Lord; my heart and my flesh cry out for the living God.

Ps 119:10 I seek you with all my heart; do not let me stray from your commands.

Ps 130:5 I wait for the Lord, my soul waits, and in his word I put my hope. ⁶My soul waits for the Lord more than watchmen wait for the morning, more than watchmen wait for the morning.

The beloved for her lover—

SS 3:1 All night long on my bed I looked for the one my heart loves; I looked for him but did not find him. ²I will get up now and go about the city, through its streets and squares; I will search for the one my heart loves. So I looked for him but did not find him. ³The watchmen found me as they made their rounds in the city. "Have you seen the one my heart loves?" ⁴Scarcely had I passed them when I found the one my heart loves. I held him and would not let him go till I had brought him to my mother's house, to the room of the one who conceived me.

Daniel—

Da 9:3 So I turned to the Lord God and pleaded with him in prayer and petition, in fasting, and in sackcloth and ashes. (+Da 9:4)

The Magi (Mt 2:1-2). Cornelius, the Centurion (Ac 10:7,30-33).

See Backsliders; Penitent; Sin, Confession of; Sin, Forgiveness of; Zeal.

SEEKING GOD [*1329, 1335, 2011, 2704+, 8838, 1699, 2426].

NIV+ See SEEKERS

Commanded (Isa 55:6; Mt 7:7).

Includes Seeking:

His name (Ps 83:16). His Word (Isa 34:16). His strength (1Ch 16:11; Ps 105:4). His commandments (1Ch 28:8; Mal 2:7). His precepts (Ps 119:45,94). His kingdom (Mt 6:33; Lk 12:31). His righteousness (Mt 6:33). Christ (Mal 3:1; Lk 2:15-16). Honor which comes from him (Jn 5:44). Justification by Christ (Gal 2:16-17). The city which God has prepared (Heb 11:10,16; 13:14). By prayer (Job 8:5; Da 9:3). In his house (Dt 12:5; Ps 27:4).

Should Be:

Immediate (Hos 10:12). Evermore (Ps 105:4). While he may be found (Isa 55:6). With the heart (Dt 4:29; 1Ch 22:19). In the day of trouble (Ps 77:2).

Ensures:

His being found (Dt 4:29; 1Ch 28:9; Pr 8:17; Jer 29:13). His favor (La 3:25). His protection (Ezr 8:22). His not forsaking us (Ps 9:10). Life (Ps 69:32; Am 5:4,6). Prosperity (Job 8:5-6; Ps 34:10). Being heard by him (Ps 34:4). Understanding all things (Pr 28:5). Gifts of righteousness (Hos 10:12). Imperative upon all (Isa 8:19).

Afflictions designed to lead to (Ps 78:33-34; Hos 5:15). None, by nature, are found to be engaged in (Jas 4:2, w Ro 3:11; Lk 12:23,30).

The Saints:
Specially exhorted to (Zep 2:3). Desirous of (Job 5:8). Purpose, in heart (Ps 27:8). Prepare their hearts for (2Ch 30:19). Set their hearts to (2Ch 11:16). Engage in, with the whole heart (2Ch 15:12; Ps 119:10). Early in (Job 8:5; Ps 63:1; Isa 26:9). Earnest in (SS 3:2,4). Characterized by (Ps 24:6). Is never in vain (Isa 45:19). Blessedness of (Ps 119:2). Leads to joy (Ps 70:4; 105:3). Ends in praise (Ps 22:26). Promise connected with (Ps 69:32). Shall be rewarded (Heb 11:6).

The Wicked:
Are gone out of the way of (Ps 14:2-3, w Ro 3:11-12). Do not prepare their hearts for (2Ch 12:14). Refuse, through pride (Ps 10:4). Not led to, by affliction (Isa 9:13). Sometimes pretend to (Ezr 4:2; Isa 58:2). Rejected, when too late in (Pr 1:28). They who neglect are denounced (Isa 31:1). Punishment of those who neglect (Zep 1:4-6).

Exemplified:
Asa (2Ch 14:7). Jehoshaphat (2Ch 17:3-4). Uzziah (2Ch 26:5). Hezekiah (2Ch 31:21). Josiah (2Ch 34:3). Ezra (Ezr 7:10). David (Ps 34:4). Daniel (Da 9:3-4).

SEER [2602, 8014].
NIV+ SEER'S, SEERS
An older term for prophet (1Sa 9:9). *See Prophets.*

SEGUB [8437] (*exalted*).
1. Son of Hiel, the rebuilder of Jericho (1Ki 16:34).
2. Grandson of Judah (1Ch 2:4-5,21-22).

SEIR [8541, 8542, 8543] (*hairy, shaggy, covered with trees* BDB IDB; possibly *the place of the goats* or *the place of Esau* [Ge 25:25, BDB]; *small forest, rich forest* KB). A Horite; an ancestor of the inhabitants of the land of Seir (Ge 26:20; 1Ch 1:38).

SEIR, LAND OF and MOUNT
1. Alternate names for the region occupied by the descendants of Edom or Esau. Originally called the land of Seir (Ge 32:3), later called Edom (Ge 36:8-9), extends S from Moab on both sides of the Arabah c. one hundred miles; mountainous; in the Greek period it was called Idumea. Mt. Seir c. 3,500 feet high. "Seir" also used for people who lived in Mt. Seir (Eze 25:8).
2. Region on the border of Judah W of Kiriath Jearim (Jos 15:10).

SEIRAH, SEIRATH [8545] (*place of the goats* BDB possibly *woody hills* IDB KB; *shaggy forest* ISBE). A town in Ephraim, probably in the SE part (Jdg 3:26).

SEIZING [*296, 1608, 2616, 3769, 4374, 5162, 8964, 9530, 2138, 3195, 3284, 4389, 5197, 5275*].
NIV+ SEIZE, SEIZED, SEIZES, SEIZURES
Of property. *See Land.*

SEIZURES [4944]. An affliction resulting from demon possession (Mt. 4:24; 17:5). Some feel this is a reference to epilepsy. *See Disease.*
NIV+ SEIZE, SEIZED, SEIZES, SEIZING

SELA [6153] (*rocky crags, cliffs*).
NIV+ SELA HAMMAHLEKOTH
An Edomite city (Isa 16:1; 42:11), also called Joktheel (2Ki 14:7). *See Joktheel.* Later the capital of the Nabateans, called Petra by the Greeks. *See Nabatea, Nabateans; Petra.*

SELA HAMMAHLEKOTH,
SELA-HAMMAH-LEKOTH [6154] (*slippery rock* BDB).
NIV+ SELA
A cliff in the wilderness of Maon (1Sa 23:28).

SELAH [6138] This term appears seventy-one times in the and in Hab 3:3,9,13. Its meaning is not clear. Possibly it signified a pause in the vocal music while an instrumental interlude played.
See Music, Symbols Used in.

SELED [6135] (*jump for joy*). A descendant of Jerahmeel (1Ch 2:30).

SELEUCIA [4942]. A seaport of Syrian Antioch, founded by Seleucus I in 300 B.C. (Ac 13:4).

SELEUCIDS A dynasty of rulers of the kingdom of Syria (it included Babylonia, Bactria, Persia, Syria, and part of Asia Minor), descended from Seleucus I, a general of Alexander the Great. It lasted from 312 to 64 B.C., when the Romans took it over. One of them, Antiochus Epiphanes, precipitated the Maccabean War by trying forcibly to Hellenize the Jews. *See Testaments, Time Between.*

SELF-CONDEMNATION [896].
NIV+ CONDEMN, SELF-CONDEMNED

1Ki 8:31 "When a man wrongs his neighbor and is required to take an oath and he comes and swears the oath before your altar in this temple, ³²then hear from heaven and act. Judge between your servants, condemning the guilty and bringing down on his own head what he has done. Declare the innocent not guilty, and so establish his innocence.
Job 9:20 Even if I were innocent, my mouth would condemn me; if I were blameless, it would pronounce me guilty.
Pr 5:12 You will say, "How I hated discipline! How my heart spurned correction! ¹³I would not obey my teachers or listen to my instructors.
Mt 23:31 So you testify against yourselves that you are the descendants of those who murdered the prophets.
Ro 2:1 You, therefore, have no excuse, you who pass judgment on someone else, for at whatever point you judge the other, you are condemning yourself, because you who pass judgment do the same things. (+1Jn 3:20; Rev 1:7)

Parables of: (Mt 21:33-41)
Mt 25:24 "Then the man who had received the one talent came. 'Master,' he said, 'I knew that you are a hard man, harvesting where you have not sown and gathering where you have not scattered seed. ²⁵So I was afraid and went out and hid your talent in the ground. See, here is what belongs to you.'
²⁶"His master replied, 'You wicked, lazy servant! So you knew that I harvest where I have not sown and gather where I have not scattered seed? ²⁷Well then, you should have put my money on deposit with the bankers, so that when I returned I would have received it back with interest.
Mk 12:1 He then began to speak to them in parables: "A man planted a vineyard. He put a wall around it, dug a pit for the winepress and built a watchtower. Then he rented the vineyard to some farmers and went away on a journey.

[2]At harvest time he sent a servant to the tenants to collect from them some of the fruit of the vineyard. [3]But they seized him, beat him and sent him away empty-handed. [4]Then he sent another servant to them; they struck this man on the head and treated him shamefully. [5]He sent still another, and that one they killed. He sent many others; some of them they beat, others they killed.

[6]"He had one left to send, a son, whom he loved. He sent him last of all, saying, 'They will respect my son.'

[7]"But the tenants said to one another, 'This is the heir. Come, let's kill him, and the inheritance will be ours.' [8]So they took him and killed him, and threw him out of the vineyard.

[9]"What then will the owner of the vineyard do? He will come and kill those tenants and give the vineyard to others.

[10]Haven't you read this scripture:

"'The stone the builders rejected has become the capstone; [11]the Lord has done this, and it is marvelous in our eyes'?"

[12]Then they looked for a way to arrest him because they knew he had spoken the parable against them. But they were afraid of the crowd; so they left him and went away. (+Lk 19:21-22)

Instances of:

Achan (Jos 7:19-25).

David (1Sa 24:1-15; 26:1-20; 2Sa 12:5-7)—

2Sa 24:17 When David saw the angel who was striking down the people, he said to the LORD, "I am the one who has sinned and done wrong. These are but sheep. What have they done? Let your hand fall upon me and my family."

Ahab (1Ki 20:39-42). Jonah (Jnh 1:12).

Those who condemned the woman—

Jn 8:9 At this, those who heard began to go away one at a time, the older ones first, until only Jesus was left, with the woman still standing there.

See Self-Incrimination; Remorse; Repentance.

SELF-CONFIDENCE *See Confidence, False.*

SELF-CONTROL [4200+5110+8120, *202, 203, 1602, 3768, 5404, 5407, 5409*].

NIV+SELF-CONTROLLED

A Virtue:

Without self-control temptation and evil may freely assault a person (Pr 25:28). Of Saul (1Sa 10:27). Of David (1Sa 24:1-15; 26:1-20). Of Jesus (Mt 26:62-63; 27:12-14). Paul instructed concerning self-control in relation to righteousness (Ac 24:25), the marriage bed (1Co 7:5); as a fruit of the Spirit (Gal 5:23); in contrast to the godlessness of the last days (1Th 5:8; 2Ti 3:3; 2Ti 1:6). Overseers and deacons must have a life that is characterized by self-control (1Ti 3:2; Tit 1:8). Taught by leaders and exemplified by older believers (Tit 2:2,5-6); taught by the grace of God (Tit 2:12). Peter lists self-control as one of the qualities of a godly life (2Pe 1:6). A believer should continually be prepared for Christ's return, exhibiting a self-controlled life (1Pe 1:13; 4:7). Be self-controlled and prepared for the devil, who prowls about looking for those who have a false sense of security which therefore make them prime candidates for his trap in the world's system (1Pe 4:7).

Sexual Self-control:

Vow of—

Job 31:1 "I made a covenant with my eyes not to look lustfully at a girl.

Commanded—

Mt 5:27 "You have heard that it was said, 'Do not commit adultery.' [28]But I tell you that anyone who looks at a woman lustfully has already committed adultery with her in his heart.

Ro 13:13 Let us behave decently, as in the daytime, not in orgies and drunkenness, not in sexual immorality and debauchery, not in dissension and jealousy.

1Co 7:1 Now for the matters you wrote about: It is good for a man not to marry. [2]But since there is so much immorality, each man should have his own wife, and each woman her own husband. [3]The husband should fulfill his marital duty to his wife, and likewise the wife to her husband. [4]The wife's body does not belong to her alone but also to her husband. In the same way, the husband's body does not belong to him alone but also to his wife. [5]Do not deprive each other except by mutual consent and for a time, so that you may devote yourselves to prayer. Then come together again so that Satan will not tempt you because of your lack of self-control. [6]I say this as a concession, not as a command. [7]I wish that all men were as I am. But each man has his own gift from God; one has this gift, another has that.

[8]Now to the unmarried and the widows I say: It is good for them to stay unmarried, as I am. [9]But if they cannot control themselves, they should marry, for it is better to marry than to burn with passion.

1Co 7:25 Now about virgins: I have no command from the Lord, but I give a judgment as one who by the Lord's mercy is trustworthy. [26]Because of the present crisis, I think that it is good for you to remain as you are. [27]Are you married? Do not seek a divorce. Are you unmarried? Do not look for a wife. [28]But if you do marry, you have not sinned; and if a virgin marries, she has not sinned. But those who marry will face many troubles in this life, and I want to spare you this.

[29]What I mean, brothers, is that the time is short. From now on those who have wives should live as if they had none;

1Co 7:36 If anyone thinks he is acting improperly toward the virgin he is engaged to, and if she is getting along in years and he feels he ought to marry, he should do as he wants. He is not sinning. They should get married. [37]But the man who has settled the matter in his own mind, who is under no compulsion but has control over his own will, and who has made up his mind not to marry the virgin— this man also does the right thing. [38]So then, he who marries the virgin does right, but he who does not marry her does even better.

Col 3:5 Put to death, therefore, whatever belongs to your earthly nature: sexual immorality, impurity, lust, evil desires and greed, which is idolatry.

1Ti 4:12 Don't let anyone look down on you because you are young, but set an example for the believers in speech, in life, in love, in faith and in purity.

1Ti 5:1 Do not rebuke an older man harshly, but exhort him as if he were your father. Treat younger men as brothers, [2]older women as mothers, and younger women as sisters, with absolute purity.

Instances of:

Joseph (Ge 39:7-12). Uriah (2Sa 11:8-13). Boaz (Ru 3:6-13). Joseph, husband of Mary (Mt 1:24-25).

Eunuchs—

Mt 19:12 For some are eunuchs because they were born that way; others were made that way by men; and others have renounced marriage because of the kingdom of heaven. The one who can accept this should accept it."

Paul (1Co 7:8)—

1Co 9:27 No, I beat my body and make it my slave so that after I have preached to others, I myself will not be disqualified for the prize.

Believers—

Rev 14:1 Then I looked, and there before me was the Lamb, standing on Mount Zion, and with him 144,000 who had his name and his Father's name written on their foreheads.

Rev 14:4 These are those who did not defile themselves with women, for they kept themselves pure. They follow the Lamb wherever he goes. They were purchased from among men and offered as firstfruits to God and the Lamb. ⁵No lie was found in their mouths; they are blameless.

See Abstinence; Chastity; Discipline; Graces, Christian; Patience; Rashness; Self-Discipline; Tact.

SELF-DECEPTION (Jas 1:26). *See Confidence, False; Security, False.*

SELF-DEFENSE Accused heard in (Mt 27:11-14; Mk 15:2-5; Lk 23:3; Jn 7:51; Ac 2:37-40; 22; 23; 24:10-21; 26). *See Defense.*

SELF-DELUSION A characteristic of the wicked (Ps 49:18). Prosperity frequently leads to (Ps 30:6; Hos 12:8; Lk 12:17-19). Obstinate sinners often given up to (Ps 81:11-12; Hos 4:17; 2Th 2:10-11).

Exhibited in thinking that:

Our own ways are right (Pr 14:12), we should adhere to established wicked practices (Jer 44:17), we are pure (Pr 30:12), we are better than others (Lk 18:11), we are rich in spiritual things (Rev 3:17), we may have peace while in sin (Dt 29:19), we are above adversity (Ps 10:6), gifts entitle us to heaven (Mt 7:21-22), privileges entitle us to heaven (Mt 3:9; Lk 13:25-26), God will not punish our sins (Jer 5:12), Christ will not come to judge (2Pe 3:4), our lives will be prolonged (Isa 56:12; Lk 12:19; Jas 4:13).

Frequently persevered in to the last (Mt 7:22; 25:11-12; Lk 13:24-25). Fatal consequences of (Mt 7:23; 24:48-51; Lk 12:20; 1Th 5:3).

Exemplified:

Ahab (1Ki 20:27,34). Israelites (Hos 12:8). Jews (Jn 8:33,41). Church of Laodicea (Rev 3:17).

See Confidence, False; Security, False.

SELF-DENIAL

Lk 21:2 He also saw a poor widow put in two very small copper coins. ³"I tell you the truth," he said, "this poor widow has put in more than all the others. ⁴All these people gave their gifts out of their wealth; but she out of her poverty put in all she had to live on."

1Co 6:12 "Everything is permissible for me"—but not everything is beneficial. "Everything is permissible for me"—but I will not be mastered by anything.

1Co 9:12 If others have this right of support from you, shouldn't we have it all the more? But we did not use this right. On the contrary, we put up with anything rather than hinder the gospel of Christ.

1Co 9:15 But I have not used any of these rights. And I am not writing this in the hope that you will do such things for me. I would rather die than have anyone deprive me of this boast.

1Co 9:18 What then is my reward? Just this: that in

preaching the gospel I may offer it free of charge, and so not make use of my rights in preaching it.

¹⁹Though I am free and belong to no man, I make myself a slave to everyone, to win as many as possible.

1Co 9:23 I do all this for the sake of the gospel, that I may share in its blessings.

1Co 9:25 Everyone who competes in the games goes into strict training. They do it to get a crown that will not last; but we do it to get a crown that will last forever. ²⁶Therefore I do not run like a man running aimlessly; I do not fight like a man beating the air. ²⁷No, I beat my body and make it my slave so that after I have preached to others, I myself will not be disqualified for the prize. (+1Co 10:23-24)

2Co 6:3 We put no stumbling block in anyone's path, so that our ministry will not be discredited.

Php 2:4 Each of you should look not only to your own interests, but also to the interests of others. (+Php 2:5-8)

Php 3:7 But whatever was to my profit I now consider loss for the sake of Christ. ⁸What is more, I consider everything a loss compared to the surpassing greatness of knowing Christ Jesus my Lord, for whose sake I have lost all things. I consider them rubbish, that I may gain Christ ⁹and be found in him, not having a righteousness of my own that comes from the law, but that which is through faith in Christ—the righteousness that comes from God and is by faith.

2Ti 2:4 No one serving as a soldier gets involved in civilian affairs—he wants to please his commanding officer.

Tit 2:12 It teaches us to say "No" to ungodliness and worldly passions, and to live self-controlled, upright and godly lives in this present age,

Heb 13:13 Let us, then, go to him outside the camp, bearing the disgrace he bore.

Rev 12:11 They overcame him by the blood of the Lamb and by the word of their testimony; they did not love their lives so much as to shrink from death.

Parables of:

Mt 13:44 "The kingdom of heaven is like treasure hidden in a field. When a man found it, he hid it again, and then in his joy went and sold all he had and bought that field.

⁴⁵"Again, the kingdom of heaven is like a merchant looking for fine pearls. ⁴⁶When he found one of great value, he went away and sold everything he had and bought it.

Mt 18:8 If your hand or your foot causes you to sin cut it off and throw it away. It is better for you to enter life maimed or crippled than to have two hands or two feet and be thrown into eternal fire. ⁹And if your eye causes you to sin, gouge it out and throw it away. It is better for you to enter life with one eye than to have two eyes and be thrown into the fire of hell. (+Mk 9:43)

In Respect to:

Appetite—

Pr 23:2 and put a knife to your throat if you are given to gluttony.

Da 10:3 I ate no choice food; no meat or wine touched my lips; and I used no lotions at all until the three weeks were over.

Sinful pleasures—

Mt 5:29 If your right eye causes you to sin, gouge it out and throw it away. It is better for you to lose one part of your body than for your whole body to be thrown into hell. ³⁰And if your right hand causes you to sin, cut it off and throw it away. It is better for you to lose one part of your body than for your whole body to go into hell. (+Mt 18:8-9; Mk 9:43)

Carnality—

Ro 6:6 For we know that our old self was crucified with him so that the body of sin might be done away with, that we should no longer be slaves to sin—

Ro 8:12 Therefore, brothers, we have an obligation—but it is not to the sinful nature, to live according to it. [13]For if you live according to the sinful nature, you will die; but if by the Spirit you put to death the misdeeds of the body, you will live,

Ro 8:35 Who shall separate us from the love of Christ? Shall trouble or hardship or persecution or famine or nakedness or danger or sword? [36]As it is written: "For your sake we face death all day long; we are considered as sheep to be slaughtered."

Ro 13:14 Rather, clothe yourselves with the Lord Jesus Christ, and do not think about how to gratify the desires of the sinful nature. (+1Co 9:27)

Gal 5:16 So I say, live by the Spirit, and you will not gratify the desires of the sinful nature. [17]For the sinful nature desires what is contrary to the Spirit, and the Spirit what is contrary to the sinful nature. They are in conflict with each other, so that you do not do what you want.

Gal 5:24 Those who belong to Christ Jesus have crucified the sinful nature with its passions and desires.

Col 3:5 Put to death, therefore, whatever belongs to your earthly nature: sexual immorality, impurity, lust, evil desires and greed, which is idolatry. (+Tit 2:12)

1Pe 2:11 Dear friends, I urge you, as aliens and strangers in the world, to abstain from sinful desires, which war against your soul. [12]Live such good lives among the pagans that, though they accuse you of doing wrong, they may see your good deeds and glorify God on the day he visits us.

1Pe 2:14 or to governors, who are sent by him to punish those who do wrong and to commend those who do right. [15]For it is God's will that by doing good you should silence the ignorant talk of foolish men. [16]Live as free men, but do not use your freedom as a cover-up for evil; live as servants of God.

Required of Christ's disciples:

Mt 8:19 Then a teacher of the law came to him and said, "Teacher, I will follow you wherever you go."

[20]Jesus replied, "Foxes have holes and birds of the air have nests, but the Son of Man has no place to lay his head."

[21]Another disciple said to him, "Lord, first let me go and bury my father."

[22]But Jesus told him, "Follow me, and let the dead bury their own dead."

Mt 10:37 "Anyone who loves his father or mother more than me is not worthy of me; anyone who loves his son or daughter more than me is not worthy of me; [38]and anyone who does not take his cross and follow me is not worthy of me. [39]Whoever finds his life will lose it, and whoever loses his life for my sake will find it.

Mt 16:24 Then Jesus said to his disciples, "If anyone would come after me, he must deny himself and take up his cross and follow me. [25]For whoever wants to save his life will lose it, but whoever loses his life for me will find it.

Mt 19:12 For some are eunuchs because they were born that way; others were made that way by men; and others have renounced marriage because of the kingdom of heaven. The one who can accept this should accept it."

Mt 19:21 Jesus answered, "If you want to be perfect, go, sell your possessions and give to the poor, and you will have treasure in heaven. Then come, follow me." (+Mk 2:14; 8:34-35; 10:29; Lk 5:11; 9:23-24,57-58; 12:33)

Lk 14:26 "If anyone comes to me and does not hate his father and mother, his wife and children, his brothers and sisters—yes, even his own life—he cannot be my disciple. [27]And anyone who does not carry his cross and follow me cannot be my disciple.

Lk 14:33 In the same way, any of you who does not give up everything he has cannot be my disciple.

Lk 18:27 Jesus replied, "What is impossible with men is possible with God."

[28]Peter said to him, "We have left all we had to follow you!"

[29]"I tell you the truth," Jesus said to them, "no one who has left home or wife or brothers or parents or children for the sake of the kingdom of God [30]will fail to receive many times as much in this age and, in the age to come, eternal life."

Jn 12:25 The man who loves his life will lose it, while the man who hates his life in this world will keep it for eternal life. (+2Ti 2:4; Heb 13:13)

1Pe 4:1 Therefore, since Christ suffered in his body, arm yourselves also with the same attitude, because he who has suffered in his body is done with sin.

3Jn 7 It was for the sake of the Name that they went out, receiving no help from the pagans.

For a brother's sake—

Ro 14:1 Accept him whose faith is weak, without passing judgment on disputable matters. [2]One man's faith allows him to eat everything, but another man, whose faith is weak, eats only vegetables. [3]The man who eats everything must not look down on him who does not, and the man who does not eat everything must not condemn the man who does, for God has accepted him. [4]Who are you to judge someone else's servant? To his own master he stands or falls. And he will stand, for the Lord is able to make him stand.

[5]One man considers one day more sacred than another; another man considers every day alike. Each one should be fully convinced in his own mind. [6]He who regards one day as special, does so to the Lord. He who eats meat, eats to the Lord, for he gives thanks to God; and he who abstains, does so to the Lord and gives thanks to God. [7]For none of us lives to himself alone and none of us dies to himself alone. [8]If we live, we live to the Lord; and if we die, we die to the Lord. So, whether we live or die, we belong to the Lord.

[9]For this very reason, Christ died and returned to life so that he might be the Lord of both the dead and the living. [10]You, then, why do you judge your brother? Or why do you look down on your brother? For we will all stand before God's judgment seat. [11]It is written:

"'As surely as I live,' says the Lord, 'every knee will bow before me; every tongue will confess to God.'"

[12]So then, each of us will give an account of himself to God.

[13]Therefore let us stop passing judgment on one another. Instead, make up your mind not to put any stumbling block or obstacle in your brother's way. [14]As one who is in the Lord Jesus, I am fully convinced that no food is unclean in itself. But if anyone regards something as unclean, then for him it is unclean. [15]If your brother is distressed because of what you eat, you are no longer acting in love. Do not by your eating destroy your brother for whom Christ died.

[16]Do not allow what you consider good to be spoken of as evil. [17]For the kingdom of God is not a matter of eating and drinking, but of righteousness, peace and joy in the Holy Spirit, [18]because anyone who serves Christ in this way is pleasing to God and approved by men.

[19]Let us therefore make every effort to do what leads to peace and to mutual edification. [20]Do not destroy the work of God for the sake of food. All food is clean, but it is wrong for a man to eat anything that causes someone else to stumble. [21]It is better not to eat meat or drink wine or to do anything else that will cause your brother to fall.

[22]So whatever you believe about these things keep between yourself and God. Blessed is the man who does not condemn himself by what he approves.

Ro 15:1 We who are strong ought to bear with the failings of the weak and not to please ourselves. [2]Each of us should please his neighbor for his good, to build him up. [3]For even Christ did not please himself but, as it is written: "The insults of those who insult you have fallen on me." [4]For everything that was written in the past was written to teach us, so that through endurance and the encouragement of the Scriptures we might have hope.

[5]May the God who gives endurance and encouragement give you a spirit of unity among yourselves as you follow Christ Jesus,

1Co 8:10 For if anyone with a weak conscience sees you who have this knowledge eating in an idol's temple, won't he be emboldened to eat what has been sacrificed to idols? [11]So this weak brother, for whom Christ died, is destroyed by your knowledge. [12]When you sin against your brothers in this way and wound their weak conscience, you sin against Christ. (+1Co 8:13)

1Co 10:23 "Everything is permissible"—but not everything is beneficial. "Everything is permissible"—but not everything is constructive. [24]Nobody should seek his own good, but the good of others. (+Php 2:4)

For the sake of the ministry (2Co 6:3). Christ's teachings concerning (Mk 12:43-44; Lk 21:2-4).

Instances of:

Abraham, when he accorded to Lot his preference for the grazing lands of Canaan (Ge 13:9; 17:8)

Abraham, in offering Isaac—

Ge 22:12 "Do not lay a hand on the boy," he said. "Do not do anything to him. Now I know that you fear God, because you have not withheld from me your son, your only son."

Moses, in choosing suffering over pleasure (Heb 11:25), in taking no compensation from the Israelites (Nu 16:15). Samuel, in his administration of justice (1Sa 12:3-4). The widow of Zarephath, in sharing with Elijah the last of her sustenance (1Ki 17:12-15).

David, in paying for the threshing floor—

2Sa 24:24 But the king replied to Araunah, "No, I insist on paying you for it. I will not sacrifice to the LORD my God burnt offerings that cost me nothing." So David bought the threshing floor and the oxen and paid fifty shekels of silver for them.

The psalmist—

Ps 132:3 "I will not enter my house or go to my bed— [4]I will allow no sleep to my eyes, no slumber to my eyelids, [5]till I find a place for the LORD, a dwelling for the Mighty One of Jacob."

Daniel, in refusing royal food (Da 1:8), in refusing rewards from Belshazzar (Da 5:16-17). Esther, in risking her life for her people (Est 4:16). The Recabites, in

refusing wine or fermented drink, or even to plant vineyards (Jer 35:6-7).

Peter and other apostles, in abandoning their vocations to follow Jesus (Mt 4:20; 9:9; Mk 1:16-20; 2:14)—

Lk 5:11 So they pulled their boats up on shore, left everything and followed him.

Lk 5:27 After this, Jesus went out and saw a tax collector by the name of Levi sitting at his tax booth. "Follow me," Jesus said to him, [28]and Levi got up, left everything and followed him.

In forsaking all (Mt 19:27; Mk 10:28; Lk 5:28). The widow, who cast all into the treasury (Lk 21:4). The early Christians, in having everything in common (Ac 2:44-45; 4:34). Joseph, in selling his possessions and giving all to the apostles (Ac 4:36-37).

Paul (1Co 10:23-24)—

Gal 2:20 I have been crucified with Christ and I no longer live, but Christ lives in me. The life I live in the body, I live by faith in the Son of God, who loved me and gave himself for me.

Gal 6:14 May I never boast except in the cross of our Lord Jesus Christ, through which the world has been crucified to me, and I to the world.

Paul, in not counting even his life valuable to himself—

Ac 20:24 However, I consider my life worth nothing to me, if only I may finish the race and complete the task the Lord Jesus has given me—the task of testifying to the gospel of God's grace.

Ac 21:13 Then Paul answered, "Why are you weeping and breaking my heart? I am ready not only to be bound, but also to die in Jerusalem for the name of the Lord Jesus." (+Php 3:7-8)

In laboring for his own support while he taught (Ac 20:34-35; 1Co 4:12; 10:33), in not exercising his authority (1Co 6:12; 9:12,15,18-19,23-27).

See Cross; Humility.

SELF-DISCIPLINE [5406]. Needed: Not to give in to sin (Ro 6:12-14); to "run the race" of life according to the rules (1Co 9:24-27; 2Ti 2:1-7). Contrasted to timidity (2Ti 1:7). *See Self-Control.*

SELF-EXALTATION

Christian attitude toward—

2Co 10:5 We demolish arguments and every pretension that sets itself up against the knowledge of God, and we take captive every thought to make it obedient to Christ.

2Co 10:17 But, "Let him who boasts boast in the Lord." [18]For it is not the one who commends himself who is approved, but the one whom the Lord commends.

Christ's teaching concerning (Mk 12:38).

Parables of—

Lk 14:7 When he noticed how the guests picked the places of honor at the table, he told them this parable: [8]"When someone invites you to a wedding feast, do not take the place of honor, for a person more distinguished than you may have been invited. [9]If so, the host who invited both of you will come and say to you, 'Give this man your seat.' Then, humiliated, you will have to take the least important place. [10]But when you are invited, take the lowest place, so that when your host comes, he will say to you, 'Friend, move up to a better place.' Then you will be honored in the presence of all your fellow guests. [11]For everyone who exalts himself will be humbled, and he who humbles himself will be exalted."

Self-deception of—

Isa 5:21 Woe to those who are wise in their own eyes and clever in their own sight. (+1Co 3:18; 8:2)

Gal 6:3 If anyone thinks he is something when he is nothing, he deceives himself.

Punishment for—

Eze 31:10 "'Therefore this is what the Sovereign LORD says: Because it towered on high, lifting its top above the thick foliage, and because it was proud of its height, ¹¹I handed it over to the ruler of the nations, for him to deal with according to its wickedness. I cast it aside, ¹²and the most ruthless of foreign nations cut it down and left it. Its boughs fell on the mountains and in all the valleys; its branches lay broken in all the ravines of the land. All the nations of the earth came out from under its shade and left it. ¹³All the birds of the air settled on the fallen tree, and all the beasts of the field were among its branches. ¹⁴Therefore no other trees by the waters are ever to tower proudly on high, lifting their tops above the thick foliage. No other trees so well-watered are ever to reach such a height; they are all destined for death, for the earth below, among mortal men, with those who go down to the pit.

Ob 3 The pride of your heart has deceived you, you who live in the clefts of the rocks and make your home on the heights, you who say to yourself, 'Who can bring me down to the ground?' ⁴Though you soar like the eagle and make your nest among the stars, from there I will bring you down," declares the LORD.

Instances of:

Job—

Job 12:3 But I have a mind as well as you; I am not inferior to you. Who does not know all these things?

Pharaoh (Ex 9:17). Korah, Dathan, and Abiram (Nu 16:1-11). Sennacherib (2Ch 32:9-19). Prince of Tyre, making himself God (Eze 28:2,9-10). Nebuchadnezzar (Da 4:30; 5:20). Belshazzar (Da 5:22-23). Simon the sorcerer (Ac 8:9-11). Herod, when deified by the people (Ac 12:20-23).

The man of lawlessness—

2Th 2:4 He will oppose and will exalt himself over everything that is called God or is worshiped, so that he sets himself up in God's temple, proclaiming himself to be God.

See Pride; Self-Righteousness.

SELF-EXAMINATION

Commanded:

Ps 4:4 In your anger do not sin; when you are on your beds, search your hearts and be silent. *Selah*

Hag 1:7 This is what the LORD Almighty says: "Give careful thought to your ways.

1Co 11:28 A man ought to examine himself before he eats of the bread and drinks of the cup.

1Co 11:31 But if we judged ourselves, we would not come under judgment.

2Co 13:5 Examine yourselves to see whether you are in the faith; test yourselves. Do you not realize that Christ Jesus is in you—unless, of course, you fail the test?

Gal 6:4 Each one should test his own actions. Then he can take pride in himself, without comparing himself to somebody else,

By Inference:

Jer 17:9 The heart is deceitful above all things and beyond cure. Who can understand it?

Conversion as a Result of (Ps 119:59)

La 3:40 Let us examine our ways and test them, and let us return to the LORD.

Exemplified by:

Job—

Job 13:23 How many wrongs and sins have I committed? Show me my offense and my sin.

David—

Ps 19:2 Day after day they pour forth speech; night after night they display knowledge.

Ps 26:2 Test me, O LORD, and try me, examine my heart and my mind;

Ps 139:23 Search me, O God, and know my heart; test me and know my anxious thoughts. ²⁴See if there is any offensive way in me, and lead me in the way everlasting.

The Psalmist—

Ps 77:6 I remembered my songs in the night. My heart mused and my spirit inquired:

Ps 119:59 I have considered my ways and have turned my steps to your statutes.

The disciples—

Mt 26:22 They were very sad and began to say to him one after the other, "Surely not I, Lord?" (+Mk 14:19)

See Meditation; Repentance; Sin, Confession of.

SELF-INCRIMINATION

Under ancient customs, accused persons were required to give self-incriminating testimonies of guilt of the offense charged and were, on occasions, scourged to force self-incriminating testimony whether guilty or innocent (Nu 5:11-27; 2Sa 1:10,16; 1Ki 8:31-32; 2Ch 6:22; Ac 22:24).

Instances of: Achan (Jos 8:19-25).
See Self-Condemnation.

SELF-INDULGENCE [202, 5059].

Instances of:

Solomon (Ecc 2:10). The rich fool (Lk 12:16-20). The rich man as contrasted to Lazarus (Lk 16:19).
See Gluttony; Idleness; Slothfulness; also, Self-Denial.

SELFISHNESS [1299, 9294, 2249].

NIV+ SELFISH

Denounced:

Admonitions against—

Lk 6:32 "If you love those who love you, what credit is that to you? Even 'sinners' love those who love them. ³³And if you do good to those who are good to you, what credit is that to you? Even 'sinners' do that. ³⁴And if you lend to those from whom you expect repayment, what credit is that to you? Even 'sinners' lend to 'sinners,' expecting to be repaid in full.

Ro 14:15 If your brother is distressed because of what you eat, you are no longer acting in love. Do not by your eating destroy your brother for whom Christ died.

Ro 15:1 We who are strong ought to bear with the failings of the weak and not to please ourselves. ²Each of us should please his neighbor for his good, to build him up. ³For even Christ did not please himself but, as it is written: "The insults of those who insult you have fallen on me."

1Co 10:24 Nobody should seek his own good, but the good of others.

Gal 6:2 Carry each other's burdens, and in this way you will fulfill the law of Christ.

Php 2:4 Each of you should look not only to your own interests, but also to the interests of others.

Christ's example against (Ro 15:3)—

2Co 5:15 And he died for all, that those who live should no longer live for themselves but for him who died for them and was raised again. (+Php 2:5-8)

Judged—

Pr 18:17 The first to present his case seems right, till another comes forward and questions him.

Pr 24:11 Rescue those being led away to death; hold back those staggering toward slaughter. [12]If you say, "But we knew nothing about this," does not he who weighs the heart perceive it? Does not he who guards your life know it? Will he not repay each person according to what he has done?

Hag 1:4 "Is it a time for you yourselves to be living in your paneled houses, while this house remains a ruin?"

Hag 1:9 "You expected much, but see, it turned out to be little. What you brought home, I blew away. Why?" declares the LORD Almighty. "Because of my house, which remains a ruin, while each of you is busy with his own house. [10]Therefore, because of you the heavens have withheld their dew and the earth its crops.

Exemplified by:

Corrupt officials—

Mic 3:11 Her leaders judge for a bribe, her priests teach for a price, and her prophets tell fortunes for money. Yet they lean upon the LORD and say, "Is not the LORD among us? No disaster will come upon us."

Corrupt priests and prophets—

Eze 34:18 Is it not enough for you to feed on the good pasture? Must you also trample the rest of your pasture with your feet? Is it not enough for you to drink clear water? Must you also muddy the rest with your feet?

Zec 7:6 And when you were eating and drinking, were you not just feasting for yourselves?

Those who accumulate too much—

Pr 11:26 People curse the man who hoards grain, but blessing crowns him who is willing to sell. (+Isa 5:8)

Mt 19:21 Jesus answered, "If you want to be perfect, go, sell your possessions and give to the poor, and you will have treasure in heaven. Then come, follow me."

[22]When the young man heard this, he went away sad, because he had great wealth.

The self-indulgent (Ro 14:15)—

2Ti 3:2 People will be lovers of themselves, lovers of money, boastful, proud, abusive, disobedient to their parents, ungrateful, unholy, [3]without love, unforgiving, slanderous, without self-control, brutal, not lovers of the good, [4]treacherous, rash, conceited, lovers of pleasure rather than lovers of God—

Those unsympathetic with the unfortunate—

Pr 28:27 He who gives to the poor will lack nothing, but he who closes his eyes to them receives many curses.

Jas 2:15 Suppose a brother or sister is without clothes and daily food. [16]If one of you says to him, "Go, I wish you well; keep warm and well fed," but does nothing about his physical needs, what good is it?

1Jn 3:17 If anyone has material possessions and sees his brother in need but has no pity on him, how can the love of God be in him?

Cain—

Ge 4:9 Then the LORD said to Cain, "Where is your brother Abel?" "I don't know," he replied. "Am I my brother's keeper?"

The Gadites and Reubenites—

Nu 32:6 Moses said to the Gadites and Reubenites, "Shall your countrymen go to war while you sit here?

David's friends—

Ps 38:11 My friends and companions avoid me because of my wounds; my neighbors stay far away.

The Israelites (Hag 1:4)—

Mal 1:10 "Oh, that one of you would shut the temple doors, so that you would not light useless fires on my altar! I am not pleased with you," says the LORD Almighty, "and I will accept no offering from your hands.

Early Christians—

Php 2:20 I have no one else like him, who takes a genuine interest in your welfare. [21]For everyone looks out for his own interests, not those of Jesus Christ.

See Liberality; Poor; Unselfishness.

SELF-RIGHTEOUSNESS

Described as:

Assertive—

Pr 20:6 Many a man claims to have unfailing love, but a faithful man who can find?

Mt 7:22 Many will say to me on that day, 'Lord, Lord, did we not prophesy in your name, and in your name drive out demons and perform many miracles?' [23]Then I will tell them plainly, 'I never knew you. Away from me, you evildoers!'

Delusive—

Pr 12:15 The way of a fool seems right to him, but a wise man listens to advice.

Pr 16:2 All a man's ways seem innocent to him, but motives are weighed by the LORD.

Pr 21:2 All a man's ways seem right to him, but the LORD weighs the heart. (+Pr 28:26; Isa 28:20)

Isa 50:11 But now, all you who light fires and provide yourselves with flaming torches, go, walk in the light of your fires and of the torches you have set ablaze. This is what you shall receive from my hand: You will lie down in torment.

Isa 64:6 All of us have become like one who is unclean, and all our righteous acts are like filthy rags; we all shrivel up like a leaf, and like the wind our sins sweep us away.

Hos 12:8 Ephraim boasts, "I am very rich; I have become wealthy. With all my wealth they will not find in me any iniquity or sin." (+Mt 7:22-23)

Mt 22:12 'Friend,' he asked, 'how did you get in here without wedding clothes?' The man was speechless.

[13]"Then the king told the attendants, 'Tie him hand and foot, and throw him outside, into the darkness, where there will be weeping and gnashing of teeth.' (+Gal 6:3)

Denounced:

Job 12:2 "Doubtless you are the people, and wisdom will die with you!

Pr 25:14 Like clouds and wind without rain is a man who boasts of gifts he does not give.

Pr 25:27 It is not good to eat too much honey, nor is it honorable to seek one's own honor.

Pr 26:12 Do you see a man wise in his own eyes? There is more hope for a fool than for him. (+Pr 30:12-13)

Isa 5:21 Woe to those who are wise in their own eyes and clever in their own sight.

Isa 65:3 a people who continually provoke me to my very face, offering sacrifices in gardens and burning incense on altars of brick; [4]who sit among the graves and spend their nights keeping secret vigil; who eat the flesh of pigs, and whose pots hold broth of unclean meat; [5]who say, 'Keep away; don't come near me, for I am too sacred for you!' Such people are smoke in my nostrils, a fire that keeps burning all day.

Jer 2:13 "My people have committed two sins: They have forsaken me, the spring of living water, and have dug their own cisterns, broken cisterns that cannot hold water.

Jer 2:22 Although you wash yourself with soda and use an abundance of soap, the stain of your guilt is still before me," declares the Sovereign LORD. ²³"How can you say, 'I am not defiled; I have not run after the Baals'? See how you behaved in the valley; consider what you have done. You are a swift she-camel running here and there,

Jer 2:34 On your clothes men find the lifeblood of the innocent poor, though you did not catch them breaking in. Yet in spite of all this ³⁵you say, 'I am innocent; he is not angry with me.' But I will pass judgment on you because you say, 'I have not sinned.'

Jer 8:8 "'How can you say, "We are wise, for we have the law of the LORD," when actually the lying pen of the scribes has handled it falsely?

Eze 33:24 "Son of man, the people living in those ruins in the land of Israel are saying, 'Abraham was only one man, yet he possessed the land. But we are many; surely the land has been given to us as our possession.' ²⁵Therefore say to them, 'This is what the Sovereign LORD says: Since you eat meat with the blood still in it and look to your idols and shed blood, should you then possess the land? ²⁶You rely on your sword, you do detestable things, and each of you defiles his neighbor's wife. Should you then possess the land?'

Am 6:13 you who rejoice in the conquest of Lo Debar and say, "Did we not take Karnaim by our own strength?"

Mt 9:10 While Jesus was having dinner at Matthew's house, many tax collectors and "sinners" came and ate with him and his disciples. ¹¹When the Pharisees saw this, they asked his disciples, "Why does your teacher eat with tax collectors and 'sinners'?"

¹²On hearing this, Jesus said, "It is not the healthy who need a doctor, but the sick. ¹³But go and learn what this means: 'I desire mercy, not sacrifice.' For I have not come to call the righteous, but sinners." (+Mk 2:16; 8:15; Lk 5:30; 16:14-15; 18:9-14; 22:12-13)

Lk 23:29 For the time will come when you will say, 'Blessed are the barren women, the wombs that never bore and the breasts that never nursed!' ³⁰Then

"'they will say to the mountains, "Fall on us!" and to the hills, "Cover us!"'

³¹For if men do these things when the tree is green, what will happen when it is dry?" (+Ro 11:19-21)

Admonitions against—

Dt 9:4 After the LORD your God has driven them out before you, do not say to yourself, "The LORD has brought me here to take possession of this land because of my righteousness." No, it is on account of the wickedness of these nations that the LORD is going to drive them out before you. ⁵It is not because of your righteousness or your integrity that you are going in to take possession of their land; but on account of the wickedness of these nations, the LORD your God will drive them out before you, to accomplish what he swore to your fathers, to Abraham, Isaac and Jacob. ⁶Understand, then, that it is not because of your righteousness that the LORD your God is giving you this good land to possess, for you are a stiff-necked people.

1Sa 2:9 He will guard the feet of his saints, but the wicked will be silenced in darkness. "It is not by strength that one prevails;

Pr 27:2 Let another praise you, and not your own mouth; someone else, and not your own lips.

Pr 27:21 The crucible for silver and the furnace for gold, but man is tested by the praise he receives.

Jer 7:4 Do not trust in deceptive words and say, "This is the temple of the LORD, the temple of the LORD, the temple of the LORD!"

Hab 2:4 "See, he is puffed up; his desires are not upright—but the righteous will live by his faith— (+2Co 1:9; 10:17-18)

Judgments against—

Pr 14:12 There is a way that seems right to a man, but in the end it leads to death.

Isa 28:17 I will make justice the measuring line and righteousness the plumb line; hail will sweep away your refuge, the lie, and water will overflow your hiding place. (+Isa 50:11; Jer 8:8)

Jer 49:4 Why do you boast of your valleys, boast of your valleys so fruitful? O unfaithful daughter, you trust in your riches and say, 'Who will attack me?'

Jer 49:16 The terror you inspire and the pride of your heart have deceived you, you who live in the clefts of the rocks, who occupy the heights of the hill. Though you build your nest as high as the eagle's, from there I will bring you down," declares the LORD.

Zep 3:11 On that day you will not be put to shame for all the wrongs you have done to me, because I will remove from this city those who rejoice in their pride. Never again will you be haughty on my holy hill.

Proverbs concerning (Pr 12:15; 14:12; 16:2; 20:6; 21:2; 25:14,27; 26:12; 27:2,21)—

Pr 28:13 He who conceals his sins does not prosper, but whoever confesses and renounces them finds mercy.

Pr 28:26 He who trusts in himself is a fool, but he who walks in wisdom is kept safe.

Pr 30:12 those who are pure in their own eyes and yet are not cleansed of their filth; ¹³those whose eyes are ever so haughty, whose glances are so disdainful;

Parables concerning—

Lk 7:36 Now one of the Pharisees invited Jesus to have dinner with him, so he went to the Pharisee's house and reclined at the table. ³⁷When a woman who had lived a sinful life in that town learned that Jesus was eating at the Pharisee's house, she brought an alabaster jar of perfume, ³⁸and as she stood behind him at his feet weeping, she began to wet his feet with her tears. Then she wiped them with her hair, kissed them and poured perfume on them.

³⁹When the Pharisee who had invited him saw this, he said to himself, "If this man were a prophet, he would know who is touching him and what kind of woman she is—that she is a sinner."

⁴⁰Jesus answered him, "Simon, I have something to tell you."

"Tell me, teacher," he said.

⁴¹"Two men owed money to a certain moneylender. One owed him five hundred denarii, and the other fifty. ⁴²Neither of them had the money to pay him back, so he canceled the debts of both. Now which of them will love him more?"

⁴³Simon replied, "I suppose the one who had the bigger debt canceled."

"You have judged correctly," Jesus said.

⁴⁴Then he turned toward the woman and said to Simon, "Do you see this woman? I came into your house. You did not give me any water for my feet, but she wet my feet with her tears and wiped them with her hair. ⁴⁵You did not give me a kiss, but this woman, from the time I entered, has not stopped kissing my feet. ⁴⁶You did not put oil on

my head, but she has poured perfume on my feet. [47]Therefore, I tell you, her many sins have been forgiven—for she loved much. But he who has been forgiven little loves little."

[48]Then Jesus said to her, "Your sins are forgiven."

[49]The other guests began to say among themselves, "Who is this who even forgives sins?"

[50]Jesus said to the woman, "Your faith has saved you; go in peace."

Lk 10:25 On one occasion an expert in the law stood up to test Jesus. "Teacher," he asked, "what must I do to inherit eternal life?"

[26]"What is written in the Law?" he replied. "How do you read it?"

[27]He answered: "'Love the Lord your God with all your heart and with all your soul and with all your strength and with all your mind'; and, 'Love your neighbor as yourself.'"

[28]"You have answered correctly," Jesus replied. "Do this and you will live."

[29]But he wanted to justify himself, so he asked Jesus, "And who is my neighbor?"

[30]In reply Jesus said: "A man was going down from Jerusalem to Jericho, when he fell into the hands of robbers. They stripped him of his clothes, beat him and went away, leaving him half dead. [31]A priest happened to be going down the same road, and when he saw the man, he passed by on the other side. [32]So too, a Levite, when he came to the place and saw him, passed by on the other side. [33]But a Samaritan, as he traveled, came where the man was; and when he saw him, he took pity on him. [34]He went to him and bandaged his wounds, pouring on oil and wine. Then he put the man on his own donkey, took him to an inn and took care of him. [35]The next day he took out two silver coins and gave them to the innkeeper. 'Look after him,' he said, 'and when I return, I will reimburse you for any extra expense you may have.'

[36]"Which of these three do you think was a neighbor to the man who fell into the hands of robbers?"

[37]The expert in the law replied, "The one who had mercy on him."

Jesus told him, "Go and do likewise."

Lk 15:25 "Meanwhile, the older son was in the field. When he came near the house, he heard music and dancing. [26]So he called one of the servants and asked him what was going on. [27]'Your brother has come,' he replied, 'and your father has killed the fattened calf because he has him back safe and sound.'

[28]"The older brother became angry and refused to go in. So his father went out and pleaded with him. [29]But he answered his father, 'Look! All these years I've been slaving for you and never disobeyed your orders. Yet you never gave me even a young goat so I could celebrate with my friends. [30]But when this son of yours who has squandered your property with prostitutes comes home, you kill the fattened calf for him!'

[31]"'My son,' the father said, 'you are always with me, and everything I have is yours. [32]But we had to celebrate and be glad, because this brother of yours was dead and is alive again; he was lost and is found.'" (+Lk 18:9-14)

Paul's instruction regarding—

Ro 2:17 Now you, if you call yourself a Jew; if you rely on the law and brag about your relationship to God; [18]if you know his will and approve of what is superior because you are instructed by the law; [19]if you are convinced that you are a guide for the blind, a light for those who are in the dark, [20]an instructor of the foolish, a teacher of infants, because you have in the law the embodiment of knowledge and truth—

Ro 3:27 Where, then, is boasting? It is excluded. On what principle? On that of observing the law? No, but on that of faith.

Ro 10:3 Since they did not know the righteousness that comes from God and sought to establish their own, they did not submit to God's righteousness.

Ro 11:19 You will say then, "Branches were broken off so that I could be grafted in." [20]Granted. But they were broken off because of unbelief, and you stand by faith. Do not be arrogant, but be afraid. [21]For if God did not spare the natural branches, he will not spare you either.

2Co 1:9 Indeed, in our hearts we felt the sentence of death. But this happened that we might not rely on ourselves but on God, who raises the dead.

2Co 10:17 But, "Let him who boasts boast in the Lord." [18]For it is not the one who commends himself who is approved, but the one whom the Lord commends.

Gal 6:3 If anyone thinks he is something when he is nothing, he deceives himself.

Instances of:

Job accused of—

Job 11:4 You say to God, 'My beliefs are flawless and I am pure in your sight.'

Job 32:1 So these three men stopped answering Job, because he was righteous in his own eyes. [2]But Elihu son of Barakel the Buzite, of the family of Ram, became very angry with Job for justifying himself rather than God.

Job 33:8 "But you have said in my hearing—I heard the very words— [9]'I am pure and without sin; I am clean and free from guilt.'

Job 35:2 "Do you think this is just? You say, 'I will be cleared by God.'

Job 35:7 If you are righteous, what do you give to him, or what does he receive from your hand? [8]Your wickedness affects only a man like yourself, and your righteousness only the sons of men.

Israelites—

Nu 16:3 They came as a group to oppose Moses and Aaron and said to them, "You have gone too far! The whole community is holy, every one of them, and the LORD is with them. Why then do you set yourselves above the LORD's assembly?" (+Ro 2:17-20; 10:3)

Saul (1Sa 15:13-21).

The wicked—

Ps 10:5 His ways are always prosperous; he is haughty and your laws are far from him; he sneers at all his enemies. [6]He says to himself, "Nothing will shake me; I'll always be happy and never have trouble."

Pharisees (Mt 9:10-13; Mk 2:16-17; Lk 5:30; 7:39)—

Lk 15:2 But the Pharisees and the teachers of the law muttered, "This man welcomes sinners and eats with them."

Lk 16:14 The Pharisees, who loved money, heard all this and were sneering at Jesus. [15]He said to them, "You are the ones who justify yourselves in the eyes of men, but God knows your hearts. What is highly valued among men is detestable in God's sight.

Lk 18:9 To some who were confident of their own righteousness and looked down on everybody else, Jesus told this parable: [10]"Two men went up to the temple to pray, one a Pharisee and the other a tax collector. [11]The Pharisee stood up and prayed about himself: 'God, I thank you that

I am not like other men—robbers, evildoers, adulterers—or even like this tax collector. [12]I fast twice a week and give a tenth of all I get.'

[13]"But the tax collector stood at a distance. He would not even look up to heaven, but beat his breast and said, 'God, have mercy on me, a sinner.'

[14]"I tell you that this man, rather than the other, went home justified before God. For everyone who exalts himself will be humbled, and he who humbles himself will be exalted." (+Jn 9:28-38)

Jn 9:39 Jesus said, "For judgment I have come into this world, so that the blind will see and those who see will become blind."

[40]Some Pharisees who were with him heard him say this and asked, "What? Are we blind too?"

[41]Jesus said, "If you were blind, you would not be guilty of sin; but now that you claim you can see, your guilt remains.

The rich young ruler—

Mt 19:16 Now a man came up to Jesus and asked, "Teacher, what good thing must I do to get eternal life?"

[17]"Why do you ask me about what is good?" Jesus replied. "There is only One who is good. If you want to enter life, obey the commandments."

[18]"Which ones?" the man inquired.

Jesus replied, "'Do not murder, do not commit adultery, do not steal, do not give false testimony, [19]honor your father and mother,' and 'love your neighbor as yourself.'"

[20]"All these I have kept," the young man said. "What do I still lack?"

[21]Jesus answered, "If you want to be perfect, go, sell your possessions and give to the poor, and you will have treasure in heaven. Then come, follow me."

[22]When the young man heard this, he went away sad, because he had great wealth. (+Mk 10:17-22; Lk 18:18-23)

The lawyer (Lk 10:25-29).

Church of Laodicea—

Rev 3:17 You say, 'I am rich; I have acquired wealth and do not need a thing.' But you do not realize that you are wretched, pitiful, poor, blind and naked. [18]I counsel you to buy from me gold refined in the fire, so you can become rich; and white clothes to wear, so you can cover your shameful nakedness; and salve to put on your eyes, so you can see.

See Hypocrisy; Self-Exaltation.

SELF-WILL Stubbornness. Forbidden (2Ch 30:8; Ps 75:5).

Proceeds From:

Unbelief (2Ki 17:14), pride (Ne 9:16,29), an evil heart (Jer 7:24). God knows (Isa 48:4). Exhibited in refusing to listen to God (Pr 1:24), refusing to listen to the messengers of God (1Sa 8:19; Jer 44:16; Zec 7:11), refusing to walk in the ways of God (Ne 9:17; Isa 42:24; Ps 78:10), refusing to listen to parents (Dt 21:18-19), refusing to receive correction (Dt 21:18; Jer 5:3; 7:28), rebelling against God (Dt 31:27; Ps 78:8), resisting the Holy Spirit (Ac 7:51), walking in the counsels of an evil heart (Jer 7:24, w Jer 23:17), hardening the neck (Ne 9:16), hardening the heart (2Ch 36:13), going backward and not forward (Jer 7:24), heinousness of (1Sa 15:23).

Ministers should be without (Tit 1:7), warn their people against (Heb 3:7-12), pray that their people may be forgiven for (Ex 34:9; Dt 9:27). Characteristic of the wicked

(Pr 7:11; 2Pe 2:10). The wicked will not cease from (Jdg 2:19). Punishment for (Dt 21:21; Pr 29:1).

Illustrated: (Ps 32:9; Jer 31:18).

Exemplified:

Simeon and Levi (Ge 49:6). Israelites (Ex 32:9; Dt 9:6,13). Saul (1Sa 15:19-23). David (2Sa 24:4). Josiah (2Ch 35:22). Zedekiah (2Ch 36:13).

See Obduracy.

SELVEDGE NIV The "edge" of each of the two curtains which covered the boards of the tabernacle (Ex 26:4; 36:11).

SEM *See Shem.*

SEMAKIAH, SEMACHIAH [6165] (*Yahweh sustains, consecrates*). The son of Shemaiah (1Ch 26:7).

SEMEI *See Shimei, 18.*

SEMEIN [4946] (*Yahweh has heard*). An ancestor of Christ (Lk 3:26).

SEMITES (*of Shem*). A diverse group of ancient peoples whose languages are related, belonging to the Semitic family of languages; their world was the Fertile Crescent.

The principal Semitic peoples of ancient times: Akkadians—including Babylonians and Assyrians; Arameans; Canaanites—including Edomites, Ammonites, and Moabites; Hebrews; Arabs; Ethiopians (Ge 10:22-31).

SENAAH [6171]. Descendants of Senaah (sometimes spelled Hassenaah), returned with Zerubbabel (Ezr 2:35; Ne 7:38).

SENATE *See Elders, Council of.*

SENATOR *See Elders; Occupations and Professions.*

SENEH [6175] (*thorny* BDB; possibly *[cliff shaped like] a tooth* IDB). A rock protecting the garrison of the Philistines at Micmash (1Sa 14:5).

SENIR [8536].

NIV+ HERMON

The Amorite name of Mt. Hermon (Dt 3:9; 1Ch 5:23; SS 4:8; Eze 27:5).

SENNACHERIB [6178] (*[pagan moon god] Sin has increased the brothers* BDB ISBE; *Sin replace the [lost] brothers!* IDB).

NIV+ SENNACHERIB'S

The king of Assyria (705-681 B.C.), the son and successor of Sargon II; a great builder and conqueror; invaded Judah in the time of Hezekiah, but his army was miraculously destroyed (2Ki 18; 19; Isa 36; 37). Accounts of his campaigns recorded on clay prisms survive.

SENSUALITY [816, 2952, 4922].

NIV+ SENSUAL

Ecc 2:24 A man can do nothing better than to eat and drink and find satisfaction in his work. This too, I see, is from the hand of God,

Ecc 8:15 So I commend the enjoyment of life, because nothing is better for a man under the sun than to eat and drink and be glad. Then joy will accompany him in his work all the days of the life God has given him under the sun.

Ecc 11:9 Be happy, young man, while you are young, and let your heart give you joy in the days of your youth.

Follow the ways of your heart and whatever your eyes see, but know that for all these things God will bring you to judgment.

Of the Glutton:

Isa 22:13 But see, there is joy and revelry, slaughtering of cattle and killing of sheep, eating of meat and drinking of wine! "Let us eat and drink," you say, "for tomorrow we die!"

Of the Drunkard:

Isa 56:12 "Come," each one cries, "let me get wine! Let us drink our fill of beer! And tomorrow will be like today, or even far better."

Of the Selfish Rich:

Lk 12:19 And I'll say to myself, "You have plenty of good things laid up for many years. Take life easy; eat, drink and be merry."'

²⁰"But God said to him, 'You fool! This very night your life will be demanded from you. Then who will get what you have prepared for yourself?'

Lk 16:25 "But Abraham replied, 'Son, remember that in your lifetime you received your good things, while Lazarus received bad things, but now he is comforted here and you are in agony.

Epicurean Philosophy Justifies (Isa 22:13):

1Co 15:32 If I fought wild beasts in Ephesus for merely human reasons, what have I gained? If the dead are not raised, "Let us eat and drink, for tomorrow we die."

Admonition Against:

Jas 5:5 You have lived on earth in luxury and self-indulgence. You have fattened yourselves in the day of slaughter.

Warning Against:

Jude 18 They said to you, "In the last times there will be scoffers who will follow their own ungodly desires." ¹⁹These are the men who divide you, who follow mere natural instincts and do not have the Spirit.

See Adultery; Drunkenness; Fornication; Gluttony; Homosexual; Lasciviousness; Self-Indulgence; also, Abstinence; Continence; Self-Denial; Temperance.

SENTRY [5874].

NIV+ SENTRIES

See Watchman.

SENUAH (*sons of the hated [rejected] woman, i.e., the poor class* BDB). *See Hassenuah.*

SEORIM [8556] (*one born at the time of the barley [harvest]*). A descendant of Aaron; head of the fourth course of priests (1Ch 24:1-8).

SEPHAR [6223]. A mountain in Arabia (Ge 10:30).

SEPHARAD [6224]. A place to which the inhabitants of Jerusalem were exiled (Ob 20); possibly Sardis or Sparta.

SEPHARVAIM [6226].

NIV+ SEPHARVITES

An Assyrian city, from which the king of Assyria colonized Samaria (2Ki 17:24,31; 18:34; 19:13; Isa 36:19; 37:13).

SEPHARVITES [6227].

NIV+ SEPHARVAIM

The people of Sepharvaim (2Ki 17:31).

SEPHER *See Kiriath Sepher.*

SEPTUAGINT (*seventy*). A translation of the OT into Greek, prepared in Alexandria in the second and third centuries B.C. *See Testaments, Time Between; Texts and Versions.*

SEPULCHRE *See Burial.*

SEPULCHRE, CHURCH OF THE HOLY One of

two main sites identified as the tomb of Jesus; built by Constantine in A.D. 325.

SERAH [8580] (*one who explains, opens, extends* IDB; *abundance* ISBE KB). *See Sarah, 2.*

SERAIAH [8588, 8589] (*Yahweh persists* BDB ISBE; *Yahweh is prince* IDB; *Yahweh contends* KB).

NIV+ SERAIAH'S

1. David's secretary. Probably the same as Sheva, Shisha, and Shavsha. (2Sa 8:17; 20:25; 1Ki 4:3; 1Ch 18:16).

2. Chief priest at the time of the taking of Jerusalem (2Ki 25:18). Father of Ezra (Ezr 7:1). Slain by Nebuchadnezzar (2Ki 25:18-21; Jer 52:24-27).

3. An Israelite captain who surrendered to Gedaliah (2Ki 25:23; Jer 40:8).

4. The son of Kenaz (1Ch 4:13-14).

5. A Simeonite (1Ch 4:35).

6. A priest who returned from the Babylonian captivity (Ezr 2:2; Ne 12:1,12). Called Azariah (Ne 7:7).

7. One who sealed the covenant with Nehemiah (Ne 10:2). Possibly identical with 6, above.

8. A ruler of the temple after the Captivity (Ne 11:11).

9. The son of Azriel. Commanded by King Jehoiakim to seize Jeremiah (Jer 36:26).

10. A servant of Zedekiah (Jer 51:59,61).

SERAPHS, SERAPHIM [8597] (*burning ones, [winged] serpents*).

Celestial beings whom Isaiah saw standing before the enthroned Lord (Isa 6:2-3,6-7). Possibly the same as the "living creatures" (Rev 4:6-9).

SERED, SEREDITE [6237, 6238].

The son of Zebulun and his descendants (Ge 46:14; Nu 26:26).

SERGEANTS NIV "officers." *See Occupations and Professions.*

SERGIUS PAULUS [4950]. A Roman deputy and convert of Paul (Ac 13:7-12).

SERMON ON THE MOUNT

The Sermon on the Mount is the first of five great discourses in Matthew (chs. 5-7; 10; 13; 18; 24-25). It contains three types of material: (1) beatitudes, or declarations of blessedness (5:1-12), (2) ethical admonitions (5:13-20; 6:1-7:23) and (3) contrasts between Jesus' ethical teaching and Jewish legalistic traditions (5:21-48). The sermon ends with a short parable stressing the importance of practicing what has just been taught (7:24-27) and an expression of amazement by the crowds at the authority with which Jesus spoke (7:28-29).

Opinion differs as to whether the sermon is a summary of what Jesus taught on one occasion or a compilation of teachings presented on numerous occasions. Matthew possibly took a single sermon and expanded it with other relevant teachings of Jesus. Thirty-four of the verses in

Matthew's account of the sermon occur in different contexts in Luke than the so-called "Sermon on the Plain" (Lk 6:17-49).

The Sermon on the Mount's call to moral and ethical living is so high that some have dismissed it as being completely unrealistic or have projected its fulfillment to the future kingdom. There is no doubt, however, that Jesus (and Matthew) gave the sermon as a standard for all Christians, realizing that its demands cannot be met in our own power. It is also true that Jesus occasionally used hyperbole to make his point. For example, Jesus is not teaching self-mutilation (Mt 5:29-30), for even a blind man can lust. The point is that we should deal as drastically with sin as necessary.

SERPENT [5729, 7352, 8597, 9490, *4058*].

NIV+ SERPENT'S, SERPENTS, SNAKE, SNAKES

Satan appears in the form of, to Eve (Ge 3:1-15; 2Co 11:3). Subtlety of (Ge 3:1; Ecc 10:8; Mt 10:16). Curse upon (Ge 3:14-15; 49:17). Metaphorically feeds on the dust (Ge 3:14; Isa 65:25; Mic 7:17). Unfit for food (Mt 7:10). Venom of (Dt 32:24,33; Job 20:16; Ps 58:4; 140:3; Pr 23:31-32; Ac 28:5-6). The staff of Moses transformed into (Ex 4:3; 7:15). Poisonous, sent as a plague upon the Israelites (Nu 21:6-7; Dt 8:15; 1Co 10:9); the wound of miraculously healed by looking upon the bronze image set up by Moses (Nu 21:8-9). Charming of (Ps 58:4-5; Ecc 10:11; Jer 8:17). Mentioned in Solomon's riddle (Pr 30:19). Constriction of (Rev 9:19). Sea serpent (Am 9:3). The seventy-two given power over (Lk 10:19). The apostles given power over (Mk 16:18; Ac 28:5).

Figurative: (Pr 23:32; Isa 14:29).

See Adder; Cobra; Dragon; Viper.

SERUG [8578, *4952*] (*descendant* i.e., *younger branch* BDB). An ancestor of Abraham (Ge 11:20-23; 1Ch 1:26). Called Serug (Lk 3:35).

SERVANT [*408, 563, 5853, 5855, 5987, 6269, 9148, 9250, 10523, *1356, 1527, 1528, 3313, 3860, 4087, 4090, 5281, 5677*].

NIV+ MAIDSERVANT, MAIDSERVANTS, MANSERVANT, MENSERVANTS, SERVANT'S, SERVANTS, SERVANTS'

Distinguished as a bondservant (who was a slave) and hired servant.

Laws of Moses concerning—

Ex 20:10 but the seventh day is a Sabbath to the LORD your God. On it you shall not do any work, neither you, nor your son or daughter, nor your manservant or maidservant, nor your animals, nor the alien within your gates. (+Ex 21:1-11,20-21,26-27,32; Lev 19:20-22; 25:6,10,35-38)

Lev 25:39 "'If one of your countrymen becomes poor among you and sells himself to you, do not make him work as a slave. [40]He is to be treated as a hired worker or a temporary resident among you; he is to work for you until the Year of Jubilee. [41]Then he and his children are to be released, and he will go back to his own clan and to the property of his forefathers. (+Lev 25:42-55; Dt 5:14; 15:12,14,18; 24:7)

Kidnapping and slave trading forbidden (Dt 21:10-14; 24:7; 1Ti 1:10; Rev 18:13). Fugitive, not to be returned to master (Dt 23:15-16). David erroneously supposed to be a fugitive slave (1Sa 25:10).

Instances of fugitive: Hagar, commanded by an angel to return to her mistress (Ge 16:9). Sought by Shimei (1Ki 2:39-41). Interceded for, by Paul (Phm 10-21).

Rights of those born to a master (Ge 14:14; 17:13,27; Ex 21:4; Pr 29:21; Ecc 2:7; Jer 2:14).

Bought and sold (Ge 17:13,27; 37:28,36; 39:17; Lev 22:11; Dt 28:68; Est 7:4; Eze 27:13; Joel 3:6; Am 8:6; Rev 18:13). Captives of war made (Dt 20:14; 21:10-14; 2Ki 5:2; 2Ch 28:8,10; La 5:13), captive bondservants shared by priests and Levites (Nu 31:28-47). Thieves punished by being made (Ge 43:18; Ex 22:3). Defaulting debtors made (Lev 25:39; Mt 18:25). Children of defaulting debtors sold for (2Ki 4:1-7). Voluntary servitude of (Lev 25:47; Dt 15:16-17; Jos 9:11-21). Given as dowry (Ge 29:24,29). Owned by priests (Lev 22:11; Mk 14:66). Slaves owned slaves (2Sa 9:10). The master might marry or give in marriage (Ex 21:7-10; Dt 21:10-14; 1Ch 2:34-35). Taken in concubinage (Ge 16:1-2,6; 30:3,9). Used as soldiers by Abraham (Ge 14:14).

Must be circumcised (Ge 17:13,27; Ex 12:44). Must enjoy religious privileges with the master's household (Dt 12:12,18; 16:11,14; 29:10-11). Must have rest on the Sabbath (Ex 20:10; 23:12; Dt 5:14).

Bond service threatened, as a national punishment, for disobedience of Israel (Dt 28:68; Joel 3:7-8). Degrading influences of bondage exemplified by cowardice (Ex 14:11-12; 16:3; Jdg 5:16-18,23).

Social status of: (Mt 10:24-25)

Lk 17:7 "Suppose one of you had a servant plowing or looking after the sheep. Would he say to the servant when he comes in from the field, 'Come along now and sit down to eat'? [8]Would he not rather say, 'Prepare my supper, get yourself ready and wait on me while I eat and drink; after that you may eat and drink'? [9]Would he thank the servant because he did what he was told to do?

Lk 22:27 For who is greater, the one who is at the table or the one who serves? Is it not the one who is at the table? But I am among you as one who serves.

Jn 13:16 I tell you the truth, no servant is greater than his master, nor is a messenger greater than the one who sent him.

Equal status of, with other disciples of Jesus—

1Co 7:21 Were you a slave when you were called? Don't let it trouble you—although if you can gain your freedom, do so. [22]For he who was a slave when he was called by the Lord is the Lord's freedman; similarly, he who was a free man when he was called is Christ's slave. (+1Co 12:13; Gal 3:28; Eph 6:8)

Proverbs concerning:

Pr 12:9 Better to be a nobody and yet have a servant than pretend to be somebody and have no food.

Pr 13:17 A wicked messenger falls into trouble, but a trustworthy envoy brings healing.

Pr 17:2 A wise servant will rule over a disgraceful son, and will share the inheritance as one of the brothers.

Pr 19:10 It is not fitting for a fool to live in luxury—how much worse for a slave to rule over princes!

Pr 25:13 Like the coolness of snow at harvest time is a trustworthy messenger to those who send him; he refreshes the spirit of his masters.

Pr 26:6 Like cutting off one's feet or drinking violence is the sending of a message by the hand of a fool.

Pr 27:18 He who tends a fig tree will eat its fruit, and he who looks after his master will be honored.

Pr 27:27 You will have plenty of goats' milk to feed you and your family and to nourish your servant girls.

Pr 29:19 A servant cannot be corrected by mere words; though he understands, he will not respond.

Pr 29:21 If a man pampers his servant from youth, he will bring grief in the end.

Pr 30:10 "Do not slander a servant to his master, or he will curse you, and you will pay for it.

Pr 30:21 "Under three things the earth trembles, under four it cannot bear up: ²²a servant who becomes king, a fool who is full of food, ²³an unloved woman who is married, and a maidservant who displaces her mistress.

Parables of:

Mt 24:45 "Who then is the faithful and wise servant, whom the master has put in charge of the servants in his household to give them their food at the proper time? ⁴⁶It will be good for that servant whose master finds him doing so when he returns. ⁴⁷I tell you the truth, he will put him in charge of all his possessions. ⁴⁸But suppose that servant is wicked and says to himself, 'My master is staying away a long time,' ⁴⁹and he then begins to beat his fellow servants and to eat and drink with drunkards. ⁵⁰The master of that servant will come on a day when he does not expect him and at an hour he is not aware of. ⁵¹He will cut him to pieces and assign him a place with the hypocrites, where there will be weeping and gnashing of teeth.

Lk 12:35 "Be dressed ready for service and keep your lamps burning, ³⁶like men waiting for their master to return from a wedding banquet, so that when he comes and knocks they can immediately open the door for him. ³⁷It will be good for those servants whose master finds them watching when he comes. I tell you the truth, he will dress himself to serve, will have them recline at the table and will come and wait on them. ³⁸It will be good for those servants whose master finds them ready, even if he comes in the second or third watch of the night. ³⁹But understand this: If the owner of the house had known at what hour the thief was coming, he would not have let his house be broken into. ⁴⁰You also must be ready, because the Son of Man will come at an hour when you do not expect him."

⁴¹Peter asked, "Lord, are you telling this parable to us, or to everyone?"

⁴²The Lord answered, "Who then is the faithful and wise manager, whom the master puts in charge of his servants to give them their food allowance at the proper time? ⁴³It will be good for that servant whom the master finds doing so when he returns. ⁴⁴I tell you the truth, he will put him in charge of all his possessions. ⁴⁵But suppose the servant says to himself, 'My master is taking a long time in coming,' and he then begins to beat the menservants and maidservants and to eat and drink and get drunk. ⁴⁶The master of that servant will come on a day when he does not expect him and at an hour he is not aware of. He will cut him to pieces and assign him a place with the unbelievers.

⁴⁷"That servant who knows his master's will and does not get ready or does not do what his master wants will be beaten with many blows. ⁴⁸But the one who does not know and does things deserving punishment will be beaten with few blows. From everyone who has been given much, much will be demanded; and from the one who has been entrusted with much, much more will be asked.

Lk 16:1 Jesus told his disciples: "There was a rich man whose manager was accused of wasting his possessions. ²So he called him in and asked him, 'What is this I hear about you? Give an account of your management, because you cannot be manager any longer.'

³"The manager said to himself, 'What shall I do now? My master is taking away my job. I'm not strong enough to dig, and I'm ashamed to beg— ⁴I know what I'll do so that,

when I lose my job here, people will welcome me into their houses.'

⁵"So he called in each one of his master's debtors. He asked the first, 'How much do you owe my master?'

⁶"'Eight hundred gallons of olive oil,' he replied.

"The manager told him, 'Take your bill, sit down quickly, and make it four hundred.'

⁷"Then he asked the second, 'And how much do you owe?'

"'A thousand bushels of wheat,' he replied. "He told him, 'Take your bill and make it eight hundred.'

⁸"The master commended the dishonest manager because he had acted shrewdly. For the people of this world are more shrewd in dealing with their own kind than are the people of the light. ⁹I tell you, use worldly wealth to gain friends for yourselves, so that when it is gone, you will be welcomed into eternal dwellings.

¹⁰"Whoever can be trusted with very little can also be trusted with much, and whoever is dishonest with very little will also be dishonest with much. ¹¹So if you have not been trustworthy in handling worldly wealth, who will trust you with true riches? ¹²And if you have not been trustworthy with someone else's property, who will give you property of your own?

¹³"No servant can serve two masters. Either he will hate the one and love the other, or he will be devoted to the one and despise the other. You cannot serve both God and Money."

Conspiracy by. *See Conspiracy.*

Cruelty to:

Hagar (Ge 16:1-5)—

Ge 16:6 "Your servant is in your hands," Abram said. "Do with her whatever you think best." Then Sarai mistreated Hagar; so she fled from her.

⁷The angel of the LORD found Hagar near a spring in the desert; it was the spring that is beside the road to Shur. ⁸And he said, "Hagar, servant of Sarai, where have you come from, and where are you going?"

"I'm running away from my mistress Sarai," she answered. ⁹Then the angel of the LORD told her, "Go back to your mistress and submit to her." (+Ge 16:10-21; Gal 4:22-31)

The Israelites (Ex 1:8-22; 2:1-4; 5:7-9; Ac 7:19,34). Sick, abandoned (1Sa 30:13).

Admonitions against cruelty to—

Jer 22:13 "Woe to him who builds his palace by unrighteousness, his upper rooms by injustice, making his countrymen work for nothing, not paying them for their labor.

Instances of cruelty to: Joseph (Ge 37:26-28,36). Israelites (Ex 1:10-22; 5:7-14; Dt 6:12,21). Gibeonites (Jos 9:22-27). Canaanites (1Ki 9:21). Jews in Babylon (2Ch 36:20; Est 1:1-10). Freeing of (2Ch 36:23; Ezr 1:1-4).

Duties of:

To be faithful—

1Co 4:2 Now it is required that those who have been given a trust must prove faithful.

Obedient—

Mt 8:9 For I myself am a man under authority, with soldiers under me. I tell this one, 'Go,' and he goes; and that one, 'Come,' and he comes. I say to my servant, 'Do this,' and he does it."

Eph 6:5 Slaves, obey your earthly masters with respect and fear, and with sincerity of heart, just as you would obey Christ. ⁶Obey them not only to win their favor when their eye is on you, but like slaves of Christ, doing the will of God from your heart. [7]Serve wholeheartedly, as if you were serving the Lord, not men, [8]because you know that the Lord will reward everyone for whatever good he does, whether he is slave or free.

[9]And masters, treat your slaves in the same way. Do not threaten them, since you know that he who is both their Master and yours is in heaven, and there is no favoritism with him.

Col 3:22 Slaves, obey your earthly masters in everything; and do it, not only when their eye is on you and to win their favor, but with sincerity of heart and reverence for the Lord. [23]Whatever you do, work at it with all your heart, as working for the Lord, not for men, [24]since you know that you will receive an inheritance from the Lord as a reward. It is the Lord Christ you are serving. [25]Anyone who does wrong will be repaid for his wrong, and there is no favoritism.

Tit 2:9 Teach slaves to be subject to their masters in everything, to try to please them, not to talk back to them, [10]and not to steal from them, but to show that they can be fully trusted, so that in every way they will make the teaching about God our Savior attractive.

1Pe 2:18 Slaves, submit yourselves to your masters with all respect, not only to those who are good and considerate, but also to those who are harsh. [19]For it is commendable if a man bears up under the pain of unjust suffering because he is conscious of God. [20]But how is it to your credit if you receive a beating for doing wrong and endure it? But if you suffer for doing good and you endure it, this is commendable before God.

To honor masters—

Mal 1:6 "A son honors his father, and a servant his master. If I am a father, where is the honor due me? If I am a master, where is the respect due me?" says the LORD Almighty. "It is you, O priests, who show contempt for my name. "But you ask, 'How have we shown contempt for your name?'

1Ti 6:1 All who are under the yoke of slavery should consider their masters worthy of full respect, so that God's name and our teaching may not be slandered. [2]Those who have believing masters are not to show less respect for them because they are brothers. Instead, they are to serve them even better, because those who benefit from their service are believers, and dear to them. These are the things you are to teach and urge on them.

Warning to—

Zep 1:9 On that day I will punish all who avoid stepping on the threshold, who fill the temple of their gods with violence and deceit.

Figurative: (Lev 25:42,55; Ps 116:16)

Isa 52:3 For this is what the LORD says: "You were sold for nothing, and without money you will be redeemed." (+Mt 24:45,51; Lk 12:35-48; 16:1-13; 17:7-9; Jn 8:32-35; Ro 6:16-22; 1Co 4:1-2; 7:21-23; Gal 5:13; 1Pe 2:16; 2Pe 2:19; Rev 7:3)

Good, Instances of:

Joseph (Ge 39:2-20; 41:9-57; Ac 7:10), Elisha (2Ki 2:1-6). Servants of Abraham (Ge 24), of Boaz (Ru 2:4), of Jonathan (1Sa 14:7), of Abigail (1Sa 25:14-17), of David (2Sa 12:18; 15:15,21), of Ziba (2Sa 9), of Naaman (2Ki 5:2-3,13), of Nehemiah (Ne 4:16,23), of centurion (Mt 8:9), of Cornelius (Ac 10:7), Onesimus (Phm 11). Servants in the parable of the pounds and talents (Mt 25:14-23; Lk 19:12-19).

Kindness to:

Ps 123:2 As the eyes of slaves look to the hand of their master, as the eyes of a maid look to the hand of her mistress, so our eyes look to the LORD our God, till he shows us his mercy. (+Pr 29:21)

Commanded (Lev 25:43; Eph 6:9).

Exemplified by Job—

Job 19:15 My guests and my maidservants count me a stranger; they look upon me as an alien. [16]I summon my servant, but he does not answer, though I beg him with my own mouth.

Job 31:13 "If I have denied justice to my menservants and maidservants when they had a grievance against me, [14]what will I do when God confronts me? What will I answer when called to account?

By Boaz (Ru 2:4), by the centurion (Mt 8:8-13; Lk 7:2-10), by Paul (Phm 1-21).

Redeemed—

Ne 5:8 and said: "As far as possible, we have bought back our Jewish brothers who were sold to the Gentiles. Now you are selling your brothers, only for them to be sold back to us!" They kept quiet, because they could find nothing to say.

Freed (2Ch 36:23; Ezr 1:1-4)—

Jer 34:8 The word came to Jeremiah from the LORD after King Zedekiah had made a covenant with all the people in Jerusalem to proclaim freedom for the slaves. [9]Everyone was to free his Hebrew slaves, both male and female; no one was to hold a fellow Jew in bondage. [10]So all the officials and people who entered into this covenant agreed that they would free their male and female slaves and no longer hold them in bondage. They agreed, and set them free. [11]But afterward they changed their minds and took back the slaves they had freed and enslaved them again.

[12]Then the word of the LORD came to Jeremiah: [13]"This is what the LORD, the God of Israel, says: I made a covenant with your forefathers when I brought them out of Egypt, out of the land of slavery. I said, [14]'Every seventh year each of you must free any fellow Hebrew who has sold himself to you. After he has served you six years, you must let him go free.' Your fathers, however, did not listen to me or pay attention to me. [15]Recently you repented and did what is right in my sight: Each of you proclaimed freedom to his countrymen. You even made a covenant before me in the house that bears my Name. [16]But now you have turned around and profaned my name; each of you has taken back the male and female slaves you had set free to go where they wished. You have forced them to become your slaves again.

[17]"Therefore, this is what the LORD says: You have not obeyed me; you have not proclaimed freedom for your fellow countrymen. So I now proclaim 'freedom' for you, declares the LORD—'freedom' to fall by the sword, plague and famine. I will make you abhorrent to all the kingdoms of the earth. (+Jer 34:18-22; Ac 6:9; 1Co 7:21)

Called Freedmen (Ac 6:9).

Tact in management of—

Ecc 7:21 Do not pay attention to every word people say, or you may hear your servant cursing you—

Wicked and Unfaithful, Instances of:

Jeroboam (1Ki 11:26), Gehazi (2Ki 5:20-27), Zimri (1Ki 16:9-10; 2Ki 9:31), Onesimus (Phm 11).

Servants of Abraham and Lot (Ge 3:7). Of Abimelech (Ge 21:25). of Ziba (2Sa 16:1-4, w 2Sa 19:26-27). Of Absalom (2Sa 13:28-29; 14:30). Of Shimei (1Ki 2:39). Of

Joash (2Ki 12:19-21). Of Amon (2Ki 21:23). Of Job (Job 19:15-16). In the parable of the talents and pounds (Mt 25:24-30; Lk 19:20-26). In the parable of the vineyard (Mt 21:33-41; Mk 12:1-9).

See Employee; Employer; Master.

Hired Workers:

Jacob (Ge 29:15; 30:26), reemployed (Ge 30:27-34; 31:6-7,41). Parable of laborers for a vineyard (Mt 20:1-15). Of the father of the prodigal son (Lk 15:17,19), of the prodigal son (Lk 15:5-19).

Kindness to (Ru 2:4). Treatment of, more considerable than that accorded slaves (Lev 25:53). Await employment in the marketplace (Mt 20:1-3).

Mercenary—
Job 7:2 Like a slave longing for the evening shadows, or a hired man waiting eagerly for his wages,

Unfaithful (Jn 10:12-13).

Rights of Hired Workers:

Receive wages—
Mt 10:10 take no bag for the journey, or extra tunic, or sandals or a staff; for the worker is worth his keep. (+Lk 10:7)
Ro 4:4 Now when a man works, his wages are not credited to him as a gift, but as an obligation.
1Ti 5:18 For the Scripture says, "Do not muzzle the ox while it is treading out the grain," and "The worker deserves his wages."
Jas 5:4 Look! The wages you failed to pay the workmen who mowed your fields are crying out against you. The cries of the harvesters have reached the ears of the Lord Almighty.

Daily payment of wages—
Lev 19:13 "'Do not defraud your neighbor or rob him. "'Do not hold back the wages of a hired man overnight.
Dt 24:15 Pay him his wages each day before sunset, because he is poor and is counting on it. Otherwise he may cry to the LORD against you, and you will be guilty of sin.

Share in spontaneous products of land in the seventh year (Lev 25:6). Wages of, paid in a portion of the flocks or products (Ge 30:31-32; 2Ch 2:10), or in money (Mt 20:2,9-10).

Oppression of, forbidden—
Dt 24:14 Do not take advantage of a hired man who is poor and needy, whether he is a brother Israelite or an alien living in one of your towns.
Col 4:1 Masters, provide your slaves with what is right and fair, because you know that you also have a Master in heaven.

Oppressors of, punished—
Mal 3:5 "So I will come near to you for judgment. I will be quick to testify against sorcerers, adulterers and perjurers, against those who defraud laborers of their wages, who oppress the widows and the fatherless, and deprive aliens of justice, but do not fear me," says the LORD Almighty.

See Master, of Servants; Wages.

SERVANT OF THE LORD
NIV+ See SERVANT

Agent of the LORD such as the patriarchs (Ex 32:13), Moses (Nu 12:7f), and the prophets (Zec 1:6).

Used as a title for the Messiah in Isaiah 40-66. The NT applies Isaiah's Servant passages to Jesus (Isa 42:1-4; Mt 12:16-21).

See Jesus the Christ, Messiah; Obedience of.

SERVICE [*2118, 3655, 3656, 3912, 4200+, 5466, 6268, 6269, 6275, 6641, 7372, 8492, 9068, 9149, 9250, 10586, *1354, 1355, 1526, 3302, 3311*].

NIV+ SERVE, SERVED, SERVES, SERVICES, SERVING, SERVITUDE

Refers to all sorts of work from the most inferior and menial to the most honored and exalted (Lev 23:7f; Nu 3:6ff).

SERVITOR *See Occupations and Professions; Servant.*

SETH [9269, 4953] (*determined, granted, Ge 4:25; restitution* KB).

1. The third son of Adam and Eve, born after the murder of Abel. Name is a play on "granted," Eve said, "God has granted me another child in place of Abel, since Cain killed him" (Ge 4:25). It was through Seth that the genealogy of Noah passed (Ge 4:25-26; 5:3,8; 1Ch 1:1; Lk 3:38).

2. *See Sheth..*

SETHUR [6256] (*concealed [by deity]* IDB). One of the twelve spies (Nu 13:13).

SEVEN [8651, 8679, 8685, 10696, *2231, 2232, 2233*].

NIV+ SEVENFOLD, SEVENS, SEVENTH

Interesting facts concerning the number.

Days:

Week consists of (Ge 2:3; Ex 20:11; Dt 5:13-14). Noah in the ark before the Flood (Ge 7:4,10), remains in the ark after sending out the dove (Ge 8:10-12). Mourning for Jacob lasted (Ge 50:10), of Job (Job 2:13). The plague of bloody waters in Egypt lasted (Ex 7:25). The Israelites circled Jericho (Jos 6:4). The Passover lasted (Ex 12:15). Saul directed by Samuel to wait at Gilgal for the prophet's command (1Sa 10:8; 13:8). The elders of Jabesh Gilead ask for a truce (1Sa 10:8; 13:8). Dedication of temple lasted double (1Ki 8:65). Ezekiel sits by the Kebar River in astonishment (Eze 3:15). The Feast of Tabernacles lasted (Lev 23:34,42). Consecration of priests and altars lasted (Ex 29:30,35; Eze 43:25-26). Defilements lasted (Lev 12:2; 13:4). Fasts of (1Sa 31:13; 2Sa 12:16, 18,22). The firstborn of flocks and sheep shall remain with the mother before being offered (Ex 22:30). The feast of Xerxes continued (Est 1:5). Paul stayed at Tyre (Ac 21:4), at Puteoli (Ac 28:14).

Weeks:

In Daniel's vision concerning the coming of the Messiah (Da 9:25). Ten times (Da 9:24-27). The period between the Passover and Pentecost (Lev 23:15).

Months:

Holy convocations in the seventh month (Lev 23:24-44; Nu 29; Eze 45:25).

Years:

Jacob serves for each of his wives (Ge 29:15-30). Of plenty (Ge 41:1-32,53). Famine lasted in Egypt (Ge 41:1-32,54-56), in Canaan (2Sa 24:13; 2Ki 8:1). Insanity of Nebuchadnezzar (Da 4:32). Seven times, the period between the Jubilees (Lev 25:8).

Miscellaneous Sevens:

Of clean beasts taken into the ark (Ge 7:2). Abraham gives Abimelech seven lambs (Ge 21:28). Rams and bulls required in sacrifices (Lev 23:18; Nu 23:1; 29:32; 1Ch 15:26; Eze 45:23). Blood sprinkling seven times (Lev 4:6; 14:7), oil (Lev 14:16). Seven cows and seven heads of grain in Pharaoh's vision (Ge 41:2-7). Israelites marched around Jericho seven times, on the seventh day sounding seven trumpets (Jos 6:4). Elisha's servant looked seven times for the appearance of rain (1Ki 18:43). Naaman was required to wash in the Jordan seven times (2Ki 5:10). Seven steps in the temple seen in Ezekiel's vision (Eze 40:22,26). The heat of Nebuchadnezzar's furnace intensified sevenfold (Da 3:19). The light of the sun intensified sevenfold (Isa 30:26). The threatened sevenfold punishment of Israel (Lev 26:18-21). Silver purified seven times (Ps 12:6). Worshiping seven times a day (Ps 119:164). Seven eunuchs at the court of Xerxes (Est 1:10), seven princes (Est 1:14). Seven counselors at the court of Artaxerxes (Ezr 7:14). Seven maidens given to Esther (Est 2:9). Symbolic of many sons (Ru 4:15; 1Sa 2:5; Jer 15:9), of liberality (Ecc 11:1-2). Seven wise men (Pr 26:16). Seven women shall seek polyandrous marriage (Isa 4:1). Seven shepherds to be sent forth against Assyria (Mic 5:5-6). Seven lamps and pipes (Zec 4:2). *See Seven Words From the Cross.* Seven ministers in the apostolic church (Ac 6:3). Seven churches in Asia (Rev 1:4,20). Seven seals (Rev 5:1). Seven thunders (Rev 10:3). Seven heads and seven crowns (Rev 12:3; 13:1; 17:9). Seven kings (Rev 17:10). Seven stars (Rev 1:16,20; 3:1; Am 5:8). Seven spirits (Rev 1:4; 3:1; 4:5; 5:6). Seven eyes of the Lord (Zec 3:9; 4:10; Rev 5:6). Seven golden lampstands (Rev 1:12). Seven angels with seven trumpets (Rev 8:2). Seven plagues (Rev 15:1). Seven horns and seven eyes (Rev 5:6). Seven angels with seven plagues (Rev 15:6). Seven golden bowls (Rev 15:7). Scarlet colored beast having seven heads (Rev 17:3,7).

SEVEN WORDS FROM THE CROSS

The seven statements Jesus made from the cross. No single gospel account recounts them all:

"Father, forgive them, for they do not know what they are doing." (Lk 23:34)

"I tell you the truth, today you will be with me in paradise." (Lk 23:43)

"Dear woman, here is your son," and to the disciple "Here is your mother." (Jn 19:26-27)

"My God, my God, why have you forsaken me?" (Mt 27:46-47; Mk 15:34-36)

"I am thirsty." (Jn 19:28)

"It is finished." (Jn 19:30)

"Father, into your hands I commit my spirit." (Lk 23:46; cf.Mt 27:50; Mk 15:37)

SEVENTY [8679, *1573*].
NIV+ 70

Seventy descendants of Jacob in Egypt (Ex 1:5; Dt 10:22). The council of the Israelites composed of seventy elders (Ex 24:1,9; Nu 11:16,24-25). Seventy-two (KJV seventy) disciples sent forth by Jesus (Lk 10:1-17). The Jews in captivity in Babylon seventy years (Jer 25:11-12; 29:10; Da 9:2; Zec 1:12; 7:5).
See Israel.

SEVENTY WEEKS, THE The name applied to a period of time (probably 490 years) referred to in Daniel (Da 9:24-27).

SEVENTY-TWO, THE Seventy-two (KJV seventy) disciples were sent on a preaching mission by Jesus (Lk 10:1-17).

SEXUAL PURITY *See Chastity; Self-Control.*

SEXUAL RELATIONS *See Adultery; Bestiality; Fornication; Homosexual; Incest; Prostitute; Rape.*

SHAALABBIN [9125] (*site of foxes*). Town between Ir Shemesh and Aijalon (Jos 19:42).

SHAALBIM [9124] (site of foxes). A town, probably in central Israel, won by Danites from Amorites (Jdg 1:35).

SHAALBONITE [9126]. Designation of Eliahba, one of David's mighty men (2Sa 23:32; 1Ch 11:33)

SHAALIM, LAND OF [9127] (possibly *[land of] hollow depth* KB). A region probably near the N boundary of Benjamin's territory (1Sa 9:4).

SHAAPH [9131].
1. Son of Jahdai (1Ch 2:47).
2. Son of Caleb (1Ch 2:49).

SHAARAIM, SHARAIM [9139] (*double gates*).
1. A town in Judah (Jos 15:36; 1Sa 17:52).
2. A town in Simeon (1Ch 4:31), "Sharuhen" (Jos 19:6), and "Shilhim" (Jos 15:32).

SHAASHGAZ [9140]. A eunuch of Xerxes' court (Est 2:14).

SHABBETHAI [8703] (*one born at Sabbath* ISBE KB).
1. A Levite, assistant to Ezra (Ezr 10:15).
2. An expounder of the Law (Ne 8:7).
3. A chief Levite, attendant of the temple (Ne 11:16).

SHACHIA *See Sakia.*

SHACKLES [3890, 4591, 4593, 5733, 6040]. Made of bronze (Jdg 16:21; 2Ki 25:7; 2Ch 33:11; 36:6; Jer 39:7; 52:11). Used for securing prisoners (2Ch 33:11; 36:6; Mk 5:4). *See Chains; Fetters.*

SHADDAI [8724] (*the Mountain One* IDB; other suggestions: 1. *mountain* 2. *maternal goddess of many breasts* 3. *self-sufficient* 4. *an Akkadian spirit, Shad* 5. *almighty, omnipotent* KB).

Shaddai is used forty-eight times as a name of God, thirty-two times in Job (Job 5:17; 6:4,14; etc.), seven times in the compound name *El Shaddai*. The NIV consistently translates *Shaddai* as "Almighty" (Ge 17:1; Ps 91:1).
See God, Names of, Shaddai.

SHADOW [694, 696, 7498, 7511, 7516, *5014, 5572*].
NIV+ SHADOWS

Used literally, figuratively (1Ch 29:15; Ps 17:8; Isa 30:3), theologically (Col 2:17; Heb 8:5; 10:1).

SHADOW OF DEATH *See Darkness.*

SHADRACH [8731, 10701] (*servant of [pagan moon god] Aku*).

His Hebrew name was Hananiah. He was taken as a captive to Babylon with Daniel, Mishael, and Azariah, where each one was given a Babylonian name (Da 1:6-20; 2:17,49; 3:12-30). Hananiah was renamed Shadrach.

Shadrach, Meshach, and Abednego were chosen to learn the language and the ways of the Chaldeans (Babylonians) so that they could enter the king's service (Da 1:3-5,17-20), c. 605 B.C. These three were eventually thrown into Nebuchadnezzar's furnace because they refused to bow down and worship the huge golden image that he had made (Da 3:1,4-6,8-30).

SHAFT [5707, 6770, 7562, 7866, *5853*].
1. Stem of the gold lampstand (Ex 25:31; 37:17).

2. Shaft of a spear (1Sa 17:7).

3. Water (2Sa 5:8) or mine shaft (Job 28:4).

SHAGEE, SHAGE [8707] (*wanderer, meanderer [like feeding sheep]*). The father of Jonathan, one of David's guard (1Ch 11:34).

SHAHAR *See Zereth Shahar.*

SHAHARAIM [8844] (*one born at early [reddish] dawn* KB). A Benjamite (1Ch 8:8).

SHAHAZUMAH, SHAHAZIMAH [8833] (*elevated place*). A city in Issachar (Jos 19:22).

SHALEM (*peace* or *safe*). See Paddan Aram, Padan-Aram, 2.

SHALIM, LAND OF *See Shaalim, Land of.*

SHALISHA [8995] (*a third part*). A district bordering on the Mount Ephraim (1Sa 9:4).

SHALISHAH *See Baal Shalishah.*

SHALLEKETH, SHALLECHETH [8962] (possibly *[gate of] sending forth* BDB). One of the gates of the temple (1Ch 26:16).

SHALLUM [8935] (*peace, well being, prosperity*).
NIV+ SHALLUM'S

1. The son of Naphtali (1Ch 7:13), "Shillem" (Ge 46:24; Nu 26:48-49). See Shillem, Shillemite.

2. The son of Shaul (1Ch 4:25).

3. The son of Sismai (1Ch 2:40-41).

4. The son of Korah chief of the gatekeepers (1Ch 9:17,19,31; Ne 7:45), "Meshelemiah" (1Ch 26:1), "Shelemiah" (1Ch 26:14).

5. The son of Zadok (1Ch 6:12f), "Meshullam" (1Ch 9:11; Ne 11:11).

6. A king of Israel (2Ki 15:10-15).

7. The father of Jehizkiah (2Ch 28:12).

8. Husband of the prophetess Huldah (2Ki 22:14).

9. The king of Judah (1Ch 3:15), better known as Jehoahaz II.

10. The uncle of Jeremiah (Jer 32:7).

11. The father of Maaseiah (Jer 35:4).

12. A Levite who divorced his foreign wife (Ezr 10:24).

13. A man who divorced his foreign wife (Ezr 10:42).

14. A ruler who helped build Jerusalem's walls (Ne 3:12).

SHALLUN [8937] (*recompense*). A Jew who repaired a gate of Jerusalem (Ne 3:15).

SHALMAI [8978] (perhaps *Yahweh is well-being*). An ancestor of the temple servants that returned with Zerubbabel (Ezr 2:46; Ne 7:48).

SHALMAN [8986] (abbreviation of *Shalmaneser* IDB ISBE). Either a contraction of Shalmaneser or the Moabite king Salamanu (Hos 10:14).

SHALMANESER [8987] (*the god Shulman is chief,* or *Sulmanu is leader*).
NIV+ SHALMANESER'S

The title of five Assyrian kings, of whom one is mentioned in the OT, another refers to an Israelite king.

1. Shalmaneser III (859-824 B.C.), the son of Ashurnasirpal; inscription left by him says that he opposed Ben-Hadad of Damascus and Ahab of Israel, and made Israel tributary.

2. Shalmaneser V (726-722 B.C.), the son of Tiglath-Pileser; received tribute from Hoshea; besieged Samaria and carried the N tribes of Israel into captivity (2Ki 17:3; 18:9), "Shalman" (Hos 10:14).

SHAMA [9052] (*one obedient [to Yahweh]*). One of David's heroes (1Ch 11:44).

SHAMARIAH *See Shemariah, 2.*

SHAMBLES NIV "meat market" (1Co 10:25).

SHAME [*1017, 1019, 1425, 2365, 3075, 4007, 4009, 4583, 6872, 7830, *158, 1959, 2875*].
NIV+ ASHAMED, SHAMED, SHAMEFUL, SHAMEFULLY, SHAMELESS, SHAMELESSLY, SHAMING

Of Adam and Eve: no shame before the Fall (Ge 2:25), but after (Ge 3:10). Jesus is ashamed of those who deny him (Mk 8:38; Lk 9:26). Of believers who do not continue in Christ (1Jn 2:28). Of the cross (Heb 12:2).

Destitute of, the Israelites when they worshiped the golden calf (Ex 32:25), the unjust (Zep 3:5).

SHAMED *See Shemed.*

SHAMELESSNESS [1017+4202, 2365].
NIV+ See SHAME

Of the wicked (Jer 6:15; 8:12; Zep 3:5).

SHAMER

1. *See Shemer.*

2. *See Shemer; Shomer, 2.*

SHAMGAR [9011] (*[the pagan Hurrian god] Shimke gave [a son]* IDB). The son of Anath; judge; killed 600 Philistines with an oxgoad (Jdg 3:31; 5:6).

SHAMHUTH [9016] (possibly *one born at a time of a horrible event* KB). David's fifth divisional commander of the army (1Ch 27:8). *See Shammah, 4.*

SHAMIR [9033, 9034] (possibly *thorny* or *emery [flint]*).

1. A town in Judah c. thirteen miles SW of Hebron (Jos 15:48).

2. A town in Ephraim; the home of Tola (Jdg 10:1f).

3. A temple attendant (1Ch 24:24).

SHAMMA [9007] (*astonishment*). The son of Zophah, an Asherite (1Ch 7:37).

SHAMMAH [9007, 9015] (*waste*).

1. The grandson of Esau (Ge 36:13,17; 1Ch 1:37).

2. The brother of David (1Sa 16:9; 17:13), also called Shimea (1Ch 20:7) and Shimeah (2Sa 13:3,32).

3. One of David's mighty men (2Sa 23:11), also called Shagee (1Ch 11:34).

4. Another of David's mighty men (2Sa 23:33), also called Shammoth (1Ch 11:27) and Shamhuth (1Ch 27:8). May be the same as 3.

SHAMMAI [9025] (*Yahweh has heard*).
NIV+ SHAMMAI'S

1. The son of Onam (1Ch 2:28,32).

2. The father of Maon (1Ch 2:44-45).

3. The son of Ezra (1Ch 4:17).

SHAMMOTH [9021] (*desolation*). One of David's mighty men (1Ch 11:27), apparently the same as Shammah, 4 (2Sa 23:25) and Shamhuth (1Ch 27:8).

SHAMMUA [9018, 9055] (possibly *[Yahweh] hears* KB; *rumor,* ZPEB).

1. The son of Zaccur; Reubenite spy (Nu 13:4).

2. The son of David and Bathsheba (2Sa 5:14; 1Ch 14:4).

3. A Levite; the father of Abda (Ne 11:17), also called Shemaiah (1Ch 9:16).

4. A priest (1Ch 24:14; Ne 12:6,18).

SHAMMUAH *See Shammua, 2.*

SHAMSHERAI [9091] (a combination of *Shemesh [pagan sun god]* and *Shamar [guard]*). The son of Jeroham (1Ch 8:26).

SHAN *See Beth Shan.*

SHAPHAM [9171]. A chief of Gad (1Ch 5:12).

SHAPHAN [9177] (*rock badger*).

1. A secretary of King Josiah (2Ki 22:3-14; 2Ch 34:8-20). The father of Gemariah (Jer 36:10-12).

2. The father of Ahikam and the grandfather of Gedaliah (2Ki 22:12; 25:22; 2Ch 34:20; Jer 26:24; 39:14; 40:5,9,11; 41:2; 43:6).

3. The father of Elasah (Jer 29:3).

4. The father of Jaazaniah (Eze 8:11).

SHAPHAT [9151] (*he judges*).

1. A Simeonite spy (Nu 13:5).

2. The father of Elisha the prophet (1Ki 19:16,19).

3. A Gadite chief in Bashan (1Ch 5:12).

4. A herdsman of David (1Ch 27:29).

5. The son of Shemaiah (1Ch 3:22).

SHAPHER *See Shepher, Mount.*

SHAPHIR [9160] (*lovely*). A town probably in SW Israel (Mic 1:10-15).

SHARAI [9232]. A descendant of Bani who divorced his Gentile wife (Ezr 10:40).

SHARAIM *See Shaaraim, Sharaim, 1.*

SHARAR [9243] (*firm*). The father of one of David's mighty men (2Sa 23:33), "Sacar" (1Ch 11:35).

See Sacar, 1.

SHARE [*430, 2475, 2490, 2745, 2750, 2976, 4950, 5989, *3123, 3125, 3126, 3556, 3561, 3576, 3581, 5170*].

NIV+ SHARED, SHARERS, SHARES, SHARING

Plowshare (1Sa 13:20).

SHAREZER [8570] (*[pagan god] protect the king!*).

1. The son of the Assyrian king Sennacherib (2Ki 19:37; Isa 37:38).

2. Contemporary of Zechariah the prophet (Zec 7:2).

SHARON [9227, *4926*] (*plain, level country*).

NIV+ SHARONITE

1. Israel coastal plain between Joppa and Mount Carmel (1Ch 27:29; Isa 35:2; Ac 9:35).

2. Suburbs of Sharon possessed by the tribe of Gad (1Ch 5:16).

3. *See Lasharon.*

4. Figurative of fruitfulness, glory, peace (Isa 35:2; 65:10).

SHARONITE [9228] (*of Sharon*).

NIV+ SHARON

Shitrai, in charge of David's herds in Sharon (1Ch 27:29).

SHARUHEN [9226]. A Simeonite town in Judah's territory (Jos 19:6). Apparently the same as Shilhim (Jos 15:32), and Shaaraim (1Ch 4:31); possibly identified with Tell el-Farah.

SHASHAI [9258] (*noble*). A descendant of Bani, who put away his Gentile wife (Ezr 10:40).

SHASHAK [9265]. A Benjamite (1Ch 8:14,25).

SHAUL, SHAULITE [8620, 8621] (*asked,* possibly *dedicated to God*).

NIV+ SHAUL'S

1. The son of Simeon and his descendants (Ge 46:10; Ex 6:15; Nu 26:13; 1Ch 4:24).

2. An ancient king of Edom (Ge 36:37; 1Ch 1:48-49).

3. Son of Uzziah (1Ch 6:24).

SHAVEH KIRIATHAIM, SHAVEH-KIRIATHAIM [8754] (*level plain of two towns*).

NIV+ KIRIATHAIM, SHAVEH

The plain where Kedorlaomer defeated the Emites (Ge 14:5), probably on the E of the Dead Sea (Nu 32:37).

SHAVEH, VALLEY OF [8753] (*level valley*). The valley where, after rescuing his nephew Lot, Abraham met the king of Sodom (Ge 14:17).

SHAVING [*1605, 1662, 6296, 7942, 7947, *3834*].

NIV+ SHAVE, SHAVED

The priests and Nazirites were prohibited from shaving (Lev 21:5; Nu 6:5), Hebrews generally wore beards. Shaving was often done for religious reasons, as an act of contrition (Job 1:20), consecration for Levites (Nu 6:9; 8:7), cleansing for lepers (Lev 14:8f; 13:32ff), also as an act of contempt (2Sa 10:4).

SHAVSHA [8807]. David's secretary (1Ch 18:16), also called Shisha (1Ki 4:3), Seraiah (2Sa 8:17), and Sheva (2Sa 20:25).

SHEAF [524, 1538, 6658, 6684].

NIV+ SHEAVES

A handful of grain left behind by the reaper, gathered and bound by women and children, and later taken to the threshing-floor (Jer 9:22; Ru 2:7,15). Some sheaves were left behind for the poor (Dt 24:19).

SHEAL [8627] (*May God grant!, asking*). A descendant of Bani, who put away his Gentile wife (Ezr 10:29).

SHEALTIEL [8630, 9003, 10691, *4886*] (*I have asked [him] of God [El]* BDB ISBE KB; possibly *God [El] is a shield, God [El] is a victor* IDB).

1. Father of Zerubbabel and an ancestor of Jesus (1Ch 3:17; Ezr 3:2,8; 5:2; Ne 12:1; Hag 1:1,12,14; 2:2,23).

2. A son of Jehoiachin, king of Judah (Mt 1:12), or of Neri (Lk 3:27). He may have been the real son of Neri, but only the legal heir of Jehoiachin.

SHEARIAH [9138] (possibly *Yahweh breaks*). The son of Azel; descendant of Jonathan (1Ch 8:38; 9:44).

SHEARING HOUSE *See Beth Eked.*

SHEAR-JASHUB [8639] (*a remnant will return*). The symbolic name of Isaiah's oldest son (Isa 7:3; 8:18).

SHEBA [8644, 8680, 8681] (*seven* or *oath*).

1. The son of Raamah (Ge 10:7; 1Ch 1:9).
2. The son of Joktan (Ge 10:28; 1Ch 1:22).
3. The son of Jokshan (Ge 25:3; 1Ch 1:32).
4. A Benjamite who led an insurrection against David (2Sa 20).
5. A Gadite (1Ch 5:13).
6. A city of Simeon (Jos 19:2).
7. Queen of, visits Solomon (1Ki 10:1-13; 2Ch 9:1-12). Kings of, bring gifts to Solomon (Ps 72:10). Rich in gold (Ps 72:15), incense (Jer 6:20). Merchandise of (Eze 27:22-23; 38:13). Prophecies concerning the people of, coming into the kingdom of Messiah (Isa 60:6).

See Sabeans; Seba.

SHEBAH *See Shibah.*

SHEBAM *See Sebam.*

SHEBANIAH [8676, 8677].

1. Trumpeter priest (1Ch 15:24).
2. Levite who signed covenant with Nehemiah (Ne 9:4-5; 10:10).
3. Another Levite who signed a covenant (Ne 10:12).
4. A priest who signed a covenant (Ne 10:4).
5. Priest (Ne 12:14).

SHEBARIM (*quarry*). A place, called the "stone quarries" in the NIV, near Ai to which Israelite soldiers were chased (Jos 7:5, ftn).

See Quarries; Stones.

SHEBAT [8658] (*[the month of] destroying [rain]*). Month eleven in sacred sequence (Zec 1:7), month five in civil sequence. Winter (January-February). *See Month, 11.*

SHEBER [8693] (possibly *lion* IDB; possibly *breaking* or *crushing* or *roughly broken grain* KB). The son of Caleb (not the Israelite spy of the land of Canaan) (1Ch 2:48).

SHEBNA, SHEBNAH [8674, 8675] (*[Yahweh] return now* IDB).

1. A scribe of Hezekiah (2Ki 18:18,26,37; 19:2; Isa 36:3,11,22; 37:2).
2. An official of the king (Isa 22:15-19).

SHEBUEL (possibly *captive of God [El]* or *God [El] restores*). *See Shubael.*

SHECANIAH, SHECHANIAH [8908, 8909] (*Yahweh has taken up his abode*).

NIV+ SHECANIAH'S

1. The head of the tenth course of priests in the days of David (1Ch 24:11).
2. Levite (2Ch 31:15).
3. Descendant of David (1Ch 3:21-22).
4. Man who returned with Ezra (Ezr 8:3).
5. Another man who returned with Ezra (Ezr 8:5).
6. Man who proposed to Ezra that foreign wives be put away (Ezr 10:2-4).
7. Keeper of E gate of Jerusalem in the time of Nehemiah (Ne 3:29).
8. The father-in-law of Tobiah the foe of Nehemiah (Ne 6:18).
9. The chief priest who returned with Zerubbabel (Ne 12:3).

SHECHEM, SHECHEMITE [8901, 8902, 8903, 8904, 5374] (possibly *shoulder [saddle of a hill]* BDB; *shoulders [and upper part of the back]* KB).

NIV+ SHECHEM'S

1. A district in the central part of the land of Canaan. Abraham dwells in (Ge 12:6). Jacob buys a piece of ground in, and builds an altar (Ge 33:18-20). The flocks and herds of Jacob kept in (Ge 37:12-14). Joseph buried in (Jos 24:32). Jacob buried in (Ac 7:16, w Ge 50:13).
2. Also called Sychar, a city of refuge in Mount Ephraim (Jos 20:7; 21:21; Jdg 21:19). Joshua assembled the tribes of Israel at, with all their elders, chiefs, and judges, and presented them before the Lord (Jos 24:1-28). Joshua buried at (Jos 24:30-32). Abimelech made king at (Jdg 8:31; 9). Rehoboam crowned at (1Ki 12:1). Destroyed by Abimelech (Jdg 9:45), rebuilt by Jeroboam (1Ki 12:25). Men of, slain by Ishmael (Jer 41:5). Jesus visits; disciples made in (Jn 4:1-42).
3. Son of Hamor; seduces Jacob's daughter; slain by Jacob's sons (Ge 33:19; 34; Jos 24:32; Jdg 9:28).
4. Descendant of Manasseh and his clan (Nu 26:31; Jos 17:2).
5. Son of Shemida (1Ch 7:19).

SHECHINAH *See Shekinah.*

SHEDEUR [8725] (*Shaddai is light*, or *Shaddai is fire*). Reubenite; father of Elizur (Nu 1:5; 2:10; 7:30; 10:18).

SHEEP [1374, 2378, 3897, 4166, 5924, 6373, 6402, 7366, 7892, 8161, 8445, 9068, *885, 4477, 4583, 4585*].

NIV+ SHEEP'S, SHEEPSKINS

Offered in sacrifice, by Abel (Ge 4:4), by Noah (Ge 8:20), by Abraham (Ge 22:13). *See Offerings.* Required in the Mosaic offerings. *See Offerings.* The land of Bashan adapted to the raising of (Dt 32:14), Bozrah (Mic 2:12), Kedar (Eze 27:21), Nebaioth (Isa 60:7), Sharon (Isa 65:10). Jacob's management of (Ge 30:32-40). Milk of, used for food (Dt 32:14). Shearing of (Ge 31:19; 38:12-17; Isa 53:7), feasting at the time of shearing (1Sa 25:11,36; 2Sa 13:23). First fleece of, belonged to priests and Levites (Dt 18:4). Tribute paid in (2Ki 3:4; 1Ch 5:21; 2Ch 17:11).

Figurative:

(1Ch 21:17; Ps 74:1; Jer 13:20). Of backsliders (Jer 50:6). Of lost sinners (Mt 9:36; 10:6). Of the righteous (Jer 50:17; Eze 34; Mt 26:31; Mk 14:27; Jn 10:1-16). Of the defenselessness of ministers (Mt 10:16).

Parable of the lost (Mt 18:11-13; Lk 15:4-7).

SHEEP GATE An ancient gate of Jerusalem (Ne 3:1, 32; 12:39; Jn 5:2).

SHEEP MARKET NIV "Sheep Gate" (Jn 5:2).

SHEEP PEN [1312, 4813, *885*]. Enclosure for protection of sheep (Nu 32:16; Jdg 5:16; 1Sa 24:3; Jn 10:1,16).

SHEEPMASTER *See Occupations and Professions; Shepherd.*

SHEEP-SHEARER [1605].

NIV+ SHEEPSHEARERS, SHEEP-SHEARING

See Occupations and Professions.

SHEERAH, SHERAH [8641] (*blood relationship* or *female relative* IDB; *remainder* KB).

NIV+ UZZEN SHEERAH

The daughter of Ephraim; the descendants built three villages (1Ch 7:24).

SHEET [5012, 7063, *3855, 5007*].

NIV+ SHEETS

A large piece of linen (Ac 10:11; 11:5).

SHEHARIAH [8843] (*he seeks Yahweh*). The son of Jeroham; Benjamite (1Ch 8:26).

SHEKEL [4084, 7088, 9203] (*weight*).

NIV+ SHEKELS

A weight, equal to twenty gerahs (Ex 30:13; Nu 3:47; Eze 45:12). Used to weigh silver (Jos 7:21; Jdg 8:26; 17:2-3). Fractions of, used in currency (Ex 30:13; 1Sa 9:8; Ne 10:32). Used to weigh gold (Ge 24:22; Nu 7:14,20-86; Jos 7:21; 1Ki 10:16), cinnamon (Ex 30:23), hair (2Sa 14:26), iron (1Sa 17:7), myrrh (Ex 30:23), rations (Eze 4:10). Fines paid in (Dt 22:19,29). Fees paid in (1Sa 9:8). Sanctuary revenues paid in (Ex 30:13; Ne 10:32).

Of different standards: Of the sanctuary (Ex 30:13), of the king's weight (2Sa 14:26). Corrupted (Am 8:5).

SHEKINAH Jewish term for the dwelling presence of God's glory (Ex 25:22; Lev 16:2; 2Sa 6:2; 2Ki 19:14-15; Ps 80:1; Isa 37:16; Eze 9:3; 10:18; Heb 9:5). Not used in the Bible.

SHELAH [8925, 8941, 8989, *4885*] (*missile [a weapon], sprout* ISBE).

NIV+ SHELANITE

1. Son of Arphaxad and ancestor of Joseph (Ge 10:24; 11:12-15; 1Ch 1:18,24; Lk 3:35).

2. Son of Judah (Ge 38:5,11,14,26; 46:12; Nu 26:20; 1Ch 2:3; 4:21).

3. The father of Zechariah (Ne 11:5).

SHELANITE [8989]. (*missile [a weapon], sprout* ISBE).

NIV+ SHELAH

Descendants of Shelah (Nu 26:20). See Shelah, 2. Apparently called Shilonites (1Ch 9:5). See Shilonite(s), 2.

SHELEMIAH [8982, 8983] (*Yahweh pays back*, possibly *restores peace offering of Yahweh*).

1. Doorkeeper of tabernacle (1Ch 26:14), in previous verses of this chapter he is called "Meshelemiah."

2. Son of Cushi (Jer 36:14).

3. Man sent to arrest Jeremiah (Jer 36:26).

4. Father of a man whom Zedekiah sent to Jeremiah to ask his prayers (Jer 37:3).

5. The son of Hananiah (Jer 37:13).

6. Two men who divorced foreign wives (Ezr 10:39,41).

7. Father of Hananiah (Ne 3:30).

8. Priest; treasurer (Ne 13:13).

SHELEPH [8991] (*one plucked out, drawn out*). The son of Joktan (Ge 10:26; 1Ch 1:20).

SHELESH [8994] (*triplet* KB; possibly *obedient* or *gentle* IDB). The son of Helem (1Ch 7:35).

SHELISHIYAH See Eglath Shelishiyah.

SHELOMI [8979] (*at peace*). The father of Ahihud, Asherite prince (Nu 34:27).

SHELOMITH [8984, 8985] (*at peace*).

1. Daughter of Dibri; her son was killed for blasphemy (Lev 24:10-12,23).

2. The daughter of Zerubbabel (1Ch 3:19).

3. Cousin of Moses (1Ch 23:18).

4. A descendant of Moses (1Ch 26:25).

5. Child of Rehoboam (2Ch 11:20).

6. An ancestor of a family that returned with Ezra (Ezr 8:10).

SHELOMOTH [8977] (*at peace*).

1. Gershonite Levite (1Ch 23:9).

2. Izharite Levite (1Ch 24:22).

SHELUMIEL [8981] (*God [El] is [my] peace*). The son of Zurishaddai and leader of Simeon in the time of Moses (Nu 1:6; 2:12; 7:36,41; 10:19).

SHEM [9006, *4954*] (*name, fame*). The son of Noah. Preserved in the ark (Ge 5:32; 6:10; 7:13; 9:18; 1Ch 1:4). His filial conduct (Ge 9:23-27). The descendants of (Ge 10:1,21-31; 11:10-29; 1Ch 1:17-54). In genealogy of Jesus (Lk 3:36).

SHEMA [9050, 9054] (*he hears*).

1. A town in S Judah (Jos 15:26).

2. The son of Hebron (1Ch 2:43-44).

3. The son of Joel (1Ch 5:8).

4. A Benjamite (1Ch 8:13).

5. An assistant of Ezra (Ne 8:4).

6. The Hebrew name for, "Hear, O Israel: The LORD our God, the LORD is one" (Dt 6:4, ftn).

SHEMAAH [9057] (possibly *Yahweh hears*). The father of Ahiezer and Joash, soldiers of David (1Ch 12:3).

SHEMAIAH [9061, 9062] (*Yahweh hears*).

NIV+ SHEMAIAH'S

1. Simeonite prince (1Ch 4:37).

2. Reubenite (1Ch 5:4), possibly the same as Shema of (1Ch 5:8).

3. The chief Levite (1Ch 15:8,11).

4. A Levite scribe (1Ch 24:6).

5. The son of Obed-Edom (1Ch 26:4,6-7).

6. A prophet who forbade Rehoboam to war against Israel (1Ki 12:22-24).

7. A descendant of David (1Ch 3:22).

8. A Merarite Levite (1Ch 9:14; Ne 12:18).

9. A Levite who returned from exile (1Ch 9:16). Also called Shammua (Ne 11:17).

10. A Levite (2Ch 17:8).

11. A Levite who cleansed the temple (2Ch 29:14).

12. A Levite who assisted in the distribution of food (2Ch 31:15).

13. A Levite in the days of Josiah (2Ch 35:9).

14. A Levite who returned with Ezra (Ezr 8:13).

15. One whom Ezra sent back for ministers (Ezr 8:16), possibly the same as (Ezr 8:13).

16. A priest who divorced his foreign wife (Ezr 10:21).

17. Another priest who divorced his foreign wife (Ezr 10:31).

18-23. Men who played various roles in Nehemiah's rebuilding and in the dedication of the Jerusalem wall (Ne 3:29; 6:10ff; 10:8; 12:6,18,34,35,36,42).

24. The father of Uriah the prophet (Jer 26:20).

25. A false prophet who fought against Jeremiah (Jer 29:24-32).

26. The father of Delaiah, a prince in the days of Jehoiakim (Jer 36:12).

SHEMARIAH [9079, 9080] (*Yahweh guards, preserves*).

1. One of David's mighty men (1Ch 12:5).

2. The son of Rehoboam, king of Judah (2Ch 11:19).

3. A man who put away his foreign wife (Ezr 10:32).

4. Another man who put away his foreign wife (Ezr 10:41).

SHEMEBER [9008]. The king of Zeboiim, a city near the Dead Sea (Ge 14:2).

SHEMED [9013] (*destruction*). The son of Elpaal (1Ch 8:12).

SHEMER [9070] (possibly *watch* IDB; possibly *sediment of wine from which clear wine is made* KB). See *Shomer, 1,3,4.*

SHEMESH See *Beth Shemesh; En Shemesh; Ir Shemesh.*

SHEMIDA, SHEMIDAITE, SHEMIDAH [9026, 9027] (possibly *the name knows* BDB KB; possibly *[pagan god] Eshmun has known* IDB). The son of Gilead; a family descended from Shemida (Nu 26:32; Jos 17:2; 1Ch 7:19).

SHEMINITH [9030] (*eight [strings]*). A musical term of uncertain meaning, possibly "octave" (1Ch 15:21; Ps 6; 12, titles).

See *Music, Symbols Used in.*

SHEMIRAMOTH [9035] (*heights, heavens* BDB; possibly *proper name of a pagan goddess* KB).
  1. A Levite musician (1Ch 15:18,20; 16:5).
  2. A Levite sent by Jehoshaphat to instruct the people in the law (2Ch 17:8).

SHEMUEL [9017] (possibly *his name is God [El]* BDB IDB ISBE; *the unnamed god is El* KB; *heard of God [El]* KD).
  1. A Simeonite leader (Nu 34:20).
  2. See *Samuel, 2.*

SHEN [9095] (*tooth, crag [of rock]*). An unidentified site near which Samuel erected the stone "Ebenezer" (1Sa 7:12).

SHENAZZAR, SHENAZAR [9100] (*may [the moon god] Sin protect*). The son of Jehoiachin (1Ch 3:18).

SHENIR See *Senir.*

SHEOL (possibly *place of inquiry [of the dead]* BDB; *desolate place, no-country underworld* KB). The OT name for the place of departed souls, corresponding to the NT word "Hades." When translated "hell" it refers to the place of punishment, but when translated "grave" the reference is to the souls of good men. It often means the place or state of the soul between death and resurrection. The clearest indication of different conditions in Sheol is in Christ's parable of the rich man and Lazarus (Lk 16:19-31).

SHEPHAM [9172] (*nakedness*). The place in NE of Canaan, near Sea of Galilee (Nu 34:10-11).

SHEPHATIAH, SHEPHATHIAH [9152, 9153] (*Yahweh has judged*).
  1. The son of David (2Sa 3:4).
  2. The son of Reuel (1Ch 9:8).
  3. One of David's mighty men (1Ch 12:5).
  4. A Simeonite prince (1Ch 27:16).
  5. The son of King Jehoshaphat (2Ch 21:2).
  6. The founder of a family which returned with Zerubbabel (Ezr 2:4).

7. One of the children of Solomon's servants whose descendants returned with Zerubbabel (Ezr 2:57).

8. One whose descendants returned with Ezra (Ezr 8:8). May be the same as (Ezr 2:57).

9. The son of Mahalalel (Ne 11:4).

10. The prince who wanted Jeremiah to be put to death for prophesying (Jer 38:1).

SHEPHELAH, THE (*lowland*). Hilly country between the mountains of Judah and the maritime plain S of the plain of Sharon, extending through the country of Philistia along the Mediterranean (Jos 12:8).

SHEPHER, MOUNT [9184]. A mountain, camping place of the Israelites in the desert (Nu 33:23-24).

SHEPHERD [1012, 5924, 7695, 8286, 8657, 9068, 799, 4477, 4478].
  NIV+ SHEPHERD'S, SHEPHERDED, SHEPHERDESS, SHEPHERDS
  One who cares for flocks (Ge 31:38-40; Ps 78:52-53; Jer 31:10; Am 3:12; Lk 2:8). David defends his flock against a lion and a bear (1Sa 17:34-35). Causes the flock to rest (Ps 23:2; SS 1:7; Jer 33:12). Numbers the flock (Lev 27:32; Jer 33:13). Knows his flock by name (Jos 10:3-5). Keeps the sheep and goats apart (Mt 25:32). Waters the flocks (Ge 29:2-10). Keeps the flocks in folds (Nu 32:16; 1Sa 24:3; 2Sa 7:8; Jn 10:1). Watch towers of (2Ch 26:10; Mic 4:8). Dogs of (Job 30:1). Was an abomination to the Egyptians (Ge 46:34). Angels appeared to (Lk 2:8-20).
  Instances of:
  Abel (Ge 4:2). Rachel (Ge 29:9). Daughters of Jethro (Ex 2:16). Moses (Ex 3:1). David (1Sa 16:11; 2Sa 7:8; Ps 78:70).
  Figurative:
  (Ge 49:24). Of prophets, priests, Levites, and civil authorities (Eze 34). Of Cyrus (Isa 44:28). Of Yahweh (Ps 23; Isa 40:11). Of Christ (Zec 13:7; Mt 26:31; Mk 14:27; Jn 10:1-16; Heb 13:20; 1Pe 2:25).

SHEPHI See *Shepho.*

SHEPHO [9143] (possibly *track, bare ways formed without human work by the traffic caravans* KB). Early descendant of Seir (Ge 36:23; 1Ch 1:40).

SHEPHUPHAN [9146] (perhaps *serpent*). The son of Bela (1Ch 8:5).

SHERAH See *Sheerah.*

SHERD See *Potsherd*

SHEREBIAH [9221] (possibly *Yahweh has sent burning heat* BDB).
  NIV+ SHEREBIAH'S
  1. A prominent Levite in Ezra's time (Ezr 8:18,24).
  2. Covenanter with Nehemiah (Ne 10:12).
  3. Levite who returned with Zerubbabel (Ne 12:8).
  4. The chief Levite (Ne 12:24).

SHERESH [9246] (*root, rootstock, sucker [of a plant]*). The son of Makir (1Ch 7:16).

SHEREZER See *Sharezer.*

SHERIFF (Da 3:2-3). See *Magistrates.*

SHESHACH [9263] (cryptogram for *Babel [Babylon]*). Perhaps a cryptogram for "Babel" or "Babylon" (Jer 25:26, ftn; 51:41, ftn).

SHESHAI [9259] (possibly *sixth [child]*). The son of Anak (Nu 13:22; Jos 15:14; Jdg 1:10).

SHESHAN [9264]. A descendant of Jerahmeel (1Ch 2:31,34-35).

SHESHBAZZAR [9256, 10746] (*may [the pagan moon god named] Sin protect [the father]*).

A Jewish official whom Cyrus made deputy governor of Judah and who helped lay the foundation of the temple (Ezr 1:8,11; 5:14,16). Some believe that Sheshbazzar and Zerubbabel were the same person for the following reasons:

1. Both were governors (Ezr 5:14; Hag 1:1; 2:2).

2. Both are said to have laid the foundation of the temple (Ezr 3:2-8; 5:16; Hag 1:14-15; Zec 4:6-10).

3. Jews in Babylon were often given "official" Babylonian names (cf. Da 1:7).

4. Josephus (*Antiq.*, 11.1.3) seems to identify Sheshbazzar with Zerubbabel.

Others point out, however:

1. The Apocrypha distinguishes between the two men (1Es 6:18).

2. Sheshbazzar was likely an elderly man at the time of the return, while Zerubbabel was probably a younger contemporary.

3. Sheshbazzar may have been viewed as the official governor, while Zerubbabel served as the popular leader (Ezr 3:8-11).

4. Whereas the high priest Jeshua is associated with Zerubbabel, no priest is associated with Sheshbazzar.

5. Although Sheshbazzar presided over the foundation of the temple in 536 B.C., so little was accomplished that Zerubbabel had to preside over a second foundation sixteen years later (Hag 1:14-15; Zec 4:6-10).

Others identify Sheshbazzar with Shenazzar (1Ch 3:18), the fourth son of King Jehoiachin. Zerubbabel would then have been Sheshbazzar's nephew (compare 3:2 with 1Ch 3:18). *See Zerubbabel.*

SHETH [9269] (*sons of tumult*, or *sons of pride, compensation*). A designation for Moab (Nu 24:17).

SHETHAR [9285]. A prince of Persia (Est 1:14).

SHETHAR-BOZENAI, SHETHAR BOZENAI

[10750] (*delivering the kingdom*). Persian official who tried to hinder Jews (Ezr 5:3,6).

SHEVA [8737] (*vanity, emptiness* IDB; *one who will emulate* IDB KB).

1. David's scribe (2Sa 20:25), perhaps the same as "Seraiah" (1Ch 2:49). *See Seraiah, 1.*

2. The son of Caleb (1Ch 2:49).

SHEWBREAD *See Bread, Consecrated.*

SHIBAH [8683] (possibly *seven* BDB ISBE; possibly *oath* BDB IDB; *plenty* KB). The name of the well dug by Isaac's servants. A town of Beersheba named from this well (Ge 26:31-33, ftn). Called Beersheba in NIV.

SHIBBOLETH [8672] (*flowing stream* BDB KB; or *ear of grain* IDB). A word differently pronounced on the two sides of the Jordan, and was used by the men of Gilead to determine whether the speaker was of Ephraim or not. Those who said "Sibboleth" instead of "Shibboleth" were killed. Forty-two thousand Ephraimites were killed at the fords of the Jordan at that time (Jdg 12:5-6).

SHIBMAH *See Sibmah.*

SHICRON *See Shikkeron.*

SHIELD [1713, 2910, 4059, 4482, 6114, 6116, 6317, 7558, 8949, 2599].

NIV+ SHIELDED, SHIELDING, SHIELDS

Defensive Armor:

Different kinds of (Ps 35:2; Eze 38:4). Used by Saul (2Sa 1:21), by the Benjamites (2Ch 14:8; 17:17). Uzziah equipped the Israelites with (2Ch 26:14). Made of bronze (1Ki 14:27), of gold (2Sa 8:7; 1Ki 10:16-17; 2Ch 9:15-16), of wood (Eze 39:9-10). Stored in armories (1Ki 10:17; 2Ch 11:12; 32:5,27), in the tabernacle (2Ki 11:10; 2Ch 23:9). Covered when not in use (Isa 22:6). Painted red (Na 2:3). *See Armor.*

Figurative:

Of God's protection (Ge 15:1; Dt 33:29; 2Sa 22:3,36; Ps 5:12; 18:2,35; 33:20; 59:11; 84:9,11; 89:18; Pr 30:5). Of God's truth (Ps 91:4). Of kings (Ps 47:9). Of an entire army (Jer 46:3).

SHIGGAION [8710] (*go astray, wander [i.e., a wild, passionate song, with rapid changes in rhythm]* BDB; possibly Akkadian for *dirge* KB). A musical term of unknown meaning found in the heading of (Ps 7).

See Music, Symbols Used in.

SHIGIONOTH [8710] (*go astray, wander [i.e., a wild, passionate song, with rapid changes in rhythm]* BDB; possibly Akkadian for *dirge* KB). The plural of *shiggaion*. The heading of Habakkuk's psalm (Hab 3:1).

See Music, Symbols Used in.

SHIHON *See Shion.*

SHIHOR [8865] (possibly *black water* BDB; Egyptian *Canal of [pagan god] Horus* KB).

NIV+ SHIHOR LIBNATH

May refer to the Nile, a stream which separated Egypt from Israel, or a branch of the Nile (Jos 13:3; 1Ch 13:5; Isa 23:3; Jer 2:18).

SHIHOR LIBNATH, SHIHOR-LIBNATH

[8866].

NIV+ SHIHOR

A small stream on the S border of Asher (Jos 19:26).

SHIKKERON [8914] (possibly *drunkenness* IDB; *hog bean plant* IDB). A town on the N boundary of Judah (Jos 15:11).

SHILHI [8944] (possibly *[my] javelin [thrower?]* IDB KB). Father-in-law of Jehoshaphat, king of Judah (1Ki 22:42; 2Ch 20:31).

SHILHIM [8946]. A city of Judah (Jos 15:32).

SHILLEM, SHILLEMITE [8973, 8980] (*recompense* BDB IDB; possibly *whole, healthy, complete* KB). The son of Naphtali (Ge 46:24; 1Ch 7:13), and his descendants (Nu 26:49).

SHILOAH [8942]. A stream or pool (Isa 8:6). Probably identical with Siloah and Siloam. *See Siloam, Pool of.*

SHILOH [8870, 8872, 8926, 8931].

NIV+ TAANATH SHILOH

1. A city in Ephraim, c. twelve miles N and E of Bethel where the tabernacle remained from the time of Joshua to

the days of Samuel (Jdg 21:19; 1Sa 4:3), Benjamites kidnapped wives (Jdg 21:15-24), residence of Eli and Samuel (1Sa 3:21), home of the prophet Ahijah (1Ki 14:3), a ruin in Jeremiah's time (Jer 7:12,14).

2. A word of uncertain meaning regarded by many Jews and Christians as a reference to the Messiah; the NIV has "until he comes to whom it belongs" (Ge 49:10, ftn).

SHILONI See Shelah, 3.

SHILONITE(S) [8872] (of Shiloh).

1. A man of Shiloh (1Ki 12:15; 15:29; 2Ch 9:29; 10:15).
2. Apparently denotes a descendant of Shelah (1Ch 9:5). See Shelanite.

SHILSHAH [8996] (possibly obedient or gentle IDB; third [part, child?], triplet KB). An Asherite; the son of Zophah (1Ch 7:37).

SHIMEA [9055] (he has heard or he is obedient).

1. Brother of David (1Ch 20:7). Perhaps the same as "Shammah" (1Sa 16:9), "Shimeah" (2Sa 21:21).
2. The son of David and Bathsheba (1Ch 3:5).
3. A Merarite Levite (1Ch 6:30).
4. A Gershonite Levite (1Ch 6:39).

SHIMEAH [9009, 9056] (he has heard or he is obedient).

1. The brother of David (2Sa 13:3,32; 21:21).
2. A Benjamite (1Ch 8:32), "Shimeam" (1Ch 9:38).

SHIMEAM [9010]. See Shimeah, 2.

SHIMEATH [9064] (guardian, watcher).
NIV+SHIMEATHITES

The mother of an assassin of King Joash (2Ki 12:21; 2Ch 24:26).

SHIMEATHITES [9065].
NIV+SHIMEATH

A family of scribes (1Ch 2:55).

SHIMEI, SHIMEITES [9059, 9060] (Yahweh has heard, or famous).
NIV+SHIMEI'S

1. Son of Gershon (Ex 6:17; Nu 3:18; 1Ch 6:17; 23:7,10) and his descendants (Nu 3:21).
2. A Benjamite. Curses David; David's magnanimity toward (2Sa 16:5-13; 19:16-23, w 1Ki 2:36-46).
3. An officer of David (1Ki 1:8).
4. One of Solomon's district governors (1Ki 4:18).
5. A son of Jesse (1Ch 2:13).
6. The grandson of Jehoiachin (1Ch 3:19).
7. The son of Zaccur (1Ch 4:26-27).
8. A Reubenite. The son of Gog (1Ch 5:4).
9. A Merarite. The son of Libni (1Ch 6:29).
10. A Gershonite. The son of Jahath (1Ch 6:42).
11. The father of a family in Benjamin (1Ch 8:21).
12. A Levite (1Ch 23:9).
13. A leader of singers in the time of David (1Ch 25:17).
14. David's overseer of vineyards (1Ch 27:27).
15. A son of Heman (2Ch 29:14).
16. A Levite. The treasurer of tithes and offerings in the time of Hezekiah (2Ch 31:12-13).
17. A Levite who put away his Gentile wife (Ezr 10:23).
18. The name of two Israelites who put away Gentile wives (Ezr 10:33,38).
19. A Benjamite. The grandfather of Mordecai (Est 2:5).

20. The ancestor of a family (Zec 12:13). Possibly identical with 1.

SHIMEON [9058] (possibly offspring of hyena and wolf BDB KB). An Israelite who divorced his Gentile wife (Ezr 10:31).

SHIMHI See Shimei, 11.

SHIMI See Shimei, 1.

SHIMMA See Shimea, 1.

SHIMON [8873]. A man of Judah (1Ch 4:20).

SHIMRATH [9086] (guardian, watchman). The son of Shimei (1Ch 8:21).

SHIMRI [9078] (Yahweh guards, preserves).

1. The son of Shemaiah; a Simeonite (1Ch 4:37).
2. The father of Jediael and Joha, two of David's mighty men (1Ch 11:45).
3. A Merarite Levite doorkeeper (1Ch 26:10).
4. A Levite who assisted in cleansing the temple (2Ch 29:13).

SHIMRITH [9083] (guardianess, watch woman). A Moabitess; the mother of Jehozabad who helped kill Joash, king of Judah (2Ch 24:26), "Shomer" (2Ki 12:21).

SHIMROM See Shimron, 1.

SHIMRON, SHIMRONITE [9074, 9075, 9084] (guardian, watchman).
NIV+ SHIMRON MERON

1. The son of Issachar (Ge 46:13; 1Ch 7:1) and his descendants (Nu 26:24).
2. A town in N Canaan whose king fought Joshua (Jos 11:1ff); probably Shimron Meron. See Shimron Meron, Simron-Meron.

SHIMRON MERON, SHIMRON-MERON [9077].
NIV+ SHIMRON

A city conquered by Joshua (Jos 12:20). Probably identical with Shimron, 2. See Shimron, 2.

SHIMSHAI [10729] (one given to [pagan sun god] Shemesh). A scribe who tried to hinder the Jews in rebuilding the temple (Ezr 4:8-9,17,23).

SHINAB [9098] ([pagan god] Sin is his father). The king of Admah. A Canaanite city, later destroyed (Ge 14:2).

SHINAR [824+9114, 9114]. An alluvial plain of Babylonia in which lay the cities of Babel, Erech, Akkad, and Calneh (Ge 10:10), the Tower of Babel was built there (Ge 11:1-9), Amraphel, king of Shinar, invaded Canaan (Ge 14:1,9). Elsewhere rendered Babylon(ia): Nebuchadnezzar transported the temple treasures to (Da 1:2, ftn), Jews exiled to (Zec 5:11, ftn).

SHION [8858]. A town in Issachar near Nazareth (Jos 19:19).

SHIP [641+9576, 641, 7469, 3729, 3730, 4434, 4450].
NIV+ SHIP'S, SHIPS, SHIPWRECK, SHIPWRECKED, SHIPWRIGHTS

Built, by Noah (Ge 6:13-22), by Solomon (1Ki 9:26; 2Ch 8:17), by Jehoshaphat (1Ki 22:48; 2Ch 20:35-36), of cypress wood (Ge 6:14), of fir wood (Eze 27:5), of papyrus (Isa 18:2), sealed with pitch (Ge 6:15).

Equipped with, rudder (Ac 27:40; Jas 3:4), rigging (Isa 33:23; Ac 27:19), sails (Isa 33:23; Ac 27:1,9,17,40), embroidered sails (Eze 27:7), masts (Isa 33:23; Eze 27:5), oars (Jnh 1:13; Mk 6:48), figurehead (Ac 28:11), anchor (Ac 27:29-30,40; Heb 6:19), lifeboats (Ac 27:30,32).

Used, in commerce (Ac 21:3; 27:10), in commerce with Tarshish (1Ki 22:48; Isa 60:9; Jnh 1:3), with Ophir (1Ki 10:11; 2Ch 8:18), with Adramyttium (Ac 27:2), for passenger traffic (Isa 60:9; Jnh 1:3; Ac 20:13; 27:2,37; 28:11).

Repaired by caulking (Eze 27:9).

Wrecked, at Ezion Geber (1Ki 22:48; 2Ch 20:35-37), at Malta (Ac 27:14-44).

Warships used by Kittim (Nu 24:24; Da 11:30).
See Mariner.

SHIPHI [9181] (*flowing abundance*). The father of Ziza (1Ch 4:37).

SHIPHMITE [9175] (*family name of Zabdi*). Vineyard overseer (1Ch 27:27).

SHIPHRAH [9186] (*beautiful, fair*). A Hebrew midwife who saved Hebrew boy babies (Ex 1:15-21).

SHIPHTAN [9154] (*he has judged*). The father of the representative of Ephraim on the committee which divided the promised land among the Israelites (Nu 34:24).

SHISHA [8881]. The father of two of Solomon's secretaries (1Ki 4:3), may be identical with Seraiah (2Sa 8:17), Sheva (2Sa 20:25), and Shavsha (1Ch 18:16).

SHISHAK [8882]. The first Egyptian Pharaoh mentioned by name in the Bible; the founder of the twenty-second dynasty (945-924 B.C.), gave refuge to Jeroboam (1Ki 11:40), invaded Jerusalem in the reign of Rehoboam (1Ki 14:25f).

SHITRAI [8855] (*scribe, officer*). A chief shepherd of David (1Ch 27:29).

SHITTAH *See Beth Shittah.*

SHITTAH TREE NIV "acacia." *See Acacia Wood; Plants of the Bible; Tree.*

SHITTIM [8850] (*acacia trees*).
NIV+ ABEL SHITTIM
1. Also called Abel Shittim (Nu 33:49). A camping place of Israel (Nu 25:1; 33:49). Joshua sends spies from (Jos 2:1). Valley of (Joel 3:18). Balaam prophesies in (Mic 6:5). *See Abel Shittim.*
2. Hebrew for acacia (Joel 3:18).
See Acacia Wood.

SHIZA [8862]. A Reubenite. The father of one of David's mighty men (1Ch 11:42).

SHOA [8778] (*rich*). People mentioned in association with the Babylonians, Chaldeans, and Assyrians (Eze 23:23). May be Sutu of Amarna letters.

SHOBAB [8744] (*one who turns back, repents*).
1. The grandson for Hezron (1Ch 2:18).
2. The son of David (2Sa 5:14; 1Ch 3:5; 14:4).

SHOBACH [8747]. The captain of the host of Hadadezer. Slain by David's army (2Sa 10:16,18). Also called Shophach (1Ch 19:16,18).

SHOBAI [8662] (possibly *captive* or *Yahweh returns*). A gatekeeper, whose descendants returned to Jerusalem with Zerubbabel (Ezr 2:42; Ne 7:45).

SHOBAL [8748] (perhaps a nickname *basket*).
1. Chief of the Horites (Ge 36:20,23,29).
2. Ephrathite; founder of Kiriath Jearim (1Ch 2:50,52).
3. Grandson of Judah (1Ch 4:1-2).

SHOBEK [8749] (*victor* IDB). A Jew who sealed the covenant with Nehemiah (Ne 10:24).

SHOBI [8661] (possibly *captive* or *Yahweh returns*). The son of Nahash. Brought supplies to David in his flight from Absalom (2Sa 17:27).

SHOCHO *See Soco, 2.*

SHOE *See Sandal.*

SHOFAR (*ram horn*). A trumpet of ram's horn (Jos 6:4-6,8,13). *See Trumpet.*

SHOHAM [8733] (*carnelian [precious stone]*). A Merarite (1Ch 24:27).

SHOMER [9071] (*guardian, watchman*).
1. A man who sold the hill of Samaria to Omri, king of Israel (1Ki 16:24).
2. The father of Jehozabad, conspirator of Joash of Judah (2Ki 12:20-21).
3. A Merarite Levite (1Ch 6:46).
4. The great-grandson of Asher (1Ch 7:32,34).

SHOPHACH [8791]. A Syrian general slain by David (1Ch 19:16,18), "Shobach" (2Sa 10:16).

SHOPHAN *See Atroth Shophan.*

SHORE [362, 824, 3338, 8557, *129, 302, 839, 1178, 4305*].
NIV+ ASHORE, SHORELANDS, SHORES
Coast line or beach (Jos 15:2; Jdg 5:17; Mt 13:2).

SHOSHANNIM NIV "Lilies." *See Music, Symbols Used in.*

SHOULDER [2432, 4190, 7418, 8900, *6049*].
NIV+ SHOULDERS
The shoulder of a sacrificed ox or sheep went to the priest as his portion (Dt 18:8), the sacred furniture of the tabernacle had to be carried upon the shoulders (Nu 7:6-9).

SHOULDER PIECE
1. Part of the ephod in which the front and the back were joined together (Ex 28:7-8).
2. A piece of meat taken from the shoulder of an animal (Eze 24:4).

SHOUTING [*606, 2116, 6699, 7412, 7754, 7924, 8131, 8262, 8264, 9558, *1066, 2215, 3189, 3198, 3306*].
NIV+ SHOUT, SHOUTED, SHOUTS
In Joy and Praise:
1Ch 15:28 So all Israel brought up the ark of the covenant of the LORD with shouts, with the sounding of rams' horns and trumpets, and of cymbals, and the playing of lyres and harps.

2Ch 15:12 They entered into a covenant to seek the LORD, the God of their fathers, with all their heart and soul. [13]All who would not seek the LORD, the God of Israel, were to be put to death, whether small or great, man or woman.

¹⁴They took an oath to the LORD with loud acclamation, with shouting and with trumpets and horns.

Ezr 3:11 With praise and thanksgiving they sang to the LORD:

"He is good; his love to Israel endures forever."

And all the people gave a great shout of praise to the LORD, because the foundation of the house of the LORD was laid. ¹²But many of the older priests and Levites and family heads, who had seen the former temple, wept aloud when they saw the foundation of this temple being laid, while many others shouted for joy. ¹³No one could distinguish the sound of the shouts of joy from the sound of weeping, because the people made so much noise. And the sound was heard far away.

Ps 47:1 Clap your hands, all you nations; shout to God with cries of joy.

Isa 12:6 Shout aloud and sing for joy, people of Zion, for great is the Holy One of Israel among you."

Lk 17:15 One of them, when he saw he was healed, came back, praising God in a loud voice.

Lk 19:37 When he came near the place where the road goes down the Mount of Olives, the whole crowd of disciples began joyfully to praise God in loud voices for all the miracles they had seen:

³⁸"Blessed is the king who comes in the name of the Lord!"

"Peace in heaven and glory in the highest!"

³⁹Some of the Pharisees in the crowd said to Jesus, "Teacher, rebuke your disciples!"

⁴⁰"I tell you," he replied, "if they keep quiet, the stones will cry out." ⁴¹As he approached Jerusalem and saw the city, he wept over it

Ac 3:8 He jumped to his feet and began to walk. Then he went with them into the temple courts, walking and jumping, and praising God. ⁹When all the people saw him walking and praising God,

Rev 5:12 In a loud voice they sang: "Worthy is the Lamb, who was slain, to receive power and wealth and wisdom and strength and honor and glory and praise!"

¹³Then I heard every creature in heaven and on earth and under the earth and on the sea, and all that is in them, singing: "To him who sits on the throne and to the Lamb be praise and honor and glory and power, for ever and ever!"

¹⁴The four living creatures said, "Amen," and the elders fell down and worshiped.

See Clap; Praise; Worship.

In Battle: (Jos 6:20; Jdg 7:18; 1Sa 17:20,52; 2Ch 13:15).

SHOVEL [3582, 4665].

NIV+ SHOVELS

A utensil in the tabernacle (Ex 27:3; 38:3; Nu 4:14), temple (1Ki 7:40; Jer 52:18).

SHOWBREAD *See Bread, Consecrated.*

SHRINE [1074, 1195, 2215, 2540, 5219, 6109, 6551, 7728, 8229, *3724*, *5008*].

NIV+ SHRINES

Places of idolatrous worship, often a high place (Eze 16:24-25,31,39). Frequented by temple prostitutes (Ge 38:21-22; Dt 23:17; Hos 4:14), including male prostitutes (1Ki 14:24; 15:12; 22:46; 2Ki 23:7; Job 36:14). A shrine also refers to an idolatrous symbol, certain small idol houses, made by the silversmith, Demetrius, and sold to the worshipers of the Temple of Diana (Ac 19:24).

See Artemis; Groves; High Places; Idolatry; Prostitute.

SHRIVELED HAND [3312, *3830*, *3831*]. As a judgment (1Ki 13:4). Jesus heals on the Sabbath (Mt 12:10-13 w Mk 3:1-6; Lk 6:6-11). *See Disease.*

SHROUD [2502, 4059, 4287, 8492]. A sheet to cover the dead (Isa 25:7).

SHRUB *See Plants of the Bible.*

SHUA [8781, 8783] (*prosperity* ISBE).

1. A Canaanite whose daughter became Judah's wife (Ge 38:2,12).

2. Heber's daughter (1Ch 7:32).

SHUAH [8756] (*depression, lowland [an Aramean land on the Euphrates River]*).

1. The son of Abraham by Keturah (Ge 25:2; 1Ch 1:32).

2. *See Shua, 1.*

3. *See Shuhah.*

SHUAL [8786, 8787] (*fox or jackal*).

NIV+ HAZAR SHUAL

1. District near Micmash (1Sa 13:17).

2. The son of Zophah (1Ch 7:36).

SHUBAEL [8649, 8742] (possibly *captive of God [El]*, or *God [El] restores*).

1. The son of Gershom son of Moses (1Ch 23:16; 26:24).

2. The son of Amram (1Ch 24:20).

3. A singer, the son of Heman (1Ch 25:4,20).

SHUHAH [8758] (*pit, depression*).

NIV+ SHUHAH'S

Kelub's brother (1Ch 4:11).

SHUHAM, SHUHAMITE [8761, 8762]. The son of Dan and his clan (Nu 26:42-43); also called Hushim (Ge 46:23). *See Hushim, 1.*

SHUHITE [8760] (*of Shuah*). Bildad, one of Job's friends (Job 2:11; 8:1; 18:1; 25:1); possibly a descendant of Shuah, 1.

SHULAMMITE, SHULAMITE [8769] (*peaceful*). A designation of the beloved in the Song of Songs (SS 6:13); possibly the same as Shunammite.

SHUMATHITES [9092] (*garlic*). Family of Kiriath Jearim (1Ch 2:53).

SHUNAMMITE [8774].

1. A person from Shunem. Abishag, the woman who nourished David (1Ki 1:3), desired by Adonijah as wife (1Ki 2:13-25).

2. A woman who gave hospitality to Elisha and whose son he raised to life (2Ki 4:8-37).

SHUNEM [8773]. A city of Issachar (Job 19:18), three-and-a-half miles N of Jezreel; the site of a Philistine encampment before battle (1Sa 28:4), the home of Abishag, David's nurse (1Ki 1:3), home of a woman who befriended Elisha (2Ki 4:8-37).

SHUNI, SHUNITE [8771, 8772]. The son of Gad (Ge 46:16) and his clan (Nu 26:15).

SHUPHAM, SHUPHAMITE [8792, 8793]. The son of Benjamin and progenitor of Shuphamites (Nu 26:39). May be the same as Shephuphan (1Ch 8:5).

SHUPPIM [9157].

　1. A Levite (1Ch 26:16).

　2. See Shuppites.

SHUPPITES [9158]. Descendants of Ir (1Ch 7:12, 15).

SHUR [8804] (*wall*). A wilderness southwest of Israel (Ge 16:7; 20:1; 25:18; Ex 15:22; 1Sa 15:7; 27:8).

SHUSHAN See Susa.

SHUSHAN-EDUTH (*lily of testimony*). See *Music, Symbols Used in*.

SHUTHELAH, SHUTHALHITE, SHUTHELAHITE [8811, 9279].

　1. The son of Ephraim and his clan (Nu 26:35-36).

　2. The son of Zabad; father of Ezer and Elead (1Ch 7:21).

SHUTTLE [756]. Part of a weaving loom; used as a figure of the shortness of life (Job 7:6).

SIA [6103] (*assembly*). Progenitor of the temple servants that returned with Zerubbabel (Ne 7:47), "Siaha" (Ezr 2:44).

SIAHA [6104]. See *Sia*.

SIBBECAI, SIBBECHAI [6021]. One of David's mighty men, designated "Hushathite" (2Sa 21:18; 1Ch 11:29; 20:4; 27:11), killed the Philistine "Saph" (2Sa 21:18).

SIBBOLETH [6027]. See *Shibboleth*.

SIBMAH [8424]. A city of Reuben (Nu 32:38; Jos 13:19; Isa 16:8-9; Jer 48:32). Apparently also called Sebam (Nu 32:3).

SIBRAIM [6028]. A place on the N boundary of Israel (Eze 47:16).

SICHEM See *Shechem, 1*.

SICILY An island lying off the "toe" of Italy, visited by Paul (Ac 28:12). See *Syracuse*.

SICK, THE [108, 2703, 5823, *779, 819+2400, 820, 822, 2400+2809, 2827, 2879*].

　NIV+ See DISEASE, SICKNESS

　Visiting (Ps 41:6). Visiting, a duty (Mt 25:36,43; Jas 1:27). See *Afflicted; Affliction; Disease*.

SICKLE [3058, 4478, *1535*] (*reaping hook*).

　NIV+ SICKLES

　A tool used for cutting grain, sometimes also for pruning (Dt 16:9; Joel 3:13; Mk 4:29). Used figuratively for God's judgment (Joel 3:13; Rev 14:14).

SICKNESS [2716, 4700, 4701, *819, 820+3798, 3433*].

　NIV+ SICK, SICKNESSES

　Figurative of sin and judgment (Isa 1:5-6; Hos 5:13). See *Affliction; Disease; Sick, The*.

SIDDIM, VALLEY OF [8443] (possibly *valley of furrows, valley of demons* BDB; *valley of bordering furrows* KB). Vale of, a valley of uncertain location. Scene of the king of Sodom (Ge 14:3,8,10).

SIDON [7477, 7479, *4972, 4973*] (*fishery*).

　NIV+ GREATER SIDON, SIDONIANS

　1. The son of Canaan (Ge 10:15; 1Ch 1:13).

2. A city on the northern boundary of the Canaanites, twenty-two miles N of Tyre (Ge 10:19). Designated by Jacob as the border of Zebulun (Ge 49:13). Was on the northern boundary of Asher (Jos 19:28; 2Sa 24:6). Belonged to the land of Israel according to the promise (Jos 13:6). Inhabitants of lived in security (Jdg 18:7). Israelites failed to make the conquest of (Jdg 1:31; 3:3). The inhabitants of, contributed cedar for the first and second temple (1Ki 5:6; 1Ch 22:4; Ezr 3:7). Solomon marries a woman of (1Ki 11:1). Chief gods were Baal and Ashtoreth (1Ki 11:5,33; 2Ki 23:13). Jezebel, wife of King Ahab, was a daughter of a king of Sidon (1Ki 16:31). People of, come to hear Jesus (Mk 3:8; Lk 6:17). Inhabitants of, offend Herod (Ac 12:20-23).

Commerce of (Isa 23:2,4,12). Seamen of (Eze 27:8). Prophecies concerning (Jer 25:15-22; 27:3-11; 47:4; Eze 28:21-23; 32:30; Joel 3:4-8). Jesus visits the region of, and heals the daughter of the Syrian Phoenician woman (Mt 15:21-28; Mk 7:24-31). Visited by Paul (Ac 27:3).

SIEGE [369+784, 1032, 1911, 2006, 2837+6584, 5189, 5193, 6149, 6164, 7443, 7674, 9068].

　NIV+ BESIEGE, BESIEGED, BESIEGES, BESIEGING, SIEGEWORKS

　An offer of peace must be made to the city before beginning (Dt 20:10-12). Conducted by erecting embankments parallel to the walls of the besieged city (Dt 20:19-20; Isa 29:3; 37:33). Battering rams used in. See *Battering Ram*. Distress of the inhabitants during (2Ki 6:24-29; 25:3; Isa 9:20; 36:12; Jer 19:9). Cannibalism in (2Ki 6:28-29).

Instances of:

　Of Jericho (Jos 6). Rabbah (2Sa 11:1), Abel (2Sa 20:15), Gibbethon (1Ki 15:27), Tirzah (1Ki 16:17). Jerusalem, by the children of Judah (Jdg 1:8), by David (2Sa 5:6,9), by Rezin, king of Syria, and Pekah, son of Remaliah, king of Israel (2Ki 16:5), by Nebuchadnezzar (2Ki 24:10-11; Da 1:1; 2Ki 25:1-3; Jer 52), by Sennacherib (2Ch 32:1-23). Samaria (1Ki 20:1; 2Ki 6:24; 17:5; 18:9-11).

SIEVE [3895, 5864]. A sifting device for grain; made of reeds, horsehair, or strings (Isa 30:28; Am 9:9). Also used figuratively (Lk 22:31).

SIGN [226, 253, 4603, 5727, 5812, 7483, 9338, *1893, 4956, 5518*].

　NIV+ SIGNED, SIGNS

　A miracle to confirm faith (Mt 12:38; 16:4; 24:30; Mk 8:11-12; 13:4; Jn 2:11; 3:2; 4:48). Asked for by, and given to Abraham (Ge 15:8-17), Moses (Ex 4:1-9), Gideon (Jdg 6:17,36-40), Hezekiah (2Ki 20:8), Zechariah (Lk 1:18). Given to Jeroboam (1Ki 13:3-5).

　A token of coming events (Mt 16:3-4; 24:3). See *Miracles*.

SIGNAL [4911, 5368, 5812, 8131, 9239, 9546, 10084, *1935, 4956, 5361*].

　NIV+ SIGNALED, SIGNALING, SIGNALS

　Used in war (Isa 18:3). See *Armies; Ensign; Trumpet*.

SIGNET [2597, 3192, 10536]. See *Seal*.

SIHON [6095].

　NIV+ SIHON'S

　King of the Amorites. His seat of government at Heshbon (Nu 21:26). The proverbial chant celebrating the victory of Sihon over the Moabites (Nu 21:26-30). Conquest of his kingdom by the Israelites (Nu 21:21-25; Dt 2:24-37; 3:2,6,8).

SIHOR *See Shihor.*

SILAS [*4976, 4977*] (*asked,* possibly *dedicated to God*). Also called Silvanus (1Th 1:1, ftn). Sent to Paul, in Antioch, from Jerusalem (Ac 15:22-34). Becomes Paul's companion (Ac 15:40-41; 2Co 1:19; 1Th 1:1; 2Th 1:1). Imprisoned with Paul in Philippi (Ac 16:19-40). Driven, with Paul, from Thessalonica (Ac 17:4-10). Left by Paul at Berea (Ac 17:14). Rejoins Paul at Corinth (Ac 17:15; 18:5). Carries Peter's epistle to Asia Minor (1Pe 5:12).

SILENT YEARS, FOUR HUNDRED *See Testaments, Time Between.*

SILK [*4986*]. Wearing apparel made of (Pr 31:22; Eze 16:10,13). Merchandise of (Rev 18:22). *See Linen.*

SILLA [*6133*] (*embankment*). A place of uncertain location (2Ki 12:20).

SILOAH *See Siloam.*

SILOAM, POOL OF [*8940, 4978*] (*sent*). A reservoir located within the city walls of Jerusalem at the S end of the Tyropean Valley; receives water through a 1,780-foot tunnel from En Rogel (Ne 3:15; Lk 13:4; Jn 9:7,11), constructed by Hezekiah in the late eighth century B.C. "Shiloah" (Isa 8:6). The pool today is called Birket Silwan and a nearby village is Silwan. *See Siloam, Village of.*

SILOAM, TOWER OF Probably part of the fortification system of the Jerusalem wall, near the pool of Siloam (Lk 13:4).

SILOAM, VILLAGE OF Not mentioned in the Bible; the modern village (Silwan) situated across the valley E of the Gihon Spring.

SILVANUS *See Silas.*

SILVER [*4084, 7988, 10362, 735, 736, 738, 1324, 1534*] (*pale, white*). From Tarshish (Eze 27:12). Refining of (Pr 17:3; 25:4; 26:23; Eze 22:18-22; Jer 6:29-30; Zec 13:9; Mal 3:3). *See Refining.* Used for money (Ge 13:2; 17:12; 20:16; 23:13-16; Am 8:6; Mt 10:9; 26:15; Mk 14:11; Ac 19:19). *See Money.* For ornamentation of, and in the manufacture of, the utensils for the tabernacle (Ex 26:19; 27:17; 35:24; 36:24; 38:25; Nu 7:13,19,25,31,37, 43,49,55,61,67,73,79,85), of the temple (1Ch 28:14; 29:2-5; Ezr 5:14; 6:5; 8:26; Da 5:2). Cups made of (Ge 44:2), trumpets (Nu 10:2), cords (Ecc 12:6), chains (Isa 40:19), shrines (Ac 19:24), idols (Ex 20:23; Isa 30:22; Hos 13:2), baskets, or filigree (Pr 25:11), jewels (SS 1:11). *See Jewel, Jewelry.* Towers, figurative (SS 8:9).

Vessels of (Nu 7:85; 1Ki 10:25; 2Sa 8:10; 2Ki 12:13; 1Ch 18:10; 2Ch 24:14; Ezr 1:6; 5:14; 6:5; 8:26; Da 5:2; 11:8).

Abundance of (1Ki 10:27; 1Ch 22:14; 29:2-7; 2Ch 1:15; Ecc 2:8; Isa 2:7). Dross from (Pr 25:4; 26:23). Rejected (Jer 6:30). Workers in (2Ch 2:14; Ac 19:24). *See Smith.*

Symbolic: (Da 2:32,35).

SILVERSMITH [*7671, 737*]. (Ac 19:24). *See Smith.*

SIMEON [*1201+9058, 9058, 9063, 5208*] (*he has heard or obedient one*).
NIV+ SIMEONITE, SIMEONITES
1. The son of Jacob (Ge 29:33; 35:23; Ex 1:1-2; 1Ch

2:1). With Levi avenges upon the Shechemites the seduction of Dinah (Ge 34; 49:5-7). Goes down to Egypt to buy grain; is bound by Joseph and detained (Ge 42:24,36; 43:23). His sons (Ge 46:10; Ex 6:15; 1Ch 4:24-37). Descendants of (Nu 26:12-14).
See below, Tribe of.
2. Tribe of: Military enrollment of, at Sinai (Nu 1:22-23; 2:13), in the plains of Moab (Nu 26:14). Place of, in camp and march (Nu 2:12; 10:18-19). Inheritance allotted to (Jos 19:1-9; Jdg 1:3-17; 1Ch 4:24-43). Stood on Mount Gerizim to bless at the time of the rehearsal of the law (Dt 27:12). Joined with the people of Judah and Benjamin in the renewal of the Passover (2Ch 15:9, w 15:1-15). Idolatry of (2Ch 34:6, w 34:1-7).
See Israel.
3. A devout man in Jerusalem. Blesses Jesus in the temple (Lk 2:25-35).
4. An ancestor of Jesus (Lk 3:30).
5. A disciple. Also called Niger (Ac 13:1).
6. Hebrew name of Peter (Ac 15:14, ftn). *See Peter, Simon.*

SIMEONITE(S) [*1201+9058, 9058, 9063*] (*of Simeon*).
NIV+ SIMEON
A member of the tribe of Simeon.

SIMILITUDE (*likeness*). Pattern, resemblance, similarity (Nu 12:8; 2Ch 4:3; Ps 106:20; Heb 7:15).

SIMON [*1639+4981, 4981, 5208*] (*he has heard or obedient one*).
NIV+ PETER, SIMON'S
1. *See Peter, Simon.*
2. One of the twelve apostles. Called the Zealot (Mt 10:4; Mk 3:18; Lk 6:15; Ac 1:13). *See Zealot.*
3. A brother of Jesus (Mt 13:55; Mk 6:3).
4. A leper. Jesus dines with (Mt 26:6; Mk 14:3).
5. A man of Cyrene. Compelled to carry Jesus' cross (Mt 27:32; Mk 15:21; Lk 23:26).
6. A Pharisee. Jesus dines with (Lk 7:36-44).
7. The father of Judas Iscariot (Jn 6:71; 12:4; 13:2,26).
8. A sorcerer. Converted by Philip; rebuked by Peter (Ac 8:9-13,18-24).
9. A tanner. Peter lodges with (Ac 9:43; 10:6,17,32).

SIMON MACCABEUS Hasmonean ruler in Israel (143-134 B.C.).

SIMONY Ecclesiastical corruption, named after Simon the sorceror (Ac 8:9-19).

SIMPLE [*7331, 7343, 7344, 7785, 7837*].
NIV+ SIMPLEHEARTED, SIMPLY
Naive; easily led into wrong-doing (Ps 19:7; 119:130; Pr 7:7).

SIMRI *See Shimri, 3.*

SIN [**2627, 2628, 2629, 2631, 2633, 6097, 6404, 6411, 7321, 7322, 8273, 279, 280, 281, 283, 4183, 4579, 4922, 4997, 4998*].
NIV+ SIN'S, SINFUL, SINFULNESS, SINNED, SINNER, SINNER'S, SINNERS, SINNING, SINS
Adamic:
Original, of Adam (Ge 3:6; Hos 6:7; Ro 5:12,15-19).
Sin Nature:
The inherited tendencies to evil (Mt 7:17-18; 12:33-35;

Mk 7:20-23; Lk 6:45; Ro 6:6; 7:17,20,23,25; 8:3,5-7; Gal 5:16-17; Eph 2:3; Jas 1:14)—

Jas 4:17 Anyone, then, who knows the good he ought to do and doesn't do it, sins.

Defined:

Transgressing the law (Hos 6:8; Mt 5:28; 1Co 8:12)—

Heb 12:15 See to it that no one misses the grace of God and that no bitter root grows up to cause trouble and defile many.

Jas 2:10 For whoever keeps the whole law and yet stumbles at just one point is guilty of breaking all of it. [11]For he who said, "Do not commit adultery," also said, "Do not murder." If you do not commit adultery but do commit murder, you have become a lawbreaker. (+Jas 4:17)

1Jn 3:4 Everyone who sins breaks the law; in fact, sin is lawlessness.

1Jn 5:17 All wrongdoing is sin, and there is sin that does not lead to death.

Turning away from God—

Dt 29:18 Make sure there is no man or woman, clan or tribe among you today whose heart turns away from the LORD our God to go and worship the gods of those nations; make sure there is no root among you that produces such bitter poison.

Ps 95:10 For forty years I was angry with that generation; I said, "They are a people whose hearts go astray, and they have not known my ways."

Not seeking God—

2Ch 12:14 He did evil because he had not set his heart on seeking the LORD.

Foolish thoughts—

Pr 24:8 He who plots evil will be known as a schemer. [9]The schemes of folly are sin, and men detest a mocker.

Self-deception (Isa 42:20).

That which is not of faith—

Ro 14:23 But the man who has doubts is condemned if he eats, because his eating is not from faith; and everything that does not come from faith is sin.

See Atonement; Conviction, of Sin; Depravity; Regeneration; Repentance; Reprobacy; Salvation; Sanctification; Wicked, Punishment of.

Against the body—

Ecc 5:6 Do not let your mouth lead you into sin. And do not protest to the [temple] messenger, "My vow was a mistake." Why should God be angry at what you say and destroy the work of your hands?

Against knowledge (Pr 26:11; Lk 12:47-48; Jn 9:41; 15:22; Ro 1:21,32; 2:17-23; Heb 10:26; Jas 4:17; 2Pe 2:21-22). *See Ignorance, Sins of.* Attempts to cover, vain (Ge 3:10; Job 31:33; Isa 29:15; 59:6).

Christ's description of (Mt 5:2-20)—

Jn 8:34 Jesus replied, "I tell you the truth, everyone who sins is a slave to sin.

Jn 8:44 You belong to your father, the devil, and you want to carry out your father's desire. He was a murderer from the beginning, not holding to the truth, for there is no truth in him. When he lies, he speaks his native language, for he is a liar and the father of lies.

Deceitful—

Heb 3:13 But encourage one another daily, as long as it is called Today, so that none of you may be hardened by sin's deceitfulness.

Defiles (Ps 51:2,7; Isa 1:18; Heb 12:15; 1Jn 1:7). *See*

Defilement. Degrees in (Lk 7:41-47; 12:47-48). Dominion of (Ro 3:9).

Enslaves (Jn 8:34; Ro 6:16; 2Pe 2:19).

Fools mock at (Pr 14:9).

Little sins (SS 2:15).

Magnitude of—

Job 22:5 Is not your wickedness great? Are not your sins endless?

Ps 25:11 For the sake of your name, O LORD, forgive my iniquity, though it is great.

None in heaven (Rev 22:3-4).

Parable of (Mt 13:24-25,33,39). Paul's discussion of the responsibility for (Ro 2-9). Pleasures of (Jn 20:12-16; 21:12-13; Lk 8:14; Heb 11:25). *See Pleasure, Worldly.*

Reproach to God (2Sa 12:14).

Secret sins (Ps 19:12; 44:22; 64:2; 90:8; Ecc 12:14; Eze 8:12; 11:5; Mt 10:26; Lk 8:17; 12:2-3; Jn 3:20; Ro 2:16; Eph 5:12).

Sinfulness of (Job 22:5; Ps 25:11; Isa 1:18)—

Ro 7:13 Did that which is good, then, become death to me? By no means! But in order that sin might be recognized as sin, it produced death in me through what was good, so that through the commandment sin might become utterly sinful.

To be hated (Dt 7:26; Ps 119:113).

Confession of: (1Ki 8:47; Pr 28:13).

Signified by placing hands on the head of the offering (Lev 3:2,13; 4:4,15,24,29,33; 16:21; Nu 8:12).

Illustrated in parables, of the prodigal son—

Lk 15:17 "When he came to his senses, he said, 'How many of my father's hired men have food to spare, and here I am starving to death! [18]I will set out and go back to my father and say to him: Father, I have sinned against heaven and against you. [19]I am no longer worthy to be called your son; make me like one of your hired men.' [20]So he got up and went to his father.

"But while he was still a long way off, his father saw him and was filled with compassion for him; he ran to his son, threw his arms around him and kissed him.

[21]"The son said to him, 'Father, I have sinned against heaven and against you. I am no longer worthy to be called your son.'

Of the Pharisee and the tax collector (Lk 18:13).

To God, commanded (Lev 5:5-10)—

Lev 16:21 He is to lay both hands on the head of the live goat and confess over it all the wickedness and rebellion of the Israelites—all their sins—and put them on the goat's head. He shall send the goat away into the desert in the care of a man appointed for the task.

To saints, commanded—

Jas 5:16 Therefore confess your sins to each other and pray for each other so that you may be healed. The prayer of a righteous man is powerful and effective.

1Jn 1:8 If we claim to be without sin, we deceive ourselves and the truth is not in us. [9]If we confess our sins, he is faithful and just and will forgive us our sins and purify us from all unrighteousness. [10]If we claim we have not sinned, we make him out to be a liar and his word has no place in our lives.

To God, exemplified by Israel—

Nu 14:40 Early the next morning they went up toward the high hill country. "We have sinned," they said. "We will go up to the place the LORD promised." (+Jdg 10:10; 1Sa 7:6)

By Saul (1Sa 15:2,4)

By David (2Sa 12:13)—

2Sa 24:10 David was conscience-stricken after he had counted the fighting men, and he said to the LORD, "I have sinned greatly in what I have done. Now, O LORD, I beg you, take away the guilt of your servant. I have done a very foolish thing."

2Sa 24:17 When David saw the angel who was striking down the people, he said to the LORD, "I am the one who has sinned and done wrong. These are but sheep. What have they done? Let your hand fall upon me and my family." (+1Ch 21:17)

By the psalmist—

Ps 32:5 Then I acknowledged my sin to you and did not cover up my iniquity. I said, "I will confess my transgressions to the LORD"—and you forgave the guilt of my sin. *Selah*

Ps 38:3 Because of your wrath there is no health in my body; my bones have no soundness because of my sin. [4]My guilt has overwhelmed me like a burden too heavy to bear.

Ps 38:18 I confess my iniquity; I am troubled by my sin.

Ps 40:11 Do not withhold your mercy from me, O LORD; may your love and your truth always protect me. [12]For troubles without number surround me; my sins have overtaken me, and I cannot see. They are more than the hairs of my head, and my heart fails within me.

Ps 41:4 I said, "O LORD, have mercy on me; heal me, for I have sinned against you."

Ps 51:2 Wash away all my iniquity and cleanse me from my sin.

[3]For I know my transgressions, and my sin is always before me. [4]Against you, you only, have I sinned and done what is evil in your sight, so that you are proved right when you speak and justified when you judge. [5]Surely I was sinful at birth, sinful from the time my mother conceived me.

Ps 69:5 You know my folly, O God; my guilt is not hidden from you.

Ps 73:21 When my heart was grieved and my spirit embittered, [22]I was senseless and ignorant; I was a brute beast before you.

Ps 119:59 I have considered my ways and have turned my steps to your statutes. [60]I will hasten and not delay to obey your commands.

Ps 119:176 I have strayed like a lost sheep. Seek your servant, for I have not forgotten your commands.

By the Jews—

2Ch 29:6 Our fathers were unfaithful; they did evil in the eyes of the LORD our God and forsook him. They turned their faces away from the LORD's dwelling place and turned their backs on him.

Ezr 9:4 Then everyone who trembled at the words of the God of Israel gathered around me because of this unfaithfulness of the exiles. And I sat there appalled until the evening sacrifice.

[5]Then, at the evening sacrifice, I rose from my self-abasement, with my tunic and cloak torn, and fell on my knees with my hands spread out to the LORD my God [6]and prayed:

"O my God, I am too ashamed and disgraced to lift up my face to you, my God, because our sins are higher than our heads and our guilt has reached to the heavens. [7]From the days of our forefathers until now, our guilt has been great. Because of our sins, we and our kings and our priests have been subjected to the sword and captivity, to pillage and humiliation at the hand of foreign kings, as it is today.

Ezr 9:10 "But now, O our God, what can we say after this? For we have disregarded the commands [11]you gave through your servants the prophets when you said: 'The land you are entering to possess is a land polluted by the corruption of its peoples. By their detestable practices they have filled it with their impurity from one end to the other. [12]Therefore, do not give your daughters in marriage to their sons or take their daughters for your sons. Do not seek a treaty of friendship with them at any time, that you may be strong and eat the good things of the land and leave it to your children as an everlasting inheritance.'

[13]"What has happened to us is a result of our evil deeds and our great guilt, and yet, our God, you have punished us less than our sins have deserved and have given us a remnant like this. [14]Shall we again break your commands and intermarry with the peoples who commit such detestable practices? Would you not be angry enough with us to destroy us, leaving us no remnant or survivor? [15]O LORD, God of Israel, you are righteous! We are left this day as a remnant. Here we are before you in our guilt, though because of it not one of us can stand in your presence."

Ne 9:2 Those of Israelite descent had separated themselves from all foreigners. They stood in their places and confessed their sins and the wickedness of their fathers. [3]They stood where they were and read from the Book of the Law of the LORD their God for a quarter of the day, and spent another quarter in confession and in worshiping the LORD their God. (+Ne 9:5-32)

Ne 9:33 In all that has happened to us, you have been just; you have acted faithfully, while we did wrong. [34]Our kings, our leaders, our priests and our fathers did not follow your law; they did not pay attention to your commands or the warnings you gave them. [35]Even while they were in their kingdom, enjoying your great goodness to them in the spacious and fertile land you gave them, they did not serve you or turn from their evil ways. (+Ne 9:36-38)

Ps 106:6 We have sinned, even as our fathers did; we have done wrong and acted wickedly.

Isa 26:13 O LORD, our God, other lords besides you have ruled over us, but your name alone do we honor.

Isa 59:12 For our offenses are many in your sight, and our sins testify against us. Our offenses are ever with us, and we acknowledge our iniquities: [13]rebellion and treachery against the LORD, turning our backs on our God, fomenting oppression and revolt, uttering lies our hearts have conceived. [14]So justice is driven back, and righteousness stands at a distance; truth has stumbled in the streets, honesty cannot enter. [15]Truth is nowhere to be found, and whoever shuns evil becomes a prey. The LORD looked and was displeased that there was no justice.

Isa 64:5 You come to the help of those who gladly do right, who remember your ways. But when we continued to sin against them, you were angry. How then can we be saved? [6]All of us have become like one who is unclean, and all our righteous acts are like filthy rags; we all shrivel up like a leaf, and like the wind our sins sweep us away. [7]No one calls on your name or strives to lay hold of you; for you have hidden your face from us and made us waste away because of our sins.

Jer 3:21 A cry is heard on the barren heights, the weeping and pleading of the people of Israel, because they have perverted their ways and have forgotten the LORD their God.

[22]"Return, faithless people; I will cure you of backsliding."

"Yes, we will come to you, for you are the LORD our God.

Jer 3:25 Let us lie down in our shame, and let our disgrace cover us. We have sinned against the LORD our God, both we and our fathers; from our youth till this day we have not obeyed the LORD our God."

Jer 8:14 "Why are we sitting here? Gather together! Let us flee to the fortified cities and perish there! For the LORD our God has doomed us to perish and given us poisoned water to drink, because we have sinned against him. ¹⁵We hoped for peace but no good has come, for a time of healing but there was only terror.

Jer 14:7 Although our sins testify against us, O LORD, do something for the sake of your name. For our backsliding is great; we have sinned against you.

Jer 14:20 O LORD, we acknowledge our wickedness and the guilt of our fathers; we have indeed sinned against you.

Jer 31:18 "I have surely heard Ephraim's moaning: 'You disciplined me like an unruly calf, and I have been disciplined. Restore me, and I will return, because you are the LORD my God. ¹⁹After I strayed, I repented; after I came to understand, I beat my breast. I was ashamed and humiliated because I bore the disgrace of my youth.'

La 3:40 Let us examine our ways and test them, and let us return to the LORD. ⁴¹Let us lift up our hearts and our hands to God in heaven, and say: ⁴²"We have sinned and rebelled and you have not forgiven.

Da 9:5 we have sinned and done wrong. We have been wicked and have rebelled; we have turned away from your commands and laws. ⁶We have not listened to your servants the prophets, who spoke in your name to our kings, our princes and our fathers, and to all the people of the land.

Da 9:8 O LORD, we and our kings, our princes and our fathers are covered with shame because we have sinned against you. ⁹The Lord our God is merciful and forgiving, even though we have rebelled against him; ¹⁰we have not obeyed the LORD our God or kept the laws he gave us through his servants the prophets. ¹¹All Israel has transgressed your law and turned away, refusing to obey you.

"Therefore the curses and sworn judgments written in the Law of Moses, the servant of God, have been poured out on us, because we have sinned against you.

Da 9:15 "Now, O Lord our God, who brought your people out of Egypt with a mighty hand and who made for yourself a name that endures to this day, we have sinned, we have done wrong.

By Job—

Job 7:20 If I have sinned, what have I done to you, O watcher of men? Why have you made me your target? Have I become a burden to you?

Job 9:20 Even if I were innocent, my mouth would condemn me; if I were blameless, it would pronounce me guilty.

Job 13:23 How many wrongs and sins have I committed? Show me my offense and my sin.

Job 40:4 "I am unworthy—how can I reply to you? I put my hand over my mouth.

Job 42:5 My ears had heard of you but now my eyes have seen you. ⁶Therefore I despise myself and repent in dust and ashes."

By Isaiah—

Isa 6:5 "Woe to me!" I cried. "I am ruined! For I am a man of unclean lips, and I live among a people of unclean lips, and my eyes have seen the King, the LORD Almighty."

By Jeremiah—

La 1:18 "The LORD is righteous, yet I rebelled against his

command. Listen, all you peoples; look upon my suffering. My young men and maidens have gone into exile.

¹⁹"I called to my allies but they betrayed me. My priests and my elders perished in the city while they searched for food to keep themselves alive.

²⁰"See, O LORD, how distressed I am! I am in torment within, and in my heart I am disturbed, for I have been most rebellious. Outside, the sword bereaves; inside, there is only death.

By Paul—

1Co 15:9 For I am the least of the apostles and do not even deserve to be called an apostle, because I persecuted the church of God.

Consequences of:

Look on the face (Isa 3:9). Guilty fear (Ge 3:7-10; Pr 10:24; 25:1). Depraved conscience (Pr 30:20). Judgment (Jer 5:25). Trouble (Isa 57:20-21; Jer 4:18).

Effects upon children—

Ex 20:5 You shall not bow down to them or worship them; for I, the LORD your God, am a jealous God, punishing the children for the sin of the fathers to the third and fourth generation of those who hate me, (+Ex 34:7)

Lev 26:39 Those of you who are left will waste away in the lands of their enemies because of their sins; also because of their fathers' sins they will waste away. (+Lev 26:40)

Nu 14:33 Your children will be shepherds here for forty years, suffering for your unfaithfulness, until the last of your bodies lies in the desert. (+Dt 5:9)

Ps 21:10 You will destroy their descendants from the earth, their posterity from mankind.

Ps 37:28 For the LORD loves the just and will not forsake his faithful ones. They will be protected forever, but the offspring of the wicked will be cut off;

Ps 109:9 May his children be fatherless and his wife a widow. ¹⁰May his children be wandering beggars; may they be driven from their ruined homes.

Pr 14:11 The house of the wicked will be destroyed, but the tent of the upright will flourish.

Isa 14:20 you will not join them in burial, for you have destroyed your land and killed your people. The offspring of the wicked will never be mentioned again.

²¹Prepare a place to slaughter his sons for the sins of their forefathers; they are not to rise to inherit the land and cover the earth with their cities.

²²"I will rise up against them," declares the LORD Almighty. "I will cut off from Babylon her name and survivors, her offspring and descendants," declares the LORD. (+Isa 65:7)

Jer 32:18 You show love to thousands but bring the punishment for the fathers' sins into the laps of their children after them. O great and powerful God, whose name is the LORD Almighty,

La 5:7 Our fathers sinned and are no more, and we bear their punishment.

Ro 5:12 Therefore, just as sin entered the world through one man, and death through sin, and in this way death came to all men, because all sinned— ¹³for before the law was given, sin was in the world. But sin is not taken into account when there is no law. ¹⁴Nevertheless, death reigned from the time of Adam to the time of Moses, even over those who did not sin by breaking a command, as did Adam, who was a pattern of the one to come.

¹⁵But the gift is not like the trespass. For if the many died by the trespass of the one man, how much more did God's grace and the gift that came by the grace of the one man,

Jesus Christ, overflow to the many! [16]Again, the gift of God is not like the result of the one man's sin: The judgment followed one sin and brought condemnation, but the gift followed many trespasses and brought justification. [17]For if, by the trespass of the one man, death reigned through that one man, how much more will those who receive God's abundant provision of grace and of the gift of righteousness reign in life through the one man, Jesus Christ.

[18]Consequently, just as the result of one trespass was condemnation for all men, so also the result of one act of righteousness was justification that brings life for all men.

[19]For just as through the disobedience of the one man the many were made sinners, so also through the obedience of the one man the many will be made righteous. [20]The law was added so that the trespass might increase. But where sin increased, grace increased all the more, [21]so that, just as sin reigned in death, so also grace might reign through righteousness to bring eternal life through Jesus Christ our Lord.

Attributed to Job's children because of Job's alleged wickedness—

Job 5:4 His children are far from safety, crushed in court without a defender.

Job 18:19 He has no offspring or descendants among his people, no survivor where once he lived.

Job 21:19 [It is said,] 'God stores up a man's punishment for his sons.' Let him repay the man himself, so that he will know it!

Punishment for, not brought upon children (Dt 24:16; 2Ki 14:6; 2Ch 25:4)—

Jer 31:29 "In those days people will no longer say,

'The fathers have eaten sour grapes, and the children's teeth are set on edge.'

[30]Instead, everyone will die for his own sin; whoever eats sour grapes—his own teeth will be set on edge. (+Eze 18:2-4,20)

No escape from (Ge 3:8-19; Isa 28:18-22; Am 9:2-4; Mt 23:33; Heb 2:3). *See Punishment, No Escape From; Wicked.*

Conviction of:

Produced by dreams (Job 33:14-17), by visions (Ac 9:3-9), by afflictions (Job 33:18-20; La 1:20; Lk 15:17-21), by adversity (Ps 107:4-6,10-14,17-20,23-30), by the Gospel (Ac 2:37), by religious testimony (1Co 14:24-25), by the conscience (Jn 8:9; Ro 2:15), by the Holy Spirit (Jn 16:7-11). *See Conviction, of Sin; Repentance, Instances of.*

Forgiveness of: (Ac 26:18; Eph 1:7).

Promised—

Ex 34:6 And he passed in front of Moses, proclaiming, "The LORD, the LORD, the compassionate and gracious God, slow to anger, abounding in love and faithfulness, [7]maintaining love to thousands, and forgiving wickedness, rebellion and sin. Yet he does not leave the guilty unpunished; he punishes the children and their children for the sin of the fathers to the third and fourth generation."

Lev 4:20 and do with this bull just as he did with the bull for the sin offering. In this way the priest will make atonement for them, and they will be forgiven.

Lev 4:26 He shall burn all the fat on the altar as he burned the fat of the fellowship offering. In this way the priest will make atonement for the man's sin, and he will be forgiven. (+Lev 4:31,35)

Lev 5:4 "'Or if a person thoughtlessly takes an oath to do anything, whether good or evil—in any matter one might

carelessly swear about—even though he is unaware of it, in any case when he learns of it he will be guilty.

[5]"'When anyone is guilty in any of these ways, he must confess in what way he has sinned [6]and, as a penalty for the sin he has committed, he must bring to the LORD a female lamb or goat from the flock as a sin offering; and the priest shall make atonement for him for his sin.

[7]"'If he cannot afford a lamb, he is to bring two doves or two young pigeons to the LORD as a penalty for his sin—one for a sin offering and the other for a burnt offering. [8]He is to bring them to the priest, who shall first offer the one for the sin offering. He is to wring its head from its neck, not severing it completely, [9]and is to sprinkle some of the blood of the sin offering against the side of the altar; the rest of the blood must be drained out at the base of the altar. It is a sin offering. [10]The priest shall then offer the other as a burnt offering in the prescribed way and make atonement for him for the sin he has committed, and he will be forgiven. (+Lev 5:11-13; Nu 14:18; 15:25; Dt 4)

Ps 130:4 But with you there is forgiveness; therefore you are feared.

Isa 1:6 From the sole of your foot to the top of your head there is no soundness—only wounds and welts and open sores, not cleansed or bandaged or soothed with oil. (+Isa 1:7-17)

Isa 1:18 "Come now, let us reason together," says the LORD. "Though your sins are like scarlet, they shall be as white as snow; though they are red as crimson, they shall be like wool.

Isa 43:25 "I, even I, am he who blots out your transgressions, for my own sake, and remembers your sins no more. [26]Review the past for me, let us argue the matter together; state the case for your innocence.

Isa 44:21 "Remember these things, O Jacob, for you are my servant, O Israel. I have made you, you are my servant; O Israel, I will not forget you. [22]I have swept away your offenses like a cloud, your sins like the morning mist. Return to me, for I have redeemed you."

Isa 55:6 Seek the LORD while he may be found; call on him while he is near. [7]Let the wicked forsake his way and the evil man his thoughts. Let him turn to the LORD, and he will have mercy on him, and to our God, for he will freely pardon.

Jer 31:34 No longer will a man teach his neighbor, or a man his brother, saying, 'Know the LORD,' because they will all know me, from the least of them to the greatest," declares the LORD. "For I will forgive their wickedness and will remember their sins no more."

Jer 33:8 I will cleanse them from all the sin they have committed against me and will forgive all their sins of rebellion against me. (+Eze 18:21-22)

Eze 33:14 And if I say to the wicked man, 'You will surely die,' but he then turns away from his sin and does what is just and right— [15]if he gives back what he took in pledge for a loan, returns what he has stolen, follows the decrees that give life, and does no evil, he will surely live; he will not die. [16]None of the sins he has committed will be remembered against him. He has done what is just and right; he will surely live.

Mt 12:31 And so I tell you, every sin and blasphemy will be forgiven men, but the blasphemy against the Spirit will not be forgiven.

Mk 3:28 I tell you the truth, all the sins and blasphemies of men will be forgiven them.

Heb 8:12 For I will forgive their wickedness and will remember their sins no more."

Heb 10:17 Then he adds: "Their sins and lawless acts I will remember no more."

Jas 5:15 And the prayer offered in faith will make the sick person well; the Lord will raise him up. If he has sinned, he will be forgiven.

1Jn 1:7 But if we walk in the light, as he is in the light, we have fellowship with one another, and the blood of Jesus, his Son, purifies us from all sin.

1Jn 1:9 If we confess our sins, he is faithful and just and will forgive us our sins and purify us from all unrighteousness.

Blessedness of—

Ps 32:1 Blessed is he whose transgressions are forgiven, whose sins are covered. [2]Blessed is the man whose sin the LORD does not count against him and in whose spirit is no deceit.

Ro 4:7 "Blessed are they whose transgressions are forgiven, whose sins are covered. [8]Blessed is the man whose sin the Lord will never count against him."

Instances of Forgiveness:

Israelites—

Nu 14:20 The LORD replied, "I have forgiven them, as you asked.

Ps 85:2 You forgave the iniquity of your people and covered all their sins. *Selah* [3]You set aside all your wrath and turned from your fierce anger.

Ps 99:8 O LORD our God, you answered them; you were to Israel a forgiving God, though you punished their misdeeds.

Ps 103:12 as far as the east is from the west, so far has he removed our transgressions from us.

David—

2Sa 12:13 Then David said to Nathan, "I have sinned against the LORD." Nathan replied, "The LORD has taken away your sin. You are not going to die.

Ps 32:5 Then I acknowledged my sin to you and did not cover up my iniquity. I said, "I will confess my transgressions to the LORD"—and you forgave the guilt of my sin. *Selah*

Isaiah—

Isa 6:7 With it he touched my mouth and said, "See, this has touched your lips; your guilt is taken away and your sin atoned for."

Paralytic (Mt 9:2,6; Mk 2:5; Lk 5:20,24).

The prostitute (Lk 7:48)—

Jn 8:11 "No one, sir," she said. "Then neither do I condemn you," Jesus declared. "Go now and leave your life of sin."

Believers—

Col 2:13 When you were dead in your sins and in the uncircumcision of your sinful nature, God made you alive with Christ. He forgave us all our sins,

Conditions of Forgiveness:

Repentance (Mt 3:6)—

Lk 3:3 He went into all the country around the Jordan, preaching a baptism of repentance for the forgiveness of sins. (+Lk 13:3,5)

Ac 2:38 Peter replied, "Repent and be baptized, every one of you, in the name of Jesus Christ for the forgiveness of your sins. And you will receive the gift of the Holy Spirit. (+Ac 3:19)

Faith—

Ac 10:36 You know the message God sent to the people of Israel, telling the good news of peace through Jesus Christ, who is Lord of all.

Ac 10:43 All the prophets testify about him that everyone who believes in him receives forgiveness of sins through his name."

Ac 13:38 "Therefore, my brothers, I want you to know that through Jesus the forgiveness of sins is proclaimed to you. [39]Through him everyone who believes is justified from everything you could not be justified from by the law of Moses.

Ac 26:16 'Now get up and stand on your feet. I have appeared to you to appoint you as a servant and as a witness of what you have seen of me and what I will show you. [17]I will rescue you from your own people and from the Gentiles. I am sending you to them [18]to open their eyes and turn them from darkness to light, and from the power of Satan to God, so that they may receive forgiveness of sins and a place among those who are sanctified by faith in me.'

Confession of sins (1Jn 1:7,9).

Parable of—

Mt 18:23 "Therefore, the kingdom of heaven is like a king who wanted to settle accounts with his servants. [24]As he began the settlement, a man who owed him ten thousand talents was brought to him. [25]Since he was not able to pay, the master ordered that he and his wife and his children and all that he had be sold to repay the debt.

[26]"The servant fell on his knees before him. 'Be patient with me,' he begged, 'and I will pay back everything.' [27]The servant's master took pity on him, canceled the debt and let him go.

Through the shedding of blood—

Heb 9:22 In fact, the law requires that nearly everything be cleansed with blood, and without the shedding of blood there is no forgiveness.

Spirit of—

Mt 6:12 Forgive us our debts, as we also have forgiven our debtors.

Mt 6:14 For if you forgive men when they sin against you, your heavenly Father will also forgive you. [15]But if you do not forgive men their sins, your Father will not forgive your sins. (+Mt 18:35)

Mk 11:25 And when you stand praying, if you hold anything against anyone, forgive him, so that your Father in heaven may forgive you your sins."

The mission of Christ to secure—

Mt 1:21 She will give birth to a son, and you are to give him the name Jesus, because he will save his people from their sins."

Mt 26:28 This is my blood of the covenant, which is poured out for many for the forgiveness of sins.

Lk 24:47 and repentance and forgiveness of sins will be preached in his name to all nations, beginning at Jerusalem.

1Jn 2:1 My dear children, I write this to you so that you will not sin. But if anybody does sin, we have one who speaks to the Father in our defense—Jesus Christ, the Righteous One. [2]He is the atoning sacrifice for our sins, and not only for ours but also for the sins of the whole world.

1Jn 2:12 I write to you, dear children, because your sins have been forgiven on account of his name.

Rev 1:5 and from Jesus Christ, who is the faithful witness, the firstborn from the dead, and the ruler of the kings of the earth. To him who loves us and has freed us from our sins by his blood,

Prayer for—

Ps 19:12 Who can discern his errors? Forgive my hidden faults.

Ps 25:7 Remember not the sins of my youth and my rebellious ways; according to your love remember me, for you are good, O LORD.

Ps 25:11 For the sake of your name, O LORD, forgive my iniquity, though it is great.

Ps 51:9 Hide your face from my sins and blot out all my iniquity.

Ps 79:9 Help us, O God our Savior, for the glory of your name; deliver us and forgive our sins for your name's sake.

Intercessory prayer for (1Ki 8:22-31)—

1Ki 8:32 then hear from heaven and act. Judge between your servants, condemning the guilty and bringing down on his own head what he has done. Declare the innocent not guilty, and so establish his innocence.

³³"When your people Israel have been defeated by an enemy because they have sinned against you, and when they turn back to you and confess your name, praying and making supplication to you in this temple, (+1Ki 8:34-50)

Apostolic—

Jn 20:23 If you forgive anyone his sins, they are forgiven; if you do not forgive them, they are not forgiven."

See Atonement; Conviction, of Sin; Offerings; Repentance.

From the Heart:

Isa 44:20 He feeds on ashes, a deluded heart misleads him; he cannot save himself, or say, "Is not this thing in my right hand a lie?"

Jer 7:24 But they did not listen or pay attention; instead, they followed the stubborn inclinations of their evil hearts. They went backward and not forward.

Jer 17:9 The heart is deceitful above all things and beyond cure. Who can understand it?

Eze 20:16 because they rejected my laws and did not follow my decrees and desecrated my Sabbaths. For their hearts were devoted to their idols.

Mt 5:28 But I tell you that anyone who looks at a woman lustfully has already committed adultery with her in his heart. (+Mt 7:17-18)

Mt 12:33 "Make a tree good and its fruit will be good, or make a tree bad and its fruit will be bad, for a tree is recognized by its fruit. ³⁴You brood of vipers, how can you who are evil say anything good? For out of the overflow of the heart the mouth speaks. ³⁵The good man brings good things out of the good stored up in him, and the evil man brings evil things out of the evil stored up in him.

Mt 15:8 "'These people honor me with their lips, but their hearts are far from me.

Mt 15:11 What goes into a man's mouth does not make him 'unclean,' but what comes out of his mouth, that is what makes him 'unclean.'"

Mt 15:16 "Are you still so dull?" Jesus asked them. ¹⁷"Don't you see that whatever enters the mouth goes into the stomach and then out of the body? ¹⁸But the things that come out of the mouth come from the heart, and these make a man 'unclean.' ¹⁹For out of the heart come evil thoughts, murder, adultery, sexual immorality, theft, false testimony, slander. (+Lk 6:45)

Of the tongue (Ecc 5:6). In thought (Pr 24:9). In secret (Ps 19:12; 90:8; Ecc 12:14; Eze 8:12; Jn 3:20; Ro 2:16; Eph 5:12). Against conscience (Ro 14:23). Against knowledge (Lk 12:47-48; Jn 9:41; 15:22; Ro 1:21,32; 2:17-23; Heb 10:26; Jas 4:17; 2Pe 2:21-22).

Fruits of:

Dt 29:18 Make sure there is no man or woman, clan or tribe among you today whose heart turns away from the LORD our God to go and worship the gods of those nations; make sure there is no root among you that produces such bitter poison.

Mk 7:21 For from within, out of men's hearts, come evil thoughts, sexual immorality, theft, murder, adultery, ²²greed, malice, deceit, lewdness, envy, slander, arrogance and folly. ²³All these evils come from inside and make a man 'unclean.'"

1Co 3:3 You are still worldly. For since there is jealousy and quarreling among you, are you not worldly? Are you not acting like mere men?

1Co 6:9 Do you not know that the wicked will not inherit the kingdom of God? Do not be deceived: Neither the sexually immoral nor idolaters nor adulterers nor male prostitutes nor homosexual offenders ¹⁰nor thieves nor the greedy nor drunkards nor slanderers nor swindlers will inherit the kingdom of God. ¹¹And that is what some of you were. But you were washed, you were sanctified, you were justified in the name of the Lord Jesus Christ and by the Spirit of our God.

Gal 5:19 The acts of the sinful nature are obvious: sexual immorality, impurity and debauchery; ²⁰idolatry and witchcraft; hatred, discord, jealousy, fits of rage, selfish ambition, dissensions, factions ²¹and envy; drunkenness, orgies, and the like. I warn you, as I did before, that those who live like this will not inherit the kingdom of God.

1Pe 4:3 For you have spent enough time in the past doing what pagans choose to do—living in debauchery, lust, drunkenness, orgies, carousing and detestable idolatry. (+Jas 5:11)

Fruits of original sin—

Ge 3:7 Then the eyes of both of them were opened, and they realized they were naked; so they sewed fig leaves together and made coverings for themselves.

⁸Then the man and his wife heard the sound of the LORD God as he was walking in the garden in the cool of the day, and they hid from the LORD God among the trees of the garden. ⁹But the LORD God called to the man, "Where are you?"

¹⁰He answered, "I heard you in the garden, and I was afraid because I was naked; so I hid."

¹¹And he said, "Who told you that you were naked? Have you eaten from the tree that I commanded you not to eat from?"

¹²The man said, "The woman you put here with me—she gave me some fruit from the tree, and I ate it."

¹³Then the LORD God said to the woman, "What is this you have done?" The woman said, "The serpent deceived me, and I ate."

¹⁴So the LORD God said to the serpent, "Because you have done this, "Cursed are you above all the livestock and all the wild animals! You will crawl on your belly and you will eat dust all the days of your life. ¹⁵And I will put enmity between you and the woman, and between your offspring and hers; he will crush your head, and you will strike his heel."

¹⁶To the woman he said, "I will greatly increase your pains in childbearing; with pain you will give birth to children. Your desire will be for your husband, and he will rule over you."

¹⁷To Adam he said, "Because you listened to your wife and ate from the tree about which I commanded you, 'You must not eat of it,' "Cursed is the ground because of you;

through painful toil you will eat of it all the days of your life. **¹⁸**It will produce thorns and thistles for you, and you will eat the plants of the field. **¹⁹**By the sweat of your brow you will eat your food until you return to the ground, since from it you were taken; for dust you are and to dust you will return."

²⁰Adam named his wife Eve, because she would become the mother of all the living.

²¹The LORD God made garments of skin for Adam and his wife and clothed them. **²²**And the LORD God said, "The man has now become like one of us, knowing good and evil. He must not be allowed to reach out his hand and take also from the tree of life and eat, and live forever." **²³**So the LORD God banished him from the Garden of Eden to work the ground from which he had been taken. **²⁴**After he drove the man out, he placed on the east side of the Garden of Eden cherubim and a flaming sword flashing back and forth to guard the way to the tree of life.

Ge 4:9 Then the LORD said to Cain, "Where is your brother Abel?"

"I don't know," he replied. "Am I my brother's keeper?"

¹⁰The LORD said, "What have you done? Listen! Your brother's blood cries out to me from the ground. **¹¹**Now you are under a curse and driven from the ground, which opened its mouth to receive your brother's blood from your hand. **¹²**When you work the ground, it will no longer yield its crops for you. You will be a restless wanderer on the earth."

¹³Cain said to the LORD, "My punishment is more than I can bear.

Ro 5:12 Therefore, just as sin entered the world through one man, and death through sin, and in this way death came to all men, because all sinned— **¹³**for before the law was given, sin was in the world. But sin is not taken into account when there is no law. **¹⁴**Nevertheless, death reigned from the time of Adam to the time of Moses, even over those who did not sin by breaking a command, as did Adam, who was a pattern of the one to come.

¹⁵But the gift is not like the trespass. For if the many died by the trespass of the one man, how much more did God's grace and the gift that came by the grace of the one man, Jesus Christ, overflow to the many! **¹⁶**Again, the gift of God is not like the result of the one man's sin: The judgment followed one sin and brought condemnation, but the gift followed many trespasses and brought justification. **¹⁷**For if, by the trespass of the one man, death reigned through that one man, how much more will those who receive God's abundant provision of grace and of the gift of righteousness reign in life through the one man, Jesus Christ.

¹⁸Consequently, just as the result of one trespass was condemnation for all men, so also the result of one act of righteousness was justification that brings life for all men. **¹⁹**For just as through the disobedience of the one man the many were made sinners, so also through the obedience of the one man the many will be made righteous.

²⁰The law was added so that the trespass might increase. But where sin increased, grace increased all the more, **²¹**so that, just as sin reigned in death, so also grace might reign through righteousness to bring eternal life through Jesus Christ our Lord.

God's anger (Jer 7:19). Moral insensibility (Pr 30:20).

No peace—

Isa 57:20 But the wicked are like the tossing sea, which cannot rest, whose waves cast up mire and mud. **²¹**"There is no peace," says my God, "for the wicked."

Shame—

Pr 3:35 The wise inherit honor, but fools he holds up to shame.

Withholding of God's goodness—

Jer 7:19 But am I the one they are provoking? declares the LORD. Are they not rather harming themselves, to their own shame?

Destruction and death—

Ge 6:5 The LORD saw how great man's wickedness on the earth had become, and that every inclination of the thoughts of his heart was only evil all the time. **⁶**The LORD was grieved that he had made man on the earth, and his heart was filled with pain. **⁷**So the LORD said, "I will wipe mankind, whom I have created, from the face of the earth—men and animals, and creatures that move along the ground, and birds of the air—for I am grieved that I have made them."

1Ki 13:33 Even after this, Jeroboam did not change his evil ways, but once more appointed priests for the high places from all sorts of people. Anyone who wanted to become a priest he consecrated for the high places. **³⁴**This was the sin of the house of Jeroboam that led to its downfall and to its destruction from the face of the earth.

Job 5:2 Resentment kills a fool, and envy slays the simple.

Ps 5:10 Declare them guilty, O God! Let their intrigues be their downfall. Banish them for their many sins, for they have rebelled against you.

Ps 94:23 He will repay them for their sins and destroy them for their wickedness; the LORD our God will destroy them.

Pr 5:22 The evil deeds of a wicked man ensnare him; the cords of his sin hold him fast. **²³**He will die for lack of discipline, led astray by his own great folly. (+Pr 10:24,29-31; 11:18-19,27,29)

Isa 3:9 The look on their faces testifies against them; they parade their sin like Sodom; they do not hide it. Woe to them! They have brought disaster upon themselves.

Isa 3:11 Woe to the wicked! Disaster is upon them! They will be paid back for what their hands have done.

Isa 9:18 Surely wickedness burns like a fire; it consumes briers and thorns, it sets the forest thickets ablaze, so that it rolls upward in a column of smoke.

Isa 14:21 Prepare a place to slaughter his sons for the sins of their forefathers; they are not to rise to inherit the land and cover the earth with their cities.

Jer 14:16 And the people they are prophesying to will be thrown out into the streets of Jerusalem because of the famine and sword. There will be no one to bury them or their wives, their sons or their daughters. I will pour out on them the calamity they deserve.

Jer 21:14 I will punish you as your deeds deserve, declares the LORD. I will kindle a fire in your forests that will consume everything around you.' "

Eze 11:21 But as for those whose hearts are devoted to their vile images and detestable idols, I will bring down on their own heads what they have done, declares the Sovereign LORD."

Eze 22:31 So I will pour out my wrath on them and consume them with my fiery anger, bringing down on their own heads all they have done, declares the Sovereign LORD." (+Eze 23:31-35)

Hos 12:14 But Ephraim has bitterly provoked him to anger; his Lord will leave upon him the guilt of his bloodshed and will repay him for his contempt.

Hos 13:9 "You are destroyed, O Israel, because you are against me, against your helper. (+Ro 6:23)

The same as sown—

Job 4:8 As I have observed, those who plow evil and those who sow trouble reap it.

Job 13:26 For you write down bitter things against me and make me inherit the sins of my youth.

Job 20:11 The youthful vigor that fills his bones will lie with him in the dust.

Ps 9:15 The nations have fallen into the pit they have dug; their feet are caught in the net they have hidden. [16]The LORD is known by his justice; the wicked are ensnared by the work of their hands. *Higgaion. Selah*

Ps 10:2 In his arrogance the wicked man hunts down the weak, who are caught in the schemes he devises.

Ps 141:10 Let the wicked fall into their own nets, while I pass by in safety.

Pr 1:31 they will eat the fruit of their ways and be filled with the fruit of their schemes. (+Pr 11:5-7; 12:13,14-21,26; 22:8)

Isa 50:11 But now, all you who light fires and provide yourselves with flaming torches, go, walk in the light of your fires and of the torches you have set ablaze. This is what you shall receive from my hand: You will lie down in torment.

Jer 4:18 "Your own conduct and actions have brought this upon you. This is your punishment. How bitter it is! How it pierces to the heart!" (+Jer 21:14; Eze 11:21)

Hos 8:7 "They sow the wind and reap the whirlwind. The stalk has no head; it will produce no flour. Were it to yield grain, foreigners would swallow it up.

Hos 10:13 But you have planted wickedness, you have reaped evil, you have eaten the fruit of deception. Because you have depended on your own strength and on your many warriors,

Mic 7:13 The earth will become desolate because of its inhabitants, as the result of their deeds.

Ro 7:5 For when we were controlled by the sinful nature, the sinful passions aroused by the law were at work in our bodies, so that we bore fruit for death.

Gal 6:7 Do not be deceived: God cannot be mocked. A man reaps what he sows. [8]The one who sows to please his sinful nature, from that nature will reap destruction; the one who sows to please the Spirit, from the Spirit will reap eternal life.

Proverbs concerning (Pr 1:31; 3:35; 5:22-23)—

Pr 8:36 But whoever fails to find me harms himself; all who hate me love death."

Pr 10:24 What the wicked dreads will overtake him; what the righteous desire will be granted.

Pr 10:29 The way of the LORD is a refuge for the righteous, but it is the ruin of those who do evil.

[30]The righteous will never be uprooted, but the wicked will not remain in the land. [31]The mouth of the righteous brings forth wisdom, but a perverse tongue will be cut out.

Pr 11:5 The righteousness of the blameless makes a straight way for them, but the wicked are brought down by their own wickedness.

[6]The righteousness of the upright delivers them, but the unfaithful are trapped by evil desires.

[7]When a wicked man dies, his hope perishes; all he expected from his power comes to nothing.

Pr 11:18 The wicked man earns deceptive wages, but he who sows righteousness reaps a sure reward.

[19]The truly righteous man attains life, but he who pursues evil goes to his death.

Pr 11:27 He who seeks good finds goodwill, but evil comes to him who searches for it.

Pr 11:29 He who brings trouble on his family will inherit only wind, and the fool will be servant to the wise.

Pr 12:13 An evil man is trapped by his sinful talk, but a righteous man escapes trouble.

[14]From the fruit of his lips a man is filled with good things as surely as the work of his hands rewards him.

Pr 12:21 No harm befalls the righteous, but the wicked have their fill of trouble.

Pr 12:26 A righteous man is cautious in friendship, but the way of the wicked leads them astray.

Pr 13:5 The righteous hate what is false, but the wicked bring shame and disgrace.

[6]Righteousness guards the man of integrity, but wickedness overthrows the sinner.

Pr 13:15 Good understanding wins favor, but the way of the unfaithful is hard.

Pr 22:8 He who sows wickedness reaps trouble, and the rod of his fury will be destroyed.

Pr 28:1 The wicked man flees though no one pursues, but the righteous are as bold as a lion.

Pr 29:6 An evil man is snared by his own sin, but a righteous one can sing and be glad.

Pr 30:20 "This is the way of an adulteress: She eats and wipes her mouth and says, 'I've done nothing wrong.'

Moved to:

By the devil—

Mt 13:24 Jesus told them another parable: "The kingdom of heaven is like a man who sowed good seed in his field. [25]But while everyone was sleeping, his enemy came and sowed weeds among the wheat, and went away.

Mt 13:38 The field is the world, and the good seed stands for the sons of the kingdom. The weeds are the sons of the evil one, [39]and the enemy who sows them is the devil. The harvest is the end of the age, and the harvesters are angels. (+Jn 8:34,44)

Eph 2:1 As for you, you were dead in your transgressions and sins, [2]in which you used to live when you followed the ways of this world and of the ruler of the kingdom of the air, the spirit who is now at work in those who are disobedient.

1Jn 3:6 No one who lives in him keeps on sinning. No one who continues to sin has either seen him or known him.

1Jn 3:8 He who does what is sinful is of the devil, because the devil has been sinning from the beginning. The reason the Son of God appeared was to destroy the devil's work. [9]No one who is born of God will continue to sin, because God's seed remains in him; he cannot go on sinning, because he has been born of God. [10]This is how we know who the children of God are and who the children of the devil are: Anyone who does not do what is right is not a child of God; nor is anyone who does not love his brother.

1Jn 3:15 Anyone who hates his brother is a murderer, and you know that no murderer has eternal life in him.

By the fallen nature (Gal 5:16-17; Eph 2:3)—

Jas 1:14 but each one is tempted when, by his own evil desire, he is dragged away and enticed. [15]Then, after desire has conceived, it gives birth to sin; and sin, when it is full-grown, gives birth to death.

Jas 4:1 What causes fights and quarrels among you? Don't they come from your desires that battle within you? [2]You want something but don't get it. You kill and covet, but you cannot have what you want. You quarrel and fight. You do not have, because you do not ask God. [3]When you ask, you do not receive, because you ask with wrong motives, that you may spend what you get on your pleasures.

Known:

To God—

Ge 3:11 And he said, "Who told you that you were naked? Have you eaten from the tree that I commanded you not to eat from?"

Ge 4:10 The LORD said, "What have you done? Listen! Your brother's blood cries out to me from the ground.

Ge 18:13 Then the LORD said to Abraham, "Why did Sarah laugh and say, 'Will I really have a child, now that I am old?'

Ex 16:8 Moses also said, "You will know that it was the LORD when he gives you meat to eat in the evening and all the bread you want in the morning, because he has heard your grumbling against him. Who are we? You are not grumbling against us, but against the LORD."

⁹Then Moses told Aaron, "Say to the entire Israelite community, 'Come before the LORD, for he has heard your grumbling.'" (+Ex 16:12)

Nu 12:2 "Has the LORD spoken only through Moses?" they asked. "Hasn't he also spoken through us?" And the LORD heard this.

Nu 14:26 The LORD said to Moses and Aaron: ²⁷"How long will this wicked community grumble against me? I have heard the complaints of these grumbling Israelites.

Dt 1:34 When the LORD heard what you said, he was angry and solemnly swore:

Dt 31:21 And when many disasters and difficulties come upon them, this song will testify against them, because it will not be forgotten by their descendants. I know what they are disposed to do, even before I bring them into the land I promised them on oath."

Dt 32:34 "Have I not kept this in reserve and sealed it in my vaults? (+Jos 7:10-15; Job 7:10-15)

Job 10:14 If I sinned, you would be watching me and would not let my offense go unpunished.

Job 11:11 Surely he recognizes deceitful men; and when he sees evil, does he not take note?

Job 13:27 You fasten my feet in shackles; you keep close watch on all my paths by putting marks on the soles of my feet.

Job 14:16 Surely then you will count my steps but not keep track of my sin. ¹⁷My offenses will be sealed up in a bag; you will cover over my sin.

Job 20:27 The heavens will expose his guilt; the earth will rise up against him. (+Job 24:23)

Job 34:21 "His eyes are on the ways of men; he sees their every step. ²²There is no dark place, no deep shadow, where evildoers can hide.

Job 34:25 Because he takes note of their deeds, he overthrows them in the night and they are crushed.

Ps 44:20 If we had forgotten the name of our God or spread out our hands to a foreign god, ²¹would not God have discovered it, since he knows the secrets of the heart?

Ps 69:5 You know my folly, O God; my guilt is not hidden from you.

Ps 90:8 You have set our iniquities before you, our secret sins in the light of your presence.

Ps 94:11 The LORD knows the thoughts of man; he knows that they are futile.

Ecc 5:8 If you see the poor oppressed in a district, and justice and rights denied, do not be surprised at such things; for one official is eyed by a higher one, and over them both are others higher still.

Isa 29:15 Woe to those who go to great depths to hide their plans from the LORD, who do their work in darkness and think, "Who sees us? Who will know?"

Jer 2:22 Although you wash yourself with soda and use an abundance of soap, the stain of your guilt is still before me," declares the Sovereign LORD.

Jer 16:17 My eyes are on all their ways; they are not hidden from me, nor is their sin concealed from my eyes.

Jer 29:23 For they have done outrageous things in Israel; they have committed adultery with their neighbors' wives and in my name have spoken lies, which I did not tell them to do. I know it and am a witness to it," declares the LORD.

Eze 21:24 "Therefore this is what the Sovereign LORD says: 'Because you people have brought to mind your guilt by your open rebellion, revealing your sins in all that you do—because you have done this, you will be taken captive.

Hos 5:3 I know all about Ephraim; Israel is not hidden from me. Ephraim, you have now turned to prostitution; Israel is corrupt.

Hos 7:2 but they do not realize that I remember all their evil deeds. Their sins engulf them; they are always before me.

Am 5:12 For I know how many are your offenses and how great your sins. You oppress the righteous and take bribes and you deprive the poor of justice in the courts.

Am 9:1 I saw the Lord standing by the altar, and he said: "Strike the tops of the pillars so that the thresholds shake. Bring them down on the heads of all the people; those who are left I will kill with the sword. Not one will get away, none will escape. ²Though they dig down to the depths of the grave, from there my hand will take them. Though they climb up to the heavens, from there I will bring them down. ³Though they hide themselves on the top of Carmel, there I will hunt them down and seize them. Though they hide from me at the bottom of the sea, there I will command the serpent to bite them. ⁴Though they are driven into exile by their enemies, there I will command the sword to slay them. I will fix my eyes upon them for evil and not for good."

Am 9:8 "Surely the eyes of the Sovereign LORD are on the sinful kingdom. I will destroy it from the face of the earth—yet I will not totally destroy the house of Jacob," declares the LORD.

Hab 2:11 The stones of the wall will cry out, and the beams of the woodwork will echo it.

Mal 2:14 You ask, "Why?" It is because the LORD is acting as the witness between you and the wife of your youth, because you have broken faith with her, though she is your partner, the wife of your marriage covenant.

Mt 10:26 "So do not be afraid of them. There is nothing concealed that will not be disclosed, or hidden that will not be made known.

To Jesus—

Mt 26:46 Rise, let us go! Here comes my betrayer!"

Lk 6:8 But Jesus knew what they were thinking and said to the man with the shriveled hand, "Get up and stand in front of everyone." So he got up and stood there.

Jn 4:17 "I have no husband," she replied.

Jesus said to her, "You are right when you say you have no husband. ¹⁸The fact is, you have had five husbands, and the man you now have is not your husband. What you have just said is quite true."

¹⁹"Sir," the woman said, "I can see that you are a prophet.

Jn 5:42 but I know you. I know that you do not have the love of God in your hearts.

Jn 6:64 Yet there are some of you who do not believe." For Jesus had known from the beginning which of them did not believe and who would betray him.

Jn 13:11 For he knew who was going to betray him, and that was why he said not every one was clean.

Rev 2:23 I will strike her children dead. Then all the churches will know that I am he who searches hearts and minds, and I will repay each of you according to your deeds.

To the Holy Spirit (Ac 5:3-11).

See God, Omniscient; Jesus the Christ, Omniscience of.

Love of:

Job 15:16 how much less man, who is vile and corrupt, who drinks up evil like water!

Job 20:12 "Though evil is sweet in his mouth and he hides it under his tongue, ¹³though he cannot bear to let it go and keeps it in his mouth,

Pr 2:14 who delight in doing wrong and rejoice in the perverseness of evil, (+Pr 4:16)

Pr 4:17 They eat the bread of wickedness and drink the wine of violence.

Pr 10:23 A fool finds pleasure in evil conduct, but a man of understanding delights in wisdom.

Pr 16:30 He who winks with his eye is plotting perversity; he who purses his lips is bent on evil.

Pr 26:11 As a dog returns to its vomit, so a fool repeats his folly.

Jer 14:10 This is what the LORD says about this people: "They greatly love to wander; they do not restrain their feet. So the LORD does not accept them; he will now remember their wickedness and punish them for their sins."

Eze 20:16 because they rejected my laws and did not follow my decrees and desecrated my Sabbaths. For their hearts were devoted to their idols.

Hos 4:8 They feed on the sins of my people and relish their wickedness.

Hos 9:10 "When I found Israel, it was like finding grapes in the desert; when I saw your fathers, it was like seeing the early fruit on the fig tree. But when they came to Baal Peor, they consecrated themselves to that shameful idol and became as vile as the thing they loved.

Mic 7:3 Both hands are skilled in doing evil; the ruler demands gifts, the judge accepts bribes, the powerful dictate what they desire—they all conspire together.

Jn 3:19 This is the verdict: Light has come into the world, but men loved darkness instead of light because their deeds were evil. ²⁰Everyone who does evil hates the light, and will not come into the light for fear that his deeds will be exposed.

Jn 12:43 for they loved praise from men more than praise from God.

1Pe 3:19 through whom also he went and preached to the spirits in prison ²⁰who disobeyed long ago when God waited patiently in the days of Noah while the ark was being built. In it only a few people, eight in all, were saved through water,

2Pe 2:22 Of them the proverbs are true: "A dog returns to its vomit," and, "A sow that is washed goes back to her wallowing in the mud."

See Reprobacy; Wicked, Described As.

National, Punishment of:

Ge 6:5 The LORD saw how great man's wickedness on the earth had become, and that every inclination of the thoughts of his heart was only evil all the time. ⁶The LORD was grieved that he had made man on the earth, and his heart was filled with pain. ⁷So the LORD said, "I will wipe mankind, whom I have created, from the face of the earth—men and animals, and creatures that move along the ground, and birds of the air—for I am grieved that I have made them."

Ge 7:21 Every living thing that moved on the earth perished—birds, livestock, wild animals, all the creatures that swarm over the earth, and all mankind. ²²Everything on dry land that had the breath of life in its nostrils died.

Lev 26:14 " 'But if you will not listen to me and carry out all these commands, ¹⁵and if you reject my decrees and abhor my laws and fail to carry out all my commands and so violate my covenant, ¹⁶then I will do this to you: I will bring upon you sudden terror, wasting diseases and fever that will destroy your sight and drain away your life. You will plant seed in vain, because your enemies will eat it. ¹⁷I will set my face against you so that you will be defeated by your enemies; those who hate you will rule over you, and you will flee even when no one is pursuing you.

¹⁸" 'If after all this you will not listen to me, I will punish you for your sins seven times over. ¹⁹I will break down your stubborn pride and make the sky above you like iron and the ground beneath you like bronze. ²⁰Your strength will be spent in vain, because your soil will not yield its crops, nor will the trees of the land yield their fruit.

²¹" 'If you remain hostile toward me and refuse to listen to me, I will multiply your afflictions seven times over, as your sins deserve. ²²I will send wild animals against you, and they will rob you of your children, destroy your cattle and make you so few in number that your roads will be deserted.

²³" 'If in spite of these things you do not accept my correction but continue to be hostile toward me, ²⁴I myself will be hostile toward you and will afflict you for your sins seven times over. ²⁵And I will bring the sword upon you to avenge the breaking of the covenant. When you withdraw into your cities, I will send a plague among you, and you will be given into enemy hands. ²⁶When I cut off your supply of bread, ten women will be able to bake your bread in one oven, and they will dole out the bread by weight. You will eat, but you will not be satisfied.

²⁷" 'If in spite of this you still do not listen to me but continue to be hostile toward me, ²⁸then in my anger I will be hostile toward you, and I myself will punish you for your sins seven times over. ²⁹You will eat the flesh of your sons and the flesh of your daughters. ³⁰I will destroy your high places, cut down your incense altars and pile your dead bodies on the lifeless forms of your idols, and I will abhor you. ³¹I will turn your cities into ruins and lay waste your sanctuaries, and I will take no delight in the pleasing aroma of your offerings. ³²I will lay waste the land, so that your enemies who live there will be appalled. ³³I will scatter you among the nations and will draw out my sword and pursue you. Your land will be laid waste, and your cities will lie in ruins. ³⁴Then the land will enjoy its sabbath years all the time that it lies desolate and you are in the country of your enemies; then the land will rest and enjoy its sabbaths. ³⁵All the time that it lies desolate, the land will have the rest it did not have during the sabbaths you lived in it.

³⁶" 'As for those of you who are left, I will make their hearts so fearful in the lands of their enemies that the sound of a windblown leaf will put them to flight. They will run as though fleeing from the sword, and they will fall, even though no one is pursuing them. ³⁷They will stumble over one another as though fleeing from the sword, even though no one is pursuing them. So you will not be able to stand before your enemies. ³⁸You will perish

among the nations; the land of your enemies will devour you.

Dt 9:5 It is not because of your righteousness or your integrity that you are going in to take possession of their land; but on account of the wickedness of these nations, the LORD your God will drive them out before you, to accomplish what he swore to your fathers, to Abraham, Isaac and Jacob.

Job 34:29 But if he remains silent, who can condemn him? If he hides his face, who can see him? Yet he is over man and nation alike, **30**to keep a godless man from ruling, from laying snares for the people.

Isa 19:4 I will hand the Egyptians over to the power of a cruel master, and a fierce king will rule over them," declares the Lord, the LORD Almighty.

Jer 12:17 But if any nation does not listen, I will completely uproot and destroy it," declares the LORD.

Jer 25:31 The tumult will resound to the ends of the earth, for the LORD will bring charges against the nations; he will bring judgment on all mankind and put the wicked to the sword,'" declares the LORD.

32This is what the LORD Almighty says:

"Look! Disaster is spreading from nation to nation; a mighty storm is rising from the ends of the earth."

33At that time those slain by the LORD will be everywhere—from one end of the earth to the other. They will not be mourned or gathered up or buried, but will be like refuse lying on the ground.

34Weep and wail, you shepherds; roll in the dust, you leaders of the flock. For your time to be slaughtered has come; you will fall and be shattered like fine pottery. **35**The shepherds will have nowhere to flee, the leaders of the flock no place to escape. **36**Hear the cry of the shepherds, the wailing of the leaders of the flock, for the LORD is destroying their pasture. **37**The peaceful meadows will be laid waste because of the fierce anger of the LORD. **38**Like a lion he will leave his lair, and their land will become desolate because of the sword of the oppressor and because of the LORD's fierce anger.

Jer 46:28 Do not fear, O Jacob my servant, for I am with you," declares the LORD. "Though I completely destroy all the nations among which I scatter you, I will not completely destroy you. I will discipline you but only with justice; I will not let you go entirely unpunished."

Eze 16:49 "'Now this was the sin of your sister Sodom: She and her daughters were arrogant, overfed and unconcerned; they did not help the poor and needy. **50**They were haughty and did detestable things before me. Therefore I did away with them as you have seen."

Jnh 1:2 "Go to the great city of Nineveh and preach against it, because its wickedness has come up before me."

See Government; Nation.

Instances of:

The Sodomites (Ge 18:20). Egyptians (Ex 7-14). *See Egypt.* Israelites (Lev 26:14-39; Dt 32:30; 2Sa 21:1; 24:1; 2Ki 24:3-4,20; 2Ch 36:21; Ezr 9; Ne 9:36-37; Isa 1:21-23; 3:4,8; 5; 59:1-15; Jer 2; 5; 6; 9; 23; 30:11-15; La 1:3,8,14; 4:6; Eze 2; 7; 22; 24:6-14; 28:18; 33:25-26; 36:16-20; 39:23-24; 44:4-14; Hos 4:1-11; 6:8-10; 7:1-7; 13; Am 2; 5; Mic 6; 7:2-6). Babylon (Jer 50:45-46; 51). *See Babylon; See also prophecies cited under Assyria; Damascus; Edom; Elam; Ethiopia; Philistines; Syria.*

Not imputed:

To righteous (Ps 32:2; Ro 4:6-8), to ignorant (Ro 4:15; 5:13), to redeemed (2Co 5:19).

Progressive:

(Dt 29:19; 1Ki 16:31; Ps 1:1; Isa 5:18; 30:1; Jer 9:3; 16:11-12; Hos 13:2; 2Ti 3:13; Jas 1:14-15). Progressiveness exemplified in Joseph's brothers, from jealousy (Ge 37:4), to conspiracy (Ge 37:18), to murder (Ge 37:20). *See also, Cain; Abel.* Retroactive (Ps 7:15-16; 9:15-16; 10:2; 94:23; Pr 1:31; 5:22-23; 8:36; 11:5-6,27,29; Isa 3:9,11; Jer 2:19; 4:8; 7:19). A root of bitterness (Dt 29:18; Heb 12:15).

Punishment of:

Ge 2:17 but you must not eat from the tree of the knowledge of good and evil, for when you eat of it you will surely die."

Ge 3:16 To the woman he said, "I will greatly increase your pains in childbearing; with pain you will give birth to children. Your desire will be for your husband, and he will rule over you."

17To Adam he said, "Because you listened to your wife and ate from the tree about which I commanded you, 'You must not eat of it,' "Cursed is the ground because of you; through painful toil you will eat of it all the days of your life. **18**It will produce thorns and thistles for you, and you will eat the plants of the field. **19**By the sweat of your brow you will eat your food until you return to the ground, since from it you were taken; for dust you are and to dust you will return." (+Ge 4:10-14)

Ge 6:5 The LORD saw how great man's wickedness on the earth had become, and that every inclination of the thoughts of his heart was only evil all the time. **6**The LORD was grieved that he had made man on the earth, and his heart was filled with pain. **7**So the LORD said, "I will wipe mankind, whom I have created, from the face of the earth—men.and animals, and creatures that move along the ground, and birds of the air—for I am grieved that I have made them."

Ge 18:20 Then the LORD said, "The outcry against Sodom and Gomorrah is so great and their sin so grievous

Ge 19:13 because we are going to destroy this place. The outcry to the LORD against its people is so great that he has sent us to destroy it."

Ex 32:33 The LORD replied to Moses, "Whoever has sinned against me I will blot out of my book. **34**Now go, lead the people to the place I spoke of, and my angel will go before you. However, when the time comes for me to punish, I will punish them for their sin."

Ex 34:7 maintaining love to thousands, and forgiving wickedness, rebellion and sin. Yet he does not leave the guilty unpunished; he punishes the children and their children for the sin of the fathers to the third and fourth generation." (+Lev 19:8)

Lev 26:14 "'But if you will not listen to me and carry out all these commands, **15**and if you reject my decrees and abhor my laws and fail to carry out all my commands and so violate my covenant, **16**then I will do this to you: I will bring upon you sudden terror, wasting diseases and fever that will destroy your sight and drain away your life. You will plant seed in vain, because your enemies will eat it. **17**I will set my face against you so that you will be defeated by your enemies; those who hate you will rule over you, and you will flee even when no one is pursuing you.

18"'If after all this you will not listen to me, I will punish you for your sins seven times over. **19**I will break down your stubborn pride and make the sky above you like iron and the ground beneath you like bronze. **20**Your strength will be spent in vain, because your soil will not yield its crops, nor will the trees of the land yield their fruit. **21**"'If you remain hostile toward me and refuse to listen to me, I will multiply your afflictions seven times over, as your sins deserve.

Nu 15:30 "'But anyone who sins defiantly, whether native-born or alien, blasphemes the LORD, and that person must be cut off from his people. **31**Because he has despised the LORD's word and broken his commands, that person must surely be cut off; his guilt remains on him.'"

Nu 32:23 "But if you fail to do this, you will be sinning against the LORD; and you may be sure that your sin will find you out. (+Dt 28:15-68; 1Ki 13:33-34; 1Ch 21:7-27)

Job 21:17 "Yet how often is the lamp of the wicked snuffed out? How often does calamity come upon them, the fate God allots in his anger?

Ps 95:10 For forty years I was angry with that generation; I said, "They are a people whose hearts go astray, and they have not known my ways." **11**So I declared on oath in my anger, "They shall never enter my rest." (+Pr 1:24-32)

Jer 44:2 "This is what the LORD Almighty, the God of Israel, says: You saw the great disaster I brought on Jerusalem and on all the towns of Judah. Today they lie deserted and in ruins **3**because of the evil they have done. They provoked me to anger by burning incense and by worshiping other gods that neither they nor you nor your fathers ever knew. (+Jer 44:4)

Jer 44:5 But they did not listen or pay attention; they did not turn from their wickedness or stop burning incense to other gods. **6**Therefore, my fierce anger was poured out; it raged against the towns of Judah and the streets of Jerusalem and made them the desolate ruins they are today. (+Eze 18:4; Mt 25:41,46; Ro 6:23)

See Punishment; Wicked, Punishment of.

Pollution of:

Typified, by the defilement caused by touching any unclean thing (Lev 5:2-3; 11:24-28,31; 22:5), by eating any unclean thing (Lev 11:41-47), by touching a dead body (Lev 21:1; Nu 5:2; 9:6,10; 19:11,13,16; 31:19), by skin diseases (Lev 13:3,8,11,20,25,27,30,36,44-46,51,55; 14:44; Nu 5:2-3), by sexual impurities (Lev 15:1-33; 22:4; Dt 23:10-11).

Repentance for:

Commanded (2Ch 30:7-9; Job 36:10; Ps 34:14; Pr 1:22-23; Isa 22:12; 31:6; 44:22; 55:6-7; Jer 3:4,12-14,19; 6:8, 16; 18:11; 25:5; 26:13; 35:15; Eze 14:6; 18:30-32; 33:10-12; Da 4:27; Hos 6:1; 10:12; 14:1-2; Joel 1:14; 2:12-13,15-18; Am 4:12; Jnh 3:8-9; Zec 1:3; Mt 4:17; Mk 1:15; 6:12; Ac 2:38,40; 3:19; 8:22; 17:30; 20:21; Jas 4:8-10; Rev 2:5,16; 3:2-3,19).

Gift, of God (2Ti 2:25), of Christ (Ac 5:31). Tribulation leads to (Dt 4:30; 1Ki 8:33-50; 2Ch 6:36-39; Ps 107:4-6,10-14,17-20,23-30). Goodness of God leads to (Ro 2:4).

A condition of pardon (Lev 26:40-42; Dt 4:29-31; 30:1-3; 2Ch 7:14; Ne 1:9; Pr 28:13; Jer 7:5-7; 36:3; Eze 18:21-23,27-28,30-31; Mal 3:7; 1Jn 1:9).

Repugnant:

To God—

Ge 6:6 The LORD was grieved that he had made man on the earth, and his heart was filled with pain. **7**So the LORD said, "I will wipe mankind, whom I have created, from the face of the earth—men and animals, and creatures that move along the ground, and birds of the air—for I am grieved that I have made them." (+Lev 18:24-30)

Nu 22:32 The angel of the LORD asked him, "Why have you beaten your donkey these three times? I have come here to oppose you because your path is a reckless one before me.

Dt 25:16 For the LORD your God detests anyone who does these things, anyone who deals dishonestly.

Dt 32:19 The LORD saw this and rejected them because he was angered by his sons and daughters.

2Sa 11:27 After the time of mourning was over, David had her brought to his house, and she became his wife and bore him a son. But the thing David had done displeased the LORD.

1Ki 14:22 Judah did evil in the eyes of the LORD. By the sins they committed they stirred up his jealous anger more than their fathers had done.

Ps 5:4 You are not a God who takes pleasure in evil; with you the wicked cannot dwell. **5**The arrogant cannot stand in your presence; you hate all who do wrong. **6**You destroy those who tell lies; bloodthirsty and deceitful men the LORD abhors.

Ps 10:3 He boasts of the cravings of his heart; he blesses the greedy and reviles the LORD.

Ps 11:5 The LORD examines the righteous, but the wicked and those who love violence his soul hates.

Ps 78:59 When God heard them, he was very angry; he rejected Israel completely.

Ps 95:10 For forty years I was angry with that generation; I said, "They are a people whose hearts go astray, and they have not known my ways."

Ps 106:40 Therefore the LORD was angry with his people and abhorred his inheritance.

Pr 3:32 for the LORD detests a perverse man but takes the upright into his confidence.

Pr 6:16 There are six things the LORD hates, seven that are detestable to him: **17**haughty eyes, a lying tongue, hands that shed innocent blood, **18**a heart that devises wicked schemes, feet that are quick to rush into evil, **19**a false witness who pours out lies and a man who stirs up dissension among brothers. (+Pr 11:20)

Pr 15:8 The LORD detests the sacrifice of the wicked, but the prayer of the upright pleases him.

9The LORD detests the way of the wicked but he loves those who pursue righteousness.

Pr 15:26 The LORD detests the thoughts of the wicked, but those of the pure are pleasing to him.

Pr 21:27 The sacrifice of the wicked is detestable—how much more so when brought with evil intent!

Isa 43:24 You have not bought any fragrant calamus for me, or lavished on me the fat of your sacrifices. But you have burdened me with your sins and wearied me with your offenses.

Jer 25:7 "But you did not listen to me," declares the LORD, "and you have provoked me with what your hands have made, and you have brought harm to yourselves."

Jer 44:4 Again and again I sent my servants the prophets, who said, 'Do not do this detestable thing that I hate!'

Jer 44:21 "Did not the LORD remember and think about the incense burned in the towns of Judah and the streets of Jerusalem by you and your fathers, your kings and your officials and the people of the land? **22**When the LORD could no longer endure your wicked actions and the detestable things you did, your land became an object of cursing and a desolate waste without inhabitants, as it is today.

Hab 1:13 Your eyes are too pure to look on evil; you cannot tolerate wrong. Why then do you tolerate the treacherous? Why are you silent while the wicked swallow up those more righteous than themselves?

Zec 8:17 do not plot evil against your neighbor, and do not love to swear falsely. I hate all this," declares the LORD.

Lk 16:15 He said to them, "You are the ones who justify yourselves in the eyes of men, but God knows your hearts. What is highly valued among men is detestable in God's sight. *See God, Holiness of.*

To Christ—

Rev 2:6 But you have this in your favor: You hate the practices of the Nicolaitans, which I also hate.

Rev 2:15 Likewise you also have those who hold to the teaching of the Nicolaitans.

To the righteous—

Ge 39:7 and after a while his master's wife took notice of Joseph and said, "Come to bed with me!"

8But he refused. "With me in charge," he told her, "my master does not concern himself with anything in the house; everything he owns he has entrusted to my care. **9**No one is greater in this house than I am. My master has withheld nothing from me except you, because you are his wife. How then could I do such a wicked thing and sin against God?"

Dt 7:26 Do not bring a detestable thing into your house or you, like it, will be set apart for destruction. Utterly abhor and detest it, for it is set apart for destruction.

Job 1:1 In the land of Uz there lived a man whose name was Job. This man was blameless and upright; he feared God and shunned evil.

Job 21:16 But their prosperity is not in their own hands, so I stand aloof from the counsel of the wicked.

Job 22:18 Yet it was he who filled their houses with good things, so I stand aloof from the counsel of the wicked.

Ps 26:5 I abhor the assembly of evildoers and refuse to sit with the wicked.

Ps 26:9 Do not take away my soul along with sinners, my life with bloodthirsty men,

Ps 84:10 Better is one day in your courts than a thousand elsewhere; I would rather be a doorkeeper in the house of my God than dwell in the tents of the wicked.

Ps 101:3 I will set before my eyes no vile thing. The deeds of faithless men I hate; they will not cling to me.

4Men of perverse heart shall be far from me; I will have nothing to do with evil.

Ps 101:7 No one who practices deceit will dwell in my house; no one who speaks falsely will stand in my presence.

Ps 119:104 I gain understanding from your precepts; therefore I hate every wrong path.

Ps 119:113 I hate double-minded men, but I love your law. (+Ps 119:128)

Ps 119:163 I hate and abhor falsehood but I love your law.

Ps 120:2 Save me, O LORD, from lying lips and from deceitful tongues.

Ps 120:5 Woe to me that I dwell in Meshech, that I live among the tents of Kedar! **6**Too long have I lived among those who hate peace. **7**I am a man of peace; but when I speak, they are for war.

Ps 139:19 If only you would slay the wicked, O God! Away from me, you bloodthirsty men! **20**They speak of you with evil intent; your adversaries misuse your name. **21**Do I not hate those who hate you, O LORD, and abhor those who rise up against you? **22**I have nothing but hatred for them; I count them my enemies.

Pr 8:13 To fear the LORD is to hate evil; I hate pride and arrogance, evil behavior and perverse speech.

Pr 29:27 The righteous detest the dishonest; the wicked detest the upright.

Jer 9:2 Oh, that I had in the desert a lodging place for travelers, so that I might leave my people and go away from them; for they are all adulterers, a crowd of unfaithful people.

Ro 7:15 I do not understand what I do. For what I want to do I do not do, but what I hate I do.

Ro 7:19 For what I do is not the good I want to do; no, the evil I do not want to do—this I keep on doing.

Ro 7:23 but I see another law at work in the members of my body, waging war against the law of my mind and making me a prisoner of the law of sin at work within my members. **24**What a wretched man I am! Who will rescue me from this body of death?

2Pe 2:7 and if he rescued Lot, a righteous man, who was distressed by the filthy lives of lawless men **8**(for that righteous man, living among them day after day, was tormented in his righteous soul by the lawless deeds he saw and heard)—

Jude 23 snatch others from the fire and save them; to others show mercy, mixed with fear—hating even the clothing stained by corrupted flesh.

Rev 2:2 I know your deeds, your hard work and your perseverance. I know that you cannot tolerate wicked men, that you have tested those who claim to be apostles but are not, and have found them false. *See Holiness.*

Separates From God:

Dt 31:17 On that day I will become angry with them and forsake them; I will hide my face from them, and they will be destroyed. Many disasters and difficulties will come upon them, and on that day they will ask, 'Have not these disasters come upon us because our God is not with us?' **18**And I will certainly hide my face on that day because of all their wickedness in turning to other gods. (+Jos 7:12; 2Ch 24:20)

Ps 78:59 When God heard them, he was very angry; he rejected Israel completely. **60**He abandoned the tabernacle of Shiloh, the tent he had set up among men. **61**He sent [the ark of] his might into captivity, his splendor into the hands of the enemy.

Isa 59:1 Surely the arm of the LORD is not too short to save, nor his ear too dull to hear. **2**But your iniquities have separated you from your God; your sins have hidden his face from you, so that he will not hear.

Isa 64:7 No one calls on your name or strives to lay hold of you; for you have hidden your face from us and made us waste away because of our sins.

Eze 23:18 When she carried on her prostitution openly and exposed her nakedness, I turned away from her in disgust, just as I had turned away from her sister.

Hos 9:12 Even if they rear children, I will bereave them of every one. Woe to them when I turn away from them!

Am 3:2 "You only have I chosen of all the families of the earth; therefore I will punish you for all your sins." **3**Do two walk together unless they have agreed to do so?

Mic 3:4 Then they will cry out to the LORD, but he will not answer them. At that time he will hide his face from them because of the evil they have done. (+Mt 7:23; 25:41)

Lk 13:27 "But he will reply, 'I don't know you or where you come from. Away from me, all you evildoers!'

Ro 8:7 the sinful mind is hostile to God. It does not submit to God's law, nor can it do so.

Heb 12:14 Make every effort to live in peace with all men and to be holy; without holiness no one will see the Lord. *See God, Holiness of; Wicked, Punishment of.*

Works spiritual death (Ro 5:12,21; 6:21,23; 7:13; Eph 2:1; Jas 1:15).

By the righteous, dishonors God (2Sa 12:14), a reproach (2Sa 12:14).

Against the Holy Spirit, unpardonable (Mt 12:31; Mk 3:29; Lk 12:10; 1Jn 5:16-17).

Typified:

The design of the Mosaic ordinances was to impress the Israelites, and through them the consciences of all people for all time, with the offensiveness of sin. To produce this effect the Mosaic law contained numerous types of sin, the design of which was to teach that sin is repugnant to God, and that it separates from God and from the righteous. Hence, we find many object lessons about uncleanness and defilement, blemishes, separation from the congregation, atonements from the congregation, atonements and atoning sacrifices, washings and purifications; all of which were designed to typify the corruption of sin and the necessity, in order to please a holy Yahweh, that sin must be purged and the heart purified.

By blemishes that disqualified animals for sacrifices (Ex 12:5; Lev 1:10; 3:1,6; 4:3,23; 5:15; 6:6; 9:2-3; 22:19-22; Nu 28:3,9,11,19,31; 29:2,8,13,17,20,23,26,29,32,36). By blemishes of priests, disqualifying them from performing sacred offices (Lev 21:17-23). By unclean animals (Lev 11:1-47; 20:25; Dt 14:3-20).

Its effect, in separating the wicked from God and from the righteous, by excluding the defiled and unclean from the congregation (Lev 7:20,25,27; 13:5,26,33; 15:19; 17:9-10,15; 18:29; 19:8; 20:3-6; Nu 5:2-3; 19:20; Dt 23:10-11).

Words for:

Missing the mark (Ro 5:12). Overstepping the boundary, or trespassing (Ro 4:15). Blunder, or offense (Ro 5:15). Disobedience, or disregard (Ro 5:19). Unrighteousness (Ro 1:18). Ungodliness (Ro 1:18). Lawlessness (Tit 2:14).

SIN, CITY OF *See Pelusium.*

SIN, DESERT OF *(desert of clay* or possibly *desert of Sin [pagan moon god]).* The wilderness through which the Israelites passed; between Elim and Mount Sinai (Ex 16:1; 17:1; Nu 33:11-12).

SIN MONEY NIV "money from ... sin offerings" (2Ki 12:16). *See Blood Money.*

SINA *See Sinai.*

SINAI, MOUNT OF; DESERT OF [6099, 4982] *(Sin [pagan moon god]; glare [from white chalk]* ISBE).

1. A mountain in the peninsula E of the Red Sea. Israelites arrive at in their wanderings in the wilderness (Ex 19:2; Dt 1:2). The law delivered to Moses upon (Ex 19:3-25; 20; 24:12-18; 32:15-16; 34:2-4; Lev 7:38; 25:1; 26:46; 27:34; Nu 3:1; Dt 4:15; 5:26; 29:1; 33:2; Ne 9:13; Ps 68:8,17; Mal 4:4; Ac 7:30,38).

God establishes a covenant (Ex 19-24). *See Covenants, Major in the Old Testament.*

Figurative of the law (Gal 4:24-25).

See Horeb; Israel, Israelites.

2. Desert of. Israelites journeyed in (Nu 10:12), kept the Passover in (Nu 9:1-5), numbered in (Nu 26:64).

SINCERITY [*537, 605, 1636].

NIV+ SINCERE, SINCERELY

Does not exempt from guilt (Ge 20). *See Ignorance, Sins of.* Forgiveness of enemies must be sincere (Mt 18:35). Servants must render honest service (Eph 6:5-7).

Whatever is done must be in (1Co 10:31). Jesus was an example of (1Pe 2:22). Ministers should be examples of (Tit 2:7). Opposed to human wisdom (2Co 1:12).

Should characterize our love to God (2Co 8:8,24), our love to Jesus (Eph 6:24), our service to God (Jos 24:14), our faith (1Ti 1:5), our love to one another (Ro 12:9; 1Pe 1:22; 1Jn 3:18), our whole conduct (2Co 1:12), the preaching of the Gospel (2Co 2:17; 1Th 2:3-5).

A characteristic of the doctrines of the Gospel (1Pe 2:2). The Gospel sometimes preached without (Php 1:16). The wicked devoid of (Ps 5:9; 55:21). Exhortations to (1Co 5:8; 1Pe 2:1). Blessedness of (Ps 32:2).

Exemplified:

By men of Zebulun (1Ch 12:33). By Hezekiah (Isa 38:3). By Nathanael (Jn 1:47). By Paul (2Co 1:12). By Timothy (2Ti 1:5). By Lois and Eunice (2Ti 1:5).

SINEW [1630, *5278*].

NIV+ SINEWS

Tendon, in contrast to bone structure (Ge 32:32; Job 40:17; Eze 37:6-8).

SINFULNESS [222, 2627, 2628, 2629, 2633, 3202+ 4202, 6411, 7322, 8278, *279, 281, 283, 2123, 4505, 4920, 4922*].

NIV+ See SIN

Universal (1Ki 8:46; 2Ch 6:36; Ps 14:3; Ecc 7:20; Ro 3:23; 11:32; 1Jn 1:8,10). *See Depravity; Sin.*

SINGERS [2952, 5834, 8876, 8877, 10234]. *See Music.*

SINGLE EYE NIV "good eye"; connotes generosity (Mt 6:22). *See Eye.*

SINIM *See Aswan.*

SINITES [6098]. A tribe of Canaanites (Ge 10:17; 1Ch 1:15).

SINLESSNESS

Ps 119:3 They do nothing wrong; they walk in his ways.

The believer's goal—

Php 1:9 And this is my prayer: that your love may abound more and more in knowledge and depth of insight, [10]so that you may be able to discern what is best and may be pure and blameless until the day of Christ, [11]filled with the fruit of righteousness that comes through Jesus Christ—to the glory and praise of God.

1Th 3:13 May he strengthen your hearts so that you will be blameless and holy in the presence of our God and Father when our Lord Jesus comes with all his holy ones.

1Th 5:23 May God himself, the God of peace, sanctify you through and through. May your whole spirit, soul and body be kept blameless at the coming of our Lord Jesus Christ.

1Pe 4:1 Therefore, since Christ suffered in his body, arm yourselves also with the same attitude, because he who has suffered in his body is done with sin. [2]As a result, he does not live the rest of his earthly life for evil human desires, but rather for the will of God.

1Jn 3:6 No one who lives in him keeps on sinning. No one who continues to sin has either seen him or known him.

1Jn 3:9 No one who is born of God will continue to sin, because God's seed remains in him; he cannot go on sinning, because he has been born of God. (+1Jn 5:18)

Impossible to attain—

1Jn 1:8 If we claim to be without sin, we deceive ourselves and the truth is not in us.

1Jn 1:10 If we claim we have not sinned, we make him out to be a liar and his word has no place in our lives.

SINNER [2627, 2629, 2633, 7321, *283, 283+467, 283+476, 1794, 4126*]. *See Wicked.*

SIN OFFERING [2627, 2631, 2633, 10260, *281*].

Was offered:

For sins of ignorance (Lev 4:2,13,22,27). At the consecration of priests (Ex 29:10,14; Lev 8:14). At the consecration of Levites (Nu 8:8). At the expiration of a Nazirite's vow (Nu 6:14). On the Day of Atonement (Lev 16:3,9). Was a most holy sacrifice (Lev 6:25,29). Probable origin of (Ge 4:4,7).

Consisted of:

A young bull for priests (Lev 4:3; 9:2,8; 16:3,6). A young bull or he-goat for the congregation (Lev 4:14; 16:9; 2Ch 29:23). A male goat for a ruler (Lev 4:23). A female goat or female lamb for a private person (Lev 4:28,32). Sins of the offerer transferred to, by laying on of hands (Lev 4:4,15,24,29; 2Ch 29:23). Was killed in the same place as the burnt offering (Lev 4:24; 6:25).

The blood of:

For a priest or for the congregation, brought by the priest into the tabernacle (Lev 4:5,16). For the priest or for the congregation, sprinkled seven times before the Lord, outside the veil, by the priest with his finger (Lev 4:6,17). For a priest or for the congregation, put upon the horns of the altar of incense (Lev 4:7,18). For a ruler or for a private person put upon the horns of the altar of burnt offering by the priest with his finger (Lev 4:25,30). In every case poured at the foot of the altar of burnt offering (Lev 4:7,18,30; 9:9). Fat, kidneys, etc. burned on the altar of burnt offering (Lev 4:8-10,19,26,31; 9:10).

When for a priest or the congregation, the skin, carcass, burned without the camp (Lev 4:11-12,21; 6:30; 9:11). Was eaten by the priests in a holy place when its blood had not been brought into the tabernacle (Lev 6:26,29, w 30). Aaron rebuked for burning and not eating that of the congregation, its blood not having been brought into the tabernacle (Lev 10:16-18, w 9:9,15). Whatever touched the flesh of, was rendered holy (Lev 6:27). Garments sprinkled with the blood of, to be washed (Lev 6:27). Laws respecting the vessels used for boiling the flesh of (Lev 6:28). Was typical of Christ's sacrifice (2Co 5:21; Heb 13:11-13).

SION *See Siyon, Mount; Zion.*

SIPHMOTH [8560]. A city of Judah (1Sa 30:28).

SIPPAI [5205]. A Philistine giant (1Ch 20:4). Called Saph (2Sa 21:18).

SIRACH, SON OF The author of Ecclesiasticus also known as the Wisdom of Jesus ben Sirach; wrote c. 190-170 B.C. *See Apocrypha.*

SIRAH [6241]. A well, c. one mile N of Hebron (2Sa 3:26).

SIRION [8590] (*coat of mail*).
NIV+ HERMON
A Sidonian name of Mount Hermon (Dt 3:9; Ps 29:6). *See Hermon, Mount; Siyon, Mount.*

SISAMAI *See Sismai.*

SISERA [6102].
NIV+ SISERA'S
1. Captain of the army of Jabin, king of Hazor; defeated in battle by Barak; slain by Deborah (Jdg 4:5; 1Sa 12:9; Ps 83:9).
2. Ancestor of the temple servants who returned with Zerubbabel (Ezr 2:53; Ne 7:55).

SISMAI [6183] (possibly *belonging to Sisam [pagan god]*). The son of Eleasah (1Ch 2:40).

SISTER [295, 1426, 1860, 3304, *80*].
NIV+ SISTER-IN-LAW, SISTER'S, SISTERS
1. A full or half-sister (Ge 20:12; Dt 27:22).
2. Wife (SS 4:9).
3. A woman of the same country or tribe (Nu 25:18).
4. Blood relatives (Mt 13:56; Mk 6:3).
5. Female fellow Christian (Ro 16:1; 2Jn 15).

SISTRUMS [4983]. Percussion instruments (2Sa 6:5). *See Music, Instruments of.*

SITHRI [6262] (possibly *Yahweh is my hiding place*). Kohathite Levite; cousin of Aaron and Moses (Ex 6:22).

SITNAH [8479] (*hostility*). A well dug by Isaac between Gerar and Rehoboth (Ge 26:21).

SIVAN [6094]. Month three in sacred sequence (Est 8:9), month nine in civil sequence. Time of the wheat harvest (May-June) and the Feast of Weeks or Pentecost (Dt 16:9-12). *See Month, 3.*

SIYON, MOUNT [8481].
NIV+ HERMON
A name of Mount Hermon (Dt 4:48, ftn w 3:9). *See Hermon, Mount; Sirion.*

SKEPTICISM (Job 21:15; 22:17; Ps 14:1; 53:1; Zep 1:12; Mal 3:14). Of Pharaoh (Ex 5:2). Of Thomas (Jn 20:25-28). *See Unbelief.*

SKILL [*682, 1067, 2681, 2682, 2683, 3110, 3359, 4542, 5492*].
NIV+ SKILLED, SKILLFUL, SKILLFULLY, SKILLS
Examples of (Ex 28:3; 31:3; 35:35; 38:23; 1Ki 7:14; 1Ch 22:15; 2Ch 2:13; 26:15).

SKIN [1414, 1654, 2293, 2827, 5532, 5574, 6425+, 7320, 7665, 7669, *829*].
NIV+ SKINNED, SKINS, SMOOTH-SKINNED
Clothes of (Ge 3:21). For covering the tabernacle (Ex 25:5; Nu 4:8-14). Diseases of (Lev 13:38-39; Dt 28:27,35; Job 7:5). *See Boil; Leprosy.*

SKINK [2793]. Unclean for food (Lev 11:30). *See Animals.*

SKIRT [8670, 8767].
NIV+ SKIRTS
See Dress.

SKULL [1653, 7721, *3191*].
NIV+ SKULLS
See Golgotha.

SKY [8836, 9028, 10723, *113, 4041*].
NIV+ SKIES
Clouds, firmament; also used figuratively (Dt 33:26).

SLANDER [224, 1804, 1819, 1984+5989, 4387, 8078, 8215, 8476, 8806, *1059, 1060, 2895, 2896, 3367*].

NIV+ SLANDERED, SLANDERER, SLANDERERS, SLANDERING, SLANDEROUS, SLANDEROUSLY, SLANDERS

Characteristics of:

Comes from the evil heart (Lk 6:45). Often arises from hatred (Ps 109:3). Idleness leads to (1Ti 5:13).

The wicked addicted to—

Ps 50:20 You speak continually against your brother and slander your own mother's son.

Hypocrites addicted to (Pr 11:9). A characteristic of the devil (Rev 12:10). The wicked love (Ps 52:4).

They who indulge in, are fools—

Pr 10:18 He who conceals his hatred has lying lips, and whoever spreads slander is a fool.

Women warned against (Tit 2:3). Ministers' wives should avoid (1Ti 3:11). Christ was exposed to (Ps 35:11; Mt 26:60). Rulers exposed to (Jude 8). Ministers exposed to (Ro 3:8; 2Co 6:8). The nearest relations exposed to (Ps 50:20). Saints exposed to (Ps 38:12; 109:2; 1Pe 4:4).

Saints should, keep their tongues from (Ps 34:13, w 1Pe 3:10), lay aside (Eph 4:31), be warned against (Tit 3:1-2), give no occasion for (1Pe 2:12; 3:16)

Return good for—

1Co 4:13 when we are slandered, we answer kindly. Up to this moment we have become the scum of the earth, the refuse of the world.

Blessed in enduring (Mt 5:11), characterized as avoiding (Ps 15:1,3).

Should not be listened to (1Sa 24:9)

Causes anger—

Pr 25:23 As a north wind brings rain, so a sly tongue brings angry looks.

A fruit of wickedness—

Ro 1:29 They have become filled with every kind of wickedness, evil, greed and depravity. They are full of envy, murder, strife, deceit and malice. They are gossips, [30]slanderers, God-haters, insolent, arrogant and boastful; they invent ways of doing evil; they disobey their parents;

2Co 12:20 For I am afraid that when I come I may not find you as I want you to be, and you may not find me as you want me to be. I fear that there may be quarreling, jealousy, outbursts of anger, factions, slander, gossip, arrogance and disorder. (+2Pe 2:10)

Forbidden—

Ex 23:1 "Do not spread false reports. Do not help a wicked man by being a malicious witness. (+1Ti 3:11; Tit 2:3; 3:2)

Jas 4:11 Brothers, do not slander one another. Anyone who speaks against his brother or judges him speaks against the law and judges it. When you judge the law, you are not keeping it, but sitting in judgment on it.

1Pe 2:1 Therefore, rid yourselves of all malice and all deceit, hypocrisy, envy, and slander of every kind.

Punishment for (Dt 19:16-21):

Dt 22:13 If a man takes a wife and, after lying with her, dislikes her [14]and slanders her and gives her a bad name, saying, "I married this woman, but when I approached her, I did not find proof of her virginity," [15]then the girl's father and mother shall bring proof that she was a virgin to the town elders at the gate. [16]The girl's father will say to the elders, "I gave my daughter in marriage to this man, but he dislikes her. [17]Now he has slandered her and said, 'I did not find your daughter to be a virgin.' But here is the proof of my daughter's virginity." Then her parents shall display the cloth before the elders of the town, [18]and the elders shall take the man and punish him. [19]They shall fine him a hundred shekels of silver and give them to the girl's father, because this man has given an Israelite virgin a bad name. She shall continue to be his wife; he must not divorce her as long as he lives.

Ps 101:5 Whoever slanders his neighbor in secret, him will I put to silence; whoever has haughty eyes and a proud heart, him will I not endure.

1Co 6:10 nor thieves nor the greedy nor drunkards nor slanderers nor swindlers will inherit the kingdom of God.

Instances of:

Joseph, by Potiphar's wife (Ge 39:14-18). Land of Canaan misrepresented by the spies (Nu 14:36). Of Mephibosheth, by Ziba (2Sa 16:3; 19:24-30).

Of David, by his enemies (Ps 31:13; 35:21)—

Ps 41:5 My enemies say of me in malice, "When will he die and his name perish?" [6]Whenever one comes to see me, he speaks falsely, while his heart gathers slander; then he goes out and spreads it abroad.

[7]All my enemies whisper together against me; they imagine the worst for me, saying, [8]"A vile disease has beset him; he will never get up from the place where he lies." [9]Even my close friend, whom I trusted, he who shared my bread, has lifted up his heel against me. (+Ps 64:3; 140:3)

Of Naboth, by Jezebel (1Ki 21:9-14).

Of Jeremiah, by the Jews—

Jer 6:28 They are all hardened rebels, going about to slander. They are bronze and iron; they all act corruptly. (+Jer 18:18)

Of the Jews, of one another—

Jer 9:4 "Beware of your friends; do not trust your brothers. For every brother is a deceiver, and every friend a slanderer.

Of Jesus, by the Jews falsely charging that he was a drunkard (Mt 11:19), that he blasphemed (Mk 14:64; Jn 5:18), that he had a devil (Jn 8:48,52; 10:20), that he was seditious (Lk 22:65; 23:5), that he was a king (Lk 23:2; Jn 18:37, w 19:1-5). Of Paul. *See Paul.*

Effects of:

Separating friends (Pr 16:28; 17:9), deadly wounds (Pr 18:8; 26:22), strife (Pr 26:20), discord among brothers (Pr 6:19), murder (Ps 31:13; Eze 22:9). End of, is wicked madness (Ecc 10:13). People shall give account for (Mt 12:36).

The Tongue:

Job 5:21 You will be protected from the lash of the tongue, and need not fear when destruction comes.

Is venomous (Ps 140:3; Ecc 10:11), is destructive (Pr 11:9).

See Accusation, False; Backbiting; False Witness; Falsehood; Speaking or Speech, Evil.

SLAVE, SLAVERY [*563, 4989, 5601, 6268, 6269, 6275, 6683, 6806, 9148, *1525, 1526, 1528, 1529, 1530, 4087*].

NIV+ ENSLAVE, ENSLAVED, ENSLAVES, ENSLAVING, SLAVES, SLAVING

Both the OT and the NT included regulations for societal situations such as slavery and divorce (Dt 24:1-4), which were the results of the hardness of hearts (Mt 19:8). Such regulations did not encourage or condone such situations but were divinely given, practical ways of dealing with the realities of the day.

See Servant.

SLAYER, THE [2222].

NIV+ SLAIN, SLAY, SLAYS, SLEW

NIV "one accused of murder" (Nu 35:11-28; Dt 4:42; 19:3-6; Jos 20:3). *See Cities of Refuge.*

SLEEP [*448+995, 3359, 3822, 3825, 5670, 8101, 8886, 9104, 9554, 10733, *2761, 3121*].

NIV+ ASLEEP, SLEEPER, SLEEPING, SLEEPLESS, SLEEPS, SLEEPY, SLEPT

From God (Ps 127:2). Of the sluggard (Pr 6:9-10). Of Jesus (Mt 8:24; Mk 4:38; Lk 8:23). A symbol of death (Job 14:12; Mt 9:24; Mk 5:39; Lk 8:52; Jn 11:11-12; 1Th 4:14). *See Death, Physical.*

SLIME [1014+8622, 8846].

NIV+ SLIMY

Slime pit (Job 9:31; Ps 40:2). *See Caulkers; Pitch; Tar.*

SLING [74+928+2021, 5275, 7843, 7845, 7847].

NIV+ SLINGS, SLINGSTONES, SLUNG

Used for throwing stones (Pr 26:8). David slays Goliath with (1Sa 17:40-50). Dexterous use of (Jdg 20:16; 2Ki 3:25; 2Ch 26:14).

SLIP [3655, 4572, 4880, 5048, 5742, 6073, 7520, *1728, 1767, 4208*].

NIV+ SLIPPED, SLIPPERY, SLIPPING, SLIPS

A cutting from a plant (Isa 17:10).

SLOTHFULNESS

Character of the Sluggard:

Pr 10:4 Lazy hands make a man poor, but diligent hands bring wealth.

[5]He who gathers crops in summer is a wise son, but he who sleeps during harvest is a disgraceful son.

Pr 10:26 As vinegar to the teeth and smoke to the eyes, so is a sluggard to those who send him. (+Pr 13:4; 15:19; 18:9; 19:15,24; 20:4; 21:25; 22:13; 23:21; 24:30-34; 26:13-16)

Isa 56:10 Israel's watchmen are blind, they all lack knowledge; they are all mute dogs, they cannot bark; they lie around and dream, they love to sleep.

Results in:

Poverty (Pr 10:4-5)—

Pr 12:24 Diligent hands will rule, but laziness ends in slave labor.

Pr 12:27 The lazy man does not roast his game, but the diligent man prizes his possessions.

Pr 13:4 The sluggard craves and gets nothing, but the desires of the diligent are fully satisfied.

Pr 15:19 The way of the sluggard is blocked with thorns, but the path of the upright is a highway.

Pr 18:9 One who is slack in his work is brother to one who destroys.

Pr 19:15 Laziness brings on deep sleep, and the shiftless man goes hungry.

Pr 19:24 The sluggard buries his hand in the dish; he will not even bring it back to his mouth!

Pr 20:4 A sluggard does not plow in season; so at harvest time he looks but finds nothing.

Pr 21:25 The sluggard's craving will be the death of him, because his hands refuse to work.

Pr 23:21 for drunkards and gluttons become poor, and drowsiness clothes them in rags.

Pr 24:30 I went past the field of the sluggard, past the vineyard of the man who lacks judgment; [31]thorns had come up everywhere, the ground was covered with weeds,

and the stone wall was in ruins. [32]I applied my heart to what I observed and learned a lesson from what I saw: [33]A little sleep, a little slumber, a little folding of the hands to rest— [34]and poverty will come on you like a bandit and scarcity like an armed man.

Pr 26:13 The sluggard says, "There is a lion in the road, a fierce lion roaming the streets!"

[14]As a door turns on its hinges, so a sluggard turns on his bed.

[15]The sluggard buries his hand in the dish; he is too lazy to bring it back to his mouth.

[16]The sluggard is wiser in his own eyes than seven men who answer discreetly.

Ecc 10:18 If a man is lazy, the rafters sag; if his hands are idle, the house leaks.

Condemnation—

Mt 25:26 "His master replied, 'You wicked, lazy servant! So you knew that I harvest where I have not sown and gather where I have not scattered seed? [27]Well then, you should have put my money on deposit with the bankers, so that when I returned I would have received it back with interest.

Condemned:

The ant, an example against—

Pr 6:6 Go to the ant, you sluggard; consider its ways and be wise! [7]It has no commander, no overseer or ruler, [8]yet it stores its provisions in summer and gathers its food at harvest.

[9]How long will you lie there, you sluggard? When will you get up from your sleep? [10]A little sleep, a little slumber, a little folding of the hands to rest— [11]and poverty will come on you like a bandit and scarcity like an armed man.

Christians are not to be lazy—

Ro 12:11 Never be lacking in zeal, but keep your spiritual fervor, serving the Lord.

2Th 3:10 For even when we were with you, we gave you this rule: "If a man will not work, he shall not eat."

[11]We hear that some among you are idle. They are not busy; they are busybodies. [12]Such people we command and urge in the Lord Jesus Christ to settle down and earn the bread they eat.

Heb 6:12 We do not want you to become lazy, but to imitate those who through faith and patience inherit what has been promised.

See Idleness; Industry.

SLOW [*336, 800, *1096*].

NIV+ SLOWLY, SLOWNESS

Always refers to the passions in the OT (Ne 9:17; Ps 103:8; 145:8).

SLUG [8671]. Melting away (Ps 58:8). *See Animals.*

SLUGGARD [6789].

NIV+ SLUGGARD'S

See Idleness; Laziness; Slothfulness.

SMITH A worker in metals. Tubal-Cain (Ge 4:22). Bezalel (Ex 31:1-11). The Philistines (1Sa 13:19). Jewish, carried captive to Babylon (2Ki 24:14; Jer 24:1). The manufacturers of idols (Isa 41:7; 44:12). Genius of, from God (Ex 31:3-5; 35:30-35; Isa 54:16).

SMITING *See Assault and Battery.*

SMITING AND SCOURGING OF JESUS *See Flog, Flogging.*

SMOKE [5366, 5368, 6727, 6939, 6940, 6942, 7798, *2837*].

NIV+ SMOKING

Figurative: (Isa 6:4; Hos 13:3).

SMYRNA [*5044*]. An ancient seaport on the W coast of Asia Minor forty miles N of Ephesus; the seat of an important Christian church (Rev 1:11; 2:8-11).

SNAIL NIV "skink" (Lev 11:30), "slug" (Ps 58:8). *See Animals.*

SNAKE *See Serpent.*

SNARE [1335, 3338, 3687, 4613, 5178, 5180, 7062, 7545, 8407, 8938, *4075*].

NIV+ ENSNARE, ENSNARED, SNARED, SNARES

A device for catching birds and animals (Ps 124:7), also used figuratively (Ps 91:3).

SNIFF [5870, 8634].

NIV+ SNIFFING

Smelling the wind (Jer 2:24). Showing contempt for God's sacrifices (Mal 1:13).

SNOUT [678]. Long projecting nose of a beast, as of a pig (Pr 11:22).

SNOW [8919, 8920, 10758, *5946*].

NIV+ SNOWS, SNOWY

Falls in elevated areas of Israel in January and February, but soon melts; Mt. Hermon covered with snow even in summer; used for cooling purposes. Used figuratively for righteousness and purity (Isa 1:18; Ps 51:7; Mt 28:3; Rev 1:14).

SNUFF [1980, 3882, *4931*]. *See Sniff.*

SNUFFDISHES NIV "trays" for the lamps of the tabernacle and temple. *See Wick Trimmers.*

SNUFFERS *See Wick Trimmers.*

SO [6046]. A king of Egypt with whom Hoshea, king of Israel, made an alliance, so bringing down the wrath of Assyria upon Israel (2Ki 17:4), possibly Oskoron.

SOAP [1383, 8921]. In a modern sense was unknown in OT times, but launderers made a cleansing material compounded from vegetable alkali (Jer 2:22; Mal 3:2). *See Soda.*

SOBERMINDEDNESS [*5404*]. Commanded (Ro 12:3; 1Pe 1:13; 4:7; 5:8), to women (1Ti 3:11; Tit 2:4-5), to men (Tit 2:2,6), to ministers (1Ti 3:2; Tit 1:8).

SOBRIETY [3516+3655, *5404*].

NIV+ SOBER

Commanded (1Pe 1:13; 5:8). The Gospel designed to teach (Tit 2:12). With watchfulness (1Th 5:6). With prayer (1Pe 4:7). Required in ministers (1Ti 3:2-3; Tit 1:8), wives of ministers (1Ti 3:11), aged men (Tit 2:2), young men (Tit 2:6), young women (Tit 2:4), all saints (1Th 5:6,8). Women should exhibit in dress (1Ti 2:9). We should estimate our character and talents with (Ro 12:3). We should live in (Tit 2:12). Motive for (1Pe 4:7; 5:8).

See Temperance; Drunkenness; Self-Control.

SOCO [8459] (perhaps *thorny place*).

1. Son of Heber (1Ch 4:18).

2. A city in Judah, built by Rehoboam (2Ch 11:7; 28:18).

SOCOH, SOCHO, SOCHOH [8458] (possibly *thorny place* IDB).

1. A town in Judah (Jos 15:35; 1Sa 17:1; 1Ki 4:10), NW of Adullam; identified with Khirbet Shuweikeh.

2. Another city by this name ten miles SW of Hebron (Jos 15:48).

SODA [1342, 6003]. A mixture of washing and baking sodas found in deposits around alkali lakes of Egypt. Used to make soap (Job 9:30; Pr 25:20; Jer 2:22). *See Soap.*

SODI [6052] (*Yahweh confides*). The father of a Zebulun spy (Nu 13:10).

SODOM [6042, *1178+5047, 5047*]. Situated in the plain of the Jordan (Ge 13:10). The southeastern limit of the Canaanites (Ge 10:19). Lot dwells at (Ge 13:12). The king of, joins other kings of the nations resisting the invasion of Kedorlaomer (Ge 14:1-12). Wickedness of the inhabitants of (Ge 13:13; 19:4-13; Dt 32:32; Isa 3:9; Jer 23:14; La 4:6; Eze 16:46,48-49; Jude 7). Abraham's intercession for (Ge 18:16-33). Destroyed on account of the wickedness of the people (Ge 19:1-29; Dt 29:23; Isa 13:19; Jer 49:18; 50:40; La 4:6; Am 4:11; Zep 2:9; Mt 10:15; Lk 17:29; Ro 9:29; 2Pe 2:6).

Figurative:

Of wickedness (Dt 23:17; 32:32; Isa 1:10; Eze 16:46-56).

SODOMITES. (*of Sodom*). Inhabitants of Sodom. Wickedness of (Ge 19:4-14). Destroyed by fire as a judgment (Ge 19:24-25). To be judged according to opportunity (Mt 11:24; Lk 10:12). *See Homosexual.*

SODOMY *See Homosexual.*

SOJOURNERS Temporary residents (Ge 12:10; 20:1; 21:34; 47:4; Lev 18:26; 20:2; 25:40; Nu 15:15; Dt 26:5; Jdg 17:7; Ru 1:1; Heb 11:9).

SOLDER *See Welding.*

SOLDIERS [*408+4878, 408+7372, 1201+2657, 1475, 2657, 6639, 8081, *5061, 5129, 5132, 5369*].

NIV+ SOLDIER

Military enrollment of Israel in the wilderness of Sinai (Nu 1; 2), in the plains of Moab (Nu 26). Levies of, in the ration of one man to ten subject to duty (Jdg 20:10). Dressed in scarlet (Na 2:3). Cowards, excused from duty as (Dt 20:8; Jdg 7:3). Others exempt from service (Dt 20:5-9; 24:5). Come to John (Lk 3:14). Mock Jesus (Mt 27:27-31; Mk 15:16-20; Lk 23:11,36-37). Officers concerned in the betrayal of Jesus (Lk 22:4). Crucified Jesus (Mt 27:27,31-37; Mk 15:16-24; Jn 19:23-24). Guard the tomb (Mt 27:65; 28:11-15). Guard prisoners (Ac 12:4-6; 28:16). Maintain the peace (Ac 21:31-35). Their duty as sentinels (Ac 12:19). Perform escort duty (Ac 21:31-33, 35; 22:24-28; 23:23,31-33; 27:1,31,42-43; 28:16).

Figurative:

Of the divine protection (Isa 59:16-17). Of the Christian (Eph 6:11-17; 2Ti 2:3). *See Armies.*

SOLOMON [8976, *5048*] (*peace, well being*).

NIV+ SOLOMON'S

Son of David by Bathsheba (2Sa 12:24; 1Ki 1:13,17,21). Named Jedidiah, by Nathan the prophet (2Sa

12:24-25). Ancestor of Joseph (Mt 1:6). Succeeds David to the throne of Israel (1Ki 1:11-48; 2:12; 1Ch 23:1; 28; Ecc 1:12). Anointed king a second time (1Ch 29:22). His prayer for wisdom and his vision (1Ki 3:5-14; 2Ch 1:7-12). Covenant renewed in a vision after the dedication of the temple (1Ki 9:1-9; 2Ch 7:12-22). His rigorous reign (1Ki 2).

Builds the temple (1Ki 5; 6; 9:10; 1Ch 6:10; 2Ch 2; 3; 4; 7:11; Jer 52:20; Ac 7:45-47). Dedicates the temple (1Ki 8; 2Ch 6). Renews the courses of the priests and Levites and the forms of service according to the regulations of David (2Ch 8:12-16; 35:4; Ne 12:45).

Builds his palace (1Ki 3:1; 7:1,8; 9:10; 2Ch 7:11; 8:1; Ecc 2:4), his house of the forest of Lebanon (1Ki 7:2-7), for Pharaoh's daughter (1Ki 7:8-12; 9:24; 2Ch 8:11; Ecc 2:4). Ivory throne of (1Ki 7:7; 10:18-20). Porches of judgment (1Ki 7:7). Builds Millo, the wall of Jerusalem; the cities of Hazor, Megiddo, Gezer, Beth Horon, Baalath, Tadmor; store cities and cities for chariots and for cavalry (1Ki 9:15-19; 2Ch 9:25). Provides an armory (1Ki 10:16-17). Plants vineyards and orchards of all kinds of fruit trees; makes pools (Ecc 2:4-6), imports apes and baboons (1Ki 10:22). Drinking vessels of his houses (1Ki 10:21; 2Ch 9:20). Musicians and musical instruments of his court (1Ki 10:12; 2Ch 9:11; Ecc 2:8). The splendor of his court (1Ki 10:5-9,12; 2Ch 9:3-8; Ecc 2:9; Mt 6:29; Lk 12:27).

Commerce of (1Ki 9:28; 10:11-12,22,28-29; 2Ch 1:16-17; 8:17-18; 9:13-22,28). Presents received by (1Ki 10:10; 2Ch 9:9,23-24). Is visited by the queen of Sheba (1Ki 10:1-13; 2Ch 9:1-12). Wealth of (1Ki 9; 10:10,14-15, 23,27; 2Ch 1:15; 9:1,9,13,24,27; Ecc 1:16). Has seven hundred wives and three hundred concubines (1Ki 11:3, w Dt 17:17); their influence over him (1Ki 11:3). Marries one of Pharaoh's daughters (1Ki 3:1). Builds idolatrous temples (1Ki 11:1-8; 2Ki 23:13). His idolatry (1Ki 3:3-4; 2Ki 23:13; Ne 13:26).

Extent of his dominions (1Ki 4:21,24; 8:65; 2Ch 7:8; 9:26). Receives tribute (1Ki 4:21; 9:21; 2Ch 8:8). Officers of (1Ki 2:35; 4:1-19; 2Ch 8:9-10). His suppliers (1Ki 4:7-19). Divides his kingdom into subsistence departments; the daily subsistence rate for his court (1Ki 4:7-23, 27-28).

Military equipment of (1Ki 4:26,28; 10:16-17,26,28; 2Ch 1:14; 9:25, w Dt 17:15-16). Cedes certain cities to Hiram (1Ki 9:10-13; 2Ch 8:2). Wisdom and fame of (1Ki 4:29-34; 10:3-4,8,23-24; 1Ch 29:24-25; 2Ch 9:2-7,22-23; Ecc 1:16; Mt 12:42). Piety of (1Ki 3:5-15; 4:29; 8). Beloved of God (2Sa 12:24). Justice of, illustrated in his judgment of the two harlots (1Ki 3:16-28). Oppressions of (1Ki 12:4; 2Ch 10:4).

Reigns forty years (2Ch 9:30). Death of (2Ch 9:29-31).

Prophecies concerning (2Sa 7:12-16; 1Ki 11:9-13; 1Ch 17:11-14; 28:6-7; Ps 132:11).

A type of Christ (Ps 45:2-17; 72).

SOLOMON, SONG OF *See Song of Solomon, Song of Songs.*

SOLOMON'S POOLS Three pools near Jerusalem from which water was brought by means of aqueducts to Jerusalem (Ecc 2:6). They are still in use.

SOLOMON'S PORCH Colonnade built by Solomon on the E side of the temple area (Jn 10:23; Ac 3:11; 5:12).

SOLOMON'S SERVANTS Slaves used by Solomon in his temple for menial tasks; their descendants

returning from Babylon under Zerubbabel (Ezr 2:55,58; Ne 7:57,60; 11:3).

SOLOMON'S TEMPLE *See Temple.*

SON [132, 408, 1201, 1337, 2351, 3495, 3528, 3529, 10120, *271, 980, 3666, 3836, 4757, 5451, 5626*].

NIV+ GRANDSON, GRANDSONS, SON'S, SON-IN-LAW, SONS, SONS', SONS-IN-LAW, SONSHIP

1. A direct male offspring (Ge 4:25,26).
2. A male descendant generations removed (Mt 1:1).
3. The member of a guild or profession (1Ki 20:35).
4. Spiritual son (1Ti 1:18).
5. Address to a younger man (1Sa 3:6).
6. Adopted son (Ex 2:10).
7. Native (La 4:2).
8. Possessor of a quality (Jn 12:36).
9. Used of Jesus in a unique sense. *See One and Only; Son of God; Son of Man.*

SON OF GOD A title of Jesus referring to His equality, eternity, and consubstantiality with the Father and the Spirit in the eternal Triune Godhead (Jn 5:18,23,36). Christ claimed to be eternal, equal and of the same substance as the Father. He is uniquely God's son. *See Jesus the Christ, Son of God; One and Only.*

SON OF MAN

1. A human being (Eze 2:1,3,8ff; Ps 8:4).
2. Used in a messianic sense (Da 7:13-14). Jesus applies the term to himself many times in the Gospels (Mt 8:20; 9:6; 10:23; 11:19; 12:8, etc). Sometimes he uses it in connection with his earthly mission, but he also uses it when describing his final triumph as Redeemer and Judge (Mt 16:27f; 19:28; 24:30; 25:31). The phrase identifies him with humanity (cf. Heb 2:14-18) and with the heavenly Son of Man (Da 7:13-14). *See Jesus the Christ, Son of Man.*

SONG [2369, 2379, 5593, 5631, 7754, 8262, 8264, 8876, 8877, 8878, *6046*].

NIV+ SANG, SING, SINGER, SINGERS, SINGING, SINGS, SONGS, SUNG

Sung at the Passover (Mt 26:30; Mk 14:26). Didactic (Dt 32). *See Psalms, Topically Arranged.* Personification of the church (SS 1-8). Of Moses (Ex 15:1-19). Of Deborah and Barak (Jdg 5). Of Hannah (1Sa 2:1-10). Of David (2Sa 22:2-51; 23:1-7). Of Mary (Lk 1:46-55). Of Moses and the Lamb (Rev 15:3-4). New (Ps 33:3; 40:3). Prophetic. *See Psalms, Topically Arranged.* Spiritual, singing of, commanded (Eph 5:19; Col 3:16). Of praise. *See Poetry; Praise; Psalms, Topically Arranged; Thankfulness.* Of redemption (Rev 5:9-10). Of the redeemed (Rev 14:2-5). Of thanksgiving. *See Psalms, Topically Arranged; Thankfulness.* War (Ex 15:1-21; Nu 21:27-30; Jdg 5; 2Sa 1:19-27; 22). Solomon wrote one thousand and five (1Ki 4:32).

See Poetry; Praise; Psalms, Topically Arranged.

SONG OF DEGREES *See Ascents, Songs of; Music.*

SONG OF SOLOMON, SONG OF SONGS

Author: Verse 1 appears to ascribe authorship to Solomon

Date: In the tenth century B.C. during Solomon's reign

Outline:

I. Title (1:1).
II. First Meeting (1:2-2:7).

III. Second Meeting (2:8-3:5).

IV. Third Meeting (3:6-5:1).

V. Fourth Meeting (5:2-6:3).

VI. Fifth Meeting (6:4-8:4).

VII. Literary Climax (8:5-7).

VIII. Conclusion (8:8-14).

SONG OF THE THREE HEBREW CHILDREN
An addition to the book of Daniel found in the OT Apocrypha. Anonymous; written before 100 B.C.

SON-IN-LAW [3161, 3163].
NIV+ See SON

Unjust, Jacob (Ge 30:37-42). Faithful, Peter (Mk 1:29-30; Lk 4:38).

SONS OF GOD, CHILDREN OF GOD
Any personal creatures of God: angelic beings (Job 1:6; 2:1; 38:7), the entire human race (Ac 17:28), the regenerate as distinguished from the unregenerate (1Jn 3:10). The "sons of God" (Ge 6:1-4).

SONS OF THE PROPHETS
NIV usually "company of the prophets." Members of prophetic guilds or schools; gathered around great prophets like Samuel and Elijah for common worship, united prayer, religious fellowship, and instruction of the people (1Sa 10:5,10; 2Ki 4:38,40). In the times of Elijah and Elisha they lived together at Bethel, Jericho, and Gilgal (2Ki 2:3,5; 4:38). *See School.*

SOOTHSAYER, SOOTHSAYING [6726, 7876].
NIV+ SOOTHSAYERS'

One claiming power to foretell future events (Jos 13:22; Jer 27:9), interpret dreams (Da 4:7), and reveal secrets (Da 2:27).

SOOTHSAYERS' TREE [6726].
A pagan shrine near Shechem (Jdg 9:37), possibly the great tree of Moreh (Ge 12:6).

SOP
NIV "piece of bread" used to dip food from a common platter (Jn 13:26-27).

SOPATER [5396] (saving one's father).
Berean Christian; companion of Paul (Ac 20:4).

SOPHERETH [6072] (scribe).
A servant of Solomon, whose descendants returned from captivity to Jerusalem (Ne 7:57).

See Hassophereth.

SORCERY [4175, 4176, 4177, 5727, 5728, 6726, 3405, 3407, 4319].
NIV+ SORCERER, SORCERERS, SORCERESS, SORCERIES

Divination by an alleged assistance of evil spirits. Forbidden (Lev 19:26-28,31; 20:6; Dt 18:9-14). Denounced (Isa 8:19; Mal 3:5).

Practiced: By, the Egyptians (Isa 19:3,11-12), the magicians (Ex 7:11,22; 8:7,18), Balaam (Nu 22:6; 23:23, w 22; 23), Jezebel (2Ki 9:22), the Ninevites (Na 3:4-5), the Babylonians (Isa 47:9-13; Eze 21:21-22; Da 2:2,10,27), Belshazzar (Da 5:7,15), Simon the sorceror (Ac 8:9,11), Elymas (Ac 13:8), the young woman at Philippi (Ac 16:16), vagabond Jews (Ac 19:13), sons of Sceva (Ac 19:14-15), astrologers (Jer 10:2; Mic 3:6-7), false prophets (Jer 14:14; 27:9; 29:8-9; Eze 13:6-9; 22:28; Mt 24:24).

To cease (Eze 12:23-24; 13:23; Mic 5:12).

Messages of, false (Eze 21:29; Zec 10:2; 2Th 2:9).

Diviners shall be confounded (Mic 3:7). Belongs to the works of the flesh (Gal 5:20). Wickedness of (1Sa 15:23). Vainness of (Isa 44:25). Punishment for (Ex 22:18; Lev 20:27; Dt 13:5). Divining by familiar spirits (Lev 20:27; 1Ch 10:13; 2Ch 33:6; Isa 8:19; 19:3; 29:4), by entrails (Eze 21:21), by images (2Ki 23:24; Eze 21:21), by rods (Hos 4:12).

Saul consulted the medium of Endor (1Sa 28:7-25).

Books of, destroyed (Ac 19:19).

SORE [1734, 2307, 3539, 4649, 4804, 5596, 8558, 8825, 1814, 1815].
Laws to determine whether clean or unclean (Lev 13). Festering sores disqualified from priesthood (Lev 21:20) or acceptable offering (Lev 22:22). Figurative of judgment for sin (Jer 30:13). *See Disease.*

SOREK, VALLEY OF [8604] ([blood red grapes];
hence, *choice vines*). A valley in the Philistine territory c. eight-and-a-half miles S of Joppa (Jdg 16:4).

SORROW [16, 65, 224, 1790, 3326, 4088, 9342, 3382, 3383, 3851, 4337].
NIV+ SORROWFUL, SORROWS

God takes notice of Hagar's (Ge 21:17-20), Israelites (Ex 3:7-10).

For sin (2Co 7:10-11). *See Repentance; Sin, Confession of.*

No sorrow in heaven (Rev 21:4). "Sorrow and sighing will flee away" (Isa 35:10).

Of Hannah (1Sa 1:15). Of David for Absalom (2Sa 18:33; 19:1-8). Of Mary and Martha (Jn 11:19-40). Jeremiah (La 1:12). Jesus (Isa 53:11; Mt 26:37-44; Mk 14:34-42; Lk 22:42-44).

From bereavement: Of Jacob for Joseph (Ge 37:34-35), for Benjamin (Ge 43:14).

Of the lost (Mt 8:12; 13:42,50; 22:13; 24:51; 25:30; Lk 13:28; 16:23). *See Wicked, Punishment of.*

See Affliction, Consolation Under; Suffering.

SOSIPATER [5399] (saving ones father).
Kinsman of Paul (Ro 16:21).

SOSTHENES [5398].
1. Chief ruler of the synagogue in Corinth (Ac 18:17).

2. A Christian with whom Paul wrote the first letter to the Corinthians (1Co 1:1).

SOTAI [6055].
A servant of Solomon whose descendants returned from captivity to Jerusalem (Ezr 2:55; Ne 7:57).

SOUL [2855+5929, 3869+4222, 3883, 5883, 6034].
NIV+ SOULS

The immortal, nonmaterial part of a human being (Mt 10:28; Rev 6:9; 20:4). Can represent the whole person (Jdg 5:21) or one's life (Job 33:18; Ps 26:9). Used with heart to represent the will and emotions (Dt 4:29; 6:4). *See Immortality; Mankind, A Spirit; Spirit.*

SOUNDING [*1075]. In navigation (Ac 27:28).

SOUTH [1999, 3542, 3545, 3556, 5582+, 9402+, 2381, 3540, 3803].
NIV+ SOUTHERN, SOUTHERNMOST, SOUTHLAND, SOUTHWARD

1. A direction of the compass (Ge 13:14).

2. The Negev, an indefinite area lying between Israel and Egypt (Ge 12:9; 13:1; 1Sa 27:8-12; 2Ch 28:18).

SOVEREIGNTY OF GOD [123, 151, 10424, 10718, *1305*].

NIV+ SOVEREIGN

The supreme authority of God. He is not subject to any power or law which could be conceived as superior to or other than himself (Isa 45:9; Ro 9:20-21).

See God, Sovereign; Jesus the Christ, King.

SOWER [2445, 2446+5433, 3655, 4669, 7046, *2178, 5062, 5725*].

NIV+ SOW, SOWED, SOWING, SOWN, SOWS

Parable of the (Mt 13:3-8; Mk 4:3-20; Lk 8:5-8). Sowing (Ecc 11:4; Isa 28:25).

Figurative:

(Ps 126:5; Pr 11:18; Isa 32:20; Hos 8:7; 10:12; Gal 6:7-8).

SPAIN [*5056*]. The westernmost peninsula of Europe. Paul hoped to visit this Roman province (Ro 15:24,28).

SPAN [2455, 2698, 3427, 8145]. About nine or ten inches (Ex 28:16; 39:9).

SPARROW [7606, *5141*].

NIV+ SPARROWS

Nests of (Ps 84:3). Two sold for a penny (Mt 10:29; Lk 12:6).

SPEAKING OR SPEECH [*522, 606, 608, 614, 1819, 1821, 2047, 3120, 4863, 5583, 7023, 7754, 8488, 8557, 10425, *238, 2895, 3281, 3306, 3364, 3455, 4231, 4245*].

NIV+ SPEAK, SPEAKER, SPEAKS, SPOKE, SPOKEN, SPOKESMAN, SPOKESMEN

Evil: (Ps 10:8)

Ps 52:2 Your tongue plots destruction; it is like a sharpened razor, you who practice deceit. ³You love evil rather than good, falsehood rather than speaking the truth. *Selah* ⁴You love every harmful word, O you deceitful tongue!

Isa 32:6 For the fool speaks folly, his mind is busy with evil: He practices ungodliness and spreads error concerning the LORD; the hungry he leaves empty and from the thirsty he withholds water. ⁷The scoundrel's methods are wicked, he makes up evil schemes to destroy the poor with lies, even when the plea of the needy is just.

Jer 20:10 I hear many whispering, "Terror on every side! Report him! Let's report him!" All my friends are waiting for me to slip, saying, "Perhaps he will be deceived; then we will prevail over him and take our revenge on him."

Jude 8 In the very same way, these dreamers pollute their own bodies, reject authority and slander celestial beings.

Jude 10 Yet these men speak abusively against whatever they do not understand; and what things they do understand by instinct, like unreasoning animals—these are the very things that destroy them.

Causes strife (Pr 15:1; 16:27-28; 17:9; 25:23).

Characteristic of mankind—

Ro 1:29 They have become filled with every kind of wickedness, evil, greed and depravity. They are full of envy, murder, strife, deceit and malice. They are gossips, ³⁰slanderers, God-haters, insolent, arrogant and boastful; they invent ways of doing evil; they disobey their parents;

Ro 3:13 "Their throats are open graves; their tongues practice deceit." "The poison of vipers is on their lips." ¹⁴"Their mouths are full of cursing and bitterness."

Not characteristic of a Christian—

Eph 4:25 Therefore each of you must put off falsehood and speak truthfully to his neighbor, for we are all members of one body.

Eph 4:29 Do not let any unwholesome talk come out of your mouths, but only what is helpful for building others up according to their needs, that it may benefit those who listen.

Eph 4:31 Get rid of all bitterness, rage and anger, brawling and slander, along with every form of malice.

Eph 5:4 Nor should there be obscenity, foolish talk or coarse joking, which are out of place, but rather thanksgiving.

Tit 3:2 to slander no one, to be peaceable and considerate, and to show true humility toward all men.

Jas 1:26 If anyone considers himself religious and yet does not keep a tight rein on his tongue, he deceives himself and his religion is worthless.

Jas 3:5 Likewise the tongue is a small part of the body, but it makes great boasts. Consider what a great forest is set on fire by a small spark. ⁶The tongue also is a fire, a world of evil among the parts of the body. It corrupts the whole person, sets the whole course of his life on fire, and is itself set on fire by hell.

Jas 3:8 but no man can tame the tongue. It is a restless evil, full of deadly poison.

⁹With the tongue we praise our Lord and Father, and with it we curse men, who have been made in God's likeness. ¹⁰Out of the same mouth come praise and cursing. My brothers, this should not be.

Jas 4:11 Brothers, do not slander one another. Anyone who speaks against his brother or judges him speaks against the law and judges it. When you judge the law, you are not keeping it, but sitting in judgment on it.

1Pe 2:1 Therefore, rid yourselves of all malice and all deceit, hypocrisy, envy, and slander of every kind.

1Pe 3:9 Do not repay evil with evil or insult with insult, but with blessing, because to this you were called so that you may inherit a blessing. ¹⁰For,

"Whoever would love life and see good days must keep his tongue from evil and his lips from deceitful speech.

Excludes from kingdom of heaven—

1Co 6:10 nor thieves nor the greedy nor drunkards nor slanderers nor swindlers will inherit the kingdom of God.

Hated by God—

Pr 6:16 There are six things the LORD hates, seven that are detestable to him: ¹⁷haughty eyes, a lying tongue, hands that shed innocent blood, ¹⁸a heart that devises wicked schemes, feet that are quick to rush into evil, ¹⁹a false witness who pours out lies and a man who stirs up dissension among brothers.

Pr 8:13 To fear the LORD is to hate evil; I hate pride and arrogance, evil behavior and perverse speech.

Punishment for—

Ps 12:3 May the LORD cut off all flattering lips and every boastful tongue ⁴that says, "We will triumph with our tongues; we own our lips—who is our master?" (+Ps 52:1-4)

Forbidden—

Ex 22:28 "Do not blaspheme God or curse the ruler of your people.

Ps 34:13 keep your tongue from evil and your lips from speaking lies.

Pr 4:24 Put away perversity from your mouth; keep corrupt talk far from your lips. (+Pr 6:16-19)

Mt 5:22 But I tell you that anyone who is angry with his brother will be subject to judgment. Again, anyone who says to his brother, 'Raca,' is answerable to the Sanhedrin.

But anyone who says, 'You fool!' will be in danger of the fire of hell.

Mt 5:37 Simply let your 'Yes' be 'Yes,' and your 'No,' 'No'; anything beyond this comes from the evil one.

Mt 12:34 You brood of vipers, how can you who are evil say anything good? For out of the overflow of the heart the mouth speaks. **35**The good man brings good things out of the good stored up in him, and the evil man brings evil things out of the evil stored up in him. **36**But I tell you that men will have to give account on the day of judgment for every careless word they have spoken. **37**For by your words you will be acquitted, and by your words you will be condemned."

Ac 23:5 Paul replied, "Brothers, I did not realize that he was the high priest; for it is written: 'Do not speak evil about the ruler of your people.'" (+Eph 4:25,29,31; Tit 3:2; Jas 1:26; 3:5-6,8-10; 4:11; 1Pe 2:1; 3:9-10)

Proverbs concerning (Pr 4:24; 6:16-19; 8:13)—

Pr 10:11 The mouth of the righteous is a fountain of life, but violence overwhelms the mouth of the wicked.

Pr 10:19 When words are many, sin is not absent, but he who holds his tongue is wise.

Pr 10:31 The mouth of the righteous brings forth wisdom, but a perverse tongue will be cut out.

32The lips of the righteous know what is fitting, but the mouth of the wicked only what is perverse.

Pr 11:11 Through the blessing of the upright a city is exalted, but by the mouth of the wicked it is destroyed.

Pr 12:5 The plans of the righteous are just, but the advice of the wicked is deceitful.

6The words of the wicked lie in wait for blood, but the speech of the upright rescues them.

Pr 12:13 An evil man is trapped by his sinful talk, but a righteous man escapes trouble.

Pr 12:17 A truthful witness gives honest testimony, but a false witness tells lies.

18Reckless words pierce like a sword, but the tongue of the wise brings healing.

19Truthful lips endure forever, but a lying tongue lasts only a moment.

Pr 13:3 He who guards his lips guards his life, but he who speaks rashly will come to ruin.

Pr 14:25 A truthful witness saves lives, but a false witness is deceitful.

Pr 15:1 A gentle answer turns away wrath, but a harsh word stirs up anger.

Pr 15:4 The tongue that brings healing is a tree of life, but a deceitful tongue crushes the spirit.

Pr 15:28 The heart of the righteous weighs its answers, but the mouth of the wicked gushes evil.

Pr 16:27 A scoundrel plots evil, and his speech is like a scorching fire.

28A perverse man stirs up dissension, and a gossip separates close friends.

Pr 17:4 A wicked man listens to evil lips; a liar pays attention to a malicious tongue.

Pr 17:9 He who covers over an offense promotes love, but whoever repeats the matter separates close friends.

Pr 17:20 A man of perverse heart does not prosper; he whose tongue is deceitful falls into trouble.

Pr 18:8 The words of a gossip are like choice morsels; they go down to a man's inmost parts.

Pr 18:21 The tongue has the power of life and death, and those who love it will eat its fruit.

Pr 18:23 A poor man pleads for mercy, but a rich man answers harshly.

Pr 19:1 Better a poor man whose walk is blameless than a fool whose lips are perverse.

Pr 19:22 What a man desires is unfailing love; better to be poor than a liar.

23The fear of the Lord leads to life: Then one rests content, untouched by trouble.

Pr 24:2 for their hearts plot violence, and their lips talk about making trouble.

Pr 25:23 As a north wind brings rain, so a sly tongue brings angry looks.

Pr 26:20 Without wood a fire goes out; without gossip a quarrel dies down.

21As charcoal to embers and as wood to fire, so is a quarrelsome man for kindling strife.

22The words of a gossip are like choice morsels; they go down to a man's inmost parts.

23Like a coating of glaze over earthenware are fervent lips with an evil heart.

Pr 26:28 A lying tongue hates those it hurts, and a flattering mouth works ruin.

Ecc 10:11 If a snake bites before it is charmed, there is no profit for the charmer.

Ecc 10:20 Do not revile the king even in your thoughts, or curse the rich in your bedroom, because a bird of the air may carry your words, and a bird on the wing may report what you say.

Prayers for deliverance from curse of—

Ps 64:2 Hide me from the conspiracy of the wicked, from that noisy crowd of evildoers.

3They sharpen their tongues like swords and aim their words like deadly arrows. **4**They shoot from ambush at the innocent man; they shoot at him suddenly, without fear.

5They encourage each other in evil plans, they talk about hiding their snares; they say, "Who will see them?"

Ps 70:3 May those who say to me, "Aha! Aha!" turn back because of their shame.

Ps 120:1 I call on the Lord in my distress, and he answers me. **2**Save me, O Lord, from lying lips and from deceitful tongues.

3What will he do to you, and what more besides, O deceitful tongue? **4**He will punish you with a warrior's sharp arrows, with burning coals of the broom tree.

5Woe to me that I dwell in Meshech, that I live among the tents of Kedar! **6**Too long have I lived among those who hate peace. **7**I am a man of peace; but when I speak, they are for war.

Self-accusation: Solomon—

Ecc 7:22 for you know in your heart that many times you yourself have cursed others.

Isaiah—

Isa 6:5 "Woe to me!" I cried. "I am ruined! For I am a man of unclean lips, and I live among a people of unclean lips, and my eyes have seen the King, the Lord Almighty."

Paul (Ac 23:5).

Instances of:

Against Job—

Job 19:18 Even the little boys scorn me; when I appear, they ridicule me.

Against Lot, those of Sodom—

2Pe 2:7 and if he rescued Lot, a righteous man, who was distressed by the filthy lives of lawless men **8**(for that righteous man, living among them day after day, was tormented in his righteous soul by the lawless deeds he saw and heard)—

2Pe 2:10 This is especially true of those who follow the corrupt desire of the sinful nature and despise authority. Bold and arrogant, these men are not afraid to slander celestial beings;

Against Moses—

Ps 106:33 for they rebelled against the Spirit of God, and rash words came from Moses' lips.

Against the psalmists—

Ps 35:21 They gape at me and say, "Aha! Aha! With our own eyes we have seen it."

Ps 41:5 My enemies say of me in malice, "When will he die and his name perish?" ⁶Whenever one comes to see me, he speaks falsely, while his heart gathers slander; then he goes out and spreads it abroad.

⁷All my enemies whisper together against me; they imagine the worst for me, saying, ⁸"A vile disease has beset him; he will never get up from the place where he lies." ⁹Even my close friend, whom I trusted, he who shared my bread, has lifted up his heel against me.

Ps 69:12 Those who sit at the gate mock me, and I am the song of the drunkards.

Ps 69:26 For they persecute those you wound and talk about the pain of those you hurt.

Ps 102:8 All day long my enemies taunt me; those who rail against me use my name as a curse.

Ps 119:23 Though rulers sit together and slander me, your servant will meditate on your decrees.

Against the church, those of the circumcision—

Tit 1:10 For there are many rebellious people, mere talkers and deceivers, especially those of the circumcision group. ¹¹They must be silenced, because they are ruining whole households by teaching things they ought not to teach—and that for the sake of dishonest gain.

False teachers (Jude 8,10).

See Accusation, False; Blasphemy; Busybody; Falsehood; Flattery; Slander; Talebearer; Uncharitableness.

Foolish:

Job 13:5 If only you would be altogether silent! For you, that would be wisdom.

Job 16:3 Will your long-winded speeches never end? What ails you that you keep on arguing? ⁴I also could speak like you, if you were in my place; I could make fine speeches against you and shake my head at you.

Job 38:2 "Who is this that darkens my counsel with words without knowledge?

Accountable to God—

Mt 12:36 But I tell you that men will have to give account on the day of judgment for every careless word they have spoken. ³⁷For by your words you will be acquitted, and by your words you will be condemned."

Forbidden (Pr 30:18). Not characteristic of a Christian (Eph 5:4).

Proverbs concerning—

Pr 10:14 Wise men store up knowledge, but the mouth of a fool invites ruin.

Pr 12:23 A prudent man keeps his knowledge to himself, but the heart of fools blurts out folly.

Pr 13:3 He who guards his lips guards his life, but he who speaks rashly will come to ruin.

Pr 14:3 A fool's talk brings a rod to his back, but the lips of the wise protect them.

Pr 15:2 The tongue of the wise commends knowledge, but the mouth of the fool gushes folly.

Pr 15:7 The lips of the wise spread knowledge; not so the hearts of fools.

Pr 15:14 The discerning heart seeks knowledge, but the mouth of a fool feeds on folly.

Pr 18:6 A fool's lips bring him strife, and his mouth invites a beating.

⁷A fool's mouth is his undoing, and his lips are a snare to his soul.

Pr 18:13 He who answers before listening—that is his folly and his shame.

Pr 26:4 Do not answer a fool according to his folly, or you will be like him yourself.

Pr 26:7 Like a lame man's legs that hang limp is a proverb in the mouth of a fool.

Pr 26:9 Like a thornbush in a drunkard's hand is a proverb in the mouth of a fool.

Pr 29:11 A fool gives full vent to his anger, but a wise man keeps himself under control.

Pr 29:20 Do you see a man who speaks in haste? There is more hope for a fool than for him.

Pr 30:10 "Do not slander a servant to his master, or he will curse you, and you will pay for it.

Ecc 5:3 As a dream comes when there are many cares, so the speech of a fool when there are many words. (+Ecc 5:5)

Ecc 10:13 At the beginning his words are folly; at the end they are wicked madness— ¹⁴and the fool multiplies words. No one knows what is coming—who can tell him what will happen after him?

See Fool.

Wise:

Job 16:5 But my mouth would encourage you; comfort from my lips would bring you relief.

Job 27:4 my lips will not speak wickedness, and my tongue will utter no deceit.

Am 5:13 Therefore the prudent man keeps quiet in such times, for the times are evil.

Zep 3:13 The remnant of Israel will do no wrong; they will speak no lies, nor will deceit be found in their mouths. They will eat and lie down and no one will make them afraid."

Zec 8:16 These are the things you are to do: Speak the truth to each other, and render true and sound judgment in your courts; (+Rev 14:17)

As good as nails (Ecc 12:11). Precious as jewels (Pr 20:16).—

Edifying (Eph 4:29).

Rewards of—

Ps 15:1 LORD, who may dwell in your sanctuary? Who may live on your holy hill?

²He whose walk is blameless and who does what is righteous, who speaks the truth from his heart ³and has no slander on his tongue, who does his neighbor no wrong and casts no slur on his fellowman,

Ps 50:23 He who sacrifices thank offerings honors me, and he prepares the way so that I may show him the salvation of God." (+Pr 14:3; 22:11)

Of the ideal woman (Pr 31:26).

Admonitions concerning, to believers—

Eph 4:22 You were taught, with regard to your former way of life, to put off your old self, which is being corrupted by its deceitful desires;

Eph 4:25 Therefore each of you must put off falsehood and speak truthfully to his neighbor, for we are all members of one body.

Eph 4:29 Do not let any unwholesome talk come out of your mouths, but only what is helpful for building others up according to their needs, that it may benefit those who listen.

Php 1:27 Whatever happens, conduct yourselves in a manner worthy of the gospel of Christ. Then, whether I come and see you or only hear about you in my absence, I will know that you stand firm in one spirit, contending as one man for the faith of the gospel

Col 4:6 Let your conversation be always full of grace, seasoned with salt, so that you may know how to answer everyone.

Jas 1:19 My dear brothers, take note of this: Everyone should be quick to listen, slow to speak and slow to become angry,

Jas 1:26 If anyone considers himself religious and yet does not keep a tight rein on his tongue, he deceives himself and his religion is worthless.

Jas 3:2 We all stumble in many ways. If anyone is never at fault in what he says, he is a perfect man, able to keep his whole body in check.

Jas 3:13 Who is wise and understanding among you? Let him show it by his good life, by deeds done in the humility that comes from wisdom.

1Pe 2:12 Live such good lives among the pagans that, though they accuse you of doing wrong, they may see your good deeds and glorify God on the day he visits us.

1Pe 3:15 But in your hearts set apart Christ as Lord. Always be prepared to give an answer to everyone who asks you to give the reason for the hope that you have. But do this with gentleness and respect, 16keeping a clear conscience, so that those who speak maliciously against your good behavior in Christ may be ashamed of their slander.

Christ's words concerning (Mt 12:35)—

Mt 12:37 For by your words you will be acquitted, and by your words you will be condemned."

Lk 6:45 The good man brings good things out of the good stored up in his heart, and the evil man brings evil things out of the evil stored up in his heart. For out of the overflow of his heart his mouth speaks.

Of psalmists—

Ps 37:30 The mouth of the righteous man utters wisdom, and his tongue speaks what is just.

Ps 39:1 I said, "I will watch my ways and keep my tongue from sin; I will put a muzzle on my mouth as long as the wicked are in my presence."

Ps 77:12 I will meditate on all your works and consider all your mighty deeds.

Ps 119:13 With my lips I recount all the laws that come from your mouth.

Ps 119:27 Let me understand the teaching of your precepts; then I will meditate on your wonders.

Ps 119:46 I will speak of your statutes before kings and will not be put to shame,

Ps 119:54 Your decrees are the theme of my song wherever I lodge.

Ps 119:172 May my tongue sing of your word, for all your commands are righteous.

Ps 141:3 Set a guard over my mouth, O Lord; keep watch over the door of my lips.

Ps 145:5 They will speak of the glorious splendor of your majesty, and I will meditate on your wonderful works. 6They will tell of the power of your awesome works, and I will proclaim your great deeds. 7They will celebrate your abundant goodness and joyfully sing of your righteousness.

Ps 145:11 They will tell of the glory of your kingdom and

speak of your might, 12so that all men may know of your mighty acts and the glorious splendor of your kingdom.

Proverbs concerning—

Pr 10:11 The mouth of the righteous is a fountain of life, but violence overwhelms the mouth of the wicked.

Pr 10:13 Wisdom is found on the lips of the discerning, but a rod is for the back of him who lacks judgment.

Pr 10:19 When words are many, sin is not absent, but he who holds his tongue is wise.

20The tongue of the righteous is choice silver, but the heart of the wicked is of little value.

21The lips of the righteous nourish many, but fools die for lack of judgment.

Pr 10:31 The mouth of the righteous brings forth wisdom, but a perverse tongue will be cut out.

32The lips of the righteous know what is fitting, but the mouth of the wicked only what is perverse.

Pr 11:12 A man who lacks judgment derides his neighbor, but a man of understanding holds his tongue.

13A gossip betrays a confidence, but a trustworthy man keeps a secret.

14For lack of guidance a nation falls, but many advisers make victory sure.

Pr 12:6 The words of the wicked lie in wait for blood, but the speech of the upright rescues them.

Pr 12:14 From the fruit of his lips a man is filled with good things as surely as the work of his hands rewards him.

Pr 12:16 A fool shows his annoyance at once, but a prudent man overlooks an insult.

17A truthful witness gives honest testimony, but a false witness tells lies.

18Reckless words pierce like a sword, but the tongue of the wise brings healing.

19Truthful lips endure forever, but a lying tongue lasts only a moment.

20There is deceit in the hearts of those who plot evil, but joy for those who promote peace.

Pr 12:23 A prudent man keeps his knowledge to himself, but the heart of fools blurts out folly.

Pr 13:2 From the fruit of his lips a man enjoys good things, but the unfaithful have a craving for violence.

3He who guards his lips guards his life, but he who speaks rashly will come to ruin.

Pr 14:3 A fool's talk brings a rod to his back, but the lips of the wise protect them.

Pr 15:1 A gentle answer turns away wrath, but a harsh word stirs up anger.

2The tongue of the wise commends knowledge, but the mouth of the fool gushes folly.

Pr 15:4 The tongue that brings healing is a tree of life, but a deceitful tongue crushes the spirit.

Pr 15:7 The lips of the wise spread knowledge; not so the hearts of fools.

Pr 15:23 A man finds joy in giving an apt reply—and how good is a timely word!

Pr 15:26 The Lord detests the thoughts of the wicked, but those of the pure are pleasing to him.

Pr 15:28 The heart of the righteous weighs its answers, but the mouth of the wicked gushes evil.

Pr 16:21 The wise in heart are called discerning, and pleasant words promote instruction.

Pr 16:23 A wise man's heart guides his mouth, and his lips promote instruction.

24Pleasant words are a honeycomb, sweet to the soul and healing to the bones.

Pr 17:7 Arrogant lips are unsuited to a fool—how much worse lying lips to a ruler!

Pr 17:27 A man of knowledge uses words with restraint, and a man of understanding is even-tempered.

28Even a fool is thought wise if he keeps silent, and discerning if he holds his tongue.

Pr 18:4 The words of a man's mouth are deep waters, but the fountain of wisdom is a bubbling brook.

Pr 18:20 From the fruit of his mouth a man's stomach is filled; with the harvest from his lips he is satisfied.

Pr 19:1 Better a poor man whose walk is blameless than a fool whose lips are perverse.

Pr 20:15 Gold there is, and rubies in abundance, but lips that speak knowledge are a rare jewel.

Pr 21:23 He who guards his mouth and his tongue keeps himself from calamity.

Pr 22:11 He who loves a pure heart and whose speech is gracious will have the king for his friend.

Pr 24:6 for waging war you need guidance, and for victory many advisers.

Pr 25:11 A word aptly spoken is like apples of gold in settings of silver.

Pr 25:15 Through patience a ruler can be persuaded, and a gentle tongue can break a bone.

Pr 26:5 Answer a fool according to his folly, or he will be wise in his own eyes.

Pr 29:11 A fool gives full vent to his anger, but a wise man keeps himself under control.

Pr 31:26 She speaks with wisdom, and faithful instruction is on her tongue.

Ecc 3:7 a time to tear and a time to mend, a time to be silent and a time to speak,

Ecc 9:17 The quiet words of the wise are more to be heeded than the shouts of a ruler of fools.

Ecc 10:12 Words from a wise man's mouth are gracious, but a fool is consumed by his own lips.

Ecc 12:9 Not only was the Teacher wise, but also he imparted knowledge to the people. He pondered and searched out and set in order many proverbs. **10**The Teacher searched to find just the right words, and what he wrote was upright and true.

11The words of the wise are like goads, their collected sayings like firmly embedded nails—given by one Shepherd.

Prayer concerning (Ps 141:3).

See Wisdom

SPEAR [1360, 2851, 3959, 4751, 7528, 8242, *3365*].

NIV+ SPEARHEAD, SPEARMEN, SPEARS

Spears and javelins differed in weight and size but had similar uses.

An implement of war (2Ki 11:10; Ne 4:13). Goliath's (1Sa 17:7). Saul's (1Sa 18:10-11). Stored in the temple (2Ch 23:9). To be changed into pruning hooks (Isa 2:4; Mic 4:3). Pruning hooks to be beaten into (Joel 3:10). Thrust into Jesus' side (Zec 12:10; Jn 19:34; 20:27; Rev 1:7). For catching fish (Job 41:7,26). *See Armory.*

SPECK [2847]. Particle of dust or splinter of wood in one's eye, figurative of improper judgment (Mt 7:3-5; Lk 6:41-42). *See Judgment.*

SPECKLED [5923, 7380]. Mottled in color (Ge 30:25-43). *See Streaked.*

SPELT [4081]. A small grain grown in Egypt (Ex 9:32). Cultivated in Canaan (Isa 28:25). Used in bread (Eze 4:9).

SPERMATORRHEA A disease of the genitals (possibly Lev 15:16).

SPICES [86, 1411, 5008, 5350, 5780, 6160, 8380, *319*, *808*, *2455*].

NIV+ SPICE, SPICED, SPICE-LADEN

In the formula for the sacred oil (Ex 25:6; 35:8). Stores of (2Ki 20:13). Used in the temple (1Ch 9:29). Exported from Gilead (Ge 37:25). Sent as a present by Jacob to Joseph (Ge 43:11). Presented by the queen of Sheba to Solomon (1Ki 10:2,10). Sold in the markets of Tyre (Eze 27:22). Used in the embalming of Asa (2Ch 16:14). Prepared for embalming the body of Jesus (Mk 16:1; Lk 23:56; 24:1; Jn 19:39-40).

SPIDER [6571].

NIV+ SPIDER'S

Web of, figurative of the hope of the hypocrite (Job 8:14; Isa 59:5).

SPIES [4855, 8078, 9068, *34*, *1588*, *2946*].

NIV+ SPY, SPIED, SPYING

(Ge 42:9). Sent to investigate Canaan (Nu 13), Jazer (Nu 21:32), Jericho (Jos 2:1). Used by David (1Sa 26:4), at the court of Absalom (2Sa 15:10; 17:1-17). Pharisees acted as (Lk 20:20). In the church of Galatia (Gal 2:4). *See Reconnaissance.*

SPIKENARD *See Nard; Perfume, 2.*

SPINDLE [7134].

NIV+ See SPINNING

Implement used in spinning (Ex 35:24; Pr 31:19).

SPINNING [755, 3211, 4757, *3756*].

NIV+ SPIN, SPINDLE, SPUN

By hand (Ex 35:25; Pr 31:19).

SPIRIT [200, 466, 4000, 4213, 5883, 5972, 8120, 10658, *899+3836+5858*, *4460*, *5249*, *6035*] (*breath, wind, spirit*).

NIV+ SPIRIT'S, SPIRITIST, SPIRITISTS, SPIRITS, SPIRITUAL, SPIRITUALLY

The immortal, nonmaterial part of a human being, similar to the soul (Job 7:11). Represents one's lifeforce or strength (Ge 45:27; Jas 2:26), character (Nu 14:24; Dt 2:30; 1Pe 3:4), desire (2Sa 13:39), heart or emotions (Ps 73:21; 77:6). The self is often called "spirit" when the direct relationship of the individual to God is the point of emphasis (2Ti 4:22; Phm 25). *See Ghost; Immortality; Mankind, A Spirit; Soul.*

SPIRIT, HOLY *See Holy Spirit.*

SPIRITISTS [3362].

NIV+ SPIRITIST

Divination by means of communication with the spirit of the dead (necromancy) was known and practiced in the ancient Near East.

Consulting of:

Forbidden (Lev 19:31; 20:6,27; Dt 18:10-11), vain (Isa 8:19; 19:3). Those who consulted, to be cut off (Lev 20:6, 27).

Instances of Consulting of:

Saul (1Sa 28:3-25; 1Ch 10:13-14). Manasseh (2Ki 21:6; 2Ch 33:6). A slave girl (Ac 16:16-18).

See Demons; Medium; Necromancer, Necromancy; Sorcery; Witchcraft.

SPIRITS IN PRISON Those who in the days of Noah refused his message (1Pe 3:18-20; 4:6). The exact interpretation of this passage is strongly debated.

SPIRITS [356, 8120, 8327, *4460*]. *See Demons.*

SPIRITUAL ADOPTION *See Adoption, Spiritual.*

SPIRITUAL BLESSINGS *See Blessings, Spiritual; Holy Spirit; Sanctification.*

SPIRITUAL BLINDNESS Blindness, Spiritual.

SPIRITUAL BOASTING (Ro 11:18-21). Incompatible, with faith (Ro 3:27; Eph 2:8-10), with humility (1Co 1:29, w 1:17-31; 4:6-7; 2Co 10:12-16).

In the Lord, approved (Jer 9:24; 2Co 10:17-18; Gal 6:14).

See Boasting, Spiritual.

SPIRITUAL DEATH Alienation from the life of God; a state of condemnation (Ro 7:9,11; 8:5-6,13; Eph 4:18).

Making alive from (Jn 5:24-26; Ro 5:12,15; Eph 2:1,5-6; 5:14; Col 2:13).

See Death, Physical; Second Death.

SPIRITUAL DESIRE *See Desire, Spiritual.*

SPIRITUAL DILIGENCE *See Zeal.*

SPIRITUAL GIFTS Extraordinary gifts of the Spirit given to Christians to equip them for the service of the Church (Ro 11:29; 12:6-8; 1Co 12:4-11,28-30; Eph 4:7-11; 1Pe 4:10-11).

See Charism, Charisma, Charismata; Holy Spirit; Tongues, Gift of.

SPIRITUAL HUNGER *See Hunger, Figurative.*

SPIRITUAL PEACE (Isa 27:5; 54:1,10,13; 55:2,12; 57:19; Eze 34:25; Lk 2:14,29; Ro 5:1; 1Co 14:33). Christ's kingdom, a kingdom of (Isa 9:6; 11:6-9,13; Mic 5:5; Lk 1:79; Ac 10:36).

See Peace, Spiritual.

SPIRITUAL PURIFICATION (Ps 65:3; 73:1; Pr 20:9; Jn 13:8-9).

By corrective judgments (Isa 4:3-4). By mercy and truth (Pr 16:6). By the Holy Spirit (1Co 6:11; Tit 3:5-6). By the blood of Christ (Heb 1:3; 9:14; 2Pe 1:9; 1Jn 1:7; Rev 1:5; 7:14).

Of the Church (Eph 5:26).

Commanded (Isa 1:16; Mt 23:26; Ac 22:16; 1Co 5:7; 2Co 7:1; Heb 10:22; Jas 4:8).

Promised (Isa 1:18; Jer 33:8; Eze 36:25; Da 12:10; Zec 13:1; 1Jn 1:9). Prayer for (Ps 51:2,7; 79:9).

See Purification; Sanctification.

SPIRITUAL UNDERSTANDING (Mt 13:23; Lk 10:21-22; Jn 7:17).

Of apostles (Mt 13:16-17; Lk 8:10; 10:23-24). Of Peter (Mt 16:16-17). Of Mary (Lk 10:39,42).

Lacking, in disciples (Mt 15:15-16; Lk 24:25), in Jews (Mt 13:11-16; Jn 6:26,41,52; 9:28-29,39-41; 12:27-40; Ac 28:24-27).

Commanded:

Concerning, the importance of preaching (Mt 11:13-15), the importance of parables (Mt 13:9,43; Lk 8:8), the character of the disciples of Jesus (Lk 14:33-35), the Holy Spirit's message to the churches (Rev 2:7).

See Wisdom, Spiritual.

SPIRITUALISM *See Necromancer; Sorcery.*

SPIRITUALITY

NIV+ See SPIRIT

Described as the great and enduring good (Lk 10:42), as love and devotion to God (Dt 6:5; Jos 22:5; 1Ki 8:23; Ps 1:2; 51:6).

Brings peace (Isa 26:3; Jer 33:6; Ro 8:6; 14:17), indifference to worldly good (1Co 7:29-31; Col 3:1-3), thirst for heavenly blessings (Mt 5:6; Jn 6:27).

Is produced by the indwelling of the Holy Spirit (Jn 14:16-17; Ro 8:4).

SPITTING [3762, 7794, 8371, 8394, 9531, *1840, 1870, 4772*].

NIV+ SPIT, SPITS

In the face, as an indignity (Nu 12:14; Dt 25:9; Job 30:10; Mt 26:67; 27:30). Jesus used spittle in healing (Mk 7:33; 8:23).

SPOILS [4917, 8965, *660, 5036*].

NIV+ BOOTY, DESPOIL, PLUNDER, SPOIL, SPOILS

Of war (Ge 14:11-12; Nu 31:9-10; Dt 2:35). Divided between the combatants and noncombatants of the Israelites, including priests and Levites (Nu 31:25-54; 1Sa 30:24). Dedicated to the Lord (1Sa 15:15; 1Ch 26:27; 2Ch 15:11).

SPOKES [3140].

NIV+ SPOKE

Rods connecting the rim of a wheel with the hub. Basins for washing of sacrifices were set on bases moving upon wheels. The spokes were part of these wheels (1Ki 7:27-33).

SPONGE [*5074*]. (Mt 27:48; Mk 15:36; Jn 19:29).

SPOONS Of the tabernacle (Ex 25:29; Nu 4:7; 7). Of the temple (1Ki 7:50; 2Ch 4:22).

SPOT [994, 1353, 2494, 3229, 5226, 9393, *834, 5536*].

NIV+ SPOTLESS, SPOTS, SPOTTED

Blemish, blot (SS 4:7; Job 11:15; Lev 24:19ff; Pr 9:7; Jude 23).

SPOUSE *See Bride; Marriage.*

SPREAD, SPREADING [*1819, 2118, 2143, 2430, 3655, 5417, 5427, 5742, 5759, 5951, 5989, 6296, 6885, 7233, 7287, 7298, 7313, 8316, 8392, *889, 1424, 2002, 5143*].

NIV+ OUTSPREAD, SPREADING, SPREADS, WIDESPREAD

Scatter, disperse (Mt 21:8; Mk 1:28).

SPRING [*1657, 3655, 4432, 4784, 4919, 5078, 5227, 6524, 6590, 7255, 7541, 9102+9588, 9333, *4380*].

NIV+ SPRANG, SPRINGING, SPRINGS, SPRINGTIME, SPRUNG, WELLSPRING

1. Season of, promised annual return of (Ge 8:22). Described (Pr 27:25; SS 2:11-13).

2. Of water. Hot (Ge 36:24).

Figurative:

Muddied or salty (Pr 25:26; Jas 3:11).

See Wells.

SPRINKLING [*2450, 4670, 5684, 6590, *4822, 4823*].

NIV+ SPRINKLE, SPRINKLED, SPRINKLES

Of blood (Lev 14:7,51; 16:14; Heb 9:13,19,21; 11:28;

1Pe 1:2). *See Blood*. Of water (Nu 8:7; Eze 36:25; Heb 9:19; 10:22).

STABILITY [6641].

Of Character:

Ps 57:7 My heart is steadfast, O God, my heart is steadfast; I will sing and make music. (+Ps 108:1; 112:7)

Rewarded:

Mt 10:22 All men will hate you because of me, but he who stands firm to the end will be saved. (+Mt 24:13)

Mk 4:20 Others, like seed sown on good soil, hear the word, accept it, and produce a crop—thirty, sixty or even a hundred times what was sown."

2Th 3:3 But the Lord is faithful, and he will strengthen and protect you from the evil one.

Commanded:

1Co 7:20 Each one should remain in the situation which he was in when God called him.

1Co 15:58 Therefore, my dear brothers, stand firm. Let nothing move you. Always give yourselves fully to the work of the Lord, because you know that your labor in the Lord is not in vain.

2Th 2:15 So then, brothers, stand firm and hold to the teachings we passed on to you, whether by word of mouth or by letter.

Heb 10:23 Let us hold unswervingly to the hope we profess, for he who promised is faithful.

Heb 13:9 Do not be carried away by all kinds of strange teachings. It is good for our hearts to be strengthened by grace, not by ceremonial foods, which are of no value to those who eat them.

Jas 1:23 Anyone who listens to the word but does not do what it says is like a man who looks at his face in a mirror [24]and, after looking at himself, goes away and immediately forgets what he looks like. [25]But the man who looks intently into the perfect law that gives freedom, and continues to do this, not forgetting what he has heard, but doing it—he will be blessed in what he does.

Rev 22:11 Let him who does wrong continue to do wrong; let him who is vile continue to be vile; let him who does right continue to do right; and let him who is holy continue to be holy."

See Character; Decision; Perseverance.

STABLE *See Pasture.*

STACHYS [5093] (*head of grain*). A Christian in Rome (Ro 16:9).

STACTE *See Gum Resin.*

STADIA [5084]. Plural of *stadion*, about 202 yards (Rev 14:20; 21:16).

STAFF, STAVES [1475, 2980, 4751, 4957, 5234, 5475, 6469, 8657, *2812, 4811*]. *See Rod.*

STAIRS [4294, 5090, 5092, 6150].

NIV+ DOWNSTAIRS, STAIRWAY, UPSTAIRS

Steps leading to an upper chamber (1Ki 6:8; Ac 21:40), or some other elevated place (Ne 9:4; Eze 40:6; 43:17). Jacob's vision of a stairway from earth to heaven (Ge 28:10-22). The sign to Hezekiah on the stairway of Ahaz (1Ki 20:1-12).

STAKE [928, 3845].

NIV+ STAKES

Tent-pin or tent-pole (Ex 27:19; Isa 33:20).

STALL [774, 1074, 5272, 8348, *5764*].

NIV+ STALLS, STALL-FED

A place for care of livestock or compartment in a stable for one animal (2Ch 32:28). Solomon's barns provided stalls for 4,000 horses (2Ch 9:25).

STAMMERING [6589]. (Isa 32:4; 33:19). Of Moses (Ex 4:10).

STANDARD [74, 253, 1840, 4500, 5477, 5504, 5812, *2848, 3836+4922*].

NIV+ STANDARDS

An ensign used by each of the tribes of Israel in camp and march (Nu 1:52; 2:2). Banners used as (Ps 20:5; SS 6:4,10). Used in war (Jer 4:21). Used to signal the route to defended cities (Jer 4:6), to call attention to news (Jer 50:2; 51:12).

See Armies; Banner; Ensign.

Figurative: (Isa 49:22; 62:10; Jer 4:6).

STARS [2122, 3919, 7372, 9028, *843, 849, 5891, 5892*].

NIV+ STAR, STARGAZERS, STARRY

Created by God (Ge 1:16; Job 26:13; Ps 8:3; 33:6; 136:7,9; Am 5:8). Differ in splendor (1Co 15:41). Worship of, forbidden (Dt 4:19). Worshiped (2Ki 17:16; 21:3; 23:5; Jer 19:13; Am 5:26; Zep 1:5; Ac 7:42-43). Constellations of (Isa 13:10), Orion (Job 9:9; Am 5:8), serpent (Job 26:13). Planets (2Ki 23:5), the morning star (Job 38:7; Rev 2:28; 22:16). Darkening of (Job 9:7; Ecc 12:2; Isa 13:10; 34:4; Joel 2:10; 3:15; Rev 8:11-12). Comets (Jude 13). Falling of (Da 8:10; 9:1; 12:4). Guides the wise men (Mt 2:2,7,9-10).

Figurative:

Of the deliverer (Nu 24:17). Seven stars of the seven churches (Rev 1:16,20). Crown of twelve stars (Rev 12:1). Of Jesus (Rev 22:16).

STATE *See Church, The Body of Believers, State; Government.*

STATECRAFT Wisdom in (Pr 28:2). School in (Da 1:3-5). Skilled in.

Instances of:

Joseph (Ge 47:15-26), Samuel (1Sa 11:12-15), Nathan (1Ki 1:11-14), Jeroboam (1Ki 12:26-33), Daniel. *See Daniel.*

See Government; Kings; Rulers.

STATURE [1541, 7757, *2461*]. Natural height of an animal body (2Sa 21:20; Isa 45:14; Lk 19:3).

STAVES Used as weapons (Mt 26:47; Mk 14:43).

Symbolic: (Zec 11:7-14).

STEADFASTNESS [3922, 6164, *2530*].

NIV+ STEADFAST, STEADFASTLY

(Ps 57:7; 108:1; 112:7; Ro 14:4; 1Th 3:8; Col 1:23; Jas 1:25).

Commanded (1Co 7:20; 15:58; 16:13; Gal 6:1; Eph 6:11,13-14; Php 1:27; 4:1; 1Th 5:21; 2Th 2:15; 3:13; Heb 10:23; 13:9; Jas 1:25; 1Pe 5:9).

Rewards of:

(Mt 10:22; 24:13; Mk 13:13; Rev 2:7,10-11,17,25-28; 3:5,11-12,21; 21:17).

See Decision; Perseverance; Stability.

STEALING [665, 1608, 1704, 2118, 8845, *3096, 3802*].

NIV+ STEAL, STEALING, STEALS, STOLE, STOLEN

See Theft.

STEEL Steel is not mentioned in the Bible. *See Bronze.*

STELE (*erect block* or *shaft*). Narrow, upright slab of stone with an inscription cut on it to commemorate an event, mark a grave, or give a votive likeness of a deity. Prevalent especially in Egypt and Greece.

STEPHANAS [*5107*] (*victor's wreath*). A Christian in Corinth, whose household Paul baptized (1Co 1:16; 16:15,17).

STEPHEN [*5108*] (*victor's wreath*). A Christian martyr. Appointed one of the committee of seven to oversee power of (Ac 6:5,8-10). False charges against (Ac 6:11-15). Defense of (Ac 7). Stoned (Ac 7:54-60; 8:1; 22:20). Burial of (Ac 8:2). Gentle and forgiving spirit of (Ac 7:59-60).

STERILITY [6829].

NIV+ STERILE

Of women. *See Barrenness.*

STEW [5686]. Soup of vegetables and meat (Ge 25:29-30,34; 2Ki 4:38-39).

STEWARD [1074+8042, 5853, 6125].

NIV+ STEWARDS

(Ge 15:2; 43:19; 1Ch 28:1; Lk 8:3).

Figurative:

The faithful steward described (Lk 12:35-38,42). The unfaithful, described (Lk 16:1-8). The parable of the pounds (Lk 19:12-27), of the talents (Mt 25:14-30). Must be faithful (1Co 4:1-2; Tit 1:7; 1Pe 4:10).

STEWARDSHIP Of the Gospel (1Co 9:17; Gal 2:7; Col 1:25; 1Th 2:4; 1Ti 1:11; Tit 1:3).

STICKS [*202, 5234, 6770, 8657, 2812*].

NIV+ STICKING, STICKS

Used as cymbals (Eze 37:16).

STIFF-NECKED [6902+7996, 6902+7997, *5019*].

See Impenitence; Obduracy.

STOCK [2446, 4551, 7212, *3833*].

NIV+ STOCKS

1. Wooden idol worshiped by apostate Israel (Isa 44:19; Jer 2:27).

2. Family (Lev 25:47; Isa 40:24; Ac 13:26; Php 3:5).

3. Instrument of punishment in which head, hands, and feet were fastened (2Ch 16:10; Jer 20:2; Job 13:27).

STOICISM [*5121*].

NIV+ STOIC

A Grecian philosophy, inculcating doctrines of severe morality, self-denial, and inconvenient services.

Scripture analogies to: John the Baptist, wears camel's hair and subsists on locusts and wild honey (Mt 3:4), comes "neither eating nor drinking" (Mt 11:18; Lk 7:33). Jesus requires self-denial and crosses (Mt 10:38-39; 16:24; Mk 8:34-35; Lk 9:23-26; 14:27), the subordination of natural affection (Mt 10:37; Lk 14:26). Paul teaches that the "law of my mind" is at war with the "law of sin at work within my members" (Ro 7:23, w 7:14-24), that the body

must be kept under (1Co 9:27), advises celibacy (1Co 7:1-9,25-26,32-33,39-40).

School of, at Athens (Ac 17:18).

See Aratus; Asceticism; Cleanthes.

STOICS (*[learners on the painted] porch*). *See Aratus; Asceticism; Cleanthes; Stoicism.*

STOMACHER NIV "fine clothing" (Isa 3:24).

STONES [*74, 1473, 1607, 5167, 6232, 8083, 10006, 3342, 3343, 3344, 3345*].

NIV+ CAPSTONE, CORNERSTONE, CORNERSTONES, FIELDSTONES, MILLSTONE, MILLSTONES, SLINGSTONES, STONE'S, STONECUTTERS, STONED, STONEMASONS, STONING, TOMBSTONE

Commandments engraved upon (Ex 24:12; 31:18; 34:1-4; Dt 4:13; 5:22; 9:9-11; 10:1-3). The law of Moses written upon (Jos 8:32). Houses built of (Isa 9:10; Am 5:11). Temple built of (1Ki 5:17-18; 7:9-12; Mt 24:2; Lk 19:44; 21:5-6). Prepared in the quarries (1Ki 6:7). Hewn (Ex 34:1; Dt 10:1; 1Ki 5:17; 6:36; 7:9; 2Ki 12:12; 22:6; 1Ch 22:2; 2Ch 34:11; La 3:9). Sawn (1Ki 7:9). Stone-masons (1Ki 5:18; 2Ki 12:12; 1Ch 22:15).

City walls built of (Ne 4:3). Memorial pillars of (Ge 28:18-22; 31:45-52; Jos 4:2-9,20-24; 24:25; 1Sa 7:12). Great, as landmarks, Abel (1Sa 6:18), Ezel (1Sa 20:19), Zoheleth (1Ki 1:9).

Cast upon accursed ground (2Ki 3:19,25). Used in building altars (Jos 8:31), for weighing (Lev 19:36), for closing tombs (Mt 27:60; Mk 15:46; 16:3). Tombs cut in (Mt 27:60; Mk 15:46; 16:3). Idols made of (Dt 4:28; 28:36,64; 29:17; 2Ki 19:18; Isa 37:19; Eze 20:32).

Great, in Solomon's temple (1Ki 5:17-18; 7:9-12). Magnificent, in Herod's (Mk 13:1). Skill in throwing (Jdg 20:16; 1Ch 12:2). *See Sling.*

See Adamant; Chalcedony; Marble; Onyx; Pillar.

See below, Precious.

Figurative:

(Ge 49:24; Zec 3:9). Of temptation, "a stone that causes men to stumble" (Isa 8:14; Ro 9:33; 1Pe 2:8). Of Christ, "a tested stone, a precious cornerstone for a sure foundation" (Isa 28:16), of Christ's rejection, the rejected corner stone (Ps 118:22; Mt 21:42-44; Mk 12:10; Lk 20:17-18; Ac 4:11; 1Pe 2:4), the true foundation (Isa 28:16; Mt 16:18; 1Co 3:11; Eph 2:20; Rev 21:14). Of Christ, the source of spiritual water (1Co 10:4). Of the impenitent heart (Eze 36:26). Of the witness of the Spirit, the white stone (Rev 2:17).

Symbolic:

Of the kingdom of Christ (Da 2:34,45).

Precious:

In the breastplate and ephod (Ex 28:9-21; 39:6-14). Voluntary offerings of, by the Israelites for the breastplate and ephod (Ex 35:27). Exported from Sheba (1Ki 10:2,10; 2Ch 9:9-10; Eze 27:22), Ophir (1Ki 10:11). Partial catalog of (Eze 28:13). Seen in the foundation of the New Jerusalem in John's apocalyptic vision (Rev 21:19-20).

In kings' crowns (2Sa 12:30; 1Ch 20:2).

Figurative: (Isa 54:11-12).

See Adamant; Agate; Amber; Amethyst; Bdellium; Beryl; Carbuncle; Carnelian; Chalcedony; Chrysolite; Chrysoprase; Coral; Crystal; Diamond; Emerald; Flint; Glowing Metal; Hardest Stone; Jacinth; Jasper; Minerals of the Bible, 1; Onyx; Pearl; Ruby; Sapphire; Sardius; Sardonyx; Topaz; Turquoise.

STONING [*6232, 8083+, *3342, 3344].

NIV+ See STONE

The ordinary form of capital punishment prescribed by Hebrew law (Lev 20:2) for blasphemy (Lev 24:16), idolatry (Dt 13:6-10), desecration of the Sabbath day (Ex 31:15; 35:2; Nu 15:32-36), human sacrifice (Lev 20:2), occultism (Lev 20:27).

Unlike unintentional sins, for which there are provisions of God's mercy, one who sets his hand defiantly to despise the word of God and to blaspheme his name must be punished. The one who sins defiantly (literally "with a high hand"), whether in the case of the willful blasphemer (Ex 20:7; 22:28; Lev 24:11-16), or the Sabbath-breaker (Ex 31:12-15; 35:2), was guilty of high-handed rebellion and was judged with death (Nu 15:30-31,32-36).

Execution took place outside city (Lev 24:14; 1Ki 21:10,13; Ac 7:58).

See Assault and Battery; Bruise, Bruises; Flog, Flogging; Lashes; Scourging; Stripes.

STOOL [78].

NIV+ FOOTSTOOL

(2Ki 4:10).

Footstool:

Figurative: Of the earth (Isa 66:1; Mt 5:35; Ac 7:49), temple (1Ch 28:2; La 2:1), sanctuary (Ps 99:5; 132:7), enemies of Jesus (Ps 110:1; Mt 22:44; Mk 12:36; Lk 20:43; Ac 2:35; Heb 1:13).

See Footstool.

STORE CITIES [*5016]. Supply depots for provisions and arms (1Ki 9:15-19; 2Ch 8:4-6; 16:4).

STOREHOUSE [238, 238, 667, 1074+]. Place for keeping treasures, supplies, and equipment (Dt 28:8; 1Ch 29:16; 2Ch 31:10; Mal 3:10). *See Barn; Granary.*

STORK [2884] *(kindly, loyal one).* Forbidden as food (Lev 11:19). Nest of, in fir trees (Ps 104:17). Migratory (Jer 8:7).

Figurative: (Zec 5:9).

STOVE Household stoves usually made of clay; were small and portable, burning charcoal; the well-to-do had metal stoves or braziers (Jer 36:22ff).

STRAIGHT [448+6298+7156, 3837, 3838, 3841, 4200+5790, 4200, 4793, 4797, 5019, 5584, 6590, 9461, 867, 1838, 2312, 2316, 2318].

NIV+ STRAIGHTEN, STRAIGHTENED

Name of a street in Damascus (Ac 9:11).

Figurative:

Of righteousness, "straight paths" (Isa 40:3-4; Mt 3:3; Heb 12:13).

STRAIT GATE *See Gates, Figurative.*

STRAKES Archaic word for:

1. "White stripes" (Ge 30:37). *See Stripes, 4.*
2. "Greenish or reddish depressions" (Lev 14:37).

STRANGERS [1591, 1731, 2319, 2424, 3359+4202, 5796, 5799, 9369, 259, 3828, 4215, 4229, 4230, 5810].

NIV+ ESTRANGED, STRANGE, STRANGER, STRANGER'S, STRANGERS

Mosaic law relating to: Authorized bondservice of (Lev 25:44-45), usury of (Dt 15:3; 23:20), sale to, of flesh of animals that had died (Dt 14:21), forbid their being made

kings over Israel (Dt 17:15), their eating the Passover (Ex 12:43,48), their eating things offered in sacrifice (Ex 29:33; Lev 22:10,12,25), their blaspheming (Lev 24:16), their approaching the tabernacle (Nu 1:51), their eating blood (Lev 17:10), injustice to (Ex 12:49; Lev 24:22; Nu 9:14; Dt 1:16; Jer 22:3), oppression of, forbidden (Ex 22:21; Lev 23:9; Dt 24:14,17; 27:19; Jer 22:3). Instances of oppression of (Eze 22:29; Mal 3:5).

Required to observe the Sabbath (Ex 20:10; 23:12). Might offer sacrifices (Lev 17:8; 22:18-19). Were buried in separate burial places (Mt 27:7).

Kindness to, required (Lev 19:33-34). Love of, commanded (Dt 10:18-19). Abhorrence of, forbidden (Dt 23:7). Marriage with, forbidden (Dt 25:5). Hospitality to. *See Hospitality.*

See Alms; Foreigner; Heathen; Proselyte.

STRANGLE [2871, 4725, *4465].

NIV+ STRANGLED, STRANGLING

To deprive of life by choking. Israelites were forbidden to eat flesh from strangled animals (Lev 17:12). At the Jerusalem council even Jewish Christians were forbidden to eat such meat (Ac 15:20).

STRATEGY [6783]. In war (Ge 14:14-15; 32:7-8; Jos 8:3-25; Jdg 7:16-23; 20:29-43; 2Sa 15:32-34, w 17:7-14; Ne 6; Isa 15:1; Jer 6:5).

See Ambush; Armies.

STRAW [5495, 7990, 9320, *2811]. Used for feed (Ge 24:32; Isa 65:25), for brick (Ex 5:7).

STRAY [5610, 5615, 5742, 6073, 8178, 8706, 8740, 8938, 9494].

NIV+ ASTRAY, STRAYED, STRAYING, STRAYS

Animals straying to be returned (Ex 23:4; Dt 22:1-3). Instances of animals straying, Kish's (1Sa 9).

STREAKED [6819]. Mottled or blotchy of color, characterizing Laban's sheep (Ge 30:35; 31:8,12). *See Speckled.*

STREAM OF EGYPT *See River of Egypt.*

STREETS [*2006, 2575, 8148, 8798, 3847, 4423, 4860].

NIV+ STREET

(Pr 1:20; Na 2:4; Mk 6:56; Lk 14:21; Ac 9:11).

STRENGTH [*226, 579, 599, 1475, 1476, 1504, 1524, 2006, 2432, 2616, 2616, 2617, 2621, 2657, 3338, 3946, 4097, 4394, 6434, 6437, 6786, 8435, 9361, 10768, 10772, 1011, 1540, 1543, 1904, 1932, 2185, 2708, 2709, 2710, 3194, 3489, 3869, 5105, 5114].

NIV+ STRENGTHEN, STRENGTHENED,
STRENGTHENING, STRENGTHENS, STRONG,
STRONGER, STRONGEST, STRONGLY

A title given Yahweh (1Sa 15:29). Spiritual. *See Power, Spiritual.*

STRIFE [4506, 5175, 8190, 2251].

NIV+ STRIVE, STRIVES, STRIVING

General:

Ps 55:9 Confuse the wicked, O Lord, confound their speech, for I see violence and strife in the city.

Ps 80:6 You have made us a source of contention to our neighbors, and our enemies mock us.

Hated by God (Isa 58:4)—

Hab 1:3 Why do you make me look at injustice? Why do

you tolerate wrong? Destruction and violence are before me; there is strife, and conflict abounds.

Punishment for—

Isa 41:11 "All who rage against you will surely be ashamed and disgraced; those who oppose you will be as nothing and perish. ¹²Though you search for your enemies, you will not find them. Those who wage war against you will be as nothing at all.

Ro 2:8 But for those who are self-seeking and who reject the truth and follow evil, there will be wrath and anger. (+Ro 2:9)

Correction of—

Mt 18:15 "If your brother sins against you, go and show him his fault, just between the two of you. If he listens to you, you have won your brother over. ¹⁶But if he will not listen, take one or two others along, so that 'every matter may be established by the testimony of two or three witnesses.' ¹⁷If he refuses to listen to them, tell it to the church; and if he refuses to listen even to the church, treat him as you would a pagan or a tax collector.

Christ brings—

Mt 10:34 "Do not suppose that I have come to bring peace to the earth. I did not come to bring peace, but a sword. ³⁵For I have come to turn "'a man against his father, a daughter against her mother, a daughter-in-law against her mother-in-law— ³⁶a man's enemies will be the members of his own household.'

Lk 12:51 Do you think I came to bring peace on earth? No, I tell you, but division. ⁵²From now on there will be five in one family divided against each other, three against two and two against three. ⁵³They will be divided, father against son and son against father, mother against daughter and daughter against mother, mother-in-law against daughter-in-law and daughter-in-law against mother-in-law."

Lk 12:58 As you are going with your adversary to the magistrate, try hard to be reconciled to him on the way, or he may drag you off to the judge, and the judge turn you over to the officer, and the officer throw you into prison. ⁵⁹I tell you, you will not get out until you have paid the last penny."

Domestic (Pr 19:13; 21:19; 25:24).

Caused by:

Busybodies (Pr 26:20)

Perversity—

Pr 16:28 A perverse man stirs up dissension, and a gossip separates close friends.

Hatred (Pr 10:12)

Lusts—

Jas 4:1 What causes fights and quarrels among you? Don't they come from your desires that battle within you? ²You want something but don't get it. You kill and covet, but you cannot have what you want. You quarrel and fight. You do not have, because you do not ask God.

Pride (Pr 13:10), scornfulness (Pr 22:10), wrath (Pr 15:18; 29:22; 30:33), excessive indulgence in the use of intoxicating drinks (Pr 23:29-30).

Destructive to Those Involved Therein:

Mt 12:25 Jesus knew their thoughts and said to them, "Every kingdom divided against itself will be ruined, and every city or household divided against itself will not stand.

Mk 3:24 If a kingdom is divided against itself, that kingdom cannot stand. ²⁵If a house is divided against itself, that house cannot stand. (+Lk 11:17)

Exhortations against:

Ge 13:8 So Abram said to Lot, "Let's not have any quarreling between you and me, or between your herdsmen and mine, for we are brothers.

Ge 45:24 Then he sent his brothers away, and as they were leaving he said to them, "Don't quarrel on the way!"

Ps 31:20 In the shelter of your presence you hide them from the intrigues of men; in your dwelling you keep them safe from accusing tongues.

Pr 3:30 Do not accuse a man for no reason—when he has done you no harm. (+Pr 17:14; 25:8)

Mt 5:25 "Settle matters quickly with your adversary who is taking you to court. Do it while you are still with him on the way, or he may hand you over to the judge, and the judge may hand you over to the officer, and you may be thrown into prison.

Mt 5:39 But I tell you, Do not resist an evil person. If someone strikes you on the right cheek, turn to him the other also. ⁴⁰And if someone wants to sue you and take your tunic, let him have your cloak as well. ⁴¹If someone forces you to go one mile, go with him two miles.

Ro 12:18 If it is possible, as far as it depends on you, live at peace with everyone.

Ro 13:13 Let us behave decently, as in the daytime, not in orgies and drunkenness, not in sexual immorality and debauchery, not in dissension and jealousy.

Ro 14:1 Accept him whose faith is weak, without passing judgment on disputable matters.

Ro 14:19 Let us therefore make every effort to do what leads to peace and to mutual edification.

Ro 14:21 It is better not to eat meat or drink wine or to do anything else that will cause your brother to fall.

Ro 16:17 I urge you, brothers, to watch out for those who cause divisions and put obstacles in your way that are contrary to the teaching you have learned. Keep away from them. ¹⁸For such people are not serving our Lord Christ, but their own appetites. By smooth talk and flattery they deceive the minds of naive people.

1Co 4:6 Now, brothers, I have applied these things to myself and Apollos for your benefit, so that you may learn from us the meaning of the saying, "Do not go beyond what is written." Then you will not take pride in one man over against another. ⁷For who makes you different from anyone else? What do you have that you did not receive? And if you did receive it, why do you boast as though you did not?

2Co 12:20 For I am afraid that when I come I may not find you as I want you to be, and you may not find me as you want me to be. I fear that there may be quarreling, jealousy, outbursts of anger, factions, slander, gossip, arrogance and disorder.

Gal 5:15 If you keep on biting and devouring each other, watch out or you will be destroyed by each other.

Gal 5:20 idolatry and witchcraft; hatred, discord, jealousy, fits of rage, selfish ambition, dissensions, factions

Php 2:3 Do nothing out of selfish ambition or vain conceit, but in humility consider others better than yourselves.

Php 2:14 Do everything without complaining or arguing, ¹⁵so that you may become blameless and pure, children of God without fault in a crooked and depraved generation, in which you shine like stars in the universe

1Ti 3:2 Now the overseer must be above reproach, the husband of but one wife, temperate, self-controlled, respectable, hospitable, able to teach, ³not given to drunkenness, not violent but gentle, not quarrelsome, not a lover of money.

1Ti 6:3 If anyone teaches false doctrines and does not agree to the sound instruction of our Lord Jesus Christ and to godly teaching, [4]he is conceited and understands nothing. He has an unhealthy interest in controversies and quarrels about words that result in envy, strife, malicious talk, evil suspicions [5]and constant friction between men of corrupt mind, who have been robbed of the truth and who think that godliness is a means to financial gain.

1Ti 6:20 Timothy, guard what has been entrusted to your care. Turn away from godless chatter and the opposing ideas of what is falsely called knowledge, [21]which some have professed and in so doing have wandered from the faith.

Grace be with you.

2Ti 2:14 Keep reminding them of these things. Warn them before God against quarreling about words; it is of no value, and only ruins those who listen.

2Ti 2:23 Don't have anything to do with foolish and stupid arguments, because you know they produce quarrels. [24]And the Lord's servant must not quarrel; instead, he must be kind to everyone, able to teach, not resentful. [25]Those who oppose him he must gently instruct, in the hope that God will grant them repentance leading them to a knowledge of the truth,

Tit 3:1 Remind the people to be subject to rulers and authorities, to be obedient, to be ready to do whatever is good, [2]to slander no one, to be peaceable and considerate, and to show true humility toward all men.

[3]At one time we too were foolish, disobedient, deceived and enslaved by all kinds of passions and pleasures. We lived in malice and envy, being hated and hating one another.

Tit 3:9 But avoid foolish controversies and genealogies and arguments and quarrels about the law, because these are unprofitable and useless.

Jas 3:14 But if you harbor bitter envy and selfish ambition in your hearts, do not boast about it or deny the truth. [15]Such "wisdom" does not come down from heaven but is earthly, unspiritual, of the devil. [16]For where you have envy and selfish ambition, there you find disorder and every evil practice.

Abstinence from, honorable (Pr 20:3).

Prayers concerning (Ps 55:9)—

1Ti 2:8 I want men everywhere to lift up holy hands in prayer, without anger or disputing.

Proverbs concerning (Pr 3:30)—

Pr 6:12 A scoundrel and villain, who goes about with a corrupt mouth, [13]who winks with his eye, signals with his feet and motions with his fingers, [14]who plots evil with deceit in his heart—he always stirs up dissension.

Pr 6:16 There are six things the LORD hates, seven that are detestable to him: [17]haughty eyes, a lying tongue, hands that shed innocent blood, [18]a heart that devises wicked schemes, feet that are quick to rush into evil, [19]a false witness who pours out lies and a man who stirs up dissension among brothers.

Pr 10:12 Hatred stirs up dissension, but love covers over all wrongs.

Pr 13:10 Pride only breeds quarrels, but wisdom is found in those who take advice.

Pr 15:18 A hot-tempered man stirs up dissension, but a patient man calms a quarrel.

Pr 17:1 Better a dry crust with peace and quiet than a house full of feasting, with strife.

Pr 17:14 Starting a quarrel is like breaching a dam; so drop the matter before a dispute breaks out.

Pr 17:19 He who loves a quarrel loves sin; he who builds a high gate invites destruction.

Pr 18:6 A fool's lips bring him strife, and his mouth invites a beating.

Pr 18:19 An offended brother is more unyielding than a fortified city, and disputes are like the barred gates of a citadel.

Pr 19:13 A foolish son is his father's ruin, and a quarrelsome wife is like a constant dripping.

Pr 20:3 It is to a man's honor to avoid strife, but every fool is quick to quarrel.

Pr 21:19 Better to live in a desert than with a quarrelsome and ill-tempered wife.

Pr 22:10 Drive out the mocker, and out goes strife; quarrels and insults are ended.

Pr 23:29 Who has woe? Who has sorrow? Who has strife? Who has complaints? Who has needless bruises? Who has bloodshot eyes? [30]Those who linger over wine, who go to sample bowls of mixed wine.

Pr 25:8 do not bring hastily to court, for what will you do in the end if your neighbor puts you to shame?

Pr 25:24 Better to live on a corner of the roof than share a house with a quarrelsome wife.

Pr 26:17 Like one who seizes a dog by the ears is a passer-by who meddles in a quarrel not his own.

Pr 26:20 Without wood a fire goes out; without gossip a quarrel dies down.

[21]As charcoal to embers and as wood to fire, so is a quarrelsome man for kindling strife.

Pr 27:15 A quarrelsome wife is like a constant dripping on a rainy day;

Pr 28:25 A greedy man stirs up dissension, but he who trusts in the LORD will prosper.

Pr 29:22 An angry man stirs up dissension, and a hot-tempered one commits many sins.

Pr 30:33 For as churning the milk produces butter, and as twisting the nose produces blood, so stirring up anger produces strife."

See Anger; Envy; Jealousy; Malice.

Instances of:

Between Abraham and Lot's herdsmen (Ge 13:6-7), Abimelech's (Ge 21:25), Isaac's and those of Gerar (Ge 26:20-22). Laban and Jacob (Ge 31:36).

Israelites—

Dt 1:12 But how can I bear your problems and your burdens and your disputes all by myself?

Jephthah and his brothers (Jdg 11:2), and Ephraimites (Jdg 12:1-6). Israel and Judah, about David (2Sa 19:41-43). Disciples, over who might be the greatest (Mk 9:34; Lk 22:24). Jews, concerning Jesus (Jn 10:19). Christians at Antioch, about circumcision (Ac 15:2). Paul and Barnabas, about Mark (Ac 15:38-39). Pharisees and Sadducees, concerning the Resurrection (Ac 23:7-10).

Christians, at Corinth—

1Co 1:10 I appeal to you, brothers, in the name of our Lord Jesus Christ, that all of you agree with one another so that there may be no divisions among you and that you may be perfectly united in mind and thought. [11]My brothers, some from Chloe's household have informed me that there are quarrels among you. [12]What I mean is this: One of you says, "I follow Paul"; another, "I follow Apollos"; another, "I follow Cephas"; still another, "I follow Christ." **1Co 3:3** You are still worldly. For since there is jealousy and quarreling among you, are you not worldly? Are you not acting like mere men? [4]For when one says, "I follow

Paul," and another, "I follow Apollos," are you not mere men?

1Co 6:1 If any of you has a dispute with another, dare he take it before the ungodly for judgment instead of before the saints? ²Do you not know that the saints will judge the world? And if you are to judge the world, are you not competent to judge trivial cases? ³Do you not know that we will judge angels? How much more the things of this life! ⁴Therefore, if you have disputes about such matters, appoint as judges even men of little account in the church! ⁵I say this to shame you. Is it possible that there is nobody among you wise enough to judge a dispute between believers? ⁶But instead, one brother goes to law against another—and this in front of unbelievers!

⁷The very fact that you have lawsuits among you means you have been completely defeated already. Why not rather be wronged? Why not rather be cheated?

1Co 11:16 If anyone wants to be contentious about this, we have no other practice—nor do the churches of God.

¹⁷In the following directives I have no praise for you, for your meetings do more harm than good. ¹⁸In the first place, I hear that when you come together as a church, there are divisions among you, and to some extent I believe it. ¹⁹No doubt there have to be differences among you to show which of you have God's approval. (+1Co 11:20-21)

At Philippi—

Php 1:15 It is true that some preach Christ out of envy and rivalry, but others out of goodwill. ¹⁶The latter do so in love, knowing that I am put here for the defense of the gospel. (+Php 1:17)

STRIKER [*2118, 2150, 4804, 5595, 5597, 5782, 7003, 9546, 10411, *3139, 4091, 4250, 4684, 4703, 5597*].
NIV+ STRIKE, STRICKEN, STRIKES, STRIKING, STROKE, STRUCK
See Violence.

STRINGED INSTRUMENTS [5593]. *See Music.*

STRIPES [7203].
1. Wounds inflicted by scourges for punishment (Ex 21:25). *See Bruise, Bruises, 1.*

2. Authorized by Jewish law for certain offenses (Dt 25:2-3). *See Lashes, 1.*

3. Practiced also by Romans (Mt 27:26 & Jn 19:1, w Isa 53:5). Roman floggings were so brutal that sometimes the victim died before crucifixion. *See Flog, Flogging.*

4. The Hebrew terms for the words "poplar" and "white stripes" are puns on the name Laban. As Jacob had gotten the best of Esau (whose other name, Edom, means "red") by means of red stew (Ge 25:30), so he now tries to get the best of Laban (whose name means "white") by means of white branches (Ge 30:37). *See Strakes, 1.*

See also, Assault and Battery; Scourging; Stoning.

STRIVING WITH GOD Folly of (Job 9:3; 33:13; 40:2; Isa 45:9; Ro 9:20).

STRONG DRINK *See Beer; Fermented Drink; Wine.*

STUBBLE [7990]. Figurative of the wicked (Ex 15:7; Job 21:18; Ps 83:13; Isa 5:24; 40:24; 41:2; 47:14; Jer 13:24; Joel 2:5; Na 1:10; Mal 4:1).

STUBBORNNESS [4213+, 6253, 6437, 7996, 7997, 8001, 9244, *4801, 5016, 5018*].
NIV+ STUBBORN, STUBBORN-HEARTED, STUBBORNLY
See Obduracy.

STUDENTS [9441, *3412*].
NIV+ STUDY, STUDENT, STUDIED
Poverty of (2Ki 4:1). In state school (Da 1). In schools of the prophets (1Sa 19:20; 1Ki 20:35; 2Ki 2:2-3,5,7,15; 4:1). *See Instruction; School.*

STUMBLING [*1892, 4173, 4842, 5597, 9023, *4682, 4684, 4760, 4998*].
NIV+ STUMBLE, STUMBLED, STUMBLES
Figurative:
Causes of (Ps 69:6). Stone of (Isa 8:14; Ro 9:32-33; 1Pe 2:8). Stumbling block (Lev 19:14; Ps 119:165; Isa 57:14; Jer 6:21; Eze 3:20; 7:19; 14:3-4,7; Zep 1:3; Lk 11:52; Ro 11:9; 14:13; 1Co 1:23; 8:9-13; Rev 2:14).
See Temptation.

SUAH [6053] (possibly *offal, dung, viscera*). An Asherite. The son of Zophah (1Ch 7:36).

SUBJECTS [*3899, 4044, 5989, 6268, 6269, *1944, 5679, 5718*]. *See Citizens; Government; Patriotism; Rulers.*

SUBMISSION [*14, 3338+5989, 5202, 5976, 6122, 6268, 6700, 9393, *1505, 2340, 5640, 5717, 5718*].
NIV+ SUBMIT, SUBMISSIVE, SUBMITS, SUBMITTED
To authority: Jesus an example of (Mt 26:39,42; Mk 14:36; Lk 22:42; Heb 5:8).
Of Paul (1Co 16:7).
See Obedience.

SUBSTITUTION [4614, 9455].
NIV+ SUBSTITUTE
(Ge 22:13; Ex 28:38). The offering for the offerer (Lev 1:4; 16:21-22). The Levites for the firstborn of the Israelites (Nu 3:12,41,45; 8:18). The life of Ahab for that of Ben-Hadad (1Ki 20:42).
Of Christ for us (Isa 53:4-6; 1Co 5:7; 2Co 5:21; Gal 3:13; 1Pe 2:24).
See Suffering, Vicarious.

SUBURB *See Pasture.*

SUCATHITES [8460]. One of three clans of scribes who lived at Jabez (1Ch 2:55).

SUCCESSION Of priests, irregularity in (Heb 7:1-28). *See Priest.* Of kings. *See Kings.*

SUCCOTH [6111] (*booths*).
NIV+ SUCCOTH BENOTH
1. A city probably east of the Jordan. Jacob builds a house in (Ge 33:17). Allotted to Gad (Jos 13:27). People of, punished by Gideon (Jdg 8:5-8,14-16). Located near the Jordan (1Ki 7:46; 2Ch 4:17; Ps 60:6; 108:7).
2. First camping place of the Israelites on leaving Rameses (Ex 12:37; 13:20; Nu 33:5-6).

SUCCOTH BENOTH [6112].
NIV+ SUCCOTH
A pagan idol brought into Samaria after Assyria had captured it (2Ki 17:24-30).

SUCHATHITES *See Sucathites.*

SUDDEN EVENTS
NIV+ SUDDEN, SUDDENLY
(Ecc 9:12; Mal 3:1; Mt 24:27; Mk 13:36; Lk 2:13; Ac 2:2; 9:3; 16:26).

SUETONIUS A Roman writer (c. A.D. 69-140), famous for his *Lives of the Caesars.*

SUFFERING [*2118, 2703, 4799, 5186, 5253, 5951, 6700, 6713, 6714, 6715, 6740, 8317, 10472, *1181, 2568, 3465, 4077, 4248, 5224, 5309*].

NIV+ SUFFER, LONG-SUFFERING, SUFFERED, SUFFERINGS, SUFFERS

For Christ:

Promised by Christ (Mt 10:34-36; Lk 12:51-53,58-59)—

Ac 9:16 I will show him how much he must suffer for my name."

Fellowship with Christ on account of—

Php 3:10 I want to know Christ and the power of his resurrection and the fellowship of sharing in his sufferings, becoming like him in his death,

Conditions of joint heirship with Christ—

Ro 8:17 Now if we are children, then we are heirs—heirs of God and co-heirs with Christ, if indeed we share in his sufferings in order that we may also share in his glory.

¹⁸I consider that our present sufferings are not worth comparing with the glory that will be revealed in us. ¹⁹The creation waits in eager expectation for the sons of God to be revealed. ²⁰For the creation was subjected to frustration, not by its own choice, but by the will of the one who subjected it, in hope ²¹that the creation itself will be liberated from its bondage to decay and brought into the glorious freedom of the children of God.

²²We know that the whole creation has been groaning as in the pains of childbirth right up to the present time.

Ro 8:26 In the same way, the Spirit helps us in our weakness. We do not know what we ought to pray for, but the Spirit himself intercedes for us with groans that words cannot express.

A privilege—

Php 1:29 For it has been granted to you on behalf of Christ not only to believe on him, but also to suffer for him,

Rejoicing in (Ac 5:41)—

Col 1:24 Now I rejoice in what was suffered for you, and I fill up in my flesh what is still lacking in regard to Christ's afflictions, for the sake of his body, which is the church.

Motives for patient enduring of: Future glory (Ro 8:17-18; 2Co 4:8-10)—

2Co 4:11 For we who are alive are always being given over to death for Jesus' sake, so that his life may be revealed in our mortal body. ¹²So then, death is at work in us, but life is at work in you.

2Co 4:17 For our light and momentary troubles are achieving for us an eternal glory that far outweighs them all. ¹⁸So we fix our eyes not on what is seen, but on what is unseen. For what is seen is temporary, but what is unseen is eternal.

1Pe 4:13 But rejoice that you participate in the sufferings of Christ, so that you may be overjoyed when his glory is revealed. ¹⁴If you are insulted because of the name of Christ, you are blessed, for the Spirit of glory and of God rests on you.

Reigning with Christ (2Ti 2:12; Rev 22:5).

Consolations in—

2Co 1:7 And our hope for you is firm, because we know that just as you share in our sufferings, so also you share in our comfort.

Php 2:27 Indeed he was ill, and almost died. But God had

mercy on him, and not on him only but also on me, to spare me sorrow upon sorrow. ²⁸Therefore I am all the more eager to send him, so that when you see him again you may be glad and I may have less anxiety. ²⁹Welcome him in the Lord with great joy, and honor men like him, ³⁰because he almost died for the work of Christ, risking his life to make up for the help you could not give me.

2Ti 2:12 if we endure, we will also reign with him. If we disown him, he will also disown us;

1Pe 5:10 And the God of all grace, who called you to his eternal glory in Christ, after you have suffered a little while, will himself restore you and make you strong, firm and steadfast.

Patience in (1Co 4:11)—

1Co 4:12 We work hard with our own hands. When we are cursed, we bless; when we are persecuted, we endure it; ¹³when we are slandered, we answer kindly. Up to this moment we have become the scum of the earth, the refuse of the world.

2Th 1:4 Therefore, among God's churches we boast about your perseverance and faith in all the persecutions and trials you are enduring.

⁵All this is evidence that God's judgment is right, and as a result you will be counted worthy of the kingdom of God, for which you are suffering.

Jas 5:10 Brothers, as an example of patience in the face of suffering, take the prophets who spoke in the name of the Lord. (+1Pe 4:14)

See Affliction; Persecution.

Of Christ:

Purpose of his coming—

Lk 24:46 He told them, "This is what is written: The Christ will suffer and rise from the dead on the third day, ⁴⁷and repentance and forgiveness of sins will be preached in his name to all nations, beginning at Jerusalem.

Jn 6:51 I am the living bread that came down from heaven. If anyone eats of this bread, he will live forever. This bread is my flesh, which I will give for the life of the world."

Jn 10:11 "I am the good shepherd. The good shepherd lays down his life for the sheep.

Jn 10:15 just as the Father knows me and I know the Father—and I lay down my life for the sheep.

Jn 11:50 You do not realize that it is better for you that one man die for the people than that the whole nation perish."

⁵¹He did not say this on his own, but as high priest that year he prophesied that Jesus would die for the Jewish nation, ⁵²and not only for that nation but also for the scattered children of God, to bring them together and make them one.

Reason for Christ's coming—

Ro 4:25 He was delivered over to death for our sins and was raised to life for our justification.

Ro 5:6 You see, at just the right time, when we were still powerless, Christ died for the ungodly. ⁷Very rarely will anyone die for a righteous man, though for a good man someone might possibly dare to die. ⁸But God demonstrates his own love for us in this: While we were still sinners, Christ died for us.

Ro 14:15 If your brother is distressed because of what you eat, you are no longer acting in love. Do not by your eating destroy your brother for whom Christ died.

1Co 1:17 For Christ did not send me to baptize, but to

preach the gospel—not with words of human wisdom, lest the cross of Christ be emptied of its power.

[18]For the message of the cross is foolishness to those who are perishing, but to us who are being saved it is the power of God.

1Co 1:23 but we preach Christ crucified: a stumbling block to Jews and foolishness to Gentiles, [24]but to those whom God has called, both Jews and Greeks, Christ the power of God and the wisdom of God.

1Co 15:3 For what I received I passed on to you as of first importance: that Christ died for our sins according to the Scriptures,

2Co 5:14 For Christ's love compels us, because we are convinced that one died for all, and therefore all died. [15]And he died for all, that those who live should no longer live for themselves but for him who died for them and was raised again.

Gal 1:4 who gave himself for our sins to rescue us from the present evil age, according to the will of our God and Father,

Gal 2:20 I have been crucified with Christ and I no longer live, but Christ lives in me. The life I live in the body, I live by faith in the Son of God, who loved me and gave himself for me. [21]I do not set aside the grace of God, for if righteousness could be gained through the law, Christ died for nothing!"

Eph 5:2 and live a life of love, just as Christ loved us and gave himself up for us as a fragrant offering and sacrifice to God.

Eph 5:25 Husbands, love your wives, just as Christ loved the church and gave himself up for her

1Th 5:9 For God did not appoint us to suffer wrath but to receive salvation through our Lord Jesus Christ. [10]He died for us so that, whether we are awake or asleep, we may live together with him.

Heb 2:9 But we see Jesus, who was made a little lower than the angels, now crowned with glory and honor because he suffered death, so that by the grace of God he might taste death for everyone.

[10]In bringing many sons to glory, it was fitting that God, for whom and through whom everything exists, should make the author of their salvation perfect through suffering.

Heb 2:14 Since the children have flesh and blood, he too shared in their humanity so that by his death he might destroy him who holds the power of death—that is, the devil—

Heb 2:18 Because he himself suffered when he was tempted, he is able to help those who are being tempted.

Heb 5:8 Although he was a son, he learned obedience from what he suffered [9]and, once made perfect, he became the source of eternal salvation for all who obey him

Heb 9:15 For this reason Christ is the mediator of a new covenant, that those who are called may receive the promised eternal inheritance—now that he has died as a ransom to set them free from the sins committed under the first covenant.

[16]In the case of a will, it is necessary to prove the death of the one who made it,

Heb 9:28 so Christ was sacrificed once to take away the sins of many people; and he will appear a second time, not to bear sin, but to bring salvation to those who are waiting for him.

Heb 10:10 And by that will, we have been made holy through the sacrifice of the body of Jesus Christ once for all.

Heb 10:18 And where these have been forgiven, there is no longer any sacrifice for sin.

[19]Therefore, brothers, since we have confidence to enter the Most Holy Place by the blood of Jesus, [20]by a new and living way opened for us through the curtain, that is, his body,

1Pe 2:21 To this you were called, because Christ suffered for you, leaving you an example, that you should follow in his steps.

1Pe 2:24 He himself bore our sins in his body on the tree, so that we might die to sins and live for righteousness; by his wounds you have been healed.

1Pe 3:18 For Christ died for sins once for all, the righteous for the unrighteous, to bring you to God. He was put to death in the body but made alive by the Spirit,

1Pe 4:1 Therefore, since Christ suffered in his body, arm yourselves also with the same attitude, because he who has suffered in his body is done with sin.

1Jn 3:16 This is how we know what love is: Jesus Christ laid down his life for us. And we ought to lay down our lives for our brothers.

See Atonement; Jesus the Christ, Death of; Purpose of His Death; Sufferings of.

Vicarious:

Ex 9:13 Then the LORD said to Moses, "Get up early in the morning, confront Pharaoh and say to him, 'This is what the LORD, the God of the Hebrews, says: Let my people go, so that they may worship me, [14]or this time I will send the full force of my plagues against you and against your officials and your people, so you may know that there is no one like me in all the earth. [15]For by now I could have stretched out my hand and struck you and your people with a plague that would have wiped you off the earth. [16]But I have raised you up for this very purpose, that I might show you my power and that my name might be proclaimed in all the earth.

Jn 15:13 Greater love has no one than this, that he lay down his life for his friends.

Ro 9:3 For I could wish that I myself were cursed and cut off from Christ for the sake of my brothers, those of my own race,

1Pe 2:21 To this you were called, because Christ suffered for you, leaving you an example, that you should follow in his steps.

[22]"He committed no sin, and no deceit was found in his mouth."

[23]When they hurled their insults at him, he did not retaliate; when he suffered, he made no threats. Instead, he entrusted himself to him who judges justly. [24]He himself bore our sins in his body on the tree, so that we might die to sins and live for righteousness; by his wounds you have been healed.

1Jn 3:16 This is how we know what love is: Jesus Christ laid down his life for us. And we ought to lay down our lives for our brothers.

See Jesus the Christ, Sufferings of; Penalty, Vicariously Assumed; above, Suffering, Of Christ.

Instances of:

Goliath, for the Philistines (1Sa 17).

SUICIDE (Am 9:2; Rev 9:6). Temptation to, of Jesus (Mt 4:5-6; Lk 4:9-11). Of the Philippian jailer (Ac 16:27). *See Death, Physical, Desired.*

Instances of:

Samson (Jdg 16:29-30). Saul and his armor-bearer (1Sa

31:4-5; 1Ch 10:4-5). Ahithophel (2Sa 17:23). Zimri (1Ki 16:18). Judas (Mt 27:5; Ac 1:18).

SUING [*5477, 8189, 8190, 8191, *3210, 3212*].
NIV+ LAWSUIT, LAWSUITS
(Mt 5:40). *See Creditor; Debtor.*

SUKKITES, SUKKIIM [6113]. Mercenary soldiers, possibly Libyan, who joined Shishak in his invasion of Judah (2Ch 12:3).

SUKKOTH *See Succoth.*

SULFUR, SULPHUR [1730, *2520, 2523*]. Fire and, rained upon Sodom (Ge 19:24; Lk 17:29). In Israel (Dt 29:23). Figurative of God's judgment (Job 18:15; Ps 11:6; Isa 30:33; Eze 38:22; Rev 9:17-18; 14:10; 19:20; 21:8). *See Minerals of the Bible.*

SUMER One of two political divisions, Sumer and Akkad, originally comprising Babylonia.

SUMMER [5249, 7810, 7811, 10627, *2550*]. Season of, promised while the earth remains (Ge 8:22). Cool rooms for (Jdg 3:20,24; Am 3:15). Fruits of (2Sa 16:1-2; Isa 16:9; 28:4; Jer 40:10,12; 48:32; Am 8:1-2; Mic 7:1). Drought of (Ps 32:4). Given by God (Ps 74:17). The time for labor and harvest (Pr 6:6-8; 10:5; 30:25; Jer 8:20). Snow in (Pr 26:1). Threshing in (Da 2:35). Approach of (Mt 24:32; Mk 13:28; Lk 21:30).
Figurative: (Jer 8:20).

SUMMER HOUSE, SUMMER PALACE
The wealthy had separate residences for hot and cold seasons. Called a "summer house" (Am 3:15), a "summer palace" (Jdg 3:20, ftn).
See Winter Apartment, Winter House.

SUN [240, 2780, 3064, 3427, 7416, 8840, 9087, *424, 2463*].
NIV+ SUNDOWN, SUNRISE, SUNSET, SUNSHINE
Created (Ge 1:14-18; Ps 74:16; 136:7; Jer 31:35). Rising and setting of (Ecc 1:5). Diurnal motion of (Ps 19:4,6). Worship of, forbidden (Dt 4:19; 17:3). Worshiped (Job 31:26-28; Jer 8:2; Eze 6:4,6; 8:16). Kings of Judah dedicate horses to (2Ki 23:11).
Miracles concerning: Darkening of (Ex 10:21-23; Isa 5:30; 24:23; Eze 32:7; Joel 2:10,31; 3:15; Am 8:9; Mic 3:6; Mt 24:29; 27:45; Mk 13:24; 15:33; Lk 21:25; 23:44-45; Ac 2:20; Rev 6:12; 8:12; 9:2; 16:8). Stands still (Jos 10:12-13; Hab 3:11). Shadow of, goes back on Ahaz's stairway (2Ki 20:11; Isa 38:8).
Does not shine in heaven (Rev 21:23).
Figurative:
(Ps 84:11; Mal 4:2; Jdg 5:31; Isa 30:26; 60:19-20; Jer 15:9; Rev 1:16; 12:1; 19:17).

SUN, WORSHIP OF Worship of the sun found varied forms in the ancient world. Even the Israelites at times worshiped sun images (Lev 26:30; Isa 17:8). Shamash was a great sun god of the ancient Middle East. Phoenicia worshiped a sun Baal, Baal Hamon. In Egypt the center of sun worship was On, or Heliopolis, where the sun was called Re.

SUNDAY The first day of the week, commemorating the resurrection of Jesus (Jn 20:1-25), and the Day of Pentecost (Ac 2:1-41). For a time after the Ascension of Jesus the Christians met on the seventh and the first days of the week, but as the Hebrew Christian churches declined in influence, the tendency to observe the Hebrew Sabbath slowly passed. The disciples at Troas worshiped on the first day (Ac 20:7). Paul admonished the Corinthians to lay by in store as God had prospered them, doing it week by week on the first day (1Co 16:2). The term "Lord's Day" occurs (Rev 1:10).

SUN-DIAL NIV "stairway" (2Ki 20:11; Isa 38:8). *See Stairs.*

SUNSTROKE (2Ki 4:19).

SUPER-APOSTLES [*693+5663*]. Paul's critics (2Co 11:5; 12:11).

SUPEREROGATION The doctrine of excessive and meritorious righteousness (Eze 33:12-13; Lk 17:10).

SUPERSCRIPTION (*inscription*).
1. The wording on coins (Mt 22:20).
2. Words written on a board attached to the cross naming the crime of which the condemned was accused (Mk 15:26; Lk 23:38; Jn 19:19-20).
3. Titles of the Psalms. *See Music, Symbols Used in; Psalms.*

SUPERSTITION (Ac 25:19).
Instances of:
Israelites in supposing that their defeat in battle with the Philistines was due to their not having brought the ark of the covenant with them (1Sa 4:3, w 4:10-11), attributing their calamities to having stopped offering sacrifices to the Queen of Heaven (Jer 44:17-19). Philistines in refusing to step on the threshold where the image of Dagon had repeatedly fallen (1Sa 5:5).
The belief of the Syrians concerning the help of the gods (1Ki 20:23). Nebuchadnezzar in supposing that the spirit of the gods was upon Daniel (Da 4:8-9). The sailors who threw Jonah into the sea (Jnh 1:4-16). The disciples in supposing they saw a spirit when Jesus came walking upon the sea (Mt 14:26; Mk 6:49-50). Herod in imagining that John the Baptist had risen from the dead (Mk 6:14,16).
The Gadarenes on account of Jesus casting demons out of the demoniac (Mt 8:34). The disciples who were frightened at the appearance of Peter (Ac 12:14-15). The Ephesians in their sorceries (Ac 19:13-19). The people of the island of Malta in imagining Paul to be a god (Ac 28:6).
See Idolatry; Sorcery.

SUPERSTITIOUS NIV "very religious" (Ac 17:22), could either commend or criticize the Athenians.

SUPH, SUPHAH [6069, 6071] (*reeds, rushes*). The "The Red Sea" is used for these words (Nu 21:14; Dt 1:1). Suph is an unidentified region E of the Jordan; Suphah, is probably the region of the Red Sea.

SUPPER [*1268, 1270*]. *See Feasts; Eucharist.*

SUPPER, LORD'S *See Lord's Supper.*

SUPPLICATION [2858, 9382, 9384]. *See Prayer.*

SUPREME COMMANDER [9580]. Commander-in-chief of the Assyrian army (Isa 20:1; 2Ki 18:17).

SUR [6075]. The gate of the temple (2Ki 11:6).

SURETY *See Security, For Debt; Debt.*

SURFEITING Overindulgence of food or drink; dissipation (Lk 21:34).

SUSA [8809, 10704].

1. Capital of the Medo-Persian Empire (Est 1:2-3; 8:15).
2. King's palace at (Ne 1:1; Est 1:2,5; 2:5,8; 4:8,16; 8:14-15; 9:11,15).

SUSAH See Hazar Susah.

SUSANCHITES NIV "of Susa" (Ezr 4:9). See Susa.

SUSANNA [5052] (lily).

1. Woman who ministered to Christ (Lk 8:1-3).
2. Heroine of The History of Susanna, in the OT Apocrypha.

SUSI [6064] ([my] horse). A Manassite (Nu 13:11).

SUSIM See Hazar Susah.

SUSPICION [*7861, 5707]. See Accusation, False.

SWADDLING BAND Bands of cloth in which a newborn baby was wrapped (Lk 2:7,12). Used figuratively (Job 38:9).

SWALLOW [2000]. Builds its nest in the sanctuary (Ps 84:3). Chattering of, figurative of the mourning of the afflicted (Isa 38:14). Migration of (Jer 8:7).

SWAN See White Owl.

SWEARING [457, 606, 5951, 8652, 8678, 3923, 3991].
NIV+ SWEAR, SWEARS, SWORE, SWORN
See Blasphemy; God, Name of; Oath.

SWEAT [2399, 2629]. (Ge 3:19). An offense in the sanctuary (Eze 44:18). Of blood (Lk 22:44).

SWEAT, BLOODY Physical manifestation of the agony of Jesus in Gethsemane (Lk 22:44). Christ's sweat most likely did not become bloody, but "his sweat was like great drops of blood falling to the ground" as if from an open wound.

SWEET INCENSE Made of spices (Ex 25:6). See Incense.

SWEET SAVOR See Pleasing Aroma.

SWELLING [1301, 7377, 7379, 8143, 8421, 4399].
NIV+ SWELL, SWELLS, SWOLLEN
Usually "pride"; or means the flooding of the Jordan in the spring (Jer 12:5; 49:19; 50:44). It refers to the tumult of a stormy sea (Ps 46:3).

SWIFT [2590, 3616+3618, 4554, 4559, 6101, 7824, 7837, 3955, 5442].
NIV+ SWIFTER, SWIFTLY
An amphibious bird (Isa 38:14; Jer 8:7).

SWINE See Animals; Pig.

SWORD, THE [2995, 4839, 7347, 8939, 3479, 4855].
NIV+ SWORDS, SWORDSMEN
Probable origin of (Ge 3:24). Was pointed (Eze 21:15). Frequently had two edges (Ps 149:6).

Described as:
Sharp (Ps 57:4). Bright (Na 3:3). Glittering (Dt 32:41; Job 20:25). Oppressive (Jer 46:16). Hurtful (Ps 144:10). Carried in a sheath or scabbard (1Ch 21:27; Jer 47:6; Eze

21:3-5). Suspended from the belt (1Sa 17:39; 2Sa 20:8; Ne 4:18; Ps 45:3).

Was Used:
By the patriarchs (Ge 34:25; 48:22). By the Jews (Jdg 7:22; 2Sa 24:9). By heathen nations (Jdg 7:22; 1Sa 15:33). For self-defense (Lk 22:36). For destruction of enemies (Nu 21:24; Jos 6:21). For punishing criminals (1Sa 15:33; Ac 12:2). Sometimes for self-destruction (1Sa 31:4-5; Ac 16:27). Hebrews early acquainted with making of (1Sa 13:19). In time of war, plowshares made into (Joel 3:10). In time of peace, made into plowshares (Isa 2:4; Mic 4:3). Sharpened and furbished before going to war (Ps 7:12; Eze 21:9). Was brandished over the head (Eze 32:10). Was thrust through enemies (Eze 16:40). Often threatened as a punishment (Lev 26:25,33; Dt 32:25). Often sent as a punishment (Ezr 9:7; Ps 78:62). Was one of God's four sore judgments (Eze 14:21). Those slain by, communicated ceremonial uncleanness (Nu 19:16).

Illustrative:
Of the Word of God (Eph 6:17, w Heb 4:12). Of the word of Christ (Isa 49:2, w Rev 1:16). Of the justice of God (Dt 32:41; Zec 13:7). Of the protection of God (Dt 33:29). Of war and contention (Mt 10:34). Of severe and heavy calamities (Eze 5:2,17; 14:17; 21:9). Of deep mental affliction (Lk 2:35). Of the wicked (Ps 17:13). Of the tongue of the wicked (Ps 57:4; 64:3; Pr 12:18). Of persecuting spirit of the wicked (Ps 37:14). Of the end of the wicked (Pr 5:4). Of false witnesses (Pr 25:18). Of judicial authority (Ro 13:4). Drawing of illustrative of war and destruction (Lev 26:33; Eze 21:3-5). Putting into its sheath illustrative of peace and friendship (Jer 47:6). Living by illustrative of violence (Ge 27:40). Not departing from one's house illustrative of perpetual calamity (2Sa 12:10).

SYCAMINE NIV "mulberry tree" (Lk 17:6).

SYCAMORE-FIG [9204, 5191].
NIV+ FIG, SYCAMORE-FIGS
A tree. Abundant in the land of Canaan (1Ki 10:27; 2Ch 1:15; 9:27; Isa 9:10). Groves of, cared for (1Ch 27:28). Destroyed by frost (Ps 78:47). Care of (Am 7:14). Zacchaeus climbs into (Lk 19:4).

SYCHAR [5373]. A village one half mile N of Jacob's well, on the E slope of Mt. Ebal (Jn 4:5).

SYCHEM See Shechem, 1.

SYENE See Aswan.

SYMBOLS, AND SIMILITUDES [253, 2355, 3213, 4603, 5694, 531].
NIV+ SYMBOL, SYMBOLIC, SYMBOLIZES, SYMBOLS

General
Almond tree branch (Jer 1:11). Altar split apart (1Ki 13:3,5). Basket for measuring (Zec 5:6-11). Belt (Jer 13:1-7; Ac 21:11). Blood sprinkled (Ex 24:8). Book cast into Euphrates (Jer 51:63). Bow shot (1Sa 20:21-37; 2Ki 13:15-19). Bread (Mt 26:26; Mk 14:22; Lk 22:19). Breaking of clay jar (Jer 19). Change of residence (Eze 12:3-11). Childlike (Mt 18:3; Mk 10:14-15; Lk 18:16-17). Circumcision, of the covenant of Abraham (Ge 17:11; Ro 4:11). Cooking (Jer 1:13; Eze 4:9-15; 24:3-5). Curtain of the temple torn in two (Mt 27:51; Mk 15:38; Lk 23:45). Darkness (Ex 20:21; Lev 16:2; 1Ki 8:12; Ps 18:11; 97:2; Heb 12:18-19). Death [without mourning] (Eze 24:16-19). Deeds of land (Jer 32:1-16). Eating food with anxiety (Eze 12:17-20). Figs [basket of good and bad] (Jer 24). Fish

[Jonah in the] (Mt 16:4; Lk 11:29-30). Food (2Ki 19:29; Isa 37:30). Fruit [basket of] (Jer 24:1-3; Am 8:1-2).

Handwriting on the wall (Da 5:5-6,16-28). Harvest (2Ki 19:29). Invitation by enemy to approach (1Sa 14:8-12). Isaiah's children (Isa 8:18). Manna [in the desert] (Jn 6:31-58). Marrying a prostitute (Hos 1:2-9; 3:1-4). Men meeting Saul (1Sa 10:2-7). Mosaic rites [system of] (Heb 9:9-10,18-23). Mute (Eze 3:26-27; 24:27; 29:21; 33:22; Lk 1:20-22,62-64). Nakedness (Isa 20:2-4). Passover [of the sparing of the firstborn] (Ex 12:3-28). Passover [atonement made by Christ] (1Co 5:7). Pillar of cloud (Ex 13:21-22; 14:19-20; 19:9,16). Plumb line (Am 7:7-8). Posture [lie on side] (Eze 4:4-8). Pot for cooking (Eze 24:1-5). Praying toward the temple (1Ki 8:29; Da 6:10). Rainbow (Ge 9:12-13).

Sacrificial animals (Ge 15:8-11; Jn 1:29,36). Salt [gracious words] (Col 4:6). Salt, Covenant of (Nu 18:19). Scroll flying (Zec 5:2-4). Shadow on Ahaz's stairway (2Ki 20:8-11; Isa 38:7-8). Shaving head and beard (Eze 5:1-4). Siege (Eze 4:1-3). Snake of bronze [lifted up, of Christ] (Nu 21:8-9; Jn 3:14). Spiritual rest [Canaan] (Heb 3:11-12; 4:5). Star in the east (Mt 2:2). Sticks and staffs (Eze 37:16-17; Zec 11:7,10-11,14). Striken rock [of Christ] (Ex 17:6; 1Co 10:4). Tabernacle and sanctuary (Ps 15:1; Eze 37:27; Heb 8:2,5; 9:1-12,23-24). Thunder and lightning on Mount Sinai (Ex 19:9,16). Thunder and rain (1Sa 12:16-18). Trees of life and knowledge (Ge 2:9,17; 3:3,24; Rev 22:2). Unclean food [preparing of] (Eze 4:9-17). Vine (Eze 15:2; 19:10-14). Water [lapping of] (Jdg 7:4-8). Water to drink [drawing of in hospitality of] (Ge 24:13-15,42-44). Waving and Ritual offering (Ex 29:24-28; Lev 8:27-29; 9:21). Wine (Jer 25:15-17; Mt 26:27; Mk 14:23; Lk 22:17). Wine [of the atoning blood] (Mt 26:27-29; Mk 14:23-25; Lk 22:17-18,20). Wineskins (Jer 13:12; 19:1-2,10). Wounding (1Ki 20:35-40). Yokes (Jer 27:2-3; 28:10).

Of the Holy Spirit:

Water (Jn 3:5; 7:38-39), cleansing by (Eze 16:9; 36:25; Eph 5:26; Heb 10:22), making prosperous (Ps 1:3; Isa 27:3,6; 44:3-4; 58:11).

Fire (Mt 3:11), refining (Isa 4:4; Mal 3:2-3), guiding (Ex 13:21; Ps 78:14), searching (Zep 1:12, w 1Co 2:10). Flame shaped like tongues (Ac 2:3,6,11).

Wind (SS 4:16), incomprehensible (Jn 3:8; 1Co 12:11), powerful (1Ki 19:11, w Ac 2:2), quiet but present (Jn 3:8), reviving, life giving (Eze 37:9-10,14).

Oil (Ps 45:7), healing (Isa 1:6; Lk 10:34; Rev 18:13), joy causing (Isa 61:3; Heb 1:9), illuminating (Zec 4:2-3,11-13; Mt 25:3-4; 1Jn 2:20,27), consecrating (Ex 29:7; 30:30; Isa 61:1).

Rain and Dew (Ps 72:6), enriching and fertilizing (Eze 34:26-27; Hos 6:3; 10:12; 14:5), refreshing (Ps 68:9; Isa 18:4), abundant (Ps 133:3), imperceptible (2Sa 17:12, w Mk 4:26-28).

A Dove (Mt 3:16).

A Voice (Isa 6:8), speaking (Mt 10:20), guiding (Isa 30:21, w Jn 16:13), warning (Heb 3:7-11).

A Seal (Rev 7:2), impressing (Job 38:14, w 2Co 3:18), guarantee (Eph 1:13-14; 4:30; 2Co 1:22).

See Holy Spirit, Emblems of.

Washings, a symbol of purity. *See Washings; Purification.* For symbolisms of color, *See Colors, Figurative and Symbolic.*

See also, Allegory; Instruction, By Object Lessons; By Types; In Religion.

SYMEON *See Simeon.*

SYMPATHY [5653, 5714, 8171, *5217, 5218*].
NIV+ SYMPATHETIC, SYMPATHIZE, SYMPATHIZED

Ecc 7:2 It is better to go to a house of mourning than to go to a house of feasting, for death is the destiny of every man; the living should take this to heart.

Commanded: (Ro 12:15)

Jas 1:27 Religion that God our Father accepts as pure and faultless is this: to look after orphans and widows in their distress and to keep oneself from being polluted by the world.

1Pe 3:8 Finally, all of you, live in harmony with one another; be sympathetic, love as brothers, be compassionate and humble.

In Christ:

Php 2:1 If you have any encouragement from being united with Christ, if any comfort from his love, if any fellowship with the Spirit, if any tenderness and compassion, ²then make my joy complete by being like-minded, having the same love, being one in spirit and purpose.

Instances of:

David with Hanun (2Sa 10:2). The Jewish maid with Naaman (2Ki 5:1-4).

Job's friends—

Job 2:11 When Job's three friends, Eliphaz the Temanite, Bildad the Shuhite and Zophar the Naamathite, heard about all the troubles that had come upon him, they set out from their homes and met together by agreement to go and sympathize with him and comfort him. ¹²When they saw him from a distance, they could hardly recognize him; they began to weep aloud, and they tore their robes and sprinkled dust on their heads. ¹³Then they sat on the ground with him for seven days and seven nights. No one said a word to him, because they saw how great his suffering was.

Turned against Job—

Job 6:14 "A despairing man should have the devotion of his friends, even though he forsakes the fear of the Almighty.

Job 22:29 When men are brought low and you say, 'Lift them up!' then he will save the downcast.

Ebed-Melech with Jeremiah (Jer 38:7-13). Nebuchadnezzar with Daniel (Da 6:18-23).

The four friends with the crippled man whom they took to Jesus (Mk 2:3-4). Others with the helpless whom they brought to Jesus (Mt 4:24). The good Samaritan with the man who fell among robbers (Lk 10:33-35). The Jews with Martha and Mary (Jn 11:19,31,33). The people of Malta with the shipwrecked mariners (Ac 28:1-2).

See Afflicted; Afflictions; Jesus the Christ, Compassion of; Kindness; Pity; Poor.

SYNAGOGUE [697, 801, 5252] (*place of gathering*).
NIV+ SYNAGOGUES

1. Primarily an assembly (Ac 13:43; Jas 2:2). Constitutes a court of justice (Lk 12:11; Ac 9:2). Had powers of criminal courts (Mt 10:17; Mt 23:34; Ac 22:19; 26:11), of ecclesiastical courts (Jn 9:22,34; 12:42; 16:2).

2. Place of assembly. Scriptures read and expounded in (Ne 8:1-8; 9:3,5; Mt 4:23; 9:35; 13:54; Mk 1:39; Lk 4:15-33; 13:10; Jn 18:20; Ac 9:20; 13:5-44; 14:1; 15:21; 17:2, 10; 18:4,19,26).

In Jerusalem (Ac 6:9), Damascus (Ac 9:2,20), other cities (Ac 14:1; 17:1,10; 18:4). Built by Jairus (Lk 7:5),

Jesus performed healing in (Mt 12:9-13; Lk 13:11-14). Alms given in (Mt 6:2).

Of Satan (Rev 2:9; 3:9).

See Church, Place of Worship; Testaments, Time Between.

SYNAGOGUE, MEN OF THE GREAT

Or of the Great Assembly, a college of learned men supposedly organized by Nehemiah after the return from exile (Ne 8-10), to which Jewish tradition attributed the origination and authoritative promulgation of many ordinances and regulations.

SYNOPTIC GOSPELS, THE

A careful comparison of the four Gospels reveals that Matthew, Mark, and Luke are noticeably similar, while John is quite different. The first three Gospels agree extensively in language, in the material they include, and in the order in which events and sayings from the life of Christ are recorded. (Chronological order does not appear to have been rigidly followed in any of the Gospels, however). Because of this agreement, these three books are called the Synoptic Gospels (*syn*, "together with"; *optic*, "seeing"; thus "seeing together"). For an example of agreement in content see Mt 9:2-8; Mk 2:3-12; Lk 5:18-26. An instance of verbatim agreement is found in Mt 10:22a; Mk 13:13a; Lk 21:17. A mathematical comparison shows that 91 percent of Mark's Gospel is contained in Matthew, while 53 percent of Mark is found in Luke. Such agreement raises questions as to the origin of the Synoptic Gospels. Did the authors rely on a common source? Were they interdependent? Questions such as these constitute what is known as the Synoptic Problem. Several suggested solutions have been advanced:

1. *The use of oral tradition.* Some have thought that tradition had become so stereotyped that it provided a common source from which all the Gospel writers drew.

2. *The use of an early Gospel.* Some have postulated that the Synoptic authors all had access to an earlier Gospel, now lost.

3. *The use of written fragments.* Some have assumed that written fragments had been composed concerning various events from the life of Christ and that these were used by the Synoptic authors.

4. *Mutual dependence.* Some have suggested that the Synoptic writers drew from each other with the result that what they wrote was often very similar.

5. *The use of two major sources.* The most common view currently is that the Gospel of Mark and a hypothetical document, called *Quelle* (German for "source") or *Q*, were used by Matthew and Luke as sources for most of the materials included in their Gospels.

6. *The priority and use of Matthew.* Another view suggests that the other two Synoptics drew from Matthew as their main source.

7. *A combination of most of the above.* This theory assumes that the authors of the Synoptic Gospels made use of oral tradition, written fragments, mutual dependence on other Synoptic writers or on their Gospels, and the testimony of eyewitnesses.

SYNTYCHE [*5345*] (*coincidence, success*). Christian woman at Philippi (Php 4:2).

SYRACUSE [*5352*]. A city of Sicily. Paul visits (Ac 28:12).

SYRIA [*5353*].
NIV+ SYRIAN

Highlands lying between the Euphrates river and the Mediterranean Sea. Called Aram, from the son of Shem (Ge 10:22-23; Nu 23:7; 1Ch 1:17; 2:23). In the time of Abraham it seems to have embraced the region between the rivers Tigris and Euphrates (Ge 24:10, w 25:20), including Paddan Aram (Ge 25:20, ftn; 28:5).

Minor kingdoms within the region: Aram Zobah, also called Zobah (1Sa 14:47; 2Sa 8:3; 10:6,8; 1Ki 11:23; 1Ch 18:5,9; 19:6; Ps 60, title), Geshur (2Sa 15:8), Aram Rehob, also called Beth Rehob (2Sa 10:6,8), Damascus (2Sa 8:5-6; 1Ch 18:5-6), Hamath (2Sa 8:9-10).

Conquest of: By David (2Sa 8:3-13), by Jeroboam (2Ki 14:25,28), by Tiglath-Pileser, king of Assyria (2Ki 16:7-9; 18:33-34). People of, colonized in Samaria by the king of Assyria (2Ki 17:24). Confederate with Nebuchadnezzar (2Ki 24:2; Jer 39:5).

The Roman province of, included the land of Canaan (Lk 2:2-3), and Phoenicia (Mk 7:26; Ac 21:3). The fame of Jesus extended over (Mt 4:24).

Paul goes to, with letters to apprehend the Christians; is converted and begins his evangelistic ministry (Ac 9:1-31). *See Paul.*

Paul preaches in (Ac 15:41; 18:18; 21:3; Gal 1:21). Damascus, the capital of. *See Damascus.*

Wars between, and the kingdoms of Judah and Israel. *See Israel.* Prophecies concerning (Isa 7:8-16; 8:4-7; 17:1-3; Jer 1:15; 49:23-27; Am 1:3-5; Zec 9:1).

SYRIAC *See Aramaic.*

SYRIAC VERSIONS *See Texts and Versions.*

SYRIA-MAACHAH *See Aram Maacah.*

SYRIAN [*5354*].
NIV+ SYRIA

The people of Syria (Lk 4:27). *See Aram, 6; Aramaic; Syria.*

SYRIAN PHOENICIAN, SYROPHOENICIAN
[*5355*].
NIV+ PHOENICIA, SYRIA

The nationality of a woman whose daughter was cured by Jesus (Mt 15:21-28; Mk 7:24-30).

SYRTIS [*5358*]. Banks of quicksand off the coast of Libya (Ac 27:17).

T

TAANACH [9505]. A city conquered by Joshua (Jos 12:21). Allotted to Manasseh (Jos 17:11; 1Ch 7:29). Canaanites not driven from (Jos 17:12; Jdg 1:27). Assigned to the Levites (Jos 21:25). The scene of Barak's victory (Jdg 5:19). One of Solomon's district governors at (1Ki 4:12).

TAANATH SHILOH, TAANATH-SHILOH
[9304] (possibly *approach to Shiloh* IDB). Town on the NE border of Ephraim (Jos 16:6), c. ten miles E of Shechem.

TABALIAH [3189] (*Yahweh has dipped*). The son of Hosah (1Ch 26:11).

TABBAOTH [3191] (*[ornamental or signet] ring*). A family of temple servants who returned with Zerubbabel (Ezr 2:43; Ne 7:46).

TABBATH [3195] (possibly *good*). A place probably E of the Jordan between Jabesh Gilead and Succoth (Jdg 7:22).

TABEAL *See Tabeel, 2.*

TABEEL [3174, 3175] (*God [El] is good*).
1. A Persian official in Samaria (Ezr 4:7).
2. The father of one whom the kings of Syria and Israel sought to make king in Judah instead of Ahaz (Isa 7:6).

TABERAH [9323] (*burning*). An encampment of Israel in the wilderness where fire of the Lord consumed some complainers (Nu 11:1-3; Dt 9:22), the site is unidentified.

TABERNACLE [185, 5438, 6109, *5008, 5009*].
NIV+TABERNACLES
One existed before Moses received the pattern authorized on Mount Sinai (Ex 33:7-11). The one instituted by Moses was called Sanctuary (Ex 25:8), Tent of Meeting (Ex 27:21; 33:7; 2Ch 5:5), Tabernacle of the Testimony (Ex 38:21; Nu 1:50), Tent of the Testimony (Nu 17:7-8; 2Ch 24:6), Temple of the Lord (1Sa 1:9; 3:3), House of the Lord (Jos 6:24).
The pattern of, revealed to Moses (Ex 25:9; 26:30; 39:32,42-43; Ac 7:44; Heb 8:5). Materials for, voluntarily offered (Ex 25:1-8; 35:4-29; 36:3-7). Value of the substance contributed for (Ex 38:24-31). Workmen who constructed it were inspired (Ex 31:1-11; 35:30-35).
Description of: Frame (Ex 26:15-37; 36:20-38). Outer covering (Ex 25:5; 26:7-14; 36:14-19). Second covering (Ex 25:5; 26:14; 35:7,23; 36:19; 39:34). Curtains of (Ex 26:1-14,31-37; 27:9-16; 35:15,17; 36:8-19,35,37), Court of (Ex 27:9-17; 38:9-16,18; 40:8,33).
Holy Place of (Ex 26:31-37; 40:22-26; Heb 9:2-6,8). The Most Holy Place (Ex 26:33-35; 40:20-21; Heb 9:3-5,7-8).
Furniture of (Ex 25:10-40; 27:1-8,19; 37; 38:1-8). *See Altar; Ark; Atonement Cover; Bread, Consecrated; Lampstand; Cherubim.*
Completed (Ex 39:32). Dedicated (Nu 7). Sanctified (Ex 29:43; 40:9-16; Nu 7:1). Anointed with holy oil (Ex 30:25-26; Lev 8:10; Nu 7:1). Sprinkled with blood (Lev 16:15-20; Heb 9:21,23). Filled with the cloud of glory (Ex 40:34-38).
How prepared for removal during the travels of the Israelites (Nu 1:51; 4:5-15). How and by whom carried (Nu 4:5-33; 7:6-9). Strangers forbidden to enter (Nu 1:51). Duties of the Levites concerning. *See Levites.* Defilement of, punished (Lev 15:31; Nu 19:13,20; Eze 5:11; 23:38). Duties of the priests in relation to. *See Priest.* Israelites worship at (Nu 10:3; 16:19,42-43; 20:6; 25:6; 1Sa 2:22; Ps 27:4). Offerings brought to (Lev 17:4; Nu 31:54; Dt 12:5-6,11-14).
Tribes encamped around, while in the wilderness (Nu 2). All males required to appear before, three times each year (Ex 23:17). Tabernacle tax (Ex 30:11-16).
Carried in front of the Israelites in the line of march (Nu 10:33-36; Jos 3:3-6). The Lord reveals himself at (Lev 1:1; Nu 1:1; 7:89; 12:4-10; Dt 31:14-15).
Pitched at Gilgal (Jos 4:18-19), at Shiloh (Jos 18:1; 19:51; Jdg 18:31; 20:18,26-27; 21:19; 1Sa 2:14; 4:3-4; Jer 7:12,14), at Nob (1Sa 21:1-6), at Gibeon (1Ch 21:29). Renewed by David and pitched on Mount Zion (1Ch 15:1; 16:1-2; 2Ch 1:4). Solomon offers sacrifice at (2Ch 1:3-6). Brought to the temple by Solomon (2Ch 5:5, w 1Ki 8:1,4-5).
Symbol of spiritual things (Ps 15:1; Heb 8:2,5; 9:1-12,24).
See Levites; Priest; Temple.

TABERNACLES, FEAST OF [6109, *5009*]. Also called the Feast of Ingathering. Instituted (Ex 23:16; 34:22; Lev 23:34-43; Nu 29:12-40; Dt 16:13-16). Design of (Lev 23:42-43). The law read in connection with, every seventh year (Dt 31:10-12; Ne 8:18).
Observance of, after the captivity (Ezr 3:4; Ne 8:14-18), by Jesus (Jn 7:2,14). Observance of, omitted (Ne 8:17). Penalty for not observing (Zec 14:16-19).
Jeroboam institutes an idolatrous feast to correspond to, in the eighth month (1Ki 12:32-33; 1Ch 27:11).

TABITHA [*5412*] (*gazelle*). A Christian woman in Joppa; befriended poor widows; raised from dead by Peter (Ac 9:36-43).

TABLE [2200, 4990, 5121, 5492, 8947, *367, 369, 404, 2879, 2884, 4752, 5263, 5544*].
NIV+TABLES
1. Table for food (Jdg 1:7; 1Ki 2:7).
2. Lord's table = Lord's Supper (1Co 10:21).
3. "Wait on tables" (Ac 6:2) refers to distribution of food, etc., to the Christian poor.
4. Tabernacle and temple were provided with various tables (Ex 25:23-30).

TABLE OF CONSECRATED BREAD Twelve loaves of consecrated, unleavened bread were placed on a table in the Holy Place in the tabernacle and temple (Ex 25:30; Lev 24:5-9).

TABLET [4246, 4283, *4400, 4419*]
NIV+TABLETS
1. Stone or clay tablets for writing (Ex 24:12; Eze 4:1; Lk 1:63). Metaphorical (2Co 3:3). *See Tablets of the Law.*
2. *See Dress.*

TABLETS OF THE LAW Stone tablets on which Moses wrote the Ten Commandments (Ex 31:18; 32:15-16; Dt 4:13; 5:22). *See Commandments and Statutes, Of God.*

TABOR [9314].

NIV+ AZNOTH TABOR, KISLOTH TABOR

1. A mountain on the border of Issachar (Jos 19:22; Jdg 8:18; Ps 89:12; Jer 46:18; Hos 5:1). Assembling place of Barak's army (Jdg 4:6,12,14).

2. A plain located by the great tree of Tabor (1Sa 10:3),

3. A Levitical city in Zebulun (1Ch 6:77).

See Kisloth Tabor.

TABRET *See Tambourine.*

TABRIMMON, TABRIMON [3193] (*[pagan god] Rimmon is good*). The father of Ben-Hadad, king of Syria (1Ki 15:18).

TACHE *See Clasp.*

TACHMONITE *See Tahkemonite.*

TACKLE, TACKLING [5006]. The masts and rigging of a ship (Isa 33:23; Ac 27:19).

TACT [10302]. (Pr 15:1; 25:15). In preaching (1Co 9:19-22; 2Co 12:6). Of Gideon (Jdg 8:1-3). Of Saul, in managing malcontents (1Sa 10:27; 11:7,12-15). Nabal's wife (1Sa 25:18-37).

In David's popular methods: In mourning for Abner (2Sa 3:28-37), in organizing the temple music (1Ch 15:16-24), in securing popular consent to bringing the ark to Jerusalem (1Ch 13:1-4). Mephibosheth (2Sa 9:8). Joab's trick in obtaining David's consent to the return of Absalom (2Sa 14:1-22). The woman of Tekoa (2Sa 14:4-20). The wise woman of Abel (2Sa 20:16-22). Solomon, in arbitrating between the harlots (1Ki 3:24-28).

Mordecai, in concealing Esther's nationality (Est 2:10). Esther, in placating the king (Est 5-7). Paul, in circumcising Timothy (Ac 16:3), in turning the preaching of adversaries to account (Php 1:10-22), in stimulating benevolent giving (2Co 8:1-8; 9:1-5), in arraying the two religious factions of the Jews against each other when he was in trouble (Ac 23:6-10). The town clerk of Ephesus (Ac 19:35-41). The church council at Jerusalem (Ac 21:20-25).

See Wisdom.

TACTICS *See Armies; Strategy.*

TADMOR [9330] (*palm tree*). A city in the desert NE of Damascus (1Ki 9:18; 2Ch 8:4), a fabulously rich trade metropolis later called Palmyra. Magnificent ruins have been excavated.

TAHAN, TAHANITE [9380, 9385] (possibly *grace, favor*).

1. The son of Ephraim and his clan (Nu 26:35).

2. A descendant of Ephraim (1Ch 7:25).

TAHAPANES *See Tahpanhes.*

TAHASH [9392] (*a species of dolphin*). The son of Nahor and Reumah (Ge 22:24).

TAHATH [9394, 9395] (*compensation*).

1. A camping place of the Israelites (Nu 33:26-27).

2. A Kohathite (1Ch 6:24,37).

3. The name of two Ephraimites (1Ch 7:20).

TAHKEMONITE [9376]. The family of David's chief captain (2Sa 23:8); also spelled Hacmonite (1Ch 11:11).

TAHPANHES [9387] (*the fortress of Penhase [the Black Man]*). A fortress city at the E edge of the Nile Delta to which Israelites fled after the fall of Jerusalem (Jer 2:16; 43:7-9; 44:1; 46:14; Eze 30:18).

TAHPENES [9388] (title *wife of the king*). A queen of Egypt (1Ki 11:19-20).

TAHREA [9390] (possibly *clever one* BDB). The grandson of Mephibosheth (1Ch 9:41), also spelled Tarea (1Ch 8:35).

TAHTIM HODSHI, TAHTIM-HODSHI [9398]. A place E of Jordan in the land of the Hittites (2Sa 24:6).

TAILORING (Ex 31:2-3,6,10; 39:1).

TALEBEARER (*The vice of repeating damaging reports, either true or false*).

Ps 15:1 LORD, who may dwell in your sanctuary? Who may live on your holy hill?

²He whose walk is blameless and who does what is righteous, who speaks the truth from his heart ³and has no slander on his tongue, who does his neighbor no wrong and casts no slur on his fellowman,

Pr 11:13 A gossip betrays a confidence, but a trustworthy man keeps a secret.

Pr 20:19 A gossip betrays a confidence; so avoid a man who talks too much.

Separates friends:

Pr 16:28 A perverse man stirs up dissension, and a gossip separates close friends.

Pr 17:9 He who covers over an offense promotes love, but whoever repeats the matter separates close friends.

Causes:

Strife—

Pr 26:20 Without wood a fire goes out; without gossip a quarrel dies down.

Tension—

Pr 18:8 The words of a gossip are like choice morsels; they go down to a man's inmost parts.

Is Forbidden:

Lev 19:16 "'Do not go about spreading slander among your people. "'Do not do anything that endangers your neighbor's life. I am the LORD.

1Ti 5:11 As for younger widows, do not put them on such a list. For when their sensual desires overcome their dedication to Christ, they want to marry.

1Ti 5:13 Besides, they get into the habit of being idle and going about from house to house. And not only do they become idlers, but also gossips and busybodies, saying things they ought not to.

See Busybody; Gossip; Slander; Speaking, Evil.

Instances of:

Joseph (Ge 37:2). Israelites (2Sa 3:23). Tobiah (Ne 6).

See Backbiting; Slander.

TALENT [3971, 10352, 5419].

NIV+ TALENTS

A weight equal to sixty minas or about seventy-five pounds (1Ki 9:14,28; 10:10,14; Ex 25:39; 38:27). Parables of the (Mt 18:23-34; 25:15-30). *See Measure.*

TALES [1212]. Avoid myths and old wives' tales (1Ti 4:7). *See Myths.*

TALITHA KOUM, TALITHA CUMI [3182+5420]. Aramaic for "Little girl, get up!" (Mk 5:41).

TALKING [*606, 1819, 6218, 7023, 8557, *515, 1368*,
3281, 3306, 3364, 3917, 5196].
NIV+ TALK, TALKED, TALKER, TALKERS, TALKS
With God.
See Communion.

TALMAI [9440] (possibly *[my] furrow maker*).
1. A son of Anak (Nu 13:22; Jos 15:14; Jdg 1:10).
2. King of Geshur (2Sa 3:3; 13:37; 1Ch 3:2).

TALMON [3236] (perhaps *brightness*). A gatekeeper of
the temple (1Ch 9:17). Family of, returned from captivity
with Zerubbabel (Ezr 2:42; Ne 7:45; 11:19; 12:25).

TALMUD (*education, instruction*). A collection of
Jewish tradition of the early Christian centuries;
The two forms: Palestinian and Babylonian.

TAMAH *See Temah.*

TAMAR [9470, 9471, *2500*] (*date palm*).
NIV+ BAAL TAMAR, HAZAZON TAMAR
1. The wife of Er, then of Onan; mother of Perez and
Zerah (Ge 38; Mt 1:3).
2. Daughter of David; abused by his half brother Amon
(2Sa 13:1-33).
3. The daughter of Absalom (2Sa 14:27).
4. Unidentified borderland site in restored Israel (Eze
47:19; 48:28).
5. A city in Syria, more commonly known as Tadmor,
later Palmyra.

TAMARISK [869]. A tree (1Sa 22:6; 31:13), planted by
Abraham (Ge 21:33). *See Tree.*

TAMBOURINE [9512, 9528].
NIV+ TAMBOURINES
Used by Miriam (Ex 15:20), by Jephthah's daughter
(Jdg 11:34). Used in religious service (2Sa 6:5; 1Ch 13:8;
Ps 68:25; 81:2; 149:3; 150:4). Used in dances (Job 21:12).
See Music, Instruments of.

TAMIR *See Tadmor.*

TAMMUZ [9452].
1. Month four in sacred sequence, month ten in civil
sequence. Not mentioned by name in the Bible. Ezekiel
called in the fourth month (Eze 1:1); Nebuchadnezzar
breaks through the wall of Jerusalem (Jer 39:1). The time
for tending vines (June-July). *See Month, 4.*
2. The fertility god worshiped in Mesopotamia, Syria,
and Israel; corresponded to Osiris in Egypt and Adonis of
the Greeks (Eze 8:14).

TANACH *See Taanach.*

TANHUMETH [9489] (*comfort*). The father of Seraiah
(2Ki 25:23; Jer 40:8).

TANIS *See Zoar.*

TANNER, TANNING [*1114*]. Tanning is the conversion of skin into leather by removing the hair and soaking
it in tanning solution (Ex 25:5; 26:14; Ac 10:6).

TANTALIZING NIV "provoking" (1Sa 1:6-7); "taunt"
(1Ki 18:27).

TAPESTRY [763]. (Pr 7:16; 31:22). Of the tabernacle
(Ex 26:1-14,31-37; 27:9-17; 36:8-18). Gold thread woven
in (Ex 39:3). In palaces (Est 1:6; SS 1:5). In groves (2Ki
23:7). *See Curtains; Embroidery; Veil.*

TAPHATH [3264] (possibly *little child*). The daughter
of Solomon (1Ki 4:11).

TAPPUAH [9516, 9517] (*apple*).
NIV+ BETH TAPPUAH, EN TAPPUAH
1. A city of Judah (Jos 12:17; 15:34).
2. A city in Ephraim (Jos 16:8; 17:8).
3. A city near Tirzah in Samaria (2Ki 15:16); a variant
reading for Tiphsah. *See Tiphsah, 2.*
4. The son of Hebron (1Ch 2:43).

TAR [2819]. A flammable substance, asphalt (Ge 14:10).
Lumps of asphalt are often seen even today floating in the
southern end of the Dead Sea. Used as mortar in building
the Tower of Babel (Ge 11:3), and in setting the burnt brick
which formed the outer layers of the ziggurat of Ur. It was
used by Moses' mother to caulk the papyrus basket (Ex
2:3), as for the rafts and reed boats on the Euphrates.
See Caulkers; Pitch.

TARAH *See Terah, 2.*

TARALAH [9550]. A city of Benjamin between Irpeel
and Zelah (Jos 18:28).

TAREA [9308]. A son of Micah (1Ch 8:35). Called Tahrea (1Ch 9:41).

TARES *See Weeds, 2.*

TARGET [4766, 5133]. A defensive article of armor.
Made of bronze (1Sa 17:6), of gold (1Ki 10:16; 2Ch 9:15).
Used by spearmen (2Ch 14:8).
See Shield.

TARIFF *See Duty, 1.*

TARPELITES *See Tripolis.*

TARSHISH [9576, 9578] (possibly *[precious stone]
yellow jasper* BDB; possibly *greedy one* IDB; *foundry,
refinery* KB).
1. The son of Javan (Ge 10:4).
2. A place in the W Mediterranean, perhaps in Spain or
Tunisia (2Ch 9:21; 20:36-37; Ps 72:10; Jn 1:3).
3. "Ships of Tarshish"; large, seagoing trade ships (1Ki
9:26; 10:22; 22:48; 2Ch 9:21).
4. Great-grandson of Benjamin (1Ch 7:10).
5. Persian prince (Est 1:14).

TARSUS [*5432, 5433*]. Capital of Cilicia, in Asia
Minor. Paul's birthplace (Ac 9:11; 21:39; 22:3). Paul sent
to, from Jerusalem, to avoid assassination (Ac 9:30). Paul
brought from, by Barnabas (Ac 11:25-26).

TARTAK [9581]. A god worshiped by Avvites, colonists
in Samaria (2Ki 17:31).

TARTAN *See Supreme Commander.*

TASKMASTER One who burdens another with labor:
overseer (Ex 1:11; 3:7; 5:6,10,13).

TASSEL(S) [1544, 7492, *3192*]. Prescribed for garments worn by the Israelites, to remember God's commands (Nu 15:38-41; Dt 22:12). Made long by the
Pharisees (Mt 23:5).

TASTE [430, 2118, 2674, 3247, 3248, 5352, 6853,
7023, *1174*].
NIV+ TASTED, TASTELESS, TASTES, TASTING, TASTY
The sense of, lost (2Sa 19:35). Figurative (Job 27:2; Ps

34:8; 119:103; Heb 6:4-5; 1Pe 2:3); taste death (Mt 16:28; Mk 9:1; Lk 9:27; Jn 8:52; Heb 2:9). *See Savor, Savour; Savory Meat.*

TATTENAI, TATNAI [10779]. The Persian governor ordered to assist the Jews in rebuilding the temple (Ezr 5:3,6; 6:6,13).

TATTLER *See Gossip; Talebearer.*

TATTOO [7882]. Pagan custom; forbidden (Lev 19:28). *See Mark.*

TAVERNS, THREE A place, c. thirty-three miles SE of Rome where Paul met Roman Christians (Ac 28:15).

TAX [4501, 5368, 5601, 6885, 10402, *803, 3056, 3284, 5467, 5468*].
NIV+ TAXED, TAXES
Census (Ex 30:11-16; 38:26; Ne 10:32; Lk 2:1). Jesus pays (Mt 17:24-27).
Land (Ge 41:34,48; 2Ki 23:35). Land mortgaged for (Ne 5:3-4). Priests exempted from (Ge 47:26; Ezr 7:24). Paid in grain (Am 5:11; 7:1), in provisions (1Ki 4:7-28).
Personal (1Ki 9:15; 2Ki 15:19-20; 23:35). Resisted by Israelites (1Ki 12:18; 2Ch 10:18). Worldwide, levied by Caesar.
Collectors of *See Tax Collectors.*

TAX COLLECTORS [5601, *803, 3284, 5467*]
Disreputable (Isa 33:18; Da 11:20; Mt 5:46-47; 9:11; 11:19; 18:17; 21:31; Lk 18:11). Repent under the preaching of John the Baptist (Mt 21:32; Lk 3:12; 7:29). Matthew, the collector of Capernaum, becomes an apostle (Mt 9:9; 10:3; Mk 2:14; Lk 5:27). Parable concerning (Lk 18:9-14). Zacchaeus, chief among, receives Jesus into his house (Lk 19:2-10).

TEACHERS [1067, 4340, 4621, 6221, 7738, 10516, *1208, 1437, 2762, 3791, 6015*].
NIV+ TEACH, TAUGHT, TEACHER, TEACHES, TEACHING, TEACHINGS
Samuel, head of school of the prophets (1Sa 19:20). Elisha, head of, at Gilgal (2Ki 4:38).
Itinerant (2Ch 17:7-9). Of public assemblies (Ne 8:1-8,13,18). Should receive compensation (Gal 6:6).
See Instruction; Jesus, Teacher; Minister, Duties of.
False:
Admonition against (Dt 13:1-3; Mt 5:19; 7:15; 15:2-20; 23:2-33; Lk 11:38-52).
See Heresy; Minister, False and Corrupt.

TEACHING *See Instruction; Minister, Duties of.*

TEAR *See Rending.*

TEARS [1140, 1940, 1965, 4784, *1232, 3081*]
NIV+ TEAR
(Ps 6:6; 39:12; 42:3). Wash Jesus' feet (Lk 7:38,44). Observed by God (Ps 56:8; Isa 38:3-5). Wiped away (Rev 7:17). None in heaven (Rev 21:4). Figurative (Ps 80:5).

TEBAH [3182, 3183, 3187] (possibly *one born at the time or place of slaughtering* KB IDB).
1. The son of Nahor (Ge 22:24).
2. A city of Zobah, E of Anti-Lebanon Mountains (1Ch 18:7-9, ftn); a city belonging to Hadadezer, Hebrew Betah (2Sa 8:8, ftn).

TEBALIAH *See Tabaliah.*

TEBETH [3194].
Month ten in sacred sequence, month four in civil sequence (December-January). Esther taken to King Xerxes (Est 2:16). *See Month, 10.*

TECHNICALITIES Legal (Mt 12:2,10; Lk 6:2,7).

TEETH [7092, 9094, 10730, *3848*].
NIV+ TOOTH
(Pr 10:26). Gnashing of (Ps 112:10; La 2:16; Mt 8:12; 13:42,50; 22:13; 24:51; 25:30; Mk 9:18; Lk 13:28).

TEHAPHNEHES *See Tahpanhes.*

TEHINNAH [9383] (*supplication for favor*). The son of Eshton (1Ch 4:12).

TEIL TREE *See Terebinth.*

TEKEL [10770]. Weighed (Da 5:25,27).

TEKOA, TEKOITE [9541, 9542].
1. The son of Ashhur (1Ch 2:24; 4:5). Some authorities interpret these passages to mean that Ashhur colonized the town of Tekoa.
2. A city in Judah (2Ch 11:6). Home of the woman who interceded for Absalom (2Sa 14:2,4,9). Rebuilt by Rehoboam (2Ch 11:6). Desert of (2Ch 20:20). People of, work on the new wall of Jerusalem (Ne 3:5,27). Prophecy concerning (Jer 6:1). Home of Amos (Am 1:1).

TEKOAH *See Tekoa, 2.*

TEL, TELL A mound or hill that marks the site of an ancient city. Composed of accumulated debris, usually covering a number of archaeological or historical periods and showing numerous building levels or strata (Dt 13:16; Jer 30:18). In the following four place names.

TEL ABIB, TEL-ABIB [9425] (*mound of barley* ISBE; Akkadian *mound of storm tide* KB; *mound of flood* IDB). A place on the Kebar River where Ezekiel lived (Eze 3:15).

TEL ASSAR, TELASSAR [9431] (*ruined city mound of Assar*). A city or district conquered by the Assyrians (2Ki 19:12; Isa 37:12).

TEL HARSHA, TEL-HARSA [9426] (*the ruined city mound of the deaf-mute*).
NIV+ HARSHA
A place in Babylonia (Ezr 2:59; Ne 7:61).

TEL MELAH, TEL-MELAH [9427] (*ruined city and mound of salt*). Babylonian town, probably not far N of Persian Gulf (Ezr 2:59; Ne 7:61).

TELAH [9436] (*fissure, split, fracture*). The son of Rephah (1Ch 7:25).

TELAIM [3230] (*lambs*). The place where Saul mustered an army against Amalek (1Sa 15:4), may be the same as Telem in Judah (Jos 15:24).

TELEM [3234, 3235] (*brightness*).
1. A city of Judah (Jos 15:24).
2. A gatekeeper who put away his Gentile wife (Ezr 10:24).

TELL EL AMARNA *See Amarna, Tell El; Ras Shamra.*

TEMA [824+9401, 9401] (*on the right side*, hence *south country*).

1. The son of Ishmael (Ge 25:15; 1Ch 1:30).

2. A people of Arabia, probably descended from Tema, Ishmael's son (Job 6:19; Isa 21:14; Jer 25:23).

TEMAH [9457]. One of the temple servants (Ezr 2:53; Ne 7:55).

TEMAN [9403] (*on the right side*, hence *south country*).
NIV+ TEMANITE, TEMANITES

1. The grandson of Esau (Ge 36:11).

2. Edomite chief (Ge 36:42).

3. A city in NE Edom (Jer 49:7).

TEMANI, TEMANITE(S) [9404] (*on the right side*, *southern*).

NIV+ TEMAN

Inhabitant of Teman (Ge 36:34). Of Eliphaz, one of Job's friends (Job 2:11; 4:1).

TEMENI [9405] (*one from the right*, hence *southerner*). The son of Ashhur (1Ch 4:6).

TEMPER [3013, 8120].
NIV+ EVEN-TEMPERED, HOT-TEMPERED,
ILL-TEMPERED, QUICK-TEMPERED
See Anger; Malice; Self-Control.

TEMPERANCE (Php 4:5; Tit 1:8; 2Pe 1:6).

In Eating:
Pr 23:1 When you sit to dine with a ruler, note well what is before you, ²and put a knife to your throat if you are given to gluttony. ³Do not crave his delicacies, for that food is deceptive.

Pr 25:16 If you find honey, eat just enough—too much of it, and you will vomit.

In the Use of Wine:
1Ti 3:8 Deacons, likewise, are to be men worthy of respect, sincere, not indulging in much wine, and not pursuing dishonest gain. (+Tit 2:3)

Commanded:
Ro 13:14 Rather, clothe yourselves with the Lord Jesus Christ, and do not think about how to gratify the desires of the sinful nature.

1Th 5:6 So then, let us not be like others, who are asleep, but let us be alert and self-controlled. ⁷For those who sleep, sleep at night, and those who get drunk, get drunk at night. ⁸But since we belong to the day, let us be self-controlled, putting on faith and love as a breastplate, and the hope of salvation as a helmet.

1Ti 3:2 Now the overseer must be above reproach, the husband of but one wife, temperate, self-controlled, respectable, hospitable, able to teach,

Tit 2:2 Teach the older men to be temperate, worthy of respect, self-controlled, and sound in faith, in love and in endurance.

³Likewise, teach the older women to be reverent in the way they live, not to be slanderers or addicted to much wine, but to teach what is good.

Tit 2:12 It teaches us to say "No" to ungodliness and worldly passions, and to live self-controlled, upright and godly lives in this present age,

2Pe 1:5 For this very reason, make every effort to add to your faith goodness; and to goodness, knowledge; ⁶and to knowledge, self-control; and to self-control, perseverance; and to perseverance, godliness;

Practiced:
By athletes—
1Co 9:25 Everyone who competes in the games goes into strict training. They do it to get a crown that will not last; but we do it to get a crown that will last forever.

1Co 9:27 No, I beat my body and make it my slave so that after I have preached to others, I myself will not be disqualified for the prize.

By Daniel—
Da 1:8 But Daniel resolved not to defile himself with the royal food and wine, and he asked the chief official for permission not to defile himself this way.

Da 1:12 "Please test your servants for ten days: Give us nothing but vegetables to eat and water to drink. ¹³Then compare our appearance with that of the young men who eat the royal food, and treat your servants in accordance with what you see." ¹⁴So he agreed to this and tested them for ten days.

¹⁵At the end of the ten days they looked healthier and better nourished than any of the young men who ate the royal food. ¹⁶So the guard took away their choice food and the wine they were to drink and gave them vegetables instead.

See Abstinence; Drunkenness; Self-Control; Wine.

TEMPLE [395, 924, 1074, 2121, 5219, 5987, 7731, 8377, 10103, 10206, 10497, *1126, 1627, 2639, 2641, 2644, 2645, 3301, 3724, 3753, 5130, 5677*].
NIV+ TEMPLES

Solomon's:
Also called Father's House (Jn 2:16). Glorious Temple (Isa 60:7). Holy Mountain (Isa 27:13). Holy and Glorious Temple (Isa 64:11). Holy Temple (Ps 79:1; 1Ch 29:3). House of Prayer (Isa 56:7; Mt 21:13). House of God (1Ch 29:2). House of the God of Jacob (Isa 2:3). House of the Lord (Jer 28:5). Mountain of the Lord's Temple (Isa 2:2). Palatial structure (1Ch 29:1,19). Sanctuary (2Ch 20:8; 2Ch 36:17). Temple of the Lord (2Ki 11:10; 2Ch 23:9). Temple for Sacrifice (2Ch 7:12). Tent of the Testimony (2Ch 24:6). Zion (Ps 20:2; 48:12; 74:2; 87:2; Isa 2:3).

Greatness of (2Ch 2:5-6). Beauty of (Isa 64:11). Holiness of (1Ki 8:10; 9:3; La 1:10; Mt 23:17; Jn 2:14-16).

David undertakes the building of (2Sa 7:2-3; 1Ch 22:7; 28:2; Ps 132:2-5; Ac 7:46), forbidden of God because he was a warrior (2Sa 7:4-12; 1Ki 5:3; 1Ch 22:8; 28:3). Not asked for by God (2Sa 7:7). The building of, committed to Solomon (2Sa 7:13). David makes preparations of (1Ch 22; 28:14-18; 29:1-5; 2Ch 3:1; 5:1).

Solomon builds (Ac 7:47; 2Sa 7:13). Solomon conscripts laborers for the building of (1Ki 5:13-16; 2Ch 2:2,17-18). Materials for, furnished by Hiram (1Ki 5:8-18). Pattern and building of (1Ki 6; 7:13-51; 1Ch 28:11-19; 2Ch 3; 4; Ac 7:47). Time when begun (1Ki 6:1,37; 2Ch 3:2), finished (1Ki 6:38). Site of (1Ch 21:28-30; 22:1; 2Ch 3:1), where Abraham offered Isaac (Ge 22:2,4).

Materials prepared for (1Ki 5:17-18). No tools used on temple site (1Ki 6:7). Foundations of (1Ki 5:17-18; Lk 21:5).

Areas and furnishings of: Inner Sanctuary (1Ki 6:19-20; 8:6). Called the Most Holy Place (2Ch 3:8), Innermost Room (1Ki 6:27).

Most Holy Place: Description of (1Ki 6:16,19-35; 2Ch 3:8-14; 4:22). Contents of the Most Holy Place: Ark (1Ki 6:19; 8:6; 2Ch 5:2-10), cherubim (1Ki 6:23-28; 2Ch 3:10-13; 5:7-8). Called Holy Place (1Ki 8:8,10), Called the main hall (2Ch 3:5), Description of (1Ki 6:15-18; 2Ch 3:3,

5-7,14-17). *See Ark; Atonement Cover; Cherubim; Curtains; Veil.*

Holy Place (1Ki 8:8,10). Contents of the holy place: The Golden table of the Bread of Presence (1Ki 7:48; 2Ch 29:18). *See Bread, Consecrated.* Other tables of gold and silver (1Ch 28:16; 2Ch 4:18-19). Lampstands and their utensils (1Ki 7:49-50; 1Ch 28:15; 2Ch 4:7,20-22). *See Lampstand.* Altar of incense and its furniture (1Ki 6:20; 7:48,50; 1Ch 28:17-18; 2Ch 4:19,22). *See Altar of Incense.*

Porch of, called Porch of the Lord (2Ch 15:8). Dimensions of (1Ki 6:3; 2Ch 3:4). Doors of (2Ch 29:7). Overlaid with gold (2Ch 3:4). Pillars of (1Ki 7:15-22; 2Ki 11:14; 23:3; 25:17; 2Ch 3:15-17; 4:12-13).

Structure around (1Ki 6:5-10; 2Ki 11:2-3). Offerings brought to (Ne 10:37-39). Treasuries in. *See Treasure.*

Courts of: Of the priests (2Ch 4:9), inner (1Ki 6:36), surrounded by rows of stones and cedar beams (1Ki 6:36; 7:12). Contents of the courts: Altar of burnt offering (2Ch 15:8). *See Altar.* The Sea of cast metal (1Ki 7:23-37,44,46; 2Ch 4:2-5,10), ten basins (1Ki 7:38-46; 2Ch 4:6). Large court of (2Ch 4:9; Jer 19:14; 26:2).

Sabbath Canopy and royal entryway (2Ki 16:18).

Gates of: Upper gate (2Ki 15:35). New Gate (Jer 26:10; 36:10). Eastern gate (Eze 46:1,12). Gifts received at (2Ch 24:8-11).

Uses of the temple: A dwelling place of the Lord (1Ki 8:10-11,13; 9:3; 2Ki 21:7; 1Ch 29:1; 2Ch 5:13-14; 7:1-3,16; Eze 10:3-4; Mic 1:2), to contain the ark of the covenant (1Ki 8:21), for the offering of fragrant incense (2Ch 2:4), for the regular offering of consecrated bread and the burnt offerings (2Ch 2:4), for prayer and worship (1Ki 8; 2Ki 19:14-15; 2Ch 30:27; Isa 27:13; 56:7; Jer 7:2; 26:2; Eze 46:2-3,9; Zec 7:2-3; 8:21-22; Mk 11:17; Lk 1:10; 2:37; 18:10; Ac 3:1; 22:17), prayer made toward (1Ki 8:38; Da 6:10; Jnh 2:4), for weapon storage (2Ki 11:10; 2Ch 23:9-10), for refuge (2Ki 11:15; Ne 6:10-11).

Facts about: Dedication of (1Ki 8; 2Ch 5-7), services in, organized by David (1Ch 15:16; 23:24). Sacking and pillaging by Shishak (1Ki 14:25-26), by Jehoash, king of Israel (2Ki 14:14). Repaired by Jehoash, king of Judah (2Ki 12:4-14; 2Ch 24:7-14), by Josiah (2Ki 22:3-7; 2Ch 34:8-13). Ahaz changes the detailed plans (2Ki 16:10-17). Purified by Hezekiah (2Ch 29:15-19). Converted into an idolatrous shrine by Manasseh (2Ki 21:4-7; 2Ch 33:4-7).

Treasures of, used in the purchase of peace: By Asa, from Ben-Hadad (1Ki 15:18), by Jehoash, king of Judah, from Hazael (2Ki 12:18), by Hezekiah, from the king of Assyria (2Ki 18:15-16). Jews swore by (Mt 23:16-22).

Destroyed by Nebuchadnezzar, and the valuable contents carried to Babylon (2Ki 24:13; 25:9-17; 2Ch 36:7,19; Ps 79:1; Isa 64:11; Jer 27:16,19-22; 28:3; 52:13,17-23; La 2:7; 4:1; Ezr 1:7). Vessels of, used by Belshazzar (Da 5:2-3). Destruction of, foretold (Isa 66:6; Jer 27:18-22; Eze 7:22,25; Mt 24:2; Mk 13:2).

Restoration of, ordered by Cyrus (Ezr 1:7-11).

The Second:

Rebuilt by Zerubbabel (Ezr 1; 2:68-69; 3:2-13; 4; 5:2-17; 6:3-5; Ne 7:70-72; Isa 44:28; Hag 2:3). Building of, suspended (Ezr 4), resumed (Ezr 4:24; 5; 6; Hag 1:2-9; 2:15; Zec 8:9), finished (Ezr 6:14-15), dedicated (Ezr 6:15-18). Artaxerxes' favorable action toward (Ezr 7:11-28; 8:25-34).

Prophecies of its restoration (Isa 44:28; Da 8:13-14; Hag 1; 2; Zec 1:16; 4:8-10; 6:12-15; 8:9-15; Mal 3:1).

Ezekiel's Vision of a Temple: (Eze 37:26,28; 40-48).

Herod's Temple:

Forty-six years in building (Jn 2:20). Massive and beautiful stones of (Mk 13:1; Lk 21:5). Magnificence of (Mt 24:1). Beautiful gate of (Ac 3:10). Solomon's Colonnade (Jn 10:23; Ac 3:11; 5:12). Treasury of (Mk 12:41-44). Zechariah receives promise of a son (Lk 1:5-23, w 1:57-64). Jesus the infant brought to, according to the law and custom (Lk 2:21-39), Simeon blesses Jesus in (Lk 2:25-35), Anna the prophetess never left (Lk 2:36-37).

Jesus in, when a youth (Lk 2:46), taken to the highest point of, in his temptation (Mt 4:5-7; Lk 4:9-12), teaches in (Mk 11:27-33; 12:35-44; 14:49; Jn 5:14-47; 7:14-28; 8; 10:23-38; 18:20), performs miracles in (Mt 21:14-15), drives money changers from (Mt 21:12-13; Mk 11:15-17; Lk 19:45-46; Jn 2:15-16).

Officer of Temple guard (Lk 22:52; Ac 4:1; 5:24,26). Judas threw the money into (Mt 27:5). Veil of, torn at the time of the crucifixion (Mt 27:51).

The disciples worship in, after the resurrection (Lk 24:53; Ac 2:46; 3:1). Peter heals the crippled man at the gate of (Ac 3:1-16). Disciples preach in (Ac 5:20-21,42). Paul's vision in (Ac 22:17-21). Paul observes the rights of (Ac 21:26-30), is arrested in (Ac 21:33).

Prophecies concerning its destruction, by Daniel (Da 8:11-15; 11:30-31). Jesus predicts the destruction of (Mt 24; Mk 13:2; Lk 21:6).

Figurative:

Of the body of Jesus (Mt 26:61; 27:40; Jn 2:19). Of the indwelling of God (1Co 3:16-17; 2Co 6:16). Of the church (Eph 2:21; 2Th 2:4; Rev 3:12). Of the kingdom of Christ (Rev 11; 14:15,17). Of Christ, the head of the church, sending forth the forces of righteousness against the powers of evil (Rev 15:5-8; 16:1-17).

Idolatrous:

Of Dagon, at Ashdod (1Sa 5:2), of the calves, at Bethel (1Ki 12:31,33), of Rimmon, at Damascus (2Ki 5:18), of Baal, at Samaria (2Ki 10:21,27), at Babylon (2Ch 36:7; Da 1:2), of Diana, at Ephesus (Ac 19:27).

Trophies stored in (1Sa 31:10; 1Ch 10:9-10; Da 1:2). *See Tabernacle.*

TEMPLE SERVANTS [5987, 10497]. Large group of servants who performed menial tasks in the temple (1Ch 9:2; Ezr 2:43-58; 8:17-20; Ne 7:46-56), probably descended from Midianites (Nu 31:47), Gibeonites (Jos 9:23), and other captives. They are usually listed with the priests, Levites, singers, and gatekeepers (Ezr 2:70).

TEMPORAL BLESSINGS *See Blessings.*

TEMPTATION [585, 4279, 4280] (*trial, proof*).

-NIV+ TEMPT, TEMPTED, TEMPTER, TEMPTING

Has two meanings: Any attempt to entice or tempt into evil; a testing which aims at an ultimate spiritual good.

Temptation to evil:

Pr 12:26 A righteous man is cautious in friendship, but the way of the wicked leads them astray.

Ro 8:35 Who shall separate us from the love of Christ? Shall trouble or hardship or persecution or famine or nakedness or danger or sword? ³⁶As it is written:

"For your sake we face death all day long; we are considered as sheep to be slaughtered."

³⁷No, in all these things we are more than conquerors through him who loved us. ³⁸For I am convinced that neither death nor life, neither angels nor demons, neither

the present nor the future, nor any powers, ³⁹neither height nor depth, nor anything else in all creation, will be able to separate us from the love of God that is in Christ Jesus our Lord.

Called snares of death (Pr 13:14)—

Pr 14:27 The fear of the LORD is a fountain of life, turning a man from the snares of death.

The way of escape from (1Co 10:13).

Christ gives help in—

Heb 2:18 Because he himself suffered when he was tempted, he is able to help those who are being tempted.

Heb 4:15 For we do not have a high priest who is unable to sympathize with our weaknesses, but we have one who has been tempted in every way, just as we are—yet was without sin.

Rev 3:10 Since you have kept my command to endure patiently, I will also keep you from the hour of trial that is going to come upon the whole world to test those who live on the earth.

The Lord delivers from—

2Pe 2:9 if this is so, then the Lord knows how to rescue godly men from trials and to hold the unrighteous for the day of judgment, while continuing their punishment.

Benefits of:

Jas 1:2 Consider it pure joy, my brothers, whenever you face trials of many kinds, ³because you know that the testing of your faith develops perseverance. ⁴Perseverance must finish its work so that you may be mature and complete, not lacking anything.

Jas 1:12 Blessed is the man who perseveres under trial, because when he has stood the test, he will receive the crown of life that God has promised to those who love him.

1Pe 1:6 In this you greatly rejoice, though now for a little while you may have had to suffer grief in all kinds of trials. ⁷These have come so that your faith—of greater worth than gold, which perishes even though refined by fire—may be proved genuine and may result in praise, glory and honor when Jesus Christ is revealed.

Leading into:

To be avoided (Mt 5:29-30; 6:9; Mk 9:42-48; Lk 17:1)—

Ro 14:13 Therefore let us stop passing judgment on one another. Instead, make up your mind not to put any stumbling block or obstacle in your brother's way.

Ro 14:15 If your brother is distressed because of what you eat, you are no longer acting in love. Do not by your eating destroy your brother for whom Christ died.

Ro 14:21 It is better not to eat meat or drink wine or to do anything else that will cause your brother to fall.

1Co 7:5 Do not deprive each other except by mutual consent and for a time, so that you may devote yourselves to prayer. Then come together again so that Satan will not tempt you because of your lack of self-control.

1Co 8:9 Be careful, however, that the exercise of your freedom does not become a stumbling block to the weak. ¹⁰For if anyone with a weak conscience sees you who have this knowledge eating in an idol's temple, won't he be emboldened to eat what has been sacrificed to idols? ¹¹So this weak brother, for whom Christ died, is destroyed by your knowledge. ¹²When you sin against your brothers in this way and wound their weak conscience, you sin against Christ. ¹³Therefore, if what I eat causes my brother to fall into sin, I will never eat meat again, so that I will not cause him to fall.

1Co 10:28 But if anyone says to you, "This has been offered in sacrifice," then do not eat it, both for the sake of the man who told you and for conscience' sake— ²⁹the other man's conscience, I mean, not yours. For why should my freedom be judged by another's conscience? ³⁰If I take part in the meal with thankfulness, why am I denounced because of something I thank God for?

³¹So whether you eat or drink or whatever you do, do it all for the glory of God. ³²Do not cause anyone to stumble, whether Jews, Greeks or the church of God—

Prayer against being led into (Mt 6:13; 26:41; Mk 14:38)—

Lk 11:4 Forgive us our sins, for we also forgive everyone who sins against us. And lead us not into temptation.'" (+Lk 22:40)

Lk 22:46 "Why are you sleeping?" he asked them. "Get up and pray so that you will not fall into temptation."

Not to lead others into (Ro 14:13,15,21; 1Co 7:5; 8:9-13; 10:28-32).—

Instances of leading others into: Abraham, of Pharaoh (Ge 12:18-19), of Abimelech (Ge 20:9). Rebekah, of Jacob (Ge 27:6-14). Balak, of Balaam (Nu 22:5-7,16-17; 23:11-13,25-27). Eli's sons, of Israel (1Sa 2:24-25). Gideon, of Israel (Jdg 8:27). The old prophet of Bethel, of the prophet of Judah (1Ki 13:15-19). Jeroboam, of Israel (1Ki 15:30,34).

Resistance to:

Commanded—

Dt 7:25 The images of their gods you are to burn in the fire. Do not covet the silver and gold on them, and do not take it for yourselves, or you will be ensnared by it, for it is detestable to the LORD your God. (+Dt 7:26)

Pr 1:10 My son, if sinners entice you, do not give in to them. ¹¹If they say, "Come along with us; let's lie in wait for someone's blood, let's waylay some harmless soul; ¹²let's swallow them alive, like the grave, and whole, like those who go down to the pit; ¹³we will get all sorts of valuable things and fill our houses with plunder; ¹⁴throw in your lot with us, and we will share a common purse"— ¹⁵my son, do not go along with them, do not set foot on their paths; ¹⁶for their feet rush into sin, they are swift to shed blood. ¹⁷How useless to spread a net in full view of all the birds! (+Pr 1:18-19)

Pr 4:14 Do not set foot on the path of the wicked or walk in the way of evil men. ¹⁵Avoid it, do not travel on it; turn from it and go on your way. (+Pr 5:3,8)

Pr 19:27 Stop listening to instruction, my son, and you will stray from the words of knowledge.

Mt 24:42 "Therefore keep watch, because you do not know on what day your Lord will come. ⁴³But understand this: If the owner of the house had known at what time of night the thief was coming, he would have kept watch and would not have let his house be broken into. ⁴⁴So you also must be ready, because the Son of Man will come at an hour when you do not expect him.

Mt 25:13 "Therefore keep watch, because you do not know the day or the hour. (+Mt 26:41)

Mk 13:21 At that time if anyone says to you, 'Look, here is the Christ!' or, 'Look, there he is!' do not believe it. ²²For false Christs and false prophets will appear and perform signs and miracles to deceive the elect—if that were possible. (+Mk 13:33-37; 14:37-38)

Ro 6:12 Therefore do not let sin reign in your mortal body so that you obey its evil desires. ¹³Do not offer the parts of your body to sin, as instruments of wickedness, but rather offer yourselves to God, as those who have been brought from death to life; and offer the parts of your body to him as instruments of righteousness. **14**For sin shall not be your master, because you are not under law, but under grace.

Ro 12:21 Do not be overcome by evil, but overcome evil with good. (+Eph 6:11,13-17)

Jas 4:7 Submit yourselves, then, to God. Resist the devil, and he will flee from you.

1Pe 5:8 Be self-controlled and alert. Your enemy the devil prowls around like a roaring lion looking for someone to devour. **9**Resist him, standing firm in the faith, because you know that your brothers throughout the world are undergoing the same kind of sufferings. (+1Jn 4:4)

Source of resistance—

Ps 17:4 As for the deeds of men—by the word of your lips I have kept myself from the ways of the violent.

Ps 73:2 But as for me, my feet had almost slipped; I had nearly lost my foothold. **3**For I envied the arrogant when I saw the prosperity of the wicked.

4They have no struggles; their bodies are healthy and strong. **5**They are free from the burdens common to man; they are not plagued by human ills. **6**Therefore pride is their necklace; they clothe themselves with violence. **7**From their callous hearts comes iniquity; the evil conceits of their minds know no limits. **8**They scoff, and speak with malice; in their arrogance they threaten oppression. **9**Their mouths lay claim to heaven, and their tongues take possession of the earth. **10**Therefore their people turn to them and drink up waters in abundance. **11**They say, "How can God know? Does the Most High have knowledge?"

12This is what the wicked are like—always carefree, they increase in wealth.

13Surely in vain have I kept my heart pure; in vain have I washed my hands in innocence. **14**All day long I have been plagued; I have been punished every morning.

15If I had said, "I will speak thus," I would have betrayed your children. **16**When I tried to understand all this, it was oppressive to me **17**till I entered the sanctuary of God; then I understood their final destiny.

18Surely you place them on slippery ground; you cast them down to ruin. **19**How suddenly are they destroyed, completely swept away by terrors! **20**As a dream when one awakes, so when you arise, O Lord, you will despise them as fantasies.

21When my heart was grieved and my spirit embittered, **22**I was senseless and ignorant; I was a brute beast before you.

23Yet I am always with you; you hold me by my right hand. **24**You guide me with your counsel, and afterward you will take me into glory. **25**Whom have I in heaven but you? And earth has nothing I desire besides you.

Ps 94:17 Unless the LORD had given me help, I would soon have dwelt in the silence of death. **18**When I said, "My foot is slipping," your love, O LORD, supported me.

Rewards to those who resist—

Isa 33:15 He who walks righteously and speaks what is right, who rejects gain from extortion and keeps his hand from accepting bribes, who stops his ears against plots of murder and shuts his eyes against contemplating evil— **16**this is the man who will dwell on the heights, whose refuge will be the mountain fortress. His bread will be supplied, and water will not fail him. (+Jas 1:12; Rev 3:10)

Instances of Those Who Resisted Temptation:

Joseph—

Ge 39:7 and after a while his master's wife took notice of

Joseph and said, "Come to bed with me!" **8**But he refused. "With me in charge," he told her, "my master does not concern himself with anything in the house; everything he owns he has entrusted to my care. **9**No one is greater in this house than I am. My master has withheld nothing from me except you, because you are his wife. How then could I do such a wicked thing and sin against God?" **10**And though she spoke to Joseph day after day, he refused to go to bed with her or even be with her. (+Ge 39:11-12)

Balaam (Nu 22:7-18,38; 23:7-12,18-24). David (1Sa 26:5-25). The prophet of Judah (1Ki 13:7-9). Micaiah (1Ki 22:13-28). The people of Jerusalem (2Ki 18:30-36).

Job (Job 1:6-21; 2:4-10)—

Job 31:1 "I made a covenant with my eyes not to look lustfully at a girl.

Job 31:5 "If I have walked in falsehood or my foot has hurried after deceit— **6**let God weigh me in honest scales and he will know that I am blameless— **7**if my steps have turned from the path, if my heart has been led by my eyes, or if my hands have been defiled, **8**then may others eat what I have sown, and may my crops be uprooted.

9"If my heart has been enticed by a woman, or if I have lurked at my neighbor's door, **10**then may my wife grind another man's grain, and may other men sleep with her. **11**For that would have been shameful, a sin to be judged. **12**It is a fire that burns to Destruction; it would have uprooted my harvest.

13"If I have denied justice to my menservants and maidservants when they had a grievance against me, **14**what will I do when God confronts me? What will I answer when called to account? **15**Did not he who made me in the womb make them? Did not the same one form us both within our mothers?

16"If I have denied the desires of the poor or let the eyes of the widow grow weary, **17**if I have kept my bread to myself, not sharing it with the fatherless—

Job 31:19 if I have seen anyone perishing for lack of clothing, or a needy man without a garment, **20**and his heart did not bless me for warming him with the fleece from my sheep, **21**if I have raised my hand against the fatherless, knowing that I had influence in court, **22**then let my arm fall from the shoulder, let it be broken off at the joint. **23**For I dreaded destruction from God, and for fear of his splendor I could not do such things.

24"If I have put my trust in gold or said to pure gold, 'You are my security,' **25**if I have rejoiced over my great wealth, the fortune my hands had gained, **26**if I have regarded the sun in its radiance or the moon moving in splendor, **27**so that my heart was secretly enticed and my hand offered them a kiss of homage, **28**then these also would be sins to be judged, for I would have been unfaithful to God on high.

29"If I have rejoiced at my enemy's misfortune or gloated over the trouble that came to him— **30**I have not allowed my mouth to sin by invoking a curse against his life— **31**if the men of my household have never said, 'Who has not had his fill of Job's meat?'— **32**but no stranger had to spend the night in the street, for my door was always open to the traveler— **33**if I have concealed my sin as men do, by hiding my guilt in my heart **34**because I so feared the crowd and so dreaded the contempt of the clans that I kept silent and would not go outside

Job 31:38 "if my land cries out against me and all its furrows are wet with tears, **39**if I have devoured its yield without payment or broken the spirit of its tenants, **40**then let briers come up instead of wheat and weeds instead of barley." The words of Job are ended.

Recabites—

Jer 35:5 Then I set bowls full of wine and some cups before the men of the Recabite family and said to them, "Drink some wine."

6But they replied, "We do not drink wine, because our forefather Jonadab son of Recab gave us this command: 'Neither you nor your descendants must ever drink wine. **7**Also you must never build houses, sow seed or plant vineyards; you must never have any of these things, but must always live in tents. Then you will live a long time in the land where you are nomads.' (+Jer 35:8-9)

Nehemiah—

Ne 4:9 But we prayed to our God and posted a guard day and night to meet this threat.

Jesus—

Mt 4:1 Then Jesus was led by the Spirit into the desert to be tempted by the devil. **2**After fasting forty days and forty nights, he was hungry. **3**The tempter came to him and said, "If you are the Son of God, tell these stones to become bread."

4Jesus answered, "It is written: 'Man does not live on bread alone, but on every word that comes from the mouth of God.' "

5Then the devil took him to the holy city and had him stand on the highest point of the temple. **6**"If you are the Son of God," he said, "throw yourself down. For it is written:

" 'He will command his angels concerning you, and they will lift you up in their hands, so that you will not strike your foot against a stone.' "

7Jesus answered him, "It is also written: 'Do not put the Lord your God to the test.' "

8Again, the devil took him to a very high mountain and showed him all the kingdoms of the world and their splendor. **9**"All this I will give you," he said, "if you will bow down and worship me."

10Jesus said to him, "Away from me, Satan! For it is written: 'Worship the Lord your God, and serve him only.' "

11Then the devil left him, and angels came and attended him.

Mt 26:38 Then he said to them, "My soul is overwhelmed with sorrow to the point of death. Stay here and keep watch with me."

39Going a little farther, he fell with his face to the ground and prayed, "My Father, if it is possible, may this cup be taken from me. Yet not as I will, but as you will."

40Then he returned to his disciples and found them sleeping. "Could you men not keep watch with me for one hour?" he asked Peter. **41**"Watch and pray so that you will not fall into temptation. The spirit is willing, but the body is weak."

42He went away a second time and prayed, "My Father, if it is not possible for this cup to be taken away unless I drink it, may your will be done." (+Lk 4:1-3; Heb 4:15)

Heb 12:3 Consider him who endured such opposition from sinful men, so that you will not grow weary and lose heart.

4In your struggle against sin, you have not yet resisted to the point of shedding your blood.

Sources of:

Cherished pleasures (Mt 5:29-30; 18:7)—

Mt 18:8 If your hand or your foot causes you to sin cut it off and throw it away. It is better for you to enter life maimed or crippled than to have two hands or two feet and be thrown into eternal fire. **9**And if your eye causes you to sin, gouge it out and throw it away. It is better for you to enter life with one eye than to have two eyes and be thrown into the fire of hell. (+Mk 9:43-45)

Evil company—

Ex 34:12 Be careful not to make a treaty with those who live in the land where you are going, or they will be a snare among you. (+Ex 34:13-16)

Pr 2:10 For wisdom will enter your heart, and knowledge will be pleasant to your soul. **11**Discretion will protect you, and understanding will guard you.

12Wisdom will save you from the ways of wicked men, from men whose words are perverse, (+Pr 2:13-15)

Pr 2:16 It will save you also from the adulteress, from the wayward wife with her seductive words,

Adultery and sexual desires (Pr 5:1-20; 6:24-29; 7:1-27)—

Pr 9:15 calling out to those who pass by, who go straight on their way. **16**"Let all who are simple come in here!" she says to those who lack judgment. (+Pr 9:17-18)

Ecc 7:26 I find more bitter than death the woman who is a snare, whose heart is a trap and whose hands are chains. The man who pleases God will escape her, but the sinner she will ensnare.

Sinful desires—

Ro 7:5 For when we were controlled by the sinful nature, the sinful passions aroused by the law were at work in our bodies, so that we bore fruit for death.

Gal 5:17 For the sinful nature desires what is contrary to the Spirit, and the Spirit what is contrary to the sinful nature. They are in conflict with each other, so that you do not do what you want.

Jas 1:13 When tempted, no one should say, "God is tempting me." For God cannot be tempted by evil, nor does he tempt anyone; **14**but each one is tempted when, by his own evil desire, he is dragged away and enticed. **15**Then, after desire has conceived, it gives birth to sin; and sin, when it is full-grown, gives birth to death.

2Pe 2:18 For they mouth empty, boastful words and, by appealing to the lustful desires of sinful human nature, they entice people who are just escaping from those who live in error.

1Jn 2:16 For everything in the world—the cravings of sinful man, the lust of his eyes and the boasting of what he has and does—comes not from the Father but from the world. (+1Jn 2:17)

False teachers—

Mt 18:6 But if anyone causes one of these little ones who believe in me to sin, it would be better for him to have a large millstone hung around his neck and to be drowned in the depths of the sea.

7"Woe to the world because of the things that cause people to sin! Such things must come, but woe to the man through whom they come! (+Lk 17:1)

1Jn 2:26 I am writing these things to you about those who are trying to lead you astray. (+1Jn 4:1-3; Rev 2:20)

Persecutions—

Jn 16:1 "All this I have told you so that you will not go astray. **2**They will put you out of the synagogue; in fact, a time is coming when anyone who kills you will think he is offering a service to God.

Prosperity—

Dt 8:10 When you have eaten and are satisfied, praise the

LORD your God for the good land he has given you. (+Dt 8:11-17; Lk 12:16-21)

Riches (Mt 19:16-24; Mk 10:17-20)—

Mk 10:21 Jesus looked at him and loved him. "One thing you lack," he said. "Go, sell everything you have and give to the poor, and you will have treasure in heaven. Then come, follow me."

22At this the man's face fell. He went away sad, because he had great wealth.

23Jesus looked around and said to his disciples, "How hard it is for the rich to enter the kingdom of God!"

24The disciples were amazed at his words. But Jesus said again, "Children, how hard it is to enter the kingdom of God! 25It is easier for a camel to go through the eye of a needle than for a rich man to enter the kingdom of God." (+Mk 10:26-30)

1Ti 6:9 People who want to get rich fall into temptation and a trap and into many foolish and harmful desires that plunge men into ruin and destruction. 10For the love of money is a root of all kinds of evil. Some people, eager for money, have wandered from the faith and pierced themselves with many griefs.

Cares, riches and pleasures—

Mt 13:22 The one who received the seed that fell among the thorns is the man who hears the word, but the worries of this life and the deceitfulness of wealth choke it, making it unfruitful. (+Lk 8:13-14; 21:34-38)

Satan (Ge 3:1-5)—

1Ch 21:1 Satan rose up against Israel and incited David to take a census of Israel.

Mk 4:15 Some people are like seed along the path, where the word is sown. As soon as they hear it, Satan comes and takes away the word that was sown in them.

Mk 4:17 But since they have no root, they last only a short time. When trouble or persecution comes because of the word, they quickly fall away.

Lk 22:3 Then Satan entered Judas, called Iscariot, one of the Twelve.

Lk 22:31 "Simon, Simon, Satan has asked to sift you as wheat. 32But I have prayed for you, Simon, that your faith may not fail. And when you have turned back, strengthen your brothers."

2Co 2:11 in order that Satan might not outwit us. For we are not unaware of his schemes.

2Co 11:3 But I am afraid that just as Eve was deceived by the serpent's cunning, your minds may somehow be led astray from your sincere and pure devotion to Christ.

2Co 11:14 And no wonder, for Satan himself masquerades as an angel of light. 15It is not surprising, then, if his servants masquerade as servants of righteousness. Their end will be what their actions deserve.

2Co 12:7 To keep me from becoming conceited because of these surpassingly great revelations, there was given me a thorn in my flesh, a messenger of Satan, to torment me. (+Gal 4:14)

Eph 4:27 and do not give the devil a foothold.

Eph 6:11 Put on the full armor of God so that you can take your stand against the devil's schemes.

Eph 6:13 Therefore put on the full armor of God, so that when the day of evil comes, you may be able to stand your ground, and after you have done everything, to stand. 14Stand firm then, with the belt of truth buckled around your waist, with the breastplate of righteousness in place, 15and with your feet fitted with the readiness that comes from the gospel of peace. 16In addition to all this, take up the shield of faith, with which you can extinguish all the

flaming arrows of the evil one. 17Take the helmet of salvation and the sword of the Spirit, which is the word of God.

1Th 3:5 For this reason, when I could stand it no longer, I sent to find out about your faith. I was afraid that in some way the tempter might have tempted you and our efforts might have been useless.

1Ti 5:15 Some have in fact already turned away to follow Satan. (+Jas 4:7; 1Pe 5:8-9)

Rev 12:10 Then I heard a loud voice in heaven say: "Now have come the salvation and the power and the kingdom of our God, and the authority of his Christ. For the accuser of our brothers, who accuses them before our God day and night, has been hurled down.

11They overcame him by the blood of the Lamb and by the word of their testimony; they did not love their lives so much as to shrink from death.

Rev 12:17 Then the dragon was enraged at the woman and went off to make war against the rest of her offspring—those who obey God's commandments and hold to the testimony of Jesus.

Wicked men—

Pr 16:29 A violent man entices his neighbor and leads him down a path that is not good.

Pr 28:10 He who leads the upright along an evil path will fall into his own trap, but the blameless will receive a good inheritance.

Hos 7:5 On the day of the festival of our king the princes become inflamed with wine, and he joins hands with the mockers.

Am 2:12 "But you made the Nazirites drink wine and commanded the prophets not to prophesy.

Mt 5:19 Anyone who breaks one of the least of these commandments and teaches others to do the same will be called least in the kingdom of heaven, but whoever practices and teaches these commands will be called great in the kingdom of heaven.

2Ti 3:13 while evil men and impostors will go from bad to worse, deceiving and being deceived. *See Demons; Faith, Trial of; Satan.*

Warnings against yielding to:

(Ex 34:12-16)—

Dt 8:11 Be careful that you do not forget the LORD your God, failing to observe his commands, his laws and his decrees that I am giving you this day. 12Otherwise, when you eat and are satisfied, when you build fine houses and settle down, 13and when your herds and flocks grow large and your silver and gold increase and all you have is multiplied, 14then your heart will become proud and you will forget the LORD your God, who brought you out of Egypt, out of the land of slavery. (+Dt 8:15-16)

Dt 8:17 You may say to yourself, "My power and the strength of my hands have produced this wealth for me." 18But remember the LORD your God, for it is he who gives you the ability to produce wealth, and so confirms his covenant, which he swore to your forefathers, as it is today. (+Dt 8:19-20; Pr 2:10-16; 5:1-5)

Pr 5:6 She gives no thought to the way of life; her paths are crooked, but she knows it not.

7Now then, my sons, listen to me; do not turn aside from what I say. 8Keep to a path far from her, do not go near the door of her house, 9lest you give your best strength to others and your years to one who is cruel, 10lest strangers feast on your wealth and your toil enrich another man's house. 11At the end of your life you will groan, when your flesh and body are spent. 12You will say, "How I hated discipline! How my heart spurned correction! 13I would not obey my teachers or listen to my instructors. ¹⁴I have come to the brink of utter ruin in the midst of the whole assembly."

¹⁵Drink water from your own cistern, running water from your own well. ¹⁶Should your springs overflow in the streets, your streams of water in the public squares? ¹⁷Let them be yours alone, never to be shared with strangers. ¹⁸May your fountain be blessed, and may you rejoice in the wife of your youth. ¹⁹A loving doe, a graceful deer—may her breasts satisfy you always, may you ever be captivated by her love. ²⁰Why be captivated, my son, by an adulteress? Why embrace the bosom of another man's wife? ²¹For a man's ways are in full view of the LORD, and he examines all his paths.

Pr 6:27 Can a man scoop fire into his lap without his clothes being burned? ²⁸Can a man walk on hot coals without his feet being scorched? (+Pr 7:1-6)

Pr 7:7 I saw among the simple, I noticed among the young men, a youth who lacked judgment. ⁸He was going down the street near her corner, walking along in the direction of her house ⁹at twilight, as the day was fading, as the dark of night set in.

¹⁰Then out came a woman to meet him, dressed like a prostitute and with crafty intent. ¹¹(She is loud and defiant, her feet never stay at home; ¹²now in the street, now in the squares, at every corner she lurks.) ¹³She took hold of him and kissed him and with a brazen face she said:

¹⁴"I have fellowship offerings at home; today I fulfilled my vows. ¹⁵So I came out to meet you; I looked for you and have found you! ¹⁶I have covered my bed with colored linens from Egypt. ¹⁷I have perfumed my bed with myrrh, aloes and cinnamon. ¹⁸Come, let's drink deep of love till morning; let's enjoy ourselves with love! ¹⁹My husband is not at home; he has gone on a long journey. ²⁰He took his purse filled with money and will not be home till full moon."

²¹With persuasive words she led him astray; she seduced him with her smooth talk. ²²All at once he followed her like an ox going to the slaughter, like a deer stepping into a noose ²³till an arrow pierces his liver, like a bird darting into a snare, little knowing it will cost him his life. (+Pr 7:24-27; 9:15-18; Ecc 7:26)

Jer 2:25 Do not run until your feet are bare and your throat is dry. But you said, 'It's no use! I love foreign gods, and I must go after them.'

Mt 26:31 Then Jesus told them, "This very night you will all fall away on account of me, for it is written: "'I will strike the shepherd, and the sheep of the flock will be scattered.'

Mt 26:41 "Watch and pray so that you will not fall into temptation. The spirit is willing, but the body is weak." (+Mk 14:37-38; Lk 21:34-36; 22:40; 1Co 16:13; Eph 6:11,13-17; Heb 12:3-4; 1Pe 4:7; 5:8-9)

2Pe 3:17 Therefore, dear friends, since you already know this, be on your guard so that you may not be carried away by the error of lawless men and fall from your secure position. (+Rev 3:2-3)

Yielding to:

Instances of: Adam and Eve—

Ge 3:1 Now the serpent was more crafty than any of the wild animals the LORD God had made. He said to the woman, "Did God really say, 'You must not eat from any tree in the garden'?"

²The woman said to the serpent, "We may eat fruit from the trees in the garden, ³but God did say, 'You must not eat

fruit from the tree that is in the middle of the garden, and you must not touch it, or you will die.'"

⁴"You will not surely die," the serpent said to the woman. ⁵"For God knows that when you eat of it your eyes will be opened, and you will be like God, knowing good and evil."

⁶When the woman saw that the fruit of the tree was good for food and pleasing to the eye, and also desirable for gaining wisdom, she took some and ate it. She also gave some to her husband, who was with her, and he ate it. ⁷Then the eyes of both of them were opened, and they realized they were naked; so they sewed fig leaves together and made coverings for themselves.

⁸Then the man and his wife heard the sound of the LORD God as he was walking in the garden in the cool of the day, and they hid from the LORD God among the trees of the garden. ⁹But the LORD God called to the man, "Where are you?"

¹⁰He answered, "I heard you in the garden, and I was afraid because I was naked; so I hid."

¹¹And he said, "Who told you that you were naked? Have you eaten from the tree that I commanded you not to eat from?"

¹²The man said, "The woman you put here with me— she gave me some fruit from the tree, and I ate it."

¹³Then the LORD God said to the woman, "What is this you have done?" The woman said, "The serpent deceived me, and I ate." (+Ge 3:14-19)

Sarah, to lie (Ge 12:13; 18:13-15; 20:13). Isaac, to lie (Ge 26:7). Jacob to defraud Esau (Ge 27:6-13). Balaam (Nu 22:15-22; 2Pe 2:15). Achan (Jos 7:21). David, to commit adultery (2Sa 11:2-5), to number Israel (1Ch 21). Solomon, to become an idolater through the influences of his wives (1Ki 11:4; Ne 13:26). The prophet of Judah (1Ki 13:11-19). Hezekiah (2Ki 20:12-20; Isa 39:1-4,6-7). Peter (Mt 26:69-74; Mk 14:67-71; Lk 22:55-60).

Of Jesus:

(Lk 22:28). In all points as we are (Heb 4:15). By the devil (Mt 4:1-11; Mk 1:12-13; Lk 4:1-13). Before his crucifixion (Mt 26:38-42).

Test of God:

Design of, a test (Ps 66:10-13; 119:101,110; Da 12:10; Zec 13:9; 1Pe 1:6-7)—

1Pe 4:12 Dear friends, do not be surprised at the painful trial you are suffering, as though something strange were happening to you.

Of fidelity (Dt 13:1-2)—

Dt 13:3 you must not listen to the words of that prophet or dreamer. The LORD your God is testing you to find out whether you love him with all your heart and with all your soul. (+2Ch 32:31; Job 1:8-22; 2:3-10)

Of obedience (Ge 22:1-14; Dt 8:2,5; Heb 11:17).—

Benefits of (Jas 1:2-4,12; 1Pe 1:6-7).

Rewards of (Isa 33:15-16; Lk 12:35-38; Jas 1:12)—

1Jn 4:4 You, dear children, are from God and have overcome them, because the one who is in you is greater than the one who is in the world.

See Affliction; Afflictions; Faith, Trial of.

TEN [6917, 6924, 6927, 6930, 8047, 8052, 10573, 10649, *1274, 3689, 3691, 3692*].

NIV+ ONE-TENTH, TENS, TENTH, TITHE, TITHES, TWO-TENTHS

Used for an indefinite number (Ge 31:7; Lev 26:26; Nu 14:22; Zec 8:23).

TEN COMMANDMENTS *See Commandments and Statutes, Of God; Decalogue.*

TENANTS [1251, 5757, 9369, *1177*]. Evicted (Mt 21:41; Mk 12:9; Lk 20:16).

TENONS NIV "projections" on tabernacle boards to hold the boards in place (Ex 26:17).

TENSION *See Anxiety.*

TENT [182, 185, 2837, 3749, 3845, 3857, 5438, 6108, 6109, 7688, *5008, 5011, 5012, 5013*].

NIV+ TENTMAKER, TENTS, TENT-DWELLING

Used for dwelling (Ge 4:20), by Noah (Ge 9:21), by Abraham (Ge 12:8; 13:18; 18:1), by Lot (Ge 13:5), by Moses (Ex 18:7), by Israelites (Nu 24:5-6; 2Sa 20:1; 1Ki 12:16), by the Midianites (Jdg 6:5), by Cushites (Hab 3:7), by Arabs (Isa 13:20), by shepherds (Jer 6:3). Women had tents apart from men (Ge 24:67; 31:33). Used for cattle (2Ch 14:15). Manufacture of (Ac 18:3). Used as a place of worship. *See Tabernacle.*

TERAH [9561, 9562, *2508*].

1. The son of Nahor (Ge 11:24-25), father of Abraham, Nahor, Haran (Ge 11:26), idolater (Jos 24:2), went as far as Haran with Abraham (Ge 11:24-32).

2. The encampment of the Israelites in wilderness (Nu 33:27-28).

TERAPHIM *See Household Gods; Idolatry.*

TEREBINTH [461]. A small tree (Isa 6:13; Hos 4:13).

TERESH [9575] (perhaps *desire*). A Persian eunuch. Plotted against Xerxes (Est 2:21-23; 6:2).

TERRACE [4864, 8727, 8805].

NIV+ TERRACES

Steps leading up to the temple (2Ch 9:11).

TERROR [*399, 987, 988, 1166, 1243, 1286, 1287, 1593, 3006, 3010, 3154, 3169, 3707+, 4471, 4616, 4745, 6907, 7064, 7065, 10097, 10167, *5429, 5832*].

NIV+ TERRIBLE, TERRIBLY, TERRIFIED, TERRIFIES, TERRIFY, TERRIFYING, TERRORISTS, TERRORS

Extreme fear or dread; or sometimes the one who causes such agitation (Ge 35:5; Ps 55:4; 2Co 5:11).

TERTIUS [5470] (*third*). Paul's amanuensis in writing the book of Romans (Ro 16:22).

TERTULLUS [5472] (*third*). Diminutive of Tertius; lawyer employed by the Jews to state their case against Paul before Felix (Ac 24:1).

TESTAMENT

1. A covenant. *See Covenant.*

2. Testamentary disposition or will. *See Will, A Testament.*

3. Divisions of the English Bible. *See New Testament, Old Testament.*

TESTAMENTS OF THE TWELVE PROPHETS An pseudepigraphal document that claims to report the last words of the twelve sons of Jacob; probably written c. second century A.D.

TESTAMENTS, TIME BETWEEN

The time between the Testaments was one of ferment and change—a time of the realignment of traditional power blocs and the passing of a Near Eastern cultural tradition that had been dominant for almost 3,000 years.

In biblical history, the approximately 400 years that separate the time of Nehemiah from the birth of Christ are known as the intertestamental period (c. 432-5 B.C.). Sometimes called the "silent" years, they were anything but silent. The events, literature and social forces of these years would shape the world of the NT.

History:

With the Babylonian captivity, Israel ceased to be an independent nation and became a minor territory in a succession of larger empires. Very little is known about the latter years of Persian domination because the Jewish historian Josephus, our primary source for the intertestamental period, all but ignores them.

With Alexander the Great's acquisition of Israel (332 B.C.), a new and more insidious threat to Israel emerged. Alexander was committed to the creation of a world united by Greek language and culture, a policy followed by his successors. This policy, called Hellenization, had a dramatic impact on the Jews.

At Alexander's death (323 B.C.) the empire he won was divided among his generals. Two of them founded dynasties—the Ptolemies in Egypt and the Seleucids in Syria and Mesopotamia—that would contend for control of Israel for over a century.

The rule of the Ptolemies was considerate of Jewish religious sensitivities, but in 198 B.C. the Seleucids took control and paved the way for one of the most heroic periods in Jewish history.

The early Seleucid years were largely a continuation of the tolerant rule of the Ptolemies, but Antiochus IV Epiphanes (whose title means "God made manifest" and who ruled 175-164 B.C.) changed that when he attempted to consolidate his fading empire through a policy of radical Hellenization. While a segment of the Jewish aristocracy had already adopted Greek ways, the majority of Jews were outraged.

Antiochus's atrocities were aimed at the eradication of Jewish religion. He prohibited some of the central elements of Jewish practice, attempted to destroy all copies of the Torah (the Pentateuch), and required offerings to the Greek god Zeus. His crowning outrage was the erection of a statue of Zeus and the sacrificing of a pig in the Jerusalem temple itself.

Opposition to Antiochus was led by Mattathias, an elderly villager from a priestly family, and his five sons: Judas (Maccabeus), Jonathan, Simon, John, and Eleazar. Mattathias destroyed a Greek altar established in his village, Modein, and killed Antiochus's emissary. This triggered the Maccabean revolt, a 24-year war (166-142 B.C.) that resulted in the independence of Judah until the Romans took control in 63 B.C.

The victory of Mattathias's family was Pyrrhic, however. With the death of his last son, Simon, the Hasmonean dynasty that they founded soon evolved into an aristocratic, Hellenistic regime sometimes hard to distinguish from that of the Seleucids. During the reign of Simon's son, John Hyrcanus, the orthodox Jews who had supported the Maccabees fell out of favor. With only a few exceptions, the rest of the Hasmoneans supported the Jewish Hellenizers. The Pharisees were actually persecuted by Alexander Janneus (103-76 B.C.).

The Hasmonean dynasty ended when, in 63 B.C., an expanding Roman empire intervened in a dynastic clash between the two sons of Janneus, Aristobulus II and

Hyrcanus II. Pompey, the general who subdued the East for Rome, took Jerusalem after a three-month siege of the temple area, massacring priests in the performance of their duties and entering the Most Holy Place. This sacrilege began Roman rule in a way that Jews could neither forgive nor forget.

Literature:

During these unhappy years of oppression and internal strife, the Jewish people produced a sizable body of literature that both recorded and addressed their era. Three of the more significant works are the Septuagint, the Apocrypha and the Dead Sea Scrolls.

Septuagint—

Jewish legend says that seventy-two scholars, under the sponsorship of Ptolemy Philadelphus (c. 250 B.C.), were brought together on the island of Pharos, near Alexandria, where they produced a Greek translation of the OT in seventy-two days. From this tradition the Latin word for seventy, "Septuagint," became the name attached to the translation. The Roman numeral for seventy, LXX, is used as an abbreviation for it.

Behind the legend lies the probability that at least the Torah (the five books of Moses) was translated into Greek c. 250 B.C. for the use of the Greek-speaking Jews of Alexandria. The rest of the OT and some noncanonical books were also included in the LXX before the dawning of the Christian era, though it is difficult to be certain when.

The Septuagint quickly became the Bible of the Jews outside Israel who, like the Alexandrians, no longer spoke Hebrew. It would be difficult to overestimate its influence. It made the Scriptures available both to the Jews who no longer spoke their ancestral language and to the entire Greek-speaking world. It later became the Bible of the early church. Also, its widespread popularity and use contributed to the retention of the Apocrypha by some branches of Christendom.

Apocrypha—

Derived from a Greek word that means "hidden," Apocrypha has acquired the meaning "false," but in a technical sense it describes a specific body of writings. This collection consists of a variety of books and additions to canonical books that, with the exception of 2 Esdras (c. A.D. 90), were written during the intertestamental period. Their recognition as authoritative in Roman and Eastern Christianity is the result of a complex historical process.

The canon of the OT accepted by Protestants today was very likely established by the dawn of the second century A.D., though after the fall of Jerusalem and the destruction of the temple in 70. The precise scope of the OT was discussed among the Jews until the Council of Jamnia (c. 90). This Hebrew canon was not accepted by the early church, which used the Septuagint. In spite of disagreements among some of the church fathers as to which books were canonical and which were not, the Apocryphal books continued in common use by most Christians until the Reformation. During this period most Protestants decided to follow the original Hebrew canon while Rome, at the Council of Trent (1546) and more recently at the First Vatican Council (1869-70), affirmed the larger "Alexandrian" canon that includes the Apocrypha.

The Apocryphal books have retained their place primarily through the weight of ecclesiastical authority, without which they would not commend themselves as canonical literature. There is no clear evidence that Jesus or the apostles ever quoted any Apocryphal works as Scripture (Jude 14). The Jewish community that produced them repudiated them, and the historical surveys in the apostolic sermons recorded in Acts completely ignore the period they cover. Even the sober, historical account of 1 Maccabees is tarnished by numerous errors and anachronisms.

There is nothing of theological value in the Apocryphal books that cannot be duplicated in canonical Scripture, and they contain much that runs counter to its teachings. Nonetheless, this body of literature does provide a valuable source of information for the study of the intertestamental period.

Dead Sea Scrolls—

In the spring of 1947 an Arab shepherd chanced upon a cave in the hills overlooking the southwestern shore of the Dead Sea that contained what has been called "the greatest manuscript discovery of modern times."

The documents and fragments of documents found in those caves, dubbed the "Dead Sea Scrolls," included OT books, a few books of the Apocrypha, apocalyptic works, pseudepigrapha (books that purport to be the work of ancient heroes of the faith), and a number of books peculiar to the sect that produced them.

Approximately a third of the documents are Biblical, with Psalms, Deuteronomy and Isaiah—the books quoted most often in the NT—occurring most frequently. One of the most remarkable finds was a complete 24-foot-long scroll of Isaiah.

The Scrolls have made a significant contribution to the quest for a form of the OT texts most accurately reflecting the original manuscripts; they provide copies a thousand years closer to the originals than were previously known. The understanding of Biblical Hebrew and Aramaic and knowledge of the development of Judaism between the Testaments have been increased significantly. Of great importance to readers of the Bible is the demonstration of the care with which OT texts were copied, thus providing objective evidence for the general reliability of those texts.

Social Developments:

The Judaism of Jesus' day is, to a large extent, the result of changes that came about in response to the pressures of the intertestamental period.

Diaspora—

The Diaspora (dispersion) of Israel begun in the Exile accelerated during these years until a writer of the day could say that Jews filled "every land and sea."

Jews outside Israel, cut off from the temple, concentrated their religious life in the study of the Torah and the life of the synagogue (see below). The missionaries of the early church began their Gentile ministries among the Diaspora, using their Greek translation of the OT.

Sadducees—

In Israel, the Greek world made its greatest impact through the party of the Sadducees. Made up of aristocrats, it became the temple party. Because of their position, the Sadducees had a vested interest in the status quo.

Relatively few in number, they wielded disproportionate political power and controlled the high priesthood. They rejected all religious writings except the Torah, as well as any doctrine (such as the Resurrection) not found in those five books.

Synagogue—

During the Exile, Israel was cut off from the temple, divested of nationhood and surrounded by pagan religious practices. Her faith was threatened with extinction. Under these circumstances, the exiles turned their religious focus from what they had lost to what they retained—the Torah and the belief that they were God's people. They concentrated on the law rather than nationhood, on personal piety rather than sacramental rectitude, and on prayer as an acceptable replacement for the sacrifices denied to them.

When they returned from the Exile, they brought with them this new form of religious expression, as well as the synagogue (its center), and Judaism became a faith that could be practiced wherever the Torah could be carried.

The emphases on personal piety and a relationship with God, which characterized synagogue worship, not only helped preserve Judaism but also prepared the way for the Christian Gospel.

Pharisees—

As the party of the synagogue, the Pharisees strove to reinterpret the law. They built a "hedge" around it to enable Jews to live righteously before God in a world that had changed drastically since the days of Moses. Although they were comparatively few in number, the Pharisees enjoyed the support of the people and influenced popular opinion if not national policy. They were the only party to survive the destruction of the temple in A.D. 70 and were the spiritual progenitors of modern Judaism.

Essenes—

An almost forgotten Jewish sect until the discovery of the Dead Sea Scrolls, the Essenes were a small, separatist group that grew out of the conflicts of the Maccabean age. Like the Pharisees, they stressed strict legal observance, but they considered the temple priesthood corrupt and rejected much of the temple ritual and sacrificial system. Mentioned by several ancient writers, the precise nature of the Essenes is still not certain, though it is generally agreed that the Qumran community that produced the Dead Sea Scrolls was an Essene group.

Because they were convinced that they were the true remnant, these Qumran Essenes had separated themselves from Judaism at large and devoted themselves to personal purity and preparation for the final war between the "Sons of Light and the Sons of Darkness." They practiced an apocalyptic faith, looking back to the contributions of their "Teacher of Righteousness" and forward to the coming of two, and possibly three, Messiahs. The destruction of the temple in A.D. 70, however, seems to have delivered a death blow to their apocalyptic expectations.

Attempts have been made to equate aspects of the beliefs of the Qumran community with the origins of Christianity. Some have seen a prototype of Jesus in their "Teacher of Righteousness," and both John the Baptist and Jesus have been assigned membership in the sect. There is, however, only a superficial, speculative base for these conjectures.

TESTIMONY [5583, 6332, 6343, 6699, 7023, 9496, 282, 2909, 3455+3456+4005, 3455, 3456, 3457, 3459, 5125, 6018, 6019].

NIV+ TESTIFY, TESTIFIED, TESTIFIES, TESTIFYING

Commandments:

Those revealed to Moses (Ex 25:16; Dt 4:44-45; 1Ki 2:3). Kept in the ark (Ex 25:16,21). Engraved on tablets (Ex 31:18; 32:15; 38:21). Atonement cover was over (Ex 26:34; 30:6; 40:20).

Ark, called ark of (Ex 25:22; 26:34; 40:3,5,20-21). Tabernacle called tabernacle of (Nu 1:50,53; 9:19; 10:11). See Ark; Tabernacle.

See Commandments and Statutes, Of God; Decalogue.

Legal: See Evidence; Witness.

Religious:

Ps 18:49 Therefore I will praise you among the nations, O LORD; I will sing praises to your name. (+Ps 22:22; 26:12; 34:1-4,8-9; 77:12; 119:13)

Ps 119:26 I recounted my ways and you answered me; teach me your decrees. (+Ps 119:27,46,67,71)

Isa 43:10 "You are my witnesses," declares the LORD, "and my servant whom I have chosen, so that you may know and believe me and understand that I am he. Before me no god was formed, nor will there be one after me. (+Isa 44:8)

Isa 45:24 They will say of me, 'In the LORD alone are righteousness and strength.'" All who have raged against him will come to him and be put to shame.

1Co 1:5 For in him you have been enriched in every way—in all your speaking and in all your knowledge— 6because our testimony about Christ was confirmed in you.

1Co 12:3 Therefore I tell you that no one who is speaking by the Spirit of God says, "Jesus be cursed," and no one can say, "Jesus is Lord," except by the Holy Spirit. (+1Co 15:15)

Required of the righteous—

1Ch 16:8 Give thanks to the LORD, call on his name; make known among the nations what he has done. 9Sing to him, sing praise to him; tell of all his wonderful acts.

Ps 9:11 Sing praises to the LORD, enthroned in Zion; proclaim among the nations what he has done.

Isa 12:4 In that day you will say: "Give thanks to the LORD, call on his name; make known among the nations what he has done, and proclaim that his name is exalted. 5Sing to the LORD, for he has done glorious things; let this be known to all the world. 6Shout aloud and sing for joy, people of Zion, for great is the Holy One of Israel among you." (+Isa 43:10; 44:8)

Jer 51:10 "'The LORD has vindicated us; come, let us tell in Zion what the LORD our God has done.'

Mt 4:21 Going on from there, he saw two other brothers, James son of Zebedee and his brother John. They were in a boat with their father Zebedee, preparing their nets. Jesus called them,

Mt 5:15 Neither do people light a lamp and put it under a bowl. Instead they put it on its stand, and it gives light to everyone in the house. 16In the same way, let your light shine before men, that they may see your good deeds and praise your Father in heaven.

Mt 5:19 Anyone who breaks one of the least of these commandments and teaches others to do the same will be called least in the kingdom of heaven, but whoever practices and teaches these commands will be called great in the kingdom of heaven. 20For I tell you that unless your righteousness surpasses that of the Pharisees and the teachers of the law, you will certainly not enter the kingdom of heaven. (+Mk 4:21; 5:19-20; Lk 8:16)

Lk 8:39 "Return home and tell how much God has done for you." So the man went away and told all over town how much Jesus had done for him.

Lk 24:48 You are witnesses of these things.

Jn 15:27 And you also must testify, for you have been with me from the beginning.

Ac 1:8 But you will receive power when the Holy Spirit comes on you; and you will be my witnesses in Jerusalem, and in all Judea and Samaria, and to the ends of the earth."

Ac 1:22 beginning from John's baptism to the time when Jesus was taken up from us. For one of these must become a witness with us of his resurrection." (+Ac 3:15; 5:32; 13:31)

Ro 10:9 That if you confess with your mouth, "Jesus is Lord," and believe in your heart that God raised him from the dead, you will be saved. ¹⁰For it is with your heart that you believe and are justified, and it is with your mouth that you confess and are saved.

Eph 5:19 Speak to one another with psalms, hymns and spiritual songs. Sing and make music in your heart to the Lord,

2Ti 1:8 So do not be ashamed to testify about our Lord, or ashamed of me his prisoner. But join with me in suffering for the gospel, by the power of God,

1Pe 3:15 But in your hearts set apart Christ as Lord. Always be prepared to give an answer to everyone who asks you to give the reason for the hope that you have. But do this with gentleness and respect, (+1Pe 5:12)

Concerning God's, faithfulness (Ps 73:23-26,28; 89:1)

Glory—

Ps 145:11 They will tell of the glory of your kingdom and speak of your might, ¹²so that all men may know of your mighty acts and the glorious splendor of your kingdom.

Merciful providence (Ps 40:1-3; 54:7; 91:2-13; Da 4:2-3; Ac 14:15-17), righteousness (Ps 35:28; 71:16)

Salvation (Ps 30:1-6; 40:1-3; 62:1-2; 66:16-20; 71:15, 18; Gal 2:20; Php 3:4-6)—

Php 3:7 But whatever was to my profit I now consider loss for the sake of Christ. ⁸What is more, I consider everything a loss compared to the surpassing greatness of knowing Christ Jesus my Lord, for whose sake I have lost all things. I consider them rubbish, that I may gain Christ ⁹and be found in him, not having a righteousness of my own that comes from the law, but that which is through faith in Christ—the righteousness that comes from God and is by faith. ¹⁰I want to know Christ and the power of his resurrection and the fellowship of sharing in his sufferings, becoming like him in his death, ¹¹and so, somehow, to attain to the resurrection from the dead. ¹²Not that I have already obtained all this, or have already been made perfect, but I press on to take hold of that for which Christ Jesus took hold of me. ¹³Brothers, I do not consider myself yet to have taken hold of it. But one thing I do: Forgetting what is behind and straining toward what is ahead, ¹⁴I press on toward the goal to win the prize for which God has called me heavenward in Christ Jesus. (+Tit 3:3-7)

Heb 2:3 how shall we escape if we ignore such a great salvation? This salvation, which was first announced by the Lord, was confirmed to us by those who heard him.

Heb 2:12 He says, "I will declare your name to my brothers; in the presence of the congregation I will sing your praises."

Words—

Ps 119:172 May my tongue sing of your word, for all your commands are righteous.

Works (Ps 71:17,24; 145:4-7,10-12; Jer 51:10; Ac 2:11).

Concerning confidence in God (Ps 16:5-9; 18:2-3,35-36; 23:1-6; 26:6-7; 27:1-6,13; 28:6-8; 30:1-6).

Rewards of (Mt 10:32)—

Lk 12:8 "I tell you, whoever acknowledges me before men, the Son of Man will also acknowledge him before the angels of God.

Victory by—

Rev 12:11 They overcame him by the blood of the Lamb and by the word of their testimony; they did not love their lives so much as to shrink from death.

Exemplified by:

Job—

Job 19:25 I know that my Redeemer lives, and that in the end he will stand upon the earth. ²⁶And after my skin has been destroyed, yet in my flesh I will see God; ²⁷I myself will see him with my own eyes—I, and not another. How my heart yearns within me!

The psalmist—

Ps 35:28 My tongue will speak of your righteousness and of your praises all day long.

Ps 40:1 I waited patiently for the LORD; he turned to me and heard my cry. ²He lifted me out of the slimy pit, out of the mud and mire; he set my feet on a rock and gave me a firm place to stand. ³He put a new song in my mouth, a hymn of praise to our God. Many will see and fear and put their trust in the LORD.

Ps 40:9 I proclaim righteousness in the great assembly; I do not seal my lips, as you know, O LORD.

Ps 57:7 My heart is steadfast, O God, my heart is steadfast; I will sing and make music. ⁸Awake, my soul! Awake, harp and lyre! I will awaken the dawn.

⁹I will praise you, O Lord, among the nations; I will sing of you among the peoples.

Ps 116:1 I love the LORD, for he heard my voice; he heard my cry for mercy. ²Because he turned his ear to me, I will call on him as long as I live.

³The cords of death entangled me, the anguish of the grave came upon me; I was overcome by trouble and sorrow. ⁴Then I called on the name of the LORD: "O LORD, save me!"

⁵The LORD is gracious and righteous; our God is full of compassion. ⁶The LORD protects the simplehearted; when I was in great need, he saved me.

⁷Be at rest once more, O my soul, for the LORD has been good to you.

⁸For you, O LORD, have delivered my soul from death, my eyes from tears, my feet from stumbling, ⁹that I may walk before the LORD in the land of the living. ¹⁰I believed; therefore I said, "I am greatly afflicted." ¹¹And in my dismay I said, "All men are liars."

¹²How can I repay the LORD for all his goodness to me? ¹³I will lift up the cup of salvation and call on the name of the LORD. ¹⁴I will fulfill my vows to the LORD in the presence of all his people. (+Ps 116:15-19)

Nebuchadnezzar—

Da 4:34 At the end of that time, I, Nebuchadnezzar, raised my eyes toward heaven, and my sanity was restored. Then I praised the Most High; I honored and glorified him who lives forever.

His dominion is an eternal dominion; his kingdom endures from generation to generation. ³⁵All the peoples of the earth are regarded as nothing. He does as he pleases with the powers of heaven and the peoples of the earth. No one can hold back his hand or say to him: "What have you done?"

³⁶At the same time that my sanity was restored, my honor and splendor were returned to me for the glory of my kingdom. My advisers and nobles sought me out, and I was restored to my throne and became even greater than before. ³⁷Now I, Nebuchadnezzar, praise and exalt and glorify the King of heaven, because everything he does is right and all his ways are just. And those who walk in pride he is able to humble.

The woman of Sychar (Jn 4:28-30,39,41-42).

The blind man whom Jesus healed—

Jn 9:17 Finally they turned again to the blind man, "What have you to say about him? It was your eyes he opened." The man replied, "He is a prophet."

Jn 9:30 The man answered, "Now that is remarkable! You don't know where he comes from, yet he opened my eyes. [31]We know that God does not listen to sinners. He listens to the godly man who does his will. [32]Nobody has ever heard of opening the eyes of a man born blind. [33]If this man were not from God, he could do nothing."

The apostles to the resurrection of Jesus (Ac 4:33)—

1Jn 1:1 That which was from the beginning, which we have heard, which we have seen with our eyes, which we have looked at and our hands have touched—this we proclaim concerning the Word of life. [2]The life appeared; we have seen it and testify to it, and we proclaim to you the eternal life, which was with the Father and has appeared to us. [3]We proclaim to you what we have seen and heard, so that you also may have fellowship with us. And our fellowship is with the Father and with his Son, Jesus Christ. [4]We write this to make our joy complete.

The disciples at Pentecost—

Ac 2:4 All of them were filled with the Holy Spirit and began to speak in other tongues as the Spirit enabled them.

[5]Now there were staying in Jerusalem God-fearing Jews from every nation under heaven. [6]When they heard this sound, a crowd came together in bewilderment, because each one heard them speaking in his own language. [7]Utterly amazed, they asked: "Are not all these men who are speaking Galileans? [8]Then how is it that each of us hears them in his own native language? [9]Parthians, Medes and Elamites; residents of Mesopotamia, Judea and Cappadocia, Pontus and Asia, [10]Phrygia and Pamphylia, Egypt and the parts of Libya near Cyrene; visitors from Rome [11](both Jews and converts to Judaism); Cretans and Arabs—we hear them declaring the wonders of God in our own tongues!"

Peter—

Ac 4:18 Then they called them in again and commanded them not to speak or teach at all in the name of Jesus. [19]But Peter and John replied, "Judge for yourselves whether it is right in God's sight to obey you rather than God. [20]For we cannot help speaking about what we have seen and heard." (+1Pe 5:1,12)

2Pe 1:16 We did not follow cleverly invented stories when we told you about the power and coming of our Lord Jesus Christ, but we were eyewitnesses of his majesty.

John (Ac 4:18-20; 1Jn 1:1-4).

Paul's conversion (Ac 22:1-16)—

Ac 26:12 "On one of these journeys I was going to Damascus with the authority and commission of the chief priests. [13]About noon, O king, as I was on the road, I saw a light from heaven, brighter than the sun, blazing around me and my companions. [14]We all fell to the ground, and I heard a voice saying to me in Aramaic, 'Saul, Saul, why do you persecute me? It is hard for you to kick against the goads.'

[15]"Then I asked, 'Who are you, Lord?'

"'I am Jesus, whom you are persecuting,' the Lord replied. [16]'Now get up and stand on your feet. I have appeared to you to appoint you as a servant and as a witness of what you have seen of me and what I will show you. [17]I will rescue you from your own people and from the Gentiles. I am sending you to them [18]to open their eyes and turn them from darkness to light, and from the power of Satan to God, so that they may receive forgiveness of sins and a place among those who are sanctified by faith in me.'

[19]"So then, King Agrippa, I was not disobedient to the vision from heaven. [20]First to those in Damascus, then to those in Jerusalem and in all Judea, and to the Gentiles also, I preached that they should repent and turn to God and prove their repentance by their deeds. [21]That is why the Jews seized me in the temple courts and tried to kill me. [22]But I have had God's help to this very day, and so I stand here and testify to small and great alike. I am saying nothing beyond what the prophets and Moses said would happen— [23]that the Christ would suffer and, as the first to rise from the dead, would proclaim light to his own people and to the Gentiles."

Paul's devotion to Christ (1Co 13:1)—

Php 3:4 though I myself have reasons for such confidence.

If anyone else thinks he has reasons to put confidence in the flesh, I have more: [5]circumcised on the eighth day, of the people of Israel, of the tribe of Benjamin, a Hebrew of Hebrews; in regard to the law, a Pharisee; [6]as for zeal, persecuting the church; as for legalistic righteousness, faultless.

[7]But whatever was to my profit I now consider loss for the sake of Christ. [8]What is more, I consider everything a loss compared to the surpassing greatness of knowing Christ Jesus my Lord, for whose sake I have lost all things. I consider them rubbish, that I may gain Christ [9]and be found in him, not having a righteousness of my own that comes from the law, but that which is through faith in Christ—the righteousness that comes from God and is by faith. [10]I want to know Christ and the power of his resurrection and the fellowship of sharing in his sufferings, becoming like him in his death, [11]and so, somehow, to attain to the resurrection from the dead.

[12]Not that I have already obtained all this, or have already been made perfect, but I press on to take hold of that for which Christ Jesus took hold of me. [13]Brothers, I do not consider myself yet to have taken hold of it. But one thing I do: Forgetting what is behind and straining toward what is ahead, [14]I press on toward the goal to win the prize for which God has called me heavenward in Christ Jesus.

Paul's confidence in Christ—

2Co 4:13 It is written: "I believed; therefore I have spoken." With that same spirit of faith we also believe and therefore speak, [14]because we know that the one who raised the Lord Jesus from the dead will also raise us with Jesus and present us with you in his presence.

2Co 5:1 Now we know that if the earthly tent we live in is destroyed, we have a building from God, an eternal house in heaven, not built by human hands.

2Ti 1:12 That is why I am suffering as I am. Yet I am not ashamed, because I know whom I have believed, and am convinced that he is able to guard what I have entrusted to him for that day.

Paul's hope of the crown of righteousness—

2Ti 4:7 I have fought the good fight, I have finished the race, I have kept the faith. [8]Now there is in store for me the crown of righteousness, which the Lord, the righteous Judge, will award to me on that day—and not only to me, but also to all who have longed for his appearing.

Paul's hope of eternal life—

Tit 1:1 Paul, a servant of God and an apostle of Jesus Christ for the faith of God's elect and the knowledge of the truth that leads to godliness— [2]a faith and knowledge resting on the hope of eternal life, which God, who does not lie, promised before the beginning of time,

TETRARCH [5489, 5490] Ruler of a fourth part of a region (Mt 14:1; Lk 3:1; 9:7; Ac 13:1).

TEXTS, ANCIENT NEAR EASTERN NON-BIBLICAL TEXTS RELATING TO THE OLD TESTAMENT

Major representative examples of ancient Near Eastern nonbiblical documents that provide parallels to or shed light on various OT passages.

Amarna Letters: [Canaanite Akkadian]—*fourteenth century* B.C. Hundreds of letters, written primarily by Canaanite scribes, illuminate social, political and religious relationships between Canaan and Egypt during the reigns of Amenhotep III and Akhenaten.

Amenemope's Wisdom: [Egyptian]—*early first millennium* B.C. Thirty chapters of wisdom instruction are similar to Pr 22:17-24:22 and provide the closest external parallels to OT wisdom literature.

Atrahasis Epic: [Akkadian]—*early second millennium* B.C. A cosmological epic depicts Creation and early human history, including the Flood (cf. Ge 1-9).

Babylonian Theodicy: [Akkadian]—*early first millennium* B.C. A sufferer and his friend dialogue with each other (cf. Job).

Cyrus Cylinder: [Akkadian]—*sixth century* B.C. King Cyrus of Persia records the conquest of Babylon (cf. Da 5:30; 6:28) and boasts of his generous policies toward his new subjects and their gods.

Dead Sea Scrolls: [Hebrew, Aramaic, Greek]—*third century* B.C. *to first century* A.D. Several hundred scrolls and fragments include the oldest copies of OT books and passages.

Ebal Tablets: [Sumerian, Eblaite]—*mid-third millennium* B.C. Thousands of commercial, legal, literary, and epistolary texts describe the cultural vitality and political power of a prepatriarchal civilization in northern Syria.

Elephantine Papyri: [Aramaic]—*late fifth century* B.C. Contracts and letters document life among Israelites who fled to southern Egypt after Jerusalem was destroyed in 586 B.C.

Enuma Elish: [Akkadian]—*early second millennium* B.C. Marduk, the Babylonian god of cosmic order, is elevated to the supreme position in the pantheon. The seven-tablet epic contains an account of creation (cf. Ge 1-2).

Gezer Calendar: [Hebrew]—*tenth century* B.C. A schoolboy from west-central Israel describes the seasons, crops and farming activity of the agricultural year.

Gilgamesh Epic: [Akkadian]—*early second millennium* B.C. Gilgamesh, ruler of Uruk, experiences numerous adventures, including a meeting with Utnapishtim, the only survivor of a great deluge (cf. Ge 6-9).

Hammurapi's Code: [Akkadian]—*eighteenth century* B.C. Together with similar law codes that preceded and followed it, the Code of Hammurapi exhibits close parallels to numerous passages in the Mosaic laws of the OT.

Hymn to the Aten: [Egyptian]—*fourteenth century* B.C. The poem praises the beneficence and universality of the sun in language somewhat similar to that used in Ps 104.

Ishtar's Descent: [Akkadian]—*first millennium* B.C. The goddess Ishtar temporarily descends to the netherworld,

which is pictured in terms reminiscent of OT descriptions of Sheol.

Jehoiachin's Ration Dockets: [Akkadian]—*early sixth century* B.C. Brief texts from the reign of Nebuchadnezzar II refer to rations allotted to Judah's exiled king Jehoiachin and his sons (cf. 2Ki 25:27-30).

King Lists: [Sumerian]—*late third millennium* B.C. The reigns of Sumerian kings before the Flood are described as lasting for thousands of years, reminding us of the longevity of the pre-Flood patriarchs in Ge 5.

Lachish Letters: [Hebrew]—*early sixth century* B.C. Inscriptions on pottery fragments vividly portray the desperate days preceding the Babylonian siege of Jerusalem in 588-586 B.C. (cf. Jer 34:7).

Lamentation Over the Destruction of Ur: [Sumerian]—*early second millennium* B.C. The poem mourns the destruction of the city of Ur at the hands of the Elamites (cf. the OT book of Lamentations).

Ludlul Bel Nemeqi: [Akkadian]—*late second millennium* B.C. A suffering Babylonian nobleman describes his distress in terms faintly reminiscent of the experience of Job.

Mari Tablets: [Akkadian]—*eighteenth century* B.C. Letters and administration texts provide detailed information regarding customs, language, and personal names that reflect the culture of the OT patriarchs.

Merneptah Stele: [Egyptian]—*thirteenth century* B.C. Pharaoh Merneptah figuratively describes his victory over various peoples in western Asia, including "Israel."

Mesha Stele (*Moabite Stone*): [Moabite]—*ninth century* B.C. Mesha, king of Moab (see 2Ki 3:4), rebels against a successor of Israel's king Omri.

Murashu Tablets: [Akkadian]—*fifth century* B.C. Commercial documents describe financial transactions engaged in by Murashu and Sons, a Babylonian firm that did business with Jews and other exiles.

Mursilis's Treaty with Duppi-Tessub: [Hittite]—*mid-second millennium* B.C. King Mursilis imposes a suzerainty treaty on King Duppi-Tessub. The literary outline of this and other Hittite treaties is strikingly paralleled in OT covenants established by God with his people.

Nabonidus Chronicle: [Akkadian]—*mid-sixth century* B.C. The account describes the absence of King Nabonidus from Babylon. His son Belshazzar is therefore the regent in charge of the kingdom (cf. Da 5:29-30).

Nebuchadnezzar Chronicle: [Akkadian]—*early sixth century* B.C. A chronicle from the reign of Nebuchadnezzar II includes the Babylonian account of the siege of Jerusalem in 597 B.C. (2Ki 24:10-17).

Nuzi Tablets: [Akkadian]—*mid-second millennium* B.C. Adoption, birthright-sale and other legal documents graphically illustrate OT patriarchal customs current centuries earlier.

Pessimistic Dialogue: [Akkadian]—*early first millennium* B.C. A master and his servant discuss the pros and cons of various activities (cf. Ecc 1-2).

Ras Shamra Tablets: [Ugaritic]—*fifteenth century* B.C. Canaanite deities and rulers experience adventures in epics that enrich our understanding of Canaanite mythology and religion and of OT poetry.

Sargon Legend: [Akkadian]—*first millennium* B.C. Sargon I (the Great), ruler of Akkad in the late third millennium B.C. claims to have been rescued as an infant from a reed basket found floating in a river (cf. Ex 2).

Sargon's Display Inscription: [Akkadian]—*eighth century* B.C. Sargon II takes credit for the conquest of Samaria in 722/721 B.C. and states that he captured and exiled 27,290 Israelites.

Sennacherib's Prism: [Akkadian]—*early seventh century* B.C. Sennacherib vividly describes his siege of Jerusalem in 701 B.C., making Hezekiah a prisoner in his own royal city (but cf. 2Ki 19:35-37).

Seven Lean Years Tradition: [Egyptian]—*second century* B.C. Egypt experiences seven years of low Nile levels and famine, which, by a contractual agreement between Pharaoh Djoser (twenty-eighth century B.C.) and a god, will be followed by prosperity (cf. Ge 41).

Shalmaneser's Black Obelisk: [Akkadian]—*ninth century* B.C. Israel's king Jehu (or his servant) presents tribute to Assyria's king Shalmaneser III. Additional Assyrian and Babylonian texts refer to other kings of Israel and Judah.

Shishak's Geographical List: [Egyptian]—*tenth century* B.C. Pharaoh Shishak lists the cities that he captured or made tributary during his campaign in Judah and Israel (cf. 1Ki 14:25-26).

Siloam Inscription: [Hebrew]—*late eighth century* B.C. A Judahite workman describes the construction of an underground conduit to guarantee Jerusalem's water supply during Hezekiah's reign (cf. 2Ki 20:20; 2Ch 32:30).

Sinuhe's Story: [Egyptian]—*twentieth to nineteenth centuries* B.C. An Egyptian official of the twelfth dynasty goes into voluntary exile in Syria and Canaan during the OT patriarchal period.

Tale of Two Brothers: [Egyptian]—*thirteenth century* B.C. A young man rejects the amorous advances of his older brother's wife (cf. Ge 39).

Wenamun's Journey: [Egyptian]—*eleventh century* B.C. An official of the Temple of Amun at Thebes in Egypt is sent to Byblos in Canaan to buy lumber for the ceremonial barge of his god.

TEXTS AND VERSIONS

Old Testament

Major Hebrew texts—

1. The oldest copies of the Hebrew OT are the famous Dead Sea Scrolls, dating from 250 B.C. to c. A.D. 70. *See Dead Sea Scrolls; Testaments, Time Between.*

2. Portions of the OT text include the Nash Papyrus (second century B.C.) and the Cairo Genizah fragments (sixth to ninth centuries A.D.).

3. The Masoretes preserved and standardized the Hebrew text between the sixth and tenth centuries A.D.. The oldest examples of this text type include the Cairo Codex of the Prophets (895), the Aleppo Codex (c. 900-925) and the Leningrad Codex (1008).

4. The Samaritan Pentateuch (eleventh century A.D.).

Major versions—

1. Greek: Septuagint (250-100 B.C.); second century A.D. versions by Aquila, Theodotion, and Symmachus; by Origen c. A.D. 240.

2. Aramaic (first to fifth century A.D.).

3. Syriac (second or third century A.D.).

4. Latin: Old Latin (second century A.D.), Jerome's Vulgate (383-405 A.D.).

New Testament:

Major Greek texts—

Greek manuscripts of portions or of the whole of the NT total nearly 5,000. Of these, c. 70 are papyri, 250 uncials, 2,500 minuscules, and 1,800 lectionaries.

1. Fragments and books on papyrus date back to the second century A.D., such as Bodmer Papyrus p^{66} of John.

2. Codex Sinaiticus (fourth century) contains the entire NT.

3. Codicies Alexandrinus (fifth century) and Vaticanus are nearly complete.

4. Quotations from the early church fathers also provide an ancient witness to the NT.

Major versions—

1. Latin (second to fourth centuries).

2. Syriac (second to sixth centuries).

3. Coptic (second and third centuries).

THADDAEUS [*2497*] (possibly *breast nipple*). One of the 12 apostles (Mt 10:3; Mk 3:18). This name does not appear in (Lk 6:16; Ac 1:13), the name "Judas son of James" occurs instead. Little is known about him.

See Lebbaeus.

THAHASH *See Tahash.*

THAMAH *See Temah.*

THAMAR *See Tamar, 1.*

THANK OFFERINGS *See Offerings.*

THANKFULNESS [*3344, 9343, 10312, 2328, 2373, 2374, 5921*].

NIV+ THANK, THANKED, THANKFUL, THANKING, THANKS, THANKSGIVING

To God:

Commanded or required—

Ge 35:1 Then God said to Jacob, "Go up to Bethel and settle there, and build an altar there to God, who appeared to you when you were fleeing from your brother Esau."

Ex 12:14 "This is a day you are to commemorate; for the generations to come you shall celebrate it as a festival to the LORD—a lasting ordinance.

Ex 12:17 "Celebrate the Feast of Unleavened Bread, because it was on this very day that I brought your divisions out of Egypt. Celebrate this day as a lasting ordinance for the generations to come.

Ex 12:42 Because the LORD kept vigil that night to bring them out of Egypt, on this night all the Israelites are to keep vigil to honor the LORD for the generations to come.

Ex 13:3 Then Moses said to the people, "Commemorate this day, the day you came out of Egypt, out of the land of slavery, because the LORD brought you out of it with a mighty hand. Eat nothing containing yeast.

Ex 13:8 On that day tell your son, 'I do this because of what the LORD did for me when I came out of Egypt.' ⁹This observance will be for you like a sign on your hand and a reminder on your forehead that the law of the LORD is to be on your lips. For the LORD brought you out of Egypt with his mighty hand. ¹⁰You must keep this ordinance at the appointed time year after year.

Ex 13:14 "In days to come, when your son asks you, 'What does this mean?' say to him, 'With a mighty hand the LORD brought us out of Egypt, out of the land of slavery. ¹⁵When Pharaoh stubbornly refused to let us go, the LORD killed every firstborn in Egypt, both man and animal. This is why I sacrifice to the LORD the first male offspring of every womb and redeem each of my firstborn sons.' ¹⁶And it will be like a sign on your hand and a symbol on your forehead that the LORD brought us out of Egypt with his mighty hand."

Ex 16:32 Moses said, "This is what the LORD has commanded: 'Take an omer of manna and keep it for the generations to come, so they can see the bread I gave you to eat in the desert when I brought you out of Egypt.'"

Ex 34:26 "Bring the best of the firstfruits of your soil to the house of the LORD your God. "Do not cook a young goat in its mother's milk."

Lev 19:24 In the fourth year all its fruit will be holy, an offering of praise to the LORD.

Lev 23:14 You must not eat any bread, or roasted or new grain, until the very day you bring this offering to your God. This is to be a lasting ordinance for the generations to come, wherever you live.

Dt 12:18 Instead, you are to eat them in the presence of the LORD your God at the place the LORD your God will choose—you, your sons and daughters, your menservants and maidservants, and the Levites from your towns—and you are to rejoice before the LORD your God in everything you put your hand to.

Dt 16:9 Count off seven weeks from the time you begin to put the sickle to the standing grain. ¹⁰Then celebrate the Feast of Weeks to the LORD your God by giving a freewill offering in proportion to the blessings the LORD your God has given you. ¹¹And rejoice before the LORD your God at the place he will choose as a dwelling for his Name—you, your sons and daughters, your menservants and maidservants, the Levites in your towns, and the aliens, the fatherless and the widows living among you. ¹²Remember that you were slaves in Egypt, and follow carefully these decrees.

¹³Celebrate the Feast of Tabernacles for seven days after you have gathered the produce of your threshing floor and your winepress. ¹⁴Be joyful at your Feast—you, your sons and daughters, your menservants and maidservants, and the Levites, the aliens, the fatherless and the widows who live in your towns. ¹⁵For seven days celebrate the Feast to the LORD your God at the place the LORD will choose. For the LORD your God will bless you in all your harvest and in all the work of your hands, and your joy will be complete.

Dt 26:10 and now I bring the firstfruits of the soil that you, O LORD, have given me." Place the basket before the LORD your God and bow down before him.

Jdg 5:11 the voice of the singers at the watering places. They recite the righteous acts of the LORD, the righteous acts of his warriors in Israel. "Then the people of the LORD went down to the city gates.

Ps 50:14 Sacrifice thank offerings to God, fulfill your vows to the Most High, ¹⁵and call upon me in the day of trouble; I will deliver you, and you will honor me."

Commanded—

Ps 48:11 Mount Zion rejoices, the villages of Judah are glad because of your judgments.

Ps 106:1 Praise the LORD. Give thanks to the LORD, for he is good; his love endures forever.

Pr 3:9 Honor the LORD with your wealth, with the firstfruits of all your crops; ¹⁰then your barns will be filled to overflowing, and your vats will brim over with new wine.

Ecc 7:14 When times are good, be happy; but when times are bad, consider: God has made the one as well as the other. Therefore, a man cannot discover anything about his future.

Isa 48:20 Leave Babylon, flee from the Babylonians! Announce this with shouts of joy and proclaim it. Send it out to the ends of the earth; say, "The LORD has redeemed his servant Jacob."

Joel 2:26 You will have plenty to eat, until you are full, and you will praise the name of the LORD your God, who has worked wonders for you; never again will my people be shamed.

Ro 2:4 Or do you show contempt for the riches of his kindness, tolerance and patience, not realizing that God's kindness leads you toward repentance?

Ro 15:27 They were pleased to do it, and indeed they owe it to them. For if the Gentiles have shared in the Jews' spiritual blessings, they owe it to the Jews to share with them their material blessings. (+Eph 1:16)

Eph 5:4 Nor should there be obscenity, foolish talk or coarse joking, which are out of place, but rather thanksgiving.

Eph 5:19 Speak to one another with psalms, hymns and spiritual songs. Sing and make music in your heart to the Lord, ²⁰always giving thanks to God the Father for everything, in the name of our Lord Jesus Christ.

Php 4:6 Do not be anxious about anything, but in everything, by prayer and petition, with thanksgiving, present your requests to God.

Col 1:12 giving thanks to the Father, who has qualified you to share in the inheritance of the saints in the kingdom of light.

Col 2:7 rooted and built up in him, strengthened in the faith as you were taught, and overflowing with thankfulness.

Col 3:15 Let the peace of Christ rule in your hearts, since as members of one body you were called to peace. And be thankful. ¹⁶Let the word of Christ dwell in you richly as you teach and admonish one another with all wisdom, and as you sing psalms, hymns and spiritual songs with gratitude in your hearts to God. ¹⁷And whatever you do, whether in word or deed, do it all in the name of the Lord Jesus, giving thanks to God the Father through him.

Col 4:2 Devote yourselves to prayer, being watchful and thankful. (+1Th 5:18)

Heb 13:15 Through Jesus, therefore, let us continually offer to God a sacrifice of praise—the fruit of lips that confess his name.

Jas 1:9 The brother in humble circumstances ought to take pride in his high position.

Exhorted—

Ps 98:1 Sing to the LORD a new song, for he has done marvelous things; his right hand and his holy arm have worked salvation for him.

Ps 105:1 Give thanks to the LORD, call on his name; make known among the nations what he has done.

Ps 105:5 Remember the wonders he has done, his miracles, and the judgments he pronounced.

Ps 105:42 For he remembered his holy promise given to his servant Abraham. ⁴³He brought out his people with rejoicing, his chosen ones with shouts of joy; ⁴⁴he gave them the lands of the nations, and they fell heir to what others had toiled for— ⁴⁵that they might keep his precepts and observe his laws.

Praise the LORD.

Ps 107:1 Give thanks to the LORD, for he is good; his love endures forever. ²Let the redeemed of the LORD say this—those he redeemed from the hand of the foe,

Ps 107:15 Let them give thanks to the LORD for his unfailing love and his wonderful deeds for men,

Ps 107:22 Let them sacrifice thank offerings and tell of his works with songs of joy.

Ps 107:42 The upright see and rejoice, but all the wicked shut their mouths.

⁴³Whoever is wise, let him heed these things and consider the great love of the LORD.

Ps 118:1 Give thanks to the LORD, for he is good; his love endures forever.

Ps 118:4 Let those who fear the LORD say: "His love endures forever." (+Col 3:15)

1Ti 2:1 I urge, then, first of all, that requests, prayers, intercession and thanksgiving be made for everyone—

1Ti 4:3 They forbid people to marry and order them to abstain from certain foods, which God created to be received with thanksgiving by those who believe and who know the truth. ⁴For everything God created is good, and nothing is to be rejected if it is received with thanksgiving, ⁵because it is consecrated by the word of God and prayer.

Jesus set an example of (Mt 11:25; 15:36; 26:27; Mk 8:6-7; 14:23; Lk 22:17,19; Jn 6:11,23; 11:41).

Should be offered, to God (Ps 30:4; 50:14; 75:1; 92:1; 97:12; 106:1; 118:1; 2Co 9:11; Eph 5:4,19-20; Php 4:6; Col 1:12; 2:7; 3:15-17; 4:2; 1Th 5:18; 1Ti 2:1; Heb 13:15), through Christ (Ro 1:8; Col 3:17; Heb 13:15), in the name of Christ (Eph 5:20), in behalf of ministers (2Co 1:11), in private worship (Da 6:10), in public (1Ch 23:30; 25:3; Ne 11:17; Ps 35:18), in everything (1Th 5:18), upon the completion of great undertakings (Ne 12:31,40), before taking food (Mt 14:19; Mk 8:9; Lk 24:30; Jn 6:11; Ac 27:35), always (Eph 1:16; 5:20; 1Th 1:2), as the remembrance of God's holiness (Ps 30:4; 97:12).

For: The goodness and mercy of God (Ps 68:19; 79:13; 89:1; 100:4; 106:1; 107:1; 116:12-14,17; 136:1-3; Isa 63:7), the gift of Christ (2Co 9:15), Christ's power and reign (Rev 11:17), the reception and effectual working of the word of God in others (1Th 2:13), deliverance, from adversity (Ps 31:7,21; 35:9-10; 44:7-8; 54:6-7; 66:8-9,12-16,20; 98:1), through Christ, from indwelling sin (Ro 7:23-25), providential deliverance (Ex 12:14,17,42; 13:3,8-10,14-16; Jdg 5:11; Ps 105:1-45; 107:1-2,15,22,42-43; 136:1-26; Joel 2:26), victory over death and the grave (1Co 15:57), wisdom and might (Da 2:23), the triumph of the Gospel (2Co 2:14), the conversion of others (Ro 6:17), faith exhibited by others (Ro 1:8; 2Th 1:3), love exhibited by others (2Th 1:3), the grace bestowed on others (1Co 1:4; Php 1:3-5; Col 1:3-6), the zeal exhibited by others (2Co 8:16), nearness of God's presence (Ps 75:1), appointment to the ministry (1Ti 1:12), willingness to offer our property for God's service (1Ch 29:6-14), the supply of our bodily wants (Ro 14:6-7; 1Ti 4:3-4), all men (1Ti 2:1), all things (2Co 9:11; Eph 5:20), temporal blessings (Ro 14:6-7; 1Ti 4:3-5).

Should be accompanied by intercession for others (1Ti 2:1; 2Ti 1:3; Phm 4). Should always accompany prayer (Ne 11:17; Php 4:6; Col 4:2). Should always accompany praise (Ps 92:1; Heb 13:15). Expressed in psalms (1Ch 16:7). Ministers appointed to offer, in public (1Ch 16:4,7; 23:30; 2Ch 31:2).

Saints, exhorted to (Ps 105:1; Col 3:15), resolve to offer (Ps 18:49; 30:12), habitually offer (Da 6:10), offer sacrifices of (Ps 116:17), abound in the faith with (Col 2:7), magnify God by (Ps 95:2), come before God with (Ps 95:2), should enter God's gates with (Ps 100:4). Of hypocrites, full of boasting (Lk 18:11). The wicked averse to (Ro 1:21).

Of the heavenly host (Rev 4:9; 7:11-12; 11:16-17).

Cultivated, by the Feast of Tabernacles (Dt 16:9-15), by thank offerings (Ex 34:26; Lev 19:24; 23:14; Dt 12:18; 26:10; Pr 3:9-10), by songs (1Ch 16:7-36; Ps 95:2; 100).

Instances of:

Eve (Ge 4:1,25). Noah (Ge 8:20). Melchizedek (Ge 14:20). Lot (Ge 19:19). Abraham (Ge 12:7). Sarah (Ge 21:6-7). Abraham's servant (Ge 24:27). Isaac (Ge 26:22). Leah (Ge 29:32-35). Rachel (Ge 30:6).

Jacob—

Ge 32:10 I am unworthy of all the kindness and faithfulness you have shown your servant. I had only my staff when I crossed this Jordan, but now I have become two groups. (+Ge 35:3,7)

Ge 48:11 Israel said to Joseph, "I never expected to see your face again, and now God has allowed me to see your children too."

Ge 48:15 Then he blessed Joseph and said, "May the God before whom my fathers Abraham and Isaac walked, the God who has been my shepherd all my life to this day, ¹⁶the Angel who has delivered me from all harm—may he bless these boys. May they be called by my name and the names of my fathers Abraham and Isaac, and may they increase greatly upon the earth."

Joseph (Ge 41:51-52).

Moses—

Ex 15:1 Then Moses and the Israelites sang this song to the LORD: "I will sing to the LORD, for he is highly exalted. The horse and its rider he has hurled into the sea. ²The LORD is my strength and my song; he has become my salvation. He is my God, and I will praise him, my father's God, and I will exalt him. ³The LORD is a warrior; the LORD is his name. ⁴Pharaoh's chariots and his army he has hurled into the sea. The best of Pharaoh's officers are drowned in the Red Sea. ⁵The deep waters have covered them; they sank to the depths like a stone.

⁶"Your right hand, O LORD, was majestic in power. Your right hand, O LORD, shattered the enemy. ⁷In the greatness of your majesty you threw down those who opposed you. You unleashed your burning anger; it consumed them like stubble. ⁸By the blast of your nostrils the waters piled up. The surging waters stood firm like a wall; the deep waters congealed in the heart of the sea.

⁹"The enemy boasted, 'I will pursue, I will overtake them. I will divide the spoils; I will gorge myself on them. I will draw my sword and my hand will destroy them.' ¹⁰But you blew with your breath, and the sea covered them. They sank like lead in the mighty waters.

¹¹"Who among the gods is like you, O LORD? Who is like you—majestic in holiness, awesome in glory, working wonders? ¹²You stretched out your right hand and the earth swallowed them.

¹³"In your unfailing love you will lead the people you have redeemed. In your strength you will guide them to your holy dwelling. ¹⁴The nations will hear and tremble; anguish will grip the people of Philistia. ¹⁵The chiefs of Edom will be terrified, the leaders of Moab will be seized with trembling, the people of Canaan will melt away; ¹⁶terror and dread will fall upon them. By the power of your arm they will be as still as a stone—until your people pass by, O LORD, until the people you bought pass by. ¹⁷You will bring them in and plant them on the mountain of your inheritance—the place, O LORD, you made for

your dwelling, the sanctuary, O Lord, your hands established. [18]The LORD will reign for ever and ever."

Miriam—

Ex 15:19 When Pharaoh's horses, chariots and horsemen went into the sea, the LORD brought the waters of the sea back over them, but the Israelites walked through the sea on dry ground. [20]Then Miriam the prophetess, Aaron's sister, took a tambourine in her hand, and all the women followed her, with tambourines and dancing. [21]Miriam sang to them:

"Sing to the LORD, for he is highly exalted. The horse and its rider he has hurled into the sea."

Jethro (Ex 18:10). Israel (Ex 4:31; 15:1-18; Nu 21:17; 31:49-54; 1Ch 29:22). Deborah (Jdg 5). Hannah (1Sa 1:27-28; 2:1-10). Samuel (1Sa 7:12).

David (2Sa 6:21)—

1Ch 29:13 Now, our God, we give you thanks, and praise your glorious name.

Solomon (1Ki 8:15)—

1Ki 8:56 "Praise be to the LORD, who has given rest to his people Israel just as he promised. Not one word has failed of all the good promises he gave through his servant Moses. (+2Ch 6:4)

Queen of Sheba (1Ki 10:9). Hiram (2Ch 2:12). Jehoshaphat's army (2Ch 20:27-28).

Ezra—

Ezr 7:27 Praise be to the LORD, the God of our fathers, who has put it into the king's heart to bring honor to the house of the LORD in Jerusalem in this way

The Levites (2Ch 5:12-13; Ne 9:4-38). The Jews (Ne 12:31,40,43).

The psalmist—

Ps 9:1 I will praise you, O LORD, with all my heart; I will tell of all your wonders. [2]I will be glad and rejoice in you; I will sing praise to your name, O Most High.

Ps 9:4 For you have upheld my right and my cause; you have sat on your throne, judging righteously.

Ps 13:6 I will sing to the LORD, for he has been good to me.

Ps 22:23 You who fear the LORD, praise him! All you descendants of Jacob, honor him! Revere him, all you descendants of Israel! [24]For he has not despised or disdained the suffering of the afflicted one; he has not hidden his face from him but has listened to his cry for help.

[25]From you comes the theme of my praise in the great assembly; before those who fear you will I fulfill my vows.

Ps 26:7 proclaiming aloud your praise and telling of all your wonderful deeds.

Ps 28:7 The LORD is my strength and my shield; my heart trusts in him, and I am helped. My heart leaps for joy and I will give thanks to him in song.

Ps 30:1 I will exalt you, O LORD, for you lifted me out of the depths and did not let my enemies gloat over me.

Ps 30:3 O LORD, you brought me up from the grave; you spared me from going down into the pit.

Ps 30:11 You turned my wailing into dancing; you removed my sackcloth and clothed me with joy, [12]that my heart may sing to you and not be silent. O LORD my God, I will give you thanks forever.

Ps 31:7 I will be glad and rejoice in your love, for you saw my affliction and knew the anguish of my soul. (+Ps 31:21)

Ps 35:9 Then my soul will rejoice in the LORD and delight in his salvation. [10]My whole being will exclaim, "Who is like you, O LORD? You rescue the poor from those too strong for them, the poor and needy from those who rob them."

Ps 35:18 I will give you thanks in the great assembly; among throngs of people I will praise you.

Ps 40:2 He lifted me out of the slimy pit, out of the mud and mire; he set my feet on a rock and gave me a firm place to stand. [3]He put a new song in my mouth, a hymn of praise to our God. Many will see and fear and put their trust in the LORD.

Ps 40:5 Many, O LORD my God, are the wonders you have done. The things you planned for us no one can recount to you; were I to speak and tell of them, they would be too many to declare.

Ps 41:11 I know that you are pleased with me, for my enemy does not triumph over me. [12]In my integrity you uphold me and set me in your presence forever.

Ps 44:7 but you give us victory over our enemies, you put our adversaries to shame. [8]In God we make our boast all day long, and we will praise your name forever. *Selah*

Ps 54:6 I will sacrifice a freewill offering to you; I will praise your name, O LORD, for it is good. [7]For he has delivered me from all my troubles, and my eyes have looked in triumph on my foes.

Ps 56:12 I am under vows to you, O God; I will present my thank offerings to you. [13]For you have delivered me from death and my feet from stumbling, that I may walk before God in the light of life.

Ps 59:16 But I will sing of your strength, in the morning I will sing of your love; for you are my fortress, my refuge in times of trouble.

[17]O my Strength, I sing praise to you; you, O God, are my fortress, my loving God.

Ps 66:8 Praise our God, O peoples, let the sound of his praise be heard; [9]he has preserved our lives and kept our feet from slipping.

Ps 66:12 You let men ride over our heads; we went through fire and water, but you brought us to a place of abundance.

[13]I will come to your temple with burnt offerings and fulfill my vows to you— [14]vows my lips promised and my mouth spoke when I was in trouble. [15]I will sacrifice fat animals to you and an offering of rams; I will offer bulls and goats. *Selah*

[16]Come and listen, all you who fear God; let me tell you what he has done for me.

Ps 66:20 Praise be to God, who has not rejected my prayer or withheld his love from me!

Ps 68:19 Praise be to the Lord, to God our Savior, who daily bears our burdens. *Selah*

Ps 71:15 My mouth will tell of your righteousness, of your salvation all day long, though I know not its measure.

Ps 71:23 My lips will shout for joy when I sing praise to you—I, whom you have redeemed. [24]My tongue will tell of your righteous acts all day long, for those who wanted to harm me have been put to shame and confusion.

Ps 79:13 Then we your people, the sheep of your pasture, will praise you forever; from generation to generation we will recount your praise.

Ps 89:1 I will sing of the LORD's great love forever; with my mouth I will make your faithfulness known through all generations.

Ps 92:1 It is good to praise the LORD and make music to your name, O Most High, [2]to proclaim your love in the morning and your faithfulness at night,

Ps 92:4 For you make me glad by your deeds, O LORD; I sing for joy at the works of your hands.

Ps 98:1 Sing to the LORD a new song, for he has done marvelous things; his right hand and his holy arm have worked salvation for him.

Ps 100:4 Enter his gates with thanksgiving and his courts with praise; give thanks to him and praise his name.

Ps 102:18 Let this be written for a future generation, that a people not yet created may praise the LORD: ¹⁹"The LORD looked down from his sanctuary on high, from heaven he viewed the earth, ²⁰to hear the groans of the prisoners and release those condemned to death."

Ps 104:1 Praise the LORD, O my soul. O LORD my God, you are very great; you are clothed with splendor and majesty.

Ps 116:12 How can I repay the LORD for all his goodness to me? ¹³I will lift up the cup of salvation and call on the name of the LORD. ¹⁴I will fulfill my vows to the LORD in the presence of all his people.

Ps 116:17 I will sacrifice a thank offering to you and call on the name of the LORD.

Ps 119:65 Do good to your servant according to your word, O LORD.

Ps 119:108 Accept, O LORD, the willing praise of my mouth, and teach me your laws.

Ps 136:1 Give thanks to the LORD, for he is good. *His love endures forever.* ²Give thanks to the God of gods. *His love endures forever.* ³Give thanks to the Lord of lords: *His love endures forever.*

⁴to him who alone does great wonders, *His love endures forever.* ⁵who by his understanding made the heavens, *His love endures forever.* ⁶who spread out the earth upon the waters, *His love endures forever.* ⁷who made the great lights—*His love endures forever.* ⁸the sun to govern the day, *His love endures forever.* ⁹the moon and stars to govern the night; *His love endures forever.*

¹⁰to him who struck down the firstborn of Egypt *His love endures forever.* ¹¹and brought Israel out from among them *His love endures forever.* ¹²with a mighty hand and outstretched arm; *His love endures forever.*

¹³to him who divided the Red Sea asunder *His love endures forever.* ¹⁴and brought Israel through the midst of it, *His love endures forever.* ¹⁵but swept Pharaoh and his army into the Red Sea; *His love endures forever.*

¹⁶to him who led his people through the desert, *His love endures forever.* ¹⁷who struck down great kings, *His love endures forever.* ¹⁸and killed mighty kings—*His love endures forever.* ¹⁹Sihon king of the Amorites *His love endures forever.* ²⁰and Og king of Bashan—*His love endures forever.* ²¹and gave their land as an inheritance, *His love endures forever.* ²²an inheritance to his servant Israel; *His love endures forever.*

²³to the One who remembered us in our low estate *His love endures forever.* ²⁴and freed us from our enemies, *His love endures forever.* ²⁵and who gives food to every creature. *His love endures forever.*

²⁶Give thanks to the God of heaven. *His love endures forever.*

Isaiah—

Isa 63:7 I will tell of the kindnesses of the LORD, the deeds for which he is to be praised, according to all the LORD has done for us—yes, the many good things he has done for the house of Israel, according to his compassion and many kindnesses.

Daniel—

Da 2:23 I thank and praise you, O God of my fathers: You have given me wisdom and power, you have made known

to me what we asked of you, you have made known to us the dream of the king."

Da 6:22 My God sent his angel, and he shut the mouths of the lions. They have not hurt me, because I was found innocent in his sight. Nor have I ever done any wrong before you, O king."

Nebuchadnezzar—

Da 4:2 It is my pleasure to tell you about the miraculous signs and wonders that the Most High God has performed for me.

Da 4:34 At the end of that time, I, Nebuchadnezzar, raised my eyes toward heaven, and my sanity was restored. Then I praised the Most High; I honored and glorified him who lives forever. His dominion is an eternal dominion; his kingdom endures from generation to generation.

The mariners (Jnh 1:16). Jonah (Jnh 2:9). The shepherds (Lk 2:20). Simeon (Lk 2:28). Anna (Lk 2:38).

Those whom Jesus healed: The paralyzed man (Lk 5:25), the demoniac (Lk 8:39), the woman bent with infirmity (Lk 13:13), one of the ten lepers (Lk 17:15-16), blind Bartimaeus (Lk 18:43), the centurion for his son (Jn 4:53).

The lame man healed by Peter (Ac 3:8).

Early Christians—

Ac 2:46 Every day they continued to meet together in the temple courts. They broke bread in their homes and ate together with glad and sincere hearts, ⁴⁷praising God and enjoying the favor of all the people. And the Lord added to their number daily those who were being saved.

Paul (Ac 27:35)—

Ac 28:15 The brothers there had heard that we were coming, and they traveled as far as the Forum of Appius and the Three Taverns to meet us. At the sight of these men Paul thanked God and was encouraged. (+Ro 1:8; 6:17; 1Co 1:4; 2Co 2:14; Php 1:3-5)

Col 1:3 We always thank God, the Father of our Lord Jesus Christ, when we pray for you, (+Col 1:4-6; 2Th 1:3)

1Ti 1:12 I thank Christ Jesus our Lord, who has given me strength, that he considered me faithful, appointing me to his service.

See Joy; Praise; Psalms; Worship.

Of Man to Man:

The Israelites, to Joshua (Jos 19:49-50). The spies, to Rahab (Jos 6:22-25). Saul, to the Kenites (1Sa 15:6). Naomi, to Boaz (Ru 2:19-20). David, to the men of Jabesh Gilead (2Sa 2:5-7), to Hanun (2Sa 10:2), to Barzillai (1Ki 2:7). Paul, to Phoebe (Ro 16:1-4), to Onesiphorus (2Ti 1:16-18). The people of Malta, to Paul (Ac 28:10).

THANKSGIVING [2117, 3344, 9343, *2330, 2374*].

NIV+ See THANK

By Jesus (Mt 11:25; 15:36; 26:27; Mk 8:6-7; 14:23; Lk 22:17,19; Jn 6:11,23; 11:41).

For food:

Commonly called "grace" (1Sa 9:13; Mt 14:19; 15:36; Mk 6:41; 8:6-7; Lk 9:16; 24:30; Jn 6:11,23; Ac 27:35; Ro 14:6; 1Co 10:30-31; 1Ti 4:3-5).

Instances of:

Jesus (Mt 14:19; Mk 8:6-7). Paul (Ac 27:35).
See Praise; Prayer, Thanksgiving; Thankfulness.

THARA *See Terah, 2.*

THARSHISH *See Trade and Travel; Tarshish, 2,4.*

THEATER [2519]. A place for dramatic and musical performances (Ac 19:29,31).

THEBES [5530, 5531] (*town, village*). Capital of Egypt during the eighteenth dynasty (KJV "No"); on the E bank of the Nile; famous for temples; cult center of the god Amon (Jer 46:25), denounced by prophets (Jer 46:25; Eze 30:14-16).

THEBEZ [9324]. A city in Ephraim about halfway from Beth Shan to Shechem; Abimelech, the son of Gideon, slain there (Jdg 9:50; 2Sa 11:21).

THEFT [1706, *3092, 3113*].

NIV+ STEAL, STEALING, STEALS, STOLE, STOLEN, THIEF

Na 3:1 Woe to the city of blood, full of lies, full of plunder, never without victims!

Mt 6:19 "Do not store up for yourselves treasures on earth, where moth and rust destroy, and where thieves break in and steal. ²⁰But store up for yourselves treasures in heaven, where moth and rust do not destroy, and where thieves do not break in and steal.

Mt 15:19 For out of the heart come evil thoughts, murder, adultery, sexual immorality, theft, false testimony, slander. (+Mk 7:21-22)

Ro 2:21 you, then, who teach others, do you not teach yourself? You who preach against stealing, do you steal?

Rev 9:21 Nor did they repent of their murders, their magic arts, their sexual immorality or their thefts.

Forbidden:

Ex 20:15 "You shall not steal.

Lev 19:11 " 'Do not steal. " 'Do not lie. " 'Do not deceive one another.

Lev 19:13 " 'Do not defraud your neighbor or rob him. " 'Do not hold back the wages of a hired man overnight. (+Dt 5:19)

Dt 23:24 If you enter your neighbor's vineyard, you may eat all the grapes you want, but do not put any in your basket. ²⁵If you enter your neighbor's grainfield, you may pick kernels with your hands, but you must not put a sickle to his standing grain.

Ps 62:10 Do not trust in extortion or take pride in stolen goods; though your riches increase, do not set your heart on them. (+Mt 19:18; Lk 18:20; Ro 13:9)

Eph 4:28 He who has been stealing must steal no longer, but must work, doing something useful with his own hands, that he may have something to share with those in need.

Tit 2:10 and not to steal from them, but to show that they can be fully trusted, so that in every way they will make the teaching about God our Savior attractive.

1Pe 4:15 If you suffer, it should not be as a murderer or thief or any other kind of criminal, or even as a meddler.

Penalty for:

Ex 21:16 "Anyone who kidnaps another and either sells him or still has him when he is caught must be put to death.

Ex 22:1 "If a man steals an ox or a sheep and slaughters it or sells it, he must pay back five head of cattle for the ox and four sheep for the sheep.

²"If a thief is caught breaking in and is struck so that he dies, the defender is not guilty of bloodshed; ³but if it happens after sunrise, he is guilty of bloodshed. "A thief must certainly make restitution, but if he has nothing, he must be sold to pay for his theft.

⁴"If the stolen animal is found alive in his possession— whether ox or donkey or sheep—he must pay back double.

Ex 22:10 "If a man gives a donkey, an ox, a sheep or any other animal to his neighbor for safekeeping and it dies or

is injured or is taken away while no one is looking, ¹¹the issue between them will be settled by the taking of an oath before the LORD that the neighbor did not lay hands on the other person's property. The owner is to accept this, and no restitution is required. ¹²But if the animal was stolen from the neighbor, he must make restitution to the owner. ¹³If it was torn to pieces by a wild animal, he shall bring in the remains as evidence and he will not be required to pay for the torn animal.

¹⁴"If a man borrows an animal from his neighbor and it is injured or dies while the owner is not present, he must make restitution. ¹⁵But if the owner is with the animal, the borrower will not have to pay. If the animal was hired, the money paid for the hire covers the loss.

Lev 6:2 "If anyone sins and is unfaithful to the LORD by deceiving his neighbor about something entrusted to him or left in his care or stolen, or if he cheats him, ³or if he finds lost property and lies about it, or if he swears falsely, or if he commits any such sin that people may do— ⁴when he thus sins and becomes guilty, he must return what he has stolen or taken by extortion, or what was entrusted to him, or the lost property he found, ⁵or whatever it was he swore falsely about. He must make restitution in full, add a fifth of the value to it and give it all to the owner on the day he presents his guilt offering.

Pr 6:30 Men do not despise a thief if he steals to satisfy his hunger when he is starving. ³¹Yet if he is caught, he must pay sevenfold, though it costs him all the wealth of his house.

Zec 5:3 And he said to me, "This is the curse that is going out over the whole land; for according to what it says on one side, every thief will be banished, and according to what it says on the other, everyone who swears falsely will be banished. (+Mt 27:38,44)

Mk 15:27 They crucified two robbers with him, one on his right and one on his left.

Restitution for things stolen required of the penitent (Eze 33:15).

Instances of:

Rachel, of the household gods (Ge 31:19,34-35). Achan (Jos 7:11). Micah (Jdg 17:2). The spies of Laish (Jdg 18:14-27).

Israelites—

Eze 22:29 The people of the land practice extortion and commit robbery; they oppress the poor and needy and mistreat the alien, denying them justice.

Hos 4:1 Hear the word of the LORD, you Israelites, because the LORD has a charge to bring against you who live in the land: "There is no faithfulness, no love, no acknowledgment of God in the land. ²There is only cursing, lying and murder, stealing and adultery; they break all bounds, and bloodshed follows bloodshed.

Judas (Jn 12:6).

See Dishonesty; Robbery; Thief, Thieves.

THELASAR *See Tel Assar, Telassar.*

THEOCRACY (*rule of God*). Established (Ex 19:8; 24:3,7; Dt 5:25-29; 33:2-5; Jdg 8:23; 1Sa 12:12). Rejected by Israel (1Sa 8:7,19; 10:19; 2Ch 13:8).

See God, Sovereign; Government.

THEOLOGY *See God.*

THEOPHANY (*appearance of God*). Visible appearance of God, generally in human form (Ge 3:8; 4; 28:10-17).

THEOPHILUS [*2541*] (*friend of God*). A man to whom the Gospel of Luke and Acts of the Apostles are addressed (Lk 1:3; Ac 1:1). Nothing is known of him.

THESSALONIANS, 1 and 2

1 Thessalonians:

Author: The Apostle Paul

Date: c. A.D. 51

Outline:

I. The Thanksgiving for the Thessalonians (ch 1).
 A. The Grounds for the Thanksgiving (1:1-4).
 B. The Genuineness of the Grounds (1:5-10).
II. The Defense of the Apostolic Actions and Absence (chs. 2-3).
 A. The Defense of the Apostolic Actions (2:1-16).
 B. The Defense of the Apostolic Absence (2:17-3:10).
 C. The Prayer (3:11-13).
III. The Exhortations to the Thessalonians (4:1-5:22).
 A. Primarily concerning Personal Life (4:1-12).
 B. Concerning the Coming of Christ (4:13-5:11).
 C. Primarily concerning Church Life (5:12-22).
IV. The Concluding Prayer, Greetings and Benediction (5:23-28).

2 Thessalonians:

Author: The Apostle Paul

Date: c. A.D. 51 or 52

Outline:

I. Introduction (ch. 1).
 A. Salutation (1:1-2).
 B. Thanksgiving for Their Faith, Love and Perseverance (1:3-10).
 C. Intercession for Their Spiritual Progress (1:11-12).
II. Instruction (ch. 2).
 A. Prophecy regarding the Day of the Lord (2:1-12).
 B. Thanksgiving for Their Election and Calling (Their Position) (2:13-15).
 C. Prayer for Their Service and Testimony (Their Practice) (2:16-17).
III. Injunctions (ch. 3).
 A. Call to Prayer (3:1-3).
 B. Charge to Discipline for the Disorderly and Lazy (3:4-15).
 C. Conclusion, Greeting and Benediction (3:16-18).

THESSALONICA [*2552, 2553*].

NIV+ THESSALONIANS

A city of Macedonia. Paul visits (Ac 17:1; Php 4:16). People of, accompany Paul (Ac 20:4; 27:2). Paul writes to Christians in (1Th 1:1; 2Th 1:1). Demas goes to (2Ti 4:10).

THEUDAS [*2554*] (*gift of God*). A Jew who led a rebellion against Rome (Ac 5:36-37).

THICKET [1454, 2560, 3091, 3623, 6019, 6020, 6109, 6266].

NIV+ THICKETS

(1Sa 13:6; Jer 4:7).

THIEF, THIEVES [1704, 1705, *3095*].

NIV+ See THEFT

In Mosaic law, punishment of thieves was very severe (Ex 22:1-4).

Penalty for (Dt 24:7; Pr 6:30-31; Eze 18:10,13; Zec 5:3; Mt 27:38,44; Mk 15:27).

Collusion with (Ps 50:18). Excluded from the kingdom

of God (1Co 6:10). Desecrated the temple (Mt 21:13; Mk 11:17; Lk 19:45-46). Disgraceful (Jer 2:26). Worship of, offensive to God (Jer 7:9-10).

Christ's coming again as unexpected as (Rev 3:3).

Figurative: (Ob 5; Jn 10:1).

See Theft.

THIGH [3751, 7066, 8797, 10334, *3611*].

NIV+ THIGHS

To put one's hand under the thigh of another was to enhance the sacredness of an oath (Ge 24:2,9; 47:29).

THIMNATHAH *See Timnah.*

THIRST [5883, 6546, 7532, 7533, 7534, 7536, 8115, *1498, 1499*].

NIV+ THIRSTS, THIRSTY

Figurative of the ardent desire of the devout mind (Ps 42:1-4; 63:1; 143:6; Isa 55:1; Am 8:11-13; Mt 5:6; Jn 4:14-15; 7:37; Rev 21:6; 22:17).

See Desire, Spiritual; Diligence; Hunger, Figurative; Zeal.

THISTLE [1998, 2560, *5560*].

NIV+ THISTLES

Exists in many varieties in Israel. Used figuratively for trouble, desolation, judgment, wickedness (Nu 33:55; Pr 24:31; 15:19; Isa 5:6; 2Co 12:7).

THOMAS [*2605*] (*twin*). Called Didymus. One of the twelve apostles (Mt 10:3; Mk 3:18; Lk 6:15). Present at the raising of Lazarus (Jn 11:16). Asks Jesus the way to the Father's house (Jn 14:5). Absent when Jesus first appeared to the disciples after the Resurrection (Jn 20:24). Skepticism of (Jn 20:25). Sees Jesus after the Resurrection (Jn 20:26-29; 21:1-2). Lives with the other apostles in Jerusalem (Ac 1:13-14). Loyalty of, to Jesus (Jn 11:16; 20:28).

THOMAS, GOSPEL OF A Gnostic gospel consisting entirely of sayings attributed to Jesus; dated c. A.D. 140; found at Nag Hammadi in Egypt in 1945.

THONG [3857, 8579, *2666*].

NIV+ THONGS

Strap to fasten a sandal to the foot. Used figuratively of something small and insignificant (Ge 14:23; Isa 5:27). Untying of, an act of humble service (Mk 1:7; Lk 3:16).

THORN [353, 2537, 2560, 5004, 6106, 6141, 7553, 7564, 7764, 7853, 8885, *180, 181, 5022*].

NIV+ THORNBUSH, THORNBUSHES, THORNS

The ground cursed with (Ge 3:18). Used as an awl (Job 41:2), for fuel (Ps 58:9; 118:12; Ecc 7:6). Hedges formed of (Hos 2:6; Mic 7:4). Crown of, mockingly put on Jesus' head (Mt 27:29; Mk 15:17; Jn 19:2,5).

Figurative:

Of afflictions (Nu 33:55; 2Co 12:7). Of the adversities of the wicked (Pr 22:5). Of the evils that spring from the heart to choke the truth (Mt 13:7,22).

THORN IN THE FLESH [*5022*].

NIV+ See THORN

Paul's description of a physical ailment from which he prayed to be relieved (2Co 12:7). What it was is not known.

THOUGHTS, GOD'S (Ps 40:5,17; 139:17; Isa 55:9; Jer 29:11).

THOUSAND [*547, 8047, 8052, 10038, 10649, *3689, 3692, 4295, 5483, 5942, 5943*].

NIV+ THOUSANDS, 1000

Often used symbolically in the Bible. In the OT sometimes means "many" (1Sa 21:11; 2Ch 15:11), "family" (Nu 10:4).

THOUSAND YEARS As a day to the Lord (Ps 90:4; 2Pe 3:8). Satan bound (Rev 20:1-3). The reign of Christ (Rev 20:4-6). *See Millennium.*

THRACE Kingdom and later a Roman province, in SE Europe, E of Macedonia (2Mc 12:35).

THREAD [2562, 9106].

NIV+ THREADS

(Ge 14:23; Jdg 16:21; SS 4:3).

THREATENINGS [*1722, 1819, 1821, 9412, *581*].

NIV+ THREAT, THREATEN, THREATENED, THREATS

Of God against the wicked (Lev 26:16; Jos 23:15; 1Sa 12:25; 1Ki 9:7; Ps 7:12; Isa 14:23; 66:4; Mal 3:5).

THREE HOLY CHILDREN, SONG OF

Apocryphal additions to the OT book of Daniel; probably written in the first century B.C.

THREE TAVERNS [5553]. A town in Italy. Roman Christians meet Paul in (Ac 28:15).

THRESHING [1755, 1889, 1912, 2468, 3023, 4617, 6322, 10010, *272*].

NIV+ THRESH, THRESHED, THRESHER, THRESHES

By beating (Ru 2:17), by treading (Dt 25:4; Isa 25:10; Hos 10:11; 1Co 9:9; 1Ti 5:18). With instruments of wood (2Sa 24:22), of iron (Am 1:3), with a cart wheel (Isa 28:27-28). Floors for (Ge 50:10-11; Jdg 6:37; Ru 3:2-14; 1Sa 23:1; 2Sa 6:6; Hos 9:2; Joel 2:24). Floor of Araunah bought by David for a place of sacrifice (2Sa 24:16-25). Floor for, in barns (2Ki 6:27).

THRESHING FLOOR [1755, *272*]. A place where grain was threshed, usually clay soil packed to a hard, smooth surface (Dt 25:4; Isa 28:27; 1Co 9:9).

THRESHOLD [5159, 6197].

NIV+ THRESHOLDS

A piece of wood or stone at the bottom of a door, which has to be crossed on entering a house.

THRONE [2292, 3782, 4058, 4632, 4887, 10372, 10424, *1037, 2585*] (*judgment seat*).

NIV+ DETHRONED, ENTHRONED, ENTHRONES, THRONES

Of Pharaoh (Ge 41:40; Ex 11:5). Of David (1Ki 2:12,24; Ps 132:11-12; Isa 9:7; Jer 13:13; 17:25; Lk 1:32). Of Solomon (1Ki 2:19; 2Ch 9:17-19). Of ivory (1Ki 10:18-20). Of Solomon, called the throne of the LORD (1Ch 29:23). Of Herod (Ac 12:21). Of Israel (1Ki 8:20; 10:9; 2Ch 6:10).

Abdicated by David (1Ki 1:32-40).

Figurative:

Anthropomorphic use of: Of God (2Ch 18:18; Ps 9:4,7; 11:4; 47:8; 89:14; 97:2; 103:19; Isa 6:1; 66:1; Mt 5:34; 23:22; Heb 8:1; 12:2; Rev 14:3,5), of Christ (Mt 19:28; 25:31; Ac 2:30; Rev 1:4; 3:21; 4:2-10; 7:9-17; 19:4; 21:5; 22:3).

THRUSH A bird (Isa 38:14; Jer 8:7). *See Birds.*

THUMB [984+3338, 991].

NIV+ THUMBS

Blood put on, in consecration (Ex 29:20; Lev 8:23), in purification (Lev 14:14,25). Oil put on (Lev 14:17,28). Of prisoners cut off (Jdg 1:6-7). *See Hand.*

THUMMIM [9460]. *See Urim and Thummim.*

THUNDER [2150, 2162, 7754, 8275, 8306, 8308, 9583, *1103, 5889*].

NIV+ THUNDERED, THUNDERING, THUNDERS

Sent as a plague upon the Egyptians (Ex 9:3-24), the Philistines, in battle with the Israelites (1Sa 7:10). Sent as a judgment (Isa 29:6). On Sinai (Ex 19:16; Ps 77:18; Heb 12:18-19). A token of divine anger (1Sa 12:17-18). A manifestation of divine power (Job 26:14; Ps 77:18). Sons of Zebedee called sons of (Mk 3:17).

THUNDER, SONS OF A title given James and John by Jesus (Mk 3:17).

THUTMOSE (*[Egyptian god] Thoth is born*). The name of four kings of Egypt of the eighteenth dynasty, centering in Thebes. Under their rule, Egypt attained her greatest power. Thutmose III may have been the Pharaoh who enslaved the Hebrews (Ex 1:8).

THYATIRA [2587]. A city in the Roman province of Asia; on the boundary of Lydia and Mysia; noted for weaving and dyeing (Ac 16:14; Rev 2:18-29).

THYINE *See Citron Wood.*

TIARAS [7566]. (Isa 3:23). *See Crown; Jewel, Jewelry.*

TIBERIAS [5500].

NIV+ GALILEE

A city on the W shore of the Sea of Galilee; built by Herod Antipas and named for the emperor Tiberius; a famous health resort; after A.D. 70 it became a center of rabbinic learning. Modern Tabariya.

TIBERIAS, SEA OF *See Sea of Galilee.*

TIBERIUS [5501]. The second Roman emperor (A.D. 14-37); reigning emperor at the time of Christ's death (Lk 3:1).

TIBHATH *See Tebah, 2.*

TIBNI [9321]. The son of Ginath; unsuccessful competitor for the throne of Israel (1Ki 16:21).

TIDAL [9331]. King of Goiim; confederate of Kedorlaomer (Ge 14:1-17).

TIGLATH-PILESER, TILGATH-PILNESER

[9325, 9433] (*my trust is in the son of [the temple] Esharra*).

NIV+ PUL

A famous Assyrian king (745-727 B.C.); great conqueror; received tribute from King Azariah of Judah and King Menahem of Samaria (2Ki 15:19-20), Ahaz secured his help against Pekah of Israel and Rezin of Syria; deported Trans-Jordanian Israelites (1Ch 5:6,26), Ahaz gave tribute to him (2Ch 28:20-21).

TIGRIS [2538] (*arrow*). One of the two great rivers of the Mesopotamian area; 1,150 miles long (Ge 2:14; Da 10:4).

TIKVAH [9537] (*hope*).

1. Father-in-law of the prophetess Huldah (2Ki 22:14). *See Tokhath.*

2. Father of Jahzeiah (Ezr 10:15).

TILE [*3041*].

NIV+ TILES

Ceiling tiles (Lk 5:19).

TILGATH-PILNESER *See Tiglath-Pileser.*

TILON [9400]. The son of Shimon (1Ch 4:20).

TIMAEUS, TIMEUS [5505] (*precious, valuable*).

NIV+ BARTIMEAUS

The father of Bartimaeus (Mk 10:46).

TIMBREL *See Tambourine.*

TIME [*255, 339+, 801, 928, 1887+, 2256, 2375, 2725, 2976, 3338, 3427, 4595, 4951, 6388, 6409, 6961, 7193, 8049, 8079, 9108, 9378, 10232, 10317, 10530, 10530, 275, 1309, 1671, 2093, 2232, 2453, 2465, 2789, 4121, 4490, 4537, 4625, 4672, 5538, 5565, 5568, 5988, 5989, 6052*].

NIV+ TIMELY, TIMES

In the early biblical period, time was marked by sunrise and sunset, phases of the moon, seasons, and years (Ge 1:14). *See Calendar.*

Ancient people had no method of reckoning long periods of time. They dated from great and well-known events, like the Exodus, the Babylonian Exile, the earthquake (Am 1:1), and especially the reigns of kings (1Ki 15:1; Hag 1:1). The year was lunar (354 days, 8 hours, 38 seconds), divided into twelve lunar months, with seven intercalary months added over nineteen years. The Hebrew month began with the new moon. Early Hebrews gave the months names; later they used numbers; and after the Exile they used Babylonian names. *See Month.*

Months were divided by the Jews into weeks of seven days, ending with the Sabbath (Ex 20:11; Dt 5:14-15). Days were divided into twenty-four hours of sixty minutes of sixty seconds. The Roman day began at midnight and had twelve hours (Jn 11:9), the Hebrew day was reckoned from sunset. Night was divided into watches. At first the Hebrews had three watches; in the time of Christ there were four. *See Day; Watches of the Night.*

TIMES, OBSERVER OF A person who has a superstitious regard for days regarded as lucky or unlucky, as decided by astrology (Dt 18:8-14).

TIMNA [9465] (*lot, portion*).

1. Concubine of Eliphaz (Ge 36:12).

2. Sister of Lotan (Ge 36:22).

3. Chieftain of Edom (Ge 36:40).

4. Son of Eliphaz (1Ch 1:36).

TIMNAH, TIMNATH [9463] (*lot, portion*).

NIV+ TIMNITE'S

1. A town about 4-and-a-half miles west of Beth Shemesh (Ge 38:12-14; 2Ch 28:18).

2. A town on the border of Judah approximately three miles SW of Beth Shemesh (Jos 15:10), possibly modern Tell Batash.

3. A town in the hill country of Judah (Jos 15:57), possibly the same as 1.

4. A Philistine town (Jdg 14:1-5), possibly the same as 1.

TIMNATH *See Timnah.*

TIMNATH HERES, TIMNATH-HERES [9466] (*place of the sun [worship]*).

NIV+ HERES

A city in the hill country of Ephraim (Jdg 2:9).

TIMNATH SERAH, TIMNATH-SERAH [9467] (*place of the sun [worship]*).

NIV+ SERAH

Given to Joshua (Jos 19:50). Joshua buried in (Jos 24:30). Modern Khirbet Tibnah.

TIMNITE [9464].

NIV+ TIMNAH, TIMNITE'S

A native of Timnah (Jdg 15:3-6).

TIMON [*5511*] (*precious, valuable*). One of seven ministers (Ac 6:5).

TIMOTHEUS *See Timothy.*

TIMOTHY [5510] (*precious one of God*). Parentage of (Ac 16:1). Reputation and Christian faith of (Ac 16:2; 1Co 4:17; 16:10; 2Ti 1:5; 3:15). Circumcised; becomes Paul's companion (Ac 16:3; 1Th 3:2). Left by Paul at Berea (Ac 17:14). Rejoins Paul at Corinth (Ac 17:15; 18:5). Sent into Macedonia (Ac 19:22). Rejoined by Paul; accompanies Paul to Asia (Ac 20:1-4). Sent to the Corinthians (1Co 4:17; 16:10-11). Preaches to the Corinthians (2Co 1:19). Sent to the Philippians (Php 2:19,23). Sent to the Thessalonians (1Th 3:2,6). Sent by Paul in Ephesus (1Ti 1:3).

Joins Paul in the Epistle to the Philippians (Php 1:1), to the Colossians (Col 1:1-2), to the Thessalonians (1Th 1:1; 2Th 1:1), to Philemon (Phm 1).

Zeal of (Php 2:19-22; 1Ti 6:12). Power of (1Ti 4:14; 2Ti 1:6). Paul's love for (1Co 4:17; Php 2:22; 1Ti 1:2,18; 2Ti 1:2-4). Paul writes to (1Ti 1:1-2; 2Ti 1:1-2).

TIMOTHY, 1 and 2

1 Timothy:

Author: The Apostle Paul

Date: c. A.D 63-65

Outline:

I. Salutation (1:1-2).

II. Warning against False Teachers (1:3-11).

  A. The Nature of the Heresy (1:3-7).

  B. The Purpose of the Law (1:8-11).

III. The Lord's Grace to Paul (1:12-17).

IV. The Purpose of Paul's Instructions to Timothy (1:18-20).

V. Instructions concerning the Administration of the Church (chs. 2-3).

  A. Public Worship (ch. 2).

    1. Prayer in public worship (2:1-8).

    2. Women in public worship (2:9-15).

  B. Qualifications for Church Officers (3:1-13).

    1. Overseers (3:1-7).

    2. Deacons (3:8-13).

  C. Purpose of These Instructions (3:14-16).

VI. Methods of Dealing with False Teaching (ch. 4).

  A. False Teaching Described (4:1-5).

  B. Methods of Dealing with It Explained (4:6-16).

VII. Methods of Dealing with Different Groups in the Church (5:1-6:2).

  A. The Older and Younger (5:1-2).

  B. Widows (5:3-16).

C. Elders (5:17-25).

D. Slaves (6:1-2).

VIII. Miscellaneous Matters (6:3-19).

A. False Teachers (6:3-5).

B. Love of Money (6:6-10).

C. Charge to Timothy (6:11-16).

D. The Rich (6:17-19).

IX. Concluding Appeal (6:20-21).

2 Timothy:

Author: The Apostle Paul

Date: c. A.D. 66-67

Outline:

I. Introduction (1:1-4).

II. Paul's Concern for Timothy (1:5-14).

III. Paul's Situation (1:15-18).

IV. Special Instructions to Timothy (ch. 2).

A. Call for Endurance (2:1-13).

B. Warning about Foolish Controversies (2:14-26).

V. Warning about the Last Days (ch. 3).

A. Terrible Times (3:1-9).

B. Means of Combating Them (3:10-17).

VI. Paul's Departing Remarks (4:1-8).

A. Charge to Preach the Word (4:1-5).

B. Paul's Victorious Prospect (4:6-8).

VII. Final Requests and Greetings (4:9-22).

See Church, The Body of Believers, Qualifications for Elders/Overseers and Deacons; Missionary Journeys of Paul; Pastoral Epistles.

TIN [974]. (Nu 31:22; Eze 22:18,20; 27:12).

TINKLING The sound of small bells worn by women on chain fastened to anklets (Isa 3:16).

TIPHSAH [9527].

1. City on Euphrates (1Ki 4:24).

2. A town, apparently not far from Tirzah in Samaria (2Ki 15:16); some versions have Tappuah. *See Tappuah, 3.*

TIRAS [9410]. The son of Japheth (Ge 10:2; 1Ch 1:5).

TIRATHITES [9571]. A family of scribes in Jabez (1Ch 2:55).

TIRE [3333, 3615, 3878, 6546, 7918, *1591, 3159*] (*head-dress*).

NIV+ TIRED

Ornamental headdress (Eze 24:17,23; Isa 3:20; 61:10).

TIRHAKAH [9555]. An Egyptian king, third of the twenty-fifth dynasty; defeated by Sennacherib (2Ki 19:9; Isa 37:9), and later by Esarhaddon and Ashurbanipal.

TIRHANAH [9563]. The son of Caleb and Maacah (1Ch 2:48).

TIRIA [9409]. The son of Jehallelel (1Ch 4:16).

TIRSHATHA *See Governor.*

TIRZAH [9573, 9574] (*pleasant one* or *compensation*).

1. A daughter of Zelophehad (Nu 26:33; 36:11; Jos 17:3). Special legislation in regard to the inheritance of (Nu 27:1-11; 36; Jos 17:3-4).

2. A city of Canaan. Captured by Joshua (Jos 12:24). Becomes the residence of the kings of Israel (1Ki 14:17; 15:21,33; 16:6,8-9,15,17,23). Royal residence moved from (1Ki 16:23-24). Base of military operations of Menahem (2Ki 15:14,16). Beauty of (SS 6:4).

TISHBE, TISHBITE [9585, 9586]. The designation of Elijah (1Ki 17:1), probably to be identified with modern el-Istib, little W of Mahanaim.

TISHRI *See Ethanim; Month, 7.*

TITHES [5130, 6923] (*a tenth*).

NIV+ See TEN, TITHE

Paid by Abraham to Melchizedek (Ge 14:20; Heb 7:2-6). Jacob vows a tenth of all his property to God (Ge 28:22).

Mosaic laws instituting (Lev 27:30-33; Nu 18:21-24; Dt 12:6-7,17,19; 14:22-29; 26:12-15). Customs relating to (Ne 10:37-38; Am 4:4; Heb 7:5-9). Tithe of tithes for priests (Nu 18:26; Ne 10:38). Stored in the temple (Ne 10:38-39; 12:44; 13:5,12; 2Ch 31:11-12; Mal 3:10).

Payment of, resumed in Hezekiah's reign (2Ch 31:5-10). Under Nehemiah (Ne 13:12). Withheld (Ne 13:10; Mal 3:8).

Customary in later times (Mt 23:23; Lk 11:42; 18:12). Observed by idolaters (Am 4:4-5).

See Alms; Beneficence; Giving; Liberality; Tax.

TITLE [4033, *3950*]. To real estate. *See Land.*

TITLES AND NAMES

Of God: *See God, Names of.*

Titles and Names of Christ:

Adam, Last (1Co 15:45). Almighty (Rev 1:8). Alpha and Omega (Rev 1:8; 22:13). Amen (Rev 3:14). Angel of his presence (Isa 63:9). Angel of the Lord (Ex 3:2; Jdg 13:15-18). Angel (Ge 48:16; Ex 23:20-21). Anointed One (Da 9:25; Jn 1:41). Apostle (Heb 3:1). Arm of the Lord (Isa 51:9; 53:1). Author of life (Ac 3:15). Author and Perfecter of our faith (Heb 2:10; 12:2). Blessed and only Ruler (1Ti 6:15). Branch (Jer 23:5; Zec 3:8; 6:12). Bread of Life (Jn 6:35,48). Chief Shepherd (1Pe 5:4). Chief Cornerstone (Eph 2:20; 1Pe 2:6). Chosen One of God (Isa 42:1). Christ of God (Lk 9:20). Commander of the Lord's army (Jos 5:14-15). Commander (Isa 55:4). Consolation of Israel (Lk 2:25). Counselor (Isa 9:6). David (Jer 30:9; Eze 34:23). Defender (1Jn 2:1). Deliverer (Ro 11:26). Door (Jn 10:7). Eternal life (1Jn 1:2; 5:20). Everlasting Father (Isa 9:6). Faithful witness (Rev 1:5; 3:14). First and Last (Rev 1:17; 2:8). Firstborn of the dead (Rev 1:5). Firstborn of all creation (Col 1:15). Glory of the Lord (Isa 40:5). God over all (Ro 9:5). God (Isa 40:9; Jn 20:28). Good Shepherd (Jn 10:14). Great High Priest (Heb 4:14). Guarantee (Heb 7:22). Head of the Church (Eph 5:23; Col 1:18). Heir of all things (Heb 1:2). Holy One of God (Mk 1:24). Holy One (Ps 16:10, w Ac 2:27,31). Holy One of Israel (Isa 41:14). Horn of salvation (Lk 1:69). I Am (Ex 3:14, w Rev 1:8; 22:13). Immanuel (Isa 7:14, w Mt 1:23). Israel's Ruler (Mic 5:1). Jesus (Mt 1:21; 1Th 1:10). King of the Jews (Mt 2:2). King of Israel (Jn 1:49). King of Kings (1Ti 6:15; Rev 17:14). King of the ages (Rev 15:3). King (Zec 9:9, w Mt 21:5). Lamb of God (Jn 1:29,36). Lamb (Rev 5:6,12; 13:8; 21:22; 22:3). Lawgiver (Isa 33:22). Leader (Isa 55:4). Life (Jn 14:6; Col 3:4; 1Jn 1:2). Light of the world (Jn 8:12). Lion of the tribe of Judah (Rev 5:5). Lord of all (Ac 10:36). Lord of glory (1Co 2:8). Lord our righteousness (Jer 23:6). Lord God Almighty (Rev 15:3). Lord God of the prophets (Rev 22:6). Mediator (1Ti 2:5). Mighty One of Jacob (Isa 60:16). Mighty God (Isa 9:6). Morning Star (Rev 22:16). Nazarene (Mt 2:23). One and Only (Jn 1:14). One Before Us (Heb 6:20). Our Passover (1Co 5:7). Prince of peace (Isa 9:6). Prophet (Lk 24:19; Jn

7:40). Ransom (1Ti 2:6). Redeemer (Job 19:25; Isa 59:20; 60:16). Resurrection and life (Jn 11:25). Righteous One (Ac 7:52). Rock (1Co 10:4). Root of Jesse (Isa 11:10). Root of David (Rev 22:16). Root and Offspring of David (Rev 22:16). Ruler of the kings of the earth (Rev 1:5). Ruler of the creation of God (Rev 3:14). Ruler over Israel (Mic 5:2). Ruler (Mt 2:6). Savior (2Pe 2:20; 3:18). Servant (Isa 42:1; 52:13). Shepherd and Overseer of Souls (1Pe 2:25). Son of the Most High (Lk 1:32). Son of man (Jn 5:27; 6:37). Son of David (Mt 9:27). Son of God (Lk 1:35; Jn 1:49). Son of the Blessed One (Mk 14:61). Star (Nu 24:17). Sun of righteousness (Mal 4:2). The desired of all nations (Hag 2:7). True Light (Jn 1:9). True Vine (Jn 15:1). True God (1Jn 5:20). Truth (Jn 14:6). Way (Jn 14:6). Wisdom (Pr 8:12). Witness (Isa 55:4). Wonderful (Isa 9:6). Word of Life (1Jn 1:1). Word (Jn 1:1; 1Jn 5:7). Word of God (Rev 19:13).

Titles and Names of the Church:

Assembly of the saints (Ps 89:7). Assembly of the saints (Ps 149:1). Body of Christ (Eph 1:22-23; Col 1:24). Bride of Christ (Rev 21:9). Church of the Firstborn (Heb 12:23). Church of the firstborn (Heb 12:23). Church of the Living God (1Ti 3:15). Church of God (Ac 20:28). City of the Living God (Heb 12:22). Council of the upright (Ps 111:1). Dwelling of God (Eph 2:22). Family in heaven and on earth (Eph 3:15). Flock of God (Eze 34:15; 1Pe 5:2). Flock of Christ (Jn 10:16). God's field (1Co 3:9). God's inheritance (Joel 3:2; 1Pe 5:3). God's building (1Co 3:9). Golden lampstand (Rev 1:20). Holy City (Rev 21:2). House of the God of Jacob (Isa 2:3). House of Christ (Heb 3:6). House(hold) of God (1Ti 3:15; Heb 10:21; Eph 2:19). Inheritance (Ps 28:9; Isa 19:25). Israel of God (Gal 6:16). Lamb's bride (Rev 19:7; 21). Mount Zion (Ps 2:6; Heb 12:22). Mountain of the Lord's house (Isa 2:2). New Jerusalem (Rev 21:2). Pillar and foundation of the truth (1Ti 3:15). Portion of the Lord (Dt 32:9). Princess (Ps 45:13). Sanctuary of God (Ps 114:2). Shoot of God's Planting (Isa 60:21). Sought After, the City no longer Deserted (Isa 62:12). Spiritual house (1Pe 2:5). Temple of the Living God (2Co 6:16). Temple of God (1Co 3:16-17). Vineyard (Jer 12:10; Mt 21:41).

Titles and Names of the Devil:

Abaddon (Rev 9:11). Accuser of our brothers (Rev 12:10). Ancient serpent (Rev 12:9; 20:2). Angel of the Abyss (Rev 9:11). Apollyon (Rev 9:11). Beelzebub (Mt 12:24). Belial (2Co 6:15). Coiling serpent (Isa 27:1). Dominion of darkness (Col 1:13). Dragon (Isa 27:1; Rev 20:2). Enemy (Mt 13:39; 1Pe 5:8). Evil one (Mt 13:19,38). Evil spirit (1Sa 16:14; Mt 12:43). Father of lies (Jn 8:44). Gliding serpent (Isa 27:1). God of this age (2Co 4:4). Leviathan (Isa 27:1). Liar (Jn 8:44). Lying spirit (1Ki 22:22). Murderer (Jn 8:44). Powers of this dark world (Eph 6:12). Prince of demons (Mt 12:24). Prince of this world (Jn 14:30). Red dragon (Rev 12:3). Ruler of the kingdom of the air (Eph 2:2). Satan (1Ch 21:1; Job 1:6). Serpent (Ge 3:4,14; 2Co 11:3). Spirit that works in those disobedient (Eph 2:2). Tempter (Mt 4:3; 1Th 3:5).

Titles and Names of the Holy Spirit:

Breath of the Almighty (Job 33:4). Counselor (Jn 14:16,26; 15:26). Eternal Spirit (Heb 9:14). God (Ac 5:3-4). Good Spirit (Ne 9:20; Ps 143:10). Holy Spirit (Ps 51:11; Lk 11:13; Eph 1:13; 4:30). Power of the Most High (Lk 1:35). Sevenfold Spirit (Rev 1:4 ftn). Spirit of fear of the Lord (Isa 11:2). Spirit of knowledge (Isa 11:2). Spirit of understanding (Isa 11:2). Spirit of power (Isa 11:2).

Spirit of truth (Jn 14:17; 15:26). Spirit of holiness (Ro 1:4). Spirit of glory (1Pe 4:14). Spirit of fire (Isa 4:4). Spirit of judgment (Isa 4:4; 28:6). Spirit of revelation (Eph 1:17). Spirit, The (Mt 4:1; Jn 3:6; 1Ti 4:1). Spirit of counsel (Isa 11:2). Spirit of Christ (Ro 8:9; 1Pe 1:11). Spirit of the Father (Mt 10:20). Spirit of God (Ge 1:2; 1Co 2:11; Job 33:4). Spirit of the Lord (Isa 11:2; Ac 5:9). Spirit of wisdom (Isa 11:2; Eph 1:17). Spirit of his Son (Gal 4:6). Spirit of sonship (Ro 8:15). Spirit of life (Ro 8:2; Rev 11:11). Spirit of prophecy (Rev 19:10). Spirit of grace (Zec 12:10; Heb 10:29). Willing Spirit (Ps 51:12).

Titles and Names of Ministers:

Administers of the grace of God (1Pe 4:10). Ambassadors for Christ (2Co 5:20). Apostles of Jesus Christ (Tit 1:1). Apostles (Lk 6:13; Eph 4:11; Rev 18:20). Deacons (Ac 6:1ff; 1Ti 3:8; Php 1:1). Elders (1Ti 5:17; 1Pe 5:1). Entrusted with the secrets of God (1Co 4:1). Entrusted with God's work (Tit 1:7). Evangelists (Eph 4:11; 2Ti 4:5). Fellow workers with God (2Co 6:1). Fishers of men (Mt 4:19; Mk 1:17). messengers of the Church (Rev 1:20; 2:1 ftn). Messenger of the Lord Almighty (Mal 2:7). Ministers of the New Covenant (2Co 3:6). Ministers in the sanctuary (Eze 45:4). Ministers of the Lord (Joel 2:17). Ministers of Christ (Ro 15:16; 1Co 4:1). Overseers (Ac 20:28). overseers (Php 1:1; 1Ti 3:1; Tit 1:7). Pastors (Jer 3:15; Eph 4:11). Preachers (Ro 10:14; 1Ti 2:7). Representatives of the Church (2Co 8:23). Servant of the Church (Col 1:24-25). Servant of this gospel (Eph 3:7; Col 1:23). Servants of the word (Lk 1:2). Servants of the Church (2Co 4:5). Servants of righteousness (2Co 11:15). Servants of God (2Co 6:4). Servants of God (Tit 1:1; Jas 1:1). Servants of the Lord (2Ti 2:24). Servants of Jesus Christ (Php 1:1; Jude 1). Shepherds (Jer 23:4). Soldiers of Christ (Php 2:25; 2Ti 2:3). Stars (Rev 1:20; 2:1). Teachers (Isa 30:20; Eph 4:11). Watchmen (Isa 62:6; Eze 33:7). Witnesses (Ac 1:8; 5:32; 26:16). Workers (Mt 9:38, w Phm 1; 1Th 2:2).

Titles and Names of Saints:

Believers (Ac 5:14; 1Ti 4:12). Blessed by the Father (Mt 25:34). Blessed by the Lord (Ge 24:31; 26:29). Brothers (Mt 23:8; Ac 12:17). Brothers of Christ (Lk 8:21; Jn 20:17). Called to belong to Jesus Christ (Ro 1:6). Children of Abraham (Gal 3:7). Children (Jn 13:33; 1Jn 2:1). Children of the free woman (Gal 4:31). Children of promise (Ro 9:8; Gal 4:28). Children of the Lord (Dt 14:1). Children of the resurrection (Lk 20:36). Children of God (Jn 1:12; Php 2:15; 1Jn 3:1-2). Children of God (Jn 11:52; 1Jn 3:10). Chosen instrument (Ac 9:15). Chosen ones (1Ch 16:13). Chosen people (1Pe 2:9). Chosen of God (Col 3:12; Tit 1:1). Christians (Ac 11:26; 26:28). co-heirs with Christ (Ro 8:17). Dear brothers (1Co 15:58; Jas 2:5). Dearly loved children (Eph 5:1). Disciples of Christ (Jn 8:31; 15:8). Faithful brothers in Christ (Col 1:2). Faithful in the land, The (Ps 101:6). Faithful, The (Ps 12:1). Fellow citizens with God's people (Eph 2:19). Fellow servants (Rev 6:11). freedman (1Co 7:22). Friends of God (2Ch 20:7; Jas 2:23). Friends of Christ (Jn 15:15). Glorious ones (Ps 16:3). Godly, The (Ps 4:3; 2Pe 2:9). Guests of the bridegroom (Mt 9:15). Heirs with you of the gracious gift of life (1Pe 3:7). Heirs of God (Ro 8:17; Gal 4:7). Heirs together with Israel (Eph 3:6). Heirs of promise (Heb 6:17; Gal 3:29). Holy brothers (Heb 3:1). Holy people (Dt 26:19; Isa 62:12). Holy nation (Ex 19:6; 1Pe 2:9). Holy priesthood (1Pe 2:5). Inheritors of salvation (Heb 1:14). Inheritors of the kingdom (Jas 2:5). Instrument for noble purposes (2Ti 2:21). Kingdom of priests (Ex 19:6). Kings and priests to serve God (Rev 1:6). Lambs (Isa 40:11; Jn 21:15). Letter from Christ (2Co 3:3). Light of the world (Mt 5:14). Living stones (1Pe 2:5). Loved of God (Ro 1:7). Man of God (1Ti 6:11; 2Ti 3:17). Members of Christ (1Co 6:15; Eph 5:30). Oaks of righteousness (Isa 61:3). Obedient children (1Pe 1:14). Objects of mercy (Ro 9:23). People close to God's heart (Ps 148:14). People of God (Heb 4:9; 1Pe 2:10). People saved by the Lord (Dt 33:29). People of Zion (Ps 149:2; Joel 2:23). Pillars in the temple of God (Rev 3:12). Ransomed of the Lord (Isa 35:10; Isa 51:11). Righteous, The (Hab 2:4). Royal priesthood (1Pe 2:9). Salt of the earth (Mt 5:13). Sheep of Christ (Jn 10:1-16; 21:16). Slaves of Christ (1Co 7:22; Eph 6:6). Slaves to Righteousness (Ro 6:18). Sons of the Living God (Ro 9:26). Sons of Jacob (Ps 105:6). Sons of the Most High (Lk 6:35). Sons of light (Lk 16:8; Eph 5:8; 1Th 5:5). Sons of the day (1Th 5:5). Sons of the Father (Mt 5:45). Sons of the kingdom (Mt 13:38). Treasured possession (Ex 19:5; Dt 14:2; Tit 2:14; 1Pe 2:9). Witnesses for God (Isa 44:8).

Titles and Names of the Wicked:

Accursed brood (2Pe 2:14). Base and nameless brood (Job 30:8). Brood of rebels (Isa 57:4). Brood of evildoers (Isa 1:4; 14:20). Brood of vipers (Mt 3:7; 12:34). Child of the devil (Ac 13:10; 1Jn 3:10). Children unwilling to hear the Lord's instruction (Isa 30:9). Children unfaithful (Dt 32:20). Children given to corruption (Isa 1:4). Clasp hands with Pagans (Isa 2:6). Corrupt generation (Ac 2:40). Crooked and depraved generation (Php 2:15). Deceitful children (Isa 30:9). Disobedient ones (Eph 2:2; Col 3:6). Enemies of God (Ps 37:20; Jas 4:4). Enemies of the cross of Christ (Php 3:18). Enemies of everything right (Ac 13:10). Evil men (Ps 37:1; Pr 4:14; 2Ti 3:13). Evil generation (Dt 1:35). Evildoer (Ps 101:8; Pr 17:4; Ps 28:3; 36:12). Evildoers (Hos 10:9). Failers of a test (2Co 13:5-7). Fools (Pr 1:7; Ro 1:22). Foreigners (Ps 144:7). God-haters (Ps 81:15; Ro 1:30). Hardened rebels (Jer 6:28). Invent ways of doing evil (Ro 1:30). Men of this world (Ps 17:14). Mockers (Ps 1:1). Natural children (Ro 9:8). Objects of wrath (Ro 9:22). Objects of wrath (Eph 2:3). Obstinate children (Eze 2:4; Isa 30:1; 65:2). Offspring of Liars (Isa 57:4). Offspring of the wicked (Ps 37:28; Isa 14:20). Opposers of the Lord (1Sa 2:10). People loaded with guilt (Isa 1:4). people of this world (Lk 16:8). Perverse generation (Dt 32:20; Mt 17:17). Proud, The (Job 41:34). Rebellious people (Isa 30:9). Rebellious house (Eze 2:5,8; 12:2). Senseless children (Jer 4:22). Sinful generation (Mk 8:38). Sinners (Ps 26:9; Pr 1:10; Ps 37:38). Slaves to sin (Jn 8:34; Ro 6:20). Slaves of Depravity (2Pe 2:19). Snakes (Mt 23:33). Son of hell (Mt 23:15). Sons of the evil one (Mt 13:38). Stubborn and rebellious generation (Ps 78:8). Transgressors (Ps 51:13). Warped and crooked generation (Dt 32:5). Wicked men (Dt 13:13; 2Ch 13:7). Wicked traitors (Ps 59:5). Wicked generation (Mt 12:45; 16:4). Wicked servants (Mt 25:26). Wicked and adulterous generation (Mt 12:39). Wicked of the earth (Ps 75:8). Wicked people (2Sa 7:10). Worthless servants (Mt 25:30). Wrongdoers (1Pe 2:14). *See also Wicked, Compared With.*

TITTLE NIV "the least stroke of a pen"; figurative of the smallest details of the law (Mt 5:18; Lk 16:17).

TITUS [*5519*]. A Greek companion of Paul. Paul's love for (2Co 2:13; 7:6-7,13-14; 8:23; Tit 1:4). With Paul in Macedonia (2Co 7:5-6). Affection of, for the Corinthians

(2Co 7:15). Sent to Corinth (2Co 8:6,16-22; 12:17-18). Character of (2Co 12:18). Accompanies Paul to Jerusalem (Gal 2:1-3, w Ac 15:1-29). Left by Paul in Crete (Tit 1:5), to rejoin him in Nicopolis (Tit 3:12). Paul writes to (Tit 1:1-4). With Paul in Rome; goes to Dalmatia (2Ti 4:10).

TITUS, EPISTLE TO

Author: The apostle Paul

Date: Probably between A.D. 63 and 65

Outline:
I. Salutation (1:1-4).
II. Concerning Elders (1:5-9).
   A. Reasons for Leaving Titus in Crete (1:5).
   B. Qualifications of Elders (1:6-9).
III. Concerning False Teachers (1:10-16).
IV. Concerning Various Groups in the Congregations (ch. 2).
   A. The Instructions to Different Groups (2:1-10).
   B. The Foundation for Christian Living (2:11-14).
   C. The Duty of Titus (2:15).
V. Concerning Believers in General (3:1-8).
   A. Obligations as Citizens (3:1-2).
   B. Motives for Godly Conduct (3:3-8).
VI. Concerning Response to Spiritual Error (3:9-11).
VII. Conclusion (3:12-15).

   See Church, The Body of Believers, Qualifications for Elders/Overseers and Deacons; Missionary Journeys of Paul; Pastoral Epistles.

TITUS, FLAVIUS VESPASIANUS A Roman emperor (A.D. 79-81); captured and destroyed Jerusalem in A.D. 70.

TITUS JUSTUS *See Justus.*

TIZITE [9407]. The designation of Joha, one of David's soldiers (1Ch 11:45).

TOAH [9346]. An ancestor of Samuel (1Ch 6:34), probably the same as "Nahath" (1Ch 6:26), and perhaps "Tohu" (1Sa 1:1). *See Nahath, 2; Tohu.*

TOB [3204] (*good*).
   1. A district in Syria, extending NE from Gilead, to which Jephthah fled (Jdg 11:3,5).
   2. Place in Israel which supplied Ammonites with soldiers against David (2Sa 10:6,8).

TOB-ADONIJAH [3207] (*good is [my] lord Yahweh*). A Levite sent by Jehoshaphat to instruct the people in the law (2Ch 17:8).

TOBIAH [3209] (*Yahweh is good*).
   NIV+ TOBIAH'S
   1. An ancestor of a family of Babylonian captives (Ezr 2:60; Ne 7:62).
   2. An enemy of the Jews in the time of Nehemiah. Opposes the rebuilding of the wall of Jerusalem (Ne 2:10, 19; 4:3,7-8). Conspires to injure and intimidate Nehemiah (Ne 6:1-14,19). Subverts nobles of Judah (Ne 6:17-18). Allies himself with Eliashib, the priest (Ne 13:4-9).

TOBIJAH [3209, 3210] (*Yahweh is good*).
   1. A Levite chosen by Jehoshaphat to instruct the people in the law (2Ch 17:8).
   2. A captive in Babylon (Zec 6:10,14).

TOBIT, BOOK OF *See Apocrypha.*

TOCHEN *See Token, 2.*

TOE [720, 991, 8079, 10064].

NIV+ TOES

Anointed in consecration (Ex 29:20; Lev 8:23-24), in purification (Lev 14:14,17,25,28). Of prisoners of war cut off (Jdg 1:6-7). Six, on each foot (2Sa 21:20; 1Ch 20:6).

TOGARMAH [9328].

NIV+ BETH TOGARMAH

Son of Gomer (Ge 10:3; 1Ch 1:6). Descendants of (Eze 27:14; 38:6).

TOHU [9375]. An ancestor of Samuel (1Sa 1:1), probably the same as "Nahath" (1Ch 6:26), and perhaps "Toah" (1Ch 6:34). See Nahath, 2; Toah.

TOI See Tou.

TOKEN [9421] (measure).

1. A sign (Ex 3:12). Sun and moon for time and seasons (Ge 1:14). The mark of Cain (Ge 4:15). Rainbow, that the world might no more be destroyed by a flood (Ge 9:12-17). Circumcision, of the covenant of Abraham (Ge 17:11). Presents (Ge 21:27,30). Miracles of Moses, of the divine authority of his missions (Ex 4:1-9). Blood of the Passover lamb (Ex 12:13). The Passover (Ex 13:9). Consecration of the firstborn (Ex 13:14-16). The Sabbath (Ex 31:13,17), a fringe (Nu 15:38-40). Scarlet thread (Jos 2:18,21). Cover of the altar (Nu 16:38-40). Aaron's rod (Nu 17:10). Memorial stones (Jos 4:2-9). Dew on Gideon's fleece (Jdg 6:36-40). Prayer for tokens of mercy (Ps 86:17).

See Miracles.

2. A city in Simeon (1Ch 4:32).

TOKHATH [9534]. Father-in-law of Huldah the prophetess; also called Tokhath (2Ch 34:22, ftn). See Tikvah.

TOLA, TOLAITE [9356, 9358] (worm of scarlet).

1. The son of Issachar (Ge 46:13).

2. Judged Israel twenty-three years (Jdg 10:1-2).

TOLAD [9351]. City of Simeon (1Ch 4:29).

TOLERANCE [5564, 5663, 6641, 496, 918, 1002].

NIV+ TOLERATE, TOLERATED

Religious (Mic 4:4-5; Mk 9:38-40; Lk 9:49-50; Ac 17:11; 28:31; Ro 14; 1Co 10:28-32). See Intolerance.

TOLL See Tribute; Tax.

TOMB [1074, 1539, 7690, 7700, 3645, 3646, 5439].

NIV+ TOMBS

A burial place. Most Hebrew burying sites were unmarked; some kings were buried in a vault in Jerusalem (2Sa 2:32; Ne 2:3). Tombs of NT times were natural or man-made caves, sealed with circular stones weighing from one to three tons (Lk 24:2; Jn 20:1). See Grave; Pillar; Tombstone.

TOMBSTONE [7483].

NIV+ STONE, TOMB

At the tomb of the man of God from Judah (2Ki 23:17). A pillar at Rachel's grave (Ge 35:20). See Pillar.

TONGS [4920]. Used to tend the lamps in the temple (1Ki 7:49). In Isaiah's vision (Isa 6:6). See Wick Trimmers.

TONGUE [2674, 3087, 3883, 4357, 4383, 8557, 1185, 2280].

NIV+ TONGUES

Language (Ge 10:5,20; Isa 66:18; Rev 7:9). Confusion of (Ge 11:1-9). Gift of (Ac 2:1-18,33; 10:46; 19:6; 1Co 12:10,28,30; 14).

Chattering (Pr 10:8,19). Restrained by wisdom (Pr 17:27; 21:23; Ecc 3:7). Hasty (Pr 29:20).

An evil. See Speaking, Evil; Slander.

TONGUES, CONFUSION OF Punishment by God for arrogant attempt to build tower reaching to heaven (Ge 11:1-9).

TONGUES, GIFT OF A spiritual gift (Mk 16:17; Ac 2:1-13; 10:44-46; 19:6; 1Co 12; 14). The gift appeared on the day of Pentecost with the outpouring of the Holy Spirit on the assembled believers (Ac 2:1-13). The phenomenon appeared again in the home of Cornelius (Ac 10:44-11:17), at Ephesus (Ac 19:6), and in the church at Corinth (1Co 12; 14). Instruction regarding the use of tongues in worship(1Co 12-14).

TONGUES OF FIRE One of the phenomena that occurred at the outpouring of the Holy Spirit on the Day of Pentecost. Symbolic of the Holy Spirit who came in power on the church (Ac 2:3).

TOOLS [1366, 2995, 3032, 3086, 3998, 5108, 6485].

NIV+ TOOL

The following kinds are mentioned in the Bible: cutting, boring, forks and shovels, carpentry, drawing, measuring, tilling, metal-working, stone-working.

TOOTH [9094, 3848].

NIV+ TEETH

Both human and animal teeth are mentioned (Nu 11:33; Dt 32:24), figurative use is common: cleanness of teeth, famine (Am 4:6), gnashing of teeth, rage and despair (Job 16:9), oppression (Pr 30:14), plenty (Ge 49:12).

TOPAZ [7077, 5535].

1. A precious stone (Eze 28:13; Rev 21:20).

2. In the priestly breastplate (Ex 28:17; 39:10).

Figurative:

As compared to the price of wisdom, the topaz cannot compare (Job 28:19).

Symbolic:

Seen in the foundation of the Holy City, the New Jerusalem (Rev 21:20).

See Minerals of the Bible, 1; Stones.

TOPHEL [9523] (cement). A place in the wilderness where Moses addressed the Israelites (Dt 1:1), possibly modern el-Tafila, fifteen miles SE of the Dead Sea.

TOPHETH, TOPHET [9532, 9533]. A place in the valley of the sons of Hinnom or Ben Hinnom (2Ki 23:10). Israelite children burned in sacrifice to Molech there (2Ki 23:10; Jer 7:31-32; 19:6,11-14; 32:35; cf. 2Ch 28:3; 33:6). Destroyed by Josiah (2Ki 23:10). Horror of (Isa 30:33).

See Ben Hinnom; Hinnom, Valley of.

TOPOGRAPHY Of Canaan (Jos 13:15-33; 15; 18:9).

TORAH [9368; NT nomos: 3795]. Divine law (Ex 13:9); instruction (Ex 16:4,28); the Law of Moses (1Ki 2:3); the Book of the Law (Dt 28:61); the entire Jewish Scriptures (Jn 10:34). See Law.

TORCHES [2338, 4365, *3286, 5749*]. (Jdg 7:16; 15:4; Na 2:3; Jn 18:3).

TORMENTOR [3324, 9354].
NIV+ TORMENT, TORMENTED, TORMENTING, TORMENTORS
Conquerors of Israel (Ps 137:3; Isa 51:23). Abusive jailers (Mt 18:34).

TORMENTS [*1286, 2813, 3324, *989, 990, 992*].
NIV+ See TORMENTOR
Of the wicked (Lk 16:23-28; Rev 14:10-11).
See Wicked, Punishment of.

TORTOISE *See Lizard.*

TOTAL ABSTINENCE *See Abstinence.*

TOU [9495, 9497]. King of Hamath who congratulated David for victory over Hadadezer (2Sa 8:9-11; 1Ch 18:9-10).

TOW NIV "thong, tinder, wick." Short fibers of flax or hemp (Jdg 16:9; Isa 1:31; 43:17).

TOWEL [*3317*]. A cloth for wiping and drying (Jn 13:4-5).

TOWER [859, 1032, 1467, 1468, 1469, 3227, 4463, 5164, 7610, 8123, *4788*].
NIV+ TOWERED, TOWERING, TOWERS, WATCHTOWER, WATCHTOWERS
Of Babel (Ge 11:1-9). Of Eder (Ge 35:21). Peniel (Jdg 8:8-9,17). Of Shechem (Jdg 9:46,49). Of the Hundred (Ne 3:1; 12:39). Of Hananel (Ne 3:1; 12:39; Jer 31:38; Zec 14:10). Of David (SS 4:4). Of Aswan (Eze 29:10). Of Siloam (Lk 13:4). In the walls of Jerusalem (2Ch 26:9; 32:5; Ne 12:38-39). Of other cities (2Ch 14:7).
In the desert (2Ch 26:10). For watchmen or sentinels (2Ki 9:17; 18:8). As fortress (Mt 21:33).
Parable of (Lk 14:28-29).
See Fortification; Ziggurat.
Figurative:
Of divine protection (2Sa 22:3,51; Ps 18:2; 61:3; 144:2; Pr 18:10).

TOWN [*6551, 7953, 9133, *4484*].
NIV+ HOMETOWN, TOWNS, TOWNSMEN, TOWNSPEOPLE
In ancient times, large cities had towns or villages surrounding them for protection (Nu 21:25,32; Jos 15:45-47), sometimes it means an unwalled town (Dt 3:5; 1Sa 16:4).

TOWNCLERK *See City Clerk.*

TRACONITIS, TRACHONITIS [*5551*] (*rough, stony district*). An area of c. 370 sq. miles S of Damascus; tetrarchy of Philip (Lk 3:1).

TRADE AND TRAVEL
NIV+ TRADE, TRADED, TRADERS, TRADES, TRADING
Trade in the OT:
Ur of the Chaldeans a trading port; Egypt, from earliest times, a great trading nation (Ge 37:25). First organized commerce of Hebrew people was under Solomon, who formed a partnership with the great mercantile cities of Tyre and Sidon (1Ki 9:27-28; 10:11); after the death of Solomon, Israel again became an agricultural nation.
Trade in the NT:
Jewish trade and commerce have small place in the

Gospels. Through the NT times, trade, in the wider sense of the word, was in the hands of Rome and of Italy.
Travel:
Motives for travel: Trade, colonization, exploration, migration, pilgrimage, preaching, courier service, exile. Travel had serious hazards (Ac 27-28; 2Co 11:25-27); was facilitated by wonderful Roman roads, some of which still are used. Regular passenger service by land or sea was unknown.

TRADE GUILDS Societies of tradesmen organized chiefly for the purpose of social interaction (Ac 19), not trade unions in the modern sense.

TRADERS [2493, 4048, 6086, 8217, *435*]. *See Commerce; Merchant.*

TRADITION [2976, 4600, *4142, 4161*].
NIV+ TRADITIONS
The decisions and minor precepts taught by Paul (1Co 11:2; 2Th 2:15; 3:6).
Commandments of men (Mt 12:1-8; 15:2-6; Mk 7:3-9; Lk 6:1-11; Col 2:8; 1Pe 1:18). Not authoritative (Mt 15:3-20; 1Ti 1:4; 4:7). *See Commandments and Statutes, of Men.*

TRAFFIC [6086].
NIV+ TRAFFICKED
Commerce suspended on the Sabbath (Ne 13:15-22).

TRAIN [*2852, 4340, 8647, 8767, *168, 169, 1214, 4082*].
NIV+ TRAINED, TRAINING, TRAINS, WELL-TRAINED
1. Retinue of a monarch (Ps 68:18).
2. Skirt of a robe (Isa 6:1).
3. To educate or discipline (2Sa 22:35; Pr 22:6).

TRAITOR [953, 8004, 8745, *4140, 4595*].
NIV+ See TREASON
Judas (Mt 26:14-16,46-50; Mk 14:10-11,43-45; Lk 22:3-6,21-23,47-48; Jn 13:2,27-30; 18:2-8,13).
See Treason.

TRAMP NIV "bandit" (Pr 6:11).

TRANCE [*1749*] (*a throwing of the mind out of its normal state*). A mental state in which the senses are partially or wholly suspended and the person is unconscious of his environment while he contemplates some extraordinary object (Ac 10:9-16; 22:17-21).

TRANS-EUPHRATES [2021+5643+6298, 10002+10468+10526, 10191+10468+10526].
NIV+ EUPHRATES
The region beyond the Euphrates; from the Persian perpective it included Israel and its neighbors (Ezr 4:10-20; 5:6; 6:6).

TRANSFIGURATION [*3565*].
NIV+ TRANSFIGURED
Of Moses (Ex 34:29-35). Of Jesus (Mt 17:2-9; Mk 9:2-10; Lk 9:29-36; 2Pe 1:16-18). Of Stephen (Ac 6:15). *See Translation.*

TRANSGRESSION [6296, 7321, 7322, *490, 491, 4126, 4183*].
NIV+ TRANSGRESSED, TRANSGRESSIONS, TRANSGRESSORS
Breaking of a law (Pr 17:19; Ro 4:15). *See Sin.*

TRANSJORDAN, TRANS-JORDAN (*beyond*
[East of] the Jordan). A large plateau E of Jordan, com-
prised in modern Hashemite Kingdom of Jordan; in the NT
times, the Perea and the Decapolis; in OT times, Moab,
Ammon, Gilead, and Bashan. Associated with Moses;
Joshua; the tribes of Reuben, Gad, and Manasseh; David;
Nabateans.

TRANSLATION [10597, *1450, 2257*].
NIV+ TRANSLATED

Removal from earth to heaven. Of Enoch (Ge 5:24; Heb
11:5). Of Elijah (2Ki 2:1-12). Of Jesus (Mk 16:19; Lk
24:51; Ac 1:9-11). Desired by Paul (2Co 5:4).

TRANSLATIONS OF THE BIBLE Ancient: *See*
Texts and Versions.

TRANSPORTATION In ancient times done chiefly
by camels, donkeys, horses, and boats.

TRAP [744, 3052, 3704, 4334, 4613, 4650, 4892, 5422,
5943, 7062, 7072, 8407, 8819, 8827, 9530, *2138, 2560,
4074, 4075, 4279*].
NIV+ TRAPPED, TRAPS

(Jos 23:13; Job 18:10; Jer 5:26).

TRAVAIL Pangs of childbirth (Ge 35:16; 38:27; 1Sa
4:19), trouble (Isa 23:4; 54:1), to be weak or sick (Jer
4:31), weariness (Ex 18:8).

TRAVEL [*782, 2006, 2143, 5023, 6296, *1451, 2262,
5321*].
NIV+ TRAVELED, TRAVELER, TRAVELERS, TRAVELING,
TRAVELS
See Trade and Travel.

TREACHERY [954, 956, 3950, 5085+5086, 5327,
2947, 4595*].
NIV+ See TREASON

(Jer 9:8). Of Rahab to her people (Jos 2). Of the man of
Bethel (Jdg 1:24-25). Of Jael (Jdg 4:18-21). Of
Shechemites (Jdg 9:23). Of Joab (2Sa 3:26-27). Of Baanah
and Recab (2Sa 4:6). Of David to Uriah (2Sa 11). Of Joab
to Amasa (2Sa 20:9-10). Of Jehu (2Ki 10:18-28). Of the
enemies of Nehemiah (Ne 6).
See Conspiracy; Treason.

TREASON [8004].
NIV+ TRAITOR, TRAITORS, TREACHEROUS,
TREACHEROUSLY, TREACHERY

Instances of:
Of Aaron and Miriam against Moses (Nu 12:1-11). Of
Korah, Dathan, and Abiram against Moses and Aaron (Nu
16:1-33). Of Rahab against Jericho (Jos 2). Of the betrayer
of Bethel (Jdg 1:24-25). Of the Shechemites against Abimelech (Jdg 9:22-25). Of the Ephraimites against Jephthah
(Jdg 12:1-4). Of the Israelites against Saul (1Sa 10:27),
against Rehoboam (1Ki 12:16-19). Of the Egyptian servant against the Amalekites (1Sa 30:15-16). Of Abner
against Ish-Bosheth (2Sa 3:6-21). Of Jehoiada against
Athaliah (2Ki 11:14-16). Of Absalom against his father.
See Absalom.

Death penalty for (Est 2:23).
Jesus falsely accused of (Mt 27:11,29-30; Lk 23:2-3,38;
Jn 19:12,14-15,19). Paul falsely accused of (Ac 17:7).

David's amnesty of the traitors (2Sa 19:16-23), to
Amasa (2Sa 19:13).
See Conspiracy; Treachery.

TREASURE [*238, 1709, 2773, 2890, 4718, 4759,
4837, 6035, 7621, 10133, *1126, 2565*].
NIV+ TREASURED, TREASURER, TREASURERS,
TREASURES, TREASURIES, TREASURY

A thing of highly estimated value. Money (Ge 42:25,27-
28,35; 43:23, w 43:18,21-22). Valuables of the temple and
royal residence (1Ki 14:26; 2Ki 20:13).

Cannot save life (Job 20:20). Jesus forbids the hoarding
of (Mt 6:19; 19:21; Lk 12:33). Hidden (Mt 13:44).

Figurative:
Of God's people (Ex 19:5; Dt 7:6). Of wisdom (Pr 2:4;
24:4; Col 2:3). Of spiritual understanding (Mt 13:52; Col
2:3). Of spiritual calling (2Co 4:6-7).

Treasures in heaven (Mt 6:19-21; 19:21; Lk 12:33-34).
Gospel called (2Co 4:7). Parables of (Mt 13:44,52).

TREASURE CITIES NIV "store cities" for Pharaoh
(Ex 1:11).

TREASURE HOUSE *See Treasury.*

TREASURER [1601, 4837, 10133, 10139].
NIV+ See TREASURE

One trusted with charge of the treasury. *See Treasury.*
Of the temple (2Ki 12:5,7). Of Persia (Ezr 1:8; 7:21). Of
Babylon (Da 3:2,3).

TREASURY [238, 1709, 10103, 10148, 10479, *1125,
1126, 3168*].
NIV+ See TREASURE

Of kings (2Ki 14:14; 2Ch 32:27-28; Ezr 1:7-8; Est 3:9).
Records preserved in (Ezr 6:1). *See Archives.* Treasurer in
charge of (Ezr 7:20-21). *See Treasurer.*

Tabernacle used for (Jos 6:19,24). Solomon's temple
used for (1Ki 7:51; 2Ki 12:4-14,18; 22:4-5; 1Ch 28:11-12;
Mt 27:6; Mk 12:41,43; Lk 21:1; Jn 8:20). Under the charge
of the Levites (1Ch 26:20). Storerooms provided in the
temple for various kinds of offerings (Ne 10:38-39;
13:5,9,12; Mal 3:10). Priests and Levites in charge of (1Ch
9:26; 26:20-28; Ne 12:44; 13:13). Pagan temples used for
(Da 1:2).

TREATY [1382, 2256+3208+8934, 4162, 8966].
Between nations: Israelites and Gibeonites (Jos 9:3-15),
Judah and Syria (1Ki 15:19). Cession of territory by (1Ki
9:10-14; 20:34). Sacredness of (Jos 9:16-21, w 2:8-21).

Reciprocity (1Ki 5:1-12). With idolatrous nations forbidden (Ex 34:12,15).
See Covenant.

TREE [100, 461, 471, 869, 1360, 2339, 6770, 7771,
8232, 8316, 8413, 9196, 9300, 9469, 9474, 9515, 10027,
66, 1285, 1777, 2814, 3833, 5189, 5190, 5191*].
NIV+ TREES

Israel in ancient times was far more wooded than today.
Over 25 different kinds of trees have been identified as
having grown in the Holy Land. Trees were venerated by
heathen people; Hebrews forbidden to plant a tree near a
sacred altar (Dt 16:21). Known by its fruit (Mt 7:17-19; Lk
6:43-44).

Specific Trees:
Acacia tree (Ex 25:10ff). Algum tree (2Ch 2:8; 9:11).
Almond tree (Ge 30:37; Ex 25:33-36; Ecc 12:5; Jer 1:11).
Almug tree (1Ki 10:11,12; 2Ch. 2:8; 9:10 ftn). Apple tree
(SS 2:3; 8:5; Joel 1:12). Balsam trees (2Sa 5:23-24).
Broom tree (1Ki 19:3-4; Job 30:4; Ps 120:4). Cedar Wood
(Lev 14:4,6,49,51,52; 2Sa 5:11; 2Sa 7:2; 1Ki 4:33). Citron

Wood (Rev 18:12). Cypress Wood (Ge 6:14; Isa 44:14, 60:13; Eze 27:6). Fig tree (Dt 8:7). Fir (Isa 41:19; 60:13; SS 1:17. Fruit trees (Ge 1:29; Lev 19:23). Incense tree (SS 4:14). Mulberry tree (Lk 17:6). Mustard tree (Mt 13:32; Lk 13:18). Myrtle tree (Ne 8:15). Nut trees (SS 6:11). Oak (Ge 35:4; Zec 11:2; Eze 6:13). Olive tree (Jdg 9:8; Job 15:33; Ps 52:8; Isa 17:6; Isa 41:19). Palm trees (Ex 15:27). Pine tree (1Ki 5:10; Ps 104:17 ;Isa 60:13). Pistachio (Ge 43:11). Plane tree (Ge 30:37; Eze 31:8). Pomegranate (Dt 8:8; 1Sa 14:2). Poplars (Ge 30:37; Lev 23:40; Job 40:22; Ps 137:2; Isa 15:7, 44:4). Sycamore-fig tree (1Ki 10:27; 1Ch 27:28; 2Ch 1:15; Am 7:14; Lk 19:4). Tamarisk tree (Ge 21:33; 1Sa 22:6; 31:13). Terebinth (Isa 6:13; Hos 4:13).

Generic and Symbolic Trees:

Bad tree (Mt 7:18; 12:33; Lk 6:43). Eden trees (Eze 31:9, 18). Execution tree (Dt 21:23; Ac 5:30; 10:39; 13:29). Field trees (Isa 55:12). Forest trees (1Ch 16:33; Ps 96:12). Good tree (2Ki 3:19, 25; Mt 7:17, 12:33; Lk 6:43). Great trees (Ge 13:18; 14:13; Jos 19:33). Great tree (Ge 12:6). Green tree (Ps 37:35; Lk 23:30). Tree of Knowledge (Ge 2:9). Leafy tree (Eze 20:28). Tree of Life (Ge 3:22-24; Pr 3:18,11:30, 13:12; 15:4; Rev 2:7; 22:2, 19). Lofty trees (Isa 10:33). Shade tree (Ne 8:15). Spreading tree (Dt 12:2; 1Ki 14:23; 2Ki 16:4, 17:10). Wild olive tree (Ro 11:24). Of Nebuchadnezzar (Da 4:1-27).

See Plants of the Bible; Tree of Knowledge; Tree of Life.

TREE OF KNOWLEDGE A special tree in the garden of Eden, set apart by the Lord as an instrument to test the obedience of Adam and Eve (Ge 2:9,17; 3:3-6,11-12,17).

TREE OF LIFE Another special tree in the Garden of Eden; its fruit conferred immortality on persons eating it (Ge 2:9; 3:22,24; Rev 22:2).

TRENCH [3022, 9498]. Rampart, entrenchment (2Sa 20:15; 1Sa 17:20; 26:5).

TRES TABERNAE *See Three Taverns.*

TRESPASS [*4183*].

NIV+ TRESPASSES

(Ex 22:9). Of an ox (Ex 21:28-36). Of a brother (Mt 18:15-18; Lk 17:3-4). Creditor shall not enter a debtor's house to take a pledge (Dt 24:10). *See Sin.*

TRESPASS OFFERING *See Guilt Offering; Offerings.*

TRIAL [4999, 5477, 6641, 9149, *72, 185, 2568+, 3212, 4225, 4280*].

NIV+ TRIALS

Before court (Lev 24:10-14). Right of (Jn 7:51; Ac 16:37-39; 22:25-30).

See Court, Of Law; Justice; Prisoners.

TRIAL OF JESUS Betrayed by Judas into the hands of the Jewish religious leaders, Jesus was first brought before Annas, former high priest, and father-in-law of the current high priest Caiaphas, for a brief examination (Jn 18:13); then before dawn he appeared before the Sanhedrin in the palace of Caiaphas, where he was questioned and insulted (Mk 14:60-65; Lk 22:63-64); at dawn he appeared before the Sanhedrin again and was condemned to death (Lk 22:66-70); next he was brought by the Sanhedrin before Pilate, who after an examination pronounced

him innocent (Jn 18:33-38), but the Jews would not hear of his being released. Pilate therefore sent him to Herod Antipas, who was also present for the Passover, on the plea that he belonged to Herod's jurisdiction. Herod, however, merely mocked Jesus and returned him to Pilate uncondemned (Lk 23:2-12); Pilate then gave the Jews the opportunity of choosing for release either Barabbas or Jesus, and the Jews chose Barabbas; another attempt by Pilate to have Jesus released met with failure, for the Jews threatened him if he did not carry out their wishes; after the Roman soldiers flogged and mocked Jesus, he was crucified (Mk 15:16-20).

See Jesus, History of.

TRIBE, TRIBES [1074, 1201, 1228, 4722, 4751, 4985, 7259, 7470, 8657, 10694, *1559, 5876*].

NIV+ HALF-TRIBE, TRIBAL

The tribes of Israel were descended from the twelve sons of Jacob, with Joseph's sons, Ephraim and Manasseh forming two, while no tribal territory was allotted to Levi (Ge 48:5; Nu 26:5-51; Jos 13:7-33; 15-19). The leaders of the tribes are called by various names: princes, rulers, heads, chiefs (Ex 34:31; Nu 1:16; Ge 36:1ff); before the Israelites entered the promised land two tribes, Reuben and Gad, and half of Manasseh chose to settle on the E side of the Jordan (Nu 32:33). During the period of the Judges in Israel, the tribes were each one a law to themselves. When David became king over the whole land the 12 tribes were unified. He appointed a captain over each tribe (1Ch 27:16-22). The captivities wiped out tribal distinctions.

TRIBULATION, GREAT TRIBULATION

[*2568*]. A period of suffering sent from God upon the earth at the end time because of its awful wickedness (Da 12:1; Mt 24:21).

TRIBUTE [4830, 4966, 4989, 5362, 5957, 10107]. From conquered nations (Jos 16:10; Jdg 1:30-33; 2Ki 15:19; 23:35; Mt 17:24-27; 22:15-22; Lk 2:1-5). By Arabs to Solomon (2Ch 9:14), to Jehoshaphat (2Ch 17:11).

See Duty; Levy; Tax.

TRIMMERS, WICK [4662, 4920]. *Wick Trimmers.*

TRINITY, HOLY (*triad, union of three*).

The word "trinity" is not used in the Bible. Plurality in the unity of God is implied in the OT; Father, Son, and Spirit are all called "God" in the NT.

Implied in the Old Testament:

God speaks of self in the plural—

Ge 1:26 Then God said, "Let us make man in our image, in our likeness, and let them rule over the fish of the sea and the birds of the air, over the livestock, over all the earth, and over all the creatures that move along the ground."

Ge 3:22 And the LORD God said, "The man has now become like one of us, knowing good and evil. He must not be allowed to reach out his hand and take also from the tree of life and eat, and live forever."

Isa 6:3 And they were calling to one another: "Holy, holy, holy is the LORD Almighty; the whole earth is full of his glory."

Isa 6:8 Then I heard the voice of the Lord saying, "Whom shall I send? And who will go for us?" And I said, "Here am I. Send me!"

LORD, Servant, and Spirit—

Isa 11:2 The Spirit of the LORD will rest on him—the Spirit of wisdom and of understanding, the Spirit of counsel and of power, the Spirit of knowledge and of the fear of the LORD— ³and he will delight in the fear of the LORD. He will not judge by what he sees with his eyes, or decide by what he hears with his ears;

Isa 42:1 "Here is my servant, whom I uphold, my chosen one in whom I delight; I will put my Spirit on him and he will bring justice to the nations. (+Mt 12:48)

Isa 48:16 "Come near me and listen to this: "From the first announcement I have not spoken in secret; at the time it happens, I am there." And now the Sovereign LORD has sent me, with his Spirit.

Tri-holiness of God suggests—

(Isa 6:3) And they were calling to one another: "Holy, holy, holy is the LORD Almighty; the whole earth is full of his glory." (+Rev 4:8)

Implied in the NT:

Father, Son, and Spirit—

Mt 28:19 Therefore go and make disciples of all nations, baptizing them in the name of the Father and of the Son and of the Holy Spirit,

Lk 3:22 and the Holy Spirit descended on him in bodily form like a dove. And a voice came from heaven: "You are my Son, whom I love; with you I am well pleased." (+Mt 3:16)

Jn 3:34 For the one whom God has sent speaks the words of God, for God gives the Spirit without limit. ³⁵The Father loves the Son and has placed everything in his hands.

Jn 14:16 And I will ask the Father, and he will give you another Counselor to be with you forever— ¹⁷the Spirit of truth. The world cannot accept him, because it neither sees him nor knows him. But you know him, for he lives with you and will be in you.

Jn 14:26 But the Counselor, the Holy Spirit, whom the Father will send in my name, will teach you all things and will remind you of everything I have said to you.

Jn 15:26 "When the Counselor comes, whom I will send to you from the Father, the Spirit of truth who goes out from the Father, he will testify about me.

Jn 16:7 But I tell you the truth: It is for your good that I am going away. Unless I go away, the Counselor will not come to you; but if I go, I will send him to you.

Jn 16:13 But when he, the Spirit of truth, comes, he will guide you into all truth. He will not speak on his own; he will speak only what he hears, and he will tell you what is yet to come. ¹⁴He will bring glory to me by taking from what is mine and making it known to you. ¹⁵All that belongs to the Father is mine. That is why I said the Spirit will take from what is mine and make it known to you.

Ac 1:2 until the day he was taken up to heaven, after giving instructions through the Holy Spirit to the apostles he had chosen.

Ac 1:4 On one occasion, while he was eating with them, he gave them this command: "Do not leave Jerusalem, but wait for the gift my Father promised, which you have heard me speak about. ⁵For John baptized with water, but in a few days you will be baptized with the Holy Spirit."

Ac 2:33 Exalted to the right hand of God, he has received from the Father the promised Holy Spirit and has poured out what you now see and hear.

Ac 10:36 You know the message God sent to the people of Israel, telling the good news of peace through Jesus Christ, who is Lord of all. ³⁷You know what has happened throughout Judea, beginning in Galilee after the baptism

that John preached— ³⁸how God anointed Jesus of Nazareth with the Holy Spirit and power, and how he went around doing good and healing all who were under the power of the devil, because God was with him.

Ro 1:3 regarding his Son, who as to his human nature was a descendant of David, ⁴and who through the Spirit of holiness was declared with power to be the Son of God by his resurrection from the dead: Jesus Christ our Lord.

Ro 8:9 You, however, are controlled not by the sinful nature but by the Spirit, if the Spirit of God lives in you. And if anyone does not have the Spirit of Christ, he does not belong to Christ. ¹⁰But if Christ is in you, your body is dead because of sin, yet your spirit is alive because of righteousness. ¹¹And if the Spirit of him who raised Jesus from the dead is living in you, he who raised Christ from the dead will also give life to your mortal bodies through his Spirit, who lives in you.

Ro 8:26 In the same way, the Spirit helps us in our weakness. We do not know what we ought to pray for, but the Spirit himself intercedes for us with groans that words cannot express. ²⁷And he who searches our hearts knows the mind of the Spirit, because the Spirit intercedes for the saints in accordance with God's will.

1Co 12:3 Therefore I tell you that no one who is speaking by the Spirit of God says, "Jesus be cursed," and no one can say, "Jesus is Lord," except by the Holy Spirit. ⁴There are different kinds of gifts, but the same Spirit. ⁵There are different kinds of service, but the same Lord. ⁶There are different kinds of working, but the same God works all of them in all men.

2Co 1:21 Now it is God who makes both us and you stand firm in Christ. He anointed us, ²²set his seal of ownership on us, and put his Spirit in our hearts as a deposit, guaranteeing what is to come. (+2Co 5:5)

2Co 13:14 May the grace of the Lord Jesus Christ, and the love of God, and the fellowship of the Holy Spirit be with you all.

Gal 4:4 But when the time had fully come, God sent his Son, born of a woman, born under law,

Gal 4:6 Because you are sons, God sent the Spirit of his Son into our hearts, the Spirit who calls out, "Abba, Father."

2Th 2:13 But we ought always to thank God for you, brothers loved by the Lord, because from the beginning God chose you to be saved through the sanctifying work of the Spirit and through belief in the truth. ¹⁴He called you to this through our gospel, that you might share in the glory of our Lord Jesus Christ.

2Th 2:16 May our Lord Jesus Christ himself and God our Father, who loved us and by his grace gave us eternal encouragement and good hope,

1Ti 3:16 Beyond all question, the mystery of godliness is great: He appeared in a body, was vindicated by the Spirit, was seen by angels, was preached among the nations, was believed on in the world, was taken up in glory.

Tit 3:4 But when the kindness and love of God our Savior appeared, ⁵he saved us, not because of righteous things we had done, but because of his mercy. He saved us through the washing of rebirth and renewal by the Holy Spirit, ⁶whom he poured out on us generously through Jesus Christ our Savior,

Heb 9:14 How much more, then, will the blood of Christ, who through the eternal Spirit offered himself unblemished to God, cleanse our consciences from acts that lead to death, so that we may serve the living God!

1Pe 1:2 who have been chosen according to the

foreknowledge of God the Father, through the sanctifying work of the Spirit, for obedience to Jesus Christ and sprinkling by his blood: Grace and peace be yours in abundance.

1Pe 3:18 For Christ died for sins once for all, the righteous for the unrighteous, to bring you to God. He was put to death in the body but made alive by the Spirit,

1Jn 5:6 This is the one who came by water and blood—Jesus Christ. He did not come by water only, but by water and blood. And it is the Spirit who testifies, because the Spirit is the truth. 7For there are three that testify:

Tri-holiness of God suggests (Isa 6:3)—

Rev 4:8 Each of the four living creatures had six wings and was covered with eyes all around, even under his wings. Day and night they never stop saying: "Holy, holy, holy is the Lord God Almighty, who was, and is, and is to come."

Relationships Within the Godhead:

God and the Holy Spirit (Isa 42:1; 48:16)—

Isa 63:9 In all their distress he too was distressed, and the angel of his presence saved them. In his love and mercy he redeemed them; he lifted them up and carried them all the days of old. 10Yet they rebelled and grieved his Holy Spirit. So he turned and became their enemy and he himself fought against them.

1Co 2:10 but God has revealed it to us by his Spirit. The Spirit searches all things, even the deep things of God.

11For who among men knows the thoughts of a man except the man's spirit within him? In the same way no one knows the thoughts of God except the Spirit of God.

1Co 6:19 Do you not know that your body is a temple of the Holy Spirit, who is in you, whom you have received from God? You are not your own;

Jesus and the Holy Spirit—

Isa 61:1 The Spirit of the Sovereign Lord is on me, because the Lord has anointed me to preach good news to the poor. He has sent me to bind up the brokenhearted, to proclaim freedom for the captives and release from darkness for the prisoners, 2to proclaim the year of the Lord's favor and the day of vengeance of our God, to comfort all who mourn, 3and provide for those who grieve in Zion—to bestow on them a crown of beauty instead of ashes, the oil of gladness instead of mourning, and a garment of praise instead of a spirit of despair. They will be called oaks of righteousness, a planting of the Lord for the display of his splendor. (+Lk 4:18)

Mt 1:18 This is how the birth of Jesus Christ came about: His mother Mary was pledged to be married to Joseph, but before they came together, she was found to be with child through the Holy Spirit.

Mt 1:20 But after he had considered this, an angel of the Lord appeared to him in a dream and said, "Joseph son of David, do not be afraid to take Mary home as your wife, because what is conceived in her is from the Holy Spirit.

Mt 12:28 But if I drive out demons by the Spirit of God, then the kingdom of God has come upon you. (+Mt 28:19)

Lk 1:35 The angel answered, "The Holy Spirit will come upon you, and the power of the Most High will overshadow you. So the holy one to be born will be called the Son of God.

Lk 4:1 Jesus, full of the Holy Spirit, returned from the Jordan and was led by the Spirit in the desert,

Lk 4:14 Jesus returned to Galilee in the power of the Spirit, and news about him spread through the whole countryside.

Jn 1:32 Then John gave this testimony: "I saw the Spirit come down from heaven as a dove and remain on him. 33I would not have known him, except that the one who sent me to baptize with water told me, 'The man on whom you see the Spirit come down and remain is he who will baptize with the Holy Spirit.'

Jn 7:39 By this he meant the Spirit, whom those who believed in him were later to receive. Up to that time the Spirit had not been given, since Jesus had not yet been glorified.

Jn 20:22 And with that he breathed on them and said, "Receive the Holy Spirit.

1Co 8:6 yet for us there is but one God, the Father, from whom all things came and for whom we live; and there is but one Lord, Jesus Christ, through whom all things came and through whom we live.

2Co 3:17 Now the Lord is the Spirit, and where the Spirit of the Lord is, there is freedom.

Php 1:19 for I know that through your prayers and the help given by the Spirit of Jesus Christ, what has happened to me will turn out for my deliverance.

Col 2:2 My purpose is that they may be encouraged in heart and united in love, so that they may have the full riches of complete understanding, in order that they may know the mystery of God, namely, Christ,

See Angel [of the Lord]; God; Holy Spirit; Jesus the Christ, Deity of.

TRIPOLIS [10305]. People sent as colonists to Samaria by the Assyrians (Ezr 4:9-10).

TRIUMPH [1452, 1504, 2116+6702, 2616, 3523, 5627, 6451, 6600, 6636, 8123, 8131, 8934, *2581, 3771*] (*to lead in triumph*).

> NIV+ TRIUMPHAL, TRIUMPHANT, TRIUMPHED, TRIUMPHING, TRIUMPHS

In Roman times a magnificent procession in honor of a victorious general (2Co 2:14; Col 2:15).

TRIUMPHAL ENTRY OF JESUS Into Jerusalem (Ps 118:26; Zec 9:9; Mt 21:5,8-10; Mk 11:7-11; Lk 19:35-38; Jn 12:12-13).

TROAS [*5590*]. A chief city and port of the Roman Province of Asia, on the Aegean coast, c. ten miles from the ruins of ancient Troy; known as Alexandria Troas (Ac 16:8; 20:5; 2Co 2:12).

TROGYLLIUM A promontory thrusting SW from the Asian mainland N of Miletus, opposite the island of Samos (Ac 20:15, KJV).

TROPHIES Goliath's head and armor (1Sa 17:54; 21:9), Saul's (1Sa 31:8-10). Placed in temples. *See Temple.*

TROPHIMUS [*5576*] (*nourished [child]*). An Ephesian companion of Paul. Accompanies Paul from Greece to Asia (Ac 20:4). With Paul in Jerusalem; made the occasion of an attack on Paul (Ac 21:27-30). Left ill at Miletus (2Ti 4:20).

TROUBLE [*1314, 6579, 6662, 7192, 7639, 7650, 7674, 8273, 8288, 8288, 8317, *86, 1943, 2567, 2568, 5429*].

> NIV+ TROUBLED, TROUBLEMAKER, TROUBLEMAKERS, TROUBLER, TROUBLES, TROUBLESOME, TROUBLING

Being Anxious: Forbidden—

Mt 6:25 "Therefore I tell you, do not worry about your

life, what you will eat or drink; or about your body, what you will wear. Is not life more important than food, and the body more important than clothes? ²⁶Look at the birds of the air; they do not sow or reap or store away in barns, and yet your heavenly Father feeds them. Are you not much more valuable than they? ²⁷Who of you by worrying can add a single hour to his life?

²⁸"And why do you worry about clothes? See how the lilies of the field grow. They do not labor or spin. ²⁹Yet I tell you that not even Solomon in all his splendor was dressed like one of these. ³⁰If that is how God clothes the grass of the field, which is here today and tomorrow is thrown into the fire, will he not much more clothe you, O you of little faith? ³¹So do not worry, saying, 'What shall we eat?' or 'What shall we drink?' or 'What shall we wear?' ³²For the pagans run after all these things, and your heavenly Father knows that you need them. ³³But seek first his kingdom and his righteousness, and all these things will be given to you as well. ³⁴Therefore do not worry about tomorrow, for tomorrow will worry about itself. Each day has enough trouble of its own.

Php 4:6 Do not be anxious about anything, but in everything, by prayer and petition, with thanksgiving, present your requests to God.

Remedy for Anxiety—

Jn 16:6 Because I have said these things, you are filled with grief. ⁷But I tell you the truth: It is for your good that I am going away. Unless I go away, the Counselor will not come to you; but if I go, I will send him to you.

1Pe 5:7 Cast all your anxiety on him because he cares for you.

See Affliction; Anxiety; Suffering.

Instances of:

Israelites at the Red Sea (Ex 14:10-12), about water (Ex 15:23-25; 17:2-3; Nu 20:1-13), food (Ex 16:2-3; Nu 11:4-33). When Moses remained on Mount Sinai (Ex 32:1). When the spies brought their adverse report (Nu 13:28-29,31-33; 14:1-4, w 14:4-12). Elijah, under the broom tree and in the cave (1Ki 19:4-15). The disciples, as to how the multitude could be fed (Mt 14:15; Mk 6:37), in the tempest, when Jesus was asleep in the ship (Mt 8:23-26; Mk 4:36-39; Lk 8:22-24), when Jesus was crucified (Lk 24:4-9,24-31,36-40). Mary at the tomb (Jn 20:11-17). The people in the shipwreck (Ac 27:22-25,30-36).

TRUCE In battle (2Sa 2:26-31).

TRUMPET [2955, 2956, 8795, 9540, 9546, 9558, *4894, 4895*].

NIV+ TRUMPETERS, TRUMPETS

Made of ram's horn (Jos 6:4-6,8,13), of silver (Nu 10:2). Uses of, prescribed by Moses (Nu 10:1-10). Used in war (Job 39:24-25; Jer 4:19; 6:1,17; 42:14; 51:27; Eze 7:14; Am 2:2; 3:6; Zep 1:16; 1Co 14:8). To summon soldiers, by Phinehas (Nu 31:6), by Ehud (Jdg 3:27), by Gideon (Jdg 6:34), by Saul (1Sa 13:3), by Joab (2Sa 2:28; 18:16; 20:22), by Absalom (2Sa 15:10), by Sheba (2Sa 20:1), by Nehemiah (Ne 4:18,20). Gideon's soldiers (Jdg 7:8-22). In war, of Abijah (2Ch 13:12,14). In the siege of Jericho (Jos 6:4-20).

Sounded in time of danger (Eze 33:3-6; Joel 2:1).

Used at Sinai (Ex 19:13-19; 20:18; Heb 12:19), on the Day of Atonement (Isa 27:13), at the Jubilee (Lev 25:9), at the bringing up of the ark (2Sa 6:5,15; 1Ch 13:8; 15:28), the anointing of kings (1Ki 1:34,39; 2Ki 9:13; 11:14), dedication of Solomon's temple (2Ch 5:12-13; 7:6), in

worship (1Ch 15:24; 16:42; 25:5; Ps 81:3-4), at Jehoshaphat's triumph (2Ch 20:28), at the foundation of the second temple (Ezr 3:10-11), at the dedication of the wall (Ne 12:35,41).

Figurative:

(Isa 27:13; Eze 33:3; Joel 2:1; Zec 9:14; Mt 6:2).

Symbolic:

(Mt 24:31; 1Co 15:52; 1Th 4:16; Rev 1:10; 4:1; 8; 9:1-14; 10:7; 11:15).

See Horn; Music, Instruments of.

TRUMPETS, FEAST OF When and how observed (Lev 23:24-25; Nu 29:1-6). Celebrated after the captivity with joy (Ne 8:2,9-12).

See Feasts.

TRUST [*575, 586, 1053, 2879, 4073, 4440, 7747, 10041, *3874, 4275, 4409, 4412*].

NIV+ ENTRUST, ENTRUSTED, TRUSTED, TRUSTEES, TRUSTFULLY, TRUSTING, TRUSTS, TRUSTWORTHY

See Faith.

TRUSTEE [*3874*].

NIV+ See TRUST, TRUSTEES

Mosaic law concerning (Ex 22:7-13; Lev 6:2-7). The parable of the pounds (Mt 25:14-28; Lk 19:12-27).

See Steward.

TRUTH [*575, 586, 589, 597, 622, 995, 4027, 7406, 7999, 9214, 10327, *237, 238, 239, 240, 242, 297, 1188, 4048*].

NIV+ TRUE, TRULY, TRUTHFUL, TRUTHFULLY, TRUTHFULNESS, TRUTHS

Truth and faithful(ness) are translated from the same Hebrew and Greek words. *See Faithfulness.*

Characterists of:

Ps 85:10 Love and faithfulness meet together; righteousness and peace kiss each other. ¹¹Faithfulness springs forth from the earth, and righteousness looks down from heaven.

Precious (Pr 23:23). Preserves (Ps 46:11; 61:7; 91:4; Pr 20:28). Purifies (Pr 16:6; 1Pe 1:22).

Sanctifies—

Jn 17:17 Sanctify them by the truth; your word is truth.

Jn 17:19 For them I sanctify myself, that they too may be truly sanctified. (+2Th 2:13)

Brings freedom—

Jn 8:32 Then you will know the truth, and the truth will set you free."

Reaches to the clouds—

Ps 57:10 For great is your love, reaching to the heavens; your faithfulness reaches to the skies.

Ps 108:4 For great is your love, higher than the heavens; your faithfulness reaches to the skies.

Endures forever—

Ps 100:5 For the LORD is good and his love endures forever; his faithfulness continues through all generations. (+Ps 117:2)

Ways of the Lord in (Ps 25:10).—

The foundation of which Christ is the cornerstone (Eph 2:20).

Came by Jesus Christ (Jn 1:17; 8:45)—

Jn 14:6 Jesus answered, "I am the way and the truth and the life. No one comes to the Father except through me.

Jn 18:37 "You are a king, then!" said Pilate. Jesus answered, "You are right in saying I am a king. In fact, for this reason I was born, and for this I came into the world, to testify to the truth. Everyone on the side of truth listens to me."

[38]"What is truth?" Pilate asked. With this he went out again to the Jews and said, "I find no basis for a charge against him. (+Eph 2:20)

Revealed to the righteous—

Ps 57:3 He sends from heaven and saves me, rebuking those who hotly pursue me; *Selah* God sends his love and his faithfulness. (+Ps 86:11)

Word of God called the word of (Jn 17:17; Eph 1:13; Col 1:5; 2Ti 2:15; Jas 1:18)

Scripture of—

Da 10:21 but first I will tell you what is written in the Book of Truth. (No one supports me against them except Michael, your prince.

Acceptance of, necessary to salvation (2Th 2:12-13; 1Ti 2:4; 2Ti 2:25; 3:7; Heb 10:26).

Rejection of, brings condemnation (2Th 2:10-12; Tit 1:14).

To be taught by parents to children (Isa 38:19). Church is the pillar of (1Ti 3:15).

Believers should worship God in (Jn 4:24, w Ps 145:18), serve God in (Jos 24:14; 1Sa 12:24), walk before God in (1Ki 2:4; 2Ki 20:3), keep religious feasts with (1Co 5:8), value as inestimable (Pr 23:23), love (Zec 8:19), rejoice in (1Co 13:6), speak to one another (Zec 8:16; Eph 4:25), execute judgment with (Zec 8:16), meditate upon (Php 4:8), bind about the neck (Pr 3:3), write upon the tables of the heart (Pr 3:3).

The fruit of the light (Eph 5:9).

They who speak, show righteousness (Pr 12:17), are the delight of God (Pr 12:22), will be established forever (Pr 2:1).

The wicked are destitute of truth—

Isa 59:14 So justice is driven back, and righteousness stands at a distance; truth has stumbled in the streets, honesty cannot enter. [15]Truth is nowhere to be found, and whoever shuns evil becomes a prey. The LORD looked and was displeased that there was no justice. (+Da 9:13; Hos 4:1; 1Ti 6:5)

The wicked resist (2Ti 3:8; 4:4), turn away from (2Ti 4:4), speak not (Jer 9:5), plead not for (Isa 59:4), are not valiant for (Jer 9:3), punished for lack of (Jer 9:5,9; Hos 4:1,3). *See Wicked.*

The Gospel:

Came by Christ (Jn 1:17). Is in Christ (1Ti 2:7). John bore witness to (Jn 5:33). Is according to godliness (Tit 1:1). Is sanctifying (Jn 17:17,19). Is purifying (1Pe 1:22). Is part of the Christian armor (Eph 6:14). Revealed abundantly to saints (Jer 33:6). Abides continually with saints (2Jn 2). Should be acknowledged (2Ti 2:25). Should be believed (2Th 2:12-13; 1Ti 4:3). Should be obeyed (Ro 2:8; Gal 3:1). Should be loved (2Th 2:10). Should be manifested (2Co 4:2). Should be rightly divided (2Ti 2:15). The church is the pillar and ground of (1Ti 3:15). The devil is devoid of (Jn 8:44).

Of the Gospel:

(2Ti 4:3-4; Tit 1:1,14; 2:1; Jas 1:18,21,23,25; 2:13; 5:19; 1Pe 1:22-25; 2:2,8; 3:1; 5:12; 2Pe 1:12). *See God, Truth.*

Of God:

Is one of his attributes—

Dt 32:4 He is the Rock, his works are perfect, and all his ways are just. A faithful God who does no wrong, upright and just is he.

Isa 65:16 Whoever invokes a blessing in the land will do so by the God of truth; he who takes an oath in the land will swear by the God of truth. For the past troubles will be forgotten and hidden from my eyes.

He keeps, forever (Ps 146:6)

Abundant—

Ex 34:6 And he passed in front of Moses, proclaiming, "The LORD, the LORD, the compassionate and gracious God, slow to anger, abounding in love and faithfulness,

Inviable (Nu 23:19; Tit 1:2), enduring to all generations (Ps 100:5). Exhibited in his ways (Rev 15:3)

Works—

Ps 33:4 For the word of the LORD is right and true; he is faithful in all he does. (+Ps 111:7; Da 4:37)

Judicial statutes (Ps 19:9), word (Ps 119:160; Jn 17:17), fulfillment of promises in Christ (2Co 1:20)

Fulfillment of His covenant—

Mic 7:20 You will be true to Jacob, and show mercy to Abraham, as you pledged on oath to our fathers in days long ago.

Dealings with saints (Ps 25:10), deliverance of saints (Ps 57:3), punishment of the wicked (Rev 16:7). Is a shield and buckler to saints (Ps 91:4).

We should confide in—

Ps 31:5 Into your hands I commit my spirit; redeem me, O LORD, the God of truth. (+Tit 1:2)

Plead in prayer (Ps 89:49). Pray for its manifestation to ourselves (2Ch 6:17). Pray for its exhibition to others (2Sa 2:6). Make known, to others (Isa 38:19). Magnify (Ps 71:22; 138:2). Is denied by the devil (Ge 3:4-5), the self-righteous (1Jn 1:10), unbelievers (1Jn 5:10).

Often linked with his mercy (Ps 85:10-11; 93:3; 100:5).

Attribute:

Of God (Ex 34:6; Dt 32:4; Ps 31:5)—

Ps 40:10 I do not hide your righteousness in my heart; I speak of your faithfulness and salvation. I do not conceal your love and your truth from the great assembly. (+Ps 40:11; 71:22)

Ps 86:15 But you, O Lord, are a compassionate and gracious God, slow to anger, abounding in love and faithfulness.

Ps 89:14 Righteousness and justice are the foundation of your throne; love and faithfulness go before you. (+Ps 115:1; 117:2; 138:2; 146:6)

Isa 25:1 O LORD, you are my God; I will exalt you and praise your name, for in perfect faithfulness you have done marvelous things, things planned long ago. (+Isa 65:16; Jer 4:2)

Jer 5:3 O LORD, do not your eyes look for truth? You struck them, but they felt no pain; you crushed them, but they refused correction. They made their faces harder than stone and refused to repent.

Exhibited in His government (Ps 119:151)

In His judgments—

Ps 96:13 they will sing before the LORD, for he comes, he comes to judge the earth. He will judge the world in righteousness and the peoples in his truth.

Ro 2:2 Now we know that God's judgment against those who do such things is based on truth.

In His word (Jn 17:19)

In His works (Ps 111:7-8)—

Da 4:37 Now I, Nebuchadnezzar, praise and exalt and glorify the King of heaven, because everything he does is right and all his ways are just. And those who walk in pride he is able to humble.

Of Christ:

Jn 1:14 The Word became flesh and made his dwelling among us. We have seen his glory, the glory of the One and Only, who came from the Father, full of grace and truth. (+Jn 14:6)

Of the Holy Spirit:

Jn 14:17 the Spirit of truth. The world cannot accept him, because it neither sees him nor knows him. But you know him, for he lives with you and will be in you.

Jn 16:13 But when he, the Spirit of truth, comes, he will guide you into all truth. He will not speak on his own; he will speak only what he hears, and he will tell you what is yet to come. (+1Jn 5:7-8)

Grace of the Righteous:

Ps 51:6 Surely you desire truth in the inner parts; you teach me wisdom in the inmost place. (+Pr 3:3; Jn 3:21; 3Jn 3)

Righteous, should be prepared with (Eph 6:14), should know (1Ti 4:3; 1Jn 2:21; 3:19; 4:6), should love (Zec 8:19; 2Th 2:10), should rejoice in (1Co 13:6), should meditate upon (Php 4:8).

TRUTHFULNESS [574, 575, 622, *237, 239*].

NIV+ See TRUTH

Commended (Pr 12:17,19). Commanded (Zec 8:16; Eph 4:25; Col 3:9). Magistrates should be men of (Ex 18:21). Fearlessness in (2Co 12:6; Gal 4:16). Of Job (Job 27:4; 36:4).

Wicked, lack (Jer 9:5). Satan, devoid of (Jn 8:44). *See Satan; Wicked.*

TRYPHENA [*5586*] (*dainty*). A Christian woman friend of Paul's in Rome (Ro 16:12).

TRYPHOSA [*5589*] (*delicate*). A Christian woman friend of Paul's in Rome (Ro 16:12).

TUBAL [9317]. The son of Japheth (Ge 10:2; 1Ch 1:5). Descendants of, become a nation (Isa 66:19; Eze 27:13; 32:26; 38:2-3; 39:1).

TUBAL-CAIN [9340].

NIV+ TUBAL-CAIN'S

The son of Lamech and Zillah; worker in bronze and iron (Ge 4:22).

TUMBLEWEED [1650]. Symbolic of wicked blown away in judgment (Ps 83:13; Isa 17:13). *See Plants of the Bible.*

TUMOR [3224, 6754].

NIV+ TUMORS

A disease with which the Philistines were afflicted (1Sa 5:6,9,12; 6:4-5,11,17). *See Disease; Hemorrhoids.*

TUNIC [955, 4189, 4230+4496, 4496, *5945*].

NIV+ TUNICS

A shirtlike garment worn by men and women under other clothes in Bible times. Worn by priests (Ex 28:4,39-40). Saul offers his to David (1Sa 17:38-39), as does Jonathan (1Sa 18:4). *See Dress.*

TURBAN [3178, 5200, 6996, 7565, 10368].

NIV+ TURBANS

Headcovering. Worn by the high priest (Ex 28:3,37-39),

by other priests (Eze 44:18), by royalty (Eze 21:26). *See Headbands.*

TURQUOISE [5876, 7037]. In the high priest's breast-piece (Ex 28:18; 39:11), in the temple (1Ch 29:2). Commerce in (Eze 27:16). *See Minerals of the Bible; Stones.*

TURTLE, TURTLEDOVE *See Dove, Turtle.*

TUTOR (2Ki 10:1; Ac 22:3; Gal 4:1-2).

TWELVE, THE *See Apostles.*

TWILIGHT [1068+2021+6847, 5974].

NIV+ LIGHT

(1Sa 30:17; 2Ki 7:5; Job 3:9; Eze 12:6).

TWINS [9298, 9339, *1483*].

NIV+ TWIN

Jacob and Esau (Ge 25:24-26). Perez and Zerah (Ge 38:27-30). *See Castor and Pollux.*

TWO-AND-A-HALF TRIBES [2256+2942+9109] Reuben, Gad, and half of Manasseh settled in the Trans-Jordan (Jos 14:3).

TYCHICUS [*5608*] (*good fortune*). An Asian companion of Paul. Accompanies Paul from Greece to Asia (Ac 20:4). With Paul in Nicopolis (Tit 3:12), in Rome (Eph 6:21-22; Col 4:7-8). Sent to Ephesus (Eph 6:21-22; 2Ti 4:12), to Colosse (Col 4:7-8).

TYPES.

Miscellaneous:

Bride, a type of the church (Rev 21:2,9; 22:17). The sanctuary a type of the heavenly sanctuary (Ex 40:2,24; Heb 8:2,5; 9:1-12). The saving of Noah and his family, of the salvation through the Gospel (1Pe 3:20-21).

Defilement a type of sin. *See Defilement; Purification.* Leaven a type of sin. *See Leaven.* Washings a type of purification. *See Washings.*

See Allegory; Parable; Symbols and Similitudes.

Of Sin: *See Blemish; Defilement; Leaven.*

Of the Savior:

(Col 2:17; Heb 9:7-15,18-28; 10:1-10). High priest, typical of the mediatorship (Ex 28:1,12,29-30,38; Lev 16:15; Zec 6:12-13, w Heb 5; 8:2; 10:21). The institutions ordained by Moses (Mt 26:54; Lk 24:25-27,44-47; Col 2:14-17; Heb 10:1-14). The sacrifices (Lev 4:2-3,12; Heb 9:7-15,18-25; 10:1-22,29; 13:11-13; 1Pe 1:19; Rev 5:6). The morning and evening sacrifice (Jn 1:29,36). The red heifer (Nu 19:2-6, w Heb 9:13-14). The Passover lamb (1Co 5:7). The bronze altar (Ex 27:1-2, w Heb 13:10). The bronze basin (Ex 30:18-20, w Zec 13:1; Eph 5:26-27). Atonement cover (Ex 25:17-22, w Heb 4:16). The veil (Ex 40:21; 2Ch 3:14, w Heb 10:20). Manna (Jn 6:32-35; 1Co 10:3). Cities of refuge (Nu 35:6, w Heb 6:18). Bronze snake (Nu 21:9; Jn 3:14-15). Tree of life (Ge 2:9, w Jn 1:4; Rev 22:2).

Adam (Ro 5:14; 1Co 15:45). Abel (Ge 4:8,10, w Heb 12:24). Noah (Ge 5:29, w 2Co 1:5). Melchizedek (Heb 7:1-17). Moses (Dt 18:15,18; Ac 3:20,22; 7:37; Heb 3:2-6). David (2Sa 8:15; Ps 89:19-20; Eze 37:24; Php 2:9). Eliakim (Isa 22:20-22; Rev 3:7). Jonah (Jnh 1:17, w Mt 12:40).

TYRANNUS [*5598*] (*ruler*). A Greek teacher in whose school Paul preached after he was expelled from the synagogue (Ac 19:9).

TYRANNY [6945].

NIV+ TYRANNICAL

Pr 28:16 A tyrannical ruler lacks judgment, but he who hates ill-gotten gain will enjoy a long life. (+Isa 54:11-14) *See Government.*

TYRE, TYRIANS [7450, 7660, *5601, 5602*] (*rocky place*).

1. Kingdom of; Hiram, king of (1Ki 5:1-2; 2Ch 2:3). Sends material to David for his palace (2Ch 2:3). Men and materials sent from, to Solomon, for the building of the temple and palaces (1Ki 5:1-11; 9:10-11; 2Ch 2:3-16).
See Hiram.

2. City of. Situated on the shore of the Mediterranean. On the northern boundary of Asher (Jos 19:29). Pleasant site of (Hos 9:13). Fortified (Jos 19:29; 2Sa 24:7). Commerce of (1Ki 9:26-28; 10:11; Isa 23; Eze 27; 28:1-19; Zec 9:2; Ac 21:3). Merchants of (Isa 23:8). Antiquity of (Isa 23:7). Riches of (Isa 23:8; Zec 9:3). Besieged by Nebuchadnezzar (Eze 26:7; 29:18).

Jesus goes to the coasts of (Mt 15:21). Heals the daughter of the Syrian Phoenician woman near (Mt 15:21-28; Mk 7:24-31). Multitudes from, come to hear Jesus and to be healed of their diseases (Mk 3:8; Lk 6:17). Herod's hostility toward (Ac 12:20-23). Paul visits (Ac 21:3-7).

To be judged according to its opportunity and privileges (Mt 11:21-22; Lk 10:13-14).

Prophecies relating to (Ps 45:12; 87:4; Isa 23; Jer 25:22; 27:1-11; 47:4; Eze 26-28; Joel 3:4-8; Am 1:9-10; Zec 9:2-4).

TYROPEON VALLEY (*valley of the cheese makers*).
A valley in Jerusalem separating W and E hills and joining Kidron and Hinnom valleys on the S.

U

UCAL [432] (possibly *I am consumed*, or *I cease*). An obscure word; usually taken as son or pupil of Agur (Pr 30:1).

UEL [198] (possibly *will of El [God]* BDB KB). An Israelite who divorced his Gentile wife (Ezr 10:34).

UGARIT *See Amarna, Tell El; Ras Shamra; Texts, Ancient Near Eastern Non-Biblical Texts Relating to the Old Testament.*

ULAI [217]. A river in Elam near Susa on whose bank Daniel saw a vision (Da 8:2,16).

ULAM [220] (*first, leader*).
1. The son of Sheresh (1Ch 7:16-17).
2. The son of Eshek (1Ch 8:39-40).

ULLA [6587]. An Asherite (1Ch 7:39).

UMMAH [6646]. A city of Asher (Jos 19:30).

UNBELIEF [*602*].
NIV+ UNBELIEVER, UNBELIEVERS, UNBELIEVING

Characteristic of:

Hardens the heart—

Ps 95:8 do not harden your hearts as you did at Meribah, as you did that day at Massah in the desert, **9**where your fathers tested and tried me, though they had seen what I did. **10**For forty years I was angry with that generation; I said, "They are a people whose hearts go astray, and they have not known my ways." **11**So I declared on oath in my anger, "They shall never enter my rest."
Heb 3:12 See to it, brothers, that none of you has a sinful, unbelieving heart that turns away from the living God.
Heb 3:16 Who were they who heard and rebelled? Were they not all those Moses led out of Egypt? **17**And with whom was he angry for forty years? Was it not with those who sinned, whose bodies fell in the desert? **18**And to whom did God swear that they would never enter his rest if not to those who disobeyed? **19**So we see that they were not able to enter, because of their unbelief.
Ac 19:9 But some of them became obstinate; they refused to believe and publicly maligned the Way. So Paul left them. He took the disciples with him and had discussions daily in the lecture hall of Tyrannus.

Rejects Christ—

Isa 53:1 Who has believed our message and to whom has the arm of the LORD been revealed? **2**He grew up before him like a tender shoot, and like a root out of dry ground. He had no beauty or majesty to attract us to him, nothing in his appearance that we should desire him. **3**He was despised and rejected by men, a man of sorrows, and familiar with suffering. Like one from whom men hide their faces he was despised, and we esteemed him not. (+Jn 12:38)
Mk 6:3 Isn't this the carpenter? Isn't this Mary's son and the brother of James, Joseph, Judas and Simon? Aren't his sisters here with us?" And they took offense at him.
Mk 6:6 And he was amazed at their lack of faith. Then Jesus went around teaching from village to village.

Jn 1:11 He came to that which was his own, but his own did not receive him.
Jn 5:38 nor does his word dwell in you, for you do not believe the one he sent.
Jn 5:40 yet you refuse to come to me to have life.
Jn 5:44 How can you believe if you accept praise from one another, yet make no effort to obtain the praise that comes from the only God?
Jn 5:46 If you believed Moses, you would believe me, for he wrote about me. **47**But since you do not believe what he wrote, how are you going to believe what I say?"
Jn 10:25 Jesus answered, "I did tell you, but you do not believe. The miracles I do in my Father's name speak for me, **26**but you do not believe because you are not my sheep.

Displeases God—

Ps 78:19 They spoke against God, saying, "Can God spread a table in the desert? **20**When he struck the rock, water gushed out, and streams flowed abundantly. But can he also give us food? Can he supply meat for his people?" **21**When the LORD heard them, he was very angry; his fire broke out against Jacob, and his wrath rose against Israel, **22**for they did not believe in God or trust in his deliverance.
Heb 11:6 And without faith it is impossible to please God, because anyone who comes to him must believe that he exists and that he rewards those who earnestly seek him.

Makes God a liar—

1Jn 5:10 Anyone who believes in the Son of God has this testimony in his heart. Anyone who does not believe God has made him out to be a liar, because he has not believed the testimony God has given about his Son.

Does not nullify God's faithfulness—

Ro 3:3 What if some did not have faith? Will their lack of faith nullify God's faithfulness? **4**Not at all! Let God be true, and every man a liar. As it is written: "So that you may be proved right when you speak and prevail when you judge."

Allows God to extend his mercy—

Ro 11:20 Granted. But they were broken off because of unbelief, and you stand by faith. Do not be arrogant, but be afraid.
Ro 11:30 Just as you who were at one time disobedient to God have now received mercy as a result of their disobedience, **31**so they too have now become disobedient in order that they too may now receive mercy as a result of God's mercy to you. **32**For God has bound all men over to disobedience so that he may have mercy on them all.

Characteristic of all mankind (Ro 11:20,30-32)—

2Th 3:2 And pray that we may be delivered from wicked and evil men, for not everyone has faith.

Leads to:

Defeat—

Isa 7:9 The head of Ephraim is Samaria, and the head of Samaria is only Remaliah's son. If you do not stand firm in your faith, you will not stand at all.'"

Destruction (Ro 11:20)—

2Th 2:12 and so that all will be condemned who have not believed the truth but have delighted in wickedness.

Reproof—

Jn 16:8 When he comes, he will convict the world of guilt in regard to sin and righteousness and judgment: **9**in regard to sin, because men do not believe in me;

Condemnation—

Ro 14:23 But the man who has doubts is condemned if he eats, because his eating is not from faith; and everything that does not come from faith is sin.

Rejection—

1Pe 2:7 Now to you who believe, this stone is precious. But to those who do not believe,

"The stone the builders rejected has become the capstone," **8**and,

"A stone that causes men to stumble and a rock that makes them fall."

They stumble because they disobey the message—which is also what they were destined for.

Instability—

Jas 1:6 But when he asks, he must believe and not doubt, because he who doubts is like a wave of the sea, blown and tossed by the wind. **7**That man should not think he will receive anything from the Lord;

Caused by Spiritual Blindness: (Isa 6:9-10)

Mt 13:13 This is why I speak to them in parables:

"Though seeing, they do not see; though hearing, they do not hear or understand.

14In them is fulfilled the prophecy of Isaiah:

"'You will be ever hearing but never understanding; you will be ever seeing but never perceiving. **15**For this people's heart has become calloused; they hardly hear with their ears, and they have closed their eyes. Otherwise they might see with their eyes, hear with their ears, understand with their hearts and turn, and I would heal them.'

Mt 13:58 And he did not do many miracles there because of their lack of faith.

Lk 13:34 "O Jerusalem, Jerusalem, you who kill the prophets and stone those sent to you, how often I have longed to gather your children together, as a hen gathers her chicks under her wings, but you were not willing!

Lk 19:41 As he approached Jerusalem and saw the city, he wept over it **42**and said, "If you, even you, had only known on this day what would bring you peace—but now it is hidden from your eyes.

Jn 12:37 Even after Jesus had done all these miraculous signs in their presence, they still would not believe in him.

Jn 12:39 For this reason they could not believe, because, as Isaiah says elsewhere:

40"He has blinded their eyes and deadened their hearts, so they can neither see with their eyes, nor understand with their hearts, nor turn—and I would heal them."

Jn 12:47 "As for the person who hears my words but does not keep them, I do not judge him. For I did not come to judge the world, but to save it.

Admonitions Against:

Ac 13:40 Take care that what the prophets have said does not happen to you:

41"'Look, you scoffers, wonder and perish, for I am going to do something in your days that you would never believe, even if someone told you.'"

2Co 6:14 Do not be yoked together with unbelievers. For what do righteousness and wickedness have in common? Or what fellowship can light have with darkness? **15**What harmony is there between Christ and Belial? What does a believer have in common with an unbeliever? **16**What agreement is there between the temple of God and idols? For we are the temple of the living God. As God has said: "I will live with them and walk among them, and I will be their God, and they will be my people." (+Heb 3:12,16-19)

Heb 4:1 Therefore, since the promise of entering his rest still stands, let us be careful that none of you be found to have fallen short of it. **2**For we also have had the gospel preached to us, just as they did; but the message they heard was of no value to them, because those who heard did not

combine it with faith. **3**Now we who have believed enter that rest, just as God has said,

"So I declared on oath in my anger, 'They shall never enter my rest.'" And yet his work has been finished since the creation of the world.

Heb 4:6 It still remains that some will enter that rest, and those who formerly had the gospel preached to them did not go in, because of their disobedience.

Heb 4:11 Let us, therefore, make every effort to enter that rest, so that no one will fall by following their example of disobedience.

Heb 12:25 See to it that you do not refuse him who speaks. If they did not escape when they refused him who warned them on earth, how much less will we, if we turn away from him who warns us from heaven?

Illustrated:

Ro 10:6 But the righteousness that is by faith says: "Do not say in your heart, 'Who will ascend into heaven?'" (that is, to bring Christ down) **7**"or 'Who will descend into the deep?'" (that is, to bring Christ up from the dead).

Ro 10:16 But not all the Israelites accepted the good news. For Isaiah says, "Lord, who has believed our message?"

2Pe 3:4 They will say, "Where is this 'coming' he promised? Ever since our fathers died, everything goes on as it has since the beginning of creation."

Parable of (Mk 4:24-25)—

Lk 8:12 Those along the path are the ones who hear, and then the devil comes and takes away the word from their hearts, so that they may not believe and be saved.

Lk 8:18 Therefore consider carefully how you listen. Whoever has will be given more; whoever does not have, even what he thinks he has will be taken from him."

Lk 14:16 Jesus replied: "A certain man was preparing a great banquet and invited many guests. **17**At the time of the banquet he sent his servant to tell those who had been invited, 'Come, for everything is now ready.'

18"But they all alike began to make excuses. The first said, 'I have just bought a field, and I must go and see it. Please excuse me.'

19"Another said, 'I have just bought five yoke of oxen, and I'm on my way to try them out. Please excuse me.'

20"Still another said, 'I just got married, so I can't come.'

21"The servant came back and reported this to his master. Then the owner of the house became angry and ordered his servant, 'Go out quickly into the streets and alleys of the town and bring in the poor, the crippled, the blind and the lame.'

22"'Sir,' the servant said, 'what you ordered has been done, but there is still room.'

23"Then the master told his servant, 'Go out to the roads and country lanes and make them come in, so that my house will be full. **24**I tell you, not one of those men who were invited will get a taste of my banquet.'"

At Christ's second coming—

Lk 18:8 I tell you, he will see that they get justice, and quickly. However, when the Son of Man comes, will he find faith on the earth?"

The spirit of the antichrist—

1Jn 2:22 Who is the liar? It is the man who denies that Jesus is the Christ. Such a man is the antichrist—he denies the Father and the Son. **23**No one who denies the Son has the Father; whoever acknowledges the Son has the Father also.

1Jn 4:3 but every spirit that does not acknowledge Jesus is not from God. This is the spirit of the antichrist, which you have heard is coming and even now is already in the world.

Used as an excuse by Moses—

Ex 4:1 Moses answered, "What if they do not believe me or listen to me and say, 'The LORD did not appear to you'?"

UNBELIEVERS [578, 602, 603].

NIV+ See UNBELIEF

Are spiritually blind (Jn 14:17; 1Co 2:14; 2Pe 3:4-7). Are impure (Tit 1:15). Make God a liar (1Jn 5:10). Will not be convinced (Lk 16:31; 22:67; Jn 4:48; 12:37-40). God's forbearance toward (Ro 10:16,21). Shall be destroyed (Jer 5:12-14; Mt 10:14-15; Lk 12:46; Jn 8:24; 12:48; Ac 13:41; 1Co 1:18; 2Th 2:11-12; Jude 5-7; Rev 21:8). Tongues a sign to (1Co 14:22).

Instances of:

Eve (Ge 3:4-6). Moses (Nu 11:21-23) and Aaron (Nu 20:12). Israelites (Dt 9:23; 2Ki 17:14; Ps 78; 106:7,24; Isa 58:3; Mal 1:2,7). Naaman (2Ki 5:12). Samaritan lord (2Ki 7:2). Disciples (Mt 17:17; Lk 24:11,25). Zechariah (Lk 1:20). Chief priests (Mt 21:32; Lk 22:67). The Jews (Mt 11:16-19; Mk 1:45; 2:6-11; 8:11-12; 15:29-32; Lk 7:31-35; Jn 5:38,40,43,46-47; Ac 22:18; 28:24). Disciples (Mt 17:20; Mk 4:38,40; 16:14,16; Lk 24:11,21,25-26,36-45; Jn 6:36,60-62,64,66,70-71). The father of a child possessed with a spirit confesses (Mk 9:24). Brothers of Christ (Jn 7:5). Thomas (Jn 20:25). Jews of Iconium (Ac 14:2). Thessalonian Jews (Ac 17:5). Jews in Jerusalem (Ro 15:31). Ephesians (Ac 19:9). Saul (1Ti 1:13). People of Jericho (Heb 11:31).

UNBELIEVING ISRAELITES Destroyed (Nu 14:11,13-39; 32:11; Dt 1:34-35; Ps 95:11; 106:26; 1Co 10:5,10; Heb 3:17; Jude 5).

UNBLEMISHED [320]. Offerings must be (Ex 12:5; Lev 22:21; Eph 5:27; 1Pe 1:19).

UNCHARITABLENESS

Isa 29:21 those who with a word make a man out to be guilty, who ensnare the defender in court and with false testimony deprive the innocent of justice.

Admonitions against:

Mt 7:1 "Do not judge, or you too will be judged. ²For in the same way you judge others, you will be judged, and with the measure you use, it will be measured to you.

³"Why do you look at the speck of sawdust in your brother's eye and pay no attention to the plank in your own eye? ⁴How can you say to your brother, 'Let me take the speck out of your eye,' when all the time there is a plank in your own eye? ⁵You hypocrite, first take the plank out of your own eye, and then you will see clearly to remove the speck from your brother's eye. (+Lk 6:37-42)

Lk 12:57 "Why don't you judge for yourselves what is right?

Jn 7:24 Stop judging by mere appearances, and make a right judgment."

Jn 8:7 When they kept on questioning him, he straightened up and said to them, "If any one of you is without sin, let him be the first to throw a stone at her."

Ro 2:1 You, therefore, have no excuse, you who pass judgment on someone else, for at whatever point you judge the other, you are condemning yourself, because you who pass judgment do the same things.

Ro 14:1 Accept him whose faith is weak, without passing judgment on disputable matters. ²One man's faith allows him to eat everything, but another man, whose faith is weak, eats only vegetables. ³The man who eats everything must not look down on him who does not, and the man who does not eat everything must not condemn the man who does, for God has accepted him. ⁴Who are you to judge someone else's servant? To his own master he stands or falls. And he will stand, for the Lord is able to make him stand.

⁵One man considers one day more sacred than another; another man considers every day alike. Each one should be fully convinced in his own mind. ⁶He who regards one day as special, does so to the Lord. He who eats meat, eats to the Lord, for he gives thanks to God; and he who abstains, does so to the Lord and gives thanks to God. ⁷For none of us lives to himself alone and none of us dies to himself alone. ⁸If we live, we live to the Lord; and if we die, we die to the Lord. So, whether we live or die, we belong to the Lord.

⁹For this very reason, Christ died and returned to life so that he might be the Lord of both the dead and the living. ¹⁰You, then, why do you judge your brother? Or why do you look down on your brother? For we will all stand before God's judgment seat. ¹¹It is written:

"'As surely as I live,' says the Lord, 'every knee will bow before me; every tongue will confess to God.'"

¹²So then, each of us will give an account of himself to God.

¹³Therefore let us stop passing judgment on one another. Instead, make up your mind not to put any stumbling block or obstacle in your brother's way. ¹⁴As one who is in the Lord Jesus, I am fully convinced that no food is unclean in itself. But if anyone regards something as unclean, then for him it is unclean. ¹⁵If your brother is distressed because of what you eat, you are no longer acting in love. Do not by your eating destroy your brother for whom Christ died.

1Co 4:3 I care very little if I am judged by you or by any human court; indeed, I do not even judge myself. ⁴My conscience is clear, but that does not make me innocent. It is the Lord who judges me. ⁵Therefore judge nothing before the appointed time; wait till the Lord comes. He will bring to light what is hidden in darkness and will expose the motives of men's hearts. At that time each will receive his praise from God.

1Co 4:7 For who makes you different from anyone else? What do you have that you did not receive? And if you did receive it, why do you boast as though you did not?

1Co 13:1 If I speak in the tongues of men and of angels, but have not love, I am only a resounding gong or a clanging cymbal. ²If I have the gift of prophecy and can fathom all mysteries and all knowledge, and if I have a faith that can move mountains, but have not love, I am nothing. ³If I give all I possess to the poor and surrender my body to the flames, but have not love, I gain nothing.

⁴Love is patient, love is kind. It does not envy, it does not boast, it is not proud. ⁵It is not rude, it is not self-seeking, it is not easily angered, it keeps no record of wrongs. ⁶Love does not delight in evil but rejoices with the truth.

Forbidden:

Jas 4:11 Brothers, do not slander one another. Anyone who speaks against his brother or judges him speaks against the law and judges it. When you judge the law, you are not keeping it, but sitting in judgment on it. ¹²There is only one Lawgiver and Judge, the one who is able to save and destroy. But you—who are you to judge your neighbor?

See Accusation, False; Charitableness; Judgment; Slander; Speaking, Evil; Talebearer.

Instances of:

The Israelites toward Moses, charging him with having made them abhorred by the Egyptians (Ex 5:21), charging him with bringing them out of Egypt to die (Ex 14:11-12), in murmuring against Moses. *See Murmuring, Instances of.*

The tribes west of Jordan toward the two and a half tribes (Nu 32:1-33; Jos 22:11-31). Of Eli toward Hannah (1Sa 1:14-17).

Eliab toward David, charging him with presumption, when he offered to fight Goliath (1Sa 17:28). Princes of Ammon toward David, when he sent commissioners to convey his sympathy to Hanun (2Sa 10:3). Bildad toward Job (Job 8). Eliphaz toward Job (Job 15; 22; 42:7-8). Zophar toward Job (Job 11:1-6; 20). Nathanael, when he said, "Can any good thing come out of Nazareth" (Jn 1:46). The Jews, charging Paul with teaching contrary to the law and against the temple (Ac 21:28).

UNCIAL LETTERS A style of handwriting that uses capitals for most letters. Early Greek manuscripts of the NT were written in uncials.

UNCIRCUMCISED [6888, *213+*, *598*, *2177*].

NIV+ UNCIRCUMCISION

1. One who has not submitted to the Jewish rite of circumcision.

2. Gentiles (Ge 34:14; Jdg 14:3; Ro 4:9).

3. One whose heart is not open to God (Jer 4:4; 6:10; Ac 7:51).

UNCLE [278, 1856].

NIV+ UNCLE'S

1. Brother of one's father or mother (2Ki 24:17).

2. Any kinsman on father's side (Lev 10:4; Am 6:10).

UNCLEAN, UNCLEANNESS [*1458, 3237, 3238, 3240, 5614, 7002, *176*, *3123*, *3124*].

1. Two kinds of uncleanness: Moral and ceremonial.

2. Foods regarded as unclean in the OT: Animals that did not chew the cud and have a split hoof; animals and birds that eat blood or carrion; anything strangled or that died of itself (Lev 11:1-8,26-28); water creatures without scales and fins (Lev 11:9-12); insects without hind legs for jumping (Lev 11).

3. Other forms of ceremonial uncleanness; contact with the dead (Lev 11:24-40; 17:15; Nu 19:16-22), leprosy (Lev 13; 14; Nu 5:2), sexual discharge (Lev 15:16-33), childbirth (Lev 12:6-8). In Christianity uncleanness is moral, not ceremonial.

See Purification.

UNCLOTHED [*1694*]. Figurative (Mt 22:11; 2Co 5:3; Rev 3:17; 16:15).

UNCTION *See Anointing.*

UNDEFILED Any person or thing not tainted with moral evil (Ps 119:1; Heb 7:26; 13:4; 1Pe 1:4).

UNDERGARMENTS [4829, *5945*]. For the priests (Ex 28:42; 39:28; Lev 6:10; 16:4; Eze 44:18). Of Jesus (Jn 19:23). *See Dress.*

UNDERSETTERS NIV "Supports" for the movable stands in Solomon's temple (1Ki 7:30,34).

UNFAITHFULNESS [574+4202, 953, 957, 2388, 2393, 2394, 3950, 5085, 5086, 5538, 8745, *4518*].

NIV+ UNFAITHFUL, UNFAITHFULLY

Characteristics of:

Unfaithful in little, unfaithful in much—

Lk 16:10 "Whoever can be trusted with very little can also be trusted with much, and whoever is dishonest with very little will also be dishonest with much. 11So if you have not been trustworthy in handling worldly wealth, who will trust you with true riches? 12And if you have not been trustworthy with someone else's property, who will give you property of your own?

Brings spiritual bankruptcy—

Mt 13:12 Whoever has will be given more, and he will have an abundance. Whoever does not have, even what he has will be taken from him. (+Mt 25:29)

Brings destruction—

Jn 15:2 He cuts off every branch in me that bears no fruit, while every branch that does bear fruit he prunes so that it will be even more fruitful.

Brings condemnation (Lk 19:12-27; Mt 25:41-46).

God rewards accordingly—

Pr 24:11 Rescue those being led away to death; hold back those staggering toward slaughter. 12If you say, "But we knew nothing about this," does not he who weighs the heart perceive it? Does not he who guards your life know it? Will he not repay each person according to what he has done?

Mt 25:8 The foolish ones said to the wise, 'Give us some of your oil; our lamps are going out.'

9"'No,' they replied, 'there may not be enough for both us and you. Instead, go to those who sell oil and buy some for yourselves.'

10"But while they were on their way to buy the oil, the bridegroom arrived. The virgins who were ready went in with him to the wedding banquet. And the door was shut.

11"Later the others also came. 'Sir! Sir!' they said. 'Open the door for us!'

12"But he replied, 'I tell you the truth, I don't know you.'

13"Therefore keep watch, because you do not know the day or the hour.

Mt 25:24 "Then the man who had received the one talent came. 'Master,' he said, 'I knew that you are a hard man, harvesting where you have not sown and gathering where you have not scattered seed. 25So I was afraid and went out and hid your talent in the ground. See, here is what belongs to you.'

26"His master replied, 'You wicked, lazy servant! So you knew that I harvest where I have not sown and gather where I have not scattered seed? 27Well then, you should have put my money on deposit with the bankers, so that when I returned I would have received it back with interest.

28"'Take the talent from him and give it to the one who has the ten talents. 29For everyone who has will be given more, and he will have an abundance. Whoever does not have, even what he has will be taken from him. 30And throw that worthless servant outside, into the darkness, where there will be weeping and gnashing of teeth.'

Mt 25:41 "Then he will say to those on his left, 'Depart from me, you who are cursed, into the eternal fire prepared for the devil and his angels. 42For I was hungry and you gave me nothing to eat, I was thirsty and you gave me nothing to drink, 43I was a stranger and you did not invite me in, I needed clothes and you did not clothe me, I was sick and in prison and you did not look after me.'

44"They also will answer, 'Lord, when did we see you hungry or thirsty or a stranger or needing clothes or sick or in prison, and did not help you?'

45"He will reply, 'I tell you the truth, whatever you did not do for one of the least of these, you did not do for me.'

46"Then they will go away to eternal punishment, but the righteous to eternal life."

Denounced:

In the parables of the vineyard—

Isa 5:1 I will sing for the one I love a song about his vineyard: My loved one had a vineyard on a fertile hillside. 2He dug it up and cleared it of stones and planted it with the choicest vines. He built a watchtower in it and cut out a winepress as well. Then he looked for a crop of good grapes, but it yielded only bad fruit.

3"Now you dwellers in Jerusalem and men of Judah, judge between me and my vineyard. 4What more could have been done for my vineyard than I have done for it? When I looked for good grapes, why did it yield only bad? 5Now I will tell you what I am going to do to my vineyard: I will take away its hedge, and it will be destroyed; I will break down its wall, and it will be trampled. 6I will make it a wasteland, neither pruned nor cultivated, and briers and thorns will grow there. I will command the clouds not to rain on it."

7The vineyard of the LORD Almighty is the house of Israel, and the men of Judah are the garden of his delight. And he looked for justice, but saw bloodshed; for righteousness, but heard cries of distress.

Mt 21:33 "Listen to another parable: There was a landowner who planted a vineyard. He put a wall around it, dug a winepress in it and built a watchtower. Then he rented the vineyard to some farmers and went away on a journey. 34When the harvest time approached, he sent his servants to the tenants to collect his fruit.

35"The tenants seized his servants; they beat one, killed another, and stoned a third. 36Then he sent other servants to them, more than the first time, and the tenants treated them the same way. 37Last of all, he sent his son to them. 'They will respect my son,' he said.

38"But when the tenants saw the son, they said to each other, 'This is the heir. Come, let's kill him and take his inheritance.' 39So they took him and threw him out of the vineyard and killed him.

40"Therefore, when the owner of the vineyard comes, what will he do to those tenants?"

41"He will bring those wretches to a wretched end," they replied, "and he will rent the vineyard to other tenants, who will give him his share of the crop at harvest time."

42Jesus said to them, "Have you never read in the Scriptures:

"'The stone the builders rejected has become the capstone; the Lord has done this, and it is marvelous in our eyes'?

43"Therefore I tell you that the kingdom of God will be taken away from you and given to a people who will produce its fruit. (+Mk 12:1-9)

In the parable of the empty vine—

Hos 10:1 Israel was a spreading vine; he brought forth fruit for himself. As his fruit increased, he built more altars; as his land prospered, he adorned his sacred stones. 2Their heart is deceitful, and now they must bear their guilt. The LORD will demolish their altars and destroy their sacred stones.

In the parable of the slothful servant (Mt 25:24-30; Lk 19:20-27).

Illustrated:

By the unfruitful tree—

Mt 3:10 The ax is already at the root of the trees, and every tree that does not produce good fruit will be cut down and thrown into the fire. (+Mk 11:13-14)

By the unfruitful branch (Jn 15:2,4,6)

By blindness—

2Pe 1:8 For if you possess these qualities in increasing measure, they will keep you from being ineffective and unproductive in your knowledge of our Lord Jesus Christ. 9But if anyone does not have them, he is nearsighted and blind, and has forgotten that he has been cleansed from his past sins.

See Sin, Fruits of; Unfruitfulness; also, Righteousness, Fruits of.

Of friends: *See Friends, False.*

UNFRUITFULNESS [182].

NIV+ UNFRUITFUL

Punished:

Parable of the unfruitful vineyard (Isa 5:1-10)

Mt 3:10 The ax is already at the root of the trees, and every tree that does not produce good fruit will be cut down and thrown into the fire. (+Lk 3:9)

Mt 7:19 Every tree that does not bear good fruit is cut down and thrown into the fire. (+Mt 13:3)

Mt 13:4 As he was scattering the seed, some fell along the path, and the birds came and ate it up. 5Some fell on rocky places, where it did not have much soil. It sprang up quickly, because the soil was shallow. 6But when the sun came up, the plants were scorched, and they withered because they had no root. 7Other seed fell among thorns, which grew up and choked the plants. (+Mk 4:3-7,14-19; Lk 8:4-14)

Mt 21:19 Seeing a fig tree by the road, he went up to it but found nothing on it except leaves. Then he said to it, "May you never bear fruit again!" Immediately the tree withered.

20When the disciples saw this, they were amazed. "How did the fig tree wither so quickly?" they asked. (+Mk 11:13; Lk 3:9)

Lk 13:6 Then he told this parable: "A man had a fig tree, planted in his vineyard, and he went to look for fruit on it, but did not find any. 7So he said to the man who took care of the vineyard, 'For three years now I've been coming to look for fruit on this fig tree and haven't found any. Cut it down! Why should it use up the soil?' 8"'Sir,' the man replied, 'leave it alone for one more year, and I'll dig around it and fertilize it. 9If it bears fruit next year, fine! If not, then cut it down.'"

Jn 15:2 He cuts off every branch in me that bears no fruit, while every branch that does bear fruit he prunes so that it will be even more fruitful.

Jn 15:4 Remain in me, and I will remain in you. No branch can bear fruit by itself; it must remain in the vine. Neither can you bear fruit unless you remain in me.

Jn 15:6 If anyone does not remain in me, he is like a branch that is thrown away and withers; such branches are picked up, thrown into the fire and burned.

See Sin, Fruits of; Unfaithfulness; also, Righteousness, Fruits of.

UNGODLY [2868, 2869, 2870, 2883+4202, 8401, *96*, *813*, *814*, *815*].

NIV+ UNGODLINESS

To be avoided (Ps 1:1). Seem to materially prosper (Ps 73:11). Judged (Ps 1:6; 3:7; 2Pe 3:7). Christ died for (Ro 5:6), therefore God justifies (Ro 4:5). Law made for (1Ti 1:9).

See Wicked.

UNICORN *See Wild Ox.*

UNION [2482, *1182*].

NIV+ REUNITED, UNISON, UNITE, UNITED, UNITES, UNITY

Advantages of (Pr 15:22; Ecc 4:9-12).

Of the righteous: *See Unity, Of the Righteous; Righteous, Union of, with Christ.*

UNITY [285, 3480, *1651*, *1942*].

NIV+ See UNITE

Of the Godhead: *See God, Unity of.*

Of the righteous:

Advantages of (Pr 15:22; Ecc 4:9-12).

Fraternal—

Mt 23:8 "But you are not to be called 'Rabbi,' for you have only one Master and you are all brothers.

Of the righteous—

Ps 133:1 How good and pleasant it is when brothers live together in unity!

Isa 52:8 Listen! Your watchmen lift up their voices; together they shout for joy. When the LORD returns to Zion, they will see it with their own eyes.

Ac 4:32 All the believers were one in heart and mind. No one claimed that any of his possessions was his own, but they shared everything they had.

Commanded among Christians—

Ro 12:16 Live in harmony with one another. Do not be proud, but be willing to associate with people of low position. Do not be conceited.

Ro 14:19 Let us therefore make every effort to do what leads to peace and to mutual edification.

Ro 15:5 May the God who gives endurance and encouragement give you a spirit of unity among yourselves as you follow Christ Jesus, ⁶so that with one heart and mouth you may glorify the God and Father of our Lord Jesus Christ.

1Co 1:10 I appeal to you, brothers, in the name of our Lord Jesus Christ, that all of you agree with one another so that there may be no divisions among you and that you may be perfectly united in mind and thought.

2Co 13:11 Finally, brothers, good-by. Aim for perfection, listen to my appeal, be of one mind, live in peace. And the God of love and peace will be with you.

Eph 4:3 Make every effort to keep the unity of the Spirit through the bond of peace.

Php 1:27 Whatever happens, conduct yourselves in a manner worthy of the gospel of Christ. Then, whether I come and see you or only hear about you in my absence, I will know that you stand firm in one spirit, contending as one man for the faith of the gospel

Php 2:2 then make my joy complete by being like-minded, having the same love, being one in spirit and purpose.

Php 3:16 Only let us live up to what we have already attained.

¹⁷Join with others in following my example, brothers, and take note of those who live according to the pattern we gave you.

1Pe 3:8 Finally, all of you, live in harmony with one another; be sympathetic, love as brothers, be compassionate and humble.

Christ's prayer for, of the church (Jn 17:11,21-23).

See Communion; Fellowship; One Another.

UNKNOWN GOD Inscription on an altar at Athens dedicated to an unknown god that worshipers did not want to overlook (Ac 17:23).

UNKNOWN TONGUE KJV "unknown" is a translator's insertion (in italics) for the term normally rendered simply "tongues" (1Co 14:2,4,13-14,19,27). *See Tongues, Gift of.*

UNLEARNED Illiterate (Ac 4:13; 2Pe 3:16), nonprofessional (1Co 14:16,23f).

UNLEAVENED [5174, *109*]. Unmixed with yeast (1Co 5:7-8).

UNLEAVENED BREAD Bread made without yeast (Ex 12:8).

UNLEAVENED BREAD, FEAST OF *See Feasts.*

UNNI [6716] (*Yahweh has answered*).

1. A Levite; musician (1Ch 15:18,20).

2. A Levite; musician (Ne 12:9).

UNPARDONABLE SIN Blasphemy against the Holy Spirit (Mt 12:31-32; Mk 3:28-29; Lk 12:10); either attributing to Satan the work of the Holy Spirit through Jesus, or rejecting the testimony of the Holy Spirit regarding the person and work of Jesus Christ. Possibly the same as the sin that leads to death (1Jn 5:16-17).

Instances of unpardoned sin: Israel (Nu 14:26-45), Eli's house (1Sa 3:14).

UNSELFISHNESS

Commanded:

In the royal law—

Jas 2:8 If you really keep the royal law found in Scripture, "Love your neighbor as yourself," you are doing right.

In the church—

Ro 12:10 Be devoted to one another in brotherly love. Honor one another above yourselves.

Ro 15:1 We who are strong ought to bear with the failings of the weak and not to please ourselves.

1Co 10:24 Nobody should seek his own good, but the good of others. (+Gal 6:2)

Php 2:3 Do nothing out of selfish ambition or vain conceit, but in humility consider others better than yourselves. ⁴Each of you should look not only to your own interests, but also to the interests of others.

Inspired by:

Love—

1Co 13:4 Love is patient, love is kind. It does not envy, it does not boast, it is not proud. ⁵It is not rude, it is not self-seeking, it is not easily angered, it keeps no record of wrongs.

Jesus' love—

2Co 5:14 For Christ's love compels us, because we are convinced that one died for all, and therefore all died. ¹⁵And he died for all, that those who live should no longer live for themselves but for him who died for them and was raised again.

Instances of:

Abraham (Ge 13:9; 14:23-24). King of Sodom (Ge 14:21). Hittites (Ge 23:6,11). Judah (Ge 44:33-34). Moses (Nu 11:29; 14:12-19). Gideon (Jdg 8:22-23). Saul (1Sa 11:12-13). Jonathan (1Sa 23:17-18). David (1Sa 24:17; 2Sa 15:19-20; 23:16-17; 1Ch 21:17; Ps 69:6). Araunah (2Sa 24:22-24). Nehemiah (Ne 5:14-18). Jews (Est 9:15). Daniel (Da 5:17). Jonah (Jnh 1:12-13). Joseph (Mt 1:19).

Jesus—

Ro 15:3 For even Christ did not please himself but, as it is written: "The insults of those who insult you have fallen on me."

2Co 8:9 For you know the grace of our Lord Jesus Christ, that though he was rich, yet for your sakes he became poor, so that you through his poverty might become rich.

The disciples (Ac 4:34-35). Priscilla and Aquila (Ro 16:3-4).

Paul—

1Co 10:33 even as I try to please everybody in every way. For I am not seeking my own good but the good of many, so that they may be saved. (+Php 1:18; 4:17; 2Th 3:8)

Philemon (Phm 13-14). Onesiphorus (2Ti 1:16-18).

See Charitableness; Fellowship; Fraternity; Selfishness.

UNTEMPERED MORTAR *See Whitewash.*

UNWORTHINESS [7781, 7837, *397, 945*].

NIV+ UNWORTHY

(Mt 10:37; 22:8; Ac 13:46).

UPHARSIN *See Parsin.*

UPHAZ [233]. A place where gold was obtained (Jer 10:9; Da 10:5), location unknown. Perhaps "Ophir" should be read. *See Ophir, 2.*

UPPER CHAMBER, UPPER ROOM [6608, *333*]. A room built on the wall or roof of a house (1Ki 17:19; Ac 20:9); scene of the Lord's Last Supper (Mk 14:15; Lk 22:12).

UPPER EGYPT [7356]. Pathros; southern Egypt. Israelite captives in (Isa 11:11, ftn; Jer 44:1,15; Eze 29:14). Prophecy against (Eze 30:14). *See Egypt.*

UPRIGHTNESS [2341, 3837, 3838, 3841, 3842, 4793, 4797, 5791, 5893, 6641, 7404, *1465, 1469*].

NIV+ UPRIGHT, UPRIGHTLY, UPRIGHTS

See Righteousness.

UR [243, 244] (*flame, light*). Father of Eliphal (1Ch 11:35). Possibly the same as Ahasbai (2Sa 23:34). *See Ahasbai.*

UR OF THE CHALDEANS, UR OF THE CHALDEES A city in S Mesopotamia, c. 140 miles SE of old Babylon; the early home of Abraham (Ge 11:28,31; 15:7; Ne 9:7).

URBANUS, URBANE [4042] (*refined, elegant*). A Roman Christian (Ro 16:9).

URI [247, 788] (*Yahweh is [my] flame, light*).

1. The father of Bezalel (Ex 31:2; 35:20; 38:22; 1Ch 2:20; 2Ch 1:5).

2. The father of Geber (1Ki 4:19).

3. The temple gatekeeper who divorced his foreign wife (Ezr 10:24).

URIAH, URIAS, URIJAH [249, 250, *4043*] (*Yahweh is [my] flame, light*).

NIV+ URIAH'S

1. A Hittite; the husband of Bathsheba (2Sa 11:3).

2. High priest during the reign of Ahaz of Judah, for whom he built a pagan altar in the temple (2Ki 16:10-16).

3. A priest who aided Ezra (Ne 8:4).

4. The father of Meremoth (Ezr 8:33; Ne 3:4).

5. The son of Shemaiah, a prophet of Kiriath Jearim, in the time of Jehoiakim. Prophesies against Judah (Jer 26:20). Fled to Egypt; taken; slain by Jehoiakim (Jer 26:21-23).

URIEL [248] (*God [El] is [my] flame, light*).

1. A Kohathite Levite (1Ch 6:24).

2. A chief of the Kohathites who assisted in bringing the ark from the house of Obed-Edom (1Ch 15:5,11).

3. The father of Maacah, wife of Rehoboam (2Ch 13:2, ftn).

URIJAH *See Uriah, Urias, Urijah.*

URIM AND THUMMIM [242] (*lights and perfections*). Signifying light and perfection. In the breastplate (Ex 28:30; Lev 8:8). Eleazar to ask counsel for Joshua, after the judgment of (Nu 27:21). Priests only might interpret (Dt 33:8; Ezr 2:63; Ne 7:65). Israelites consult (Jdg 1:1; 20:18,23). Withheld answer from King Saul (1Sa 28:6).

USURPATION

Of Political Functions:

By Absalom (2Sa 15:1-12). By Adonijah (1Ki 1:5-9). By Baasha (1Ki 15:27-28). By Zimri (1Ki 16:9-10). By Jehu (2Ki 9:11-37). By Athaliah (2Ki 11:1-16). By Shallum (2Ki 15:10). *See Rebellion.*

In Ecclesiastical Affairs:

By Saul, in assuming priestly functions (1Sa 13:8-14). By Solomon, in thrusting Abiathar out of the priesthood (1Ki 2:26-27). By Uzziah, in assuming priestly offices (2Ch 26:16-21). By Ahaz (2Ki 16:12-13).

See Church, The Body of Believers, State; Government, Ecclesiastical.

Of Executive Power:

In ordering Naboth's death and confiscation of his vineyard (1Ki 21:7-19). In the scheme of Joseph to dispossess the Egyptians of their real and personal property (Ge 47:13-26). Of Pharaoh, making bondservants of the Israelites (Ex 1:9-22). Moses accused of (Nu 16:3).

USURY [5391, 5957, 5968]. Interest, not necessarily unreasonable exaction, but all income from loans. Forbidden (Ex 22:25; Lev 25:35-37; Dt 23:19; Ps 15:5; Pr 28:8; Jer 15:10; Eze 18:8,13,17; 22:12). Exaction of, rebuked (Ne 5:1-13). Authorized, of strangers (Dt 23:20). Exacted by the Jews (Eze 22:12).

Just men innocent of the vice of requiring (Eze 18:8).

See Interest; Money.

UTHAI [6433] (possibly *superiority of Yahweh* IDB; possibly *[my] restoration* KB).

1. The son of Ammihud (1Ch 9:4).

2. A man who returned with Ezra (Ezr 8:14).

UZ [824+6420, 6419, 6420].

1. The son of Nahor (Ge 22:21).

2. The son of Aram (Ge 10:23; 1Ch 1:17).

3. The son of Dishan (Ge 36:28).

4. The country in which Job lived (Job 1:1); the site is uncertain.

UZAI [206] (*Yahweh has given ear, listened*). Father of Palal (Ne 3:25).

UZAL [207].

1. The son of Joktan (Ge 10:27; 1Ch 1:21).

2. A region, perhaps Yemen or the area between Haran and the Tigris (Eze 27:19).

UZZA [6438] (*strength*).

1. The son of Shimei (1Ch 6:29).

2. The son of Ehud (1Ch 8:7).

3. The owner or caretaker of a garden in which Manasseh and Amon were buried (2Ki 21:18,26).

4. One whose children returned under Zerubbabel (Ezr 2:49; Ne 7:51).

UZZA, GARDEN OF [6438]. A garden in which Manasseh and his son were buried (2Ki 21:18,26).

UZZAH [6438, 6446] (*strong, fierce one*). The son of Abinadab; slain for touching the ark to steady it when the oxen carrying it stumbled (2Sa 6:3-8; 1Ch 13:6-11).

UZZEN SHEERAH, UZZEN-SHERAH [267] (perhaps *ear of Sheerah*). A town built by Ephraim's daughter Sheerah (1Ch 7:24).

UZZI [6454] (*Yahweh is [my] strength*).

1. Descendant of Aaron (1Ch 6:5,51; Ezr 7:4).

2. The grandson of Issachar (1Ch 7:2-3).

3. A Benjamite (1Ch 7:7).

4. The father of Elah (1Ch 9:8).

5. An overseer of the Levites (Ne 11:22).

6. A priest in the family of Jedaiah (Ne 12:19).

UZZIA [6455] (*[my] strength* or *Yahweh is [my] strength*). One of David's mighty men (1Ch 11:44).

UZZIAH [6459, 6460, *3852*] (*Yahweh is [my] strength*). NIV+ AZARIAH, UZZIAH'S

1. Also called Azariah. The king of Judah (2Ki 14:21; 15:1-2; 2Ch 26:1,3). Rebuilds Elath (2Ki 14:22; 2Ch 26:2). Reigns righteously (2Ki 15:3; 2Ch 26:4-5). Defeats the Philistines (2Ch 26:6-7). Takes tribute from the Ammonites; strengthens the kingdom (2Ch 26:8). Strengthens the fortifications of Jerusalem (2Ch 26:9). Promotes cattle raising and agriculture (2Ch 26:10). Military establishment of (2Ch 26:11-15). Is presumptuous in burning incense; stricken with leprosy; quarantined (2Ch 26:16-21; 2Ki 15:5). Jotham regent during quarantine of (2Ki 15:5; 2Ch 26:21). Death of (2Ki 15:7; 2Ch 26:23). History of, written by Isaiah (2Ch 26:22; Isa 1:1). Earthquake in the reign of (Am 1:1; Zec 14:5). An ancestor of Jesus and listed in Matthew's record of Jesus' genealogy (Mt 1:8-9).

2. The son of Uriel (1Ch 6:24).

3. The father of Jonathan (1Ch 27:25).

4. A priest who divorced his Gentile wife (Ezr 10:21).

5. The father of Athaiah (Ne 11:4).

UZZIEL, UZZIELITES [6457, 6458] (*God [El] is [my] strength*).

1. A Kohathite Levite (Ex 6:18,22; Lev 10:4).

2. The son of Ishi; Simeonite (1Ch 4:42).

3. Head of Benjamite family (1Ch 7:7).

4. The son of Heman (1Ch 25:4), also known as Azarel (1Ch 25:18). *See Azarel, 2.*

5. A Levite who helped in cleansing the temple (2Ch 29:14-19).

6. The son of Harhaiah (Ne 3:8). Anyone descended from Uzziel, the Levite, was known as an Uzzielite (Nu 3:27; 1Ch 15:10; 26:23).

V

VAGABOND NIV "wanderer, wandering." A word used in a curse pronounced upon Cain (Ge 4:12,14), in an imprecatory prayer of David (Ps 109:10), and of professional exorcists (Ac 19:13).

VAIL *See Curtains; Veil.*

VAIN REPETITIONS *See Babbling.*

VAIZATHA, VAJEZATHA [2262] (possibly *given of the best one* BDB). The son of Haman (Est 9:9).

VALLEY, VALE [692, 1326, 1628, 5707, 6677, *5754, 5929*].

NIV+ VALLEYS

Low-lying ground; plain, ravine, gorge, a wadi (Dt 34:6; Jos 10:40; Lk 3:5).

Mentioned in Scripture:

Achor (Jos 7:24; Isa 65:10; Hos 2:15). Aijalon (Jos 10:12). Baca (Ps 84:6). Beracah (2Ch 20:26). Bokim (Jdg 2:5). Craftsmen (1Ch 4:14, ftn). Elah (1Sa 17:2; 21:9). Emek Keziz (Jos 18:21). Eshcol (Nu 32:9; Dt 1:24). Gad (2Sa 24:5). Gerar (Ge 26:17). Gibeon (Isa 28:21). Hebron (Ge 37:14). Ben Hinnom or Tophet (Jos 18:16; 2Ki 23:10; 2Ch 28:3; Jer 7:32). Hamon Gog (Eze 39:11). Iphtah El (Jos 19:14,27). Jehoshaphat or decision (Joel 3:2,14). Jericho (Dt 34:3). Jezreel (Hos 1:5). King's Valley (Ge 14:17; 2Sa 18:18). Lebanon (Jos 11:17). Megiddo (2Ch 35:22; Zec 12:11). Moab, where Moses was buried (Dt 34:6). Rephaim (Jos 15:8; 18:16; 2Sa 5:18; Isa 17:5). Salt (2Sa 8:13; 2Ki 14:17). Shaveh (Ge 14:17; 2Sa 18:18). Shittim (Joel 3:18). Siddim (Ge 14:3,8,10). Sorek (Jdg 16:4). Succoth (Ps 60:6). Zeboim (1Sa 13:18; Ne 11:34). Zephathah (2Ch 14:10). Zered (Nu 21:12).

VALLEY GATE A gate in the Jerusalem walls (Ne 2:13; 3:13; 12:31,38), location uncertain.

VALOR, VALOUR [52+4213, 2657].

NIV+ VALIANT, VALIANTLY

See Courage.

VANIAH [2264] (possibly *worthy of love* IDB). A man who divorced his foreign wife (Ezr 10:36).

VANITY [401, 448+2855, 2039, 4200+8198, 4202, 8198, 8736, 9214, 9332, *1632, 3029, 3031, 3472*].

NIV+ VAIN

1. Archaic word meaning "temporary" or "meaningless":

"Temporary, a breath." Every human is but a breath (Ps 39:5,11; 62:9; 144:4). Beauty is fleeting (Ps 39:11; Pr 31:30). Wealth acquired by lies (Pr 21:6).

"Futile, meaningless, in vain, worthless." A consequence of the fall (Ro 8:20). Human life (Job 7:16; Ecc 6:12), youth and vigor (Ecc 11:10), thoughts (Ps 94:11), help (Ps 60:11; La 4:17). Worldly wisdom (Ecc 2:15,21; 1Co 3:20), pleasure (Ecc 2:1-3,10-11), activity (Ps 39:6; 127:2), achievement (Ecc 2:11; 4:4), possessions (Ecc 2:4-11). Accumulating wealth (Ecc 2:26; 4:8), love of wealth (Ecc 5:10; 6:2). Everything (Ecc 1:2). Foolish controversies (1Ti 1:6-7; 6:20; 2Ti 2:14,16; Tit 3:9). The conduct of

the ungodly (1Pe 1:18). The religion of hypocrites (Isa 1:13; Jas 1:26), pagans (Mt 6:7). Faith without works is (Jas 2:14).

The wicked, especially characterized by (Job 11:11). Fools follow those given to (Pr 12:11), leading to poverty (Pr 28:19). Saints hate the thoughts of (Ps 119:113), pray to be kept from (Ps 119:37; Pr 30:8), avoid (Ps 24:4), avoid those given to (Ps 26:4).

2. *See Pride.*

VASHNI KJV Samuel's firstborn (1Ch 6:28). NIV follows the LXX and supplies "Joel" as the firstborn (cf. 1Sa 6:33; 8:2; 15:17), rendering *vashni* as "the second." *See Joel, 1.*

VASHTI [2267] (*one beautiful, desired*). The wife of Xerxes; queen of Persia; divorced (Est 1:19).

VEDAN A place whose merchants traded with Tyre (Eze 27:19, NRSV). Translated as the Hebrew conjunction *vav* and the proper name Danites/Dan in the NIV and KJV. *See Dan, 2.*

VEGETARIANS Persons who eat no meat. Daniel chooses to eat only vegetables (Da 1:11-16). Christians are not to judge or be judged by diet (Ro 14).

VEGETATION [2013, 6912, 7542]. Created the third day (Ge 1:11; 2:5). For food (Ge 1:29-30).

VEIL [4485, 5003, 5029, 6260, 6486, 7539, 7581, 8304, *2820, 2821*].

NIV+ VEILED, VEILS

1. Scarf used for concealment or for protection against the elements (Ge 24:65; 1Co 11:4-16). Worn by Rebekah (Ge 24:65), by Tamar (Ge 38:14,19), by Moses, to screen his face when he descended from Mount Sinai (Ex 34:33, 35). Metaphoric of failing to understand the Gospel (2Co 3:14-18; 4:3-4)

2. *See Curtains.*

VEIN NIV "mine" for silver (Job 28:1). *See Mines, Mining.*

VENERATION For parents (Ge 48:15-16).

See Old Age; Parents; Reverence.

VENGEANCE [1947, 5933, 5934, 5935].

NIV+ AVENGE, AVENGED, AVENGER, AVENGES, AVENGING, REVENGE

Any punishment meted out in the sense of retribution (Jdg 15:7; Jer 11:20; 20:12). It belongs to God (Dt 32:35-36; Ps 94:1; Lk 18:7-8; Ro 12:19; 2Th 1:6; Heb 10:30; Rev 6:10).

Instances of:

Sons of Jacob on Hamor and Shechem (Ge 34:20-31).

See Judgments; Revenge; Retaliation.

VENISON NIV "(wild) game," taken in hunting (Ge 25:28; 27:5-33).

VENTRILOQUISM Possibly a trick of mediums and spiritists (Isa 29:4).

VERDICT [1821+5477, 5477, 6783, 10690, *3213*]. Against Jesus (Mt 26:66; 27:24-26; Mk 15:15; Lk 23:24; Jn 19:16). *See Court, Of Law.*

VERMILION *See Red.*

VERSIONS OF THE BIBLE Ancient: *See Texts and Versions.*

VESSEL [3998, 8500].

NIV+ VESSELS

Any material thing which may be used for any purpose, whether a tool, implement, weapon, or receptacle (Isa 22:24; 52:11; 66:20). A ship (Isa 2:16).

KJV "earthen vessels" is NIV "jars of clay" (2Co 4:7). *See Jar(s)*. KJV "weaker vessel" is NIV "weaker partner" (1Pe 3:7). *See Women*.

VESTMENTS [4252].

NIV+ VESTMENT

Of priests. *See Priest*.

VESTRY *See Wardrobe.*

VESTURE An archaic word for garments (Ge 41:42; Dt 22:12; Ps 22:18). Sometimes used metaphorically (Ps 102:26; Heb 1:12).

See Cloak; Clothing; Dress; Robe.

VIA DOLOROSA The traditional route which our Lord traveled on the day of his crucifixion from the judgment seat of Pilate to the place of his crucifixion (Mt 27:26,31,33).

VIAL *See Bowl.*

VICARIOUS DEATH The ram for Isaac (Ge 22:13). Jesus for sinners. *See Jesus the Christ, Death of; Mission of; Savior; Sufferings of; also, Atonement; Suffering, Vicarious.*

VICEGERENCY Imputed authority. Of Elisha, in miraculously rewarding the Shunammite (2Ki 4:16-17), in cursing Gehazi (2Ki 5:27). Of the apostles (Mt 16:19; 18:18; Jn 20:23).

VICTORIES [928+3338+5989, 1476, 2657, 3523, 3802, 3828, 3829, 4804, 5782, 9370, 9591, *3772, 3777*].

NIV+ VICTOR'S, VICTORIOUS, VICTORIOUSLY, VICTORY

In battle, from God (Ps 55:18; 76:5-6). Celebrated in song (Jdg 5; 2Sa 22), by women (1Sa 18:6-7; 2Sa 1:20). *See Armies; War.*

VICTUAL Food.

VIGILANCE [5915, 9081].

NIV+ VIGIL

Instances of: The LORD in the Exodus (Ex 12:42). King of Jericho (Jos 2:1-3). *See Watchman.*

VILLAGE [1426, 2958, 4099, 4107, 4108, 6551, 7253, *3267, 3268, 4484*].

NIV+ VILLAGES

Villages were usually grouped around a fortified town to which the people could flee in a time of war (2Ch 8:18).

VINE [339+6618, 1201+7238, 1728, 2367, 4144, 5687, 7813, 8602, 8603, *306*].

NIV+ VINES, VINEYARD, VINEYARDS, VINTAGE

Degeneracy of (Jer 2:21). Fable of (Jdg 9:12-13). Pruned (Isa 5:6; Jn 15:1-5). Parables of (Ps 80:8-14; Eze 17:6-10; 19:10-14). *See Vineyards.*

Symbolic: (Jn 15:1-5).

VINEGAR [2810, *3954*]. A sour wine. Forbidden to the Nazirites (Nu 6:3). Used with food (Ru 2:14; Ps 69:21; Pr 10:26; 25:20). Offered to Christ on the cross (Mt 27:34,48; Jn 19:29, w Mk 15:23).

VINEYARDS [1292, 4142, 4144, 9224, *307, 308*].

NIV+ VINE, VINEYARD

Origin and antiquity of (Ge 9:20). The design of planting (Ps 107:37; 1Co 9:7). Frequently walled or fenced with hedges (Nu 22:24; Pr 24:31; Isa 5:2,5). Cottages built in, for the keepers (Isa 1:8). Provided with the apparatus for making wine (Isa 5:2; Mt 21:33). The stones carefully gathered out of (Isa 5:2).

Laws Respecting:

Not to be planted with different kinds of seed (Dt 22:9). Not to be cultivated during the sabbatical year (Ex 23:11; Lev 25:4). The spontaneous fruit of, not to be gathered the sabbatical or jubilee year (Lev 25:5,11). Compensation in kind to be made for injury done to (Ex 22:5). Strangers entering, allowed to eat the fruit of, but not to take any away (Dt 23:24). The gleaning of, to be left for the poor (Lev 19:10; Dt 24:21). The fruit of new, not to be eaten for three years (Lev 19:23). The fruit of new, to be holy to the Lord in the fourth year (Lev 19:24). The fruit of new, to be eaten by the owners from the fifth year (Lev 19:25). Planters of, not liable to military service till they had eaten of the fruit (Dt 20:6). Frequently rented out to tenant farmers (SS 8:11; Mt 21:33). Rent of, frequently paid by part of the fruit (Mt 21:34). Were often mortgaged (Ne 5:3-4). Estimated rent of (SS 8:11; Isa 7:23). Estimated profit arising from, to the cultivators (SS 8:12). The poor engaged in the culture of (2Ki 25:12; Isa 61:5). Members of the family often wrought in (SS 1:6; Mt 21:28-30). Mode of hiring and paying laborers for working in (Mt 20:1-2). Of the kings of Israel superintended by officers of state (1Ch 27:27).

The Vintage or Ingathering of:

Was a time of great rejoicing (Isa 16:10). Sometimes continued to the time of the sowing seed (Lev 26:5). Failure in, occasioned great grief (Isa 16:9-10). Of red grapes particularly esteemed (Isa 27:2). The produce of, was frequently destroyed by enemies (Jer 48:32). The whole produce of, often destroyed by insects (Dt 28:39; Am 4:9). In unfavorable seasons produced but little wine (Isa 5:10; Hag 1:9,11). The wicked judicially deprived of the enjoyment of (Am 5:11; Zep 1:13). The Recabites forbidden to plant (Jer 35:7-9). Of the slothful man neglected and laid waste (Pr 24:30-31).

Illustrative:

Of Israel (Isa 5:7; 27:2; Jer 12:10; Mt 21:23).

VINEYARDS, PLAIN OF THE *See Abel Keramim.*

VINTAGE [4142].

NIV+ VINE

(Lev 26:5; Jdg 8:2; Isa 16:10; 24:13; 32:10; Jer 48:32; Mic 7:1). *See Vine; Vineyards.*

VIOL *See Lyre; Music, Instruments of.*

VIOLENCE [*2803, 2805, 6449, 7265, 8719, 1040, 1042, 44385616*].

NIV+ VIOLENT, VIOLENTLY

A cause of the Flood (Ge 6:11-13). Prayer for deliverance from (2Sa 22:49; Ps 7:9; Hab 1:2-3). Divorce (Mal 2:16). An overseer must not be (1Ti 3:3; Tit 1:7).

VIPER [6582, 7625, 7626, 9159, *835, 2399*].

NIV+ VIPER'S, VIPERS

A poisonous snake (Dt 32:24; Isa 59:5). Fastens on Paul's hand (Ac 28:3).

Figurative (Ge 49:17; Ps 140:3; Pr 23:32; Mt 3:7; 23:33; Lk 3:7).

See Adder; Cobra; Serpent.

VIRGIN [408+3359+4202, 1435, 1436, 2351+3359+5435, 6625, *4221*].

NIV+ VIRGIN'S, VIRGINITY, VIRGINS

Proofs of (Dt 22:13-21). Dowry of (Ex 22:17). Character of, to be protected (Dt 22:17-21,23-24). Betrothal of, a quasi-marriage (Dt 22:23-24). Distinguishing apparel of (2Sa 13:18). Priests might marry none but (Lev 21:14). Mourn in the temple (La 1:4; 2:10). Virginity of, bewailed (Jdg 11:37-39). Parable of the wise and foolish (Mt 25:1-13). Mother of Jesus (Isa 7:14; Mt 1:23; Lk 1:27). Advised by Paul not to marry (1Co 7).

Figurative:

Of the Church (Isa 62:5; Jer 14:17; 31:4,13; 2Co 11:2). Of personal purity (1Co 7:25,37; Rev 14:4).

VIRGIN BIRTH
The NT teaching that Jesus Christ became a human being without the mediation of an earthly father, not born by means of sexual intercourse, but as a result of the supernatural overshadowing of the Holy Spirit (Mt 1:18-25; Lk 1:26-2:7).

VIRGINITY *See Virgin.*

VIRTUE
Positive character traits (Col 3:12-14). *See Character.*

VISION [2600, 2606, 2607, 2608, 2612, 4690, 5260, 5261, 8011, 8015, 10255, 10256, *3965, 3969+3972, 3969, 3970*].

NIV+ VISIONS

A mode of revelation (Nu 12:6; 1Sa 3:1; 2Ch 26:5; Ps 89:19; Pr 29:18; Jer 14:14; 23:16; Da 1:17; Hos 12:10; Joel 2:28; Ob 1; Hab 2:2; Ac 2:17).

Of Abraham, concerning his descendants (Ge 15:1-17). Of Jacob, of the stairway with ascending and descending angels (Ge 28:12), at Beersheba (Ge 46:2). Of Joshua, of the captain of the Lord's host (Jos 5:13-15). Of Moses, of the burning bush (Ex 3:2), of the glory of God (Ex 24:9-11; 33:18-23).

Of the Israelites, of the manifestation of the glory of God (Ex 24:10,17; Heb 12:18-21). Of Balaam, in a trance. *See Balaam.* Of Elisha, at the translation of Elijah (2Ki 2:11). Of Elisha's servant, of the chariots of the Lord (2Ki 6:17). Of Micaiah, of the defeat of the Israelites; of the Lord on his throne; and of a lying spirit (1Ki 22:17-23; 2Ch 18:16-22). Of David, of the angel of the Lord by the threshing floor of Araunah (1Ch 21:15-18, ftn v.15). *See Araunah.* Of Job, of a spirit (Job 4:12-16). Of Isaiah, of the Lord and his glory in the temple (Isa 6), of the valley of vision (Isa 22). Of Jeremiah, of an almond rod (Jer 1:11), of the boiling pot (Jer 1:13).

Of Ezekiel, of the glory of God (Eze 1:3,12-14; 3:23), of the scroll (Eze 2:9), of the man of fire (Eze 8-9), of the coals of fire (Eze 10:1-7), of the dry bones (Eze 37:1-14), of the city and temple (Eze 40-48), of the waters (Eze 47:1-12).

Of Daniel, of the four beasts (Da 7), of the Ancient of Days (Da 7:9-27), of the ram and the goat (Da 8), of the angel (Da 10).

Of Amos, of grasshoppers (Am 7:1-2), of fire (Am 7:4), of a plumb line (Am 7:7-8), of summer fruit (Am 8:1-2), of the temple (Am 9:1).

Of Zechariah, of horses (Zec 1:8-11), of horns and carpenters (Zec 1:18-21), of the high priest (Zec 3:1-5), of

the golden lampstand (Zec 4), of the flying scroll (Zec 5:1-4), of the mountains and chariots (Zec 6:1-8).

Of Zechariah, in the temple (Lk 1:13-22). Of John the Baptist, at the baptism of Jesus (Mt 3:16; Mk 1:10; Lk 3:22; Jn 1:32-34). Peter, James, and John, of the transfiguration of Jesus and the appearance of Moses and Elijah (Mt 17:1-9; Lk 9:28-36). Of the people, of the tongues of fire at Pentecost (Ac 2:2-3). Of Stephen, of Christ (Ac 7:55-56). Of Paul, of Christ, on the way to Damascus (Ac 9:3-6; 1Co 9:1), of Ananias (Ac 9:12), of a man of Macedonia, saying, "Come over to Macedonia and help us" (Ac 16:9), in Corinth (Ac 18:9-10), in a trance (Ac 22:17-21), of paradise (2Co 12:1-4). Of Ananias, of Christ (Ac 9:10-12). Of Cornelius, the centurion, of an angel (Ac 10:3). Of Peter, of the sheet let down from heaven (Ac 10:9-18).

Of John on the Isle of Patmos—

Of Christ and the golden lampstands (Rev 1:10-20), the open door (Rev 4:1), a rainbow and throne (Rev 4:2-3), twenty-four elders (Rev 4:4), seven lamps (Rev 4:5), sea of glass (Rev 4:6), four living creatures (Rev 4:6-8), book with seven seals (Rev 5:1-5), golden bowls (Rev 5:8), of the six seals (Rev 6), four horses (Rev 6:2-8), earthquake and celestial phenomena (Rev 6:12-14), four angels (Rev 7:1), sealing of the 144,00 (Rev 7:2-8), of the seventh seal and seven angels (Rev 8-11), of the censer (Rev 8:5), hail and fire (Rev 8:7), mountain cast into the sea (Rev 8:8-9), falling star (Rev 8:10-11; 9:1), the third part of sun and moon and stars darkened (Rev 8:12), bottomless pit (Rev 9:2), locusts (Rev 9:3-11), four angels loosed from the Euphrates (Rev 9:14), army of horsemen (Rev 9:16-19), angel having a book (Rev 10:1-10), seven thunders (Rev 10:3-4), measurement of the temple (Rev 11:1-2), two witnesses (Rev 11:3-12), court of the Gentiles (Rev 11:2), two olive trees and two lampstands (Rev 11:4), the beast out of the bottomless pit (Rev 11:7), fall of the city (Rev 11:13), second and third woes (Rev 11:14), a woman clothed with the sun and the birth of the male child (Rev 12), a red dragon (Rev 12:4-17), war in heaven (Rev 12:7-9), the beast rising out of the sea (Rev 13:1-10), the beast coming out of the earth (Rev 13:11-18), the Lamb on Mount Zion (Rev 14:1-5), the angel having the everlasting gospel (Rev 14:6-7), the angel proclaiming the fall of Babylon (Rev 14:8-13), the Son of man with a sickle (Rev 14:14-16), an angel reaping the harvest (Rev 14:14-20), angel coming out of the temple (Rev 14:17-19), an angel having power over fire (Rev 14:18), the vine and the winepress (Rev 14:18-20), angels with the seven last plagues (Rev 15), sea of glass (Rev 15:2), temple opened (Rev 15:5), the plague upon the people who had the mark of the beast (Rev 16:2), sea turned into blood (Rev 16:3), the seven angels with the seven bowls of the wrath of God (Rev 16-17), destruction of Babylon (Rev 18), of the multitude praising (Rev 19:1-9), of him who is faithful and true riding a white horse (Rev 19:11-16), an angel in the sun (Rev 19:17-21), Satan bound a thousand years (Rev 20:1-3), thrones of judgment, and the resurrection, and the freeing of Satan (Rev 20:1-10), the great white throne (Rev 20:11), opening of the Book of Life (Rev 20:12), death and hell (Rev 20:14), New Jerusalem (Rev 21), river of life (Rev 22:1), Tree of Life (Rev 22:2). *See Revelation, Book of.*

VISITATION
A divine visit for purpose of rewarding or punishing people for their deeds (Jer 10:15; Lk 19:44; 1Pe 2:12).

VISITORS [2111, 4228].

NIV+ VISITOR

See Guest.

VOICE, OF GOD (Eze 1:24,28; 10:5; Jn 5:37; 12:28-30; Ac 7:31; 9:4,7; 26:14-15).

See Anthropomorphisms.

VOLCANOES Smoking or flaming mountains symbolic of God's presence (Dt 4:11; 5:23; Jdg 5:5; Ps 97:5; 104:32; 144:5; Isa 34:9-10; 64:1-3; Jer 51:25; Mic 1:4; Na 1:5-6).

See Earthquakes; Mountain.

VOLUPTUOUSNESS *See Lasciviousness; Sensuality.*

VOPHSI [2265]. The father of Nahbi (Nu 13:14).

VOWS [5623, 5624, 5883+6886, 7023+7198, 2376].

NIV+ VOW, VOWED

A Part of Israel's Worship:

Ps 22:25 From you comes the theme of my praise in the great assembly; before those who fear you will I fulfill my vows.

Ps 61:8 Then will I ever sing praise to your name and fulfill my vows day after day.

Ps 65:1 Praise awaits you, O God, in Zion; to you our vows will be fulfilled.

Heard by God:

Ps 61:5 For you have heard my vows, O God; you have given me the heritage of those who fear your name.

Obligatory: (Nu 30:2)

Dt 23:21 If you make a vow to the LORD your God, do not be slow to pay it, for the LORD your God will certainly demand it of you and you will be guilty of sin. ²²But if you refrain from making a vow, you will not be guilty. ²³Whatever your lips utter you must be sure to do, because you made your vow freely to the LORD your God with your own mouth.

Job 22:27 You will pray to him, and he will hear you, and you will fulfill your vows.

Ps 50:14 Sacrifice thank offerings to God, fulfill your vows to the Most High,

Ps 56:12 I am under vows to you, O God; I will present my thank offerings to you.

Ps 66:13 I will come to your temple with burnt offerings and fulfill my vows to you— ¹⁴vows my lips promised and my mouth spoke when I was in trouble.

Ps 76:11 Make vows to the LORD your God and fulfill them; let all the neighboring lands bring gifts to the One to be feared.

Ecc 5:4 When you make a vow to God, do not delay in fulfilling it. He has no pleasure in fools; fulfill your vow. ⁵It is better not to vow than to make a vow and not fulfill it.

Na 1:15 Look, there on the mountains, the feet of one who brings good news, who proclaims peace! Celebrate your festivals, O Judah, and fulfill your vows. No more will the wicked invade you; they will be completely destroyed.

In Affliction:

Ps 116:14 I will fulfill my vows to the LORD in the presence of all his people.

¹⁵Precious in the sight of the LORD is the death of his saints. ¹⁶O LORD, truly I am your servant; I am your servant, the son of your maidservant; you have freed me from my chains.

¹⁷I will sacrifice a thank offering to you and call on the name of the LORD. ¹⁸I will fulfill my vows to the LORD in the presence of all his people, ¹⁹in the courts of the house of the LORD—in your midst, O Jerusalem.

Praise the LORD.

Rash Vows:

Pr 20:25 It is a trap for a man to dedicate something rashly and only later to consider his vows.

Ecc 5:6 Do not let your mouth lead you into sin. And do not protest to the [temple] messenger, "My vow was a mistake." Why should God be angry at what you say and destroy the work of your hands?

By Jephthah (Jdg 11:29-40), by Israelites (Jdg 20:7-11).

Mosaic Laws Concerning:

Must be voluntary—

Lev 22:18 "Speak to Aaron and his sons and to all the Israelites and say to them: 'If any of you—either an Israelite or an alien living in Israel—presents a gift for a burnt offering to the LORD, either to fulfill a vow or as a freewill offering, ¹⁹you must present a male without defect from the cattle, sheep or goats in order that it may be accepted on your behalf. ²⁰Do not bring anything with a defect, because it will not be accepted on your behalf. ²¹When anyone brings from the herd or flock a fellowship offering to the LORD to fulfill a special vow or as a freewill offering, it must be without defect or blemish to be acceptable. ²²Do not offer to the LORD the blind, the injured or the maimed, or anything with warts or festering or running sores. Do not place any of these on the altar as an offering made to the LORD by fire. ²³You may, however, present as a freewill offering an ox or a sheep that is deformed or stunted, but it will not be accepted in fulfillment of a vow. ²⁴You must not offer to the LORD an animal whose testicles are bruised, crushed, torn or cut. You must not do this in your own land, ²⁵and you must not accept such animals from the hand of a foreigner and offer them as the food of your God. They will not be accepted on your behalf, because they are deformed and have defects.'" (+Lev 23:37-38)

Nu 15:2 "Speak to the Israelites and say to them: 'After you enter the land I am giving you as a home ³and you present to the LORD offerings made by fire, from the herd or the flock, as an aroma pleasing to the LORD—whether burnt offerings or sacrifices, for special vows or freewill offerings or festival offerings— ⁴then the one who brings his offering shall present to the LORD a grain offering of a tenth of an ephah of fine flour mixed with a quarter of a hin of oil. ⁵With each lamb for the burnt offering or the sacrifice, prepare a quarter of a hin of wine as a drink offering.

⁶"'With a ram prepare a grain offering of two-tenths of an ephah of fine flour mixed with a third of a hin of oil, ⁷and a third of a hin of wine as a drink offering. Offer it as an aroma pleasing to the LORD.

⁸"'When you prepare a young bull as a burnt offering or sacrifice, for a special vow or a fellowship offering to the LORD, ⁹bring with the bull a grain offering of three-tenths of an ephah of fine flour mixed with half a hin of oil. ¹⁰Also bring half a hin of wine as a drink offering. It will be an offering made by fire, an aroma pleasing to the LORD. ¹¹Each bull or ram, each lamb or young goat, is to be prepared in this manner. ¹²Do this for each one, for as many as you prepare.

¹³"'Everyone who is native-born must do these things in this way when he brings an offering made by fire as an

aroma pleasing to the LORD. [14]For the generations to come, whenever an alien or anyone else living among you presents an offering made by fire as an aroma pleasing to the LORD, he must do exactly as you do. [15]The community is to have the same rules for you and for the alien living among you; this is a lasting ordinance for the generations to come. You and the alien shall be the same before the LORD: [16]The same laws and regulations will apply both to you and to the alien living among you.'" (+Nu 29:39)

Must be performed—

Lev 5:4 "'Or if a person thoughtlessly takes an oath to do anything, whether good or evil—in any matter one might carelessly swear about—even though he is unaware of it, in any case when he learns of it he will be guilty.

[5]"'When anyone is guilty in any of these ways, he must confess in what way he has sinned [6]and, as a penalty for the sin he has committed, he must bring to the LORD a female lamb or goat from the flock as a sin offering; and the priest shall make atonement for him for his sin.

[7]"'If he cannot afford a lamb, he is to bring two doves or two young pigeons to the LORD as a penalty for his sin—one for a sin offering and the other for a burnt offering. [8]He is to bring them to the priest, who shall first offer the one for the sin offering. He is to wring its head from its neck, not severing it completely, [9]and is to sprinkle some of the blood of the sin offering against the side of the altar; the rest of the blood must be drained out at the base of the altar. It is a sin offering. [10]The priest shall then offer the other as a burnt offering in the prescribed way and make atonement for him for the sin he has committed, and he will be forgiven.

[11]"'If, however, he cannot afford two doves or two young pigeons, he is to bring as an offering for his sin a tenth of an ephah of fine flour for a sin offering. He must not put oil or incense on it, because it is a sin offering. [12]He is to bring it to the priest, who shall take a handful of it as a memorial portion and burn it on the altar on top of the offerings made to the LORD by fire. It is a sin offering. [13]In this way the priest will make atonement for him for any of these sins he has committed, and he will be forgiven. The rest of the offering will belong to the priest, as in the case of the grain offering.'"

Nu 30:2 When a man makes a vow to the LORD or takes an oath to obligate himself by a pledge, he must not break his word but must do everything he said.

[3]"When a young woman still living in her father's house makes a vow to the LORD or obligates herself by a pledge [4]and her father hears about her vow or pledge but says nothing to her, then all her vows and every pledge by which she obligated herself will stand. [5]But if her father forbids her when he hears about it, none of her vows or the pledges by which she obligated herself will stand; the LORD will release her because her father has forbidden her.

[6]"If she marries after she makes a vow or after her lips utter a rash promise by which she obligates herself [7]and her husband hears about it but says nothing to her, then her vows or the pledges by which she obligated herself will stand. [8]But if her husband forbids her when he hears about it, he nullifies the vow that obligates her or the rash promise by which she obligates herself, and the LORD will release her.

[9]"Any vow or obligation taken by a widow or divorced woman will be binding on her.

[10]"If a woman living with her husband makes a vow or obligates herself by a pledge under oath [11]and her husband hears about it but says nothing to her and does not forbid her, then all her vows or the pledges by which she obligated herself will stand. [12]But if her husband nullifies them when he hears about them, then none of the vows or pledges that came from her lips will stand. Her husband has nullified them, and the LORD will release her. [13]Her husband may confirm or nullify any vow she makes or any sworn pledge to deny herself. [14]But if her husband says nothing to her about it from day to day, then he confirms all her vows or the pledges binding on her. He confirms them by saying nothing to her when he hears about them. [15]If, however, he nullifies them some time after he hears about them, then he is responsible for her guilt."

[16]These are the regulations the LORD gave Moses concerning relationships between a man and his wife, and between a father and his young daughter still living in his house. *See above, Obligatory.* Estimation of the redemption price of things offered in vows, to be made by the priest, according to age and sex of the person making the offering (Lev 27:1-13). The redemptive price of the offering of real estate, to be valued by the priest (Lev 27:14-15), of a field (Lev 27:16-25).

Of women (Nu 30:3-16). Of Nazirites (Nu 6:1-21). Unintentional (Lev 5:4-5). Offerings devoted under (Lev 5:6-13; 7:16-18; 27:1-25; Nu 15:2-16). Things offered in, must be perfect (Lev 22:18-25).

Edible things offered in, to be eaten the same day they were offered (Lev 7:16-18). Things offered in, to be brought to the tabernacle or temple (Dt 12:6,11,17-18,26), belonged to the priests (Nu 18:14).

Things forbidden to pay a vow—

Dt 23:18 You must not bring the earnings of a female prostitute or of a male prostitute into the house of the LORD your God to pay any vow, because the LORD your God detests them both.

A minor, of himself (Mk 7:11-13).

See Contract; Covenant.

Instances of:

Of Jacob—

Ge 28:20 Then Jacob made a vow, saying, "If God will be with me and will watch over me on this journey I am taking and will give me food to eat and clothes to wear [21]so that I return safely to my father's house, then the LORD will be my God [22]and this stone that I have set up as a pillar will be God's house, and of all that you give me I will give you a tenth."

Of the mother of Micah, in the dedication of silver for the making of an idol (Jdg 17:2-3). Of Hannah, to consecrate to the Lord the child for which she prayed (1Sa 1:11, w 1:27-28). Of Elkanah (1Sa 1:21). Of Absalom (2Sa 15:7-8). Of Job, not to entertain thoughts of fornication (Job 31:1). Of David (Ps 132:2). Of Ananias and Sapphira, in the dedication of the proceeds of the sale of their land (Ac 5:1-11). Of the Jews, to kill Paul (Ac 23:12-15).

Of Jephthah, and of the Israelites. *See above, Rash Vows.*

See Nazirite(s), Nazarite(s).

VULTURE [370, 5979, 6465, 7272, *108*].

NIV+ VULTURES

The name given to several kinds of large birds of prey, usually feeding on carrion; unclean for food (Lev 11:13; Dt 14:12; Mic 1:16; Hab 1:8).

W

WADI [5707, 5711] (*ravine, valley*). A valley which forms the bed of a stream during the winter, but which dries up in the summer (Ge 26:19).

WADI OF EGYPT *See River of Egypt.*

WAFERS [7613, 8386].

NIV+ WAFER

Thin cakes (Ex 16:31; 1Ch 23:29).

WAGES [924, 5382, 7189, 7190, 8509, 8510, *1324, 3635, 4072*].

NIV+ WAGE

General:

Of Jacob (Ge 29:15-30; 30:28-34; 31:7,41). Parable concerning (Mt 20:1-15).

Laborer entitled to—

Dt 25:4 Do not muzzle an ox while it is treading out the grain. (+Mt 10:10)

Lk 10:7 Stay in that house, eating and drinking whatever they give you, for the worker deserves his wages. Do not move around from house to house.

Ro 4:4 Now when a man works, his wages are not credited to him as a gift, but as an obligation.

Must be just—

Col 4:1 Masters, provide your slaves with what is right and fair, because you know that you also have a Master in heaven.

Must be paid promptly—

Lev 19:13 "'Do not defraud your neighbor or rob him. "'Do not hold back the wages of a hired man overnight.

Dt 24:15 Pay him his wages each day before sunset, because he is poor and is counting on it. Otherwise he may cry to the LORD against you, and you will be guilty of sin.

Withholding of, denounced—

Jer 22:13 "Woe to him who builds his palace by unrighteousness, his upper rooms by injustice, making his countrymen work for nothing, not paying them for their labor.

Mal 3:5 "So I will come near to you for judgment. I will be quick to testify against sorcerers, adulterers and perjurers, against those who defraud laborers of their wages, who oppress the widows and the fatherless, and deprive aliens of justice, but do not fear me," says the LORD Almighty.

Jas 5:4 Look! The wages you failed to pay the workmen who mowed your fields are crying out against you. The cries of the harvesters have reached the ears of the Lord Almighty.

Wasting of, denounced—

Hag 1:6 You have planted much, but have harvested little. You eat, but never have enough. You drink, but never have your fill. You put on clothes, but are not warm. You earn wages, only to put them in a purse with holes in it."

Contentment with, commanded—

Lk 3:14 Then some soldiers asked him, "And what should we do?" He replied, "Don't extort money and don't accuse people falsely—be content with your pay."

Figurative:

Ro 6:23 For the wages of sin is death, but the gift of God is eternal life in Christ Jesus our Lord.

WAGON [1649, 7369].

NIV+ WAGONS

Used to carry supplies (Isa 66:20; Eze 23:24; 26:10). *See Cart, Carts.*

WAHEB [2259]. If this is a proper noun then it is an unknown place in Moab. Its meaning is uncertain (Nu 21:14).

WAIL [*1134, 3536, 3538, 5027, 5631, 7591, *3081*].

NIV+ WAILED, WAILING, WAILS

In ancient funeral processions wailing relatives and hired mourners and musicians preceded body to grave (Jer 9:17-21; Am 5:16; Mt 9:23). Of the wicked (Mt 13:42).

WAITING [*741, 2565, 2675, 3498, 3782, 4538, 5893, 6218, 6641, 7595, 7747, 8432, 9068, *587, 1354, 1683, 1910, 2705, 4657, 4659*].

NIV+ AWAIT, AWAITS, AWAITING, WAITED, WAITS

Upon God: As the God of providence (Jer 14:22), as the God of salvation (Ps 25:5), as the giver of all temporal blessings (Ps 104:27-28; 145:15-16).

For mercy (Ps 123:2), pardon (Ps 39:7-8), the consolation of Israel (Lk 2:25), salvation (Ge 49:18; Ps 62:1-2), guidance and teaching (Ps 25:5), protection (Ps 33:20; 59:9-10), the fulfillment of his word (Hab 2:3), the fulfillment of his promises (Ac 1:4), hope of righteousness by faith (Gal 5:5), coming of Christ (1Co 1:7; 1Th 1:10). Is good (Ps 52:9). God calls us to (Zep 3:8). Exhortations and encouragements to (Ps 27:14; 37:7; Hos 12:6).

Should be with the soul (Ps 62:1,5), with earnest desire (Ps 130:6), with patience (Ps 37:7; 40:1), with resignation (La 3:26), with hope in his word (Ps 130:5), with full confidence (Mic 7:7), continually (Hos 12:6), all the day (Ps 25:5), specially in adversity (Ps 59:1-9; Isa 8:17), in the way of his judgments (Isa 26:8). Saints resolve on (Ps 52:9; 59:9). Saints have expectation from (Ps 62:5). Saints plead, in prayer (Ps 25:21; Isa 33:2). The patience of saints often tried in (Ps 69:3).

They who engage in, wait upon him only (Ps 62:5), are heard (Ps 40:1), are blessed (Isa 30:18; Da 12:12), experience his goodness (La 3:24-26), shall not be ashamed (Ps 25:3; Isa 49:23), shall renew their strength (Isa 40:31), shall inherit the earth (Ps 37:9), shall be saved (Pr 20:22; Isa 25:9), shall rejoice in salvation (Isa 25:9), shall receive the glorious things prepared by God for them (Isa 64:4). Predicted of the Gentiles (Isa 42:4; 60:9). Illustrated (Ps 123:2; Lk 12:36; Jas 5:7).

Exemplified:

Jacob (Ge 49:18), David (Ps 39:7), Isaiah (Isa 8:17), Micah (Mic 7:7), Joseph (Mk 15:43).
Faith; Hope.

WALKING [*886, 2006, 2143, 6015, 6296, 7575, 10207, *1451, 4135, 4344, 4513*].

NIV+ WALK, WALKED, WALKS

With God—a Godly Lifestyle:

According to his commands (Dt 5:33; Ps 1; Jer 7:23); in his ways (Dt 28:9; Jos 22:5); in the old paths (Jer 6:16); as taught by him (1Ki 8:36; Isa 2:3; 30:21); uprightly (Pr 2:7); in his statutes and judgments (Eze 37:24); in newness of life (Ro 6:4); not after the flesh, but after the Spirit (Ro 8:1; Gal 5:16); honestly, as in the day (Ro 13:13); by faith, not by sight (2Co 5:7); in love, following Christ (Eph 5:2); worthy of the Lord (Col 1:10); in Christ (Col 2:6); by the gospel rule (Php 3:16); in the light, as God is (1Jn 1:7); in white clothing (Rev 3:4); in the light of heaven (Rev 21:24).

Instances of: Enoch (Ge 5:24), Noah (Ge 6:9).

WALLED CITIES Settlements were enclosed with walls for protection against invasion (Lev 25:29-31; 1Ki 4:13). *See Walls.*

WALLS [382, 1074, 1230, 1290, 1473, 1553, 1555, 1556, 2570, 2658, 2666, 4185, 4190, 4321, 5243, 5603, 6017, 7252, 7288, 7815, 10376, 10703, *3546, 5446, 5526, 5850*].

NIV+ WALL, WALLED

Of the cities: Of Bashan, destroyed by the Israelites (Dt 3:5-6). Of Jericho (Jos 2:15; 6). Of Jerusalem. *See Jerusalem.* Of Babylon (Jer 51:44), broad (Jer 51:58). Of Beth Shan (1Sa 31:10). Of Rabbah (2Sa 11:20). Of Abel (2Sa 20:15,21).

Houses built upon (Jos 2:15). Double (2Ki 25:4; Isa 22:11). Sentinels on. *See Watchman.*

Figurative:

Of the New Jerusalem (Rev 21:12,14,17-21).

WAR [*1741, 2995, 4309, 4878, 7304, 7372, 7930, 8131, 8569, 9558, *4482, 4483, 5129*].

NIV+ WARFARE, WARRIOR, WARRIOR'S, WARRIORS, WARS

Divine approval of (2Sa 22:35). Civil (Jdg 12:1-6; 20; 2Sa 2:12-31; 3:1; 20; 1Ki 14:30; 16:21; Isa 19:2), forbidden (2Ch 11:4), averted (Jos 22:11-34). Enemy harangued by general of opposing side (2Ki 18:19-36; 2Ch 13:4-12). Of extermination (Nu 31:7-17; Dt 2:33-34; 3:6; 20:13-18; Jos 6:21,24; 8:24-25; 10:2-40; 11:11-23; 1Sa 15:3-9; 27:8-11).

God in (Ex 14:13-14; Dt 1:30; 3:21-22; 7:17-24; 20:1,4; 31:6-8,23; 32:29-30; Jos 1:1,5-7,9; Jdg 1:2; 6:16; 7:9; 11:29; 1Sa 17:45-47; 19:5; 30:7-8; 2Sa 5:22-24; 22:18; 1Ki 20:28; Ps 18:34; 76:3; Jer 46:15; Am 5:8-9; Zec 10:5). God uses, as a judgment (Ex 23:24; Lev 26:17,31-39; Dt 28:25-68; 32:30; Jdg 2:14; 2Ki 15:37; 1Ch 5:22,26; 21:12; 2Ch 12:1-12; 15:6; 24:23-24; 33:11; 36; Job 19:29; Ps 44:9-16; 60:1-3; 105:25; Isa 5:1-8,25-30; 9:8-12; 13:3-4,9; 19:2; 34:2-6; 43:28; 45:7; Jer 12:7,12; 46:15-17,21; 47:6-7; 48:10; 49:5; 50:25; Eze 23:22-25; Am 3:6; 4:11; Zep 1:7-18; Zec 8:10; 14:2).

Repugnant to God (1Ch 22:8-9; Ps 68:30; 120:6-7; Rev 13:10). God sends panic in (Ex 15:14-16), threatens defeat in (Dt 32:25; 1Sa 2:10; 2Ch 18:12-16; Isa 30:15-17; Eze 15:6-8; 21:9-17), inflicts defeat in (Jos 7:12-13; 2Ch 12:5-8; 24:23-24; Ps 48:4-7; Pr 11:14; 20:18). Wisdom required in (Pr 21:22; 24:6; Ecc 9:14-18; Lk 14:31-32).

Tumult of (Am 2:2). Slain in, neglected (Isa 14:19; 18:6). Evils of (2Sa 2:26; Ps 46:8; 79:1-3; 137:9; Isa 3:5, 25-26; 5:29-30; 6:11-12; 9:5,19-21; 13:15-16; 15; 16:9-10; 18:6; 19:2-16; 32:13-14; 33:8-9; 34:7-15; Jer 4:19-31; 5:16-17; 6:24-26; 7:33-34; 8:16-17; 9:10-21; 10:20; 13:14; 14:18; 15:8-9; 19:7-9; 25:33; 46:3-12; 47:3; 48:28, 33; 51:30-58; La 1-5; Eze 33:27; 39:17-19; Hos 10:14; 13:16; Joel 2:2-10; Am 1:13; 6:9-10; 8:3; Na 2:10; 3:3,10; Zec 14:2; Lk 21:20-26; Rev 19:17-18).

To cease (Ps 46:9; Isa 2:4; Mic 4:3).

Wars and rumors of (Mt 24:6; Mk 13:7; Lk 21:9).

See Armies; Armor; Fort; Soldiers; Strategy; Tower; Watchman.

Figurative:

Warfare of saints: Is not after the flesh (2Co 10:3). Is a good warfare (1Ti 1:18-19). Called the good fight of faith (1Ti 6:12).

Is against the devil (Ge 3:15; 2Co 2:11; Eph 6:12; Jas 4:7; 1Pe 5:8; Rev 12:17), the flesh (Ro 7:23; 1Co 9:25-27; 2Co 12:7; Gal 5:17; 1Pe 2:11), enemies (Ps 38:19; 56:2; 59:3), the world (Jn 16:33; 1Jn 5:4-5), death (1Co 15:26, w Heb 2:14-15).

Often arises from the opposition of friends or relatives (Mic 7:6; Mt 10:35-36). To be carried on under Christ, as our Captain (Heb 2:10), under the Lord's banner (Ps 60:4), with faith (1Ti 1:18-19), with a good conscience (1Ti 1:18-19), with steadfastness in the faith (1Co 16:13; 1Pe 5:9, w Heb 10:23), with earnestness (Jude 3), with watchfulness (1Co 16:13; 1Pe 5:8), with sobriety (1Th 5:6; 1Pe 5:8), with endurance of hardness (2Ti 2:3,10), with self-denial (1Co 9:25-27), with confidence in God (Ps 27:1-3), with prayer (Ps 35:1-3; Eph 6:18), without earthly entanglements (2Ti 2:4). Mere professors do not maintain (Jer 9:3).

Saints are all engaged in (Php 1:30), must stand firm in (Eph 6:13-14), exhorted to diligence in (1Ti 6:12; Jude 3). encouraged in (Isa 41:11-12; 51:12; Mic 7:8; 1Jn 4:4), helped by God in (Ps 118:13; Isa 41:13-14), protected by God in (Ps 140:7), comforted by God in (2Co 7:5-6), strengthened by God in (Ps 20:2; 27:14; Isa 41:10), strengthened by Christ in (2Co 12:9; 2Ti 4:17), delivered by Christ in (2Ti 4:18), thank God for victory in (Ro 7:25; 1Co 15:57).

Armor for: A belt of truth (Eph 6:14), the breastplate of righteousness (Eph 6:14), readiness from the gospel (Eph 6:15), shield of faith (Eph 6:16), helmet of salvation (Eph 6:17; 1Th 5:8), sword of the Spirit (Eph 6:17). Called armor of God (Eph 6:11), weapons of righteousness (2Co 6:7), armor of light (Ro 13:12), not weapons of the world (2Co 10:4). Mighty through God (2Co 10:4-5), the whole is required (Eph 6:13), must be put on (Ro 13:12; Eph 6:11), to be on the right hand and the left (2Co 6:7).

Victory in, is from God (1Co 15:57; 2Co 2:14), through Christ (Ro 7:25; 1Co 15:57; 2Co 12:9; Rev 12:11), by faith (Heb 11:33-37; 1Jn 5:4-5), over the devil (Ro 16:20; 1Jn 2:14), over the flesh (Ro 7:24-25; Gal 5:24), over the world (1Jn 5:4-5), over all that exalts itself (2Co 10:5), over death and the grave (Isa 25:8; 26:19; Hos 13:14; 1Co 15:54-55), triumphant (Ro 8:37; 2Co 10:5).

They who overcome in, shall eat of the hidden manna (Rev 2:17), eat of the tree of life (Rev 2:7), be clothed in white garments (Rev 3:5), be pillars in the temple of God (Rev 3:12), sit with Christ in his throne (Rev 3:21), have a white stone and on it a new name written (Rev 2:17), have power over the nations (Rev 2:26), have the name of God written upon them by Christ (Rev 3:12), have God as their God (Rev 21:7), have the morning star (Rev 2:28), inherit all things (Rev 21:7), be confessed by Christ before God the Father (Rev 3:5), be sons of God (Rev 21:7), not be hurt by the second death (Rev 2:11), not have their names blotted out of the book of life (Rev 3:5).

Symbolized by a red horse (Rev 6:4).

In Heaven:

Symbolic (Rev 12:7).

WAR SONGS Celebrating the destruction of Pharaoh's army (Ex 15:1-21); victory over Sihon, king of the

Amorites (Nu 21:24-30); victory over Sisera (Jdg 5); David's victories over his enemies and his deliverance from Saul (2Sa 22).

David's lament over the defeat of Saul (2Sa 1:19-27).

WARDROBE [955, 4921]. Place where royal or ceremonial garments were kept (2Ki 10:22; 22:14; 34:22). *See Dress.*

WARFARE [4878, 6009]. *See War, Figurative; In Heaven.*

WARNING [*606, 1819, 2302, 3579, 4592, 5583, 6386, *1371, 1839, 2203, 3805, 4625, 5683, 5976*]. *See Wicked, Warned.*

WARRIORS [52, 408+2657, 1201+2657, 1475, 1476, 2514, 6008, 6883, 7250, 7251, 7940].

NIV+ See WAR

(Nu 32:17; Jos 4:13; 1Ch 8:40; 12:2,8,21; 2Ch 14:8; 17:18; 25:5; 26:13).

WARTS [3301]. Unacceptable on a sacrificial animal (Lev 22:22).

WASHERMAN'S FIELD [3891]. A field outside Jerusalem where fullers or launderers washed the cloth that they were processing (2Ki 18:17; Isa 7:3; 36:2).

WASHING [1342, 8175, 8177, *968, 2752, 3373, 3782, 4459*].

NIV+ WASH, WASHED, WASHERMAN'S, WASHINGS, WHITEWASH, WHITEWASHED

Of hands, a token of innocency (Dt 21:6; Ps 26:6; 73:13; Mt 27:24).

See Washing; Purification.

Figurative:

Of regeneration (Ps 51:7; Pr 30:12; Isa 1:16; 4:4; Zec 13:1; 1Co 6:11; Eph 5:26; Tit 3:5).

WASHINGS [*968*].

NIV+ See WASH

(Ex 19:10,14; Mt 15:2; Mk 7:2-5,8-9; Lk 11:38; Heb 9:10). Of priests (Ex 29:4; 30:18-21; 40:12,31-32; Lev 8:6; 16:4,24,26,28; Nu 19:7-10,19; 2Ch 4:6).

Of burnt offerings (Lev 1:9,13; 9:14; 2Ch 4:6). Of the dead (Ac 9:37). Of infants (Eze 16:4). Of the face (Mt 6:17). Of feet (Ge 18:4; 19:2; 24:32; 43:24; Ex 30:19,21; 40:31; Jdg 19:21; 2Sa 11:8; SS 5:3; Lk 7:38,44; Jn 13:5; 1Ti 5:10). Of hands (Ex 30:18-21; 40:30-32). Of the hands, as a token of innocency (Dt 21:6; Ps 26:6; Mt 27:24).

For defilement of, lepers (Lev 14:8-9), those having bloody issue (Lev 15:5-13), those having eaten that which died (Lev 17:15-16).

Traditions of, not observed by Jesus (Lk 11:38-39).

Figurative:

Of baptism—

Ac 22:16 And now what are you waiting for? Get up, be baptized and wash your sins away, calling on his name.'

Of believers—

1Co 6:11 And that is what some of you were. But you were washed, you were sanctified, you were justified in the name of the Lord Jesus Christ and by the Spirit of our God. (+Tit 3:5)

Heb 1:3 The Son is the radiance of God's glory and the exact representation of his being, sustaining all things by his powerful word. After he had provided purification for

sins, he sat down at the right hand of the Majesty in heaven.

Heb 9:14 How much more, then, will the blood of Christ, who through the eternal Spirit offered himself unblemished to God, cleanse our consciences from acts that lead to death, so that we may serve the living God!

2Pe 1:9 But if anyone does not have them, he is nearsighted and blind, and has forgotten that he has been cleansed from his past sins.

1Jn 1:7 But if we walk in the light, as he is in the light, we have fellowship with one another, and the blood of Jesus, his Son, purifies us from all sin.

1Jn 1:9 If we confess our sins, he is faithful and just and will forgive us our sins and purify us from all unrighteousness.

Of bodies (Heb 10:22). Of the Church (Eph 5:26). Of conscience (Heb 9:14; 10:22).

Of hands—

Ps 73:13 Surely in vain have I kept my heart pure; in vain have I washed my hands in innocence.

Jas 4:8 Come near to God and he will come near to you. Wash your hands, you sinners, and purify your hearts, you double-minded.

Of leaven (1Co 5:7). Of robes (Rev 7:14; 22:14).

Of sin:

Corporate—

Ps 79:9 Help us, O God our Savior, for the glory of your name; deliver us and forgive our sins for your name's sake.

Isa 1:16 wash and make yourselves clean. Take your evil deeds out of my sight! Stop doing wrong, (+Isa 1:18)

Isa 4:3 Those who are left in Zion, who remain in Jerusalem, will be called holy, all who are recorded among the living in Jerusalem. ⁴The Lord will wash away the filth of the women of Zion; he will cleanse the bloodstains from Jerusalem by a spirit of judgment and a spirit of fire.

Da 12:10 Many will be purified, made spotless and refined, but the wicked will continue to be wicked. None of the wicked will understand, but those who are wise will understand. (+Zec 13:1; Jn 13:8; 2Co 7:1; Rev 1:5)

General—

Pr 16:6 Through love and faithfulness sin is atoned for; through the fear of the LORD a man avoids evil.

Personal—

Ps 51:2 Wash away all my iniquity and cleanse me from my sin.

Ps 65:3 When we were overwhelmed by sins, you forgave our transgressions.

Pr 20:9 Who can say, "I have kept my heart pure; I am clean and without sin"? (+Jn 13:8; 2Pe 1:9; 1Jn 1:7,9)

By Christ, work and blood of (Eph 5:26)—

Tit 3:5 he saved us, not because of righteous things we had done, but because of his mercy. He saved us through the washing of rebirth and renewal by the Holy Spirit, ⁶whom he poured out on us generously through Jesus Christ our Savior, (+Heb 1:3; 9:14; 1Jn 1:7)

Rev 1:5 and from Jesus Christ, who is the faithful witness, the firstborn from the dead, and the ruler of the kings of the earth. To him who loves us and has freed us from our sins by his blood,

Rev 7:14 I answered, "Sir, you know." And he said, "These are they who have come out of the great tribulation; they have washed their robes and made them white in the blood of the Lamb.

See Defilement; Fuller; Purification; Regeneration; Soap.

WASTE PLACES [1429, 2999, 3810, 4497, 5118, 5409, 6858, 9014, 9039, 9332].

　NIV+ WASTELAND, WASTELANDS

　Restored (Isa 35:1; 41:19; 44:26; 49:19; 51:3; 52:9; 58:12; 61:4; Eze 36:10).

WATCH [*874, 3359, 5564, 5915, 6524, 7595, 7595, 8011, 9068, 9193, 9207, 10255, *70*, *1063*, *1213*, *2426*, *2555*, *3972*, *4190*, *4668*, *5023*, *5871*].

　NIV+ WATCHED, WATCHER, WATCHES, WATCHFUL, WATCHING, WATCHMAN, WATCHMEN

　A man or group of men set to guard a city, crops, etc. (Ne 4:9; Mt 27:62-66).

WATCHES OF THE NIGHT Divisions into which hours of the night were divided. Jews had a threefold division; Romans, fourfold (Jdg 7:19; Mk 6:48). *See Time.*

WATCHFULNESS [7219, *1213*].

　NIV+ See WATCH

Ps 102:7 I lie awake; I have become like a bird alone on a roof.

Hab 2:1 I will stand at my watch and station myself on the ramparts; I will look to see what he will say to me, and what answer I am to give to this complaint.

1Co 9:27 No, I beat my body and make it my slave so that after I have preached to others, I myself will not be disqualified for the prize.

Over the Tongue—

Ps 39:1 I said, "I will watch my ways and keep my tongue from sin; I will put a muzzle on my mouth as long as the wicked are in my presence."

Ps 141:3 Set a guard over my mouth, O LORD; keep watch over the door of my lips. (+Jas 3:5-8)

In Prayer:

Ne 4:9 But we prayed to our God and posted a guard day and night to meet this threat.

Mt 26:41 "Watch and pray so that you will not fall into temptation. The spirit is willing, but the body is weak." (+Mk 13:33)

Eph 6:18 And pray in the Spirit on all occasions with all kinds of prayers and requests. With this in mind, be alert and always keep on praying for all the saints.

Col 4:2 Devote yourselves to prayer, being watchful and thankful.

1Pe 4:7 The end of all things is near. Therefore be clear minded and self-controlled so that you can pray.

Commanded: (Dt 4:15; 6:17)

Jos 22:5 But be very careful to keep the commandment and the law that Moses the servant of the LORD gave you: to love the LORD your God, to walk in all his ways, to obey his commands, to hold fast to him and to serve him with all your heart and all your soul."

Jos 23:11 So be very careful to love the LORD your God.

1Ki 2:3 and observe what the LORD your God requires: Walk in his ways, and keep his decrees and commands, his laws and requirements, as written in the Law of Moses, so that you may prosper in all you do and wherever you go, (+1Ki 2:4)

1Ki 8:25 "Now LORD, God of Israel, keep for your servant David my father the promises you made to him when you said, 'You shall never fail to have a man to sit before me on the throne of Israel, if only your sons are careful in all they do to walk before me as you have done.'

2Ch 19:7 Now let the fear of the LORD be upon you. Judge

carefully, for with the LORD our God there is no injustice or partiality or bribery."

Job 36:18 Be careful that no one entices you by riches; do not let a large bribe turn you aside. [19]Would your wealth or even all your mighty efforts sustain you so you would not be in distress? [20]Do not long for the night, to drag people away from their homes. [21]Beware of turning to evil, which you seem to prefer to affliction.

Pr 8:34 Blessed is the man who listens to me, watching daily at my doors, waiting at my doorway.

Pr 16:17 The highway of the upright avoids evil; he who guards his way guards his life.

Na 2:1 An attacker advances against you, [Nineveh]. Guard the fortress, watch the road, brace yourselves, marshal all your strength!

Mt 18:10 "See that you do not look down on one of these little ones. For I tell you that their angels in heaven always see the face of my Father in heaven. (+Mt 24:42-51)

Mt 25:13 "Therefore keep watch, because you do not know the day or the hour.

Mk 4:24 "Consider carefully what you hear," he continued. "With the measure you use, it will be measured to you—and even more.

Mk 13:32 "No one knows about that day or hour, not even the angels in heaven, nor the Son, but only the Father. [33]Be on guard! Be alert! You do not know when that time will come. [34]It's like a man going away: He leaves his house and puts his servants in charge, each with his assigned task, and tells the one at the door to keep watch.

[35]"Therefore keep watch because you do not know when the owner of the house will come back—whether in the evening, or at midnight, or when the rooster crows, or at dawn. [36]If he comes suddenly, do not let him find you sleeping. [37]What I say to you, I say to everyone: 'Watch!' " (+Lk 8:18; 11:35; 12:35-40; 17:3; 21:34-36; Ro 11:20)

1Co 10:12 So, if you think you are standing firm, be careful that you don't fall!

1Co 11:28 A man ought to examine himself before he eats of the bread and drinks of the cup.

1Co 16:13 Be on your guard; stand firm in the faith; be men of courage; be strong.

Gal 6:1 Brothers, if someone is caught in a sin, you who are spiritual should restore him gently. But watch yourself, or you also may be tempted.

Eph 5:15 Be very careful, then, how you live—not as unwise but as wise, (+Col 2:8)

1Th 5:4 But you, brothers, are not in darkness so that this day should surprise you like a thief.

1Th 5:6 So then, let us not be like others, who are asleep, but let us be alert and self-controlled.

1Th 5:21 Test everything. Hold on to the good.

Heb 2:1 We must pay more careful attention, therefore, to what we have heard, so that we do not drift away.

1Pe 5:8 Be self-controlled and alert. Your enemy the devil prowls around like a roaring lion looking for someone to devour.

2Pe 1:19 And we have the word of the prophets made more certain, and you will do well to pay attention to it, as to a light shining in a dark place, until the day dawns and the morning star rises in your hearts.

1Jn 5:18 We know that anyone born of God does not continue to sin; the one who was born of God keeps him safe, and the evil one cannot harm him.

　Upon Israel—

Dt 27:9 Then Moses and the priests, who are Levites, said to all Israel, "Be silent, O Israel, and listen! You have now become the people of the LORD your God.

Upon young men—

Ps 119:9 How can a young man keep his way pure? By living according to your word.

Pr 4:23 Above all else, guard your heart, for it is the wellspring of life. (+Pr 4:24)

Pr 4:25 Let your eyes look straight ahead, fix your gaze directly before you. ²⁶Make level paths for your feet and take only ways that are firm. (+Pr 4:27)

Upon married men—

Mal 2:15 Has not [the LORD] made them one? In flesh and spirit they are his. And why one? Because he was seeking godly offspring. So guard yourself in your spirit, and do not break faith with the wife of your youth.

Upon ministers (Ac 20:28-31; 1Co 3:10; Col 4:2)—

1Ti 4:16 Watch your life and doctrine closely. Persevere in them, because if you do, you will save both yourself and your hearers.

2Ti 4:5 But you, keep your head in all situations, endure hardship, do the work of an evangelist, discharge all the duties of your ministry.

Over motives—

Mt 6:1 "Be careful not to do your 'acts of righteousness' before men, to be seen by them. If you do, you will have no reward from your Father in heaven. (+Mt 6:2-5)

Over conscience—

Lk 11:35 See to it, then, that the light within you is not darkness.

Over the heart (Pr 4:23)—

Pr 28:26 He who trusts in himself is a fool, but he who walks in wisdom is kept safe.

Against: Hypocrisy—

Mt 16:6 "Be careful," Jesus said to them. "Be on your guard against the yeast of the Pharisees and Sadducees."

Apostasy—

2Jn 8 Watch out that you do not lose what you have worked for, but that you may be rewarded fully.

Lethargy—

Ro 13:11 And do this, understanding the present time. The hour has come for you to wake up from your slumber, because our salvation is nearer now than when we first believed.

1Pe 1:13 Therefore, prepare your minds for action; be self-controlled; set your hope fully on the grace to be given you when Jesus Christ is revealed.

1Pe 1:17 Since you call on a Father who judges each man's work impartially, live your lives as strangers here in reverent fear.

Backsliding—

Dt 4:9 Only be careful, and watch yourselves closely so that you do not forget the things your eyes have seen or let them slip from your heart as long as you live. Teach them to your children and to their children after them.

Dt 4:23 Be careful not to forget the covenant of the LORD your God that he made with you; do not make for yourselves an idol in the form of anything the LORD your God has forbidden.

Heb 3:12 See to it, brothers, that none of you has a sinful, unbelieving heart that turns away from the living God.

Heb 12:15 See to it that no one misses the grace of God and that no bitter root grows up to cause trouble and defile many.

Jude 20 But you, dear friends, build yourselves up in your most holy faith and pray in the Holy Spirit. ²¹Keep your-

selves in God's love as you wait for the mercy of our Lord Jesus Christ to bring you to eternal life.

Rev 3:2 Wake up! Strengthen what remains and is about to die, for I have not found your deeds complete in the sight of my God. ³Remember, therefore, what you have received and heard; obey it, and repent. But if you do not wake up, I will come like a thief, and you will not know at what time I will come to you.

Rev 3:11 I am coming soon. Hold on to what you have, so that no one will take your crown.

Worldliness—

1Co 7:29 What I mean, brothers, is that the time is short. From now on those who have wives should live as if they had none; ³⁰those who mourn, as if they did not; those who are happy, as if they were not; those who buy something, as if it were not theirs to keep; ³¹those who use the things of the world, as if not engrossed in them. For this world in its present form is passing away.

Covetousness (Mt 24:42-47; Mk 13:33-37)—

Lk 12:15 Then he said to them, "Watch out! Be on your guard against all kinds of greed; a man's life does not consist in the abundance of his possessions."

Lk 12:35 "Be dressed ready for service and keep your lamps burning, ³⁶like men waiting for their master to return from a wedding banquet, so that when he comes and knocks they can immediately open the door for him. ³⁷It will be good for those servants whose master finds them watching when he comes. I tell you the truth, he will dress himself to serve, will have them recline at the table and will come and wait on them. ³⁸It will be good for those servants whose master finds them ready, even if he comes in the second or third watch of the night. ³⁹But understand this: If the owner of the house had known at what hour the thief was coming, he would not have let his house be broken into. ⁴⁰You also must be ready, because the Son of Man will come at an hour when you do not expect him."

Idolatry—

Ex 23:13 "Be careful to do everything I have said to you. Do not invoke the names of other gods; do not let them be heard on your lips. (+Dt 4:23)

Dt 11:16 Be careful, or you will be enticed to turn away and worship other gods and bow down to them.

Dt 12:13 Be careful not to sacrifice your burnt offerings anywhere you please.

Evil associations—

Ex 34:12 Be careful not to make a treaty with those who live in the land where you are going, or they will be a snare among you.

Php 3:2 Watch out for those dogs, those men who do evil, those mutilators of the flesh.

2Pe 3:17 Therefore, dear friends, since you already know this, be on your guard so that you may not be carried away by the error of lawless men and fall from your secure position.

False teachers (Mt 7:15)—

Mk 13:22 For false Christs and false prophets will appear and perform signs and miracles to deceive the elect—if that were possible. ²³So be on your guard; I have told you everything ahead of time.

Ac 20:28 Keep watch over yourselves and all the flock of which the Holy Spirit has made you overseers. Be shepherds of the church of God, which he bought with his own blood. ²⁹I know that after I leave, savage wolves will come in among you and will not spare the flock. ³⁰Even from your own number men will arise and distort the truth in order to draw away disciples after them. ³¹So be on your guard! Remember that for three years I never stopped warning each of you night and day with tears. (+1Jn 4:1)

Deceivers—

Mt 24:4 Jesus answered: "Watch out that no one deceives you.

See Temptation.

WATCHMAN [5915, 7595, 9068, *2601*].

NIV+ See WATCH

A sentinel. On the walls of cities (SS 3:3; 5:7), of Jerusalem (2Sa 13:34; 18:24-25; Ne 4:9; 7:3; Isa 52:8; 62:6), of Babylon (Jer 51:12). On towers (2Ki 9:17; 2Ch 20:24; Isa 21:5-12; Jer 31:6). At the gates of the temple (2Ki 11:6-7). Alarm of, given by trumpets (Eze 33:3-6). Unfaithfulness in the discharge of duty of, punished by death (Eze 33:6; Mt 28:14; Ac 12:19). *See Guard.*

WATER [1926, 3722, 4763, 4784, 5482, 5574, 5635, 5689, 7562, 8612, 8796, 9197, *533, 536, 1184, 2498, 4395, 4540, 5620, 5621, 5623*].

NIV+ WATER'S, WATERCOURSE, WATERED, WATERFALLS, WATERING, WATERLESS, WATERS, WATERY, WELL-WATERED

Creation of (Ps 148:4-5). Covered the whole earth (Ge 1:9). Daily allowance of (Eze 4:11). City waterworks (2Ki 20:20). Vision of, by Ezekiel (Eze 47:1-5). Of separation (Nu 19:2-22). Libation of (1Sa 7:6). Irrigation with. *See Irrigation.* Miraculously supplied to the Israelites (Ex 17:1,6; Nu 20:11), to Samson (Jdg 15:19), to Jehoshaphat's army (2Ki 3:16-20). Purified by Elisha (2Ki 2:19-22). Red Sea divided (Ex 14:21-22), the Jordan River (Jos 3:14-17; 2Ki 2:6-8,14). Jesus walks on (Mt 14:25). Changed to wine (Jn 2:1-11), to blood (Rev 16:3-5).

Figurative:

Water of life (Jn 4:14; 7:37-39; Rev 21:6; 22:17). Of affliction (2Sa 22:17; Ps 69:1; Isa 30:20; 43:2). Of salvation (Isa 12:3; 49:10; 55:1; Eze 36:25; Jn 4:10; 7:38). Domestic love (Pr 5:15).

Symbolic: (Isa 8:7; Rev 8:11; 12:15; 16:4; 17:1,15).

WATER JAR Clay or stone jars for carrying or holding water (Ru 2:9; Jn 2:6-7; 4:28). *See Jar(s).*

WATER OF BITTERNESS Water mingled with dust which a woman suspected of unfaithfulness was expected to drink to prove her innocence (Nu 5:12-31).

WATER OF SEPARATION Water for removal of impurity (Nu 19:9,13,20-21; 31:23).

WATERSPOUT NIV "waterfalls" (Ps 42:7).

WATERWAY See Aqueduct.

WAVE OFFERING Sacrificial portion waved before the Lord (Ex 29:24-27; Lev 7:30; 8:27-29). *See Offerings.*

WAVES [1195, 1644, 1922, 3338, 4784, 5403, *2498, 3115, 3246*]. *See Sea, Waves of.*

WAX [1880]. (Ps 22:14; 68:2; 97:5; Mic 1:4).

WAY [*448, 784, 1821, 2006, 2143, 2256, 3869, 3970, 4027, 5477, 6330, 8938, 10068, *419, 2262, 2426, 3847, 3931, 4048, 4513, 4636, 6058*].

NIV+ AWAY, WAYS

Figurative:

Of holiness (Ps 16:11; Isa 35:8-9; Jer 6:16; Hos 14:9). Of righteousness, narrow (Mt 7:14). Of sin, broad (Mt

7:13). Jesus the (Jn 14:6; Heb 9:8). Doctrines taught by Christ (Ac 9:2; 19:23; 22:4; 24:14,22).

WAYFARING MAN Traveler (Jdg 19:17; 2Sa 12:4; Isa 33:8; 35:8).

WAYS OF GOD Perfect (Ps 18:30), righteous or just (Ps 145:17; Da 4:37; Hos 14:9; Rev 15:3), higher than human ways (Isa 55:9), eternal (Hab 3:6).

WEAK [*1924, 2143, 2703, 3908, 6714, 6949, 8205, *819, 820, 822*].

NIV+ WEAKENED, WEAKENING, WEAKER, WEAKEST, WEAKLING, WEAKNESS, WEAKNESSES

Duty of the strong to (Job 4:3-4; Isa 35:3-7; Mt 25:35, 40; Ro 14:1-23; 15:1-3; 1Co 8:7-13; 9:22; 2Co 11:29; Gal 6:1-2; Jas 5:19-20). *See Kindness.*

WEALTH [*226, 1524, 1540, 2104, 2162, 2657, 3856, 3860, 3877, 3883, 3946, 6938, 6947, 6948, 8214, *3228, 3440, 4355, 4454, 4456, 4458*].

NIV+ WEALTHY

Abundance of possessions, whether material, social, or spiritual. In early history of Israel, wealth consisted largely of flocks and herds, silver and gold, bronze, iron, and clothing (Jos 22:8). God taught Israel that he was the giver of their wealth (Dt 8:18), taught them to be generous (Pr 11:24). Jesus did not condemn wealth but stressed the difficulty of the rich in entering the kingdom of God (Mt 19:24; Lk 16:19-31).

WEAN, WEANING [1694].

NIV+ WEANED

To wean is to accustom a child to depend upon other food than its mother's milk; celebrated by a feast (Ge 21:8), and with an offering (1Sa 1:24).

WEAPONS [2210, 2723, 2995, 3998, 5977, 8939, *3960*].

NIV+ WEAPON

See Armor.

WEASEL [2700]. A small, carnivorous animal, allied to the ferret; for Israelites, unclean (Lev 11:29).

WEATHER [*2304*]. There is no Hebrew word corresponding to "weather," but the Israelites were keenly aware of weather phenomena. The great topographical diversity of Israel assures a variety of weather on a given day: on the top of Mt. Hermon (9,232 feet above sea level) there is snow on the ground the year round; while at Jericho (800 feet below sea level) the heat is oppressive in summer, and the region around the Dead Sea (1,290 feet below sea level) is intolerable in summer. On the coast even the hottest summer day is made bearable by refreshing breezes from the Mediterranean. Signs of (Mt 16:2-3). Sayings concerning (Job 37:9,17,22). *See Meteorology.*

WEAVING [755, 756, 8687].

NIV+ INTERWOVEN, WEAVE, WEAVER, WEAVER'S, WEAVERS, WOVE, WOVEN

(Isa 19:9; 38:12). Bezalel skilled in (Ex 35:35). Wrought by women (2Ki 23:7). Of the ephod (Ex 28:32; 39:22). Of coats (Ex 39:27).

Weaver's shuttle (Job 7:6), beam (Jdg 16:14; 2Sa 21:19; 1Ch 11:23).

WEDDING [2146, 3164, 3353, 8005, 8287, 8933, *1141*]. A joyous occasion, celebrated with music, feasting,

drinking of wine, joking; after the Exile written contracts were drawn up and sealed; bridegroom went to the bride's home with friends and escorted her to his own house (Mt 25:7); festive apparel expected of guests; festivities lasted one or two weeks (Ge 29:27; Jdg 14:12).

WEDGE [4383]. A bar of gold (Jos 7:21,24).

WEEDING (Mt 13:28).

WEEDS [947, 3017, 8032, *2429, 5198*].
NIV+ WEED

1. A general term for obnoxious plants (Job 31:40).

2. Probably bearded darnel, a poisonous plant resembling wheat (Mt 13:25-30).

WEEK [*8651, *4879, 4879*]. *See Calendar; Time.*

WEEKS, FEAST OF [8651]. Pentecost, celebrated fifty days after the sheaf waving on the sixteenth of Nisan (Ex 34:18-26).

WEEPING [*1134, 1140, 5027, *3081, 3088*].
NIV+ WEEP, WEEPS, WEPT

(Ro 12:15; 1Co 7:30). In perdition, the outer darkness (Mt 8:12; 22:13; 24:51; 25:30). None in heaven (Rev 7:17). Penitential (Jer 50:4; Joel 2:12).

Instances of Penitential:

The Israelites (Jdg 2:4-5). Peter (Mt 26:75; Mk 14:72; Lk 22:62). While doing good (Ps 126:5-6). For others (Jer 9:1). On account of tribulation (Jer 22:10; Am 5:16-17).

Instances of:

Of Abraham for Sarah (Ge 23:2). Of Esau (Ge 27:38). Of Jacob and Esau (Ge 33:4). Of Jacob (Ge 37:35). Of Joseph (Ge 42:24; 43:30; 45:2,14; 46:29; 50:1,17). Of Hannah (1Sa 1:7). Of Jonathan and David (1Sa 20:41). Of David (2Sa 1:17; 3:32; 13:36; 15:23,30; 18:33). Of Hezekiah (2Ki 20:3; Isa 38:3). Of Jesus, over Jerusalem (Lk 19:41), at the grave of Lazarus (Jn 11:35). Of Mary, when she washed the feet of Jesus (Lk 7:38; Jn 11:2,33). Of Mary Magdalene (Jn 20:11). Of Paul (Ac 20:19; Php 3:18).

WEIGHTS AND MEASURES Balances were used for scales (Lev 19:36; Pr 16:11), and stones for weights (Lev 19:36).

For biblical weights and measures, *See Measure.*

WELDING [1817]. A process used to join metals together (Isa 41:7).

WELLS [931, 1014, 5078, 7769, *4380, 5853*].
NIV+ WELL, WELLSPRING

The occasion of feuds: between Abraham and Abimelech (Ge 21:25-30), between Isaac and Abimelech (Ge 26:15-22,32-33). Of Jacob (Jn 4:6). Of Solomon (Ecc 2:6). Of Uzziah (2Ch 26:10). Of Hezekiah. *See Gihon.* At Haran (Ge 24:16).

Figurative:

Of salvation (Isa 12:3; Jn 4:14). Without water (Jer 15:18; 2Pe 2:17).

See Spring.

WEN *See Warts.*

WEST [294, 339, 340, 2025+5115, 3542+, 4427+9087, 5115, 6298+, *1553*].
NIV+ NORTHWEST, SOUTHWEST, WESTERN, WESTWARD

Used figuratively with "east" to denote great distance (Ps 103:12).

WHALE *See Fish; Sea Monster.*

WHEAT [1339, 2636, 10272, *4992, 5965*]. (Rev 6:6). Grown in Israel (1Ki 5:11; Ps 81:16; 147:14). Offerings of (Nu 18:12). Prophecy of the sale of a measure of, for a penny (Rev 6:6).

Parables of (Mt 13:25; Lk 16:7). Winnowing of (Mt 3:12; Lk 3:17). Ground in a mortar (Pr 27:22). Chaff of (Jer 23:28; Mt 3:12; Lk 3:17). Growth of, figurative of vicarious death (Jn 12:24).

Figurative:

Of God's mercy (Ps 81:16; 147:14). Of self-righteousness (Jer 12:13).

WHEEL [78, 236, 1649, 1651, 10143, 2200+3338].
NIV+ WHEELS

Potter's (Jer 18:3).

Figurative: (Pr 20:26; Ecc 12:6).

Symbolic: (Eze 1:15-21; 3:13; 10:9-19; 11:22).

WHELP *See Cub.*

WHIP [8765, 8849, *4811, 5848*].
NIV+ WHIPS

(1Ki 12:11; Pr 26:3; Na 3:2).

WHIRLWIND [1649, 6070, 6192, 6193, 6194, 8120].
NIV+ WHIRLWINDS, WIND

Destructive (Pr 1:27). From the south in the land of Uz (Job 37:9), in the valley of the Euphrates (Isa 21:1), in the land of Canaan (Zec 9:14). From the north (Eze 1:4). Elijah translated in (2Ki 2:1,11). God answered Job in (Job 38:1).

See Meteorology.

Figurative:

Of the judgment of God (Jer 23:19; 30:23). Of the fruits of unrighteousness (Hos 8:7). Of divine judgments (Eze 1:4).

WHISPER [1804, 1821, 1960+7754, 1960, 4317, 4318+7440, 7627, 8557, 9066, *1197, 1198, 3281*]. *See Busybody; Slander; Talebearer.*

WHISPERER
NIV+ WHISPER, WHISPERED, WHISPERING

A slanderer (Ro 1:29; 2Co 12:20).

See Slander; Speaking, Evil.

WHITE [1009, 2580, 4235, 4237, 7467, 8202, 8484, 9492, 10254, 10490, *3326, 3328*].
NIV+ REDDISH-WHITE, WHITER

See Colors, Figurative and Symbolic.

WHITE OWL Forbidden as food (Lev 11:18; Dt 14:16). *See Owl.*

WHITEWASH [3212, 3225, 9521, *3154*].
NIV+ WHITEWASHED

Used to "repair" a flimsy wall (Eze 13:10-16). Whitewashed tomb or wall a picture of hypocrisy (Mt 23:27-28; Ac 23:3).

WHOEVER Of condemnation (Ex 32:33; Dt 18:19; Mt 5:22; Jn 8:34; Ro 2:1; 1Jn 2:23; 3:4,10,15; 2Jn 9).

Of salvation (Lk 12:8; Jn 4:14; Ac 10:43; 1Jn 5:1; Rev 22:17).

WHORE *See Adultery; Fornication; Prostitute.*

WHOREDOM *See Idolatry; Fornication; Prostitute.*

WHOREMONGER *See Adultery; Sensuality.*

WICK TRIMMERS [4662, 4920]. Used to trim and adjust the wicks of the lamps in the temple and the tabernacle (Ex 37:23; Nu 4:9; 1Ki 7:50; 2Ki 12:13; 25:14; 2Ch 4:22; Jer 52:18).

WICKED [*1175, 2365, 4659, 6405, 6406, 6411, 8273, 8278, 8288, 8317, 8399, 8400, 8401, 8402, *94, 96, 490, 2805, 4505*].

NIV+ OVERWICKED, WICKEDLY, WICKEDNESS

God is angry with (Ps 5:5-6; 7:11; Ro 9:13; 1Co 10:5). Spirit of God withdrawn from (Ge 6:3; Hos 4:17-19; Ro 1:24,26,28). Hate the righteous (Mt 5:11-12; Lk 6:22-23). Worship of, offensive to God (Ps 50:16-17; Isa 1:10-15).

Present and future state of the wicked and righteous contrasted (Job 8; Ps 49). *See below.*

Prosperity of (Job 5:3-5; 12:6; 15:21-23,27,29; 20:5,22; 21:7-13; Ps 37:1,35-36; 49:10-15; 73:3-22; 92:6-7; Ecc 8:12-13; Jer 12:1-2; Hab 1:3-4,13-17; Mal 3:15). Hate reproof (1Ki 22:8; 2Ch 18:7). God's mercy to (Job 33:14-30), love for (Dt 5:29; 32:29; Mt 18:11-14; Jn 3:16-17; Ro 5:8; 1Jn 3:16; 4:9-10). Dread God (Job 18:11). Eliphaz's exhortation to (Job 22:21-30). Temporal punishment of (Job 15:20-35; 18:5-21; 20:5-29; 21:7-33; 24:2-24; 27:13-23; Jer 5:25; Eze 11:10; 12:19-20; Zec 14:17-19). False hope to (Job 8:13-18).

Gospel invitation to, illustrated by the parables of the householder (Mt 20:1-16), and marriage supper (Mt 22:1-14).

Warned (Jer 7:13-15,23-25; 25:4-6; 26:2-7,12-13; 29:17-19; Eze 33:8; Da 4:4-27; 5:4-29; Zep 2:1-2; Lk 3:7-9; 1Co 10:11; Jude 4-7; Rev 3:1-3,16-19). Terrors of, at the judgment (Rev 1:7). Death of (Ps 49:14; 73:4).

Compared With:

Ashes under the feet (Mal 4:3), bad fish (Mt 13:48), bad trees (Lk 6:43), beasts (Ps 49:12; 2Pe 2:12), the blind (Zep 1:17; Mt 15:14), bronze and iron (Jer 6:28; Eze 22:18), briers and thorns (Isa 55:13; Eze 2:6), bulls of Bashan (Ps 22:12), burning thorns (Ps 118:12), bushes in the wastelands (Jer 17:6), chaff (Job 21:18; Ps 1:4; Mt 3:12), clouds without rain (Jude 12), corpses trampled underfoot (Isa 14:19), deaf cobras (Ps 58:4), dogs (Pr 26:11; Mt 7:6; 2Pe 2:22), dross (Ps 119:119; Eze 22:18-19), early dew that passes away (Hos 13:3), earthenware coated with glaze (Pr 26:23), fading leaves (Isa 1:30), fiery furnace (Ps 21:9; Hos 7:4), fools building upon sand (Mt 7:26), fuel for the fire (Isa 9:19), garden without water (Isa 1:30), goats (Mt 25:32), grass that withers (2Ki 19:26; Ps 37:2; 92:7), green plants that die away (Ps 37:2), horses charging into the battle (Jer 8:6), idols (Ps 115:8), lions hungry for prey (Ps 17:12), melting wax (Ps 68:2), morning mist (Hos 13:3), moth-eaten garments (Isa 50:9; 51:8), pigs (Mt 7:6), poor figs (Jer 24:8), rejected branches (Isa 14:19), rejected silver (Jer 6:30; Mt 23:33), rocky places (Mt 13:5), scorpions (Eze 2:6), serpents (Ps 58:4; Mt 23:33), smoke through a window (Hos 13:3), sows (2Pe 2:22), springs without water (2Pe 2:17), storms sweeping by (Pr 10:25), straw before the wind (Job 21:18), stubble (Mal 4:1), tossing sea (Isa

57:20), tumbleweeds (Ps 83:13), visions of the night (Job 20:8), wandering stars (Jude 13), wayward children (Mt 11:16), weeds (Mt 13:38), whitewashed tombs (Mt 23:27), wild waves of the sea (Jude 13), wild donkey's colts (Job 11:12).

See Base Fellows; Impenitence; Obduracy; Penitence; Reprobate; Reprobacy; Seekers; Sin, Confession of.

Contrasted With The Righteous:

Ps 1:1 Blessed is the man who does not walk in the counsel of the wicked or stand in the way of sinners or sit in the seat of mockers. [2]But his delight is in the law of the Lord, and on his law he meditates day and night. [3]He is like a tree planted by streams of water, which yields its fruit in season and whose leaf does not wither. Whatever he does prospers.

[4]Not so the wicked! They are like chaff that the wind blows away. [5]Therefore the wicked will not stand in the judgment, nor sinners in the assembly of the righteous.

[6]For the Lord watches over the way of the righteous, but the way of the wicked will perish.

Ps 11:5 The Lord examines the righteous, but the wicked and those who love violence his soul hates.

Ps 17:14 O Lord, by your hand save me from such men, from men of this world whose reward is in this life. You still the hunger of those you cherish; their sons have plenty, and they store up wealth for their children.

[15]And I—in righteousness I will see your face; when I awake, I will be satisfied with seeing your likeness.

Ps 32:10 Many are the woes of the wicked, but the Lord's unfailing love surrounds the man who trusts in him.

Ps 37:17 for the power of the wicked will be broken, but the Lord upholds the righteous.

[18]The days of the blameless are known to the Lord, and their inheritance will endure forever. [19]In times of disaster they will not wither; in days of famine they will enjoy plenty.

[20]But the wicked will perish: The Lord's enemies will be like the beauty of the fields, they will vanish—vanish like smoke.

[21]The wicked borrow and do not repay, but the righteous give generously; [22]those the Lord blesses will inherit the land, but those he curses will be cut off.

Ps 37:37 Consider the blameless, observe the upright; there is a future for the man of peace. [38]But all sinners will be destroyed; the future of the wicked will be cut off.

Ps 73:1 Surely God is good to Israel, to those who are pure in heart.

[2]But as for me, my feet had almost slipped; I had nearly lost my foothold. [3]For I envied the arrogant when I saw the prosperity of the wicked.

[4]They have no struggles; their bodies are healthy and strong. [5]They are free from the burdens common to man; they are not plagued by human ills. [6]Therefore pride is their necklace; they clothe themselves with violence. [7]From their callous hearts comes iniquity; the evil conceits of their minds know no limits. [8]They scoff, and speak with malice; in their arrogance they threaten oppression. [9]Their mouths lay claim to heaven, and their tongues take possession of the earth. [10]Therefore their people turn to them and drink up waters in abundance. [11]They say, "How can God know? Does the Most High have knowledge?"

[12]This is what the wicked are like—always carefree, they increase in wealth.

[13]Surely in vain have I kept my heart pure; in vain have I washed my hands in innocence. [14]All day long I have been plagued; I have been punished every morning.

¹⁵If I had said, "I will speak thus," I would have betrayed your children. ¹⁶When I tried to understand all this, it was oppressive to me ¹⁷till I entered the sanctuary of God; then I understood their final destiny.

¹⁸Surely you place them on slippery ground; you cast them down to ruin. ¹⁹How suddenly are they destroyed, completely swept away by terrors! ²⁰As a dream when one awakes, so when you arise, O Lord, you will despise them as fantasies.

²¹When my heart was grieved and my spirit embittered, ²²I was senseless and ignorant; I was a brute beast before you.

²³Yet I am always with you; you hold me by my right hand. ²⁴You guide me with your counsel, and afterward you will take me into glory. ²⁵Whom have I in heaven but you? And earth has nothing I desire besides you. ²⁶My flesh and my heart may fail, but God is the strength of my heart and my portion forever.

²⁷Those who are far from you will perish; you destroy all who are unfaithful to you. ²⁸But as for me, it is good to be near God. I have made the Sovereign LORD my refuge; I will tell of all your deeds.

Ps 75:10 I will cut off the horns of all the wicked, but the horns of the righteous will be lifted up.

Ps 91:7 A thousand may fall at your side, ten thousand at your right hand, but it will not come near you. ⁸You will only observe with your eyes and see the punishment of the wicked.

Ps 107:33 He turned rivers into a desert, flowing springs into thirsty ground, ³⁴and fruitful land into a salt waste, because of the wickedness of those who lived there. ³⁵He turned the desert into pools of water and the parched ground into flowing springs; ³⁶there he brought the hungry to live, and they founded a city where they could settle. ³⁷They sowed fields and planted vineyards that yielded a fruitful harvest; ³⁸he blessed them, and their numbers greatly increased, and he did not let their herds diminish.

Ps 125:5 But those who turn to crooked ways the LORD will banish with the evildoers. Peace be upon Israel. (+Pr 2:21-22; 3:32-33; 4:16-19; 10:3)

Pr 10:6 Blessings crown the head of the righteous, but violence overwhelms the mouth of the wicked.

Pr 10:9 The man of integrity walks securely, but he who takes crooked paths will be found out. (+Pr 10:11,16,20)

Pr 10:21 The lips of the righteous nourish many, but fools die for lack of judgment.

Pr 10:23 A fool finds pleasure in evil conduct, but a man of understanding delights in wisdom.

²⁴What the wicked dreads will overtake him; what the righteous desire will be granted.

²⁵When the storm has swept by, the wicked are gone, but the righteous stand firm forever.

Pr 10:28 The prospect of the righteous is joy, but the hopes of the wicked come to nothing.

²⁹The way of the LORD is a refuge for the righteous, but it is the ruin of those who do evil.

³⁰The righteous will never be uprooted, but the wicked will not remain in the land. (+Pr 10:31)

Pr 10:32 The lips of the righteous know what is fitting, but the mouth of the wicked only what is perverse.

Pr 11:3 The integrity of the upright guides them, but the unfaithful are destroyed by their duplicity.

Pr 11:5 The righteousness of the blameless makes a straight way for them, but the wicked are brought down by their own wickedness.

⁶The righteousness of the upright delivers them, but the unfaithful are trapped by evil desires.

Pr 11:8 The righteous man is rescued from trouble, and it comes on the wicked instead. (+Pr 11:9)

Pr 11:10 When the righteous prosper, the city rejoices; when the wicked perish, there are shouts of joy.

¹¹Through the blessing of the upright a city is exalted, but by the mouth of the wicked it is destroyed.

Pr 11:18 The wicked man earns deceptive wages, but he who sows righteousness reaps a sure reward.

¹⁹The truly righteous man attains life, but he who pursues evil goes to his death.

²⁰The LORD detests men of perverse heart but he delights in those whose ways are blameless.

²¹Be sure of this: The wicked will not go unpunished, but those who are righteous will go free.

Pr 11:23 The desire of the righteous ends only in good, but the hope of the wicked only in wrath.

Pr 11:31 If the righteous receive their due on earth, how much more the ungodly and the sinner! (+Pr 12:2)

Pr 12:3 A man cannot be established through wickedness, but the righteous cannot be uprooted.

Pr 12:5 The plans of the righteous are just, but the advice of the wicked is deceitful.

⁶The words of the wicked lie in wait for blood, but the speech of the upright rescues them.

⁷Wicked men are overthrown and are no more, but the house of the righteous stands firm. (+Pr 12:10,12)

Pr 12:13 An evil man is trapped by his sinful talk, but a righteous man escapes trouble.

Pr 12:21 No harm befalls the righteous, but the wicked have their fill of trouble.

Pr 12:26 A righteous man is cautious in friendship, but the way of the wicked leads them astray. (+Pr 13:5)

Pr 13:6 Righteousness guards the man of integrity, but wickedness overthrows the sinner. (+Pr 13:9)

Pr 13:17 A wicked messenger falls into trouble, but a trustworthy envoy brings healing.

Pr 13:21 Misfortune pursues the sinner, but prosperity is the reward of the righteous.

²²A good man leaves an inheritance for his children's children, but a sinner's wealth is stored up for the righteous. (+Pr 13:25; 14:2,11)

Pr 14:19 Evil men will bow down in the presence of the good, and the wicked at the gates of the righteous.

Pr 14:22 Do not those who plot evil go astray? But those who plan what is good find love and faithfulness.

Pr 14:32 When calamity comes, the wicked are brought down, but even in death the righteous have a refuge.

Pr 15:6 The house of the righteous contains great treasure, but the income of the wicked brings them trouble. (+Pr 15:8-9,28-29; 21:15)

Pr 21:18 The wicked become a ransom for the righteous, and the unfaithful for the upright.

Pr 21:26 All day long he craves for more, but the righteous give without sparing. (+Pr 21:29)

Pr 22:5 In the paths of the wicked lie thorns and snares, but he who guards his soul stays far from them. (+Pr 22:8-9; 24:16)

Pr 28:1 The wicked man flees though no one pursues, but the righteous are as bold as a lion.

Pr 28:4 Those who forsake the law praise the wicked, but those who keep the law resist them.

⁵Evil men do not understand justice, but those who seek the LORD understand it fully.

Pr 28:13 He who conceals his sins does not prosper, but whoever confesses and renounces them finds mercy. ¹⁴Blessed is the man who always fears the LORD, but he who hardens his heart falls into trouble.

Pr 28:18 He whose walk is blameless is kept safe, but he whose ways are perverse will suddenly fall. (+Pr 29:2,6-7,27)

Isa 32:1 See, a king will reign in righteousness and rulers will rule with justice. ²Each man will be like a shelter from the wind and a refuge from the storm, like streams of water in the desert and the shadow of a great rock in a thirsty land.

³Then the eyes of those who see will no longer be closed, and the ears of those who hear will listen. ⁴The mind of the rash will know and understand, and the stammering tongue will be fluent and clear. ⁵No longer will the fool be called noble nor the scoundrel be highly respected. ⁶For the fool speaks folly, his mind is busy with evil: He practices ungodliness and spreads error concerning the LORD; the hungry he leaves empty and from the thirsty he withholds water. ⁷The scoundrel's methods are wicked, he makes up evil schemes to destroy the poor with lies, even when the plea of the needy is just. ⁸But the noble man makes noble plans, and by noble deeds he stands.

Isa 65:13 Therefore this is what the Sovereign LORD says: "My servants will eat, but you will go hungry; my servants will drink, but you will go thirsty; my servants will rejoice, but you will be put to shame. ¹⁴My servants will sing out of the joy of their hearts, but you will cry out from anguish of heart and wail in brokenness of spirit.

Mal 3:18 And you will again see the distinction between the righteous and the wicked, between those who serve God and those who do not.

Ro 2:7 To those who by persistence in doing good seek glory, honor and immortality, he will give eternal life. ⁸But for those who are self-seeking and who reject the truth and follow evil, there will be wrath and anger. ⁹There will be trouble and distress for every human being who does evil: first for the Jew, then for the Gentile; ¹⁰but glory, honor and peace for everyone who does good: first for the Jew, then for the Gentile.

Eph 2:12 remember that at that time you were separate from Christ, excluded from citizenship in Israel and foreigners to the covenants of the promise, without hope and without God in the world. ¹³But now in Christ Jesus you who once were far away have been brought near through the blood of Christ.

¹⁴For he himself is our peace, who has made the two one and has destroyed the barrier, the dividing wall of hostility,

Php 2:15 so that you may become blameless and pure, children of God without fault in a crooked and depraved generation, in which you shine like stars in the universe

1Th 5:5 You are all sons of the light and sons of the day. We do not belong to the night or to the darkness. ⁶So then, let us not be like others, who are asleep, but let us be alert and self-controlled. ⁷For those who sleep, sleep at night, and those who get drunk, get drunk at night. ⁸But since we belong to the day, let us be self-controlled, putting on faith and love as a breastplate, and the hope of salvation as a helmet.

Tit 1:15 To the pure, all things are pure, but to those who are corrupted and do not believe, nothing is pure. In fact, both their minds and consciences are corrupted.

1Pe 4:17 For it is time for judgment to begin with the family of God; and if it begins with us, what will the outcome be for those who do not obey the gospel of God? ¹⁸And,

"If it is hard for the righteous to be saved, what will become of the ungodly and the sinner?"

1Jn 1:6 If we claim to have fellowship with him yet walk in the darkness, we lie and do not live by the truth. ⁷But if we walk in the light, as he is in the light, we have fellowship with one another, and the blood of Jesus, his Son, purifies us from all sin.

1Jn 3:3 Everyone who has this hope in him purifies himself, just as he is pure.

⁴Everyone who sins breaks the law; in fact, sin is lawlessness. ⁵But you know that he appeared so that he might take away our sins. And in him is no sin. ⁶No one who lives in him keeps on sinning. No one who continues to sin has either seen him or known him.

⁷Dear children, do not let anyone lead you astray. He who does what is right is righteous, just as he is righteous. ⁸He who does what is sinful is of the devil, because the devil has been sinning from the beginning. The reason the Son of God appeared was to destroy the devil's work. ⁹No one who is born of God will continue to sin, because God's seed remains in him; he cannot go on sinning, because he has been born of God. ¹⁰This is how we know who the children of God are and who the children of the devil are: Anyone who does not do what is right is not a child of God; nor is anyone who does not love his brother.

¹¹This is the message you heard from the beginning: We should love one another. ¹²Do not be like Cain, who belonged to the evil one and murdered his brother. And why did he murder him? Because his own actions were evil and his brother's were righteous. ¹³Do not be surprised, my brothers, if the world hates you. ¹⁴We know that we have passed from death to life, because we love our brothers. Anyone who does not love remains in death. ¹⁵Anyone who hates his brother is a murderer, and you know that no murderer has eternal life in him.

¹⁶This is how we know what love is: Jesus Christ laid down his life for us. And we ought to lay down our lives for our brothers. ¹⁷If anyone has material possessions and sees his brother in need but has no pity on him, how can the love of God be in him?

Described as: (Job 8:13-17)

Job 15:16 how much less man, who is vile and corrupt, who drinks up evil like water!

Job 15:20 All his days the wicked man suffers torment, the ruthless through all the years stored up for him. ²¹Terrifying sounds fill his ears; when all seems well, marauders attack him. ²²He despairs of escaping the darkness; he is marked for the sword. ²³He wanders about—food for vultures; he knows the day of darkness is at hand. ²⁴Distress and anguish fill him with terror; they overwhelm him, like a king poised to attack, ²⁵because he shakes his fist at God and vaunts himself against the Almighty, ²⁶defiantly charging against him with a thick, strong shield.

²⁷"Though his face is covered with fat and his waist bulges with flesh, ²⁸he will inhabit ruined towns and houses where no one lives, houses crumbling to rubble. ²⁹He will no longer be rich and his wealth will not endure, nor will his possessions spread over the land. ³⁰He will not escape the darkness; a flame will wither his shoots, and the breath of God's mouth will carry him away. ³¹Let him not deceive himself by trusting what is worthless, for he will get nothing in return. ³²Before his time he will be paid in full, and his branches will not flourish. ³³He will be like a

vine stripped of its unripe grapes, like an olive tree shedding its blossoms. [34]For the company of the godless will be barren, and fire will consume the tents of those who love bribes. [35]They conceive trouble and give birth to evil; their womb fashions deceit."

Ps 10:4 In his pride the wicked does not seek him; in all his thoughts there is no room for God. [5]His ways are always prosperous; he is haughty and your laws are far from him; he sneers at all his enemies. [6]He says to himself, "Nothing will shake me; I'll always be happy and never have trouble." [7]His mouth is full of curses and lies and threats; trouble and evil are under his tongue. [8]He lies in wait near the villages; from ambush he murders the innocent, watching in secret for his victims. [9]He lies in wait like a lion in cover; he lies in wait to catch the helpless; he catches the helpless and drags them off in his net. [10]His victims are crushed, they collapse; they fall under his strength. [11]He says to himself, "God has forgotten; he covers his face and never sees."

Ps 36:1 An oracle is within my heart concerning the sinfulness of the wicked: There is no fear of God before his eyes. [2]For in his own eyes he flatters himself too much to detect or hate his sin. [3]The words of his mouth are wicked and deceitful; he has ceased to be wise and to do good. [4]Even on his bed he plots evil; he commits himself to a sinful course and does not reject what is wrong.

Ps 73:4 They have no struggles; their bodies are healthy and strong. [5]They are free from the burdens common to man; they are not plagued by human ills. [6]Therefore pride is their necklace; they clothe themselves with violence. [7]From their callous hearts comes iniquity; the evil conceits of their minds know no limits. [8]They scoff, and speak with malice; in their arrogance they threaten oppression. [9]Their mouths lay claim to heaven, and their tongues take possession of the earth. [10]Therefore their people turn to them and drink up waters in abundance. [11]They say, "How can God know? Does the Most High have knowledge?"

[12]This is what the wicked are like—always carefree, they increase in wealth.

Isa 59:2 But your iniquities have separated you from your God; your sins have hidden his face from you, so that he will not hear. [3]For your hands are stained with blood, your fingers with guilt. Your lips have spoken lies, and your tongue mutters wicked things. [4]No one calls for justice; no one pleads his case with integrity. They rely on empty arguments and speak lies; they conceive trouble and give birth to evil. [5]They hatch the eggs of vipers and spin a spider's web. Whoever eats their eggs will die, and when one is broken, an adder is hatched. [6]Their cobwebs are useless for clothing; they cannot cover themselves with what they make. Their deeds are evil deeds, and acts of violence are in their hands. [7]Their feet rush into sin; they are swift to shed innocent blood. Their thoughts are evil thoughts; ruin and destruction mark their ways. [8]The way of peace they do not know; there is no justice in their paths. They have turned them into crooked roads; no one who walks in them will know peace.

Jer 2:22 Although you wash yourself with soda and use an abundance of soap, the stain of your guilt is still before me," declares the Sovereign LORD. [23]"How can you say, 'I am not defiled; I have not run after the Baals'? See how you behaved in the valley; consider what you have done. You are a swift she-camel running here and there, [24]a wild donkey accustomed to the desert, sniffing the wind in her craving—in her heat who can restrain her? Any males that pursue her need not tire themselves; at mating time they

will find her. [25]Do not run until your feet are bare and your throat is dry. But you said, 'It's no use! I love foreign gods, and I must go after them.'

Abomination—

Pr 13:9 The light of the righteous shines brightly, but the lamp of the wicked is snuffed out.

Pr 15:9 The LORD detests the way of the wicked but he loves those who pursue righteousness.

Hos 9:10 "When I found Israel, it was like finding grapes in the desert; when I saw your fathers, it was like seeing the early fruit on the fig tree. But when they came to Baal Peor, they consecrated themselves to that shameful idol and became as vile as the thing they loved.

Alienated—

Col 1:21 Once you were alienated from God and were enemies in your minds because of your evil behavior.

Beasts—

Ps 49:20 A man who has riches without understanding is like the beasts that perish.

Dogs—

Ps 59:6 They return at evening, snarling like dogs, and prowl about the city. (+2Pe 2:22; Rev 22:15)

Horse rushing into battle—

Jer 8:6 I have listened attentively, but they do not say what is right. No one repents of his wickedness, saying, "What have I done?" Each pursues his own course like a horse charging into battle.

Blind (Eze 12:2).

Carnal—

Ro 8:5 Those who live according to the sinful nature have their minds set on what that nature desires; but those who live in accordance with the Spirit have their minds set on what the Spirit desires.

Ro 8:7 the sinful mind is hostile to God. It does not submit to God's law, nor can it do so. [8]Those controlled by the sinful nature cannot please God.

Ro 9:8 In other words, it is not the natural children who are God's children, but it is the children of the promise who are regarded as Abraham's offspring.

Children of the devil (Jn 8:44)—

Ac 13:10 "You are a child of the devil and an enemy of everything that is right! You are full of all kinds of deceit and trickery. Will you never stop perverting the right ways of the Lord?

1Jn 3:10 This is how we know who the children of God are and who the children of the devil are: Anyone who does not do what is right is not a child of God; nor is anyone who does not love his brother.

Perverse (Jer 9:6; Ro 1:21; 2:4-5)—

Php 2:15 so that you may become blameless and pure, children of God without fault in a crooked and depraved generation, in which you shine like stars in the universe

Despising God (Job 21:14; Ro 11:28).

Contentious—

Ro 2:8 But for those who are self-seeking and who reject the truth and follow evil, there will be wrath and anger.

Corrupt—

Ps 53:1 The fool says in his heart, "There is no God." They are corrupt, and their ways are vile; there is no one who does good. (+Ps 73:8; Isa 59:3; Jer 2:22)

Eze 16:47 You not only walked in their ways and copied their detestable practices, but in all your ways you soon became more depraved than they.

Eze 20:16 because they rejected my laws and did not

follow my decrees and desecrated my Sabbaths. For their hearts were devoted to their idols.

Mic 7:2 The godly have been swept from the land; not one upright man remains. All men lie in wait to shed blood; each hunts his brother with a net. ³Both hands are skilled in doing evil; the ruler demands gifts, the judge accepts bribes, the powerful dictate what they desire—they all conspire together. ⁴The best of them is like a brier, the most upright worse than a thorn hedge. The day of your watchmen has come, the day God visits you. Now is the time of their confusion. (+Tit 1:15)

Loving darkness (Jn 3:19-20).

Dead in sin—

Eph 2:1 As for you, you were dead in your transgressions and sins, ²in which you used to live when you followed the ways of this world and of the ruler of the kingdom of the air, the spirit who is now at work in those who are disobedient. ³All of us also lived among them at one time, gratifying the cravings of our sinful nature and following its desires and thoughts. Like the rest, we were by nature objects of wrath.

1Jn 3:14 We know that we have passed from death to life, because we love our brothers. Anyone who does not love remains in death.

Delighting in lies (Ps 62:4)

In perversity—

Pr 2:13 who leave the straight paths to walk in dark ways, ¹⁴who delight in doing wrong and rejoice in the perverseness of evil, ¹⁵whose paths are crooked and who are devious in their ways. ¹⁶It will save you also from the adulteress, from the wayward wife with her seductive words, ¹⁷who has left the partner of her youth and ignored the covenant she made before God. ¹⁸For her house leads down to death and her paths to the spirits of the dead. ¹⁹None who go to her return or attain the paths of life.

Defiled—

Tit 1:15 To the pure, all things are pure, but to those who are corrupted and do not believe, nothing is pure. In fact, both their minds and consciences are corrupted. ¹⁶They claim to know God, but by their actions they deny him. They are detestable, disobedient and unfit for doing anything good.

Depraved—

Isa 1:4 Ah, sinful nation, a people loaded with guilt, a brood of evildoers, children given to corruption! They have forsaken the LORD; they have spurned the Holy One of Israel and turned their backs on him.

⁵Why should you be beaten anymore? Why do you persist in rebellion? Your whole head is injured, your whole heart afflicted. ⁶From the sole of your foot to the top of your head there is no soundness—only wounds and welts and open sores, not cleansed or bandaged or soothed with oil. (+Jer 17:9)

Jer 30:12 "This is what the LORD says: "'Your wound is incurable, your injury beyond healing. ¹³There is no one to plead your cause, no remedy for your sore, no healing for you. ¹⁴All your allies have forgotten you; they care nothing for you. I have struck you as an enemy would and punished you as would the cruel, because your guilt is so great and your sins so many. ¹⁵Why do you cry out over your wound, your pain that has no cure? Because of your great guilt and many sins I have done these things to you.

Ro 1:20 For since the creation of the world God's invisible qualities—his eternal power and divine nature—have been clearly seen, being understood from what has been made, so that men are without excuse.

²¹For although they knew God, they neither glorified him as God nor gave thanks to him, but their thinking became futile and their foolish hearts were darkened. ²²Although they claimed to be wise, they became fools ²³and exchanged the glory of the immortal God for images made to look like mortal man and birds and animals and reptiles.

²⁴Therefore God gave them over in the sinful desires of their hearts to sexual impurity for the degrading of their bodies with one another. ²⁵They exchanged the truth of God for a lie, and worshiped and served created things rather than the Creator—who is forever praised. Amen.

²⁶Because of this, God gave them over to shameful lusts. Even their women exchanged natural relations for unnatural ones. ²⁷In the same way the men also abandoned natural relations with women and were inflamed with lust for one another. Men committed indecent acts with other men, and received in themselves the due penalty for their perversion.

²⁸Furthermore, since they did not think it worthwhile to retain the knowledge of God, he gave them over to a depraved mind, to do what ought not to be done. ²⁹They have become filled with every kind of wickedness, evil, greed and depravity. They are full of envy, murder, strife, deceit and malice. They are gossips, ³⁰slanderers, God-haters, insolent, arrogant and boastful; they invent ways of doing evil; they disobey their parents; ³¹they are senseless, faithless, heartless, ruthless. ³²Although they know God's righteous decree that those who do such things deserve death, they not only continue to do these very things but also approve of those who practice them.

Ro 3:10 As it is written: "There is no one righteous, not even one; ¹¹there is no one who understands, no one who seeks God. ¹²All have turned away, they have together become worthless; there is no one who does good, not even one." ¹³"Their throats are open graves; their tongues practice deceit." "The poison of vipers is on their lips." ¹⁴"Their mouths are full of cursing and bitterness." ¹⁵"Their feet are swift to shed blood; ¹⁶ruin and misery mark their ways, ¹⁷and the way of peace they do not know." ¹⁸"There is no fear of God before their eyes."

1Ti 1:9 We also know that law is made not for the righteous but for lawbreakers and rebels, the ungodly and sinful, the unholy and irreligious; for those who kill their fathers or mothers, for murderers, ¹⁰for adulterers and perverts, for slave traders and liars and perjurers—and for whatever else is contrary to the sound doctrine

2Ti 3:2 People will be lovers of themselves, lovers of money, boastful, proud, abusive, disobedient to their parents, ungrateful, unholy, ³without love, unforgiving, slanderous, without self-control, brutal, not lovers of the good, ⁴treacherous, rash, conceited, lovers of pleasure rather than lovers of God— ⁵having a form of godliness but denying its power. Have nothing to do with them.

⁶They are the kind who worm their way into homes and gain control over weak-willed women, who are loaded down with sins and are swayed by all kinds of evil desires, ⁷always learning but never able to acknowledge the truth. ⁸Just as Jannes and Jambres opposed Moses, so also these men oppose the truth—men of depraved minds, who, as far as the faith is concerned, are rejected. ⁹But they will not get very far because, as in the case of those men, their folly will be clear to everyone.

2Ti 3:13 while evil men and impostors will go from bad to worse, deceiving and being deceived. (+Tit 3:2)

2Pe 2:10 This is especially true of those who follow the corrupt desire of the sinful nature and despise authority.

Bold and arrogant, these men are not afraid to slander celestial beings;

2Pe 2:12 But these men blaspheme in matters they do not understand. They are like brute beasts, creatures of instinct, born only to be caught and destroyed, and like beasts they too will perish.

[13]They will be paid back with harm for the harm they have done. Their idea of pleasure is to carouse in broad daylight. They are blots and blemishes, reveling in their pleasures while they feast with you. [14]With eyes full of adultery, they never stop sinning; they seduce the unstable; they are experts in greed—an accursed brood! [15]They have left the straight way and wandered off to follow the way of Balaam son of Beor, who loved the wages of wickedness. [16]But he was rebuked for his wrongdoing by a donkey—a beast without speech—who spoke with a man's voice and restrained the prophet's madness.

[17]These men are springs without water and mists driven by a storm. Blackest darkness is reserved for them. [18]For they mouth empty, boastful words and, by appealing to the lustful desires of sinful human nature, they entice people who are just escaping from those who live in error. [19]They promise them freedom, while they themselves are slaves of depravity—for a man is a slave to whatever has mastered him.

Jude 12 These men are blemishes at your love feasts, eating with you without the slightest qualm—shepherds who feed only themselves. They are clouds without rain, blown along by the wind; autumn trees, without fruit and uprooted—twice dead. [13]They are wild waves of the sea, foaming up their shame; wandering stars, for whom blackest darkness has been reserved forever.

Destitute of faithfulness—

Ps 5:9 Not a word from their mouth can be trusted; their heart is filled with destruction. Their throat is an open grave; with their tongue they speak deceit.

Destitute of the love of God—

Jn 5:42 but I know you. I know that you do not have the love of God in your hearts.

Devilish—

1Jn 3:8 He who does what is sinful is of the devil, because the devil has been sinning from the beginning. The reason the Son of God appeared was to destroy the devil's work.

Devisers of evil—

Ps 52:1 Why do you boast of evil, you mighty man? Why do you boast all day long, you who are a disgrace in the eyes of God? [2]Your tongue plots destruction; it is like a sharpened razor, you who practice deceit. [3]You love evil rather than good, falsehood rather than speaking the truth. *Selah* [4]You love every harmful word, O you deceitful tongue!

Ps 64:3 They sharpen their tongues like swords and aim their words like deadly arrows. [4]They shoot from ambush at the innocent man; they shoot at him suddenly, without fear.

[5]They encourage each other in evil plans, they talk about hiding their snares; they say, "Who will see them?" [6]They plot injustice and say, "We have devised a perfect plan!" Surely the mind and heart of man are cunning.

Pr 4:16 For they cannot sleep till they do evil; they are robbed of slumber till they make someone fall.

Pr 6:12 A scoundrel and villain, who goes about with a corrupt mouth, [13]who winks with his eye, signals with his feet and motions with his fingers, [14]who plots evil with deceit in his heart—he always stirs up dissension. [15]There-

fore disaster will overtake him in an instant; he will suddenly be destroyed—without remedy.

Pr 10:23 A fool finds pleasure in evil conduct, but a man of understanding delights in wisdom.

Isa 32:6 For the fool speaks folly, his mind is busy with evil: He practices ungodliness and spreads error concerning the LORD; the hungry he leaves empty and from the thirsty he withholds water. [7]The scoundrel's methods are wicked, he makes up evil schemes to destroy the poor with lies, even when the plea of the needy is just.

Jer 4:22 "My people are fools; they do not know me. They are senseless children; they have no understanding. They are skilled in doing evil; they know not how to do good."

Enemies (Ro 5:10; Col 1:21).

Filthy—

Ezr 9:11 you gave through your servants the prophets when you said: 'The land you are entering to possess is a land polluted by the corruption of its peoples. By their detestable practices they have filled it with their impurity from one end to the other.

Full of bitterness—

Ac 8:23 For I see that you are full of bitterness and captive to sin."

Uncircumcised (Isa 52:1; Jer 6:10; Eze 28:10; 31:18; 32:19-32). Uncircumcised of heart (Lev 26:41; Eze 44:7; Ac 7:51), of lips (Ex 6:12).

Disobedient—

Jer 11:8 But they did not listen or pay attention; instead, they followed the stubbornness of their evil hearts. So I brought on them all the curses of the covenant I had commanded them to follow but that they did not keep.'" (+Tit 1:16)

Alienated from God (Col 1:21).

Full of bitterness and venom—

Dt 32:32 Their vine comes from the vine of Sodom and from the fields of Gomorrah. Their grapes are filled with poison, and their clusters with bitterness. [33]Their wine is the venom of serpents, the deadly poison of cobras.

Ps 58:3 Even from birth the wicked go astray; from the womb they are wayward and speak lies. [4]Their venom is like the venom of a snake, like that of a cobra that has stopped its ears, [5]that will not heed the tune of the charmer, however skillful the enchanter may be.

Grievous sinners—

Ge 13:13 Now the men of Sodom were wicked and were sinning greatly against the LORD.

Ge 18:20 Then the LORD said, "The outcry against Sodom and Gomorrah is so great and their sin so grievous

Job 22:5 Is not your wickedness great? Are not your sins endless? (+Isa 1:4-6)

Hating: correction—

Pr 15:10 Stern discipline awaits him who leaves the path; he who hates correction will die.

Am 5:10 you hate the one who reproves in court and despise him who tells the truth.

Instruction—

Ps 50:17 You hate my instruction and cast my words behind you.

Pr 1:29 Since they hated knowledge and did not choose to fear the LORD, [30]since they would not accept my advice and spurned my rebuke,

The light—

Jn 3:20 Everyone who does evil hates the light, and will not come into the light for fear that his deeds will be exposed.

Being in moral darkness—

Mt 4:16 the people living in darkness have seen a great light; on those living in the land of the shadow of death a light has dawned."

Mt 6:23 But if your eyes are bad, your whole body will be full of darkness. If then the light within you is darkness, how great is that darkness!

Lk 1:79 to shine on those living in darkness and in the shadow of death, to guide our feet into the path of peace."

Eph 4:17 So I tell you this, and insist on it in the Lord, that you must no longer live as the Gentiles do, in the futility of their thinking. [18]They are darkened in their understanding and separated from the life of God because of the ignorance that is in them due to the hardening of their hearts.

Not knowing the way of the Lord (Jer 5:4).

Lewd—

Jer 11:15 "What is my beloved doing in my temple as she works out her evil schemes with many? Can consecrated meat avert [your punishment]? When you engage in your wickedness, then you rejoice."

Lost—

Lk 19:10 For the Son of Man came to seek and to save what was lost."

Loving wickedness—

Ps 7:14 He who is pregnant with evil and conceives trouble gives birth to disillusionment.

Jer 14:10 This is what the LORD says about this people: "They greatly love to wander; they do not restrain their feet. So the LORD does not accept them; he will now remember their wickedness and punish them for their sins."

Hos 4:8 They feed on the sins of my people and relish their wickedness.

Mic 3:2 you who hate good and love evil; who tear the skin from my people and the flesh from their bones;

Malicious toward the righteous—

Ps 37:12 The wicked plot against the righteous and gnash their teeth at them;

Ps 94:3 How long will the wicked, O LORD, how long will the wicked be jubilant?

[4]They pour out arrogant words; all the evildoers are full of boasting. [5]They crush your people, O LORD; they oppress your inheritance. [6]They slay the widow and the alien; they murder the fatherless. [7]They say, "The LORD does not see; the God of Jacob pays no heed."

[8]Take heed, you senseless ones among the people; you fools, when will you become wise? (+Ps 140:9)

Mocking sin—

Pr 14:9 Fools mock at making amends for sin, but goodwill is found among the upright.

Obdurate (Ps 10:4,11; Pr 1:29-30)—

Isa 26:10 Though grace is shown to the wicked, they do not learn righteousness; even in a land of uprightness they go on doing evil and regard not the majesty of the LORD. [11]O LORD, your hand is lifted high, but they do not see it. Let them see your zeal for your people and be put to shame; let the fire reserved for your enemies consume them.

Eze 3:7 But the house of Israel is not willing to listen to you because they are not willing to listen to me, for the whole house of Israel is hardened and obstinate.

Outsiders—

Mk 4:11 He told them, "The secret of the kingdom of God has been given to you. But to those on the outside everything is said in parables

Past feeling—

Eph 4:19 Having lost all sensitivity, they have given themselves over to sensuality so as to indulge in every kind of impurity, with a continual lust for more.

Progressing in wickedness—

Isa 30:1 "Woe to the obstinate children," declares the LORD, "to those who carry out plans that are not mine, forming an alliance, but not by my Spirit, heaping sin upon sin;

Isa 30:10 They say to the seers, "See no more visions!" and to the prophets, "Give us no more visions of what is right! Tell us pleasant things, prophesy illusions. [11]Leave this way, get off this path, and stop confronting us with the Holy One of Israel!" (+Jer 9:3; 2Ti 3:13)

Rebellious—

Dt 9:24 You have been rebellious against the LORD ever since I have known you.

Sensual (Php 3:19; Jude 19).

Servants of sin—

Jn 8:34 Jesus replied, "I tell you the truth, everyone who sins is a slave to sin.

Shameful—

Eph 5:11 Have nothing to do with the fruitless deeds of darkness, but rather expose them. [12]For it is shameful even to mention what the disobedient do in secret.

Shameless—

Jer 6:15 Are they ashamed of their loathsome conduct? No, they have no shame at all; they do not even know how to blush. So they will fall among the fallen; they will be brought down when I punish them," says the LORD. (+Jer 8:12)

Zep 3:5 The LORD within her is righteous; he does no wrong. Morning by morning he dispenses his justice, and every new day he does not fail, yet the unrighteous know no shame.

Unscrupulous—

Job 24:2 Men move boundary stones; they pasture flocks they have stolen. [3]They drive away the orphan's donkey and take the widow's ox in pledge. [4]They thrust the needy from the path and force all the poor of the land into hiding. [5]Like wild donkeys in the desert, the poor go about their labor of foraging food; the wasteland provides food for their children. [6]They gather fodder in the fields and glean in the vineyards of the wicked. [7]Lacking clothes, they spend the night naked; they have nothing to cover themselves in the cold. [8]They are drenched by mountain rains and hug the rocks for lack of shelter. [9]The fatherless child is snatched from the breast; the infant of the poor is seized for a debt. [10]Lacking clothes, they go about naked; they carry the sheaves, but still go hungry. [11]They crush olives among the terraces; they tread the winepresses, yet suffer thirst. [12]The groans of the dying rise from the city, and the souls of the wounded cry out for help. But God charges no one with wrongdoing.

[13]"There are those who rebel against the light, who do not know its ways or stay in its paths. [14]When daylight is gone, the murderer rises up and kills the poor and needy; in the night he steals forth like a thief. [15]The eye of the adulterer watches for dusk; he thinks, 'No eye will see me,' and he keeps his face concealed. [16]In the dark, men break into houses, but by day they shut themselves in; they want nothing to do with the light. [17]For all of them, deep darkness is their morning; they make friends with the terrors of darkness.

[18]"Yet they are foam on the surface of the water; their

portion of the land is cursed, so that no one goes to the vineyards. ¹⁹As heat and drought snatch away the melted snow, so the grave snatches away those who have sinned. ²⁰The womb forgets them, the worm feasts on them; evil men are no longer remembered but are broken like a tree. ²¹They prey on the barren and childless woman, and to the widow show no kindness. ²²But God drags away the mighty by his power; though they become established, they have no assurance of life. ²³He may let them rest in a feeling of security, but his eyes are on their ways. ²⁴For a little while they are exalted, and then they are gone; they are brought low and gathered up like all others; they are cut off like heads of grain. (+Ps 10:4-10)

Isa 5:18 Woe to those who draw sin along with cords of deceit, and wickedness as with cart ropes, ¹⁹to those who say, "Let God hurry, let him hasten his work so we may see it. Let it approach, let the plan of the Holy One of Israel come, so we may know it."

²⁰Woe to those who call evil good and good evil, who put darkness for light and light for darkness, who put bitter for sweet and sweet for bitter.

²¹Woe to those who are wise in their own eyes and clever in their own sight.

²²Woe to those who are heroes at drinking wine and champions at mixing drinks, ²³who acquit the guilty for a bribe, but deny justice to the innocent.

Jer 5:26 "Among my people are wicked men who lie in wait like men who snare birds and like those who set traps to catch men. ²⁷Like cages full of birds, their houses are full of deceit; they have become rich and powerful ²⁸and have grown fat and sleek. Their evil deeds have no limit; they do not plead the case of the fatherless to win it, they do not defend the rights of the poor. (+Jer 9:2)

Jer 9:3 "They make ready their tongue like a bow, to shoot lies; it is not by truth that they triumph in the land. They go from one sin to another; they do not acknowledge me," declares the LORD. ⁴"Beware of your friends; do not trust your brothers. For every brother is a deceiver, and every friend a slanderer. ⁵Friend deceives friend, and no one speaks the truth. They have taught their tongues to lie; they weary themselves with sinning. ⁶You live in the midst of deception; in their deceit they refuse to acknowledge me," declares the LORD.

Sold to work iniquity—

1Ki 21:20 Ahab said to Elijah, "So you have found me, my enemy!" "I have found you," he answered, "because you have sold yourself to do evil in the eyes of the LORD."

Stiff-necked—

Dt 9:13 And the LORD said to me, "I have seen this people, and they are a stiff-necked people indeed! (+Ac 7:51)

Under condemnation—

Jn 3:18 Whoever believes in him is not condemned, but whoever does not believe stands condemned already because he has not believed in the name of God's one and only Son. ¹⁹This is the verdict: Light has come into the world, but men loved darkness instead of light because their deeds were evil.

Unclean (Ezr 9:11)—

Job 14:4 Who can bring what is pure from the impure? No one!

Hag 2:14 Then Haggai said, "'So it is with this people and this nation in my sight,' declares the LORD. 'Whatever they do and whatever they offer there is defiled.

Ungodly (Ro 5:6), without strength (Ro 5:6).

Vomit—

Lev 18:25 Even the land was defiled; so I punished it for its sin, and the land vomited out its inhabitants. (cf. Rev 3:16)

Wretched, miserable, poor, blind, naked—

Rev 3:17 You say, 'I am rich; I have acquired wealth and do not need a thing.' But you do not realize that you are wretched, pitiful, poor, blind and naked. ¹⁸I counsel you to buy from me gold refined in the fire, so you can become rich; and white clothes to wear, so you can cover your shameful nakedness; and salve to put on your eyes, so you can see.

Happiness of:

Sensual (Isa 22:13; 56:12). Limited to this life (Lk 16:25). Ends suddenly (Job 21:12-13; Lk 12:19-20).

Hope of:

Shall perish (Job 8:13; 11:20; 27:8; Pr 10:28).

Miscellany concerning:

Hate reproof (1Ki 22:8; 2Ch 18:7). God's mercy to (Job 33:14-30). God's love for (Dt 5:29; 32:29; Mt 18:12-14; Jn 3:16-17; Ro 5:8; 1Jn 4:9-10).

Gospel invitation to, illustrated by the parables of the householder (Mt 20:1-16), and marriage supper (Mt 22:1-14).

Terrors of, at the judgment (Rev 1:7). Death of (Ps 49:14; 73:3-4,17-19).

Prayers of:

Abominable to God—

Pr 15:8 The LORD detests the sacrifice of the wicked, but the prayer of the upright pleases him.

Pr 15:29 The LORD is far from the wicked but he hears the prayer of the righteous. (+Pr 21:27)

Pr 28:9 If anyone turns a deaf ear to the law, even his prayers are detestable.

Not answered—

Dt 1:45 You came back and wept before the LORD, but he paid no attention to your weeping and turned a deaf ear to you. (+1Sa 28:6)

2Sa 22:42 They cried for help, but there was no one to save them—to the LORD, but he did not answer.

Job 27:9 Does God listen to his cry when distress comes upon him?

Job 35:12 He does not answer when men cry out because of the arrogance of the wicked. ¹³Indeed, God does not listen to their empty plea; the Almighty pays no attention to it.

Ps 18:41 They cried for help, but there was no one to save them—to the LORD, but he did not answer.

Ps 66:18 If I had cherished sin in my heart, the Lord would not have listened;

Pr 1:24 But since you rejected me when I called and no one gave heed when I stretched out my hand, ²⁵since you ignored all my advice and would not accept my rebuke, ²⁶I in turn will laugh at your disaster; I will mock when calamity overtakes you— ²⁷when calamity overtakes you like a storm, when disaster sweeps over you like a whirlwind, when distress and trouble overwhelm you.

²⁸"Then they will call to me but I will not answer; they will look for me but will not find me.

Pr 21:13 If a man shuts his ears to the cry of the poor, he too will cry out and not be answered.

Pr 21:27 The sacrifice of the wicked is detestable—how much more so when brought with evil intent!

Isa 1:15 When you spread out your hands in prayer, I will hide my eyes from you; even if you offer many prayers, I will not listen. Your hands are full of blood;

Isa 59:2 But your iniquities have separated you from your God; your sins have hidden his face from you, so that he will not hear.

Jer 11:11 Therefore this is what the LORD says: 'I will bring on them a disaster they cannot escape. Although they cry out to me, I will not listen to them.

Jer 14:12 Although they fast, I will not listen to their cry; though they offer burnt offerings and grain offerings, I will not accept them. Instead, I will destroy them with the sword, famine and plague."

Jer 18:17 Like a wind from the east, I will scatter them before their enemies; I will show them my back and not my face in the day of their disaster."

La 3:8 Even when I call out or cry for help, he shuts out my prayer.

La 3:44 You have covered yourself with a cloud so that no prayer can get through.

Eze 8:18 Therefore I will deal with them in anger; I will not look on them with pity or spare them. Although they shout in my ears, I will not listen to them."

Eze 20:3 "Son of man, speak to the elders of Israel and say to them, 'This is what the Sovereign LORD says: Have you come to inquire of me? As surely as I live, I will not let you inquire of me, declares the Sovereign LORD.'

Eze 20:31 When you offer your gifts—the sacrifice of your sons in the fire—you continue to defile yourselves with all your idols to this day. Am I to let you inquire of me, O house of Israel? As surely as I live, declares the Sovereign LORD, I will not let you inquire of me.

Hos 5:6 When they go with their flocks and herds to seek the LORD, they will not find him; he has withdrawn himself from them.

Mic 3:4 Then they will cry out to the LORD, but he will not answer them. At that time he will hide his face from them because of the evil they have done.

Zec 7:13 "'When I called, they did not listen; so when they called, I would not listen,' says the LORD Almighty.

Mal 1:9 "Now implore God to be gracious to us. With such offerings from your hands, will he accept you?"—says the LORD Almighty.

Mal 2:11 Judah has broken faith. A detestable thing has been committed in Israel and in Jerusalem: Judah has desecrated the sanctuary the LORD loves, by marrying the daughter of a foreign god. ¹²As for the man who does this, whoever he may be, may the LORD cut him off from the tents of Jacob—even though he brings offerings to the LORD Almighty.

¹³Another thing you do: You flood the LORD's altar with tears. You weep and wail because he no longer pays attention to your offerings or accepts them with pleasure from your hands.

Jn 9:31 We know that God does not listen to sinners. He listens to the godly man who does his will.

Jas 1:6 But when he asks, he must believe and not doubt, because he who doubts is like a wave of the sea, blown and tossed by the wind. ⁷That man should not think he will receive anything from the Lord;

Jas 4:3 When you ask, you do not receive, because you ask with wrong motives, that you may spend what you get on your pleasures.

1Pe 3:7 Husbands, in the same way be considerate as you live with your wives, and treat them with respect as the weaker partner and as heirs with you of the gracious gift of life, so that nothing will hinder your prayers.

On behalf of, not answered—

Dt 3:26 But because of you the LORD was angry with me and would not listen to me. "That is enough," the LORD said. "Do not speak to me anymore about this matter.

Jer 15:11 The LORD said, "Surely I will deliver you for a good purpose; surely I will make your enemies plead with you in times of disaster and times of distress.

Prosperity of:

(Job 12:6; 21:7-13; Ps 73:3-12; Jer 12:1-2; Mal 3:15). Brief (Job 5:3-5; 15:21,23,27,29; 20:5,22-23; 21:17-18; 24:24; Ps 37:35-36; 49:10-14; 73:18-19; 92:7; Ecc 8:12-13).

Punishment of:

Ge 4:7 If you do what is right, will you not be accepted? But if you do not do what is right, sin is crouching at your door; it desires to have you, but you must master it."

Ex 20:5 You shall not bow down to them or worship them; for I, the LORD your God, am a jealous God, punishing the children for the sin of the fathers to the third and fourth generation of those who hate me, (+Ex 34:7)

Nu 32:23 "But if you fail to do this, you will be sinning against the LORD; and you may be sure that your sin will find you out.

1Sa 3:11 And the LORD said to Samuel: "See, I am about to do something in Israel that will make the ears of everyone who hears of it tingle. ¹²At that time I will carry out against Eli everything I spoke against his family—from beginning to end. ¹³For I told him that I would judge his family forever because of the sin he knew about; his sons made themselves contemptible, and he failed to restrain them. ¹⁴Therefore, I swore to the house of Eli, 'The guilt of Eli's house will never be atoned for by sacrifice or offering.'"

2Sa 3:39 And today, though I am the anointed king, I am weak, and these sons of Zeruiah are too strong for me. May the LORD repay the evildoer according to his evil deeds!"

2Sa 7:14 I will be his father, and he will be my son. When he does wrong, I will punish him with the rod of men, with floggings inflicted by men.

2Sa 22:27 to the pure you show yourself pure, but to the crooked you show yourself shrewd. ²⁸You save the humble, but your eyes are on the haughty to bring them low.

2Sa 23:6 But evil men are all to be cast aside like thorns, which are not gathered with the hand. ⁷Whoever touches thorns uses a tool of iron or the shaft of a spear; they are burned up where they lie."

1Ki 21:20 Ahab said to Elijah, "So you have found me, my enemy!"

"I have found you," he answered, "because you have sold yourself to do evil in the eyes of the LORD.

²¹"I am going to bring disaster on you. I will consume your descendants and cut off from Ahab every last male in Israel—slave or free.

Job 8:20 "Surely God does not reject a blameless man or strengthen the hands of evildoers.

Job 8:22 Your enemies will be clothed in shame, and the tents of the wicked will be no more."

Job 11:20 But the eyes of the wicked will fail, and escape will elude them; their hope will become a dying gasp."

Job 18:5 "The lamp of the wicked is snuffed out; the flame of his fire stops burning. ⁶The light in his tent becomes dark; the lamp beside him goes out. ⁷The vigor of his step is weakened; his own schemes throw him down. ⁸His feet thrust him into a net and he wanders into its mesh.

⁹A trap seizes him by the heel; a snare holds him fast. ¹⁰A noose is hidden for him on the ground; a trap lies in his path. ¹¹Terrors startle him on every side and dog his every step. ¹²Calamity is hungry for him; disaster is ready for him when he falls. ¹³It eats away parts of his skin; death's firstborn devours his limbs. ¹⁴He is torn from the security of his tent and marched off to the king of terrors. ¹⁵Fire resides in his tent; burning sulfur is scattered over his dwelling. ¹⁶His roots dry up below and his branches wither above. ¹⁷The memory of him perishes from the earth; he has no name in the land. ¹⁸He is driven from light into darkness and is banished from the world. ¹⁹He has no offspring or descendants among his people, no survivor where once he lived. ²⁰Men of the west are appalled at his fate; men of the east are seized with horror. ²¹Surely such is the dwelling of an evil man; such is the place of one who knows not God."

Job 19:29 you should fear the sword yourselves; for wrath will bring punishment by the sword, and then you will know that there is judgment."

Job 21:7 Why do the wicked live on, growing old and increasing in power? ⁸They see their children established around them, their offspring before their eyes. ⁹Their homes are safe and free from fear; the rod of God is not upon them. ¹⁰Their bulls never fail to breed; their cows calve and do not miscarry. ¹¹They send forth their children as a flock; their little ones dance about. ¹²They sing to the music of tambourine and harp; they make merry to the sound of the flute. ¹³They spend their years in prosperity and go down to the grave in peace. ¹⁴Yet they say to God, 'Leave us alone! We have no desire to know your ways. ¹⁵Who is the Almighty, that we should serve him? What would we gain by praying to him?' ¹⁶But their prosperity is not in their own hands, so I stand aloof from the counsel of the wicked.

¹⁷"Yet how often is the lamp of the wicked snuffed out? How often does calamity come upon them, the fate God allots in his anger? ¹⁸How often are they like straw before the wind, like chaff swept away by a gale? ¹⁹[It is said,] 'God stores up a man's punishment for his sons.' Let him repay the man himself, so that he will know it! ²⁰Let his own eyes see his destruction; let him drink of the wrath of the Almighty. ²¹For what does he care about the family he leaves behind when his allotted months come to an end?

²²"Can anyone teach knowledge to God, since he judges even the highest? ²³One man dies in full vigor, completely secure and at ease, ²⁴his body well nourished, his bones rich with marrow. ²⁵Another man dies in bitterness of soul, never having enjoyed anything good. ²⁶Side by side they lie in the dust, and worms cover them both.

²⁷"I know full well what you are thinking, the schemes by which you would wrong me. ²⁸You say, 'Where now is the great man's house, the tents where wicked men lived?' ²⁹Have you never questioned those who travel? Have you paid no regard to their accounts— ³⁰that the evil man is spared from the day of calamity, that he is delivered from the day of wrath? ³¹Who denounces his conduct to his face? Who repays him for what he has done? ³²He is carried to the grave, and watch is kept over his tomb. ³³The soil in the valley is sweet to him; all men follow after him, and a countless throng goes before him.

Job 27:13 "Here is the fate God allots to the wicked, the heritage a ruthless man receives from the Almighty: ¹⁴However many his children, their fate is the sword; his offspring will never have enough to eat. ¹⁵The plague will bury those who survive him, and their widows will not

weep for them. ¹⁶Though he heaps up silver like dust and clothes like piles of clay, ¹⁷what he lays up the righteous will wear, and the innocent will divide his silver. ¹⁸The house he builds is like a moth's cocoon, like a hut made by a watchman. ¹⁹He lies down wealthy, but will do so no more; when he opens his eyes, all is gone. ²⁰Terrors overtake him like a flood; a tempest snatches him away in the night. ²¹The east wind carries him off, and he is gone; it sweeps him out of his place. ²²It hurls itself against him without mercy as he flees headlong from its power. ²³It claps its hands in derision and hisses him out of his place.

Job 36:12 But if they do not listen, they will perish by the sword and die without knowledge.

Job 36:17 But now you are laden with the judgment due the wicked; judgment and justice have taken hold of you.

Ps 3:7 Arise, O Lord! Deliver me, O my God! Strike all my enemies on the jaw; break the teeth of the wicked.

Ps 5:5 The arrogant cannot stand in your presence; you hate all who do wrong.

Ps 18:14 He shot his arrows and scattered [the enemies], great bolts of lightning and routed them. (+Ps 18:26-27)

Ps 36:12 See how the evildoers lie fallen—thrown down, not able to rise!

Ps 37:1 Do not fret because of evil men or be envious of those who do wrong; ²for like the grass they will soon wither, like green plants they will soon die away.

Ps 37:9 For evil men will be cut off, but those who hope in the Lord will inherit the land. ¹⁰A little while, and the wicked will be no more; though you look for them, they will not be found.

Ps 37:17 for the power of the wicked will be broken, but the Lord upholds the righteous.

Ps 37:20 But the wicked will perish: The Lord's enemies will be like the beauty of the fields, they will vanish—vanish like smoke.

Ps 37:22 those the Lord blesses will inherit the land, but those he curses will be cut off.

Ps 37:34 Wait for the Lord and keep his way. He will exalt you to inherit the land; when the wicked are cut off, you will see it.

³⁵I have seen a wicked and ruthless man flourishing like a green tree in its native soil, ³⁶but he soon passed away and was no more; though I looked for him, he could not be found.

³⁷Consider the blameless, observe the upright; there is a future for the man of peace. ³⁸But all sinners will be destroyed; the future of the wicked will be cut off.

Ps 64:7 But God will shoot them with arrows; suddenly they will be struck down. ⁸He will turn their own tongues against them and bring them to ruin; all who see them will shake their heads in scorn.

Ps 73:18 Surely you place them on slippery ground; you cast them down to ruin. ¹⁹How suddenly are they destroyed, completely swept away by terrors! ²⁰As a dream when one awakes, so when you arise, O Lord, you will despise them as fantasies.

Ps 73:27 Those who are far from you will perish; you destroy all who are unfaithful to you.

Ps 91:8 You will only observe with your eyes and see the punishment of the wicked.

Ps 97:3 Fire goes before him and consumes his foes on every side.

Ps 107:17 Some became fools through their rebellious ways and suffered affliction because of their iniquities.

Ps 107:33 He turned rivers into a desert, flowing springs into thirsty ground, [34]and fruitful land into a salt waste, because of the wickedness of those who lived there.

Ps 119:21 You rebuke the arrogant, who are cursed and who stray from your commands.

Ps 119:118 You reject all who stray from your decrees, for their deceitfulness is in vain. [119]All the wicked of the earth you discard like dross; therefore I love your statutes.

Ps 119:155 Salvation is far from the wicked, for they do not seek out your decrees.

Ps 129:4 But the LORD is righteous; he has cut me free from the cords of the wicked.

Ps 146:9 The LORD watches over the alien and sustains the fatherless and the widow, but he frustrates the ways of the wicked.

Ps 147:6 The LORD sustains the humble but casts the wicked to the ground.

Pr 3:33 The LORD's curse is on the house of the wicked, but he blesses the home of the righteous.

Pr 10:3 The LORD does not let the righteous go hungry but he thwarts the craving of the wicked.

Pr 10:6 Blessings crown the head of the righteous, but violence overwhelms the mouth of the wicked.

[7]The memory of the righteous will be a blessing, but the name of the wicked will rot. (+Pr 10:8)

Pr 10:14 Wise men store up knowledge, but the mouth of a fool invites ruin.

Pr 10:24 What the wicked dreads will overtake him; what the righteous desire will be granted.

[25]When the storm has swept by, the wicked are gone, but the righteous stand firm forever.

Pr 10:27 The fear of the LORD adds length to life, but the years of the wicked are cut short.

[28]The prospect of the righteous is joy, but the hopes of the wicked come to nothing.

[29]The way of the LORD is a refuge for the righteous, but it is the ruin of those who do evil.

[30]The righteous will never be uprooted, but the wicked will not remain in the land.

[31]The mouth of the righteous brings forth wisdom, but a perverse tongue will be cut out.

Pr 11:3 The integrity of the upright guides them, but the unfaithful are destroyed by their duplicity.

Pr 11:5 The righteousness of the blameless makes a straight way for them, but the wicked are brought down by their own wickedness.

[6]The righteousness of the upright delivers them, but the unfaithful are trapped by evil desires.

[7]When a wicked man dies, his hope perishes; all he expected from his power comes to nothing.

[8]The righteous man is rescued from trouble, and it comes on the wicked instead.

Pr 11:19 The truly righteous man attains life, but he who pursues evil goes to his death.

Pr 11:21 Be sure of this: The wicked will not go unpunished, but those who are righteous will go free.

Pr 11:23 The desire of the righteous ends only in good, but the hope of the wicked only in wrath.

Pr 11:31 If the righteous receive their due on earth, how much more the ungodly and the sinner!

Pr 13:2 From the fruit of his lips a man enjoys good things, but the unfaithful have a craving for violence.

Pr 13:5 The righteous hate what is false, but the wicked bring shame and disgrace.

[6]Righteousness guards the man of integrity, but wickedness overthrows the sinner.

Pr 13:9 The light of the righteous shines brightly, but the lamp of the wicked is snuffed out.

Pr 13:21 Misfortune pursues the sinner, but prosperity is the reward of the righteous.

Pr 13:25 The righteous eat to their hearts' content, but the stomach of the wicked goes hungry.

Pr 14:12 There is a way that seems right to a man, but in the end it leads to death.

Pr 14:19 Evil men will bow down in the presence of the good, and the wicked at the gates of the righteous.

Pr 14:32 When calamity comes, the wicked are brought down, but even in death the righteous have a refuge.

Pr 16:4 The LORD works out everything for his own ends—even the wicked for a day of disaster.

[5]The LORD detests all the proud of heart. Be sure of this: They will not go unpunished.

Pr 22:5 In the paths of the wicked lie thorns and snares, but he who guards his soul stays far from them.

Pr 22:23 for the LORD will take up their case and will plunder those who plunder them.

Ecc 8:12 Although a wicked man commits a hundred crimes and still lives a long time, I know that it will go better with God-fearing men, who are reverent before God. [13]Yet because the wicked do not fear God, it will not go well with them, and their days will not lengthen like a shadow.

Isa 3:11 Woe to the wicked! Disaster is upon them! They will be paid back for what their hands have done.

Isa 26:21 See, the LORD is coming out of his dwelling to punish the people of the earth for their sins. The earth will disclose the blood shed upon her; she will conceal her slain no longer.

Jer 21:14 I will punish you as your deeds deserve, declares the LORD. I will kindle a fire in your forests that will consume everything around you.'"

Jer 36:31 I will punish him and his children and his attendants for their wickedness; I will bring on them and those living in Jerusalem and the people of Judah every disaster I pronounced against them, because they have not listened.'" (+La 3:39)

Eze 3:18 When I say to a wicked man, 'You will surely die,' and you do not warn him or speak out to dissuade him from his evil ways in order to save his life, that wicked man will die for his sin, and I will hold you accountable for his blood. [19]But if you do warn the wicked man and he does not turn from his wickedness or from his evil ways, he will die for his sin; but you will have saved yourself. [20]"Again, when a righteous man turns from his righteousness and does evil, and I put a stumbling block before him, he will die. Since you did not warn him, he will die for his sin. The righteous things he did will not be remembered, and I will hold you accountable for his blood.

Eze 18:1 The word of the LORD came to me: [2]"What do you people mean by quoting this proverb about the land of Israel:

"'The fathers eat sour grapes, and the children's teeth are set on edge'?

[3]"As surely as I live, declares the Sovereign LORD, you will no longer quote this proverb in Israel. [4]For every living soul belongs to me, the father as well as the son—both alike belong to me. The soul who sins is the one who will die.

[5]"Suppose there is a righteous man who does what is just and right. [6]He does not eat at the mountain shrines or look to the idols of the house of Israel. He does not defile his neighbor's wife or lie with a woman during her period.

[7]He does not oppress anyone, but returns what he took in pledge for a loan. He does not commit robbery but gives his food to the hungry and provides clothing for the naked. [8]He does not lend at usury or take excessive interest. He withholds his hand from doing wrong and judges fairly between man and man. [9]He follows my decrees and faithfully keeps my laws. That man is righteous; he will surely live, declares the Sovereign LORD.

[10]"Suppose he has a violent son, who sheds blood or does any of these other things [11](though the father has done none of them):

"He eats at the mountain shrines. He defiles his neighbor's wife. [12]He oppresses the poor and needy. He commits robbery. He does not return what he took in pledge. He looks to the idols. He does detestable things. [13]He lends at usury and takes excessive interest.

Will such a man live? He will not! Because he has done all these detestable things, he will surely be put to death and his blood will be on his own head.

[14]"But suppose this son has a son who sees all the sins his father commits, and though he sees them, he does not do such things:

[15]"He does not eat at the mountain shrines or look to the idols of the house of Israel. He does not defile his neighbor's wife. [16]He does not oppress anyone or require a pledge for a loan. He does not commit robbery but gives his food to the hungry and provides clothing for the naked. [17]He withholds his hand from sin and takes no usury or excessive interest. He keeps my laws and follows my decrees.

He will not die for his father's sin; he will surely live. [18]But his father will die for his own sin, because he practiced extortion, robbed his brother and did what was wrong among his people.

[19]"Yet you ask, 'Why does the son not share the guilt of his father?' Since the son has done what is just and right and has been careful to keep all my decrees, he will surely live. [20]The soul who sins is the one who will die. The son will not share the guilt of the father, nor will the father share the guilt of the son. The righteousness of the righteous man will be credited to him, and the wickedness of the wicked will be charged against him.

[21]"But if a wicked man turns away from all the sins he has committed and keeps all my decrees and does what is just and right, he will surely live; he will not die. [22]None of the offenses he has committed will be remembered against him. Because of the righteous things he has done, he will live. [23]Do I take any pleasure in the death of the wicked? declares the Sovereign LORD. Rather, am I not pleased when they turn from their ways and live?

[24]"But if a righteous man turns from his righteousness and commits sin and does the same detestable things the wicked man does, will he live? None of the righteous things he has done will be remembered. Because of the unfaithfulness he is guilty of and because of the sins he has committed, he will die.

[25]"Yet you say, 'The way of the Lord is not just.' Hear, O house of Israel: Is my way unjust? Is it not your ways that are unjust? [26]If a righteous man turns from his righteousness and commits sin, he will die for it; because of the sin he has committed he will die. [27]But if a wicked man turns away from the wickedness he has committed and does what is just and right, he will save his life. [28]Because he considers all the offenses he has committed and turns away from them, he will surely live; he will not die. [29]Yet the house of Israel says, 'The way of the Lord is not just.'

Are my ways unjust, O house of Israel? Is it not your ways that are unjust?

[30]"Therefore, O house of Israel, I will judge you, each one according to his ways, declares the Sovereign LORD. Repent! Turn away from all your offenses; then sin will not be your downfall. [31]Rid yourselves of all the offenses you have committed, and get a new heart and a new spirit. Why will you die, O house of Israel? [32]For I take no pleasure in the death of anyone, declares the Sovereign LORD. Repent and live!

Eze 33:7 "Son of man, I have made you a watchman for the house of Israel; so hear the word I speak and give them warning from me. [8]When I say to the wicked, 'O wicked man, you will surely die,' and you do not speak out to dissuade him from his ways, that wicked man will die for his sin, and I will hold you accountable for his blood. [9]But if you do warn the wicked man to turn from his ways and he does not do so, he will die for his sin, but you will have saved yourself.

[10]"Son of man, say to the house of Israel, 'This is what you are saying: "Our offenses and sins weigh us down, and we are wasting away because of them. How then can we live?"' [11]Say to them, 'As surely as I live, declares the Sovereign LORD, I take no pleasure in the death of the wicked, but rather that they turn from their ways and live. Turn! Turn from your evil ways! Why will you die, O house of Israel?'

[12]"Therefore, son of man, say to your countrymen, 'The righteousness of the righteous man will not save him when he disobeys, and the wickedness of the wicked man will not cause him to fall when he turns from it. The righteous man, if he sins, will not be allowed to live because of his former righteousness.' [13]If I tell the righteous man that he will surely live, but then he trusts in his righteousness and does evil, none of the righteous things he has done will be remembered; he will die for the evil he has done. [14]And if I say to the wicked man, 'You will surely die,' but he then turns away from his sin and does what is just and right— [15]if he gives back what he took in pledge for a loan, returns what he has stolen, follows the decrees that give life, and does no evil, he will surely live; he will not die. [16]None of the sins he has committed will be remembered against him. He has done what is just and right; he will surely live.

[17]"Yet your countrymen say, 'The way of the Lord is not just.' But it is their way that is not just. [18]If a righteous man turns from his righteousness and does evil, he will die for it. [19]And if a wicked man turns away from his wickedness and does what is just and right, he will live by doing so. [20]Yet, O house of Israel, you say, 'The way of the Lord is not just.' But I will judge each of you according to his own ways."

Hos 14:9 Who is wise? He will realize these things. Who is discerning? He will understand them. The ways of the LORD are right; the righteous walk in them, but the rebellious stumble in them.

Am 3:2 "You only have I chosen of all the families of the earth; therefore I will punish you for all your sins."

Mic 2:3 Therefore, the LORD says: "I am planning disaster against this people, from which you cannot save yourselves. You will no longer walk proudly, for it will be a time of calamity.

Mic 6:13 Therefore, I have begun to destroy you, to ruin you because of your sins.

Mt 15:13 He replied, "Every plant that my heavenly Father has not planted will be pulled up by the roots. (w Jn 15:2)

Ro 1:18 The wrath of God is being revealed from heaven against all the godlessness and wickedness of men who suppress the truth by their wickedness,

Ro 2:5 But because of your stubbornness and your unrepentant heart, you are storing up wrath against yourself for the day of God's wrath, when his righteous judgment will be revealed.

Ro 2:8 But for those who are self-seeking and who reject the truth and follow evil, there will be wrath and anger. ⁹There will be trouble and distress for every human being who does evil: first for the Jew, then for the Gentile;

Col 3:25 Anyone who does wrong will be repaid for his wrong, and there is no favoritism.

1Th 1:10 and to wait for his Son from heaven, whom he raised from the dead—Jesus, who rescues us from the coming wrath.

1Pe 3:12 For the eyes of the Lord are on the righteous and his ears are attentive to their prayer, but the face of the Lord is against those who do evil."

2Pe 2:3 In their greed these teachers will exploit you with stories they have made up. Their condemnation has long been hanging over them, and their destruction has not been sleeping.

⁴For if God did not spare angels when they sinned, but sent them to hell, putting them into gloomy dungeons to be held for judgment; ⁵if he did not spare the ancient world when he brought the flood on its ungodly people, but protected Noah, a preacher of righteousness, and seven others; ⁶if he condemned the cities of Sodom and Gomorrah by burning them to ashes, and made them an example of what is going to happen to the ungodly; ⁷and if he rescued Lot, a righteous man, who was distressed by the filthy lives of lawless men ⁸(for that righteous man, living among them day after day, was tormented in his righteous soul by the lawless deeds he saw and heard)— ⁹if this is so, then the Lord knows how to rescue godly men from trials and to hold the unrighteous for the day of judgment, while continuing their punishment.

2Pe 2:12 But these men blaspheme in matters they do not understand. They are like brute beasts, creatures of instinct, born only to be caught and destroyed, and like beasts they too will perish.

¹³They will be paid back with harm for the harm they have done. Their idea of pleasure is to carouse in broad daylight. They are blots and blemishes, reveling in their pleasures while they feast with you. ¹⁴With eyes full of adultery, they never stop sinning; they seduce the unstable; they are experts in greed—an accursed brood! ¹⁵They have left the straight way and wandered off to follow the way of Balaam son of Beor, who loved the wages of wickedness. ¹⁶But he was rebuked for his wrongdoing by a donkey—a beast without speech—who spoke with a man's voice and restrained the prophet's madness.

¹⁷These men are springs without water and mists driven by a storm. Blackest darkness is reserved for them.

Jude 5 Though you already know all this, I want to remind you that the Lord delivered his people out of Egypt, but later destroyed those who did not believe. ⁶And the angels who did not keep their positions of authority but abandoned their own home—these he has kept in darkness, bound with everlasting chains for judgment on the great Day. ⁷In a similar way, Sodom and Gomorrah and the surrounding towns gave themselves up to sexual immorality and perversion. They serve as an example of those who suffer the punishment of eternal fire.

Rev 14:10 he, too, will drink of the wine of God's fury,

which has been poured full strength into the cup of his wrath. He will be tormented with burning sulfur in the presence of the holy angels and of the Lamb. ¹¹And the smoke of their torment rises for ever and ever. There is no rest day or night for those who worship the beast and his image, or for anyone who receives the mark of his name."

By chastisements—

Ps 89:32 I will punish their sin with the rod, their iniquity with flogging;

1Co 5:5 hand this man over to Satan, so that the sinful nature may be destroyed and his spirit saved on the day of the Lord.

1Ti 1:20 Among them are Hymenaeus and Alexander, whom I have handed over to Satan to be taught not to blaspheme.

Judgments—

Ex 32:35 And the LORD struck the people with a plague because of what they did with the calf Aaron had made.

Lev 26:14 "'But if you will not listen to me and carry out all these commands, (+Lev 26:15)

Lev 26:16 then I will do this to you: I will bring upon you sudden terror, wasting diseases and fever that will destroy your sight and drain away your life. You will plant seed in vain, because your enemies will eat it. ¹⁷I will set my face against you so that you will be defeated by your enemies; those who hate you will rule over you, and you will flee even when no one is pursuing you.

¹⁸" 'If after all this you will not listen to me, I will punish you for your sins seven times over. (+Lev 26:19-39)

Dt 11:26 See, I am setting before you today a blessing and a curse— (+Dt 11:27)

Dt 11:28 the curse if you disobey the commands of the LORD your God and turn from the way that I command you today by following other gods, which you have not known. (+Dt 28:15-19)

Dt 28:20 The LORD will send on you curses, confusion and rebuke in everything you put your hand to, until you are destroyed and come to sudden ruin because of the evil you have done in forsaking him. (+Dt 28:21-68)

Dt 30:15 See, I set before you today life and prosperity, death and destruction. (+Dt 30:18)

Dt 30:19 This day I call heaven and earth as witnesses against you that I have set before you life and death, blessings and curses. Now choose life, so that you and your children may live

Job 20:5 that the mirth of the wicked is brief, the joy of the godless lasts but a moment. ⁶Though his pride reaches to the heavens and his head touches the clouds, ⁷he will perish forever, like his own dung; those who have seen him will say, 'Where is he?' ⁸Like a dream he flies away, no more to be found, banished like a vision of the night. ⁹The eye that saw him will not see him again; his place will look on him no more. ¹⁰His children must make amends to the poor; his own hands must give back his wealth. ¹¹The youthful vigor that fills his bones will lie with him in the dust.

¹²"Though evil is sweet in his mouth and he hides it under his tongue, ¹³though he cannot bear to let it go and keeps it in his mouth, ¹⁴yet his food will turn sour in his stomach; it will become the venom of serpents within him. ¹⁵He will spit out the riches he swallowed; God will make his stomach vomit them up. ¹⁶He will suck the poison of serpents; the fangs of an adder will kill him. ¹⁷He will not enjoy the streams, the rivers flowing with honey and cream. ¹⁸What he toiled for he must give back uneaten; he will not enjoy the profit from his trading. ¹⁹For he has

oppressed the poor and left them destitute; he has seized houses he did not build.

20"Surely he will have no respite from his craving; he cannot save himself by his treasure. **21**Nothing is left for him to devour; his prosperity will not endure. **22**In the midst of his plenty, distress will overtake him; the full force of misery will come upon him. **23**When he has filled his belly, God will vent his burning anger against him and rain down his blows upon him. **24**Though he flees from an iron weapon, a bronze-tipped arrow pierces him. **25**He pulls it out of his back, the gleaming point out of his liver. Terrors will come over him; **26**total darkness lies in wait for his treasures. A fire unfanned will consume him and devour what is left in his tent. **27**The heavens will expose his guilt; the earth will rise up against him. **28**A flood will carry off his house, rushing waters on the day of God's wrath. **29**Such is the fate God allots the wicked, the heritage appointed for them by God."

Ps 11:6 On the wicked he will rain fiery coals and burning sulfur; a scorching wind will be their lot.

Ps 21:9 At the time of your appearing you will make them like a fiery furnace. In his wrath the LORD will swallow them up, and his fire will consume them. **10**You will destroy their descendants from the earth, their posterity from mankind.

Ps 39:11 You rebuke and discipline men for their sin; you consume their wealth like a moth—each man is but a breath. *Selah*

Ps 75:8 In the hand of the LORD is a cup full of foaming wine mixed with spices; he pours it out, and all the wicked of the earth drink it down to its very dregs.

Ps 78:49 He unleashed against them his hot anger, his wrath, indignation and hostility—a band of destroying angels. **50**He prepared a path for his anger; he did not spare them from death but gave them over to the plague. (+Ps 78:51)

Isa 5:11 Woe to those who rise early in the morning to run after their drinks, who stay up late at night till they are inflamed with wine. **12**They have harps and lyres at their banquets, tambourines and flutes and wine, but they have no regard for the deeds of the LORD, no respect for the work of his hands. **13**Therefore my people will go into exile for lack of understanding; their men of rank will die of hunger and their masses will be parched with thirst. **14**Therefore the grave enlarges its appetite and opens its mouth without limit; into it will descend their nobles and masses with all their brawlers and revelers.

Isa 5:24 Therefore, as tongues of fire lick up straw and as dry grass sinks down in the flames, so their roots will decay and their flowers blow away like dust; for they have rejected the law of the LORD Almighty and spurned the word of the Holy One of Israel.

Isa 9:18 Surely wickedness burns like a fire; it consumes briers and thorns, it sets the forest thickets ablaze, so that it rolls upward in a column of smoke.

Isa 10:3 What will you do on the day of reckoning, when disaster comes from afar? To whom will you run for help? Where will you leave your riches? (+Isa 13:9,11,14-22)

Isa 24:17 Terror and pit and snare await you, O people of the earth. **18**Whoever flees at the sound of terror will fall into a pit; whoever climbs out of the pit will be caught in a snare. The floodgates of the heavens are opened, the foundations of the earth shake.

Isa 28:18 Your covenant with death will be annulled; your agreement with the grave will not stand. When the overwhelming scourge sweeps by, you will be beaten down by it. **19**As often as it comes it will carry you away; morning after morning, by day and by night, it will sweep through." The understanding of this message will bring sheer terror.

20The bed is too short to stretch out on, the blanket too narrow to wrap around you. **21**The LORD will rise up as he did at Mount Perazim, he will rouse himself as in the Valley of Gibeon—to do his work, his strange work, and perform his task, his alien task. **22**Now stop your mocking, or your chains will become heavier; the Lord, the LORD Almighty, has told me of the destruction decreed against the whole land.

Isa 65:12 I will destine you for the sword, and you will all bend down for the slaughter; for I called but you did not answer, I spoke but you did not listen. You did evil in my sight and chose what displeases me."

13Therefore this is what the Sovereign LORD says: "My servants will eat, but you will go hungry; my servants will drink, but you will go thirsty; my servants will rejoice, but you will be put to shame. **14**My servants will sing out of the joy of their hearts, but you will cry out from anguish of heart and wail in brokenness of spirit. (+Isa 65:15; Jer 5:25)

Jer 8:12 Are they ashamed of their loathsome conduct? No, they have no shame at all; they do not even know how to blush. So they will fall among the fallen; they will be brought down when they are punished, says the LORD.

13"'I will take away their harvest, declares the LORD. There will be no grapes on the vine. There will be no figs on the tree, and their leaves will wither. What I have given them will be taken from them.'"

14"Why are we sitting here? Gather together! Let us flee to the fortified cities and perish there! For the LORD our God has doomed us to perish and given us poisoned water to drink, because we have sinned against him.

Jer 8:20 "The harvest is past, the summer has ended, and we are not saved."

21Since my people are crushed, I am crushed; I mourn, and horror grips me. **22**Is there no balm in Gilead? Is there no physician there? Why then is there no healing for the wound of my people?

Jer 14:10 This is what the LORD says about this people: "They greatly love to wander; they do not restrain their feet. So the LORD does not accept them; he will now remember their wickedness and punish them for their sins."

Jer 14:12 Although they fast, I will not listen to their cry; though they offer burnt offerings and grain offerings, I will not accept them. Instead, I will destroy them with the sword, famine and plague."

Jer 25:31 The tumult will resound to the ends of the earth, for the LORD will bring charges against the nations; he will bring judgment on all mankind and put the wicked to the sword,'" declares the LORD. (+Jer 44:2-14)

Jer 44:23 Because you have burned incense and have sinned against the LORD and have not obeyed him or followed his law or his decrees or his stipulations, this disaster has come upon you, as you now see." (+Jer 44:24-29; 49:10)

La 3:39 Why should any living man complain when punished for his sins?

La 4:22 O Daughter of Zion, your punishment will end; he will not prolong your exile. But, O Daughter of Edom, he will punish your sin and expose your wickedness.

La 5:16 The crown has fallen from our head. Woe to us, for we have sinned! **17**Because of this our hearts are faint, because of these things our eyes grow dim

Eze 5:4 Again, take a few of these and throw them into the fire and burn them up. A fire will spread from there to the whole house of Israel.

Eze 5:8 "Therefore this is what the Sovereign LORD says: I myself am against you, Jerusalem, and I will inflict punishment on you in the sight of the nations. ⁹Because of all your detestable idols, I will do to you what I have never done before and will never do again. ¹⁰Therefore in your midst fathers will eat their children, and children will eat their fathers. I will inflict punishment on you and will scatter all your survivors to the winds. ¹¹Therefore as surely as I live, declares the Sovereign LORD, because you have defiled my sanctuary with all your vile images and detestable practices, I myself will withdraw my favor; I will not look on you with pity or spare you. ¹²A third of your people will die of the plague or perish by famine inside you; a third will fall by the sword outside your walls; and a third I will scatter to the winds and pursue with drawn sword.

¹³"Then my anger will cease and my wrath against them will subside, and I will be avenged. And when I have spent my wrath upon them, they will know that I the LORD have spoken in my zeal.

¹⁴"I will make you a ruin and a reproach among the nations around you, in the sight of all who pass by. ¹⁵You will be a reproach and a taunt, a warning and an object of horror to the nations around you when I inflict punishment on you in anger and in wrath and with stinging rebuke. I the LORD have spoken. ¹⁶When I shoot at you with my deadly and destructive arrows of famine, I will shoot to destroy you. I will bring more and more famine upon you and cut off your supply of food. ¹⁷I will send famine and wild beasts against you, and they will leave you childless. Plague and bloodshed will sweep through you, and I will bring the sword against you. I the LORD have spoken."

Eze 9:5 As I listened, he said to the others, "Follow him through the city and kill, without showing pity or compassion. ⁶Slaughter old men, young men and maidens, women and children, but do not touch anyone who has the mark. Begin at my sanctuary." So they began with the elders who were in front of the temple.

⁷Then he said to them, "Defile the temple and fill the courts with the slain. Go!" So they went out and began killing throughout the city.

Eze 9:10 So I will not look on them with pity or spare them, but I will bring down on their own heads what they have done."

Eze 20:8 "'But they rebelled against me and would not listen to me; they did not get rid of the vile images they had set their eyes on, nor did they forsake the idols of Egypt. So I said I would pour out my wrath on them and spend my anger against them in Egypt.

Eze 22:14 Will your courage endure or your hands be strong in the day I deal with you? I the LORD have spoken, and I will do it.

Eze 22:20 As men gather silver, copper, iron, lead and tin into a furnace to melt it with a fiery blast, so will I gather you in my anger and my wrath and put you inside the city and melt you. ²¹I will gather you and I will blow on you with my fiery wrath, and you will be melted inside her.

Eze 22:31 So I will pour out my wrath on them and consume them with my fiery anger, bringing down on their own heads all they have done, declares the Sovereign LORD."

Eze 24:13 "'Now your impurity is lewdness. Because I tried to cleanse you but you would not be cleansed from your impurity, you will not be clean again until my wrath against you has subsided.

¹⁴"'I the LORD have spoken. The time has come for me to act. I will not hold back; I will not have pity, nor will I relent. You will be judged according to your conduct and your actions, declares the Sovereign LORD.'"

Hos 2:9 "Therefore I will take away my grain when it ripens, and my new wine when it is ready. I will take back my wool and my linen, intended to cover her nakedness. ¹⁰So now I will expose her lewdness before the eyes of her lovers; no one will take her out of my hands. ¹¹I will stop all her celebrations: her yearly festivals, her New Moons, her Sabbath days—all her appointed feasts. ¹²I will ruin her vines and her fig trees, which she said were her pay from her lovers; I will make them a thicket, and wild animals will devour them. ¹³I will punish her for the days she burned incense to the Baals; she decked herself with rings and jewelry, and went after her lovers, but me she forgot," declares the LORD.

Hos 5:4 "Their deeds do not permit them to return to their God. A spirit of prostitution is in their heart; they do not acknowledge the LORD. ⁵Israel's arrogance testifies against them; the Israelites, even Ephraim, stumble in their sin; Judah also stumbles with them. ⁶When they go with their flocks and herds to seek the LORD, they will not find him; he has withdrawn himself from them.

Hos 5:9 Ephraim will be laid waste on the day of reckoning. Among the tribes of Israel I proclaim what is certain.

Hos 9:7 The days of punishment are coming, the days of reckoning are at hand. Let Israel know this. Because your sins are so many and your hostility so great, the prophet is considered a fool, the inspired man a maniac.

Hos 9:9 They have sunk deep into corruption, as in the days of Gibeah. God will remember their wickedness and punish them for their sins.

Hos 9:15 "Because of all their wickedness in Gilgal, I hated them there. Because of their sinful deeds, I will drive them out of my house. I will no longer love them; all their leaders are rebellious.

Joel 2:1 Blow the trumpet in Zion; sound the alarm on my holy hill. Let all who live in the land tremble, for the day of the LORD is coming. It is close at hand— ²a day of darkness and gloom, a day of clouds and blackness. Like dawn spreading across the mountains a large and mighty army comes, such as never was of old nor ever will be in ages to come.

Joel 3:13 Swing the sickle, for the harvest is ripe. Come, trample the grapes, for the winepress is full and the vats overflow—so great is their wickedness!"

¹⁴Multitudes, multitudes in the valley of decision! For the day of the LORD is near in the valley of decision. ¹⁵The sun and moon will be darkened, and the stars no longer shine. ¹⁶The LORD will roar from Zion and thunder from Jerusalem; the earth and the sky will tremble. But the LORD will be a refuge for his people, a stronghold for the people of Israel.

Am 5:18 Woe to you who long for the day of the LORD! Why do you long for the day of the LORD? That day will be darkness, not light. ¹⁹It will be as though a man fled from a lion only to meet a bear, as though he entered his house and rested his hand on the wall only to have a snake bite him. ²⁰Will not the day of the LORD be darkness, not light—pitch-dark, without a ray of brightness? (+Lk 12:46)

1Co 10:5 Nevertheless, God was not pleased with most of them; their bodies were scattered over the desert.

⁶Now these things occurred as examples to keep us from setting our hearts on evil things as they did. ⁷Do not be idolaters, as some of them were; as it is written: "The people sat down to eat and drink and got up to indulge in pagan revelry." ⁸We should not commit sexual immorality, as some of them did—and in one day twenty-three thousand of them died. ⁹We should not test the Lord, as some of them did—and were killed by snakes. ¹⁰And do not grumble, as some of them did—and were killed by the destroying angel.

¹¹These things happened to them as examples and were written down as warnings for us, on whom the fulfillment of the ages has come.

1Ti 5:24 The sins of some men are obvious, reaching the place of judgment ahead of them; the sins of others trail behind them. (+Heb 10:26)

Heb 10:27 but only a fearful expectation of judgment and of raging fire that will consume the enemies of God. ²⁸Anyone who rejected the law of Moses died without mercy on the testimony of two or three witnesses. ²⁹How much more severely do you think a man deserves to be punished who has trampled the Son of God under foot, who has treated as an unholy thing the blood of the covenant that sanctified him, and who has insulted the Spirit of grace? ³⁰For we know him who said, "It is mine to avenge; I will repay," and again, "The Lord will judge his people." ³¹It is a dreadful thing to fall into the hands of the living God.

1Pe 4:17 For it is time for judgment to begin with the family of God; and if it begins with us, what will the outcome be for those who do not obey the gospel of God? ¹⁸And,

"If it is hard for the righteous to be saved, what will become of the ungodly and the sinner?"

Sorrow—

Ge 3:16 To the woman he said,

"I will greatly increase your pains in childbearing; with pain you will give birth to children. Your desire will be for your husband, and he will rule over you."

¹⁷To Adam he said, "Because you listened to your wife and ate from the tree about which I commanded you, 'You must not eat of it,'

"Cursed is the ground because of you; through painful toil you will eat of it all the days of your life. ¹⁸It will produce thorns and thistles for you, and you will eat the plants of the field. ¹⁹By the sweat of your brow you will eat your food until you return to the ground, since from it you were taken; for dust you are and to dust you will return."

Job 15:20 All his days the wicked man suffers torment, the ruthless through all the years stored up for him. ²¹Terrifying sounds fill his ears; when all seems well, marauders attack him. ²²He despairs of escaping the darkness; he is marked for the sword. ²³He wanders about—food for vultures; he knows the day of darkness is at hand. ²⁴Distress and anguish fill him with terror; they overwhelm him, like a king poised to attack,

Ps 32:10 Many are the woes of the wicked, but the Lord's unfailing love surrounds the man who trusts in him.

Ecc 2:26 To the man who pleases him, God gives wisdom, knowledge and happiness, but to the sinner he gives the task of gathering and storing up wealth to hand it over to the one who pleases God. This too is meaningless, a chasing after the wind.

Isa 50:11 But now, all you who light fires and provide yourselves with flaming torches, go, walk in the light of your fires and of the torches you have set ablaze. This is

what you shall receive from my hand: You will lie down in torment.

Trouble—

Isa 48:22 "There is no peace," says the Lord, "for the wicked."

Isa 57:20 But the wicked are like the tossing sea, which cannot rest, whose waves cast up mire and mud. ²¹"There is no peace," says my God, "for the wicked."

Being rejected of the Lord—

1Ch 28:9 "And you, my son Solomon, acknowledge the God of your father, and serve him with wholehearted devotion and with a willing mind, for the Lord searches every heart and understands every motive behind the thoughts. If you seek him, he will be found by you; but if you forsake him, he will reject you forever.

2Ch 15:2 He went out to meet Asa and said to him, "Listen to me, Asa and all Judah and Benjamin. The Lord is with you when you are with him. If you seek him, he will be found by you, but if you forsake him, he will forsake you.

Mt 10:33 But whoever disowns me before men, I will disown him before my Father in heaven. (+Mk 8:38; Lk 9:26)

Lk 13:27 "But he will reply, 'I don't know you or where you come from. Away from me, all you evildoers!'

²⁸"There will be weeping there, and gnashing of teeth, when you see Abraham, Isaac and Jacob and all the prophets in the kingdom of God, but you yourselves thrown out. (+Mt 7:23; Jn 8:21)

2Ti 2:12 if we endure, we will also reign with him. If we disown him, he will also disown us; ¹³if we are faithless, he will remain faithful, for he cannot disown himself.

Heb 6:8 But land that produces thorns and thistles is worthless and is in danger of being cursed. In the end it will be burned.

Being excluded from the kingdom of heaven—

1Co 6:9 Do you not know that the wicked will not inherit the kingdom of God? Do not be deceived: Neither the sexually immoral nor idolaters nor adulterers nor male prostitutes nor homosexual offenders ¹⁰nor thieves nor the greedy nor drunkards nor slanderers nor swindlers will inherit the kingdom of God.

Gal 5:19 The acts of the sinful nature are obvious: sexual immorality, impurity and debauchery; ²⁰idolatry and witchcraft; hatred, discord, jealousy, fits of rage, selfish ambition, dissensions, factions ²¹and envy; drunkenness, orgies, and the like. I warn you, as I did before, that those who live like this will not inherit the kingdom of God.

Eph 5:5 For of this you can be sure: No immoral, impure or greedy person—such a man is an idolater—has any inheritance in the kingdom of Christ and of God. (+Rev 21:27; 22:19)

Being blotted from God's book—

Ex 32:33 The Lord replied to Moses, "Whoever has sinned against me I will blot out of my book.

Destruction—

Ge 6:3 Then the Lord said, "My Spirit will not contend with man forever, for he is mortal; his days will be a hundred and twenty years."

Ge 6:7 So the Lord said, "I will wipe mankind, whom I have created, from the face of the earth—men and animals, and creatures that move along the ground, and birds of the air—for I am grieved that I have made them."

Ge 6:12 God saw how corrupt the earth had become, for all the people on earth had corrupted their ways. ¹³So God said to Noah, "I am going to put an end to all people, for the earth is filled with violence because of them. I am surely going to destroy both them and the earth.

Nu 15:31 Because he has despised the LORD's word and broken his commands, that person must surely be cut off; his guilt remains on him.'"

Dt 7:9 Know therefore that the LORD your God is God; he is the faithful God, keeping his covenant of love to a thousand generations of those who love him and keep his commands. [10]But those who hate him he will repay to their face by destruction; he will not be slow to repay to their face those who hate him.

1Sa 12:25 Yet if you persist in doing evil, both you and your king will be swept away."

1Ch 10:13 Saul died because he was unfaithful to the LORD; he did not keep the word of the LORD and even consulted a medium for guidance, [14]and did not inquire of the LORD. So the LORD put him to death and turned the kingdom over to David son of Jesse.

Job 4:8 As I have observed, those who plow evil and those who sow trouble reap it. [9]At the breath of God they are destroyed; at the blast of his anger they perish.

Job 31:3 Is it not ruin for the wicked, disaster for those who do wrong?

Ps 2:9 You will rule them with an iron scepter; you will dash them to pieces like pottery."

Ps 7:11 God is a righteous judge, a God who expresses his wrath every day. [12]If he does not relent, he will sharpen his sword; he will bend and string his bow. [13]He has prepared his deadly weapons; he makes ready his flaming arrows.

Ps 9:5 You have rebuked the nations and destroyed the wicked; you have blotted out their name for ever and ever.

Ps 9:17 The wicked return to the grave, all the nations that forget God.

Ps 34:16 the face of the LORD is against those who do evil, to cut off the memory of them from the earth.

Ps 34:21 Evil will slay the wicked; the foes of the righteous will be condemned.

Ps 52:5 Surely God will bring you down to everlasting ruin: He will snatch you up and tear you from your tent; he will uproot you from the land of the living. *Selah*

Ps 55:19 God, who is enthroned forever, will hear them and afflict them—*Selah* men who never change their ways and have no fear of God.

Ps 55:23 But you, O God, will bring down the wicked into the pit of corruption; bloodthirsty and deceitful men will not live out half their days. But as for me, I trust in you.

Ps 92:7 that though the wicked spring up like grass and all evildoers flourish, they will be forever destroyed.

Ps 92:9 For surely your enemies, O LORD, surely your enemies will perish; all evildoers will be scattered.

Ps 94:13 you grant him relief from days of trouble, till a pit is dug for the wicked.

Ps 94:23 He will repay them for their sins and destroy them for their wickedness; the LORD our God will destroy them.

Ps 101:8 Every morning I will put to silence all the wicked in the land; I will cut off every evildoer from the city of the LORD.

Ps 104:35 But may sinners vanish from the earth and the wicked be no more. Praise the LORD, O my soul. Praise the LORD.

Ps 106:18 Fire blazed among their followers; a flame consumed the wicked.

Ps 106:43 Many times he delivered them, but they were bent on rebellion and they wasted away in their sin.

Ps 145:20 The LORD watches over all who love him, but all the wicked he will destroy.

Pr 2:22 but the wicked will be cut off from the land, and the unfaithful will be torn from it.

Pr 12:7 Wicked men are overthrown and are no more, but the house of the righteous stands firm.

Pr 21:12 The Righteous One takes note of the house of the wicked and brings the wicked to ruin.

Pr 21:15 When justice is done, it brings joy to the righteous but terror to evildoers.

[16]A man who strays from the path of understanding comes to rest in the company of the dead.

Pr 24:20 for the evil man has no future hope, and the lamp of the wicked will be snuffed out.

Isa 11:4 but with righteousness he will judge the needy, with justice he will give decisions for the poor of the earth. He will strike the earth with the rod of his mouth; with the breath of his lips he will slay the wicked. (+Isa 13:8)

Isa 64:5 You come to the help of those who gladly do right, who remember your ways. But when we continued to sin against them, you were angry. How then can we be saved? [6]All of us have become like one who is unclean, and all our righteous acts are like filthy rags; we all shrivel up like a leaf, and like the wind our sins sweep us away. [7]No one calls on your name or strives to lay hold of you; for you have hidden your face from us and made us waste away because of our sins.

Jer 13:14 I will smash them one against the other, fathers and sons alike, declares the LORD. I will allow no pity or mercy or compassion to keep me from destroying them.'"

Jer 13:16 Give glory to the LORD your God before he brings the darkness, before your feet stumble on the darkening hills. You hope for light, but he will turn it to thick darkness and change it to deep gloom.

Jer 13:22 And if you ask yourself, "Why has this happened to me?"—it is because of your many sins that your skirts have been torn off and your body mistreated.

Eze 25:7 therefore I will stretch out my hand against you and give you as plunder to the nations. I will cut you off from the nations and exterminate you from the countries. I will destroy you, and you will know that I am the LORD.'"

Hos 7:12 When they go, I will throw my net over them; I will pull them down like birds of the air. When I hear them flocking together, I will catch them. [13]Woe to them, because they have strayed from me! Destruction to them, because they have rebelled against me! I long to redeem them but they speak lies against me.

Am 8:14 They who swear by the shame of Samaria, or say, 'As surely as your god lives, O Dan,' or, 'As surely as the god of Beersheba lives'—they will fall, never to rise again."

Na 1:2 The LORD is a jealous and avenging God; the LORD takes vengeance and is filled with wrath. The LORD takes vengeance on his foes and maintains his wrath against his enemies.

Na 1:8 but with an overwhelming flood he will make an end of [Nineveh]; he will pursue his foes into darkness.

[9]Whatever they plot against the LORD he will bring to an end; trouble will not come a second time. [10]They will be entangled among thorns and drunk from their wine; they will be consumed like dry stubble.

Zep 1:12 At that time I will search Jerusalem with lamps and punish those who are complacent, who are like wine left on its dregs, who think, 'The LORD will do nothing, either good or bad.' [13]Their wealth will be plundered, their houses demolished. They will build houses but not live in them; they will plant vineyards but not drink the wine.

[14]"The great day of the LORD is near—near and coming quickly. Listen! The cry on the day of the LORD will be bitter, the shouting of the warrior there. [15]That day will be a day of wrath, a day of distress and anguish, a day of trouble and ruin, a day of darkness and gloom, a day of clouds and blackness, [16]a day of trumpet and battle cry against the fortified cities and against the corner towers. [17]I will bring distress on the people and they will walk like blind men, because they have sinned against the LORD. Their blood will be poured out like dust and their entrails like filth. [18]Neither their silver nor their gold will be able to save them on the day of the LORD's wrath. In the fire of his jealousy the whole world will be consumed, for he will make a sudden end of all who live in the earth."

Zec 5:2 He asked me, "What do you see?"

I answered, "I see a flying scroll, thirty feet long and fifteen feet wide."

[3]And he said to me, "This is the curse that is going out over the whole land; for according to what it says on one side, every thief will be banished, and according to what it says on the other, everyone who swears falsely will be banished. [4]The LORD Almighty declares, 'I will send it out, and it will enter the house of the thief and the house of him who swears falsely by my name. It will remain in his house and destroy it, both its timbers and its stones.'"

Mal 4:1 "Surely the day is coming; it will burn like a furnace. All the arrogant and every evildoer will be stubble, and that day that is coming will set them on fire," says the LORD Almighty. "Not a root or a branch will be left to them.

Mt 3:10 The ax is already at the root of the trees, and every tree that does not produce good fruit will be cut down and thrown into the fire.

Mt 3:12 His winnowing fork is in his hand, and he will clear his threshing floor, gathering his wheat into the barn and burning up the chaff with unquenchable fire." (+Lk 3:17)

Mt 7:13 "Enter through the narrow gate. For wide is the gate and broad is the road that leads to destruction, and many enter through it. (+Mt 7:19)

Mt 10:28 Do not be afraid of those who kill the body but cannot kill the soul. Rather, be afraid of the One who can destroy both soul and body in hell. (+Lk 12:4-5)

Mt 21:41 "He will bring those wretches to a wretched end," they replied, "and he will rent the vineyard to other tenants, who will give him his share of the crop at harvest time."

Mt 21:44 He who falls on this stone will be broken to pieces, but he on whom it falls will be crushed." (+Mk 12:1-9; Lk 20:16,18)

Mt 24:50 The master of that servant will come on a day when he does not expect him and at an hour he is not aware of. [51]He will cut him to pieces and assign him a place with the hypocrites, where there will be weeping and gnashing of teeth.

Lk 9:24 For whoever wants to save his life will lose it, but whoever loses his life for me will save it. [25]What good is it for a man to gain the whole world, and yet lose or forfeit his very self? (+Mt 16:26; Mk 8:36)

Lk 19:27 But those enemies of mine who did not want me to be king over them—bring them here and kill them in front of me.'"

Jn 5:29 and come out—those who have done good will

rise to live, and those who have done evil will rise to be condemned.

Ac 3:23 Anyone who does not listen to him will be completely cut off from among his people.' (+Ro 2:12)

Ro 9:22 What if God, choosing to show his wrath and make his power known, bore with great patience the objects of his wrath—prepared for destruction?

1Co 3:17 If anyone destroys God's temple, God will destroy him; for God's temple is sacred, and you are that temple.

Php 3:19 Their destiny is destruction, their god is their stomach, and their glory is in their shame. Their mind is on earthly things.

1Th 5:3 While people are saying, "Peace and safety," destruction will come on them suddenly, as labor pains on a pregnant woman, and they will not escape.

2Th 2:8 And then the lawless one will be revealed, whom the Lord Jesus will overthrow with the breath of his mouth and destroy by the splendor of his coming. [9]The coming of the lawless one will be in accordance with the work of Satan displayed in all kinds of counterfeit miracles, signs and wonders, [10]and in every sort of evil that deceives those who are perishing. They perish because they refused to love the truth and so be saved.

Sudden destruction—

Pr 6:15 Therefore disaster will overtake him in an instant; he will suddenly be destroyed—without remedy.

Pr 24:22 for those two will send sudden destruction upon them, and who knows what calamities they can bring?

Pr 28:18 He whose walk is blameless is kept safe, but he whose ways are perverse will suddenly fall.

Pr 29:1 A man who remains stiff-necked after many rebukes will suddenly be destroyed—without remedy.

Everlasting destruction—

2Th 1:9 They will be punished with everlasting destruction and shut out from the presence of the Lord and from the majesty of his power

Everlasting contempt—

Da 12:2 Multitudes who sleep in the dust of the earth will awake: some to everlasting life, others to shame and everlasting contempt.

Everlasting fire (Isa 28:18-22)—

Mt 18:8 If your hand or your foot causes you to sin cut it off and throw it away. It is better for you to enter life maimed or crippled than to have two hands or two feet and be thrown into eternal fire. [9]And if your eye causes you to sin, gouge it out and throw it away. It is better for you to enter life with one eye than to have two eyes and be thrown into the fire of hell.

Mt 25:41 "Then he will say to those on his left, 'Depart from me, you who are cursed, into the eternal fire prepared for the devil and his angels. (+Mk 9:43; Rev 20:15; 21:8)

Death—

Ge 2:17 but you must not eat from the tree of the knowledge of good and evil, for when you eat of it you will surely die."

Ps 1:4 Not so the wicked! They are like chaff that the wind blows away. [5]Therefore the wicked will not stand in the judgment, nor sinners in the assembly of the righteous.

[6]For the LORD watches over the way of the righteous, but the way of the wicked will perish. (+Pr 16:25)

Pr 19:16 He who obeys instructions guards his life, but he who is contemptuous of his ways will die.

Hos 13:1 When Ephraim spoke, men trembled; he was

exalted in Israel. But he became guilty of Baal worship and died.

Hos 13:3 Therefore they will be like the morning mist, like the early dew that disappears, like chaff swirling from a threshing floor, like smoke escaping through a window.

Am 9:1 I saw the Lord standing by the altar, and he said: "Strike the tops of the pillars so that the thresholds shake. Bring them down on the heads of all the people; those who are left I will kill with the sword. Not one will get away, none will escape. ²Though they dig down to the depths of the grave, from there my hand will take them. Though they climb up to the heavens, from there I will bring them down. ³Though they hide themselves on the top of Carmel, there I will hunt them down and seize them. Though they hide from me at the bottom of the sea, there I will command the serpent to bite them. ⁴Though they are driven into exile by their enemies, there I will command the sword to slay them. I will fix my eyes upon them for evil and not for good." ⁵The Lord, the LORD Almighty, he who touches the earth and it melts, and all who live in it mourn—the whole land rises like the Nile, then sinks like the river of Egypt—

Am 9:10 All the sinners among my people will die by the sword, all those who say, 'Disaster will not overtake or meet us.'

Ro 5:12 Therefore, just as sin entered the world through one man, and death through sin, and in this way death came to all men, because all sinned—

Ro 5:21 so that, just as sin reigned in death, so also grace might reign through righteousness to bring eternal life through Jesus Christ our Lord.

Ro 6:16 Don't you know that when you offer yourselves to someone to obey him as slaves, you are slaves to the one whom you obey—whether you are slaves to sin, which leads to death, or to obedience, which leads to righteousness?

Ro 6:21 What benefit did you reap at that time from the things you are now ashamed of? Those things result in death!

Ro 8:2 because through Christ Jesus the law of the Spirit of life set me free from the law of sin and death.

Ro 8:6 The mind of sinful man is death, but the mind controlled by the Spirit is life and peace;

Ro 8:13 For if you live according to the sinful nature, you will die; but if by the Spirit you put to death the misdeeds of the body, you will live,

1Co 15:21 For since death came through a man, the resurrection of the dead comes also through a man. ²²For as in Adam all die, so in Christ all will be made alive.

2Co 7:10 Godly sorrow brings repentance that leads to salvation and leaves no regret, but worldly sorrow brings death.

Gal 6:8 The one who sows to please his sinful nature, from that nature will reap destruction; the one who sows to please the Spirit, from the Spirit will reap eternal life.

1Jn 3:14 We know that we have passed from death to life, because we love our brothers. Anyone who does not love remains in death. ¹⁵Anyone who hates his brother is a murderer, and you know that no murderer has eternal life in him.

Jas 1:15 Then, after desire has conceived, it gives birth to sin; and sin, when it is full-grown, gives birth to death.

Jas 5:20 remember this: Whoever turns a sinner from the error of his way will save him from death and cover over a multitude of sins.

Rev 2:22 So I will cast her on a bed of suffering, and I will make those who commit adultery with her suffer intensely, unless they repent of her ways. ²³I will strike her children dead. Then all the churches will know that I am he who searches hearts and minds, and I will repay each of you according to your deeds.

The second death (Rev 21:8).

Condemnation to hell—

Mt 23:33 "You snakes! You brood of vipers! How will you escape being condemned to hell?

Mk 16:16 Whoever believes and is baptized will be saved, but whoever does not believe will be condemned.

Jn 3:15 that everyone who believes in him may have eternal life.

¹⁶"For God so loved the world that he gave his one and only Son, that whoever believes in him shall not perish but have eternal life.

Jn 3:18 Whoever believes in him is not condemned, but whoever does not believe stands condemned already because he has not believed in the name of God's one and only Son.

Jn 3:36 Whoever believes in the Son has eternal life, but whoever rejects the Son will not see life, for God's wrath remains on him."

Being cast into outer darkness—

Mt 8:12 But the subjects of the kingdom will be thrown outside, into the darkness, where there will be weeping and gnashing of teeth."

Mt 22:13 "Then the king told the attendants, 'Tie him hand and foot, and throw him outside, into the darkness, where there will be weeping and gnashing of teeth.'

Mt 25:30 And throw that worthless servant outside, into the darkness, where there will be weeping and gnashing of teeth.'

The last judgments—

Rev 6:15 Then the kings of the earth, the princes, the generals, the rich, the mighty, and every slave and every free man hid in caves and among the rocks of the mountains. ¹⁶They called to the mountains and the rocks, "Fall on us and hide us from the face of him who sits on the throne and from the wrath of the Lamb! ¹⁷For the great day of their wrath has come, and who can stand?"

Rev 9:4 They were told not to harm the grass of the earth or any plant or tree, but only those people who did not have the seal of God on their foreheads. ⁵They were not given power to kill them, but only to torture them for five months. And the agony they suffered was like that of the sting of a scorpion when it strikes a man. ⁶During those days men will seek death, but will not find it; they will long to die, but death will elude them.

Rev 9:15 And the four angels who had been kept ready for this very hour and day and month and year were released to kill a third of mankind.

Rev 9:18 A third of mankind was killed by the three plagues of fire, smoke and sulfur that came out of their mouths.

Rev 11:18 The nations were angry; and your wrath has come. The time has come for judging the dead, and for rewarding your servants the prophets and your saints and those who reverence your name, both small and great— and for destroying those who destroy the earth."

Rev 16:2 The first angel went and poured out his bowl on the land, and ugly and painful sores broke out on the people who had the mark of the beast and worshiped his image.

³The second angel poured out his bowl on the sea, and it

turned into blood like that of a dead man, and every living thing in the sea died.

⁴The third angel poured out his bowl on the rivers and springs of water, and they became blood. ⁵Then I heard the angel in charge of the waters say:

"You are just in these judgments, you who are and who were, the Holy One, because you have so judged; ⁶for they have shed the blood of your saints and prophets, and you have given them blood to drink as they deserve."

⁷And I heard the altar respond:

"Yes, Lord God Almighty, true and just are your judgments."

⁸The fourth angel poured out his bowl on the sun, and the sun was given power to scorch people with fire. ⁹They were seared by the intense heat and they cursed the name of God, who had control over these plagues, but they refused to repent and glorify him.

¹⁰The fifth angel poured out his bowl on the throne of the beast, and his kingdom was plunged into darkness. Men gnawed their tongues in agony ¹¹and cursed the God of heaven because of their pains and their sores, but they refused to repent of what they had done.

¹²The sixth angel poured out his bowl on the great river Euphrates, and its water was dried up to prepare the way for the kings from the East. ¹³Then I saw three evil spirits that looked like frogs; they came out of the mouth of the dragon, out of the mouth of the beast and out of the mouth of the false prophet. ¹⁴They are spirits of demons performing miraculous signs, and they go out to the kings of the whole world, to gather them for the battle on the great day of God Almighty.

¹⁵"Behold, I come like a thief! Blessed is he who stays awake and keeps his clothes with him, so that he may not go naked and be shamefully exposed."

¹⁶Then they gathered the kings together to the place that in Hebrew is called Armageddon.

¹⁷The seventh angel poured out his bowl into the air, and out of the temple came a loud voice from the throne, saying, "It is done!" ¹⁸Then there came flashes of lightning, rumblings, peals of thunder and a severe earthquake. No earthquake like it has ever occurred since man has been on earth, so tremendous was the quake. ¹⁹The great city split into three parts, and the cities of the nations collapsed. God remembered Babylon the Great and gave her the cup filled with the wine of the fury of his wrath. ²⁰Every island fled away and the mountains could not be found. ²¹From the sky huge hailstones of about a hundred pounds each fell upon men. And they cursed God on account of the plague of hail, because the plague was so terrible. (+Rev 18:5)

Rev 19:15 Out of his mouth comes a sharp sword with which to strike down the nations. "He will rule them with an iron scepter." He treads the winepress of the fury of the wrath of God Almighty.

Rev 19:17 And I saw an angel standing in the sun, who cried in a loud voice to all the birds flying in midair, "Come, gather together for the great supper of God, ¹⁸so that you may eat the flesh of kings, generals, and mighty men, of horses and their riders, and the flesh of all people, free and slave, small and great."

¹⁹Then I saw the beast and the kings of the earth and their armies gathered together to make war against the rider on the horse and his army. ²⁰But the beast was captured, and with him the false prophet who had performed the miraculous signs on his behalf. With these signs he had deluded those who had received the mark of the beast and

worshiped his image. The two of them were thrown alive into the fiery lake of burning sulfur. ²¹The rest of them were killed with the sword that came out of the mouth of the rider on the horse, and all the birds gorged themselves on their flesh.

Rev 20:10 And the devil, who deceived them, was thrown into the lake of burning sulfur, where the beast and the false prophet had been thrown. They will be tormented day and night for ever and ever.

Rev 20:15 If anyone's name was not found written in the book of life, he was thrown into the lake of fire.

Rev 21:8 But the cowardly, the unbelieving, the vile, the murderers, the sexually immoral, those who practice magic arts, the idolaters and all liars—their place will be in the fiery lake of burning sulfur. This is the second death."

Rev 21:27 Nothing impure will ever enter it, nor will anyone who does what is shameful or deceitful, but only those whose names are written in the Lamb's book of life.

Rev 22:19 And if anyone takes words away from this book of prophecy, God will take away from him his share in the tree of life and in the holy city, which are described in this book.

Everlasting—

Mt 25:46 "Then they will go away to eternal punishment, but the righteous to eternal life." (+Rev 14:10-11; 20:10)

Degrees in (Mt 10:15; 11:22,24)—

Mk 12:40 They devour widows' houses and for a show make lengthy prayers. Such men will be punished most severely."

No escape from—

Job 34:22 There is no dark place, no deep shadow, where evildoers can hide. (+1Th 5:3; Heb 2:3)

Punishment Illustrated in Parables:

The weeds (Mt 13:24-29)—

Mt 13:30 Let both grow together until the harvest. At that time I will tell the harvesters: First collect the weeds and tie them in bundles to be burned; then gather the wheat and bring it into my barn.'"

Mt 13:38 The field is the world, and the good seed stands for the sons of the kingdom. The weeds are the sons of the evil one, ³⁹and the enemy who sows them is the devil. The harvest is the end of the age, and the harvesters are angels.

⁴⁰"As the weeds are pulled up and burned in the fire, so it will be at the end of the age. ⁴¹The Son of Man will send out his angels, and they will weed out of his kingdom everything that causes sin and all who do evil. ⁴²They will throw them into the fiery furnace, where there will be weeping and gnashing of teeth.

Mt 13:49 This is how it will be at the end of the age. The angels will come and separate the wicked from the righteous ⁵⁰and throw them into the fiery furnace, where there will be weeping and gnashing of teeth.

The talents (Mt 25:14-30)

The barren fig tree—

Lk 13:6 Then he told this parable: "A man had a fig tree, planted in his vineyard, and he went to look for fruit on it, but did not find any. ⁷So he said to the man who took care of the vineyard, 'For three years now I've been coming to look for fruit on this fig tree and haven't found any. Cut it down! Why should it use up the soil?' (+Lk 13:8-9)

The man who built his house on the sand—

Mt 7:26 But everyone who hears these words of mine and does not put them into practice is like a foolish man who built his house on sand. ²⁷The rain came down, the streams rose, and the winds blew and beat against that house, and it fell with a great crash." (+Lk 6:49)

Lazarus and the rich man—

Lk 16:22 "The time came when the beggar died and the angels carried him to Abraham's side. The rich man also died and was buried. ²³In hell, where he was in torment, he looked up and saw Abraham far away, with Lazarus by his side. ²⁴So he called to him, 'Father Abraham, have pity on me and send Lazarus to dip the tip of his finger in water and cool my tongue, because I am in agony in this fire.'

²⁵"But Abraham replied, 'Son, remember that in your lifetime you received your good things, while Lazarus received bad things, but now he is comforted here and you are in agony. ²⁶And besides all this, between us and you a great chasm has been fixed, so that those who want to go from here to you cannot, nor can anyone cross over from there to us.'

²⁷"He answered, 'Then I beg you, father, send Lazarus to my father's house, ²⁸for I have five brothers. Let him warn them, so that they will not also come to this place of torment.'

Woes Against the Wicked: (Isa 5:8,11,18-23)

Mt 26:24 The Son of Man will go just as it is written about him. But woe to that man who betrays the Son of Man! It would be better for him if he had not been born." (+Mk 14:21; Lk 11:52)

Lk 17:1 Jesus said to his disciples: "Things that cause people to sin are bound to come, but woe to that person through whom they come. ²It would be better for him to be thrown into the sea with a millstone tied around his neck than for him to cause one of these little ones to sin. (+Lk 22:22)

Jude 11 Woe to them! They have taken the way of Cain; they have rushed for profit into Balaam's error; they have been destroyed in Korah's rebellion.

God has no pleasure in the death of (Eze 18:23; 33:11). *See Punishment.*

Warned:

(Jer 7:13-15,23-25; 25:4-6; 26:2-7,12-13; 29:17-19; Eze 33:8; Da 4:4-27; 5:4-29; Zep 2:1-2; Lk 3:7-9; 1Co 10:11; Rev 3:1-3,16-19).

See Hell; Judgments; Punishment.

WIDOW [530, 531, 851+4637, 851, 3304, *1222, 5939*].
NIV+ WIDOW'S, WIDOWHOOD, WIDOWS, WIDOWS'

Mosaic Laws Concerning:

High priest forbidden to marry (Lev 21:14). Supported by father, when daughter of priest (Lev 22:13). Vows of, binding (Nu 30:9).

Entitled to glean in the orchards and harvest fields—

Dt 24:19 When you are harvesting in your field and you overlook a sheaf, do not go back to get it. Leave it for the alien, the fatherless and the widow, so that the LORD your God may bless you in all the work of your hands. ²⁰When you beat the olives from your trees, do not go over the branches a second time. Leave what remains for the alien, the fatherless and the widow. ²¹When you harvest the grapes in your vineyard, do not go over the vines again. Leave what remains for the alien, the fatherless and the widow.

Levirate marriage of—

Dt 25:5 If brothers are living together and one of them dies without a son, his widow must not marry outside the family. Her husband's brother shall take her and marry her and fulfill the duty of a brother-in-law to her. ⁶The first son

she bears shall carry on the name of the dead brother so that his name will not be blotted out from Israel.

⁷However, if a man does not want to marry his brother's wife, she shall go to the elders at the town gate and say, "My husband's brother refuses to carry on his brother's name in Israel. He will not fulfill the duty of a brother-in-law to me." ⁸Then the elders of his town shall summon him and talk to him. If he persists in saying, "I do not want to marry her," ⁹his brother's widow shall go up to him in the presence of the elders, take off one of his sandals, spit in his face and say, "This is what is done to the man who will not build up his brother's family line." ¹⁰That man's line shall be known in Israel as The Family of the Unsandaled.

Care of commanded—

Dt 14:28 At the end of every three years, bring all the tithes of that year's produce and store it in your towns, ²⁹so that the Levites (who have no allotment or inheritance of their own) and the aliens, the fatherless and the widows who live in your towns may come and eat and be satisfied, and so that the LORD your God may bless you in all the work of your hands.

Dt 16:11 And rejoice before the LORD your God at the place he will choose as a dwelling for his Name—you, your sons and daughters, your menservants and maidservants, the Levites in your towns, and the aliens, the fatherless and the widows living among you.

Dt 16:14 Be joyful at your Feast—you, your sons and daughters, your menservants and maidservants, and the Levites, the aliens, the fatherless and the widows who live in your towns.

Isa 1:17 learn to do right! Seek justice, encourage the oppressed. Defend the cause of the fatherless, plead the case of the widow.

Jer 7:6 if you do not oppress the alien, the fatherless or the widow and do not shed innocent blood in this place, and if you do not follow other gods to your own harm, ⁷then I will let you live in this place, in the land I gave your forefathers for ever and ever.

Kindness to:

Exemplified by Job—

Job 29:13 The man who was dying blessed me; I made the widow's heart sing.

Job 31:16 "If I have denied the desires of the poor or let the eyes of the widow grow weary,

Job 31:22 then let my arm fall from the shoulder, let it be broken off at the joint.

God, the friend of—

Dt 10:18 He defends the cause of the fatherless and the widow, and loves the alien, giving him food and clothing.

Ps 68:5 A father to the fatherless, a defender of widows, is God in his holy dwelling.

Ps 146:9 The LORD watches over the alien and sustains the fatherless and the widow, but he frustrates the ways of the wicked.

Pr 15:25 The LORD tears down the proud man's house but he keeps the widow's boundaries intact.

Jer 49:11 Leave your orphans; I will protect their lives. Your widows too can trust in me."

Care of in the church—

Ac 6:1 In those days when the number of disciples was increasing, the Grecian Jews among them complained against the Hebraic Jews because their widows were being overlooked in the daily distribution of food.

1Ti 5:3 Give proper recognition to those widows who are really in need. ⁴But if a widow has children or grandchildren, these should learn first of all to put their religion into practice by caring for their own family and so repaying their parents and grandparents, for this is pleasing to God. **⁵**The widow who is really in need and left all alone puts her hope in God and continues night and day to pray and to ask God for help. **⁶**But the widow who lives for pleasure is dead even while she lives.

1Ti 5:9 No widow may be put on the list of widows unless she is over sixty, has been faithful to her husband, **¹⁰**and is well known for her good deeds, such as bringing up children, showing hospitality, washing the feet of the saints, helping those in trouble and devoting herself to all kinds of good deeds.

¹¹As for younger widows, do not put them on such a list. For when their sensual desires overcome their dedication to Christ, they want to marry. **¹²**Thus they bring judgment on themselves, because they have broken their first pledge. **1Ti 5:16** If any woman who is a believer has widows in her family, she should help them and not let the church be burdened with them, so that the church can help those widows who are really in need.

Jas 1:27 Religion that God our Father accepts as pure and faultless is this: to look after orphans and widows in their distress and to keep oneself from being polluted by the world.

Oppression of:

Job 22:9 And you sent widows away empty-handed and broke the strength of the fatherless.

Job 24:3 They drive away the orphan's donkey and take the widow's ox in pledge.

Job 24:21 They prey on the barren and childless woman, and to the widow show no kindness.

Ps 94:6 They slay the widow and the alien; they murder the fatherless.

Isa 1:23 Your rulers are rebels, companions of thieves; they all love bribes and chase after gifts. They do not defend the cause of the fatherless; the widow's case does not come before them. (+Eze 22:7)

Mk 12:40 They devour widows' houses and for a show make lengthy prayers. Such men will be punished most severely." (+Lk 20:47)

Oppression of, forbidden—

Ex 22:22 "Do not take advantage of a widow or an orphan. **²³**If you do and they cry out to me, I will certainly hear their cry. **²⁴**My anger will be aroused, and I will kill you with the sword; your wives will become widows and your children fatherless.

Dt 24:17 Do not deprive the alien or the fatherless of justice, or take the cloak of the widow as a pledge.

Dt 27:19 "Cursed is the man who withholds justice from the alien, the fatherless or the widow." Then all the people shall say, "Amen!"

Isa 10:2 to deprive the poor of their rights and withhold justice from the oppressed of my people, making widows their prey and robbing the fatherless.

Jer 22:3 This is what the LORD says: Do what is just and right. Rescue from the hand of his oppressor the one who has been robbed. Do no wrong or violence to the alien, the fatherless or the widow, and do not shed innocent blood in this place.

Zec 7:10 Do not oppress the widow or the fatherless, the alien or the poor. In your hearts do not think evil of each other.'

Mal 3:5 "So I will come near to you for judgment. I will be quick to testify against sorcerers, adulterers and perjurers, against those who defraud laborers of their wages,

who oppress the widows and the fatherless, and deprive aliens of justice, but do not fear me," says the LORD Almighty.

Widow's dowry. *See Dowry.*

Instances of:

Naomi (Ru 1:3). Ruth (Ru 1-4). The widow of Zarephath, who sustained Elijah during a famine (1Ki 17). The woman whose sons Elisha saved from being sold for debt (2Ki 4:1-7). Anna (Lk 2:36-37). The woman who gave two mites in the temple (Mk 12:41-44; Lk 21:2), of Nain, whose only son Jesus raised from the dead (Lk 7:11-15).

Remarriage of, authorized (Ro 7:3; 1Co 7:39; 1Ti 5:14). Remarriage of discouraged (1Co 7:8-9).

Qualifications for widows in 1Ti 5:3-16 may indicate a church office.

See Levirate Marriage; Marriage; Women.

WIFE [851+, 3304, 7675, *1222+, 3836*].

NIV+ WIFE'S, WIVES, WIVES'

Described:

Called a helper (Ge 2:18,20), desire of the eyes (Eze 24:10).

Compared to a fruitful vine—

Ps 128:3 Your wife will be like a fruitful vine within your house; your sons will be like olive shoots around your table.

The judgment denounced against Eve—

Ge 3:16 To the woman he said, "I will greatly increase your pains in childbearing; with pain you will give birth to children. Your desire will be for your husband, and he will rule over you."

Contentious—

Pr 19:13 A foolish son is his father's ruin, and a quarrelsome wife is like a constant dripping. (+Pr 21:9,19)

Pr 25:24 Better to live on a corner of the roof than share a house with a quarrelsome wife.

Instances of: Zipporah (Ex 4:25), Peninnah (1Sa 1:6-7). Loyal, Jacob's (Ge 31:14-16).

Unfaithful (Nu 5:12-31). Instances of: Potiphar's (Ge 39:7), Bathsheba (2Sa 11:2-5).

Prudent—

Pr 19:14 Houses and wealth are inherited from parents, but a prudent wife is from the LORD.

Tactful: Abigail (1Sa 25:3,14-34), Esther (Est 5:5-8; 7:1-4).

Virtuous—

Pr 12:4 A wife of noble character is her husband's crown, but a disgraceful wife is like decay in his bones.

Pr 31:10 A wife of noble character who can find? She is worth far more than rubies.

¹¹Her husband has full confidence in her and lacks nothing of value. **¹²**She brings him good, not harm, all the days of her life.

Incorruptible or strong-willed: Vashti (Est 1:10-12).

Wise—

Pr 14:1 The wise woman builds her house, but with her own hands the foolish one tears hers down.

Beloved, by Isaac (Ge 24:67), by Jacob (Ge 29:30). Hated (Ge 29:31-33).

Marrying of:

Commended—

Pr 18:22 He who finds a wife finds what is good and receives favor from the LORD. (+1Co 7:2)

1Ti 5:14 So I counsel younger widows to marry, to have

children, to manage their homes and to give the enemy no opportunity for slander.

Bought (Ge 29:18-30; 31:41; Ex 21:7-11; Ru 4:10). Obtained by kidnapping (Jdg 21:21). Procured (Ge 24; 34:4-10; 38:6).

Duty:

Husband to wife (1Co 7:2-5)—

1Co 7:27 Are you married? Do not seek a divorce. Are you unmarried? Do not look for a wife.

Eph 5:25 Husbands, love your wives, just as Christ loved the church and gave himself up for her

Eph 5:28 In this same way, husbands ought to love their wives as their own bodies. He who loves his wife loves himself.

Eph 5:31 "For this reason a man will leave his father and mother and be united to his wife, and the two will become one flesh."

Eph 5:33 However, each one of you also must love his wife as he loves himself, and the wife must respect her husband. (+Col 3:19)

1Pe 3:7 Husbands, in the same way be considerate as you live with your wives, and treat them with respect as the weaker partner and as heirs with you of the gracious gift of life, so that nothing will hinder your prayers.

Wife to husband: To be obedient—

1Co 14:34 women should remain silent in the churches. They are not allowed to speak, but must be in submission, as the Law says. ³⁵If they want to inquire about something, they should ask their own husbands at home; for it is disgraceful for a woman to speak in the church.

Eph 5:22 Wives, submit to your husbands as to the Lord.

Eph 5:24 Now as the church submits to Christ, so also wives should submit to their husbands in everything.

Col 3:18 Wives, submit to your husbands, as is fitting in the Lord.

Tit 2:5 to be self-controlled and pure, to be busy at home, to be kind, and to be subject to their husbands, so that no one will malign the word of God.

1Pe 3:1 Wives, in the same way be submissive to your husbands so that, if any of them do not believe the word, they may be won over without words by the behavior of their wives,

1Pe 3:6 like Sarah, who obeyed Abraham and called him her master. You are her daughters if you do what is right and do not give way to fear.

To be affectionate—

Tit 2:4 Then they can train the younger women to love their husbands and children,

To be faithful (Tit 3:11).

Relation of, to the husband—

Ge 2:18 The LORD God said, "It is not good for the man to be alone. I will make a helper suitable for him."

Ge 2:23 The man said, "This is now bone of my bones and flesh of my flesh; she shall be called 'woman,' for she was taken out of man."

²⁴For this reason a man will leave his father and mother and be united to his wife, and they will become one flesh.

1Co 7:2 But since there is so much immorality, each man should have his own wife, and each woman her own husband. ³The husband should fulfill his marital duty to his wife, and likewise the wife to her husband. ⁴The wife's body does not belong to her alone but also to her husband. In the same way, the husband's body does not belong to him alone but also to his wife. ⁵Do not deprive each other except by mutual consent and for a time, so that you may

devote yourselves to prayer. Then come together again so that Satan will not tempt you because of your lack of self-control. (+1Co 7:10)

1Co 7:11 But if she does, she must remain unmarried or else be reconciled to her husband. And a husband must not divorce his wife.

1Co 7:13 And if a woman has a husband who is not a believer and he is willing to live with her, she must not divorce him.

1Co 7:39 A woman is bound to her husband as long as he lives. But if her husband dies, she is free to marry anyone she wishes, but he must belong to the Lord.

1Co 11:3 Now I want you to realize that the head of every man is Christ, and the head of the woman is man, and the head of Christ is God.

1Co 11:8 For man did not come from woman, but woman from man; ⁹neither was man created for woman, but woman for man.

1Co 11:11 In the Lord, however, woman is not independent of man, nor is man independent of woman. ¹²For as woman came from man, so also man is born of woman. But everything comes from God.

Domestic duties of (Ge 18:6)—

Pr 31:13 She selects wool and flax and works with eager hands. ¹⁴She is like the merchant ships, bringing her food from afar. ¹⁵She gets up while it is still dark; she provides food for her family and portions for her servant girls. ¹⁶She considers a field and buys it; out of her earnings she plants a vineyard. ¹⁷She sets about her work vigorously; her arms are strong for her tasks. ¹⁸She sees that her trading is profitable, and her lamp does not go out at night. ¹⁹In her hand she holds the distaff and grasps the spindle with her fingers. ²⁰She opens her arms to the poor and extends her hands to the needy. ²¹When it snows, she has no fear for her household; for all of them are clothed in scarlet. ²²She makes coverings for her bed; she is clothed in fine linen and purple. ²³Her husband is respected at the city gate, where he takes his seat among the elders of the land. ²⁴She makes linen garments and sells them, and supplies the merchants with sashes. ²⁵She is clothed with strength and dignity; she can laugh at the days to come. ²⁶She speaks with wisdom, and faithful instruction is on her tongue. ²⁷She watches over the affairs of her household and does not eat the bread of idleness.

Vows of (Nu 30:6-16).

See Vow.

Instances of Evil Influence of, Upon Husbands:

Eve (Ge 3:6,12). Solomon's wives (1Ki 11:1-8; Ne 13:26). Jezebel (1Ki 21:25; 2Ki 9:30-37). Haman's (Est 5:14). Herodias (Mt 14:3,6-11; Mk 6:17,24-28).

See Husband; Marriage; Parents; Widow; Women.

WILD OX [8028]. A powerful animal (Nu 23:22; 24:8; Ps 92:9); two-horned (Dt 33:17); wild and difficult to catch (Job 39:9-12; Ps 29:6); KJV "unicorn." *See Animals.*

WILDERNESS [4497, 6858].

NIV+ WILD

Wandering of the Israelites in. *See Israel.* Typical of the sinner's state (Dt 32:10). Jesus' temptation in (Mt 4:1; Mk 1:12-13; Lk 4:1).

See Deserts.

WILL [*2911, 2914, 4213, 8356, 10668, *1087, 1088, 1089, 2525, 2526, 2527*].

NIV+ FREEWILL, WEAK-WILLED, WILLFUL, WILLFULLY, WILLING, WILLINGLY, WILLINGNESS, WILLS

The Mental Faculty:

Freedom of, recognized by God (Ge 4:6-10; Dt 5:29; 1Ki 20:42; Isa 1:18-20; 43:26; Jer 36:3,7; Jn 7:17).

See *Blessings, Spiritual, Contingent Upon Obedience; Choice; Contingencies.*

Of God:

The supreme rule of duty (Mt 6:10)—

Mt 12:50 For whoever does the will of my Father in heaven is my brother and sister and mother." (+Mk 3:35)

Mt 26:39 Going a little farther, he fell with his face to the ground and prayed, "My Father, if it is possible, may this cup be taken from me. Yet not as I will, but as you will."

Mt 26:42 He went away a second time and prayed, "My Father, if it is not possible for this cup to be taken away unless I drink it, may your will be done." (+Mk 14:36; Lk 22:42)

Jn 4:34 "My food," said Jesus, "is to do the will of him who sent me and to finish his work.

Jn 5:30 By myself I can do nothing; I judge only as I hear, and my judgment is just, for I seek not to please myself but him who sent me.

Jn 6:38 For I have come down from heaven not to do my will but to do the will of him who sent me. ³⁹And this is the will of him who sent me, that I shall lose none of all that he has given me, but raise them up at the last day. ⁴⁰For my Father's will is that everyone who looks to the Son and believes in him shall have eternal life, and I will raise him up at the last day."

Ro 12:2 Do not conform any longer to the pattern of this world, but be transformed by the renewing of your mind. Then you will be able to test and approve what God's will is—his good, pleasing and perfect will. (+Eph 5:17)

Plans of the righteous subject to—

Ac 18:21 But as he left, he promised, "I will come back if it is God's will." Then he set sail from Ephesus. (+Ro 1:10)

Ro 15:32 so that by God's will I may come to you with joy and together with you be refreshed.

1Co 4:19 But I will come to you very soon, if the Lord is willing, and then I will find out not only how these arrogant people are talking, but what power they have.

1Co 16:7 I do not want to see you now and make only a passing visit; I hope to spend some time with you, if the Lord permits.

Heb 6:3 And God permitting, we will do so. (+Jas 4:15)

"Lord's prayer" concerns (Mt 6:10)—

Lk 11:2 He said to them, "When you pray, say: " 'Father, hallowed be your name, your kingdom come. *See Agency.*

Reasons for wanting to know: Love for God (Jn 14:15, 21,23-24), desire to please God (1Jn 3:22). Blessings in this life (1Pe 3:10-12), rewards in the future life (1Co 3:10-15; 2Ti 4:8; Heb 10:35). Avoid discipline (1Co 3:16-17; 11:31-32; 1Pe 4:17). Good example to other believers (1Co 4:16; 1Th 1:7; 2Th 3:9; Heb 13:7). Will not be ashamed at the Second Coming (1Jn 2:28). Glorify God (1Co 10:31; Col 3:17,23; Heb 12:10; 2Pe 1:4).

Defined: God's purpose (2Ti 1:9, w Eph 1:9), God's plan (1Co 12:11; 2Co 1:15; Jas 3:4), God's will (Ac 27:12; Eph 1:11). *See above, The Supreme Rule of Duty.*

Obligation to know (Eph 5:15-17).

How God reveals: Through his Word (Ps 119:105; 2Ti

3:16-17). Through control of thoughts, indirectly (2Co 7:8-11; 12:7; 1Pe 1:6-7; 4:12-13; Jas 1:2-4), directly (Pr 16:1,9; 21:1; Eph 2:13), through Satan (Job 1:12; 2:6). Through the control of circumstances (Pr 16:9; 20:24; Ac 2:23; 4:28; Eph 1:11). Until revelation is complete, through dreams (Ge 20:3,6; 31:11,24; 1Ki 3:5; Mt 2:12-13) and visions (Ge 15:1; Zec 1:7-8; Ac 10:10-11).

Prerequisites: Spiritual maturity (Isa 55:8-9; 1Co 2:7; Eph 4:14; Col 1:9; 1Ti 3:6; Heb 5:13-14; 13:21), through the teaching ministry of the Holy Spirit (Jn 16:13-14; 1Co 2:12-14; 1Jn 2:27), through application in testings (Php 3:15; Heb 5:14; 12:7,11; Jas 1:2-5). Yieldedness or self-denial (Ro 6:13,19; 12:1; 1Pe 2:9; Rev 1:6), discipleship (Mt 16:24; Mk 8:34; Lk 9:23). Desire to know God's will (Jn 7:17), to do it (Mk 4:24-25; Ac 10:22,35,44,47; 1Jn 2:11). Willingness to obey daily (Mt 16:24; Mk 8:34; Lk 9:23; Ro 6:16; Php 2:13; 2Pe 2:19). Faith (Ps 37:5; Pr 3:5-6; Ro 14:23; 2Co 5:7; Php 2:13; Heb 11:17,27). Patience (Ps 37:7; Jas 1:5-6). Common sense (Tit 2:12). Peace of God (Col 3:15). A clear conscience (Ro 14:23).

A Testament:

Of Abraham (Ge 25:5-6). Jacob (Ge 48:49). David (1Ki 2:1-9). Jehoshaphat (2Ch 21:3). May not be annulled (Gal 3:15). In force after death only (Heb 9:16-17). *See Testament; Wills.*

WILLFULNESS *See Obduracy; Self-Will.*

WILLOW [7628]. A type of tree growing along the brook or near water; several species in Israel; symbol of joy (Lev 23:40; Job 40:22), sorrow (Ps 137:2).

WILLOWS, BROOK OF THE *See Poplars, Ravine of.*

WILLS

NIV+ See WILL

Statements, oral or written in a form, to which law courts give effect, by which property may be disposed of after death (Heb 9:16-17). *See Covenant; Will, A Testament.*

WIMPLE *See Cloak.*

WIND [1999, 6193, 7600, 7708, 8120, 8551, 9402, 10658, *448, 449, 3803, 4460, 4463, 4466*].

NIV+ WINDBLOWN, WINDING, WINDS, WINDSTORM, WOUND

Characterized:

Blasting (2Ki 19:7,35).

East: Hot and blasting in Egypt (Ge 41:6), in the valley of the Euphrates (Eze 19:12), in Canaan (Hos 13:15; Lk 12:55), at Nineveh (Jnh 4:8), tempestuous in Uz (Job 27:21).

West: Took away the plague of locusts from the land of Egypt (Ex 10:19).

North: Free from humidity in Canaan (Pr 25:23).

South: Soothing (Job 37:17), tempestuous (Job 37:9), purifying (Job 37:21).

Figurative:

(Hos 4:19). Of the judgments of God (Jer 22:22; Hos 13:15; Mt 7:25). Of the Spirit (Jn 3:8). Of heresy (Eph 4:14).

WINDOW [748, 2707, 9209, 10348, *2600*].

NIV+ WINDOWS

An opening in a wall (Ge 6:16; 26:8; Jos 2:15,21; 1Ki 6:4; Eze 40:16-36; Ac 20:9).

WINE [1074+8042, 2810, 3516, 3676, 4641, 4932, 6011, 6747, 9069, 9197, 9408, 10271, *1183, 3885, 3954*].

NIV+ WINEPRESS, WINEPRESSES, WINES, WINESKIN, WINESKINS

General

Made from grapes (Ge 49:11; Jer 40:10,12), from pomegranates (SS 8:2). Kept in wineskins (Jos 9:4,13; Job 32:19; Jer 13:12; Mt 9:17; Lk 5:37-38), in jars (Jer 48:12), in vats (1Ch 27:27), in buildings (2Ch 32:28). Commerce in (Rev 18:13). Banquets of (Est 5:6).

Plentiful in Canaan—

Dt 33:28 So Israel will live in safety alone; Jacob's spring is secure in a land of grain and new wine, where the heavens drop dew.

2Ki 18:32 until I come and take you to a land like your own, a land of grain and new wine, a land of bread and vineyards, a land of olive trees and honey. Choose life and not death! "Do not listen to Hezekiah, for he is misleading you when he says, 'The LORD will deliver us.'

Fermented (Lev 10:9; Nu 6:3)—

Dt 14:26 Use the silver to buy whatever you like: cattle, sheep, wine or other fermented drink, or anything you wish. Then you and your household shall eat there in the presence of the LORD your God and rejoice. (+Dt 29:6)

New wine, a staple—

Hos 2:8 She has not acknowledged that I was the one who gave her the grain, the new wine and oil, who lavished on her the silver and gold—which they used for Baal.

Hos 2:22 and the earth will respond to the grain, the new wine and oil, and they will respond to Jezreel.

Hos 7:14 They do not cry out to me from their hearts but wail upon their beds. They gather together for grain and new wine but turn away from me.

Joel 2:24 The threshing floors will be filled with grain; the vats will overflow with new wine and oil.

Hag 1:11 I called for a drought on the fields and the mountains, on the grain, the new wine, the oil and whatever the ground produces, on men and cattle, and on the labor of your hands." (+Mk 2:22; Lk 5:37-39)

Aged wine, a delicacy—

Isa 25:6 On this mountain the LORD Almighty will prepare a feast of rich food for all peoples, a banquet of aged wine—the best of meats and the finest of wines. (+Jer 48:11)

Old wine (Lk 5:39).

Positive Use of:

Offered with sacrifices (Ex 29:40; Lev 23:13; Nu 15:5,10; 18:12; 28:7,14; Dt 14:23)—

Ne 10:39 The people of Israel, including the Levites, are to bring their contributions of grain, new wine and oil to the storerooms where the articles for the sanctuary are kept and where the ministering priests, the gatekeepers and the singers stay. "We will not neglect the house of our God."

For enjoyment—

Ps 4:7 You have filled my heart with greater joy than when their grain and new wine abound.

Ps 104:15 wine that gladdens the heart of man, oil to make his face shine, and bread that sustains his heart.

Pr 31:6 Give beer to those who are perishing, wine to those who are in anguish; ⁷let them drink and forget their poverty and remember their misery no more.

Ecc 2:3 I tried cheering myself with wine, and embracing folly—my mind still guiding me with wisdom. I wanted to see what was worthwhile for men to do under heaven during the few days of their lives.

Isa 25:6 On this mountain the LORD Almighty will prepare a feast of rich food for all peoples, a banquet of aged wine—the best of meats and the finest of wines.

Zec 9:17 How attractive and beautiful they will be! Grain will make the young men thrive, and new wine the young women.

Zec 10:7 The Ephraimites will become like mighty men, and their hearts will be glad as with wine. Their children will see it and be joyful; their hearts will rejoice in the LORD.

Recommended by Paul to Timothy—

1Ti 5:23 Stop drinking only water, and use a little wine because of your stomach and your frequent illnesses.

Given by Melchizedek to Abraham (Ge 14:18). Used at meals (Mt 26:27-29; Mk 14:23). Made by Jesus at the marriage feast in Cana (Jn 2:9-10). Used in the Lord's Supper (Mt 26:27-29; Lk 22:17-20). Given to Jesus at the Crucifixion, possibly as a pain killer (Mt 27:48; Mk 15:23; Lk 23:36; Jn 19:29).

Negative Use of:

Drunkenness condemned—

Pr 20:1 Wine is a mocker and beer a brawler; whoever is led astray by them is not wise.

Isa 5:11 Woe to those who rise early in the morning to run after their drinks, who stay up late at night till they are inflamed with wine.

Isa 5:22 Woe to those who are heroes at drinking wine and champions at mixing drinks,

Isa 24:9 No longer do they drink wine with a song; the beer is bitter to its drinkers.

Isa 28:1 Woe to that wreath, the pride of Ephraim's drunkards, to the fading flower, his glorious beauty, set on the head of a fertile valley—to that city, the pride of those laid low by wine!

Isa 28:3 That wreath, the pride of Ephraim's drunkards, will be trampled underfoot.

Isa 28:7 And these also stagger from wine and reel from beer: Priests and prophets stagger from beer and are befuddled with wine; they reel from beer, they stagger when seeing visions, they stumble when rendering decisions.

Isa 56:12 "Come," each one cries, "let me get wine! Let us drink our fill of beer! And tomorrow will be like today, or even far better." (+Jer 23:9)

Hos 4:11 to prostitution, to old wine and new, which take away the understanding (+Joel 1:5)

Am 6:6 You drink wine by the bowlful and use the finest lotions, but you do not grieve over the ruin of Joseph.

Hab 2:5 indeed, wine betrays him; he is arrogant and never at rest. Because he is as greedy as the grave and like death is never satisfied, he gathers to himself all the nations and takes captive all the peoples.

Eph 5:18 Do not get drunk on wine, which leads to debauchery. Instead, be filled with the Spirit.

1Ti 3:8 Deacons, likewise, are to be men worthy of respect, sincere, not indulging in much wine, and not pursuing dishonest gain.

Tit 2:3 Likewise, teach the older women to be reverent in the way they live, not to be slanderers or addicted to much wine, but to teach what is good.

Addiction and craving condemned—

Pr 21:17 He who loves pleasure will become poor; whoever loves wine and oil will never be rich.

Pr 23:29 Who has woe? Who has sorrow? Who has strife? Who has complaints? Who has needless bruises? Who has bloodshot eyes? ³⁰Those who linger over wine, who go to sample bowls of mixed wine. ³¹Do not gaze at wine when it is red, when it sparkles in the cup, when it goes down smoothly! ³²In the end it bites like a snake and poisons like a viper.

Joel 1:5 Wake up, you drunkards, and weep! Wail, all you drinkers of wine; wail because of the new wine, for it has been snatched from your lips.

Children sold for—

Joel 3:3 They cast lots for my people and traded boys for prostitutes; they sold girls for wine that they might drink.

Instances of drunkenness—

Noah (Ge 9:21), Lot (Ge 19:32), Joseph and his brothers (Ge 43:34), Nabal (1Sa 25:36), Amnon (2Sa 13:28-29), Xerxes (Est 1:10), kings of Israel (Hos 7:5). Falsely charged against Jesus (Mt 11:19; Lk 7:34) and the disciples (Ac 2:13).

Abstinence From:

Required of Levites while on duty—

Lev 10:9 "You and your sons are not to drink wine or other fermented drink whenever you go into the Tent of Meeting, or you will die. This is a lasting ordinance for the generations to come.

Eze 44:21 No priest is to drink wine when he enters the inner court.

Required of Nazirites during their·vow—

Nu 6:3 he must abstain from wine and other fermented drink and must not drink vinegar made from wine or from other fermented drink. He must not drink grape juice or eat grapes or raisins.

Required of Samson's mother during her pregnancy—

Jdg 13:4 Now see to it that you drink no wine or other fermented drink and that you do not eat anything unclean, ⁵because you will conceive and give birth to a son. No razor may be used on his head, because the boy is to be a Nazirite, set apart to God from birth, and he will begin the deliverance of Israel from the hands of the Philistines." *See Nazirite(s), Nazarite(s).*

Required of kings and rulers—

Pr 31:4 "It is not for kings, O Lemuel— not for kings to drink wine, not for rulers to crave beer, ⁵lest they drink and forget what the law decrees, and deprive all the oppressed of their rights.

Required of John the Baptist—

Lk 1:15 for he will be great in the sight of the Lord. He is never to take wine or other fermented drink, and he will be filled with the Holy Spirit even from birth.

Chosen by Daniel to avoid defilement (Da 1:8-20), in mouring (Da 10:3). Chosen by the Recabites to honor a vow (Jer 35:6,8,14,16). With bread, denied to the Israelites in the desert (Dt 29:6). Temperance allowed the quests at Xerxes' banquet (Est 1:8).

Chosen, for the sake of the weaker brother—

Ro 14:21 It is better not to eat meat or drink wine or to do anything else that will cause your brother to fall.

Possibly abstained from by Timothy (1Ti 5:23).

Figurative:

Of, the divine judgments (Ps 60:3; 75:8; Jer 51:7; Rev 14:10; 16:19), the joy of wisdom (Pr 9:2,5), the joys of religion (Isa 25:6; 55:1; Joel 2:19), abominations (Rev 14:9; 17:2; 18:3).

Symbolic:

Of the blood of Jesus (Mt 26:28; Mk 14:23-24; Lk 22:20; Jn 6:53-56).

See Abstinence; Drunkenness; Vine; Vineyards.

WINEBIBBER *See Drunkard; Drunkenness; Wine.*

WINEPRESS [1780, 3676, 7053, *3332, 5700*].

NIV+ See WINE

(Nu 18:27,30; Dt 15:14; Jdg 6:11). In vineyards (Isa 5:2; Mt 21:33; Mk 12:1).

Figurative:

Treading the winepress of the judgments of God (Isa 63:2-3; La 1:15; Rev 14:19-20).

WINESKIN [199, 2827, 5532, 5574, *829*].

NIV+ See WINE

Made of tanned whole skins of animals (Mt 9:17). *See Wine.*

WING [88, 4053, 6416, 10149, *4763*].

NIV+ WINGED, WINGS, WINGSPAN

Often used figuratively (Ps 18:10; 55:6; 68:13; Pr 23:5; Mt 23:37).

WINNOW [2430].

NIV+ WINNOWING, WINNOWS

Figurative:

Of Israel in destroying its enemies (Isa 41:15-16). God's judgment separating evil men from good (Jer 15:7; 51:2). The character of a good king, not all kings (Pr 20:8; 20:26).

WINNOWING [2430, 4665, *4768*].

NIV+ See WINNOW

Separating kernels of threshed grain from chaff; done by shaking bunches of grain into air so that the kernels fall to the ground, while the chaff is blown away by the wind (Ru 3:2).

Figurative:

(Mt 3:12; Lk 3:17).

WINTER [1773, 3069, 3074, 6255, *4199, 4200, 5930*].

NIV+ WINTERED

Annual return of, shall never cease (Ge 8:22). Plowing in, in Canaan (Pr 20:4). Rainy season in, in Canaan (SS 2:11). Shipping suspended in, on the Mediterranean Sea (Ac 27:12; 28:11). Paul remains for one, at Nicopolis (Tit 3:12). Summer and winter houses (Jer 36:22; Am 3:15).

See Meteorology.

WINTER APARTMENT, WINTER HOUSE The wealthy had separate residences for hot and cold seasons. Called a "winter apartment" (Jer 36:22), a "winter house" (Am 3:15).

See Summer House, Summer Palace.

WISDOM [1069, 2681, 2682, 2683, 2684, 4213, 4220, 8505, 8507, 9312, 9370, 10265, 10266, 10539, *5053, 5054, 5055, 5317, 5860, 5861*].

NIV+ OVERWISE, WISELY, WISDOM, WISE, WISER, WISEST

Job 32:9 It is not only the old who are wise, not only the aged who understand what is right.

Ps 2:10 Therefore, you kings, be wise; be warned, you rulers of the earth. (+Ps 90:12)

Pr 2:1 My son, if you accept my words and store up my commands within you, ²turning your ear to wisdom and applying your heart to understanding, ³and if you call out for insight and cry aloud for understanding, ⁴and if you look for it as for silver and search for it as for hidden treasure, ⁵then you will understand the fear of the LORD and find the knowledge of God. ⁶For the LORD gives wisdom, and from his mouth come knowledge and understanding. ⁷He holds victory in store for the upright, he is a shield to those whose walk is blameless, ⁸for he guards the course of the just and protects the way of his faithful ones.

⁹Then you will understand what is right and just and fair—every good path. ¹⁰For wisdom will enter your heart, and knowledge will be pleasant to your soul.

¹¹Discretion will protect you, and understanding will guard you.

¹²Wisdom will save you from the ways of wicked men, from men whose words are perverse, ¹³who leave the straight paths to walk in dark ways, ¹⁴who delight in doing wrong and rejoice in the perverseness of evil, ¹⁵whose paths are crooked and who are devious in their ways.

¹⁶It will save you also from the adulteress, from the wayward wife with her seductive words, ¹⁷who has left the partner of her youth and ignored the covenant she made before God. ¹⁸For her house leads down to death and her paths to the spirits of the dead. ¹⁹None who go to her return or attain the paths of life.

²⁰Thus you will walk in the ways of good men and keep to the paths of the righteous. (+Pr 4:18-20)

Pr 7:4 Say to wisdom, "You are my sister," and call understanding your kinsman; (+Pr 9:1-6)

Pr 10:13 Wisdom is found on the lips of the discerning, but a rod is for the back of him who lacks judgment.

Pr 10:21 The lips of the righteous nourish many, but fools die for lack of judgment.

Pr 10:23 A fool finds pleasure in evil conduct, but a man of understanding delights in wisdom.

Pr 12:1 Whoever loves discipline loves knowledge, but he who hates correction is stupid.

Pr 12:8 A man is praised according to his wisdom, but men with warped minds are despised.

Pr 12:15 The way of a fool seems right to him, but a wise man listens to advice.

Pr 13:14 The teaching of the wise is a fountain of life, turning a man from the snares of death.

¹⁵Good understanding wins favor, but the way of the unfaithful is hard.

¹⁶Every prudent man acts out of knowledge, but a fool exposes his folly.

Pr 14:6 The mocker seeks wisdom and finds none, but knowledge comes easily to the discerning.

⁷Stay away from a foolish man, for you will not find knowledge on his lips.

⁸The wisdom of the prudent is to give thought to their ways, but the folly of fools is deception.

Pr 14:16 A wise man fears the LORD and shuns evil, but a fool is hotheaded and reckless. (+Pr 14:18)

Pr 14:33 Wisdom reposes in the heart of the discerning and even among fools she lets herself be known. (+Pr 15:2)

Pr 15:7 The lips of the wise spread knowledge; not so the hearts of fools.

Pr 15:14 The discerning heart seeks knowledge, but the mouth of a fool feeds on folly.

Pr 15:33 The fear of the LORD teaches a man wisdom, and humility comes before honor.

Pr 16:16 How much better to get wisdom than gold, to choose understanding rather than silver!

Pr 16:20 Whoever gives heed to instruction prospers, and blessed is he who trusts in the LORD.

²¹The wise in heart are called discerning, and pleasant words promote instruction.

²²Understanding is a fountain of life to those who have it, but folly brings punishment to fools.

²³A wise man's heart guides his mouth, and his lips promote instruction.

²⁴Pleasant words are a honeycomb, sweet to the soul and healing to the bones.

Pr 17:10 A rebuke impresses a man of discernment more than a hundred lashes a fool.

Pr 17:24 A discerning man keeps wisdom in view, but a fool's eyes wander to the ends of the earth.

Pr 18:15 The heart of the discerning acquires knowledge; the ears of the wise seek it out.

Pr 19:8 He who gets wisdom loves his own soul; he who cherishes understanding prospers.

Pr 19:20 Listen to advice and accept instruction, and in the end you will be wise.

Pr 21:11 When a mocker is punished, the simple gain wisdom; when a wise man is instructed, he gets knowledge. (+Ecc 8:1,5)

Ecc 9:13 I also saw under the sun this example of wisdom that greatly impressed me: ¹⁴There was once a small city with only a few people in it. And a powerful king came against it, surrounded it and built huge siegeworks against it. ¹⁵Now there lived in that city a man poor but wise, and he saved the city by his wisdom. But nobody remembered that poor man. ¹⁶So I said, "Wisdom is better than strength." But the poor man's wisdom is despised, and his words are no longer heeded.

¹⁷The quiet words of the wise are more to be heeded than the shouts of a ruler of fools. ¹⁸Wisdom is better than weapons of war, but one sinner destroys much good.

Ecc 10:12 Words from a wise man's mouth are gracious, but a fool is consumed by his own lips.

Ecc 12:11 The words of the wise are like goads, their collected sayings like firmly embedded nails—given by one Shepherd.

Isa 11:9 They will neither harm nor destroy on all my holy mountain, for the earth will be full of the knowledge of the LORD as the waters cover the sea.

Isa 29:24 Those who are wayward in spirit will gain understanding; those who complain will accept instruction."

Mt 11:19 The Son of Man came eating and drinking, and they say, 'Here is a glutton and a drunkard, a friend of tax collectors and "sinners."' But wisdom is proved right by her actions."

Lk 1:17 And he will go on before the Lord, in the spirit and power of Elijah, to turn the hearts of the fathers to their children and the disobedient to the wisdom of the righteous—to make ready a people prepared for the Lord." (+Lk 7:35; 21:15; Jas 1:5)

Commended:

Pr 3:13 Blessed is the man who finds wisdom, the man who gains understanding, ¹⁴for she is more profitable than silver and yields better returns than gold. ¹⁵She is more precious than rubies; nothing you desire can compare with her. ¹⁶Long life is in her right hand; in her left hand are riches and honor. ¹⁷Her ways are pleasant ways, and all her paths are peace. ¹⁸She is a tree of life to those who embrace her; those who lay hold of her will be blessed.

¹⁹By wisdom the LORD laid the earth's foundations, by understanding he set the heavens in place; ²⁰by his knowledge the deeps were divided, and the clouds let drop the dew.

²¹My son, preserve sound judgment and discernment, do not let them out of your sight; ²²they will be life for you, an

ornament to grace your neck. ²³Then you will go on your way in safety, and your foot will not stumble; ²⁴when you lie down, you will not be afraid; when you lie down, your sleep will be sweet. ²⁵Have no fear of sudden disaster or of the ruin that overtakes the wicked, ²⁶for the LORD will be your confidence and will keep your foot from being snared. (+Pr 24:3-7; Ecc 7:11-12,19; 10:1,12)

Is Above Value:

Job 28:12 "But where can wisdom be found? Where does understanding dwell? ¹³Man does not comprehend its worth; it cannot be found in the land of the living. ¹⁴The deep says, 'It is not in me'; the sea says, 'It is not with me.' ¹⁵It cannot be bought with the finest gold, nor can its price be weighed in silver. ¹⁶It cannot be bought with the gold of Ophir, with precious onyx or sapphires. ¹⁷Neither gold nor crystal can compare with it, nor can it be had for jewels of gold. ¹⁸Coral and jasper are not worthy of mention; the price of wisdom is beyond rubies. ¹⁹The topaz of Cush cannot compare with it; it cannot be bought with pure gold. (+Pr 3:13-15; 16:16)

Personified:

Pr 1:20 Wisdom calls aloud in the street, she raises her voice in the public squares; ²¹at the head of the noisy streets she cries out, in the gateways of the city she makes her speech:

²²"How long will you simple ones love your simple ways? How long will mockers delight in mockery and fools hate knowledge? ²³If you had responded to my rebuke, I would have poured out my heart to you and made my thoughts known to you. ²⁴But since you rejected me when I called and no one gave heed when I stretched out my hand, ²⁵since you ignored all my advice and would not accept my rebuke, ²⁶I in turn will laugh at your disaster; I will mock when calamity overtakes you— ²⁷when calamity overtakes you like a storm, when disaster sweeps over you like a whirlwind, when distress and trouble overwhelm you.

²⁸"Then they will call to me but I will not answer; they will look for me but will not find me. ²⁹Since they hated knowledge and did not choose to fear the LORD, ³⁰since they would not accept my advice and spurned my rebuke, ³¹they will eat the fruit of their ways and be filled with the fruit of their schemes. ³²For the waywardness of the simple will kill them, and the complacency of fools will destroy them; ³³but whoever listens to me will live in safety and be at ease, without fear of harm."

Pr 8:1 Does not wisdom call out? Does not understanding raise her voice? ²On the heights along the way, where the paths meet, she takes her stand; ³beside the gates leading into the city, at the entrances, she cries aloud: ⁴"To you, O men, I call out; I raise my voice to all mankind. ⁵You who are simple, gain prudence; you who are foolish, gain understanding. ⁶Listen, for I have worthy things to say; I open my lips to speak what is right. ⁷My mouth speaks what is true, for my lips detest wickedness. ⁸All the words of my mouth are just; none of them is crooked or perverse. ⁹To the discerning all of them are right; they are faultless to those who have knowledge. ¹⁰Choose my instruction instead of silver, knowledge rather than choice gold, ¹¹for wisdom is more precious than rubies, and nothing you desire can compare with her.

¹²"I, wisdom, dwell together with prudence; I possess knowledge and discretion. ¹³To fear the LORD is to hate evil; I hate pride and arrogance, evil behavior and perverse speech. ¹⁴Counsel and sound judgment are mine; I have

understanding and power. ¹⁵By me kings reign and rulers make laws that are just; ¹⁶by me princes govern, and all nobles who rule on earth. ¹⁷I love those who love me, and those who seek me find me. ¹⁸With me are riches and honor, enduring wealth and prosperity. ¹⁹My fruit is better than fine gold; what I yield surpasses choice silver. ²⁰I walk in the way of righteousness, along the paths of justice, ²¹bestowing wealth on those who love me and making their treasuries full.

²²"The LORD brought me forth as the first of his works, before his deeds of old; ²³I was appointed from eternity, from the beginning, before the world began. ²⁴When there were no oceans, I was given birth, when there were no springs abounding with water; ²⁵before the mountains were settled in place, before the hills, I was given birth, ²⁶before he made the earth or its fields or any of the dust of the world. ²⁷I was there when he set the heavens in place, when he marked out the horizon on the face of the deep, ²⁸when he established the clouds above and fixed securely the fountains of the deep, ²⁹when he gave the sea its boundary so the waters would not overstep his command, and when he marked out the foundations of the earth. ³⁰Then I was the craftsman at his side. I was filled with delight day after day, rejoicing always in his presence, ³¹rejoicing in his whole world and delighting in mankind.

³²"Now then, my sons, listen to me; blessed are those who keep my ways. ³³Listen to my instruction and be wise; do not ignore it. ³⁴Blessed is the man who listens to me, watching daily at my doors, waiting at my doorway. ³⁵For whoever finds me finds life and receives favor from the LORD. ³⁶But whoever fails to find me harms himself; all who hate me love death."

Pr 9:1 Wisdom has built her house; she has hewn out its seven pillars. ²She has prepared her meat and mixed her wine; she has also set her table. ³She has sent out her maids, and she calls from the highest point of the city. ⁴"Let all who are simple come in here!" she says to those who lack judgment. ⁵"Come, eat my food and drink the wine I have mixed. ⁶Leave your simple ways and you will live; walk in the way of understanding. (+Pr 9:7-8)

Pr 9:9 Instruct a wise man and he will be wiser still; teach a righteous man and he will add to his learning.

¹⁰"The fear of the LORD is the beginning of wisdom, and knowledge of the Holy One is understanding. ¹¹For through me your days will be many, and years will be added to your life. ¹²If you are wise, your wisdom will reward you; if you are a mocker, you alone will suffer." (+Pr 9:13-18)

Spiritual:

Dt 32:29 If only they were wise and would understand this and discern what their end will be!

Job 5:27 "We have examined this, and it is true. So hear it and apply it to yourself."

Job 8:8 "Ask the former generations and find out what their fathers learned,

Job 8:10 Will they not instruct you and tell you? Will they not bring forth words from their understanding?

Job 12:2 "Doubtless you are the people, and wisdom will die with you! ³But I have a mind as well as you; I am not inferior to you. Who does not know all these things?

Job 12:7 "But ask the animals, and they will teach you, or the birds of the air, and they will tell you; ⁸or speak to the earth, and it will teach you, or let the fish of the sea inform you. ⁹Which of all these does not know that the hand of the LORD has done this? ¹⁰In his hand is the life of every creature and the breath of all mankind. ¹¹Does not the ear test words as the tongue tastes food? ¹²Is not wisdom found among the aged? Does not long life bring understanding?

¹³"To God belong wisdom and power; counsel and understanding are his.

Job 12:16 To him belong strength and victory; both deceived and deceiver are his. ¹⁷He leads counselors away stripped and makes fools of judges.

Job 12:22 He reveals the deep things of darkness and brings deep shadows into the light.

The fear of the Lord is the beginning of—

Ps 111:10 The fear of the LORD is the beginning of wisdom; all who follow his precepts have good understanding. To him belongs eternal praise.

Pr 1:7 The fear of the LORD is the beginning of knowledge, but fools despise wisdom and discipline. (+Pr 9:10)

Isa 33:6 He will be the sure foundation for your times, a rich store of salvation and wisdom and knowledge; the fear of the LORD is the key to this treasure.

Is revealed to the obedient—

Ps 107:43 Whoever is wise, let him heed these things and consider the great love of the LORD.

Pr 28:5 Evil men do not understand justice, but those who seek the LORD understand it fully.

Pr 28:7 He who keeps the law is a discerning son, but a companion of gluttons disgraces his father. (+Pr 29:3; Ecc 8:5)

Da 12:3 Those who are wise will shine like the brightness of the heavens, and those who lead many to righteousness, like the stars for ever and ever. ⁴But you, Daniel, close up and seal the words of the scroll until the time of the end. Many will go here and there to increase knowledge."

Da 12:10 Many will be purified, made spotless and refined, but the wicked will continue to be wicked. None of the wicked will understand, but those who are wise will understand.

Hos 6:3 Let us acknowledge the LORD; let us press on to acknowledge him. As surely as the sun rises, he will appear; he will come to us like the winter rains, like the spring rains that water the earth."

Hos 6:6 For I desire mercy, not sacrifice, and acknowledgment of God rather than burnt offerings.

Hos 14:9 Who is wise? He will realize these things. Who is discerning? He will understand them. The ways of the LORD are right; the righteous walk in them, but the rebellious stumble in them.

Mt 6:22 "The eye is the lamp of the body. If your eyes are good, your whole body will be full of light. ²³But if your eyes are bad, your whole body will be full of darkness. If then the light within you is darkness, how great is that darkness! (+Lk 11:34-36)

Jn 7:17 If anyone chooses to do God's will, he will find out whether my teaching comes from God or whether I speak on my own.

Jn 10:4 When he has brought out all his own, he goes on ahead of them, and his sheep follow him because they know his voice.

Jn 10:14 "I am the good shepherd; I know my sheep and my sheep know me—

1Co 2:6 We do, however, speak a message of wisdom among the mature, but not the wisdom of this age or of the rulers of this age, who are coming to nothing. ⁷No, we speak of God's secret wisdom, a wisdom that has been hidden and that God destined for our glory before time began. ⁸None of the rulers of this age understood it, for if

they had, they would not have crucified the Lord of glory. ⁹However, as it is written:

"No eye has seen, no ear has heard, no mind has conceived what God has prepared for those who love him"—

¹⁰but God has revealed it to us by his Spirit. The Spirit searches all things, even the deep things of God.

1Co 8:3 But the man who loves God is known by God.

1Jn 4:6 We are from God, and whoever knows God listens to us; but whoever is not from God does not listen to us. This is how we recognize the Spirit of truth and the spirit of falsehood.

Exemplified—

Ps 9:10 Those who know your name will trust in you, for you, LORD, have never forsaken those who seek you.

Ps 76:1 In Judah God is known; his name is great in Israel.

Pr 1:5 let the wise listen and add to their learning, and let the discerning get guidance—

Pr 11:12 A man who lacks judgment derides his neighbor, but a man of understanding holds his tongue.

Mt 7:24 "Therefore everyone who hears these words of mine and puts them into practice is like a wise man who built his house on the rock. ²⁵The rain came down, the streams rose, and the winds blew and beat against that house; yet it did not fall, because it had its foundation on the rock.

Mt 25:1 "At that time the kingdom of heaven will be like ten virgins who took their lamps and went out to meet the bridegroom. ²Five of them were foolish and five were wise. ³The foolish ones took their lamps but did not take any oil with them. ⁴The wise, however, took oil in jars along with their lamps. ⁵The bridegroom was a long time in coming, and they all became drowsy and fell asleep.

⁶"At midnight the cry rang out: 'Here's the bridegroom! Come out to meet him!'

⁷"Then all the virgins woke up and trimmed their lamps. ⁸The foolish ones said to the wise, 'Give us some of your oil; our lamps are going out.'

⁹"'No,' they replied, 'there may not be enough for both us and you. Instead, go to those who sell oil and buy some for yourselves.'

¹⁰"But while they were on their way to buy the oil, the bridegroom arrived. The virgins who were ready went in with him to the wedding banquet. And the door was shut.

¹¹"Later the others also came. 'Sir! Sir!' they said. 'Open the door for us!'

¹²"But he replied, 'I tell you the truth, I don't know you.'

¹³"Therefore keep watch, because you do not know the day or the hour.

Mk 12:32 "Well said, teacher," the man replied. "You are right in saying that God is one and there is no other but him. ³³To love him with all your heart, with all your understanding and with all your strength, and to love your neighbor as yourself is more important than all burnt offerings and sacrifices."

³⁴When Jesus saw that he had answered wisely, he said to him, "You are not far from the kingdom of God." And from then on no one dared ask him any more questions. (+Ac 6:10)

Ro 15:14 I myself am convinced, my brothers, that you yourselves are full of goodness, complete in knowledge and competent to instruct one another.

1Co 13:11 When I was a child, I talked like a child, I thought like a child, I reasoned like a child. When I became a man, I put childish ways behind me.

Php 3:7 But whatever was to my profit I now consider loss for the sake of Christ. ⁸What is more, I consider everything a loss compared to the surpassing greatness of knowing Christ Jesus my Lord, for whose sake I have lost all things. I consider them rubbish, that I may gain Christ

Php 3:10 I want to know Christ and the power of his resurrection and the fellowship of sharing in his sufferings, becoming like him in his death,

1Th 5:4 But you, brothers, are not in darkness so that this day should surprise you like a thief. ⁵You are all sons of the light and sons of the day. We do not belong to the night or to the darkness.

Jas 3:13 Who is wise and understanding among you? Let him show it by his good life, by deeds done in the humility that comes from wisdom.

Parable of (Mt 25:1-13).

Exhortations to attain to (Pr 2:1-20)—

Pr 4:4 he taught me and said, "Lay hold of my words with all your heart; keep my commands and you will live. ⁵Get wisdom, get understanding; do not forget my words or swerve from them. ⁶Do not forsake wisdom, and she will protect you; love her, and she will watch over you. ⁷Wisdom is supreme; therefore get wisdom. Though it cost all you have, get understanding. ⁸Esteem her, and she will exalt you; embrace her, and she will honor you. ⁹She will set a garland of grace on your head and present you with a crown of splendor."

¹⁰Listen, my son, accept what I say, and the years of your life will be many. ¹¹I guide you in the way of wisdom and lead you along straight paths. ¹²When you walk, your steps will not be hampered; when you run, you will not stumble. ¹³Hold on to instruction, do not let it go; guard it well, for it is your life.

Pr 4:18 The path of the righteous is like the first gleam of dawn, shining ever brighter till the full light of day. ¹⁹But the way of the wicked is like deep darkness; they do not know what makes them stumble.

²⁰My son, pay attention to what I say; listen closely to my words.

Pr 22:17 Pay attention and listen to the sayings of the wise; apply your heart to what I teach, ¹⁸for it is pleasing when you keep them in your heart and have all of them ready on your lips. ¹⁹So that your trust may be in the LORD, I teach you today, even you. ²⁰Have I not written thirty sayings for you, sayings of counsel and knowledge, ²¹teaching you true and reliable words, so that you can give sound answers to him who sent you?

Pr 23:12 Apply your heart to instruction and your ears to words of knowledge.

Pr 23:19 Listen, my son, and be wise, and keep your heart on the right path.

Pr 23:23 Buy the truth and do not sell it; get wisdom, discipline and understanding.

Pr 24:13 Eat honey, my son, for it is good; honey from the comb is sweet to your taste. ¹⁴Know also that wisdom is sweet to your soul; if you find it, there is a future hope for you, and your hope will not be cut off.

Ro 16:19 Everyone has heard about your obedience, so I am full of joy over you; but I want you to be wise about what is good, and innocent about what is evil. (+1Co 8:3)

1Co 14:20 Brothers, stop thinking like children. In regard to evil be infants, but in your thinking be adults.

2Co 8:7 But just as you excel in everything—in faith, in speech, in knowledge, in complete earnestness and in your love for us—see that you also excel in this grace of giving.

Eph 5:15 Be very careful, then, how you live—not as unwise but as wise, ¹⁶making the most of every oppor-

tunity, because the days are evil. ¹⁷Therefore do not be foolish, but understand what the Lord's will is.

Col 3:10 and have put on the new self, which is being renewed in knowledge in the image of its Creator.

Col 3:16 Let the word of Christ dwell in you richly as you teach and admonish one another with all wisdom, and as you sing psalms, hymns and spiritual songs with gratitude in your hearts to God. (+2Pe 3:18)

See Knowledge; Speaking or Speech, Wise.

From God—

Ex 4:12 Now go; I will help you speak and will teach you what to say." (+Ex 8:4)

Ex 8:10 "Tomorrow," Pharaoh said. Moses replied, "It will be as you say, so that you may know there is no one like the LORD our God.

Dt 4:5 See, I have taught you decrees and laws as the LORD my God commanded me, so that you may follow them in the land you are entering to take possession of it. ⁶Observe them carefully, for this will show your wisdom and understanding to the nations, who will hear about all these decrees and say, "Surely this great nation is a wise and understanding people."

Dt 4:35 You were shown these things so that you might know that the LORD is God; besides him there is no other. ³⁶From heaven he made you hear his voice to discipline you. On earth he showed you his great fire, and you heard his words from out of the fire.

Dt 29:4 But to this day the LORD has not given you a mind that understands or eyes that see or ears that hear.

1Ch 22:12 May the LORD give you discretion and understanding when he puts you in command over Israel, so that you may keep the law of the LORD your God.

Ne 9:20 You gave your good Spirit to instruct them. You did not withhold your manna from their mouths, and you gave them water for their thirst.

Job 4:3 Think how you have instructed many, how you have strengthened feeble hands.

Job 11:5 Oh, how I wish that God would speak, that he would open his lips against you (+Job 11:6)

Job 22:21 "Submit to God and be at peace with him; in this way prosperity will come to you. ²²Accept instruction from his mouth and lay up his words in your heart.

Job 28:20 "Where then does wisdom come from? Where does understanding dwell? ²¹It is hidden from the eyes of every living thing, concealed even from the birds of the air. ²²Destruction and Death say, 'Only a rumor of it has reached our ears.' ²³God understands the way to it and he alone knows where it dwells, ²⁴for he views the ends of the earth and sees everything under the heavens. ²⁵When he established the force of the wind and measured out the waters, ²⁶when he made a decree for the rain and a path for the thunderstorm, ²⁷then he looked at wisdom and appraised it; he confirmed it and tested it. ²⁸And he said to man, 'The fear of the Lord—that is wisdom, and to shun evil is understanding.'"

Job 32:7 I thought, 'Age should speak; advanced years should teach wisdom.' ⁸But it is the spirit in a man, the breath of the Almighty, that gives him understanding. (+Job 33:16)

Job 35:10 But no one says, 'Where is God my Maker, who gives songs in the night, ¹¹who teaches more to us than to the beasts of the earth and makes us wiser than the birds of the air?' (+Job 36:22)

Job 38:36 Who endowed the heart with wisdom or gave understanding to the mind? ³⁷Who has the wisdom to count the clouds? Who can tip over the water jars of the heavens

Ps 16:7 I will praise the Lord, who counsels me; even at night my heart instructs me.

Ps 19:1 The heavens declare the glory of God; the skies proclaim the work of his hands. ²Day after day they pour forth speech; night after night they display knowledge.

Ps 25:8 Good and upright is the Lord; therefore he instructs sinners in his ways. ⁹He guides the humble in what is right and teaches them his way.

Ps 25:12 Who, then, is the man that fears the Lord? He will instruct him in the way chosen for him.

Ps 25:14 The Lord confides in those who fear him; he makes his covenant known to them.

Ps 32:8 I will instruct you and teach you in the way you should go; I will counsel you and watch over you.

Ps 36:9 For with you is the fountain of life; in your light we see light.

Ps 51:6 Surely you desire truth in the inner parts; you teach me wisdom in the inmost place.

Ps 71:17 Since my youth, O God, you have taught me, and to this day I declare your marvelous deeds.

Ps 94:12 Blessed is the man you discipline, O Lord, the man you teach from your law;

Ps 112:4 Even in darkness light dawns for the upright, for the gracious and compassionate and righteous man.

Ps 119:130 The unfolding of your words gives light; it gives understanding to the simple.

Pr 1:23 If you had responded to my rebuke, I would have poured out my heart to you and made my thoughts known to you.

Pr 2:6 For the Lord gives wisdom, and from his mouth come knowledge and understanding. ⁷He holds victory in store for the upright, he is a shield to those whose walk is blameless,

Pr 3:5 Trust in the Lord with all your heart and lean not on your own understanding; ⁶in all your ways acknowledge him, and he will make your paths straight.

Ecc 2:26 To the man who pleases him, God gives wisdom, knowledge and happiness, but to the sinner he gives the task of gathering and storing up wealth to hand it over to the one who pleases God. This too is meaningless, a chasing after the wind.

Isa 2:3 Many peoples will come and say, "Come, let us go up to the mountain of the Lord, to the house of the God of Jacob. He will teach us his ways, so that we may walk in his paths." The law will go out from Zion, the word of the Lord from Jerusalem.

Isa 11:1 A shoot will come up from the stump of Jesse; from his roots a Branch will bear fruit. ²The Spirit of the Lord will rest on him—the Spirit of wisdom and of understanding, the Spirit of counsel and of power, the Spirit of knowledge and of the fear of the Lord— ³and he will delight in the fear of the Lord. He will not judge by what he sees with his eyes, or decide by what he hears with his ears;

Isa 30:21 Whether you turn to the right or to the left, your ears will hear a voice behind you, saying, "This is the way; walk in it."

Isa 42:6 "I, the Lord, have called you in righteousness; I will take hold of your hand. I will keep you and will make you to be a covenant for the people and a light for the Gentiles, ⁷to open eyes that are blind, to free captives from prison and to release from the dungeon those who sit in darkness.

Isa 42:16 I will lead the blind by ways they have not

known, along unfamiliar paths I will guide them; I will turn the darkness into light before them and make the rough places smooth. These are the things I will do; I will not forsake them.

Isa 48:17 This is what the Lord says—your Redeemer, the Holy One of Israel: "I am the Lord your God, who teaches you what is best for you, who directs you in the way you should go.

Isa 54:13 All your sons will be taught by the Lord, and great will be your children's peace.

Jer 9:23 This is what the Lord says: "Let not the wise man boast of his wisdom or the strong man boast of his strength or the rich man boast of his riches, ²⁴but let him who boasts boast about this: that he understands and knows me, that I am the Lord, who exercises kindness, justice and righteousness on earth, for in these I delight," declares the Lord.

Jer 24:7 I will give them a heart to know me, that I am the Lord. They will be my people, and I will be their God, for they will return to me with all their heart.

Da 1:17 To these four young men God gave knowledge and understanding of all kinds of literature and learning. And Daniel could understand visions and dreams of all kinds.

Da 2:21 He changes times and seasons; he sets up kings and deposes them. He gives wisdom to the wise and knowledge to the discerning. ²²He reveals deep and hidden things; he knows what lies in darkness, and light dwells with him. ²³I thank and praise you, O God of my fathers: You have given me wisdom and power, you have made known to me what we asked of you, you have made known to us the dream of the king."

Da 11:32 With flattery he will corrupt those who have violated the covenant, but the people who know their God will firmly resist him.

³³"Those who are wise will instruct many, though for a time they will fall by the sword or be burned or captured or plundered.

Mt 11:25 At that time Jesus said, "I praise you, Father, Lord of heaven and earth, because you have hidden these things from the wise and learned, and revealed them to little children. ²⁶Yes, Father, for this was your good pleasure.

²⁷"All things have been committed to me by my Father. No one knows the Son except the Father, and no one knows the Father except the Son and those to whom the Son chooses to reveal him.

Mt 13:11 He replied, "The knowledge of the secrets of the kingdom of heaven has been given to you, but not to them.

Mt 16:16 Simon Peter answered, "You are the Christ, the Son of the living God."

¹⁷Jesus replied, "Blessed are you, Simon son of Jonah, for this was not revealed to you by man, but by my Father in heaven.

Lk 1:76 And you, my child, will be called a prophet of the Most High; for you will go on before the Lord to prepare the way for him, ⁷⁷to give his people the knowledge of salvation through the forgiveness of their sins, ⁷⁸because of the tender mercy of our God, by which the rising sun will come to us from heaven ⁷⁹to shine on those living in darkness and in the shadow of death, to guide our feet into the path of peace."

Lk 12:11 "When you are brought before synagogues, rulers and authorities, do not worry about how you will defend yourselves or what you will say, ¹²for the Holy Spirit will teach you at that time what you should say."

Lk 21:15 For I will give you words and wisdom that none of your adversaries will be able to resist or contradict.

Lk 24:32 They asked each other, "Were not our hearts burning within us while he talked with us on the road and opened the Scriptures to us?"

Lk 24:45 Then he opened their minds so they could understand the Scriptures.

Jn 1:1 In the beginning was the Word, and the Word was with God, and the Word was God.

Jn 1:4 In him was life, and that life was the light of men. ⁵The light shines in the darkness, but the darkness has not understood it.

Jn 1:7 He came as a witness to testify concerning that light, so that through him all men might believe. ⁸He himself was not the light; he came only as a witness to the light. ⁹The true light that gives light to every man was coming into the world.

Jn 1:17 For the law was given through Moses; grace and truth came through Jesus Christ.

Jn 6:45 It is written in the Prophets: 'They will all be taught by God.' Everyone who listens to the Father and learns from him comes to me.

Jn 8:12 When Jesus spoke again to the people, he said, "I am the light of the world. Whoever follows me will never walk in darkness, but will have the light of life."

Jn 8:31 To the Jews who had believed him, Jesus said, "If you hold to my teaching, you are really my disciples. ³²Then you will know the truth, and the truth will set you free."

Jn 9:5 While I am in the world, I am the light of the world."

Jn 9:39 Jesus said, "For judgment I have come into this world, so that the blind will see and those who see will become blind."

Jn 12:46 I have come into the world as a light, so that no one who believes in me should stay in darkness.

Jn 14:7 If you really knew me, you would know my Father as well. From now on, you do know him and have seen him."

Jn 16:13 But when he, the Spirit of truth, comes, he will guide you into all truth. He will not speak on his own; he will speak only what he hears, and he will tell you what is yet to come. ¹⁴He will bring glory to me by taking from what is mine and making it known to you.

Jn 17:3 Now this is eternal life: that they may know you, the only true God, and Jesus Christ, whom you have sent.

Jn 17:6 "I have revealed you to those whom you gave me out of the world. They were yours; you gave them to me and they have obeyed your word. ⁷Now they know that everything you have given me comes from you. ⁸For I gave them the words you gave me and they accepted them. They knew with certainty that I came from you, and they believed that you sent me.

Jn 17:25 "Righteous Father, though the world does not know you, I know you, and they know that you have sent me. ²⁶I have made you known to them, and will continue to make you known in order that the love you have for me may be in them and that I myself may be in them."

Jn 18:37 "You are a king, then!" said Pilate. Jesus answered, "You are right in saying I am a king. In fact, for this reason I was born, and for this I came into the world, to testify to the truth. Everyone on the side of truth listens to me."

Ro 1:19 since what may be known about God is plain to them, because God has made it plain to them. ²⁰For since the creation of the world God's invisible qualities—his eternal power and divine nature—have been clearly seen, being understood from what has been made, so that men are without excuse.

1Co 1:30 It is because of him that you are in Christ Jesus, who has become for us wisdom from God—that is, our righteousness, holiness and redemption.

1Co 2:9 However, as it is written: "No eye has seen, no ear has heard, no mind has conceived what God has prepared for those who love him"—

1Co 2:11 For who among men knows the thoughts of a man except the man's spirit within him? In the same way no one knows the thoughts of God except the Spirit of God. ¹²We have not received the spirit of the world but the Spirit who is from God, that we may understand what God has freely given us. ¹³This is what we speak, not in words taught us by human wisdom but in words taught by the Spirit, expressing spiritual truths in spiritual words. ¹⁴The man without the Spirit does not accept the things that come from the Spirit of God, for they are foolishness to him, and he cannot understand them, because they are spiritually discerned.

1Co 12:8 To one there is given through the Spirit the message of wisdom, to another the message of knowledge by means of the same Spirit,

2Co 3:15 Even to this day when Moses is read, a veil covers their hearts.

2Co 4:6 For God, who said, "Let light shine out of darkness," made his light shine in our hearts to give us the light of the knowledge of the glory of God in the face of Christ.

Gal 4:9 But now that you know God—or rather are known by God—how is it that you are turning back to those weak and miserable principles? Do you wish to be enslaved by them all over again?

Eph 4:11 It was he who gave some to be apostles, some to be prophets, some to be evangelists, and some to be pastors and teachers, ¹²to prepare God's people for works of service, so that the body of Christ may be built up ¹³until we all reach unity in the faith and in the knowledge of the Son of God and become mature, attaining to the whole measure of the fullness of Christ. (+Php 3:15)

Col 1:26 the mystery that has been kept hidden for ages and generations, but is now disclosed to the saints. ²⁷To them God has chosen to make known among the Gentiles the glorious riches of this mystery, which is Christ in you, the hope of glory.

²⁸We proclaim him, admonishing and teaching everyone with all wisdom, so that we may present everyone perfect in Christ.

1Ti 2:4 who wants all men to be saved and to come to a knowledge of the truth.

2Ti 1:7 For God did not give us a spirit of timidity, but a spirit of power, of love and of self-discipline.

2Ti 3:15 and how from infancy you have known the holy Scriptures, which are able to make you wise for salvation through faith in Christ Jesus.

Jas 3:17 But the wisdom that comes from heaven is first of all pure; then peace-loving, considerate, submissive, full of mercy and good fruit, impartial and sincere.

2Pe 1:2 Grace and peace be yours in abundance through the knowledge of God and of Jesus our Lord.

³His divine power has given us everything we need for life and godliness through our knowledge of him who called us by his own glory and goodness. ⁴Through these he has given us his very great and precious promises, so that through them you may participate in the divine nature

and escape the corruption in the world caused by evil desires.

5For this very reason, make every effort to add to your faith goodness; and to goodness, knowledge;

2Pe 1:8 For if you possess these qualities in increasing measure, they will keep you from being ineffective and unproductive in your knowledge of our Lord Jesus Christ.

2Pe 1:12 So I will always remind you of these things, even though you know them and are firmly established in the truth you now have.

2Pe 3:18 But grow in the grace and knowledge of our Lord and Savior Jesus Christ. To him be glory both now and forever! Amen.

1Jn 2:20 But you have an anointing from the Holy One, and all of you know the truth.

1Jn 2:27 As for you, the anointing you received from him remains in you, and you do not need anyone to teach you. But as his anointing teaches you about all things and as that anointing is real, not counterfeit—just as it has taught you, remain in him.

1Jn 5:20 We know also that the Son of God has come and has given us understanding, so that we may know him who is true. And we are in him who is true—even in his Son Jesus Christ. He is the true God and eternal life. *See God, Wisdom of.*

Exemplified: Of Joseph (Ge 41:16,25-39; Ac 7:10). Of Moses (Ac 7:22). Of Bezalel (Ex 31:3-5; 35:31-35; 36:1). Of Oholiab (Ex 31:6; 35:34-35; 36:1), of other skilled artisans (Ex 36:2), of women (Ex 35:26). Of Hiram (1Ki 7:14; 2Ch 2:14). Of Solomon (1Ki 3:12,16-28; 4:29-34; 5:12; 10:24). Of Ethan, Heman, Calcol, and Darda (1Ki 4:31). Of the princes of Issachar (1Ch 12:32). Of Ezra (Ezr 7:25). Of Daniel (Da 1:17; 5:14). Of Paul (2Pe 3:15). Of the Magi (Mt 2:1-12).

Prayer for—

Nu 27:21 He is to stand before Eleazar the priest, who will obtain decisions for him by inquiring of the Urim before the LORD. At his command he and the entire community of the Israelites will go out, and at his command they will come in."

Jdg 20:18 The Israelites went up to Bethel and inquired of God. They said, "Who of us shall go first to fight against the Benjamites?" The LORD replied, "Judah shall go first." (+Jdg 20:23,26-28)

1Ki 3:7 "Now, O LORD my God, you have made your servant king in place of my father David. But I am only a little child and do not know how to carry out my duties.

1Ki 3:9 So give your servant a discerning heart to govern your people and to distinguish between right and wrong. For who is able to govern this great people of yours?"

1Ki 8:36 then hear from heaven and forgive the sin of your servants, your people Israel. Teach them the right way to live, and send rain on the land you gave your people for an inheritance. (+2Ch 1:10)

Job 34:32 Teach me what I cannot see; if I have done wrong, I will not do so again.'

Ps 5:8 Lead me, O LORD, in your righteousness because of my enemies—make straight your way before me.

Ps 25:4 Show me your ways, O LORD, teach me your paths; **5**guide me in your truth and teach me, for you are God my Savior, and my hope is in you all day long.

Ps 27:11 Teach me your way, O LORD; lead me in a straight path because of my oppressors.

Ps 31:3 Since you are my rock and my fortress, for the sake of your name lead and guide me.

Ps 39:4 "Show me, O LORD, my life's end and the number of my days; let me know how fleeting is my life.

Ps 43:3 Send forth your light and your truth, let them guide me; let them bring me to your holy mountain, to the place where you dwell.

Ps 86:11 Teach me your way, O LORD, and I will walk in your truth; give me an undivided heart, that I may fear your name.

Ps 90:12 Teach us to number our days aright, that we may gain a heart of wisdom.

Ps 119:12 Praise be to you, O LORD; teach me your decrees.

Ps 119:18 Open my eyes that I may see wonderful things in your law. **19**I am a stranger on earth; do not hide your commands from me.

Ps 119:26 I recounted my ways and you answered me; teach me your decrees. **27**Let me understand the teaching of your precepts; then I will meditate on your wonders.

Ps 119:33 Teach me, O LORD, to follow your decrees; then I will keep them to the end. **34**Give me understanding, and I will keep your law and obey it with all my heart.

Ps 119:66 Teach me knowledge and good judgment, for I believe in your commands.

Ps 119:68 You are good, and what you do is good; teach me your decrees.

Ps 119:73 Your hands made me and formed me; give me understanding to learn your commands.

Ps 119:80 May my heart be blameless toward your decrees, that I may not be put to shame.

Ps 119:124 Deal with your servant according to your love and teach me your decrees. **125**I am your servant; give me discernment that I may understand your statutes.

Ps 119:135 Make your face shine upon your servant and teach me your decrees.

Ps 119:144 Your statutes are forever right; give me understanding that I may live.

Ps 119:169 May my cry come before you, O LORD; give me understanding according to your word.

Ps 119:171 May my lips overflow with praise, for you teach me your decrees.

Ps 139:24 See if there is any offensive way in me, and lead me in the way everlasting.

Eph 1:16 I have not stopped giving thanks for you, remembering you in my prayers. **17**I keep asking that the God of our Lord Jesus Christ, the glorious Father, may give you the Spirit of wisdom and revelation, so that you may know him better. **18**I pray also that the eyes of your heart may be enlightened in order that you may know the hope to which he has called you, the riches of his glorious inheritance in the saints, **19**and his incomparably great power for us who believe. That power is like the working of his mighty strength,

Eph 3:14 For this reason I kneel before the Father, **15**from whom his whole family in heaven and on earth derives its name. **16**I pray that out of his glorious riches he may strengthen you with power through his Spirit in your inner being, **17**so that Christ may dwell in your hearts through faith. And I pray that you, being rooted and established in love, **18**may have power, together with all the saints, to grasp how wide and long and high and deep is the love of Christ, **19**and to know this love that surpasses knowledge—that you may be filled to the measure of all the fullness of God.

Eph 6:18 And pray in the Spirit on all occasions with all kinds of prayers and requests. With this in mind, be alert and always keep on praying for all the saints.

[19]Pray also for me, that whenever I open my mouth, words may be given me so that I will fearlessly make known the mystery of the gospel, [20]for which I am an ambassador in chains. Pray that I may declare it fearlessly, as I should.

Php 1:9 And this is my prayer: that your love may abound more and more in knowledge and depth of insight,

Col 1:9 For this reason, since the day we heard about you, we have not stopped praying for you and asking God to fill you with the knowledge of his will through all spiritual wisdom and understanding. [10]And we pray this in order that you may live a life worthy of the Lord and may please him in every way: bearing fruit in every good work, growing in the knowledge of God,

Col 2:1 I want you to know how much I am struggling for you and for those at Laodicea, and for all who have not met me personally. [2]My purpose is that they may be encouraged in heart and united in love, so that they may have the full riches of complete understanding, in order that they may know the mystery of God, namely, Christ, [3]in whom are hidden all the treasures of wisdom and knowledge.

Col 4:2 Devote yourselves to prayer, being watchful and thankful. [3]And pray for us, too, that God may open a door for our message, so that we may proclaim the mystery of Christ, for which I am in chains. [4]Pray that I may proclaim it clearly, as I should.

2Ti 2:7 Reflect on what I am saying, for the Lord will give you insight into all this.

Jas 1:5 If any of you lacks wisdom, he should ask God, who gives generously to all without finding fault, and it will be given to him.

To be possessed in humility (Jer 9:23-24; Jas 3:13). *See Desire, Spiritual.* Solomon's prayer for. *See Solomon.*

Promised (Jn 8:22). Opportunity to obtain, forfeited (Pr 1:24-31). Shall become universal.

Worldly:

Job 4:18 If God places no trust in his servants, if he charges his angels with error, [19]how much more those who live in houses of clay, whose foundations are in the dust, who are crushed more readily than a moth! [20]Between dawn and dusk they are broken to pieces; unnoticed, they perish forever. [21]Are not the cords of their tent pulled up, so that they die without wisdom?'

Job 5:13 He catches the wise in their craftiness, and the schemes of the wily are swept away.

Job 11:2 "Are all these words to go unanswered? Is this talker to be vindicated?

Job 11:12 But a witless man can no more become wise than a wild donkey's colt can be born a man.

Job 37:24 Therefore, men revere him, for does he not have regard for all the wise in heart?"

Desired by Eve—

Ge 3:6 When the woman saw that the fruit of the tree was good for food and pleasing to the eye, and also desirable for gaining wisdom, she took some and ate it. She also gave some to her husband, who was with her, and he ate it. [7]Then the eyes of both of them were opened, and they realized they were naked; so they sewed fig leaves together and made coverings for themselves.

Misleading—

Pr 21:30 There is no wisdom, no insight, no plan that can succeed against the LORD. (+Isa 47:10)

1Co 8:1 Now about food sacrificed to idols: We know that we all possess knowledge. Knowledge puffs up, but love builds up. [2]The man who thinks he knows something does not yet know as he ought to know.

Ending in death—

Pr 16:25 There is a way that seems right to a man, but in the end it leads to death.

Folly of—

Ecc 2:1 I thought in my heart, "Come now, I will test you with pleasure to find out what is good." But that also proved to be meaningless. [2]"Laughter," I said, "is foolish. And what does pleasure accomplish?" [3]I tried cheering myself with wine, and embracing folly—my mind still guiding me with wisdom. I wanted to see what was worthwhile for men to do under heaven during the few days of their lives.

[4]I undertook great projects: I built houses for myself and planted vineyards. [5]I made gardens and parks and planted all kinds of fruit trees in them. [6]I made reservoirs to water groves of flourishing trees. [7]I bought male and female slaves and had other slaves who were born in my house. I also owned more herds and flocks than anyone in Jerusalem before me. [8]I amassed silver and gold for myself, and the treasure of kings and provinces. I acquired men and women singers, and a harem as well—the delights of the heart of man. [9]I became greater by far than anyone in Jerusalem before me. In all this my wisdom stayed with me.

[10]I denied myself nothing my eyes desired; I refused my heart no pleasure. My heart took delight in all my work, and this was the reward for all my labor. [11]Yet when I surveyed all that my hands had done and what I had toiled to achieve, everything was meaningless, a chasing after the wind; nothing was gained under the sun.

[12]Then I turned my thoughts to consider wisdom, and also madness and folly. What more can the king's successor do than what has already been done? [13]I saw that wisdom is better than folly, just as light is better than darkness. [14]The wise man has eyes in his head, while the fool walks in the darkness; but I came to realize that the same fate overtakes them both.

[15]Then I thought in my heart,

"The fate of the fool will overtake me also. What then do I gain by being wise?" I said in my heart, "This too is meaningless." [16]For the wise man, like the fool, will not be long remembered; in days to come both will be forgotten. Like the fool, the wise man too must die!

[17]So I hated life, because the work that is done under the sun was grievous to me. All of it is meaningless, a chasing after the wind. [18]I hated all the things I had toiled for under the sun, because I must leave them to the one who comes after me. [19]And who knows whether he will be a wise man or a fool? Yet he will have control over all the work into which I have poured my effort and skill under the sun. This too is meaningless. [20]So my heart began to despair over all my toilsome labor under the sun. [21]For a man may do his work with wisdom, knowledge and skill, and then he must leave all he owns to someone who has not worked for it. This too is meaningless and a great misfortune. [22]What does a man get for all the toil and anxious striving with which he labors under the sun? [23]All his days his work is pain and grief; even at night his mind does not rest. This too is meaningless.

[24]A man can do nothing better than to eat and drink and find satisfaction in his work. This too, I see, is from the hand of God, [25]for without him, who can eat or find enjoyment? [26]To the man who pleases him, God gives wisdom, knowledge and happiness, but to the sinner he gives the

task of gathering and storing up wealth to hand it over to the one who pleases God. This too is meaningless, a chasing after the wind.

Ecc 7:11 Wisdom, like an inheritance, is a good thing and benefits those who see the sun. ¹²Wisdom is a shelter as money is a shelter, but the advantage of knowledge is this: that wisdom preserves the life of its possessor.

¹³Consider what God has done: Who can straighten what he has made crooked?

Ecc 7:16 Do not be overrighteous, neither be overwise— why destroy yourself? ¹⁷Do not be overwicked, and do not be a fool—why die before your time? ¹⁸It is good to grasp the one and not let go of the other. The man who fears God will avoid all [extremes].

¹⁹Wisdom makes one wise man more powerful than ten rulers in a city.

²⁰There is not a righteous man on earth who does what is right and never sins.

²¹Do not pay attention to every word people say, or you may hear your servant cursing you— ²²for you know in your heart that many times you yourself have cursed others.

²³All this I tested by wisdom and I said, "I am determined to be wise"—but this was beyond me. ²⁴Whatever wisdom may be, it is far off and most profound—who can discover it? ²⁵So I turned my mind to understand, to investigate and to search out wisdom and the scheme of things and to understand the stupidity of wickedness and the madness of folly.

Ecc 8:1 Who is like the wise man? Who knows the explanation of things? Wisdom brightens a man's face and changes its hard appearance.

Ecc 8:16 When I applied my mind to know wisdom and to observe man's labor on earth—his eyes not seeing sleep day or night— ¹⁷then I saw all that God has done. No one can comprehend what goes on under the sun. Despite all his efforts to search it out, man cannot discover its meaning. Even if a wise man claims he knows, he cannot really comprehend it.

Jer 8:7 Even the stork in the sky knows her appointed seasons, and the dove, the swift and the thrush observe the time of their migration. But my people do not know the requirements of the LORD.

⁸"'How can you say, "We are wise, for we have the law of the LORD," when actually the lying pen of the scribes has handled it falsely? ⁹The wise will be put to shame; they will be dismayed and trapped. Since they have rejected the word of the LORD, what kind of wisdom do they have?

Jer 49:7 Concerning Edom: This is what the LORD Almighty says: "Is there no longer wisdom in Teman? Has counsel perished from the prudent? Has their wisdom decayed?

Mt 6:23 But if your eyes are bad, your whole body will be full of darkness. If then the light within you is darkness, how great is that darkness!

Ro 1:21 For although they knew God, they neither glorified him as God nor gave thanks to him, but their thinking became futile and their foolish hearts were darkened. ²²Although they claimed to be wise, they became fools ²³and exchanged the glory of the immortal God for images made to look like mortal man and birds and animals and reptiles.

Increases sorrow—

Ecc 1:18 For with much wisdom comes much sorrow; the more knowledge, the more grief.

Isa 47:10 You have trusted in your wickedness and have said, 'No one sees me.' Your wisdom and knowledge mislead you when you say to yourself, 'I am, and there is none besides me.' ¹¹Disaster will come upon you, and you will not know how to conjure it away. A calamity will fall upon you that you cannot ward off with a ransom; a catastrophe you cannot foresee will suddenly come upon you.

Denounced—

2Co 1:12 Now this is our boast: Our conscience testifies that we have conducted ourselves in the world, and especially in our relations with you, in the holiness and sincerity that are from God. We have done so not according to worldly wisdom but according to God's grace.

Woe denounced against—

Isa 5:21 Woe to those who are wise in their own eyes and clever in their own sight.

Shall perish—

Isa 29:14 Therefore once more I will astound these people with wonder upon wonder; the wisdom of the wise will perish, the intelligence of the intelligent will vanish." ¹⁵Woe to those who go to great depths to hide their plans from the LORD, who do their work in darkness and think, "Who sees us? Who will know?" ¹⁶You turn things upside down, as if the potter were thought to be like the clay! Shall what is formed say to him who formed it, "He did not make me"? Can the pot say of the potter, "He knows nothing"?

Illustration of—

Mt 7:24 "Therefore everyone who hears these words of mine and puts them into practice is like a wise man who built his house on the rock. ²⁵The rain came down, the streams rose, and the winds blew and beat against that house; yet it did not fall, because it had its foundation on the rock. ²⁶But everyone who hears these words of mine and does not put them into practice is like a foolish man who built his house on sand. ²⁷The rain came down, the streams rose, and the winds blew and beat against that house, and it fell with a great crash."

Lk 16:8 "The master commended the dishonest manager because he had acted shrewdly. For the people of this world are more shrewd in dealing with their own kind than are the people of the light.

Council of others commanded—

Pr 15:22 Plans fail for lack of counsel, but with many advisers they succeed.

Pr 20:18 Make plans by seeking advice; if you wage war, obtain guidance.

Pr 24:3 By wisdom a house is built, and through understanding it is established; ⁴through knowledge its rooms are filled with rare and beautiful treasures.

⁵A wise man has great power, and a man of knowledge increases strength; ⁶for waging war you need guidance, and for victory many advisers.

⁷Wisdom is too high for a fool; in the assembly at the gate he has nothing to say.

Wise application of, profitable—

Ecc 10:10 If the ax is dull and its edge unsharpened, more strength is needed but skill will bring success.

Isa 28:24 When a farmer plows for planting, does he plow continually? Does he keep on breaking up and harrowing the soil? ²⁵When he has leveled the surface, does he not sow caraway and scatter cummin? Does he not plant wheat in its place, barley in its plot, and spelt in its field? ²⁶His God instructs him and teaches him the right way.

²⁷Caraway is not threshed with a sledge, nor is a

cartwheel rolled over cummin; caraway is beaten out with a rod, and cummin with a stick. ²⁸Grain must be ground to make bread; so one does not go on threshing it forever. Though he drives the wheels of his threshing cart over it, his horses do not grind it. ²⁹All this also comes from the LORD Almighty, wonderful in counsel and magnificent in wisdom.

Admonitions against—

Pr 3:7 Do not be wise in your own eyes; fear the LORD and shun evil.

Col 2:8 See to it that no one takes you captive through hollow and deceptive philosophy, which depends on human tradition and the basic principles of this world rather than on Christ.

1Ti 6:20 Timothy, guard what has been entrusted to your care. Turn away from godless chatter and the opposing ideas of what is falsely called knowledge, ²¹which some have professed and in so doing have wandered from the faith.

Grace be with you.

Admonitions against glorying in—

Jer 9:23 This is what the LORD says: "Let not the wise man boast of his wisdom or the strong man boast of his strength or the rich man boast of his riches, ²⁴but let him who boasts boast about this: that he understands and knows me, that I am the LORD, who exercises kindness, justice and righteousness on earth, for in these I delight," declares the LORD.

Heavenly things not discerned by—

Mt 11:25 At that time Jesus said, "I praise you, Father, Lord of heaven and earth, because you have hidden these things from the wise and learned, and revealed them to little children. (+Lk 10:21)

Gospel not to be preached with—

1Co 1:17 For Christ did not send me to baptize, but to preach the gospel—not with words of human wisdom, lest the cross of Christ be emptied of its power.

¹⁸For the message of the cross is foolishness to those who are perishing, but to us who are being saved it is the power of God. ¹⁹For it is written:

"I will destroy the wisdom of the wise; the intelligence of the intelligent I will frustrate."

²⁰Where is the wise man? Where is the scholar? Where is the philosopher of this age? Has not God made foolish the wisdom of the world? ²¹For since in the wisdom of God the world through its wisdom did not know him, God was pleased through the foolishness of what was preached to save those who believe. ²²Jews demand miraculous signs and Greeks look for wisdom, ²³but we preach Christ crucified: a stumbling block to Jews and foolishness to Gentiles, ²⁴but to those whom God has called, both Jews and Greeks, Christ the power of God and the wisdom of God. ²⁵For the foolishness of God is wiser than man's wisdom, and the weakness of God is stronger than man's strength.

²⁶Brothers, think of what you were when you were called. Not many of you were wise by human standards; not many were influential; not many were of noble birth. **1Co 2:1** When I came to you, brothers, I did not come with eloquence or superior wisdom as I proclaimed to you the testimony about God. ²For I resolved to know nothing while I was with you except Jesus Christ and him crucified. ³I came to you in weakness and fear, and with much trembling. ⁴My message and my preaching were not with wise and persuasive words, but with a demonstration

of the Spirit's power, ⁵so that your faith might not rest on men's wisdom, but on God's power.

⁶We do, however, speak a message of wisdom among the mature, but not the wisdom of this age or of the rulers of this age, who are coming to nothing. ⁷No, we speak of God's secret wisdom, a wisdom that has been hidden and that God destined for our glory before time began. ⁸None of the rulers of this age understood it, for if they had, they would not have crucified the Lord of glory. ⁹However, as it is written:

"No eye has seen, no ear has heard, no mind has conceived what God has prepared for those who love him"—

¹⁰but God has revealed it to us by his Spirit.

The Spirit searches all things, even the deep things of God. ¹¹For who among men knows the thoughts of a man except the man's spirit within him? In the same way no one knows the thoughts of God except the Spirit of God. ¹²We have not received the spirit of the world but the Spirit who is from God, that we may understand what God has freely given us. ¹³This is what we speak, not in words taught us by human wisdom but in words taught by the Spirit, expressing spiritual truths in spiritual words. ¹⁴The man without the Spirit does not accept the things that come from the Spirit of God, for they are foolishness to him, and he cannot understand them, because they are spiritually discerned.

To be renounced in order to attain spiritual wisdom—

1Co 3:18 Do not deceive yourselves. If any one of you thinks he is wise by the standards of this age, he should become a "fool" so that he may become wise. ¹⁹For the wisdom of this world is foolishness in God's sight. As it is written: "He catches the wise in their craftiness"; ²⁰and again, "The Lord knows that the thoughts of the wise are futile."

Of God. *See God, Wisdom of.*

Of Jesus. *See Jesus the Christ, Wisdom of.*

WISDOM OF JESUS, SON OF SIRACH *See Apocrypha.*

WISDOM OF SOLOMON *See Apocrypha.*

WISE MEN
NIV+ See MAGI, WISE

1. Men of understanding and skill in ordinary affairs (Pr 1:5; Job 15:2; Ps 49:10), came to be recognized as a distinct class, listed with priests and prophets (Jer 18:18), and also found outside Israel (Ge 41:8; Ex 7:11; Da 2:12-5:15).

2. The Magi (Mt 2:1-12), astrologers who came from the East. Their number and names are not given in Scripture. *See Magi.*

WITCH
NIV+ BEWITCHED, WITCHCRAFT

One (usually a woman) in league with evil spirits who practices witchcraft, sorcery, and divination; condemned by law (Ex 22:18; Dt 18:9-14; 1Sa 28:3,9; 2Ki 23:24; Isa 8:19; Ac 19:18-19). *See Divination; Medium; Sorcery; Spiritists; Witchcraft.*

WITCHCRAFT [4175, 4176, 5758].
NIV+ BEWITCHED

Detestable to God (Dt 18:9-13; 2Ki 9:22; 2Ch 33:6; Na 3:4; Gal 5:19). To be destroyed (Mic 5:12).

See Divination; Sorcery; Spiritists; Witch.

WITHE NIV "thong" (Jdg 16:7-9).

WITHERED HAND Hand wasted away through some form of atrophy (Mk 3:1-6).

WITNESS [1068+9048, 6332, 6338, 6386, 7032, *3455, 3456, 3457, 3459, 5210, 6019, 6020*].

NIV+ EYEWITNESSES, WITNESSED, WITNESSES

(Lev 5:1; Pr 18:17). Qualified by oath (Ex 22:11; Nu 5:19,21; 1Ki 8:31-32), by laying hands on the accused (Lev 24:14). Two necessary to establish a fact (Nu 35:30; Dt 17:6; 19:15; Mt 18:16; Jn 8:17; 2Co 13:1; 1Ti 5:19; Heb 10:28). Required to cast the first stone in executing sentence (Dt 13:9; 17:5-7; Ac 7:58).

To the transfer of land (Ge 21:25-30; 23:11,16-18; Ru 4:1-9; Jer 32:9-12,25,44). To marriage (Ru 4:10-11; Isa 8:2-3). Incorruptible (Ps 15:4). Corrupted by money (Mt 28:11-15; Ac 6:11,13).

Figurative:

Of instruction in righteousness (Rev 11:3).

See Court, Of Law; Evidence; Falsehood; False Witness; Holy Spirit; Testimony, Religious.

WITNESS OF THE SPIRIT Direct, personal communication by the Holy Spirit that we are children of God (Ro 8:15-16), or some other truth (Ac 20:23; 1Ti 4:1).

WITNESSING FOR CHRIST (Lk 2:17,38; 24:48; Ac 1:8; 10:39; 22:15; 23:11; 26:22).

Of John the Baptist (Jn 1:15; 3:26). Of the apostles (Jn 15:27; 19:35; Ac 10:39-43; 1Jn 1:1-5), to his resurrection (Ac 1:22; 2:32; 3:15; 4:33; 5:32; 1Co 15:3-8).

WIZARD *See Spiritists.*

WOLF [2269, *3380*].

NIV+ WOLVES

Ravenous (Ge 49:27; Jer 5:6; Eze 22:27; Zep 3:3; Jn 10:12).

Figurative:

Of the enemies of the righteous (Mt 7:15; 10:16; Jn 10:12; Ac 20:29). Of the reconciling power of the gospel (Isa 11:6).

WOMEN [*851, 1426, 1435, 3251, 5922, 9148, *1222, 4087*].

NIV+ WOMAN, WOMAN'S, WOMEN'S

General:

Creation of (Ge 1:27)—

Ge 2:21 So the LORD God caused the man to fall into a deep sleep; and while he was sleeping, he took one of the man's ribs and closed up the place with flesh. ²²Then the LORD God made a woman from the rib he had taken out of the man, and he brought her to the man.

Named—

Ge 2:23 The man said, "This is now bone of my bones and flesh of my flesh; she shall be called 'woman,' for she was taken out of man."

Fall of and curse upon (Ge 3:1-15)—

Ge 3:16 To the woman he said, "I will greatly increase your pains in childbearing; with pain you will give birth to children. Your desire will be for your husband, and he will rule over you." (+2Co 11:3; 1Ti 2:14)

Promise to (Ge 3:15).

Took part in ancient worship (Ex 15:20-21; 38:8; 1Sa 2:22), in choir (1Ch 25:5-6; Ezr 2:65; Ne 7:67). Served at the entrance to the Tent of Meeting (Ex 38:8; 1Sa 2:22). Consecrated jewels to tabernacle (Ex 35:22), mirrors (Ex 38:8). Required to attend the reading of the law (Dt 31:12;

Jos 8:35). Ministered in the tabernacle (Ex 38:8; 1Sa 2:22). Religious privileges of, among early Christians (Ac 1:14; 12:12-13; 1Co 11:5; 14:34; 1Ti 2:11).

Purifications of after menstruation (Lev 15:19-33; 2Sa 11:4), childbirth (Lev 12; Lk 2:22). Difference in ceremonies made between male and female children (Lev 12). Vows of (Nu 30:3-16).

Had their own tents (Ge 24:67; 31:33). Domestic duties of (Ge 18:6; Pr 31:15-19; Mt 24:41). Cooked (Ge 18:6). Spun (Ex 35:25-26; 1Sa 2:19; Pr 31:19-24). Embroidered (Pr 31:22). Made garments (1Sa 2:19; Ac 9:39). Gleaned (Ru 2:7-8,15-23). Kept vineyards (SS 1:6). Tended flocks and herds (Ge 24:11,13-14,19-20; 29:9; Ex 2:16). Worked in fields (Isa 27:11; Eze 26:6,8). Doorkeeper (Mt 26:69; Jn 18:16-17; Ac 12:13-14). Did not serve in army (Isa 19:16; Jer 50:37; 51:30; Na 3:13).

Veiled the face (Ge 24:65), *See Veil.* Forbidden to wear men's clothing (Dt 22:5). Ornaments of (Isa 3:16-23; Jer 3:32). Wore hair long (1Co 11:5-15). Commended for modesty in dress (1Ti 2:9-10; 1Pe 3:3-6).

Compassionate to her children (Isa 49:15), rejoice with dancing (Jdg 11:34; 21:21; Jer 31:13), courteous to strangers (Ge 24:17-20), wise (1Sa 25:3; 2Sa 20:16-22), weaker partner but co-heir (1Pe 3:7).

Property rights of: In inheritance (Nu 27:1-11; 36; Jos 17:3-6; Job 42:15), to sell real estate (Ru 4:3-9).

First to sin (Ge 3:6). Last at the cross (Mt 27:55-56; Mk 15:40-41). First at the tomb (Mk 15:46-47; 16:1-6; Lk 23:27-28,49,55-56; 24:1-10). First to whom the risen Lord appeared (Mk 16:9; Jn 20:14-18). Converted by preaching of Paul (Ac 16:14-15; 17:4,12,34).

Virtuous, held in high estimation (Ru 3:11)—

Pr 11:16 A kindhearted woman gains respect, but ruthless men gain only wealth.

Pr 11:22 Like a gold ring in a pig's snout is a beautiful woman who shows no discretion.

Pr 12:4 A wife of noble character is her husband's crown, but a disgraceful wife is like decay in his bones. (+Pr 14:1; 31:10-30) *See below, Good.*

Zealous in promoting superstition and idolatry (Jer 7:18; Eze 13:17,23). Active in instigating iniquity (Nu 31:15-16; 1Ki 21:25; Ne 13:26). Guilty of lesbianism (Ro 1:26). *See below, Wicked.*

Could not marry without consent of parents, father (Ge 24:3-4; 34:6; Ex 22:17; Jos 3:16-17; 1Sa 17:25; 18:17-27). Not to be given in marriage considered a calamity (Jdg 11:37; Ps 78:63; Isa 4:1). When charged with infidelity, guilt or innocence was determined by trial (Nu 5:12-31). Sold for husband's debts (Mt 18:25). Taken captive (Nu 31:9,15,17-18,35; La 1:18; Eze 30:17-18).

Punishment to be inflicted on men for seducing, when betrothed (Dt 22:23-27). Punishment for seducing, when not betrothed (Ex 22:16-17; Dt 22:28-29). Protected during menstruation (Lev 18:19; 20:18). Treated with cruelty in war (Dt 32:25; La 2:21; 5:11).

In Leadership:

Rulers of nations—

Deborah, judge and prophetess (Jdg 4:4); Athaliah, queen of Judah (2Ki 11:1-16; 2Ch 22:2-3,10-12; 23:1-15); Jezebel, queen of Israel (1Ki 16:31); as rulers in Israel (Isa 3:12); Queen of Sheba (1Ki 10:1-13; 2Ch 9:1-9,12); Esther, queen of Persia (Est 2:17); Candace, queen of Ethiopia (Ac 8:27).

Patriots—

Miriam (Ex 15:20), Deborah (Jdg 4:4-16; 5), women of

Israel (1Sa 18:6), of Thebez (Jdg 9:50), of Abel (2Sa 20:16-22), Esther (Est 4:4-17; 5:1-8; 7:1-6; 8:1-8), of the Philistines (2Sa 1:20). Aid in defensive operations (Jdg 9:53).

Influential in public affairs—

The wise woman from Tekoa (2Sa 14:1-21), Bathsheba (1Ki 1:15-21), Jezebel (1Ki 21:7-15,25), Athaliah (2Ki 11:1,3; 2Ch 21:6; 22:3), Huldah (2Ki 22:14-20; 2Ch 34:22-28), the queen of Babylon (Da 5:9-13), Pilate's wife (Mt 27:19).

Poets—

Miriam (Ex 15:21), Deborah (Jdg 5), Hannah (1Sa 2:1-10), Elizabeth (Lk 1:42-45), Mary (Lk 1:46-55).

Prophets—

Miriam (Ex 15:20-21; Mic 6:4), Deborah (Jdg 4:4-5), Huldah (2Ki 22:14-20; 2Ch 34:22-28), Anna (Lk 2:36-38), Philip's daughters (Ac 21:9).

False prophets and mediums—

The medium at Endor (1Sa 28:7-25), false prophets (Eze 13:17-23), Noadiah the prophetess (Ne 6:14).

In business (1Ch 7:24; Pr 31:14-18,24).

In the church—

Present at the selection of Matthias (Ac 1:13-26), present at Pentecost (Ac 2:1-18), churches met in women's homes (Ac 12:12; 16:40; Ro 16:3-5; 1Co 1:11; 16:19; Col 4:15; 2Jn), teachers (Ac 18:26; Tit 2:3-5), deaconesses or wives of deacons (Ro 16:1-2; 1Ti 3:11), and if Junias was a woman, apostles (Ro 16:7). Widow may have been a church office (1Ti 5:1-16).

Social Status of:

In Persia (Est 1:10-19)—

Est 1:20 Then when the king's edict is proclaimed throughout all his vast realm, all the women will respect their husbands, from the least to the greatest." [21]The king and his nobles were pleased with this advice, so the king did as Memucan proposed. [22]He sent dispatches to all parts of the kingdom, to each province in its own script and to each people in its own language, proclaiming in each people's tongue that every man should be ruler over his own household. (+Da 5:1-12)

In Roman empire (Ac 24:24; 25:13,23; 26:30).

Paul's precepts concerning women in the church—

Gal 3:28 There is neither Jew nor Greek, slave nor free, male nor female, for you are all one in Christ Jesus.

1Co 11:5 And every woman who prays or prophesies with her head uncovered dishonors her head—it is just as though her head were shaved. [6]If a woman does not cover her head, she should have her hair cut off; and if it is a disgrace for a woman to have her hair cut or shaved off, she should cover her head. [7]A man ought not to cover his head, since he is the image and glory of God; but the woman is the glory of man. [8]For man did not come from woman, but woman from man; [9]neither was man created for woman, but woman for man. [10]For this reason, and because of the angels, the woman ought to have a sign of authority on her head. [11]In the Lord, however, woman is not independent of man, nor is man independent of woman. [12]For as woman came from man, so also man is born of woman. But everything comes from God. [13]Judge for yourselves: Is it proper for a woman to pray to God with her head uncovered? [14]Does not the very nature of things teach you that if a man has long hair, it is a disgrace to him, [15]but that if a woman has long hair, it is her glory? For long hair is given to her as a covering.

1Co 14:34 women should remain silent in the churches. They are not allowed to speak, but must be in submission, as the Law says. [35]If they want to inquire about something, they should ask their own husbands at home; for it is disgraceful for a woman to speak in the church. (+Eph 5:22-24; Col 3:18)

1Ti 2:9 I also want women to dress modestly, with decency and propriety, not with braided hair or gold or pearls or expensive clothes, [10]but with good deeds, appropriate for women who profess to worship God. [11]A woman should learn in quietness and full submission. [12]I do not permit a woman to teach or to have authority over a man; she must be silent.

1Ti 3:11 In the same way, their wives are to be women worthy of respect, not malicious talkers but temperate and trustworthy in everything.

1Ti 5:1 Do not rebuke an older man harshly, but exhort him as if he were your father. Treat younger men as brothers, [2]older women as mothers, and younger women as sisters, with absolute purity. [3]Give proper recognition to those widows who are really in need. [4]But if a widow has children or grandchildren, these should learn first of all to put their religion into practice by caring for their own family and so repaying their parents and grandparents, for this is pleasing to God. [5]The widow who is really in need and left all alone puts her hope in God and continues night and day to pray and to ask God for help. [6]But the widow who lives for pleasure is dead even while she lives. [7]Give the people these instructions, too, so that no one may be open to blame. [8]If anyone does not provide for his relatives, and especially for his immediate family, he has denied the faith and is worse than an unbeliever. [9]No widow may be put on the list of widows unless she is over sixty, has been faithful to her husband, [10]and is well known for her good deeds, such as bringing up children, showing hospitality, washing the feet of the saints, helping those in trouble and devoting herself to all kinds of good deeds. [11]As for younger widows, do not put them on such a list. For when their sensual desires overcome their dedication to Christ, they want to marry. [12]Thus they bring judgment on themselves, because they have broken their first pledge. [13]Besides, they get into the habit of being idle and going about from house to house. And not only do they become idlers, but also gossips and busybodies, saying things they ought not to. [14]So I counsel younger widows to marry, to have children, to manage their homes and to give the enemy no opportunity for slander. [15]Some have in fact already turned away to follow Satan. [16]If any woman who is a believer has widows in her family, she should help them and not let the church be burdened with them, so that the church can help those widows who are really in need.

Tit 2:3 Likewise, teach the older women to be reverent in the way they live, not to be slanderers or addicted to much wine, but to teach what is good. [4]Then they can train the younger women to love their husbands and children, [5]to be self-controlled and pure, to be busy at home, to be kind, and to be subject to their husbands, so that no one will malign the word of God.

See Widow; Wife. See also, Husbands; Parents.

Good:

Good wife, from the Lord—

Pr 18:22 He who finds a wife finds what is good and receives favor from the LORD.

Pr 19:13 A foolish son is his father's ruin, and a quarrelsome wife is like a constant dripping.

¹⁴Houses and wealth are inherited from parents, but a prudent wife is from the LORD. (+Pr 12:4)

Pr 31:10 A wife of noble character who can find? She is worth far more than rubies. ¹¹Her husband has full confidence in her and lacks nothing of value. ¹²She brings him good, not harm, all the days of her life. ¹³She selects wool and flax and works with eager hands. ¹⁴She is like the merchant ships, bringing her food from afar. ¹⁵She gets up while it is still dark; she provides food for her family and portions for her servant girls. ¹⁶She considers a field and buys it; out of her earnings she plants a vineyard. ¹⁷She sets about her work vigorously; her arms are strong for her tasks. ¹⁸She sees that her trading is profitable, and her lamp does not go out at night. ¹⁹In her hand she holds the distaff and grasps the spindle with her fingers. ²⁰She opens her arms to the poor and extends her hands to the needy. ²¹When it snows, she has no fear for her household; for all of them are clothed in scarlet. ²²She makes coverings for her bed; she is clothed in fine linen and purple. ²³Her husband is respected at the city gate, where he takes his seat among the elders of the land. ²⁴She makes linen garments and sells them, and supplies the merchants with sashes. ²⁵She is clothed with strength and dignity; she can laugh at the days to come. ²⁶She speaks with wisdom, and faithful instruction is on her tongue. ²⁷She watches over the affairs of her household and does not eat the bread of idleness. ²⁸Her children arise and call her blessed; her husband also, and he praises her: ²⁹"Many women do noble things, but you surpass them all." ³⁰Charm is deceptive, and beauty is fleeting; but a woman who fears the LORD is to be praised. ³¹Give her the reward she has earned, and let her works bring her praise at the city gate. (+1Ti 2:9-10; 3:11; 5:3-16; Tit 2:3-5)

Virtuous (Ru 3:11; Pr 11:16,22; 12:4; 14:1). Affectionate (2Sa 1:26), to offspring (Isa 49:15). Illustrated by the five wise virgins (Mt 25:1-10).

Instances of—

Deborah, a judge, prophetess, and military leader (Jdg 4:5). Mother of Samson (Jdg 13:23). Naomi (Ru 1:2; 3:1; 4:14-17). Ruth (Ru 1:4,14-22, & Ru 2-4). Hannah, the mother of Samuel (1Sa 1:9-18,24-28). Widow of Zarephath, who fed Elijah during the famine (1Ki 17:8-24). The Shunammite, who gave hospitality to Elisha (2Ki 4:8-38). Vashti (Est 1:11-12). Esther (Est 4:15-17; 5:1-8; 7:1-6; 8:1-8). Mary (Lk 1:26-38). Elizabeth (Lk 1:6,41-45). Anna (Lk 2:37). The widow who cast her mite into the treasury (Mk 12:41-44; Lk 21:2-4). Mary and Martha (Mk 14:3-9; Lk 10:42; Jn 11:5). Mary Magdalene (Mk 16:1; Lk 8:2; Jn 20:1-2,11-16). Pilate's wife (Mt 27:19). Dorcas (Ac 9:36). Lydia (Ac 19:14). Priscilla (Ac 18:26). Phoebe (Ro 16:1-2). Julia (Ro 16:15). Mary (Ro 16:6). Lois and Eunice (2Ti 1:5). Philippians (Php 4:3). The chosen lady (2Jn).

Figurative—

Of the church of Christ (Ps 45:2-15; Gal 4:26; Rev 12:1). Of saints (Mt 25:1-4; 2Co 11:2; Rev 14:4).

Wicked:

(2Ki 9:30-37; 23:7; Jer 44:15-19,25; Eze 8:14; Ro 1:26). Zeal of, in licentious practices of idolatry (2Ki 23:7; Hos 4:13-14), in promoting superstition and idolatry (Jer 7:18; Eze 13:17,23). Careless (Isa 32:9-11).

Contentious—

Pr 27:15 A quarrelsome wife is like a constant dripping on a rainy day; ¹⁶restraining her is like restraining the wind or grasping oil with the hand.

Fond of self-indulgence—

Isa 32:9 You women who are so complacent, rise up and listen to me; you daughters who feel secure, hear what I have to say! ¹⁰In little more than a year you who feel secure will tremble; the grape harvest will fail, and the harvest of fruit will not come. ¹¹Tremble, you complacent women; shudder, you daughters who feel secure! Strip off your clothes, put sackcloth around your waists.

Of ornaments (Jer 2:32).

Subtle and deceitful (Pr 6:24-29,32-35; 7:6-27)—

Ecc 7:26 I find more bitter than death the woman who is a snare, whose heart is a trap and whose hands are chains. The man who pleases God will escape her, but the sinner she will ensnare.

Weak-willed—

2Ti 3:6 They are the kind who worm their way into homes and gain control over weak-willed women, who are loaded down with sins and are swayed by all kinds of evil desires,

Active in instigating iniquity (Nu 31:15-16; 1Ki 21:25; Ne 13:26). Idolatrous (Nu 31:15-16; 2Ki 23:7; Ne 13:26; Jer 7:18). Gossips (1Ti 5:11-13). Haughty and vain (Isa 3:16). Odious (Pr 30:23). Guileful and licentious (Pr 2:16-19; 5:3-20; 6:24-29,32-35; 7:6-27; Ecc 7:26; Eze 16:32; Ro 1:26). Commits forgery (1Ki 21:8). Subtle and deceitful (Pr 6:24-29,32-35; 7:6-27; Ecc 7:26). Illustrated by the five foolish virgins (Mt 25:1-12).

Instances of Wicked—

Eve, in yielding to temptation and seducing her husband (Ge 3:6; 1Ti 2:14). Sarah, in her jealousy and malice toward Hagar (Ge 21:9-11, w 21:12-21). Lot's wife, in her rebellion against her situation, and against the destruction of Sodom (Ge 19:26; Lk 17:32). The daughters of Lot, in their incestuous lust (Ge 19:31-38). Rebekah, in her partiality for Jacob and her actions to secure for him Isaac's blessing (Ge 27:11-17). Rachel, in her jealousy of Leah (Ge 30:1), in stealing images (Ge 31:19,34). Leah in her imitation of Rachel in the matter of children (Ge 30:9-18). Tamar, in her adultery (Ge 38:14-24). Potiphar's wife, in her lust and slander against Joseph (Ge 39:7-20).

Miriam, in her sedition with Aaron against Moses (Nu 12). Rahab, in her harlotry (Jos 2:1). Delilah, in her conspiracy against Samson (Jdg 16:4-20). Peninnah, the wife of Elkanah, in her jealous taunting of Hannah (1Sa 1:4-8). The Midianite woman in the camp of Israel, taken in adultery (Nu 25:6-8).

Michal, in her derision of David's religious zeal (2Sa 6:16,20-23). Bathsheba, in her adultery and in becoming the wife of her husband's murderer (2Sa 11:4-5,27; 12:9-10). Solomon's wives, in their idolatrous and wicked influence over Solomon (1Ki 11:1-11; Ne 13:26). Jezebel, in her persecution and destruction of the prophets of the Lord (1Ki 18:4,13); in her persecution of Elijah (1Ki 19:2),;in her conspiracy against Naboth to despoil him of his vineyard (1Ki 21:1-16); in her evil influence over Ahab (1Ki 21:25, w 21:17-27, & 2Ki 9:30-37). The cannibal mothers of Samaria (2Ki 6:28-29). Athaliah, in destroying the royal household and usurping the throne (2Ki 11:1-16; 2Ch 22:10,12; 23:12-15).

Noadiah, a false prophetess, in troubling the Jews when they were restoring Jerusalem (Ne 6:14). Haman's wife, in counseling him to hang Mordecai (Est 5:14; 6:13). Job's wife, in counseling him to curse God (Job 2:9; 19:17). The idolatrous wife of Hosea (Hos 1:2-3; 3:1).

Herodias, in her incestuous marriage with Herod (Mt

14:3-4; Mk 6:17-19; Lk 3:19) and causing the death of John the Baptist (Mt 14:6-11; Mk 6:24-28). The daughter of Herodias, in her complicity with her mother in causing the death of John the Baptist (Mt 14:8; Mk 6:18-28). Sapphira, in her blasphemous falsehood (Ac 5:2-10).

Figurative:

Of backsliding (Jer 6:2; Rev 17:4,18). Of the wicked (Isa 32:9,11; Mt 25:1-13).

Symbolic:

Of wickedness (Zec 5:7-8; Rev 17; 19:2).
See Widow; Wife.

WONDERFUL [7098, 7099, 7100, *1902, 2514, 2515*].

NIV+ WONDER, WONDERED, WONDERFULLY, WONDERING, WONDERS, WONDROUS

The acts of God (1Ch 16:9; Ps 26:7; 107:8,15,21,24,31). The name of God is (Jdg 13:18, ftn). A name of the Messiah (Isa 9:6).
See Jesus the Christ, Names of; Titles and Names.

WOOL [1600, 7547, 9106+9357, 10556, *2250*].

NIV+ WOOLEN

Used for clothing (Lev 13:47-52,59; Pr 31:13; Eze 34:3; 44:17). Prohibited in the priest's temple dress (Eze 44:17). Mixing of, with other fabrics forbidden (Lev 19:19; Dt 22:11). Fleece of (Jdg 6:37). First fleece of, belonged to the priests (Dt 18:4).

WORD [*3364*].

NIV+ BYWORD, WORDS

A title of Jesus (Jn 1:1,14; 1Jn 5:7; Rev 19:13). *See Jesus the Christ, Names of; Logos.*

WORD OF GOD

Written Word; the Bible:

Called: Book (Ps 40:7; Rev 22:19)

Book of the Lord—
Isa 34:16 Look in the scroll of the LORD and read: None of these will be missing, not one will lack her mate. For it is his mouth that has given the order, and his Spirit will gather them together.

Book of the Law (Ne 8:3; Gal 3:10)

Holy Scriptures (Ro 1:2)—
2Ti 3:15 and how from infancy you have known the holy Scriptures, which are able to make you wise for salvation through faith in Christ Jesus.

Law of the Lord—
Ps 1:2 But his delight is in the law of the LORD, and on his law he meditates day and night. (+Isa 30:9)

Oracles (Zec 9:1; 12:1; Mal 1:1)

Scriptures—
1Co 15:3 For what I received I passed on to you as of first importance: that Christ died for our sins according to the Scriptures,

Scriptures of Truth—
Da 10:21 but first I will tell you what is written in the Book of Truth. (No one supports me against them except Michael, your prince.

Sword of the Spirit—
Eph 6:17 Take the helmet of salvation and the sword of the Spirit, which is the word of God.

The Word—
Jas 1:21 Therefore, get rid of all moral filth and the evil that is so prevalent and humbly accept the word planted in you, which can save you.

[22]Do not merely listen to the word, and so deceive

yourselves. Do what it says. [23]Anyone who listens to the word but does not do what it says is like a man who looks at his face in a mirror (+1Pe 2:2)

Word of God—
Lk 11:28 He replied, "Blessed rather are those who hear the word of God and obey it."
Heb 4:12 For the word of God is living and active. Sharper than any double-edged sword, it penetrates even to dividing soul and spirit, joints and marrow; it judges the thoughts and attitudes of the heart.

Good Word of God—
Heb 6:5 who have tasted the goodness of the word of God and the powers of the coming age,

Word of Christ—
Col 3:16 Let the word of Christ dwell in you richly as you teach and admonish one another with all wisdom, and as you sing psalms, hymns and spiritual songs with gratitude in your hearts to God.

Word of Life—
Php 2:16 as you hold out the word of life—in order that I may boast on the day of Christ that I did not run or labor for nothing.

Word of Truth—
Pr 22:21 teaching you true and reliable words, so that you can give sound answers to him who sent you?
Eph 1:13 And you also were included in Christ when you heard the word of truth, the gospel of your salvation. Having believed, you were marked in him with a seal, the promised Holy Spirit,
2Ti 2:15 Do your best to present yourself to God as one approved, a workman who does not need to be ashamed and who correctly handles the word of truth.
Jas 1:18 He chose to give us birth through the word of truth, that we might be a kind of firstfruits of all he created.

Compared to: A lamp (Ps 119:105)—
Pr 6:23 For these commands are a lamp, this teaching is a light, and the corrections of discipline are the way to life,

Fire—
Jer 23:29 "Is not my word like fire," declares the LORD, "and like a hammer that breaks a rock in pieces?

Seed (Mt 13:38,18-22)—
Mt 13:23 But the one who received the seed that fell on good soil is the man who hears the word and understands it. He produces a crop, yielding a hundred, sixty or thirty times what was sown." (+Mt 13:37)
Mt 13:38 The field is the world, and the good seed stands for the sons of the kingdom. The weeds are the sons of the evil one, (+Mk 4:3-19)
Mk 4:20 Others, like seed sown on good soil, hear the word, accept it, and produce a crop—thirty, sixty or even a hundred times what was sown." (+Mk 4:26-32; Lk 8:5-10)
Lk 8:11 "This is the meaning of the parable: The seed is the word of God. [12]Those along the path are the ones who hear, and then the devil comes and takes away the word from their hearts, so that they may not believe and be saved. [13]Those on the rock are the ones who receive the word with joy when they hear it, but they have no root. They believe for a while, but in the time of testing they fall away. [14]The seed that fell among thorns stands for those who hear, but as they go on their way they are choked by life's worries, riches and pleasures, and they do not mature. [15]But the seed on good soil stands for those with a noble and good heart, who hear the word, retain it, and by persevering produce a crop.

To a two-edged sword (Heb 4:12).

To be publicly read (Ex 24:7)—

Dt 31:11 when all Israel comes to appear before the LORD your God at the place he will choose, you shall read this law before them in their hearing. [12]Assemble the people—men, women and children, and the aliens living in your towns—so they can listen and learn to fear the LORD your God and follow carefully all the words of this law. [13]Their children, who do not know this law, must hear it and learn to fear the LORD your God as long as you live in the land you are crossing the Jordan to possess." (+Jos 8:33-35; 2Ki 23:2; 2Ch 17:7-9; Ne 8:1-8,13,18)

Isa 2:3 Many peoples will come and say, "Come, let us go up to the mountain of the LORD, to the house of the God of Jacob. He will teach us his ways, so that we may walk in his paths." The law will go out from Zion, the word of the LORD from Jerusalem. (+Jer 36:6; Ac 13:15,27; Col 4:16; 1Th 5:27)

Instruction of, to be desired (Ps 119:18-19). The people stood and responded saying "Amen" (Ex 24:7; Dt 27:12-26; Ne 8:5-6).

Publicly expounded (Ne 8:8)

By Jesus (Lk 4:16-21)—

Lk 4:22 All spoke well of him and were amazed at the gracious words that came from his lips. "Isn't this Joseph's son?" they asked. (+Lk 4:23-27; 24:27)

Lk 24:45 Then he opened their minds so they could understand the Scriptures.

Jn 2:22 After he was raised from the dead, his disciples recalled what he had said. Then they believed the Scripture and the words that Jesus had spoken.

By the apostles (Ac 2:16-47)—

Ac 8:32 The eunuch was reading this passage of Scripture: "He was led like a sheep to the slaughter, and as a lamb before the shearer is silent, so he did not open his mouth.

Ac 8:35 Then Philip began with that very passage of Scripture and told him the good news about Jesus. (+Ac 17:2; 28:23)

Searched—

Ac 17:11 Now the Bereans were of more noble character than the Thessalonians, for they received the message with great eagerness and examined the Scriptures every day to see if what Paul said was true.

Searching of, commanded (Isa 34:16)—

Jn 5:39 You diligently study the Scriptures because you think that by them you possess eternal life. These are the Scriptures that testify about me, (+Jn 7:52)

To be studied (2Ti 2:15)—

1Pe 2:2 Like newborn babies, crave pure spiritual milk, so that by it you may grow up in your salvation, [3]now that you have tasted that the Lord is good.

Various portions to be compared (2Pe 2:20).

Obeyed (Dt 4:5-6; 29:29)—

Ps 78:1 O my people, hear my teaching; listen to the words of my mouth.

Ps 78:7 Then they would put their trust in God and would not forget his deeds but would keep his commands. (+Isa 34:16)

Eze 44:5 The LORD said to me, "Son of man, look carefully, listen closely and give attention to everything I tell you concerning all the regulations regarding the temple of the LORD. Give attention to the entrance of the temple and all the exits of the sanctuary.

Hab 2:2 Then the LORD replied: "Write down the revela-

tion and make it plain on tablets so that a herald may run with it.

Mt 7:24 "Therefore everyone who hears these words of mine and puts them into practice is like a wise man who built his house on the rock. [25]The rain came down, the streams rose, and the winds blew and beat against that house; yet it did not fall, because it had its foundation on the rock. (+Lk 6:47-48; 11:28)

Ro 16:26 but now revealed and made known through the prophetic writings by the command of the eternal God, so that all nations might believe and obey him—

1Co 11:2 I praise you for remembering me in everything and for holding to the teachings, just as I passed them on to you.

1Th 4:1 Finally, brothers, we instructed you how to live in order to please God, as in fact you are living. Now we ask you and urge you in the Lord Jesus to do this more and more. [2]For you know what instructions we gave you by the authority of the Lord Jesus.

2Th 2:14 He called you to this through our gospel, that you might share in the glory of our Lord Jesus Christ. [15]So then, brothers, stand firm and hold to the teachings we passed on to you, whether by word of mouth or by letter.

Heb 2:1 We must pay more careful attention, therefore, to what we have heard, so that we do not drift away. [2]For if the message spoken by angels was binding, and every violation and disobedience received its just punishment, [3]how shall we escape if we ignore such a great salvation? This salvation, which was first announced by the Lord, was confirmed to us by those who heard him.

Jas 1:25 But the man who looks intently into the perfect law that gives freedom, and continues to do this, not forgetting what he has heard, but doing it—he will be blessed in what he does.

2Pe 3:1 Dear friends, this is now my second letter to you. I have written both of them as reminders to stimulate you to wholesome thinking. [2]I want you to recall the words spoken in the past by the holy prophets and the command given by our Lord and Savior through your apostles.

Jude 3 Dear friends, although I was very eager to write to you about the salvation we share, I felt I had to write and urge you to contend for the faith that was once for all entrusted to the saints.

Jude 17 But, dear friends, remember what the apostles of our Lord Jesus Christ foretold.

Rev 1:3 Blessed is the one who reads the words of this prophecy, and blessed are those who hear it and take to heart what is written in it, because the time is near.

Believed—

Mk 1:15 "The time has come," he said. "The kingdom of God is near. Repent and believe the good news!"

1Jn 5:11 And this is the testimony: God has given us eternal life, and this life is in his Son.

1Jn 5:13 I write these things to you who believe in the name of the Son of God so that you may know that you have eternal life.

Longing for (Ps 119:20,131)—

Am 8:11 "The days are coming," declares the Sovereign LORD, "when I will send a famine through the land—not a famine of food or a thirst for water, but a famine of hearing the words of the LORD. [12]Men will stagger from sea to sea and wander from north to east, searching for the word of the LORD, but they will not find it.

[13]"In that day "the lovely young women and strong young men will faint because of thirst.

Walking after (Ps 119:30).

Psalm of (Ps 119:1-8)—

Ps 119:9 How can a young man keep his way pure? By living according to your word. (+Ps 119:10)

Ps 119:11 I have hidden your word in my heart that I might not sin against you. [12]Praise be to you, O LORD; teach me your decrees. (+Ps 119:13)

Ps 119:14 I rejoice in following your statutes as one rejoices in great riches. [15]I meditate on your precepts and consider your ways. [16]I delight in your decrees; I will not neglect your word. (+Ps 119:17)

Ps 119:18 Open my eyes that I may see wonderful things in your law. [19]I am a stranger on earth; do not hide your commands from me. [20]My soul is consumed with longing for your laws at all times. (+Ps 119:21-22)

Ps 119:23 Though rulers sit together and slander me, your servant will meditate on your decrees. [24]Your statutes are my delight; they are my counselors.

[25]I am laid low in the dust; preserve my life according to your word. (+Ps 119:26-27)

Ps 119:28 My soul is weary with sorrow; strengthen me according to your word. (+Ps 119:29)

Ps 119:30 I have chosen the way of truth; I have set my heart on your laws. [31]I hold fast to your statutes, O LORD; do not let me be put to shame. (+Ps 119:32)

Ps 119:33 Teach me, O LORD, to follow your decrees; then I will keep them to the end. (+Ps 119:34)

Ps 119:35 Direct me in the path of your commands, for there I find delight. (+Ps 119:36-40)

Ps 119:41 May your unfailing love come to me, O LORD, your salvation according to your promise; (+Ps 119:42-44)

Ps 119:45 I will walk about in freedom, for I have sought out your precepts. [46]I will speak of your statutes before kings and will not be put to shame, [47]for I delight in your commands because I love them. [48]I lift up my hands to your commands, which I love, and I meditate on your decrees.

[49]Remember your word to your servant, for you have given me hope. [50]My comfort in my suffering is this: Your promise preserves my life. [51]The arrogant mock me without restraint, but I do not turn from your law. [52]I remember your ancient laws, O LORD, and I find comfort in them. (+Ps 119:53)

Ps 119:54 Your decrees are the theme of my song wherever I lodge. (+Ps 119:55-60)

Ps 119:61 Though the wicked bind me with ropes, I will not forget your law. (+Ps 119:62-65)

Ps 119:66 Teach me knowledge and good judgment, for I believe in your commands. [67]Before I was afflicted I went astray, but now I obey your word. (+Ps 119:68-69)

Ps 119:70 Their hearts are callous and unfeeling, but I delight in your law. (+Ps 119:71)

Ps 119:72 The law from your mouth is more precious to me than thousands of pieces of silver and gold. (+Ps 119:73)

Ps 119:74 May those who fear you rejoice when they see me, for I have put my hope in your word. (+Ps 119:75)

Ps 119:76 May your unfailing love be my comfort, according to your promise to your servant. [77]Let your compassion come to me that I may live, for your law is my delight. [78]May the arrogant be put to shame for wronging me without cause; but I will meditate on your precepts. (+Ps 119:80)

Ps 119:81 My soul faints with longing for your salvation, but I have put my hope in your word. [82]My eyes fail, looking for your promise; I say, "When will you comfort me?" [83]Though I am like a wineskin in the smoke, I do not forget your decrees. (+Ps 119:84-85)

Ps 119:86 All your commands are trustworthy; help me, for men persecute me without cause. (+Ps 119:87-88)

Ps 119:89 Your word, O LORD, is eternal; it stands firm in the heavens. (+Ps 119:90-91)

Ps 119:92 If your law had not been my delight, I would have perished in my affliction. [93]I will never forget your precepts, for by them you have preserved my life. (+Ps 119:94-95)

Ps 119:96 To all perfection I see a limit; but your commands are boundless.

[97]Oh, how I love your law! I meditate on it all day long. [98]Your commands make me wiser than my enemies, for they are ever with me. [99]I have more insight than all my teachers, for I meditate on your statutes. [100]I have more understanding than the elders, for I obey your precepts. (+Ps 119:101-102)

Ps 119:103 How sweet are your words to my taste, sweeter than honey to my mouth! [104]I gain understanding from your precepts; therefore I hate every wrong path.

[105]Your word is a lamp to my feet and a light for my path. (+Ps 119:106-108)

Ps 119:109 Though I constantly take my life in my hands, I will not forget your law. (+Ps 119:110)

Ps 119:111 Your statutes are my heritage forever; they are the joy of my heart. (+Ps 119:112)

Ps 119:113 I hate double-minded men, but I love your law. (+Ps 119:114)

Ps 119:115 Away from me, you evildoers, that I may keep the commands of my God! (+Ps 119:116-118)

Ps 119:119 All the wicked of the earth you discard like dross; therefore I love your statutes. (+Ps 119:120-126)

Ps 119:127 Because I love your commands more than gold, more than pure gold, [128]and because I consider all your precepts right, I hate every wrong path.

[129]Your statutes are wonderful; therefore I obey them. [130]The unfolding of your words gives light; it gives understanding to the simple. [131]I open my mouth and pant, longing for your commands. (+Ps 119:132)

Ps 119:133 Direct my footsteps according to your word; let no sin rule over me. (+Ps 119:134-137)

Ps 119:138 The statutes you have laid down are righteous; they are fully trustworthy. (+Ps 119:139)

Ps 119:140 Your promises have been thoroughly tested, and your servant loves them. [141]Though I am lowly and despised, I do not forget your precepts. [142]Your righteousness is everlasting and your law is true. [143]Trouble and distress have come upon me, but your commands are my delight. [144]Your statutes are forever right; give me understanding that I may live. (+Ps 119:145-147)

Ps 119:148 My eyes stay open through the watches of the night, that I may meditate on your promises. (+Ps 119:149-150)

Ps 119:151 Yet you are near, O LORD, and all your commands are true. [152]Long ago I learned from your statutes that you established them to last forever.

[153]Look upon my suffering and deliver me, for I have not forgotten your law. (+Ps 119:154-156)

Ps 119:157 Many are the foes who persecute me, but I have not turned from your statutes. [158]I look on the faithless with loathing, for they do not obey your word. [159]See how I love your precepts; preserve my life, O LORD, according to your love. [160]All your words are true; all your righteous laws are eternal.

[161]Rulers persecute me without cause, but my heart

trembles at your word. ¹⁶²I rejoice in your promise like one who finds great spoil. ¹⁶³I hate and abhor falsehood but I love your law. (+Ps 119:164)

Ps 119:165 Great peace have they who love your law, and nothing can make them stumble. (+Ps 119:166)

Ps 119:167 I obey your statutes, for I love them greatly. (+Ps 119:168-171)

Ps 119:172 May my tongue sing of your word, for all your commands are righteous. ¹⁷³May your hand be ready to help me, for I have chosen your precepts. ¹⁷⁴I long for your salvation, O Lord, and your law is my delight. (+Ps 119:175-176)

To be: In the heart—

Dt 30:11 Now what I am commanding you today is not too difficult for you or beyond your reach. ¹²It is not up in heaven, so that you have to ask, "Who will ascend into heaven to get it and proclaim it to us so we may obey it?" ¹³Nor is it beyond the sea, so that you have to ask, "Who will cross the sea to get it and proclaim it to us so we may obey it?" ¹⁴No, the word is very near you; it is in your mouth and in your heart so you may obey it.

Job 22:22 Accept instruction from his mouth and lay up his words in your heart.

Ps 37:31 The law of his God is in his heart; his feet do not slip.

Ps 40:8 I desire to do your will, O my God; your law is within my heart." (+Ps 119:11)

Pr 6:20 My son, keep your father's commands and do not forsake your mother's teaching. ²¹Bind them upon your heart forever; fasten them around your neck.

Isa 51:7 "Hear me, you who know what is right, you people who have my law in your hearts: Do not fear the reproach of men or be terrified by their insults.

Eze 3:10 And he said to me, "Son of man, listen carefully and take to heart all the words I speak to you. (+Ro 10:6-8)

Meditated upon—

Jos 1:8 Do not let this Book of the Law depart from your mouth; meditate on it day and night, so that you may be careful to do everything written in it. Then you will be prosperous and successful. (+Ps 1:2; 119:15,23,48,78,97, 99,148)

Worn on the hand and forehead—

Ex 13:9 This observance will be for you like a sign on your hand and a reminder on your forehead that the law of the Lord is to be on your lips. For the Lord brought you out of Egypt with his mighty hand.

Dt 6:8 Tie them as symbols on your hands and bind them on your foreheads. (+Dt 11:18)

Written on the doorframes—

Dt 6:9 Write them on the doorframes of your houses and on your gates. (+Dt 11:20)

In public places—

Dt 27:2 When you have crossed the Jordan into the land the Lord your God is giving you, set up some large stones and coat them with plaster. ³Write on them all the words of this law when you have crossed over to enter the land the Lord your God is giving you, a land flowing with milk and honey, just as the Lord, the God of your fathers, promised you.

Dt 27:8 And you shall write very clearly all the words of this law on these stones you have set up." (+Jos 8:32)

Studied by rulers—

Dt 17:18 When he takes the throne of his kingdom, he is to write for himself on a scroll a copy of this law, taken from that of the priests, who are Levites. ¹⁹It is to be with him,

and he is to read it all the days of his life so that he may learn to revere the Lord his God and follow carefully all the words of this law and these decrees (+Jos 1:8)

Taught to children—

Dt 6:7 Impress them on your children. Talk about them when you sit at home and when you walk along the road, when you lie down and when you get up. (+Dt 11:19; 21:12-13)

Ps 78:5 He decreed statutes for Jacob and established the law in Israel, which he commanded our forefathers to teach their children,

Placed inside of the ark of the covenant (Ex 40:20), beside the ark (Dt 31:26), read in public assemblies (Dt 31:11), *See above, In Public Places.*

Taught in the Psalms—

Dt 31:19 "Now write down for yourselves this song and teach it to the Israelites and have them sing it, so that it may be a witness for me against them.

Dt 31:21 And when many disasters and difficulties come upon them, this song will testify against them, because it will not be forgotten by their descendants. I know what they are disposed to do, even before I bring them into the land I promised them on oath." (+Ps 119:54)

Used for teaching and admonishing one another—

1Co 10:11 These things happened to them as examples and were written down as warnings for us, on whom the fulfillment of the ages has come. (+Col 3:16)

Instruction—

2Ti 3:16 All Scripture is God-breathed and is useful for teaching, rebuking, correcting and training in righteousness, ¹⁷so that the man of God may be thoroughly equipped for every good work.

Not to be: Added to nor taken from—

Dt 4:2 Do not add to what I command you and do not subtract from it, but keep the commands of the Lord your God that I give you. (+Dt 12:32; Pr 30:6)

Rev 22:18 I warn everyone who hears the words of the prophecy of this book: If anyone adds anything to them, God will add to him the plagues described in this book. ¹⁹And if anyone takes words away from this book of prophecy, God will take away from him his share in the tree of life and in the holy city, which are described in this book.

Handled deceitfully (2Co 4:2)

Broken—

Jn 10:35 If he called them 'gods,' to whom the word of God came—and the Scripture cannot be broken—

Nature of: comforting (Ps 119:28,50,52,76,83,92).

Delight of the righteous—

Job 23:12 I have not departed from the commands of his lips; I have treasured the words of his mouth more than my daily bread. (+Ps 1:2; 119:16,24,35,77,103,143,162,174)

Desired more than gold (Ps 119:72,127).

Edifying (Ps 119:98,99,104,130)—

Ac 20:32 "Now I commit you to God and to the word of his grace, which can build you up and give you an inheritance among all those who are sanctified.

Ro 4:23 The words "it was credited to him" were written not for him alone, ²⁴but also for us, to whom God will credit righteousness—for us who believe in him who raised Jesus our Lord from the dead.

Ro 15:4 For everything that was written in the past was written to teach us, so that through endurance and the encouragement of the Scriptures we might have hope.

1Ti 4:6 If you point these things out to the brothers, you will be a good minister of Christ Jesus, brought up in the truths of the faith and of the good teaching that you have followed.

1Jn 2:7 Dear friends, I am not writing you a new command but an old one, which you have had since the beginning. This old command is the message you have heard. [8]Yet I am writing you a new command; its truth is seen in him and you, because the darkness is passing and the true light is already shining.

1Jn 2:12 I write to you, dear children, because your sins have been forgiven on account of his name.

1Jn 2:14 I write to you, fathers, because you have known him who is from the beginning. I write to you, young men, because you are strong, and the word of God lives in you, and you have overcome the evil one.

1Jn 2:21 I do not write to you because you do not know the truth, but because you do know it and because no lie comes from the truth.

Effective—

Isa 55:11 so is my word that goes out from my mouth: It will not return to me empty, but will accomplish what I desire and achieve the purpose for which I sent it.

Enduring forever (Ps 119:89,138,152)—

Isa 40:8 The grass withers and the flowers fall, but the word of our God stands forever."

Mk 13:31 Heaven and earth will pass away, but my words will never pass away.

Lk 16:17 It is easier for heaven and earth to disappear than for the least stroke of a pen to drop out of the Law.

1Pe 1:23 For you have been born again, not of perishable seed, but of imperishable, through the living and enduring word of God. [24]For,

"All men are like grass, and all their glory is like the flowers of the field; the grass withers and the flowers fall, [25]but the word of the Lord stands forever."

And this is the word that was preached to you.

Full of hope (Ps 119:81)—

Col 1:5 the faith and love that spring from the hope that is stored up for you in heaven and that you have already heard about in the word of truth, the gospel

Full of joy—

Jer 15:16 When your words came, I ate them; they were my joy and my heart's delight, for I bear your name, O LORD God Almighty.

1Jn 1:4 We write this to make our joy complete.

Inspiration of—

Ex 19:7 So Moses went back and summoned the elders of the people and set before them all the words the LORD had commanded him to speak.

Ex 20:1 And God spoke all these words:

Ex 24:3 When Moses went and told the people all the LORD's words and laws, they responded with one voice, "Everything the LORD has said we will do." [4]Moses then wrote down everything the LORD had said. He got up early the next morning and built an altar at the foot of the mountain and set up twelve stone pillars representing the twelve tribes of Israel.

Ex 24:12 The LORD said to Moses, "Come up to me on the mountain and stay here, and I will give you the tablets of stone, with the law and commands I have written for their instruction."

Ex 31:18 When the LORD finished speaking to Moses on Mount Sinai, he gave him the two tablets of the Testimony, the tablets of stone inscribed by the finger of God.

Ex 32:16 The tablets were the work of God; the writing was the writing of God, engraved on the tablets.

Ex 34:27 Then the LORD said to Moses, "Write down these words, for in accordance with these words I have made a covenant with you and with Israel."

Ex 34:32 Afterward all the Israelites came near him, and he gave them all the commands the LORD had given him on Mount Sinai.

Lev 26:46 These are the decrees, the laws and the regulations that the LORD established on Mount Sinai between himself and the Israelites through Moses.

Dt 4:5 See, I have taught you decrees and laws as the LORD my God commanded me, so that you may follow them in the land you are entering to take possession of it.

Dt 4:10 Remember the day you stood before the LORD your God at Horeb, when he said to me, "Assemble the people before me to hear my words so that they may learn to revere me as long as they live in the land and may teach them to their children."

Dt 4:14 And the LORD directed me at that time to teach you the decrees and laws you are to follow in the land that you are crossing the Jordan to possess.

2Ki 17:13 The LORD warned Israel and Judah through all his prophets and seers: "Turn from your evil ways. Observe my commands and decrees, in accordance with the entire Law that I commanded your fathers to obey and that I delivered to you through my servants the prophets."

2Ch 33:18 The other events of Manasseh's reign, including his prayer to his God and the words the seers spoke to him in the name of the LORD, the God of Israel, are written in the annals of the kings of Israel.

Ps 99:7 He spoke to them from the pillar of cloud; they kept his statutes and the decrees he gave them.

Ps 147:19 He has revealed his word to Jacob, his laws and decrees to Israel.

Isa 34:16 Look in the scroll of the LORD and read: None of these will be missing, not one will lack her mate. For it is his mouth that has given the order, and his Spirit will gather them together.

Isa 59:21 "As for me, this is my covenant with them," says the LORD. "My Spirit, who is on you, and my words that I have put in your mouth will not depart from your mouth, or from the mouths of your children, or from the mouths of their descendants from this time on and forever," says the LORD.

Jer 30:2 "This is what the LORD, the God of Israel, says: 'Write in a book all the words I have spoken to you.

Jer 36:1 In the fourth year of Jehoiakim son of Josiah king of Judah, this word came to Jeremiah from the LORD: [2]"Take a scroll and write on it all the words I have spoken to you concerning Israel, Judah and all the other nations from the time I began speaking to you in the reign of Josiah till now.

Jer 36:27 After the king burned the scroll containing the words that Baruch had written at Jeremiah's dictation, the word of the LORD came to Jeremiah: [28]"Take another scroll and write on it all the words that were on the first scroll, which Jehoiakim king of Judah burned up.

Jer 36:32 So Jeremiah took another scroll and gave it to the scribe Baruch son of Neriah, and as Jeremiah dictated, Baruch wrote on it all the words of the scroll that Jehoiakim king of Judah had burned in the fire. And many similar words were added to them. (+Jer 51:59-64)

Eze 11:25 and I told the exiles everything the LORD had shown me.

Da 10:21 but first I will tell you what is written in the

Book of Truth. (No one supports me against them except Michael, your prince.

Hos 8:12 I wrote for them the many things of my law, but they regarded them as something alien.

Zec 7:12 They made their hearts as hard as flint and would not listen to the law or to the words that the LORD Almighty had sent by his Spirit through the earlier prophets. So the LORD Almighty was very angry.

Ac 1:16 and said, "Brothers, the Scripture had to be fulfilled which the Holy Spirit spoke long ago through the mouth of David concerning Judas, who served as guide for those who arrested Jesus—

Ac 28:25 They disagreed among themselves and began to leave after Paul had made this final statement: "The Holy Spirit spoke the truth to your forefathers when he said through Isaiah the prophet:

Ro 3:1 What advantage, then, is there in being a Jew, or what value is there in circumcision? ²Much in every way! First of all, they have been entrusted with the very words of God.

1Co 2:12 We have not received the spirit of the world but the Spirit who is from God, that we may understand what God has freely given us. ¹³This is what we speak, not in words taught us by human wisdom but in words taught by the Spirit, expressing spiritual truths in spiritual words.

1Co 14:37 If anybody thinks he is a prophet or spiritually gifted, let him acknowledge that what I am writing to you is the Lord's command.

Eph 6:17 Take the helmet of salvation and the sword of the Spirit, which is the word of God.

1Th 2:13 And we also thank God continually because, when you received the word of God, which you heard from us, you accepted it not as the word of men, but as it actually is, the word of God, which is at work in you who believe.

2Ti 3:16 All Scripture is God-breathed and is useful for teaching, rebuking, correcting and training in righteousness, ¹⁷so that the man of God may be thoroughly equipped for every good work.

Heb 1:1 In the past God spoke to our forefathers through the prophets at many times and in various ways, ²but in these last days he has spoken to us by his Son, whom he appointed heir of all things, and through whom he made the universe.

Heb 3:7 So, as the Holy Spirit says: "Today, if you hear his voice, ⁸do not harden your hearts as you did in the rebellion, during the time of testing in the desert,

Heb 4:12 For the word of God is living and active. Sharper than any double-edged sword, it penetrates even to dividing soul and spirit, joints and marrow; it judges the thoughts and attitudes of the heart.

2Pe 1:21 For prophecy never had its origin in the will of man, but men spoke from God as they were carried along by the Holy Spirit.

2Pe 3:2 I want you to recall the words spoken in the past by the holy prophets and the command given by our Lord and Savior through your apostles.

2Pe 3:15 Bear in mind that our Lord's patience means salvation, just as our dear brother Paul also wrote you with the wisdom that God gave him.

Rev 1:1 The revelation of Jesus Christ, which God gave him to show his servants what must soon take place. He made it known by sending his angel to his servant John, ²who testifies to everything he saw—that is, the word of God and the testimony of Jesus Christ.

Rev 1:11 which said: "Write on a scroll what you see and send it to the seven churches: to Ephesus, Smyrna, Pergamum, Thyatira, Sardis, Philadelphia and Laodicea."

Rev 1:17 When I saw him, I fell at his feet as though dead. Then he placed his right hand on me and said: "Do not be afraid. I am the First and the Last. ¹⁸I am the Living One; I was dead, and behold I am alive for ever and ever! And I hold the keys of death and Hades.

¹⁹"Write, therefore, what you have seen, what is now and what will take place later.

Rev 2:7 He who has an ear, let him hear what the Spirit says to the churches. To him who overcomes, I will give the right to eat from the tree of life, which is in the paradise of God.

Rev 22:6 The angel said to me, "These words are trustworthy and true. The Lord, the God of the spirits of the prophets, sent his angel to show his servants the things that must soon take place."

⁷"Behold, I am coming soon! Blessed is he who keeps the words of the prophecy in this book."

⁸I, John, am the one who heard and saw these things. And when I had heard and seen them, I fell down to worship at the feet of the angel who had been showing them to me.

Life giving (Ps 119:25,93; Jas 1:18; 1Pe 1:23). Living (Heb 4:12). Loved (Ps 119:47-48,70,97,111,113,119,159, 163,167). Part of the Christian armor (Eph 6:17).

Perfect—

Ps 19:7 The law of the LORD is perfect, reviving the soul. The statutes of the LORD are trustworthy, making wise the simple.

Jas 1:24 and, after looking at himself, goes away and immediately forgets what he looks like.

Powerful—

Lk 1:37 For nothing is impossible with God." (+Heb 4:12)

Praiseworthy—

Ps 56:4 In God, whose word I praise, in God I trust; I will not be afraid. What can mortal man do to me?

Pure—

Ps 12:6 And the words of the LORD are flawless, like silver refined in a furnace of clay, purified seven times.

Ps 19:8 The precepts of the LORD are right, giving joy to the heart. The commands of the LORD are radiant, giving light to the eyes. (+Ps 119:140)

Pr 30:5 "Every word of God is flawless; he is a shield to those who take refuge in him.

Restraining—

Ps 17:4 As for the deeds of men—by the word of your lips I have kept myself from the ways of the violent. (+Ps 119:11)

Revered (Ps 119:161)—

Ps 138:2 I will bow down toward your holy temple and will praise your name for your love and your faithfulness, for you have exalted above all things your name and your word.

Sanctifying—

Jn 15:3 You are already clean because of the word I have spoken to you.

Jn 17:17 Sanctify them by the truth; your word is truth.

Jn 17:19 For them I sanctify myself, that they too may be truly sanctified.

Eph 5:26 to make her holy, cleansing her by the washing with water through the word,

1Ti 4:5 because it is consecrated by the word of God and prayer.

Spirit and life—

Jn 6:63 The Spirit gives life; the flesh counts for nothing. The words I have spoken to you are spirit and they are life.

Spiritual food, bread—

Dt 8:3 He humbled you, causing you to hunger and then feeding you with manna, which neither you nor your fathers had known, to teach you that man does not live on bread alone but on every word that comes from the mouth of the LORD. (+Mt 4:4)

Standard of righteous (Ps 119:138,144,172)—

Isa 8:20 To the law and to the testimony! If they do not speak according to this word, they have no light of dawn.

Trustworthy (Ps 19:7)—

Ps 19:9 The fear of the LORD is pure, enduring forever. The ordinances of the LORD are sure and altogether righteous.

Ps 33:4 For the word of the LORD is right and true; he is faithful in all he does.

Ps 33:6 By the word of the LORD were the heavens made, their starry host by the breath of his mouth.

Ps 93:5 Your statutes stand firm; holiness adorns your house for endless days, O LORD.

Ps 111:7 The works of his hands are faithful and just; all his precepts are trustworthy. **⁸**They are steadfast for ever and ever, done in faithfulness and uprightness. (+Ps 119:86)

Truth (Ps 119:142,151,160; 1Th 2:13; Jas 1:18). Wonderful (Ps 119:129).

Bears the test of criticism and experience—

2Sa 22:31 "As for God, his way is perfect; the word of the LORD is flawless. He is a shield for all who take refuge in him. (+Ps 18:30)

Cleanses life of youth (Ps 119:9). Convicts of sin (2Ki 22:9-13; 2Ch 17:7-10; 34:14-33). Gives peace (Ps 119:165).

Inspires faith—

Ro 10:17 Consequently, faith comes from hearing the message, and the message is heard through the word of Christ.

Heb 11:3 By faith we understand that the universe was formed at God's command, so that what is seen was not made out of what was visible.

Makes free (Ps 119:45)—

Jn 8:32 Then you will know the truth, and the truth will set you free."

Makes wise (Ps 119:99; 2Ti 3:15). Rejoices the heart (Ps 119:111; Jer 15:16).

Spirit of, gives life—

2Co 3:6 He has made us competent as ministers of a new covenant—not of the letter but of the Spirit; for the letter kills, but the Spirit gives life.

Standard of judgment, the world to be judged by (Jn 12:48; Ro 2:16). Works salvation (1Th 2:13; 1Pe 1:23).

Fulfilled by Jesus—

Mt 5:17 "Do not think that I have come to abolish the Law or the Prophets; I have not come to abolish them but to fulfill them. (+Lk 24:27; Jn 19:24)

Testify of Jesus (Jn 5:39)—

Jn 20:31 But these are written that you may believe that Jesus is the Christ, the Son of God, and that by believing you may have life in his name. (+Ac 10:43; 18:28; 1Co 15:3)

Heb 10:7 Then I said, 'Here I am—it is written about me in the scroll—I have come to do your will, O God.'" *See Jesus the Christ, Prophecies Concerning.*

Ignorance of:

Mt 22:29 Jesus replied, "You are in error because you do not know the Scriptures or the power of God.

Mk 12:24 Jesus replied, "Are you not in error because you do not know the Scriptures or the power of God?

Disbelief in—

Lk 16:31 "He said to him, 'If they do not listen to Moses and the Prophets, they will not be convinced even if someone rises from the dead.'" (+Lk 24:25; Jn 5:46-47; 8:37; 2Ti 4:3-4; 1Pe 2:8)

2Pe 3:15 Bear in mind that our Lord's patience means salvation, just as our dear brother Paul also wrote you with the wisdom that God gave him. **¹⁶**He writes the same way in all his letters, speaking in them of these matters. His letters contain some things that are hard to understand, which ignorant and unstable people distort, as they do the other Scriptures, to their own destruction.

Rejected by the wicked—

Ps 50:16 But to the wicked, God says: "What right have you to recite my laws or take my covenant on your lips? **¹⁷**You hate my instruction and cast my words behind you.

Pr 1:29 Since they hated knowledge and did not choose to fear the LORD,

Pr 13:13 He who scorns instruction will pay for it, but he who respects a command is rewarded.

Isa 5:24 Therefore, as tongues of fire lick up straw and as dry grass sinks down in the flames, so their roots will decay and their flowers blow away like dust; for they have rejected the law of the LORD Almighty and spurned the word of the Holy One of Israel.

Isa 28:9 "Who is it he is trying to teach? To whom is he explaining his message? To children weaned from their milk, to those just taken from the breast? **¹⁰**For it is: Do and do, do and do, rule on rule, rule on rule; a little here, a little there."

¹¹Very well then, with foreign lips and strange tongues God will speak to this people, **¹²**to whom he said, "This is the resting place, let the weary rest"; and, "This is the place of repose"—but they would not listen. **¹³**So then, the word of the LORD to them will become: Do and do, do and do, rule on rule, rule on rule; a little here, a little there—so that they will go and fall backward, be injured and snared and captured.

¹⁴Therefore hear the word of the LORD, you scoffers who rule this people in Jerusalem.

Isa 30:9 These are rebellious people, deceitful children, children unwilling to listen to the LORD's instruction. **¹⁰**They say to the seers, "See no more visions!" and to the prophets, "Give us no more visions of what is right! Tell us pleasant things, prophesy illusions. **¹¹**Leave this way, get off this path, and stop confronting us with the Holy One of Israel!"

Isa 53:1 Who has believed our message and to whom has the arm of the LORD been revealed?

Jer 6:10 To whom can I speak and give warning? Who will listen to me? Their ears are closed so they cannot hear. The word of the LORD is offensive to them; they find no pleasure in it.

Jer 8:9 The wise will be put to shame; they will be dismayed and trapped. Since they have rejected the word of the LORD, what kind of wisdom do they have?

Hos 8:12 I wrote for them the many things of my law, but they regarded them as something alien.

Am 2:12 "But you made the Nazirites drink wine and commanded the prophets not to prophesy.

Mic 2:6 "Do not prophesy," their prophets say. "Do not

prophesy about these things; disgrace will not overtake us."

Mk 7:9 And he said to them: "You have a fine way of setting aside the commands of God in order to observe your own traditions!

Mk 7:13 Thus you nullify the word of God by your tradition that you have handed down. And you do many things like that." (+Lk 16:31)

Lk 24:25 He said to them, "How foolish you are, and how slow of heart to believe all that the prophets have spoken!

Jn 3:20 Everyone who does evil hates the light, and will not come into the light for fear that his deeds will be exposed.

Jn 5:46 If you believed Moses, you would believe me, for he wrote about me. **47**But since you do not believe what he wrote, how are you going to believe what I say?"

Jn 8:37 I know you are Abraham's descendants. Yet you are ready to kill me, because you have no room for my word.

Jn 8:45 Yet because I tell the truth, you do not believe me! (+Ac 13:46)

1Co 1:18 For the message of the cross is foolishness to those who are perishing, but to us who are being saved it is the power of God.

1Co 1:22 Jews demand miraculous signs and Greeks look for wisdom, **23**but we preach Christ crucified: a stumbling block to Jews and foolishness to Gentiles,

2Ti 4:3 For the time will come when men will not put up with sound doctrine. Instead, to suit their own desires, they will gather around them a great number of teachers to say what their itching ears want to hear. **4**They will turn their ears away from the truth and turn aside to myths.

1Pe 2:8 and, "A stone that causes men to stumble and a rock that makes them fall." They stumble because they disobey the message—which is also what they were destined for.

2Pe 3:15 Bear in mind that our Lord's patience means salvation, just as our dear brother Paul also wrote you with the wisdom that God gave him. **16**He writes the same way in all his letters, speaking in them of these matters. His letters contain some things that are hard to understand, which ignorant and unstable people distort, as they do the other Scriptures, to their own destruction.

Rev 22:19 And if anyone takes words away from this book of prophecy, God will take away from him his share in the tree of life and in the holy city, which are described in this book.

See Commandments and Statutes, Of God.

WORDS [*606, 609, 614, 1819, 1821, 4383, 4863, 7023, 7754, 8938, 9048, 10418, *3364, 3306, 3359, 4048, 4839, 5125, 5889*].

NIV+ BYWORD, WORD

Of Jesus:

Gracious (Lk 4:22), spirit and life (Jn 6:63), eternal life (Jn 6:68), shall judge (Jn 12:47-48).

Of the wise:

As goads, and as nails well fastened (Ecc 12:11), gracious (Ecc 10:12). Spoken in season (Pr 15:23; Isa 50:4). Fitly spoken, like apples of gold in settings of silver (Pr 25:11). Of the perfect man, gentle (Jas 3:2).

Should be acceptable to God (Ps 19:14).

Of the teacher, should be plain (1Co 14:9,19). Unprofitable, to be avoided (2Ti 2:14). Unspeakable, heard by Paul in paradise (2Co 12:4). Vain, not to be regarded (Ex 5:9; Eph 5:6), like a tempest (Job 8:2). Without

knowledge, darken counsel (Job 38:2). Idle, account must be given for in the day of judgment (Mt 12:36-37). Hasty, folly of (Pr 29:20). In a multitude of, is sin (Pr 10:19). Fool known by the multitude of (Ecc 5:3), will swallow himself (Ecc 10:12-14). Seditious, deceive the simple (Ro 16:18). Deceitful, are a snare to him who utters them (Pr 6:2). Of the hypocrite, softer than oil (Ps 55:21). Of the talebearer, wounds to the soul (Pr 18:8).

See Busybody; Slander; Speaking, Evil; Talebearer.

WORK [*1215, 1911, 2006, 3098, 3330, 3828, 4144, 4856, 5126, 6268, 6275, 6662, 6913, 6913, 7188, 7189, 7190, 7258, 7756, 8391, 8502, 8697, 10525, *1918, 1919, 2237, 2239, 2240, 2435, 3159, 3160, 4472, 5300, 5301*].

NIV+ HARDWORKING, METALWORKER, WORKED, WORKER, WORKERS, WORKING, WORKMAN, WORKMAN'S, WORKMANSHIP, WORKMEN, WORKS

See Industry; Labor.

WORKS, GOOD [*1911, 2006, 5126, 6268, 6913, 7188, 7189, *1919, 2240, 2435*].

General:

2Co 9:8 And God is able to make all grace abound to you, so that in all things at all times, having all that you need, you will abound in every good work.

Eph 2:10 For we are God's workmanship, created in Christ Jesus to do good works, which God prepared in advance for us to do.

Php 2:13 for it is God who works in you to will and to act according to his good purpose.

Col 1:10 And we pray this in order that you may live a life worthy of the Lord and may please him in every way: bearing fruit in every good work, growing in the knowledge of God,

1Th 1:3 We continually remember before our God and Father your work produced by faith, your labor prompted by love, and your endurance inspired by hope in our Lord Jesus Christ.

1Th 1:7 And so you became a model to all the believers in Macedonia and Achaia. **8**The Lord's message rang out from you not only in Macedonia and Achaia—your faith in God has become known everywhere. Therefore we do not need to say anything about it,

2Th 2:17 encourage your hearts and strengthen you in every good deed and word.

2Ti 2:21 If a man cleanses himself from the latter, he will be an instrument for noble purposes, made holy, useful to the Master and prepared to do any good work.

Jas 1:22 Do not merely listen to the word, and so deceive yourselves. Do what it says. **23**Anyone who listens to the word but does not do what it says is like a man who looks at his face in a mirror **24**and, after looking at himself, goes away and immediately forgets what he looks like. **25**But the man who looks intently into the perfect law that gives freedom, and continues to do this, not forgetting what he has heard, but doing it—he will be blessed in what he does.

26If anyone considers himself religious and yet does not keep a tight rein on his tongue, he deceives himself and his religion is worthless. **27**Religion that God our Father accepts as pure and faultless is this: to look after orphans and widows in their distress and to keep oneself from being polluted by the world.

Jas 3:17 But the wisdom that comes from heaven is first of all pure; then peace-loving, considerate, submissive, full of mercy and good fruit, impartial and sincere.

[18]Peacemakers who sow in peace raise a harvest of righteousness.

Jesus an example of (Jn 10:32; Ac 10:38).

Holy women should manifest—

1Ti 2:10 but with good deeds, appropriate for women who profess to worship God.

1Ti 5:10 and is well known for her good deeds, such as bringing up children, showing hospitality, washing the feet of the saints, helping those in trouble and devoting herself to all kinds of good deeds.

God remembers (Ne 13:14; Heb 6:9)—

Heb 6:10 God is not unjust; he will not forget your work and the love you have shown him as you have helped his people and continue to help them.

Shall be brought into judgment (Ecc 12:14, w 2Co 5:10). In the judgment, will be an evidence of faith (Mt 25:34-40, w Jas 2:14-20). Ministers should be patterns of (Tit 2:7). Ministers should exhort to (1Ti 6:17-18; Tit 3:1,8,14). God is glorified by (Jn 15:8). Designed to lead others to glorify God (Mt 5:16; 1Pe 2:12). A blessing attends (Jas 1:25). Of the righteous, are manifest (1Ti 5:25).

Parables relating to: The talents and pounds (Mt 25:14-29; Lk 19:12-27), the laborers in the vineyard (Mt 20:11-15), the two sons (Mt 21:28-31), the barren fig tree (Lk 13:6-9).

In humanitarian service (Eze 18:7-8)—

Mt 10:42 And if anyone gives even a cup of cold water to one of these little ones because he is my disciple, I tell you the truth, he will certainly not lose his reward." (+Mt 25:35-46; Jas 1:27)

Manifest faith—

Ps 37:3 Trust in the LORD and do good; dwell in the land and enjoy safe pasture.

Mt 19:16 Now a man came up to Jesus and asked, "Teacher, what good thing must I do to get eternal life?"

[17]"Why do you ask me about what is good?" Jesus replied. "There is only One who is good. If you want to enter life, obey the commandments."

[18]"Which ones?" the man inquired.

Jesus replied, " 'Do not murder, do not commit adultery, do not steal, do not give false testimony, [19]honor your father and mother,' and 'love your neighbor as yourself.' "

[20]"All these I have kept," the young man said. "What do I still lack?"

[21]Jesus answered, "If you want to be perfect, go, sell your possessions and give to the poor, and you will have treasure in heaven. Then come, follow me."

Ro 2:13 For it is not those who hear the law who are righteous in God's sight, but it is those who obey the law who will be declared righteous.

Gal 6:4 Each one should test his own actions. Then he can take pride in himself, without comparing himself to somebody else, (+Jas 2:14-26)

Commanded: (Ps 37:3)

Mt 3:8 Produce fruit in keeping with repentance. (+Jn 14:2-8,14)

To ministers (Tit 2:7), women professing godliness (1Ti 2:10), widows (1Ti 5:10)

To Christians (Mt 5:16)—

Col 3:13 Bear with each other and forgive whatever grievances you may have against one another. Forgive as the Lord forgave you.

Tit 3:1 Remind the people to be subject to rulers and authorities, to be obedient, to be ready to do whatever is

good, [2]to slander no one, to be peaceable and considerate, and to show true humility toward all men.

Tit 3:8 This is a trustworthy saying. And I want you to stress these things, so that those who have trusted in God may be careful to devote themselves to doing what is good. These things are excellent and profitable for everyone.

Tit 3:14 Our people must learn to devote themselves to doing what is good, in order that they may provide for daily necessities and not live unproductive lives.

Heb 10:24 And let us consider how we may spur one another on toward love and good deeds. (+Jas 1:22-27)

Jas 3:13 Who is wise and understanding among you? Let him show it by his good life, by deeds done in the humility that comes from wisdom. (+1Pe 2:12)

To the rich—

1Ti 6:18 Command them to do good, to be rich in good deeds, and to be generous and willing to share.

To be done without a show—

Mt 6:1 "Be careful not to do your 'acts of righteousness' before men, to be seen by them. If you do, you will have no reward from your Father in heaven.

[2]"So when you give to the needy, do not announce it with trumpets, as the hypocrites do in the synagogues and on the streets, to be honored by men. I tell you the truth, they have received their reward in full. [3]But when you give to the needy, do not let your left hand know what your right hand is doing, [4]so that your giving may be in secret. Then your Father, who sees what is done in secret, will reward you.

Following the example of the faithful (Heb 10-14).

Zeal in—

Tit 2:14 who gave himself for us to redeem us from all wickedness and to purify for himself a people that are his very own, eager to do what is good.

Remembered by God:

Dt 6:25 And if we are careful to obey all this law before the LORD our God, as he has commanded us, that will be our righteousness."

Dt 24:13 Return his cloak to him by sunset so that he may sleep in it. Then he will thank you, and it will be regarded as a righteous act in the sight of the LORD your God.

Ps 106:30 But Phinehas stood up and intervened, and the plague was checked. [31]This was credited to him as righteousness for endless generations to come.

Jer 22:15 "Does it make you a king to have more and more cedar? Did not your father have food and drink? He did what was right and just, so all went well with him. [16]He defended the cause of the poor and needy, and so all went well. Is that not what it means to know me?" declares the LORD.

Eze 18:5 "Suppose there is a righteous man who does what is just and right. [6]He does not eat at the mountain shrines or look to the idols of the house of Israel. He does not defile his neighbor's wife or lie with a woman during her period. [7]He does not oppress anyone, but returns what he took in pledge for a loan. He does not commit robbery but gives his food to the hungry and provides clothing for the naked. [8]He does not lend at usury or take excessive interest. He withholds his hand from doing wrong and judges fairly between man and man. [9]He follows my decrees and faithfully keeps my laws. That man is righteous; he will surely live, declares the Sovereign LORD. (+Mt 6:1-4)

Mt 18:5 "And whoever welcomes a little child like this in my name welcomes me. (+Mt 25:34-36)

Jn 15:2 He cuts off every branch in me that bears no fruit, while every branch that does bear fruit he prunes so that it will be even more fruitful. ³You are already clean because of the word I have spoken to you. ⁴Remain in me, and I will remain in you. No branch can bear fruit by itself; it must remain in the vine. Neither can you bear fruit unless you remain in me. ⁵"I am the vine; you are the branches. If a man remains in me and I in him, he will bear much fruit; apart from me you can do nothing. ⁶If anyone does not remain in me, he is like a branch that is thrown away and withers; such branches are picked up, thrown into the fire and burned. ⁷If you remain in me and my words remain in you, ask whatever you wish, and it will be given you. ⁸This is to my Father's glory, that you bear much fruit, showing yourselves to be my disciples.

Jn 15:14 You are my friends if you do what I command.

Ac 10:14 "Surely not, Lord!" Peter replied. "I have never eaten anything impure or unclean."

Ac 10:38 how God anointed Jesus of Nazareth with the Holy Spirit and power, and how he went around doing good and healing all who were under the power of the devil, because God was with him. (+Heb 6:9-10)

Rev 14:13 Then I heard a voice from heaven say, "Write: Blessed are the dead who die in the Lord from now on." "Yes," says the Spirit, "they will rest from their labor, for their deeds will follow them."

Rev 22:14 "Blessed are those who wash their robes, that they may have the right to the tree of life and may go through the gates into the city.

Glorify God:

Mt 25:34 "Then the King will say to those on his right, 'Come, you who are blessed by my Father; take your inheritance, the kingdom prepared for you since the creation of the world. ³⁵For I was hungry and you gave me something to eat, I was thirsty and you gave me something to drink, I was a stranger and you invited me in, ³⁶I needed clothes and you clothed me, I was sick and you looked after me, I was in prison and you came to visit me.'

³⁷"Then the righteous will answer him, 'Lord, when did we see you hungry and feed you, or thirsty and give you something to drink? ³⁸When did we see you a stranger and invite you in, or needing clothes and clothe you? ³⁹When did we see you sick or in prison and go to visit you?'

⁴⁰"The King will reply, 'I tell you the truth, whatever you did for one of the least of these brothers of mine, you did for me.'

⁴¹"Then he will say to those on his left, 'Depart from me, you who are cursed, into the eternal fire prepared for the devil and his angels. ⁴²For I was hungry and you gave me nothing to eat, I was thirsty and you gave me nothing to drink, ⁴³I was a stranger and you did not invite me in, I needed clothes and you did not clothe me, I was sick and in prison and you did not look after me.'

⁴⁴"They also will answer, 'Lord, when did we see you hungry or thirsty or a stranger or needing clothes or sick or in prison, and did not help you?'

⁴⁵"He will reply, 'I tell you the truth, whatever you did not do for one of the least of these, you did not do for me.'

⁴⁶"Then they will go away to eternal punishment, but the righteous to eternal life." (+Jn 15:2-8,14)

1Co 3:6 I planted the seed, Apollos watered it, but God made it grow. ⁷So neither he who plants nor he who waters is anything, but only God, who makes things grow. ⁸The man who plants and the man who waters have one pur-

pose, and each will be rewarded according to his own labor. ⁹For we are God's fellow workers; you are God's field, God's building.

Php 1:11 filled with the fruit of righteousness that comes through Jesus Christ—to the glory and praise of God.

Heb 13:21 equip you with everything good for doing his will, and may he work in us what is pleasing to him, through Jesus Christ, to whom be glory for ever and ever. Amen.

Scriptures given for (Tit 2:14).

Insufficient for Salvation:

Ps 49:7 No man can redeem the life of another or give to God a ransom for him— ⁸the ransom for a life is costly, no payment for it is ever enough—

Ps 127:1 Unless the LORD builds the house, its builders labor in vain. Unless the LORD watches over the city, the watchmen stand guard in vain. ²In vain you rise early and stay up late, toiling for food to eat—for he grants sleep to those he loves.

Ecc 1:14 I have seen all the things that are done under the sun; all of them are meaningless, a chasing after the wind. (+Isa 13:14)

Isa 57:12 I will expose your righteousness and your works, and they will not benefit you.

Isa 64:6 All of us have become like one who is unclean, and all our righteous acts are like filthy rags; we all shrivel up like a leaf, and like the wind our sins sweep us away.

Eze 7:19 They will throw their silver into the streets, and their gold will be an unclean thing. Their silver and gold will not be able to save them in the day of the LORD's wrath. They will not satisfy their hunger or fill their stomachs with it, for it has made them stumble into sin.

Eze 33:12 "Therefore, son of man, say to your countrymen, 'The righteousness of the righteous man will not save him when he disobeys, and the wickedness of the wicked man will not cause him to fall when he turns from it. The righteous man, if he sins, will not be allowed to live because of his former righteousness.' ¹³If I tell the righteous man that he will surely live, but then he trusts in his righteousness and does evil, none of the righteous things he has done will be remembered; he will die for the evil he has done. ¹⁴And if I say to the wicked man, 'You will surely die,' but he then turns away from his sin and does what is just and right— ¹⁵if he gives back what he took in pledge for a loan, returns what he has stolen, follows the decrees that give life, and does no evil, he will surely live; he will not die. ¹⁶None of the sins he has committed will be remembered against him. He has done what is just and right; he will surely live.

¹⁷"Yet your countrymen say, 'The way of the Lord is not just.' But it is their way that is not just. ¹⁸If a righteous man turns from his righteousness and does evil, he will die for it. ¹⁹And if a wicked man turns away from his wickedness and does what is just and right, he will live by doing so.

Da 9:18 Give ear, O God, and hear; open your eyes and see the desolation of the city that bears your Name. We do not make requests of you because we are righteous, but because of your great mercy.

Mt 5:20 For I tell you that unless your righteousness surpasses that of the Pharisees and the teachers of the law, you will certainly not enter the kingdom of heaven.

Lk 17:7 "Suppose one of you had a servant plowing or looking after the sheep. Would he say to the servant when he comes in from the field, 'Come along now and sit down to eat'? ⁸Would he not rather say, 'Prepare my supper, get yourself ready and wait on me while I eat and drink; after that you may eat and drink'? ⁹Would he thank the servant because he did what he was told to do? ¹⁰So you also, when you have done everything you were told to do, should say, 'We are unworthy servants; we have only done our duty.'"

Lk 18:9 To some who were confident of their own righteousness and looked down on everybody else, Jesus told this parable: ¹⁰"Two men went up to the temple to pray, one a Pharisee and the other a tax collector. ¹¹The Pharisee stood up and prayed about himself: 'God, I thank you that I am not like other men—robbers, evildoers, adulterers—or even like this tax collector. ¹²I fast twice a week and give a tenth of all I get.'

¹³"But the tax collector stood at a distance. He would not even look up to heaven, but beat his breast and said, 'God, have mercy on me, a sinner.'

¹⁴"I tell you that this man, rather than the other, went home justified before God. For everyone who exalts himself will be humbled, and he who humbles himself will be exalted."

Ac 13:39 Through him everyone who believes is justified from everything you could not be justified from by the law of Moses.

Ro 3:20 Therefore no one will be declared righteous in his sight by observing the law; rather, through the law we become conscious of sin.

²¹But now a righteousness from God, apart from law, has been made known, to which the Law and the Prophets testify.

Ro 4:1 What then shall we say that Abraham, our forefather, discovered in this matter? ²If, in fact, Abraham was justified by works, he had something to boast about—but not before God. ³What does the Scripture say? "Abraham believed God, and it was credited to him as righteousness."

⁴Now when a man works, his wages are not credited to him as a gift, but as an obligation. ⁵However, to the man who does not work but trusts God who justifies the wicked, his faith is credited as righteousness. ⁶David says the same thing when he speaks of the blessedness of the man to whom God credits righteousness apart from works:

⁷"Blessed are they whose transgressions are forgiven, whose sins are covered. ⁸Blessed is the man whose sin the Lord will never count against him."

⁹Is this blessedness only for the circumcised, or also for the uncircumcised? We have been saying that Abraham's faith was credited to him as righteousness. ¹⁰Under what circumstances was it credited? Was it after he was circumcised, or before? It was not after, but before! ¹¹And he received the sign of circumcision, a seal of the righteousness that he had by faith while he was still uncircumcised. So then, he is the father of all who believe but have not been circumcised, in order that righteousness might be credited to them. ¹²And he is also the father of the circumcised who not only are circumcised but who also walk in the footsteps of the faith that our father Abraham had before he was circumcised.

¹³It was not through law that Abraham and his offspring received the promise that he would be heir of the world, but through the righteousness that comes by faith. ¹⁴For if those who live by law are heirs, faith has no value and the promise is worthless, ¹⁵because law brings wrath. And where there is no law there is no transgression.

¹⁶Therefore, the promise comes by faith, so that it may be by grace and may be guaranteed to all Abraham's offspring—not only to those who are of the law but also to those who are of the faith of Abraham. He is the father of

us all. ¹⁷As it is written: "I have made you a father of many nations." He is our father in the sight of God, in whom he believed—the God who gives life to the dead and calls things that are not as though they were.

¹⁸Against all hope, Abraham in hope believed and so became the father of many nations, just as it had been said to him, "So shall your offspring be." ¹⁹Without weakening in his faith, he faced the fact that his body was as good as dead—since he was about a hundred years old—and that Sarah's womb was also dead. ²⁰Yet he did not waver through unbelief regarding the promise of God, but was strengthened in his faith and gave glory to God, ²¹being fully persuaded that God had power to do what he had promised. ²²This is why "it was credited to him as righteousness." ²³The words "it was credited to him" were written not for him alone, ²⁴but also for us, to whom God will credit righteousness—for us who believe in him who raised Jesus our Lord from the dead. ²⁵He was delivered over to death for our sins and was raised to life for our justification.

Ro 8:3 For what the law was powerless to do in that it was weakened by the sinful nature, God did by sending his own Son in the likeness of sinful man to be a sin offering. And so he condemned sin in sinful man,

Ro 9:16 It does not, therefore, depend on man's desire or effort, but on God's mercy.

Ro 9:31 but Israel, who pursued a law of righteousness, has not attained it. ³²Why not? Because they pursued it not by faith but as if it were by works. They stumbled over the "stumbling stone."

Ro 11:6 And if by grace, then it is no longer by works; if it were, grace would no longer be grace.

1Co 13:1 If I speak in the tongues of men and of angels, but have not love, I am only a resounding gong or a clanging cymbal. ²If I have the gift of prophecy and can fathom all mysteries and all knowledge, and if I have a faith that can move mountains, but have not love, I am nothing. ³If I give all I possess to the poor and surrender my body to the flames, but have not love, I gain nothing.

Gal 2:16 know that a man is not justified by observing the law, but by faith in Jesus Christ. So we, too, have put our faith in Christ Jesus that we may be justified by faith in Christ and not by observing the law, because by observing the law no one will be justified.

Gal 2:21 I do not set aside the grace of God, for if righteousness could be gained through the law, Christ died for nothing!"

Gal 3:10 All who rely on observing the law are under a curse, for it is written: "Cursed is everyone who does not continue to do everything written in the Book of the Law." ¹¹Clearly no one is justified before God by the law, because, "The righteous will live by faith." ¹²The law is not based on faith; on the contrary, "The man who does these things will live by them."

Gal 3:21 Is the law, therefore, opposed to the promises of God? Absolutely not! For if a law had been given that could impart life, then righteousness would certainly have come by the law.

Gal 4:9 But now that you know God—or rather are known by God—how is it that you are turning back to those weak and miserable principles? Do you wish to be enslaved by them all over again? ¹⁰You are observing special days and months and seasons and years! ¹¹I fear for you, that somehow I have wasted my efforts on you.

Gal 5:2 Mark my words! I, Paul, tell you that if you let yourselves be circumcised, Christ will be of no value to you at all.

Gal 5:4 You who are trying to be justified by law have been alienated from Christ; you have fallen away from grace.

Gal 5:6 For in Christ Jesus neither circumcision nor uncircumcision has any value. The only thing that counts is faith expressing itself through love.

Gal 5:18 But if you are led by the Spirit, you are not under law.

Gal 6:15 Neither circumcision nor uncircumcision means anything; what counts is a new creation.

Eph 2:8 For it is by grace you have been saved, through faith—and this not from yourselves, it is the gift of God— ⁹not by works, so that no one can boast.

Php 3:3 For it is we who are the circumcision, we who worship by the Spirit of God, who glory in Christ Jesus, and who put no confidence in the flesh— ⁴though I myself have reasons for such confidence.

If anyone else thinks he has reasons to put confidence in the flesh, I have more: ⁵circumcised on the eighth day, of the people of Israel, of the tribe of Benjamin, a Hebrew of Hebrews; in regard to the law, a Pharisee; ⁶as for zeal, persecuting the church; as for legalistic righteousness, faultless.

⁷But whatever was to my profit I now consider loss for the sake of Christ. ⁸What is more, I consider everything a loss compared to the surpassing greatness of knowing Christ Jesus my Lord, for whose sake I have lost all things. I consider them rubbish, that I may gain Christ ⁹and be found in him, not having a righteousness of my own that comes from the law, but that which is through faith in Christ—the righteousness that comes from God and is by faith.

Col 2:20 Since you died with Christ to the basic principles of this world, why, as though you still belonged to it, do you submit to its rules: ²¹"Do not handle! Do not taste! Do not touch!"? ²²These are all destined to perish with use, because they are based on human commands and teachings. ²³Such regulations indeed have an appearance of wisdom, with their self-imposed worship, their false humility and their harsh treatment of the body, but they lack any value in restraining sensual indulgence.

2Ti 1:9 who has saved us and called us to a holy life—not because of anything we have done but because of his own purpose and grace. This grace was given us in Christ Jesus before the beginning of time,

Tit 3:4 But when the kindness and love of God our Savior appeared, ⁵he saved us, not because of righteous things we had done, but because of his mercy. He saved us through the washing of rebirth and renewal by the Holy Spirit,

Heb 4:3 Now we who have believed enter that rest, just as God has said,

"So I declared on oath in my anger, 'They shall never enter my rest.'"

And yet his work has been finished since the creation of the world. ⁴For somewhere he has spoken about the seventh day in these words: "And on the seventh day God rested from all his work." ⁵And again in the passage above he says, "They shall never enter my rest."

⁶It still remains that some will enter that rest, and those who formerly had the gospel preached to them did not go in, because of their disobedience. ⁷Therefore God again set a certain day, calling it Today, when a long time later he spoke through David, as was said before:

"Today, if you hear his voice, do not harden your hearts."

⁸For if Joshua had given them rest, God would not have spoken later about another day. ⁹There remains, then, a Sabbath-rest for the people of God; ¹⁰for anyone who enters God's rest also rests from his own work, just as God did from his.

Heb 6:1 Therefore let us leave the elementary teachings about Christ and go on to maturity, not laying again the foundation of repentance from acts that lead to death, and of faith in God, ²instruction about baptisms, the laying on of hands, the resurrection of the dead, and eternal judgment.

Heb 9:1 Now the first covenant had regulations for worship and also an earthly sanctuary. ²A tabernacle was set up. In its first room were the lampstand, the table and the consecrated bread; this was called the Holy Place. ³Behind the second curtain was a room called the Most Holy Place, ⁴which had the golden altar of incense and the gold-covered ark of the covenant. This ark contained the gold jar of manna, Aaron's staff that had budded, and the stone tablets of the covenant. ⁵Above the ark were the cherubim of the Glory, overshadowing the atonement cover. But we cannot discuss these things in detail now.

⁶When everything had been arranged like this, the priests entered regularly into the outer room to carry on their ministry. ⁷But only the high priest entered the inner room, and that only once a year, and never without blood, which he offered for himself and for the sins the people had committed in ignorance. ⁸The Holy Spirit was showing by this that the way into the Most Holy Place had not yet been disclosed as long as the first tabernacle was still standing. ⁹This is an illustration for the present time, indicating that the gifts and sacrifices being offered were not able to clear the conscience of the worshiper. ¹⁰They are only a matter of food and drink and various ceremonial washings—external regulations applying until the time of the new order.

¹¹When Christ came as high priest of the good things that are already here, he went through the greater and more perfect tabernacle that is not man-made, that is to say, not a part of this creation. ¹²He did not enter by means of the blood of goats and calves; but he entered the Most Holy Place once for all by his own blood, having obtained eternal redemption. ¹³The blood of goats and bulls and the ashes of a heifer sprinkled on those who are ceremonially unclean sanctify them so that they are outwardly clean. ¹⁴How much more, then, will the blood of Christ, who through the eternal Spirit offered himself unblemished to God, cleanse our consciences from acts that lead to death, so that we may serve the living God!

Jas 2:10 For whoever keeps the whole law and yet stumbles at just one point is guilty of breaking all of it. ¹¹For he who said, "Do not commit adultery," also said, "Do not murder." If you do not commit adultery but do commit murder, you have become a lawbreaker.

Hypocritical (Mt 6:1-4).

Under the Law:

(Lev 18:5; Eze 20:11,13,20; Lk 10:28; Ro 10:5; Gal 3:12).

WORKS OF GOD In creation (Job 9:8-9; Ps 8:3-5; 89:11; 136:5-9; 139:13-14; 148:4-5; Ecc 3:11; Jer 10:12), good (Ge 1:10,18,21,25). Faithful (Ps 33:4). Wonderful (Ps 26:7; 40:5). Incomparable (Ps 86:8). In his overruling providence in human affairs (Ps 26:7; 40:5; 66:3; 75:1; 111:2,4,6; 118:17; 145:4-17).

See also, God, Works of.

WORLD [824, 2535, 2698, 9315, 10075, *172, 1178, 3179, 3180, 3232, 3876, 4246, 4920, 4922*].

NIV+ WORLD'S, WORLDLY

1. Universe (Jn 1:10).
2. Human race (Ps 9:8; 96:13; Ac 17:31).
3. Unregenerate humanity (Jn 15:18; 1Jn 2:15).
4. Roman Empire (Lk 2:1).

WORLDLINESS [*94, 96, 3176, 3180+3836, 4920, 4921, 4922*].

NIV+ WORLDLY

Described:

Ecc 1:8 All things are wearisome, more than one can say. The eye never has enough of seeing, nor the ear its fill of hearing.

Ecc 8:15 So I commend the enjoyment of life, because nothing is better for a man under the sun than to eat and drink and be glad. Then joy will accompany him in his work all the days of the life God has given him under the sun. (+Isa 56:12)

Jn 15:19 If you belonged to the world, it would love you as its own. As it is, you do not belong to the world, but I have chosen you out of the world. That is why the world hates you.

Tit 3:3 At one time we too were foolish, disobedient, deceived and enslaved by all kinds of passions and pleasures. We lived in malice and envy, being hated and hating one another.

2Pe 2:12 But these men blaspheme in matters they do not understand. They are like brute beasts, creatures of instinct, born only to be caught and destroyed, and like beasts they too will perish.

¹³They will be paid back with harm for the harm they have done. Their idea of pleasure is to carouse in broad daylight. They are blots and blemishes, reveling in their pleasures while they feast with you. ¹⁴With eyes full of adultery, they never stop sinning; they seduce the unstable; they are experts in greed—an accursed brood! ¹⁵They have left the straight way and wandered off to follow the way of Balaam son of Beor, who loved the wages of wickedness.

2Pe 2:18 For they mouth empty, boastful words and, by appealing to the lustful desires of sinful human nature, they entice people who are just escaping from those who live in error. (+2Pe 2:19)

Proverbial theme—

Isa 22:13 But see, there is joy and revelry, slaughtering of cattle and killing of sheep, eating of meat and drinking of wine! "Let us eat and drink," you say, "for tomorrow we die!"

Lk 12:19 And I'll say to myself, "You have plenty of good things laid up for many years. Take life easy; eat, drink and be merry."'

1Co 15:32 If I fought wild beasts in Ephesus for merely human reasons, what have I gained? If the dead are not raised, "Let us eat and drink, for tomorrow we die."

Tends to poverty—

Pr 21:17 He who loves pleasure will become poor; whoever loves wine and oil will never be rich.

Hag 1:6 You have planted much, but have harvested little. You eat, but never have enough. You drink, but never have your fill. You put on clothes, but are not warm. You earn wages, only to put them in a purse with holes in it."

Fatal to spirituality (Gal 6:8)—

Php 3:19 Their destiny is destruction, their god is their stomach, and their glory is in their shame. Their mind is on earthly things.

1Ti 5:6 But the widow who lives for pleasure is dead even while she lives.

Chokes the Word (Mt 13:22; Mk 4:19)—

Lk 8:14 The seed that fell among thorns stands for those who hear, but as they go on their way they are choked by life's worries, riches and pleasures, and they do not mature.

Leads to:

The rejection of the Gospel (Mt 22:2-6)—

Lk 14:17 At the time of the banquet he sent his servant to tell those who had been invited, 'Come, for everything is now ready.'

¹⁸"But they all alike began to make excuses. The first said, 'I have just bought a field, and I must go and see it. Please excuse me.'

¹⁹"Another said, 'I have just bought five yoke of oxen, and I'm on my way to try them out. Please excuse me.'

²⁰"Still another said, 'I just got married, so I can't come.'

²¹"The servant came back and reported this to his master. Then the owner of the house became angry and ordered his servant, 'Go out quickly into the streets and alleys of the town and bring in the poor, the crippled, the blind and the lame.'

²²"'Sir,' the servant said, 'what you ordered has been done, but there is still room.'

²³"Then the master told his servant, 'Go out to the roads and country lanes and make them come in, so that my house will be full. ²⁴I tell you, not one of those men who were invited will get a taste of my banquet.'"

The rejection of Christ—

Jn 5:44 How can you believe if you accept praise from one another, yet make no effort to obtain the praise that comes from the only God?

Jn 12:43 for they loved praise from men more than praise from God.

Moral insensibility (Isa 22:13)—

Isa 32:9 You women who are so complacent, rise up and listen to me; you daughters who feel secure, hear what I have to say! ¹⁰In little more than a year you who feel secure will tremble; the grape harvest will fail, and the harvest of fruit will not come. ¹¹Tremble, you complacent women; shudder, you daughters who feel secure! Strip off your clothes, put sackcloth around your waists.

Isa 47:7 You said, 'I will continue forever—the eternal queen!' But you did not consider these things or reflect on what might happen.

⁸"Now then, listen, you wanton creature, lounging in your security and saying to yourself, 'I am, and there is none besides me. I will never be a widow or suffer the loss of children.' ⁹Both of these will overtake you in a moment, on a single day: loss of children and widowhood. They will come upon you in full measure, in spite of your many sorceries and all your potent spells.

Death—

Pr 14:12 There is a way that seems right to a man, but in the end it leads to death.

¹³Even in laughter the heart may ache, and joy may end in grief.

Prosperity of is Short-Lived—

Job 20:4 "Surely you know how it has been from of old,

ever since man was placed on the earth, [5]that the mirth of the wicked is brief, the joy of the godless lasts but a moment. [6]Though his pride reaches to the heavens and his head touches the clouds, [7]he will perish forever, like his own dung; those who have seen him will say, 'Where is he?' [8]Like a dream he flies away, no more to be found, banished like a vision of the night. [9]The eye that saw him will not see him again; his place will look on him no more. [10]His children must make amends to the poor; his own hands must give back his wealth. [11]The youthful vigor that fills his bones will lie with him in the dust.

[12]"Though evil is sweet in his mouth and he hides it under his tongue, [13]though he cannot bear to let it go and keeps it in his mouth, [14]yet his food will turn sour in his stomach; it will become the venom of serpents within him. [15]He will spit out the riches he swallowed; God will make his stomach vomit them up. [16]He will suck the poison of serpents; the fangs of an adder will kill him. [17]He will not enjoy the streams, the rivers flowing with honey and cream. [18]What he toiled for he must give back uneaten; he will not enjoy the profit from his trading. [19]For he has oppressed the poor and left them destitute; he has seized houses he did not build.

[20]"Surely he will have no respite from his craving; he cannot save himself by his treasure. [21]Nothing is left for him to devour; his prosperity will not endure. [22]In the midst of his plenty, distress will overtake him; the full force of misery will come upon him. [23]When he has filled his belly, God will vent his burning anger against him and rain down his blows upon him. [24]Though he flees from an iron weapon, a bronze-tipped arrow pierces him. [25]He pulls it out of his back, the gleaming point out of his liver. Terrors will come over him; [26]total darkness lies in wait for his treasures. A fire unfanned will consume him and devour what is left in his tent. [27]The heavens will expose his guilt; the earth will rise up against him. [28]A flood will carry off his house, rushing waters on the day of God's wrath. [29]Such is the fate God allots the wicked, the heritage appointed for them by God."

Job 21:11 They send forth their children as a flock; their little ones dance about. [12]They sing to the music of tambourine and harp; they make merry to the sound of the flute. [13]They spend their years in prosperity and go down to the grave in peace. [14]Yet they say to God, 'Leave us alone! We have no desire to know your ways. [15]Who is the Almighty, that we should serve him? What would we gain by praying to him?'

Ps 49:16 Do not be overawed when a man grows rich, when the splendor of his house increases; [17]for he will take nothing with him when he dies, his splendor will not descend with him. [18]Though while he lived he counted himself blessed—and men praise you when you prosper—

Isa 24:7 The new wine dries up and the vine withers; all the merrymakers groan. [8]The gaiety of the tambourines is stilled, the noise of the revelers has stopped, the joyful harp is silent. [9]No longer do they drink wine with a song; the beer is bitter to its drinkers. [10]The ruined city lies desolate; the entrance to every house is barred. [11]In the streets they cry out for wine; all joy turns to gloom, all gaiety is banished from the earth.

Isa 28:4 That fading flower, his glorious beauty, set on the head of a fertile valley, will be like a fig ripe before harvest—as soon as someone sees it and takes it in his hand, he swallows it.

Prayer Regarding:

Ps 73:2 But as for me, my feet had almost slipped; I had

nearly lost my foothold. [3]For I envied the arrogant when I saw the prosperity of the wicked.

[4]They have no struggles; their bodies are healthy and strong. [5]They are free from the burdens common to man; they are not plagued by human ills. [6]Therefore pride is their necklace; they clothe themselves with violence. [7]From their callous hearts comes iniquity; the evil conceits of their minds know no limits. [8]They scoff, and speak with malice; in their arrogance they threaten oppression. [9]Their mouths lay claim to heaven, and their tongues take possession of the earth. [10]Therefore their people turn to them and drink up waters in abundance. [11]They say, "How can God know? Does the Most High have knowledge?"

[12]This is what the wicked are like—always carefree, they increase in wealth.

[13]Surely in vain have I kept my heart pure; in vain have I washed my hands in innocence. [14]All day long I have been plagued; I have been punished every morning.

[15]If I had said, "I will speak thus," I would have betrayed your children. [16]When I tried to understand all this, it was oppressive to me [17]till I entered the sanctuary of God; then I understood their final destiny.

[18]Surely you place them on slippery ground; you cast them down to ruin. [19]How suddenly are they destroyed, completely swept away by terrors! [20]As a dream when one awakes, so when you arise, O Lord, you will despise them as fantasies.

[21]When my heart was grieved and my spirit embittered, [22]I was senseless and ignorant; I was a brute beast before you.

Parables of:

Lk 16:1 Jesus told his disciples: "There was a rich man whose manager was accused of wasting his possessions. [2]So he called him in and asked him, 'What is this I hear about you? Give an account of your management, because you cannot be manager any longer.'

[3]"The manager said to himself, 'What shall I do now? My master is taking away my job. I'm not strong enough to dig, and I'm ashamed to beg— [4]I know what I'll do so that, when I lose my job here, people will welcome me into their houses.'

[5]"So he called in each one of his master's debtors. He asked the first, 'How much do you owe my master?'

[6]"'Eight hundred gallons of olive oil,' he replied.

"The manager told him, 'Take your bill, sit down quickly, and make it four hundred.'

[7]"Then he asked the second, 'And how much do you owe?'

"'A thousand bushels of wheat,' he replied.

"He told him, 'Take your bill and make it eight hundred.'

[8]"The master commended the dishonest manager because he had acted shrewdly. For the people of this world are more shrewd in dealing with their own kind than are the people of the light. [9]I tell you, use worldly wealth to gain friends for yourselves, so that when it is gone, you will be welcomed into eternal dwellings.

[10]"Whoever can be trusted with very little can also be trusted with much, and whoever is dishonest with very little will also be dishonest with much. [11]So if you have not been trustworthy in handling worldly wealth, who will trust you with true riches? [12]And if you have not been trustworthy with someone else's property, who will give you property of your own?

[13]"No servant can serve two masters. Either he will hate the one and love the other, or he will be devoted to the one

and despise the other. You cannot serve both God and Money."

Lk 16:19 "There was a rich man who was dressed in purple and fine linen and lived in luxury every day. **20**At his gate was laid a beggar named Lazarus, covered with sores **21**and longing to eat what fell from the rich man's table. Even the dogs came and licked his sores.

22"The time came when the beggar died and the angels carried him to Abraham's side. The rich man also died and was buried. **23**In hell, where he was in torment, he looked up and saw Abraham far away, with Lazarus by his side. **24**So he called to him, 'Father Abraham, have pity on me and send Lazarus to dip the tip of his finger in water and cool my tongue, because I am in agony in this fire.'

25"But Abraham replied, 'Son, remember that in your lifetime you received your good things, while Lazarus received bad things, but now he is comforted here and you are in agony.

Vanity of:

Ecc 2:1 I thought in my heart, "Come now, I will test you with pleasure to find out what is good." But that also proved to be meaningless. **2**"Laughter," I said, "is foolish. And what does pleasure accomplish?" **3**I tried cheering myself with wine, and embracing folly—my mind still guiding me with wisdom. I wanted to see what was worthwhile for men to do under heaven during the few days of their lives.

4I undertook great projects: I built houses for myself and planted vineyards. **5**I made gardens and parks and planted all kinds of fruit trees in them. **6**I made reservoirs to water groves of flourishing trees. **7**I bought male and female slaves and had other slaves who were born in my house. I also owned more herds and flocks than anyone in Jerusalem before me. **8**I amassed silver and gold for myself, and the treasure of kings and provinces. I acquired men and women singers, and a harem as well—the delights of the heart of man. **9**I became greater by far than anyone in Jerusalem before me. In all this my wisdom stayed with me.

10I denied myself nothing my eyes desired; I refused my heart no pleasure. My heart took delight in all my work, and this was the reward for all my labor. **11**Yet when I surveyed all that my hands had done and what I had toiled to achieve, everything was meaningless, a chasing after the wind; nothing was gained under the sun.

12Then I turned my thoughts to consider wisdom, and also madness and folly. What more can the king's successor do than what has already been done?

Ecc 6:11 The more the words, the less the meaning, and how does that profit anyone?

12For who knows what is good for a man in life, during the few and meaningless days he passes through like a shadow? Who can tell him what will happen under the sun after he is gone?

Admonitions Against:

Pr 23:20 Do not join those who drink too much wine or gorge themselves on meat, **21**for drunkards and gluttons become poor, and drowsiness clothes them in rags.

Pr 27:1 Do not boast about tomorrow, for you do not know what a day may bring forth.

Pr 27:7 He who is full loathes honey, but to the hungry even what is bitter tastes sweet. (+Ecc 7:2-4)

Ecc 11:9 Be happy, young man, while you are young, and let your heart give you joy in the days of your youth. Follow the ways of your heart and whatever your eyes see,

but know that for all these things God will bring you to judgment. **10**So then, banish anxiety from your heart and cast off the troubles of your body, for youth and vigor are meaningless. (+Hos 9:1,11,13)

Am 6:3 You put off the evil day and bring near a reign of terror. **4**You lie on beds inlaid with ivory and lounge on your couches. You dine on choice lambs and fattened calves. **5**You strum away on your harps like David and improvise on musical instruments. **6**You drink wine by the bowlful and use the finest lotions, but you do not grieve over the ruin of Joseph. **7**Therefore you will be among the first to go into exile; your feasting and lounging will end.

Am 8:10 I will turn your religious feasts into mourning and all your singing into weeping. I will make all of you wear sackcloth and shave your heads. I will make that time like mourning for an only son and the end of it like a bitter day.

Mic 2:10 Get up, go away! For this is not your resting place, because it is defiled, it is ruined, beyond all remedy.

Mic 6:14 You will eat but not be satisfied; your stomach will still be empty. You will store up but save nothing, because what you save I will give to the sword. (+Mt 6:19,24)

Mt 6:25 "Therefore I tell you, do not worry about your life, what you will eat or drink; or about your body, what you will wear. Is not life more important than food, and the body more important than clothes? **26**Look at the birds of the air; they do not sow or reap or store away in barns, and yet your heavenly Father feeds them. Are you not much more valuable than they? **27**Who of you by worrying can add a single hour to his life?

28"And why do you worry about clothes? See how the lilies of the field grow. They do not labor or spin. **29**Yet I tell you that not even Solomon in all his splendor was dressed like one of these. **30**If that is how God clothes the grass of the field, which is here today and tomorrow is thrown into the fire, will he not much more clothe you, O you of little faith? **31**So do not worry, saying, 'What shall we eat?' or 'What shall we drink?' or 'What shall we wear?' **32**For the pagans run after all these things, and your heavenly Father knows that you need them. **33**But seek first his kingdom and his righteousness, and all these things will be given to you as well. **34**Therefore do not worry about tomorrow, for tomorrow will worry about itself. Each day has enough trouble of its own.

Mt 16:26 What good will it be for a man if he gains the whole world, yet forfeits his soul? Or what can a man give in exchange for his soul? (+Mt 24:28; Mk 8:36-37; Lk 17:26-29,33)

Lk 21:34 "Be careful, or your hearts will be weighed down with dissipation, drunkenness and the anxieties of life, and that day will close on you unexpectedly like a trap. (+Jn 12:25)

Ro 12:2 Do not conform any longer to the pattern of this world, but be transformed by the renewing of your mind. Then you will be able to test and approve what God's will is—his good, pleasing and perfect will.

1Co 7:29 What I mean, brothers, is that the time is short. From now on those who have wives should live as if they had none; **30**those who mourn, as if they did not; those who are happy, as if they were not; those who buy something, as if it were not theirs to keep; **31**those who use the things of the world, as if not engrossed in them. For this world in its present form is passing away.

1Co 10:6 Now these things occurred as examples to keep us from setting our hearts on evil things as they did.

Col 3:2 Set your minds on things above, not on earthly things.

Col 3:5 Put to death, therefore, whatever belongs to your earthly nature: sexual immorality, impurity, lust, evil desires and greed, which is idolatry.

2Ti 2:4 No one serving as a soldier gets involved in civilian affairs—he wants to please his commanding officer.

2Ti 2:22 Flee the evil desires of youth, and pursue righteousness, faith, love and peace, along with those who call on the Lord out of a pure heart.

2Ti 3:2 People will be lovers of themselves, lovers of money, boastful, proud, abusive, disobedient to their parents, ungrateful, unholy, ³without love, unforgiving, slanderous, without self-control, brutal, not lovers of the good, ⁴treacherous, rash, conceited, lovers of pleasure rather than lovers of God— ⁵having a form of godliness but denying its power. Have nothing to do with them.

⁶They are the kind who worm their way into homes and gain control over weak-willed women, who are loaded down with sins and are swayed by all kinds of evil desires, ⁷always learning but never able to acknowledge the truth. (+2Ti 3:8-9)

Tit 2:12 It teaches us to say "No" to ungodliness and worldly passions, and to live self-controlled, upright and godly lives in this present age,

Jas 2:1 My brothers, as believers in our glorious Lord Jesus Christ, don't show favoritism. ²Suppose a man comes into your meeting wearing a gold ring and fine clothes, and a poor man in shabby clothes also comes in. ³If you show special attention to the man wearing fine clothes and say, "Here's a good seat for you," but say to the poor man, "You stand there" or "Sit on the floor by my feet," ⁴have you not discriminated among yourselves and become judges with evil thoughts?

Jas 4:4 You adulterous people, don't you know that friendship with the world is hatred toward God? Anyone who chooses to be a friend of the world becomes an enemy of God.

Jas 4:9 Grieve, mourn and wail. Change your laughter to mourning and your joy to gloom.

Jas 5:5 You have lived on earth in luxury and self-indulgence. You have fattened yourselves in the day of slaughter.

1Pe 1:14 As obedient children, do not conform to the evil desires you had when you lived in ignorance.

1Pe 1:24 For, "All men are like grass, and all their glory is like the flowers of the field; the grass withers and the flowers fall,

1Pe 2:11 Dear friends, I urge you, as aliens and strangers in the world, to abstain from sinful desires, which war against your soul. (+1Pe 4:1-2)

1Pe 4:3 For you have spent enough time in the past doing what pagans choose to do—living in debauchery, lust, drunkenness, orgies, carousing and detestable idolatry. ⁴They think it strange that you do not plunge with them into the same flood of dissipation, and they heap abuse on you.

1Jn 2:15 Do not love the world or anything in the world. If anyone loves the world, the love of the Father is not in him. ¹⁶For everything in the world—the cravings of sinful man, the lust of his eyes and the boasting of what he has and does—comes not from the Father but from the world. ¹⁷The world and its desires pass away, but the man who does the will of God lives forever.

Denounced (Isa 5:11-12; 47:8-9)—

Jude 11 Woe to them! They have taken the way of Cain; they have rushed for profit into Balaam's error; they have been destroyed in Korah's rebellion.

¹²These men are blemishes at your love feasts, eating with you without the slightest qualm—shepherds who feed only themselves. They are clouds without rain, blown along by the wind; autumn trees, without fruit and uprooted—twice dead. ¹³They are wild waves of the sea, foaming up their shame; wandering stars, for whom blackest darkness has been reserved forever.

Jude 16 These men are grumblers and faultfinders; they follow their own evil desires; they boast about themselves and flatter others for their own advantage.

Jude 19 These are the men who divide you, who follow mere natural instincts and do not have the Spirit.

Moses' choice against—

Heb 11:24 By faith Moses, when he had grown up, refused to be known as the son of Pharaoh's daughter. ²⁵He chose to be mistreated along with the people of God rather than to enjoy the pleasures of sin for a short time. ²⁶He regarded disgrace for the sake of Christ as of greater value than the treasures of Egypt, because he was looking ahead to his reward.

Instances of:

Antediluvians—

Mt 24:38 For in the days before the flood, people were eating and drinking, marrying and giving in marriage, up to the day Noah entered the ark; ³⁹and they knew nothing about what would happen until the flood came and took them all away. That is how it will be at the coming of the Son of Man. (+Lk 17:26-27)

Sodomites (Lk 17:28-29). Esau (Ge 25:31-34; Heb 12:16). Jacob (Ge 25:31-34; 27:36; 30:37-43). Judah (Ge 37:26-27).

Israelites—

1Sa 8:19 But the people refused to listen to Samuel. "No!" they said. "We want a king over us. ²⁰Then we will be like all the other nations, with a king to lead us and to go out before us and fight our battles."

Balaam (2Pe 2:15; Jude 11, w Nu 22; 23; 24). Eli's sons (1Sa 2:12-17). Gehazi (2Ki 5:20-27). Herod (Mt 14:6-7).

The disciples—

Mt 18:1 At that time the disciples came to Jesus and asked, "Who is the greatest in the kingdom of heaven?"

²He called a little child and had him stand among them. ³And he said: "I tell you the truth, unless you change and become like little children, you will never enter the kingdom of heaven. ⁴Therefore, whoever humbles himself like this child is the greatest in the kingdom of heaven. (+Mk 9:34; Lk 9:46-48)

The rich fool (Lk 12:16-21). Dives (Lk 16:19-25). The worldly steward (Lk 16:1-13). Cretans (Tit 1:12).

See Worldly Pleasure.

WORLDLY CARE *See Anxiety.*

WORLDLY PLEASURE (Job 20:12; Ecc 7:4; Isa 22:13; 2Ti 3:4; Tit 3:3). Rejected by Moses (Heb 11:25). To be rejected by the righteous (1Pe 4:3-4). Brings poverty (Pr 21:17). Chokes righteousness (Lk 8:14). Leads to suffering (Isa 47:8-9; 2Pe 3:13), spiritual death (1Ti 5:6). Denounced (Isa 5:11-12; Jas 5:5). Folly of (Ecc 1:17; 2:1-13).

See Worldliness.

WORLDLY WISDOM Desired by Eve (Ge 3:6-7).

Misleading (Isa 47:10). Increases sorrow (Ecc 1:18). Shall perish (Isa 29:14). Heavenly things not discerned by (Mt 11:25; Lk 10:21). Gospel not to be preached with (1Co 1:17-26; 2:1-14). To be renounced in order to attain spiritual wisdom (1Co 3:18-20).

Admonitions against (Col 2:8; 1Ti 6:20-21). Admonitions against glorying in (Jer 9:23-24).

See Wisdom.

WORM [6182, 8231, 9357, *1905, 5037, 5038*].
NIV+ WORMS

Low form of life (Ex 16:24; Isa 51:8; Ac 12:23), used metaphorically of mankind's insignificance (Job 25:6; Isa 41:14).

WORMWOOD [*952*]. Bitter plant that grows in wastelands; name of a star that turns water bitter (Rev 8:11).

WORSHIP [*1251, 2556, 3707, 3710, 6268, 6913, 7537, 10504, 10586, *3301, 3302, 4686, 4934, 4936*].
NIV+ WORSHIPED, WORSHIPER, WORSHIPERS, WORSHIPING, WORSHIPS

General:

To be rendered to God only (Ex 20:3; Dt 5:7; 6:13; Mt 4:10)—

Lk 4:8 Jesus answered, "It is written: 'Worship the Lord your God and serve him only.'" (+Ac 10:26; 14:15; Col 2:18; Rev 19:10; 22:8)

Not needed by God—

Ac 17:24 "The God who made the world and everything in it is the Lord of heaven and earth and does not live in temples built by hands. ²⁵And he is not served by human hands, as if he needed anything, because he himself gives all men life and breath and everything else.

Divine presence in (Ex 29:42)—

Ex 29:43 there also I will meet with the Israelites, and the place will be consecrated by my glory. (+Ex 40:34-35; Lev 19:30; Nu 17:4; 1Ki 8:3-11)

2Ch 5:13 The trumpeters and singers joined in unison, as with one voice, to give praise and thanks to the LORD. Accompanied by trumpets, cymbals and other instruments, they raised their voices in praise to the LORD and sang: "He is good; his love endures forever."

Then the temple of the LORD was filled with a cloud, ¹⁴and the priests could not perform their service because of the cloud, for the glory of the LORD filled the temple of God.

Ps 77:13 Your ways, O God, are holy. What god is so great as our God? (+Ps 84:4; Isa 56:7)

Mt 18:20 For where two or three come together in my name, there am I with them."

Ac 2:1 When the day of Pentecost came, they were all together in one place. ²Suddenly a sound like the blowing of a violent wind came from heaven and filled the whole house where they were sitting. ³They saw what seemed to be tongues of fire that separated and came to rest on each of them. ⁴All of them were filled with the Holy Spirit and began to speak in other tongues as the Spirit enabled them.

Heb 10:25 Let us not give up meeting together, as some are in the habit of doing, but let us encourage one another—and all the more as you see the Day approaching.

Origin of (Ge 4:26). Of Jesus. *See Jesus the Christ, Worship of.*

Acceptable to God (Ge 4:4; 8:21). Of the wicked, rejected (Ge 4:5,7). *See Prayer, of the Wicked.* "Iniquity of the holy things" (Ex 28:38).

Sanctuary instituted for—

Ex 25:8 "Then have them make a sanctuary for me, and I will dwell among them.

Ex 25:22 There, above the cover between the two cherubim that are over the ark of the Testimony, I will meet with you and give you all my commands for the Israelites. (+Ex 29:43; 40:34-35; Nu 17:4)

Summons to:

Ps 95:6 Come, let us bow down in worship, let us kneel before the LORD our Maker;

Isa 2:3 Many peoples will come and say, "Come, let us go up to the mountain of the LORD, to the house of the God of Jacob. He will teach us his ways, so that we may walk in his paths." The law will go out from Zion, the word of the LORD from Jerusalem. (+Mic 4:2)

Commanded:

Ge 35:1 Then God said to Jacob, "Go up to Bethel and settle there, and build an altar there to God, who appeared to you when you were fleeing from your brother Esau." (+Ex 15:1)

Ex 23:17 "Three times a year all the men are to appear before the Sovereign LORD.

¹⁸"Do not offer the blood of a sacrifice to me along with anything containing yeast.

"The fat of my festival offerings must not be kept until morning. (+Ex 34:23)

Dt 12:5 But you are to seek the place the LORD your God will choose from among all your tribes to put his Name there for his dwelling. To that place you must go; ⁶there bring your burnt offerings and sacrifices, your tithes and special gifts, what you have vowed to give and your freewill offerings, and the firstborn of your herds and flocks. ⁷There, in the presence of the LORD your God, you and your families shall eat and shall rejoice in everything you have put your hand to, because the LORD your God has blessed you.

Dt 12:11 Then to the place the LORD your God will choose as a dwelling for his Name—there you are to bring everything I command you: your burnt offerings and sacrifices, your tithes and special gifts, and all the choice possessions you have vowed to the LORD. ¹²And there rejoice before the LORD your God, you, your sons and daughters, your menservants and maidservants, and the Levites from your towns, who have no allotment or inheritance of their own.

Dt 16:6 except in the place he will choose as a dwelling for his Name. There you must sacrifice the Passover in the evening, when the sun goes down, on the anniversary of your departure from Egypt. ⁷Roast it and eat it at the place the LORD your God will choose. Then in the morning return to your tents. ⁸For six days eat unleavened bread and on the seventh day hold an assembly to the LORD your God and do no work.

Dt 31:11 when all Israel comes to appear before the LORD your God at the place he will choose, you shall read this law before them in their hearing. ¹²Assemble the people—men, women and children, and the aliens living in your towns—so they can listen and learn to fear the LORD your God and follow carefully all the words of this law. ¹³Their children, who do not know this law, must hear it and learn to fear the LORD your God as long as you live in the land you are crossing the Jordan to possess."

Dt 33:19 They will summon peoples to the mountain and there offer sacrifices of righteousness; they will feast on the abundance of the seas, on the treasures hidden in the sand."

2Ki 17:36 But the LORD, who brought you up out of Egypt with mighty power and outstretched arm, is the one you must worship. To him you shall bow down and to him offer sacrifices.

1Ch 16:29 ascribe to the LORD the glory due his name. Bring an offering and come before him; worship the LORD in the splendor of his holiness.

Ne 10:39 The people of Israel, including the Levites, are to bring their contributions of grain, new wine and oil to the storerooms where the articles for the sanctuary are kept and where the ministering priests, the gatekeepers and the singers stay. "We will not neglect the house of our God."

Ps 29:2 Ascribe to the LORD the glory due his name; worship the LORD in the splendor of his holiness.

Ps 45:11 The king is enthralled by your beauty; honor him, for he is your lord.

Ps 76:11 Make vows to the LORD your God and fulfill them; let all the neighboring lands bring gifts to the One to be feared.

Ps 96:8 Ascribe to the LORD the glory due his name; bring an offering and come into his courts. ⁹Worship the LORD in the splendor of his holiness; tremble before him, all the earth.

Ps 97:7 All who worship images are put to shame, those who boast in idols—worship him, all you gods!

Ps 99:5 Exalt the LORD our God and worship at his footstool; he is holy.

Isa 12:5 Sing to the LORD, for he has done glorious things; let this be known to all the world. ⁶Shout aloud and sing for joy, people of Zion, for great is the Holy One of Israel among you."

Isa 49:13 Shout for joy, O heavens; rejoice, O earth; burst into song, O mountains! For the LORD comforts his people and will have compassion on his afflicted ones.

Isa 52:9 Burst into songs of joy together, you ruins of Jerusalem, for the LORD has comforted his people, he has redeemed Jerusalem.

Jer 31:11 For the LORD will ransom Jacob and redeem them from the hand of those stronger than they. ¹²They will come and shout for joy on the heights of Zion; they will rejoice in the bounty of the LORD—the grain, the new wine and the oil, the young of the flocks and herds. They will be like a well-watered garden, and they will sorrow no more.

Joel 1:14 Declare a holy fast; call a sacred assembly. Summon the elders and all who live in the land to the house of the LORD your God, and cry out to the LORD.

¹⁵Alas for that day! For the day of the LORD is near; it will come like destruction from the Almighty.

Joel 2:15 Blow the trumpet in Zion, declare a holy fast, call a sacred assembly. ¹⁶Gather the people, consecrate the assembly; bring together the elders, gather the children, those nursing at the breast. Let the bridegroom leave his room and the bride her chamber. ¹⁷Let the priests, who minister before the LORD, weep between the temple porch and the altar. Let them say, "Spare your people, O LORD. Do not make your inheritance an object of scorn, a byword among the nations. Why should they say among the peoples, 'Where is their God?'"

Na 1:15 Look, there on the mountains, the feet of one who brings good news, who proclaims peace! Celebrate your festivals, O Judah, and fulfill your vows. No more will the wicked invade you; they will be completely destroyed.

Hag 1:8 Go up into the mountains and bring down timber and build the house, so that I may take pleasure in it and be honored," says the LORD.

Zec 14:16 Then the survivors from all the nations that have attacked Jerusalem will go up year after year to worship the King, the LORD Almighty, and to celebrate the Feast of Tabernacles. ¹⁷If any of the peoples of the earth do not go up to Jerusalem to worship the King, the LORD Almighty, they will have no rain. ¹⁸If the Egyptian people do not go up and take part, they will have no rain. The LORD will bring on them the plague he inflicts on the nations that do not go up to celebrate the Feast of Tabernacles.

Mt 8:4 Then Jesus said to him, "See that you don't tell anyone. But go, show yourself to the priest and offer the gift Moses commanded, as a testimony to them." (+Mk 1:44; Lk 4:8; 5:14)

1Ti 2:8 I want men everywhere to lift up holy hands in prayer, without anger or disputing.

Heb 10:25 Let us not give up meeting together, as some are in the habit of doing, but let us encourage one another—and all the more as you see the Day approaching.

Heb 12:28 Therefore, since we are receiving a kingdom that cannot be shaken, let us be thankful, and so worship God acceptably with reverence and awe,

Rev 14:7 He said in a loud voice, "Fear God and give him glory, because the hour of his judgment has come. Worship him who made the heavens, the earth, the sea and the springs of water."

Rev 19:10 At this I fell at his feet to worship him. But he said to me, "Do not do it! I am a fellow servant with you and with your brothers who hold to the testimony of Jesus. Worship God! For the testimony of Jesus is the spirit of prophecy."

Attitudes in:

Bowing—

Ex 34:8 Moses bowed to the ground at once and worshiped. (+2Ch 20:18)

Prostration (Ge 17:3; Mk 3:11).

Prayer in. *See Prayer.*

Benedictions pronounced. *See Benedictions.*

With music (2Ch 5:13-14)—

Ezr 3:10 When the builders laid the foundation of the temple of the LORD, the priests in their vestments and with trumpets, and the Levites (the sons of Asaph) with cymbals, took their places to praise the LORD, as prescribed by David king of Israel. ¹¹With praise and thanksgiving they sang to the LORD: "He is good; his love to Israel endures forever."

And all the people gave a great shout of praise to the LORD, because the foundation of the house of the LORD was laid.

Ps 100:1 Shout for joy to the LORD, all the earth. ²Worship the LORD with gladness; come before him with joyful songs.

Ps 126:1 When the LORD brought back the captives to Zion, we were like men who dreamed. ²Our mouths were filled with laughter, our tongues with songs of joy. Then it was said among the nations, "The LORD has done great things for them." ³The LORD has done great things for us, and we are filled with joy.

Isa 30:29 And you will sing as on the night you celebrate a holy festival; your hearts will rejoice as when people go up with flutes to the mountain of the LORD, to the Rock of Israel.

Isa 38:20 The LORD will save me, and we will sing with stringed instruments all the days of our lives in the temple of the LORD.

Rendering praise—

Ps 22:22 I will declare your name to my brothers; in the congregation I will praise you.

Ps 138:2 I will bow down toward your holy temple and will praise your name for your love and your faithfulness, for you have exalted above all things your name and your word.

Ps 149:1 Praise the LORD. Sing to the LORD a new song, his praise in the assembly of the saints.

Thanksgiving—

Ps 35:18 I will give you thanks in the great assembly; among throngs of people I will praise you.

Ps 100:4 Enter his gates with thanksgiving and his courts with praise; give thanks to him and praise his name. (+Ps 116:17)

In spirit and in truth—

Jn 4:23 Yet a time is coming and has now come when the true worshipers will worship the Father in spirit and truth, for they are the kind of worshipers the Father seeks. ²⁴God is spirit, and his worshipers must worship in spirit and in truth." (+1Co 14:15)

Php 3:3 For it is we who are the circumcision, we who worship by the Spirit of God, who glory in Christ Jesus, and who put no confidence in the flesh—

Renews strength—

Isa 40:31 but those who hope in the LORD will renew their strength. They will soar on wings like eagles; they will run and not grow weary, they will walk and not be faint.

Loved by God's people—

Ps 27:4 One thing I ask of the LORD, this is what I seek: that I may dwell in the house of the LORD all the days of my life, to gaze upon the beauty of the LORD and to seek him in his temple.

Ps 84:1 How lovely is your dwelling place, O LORD Almighty! ²My soul yearns, even faints, for the courts of the LORD; my heart and my flesh cry out for the living God.

³Even the sparrow has found a home, and the swallow a nest for herself, where she may have her young—a place near your altar, O LORD Almighty, my King and my God. ⁴Blessed are those who dwell in your house; they are ever praising you. *Selah*

Ps 84:10 Better is one day in your courts than a thousand elsewhere; I would rather be a doorkeeper in the house of my God than dwell in the tents of the wicked.

Zec 8:21 and the inhabitants of one city will go to another and say, 'Let us go at once to entreat the LORD and seek the LORD Almighty. I myself am going.'

Reward of—

Ps 65:4 Blessed are those you choose and bring near to live in your courts! We are filled with the good things of your house, of your holy temple.

Ps 92:13 planted in the house of the LORD, they will flourish in the courts of our God. ¹⁴They will still bear fruit in old age, they will stay fresh and green,

Ps 122:1 I rejoiced with those who said to me, "Let us go to the house of the LORD."

Preparation for—

Ex 19:10 And the LORD said to Moses, "Go to the people and consecrate them today and tomorrow. Have them wash their clothes ¹¹and be ready by the third day, because on that day the LORD will come down on Mount Sinai in the sight of all the people. ¹²Put limits for the people around the mountain and tell them, 'Be careful that you do not go up the mountain or touch the foot of it. Whoever touches the mountain shall surely be put to death. ¹³He

shall surely be stoned or shot with arrows; not a hand is to be laid on him. Whether man or animal, he shall not be permitted to live.' Only when the ram's horn sounds a long blast may they go up to the mountain."

Ex 19:21 and the LORD said to him, "Go down and warn the people so they do not force their way through to see the LORD and many of them perish. ²²Even the priests, who approach the LORD, must consecrate themselves, or the LORD will break out against them."

²³Moses said to the LORD, "The people cannot come up Mount Sinai, because you yourself warned us, 'Put limits around the mountain and set it apart as holy.'"

²⁴The LORD replied, "Go down and bring Aaron up with you. But the priests and the people must not force their way through to come up to the LORD, or he will break out against them."

Ex 20:24 "'Make an altar of earth for me and sacrifice on it your burnt offerings and fellowship offerings, your sheep and goats and your cattle. Wherever I cause my name to be honored, I will come to you and bless you. ²⁵If you make an altar of stones for me, do not build it with dressed stones, for you will defile it if you use a tool on it.

Ex 30:19 Aaron and his sons are to wash their hands and feet with water from it.

Ex 30:21 they shall wash their hands and feet so that they will not die. This is to be a lasting ordinance for Aaron and his descendants for the generations to come."

Lev 10:3 Moses then said to Aaron, "This is what the LORD spoke of when he said: "'Among those who approach me I will show myself holy; in the sight of all the people I will be honored.'" Aaron remained silent.

Ps 26:6 I wash my hands in innocence, and go about your altar, O LORD,

Isa 56:6 And foreigners who bind themselves to the LORD to serve him, to love the name of the LORD, and to worship him, all who keep the Sabbath without desecrating it and who hold fast to my covenant— ⁷these I will bring to my holy mountain and give them joy in my house of prayer. Their burnt offerings and sacrifices will be accepted on my altar; for my house will be called a house of prayer for all nations."

Zep 3:18 "The sorrows for the appointed feasts I will remove from you; they are a burden and a reproach to you.

Mal 3:3 He will sit as a refiner and purifier of silver; he will purify the Levites and refine them like gold and silver. Then the LORD will have men who will bring offerings in righteousness, ⁴and the offerings of Judah and Jerusalem will be acceptable to the LORD, as in days gone by, as in former years.

Requirements of—

Ps 24:3 Who may ascend the hill of the LORD? Who may stand in his holy place? ⁴He who has clean hands and a pure heart, who does not lift up his soul to an idol or swear by what is false. ⁵He will receive blessing from the LORD and vindication from God his Savior. ⁶Such is the generation of those who seek him, who seek your face, O God of Jacob. *Selah* (+Ps 51:18)

Ps 51:19 Then there will be righteous sacrifices, whole burnt offerings to delight you; then bulls will be offered on your altar.

Proprieties in—

Ecc 5:1 Guard your steps when you go to the house of God. Go near to listen rather than to offer the sacrifice of fools, who do not know that they do wrong.

²Do not be quick with your mouth, do not be hasty in

your heart to utter anything before God. God is in heaven and you are on earth, so let your words be few.

1Co 11:13 Judge for yourselves: Is it proper for a woman to pray to God with her head uncovered?

1Co 11:20 When you come together, it is not the Lord's Supper you eat, ²¹for as you eat, each of you goes ahead without waiting for anybody else. One remains hungry, another gets drunk. ²²Don't you have homes to eat and drink in? Or do you despise the church of God and humiliate those who have nothing? What shall I say to you? Shall I praise you for this? Certainly not! (+1Co 14:2-14)

1Co 14:15 So what shall I do? I will pray with my spirit, but I will also pray with my mind; I will sing with my spirit, but I will also sing with my mind. ¹⁶If you are praising God with your spirit, how can one who finds himself among those who do not understand say "Amen" to your thanksgiving, since he does not know what you are saying? ¹⁷You may be giving thanks well enough, but the other man is not edified. (+1Co 14:18-19)

Reverence in—

Ex 3:5 "Do not come any closer," God said. "Take off your sandals, for the place where you are standing is holy ground." (+Ex 19:10-12,21-24)

Ex 24:1 Then he said to Moses, "Come up to the LORD, you and Aaron, Nadab and Abihu, and seventy of the elders of Israel. You are to worship at a distance, ²but Moses alone is to approach the LORD; the others must not come near. And the people may not come up with him." (+Ecc 5:1)

Hab 2:20 But the LORD is in his holy temple; let all the earth be silent before him."

Private (Mt 6:6; 14:23; Lk 6:12).

At night (Isa 30:29; Ac 16:25). Jesus prays at night (Lk 6:12). In the temple (Jer 26:2; Lk 18:10; 24:53; Ac 3:1).

In the heavenly temple—

Rev 11:1 I was given a reed like a measuring rod and was told, "Go and measure the temple of God and the altar, and count the worshipers there.

In private homes (Ac 1:13-14; 5:42; 12:12; 20:7-9; Ro 16:5; 1Co 16:19; Col 4:15; Phm 2). Anywhere (Jn 4:21-24). To become universal (Isa 45:23; Ro 14:11; Php 2:10).

Of Hypocrites, Despised by God:

Isa 1:11 "The multitude of your sacrifices—what are they to me?" says the LORD. "I have more than enough of burnt offerings, of rams and the fat of fattened animals; I have no pleasure in the blood of bulls and lambs and goats. ¹²When you come to appear before me, who has asked this of you, this trampling of my courts? ¹³Stop bringing meaningless offerings! Your incense is detestable to me. New Moons, Sabbaths and convocations—I cannot bear your evil assemblies. ¹⁴Your New Moon festivals and your appointed feasts my soul hates. They have become a burden to me; I am weary of bearing them. ¹⁵When you spread out your hands in prayer, I will hide my eyes from you; even if you offer many prayers, I will not listen. Your hands are full of blood;

Isa 29:13 The Lord says: "These people come near to me with their mouth and honor me with their lips, but their hearts are far from me. Their worship of me is made up only of rules taught by men. ¹⁴Therefore once more I will astound these people with wonder upon wonder; the wisdom of the wise will perish, the intelligence of the intelligent will vanish." ¹⁵Woe to those who go to great depths to hide their plans from the LORD, who do their work in darkness and think, "Who sees us? Who will know?"

¹⁶You turn things upside down, as if the potter were thought to be like the clay! Shall what is formed say to him who formed it, "He did not make me"? Can the pot say of the potter, "He knows nothing"?

Hos 6:6 For I desire mercy, not sacrifice, and acknowledgment of God rather than burnt offerings.

Am 5:21 "I hate, I despise your religious feasts; I cannot stand your assemblies. ²²Even though you bring me burnt offerings and grain offerings, I will not accept them. Though you bring choice fellowship offerings, I will have no regard for them. ²³Away with the noise of your songs! I will not listen to the music of your harps. ²⁴But let justice roll on like a river, righteousness like a never-failing stream!

Of the wicked, rejected (Ge 4:5,7).

Family: (Dt 16:11,14).

Of Abraham (Ge 12:7-8; 13:4,18).

Of Jacob—

Ge 35:2 So Jacob said to his household and to all who were with him, "Get rid of the foreign gods you have with you, and purify yourselves and change your clothes. ³Then come, let us go up to Bethel, where I will build an altar to God, who answered me in the day of my distress and who has been with me wherever I have gone."

Of Job (Job 1:5). Of the Philippian jailer (Ac 16:34).

National:

Rev 15:4 Who will not fear you, O Lord, and bring glory to your name? For you alone are holy. All nations will come and worship before you, for your righteous acts have been revealed."

The whole nation required to assemble for, including men, women, children, servants, and strangers (Dt 16:11; 31:11-13), in Mount Gerizim and Mount Ebal (Jos 8:32-35). The word of God read in public assemblies (Ex 24:7; Dt 27:12-26; 31:11-13; Jos 8:33-35; 2Ki 23:1-3; Ne 8:1-8,13-18; Mt 21:23; Lk 4:16-17).

Of angels, forbidden (Rev 19:10; 22:8-9).

See Affliction, Prayer Under; Blasphemy; Children; Church, The Body of Believers; Consecration; Dedication; Idolatry; Instruction, in Religion; Levites; Minister; Music; Offerings; Praise; Prayer; Preaching; Priest; Psalms; Religion; Sacrilege; Servant; Strangers; Tabernacle; Temple; Thanksgiving; Women; Word of God; Young Men.

Instances of:

Israel (Ex 15:1)—

Ex 15:2 The LORD is my strength and my song; he has become my salvation. He is my God, and I will praise him, my father's God, and I will exalt him.

Ps 107:6 Then they cried out to the LORD in their trouble, and he delivered them from their distress. ⁷He led them by a straight way to a city where they could settle. ⁸Let them give thanks to the LORD for his unfailing love and his wonderful deeds for men,

Ps 107:32 Let them exalt him in the assembly of the people and praise him in the council of the elders.

Moses (Ex 34:8).

Solomon—

2Ch 7:1 When Solomon finished praying, fire came down from heaven and consumed the burnt offering and the sacrifices, and the glory of the LORD filled the temple.

Priests and Levites—

2Ch 30:27 The priests and the Levites stood to bless the people, and God heard them, for their prayer reached heaven, his holy dwelling place.

Psalmists—

Ps 5:7 But I, by your great mercy, will come into your house; in reverence will I bow down toward your holy temple.

Ps 42:4 These things I remember as I pour out my soul: how I used to go with the multitude, leading the procession to the house of God, with shouts of joy and thanksgiving among the festive throng.

Ps 48:9 Within your temple, O God, we meditate on your unfailing love.

Ps 55:14 with whom I once enjoyed sweet fellowship as we walked with the throng at the house of God.

Ps 63:1 O God, you are my God, earnestly I seek you; my soul thirsts for you, my body longs for you, in a dry and weary land where there is no water.

²I have seen you in the sanctuary and beheld your power and your glory.

Ps 66:4 All the earth bows down to you; they sing praise to you, they sing praise to your name." *Selah*

Ps 66:13 I will come to your temple with burnt offerings and fulfill my vows to you— ¹⁴vows my lips promised and my mouth spoke when I was in trouble.

Ps 89:7 In the council of the holy ones God is greatly feared; he is more awesome than all who surround him.

Ps 93:5 Your statutes stand firm; holiness adorns your house for endless days, O LORD.

Ps 103:1 Praise the LORD, O my soul; all my inmost being, praise his holy name. ²Praise the LORD, O my soul, and forget not all his benefits— ³who forgives all your sins and heals all your diseases, ⁴who redeems your life from the pit and crowns you with love and compassion,

Ps 116:12 How can I repay the LORD for all his goodness to me? ¹³I will lift up the cup of salvation and call on the name of the LORD. ¹⁴I will fulfill my vows to the LORD in the presence of all his people.

Ps 116:17 I will sacrifice a thank offering to you and call on the name of the LORD.

Ps 119:108 Accept, O LORD, the willing praise of my mouth, and teach me your laws.

Ps 132:7 "Let us go to his dwelling place; let us worship at his footstool—

Ps 132:13 For the LORD has chosen Zion, he has desired it for his dwelling: ¹⁴"This is my resting place for ever and ever; here I will sit enthroned, for I have desired it—

Isaiah (Isa 49:13; 52:9).

WORSHIPERS [*6985, *3302, *4686, *4687, *4936*].

NIV+ See WORSHIP

Examples of (Ge 22:5; 24:26; Ex 34:8; Jos 5:14; Jdg 7:15; 1Sa 1:28; 2Sa 12:20; 2Ch 7:3; Ne 8:6; Job 1:20; Rev 4:10; 7:11; 11:16).

WOUNDS [928+995, 2467, 2726, 3872, 4731, 4804, 5596, 5782, 6780, 7206, *3698, 4435, 5546*].

NIV+ WOUND

Treatment of (Pr 20:30; Isa 1:6; Lk 10:34). By Jesus' wounds we are healed (Isa 53:5; 1Pe 2:24).

WRATH [399, 678, 2404, 2405, 2408, 2779, 3019, 5757, 6301, 6552, 7288, 7911, 7912, 8075, 10634, *2596, 3973*].

NIV+ See ANGER, FURY

1. Anger of people (Ge 30:2; 1Sa 17:28), may be evil (2Co 12:20), or a reaction to evil (1Sa 20:34), or a work of the flesh (Gal 5:20). *See Anger.*

2. Anger of God—reaction of a righteous God against sinful people and evil in all forms (Dt 9:7; Isa 13:9; Ro 1:18; Eph 5:6; Rev 14:10,19). *See Anger of God.*

WREATHS [4324, 6498, *5098*].

NIV+ WREATH

Decorating the tabernacle and temple (Ex 28:14; 1Ki 7:17; 2Ch 4:12).

WRESTLE [84, 8883, *76*].

NIV+ WRESTLED, WRESTLING

To contend by grappling with an opponent (Ge 32:24-25), used figuratively (Ge 30:8; Eph 6:12).

WRITING [*1821, 4180, 4181, 4844, 6219, 6221, 10375, 10673, *1207, 1210, 1211, 1582, 2107, 2108, 2182, 4592*].

NIV+ WRITE, WRITER, WRITES, WRITINGS, WRITTEN, WROTE

Discovered to be in use in Mesopotamia as early as 3200 B.C., its development credited to the Sumerians. They had a primitive, nonalphabetic linear writing, not phonetic but pictographic, ideas being recorded by means of pictures of sense-symbols, rather than by sounds-symbols. The next stage in the history of writing was the introduction of the phonogram, or the type of sign which indicates a sound, and afterward came alphabetic scripts. The Egyptians first developed an alphabetic system of writing. Hebrews derived their alphabet from Phoenicians. Semitic writing dating between 1900 and 1500 B.C. has been found at Serabit el-Khadim in Sinai. Greeks received their alphabet from Phoenicians and Arameans.

Writing mentioned in Bible (Ex 17:14). Ten Commandments written with the finger of God (Ex 31:18; 32:15-16). Ancient writing materials: clay, wax, wood, metal, plaster (Dt 27:2-3; Jos 8:32; Lk 1:63), later, parchment (2Ti 4:13), and papyrus (2Jn 12). Instruments of writing: reed on papyrus and parchment; stylus on hard material (Ex 32:4).

See Book; Engraving; Ink; Letters; Pen; Tablet, 1.

WRITING KIT In Ezekiel's vision (Eze 9:2-3,11).

X

XERXES [347].

1. Xerxes is a transliteration of the Greek form of the Persian name Khshayarshan; KJV Ahasuerus. The king of Persia mentioned in the book of Esther and Ezr 4:6. Xerxes succeeded his father Darius I the Great and reigned from 486 to 465 B.C.

2. Father of Darius the Mede (Da 9:1).

Y

YAHWEH [3363, 3378] (*He who is [I am] or He who causes to be*) .

NIV+ †LORD

The Hebrew personal name for God, Yahweh, is translated in the NIV as LORD. God revealed his name as "I AM WHO I AM," his eternal covenant name implying self-existence and saving presence (Ex 3:14-17).

YHWH is often called the "tetragrammaton," referring to the "four letters" or consonants of Yahweh.

See God, Names of, Yahweh; Jehovah.

YARMUK, WADI EL Stream six miles SE of Sea of Galilee flowing into Jordan, marked S boundary of Bashan.

YARN [9106+9357, 9418].

1. Blue, purple, and scarlet yarn used to embroider the tabernacle and priestly garments (Ex 25:4; 26:1; 28:5), in the temple (1Ch 2:7,14; 3:14). Used in cleaning sacrifices (Lev 14:4,6,49,51-52).

2. *See Kue.*

YAUDI [3373]. A place in N Aram or the same as Judah (2Ki 14:28, ftn).

YEAR [*2645, 3427, 9102, 10732, *1454, 1929, 2291, 2465, 4373, 5478*].

NIV+ YEAR-OLD, YEAR'S, YEARLING, YEARLY, YEARS

(Ge 1:14). Divided into months (Ex 12:2; Nu 10:10; 28:11). *See Month.*

Annual feasts (Lev 25:5). *See Feasts.*

Redemption of houses sold, limited to one (Lev 25:29-30). Land to rest one, in seven (Lev 25:5). Of release (Dt 15:9).

Age computed by: of Abraham (Ge 25:7), of Jacob (Ge 47:9). *See Longevity.*

A thousand, with the Lord as one day (Ps 90:4; 2Pe 3:8). Satan to be bound a thousand (Rev 20:2-4,7).

See Jubilee; Millennium; Time.

YEAST [2806, 2809, 4721, 5174, 8419, *109, 2434*]. See Leaven.

YHWH See Lord; Yahweh.

YOKE [3998, 4573, 4574, 4593, 6026, 6296, 6585, 7537, 7538, *2282, 2414, 2433*].

NIV+ YOKED, YOKEFELLOW, YOKES

Wooden frame for joining two draft animals; a wooden bar held on neck by thongs around neck (Nu 19:2; Dt 21:3). Yoke of oxen is a pair (1Sa 14:14; Lk 14:19).

Figurative of:

Oppression (Lev 26:13; 1Ki 12:4; 2Ch 10:4,9-11; Isa 9:4; 10:27; Jer 28:2,4,10; 30:8), the bondage of sin (La 1:14), burdensome ordinances (Ac 15:10; Gal 5:1), discipleship to Christ (Mt 11:29-30), discipline (La 3:27).

Removal of, figurative of deliverance (Ge 27:40; Jer 2:20; Mt 11:29-30).

YOKEFELLOW [*5187*] (*yoked together*).

NIV+ YOKE, YOKES

Person united to another by close bonds, as in marriage or labor (Php 4:3, ftn).

YOM KIPPUR Hebrew for "Day of Atonement." *See Feasts.*

YOUNG MEN, WOMEN [*711, 1033, 1201, 1426, 1435, 1531, 3528, 3529, 4097, 5830, 5853, 5855, 6402, 7228, 7262, 7582, 7582, 7783, 7785, *3733, 3734, 3742*].

NIV+ YOUNGER, YOUNGEST, YOUTH, YOUTHFUL, YOUTHS

Wise and Foolish; Young Men and Women:

Wise, exemplified in Moses' wise choice—

Ex 24:3 When Moses went and told the people all the LORD's words and laws, they responded with one voice, "Everything the LORD has said we will do." [4]Moses then wrote down everything the LORD had said. He got up early the next morning and built an altar at the foot of the mountain and set up twelve stone pillars representing the twelve tribes of Israel.

[5]Then he sent young Israelite men, and they offered burnt offerings and sacrificed young bulls as fellowship offerings to the LORD.

Heb 11:24 By faith Moses, when he had grown up, refused to be known as the son of Pharaoh's daughter. [25]He chose to be mistreated along with the people of God rather than to enjoy the pleasures of sin for a short time. [26]He regarded disgrace for the sake of Christ as of greater value than the treasures of Egypt, because he was looking ahead to his reward.

Wise, a comfort to parents—

Note: In the following proverbs throughout this entry, "son" can be read as an inclusive term for both male and female children.

Pr 10:1 The proverbs of Solomon: A wise son brings joy to his father, but a foolish son grief to his mother.

Pr 15:20 A wise son brings joy to his father, but a foolish man despises his mother.

Pr 29:3 A man who loves wisdom brings joy to his father, but a companion of prostitutes squanders his wealth.

Foolish, a sorrow to parents (Pr 10:1)—

Pr 17:25 A foolish son brings grief to his father and bitterness to the one who bore him.

Pr 19:13 A foolish son is his father's ruin, and a quarrelsome wife is like a constant dripping.

Pr 19:26 He who robs his father and drives out his mother is a son who brings shame and disgrace.

Pr 28:7 He who keeps the law is a discerning son, but a companion of gluttons disgraces his father.

Wise and foolish, contrasted (Pr 10:1)—

Pr 13:1 A wise son heeds his father's instruction, but a mocker does not listen to rebuke. (+Pr 15:20)

See below, Folly of.

Admonitions to:

Pr 3:1 My son, do not forget my teaching, but keep my commands in your heart, ²for they will prolong your life many years and bring you prosperity.

³Let love and faithfulness never leave you; bind them around your neck, write them on the tablet of your heart. ⁴Then you will win favor and a good name in the sight of God and man.

⁵Trust in the LORD with all your heart and lean not on your own understanding;

Pr 4:20 My son, pay attention to what I say; listen closely to my words. ²¹Do not let them out of your sight, keep them within your heart; ²²for they are life to those who find them and health to a man's whole body. ²³Above all else, guard your heart, for it is the wellspring of life. ²⁴Put away perversity from your mouth; keep corrupt talk far from your lips. ²⁵Let your eyes look straight ahead, fix your gaze directly before you. ²⁶Make level paths for your feet and take only ways that are firm. ²⁷Do not swerve to the right or the left; keep your foot from evil.

Pr 6:1 My son, if you have put up security for your neighbor, if you have struck hands in pledge for another, ²if you have been trapped by what you said, ensnared by the words of your mouth, ³then do this, my son, to free yourself, since you have fallen into your neighbor's hands: Go and humble yourself; press your plea with your neighbor! ⁴Allow no sleep to your eyes, no slumber to your eyelids. ⁵Free yourself, like a gazelle from the hand of the hunter, like a bird from the snare of the fowler.

Pr 6:20 My son, keep your father's commands and do not forsake your mother's teaching. ²¹Bind them upon your heart forever; fasten them around your neck. ²²When you walk, they will guide you; when you sleep, they will watch over you; when you awake, they will speak to you. ²³For these commands are a lamp, this teaching is a light, and the corrections of discipline are the way to life, ²⁴keeping you from the immoral woman, from the smooth tongue of the wayward wife. ²⁵Do not lust in your heart after her beauty or let her captivate you with her eyes,

Pr 19:27 Stop listening to instruction, my son, and you will stray from the words of knowledge.

Pr 23:15 My son, if your heart is wise, then my heart will be glad; ¹⁶my inmost being will rejoice when your lips speak what is right.

¹⁷Do not let your heart envy sinners, but always be zealous for the fear of the LORD. ¹⁸There is surely a future hope for you, and your hope will not be cut off.

¹⁹Listen, my son, and be wise, and keep your heart on the right path. ²⁰Do not join those who drink too much wine or gorge themselves on meat, ²¹for drunkards and gluttons become poor, and drowsiness clothes them in rags. (+Pr 23:22-23,25-26)

Pr 24:1 Do not envy wicked men, do not desire their company; ²for their hearts plot violence, and their lips talk about making trouble.

³By wisdom a house is built, and through understanding it is established; ⁴through knowledge its rooms are filled with rare and beautiful treasures.

⁵A wise man has great power, and a man of knowledge increases strength; ⁶for waging war you need guidance, and for victory many advisers.

⁷Wisdom is too high for a fool; in the assembly at the gate he has nothing to say.

⁸He who plots evil will be known as a schemer. ⁹The schemes of folly are sin, and men detest a mocker.

¹⁰If you falter in times of trouble, how small is your strength!

¹¹Rescue those being led away to death; hold back those staggering toward slaughter. ¹²If you say, "But we knew nothing about this," does not he who weighs the heart perceive it? Does not he who guards your life know it? Will he not repay each person according to what he has done?

Pr 24:15 Do not lie in wait like an outlaw against a righteous man's house, do not raid his dwelling place; ¹⁶for though a righteous man falls seven times, he rises again, but the wicked are brought down by calamity.

¹⁷Do not gloat when your enemy falls; when he stumbles, do not let your heart rejoice, ¹⁸or the LORD will see and disapprove and turn his wrath away from him.

¹⁹Do not fret because of evil men or be envious of the wicked, ²⁰for the evil man has no future hope, and the lamp of the wicked will be snuffed out.

²¹Fear the LORD and the king, my son, and do not join with the rebellious, ²²for those two will send sudden destruction upon them, and who knows what calamities they can bring?

²³These also are sayings of the wise: To show partiality in judging is not good: ²⁴Whoever says to the guilty, "You are innocent"—peoples will curse him and nations denounce him. ²⁵But it will go well with those who convict the guilty, and rich blessing will come upon them.

²⁶An honest answer is like a kiss on the lips.

²⁷Finish your outdoor work and get your fields ready; after that, build your house.

²⁸Do not testify against your neighbor without cause, or use your lips to deceive. ²⁹Do not say, "I'll do to him as he has done to me; I'll pay that man back for what he did."

³⁰I went past the field of the sluggard, past the vineyard of the man who lacks judgment; ³¹thorns had come up everywhere, the ground was covered with weeds, and the stone wall was in ruins. ³²I applied my heart to what I observed and learned a lesson from what I saw: ³³A little sleep, a little slumber, a little folding of the hands to rest— ³⁴and poverty will come on you like a bandit and scarcity like an armed man.

Pr 27:11 Be wise, my son, and bring joy to my heart; then I can answer anyone who treats me with contempt.

Against lust—

2Ti 2:22 Flee the evil desires of youth, and pursue righteousness, faith, love and peace, along with those who call on the Lord out of a pure heart. ²³Don't have anything to do with foolish and stupid arguments, because you know they produce quarrels.

Against drunkenness (Pr 23:20-21)—

Pr 23:29 Who has woe? Who has sorrow? Who has strife? Who has complaints? Who has needless bruises? Who has bloodshot eyes? ³⁰Those who linger over wine, who go to sample bowls of mixed wine. ³¹Do not gaze at wine when it is red, when it sparkles in the cup, when it goes down smoothly! ³²In the end it bites like a snake and poisons like a viper. ³³Your eyes will see strange sights and your mind imagine confusing things. ³⁴You will be like one sleeping on the high seas, lying on top of the rigging. ³⁵"They hit me," you will say, "but I'm not hurt! They beat me, but I don't feel it! When will I wake up so I can find another drink?"

Against loving the world—

1Jn 2:13 I write to you, fathers, because you have known him who is from the beginning. I write to you, young men, because you have overcome the evil one. I write to you, dear children, because you have known the Father. ¹⁴I write to you, fathers, because you have known him who is from the beginning. I write to you, young men, because you are strong, and the word of God lives in you, and you have overcome the evil one.

¹⁵Do not love the world or anything in the world. If anyone loves the world, the love of the Father is not in him. ¹⁶For everything in the world—the cravings of sinful man, the lust of his eyes and the boasting of what he has and does—comes not from the Father but from the world. ¹⁷The world and its desires pass away, but the man who does the will of God lives forever.

Against the snares of the adulteress—

Pr 5:3 For the lips of an adulteress drip honey, and her speech is smoother than oil; ⁴but in the end she is bitter as gall, sharp as a double-edged sword. ⁵Her feet go down to death; her steps lead straight to the grave. ⁶She gives no thought to the way of life; her paths are crooked, but she knows it not.

⁷Now then, my sons, listen to me; do not turn aside from what I say. ⁸Keep to a path far from her, do not go near the door of her house, ⁹lest you give your best strength to others and your years to one who is cruel, ¹⁰lest strangers feast on your wealth and your toil enrich another man's house. ¹¹At the end of your life you will groan, when your flesh and body are spent. ¹²You will say, "How I hated discipline! How my heart spurned correction! ¹³I would not obey my teachers or listen to my instructors. ¹⁴I have come to the brink of utter ruin in the midst of the whole assembly." (+Pr 6:24-35)

Pr 7:1 My son, keep my words and store up my commands within you. ²Keep my commands and you will live; guard my teachings as the apple of your eye. ³Bind them on your fingers; write them on the tablet of your heart. ⁴Say to wisdom, "You are my sister," and call understanding your kinsman; ⁵they will keep you from the adulteress, from the wayward wife with her seductive words.

⁶At the window of my house I looked out through the lattice. ⁷I saw among the simple, I noticed among the young men, a youth who lacked judgment. ⁸He was going down the street near her corner, walking along in the direction of her house ⁹at twilight, as the day was fading, as the dark of night set in.

¹⁰Then out came a woman to meet him, dressed like a prostitute and with crafty intent. ¹¹(She is loud and defiant, her feet never stay at home; ¹²now in the street, now in the squares, at every corner she lurks.) ¹³She took hold of him and kissed him and with a brazen face she said:

¹⁴"I have fellowship offerings at home; today I fulfilled my vows. ¹⁵So I came out to meet you; I looked for you and have found you! ¹⁶I have covered my bed with colored linens from Egypt. ¹⁷I have perfumed my bed with myrrh, aloes and cinnamon. ¹⁸Come, let's drink deep of love till morning; let's enjoy ourselves with love! ¹⁹My husband is not at home; he has gone on a long journey. ²⁰He took his purse filled with money and will not be home till full moon."

²¹With persuasive words she led him astray; she seduced him with her smooth talk. ²²All at once he followed her like an ox going to the slaughter, like a deer stepping into a noose ²³till an arrow pierces his liver, like a bird darting into a snare, little knowing it will cost him his life.

²⁴Now then, my sons, listen to me; pay attention to what I say. ²⁵Do not let your heart turn to her ways or stray into her paths. ²⁶Many are the victims she has brought down; her slain are a mighty throng. ²⁷Her house is a highway to the grave, leading down to the chambers of death.

Pr 23:27 for a prostitute is a deep pit and a wayward wife is a narrow well. ²⁸Like a bandit she lies in wait, and multiplies the unfaithful among men. (+Pr 31:1-3)

Against the enticements of sinners—

Pr 1:10 My son, if sinners entice you, do not give in to them. ¹¹If they say, "Come along with us; let's lie in wait for someone's blood, let's waylay some harmless soul; ¹²let's swallow them alive, like the grave, and whole, like those who go down to the pit; ¹³we will get all sorts of valuable things and fill our houses with plunder; ¹⁴throw in your lot with us, and we will share a common purse"— ¹⁵my son, do not go along with them, do not set foot on their paths; ¹⁶for their feet rush into sin, they are swift to shed blood.

Against evil companions—

Pr 2:12 Wisdom will save you from the ways of wicked men, from men whose words are perverse, ¹³who leave the straight paths to walk in dark ways, ¹⁴who delight in doing wrong and rejoice in the perverseness of evil, ¹⁵whose paths are crooked and who are devious in their ways.

Pr 4:14 Do not set foot on the path of the wicked or walk in the way of evil men. ¹⁵Avoid it, do not travel on it; turn from it and go on your way. (+Pr 24:1-2)

Exhortations to:

Be sober-minded—

Tit 2:6 Similarly, encourage the young men to be self-controlled.

Be an example of piety—

1Ti 4:12 Don't let anyone look down on you because you are young, but set an example for the believers in speech, in life, in love, in faith and in purity.

Keep the heart with all diligence (Pr 4:23).

Paying attention to God's word—

Ps 119:9 How can a young man keep his way pure? By living according to your word.

Seek wisdom—

Pr 2:1 My son, if you accept my words and store up my commands within you, ²turning your ear to wisdom and applying your heart to understanding, ³and if you call out for insight and cry aloud for understanding, ⁴and if you look for it as for silver and search for it as for hidden treasure, ⁵then you will understand the fear of the LORD and find the knowledge of God. ⁶For the LORD gives wisdom, and from his mouth come knowledge and understanding. ⁷He holds victory in store for the upright, he is a shield to those whose walk is blameless, ⁸for he guards the course of the just and protects the way of his faithful ones. **Pr 3:13** Blessed is the man who finds wisdom, the man who gains understanding, ¹⁴for she is more profitable than silver and yields better returns than gold. ¹⁵She is more precious than rubies; nothing you desire can compare with her. ¹⁶Long life is in her right hand; in her left hand are riches and honor. ¹⁷Her ways are pleasant ways, and all her paths are peace. ¹⁸She is a tree of life to those who embrace her; those who lay hold of her will be blessed.

¹⁹By wisdom the LORD laid the earth's foundations, by understanding he set the heavens in place; ²⁰by his knowledge the deeps were divided, and the clouds let drop the dew.

²¹My son, preserve sound judgment and discernment, do

not let them out of your sight; ²²they will be life for you, an ornament to grace your neck. ²³Then you will go on your way in safety, and your foot will not stumble;

Pr 4:5 Get wisdom, get understanding; do not forget my words or swerve from them. ⁶Do not forsake wisdom, and she will protect you; love her, and she will watch over you. ⁷Wisdom is supreme; therefore get wisdom. Though it cost all you have, get understanding. ⁸Esteem her, and she will exalt you; embrace her, and she will honor you. ⁹She will set a garland of grace on your head and present you with a crown of splendor."

¹⁰Listen, my son, accept what I say, and the years of your life will be many. ¹¹I guide you in the way of wisdom and lead you along straight paths. ¹²When you walk, your steps will not be hampered; when you run, you will not stumble. ¹³Hold on to instruction, do not let it go; guard it well, for it is your life.

Pr 24:13 Eat honey, my son, for it is good; honey from the comb is sweet to your taste. ¹⁴Know also that wisdom is sweet to your soul; if you find it, there is a future hope for you, and your hope will not be cut off.

Obey parents (Pr 6:20-23)—

Pr 23:22 Listen to your father, who gave you life, and do not despise your mother when she is old. ²³Buy the truth and do not sell it; get wisdom, discipline and understanding. ²⁴The father of a righteous man has great joy; he who has a wise son delights in him. ²⁵May your father and mother be glad; may she who gave you birth rejoice!

²⁶My son, give me your heart and let your eyes keep to my ways,

Obey the Lord (Pr 3:5)—

Pr 3:6 in all your ways acknowledge him, and he will make your paths straight.

⁷Do not be wise in your own eyes; fear the LORD and shun evil. ⁸This will bring health to your body and nourishment to your bones.

⁹Honor the LORD with your wealth, with the firstfruits of all your crops; ¹⁰then your barns will be filled to overflowing, and your vats will brim over with new wine.

¹¹My son, do not despise the LORD's discipline and do not resent his rebuke, ¹²because the LORD disciplines those he loves, as a father the son he delights in.

Praise the Lord—

Ps 148:12 young men and maidens, old men and children. ¹³Let them praise the name of the LORD, for his name alone is exalted; his splendor is above the earth and the heavens.

Glory of:

Pr 20:29 The glory of young men is their strength, gray hair the splendor of the old.

Folly of, Exemplified:

Esau (Ge 25:31-34; Heb 12:16-17),

Rehoboam's counselors—

1Ki 12:8 But Rehoboam rejected the advice the elders gave him and consulted the young men who had grown up with him and were serving him. ⁹He asked them, "What is your advice? How should we answer these people who say to me, 'Lighten the yoke your father put on us'?"

¹⁰The young men who had grown up with him replied, "Tell these people who have said to you, 'Your father put a heavy yoke on us, but make our yoke lighter'—tell them, 'My little finger is thicker than my father's waist. ¹¹My father laid on you a heavy yoke; I will make it even heavier. My father scourged you with whips; I will scourge you with scorpions.'"

Rehoboam—

1Ki 12:13 The king answered the people harshly. Rejecting the advice given him by the elders, ¹⁴he followed the advice of the young men and said, "My father made your yoke heavy; I will make it even heavier. My father scourged you with whips; I will scourge you with scorpions."

The rich young ruler—

Mt 19:16 Now a man came up to Jesus and asked, "Teacher, what good thing must I do to get eternal life?"

¹⁷"Why do you ask me about what is good?" Jesus replied. "There is only One who is good. If you want to enter life, obey the commandments."

¹⁸"Which ones?" the man inquired.

Jesus replied, "'Do not murder, do not commit adultery, do not steal, do not give false testimony, ¹⁹honor your father and mother,' and 'love your neighbor as yourself.'"

²⁰"All these I have kept," the young man said. "What do I still lack?"

²¹Jesus answered, "If you want to be perfect, go, sell your possessions and give to the poor, and you will have treasure in heaven. Then come, follow me."

²²When the young man heard this, he went away sad, because he had great wealth. (+Mk 10:17-22; Lk 18:18-23)

The prodigal son—

Lk 15:11 Jesus continued: "There was a man who had two sons. ¹²The younger one said to his father, 'Father, give me my share of the estate.' So he divided his property between them.

¹³"Not long after that, the younger son got together all he had, set off for a distant country and there squandered his wealth in wild living. ¹⁴After he had spent everything, there was a severe famine in that whole country, and he began to be in need. ¹⁵So he went and hired himself out to a citizen of that country, who sent him to his fields to feed pigs. ¹⁶He longed to fill his stomach with the pods that the pigs were eating, but no one gave him anything.

¹⁷"When he came to his senses, he said, 'How many of my father's hired men have food to spare, and here I am starving to death! ¹⁸I will set out and go back to my father and say to him: Father, I have sinned against heaven and against you. ¹⁹I am no longer worthy to be called your son; make me like one of your hired men.' ²⁰So he got up and went to his father.

"But while he was still a long way off, his father saw him and was filled with compassion for him; he ran to his son, threw his arms around him and kissed him.

²¹"The son said to him, 'Father, I have sinned against heaven and against you. I am no longer worthy to be called your son.'

²²"But the father said to his servants, 'Quick! Bring the best robe and put it on him. Put a ring on his finger and sandals on his feet. ²³Bring the fattened calf and kill it. Let's have a feast and celebrate. ²⁴For this son of mine was dead and is alive again; he was lost and is found.' So they began to celebrate.

²⁵"Meanwhile, the older son was in the field. When he came near the house, he heard music and dancing. ²⁶So he called one of the servants and asked him what was going on. ²⁷'Your brother has come,' he replied, 'and your father has killed the fattened calf because he has him back safe and sound.'

²⁸"The older brother became angry and refused to go in. So his father went out and pleaded with him. ²⁹But he answered his father, 'Look! All these years I've been

slaving for you and never disobeyed your orders. Yet you never gave me even a young goat so I could celebrate with my friends. ³⁰But when this son of yours who has squandered your property with prostitutes comes home, you kill the fattened calf for him!'

³¹"'My son,' the father said, 'you are always with me, and everything I have is yours. ³²But we had to celebrate and be glad, because this brother of yours was dead and is alive again; he was lost and is found.'"

Instances of Religious:

See Joseph, 1; Joshua; Samuel; David; Solomon; Uriah.

See also, Children; Parents.

Z

ZAANAIM *See Zaanannim.*

ZAANAN [7367]. A place of uncertain location (Mic 1:11).

ZAANANNIM [7588]. A plain near Kedesh (Jos 19:33; Jdg 4:11).

ZAAVAN [2401] (possibly *trembling, terror*). A son of Ezer (Ge 36:27; 1Ch 1:42).

ZABAD [2274] (*he bestows*).
1. Son of Nathan (1Ch 2:36-37).
2. An Ephraimite (1Ch 7:21).
3. One of David's valiant men (1Ch 11:41).
4. An assassin of King Joash (2Ch 24:26). Also called Jozabad (2Ki 12:21). *See Jozabad, 1.*
5. Three Israelites who divorced their Gentile wives (Ezr 10:27,33,43).

ZABBAI [2287] (perhaps *God has given*).
1. Son of Bebai (Ezr 10:28).
2. Father of Baruch (Ne 3:20).

ZABBUD *See Zaccur, 5.*

ZABDI [2275] (*Yahweh bestows*).
1. Father of Carmi (Jos 7:1,17-18, ftn). *See Zimri, 3.*
2. A Benjamite (1Ch 8:19).
3. A Shiphmite in charge of David's wine vats (1Ch 27:27).
4. Son of Asaph (Ne 11:17).

ZABDIEL [2276] (*God [El] bestows*).
1. Father of Jashobeam (1Ch 27:2).
2. An chief officer of 128 able men who lived in Jerusalem (Ne 11:14).

ZABUD [2280] (*[he has] bestowed upon*). A chief officer of Solomon (1Ki 4:5).

ZABULON *See Zebulun.*

ZACCAI [2347] (*Yahweh has remembered*, or perhaps *Yahweh remember*). A Jew whose descendants returned from the Exile (Ezr 2:9; Ne 7:14).

ZACCHAEUS [2405] (*righteous, pure one*). Chief tax collector; climbed sycamore tree to see Jesus and became his disciple (Lk 19:8).

ZACCUR, ZACCHUR [2346] (*remembering*).
1. Father of Reubenite spy, Shammua (Nu 13:4).
2. Simeonite (1Ch 4:26).
3. Son of Merari (1Ch 24:27).
4. Son of Asaph; musician (1Ch 25:1-2; Ne 12:35).
5. A returned exile (Ezr 8:14).
6. Son of Imri who helped rebuild walls of Jerusalem (Ne 3:2).
7. Man who sealed covenant with Nehemiah (Ne 10:12).
8. Father of Hanan (Ne 13:13).

ZACHARIAH *See Zechariah, 1 & 15.*

ZACHARIAS *See Zechariah, 30 & 31.*

ZACHER *See Zeker.*

ZADOC *See Zadok, 10.*

ZADOK [7401, 4882] (*righteous one*).
NIV+ ZADOKITES
1. High priest in time of David's reign (2Sa 19:11; 20:25; 1Ch 15:11; 16:39). Removes the ark from Jerusalem at the time of Absalom's usurpation; returns with it at David's command (2Sa 15:24-36; 17:15,17-21). Stands aloof from Adonijah at the time of his attempted usurpation (1Ki 1:8,26). Summoned by David to anoint Solomon (1Ki 1:32-40,44-45). Performs the function of high priest after Abiathar was deposed by Solomon (1Ki 2:35; 1Ch 29:22).
2. Father of Jerusha (2Ki 15:33; 2Ch 27:1).
3. Son of Ahitub (1Ch 6:12).
4. A man of valor (1Ch 12:28).
5. Son of Baana (Ne 3:4).
6. A priest (Ne 3:29).
7. A returned exile (Ne 10:21).
8. Son of Meraioth (Ne 11:11).
9. A treasurer of the temple (Ne 13:13).
10. Descendant of Zerubbabel and an ancestor of Jesus (Mt 1:14).

ZAHAM [2300] (*putrid, loathsome*). Grandson of Solomon (2Ch 11:19).

ZAHAR [7466]. An area NW of Damascus (Eze 27:18); modern Sahra.

ZAIR [7583] (*small, insignificant*, hence *narrow pass*). Village E of Dead Sea where Jehoram NIV, broke through the lines of the Edomites (2Ki 8:21).

ZALAPH [7523] (*low, prickly shrub [caper plant]*). Father of man who helped Nehemiah repair walls (Ne 3:30).

ZALMON [7514, 7515] (*in his image, a copy; black hill*).
1. Forest near Shechem (Jdg 9:48).
2. One of David's mighty men (2Sa 23:28), called "Ilai the Ahohite" (1Ch 11:29).

ZALMONAH [7517] (*dark, gloomy, shaded place*). Encampment of Israelites in wilderness, SE of Edom (Nu 33:41-42).

ZALMUNNA [7518] (*protection refused*). King of Midian (Jdg 8:5-21; Ps 83:11).

ZAMZUMMITES, ZAMZUMMIM [2368] (*babblers*). Ammonite name for Rephaites (Dt 2:20), lived E of Jordan. May be same as Zuzites (Ge 14:5). *See Rephaites; Zuzites, Zuzim.*

ZANOAH [2391, 2392] (*rejected*).
1. A city of western Judah (Jos 15:34; Ne 3:13; 11:30).
2. A city of eastern Judah (Jos 15:56).
3. A descendant of Caleb (1Ch 4:18).

ZAPHENATH-PANEAH [7624] (*the [pagan] god speaks and he [the newborn] lives*). Name given to Joseph by Pharaoh (Ge 41:45).

ZAPHON [7601] (possibly *North* or *[proper name of a god], Zephon*). Territory E of Jordan assigned to Gad (Jos 13:27); possibly modern Amateh.

ZARA, ZARAH *See Zerah.*

ZAREAH A city of Judah (Ne 11:29). *See Zorah.*

ZAREATHITES *See Zorathites.*

ZARED *See Zered.*

ZAREDA *See Zereda, Zeredah.*

ZAREPHATH [7673, *4919*] (possibly *smelting place* BDB; *place of pigmenting, staining* KB). A city between Tyre and Sidon. Elijah performs two miracles in (1Ki 17:8-24; Lk 4:26).

ZARETHAN [7681]. Place in Ephraim or Manasseh near Beth Shan and Adam (Jos 3:16; 1Ki 4:12), and near Succoth (1Ki 7:46; 2Ch 4:17). Exact site not known.

ZARETH-SHAHAR *See Zereth Shahar.*

ZARHITES *See Zerahite(s).*

ZARTANAH, ZARTHAN *See Zarethan.*

ZATTU, ZATTHU [2456].

1. One whose descendants returned with Zerubbabel (Ezr 2:8; 10:27; Ne 7:13).

2. One who sealed the covenant with Nehemiah (Ne 10:14). Probably the same as 1.

ZAVAN *See Zaavan.*

ZAZA [2321] (*a form of a shortened nick name; term of endearment*). Son of Jonathan (1Ch 2:33).

ZEAL [3013, 5883, 7861, 7863, *2419, 2420, 2421, 5080, 5082*] (*zeal, jealousy*).
    NIV+ ZEALOUS, ZEALOUSLY

General:

    Without love, unprofitable—

1Co 13:3 If I give all I possess to the poor and surrender my body to the flames, but have not love, I gain nothing.

    Without knowledge (Nu 11:27-28; Jdg 11:30-31,34-35)—

Ecc 7:16 Do not be overrighteous, neither be overwise—why destroy yourself?

Mt 8:19 Then a teacher of the law came to him and said, "Teacher, I will follow you wherever you go."

    20Jesus replied, "Foxes have holes and birds of the air have nests, but the Son of Man has no place to lay his head." (+Lk 9:57-58)

Jn 16:2 They will put you out of the synagogue; in fact, a time is coming when anyone who kills you will think he is offering a service to God.

Ac 21:20 When they heard this, they praised God. Then they said to Paul: "You see, brother, how many thousands of Jews have believed, and all of them are zealous for the law.

Ro 10:2 For I can testify about them that they are zealous for God, but their zeal is not based on knowledge. 3Since they did not know the righteousness that comes from God and sought to establish their own, they did not submit to God's righteousness.

Gal 1:13 For you have heard of my previous way of life in Judaism, how intensely I persecuted the church of God and tried to destroy it. 14I was advancing in Judaism beyond many Jews of my own age and was extremely zealous for the traditions of my fathers.

    Wisdom of—

Pr 11:30 The fruit of the righteous is a tree of life, and he who wins souls is wise.

    Required—

Isa 62:6 I have posted watchmen on your walls, O Jerusalem; they will never be silent day or night. You who call on the LORD, give yourselves no rest, 7and give him no rest till he establishes Jerusalem and makes her the praise of the earth.

Mt 5:13 "You are the salt of the earth. But if the salt loses its saltiness, how can it be made salty again? It is no longer good for anything, except to be thrown out and trampled by men.

    14"You are the light of the world. A city on a hill cannot be hidden. 15Neither do people light a lamp and put it under a bowl. Instead they put it on its stand, and it gives light to everyone in the house. 16In the same way, let your light shine before men, that they may see your good deeds and praise your Father in heaven. (+Mk 4:21-22; Lk 8:16-17)

Ac 10:42 He commanded us to preach to the people and to testify that he is the one whom God appointed as judge of the living and the dead.

1Co 15:58 Therefore, my dear brothers, stand firm. Let nothing move you. Always give yourselves fully to the work of the Lord, because you know that your labor in the Lord is not in vain.

Tit 2:14 who gave himself for us to redeem us from all wickedness and to purify for himself a people that are his very own, eager to do what is good.

Tit 3:1 Remind the people to be subject to rulers and authorities, to be obedient, to be ready to do whatever is good,

    Commanded—

Jos 24:15 But if serving the LORD seems undesirable to you, then choose for yourselves this day whom you will serve, whether the gods your forefathers served beyond the River, or the gods of the Amorites, in whose land you are living. But as for me and my household, we will serve the LORD."

    16Then the people answered, "Far be it from us to forsake the LORD to serve other gods!

Ezr 7:23 Whatever the God of heaven has prescribed, let it be done with diligence for the temple of the God of heaven. Why should there be wrath against the realm of the king and of his sons?

Ps 60:4 But for those who fear you, you have raised a banner to be unfurled against the bow. *Selah*

Ps 96:2 Sing to the LORD, praise his name; proclaim his salvation day after day.

Ecc 9:10 Whatever your hand finds to do, do it with all your might, for in the grave, where you are going, there is neither working nor planning nor knowledge nor wisdom.

Isa 60:1 "Arise, shine, for your light has come, and the glory of the LORD rises upon you.

Hag 2:4 But now be strong, O Zerubbabel,' declares the LORD. 'Be strong, O Joshua son of Jehozadak, the high priest. Be strong, all you people of the land,' declares the LORD, 'and work. For I am with you,' declares the LORD Almighty.

Ro 12:11 Never be lacking in zeal, but keep your spiritual fervor, serving the Lord.

1Co 7:29 What I mean, brothers, is that the time is short. From now on those who have wives should live as if they had none; 30those who mourn, as if they did not; those who are happy, as if they were not; those who buy something, as if it were not theirs to keep; 31those who use the things of the world, as if not engrossed in them. For this world in its present form is passing away.

[32]I would like you to be free from concern. An unmarried man is concerned about the Lord's affairs—how he can please the Lord. [33]But a married man is concerned about the affairs of this world—how he can please his wife— [34]and his interests are divided. An unmarried woman or virgin is concerned about the Lord's affairs: Her aim is to be devoted to the Lord in both body and spirit. But a married woman is concerned about the affairs of this world—how she can please her husband. [35]I am saying this for your own good, not to restrict you, but that you may live in a right way in undivided devotion to the Lord.

Gal 6:9 Let us not become weary in doing good, for at the proper time we will reap a harvest if we do not give up.

Eph 5:15 Be very careful, then, how you live—not as unwise but as wise, [16]making the most of every opportunity, because the days are evil. (+Eph 6:10-13)

Eph 6:14 Stand firm then, with the belt of truth buckled around your waist, with the breastplate of righteousness in place, [15]and with your feet fitted with the readiness that comes from the gospel of peace. [16]In addition to all this, take up the shield of faith, with which you can extinguish all the flaming arrows of the evil one. [17]Take the helmet of salvation and the sword of the Spirit, which is the word of God. [18]And pray in the Spirit on all occasions with all kinds of prayers and requests. With this in mind, be alert and always keep on praying for all the saints.

[19]Pray also for me, that whenever I open my mouth, words may be given me so that I will fearlessly make known the mystery of the gospel, [20]for which I am an ambassador in chains. Pray that I may declare it fearlessly, as I should.

Php 1:27 Whatever happens, conduct yourselves in a manner worthy of the gospel of Christ. Then, whether I come and see you or only hear about you in my absence, I will know that you stand firm in one spirit, contending as one man for the faith of the gospel [28]without being frightened in any way by those who oppose you. This is a sign to them that they will be destroyed, but that you will be saved—and that by God.

Col 4:5 Be wise in the way you act toward outsiders; make the most of every opportunity. (+2Th 3:13; Heb 12:1-2)

Heb 13:13 Let us, then, go to him outside the camp, bearing the disgrace he bore. [14]For here we do not have an enduring city, but we are looking for the city that is to come.

[15]Through Jesus, therefore, let us continually offer to God a sacrifice of praise—the fruit of lips that confess his name.

1Pe 2:2 Like newborn babies, crave pure spiritual milk, so that by it you may grow up in your salvation, (+2Pe 1:10-11)

2Pe 3:14 So then, dear friends, since you are looking forward to this, make every effort to be found spotless, blameless and at peace with him.

Jude 3 Dear friends, although I was very eager to write to you about the salvation we share, I felt I had to write and urge you to contend for the faith that was once for all entrusted to the saints.

Jude 22 Be merciful to those who doubt; [23]snatch others from the fire and save them; to others show mercy, mixed with fear—hating even the clothing stained by corrupted flesh.

Rev 3:19 Those whom I love I rebuke and discipline. So be earnest, and repent.

Expected—

Hab 2:2 Then the LORD replied: "Write down the revelation and make it plain on tablets so that a herald may run with it.

Zec 14:20 On that day HOLY TO THE LORD will be inscribed on the bells of the horses, and the cooking pots in the LORD's house will be like the sacred bowls in front of the altar. [21]Every pot in Jerusalem and Judah will be holy to the LORD Almighty, and all who come to sacrifice will take some of the pots and cook in them. And on that day there will no longer be a Canaanite in the house of the LORD Almighty.

2Co 4:8 We are hard pressed on every side, but not crushed; perplexed, but not in despair; [9]persecuted, but not abandoned; struck down, but not destroyed. [10]We always carry around in our body the death of Jesus, so that the life of Jesus may also be revealed in our body.

2Co 4:13 It is written: "I believed; therefore I have spoken." With that same spirit of faith we also believe and therefore speak,

2Co 4:16 Therefore we do not lose heart. Though outwardly we are wasting away, yet inwardly we are being renewed day by day. [17]For our light and momentary troubles are achieving for us an eternal glory that far outweighs them all. [18]So we fix our eyes not on what is seen, but on what is unseen. For what is seen is temporary, but what is unseen is eternal.

Gal 4:18 It is fine to be zealous, provided the purpose is good, and to be so always and not just when I am with you.

Php 2:15 so that you may become blameless and pure, children of God without fault in a crooked and depraved generation, in which you shine like stars in the universe

Rewards of—

Da 12:3 Those who are wise will shine like the brightness of the heavens, and those who lead many to righteousness, like the stars for ever and ever. (+Mt 25:21,23; Lk 19:17-19)

Jas 5:20 remember this: Whoever turns a sinner from the error of his way will save him from death and cover over a multitude of sins.

Exemplified in:

Moses (Ex 2:12; 11:8; 32:19-20)—

Ex 32:31 So Moses went back to the LORD and said, "Oh, what a great sin these people have committed! They have made themselves gods of gold. [32]But now, please forgive their sin—but if not, then blot me out of the book you have written."

Nu 10:29 Now Moses said to Hobab son of Reuel the Midianite, Moses' father-in-law, "We are setting out for the place about which the LORD said, 'I will give it to you.' Come with us and we will treat you well, for the LORD has promised good things to Israel."

Nu 11:29 But Moses replied, "Are you jealous for my sake? I wish that all the LORD's people were prophets and that the LORD would put his Spirit on them!"

Dt 9:18 Then once again I fell prostrate before the LORD for forty days and forty nights; I ate no bread and drank no water, because of all the sin you had committed, doing what was evil in the LORD's sight and so provoking him to anger. [19]I feared the anger and wrath of the LORD, for he was angry enough with you to destroy you. But again the LORD listened to me.

Phinehas (Nu 25:7-13; Ps 106:30).

Joshua (Nu 11:27-29; Jos 7:6)—

Jos 24:14 "Now fear the LORD and serve him with all

faithfulness. Throw away the gods your forefathers worshiped beyond the River and in Egypt, and serve the LORD. [15]But if serving the LORD seems undesirable to you, then choose for yourselves this day whom you will serve, whether the gods your forefathers served beyond the River, or the gods of the Amorites, in whose land you are living. But as for me and my household, we will serve the LORD."

[16]Then the people answered, "Far be it from us to forsake the LORD to serve other gods!

Gideon (Jdg 6:11-32). Jephthah (Jdg 11:30-31,34-39). Samuel (1Sa 12:23; 15:11,35; 16:1).

David—

1Sa 17:26 David asked the men standing near him, "What will be done for the man who kills this Philistine and removes this disgrace from Israel? Who is this uncircumcised Philistine that he should defy the armies of the living God?" (+2Sa 6; 7:2; 8:11-12)

2Sa 24:24 But the king replied to Araunah, "No, I insist on paying you for it. I will not sacrifice to the LORD my God burnt offerings that cost me nothing." So David bought the threshing floor and the oxen and paid fifty shekels of silver for them.

1Ch 29:17 I know, my God, that you test the heart and are pleased with integrity. All these things have I given willingly and with honest intent. And now I have seen with joy how willingly your people who are here have given to you.

Ps 40:8 I desire to do your will, O my God; your law is within my heart."

[9]I proclaim righteousness in the great assembly; I do not seal my lips, as you know, O LORD. [10]I do not hide your righteousness in my heart; I speak of your faithfulness and salvation. I do not conceal your love and your truth from the great assembly.

Ps 42:1 As the deer pants for streams of water, so my soul pants for you, O God. [2]My soul thirsts for God, for the living God. When can I go and meet with God?

Ps 51:13 Then I will teach transgressors your ways, and sinners will turn back to you.

Ps 69:7 For I endure scorn for your sake, and shame covers my face. [8]I am a stranger to my brothers, an alien to my own mother's sons; [9]for zeal for your house consumes me, and the insults of those who insult you fall on me.

Ps 71:17 Since my youth, O God, you have taught me, and to this day I declare your marvelous deeds. [18]Even when I am old and gray, do not forsake me, O God, till I declare your power to the next generation, your might to all who are to come.

Solomon (1Ki 8:31-42)—

1Ki 8:43 then hear from heaven, your dwelling place, and do whatever the foreigner asks of you, so that all the peoples of the earth may know your name and fear you, as do your own people Israel, and may know that this house I have built bears your Name. (+1Ki 8:44-53; 2Ch 6:22-42)

Elijah (1Ki 19:10). Obadiah (1Ki 18:3-4).

Micaiah—

1Ki 22:14 But Micaiah said, "As surely as the LORD lives, I can tell him only what the LORD tells me."

Jehu (2Ki 9:10). Jehoiada (2Ki 11:4-17; 2Ch 23:1-17).

Asa (1Ki 15:11-13)—

1Ki 15:14 Although he did not remove the high places, Asa's heart was fully committed to the LORD all his life. (+1Ki 15:15; 2Ch 14:1-5,15)

Israelites—

2Ch 15:15 All Judah rejoiced about the oath because they

had sworn it wholeheartedly. They sought God eagerly, and he was found by them. So the LORD gave them rest on every side.

Eze 9:4 and said to him, "Go throughout the city of Jerusalem and put a mark on the foreheads of those who grieve and lament over all the detestable things that are done in it."

Jehoshaphat (2Ch 17:3-10,19).

Isaiah—

Isa 6:8 Then I heard the voice of the Lord saying, "Whom shall I send? And who will go for us?" And I said, "Here am I. Send me!"

Isa 62:1 For Zion's sake I will not keep silent, for Jerusalem's sake I will not remain quiet, till her righteousness shines out like the dawn, her salvation like a blazing torch.

Hezekiah (Isa 37:1). Josiah (2Ki 22:11-13; 2Ch 34:3-7,29-33).

Priests—

Eze 44:15 "'But the priests, who are Levites and descendants of Zadok and who faithfully carried out the duties of my sanctuary when the Israelites went astray from me, are to come near to minister before me; they are to stand before me to offer sacrifices of fat and blood, declares the Sovereign LORD.

Ezra (Ezr 7:10; 9:10; Ne 8:1-6,13,18). Nehemiah (Ne 4; 5; 13:7-9,15-28).

Job—

Job 16:19 Even now my witness is in heaven; my advocate is on high.

Psalmist—

Ps 119:53 Indignation grips me because of the wicked, who have forsaken your law.

Ps 119:126 It is time for you to act, O LORD; your law is being broken.

Ps 119:136 Streams of tears flow from my eyes, for your law is not obeyed.

Ps 119:139 My zeal wears me out, for my enemies ignore your words.

Ps 119:158 I look on the faithless with loathing, for they do not obey your word.

Jeremiah—

Jer 9:1 Oh, that my head were a spring of water and my eyes a fountain of tears! I would weep day and night for the slain of my people. [2]Oh, that I had in the desert a lodging place for travelers, so that I might leave my people and go away from them; for they are all adulterers, a crowd of unfaithful people.

[3]"They make ready their tongue like a bow, to shoot lies; it is not by truth that they triumph in the land. They go from one sin to another; they do not acknowledge me," declares the LORD.

Jer 13:17 But if you do not listen, I will weep in secret because of your pride; my eyes will weep bitterly, overflowing with tears, because the LORD's flock will be taken captive.

Jer 18:20 Should good be repaid with evil? Yet they have dug a pit for me. Remember that I stood before you and spoke in their behalf to turn your wrath away from them.

Jer 20:9 But if I say, "I will not mention him or speak any more in his name," his word is in my heart like a fire, a fire shut up in my bones. I am weary of holding it in; indeed, I cannot. (+Jer 25:3-4; 26:12-15)

Three Hebrews—

Da 3:17 If we are thrown into the blazing furnace, the God we serve is able to save us from it, and he will rescue us from your hand, O king. **¹⁸**But even if he does not, we want you to know, O king, that we will not serve your gods or worship the image of gold you have set up."

Habakkuk—

Hab 1:2 How long, O LORD, must I call for help, but you do not listen? Or cry out to you, "Violence!" but you do not save? (+Hab 1:3-4)

Old Testament faithful (Heb 11).

Jesus (Mt 23:27)—

Lk 19:41 As he approached Jerusalem and saw the city, he wept over it

Jn 4:34 "My food," said Jesus, "is to do the will of him who sent me and to finish his work. **³⁵**Do you not say, 'Four months more and then the harvest'? I tell you, open your eyes and look at the fields! They are ripe for harvest.

Jn 9:4 As long as it is day, we must do the work of him who sent me. Night is coming, when no one can work.

Anna (Lk 2:38).

Andrew and Philip—

Jn 1:41 The first thing Andrew did was to find his brother Simon and tell him, "We have found the Messiah" (that is, the Christ). **⁴²**And he brought him to Jesus. Jesus looked at him and said, "You are Simon son of John. You will be called Cephas" (which, when translated, is Peter). (+Jn 1:43-44)

Jn 1:45 Philip found Nathanael and told him, "We have found the one Moses wrote about in the Law, and about whom the prophets also wrote—Jesus of Nazareth, the son of Joseph."

⁴⁶"Nazareth! Can anything good come from there?" Nathanael asked.

"Come and see," said Philip.

Apostles—

Mk 16:20 Then the disciples went out and preached everywhere, and the Lord worked with them and confirmed his word by the signs that accompanied it.

Ac 4:31 After they prayed, the place where they were meeting was shaken. And they were all filled with the Holy Spirit and spoke the word of God boldly.

Ac 4:33 With great power the apostles continued to testify to the resurrection of the Lord Jesus, and much grace was upon them all. (+Ac 5:21,25,29-32,41)

Ac 5:42 Day after day, in the temple courts and from house to house, they never stopped teaching and proclaiming the good news that Jesus is the Christ.

Ac 8:4 Those who had been scattered preached the word wherever they went. (+Ac 8:25,30)

Ac 8:35 Then Philip began with that very passage of Scripture and told him the good news about Jesus. (+Ac 8:40; 11:19-20,24,26)

Two blind men proclaiming the miracle of healing, contrary to the injunction of Jesus (Mt 9:30-31). The restored leper (Mk 1:44-45).

Man delivered of demons (Mk 5:19-20)—

Mk 5:20 So the man went away and began to tell in the Decapolis how much Jesus had done for him. And all the people were amazed.

Peter (Mt 16:22)—

Mk 14:29 Peter declared, "Even if all fall away, I will not."

³⁰"I tell you the truth," Jesus answered, "today—yes, tonight—before the rooster crows twice you yourself will disown me three times."

³¹But Peter insisted emphatically, "Even if I have to die

with you, I will never disown you." And all the others said the same.

Lk 22:33 But he replied, "Lord, I am ready to go with you to prison and to death." (+Ac 2:14-40; 3:12-26; 4:2,8-12)

Ac 4:18 Then they called them in again and commanded them not to speak or teach at all in the name of Jesus. **¹⁹**But Peter and John replied, "Judge for yourselves whether it is right in God's sight to obey you rather than God. **²⁰**For we cannot help speaking about what we have seen and heard." (+Ac 5:29-32)

2Pe 1:12 So I will always remind you of these things, even though you know them and are firmly established in the truth you now have. **¹³**I think it is right to refresh your memory as long as I live in the tent of this body, (+2Pe 1:14)

2Pe 1:15 And I will make every effort to see that after my departure you will always be able to remember these things.

Samaritan woman (Jn 4:28-30,39).

Paul: For the evangelization of the Jews—

Ro 9:1 I speak the truth in Christ—I am not lying, my conscience confirms it in the Holy Spirit— **²**I have great sorrow and unceasing anguish in my heart. **³**For I could wish that I myself were cursed and cut off from Christ for the sake of my brothers, those of my own race,

Ro 10:1 Brothers, my heart's desire and prayer to God for the Israelites is that they may be saved. (+Ro 11:14)

Paul: In his ministry—

Ac 9:20 At once he began to preach in the synagogues that Jesus is the Son of God. (+Ac 9:21-29; 14:1-21)

Ac 14:22 strengthening the disciples and encouraging them to remain true to the faith. "We must go through many hardships to enter the kingdom of God," they said. (+Ac 14:23-28; 15:25)

Ac 15:26 men who have risked their lives for the name of our Lord Jesus Christ.

Ac 17:16 While Paul was waiting for them in Athens, he was greatly distressed to see that the city was full of idols. **¹⁷**So he reasoned in the synagogue with the Jews and the God-fearing Greeks, as well as in the marketplace day by day with those who happened to be there. (+Ac 17:22-31; 19:8-10)

Ac 20:18 When they arrived, he said to them: "You know how I lived the whole time I was with you, from the first day I came into the province of Asia. **¹⁹**I served the Lord with great humility and with tears, although I was severely tested by the plots of the Jews. **²⁰**You know that I have not hesitated to preach anything that would be helpful to you but have taught you publicly and from house to house. **²¹**I have declared to both Jews and Greeks that they must turn to God in repentance and have faith in our Lord Jesus.

²²"And now, compelled by the Spirit, I am going to Jerusalem, not knowing what will happen to me there. **²³**I only know that in every city the Holy Spirit warns me that prison and hardships are facing me. **²⁴**However, I consider my life worth nothing to me, if only I may finish the race and complete the task the Lord Jesus has given me—the task of testifying to the gospel of God's grace.

Ac 20:26 Therefore, I declare to you today that I am innocent of the blood of all men. **²⁷**For I have not hesitated to proclaim to you the whole will of God.

Ac 20:31 So be on your guard! Remember that for three years I never stopped warning each of you night and day with tears.

Ac 20:33 I have not coveted anyone's silver or gold or clothing. **³⁴**You yourselves know that these hands of mine have supplied my own needs and the needs of my companions. (+Ac 21:13; 24:14-24)

Ac 24:25 As Paul discoursed on righteousness, self-control and the judgment to come, Felix was afraid and said, "That's enough for now! You may leave. When I find it convenient, I will send for you." (+Ac 26:1-18)

Ac 26:19 "So then, King Agrippa, I was not disobedient to the vision from heaven. ²⁰First to those in Damascus, then to those in Jerusalem and in all Judea, and to the Gentiles also, I preached that they should repent and turn to God and prove their repentance by their deeds. (+Ac 26:21)

Ac 26:22 But I have had God's help to this very day, and so I stand here and testify to small and great alike. I am saying nothing beyond what the prophets and Moses said would happen— ²³that the Christ would suffer and, as the first to rise from the dead, would proclaim light to his own people and to the Gentiles." (+Ac 26:28)

Ac 26:29 Paul replied, "Short time or long—I pray God that not only you but all who are listening to me today may become what I am, except for these chains."

Ac 28:23 They arranged to meet Paul on a certain day, and came in even larger numbers to the place where he was staying. From morning till evening he explained and declared to them the kingdom of God and tried to convince them about Jesus from the Law of Moses and from the Prophets.

Ac 28:30 For two whole years Paul stayed there in his own rented house and welcomed all who came to see him. ³¹Boldly and without hindrance he preached the kingdom of God and taught about the Lord Jesus Christ.

Ro 1:1 Paul, a servant of Christ Jesus, called to be an apostle and set apart for the gospel of God—

Ro 1:8 First, I thank my God through Jesus Christ for all of you, because your faith is being reported all over the world. ⁹God, whom I serve with my whole heart in preaching the gospel of his Son, is my witness how constantly I remember you

Ro 1:14 I am obligated both to Greeks and non-Greeks, both to the wise and the foolish. ¹⁵That is why I am so eager to preach the gospel also to you who are at Rome. (+Ro 15:15-17)

Ro 15:18 I will not venture to speak of anything except what Christ has accomplished through me in leading the Gentiles to obey God by what I have said and done— ¹⁹by the power of signs and miracles, through the power of the Spirit. So from Jerusalem all the way around to Illyricum, I have fully proclaimed the gospel of Christ. ²⁰It has always been my ambition to preach the gospel where Christ was not known, so that I would not be building on someone else's foundation. ²¹Rather, as it is written:

"Those who were not told about him will see, and those who have not heard will understand." (+Ro 15:22-32; 1Co 4:1-11)

1Co 4:12 We work hard with our own hands. When we are cursed, we bless; when we are persecuted, we endure it; ¹³when we are slandered, we answer kindly. Up to this moment we have become the scum of the earth, the refuse of the world. (+1Co 4:14-21; 9:12-15)

1Co 9:16 Yet when I preach the gospel, I cannot boast, for I am compelled to preach. Woe to me if I do not preach the gospel! (+1Co 9:17)

1Co 9:18 What then is my reward? Just this: that in preaching the gospel I may offer it free of charge, and so not make use of my rights in preaching it. ¹⁹Though I am free and belong to no man, I make myself a slave to everyone, to win as many as possible. (+1Co 9:20-21)

1Co 9:22 To the weak I became weak, to win the weak. I have become all things to all men so that by all possible means I might save some. ²³I do all this for the sake of the gospel, that I may share in its blessings. (+1Co 9:24-26)

1Co 9:27 No, I beat my body and make it my slave so that after I have preached to others, I myself will not be disqualified for the prize.

2Co 1:12 Now this is our boast: Our conscience testifies that we have conducted ourselves in the world, and especially in our relations with you, in the holiness and sincerity that are from God. We have done so not according to worldly wisdom but according to God's grace. (+2Co 1:17-19)

2Co 5:9 So we make it our goal to please him, whether we are at home in the body or away from it.

2Co 5:11 Since, then, we know what it is to fear the Lord, we try to persuade men. What we are is plain to God, and I hope it is also plain to your conscience.

2Co 5:13 If we are out of our mind, it is for the sake of God; if we are in our right mind, it is for you. ¹⁴For Christ's love compels us, because we are convinced that one died for all, and therefore all died.

2Co 5:20 We are therefore Christ's ambassadors, as though God were making his appeal through us. We implore you on Christ's behalf: Be reconciled to God.

2Co 6:3 We put no stumbling block in anyone's path, so that our ministry will not be discredited. ⁴Rather, as servants of God we commend ourselves in every way: in great endurance; in troubles, hardships and distresses; ⁵in beatings, imprisonments and riots; in hard work, sleepless nights and hunger; ⁶in purity, understanding, patience and kindness; in the Holy Spirit and in sincere love; ⁷in truthful speech and in the power of God; with weapons of righteousness in the right hand and in the left; (+2Co 6:8-10)

2Co 6:11 We have spoken freely to you, Corinthians, and opened wide our hearts to you. (+2Co 11:16-21)

2Co 11:22 Are they Hebrews? So am I. Are they Israelites? So am I. Are they Abraham's descendants? So am I. ²³Are they servants of Christ? (I am out of my mind to talk like this.) I am more. I have worked much harder, been in prison more frequently, been flogged more severely, and been exposed to death again and again. ²⁴Five times I received from the Jews the forty lashes minus one. ²⁵Three times I was beaten with rods, once I was stoned, three times I was shipwrecked, I spent a night and a day in the open sea, ²⁶I have been constantly on the move. I have been in danger from rivers, in danger from bandits, in danger from my own countrymen, in danger from Gentiles; in danger in the city, in danger in the country, in danger at sea; and in danger from false brothers. ²⁷I have labored and toiled and have often gone without sleep; I have known hunger and thirst and have often gone without food; I have been cold and naked. ²⁸Besides everything else, I face daily the pressure of my concern for all the churches. ²⁹Who is weak, and I do not feel weak? Who is led into sin, and I do not inwardly burn?

³⁰If I must boast, I will boast of the things that show my weakness. ³¹The God and Father of the Lord Jesus, who is to be praised forever, knows that I am not lying. ³²In Damascus the governor under King Aretas had the city of the Damascenes guarded in order to arrest me. ³³But I was lowered in a basket from a window in the wall and slipped through his hands. (+2Co 12:10-19)

2Co 12:20 For I am afraid that when I come I may not find you as I want you to be, and you may not find me as you want me to be. I fear that there may be quarreling, jealousy, outbursts of anger, factions, slander, gossip, arrogance and disorder. [21]I am afraid that when I come again my God will humble me before you, and I will be grieved over many who have sinned earlier and have not repented of the impurity, sexual sin and debauchery in which they have indulged.

Gal 1:15 But when God, who set me apart from birth and called me by his grace, was pleased [16]to reveal his Son in me so that I might preach him among the Gentiles, I did not consult any man,

Gal 2:2 I went in response to a revelation and set before them the gospel that I preach among the Gentiles. But I did this privately to those who seemed to be leaders, for fear that I was running or had run my race in vain.

Gal 4:19 My dear children, for whom I am again in the pains of childbirth until Christ is formed in you,

Eph 6:20 for which I am an ambassador in chains. Pray that I may declare it fearlessly, as I should.

Php 1:18 But what does it matter? The important thing is that in every way, whether from false motives or true, Christ is preached. And because of this I rejoice. Yes, and I will continue to rejoice,

Php 1:20 I eagerly expect and hope that I will in no way be ashamed, but will have sufficient courage so that now as always Christ will be exalted in my body, whether by life or by death.

Php 1:24 but it is more necessary for you that I remain in the body. [25]Convinced of this, I know that I will remain, and I will continue with all of you for your progress and joy in the faith,

Php 1:27 Whatever happens, conduct yourselves in a manner worthy of the gospel of Christ. Then, whether I come and see you or only hear about you in my absence, I will know that you stand firm in one spirit, contending as one man for the faith of the gospel (+Php 2:16-17)

Php 3:4 though I myself have reasons for such confidence.

If anyone else thinks he has reasons to put confidence in the flesh, I have more: [5]circumcised on the eighth day, of the people of Israel, of the tribe of Benjamin, a Hebrew of Hebrews; in regard to the law, a Pharisee; [6]as for zeal, persecuting the church; as for legalistic righteousness, faultless.

[7]But whatever was to my profit I now consider loss for the sake of Christ. [8]What is more, I consider everything a loss compared to the surpassing greatness of knowing Christ Jesus my Lord, for whose sake I have lost all things. I consider them rubbish, that I may gain Christ [9]and be found in him, not having a righteousness of my own that comes from the law, but that which is through faith in Christ—the righteousness that comes from God and is by faith. [10]I want to know Christ and the power of his resurrection and the fellowship of sharing in his sufferings, becoming like him in his death, [11]and so, somehow, to attain to the resurrection from the dead.

[12]Not that I have already obtained all this, or have already been made perfect, but I press on to take hold of that for which Christ Jesus took hold of me. [13]Brothers, I do not consider myself yet to have taken hold of it. But one thing I do: Forgetting what is behind and straining toward what is ahead, [14]I press on toward the goal to win the prize for which God has called me heavenward in Christ Jesus.

[15]All of us who are mature should take such a view of things. And if on some point you think differently, that too God will make clear to you. [16]Only let us live up to what we have already attained.

Col 1:28 We proclaim him, admonishing and teaching everyone with all wisdom, so that we may present everyone perfect in Christ. [29]To this end I labor, struggling with all his energy, which so powerfully works in me.

Col 2:1 I want you to know how much I am struggling for you and for those at Laodicea, and for all who have not met me personally. (+Col 2:5)

1Th 1:5 because our gospel came to you not simply with words, but also with power, with the Holy Spirit and with deep conviction. You know how we lived among you for your sake. [6]You became imitators of us and of the Lord; in spite of severe suffering, you welcomed the message with the joy given by the Holy Spirit.

1Th 2:2 We had previously suffered and been insulted in Philippi, as you know, but with the help of our God we dared to tell you his gospel in spite of strong opposition. [3]For the appeal we make does not spring from error or impure motives, nor are we trying to trick you. [4]On the contrary, we speak as men approved by God to be entrusted with the gospel. We are not trying to please men but God, who tests our hearts. [5]You know we never used flattery, nor did we put on a mask to cover up greed—God is our witness. [6]We were not looking for praise from men, not from you or anyone else.

As apostles of Christ we could have been a burden to you,

1Th 2:8 We loved you so much that we were delighted to share with you not only the gospel of God but our lives as well, because you had become so dear to us. [9]Surely you remember, brothers, our toil and hardship; we worked night and day in order not to be a burden to anyone while we preached the gospel of God to you.

[10]You are witnesses, and so is God, of how holy, righteous and blameless we were among you who believed. [11]For you know that we dealt with each of you as a father deals with his own children,

2Th 3:7 For you yourselves know how you ought to follow our example. We were not idle when we were with you, [8]nor did we eat anyone's food without paying for it. On the contrary, we worked night and day, laboring and toiling so that we would not be a burden to any of you. [9]We did this, not because we do not have the right to such help, but in order to make ourselves a model for you to follow. (+2Ti 1:3,7,11-13)

Paul: In his piety (1Co 4:12; 10:33; 15:31; 2Co 4:8-12)—

2Co 4:13 It is written: "I believed; therefore I have spoken." With that same spirit of faith we also believe and therefore speak, (+2Co 4:14-18; 11:22-33; 12:10; Php 3:4-16; 4:11-12,17)

2Ti 3:10 You, however, know all about my teaching, my way of life, my purpose, faith, patience, love, endurance, [11]persecutions, sufferings—what kinds of things happened to me in Antioch, Iconium and Lystra, the persecutions I endured. Yet the Lord rescued me from all of them.

Paul: In providing self-support (Ac 20:33-34; 1Co 4:12; 2Co 11:7-12; 2Th 3:7-9)

Paul: In suffering for Christ (Ac 21:13; 2Co 6:4-5,8-10; 11:22-33)—

2Co 12:10 That is why, for Christ's sake, I delight in weaknesses, in insults, in hardships, in persecutions, in difficulties. For when I am weak, then I am strong.

2Co 12:14 Now I am ready to visit you for the third time, and I will not be a burden to you, because what I want is not your possessions but you. After all, children should not have to save up for their parents, but parents for their children. [15]So I will very gladly spend for you everything I have and expend myself as well. If I love you more, will you love me less?

2Co 12:21 I am afraid that when I come again my God will humble me before you, and I will be grieved over many who have sinned earlier and have not repented of the impurity, sexual sin and debauchery in which they have indulged. (+2Ti 2:9-10; 3:10-11)

Paul and Barnabas (Ac 14:14-15).

Timothy—

Php 2:22 But you know that Timothy has proved himself, because as a son with his father he has served with me in the work of the gospel.

Phoebe (Ro 16:1-2).

Epaphroditus—

Php 2:26 For he longs for all of you and is distressed because you heard he was ill.

Php 2:30 because he almost died for the work of Christ, risking his life to make up for the help you could not give me.

Corinthians—

1Co 14:12 So it is with you. Since you are eager to have spiritual gifts, try to excel in gifts that build up the church.

2Co 7:11 See what this godly sorrow has produced in you: what earnestness, what eagerness to clear yourselves, what indignation, what alarm, what longing, what concern, what readiness to see justice done. At every point you have proved yourselves to be innocent in this matter.

2Co 9:2 For I know your eagerness to help, and I have been boasting about it to the Macedonians, telling them that since last year you in Achaia were ready to give; and your enthusiasm has stirred most of them to action.

Thessalonians—

1Th 1:2 We always thank God for all of you, mentioning you in our prayers. ³We continually remember before our God and Father your work produced by faith, your labor prompted by love, and your endurance inspired by hope in our Lord Jesus Christ.

⁴For we know, brothers loved by God, that he has chosen you, ⁵because our gospel came to you not simply with words, but also with power, with the Holy Spirit and with deep conviction. You know how we lived among you for your sake. ⁶You became imitators of us and of the Lord; in spite of severe suffering, you welcomed the message with the joy given by the Holy Spirit. ⁷And so you became a model to all the believers in Macedonia and Achaia. ⁸The Lord's message rang out from you not only in Macedonia and Achaia—your faith in God has become known everywhere. Therefore we do not need to say anything about it,

Ephesians (Rev 2:2-3,6).

Christian Jews—

Heb 10:34 You sympathized with those in prison and joyfully accepted the confiscation of your property, because you knew that you yourselves had better and lasting possessions.

John (Ac 4:8-12)—

Ac 4:13 When they saw the courage of Peter and John and realized that they were unschooled, ordinary men, they were astonished and they took note that these men had been with Jesus. (+Ac 4:18-20)

3Jn 4 I have no greater joy than to hear that my children are walking in the truth.

Rev 5:4 I wept and wept because no one was found who was worthy to open the scroll or look inside.

In Punishing the Wicked:

Moses and Levites (Ex 32:20,26-29). Phinehas (Nu 25:11-13; Ps 106:30-31). Israelites (Jos 22:11-20; Jdg 20). Samuel (1Sa 15:33). David (2Sa 1:14; 4:9-12). Elijah (1Ki 18:40). Jehu (2Ki 10:15-28). Jehoiada (2Ki 11:18). Josiah (2Ki 23:20).

In Reproving Iniquity: *See Reproof, Faithfulness in.*

ZEALOT [*2421, 2831*]. Member of Jewish patriotic party started to resist Roman rule over Israel; violent; fanatical.

ZEALOT, SIMON THE [*2421, 2831*]. An apostle (Mt 10:4; Mk 3:18; Lk 6:15; Ac 1:13), was known either for religious zeal or for membership in the party of the Zealots. *See Simon, 2; Zealot.*

ZEBADIAH [2277, 2278] (*Yahweh bestows*).
1. Benjamite (1Ch 8:15).
2. Another Benjamite (1Ch 8:17).
3. Ambidextrous Benjamite soldier of David (1Ch 12:1-2,7).
4. Korahite gatekeeper (1Ch 26:2).
5. Son of Asahel (1Ch 27:7).
6. Levite sent by Jehoshaphat to teach law to residents of Judah (2Ch 17:8).
7. Son of Ishmael; head of Jehoshaphat's affairs (2Ch 19:11).
8. Son of Michael; returned with Ezra (Ezr 8:8).
9. Son of Immer; priest who divorced foreign wife (Ezr 10:20).

ZEBAH [2286] (*sacrifice*). King of Midian defeated and slain by Gideon (Jdg 8:10,12,18,21; Ps 83:11).

ZEBAIM (*gazelles*). Native dwelling place of "sons of Pokereth-Hazzebaim" who returned with Zerubbabel (Ezr 2:57; Ne 7:59). Perhaps the same as Zeboim.
See Zeboiim, Zeboim.

ZEBEDEE [*2411*] (*Yahweh bestows*).
NIV+ ZEBEDEE'S
Father of James and John (Mt 4:21; 20:20; 27:56; Mk 1:20).

ZEBIDAH [2288] (*given*). Wife of Josiah, king of Judah (2Ki 23:36).

ZEBINA [2289] (*one bought, purchased*). Son of Nebo (Ezr 10:43).

ZEBOIIM, ZEBOIM [7375, 7391] (*hyenas*).
1. Called Zeboiim: One of the cities in the valley of Siddim (Ge 10:19; 14:2,8; Dt 29:23; Hos 11:8).
2. Called Zeboim: A city and valley in Benjamin (1Sa 13:18; Ne 11:34).

ZEBUDAH *See Zebidah.*

ZEBUL [2291] (*elevation, height, lofty [temple]*). An officer of Abimelech (Jdg 9:28-41).

ZEBULONITES *See Zebulun.*

ZEBULUN, ZEBULUNITE [1201+2282, 2282, 2283, 2404] (*honor* Ge. 30:20 ISBE).
1. Son of Jacob and Leah (Ge 30:20; 35:23; 46:14; 49:13; Ex 1:3; 1Ch 2:1). Descendants of (Ge 46:14; Nu 26:26-27).
2. Tribe of. Place of, in march and camp (Nu 2:3,7; 10:14,16). Territory awarded to (Ge 49:13; Jos 19:10-16;

Mt 4:13). Aboriginal inhabitants of the territory of, not expelled (Jdg 1:30). Levitical cities of (Jos 21:34-35; 1Ch 6:77). Moses' benediction upon (Dt 33:18-19).

Loyalty of, in resisting the enemies of Israel: With Barak against Sisera (Jdg 4:6,10; 5:14,18), with Gideon against the Midianites (Jdg 6:35), with David when made king over Israel (1Ch 12:33,38-40). Joins with Hezekiah in renewing the Passover (2Ch 30:11,18). Conquest of, by Tiglath-Pileser; carried to Assyria into captivity (2Ki 15:29; Isa 9:1). Jesus lived in the land of (Mt 4:15). Twelve thousand sealed (Rev 7:8).

See Israel.

ZECHARIAH [2357, 2358, 10230, *2408*] (*Yahweh remembers*).

NIV+ZECHARIAH'S

1. Son of Jeroboam II, and last of the house of Jehu, whose reign lasted six months (2Ki 10:30; 14:29; 15:8-12).

2. Reubenite chief (1Ch 5:7).

3. Korahite, son of Meshelemiah (1Ch 9:21; 26:2,14).

4. Benjamite (1Ch 9:37).

5. Levite; musician (1Ch 15:20; 16:5).

6. Priest; trumpeter (1Ch 15:24).

7. Levite (1Ch 24:25).

8. Merarite Levite (1Ch 26:11).

9. Manassite chief; father of Iddo (1Ch 27:21).

10. Prince who taught in cities of Judah (2Ch 17:7).

11. Father of prophet Jahaziel (2Ch 20:14).

12. Son of Jehoshaphat; killed by Jehoram (2Ch 21:2-4).

13. Son of Jehoiada, the high priest; stoned (2Ch 24:20-22).

14. Prophet in reign of Uzziah (2Ch 26:5).

15. Grandfather of Hezekiah and father of Abijah, wife of Ahaz (2Ki 18:2; 2Ch 29:1).

16. Levite; son of Asaph (2Ch 29:13).

17. Kohathite who assisted in repair of temple in days of Josiah (2Ch 34:12).

18. Temple ruler (2Ch 35:8).

19. Man who returned with Ezra (Ezr 8:3).

20. Another man who returned with Ezra (Ezr 8:11).

21. Adviser of Ezra (Ne 8:4; Ezr 8:15-16).

22. Man who divorced foreign wife (Ezr 10:26).

23. Judahite (Ne 11:4).

24. Another Judahite (Ne 11:5).

25. Son of Pashhur; aided rebuilding of walls (Ne 11:12).

26. Son of Iddo; priest (Ne 12:16).

27. Priest; son of Jonathan; trumpeter (Ne 12:35,41).

28. Son of Jeberekiah (Isa 8:2).

29. Prophet; son of Berekiah and grandson of Iddo (Zec 1:1), returned with Zerubbabel; contemporary with Haggai.

30. Father of John the Baptist (Lk 1:5), righteous priest; angel announced to him he would have a son (Lk 1:5-80).

31. Son of Berekiah; slain between altar and temple (Mt 23:35; Lk 11:51).

ZECHARIAH, BOOK OF

Author: Zechariah son of Berekiah

Dates (correlated with Haggai and Ezra):

1. Haggai's first message (Hag 1:1-11; Ezr 5:1): Aug. 29, 520 B.C.

2. Resumption of the building of the temple (Hag 1:12-15; Ezr 5:2): Sept. 21, 520

3. Haggai's second message (Hag 2:1-9): Oct. 17, 520

4. Beginning of Zechariah's preaching (1:1-6): Oct./Nov., 520

5. Haggai's third message (Hag 2:10-19): Dec. 18, 520

6. Haggai's fourth message (Hag 2:20-23): Dec. 18, 520

7. Tattenai's letter to Darius concerning the rebuilding of the temple (Ezr 5:3-6:14).: 519-518

8. Zechariah's eight night visions (1:7-6:8): Feb 15, 519

9. Joshua crowned (6:9-15): Feb 16 (?), 519

10. Repentance urged, blessings promised (chs. 7-8).: Dec. 7, 518

11. Dedication of the temple (Ezr 6:15-18): Mar. 12, 516

12. Zechariah's final prophecy (chs. 9-14): After 480 (?)

Outline:

Part I (chs. 1-8):

I. Introduction (1:1-6).
  A. The Date and the Author's Name (1:1).
  B. A Call to Repentance (1:2-6).

II. A Series of Eight Night Visions (1:7-6:8).
  A. The Horseman among the Myrtle Trees (1:7-17).
  B. The Four Horns and the Four Craftsmen (1:18-21).
  C. A Man with a Measuring Line (ch. 2).
  D. Clean Garments for the High Priest (ch. 3).
  E. The Gold Lampstand and the Two Olive Trees (ch. 4).
  F. The Flying Scroll (5:1-4).
  G. The Woman in a Basket (5:5-11).
  H. The Four Chariots (6:1-8).

III. The Symbolic Crowning of Joshua the High Priest (6:9-15).

IV. The Problem of Fasting and the Promise of the Future (chs. 7-8).
  A. The Question by the Delegation from Bethel (7:1-3).
  B. The Rebuke by the Lord (7:4-7).
  C. The Command to Repent (7:8-14).
  D. The Restoration of Israel to God's Favor (8:1-17).
  E. Kingdom Joy and Jewish Favor (8:18-23).

Part II (chs. 9-14):

V. Two Prophetic Oracles: The Great Messianic Future and the Full Realization of God's Kingdom (chs. 9-14).
  A. The First Oracle: The Advent and Rejection of the Messiah (chs. 9-11).
    1. The advent of the Messianic King (chs. 9-10).
    2. The rejection of the Messianic Shepherd-King (ch. 11).
  B. The Second Oracle: The Advent and Reception of the Messiah (chs. 12-14).
    1. The deliverance and conversion of Israel (chs. 12-13).
    2. The Messiah's coming and his kingdom (ch. 14).
    See Prophets, The Minor.

ZEDAD [7398] (*a siding*). A place near Hamath (Nu 34:8; Eze 47:15).

ZEDEKIAH [7408, 7409] (*Yahweh is [my] righteousness*).

NIV+ZEDEKIAH'S

1. Made king of Judah by Nebuchadnezzar (2Ki 24:17-18; 1Ch 3:15; 2Ch 36:10; Jer 37:1). Breaks his allegiance to Nebuchadnezzar (2Ki 24:20; 2Ch 36:13; Jer 52:3; Eze 17:12-21). Forms an alliance with the king of Egypt (Eze 17:11-18). The allegiance denounced by Jeremiah (2Ch 36:12; Jer 21; 24:8-10; 27:12-22; 32:3-5; 34; 37:7-10,17; 38:14-28), by Ezekiel (Eze 12:10-16; 17:12-21).

Imprisons Jeremiah on account of his denunciations (Jer 32:2-3; 37:15-21; 38:5-28). Seeks the intercession of Jeremiah with God in his behalf (Jer 21:1-3; 37:3; 28:14-27). Wicked reign of (2Ki 24:19-20; 2Ch 36:12-13; Jer 37:2; 38:5,19,24-26; 52:2). Nebuchadnezzar destroys the city and temple, takes him captive to Babylon, blinds his eyes, slays his sons (2Ki 25:1-10; 2Ch 36:17-20; Jer 1:3; 32:1-2; 39:1-10; 51:59; 52:4-30).

2. Grandson of Jehoiakim (1Ch 3:16).

3. A chief prince of the exiles who returned to Jerusalem (Ne 10:1).

4. A false prophet (Jer 29:21-23).

5. A prince of Judah (Jer 36:12).

6. A false prophet. Prophesies to Ahab victory over the Syrians, instead of defeat (1Ki 22:11; 2Ch 18:10). Smites Micaiah, the true prophet (1Ki 22:24; 2Ch 18:23).

ZEEB [2270] (*wolf*). A prince of Midian (Jdg 7:25; 8:3; Ps 83:11).

ZEKER [2353] (*memorial*). Son of Jeiel (1Ch 8:31), called Zechariah (1Ch 9:37). *See Zechariah, 4.*

ZELA [7521] (*side, slope*). Saul buried in (2Sa 21:14).

ZELAH [7522] (*side, slope*). A city in Benjamin (Jos 18:28).

ZELEK [7530] (*cry aloud* KB). An Ammonite (2Sa 23:37; 1Ch 11:39).

ZELOPHEHAD [7524] (*shadow of dread, terror* [i.e., *protection from dread and terror*]).

NIV+ ZELOPHEHAD'S

Grandson of Gilead. His daughters petition for his inheritance (Nu 27:1-11; 36; Jos 17:3-6; 1Ch 7:15).

ZELOTES *See Zealot.*

ZELZAH [7525]. A city of Benjamin (1Sa 10:2).

ZEMARAIM [7549] (possibly *double peak* KB).

1. Town c. four miles N of Jericho assigned to tribe of Benjamin (Jos 18:22).

2. Mountain in Ephraim upon which King Abijah rebuked King Jeroboam (2Ch 13:4).

ZEMARITES [7548] (*[snow, wool] white; possibly peak, height*). A tribe descended from Canaan (Ge 10:18; 1Ch 1:16).

ZEMIRAH, ZEMIRA [2371] (possibly *song [with instrumental accompaniment]* KB; possibly *Yahweh has helped* IDB). Grandson of Benjamin (1Ch 7:8).

ZENAN [7569] (*place of flocks*). A city of Judah (Jos 15:37).

ZENAS [2424] (*gift of Zeus*). A Christian believer and lawyer (Tit 3:13).

ZEPHANIAH [7622, 7623] (*Yahweh has hidden [to shelter]* or *Yahweh has hidden [as a treasure]*).

1. Ancestor of prophet Samuel (1Ch 6:36).

2. Author of book of Zephaniah (Zep 1:1), of royal descent; principal work done in Josiah's reign; contemporaries were Nahum and Habakkuk.

3. Priest, son of Maaseiah (2Ki 25:18-21; Jer 21:1),

4. Father of a Josiah to whom God sent the prophet Zechariah (Zec 6:10).

ZEPHANIAH, BOOK OF

Author: The prophet Zephaniah

Date: Probably between 640 and 627 B.C.

Outline:

I. Introduction (1:1-3).
   A. Title: The Prophet Identified (1:1).
   B. Prologue: Double Announcement of Total Judgment (1:2-3).
II. The Day of the Lord Coming on Judah and the Nations (1:4-18).
   A. Judgment on the Idolaters in Judah (1:4-9).
   B. Wailing throughout Jerusalem (1:10-13).
   C. The Inescapable Day of the Lord's Wrath (1:14-18).
III. God's Judgment on the Nations (2:1-3:8).
   A. Call to Repentance (2:1-3).
   B. Judgment on Philistia (2:4-7).
   C. Judgment on Moab and Ammon (2:8-11).
   D. Judgment on Cush (2:12).
   E. Judgment on Assyria (2:13-15).
   F. Judgment on Jerusalem (3:1-5).
   G. Jerusalem's Refusal to Repent (3:6-8).
IV. Redemption of the Remnant (3:9-20).
   A. The Nations Purified, the Remnant Restored, Jerusalem Purged (3:9-13).
   B. Rejoicing in the City (3:14-17).
   C. The Nation Restored (3:18-20).
   See Prophets, The Minor.

ZEPHATH [7634] (*watchtower* IDB). A Canaanite city c. twenty-two miles SW of S end of Dead Sea; destroyed by tribes of Judah and Simeon and renamed "Hormah" (Jdg 1:17, ftn).

ZEPHATHAH [7635] (*watchtower* IDB). Valley near Mareshah in W part of Judah (2Ch 14:10).

ZEPHI *See Zepho.*

ZEPHO [7598] (possibly *gaze* BDB ISBE). The grandson of Esau (Ge 36:11,15; 1Ch 1:36). Lesser known brother of Groucho, Chico, and Harpo.

ZEPHON, ZEPHONITE [7602, 7604] (possibly *gaze* BDB; possibly *look out [tower], watch* KB).

NIV+ BAAL ZEPHON

A son of Gad and his descendants (Ge 46:16; Nu 26:15).

ZER [7643]. A city in Naphtali (Jos 19:35).

ZERAH [2438, 2439, 2406] (*dawning, shining,* or *flashing [red or scarlet] light* KB).

NIV+ ZERAHITE, ZERAHITES

1. Son of Reuel (Ge 36:13,17; 1Ch 1:37).

2. Father of Jobab (Ge 36:33; 1Ch 1:44).

3. Son of Judah and Tamar (Ge 38:30; 46:12; Nu 26:20; 1Ch 2:4,6).

4. Son of Simeon (Nu 26:13; 1Ch 4:24).

5. A Gershonite (1Ch 6:21).

6. A Levite (1Ch 6:41).

7. King of Ethiopia, possibly Pharaoh Osorkon I (2Ch 14:9-15).

ZERAHIAH [2440] (*Yahweh shines brightly [red or scarlet]; Yahweh has risen [like the sun]* BDB).

1. Levite in ancestry of Ezra (1Ch 6:6,51).

2. Leader of 200 who returned with Ezra (Ezr 8:4).

ZERAHITE(S) [1201+2438, 2439] (*those who shine*).
NIV+ ZERAH

1. Descendants of Zerah, son of Judah (Nu 26:20; Jos 7:17; 1Ch 27:11,13).

2. Descendants of Zerah, son of Simeon (Nu 26:13).

ZERED, VALLEY OF, BROOK OF [2429] (*valley of [some kind of] plant*). Valley between Moab and Edom; encampment of Israel in wilderness wanderings (Nu 21:12; Dt 2:13-14).

ZEREDAH, ZEREDA [7649]. A city or district on the N of Mount Ephraim, but in Manasseh, and the birthplace of Jeroboam (1Ki 11:26).

ZEREDATHAH *See Zarethan.*

ZERERAH, ZERERATH [7678]. Part of Valley of Jezreel to which Midianites fled from Gideon (Jdg 7:22).

ZERESH [2454] (possibly *[pagan goddess] Kirisha* BDB IDB; *gold* ISBE; *mop-head* KB). Wife of Haman the Agagite (Est 5:10,14; 6:13).

ZERETH [7679] (*splendor*).
NIV+ ZERETH SHAHAR

Son of Ashhur (1Ch 4:7).

ZERETH SHAHAR [7680] (*the glory of dawn*).
NIV+ ZERETH

A city in Reuben (Jos 13:19).

ZERI [7662] (*balsam* IDB). The son of Jeduthun (1Ch 25:3).

ZEROR [7657] (*money bag, pouch,* or possibly *pebbles* KB). Benjamite; great-grandfather of King Saul (1Sa 9:1).

ZERQA *See Jabbok.*

ZERUAH [7654] (*one with skin disease*). Mother of Jeroboam (1Ki 11:26).

ZERUBBABEL [2428, 10239, *2431*] (*offspring [seed] of Babylon* BDB ISBE KB; *scion* i.e., *one grafted into the [plant] of Babylon* IDB).

Directs the rebuilding of the altar and temple after his return from captivity in Babylon (Ezr 3:2-8; 4:2-3; 5:2; Hag 1:12-14). Leads the freed Jews back from Babylon (Ezr 2; Ne 12). Appoints the Levites to inaugurate the rebuilding of the temple (Ezr 3:2-8). Prophecies relating to (Hag 2:2; Zec 4:6-10). In the genealogy of Joseph (Mt 1:12; Lk 3:27).

Possibly the same as Sheshbazzar (Ezr 1:8,11; 5:14,16). *See Sheshbazzar.*

ZERUIAH [7653] (*perfumed resin* IDB KB).
NIV+ ZERUIAH'S

Sister of David (1Ch 2:16). Mother of three of David's great soldiers (1Ch 2:16; 2Sa 2:18; 3:39; 16:9-11; 17:25).

ZETHAM [2457] (possibly *olive tree*). A son of Ladan (1Ch 23:8; 26:22).

ZETHAN [2340] (*olive tree* or *one who deals in olives*). Son of Bilhan (1Ch 7:10).

ZETHAR [2458] (possibly *conqueror* BDB; *slayer* KB). Chamberlain of Xerxes (Est 1:10).

ZEUS [*2416*] (*shine, bright*). Chief of Greek gods, corresponding to Roman Jupiter (Ac 14:12-13).

ZIA [2333] (possibly *trembler* IDB). A Gadite (1Ch 5:13).

ZIBA [7471] (*gazelle*).
NIV+ ZIBA'S

Member of Saul's household staff (2Sa 9:2), appointed by David to work for Mephibosheth; slandered Mephibosheth (2Sa 19:24-30).

ZIBEON [7390] (*hyena*).

1. A Hivite (Ge 36:2,14).

2. Son of Seir (Ge 36:20,24,29; 1Ch 1:38,40).

ZIBIA [7384] (*gazelle*). Early descendant of Benjamin (1Ch 8:9).

ZIBIAH [7385] (*gazelle*). Woman of Beersheba who married King Ahaziah; mother of King Joash (2Ki 12:1; 2Ch 24:1).

ZICRI, ZICHRI [2356] (*Yahweh remembers* IDB).

1. A Levite; son of Izhar, cousin of Aaron and Moses (Ex 6:21).

2. Three Benjamites (1Ch 8:19,23,27).

3. A Levite; ancestor of Mattaniah who returned from captivity (1Ch 9:15), "Zabdi" (Ne 11:17).

4. Two chiefs in the days of David; a descendant of Eliezer (1Ch 26:25), father of Eliezer, a Reubenite (1Ch 27:16).

5. Father of Amasiah; a soldier (2Ch 17:16).

6. Father of Elishaphat (2Ch 23:1).

7. An Ephraimite; killed the son of Ahaz (2Ch 28:7).

8. Father of Joel, the overseer of the Benjamites (Ne 11:9).

9. A descendant of Abijah; a priest (Ne 12:17).

ZIDDIM [7403] (*place on the sides or flanks [of the hill]*). A city in Naphtali (Jos 19:35).

ZIDKIJAH *See Zedekiah, 3.*

ZIDON *See Sidon.*

ZIDONIANS *See Sidon.*

ZIF *See Ziv.*

ZIGGURAT (*pinnacle*). Temple tower of the Babylonians, consisting of a lofty structure in the form of a pyramid, built in successive stages, with staircases on the outside and a shrine at the top. The tower of Babel may have been a ziggurat (Ge 11:1-9). *See Pyramids; Tower.*

ZIHA [7484].

1. Head of family of temple servants that returned with Zerubbabel (Ezr 2:43; Ne 7:46).

2. Leader of the temple servants (Ne 11:21).

ZIKLAG [7637]. A city within the territory allotted to the tribe of Judah (Jos 15:31). Reallotted to the tribe of Simeon (Jos 19:5). David lives at (1Sa 27:5-6; 2Sa 1:1; 1Ch 12:1). Amalekites destroy (1Sa 30). Inhabited by the returned exiles of Judah (Ne 11:28).

ZIKRI *See Zicri, Zichri.*

ZILLAH [7500] (*[God is my] shadow [i.e., protection]*). Wife of Lamech (Ge 4:19,22-23).

ZILLETHAI, ZILTHAI [7531] (*shadow of Yahweh*).

1. A Benjamite (1Ch 8:20).

2. A captain of Manasseh (1Ch 12:20).

ZILPAH [2364] (*short nosed person* KB). Leah's hand-maid (Ge 29:24). Mother of Gad and Asher by Jacob (Ge 30:9-13; 35:26; 37:2; 46:18).

ZIMMAH [2366] (*consider, plan* ISBE).
1. A son of Jahath (1Ch 6:20).
2. Two Gershonites (1Ch 6:42; 2Ch 29:12).

ZIMRAN [2383] (*wild goats, sheep* ISBE). Son of Abraham (Ge 25:2; 1Ch 1:32).

ZIMRI [2381, 2382] (*wild goats, sheep* ISBE; possibly *awe of Yahweh* IDB).
NIV+ ZIMRI'S
1. Prince of Simeon; slain by Phinehas, grandson of Aaron, for committing adultery with Midianite woman (Nu 25:14).
2. The fifth king of N kingdom; murdered King Elah; ruled seven days (c. 885 B.C.); overthrown by Omri (1Ki 16:8-20).
3. Son of Zerah; grandson of Judah (1Ch 2:6). *See Zabdi, 1.*
4. Benjamite; father of Moza (1Ch 8:36; 9:42).
5. Unknown tribe in East (Jer 25:25).

ZIN [7554]. A desert S of Judah (Nu 13:21; 20:1; 27:14; 33:36; 34:3-4; Dt 32:51; Jos 15:1,3).

ZINA (possibly *dry place*). *See Ziza.*

ZION [7482, 4994] (*citadel*).
NIV+ ZION'S
Taken from the Jebusites by David (2Sa 5:6-9; 1Ch 11:5-7). Called thereafter "the city of David" (2Sa 5:7,9; 6:12,16; 1Ki 8:1; 1Ch 11:5,7; 15:1,29; 2Ch 5:2). Ark of the covenant placed in (2Sa 6:12,16; 1Ki 8:1; 1Ch 15:1,29; 2Ch 5:2). Removed from to Solomon's temple on Mount Moriah (1Ki 8:1; 2Ch 5:2, w 2Ch 3:1).
Collectively, the place, the forms, and the assemblies of Israelite worship (2Ki 19:21,31; Ps 9:11; 48:2,11-12; 74:2; 132:13; 137:1; Isa 35:10; 40:9; 49:14; 51:16; 52:1-2,7-8; 60:14; 62:1,11; Jer 31:6; 50:5; La 1:4; Joel 2:1,15; Mt 21:5; Jn 12:15; Ro 9:33; 11:26; 1Pe 2:6). Name of, applied to Jerusalem (Ps 87:2,5; 149:2; SS 3:11; Isa 33:14,20; Jer 9:19; 30:17; Zec 9:13). Called the city of God (Ps 87:2-3; Isa 60:14). Restoration of, promised (Isa 51:3,11,16; 52:1-2,7-8; 59:20; 60:14; Ob 17,21; Zep 3:14,16; Zec 1:14,17; 2:7,10; 8:2-3; 9:9,13). Name of, applied to the city of the redeemed (Heb 12:22; Rev 14:1).
See Church, Place of Worship; Jerusalem.

ZIOR [7486] (*small, insignificant*). Town in S Judah probably near Hebron (Jos 15:54).

ZIPH [2334, 2335].
NIV+ ZIPHITES
1. City in Negev, probably c. four miles S by E from Hebron (Jos 15:55).
2. Wilderness named from above city where David hid (1Sa 23:14-24; 26:1-2).
3. City in W Judah (2Ch 11:8).
4. Calebite family name (1Ch 2:42).
5. Judahite (1Ch 4:16).

ZIPHAH [2336]. A son of Jehallelel (1Ch 4:16).

ZIPHIMS *See Ziphites.*

ZIPHION (possibly *gaze* BDB ISBE; possibly *place of the lookout, tower* KB). *See Zephon.*

ZIPHITES [2337].
NIV+ ZIPH
Inhabitants of Ziph (1Sa 23:19; 26:1-5; Ps 54:T).

ZIPHRON [2412]. A place in the N of Israel (Nu 34:9).

ZIPPOR [7607] (*bird, swallow*). Father of Balak (Nu 22:2,4,10,16; 23:18; Jos 24:9).

ZIPPORAH [7631] (*bird, swallow*). Wife of Moses (Ex 2:16-22). Reproaches Moses (Ex 4:25-26). Separates from Moses, is brought again to him by her father (Ex 18:2-6). May have been a Cushite (Nu 12:1).

ZITHER [10630]. A stringed instrument (Da 3:5,7,10,15). *See Music, Instruments of.*

ZITHRI *See Sithri.*

ZIV [2304] (*bright [as in colorful flowers]*).
Month two in sacred sequence, month eight in civil sequence. Also called Iyyar (not in the Bible). Time of the barley harvest (April-May); the dry season begins. Solomon begins building the temple (1Ki 6:1,37). The later Passover is celebrated (Nu 9:10-11). *See Month, 2.*

ZIZ [7489] (possibly *ascent where the flowers grow*). Cliff near W side of Red Sea on way from En Gedi to Tekoa (2Ch 20:16).

ZIZA [2330, 2331] (a childish duplicated abbreviation, like "mama," as a name of endearment, IDB ISBE).
1. Simeonite; son of Shiphi (1Ch 4:37-41).
2. Son of Rehoboam and brother of Abijah, kings of Judah (2Ch 11:20).
3. A son of Shimei (1Ch 23:10-11, ftn).

ZIZAH *See Ziza, 3.*

ZOAN [7586]. A city in Egypt. Built seven years after Hebron in the land of Canaan (Nu 13:22). Prophecies concerning (Eze 30:14). Wise men from, were counselors of Pharaoh (Isa 19:11,13). Princes of (Isa 30:4).

ZOAR [7593] (*small, insignificant*).
NIV+ BELA
A city of the Moabites near the Jordan (Ge 13:10). Territory of (Dt 34:3; Isa 15:5; Jer 48:34). King of, fought against Kedorlaomer (Ge 14:2,8). Not destroyed with Sodom and Gomorrah (Ge 19:20-23,30).

ZOBAH, ZOBA [7419, 7420].
NIV+ ARAM ZOBAH, HAMATH ZOBAH
Also called Aram Zobah; Hamath Zobah. A kingdom in the N of Israel (1Sa 14:47). Conquest of, by David (2Sa 8:3-8,12; 1Ki 11:23-24; 1Ch 18:2-9). Its inhabitants mercenaries of the Ammonites against David (2Sa 10:6-19; 1Ch 19:6-19). David writes a psalm after the conquest of (Ps 60, title). Invaded by Solomon (2Ch 8:3).
See Aram Maacah; Aram Naharaim.

ZOBEBAH (*one who slithers [like a lizard]* or *one born in a covered wagon*). *See Hazzobebah.*

ZODIAC *See Constellations; Mazzaroth.*

ZOHAR [7468] (*one yellowish red, tawny*).
1. Hittite; father of Ephron from whom Abraham purchased field of Machpelah (Ge 23:8; 25:9).
2. Son of Simeon, second son of Jacob (Ge 46:10; Ex 6:15); "Zerah" (Nu 26:13; 1Ch 4:24).
3. A son of Helah, wife of Ashhur (1Ch 4:7).

ZOHELETH [2325] (*serpent*). Stone or ledge by En Rogel (1Ki 1:9).

ZOHETH [2311] (*proud*). Son of Ishi (1Ch 4:20).

ZOPHAH [7432] (*bellied jug*). Son of Helem (1Ch 7:35-36).

ZOPHAI [7433] (*[dripping, full] honeycomb*). Ancestor of Samuel the prophet (1Ch 6:26), also called Zuph (1Ch 6:35).

ZOPHAR [7436] (possibly *peep, twitter [as a bird]* KB). One of Job's three friends (Job 2:11; 11; 20; 42:7-9).

ZOPHIM [7614] (*watchers, lookouts*).
1. A place on the top of Pisgah (Nu 23:14).
2. A city on Mount Ephraim (1Sa 1:1).

ZORAH [7666]. A city of Dan or Judah (Jos 15:33; 19:41). The city of Samson (Jdg 13:2,24-25; 16:31). Representatives of the tribe of Dan sent from, to spy out the land with a view to its conquest (Jdg 18). Fortified by Rehoboam (2Ch 11:10). Repopulated after the Captivity (Ne 11:29).

ZORATHITES [7670]. Inhabitants of Zorah (1Ch 2:53).

ZOREAH *See Zorah.*

ZORITES [7668]. Judahite family, descendants of Salma (1Ch 2:54).

ZOROBABEL *See Zerubbabel.*

ZUAR [7428] (*little one*). Father of Nethanel (Nu 1:8; 2:5; 7:18,23; 10:15).

ZUPH, ZUPHITE [7431, 7434] (*honeycomb*).
1. Ancestor of the prophet Samuel (1Sa 1:1; 1Ch 6:35), also called Zophai (1Ch 6:26).
2. District in Benjamin, near N border (1Sa 9:5), Location unknown.

ZUR [7448] (*rock*).
NIV+ BETH ZUR
1. King of Midian slain by Israel (Nu 25:15; 31:8).
2. Son of Jeiel (1Ch 8:29, ftn; 8:30).

ZURIEL [7452] (*God [El] is [my] rock*). Son of Abihail, prince of Merarite Levites in wilderness (Nu 3:35).

ZURISHADDAI [7453] (*Shaddai is [my] rock*). Father of Shelumiel (Nu 1:6; 2:12; 7:36,41; 10:19).

ZUZITES, ZUZIM [2309]. (*strong nations* ISBE; *babblers* KB). A people defeated by Kedorlaomer and his allies (Ge 14:5). May be the same as Zamzummites. *See Rephaites; Zamzummites, Zamzummim.*

Index of G/K → Strong's Numbers

HEBREW OLD TESTAMENT

G/K	STRONG	G/K	STRONG	G/K	STRONG	G/K	STRONG	G/K	STRONG	G/K	STRONG
1285	1203	1397	1299	1505	1397	1613	1502	1729	1613	1848	1719
1286	1204	1398	1300	1506	1398	1618	1507	1730	1614	"	1720
1287	1205	1399	1301	1507	1402	1623	1512	1731	1616	1854	1728
1289	1207	1401	1302	1508	1403	1624	1513	1732	1615	1855	1729
1290	1208	1402	1303	1509	1404	1625	1513	1733	1617	1856	1730
1291	1209	1403	1304	1510	1405	1626	1514	1734	1618	1857	1731
1292	1210	1404	1304	1511	1406	1627	1515	1735	1619	1858	1732
1294	1211	1405	1305	1512	1407	1628	1516	1736	1619	1859	1736
1295	1212	1407	1306	1513	1408	1629	2798	1737	1620	1860	1733
1296	1213	1408	1268	"	1409	1630	1517	1738	1621	1861	1734
1298	1214	1410	1308	1514	1410	1631	1518	1739	1622	1862	1737
1299	1215	1411	1313	1516	1412	1632	1520	1741	1624	1865	1739
1301	1216	"	1314	1522	1416	1633	1521	1742	1625	1868	1742
1302	1217	1412	1315	1524	1419	1634	1522	1743	1626	1871	1744
1304	1218	1413	1319	1525	1420	1637	1524	1744	1627	1873	1746
1305	1219	1414	1320	1529	1446	1640	1527	1745	1628+3643	1874	1746
1309	1220	1415	1309	1530	1446	1642	1529	1747	1511	1880	1749
"	1222	1418	1310	1531	1423	1643	1530	1748	1630	1885	1754
1310	1221	1419	1311	1532	1425	1645	1530	1749	1631	1887	1755
1311	1221	1420	1312	1533	1424	1647	1532	1752	1634	1888	1756
1312	1223	1421	1316	1534	1426	1648	1533	1753	1636	1889	1758
1313	1224	1425	1322	1535	1427	1649	1534	1755	1637	1892	1762
1314	1226	1426	1323	1536	1428	1651	1536	1761	1642	1893	1764
1315	1225	1427	1324	1537	1429	1652	1537	1763	1644	1895	1766
1316	1226	1429	1326	1538	1430	1653	1538	1767	1648	1896	1767
1317	1227	1432	1328	1539	1430	1654	1539	1768	1647	1897	1769
1319	1229	1433	1328	1540	1431	1655	1540	1769	1649	1900	1771
1320	1230	1434	1329	1541	1432	1656	1542	1770	1650	1901	1772
1321	1231	1435	1330	1542	1433	1657	1543	1771	1651	1902	1773
1322	1232	1436	1331	1543	1435	1658	1544	1772	1652	1903	1774
1323	1233	1437	1332	1545	1436	1661	1546	1773	1653	1904	1775
1325	1235	1442	1337	1546	1436	1662	1548	1774	1654	1905	1776
1326	1237	1443	1338	1547	1437	1663	1549	1776	1654	1906	1777
1329	1239	1444	1339	1548	1438	1665	1551	1777	1657	1907	1779
1330	1241	1450	1343	1549	1439	1667	1553	1778	1658	1909	1783
1332	1242	1451	1345	1550	1440	1668	1554	1780	1660	1911	1785
1335	1245	1452	1346	1551	1441	1669	1555	1781	1661	1912	1786
1337	1248	1453	1350	1552	1442	1670	1556	1783	1662	1913	1788
1338	1249	1454	1347	1553	1443	1672	1557	1784	1667	1914	1787
1339	1250	1455	1348	1554	1445	1674	1559	1785	1663	1915	1789
1342	1253	1457	1350	1555	1444	1675	1562	1786	1664	1916	1790
1343	1254	1458	1351	"	1447	1676	1563	1787	1665	1917	1792
1349	1256	1460	1353	1556	1448	1678	1565	1788	1666	1918	1793
1351	1258	1462	1354	1557	1449	1680	1568	1790	1669	1919	1793
1352	1259	1463	1356	1558	1450	1681	1567	1794	1709	1920	1794
1353	1261	1464	1356	1562	1453	1682	1569	1795	1673	1922	1796
1354	1260	1465	1360	1565	1456	1687	1573	1796	1674	1923	1817
1355	1260	1466	1357	1570	1459	1690	1577	1799	1756	1924	1800
1356	1262	1467	1361	1573	1463	1691	1576	1800	1677	1925	1801
"	1274	1468	1362	1575	1467	1692	1578	1804	1681	1926	1802
1358	1263	"	1364	1578	1469	1693	1579	1805	1682	1930	1803
1360	1265	1469	1364	1579	1470	1694	1580	1806	1683	1931	1804
1361	1266	1470	1363	1580	1471	1695	1581	1807	1686	1932	1805
1363	1268	1473	1366	1581	1472	1696	1582	1808	1687	1933	1806
1365	1269	1474	1367	1582	1471	1697	1583	1809	1688	1934	1806
1366	1270	1475	1368	1583	1473	1699	1586	1810	1688	1935	1807
1367	1271	1476	1369	1584	1474	1700	1586	1811	1690	1936	1808
1371	1281	1477	1371	1585	1475	1701	1587	1812	1689	1939	1810
1373	1275	1478	1372	1586	1476	1702	1587	1813	1691	1942	1812
1374	1277	1479	1462	1587	1477	1703	1588	1815	1692	1943	1813
1376	1279	1480	1373	1588	1478	1704	1589	1819	1696	1944	1814
1377	1282	1481	1374	1591	1481	1705	1590	1821	1697	1947	1818
1378	1280	1482	1385	1593	1481	1706	1591	1822	1698	1948	1819
1379	1276	1483	1375	1595	1483	1707	1592	1828	1704	1952	1823
1380	1283	1484	1376	1597	1485	1708	1593	1829	1705	1954	1824
1381	1284	1485	1377	1598	1486	"	1594	1831	1706	1957	1826
1382	1285	1486	1378	1599	1487	1709	1595	1833	1708	1960	1827
1383	1287	1488	1380	1600	1488	1713	1598	1834	1709	1962	1829
1385	1288	1489	1381	1601	1489	1715	1599	1836	1710	1968	1835
1386	1290	1490	1382	1603	1492	1717	1601	1837	1712	1969	1835
1387	1292	1494	1387	1604	1493	1718	1602	1839	1713	1970	1842
1388	1293	1495	1388	1605	1494	1720	1603	1840	1714	1972	1837
1389	1294	1496	1389	1606	1495	1722	1606	1841	1715	1973	1838
1390	1294	1497	1390	1607	1496	1723	1607	1842	1716	1974	1839
1391	1295	1498	1393	1608	1497	1724	1608	1843	1717	1975	1840
1392	1296	1500	1391	1610	1498	1725	1609	1845	1735	1978	1844
1393	1296	1504	1396	1611	1500	1728	1612	1847	1719	1979	1845
1396	1298	"	1399	1612	1501						

G/K	STRONG	G/K	STRONG	G/K	STRONG	G/K	STRONG	G/K	STRONG	G/K	STRONG
4087	3707	4193	3803	4318	3908	4457	4021	4578	4136	4707	4250
4088	3708	4194	3803	4319	3814	4458	4022	4579	4137	4713	4256
4089	3708	4195	3804	"	3909	"	4030	4580	4138	4714	4257
4090	3709	4196	3805	4320	3910	4459	4023	4582	4140	4715	4258
4091	3710	4197	3806	4321	3911	4461	4023	4583	3971	4716	4259
4093	3712	4200		4322	3912	4462	4025	4586	4143	4717	4260
4094	3713	4202	3808	4324	3914	4463	4026	4587	4144	4718	4261
4095	3713	4203	3810	4325	3915	4465	4024	4588	4145	4722	4264
4096	3714	4204	3818	4326	3915	4466	4027	"	4328	4723	4265
4097	3715	4205	3819	4328	3885	4467	4028	4589	4146	4724	4266
4098	3716	4206	3811	4329	3887	4470	4031	4591	4147	4725	4267
4099	3715	4207	3812	4330	3918	4474	4033	4592	4148	4727	4269
4103	3720	4210	3815	4331	3919	4476	4035	4593	4147	4728	4270
4104	3721	4211	3816	4332	3919	4477	4037	4594	4149	4731	4273
4105	3722	4212	3817	4333	3919	4478	4038	4595	4150	4732	4274
4107	3723	4213	3820	4334	3920	4479	4039	4598	4153	4734	4276
4108	3724	4216	3833	4336	3922	4482	4043	4600	4156	4737	4279
4109	3724	4219	3822	4337	3923	4487	4044	4603	4159	4739	4281
4110	3724	4220	3823	4340	3925	4488	4046	4604	4161	"	4282
4111	3724	4222	3824	4341	3928	4490	4047	4605	4162	4740	4283
4112	3726	4228	3829	4345	3927	4491	4050	4607	4164	4742	4284
4113	3725	4229	3830	4347	3929	4494	4051	4610	4167	4743	4285
4114	3727	4230	3830	4352	3932	4496	4054	4612	4169	4744	4287
4116	3731	4233	3833	4353	3933	4497	4055	4613	4170	4746	4289
4117	3730	4234	3833	4355	3935	4498	4057	4614	4171	4751	4294
4118	3732	4235	3835	4356	3936	4499	4057	4616	4172	4753	4296
4119	3733	4236	3835	4357	3937	"	4058	4617	4173	4754	4297
4120	3733	4237	3836	4360	3939	"	4059	4618	4174	4757	4299
4121	3733	4238	3837	4361	6030	4500	4060	4619	4175	4759	4301
4123	3734	4239	3837	4362	3886	4501	4060	4621	4175	4760	4302
4126	3739	4242	3839	4365	3940	4503	4063	4622	4176	4761	4303
4131	3742	4243	3841	4366	3941	4506	4066	4623	4177	4762	4304
4132	3743	4244	3842	4370	3887	"	4079	4625	4180	4763	4305
4134	3747	4245	3838	4371	3944	"	4090	4628	4182	4764	4306
4135	3748	4246	3840	4373	3946	4507	4068	4629	4183	4765	4308
4137	3750	"	3843	4374	3947	4509	4071	4632	4186	4766	4307
4138	3751	4247	3828	4375	3948	4512	4074	4633	4187	4767	4309
4139	3752	4248	3844	4376	3949	4513	4075	4634	4188	4771	4314
4140	3753	4249	3845	4377	3950	4516	4081	4635	3467	4772	4311
4142	3754	4250	3846	4378	3951	4518	4080	4637	4191	4773	4312
4144	3755	4252	3847	4379	3952	4519	4082	"	4192	4775	4316
4145	3756	4253	3849	4380	3953	4520	4084	4638	4194	4776	4317
4146	3757	4254	3850	4383	3956	"	4092	4640	4196	4777	4318
4147	3758	4260	3853	4384	3957	4521	4085	4641	4197	4779	4320
4149	3759	4262	3855	4385	3958	4523	4087	4645	4199	4780	4322
4150	3760	4268	3858	4386	3959	4524	4088	4647	4201	4781	4321
4151	3760	4269	3859	4387	3960	4525	4089	4649	4205	4782	4323
4152	3759	4274	3810	4388	3962	4526	4089	4654	2142	4783	4324
4153	3761	4275	3864	4389	8289	4527	4091	4655	4208	4784	4325
"	3762	4276	3865	4393	3965	4529	4093	4657	4207	4785	4326
4154	3763	"	3866	4394	3966	4530	4129	4659	4209	4787	3243
4156	3766	4278	3867	4401	3974	4531	4130	4660	4210	4789	4158
4157	3767	4279	3868	4402	3975	4537	4100	4661	4211	4790	4330
4158	3768	4280	3869	4404	3976	4538	4102	4662	4212	4791	4331
4159	3769	4281	3870	4407	3978	4539	4103	4665	4214	4792	4332
4161	3771	4284	3872	4408	3979	4540	4104	4666	4216	4793	4334
4162	3772	4287	3875	4409	3980	4541	4105	4667	4217	4794	4335
4164	3773	4288	3876	4415	3988	4542	4106	4669	4218	4795	4338
4165	3774	4289	3877	4419	3990	4544	4108	4670	4219	4796	4337
4166	3775	4290	3878	4420	3991	"	4109	4671	4220	4797	4339
4167	3776	4291	3878	4422	3993	4546	4111	4672	4221	4798	4340
4168	3777	"	3881	4423	3994	4547	4112	4684	4230	4800	4343
4169	3778	4292	3880	4427	3996	4551	4115	4686	4232	4801	4344
4172	3781	4293	3882	"	3997	4554	4116	4687	4233	4802	4346
4173	3782	4294	3883	4428	3998	4558	4119	4688	4234	4803	4345
4175	3784	4296	3885	4429	3999	4559	4120	4689	4235	4804	4347
4176	3785	4297	3888	4432	4002	4560	4121	4690	4236	4805	4348
4177	3786	4299	3891	4436	4005	4561	4122	4692	4238	4806	4349
4180	3789	4305	3895	4437	4006	4565	4124	4694	4240	4807	4350
4181	3791	4306	3896	4438	4007	4566	4124	4695	4241	"	4369
4182	3793	4309	3898	4439	4008	4567	4125	4698	4243	4809	4352
4183	3794	4310	3898	4440	4009	4570	4127	4700	4245	4810	4353
4184	3795	4312	3899	4445	4011	4572	4131	4701	4245	4811	4354
4185	3796	4313	3902	4446	4012	4573	4132	4702	4244	4813	4356
4186	3798	4314	3903	4448	4013	4574	4133	4703	4246	4820	4363
4188	3800	4315	3905	4449	4014	4575	4134	4705	4248	4821	4364
4189	3801	4316	3906	4452	4017	4576	4135	4706	4249	4825	4363
4190	3802	4317	3907	4455	4019						

G/K	STRONG	G/K	STRONG	G/K	STRONG	G/K	STRONG	G/K	STRONG	G/K	STRONG
7764	6975	7881	7084	8015	7203	8149	7340	8266	7443	8402	7564
7766	6976	7882	7085	8017	7205	8150	7340	8267	7446	8404	7565
7769	6979	7885	7087	8018	7206	8151	7344	8270	7448	8405	7566
7771	6982	7886	7088	8020	7208	8152	7345	8271	7449	8407	7568
7773	6984	7887	7090	8023	7209	8153	7345	8273	7451	8409	7570
7776	6986	7889	7091	8025	7211	8154	7346	8275	7452	8410	7571
"	6987	7892	7094	8028	7214	8156	7348	8276	7453	8413	7574
7777	6988	7894	7096	8029	7215	8158	7350	8278	7455	8414	7575
7778	6989	7895	7097	8030	7216	8160	7347	8279	7456	8421	7613
7781	6994	7902	7100	8031	7218	8161	7353	8280	7457	8422	7638
7782	6995	7903	7101	"	7226	8162	7354	"	7458	"	7639
7783	6996	7904	7102	8032	7219	8163	7355	8282	7459	8423	7643
7785	6996	7905	7103	8033	7220	8164	7360	8286	7473	8424	7643
7787	6999	7907	7105	8037	7223	8165	7357	8287	7462	8425	7646
7789	7002	7908	7105	8040	7225	8167	7358	8288	7465	8432	7663
7790	7003	7911	7107	8041	7227	8168	7360	8291	7463	8435	7682
7792	7004	7912	7110	8042	7227	8171	7356	8293	7466	8437	7687
7793	7005	7917	7114	8043	7228	8175	7364	8294	7467	8440	7702
7794	6958	7918	7114	8044	7230	8177	7367	8298	7472	8441	7704
"	7006	7919	7115	8047	7233	8178	7368	8304	7479	8442	7704
7798	7008	7924	7121	8049	7235	8185	7374	8305	7480	8443	7708
7801	6969	7926	7124	8051	7237	8187	7376	8306	7481	8445	2089
7803	7014	7927	6981	8052	7239	8189	7378	8308	7482	"	7716
7804	7014	7930	7128	8053	7241	8190	7379	8309	7483	8446	7717
7805	7014	7933	7133	8054	7242	8191	7379	8311	7484	8448	7720
7806	7015	7935	7134	8055	7243	8192	7380	8313	7485	8452	7742
7807	7016	7936	7136	8056	7245	8193	7306	8314	7486	8455	7753
7808	7017	7938	7135	8058	7247	8194	7381	8316	7488	8458	7755
7809	7018	7940	7138	8064	7254	8195	7383	8317	7489	8459	7755
7810	6974	7942	7139	8067	7256	8196	7384	8319	7491	8460	7756
7811	7019	"	7144	8069	7257	8198	7385	8323	7494	8464	7797
7813	7021	7943	7140	8070	7258	8199	7386	8324	7495	8466	7811
7815	7023	7944	7142	8071	7259	8200	7387	8325	7498	8468	7814
7816	7024	7945	7143	8072	7262	8202	7388	8327	7496	8471	7832
7817	7024	7946	7141	8073	7263	8203	7389	8328	7497	8475	7852
7818	7025	7947	7146	8074	7264	8204	7391	8329	7497	8476	7853
7819	7025	7948	7145	8075	7267	8205	7390	8330	7501	8477	7854
7820	7026	7949	7146	8078	7270	8206	7392	8332	7503	8479	7856
7821	7027	7950	7147	"	8637	8207	7393	8334	7498	8481	7865
7822	7028	7953	7151	8079	7272	8208	7395	8335	7510	8484	7872
7823	7029	7954	7152	8081	7273	8209	7394	8336	7505	8487	7875
7824	7031	7955	2696+7152	8082	7274	8210	7396	8338	7506	8488	7878
7829	7034	7957	7153	8083	7275	8211	7394	8340	7508	8489	7880
7830	7036	7959	7153	8084	7276	8212	7397	8341	7509	8490	7879
7831	7037	7960	7155	8085	7278	8213	7398	8347	7516	8491	7881
7833	7039	7961	7157	8087	5372	8214	7399	8348	7517	8492	7760
7834	7040	7962	7158	"	7279	8215	7400	8353	7520	"	7787
7835	7041	7963	7158	8088	7280	8217	7402	8354	7521	8497	7906
7837	7043	7964	7156	8089	7280	8218	7403	8356	7522	8499	7634
7839	7045	7966	7160	8092	7281	8219	7404	8357	7523	8500	7914
7840	7046	7967	7161	8097	7287	8222	7407	8358	7524	8501	7915
7841	7047	7968	7163	8099	7288	8224	7409	8359	7525	8502	7916
7843	7049	7971	7165	8100	7289	8226	7410	8360	7526	"	7917
7844	7049	7973	7167	8101	7290	8228	7411	8363	7529	8505	7919
7845	7050	7975	7169	8102	1721	8229	7413	8364	7530	8507	7922
7847	7051	7978	7173	8103	7291	8230	7414	8366	7532	8509	7937
7850	7054	7980	7174	8104	7292	8231	7415	8367	7531	8510	7939
7851	7055	7985	7177	8105	7293	8232	7416	8368	7533	8511	7940
7852	7056	7986	7178	"	7294	8233	7417	8371	7536	8513	7958
7853	7057	7988	7192	8108	7303	8234	7417	8376	7540	8514	8007
"	7063	7989	7193	8115	7301	8235	7417	8377	7541	8515	8008
7854	7058	7990	7179	8120	7307	8236	7428	8378	7542	8517	8012
7860	7064	7991	7180	8123	7311	8240	7433	8379	7543	8520	8040
7861	7065	7992	7181	8124	7312	8242	7420	8380	7544	"	8041
7862	7067	7996	7185	8126	7316	8243	7422	8384	7548	8521	8041
7863	7068	7997	7186	8131	7321	8244	7423	8385	7549	8522	8042
7864	7069	7999	7189	8132	7323	8245	7423	8386	7550	8523	8055
7865	7069	8000	7189	8133	7326	8248	7425	8387	7551	8524	8056
7866	7070	8001	7190	8134	7327	8251	7320	8388	7552	8525	8057
7867	7071	8002	7191	8137	7332	8254	7431	8389	7552	8528	8072
7868	7072	8003	7194	8138	7333	8255	7432	8390	7552	8529	8071
7869	7073	8004	7195	8139	7331	8256	7434	8391	7553	8532	8079
7870	7074	8005	7196	8142	7336	8257	7437	8392	7554	8533	8130
7872	7076	8008	7198	8143	7337	8258	7435	8394	7556	8534	8135
7873	7077	8011	7200	8145	7341	8262	7440	8395	7557	8536	8149
7875	7079	"	7202	8146	7342	8263	7441	8399	7561	8538	8163
7876	7080	8012	7201	8147	7343	8264	7442	8400	7562	8539	8163
7877	7081	8014	7203	8148	7339	"	7444	8401	7563	8541	8165

G/K	STRONG	G/K	STRONG	G/K	STRONG	G/K	STRONG	G/K	STRONG	G/K	STRONG
8542	8165	8674	7644	8793	7781	8907	7934	9018	8051	9140	8190
8543	8165	8675	7644	8795	7782	8908	7935	9019	8052	9141	8191
8545	8167	8676	7645	8796	7783	8909	7935	9021	8054	9143	8195
8551	8178	8677	7645	8797	7785	8910	7937	9023	8058	9146	8197
8552	8181	8678	7650	8798	7784	8911	7941	9024	8059	9147	8194
8553	8185	8679	7651	8802	7794	8912	7937	9025	8060	9148	8198
8555	8184	8680	7652	8804	7793	8913	7943	9026	8061	9149	8199
8556	8188	8681	7652	8805	7791	8914	7942	9027	8062	9150	8201
8557	8193	8683	7656	8806	8324	8919	7949	9028	8064	9151	8202
8558	5596	8685	7658	8807	7798	8920	7950	9030	8067	9152	8203
8559	8222	8687	7660	8808	7799	8921	7950	9031	8068	9153	8203
8560	8224	8690	7666	8809	7800	8922	7951	9032	8068	9154	8204
8562	5606	8691	7667	8811	7803	8925	7956	9033	8069	9155	8205
8566	8242	8692	7668	8815	7809	8926	7887	9034	8069	9157	8206
8569	8269	8693	7669	8816	7810	8931	7887	9035	8070	9159	8207
8570	8272	8694	7667	8820	7817	8932	7962	9037	8074	9160	8208
8574	8279	8696	7671	8822	7819	8933	7964	9039	8077	9165	8216
8576	8282	8697	7673	"	7820	8934	7965	9041	8078	9166	8217
8577	8283	8701	7676	8825	7822	8935	7967	9042	8080	9170	8220
8578	8286	8702	7677	8827	7825	8936	7966	9043	8081	9171	8223
8580	8294	8703	7678	8828	7826	8937	7968	9048	8085	9172	8221
8584	8297	8704	7683	8829	7827	8938	7971	9050	8087	9175	8225
8585	8299	8705	7684	8830	7828	8939	7973	9051	8088	9176	8227
8587	8301	8706	7686	8831	7829	8940	7975	9052	8091	9177	8227
8588	8304	8707	7681	8833	7831	8941	7974	9053	8089	9180	8229
8589	8304	8709	7691	8835	7833	8942	7975	9054	8090	9181	8230
8590	8303	8710	7692	8836	7834	8944	7977	9055	8092	9184	8234
8594	8311	8711	7693	8837	7835	8946	7978	9056	8093	9185	8235
8595	8312	8712	7694	8838	7836	8947	7979	9057	8094	9186	8236
8596	8313	8713	7696	8839	7838	8949	7982	9058	8095	9191	8240
8597	8314	8714	7697	8840	7837	8955	7991	9059	8096	9193	8245
8598	8315	8717	7700	8843	7841	8956	7991	9060	8097	9196	8247
8599	8316	8720	7703	8844	7842	8957	7991	9061	8098	9197	8248
8602	8291	"	7736	8845	516	8959	7993	9062	8098	9198	8249
8603	8321	8721	7705	"	7843	8960	7994	9063	8099	"	8250
8604	7796	8724	7706	8846	7845	8962	7996	9064	8100	9199	8251
"	8291	8725	7707	8847	7848	8964	7997	9065	8101	9202	8254
8606	7786	8727	7709	8849	7850	8965	7998	9066	8102	9203	8255
"	8323	8731	7714	8850	7851	8966	7999	9068	8104	9204	8256
8607	8342	8732	7718	8851	7857	8969	8003	9069	8105	9207	8259
8611	7945	8733	7719	8852	7858	8970	8004	9070	8106	9209	8261
8612	7579	8736	7723	8853	7860	8973	8006	9071	7763	9210	8262
8619	7585	8737	7724	8855	7861	8976	8010	9074	8110	9213	8266
8620	7586	8740	7725	8856	7862	8977	8013	9075	8110	9214	8267
8621	7587	8742	7619	8858	7866	8978	8073	9076	8111	9217	8285
8622	7588	8744	7727	8862	7877	8979	8015	9077	8112	9219	8270
8624	7589	8745	7728	8864	7882	8980	8016	9078	8113	9220	8273
8626	7592	8746	7729	8865	7883	8981	8017	9079	8114	9221	8274
8627	7594	8747	7731	8866	7884	8982	8018	9080	8114	9222	8275
8629	7596	8748	7732	8868	7885	8983	8018	9083	8116	9224	8281
8630	7597	8749	7733	8870	7887	8984	8019	9084	8117	"	8284
8631	7599	8750	7737	8872	7888	8985	8019	9085	8118	9226	8287
8636	7604	8753	7740	8873	7889	8986	8020	9086	8119	9227	8289
8637	7605	8754	7741	8876	7891	8987	8022	9087	8121	9232	8298
8638	7607	8756	7744	8877	7892	8989	8023	9088	8123	9233	8302
8639	7610	8757	7745	8878	7892	"	8024	9091	8125	9234	8302
8641	7609	8758	7746	8880	7893	8990	8025	9092	8126	9238	8318
8642	7611	8760	7747	8881	7894	8991	8026	9094	8127	9239	8319
8644	7614	8761	7748	8882	7895	8994	8028	9095	8129	9240	8322
8645	7615	8762	7749	8883	7896	8995	8031	9098	8134	9243	8325
8647	7617	8765	7752	8886	7901	8996	8030	9100	8137	9244	8307
8648	7618	8767	7757	8890	7908	8997	8032	9101	8132	9245	8327
8649	7619	8769	7759	8891	7909	9000	8029	9102	8141	9246	8329
8651	7620	8770	7762	8892	7909	9003	7597	9104	8142	9247	8326
8652	7621	8771	7764	8893	7910	9005	8034	9105	8143	"	8328
8654	7622	8772	7765	8894	7911	9006	8035	9106	8144	9249	8333
8655	7623	8773	7766	8895	7913	9007	8037	9114	8152	9250	8334
8657	7626	8774	7767	8897	7921	9008	8038	9120	8159	9253	8336
8658	7627	8775	7768	8898	7923	9009	8039	9124	8169	9254	8336
8660	7628	8778	7772	8899	7925	9010	8043	9125	8169	9256	8339
8661	7629	8781	7770	8900	7926	9011	8044	9126	8170	9259	8344
8662	7630	8783	7774	"	7929	9012	8045	9127	8171	9263	8347
8664	7633	8785	7776	8901	7927	9013	8106	9130	8173	9264	8348
8667	7636	8786	7777	8902	7927	9014	8047	9131	8174	9265	8349
8668	7637	8787	7777	8903	7928	9015	8048	9133	8179	9266	8350
8669	7622	8788	7778	8904	7930	9016	8049	9138	8187	9269	8352
8670	7640	8791	7780	8905	7931	9017	8050	9139	8189		
8672	7641	8792	8197	"	7933						

G/K	STRONG	G/K	STRONG	G/K	STRONG	G/K	STRONG	G/K	STRONG	G/K	STRONG
9271	8356	9389	8473	9498	8585	10030	399	10234	2171	10418	4406
9272	8354	9390	8475	9499	8585	10033	426	10239	2217	10419	4415
9275	8358	9391	8476	9503	8588	10038	506	10245	2269	10420	4416
9276	8360	9392	8477	9505	8590	10039	521	10247	2292	10421	4430
9278	8362	9393	8478	9506	8591	10040	524	10249	2306	10423	4433
9279	8364	9394	8480	9507	5774	10041	540	10254	2358	10424	4437
9285	8369	9395	8480	9509	8593	10054	613	10255	2370	10428	4484
9293	8377	9398	8483	9510	8594	10055	620	10263	2423	10430	4486
9294	8378	9400	8436	9511	8595	10056	629	10264	2429	10435	4577
9298	8382	9401	8485	9512	8596	10057	633	10265	2445	10437	4756
9300	8384	9402	8486	9514	8597	10058	636	10266	2452	10439	4779
9302	8386	9403	8487	9515	8598	10060	670	10267	2493	10441	4873
9304	8387	9404	8489	9516	8599	10063	674	10271	2562	10442	4887
9306	8388	9405	8488	9517	8599	10064	677	10272	2591	10444	4903
9307	8389	9407	8491	9523	8603	10066	711	10273	2597	10446	4953
9308	8390	9408	8492	9525	8605	10068	735	10275	2608	10447	4961
9309	839	9409	8493	9527	8607	10069	738	10279	2635	10448	4978
"	8391	9410	8494	9528	8608	10070	746	10282	2749	10451	5013
9310	8392	9412	8496	9530	8610	10072	755	10284	2783	10452	5017
9311	8393	"	8501	9531	8611	10074	756	10286	2816	10453	5020
9312	8394	9413	8497	9532	8612	10075	772	10296	2906	10454	5023
9314	8396	9418	8504	9533	8613	10077	778	10299	2920	10455	5029
9315	8398	9419	8505	9535	8615	10078	783	10301	2939	10461	5069
9316	8397	9421	8507	9536	8615	10079	787	10302	2942	10468	5103
9317	8422	9425	8512	9537	8616	10081	826	10303	2953	10471	5135
9320	8401	9426	8521	9540	8619	10083	849	10305	2967	10473	5174
9321	8402	9427	8528	9541	8620	10084	852	10309	3007	10480	5245
9322	8403	9431	8515	9542	8621	10086	861	10311	3028	10483	5261
9323	8404	9433	8407	9546	8628	10093	895	10312	3029	10490	5343
9324	8405	9434	8518	9550	8634	10094	896	10313	3046	10492	5376
9325	8407	9436	8520	9552	8636	10103	1005	10315	3061	10495	5403
9328	8425	9437	8522	9553	8638	10105	1113	10316	3062	10496	5407
9329	8410	9438	2048	9554	8639	10107	1093	10317	3118	10504	5457
9330	8412	9439	8525	9555	8640	10108	1096	10318	3136	10507	5481
9331	8413	9440	8526	9556	8641	10109	1113	10322	3221	10515	5609
9332	8414	9441	8527	9558	8643	10111	1124	10327	3330	10516	5613
9333	8415	9442	8519	9560	8645	10112	1147	10331	3367	10517	5622
9334	8417	9443	8529	9561	8646	10114	1156	10332	3390	10518	5632
9335	8416	9447	8535	9562	8646	10117	1236	10333	3393	10523	5649
9337	8419	9448	8537	9563	8647	10119	1251	10334	3410	10524	5665
9338	8420	9449	8539	9567	8649	10120	1247	10335	3479	10525	5673
9339	8380	9450	8538	9571	8654	10122	1289	10336	3443	10526	5675
9340	8423	9451	8541	9572	8655	10123	1291	10338	3488	10529	5714
9342	8424	9452	8542	9573	8656	10125	1321	10347	3549	10533	5776
9343	8426	9453	8543	9574	8656	10126	1325	10348	3551	10534	5784
9344	8427	9454	8544	9575	8657	10129	1358	10350	3567	10535	5796
9346	8430	9455	8545	9576	8659	10133	1411	10352	3604	10536	5824
9350	8433	9457	8547	9577	8658	10137	1519	10353	3606	10537	5831
9351	8434	9458	8548	9578	8659	10139	1490	10354	3635	10538	5839
9352	8435	9459	8549	9581	8662	10140	1505	10362	3702	10539	5843
9354	8437	9460	8550	9583	8663	10142	1528	10367	3734	10540	5870
9355	8438	9462	8552	9585	8664	10143	1535	10368	3737	10541	5894
9356	8439	9463	8553	9586	8664	10145	1547	10370	3744	10546	5943
9357	8438	9464	8554	9591	8668	10149	1611	10372	3764	10548	5946
9358	8440	9465	8555	9592	8669	10150	1635	10373	3779	10550	5957
9359	8441	9466	8556			10151	1655	10375	3792	10551	5962
9360	8442	9467	8556			10155	1678	10376	3797	10556	6015
9365	8446	9469	8558	**ARAMAIC**		10160	1722	10381	3825	10560	6050
9366	8447	9470	8559	**OLD**		10164	1757	10382	3831	10561	6056
"	8448	9471	8559	**TESTAMENT**		10166	1761	10383	3848	10562	6065
9367	8449	9472	8560			10167	1763	10387	3879	10572	6211
9368	8451	9474	8561			10170	1780	10389	3900	10573	6236
"	8452	9475	8562			10180	1836	10390	3904	10585	6392
9369	8453	9478	8565			10181	1841	10391	3916	10586	6399
9370	8454	"	8568	10002		10183	1859	10392	3961	10588	6433
9373	8457	9482	8570	10003	2	10184	1868	10396	3977	10590	6460
9375	8459	9486	8574	10004	4	10186	1882	10398	3984	10591	6523
9376	8461	9487	8575	10006	69	10187	1883	10399	4040	10593	6537
9379	8464	9488	8575	10007	104	10191		10401	4056	10594	6540
9380	8465	9489	8576	10009	144	10198	1922	10402	4061	10595	6543
9381	8466	9490	8577	10010	147	10206	1965	10404	4076	10597	6568
9382	8467	9491	8580	10012	149	10207	1981	"	4077	10599	6590
9383	8468	9492	8580	10017	252	10208	1983	10406	4083	10600	6591
9384	8469	9493	8581	10019	280	10212	2002	10410	4203	10601	6600
9385	8466	9494	8582	10020	307	10228	2122	10411	4223	10611	6676
"	8470	9495	8583	10021	311	10229	2136	10414	4333	10612	6739
9387	8471	9496	8584	10026	324	10230	2148	10415	4336	10614	6755
9388	8472	9497	8583			10232	2166	10417	4398	10615	6841

G/K	STRONG	G/K	STRONG	G/K	STRONG	G/K	STRONG	G/K	STRONG	G/K	STRONG
2263	2065	2432	2217	2591	2367	2716	2486	2905	2645	3117	2833
2264	2066	2433	2218	2593	2369	2718	2488	2906	2646	3118	2834
2266	2068	2435	2220	2596	2372	2720	2489	2907	2647	3119	2835
"	5315	2439	2224	2598	2374	2721	2489	2909	2649	3120	2836
2268	2069	2442	2226	2599	2375	"	2490	2915	2655	3121	2837
2269	2072	2455	2238	2600	2376	2722	2491	2925	2665	3123	2839
2270	2073	2456	2239	2601	2377	2725	5601	2932	2671	3124	2840
2272	2074	2459	2242	2603	2379	2727	2493	2933	2672	3126	2842
2279	2083	2460	2243	2605	2381	2729	2494	2934	2673	3128	2844
2280	2084	2461	2244	2606	2382	2731	2495	2936	2675	3130	2845
2281	2085	2463	2246	2608	2383	2732	2496	2941	2680	3132	2847
2282	2086	2464	2247	2609	2384	2733	2497	2943	2682	3135	2850
2283	2087	2465	2250	2610	2385	2734	2498	2946	2685	3139	2852
2291	2094	2469	2256	2612	2387	2736	2500	2947	2686	3140	2853
2293	2096	2473	2261	2613	2388	2737	2501	2952	2691	3142	2855
2294	2097	2474	2262	2614	2389	2738	2501	2967	2704	3145	2857
2295	2098	2476	2264	2616	2391	2739	2502	2968	2705	3148	2861
2296	2099	2477	2265	2618	2393	2748	2508	2969	2706	3155	2868
2300	2103	2478	2266	2619	2394	2751	2511	2970	2707	3156	2869
2302	2104	2479	2267	2620	2395	2752	2512	2973	2709	3159	2872
2304	2105	2480	2268	2628	2401	2754	2513	2983	2719	3160	2873
2305	2106	2481	2269	2629	2402	2755	2514	2989	2723	3161	2874
2306	2107	2487	2274	2630	2403	2756	2515	2991	2725	3165	2876
2307	2108	2497	2280	2631	2404	2757	2516	3007	2802	3167	2878
2309	2110	2498	2281	2632	2405	2764	2521	3013	2743	3169	2879
2313	2114	2499	2282	2634	2407	2779	2532	3016	2744	3172	2882
2320	2119	2500	2283	2635	2408	2780	2533	3017	2745	3173	2883
2321	2120	2503	2286	2637	2410	2782	2535	3018	2746	3174	2884
2323	2122	2505	2288	2639	2411	2783	2536	3019	2584	3175	2885
2325	2124	2506	2289	2643	2415	2789	2540	3020	2747	3176	2886
2327	2126	2507	2290	2646	2418	2790	2541	3022	2748	3179	2888
2328	2127	2508	2291	2647	2419	2791	2542	3025	2751	3180	2889
2330	2129	2509	2292	2649	2421	2794	2545	3029	2754	3181	2890
2331	2130	2510	2293	2650	2422	2798	2549	3030	2755	3182	2891
2332	2131	2513	2296	2651	2423	2799	2550	3034	2759	3184	2892
2336	2135	2514	2297	2652	2424	2800	2551	3035	2760	3189	2896
2337	2136	2515	2298	2653	2425	2803	2554	3038	2763	3190	2897
2339	2145	2516	2299	2658	2430	2804	2555	3041	2766	3191	2898
2350	2148	2519	2302	2659	2431	2805	2556	3043	2768	3195	2902
2354	2150	2520	2303	2660	2432	2806	2557	3047	2772	3197	2904
2355	2151	2522	2305	2661	2433	2808	2559	3051	2776	3200	2907
2356	2152	2523	2306	2662	2434	2811	2562	3055	5392	3204	2911
2357	2153	2525	2307	2663	2435	2812	2563	3056	2778	3205	2912
2359	2155	2526	2308	2665	2437	2813	2564	3057	2779	3206	2913
2362	2157	2527	2309	2666	2438	2816	2568	3058	2780	3207	2914
2366	2161	2528	2310	2667	2439	2819	2566	3061	2783	3208	2915
2371	2166	2529	2310	2668	2440	"	2570	3063	2785	3209	2916
2373	2168	2530	2311	2669	2441	2820	2571	3064	2786	3210	2917
2374	2169	2531	2312	2673	2445	2822	2573	3066	2787	3211	2918
2376	2171	2534	2314	2674	2446	2823	2574	3067	2788	3212	2919
2381	2176	2536	2316	2675	2447	2825	2575	3069	2790	3213	2920
2386	2180	2537	2317	2677	2449	2828	2578	3070	2791	3214	2921
2387	2181	2538	2318	2678	2450	2830	2580	3077	2792	3215	2922
2388	2182	2541	2321	2679	2451	2831	2581	3078	2797	3222	2929
2394	2187	2542	2322	2680	2452	2833	2582	3079	5531	3223	2930
2395	2188	2543	2323	2681	2453	2837	2586	3080	2798	3228	2933
2398	2190	2545	2325	2682	2454	2838	2587	3081	2799	3229	2934
2399	2191	2546	2326	2683	2455	2842	2591	3086	2803	3231	2936
2400	2192	2550	2330	2684	2456	2843	2590	3087	2804	3232	2937
2404	2194	2552	2331	2685	2457	2844	2592	3088	2805	3233	2938
2405	2195	2553	2332	2687	2458	2846	2594	3090	2807	3234	2939
2406	2196	2554	2333	2689	2460	2848	2596	3091	2808	3237	2942
2408	2197	2555	2334	2691	2462	2853	2600	3092	2809	3245	2948
2411	2199	2558	2337	2692	2463	2856	2602	3093	2810	3246	2949
2414	2201	2563	2342	2693	2464	2857	2603	3095	2812	3247	2950
2415	2202	2567	2346	2694	2465	2858	2604	3096	2813	3248	2951
2416	2203	2568	2347	2697	2469	2859	2605	3097	2814	3249	2952
2418	2206	2569	2348	2699	2471	2860	2606	3098	2815	3250	2953
2419	2205	2570	2349	2702	2474	2875	2617	3099	2816	3251	2954
2420	2206	2572	2350	2703	2475	2876	2618	3101	2818	3254	2956
2421	2207	2573	2351	2704	2466	2878	2620	3102	2819	3255	2957
"	2208	2576	2353	2705	2476	2879	2621	3104	2821	3256	2958
2424	2211	2579	2356	2710	2480	2881	2623	3105	2822	3262	2963
2426	2212	2580	2357	2712	2482	2883	2624	3106	2823	3264	2965
2427	2213	2582	2359	2713	2483	2886	2627	3109	2825	3267	2968
2428	2214	2587	2363	2714	2484	2898	2638	3113	2829	3268	2969
2429	2215	2588	2364	2715	2485	2903	2643	3115	2831	3270	2971
2431	2216	2589	2365			2904	2644	3116	2832	3271	2972

G/K	STRONG	G/K	STRONG	G/K	STRONG	G/K	STRONG	G/K	STRONG	G/K	STRONG
3272	2973	3397	3091	3546	3320	3730	3491	3899	3640	4106	3829
3273	2974	3399	3092	3549	3323	3731	3492	3906	3646	4110	3833
3275	2975	3400	3093	3552	3326	3732	3493	3910	3650	4111	3834
3276	2976	3402	3094	3564	3338	3733	3494	3912	3652	4112	3835
3281	2980	3404	3095	3565	3339	3734	3495	3918	3657	4120	3841
3284	2983	3405	3096	3566	3340	3735	3496	3920		4126	3847
3285	2984	3407	3097	3567	3341	3738	3498	3923	3660	4130	3850
3286	2985	3408	3098	3578	3350	3741	3561	3929	3666	4133	3853
3290	2989	3409	3099	3579	3351	3742	3501	3931	3668	4134	3854
3291	2990	3411	3100	3581	3353	3745	3504	3933	3670	4135	3855
3292	2991	3412	3101	3582	3354	3749	3507	3934	3671	4137	3857
3293	2993	3413	3102	3587	3359	3750	3508	3941	3677	4138	3858
3297	2996	3414	3156	3597	3370	3751	3509	3942	3678	4140	3860
3301	2999	3415	3158	3604	3375	3756	3514	3946	3682	4142	3862
3302	3000	3416	3159	3611	3382	3758	3516	3947	3683	4143	3863
3303	3001	3417	3103	3613	3384	3759	3517	3950	3686	4148	3868
3305	3003	3419	3105	3616	3388	3760	3518	3951	3687	4151	3870
3306	2036	3421	3107	3620	3392	3761	3519	3952	3688	4155	3874
"	2046	3423	3109	3621	3393	3762	3520	3954	3690	4156	3875
"	3004	3424	3110	3622	3394	3763	3521	3955	3691	4157	3876
"	4483	3428	3114	3626	3399	3764	3522	3958	3694	4158	3877
3307	3005	3429	3115	3627	3400	3768	3525	3959	3695	4161	3880
3310	3008	3433	3119	3631	3404	3769	3526	3960	3696	4165	3884
3316	2982	3434	3120	3634	3407	3770	3527	3972	3708	4166	3885
3317	3012	3435	3121	3635	3408	3771	3528	3973	3709	4168	3886
3318	3013	3438	3124	3636	3409	3773	3530	3974	3710	4170	3888
3319	3014	3440	3126	3637	3410	3774	3531	3978	3714	4171	3889
3320	3015	3441	3127	3638	3411	3775	3532	3979	3715	4172	3890
3321	3016	3443	3129	3639	3412	3776	3533	3991	3726	4183	3900
3322	3017	3444	3130	3640	3413	3780	3536	3995	3730	4187	3904
3324	3019	3445	3131	3641	3414	3781	3537	3997	3732	4190	3906
3325	3020	3446	3132	3643	3416	3782	3538	3998	3733	4197	3913
3326	3021	3449	3135	3645	3418	3788	3544	4001	3735	4199	3914
3328	3022	3450	3136	3646	3419	3790	3546	4003	3737	4200	3915
3329	3023	3451	3137	3648	3421	3794	3550	4004	3738	4203	3917
3330	3024	3453	3138	3654	3426	3798	3554	4014	3747	4213	3925
3332	3025	3454	3139	3655	3428	3802	3557	4017	3749	4219	3931
3334	3027	3455	3140	3656	3429	3803	3558	4029	3762	4221	3933
3337	3030	3456	3141	3657	3430	3805	3560	4033	3765	4222	3934
3338	3031	3457	3142	3658	3431	3809	3564	4039	3770	4226	3937
3339	3032	3459	3144	3659	3432	3811	3565	4041	3772	4228	3939
3340	3033	3463	3146	3661	3434	3812	3566	4042	3773	4230	3941
3342	3034	3464	3147	3662	3435	3813	3567	4043	3774	4231	3942
3343	3035	3465	3148	3666	3439	3816	3571	4044	3775	4232	3943
3344	3036	3466	3149	3669	3442	3820	3575	4045	3776	4243	3953
3345	3037	3474	3157	3671	3444	3821	3576	4047	3778	4244	3954
3346	3038	3477	3160	3673	3446	3825	3578	"	5023	4245	3955
3349	3041	3478	3161	3674	3447	3826	3579	"	5025	4246	3956
3350	3042	3479	3162	3675	3448	3827	3580	"	5026	4247	3957
3352	3044	3484	3168	3678	3452	3828	3581	"	5123	4249	3959
3356	3048	3486	3170	3684	3458	3830	3383	"	5124	4252	3962
3357	3049	3494	3178	3685	3458	3831	3584	"	5125	4253	3963
3359	3051	3499	3182	3689	3461	3833	3586	"	5126	4256	3966
3364	3056	3500	3183	3692	3463	3834	3587	"	5127	4257	3967
3365	3057	3501	3184	3693	3464	3836	3588	"	5128	4258	3968
3369	3061	3506	3188	3695	3465	"	5120	"	5129	4259	3969
3371	3065	"	3189	3696	3466	3847	3598	"	5130	4260	3964
3372	3066	3507	3190	3698	3468	3848	3599	4048	3779	4262	3971
3373	3067	3508	3199	3699	3469	3849	3600	4050	3781	4263	3972
3374	3068	3510	3192	3700	3470	3852	3604	4051	3782	4265	3974
3375	3069	3514	3194	3704	3474	3853	3605	4052	3783	4267	3976
3376	3070	3516	3195	3707	3475	3855	3607	4053	3784	4270	3979
3377	3071	3517	3196	3709	3476	3858	3609	4055	3786	4272	3980
3378	3072	3518	3197	3710	3477	3864	3614	4056	3787	4275	3982
3379	3073	3519	3198	3714	3478	3868	3618	4057	3788	4279	3985
3380	3074	3521	3200	3716	3479	3869	3619	4058	3789	4280	3986
3382	3076	3523	3202	3717	3480	3871	3618	4062	3792	4284	3990
3383	3077	3527		3718	3481	3873	3622	4063	3793	4289	3994
3384	3078	3531	3306	3720	3482	3874	3623	4066	3795	4290	3995
3385	3079	3533	3308	3722	3497	3875	3624	4067	3796	4291	3996
3386	3080	3534	3309	3723	3484	3876	3625	4070	3798	4292	3997
3388	3082	3537	3312	3724	3485	3880	3628	4072	3800	4300	4005
3390	3084	3540	3314	3725	3486	3882	3627	4077	3804	4301	4006
3391	3085	3542	3316	3726	3487	3884	3630	4082	3809	4307	4010
3392	3086	3543	3317	3727	3488	3885	3631	4084	3811	4308	4011
3394	3088	3544	3318	3729	3490	3886	3632	4086	3813	4309	4012
3395	3089	3545	3319			3891	3636	4087	3814	4311	4014
3396	3090					3898	570	4103	3828	4314	4016

G/K	STRONG	G/K	STRONG	G/K	STRONG	G/K	STRONG	G/K	STRONG	G/K	STRONG
4318	4020	4511	4196	4768	4425	4908	4547	5044	4667	5197	4815
4319	4021	4513	4198	4772	4429	4910	4549	5046	4669	5198	4816
4330	4030	4517	4201	4773	4430	4912	4551	5047	4670	5202	4820
4340	4039	4518	4202	4775	4432	4913	4552	5048	4672	5205	4823
4343	4042	4519	4203	4777	4434	4914	4553	5049	4673	5206	4824
4344	4043	4520	4204	4778	4435	4915	4554	5051	4676	5207	4825
4355	4052	4521	4205	4780	4436	4917	4556	5052	4677	5208	4826
4361	4058	4525	4209	4783	4439	4918	4557	5053	4678	5209	4827
4362	4059	4526	4210	4784	4440	4919	4558	5054	4679	5210	4828
4364	4061	4527	4211	4785	4441	4920	4559	5055	4680	5217	4834
4369	4066	4530	4213	4787	4443	4921	4560	5056	4681	5218	4835
4372	4069	4532	4215	4789	4445	4922	4561	5058	4683	5228	4844
4373	4070	4539	4221	4790	4446	4924	4563	5059	4684	5232	4847
4374	4071	4540	4222	4792	4448	4925	4564	5061	4686	5236	4850
4376	4073	4541	4223	4795		4926	4565	5062	4687	5237	4851
4377	4074	4545	4227	4796	4451	4928	4567	5063	4688	5239	4851
4379	4076	4546	4228	4798	4454	4930	4569	5064	4689	5251	4863
4380	4077	4547	4229	4801	4457	4931	4570	5065	4690	5252	4864
4385	4082	4550	4232	4805	4460	4932	4572	5066	4691	5257	4869
4388	4083	4552	4234	4806	4461	4934	4574	5068	4693	5263	4873
4389	4084	4556	4238	4808	4462	4936	4576	5069	4694	5269	4878
4394	4088	4558	4239	4811	4464	4939	4578	5072	4697	5271	4880
4395	4089	4559	4240	4814	4466	4941	4580	5073	4698	5278	4886
4397	4091	4563	4243	4815	4467	4942	4581	5074	4699	5281	4889
4399	4092	4564	4244	4819	4469	4943	4582	5075	4700	5284	4892
4402	4094	4565	4245	4820	4470	4946	4584	5080	4705	5287	4893
4403	4095	4569	4249	4821	4471	4947	4585	"	4706	5300	4903
4406	4098	4571	4251	4822	4472	4948	4586	"	4707	5301	4904
4407	4099	4589	4267	4823	4473	4950	4588	5081	4708	5303	4906
4408	4099	4590	4268	4827	4476	4952	4562	"	4709	5309	4912
4409	4100	4591	4269	4830	4478	4953	4589	5082	4710	5313	4916
4411	4102	4592	4270	4831	4479	4954	4590	5083	4711	5317	4920
4412	4103	4595	4273	4832	4480	4956	4592	5084	4712	5321	4922
4414	4105	4603	4283	4836	4484	4958	4594	5086	4955	5322	4923
4415	4106	4606	4286	4838	4486	4962	4597	5087	4714	5323	4894
4418	4108	4613	4291	4839	4487	4963	4598	5088	4715	5327	4927
4423	4113	4614	4292	4840	4488	4969	4603	5089	4716	5341	4937
4431	4123	4625	4302	4842	4489	4970	4604	5090	4717	5345	4941
4432	4124	"	4277	4844	4491	4972	4605	5091	4718	5347	4942
4434	4126	"	4280	4845	4492	4973	4606	5092	4719	5349	4944
4435	4127	4633	4309	4850	4497	4975	4608	5093	4720	5352	4946
4436	4128	4636	4311	4851	4498	4976	4609	5094	4721	5353	4947
4439	4132	4637	4312	4852	4499	4977	4610	5096	4723	5354	4948
4443	4136	4640	4315	4855	4501	4978	4611	5098	4725	5355	4949
4449	4142	4657	4327	4857	4502	4981	4613	5107	4734	5358	4950
4450	4143	4659	4328	4858	4503	4982	4614	5108	4736	5365	4957
4454	4145	4666	4335	4859	4504	4983	4615	5109	4735	5369	4961
4456	4147	4667	4336	4860	4505	4984	4616	5110	4737	5371	4963
4458	4149	4668	4337	4861	4506	4986	4596	5111	4738	5373	4965
4459	4150	4669	4338	4871	4514	4987	4577	5121	4770	5374	4966
4460	4151	4670	4339	4872	4515	4988	4618	5122	4747	5377	4969
4463	4154	4673	4341	4873	4516	4990	4619	5125	4750	5381	4972
4465	4156	4674	4342	4876	4518	4992	4621	5128	4753	5382	4973
4466	4157	4680	4346	4877	4519	4994	4622	5129	4754	5386	4976
4472	4160	4682	4348	4878	4520	4997	4624	5130	4755	5388	4978
4475	4163	4684	4350	4879	4521	4998	4625	5131	4756	5389	4979
4477	4165	4686	4352	4881	4523	5005	4630	5136	4760	5391	4981
4478	4166	4687	4353	4882	4524	5007	4632	5141	4765	5392	4982
4479	4167	4689	4355	4884	4526	5008	4633	5146	4769	5393	4983
4480	4168	4694	4358	4885	4527	5009	4634	5148	4571	5395	4985
4482	4170	4699	4362	4886	4528	5014	4639	"	4671	5396	4986
4483	4171	4709	4371	4887	4529	5016	4641	"	4675	5398	4988
4484	4172	4719	4380	4889	4532	5019	4644	"	4771	5399	4989
4486	4174	4720	4381	4890	4530	5021	4646	"	5209	5400	4990
4487	4175	4721	4382	4891	4533	5022	4647	"	5210	5401	4991
4488	4176	4725	4383	4892	4534	5023	4648	"	5213	5403	4992
4498	4118	4733	4392	4894	4536	5026	4651	"	5216	5404	4993
"	4119	4735	4394	4895	4537	5027	4652	5157	4779	5406	4995
"	4183	4737	4396	4897	4539	5028	4653	5168	4788	5412	5000
4499	4184	4739	4398	4899	4540	5030	4655	5169	4789	5419	5007
4503	4188	4743	4402	4901	4541	5031	4656	5177	4797	5420	5008
4504	4189	4745	4404	4902	4542	5033	4658	5186	4804	5425	5012
4505	4190	4746	4405	4903	4543	5036	4661	5187	4805	5428	5014
"	4191	4749	4408	4904	4544	5037	4662	5189	4807	5429	5015
4506	4192	4758	4416	4905	4545	5038	4663	5190	4808	5432	5018
4507	4193	4763	4420	4907	4546	5039	4664	5191	4809	5433	5019
4508	4194	4764	4421			5040	4665	5192	4810	5434	5020
4509	5117	4767	4424			5043	4666	5193	4811	5435	5021

G/K	STRONG	G/K	STRONG	G/K	STRONG	G/K	STRONG	G/K	STRONG	G/K	STRONG
5436	5022	5576	5161	5700	5276	5806	5377	5881	5448	5985	5546
5439	5028	5581	5165	5702	5278	5807	5378	5882	5449	5986	5547
5446	5038	5583	5167	5705	5281	5808	5379	5888	5455	5987	5548
5448	5040	5584	5168	5707	5283	5809	5380	5889	5456	5991	5552
5450	5042	5585	5169	5710	5285	5810	5381	5891	5458	5992	5553
5451	5043	5586	5170	5711	5286	5811	5382	5897	5463	5993	5554
5454	5045	5589	5173	5712	5287	5813	5384	5898	5464	5994	5555
5455	5046	5590	5174	5727	5301	5814	5385	5900	5466	5995	5556
5457	5048	5592	5176	5729	5303	5815	5386	5903	5469	5996	5557
5462	5053	5596	5179	5736	5310	5816	5387	5905	5470	6000	5560
5465	5056	5597	5180	5738	5312	5818	5389	5907	5472	6001	5561
5468	5058	5598	5181	5741	5314	5821	5392	5908	5473	6005	5564
5470	5060	5601	5183	5742	5341	5823	5393	5909	5474	6010	5567
5472	5061	5602	5184	5743	5316	5824	5394	5910	5475	6011	5568
5477	5062	5603	5185	5744	5317	5826	5396	5912	5476	6012	5569
5478	5063	5604	5186	5745	5318	5827	5397	5913	5477	6013	5570
5485	5072	5605	5187	5746	5319	5828	5399	5914	5478	6014	5571
5488	5074	5608	5190	5750	5323	5832	5401	5915	5479	6016	5573
5489	5075	5610	5191	5753	5326	5833	5402	5919	5483	6017	5574
5490	5076	5611	5192	5754	5327	5834	5403	5921	5485	6018	5576
5491	5077	5612	5193	5755	5328	5836	5404	5922	5486	6019	5577
5492	5078	5613	5194	5756	5329	5837	5405	5924	5488	6020	5575
5493	5079	5618	5199	5757	5330	5838	5406	5925	5489	6021	5578
5498	5083	5620	5201	5758	5331	5839	5407	5929	5493	6022	5579
5500	5085	5621	5202	5760	5331	5842	5410	5930	5494	6023	5580
5501	5086	5622	5203	5764	5336	5845	5413	5931	5495	6025	5582
5503	5088	5623	5204	5765	5337	5847	5415	5938	5502	6030	5587
5505	5090	5625	5206	5770	5342	5848	5416	5939	5503	6031	5588
5510	5095	5626	5207	5771	5343	5850	5418	5941	5506	6034	5590
5511	5096	5627	5208	5772	5344	5853	5421	5944	5508	6035	5591
5516	5100	5628	5211	5776	5347	5854	5422	5945	5509	6040	5596
5519	5103	5630	5214	5778	5349	5855	5423	5946	5510	6042	5598
5526	5109	5631	5215	5780	5351	5858	5426	5950	5513	6047	5604
5527	5110	5643	5229	5784	5355	5860	5428	5951	5514	6048	5605
5534	5115	5655	5240	5785	5356	5861	5429	5954	5517	6049	5606
5535	5116	5659	5241	5786	5357	5864	5432	5958	5521	6051	5609
5536	5117	5660	5242	5788	5359	5867	5435	5960	5523	6052	5610
5543	5131	5677	5257	5789	5360	5869	5436	5962	5525	6053	5611
5546	5134	5679	5259	5790	5361	5871	5438	5963	5526	6055	5613
5551	5139	5682	5262	5797	5368	5872	5439	5965	5528	6057	5614
5553	5140+4999	5683	5263	5799	5370	5873	5440	5966	5529	6058	5615
5555	5142	5685	5264	5800	5371	5874	5441	5967	5522	6060	5617
5557	5169	5687	5266	5801	5372	5875	5442	5970	5532	6064	5621
5560	5146	5689	5268	5802	5373	5876	5443	5971	5533	6065	5621
5563	5149	5694	5272	5803	5374	5877	5444	5975	5536	6067	5623
5564	5150	5695	5273	5804	5375	5878	5445	5976	5537		
5572	5157	5696	5274	5805	5376	5879	5446	5982	5543		
5575	5160	5698	2640			5880	5447	5984	5545		